COMPLETE BOOK OF COLLEGES

THE PRINCETON REVIEW

COMPLETE BOOK OF COLLEGES

Random House, Inc., New York
2004 Edition
www.PrincetonReview.com

Princeton Review Publishing, L. L. C.
2315 Broadway
New York, NY 10024
Email: bookeditor@review.com

Published in the United States by Random House, Inc., New York, and simultaneously in Canada by Random House of Canada Limited, Toronto. This is a revised edition of a book first published in 1989.

ISBN 0-375-76339-2
ISSN 1088-8594

Editorial Director: Robert Franek
Editors: Robert Franek and Erik Olson
Production Editor: Julieanna Lambert
Designer and Production Coordinator: Scott Harris

Manufactured in the United States of America on partially recycled paper.

9 8 7 6 5 4 3 2 1

2004 Edition

ACKNOWLEDGMENTS

The *Complete Book of Colleges* is the largest undergraduate guide produced by The Princeton Review. Our publication contains information on 1,669 colleges. There are many people both to thank and praise for their creativity, dedication, and attentiveness to detail: to each a well-deserved *thank you*.

My thanks go to the entire data collection staff, under the direction of David Soto. Each in his department gave their best to ensure that we had quality data from each school and to build a positive relationship with our administrative contact at each school. David and his right-hand man, Ben Zelevansky, are pros at explaining the collection process, how to use our tools, and how each schools' data is to be used, and at soothing the fears of everyone in the process. David's staff includes Yojaira Cordero, Tiffany Titus, Miguel Lopez, Nathan Firer, and Jillian Taylor. Thanks also go to our sales staff. Under the direction of Richard Strattner and Matt Doherty, our representatives invite schools to supply individual profiles to our guide; each year hundreds do. May special thanks go to our team of account executives: Josh Escott and Tore Erickson—without their efforts this book would not be the greatest resource for prospective college students available.

Scott Harris and Julieanna Lambert year after year earn my most sincere thanks. I could not have been luckier than to find a production team so efficient that no matter what the obstacle they pull together a superior product. Their savvy editing and design skills make this book a success each year; coupled with their professional manner, they both make this project a pleasure to work on as well. My thanks also goes to Chris Wujciak for his insight regarding data collection and his savvy book pouring abilities and to Erik Olson for his superior editorial eye. Lastly, a special thank you to Erica Magrey for her stylish management of this year's front matter.

Again, to all who worked so hard on this publication, thank you. Your efforts do not go unnoticed.

Robert Franek
Editorial Director

CONTENTS

FOREWORD

Welcome. You have found the best place to begin, fine-tune, and execute the search for your perfect college. Understanding that choosing a school wisely is a top priority for each prospective student, we have provided in this text a breadth of information to help you navigate the exciting, amazing, and sometimes confusing process of choosing the right college.

The design of this guidebook will allow you to narrow your search of colleges from 1,669 to a few dozen. Here you'll find all the individual college statistics you'll need to make informed choices about the competitiveness, size, location, and academic offerings of the schools available to you. In addition, you can find even more information about individual schools at The Princeton Review's website, www.PrincetonReview.com. It includes college search features, college profiles, college discussion boards, a college majors search engine, and an entire Web-based college application service.

By using this book, you can search, choose, and apply to college with the confidence of a pro, or at the very least a well-informed undergraduate hopeful! We supply the information and guidance, and you ultimately make your own decision. This guide also contains TPR's Admissions Wizard, which will aid you in finding colleges that match both your ability and preferences.

The college selection, application, and interviewing process can be overwhelming at times. It can also be a rewarding experience. For most, choosing a college is their first major life decision. I know it was mine. Remember that your college decision is yours alone, so arm yourself with the best available information. Badger teachers, friends, high school and college admissions counselors, brothers, sisters, and parents; ask them how they chose their colleges and why. The more you know when beginning the process, the more in control of the situation you'll feel.

Whatever it is that you choose as your path in life, your college selection will forever be your first step in that direction. The friends you make, the professors you meet, and the classes you take are all springboards to the next phase of your life.

I wish you much luck and success at whatever college you decide to attend. My sincere hope is that this publication and other Princeton Review tools will be helpful in the process.

Robert Franek
Editorial Director

INTRODUCTION

Before you dive into the *Complete Book of Colleges*, we want to give you some tips for your college search—especially on how to get the most out of this book and what to do once you've made your choices and are ready to apply. Since the most important thing for you to do now is to start on your search, we want to start right off by revealing the secret to getting admitted to the college of your choice.

It's almost never the focus of talk about college admission in the media, and parents and students discuss the subject all the time without even realizing that it's the crucial element to getting admitted. We're talking about matchmaking: finding colleges that have the educational and social environment you're looking for, where you are well-suited academically and have something the college is looking for in return. You have a lot more control over where you wind up going to college than you might think.

Matchmaking is a two-step process. To be most effective, you should begin with a thorough self-examination, or personal inventory. Your personal inventory is best structured in the form of a spreadsheet or chart, so that when you begin to consider your options you can check off those colleges that satisfy the various needs or wants you've identified. In this way, the best of your college choices will gradually begin to identify themselves.

Divide your inventory into two sections. One section should be biographical, including your high school course selection, GPA, SAT or ACT scores, class rank, and personal information like extracurricular activities—especially those you plan to continue in college. This will help you to assess how you stack up against each college's admissions standards and student body. The second section is a listing of the characteristics you need or want in the college you'll choose to attend. This list should include anything and everything you consider to be important, such as location, size of the student body, availability of scholarships, dormitory options, clubs and activities, even school colors if that has some kind of significance to you. This part of your inventory should grow continuously as you become more and more aware of what is important to you in your choice of colleges.

Armed with your personal inventory, you can begin to take advantage of the numerous resources available to help you narrow your choices of where to apply. There are five sources for information and advice that have become standard for most college-bound students:

1. College admissions viewbooks, videos, brochures, and catalogs

If you are a junior or senior in high school, you know more about the kinds of information these materials should include than the people who are responsible for designing and writing them. No college that spends half a million dollars on glossy literature is going to be objective about its content. In the best of this material, you can probably get a decent idea of the academic offerings and the basic admissions requirements. In all of it, you will never see any but the best looking students and the most appealing architecture on campus, nor will you hear about the tuition increases that were greater than the rate of inflation. Look this stuff over, but don't make any decisions based solely on what you read or see.

2. Your friends

No one knows colleges and universities better than the students who currently attend them. Seek out any and all of your friends, sons and daughters of family friends, and recent graduates of your high school who attend college, especially those who attend colleges that you are considering. Talk to them when they come home. Arrange to stay with them when you visit their colleges. Pick their brains for everything they know. It doesn't get any more direct and honest than this.

3. Books and college guides

There are two types of books that can be helpful to you in your search: those that discuss specific aspects of going to college, and college guides. A great narrative guide that stresses students' own opinions of colleges is our own *The Best 351 Colleges*. In addition, look at *The Fiske Guide to Colleges* or the *Yale Daily News' Insiders Guide to Colleges* for good second opinions. As for comprehensive guides—those that emphasize data over narrative content—you're holding the most up-to-date and useful one in your hands.

4. Computers

There's a lot of help out there. Using our site, PrincetonReview.com, is the best way to find the right school for you and prepare for college. For more information about our FREE online tools and features see page 10.

5. Your counselor

Since it's *critically* important, we'll say it again. Once you've developed some ideas about your personal inventory and college options, schedule a meeting with your college counselor. The more research you've done before you get together, the more help you're likely to get. Good advice comes out of thoughtful discussion, not from the expectation that your counselor will do your work. When it comes time to file applications, look over the materials and requirements together, and allow plenty of time to put forth your best.

Using College Information in the *Complete Book of Colleges* and Elsewhere

Throughout the course of your college search, you'll confront an amazing array of statistics and other data related to every college you consider. In order for all of this information to be helpful, you need to have some sense of how to interpret it. We've included a detailed key to the college entries in this book a few pages deeper into this introduction. Almost all the statistics we've compiled are self-explanatory, but there are a few that will be more useful with some elaboration.

Let's start with student/teacher ratio. Don't use it to assess average class size; they are not interchangeable terms. At almost every college, the average class size is larger than its student/teacher ratio. At many big universities, it is considerably larger. What is useful about the ratio is that it can give you an idea of how accessible your professors will be outside of the classroom. Once you are in college, you'll grow to realize just how important this is.

In the same way, the percentage of faculty that holds PhDs is useful information. When you're paying thousands of dollars in tuition each year, there's something comforting about knowing that your professors have a considerably broader and deeper grasp of what you're studying than you do. In contrast, teaching assistants (TAs) may be just one or two steps ahead of you.

Another interesting group of statistics deals with the percentage of students who go on to graduate or professional school. Never allow yourself to be overly impressed by such statistics unless you've taken the time to ponder their meaning and visited the college in question. High percentages almost always mean one of two things: that the college is an intellectual enclave that inspires students onward to further their education, or that it is a pre-professional bastion of aggressive careerists. There isn't anything inherently wrong with either one, but neither has universal appeal to prospective students. Colleges that are exceptions to this rule are rare and precious. The most misleading figures provided to prospective students are those for medical school acceptance rates. Virtually every college in the country can boast of high acceptance rates to medical school for its graduates; pre-med programs are designed to weed out those who will not be strong candidates before they even get to apply! If you're thinking about medical school, ask colleges how many of their students apply to medical school each year.

One final piece of advice about statistics relates to the college's acceptance rate. Simply knowing the percentage of applicants who are admitted each year is helpful, but it is even more helpful if you know how many applied as well. When you compare these figures to the freshman profile, you have the most accurate picture of just how tough it is to get in. An 80 percent acceptance rate doesn't mean there's an open door if you don't match up well to the academic achievements of the college's typical freshman. And when evaluating highly selective public colleges as an out-of-state applicant, remember that you will likely face a more selective evaluation than do applicants who are state residents.

A Few Final Thoughts

Once you've narrowed down your options and decided where to apply, find the applications on www.PrincetonReview.com and get to work filling them out. The admissions process is stressful enough without putting extra pressure on yourself by waiting until the last minute. The first thing you should do when you receive the necessary forms is to go over them with your college counselor. Immediately remove the recommendation forms (if they are required) and give them to the teachers and counselor who will be completing them for you. They'll have a better opportunity to write a thorough and supportive recommendation if you give them more than one night before they're due to complete them. This is also the time to make your request for official transcripts. Again, it takes time to do these things. Plan ahead.

As for completing the applications, organize yourself and all the materials. Keep everything in folders and accessible in case you need to speak with an admissions officer over the telephone. When essays and information on your extracurricular activities are required, do some outlining and rough drafts before you commit yourself to the actual forms.

Paying for college requires some of your attention too. We don't have nearly the space to go into such a complicated and stressful subject now, but it's also important that you get to work on your financial circumstances right away. As a comforting thought, keep in mind that while college is costly, few people pay the "sticker price." Regardless, you have to have your finances in order before you can get the most financial aid possible. We've developed a financial center on PrincetonReview.com to help demystify the sometimes bewildering task of financing your education. You can also find the most exhaustive strategies for financing your education in our book *Paying for College Without Going Broke*.

Last but not least, **don't take it easy during your senior year!** Colleges routinely request mid-year grades, and they expect you to continue taking challenging academic courses and keep your grades up throughout your high school career. Doing so takes you one step closer to getting good news. On behalf of The Princeton Review, have a good time and good luck. See you on campus!

HOW TO USE THIS BOOK

HOW THE *COMPLETE BOOK OF COLLEGES* IS ORGANIZED

There are two types of profiles in this book. Not every school listed will have both. All of the 1,669 colleges and universities included in this book have their own informational profiles, and each entry follows the same basic format. More than 190 of the institutions also have special two-page portraits located at the back of the book. These are written by the colleges and universities who wanted to present detailed descriptions of their campuses and programs.

Unless noted in the descriptions below, the Admissions Services Division of The Princeton Review collected all of the data presented in the informational profiles. As is customary with college guides, all data reflects figures for the academic year prior to publication, unless otherwise indicated. Since college offerings and demographics vary significantly from one institution to another and some colleges report data more thoroughly than others, few entries will include all the individual data described below.

The Heading

This section includes school name, address, telephone number, fax number, email address, Internet site, and college code numbers for both the College Board (CEEB) and the American College Testing Program (ACT) where applicable. All Internet site addresses were accurate and functioning at the time of publication. Check www.PrincetonReview.com for the most up-to-date links to colleges.

The Icons

The icons are a feature we hope will make using the *Complete Book of Colleges* easier. Icons appear under the school name and represent six categories in the following order: enrollment, tuition, environment, intercollegiate athletic division, whether the college has an application on PrincetonReview.com, and whether the college is profiled in *The Best 351 Colleges*. For a complete listing of icons and their descriptions, see page 8.

The Blurb

Describes the college or university. Includes all available data that relates to the date of founding of the school, any religious affiliation, whether the school is public or private, and campus size.

Students & Faculty

Enrollment

The total number of full-time undergraduates.

Student Body

The percentage of male, female, out-of-state, and international students, and the number of foreign countries represented.

Ethnic Representation

By percentage according to ethnic group. Figures may not add up to 100 percent, as student reporting of ethnicity is voluntary by law.

Retention and Graduation

The percentage of freshmen who return for sophomore year. The percentage of last year's seniors who entered as freshmen and graduated in four years. The percentage of graduates who pursue further study within one year. The percentage of graduates who pursue further study at law school. The percentage of graduates who pursue further study at business school. The percentage of graduates who pursue further study at medical school.

Faculty

The ratio of undergraduates to full-time faculty. The number of full-time instructional faculty. The percentage of faculty who hold PhDs. The percentage of faculty who teach undergraduates.

Academics

Degree

The types of degrees awarded to students.

Academic Requirements

Areas in which all or most students are required to complete some course work prior to graduation. Can include General Education (nonspecific), arts/fine arts, computer literacy, philosophy, foreign languages, history, humanities, mathematics, English (including composition), sciences (biological or physical), social sciences, and other requirements as specified by the school.

Classes

Number of students in an average regular class and an average lab/discussion section.

Majors with Highest Enrollment

The three most popular majors.

Disciplines with Highest Percent of Degrees Awarded

Covers arts and humanities, business, math and sciences, social sciences, education, and pre-professional enrollments. May add up to more or less than 100 percent, since not all majors fall into these broad categories and pre-professional students must also have a true major.

Special Study Options

May include accelerated program, cross registration, cooperative (work-study) program, distance learning, double major, dual enrollment, English as a second language, student exchange program (domestic), external degree program, honors program, independent study, internships, liberal arts/career combination, student-designed major, study abroad, teacher certification program, weekend college, and other options as specified by the school.

Facilities

Housing

Types of school-owned or -affiliated housing available. May include coed dorms, women's dorms, men's dorms, apartments for married students, apartments for single students, special housing for disabled students, special housing for international students, fraternity/sorority housing, cooperative housing, and other options as specified by the school. The availability of assistance in finding off-campus housing. Any housing requirements that may exist, such as freshmen being required to live on campus.

Library Holdings

The number of bound volumes, periodical subscriptions, microform items, and audiovisual titles held by the school's library.

Special Academic Facilities/Equipment

Other facilities and equipment of note (e.g., nuclear reactor, on-campus elementary school for student teachers, scanning electron microscopes, and so forth).

Extracurriculars

Activities

Standard activities available. May include choral groups, concert band, dance, drama/theater, jazz band, literary magazine, musical ensembles, musical theater, opera, pep band, radio station, student film society, student government, student newspaper, symphony orchestra, television station, yearbook.

Organizations

Total number of registered organizations, honor societies, religious organizations, fraternities (with percentage of males who are members), sororities (with percentage of females who are members).

Athletics

Intercollegiate athletics available, listed by sex.

Admissions

Selectivity Rating

The number listed for each college is The Princeton Review's exclusive rating of admissions competitiveness. It is a very general assessment determined by considering several factors, among them the schools' acceptance rate, the number of acceptees who actually enroll (yield), and the class rank and average test scores of entering first-year students. By incorporating all these factors, the rating adjusts for "self-selecting" applicant pools. *Note:* The Selectivity Rating for visual and performing arts schools are approximations only. Estimated Selectivity Ratings are included to give you a general idea of where they fit in the selectivity scale, but auditions and portfolios carry the greatest weight in admissions decisions.

Freshman Academic Profile

Average high school GPA. Class rank distribution. The percentage from public high schools. Average SAT I and/or ACT composite scores. Median range of SAT I and/or ACT composite scores. Test of English as a Foreign Language (TOEFL) requirements for international students.

Basis for Candidate Selection

The criteria considered by the admissions committee in evaluating candidates. May include secondary school record, class rank, recommendations, standardized test scores, essay, interview, extracurricular activities, talent/ability, character/personal qualities, alumni/ae relation, geographical residence, state residency, religious affiliation/commitment, minority status, volunteer work, work experience.

Freshman Admission Requirements

High school diploma/GED requirements. The number of academic units required or recommended in total and by academic subject. (Individual subject totals may not equal the total number of academic units required; in most cases, the difference is made up with electives. Check with the admissions office for any additional requirements.)

Freshman Admission Statistics

The number of students who applied, the percentage of applicants who were accepted, and the percentage of those accepted who ultimately enrolled.

Transfer Admission Requirements

Application requirements (may include high school transcript, college transcript, essay, interview, standardized tests, statement of good standing from prior school). Minimum high school GPA required. Minimum college GPA required. Lowest course grade transferable.

General Admission Information

Application fee. Application deadlines. Admission notification date. "Rolling" indicates that decisions are sent to candidates as they are made, rather than held for a common notification date. Registration policy for terms other than the fall term. Common Application participation. Credit policies for College Entrance Examination Board Advanced Placement tests. Deferred admission policy.

Costs and Financial Aid

Tuition, room & board, fees, and books.

Required Forms and Deadlines

Forms that applicants for financial aid must file, and their respective deadlines. May include FAFSA, institution's own financial aid form, CSS/Financial Aid PROFILE, business/farm supplement, state aid form, noncustodial (divorced/separated) parent's statement, and other forms specified by the school. Deadlines for filing financial aid forms.

Notification of Awards

The date that notification of financial aid awards occurs. "Rolling" indicates that notification is ongoing—the sooner you complete all of your required financial aid paperwork, the sooner you'll hear about your package.

Types of Aid

Need-based scholarships and grants may include Federal Pell, SEOG, state scholarships/grants, private scholarships, college/university gift aid from institutional funds, United Negro College Fund, Federal Nursing Scholarship, and other resources as specified by the school. Loans may include Direct Subsidized Stafford Loans, Direct Unsubsidized Stafford Loans, Direct PLUS Loans, Direct Consolidation Loan, FFEL Subsidized Stafford Loans, FFEL Unsubsidized Stafford Loans, FFEL PLUS Loans, FFEL Consolidation Loans, Federal Perkins Loans, Federal Nursing Loans, state loans, college/university loans from institutional funds, and other resources as specified by the school.

Student Employment

Availability of Federal Work-Study, a federal program that is need-based and part of most financial aid packages. Availability of part-time jobs direct from the college that are not based on need. The college's own assessment of part-time employment opportunities off campus.

Financial Aid Statistics

The percentage of freshmen who received some form of financial aid. The percentage of undergraduates who received some form of financial aid. The average amount of freshman scholarships and grants. The average amount of freshman loans. The average income from an on-campus job.

Financial Aid Phone

Don't hesitate to use it; you can bargain for a better financial aid package if the one you've been offered won't enable you to attend the school.

THE *COMPLETE BOOK OF COLLEGES* ICON SYSTEM

The icons that appear at the top of each college entry in the *Complete Book of Colleges* relate to six different categories: enrollment, tuition, environment, intercollegiate athletic division, whether the school has an application on www.PrincetonReview.com, and whether it is included in The Princeton Review's *The Best 345 Colleges*. The icons and their interpretations are indicated below.

Enrollment

Large (more than 10,000 undergraduate students)

Medium (4,000–10,000 undergraduate students)

Small (up to 4,000 undergraduate students)

Tuition

$$$ Very Expensive (tuition more than $15,000)

$$ Expensive (tuition $10,000–$15,000)

$ Moderate (tuition under $10,000)

Environment

Urban (includes cities)

Suburban

Rural (includes small towns)

Intercollegiate Athletic Division

Division I

Division II

Division III

NAIA

The Best 351 Colleges

Indicates whether the school can be found in our book, *The Best 351 Colleges*. In that book each school has a detailed profile that includes the results of our surveys regarding students' opinion about many aspects of their school and their education.

PRINCETONREVIEW.COM

PrincetonReview.com has a ton of FREE information to help you through the entire college admissions process. This book is one step in the right direction, but we can also help you **RESEARCH** more schools, **PREPARE** for the SAT/ACT, **APPLY** to college directly through our website, and learn how to **PAY** for college!

Try out **Counselor-o-Matic**, our dynamic college search engine that asks you a little bit about yourself and what you're looking for in a college and SHAZAM—it spits out schools that are Good Matches, Safeties, and Reach Schools. And it doesn't stop there. We also have relationships with thousands of colleges looking to fill their lecture halls with our PrincetonReview.com users. That's right—once you fill out Counselor-o-Matic, we can get your name in front of colleges who want YOU!

We've also got the most powerful **Scholarship Search** on the Web! And no, we won't sell your name like other popular scholarship sites.

Oh, and did we forget to mention that we have over **500 official online college applications?** Take some of the stress out of applying to college and come to PrincetonReview.com.

What do rocket scientists really study?
Find out at *www.PrincetonReview.com/college*.

AP_LIC_T_O_.

What's *that*?!?!

It's APPLICATION with P-A-I-N removed from the process.

We removed the paper, too.

With PrincetonReview.com's Online College Applications there are no endless piles to shuffle. No leaky pens, no hand cramps, no trying to figure out how many stamps to stick on that envelope.

The process is so painless, online applications practically submit themselves for you. Watch . . .

Type in your main contact information just once in our application profile and every subsequent application you file from our database—picking from hundreds of top schools—is automatically filled in with your information.

Not only are online applications:

- Faster to fill out
- Completely safe and secure
- Instantly trackable (check your application status online!)
- And . . . impossible to lose in the mail (they reach schools instantly)

But also: On PrincetonReview.com, there's no extra fee to submit your application online—our technology is totally FREE for you to use. In fact, some colleges even *waive* the application fee if you apply online.

Still have questions?

- Can I start an application now and finish it later?
- Are there easy-to-use instructions or someone I can call if I have a question? If I get stuck are there application instructions?
- Do schools *really* want to receive applications online?

Yes, yes, and yes!

It's easy to see the advantages of online applications. Almost as easy as actually applying.

Just log on and apply. It's that easy.

PrincetonReview.com—Applications without the pain.

THE ADMISSIONS WIZARD

WHAT'S THE ADMISSIONS WIZARD?

We realize that the *Complete Book of Colleges* is big, and you're not going to read through all the entries. So we've put together the following index to help you identify schools that might be interesting to you. To use it, you have to answer the following questions about your preferences. Feel free to blow off a category you don't care about—put a * instead of a letter or number in the box on the right.

Selectivity

Every college with an informational profile in the *Complete Book of Colleges* has an admissions selectivity rating between 60 and 100. This is not a measure of the academic quality of the school, but simply an indication of how tough it is to gain admission.

M If you're an A- student taking tough courses and have SAT scores over 1350 (or an ACT over 31) and a solid extracurricular record, you have a good shot at colleges with a selectivity rating of 90 or higher—the mega-selective colleges.

H You're in the top 20 percent of your high school class, and scored between 1100 and 1350 on the SAT. You have a good shot at colleges with a highly selective rating.

S You're a pretty good student (probably in the top half of your class) looking for a selective college whose students also did well in school.

N You're not looking for a selective college.

* You don't care how many people got turned away from a particular college.

Region

1 New England—Every place from Maine through Connecticut, and our Canadian schools.

2 Mid-Atlantic States—From New York south to Washington, D.C., including Pennsylvania.

3 Midwest—From Ohio west to Kansas and north to the Dakotas.

4 South—From Virginia south to Florida and west to Louisiana and Arkansas.

5 Southwest—Texas, Oklahoma, New Mexico, and Arizona.

6 West—Every place from Colorado, Wyoming, and Montana west, including Alaska and Hawaii.

* Any place that's not home.

Cost

- **e** Tuition is under $10,000 per year. (Remember: Room, board, books, and other expenses will add another $5,000 to $10,000.)
- **m** Tuition is between $10,000 and $15,000.
- **v** You're willing to pay (or borrow) tuition of over $15,000 per year.
- ***** That's my folks' problem.

Size

- **1** You want a school with 10,000 or more undergraduates. Not a bad idea; large schools generally provide more resources and satisfy more varied interests.
- **2** You want a school with 4,000 to 10,000 undergraduates. Some students feel this is a nice balance between the personal attention a small school can give and the resources a large school can offer.
- **3** You want a school with fewer than 4,000 undergraduates. These schools generally provide more personal attention; you'll rarely feel like a number.
- ***** We recommend you keep an open mind on size. Visit schools of all sizes before you narrow your choice here.

Environment

- **R** Rural schools provide plenty of fresh air, lots of space, and a more laid-back atmosphere.
- **S** Suburban schools are often in small towns within an hour or two of a good-sized city, and are always close to a mall.
- **U** Urban schools provide the widest variety of off-campus activities, such as museums, restaurants, and clubs.
- ***** This is important to some people, but again, you should look at schools of all settings before deciding. What's on the campus is often more important than what's next door.

Your search string

Now put your letters and numbers together to form your search string. It should look something like this: H6e*S (that would be a highly selective school in the West that is expensive and has a suburban setting). Now simply scan the (long) list that follows, and note the schools whose code is similar to your search string. If your search string is S2*2U, for example, you might put a check mark next to a college whose code is S2v3S, but not check off a college whose code is N4e2R. When in doubt, check it off—this will give you the widest variety of options. If you need more space for your list of target schools and Wizard-related calculations, use the notes pages at the back of the book. And remember, you're using this book to start your search, not to make any final decisions about where you should spend your next four or five years.

Enjoy your search!

THE WIZARD INDEX

Code	School	Page
H3v3R	Taylor University—Upland	690
H3v3S	Augustana College (IL)	66
H3v3S	Denison University	223, 1010
H3v3S	Earlham College	243, 1018
H3v3S	Gustavus Adolphus College	311
H3v3S	John Carroll University	354, 1068
H3v3S	Kettering University	368, 1078
H3v3S	Lawrence University	382
H3v3S	Ohio Wesleyan University	520, 1146
H3v3S	St. Norbert College	614
H3v3S	The College of Wooster	184
H3v3S	Wabash College	855
H3v3S	Wittenberg University	901, 1296
H3v3U	Beloit College	84
H3v3U	Case Western Reserve University	141, 960
H3v3U	Cleveland Institute of Music	167
H3v3U	Coe College	169
H3v3U	Hamline University	312
H3v3U	Illinois Institute of Technology	338, 1064
H4e1R	Clemson University	166
H4e1R	James Madison University	351
H4e1R	Virginia Tech	853
H4e1S	Florida State University	279
H4e1S	George Mason University	292
H4e1S	North Carolina State University	495
H4e1S	University of Alabama—Tuscaloosa	725
H4e1S	University of Florida	747
H4e1U	College of Charleston	174, 984
H4e1U	Florida A&M University	275
H4e1U	University of Arkansas—Fayetteville	728, 1242
H4e2R	Harding University	316
H4e2R	Shepherd College	636
H4e2R	University of Tennessee—Martin	817
H4e2S	University of Tennessee—Chattanooga	816
H4e2U	University of South Alabama	809
H4e3R	Berea College	88
H4e3R	Rust College	584
H4e3S	Lee University	384
H4e3S	University of North Carolina—Asheville	787
H4e3U	North Carolina School of the Arts	494
H4e3U	Spelman College	664, 1216
H4m3R	Bethany College (WV)	91
H4m3R	Gardner-Webb University	290
H4m3S	Hendrix College	323
H4m3U	Anderson College	47
H4m3U	Morehouse College	465
H4m3U	Salem College	618, 1192
H4m3U	Union University	718
H4v2S	University of Miami	771
H4v2U	Tulane University	714
H4v3R	Erskine College	265
H4v3R	Sweet Briar College	687, 1224
H4v3R	The University of the South	826
H4v3S	Oglethorpe University	514, 1142
H4v3S	Ringling School of Art & Design	574
H4v3S	Rollins College	581
H4v3S	Stetson University	680
H4v3U	Agnes Scott College	33
H4v3U	Birmingham-Southern College	96
H4v3U	Christian Brothers University	158, 974
H4v3U	Converse College	199
H4v3U	Millsaps College	449
H4v3U	Rhodes College	572
H4v3U	Wofford College	902
H5e1S	Texas A&M University—College Station	695
H5e1U	University of Texas—Austin	818
H5e2S	University of Texas—Dallas	819
H5e3R	New Mexico Institute of Mining & Technology	486
H5e3U	Texas A&M University—Galveston	696
H5m2S	TCU	691
H5m3U	Oral Roberts University	526
H5v1S	Baylor University	80
H5v2S	Southern Methodist University	653
H5v3S	Austin College	68
H5v3U	St. John's College (NM)	600
H5v3U	Trinity University	709
H5v3U	University of Dallas	742, 1244
H5v3U	University of Tulsa	828
H6e1S	California Polytechnic State University—San Luis Obispo	124
H6e1S	University of California—Davis	732
H6e1S	University of California—Riverside	734
H6e1S	University of California—Santa Cruz	736
H6e1S	University of Colorado—Boulder	740
H6e1S	Western Washington University	882
H6e1U	Brigham Young University (UT)	113
H6e1U	University of California—San Diego	735
H6e1U	University of Hawaii—Manoa	750
H6e1U	University of Oregon	795, 1256
H6e1U	University of Washington	831
H6e2R	Central Washington University	150
H6e2R	Western Oregon University	881
H6e3R	Brigham Young University (HI)	112
H6e3S	Colorado School of Mines	188
H6e3S	Oregon Institute of Technology	527
H6m3R	Northwest Nazarene University	505
H6m3S	Albertson College of Idaho	37
H6m3S	Cogswell Polytechnical College	169
H6v1U	University of Southern California	812
H6v2U	University of San Diego	806
H6v2U	University of San Francisco	807, 1262
H6v3R	Thomas Aquinas College	701
H6v3R	Walla Walla College	857
H6v3S	Art Center College of Design	56
H6v3S	Biola University	95
H6v3S	California Institute of the Arts	122
H6v3S	Lewis & Clark College	388
H6v3S	Occidental College	514
H6v3S	Pepperdine University	547
H6v3S	Regis University	569

H6v3S	Scripps College	631, 1200
H6v3S	University of Puget Sound	800
H6v3S	Whitworth College	889
H6v3U	Gonzaga University	300, 1040
H6v3U	Mount Saint Mary's College (CA)	472
H6v3U	San Francisco Art Institute	624
H6v3U	Seattle University	632, 1202
M1e3R	Middlebury College	444
M1e3S	Bates College	78
M1e3S	United States Coast Guard Academy	719
M1v1U	Boston University	104, 946
M1v2R	Dartmouth College	217, 1006
M1v2S	Boston College	103
M1v2S	Tufts University	713
M1v2U	Brown University	114
M1v2U	Harvard College	318
M1v2U	Massachusetts Institute of Technology	427
M1v2U	Yale University	906
M1v3R	Amherst College	47
M1v3R	Simon's Rock College of Bard	641
M1v3R	Williams College	896
M1v3S	Babson College	71, 924
M1v3S	Bowdoin College	105
M1v3S	Brandeis University	107
M1v3S	College of the Holy Cross	182
M1v3S	Smith College	644
M1v3S	Wellesley College	868, 1284
M1v3U	Rhode Island School of Design	571
M1v3U	Trinity College (CT)	707, 1234
M2e1S	Binghamton University (State University of New York)	95
M2e2R	State University of New York College at Geneseo	670
M2e2S	United States Naval Academy	721
M2e3R	Grove City College	309
M2e3R	St. Mary's College of Maryland	611
M2e3S	Webb Institute	866
M2e3U	Cooper Union	200
M2v1R	Cornell University	202
M2v1U	New York University	488, 1136
M2v1U	The George Washington University	293
M2v2S	Princeton University	560
M2v2U	Georgetown University	294
M2v2U	University of Pennsylvania	796
M2v3R	Bard College	76
M2v3R	Bucknell University	117
M2v3R	Colgate University	171, 982
M2v3R	Hamilton College	312
M2v3S	Bryn Mawr College	116
M2v3S	Sarah Lawrence College	626
M2v3S	Swarthmore College	686
M2v3S	Union College (NY)	717, 1236
M2v3S	Vassar College	848
M2v3U	Barnard College	77, 926
M2v3U	Eastman School of Music, University of Rochester	252
M2v3U	The Juilliard School	360
M2v3U	Yeshiva University	906
M3e1U	University of Michigan—Ann Arbor	771
M3e1U	University of Nebraska—Lincoln	781
M3e1U	University of Wisconsin—Madison	835
M3v2S	Northwestern University	508
M3v2S	University of Notre Dame	794, 1254
M3v2S	Washington University in St. Louis	863
M3v2U	University of Chicago	739
M3v3R	Carleton College	137
M3v3R	Grinnell College	309
M3v3R	Kenyon College	367, 1076
M3v3R	Oberlin College	513, 1140
M3v3S	Illinois Wesleyan University	339
M3v3S	Rose-Hulman Institute of Technology	582
M3v3S	Wheaton College (IL)	885, 1290
M3v3U	Macalester College	408
M4e1S	University of North Carolina—Chapel Hill	788
M4e1U	Georgia Institute of Technology	295
M4e2S	College of William and Mary	184
M4e2S	Mary Washington College	420
M4e3S	New College of Florida	483, 1132
M4v2S	Emory University	262, 1024
M4v2S	Wake Forest University	856
M4v2U	Duke University	241
M4v2U	Vanderbilt University	847, 1272
M4v3S	Davidson College	218, 1008
M4v3S	University of Richmond	802
M4v3S	Washington and Lee University	861
M5m3U	University of St. Thomas (TX)	805
M6e1U	University of California—Berkeley	732
M6e1U	University of California—Los Angeles	733
M6e2S	United States Air Force Academy	718, 1238
M6e3R	Deep Springs College	220
M6v2S	Stanford University	666
M6v3R	Whitman College	888, 1292
M6v3S	California Institute of Technology	122
M6v3S	Claremont McKenna College	161
M6v3S	Harvey Mudd College	319
M6v3U	Colorado College	186
N1e1S	University of Guelph	749
N1e1S	University of Waterloo	831
N1e1U	Brock University	113
N1e1U	University of Massachusetts—Boston	768
N1e1U	University of Western Ontario	833
N1e1U	York University	907
N1e2S	Central Connecticut State University	147
N1e2S	Eastern Connecticut State University	247
N1e2S	Framingham State College	282
N1e2S	Lakehead University	376
N1e2S	Rhode Island College	571
N1e2S	University of Maine—Augusta	761
N1e2S	University of Southern Maine	814
N1e2S	Western Connecticut State University	877
N1e2S	Westfield State College	882
N1e2U	University of Massachusetts—Lowell	770

Code	School	Page
N1e2U	Worcester State College	904
N1e3R	Castleton State College	142, 962
N1e3R	Johnson State College	358
N1e3R	Lyndon State College	406, 1098
N1e3R	Massachusetts College of Liberal Arts	426
N1e3R	Plymouth State College	554
N1e3R	University of Maine—Farmington	762, 1248
N1e3R	University of Maine—Fort Kent	762
N1e3R	University of Maine—Presque Isle	763
N1e3S	Fitchburg State College	274
N1e3S	Hellenic College	322
N1e3S	Husson College	336
N1e3S	Massachusetts Maritime Academy	428
N1e3U	Boston Architectural Center	103
N1e3U	University of New Hampshire—Manchester	785
N1m3R	Lyme Academy of Fine Arts	405
N1m3R	Southern Vermont College	658, 1214
N1m3R	Thomas College	701
N1m3R	Unity College	721
N1m3R	Westbrook College	876
N1m3S	Becker College	81, 932
N1m3S	Burlington College	118
N1m3S	Champlain College	153, 968
N1m3S	Lasell College	381
N1m3S	Thomas More College of Liberal Arts	703
N1m3U	Atlantic Union College	64
N1m3U	University of Bridgeport	731
N1m3U	Wentworth Institute of Technology	870
N1v2S	Roger Williams University	580
N1v2S	Sacred Heart University	592
N1v2U	Johnson & Wales University—Providence	357, 1070
N1v3R	Endicott College	263
N1v3R	Franklin Pierce College	285, 1036
N1v3R	Green Mountain College	307
N1v3R	New England College	483
N1v3R	Nichols College	492
N1v3R	Norwich University	509
N1v3S	Curry College	213
N1v3S	Elms College	257
N1v3S	Mitchell College	457
N1v3S	Montserrat College of Art	463
N1v3S	Regis College	569
N1v3S	Rivier College	575, 1172
N1v3S	Saint Joseph College (CT)	602, 1184
N1v3S	Southern New Hampshire University	654, 1212
N1v3S	Teikyo Post University	692
N1v3U	Art Institute of Boston at Lesley University	57, 920
N1v3U	Emmanuel College (MA)	261
N1v3U	Massachusetts College of Pharmacy & Health Science	427
N1v3U	Richmond, American International University in London	573
N1v3U	Wheelock College	887
N2e1S	Excelsior College	268
N2e1S	Rutgers University—University College at New Brunswick	591
N2e1S	University of Maryland, University College	767
N2e1S	West Chester University of Pennsylvania	872
N2e1U	Borough of Manhattan Community College	102
N2e1U	CUNY—Baruch College	206
N2e1U	CUNY—College of Staten Island	208
N2e1U	CUNY—Kingsborough Community College	210
N2e1U	CUNY—LaGuardia Community College	210
N2e1U	CUNY—New York City College of Technology	212
N2e1U	Queensborough Community College	564
N2e1U	Towson University	705, 1230
N2e1U	University of the District of Columbia	823
N2e2R	Bloomsburg University of Pennsylvania	99
N2e2R	Clarion University of Pennsylvania	162, 976
N2e2R	East Stroudsburg University of Pennsylvania	245
N2e2R	Edinboro University of Pennsylvania	254
N2e2R	Frostburg State University	288
N2e2R	Kutztown University of Pennsylvania	371
N2e2R	Niagara County Community College	491
N2e2R	Rowan University	583
N2e2R	Slippery Rock University of Pennsylvania	643
N2e2S	Broome Community College	114
N2e2S	California University of Pennsylvania	131
N2e2S	Erie Community College—North Campus	264
N2e2S	Plattsburgh State University	553
N2e2S	State University of New York College at Oneonta	672
N2e2S	State University of New York College at Oswego	672
N2e2S	State University of New York Empire State College	677
N2e2S	Wilmington College (DE)	897
N2e2U	CUNY—City College	208
N2e2U	CUNY—John Jay College of Criminal Justice	209
N2e2U	CUNY—Lehman College	211
N2e2U	CUNY—Medgar Evers College	211
N2e2U	CUNY—York College	213
N2e2U	Mohawk Valley Community College	458
N2e2U	Rutgers University—University College at Newark	592
N2e3R	Alfred State College (State University of New York)	40
N2e3R	Mansfield University of Pennsylvania	414
N2e3R	Mount Aloysius College	468
N2e3R	Pennsylvania State University—Hazleton	542
N2e3R	State University of New York College at Potsdam	673
N2e3R	State University of New York College of A&T at Cobleskill	674
N2e3R	State University of New York College of A&T at Morrisville	675
N2e3R	State University of New York College of Technology at Canton	676
N2e3R	Sullivan County Community College	685
N2e3S	Baptist Bible College and Seminary of Pennsylvania	74
N2e3S	Bowie State University	105
N2e3S	Delaware State University	221
N2e3S	Erie Community College—South Campus	265
N2e3S	Goldey-Beacom College	300
N2e3S	Gratz College	307
N2e3S	Pennsylvania State University—Abington	538
N2e3S	Pennsylvania State University—Altoona	538

N3e2S	Missouri Southern State College	455
N3e2S	Missouri Western State College	457
N3e2S	Northern Michigan University	502
N3e2S	Pittsburg State University	552
N3e2S	University of Nebraska—Kearney	781
N3e2S	University of Southern Indiana	813
N3e2U	Chicago State University	156
N3e2U	Indiana University Northwest	343
N3e2U	Indiana University South Bend	345
N3e2U	Purdue University—Calumet	562
N3e2U	Washburn University	860
N3e3R	Barclay College	76
N3e3R	Circleville Bible College	160
N3e3R	Dakota State University	214
N3e3R	Hannibal-LaGrange College	315
N3e3R	Medcenter One College of Nursing	433
N3e3R	Minot State University—Bottineau	452
N3e3R	Northern State University	502
N3e3R	Peru State College	548
N3e3R	Presentation College	559
N3e3R	Purdue University—North Central	562
N3e3R	University of Illinois—Springfield	754
N3e3R	University of Minnesota—Crookston	773
N3e3R	University of Rio Grande	803
N3e3R	Valley City State University	846
N3e3R	Wayne State College	864
N3e3S	Allen College	42
N3e3S	Black Hills State University	97
N3e3S	Grand Rapids Baptist Seminary	305
N3e3S	Indiana University—Kokomo	342
N3e3S	Laura and Alvin Siegal College of Judaic Studies	381
N3e3S	Lincoln University (MO)	392
N3e3S	Madonna University	409
N3e3S	Ohio University—Southern	518
N3e3S	Ohio University—Zanesville	519
N3e3S	Saint Mary's College of Ave Maria University (MI)	611
N3e3S	Shawnee State University	634
N3e3S	The Illinois Institute of Art Schaumburg	338
N3e3S	Union College (NE)	716
N3e3U	Bellevue University	82
N3e3U	East-West University	253
N3e3U	Evangel University	267
N3e3U	Harris-Stowe State College	317
N3e3U	Indiana University East	342
N3e3U	Lake Superior State University	375
N3e3U	Lexington College	390
N3e3U	Minot State University—Minot	452
N3e3U	Nebraska Methodist College	481
N3e3U	Palmer College of Chiropractic	536
N3e3U	Wilberforce University	891
N3m2U	Columbia College Chicago	190
N3m2U	Roosevelt University	581
N3m3R	Andrews University	48
N3m3R	Central Methodist College	148
N3m3R	Concordia University Nebraska	197
N3m3R	Iowa Wesleyan College	348
N3m3R	Lakeland College	376
N3m3R	MacMurray College	408
N3m3R	Missouri Valley College	456
N3m3R	Mount Senario College	474
N3m3R	Mount Vernon Nazarene College	475
N3m3R	Muskingum College	478
N3m3R	Oakland City University	512
N3m3R	Olivet College	524
N3m3R	Southwestern College	661
N3m3R	Spring Arbor University	664
N3m3R	Sterling College	680
N3m3R	Tabor College	688
N3m3R	Tiffin University	703
N3m3R	Upper Iowa University	842
N3m3R	Urbana University	842
N3m3R	William Penn University	894
N3m3R	William Woods University	895
N3m3S	Barat College of DePaul University	75
N3m3S	Bethel College (IN)	91
N3m3S	Crown College	204
N3m3S	Kansas Wesleyan University	362
N3m3S	Kendall College	364
N3m3S	Malone College	411
N3m3S	Marian College of Fond du Lac	415
N3m3S	McPherson College	432
N3m3S	MidAmerica Nazarene University	443
N3m3S	National-Louis University	480
N3m3S	Silver Lake College	639
N3m3S	Viterbo University	854
N3m3U	Alverno College	44
N3m3U	Aurora University	67
N3m3U	Blessing-Rieman College of Nursing	98
N3m3U	College of Saint Mary	179
N3m3U	Columbia College (MO)	189
N3m3U	Grand View College	306
N3m3U	Newman University	490
N3m3U	The Franciscan University	283
N3m3U	University of Sioux Falls	808
N3m3U	Vandercook College of Music	847
N3v3R	Bluffton College	101, 944
N3v3R	Defiance College	221
N3v3R	Saint Joseph's College (IN)	603
N3v3R	Saint Mary-of-the-Woods College	609
N3v3R	Wilmington College (OH)	897
N3v3S	Anderson University	48
N3v3S	Heidelberg College	321
N3v3S	Lake Erie College	374
N3v3S	Lewis University	388, 1088
N3v3S	Millikin University	448
N3v3S	Notre Dame College (OH)	510
N3v3U	Augsburg College	65
N3v3U	Cleveland Institute of Art	167
N3v3U	Shimer College	636
N4e1R	Georgia Southern University	296

N4m3R	Mars Hill College	418
N4m3R	Midway College	445
N4m3R	Pfeiffer University	548
N4m3R	Piedmont College	550
N4m3R	Saint Andrews Presbyterian College	594
N4m3R	Saint Leo University	607
N4m3R	Salem International University	619
N4m3R	Southern Wesleyan University	658
N4m3R	Union College (KY)	716
N4m3R	Warner Southern College	859
N4m3R	Webber International University	866, 1280
N4m3S	Barton College	78
N4m3S	Belhaven College	81
N4m3S	Belmont Abbey College	83
N4m3S	High Point University	324
N4m3S	Lenoir-Rhyne College	386
N4m3S	Mercer University—Atlanta	435
N4m3S	Methodist College	439
N4m3S	North Carolina Wesleyan College	495
N4m3S	Virginia Intermont College	851
N4m3S	Wingate University	899
N4m3U	Clark Atlanta University	162
N4m3U	Dillard University	235
N4m3U	Greensboro College	308, 1046
N4m3U	Palm Beach Atlantic College	536
N4m3U	St. Thomas University	617
N4v2U	Embry Riddle Aeronautical University (FL)	259, 1020
N4v3R	Newberry College	489
N4v3S	Art Institute of Atlanta	56, 918
N4v3S	Averett University	69
N4v3S	Lynchburg College	405
N4v3S	Marymount University	423
N4v3S	Oxford College of Emory University	531
N4v3S	Virginia Wesleyan College	854
N4v3U	Johnson & Wales University—Charleston	355, 1070
N4v3U	Lynn University	406, 1100
N4v3U	University of Charleston	738
N4v3U	University of Tampa	815, 1266
N5e1R	Northern Arizona University	500
N5e1S	Sam Houston State University	621
N5e1S	Southwest Texas State University	660
N5e1S	University of Central Oklahoma	737
N5e1U	University of Houston—Downtown	752
N5e1U	University of Texas—Pan American	821
N5e2R	Northeastern State University	499
N5e2R	Prairie View A&M University	557
N5e2R	Texas A&M University—Commerce	695
N5e2S	Angelo State University	49
N5e2S	Lamar University	377
N5e2S	Southwestern Oklahoma State University	662
N5e2S	Tarleton State University	689
N5e2S	Texas Woman's University	700
N5e2S	University of Houston—Clear Lake	751
N5e2U	Arizona State University West	54
N5e2U	Cameron University	133
N5e3R	Eastern New Mexico University	250
N5e3R	Howard Payne University	332
N5e3R	Jarvis Christian College	352
N5e3R	Langston University	379
N5e3R	Oklahoma Panhandle State University	522
N5e3R	Southeastern Oklahoma State University	649
N5e3R	Sul Ross State University	685
N5e3R	University of Science and Arts of Oklahoma	807
N5e3S	Arizona State University East	53
N5e3S	East Central University	244
N5e3S	University of Central Texas	738
N5e3S	University of Houston—Victoria	753
N5e3S	Wiley College	891
N5e3U	Houston Baptist University	332
N5e3U	Huston-Tillotson College	336
N5e3U	Southwestern Christian University	661
N5e3U	Texas College	697
N5e3U	University of Texas—Houston Health Science Center	820
N5e3U	Wayland Baptist University	864
N5m3R	Schreiner University	630
N5m3S	Dallas Baptist University	216
N5m3S	Texas Lutheran University	698
N5m3U	Art Institute of Dallas	58
N5m3U	Concordia University at Austin	196
N5m3U	University of the Incarnate Word	824
N6e1S	California State University—Chico	125
N6e1S	Idaho State University	337
N6e1S	Oregon State University	527
N6e1S	Weber State University	867
N6e1U	California State University—Fresno	126
N6e1U	California State University—Long Beach	128
N6e1U	California State University—Los Angeles	128
N6e1U	California State University—Northridge	129
N6e1U	California State University—San Bernardino	130
N6e1U	Metropolitan State College of Denver	441
N6e1U	Portland State University	557
N6e1U	University of Montana College of Technology	778
N6e1U	University of Nevada—Reno	783
N6e1U	Utah State University	844
N6e2R	Eastern Washington University	251
N6e2R	Fort Lewis College	281
N6e2R	Humboldt State University	333
N6e2S	California State University—Bakersfield	125
N6e2S	California State University—Hayward	127
N6e2S	California State University—San Marcos	130
N6e2S	Southern Utah University	657
N6e2S	University of Alaska—Fairbanks	727
N6e2U	California State University—Dominguez Hills	126
N6e2U	National University	479
N6e2U	University of Southern Colorado	813
N6e3R	Adams State College	31
N6e3R	Colorado Mountain College—Alpine Campus	187
N6e3R	Colorado Mountain College—Spring Valley	187
N6e3R	Colorado Mountain College—Timberline Campus	187

S2e3U	Saint Francis College (NY)	598
S2m3S	Gannon University	290
S2m3S	Mercyhurst College	436
S2m3S	Nyack College	512
S2m3S	Philadelphia Biblical University	549
S2m3S	St. Thomas Aquinas College	616
S2m3U	Marymount Manhattan College	423
S2m3U	The College of Saint Rose	179
S2m3U	Trinity College (DC)	708
S2v1U	Drexel University	240
S2v2S	Hofstra University	327
S2v2S	Rider University	573, 1168
S2v2S	Seton Hall University	632, 1204
S2v2U	Duquesne University	242
S2v2U	Metropolitan College of New York (formerly Audrey Cohen)	440, 1116
S2v2U	Pace University—New York City	531
S2v3R	Alfred University	41
S2v3R	Houghton College	331
S2v3R	Juniata College	360
S2v3R	Keuka College	369
S2v3R	Lebanon Valley College	384
S2v3R	Mount Saint Mary's College (MD)	473
S2v3R	St. Bonaventure University	596
S2v3R	Washington College	862, 1278
S2v3S	Albright College	38
S2v3S	Arcadia University	52, 916
S2v3S	Cabrini College	119
S2v3S	Caldwell College	120, 956
S2v3S	College of Notre Dame of Maryland	177, 990
S2v3S	Concordia College (NY)	195
S2v3S	DeSales University	225
S2v3S	Eastern College	247
S2v3S	Elizabethtown College	255
S2v3S	Gwynedd-Mercy College	311
S2v3S	Hood College	330
S2v3S	King's College (PA)	370
S2v3S	Le Moyne College	383
S2v3S	Manhattan College	412
S2v3S	Manhattanville College	413
S2v3S	Marywood University	425
S2v3S	Messiah College	439, 1114
S2v3S	Moravian College	464
S2v3S	Nazareth College of Rochester	480, 1130
S2v3S	Niagara University	491, 1138
S2v3S	Roberts Wesleyan College	577
S2v3S	Saint John Fisher College	599
S2v3S	Saint Vincent College	617
S2v3S	Siena College	638, 1208
S2v3S	Susquehanna University	686
S2v3S	Washington & Jefferson College	861
S2v3S	Westminster College (PA)	884
S2v3S	Widener University	890
S2v3U	Canisius College	135
S2v3U	Columbia Union College	192

S2v3U	Eugene Lang College/New School University	266, 1026
S2v3U	Manhattan School of Music	412
S2v3U	Mannes College of Music	413, 1104
S2v3U	Moore College of Art & Design	464
S2v3U	Russell Sage College	584
S2v3U	Wagner College	856, 1274
S2v3U	Wilkes University	891
S3e1R	Northern Illinois University	501
S3e1R	Ohio University—Athens	518
S3e1R	Western Illinois University	878
S3e1S	Central Michigan University	148
S3e1S	Grand Valley State University	305, 1044
S3e1S	Illinois State University	339
S3e1S	Indiana University—Bloomington	341
S3e1S	Michigan State University	442
S3e1S	Oakland University	513
S3e1S	Purdue University—West Lafayette	563
S3e1S	Southern Illinois University—Carbondale	652
S3e1S	University of Missouri—Columbia	776
S3e1U	Eastern Michigan University	249
S3e1U	Iowa State University of Science and Technology	348
S3e1U	Ohio State University—Columbus	516
S3e1U	Southwest Missouri State University	659
S3e1U	University of Cincinnati	739
S3e1U	University of Illinois—Chicago	753
S3e1U	University of Northern Iowa	793
S3e1U	University of Wisconsin—Eau Claire	834
S3e1U	University of Wisconsin—Milwaukee	836
S3e1U	Wichita State University	889
S3e2R	Central Missouri State University	149
S3e2R	Northwest Missouri State University	504
S3e2R	Saginaw Valley State University	593
S3e2R	Southeast Missouri State University	648
S3e2R	The University of South Dakota	811
S3e2R	University of Wisconsin—Platteville	838
S3e2R	Winona State University	899
S3e2S	Park University	536
S3e2S	University of Minnesota—Duluth	773
S3e2S	University of Wisconsin—Green Bay	834
S3e2S	University of Wisconsin—River Falls	838
S3e2S	University of Wisconsin—Stevens Point	839
S3e2S	University of Wisconsin—Whitewater	840
S3e2U	Emporia State University	263
S3e2U	Franklin University	286
S3e2U	Marquette University	417
S3e2U	Minnesota State University—Moorhead	451
S3e2U	North Dakota State University	497
S3e2U	University of Michigan—Dearborn	772
S3e2U	University of Michigan—Flint	772
S3e2U	University of Missouri—Kansas City	776
S3e2U	University of Wisconsin—LaCrosse	835
S3e3R	Central State University	150
S3e3R	Chadron State College	151
S3e3R	Dickinson State University	234
S3e3R	Jamestown College	352

S3v3U	Milwaukee School of Engineering	450, 1118
S3v3U	Minneapolis College of Art and Design	450, 1120
S3v3U	North Park University	498
S3v3U	Ohio Dominican University	515
S3v3U	Otterbein College	529
S3v3U	Rockford College	579, 1174
S3v3U	Saint Xavier University	618
S3v3U	School of the Art Institute of Chicago	629, 1196
S3v3U	University of Evansville	746
S4e1R	Appalachian State University	50
S4e1R	Eastern Kentucky University	248
S4e1R	Mississippi State University	453
S4e1R	University of Mississippi	775
S4e1S	Auburn University—Auburn	64
S4e1S	Middle Tennessee State University	443
S4e1S	University of Central Florida	737
S4e1S	University of Southern Mississippi	815
S4e1S	West Virginia University	874
S4e1S	Western Kentucky University	879
S4e1U	Florida International University	277
S4e1U	University of Alabama—Birmingham	724
S4e1U	University of Kentucky	757
S4e1U	University of Louisville	760
S4e1U	University of New Orleans	786
S4e1U	University of North Florida	792
S4e1U	University of South Carolina—Columbia	810
S4e1U	University of South Florida	812
S4e1U	University of Tennessee—Knoxville	816
S4e2R	East Tennessee State University	245
S4e2R	Louisiana Tech University	400
S4e2R	State University of West Georgia	678
S4e2R	Tennessee Technological University	693
S4e2R	University of Central Arkansas	736
S4e2S	Arkansas State University	54
S4e2S	Coastal Carolina University	168
S4e2S	Murray State University	478
S4e2S	University of Alabama—Huntsville	725
S4e2S	University of North Alabama	787
S4e2S	University of West Florida	832
S4e2U	Auburn University—Montgomery	65
S4e2U	North Carolina A&T State University	493
S4e2U	Tennessee State University	693
S4e2U	University of Arkansas—Little Rock	729
S4e3R	Alice Lloyd College	41
S4e3R	Brewton-Parker College	110
S4e3R	John Brown University	353
S4e3R	Kentucky Christian College	366
S4e3R	Lincoln Memorial University	392
S4e3R	Mississippi University for Women	454
S4e3R	North Georgia College and State University	497
S4e3R	Talladega College	689
S4e3R	Toccoa Falls College	704
S4e3R	University of Montevallo	780
S4e3R	University of Virginia's College at Wise	830
S4e3R	Virginia Military Institute	852
S4e3S	Flagler College	275
S4e3S	Lander University	378
S4e3S	Louisiana College	398
S4e3S	Shenandoah University	635
S4e3S	Tougaloo College	704
S4e3S	University of Mobile	778
S4e3S	William Carey College	892
S4e3U	Brescia University	109
S4e3U	Faulkner University	271
S4e3U	Fisk University	273
S4e3U	Lane College	379
S4e3U	Miles College	446
S4e3U	Saint Augustine's College	595
S4m2S	Nova Southeastern University	511
S4m2U	Hampton University	314
S4m3R	Alderson-Broaddus College	40
S4m3R	Berry College	90
S4m3R	Campbell University	134
S4m3R	Campbellsville University	134
S4m3R	Carson-Newman College	140
S4m3R	Cumberland College	205, 1002
S4m3R	Lees-McRae College	385
S4m3R	Milligan College	447
S4m3R	Southern Adventist University	650
S4m3R	Tuskegee University	715
S4m3S	Bellarmine University	82
S4m3S	Brenau University Women's College	108
S4m3S	Catawba College	143
S4m3S	Columbia College (SC)	190
S4m3S	Florida Southern College	278
S4m3S	Kentucky Wesleyan College	367
S4m3S	King College (TN)	369
S4m3S	LaGrange College	373
S4m3S	Lambuth University	377
S4m3S	Mississippi College	453
S4m3S	Shorter College	637
S4m3S	Thomas More College	702
S4m3S	Tusculum College	714
S4m3S	Wheeling Jesuit University	887
S4m3U	Belmont University	83
S4m3U	Charleston Southern University	154
S4m3U	Huntingdon College	334
S4m3U	Memphis College of Art	434
S4m3U	Tennessee Wesleyan College	694
S4m3U	Trevecca Nazarene University	706
S4m3U	Xavier University of Louisiana	905
S4v2U	Mercer University—Macon	435, 1110
S4v2U	Savannah College of Art and Design	627, 1194
S4v3R	Asbury College	61
S4v3R	Bridgewater College	111
S4v3R	Centre College	151
S4v3R	Coker College	170
S4v3R	Eastern Mennonite University	249
S4v3R	Hampden-Sydney College	313
S4v3R	Presbyterian College	558

S4v3R	West Virginia Wesleyan College	875
S4v3S	Centenary College of Louisiana	146
S4v3S	Covenant College	203
S4v3S	Eckerd College	253
S4v3S	Elon University	258
S4v3S	Florida Institute of Technology	276
S4v3S	Georgetown College	293
S4v3S	Guilford College	310
S4v3S	Hollins University	328
S4v3S	Jacksonville University	351
S4v3S	Mary Baldwin College	420
S4v3S	Maryville College	424
S4v3S	Queens University of Charlotte	563
S4v3S	Randolph-Macon College	566
S4v3S	Roanoke College	576
S4v3S	Transylvania University	706, 1232
S4v3S	Warren Wilson College	859, 1276
S4v3U	Loyola University New Orleans	402, 1094
S5e1R	Oklahoma State University	522
S5e1S	Arizona State University	52
S5e1S	University of Oklahoma	795
S5e1S	University of Texas—San Antonio	822
S5e1U	New Mexico State University	486
S5e1U	University of Arizona	728
S5e1U	University of Houston—Houston	752
S5e1U	University of New Mexico	786
S5e1U	University of Texas—El Paso	820
S5e2S	Midwestern State University	445
S5e2S	Stephen F. Austin State University	679
S5e2S	West Texas A&M University	873
S5e2U	Texas Southern University	698
S5e3R	College of the Southwest	183
S5e3S	New Mexico Highlands University	485
S5e3S	Northwestern Oklahoma State University	507
S5e3S	Oklahoma Wesleyan University	523
S5m3S	LeTourneau University	387
S5m3S	Oklahoma Baptist University	520
S5m3S	Oklahoma Christian University	521
S5m3U	Grand Canyon University	305
S5m3U	Hardin-Simmons University	316
S5m3U	Oklahoma City University	521
S5m3U	Our Lady of the Lake University	530
S5m3U	Prescott College	559
S5m3U	St. Mary's University (TX)	612
S5m3U	Texas Wesleyan University	699
S5v3U	Embry Riddle Aeronautical University (AZ)	258
S6e1R	Washington State University	863
S6e1S	California State Polytechnic University—Pomona	124
S6e1S	Colorado State University	188
S6e1S	University of California—Irvine	733
S6e1S	University of Northern Colorado	793
S6e1U	Boise State University	102
S6e1U	California State University—Sacramento	129
S6e1U	Montana State University—Bozeman	461
S6e1U	San Diego State University	623
S6e1U	University of Montana—Missoula	779
S6e1U	University of Nevada—Las Vegas	782
S6e2R	California State University—Stanislaus	131
S6e2R	The Evergreen State College	267, 1028
S6e2R	University of Idaho	753
S6e2R	University of Wyoming	841, 1270
S6e2S	Mesa State College	438
S6e2S	Sonoma State University	645
S6e2U	Hawaii Pacific University	320, 1054
S6e2U	University of Colorado—Colorado Springs	741
S6e3S	Montana Tech of the University of Montana	462
S6e3U	Colorado Technical University	189
S6e3U	Golden Gate University	300
S6m3S	Carroll College (MT)	139
S6m3S	Fresno Pacific University	287
S6m3S	Northwest College	504
S6m3S	Notre Dame de Namur University	510
S6m3S	United States International University	719
S6m3U	Cornish College of the Arts	203
S6m3U	Pacific Northwest College of Art	533
S6v2S	Loyola Marymount University	401
S6v3R	Linfield College	394
S6v3R	Pacific Union College	534
S6v3S	Chapman University	153, 970
S6v3S	Concordia University Irvine	197
S6v3S	Master's College and Seminary	428
S6v3S	Saint Martin's College	608
S6v3S	Saint Mary's College (CA)	610
S6v3S	University of Denver	744
S6v3S	University of Judaism	756
S6v3S	University of Redlands	800
S6v3S	University of the Pacific	825
S6v3S	Western Baptist College	876
S6v3S	Westminster College (UT)	884
S6v3S	Westmont College	885
S6v3S	Whittier College	888
S6v3U	California College of Arts and Crafts	121, 958
S6v3U	Colorado Christian University	185
S6v3U	Mills College	448
S6v3U	Otis College of Art & Design	528, 1152
S6v3U	Pacific Lutheran University	533
S6v3U	San Francisco Conservatory of Music	624
S6v3U	University of Portland	799

COLLEGE DIRECTORY

ABILENE CHRISTIAN UNIVERSITY

ACU Box 29000, Abilene, TX 79699
Phone: 915-674-2650 **E-mail:** info@admissions.acu.edu **CEEB Code:** 6001
Fax: 915-674-2130 **Web:** www.acu.edu **ACT Code:** 4050

This private school, which is affiliated with the Church of Christ, was founded in 1906. It has a 208-acre campus.

STUDENTS AND FACULTY

Enrollment: 4,186. **Student Body:** Male 44%, female 56%, out-of-state 21%, international 3% (52 countries represented). **Ethnic Representation:** African American 7%, Asian 1%, Caucasian 83%, Hispanic 7%, Native American 1%. **Retention and Graduation:** 77% freshmen return for sophomore year. 27% freshmen graduate within 4 years. 28% grads go on to further study within 1 year. 2% grads pursue business degrees. 2% grads pursue law degrees. 4% grads pursue medical degrees. **Faculty:** Student/faculty ratio 18:1. 217 full-time faculty, 73% hold PhDs. 98% faculty teach undergrads.

ACADEMICS

Degrees: Associate's, bachelor's, doctoral, first professional, master's, post-bachelor's certificate, post-master's certificate, terminal, transfer. **Academic Requirements:** General education including some course work in arts/fine arts, English (including composition), foreign languages, history, humanities, mathematics, sciences (biological or physical), social science. **Classes:** 10-19 students in an average class. 10-19 students in an average lab/discussion section. **Majors with Highest Enrollment:** Accounting; elementary education and teaching; pastoral studies/counseling. **Disciplines with Highest Percentage of Degrees Awarded:** Business/marketing 21%, education 15%, interdisciplinary studies 10%, philosophy/religion/theology 7%, visual and performing arts 5%. **Special Study Options:** Cross registration, distance learning, double major, dual enrollment, English as a second language, honors program, independent study, internships, student-designed major, study abroad, teacher certification program.

FACILITIES

Housing: All-female, all-male, apartments for married students, apartments for single students, housing for disabled students. **Library Holdings:** 481,689 bound volumes. 2,439 periodicals. 1,164,685 microforms. 62,224 audiovisuals. **Special Academic Facilities/Equipment:** Museum of university's history, biblical restoration studies center, voice institute, demonstration farm and ranch, observatory. **Computers:** School-owned computers available for student use.

EXTRACURRICULARS

Activities: Choral groups, concert band, drama/theater, jazz band, literary magazine, marching band, music ensembles, musical theater, opera, radio station, student government, student newspaper, student-run film society, symphony orchestra, television station, yearbook. **Organizations:** 100 registered organizations, 14 honor societies, 9 religious organizations, 9 fraternities (20% men join), 7 sororities (23% women join). **Athletics (Intercollegiate):** *Men:* baseball, basketball, cross-country, football, indoor track, tennis, track & field. *Women:* basketball, cross-country, indoor track, softball, tennis, track & field, volleyball.

ADMISSIONS

Selectivity Rating: 81 (of 100). **Freshman Academic Profile:** Average high school GPA 3.5. 20% in top 10% of high school class, 45% in top 25% of high school class, 73% in top 50% of high school class. 85% from public high schools. Average SAT I Math 549, SAT I Math middle 50% range 480-620. Average SAT I Verbal 554, SAT I Verbal middle 50% range 490-610. Average ACT 24, ACT middle 50% range 20-27. TOEFL required of all international applicants, minimum TOEFL 525. **Basis for Candidate Selection:** *Very important factors considered include:* character/personal qualities, secondary school record, standardized test scores. *Important factors considered include:* class rank, interview, recommendations, religious affiliation/commitment, talent/ability. *Other factors considered include:* alumni/ae relation, extracurricular activities, minority status, volunteer work, work experience. **Freshman Admission Requirements:** High school diploma or GED is required. *Academic units required/recommended:* 12 total recommended; 4 English recommended, 3 math recommended, 3 science recommended, 2 science lab recommended, 2 foreign language recommended. **Freshman Admission Statistics:** 3,029 applied, 61% accepted, 50% of those accepted enrolled. **Transfer Admission Requirements:** *Items required:* high school transcript, college transcript, interview. Minimum college GPA of 2.0 required. Lowest grade transferable C. **General Admission Information:** Application fee $25. Regular application deadline August 1. Nonfall registration accepted. Credit offered for CEEB Advanced Placement tests.

COSTS AND FINANCIAL AID

Required Forms and Deadlines: FAFSA and institution's own financial aid form. Priority filing deadline March 1. **Notification of Awards:** Applicants will be notified of awards on a rolling basis beginning on or about April 1. **Types of Aid:** *Need-based scholarships/grants:* Pell, SEOG, state scholarships/grants, private scholarships, the school's own gift aid, United Negro College Fund. *Loans:* FFEL Subsidized Stafford, FFEL Unsubsidized Stafford, FFEL PLUS, Federal Perkins, state loans, college/university loans from institutional funds. **Student Employment:** Federal Work-Study Program available. Institutional employment available. Off-campus job opportunities are good. **Financial Aid Statistics:** 55% freshmen, 53% undergrads receive some form of aid. Average freshman grant $7,210. Average freshman loan $4,512. Average income from on-campus job $1,556. **Financial Aid Phone:** 915-674-2643.

ACADEMY OF ART COLLEGE

79 New Montgomery Street, San Francisco, CA 94105
Phone: 415-274-2222 **E-mail:** info@academyart.edu
Fax: 415-263-4130 **Web:** www.academyart.edu **ACT Code:** 155

This private school was founded in 1929. It has a 20-acre campus.

STUDENTS AND FACULTY

Enrollment: 5,435. **Student Body:** Male 54%, female 46%, out-of-state 37%, international 23%. **Ethnic Representation:** African American 4%, Asian 22%, Caucasian 49%, Hispanic 11%, Native American 1%. **Retention and Graduation:** 80% freshmen return for sophomore year. 28% freshmen graduate within 4 years. **Faculty:** Student/faculty ratio 15:1. 84 full-time faculty, 4% hold PhDs. 80% faculty teach undergrads.

ACADEMICS

Degrees: Associate's, bachelor's, certificate, master's. **Academic Requirements:** General education including some course work in arts/fine arts, computer literacy, English (including composition), history, humanities. **Classes:** Under 10 students in an average class. **Majors with Highest Enrollment:** Computer graphics; fashion/apparel design; cinematography and film/video production. **Disciplines with Highest Percentage of Degrees Awarded:** Visual and performing arts 100%. **Special Study Options:** Accelerated program, cooperative (work-study) program, distance learning, English as a second language, independent study, internships, study abroad, weekend college, portfolio development, personal enrichment program.

FACILITIES

Housing: Coed, all-female, all-male, apartments for married students, apartments for single students. **Library Holdings:** 18,573 bound volumes. 276 periodicals. 0 microforms. 87,175 audiovisuals. **Special Academic Facilities/Equipment:** 4 art galleries (public) for display of student work. **Computers:** School-owned computers available for student use.

EXTRACURRICULARS

Activities: Concert band, dance, drama/theater, musical theater, student newspaper. **Organizations:** 12 registered organizations. **Athletics (Intercollegiate):** *Men:* baseball, basketball, soccer, volleyball. *Women:* soccer, volleyball.

ADMISSIONS

Selectivity Rating: 60 (of 100). **Freshman Academic Profile:** Average high school GPA 2.8. **Basis for Candidate Selection:** *Important factors considered include:* interview. *Other factors considered include:* secondary school record. **Freshman Admission Requirements:** High school diploma or GED is required. **Freshman Admission Statistics:** 799 applied, 100% accepted, 81% of those accepted enrolled. **Transfer Admission Requirements:** *Items required:* high school transcript, college transcript, interview. Minimum college GPA of 2.0 required. Lowest grade transferable C. **General Admission Information:** Application fee $100. Nonfall registration accepted. Admission may be deferred for a maximum of 2 years.

COSTS AND FINANCIAL AID

Tuition $12,000. Room & board $8,958. Required fees $300. Average book expense $864. **Required Forms and Deadlines:** FAFSA and institution's own financial aid form. No deadline for regular filing. Priority filing deadline July 10. **Notification of Awards:** Applicants will be notified of awards on a rolling basis. **Types of Aid:** *Need-based scholarships/grants:* Pell, SEOG, state scholarships/grants. *Loans:* Direct Subsidized Stafford, Direct Unsubsidized Stafford, Direct PLUS, FFEL Subsidized Stafford, FFEL Unsubsidized Stafford, FFEL PLUS. **Student Employment:** Federal Work-Study Program available. Off-campus job opportunities are good. **Financial Aid Statistics:** 43% freshmen, 37% undergrads receive some form of aid. Average freshman grant $1,500. Average freshman loan $6,625. **Financial Aid Phone:** 415-274-2223.

See page 910.

ACADIA UNIVERSITY

Admissions Office, Wolfville, NS BOP 1XO
Phone: 902-585-1222 **E-mail:** admissions@acadiau.ca
Fax: 902-585-1081 **Web:** www.acadiau.ca

This public school was founded in 1838. It has a 200-acre campus.

STUDENTS AND FACULTY

Enrollment: 3,841. **Student Body:** Male 44%, female 56%. **Retention and Graduation:** 82% freshmen return for sophomore year. **Faculty:** Student/faculty ratio 15:1. 242 full-time faculty, 97% hold PhDs. 100% faculty teach undergrads.

ACADEMICS

Degrees: Bachelor's, certificate, diploma, master's. **Academic Requirements:** General education including some course work in arts/fine arts, English (including composition), humanities, sciences (biological or physical), social science. **Majors with Highest Enrollment:** Computer science; biology/biological sciences, general; business administration/management. **Disciplines with Highest Percentage of Degrees Awarded:** Education 17%, business/marketing 14%, social sciences and history 12%, parks and recreation 10%, biological life sciences 7%. **Special Study Options:** Cooperative (work-study) program, distance learning, double major, student exchange program (domestic), honors program, independent study, internships, study abroad.

FACILITIES

Housing: Coed, all-female, all-male, apartments for single students, housing for disabled students. **Library Holdings:** 822,030 bound volumes. 3,369 periodicals. 406,738 microforms. 5,358 audiovisuals. **Computers:** *Recommended operating system:* Windows 95. School-owned computers available for student use.

EXTRACURRICULARS

Activities: Choral groups, concert band, dance, drama/theater, jazz band, literary magazine, music ensembles, pep band, radio station, student government, student newspaper, symphony orchestra, yearbook. **Organizations:** 60 registered organizations, 3 religious organizations. **Athletics (Intercollegiate):** *Men:* basketball, cheerleading, football, ice hockey, rugby, soccer, swimming, volleyball. *Women:* basketball, cheerleading, ice hockey, rugby, soccer, swimming, volleyball.

ADMISSIONS

Selectivity Rating: 63 (of 100). **Freshman Academic Profile:** 80% from public high schools. TOEFL required of all international applicants, minimum TOEFL 550. **Basis for Candidate Selection:** *Very important factors considered include:* secondary school record. *Important factors considered include:* recommendations, talent/ability. *Other factors considered include:* character/personal qualities, class rank, extracurricular activities, geographical residence, standardized test scores, volunteer work, work experience. **Freshman Admission Requirements:** High school diploma is required and GED is not accepted. *Academic units required/recommended:* 6 total required; 6 total recommended; 1 English required, 1 English recommended, 1 math required, 2 math recommended, 1 science recommended, 1 foreign language recommended, 1 social studies recommended, 1 history recommended, 2 elective recommended. **Transfer Admission Requirements:** *Items required:* college transcript. **General Admission Information:** Application fee $25. Priority application deadline March 15. Nonfall registration accepted. Admission may be deferred for a maximum of 1 year. Credit and/or placement offered for CEEB Advanced Placement tests.

COSTS AND FINANCIAL AID

In-state tuition $9,700. Out-of-state tuition $9,700. Room & board $5,260. Required fees $298. Average book expense $800. **Notification of Awards:** Applicants will be notified of awards on or about April 15. **Types of Aid:** *Loans:* Direct Subsidized Stafford, Direct Unsubsidized Stafford, Direct PLUS. **Student Employment:** Off-campus job opportunities are excellent. **Financial Aid Phone:** 902-585-1574.

ADAMS STATE COLLEGE

Office of Admissions, Alamosa, CO 81102
Phone: 719-587-7712 **E-mail:** ascadmit@adams.edu **CEEB Code:** 4001
Fax: 719-587-7522 **Web:** www.adams.edu **ACT Code:** 496

This public school was founded in 1921. It has a 90-acre campus.

STUDENTS AND FACULTY

Enrollment: 2,164. **Student Body:** Male 45%, female 55%, out-of-state 18%, international students represent 4 countries. **Ethnic Representation:** African American 3%, Asian 1%, Caucasian 67%, Hispanic 26%, Native American 2%. **Retention and Graduation:** 59% freshmen return for sophomore year. 14% freshmen graduate within 4 years. 21% grads go on to further study within 1 year. 7% grads pursue business degrees. 1% grads pursue law degrees. 4% grads pursue medical degrees. **Faculty:** Student/faculty ratio 19:1. 100 full-time faculty, 77% hold PhDs. 89% faculty teach undergrads.

ACADEMICS

Degrees: Associate's, bachelor's, master's. **Academic Requirements:** General education including some course work in arts/fine arts, computer literacy, English (including composition), history, humanities, mathematics, sciences (biological or physical), social science, wellness. Computer literacy is a proficiency requirement—may be met by passing a class or an examination. **Classes:** 10-19 students in an average class. Under 10 students in an average lab/discussion section. **Disciplines with Highest Percentage of Degrees Awarded:** Business/marketing 21%, parks and recreation 16%, liberal arts/general studies 15%, social sciences and history 11%, psychology 9%. **Special Study Options:** Accelerated program, distance learning, double major, honors program, independent study, internships, study abroad, teacher certification program, ACS Achieve-High School dual enrollment when admitted.

FACILITIES

Housing: Coed, all-female, all-male, apartments for married students, apartments for single students, Learning Community. **Library Holdings:** 543,625 bound volumes. 574 periodicals. 768,699 microforms. 2,119 audiovisuals. **Special Academic Facilities/Equipment:** Luther Bean Museum, Hatfield Gallery, Gallery 114, Leon Memorial Music Hall. **Computers:** School-owned computers available for student use.

EXTRACURRICULARS

Activities: Choral groups, concert band, dance, drama/theater, jazz band, literary magazine, marching band, music ensembles, musical theater, pep band, radio station, student government, student newspaper. **Organizations:** 42 registered organizations. **Athletics (Intercollegiate):** *Men:* basketball, cross-country, football, golf, indoor track, track & field, wrestling. *Women:* basketball, cross-country, indoor track, softball, track & field, volleyball.

ADMISSIONS

Selectivity Rating: 63 (of 100). **Freshman Academic Profile:** Average high school GPA 3.1. 10% in top 10% of high school class, 31% in top 25% of high school class, 63% in top 50% of high school class. Average SAT I Math 480, SAT I Math middle 50% range 430-560. Average SAT I Verbal 490, SAT I Verbal middle 50% range 440-570. Average ACT 21.5, ACT middle 50% range 18-22. TOEFL required of all international applicants, minimum TOEFL 550. **Basis for Candidate Selection:** *Very important factors considered include:* secondary school record, standardized test scores. *Other factors considered include:* character/personal qualities, class rank, essays, extracurricular activities, geographical residence, interview, recommendations, state residency. **Freshman Admission Requirements:** High school diploma or GED is required. *Academic units required/recommended:* 15 total required; 15 total recommended; 4 English recommended, 2 math recommended, 2 science recommended, 2 foreign language recommended, 3 social studies recommended, 1 history recommended, 1 computer applications recommended. **Freshman Admission Statistics:** 1,603 applied, 97% accepted, 35% of those accepted enrolled. **Transfer Admission Requirements:** *Items required:* college transcript. Minimum high school GPA of 2.0 required. Minimum college GPA of 2.0 required. Lowest grade transferable D. **General Admission Information:** Application fee $20. Regular application deadline August 1. Nonfall registration accepted. Admission may be deferred for a maximum of 2 years. Credit offered for CEEB Advanced Placement tests.

COSTS AND FINANCIAL AID

In-state tuition $1,712. Out-of-state tuition $6,752. Room & board $5,595. Required fees $892. Average book expense $840. **Required Forms and Deadlines:** FAFSA. Financial aid filing deadline April 15. Priority filing deadline March 1. **Notification of Awards:** Applicants will be notified of awards on a rolling basis beginning on or about May 15. **Types of Aid:** *Need-*

based scholarships/grants: Pell, SEOG, state scholarships/grants, private scholarships, the school's own gift aid. *Loans:* Direct Subsidized Stafford, Direct Unsubsidized Stafford, Direct PLUS, FFEL Subsidized Stafford, FFEL Unsubsidized Stafford, FFEL PLUS, Federal Perkins, college/university loans from institutional funds. **Student Employment:** Federal Work-Study Program available. Institutional employment available. Off-campus job opportunities are fair. **Financial Aid Statistics:** 58% freshmen, 59% undergrads receive some form of aid. Average freshman grant $955. Average freshman loan $2,625. Average income from on-campus job $922. **Financial Aid Phone:** 719-587-7306.

ADELPHI UNIVERSITY

Levermore Hall 114, South Avenue, Garden City, NY 11530
Phone: 516-877-3050 **E-mail:** admissions@adelphi.edu **CEEB Code:** 2003
Fax: 516-877-3039 **Web:** www.adelphi.edu **ACT Code:** 2664

This private school was founded in 1896. It has a 75-acre campus.

STUDENTS AND FACULTY

Enrollment: 3,746. **Student Body:** Male 28%, female 72%, out-of-state 9%, international 3% (63 countries represented). **Ethnic Representation:** African American 12%, Asian 4%, Caucasian 52%, Hispanic 8%. **Retention and Graduation:** 78% freshmen return for sophomore year. 41% freshmen graduate within 4 years. 58% grads go on to further study within 1 year. **Faculty:** Student/faculty ratio 15:1. 215 full-time faculty, 76% hold PhDs. 100% faculty teach undergrads.

ACADEMICS

Degrees: Associate's, bachelor's, doctoral, master's, post-bachelor's certificate, post-master's certificate, transfer. **Academic Requirements:** General education including some course work in arts/fine arts, English (including composition), humanities, mathematics, sciences (biological or physical), social science. **Classes:** 20-29 students in an average class. 10-19 students in an average lab/discussion section. **Majors with Highest Enrollment:** Business administration/management; social work; social sciences, general. **Disciplines with Highest Percentage of Degrees Awarded:** Business/marketing 24%, social sciences and history 17%, education 11%, visual and performing arts 9%, health professions and related sciences 8%. **Special Study Options:** Accelerated program, distance learning, double major, honors program, independent study, internships, liberal arts/career combination, student-designed major, study abroad, teacher certification program, weekend college, learning disabilities program; distance learning program is being restructured.

FACILITIES

Housing: Coed, housing for disabled students, housing for international students. **Library Holdings:** 631,023 bound volumes. 1,642 periodicals. 836,186 microforms. 44,191 audiovisuals. **Special Academic Facilities/ Equipment:** Art gallery, sculpture and ceramics studios, bronze-casting foundry, theatre, language labs. **Computers:** School-owned computers available for student use.

EXTRACURRICULARS

Activities: Choral groups, concert band, dance, drama/theater, jazz band, literary magazine, radio station, student government, student newspaper, student-run film society, yearbook. **Organizations:** 76 registered organizations, 19 honor societies, 4 religious organizations, 3 fraternities (4% men join), 7 sororities (5% women join). **Athletics (Intercollegiate):** *Men:* baseball, basketball, cross-country, golf, lacrosse, soccer, swimming, tennis, track & field. *Women:* basketball, cross-country, golf, lacrosse, soccer, softball, swimming, tennis, track & field, volleyball.

ADMISSIONS

Selectivity Rating: 66 (of 100). **Freshman Academic Profile:** Average high school GPA 3.3. 17% in top 10% of high school class, 41% in top 25% of high school class, 77% in top 50% of high school class. 70% from public high schools. Average SAT I Math 540, SAT I Math middle 50% range 480-590. Average SAT I Verbal 532, SAT I Verbal middle 50% range 480-580. TOEFL required of all international applicants, minimum TOEFL 550. **Basis for Candidate Selection:** *Very important factors considered include:* secondary school record. *Important factors considered include:* character/personal qualities, class rank, essays, extracurricular activities, standardized test scores, talent/ability, volunteer work. *Other factors considered include:* alumni/ae relation, interview, recommendations, work experience. **Freshman Admission Requirements:** High school diploma or GED is required. *Academic units required/recommended:* 16 total recommended; 4 English recommended, 3 math recommended, 3 science recommended, 2 foreign language recommended, 4 social studies recommended. **Freshman Admission Statistics:** 4,027 applied, 70% accepted, 24% of those accepted enrolled. **Transfer Admission Requirements:** *Items required:* college transcript. Minimum college GPA of 2.3 required. Lowest grade transferable C-. **General Admission Information:** Application fee $35. Nonfall registration accepted. Admission may be deferred for a maximum of 1 year. Credit and/or placement offered for CEEB Advanced Placement tests.

COSTS AND FINANCIAL AID

Tuition $16,200. Room & board $8,200. Required fees $780. Average book expense $1,000. **Required Forms and Deadlines:** FAFSA and state aid form. No deadline for regular filing. Priority filing deadline March 1. **Notification of Awards:** Applicants will be notified of awards on a rolling basis beginning on or about March 1. **Types of Aid:** *Need-based scholarships/grants:* Pell, SEOG, state scholarships/grants, private scholarships, the school's own gift aid, United Negro College Fund, Endowed, restricted funds (donor funds). *Loans:* FFEL Subsidized Stafford, FFEL Unsubsidized Stafford, FFEL PLUS, Federal Perkins, Federal Nursing, non-Federal (private) alternative loans. **Student Employment:** Federal Work-Study Program available. Institutional employment available. Off-campus job opportunities are good. **Financial Aid Statistics:** 92% freshmen, 89% undergrads receive some form of aid. Average freshman grant $5,440. Average freshman loan $3,720. **Financial Aid Phone:** 516-877-3080.

ADRIAN COLLEGE

110 South Madison Street, Adrian, MI 49221
Phone: 517-265-5161 **E-mail:** admissions@adrian.edu **CEEB Code:** 1001
Fax: 517-264-3331 **Web:** www.adrian.edu **ACT Code:** 1954

This private school, which is affiliated with the Methodist Church, was founded in 1859. It has a 100-acre campus.

STUDENTS AND FACULTY

Enrollment: 1,021. **Student Body:** Male 42%, female 58%, out-of-state 21%, international 2% (10 countries represented). **Ethnic Representation:** African American 4%, Asian 1%, Caucasian 77%, Hispanic 2%. **Retention and Graduation:** 67% freshmen return for sophomore year. 27% freshmen graduate within 4 years. 25% grads go on to further study within 1 year. **Faculty:** Student/faculty ratio 13:1. 66 full-time faculty, 92% hold PhDs. 100% faculty teach undergrads.

ACADEMICS

Degrees: Associate's, bachelor's, transfer. **Academic Requirements:** General education including some course work in arts/fine arts, English (including composition), foreign languages, history, humanities, mathematics, philosophy, sciences (biological or physical), social science, one nonwestern perspectives, one religion or philosophy. **Classes:** 10-19 students in an average class. 10-19 students in an average lab/discussion section. **Majors with Highest Enrollment:** Business administration/management; English language and literature, general; art/art studies, general. **Disciplines with Highest Percentage of Degrees Awarded:** Business/marketing 22%, visual and performing arts 16%, social sciences and history 15%, parks and recreation 8%, English 8%. **Special Study Options:** Cooperative (work-study) program, double major, dual enrollment, English as a second language, student exchange program (domestic), honors program, independent study, internships, liberal arts/career combination, student-designed major, study abroad, teacher certification program.

FACILITIES

Housing: Coed, housing for disabled students, fraternities and/or sororities. **Library Holdings:** 143,484 bound volumes. 610 periodicals. 47,028 microforms. 1,178 audiovisuals. **Special Academic Facilities/Equipment:** Art gallery, studio theatre, arboretum, education resource center, language lab, observatory, planetarium, solar greenhouse, nuclear magnetic resonance spectrometer, differential scanning calorimeter. **Computers:** School-owned computers available for student use.

EXTRACURRICULARS

Activities: Choral groups, concert band, dance, drama/theater, jazz band, literary magazine, music ensembles, musical theater, radio station, student government, student newspaper, symphony orchestra. **Organizations:** 65 registered organizations, 13 honor societies, 8 religious organizations, 4 fraternities (29% men join), 3 sororities (29% women join). **Athletics (Intercollegiate):** *Men:* baseball, basketball, cross-country, football, golf, indoor track, soccer, tennis, track & field. *Women:* basketball, cross-country, golf, indoor track, soccer, softball, tennis, track & field, volleyball.

ADMISSIONS

Selectivity Rating: 79 (of 100). **Freshman Academic Profile:** Average high school GPA 3.3. 16% in top 10% of high school class, 44% in top 25% of high school class, 78% in top 50% of high school class. Average ACT 22, ACT middle 50% range 19-23. TOEFL required of all international applicants, minimum TOEFL 475. **Basis for Candidate Selection:** *Very important factors considered include:* secondary school record. *Important factors considered include:* extracurricular activities, standardized test scores, talent/ability, volunteer work. *Other factors considered include:* character/personal qualities, class rank, interview, work experience. **Freshman Admission Requirements:** High school diploma or GED is required. *Academic units required/recommended:* 4 English recommended, 2 math recommended, 2 science recommended, 1 science lab recommended, 2 foreign language recommended, 1 social studies recommended, 1 history recommended, 3 elective recommended. **Freshman Admission Statistics:** 1,456 applied, 88% accepted, 24% of those accepted enrolled. **Transfer Admission Requirements:** *Items required:* high school transcript, college transcript. Lowest grade transferable C. **General Admission Information:** Application fee $20. Priority application deadline March 15. Regular application deadline August 1. Admission may be deferred for a maximum of 1 year. Credit and/or placement offered for CEEB Advanced Placement tests.

COSTS AND FINANCIAL AID

Tuition $15,560. Room & board $5,440. Required fees $100. Average book expense $400. **Required Forms and Deadlines:** FAFSA. Financial aid filing deadline March 1. Priority filing deadline March 1. **Notification of Awards:** Applicants will be notified of awards on a rolling basis beginning on or about March 15. **Types of Aid:** *Need-based scholarships/grants:* Pell, SEOG, state scholarships/grants, private scholarships, the school's own gift aid. *Loans:* FFEL Subsidized Stafford, FFEL Unsubsidized Stafford, FFEL PLUS, Federal Perkins. **Student Employment:** Federal Work-Study Program available. Institutional employment available. Off-campus job opportunities are good. **Financial Aid Statistics:** 84% freshmen, 76% undergrads receive some form of aid. Average freshman grant $9,665. Average freshman loan $3,625. Average income from on-campus job $1,500. **Financial Aid Phone:** 517-265-5161.

AGNES SCOTT COLLEGE

141 East College Avenue, Atlanta/Decatur, GA 30030-3797
Phone: 404-471-6285 **E-mail:** admission@agnesscott.edu **CEEB Code:** 5002
Fax: 404-471-6414 **Web:** www.agnesscott.edu **ACT Code:** 780

This private school, which is affiliated with the Presbyterian Church, was founded in 1889. It has a 100-acre campus.

STUDENTS AND FACULTY

Enrollment: 869. **Student Body:** Out-of-state 45%, international 5% (46 countries represented). **Ethnic Representation:** African American 22%, Asian 6%, Caucasian 62%, Hispanic 3%. **Retention and Graduation:** 82% freshmen return for sophomore year. 69% freshmen graduate within 4 years. 53% grads go on to further study within 1 year. 5% grads pursue law degrees. 3% grads pursue medical degrees. **Faculty:** Student/faculty ratio 10:1. 80 full-time faculty, 95% hold PhDs. 100% faculty teach undergrads.

ACADEMICS

Degrees: Bachelor's, master's, post-bachelor's certificate. **Academic Requirements:** General education including some course work in arts/fine arts, English (including composition), foreign languages, history, mathematics, philosophy, sciences (biological or physical), social science, literature, PE, social and cultural analysis, philosophy or religious studies. **Classes:** 10-19 students in an average class. 10-19 students in an average lab/discussion section. **Majors with Highest Enrollment:** English language and literature, general; biology/biological sciences, general; psychology, general. **Disciplines with Highest Percentage of Degrees Awarded:** Social sciences and history 32%, psychology 14%, biological life sciences 11%, English 10%, foreign languages and literature 9%. **Special Study Options:** Accelerated program, cross registration, double major, dual enrollment, student exchange program (domestic), independent study, internships, student-designed major, study abroad, teacher certification program, PLEN Public Policy Semester, Atlanta Semester, Woodruff Scholars Program for women beyond traditional college age, exchange program with 123 institutions in 33 countries.

FACILITIES

Housing: All-female, apartments for single students, theme houses, limited number of college-owned housing available for nontraditional-age students. **Library Holdings:** 171,891 bound volumes. 1,118 periodicals. 32,357 microforms. 17,828 audiovisuals. **Special Academic Facilities/Equipment:** Art galleries, state-of the art science building opened in January 2003, collaborative learning centers, language lab, electron microscope, observatory, 30-inch Beck telescope, planetarium, interactive learning center, multimedia presentation classrooms, instructional technology center, multimedia production facility. **Computers:** School-owned computers available for student use.

EXTRACURRICULARS

Activities: Choral groups, dance, drama/theater, jazz band, literary magazine, marching band, music ensembles, musical theater, student government, student newspaper, symphony orchestra, yearbook. **Organizations:** 60 registered organizations, 11 honor societies, 8 religious organizations. **Athletics (Intercollegiate):** *Women:* basketball, cross-country, soccer, softball, swimming, tennis, volleyball.

ADMISSIONS

Selectivity Rating: 80 (of 100). **Freshman Academic Profile:** Average high school GPA 3.7. 44% in top 10% of high school class, 70% in top 25% of high school class, 95% in top 50% of high school class. 76% from public high schools. Average SAT I Math 590, SAT I Math middle 50% range 540-650. Average SAT I Verbal 620, SAT I Verbal middle 50% range 570-680. Average ACT 26, ACT middle 50% range 23-29. TOEFL required of all international applicants, minimum TOEFL 577. **Basis for Candidate Selection:** *Very important factors considered include:* character/personal qualities, class rank, essays, recommendations, secondary school record, standardized test scores, talent/ability. *Important factors considered include:* extracurricular activities, volunteer work, work experience. *Other factors considered include:* alumni/ae relation, geographical residence, interview, minority status, state residency. **Freshman Admission Requirements:** High school diploma or GED is required. *Academic units required/recommended:* 16 total recommended; 4 English recommended, 3 math recommended, 2 science recommended, 2 science lab recommended, 2 foreign language recommended, 2 social studies recommended. **Freshman Admission Statistics:** 743 applied, 73% accepted, 43% of those accepted enrolled. **Transfer Admission Requirements:** *Items required:* high school transcript, college transcript, essay, standardized test score, statement of good standing from prior school. Minimum college GPA of 3.0 required. Lowest grade transferable C. **General Admission Information:** Application fee $35. Early decision application deadline November 15. Regular application deadline March 1. Nonfall registration accepted. Admission may be deferred for a maximum of 1 year. Credit and/or placement offered for CEEB Advanced Placement tests.

COSTS AND FINANCIAL AID

Tuition $18,850. Room & board $7,500. Required fees $150. Average book expense $700. **Required Forms and Deadlines:** FAFSA, institution's own financial aid form, state aid form, noncustodial (divorced/separated) parent's statement, business/farm supplement, and CSS PROFILE required of Early Decision applicants. Financial aid filing deadline May 1. Priority filing deadline February 15. **Notification of Awards:** Applicants will be notified of awards on a rolling basis beginning on or about March 1. **Types of Aid:** *Need-based scholarships/grants:* Pell, SEOG, state scholarships/grants, private scholarships, the school's own gift aid, Achiever. *Loans:* FFEL Subsidized Stafford, FFEL Unsubsidized Stafford, FFEL PLUS, college/university loans from institutional funds, Achiever. **Student Employment:** Federal Work-Study Program available. Institutional employment available. Off-campus job opportunities are excellent. **Financial Aid Statistics:** 73% freshmen, 67% undergrads receive some form of aid. Average freshman grant $14,757. Average freshman loan $2,459. Average income from on-campus job $1,500. **Financial Aid Phone:** 404-471-6395.

ALABAMA A&M UNIVERSITY

PO Box 908, Normal, AL 35762
Phone: 256-851-5245 **E-mail:** aboyle@asnaam.aamu.edu **CEEB Code:** 1003
Fax: 256-851-5249 **Web:** www.aamu.edu **ACT Code:** 2

This public school was founded in 1875. It has an 880-acre campus.

STUDENTS AND FACULTY

Enrollment: 4,744. **Student Body:** Male 48%, female 52%, international 4% (42 countries represented). **Ethnic Representation:** African American 95%, Caucasian 4%. **Retention and Graduation:** 71% freshmen return for sophomore year. 21% freshmen graduate within 4 years. 77% grads go on to further study within 1 year. 45% grads pursue business degrees. 2% grads pursue law degrees. 11% grads pursue medical degrees. **Faculty:** 95% faculty teach undergrads.

ACADEMICS

Degrees: Bachelor's, doctoral, master's, post-master's certificate. **Academic Requirements:** General education including some course work in arts/fine arts, computer literacy, English (including composition), foreign languages, history, humanities, mathematics, sciences (biological or physical), social science. **Special Study Options:** Cooperative (work-study) program, distance learning, honors program, independent study, study abroad, teacher certification program, weekend college.

FACILITIES

Housing: All-female, all-male. **Library Holdings:** 219,230 bound volumes. 2,439 periodicals. 633,077 microforms. 32,617 audiovisuals. **Special Academic Facilities/Equipment:** State Black Archives. **Computers:** *Recommended operating system:* UNIX. School-owned computers available for student use.

EXTRACURRICULARS

Activities: Choral groups, concert band, jazz band, literary magazine, marching band, radio station, student government, student newspaper, symphony orchestra, television station, yearbook. **Organizations:** 76 registered organizations, 14 honor societies, 3 religious organizations, 4 fraternities, 4 sororities. **Athletics (Intercollegiate):** *Men:* baseball, basketball, cross-country, football, golf, soccer, track & field. *Women:* basketball, cross-country, soccer, softball, track & field, volleyball.

ADMISSIONS

Selectivity Rating: 70 (of 100). **Freshman Academic Profile:** 90% from public high schools. Average ACT 17. TOEFL required of all international applicants, minimum TOEFL 550. **Basis for Candidate Selection:** *Very important factors considered include:* alumni/ae relation, geographical residence, standardized test scores, state residency. *Important factors considered include:* minority status. *Other factors considered include:* class rank, recommendations. **Freshman Admission Requirements:** High school diploma or GED is required. *Academic units required/recommended:* 4 English required, 3 math required, 4 science required, 2 science lab required, 2 foreign language required, 4 social studies required, 4 history required. **Freshman Admission Statistics:** 4,676 applied, 56% accepted, 55% of those accepted enrolled. **Transfer Admission Requirements:** *Items required:* high school transcript, college transcript, standardized test scores. Minimum high school GPA of 2.5 required. Minimum college GPA of 2.5 required. Lowest grade transferable C. **General Admission Information:** Application fee $10. Priority application deadline April 1. Regular application deadline July 1. Nonfall registration accepted. Admission may be deferred for a maximum of 1 year. Neither credit nor placement offered for CEEB Advanced Placement tests.

COSTS AND FINANCIAL AID

Average book expense $600. **Required Forms and Deadlines:** FAFSA and institution's own financial aid form. Priority filing deadline April 15. **Notification of Awards:** Applicants will be notified of awards on a rolling basis. **Types of Aid:** *Need-based scholarships/grants:* Pell, SEOG, state scholarships/grants, private scholarships, the school's own gift aid, United Negro College Fund. *Loans:* Direct Subsidized Stafford, Direct Unsubsidized Stafford, Direct PLUS, Federal Perkins, state loans, college/university loans from institutional funds. **Student Employment:** Federal Work-Study Program available. Institutional employment available. Off-campus job opportunities are good. **Financial Aid Statistics:** Average freshman grant $2,100. Average freshman loan $800. Average income from on-campus job $5,400. **Financial Aid Phone:** 256-851-4862.

ALABAMA STATE UNIVERSITY

915 South Jackson Street, Montgomery, AL 36104
Phone: 334-229-4291 **E-mail:** dlamar@asunet.alasu.edu
Fax: 334-229-4984 **Web:** www.alasu.edu **ACT Code:** 8

This public school was founded in 1867.

STUDENTS AND FACULTY

Enrollment: 5,125. **Student Body:** Male 41%, female 59%, out-of-state 27%. **Ethnic Representation:** African American 95%, Caucasian 4%. **Retention and Graduation:** 68% freshmen return for sophomore year. 50% grads go on to further study within 1 year. **Faculty:** Student/faculty ratio 19:1. 229 full-time faculty, 58% hold PhDs.

ACADEMICS

Degrees: Bachelor's, master's. **Academic Requirements:** General education including some course work in arts/fine arts, computer literacy, English (including composition), history, humanities, mathematics, sciences (biological or physical), social science. **Majors with Highest Enrollment:** Elementary education and teaching; criminal justice/safety studies; computer and information sciences, general. **Disciplines with Highest Percentage of Degrees Awarded:** Education 27%, business/marketing 14%, protective services/public administration 14%, computer and information sciences 11%, biological life sciences 10%. **Special Study Options:** Cooperative (work-study) program, cross registration, double major, honors program, internships, teacher certification program.

FACILITIES

Housing: All-female, all-male, apartments for single students, honor dorms. **Library Holdings:** 399,212 bound volumes. 1,308 periodicals. 2,588,453 microforms. 42,319 audiovisuals. **Special Academic Facilities/Equipment:** Levi Watkins Learning Center Special Collections. **Computers:** School-owned computers available for student use.

EXTRACURRICULARS

Activities: Choral groups, concert band, dance, drama/theater, jazz band, marching band, music ensembles, musical theater, pep band, radio station, student government, student newspaper, symphony orchestra, yearbook. **Organizations:** 64 registered organizations, 17 honor societies, 5 fraternities (8% men join), 4 sororities (6% women join). **Athletics (Intercollegiate):** *Men:* baseball, basketball, cheerleading, cross-country, football, golf, indoor track, tennis, track & field. *Women:* basketball, cheerleading, cross-country, golf, indoor track, softball, tennis, track & field, volleyball.

ADMISSIONS

Selectivity Rating: 63 (of 100). **Freshman Academic Profile:** Average high school GPA 2.6. Average SAT I Math 410, SAT I Math middle 50% range 330-440. Average SAT I Verbal 407, SAT I Verbal middle 50% range 340-440. Average ACT 16, ACT middle 50% range 14-17. TOEFL required of all international applicants, minimum TOEFL 500. **Basis for Candidate Selection:** *Very important factors considered include:* secondary school record. *Important factors considered include:* class rank, standardized test scores. *Other factors considered include:* recommendations. **Freshman Admission Requirements:** High school diploma or GED is required. *Academic units required/recommended:* 11 total recommended; 3 English recommended, 2 math recommended, 2 science recommended, 2 foreign language recommended, 2 social studies recommended. **Freshman Admission Statistics:** 8,148 applied, 41% accepted, 41% of those accepted enrolled. **Transfer Admission Requirements:** *Items required:* college transcript. Minimum high school GPA of 2.0 required. Minimum college GPA of 2.0 required. Lowest grade transferable C. **General Admission Information:** Priority application deadline February 28. Regular application deadline July 30. Nonfall registration accepted. Admission may be deferred. Credit and/or placement offered for CEEB Advanced Placement tests.

COSTS AND FINANCIAL AID

In-state tuition $2,904. Out-of-state tuition $5,808. Room & board $3,700. Required fees $0. Average book expense $800. **Required Forms and Deadlines:** FAFSA and state aid form. No deadline for regular filing. Priority filing deadline May 1. **Notification of Awards:** Applicants will be notified of awards on a rolling basis beginning on or about May 15. **Types of Aid:** *Need-based scholarships/grants:* Pell, SEOG, state scholarships/grants, private scholarships, the school's own gift aid. *Loans:* FFEL Subsidized Stafford, FFEL Unsubsidized Stafford, FFEL PLUS, Federal Perkins. **Student Employment:** Federal Work-Study Program available. Institutional employment available. Off-campus job opportunities are good. **Financial Aid Statistics:** 82% freshmen, 82% undergrads receive some form of aid. Average freshman grant $2,364. Average freshman loan $4,466. Average income from on-campus job $2,400. **Financial Aid Phone:** 334-229-4862.

ALASKA PACIFIC UNIVERSITY

4101 University Drive, Anchorage, AK 99508
Phone: 907-564-8248 **E-mail:** rfi@alaskapacific.edu
Fax: 907-562-4276 **Web:** www.alaskapacific.edu

This private school was founded in 1957. It has a 170-acre campus.

STUDENTS AND FACULTY

Enrollment: 478. **Student Body:** Male 30%, female 70%, out-of-state 25%, international 1%. **Ethnic Representation:** African American 5%, Asian 4%, Caucasian 65%, Hispanic 4%, Native American 19%. **Retention and Graduation:** 70% freshmen return for sophomore year. 24% freshmen graduate within 4 years. **Faculty:** Student/faculty ratio 8:1. 28 full-time faculty, 85% hold PhDs. 99% faculty teach undergrads.

ACADEMICS

Degrees: Associate's, bachelor's, certificate, master's. **Academic Requirements:** General education including some course work in English (including composition), foreign languages, humanities, mathematics, sciences (biological or physical), social science, ethics and/or religion. **Classes:** Under 10 students in an average class. 30-39 students in an average lab/discussion section. **Majors with Highest Enrollment:** Business administration/management; environmental science; elementary education and teaching. **Disciplines with Highest Percentage of Degrees Awarded:** Business/marketing 31%, protective services/public administration 11%, natural resources/environmental sciences 8%, education 7%, psychology 7%. **Special Study Options:** Distance learning, double major, independent study, internships, student-designed major, study abroad, teacher certification program.

FACILITIES

Housing: Coed, cooperative housing. **Library Holdings:** 1,172,669 bound volumes. 3,514 periodicals. 521,872 microforms. 8,847 audiovisuals. **Special Academic Facilities/Equipment:** Alaskana collection, GIS lab, climbing wall. **Computers:** School-owned computers available for student use.

EXTRACURRICULARS

Activities: Drama/theater, literary magazine, music ensembles, student government, student newspaper, yearbook. **Organizations:** 15 registered organizations, 1 religious organization. **Athletics (Intercollegiate):** *Women:* skiing (Nordic).

ADMISSIONS

Selectivity Rating: 66 (of 100). **Freshman Academic Profile:** Average high school GPA 3.1. Average SAT I Math 502, SAT I Math middle 50% range 500-530. Average SAT I Verbal 547, SAT I Verbal middle 50% range 520-610. Average ACT 20, ACT middle 50% range 18-23. TOEFL required of all international applicants, minimum TOEFL 550. **Basis for Candidate Selection:** *Important factors considered include:* standardized test scores. *Other factors considered include:* alumni/ae relation, character/personal qualities, class rank, essays, extracurricular activities, geographical residence, interview, recommendations, state residency, talent/ability, volunteer work, work experience. **Freshman Admission Requirements:** High school diploma or GED is required. *Academic units required/recommended:* 4 English recommended, 3 math recommended, 2 science recommended, 1 science lab recommended, 2 foreign language recommended, 1 social studies recommended, 1 history recommended. **Freshman Admission Statistics:** 109 applied, 94% accepted, 23% of those accepted enrolled. **Transfer Admission Requirements:** *Items required:* college transcript, essay, statement of good standing from prior school. Minimum college GPA of 2.0 required. Lowest grade transferable C. **General Admission Information:** Application fee $25. Priority application deadline December 1. Early decision application deadline December 1. Regular application deadline February 1. Nonfall registration accepted. Admission may be deferred for a maximum of 1 year. Credit offered for CEEB Advanced Placement tests.

COSTS AND FINANCIAL AID

Tuition $14,400. Room & board $5,600. Required fees $80. Average book expense $1,200. **Required Forms and Deadlines:** FAFSA. No deadline for regular filing. Priority filing deadline April 15. **Notification of Awards:** Applicants will be notified of awards on a rolling basis beginning on or about April 15. **Types of Aid:** *Need-based scholarships/grants:* Pell, SEOG, state scholarships/grants, private scholarships, the school's own gift aid. *Loans:* Direct Subsidized Stafford, Direct Unsubsidized Stafford, Direct PLUS, state loans, college/university loans from institutional funds. **Student Employment:** Federal Work-Study Program available. Institutional employment available. Off-campus job opportunities are good. **Financial Aid Statistics:** 80% freshmen, 59% undergrads receive some form of aid. **Financial Aid Phone:** 907-564-8341.

ALBANY COLLEGE OF PHARMACY

106 New Scotland Avenue, Albany, NY 12208
Phone: 518-445-7221 **E-mail:** admissions@acp.edu **CEEB Code:** 2013
Fax: 518-445-7202 **Web:** www.acp.edu **ACT Code:** 2672

This private school was founded in 1881. It has a 1-acre campus.

STUDENTS AND FACULTY

Enrollment: 632. **Student Body:** Out-of-state 11%, international 3% (6 countries represented). **Ethnic Representation:** African American 2%, Asian 7%, Caucasian 89%, Hispanic 1%. **Retention and Graduation:** 12% grads go on to further study within 1 year. **Faculty:** Student/faculty ratio 14:1. 57 full-time faculty, 72% hold PhDs. 100% faculty teach undergrads.

ACADEMICS

Degrees: Bachelor's, first professional. **Academic Requirements:** General education including some course work in English (including composition), humanities, mathematics, sciences (biological or physical). **Classes:** 20-29 students in an average class. 30-39 students in an average lab/discussion section. **Disciplines with Highest Percentage of Degrees Awarded:** Health professions and related sciences 100%. **Special Study Options:** Accelerated program, cross registration, independent study, internships.

FACILITIES

Housing: Coed, apartments for single students, housing for disabled students. **Library Holdings:** 12,314 bound volumes. 1,399 periodicals. 28,388 microforms. 2,676 audiovisuals. **Special Academic Facilities/Equipment:** Pharmaceutical museum. **Computers:** *Recommended operating system:* Windows 95. School-owned computers available for student use.

EXTRACURRICULARS

Activities: Literary magazine, student government, student newspaper, yearbook. **Organizations:** 7 registered organizations, 1 honor society, 3 fraternities, 1 sorority. **Athletics (Intercollegiate):** *Men:* basketball, soccer. *Women:* basketball, soccer.

ADMISSIONS

Selectivity Rating: 89 (of 100). **Freshman Academic Profile:** Average high school GPA 3.4. 48% in top 10% of high school class, 77% in top 25% of high school class, 99% in top 50% of high school class. 80% from public high schools. Average SAT I Math 590. Average SAT I Verbal 550. TOEFL required of all international applicants, minimum TOEFL 600. **Basis for Candidate Selection:** *Very important factors considered include:* secondary school record. *Other factors considered include:* alumni/ae relation, class rank, essays, extracurricular activities, minority status, recommendations, standardized test scores, work experience. **Freshman Admission Requirements:** High school diploma or GED is required. *Academic units required/recommended:* 17 total required; 4 English required, 4 math required, 3 science required, 6 elective required. **Freshman Admission Statistics:** 498 applied, 61% accepted, 56% of those accepted enrolled. **Transfer Admission Requirements:** *Items required:* high school transcript, college transcript, essay, standardized test scores. Minimum college GPA of 3.2 required. Lowest grade transferable C. **General Admission Information:** Application fee $50. Priority application deadline February 1. Credit offered for CEEB Advanced Placement tests.

COSTS AND FINANCIAL AID

Tuition $14,700. Room & board $5,250. Required fees $242. Average book expense $700. **Required Forms and Deadlines:** FAFSA. No deadline for regular filing. Priority filing deadline February 1. **Notification of Awards:** Applicants will be notified of awards on or about April 1. **Types of Aid:** *Need-based scholarships/grants:* state scholarships/grants, the school's own gift aid. *Loans:* Direct Subsidized Stafford, Direct Unsubsidized Stafford, Direct PLUS, FFEL Subsidized Stafford, FFEL PLUS, Federal Perkins, college/university loans from institutional funds. **Student Employment:** Federal Work-Study Program available. Institutional employment available. Off-campus job opportunities are good. **Financial Aid Phone:** 518-445-7256.

ALBANY STATE UNIVERSITY

504 College Drive, Albany, GA 31705
Phone: 229-430-4646 **E-mail:** fsuttles@asurams.edu **CEEB Code:** 5004
Fax: 229-430-3936 **Web:** www.asurams.edu **ACT Code:** 782

This public school was founded in 1903. It has a 206-acre campus.

STUDENTS AND FACULTY

Enrollment: 3,015. **Student Body:** Male 33%, female 67%, international 4%. **Ethnic Representation:** African American 95%, Caucasian 5%, Hispanic 1%. **Retention and Graduation:** 84% freshmen return for sophomore year. 7% freshmen graduate within 4 years. **Faculty:** Student/faculty ratio 20:1. 40% faculty teach undergrads.

ACADEMICS

Degrees: Bachelor's, master's, post-master's certificate. **Academic Requirements:** General education including some course work in arts/fine arts, computer literacy, sciences (biological or physical), social science. **Majors with Highest Enrollment:** Criminal justice/safety studies; business administration/management; nursing/registered nurse training (RN, ASN, BSN, MSN). **Disciplines with Highest Percentage of Degrees Awarded:** Education 20%, business/marketing 17%, protective services/public administration 17%, health professions and related sciences 14%, social sciences and history 12%.

Special Study Options: Distance learning, dual enrollment, honors program, internships, weekend college.

FACILITIES

Housing: All-female, all-male, housing for disabled students. **Library Holdings:** 169,150 bound volumes. 617 periodicals. 691,524 microforms. 2,637 audiovisuals. **Computers:** *Recommended operating system:* UNIX. School-owned computers available for student use.

EXTRACURRICULARS

Activities: Choral groups, concert band, dance, drama/theater, jazz band, marching band, music ensembles, pep band, student government, student newspaper, student-run film society, yearbook. **Organizations:** 47 registered organizations, 5 honor societies, 4 religious organizations, 3 fraternities, 3 sororities. **Athletics (Intercollegiate):** *Men:* baseball, basketball, cross-country, football, track & field. *Women:* basketball, cross-country, softball, tennis, track & field, volleyball.

ADMISSIONS

Selectivity Rating: 63 (of 100). **Freshman Academic Profile:** Average high school GPA 2.6. 4% in top 10% of high school class, 11% in top 25% of high school class, 27% in top 50% of high school class. Average SAT I Math 450. Average SAT I Verbal 450. Average ACT 17. TOEFL required of all international applicants, minimum TOEFL 523. **Basis for Candidate Selection:** *Very important factors considered include:* secondary school record, standardized test scores. **Freshman Admission Requirements:** High school diploma or GED is required. *Academic units required/recommended:* 16 total required; 4 English required, 4 math required, 3 science lab required, 2 foreign language required, 1 social studies required, 2 history required. **Freshman Admission Statistics:** 2,233 applied, 57% accepted, 50% of those accepted enrolled. **Transfer Admission Requirements:** *Items required:* college transcript, statement of good standing from prior school. Minimum high school GPA of 2.0 required. Minimum college GPA of 2.0 required. Lowest grade transferable C. **General Admission Information:** Application fee $20. Priority application deadline July 1. Regular application deadline July 1. Nonfall registration accepted. Admission may be deferred for a maximum of 1 year. Credit and/or placement offered for CEEB Advanced Placement tests.

COSTS AND FINANCIAL AID

Required Forms and Deadlines: FAFSA and institution's own financial aid form. **Notification of Awards:** Applicants will be notified of awards on a rolling basis. **Types of Aid:** *Need-based scholarships/grants:* Pell, SEOG, state scholarships/grants, private scholarships, the school's own gift aid, Federal Nursing, Thurgood Marshall Scholarship. **Student Employment:** Federal Work-Study Program available. Off-campus job opportunities are good. **Financial Aid Phone:** 229-430-4650.

ALBERT A. LIST COLLEGE OF JEWISH STUDIES AT JEWISH THEOLOGICAL SEMINARY

3080 Broadway, Box 32, New York, NY 10027
Phone: 212-678-8832 **E-mail:** lcadmissions@jtsa.edu **CEEB Code:** 2339
Fax: 212-678-8947 **Web:** www.jtsa.edu **ACT Code:** 2776

This private school, which is affiliated with the Jewish faith, was founded in 1886. It has a 1-acre campus.

STUDENTS AND FACULTY

Enrollment: 435. **Student Body:** Male 45%, female 55%, out-of-state 75%, international students represent 5 countries. **Faculty:** 70% faculty teach undergrads.

ACADEMICS

Degrees: Bachelor's, doctoral, first professional, master's. **Academic Requirements:** General education including some course work in arts/fine arts, English (including composition), foreign languages, history, humanities, mathematics, philosophy, sciences (biological or physical), social science. **Majors with Highest Enrollment:** Jewish/Judaic studies; philosophy and religion; Bible/biblical studies. **Disciplines with Highest Percentage of Degrees Awarded:** Philosophy/religion/theology 100%. **Special Study Options:** Accelerated program, cross registration, distance learning, dual enrollment, honors program, independent study, internships, student-designed major, study abroad.

FACILITIES

Housing: Coed, apartments for married students, apartments for single students, fraternities and/or sororities. **Special Academic Facilities/Equipment:** The Jewish Museum and the rare book room of the library.

EXTRACURRICULARS

Activities: Choral groups, concert band, dance, drama/theater, jazz band, literary magazine, music ensembles, musical theater, radio station, student government, student newspaper, yearbook. **Organizations:** 6 honor societies, 8 religious organizations, 10% men join fraternities, 10% women join sororities. **Athletics (Intercollegiate):** *Men:* baseball, basketball, crew, soccer, tennis, track & field, volleyball. *Women:* baseball, basketball, crew, soccer, tennis, track & field, volleyball.

ADMISSIONS

Selectivity Rating: 60 (of 100). **Freshman Academic Profile:** Average high school GPA 3.8. 100% in top 50% of high school class. 73% from public high schools. Average SAT I Math 659. Average SAT I Verbal 689. Average ACT 29. TOEFL required of all international applicants, minimum TOEFL 600. **Basis for Candidate Selection:** *Very important factors considered include:* essays, interview, secondary school record, standardized test scores. *Important factors considered include:* character/personal qualities, recommendations, talent/ability. *Other factors considered include:* alumni/ae relation, class rank, extracurricular activities, geographical residence, volunteer work, work experience. **Freshman Admission Requirements:** High school diploma or GED is required. *Academic units required/recommended:* 4 English recommended, 3 math recommended, 3 science recommended, 3 foreign language recommended, 3 social studies recommended, 3 history recommended, 3 elective recommended. **Freshman Admission Statistics:** 135 applied, 53% accepted, 71% of those accepted enrolled. **Transfer Admission Requirements:** *Items required:* high school transcript, college transcript, essay, standardized test scores. **General Admission Information:** Application fee $65. Early decision application deadline November 15. Regular application deadline February 15. Nonfall registration accepted. Admission may be deferred for a maximum of 1 year. Credit and/or placement offered for CEEB Advanced Placement tests.

COSTS AND FINANCIAL AID

Tuition $8,320. Room & board $6,450. Required fees $170. Average book expense $700. **Required Forms and Deadlines:** FAFSA, institution's own financial aid form, and CSS/Financial Aid PROFILE. Financial aid filing deadline March 1. Priority filing deadline March 1. **Notification of Awards:** Applicants will be notified of awards on a rolling basis beginning on or about March 15. **Types of Aid:** *Loans:* Direct Subsidized Stafford, Direct Unsubsidized Stafford, college/university loans from institutional funds. **Student Employment:** Federal Work-Study Program available. Institutional employment available. Off-campus job opportunities are excellent. **Financial Aid Phone:** 212-678-8007.

ALBERTA COLLEGE OF ART & DESIGN

1407 14 Avenue NW, Calgary, AB T2N 4R3
Phone: 403-284-7678 **E-mail:** admissions@acad.ab.ca
Fax: 403-284-7644 **Web:** www.acad.ab.ca

This public school was founded in 1926.

STUDENTS AND FACULTY

Enrollment: 955. **Faculty:** 100% faculty teach undergrads.

ACADEMICS

Degrees: Bachelor's, diploma. **Academic Requirements:** General education including some course work in arts/fine arts, English (including composition), humanities, social science. **Majors with Highest Enrollment:** Drawing; painting; sculpture. **Special Study Options:** Cross registration, honors program, study abroad.

FACILITIES

Housing: Assisted off-campus housing search. **Library Holdings:** 24,000 bound volumes. 85 periodicals. **Special Academic Facilities/Equipment:** 2 art galleries. **Computers:** School-owned computers available for student use.

EXTRACURRICULARS

Activities: Student government. **Athletics (Intercollegiate):** *Men:* basketball, ice hockey, volleyball. *Women:* basketball, volleyball.

ADMISSIONS

Selectivity Rating: 60 (of 100). **Freshman Academic Profile:** TOEFL required of all international applicants, minimum TOEFL 560. **Basis for Candidate Selection:** *Very important factors considered include:* talent/ability. *Other factors considered include:* character/personal qualities, class rank, essays, extracurricular activities, recommendations, secondary school record, standardized test scores, work experience. **Freshman Admission Requirements:** High school diploma is required and GED is not accepted. *Academic units required/recommended:* 4 English required, 4 social studies required. **Transfer Admission Requirements:** *Items required:* college transcript, essay. **General Admission Information:** Application fee $25. Early decision application deadline March 1. Regular application deadline April 1.

COSTS AND FINANCIAL AID

In-state tuition $9,133. Out-of-state tuition $9,133. Room & board $10,200. Required fees $433. Average book expense $2,200. **Required Forms and Deadlines:** FAFSA. **Student Employment:** Off-campus job opportunities are good. **Financial Aid Phone:** 403-284-7685.

ALBERTSON COLLEGE OF IDAHO

2112 Cleveland Boulevard, Caldwell, ID 83605
Phone: 208-459-5305 **E-mail:** admission@albertson.edu **CEEB Code:** 4060
Fax: 208-459-5757 **Web:** www.albertson.edu **ACT Code:** 916

This private school was founded in 1891. It has a 43-acre campus.

STUDENTS AND FACULTY

Enrollment: 841. **Student Body:** Male 45%, female 55%, out-of-state 25%, international 2%. **Ethnic Representation:** Asian 4%, Caucasian 80%, Hispanic 5%, Native American 1%. **Retention and Graduation:** 76% freshmen return for sophomore year. 47% freshmen graduate within 4 years. **Faculty:** Student/faculty ratio 10:1. 71 full-time faculty, 92% hold PhDs. 100% faculty teach undergrads.

ACADEMICS

Degrees: Bachelor's, master's. **Academic Requirements:** General education including some course work in arts/fine arts, English (including composition), history, humanities, mathematics, philosophy, sciences (biological or physical), social science, personal fitness, religion. **Classes:** Under 10 students in an average class. **Majors with Highest Enrollment:** Business administration/management; biology/biological sciences, general; psychology, general. **Disciplines with Highest Percentage of Degrees Awarded:** Social sciences and history 19%, business/marketing 17%, biological life sciences 16%, psychology 10%, visual and performing arts 8%. **Special Study Options:** Cross registration, double major, dual enrollment, student exchange program (domestic), honors program, independent study, internships, liberal arts/career combination, student-designed major, study abroad, teacher certification program.

FACILITIES

Housing: Coed, all-female, apartment-style dormitories; honors residence available for students with superior academic records. Freshmen and sophomores under age 21 must live on campus unless living with parents or relatives. **Library Holdings:** 183,308 bound volumes. 703 periodicals. 17,000 microforms. 1,717 audiovisuals. **Special Academic Facilities/Equipment:** Art and natural history museums, gem and mineral collections, observatory, planetarium, nuclear magnetic resonance spectrometer, gas chromatograph, gamma camera, graphic computer, art gallery. **Computers:** *Recommended operating system:* Windows NT/2000. School-owned computers available for student use.

EXTRACURRICULARS

Activities: Choral groups, concert band, dance, drama/theater, jazz band, literary magazine, music ensembles, musical theater, opera, pep band, radio station, student government, student newspaper, student-run film society, symphony orchestra, yearbook. **Organizations:** 60 registered organizations, 4 honor societies, 3 religious organizations, 3 fraternities (20% men join), 4 sororities (15% women join). **Athletics (Intercollegiate):** *Men:* baseball, basketball, golf, skiing (alpine), soccer. *Women:* basketball, golf, skiing (alpine), soccer, softball, tennis, volleyball.

ADMISSIONS

Selectivity Rating: 81 (of 100). **Freshman Academic Profile:** Average high school GPA 3.6. 33% in top 10% of high school class, 66% in top 25% of high school class, 90% in top 50% of high school class. Average SAT I Math 563, SAT I Math middle 50% range 510-616. Average SAT I Verbal 571, SAT I Verbal middle 50% range 510-630. Average ACT 24, ACT middle 50% range 21-26. TOEFL required of all international applicants, minimum TOEFL 550. **Basis for Candidate Selection:** *Very important factors considered include:* extracurricular activities, secondary school record. *Important factors considered include:* character/personal qualities, essays, geographical residence, interview, recommendations, standardized test scores, volunteer work, work experience. *Other factors considered include:* alumni/ae relation, class rank, talent/ability. **Freshman Admission Requirements:** High school diploma or GED is required. *Academic units required/recommended:* 12 total recommended; 4 English required, 4 English recommended, 3 math required, 3 math recommended, 2 science required, 3 science recommended, 2 science lab recommended, 2 foreign language recommended, 3 social studies required, 3 social studies recommended, 3 history required, 3 history recommended. **Freshman Admission Statistics:** 950 applied, 77% accepted, 35% of those accepted enrolled. **Transfer Admission Requirements:** *Items required:* college transcript, essay, statement of good standing from prior school. Minimum college GPA of 2.2 required. Lowest grade transferable C. **General Admission Information:** Application fee $50. Priority application deadline February 15. Regular application deadline June 1. Nonfall registration accepted. Credit and/or placement offered for CEEB Advanced Placement tests.

COSTS AND FINANCIAL AID

Tuition $13,900. Room & board $5,015. Required fees $600. Average book expense $650. **Required Forms and Deadlines:** FAFSA and institution's own financial aid form. Priority filing deadline February 15. **Notification of Awards:** Applicants will be notified of awards on a rolling basis beginning on or about April 1. **Types of Aid:** *Need-based scholarships/grants:* Pell, SEOG, state scholarships/grants, private scholarships, the school's own gift aid. *Loans:* FFEL Subsidized Stafford, FFEL Unsubsidized Stafford, FFEL PLUS, Federal Perkins, alternative loans. **Student Employment:** Federal Work-Study Program available. Institutional employment available. Off-campus job opportunities are good. **Financial Aid Statistics:** 72% freshmen, 69% undergrads receive some form of aid. Average freshman grant $11,255. Average freshman loan $3,420. **Financial Aid Phone:** 208-459-5308.

ALBERTUS MAGNUS COLLEGE

700 Prospect Street, New Haven, CT 06511
Phone: 203-773-8501 **E-mail:** admissions@albertus.edu
Fax: 203-773-5248 **Web:** www.albertus.edu **ACT Code:** 549

This private school, which is affiliated with the Roman Catholic Church, was founded in 1925. It has a 45-acre campus.

STUDENTS AND FACULTY

Enrollment: 1,720. **Student Body:** Male 34%, female 66%, out-of-state 24%, international students represent 3 countries. **Ethnic Representation:** African American 20%, Asian 1%, Caucasian 69%, Hispanic 7%. **Retention and Graduation:** 40% grads go on to further study within 1 year. 20% grads pursue business degrees. 5% grads pursue law degrees. 5% grads pursue medical degrees. **Faculty:** 100% faculty teach undergrads.

ACADEMICS

Degrees: Associate's, bachelor's, master's, transfer. **Academic Requirements:** General education including some course work in arts/fine arts, English (including composition), humanities, mathematics, philosophy, sciences (biological or physical), social science. **Special Study Options:** Cross registration, double major, English as a second language, honors program, independent study, internships, study abroad.

FACILITIES

Housing: Coed, all-female. **Library Holdings:** 538 periodicals. 5,638 microforms. 817 audiovisuals. **Special Academic Facilities/Equipment:** Margart McDonough Art Gallery. **Computers:** *Recommended operating system:* Windows 95. School-owned computers available for student use.

EXTRACURRICULARS

Activities: Choral groups, drama/theater, literary magazine, musical theater, student government, student newspaper, yearbook. **Organizations:** 12 registered organizations, 1 honor society, 1 religious organization. **Athletics (Intercollegiate):** *Men:* baseball, basketball, cross-country, lacrosse, soccer, tennis. *Women:* basketball, cross-country, lacrosse, softball, tennis, volleyball.

ADMISSIONS

Selectivity Rating: 81 (of 100). **Freshman Academic Profile:** Average high school GPA 2.9. 18% in top 10% of high school class, 40% in top 25% of high school class, 35% in top 50% of high school class. 70% from public high schools. Average SAT I Math 570. Average SAT I Verbal 615. TOEFL required of all international applicants, minimum TOEFL 550. **Basis for Candidate Selection:** *Very important factors considered include:* secondary school record. *Important factors considered include:* class rank, extracurricular activities, interview, recommendations, standardized test scores. *Other factors considered include:* alumni/ae relation, character/personal qualities, talent/ability.

Freshman Admission Requirements: High school diploma or GED is required. *Academic units required/recommended:* 16 total required; 4 English required, 3 math recommended, 1 science recommended, 2 foreign language recommended, 1 social studies recommended, 1 history recommended. **Freshman Admission Statistics:** 277 applied, 93% accepted. **General Admission Information:** Application fee $35. Nonfall registration accepted. Admission may be deferred for a maximum of 1 year. Credit and/or placement offered for CEEB Advanced Placement tests.

COSTS AND FINANCIAL AID

Tuition $13,908. Room & board $6,512. Required fees $435. Average book expense $500. **Required Forms and Deadlines:** FAFSA and institution's own financial aid form. Priority filing deadline March 15. **Notification of Awards:** Applicants will be notified of awards on a rolling basis beginning on or about March 1. **Types of Aid:** *Need-based scholarships/grants:* Pell, SEOG, state scholarships/grants, the school's own gift aid. *Loans:* FFEL Subsidized Stafford, FFEL Unsubsidized Stafford, FFEL PLUS, Federal Perkins. **Student Employment:** Federal Work-Study Program available. Institutional employment available. Off-campus job opportunities are good. **Financial Aid Statistics:** 38% freshmen, 41% undergrads receive some form of aid. Average freshman grant $8,000. Average freshman loan $2,625. **Financial Aid Phone:** 203-773-8508.

ALBION COLLEGE

611 East Porter, Albion, MI 49224

Phone: 517-629-0321 **E-mail:** admissions@albion.edu **CEEB Code:** 1007

Fax: 517-629-0569 **Web:** www.albion.edu **ACT Code:** 1956

This private school, which is affiliated with the Methodist Church, was founded in 1835. It has a 225-acre campus.

STUDENTS AND FACULTY

Enrollment: 1,548. **Student Body:** Male 44%, female 56%, out-of-state 9%, international 1% (19 countries represented). **Ethnic Representation:** African American 2%, Asian 2%, Caucasian 86%. **Retention and Graduation:** 86% freshmen return for sophomore year. 70% freshmen graduate within 4 years. 40% grads go on to further study within 1 year. 1% grads pursue business degrees. 6% grads pursue law degrees. 18% grads pursue medical degrees. **Faculty:** Student/faculty ratio 12:1. 121 full-time faculty, 92% hold PhDs. 100% faculty teach undergrads.

ACADEMICS

Degrees: Bachelor's. **Academic Requirements:** General education including some course work in arts/fine arts, humanities, sciences (biological or physical), social science. **Classes:** 10-19 students in an average class. 10-19 students in an average lab/discussion section. **Majors with Highest Enrollment:** Business administration/management; English language and literature, general; biology/biological sciences, general. **Disciplines with Highest Percentage of Degrees Awarded:** Business/marketing 27%, social sciences and history 16%, biological life sciences 10%, English 10%, psychology 8%. **Special Study Options:** Accelerated program, cooperative (work-study) program, double major, dual enrollment, student exchange program (domestic), honors program, independent study, internships, liberal arts/career combination, student-designed major, study abroad, teacher certification program, Environmental Institute, Ford Institute for Public Service, Gerstacher Liberal Arts Program in Professional Management.

FACILITIES

Housing: Coed, all-female, all-male, apartments for single students, housing for disabled students, housing for international students, fraternities and/or sororities, cooperative housing. **Library Holdings:** 355,040 bound volumes. 1,743 periodicals. 67,188 microforms. 6,040 audiovisuals. **Special Academic Facilities/Equipment:** Visual arts museum, nature center, electron microscope, geographic information systems/computer-aided mapping lab, observatory. **Computers:** *Recommended operating system:* Windows 2000. School-owned computers available for student use.

EXTRACURRICULARS

Activities: Choral groups, concert band, dance, drama/theater, jazz band, marching band, music ensembles, musical theater, opera, pep band, radio station, student government, student newspaper, symphony orchestra, yearbook. **Organizations:** 122 registered organizations, 4 honor societies, 6 religious organizations, 5 fraternities (40% men join), 6 sororities (40% women join). **Athletics (Intercollegiate):** *Men:* baseball, basketball, cross-country, diving, football, golf, soccer, swimming, tennis, track & field. *Women:* basketball, cheerleading, cross-country, diving, golf, soccer, softball, swimming, tennis, track & field, volleyball.

ADMISSIONS

Selectivity Rating: 80 (of 100). **Freshman Academic Profile:** Average high school GPA 3.5. 31% in top 10% of high school class, 63% in top 25% of high school class, 88% in top 50% of high school class. 72% from public high schools. Average SAT I Math 582, SAT I Math middle 50% range 520-630. Average SAT I Verbal 562, SAT I Verbal middle 50% range 510-640. Average ACT 25, ACT middle 50% range 22-27. TOEFL required of all international applicants, minimum TOEFL 550. **Basis for Candidate Selection:** *Very important factors considered include:* character/personal qualities, extracurricular activities, interview, secondary school record, standardized test scores, talent/ability, volunteer work. *Important factors considered include:* alumni/ae relation, class rank, essays, geographical residence, minority status, recommendations. *Other factors considered include:* work experience. **Freshman Admission Requirements:** High school diploma or GED is required. *Academic units required/recommended:* 15 total required; 17 total recommended; 4 English required, 4 English recommended, 2 math required, 3 math recommended, 2 science required, 3 science recommended, 1 science lab required, 2 foreign language recommended, 3 social studies required, 1 history required, 3 elective required. **Freshman Admission Statistics:** 1,297 applied, 87% accepted, 40% of those accepted enrolled. **Transfer Admission Requirements:** *Items required:* high school transcript, college transcript, statement of good standing from prior school. Minimum high school GPA of 3.0 required. Minimum college GPA of 2.5 required. Lowest grade transferable C. **General Admission Information:** Application fee $20. Priority application deadline April 1. Early decision application deadline November 15. Regular application deadline May 1. Nonfall registration accepted. Admission may be deferred for a maximum of 1 year. Credit and/or placement offered for CEEB Advanced Placement tests.

COSTS AND FINANCIAL AID

Tuition $19,390. Room & board $5,604. Required fees $230. Average book expense $650. **Required Forms and Deadlines:** FAFSA. Priority filing deadline February 15. **Notification of Awards:** Applicants will be notified of awards on a rolling basis beginning on or about March 15. **Types of Aid:** *Need-based scholarships/grants:* Pell, SEOG, state scholarships/grants, private scholarships, the school's own gift aid. *Loans:* Direct Subsidized Stafford, Direct Unsubsidized Stafford, FFEL Subsidized Stafford, FFEL Unsubsidized Stafford, FFEL PLUS, Federal Perkins, state loans. **Student Employment:** Federal Work-Study Program available. Institutional employment available. Off-campus job opportunities are good. **Financial Aid Statistics:** 65% freshmen, 60% undergrads receive some form of aid. Average freshman grant $16,823. Average freshman loan $2,610. Average income from on-campus job $1,238. **Financial Aid Phone:** 517-629-0440.

ALBRIGHT COLLEGE

PO Box 15234, 13th and Bern Streets, Reading, PA 19612-5234

Phone: 610-921-7512 **E-mail:** admissions@albright.edu **CEEB Code:** 2004

Fax: 610-921-7294 **Web:** www.albright.edu **ACT Code:** 2004

This private school, which is affiliated with the Methodist Church, was founded in 1856. It has a 110-acre campus.

STUDENTS AND FACULTY

Enrollment: 2,076. **Student Body:** Male 44%, female 56%, out-of-state 29%, international 4% (22 countries represented). **Ethnic Representation:** African American 9%, Asian 2%, Caucasian 82%, Hispanic 3%. **Retention and Graduation:** 76% freshmen return for sophomore year. 61% freshmen graduate within 4 years. 23% grads go on to further study within 1 year. 5% grads pursue business degrees. 9% grads pursue law degrees. 7% grads pursue medical degrees. **Faculty:** Student/faculty ratio 13:1. 95 full-time faculty, 81% hold PhDs. 100% faculty teach undergrads.

ACADEMICS

Degrees: Bachelor's, certificate, master's. **Academic Requirements:** General education including some course work in arts/fine arts, computer literacy, English (including composition), foreign languages, history, humanities, mathematics, philosophy, sciences (biological or physical), social science, interdisciplinary. **Classes:** 10-19 students in an average class. 10-19 students in an average lab/discussion section. **Majors with Highest Enrollment:** Psychology, general; business administration/management; elementary education and teaching. **Disciplines with Highest Percentage of Degrees Awarded:** Business/marketing 42%, psychology 20%, social sciences and history 10%, education 8%, biological life sciences 4%. **Special Study Options:** Accelerated program, cross registration, double major, dual enrollment, English as a second language, student exchange program (domestic), honors program, independent study, internships, liberal arts/career combination, student-designed major, study abroad, teacher certification program.

FACILITIES

Housing: Coed, apartments for single students, honors/special-interest. **Library Holdings:** 214,834 bound volumes. 784 periodicals. 78,952 microforms. 28,988 audiovisuals. **Special Academic Facilities/Equipment:** Freedman Art Gallery. **Computers:** School-owned computers available for student use.

EXTRACURRICULARS

Activities: Choral groups, concert band, dance, drama/theater, jazz band, literary magazine, music ensembles, musical theater, radio station, student government, student newspaper, yearbook. **Organizations:** 84 registered organizations, 10 honor societies, 3 religious organizations, 4 fraternities (25% men join), 3 sororities (30% women join). **Athletics (Intercollegiate):** *Men:* baseball, basketball, cheerleading, cross-country, football, golf, indoor track, soccer, swimming, tennis, track & field, wrestling. *Women:* basketball, cheerleading, cross-country, field hockey, indoor track, soccer, softball, swimming, tennis, track & field, volleyball.

ADMISSIONS

Selectivity Rating: 74 (of 100). **Freshman Academic Profile:** Average high school GPA 3.0. 20% in top 10% of high school class, 43% in top 25% of high school class, 74% in top 50% of high school class. 71% from public high schools. Average SAT I Math 510, SAT I Math middle 50% range 450-570. Average SAT I Verbal 514, SAT I Verbal middle 50% range 450-570. Average ACT 22. TOEFL required of all international applicants, minimum TOEFL 530. **Basis for Candidate Selection:** *Very important factors considered include:* secondary school record. *Important factors considered include:* character/personal qualities, class rank, essays, recommendations, standardized test scores. *Other factors considered include:* alumni/ae relation, extracurricular activities, talent/ability, volunteer work, work experience. **Freshman Admission Requirements:** High school diploma or GED is required. *Academic units required/recommended:* 16 total required; 20 total recommended; 4 English required, 4 English recommended, 2 math required, 3 math recommended, 3 science required, 4 science recommended, 1 science lab required, 2 science lab recommended, 2 foreign language required, 3 foreign language recommended, 2 social studies required, 2 social studies recommended, 1 history required, 2 history recommended, 2 elective required, 2 elective recommended. **Freshman Admission Statistics:** 2,589 applied, 73% accepted, 24% of those accepted enrolled. **Transfer Admission Requirements:** *Items required:* college transcript, essay, statement of good standing from prior school. Minimum college GPA of 2.0 required. Lowest grade transferable C-. **General Admission Information:** Application fee $25. Priority application deadline March 1. Nonfall registration accepted. Admission may be deferred for a maximum of 1 year. Credit and/or placement offered for CEEB Advanced Placement tests.

COSTS AND FINANCIAL AID

Tuition $21,790. Room & board $6,809. Required fees $550. Average book expense $800. **Required Forms and Deadlines:** FAFSA. No deadline for regular filing. **Notification of Awards:** Applicants will be notified of awards on a rolling basis beginning on or about March 1. **Types of Aid:** *Need-based scholarships/grants:* Pell, SEOG, state scholarships/grants, private scholarships, the school's own gift aid. *Loans:* FFEL Subsidized Stafford, FFEL Unsubsidized Stafford, FFEL PLUS, Federal Perkins, private loans. **Student Employment:** Federal Work-Study Program available. Institutional employment available. Off-campus job opportunities are good. **Financial Aid Statistics:** 85% freshmen, 66% undergrads receive some form of aid. Average freshman grant $14,092. Average freshman loan $6,649. Average income from on-campus job $1,100. **Financial Aid Phone:** 610-921-7515.

ALCORN STATE UNIVERSITY

1000 ASU Drive #300, Alcorn State, MS 39096
Phone: 601-877-6147 **E-mail:** ebarnes@lorman.alcorn.edu **CEEB Code:** 1008
Fax: 601-877-6347 **Web:** www.alcorn.edu **ACT Code:** 2176

This public school was founded in 1871. It has a 1,756-acre campus.

STUDENTS AND FACULTY

Enrollment: 2,522. **Student Body:** Male 40%, female 60%, out-of-state 17%, international 2% (14 countries represented). **Ethnic Representation:** African American 95%, Caucasian 5%. **Retention and Graduation:** 71% freshmen return for sophomore year. 28% freshmen graduate within 4 years. 38% grads go on to further study within 1 year. **Faculty:** Student/faculty ratio 16:1. 172 full-time faculty, 61% hold PhDs.

ACADEMICS

Degrees: Associate's, bachelor's, master's, post-master's certificate. **Academic Requirements:** General education including some course work in arts/fine arts, computer literacy, English (including composition), history, humanities, mathematics, sciences (biological or physical), social science, oral communication, physical education, student adjustment. **Classes:** 20-29 students in an average class. Under 10 students in an average lab/discussion section. **Majors with Highest Enrollment:** Elementary education and teaching; biology/biological sciences, general; liberal arts and sciences/liberal studies. **Disciplines with Highest Percentage of Degrees Awarded:** Liberal arts/general studies 27%, business/marketing 11%, biological life sciences 11%, health professions and related sciences 10%, education 8%. **Special Study Options:** Accelerated program, cooperative (work-study) program, distance learning, double major, honors program, independent study, internships, liberal arts/career combination, teacher certification program; undergrads may take grad-level classes.

FACILITIES

Housing: Coed, all-female, all-male. **Library Holdings:** 195,433 bound volumes. 1,046 periodicals. 506,148 microforms. 9,908 audiovisuals. **Special Academic Facilities/Equipment:** Honors resident hall. **Computers:** *Recommended operating system:* Windows 2000/Windows XP. School-owned computers available for student use.

EXTRACURRICULARS

Activities: Choral groups, concert band, dance, drama/theater, jazz band, marching band, music ensembles, radio station, student government, student newspaper, television station, yearbook. **Organizations:** 6 honor societies, 13 religious organizations, 4 fraternities (15% men join), 4 sororities (30% women join). **Athletics (Intercollegiate):** *Men:* baseball, basketball, cross-country, football, golf, tennis, track & field. *Women:* basketball, cross-country, golf, soccer, softball, tennis, track & field, volleyball.

ADMISSIONS

Selectivity Rating: 63 (of 100). **Freshman Academic Profile:** 99% from public high schools. Average ACT 18, ACT middle 50% range 17-20. TOEFL required of all international applicants, minimum TOEFL 525. **Basis for Candidate Selection:** *Very important factors considered include:* class rank, secondary school record. *Important factors considered include:* standardized test scores. *Other factors considered include:* interview, minority status, recommendations. **Freshman Admission Requirements:** High school diploma or GED is required. *Academic units required/recommended:* 15 total required; 4 English required, 3 math required, 3 science required, 2 science lab required, 1 foreign language recommended, 3 social studies required, 2 elective required. **Freshman Admission Statistics:** 3,887 applied, 21% accepted, 53% of those accepted enrolled. **Transfer Admission Requirements:** *Items required:* college transcript, statement of good standing from prior school. Minimum college GPA of 2.0 required. Lowest grade transferable C. **General Admission Information:** Nonfall registration accepted. Admission may be deferred. Credit and/or placement offered for CEEB Advanced Placement tests.

COSTS AND FINANCIAL AID

In-state tuition $3,459. Out-of-state tuition $7,965. Room & board $3,538. Average book expense $1,000. **Required Forms and Deadlines:** FAFSA and institution's own financial aid form. Priority filing deadline April 1. **Notification of Awards:** Applicants will be notified of awards on a rolling basis beginning on or about April 1. **Types of Aid:** *Need-based scholarships/grants:* Pell, SEOG, state scholarships/grants, private scholarships, the school's own gift aid. *Loans:* Direct Subsidized Stafford, Direct Unsubsidized Stafford, Direct PLUS. **Student Employment:** Federal Work-Study Program available. Institutional employment available. Off-campus job opportunities are poor. **Financial Aid Statistics:** 97% freshmen, 96% undergrads receive some form of aid. Average income from on-campus job $500. **Financial Aid Phone:** 601-877-6190.

ALDERSON-BROADDUS COLLEGE

PO Box 2003, Philippi, WV 26416
Phone: 800-263-1549 **E-mail:** admissions@ab.edu
Fax: 304-457-6239 **Web:** www.ab.edu

This private school, which is affiliated with the American Baptist Church, was founded in 1871. It has a 120-acre campus.

STUDENTS AND FACULTY

Enrollment: 741. **Student Body:** Male 36%, female 64%, out-of-state 40%, international 1% (6 countries represented). **Ethnic Representation:** African American 3%, Asian 2%, Caucasian 87%, Hispanic 1%, Native American 1%. **Retention and Graduation:** 60% freshmen return for sophomore year. 42% grads go on to further study within 1 year. 6% grads pursue business degrees. 8% grads pursue law degrees. 8% grads pursue medical degrees. **Faculty:** Student/faculty ratio 13:1. 59 full-time faculty, 44% hold PhDs. 100% faculty teach undergrads.

ACADEMICS

Degrees: Associate's, bachelor's, certificate, master's. **Academic Requirements:** General education including some course work in arts/fine arts, computer literacy, English (including composition), foreign languages, history, humanities, mathematics, philosophy, sciences (biological or physical), social science. **Majors with Highest Enrollment:** Music teacher education; nursing/registered nurse training (RN, ASN, BSN, MSN); health professions and related sciences. **Special Study Options:** Double major, honors program, independent study, internships, study abroad, teacher certification program.

FACILITIES

Housing: Coed, all-female, apartments for married students, apartments for single students, fraternities and/or sororities. **Library Holdings:** 85,000 bound volumes. 560 periodicals. 10,000 microforms. 5,000 audiovisuals. **Special Academic Facilities/Equipment:** 2 art gallerys in new main hall.

EXTRACURRICULARS

Activities: Choral groups, concert band, drama/theater, jazz band, literary magazine, music ensembles, radio station, student government, student newspaper, television station, yearbook. **Organizations:** 44 registered organizations, 4 religious organizations. **Athletics (Intercollegiate):** *Men:* baseball, basketball, cross-country, soccer, track & field. *Women:* basketball, cross-country, softball, track & field, volleyball.

ADMISSIONS

Selectivity Rating: 73 (of 100). **Freshman Academic Profile:** Average high school GPA 3.3. 25% in top 10% of high school class, 50% in top 25% of high school class, 25% in top 50% of high school class. Average SAT I Math 475, SAT I Math middle 50% range 410-620. Average SAT I Verbal 530, SAT I Verbal middle 50% range 470-650. Average ACT 20, ACT middle 50% range 18-29. TOEFL required of all international applicants, minimum TOEFL 500. **Basis for Candidate Selection:** *Very important factors considered include:* secondary school record, standardized test scores, talent/ability. *Other factors considered include:* alumni/ae relation, character/personal qualities, extracurricular activities, interview, minority status, recommendations, religious affiliation/commitment, volunteer work, work experience. **Freshman Admission Requirements:** High school diploma or GED is required. *Academic units required/recommended:* 15 total recommended; 4 English recommended, 3 math recommended, 3 science recommended, 2 science lab recommended, 1 foreign language recommended, 2 social studies recommended. **Freshman Admission Statistics:** 916 applied, 70% accepted, 38% of those accepted enrolled. **Transfer Admission Requirements:** *Items required:* college transcript. Minimum college GPA of 2.0 required. Lowest grade transferable C. **General Admission Information:** Application fee $10. Priority application deadline March 1. Regular application deadline August 1. Nonfall registration accepted. Admission may be deferred for a maximum of 1 year. Credit and/or placement offered for CEEB Advanced Placement tests.

COSTS AND FINANCIAL AID

Tuition $14,830. Room & board $5,230. Required fees $165. Average book expense $690. **Required Forms and Deadlines:** FAFSA. Financial aid filing deadline August 1. Priority filing deadline March 1. **Notification of Awards:** Applicants will be notified of awards on a rolling basis beginning on or about February 1. **Types of Aid:** *Need-based scholarships/grants:* Pell, SEOG, state scholarships/grants, private scholarships, the school's own gift aid. *Loans:* Direct Subsidized Stafford, Direct Unsubsidized Stafford, Direct PLUS, Federal Perkins, Federal Nursing. **Student Employment:** Federal Work-Study Program available. Institutional employment available. Off-campus job opportunities are fair. **Financial Aid Statistics:** Average freshman grant $4,000. Average freshman loan $4,625. Average income from on-campus job $1,400. **Financial Aid Phone:** 304-457-6254.

ALFRED STATE COLLEGE (STATE UNIVERSITY OF NEW YORK)

Huntington Administration Bldg., Alfred, NY 14802
Phone: 800-425-3733 **E-mail:** admissions@alfredstate.edu **CEEB Code:** 2522
Fax: 607-587-4299 **Web:** www.alfredstate.edu **ACT Code:** 2910

This public school was founded in 1908. It has an 840-acre campus.

STUDENTS AND FACULTY

Enrollment: 3,296. **Student Body:** Male 66%, female 34%, out-of-state 6%, international 2%. **Ethnic Representation:** African American 5%, Caucasian 91%, Hispanic 2%, Native American 1%. **Retention and Graduation:** 38% grads go on to further study within 1 year. **Faculty:** Student/faculty ratio 20:1. 161 full-time faculty, 13% hold PhDs.

ACADEMICS

Degrees: Associate's, bachelor's, certificate. **Academic Requirements:** General education including some course work in English (including composition), humanities, mathematics, sciences (biological or physical), social science. **Majors with Highest Enrollment:** Information technology; civil engineering technologies/technicians; electrical, electronic, and communications engineering technology/technician. **Special Study Options:** Cooperative (work-study) program, cross registration, distance learning, honors program, independent study, internships, student-designed major, Internet courses.

FACILITIES

Housing: Coed, housing for disabled students, suites, corridor, singles, smoke-free, over 21 years, over 24 years, wellness living, quiet study, same curriculum housing, baccalaureate, single-room options, and computer lifestyle. **Library Holdings:** 71,243 bound volumes. 594 periodicals. 76,431 microforms. 2,357 audiovisuals. **Computers:** School-owned computers available for student use.

EXTRACURRICULARS

Activities: Choral groups, concert band, drama/theater, jazz band, literary magazine, music ensembles, musical theater, radio station, student government, student newspaper, symphony orchestra, yearbook. **Organizations:** 60 registered organizations, 2 honor societies, 3 fraternities, 3 sororities. **Athletics (Intercollegiate):** *Men:* baseball, basketball, cheerleading, cross-country, football, lacrosse, soccer, swimming, track & field, wrestling. *Women:* basketball, cheerleading, cross-country, soccer, softball, swimming, track & field, volleyball.

ADMISSIONS

Selectivity Rating: 63 (of 100). **Freshman Academic Profile:** Average high school GPA 2.5. Average SAT I Math 470. Average SAT I Verbal 470. Average ACT 19. TOEFL required of all international applicants, minimum TOEFL 500. **Basis for Candidate Selection:** *Very important factors considered include:* secondary school record. *Important factors considered include:* class rank, interview. *Other factors considered include:* alumni/ae relation, character/personal qualities, essays, extracurricular activities, recommendations, standardized test scores, talent/ability, volunteer work, work experience. **Freshman Admission Requirements:** High school diploma or GED is required. *Academic units required/recommended:* 4 English recommended, 4 math recommended, 4 science recommended, 4 social studies recommended. **Freshman Admission Statistics:** 4,153 applied, 69% accepted, 54% of those accepted enrolled. **Transfer Admission Requirements:** *Items required:* high school transcript, college transcript, statement of good standing from prior school. Minimum high school GPA of 2.4 required. Minimum college GPA of 2.4 required. Lowest grade transferable C. **General Admission Information:** Application fee $40. Priority application deadline November 2. Nonfall registration accepted. Admission may be deferred.

COSTS AND FINANCIAL AID

In-state tuition $3,200. Out-of-state tuition $5,000. Room & board $5,746. Required fees $790. Average book expense $600. **Required Forms and Deadlines:** FAFSA. No deadline for regular filing. Priority filing deadline January 3. **Notification of Awards:** Applicants will be notified of awards on a rolling basis beginning on or about March 3. **Types of Aid:** *Need-based scholarships/grants:* Pell, SEOG, state scholarships/grants, private scholarships, the school's own gift aid. *Loans:* Direct Subsidized Stafford, Direct Unsubsidized Stafford, Direct PLUS, FFEL Subsidized Stafford, FFEL Unsubsidized Stafford, FFEL PLUS, Federal Perkins, Federal Nursing. **Student Employment:** Federal Work-Study Program available. Institutional employment available. Off-campus job opportunities are fair. **Financial Aid Phone:** 800-425-3733.

ALFRED UNIVERSITY

Alumni Hall, One Saxon Drive, Alfred, NY 14802-1205
Phone: 607-871-2115 **E-mail:** admwww@alfred.edu **CEEB Code:** 2005
Fax: 607-871-2198 **Web:** www.alfred.edu **ACT Code:** 2666

This private school was founded in 1836. It has a 232-acre campus.

STUDENTS AND FACULTY

Enrollment: 2,080. **Student Body:** Male 48%, female 52%, out-of-state 35%, international 2%. **Ethnic Representation:** African American 5%, Asian 2%, Caucasian 78%, Hispanic 4%, Native American 1%. **Retention and Graduation:** 77% freshmen return for sophomore year. 50% freshmen graduate within 4 years. 22% grads go on to further study within 1 year. **Faculty:** Student/faculty ratio 12:1. 180 full-time faculty. 100% faculty teach undergrads.

ACADEMICS

Degrees: Bachelor's, doctoral, master's, post-master's certificate. **Academic Requirements:** General education including some course work in arts/fine arts, English (including composition), foreign languages, history, mathematics, philosophy, sciences (biological or physical), social science. Please note that general education requirements vary by college within the university. **Classes:** 10-19 students in an average class. 10-19 students in an average lab/discussion section. **Majors with Highest Enrollment:** Business administration/management; ceramic sciences and engineering; fine/studio arts, general. **Disciplines with Highest Percentage of Degrees Awarded:** Visual and performing arts 26%, engineering/engineering technology 18%, business/marketing 16%, education 8%, psychology 8%. **Special Study Options:** Cooperative (work-study) program, cross registration, double major, honors program, independent study, internships, liberal arts/career combination, student-designed major, study abroad.

FACILITIES

Housing: All-female, all-male, apartments for single students, theme housing (e.g., Environmental Studies House, Language House, etc.). **Library Holdings:** 323,944 bound volumes. 94,298 microforms. 162,938 audiovisuals. **Special Academic Facilities/Equipment:** Art museums, carillon, language labs, electron microscope, observatory, extensive engineering equipment, performing arts center. **Computers:** *Recommended operating system:* Windows XP. School-owned computers available for student use.

EXTRACURRICULARS

Activities: Choral groups, concert band, dance, drama/theater, literary magazine, music ensembles, musical theater, pep band, radio station, student government, student newspaper, student-run film society, television station, yearbook. **Organizations:** 105 registered organizations, 12 honor societies, 2 religious organizations. **Athletics (Intercollegiate):** *Men:* basketball, cross-country, diving, equestrian, football, golf, indoor track, lacrosse, skiing (alpine), skiing (Nordic), soccer, swimming, tennis, track & field. *Women:* basketball, cross-country, diving, equestrian, golf, indoor track, lacrosse, skiing (alpine), skiing (Nordic), soccer, softball, swimming, tennis, track & field, volleyball.

ADMISSIONS

Selectivity Rating: 77 (of 100). **Freshman Academic Profile:** 23% in top 10% of high school class, 51% in top 25% of high school class, 83% in top 50% of high school class. SAT I Math middle 50% range 490-610. SAT I Verbal middle 50% range 490-610. ACT middle 50% range 23-27. TOEFL required of all international applicants, minimum TOEFL 550. **Basis for Candidate Selection:** *Very important factors considered include:* character/personal qualities, class rank, extracurricular activities, recommendations, secondary school record. *Important factors considered include:* essays, standardized test scores, volunteer work. *Other factors considered include:* interview, talent/ability, work experience. **Freshman Admission Requirements:** High school diploma or GED is required. *Academic units required/recommended:* 16 total required; 4 English required, 2 math required, 4 math recommended, 2 science required, 3 science recommended, 2 science lab required, 3 science lab recommended, 2 social studies required, 3 social studies recommended. **Freshman Admission Statistics:** 1,951 applied, 73% accepted, 33% of those accepted enrolled. **Transfer Admission Requirements:** *Items required:* college transcript, statement of good standing from prior school. Minimum college GPA of 2.5 required. Lowest grade transferable C. **General Admission Information:** Application fee $40. Priority application deadline February 1. Early decision application deadline December 1. Nonfall registration accepted. Admission may be deferred for a maximum of 2 years.

COSTS AND FINANCIAL AID

Tuition $19,918. Room & board $8,016. Required fees $698. Average book expense $700. **Required Forms and Deadlines:** FAFSA, institution's own financial aid form, state aid form, noncustodial (divorced/separated) parent's statement, and business/farm supplement. No deadline for regular filing. **Notification of Awards:** Applicants will be notified of awards on a rolling basis beginning on or about February 1. **Types of Aid:** *Need-based scholarships/grants:* Pell, SEOG, state scholarships/grants, private scholarships, the school's own gift aid. *Loans:* FFEL Subsidized Stafford, FFEL Unsubsidized Stafford, FFEL PLUS, Federal Perkins, college/university loans from institutional funds, private alternative loans. **Student Employment:** Federal Work-Study Program available. Institutional employment available. Off-campus job opportunities are fair. **Financial Aid Statistics:** 81% freshmen, 80% undergrads receive some form of aid. **Financial Aid Phone:** 607-871-2159.

ALICE LLOYD COLLEGE

100 Purpose Road, Pippa Passes, KY 41844
Phone: 606-368-6036 **E-mail:** admissions@alc.edu **CEEB Code:** 1098
Fax: 606-368-6215 **Web:** www.alc.edu **ACT Code:** 1502

This private school was founded in 1923. It has a 225-acre campus.

STUDENTS AND FACULTY

Enrollment: 577. **Student Body:** Male 45%, female 55%, out-of-state 18%, international 1% (4 countries represented). **Ethnic Representation:** Asian 1%, Caucasian 98%, Hispanic 1%. **Retention and Graduation:** 55% freshmen return for sophomore year. 21% freshmen graduate within 4 years. 55% grads go on to further study within 1 year. 10% grads pursue business degrees. 5% grads pursue law degrees. 5% grads pursue medical degrees. **Faculty:** Student/faculty ratio 19:1. 27 full-time faculty, 55% hold PhDs. 100% faculty teach undergrads.

ACADEMICS

Degrees: Bachelor's. **Academic Requirements:** General education including some course work in arts/fine arts, computer literacy, English (including composition), foreign languages, history, humanities, mathematics, philosophy, sciences (biological or physical), social science. **Classes:** 20-29 students in an average class. **Disciplines with Highest Percentage of Degrees Awarded:** Education 42%, biological life sciences 21%, business/marketing 20%, social sciences and history 11%, English 4%. **Special Study Options:** Cooperative (work-study) program, double major, honors program, independent study, internships, liberal arts/career combination, study abroad, teacher certification program.

FACILITIES

Housing: All-female, all-male. **Library Holdings:** 74,216 bound volumes. 118 periodicals. 3,600 microforms. 1,225 audiovisuals. **Special Academic Facilities/Equipment:** Photographic archives, oral history museum, Appalachian collection, on-campus daycare center, kindergarten, elementary and secondary school. **Computers:** School-owned computers available for student use.

EXTRACURRICULARS

Activities: Choral groups, drama/theater, music ensembles, musical theater, pep band, radio station, student government, student newspaper, television station, yearbook. **Organizations:** 16 registered organizations, 2 honor societies, 1 religious organization. **Athletics (Intercollegiate):** *Men:* baseball, basketball, cheerleading, cross-country, golf, tennis. *Women:* basketball, cheerleading, cross-country, golf, softball, tennis.

ADMISSIONS

Selectivity Rating: 76 (of 100). **Freshman Academic Profile:** Average high school GPA 3.3. 90% from public high schools. Average SAT I Math 450. Average SAT I Verbal 415. ACT middle 50% range 18-26. TOEFL required of all international applicants, minimum TOEFL 550. **Basis for Candidate Selection:** *Very important factors considered include:* character/personal qualities, geographical residence, secondary school record, standardized test scores. *Important factors considered include:* alumni/ae relation, class rank, recommendations, state residency. *Other factors considered include:* essays, extracurricular activities, interview, talent/ability, volunteer work, work experience. **Freshman Admission Requirements:** High school diploma or GED is required. *Academic units required/recommended:* 12 total required; 16 total recommended; 4 English required, 4 English recommended, 3 math required, 3 math recommended, 2 science required, 2 science recommended, 2 foreign language recommended, 2 social studies required, 2 social studies recommended, 1 history required. **Freshman Admission Statistics:** 880 applied, 58% accepted, 37% of those accepted enrolled. **Transfer Admission Requirements:** *Items required:* high school transcript, college transcript, standardized test scores. Minimum college GPA of 2.0 required. Lowest grade transferable C. **General Admission Information:** Priority application deadline July 1. Early decision application deadline May 1. Nonfall registration accepted. Credit and/or placement offered for CEEB Advanced Placement tests.

COSTS AND FINANCIAL AID

Room & board $3,180. Required fees $790. Average book expense $850. **Required Forms and Deadlines:** FAFSA. Priority filing deadline March 15. **Notification of Awards:** Applicants will be notified of awards on a rolling basis. **Types of Aid:** *Need-based scholarships/grants:* Pell, SEOG, state scholarships/grants, private scholarships, the school's own gift aid. *Loans:* FFEL Subsidized Stafford, FFEL Unsubsidized Stafford, FFEL PLUS, Federal Perkins, state loans, college/university loans from institutional funds. **Student Employment:** Federal Work-Study Program available. Off-campus job opportunities are fair. **Financial Aid Statistics:** 84% freshmen, 83% undergrads receive some form of aid. Average freshman grant $7,182. Average freshman loan $1,210. **Financial Aid Phone:** 606-368-6059.

ALLEGHENY COLLEGE

Office of Admissions, Allegheny College, Meadville, PA 16335
Phone: 814-332-4351 **E-mail:** admiss@allegheny.edu **CEEB Code:** 2006
Fax: 814-337-0431 **Web:** www.allegheny.edu **ACT Code:** 3520

This private school was founded in 1815. It has a 254-acre campus.

STUDENTS AND FACULTY

Enrollment: 1,924. **Student Body:** Male 48%, female 52%, out-of-state 32%, international 1% (16 countries represented). **Ethnic Representation:** African American 2%, Asian 2%, Caucasian 95%, Hispanic 1%. **Retention and Graduation:** 83% freshmen return for sophomore year. 66% freshmen graduate within 4 years. 31% grads go on to further study within 1 year. 3% grads pursue business degrees. 6% grads pursue law degrees. 3% grads pursue medical degrees. **Faculty:** Student/faculty ratio 14:1. 133 full-time faculty, 91% hold PhDs. 100% faculty teach undergrads.

ACADEMICS

Degrees: Bachelor's. **Academic Requirements:** Students must major in one academic division, minor in another, and complete 8 credits from the third academic division. **Classes:** 10-19 students in an average class. 10-19 students in an average lab/discussion section. **Majors with Highest Enrollment:** Biology/biological sciences, general; psychology, general; economics, general. **Disciplines with Highest Percentage of Degrees Awarded:** Social sciences and history 25%, biological life sciences 20%, psychology 11%, communications/communication technologies 8%, natural resources/environmental sciences 8%. **Special Study Options:** Double major, independent study, internships, student-designed major, study abroad, cooperative program in teacher education. Marine sciences semester with Duke University; 3-2 liberal arts/career combination programs in engineering with Columbia University, Case Western Reserve University, University of Pittsburgh, Duke University, Washington University; 3-4 bachelor's/doctorate program in nursing with Case Western Reserve University; 3-1 program in allied health with Rochester General Hospital School of Medical Technology-University of Rochester.

FACILITIES

Housing: Coed, all-female, all-male, apartments for single students, housing for disabled students, housing for international students, fraternities and/or sororities, theme houses (e.g., foreign language, jazz, writers, Afro-American cultural, meditation and mindfulness, ecology, arts, Athena, faith & social justice, international, social awareness, gay pride). **Library Holdings:** 279,648 bound volumes. 3,500 periodicals. 495,557 microforms. 7,051 audiovisuals. **Special Academic Facilities/Equipment:** 283-acre Bousson Environmental Research Reserve, 80-acre protected forest, world's largest solid-volume glass sculpture grouping, The Academic Village (theme-based student apartments), state-of-the-art, nationally acclaimed science complex, videoconference facilities, planetarium, observatory, GIS lab, state-of-the-art language-learning center, smart classrooms, radio and television studios, recently renovated dance studios and performance spaces, art galleries. **Computers:** *Recommended operating system:* Windows 95. School-owned computers available for student use.

EXTRACURRICULARS

Activities: Choral groups, concert band, dance, drama/theater, jazz band, literary magazine, music ensembles, musical theater, radio station, student government, student newspaper, symphony orchestra, television station, yearbook. **Organizations:** 107 registered organizations, 13 honor societies, 6 religious organizations, 5 fraternities (17% men join), 4 sororities (30% women join). **Athletics (Intercollegiate):** *Men:* baseball, basketball, cross-country, diving, football, golf, indoor track, soccer, swimming, tennis, track & field. *Women:* basketball, cross-country, diving, indoor track, lacrosse, soccer, softball, swimming, tennis, track & field, volleyball.

ADMISSIONS

Selectivity Rating: 87 (of 100). **Freshman Academic Profile:** Average high school GPA 3.7. 40% in top 10% of high school class, 74% in top 25% of high school class, 94% in top 50% of high school class. 85% from public high schools. Average SAT I Math 600, SAT I Math middle 50% range 550-650. Average SAT I Verbal 598, SAT I Verbal middle 50% range 550-650. Average ACT 25, ACT middle 50% range 23-27. TOEFL required of all international applicants, minimum TOEFL 550. **Basis for Candidate Selection:** *Very important factors considered include:* class rank, secondary school record. *Important factors considered include:* character/personal qualities, extracurricular activities, interview, recommendations, standardized test scores. *Other factors considered include:* alumni/ae relation, essays, geographical residence, minority status, talent/ability, volunteer work, work experience. **Freshman Admission Requirements:** High school diploma or GED is required. *Academic units required/recommended:* 16 total required; 4 English required, 3 math required, 3 science required, 2 foreign language required, 3 social studies required, 1 elective required. **Freshman Admission Statistics:** 2,612 applied, 80% accepted, 26% of those accepted enrolled. **Transfer Admission Requirements:** *Items required:* high school transcript, college transcript, essay, standardized test score, statement of good standing from prior school. Minimum high school GPA of 2.5 required. Minimum college GPA of 2.5 required. Lowest grade transferable C. **General Admission Information:** Application fee $35. Early decision application deadline January 15. Regular application deadline February 15. Nonfall registration accepted. Admission may be deferred for a maximum of 1 year. Credit and/or placement offered for CEEB Advanced Placement tests.

COSTS AND FINANCIAL AID

Tuition $22,210. Room & board $5,290. Required fees $280. Average book expense $670. **Required Forms and Deadlines:** FAFSA. No deadline for regular filing. Priority filing deadline February 15. **Notification of Awards:** Applicants will be notified of awards on a rolling basis beginning on or about March 1. **Types of Aid:** *Need-based scholarships/grants:* Pell, SEOG, state scholarships/grants, private scholarships, the school's own gift aid. *Loans:* FFEL Subsidized Stafford, FFEL Unsubsidized Stafford, FFEL PLUS, Federal Perkins, state loans, private loans from commercial lenders. **Student Employment:** Federal Work-Study Program available. Institutional employment available. Off-campus job opportunities are excellent. **Financial Aid Statistics:** 74% freshmen, 72% undergrads receive some form of aid. Average freshman grant $14,266. Average freshman loan $3,062. Average income from on-campus job $939. **Financial Aid Phone:** 800-835-7780.

ALLEN COLLEGE

1825 Logan Avenue, Waterloo, IA 50703
Phone: 319-226-2002 **E-mail:** HagedoLE@IHS.org
Fax: 319-226-2051 **Web:** www.allencollege.edu **ACT Code:** 30691

This private school was founded in 1989.

STUDENTS AND FACULTY

Enrollment: 238. **Student Body:** Out-of-state 1%. **Ethnic Representation:** African American 1%, Caucasian 97%, Hispanic 1%. **Retention and Graduation:** 68% freshmen return for sophomore year. 46% freshmen graduate within 4 years. 10% grads go on to further study within 1 year. **Faculty:** Student/faculty ratio 10:1. 20 full-time faculty, 15% hold PhDs. 100% faculty teach undergrads.

ACADEMICS

Degrees: Associate's, bachelor's, master's, post-master's certificate. **Academic Requirements:** General education including some course work in English (including composition), humanities, sciences (biological or physical), social science. **Classes:** 10-19 students in an average class. Under 10 students in an average lab/discussion section. **Majors with Highest Enrollment:** Nursing/registered nurse training (RN, ASN, BSN, MSN); family practice nurse, nurse practitioner; health services/allied health, general. **Disciplines with Highest Percentage of Degrees Awarded:** Health professions and related sciences 100%. **Special Study Options:** Cooperative (work-study) program, distance learning, independent study, internships.

FACILITIES

Housing: Housing available at a cooperating institution. **Library Holdings:** 2,500 bound volumes. 105 periodicals. 0 microforms. 515 audiovisuals. **Computers:** School-owned computers available for student use.

EXTRACURRICULARS

Activities: Student government, student newspaper, yearbook. **Organizations:** 4 registered organizations, 1 religious organization.

ADMISSIONS

Selectivity Rating: 60 (of 100). **Freshman Academic Profile:** Average high school GPA 3.5. 21% in top 10% of high school class, 42% in top 25% of high school class, 100% in top 50% of high school class. Average ACT 22, ACT middle 50% range 20-23. TOEFL required of all international applicants, minimum TOEFL 550. **Basis for Candidate Selection:** *Very important factors considered include:* class rank, secondary school record, standardized test scores. *Important factors considered include:* essays, recommendations. *Other factors considered include:* character/personal qualities, interview. **Freshman Admission Requirements:** High school diploma or GED is required. *Academic units required/recommended:* 8 English required, 6 math required, 6 science required, 6 social studies required. **Freshman Admission Statistics:** 67 applied, 43% accepted, 93% of those accepted enrolled. **Transfer Admission Requirements:** *Items required:* high school transcript, college transcript, essay, standardized test scores. Lowest grade transferable C. **General Admission Information:** Application fee $20. Priority application deadline August 1. Nonfall registration accepted. Admission may be deferred. Credit offered for CEEB Advanced Placement tests.

COSTS AND FINANCIAL AID

Tuition $7,967. Room & board $4,410. Required fees $745. Average book expense $776. **Required Forms and Deadlines:** FAFSA and institution's own financial aid form. No deadline for regular filing. Priority filing deadline June 30. **Notification of Awards:** Applicants will be notified of awards on a rolling basis beginning on or about March 15. **Types of Aid:** *Need-based scholarships/grants:* Pell, SEOG, state scholarships/grants, private scholarships, the school's own gift aid, Federal Nursing. *Loans:* Direct Subsidized Stafford, Direct Unsubsidized Stafford, Direct PLUS, Federal Perkins, Federal Nursing, college/university loans from institutional funds, alternative loans. **Student Employment:** Federal Work-Study Program available. Institutional employment available. Off-campus job opportunities are excellent. **Financial Aid Statistics:** 74% freshmen, 74% undergrads receive some form of aid. Average freshman grant $4,056. Average freshman loan $2,588. **Financial Aid Phone:** 319-226-2003.

ALMA COLLEGE

614 West Superior Street, Alma, MI 48801-1599
Phone: 989-463-7139 **E-mail:** admissions@alma.edu **CEEB Code:** 1010
Fax: 989-463-7057 **Web:** www.alma.edu **ACT Code:** 1958

This private school, which is affiliated with the Presbyterian Church, was founded in 1886. It has a 125-acre campus.

STUDENTS AND FACULTY

Enrollment: 1,317. **Student Body:** Male 43%, female 57%, out-of-state 4%, international 1% (8 countries represented). **Ethnic Representation:** African American 1%, Asian 2%, Caucasian 95%, Hispanic 1%, Native American 1%. **Retention and Graduation:** 83% freshmen return for sophomore year. 55% freshmen graduate within 4 years. 40% grads go on to further study within 1 year. 8% grads pursue law degrees. 5% grads pursue medical degrees. **Faculty:** Student/faculty ratio 12:1. 92 full-time faculty, 84% hold PhDs. 100% faculty teach undergrads.

ACADEMICS

Degrees: Bachelor's. **Academic Requirements:** General education including some course work in arts/fine arts, English (including composition), foreign languages, history, humanities, mathematics, philosophy, sciences (biological or physical), social science. **Classes:** 10-19 students in an average class. 10-19 students in an average lab/discussion section. **Majors with Highest Enrollment:** Business administration/management; education, general; biology/biological sciences, general. **Disciplines with Highest Percentage of Degrees Awarded:** Business/marketing 16%, social sciences and history 14%, education 11%, biological life sciences 10%, health professions and related sciences 10%. **Special Study Options:** Double major, dual enrollment, English as a second language, student exchange program (domestic), independent study, internships, student-designed major, study abroad, teacher certification program.

FACILITIES

Housing: Coed, all-female, apartments for single students, housing for international students, fraternities and/or sororities, academic theme houses. **Library Holdings:** 246,649 bound volumes. 1,157 periodicals. 242,879 microforms. 7,962 audiovisuals. **Special Academic Facilities/Equipment:** Music and arts centers, science lab, planetarium, a DNA synthesizer and sequencer, and a multinuclear magnetic resonance spectrometer. **Computers:** School-owned computers available for student use.

EXTRACURRICULARS

Activities: Choral groups, dance, drama/theater, jazz band, literary magazine, marching band, music ensembles, radio station, student government, student newspaper, symphony orchestra, yearbook. **Organizations:** 127 registered organizations, 18 honor societies, 3 religious organizations, 5 fraternities (25% men join), 5 sororities (39% women join). **Athletics (Intercollegiate):** *Men:* baseball, basketball, cross-country, diving, football, golf, soccer, swimming, tennis, track & field. *Women:* basketball, cross-country, diving, golf, soccer, softball, swimming, tennis, track & field, volleyball.

ADMISSIONS

Selectivity Rating: 78 (of 100). **Freshman Academic Profile:** Average high school GPA 3.4. 33% in top 10% of high school class, 64% in top 25% of high school class, 93% in top 50% of high school class. 93% from public high schools. Average ACT 25, ACT middle 50% range 22-27. TOEFL required of all international applicants, minimum TOEFL 525. **Basis for Candidate Selection:** *Very important factors considered include:* secondary school record, standardized test scores. *Important factors considered include:* class rank, essays. *Other factors considered include:* alumni/ae relation, character/personal qualities, extracurricular activities, interview, recommendations, talent/ability, volunteer work. **Freshman Admission Requirements:** High school diploma or GED is required. *Academic units required/recommended:* 16 total required; 4 English required, 3 math required, 3 science required, 2 foreign language recommended, 3 social studies required. **Freshman Admission Statistics:** 1,502 applied, 79% accepted, 28% of those accepted enrolled. **Transfer Admission Requirements:** *Items required:* high school transcript, college transcript, standardized test scores, statement of good standing from prior school. Minimum high school GPA of 3.0 required. Minimum college GPA of 2.0 required. Lowest grade transferable C. **General Admission Information:** Application fee $25. Priority application deadline March 1. Nonfall registration accepted. Admission may be deferred for a maximum of 1 year. Credit and/or placement offered for CEEB Advanced Placement tests.

COSTS AND FINANCIAL AID

Tuition $18,684. Room & board $6,712. Required fees $170. Average book expense $700. **Required Forms and Deadlines:** FAFSA. No deadline for regular filing. Priority filing deadline February 21. **Notification of Awards:** Applicants will be notified of awards on a rolling basis beginning on or about March 1. **Types of Aid:** *Need-based scholarships/grants:* Pell, SEOG, state scholarships/grants, private scholarships, the school's own gift aid. *Loans:* Direct Subsidized Stafford, Direct Unsubsidized Stafford, Direct PLUS, Federal Perkins, state loans, college/university loans from institutional funds, alternative loans. **Student Employment:** Federal Work-Study Program available. Institutional employment available. Off-campus job opportunities are fair. **Financial Aid Statistics:** 73% freshmen, 78% undergrads receive some form of aid. Average freshman grant $9,071. Average freshman loan $3,615. Average income from on-campus job $800. **Financial Aid Phone:** 989-463-7347.

ALVERNIA COLLEGE

400 St. Bernardine Street, Reading, PA 19607
Phone: 610-796-8220 **E-mail:** admissions@alvernia.edu
Fax: 610-796-8336 **Web:** www.alvernia.edu

This private school, which is affiliated with the Roman Catholic Church, was founded in 1958. It has an 80-acre campus.

STUDENTS AND FACULTY

Enrollment: 1,781. **Student Body:** Male 34%, female 66%, out-of-state 8%. **Ethnic Representation:** African American 10%, Asian 2%, Caucasian 81%, Hispanic 4%. **Retention and Graduation:** 81% freshmen return for sophomore year. **Faculty:** Student/faculty ratio 14:1. 58 full-time faculty, 52% hold PhDs. 100% faculty teach undergrads.

ACADEMICS

Degrees: Associate's, bachelor's, certificate, master's, post-bachelor's certificate. **Academic Requirements:** General education including some course work in arts/fine arts, computer literacy, English (including composition), foreign languages, history, humanities, mathematics, philosophy, sciences (biological or physical), social science. **Classes:** 10-19 students in an average class. 10-19 students in an average lab/discussion section. **Majors with Highest Enrollment:** Criminal justice/law enforcement administration; substance abuse/

addiction counseling; elementary education and teaching. **Disciplines with Highest Percentage of Degrees Awarded:** Business/marketing 27%, education 16%, protective services/public administration 14%, health professions and related sciences 13%, computer and information sciences 8%. **Special Study Options:** Accelerated program, cooperative (work-study) program, cross registration, double major, honors program, independent study, internships, student-designed major, teacher certification program.

FACILITIES

Housing: Coed, all-female. **Library Holdings:** 89,399 bound volumes. 378 periodicals. 1,036 microforms. 7,766 audiovisuals. **Computers:** *Recommended operating system:* Windows NT/2000. School-owned computers available for student use.

EXTRACURRICULARS

Activities: Choral groups, drama/theater, literary magazine, music ensembles, musical theater, student government, student newspaper, yearbook. **Organizations:** 35 registered organizations, 5 honor societies, 5 religious organizations. **Athletics (Intercollegiate):** *Men:* baseball, basketball, cross-country, golf, soccer, tennis, volleyball. *Women:* basketball, cheerleading, cross-country, field hockey, soccer, softball, tennis, volleyball.

ADMISSIONS

Selectivity Rating: 63 (of 100). **Freshman Academic Profile:** Average high school GPA 3.0. 8% in top 10% of high school class, 27% in top 25% of high school class, 48% in top 50% of high school class. 72% from public high schools. Average SAT I Math 434, SAT I Math middle 50% range 430-510. Average SAT I Verbal 440, SAT I Verbal middle 50% range 420-520. ACT middle 50% range 15-22. TOEFL required of all international applicants, minimum TOEFL 550. **Basis for Candidate Selection:** *Very important factors considered include:* interview, secondary school record, standardized test scores. *Important factors considered include:* extracurricular activities, recommendations. *Other factors considered include:* character/personal qualities, class rank, essays, volunteer work, work experience. **Freshman Admission Requirements:** High school diploma or GED is required. *Academic units required/recommended:* 4 English required, 2 math required, 2 science required, 1 science lab required, 2 foreign language required, 2 social studies required, 4 elective required. **Freshman Admission Statistics:** 692 applied, 80% accepted, 46% of those accepted enrolled. **Transfer Admission Requirements:** *Items required:* high school transcript, college transcript. Minimum college GPA of 2.0 required. Lowest grade transferable C. **General Admission Information:** Application fee $25. Nonfall registration accepted. Admission may be deferred for a maximum of 1 year. Neither credit nor placement offered for CEEB Advanced Placement tests.

COSTS AND FINANCIAL AID

Required Forms and Deadlines: FAFSA. Financial aid filing deadline April 1. Priority filing deadline April 1. **Notification of Awards:** Applicants will be notified of awards on a rolling basis beginning on or about March 1. **Types of Aid:** *Need-based scholarships/grants:* Pell, SEOG, state scholarships/grants, private scholarships, the school's own gift aid. *Loans:* FFEL Subsidized Stafford, FFEL Unsubsidized Stafford, FFEL PLUS, Federal Perkins, college/university loans from institutional funds, O'Rourke Nursing Loans, Health Professions Loans. **Student Employment:** Federal Work-Study Program available. Institutional employment available. Off-campus job opportunities are excellent. **Financial Aid Statistics:** 77% freshmen receive some form of aid. **Financial Aid Phone:** 610-796-8215.

ALVERNO COLLEGE

3400 South 43rd Street, PO Box 343922, Milwaukee, WI 53219
Phone: 414-382-6100 **E-mail:** admissions@alverno.edu **CEEB Code:** 1012
Fax: 414-382-6354 **Web:** www.alverno.edu **ACT Code:** 4558

This private school, which is affiliated with the Roman Catholic Church, was founded in 1887. It has a 46-acre campus.

STUDENTS AND FACULTY

Enrollment: 1,800. **Student Body:** Out-of-state 2%, international 1%. **Ethnic Representation:** African American 27%, Asian 3%, Caucasian 60%, Hispanic 8%, Native American 1%. **Retention and Graduation:** 72% freshmen return for sophomore year. 7% grads go on to further study within 1 year. 2% grads pursue business degrees. 1% grads pursue law degrees. 1% grads pursue medical degrees. **Faculty:** Student/faculty ratio 14:1. 100 full-time faculty, 90% hold PhDs. 100% faculty teach undergrads.

ACADEMICS

Degrees: Associate's, bachelor's, master's. **Academic Requirements:** General education including some course work in arts/fine arts, computer literacy, English (including composition), history, humanities, mathematics, philosophy, sciences (biological or physical), social science, communications. **Classes:** 20-29 students in an average class. 10-19 students in an average lab/discussion section. **Disciplines with Highest Percentage of Degrees Awarded:** Business/marketing 27%, communications/communication technologies 16%, health professions and related sciences 16%, education 14%, social sciences and history 7%. **Special Study Options:** Double major, internships, study abroad, teacher certification program, weekend college. College Transition Program allows some students to take a semester of college-prepatory courses that they may have missed in high school or prior colleges.

FACILITIES

Housing: All-female, semi-apartment living within residence halls available to older students. **Library Holdings:** 92,076 bound volumes. 1,001 periodicals. 248,124 microforms. 34,795 audiovisuals. **Special Academic Facilities/Equipment:** Art gallery, career development center, fitness center. **Computers:** School-owned computers available for student use.

EXTRACURRICULARS

Activities: Choral groups, dance, drama/theater, literary magazine, music ensembles, pep band, student newspaper. **Organizations:** 29 registered organizations, 3 honor societies, 1 religious organization, 1 sorority. **Athletics (Intercollegiate):** *Women:* basketball, cross-country, soccer, softball, volleyball.

ADMISSIONS

Selectivity Rating: 63 (of 100). **Freshman Academic Profile:** 60% from public high schools. Average ACT 20. TOEFL required of all international applicants, minimum TOEFL 500. **Basis for Candidate Selection:** *Very important factors considered include:* secondary school record. *Important factors considered include:* class rank, essays, standardized test scores. *Other factors considered include:* character/personal qualities, extracurricular activities, interview, recommendations, talent/ability. **Freshman Admission Requirements:** High school diploma or GED is required. *Academic units required/recommended:* 17 total required; 4 English recommended, 3 math recommended, 3 science recommended, 2 foreign language recommended, 3 social studies recommended. **Freshman Admission Statistics:** 667 applied, 82% accepted, 36% of those accepted enrolled. **Transfer Admission Requirements:** *Items required:* high school transcript, college transcript, essay. Minimum college GPA of 2.0 required. Lowest grade transferable C. **General Admission Information:** Application fee $20. Nonfall registration accepted. Admission may be deferred for a maximum of 4 years. Credit and/or placement offered for CEEB Advanced Placement tests.

COSTS AND FINANCIAL AID

Tuition $12,000. Room & board $4,780. Required fees $150. Average book expense $800. **Required Forms and Deadlines:** FAFSA, institution's own financial aid form, income tax forms if chosen for verification, and Alverno Institutional Application. No deadline for regular filing. Priority filing deadline April 1. **Notification of Awards:** Applicants will be notified of awards on a rolling basis beginning on or about April 15. **Types of Aid:** *Need-based scholarships/grants:* Pell, SEOG, state scholarships/grants, private scholarships, the school's own gift aid, transfer scholarships. *Loans:* FFEL Subsidized Stafford, FFEL Unsubsidized Stafford, FFEL PLUS, Federal Perkins. **Student Employment:** Federal Work-Study Program available. Institutional employment available. Off-campus job opportunities are good. **Financial Aid Statistics:** Average freshman grant $7,758. Average freshman loan $3,800. Average income from on-campus job $1,200. **Financial Aid Phone:** 414-382-6046.

AMERICAN ACADEMY FOR DRAMATIC ARTS—EAST

120 Madison Avenue, New York, NY 10016
Phone: 212-686-0620 **E-mail:** admissions-ny@aada.org
Fax: 212-696-1284 **Web:** www.aada.org

This private school was founded in 1884.

STUDENTS AND FACULTY

Enrollment: 221. **Faculty:** Student/faculty ratio 15:1. 12 full-time faculty.

ACADEMICS

Degrees: Associate's, terminal. **Classes:** 10-19 students in an average class.

ADMISSIONS

Selectivity Rating: 60 (of 100). **Freshman Academic Profile:** 26% from public high schools. **Basis for Candidate Selection:** *Very important factors considered include:* interview, talent/ability. *Important factors considered include:* recommendations. *Other factors considered include:* alumni/ae relation, character/personal qualities, essays, secondary school record, work experience. **Freshman Admission Requirements:** High school diploma or GED is required. **Freshman Admission Statistics:** 458 applied. **General Admission Information:** Application fee $50. Nonfall registration accepted. Admission may be deferred for a maximum of 1 year.

COSTS AND FINANCIAL AID

Tuition $12,200. Required fees $400. Average book expense $400. **Required Forms and Deadlines:** FAFSA. **Types of Aid:** *Need-based scholarships/grants:* Pell, SEOG, state scholarships/grants, private scholarships. *Loans:* FFEL Subsidized Stafford, FFEL Unsubsidized Stafford, FFEL PLUS. **Student Employment:** Federal Work-Study Program available. Institutional employment available. Off-campus job opportunities are good. **Financial Aid Statistics:** 64% freshmen, 77% undergrads receive some form of aid. Average freshman grant $3,250. Average freshman loan $6,330. Average income from on-campus job $2,340. **Financial Aid Phone:** 212-686-0250.

AMERICAN ACADEMY FOR DRAMATIC ARTS—WEST

1336 N. LaBrea Avenue, Hollywood, CA 90028
Phone: 800-222-2867 **E-mail:** admissions-ca@aada.org
Fax: 626-229-9977 **Web:** www.aada.org

This private school was founded in 1884. It has a 2-acre campus.

STUDENTS AND FACULTY

Enrollment: 104. **Student Body:** International 4%. **Ethnic Representation:** African American 11%, Caucasian 69%, Hispanic 17%. **Faculty:** Student/faculty ratio 12:1.

ACADEMICS

Degrees: Associate's, terminal. **Classes:** 10-19 students in an average class. 10-19 students in an average lab/discussion section.

FACILITIES

Computers: School-owned computers available for student use.

ADMISSIONS

Selectivity Rating: 63 (of 100). **Basis for Candidate Selection:** *Very important factors considered include:* interview, talent/ability. *Important factors considered include:* recommendations. *Other factors considered include:* alumni/ae relation, character/personal qualities, essays, extracurricular activities, secondary school record, work experience. **Freshman Admission Requirements:** High school diploma or GED is required. **Freshman Admission Statistics:** 230 applied, 79% accepted, 57% of those accepted enrolled. **Transfer Admission Requirements:** *Items required:* high school transcript, college transcript, essay, interview. **General Admission Information:** Application fee $50. Nonfall registration accepted. Admission may be deferred for a maximum of 1 year.

COSTS AND FINANCIAL AID

Tuition $11,700. **Required Forms and Deadlines:** FAFSA. **Student Employment:** Federal Work-Study Program available. Institutional employment available. Off-campus job opportunities are good. **Financial Aid Statistics:** 64% freshmen, 53% undergrads receive some form of aid. Average freshman grant $2,950. Average freshman loan $6,000. Average income from on-campus job $1,510. **Financial Aid Phone:** 800-222-2867.

AMERICAN INTERNATIONAL COLLEGE

1000 State Street, Springfield, MA 01109-3184
Phone: 413-205-3201 **E-mail:** inquiry@www.aic.edu **CEEB Code:** 3002
Fax: 413-205-3948 **Web:** www.aic.edu **ACT Code:** 1772

This private school was founded in 1885. It has a 58-acre campus.

STUDENTS AND FACULTY

Enrollment: 1,426. **Student Body:** Out-of-state 44%, international 6%. **Ethnic Representation:** African American 11%, Asian 4%, Caucasian 81%, Hispanic 4%. **Retention and Graduation:** 68% freshmen return for sophomore year. 31% grads go on to further study within 1 year. 15% grads pursue business degrees. 5% grads pursue law degrees. 2% grads pursue medical degrees. **Faculty:** 100% faculty teach undergrads.

ACADEMICS

Degrees: Associate's, bachelor's, certificate, doctoral, master's, terminal. **Special Study Options:** Study abroad, off-campus study in Washington, DC, undergrads may take grad-level courses.

FACILITIES

Housing: Coed, apartments for single students. **Library Holdings:** 126,000 bound volumes. 390 periodicals. 84,100 microforms. **Special Academic Facilities/Equipment:** Centers for child development, cultural arts, and human technology. **Computers:** School-owned computers available for student use.

EXTRACURRICULARS

Organizations: 8% men join fraternities, 9% women join sororities. **Athletics (Intercollegiate):** *Men:* baseball, basketball, football, golf, ice hockey, lacrosse, soccer, tennis, wrestling. *Women:* basketball, softball, tennis, volleyball.

ADMISSIONS

Selectivity Rating: 77 (of 100). **Freshman Academic Profile:** Average high school GPA 2.7. 9% in top 10% of high school class, 22% in top 25% of high school class, 67% in top 50% of high school class. 79% from public high schools. Average SAT I Math 487, SAT I Math middle 50% range 430-520. Average SAT I Verbal 456, SAT I Verbal middle 50% range 430-560. TOEFL required of all international applicants, minimum TOEFL 500. **Freshman Admission Requirements:** High school diploma is required and GED is not accepted. *Academic units required/recommended:* 15 total required; 4 English required, 2 math required, 2 science required, 2 foreign language recommended, 1 social studies required, 1 history required, 5 elective required. **Transfer Admission Requirements:** Minimum college GPA of 2.0 required. Lowest grade transferable C. **General Admission Information:** Early decision application deadline March 1. Regular application deadline rolling. Nonfall registration accepted. Credit and/or placement offered for CEEB Advanced Placement tests.

COSTS AND FINANCIAL AID

Tuition $11,800. Room & board $5,692. Required fees $652. Average book expense $550. **Required Forms and Deadlines:** FAFSA and institution's own financial aid form. **Notification of Awards:** Applicants will be notified of awards on or about March 1. **Types of Aid:** *Need-based scholarships/grants:* Pell, SEOG, state scholarships/grants, private scholarships, the school's own gift aid, Federal Nursing. *Loans:* FFEL Subsidized Stafford, FFEL Unsubsidized Stafford, FFEL PLUS, Federal Perkins, Federal Nursing, college/university loans from institutional funds. **Student Employment:** Federal Work-Study Program available. Institutional employment available. Off-campus job opportunities are good. **Financial Aid Statistics:** Average freshman grant $5,590. Average freshman loan $2,354. Average income from on-campus job $1,200. **Financial Aid Phone:** 413-747-6259.

AMERICAN UNIVERSITY

   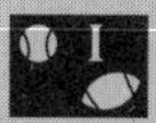 

4400 Massachusetts Avenue, NW, Washington, DC 20016-8001
Phone: 202-885-6000 **E-mail:** afa@american.edu **CEEB Code:** 5007
Fax: 202-885-1025 **Web:** www.american.edu **ACT Code:** 648

This private school, which is affiliated with the Methodist Church, was founded in 1893. It has an 84-acre campus.

STUDENTS AND FACULTY

Enrollment: 5,872. **Student Body:** Male 39%, female 61%, out-of-state 93%, international 8%. **Ethnic Representation:** African American 6%, Asian 5%, Caucasian 65%, Hispanic 5%. **Retention and Graduation:** 87% freshmen return for sophomore year. 73% grads go on to further study within 1 year. **Faculty:** Student/faculty ratio 15:1. 476 full-time faculty, 96% hold PhDs. 95% faculty teach undergrads.

ACADEMICS

Degrees: Associate's, bachelor's, certificate, doctoral, first professional, master's, post-bachelor's certificate, terminal. **Academic Requirements:** General education including some course work in arts/fine arts, English (including composition), humanities, mathematics, sciences (biological or physical), social science. The general education program requires course work in five curricular areas: the creative arts, traditions that shape the western world, international and intercultural experience, social institutions and behavior, and the natural sciences. **Majors with Highest Enrollment:** Business administration/management; international relations and affairs; political science and government, general. **Disciplines with Highest Percentage of Degrees Awarded:** Social sciences and history 35%, business/marketing 20%, communications/communication technologies 15%, protective services/public administration 7%, psychology 4%. **Special Study Options:** Accelerated program, cooperative (work-study) program, cross registration, double major, student exchange program (domestic), honors program, independent study, internships, student-designed major, study abroad, teacher certification program, weekend college. Summer programs include pre-college programs in leadership, college writing skills, and the media (script writing, photography, video production, news writing); a swim school; institutes in human rights in the 21st century; nuclear studies; the Civil War; peace, conflict resolution and development; Washington Semester Summer Internship Program; Film and Video Institute; TESOL Institute; summer study abroad programs in Cuba (politics), Southeast Asia (globalization), and Japan (nuclear studies); summer internship opportunities in Brussels, London, Madrid, Santiago, South Africa, Berlin/Prague, Prague (photography), Monterrey, Mexico (NAFTA); and Washington Internships for Native Students (WINS).

FACILITIES

Housing: Coed, apartments for single students, housing for international students, honors floors, community service floor. Intercultural/international hall available. Housing for handicapped students handled individually. Single-sex floors & wings of coed dorm; some suites. Off-campus university apartments for transfers and graduate students. **Library Holdings:** 763,000 bound volumes. 3,100 periodicals. 1,076,000 microforms. 43,000 audiovisuals. **Special Academic Facilities/Equipment:** Student-run radio and TV facilities, Watkins Art Gallery, Katzen Art Center (2004), Experimental Theatre, Greenberg Theatre, Friedheim Journalism Center, William I Jacobs Fitness Center, language resource center, multimedia center, audiotechnology lab, UNIX and Oracle labs, Kay Spiritual Life Center (interdenominational). **Computers:** School-owned computers available for student use.

EXTRACURRICULARS

Activities: Choral groups, dance, drama/theater, jazz band, literary magazine, music ensembles, musical theater, opera, pep band, radio station, student government, student newspaper, student-run film society, symphony orchestra, television station, yearbook. **Organizations:** 111 registered organizations, 15 honor societies, 10 religious organizations, 10 fraternities (17% men join), 12 sororities (18% women join). **Athletics (Intercollegiate):** *Men:* basketball, cross-country, diving, golf, indoor track, soccer, swimming, tennis, track & field, wrestling. *Women:* basketball, cross-country, diving, field hockey, indoor track, lacrosse, soccer, swimming, tennis, track & field, volleyball.

ADMISSIONS

Selectivity Rating: 83 (of 100). **Freshman Academic Profile:** Average high school GPA 3.3. 31% in top 10% of high school class, 66% in top 25% of high school class, 97% in top 50% of high school class. Average SAT I Math 600, SAT I Math middle 50% range 550-650. Average SAT I Verbal 613, SAT I Verbal middle 50% range 560-670. Average ACT 27. TOEFL required of all international applicants, minimum TOEFL 550. **Basis for Candidate Selection:** *Very important factors considered include:* secondary school record, standardized test scores. *Important factors considered include:* class rank, essays, extracurricular activities, recommendations, volunteer work. *Other factors considered include:* alumni/ae relation, character/personal qualities, interview, minority status, talent/ability, work experience. **Freshman Admission Requirements:** High school diploma or GED is required. *Academic units required/recommended:* 16 total required; 20 total recommended; 4 English required, 3 math required, 4 math recommended, 2 science required, 4 science recommended, 2 science lab required, 2 foreign language required, 3 foreign language recommended, 2 social studies required, 4 social studies recommended, 4 elective recommended. **Freshman Admission Statistics:** 9,879 applied, 63% accepted, 21% of those accepted enrolled. **Transfer Admission Requirements:** *Items required:* college transcript, essay. Minimum college GPA of 2.0 required. Lowest grade transferable C. **General Admission Information:** Application fee $45. Early decision application deadline November 15. Regular application deadline February 1. Nonfall registration accepted. Admission may be deferred for a maximum of 1 year. Credit and/or placement offered for CEEB Advanced Placement tests.

COSTS AND FINANCIAL AID

Tuition $23,068. Room & board $9,488. Required fees $387. Average book expense $600. **Required Forms and Deadlines:** FAFSA and institution's own financial aid form. Financial aid filing deadline March 1. **Notification of Awards:** Applicants will be notified of awards on or about April 1. **Types of Aid:** *Need-based scholarships/grants:* Pell, SEOG, state scholarships/grants, private scholarships, the school's own gift aid. *Academic merit scholarships:* Presidential Scholarships, Dean's Scholarships, Frederick Douglass Scholarships, Leadership Scholarships, Phi Theta Kappa Scholarships (transfers only) Tuition Exchange Scholarships, United Methodist Scholarships, and other private/restricted scholarships are awarded by the Undergraduate Admissions Office. Most scholarships do not require a separate application and are renewable for up to three years if certain criteria are met. *Loans:* Direct Subsidized Stafford, Direct Unsubsidized Stafford, Direct PLUS, Federal Perkins, college/university loans from institutional funds. **Student Employment:** Federal Work-Study Program available. Institutional employment available. Off-campus job opportunities are excellent. **Financial Aid Statistics:** 49% freshmen, 44% undergrads receive some form of aid. Average freshman grant $12,333. Average freshman loan $5,791. Average income from on-campus job $1,300. **Financial Aid Phone:** 202-885-6100.

THE AMERICAN UNIVERSITY OF PARIS

950 South Cherry Street, Suite 210, Denver, CO 80246
Phone: 303-757-6333 **E-mail:** usoffice@aup.edu **CEEB Code:** 866
Fax: 303-757-6444 **Web:** www.aup.edu **ACT Code:** 5295

This private school was founded in 1962.

STUDENTS AND FACULTY

Enrollment: 900. **Student Body:** International students represent 96 countries. **Faculty:** Student/faculty ratio 13:1. 51 full-time faculty, 72% hold PhDs. 100% faculty teach undergrads.

ACADEMICS

Degrees: Bachelor's. **Academic Requirements:** General education including some course work in English (including composition), foreign languages, humanities, sciences (biological or physical). **Majors with Highest Enrollment:** Business administration/management; English language and literature/letters; international relations and affairs. **Special Study Options:** Double major, student exchange program (domestic), independent study, internships, study abroad.

FACILITIES

Housing: Students are housed in independent rooms or with French families. **Library Holdings:** 65,000 bound volumes. **Computers:** School-owned computers available for student use.

EXTRACURRICULARS

Activities: Drama/theater, literary magazine, musical theater, student government, student newspaper, yearbook. **Organizations:** 20 registered organizations, 4 honor societies. **Athletics (Intercollegiate):** *Men:* basketball, football, rugby, soccer, swimming, volleyball. *Women:* basketball, football, soccer, swimming, volleyball.

ADMISSIONS

Selectivity Rating: 63 (of 100). **Freshman Academic Profile:** Average SAT I Math 564. Average SAT I Verbal 587. TOEFL required of all international applicants, minimum TOEFL 600. **Basis for Candidate Selection:** *Very* *important factors considered include:* class rank, secondary school record. *Important factors considered include:* character/personal qualities, essays, extracurricular activities, recommendations, standardized test scores. *Other factors considered include:* alumni/ae relation, interview, talent/ability, volunteer work, work experience. **Freshman Admission Requirements:** High school diploma or GED is required. *Academic units required/recommended:* 4 English recommended, 2 math recommended, 2 science recommended, 1 science lab recommended, 2 foreign language recommended, 2 social studies recommended, 2 history recommended. **Freshman Admission Statistics:** 482 applied, 62% accepted, 55% of those accepted enrolled. **Transfer Admission Requirements:** *Items required:* college transcript, essay, statement of good standing from prior school. Minimum college GPA of 3.0 required. Lowest grade transferable C. **General Admission Information:** Application fee $50. Priority application deadline May 1. Nonfall registration accepted. Admission may be deferred for a maximum of 1 year. Credit and/or placement offered for CEEB Advanced Placement tests.

COSTS AND FINANCIAL AID

Tuition $19,000. Room & board $10,000. Required fees $1,516. Average book expense $1,036. **Required Forms and Deadlines:** FAFSA and institution's own financial aid form. No deadline for regular filing. **Notification of Awards:** Applicants will be notified of awards on a rolling basis. **Types of Aid:** *Need-based scholarships/grants:* the school's own gift aid. *Loans:* FFEL Subsidized Stafford, FFEL Unsubsidized Stafford, FFEL PLUS. **Student Employment:** Off-campus job opportunities are fair. **Financial Aid Statistics:** Average income from on-campus job $1,600.

AMHERST COLLEGE

Campus Box 2231, PO Box 5000, Amherst, MA 01002
Phone: 413-542-2328 **E-mail:** admission@amherst.edu **CEEB Code:** 3003
Fax: 413-542-2040 **Web:** www.amherst.edu **ACT Code:** 1774

This private school was founded in 1821. It has a 978-acre campus.

STUDENTS AND FACULTY

Enrollment: 1,618. **Student Body:** Out-of-state 85%, international 5% (34 countries represented). **Ethnic Representation:** African American 9%, Asian 13%, Caucasian 52%, Hispanic 8%. **Retention and Graduation:** 98% freshmen return for sophomore year. 85% freshmen graduate within 4 years. 33% grads go on to further study within 1 year. 9% grads pursue law degrees. 10% grads pursue medical degrees. **Faculty:** Student/faculty ratio 9:1. 177 full-time faculty, 91% hold PhDs. 100% faculty teach undergrads.

ACADEMICS

Degrees: Bachelor's. **Classes:** 10-19 students in an average class. Under 10 students in an average lab/discussion section. **Majors with Highest Enrollment:** English language and literature, general; economics, general; political science and government, general. **Disciplines with Highest Percentage of Degrees Awarded:** Social sciences and history 26%, foreign languages and literature 11%, English 11%, psychology 10%, visual and performing arts 8%. **Special Study Options:** Cross registration, double major, student exchange program (domestic), honors program, independent study, student-designed major, study abroad, teacher certification program.

FACILITIES

Housing: Coed, all-female, all-male, cooperative housing, French/Spanish language house, German/Russian language house, Latino culture house, African American culture house, health and wellness quarter. **Library Holdings:** 977,379 bound volumes. 5,348 periodicals. 29,481 microforms. 32,460 audiovisuals. **Special Academic Facilities/Equipment:** Art, natural history, geology, and natural science museums, language labs, observatory, planetarium, the Amherst Center for Russian Culture. **Computers:** School-owned computers available for student use.

EXTRACURRICULARS

Activities: Choral groups, concert band, dance, drama/theater, jazz band, literary magazine, music ensembles, musical theater, opera, radio station, student government, student newspaper, student-run film society, symphony orchestra, television station, yearbook. **Organizations:** 100 registered organizations, 2 honor societies, 7 religious organizations. **Athletics (Intercollegiate):** *Men:* baseball, basketball, cross-country, diving, football, golf, ice hockey, indoor track, lacrosse, soccer, squash, swimming, tennis, track & field. *Women:* basketball, cross-country, diving, field hockey, golf, ice hockey, indoor track, lacrosse, soccer, softball, squash, swimming, tennis, track & field, volleyball.

ADMISSIONS

Selectivity Rating: 99 (of 100). **Freshman Academic Profile:** 82% in top 10% of high school class, 98% in top 25% of high school class, 100% in top 50% of high school class. 60% from public high schools. Average SAT I Math 707, SAT I Math middle 50% range 650-770. Average SAT I Verbal 710, SAT I Verbal middle 50% range 660-770. Average ACT 30, ACT middle 50% range 28-33. TOEFL required of all international applicants, minimum TOEFL 600. **Basis for Candidate Selection:** *Very important factors considered include:* character/personal qualities, essays, extracurricular activities, recommendations, secondary school record, standardized test scores, talent/ability. *Important factors considered include:* alumni/ae relation, class rank, volunteer work. *Other factors considered include:* geographical residence, state residency, work experience. **Freshman Admission Requirements:** High school diploma or equivalent is not required. *Academic units required/recommended:* 4 English recommended, 4 math recommended, 3 science recommended, 1 science lab recommended, 4 foreign language recommended, 2 social studies recommended, 2 history recommended. **Freshman Admission Statistics:** 5,238 applied, 18% accepted. **Transfer Admission Requirements:** *Items required:* high school transcript, college transcript, essay, statement of good standing from prior school. Minimum college GPA of 3.5 required. Lowest grade transferable C. **General Admission Information:** Application fee $55. Early decision application deadline November 15. Regular application deadline December 31. Admission may be deferred for a maximum of 1 year. Neither credit nor placement offered for CEEB Advanced Placement tests.

COSTS AND FINANCIAL AID

Tuition $27,800. Room & board $7,380. Required fees $510. Average book expense $850. **Required Forms and Deadlines:** FAFSA, CSS/Financial Aid PROFILE, noncustodial (divorced/separated) parent's statement, business/farm supplement, income tax returns, W-2 forms (or other wage statements). Financial aid filing deadline February 15. **Notification of Awards:** Applicants will be notified of awards on or about April 8. **Types of Aid:** *Need-based scholarships/grants:* Pell, SEOG, state scholarships/grants, private scholarships, the school's own gift aid. *Loans:* Direct Subsidized Stafford, Direct Unsubsidized Stafford, Direct PLUS, Federal Perkins, college/university loans from institutional funds. **Student Employment:** Federal Work-Study Program available. Institutional employment available. Off-campus job opportunities are good. **Financial Aid Statistics:** 47% freshmen, 49% undergrads receive some form of aid. Average freshman grant $25,534. Average freshman loan $2,150. Average income from on-campus job $1,450. **Financial Aid Phone:** 413-542-2296.

ANDERSON COLLEGE

316 Boulevard, Anderson, SC 29621
Phone: 864-231-5607 **E-mail:** admissions@ac.edu **CEEB Code:** 5008
Fax: 864-231-2033 **Web:** www.ac.edu **ACT Code:** 3832

This private school was founded in 1911. It has a 56-acre campus.

STUDENTS AND FACULTY

Enrollment: 1,639. **Student Body:** Male 35%, female 65%, out-of-state 10%, international 1%. **Ethnic Representation:** African American 12%, Caucasian 84%, Hispanic 1%. **Retention and Graduation:** 67% freshmen return for sophomore year. 12% freshmen graduate within 4 years. 15% grads go on to further study within 1 year. **Faculty:** Student/faculty ratio 14:1. 66 full-time faculty, 65% hold PhDs. 100% faculty teach undergrads.

ACADEMICS

Degrees: Bachelor's. **Academic Requirements:** General education including some course work in arts/fine arts, computer literacy, English (including composition), history, humanities, mathematics, sciences (biological or physical), social science. **Classes:** 20-29 students in an average class. **Majors with Highest Enrollment:** Education, general; business administration/management; human resources management/personnel administration, general. **Disciplines with Highest Percentage of Degrees Awarded:** Business/marketing 33%, other 22%, education 13%, visual and performing arts 10%, psychology 7%. **Special Study Options:** Accelerated program, double major, dual enrollment, honors program, independent study, internships, study abroad, teacher certification program.

FACILITIES

Housing: All-female, all-male, apartments for single students, housing for disabled students. **Library Holdings:** 65,602 bound volumes. 355 periodicals. 6,761 microforms. 4,591 audiovisuals. **Special Academic Facilities/Equipment:** Electronic classrooms, art gallery, recording studio. **Computers:** School-owned computers available for student use.

EXTRACURRICULARS

Activities: Choral groups, concert band, jazz band, literary magazine, music ensembles, musical theater, student government, student newspaper, symphony orchestra, yearbook. **Organizations:** 27 registered organizations, 1 honor society, 6 religious organizations. **Athletics (Intercollegiate):** *Men:* baseball, basketball, cross-country, equestrian, golf, soccer, tennis, track & field, wrestling. *Women:* basketball, cheerleading, cross-country, equestrian, golf, soccer, softball, tennis, track & field, volleyball.

ADMISSIONS

Selectivity Rating: 83 (of 100). **Freshman Academic Profile:** Average high school GPA 3.4. 11% in top 10% of high school class, 51% in top 25% of high school class, 79% in top 50% of high school class. 94% from public high schools. Average SAT I Math 556, SAT I Math middle 50% range 440-550. Average SAT I Verbal 543, SAT I Verbal middle 50% range 440-530. Average ACT 20, ACT middle 50% range 18-22. TOEFL required of all international applicants, minimum TOEFL 550. **Basis for Candidate Selection:** *Very important factors considered include:* secondary school record. *Important factors considered include:* class rank, standardized test scores. *Other factors considered include:* alumni/ae relation, character/personal qualities, essays, extracurricular activities, interview, recommendations. **Freshman Admission Requirements:** High school diploma or GED is required. *Academic units required/recommended:* 20 total recommended; 4 English recommended, 3 math recommended, 3 science recommended, 2 foreign language recommended, 3 social studies recommended. **Freshman Admission Statistics:** 1,011 applied, 73% accepted, 51% of those accepted enrolled. **Transfer Admission Requirements:** *Items required:* college transcript, statement of good standing from prior school. Minimum college GPA of 2.0 required. Lowest grade transferable C. **General Admission Information:** Application fee $40. Priority application deadline March 15. Regular application deadline June 30. Nonfall registration accepted. Admission may be deferred for a maximum of 1 year. Credit and/or placement offered for CEEB Advanced Placement tests.

COSTS AND FINANCIAL AID

Tuition $12,320. Room & board $5,445. Required fees $795. Average book expense $1,400. **Required Forms and Deadlines:** FAFSA. Financial aid filing deadline July 1. Priority filing deadline March 1. **Notification of Awards:** Applicants will be notified of awards on a rolling basis beginning on or about March 1. **Types of Aid:** *Need-based scholarships/grants:* Pell, SEOG, state scholarships/grants, the school's own gift aid. *Loans:* FFEL Subsidized Stafford, FFEL Unsubsidized Stafford, FFEL PLUS, Federal Perkins, college/university loans from institutional funds. **Student Employment:** Federal Work-Study Program available. Institutional employment available. Off-campus job opportunities are excellent. **Financial Aid Statistics:** 100% freshmen, 87% undergrads receive some form of aid. Average freshman grant $9,137. Average freshman loan $2,142. Average income from on-campus job $872. **Financial Aid Phone:** 864-231-2070.

ANDERSON UNIVERSITY

1100 East Fifth Street, Anderson, IN 46012
Phone: 765-641-4080 **E-mail:** info@anderson.edu **CEEB Code:** 1016
Fax: 765-641-4091 **Web:** www.anderson.edu **ACT Code:** 1174

This private school was founded in 1917. It has a 103-acre campus.

STUDENTS AND FACULTY

Enrollment: 1,977. **Student Body:** Male 40%, female 60%, out-of-state 36%, international 1% (12 countries represented). **Ethnic Representation:** African American 4%, Caucasian 94%, Hispanic 1%. **Retention and Graduation:** 76% freshmen return for sophomore year. 32% freshmen graduate within 4 years. **Faculty:** 93% faculty teach undergrads.

ACADEMICS

Degrees: Associate's, bachelor's, doctoral, master's. **Academic Requirements:** General education including some course work in arts/fine arts, English (including composition), foreign languages, humanities, mathematics, philosophy, sciences (biological or physical), social science. **Special Study Options:** Accelerated program, cross registration, double major, honors program, independent study, internships, student-designed major, study abroad, teacher certification program, summer overseas service program.

FACILITIES

Housing: All-female, all-male, apartments for married students, apartments for single students. **Library Holdings:** 280,575 bound volumes. 928 periodicals. 104,995 microforms. 65 audiovisuals. **Special Academic Facilities/Equipment:** Gustav Jeeninga Museum of Bible and Near Eastern Studies, Wilson Galleries, Archives of the Church of God.

EXTRACURRICULARS

Activities: Choral groups, concert band, drama/theater, jazz band, literary magazine, music ensembles, musical theater, opera, pep band, radio station, student government, student newspaper, symphony orchestra, yearbook. **Organizations:** 35 registered organizations, 12 honor societies, 15 religious organizations, 4 fraternities. **Athletics (Intercollegiate):** *Men:* baseball, basketball, cheerleading, cross-country, football, golf, soccer, tennis, track & field. *Women:* basketball, cheerleading, cross-country, golf, soccer, softball, tennis, track & field, volleyball.

ADMISSIONS

Selectivity Rating: 63 (of 100). **Freshman Academic Profile:** Average high school GPA 3.4. 23% in top 10% of high school class, 53% in top 25% of high school class, 85% in top 50% of high school class. Average SAT I Math 538, SAT I Math middle 50% range 480-590. Average SAT I Verbal 533, SAT I Verbal middle 50% range 480-590. Average ACT 24, ACT middle 50% range 21-26. TOEFL required of all international applicants, **Basis for Candidate Selection:** *Very important factors considered include:* recommendations. *Important factors considered include:* character/personal qualities, class rank, extracurricular activities, interview, religious affiliation/commitment, standardized test scores, volunteer work. *Other factors considered include:* alumni/ae relation, essays, minority status, secondary school record, talent/ability, work experience. **Freshman Admission Requirements:** High school diploma or GED is required. *Academic units required/recommended:* 16 total required; 20 total recommended; 4 English required, 3 math required, 2 science required, 3 science recommended, 2 science lab required, 3 science lab recommended, 2 foreign language recommended, 2 social studies required, 3 social studies recommended, 2 history required, 5 elective recommended. **Freshman Admission Statistics:** 1,552 applied, 82% accepted, 44% of those accepted enrolled. **Transfer Admission Requirements:** *Items required:* high school transcript, college transcript, standardized test scores, statement of good standing from prior school. Minimum high school GPA of 2.0 required. Minimum college GPA of 2.0 required. Lowest grade transferable C. **General Admission Information:** Application fee $20. Priority application deadline May 1. Regular application deadline August 1. Nonfall registration accepted. Admission may be deferred for a maximum of 1 year. Credit and/or placement offered for CEEB Advanced Placement tests.

COSTS AND FINANCIAL AID

Tuition $16,140. Room & board $5,260. Average book expense $580. **Required Forms and Deadlines:** FAFSA. No deadline for regular filing. Priority filing deadline March 1. **Notification of Awards:** Applicants will be notified of awards on a rolling basis beginning on or about February 15. **Types of Aid:** *Need-based scholarships/grants:* Pell, SEOG, state scholarships/grants, private scholarships, the school's own gift aid. *Loans:* FFEL Subsidized Stafford, FFEL Unsubsidized Stafford, FFEL PLUS, Federal Perkins, college/university loans from institutional funds. **Student Employment:** Federal Work-Study Program available. Institutional employment available. Off-campus job opportunities are excellent. **Financial Aid Statistics:** 79% freshmen, 76% undergrads receive some form of aid. **Financial Aid Phone:** 800-421-1026.

ANDREWS UNIVERSITY

Office of Admissions, Berrien Springs, MI 49104
Phone: 800-253-2874 **E-mail:** enroll@andrews.edu **CEEB Code:** 1030
Fax: 616-471-3228 **Web:** www.andrews.edu **ACT Code:** 1992

This private school, which is affiliated with the Seventh-Day Adventist Church, was founded in 1874. It has a 1,600-acre campus.

STUDENTS AND FACULTY

Enrollment: 1,847. **Student Body:** Male 43%, female 57%, out-of-state 42%, international 14% (82 countries represented). **Ethnic Representation:** African American 23%, Asian 11%, Caucasian 58%, Hispanic 9%. **Retention and Graduation:** 69% freshmen return for sophomore year. 24% grads go on to further study within 1 year.

ACADEMICS

Degrees: Associate's, bachelor's, doctoral, first professional, master's. **Special Study Options:** Study abroad; undergrads may take grad-level classes.

FACILITIES

Housing: All-female, all-male, apartments for married students, apartments for single students. **Library Holdings:** 659,890 bound volumes. 2,259 periodicals. 68,415 microforms. 113,727 audiovisuals. **Special Academic Facilities/**

Equipment: Audiovisual center, lab school, natural history and archaeological museums, observatory, physical therapy facilities. **Computers:** *Recommended operating system:* Mac. School-owned computers available for student use.

EXTRACURRICULARS

Activities: Choral groups, concert band, radio station, student government, student newspaper, yearbook. **Organizations:** 2 religious organizations.

ADMISSIONS

Selectivity Rating: 69 (of 100). **Freshman Academic Profile:** Average high school GPA 3.0. 14% in top 10% of high school class, 35% in top 25% of high school class, 69% in top 50% of high school class. 23% from public high schools. Average SAT I Math 510, SAT I Math middle 50% range 420-600. Average SAT I Verbal 540, SAT I Verbal middle 50% range 440-610. Average ACT 22, ACT middle 50% range 19-27. TOEFL required of all international applicants, minimum TOEFL 550. **Freshman Admission Requirements:** High school diploma or GED is required. *Academic units required/recommended:* 4 English recommended, 2 math recommended, 2 science recommended, 2 history recommended. **Transfer Admission Requirements:** Minimum college GPA of 2.0 required. Lowest grade transferable C. **General Admission Information:** Application fee $30. Early decision application deadline January 1. Regular application deadline rolling. Nonfall registration accepted. Credit offered for CEEB Advanced Placement tests.

COSTS AND FINANCIAL AID

Tuition $11,685. Room & board $3,630. Required fees $285. Average book expense $1,128. **Required Forms and Deadlines:** FAFSA, institution's own financial aid form and state aid form. **Types of Aid:** *Need-based scholarships/grants:* state scholarships/grants. *Loans:* FFEL Subsidized Stafford, FFEL PLUS. **Student Employment:** Federal Work-Study Program available. Institutional employment available. Off-campus job opportunities are good. **Financial Aid Statistics:** Average income from on-campus job $1,200. **Financial Aid Phone:** 800-253-2874.

ANGELO STATE UNIVERSITY

2601 West Avenue N, San Angelo, TX 76909
Phone: 915-942-2185 **E-mail:** admissions@angelo.edu **CEEB Code:** 6644
Fax: 915-942-2078 **Web:** www.angelo.edu **ACT Code:** 4164

This public school was founded in 1928. It has a 268-acre campus.

STUDENTS AND FACULTY

Enrollment: 5,859. **Student Body:** Male 44%, female 56%, out-of-state 3%, international 1%. **Ethnic Representation:** African American 5%, Asian 1%, Caucasian 73%, Hispanic 20%. **Retention and Graduation:** 67% freshmen return for sophomore year. 15% grads pursue business degrees. 3% grads pursue law degrees. 4% grads pursue medical degrees. **Faculty:** Student/faculty ratio 32:1. 232 full-time faculty, 70% hold PhDs.

ACADEMICS

Degrees: Associate's, bachelor's, master's. **Academic Requirements:** General education including some course work in arts/fine arts, computer literacy, English (including composition), history, mathematics, sciences (biological or physical). **Disciplines with Highest Percentage of Degrees Awarded:** Education 27%, business/marketing 19%, social sciences and history 11%, communications/communication technologies 5%, biological life sciences 5%. **Special Study Options:** Accelerated program, cooperative (work-study) program, distance learning, double major, dual enrollment, student exchange program (domestic), internships, study abroad, teacher certification program.

FACILITIES

Housing: All-female, all-male, apartments for single students. **Library Holdings:** 257,376 bound volumes. 13,300 periodicals. 648,373 microforms. 8,000 audiovisuals. **Special Academic Facilities/Equipment:** Planetarium. **Computers:** School-owned computers available for student use.

EXTRACURRICULARS

Activities: Choral groups, concert band, dance, drama/theater, jazz band, literary magazine, marching band, music ensembles, musical theater, radio station, student government, student newspaper. **Organizations:** 69 registered organizations, 18 honor societies, 8 religious organizations, 3 fraternities (2% men join), 2 sororities (4% women join). **Athletics (Intercollegiate):** *Men:* basketball, cheerleading, cross-country, football, track & field. *Women:* basketball, cheerleading, cross-country, soccer, softball, track & field, volleyball.

ADMISSIONS

Selectivity Rating: 67 (of 100). **Freshman Academic Profile:** 19% in top 10% of high school class, 43% in top 25% of high school class, 80% in top 50% of high school class. 98% from public high schools. Average SAT I Math 499, SAT I Math middle 50% range 430-560. Average SAT I Verbal 493, SAT I Verbal middle 50% range 430-600. Average ACT 21, ACT middle 50% range 20-22. TOEFL required of all international applicants, minimum TOEFL 550. **Basis for Candidate Selection:** *Very important factors considered include:* class rank, secondary school record, standardized test scores. **Freshman Admission Requirements:** High school diploma or GED is required. *Academic units required/recommended:* 23 total recommended; 4 English recommended, 3 math recommended, 3 science recommended, 2 foreign language recommended, 3 social studies recommended, 1 elective recommended. **Freshman Admission Statistics:** 3,281 applied, 71% accepted, 56% of those accepted enrolled. **Transfer Admission Requirements:** Minimum college GPA of 2.0 required. Lowest grade transferable F. **General Admission Information:** Priority application deadline August 1. Regular application deadline August 1. Nonfall registration accepted. Admission may be deferred for a maximum of 1 year. Credit offered for CEEB Advanced Placement tests.

COSTS AND FINANCIAL AID

In-state tuition $2,000. Out-of-state tuition $6,096. Room & board $4,066. Required fees $263. Average book expense $500. **Required Forms and Deadlines:** Financial aid filing deadline June 1. **Student Employment:** Federal Work-Study Program available. Institutional employment available. Off-campus job opportunities are excellent. **Financial Aid Statistics:** Average freshman grant $1,474. Average freshman loan $2,734. Average income from on-campus job $1,986. **Financial Aid Phone:** 915-942-2246.

ANNA MARIA COLLEGE

50 Sunset Lane, Box O, Paxton, MA 01612-1198
Phone: 508-849-3360 **E-mail:** admission@annamaria.edu **CEEB Code:** 3005
Fax: 508-849-3362 **Web:** www.annamaria.edu **ACT Code:** 3232

This private school, which is affiliated with the Roman Catholic Church, was founded in 1946. It has a 180-acre campus.

STUDENTS AND FACULTY

Enrollment: 803. **Student Body:** Male 36%, female 64%, out-of-state 16%, international 1% (9 countries represented). **Ethnic Representation:** African American 2%, Asian 1%, Caucasian 89%, Hispanic 2%, Native American 1%. **Retention and Graduation:** 71% freshmen return for sophomore year. 47% freshmen graduate within 4 years. **Faculty:** Student/faculty ratio 10:1. 37 full-time faculty, 41% hold PhDs. 100% faculty teach undergrads.

ACADEMICS

Degrees: Associate's, bachelor's, master's, post-bachelor's certificate, post-master's certificate. **Academic Requirements:** General education including some course work in arts/fine arts, computer literacy, English (including composition), foreign languages, history, humanities, mathematics, philosophy, sciences (biological or physical), social science. **Classes:** Under 10 students in an average class. **Majors with Highest Enrollment:** Criminal justice/law enforcement administration; human development and family studies, general; business administration/management. **Disciplines with Highest Percentage of Degrees Awarded:** Protective services/public administration 43%, education 13%, business/marketing 11%, visual and performing arts 8%, social sciences and history 6%. **Special Study Options:** Accelerated program, cooperative (work-study) program, cross registration, double major, dual enrollment, English as a second language, independent study, internships, liberal arts/career combination, student-designed major, study abroad, teacher certification program.

FACILITIES

Housing: Coed, housing for disabled students, substance-free option. **Library Holdings:** 79,039 bound volumes. 318 periodicals. 1,738 microforms. 895 audiovisuals. **Computers:** School-owned computers available for student use.

EXTRACURRICULARS

Activities: Choral groups, drama/theater, jazz band, music ensembles, pep band, student government, student newspaper, yearbook. **Organizations:** 25 registered organizations. **Athletics (Intercollegiate):** *Men:* baseball, basketball, cross-country, golf, soccer. *Women:* basketball, cheerleading, field hockey, soccer, softball, volleyball.

ADMISSIONS

Selectivity Rating: 67 (of 100). **Freshman Academic Profile:** Average high school GPA 2.7. 1% in top 10% of high school class, 14% in top 25% of high school class, 40% in top 50% of high school class. 73% from public high schools. Average SAT I Math 462, SAT I Math middle 50% range 400-530. Average SAT I Verbal 478, SAT I Verbal middle 50% range 420-530. Average ACT 18, ACT middle 50% range 16-18. TOEFL required of all international applicants, minimum TOEFL 525. **Basis for Candidate Selection:** *Very important factors considered include:* secondary school record. *Important factors considered include:* essays, extracurricular activities, recommendations, standardized test scores. *Other factors considered include:* alumni/ae relation, character/personal qualities, class rank, interview, talent/ability, volunteer work, work experience. **Freshman Admission Requirements:** High school diploma or GED is required. *Academic units required/recommended:* 19 total required; 4 English required, 3 math required, 3 science required, 1 science lab required, 2 foreign language required, 2 social studies required, 4 elective required. **Freshman Admission Statistics:** 574 applied, 83% accepted, 35% of those accepted enrolled. **Transfer Admission Requirements:** *Items required:* high school transcript, college transcript, essay, statement of good standing from prior school. Minimum college GPA of 2.0 required. Lowest grade transferable C. **General Admission Information:** Application fee $30. Priority application deadline March 1. Nonfall registration accepted. Admission may be deferred for a maximum of 1 year. Neither credit nor placement offered for CEEB Advanced Placement tests.

COSTS AND FINANCIAL AID

Average book expense $800. **Required Forms and Deadlines:** FAFSA. No deadline for regular filing. Priority filing deadline March 15. **Notification of Awards:** Applicants will be notified of awards on a rolling basis beginning on or about May 15. **Types of Aid:** *Need-based scholarships/grants:* Pell, SEOG, state scholarships/grants, private scholarships, the school's own gift aid. *Loans:* FFEL Subsidized Stafford, FFEL Unsubsidized Stafford, FFEL PLUS, Federal Perkins, state loans. **Student Employment:** Federal Work-Study Program available. Institutional employment available. Off-campus job opportunities are good. **Financial Aid Statistics:** 86% freshmen, 71% undergrads receive some form of aid. Average freshman grant $10,008. Average freshman loan $3,706. **Financial Aid Phone:** 508-849-3367.

See page 912.

ANTIOCH COLLEGE

795 Livermore Street, Yellow Spring, OH 45387
Phone: 937-769-1100 **E-mail:** admissions@antioch-college.edu **CEEB Code:** 1017
Fax: 937-769-1111 **Web:** www.antioch-college.edu **ACT Code:** 3232

This private school was founded in 1852. It has a 100-acre campus.

STUDENTS AND FACULTY

Enrollment: 581. **Student Body:** Male 39%, female 61%, out-of-state 76%, international 1%. **Ethnic Representation:** African American 6%, Asian 1%, Caucasian 66%, Hispanic 5%, Native American 1%. **Retention and Graduation:** 69% freshmen return for sophomore year. **Faculty:** Student/faculty ratio 10:1. 100% faculty teach undergrads.

ACADEMICS

Degrees: Bachelor's. **Academic Requirements:** General education including some course work in arts/fine arts, English (including composition), foreign languages, history, humanities, mathematics, philosophy, sciences (biological or physical), social science. **Disciplines with Highest Percentage of Degrees Awarded:** Interdisciplinary studies 24%, communications/communication technologies 19%, social sciences and history 14%, visual and performing arts 9%, English 8%. **Special Study Options:** Cooperative (work-study) program, cross registration, double major, independent study, internships, liberal arts/career combination, student-designed major, study abroad.

FACILITIES

Housing: Coed, all-female, all-male, apartments for married students, housing for international students. **Library Holdings:** 300,000 bound volumes. 10,504 periodicals. 48,394 microforms. 6,259 audiovisuals. **Special Academic Facilities/Equipment:** 1,000-acre nature preserve. **Computers:** School-owned computers available for student use.

EXTRACURRICULARS

Activities: Choral groups, dance, drama/theater, jazz band, literary magazine, music ensembles, musical theater, radio station, student government, student newspaper, student-run film society, symphony orchestra. **Organizations:** 16 registered organizations.

ADMISSIONS

Selectivity Rating: 72 (of 100). **Freshman Academic Profile:** Average high school GPA 3.0. TOEFL required of all international applicants, minimum TOEFL 525. **Basis for Candidate Selection:** *Very important factors considered include:* essays, interview, recommendations, secondary school record. *Important factors considered include:* character/personal qualities, talent/ability, volunteer work, work experience. *Other factors considered include:* alumni/ae relation, extracurricular activities, minority status. **Freshman Admission Requirements:** High school diploma or GED is required. *Academic units required/recommended:* 13 total recommended; 4 English recommended, 3 math recommended, 3 science recommended, 1 foreign language recommended, 1 social studies recommended, 1 history recommended. **Freshman Admission Statistics:** 504 applied, 75% accepted, 42% of those accepted enrolled. **Transfer Admission Requirements:** *Items required:* high school transcript, college transcript, essay, statement of good standing from prior school. Minimum high school GPA of 2.5 required. Minimum college GPA of 2.0 required. Lowest grade transferable C. **General Admission Information:** Application fee $35. Priority application deadline February 1. Nonfall registration accepted. Admission may be deferred for a maximum of 1 year. Credit and/or placement offered for CEEB Advanced Placement tests.

COSTS AND FINANCIAL AID

Tuition $21,826. Room & board $5,770. Required fees $913. Average book expense $2,000. **Required Forms and Deadlines:** FAFSA, institution's own financial aid form, noncustodial (divorced/separated) parent's statement, and W-2s and 1040s. Financial aid filing deadline March 3. Priority filing deadline February 3. **Notification of Awards:** Applicants will be notified of awards on a rolling basis. **Types of Aid:** *Need-based scholarships/grants:* Pell, SEOG, state scholarships/grants, private scholarships, the school's own gift aid. *Loans:* Direct Subsidized Stafford, Direct Unsubsidized Stafford, Direct PLUS, FFEL Subsidized Stafford, FFEL Unsubsidized Stafford, FFEL PLUS, Federal Perkins, college/university loans from institutional funds. **Student Employment:** Federal Work-Study Program available. Institutional employment available. Off-campus job opportunities are fair. **Financial Aid Statistics:** 76% freshmen, 84% undergrads receive some form of aid. Average freshman grant $11,534. Average freshman loan $2,625. **Financial Aid Phone:** 800-543-9436.

APPALACHIAN STATE UNIVERSITY

Office of Admissions, PO Box 32004, Boone, NC 28608-2004
Phone: 828-262-2120 **E-mail:** admissions@appstate.edu **CEEB Code:** 5010
Fax: 828-262-3296 **Web:** www.appstate.edu **ACT Code:** 3062

This public school was founded in 1899. It has a 1,100-acre campus.

STUDENTS AND FACULTY

Enrollment: 12,852. **Student Body:** Male 49%, female 51%, out-of-state 11%. **Ethnic Representation:** African American 3%, Asian 1%, Caucasian 93%, Hispanic 1%. **Retention and Graduation:** 31% freshmen graduate within 4 years. **Faculty:** Student/faculty ratio 19:1. 619 full-time faculty, 79% hold PhDs. 100% faculty teach undergrads.

ACADEMICS

Degrees: Bachelor's, doctoral, master's, post-master's certificate. **Academic Requirements:** General education including some course work in arts/fine arts, computer literacy, English (including composition), history, humanities, mathematics, sciences (biological or physical), social science. **Classes:** 20-29 students in an average class. 20-29 students in an average lab/discussion section. **Majors with Highest Enrollment:** Elementary education and teaching; psychology, general; business administration/management. **Disciplines with Highest Percentage of Degrees Awarded:** Business/marketing 21%, education 15%, communications/communication technologies 9%, social sciences and history 8%, visual and performing arts 7%. **Special Study Options:** Cooperative (work-study) program, distance learning, double major, dual enrollment, English as a second language, honors program, independent study, internships, liberal arts/career combination, student-designed major, study abroad, teacher certification program.

FACILITIES

Housing: Coed, all-female, all-male, apartments for married students, housing for disabled students, housing for international students, cooperative housing. **Library Holdings:** 533,391 bound volumes. 5,313 periodicals. 1,461,181 microforms. 75,571 audiovisuals. **Special Academic Facilities/Equipment:** Museum of Appalachian history, language lab, observatory, meteorological reporting station, Catherine Smith Gallery. **Computers:** *Recommended operating system:* Windows 98. School-owned computers available for student use.

EXTRACURRICULARS

Activities: Choral groups, concert band, dance, drama/theater, jazz band, literary magazine, marching band, music ensembles, musical theater, opera, pep band, radio station, student government, student newspaper, student-run film society, symphony orchestra, television station. **Organizations:** 213 registered organizations, 30 honor societies, 40 religious organizations, 11 fraternities (4% men join), 8 sororities (3% women join). **Athletics (Intercollegiate):** *Men:* baseball, basketball, cheerleading, cross-country, football, golf, indoor track, soccer, tennis, track & field, wrestling. *Women:* basketball, cheerleading, cross-country, field hockey, golf, indoor track, soccer, tennis, track & field, volleyball.

ADMISSIONS

Selectivity Rating: 79 (of 100). **Freshman Academic Profile:** Average high school GPA 3.7. 17% in top 10% of high school class, 52% in top 25% of high school class, 91% in top 50% of high school class. Average SAT I Math 553, SAT I Math middle 50% range 510-610. Average SAT I Verbal 548, SAT I Verbal middle 50% range 500-600. Average ACT 22, ACT middle 50% range 19-26. TOEFL required of all international applicants, minimum TOEFL 500. **Basis for Candidate Selection:** *Very important factors considered include:* class rank, secondary school record. *Important factors considered include:* standardized test scores. *Other factors considered include:* character/personal qualities, essays, extracurricular activities, geographical residence, recommendations, state residency, talent/ability, volunteer work, work experience. **Freshman Admission Requirements:** High school diploma or GED is required. *Academic units required/recommended:* 4 English required, 3 math required, 3 science required, 1 science lab required, 2 foreign language recommended, 1 social studies required, 1 history required. **Freshman Admission Statistics:** 8,874 applied, 64% accepted, 42% of those accepted enrolled. **Transfer Admission Requirements:** *Items required:* high school transcript, college transcript, statement of good standing from prior school. Minimum college GPA of 2.0 required. Lowest grade transferable D. **General Admission Information:** Application fee $45. Nonfall registration accepted. Admission may be deferred for a maximum of 1 year. Credit and/or placement offered for CEEB Advanced Placement tests.

COSTS AND FINANCIAL AID

In-state tuition $1,520. Out-of-state tuition $10,441. Room & board $4,333. Required fees $1,275. Average book expense $500. **Required Forms and Deadlines:** FAFSA. No deadline for regular filing. Priority filing deadline March 31. **Notification of Awards:** Applicants will be notified of awards on a rolling basis beginning on or about April 1. **Types of Aid:** *Need-based scholarships/grants:* Pell, SEOG, state scholarships/grants, private scholarships, the school's own gift aid. *Loans:* FFEL Subsidized Stafford, FFEL Unsubsidized Stafford, FFEL PLUS, Federal Perkins. **Student Employment:** Federal Work-Study Program available. Institutional employment available. Off-campus job opportunities are good. **Financial Aid Statistics:** 30% freshmen, 31% undergrads receive some form of aid. **Financial Aid Phone:** 828-262-2190.

AQUINAS COLLEGE (MI)

1607 Robinson Road SE, Grand Rapids, MI 49506-1799
Phone: 616-732-4460 **E-mail:** admissions@aquinas.edu **CEEB Code:** 1018
Fax: 616-732-4469 **Web:** www.aquinas.edu **ACT Code:** 1962

This private school, which is affiliated with the Roman Catholic Church, was founded in 1886. It has a 107-acre campus.

STUDENTS AND FACULTY

Enrollment: 1,991. **Student Body:** Male 34%, female 66%, out-of-state 6%, international students represent 11 countries. **Ethnic Representation:** African American 4%, Asian 1%, Caucasian 91%, Hispanic 2%. **Retention and Graduation:** 73% freshmen return for sophomore year. 33% freshmen graduate within 4 years. 13% grads go on to further study within 1 year. 15% grads pursue business degrees. 11% grads pursue law degrees. 11% grads pursue medical degrees. **Faculty:** Student/faculty ratio 16:1. 98 full-time faculty, 68% hold PhDs. 100% faculty teach undergrads.

ACADEMICS

Degrees: Associate's, bachelor's, master's. **Academic Requirements:** General education including some course work in arts/fine arts, computer literacy, English (including composition), foreign languages, history, humanities, mathematics, philosophy, sciences (biological or physical), social science. **Classes:** 10-19 students in an average class. **Majors with Highest Enrollment:** Business administration/management; English language and literature, general; liberal arts and sciences/liberal studies. **Disciplines with Highest Percentage of Degrees Awarded:** Business/marketing 28%, education 14%, social sciences and history 14%, liberal arts/general studies 7%, English 7%. **Special Study Options:** Accelerated program, cooperative (work-study) program, cross registration, distance learning, double major, dual enrollment, student exchange program (domestic), honors program, independent study, internships, liberal arts/career combination, student-designed major, study abroad, teacher certification program; service learning experiences in Costa Rica, Peru, Haiti, Mexico, and Montana; semester in Ireland program.

FACILITIES

Housing: Coed, apartments for single students, project/theme houses. **Library Holdings:** 112,458 bound volumes. 14,725 periodicals. 223,804 microforms. 4,907 audiovisuals. **Special Academic Facilities/Equipment:** Observatory and Jarecki Center for Advanced Learning featuring high-speed, two-way interactive videoconferencing for courses and a virtual connection for external experts to interact with classes (sound, video, graphics) using a laptop computer equipped with a camera that is housed in a self-contained briefcase. The package includes all the technology needed to accomplish the connection through a standard phone jack. This "virtual faculty briefcase" can be shipped to a guest lecturer at another location anywhere in the world, and he or she is able to conduct an interactive lecture or discussion with an Aquinas classroom. **Computers:** *Recommended operating system:* Windows NT/2000. School-owned computers available for student use.

EXTRACURRICULARS

Activities: Choral groups, jazz band, literary magazine, music ensembles, radio station, student government, student newspaper, yearbook. **Organizations:** 49 registered organizations, 2 honor societies, 2 religious organizations. **Athletics (Intercollegiate):** *Men:* baseball, basketball, cheerleading, cross-country, golf, indoor track, soccer, tennis, track & field. *Women:* basketball, cheerleading, cross-country, golf, indoor track, soccer, softball, tennis, track & field, volleyball.

ADMISSIONS

Selectivity Rating: 68 (of 100). **Freshman Academic Profile:** Average high school GPA 3.3. 18% in top 10% of high school class, 42% in top 25% of high school class, 67% in top 50% of high school class. 88% from public high schools. Average ACT 23, ACT middle 50% range 20-26. TOEFL required of all international applicants, minimum TOEFL 550. **Basis for Candidate Selection:** *Very important factors considered include:* class rank, secondary school record, standardized test scores. *Other factors considered include:* character/personal qualities, essays, extracurricular activities, recommendations, talent/ability, volunteer work, work experience. **Freshman Admission Requirements:** High school diploma is required and GED is not accepted. *Academic units required/recommended:* 15 total required; 4 English required, 4 math required, 3 science required, 4 social studies required. **Freshman Admission Statistics:** 1,300 applied, 79% accepted, 33% of those accepted enrolled. **Transfer Admission Requirements:** *Items required:* high school transcript, college transcript. Minimum college GPA of 2.0 required. Lowest grade transferable D. **General Admission Information:** Application fee $25. Nonfall registration accepted. Admission may be deferred for a maximum of 1 year. Credit offered for CEEB Advanced Placement tests.

COSTS AND FINANCIAL AID

Required Forms and Deadlines: FAFSA. No deadline for regular filing. Priority filing deadline February 15. **Notification of Awards:** Applicants will be notified of awards on a rolling basis beginning on or about March 1. **Types of Aid:** *Need-based scholarships/grants:* Pell, SEOG, state scholarships/grants, private scholarships, the school's own gift aid. *Loans:* FFEL Subsidized Stafford, FFEL Unsubsidized Stafford, FFEL PLUS, Federal Perkins. **Student Employment:** Federal Work-Study Program available. Institutional employment available. Off-campus job opportunities are good. **Financial Aid Statistics:** 75% freshmen, 72% undergrads receive some form of aid. Average freshman grant $12,523. Average freshman loan $2,078. Average income from on-campus job $750. **Financial Aid Phone:** 616-459-8281.

See page 914.

AQUINAS COLLEGE (TN)

4210 Harding Road, Nashville, TN 37205
Phone: 615-297-7545 **E-mail:** admissions@aquinas-tn.edu
Fax: 615-297-7970 **Web:** www.aquinas-tn.edu **ACT Code:** 3942

This private school, which is affiliated with the Roman Catholic Church, was founded in 1961. It has an 80-acre campus.

STUDENTS AND FACULTY

Enrollment: 329. **Student Body:** Male 23%, female 77%. **Faculty:** Student/faculty ratio 12:1. 21 full-time faculty, 42% hold PhDs. 100% faculty teach undergrads.

ACADEMICS

Degrees: Associate's, bachelor's, post-bachelor's certificate, terminal, transfer. **Academic Requirements:** General education including some course work in English (including composition), history, humanities, mathematics, sciences (biological or physical), social science, religion. **Special Study Options:** Liberal arts/career combination, teacher certification program, weekend college.

FACILITIES

Computers: *Recommended operating system:* Windows 95. School-owned computers available for student use.

EXTRACURRICULARS

Activities: Student government, student newspaper. **Organizations:** 5 registered organizations. **Athletics (Intercollegiate):** *Men:* baseball, basketball. *Women:* cheerleading.

ADMISSIONS

Selectivity Rating: 63 (of 100). **Freshman Academic Profile:** Average high school GPA 2.7. 7% in top 10% of high school class, 20% in top 25% of high school class, 65% in top 50% of high school class. 80% from public high schools. Average SAT I Math 380. Average SAT I Verbal 400. Average ACT 18. TOEFL required of all international applicants, minimum TOEFL 525. **Basis for Candidate Selection:** *Very important factors considered include:* secondary school record, standardized test scores. *Other factors considered include:* alumni/ae relation, character/personal qualities, extracurricular activities, interview, recommendations, work experience. **Freshman Admission Requirements:** High school diploma or GED is required. *Academic units required/recommended:* 4 English recommended, 3 math recommended, 3 science recommended, 1 foreign language recommended, 1 social studies recommended, 1 history recommended. **Freshman Admission Statistics:** 329 applied, 73% accepted, 28% of those accepted enrolled. **Transfer Admission Requirements:** *Items required:* college transcript. Minimum college GPA of 2.0 required. Lowest grade transferable C. **General Admission Information:** Application fee $10. Priority application deadline August 1. Nonfall registration accepted. Admission may be deferred for a maximum of 1 year. Credit offered for CEEB Advanced Placement tests.

COSTS AND FINANCIAL AID

Tuition $9,000. Required fees $400. Average book expense $600. **Required Forms and Deadlines:** FAFSA and institution's own financial aid form. No deadline for regular filing. Priority filing deadline February 15. **Notification of Awards:** Applicants will be notified of awards on a rolling basis beginning on or about March 1. **Types of Aid:** *Need-based scholarships/grants:* Pell, SEOG, state scholarships/grants, private scholarships, the school's own gift aid. *Loans:* FFEL Subsidized Stafford, FFEL Unsubsidized Stafford, FFEL PLUS. **Student Employment:** Federal Work-Study Program available. Off-campus job opportunities are excellent. **Financial Aid Statistics:** 87% undergrads receive some form of aid. **Financial Aid Phone:** 615-297-7545.

ARCADIA UNIVERSITY

450 South Easton Road, Glenside, PA 19038
Phone: 215-572-2910 **E-mail:** admiss@arcadia.edu **CEEB Code:** 2039
Fax: 215-572-4049 **Web:** www.arcadia.edu

This private school, which is affiliated with the Presbyterian Church, was founded in 1853. It has a 60-acre campus.

STUDENTS AND FACULTY

Enrollment: 1,649. **Student Body:** Male 28%, female 72%, out-of-state 28%, international 2%. **Ethnic Representation:** African American 12%, Asian 3%, Caucasian 83%, Hispanic 2%. **Retention and Graduation:** 76% freshmen return for sophomore year. 39% freshmen graduate within 4 years. 25% grads go on to further study within 1 year. 3% grads pursue business degrees. 2% grads pursue law degrees. 2% grads pursue medical degrees. **Faculty:** Student/faculty ratio 13:1. 104 full-time faculty. 100% faculty teach undergrads.

ACADEMICS

Degrees: Bachelor's, doctoral, master's, post-bachelor's certificate, post-master's certificate. **Academic Requirements:** General education including some course work in arts/fine arts, English (including composition), foreign languages, history, humanities, mathematics, sciences (biological or physical), social science, common core, justice—multicultural interpretations, pluralism in the United States. **Majors with Highest Enrollment:** Biology/biological sciences, general; education, general; fine/studio arts, general. **Disciplines with Highest Percentage of Degrees Awarded:** Education 19%, psychology 17%, business/marketing 15%, visual and performing arts 8%, biological life sciences 7%. **Special Study Options:** Cooperative (work-study) program, double major, English as a second language, student exchange program (domestic), honors program, independent study, internships, liberal arts/career combination, student-designed major, study abroad, teacher certification program, evening and weekend college. Off-campus study: Washington, DC; Appalachian Semester (Kentucky); Philadelphia Urban Semester. Undergrads may take grad classes.

FACILITIES

Housing: Coed, all-female, apartments for single students, housing for disabled students. **Library Holdings:** 136,903 bound volumes. 798 periodicals. 251,507 microforms. 2,861 audiovisuals. **Special Academic Facilities/Equipment:** Art gallery, language lab, observatory. **Computers:** School-owned computers available for student use.

EXTRACURRICULARS

Activities: Choral groups, drama/theater, radio station, student government, student newspaper, yearbook. **Organizations:** 40 registered organizations, 8 honor societies, 4 religious organizations. **Athletics (Intercollegiate):** *Men:* baseball, basketball, cross-country, equestrian, golf, soccer, swimming, tennis. *Women:* basketball, cheerleading, cross-country, equestrian, field hockey, lacrosse, soccer, softball, swimming, tennis, volleyball.

ADMISSIONS

Selectivity Rating: 74 (of 100). **Freshman Academic Profile:** Average high school GPA 2.9. 18% in top 10% of high school class, 52% in top 25% of high school class, 78% in top 50% of high school class. Average SAT I Math 518, SAT I Math middle 50% range 480-580. Average SAT I Verbal 530, SAT I Verbal middle 50% range 490-600. TOEFL required of all international applicants, minimum TOEFL 600. **Basis for Candidate Selection:** *Very important factors considered include:* secondary school record. *Important factors considered include:* class rank, essays, extracurricular activities, recommendations, standardized test scores. *Other factors considered include:* alumni/ae relation, character/personal qualities, interview, talent/ability, volunteer work, work experience. **Freshman Admission Requirements:** High school diploma or GED is required. *Academic units required/recommended:* 4 English recommended, 3 math recommended, 3 science recommended, 3 science lab recommended, 2 foreign language recommended, 2 social studies recommended, 2 history recommended. **Freshman Admission Statistics:** 1,642 applied, 84% accepted. **Transfer Admission Requirements:** *Items required:* college transcript, essay. Minimum college GPA of 2.5 required. Lowest grade transferable C-. **General Admission Information:** Application fee $30. Priority application deadline June 1. Early decision application deadline October 15. Regular application deadline August 1. Nonfall registration accepted. Admission may be deferred for a maximum of 1 year. Credit and/or placement offered for CEEB Advanced Placement tests.

COSTS AND FINANCIAL AID

Tuition $19,660. Room & board $8,290. Required fees $280. Average book expense $800. **Required Forms and Deadlines:** FAFSA and institution's own financial aid form. Priority filing deadline March 1. **Notification of Awards:** Applicants will be notified of awards on a rolling basis beginning on or about February 1. **Types of Aid:** *Need-based scholarships/grants:* Pell, SEOG, state scholarships/grants, private scholarships, the school's own gift aid. *Loans:* FFEL Subsidized Stafford, FFEL Unsubsidized Stafford, FFEL PLUS, Federal Perkins, college/university loans from institutional funds. **Student Employment:** Federal Work-Study Program available. Institutional employment available. Off-campus job opportunities are good. **Financial Aid Statistics:** 82% freshmen, 88% undergrads receive some form of aid. Average freshman grant $13,258. Average freshman loan $2,656. **Financial Aid Phone:** 215-572-2980.

See page 916.

ARIZONA STATE UNIVERSITY

Box 870112, Tempe, AZ 85287-0112
Phone: 480-965-7788 **E-mail:** ugradinq@asu.edu **CEEB Code:** 4007
Fax: 480-965-3610 **Web:** www.asu.edu **ACT Code:** 88

This public school was founded in 1885. It has a 722-acre campus.

STUDENTS AND FACULTY

Enrollment: 36,802. **Student Body:** Male 48%, female 52%, out-of-state 23%, international 3% (125 countries represented). **Ethnic Representation:** African American 3%, Asian 5%, Caucasian 74%, Hispanic 12%, Native American 2%. **Retention and Graduation:** 77% freshmen return for sophomore year. 26%

freshmen graduate within 4 years. **Faculty:** Student/faculty ratio 22:1. 1,730 full-time faculty, 84% hold PhDs. 75% faculty teach undergrads.

ACADEMICS

Degrees: Bachelor's, doctoral, first professional, master's, post-bachelor's certificate, post-master's certificate. **Academic Requirements:** General education including some course work in arts/fine arts, computer literacy, English (including composition), foreign languages, history, humanities, mathematics, sciences (biological or physical), social science. **Classes:** 20-29 students in an average class. 20-29 students in an average lab/discussion section. **Majors with Highest Enrollment:** Communications studies/speech communication and rhetoric; multi/interdisciplinary studies; psychology, general. **Disciplines with Highest Percentage of Degrees Awarded:** Business/marketing 19%, communications/communication technologies 9%, interdisciplinary studies 9%, engineering/engineering technology 8%, education 8%. **Special Study Options:** Accelerated program, cooperative (work-study) program, distance learning, double major, dual enrollment, student exchange program (domestic), honors program, independent study, internships, study abroad, teacher certification program.

FACILITIES

Housing: Coed, apartments for single students, housing for disabled students, fraternities and/or sororities, freshman housing. **Library Holdings:** 2,380,457 bound volumes. 28,159 periodicals. 5,733,474 microforms. 1,315,373 audiovisuals. **Special Academic Facilities/Equipment:** Art, anthropology, geology, history, and sports museums; early childhood development lab; herbarium; wind tunnel; robotics lab; semiconductor clean room; high-resolution electron microscope facility; gamma cell irradiation chamber; solar research facilities; nuclear reactor. **Computers:** School-owned computers available for student use.

EXTRACURRICULARS

Activities: Choral groups, concert band, dance, drama/theater, jazz band, literary magazine, marching band, music ensembles, musical theater, opera, pep band, radio station, student government, student newspaper, symphony orchestra, television station. **Organizations:** 450 registered organizations, 20 honor societies, 24 fraternities (6% men join), 18 sororities (7% women join). **Athletics (Intercollegiate):** *Men:* baseball, basketball, cross-country, diving, football, golf, swimming, tennis, track & field, wrestling. *Women:* basketball, cross-country, diving, golf, gymnastics, soccer, softball, swimming, tennis, track & field, volleyball, water polo.

ADMISSIONS

Selectivity Rating: 79 (of 100). **Freshman Academic Profile:** Average high school GPA 3.4. 26% in top 10% of high school class, 52% in top 25% of high school class, 83% in top 50% of high school class. Average SAT I Math 551, SAT I Math middle 50% range 490-610. Average SAT I Verbal 538, SAT I Verbal middle 50% range 480-590. Average ACT 23, ACT middle 50% range 20-26. TOEFL required of all international applicants, minimum TOEFL 500. **Basis for Candidate Selection:** *Very important factors considered include:* class rank, secondary school record, standardized test scores. *Important factors considered include:* state residency. *Other factors considered include:* essays, extracurricular activities, interview, recommendations, talent/ability. **Freshman Admission Requirements:** High school diploma or GED is required. *Academic units required/recommended:* 16 total required; 4 English required, 4 math required, 3 science required, 3 science lab required, 2 foreign language required, 1 social studies required, 1 history required. **Freshman Admission Statistics:** 18,155 applied, 85% accepted, 41% of those accepted enrolled. **Transfer Admission Requirements:** *Items required:* high school transcript, college transcript, standardized test scores. Minimum college GPA of 2.0 required. Lowest grade transferable C. **General Admission Information:** Application fee $50. Priority application deadline April 15. Nonfall registration accepted. Credit offered for CEEB Advanced Placement tests.

COSTS AND FINANCIAL AID

In-state tuition $2,508. Out-of-state tuition $11,028. Room & board $5,866. Required fees $77. Average book expense $748. **Required Forms and Deadlines:** FAFSA. Priority filing deadline March 1. **Notification of Awards:** Applicants will be notified of awards on a rolling basis beginning on or about March 15. **Types of Aid:** *Need-based scholarships/grants:* Pell, SEOG, state scholarships/grants, private scholarships, the school's own gift aid, Federal Nursing. *Loans:* Direct Subsidized Stafford, Direct Unsubsidized Stafford, Direct PLUS, FFEL PLUS, Federal Perkins. **Student Employment:** Federal Work-Study Program available. Institutional employment available. Off-campus job opportunities are good. **Financial Aid Statistics:** 32% freshmen, 37% undergrads receive some form of aid. Average freshman grant $4,638. Average freshman loan $2,636. Average income from on-campus job $2,937. **Financial Aid Phone:** 480-965-3355.

ARIZONA STATE UNIVERSITY EAST

AZ State University, PO Box 870112, Tempe, AZ 85287-0112
Phone: 480-965-7788 **E-mail:** ugradinq@asu.edu **CEEB Code:** 4007
Fax: 480-727-1008 **Web:** www.east.asu.edu **ACT Code:** 88

This public school was founded in 1994. It has a 605-acre campus.

STUDENTS AND FACULTY

Enrollment: 2,526. **Student Body:** Male 51%, female 49%, out-of-state 10%, international 2% (41 countries represented). **Ethnic Representation:** African American 2%, Asian 4%, Caucasian 77%, Hispanic 11%, Native American 2%. **Faculty:** Student/faculty ratio 16:1. 83 full-time faculty, 80% hold PhDs. 100% faculty teach undergrads.

ACADEMICS

Degrees: Bachelor's, master's, post-bachelor's certificate. **Academic Requirements:** General education including some course work in arts/fine arts, English (including composition), history, humanities, mathematics, philosophy, sciences (biological or physical), social science. **Classes:** Under 10 students in an average class. Under 10 students in an average lab/discussion section. **Disciplines with Highest Percentage of Degrees Awarded:** Engineering/engineering technology 30%, home economics and vocational home economics 19%, business/marketing 18%, education 12%, agriculture 12%. **Special Study Options:** Distance learning, double major, English as a second language, honors program, independent study, internships, liberal arts/career combination, student-designed major, study abroad, teacher certification program.

FACILITIES

Housing: Coed, apartments for married students, apartments for single students, housing for disabled students, theme housing based on academic interest, "Single Family Style" housing for students with families and single students. There is also a special dorm for freshmen. **Library Holdings:** 4,435,301 bound volumes. 206 periodicals. 315 microforms. 105 audiovisuals. **Special Academic Facilities/Equipment:** Exercise and wellness laboratory; cryo chamber; photovoltaics lab; wind tunnel & simulators; rapid prototyping lab; VHDL software; Fluke LCD hand-held oscilloscopes; high altitude simulation chamber; single & multiengine flight simulators; fleet of Baron & Beech aircraft; microelectronics teaching factory; graphics information printing factory; digital photography studio. **Computers:** School-owned computers available for student use.

EXTRACURRICULARS

Activities: Student newspaper. **Organizations:** 27 registered organizations, 3 honor societies, 2 religious organizations.

ADMISSIONS

Selectivity Rating: 63 (of 100). **Freshman Academic Profile:** Average high school GPA 3.0. 21% in top 10% of high school class, 22% in top 25% of high school class, 41% in top 50% of high school class. Average SAT I Math 536, SAT I Math middle 50% range 478-580. Average SAT I Verbal 520, SAT I Verbal middle 50% range 470-580. Average ACT 22, ACT middle 50% range 19-25. TOEFL required of all international applicants, minimum TOEFL 500. **Basis for Candidate Selection:** *Very important factors considered include:* class rank, secondary school record, standardized test scores, state residency. **Freshman Admission Requirements:** High school diploma or GED is required. *Academic units required/recommended:* 16 total required; 4 English required, 4 math required, 3 science required, 3 science lab required, 2 foreign language required, 1 social studies required, 1 history required. **Freshman Admission Statistics:** 461 applied, 73% accepted, 42% of those accepted enrolled. **Transfer Admission Requirements:** *Items required:* college transcript, standardized test scores. Lowest grade transferable C. **General Admission Information:** Application fee $45. Nonfall registration accepted. Credit offered for CEEB Advanced Placement tests.

COSTS AND FINANCIAL AID

In-state tuition $2,508. Out-of-state tuition $11,028. Room & board $4,544. Required fees $26. Average book expense $726. **Required Forms and Deadlines:** FAFSA. Priority filing deadline March 1. **Notification of Awards:** Applicants will be notified of awards on a rolling basis beginning on or about April 15. **Types of Aid:** *Need-based scholarships/grants:* Pell, SEOG, state scholarships/grants, private scholarships, the school's own gift aid. *Loans:* Direct Subsidized Stafford, Direct Unsubsidized Stafford, Direct PLUS, FFEL PLUS, Federal Perkins. **Student Employment:** Federal Work-Study Program available. Institutional employment available. Off-campus job opportunities are good. **Financial Aid Statistics:** 43% undergrads receive some form of aid. Average income from on-campus job $2,185. **Financial Aid Phone:** 480-727-1042.

ARIZONA STATE UNIVERSITY WEST

4701 West Thunderbird Road, Phoenix, AZ 85306-4908
Phone: 602-543-8123 **E-mail:** west-admissions@asu.edu **CEEB Code:** 4007
Fax: 602-543-8312 **Web:** www.west.asu.edu

This public school was founded in 1984. It has a 300-acre campus.

STUDENTS AND FACULTY

Enrollment: 5,035. **Student Body:** Male 31%, female 69%, out-of-state 2%, international 1%. **Ethnic Representation:** African American 5%, Asian 3%, Caucasian 71%, Hispanic 16%, Native American 2%. **Faculty:** Student/faculty ratio 22:1. 181 full-time faculty, 88% hold PhDs. 100% faculty teach undergrads.

ACADEMICS

Degrees: Bachelor's, master's, post-bachelor's certificate. **Academic Requirements:** General education including some course work in computer literacy, humanities, philosophy, sciences (biological or physical), social science, liberal arts and sciences. **Classes:** 30-39 students in an average class. **Majors with Highest Enrollment:** Elementary education and teaching; psychology, general; criminal justice/law enforcement administration. **Disciplines with Highest Percentage of Degrees Awarded:** Education 29%, business/marketing 26%, protective services/public administration 10%, communications/communication technologies 7%, psychology 7%. **Special Study Options:** Distance learning, double major, honors program, internships, dual degree.

FACILITIES

Library Holdings: 334,625 bound volumes. 3,318 periodicals. 1,440,132 microforms. 26,369 audiovisuals. **Computers:** *Recommended operating system:* windows XP. School-owned computers available for student use.

EXTRACURRICULARS

Activities: Drama/theater, literary magazine, student government, student newspaper. **Organizations:** 30 registered organizations, 4 honor societies.

ADMISSIONS

Selectivity Rating: 63 (of 100). **Freshman Academic Profile:** Average high school GPA 3.4. 31% in top 10% of high school class, 66% in top 25% of high school class, 92% in top 50% of high school class. Average SAT I Math 510, SAT I Math middle 50% range 450-580. Average SAT I Verbal 515, SAT I Verbal middle 50% range 470-560. Average ACT 21, ACT middle 50% range 18-24. TOEFL required of all international applicants, minimum TOEFL 500. **Basis for Candidate Selection:** *Very important factors considered include:* secondary school record, standardized test scores. *Other factors considered include:* class rank, recommendations. **Freshman Admission Requirements:** High school diploma or GED is required. *Academic units required/recommended:* 16 total required; 4 English required, 4 math required, 3 science required, 3 science lab required, 2 foreign language required, 2 social studies required, 1 history required. **Freshman Admission Statistics:** 636 applied, 85% accepted, 63% of those accepted enrolled. **Transfer Admission Requirements:** *Items required:* college transcript, statement of good standing from prior school. Minimum college GPA of 3.0 required. Lowest grade transferable C. **General Admission Information:** Application fee $50. Nonfall registration accepted. Neither credit nor placement offered for CEEB Advanced Placement tests.

COSTS AND FINANCIAL AID

In-state tuition $2,585. Out-of-state tuition $11,105. Required fees $77. Average book expense $748. **Required Forms and Deadlines:** FAFSA. No deadline for regular filing. **Notification of Awards:** Applicants will be notified of awards on a rolling basis. **Types of Aid:** *Need-based scholarships/grants:* Pell, SEOG, state scholarships/grants, private scholarships, the school's own gift aid. *Loans:* Direct Subsidized Stafford, Direct Unsubsidized Stafford, FFEL PLUS, Federal Perkins, college/university loans from institutional funds. **Student Employment:** Federal Work-Study Program available. Institutional employment available. Off-campus job opportunities are excellent. **Financial Aid Statistics:** 37% freshmen, 50% undergrads receive some form of aid. Average income from on-campus job $3,973. **Financial Aid Phone:** 602-543-8178.

ARKANSAS BAPTIST COLLEGE

 $

1600 Bishop Street, Little Rock, AR 72202
Phone: 501-374-7856 **E-mail:** ahightower@swbell.net
Fax: 501-375-9257 **Web:** arkbapcol.edu

This private school, which is affiliated with the Baptist Church, was founded in 1884.

STUDENTS AND FACULTY

Enrollment: 157. **Student Body:** Male 40%, female 60%, out-of-state 10%. **Retention and Graduation:** 4% freshmen graduate within 4 years.

ACADEMICS

Degrees: Associate's, bachelor's, certificate, transfer. **Academic Requirements:** General education including some course work in computer literacy, English (including composition), humanities, mathematics, philosophy, sciences (biological or physical), social science. **Special Study Options:** Independent study, internships, teacher certification program, weekend college.

FACILITIES

Housing: All-female, all-male. **Library Holdings:** 29,315 bound volumes. 39 periodicals. 700 microforms. 10 audiovisuals.

EXTRACURRICULARS

Activities: Choral groups, student government, yearbook.

ADMISSIONS

Selectivity Rating: 66 (of 100). **Freshman Academic Profile:** Average high school GPA 2.0. 0% in top 10% of high school class, 3% in top 25% of high school class, 5% in top 50% of high school class. **Basis for Candidate Selection:** *Important factors considered include:* secondary school record. *Other factors considered include:* alumni/ae relation, character/personal qualities, extracurricular activities, recommendations, standardized test scores, volunteer work, work experience. **Freshman Admission Requirements:** High school diploma or GED is required. *Academic units required/recommended:* 16 total required; 4 English required, 4 math required, 4 science required, 1 science lab recommended, 3 social studies required, 1 history required. **Freshman Admission Statistics:** 72 applied, 100% accepted, 22% of those accepted enrolled. **Transfer Admission Requirements:** *Items required:* high school transcript, college transcript. Minimum high school GPA of 1.5 required. Minimum college GPA of 1.7 required. Lowest grade transferable C. **General Admission Information:** Application fee $10. Nonfall registration accepted. Admission may be deferred.

COSTS AND FINANCIAL AID

Tuition $2,200. Room & board $3,000. Required fees $30. Average book expense $250. **Types of Aid:** *Loans:* FFEL Subsidized Stafford, FFEL PLUS.

ARKANSAS STATE UNIVERSITY

PO Box 1630, State University, AR 72467
Phone: 870-972-3024 **E-mail:** admissions@astate.edu **CEEB Code:** 6011
Fax: 870-910-8094 **Web:** www.astate.edu **ACT Code:** 116

This public school was founded in 1909. It has a 941-acre campus.

STUDENTS AND FACULTY

Enrollment: 9,275. **Student Body:** Male 42%, female 58%, out-of-state 10%, international 1% (51 countries represented). **Ethnic Representation:** African American 14%, Asian 1%, Caucasian 84%, Hispanic 1%. **Retention and Graduation:** 67% freshmen return for sophomore year. 14% freshmen graduate within 4 years. 3% grads go on to further study within 1 year. 2% grads pursue business degrees. 1% grads pursue law degrees. 1% grads pursue medical degrees. **Faculty:** Student/faculty ratio 19:1. 432 full-time faculty, 64% hold PhDs. 90% faculty teach undergrads.

ACADEMICS

Degrees: Associate's, bachelor's, certificate, doctoral, master's, post-bachelor's certificate, post-master's certificate. **Academic Requirements:** General education including some course work in arts/fine arts, English (including composition), history, humanities, mathematics, philosophy, sciences (biological or physical), social science, physical education. **Classes:** Under 10 students in an average class. Under 10 students in an average lab/discussion section.

Majors with Highest Enrollment: Business administration/management; accounting; early childhood education and teaching. **Disciplines with Highest Percentage of Degrees Awarded:** Business/marketing 25%, education 21%, health professions and related sciences 7%, computer and information sciences 6%, agriculture 6%. **Special Study Options:** Accelerated program, cooperative (work-study) program, distance learning, double major, dual enrollment, English as a second language, student exchange program (domestic), honors program, independent study, internships, study abroad, teacher certification program.

FACILITIES

Housing: All-female, all-male, apartments for married students, apartments for single students, fraternities and/or sororities, married and graduate student housing. **Library Holdings:** 572,674 bound volumes. 1,739 periodicals. 624,520 microforms. 10,689 audiovisuals. **Special Academic Facilities/ Equipment:** Art gallery, museum of Native American cultures and Arkansas artifacts, ecotoxicology research facility, electron microscope facility, geographic information system facility, equine center. **Computers:** School-owned computers available for student use.

EXTRACURRICULARS

Activities: Choral groups, concert band, dance, drama/theater, jazz band, marching band, music ensembles, musical theater, opera, pep band, radio station, student government, student newspaper, symphony orchestra, television station, yearbook. **Organizations:** 190 registered organizations, 81 honor societies, 16 religious organizations, 11 fraternities (15% men join), 9 sororities (11% women join). **Athletics (Intercollegiate):** *Men:* baseball, basketball, cross-country, football, golf, indoor track, track & field. *Women:* basketball, cross-country, golf, indoor track, soccer, tennis, track & field, volleyball.

ADMISSIONS

Selectivity Rating: 76 (of 100). **Freshman Academic Profile:** Average high school GPA 3.2. 96% from public high schools. Average ACT 22, ACT middle 50% range 19-25. TOEFL required of all international applicants, minimum TOEFL 500. **Basis for Candidate Selection:** *Very important factors considered include:* secondary school record, standardized test scores. *Other factors considered include:* class rank, recommendations, talent/ability. **Freshman Admission Requirements:** High school diploma or GED is required. *Academic units required/recommended:* 15 total recommended; 4 English recommended, 3 math recommended, 3 science recommended, 3 science lab recommended, 2 foreign language recommended, 1 social studies recommended, 2 history recommended. **Freshman Admission Statistics:** 2,822 applied, 73% accepted, 80% of those accepted enrolled. **Transfer Admission Requirements:** *Items required:* college transcript. Minimum high school GPA of 2.5 required. Minimum college GPA of 2.0 required. Lowest grade transferable C. **General Admission Information:** Application fee $15. Regular application deadline August 21. Nonfall registration accepted. Admission may be deferred. Credit offered for CEEB Advanced Placement tests.

COSTS AND FINANCIAL AID

In-state tuition $3,570. Out-of-state tuition $9,180. Room & board $3,410. Required fees $910. Average book expense $900. **Required Forms and Deadlines:** FAFSA and institution's own financial aid form. Financial aid filing deadline July 1. Priority filing deadline February 15. **Notification of Awards:** Applicants will be notified of awards on a rolling basis beginning on or about June 1. **Types of Aid:** *Need-based scholarships/grants:* Pell, SEOG, state scholarships/grants, private scholarships, the school's own gift aid. *Loans:* FFEL Subsidized Stafford, FFEL Unsubsidized Stafford, FFEL PLUS, Federal Perkins. **Student Employment:** Federal Work-Study Program available. Institutional employment available. Off-campus job opportunities are good. **Financial Aid Statistics:** 88% freshmen, 82% undergrads receive some form of aid. Average freshman grant $2,000. Average freshman loan $1,200. Average income from on-campus job $3,000. **Financial Aid Phone:** 870-972-2310.

ARKANSAS TECH UNIVERSITY

Doc Bryan #414, Arkansas Tech Univ., Russellville, AR 72801
Phone: 479-968-0343 **E-mail:** tech.enroll@mail.atu.edu **CEEB Code:** 6010
Fax: 479-964-0522 **Web:** www.atu.edu **ACT Code:** 114

This public school was founded in 1909. It has a 516-acre campus.

STUDENTS AND FACULTY

Enrollment: 5,457. **Student Body:** Male 47%, female 53%, out-of-state 4%, international 1% (38 countries represented). **Ethnic Representation:** African American 4%, Asian 1%, Caucasian 92%, Hispanic 2%, Native American 1%. **Retention and Graduation:** 67% freshmen return for sophomore year. 18% freshmen graduate within 4 years. **Faculty:** Student/faculty ratio 19:1. 209 full-time faculty, 67% hold PhDs. 100% faculty teach undergrads.

ACADEMICS

Degrees: Associate's, bachelor's, certificate, master's. **Academic Requirements:** General education including some course work in arts/fine arts, computer literacy, English (including composition), humanities, mathematics, sciences (biological or physical), social science, public speaking. **Classes:** 20-29 students in an average class. 20-29 students in an average lab/discussion section. **Majors with Highest Enrollment:** Computer science; physical education teaching and coaching; early childhood education and teaching. **Disciplines with Highest Percentage of Degrees Awarded:** Education 21%, business/ marketing 13%, social sciences and history 9%, health professions and related sciences 8%, computer and information sciences 7%. **Special Study Options:** Distance learning, double major, dual enrollment, external degree program, honors program, independent study, internships, teacher certification program, weekend college.

FACILITIES

Housing: Coed, all-female, all-male, apartments for single students, housing for disabled students. **Library Holdings:** 239,398 bound volumes. 1,136 periodicals. 828,218 microforms. 5,086 audiovisuals. **Special Academic Facilities/Equipment:** Arkansas Center for Energy, Natural Resources, and Environmental Studies; Crabaugh Communications Center; Museum of Prehistory and History; technology center. **Computers:** School-owned computers available for student use.

EXTRACURRICULARS

Activities: Choral groups, concert band, dance, drama/theater, jazz band, literary magazine, marching band, music ensembles, musical theater, pep band, radio station, student government, student newspaper, student-run film society, television station, yearbook. **Organizations:** 89 registered organizations, 14 honor societies, 10 religious organizations, 4 fraternities (5% men join), 2 sororities (4% women join). **Athletics (Intercollegiate):** *Men:* baseball, basketball, cheerleading, football, golf, tennis. *Women:* basketball, cheerleading, cross-country, golf, softball, tennis, volleyball.

ADMISSIONS

Selectivity Rating: 60 (of 100). **Freshman Academic Profile:** Average high school GPA 3.2. Average SAT I Math 549, SAT I Math middle 50% range 450-630. Average SAT I Verbal 491, SAT I Verbal middle 50% range 400-450. Average ACT 22, ACT middle 50% range 19-25. TOEFL required of all international applicants, minimum TOEFL 500. **Basis for Candidate Selection:** *Very important factors considered include:* secondary school record, standardized test scores. *Other factors considered include:* class rank. **Freshman Admission Requirements:** High school diploma or GED is required. *Academic units required/recommended:* 21 total required; 4 English required, 3 math required, 3 science required, 2 foreign language recommended, 1 social studies required, 3 history required, 4 elective required. **Freshman Admission Statistics:** 2,691 applied, 52% accepted, 86% of those accepted enrolled. **Transfer Admission Requirements:** *Items required:* college transcript. Minimum college GPA of 2.0 required. Lowest grade transferable C. **General Admission Information:** Nonfall registration accepted. Admission may be deferred.

COSTS AND FINANCIAL AID

In-state tuition $3,076. Out-of-state tuition $6,152. Room & board $3,576. Required fees $180. Average book expense $800. **Required Forms and Deadlines:** FAFSA. No deadline for regular filing. Priority filing deadline April 15. **Notification of Awards:** Applicants will be notified of awards on a rolling basis beginning on or about May 1. **Types of Aid:** *Need-based scholarships/ grants:* Pell, SEOG, state scholarships/grants, private scholarships, the school's own gift aid. *Loans:* FFEL Subsidized Stafford, FFEL Unsubsidized Stafford, FFEL PLUS, Federal Perkins. **Student Employment:** Federal Work-Study Program available. Institutional employment available. Off-campus job opportunities are excellent. **Financial Aid Statistics:** 58% freshmen, 56% undergrads receive some form of aid. Average freshman grant $3,350. Average freshman loan $1,942. **Financial Aid Phone:** 479-968-0399.

ARMSTRONG ATLANTIC STATE UNIVERSITY

11935 Abercorn Street, Savannah, GA 31419-1997
Phone: 912-927-5277 **E-mail:** adm-info@mail.armstrong.edu **CEEB Code:** 5012
Fax: 912-927-5462 **Web:** www.armstrong.edu **ACT Code:** 786

This public school was founded in 1935. It has a 250-acre campus.

STUDENTS AND FACULTY

Enrollment: 5,213. **Student Body:** Male 32%, female 68%, out-of-state 8%, international 2%. **Ethnic Representation:** African American 23%, Asian 3%, Caucasian 68%, Hispanic 3%. **Faculty:** Student/faculty ratio 16:1. 229 full-time faculty, 66% hold PhDs. 90% faculty teach undergrads.

ACADEMICS

Degrees: Associate's, bachelor's, master's, post-bachelor's certificate, post-master's certificate. **Academic Requirements:** General education including some course work in arts/fine arts, computer literacy, English (including composition), history, humanities, mathematics, sciences (biological or physical), social science. **Classes:** 10-19 students in an average class. Under 10 students in an average lab/discussion section. **Majors with Highest Enrollment:** Nursing/registered nurse training (RN, ASN, BSN, MSN); early childhood education and teaching; liberal arts and sciences/liberal studies. **Disciplines with Highest Percentage of Degrees Awarded:** Health professions and related sciences 29%, education 27%, liberal arts/general studies 13%, social sciences and history 10%, biological life sciences 4%. **Special Study Options:** Cooperative (work-study) program, distance learning, double major, dual enrollment, honors program, internships, study abroad, teacher certification program, weekend college.

FACILITIES

Housing: Coed. **Library Holdings:** 223,412 bound volumes. 1,166 periodicals. 666,657 microforms. 15,618 audiovisuals. **Special Academic Facilities/Equipment:** Language lab, criminal justice training center, sports medicine clinic, speech/language pathology lab.

EXTRACURRICULARS

Activities: Choral groups, concert band, drama/theater, jazz band, literary magazine, music ensembles, musical theater, pep band, student government, student newspaper, symphony orchestra. **Organizations:** 55 registered organizations, 7 honor societies, 3 religious organizations, 17 fraternity, 1 sorority. **Athletics (Intercollegiate):** *Men:* baseball, basketball, golf, tennis. *Women:* basketball, softball, tennis, volleyball.

ADMISSIONS

Selectivity Rating: 66 (of 100). **Freshman Academic Profile:** Average high school GPA 3.0. Average SAT I Math 488, SAT I Math middle 50% range 450-550. Average SAT I Verbal 499, SAT I Verbal middle 50% range 460-560. TOEFL required of all international applicants, minimum TOEFL 523. **Basis for Candidate Selection:** *Important factors considered include:* secondary school record, standardized test scores. *Other factors considered include:* geographical residence, state residency. **Freshman Admission Requirements:** High school diploma or GED is required. *Academic units required/recommended:* 4 English required, 3 math required, 3 science required, 2 science lab required, 2 foreign language required, 3 social studies required. **Freshman Admission Statistics:** 1,407 applied, 66% accepted, 73% of those accepted enrolled. **Transfer Admission Requirements:** *Items required:* college transcript. Minimum high school GPA of 1.9 required. Minimum college GPA of 1.9 required. Lowest grade transferable D. **General Admission Information:** Application fee $20. Regular application deadline July 1. Nonfall registration accepted. Admission may be deferred for a maximum of 1 year. Credit and/or placement offered for CEEB Advanced Placement tests.

COSTS AND FINANCIAL AID

In-state tuition $2,010. Out-of-state tuition $8,040. Required fees $382. Average book expense $800. **Required Forms and Deadlines:** FAFSA. No deadline for regular filing. Priority filing deadline March 15. **Notification of Awards:** Applicants will be notified of awards on a rolling basis. **Types of Aid:** *Need-based scholarships/grants:* Pell, SEOG, state scholarships/grants, private scholarships, the school's own gift aid, Federal Nursing. *Loans:* FFEL Subsidized Stafford, FFEL Unsubsidized Stafford, FFEL PLUS, state loans. **Student Employment:** Federal Work-Study Program available. Institutional employment available. Off-campus job opportunities are excellent. **Financial Aid Statistics:** 38% freshmen, 72% undergrads receive some form of aid. **Financial Aid Phone:** 912-927-5272.

ART CENTER COLLEGE OF DESIGN

 $$$ 

1700 Lida Street, Pasadena, CA 91103-1999
Phone: 626-396-2373 **E-mail:** admissions@artcenter.edu **CEEB Code:** 4009
Fax: 626-795-0578 **Web:** www.artcenter.edu

This private school was founded in 1930. It has a 175-acre campus.

STUDENTS AND FACULTY

Enrollment: 1,406. **Student Body:** Out-of-state 23%, international 17% (36 countries represented). **Ethnic Representation:** African American 2%, Asian 39%, Caucasian 47%, Hispanic 11%, Native American 1%. **Retention and Graduation:** 92% freshmen return for sophomore year. 60% freshmen graduate within 4 years. **Faculty:** Student/faculty ratio 12:1. 66 full-time faculty. 98% faculty teach undergrads.

ACADEMICS

Degrees: Bachelor's, master's. **Academic Requirements:** General education including some course work in arts/fine arts, computer literacy, English (including composition), history, humanities, philosophy, sciences (biological or physical), social science, art history. **Classes:** 10-19 students in an average class. **Majors with Highest Enrollment:** Industrial design; graphic design; illustration. **Disciplines with Highest Percentage of Degrees Awarded:** Visual and performing arts 100%. **Special Study Options:** Independent study, internships.

FACILITIES

Library Holdings: 76,000 bound volumes. 400 periodicals. 560 microforms. 5,265 audiovisuals. **Special Academic Facilities/Equipment:** 2 art galleries. **Computers:** *Recommended operating system:* Mac. School-owned computers available for student use.

EXTRACURRICULARS

Activities: Student government. **Organizations:** 12 registered organizations.

ADMISSIONS

Selectivity Rating: 86 (of 100). **Freshman Academic Profile:** Average high school GPA 3.3. TOEFL required of all international applicants, minimum TOEFL 550. **Basis for Candidate Selection:** *Very important factors considered include:* essays, secondary school record, talent/ability. *Important factors considered include:* character/personal qualities, class rank, extracurricular activities, volunteer work, work experience. *Other factors considered include:* alumni/ae relation, interview, minority status, recommendations, standardized test scores. **Freshman Admission Requirements:** High school diploma or GED is required. **Freshman Admission Statistics:** 1,120 applied, 66% accepted, 65% of those accepted enrolled. **Transfer Admission Requirements:** *Items required:* college transcript, essay. Minimum college GPA of 3.0 required. Lowest grade transferable C. **General Admission Information:** Application fee $45. Nonfall registration accepted. Admission may be deferred. Credit offered for CEEB Advanced Placement tests.

COSTS AND FINANCIAL AID

Tuition $22,148. **Required Forms and Deadlines:** FAFSA. No deadline for regular filing. Priority filing deadline March 1. **Notification of Awards:** Applicants will be notified of awards on a rolling basis. **Types of Aid:** *Need-based scholarships/grants:* Pell, SEOG, state scholarships/grants, private scholarships, the school's own gift aid. *Loans:* Direct Subsidized Stafford, Direct PLUS, Federal Perkins. **Student Employment:** Federal Work-Study Program available. Institutional employment available. Off-campus job opportunities are fair. **Financial Aid Statistics:** 73% freshmen, 77% undergrads receive some form of aid. Average freshman grant $2,977. Average freshman loan $4,175. **Financial Aid Phone:** 626-396-2215.

ART INSTITUTE OF ATLANTA

 $$$ 

6600 Peachtree Dunwoody Road, 100 Embassy Row, Atlanta, GA 30328
Phone: 770-394-8300 **E-mail:** aiaadm@aii.edu
Fax: 770-394-0008 **Web:** www.aia.artinstitute.edu **ACT Code:** 859

This private school was founded in 1949. It has a 2-acre campus.

STUDENTS AND FACULTY

Enrollment: 2,620. **Student Body:** Male 52%, female 48%, out-of-state 25%, international 3%. **Ethnic Representation:** African American 34%, Asian 4%, Caucasian 50%, Hispanic 4%. **Retention and Graduation:** 63% freshmen return for sophomore year. **Faculty:** Student/faculty ratio 18:1. 105 full-time faculty, 40% hold PhDs. 100% faculty teach undergrads.

ACADEMICS

Degrees: Associate's, bachelor's, certificate. **Academic Requirements:** General education including some course work in arts/fine arts, computer literacy, English (including composition), history, humanities, mathematics, sciences (biological or physical), social science, career development, portfolio, art foundation courses. **Classes:** 20-29 students in an average class. **Majors with Highest Enrollment:** Culinary arts/chef training; commercial and advertising art; precision production trades, general. **Disciplines with Highest Percentage of Degrees Awarded:** Visual and performing arts 84%, trade and industry 16%. **Special Study Options:** Cross registration, dual enrollment, independent study, internships, study abroad, academic remediation, advanced placement credit.

FACILITIES

Housing: Coed, apartments for married students, apartments for single students, apartment and roommate referral services. **Library Holdings:** 36,183 bound volumes. 147 periodicals. 0 microforms. 3,520 audiovisuals. **Special Academic Facilities/Equipment:** Art gallery, multicamera video studio, two digital video-editing suites, and an audio studio and control room featuring Protools stations. Professional photography studios with traditional and digital darkroom facilities containing high-end professional equipment such as the Imacon scanners, Cone Piezograph black-and-white printers, Epson 5500 printer, and Epson 10000 printer. Photographic video-editing stations consist of dual processor G4s with cinema displays that are color managed with Greytag MacBeth equipment. Culinary facilities with five teaching kitchens and a dining lab. **Computers:** School-owned computers available for student use.

EXTRACURRICULARS

Activities: Student government. **Organizations:** 16 registered organizations.

ADMISSIONS

Selectivity Rating: 63 (of 100). **Freshman Academic Profile:** TOEFL required of all international applicants, minimum TOEFL 480. **Basis for Candidate Selection:** *Very important factors considered include:* essays, interview, secondary school record, standardized test scores. *Important factors considered include:* talent/ability. *Other factors considered include:* character/personal qualities, class rank, extracurricular activities, recommendations, volunteer work, work experience. **Freshman Admission Requirements:** High school diploma or GED is required. **Transfer Admission Requirements:** *Items required:* college transcript, essay, interview. Minimum high school GPA of 2.0 required. Minimum college GPA of 2.0 required. Lowest grade transferable C. **General Admission Information:** Application fee $50. Regular application deadline October 1. Nonfall registration accepted. Admission may be deferred. Credit offered for CEEB Advanced Placement tests.

COSTS AND FINANCIAL AID

Tuition $15,648. Average book expense $1,401. **Required Forms and Deadlines:** FAFSA and state aid form. No deadline for regular filing. **Notification of Awards:** Applicants will be notified of awards on a rolling basis beginning on or about March 15. **Types of Aid:** *Need-based scholarships/grants:* Pell, SEOG, state scholarships/grants, private scholarships, the school's own gift aid. *Loans:* Direct Subsidized Stafford, Direct Unsubsidized Stafford, Direct PLUS, FFEL Subsidized Stafford, FFEL Unsubsidized Stafford, FFEL PLUS, Federal Perkins. **Student Employment:** Institutional employment available. Off-campus job opportunities are excellent. **Financial Aid Statistics:** 54% freshmen, 47% undergrads receive some form of aid. **Financial Aid Phone:** 770-394-8300.

See page 918.

ART INSTITUTE OF BOSTON AT LESLEY UNIVERSITY

700 Beacon Street, Boston, MA 02215-2598
Phone: 617-585-6700 **E-mail:** admissions@aiboston.edu **CEEB Code:** 3777
Fax: 617-437-1226 **Web:** www.aiboston.edu

This private school was founded in 1912. It has a 1-acre campus.

STUDENTS AND FACULTY

Enrollment: 519. **Student Body:** Male 44%, female 56%, out-of-state 39%, international 11% (29 countries represented). **Ethnic Representation:** African American 3%, Asian 5%, Caucasian 88%, Hispanic 3%, Native American 1%. **Retention and Graduation:** 78% freshmen return for sophomore year. 15% freshmen graduate within 4 years. 17% grads go on to further study within 1 year. **Faculty:** Student/faculty ratio 9:1. 24 full-time faculty, 83% hold PhDs. 100% faculty teach undergrads.

ACADEMICS

Degrees: Bachelor's, diploma, master's, post-bachelor's certificate. **Academic Requirements:** General education including some course work in arts/fine arts, computer literacy, English (including composition), history, humanities, social science. **Classes:** 10-19 students in an average class. **Majors with Highest Enrollment:** Graphic design; illustration; photography. **Disciplines with Highest Percentage of Degrees Awarded:** Visual and performing arts 100%. **Special Study Options:** Accelerated program, cross registration, distance learning, double major, English as a second language, student exchange program (domestic), honors program, independent study, internships, study abroad, teacher certification program, AICAD mobility program, NY Studio program, Bridge program.

FACILITIES

Housing: Coed, all-female. **Library Holdings:** 98,271 bound volumes. 739 periodicals. 785,000 microforms. 47,312 audiovisuals. **Special Academic Facilities/Equipment:** Art gallery with regular shows of prominent artists; art library; applied art facilities, including state-of-the-art photo and computer labs, animation studio, ceramics studio, wood shop, metals studio, and printmaking studio. **Computers:** *Recommended operating system:* Mac. School-owned computers available for student use.

EXTRACURRICULARS

Activities: Choral groups, dance, drama/theater, literary magazine. **Organizations:** 6 registered organizations. **Athletics (Intercollegiate):** *Women:* basketball, crew, soccer, softball, volleyball.

ADMISSIONS

Selectivity Rating: 63 (of 100). **Freshman Academic Profile:** Average high school GPA 2.9. 79% from public high schools. Average SAT I Math 500, SAT I Math middle 50% range 440-540. Average SAT I Verbal 530, SAT I Verbal middle 50% range 460-580. TOEFL required of all international applicants, minimum TOEFL 500. **Basis for Candidate Selection:** *Very important factors considered include:* character/personal qualities, secondary school record, talent/ability. *Important factors considered include:* essays, interview, recommendations, standardized test scores. *Other factors considered include:* alumni/ae relation, extracurricular activities, geographical residence, minority status, state residency, volunteer work, work experience. **Freshman Admission Requirements:** High school diploma or GED is required. *Academic units required/recommended:* 14 total recommended; 3 English required, 3 English recommended, 1 math recommended, 1 science recommended, 1 foreign language recommended, 2 social studies recommended, 2 history recommended, 2 elective recommended. **Freshman Admission Statistics:** 480 applied, 60% accepted, 41% of those accepted enrolled. **Transfer Admission Requirements:** *Items required:* high school transcript, college transcript, essay, interview. Minimum college GPA of 2.0 required. Lowest grade transferable C. **General Admission Information:** Application fee $40. Priority application deadline February 15. Nonfall registration accepted. Admission may be deferred for a maximum of 1 year. Credit and/or placement offered for CEEB Advanced Placement tests.

COSTS AND FINANCIAL AID

Tuition $16,400. Room & board $8,800. Required fees $710. Average book expense $1,575. **Required Forms and Deadlines:** FAFSA and institution's own financial aid form. No deadline for regular filing. Priority filing deadline March 12. **Notification of Awards:** Applicants will be notified of awards on a rolling basis beginning on or about April 1. **Types of Aid:** *Need-based scholarships/grants:* Pell, SEOG, state scholarships/grants, private scholarships, the school's own gift aid. *Loans:* FFEL Subsidized Stafford, FFEL Unsubsidized Stafford, FFEL PLUS, Federal Perkins, state loans. **Student Employment:** Federal Work-Study Program available. Institutional employment available. Off-campus job opportunities are excellent. **Financial Aid Statistics:** 65% freshmen, 47% undergrads receive some form of aid. Average freshman grant $4,845. Average freshman loan $3,207. Average income from on-campus job $2,241. **Financial Aid Phone:** 617-349-8710.

See page 920.

ART INSTITUTE OF COLORADO

1200 Lincoln St., Denver, CO 80203
Phone: 303-837-0825 **E-mail:** aicinfo@artinstitutes.edu
Fax: 303-860-8520 **Web:** www.aic.artinstitutes.edu **ACT Code:** 495

This proprietary school was founded in 1952.

STUDENTS AND FACULTY

Enrollment: 2,226. **Student Body:** Male 56%, female 44%, international 3%. **Ethnic Representation:** African American 3%, Asian 4%, Caucasian 52%, Hispanic 5%, Native American 1%. **Faculty:** Student/faculty ratio 20:1. 74 full-time faculty, 20% hold PhDs.

ACADEMICS

Degrees: Associate's, bachelor's, certificate, diploma. **Academic Requirements:** General education including some course work in arts/fine arts, computer literacy, English (including composition), foreign languages, history, humanities, mathematics, philosophy, sciences (biological or physical), social science. **Special Study Options:** Independent study, internships, study abroad.

FACILITIES

Housing: Apartments for single students. **Library Holdings:** 25,000 bound volumes. 250 periodicals. 0 microforms. 1,437 audiovisuals. **Computers:** School-owned computers available for student use.

EXTRACURRICULARS

Organizations: 3 honor societies.

ADMISSIONS

Selectivity Rating: 63 (of 100). **Freshman Academic Profile:** TOEFL required of all international applicants, minimum TOEFL 480. **Basis for Candidate Selection:** *Important factors considered include:* essays, interview, standardized test scores. *Other factors considered include:* secondary school record. **Freshman Admission Requirements:** High school diploma or GED is required. **Freshman Admission Statistics:** 1,163 applied, 99% accepted, 58% of those accepted enrolled. **Transfer Admission Requirements:** *Items required:* high school transcript, essay, interview. Lowest grade transferable C. **General Admission Information:** Application fee $50. Nonfall registration accepted. Admission may be deferred for a maximum of 1 year. Credit offered for CEEB Advanced Placement tests.

COSTS AND FINANCIAL AID

Room & board $5,760. Required fees $50. Average book expense $2,250. **Required Forms and Deadlines:** FAFSA and institution's own financial aid form. No deadline for regular filing. Priority filing deadline March 15. **Notification of Awards:** Applicants will be notified of awards on a rolling basis. **Types of Aid:** *Need-based scholarships/grants:* Pell, SEOG, state scholarships/grants, private scholarships, the school's own gift aid. *Loans:* FFEL Subsidized Stafford, FFEL Unsubsidized Stafford, FFEL PLUS, Federal Perkins, state loans. **Student Employment:** Federal Work-Study Program available. Institutional employment available. Off-campus job opportunities are excellent. **Financial Aid Phone:** 303-824-4757.

ART INSTITUTE OF DALLAS

8080 Park Lane # 100, Two Park North East, Dallas, TX 75231
Phone: 214-692-8080 **E-mail:** crispm@aii.edu **CEEB Code:** 2680
Fax: 214-750-9460 **ACT Code:** 4075

This private school was founded in 1964.

STUDENTS AND FACULTY

Enrollment: 1,463. **Student Body:** Male 59%, female 41%, out-of-state 97%. **Ethnic Representation:** African American 7%, Asian 3%, Caucasian 43%, Hispanic 9%. **Retention and Graduation:** 8% grads go on to further study within 1 year. **Faculty:** Student/faculty ratio 18:1. 62 full-time faculty, 20% hold PhDs. 100% faculty teach undergrads.

ACADEMICS

Degrees: Associate's, bachelor's, certificate, terminal. **Academic Requirements:** General education including some course work in arts/fine arts, computer literacy, English (including composition), humanities, mathematics, social science. **Classes:** 10-19 students in an average class. **Special Study Options:** Cross registration, dual enrollment, internships, liberal arts/career combination, study abroad.

FACILITIES

Housing: Apartments for single students. **Library Holdings:** 16,921 bound volumes. 262 periodicals. 0 microforms. 1,478 audiovisuals. **Computers:** School-owned computers available for student use.

EXTRACURRICULARS

Activities: Student government, student newspaper, student-run film society. **Organizations:** 5 registered organizations.

ADMISSIONS

Selectivity Rating: 63 (of 100). **Freshman Academic Profile:** 93% from public high schools. TOEFL required of all international applicants, minimum TOEFL 550. **Basis for Candidate Selection:** *Other factors considered include:* class rank, essays, recommendations, secondary school record, standardized test scores. **Freshman Admission Requirements:** High school diploma or GED is required. *Academic units required/recommended:* 15 total required; 15 total recommended; 4 English required, 4 English recommended, 4 math required, 4 math recommended, 2 science required, 2 science recommended, 1 foreign language required, 1 foreign language recommended, 2 social studies required, 2 social studies recommended, 2 history required, 2 history recommended. **Freshman Admission Statistics:** 855 applied, 53% accepted, 61% of those accepted enrolled. **Transfer Admission Requirements:** *Items required:* high school transcript, essay, interview, standardized test scores. Minimum college GPA of 2.0 required. Lowest grade transferable C. **General Admission Information:** Application fee $50. Nonfall registration accepted. Admission may be deferred. Credit and/or placement offered for CEEB Advanced Placement tests.

COSTS AND FINANCIAL AID

Tuition $13,770. Average book expense $950. **Required Forms and Deadlines:** FAFSA and institution's own financial aid form. No deadline for regular filing. **Types of Aid:** *Need-based scholarships/grants:* Pell, SEOG, private scholarships, the school's own gift aid. *Loans:* FFEL Subsidized Stafford, FFEL Unsubsidized Stafford, FFEL PLUS. **Student Employment:** Federal Work-Study Program available. Institutional employment available. Off-campus job opportunities are excellent. **Financial Aid Statistics:** 80% freshmen, 84% undergrads receive some form of aid. Average freshman grant $752. Average freshman loan $6,625. Average income from on-campus job $1,014. **Financial Aid Phone:** 800-275-4243.

ART INSTITUTE OF LOS ANGELES—ORANGE COUNTY

3601 Sunflower Avenue, Santa Ana, CA 92704
Phone: 714-830-0200 **E-mail:** www.admisssions@ailaoc.artinstitutes.edu
Fax: 714-556-1923

This proprietary school was founded in 2000.

ACADEMICS

Degrees: Associate's, bachelor's. **Academic Requirements:** General education including some course work in arts/fine arts, computer literacy, English (including composition), history, humanities, mathematics, philosophy, social science. **Special Study Options:** Internships.

FACILITIES

Housing: Apartments for single students.

EXTRACURRICULARS

Activities: Student newspaper.

ADMISSIONS

Selectivity Rating: 63 (of 100). **Freshman Academic Profile: Basis for Candidate Selection:** *Very important factors considered include:* essays, interview. *Important factors considered include:* secondary school record. *Other factors considered include:* class rank, standardized test scores, talent/ability. **Freshman Admission Requirements:** High school diploma or GED is required. **Freshman Admission Statistics:** 1,998 applied, 100% accepted. **Transfer Admission Requirements:** *Items required:* high school transcript, college transcript, essay. Lowest grade transferable C. **General Admission Information:** Application fee $50. Nonfall registration accepted. Admission may be deferred for a maximum of 1 year.

COSTS AND FINANCIAL AID

Required fees $150. Average book expense $125. **Required Forms and Deadlines:** FAFSA, institution's own financial aid form, and state aid form. No deadline for regular filing. **Notification of Awards:** Applicants will be notified of awards on a rolling basis beginning on or about January 1. **Types of Aid:** *Need-based scholarships/grants:* Pell, SEOG, state scholarships/grants, private scholarships, the school's own gift aid. *Loans:* Direct Subsidized Stafford, Direct Unsubsidized Stafford, Direct PLUS, FFEL Subsidized Stafford, FFEL Unsubsidized Stafford, FFEL PLUS, Federal Perkins, Creative Education Loan. **Student Employment:** Federal Work-Study Program available. Institutional employment available. Off-campus job opportunities are excellent. **Financial Aid Phone:** 888-549-3055.

ART INSTITUTE OF PITTSBURGH

420 Blvd. of the Allies, Pittsburgh, PA 15219
Phone: 412-263-6600 **E-mail:** aip_admissions@aii.edu
Fax: 412-263-6667 **Web:** www.aip.aii.edu

This public school was founded in 1921.

STUDENTS AND FACULTY

Enrollment: 2,443. **Student Body:** Male 68%, female 32%, international 2% (20 countries represented). **Ethnic Representation:** African American 9%, Caucasian 82%. **Faculty:** Student/faculty ratio 20:1. 65 full-time faculty, 1% hold PhDs. 100% faculty teach undergrads.

ACADEMICS

Degrees: Associate's, bachelor's, diploma, terminal, transfer. **Academic Requirements:** General education including some course work in arts/fine arts, computer literacy, English (including composition), mathematics. **Special Study Options:** Cooperative (work-study) program, distance learning, English as a second language, honors program, independent study, internships.

FACILITIES

Library Holdings: 13,650 bound volumes. 235 periodicals. 0 microforms. 420 audiovisuals. **Computers:** School-owned computers available for student use.

EXTRACURRICULARS

Activities: Drama/theater, student government, student newspaper, student-run film society. **Organizations:** 25 registered organizations, 1 honor society, 1 religious organization.

ADMISSIONS

Selectivity Rating: 60 (of 100). **Freshman Academic Profile: Basis for Candidate Selection:** *Very important factors considered include:* essays, interview, secondary school record. *Important factors considered include:* character/personal qualities. *Other factors considered include:* recommendations. **Freshman Admission Requirements:** High school diploma or GED is required. **Transfer Admission Requirements:** *Items required:* high school transcript, essay, interview. Minimum high school GPA of 2.0 required. Lowest grade transferable C. **General Admission Information:** Nonfall registration accepted. Admission may be deferred for a maximum of 1 year. Neither credit nor placement offered for CEEB Advanced Placement tests.

COSTS AND FINANCIAL AID

Average book expense $900. **Required Forms and Deadlines:** FAFSA, institution's own financial aid form and state aid form. No deadline for regular filing. **Notification of Awards:** Applicants will be notified of awards on a rolling basis. **Types of Aid:** *Need-based scholarships/grants:* Pell, SEOG, state scholarships/grants, private scholarships, the school's own gift aid. *Loans:* Direct Subsidized Stafford, Direct Unsubsidized Stafford, Direct PLUS, Federal Perkins, state loans, college/university loans from institutional funds. **Student Employment:** Federal Work-Study Program available. Institutional employment available. Off-campus job opportunities are excellent. **Financial Aid Phone:** 800-275-2470.

THE ART INSTITUTE OF SEATTLE

2323 Elliott Avenue, Seattle, WA 98121
Phone: 206-448-6600 **E-mail:** aisadm@aii.edu
Fax: 206-269-0275

This proprietary school was founded in 1946.

STUDENTS AND FACULTY

Enrollment: 2,525. **Student Body:** Out-of-state 15%, international students represent 25 countries. **Faculty:** 70 full-time faculty.

ACADEMICS

Degrees: Associate's, certificate, diploma. **Academic Requirements:** General education including some course work in arts/fine arts, computer literacy, English (including composition), foreign languages, history, humanities, mathematics, philosophy, sciences (biological or physical), social science. **Majors with Highest Enrollment:** Graphic design; design and applied arts; Web page, digital/multimedia, and information resources design. **Special Study Options:** English as a second language, internships, liberal arts/career combination.

FACILITIES

Housing: Apartments for married students, apartments for single students. **Special Academic Facilities/Equipment:** Gallery.

EXTRACURRICULARS

Organizations: 16 registered organizations. **Activities:** Student government, student newspaper.

ADMISSIONS

Selectivity Rating: 63 (of 100). **Transfer Admission Requirements:** High school diploma or GED is required. *Items required:* high school transcript, college transcript, essay, interview. **General Admission Information:** Application fee $50. Nonfall registration accepted.

COSTS AND FINANCIAL AID

Student Employment: Federal Work-Study Program available. Off-campus job opportunities are good. **Financial Aid Phone:** 206-239-2261.

ART INSTITUTE OF SOUTHERN CALIFORNIA

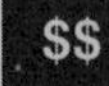

2222 Laguna Canyon Road, Laguna Beach, CA 92651
Phone: 949-376-6000 **E-mail:** admission@aisc.edu
Fax: 949-376-6009 **Web:** www.aisc.edu

STUDENTS AND FACULTY

Enrollment: 268. **Student Body:** Male 53%, female 47%, international 9%. **Ethnic Representation:** African American 2%, Asian 8%, Caucasian 73%, Hispanic 13%, Native American 1%.

ACADEMICS

Degrees: Bachelor's, certificate.

ADMISSIONS

Selectivity Rating: 60 (of 100). *Academic units required/recommended:* 16 total recommended; 4 English recommended, 3 math recommended, 3 science recommended, 2 foreign language recommended, 4 social studies recommended.

COSTS AND FINANCIAL AID

Tuition $14,285. Required fees $100. Average book expense $2,000. **Types of Aid:** *Need-based scholarships/grants:* Pell, SEOG, state scholarships/grants, private scholarships, the school's own gift aid. *Loans:* FFEL Subsidized Stafford, FFEL Unsubsidized Stafford, FFEL PLUS, Federal Perkins, college/university loans from institutional funds.

ART INSTITUTE OF WASHINGTON

1820 N Fort Myer Drive, Arlington, VA 22209
Phone: 703-358-9550
Fax: 703-358-9759

This public school was founded in 2000.

STUDENTS AND FACULTY

Enrollment: 332. **Student Body:** Male 40%, female 60%. **Faculty:** Student/faculty ratio 20:1. 100% faculty teach undergrads.

ACADEMICS

Degrees: Associate's, bachelor's. **Academic Requirements:** General education including some course work in arts/fine arts, computer literacy, English (including composition), history, mathematics, sciences (biological or physical).

ADMISSIONS

Selectivity Rating: 60 (of 100). **Freshman Academic Profile:** TOEFL required of all international applicants, minimum TOEFL 480. **Basis for Candidate Selection:** *Very important factors considered include:* essays, interview, secondary school record. **Freshman Admission Requirements:** High school diploma or GED is required. **Transfer Admission Requirements:** *Items required:* high school transcript, college transcript, essay, interview. Lowest grade transferable C. **General Admission Information:** Application fee $50. Nonfall registration accepted. Admission may be deferred.

COSTS AND FINANCIAL AID

Average book expense $125. **Required Forms and Deadlines:** FAFSA. No deadline for regular filing. **Notification of Awards:** Applicants will be notified of awards on a rolling basis. **Types of Aid:** *Need-based scholarships/grants:* Pell, SEOG. *Loans:* Direct Subsidized Stafford, Direct Unsubsidized Stafford, Direct PLUS, Federal Perkins. **Student Employment:** Off-campus job opportunities are excellent.

ART INSTITUTES INTERNATIONAL AT MINNESOTA

15 South 9th Street, Minneapolis, MN 55402
Phone: 612-332-3361 **E-mail:** kozela@aii.edu
Fax: 612-332-3934 **Web:** www.aim.artinstitutes.edu

This proprietary school was founded in 1997.

STUDENTS AND FACULTY

Enrollment: 989. **Student Body:** Male 53%, female 47%. **Ethnic Representation:** African American 2%, Asian 3%, Caucasian 34%, Hispanic 1%. **Faculty:** Student/faculty ratio 19:1. 20 full-time faculty. 100% faculty teach undergrads.

ACADEMICS

Degrees: Associate's, bachelor's, certificate, terminal. **Academic Requirements:** General education including some course work in arts/fine arts, computer literacy, English (including composition), history, mathematics, sciences (biological or physical). **Majors with Highest Enrollment:** Culinary arts/chef training; design and visual communications, general; design and applied arts. **Special Study Options:** Cooperative (work-study) program, internships, evening program, online program.

FACILITIES

Housing: Coed. **Special Academic Facilities/Equipment:** Gallery, Gourmet Gallery (student-run dining lab), learning resource center. **Computers:** School-owned computers available for student use.

EXTRACURRICULARS

Organizations: 6 registered organizations.

ADMISSIONS

Selectivity Rating: 60 (of 100). **Freshman Academic Profile:** TOEFL required of all international applicants, minimum TOEFL 500. **Freshman Admission Requirements:** High school diploma or GED is required. **Transfer Admission Requirements:** *Items required:* high school transcript, college transcript, essay, interview, standardized test scores. Lowest grade transferable C. **General Admission Information:** Application fee $50.

COSTS AND FINANCIAL AID

Average book expense $1,125. **Required Forms and Deadlines:** FAFSA, institution's own financial aid form, and state aid form. No deadline for regular filing. **Types of Aid:** *Need-based scholarships/grants:* Pell, SEOG, state scholarships/grants, the school's own gift aid. *Loans:* FFEL Subsidized Stafford, FFEL Unsubsidized Stafford, FFEL PLUS, state loans. **Student Employment:** Federal Work-Study Program available. Off-campus job opportunities are good. **Financial Aid Phone:** 612-332-3361.

ART INSTITUTES INTERNATIONAL AT PORTLAND

2000 SW Fifth Ave., Portland, OR 97201-4907
Phone: 503-228-6528 **E-mail:** alstonK@aii.edu **CEEB Code:** 7819
Fax: 503-228-4227 **Web:** www.aii.edu

This proprietary school was founded in 1963. It has a 1-acre campus.

STUDENTS AND FACULTY

Enrollment: 214. **Student Body:** Male 27%, female 73%. **Retention and Graduation:** 57% freshmen return for sophomore year. **Faculty:** 100% faculty teach undergrads.

ACADEMICS

Degrees: Associate's, bachelor's. **Academic Requirements:** General education including some course work in arts/fine arts, computer literacy, English (including composition), history, humanities, mathematics, philosophy, sciences (biological or physical), social science. **Special Study Options:** Independent study, internships.

FACILITIES

Library Holdings: 16,900 bound volumes. 115 periodicals. 300 audiovisuals. **Computers:** School-owned computers available for student use.

EXTRACURRICULARS

Organizations: 2 registered organizations.

ADMISSIONS

Selectivity Rating: 63 (of 100). **Freshman Academic Profile:** TOEFL required of all international applicants, minimum TOEFL 500. **Basis for Candidate Selection:** *Very important factors considered include:* essays, secondary school record. *Important factors considered include:* interview, talent/ability. *Other factors considered include:* character/personal qualities, class rank, extracurricular activities, recommendations, standardized test scores, work experience. **Freshman Admission Requirements:** High school diploma or GED is required. **Freshman Admission Statistics:** 51 applied, 96% accepted, 67% of those accepted enrolled. **Transfer Admission Requirements:** *Items required:* high school transcript, college transcript, essay, interview. Minimum high school GPA of 2.0 required. Minimum college GPA of 2.0 required. Lowest grade transferable C. **General Admission Information:** Application fee $50. Nonfall registration accepted. Admission may be deferred.

COSTS AND FINANCIAL AID

Average book expense $1,125. **Required Forms and Deadlines:** FAFSA. No deadline for regular filing. **Notification of Awards:** Applicants will be notified of awards on a rolling basis beginning on or about February 1. **Types of Aid:** *Need-based scholarships/grants:* Pell, SEOG, private scholarships, the school's own gift aid. *Loans:* FFEL Subsidized Stafford, FFEL Unsubsidized Stafford, FFEL PLUS, Federal Perkins. **Student Employment:** Off-campus job opportunities are excellent. **Financial Aid Statistics:** 87% freshmen, 77% undergrads receive some form of aid. **Financial Aid Phone:** 503-228-6528.

ART INSTITUTES INTERNATIONAL AT SAN FRANCISCO

1170 Market Street, San Francisco, CA 94102
Phone: 415-865-0198 **E-mail:** aisfadm@aii.edu
Fax: 415-863-6344 **Web:** www.aicasf.aii.edu

This proprietary school was founded in 1939. It has a 1-acre campus.

STUDENTS AND FACULTY

Enrollment: 346. **Student Body:** Male 56%, female 44%, out-of-state 25%, international 5%. **Ethnic Representation:** African American 6%, Asian 15%, Caucasian 32%, Hispanic 23%, Native American 2%. **Retention and Graduation:** 78% freshmen return for sophomore year. 5% grads go on to further study within 1 year. **Faculty:** Student/faculty ratio 14:1. 7 full-time faculty, 85% hold PhDs. 100% faculty teach undergrads.

ACADEMICS

Degrees: Associate's, bachelor's. **Academic Requirements:** General education including some course work in arts/fine arts, computer literacy, English (including composition), history, mathematics, sciences (biological or physical), social science. **Classes:** 10-19 students in an average class. **Disciplines with Highest Percentage of Degrees Awarded:** Visual and performing arts 100%. **Special Study Options:** Accelerated program, distance learning, internships.

FACILITIES

Housing: All housing is in an apartment complex; studio, one, and two bedrooms available with 2/2/4 roommates per apartment respectively. Apartments are available for married couples. **Computers:** School-owned computers available for student use.

EXTRACURRICULARS

Activities: Student government, student newspaper.

ADMISSIONS

Selectivity Rating: 63 (of 100). TOEFL required of all international applicants, minimum TOEFL 480. **Basis for Candidate Selection:** *Important factors considered include:* character/personal qualities, essays, interview, talent/ability. *Other factors considered include:* alumni/ae relation, class rank, extracurricular activities, recommendations, secondary school record, standardized test scores, volunteer work, work experience. **Freshman Admission Requirements:** High school diploma or GED is required. **Freshman Admission Statistics:** 205 applied, 100% accepted, 48% of those accepted enrolled. **Transfer Admission Requirements:** *Items required:* high school transcript, college transcript, essay, interview. Lowest grade transferable C. **General Admission Information:** Application fee $50. Nonfall registration accepted. Admission may be deferred for a maximum of 1 year.

COSTS AND FINANCIAL AID

Tuition $32,000. Room & board $6,459. Average book expense $1,125. **Required Forms and Deadlines:** FAFSA. Financial aid filing deadline June 30. Priority filing deadline March 1. **Notification of Awards:** Applicants will be notified of awards on a rolling basis. **Types of Aid:** *Need-based scholarships/grants:* Pell, SEOG, state scholarships/grants, private scholarships, the school's own gift aid, United Negro College Fund. *Loans:* FFEL Subsidized Stafford, FFEL Unsubsidized Stafford, FFEL PLUS, Federal Perkins, Federal Nursing, state loans, CELP, CEOL, independent loans from private organizations. **Student Employment:** Federal Work-Study Program available. Institutional employment available. Off-campus job opportunities are good. **Financial Aid Statistics:** 50% freshmen, 68% undergrads receive some form of aid. Average freshman grant $2,000. Average freshman loan $6,000. Average income from on-campus job $5,000. **Financial Aid Phone:** 415-865-0198.

ASBURY COLLEGE

1 Macklem Drive, Wilmore, KY 40390
Phone: 859-858-3511 **E-mail:** admissions@asbury.edu **CEEB Code:** 1019
Fax: 859-858-3921 **Web:** www.asbury.edu **ACT Code:** 1486

This private school was founded in 1890. It has a 400-acre campus.

STUDENTS AND FACULTY

Enrollment: 1,271. **Student Body:** Male 40%, female 60%, out-of-state 72%, international 1% (10 countries represented). **Ethnic Representation:** African American 1%, Asian 1%, Caucasian 97%, Hispanic 1%. **Retention and Graduation:** 78% freshmen return for sophomore year. 46% freshmen graduate within 4 years. **Faculty:** Student/faculty ratio 11:1. 92 full-time faculty, 75% hold PhDs. 100% faculty teach undergrads.

ACADEMICS

Degrees: Bachelor's, master's. **Academic Requirements:** General education including some course work in arts/fine arts, computer literacy, English (including composition), foreign languages, history, humanities, mathematics, philosophy, sciences (biological or physical), social science, Bible and theology. **Classes:** 10-19 students in an average class. **Majors with Highest Enrollment:** Elementary education and teaching; psychology, general; communications technologies and support services. **Disciplines with Highest Percentage of Degrees Awarded:** Education 15%, philosophy/religion/theology 15%, communications/communication technologies 13%, business/marketing 9%, psychology 8%. **Special Study Options:** Double major, internships, teacher certification program, 3-2 programs in engineering and computer science with the University of Kentucky.

FACILITIES

Housing: All-female, all-male, apartments for married students, apartments for single students, housing for disabled students, Spanish House. **Library Holdings:** 155,320 bound volumes. 14,550 periodicals. 21,485 microforms. 8,974 audiovisuals. **Special Academic Facilities/Equipment:** Art gallery, art annex, practice rooms, theatre building, Luce Physical Activities Center, TV/radio studios, and Mac lab. **Computers:** School-owned computers available for student use.

EXTRACURRICULARS

Activities: Choral groups, concert band, drama/theater, jazz band, literary magazine, music ensembles, opera, radio station, student government, student newspaper, symphony orchestra, television station, yearbook. **Organizations:** 41 registered organizations, 6 honor societies, 8 religious organizations. **Athletics (Intercollegiate):** *Men:* baseball, basketball, cross-country, diving, soccer, swimming, tennis, track & field. *Women:* basketball, cross-country, diving, soccer, softball, swimming, tennis, track & field, volleyball.

ADMISSIONS

Selectivity Rating: 75 (of 100). **Freshman Academic Profile:** Average high school GPA 3.6. 32% in top 10% of high school class, 63% in top 25% of high school class, 86% in top 50% of high school class. 65% from public high schools. Average SAT I Math 561, SAT I Math middle 50% range 500-630. Average SAT I Verbal 585, SAT I Verbal middle 50% range 523-650. Average ACT 25, ACT middle 50% range 22-27. TOEFL required of all international applicants, minimum TOEFL 550. **Basis for Candidate Selection:** *Very important factors considered include:* character/personal qualities, minority status, recommendations, religious affiliation/commitment, secondary school record, standardized test scores. *Important factors considered include:* class rank, essays, volunteer work, work experience. *Other factors considered include:* alumni/ae relation, extracurricular activities, geographical residence, state residency, talent/ability. **Freshman Admission Requirements:** High school diploma or GED is required. *Academic units required/recommended:* 17 total recommended; 4 English recommended, 4 math recommended, 3 science recommended, 2 foreign language recommended, 2 social studies recommended. **Freshman Admission Statistics:** 838 applied, 81% accepted, 48% of those accepted enrolled. **Transfer Admission Requirements:** *Items required:* high school transcript, college transcript, essay, standardized test scores. Minimum high school GPA of 2.5 required. Minimum college GPA of 2.5 required. Lowest grade transferable C-. **General Admission Information:** Application fee $30. Nonfall registration accepted. Admission may be deferred for a maximum of 1 year. Neither credit nor placement offered for CEEB Advanced Placement tests.

COSTS AND FINANCIAL AID

Tuition $16,352. Room & board $4,204. Required fees $142. Average book expense $500. **Required Forms and Deadlines:** FAFSA and institution's own financial aid form. No deadline for regular filing. Priority filing deadline March

1. **Notification of Awards:** Applicants will be notified of awards on a rolling basis beginning on or about March 1. **Types of Aid:** *Need-based scholarships/grants:* Pell, SEOG, state scholarships/grants, the school's own gift aid. *Loans:* FFEL Subsidized Stafford, FFEL Unsubsidized Stafford, FFEL PLUS, Federal Perkins, college/university loans from institutional funds, private alternative loans. **Student Employment:** Federal Work-Study Program available. Institutional employment available. Off-campus job opportunities are good. **Financial Aid Statistics:** 67% freshmen, 66% undergrads receive some form of aid. Average income from on-campus job $1,200. **Financial Aid Phone:** 859-858-3511.

ASHLAND UNIVERSITY

401 College Avenue, Ashland, OH 44805
Phone: 419-289-5052 **E-mail:** auadmsn@ashland.edu **CEEB Code:** 1021
Fax: 419-289-5999 **Web:** www.ashland.edu **ACT Code:** 3234

This private school, which is affiliated with the Church of Brethren, was founded in 1878. It has a 98-acre campus.

STUDENTS AND FACULTY

Enrollment: 2,748. **Student Body:** Male 42%, female 58%, out-of-state 5%, international 1% (28 countries represented). **Ethnic Representation:** African American 4%, Caucasian 91%, Hispanic 1%. **Retention and Graduation:** 71% freshmen return for sophomore year. 42% freshmen graduate within 4 years. 10% grads go on to further study within 1 year. 1% grads pursue business degrees. 1% grads pursue law degrees. 1% grads pursue medical degrees. **Faculty:** Student/faculty ratio 16:1. 213 full-time faculty, 82% hold PhDs.

ACADEMICS

Degrees: Associate's, bachelor's, doctoral, first professional, master's, terminal, transfer. **Academic Requirements:** General education including some course work in arts/fine arts, computer literacy, English (including composition), foreign languages, history, humanities, mathematics, philosophy, sciences (biological or physical), social science, freshman seminar, physical education, religion, communications, business/economics, interdisciplinary studies courses. **Classes:** 20-29 students in an average class. Under 10 students in an average lab/discussion section. **Majors with Highest Enrollment:** Business administration/management; education, general; biology/biological sciences, general. **Disciplines with Highest Percentage of Degrees Awarded:** Education 32%, business/marketing 21%, communications/communication technologies 7%, health professions and related sciences 6%, social sciences and history 5%. **Special Study Options:** Double major, English as a second language, honors program, independent study, internships, liberal arts/career combination, study abroad, teacher certification program, weekend college, Ashbrook Center for Public Affairs.

FACILITIES

Housing: Coed, all-female, all-male, apartments for single students, fraternities and/or sororities. Some family and consumer science majors must live in a home management residence in order to graduate. Special rooms exist for housing disabled students. One dorm is open year round for international student housing. **Library Holdings:** 205,200 bound volumes. 1,265 periodicals. 318,000 microforms. 3,550 audiovisuals. **Special Academic Facilities/Equipment:** Numismatic center, Patterson Technology Center, Coburn Art Gallery, Hugo Young Theatre, Studio Theatre, 33-room radio/television complex, media center, pre-Columbian art exhibit, Ashbrook Center. **Computers:** School-owned computers available for student use.

EXTRACURRICULARS

Activities: Choral groups, concert band, dance, drama/theater, jazz band, literary magazine, marching band, music ensembles, musical theater, pep band, radio station, student government, student newspaper, symphony orchestra, television station, yearbook. **Organizations:** 104 registered organizations, 18 honor societies, 4 religious organizations, 4 fraternities (9% men join), 5 sororities (13% women join). **Athletics (Intercollegiate):** *Men:* baseball, basketball, cross-country, football, golf, indoor track, soccer, swimming, track & field, wrestling. *Women:* basketball, cross-country, golf, indoor track, soccer, softball, swimming, tennis, track & field, volleyball.

ADMISSIONS

Selectivity Rating: 71 (of 100). **Freshman Academic Profile:** Average high school GPA 3.3. 16% in top 10% of high school class, 44% in top 25% of high school class, 74% in top 50% of high school class. 89% from public high schools. Average SAT I Math 512, SAT I Math middle 50% range 470-580. Average SAT I Verbal 510, SAT I Verbal middle 50% range 490-580. Average ACT 22, ACT middle 50% range 19-25. TOEFL required of all international applicants, minimum TOEFL 500. **Basis for Candidate Selection:** *Very important factors considered include:* secondary school record, standardized test scores. *Important factors considered include:* alumni/ae relation, character/personal qualities, class rank, essays, extracurricular activities, interview. *Other factors considered include:* geographical residence, recommendations, religious affiliation/commitment, work experience. **Freshman Admission Requirements:** High school diploma or GED is required. *Academic units required/recommended:* 3 English required, 4 English recommended, 2 math required, 3 math recommended, 2 science required, 3 science recommended, 2 foreign language recommended, 2 social studies required, 3 social studies recommended, 1 history required, 1 history recommended. **Freshman Admission Statistics:** 1,773 applied, 89% accepted. **Transfer Admission Requirements:** *Items required:* college transcript, essay. Minimum college GPA of 2.5 required. Lowest grade transferable C-. **General Admission Information:** Application fee $25. Priority application deadline November 15. Nonfall registration accepted. Admission may be deferred. Credit and/or placement offered for CEEB Advanced Placement tests.

COSTS AND FINANCIAL AID

Tuition $16,764. Room & board $6,212. Required fees $506. Average book expense $800. **Required Forms and Deadlines:** FAFSA and institution's own financial aid form. No deadline for regular filing. Priority filing deadline March 15. **Notification of Awards:** Applicants will be notified of awards on a rolling basis. **Types of Aid:** *Need-based scholarships/grants:* Pell, SEOG, state scholarships/grants, private scholarships, the school's own gift aid. *Loans:* Direct Subsidized Stafford, Direct Unsubsidized Stafford, Direct PLUS, Federal Perkins, Federal Nursing, state loans, college/university loans from institutional funds. **Student Employment:** Federal Work-Study Program available. Off-campus job opportunities are good. **Financial Aid Statistics:** 80% freshmen, 77% undergrads receive some form of aid. Average freshman grant $5,500. Average freshman loan $3,000. Average income from on-campus job $1,000. **Financial Aid Phone:** 419-289-5002.

ASSUMPTION COLLEGE

500 Salisbury Street, Worcester, MA 01609-1296
Phone: 508-767-7285 **E-mail:** admiss@assumption.edu **CEEB Code:** 3009
Fax: 508-799-4412 **Web:** www.assumption.edu **ACT Code:** 1782

This private school, which is affiliated with the Roman Catholic Church, was founded in 1904. It has a 175-acre campus.

STUDENTS AND FACULTY

Enrollment: 2,067. **Student Body:** Male 39%, female 61%, out-of-state 32%, (17 countries represented). **Ethnic Representation:** African American 1%, Asian 2%, Caucasian 86%, Hispanic 2%. **Retention and Graduation:** 79% freshmen return for sophomore year. 65% freshmen graduate within 4 years. 18% grads go on to further study within 1 year. **Faculty:** Student/faculty ratio 13:1. 140 full-time faculty, 94% hold PhDs. 100% faculty teach undergrads.

ACADEMICS

Degrees: Bachelor's, master's, post-master's certificate. **Academic Requirements:** General education including some course work in arts/fine arts, English (including composition), foreign languages, history, mathematics, philosophy, sciences (biological or physical), social science, theology. **Classes:** 10-19 students in an average class. 10-19 students in an average lab/discussion section. **Majors with Highest Enrollment:** Rehabilitation and therapeutic professions; English language and literature, general; psychology, general. **Disciplines with Highest Percentage of Degrees Awarded:** Business/marketing 22%, social sciences and history 17%, health professions and related sciences 13%, psychology 9%, English 9%. **Special Study Options:** Cross registration, double major, honors program, independent study, internships, student-designed major, study abroad, teacher certification program.

FACILITIES

Housing: Coed, all-female, housing for disabled students, freshmen dorms, living/learning center. **Library Holdings:** 103,467 bound volumes. 1,119 periodicals. 17,690 microforms. 1,450 audiovisuals. **Special Academic Facilities/Equipment:** French Institute Museum, Social and Rehabilitation Services Institute, language lab, media center, living/learning center, university transportation center, information technology center. **Computers:** School-owned computers available for student use.

EXTRACURRICULARS

Activities: Choral groups, concert band, drama/theater, literary magazine, musical theater, pep band, student government, student newspaper, student-run film society, television station, yearbook. **Organizations:** 40 registered organizations, 8 honor societies, 4 religious organizations. **Athletics (Intercollegiate):** *Men:* baseball, basketball, crew, cross-country, football, golf, ice hockey, lacrosse, soccer, tennis, track & field. *Women:* basketball, crew, cross-country, field hockey, lacrosse, soccer, softball, tennis, track & field, volleyball.

ADMISSIONS

Selectivity Rating: 81 (of 100). **Freshman Academic Profile:** Average high school GPA 3.2. 13% in top 10% of high school class, 42% in top 25% of high school class, 81% in top 50% of high school class. 64% from public high schools. Average SAT I Math 534, SAT I Math middle 50% range 490-590. Average SAT I Verbal 535, SAT I Verbal middle 50% range 490-580. Average ACT 21, ACT middle 50% range 18-23. TOEFL required of all international applicants, minimum TOEFL 200. **Basis for Candidate Selection:** *Very important factors considered include:* class rank, essays, secondary school record, standardized test scores. *Important factors considered include:* character/personal qualities, extracurricular activities, interview, recommendations, talent/ability. *Other factors considered include:* alumni/ae relation, geographical residence, minority status, volunteer work, work experience. **Freshman Admission Requirements:** High school diploma or GED is required. *Academic units required/recommended:* 18 total required; 4 English required, 3 math required, 2 science required, 2 foreign language required, 2 history required, 5 elective required. **Freshman Admission Statistics:** 2,764 applied, 77% accepted, 29% of those accepted enrolled. **Transfer Admission Requirements:** *Items required:* high school transcript, college transcript, essay, standardized test scores. Minimum college GPA of 2.5 required. Lowest grade transferable C-. **General Admission Information:** Application fee $40. Early decision application deadline November 15. Regular application deadline March 1. Nonfall registration accepted. Admission may be deferred for a maximum of 1 year. Credit and/or placement offered for CEEB Advanced Placement tests.

COSTS AND FINANCIAL AID

Tuition $19,835. Room & board $4,850. Required fees $145. Average book expense $850. **Required Forms and Deadlines:** FAFSA. Priority filing deadline February 28. **Notification of Awards:** Applicants will be notified of awards on a rolling basis beginning on or about February 15. **Types of Aid:** *Need-based scholarships/grants:* Pell, SEOG, state scholarships/grants, private scholarships, the school's own gift aid. *Loans:* FFEL Subsidized Stafford, FFEL Unsubsidized Stafford, FFEL PLUS, Federal Perkins, state loans, college/university loans from institutional funds. **Student Employment:** Federal Work-Study Program available. Institutional employment available. Off-campus job opportunities are good. **Financial Aid Statistics:** 71% freshmen, 69% undergrads receive some form of aid. Average freshman grant $9,572. Average freshman loan $3,315. Average income from on-campus job $861. **Financial Aid Phone:** 508-767-7158.

See page 922.

ATHABASCA UNIVERSITY

1 University Drive, Athabasca, AB T95 3A3
Phone: 780-675-6100 **E-mail:** admissions@athabascau.ca
Fax: 780-675-6174 **Web:** www.athabascau.ca

This public school was founded in 1970.

STUDENTS AND FACULTY

Enrollment: 20,855. **Student Body:** Out-of-state 50%. **Faculty:** 93 full-time faculty.

ACADEMICS

Degrees: Bachelor's, certificate, diploma, master's. **Majors with Highest Enrollment:** Business administration/management; organizational behavior studies; psychology, general. **Special Study Options:** Distance learning, English as a second language.

FACILITIES

Housing: Housing for disabled students, housing for international students. Students can complete studies from their home or workplace. **Library Holdings:** 135,000 bound volumes. 4,000 periodicals. 1,479 microforms. 3,345 audiovisuals. **Computers:** School-owned computers available for student use.

EXTRACURRICULARS

Activities: Student government, student newspaper.

ADMISSIONS

Selectivity Rating: 63 (of 100). **General Admission Information:** Application fee $50. Nonfall registration accepted. Admission may be deferred for a maximum of 1 year.

COSTS AND FINANCIAL AID

Types of Aid: *Need-based scholarships/grants:* Pell, SEOG, state scholarships/grants, private scholarships, the school's own gift aid. *Loans:* FFEL Subsidized Stafford, FFEL Unsubsidized Stafford, FFEL PLUS, Federal Perkins, college/university loans from institutional funds.

ATLANTA COLLEGE OF ART

1280 Peachtree Street Northeast, Atlanta, GA 30309
Phone: 404-733-5100 **E-mail:** acainfo@woodruffcenter.org **CEEB Code:** 5014
Fax: 404-733-5107 **Web:** www.aca.edu **ACT Code:** 829

This private school was founded in 1905.

STUDENTS AND FACULTY

Enrollment: 339. **Student Body:** Out-of-state 44%, international 6%. **Ethnic Representation:** African American 25%, Asian 6%, Caucasian 63%, Hispanic 3%. **Retention and Graduation:** 26% freshmen graduate within 4 years. 39% grads go on to further study within 1 year. **Faculty:** Student/faculty ratio 12:1. 24 full-time faculty. 100% faculty teach undergrads.

ACADEMICS

Degrees: Bachelor's. **Academic Requirements:** General education including some course work in arts/fine arts, English (including composition), history, humanities, mathematics, sciences (biological or physical), social science, art history. **Classes:** 10-19 students in an average class. **Disciplines with Highest Percentage of Degrees Awarded:** Visual and performing arts 100%. **Special Study Options:** Cross registration, dual enrollment, student exchange program (domestic), independent study, internships, student-designed major, study abroad.

FACILITIES

Housing: Coed. **Library Holdings:** 25,000 bound volumes. 200 periodicals. 0 microforms. 98,400 audiovisuals. **Special Academic Facilities/Equipment:** High Museum of Art, Atlanta Symphony Orchestra, Alliance Theatre. **Computers:** School-owned computers available for student use.

EXTRACURRICULARS

Activities: Student government.

ADMISSIONS

Selectivity Rating: 63 (of 100). **Freshman Academic Profile:** Average high school GPA 2.9. 5% in top 10% of high school class, 29% in top 25% of high school class, 64% in top 50% of high school class. 87% from public high schools. Average SAT I Math 471, SAT I Math middle 50% range 430-540. Average SAT I Verbal 513, SAT I Verbal middle 50% range 450-580. Average ACT 20. TOEFL required of all international applicants, minimum TOEFL 500. **Basis for Candidate Selection:** *Very important factors considered include:* essays, interview, secondary school record, talent/ability. *Important factors considered include:* class rank, recommendations, standardized test scores. *Other factors considered include:* alumni/ae relation, character/personal qualities, extracurricular activities. **Freshman Admission Requirements:** High school diploma or GED is required. *Academic units required/recommended:* 16 total recommended; 4 English recommended, 4 math recommended, 3 science recommended, 2 foreign language recommended, 3 social studies recommended, 4 elective recommended. **Freshman Admission Statistics:** 240 applied, 63% accepted, 39% of those accepted enrolled. **Transfer Admission Requirements:** *Items required:* college transcript, essay. Minimum high school GPA of 2.0 required. Minimum college GPA of 2.0 required. Lowest grade transferable C. **General Admission Information:** Application fee $30. Priority application deadline March 1. Nonfall registration accepted. Admission may be deferred for a maximum of 1 year. Credit offered for CEEB Advanced Placement tests.

COSTS AND FINANCIAL AID

Required Forms and Deadlines: FAFSA and institution's own financial aid form. Financial aid filing deadline July 15. Priority filing deadline March 15. **Notification of Awards:** Applicants will be notified of awards on a rolling basis beginning on or about April 1. **Types of Aid:** *Need-based scholarships/grants:* Pell, SEOG, state scholarships/grants, private scholarships, the school's own gift aid. *Loans:* Direct Subsidized Stafford, Direct Unsubsidized Stafford, Direct PLUS, FFEL Subsidized Stafford, FFEL Unsubsidized Stafford, FFEL PLUS. **Student Employment:** Federal Work-Study Program available. Institutional employment available. Off-campus job opportunities are excellent. **Financial Aid Statistics:** 62% freshmen, 63% undergrads receive some form of aid. Average freshman grant $12,444. Average freshman loan $3,278. **Financial Aid Phone:** 404-733-5110.

ATLANTIC UNION COLLEGE

Main Street, South Lancaster, MA 01561
Phone: 978-368-2255 **E-mail:** pubrel@atlanticuc.edu **CEEB Code:** 3010
Web: www.atlanticuc.edu **ACT Code:** 1784

This private school, which is affiliated with the Seventh-Day Adventist Church, was founded in 1882. It has a 330-acre campus.

STUDENTS AND FACULTY

Enrollment: 1,193. **Student Body:** Out-of-state 60%. **Ethnic Representation:** African American 28%, Asian 3%, Caucasian 51%, Hispanic 17%, Native American 1%. **Retention and Graduation:** 6% grads go on to further study within 1 year. 1% grads pursue law degrees. 3% grads pursue medical degrees.

ACADEMICS

Degrees: Associate's, bachelor's. **Special Study Options:** Cooperative (work-study) program, study abroad.

FACILITIES

Housing: Coed, apartments for married students. **Library Holdings:** 110,150 bound volumes. 771 periodicals. 8,867 microforms. **Special Academic Facilities/Equipment:** Art gallery, music conservatory, demonstration high school and elementary school near campus. **Computers:** *Recommended operating system:* Mac. School-owned computers available for student use.

EXTRACURRICULARS

Organizations: 2 honor societies. **Athletics (Intercollegiate):** *Men:* basketball.

ADMISSIONS

Selectivity Rating: 68 (of 100). **Freshman Academic Profile:** TOEFL required of all international applicants, minimum TOEFL 525. **Freshman Admission Requirements:** High school diploma is required and GED is not accepted. **Transfer Admission Requirements:** Minimum college GPA of 2.0 required. Lowest grade transferable C. **General Admission Information:** Early decision application deadline February 1. Regular application deadline August 1. Nonfall registration accepted.

COSTS AND FINANCIAL AID

Tuition $12,125. Room & board $3,900. Required fees $650. Average book expense $800. **Required Forms and Deadlines:** FAFSA, institution's own financial aid form, and state aid form. **Types of Aid:** *Need-based scholarships/grants:* Pell, SEOG, state scholarships/grants, private scholarships, the school's own gift aid. *Loans:* FFEL Subsidized Stafford, FFEL Unsubsidized Stafford, FFEL PLUS, Federal Perkins, college/university loans from institutional funds. **Student Employment:** Federal Work-Study Program available. Institutional employment available. Off-campus job opportunities are fair. **Financial Aid Statistics:** Average freshman grant $4,000. Average income from on-campus job $2,000. **Financial Aid Phone:** 508-368-2280.

AUBURN UNIVERSITY—AUBURN

202 Mary Martin Hall, Auburn, AL 36849-5145
Phone: 334-844-4080 **E-mail:** admissions@auburn.edu **CEEB Code:** 1005
Web: www.auburn.edu **ACT Code:** 11

This public school was founded in 1856. It has a 1,871-acre campus.

STUDENTS AND FACULTY

Enrollment: 18,922. **Student Body:** Male 52%, female 48%, out-of-state 30%, international 1% (95 countries represented). **Ethnic Representation:** African American 7%, Asian 1%, Caucasian 90%, Hispanic 1%. **Retention and Graduation:** 81% freshmen return for sophomore year. 32% freshmen graduate within 4 years. 35% grads go on to further study within 1 year. 10% grads pursue business degrees. 3% grads pursue law degrees. 8% grads pursue medical degrees. **Faculty:** Student/faculty ratio 16:1. 1,115 full-time faculty, 92% hold PhDs. 98% faculty teach undergrads.

ACADEMICS

Degrees: Bachelor's, doctoral, first professional, master's, post-master's certificate. **Academic Requirements:** General education including some course work in arts/fine arts, computer literacy, English (including composition), history, humanities, mathematics, philosophy, sciences (biological or physical), social science. **Classes:** 20-29 students in an average class. 10-19 students in an average lab/discussion section. **Disciplines with Highest Percentage of Degrees Awarded:** Business/marketing 25%, engineering/engineering technology 17%, education 9%, agriculture 6%, social sciences and history 5%. **Special Study Options:** Accelerated program, cooperative (work-study) program, distance learning, double major, dual enrollment, English as a second language, honors program, independent study, internships, liberal arts/career combination, study abroad, teacher certification program.

FACILITIES

Housing: Coed, all-female, all-male, apartments for married students, apartments for single students, housing for disabled students, fraternities and/or sororities, housing for honors students. **Library Holdings:** 2,591,255 bound volumes. 23,121 periodicals. 2,511,632 microforms. 219,454 audiovisuals. **Special Academic Facilities/Equipment:** Speech and hearing clinic, center for arts and humanities, TV studio, electron microscopes, nuclear science center, torsatron, sports museum. **Computers:** School-owned computers available for student use.

EXTRACURRICULARS

Activities: Choral groups, concert band, dance, drama/theater, jazz band, literary magazine, marching band, music ensembles, musical theater, opera, pep band, radio station, student government, student newspaper, student-run film society, symphony orchestra, television station, yearbook. **Organizations:** 300 registered organizations, 40 honor societies, 16 religious organizations, 28 fraternities (21% men join), 19 sororities (35% women join). **Athletics (Intercollegiate):** *Men:* baseball, basketball, cross-country, diving, football, golf, indoor track, swimming, tennis, track & field. *Women:* basketball, cross-country, diving, golf, gymnastics, indoor track, soccer, softball, swimming, tennis, track & field, volleyball.

ADMISSIONS

Selectivity Rating: 79 (of 100). **Freshman Academic Profile:** Average high school GPA 3.3. 26% in top 10% of high school class, 51% in top 25% of high school class, 80% in top 50% of high school class. 86% from public high schools. Average SAT I Math 563, SAT I Math middle 50% range 510-610. Average SAT I Verbal 547, SAT I Verbal middle 50% range 490-600. Average ACT 24, ACT middle 50% range 21-26. TOEFL required of all international applicants, minimum TOEFL 550. **Basis for Candidate Selection:** *Very important factors considered include:* secondary school record, standardized test scores. *Important factors considered include:* state residency. *Other factors considered include:* alumni/ae relation, geographical residence, minority status, talent/ability, volunteer work. **Freshman Admission Requirements:** High school diploma or GED is required. *Academic units required/recommended:* 12 total required; 15 total recommended; 4 English required, 4 English recommended, 3 math required, 3 math recommended, 2 science required, 3 science recommended, 1 foreign language recommended, 3 social studies required, 4 social studies recommended. **Freshman Admission Statistics:** 13,645 applied, 76% accepted, 36% of those accepted enrolled. **Transfer Admission Requirements:** *Items required:* college transcript. Minimum college GPA of 2.5 required. Lowest grade transferable C. **General Admission Information:** Application fee $25. Early decision application deadline November 1. Regular application deadline August 1. Nonfall registration accepted. Admission may be deferred for a maximum of 1 year. Credit offered for CEEB Advanced Placement tests.

COSTS AND FINANCIAL AID

In-state tuition $3,260. Out-of-state tuition $9,780. Required fees $120. Average book expense $900. **Required Forms and Deadlines:** FAFSA and institution's own financial aid form. No deadline for regular filing. Priority filing deadline March 1. **Types of Aid:** *Need-based scholarships/grants:* Pell, SEOG, state scholarships/grants, private scholarships, the school's own gift aid. *Loans:* FFEL Subsidized Stafford, FFEL Unsubsidized Stafford, FFEL PLUS, Federal Perkins, college/university loans from institutional funds. **Student Employment:** Federal Work-Study Program available. Institutional employment available. Off-campus job opportunities are excellent. **Financial Aid Statistics:** 24% freshmen, 29% undergrads receive some form of aid. Average freshman grant $6,135. Average freshman loan $2,931. Average income from on-campus job $2,250. **Financial Aid Phone:** 334-844-4367.

AUBURN UNIVERSITY—MONTGOMERY

PO Box 244023, Montgomery, AL 36124-4023
Phone: 334-244-3611 **E-mail:** mmoore@mickey.aum.edu
Fax: 334-244-3795 **Web:** www.aum.edu **ACT Code:** 57

This public school was founded in 1967. It has a 500-acre campus.

STUDENTS AND FACULTY

Enrollment: 4,329. **Student Body:** Male 37%, female 63%, out-of-state 3%, international 1% (19 countries represented). **Ethnic Representation:** African American 32%, Asian 1%, Caucasian 63%, Hispanic 2%, Native American 1%. **Faculty:** Student/faculty ratio 16:1. 179 full-time faculty, 81% hold PhDs. 98% faculty teach undergrads.

ACADEMICS

Degrees: Bachelor's, doctoral, master's, post-master's certificate. **Academic Requirements:** General education including some course work in arts/fine arts, computer literacy, English (including composition), history, humanities, mathematics, sciences (biological or physical), social science. **Classes:** 20-29 students in an average class. Under 10 students in an average lab/discussion section. **Majors with Highest Enrollment:** Nursing/registered nurse training (RN, ASN, BSN, MSN); business administration/management; elementary education and teaching. **Disciplines with Highest Percentage of Degrees Awarded:** Business/marketing 38%, education 21%, health professions and related sciences 9%, liberal arts/general studies 6%, psychology 5%. **Special Study Options:** Accelerated program, cooperative (work-study) program, cross registration, distance learning, double major, dual enrollment, English as a second language, student exchange program (domestic), honors program, independent study, internships, liberal arts/career combination, study abroad, teacher certification program, weekend college, joint PhD in public administration with Auburn University, EdD in cooperation with Auburn University.

FACILITIES

Housing: Apartments for married students, apartments for single students, housing for disabled students. **Library Holdings:** 238,322 bound volumes. 1,436 periodicals. 2,376,000 microforms. 24,743 audiovisuals. **Computers:** School-owned computers available for student use.

EXTRACURRICULARS

Activities: Choral groups, dance, drama/theater, musical theater, student government, student newspaper. **Organizations:** 62 registered organizations, 13 honor societies, 1 religious organization, 5 fraternities (6% men join), 5 sororities (4% women join). **Athletics (Intercollegiate):** *Men:* baseball, basketball, cheerleading, soccer, tennis. *Women:* basketball, cheerleading, soccer, tennis.

ADMISSIONS

Selectivity Rating: 72 (of 100). **Freshman Academic Profile:** Average ACT 20, ACT middle 50% range 17-23. TOEFL required of all international applicants, minimum TOEFL 500. **Basis for Candidate Selection:** *Very important factors considered include:* secondary school record, standardized test scores. *Other factors considered include:* recommendations. **Freshman Admission Requirements:** High school diploma or GED is required. *Academic units required/recommended:* 4 English recommended, 4 math recommended, 3 science recommended, 2 science lab recommended, 2 foreign language recommended, 2 social studies recommended, 2 history recommended. **Transfer Admission Requirements:** *Items required:* college transcript, statement of good standing from prior school. Minimum college GPA of 2.0 required. Lowest grade transferable D. **General Admission Information:** Application fee $25. Nonfall registration accepted. Admission may be deferred for a maximum of 1 year. Credit offered for CEEB Advanced Placement tests.

COSTS AND FINANCIAL AID

In-state tuition $3,390. Out-of-state tuition $10,170. Room & board $4,770. Required fees $230. Average book expense $600. **Required Forms and Deadlines:** FAFSA and institution's own financial aid form. No deadline for regular filing. Priority filing deadline March 1. **Notification of Awards:** Applicants will be notified of awards on a rolling basis beginning on or about May 1. **Types of Aid:** *Need-based scholarships/grants:* Pell, SEOG, state scholarships/grants, the school's own gift aid. *Loans:* FFEL Subsidized Stafford, FFEL Unsubsidized Stafford, FFEL PLUS, Federal Perkins. **Student Employment:** Federal Work-Study Program available. Institutional employment available. Off-campus job opportunities are good. **Financial Aid Statistics:** Average freshman loan $3,000. Average income from on-campus job $5,356. **Financial Aid Phone:** 334-244-3571.

AUGSBURG COLLEGE

2211 Riverside Avenue South, Minneapolis, MN 55454
Phone: 612-330-1001 **E-mail:** admissions@augsburg.edu **CEEB Code:** 6014
Fax: 612-330-1590 **Web:** www.augsburg.edu **ACT Code:** 2080

This private school, which is affiliated with the Lutheran Church, was founded in 1869. It has a 23-acre campus.

STUDENTS AND FACULTY

Enrollment: 2,763. **Student Body:** Male 42%, female 58%, out-of-state 10%, international 1%. **Ethnic Representation:** African American 5%, Asian 4%, Caucasian 73%, Hispanic 1%, Native American 1%. **Retention and Graduation:** 79% freshmen return for sophomore year. 39% freshmen graduate within 4 years. 17% grads go on to further study within 1 year. 2% grads pursue law degrees. 2% grads pursue medical degrees. **Faculty:** Student/faculty ratio 14:1. 147 full-time faculty, 79% hold PhDs. 99% faculty teach undergrads.

ACADEMICS

Degrees: Bachelor's, certificate, master's, post-master's certificate. **Academic Requirements:** General education including some course work in arts/fine arts, English (including composition), foreign languages, history, humanities, mathematics, sciences (biological or physical), social science. **Classes:** 10-19 students in an average class. 10-19 students in an average lab/discussion section. **Majors with Highest Enrollment:** Business administration/management; communications studies/speech communication and rhetoric; education, general. **Disciplines with Highest Percentage of Degrees Awarded:** Business/marketing 35%, education 11%, social sciences and history 9%, health professions and related sciences 8%, communications/communication technologies 6%. **Special Study Options:** Cooperative (work-study) program, cross registration, double major, dual enrollment, English as a second language, honors program, independent study, internships, student-designed major, study abroad, teacher certification program, weekend college.

FACILITIES

Housing: Coed, housing for disabled students. **Library Holdings:** 146,166 bound volumes. 754 periodicals. 19,719 microforms. 2,908 audiovisuals. **Special Academic Facilities/Equipment:** Electron microscope, center for atmospheric science research, theatre, pipe organ. **Computers:** School-owned computers available for student use.

EXTRACURRICULARS

Activities: Choral groups, concert band, drama/theater, jazz band, literary magazine, music ensembles, pep band, radio station, student government, student newspaper, symphony orchestra, yearbook. **Organizations:** 35 registered organizations, 1 honor society, 1 religious organization. **Athletics (Intercollegiate):** *Men:* baseball, basketball, cross-country, football, golf, ice hockey, indoor track, soccer, tennis, track & field, wrestling. *Women:* basketball, cheerleading, cross-country, golf, ice hockey, indoor track, soccer, softball, tennis, track & field, volleyball.

ADMISSIONS

Selectivity Rating: 67 (of 100). **Freshman Academic Profile:** Average high school GPA 3.3. 19% in top 10% of high school class, 39% in top 25% of high school class, 72% in top 50% of high school class. Average SAT I Math 525, SAT I Math middle 50% range 450-580. Average SAT I Verbal 527, SAT I Verbal middle 50% range 480-590. Average ACT 23, ACT middle 50% range 19-26. TOEFL required of all international applicants, minimum TOEFL 550. **Basis for Candidate Selection:** *Very important factors considered include:* class rank, essays, recommendations, secondary school record, standardized test scores. *Important factors considered include:* character/personal qualities, extracurricular activities. *Other factors considered include:* alumni/ae relation, interview, talent/ability, volunteer work, work experience. **Freshman Admission Requirements:** High school diploma or GED is required. *Academic units required/recommended:* 15 total required; 4 English required, 3 math required, 3 science required, 2 foreign language required, 3 social studies required, 4 social studies recommended, 2 history recommended. **Freshman Admission Statistics:** 856 applied, 80% accepted, 51% of those accepted enrolled. **Transfer Admission Requirements:** *Items required:* college transcript, essay. Minimum high school GPA of 2.5 required. Minimum college GPA of 2.5 required. Lowest grade transferable B. **General Admission Information:** Application fee $25. Priority application deadline May 1. Regular application deadline August 15. Nonfall registration accepted. Admission may be deferred for a maximum of 2 years. Credit and/or placement offered for CEEB Advanced Placement tests.

COSTS AND FINANCIAL AID

Tuition $17,825. Room & board $5,690. Required fees $368. Average book expense $800. **Required Forms and Deadlines:** FAFSA and institution's own

financial aid form. Financial aid filing deadline August 1. Priority filing deadline April 15. **Notification of Awards:** Applicants will be notified of awards on a rolling basis beginning on or about March 1. **Types of Aid:** *Need-based scholarships/grants:* Pell, SEOG, state scholarships/grants, private scholarships, the school's own gift aid. *Loans:* FFEL Subsidized Stafford, FFEL Unsubsidized Stafford, FFEL PLUS, Federal Perkins, Federal Nursing, state loans. **Student Employment:** Federal Work-Study Program available. Institutional employment available. Off-campus job opportunities are good. **Financial Aid Statistics:** 67% freshmen, 63% undergrads receive some form of aid. Average freshman grant $11,299. Average freshman loan $6,382. Average income from on-campus job $2,000. **Financial Aid Phone:** 612-330-1046.

AUGUSTA STATE UNIVERSITY

2500 Walton Way, Augusta, GA 30904-2200
Phone: 706-737-1632 **E-mail:** admissio@aug.edu **CEEB Code:** 5336
Fax: 706-667-4355 **Web:** www.aug.edu **ACT Code:** 796

This public school was founded in 1925. It has a 72-acre campus.

STUDENTS AND FACULTY

Enrollment: 5,041. **Student Body:** Male 35%, female 65%, international 1% (55 countries represented). **Ethnic Representation:** African American 27%, Asian 3%, Caucasian 67%, Hispanic 2%. **Retention and Graduation:** 7% freshmen graduate within 4 years. **Faculty:** Student/faculty ratio 19:1. 194 full-time faculty, 70% hold PhDs. 100% faculty teach undergrads.

ACADEMICS

Degrees: Associate's, bachelor's, master's, terminal, transfer. **Academic Requirements:** General education including some course work in English (including composition), foreign languages, history, humanities, mathematics, sciences (biological or physical), social science. **Classes:** 20-29 students in an average class. 20-29 students in an average lab/discussion section. **Majors with Highest Enrollment:** Early childhood education and teaching; biology/biological sciences, general; psychology, general. **Disciplines with Highest Percentage of Degrees Awarded:** Business/marketing 21%, education 17%, social sciences and history 16%, psychology 9%, computer and information sciences 7%. **Special Study Options:** Cooperative (work-study) program, cross registration, double major, dual enrollment, English as a second language, honors program, independent study, internships, study abroad, teacher certification program.

FACILITIES

Library Holdings: 430,938 bound volumes. 1,276 periodicals. 935,182 microforms. 5,807 audiovisuals. **Special Academic Facilities/Equipment:** Performing arts theater. **Computers:** *Recommended operating system:* Windows 95. School-owned computers available for student use.

EXTRACURRICULARS

Activities: Choral groups, concert band, drama/theater, jazz band, literary magazine, pep band, radio station, student government, student newspaper. **Organizations:** 60 registered organizations, 5 honor societies, 4 religious organizations, 1 fraternity (1% men join), 3 sororities (1% women join). **Athletics (Intercollegiate):** *Men:* baseball, basketball, golf, tennis. *Women:* basketball, golf, softball, tennis, volleyball.

ADMISSIONS

Selectivity Rating: 70 (of 100). **Freshman Academic Profile:** Average high school GPA 3.0. 95% from public high schools. Average SAT I Math 483, SAT I Math middle 50% range 430-540. Average SAT I Verbal 489, SAT I Verbal middle 50% range 430-550. TOEFL required of all international applicants, minimum TOEFL 500. **Basis for Candidate Selection:** *Very important factors considered include:* secondary school record, standardized test scores. **Freshman Admission Requirements:** High school diploma or GED is required. *Academic units required/recommended:* 18 total required; 4 English required, 4 math required, 3 science required, 2 foreign language required, 3 social studies required, 2 elective required. **Freshman Admission Statistics:** 1,680 applied, 66% accepted, 87% of those accepted enrolled. **Transfer Admission Requirements:** *Items required:* college transcript. Minimum college GPA of 2.0 required. Lowest grade transferable D. **General Admission Information:** Application fee $20. Regular application deadline July 19. Nonfall registration accepted. Admission may be deferred. Credit and/or placement offered for CEEB Advanced Placement tests.

COSTS AND FINANCIAL AID

Average book expense $832. **Required Forms and Deadlines:** FAFSA and institution's own financial aid form. Financial aid filing deadline May 1. Priority filing deadline April 15. **Notification of Awards:** Applicants will be notified of awards on or about June 1. **Types of Aid:** *Need-based scholarships/grants:* Pell, SEOG, state scholarships/grants, private scholarships, the school's own gift aid. *Loans:* FFEL Subsidized Stafford, FFEL Unsubsidized Stafford, FFEL PLUS, Federal Perkins, state loans, college/university loans from institutional funds, alternative loans. **Student Employment:** Federal Work-Study Program available. Institutional employment available. Off-campus job opportunities are good. **Financial Aid Statistics:** 48% freshmen, 53% undergrads receive some form of aid. Average freshman loan $3,550. **Financial Aid Phone:** 706-737-1431.

AUGUSTANA COLLEGE (IL)

639 38th Street, Rock Island, IL 61201-2296
Phone: 309-794-7341 **E-mail:** admissions@augustana.edu **CEEB Code:** 1025
Fax: 309-794-7422 **Web:** www.augustana.edu **ACT Code:** 946

This private school, which is affiliated with the Lutheran Church, was founded in 1860. It has a 115-acre campus.

STUDENTS AND FACULTY

Enrollment: 2,261. **Student Body:** Male 43%, female 57%, out-of-state 13%, international 1% (26 countries represented). **Ethnic Representation:** African American 2%, Asian 1%, Caucasian 94%, Hispanic 3%. **Retention and Graduation:** 85% freshmen return for sophomore year. 69% freshmen graduate within 4 years. 30% grads go on to further study within 1 year. 1% grads pursue business degrees. 2% grads pursue law degrees. 11% grads pursue medical degrees. **Faculty:** Student/faculty ratio 14:1. 142 full-time faculty, 90% hold PhDs. 100% faculty teach undergrads.

ACADEMICS

Degrees: Bachelor's. **Academic Requirements:** General education including some course work in arts/fine arts, English (including composition), foreign languages, history, humanities, philosophy, sciences (biological or physical), social science. **Classes:** 10-19 students in an average class. 10-19 students in an average lab/discussion section. **Majors with Highest Enrollment:** Business administration/management; biology/biological sciences, general; political science and government, general. **Disciplines with Highest Percentage of Degrees Awarded:** Business/marketing 18%, biological life sciences 18%, social sciences and history 11%, health professions and related sciences 10%, psychology 6%. **Special Study Options:** Accelerated program, cooperative (work-study) program, double major, honors program, independent study, internships, liberal arts/career combination, study abroad, teacher certification program.

FACILITIES

Housing: Coed, all-female, all-male, apartments for single students. **Library Holdings:** 190,641 bound volumes. 1,705 periodicals. 100,794 microforms. 2,019 audiovisuals. **Special Academic Facilities/Equipment:** Educational technology building, art gallery, Black culture house, Hispanic culture house, geology museum, on-campus preschool, immigration research center, scanning and transmission electron microscopes, nuclear magnetic resonance, atomic absorption and diode array mass spectrophotometers, planetarium, observatory with celestron telescope, environmental field stations. **Computers:** School-owned computers available for student use.

EXTRACURRICULARS

Activities: Choral groups, concert band, dance, drama/theater, jazz band, literary magazine, music ensembles, musical theater, opera, pep band, radio station, student government, student newspaper, symphony orchestra, yearbook. **Organizations:** 110 registered organizations, 15 honor societies, 6 religious organizations, 7 fraternities (23% men join), 6 sororities (29% women join). **Athletics (Intercollegiate):** *Men:* baseball, basketball, cross-country, diving, football, golf, indoor track, soccer, swimming, tennis, track & field, wrestling. *Women:* basketball, cheerleading, cross-country, diving, golf, indoor track, soccer, softball, swimming, tennis, track & field, volleyball.

ADMISSIONS

Selectivity Rating: 81 (of 100). **Freshman Academic Profile:** Average high school GPA 3.5. 35% in top 10% of high school class, 67% in top 25% of high school class, 95% in top 50% of high school class. 85% from public high schools. Average ACT 26, ACT middle 50% range 23-28. TOEFL required of all international applicants, minimum TOEFL 550. **Basis for Candidate Selection:** *Very important factors considered include:* class rank, secondary school record, standardized test scores. *Important factors considered include:* character/personal qualities, essays, extracurricular activities, interview, talent/ability. *Other factors considered include:* alumni/ae relation, minority status, recommendations, volunteer work, work experience. **Freshman Admission Requirements:** High school diploma or GED is required. *Academic units required/recommended:* 16 total recommended; 4 English recommended, 3 math recommended, 2 science recommended, 1 foreign language recommended, 1 social studies recommended, 1 history recommended, 4 elective recommended. **Freshman Admission Statistics:** 2,744 applied, 74% accepted, 59% of those accepted enrolled. **Transfer Admission Requirements:** *Items required:* high school transcript, college transcript, statement of good standing from prior school. Minimum college GPA of 2.0 required. Lowest grade transferable D. **General Admission Information:** Application fee $25. Priority application deadline February 1. Nonfall registration accepted. Admission may be deferred for a maximum of 1 year. Credit and/or placement offered for CEEB Advanced Placement tests.

COSTS AND FINANCIAL AID

Tuition $19,200. Room & board $5,586. Required fees $408. Average book expense $675. **Required Forms and Deadlines:** FAFSA and institution's own financial aid form. Priority filing deadline April 1. **Notification of Awards:** Applicants will be notified of awards on a rolling basis beginning on or about February 15. **Types of Aid:** *Need-based scholarships/grants:* Pell, SEOG, state scholarships/grants, private scholarships, the school's own gift aid. *Loans:* FFEL Subsidized Stafford, FFEL Unsubsidized Stafford, FFEL PLUS, Federal Perkins. **Student Employment:** Federal Work-Study Program available. Institutional employment available. Off-campus job opportunities are good. **Financial Aid Statistics:** 68% freshmen, 67% undergrads receive some form of aid. Average freshman grant $11,118. Average freshman loan $3,898. Average income from on-campus job $810. **Financial Aid Phone:** 309-794-7207.

AUGUSTANA COLLEGE (SD)

2001 South Summit Avenue, Sioux Falls, SD 57197
Phone: 605-274-5516 **E-mail:** info@augie.edu **CEEB Code:** 6015
Fax: 605-274-5518 **Web:** www.augie.edu **ACT Code:** 3902

This private school, which is affiliated with the Lutheran Church, was founded in 1860. It has a 100-acre campus.

STUDENTS AND FACULTY

Enrollment: 1,804. **Student Body:** Male 36%, female 64%, out-of-state 50%, international 2%. **Ethnic Representation:** African American 1%, Asian 1%, Caucasian 98%, Native American 1%. **Retention and Graduation:** 80% freshmen return for sophomore year. 47% freshmen graduate within 4 years. 22% grads go on to further study within 1 year. 1% grads pursue business degrees. 1% grads pursue law degrees. 3% grads pursue medical degrees. **Faculty:** Student/faculty ratio 12:1. 108 full-time faculty, 91% hold PhDs. 100% faculty teach undergrads.

ACADEMICS

Degrees: Bachelor's, master's. **Academic Requirements:** General education including some course work in arts/fine arts, computer literacy, English (including composition), foreign languages, history, humanities, mathematics, philosophy, sciences (biological or physical), social science, religion, physical education activity classes. **Classes:** 20-29 students in an average class. **Majors with Highest Enrollment:** Elementary education and teaching; business administration/management; biology/biological sciences, general. **Disciplines with Highest Percentage of Degrees Awarded:** Education 19%, business/marketing 19%, health professions and related sciences 12%, biological life sciences 9%, social sciences and history 7%. **Special Study Options:** Accelerated program, cross registration, double major, independent study, internships, student-designed major, study abroad, teacher certification program, living/learning semester in Minneapolis Modern Cities area, San Francisco Studies Term, metro-urban studies, January Abroad program through UMAIE.

FACILITIES

Housing: Coed, apartments for married students, theme houses. Housing is available for students with children. **Library Holdings:** 234,515 bound volumes. 1,085 periodicals. 85,938 microforms. 6,147 audiovisuals. **Special Academic Facilities/Equipment:** Language lab, community organization and area development center, western studies center. **Computers:** School-owned computers available for student use.

EXTRACURRICULARS

Activities: Choral groups, concert band, dance, drama/theater, jazz band, literary magazine, music ensembles, musical theater, opera, pep band, radio station, student government, student newspaper, student-run film society, symphony orchestra, yearbook. **Organizations:** 56 registered organizations, 11 honor societies, 8 religious organizations. **Athletics (Intercollegiate):** *Men:* baseball, basketball, cross-country, football, golf, indoor track, tennis, track & field, wrestling. *Women:* basketball, cheerleading, cross-country, golf, indoor track, soccer, softball, tennis, track & field, volleyball.

ADMISSIONS

Selectivity Rating: 74 (of 100). **Freshman Academic Profile:** Average high school GPA 3.5. 29% in top 10% of high school class, 58% in top 25% of high school class, 87% in top 50% of high school class. 97% from public high schools. Average SAT I Math 560, SAT I Math middle 50% range 500-620. Average SAT I Verbal 550, SAT I Verbal middle 50% range 500-600. Average ACT 25, ACT middle 50% range 22-27. TOEFL required of all international applicants, minimum TOEFL 550. **Basis for Candidate Selection:** *Very important factors considered include:* secondary school record. *Important factors considered include:* class rank, standardized test scores. *Other factors considered include:* alumni/ae relation, character/personal qualities, extracurricular activities, geographical residence, interview, minority status, recommendations, religious affiliation/commitment, state residency, talent/ability, volunteer work, work experience. **Freshman Admission Requirements:** High school diploma or GED is required. *Academic units required/recommended:* 16 total recommended; 4 English recommended, 3 math recommended, 3 science recommended, 2 foreign language recommended, 2 social studies recommended, 2 history recommended. **Freshman Admission Statistics:** 1,534 applied, 79% accepted, 38% of those accepted enrolled. **Transfer Admission Requirements:** *Items required:* college transcript. Minimum college GPA of 2.0 required. Lowest grade transferable C-. **General Admission Information:** Application fee $25. Priority application deadline February 1. Regular application deadline August 15. Nonfall registration accepted. Admission may be deferred for a maximum of 1 year. Credit offered for CEEB Advanced Placement tests.

COSTS AND FINANCIAL AID

Tuition $16,766. Room & board $5,026. Required fees $206. Average book expense $600. **Required Forms and Deadlines:** FAFSA. Priority filing deadline March 1. **Types of Aid:** *Need-based scholarships/grants:* Pell, SEOG, private scholarships, the school's own gift aid. *Loans:* FFEL Subsidized Stafford, FFEL Unsubsidized Stafford, FFEL PLUS, Federal Perkins, Federal Nursing, college/university loans from institutional funds. **Student Employment:** Federal Work-Study Program available. Institutional employment available. Off-campus job opportunities are excellent. **Financial Aid Statistics:** 72% freshmen, 70% undergrads receive some form of aid. **Financial Aid Phone:** 605-274-5216.

AURORA UNIVERSITY

347 South Gladstone Avenue, Aurora, IL 60506
Phone: 630-844-5533 **E-mail:** admission@aurora.edu **CEEB Code:** 1027
Fax: 630-844-5535 **Web:** www.aurora.edu **ACT Code:** 950

This private school was founded in 1893. It has a 27-acre campus.

STUDENTS AND FACULTY

Enrollment: 1,446. **Student Body:** Male 35%, female 65%, out-of-state 5%. **Ethnic Representation:** African American 16%, Asian 2%, Caucasian 71%, Hispanic 10%. **Retention and Graduation:** 68% freshmen return for sophomore year. 28% freshmen graduate within 4 years. 19% grads go on to further study within 1 year. **Faculty:** Student/faculty ratio 17:1. 83 full-time faculty, 78% hold PhDs.

ACADEMICS

Degrees: Bachelor's, doctoral, master's. **Academic Requirements:** General education including some course work in English (including composition), humanities, mathematics, sciences (biological or physical), social science. **Classes:** 20-29 students in an average class. 10-19 students in an average lab/discussion section. **Disciplines with Highest Percentage of Degrees Awarded:** Business/marketing 28%, protective services/public administration 19%, education 14%, psychology 8%, health professions and related sciences 8%. **Special Study Options:** Cross registration, double major, dual enrollment, student exchange program (domestic), independent study, internships, liberal arts/career combination, student-designed major, study abroad.

FACILITIES

Housing: Coed, all-female, all-male, apartments for single students. **Library Holdings:** 114,180 bound volumes. 121 periodicals. 194,087 microforms. **Special Academic Facilities/Equipment:** Center for Native American culture. **Computers:** *Recommended operating system:* Windows 95. School-owned computers available for student use.

EXTRACURRICULARS

Activities: Choral groups, dance, drama/theater, literary magazine, music ensembles, student government, student newspaper, television station, yearbook. **Organizations:** 2 religious organizations, 4 fraternities (3% men join), 5 sororities (4% women join). **Athletics (Intercollegiate):** *Men:* baseball, basketball, football, golf, soccer, tennis. *Women:* basketball, cross-country, soccer, softball, tennis, volleyball.

ADMISSIONS

Selectivity Rating: 63 (of 100). **Freshman Academic Profile:** Average ACT 21. TOEFL required of all international applicants, minimum TOEFL 550. **Basis for Candidate Selection:** *Very important factors considered include:* class rank, secondary school record, standardized test scores. *Important factors considered include:* alumni/ae relation, character/personal qualities. *Other factors considered include:* extracurricular activities, interview, recommendations, talent/ability. **Freshman Admission Requirements:** High school diploma or GED is required. *Academic units required/recommended:* 16 total required; 4 English recommended, 3 math recommended, 3 science recommended, 3 social studies recommended, 3 elective recommended. **Freshman Admission Statistics:** 1,140 applied, 57% accepted, 45% of those accepted enrolled. **Transfer Admission Requirements:** Minimum high school GPA of 2.0 required. Minimum college GPA of 2.0 required. Lowest grade transferable C. **General Admission Information:** Application fee $25. Nonfall registration accepted. Admission may be deferred. Credit and/or placement offered for CEEB Advanced Placement tests.

COSTS AND FINANCIAL AID

Tuition $13,767. Room & board $5,541. Required fees $60. Average book expense $750. **Required Forms and Deadlines:** FAFSA and state aid form. **Notification of Awards:** Applicants will be notified of awards on or about March 1. **Types of Aid:** *Need-based scholarships/grants:* state scholarships/grants. *Loans:* FFEL Subsidized Stafford, FFEL PLUS. **Student Employment:** Federal Work-Study Program available. Institutional employment available. Off-campus job opportunities are good. **Financial Aid Statistics:** 81% freshmen, 79% undergrads receive some form of aid. Average freshman grant $10,888. Average freshman loan $2,507. Average income from on-campus job $1,423. **Financial Aid Phone:** 630-844-5149.

AUSTIN COLLEGE

900 North Grand Avenue, Suite 6N, Sherman, TX 75090-4400
Phone: 903-813-3000 **E-mail:** admission@austincollege.edu **CEEB Code:** 6016
Fax: 903-813-3198 **Web:** www.austincollege.edu **ACT Code:** 4058

This private school, which is affiliated with the Presbyterian Church, was founded in 1849. It has a 70-acre campus.

STUDENTS AND FACULTY

Enrollment: 1,241. **Student Body:** Male 44%, female 56%, out-of-state 10%, international 2% (28 countries represented). **Ethnic Representation:** African American 4%, Asian 9%, Caucasian 78%, Hispanic 7%, Native American 1%. **Retention and Graduation:** 83% freshmen return for sophomore year. 74% freshmen graduate within 4 years. 45% grads go on to further study within 1 year. 2% grads pursue business degrees. 5% grads pursue law degrees. 12% grads pursue medical degrees. **Faculty:** Student/faculty ratio 13:1. 88 full-time faculty, 98% hold PhDs. 100% faculty teach undergrads.

ACADEMICS

Degrees: Bachelor's, master's. **Academic Requirements:** General education including some course work in arts/fine arts, computer literacy, English (including composition), foreign languages, history, humanities, mathematics, philosophy, sciences (biological or physical), social science, social policy, values and decision making. **Classes:** 20-29 students in an average class. 10-19 students in an average lab/discussion section. **Majors with Highest Enrollment:** Business administration/management; psychology, general; biology/biological sciences, general. **Disciplines with Highest Percentage of Degrees Awarded:** Social sciences and history 20%, psychology 14%, business/marketing 12%, biological life sciences 11%, visual and performing arts 6%. **Special Study Options:** Double major, student exchange program (domestic), honors program, independent study, internships, student-designed major, study abroad, teacher certification program, Phi Beta Kappa.

FACILITIES

Housing: Coed, all-female, all-male, apartments for single students, housing for disabled students, Jordan Language House. **Library Holdings:** 195,328 bound volumes. 1,008 periodicals. 106,224 microforms. 7,418 audiovisuals. **Special Academic Facilities/Equipment:** Tissue culture facility, high-performance numerics and graphics computing facility. **Computers:** School-owned computers available for student use.

EXTRACURRICULARS

Activities: Choral groups, dance, drama/theater, jazz band, literary magazine, music ensembles, musical theater, pep band, student government, student newspaper, symphony orchestra, yearbook. **Organizations:** 48 registered organizations, 14 honor societies, 5 religious organizations, 10 fraternities (27% men join), 7 sororities (30% women join). **Athletics (Intercollegiate):** *Men:* baseball, basketball, diving, football, golf, soccer, swimming, tennis. *Women:* basketball, diving, soccer, swimming, tennis, volleyball.

ADMISSIONS

Selectivity Rating: 84 (of 100). **Freshman Academic Profile:** Average high school GPA 3.4. 42% in top 10% of high school class, 75% in top 25% of high school class, 96% in top 50% of high school class. 89% from public high schools. Average SAT I Math 613, SAT I Math middle 50% range 570-660. Average SAT I Verbal 614, SAT I Verbal middle 50% range 560-660. Average ACT 25, ACT middle 50% range 22-28. TOEFL required of all international applicants, minimum TOEFL 550. **Basis for Candidate Selection:** *Very important factors considered include:* secondary school record. *Important factors considered include:* character/personal qualities, class rank, essays, extracurricular activities, recommendations, standardized test scores, talent/ability. *Other factors considered include:* alumni/ae relation, geographical residence, interview, minority status, religious affiliation/commitment, state residency, volunteer work, work experience. **Freshman Admission Requirements:** High school diploma or GED is required. *Academic units required/recommended:* 4 English required, 4 English recommended, 3 math required, 4 math recommended, 3 science required, 4 science recommended, 2 science lab required, 3 science lab recommended, 2 foreign language required, 3 foreign language recommended, 2 social studies required, 3 social studies recommended, 1 elective required. **Freshman Admission Statistics:** 1,140 applied, 78% accepted, 39% of those accepted enrolled. **Transfer Admission Requirements:** *Items required:* college transcript, essay, statement of good standing from prior school. Minimum college GPA of 2.5 required. Lowest grade transferable C. **General Admission Information:** Application fee $35. Priority application deadline March 1. Early decision application deadline December 1. Regular application deadline August 15. Nonfall registration accepted. Admission may be deferred for a maximum of 1 year. Credit and/or placement offered for CEEB Advanced Placement tests.

COSTS AND FINANCIAL AID

Tuition $17,740. Room & board $6,822. Required fees $160. Average book expense $800. **Required Forms and Deadlines:** FAFSA and institution's own financial aid form. Priority filing deadline April 1. **Notification of Awards:** Applicants will be notified of awards on a rolling basis beginning on or about March 1. **Types of Aid:** *Need-based scholarships/grants:* Pell, SEOG, state scholarships/grants, private scholarships, the school's own gift aid. *Loans:* FFEL Subsidized Stafford, FFEL Unsubsidized Stafford, FFEL PLUS, Federal Perkins, state loans, college/university loans from institutional funds, alternative loans, Premier Signature loans. **Student Employment:** Federal Work-Study Program available. Institutional employment available. Off-campus job opportunities are good. **Financial Aid Statistics:** 60% freshmen, 61% undergrads receive some form of aid. Average freshman grant $11,877. Average freshman loan $3,717. Average income from on-campus job $1,175. **Financial Aid Phone:** 903-813-2900.

AUSTIN PEAY STATE UNIVERSITY

PO Box 4548, Clarksville, TN 37044-4548
Phone: 931-221-7661 **E-mail:** admissions@apsu01.apsu.edu **CEEB Code:** 1028
Fax: 931-221-5994 **Web:** www.apsu.edu **ACT Code:** 3944

This public school was founded in 1927. It has a 210-acre campus.

STUDENTS AND FACULTY

Enrollment: 7,057. **Student Body:** Male 39%, female 61%, out-of-state 3%, international students represent 13 countries. **Ethnic Representation:** African American 20%, Asian 3%, Caucasian 64%, Hispanic 5%, Native American 1%. **Faculty:** Student/faculty ratio 17:1. 271 full-time faculty, 88% hold PhDs. 100% faculty teach undergrads.

ACADEMICS

Degrees: Associate's, bachelor's, certificate, master's, post-bachelor's certificate, post-master's certificate, terminal, transfer. **Academic Requirements:** General education including some course work in arts/fine arts, computer literacy, English (including composition), foreign languages, history, humanities, mathematics, philosophy, sciences (biological or physical), social science, health and human performance. **Classes:** 20-29 students in an average class. 20-29 students in an average lab/discussion section. **Disciplines with Highest Percentage of Degrees Awarded:** Business/marketing 28%, interdisciplinary studies 12%, health professions and related sciences 9%, social sciences and history 7%, communications/communication technologies 5%. **Special Study Options:** Cooperative (work-study) program, distance learning, double major, honors program, independent study, internships, study abroad, teacher certification program, Service members Opportunity College (SOC) for associate and bachelor's degrees.

FACILITIES

Housing: Coed, all-female, all-male, apartments for married students, apartments for single students, honors dorm. **Library Holdings:** 333,372 bound volumes. 1,754 periodicals. 633,432 microforms. 6,786 audiovisuals. **Special Academic Facilities/Equipment:** Art museum, biology museum, language lab, demonstration farm, 21st century classroom. **Computers:** School-owned computers available for student use.

EXTRACURRICULARS

Activities: Choral groups, concert band, drama/theater, jazz band, literary magazine, marching band, music ensembles, musical theater, radio station, student government, student newspaper, television station. **Organizations:** 50 registered organizations, 13 honor societies, 10 religious organizations, 8 fraternities (5% men join), 6 sororities (3% women join). **Athletics (Intercollegiate):** *Men:* baseball, basketball, cross-country, football, golf, tennis. *Women:* basketball, cross-country, golf, rifle, softball, tennis, track & field, volleyball.

ADMISSIONS

Selectivity Rating: 67 (of 100). **Freshman Academic Profile:** Average high school GPA 3.0. 11% in top 10% of high school class, 33% in top 25% of high school class, 66% in top 50% of high school class. 95% from public high schools. Average SAT I Math 506, SAT I Math middle 50% range 420-560. Average SAT I Verbal 490, SAT I Verbal middle 50% range 440-570. Average ACT 21, ACT middle 50% range 19-23. TOEFL required of all international applicants, minimum TOEFL 500. **Basis for Candidate Selection:** *Very important factors considered include:* secondary school record, standardized test scores. **Freshman Admission Requirements:** High school diploma or GED is required. *Academic units required/recommended:* 14 total required; 4 English required, 3 math required, 2 science required, 1 science lab required, 2 foreign language required, 1 social studies required, 1 history required. **Freshman Admission Statistics:** 2,912 applied, 45% accepted, 88% of those accepted enrolled. **Transfer Admission Requirements:** *Items required:* college transcript. Lowest grade transferable D. **General Admission Information:** Application fee $15. Regular application deadline August 15. Nonfall registration accepted. Admission may be deferred for a maximum of 1 year. Credit offered for CEEB Advanced Placement tests.

COSTS AND FINANCIAL AID

Room & board $3,350. Required fees $609. Average book expense $800. **Required Forms and Deadlines:** FAFSA. No deadline for regular filing. Priority filing deadline April 1. **Notification of Awards:** Applicants will be notified of awards on a rolling basis beginning on or about May 1. **Types of Aid:** *Need-based scholarships/grants:* Pell, SEOG, state scholarships/grants. *Loans:* FFEL Subsidized Stafford, FFEL Unsubsidized Stafford, FFEL PLUS, Federal Perkins. **Student Employment:** Federal Work-Study Program available. Institutional employment available. Off-campus job opportunities are good. **Financial Aid Statistics:** 47% freshmen, 53% undergrads receive some form of aid. **Financial Aid Phone:** 931-221-7907.

AVERETT UNIVERSITY

420 West Main Street, Danville, VA 24541
Phone: 434-791-5660 **E-mail:** admit@averett.edu **CEEB Code:** 5017
Fax: 434-797-2784 **Web:** www.averett.edu **ACT Code:** 4338

This private school was founded in 1859. It has a 25-acre campus.

STUDENTS AND FACULTY

Enrollment: 1,987. **Student Body:** Male 40%, female 60%, out-of-state 12%, international 1% (17 countries represented). **Ethnic Representation:** African American 32%, Asian 1%, Caucasian 65%, Hispanic 1%, Native American 1%. **Retention and Graduation:** 58% freshmen return for sophomore year. 28% freshmen graduate within 4 years. **Faculty:** Student/faculty ratio 14:1. 61 full-time faculty, 80% hold PhDs. 100% faculty teach undergrads.

ACADEMICS

Degrees: Associate's, bachelor's, master's, transfer. **Academic Requirements:** General education including some course work in arts/fine arts, computer literacy, English (including composition), history, humanities, mathematics, philosophy, sciences (biological or physical), social science, general education. **Classes:** 10-19 students in an average class. Under 10 students in an average lab/discussion section. **Majors with Highest Enrollment:** Business administration/management; teacher education and professional development, specific subject areas; sports and fitness administration/management. **Disciplines with Highest Percentage of Degrees Awarded:** Business/marketing 66%, education 8%, parks and recreation 5%, social sciences and history 3%, psychology 3%. **Special Study Options:** Accelerated program, double major, dual enrollment, honors program, independent study, internships, student-designed major, study abroad, teacher certification program; undergrads may take grad-level classes; accelerated adult program AS, BBA, MBA; minor in leadership studies.

FACILITIES

Housing: Coed, all-female, all-male, apartments for single students. **Library Holdings:** 130,519 bound volumes. 512 periodicals. 210,671 microforms. 84 audiovisuals. **Special Academic Facilities/Equipment:** Regional archives collection. **Computers:** School-owned computers available for student use.

EXTRACURRICULARS

Activities: Choral groups, drama/theater, literary magazine, musical theater, student government, student newspaper. **Organizations:** 28 registered organizations, 9 honor societies, 3 religious organizations, 1 fraternity (12% men join), 1 sorority (15% women join). **Athletics (Intercollegiate):** *Men:* baseball, basketball, cross-country, equestrian, football, golf, soccer, tennis. *Women:* basketball, cross-country, equestrian, lacrosse, soccer, softball, tennis, volleyball.

ADMISSIONS

Selectivity Rating: 63 (of 100). **Freshman Academic Profile:** Average high school GPA 3.0. 10% in top 10% of high school class, 21% in top 25% of high school class, 60% in top 50% of high school class. 85% from public high schools. Average SAT I Math 472, SAT I Math middle 50% range 410-520. Average SAT I Verbal 478, SAT I Verbal middle 50% range 420-530. Average ACT 18, ACT middle 50% range 15-20. TOEFL required of all international applicants, minimum TOEFL 500. **Basis for Candidate Selection:** *Very important factors considered include:* class rank, secondary school record, standardized test scores. *Important factors considered include:* recommendations. *Other factors considered include:* alumni/ae relation, character/personal qualities, essays, extracurricular activities, interview, talent/ability, volunteer work, work experience. **Freshman Admission Requirements:** High school diploma or GED is required. *Academic units required/recommended:* 15 total required; 17 total recommended; 4 English required, 4 English recommended, 2 math required, 3 math recommended, 2 science required, 3 science recommended, 2 science lab required, 2 science lab recommended, 2 foreign language recommended, 3 social studies required, 3 social studies recommended, 3 history required, 3 history recommended, 3 elective recommended. **Freshman Admission Statistics:** 687 applied, 90% accepted, 36% of those accepted enrolled. **Transfer Admission Requirements:** *Items required:* college transcript, essay, statement of good standing from prior school. Minimum college GPA of 2.0 required. Lowest grade transferable C. **General Admission Information:** Priority application deadline May 1. Regular application deadline September 1. Nonfall registration accepted. Admission may be deferred for a maximum of 2 years. Credit and/or placement offered for CEEB Advanced Placement tests.

COSTS AND FINANCIAL AID

Tuition $15,800. Room & board $5,150. Required fees $1,000. Average book expense $750. **Required Forms and Deadlines:** FAFSA and all full-time (12 or more credits hour per semester) Virginia residents must apply for VTAG (Virginia Tuition Assistance Grant). No deadline for regular filing. **Notification of Awards:** Applicants will be notified of awards on a rolling basis beginning on or about March 1. **Types of Aid:** *Need-based scholarships/grants:* Pell, SEOG, state scholarships/grants, private scholarships, the school's own gift aid. *Loans:* FFEL Subsidized Stafford, FFEL Unsubsidized Stafford, FFEL PLUS, Federal Perkins, private loans. **Student Employment:** Federal Work-Study Program available. Institutional employment available. Off-campus job opportunities are good. **Financial Aid Statistics:** 85% freshmen, 80% undergrads receive some form of aid. Average freshman grant $12,535. Average freshman loan $3,370. Average income from on-campus job $4,000. **Financial Aid Phone:** 804-791-5645.

AVILA UNIVERSITY

11901 Wornall Road, Kansas City, MO 64145-1698
Phone: 816-942-8400 **E-mail:** admissions@mail.avila.edu **CEEB Code:** 6109
Fax: 816-942-3362 **Web:** www.avila.edu **ACT Code:** 2278

This private school, which is affiliated with the Roman Catholic Church, was founded in 1916.

STUDENTS AND FACULTY

Enrollment: 1,236. **Student Body:** Male 35%, female 65%, out-of-state 28%, international 2%. **Ethnic Representation:** African American 14%, Asian 1%, Caucasian 76%, Hispanic 4%, Native American 1%. **Retention and Graduation:** 63% freshmen return for sophomore year. 23% freshmen graduate within 4 years. 40% grads go on to further study within 1 year. 15% grads pursue business degrees. 2% grads pursue law degrees. 3% grads pursue medical degrees. **Faculty:** Student/faculty ratio 13:1. 62 full-time faculty, 77% hold PhDs. 100% faculty teach undergrads.

ACADEMICS

Degrees: Bachelor's, certificate, master's. **Academic Requirements:** General education including some course work in arts/fine arts, computer literacy, English (including composition), history, mathematics, philosophy, sciences (biological or physical). **Classes:** Under 10 students in an average class. 10-19 students in an average lab/discussion section. **Majors with Highest Enrollment:** Business administration/management; nursing; communications studies/speech communication and rhetoric. **Disciplines with Highest Percentage of Degrees Awarded:** Business/marketing 29%, health professions and related sciences 19%, education 13%, communications/communication technologies 10%, visual and performing arts 7%. **Special Study Options:** Accelerated program, double major, dual enrollment, English as a second language, independent study, internships, study abroad, teacher certification program.

FACILITIES

Housing: Coed. **Computers:** School-owned computers available for student use.

EXTRACURRICULARS

Activities: Choral groups, drama/theater, literary magazine, student government, student newspaper, television station. **Organizations:** 12 religious organizations. **Athletics (Intercollegiate):** *Men:* baseball, basketball, football, soccer, volleyball. *Women:* basketball, cheerleading, golf, soccer, softball, volleyball.

ADMISSIONS

Selectivity Rating: 73 (of 100). **Freshman Academic Profile:** Average high school GPA 3.2. 17% in top 10% of high school class, 39% in top 25% of high school class, 74% in top 50% of high school class. 92% from public high schools. Average ACT 22, ACT middle 50% range 18-25. TOEFL required of all international applicants, minimum TOEFL 550. **Basis for Candidate Selection:** *Very important factors considered include:* secondary school record, standardized test scores. *Other factors considered include:* character/personal qualities, class rank, essays, extracurricular activities, interview, recommendations, talent/ability. **Freshman Admission Requirements:** High school diploma or GED is required. *Academic units required/recommended:* 16 total recommended; 4 English recommended, 3 math recommended, 2 science recommended, 1 science lab recommended, 2 foreign language recommended, 3 social studies recommended, 2 history recommended. **Freshman Admission Statistics:** 707 applied, 81% accepted, 20% of those accepted enrolled. **Transfer Admission Requirements:** *Items required:* college transcript. Minimum college GPA of 2.0 required. Lowest grade transferable C. **General Admission Information:** Nonfall registration accepted. Admission may be deferred for a maximum of 1 year.

COSTS AND FINANCIAL AID

Tuition $14,700. Room & board $5,300. Required fees $187. Average book expense $847. **Required Forms and Deadlines:** FAFSA and institution's own financial aid form. No deadline for regular filing. Priority filing deadline April 1. **Notification of Awards:** Applicants will be notified of awards on a rolling basis beginning on or about February 15. **Types of Aid:** *Need-based scholarships/grants:* Pell, SEOG, state scholarships/grants. *Loans:* FFEL Subsidized Stafford, FFEL Unsubsidized Stafford, FFEL PLUS, Federal Perkins. **Student Employment:** Federal Work-Study Program available. **Financial Aid Statistics:** 46% freshmen, 63% undergrads receive some form of aid. Average freshman grant $4,095. Average freshman loan $3,200. Average income from on-campus job $1,500.

AZUSA PACIFIC UNIVERSITY

901 East Alosta, Azusa, CA 91702
Phone: 626-812-3016 **E-mail:** admissions@apu.edu **CEEB Code:** 4596
Fax: 626-812-3096 **Web:** www.apu.edu

This private school, which is affiliated with the Christian (Nondenominational) Church, was founded in 1899. It has a 103-acre campus.

STUDENTS AND FACULTY

Enrollment: 4,217. **Student Body:** Male 36%, female 64%, out-of-state 19%, international 2% (74 countries represented). **Ethnic Representation:** African American 3%, Asian 5%, Caucasian 75%, Hispanic 12%. **Retention and Graduation:** 83% freshmen return for sophomore year. 51% freshmen graduate within 4 years. **Faculty:** Student/faculty ratio 14:1. 234 full-time faculty, 73% hold PhDs. 100% faculty teach undergrads.

ACADEMICS

Degrees: Bachelor's, doctoral, first professional, master's. **Academic Requirements:** General education including some course work in arts/fine arts, English (including composition), foreign languages, history, humanities, mathematics, philosophy, sciences (biological or physical), social science. **Classes:** Under 10 students in an average class. **Majors with Highest Enrollment:** Nursing; business, management, marketing, and related support services; liberal arts and sciences, general studies and humanities. **Disciplines with Highest Percentage of Degrees Awarded:** Business/marketing 25%, education 20%, communications/communication technologies 7%, visual and performing arts 6%, liberal arts/general studies 6%. **Special Study Options:** Accelerated program, cooperative (work-study) program, distance learning, double major, English as a second language, student exchange program (domestic), honors program, independent study, internships, study abroad, teacher certification program.

FACILITIES

Housing: Coed, all-female, all-male, apartments for single students. **Library Holdings:** 176,679 bound volumes. 14,000 periodicals. 613,038 microforms. 6,004 audiovisuals. **Special Academic Facilities/Equipment:** Electron microscope. **Computers:** School-owned computers available for student use.

EXTRACURRICULARS

Activities: Choral groups, concert band, drama/theater, jazz band, marching band, music ensembles, musical theater, opera, pep band, radio station, student government, student newspaper, symphony orchestra, television station, yearbook. **Organizations:** 36 registered organizations, 7 honor societies. **Athletics (Intercollegiate):** *Men:* baseball, basketball, cross-country, football, soccer, tennis, track & field, volleyball. *Women:* basketball, cheerleading, cross-country, soccer, softball, tennis, track & field, volleyball.

ADMISSIONS

Selectivity Rating: 69 (of 100). **Freshman Academic Profile:** Average high school GPA 3.6. 29% in top 10% of high school class, 60% in top 25% of high school class, 86% in top 50% of high school class. Average SAT I Math 561, SAT I Math middle 50% range 500-620. Average SAT I Verbal 561, SAT I Verbal middle 50% range 500-620. Average ACT 24, ACT middle 50% range 20-25. TOEFL required of all international applicants, minimum TOEFL 525. **Basis for Candidate Selection:** *Very important factors considered include:* class rank, essays, recommendations, secondary school record, standardized test scores. *Important factors considered include:* character/personal qualities, state residency. *Other factors considered include:* alumni/ae relation, extracurricular activities, interview, minority status, talent/ability, volunteer work, work experience. **Freshman Admission Requirements:** High school diploma or GED is required. *Academic units required/recommended:* 4 English recommended, 3 math recommended, 2 science recommended, 2 foreign language recommended, 1 social studies recommended, 2 history recommended. **Freshman Admission Statistics:** 2,095 applied, 72% accepted, 66% of those accepted enrolled. **Transfer Admission Requirements:** *Items required:* college transcript, essay, statement of good standing from prior school. Minimum high school GPA of 2.5 required. Minimum college GPA of 2.0 required. Lowest grade transferable C. **General Admission Information:** Application fee $45. Priority application deadline March 1. Nonfall registration accepted. Credit offered for CEEB Advanced Placement tests.

COSTS AND FINANCIAL AID

Tuition $17,140. Room & board $2,930. Required fees $454. Average book expense $1,206. **Required Forms and Deadlines:** FAFSA and institution's own financial aid form. Financial aid filing deadline July 1. Priority filing deadline March 2. **Notification of Awards:** Applicants will be notified of awards on a rolling basis beginning on or about March 1. **Types of Aid:** *Need-*

based scholarships/grants: Pell, SEOG, state scholarships/grants, private scholarships, the school's own gift aid, Federal Nursing. *Loans:* FFEL Subsidized Stafford, FFEL Unsubsidized Stafford, FFEL PLUS, Federal Perkins, Federal Nursing. **Student Employment:** Federal Work-Study Program available. Institutional employment available. Off-campus job opportunities are good. **Financial Aid Statistics:** 92% freshmen, 90% undergrads receive some form of aid. Average freshman grant $9,121. Average freshman loan $4,766. **Financial Aid Phone:** 626-812-3009.

BABSON COLLEGE

Mustard Hall, Babson Park, MA 02457
Phone: 781-239-5522 **E-mail:** ugradadmission@babson.edu **CEEB Code:** 3075
Fax: 781-239-4006 **Web:** www.babson.edu **ACT Code:** 1780

This private school was founded in 1919. It has a 370-acre campus.

STUDENTS AND FACULTY

Enrollment: 1,735. **Student Body:** Out-of-state 44%, international 19% (64 countries represented). **Ethnic Representation:** African American 3%, Asian 11%, Caucasian 57%, Hispanic 4%, Native American 1%. **Retention and Graduation:** 92% freshmen return for sophomore year. 77% freshmen graduate within 4 years. 1% grads go on to further study within 1 year. 1% grads pursue law degrees. **Faculty:** Student/faculty ratio 14:1. 169 full-time faculty, 89% hold PhDs. 100% faculty teach undergrads.

ACADEMICS

Degrees: Bachelor's, master's, post-master's certificate. **Academic Requirements:** General education including some course work in arts/fine arts, computer literacy, English (including composition), history, humanities, mathematics, sciences (biological or physical), social science. **Classes:** 30-39 students in an average class. 10-19 students in an average lab/discussion section. **Majors with Highest Enrollment:** Business administration/management. **Disciplines with Highest Percentage of Degrees Awarded:** Business/marketing 100%. **Special Study Options:** Accelerated program, cross registration, student exchange program (domestic), honors program, independent study, internships, liberal arts/career combination, student-designed major, study abroad.

FACILITIES

Housing: Coed, all-male, housing for disabled students, housing for international students, fraternities and/or sororities, substance free, theme housing. **Library Holdings:** 131,844 bound volumes. 580 periodicals. 346,868 microforms. 4,472 audiovisuals. **Special Academic Facilities/Equipment:** Babson World Globe, Roger Babson Museum, Isaac Newton Museum, Arthur Blank Center for Entrepreneurship. **Computers:** *Recommended operating system:* Windows NT/2000. School-owned computers available for student use.

EXTRACURRICULARS

Activities: Choral groups, dance, drama/theater, jazz band, music ensembles, musical theater, radio station, student government, student newspaper, yearbook. **Organizations:** 35 registered organizations, 2 honor societies, 1 religious organization, 3 fraternities, 2 sororities. **Athletics (Intercollegiate):** *Men:* baseball, basketball, cross-country, diving, golf, ice hockey, indoor track, lacrosse, skiing (alpine), soccer, swimming, tennis, track & field. *Women:* basketball, cross-country, diving, field hockey, indoor track, lacrosse, skiing (alpine), soccer, softball, swimming, tennis, track & field, volleyball.

ADMISSIONS

Selectivity Rating: 90 (of 100). **Freshman Academic Profile:** 44% in top 10% of high school class, 81% in top 25% of high school class, 100% in top 50% of high school class. 52% from public high schools. Average SAT I Math 640, SAT I Math middle 50% range 600-690. Average SAT I Verbal 600, SAT I Verbal middle 50% range 550-630. TOEFL required of all international applicants, minimum TOEFL 550. **Basis for Candidate Selection:** *Very important factors considered include:* essays, secondary school record, standardized test scores. *Important factors considered include:* class rank, recommendations. *Other factors considered include:* alumni/ae relation, character/personal qualities, extracurricular activities, geographical residence, interview, minority status, state residency, talent/ability, volunteer work, work experience. **Freshman Admission Requirements:** High school diploma or GED is required. *Academic units required/recommended:* 4 English required, 4 English recommended, 3 math required, 4 math recommended, 2 science required, 3 science recommended, 4 foreign language recommended, 2 social studies required, 3 social studies recommended. **Freshman Admission Statistics:** 2,402 applied, 48% accepted, 35% of those accepted enrolled. **Transfer Admission Requirements:** *Items required:* high school transcript, college transcript, essay, standardized test scores, statement of good standing from prior school. Lowest grade transferable C. **General Admission Information:** Application fee $50. Priority application deadline December 1. Early decision application deadline December 1. Regular application deadline February 1. Admission may be deferred for a maximum of 2 years. Credit and/or placement offered for CEEB Advanced Placement tests.

COSTS AND FINANCIAL AID

Tuition $24,544. Room & board $9,226. Required fees $0. Average book expense $658. **Required Forms and Deadlines:** FAFSA, CSS/Financial Aid PROFILE, noncustodial (divorced/separated) parent's statement, business/farm supplement, federal tax returns, W-2s, and verification worksheet. Financial aid filing deadline February 15. **Notification of Awards:** Applicants will be notified of awards on or about April 1. **Types of Aid:** *Need-based scholarships/grants:* Pell, SEOG, state scholarships/grants, the school's own gift aid. *Loans:* FFEL Subsidized Stafford, FFEL Unsubsidized Stafford, FFEL PLUS, Federal Perkins, state loans. **Student Employment:** Federal Work-Study Program available. Institutional employment available. Off-campus job opportunities are good. **Financial Aid Statistics:** 44% freshmen, 42% undergrads receive some form of aid. Average freshman grant $14,247. Average freshman loan $2,887. Average income from on-campus job $1,500. **Financial Aid Phone:** 781-239-4219.

See page 924.

BAKER COLLEGE OF FLINT

1050 West Bristol Road, Flint, MI 48507
Phone: 810-766-4000 **E-mail:** troy.crowe@baker.edu
Fax: 810-766-4255 **Web:** www.baker.edu

STUDENTS AND FACULTY

Enrollment: 5,291. **Student Body:** Male 31%, female 69%. **Ethnic Representation:** African American 25%, Asian 2%, Caucasian 70%, Hispanic 2%, Native American 1%.

ACADEMICS

Degrees: Associate's, bachelor's, certificate, diploma, master's. **Academic Requirements:** General education including some course work in computer literacy, English (including composition), mathematics. **Special Study Options:** Accelerated program, cooperative (work-study) program, distance learning, dual enrollment, internships.

ADMISSIONS

Selectivity Rating: 60 (of 100).

COSTS AND FINANCIAL AID

Tuition $5,760. Room & board $2,100. Required fees $20. Average book expense $900. **Types of Aid:** *Loans:* FFEL Subsidized Stafford, FFEL PLUS.

BAKER UNIVERSITY

Eighth and Grove, Baldwin City, KS 66006
Phone: 785-594-8307 **E-mail:** admission@bakeru.edu **CEEB Code:** 6031
Fax: 785-594-8372 **Web:** www.bakeru.edu **ACT Code:** 1386

This private school, which is affiliated with the Methodist Church, was founded in 1858. It has a 36-acre campus.

STUDENTS AND FACULTY

Enrollment: 988. **Student Body:** Male 40%, female 60%, out-of-state 24%, international 1% (4 countries represented). **Ethnic Representation:** African American 5%, Asian 1%, Caucasian 86%, Hispanic 3%, Native American 1%. **Retention and Graduation:** 72% freshmen return for sophomore year. 16% grads go on to further study within 1 year. 2% grads pursue business degrees. 1% grads pursue law degrees. 2% grads pursue medical degrees. **Faculty:** Student/faculty ratio 11:1. 69 full-time faculty, 71% hold PhDs. 100% faculty teach undergrads.

ACADEMICS

Degrees: Bachelor's. **Academic Requirements:** General education including some course work in arts/fine arts, English (including composition), history, humanities, mathematics, sciences (biological or physical), social science, critical thinking, nonwestern studies, fitness and well-being, oral communication. **Classes:** 10-19 students in an average class. 10-19 students in an average lab/discussion section. **Majors with Highest Enrollment:** Nursing/registered nurse training (RN, ASN, BSN, MSN); business/commerce, general; education. **Disciplines with Highest Percentage of Degrees Awarded:** Business/marketing 26%, health professions and related sciences 19%, education 13%, biological life sciences 9%, social sciences and history 8%. **Special Study Options:** Accelerated program, double major, honors program, independent study, internships, liberal arts/career combination, student-designed major, study abroad, teacher certification program. Interterm program (3.5 weeks in January) allows students to take classes on campus, pursue travel courses, or work in internships.

FACILITIES

Housing: Coed, all-female, all-male, apartments for single students, housing for disabled students, fraternities and/or sororities. **Library Holdings:** 84,114 bound volumes. 507 periodicals. 203,328 microforms. 1,139 audiovisuals. **Special Academic Facilities/Equipment:** Old Castle Museum, Quayle Bible Collection. **Computers:** *Recommended operating system:* Windows 95. School-owned computers available for student use.

EXTRACURRICULARS

Activities: Choral groups, concert band, drama/theater, jazz band, literary magazine, music ensembles, pep band, radio station, student government, student newspaper, television station, yearbook. **Organizations:** 60 registered organizations, 15 honor societies, 2 religious organizations, 4 fraternities (48% men join), 4 sororities (52% women join). **Athletics (Intercollegiate):** *Men:* baseball, basketball, cross-country, football, golf, soccer, tennis, track & field. *Women:* basketball, cross-country, golf, soccer, softball, tennis, track & field, volleyball.

ADMISSIONS

Selectivity Rating: 76 (of 100). **Freshman Academic Profile:** Average high school GPA 3.5. 24% in top 10% of high school class, 55% in top 25% of high school class, 84% in top 50% of high school class. 95% from public high schools. SAT I Math middle 50% range 410-652. SAT I Verbal middle 50% range 400-580. Average ACT 23, ACT middle 50% range 21-26. TOEFL required of all international applicants, minimum TOEFL 525. **Basis for Candidate Selection:** *Very important factors considered include:* recommendations, secondary school record, standardized test scores. *Important factors considered include:* class rank. *Other factors considered include:* essays. **Freshman Admission Requirements:** High school diploma or GED is required. *Academic units required/recommended:* 17 total recommended; 4 English recommended, 3 math recommended, 3 science recommended, 1 science lab recommended, 2 foreign language recommended, 3 social studies recommended. **Freshman Admission Statistics:** 844 applied, 95% accepted, 29% of those accepted enrolled. **Transfer Admission Requirements:** *Items required:* high school transcript, college transcript, standardized test scores. Minimum college GPA of 2.3 required. Lowest grade transferable C. **General Admission Information:** Application fee $20. Priority application deadline August 1. Regular application deadline rolling. Nonfall registration accepted. Admission may be deferred for a maximum of 1 year. Neither credit nor placement offered for CEEB Advanced Placement tests.

COSTS AND FINANCIAL AID

Tuition $14,210. Room & board $5,300. Required fees $430. Average book expense $900. **Required Forms and Deadlines:** FAFSA and institution's own financial aid form. No deadline for regular filing. Priority filing deadline March 1. **Notification of Awards:** Applicants will be notified of awards on a rolling basis beginning on or about February 15. **Types of Aid:** *Need-based scholarships/grants:* Pell, SEOG, state scholarships/grants, private scholarships, the school's own gift aid. *Loans:* FFEL Subsidized Stafford, FFEL Unsubsidized Stafford, FFEL PLUS, Federal Perkins, college/university loans from institutional funds. **Student Employment:** Federal Work-Study Program available. Institutional employment available. Off-campus job opportunities are good. **Financial Aid Statistics:** 75% freshmen, 74% undergrads receive some form of aid. Average freshman grant $7,381. Average freshman loan $4,125. Average income from on-campus job $900. **Financial Aid Phone:** 785-594-4595.

BALDWIN-WALLACE COLLEGE

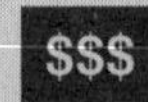

275 Eastland Rd, Berea, OH 44017
Phone: 440-826-2222 **E-mail:** admit@bw.edu **CEEB Code:** 1050
Fax: 440-826-3830 **Web:** www.bw.edu **ACT Code:** 3236

This private school, which is affiliated with the Methodist Church, was founded in 1845. It has a 100-acre campus.

STUDENTS AND FACULTY

Enrollment: 3,910. **Student Body:** Male 38%, female 62%, out-of-state 9%, international 1%. **Ethnic Representation:** African American 3%, Asian 1%, Caucasian 86%, Hispanic 2%. **Retention and Graduation:** 82% freshmen return for sophomore year. 49% freshmen graduate within 4 years. 29% grads go on to further study within 1 year. 4% grads pursue law degrees. 2% grads pursue medical degrees. **Faculty:** Student/faculty ratio 15:1. 162 full-time faculty, 77% hold PhDs. 93% faculty teach undergrads.

ACADEMICS

Degrees: Bachelor's, master's. **Academic Requirements:** General education including some course work in arts/fine arts, English (including composition), history, humanities, mathematics, philosophy, sciences (biological or physical), social science, international studies (including foreign language, study abroad, or selected courses with an international emphasis). Please note: history is part of the cultural heritage core. **Classes:** 10-19 students in an average class. 20-29 students in an average lab/discussion section. **Majors with Highest Enrollment:** Business administration/management; elementary education and teaching; sports and fitness administration/management. **Disciplines with Highest Percentage of Degrees Awarded:** Business/marketing 33%, education 16%, social sciences and history 9%, visual and performing arts 7%, psychology 5%. **Special Study Options:** Accelerated program, cross registration, distance learning, double major, dual enrollment, student exchange program (domestic), honors program, independent study, internships, liberal arts/career combination, student-designed major, study abroad, teacher certification program, weekend college. BS program in allied health fields with 3 local community colleges; 3-2 in engineering with Case Western Reserve, Columbia University, and Washington University; 3-2 in social work with Case Western Reserve; 3-2 in forestry and environmental studies with Duke University.

FACILITIES

Housing: Coed, all-female, all-male, apartments for single students, housing for disabled students, housing for international students, fraternities and/or sororities, wellness halls, Sprout houses (for single mothers and children), Carmel Living Learning Center (education-based), honors, and freshmen only. **Library Holdings:** 200,000 bound volumes. 883 periodicals. 0 microforms. 0 audiovisuals. **Special Academic Facilities/Equipment:** Art gallery, electron microscope, observatory. **Computers:** *Recommended operating system:* Windows NT/2000. School-owned computers available for student use.

EXTRACURRICULARS

Activities: Choral groups, concert band, dance, drama/theater, jazz band, literary magazine, music ensembles, musical theater, opera, pep band, radio station, student government, student newspaper, symphony orchestra, yearbook. **Organizations:** 100 registered organizations, 17 honor societies, 10 religious organizations, 6 fraternities (17% men join), 6 sororities (21% women join). **Athletics (Intercollegiate):** *Men:* baseball, basketball, cross-country, diving, football, golf, indoor track, soccer, swimming, tennis, track & field, wrestling. *Women:* basketball, cross-country, diving, golf, indoor track, soccer, softball, swimming, tennis, track & field, volleyball.

ADMISSIONS

Selectivity Rating: 70 (of 100). **Freshman Academic Profile:** Average high school GPA 3.6. 33% in top 10% of high school class, 60% in top 25% of high school class, 88% in top 50% of high school class. 85% from public high schools. Average SAT I Math 541, SAT I Math middle 50% range 500-620. Average SAT I Verbal 543, SAT I Verbal middle 50% range 480-610. Average ACT 23, ACT middle 50% range 20-26. TOEFL required of all international applicants, minimum TOEFL 500. **Basis for Candidate Selection:** *Very important factors considered include:* class rank, secondary school record. *Important factors considered include:* essays, extracurricular activities, recommendations, standardized test scores. *Other factors considered include:* alumni/ae relation, character/personal qualities, geographical residence, interview, minority status, religious affiliation/commitment, state residency, talent/ability, volunteer work, work experience. **Freshman Admission Requirements:** High school diploma or GED is required. *Academic units required/recommended:* 15 total required; 19 total recommended; 4 English required, 4 English recommended, 3 math required, 4 math recommended, 3 science required, 4 science recommended, 2 science lab required, 2 science lab recommended, 2 foreign language required, 2 foreign language recommended, 2 social studies required, 2 social studies recommended, 1 history required, 1 history recommended, 2 elective recommended. **Freshman Admission Statistics:** 2,193 applied, 84% accepted, 40% of those accepted enrolled. **Transfer Admission Requirements:** *Items required:* high school transcript, college transcript, essay. Minimum high school GPA of 2.5 required. Minimum college GPA of 2.5 required. Lowest grade transferable C. **General Admission Information:** Application fee $15. Priority application deadline May 1. Nonfall registration accepted. Admission may be deferred for a maximum of 1 year. Credit and/or placement offered for CEEB Advanced Placement tests.

COSTS AND FINANCIAL AID

Tuition $17,432. Room & board $6,022. Required fees $0. Average book expense $780. **Required Forms and Deadlines:** FAFSA. Financial aid filing deadline September 1. Priority filing deadline May 1. **Notification of Awards:** Applicants will be notified of awards on a rolling basis beginning on or about February 14. **Types of Aid:** *Need-based scholarships/grants:* Pell, SEOG, state scholarships/grants, private scholarships, the school's own gift aid. *Loans:* FFEL Subsidized Stafford, FFEL Unsubsidized Stafford, FFEL PLUS, Federal Perkins, college/university loans from institutional funds. **Student Employment:** Federal Work-Study Program available. Institutional employment available. Off-campus job opportunities are good. **Financial Aid Statistics:** 75% freshmen, 68% undergrads receive some form of aid. Average freshman grant $10,938. Average freshman loan $3,452. Average income from on-campus job $1,831. **Financial Aid Phone:** 440-826-2108.

BALL STATE UNIVERSITY

Office of Admissions, 2000 University Avenue, Muncie, IN 47306
Phone: 765-285-8300 **E-mail:** Askus@bsu.edu **CEEB Code:** 1051
Fax: 765-285-1632 **Web:** www.bsu.edu **ACT Code:** 1176

This public school was founded in 1918. It has a 955-acre campus.

STUDENTS AND FACULTY

Enrollment: 17,061. **Student Body:** Male 47%, female 53%, out-of-state 8%, international students represent 86 countries. **Ethnic Representation:** African American 6%, Asian 1%, Caucasian 89%, Hispanic 1%. **Retention and Graduation:** 77% freshmen return for sophomore year. 34% grads go on to further study within 1 year. **Faculty:** Student/faculty ratio 16:1. 896 full-time faculty, 75% hold PhDs. 96% faculty teach undergrads.

ACADEMICS

Degrees: Associate's, bachelor's, doctoral, master's, post-bachelor's certificate, post-master's certificate. **Academic Requirements:** General education including some course work in arts/fine arts, English (including composition), history, humanities, mathematics, sciences (biological or physical), social science. **Classes:** 20-29 students in an average class. 20-29 students in an average lab/discussion section. **Majors with Highest Enrollment:** Business administration/management; elementary education and teaching; physical education teaching and coaching. **Disciplines with Highest Percentage of Degrees Awarded:** Education 16%, business/marketing 13%, communications/communication technologies 11%, liberal arts/general studies 11%, social sciences and history 7%. **Special Study Options:** Cooperative (work-study) program, distance learning, double major, English as a second language, student exchange program (domestic), honors program, independent study, internships, liberal arts/career combination, study abroad, teacher certification program.

FACILITIES

Housing: Coed, all-female, all-male, apartments for married students, apartments for single students, housing for disabled students, housing for international students, fraternities and/or sororities, cooperative housing. **Library Holdings:** 1,146,899 bound volumes. 2,937 periodicals. 1,041,599 microforms. 506,303 audiovisuals. **Special Academic Facilities/Equipment:** Art gallery, museum, on-campus school (K-12), learning center, weather station, physical therapy lab, human performance lab, planetarium/observatory, wildlife and nature preserve. **Computers:** School-owned computers available for student use.

EXTRACURRICULARS

Activities: Choral groups, concert band, dance, drama/theater, jazz band, marching band, music ensembles, musical theater, opera, pep band, radio station, student government, student newspaper, student-run film society, symphony orchestra, television station, yearbook. **Organizations:** 325 registered organizations, 38 honor societies, 20 religious organizations, 20 fraternities, 15 sororities. **Athletics (Intercollegiate):** *Men:* baseball, basketball, cheerleading, cross-country, diving, football, golf, indoor track, swimming, tennis, track & field, volleyball. *Women:* basketball, cheerleading, cross-country, diving, field hockey, gymnastics, indoor track, softball, swimming, tennis, track & field, volleyball.

ADMISSIONS

Selectivity Rating: 66 (of 100). **Freshman Academic Profile:** 14% in top 10% of high school class, 44% in top 25% of high school class, 81% in top 50% of high school class. 95% from public high schools. Average SAT I Math 522, SAT I Math middle 50% range 460-580. Average SAT I Verbal 518, SAT I Verbal middle 50% range 460-570. Average ACT 22, ACT middle 50% range 20-25. TOEFL required of all international applicants, minimum TOEFL 450. **Basis for Candidate Selection:** *Very important factors considered include:* secondary school record. *Important factors considered include:* standardized test scores. *Other factors considered include:* alumni/ae relation, character/personal qualities, essays, extracurricular activities, interview, recommendations, talent/ability, volunteer work, work experience. **Freshman Admission Requirements:** High school diploma or GED is required. *Academic units required/recommended:* 4 English required, 3 math required, 3 science required, 3 foreign language recommended, 3 social studies required. **Freshman Admission Statistics:** 10,771 applied, 76% accepted, 46% of those accepted enrolled. **Transfer Admission Requirements:** *Items required:* college transcript. Minimum college GPA of 2.0 required. Lowest grade transferable C. **General Admission Information:** Application fee $25. Priority application deadline May 1. Nonfall registration accepted. Admission may be deferred for a maximum of 1 year. Credit and/or placement offered for CEEB Advanced Placement tests.

COSTS AND FINANCIAL AID

In-state tuition $4,320. Out-of-state tuition $12,100. Room & board $5,546. Required fees $380. Average book expense $840. **Required Forms and Deadlines:** FAFSA. No deadline for regular filing. Priority filing deadline March 1. **Notification of Awards:** Applicants will be notified of awards on a rolling basis beginning on or about April 15. **Types of Aid:** *Need-based scholarships/grants:* Pell, SEOG, state scholarships/grants, private scholarships, the school's own gift aid. *Loans:* Direct Subsidized Stafford, Direct Unsubsidized Stafford, Direct PLUS, Federal Perkins. **Student Employment:** Federal Work-Study Program available. Institutional employment available. Off-campus job opportunities are good. **Financial Aid Statistics:** 55% freshmen, 52% undergrads receive some form of aid. Average freshman grant $1,466. Average freshman loan $3,439. Average income from on-campus job $1,570. **Financial Aid Phone:** 800-227-4017.

BALTIMORE HEBREW UNIVERSITY

5800 Park Heights, Baltimore, MD 21215
Phone: 410-578-6967 **E-mail:** bhu@bhu.edu **CEEB Code:** 5035
Fax: 410-578-6940 **Web:** www.bhu.edu **ACT Code:** 20093

This private school was founded in 1919.

STUDENTS AND FACULTY

Enrollment: 108. **Student Body:** Male 29%, female 71%, international students represent 4 countries. **Ethnic Representation:** African American 2%, Caucasian 98%. **Retention and Graduation:** 67% freshmen return for sophomore year. 33% freshmen graduate within 4 years. **Faculty:** Student/faculty ratio 8:1. 100% faculty teach undergrads.

ACADEMICS

Degrees: Associate's, bachelor's, certificate, doctoral, master's. **Academic Requirements:** General education including some course work in English (including composition), foreign languages, history, humanities, mathematics, philosophy, sciences (biological or physical), social science, Judaic studies. **Special Study Options:** Cross registration, double major, dual enrollment, independent study, internships, study abroad, teacher certification program, English language skills program for non-native speakers.

FACILITIES

Library Holdings: 41,609 bound volumes. 154 periodicals. 2,536 microforms. 500 audiovisuals. **Special Academic Facilities/Equipment:** Joseph Meyerhoff Library, Cohen Auditorium. **Computers:** School-owned computers available for student use.

EXTRACURRICULARS

Organizations: 2 registered organizations.

ADMISSIONS

Selectivity Rating: 63 (of 100). **Freshman Academic Profile:** TOEFL required of all international applicants, minimum TOEFL 250. **Basis for Candidate Selection:** *Very important factors considered include:* interview, recommendations. *Other factors considered include:* character/personal qualities, class rank, secondary school record, standardized test scores. **Freshman Admission Requirements:** High school diploma or GED is required. **Freshman Admission Statistics:** 6 applied, 100% accepted, 67% of those accepted enrolled. **Transfer Admission Requirements:** *Items required:* college transcript. Minimum high school GPA of 2.0 required. Minimum college GPA of 2.0 required. Lowest grade transferable C. **General Admission Information:** Application fee $20. Nonfall registration accepted. Admission may be deferred for a maximum of 1 year.

COSTS AND FINANCIAL AID

Tuition $6,400. Required fees $30. Average book expense $600. **Required Forms and Deadlines:** FAFSA. No deadline for regular filing. **Notification of Awards:** Applicants will be notified of awards on a rolling basis. **Types of Aid:** *Need-based scholarships/grants:* Pell, state scholarships/grants, private scholarships, the school's own gift aid. *Loans:* FFEL Subsidized Stafford, FFEL Unsubsidized Stafford, FFEL PLUS. **Student Employment:** Off-campus job opportunities are excellent. **Financial Aid Statistics:** 100% freshmen, 87% undergrads receive some form of aid. **Financial Aid Phone:** 410-578-6913.

BAPTIST BIBLE COLLEGE AND SEMINARY OF PENNSYLVANIA

538 Venard Road, Clarks Summit, PA 18411-1297
Phone: 570-586-2400 **E-mail:** admissions@bbc.edu **CEEB Code:** 2036
Fax: 570-586-1753 **Web:** www.bbc.edu **ACT Code:** 3523

This private school, which is affiliated with the Baptist Church, was founded in 1932. It has a 121-acre campus.

STUDENTS AND FACULTY

Enrollment: 709. **Student Body:** Male 44%, female 56%, out-of-state 61%, international students represent 5 countries. **Ethnic Representation:** Asian 1%, Caucasian 98%, Hispanic 1%. **Retention and Graduation:** 42% freshmen graduate within 4 years. 15% grads go on to further study within 1 year. **Faculty:** Student/faculty ratio 25:1. 32 full-time faculty, 25% hold PhDs. 100% faculty teach undergrads.

ACADEMICS

Degrees: Associate's, bachelor's, certificate, doctoral, first professional, master's. **Academic Requirements:** General education including some course work in arts/fine arts, English (including composition), history, humanities, sciences (biological or physical). **Classes:** Under 10 students in an average class. 20-29 students in an average lab/discussion section. **Majors with Highest Enrollment:** Elementary and middle school administration/principalship; pastoral studies/counseling; youth ministry. **Disciplines with Highest Percentage of Degrees Awarded:** Philosophy/religion/theology 72%, education 26%, business/marketing 2%. **Special Study Options:** Distance learning, double major, dual enrollment, honors program, independent study, internships, study abroad, teacher certification program.

FACILITIES

Housing: All-female, all-male. **Library Holdings:** 97,139 bound volumes. 1,900 periodicals. 9,812 microforms. 22,945 audiovisuals. **Computers:** *Recommended operating system:* Windows 95. School-owned computers available for student use.

EXTRACURRICULARS

Activities: Choral groups, concert band, drama/theater, music ensembles, pep band, student government, yearbook. **Organizations:** 2 honor societies. **Athletics (Intercollegiate):** *Men:* basketball, cross-country, soccer, track & field, wrestling. *Women:* basketball, cheerleading, cross-country, soccer, softball, track & field, volleyball.

ADMISSIONS

Selectivity Rating: 63 (of 100). **Freshman Academic Profile:** Average high school GPA 3.1. 10% in top 10% of high school class, 32% in top 25% of high school class, 64% in top 50% of high school class. 39% from public high schools. Average SAT I Math 495, SAT I Math middle 50% range 430-550. Average SAT I Verbal 493, SAT I Verbal middle 50% range 430-580. Average ACT 21, ACT middle 50% range 17-24. TOEFL required of all international applicants, minimum TOEFL 500. **Basis for Candidate Selection:** *Very important factors considered include:* character/personal qualities, essays, recommendations, religious affiliation/commitment, secondary school record, standardized test scores. *Other factors considered include:* class rank, talent/ability. **Freshman Admission Requirements:** High school diploma or GED is required. **Freshman Admission Statistics:** 352 applied, 87% accepted, 54% of those accepted enrolled. **Transfer Admission Requirements:** *Items required:* high school transcript, college transcript, essay. Lowest grade transferable C. **General Admission Information:** Application fee $30. Priority application deadline May 1. Regular application deadline August 15. Nonfall registration accepted. Admission may be deferred for a maximum of 1 year. Credit offered for CEEB Advanced Placement tests.

COSTS AND FINANCIAL AID

Tuition $9,720. Room & board $4,892. Required fees $900. Average book expense $600. **Required Forms and Deadlines:** FAFSA. Financial aid filing deadline May 1. **Notification of Awards:** Applicants will be notified of awards on or about July 1. **Types of Aid:** *Need-based scholarships/grants:* Pell, state scholarships/grants, private scholarships, the school's own gift aid. *Loans:* FFEL Subsidized Stafford, FFEL Unsubsidized Stafford, FFEL PLUS. **Student Employment:** Institutional employment available. Off-campus job opportunities are excellent. **Financial Aid Statistics:** 83% freshmen, 75% undergrads receive some form of aid. Average freshman grant $1,610. Average freshman loan $3,238. Average income from on-campus job $1,917. **Financial Aid Phone:** 570-586-2400.

BAPTIST COLLEGE OF FLORIDA

5400 College Drive, Graceville, FL 32440
Phone: 850-263-3261 **E-mail:** admissions@baptistcollege.edu
Fax: 850-263-7506 **Web:** www.baptistcollege.edu **ACT Code:** 6870

This private school, which is affiliated with the Southern Baptist Church, was founded in 1943. It has a 217-acre campus.

STUDENTS AND FACULTY

Enrollment: 581. **Student Body:** Male 63%, female 37%, out-of-state 24%, international students represent 9 countries. **Ethnic Representation:** African American 7%, Asian 1%, Caucasian 88%, Hispanic 2%, Native American 1%. **Retention and Graduation:** 58% freshmen return for sophomore year. 13% freshmen graduate within 4 years. 45% grads go on to further study within 1 year. **Faculty:** Student/faculty ratio 15:1. 22 full-time faculty, 68% hold PhDs. 100% faculty teach undergrads.

ACADEMICS

Degrees: Associate's, bachelor's, terminal. **Academic Requirements:** General education including some course work in arts/fine arts, computer literacy, English (including composition), history, humanities, mathematics, philosophy, sciences (biological or physical), social science. **Classes:** 10-19 students in an average class. **Disciplines with Highest Percentage of Degrees Awarded:** Philosophy/religion/theology 74%, education 15%, visual and performing arts 11%. **Special Study Options:** Distance learning, double major, independent study, internships, teacher certification program, weekend college.

FACILITIES

Housing: All-female, all-male, apartments for married students, housing for disabled students. **Library Holdings:** 68,419 bound volumes. 484 periodicals. 39,260 microforms. 12,052 audiovisuals. **Special Academic Facilities/Equipment:** Florida Baptist Historical Society, Heritage Village. **Computers:** School-owned computers available for student use.

EXTRACURRICULARS

Activities: Choral groups, concert band, drama/theater, jazz band, music ensembles, student government. **Organizations:** 3 registered organizations, 2 religious organizations. **Athletics (Intercollegiate):** *Men:* basketball, football, soccer, softball, tennis, volleyball. *Women:* basketball, football, soccer, softball, tennis, volleyball.

ADMISSIONS

Selectivity Rating: 63 (of 100). **Freshman Academic Profile:** 86% from public high schools. SAT I Math middle 50% range 460-558. SAT I Verbal middle 50% range 483-547. ACT middle 50% range 17-23. TOEFL required of all international applicants, minimum TOEFL 500. **Basis for Candidate Selection:** *Very important factors considered include:* character/personal qualities, recommendations, religious affiliation/commitment. *Important factors considered include:* alumni/ae relation, talent/ability. *Other factors considered include:* class rank, extracurricular activities, interview, secondary school record, standardized test scores, volunteer work. **Freshman Admission Require-**

ments: High school diploma or GED is required. **Freshman Admission Statistics:** 75 applied, 87% accepted, 86% of those accepted enrolled. **Transfer Admission Requirements:** *Items required:* high school transcript, college transcript, essay. Minimum college GPA of 2.0 required. Lowest grade transferable C. **General Admission Information:** Application fee $20. Priority application deadline June 30. Regular application deadline August 1. Nonfall registration accepted. Admission may be deferred. Neither credit nor placement offered for CEEB Advanced Placement tests.

COSTS AND FINANCIAL AID

Tuition $5,400. Room & board $3,150. Required fees $200. Average book expense $600. **Required Forms and Deadlines:** FAFSA, institution's own financial aid form, state aid form, and business/farm supplement. Financial aid filing deadline April 15. Priority filing deadline April 1. **Notification of Awards:** Applicants will be notified of awards on a rolling basis beginning on or about June 15. **Types of Aid:** *Need-based scholarships/grants:* Pell, SEOG, state scholarships/grants, private scholarships, the school's own gift aid. *Loans:* FFEL Subsidized Stafford, FFEL Unsubsidized Stafford, FFEL PLUS, college/university loans from institutional funds. **Student Employment:** Federal Work-Study Program available. Institutional employment available. Off-campus job opportunities are good. **Financial Aid Statistics:** 57% freshmen, 74% undergrads receive some form of aid. Average freshman grant $1,200. Average freshman loan $2,625. Average income from on-campus job $1,600. **Financial Aid Phone:** 850-263-3261.

BARAT COLLEGE OF DEPAUL UNIVERSITY

700 East Westleigh Road, Lake Forest, IL 60045
Phone: 847-295-4260 **E-mail:** admissions@barat.edu **CEEB Code:** 1635
Fax: 847-604-6300 **Web:** www.barat.edu **ACT Code:** 952

This private school, which is affiliated with the Roman Catholic Church, was founded in 1858. It has a 30-acre campus.

STUDENTS AND FACULTY

Enrollment: 746. **Student Body:** Male 27%, female 73%, out-of-state 18%. **Ethnic Representation:** African American 9%, Asian 4%, Caucasian 65%, Hispanic 8%. **Retention and Graduation:** 85% freshmen return for sophomore year. 15% freshmen graduate within 4 years. 35% grads go on to further study within 1 year. **Faculty:** Student/faculty ratio 12:1. 40 full-time faculty, 87% hold PhDs. 100% faculty teach undergrads.

ACADEMICS

Degrees: Bachelor's, certificate, master's, post-bachelor's certificate. **Academic Requirements:** General education including some course work in arts/fine arts, computer literacy, English (including composition), foreign languages, history, humanities, mathematics, philosophy, sciences (biological or physical), social science, writing experience, and multicultural class experience. **Classes:** 10-19 students in an average class. **Disciplines with Highest Percentage of Degrees Awarded:** Business/marketing 21%, visual and performing arts 20%, health professions and related sciences 18%, education 9%, psychology 9%. **Special Study Options:** Accelerated program, cross registration, double major, dual enrollment, student exchange program (domestic), honors program, independent study, internships, liberal arts/career combination, student-designed major, study abroad, teacher certification program.

FACILITIES

Housing: Coed, all-female. **Library Holdings:** 115,000 bound volumes. 273 periodicals. 59,676 microforms. 567 audiovisuals. **Special Academic Facilities/Equipment:** Drake Theater Complex, Sister Madeline Sophie Cooney Library, Cuneo Science Building. **Computers:** School-owned computers available for student use.

EXTRACURRICULARS

Activities: Choral groups, dance, drama/theater, literary magazine, radio station, student government, student newspaper. **Organizations:** 22 registered organizations, 2 honor societies, 1 religious organization. **Athletics (Intercollegiate):** *Men:* basketball. *Women:* volleyball.

ADMISSIONS

Selectivity Rating: 68 (of 100). **Freshman Academic Profile:** Average high school GPA 3.0. 4% in top 10% of high school class, 20% in top 25% of high school class, 49% in top 50% of high school class. 60% from public high schools. Average SAT I Math 490, SAT I Math middle 50% range 470-550. Average SAT I Verbal 500, SAT I Verbal middle 50% range 520-620. Average ACT 21, ACT middle 50% range 18-24. TOEFL required of all international applicants, minimum TOEFL 500. **Basis for Candidate Selection:** *Very important factors considered include:* essays, secondary school record, standardized test scores. *Important factors considered include:* interview, recommendations, talent/ability. *Other factors considered include:* alumni/ae relation, character/personal qualities, class rank, extracurricular activities, volunteer work, work experience. **Freshman Admission Requirements:** High school diploma or GED is required. *Academic units required/recommended:* 16 total recommended; 4 English recommended, 2 math recommended, 2 science recommended, 2 foreign language recommended, 2 social studies recommended, 1 history recommended. **Freshman Admission Statistics:** 388 applied, 62% accepted, 48% of those accepted enrolled. **Transfer Admission Requirements:** *Items required:* college transcript. Minimum college GPA of 2.5 required. Lowest grade transferable C. **General Admission Information:** Application fee $20. Priority application deadline April 15. Nonfall registration accepted. Admission may be deferred for a maximum of 1 year. Credit and/or placement offered for CEEB Advanced Placement tests.

COSTS AND FINANCIAL AID

Tuition $14,630. Room & board $5,920. Required fees $0. Average book expense $840. **Required Forms and Deadlines:** FAFSA and institution's own financial aid form. No deadline for regular filing. Priority filing deadline May 30. **Notification of Awards:** Applicants will be notified of awards on a rolling basis beginning on or about March 1. **Types of Aid:** *Need-based scholarships/grants:* Pell, SEOG, state scholarships/grants, private scholarships, the school's own gift aid. *Loans:* FFEL Subsidized Stafford, FFEL Unsubsidized Stafford, FFEL PLUS, Federal Perkins. **Student Employment:** Federal Work-Study Program available. Institutional employment available. Off-campus job opportunities are good. **Financial Aid Statistics:** 44% freshmen, 31% undergrads receive some form of aid. **Financial Aid Phone:** 847-604-6279.

BARBER SCOTIA COLLEGE

145 Cabarrus Avenue, Concord, NC 28025
Phone: 704-789-2901 **E-mail:** wwhite@b-sc.edu
Fax: 704-789-2624 **Web:** www.barber-scotia.edu **ACT Code:** 3060

This private school, which is affiliated with the Presbyterian Church, was founded in 1867. It has a 40-acre campus.

STUDENTS AND FACULTY

Enrollment: 488. **Student Body:** Male 55%, female 45%, out-of-state 45%, international students represent 2 countries. **Ethnic Representation:** African American 98%, Caucasian 1%. **Retention and Graduation:** 61% freshmen return for sophomore year. 9% grads go on to further study within 1 year. 2% grads pursue business degrees. **Faculty:** 100% faculty teach undergrads.

ACADEMICS

Degrees: Bachelor's. **Academic Requirements:** General education including some course work in English (including composition), history, humanities, mathematics, sciences (biological or physical), social science. **Special Study Options:** Cooperative (work-study) program, double major, dual enrollment, honors program, internships, student-designed major, teacher certification program.

FACILITIES

Housing: All-female, all-male, apartments for married students, housing for disabled students. **Library Holdings:** 35,896 bound volumes. 225 periodicals. 80,271 microforms. 341 audiovisuals. **Special Academic Facilities/Equipment:** Barber-Scotia's African American Women's History Collection: This collection houses one of the largest bodies of documents related to African American women in the United States. Major areas of interest are the Reconstruction-Jim Crow Era. **Computers:** *Recommended operating system:* Mac. School-owned computers available for student use.

EXTRACURRICULARS

Activities: Choral groups, dance, pep band, student government, student newspaper, yearbook. **Organizations:** 18 registered organizations, 2 honor societies, 2 religious organizations, 4 fraternities (8% men join), 4 sororities (8% women join). **Athletics (Intercollegiate):** *Men:* basketball, cross-country, track & field. *Women:* basketball, cheerleading, cross-country, softball, track & field, volleyball.

ADMISSIONS

Selectivity Rating: 63 (of 100). **Freshman Academic Profile:** Average high school GPA 2.1. 3% in top 10% of high school class, 13% in top 25% of high school class, 24% in top 50% of high school class. 98% from public high schools. Average SAT I Math 341. Average SAT I Verbal 375. TOEFL required of all international applicants. **Basis for Candidate Selection:** *Very important* *factors considered include:* class rank, essays, interview, recommendations. *Important factors considered include:* extracurricular activities, secondary school record, talent/ability, volunteer work. *Other factors considered include:* alumni/ae relation, character/personal qualities, state residency. **Freshman Admission Requirements:** High school diploma or GED is required. *Academic units required/recommended:* 13 total required; 4 English required, 3 math required, 3 science required, 2 social studies required, 1 history required. **Freshman Admission Statistics:** 840 applied, 64% accepted, 32% of those accepted enrolled. **Transfer Admission Requirements:** *Items required:* college transcript. Minimum college GPA of 2.0 required. Lowest grade transferable C. **General Admission Information:** Application fee $15. Regular application deadline July 1. Nonfall registration accepted. Credit and/or placement offered for CEEB Advanced Placement tests.

COSTS AND FINANCIAL AID

Tuition $7,400. Room & board $3,500. Required fees $466. Average book expense $250. **Required Forms and Deadlines:** FAFSA. Financial aid filing deadline August 1. Priority filing deadline May 30. **Notification of Awards:** Applicants will be notified of awards on or about June 15. **Types of Aid:** *Need-based scholarships/grants:* Pell, SEOG, state scholarships/grants, private scholarships, the school's own gift aid, United Negro College Fund. *Loans:* Direct Subsidized Stafford, Direct Unsubsidized Stafford, Direct PLUS, FFEL Subsidized Stafford, FFEL Unsubsidized Stafford, FFEL PLUS. **Student Employment:** Federal Work-Study Program available. Institutional employment available. Off-campus job opportunities are excellent. **Financial Aid Statistics:** 92% freshmen, 94% undergrads receive some form of aid. Average freshman grant $6,244. **Financial Aid Phone:** 704-789-7908.

BARCLAY COLLEGE

607 N Kingman, Haviland, KS 67059-0288
Phone: 620-862-5252 **E-mail:** admissions@barclaycollege.edu
Fax: 620-862-5242 **Web:** www.barclaycollege.edu **ACT Code:** 1411

This private school, which is affiliated with the Quaker Church, was founded in 1917. It has a 17-acre campus.

STUDENTS AND FACULTY

Enrollment: 203. **Student Body:** Male 47%, female 53%, international 5%. **Ethnic Representation:** African American 60%, Asian 20%, Caucasian 10%, Hispanic 10%. **Retention and Graduation:** 66% freshmen return for sophomore year. 19% freshmen graduate within 4 years. 4% grads go on to further study within 1 year. **Faculty:** Student/faculty ratio 8:1. 8 full-time faculty, 25% hold PhDs. 100% faculty teach undergrads.

ACADEMICS

Degrees: Associate's, bachelor's. **Academic Requirements:** General education including some course work in arts/fine arts, computer literacy, English (including composition), history, humanities, mathematics, philosophy, sciences (biological or physical), social science. Everyone is required to take 30 hours of Bible and graduates with a degree in Bible along with their declared major. **Classes:** Under 10 students in an average class. Under 10 students in an average lab/discussion section. **Disciplines with Highest Percentage of Degrees Awarded:** Business/marketing 54%, philosophy/religion/theology 34%, psychology 12%. **Special Study Options:** Cooperative (work-study) program, distance learning, double major, dual enrollment, independent study, internships.

FACILITIES

Housing: All-female, all-male, housing for disabled students. **Library Holdings:** 54,505 bound volumes. 194 periodicals. 134 microforms. 552 audiovisuals. **Computers:** School-owned computers available for student use.

EXTRACURRICULARS

Activities: Choral groups, drama/theater, music ensembles, student government, yearbook. **Organizations:** 1 honor society. **Athletics (Intercollegiate):** *Men:* baseball, basketball, cheerleading, golf, soccer, tennis. *Women:* basketball, cheerleading, golf, softball, tennis, volleyball.

ADMISSIONS

Selectivity Rating: 63 (of 100). **Freshman Academic Profile:** Average high school GPA 3.1. 80% from public high schools. SAT I Math middle 50% range 350-540. SAT I Verbal middle 50% range 280-490. Average ACT 20, ACT middle 50% range 18-26. **Basis for Candidate Selection:** *Very important factors considered include:* recommendations. *Important factors considered include:* character/personal qualities, interview, religious affiliation/commitment, secondary school record, standardized test scores. *Other factors considered include:* alumni/ae relation, class rank, essays, extracurricular activities. **Freshman Admission Requirements:** High school diploma or GED is required. **Freshman Admission Statistics:** 66 applied, 73% accepted, 48% of those accepted enrolled. **Transfer Admission Requirements:** *Items required:* high school transcript, college transcript, essay, standardized test scores. Lowest grade transferable C-. **General Admission Information:** Application fee $15. Nonfall registration accepted. Credit and/or placement offered for CEEB Advanced Placement tests.

COSTS AND FINANCIAL AID

Tuition $6,240. Room & board $3,300. Required fees $955. Average book expense $500. **Required Forms and Deadlines:** FAFSA. No deadline for regular filing. Priority filing deadline March 15. **Notification of Awards:** Applicants will be notified of awards on a rolling basis beginning on or about April 15. **Types of Aid:** *Need-based scholarships/grants:* Pell, SEOG, state scholarships/grants, private scholarships, the school's own gift aid. *Loans:* FFEL Subsidized Stafford, FFEL Unsubsidized Stafford, FFEL PLUS. **Student Employment:** Federal Work-Study Program available. Institutional employment available. Off-campus job opportunities are fair. **Financial Aid Statistics:** 89% freshmen, 73% undergrads receive some form of aid. Average freshman grant $90. **Financial Aid Phone:** 316-862-5252.

BARD COLLEGE

Office of Admissions, Annandale-on-Hudson, NY 12504
Phone: 845-758-7472 **E-mail:** admission@bard.edu **CEEB Code:** 2037
Fax: 845-758-5208 **Web:** www.bard.edu **ACT Code:** 2674

This private school was founded in 1860. It has a 600-acre campus.

STUDENTS AND FACULTY

Enrollment: 1,454. **Student Body:** Male 45%, female 55%, out-of-state 76%, international 6% (48 countries represented). **Ethnic Representation:** African American 3%, Asian 4%, Caucasian 77%, Hispanic 5%, Native American 1%. **Retention and Graduation:** 89% freshmen return for sophomore year. 59% freshmen graduate within 4 years. 54% grads go on to further study within 1 year. 3% grads pursue business degrees. 5% grads pursue law degrees. 3% grads pursue medical degrees. **Faculty:** Student/faculty ratio 9:1. 113 full-time faculty, 97% hold PhDs. 100% faculty teach undergrads.

ACADEMICS

Degrees: Associate's, bachelor's, doctoral, master's. **Academic Requirements:** General education including some course work in arts/fine arts, English (including composition), foreign languages, history, humanities, mathematics, philosophy, sciences (biological or physical), social science. **Classes:** Under 10 students in an average class. **Majors with Highest Enrollment:** Visual and performing arts; English language and literature, general; social sciences, general. **Disciplines with Highest Percentage of Degrees Awarded:** Visual and performing arts 40%, English 20%, social sciences and history 17%, philosophy/religion/theology 8%, foreign languages and literature 5%. **Special Study Options:** Accelerated program, cross registration, double major, dual enrollment, student exchange program (domestic), independent study, internships, liberal arts/career combination, student-designed major, study abroad.

FACILITIES

Housing: Coed, all-female, cooperative housing. **Library Holdings:** 280,000 bound volumes. 1,322 periodicals. 9,050 microforms. 5,800 audiovisuals. **Special Academic Facilities/Equipment:** Performing arts center, gallery, art museum, collection of contemporary art, center for curatorial studies, language lab, nursery school, ecology field station, archaeology field school, economics institute. **Computers:** School-owned computers available for student use.

EXTRACURRICULARS

Activities: Choral groups, dance, drama/theater, jazz band, literary magazine, music ensembles, musical theater, opera, radio station, student government, student newspaper, student-run film society, symphony orchestra, yearbook. **Organizations:** 90 registered organizations, 5 religious organizations. **Athletics (Intercollegiate):** *Men:* basketball, cross-country, rugby, soccer, squash, tennis, volleyball. *Women:* basketball, cross-country, soccer, squash, tennis, volleyball.

ADMISSIONS

Selectivity Rating: 95 (of 100). **Freshman Academic Profile:** Average high school GPA 3.5. 64% in top 10% of high school class, 90% in top 25% of high school class, 99% in top 50% of high school class. 67% from public high schools. Average SAT I Math 630, SAT I Math middle 50% range 590-690. Average SAT I Verbal 670, SAT I Verbal middle 50% range 650-750. TOEFL required of all international applicants, minimum TOEFL 600. **Basis for Candidate Selection:** *Very important factors considered include:* character/personal qualities, essays, extracurricular activities, recommendations, secondary school record, talent/ability, volunteer work. *Important factors considered include:* work experience. *Other factors considered include:* alumni/ae relation, class rank, geographical residence, interview, minority status, religious affiliation/commitment, standardized test scores, state residency. **Freshman Admission Requirements:** High school diploma or GED is required. *Academic units required/recommended:* 4 English recommended, 4 math recommended, 4 science recommended, 4 foreign language recommended, 4 social studies recommended, 4 history recommended. **Freshman Admission Statistics:** 3,118 applied, 36% accepted, 31% of those accepted enrolled. **Transfer Admission Requirements:** *Items required:* college transcript, essay. Minimum college GPA of 3.0 required. Lowest grade transferable C. **General Admission Information:** Application fee $50. Regular application deadline January 15. Nonfall registration accepted. Admission may be deferred for a maximum of 1 year. Credit offered for CEEB Advanced Placement tests.

COSTS AND FINANCIAL AID

Tuition $26,900. Room & board $8,134. Required fees $550. Average book expense $700. **Required Forms and Deadlines:** FAFSA, CSS/Financial Aid PROFILE, state aid form, noncustodial (divorced/separated) parent's statement, and business/farm supplement. Financial aid filing deadline February 15. Priority filing deadline February 1. **Notification of Awards:** Applicants will be notified of awards on or about April 1. **Types of Aid:** *Need-based scholarships/grants:* Pell, SEOG, state scholarships/grants, private scholarships, the school's own gift aid. *Loans:* FFEL Subsidized Stafford, FFEL Unsubsidized Stafford, FFEL PLUS, Federal Perkins, college/university loans from institutional funds (for international students only). **Student Employment:** Federal Work-Study Program available. Institutional employment available. Off-campus job opportunities are fair. **Financial Aid Statistics:** 60% freshmen, 61% undergrads receive some form of aid. Average freshman grant $18,282. Average freshman loan $3,351. Average income from on-campus job $1,000. **Financial Aid Phone:** 845-758-7526.

BARNARD COLLEGE

3009 Broadway, New York, NY 10027
Phone: 212-854-2014 **E-mail:** admissions@barnard.edu **CEEB Code:** 2038
Fax: 212-854-6220 **Web:** www.barnard.edu **ACT Code:** 2718

This private school was founded in 1889. It has a 4-acre campus.

STUDENTS AND FACULTY

Enrollment: 2,297. **Student Body:** Out-of-state 64%, international 3% (35 countries represented). **Ethnic Representation:** African American 5%, Asian 20%, Caucasian 67%, Hispanic 7%, Native American 1%. **Retention and Graduation:** 93% freshmen return for sophomore year. 77% freshmen graduate within 4 years. 27% grads go on to further study within 1 year. 1% grads pursue business degrees. 5% grads pursue law degrees. 6% grads pursue medical degrees. **Faculty:** Student/faculty ratio 10:1. 185 full-time faculty, 88% hold PhDs. 100% faculty teach undergrads.

ACADEMICS

Degrees: Bachelor's. **Academic Requirements:** General education including some course work in English (including composition), foreign languages, humanities, mathematics, sciences (biological or physical), social science. **Classes:** 10-19 students in an average class. Under 10 students in an average lab/discussion section. **Majors with Highest Enrollment:** English language and literature, general; psychology, general; economics, general. **Disciplines with Highest Percentage of Degrees Awarded:** Social sciences and history 35%, psychology 12%, English 12%, visual and performing arts 10%, biological life sciences 9%. **Special Study Options:** Accelerated program, cross registration, double major, dual enrollment, student exchange program (domestic), honors program, independent study, internships, liberal arts/career combination, student-designed major, study abroad, teacher certification program, independent scholars program, BA/BS in engineering and applied science.

FACILITIES

Housing: Coed, all-female, apartments for single students, housing for disabled students, rooms modified to accommodate disabled students. **Library Holdings:** 201,566 bound volumes. 544 periodicals. 17,565 microforms. 16,403 audiovisuals. **Special Academic Facilities/Equipment:** Professional theatre, infant-toddler center, greenhouse, academic computer center. **Computers:** School-owned computers available for student use.

EXTRACURRICULARS

Activities: Choral groups, concert band, dance, drama/theater, literary magazine, marching band, music ensembles, musical theater, opera, pep band, radio station, student government, student newspaper, student-run film society, symphony orchestra, yearbook. **Organizations:** 100 registered organizations, 1 honor society. **Athletics (Intercollegiate):** *Women:* basketball, crew, cross-country, diving, fencing, field hockey, lacrosse, rugby, soccer, softball, squash, swimming, tennis, track & field, volleyball.

ADMISSIONS

Selectivity Rating: 97 (of 100). **Freshman Academic Profile:** Average high school GPA 3.9. 84% in top 10% of high school class, 98% in top 25% of high school class, 100% in top 50% of high school class. 55% from public high schools. Average SAT I Math 670, SAT I Math middle 50% range 620-700. Average SAT I Verbal 660, SAT I Verbal middle 50% range 630-710. Average ACT 29, ACT middle 50% range 27-30. TOEFL required of all international applicants, minimum TOEFL 600. **Basis for Candidate Selection:** *Very important factors considered include:* essays, recommendations, secondary school record, standardized test scores. *Important factors considered include:* class rank, extracurricular activities, talent/ability, volunteer work. *Other factors considered include:* alumni/ae relation, character/personal qualities, geographical residence, interview, minority status, state residency, work experience. **Freshman Admission Requirements:** High school diploma or equivalent is not required. *Academic units required/recommended:* 17 total recommended; 4 English recommended, 3 math recommended, 3 science recommended, 2 science lab recommended, 3 foreign language recommended, 2 social studies recommended, 2 history recommended. **Freshman Admission Statistics:** 3,686 applied, 34% accepted, 43% of those accepted enrolled. **Transfer Admission Requirements:** *Items required:* high school transcript, college transcript, essay, standardized test score, statement of good standing from prior school. Minimum college GPA of 3.0 required. Lowest grade transferable C. **General Admission Information:** Application fee $45. Early decision application deadline November 15. Regular application deadline January 1. Nonfall registration accepted. Admission may be deferred for a maximum of 1 year. Credit and/or placement offered for CEEB Advanced Placement tests.

COSTS AND FINANCIAL AID

Tuition $24,090. Room & board $10,140. Required fees $1,180. Average book expense $900. **Required Forms and Deadlines:** FAFSA, institution's own financial aid form, CSS/Financial Aid PROFILE, state aid form, noncustodial (divorced/separated) parent's statement, business/farm supplement, Parent's individual and corporate and/or partnership federal income tax returns. Financial aid filing deadline February 1. **Notification of Awards:** Applicants will be notified of awards on or about April 1. **Types of Aid:** *Need-based scholarships/grants:* Pell, SEOG, state scholarships/grants, private scholarships, the school's own gift aid, New York Higher Educational Opportunity Program. *Loans:* FFEL Subsidized Stafford, FFEL Unsubsidized Stafford, FFEL PLUS, Federal Perkins, state loans, college/university loans from institutional funds. **Student Employment:** Federal Work-Study Program available. Institutional employment available. Off-campus job opportunities are excellent. **Financial Aid Statistics:** 41% freshmen, 41% undergrads receive some form of aid. Average freshman grant $21,914. Average freshman loan $2,625. Average income from on-campus job $1,700. **Financial Aid Phone:** 212-854-2154.

See page 926.

BARRY UNIVERSITY

11300 North East Second Avenue, Miami Shores, FL 33161-6695
Phone: 305-899-3100 **E-mail:** admissions@mail.barry.edu **CEEB Code:** 5053
Fax: 305-899-2971 **Web:** www.barry.edu **ACT Code:** 718

This private school, which is affiliated with the Roman Catholic Church, was founded in 1940. It has a 122-acre campus.

STUDENTS AND FACULTY

Enrollment: 5,622. **Student Body:** Male 33%, female 67%, out-of-state 12%, international 5% (80 countries represented). **Ethnic Representation:** African American 22%, Asian 1%, Caucasian 31%, Hispanic 36%. **Retention and Graduation:** 67% freshmen return for sophomore year. 23% freshmen graduate within 4 years. **Faculty:** Student/faculty ratio 12:1. 334 full-time faculty, 81% hold PhDs.

ACADEMICS

Degrees: Bachelor's, doctoral, first professional, master's, post-bachelor's certificate, post-master's certificate. **Academic Requirements:** General education including some course work in arts/fine arts, computer literacy,

English (including composition), humanities, mathematics, philosophy, sciences (biological or physical), social science, theology, orientation, and capstone course. **Classes:** 10-19 students in an average class. **Disciplines with Highest Percentage of Degrees Awarded:** Business/marketing 21%, education 18%, liberal arts/general studies 16%, health professions and related sciences 14%, computer and information sciences 9%. **Special Study Options:** Accelerated program, distance learning, double major, dual enrollment, English as a second language, honors program, independent study, internships, study abroad, teacher certification program.

FACILITIES

Housing: Coed, all-female, all-male, housing for disabled students. **Library Holdings:** 309,192 bound volumes. 1,653 periodicals. 581,751 microforms. 5,917 audiovisuals. **Special Academic Facilities/Equipment:** Human performance lab; broadcasting studio; radio station; athletic training room; cell biology/biotechnology labs; Classroom of Tomorrow, biomechanics lab; photography lab, darkroom, and studio; language lab; athletic training room. **Computers:** *Recommended operating system:* Windows NT/2000.

EXTRACURRICULARS

Activities: Choral groups, dance, drama/theater, literary magazine, music ensembles, musical theater, radio station, student government, student newspaper, television station. **Organizations:** 67 registered organizations, 20 honor societies, 5 religious organizations, 2 fraternities, 2 sororities. **Athletics (Intercollegiate):** *Men:* baseball, basketball, golf, soccer, tennis. *Women:* basketball, crew, golf, soccer, softball, tennis, volleyball.

ADMISSIONS

Selectivity Rating: 71 (of 100). **Freshman Academic Profile:** Average high school GPA 3.0. Average SAT I Math 485, SAT I Math middle 50% range 430-540. Average SAT I Verbal 495, SAT I Verbal middle 50% range 450-540. Average ACT 20, ACT middle 50% range 18-23. TOEFL required of all international applicants, minimum TOEFL 550. **Basis for Candidate Selection:** *Very important factors considered include:* secondary school record, standardized test scores. *Important factors considered include:* character/personal qualities, interview, talent/ability. *Other factors considered include:* class rank, essays, extracurricular activities, recommendations, volunteer work, work experience. **Freshman Admission Requirements:** High school diploma or GED is required. *Academic units required/recommended:* 12 total recommended; 4 English recommended, 3 math recommended, 3 science recommended, 3 social studies recommended. **Freshman Admission Statistics:** 2,407 applied, 72% accepted, 26% of those accepted enrolled. **Transfer Admission Requirements:** *Items required:* college transcript. Lowest grade transferable C. **General Admission Information:** Application fee $30. Nonfall registration accepted. Admission may be deferred for a maximum of 1 year. Credit offered for CEEB Advanced Placement tests.

COSTS AND FINANCIAL AID

Required Forms and Deadlines: FAFSA. No deadline for regular filing. **Notification of Awards:** Applicants will be notified of awards on a rolling basis beginning on or about January 25. **Types of Aid:** *Need-based scholarships/grants:* Pell, SEOG, state scholarships/grants, private scholarships, the school's own gift aid, Federal Nursing. *Loans:* FFEL Subsidized Stafford, FFEL Unsubsidized Stafford, FFEL PLUS, Federal Perkins, Federal Nursing, college/university loans from institutional funds, alternative loans. **Student Employment:** Federal Work-Study Program available. Off-campus job opportunities are good. **Financial Aid Statistics:** 73% freshmen, 76% undergrads receive some form of aid. **Financial Aid Phone:** 305-899-3673.

See page 928.

BARTON COLLEGE

Box 5000, College Station, Wilson, NC 27893
Phone: 252-399-6317 **E-mail:** enroll@barton.edu **CEEB Code:** 5016
Fax: 252-399-6572 **Web:** www.barton.edu **ACT Code:** 3066

This private school, which is affiliated with the Disciples of Christ Church, was founded in 1902. It has a 62-acre campus.

STUDENTS AND FACULTY

Enrollment: 1,245. **Student Body:** Male 31%, female 69%, out-of-state 23%, international 2%. **Ethnic Representation:** African American 19%, Asian 1%, Caucasian 78%, Hispanic 2%. **Retention and Graduation:** 65% freshmen return for sophomore year. 29% freshmen graduate within 4 years. 12% grads go on to further study within 1 year. 2% grads pursue business degrees. 2% grads pursue law degrees. 3% grads pursue medical degrees. **Faculty:** Student/faculty ratio 14:1. 77 full-time faculty, 53% hold PhDs. 100% faculty teach undergrads.

ACADEMICS

Degrees: Bachelor's. **Academic Requirements:** General education including some course work in arts/fine arts, computer literacy, English (including composition), history, humanities, mathematics, sciences (biological or physical), social science, physical education. **Classes:** 10-19 students in an average class. **Majors with Highest Enrollment:** Nursing/registered nurse training (RN, ASN, BSN, MSN); business administration/management; mass communications/media studies. **Disciplines with Highest Percentage of Degrees Awarded:** Business/marketing 27%, health professions and related sciences 17%, protective services/public administration 14%, education 11%, biological life sciences 6%. **Special Study Options:** Cooperative (work-study) program, independent study, internships, study abroad, teacher certification program, weekend college.

FACILITIES

Housing: Coed, all-female, fraternities and/or sororities. **Library Holdings:** 336,836 bound volumes. 437 periodicals. 292,748 microforms. 3,445 audiovisuals. **Special Academic Facilities/Equipment:** TV station, art museum, music recording studio, greenhouse. **Computers:** School-owned computers available for student use.

EXTRACURRICULARS

Activities: Choral groups, concert band, drama/theater, jazz band, literary magazine, music ensembles, student government, student newspaper, symphony orchestra, television station. **Organizations:** 32 registered organizations, 5 honor societies, 3 religious organizations, 4 fraternities (5% men join), 3 sororities (9% women join). **Athletics (Intercollegiate):** *Men:* baseball, basketball, cross-country, golf, soccer, tennis. *Women:* basketball, cheerleading, cross-country, soccer, softball, tennis, volleyball.

ADMISSIONS

Selectivity Rating: 63 (of 100). **Freshman Academic Profile:** Average high school GPA 2.9. 13% in top 10% of high school class, 31% in top 25% of high school class, 65% in top 50% of high school class. 80% from public high schools. SAT I Math middle 50% range 420-560. SAT I Verbal middle 50% range 400-560. TOEFL required of all international applicants, minimum TOEFL 525. **Basis for Candidate Selection:** *Very important factors considered include:* secondary school record, standardized test scores. *Important factors considered include:* class rank. *Other factors considered include:* character/personal qualities, essays, extracurricular activities, interview, recommendations, volunteer work. **Freshman Admission Requirements:** High school diploma or GED is required. *Academic units required/recommended:* 13 total required; 18 total recommended; 4 English required, 4 English recommended, 3 math required, 3 math recommended, 2 science required, 3 science recommended, 1 science lab required, 1 science lab recommended, 2 foreign language recommended, 3 social studies recommended, 1 elective required, 3 elective recommended. **Freshman Admission Statistics:** 945 applied, 82% accepted, 39% of those accepted enrolled. **Transfer Admission Requirements:** *Items required:* statement of good standing from prior school. Minimum college GPA of 2.0 required. Lowest grade transferable D. **General Admission Information:** Application fee $25. Nonfall registration accepted. Admission may be deferred. Placement offered for CEEB Advanced Placement tests.

COSTS AND FINANCIAL AID

Tuition $13,368. Room & board $5,028. Required fees $960. Average book expense $700. **Required Forms and Deadlines:** FAFSA. No deadline for regular filing. Priority filing deadline April 1. **Notification of Awards:** Applicants will be notified of awards on a rolling basis beginning on or about February 1. **Types of Aid:** *Need-based scholarships/grants:* Pell, SEOG, state scholarships/grants, private scholarships, the school's own gift aid. *Loans:* FFEL Subsidized Stafford, FFEL Unsubsidized Stafford, FFEL PLUS, Federal Perkins. **Student Employment:** Federal Work-Study Program available. Institutional employment available. Off-campus job opportunities are good. **Financial Aid Statistics:** 67% freshmen, 62% undergrads receive some form of aid. **Financial Aid Phone:** 800-345-4973.

BATES COLLEGE

22 Andrew Road, Lewiston, ME 04240
Phone: 207-786-6000 **E-mail:** admissions@bates.edu **CEEB Code:** 3076
Fax: 207-786-6025 **Web:** www.bates.edu **ACT Code:** 1634

This private school was founded in 1855. It has a 109-acre campus.

STUDENTS AND FACULTY

Enrollment: 1,738. **Student Body:** Out-of-state 89%, international 6%. **Ethnic Representation:** African American 2%, Asian 4%, Caucasian 89%,

Hispanic 2%. **Retention and Graduation:** 94% freshmen return for sophomore year. 82% freshmen graduate within 4 years. **Faculty:** Student/faculty ratio 10:1. 163 full-time faculty, 96% hold PhDs. 100% faculty teach undergrads.

ACADEMICS

Degrees: Bachelor's. **Academic Requirements:** General education including some course work in humanities, mathematics, sciences (biological or physical), social science. **Classes:** 10-19 students in an average class. 10-19 students in an average lab/discussion section. **Majors with Highest Enrollment:** English language and literature, general; psychology, general; political science and government, general. **Disciplines with Highest Percentage of Degrees Awarded:** Social sciences and history 30%, biological life sciences 13%, psychology 8%, foreign languages and literature 8%, English 8%. **Special Study Options:** Accelerated program, double major, student exchange program (domestic), honors program, independent study, internships, liberal arts/career combination, student-designed major, study abroad, teacher certification program.

FACILITIES

Housing: Coed, all-female, all-male, chemical-free, quiet/study and theme houses. **Library Holdings:** 568,750 bound volumes. 2,311 periodicals. 301,205 microforms. 29,196 audiovisuals. **Special Academic Facilities/Equipment:** Art gallery, Edmund S. Muskie Archives, language labs, planetarium, 600-acre conservation area on seacoast for environmental studies, scanning electron microscope. **Computers:** School-owned computers available for student use.

EXTRACURRICULARS

Activities: Choral groups, concert band, dance, drama/theater, jazz band, literary magazine, music ensembles, musical theater, pep band, radio station, student government, student newspaper, student-run film society, symphony orchestra, television station, yearbook. **Organizations:** 89 registered organizations, 7 religious organizations. **Athletics (Intercollegiate):** *Men:* baseball, basketball, crew, skiing (cross-country), cross-country, diving, football, golf, indoor track, lacrosse, skiing (alpine), skiing (Nordic), soccer, squash, swimming, tennis, track & field. *Women:* basketball, crew, skiing (cross-country), cross-country, diving, field hockey, golf, indoor track, lacrosse, skiing (alpine), skiing (Nordic), soccer, softball, squash, swimming, tennis, track & field, volleyball.

ADMISSIONS

Selectivity Rating: 98 (of 100). **Freshman Academic Profile:** 62% in top 10% of high school class, 93% in top 25% of high school class, 100% in top 50% of high school class. 56% from public high schools. Average SAT I Math 677, SAT I Math middle 50% range 630-720. Average SAT I Verbal 671, SAT I Verbal middle 50% range 630-710. TOEFL required of all international applicants, minimum TOEFL 200. **Basis for Candidate Selection:** *Very important factors considered include:* character/personal qualities, class rank, essays, extracurricular activities, interview, recommendations, secondary school record, talent/ability. *Other factors considered include:* alumni/ae relation, geographical residence, minority status, religious affiliation/commitment, standardized test scores, volunteer work. **Freshman Admission Requirements:** High school diploma is required and GED is not accepted. *Academic units required/recommended:* 15 total required; 19 total recommended; 4 English required, 4 English recommended, 3 math required, 4 math recommended, 2 science required, 3 science recommended, 1 science lab required, 1 science lab recommended, 2 foreign language required, 4 foreign language recommended. **Freshman Admission Statistics:** 4,012 applied, 28% accepted, 37% of those accepted enrolled. **Transfer Admission Requirements:** *Items required:* high school transcript, college transcript, essay, statement of good standing from prior school. Lowest grade transferable C. **General Admission Information:** Application fee $60. Early decision application deadline November 15. Regular application deadline January 15. Nonfall registration accepted. Admission may be deferred for a maximum of 1 year. Credit and/or placement offered for CEEB Advanced Placement tests.

COSTS AND FINANCIAL AID

Average book expense $1,750. **Required Forms and Deadlines:** FAFSA, CSS/Financial Aid PROFILE, noncustodial (divorced/separated) parent's statement and business/farm supplement. Priority filing deadline February 1. **Notification of Awards:** Applicants will be notified of awards on or about April 2. **Types of Aid:** *Need-based scholarships/grants:* Pell, SEOG, state scholarships/grants, private scholarships, the school's own gift aid. *Loans:* FFEL Subsidized Stafford, FFEL Unsubsidized Stafford, FFEL PLUS, Federal Perkins, state loans, college/university loans from institutional funds, private alternative loans. **Student Employment:** Federal Work-Study Program available. Institutional employment available. Off-campus job opportunities are good. **Financial Aid Statistics:** 46% freshmen, 39% undergrads receive some form of aid. Average freshman grant $21,160. Average freshman loan $2,500. Average income from on-campus job $1,300. **Financial Aid Phone:** 207-786-6096.

BAY PATH COLLEGE

588 Longmeadow Street, Longmeadow, MA 01106-2292
Phone: 413-565-1331 **E-mail:** admiss@baypath.edu
Fax: 413-565-1105 **Web:** www.baypath.edu

This private school was founded in 1897. It has a 47-acre campus.

STUDENTS AND FACULTY

Enrollment: 1,055. **Student Body:** Out-of-state 40%, international 2%. **Ethnic Representation:** African American 11%, Asian 2%, Caucasian 81%, Hispanic 6%. **Retention and Graduation:** 67% freshmen return for sophomore year. **Faculty:** Student/faculty ratio 15:1. 29 full-time faculty, 62% hold PhDs. 100% faculty teach undergrads.

ACADEMICS

Degrees: Associate's, bachelor's, certificate, master's. **Academic Requirements:** General education including some course work in computer literacy, English (including composition), history, humanities, sciences (biological or physical), social science, foundations of college. **Classes:** 10-19 students in an average class. 10-19 students in an average lab/discussion section. **Majors with Highest Enrollment:** Business/commerce, general; liberal arts and sciences/liberal studies; psychology, general. **Disciplines with Highest Percentage of Degrees Awarded:** Business/marketing 35%, liberal arts/general studies 24%, psychology 19%, health professions and related sciences 13%, law/legal studies 6%. **Special Study Options:** Cooperative (work-study) program, cross registration, English as a second language, honors program, independent study, internships, study abroad, weekend college, directed study program.

FACILITIES

Housing: All-female. **Library Holdings:** 42,375 bound volumes. 200 periodicals. 4,205 microforms. 3,152 audiovisuals. **Special Academic Facilities/Equipment:** Blake Student Commons, Bashevkin Academic Development Center, Breck Fitness Center, occupational therapy laboratory, design studio, and D'Amour Hall for Business, Technology and Communications. **Computers:** *Recommended operating system:* Windows 95. School-owned computers available for student use.

EXTRACURRICULARS

Activities: Choral groups, dance, drama/theater, literary magazine, musical theater, student government, yearbook. **Organizations:** 31 registered organizations, 2 honor societies, 1 religious organization. **Athletics (Intercollegiate):** *Women:* basketball, cross-country, soccer, softball, volleyball.

ADMISSIONS

Selectivity Rating: 63 (of 100). **Freshman Academic Profile:** Average high school GPA 3.0. 5% in top 10% of high school class, 19% in top 25% of high school class, 58% in top 50% of high school class. TOEFL required of all international applicants, minimum TOEFL 500. **Basis for Candidate Selection:** *Very important factors considered include:* secondary school record, standardized test scores. *Important factors considered include:* class rank, essays, extracurricular activities, recommendations, talent/ability, volunteer work. *Other factors considered include:* character/personal qualities, work experience. **Freshman Admission Requirements:** High school diploma or GED is required. *Academic units required/recommended:* 15 total required; 17 total recommended; 4 English required, 3 math required, 4 math recommended, 3 science required, 2 science lab required, 2 foreign language required, 3 foreign language recommended, 2 social studies required, 1 history required, 2 history recommended. **Freshman Admission Statistics:** 639 applied, 67% accepted, 34% of those accepted enrolled. **Transfer Admission Requirements:** *Items required:* high school transcript, college transcript, essay, statement of good standing from prior school. Minimum college GPA of 2.0 required. Lowest grade transferable C-. **General Admission Information:** Application fee $25.

COSTS AND FINANCIAL AID

Average book expense $900. **Required Forms and Deadlines:** FAFSA and institution's own financial aid form. No deadline for regular filing. Priority filing deadline March 15. **Notification of Awards:** Applicants will be notified of awards on a rolling basis. **Types of Aid:** *Need-based scholarships/grants:* Pell, SEOG, state scholarships/grants, private scholarships, the school's own gift aid. *Loans:* Direct Subsidized Stafford, Direct Unsubsidized Stafford, Direct PLUS, FFEL Subsidized Stafford, FFEL Unsubsidized Stafford, FFEL PLUS, Federal Perkins, state loans. **Student Employment:** Federal Work-Study Program available. Off-campus job opportunities are excellent. **Financial Aid Statistics:** 85% freshmen, 84% undergrads receive some form of aid. **Financial Aid Phone:** 413-565-1345.

See page 930.

BAYLOR UNIVERSITY

 $$$   

PO Box 97056, Waco, TX 76798-7056
Phone: 254-710-3435 **E-mail:** admissions_serv_office@baylor.edu **CEEB Code:** 6032
Fax: 254-710-3436 **Web:** www.baylor.edu **ACT Code:** 4062

This private school, which is affiliated with the Baptist Church, was founded in 1845. It has a 432-acre campus.

STUDENTS AND FACULTY

Enrollment: 11,987. **Student Body:** Male 42%, female 58%, out-of-state 16%, international 2% (90 countries represented). **Ethnic Representation:** African American 6%, Asian 5%, Caucasian 78%, Hispanic 8%, Native American 1%. **Retention and Graduation:** 84% freshmen return for sophomore year. 43% freshmen graduate within 4 years. **Faculty:** Student/faculty ratio 17:1. 756 full-time faculty, 76% hold PhDs. 90% faculty teach undergrads.

ACADEMICS

Degrees: Bachelor's, doctoral, first professional, master's, post-master's certificate. **Academic Requirements:** General education including some course work in arts/fine arts, English (including composition), foreign languages, history, humanities, mathematics, sciences (biological or physical), social science, religion. **Classes:** 20-29 students in an average class. 10-19 students in an average lab/discussion section. **Majors with Highest Enrollment:** Business administration/management; biology/biological sciences, general; psychology, general. **Disciplines with Highest Percentage of Degrees Awarded:** Business/marketing 36%, education 9%, social sciences and history 7%, health professions and related sciences 7%, communications/communication technologies 6%. **Special Study Options:** Accelerated program, double major, honors program, internships, student-designed major, study abroad, teacher certification program.

FACILITIES

Housing: All-female, all-male, apartments for married students, apartments for single students, housing for disabled students, housing for international students. **Library Holdings:** 2,252,780 bound volumes. 8,429 periodicals. 2,182,670 microforms. 73,228 audiovisuals. **Special Academic Facilities/Equipment:** Language and environmental studies labs, natural science museum, high definition television, Armstrong Browning Library, Texas Collection Library, Strecker Museum/Bill & Vara Daniel Historical Village, TV station, radio station. **Computers:** School-owned computers available for student use.

EXTRACURRICULARS

Activities: Choral groups, concert band, dance, drama/theater, jazz band, literary magazine, marching band, music ensembles, musical theater, opera, pep band, radio station, student government, student newspaper, student-run film society, symphony orchestra, television station, yearbook. **Organizations:** 275 registered organizations, 35 honor societies, 13 religious organizations, 18 fraternities (15% men join), 15 sororities (17% women join). **Athletics (Intercollegiate):** *Men:* baseball, basketball, cross-country, football, golf, indoor track, tennis, track & field. *Women:* basketball, cross-country, golf, indoor track, soccer, softball, tennis, track & field, volleyball.

ADMISSIONS

Selectivity Rating: 81 (of 100). **Freshman Academic Profile:** 40% in top 10% of high school class, 68% in top 25% of high school class, 92% in top 50% of high school class. SAT I Math middle 50% range 550-650. SAT I Verbal middle 50% range 530-630. ACT middle 50% range 22-27. TOEFL required of all international applicants, minimum TOEFL 540. **Basis for Candidate Selection:** *Very important factors considered include:* class rank, secondary school record, standardized test scores. *Other factors considered include:* alumni/ae relation, character/personal qualities, essays, extracurricular activities, geographical residence, interview, recommendations, religious affiliation/commitment, state residency, talent/ability, volunteer work. **Freshman Admission Requirements:** High school diploma or GED is required. *Academic units required/recommended:* 4 English required, 3 math required, 2 science required, 2 foreign language required, 1 social studies required, 1 history required. **Freshman Admission Statistics:** 7,431 applied, 81% accepted, 43% of those accepted enrolled. **Transfer Admission Requirements:** *Items required:* college transcript, essay. Minimum high school GPA of 2.5 required. Minimum college GPA of 2.5 required. Lowest grade transferable C. **General Admission Information:** Application fee $35. Priority application deadline March 1. Nonfall registration accepted. Credit and/or placement offered for CEEB Advanced Placement tests.

COSTS AND FINANCIAL AID

Tuition $16,750. Room & board $5,434. Required fees $1,680. Average book expense $1,460. **Required Forms and Deadlines:** FAFSA. No deadline for regular filing. Priority filing deadline March 1. **Notification of Awards:** Applicants will be notified of awards on a rolling basis beginning on or about March 1. **Types of Aid:** *Need-based scholarships/grants:* Pell, SEOG, state scholarships/grants, the school's own gift aid, Federal Nursing. *Loans:* FFEL Subsidized Stafford, FFEL Unsubsidized Stafford, FFEL PLUS, Federal Perkins, Federal Nursing, state loans, college/university loans from institutional funds. **Student Employment:** Federal Work-Study Program available. Institutional employment available. Off-campus job opportunities are excellent. **Financial Aid Statistics:** 49% freshmen, 44% undergrads receive some form of aid. **Financial Aid Phone:** 254-710-2611.

BEACON COLLEGE

105 E. Main Street, Leesburg, FL 34748
Phone: 352-787-7249 **E-mail:** admissions@beaconcollege.edu
Fax: 352-787-0721 **Web:** www.beaconcollege.edu

This private school was founded in 1989.

STUDENTS AND FACULTY

Enrollment: 152. **Student Body:** Out-of-state 86%. **Ethnic Representation:** African American 11%, Asian 3%, Caucasian 83%, Hispanic 4%. **Faculty:** Student/faculty ratio 6:1. 10 full-time faculty, 40% hold PhDs.

ACADEMICS

Degrees: Associate's, bachelor's. **Academic Requirements:** General education including some course work in arts/fine arts, computer literacy, English (including composition), humanities, mathematics, sciences (biological or physical), social science. **Classes:** Under 10 students in an average class. **Disciplines with Highest Percentage of Degrees Awarded:** Human services 3%. **Special Study Options:** Cooperative (work-study) program, internships.

FACILITIES

Housing: All students live in College-leased apartments within the community of Leesburg. The College is in the process of building its own apartment complex. **Library Holdings:** 45,389 bound volumes. 161 periodicals. 0 microforms. 446 audiovisuals. **Computers:** School-owned computers available for student use.

EXTRACURRICULARS

Activities: Drama/theater, student government, yearbook.

ADMISSIONS

Selectivity Rating: 63 (of 100). **Basis for Candidate Selection:** *Very important factors considered include:* interview, recommendations. *Important factors considered include:* character/personal qualities, secondary school record. *Other factors considered include:* extracurricular activities, talent/ability, volunteer work, work experience. **Freshman Admission Requirements:** High school diploma or GED is required. **Freshman Admission Statistics:** 61 applied, 36% accepted, 64% of those accepted enrolled. **Transfer Admission Requirements:** *Items required:* high school transcript, college transcript, essay, interview. Lowest grade transferable C. **General Admission Information:** Application fee $50. Nonfall registration accepted.

COSTS AND FINANCIAL AID

Average book expense $300. **Types of Aid:** *Need-based scholarships/grants:* Pell, SEOG, state scholarships/grants, private scholarships, the school's own gift aid. *Loans:* FFEL Subsidized Stafford, FFEL Unsubsidized Stafford, FFEL PLUS, Federal Perkins, college/university loans from institutional funds. **Student Employment:** Off-campus job opportunities are good. **Financial Aid Statistics:** Average income from on-campus job $6,000. **Financial Aid Phone:** 352-787-7660.

BECKER COLLEGE

61 Sever Street, Worcester, MA 01609
Phone: 508-791-9241 **E-mail:** admissions@beckercollege.edu **CEEB Code:** 3079
Fax: 508-890-1500 **Web:** www.beckercollege.edu **ACT Code:** 1787

This private school was founded in 1784. It has a 100-acre campus.

STUDENTS AND FACULTY

Enrollment: 1,577. **Student Body:** Male 27%, female 73%, out-of-state 57%, international students represent 12 countries. **Ethnic Representation:** African American 4%, Asian 2%, Caucasian 50%, Hispanic 3%. **Retention and Graduation:** 72% freshmen return for sophomore year. 46% grads go on to further study within 1 year. **Faculty:** Student/faculty ratio 15:1. 39 full-time faculty, 23% hold PhDs. 100% faculty teach undergrads.

ACADEMICS

Degrees: Associate's, bachelor's, certificate, terminal, transfer. **Academic Requirements:** General education including some course work in computer literacy, English (including composition), humanities, mathematics, sciences (biological or physical), social science. **Majors with Highest Enrollment:** Veterinary sciences/veterinary clinical sciences, general (certificate, MS, PhD); business administration/management; psychology, general. **Disciplines with Highest Percentage of Degrees Awarded:** Business/marketing 41%, psychology 17%, parks and recreation 10%, health professions and related sciences 10%, protective services/public administration 9%. **Special Study Options:** Accelerated program, cooperative (work-study) program, cross registration, distance learning, dual enrollment, independent study, internships, liberal arts/career combination, student-designed major, study abroad, teacher certification program.

FACILITIES

Housing: Coed, all-female, all-male, housing for disabled students. **Library Holdings:** 65,000 bound volumes. 400 periodicals. 2,230 microforms. 2,900 audiovisuals. **Special Academic Facilities/Equipment:** Veterinary clinic, motion analysis lab, daycare center, preschool facility. **Computers:** School-owned computers available for student use.

EXTRACURRICULARS

Activities: Dance, radio station, student government, student newspaper, yearbook. **Organizations:** 30 registered organizations, 3 honor societies. **Athletics (Intercollegiate):** *Men:* baseball, basketball, cross-country, equestrian, golf, soccer, tennis. *Women:* basketball, cross-country, equestrian, field hockey, soccer, softball, tennis, volleyball.

ADMISSIONS

Selectivity Rating: 63 (of 100). **Freshman Academic Profile:** Average high school GPA 2.7. TOEFL required of all international applicants, minimum TOEFL 500. **Basis for Candidate Selection:** *Important factors considered include:* essays, extracurricular activities, recommendations, secondary school record, talent/ability. *Other factors considered include:* alumni/ae relation, character/personal qualities, class rank, interview, standardized test scores, volunteer work, work experience. **Freshman Admission Requirements:** High school diploma or GED is required. **Freshman Admission Statistics:** 1,309 applied, 90% accepted, 30% of those accepted enrolled. **Transfer Admission Requirements:** *Items required:* high school transcript, college transcript. Minimum high school GPA of 2.0 required. Minimum college GPA of 2.0 required. Lowest grade transferable C-. **General Admission Information:** Application fee $25. Nonfall registration accepted. Admission may be deferred for a maximum of 1 year. Credit and/or placement offered for CEEB Advanced Placement tests.

COSTS AND FINANCIAL AID

Tuition $14,200. Room & board $7,550. Required fees $970. Average book expense $1,000. **Required Forms and Deadlines:** FAFSA. No deadline for regular filing. Priority filing deadline March 15. **Notification of Awards:** Applicants will be notified of awards on a rolling basis beginning on or about March 15. **Types of Aid:** *Need-based scholarships/grants:* Pell, SEOG, state scholarships/grants, private scholarships, the school's own gift aid. *Loans:* FFEL Subsidized Stafford, FFEL Unsubsidized Stafford, FFEL PLUS, state loans. **Student Employment:** Federal Work-Study Program available. Institutional employment available. Off-campus job opportunities are good. **Financial Aid Statistics:** 86% freshmen, 88% undergrads receive some form of aid. **Financial Aid Phone:** 508-791-9241.

See page 932.

BELHAVEN COLLEGE

1500 Peachtree Street, Jackson, MS 39202
Phone: 601-968-5940 **E-mail:** admissions@belhaven.edu **CEEB Code:** 1055
Fax: 601-968-8946 **Web:** www.belhaven.edu **ACT Code:** 2180

This private school, which is affiliated with the Presbyterian Church, was founded in 1883. It has a 42-acre campus.

STUDENTS AND FACULTY

Enrollment: 1,467. **Student Body:** Male 36%, female 64%, out-of-state 30%, international 1%. **Ethnic Representation:** African American 33%, Asian 1%, Caucasian 65%, Hispanic 1%. **Retention and Graduation:** 73% freshmen return for sophomore year. 40% freshmen graduate within 4 years. **Faculty:** Student/faculty ratio 15:1. 49 full-time faculty, 85% hold PhDs. 100% faculty teach undergrads.

ACADEMICS

Degrees: Associate's, bachelor's, certificate, master's. **Academic Requirements:** General education including some course work in arts/fine arts, English (including composition), foreign languages, history, mathematics, sciences (biological or physical), biblical studies, ethics in the marketplace. **Classes:** 10-19 students in an average class. 10-19 students in an average lab/discussion section. **Disciplines with Highest Percentage of Degrees Awarded:** Business/marketing 42%, education 11%, psychology 11%, biological life sciences 8%, computer and information sciences 6%. **Special Study Options:** Accelerated program, double major, dual enrollment, English as a second language, honors program, independent study, internships, study abroad, teacher certification program.

FACILITIES

Housing: All-female, all-male. **Library Holdings:** 108,042 bound volumes. 541 periodicals. 8,965 microforms. 3,344 audiovisuals. **Computers:** School-owned computers available for student use.

EXTRACURRICULARS

Activities: Choral groups, dance, drama/theater, literary magazine, music ensembles, student government, student newspaper, yearbook. **Organizations:** 29 registered organizations, 7 honor societies, 4 religious organizations. **Athletics (Intercollegiate):** *Men:* baseball, basketball, cheerleading, cross-country, football, golf, soccer, tennis. *Women:* basketball, cheerleading, cross-country, golf, soccer, softball, tennis, volleyball.

ADMISSIONS

Selectivity Rating: 67 (of 100). **Freshman Academic Profile:** Average high school GPA 3.3. Average SAT I Math 550, SAT I Math middle 50% range 490-600. Average SAT I Verbal 580, SAT I Verbal middle 50% range 490-660. Average ACT 24, ACT middle 50% range 20-26. TOEFL required of all international applicants, minimum TOEFL 500. **Basis for Candidate Selection:** *Very important factors considered include:* standardized test scores. *Other factors considered include:* alumni/ae relation, character/personal qualities, extracurricular activities, interview, recommendations, secondary school record, talent/ability. **Freshman Admission Requirements:** High school diploma or GED is required. *Academic units required/recommended:* 16 total required; 4 English required, 2 math required, 1 science required, 2 foreign language recommended, 1 social studies required, 8 elective required. **Freshman Admission Statistics:** 524 applied, 70% accepted, 57% of those accepted enrolled. **Transfer Admission Requirements:** *Items required:* college transcript. Minimum college GPA of 2.0 required. Lowest grade transferable D. **General Admission Information:** Application fee $25. Nonfall registration accepted. Admission may be deferred for a maximum of 1 year. Credit and/or placement offered for CEEB Advanced Placement tests.

COSTS AND FINANCIAL AID

Tuition $10,990. Room & board $4,440. Required fees $610. Average book expense $1,400. **Required Forms and Deadlines:** FAFSA and state aid form. Priority filing deadline March 1. **Notification of Awards:** Applicants will be notified of awards on a rolling basis beginning on or about February 1. **Types of Aid:** *Need-based scholarships/grants:* Pell, SEOG, state scholarships/grants, private scholarships, the school's own gift aid. *Loans:* FFEL Subsidized Stafford, FFEL Unsubsidized Stafford, FFEL PLUS, Federal Perkins, state loans. **Student Employment:** Federal Work-Study Program available. Institutional employment available. Off-campus job opportunities are good. **Financial Aid Statistics:** 92% freshmen, 93% undergrads receive some form of aid. Average freshman grant $3,187. Average freshman loan $2,625. Average income from on-campus job $1,545. **Financial Aid Phone:** 601-968-5933.

BELLARMINE UNIVERSITY

2001 Newburg Road, Louisville, KY 40205
Phone: 502-452-8131 **E-mail:** admissions@bellarmine.edu **CEEB Code:** 1056
Fax: 502-452-8002 **Web:** www.bellarmine.edu **ACT Code:** 1490

This private school, which is affiliated with the Roman Catholic Church, was founded in 1950. It has a 124-acre campus.

STUDENTS AND FACULTY

Enrollment: 2,373. **Student Body:** Male 36%, female 64%, out-of-state 31%, international 1% (21 countries represented). **Ethnic Representation:** African American 3%, Asian 1%, Caucasian 94%, Hispanic 1%. **Retention and Graduation:** 83% freshmen return for sophomore year. 44% freshmen graduate within 4 years. 15% grads go on to further study within 1 year. 2% grads pursue business degrees. 2% grads pursue law degrees. 2% grads pursue medical degrees. **Faculty:** Student/faculty ratio 14:1. 101 full-time faculty, 79% hold PhDs. 98% faculty teach undergrads.

ACADEMICS

Degrees: Bachelor's, master's, post-master's certificate. **Academic Requirements:** General education including some course work in arts/fine arts, English (including composition), history, humanities, mathematics, philosophy, sciences (biological or physical), social science, theology, American experience, transcultural experience. **Classes:** 20-29 students in an average class. **Disciplines with Highest Percentage of Degrees Awarded:** Business/marketing 25%, health professions and related sciences 18%, social sciences and history 12%, psychology 9%, biological life sciences 8%. **Special Study Options:** Accelerated program, cross registration, double major, honors program, independent study, internships, study abroad, teacher certification program, Washington Semester program.

FACILITIES

Housing: Coed, all-female, all-male, housing for disabled students, suites. **Library Holdings:** 97,737 bound volumes. 1,758 periodicals. 625,768 microforms. 4,784 audiovisuals. **Special Academic Facilities/Equipment:** Art gallery, Thomas Merton Center. **Computers:** School-owned computers available for student use.

EXTRACURRICULARS

Activities: Choral groups, concert band, dance, drama/theater, jazz band, literary magazine, music ensembles, musical theater, opera, pep band, student government, student newspaper, yearbook. **Organizations:** 50 registered organizations, 6 honor societies, 3 religious organizations, 2 fraternities (3% men join), 1 sorority (3% women join). **Athletics (Intercollegiate):** *Men:* baseball, basketball, cheerleading, cross-country, golf, soccer, tennis, track & field. *Women:* basketball, cheerleading, cross-country, field hockey, golf, soccer, softball, tennis, track & field, volleyball.

ADMISSIONS

Selectivity Rating: 75 (of 100). **Freshman Academic Profile:** Average high school GPA 3.5. 28% in top 10% of high school class, 55% in top 25% of high school class, 79% in top 50% of high school class. 50% from public high schools. Average SAT I Math 576, SAT I Math middle 50% range 490-620. Average SAT I Verbal 576, SAT I Verbal middle 50% range 500-600. Average ACT 24, ACT middle 50% range 22-26. TOEFL required of all international applicants, minimum TOEFL 550. **Basis for Candidate Selection:** *Very important factors considered include:* secondary school record, standardized test scores. *Important factors considered include:* class rank, essays, extracurricular activities, recommendations, volunteer work. *Other factors considered include:* alumni/ae relation, character/personal qualities, interview, minority status, talent/ability, work experience. **Freshman Admission Requirements:** High school diploma or GED is required. *Academic units required/recommended:* 4 English required, 3 math required, 4 math recommended, 2 science required, 3 science recommended, 2 foreign language recommended, 2 social studies required. **Freshman Admission Statistics:** 974 applied, 87% accepted, 39% of those accepted enrolled. **Transfer Admission Requirements:** *Items required:* college transcript. Minimum college GPA of 2.5 required. Lowest grade transferable D. **General Admission Information:** Application fee $25. Priority application deadline January 15. Regular application deadline August 15. Nonfall registration accepted. Admission may be deferred for a maximum of 1 year. Credit offered for CEEB Advanced Placement tests.

COSTS AND FINANCIAL AID

Tuition $13,590. Room & board $4,160. Required fees $170. Average book expense $750. **Required Forms and Deadlines:** FAFSA. No deadline for regular filing. Priority filing deadline March 1. **Notification of Awards:** Applicants will be notified of awards on a rolling basis beginning on or about April 1. **Types of Aid:** *Need-based scholarships/grants:* Pell, SEOG, state scholarships/grants, the school's own gift aid. *Loans:* FFEL Subsidized Stafford, FFEL Unsubsidized Stafford, FFEL PLUS, Federal Perkins, college/university loans from institutional funds. **Student Employment:** Federal Work-Study Program available. Institutional employment available. Off-campus job opportunities are excellent. **Financial Aid Statistics:** 64% freshmen receive some form of aid. Average freshman grant $4,742. Average freshman loan $2,894. Average income from on-campus job $1,443. **Financial Aid Phone:** 502-452-8124.

BELLEVUE UNIVERSITY

1000 Galvin Road South, Bellevue, NE 68005
Phone: 402-293-3766 **E-mail:** bellevue_u@scholars.bellevue.edu
Fax: 402-293-3730 **Web:** www.bellevue.edu **ACT Code:** 2437

This private school was founded in 1966. It has a 20-acre campus.

STUDENTS AND FACULTY

Enrollment: 3,350. **Student Body:** Male 49%, female 51%, international 6%. **Ethnic Representation:** African American 6%, Asian 1%, Caucasian 88%, Hispanic 3%, Native American 1%. **Faculty:** Student/faculty ratio 23:1. 63 full-time faculty, 47% hold PhDs.

ACADEMICS

Degrees: Bachelor's, certificate, diploma, master's. **Academic Requirements:** General education including some course work in English (including composition), humanities, mathematics, sciences (biological or physical), social science, signature series. **Majors with Highest Enrollment:** Business/commerce, general; accounting; computer systems networking and telecommunications. **Disciplines with Highest Percentage of Degrees Awarded:** Business/marketing 75%, psychology 10%, computer and information sciences 8%, protective services/public administration 3%, health professions and related sciences 3%. **Special Study Options:** Accelerated program, cross registration, distance learning, double major, dual enrollment, English as a second language, independent study, internships, liberal arts/career combination, weekend college.

FACILITIES

Housing: Apartments for single students. **Library Holdings:** 84,524 bound volumes. 7,564 periodicals. 14,349 microforms. 3,314 audiovisuals. **Computers:** School-owned computers available for student use.

EXTRACURRICULARS

Activities: Literary magazine, student government, student newspaper. **Athletics (Intercollegiate):** *Men:* baseball, basketball, soccer. *Women:* soccer, softball, volleyball.

ADMISSIONS

Selectivity Rating: 68 (of 100). **Freshman Academic Profile:** 10% in top 10% of high school class, 39% in top 25% of high school class, 89% in top 50% of high school class. TOEFL required of all international applicants, minimum TOEFL 500. **Freshman Admission Requirements:** High school diploma or GED is required. *Academic units required/recommended:* 3 English recommended, 3 math recommended, 3 science recommended, 3 foreign language recommended, 3 social studies recommended, 3 history recommended, 3 elective recommended. **Transfer Admission Requirements:** *Items required:* high school transcript, college transcript. Lowest grade transferable D. **General Admission Information:** Application fee $25. Nonfall registration accepted. Admission may be deferred for a maximum of 1 year.

COSTS AND FINANCIAL AID

Tuition $4,200. Required fees $75. Average book expense $1,000. **Required Forms and Deadlines:** FAFSA and institution's own financial aid form. No deadline for regular filing. **Notification of Awards:** Applicants will be notified of awards on a rolling basis beginning on or about April 1. **Types of Aid:** *Need-based scholarships/grants:* Pell, SEOG, state scholarships/grants. *Loans:* FFEL Subsidized Stafford, FFEL Unsubsidized Stafford, FFEL PLUS. **Student Employment:** Federal Work-Study Program available. Off-campus job opportunities are good. **Financial Aid Statistics:** 84% undergrads receive some form of aid. Average freshman grant $2,421. Average freshman loan $4,106. **Financial Aid Phone:** 402-293-3816.

BELMONT ABBEY COLLEGE

100 Belmont-Mount Holly Road, Belmont, NC 28012
Phone: 704-825-6665 **E-mail:** admissions@bac.edu **CEEB Code:** 5055
Fax: 704-825-6220 **Web:** www.belmontabbeycollege.edu **ACT Code:** 3070

This private school, which is affiliated with the Roman Catholic Church, was founded in 1876. It has a 650-acre campus.

STUDENTS AND FACULTY

Enrollment: 883. **Student Body:** Male 41%, female 59%, out-of-state 32%, international 3% (16 countries represented). **Ethnic Representation:** African American 10%, Asian 1%, Caucasian 79%, Hispanic 4%. **Retention and Graduation:** 71% freshmen return for sophomore year. 34% freshmen graduate within 4 years. 20% grads go on to further study within 1 year. 15% grads pursue business degrees. 2% grads pursue law degrees. **Faculty:** Student/faculty ratio 15:1. 43 full-time faculty, 81% hold PhDs. 100% faculty teach undergrads.

ACADEMICS

Degrees: Bachelor's. **Academic Requirements:** General education including some course work in arts/fine arts, computer literacy, English (including composition), history, humanities, mathematics, philosophy, sciences (biological or physical), social science, theology, great books, international studies. **Classes:** 10-19 students in an average class. 10-19 students in an average lab/discussion section. **Disciplines with Highest Percentage of Degrees Awarded:** Business/marketing 42%, education 22%, psychology 10%, protective services/public administration 6%, health professions and related sciences 6%. **Special Study Options:** Accelerated program, cooperative (work-study) program, distance learning, double major, dual enrollment, external degree program, honors program, independent study, internships, study abroad, teacher certification program, weekend college.

FACILITIES

Housing: Coed, all-male, apartments for single students. **Library Holdings:** 206,285 bound volumes. 643 periodicals. 126,726 microforms. 6,912 audiovisuals. **Special Academic Facilities/Equipment:** Museum with rare book collection. **Computers:** *Recommended operating system:* Windows 95. School-owned computers available for student use.

EXTRACURRICULARS

Activities: Choral groups, drama/theater, literary magazine, musical theater, student government, student newspaper, student-run film society, yearbook. **Organizations:** 14 registered organizations, 5 honor societies, 1 religious organization, 5 fraternities (20% men join), 4 sororities (20% women join). **Athletics (Intercollegiate):** *Men:* baseball, basketball, cross-country, golf, soccer, tennis, wrestling. *Women:* basketball, cheerleading, cross-country, soccer, softball, tennis, volleyball.

ADMISSIONS

Selectivity Rating: 65 (of 100). **Freshman Academic Profile:** Average high school GPA 3.0. 1% in top 10% of high school class, 10% in top 25% of high school class, 39% in top 50% of high school class. 65% from public high schools. Average SAT I Math 505, SAT I Math middle 50% range 430-540. Average SAT I Verbal 508, SAT I Verbal middle 50% range 430-540. Average ACT 19, ACT middle 50% range 18-23. TOEFL required of all international applicants, minimum TOEFL 550. **Basis for Candidate Selection:** *Very important factors considered include:* character/personal qualities, secondary school record, standardized test scores. *Important factors considered include:* alumni/ae relation, class rank, extracurricular activities, interview, volunteer work. *Other factors considered include:* essays, recommendations, talent/ability, work experience. **Freshman Admission Requirements:** High school diploma or GED is required. *Academic units required/recommended:* 16 total required; 4 English required, 3 math required, 4 math recommended, 2 science required, 2 foreign language required, 3 foreign language recommended, 2 social studies required, 3 elective required. **Freshman Admission Statistics:** 1,112 applied, 70% accepted, 29% of those accepted enrolled. **Transfer Admission Requirements:** *Items required:* college transcript. Minimum college GPA of 2.0 required. Lowest grade transferable C. **General Admission Information:** Application fee $35. Regular application deadline August 2. Nonfall registration accepted. Admission may be deferred for a maximum of 1 year. Credit offered for CEEB Advanced Placement tests.

COSTS AND FINANCIAL AID

Tuition $13,358. Room & board $7,200. Required fees $672. Average book expense $750. **Required Forms and Deadlines:** FAFSA. No deadline for regular filing. Priority filing deadline April 2. **Notification of Awards:** Applicants will be notified of awards on a rolling basis beginning on or about March 10. **Types of Aid:** *Need-based scholarships/grants:* Pell, SEOG, state scholarships/grants, private scholarships, the school's own gift aid. *Loans:* Direct Subsidized Stafford, Direct Unsubsidized Stafford, Direct PLUS, Federal Perkins, state loans. **Student Employment:** Federal Work-Study Program available. Institutional employment available. Off-campus job opportunities are excellent. **Financial Aid Statistics:** 83% freshmen, 87% undergrads receive some form of aid. Average freshman grant $7,869. Average freshman loan $2,625. Average income from on-campus job $1,600. **Financial Aid Phone:** 888-222-0110.

BELMONT UNIVERSITY

1900 Belmont Boulevard, Nashville, TN 37212-3757
Phone: 615-460-6785 **E-mail:** buadmission@mail.belmont.edu **CEEB Code:** 1058
Fax: 615-460-5434 **Web:** www.belmont.edu **ACT Code:** 3946

This private school, which is affiliated with the Baptist Church, was founded in 1951. It has a 55-acre campus.

STUDENTS AND FACULTY

Enrollment: 2,800. **Student Body:** Male 40%, female 60%, out-of-state 54%, international 2% (28 countries represented). **Ethnic Representation:** African American 4%, Asian 1%, Caucasian 91%, Hispanic 1%. **Retention and Graduation:** 77% freshmen return for sophomore year. 35% freshmen graduate within 4 years. 15% grads go on to further study within 1 year. 4% grads pursue business degrees. 1% grads pursue law degrees. 2% grads pursue medical degrees. **Faculty:** Student/faculty ratio 12:1. 196 full-time faculty, 66% hold PhDs. 99% faculty teach undergrads.

ACADEMICS

Degrees: Bachelor's, doctoral, master's, post-bachelor's certificate, post-master's certificate. **Academic Requirements:** General education including some course work in arts/fine arts, computer literacy, English (including composition), foreign languages, history, humanities, mathematics, philosophy, sciences (biological or physical), social science. **Classes:** 10-19 students in an average class. Under 10 students in an average lab/discussion section. **Majors with Highest Enrollment:** Business administration/management; music performance, general; music management and merchandising. **Disciplines with Highest Percentage of Degrees Awarded:** Visual and performing arts 34%, business/marketing 20%, liberal arts/general studies 10%, health professions and related sciences 6%, communications/communication technologies 4%. **Special Study Options:** Accelerated program, cooperative (work-study) program, distance learning, double major, honors program, independent study, internships, student-designed major, study abroad, teacher certification program.

FACILITIES

Housing: Coed, all-female, all-male, apartments for married students, apartments for single students, housing for international students, international house, language house, philosophy house. **Library Holdings:** 184,835 bound volumes. 1,311 periodicals. 18,111 microforms. 26,289 audiovisuals. **Special Academic Facilities/Equipment:** Language lab, recording studio, the Belmont Mansion, Little Theatre. **Computers:** *Recommended operating system:* Windows 95. School-owned computers available for student use.

EXTRACURRICULARS

Activities: Choral groups, concert band, dance, drama/theater, jazz band, literary magazine, marching band, music ensembles, musical theater, pep band, radio station, student government, student newspaper, symphony orchestra, television station. **Organizations:** 52 registered organizations, 17 honor societies, 4 religious organizations, 2 fraternities (6% men join), 2 sororities (8% women join). **Athletics (Intercollegiate):** *Men:* baseball, basketball, cross-country, golf, soccer, tennis, track & field. *Women:* basketball, cross-country, golf, soccer, softball, tennis, track & field, volleyball.

ADMISSIONS

Selectivity Rating: 73 (of 100). **Freshman Academic Profile:** Average high school GPA 3.4. 30% in top 10% of high school class, 60% in top 25% of high school class, 90% in top 50% of high school class. 50% from public high schools. Average SAT I Math 569, SAT I Math middle 50% range 520-620. Average SAT I Verbal 579, SAT I Verbal middle 50% range 530-630. Average ACT 24, ACT middle 50% range 22-27. TOEFL required of all international applicants, minimum TOEFL 500. **Basis for Candidate Selection:** *Very important factors considered include:* class rank, secondary school record, standardized test scores. *Important factors considered include:* essays, recommendations. *Other factors considered include:* alumni/ae relation, extracurricular activities, interview, minority status, religious affiliation/commitment, talent/ability. **Freshman Admission Requirements:** High school diploma or GED is required. *Academic units required/recommended:* 18 total required; 4 English required, 3 math required, 4 math recommended, 2 science required, 3 science recommended, 2 foreign language required, 2 foreign language recommended, 2 social studies required, 2 social studies recommended. **Freshman Admission Statistics:** 1,346 applied, 78% accepted, 50% of those accepted enrolled. **Transfer Admission Requirements:** *Items required:* high school transcript, college transcript, essay, standardized test scores. Minimum college GPA of 2.0 required. Lowest grade transferable C. **General Admission Information:** Application fee $35. Priority application deadline March 15. Regular application deadline May 1. Nonfall registration accepted. Admission may be deferred for a maximum of 1 year. Credit and/or placement offered for CEEB Advanced Placement tests.

COSTS AND FINANCIAL AID

Tuition $13,690. Room & board $8,029. Required fees $760. Average book expense $850. **Required Forms and Deadlines:** FAFSA. No deadline for regular filing. Priority filing deadline March 1. **Notification of Awards:** Applicants will be notified of awards on a rolling basis beginning on or about March 15. **Types of Aid:** *Need-based scholarships/grants:* Pell, SEOG, state scholarships/grants, private scholarships, the school's own gift aid. *Loans:* FFEL Subsidized Stafford, FFEL Unsubsidized Stafford, FFEL PLUS, Federal Perkins, college/university loans from institutional funds. **Student Employment:** Federal Work-Study Program available. Institutional employment available. Off-campus job opportunities are good. **Financial Aid Statistics:** 47% freshmen, 47% undergrads receive some form of aid. Average freshman grant $2,554. Average freshman loan $2,284. Average income from on-campus job $4,000. **Financial Aid Phone:** 615-460-6403.

BELOIT COLLEGE

700 College Street, Beloit, WI 53511
Phone: 608-363-2500 **E-mail:** admiss@beloit.edu **CEEB Code:** 1059
Fax: 608-363-2075 **Web:** www.beloit.edu **ACT Code:** 4564

This private school was founded in 1846. It has a 75-acre campus.

STUDENTS AND FACULTY

Enrollment: 1,281. **Student Body:** Male 38%, female 62%, out-of-state 80%, international 8% (54 countries represented). **Ethnic Representation:** African American 4%, Asian 4%, Caucasian 86%, Hispanic 3%. **Retention and Graduation:** 89% freshmen return for sophomore year. 56% freshmen graduate within 4 years. 30% grads go on to further study within 1 year. 2% grads pursue business degrees. 2% grads pursue law degrees. 3% grads pursue medical degrees. **Faculty:** Student/faculty ratio 11:1. 99 full-time faculty, 98% hold PhDs. 100% faculty teach undergrads.

ACADEMICS

Degrees: Bachelor's. **Academic Requirements:** General education including some course work in English (including composition), humanities, sciences (biological or physical), social science. Graduates are also expected to include international, "experiential" (hands-on), and interdisciplinary credit in their course work. **Classes:** 10-19 students in an average class. **Majors with Highest Enrollment:** Creative writing; psychology, general; anthropology. **Disciplines with Highest Percentage of Degrees Awarded:** Social sciences and history 34%, English 13%, visual and performing arts 12%, biological life sciences 9%, psychology 7%. **Special Study Options:** Double major, English as a second language, student exchange program (domestic), independent study, internships, liberal arts/career combination, student-designed major, study abroad, teacher certification program. Over half of our graduates earn credit off-campus for at least a semester through our comprehensive study abroad and "field term" programs.

FACILITIES

Housing: Coed, all-female, apartments for single students, fraternities and/or sororities, cooperative housing, wide variety of special-interest housing, particularly for languages. **Library Holdings:** 183,736 bound volumes. 946 periodicals. 139,248 microforms. 7,285 audiovisuals. **Special Academic Facilities/Equipment:** Wright Museum of Art, Logan Museum of Anthropology, Center for Language Study, student-run market research company (BELMARK), Alfred S. Thompson Observatory. **Computers:** School-owned computers available for student use.

EXTRACURRICULARS

Activities: Choral groups, dance, drama/theater, jazz band, literary magazine, music ensembles, musical theater, pep band, radio station, student government, student newspaper, student-run film society, symphony orchestra, television station, yearbook. **Organizations:** 85 registered organizations, 6 honor societies, 3 religious organizations, 3 fraternities (15% men join), 2 sororities (5% women join). **Athletics (Intercollegiate):** *Men:* baseball, basketball, cross-country, football, golf, indoor track, soccer, swimming, tennis, track & field, volleyball. *Women:* basketball, cross-country, golf, indoor track, soccer, softball, swimming, tennis, track & field, volleyball.

ADMISSIONS

Selectivity Rating: 80 (of 100). **Freshman Academic Profile:** Average high school GPA 3.5. 30% in top 10% of high school class, 68% in top 25% of high school class, 95% in top 50% of high school class. 80% from public high schools. Average SAT I Math 610, SAT I Math middle 50% range 560-650. Average SAT I Verbal 640, SAT I Verbal middle 50% range 590-690. Average ACT 27, ACT middle 50% range 25-29. TOEFL required of all international applicants, minimum TOEFL 525. **Basis for Candidate Selection:** *Very important factors considered include:* essays, recommendations, secondary school record. *Important factors considered include:* class rank, interview, standardized test scores. *Other factors considered include:* alumni/ae relation, character/personal qualities, extracurricular activities, talent/ability, volunteer work, work experience. **Freshman Admission Requirements:** High school diploma or GED is required. *Academic units required/recommended:* 4 English recommended, 4 math recommended, 3 science recommended, 2 foreign language recommended, 4 social studies recommended, 4 history recommended. **Freshman Admission Statistics:** 1,677 applied, 70% accepted, 26% of those accepted enrolled. **Transfer Admission Requirements:** *Items required:* college transcript, essay, statement of good standing from prior school. Minimum college GPA of 2.5 required. Lowest grade transferable C. **General Admission Information:** Application fee $30. Priority application deadline February 1. Admission may be deferred for a maximum of 1 year. Credit and/or placement offered for CEEB Advanced Placement tests.

COSTS AND FINANCIAL AID

Tuition $23,016. Room & board $5,268. Required fees $220. Average book expense $400. **Required Forms and Deadlines:** FAFSA, institution's own financial aid form, state aid form, and CSS accepted. No deadline for regular filing. Priority filing deadline March 1. **Notification of Awards:** Applicants will be notified of awards on a rolling basis beginning on or about April 1. **Types of Aid:** *Need-based scholarships/grants:* Pell, SEOG, state scholarships/grants, private scholarships, the school's own gift aid. *Loans:* FFEL Subsidized Stafford, FFEL Unsubsidized Stafford, FFEL PLUS, Federal Perkins, college/university loans from institutional funds. **Student Employment:** Federal Work-Study Program available. Institutional employment available. Off-campus job opportunities are fair. **Financial Aid Statistics:** 71% freshmen, 70% undergrads receive some form of aid. Average freshman grant $12,956. Average freshman loan $2,920. Average income from on-campus job $1,292. **Financial Aid Phone:** 608-363-2500.

BEMIDJI STATE UNIVERSITY

1500 Birchmont Dr. NE, Deputy Hall, Bemidji, MN 56601
Phone: 218-755-2040 **E-mail:** admissions@bemidjistate.edu **CEEB Code:** 6676
Fax: 218-755-2074 **Web:** www.bemidjistate.edu **ACT Code:** 2084

This public school was founded in 1919. It has a 90-acre campus.

STUDENTS AND FACULTY

Enrollment: 4,614. **Student Body:** Male 46%, female 54%, out-of-state 9%, international 6% (48 countries represented). **Ethnic Representation:** Caucasian 56%, Native American 3%. **Retention and Graduation:** 72% freshmen return for sophomore year. 17% freshmen graduate within 4 years. 34% grads go on to further study within 1 year. 5% grads pursue business degrees. 1% grads pursue law degrees. 1% grads pursue medical degrees. **Faculty:** Student/faculty ratio 19:1. 212 full-time faculty, 82% hold PhDs. 100% faculty teach undergrads.

ACADEMICS

Degrees: Associate's, bachelor's, master's. **Academic Requirements:** General education including some course work in English (including composition), mathematics, sciences (biological or physical), social science, liberal arts required. **Classes:** Under 10 students in an average class. 20-29 students in an average lab/discussion section. **Majors with Highest Enrollment:** Business administration/management; education, general; industrial production technologies/technicians. **Disciplines with Highest Percentage of Degrees Awarded:** Education 19%, engineering/engineering technology 14%, business/marketing 13%, social sciences and history 9%, visual and performing arts 6%. **Special Study Options:** Cooperative (work-study) program, distance learning, double major, dual enrollment, English as a second language, student exchange program (domestic), external degree program, honors program, independent study, internships, liberal arts/career combination, study abroad, teacher certification program, Eurospring Semester, Sino-Summer, exchange program with other Minnesota state universities.

FACILITIES

Housing: Coed, all-female, all-male, apartments for married students, apartments for single students, housing for international students, two floors for SOTA (students older than average age). **Library Holdings:** 554,087 bound volumes. 991 periodicals. 980,000 microforms. 5,521 audiovisuals. **Special Academic Facilities/Equipment:** Aquatics lab, waterfront, C.V. Hobson Forest, Center for Research & Innovation (CRI). **Computers:** School-owned computers available for student use.

EXTRACURRICULARS

Activities: Choral groups, concert band, dance, drama/theater, jazz band, literary magazine, music ensembles, musical theater, opera, pep band, radio station, student government, student newspaper, student-run film society, symphony orchestra, television station. **Organizations:** 83 registered organizations, 1 honor society, 8 religious organizations, 2 fraternities, 1 sorority. **Athletics (Intercollegiate):** *Men:* baseball, basketball, cross-country, football, golf, ice hockey, indoor track, soccer, softball, tennis, track & field, volleyball. *Women:* basketball, cross-country, golf, ice hockey, indoor track, soccer, softball, tennis, track & field, volleyball.

ADMISSIONS

Selectivity Rating: 69 (of 100). **Freshman Academic Profile:** Average high school GPA 3.3. 10% in top 10% of high school class, 50% in top 25% of high school class, 90% in top 50% of high school class. 95% from public high schools. Average ACT 22, ACT middle 50% range 19-24. TOEFL required of all international applicants, minimum TOEFL 550. **Basis for Candidate Selection:** *Very important factors considered include:* secondary school record, standardized test scores. *Important factors considered include:* class rank, recommendations. *Other factors considered include:* essays. **Freshman Admission Requirements:** High school diploma or GED is required. *Academic units required/recommended:* 16 total required; 16 total recommended; 4 English required, 4 English recommended, 3 math required, 3 math recommended, 3 science required, 3 science recommended, 1 science lab required, 1 science lab recommended, 2 foreign language required, 2 foreign language recommended, 3 social studies required, 3 social studies recommended, 1 history required, 1 history recommended, 1 elective recommended. **Freshman Admission Statistics:** 1,338 applied, 70% accepted, 60% of those accepted enrolled. **Transfer Admission Requirements:** Minimum college GPA of 2.0 required. Lowest grade transferable C. **General Admission Information:** Application fee $20. Regular application deadline August 15. Nonfall registration accepted. Admission may be deferred for a maximum of 1 year. Placement offered for CEEB Advanced Placement tests.

COSTS AND FINANCIAL AID

In-state tuition $3,782. Out-of-state tuition $8,022. Room & board $4,597. Required fees $693. Average book expense $900. **Required Forms and Deadlines:** institution's own financial aid form. No deadline for regular filing. Priority filing deadline May 15. **Notification of Awards:** Applicants will be notified of awards on a rolling basis beginning on or about May 15. **Types of Aid:** *Need-based scholarships/grants:* Pell, SEOG, state scholarships/grants, private scholarships, the school's own gift aid. *Loans:* Direct Subsidized Stafford, Direct Unsubsidized Stafford, Direct PLUS, Federal Perkins, state loans. **Student Employment:** Federal Work-Study Program available. Institutional employment available. Off-campus job opportunities are good. **Financial Aid Statistics:** 56% freshmen, 58% undergrads receive some form of aid. Average freshman grant $3,724. Average freshman loan $2,572. Average income from on-campus job $1,825. **Financial Aid Phone:** 218-755-2034.

BENEDICT COLLEGE

Harden and Blanding Streets, Columbia, SC 29204
Phone: 803-253-5143 **E-mail:** admission@benedict.edu **CEEB Code:** 5056
Fax: 803-253-5167 **Web:** www.benedict.edu **ACT Code:** 3834

This private school, which is affiliated with the Baptist Church, was founded in 1870. It has a 20-acre campus.

STUDENTS AND FACULTY

Enrollment: 2,208. **Student Body:** Male 47%, female 53%, out-of-state 15%, international students represent 6 countries. **Ethnic Representation:** African American 100%. **Retention and Graduation:** 15% grads go on to further study within 1 year. **Faculty:** 100% faculty teach undergrads.

ACADEMICS

Degrees: Bachelor's. **Academic Requirements:** General education including some course work in arts/fine arts, English (including composition), foreign languages, history, mathematics, sciences (biological or physical), social science. **Special Study Options:** Cooperative (work-study) program, double major, dual enrollment, honors program, independent study, internships, study abroad, teacher certification program.

FACILITIES

Housing: All-female, all-male. **Library Holdings:** 134,167 bound volumes. 325 periodicals. 1,800 microforms. **Special Academic Facilities/Equipment:** Language lab. **Computers:** *Recommended operating system:* Windows 95. School-owned computers available for student use.

EXTRACURRICULARS

Activities: Choral groups, dance, marching band. **Organizations:** 2 honor societies, 5 religious organizations, 4 fraternities (5% men join), 4 sororities (8% women join). **Athletics (Intercollegiate):** *Men:* baseball, basketball, football, golf, track & field. *Women:* basketball, cheerleading, golf, softball, track & field, volleyball.

ADMISSIONS

Selectivity Rating: 65 (of 100). **Freshman Academic Profile:** 98% from public high schools. TOEFL required of all international applicants, minimum TOEFL 500. **Basis for Candidate Selection:** *Very important factors considered include:* standardized test scores. *Important factors considered include:* class rank, secondary school record. *Other factors considered include:* alumni/ae relation, character/personal qualities, essays, extracurricular activities, geographical residence, minority status, religious affiliation/commitment, state residency, volunteer work. **Freshman Admission Requirements:** High school diploma or GED is required. *Academic units required/recommended:* 20 total recommended; 4 English recommended, 3 math recommended, 2 science recommended, 4 social studies recommended, 7 elective recommended. **Freshman Admission Statistics:** 3,586 applied, 79% accepted. **Transfer Admission Requirements:** *Items required:* college transcript. Minimum college GPA of 2.0 required. Lowest grade transferable C. **General Admission Information:** Application fee $25. Regular application deadline rolling. Nonfall registration accepted. Admission may be deferred for a maximum of 3 years.

COSTS AND FINANCIAL AID

Tuition $7,284. Room & board $4,182. Required fees $594. Average book expense $850. **Required Forms and Deadlines:** FAFSA, institution's own financial aid form and state aid form. **Types of Aid:** *Need-based scholarships/grants:* United Negro College Fund. *Loans:* FFEL Subsidized Stafford, FFEL PLUS. **Student Employment:** Federal Work-Study Program available. Institutional employment available. Off-campus job opportunities are good. **Financial Aid Statistics:** Average income from on-campus job $1,600. **Financial Aid Phone:** 803-253-5143.

BENEDICTINE COLLEGE

1020 North Second Street, Atchison, KS 66002
Phone: 913-367-5340 **E-mail:** bcadmiss@benedictine.edu **CEEB Code:** 6056
Fax: 913-367-5462 **Web:** www.benedictine.edu **ACT Code:** 1444

This private school, which is affiliated with the Roman Catholic Church, was founded in 1859. It has a 100-acre campus.

STUDENTS AND FACULTY

Enrollment: 1,326. **Student Body:** Male 47%, female 53%, international 2%. **Ethnic Representation:** African American 3%, Asian 1%, Caucasian 87%, Hispanic 7%. **Retention and Graduation:** 77% freshmen return for sophomore year. 36% freshmen graduate within 4 years. 20% grads go on to further study within 1 year. 2% grads pursue business degrees. 4% grads pursue law degrees. 5% grads pursue medical degrees. **Faculty:** Student/faculty ratio 16:1. 56 full-time faculty, 78% hold PhDs. 100% faculty teach undergrads.

ACADEMICS

Degrees: Associate's, bachelor's, master's. **Academic Requirements:** General education including some course work in arts/fine arts, English (including composition), foreign languages, history, humanities, mathematics, philosophy, sciences (biological or physical), social science, religious studies. **Classes:** 20-29 students in an average class. 10-19 students in an average lab/discussion section. **Majors with Highest Enrollment:** Business administration/management;

elementary education and teaching; sociology. **Disciplines with Highest Percentage of Degrees Awarded:** Business/marketing 18%, education 17%, social sciences and history 11%, philosophy/religion/theology 9%, communications/communication technologies 8%. **Special Study Options:** Cooperative (work-study) program, double major, dual enrollment, English as a second language, independent study, internships, liberal arts/career combination, student-designed major, study abroad, teacher certification program.

FACILITIES

Housing: Coed, all-female, all-male, Off-campus college-owned housing. **Library Holdings:** 366,212 bound volumes. 501 periodicals. 36,431 microforms. 831 audiovisuals. **Special Academic Facilities/Equipment:** Language and special education labs, high tech classroom, stadium, student union. **Computers:** *Recommended operating system:* Windows 95. School-owned computers available for student use.

EXTRACURRICULARS

Activities: Choral groups, concert band, dance, drama/theater, jazz band, literary magazine, music ensembles, musical theater, student government, student newspaper, symphony orchestra, yearbook. **Organizations:** 22 registered organizations, 14 honor societies, 5 religious organizations. **Athletics (Intercollegiate):** *Men:* baseball, basketball, cheerleading, cross-country, football, golf, soccer, tennis, track & field. *Women:* basketball, cheerleading, cross-country, golf, soccer, softball, tennis, track & field, volleyball.

ADMISSIONS

Selectivity Rating: 74 (of 100). **Freshman Academic Profile:** Average high school GPA 3.4. 14% in top 10% of high school class, 34% in top 25% of high school class, 68% in top 50% of high school class. 55% from public high schools. Average SAT I Math 510, SAT I Math middle 50% range 460-600. Average SAT I Verbal 510, SAT I Verbal middle 50% range 430-583. Average ACT 23, ACT middle 50% range 19-25. TOEFL required of all international applicants, minimum TOEFL 535. **Basis for Candidate Selection:** *Very important factors considered include:* class rank, secondary school record, standardized test scores. *Other factors considered include:* alumni/ae relation, character/ personal qualities, essays, extracurricular activities, interview, minority status, recommendations, talent/ability, volunteer work, work experience. **Freshman Admission Requirements:** High school diploma or GED is required. *Academic units required/recommended:* 4 English required, 3 math required, 4 math recommended, 2 science required, 4 science recommended, 2 foreign language required, 2 social studies required, 4 social studies recommended, 2 history required, 1 elective required. **Freshman Admission Statistics:** 675 applied, 89% accepted, 47% of those accepted enrolled. **Transfer Admission Requirements:** *Items required:* high school transcript, college transcript, essay, standardized test scores. Minimum high school GPA of 2.0 required. Minimum college GPA of 2.0 required. Lowest grade transferable C. **General Admission Information:** Application fee $25. Priority application deadline March 1. Nonfall registration accepted. Admission may be deferred for a maximum of 1 year. Credit and/or placement offered for CEEB Advanced Placement tests.

COSTS AND FINANCIAL AID

Tuition $13,400. Room & board $5,630. Required fees $800. Average book expense $2,000. **Required Forms and Deadlines:** FAFSA and institution's own financial aid form. No deadline for regular filing. Priority filing deadline March 1. **Notification of Awards:** Applicants will be notified of awards on a rolling basis beginning on or about February 1. **Types of Aid:** *Need-based scholarships/grants:* Pell, SEOG, state scholarships/grants, private scholarships, the school's own gift aid. *Loans:* FFEL Subsidized Stafford, FFEL Unsubsidized Stafford, FFEL PLUS, Federal Perkins, alternative loans. **Student Employment:** Federal Work-Study Program available. Institutional employment available. Off-campus job opportunities are good. **Financial Aid Statistics:** 86% freshmen, 88% undergrads receive some form of aid. **Financial Aid Phone:** 800-467-5340.

See page 934.

BENEDICTINE UNIVERSITY

5700 College Road, Lisle, IL 60532-0900
Phone: 630-829-6300 **E-mail:** admissions@ben.edu **CEEB Code:** 1707
Fax: 630-829-6301 **Web:** www.ben.edu **ACT Code:** 1132

This private school, which is affiliated with the Roman Catholic Church, was founded in 1887. It has a 108-acre campus.

STUDENTS AND FACULTY

Enrollment: 2,044. **Student Body:** Male 40%, female 60%, out-of-state 4%, international 2%. **Ethnic Representation:** African American 10%, Asian 13%, Caucasian 51%, Hispanic 8%. **Retention and Graduation:** 78% freshmen return for sophomore year. 38% freshmen graduate within 4 years. **Faculty:** Student/faculty ratio 13:1. 90 full-time faculty, 82% hold PhDs. 83% faculty teach undergrads.

ACADEMICS

Degrees: Associate's, bachelor's, doctoral, master's, post-bachelor's certificate, transfer. **Academic Requirements:** General education including some course work in arts/fine arts, English (including composition), history, humanities, mathematics, philosophy, sciences (biological or physical), social science. **Classes:** 10-19 students in an average class. **Disciplines with Highest Percentage of Degrees Awarded:** Business/marketing 30%, biological life sciences 14%, education 11%, psychology 10%, health professions and related sciences 9%. **Special Study Options:** Accelerated program, cross registration, distance learning, double major, dual enrollment, English as a second language, honors program, independent study, internships, study abroad, teacher certification program, weekend college.

FACILITIES

Housing: Coed, all-female, all-male, apartments for married students, apartments for single students. **Library Holdings:** 166,341 bound volumes. 8,900 periodicals. 332,895 microforms. 9,349 audiovisuals. **Special Academic Facilities/Equipment:** Natural science and history museums, PhD-level exercise physiology and robotics lab. **Computers:** School-owned computers available for student use.

EXTRACURRICULARS

Activities: Choral groups, concert band, jazz band, literary magazine, music ensembles, pep band, student government, student newspaper, television station. **Organizations:** 36 registered organizations, 3 honor societies, 3 religious organizations. **Athletics (Intercollegiate):** *Men:* baseball, basketball, cross-country, diving, football, golf, soccer, swimming, tennis, track & field. *Women:* basketball, cheerleading, cross-country, diving, golf, soccer, softball, swimming, tennis, track & field, volleyball.

ADMISSIONS

Selectivity Rating: 77 (of 100). **Freshman Academic Profile:** Average high school GPA 3.4. 25% in top 10% of high school class, 51% in top 25% of high school class, 81% in top 50% of high school class. 67% from public high schools. Average ACT 22, ACT middle 50% range 21-26. TOEFL required of all international applicants, minimum TOEFL 550. **Basis for Candidate Selection:** *Very important factors considered include:* class rank, secondary school record, standardized test scores. *Other factors considered include:* essays, extracurricular activities, interview, recommendations, talent/ability. **Freshman Admission Requirements:** High school diploma or GED is required. *Academic units required/recommended:* 16 total required; 4 English required, 3 math required, 4 math recommended, 2 science required, 3 science recommended, 1 science lab required, 2 science lab recommended, 2 foreign language required, 1 history required. **Freshman Admission Statistics:** 952 applied, 74% accepted, 43% of those accepted enrolled. **Transfer Admission Requirements:** *Items required:* college transcript. Minimum high school GPA of 2.0 required. Minimum college GPA of 2.0 required. Lowest grade transferable D. **General Admission Information:** Application fee $40. Regular application deadline August 30. Nonfall registration accepted. Admission may be deferred for a maximum of 4 years. Credit and/or placement offered for CEEB Advanced Placement tests.

COSTS AND FINANCIAL AID

Tuition $16,150. Room & board $5,940. Required fees $510. Average book expense $750. **Required Forms and Deadlines:** FAFSA and institution's own financial aid form. No deadline for regular filing. **Notification of Awards:** Applicants will be notified of awards on a rolling basis beginning on or about March 1. **Types of Aid:** *Need-based scholarships/grants:* Pell, SEOG, state scholarships/grants, private scholarships, the school's own gift aid. *Loans:* FFEL Subsidized Stafford, FFEL Unsubsidized Stafford, FFEL PLUS, Federal Perkins. **Student Employment:** Federal Work-Study Program available. Institutional employment available. Off-campus job opportunities are excellent. **Financial Aid Statistics:** 71% freshmen, 63% undergrads receive some form of aid. **Financial Aid Phone:** 630-829-6105.

BENNETT COLLEGE

900 East Washinton Street, Greensboro, NC 27401
Phone: 910-370-8624 **E-mail:** admiss@bennett1.bennett.edu **CEEB Code:** 5058
Fax: 910-378-0511 **Web:** www.bennett.edu **ACT Code:** 3072

This private school, which is affiliated with the Methodist Church, was founded in 1873. It has a 55-acre campus.

STUDENTS AND FACULTY

Enrollment: 664. **Student Body:** Out-of-state 73%, international 2% (6 countries represented). **Ethnic Representation:** African American 100%. **Retention and Graduation:** 67% freshmen return for sophomore year. 29% freshmen graduate within 4 years. 30% grads go on to further study within 1 year. 5% grads pursue business degrees. 5% grads pursue law degrees. 15% grads pursue medical degrees. **Faculty:** 100% faculty teach undergrads.

ACADEMICS

Academic Requirements: General education including some course work in arts/fine arts, English (including composition), foreign languages, history, humanities, mathematics, philosophy, sciences (biological or physical), social science. **Special Study Options:** Cross registration, double major, dual enrollment, student exchange program (domestic), honors program, independent study, internships, teacher certification program.

FACILITIES

Housing: All-female, housing for disabled students. **Library Holdings:** 98,000 bound volumes. 1,607 periodicals. 93,326 microforms. 3,781 audiovisuals. **Special Academic Facilities/Equipment:** Children's House, Constance Maiteena collection, college archives, telecommunications satellite dish. **Computers:** *Recommended operating system:* Windows 3x. School-owned computers available for student use.

EXTRACURRICULARS

Activities: Choral groups, drama/theater, jazz band, literary magazine, music ensembles, student government, student newspaper, yearbook. **Organizations:** 34 registered organizations, 5 honor societies, 1 religious organization, 4 sororities (20% women join). **Athletics (Intercollegiate):** *Women:* basketball, cheerleading, cross-country, softball, swimming, tennis, track & field, volleyball.

ADMISSIONS

Selectivity Rating: 60 (of 100). **Freshman Academic Profile:** Average high school GPA 3.1. 17% in top 10% of high school class, 38% in top 25% of high school class, 67% in top 50% of high school class. 92% from public high schools. Average SAT I Math 395. Average SAT I Verbal 385. Average ACT 17. TOEFL required of all international applicants, minimum TOEFL 500. **Basis for Candidate Selection:** *Very important factors considered include:* recommendations, secondary school record, standardized test scores. *Important factors considered include:* alumni/ae relation, character/personal qualities, class rank, essays, extracurricular activities, talent/ability, volunteer work. **Freshman Admission Requirements:** High school diploma or GED is required. *Academic units required/recommended:* 16 total required; 4 English required, 2 math required, 2 science required, 1 foreign language required, 2 social studies required, 5 elective required. **Transfer Admission Requirements:** *Items required:* high school transcript, college transcript, essay, statement of good standing from prior school. Minimum high school GPA of 2.0 required. Minimum college GPA of 2.0 required. Lowest grade transferable C. **General Admission Information:** Application fee $20. Regular application deadline rolling. Nonfall registration accepted. Admission may be deferred for a maximum of 4 years. Neither credit nor placement offered for CEEB Advanced Placement tests.

COSTS AND FINANCIAL AID

Tuition $6,400. Room & board $3,525. Required fees $1,505. Average book expense $750. **Required Forms and Deadlines:** FAFSA. Financial aid filing deadline June 15. Priority filing deadline March 15. **Notification of Awards:** Applicants will be notified of awards on a rolling basis. **Types of Aid:** *Need-based scholarships/grants:* Pell, SEOG, state scholarships/grants, private scholarships, the school's own gift aid, United Negro College Fund. *Loans:* Direct Subsidized Stafford, Direct Unsubsidized Stafford, Direct PLUS, Federal Perkins, college/university loans from institutional funds. **Student Employment:** Federal Work-Study Program available. Institutional employment available. Off-campus job opportunities are good. **Financial Aid Statistics:** Average income from on-campus job $1,500. **Financial Aid Phone:** 910-370-8677.

BENNINGTON COLLEGE

Office of Admissions and Financial Aid, Bennington, VT 05201
Phone: 800-833-6845 **E-mail:** admissions@bennington.edu **CEEB Code:** 3080
Fax: 802-440-4320 **Web:** www.bennington.edu **ACT Code:** 4296

This private school was founded in 1932. It has a 550-acre campus.

STUDENTS AND FACULTY

Enrollment: 580. **Student Body:** Male 33%, female 67%, out-of-state 95%, international 9% (19 countries represented). **Ethnic Representation:** African American 1%, Asian 2%, Caucasian 90%, Hispanic 2%. **Retention and Graduation:** 84% freshmen return for sophomore year. 66% freshmen graduate within 4 years. **Faculty:** Student/faculty ratio 9:1. 61 full-time faculty, 68% hold PhDs. 100% faculty teach undergrads.

ACADEMICS

Degrees: Bachelor's, diploma, master's, post-bachelor's certificate. **Academic Requirements:** Bennington expects breadth and depth in the curriculum. **Classes:** 10-19 students in an average class. 10-19 students in an average lab/discussion section. **Majors with Highest Enrollment:** Multi/interdisciplinary studies; visual and performing arts; social sciences, general. **Disciplines with Highest Percentage of Degrees Awarded:** Visual and performing arts 49%, interdisciplinary studies 16%, social sciences and history 13%, English 13%, biological life sciences 3%. **Special Study Options:** Cooperative (work-study) program, cross registration, distance learning, double major, dual enrollment, English as a second language, student exchange program (domestic), independent study, internships, liberal arts/career combination, student-designed major, study abroad, teacher certification program. Off-campus study available at the School for Field Studies (science). Post-baccalaureate plan of study for those preparing to apply to medical or allied health sciences graduate schools.

FACILITIES

Housing: Coed, cooperative housing; 18 student houses are located on campus, with living rooms, working fireplaces, and small kitchens. One off-campus house is set up as a cooperative living space. **Library Holdings:** 128,413 bound volumes. 250 periodicals. 6,155 microforms. 40,219 audiovisuals. **Computers:** School-owned computers available for student use.

EXTRACURRICULARS

Activities: Choral groups, dance, drama/theater, literary magazine, music ensembles, musical theater, opera, radio station, student government, student newspaper, student-run film society, symphony orchestra, yearbook. **Organizations:** 20 registered organizations.

ADMISSIONS

Selectivity Rating: 84 (of 100). **Freshman Academic Profile:** Average high school GPA 3.4. 40% in top 10% of high school class, 68% in top 25% of high school class, 89% in top 50% of high school class. Average SAT I Math 568, SAT I Math middle 50% range 500-630. Average SAT I Verbal 630, SAT I Verbal middle 50% range 580-690. TOEFL required of all international applicants, minimum TOEFL 550. **Basis for Candidate Selection:** *Very important factors considered include:* character/personal qualities, essays, interview, secondary school record, talent/ability, volunteer work. *Important factors considered include:* alumni/ae relation, extracurricular activities, recommendations. *Other factors considered include:* class rank, standardized test scores, work experience. **Freshman Admission Requirements:** High school diploma or GED is required. *Academic units required/recommended:* 16 total recommended; 4 English recommended, 3 math recommended, 3 science recommended, 3 foreign language recommended, 3 social studies recommended. **Freshman Admission Statistics:** 701 applied, 70% accepted, 35% of those accepted enrolled. **Transfer Admission Requirements:** *Items required:* high school transcript, college transcript, essay, interview, standardized test score, statement of good standing from prior school. Lowest grade transferable C. **General Admission Information:** Application fee $50. Early decision application deadline November 15. Regular application deadline January 1. Nonfall registration accepted. Admission may be deferred for a maximum of 1 year. Neither credit nor placement offered for CEEB Advanced Placement tests.

COSTS AND FINANCIAL AID

Tuition $25,900. Room & board $6,700. Required fees $640. Average book expense $600. **Required Forms and Deadlines:** FAFSA, institution's own financial aid form, CSS/Financial Aid PROFILE, noncustodial (divorced/separated) parent's statement and parent and student federal tax returns and W-2s. *Note:* CSS/Financial Aid PROFILE for early decision applicants only. Priority filing deadline March 1. **Notification of Awards:** Applicants will be notified of awards on or about April 1. **Types of Aid:** *Need-based scholarships/grants:* Pell, SEOG, state scholarships/grants, private scholarships, the school's own gift aid. *Loans:* FFEL Subsidized Stafford, FFEL Unsubsidized Stafford, FFEL PLUS, college/university loans from institutional funds. **Student Employment:** Federal Work-Study Program available. Institutional employment available. Off-campus job opportunities are fair. **Financial Aid Statistics:** 64% freshmen, 59% undergrads receive some form of aid. Average freshman grant $14,500. Average freshman loan $2,977. Average income from on-campus job $1,300. **Financial Aid Phone:** 802-440-4325.

See page 936.

BENTLEY COLLEGE

Waltham, MA 02452-4705
Phone: 781-891-2244 **E-mail:** ugadmission@bentley.edu **CEEB Code:** 3096
Fax: 781-891-3414 **Web:** www.bentley.edu **ACT Code:** 1783

This private school was founded in 1917. It has a 163-acre campus.

STUDENTS AND FACULTY

Enrollment: 4,325. **Student Body:** Male 57%, female 43%, out-of-state 40%, international 8% (61 countries represented). **Ethnic Representation:** African American 4%, Asian 8%, Caucasian 78%, Hispanic 4%. **Retention and Graduation:** 93% freshmen return for sophomore year. 59% freshmen graduate within 4 years. **Faculty:** Student/faculty ratio 14:1. 250 full-time faculty, 82% hold PhDs. 100% faculty teach undergrads.

ACADEMICS

Degrees: Associate's, bachelor's, master's, post-bachelor's certificate, post-master's certificate, terminal, transfer. **Academic Requirements:** General education including some course work in computer literacy, English (including composition), history, humanities, mathematics, philosophy, sciences (biological or physical), social science. **Classes:** 20-29 students in an average class. **Majors with Highest Enrollment:** Accounting; finance, general; marketing/marketing management, general. **Disciplines with Highest Percentage of Degrees Awarded:** Business/marketing 82%, computer and information sciences 12%, interdisciplinary studies 3%, liberal arts/general studies 1%. **Special Study Options:** Accelerated program, cross registration, English as a second language, honors program, independent study, internships, liberal arts/career combination, study abroad.

FACILITIES

Housing: Coed, apartments for single students, substance-free apartments, smoke-free housing, intensive-study housing, 2 off-campus locations. **Library Holdings:** 212,573 bound volumes. 1,993 periodicals. 1,320 microforms. 4,705 audiovisuals. **Special Academic Facilities/Equipment:** Several hands-on learning labs, trading room, ACELAB (Accounting Center for Electronic Learning & Business Measurement) Observatory, Smith Academic Technology Center, marketing technologies showcase. **Computers:** *Recommended operating system:* Windows NT/2000. School-owned computers available for student use.

EXTRACURRICULARS

Activities: Choral groups, dance, drama/theater, jazz band, literary magazine, pep band, radio station, student government, student newspaper, yearbook. **Organizations:** 90 registered organizations, 8 honor societies, 5 religious organizations, 5 fraternities, 4 sororities. **Athletics (Intercollegiate):** *Men:* baseball, basketball, cross-country, football, golf, ice hockey, indoor track, lacrosse, soccer, swimming, tennis, track & field. *Women:* basketball, cross-country, field hockey, indoor track, lacrosse, soccer, softball, swimming, tennis, track & field, volleyball.

ADMISSIONS

Selectivity Rating: 81 (of 100). **Freshman Academic Profile:** 31% in top 10% of high school class, 65% in top 25% of high school class, 95% in top 50% of high school class. 70% from public high schools. Average SAT I Math 603, SAT I Math middle 50% range 560-650. Average SAT I Verbal 559, SAT I Verbal middle 50% range 520-600. ACT middle 50% range 22-26. TOEFL required of all international applicants, minimum TOEFL 550. **Basis for Candidate Selection:** *Very important factors considered include:* class rank, essays, recommendations, secondary school record, standardized test scores. *Important factors considered include:* character/personal qualities, extracurricular activities, interview, talent/ability, volunteer work, work experience. *Other factors considered include:* alumni/ae relation, geographical residence, minority status, state residency. **Freshman Admission Requirements:** High school diploma or GED is required. *Academic units required/recommended:* 17 total required; 18 total recommended; 4 English required, 4 English recommended, 4 math required, 4 math recommended, 3 science required, 3 science recommended, 2 foreign language required, 3 foreign language recommended, 2 social studies required, 2 social studies recommended. **Freshman Admission Statistics:** 5,082 applied, 46% accepted, 39% of those accepted enrolled. **Transfer Admission Requirements:** *Items required:* high school transcript, college transcript, essay. Lowest grade transferable C. **General Admission Information:** Application fee $50. Priority application deadline February 1. Early decision application deadline December 1. Regular application deadline February 1. Nonfall registration accepted. Admission may be deferred for a maximum of 1 year. Credit and/or placement offered for CEEB Advanced Placement tests.

COSTS AND FINANCIAL AID

Tuition $20,880. Room & board $9,350. Required fees $195. Average book expense $900. **Required Forms and Deadlines:** FAFSA, CSS/Financial Aid PROFILE, noncustodial (divorced/separated) parent's statement, and business/farm supplement. Financial aid filing deadline February 1. **Notification of Awards:** Applicants will be notified of awards on a rolling basis beginning on or about March 25. **Types of Aid:** *Need-based scholarships/grants:* Pell, SEOG, state scholarships/grants, private scholarships, the school's own gift aid. *Loans:* Federal Perkins, state loans. **Student Employment:** Federal Work-Study Program available. Institutional employment available. Off-campus job opportunities are excellent. **Financial Aid Statistics:** 57% freshmen, 50% undergrads receive some form of aid. Average freshman grant $15,170. Average freshman loan $2,810. Average income from on-campus job $5,376. **Financial Aid Phone:** 781-891-3441.

See page 938.

BEREA COLLEGE

CPO 2220, Berea, KY 40404
Phone: 800-326-5948 **E-mail:** admissions@berea.edu **CEEB Code:** 1060
Fax: 859-985-3512 **Web:** www.berea.edu **ACT Code:** 1492

This private school was founded in 1855. It has a 140-acre campus.

STUDENTS AND FACULTY

Enrollment: 1,578. **Student Body:** Male 41%, female 59%, out-of-state 59%, international 6% (64 countries represented). **Ethnic Representation:** African American 18%, Asian 1%, Caucasian 76%, Hispanic 1%, Native American 1%. **Retention and Graduation:** 80% freshmen return for sophomore year. 31% freshmen graduate within 4 years. **Faculty:** Student/faculty ratio 10:1. 134 full-time faculty, 85% hold PhDs. 100% faculty teach undergrads.

ACADEMICS

Degrees: Bachelor's. **Academic Requirements:** General education including some course work in arts/fine arts, English (including composition), history, humanities, mathematics, sciences (biological or physical), social science, concept of wellness. **Classes:** 10-19 students in an average class. **Majors with Highest Enrollment:** Industrial production technologies/technicians; family and consumer sciences/human sciences, general; business administration/management. **Disciplines with Highest Percentage of Degrees Awarded:** Business/marketing 14%, visual and performing arts 11%, home economics and vocational home economics 9%, engineering/engineering technology 8%, education 8%. **Special Study Options:** Double major, student exchange program (domestic), honors program, independent study, internships, student-designed major, study abroad, teacher certification program, 3-2 engineering program with Washington University, St. Louis, and University of Kentucky.

FACILITIES

Housing: All-female, all-male, apartments for married students, apartments for single-parent students; 8 small houses that hold 6-12 upperclass students. **Library Holdings:** 330,401 bound volumes. 1,069 periodicals. 128,326 microforms. 10,178 audiovisuals. **Special Academic Facilities/Equipment:** Geology museum, nursery school lab for child psychology and development majors, language labs, 1,100-acre farm, planetarium. **Computers:** School-owned computers available for student use.

EXTRACURRICULARS

Activities: Choral groups, dance, drama/theater, jazz band, literary magazine, music ensembles, pep band, student government, student newspaper, yearbook. **Organizations:** 66 registered organizations, 14 honor societies, 5 religious organizations. **Athletics (Intercollegiate):** *Men:* baseball, basketball, cross-country, golf, soccer, swimming, tennis, track & field. *Women:* basketball, cross-country, soccer, softball, swimming, tennis, track & field, volleyball.

ADMISSIONS

Selectivity Rating: 84 (of 100). **Freshman Academic Profile:** Average high school GPA 3.4. 29% in top 10% of high school class, 66% in top 25% of high school class, 94% in top 50% of high school class. Average SAT I Math 544, SAT I Math middle 50% range 480-610. Average SAT I Verbal 557, SAT I Verbal middle 50% range 480-610. Average ACT 23, ACT middle 50% range 21-26. TOEFL required of all international applicants, minimum TOEFL 500. **Basis for Candidate Selection:** *Very important factors considered include:* class rank, essays, geographical residence, minority status, secondary school record, standardized test scores. *Important factors considered include:* character/personal qualities, extracurricular activities, interview, talent/ability, volunteer work. *Other factors considered include:* recommendations, state residency, work experience. **Freshman Admission Requirements:** High school diploma or GED is required. *Academic units required/recommended:* 13 total recommended; 4 English recommended, 3 math recommended, 2 science recommended, 2 science lab recommended, 2 foreign language recommended, 1 social studies recommended, 1 history recommended. **Freshman Admission Statistics:** 1,974 applied, 24% accepted, 74% of those accepted enrolled. **Transfer Admission Requirements:** *Items required:* high school transcript, college transcript, interview. Lowest grade transferable C. **General Admission Information:** Nonfall registration accepted. Credit offered for CEEB Advanced Placement tests.

COSTS AND FINANCIAL AID

Average book expense $675. **Required Forms and Deadlines:** FAFSA. Financial aid filing deadline August 1. Priority filing deadline April 15. **Notification of Awards:** Applicants will be notified of awards on a rolling basis beginning on or about May 1. **Types of Aid:** *Need-based scholarships/grants:* Pell, SEOG, state scholarships/grants, private scholarships, the school's own gift aid. *Loans:* FFEL Subsidized Stafford, FFEL Unsubsidized Stafford, FFEL PLUS, Federal Perkins, college/university loans from institutional funds. **Student Employment:** Federal Work-Study Program available. Off-campus job opportunities are excellent. **Financial Aid Statistics:** 100% freshmen, 100% undergrads receive some form of aid. **Financial Aid Phone:** 859-985-3310.

BERKELEY COLLEGE

44 Rifle Camp Road, West Paterson, NJ 07424
Phone: 973-278-5400 **E-mail:** admissions@berkeleycollege.edu **CEEB Code:** 2061
Fax: 973-278-9141 **Web:** www.berkeleycollege.edu **ACT Code:** 2576

This proprietary school was founded in 1931.

STUDENTS AND FACULTY

Enrollment: 2,144. **Student Body:** Male 22%, female 78%, out-of-state 3%, international 1%. **Ethnic Representation:** African American 17%, Asian 4%, Caucasian 44%, Hispanic 33%. **Faculty:** Student/faculty ratio 24:1. 59 full-time faculty. 100% faculty teach undergrads.

ACADEMICS

Degrees: Associate's, bachelor's, certificate, terminal, transfer. **Academic Requirements:** General education including some course work in computer literacy, English (including composition), humanities, social science. 1 class in either mathematics or sciences is required in every associate degree program. Every baccalaureate degree program requires 2 mathematics courses and an elective in the sciences. **Majors with Highest Enrollment:** Business administration/management; marketing; accounting. **Special Study Options:** Distance learning, internships, study abroad, academic remediation, off-campus study at Berkeley College of New York City and Berkeley College of White Plains.

FACILITIES

Housing: Coed. **Library Holdings:** 49,584 bound volumes. 224 periodicals. 6,419 microforms. 2,659 audiovisuals. **Computers:** School-owned computers available for student use.

EXTRACURRICULARS

Activities: Choral groups, literary magazine, student government, student newspaper. **Organizations:** 8 registered organizations, 1 honor society.

ADMISSIONS

Selectivity Rating: 63 (of 100). **Freshman Academic Profile:** Average high school GPA 2.7. 5% in top 10% of high school class, 16% in top 25% of high school class, 60% in top 50% of high school class. TOEFL required of all international applicants, minimum TOEFL 500. **Basis for Candidate Selection:** *Very important factors considered include:* interview, secondary school record. *Important factors considered include:* standardized test scores. *Other factors considered include:* character/personal qualities, class rank, extracurricular activities, recommendations, talent/ability, volunteer work, work experience. **Freshman Admission Requirements:** High school diploma or GED is required. **Freshman Admission Statistics:** 1,458 applied, 93% accepted, 54% of those accepted enrolled. **Transfer Admission Requirements:** *Items required:* college transcript. Lowest grade transferable C. **General Admission Information:** Application fee $40. Nonfall registration accepted. Admission may be deferred. Credit and/or placement offered for CEEB Advanced Placement tests.

COSTS AND FINANCIAL AID

Room & board $8,100. Required fees $390. Average book expense $900. **Required Forms and Deadlines:** FAFSA. No deadline for regular filing. **Notification of Awards:** Applicants will be notified of awards on a rolling basis beginning on or about March 1. **Types of Aid:** *Need-based scholarships/grants:* Pell; SEOG, state scholarships/grants, private scholarships, the school's own gift aid. *Loans:* FFEL Subsidized Stafford, FFEL Unsubsidized Stafford, FFEL PLUS, state loans. **Student Employment:** Federal Work-Study Program available. Institutional employment available. Off-campus job opportunities are excellent. **Financial Aid Phone:** 973-278-5400.

See page 940.

BERKLEE COLLEGE OF MUSIC

1140 Boylston Street, Boston, MA 02215-3693
Phone: 617-747-2222 **E-mail:** admissions@berklee.edu **CEEB Code:** 3107
Fax: 617-747-2047 **Web:** www.berklee.edu **ACT Code:** 1789

This private school was founded in 1945.

STUDENTS AND FACULTY

Enrollment: 3,361. **Student Body:** Out-of-state 79%, international 32% (75 countries represented). **Ethnic Representation:** African American 6%, Asian 3%, Caucasian 73%, Hispanic 5%. **Faculty:** Student/faculty ratio 8:1. 156 full-time faculty.

ACADEMICS

Degrees: Bachelor's. **Academic Requirements:** General education including some course work in arts/fine arts, computer literacy. **Majors with Highest Enrollment:** Music performance, general; music. **Special Study Options:** Accelerated program, double major, internships, student-designed major, teacher certification program.

FACILITIES

Housing: Coed. **Library Holdings:** 28,176 bound volumes. 80 periodicals. 3,300 microforms. **Special Academic Facilities/Equipment:** Ensemble library, 10 professional recording studios, film scoring and editing studio, analog and digital music synthesis labs, 1,200-seat performance center, learning center. **Computers:** School-owned computers available for student use.

EXTRACURRICULARS

Activities: Choral groups, concert band, jazz band, music ensembles, musical theater, student government, student newspaper. **Organizations:** 63 registered organizations, 2 honor societies.

ADMISSIONS

Selectivity Rating: 81 (of 100). **Freshman Academic Profile:** TOEFL required of all international applicants, minimum TOEFL 500. **Basis for Candidate Selection:** *Very important factors considered include:* extracurricular activities, interview, recommendations, secondary school record, talent/ability. *Important factors considered include:* character/personal qualities, standardized test scores. *Other factors considered include:* alumni/ae relation, class rank, essays, geographical residence, minority status, state residency, volunteer work, work experience. **Freshman Admission Requirements:** High school diploma or GED is required. *Academic units required/recommended:* 4 English required, 1 math required, 1 science required, 1 science lab required, 2 social studies required, 6 elective required. **Transfer Admission Requirements:** *Items required:* college transcript, essay. Minimum high school GPA of 2.5 required. Minimum college GPA of 2.0 required. Lowest grade transferable C. **General Admission Information:** Application fee $75. Priority application deadline March 1. Nonfall registration accepted. Admission may be deferred for a maximum of 3 years. Credit offered for CEEB Advanced Placement tests.

COSTS AND FINANCIAL AID

Tuition $19,200. Room & board $10,280. Required fees $480. Average book expense $500. **Required Forms and Deadlines:** FAFSA and institution's own

financial aid form. **Notification of Awards:** Applicants will be notified of awards on or about April 3. **Types of Aid:** *Need-based scholarships/grants:* Pell, SEOG, state scholarships/grants, private scholarships, the school's own gift aid. *Loans:* Direct Subsidized Stafford, Direct Unsubsidized Stafford, Direct PLUS, Federal Perkins, state loans. **Student Employment:** Federal Work-Study Program available. Off-campus job opportunities are good. **Financial Aid Statistics:** Average freshman loan $2,150. Average income from on-campus job $2,000. **Financial Aid Phone:** 800-538-3844.

BERRY COLLEGE

PO Box 490159, Mount Berry, GA 30149-0159
Phone: 706-236-2215 **E-mail:** admissions@berry.edu **CEEB Code:** 5059
Fax: 706-236-2248 **Web:** www.berry.edu **ACT Code:** 798

This private school was founded in 1902.

STUDENTS AND FACULTY

Enrollment: 1,933. **Student Body:** Male 38%, female 62%, out-of-state 13%, international 1% (31 countries represented). **Ethnic Representation:** African American 2%, Asian 1%, Caucasian 95%, Hispanic 1%. **Retention and Graduation:** 3% grads pursue business degrees. 1% grads pursue law degrees. 3% grads pursue medical degrees. **Faculty:** 100% faculty teach undergrads.

ACADEMICS

Degrees: Bachelor's, master's. **Academic Requirements:** General education including some course work in arts/fine arts, computer literacy, English (including composition), history, humanities, mathematics, philosophy, sciences (biological or physical), social science. **Special Study Options:** Cooperative (work-study) program, double major, honors program, internships, student-designed major, study abroad, teacher certification program.

FACILITIES

Housing: All-female, all-male. **Library Holdings:** 255,284 bound volumes. 1,418 periodicals. 455,319 microforms. **Special Academic Facilities/ Equipment:** On-campus child development center and elementary school, Martha Berry Museum. **Computers:** *Recommended operating system:* Windows 95. School-owned computers available for student use.

EXTRACURRICULARS

Activities: Choral groups, concert band, dance, drama/theater, jazz band, literary magazine, music ensembles, student government, student newspaper, symphony orchestra, television station, yearbook. **Organizations:** 60 registered organizations, 18 honor societies, 2 religious organizations. **Athletics (Intercollegiate):** *Men:* baseball, basketball, cheerleading, crew, cross-country, golf, soccer, tennis. *Women:* basketball, cheerleading, crew, cross-country, soccer, tennis.

ADMISSIONS

Selectivity Rating: 76 (of 100). **Freshman Academic Profile:** 41% in top 10% of high school class, 73% in top 25% of high school class, 96% in top 50% of high school class. 87% from public high schools. Average SAT I Math 570, SAT I Math middle 50% range 520-620. Average SAT I Verbal 579, SAT I Verbal middle 50% range 530-640. Average ACT 25, ACT middle 50% range 23-28. TOEFL required of all international applicants, minimum TOEFL 550. **Basis for Candidate Selection:** *Very important factors considered include:* secondary school record, standardized test scores. *Important factors considered include:* extracurricular activities, interview, work experience. *Other factors considered include:* alumni/ae relation, character/personal qualities, class rank, essays, recommendations, talent/ability, volunteer work. **Freshman Admission Requirements:** High school diploma or GED is required. *Academic units required/recommended:* 4 English required, 4 math required, 3 science required, 3 science lab required, 2 foreign language required, 3 social studies required. **Freshman Admission Statistics:** 2,340 applied, 65% accepted. **Transfer Admission Requirements:** *Items required:* college transcript. Minimum college GPA of 2.5 required. Lowest grade transferable C. **General Admission Information:** Application fee $25. Priority application deadline February 1. Nonfall registration accepted. Admission may be deferred. Credit and/or placement offered for CEEB Advanced Placement tests.

COSTS AND FINANCIAL AID

Tuition $11,550. Room & board $5,700. Average book expense $600. **Required Forms and Deadlines:** FAFSA, institution's own financial aid form, and state aid form. Priority filing deadline April 1. **Notification of Awards:** Applicants will be notified of awards on a rolling basis beginning on or about April 15. **Types of Aid:** *Need-based scholarships/grants:* Pell, SEOG, state scholarships/ grants, private scholarships, the school's own gift aid. *Loans:* FFEL Subsidized Stafford, FFEL Unsubsidized Stafford, FFEL PLUS, Federal Perkins, college/ university loans from institutional funds. **Student Employment:** Federal Work-Study Program available. Institutional employment available. Off-campus job opportunities are good. **Financial Aid Statistics:** 59% freshmen, 57% undergrads receive some form of aid. Average freshman grant $8,800. Average freshman loan $2,078. Average income from on-campus job $1,850. **Financial Aid Phone:** 706-236-1714.

BETHANY COLLEGE (KS)

421 North First Street, Lindsborg, KS 67456-1897
Phone: 785-227-3311 **E-mail:** admissions@bethanylb.edu **CEEB Code:** 6034
Fax: 785-227-2004 **Web:** www.bethanylb.edu **ACT Code:** 1388

This private school, which is affiliated with the Lutheran Church, was founded in 1881. It has a 62-acre campus.

STUDENTS AND FACULTY

Enrollment: 623. **Student Body:** Male 51%, female 49%, out-of-state 39%, international 2% (11 countries represented). **Ethnic Representation:** African American 7%, Asian 1%, Caucasian 87%, Hispanic 2%, Native American 1%. **Retention and Graduation:** 73% freshmen return for sophomore year. 32% freshmen graduate within 4 years. 20% grads go on to further study within 1 year. 5% grads pursue business degrees. 2% grads pursue law degrees. 3% grads pursue medical degrees. **Faculty:** Student/faculty ratio 10:1. 44 full-time faculty, 61% hold PhDs. 100% faculty teach undergrads.

ACADEMICS

Degrees: Bachelor's. **Academic Requirements:** General education including some course work in arts/fine arts, English (including composition), history, humanities, mathematics, philosophy, sciences (biological or physical), social science. **Classes:** Under 10 students in an average class. 10-19 students in an average lab/discussion section. **Disciplines with Highest Percentage of Degrees Awarded:** Business/marketing 13%, education 12%, biological life sciences 10%, social sciences and history 9%, health professions and related sciences 9%. **Special Study Options:** Accelerated program, cooperative (work-study) program, cross registration, double major, dual enrollment, student exchange program (domestic), independent study, internships, student-designed major, teacher certification program.

FACILITIES

Housing: Coed, all-female, special-interest housing (bid on by student groups). **Library Holdings:** 86,373 bound volumes. 709 periodicals. 50,749 microforms. 2,900 audiovisuals. **Special Academic Facilities/Equipment:** Mingenback Gallery, Bethany College Archives, Plym Gallery, Sandzen Gallery. **Computers:** School-owned computers available for student use.

EXTRACURRICULARS

Activities: Choral groups, concert band, drama/theater, jazz band, music ensembles, musical theater, pep band, student government, student newspaper, symphony orchestra, yearbook. **Organizations:** 49 registered organizations, 8 honor societies, 9 religious organizations, 3 fraternities (19% men join), 3 sororities (20% women join). **Athletics (Intercollegiate):** *Men:* baseball, basketball, cheerleading, cross-country, football, golf, indoor track, soccer, tennis, track & field. *Women:* basketball, cheerleading, cross-country, indoor track, soccer, softball, tennis, track & field, volleyball.

ADMISSIONS

Selectivity Rating: 76 (of 100). **Freshman Academic Profile:** Average high school GPA 3.4. 15% in top 10% of high school class, 25% in top 25% of high school class, 79% in top 50% of high school class. 97% from public high schools. Average ACT 22, ACT middle 50% range 18-24. TOEFL required of all international applicants, minimum TOEFL 525. **Basis for Candidate Selection:** *Very important factors considered include:* secondary school record, standardized test scores. *Important factors considered include:* interview. *Other factors considered include:* character/personal qualities, class rank, essays, extracurricular activities, minority status, recommendations, talent/ability, volunteer work. **Freshman Admission Requirements:** High school diploma or GED is required. *Academic units required/recommended:* 4 English recommended, 3 math recommended, 3 science recommended, 2 science lab recommended, 2 foreign language recommended, 3 social studies recommended. **Freshman Admission Statistics:** 561 applied, 69% accepted, 38% of those accepted enrolled. **Transfer Admission Requirements:** *Items required:* high school transcript, college transcript, standardized test scores. Minimum high school GPA of 2.5 required. Minimum college GPA of 2.3 required. Lowest grade transferable D. **General Admission Information:** Application fee $20. Priority application deadline February 1. Regular application deadline July 1. Nonfall registration accepted. Neither credit nor placement offered for CEEB Advanced Placement tests.

COSTS AND FINANCIAL AID

Tuition $14,140. Room & board $4,528. Required fees $0. Average book expense $550. **Required Forms and Deadlines:** FAFSA. No deadline for regular filing. Priority filing deadline March 15. **Notification of Awards:** Applicants will be notified of awards on a rolling basis beginning on or about February 1. **Types of Aid:** *Need-based scholarships/grants:* Pell, SEOG, state scholarships/grants, private scholarships, the school's own gift aid. *Loans:* FFEL Subsidized Stafford, FFEL Unsubsidized Stafford, FFEL PLUS, Federal Perkins. **Student Employment:** Federal Work-Study Program available. Institutional employment available. Off-campus job opportunities are excellent. **Financial Aid Statistics:** 77% freshmen, 75% undergrads receive some form of aid. Average freshman grant $6,055. Average freshman loan $3,190. Average income from on-campus job $500. **Financial Aid Phone:** 785-227-3311.

BETHANY COLLEGE (WV)

Office of Admission, Bethany, WV 26032
Phone: 304-829-7611 **E-mail:** admission@bethanywv.edu **CEEB Code:** 5060
Fax: 304-829-7142 **Web:** www.bethanywv.edu **ACT Code:** 4512

This private school, which is affiliated with the Disciples of Christ Church, was founded in 1840. It has a 400-acre campus.

STUDENTS AND FACULTY

Enrollment: 887. **Student Body:** Male 51%, female 49%, out-of-state 74%, international 4%. **Ethnic Representation:** African American 2%, Asian 1%, Caucasian 96%, Hispanic 1%. **Retention and Graduation:** 79% freshmen return for sophomore year. 51% freshmen graduate within 4 years. 10% grads go on to further study within 1 year. 2% grads pursue business degrees. 4% grads pursue law degrees. 3% grads pursue medical degrees. **Faculty:** Student/faculty ratio 12:1. 66 full-time faculty, 65% hold PhDs. 100% faculty teach undergrads.

ACADEMICS

Degrees: Bachelor's. **Academic Requirements:** General education including some course work in arts/fine arts, English (including composition), foreign languages, history, humanities, mathematics, philosophy, sciences (biological or physical), social science, first-year seminar. **Classes:** 10-19 students in an average class. 10-19 students in an average lab/discussion section. **Majors with Highest Enrollment:** Mass communications/media studies; education, general; psychology, general. **Disciplines with Highest Percentage of Degrees Awarded:** Other 15%, communications/communication technologies 13%, psychology 13%, social sciences and history 9%, education 8%. **Special Study Options:** Double major, student exchange program (domestic), independent study, internships, liberal arts/career combination, student-designed major, study abroad, teacher certification program, off-campus study in Washington, DC.

FACILITIES

Housing: Coed, all-female, all-male, apartments for married students, apartments for single students, housing for disabled students, fraternities and/or sororities. **Library Holdings:** 130,696 bound volumes. 785 periodicals. 116,065 microforms. 3,101 audiovisuals. **Special Academic Facilities/Equipment:** Language lab, economics lab, media center, elementary school training center, archives center, 5 computer labs, 1,300 acres of farm and timber land. **Computers:** School-owned computers available for student use.

EXTRACURRICULARS

Activities: Choral groups, concert band, drama/theater, jazz band, literary magazine, music ensembles, musical theater, pep band, radio station, student government, student newspaper, student-run film society, television station, yearbook. **Organizations:** 38 registered organizations, 18 honor societies, 3 religious organizations, 6 fraternities (45% men join), 3 sororities (45% women join). **Athletics (Intercollegiate):** *Men:* baseball, basketball, cross-country, diving, football, indoor track, soccer, swimming, tennis, track & field. *Women:* basketball, cross-country, diving, indoor track, soccer, softball, swimming, tennis, track & field, volleyball.

ADMISSIONS

Selectivity Rating: 81 (of 100). **Freshman Academic Profile:** Average high school GPA 3.5. 20% in top 10% of high school class; 47% in top 25% of high school class, 81% in top 50% of high school class. 85% from public high schools. Average SAT I Math 517, SAT I Math middle 50% range 460-570. Average SAT I Verbal 515, SAT I Verbal middle 50% range 470-560. Average ACT 23, ACT middle 50% range 20-26. TOEFL required of all international applicants, minimum TOEFL 500. **Basis for Candidate Selection:** *Very important factors considered include:* class rank, essays, recommendations, secondary school record, standardized test scores. *Important factors considered include:* interview. *Other factors considered include:* alumni/ae relation, character/personal qualities, extracurricular activities, talent/ability, volunteer work, work experience. **Freshman Admission Requirements:** High school diploma or GED is required. *Academic units required/recommended:* 15 total required; 4 English required, 3 math required, 3 science required, 2 foreign language required, 3 social studies required. **Freshman Admission Statistics:** 977 applied, 83% accepted, 35% of those accepted enrolled. **Transfer Admission Requirements:** *Items required:* college transcript, essay, statement of good standing from prior school. Minimum college GPA of 2.0 required. Lowest grade transferable D. **General Admission Information:** Application fee $25. Nonfall registration accepted. Admission may be deferred for a maximum of 1 year. Credit and/or placement offered for CEEB Advanced Placement tests.

COSTS AND FINANCIAL AID

Tuition $12,000. Room & board $6,000. Required fees $766. Average book expense $400. **Required Forms and Deadlines:** FAFSA and institution's own financial aid form. No deadline for regular filing. Priority filing deadline April 1. **Notification of Awards:** Applicants will be notified of awards on a rolling basis beginning on or about March 1. **Types of Aid:** *Need-based scholarships/grants:* Pell, SEOG, state scholarships/grants, private scholarships, the school's own gift aid. *Loans:* Direct Subsidized Stafford, Direct Unsubsidized Stafford, Direct PLUS, Federal Perkins. **Student Employment:** Federal Work-Study Program available. Institutional employment available. Off-campus job opportunities are poor. **Financial Aid Statistics:** 88% freshmen, 88% undergrads receive some form of aid. Average freshman grant $7,000. Average freshman loan $2,650. Average income from on-campus job $1,000. **Financial Aid Phone:** 800-922-7611.

BETHEL COLLEGE (IN)

1001 W McKinley Avenue, Mishawaka, IN 46545
Phone: 574-257-3339 **E-mail:** admissions@bethelcollege.edu **CEEB Code:** 1079
Fax: 574-257-3335 **Web:** www.bethelcollege.edu **ACT Code:** 1178

This private school was founded in 1947. It has a 70-acre campus.

STUDENTS AND FACULTY

Enrollment: 1,634. **Student Body:** Male 36%, female 64%, out-of-state 27%, international 3% (14 countries represented). **Ethnic Representation:** African American 10%, Asian 1%, Caucasian 87%, Hispanic 2%. **Retention and Graduation:** 87% freshmen return for sophomore year. 40% freshmen graduate within 4 years. **Faculty:** Student/faculty ratio 17:1. 66 full-time faculty, 65% hold PhDs. 100% faculty teach undergrads.

ACADEMICS

Degrees: Associate's, bachelor's, master's, terminal. **Academic Requirements:** General education including some course work in arts/fine arts, computer literacy, English (including composition), foreign languages, history, humanities, mathematics, philosophy, sciences (biological or physical), social science, Bible/religion. **Classes:** 10-19 students in an average class. 10-19 students in an average lab/discussion section. **Majors with Highest Enrollment:** Nursing/registered nurse training (RN, ASN, BSN, MSN); business administration/management; elementary education and teaching. **Disciplines with Highest Percentage of Degrees Awarded:** Business/marketing 35%, education 17%, health professions and related sciences 14%, psychology 8%, liberal arts/general studies 8%. **Special Study Options:** Cross registration, double major, dual enrollment, independent study, internships, study abroad, teacher certification program, cooperative programs with area colleges/universities.

FACILITIES

Housing: All-female, all-male, college-owned homes, on-campus apartments that house 3-4 students, discipleship homes, and missions homes. **Library Holdings:** 106,584 bound volumes. 450 periodicals. 4,298 microforms. 3,926 audiovisuals. **Special Academic Facilities/Equipment:** Bowen Museum, Weaver Gallery. **Computers:** School-owned computers available for student use.

EXTRACURRICULARS

Activities: Choral groups, concert band, drama/theater, jazz band, literary magazine, music ensembles, musical theater, pep band, radio station, student government, student newspaper, yearbook. **Organizations:** 18 registered organizations. **Athletics (Intercollegiate):** *Men:* baseball, basketball, cheerleading, cross-country, golf, soccer, tennis, track & field, wrestling. *Women:* basketball, cheerleading, cross-country, soccer, softball, tennis, track & field, volleyball.

ADMISSIONS

Selectivity Rating: 60 (of 100). **Freshman Academic Profile:** Average high school GPA 3.3. 26% in top 10% of high school class, 54% in top 25% of high school class, 75% in top 50% of high school class. 78% from public high schools. Average SAT I Math 531, SAT I Math middle 50% range 470-580. Average SAT I Verbal 534, SAT I Verbal middle 50% range 460-600. Average ACT 23, ACT middle 50% range 21-26. TOEFL required of all international applicants, minimum TOEFL 540. **Basis for Candidate Selection:** *Very important factors considered include:* class rank, secondary school record, standardized test scores. *Important factors considered include:* character/personal qualities, essays, recommendations. *Other factors considered include:* alumni/ae relation, extracurricular activities, interview, minority status, religious affiliation/commitment, talent/ability. **Freshman Admission Requirements:** High school diploma or GED is required. *Academic units required/recommended:* 17 total recommended; 4 English recommended, 3 math recommended, 3 science recommended, 2 science lab recommended, 2 foreign language recommended, 1 social studies recommended, 1 history recommended, 2 elective recommended. **Freshman Admission Statistics:** 520 applied, 90% accepted, 91% of those accepted enrolled. **Transfer Admission Requirements:** *Items required:* high school transcript, college transcript, essay, standardized test scores. Minimum high school GPA of 2.0 required. Minimum college GPA of 2.0 required. Lowest grade transferable C-. **General Admission Information:** Application fee $25. Regular application deadline August 1. Nonfall registration accepted. Admission may be deferred for a maximum of 2 years. Credit and/or placement offered for CEEB Advanced Placement tests.

COSTS AND FINANCIAL AID

Tuition $13,990. Room & board $4,380. Required fees $530. Average book expense $1,000. **Required Forms and Deadlines:** FAFSA and institution's own financial aid form. Priority filing deadline March 1. **Notification of Awards:** Applicants will be notified of awards on a rolling basis beginning on or about March 15. **Types of Aid:** *Need-based scholarships/grants:* Pell, SEOG, state scholarships/grants, private scholarships, the school's own gift aid, Federal Nursing. *Loans:* FFEL Subsidized Stafford, FFEL Unsubsidized Stafford, FFEL PLUS, Federal Perkins, college/university loans from institutional funds. **Student Employment:** Federal Work-Study Program available. Institutional employment available. Off-campus job opportunities are excellent. **Financial Aid Statistics:** 85% freshmen, 78% undergrads receive some form of aid. Average income from on-campus job $2,000. **Financial Aid Phone:** 574-257-3316.

BETHEL COLLEGE (KS)

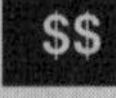

300 E 27th Street, North Newton, KS 67117-0531
Phone: 316-284-5230 **E-mail:** admissions@bethelks.edu **CEEB Code:** 6037
Fax: 316-284-5870 **Web:** www.bethelks.edu **ACT Code:** 1390

This private school, which is affiliated with the Mennonite Church, was founded in 1887. It has a 60-acre campus.

STUDENTS AND FACULTY

Enrollment: 471. **Student Body:** Male 52%, female 48%, out-of-state 38%, international 5% (12 countries represented). **Ethnic Representation:** African American 10%, Asian 2%, Caucasian 82%, Hispanic 6%. **Retention and Graduation:** 66% freshmen return for sophomore year. 25% freshmen graduate within 4 years. **Faculty:** Student/faculty ratio 9:1. 44 full-time faculty, 56% hold PhDs. 100% faculty teach undergrads.

ACADEMICS

Degrees: Bachelor's. **Academic Requirements:** General education including some course work in arts/fine arts, computer literacy, English (including composition), foreign languages, history, humanities, mathematics, philosophy, sciences (biological or physical), social science, cross cultural learning, senior capstone course focusing on basic issues of faith and life, and convocation. **Classes:** 10-19 students in an average class. Under 10 students in an average lab/discussion section. **Majors with Highest Enrollment:** Nursing/registered nurse training (RN, ASN, BSN, MSN); business administration/management; elementary education and teaching. **Disciplines with Highest Percentage of Degrees Awarded:** Business/marketing 17%, health professions and related sciences 14%, foreign languages and literature 13%, education 9%, visual and performing arts 9%. **Special Study Options:** Cooperative (work-study) program, cross registration, double major, dual enrollment, independent study, internships, liberal arts/career combination, study abroad, teacher certification program, RN outreach program.

FACILITIES

Housing: Coed, apartments for married students, apartments for single students, housing for disabled students. **Library Holdings:** 99,287 bound volumes. 560 periodicals. 12,884 microforms. 161,396 audiovisuals. **Special Academic Facilities/Equipment:** Art gallery, natural history and midwestern/Kansas history museums, 80-acre natural history field laboratory for biological studies, Mennonite Historical Library and Archives, Institute for Peace and Conflict Resolution, observatory. **Computers:** School-owned computers available for student use.

EXTRACURRICULARS

Activities: Choral groups, concert band, dance, drama/theater, jazz band, literary magazine, music ensembles, musical theater, opera, pep band, radio station, student government, student newspaper, symphony orchestra, yearbook. **Organizations:** 38 registered organizations, 3 religious organizations. **Athletics (Intercollegiate):** *Men:* basketball, football, indoor track, soccer, tennis, track & field. *Women:* basketball, indoor track, soccer, tennis, track & field, volleyball.

ADMISSIONS

Selectivity Rating: 72 (of 100). **Freshman Academic Profile:** Average high school GPA 3.3. 20% in top 10% of high school class, 43% in top 25% of high school class, 75% in top 50% of high school class. 95% from public high schools. SAT I Math middle 50% range 440-590. SAT I Verbal middle 50% range 420-500. Average ACT 24, ACT middle 50% range 19-28. TOEFL required of all international applicants, minimum TOEFL 540. **Basis for Candidate Selection:** *Very important factors considered include:* alumni/ae relation, character/personal qualities, interview, secondary school record. *Important factors considered include:* class rank, extracurricular activities, recommendations, religious affiliation/commitment, standardized test scores, talent/ability, volunteer work. *Other factors considered include:* essays, geographical residence, minority status, state residency, work experience. **Freshman Admission Requirements:** High school diploma or GED is required. *Academic units required/recommended:* 16 total recommended; 4 English recommended, 4 math recommended, 3 science recommended, 2 foreign language recommended, 3 social studies recommended. **Freshman Admission Statistics:** 488 applied, 68% accepted, 30% of those accepted enrolled. **Transfer Admission Requirements:** *Items required:* high school transcript, college transcript, statement of good standing from prior school. Minimum college GPA of 2.0 required. Lowest grade transferable D-. **General Admission Information:** Application fee $20. Priority application deadline March 1. Regular application deadline August 1. Nonfall registration accepted. Admission may be deferred for a maximum of 1 year. Credit offered for CEEB Advanced Placement tests.

COSTS AND FINANCIAL AID

Tuition $13,900. Room & board $5,900. Required fees $0. Average book expense $800. **Required Forms and Deadlines:** FAFSA. No deadline for regular filing. **Notification of Awards:** Applicants will be notified of awards on a rolling basis beginning on or about March 15. **Types of Aid:** *Need-based scholarships/grants:* Pell, SEOG, state scholarships/grants, private scholarships, the school's own gift aid. *Loans:* FFEL Subsidized Stafford, FFEL Unsubsidized Stafford, FFEL PLUS, Federal Perkins. **Student Employment:** Federal Work-Study Program available. Institutional employment available. Off-campus job opportunities are good. **Financial Aid Statistics:** 88% freshmen, 80% undergrads receive some form of aid. Average freshman grant $4,800. Average freshman loan $2,625. Average income from on-campus job $778. **Financial Aid Phone:** 800-522-1887.

BETHEL COLLEGE (MN)

3900 Bethel Drive, Saint Paul, MN 55112
Phone: 651-638-6242 **E-mail:** bcoll-admit@bethel.edu **CEEB Code:** 6038
Fax: 651-635-1490 **Web:** www.bethel.edu **ACT Code:** 2088

This private school, which is affiliated with the Baptist Church, was founded in 1947. It has a 231-acre campus.

STUDENTS AND FACULTY

Enrollment: 2,772. **Student Body:** Male 39%, female 61%, out-of-state 26%. **Ethnic Representation:** African American 2%, Asian 3%, Caucasian 94%, Hispanic 1%. **Retention and Graduation:** 86% freshmen return for sophomore year. 63% freshmen graduate within 4 years. **Faculty:** Student/faculty ratio 9:1. 155 full-time faculty, 74% hold PhDs. 100% faculty teach undergrads.

ACADEMICS

Degrees: Associate's, bachelor's, master's, post-bachelor's certificate. **Academic Requirements:** General education including some course work in arts/fine arts, English (including composition), foreign languages, history, humanities, mathematics, sciences (biological or physical), biblical/theological studies. **Classes:** 20-29 students in an average class. 10-19 students in an average lab/discussion section. **Majors with Highest Enrollment:** Elementary education and teaching; nursing/registered nurse training (RN, ASN, BSN, MSN); business administration/management. **Disciplines with Highest Percentage of Degrees Awarded:** Business/marketing 22%, health professions and related sciences 17%, education 14%, philosophy/religion/ theology 8%, social sciences and history 6%. **Special Study Options:** Accelerated program, double major, English as a second language, student exchange program (domestic), external degree program, honors program, independent study, internships, liberal arts/career combination, student-designed major, study abroad, teacher certification program.

FACILITIES

Housing: Coed, apartments for single students, housing for disabled students. **Library Holdings:** 137,000 bound volumes. 14,678 periodicals. 178,000 microforms. 12,204 audiovisuals. **Special Academic Facilities/Equipment:** Art gallery, media center, television and radio stations. **Computers:** School-owned computers available for student use.

EXTRACURRICULARS

Activities: Choral groups, concert band, drama/theater, literary magazine, music ensembles, pep band, radio station, student government, student newspaper, television station. **Organizations:** 75 registered organizations, 20 religious organizations. **Athletics (Intercollegiate):** *Men:* baseball, basketball, cross-country, football, golf, ice hockey, indoor track, soccer, tennis, track & field. *Women:* basketball, cross-country, ice hockey, indoor track, soccer, softball, tennis, track & field, volleyball.

ADMISSIONS

Selectivity Rating: 78 (of 100). **Freshman Academic Profile:** Average high school GPA 3.2. 35% in top 10% of high school class, 66% in top 25% of high school class, 93% in top 50% of high school class. Average SAT I Math 600, SAT I Math middle 50% range 520-650. Average SAT I Verbal 598, SAT I Verbal middle 50% range 530-660. Average ACT 25, ACT middle 50% range 22-28. TOEFL required of all international applicants, minimum TOEFL 525. **Basis for Candidate Selection:** *Very important factors considered include:* class rank, religious affiliation/commitment, secondary school record, standardized test scores. *Important factors considered include:* character/personal qualities, essays, interview, recommendations. *Other factors considered include:* alumni/ae relation, extracurricular activities, minority status, volunteer work. **Freshman Admission Requirements:** High school diploma or GED is required. *Academic units required/recommended:* 19 total recommended; 4 English recommended, 3 math recommended, 3 science recommended, 2 foreign language recommended, 4 social studies recommended, 3 history recommended. **Freshman Admission Statistics:** 1,460 applied, 89% accepted, 45% of those accepted enrolled. **Transfer Admission Requirements:** *Items required:* college transcript, essay. Minimum college GPA of 2.5 required. Lowest grade transferable C. **General Admission Information:** Application fee $25. Priority application deadline December 1. Regular application deadline March 1. Nonfall registration accepted. Credit and/or placement offered for CEEB Advanced Placement tests.

COSTS AND FINANCIAL AID

Required Forms and Deadlines: FAFSA and institution's own financial aid form. No deadline for regular filing. Priority filing deadline April 15. **Notification of Awards:** Applicants will be notified of awards on a rolling basis beginning on or about March 1. **Types of Aid:** *Need-based scholarships/grants:* Pell, SEOG, state scholarships/grants, private scholarships, the school's own gift aid. *Loans:* FFEL Subsidized Stafford, FFEL Unsubsidized Stafford, FFEL PLUS, Federal Perkins, state loans. **Student Employment:** Federal Work-Study Program available. Institutional employment available. Off-campus job opportunities are excellent. **Financial Aid Statistics:** 64% freshmen, 67% undergrads receive some form of aid. Average freshman grant $7,808. Average freshman loan $3,603. Average income from on-campus job $1,200. **Financial Aid Phone:** 651-638-6241.

BETHEL COLLEGE (TN)

325 Cherry Avenue, McKenzie, TN 38201
Phone: 731-352-4030 **E-mail:** admissions@bethel-college.edu **CEEB Code:** 1063
Fax: 731-352-4069 **Web:** www.bethel-college.edu

This private school was founded in 1842. It has a 100-acre campus.

STUDENTS AND FACULTY

Enrollment: 941. **Student Body:** Male 46%, female 54%, out-of-state 12%. **Retention and Graduation:** 60% freshmen return for sophomore year. 13% freshmen graduate within 4 years. **Faculty:** Student/faculty ratio 14:1. 35 full-time faculty, 51% hold PhDs. 100% faculty teach undergrads.

ACADEMICS

Degrees: Bachelor's, first professional, master's. **Academic Requirements:** General education including some course work in arts/fine arts, computer literacy, English (including composition), history, humanities, mathematics, philosophy, sciences (biological or physical), social science. **Classes:** 10-19 students in an average class. 10-19 students in an average lab/discussion section. **Disciplines with Highest Percentage of Degrees Awarded:** Business/ marketing 63%, education 11%, biological life sciences 6%, social sciences and history 4%, health professions and related sciences 4%. **Special Study Options:** Accelerated program, double major, internships, liberal arts/career combination, student-designed major, teacher certification program, weekend college.

FACILITIES

Housing: All-female, all-male, housing for international students. **Library Holdings:** 79,360 bound volumes. 468 periodicals. 2,590 microforms. 4,707 audiovisuals. **Computers:** *Recommended operating system:* Windows 98. School-owned computers available for student use.

EXTRACURRICULARS

Activities: Choral groups, drama/theater, musical theater, yearbook. **Organizations:** 30 registered organizations, 1 honor society, 4 religious organizations, 4 fraternities, 4 sororities. **Athletics (Intercollegiate):** *Men:* baseball, basketball, cheerleading, football, golf, soccer, tennis, track & field. *Women:* basketball, cheerleading, golf, soccer, softball, tennis, track & field, volleyball.

ADMISSIONS

Selectivity Rating: 60 (of 100). **Freshman Academic Profile:** 12% in top 10% of high school class, 38% in top 25% of high school class, 68% in top 50% of high school class. SAT I Math middle 50% range 440-580. SAT I Verbal middle 50% range 400-540. ACT middle 50% range 17-23. **Basis for Candidate Selection:** *Very important factors considered include:* class rank, secondary school record, standardized test scores. *Other factors considered include:* recommendations. **Freshman Admission Requirements:** High school diploma or GED is required. *Academic units required/recommended:* 4 English required, 2 math required, 2 science required, 2 social studies required. **Freshman Admission Statistics:** 452 applied, 62% accepted, 50% of those accepted enrolled. **Transfer Admission Requirements:** *Items required:* college transcript, statement of good standing from prior school. Minimum high school GPA of 1.5 required. Minimum college GPA of 1.5 required. Lowest grade transferable D. **General Admission Information:** Application fee $30. Nonfall registration accepted. Admission may be deferred for a maximum of 1 year.

COSTS AND FINANCIAL AID

Tuition $8,180. Room & board $4,740. Required fees $850. Average book expense $1,000. **Required Forms and Deadlines:** FAFSA, institution's own financial aid form, 1040, 1040A, and 1040EZ. Financial aid filing deadline August 21. Priority filing deadline March 1. **Notification of Awards:** Applicants will be notified of awards on a rolling basis beginning on or about March 1. **Types of Aid:** *Need-based scholarships/grants:* Pell, SEOG, state scholarships/grants, private scholarships, the school's own gift aid. *Loans:* FFEL Subsidized Stafford, FFEL Unsubsidized Stafford, FFEL PLUS, Federal Perkins. **Student Employment:** Federal Work-Study Program available. Institutional employment available. Off-campus job opportunities are fair. **Financial Aid Phone:** 901-352-4007.

BETHUNE-COOKMAN COLLEGE

640 Dr. Mary McLeod Bethune Boulevard, Daytona Beach, FL 32114-3099
Phone: 386-481-2600 **E-mail:** admissions@cookman.edu **CEEB Code:** 5061
Fax: 386-481-2601 **Web:** www.bethune.cookman.edu **ACT Code:** 720

This private school, which is affiliated with the Methodist Church, was founded in 1904. It has a 70-acre campus.

STUDENTS AND FACULTY

Enrollment: 2,584. **Student Body:** Male 41%, female 59%, out-of-state 28%, international 7% (35 countries represented). **Ethnic Representation:** African American 94%, Caucasian 2%, Hispanic 1%. **Retention and Graduation:** 68% freshmen return for sophomore year. 15% freshmen graduate within 4 years. 25% grads go on to further study within 1 year. 11% grads pursue business degrees. 1% grads pursue law degrees. 1% grads pursue medical degrees. **Faculty:** Student/faculty ratio 17:1. 136 full-time faculty, 55% hold PhDs. 100% faculty teach undergrads.

ACADEMICS

Degrees: Bachelor's. **Academic Requirements:** General education including some course work in arts/fine arts, computer literacy, English (including composition), foreign languages, history, humanities, mathematics, philosophy, sciences (biological or physical), social science. **Classes:** 10-19 students in an average class. Under 10 students in an average lab/discussion section. **Majors with Highest Enrollment:** Business administration/management; elementary education and teaching; corrections and criminal justice. **Disciplines with Highest Percentage of Degrees Awarded:** Business/marketing 24%, education 17%, protective services/public administration 13%, psychology 9%, social sciences and history 8%. **Special Study Options:** Accelerated program, cooperative (work-study) program, distance learning, double major, honors program, independent study, internships, study abroad, teacher certification program, weekend college.

FACILITIES

Housing: All-female, all-male. **Library Holdings:** 166,772 bound volumes. 770 periodicals. 47,125 microforms. 10,500 audiovisuals. **Special Academic Facilities/Equipment:** Historic archives, founder's home and gravesite (historic landmark), outreach center, telecommunications satellite network, art gallery/studio, audiologic recording studio, observatory. **Computers:** *Recommended operating system:* UNIX. School-owned computers available for student use.

EXTRACURRICULARS

Activities: Choral groups, concert band, drama/theater, jazz band, marching band, music ensembles, radio station, student government, student newspaper, yearbook. **Organizations:** 40 registered organizations, 9 honor societies, 2 religious organizations, 5 fraternities (3% men join), 4 sororities (5% women join). **Athletics (Intercollegiate):** *Men:* baseball, basketball, cross-country, football, golf, indoor track, tennis, track & field. *Women:* basketball, cross-country, golf, indoor track, softball, tennis, track & field, volleyball.

ADMISSIONS

Selectivity Rating: 63 (of 100). **Freshman Academic Profile:** Average high school GPA 2.8. 9% in top 10% of high school class, 23% in top 25% of high school class, 55% in top 50% of high school class. 90% from public high schools. Average SAT I Math 410. Average SAT I Verbal 410. Average ACT 16. TOEFL required of all international applicants, minimum TOEFL 550. **Basis for Candidate Selection:** *Very important factors considered include:* secondary school record, standardized test scores. *Important factors considered include:* character/personal qualities, recommendations. *Other factors considered include:* alumni/ae relation, class rank, extracurricular activities, religious affiliation/commitment, talent/ability. **Freshman Admission Requirements:** High school diploma or GED is required. *Academic units required/recommended:* 19 total required; 4 English required, 3 math required, 3 science required, 2 foreign language recommended, 1 social studies required, 2 history required, 6 elective required. **Freshman Admission Statistics:** 2,523 applied, 72% accepted, 34% of those accepted enrolled. **Transfer Admission Requirements:** *Items required:* college transcript, statement of good standing from prior school. Minimum college GPA of 2.2 required. Lowest grade transferable C. **General Admission Information:** Application fee $25. Priority application deadline June 30. Nonfall registration accepted. Admission may be deferred for a maximum of 1 year. Credit offered for CEEB Advanced Placement tests.

COSTS AND FINANCIAL AID

Tuition $9,810. Room & board $6,130. Average book expense $730. **Required Forms and Deadlines:** FAFSA. Priority filing deadline April 1. **Notification of Awards:** Applicants will be notified of awards on or about April 1. **Types of Aid:** *Need-based scholarships/grants:* Pell, SEOG, state scholarships/grants, private scholarships, the school's own gift aid, United Negro College Fund, Federal Nursing. *Loans:* Direct Subsidized Stafford, Direct Unsubsidized Stafford, Direct PLUS, FFEL PLUS, Federal Perkins. **Student Employment:** Federal Work-Study Program available. Institutional employment available. Off-campus job opportunities are good. **Financial Aid Statistics:** 97% freshmen, 87% undergrads receive some form of aid. Average freshman grant $7,200. Average freshman loan $2,600. Average income from on-campus job $1,400. **Financial Aid Phone:** 386-481-2620.

BEULAH HEIGHTS BIBLE COLLEGE

892 Berne Street SE, PO Box 18145, Atlanta, GA 30316
Phone: 404-627-2681 **E-mail:** Admissions@beulah.org
Fax: 404-627-0702 **Web:** www.beulah.org **ACT Code:** 842

This private school, which is affiliated with the Pentecostal Church, was founded in 1918. It has a 5-acre campus.

STUDENTS AND FACULTY

Enrollment: 557. **Student Body:** Male 44%, female 56%, international 13%. **Ethnic Representation:** African American 89%, Caucasian 8%, Hispanic 2%, Native American 1%. **Retention and Graduation:** 47% freshmen graduate within 4 years. 58% grads go on to further study within 1 year. 4% grads pursue business degrees. **Faculty:** Student/faculty ratio 10:1. 28 full-time faculty, 21% hold PhDs. 100% faculty teach undergrads.

ACADEMICS

Degrees: Associate's, bachelor's, certificate, diploma. **Academic Requirements:** General education including some course work in arts/fine arts, English (including composition), history, humanities, mathematics, sciences (biological or physical), social science. **Classes:** Under 10 students in an average class. **Disciplines with Highest Percentage of Degrees Awarded:** Philosophy/religion/theology 65%. **Special Study Options:** Distance learning, double major, English as a second language, independent study, internships.

FACILITIES

Housing: All-female, all-male, apartments for married students, apartments for single students. **Library Holdings:** 34,747 bound volumes. 210 periodicals. 900 audiovisuals. **Computers:** *Recommended operating system:* Windows NT/2000. School-owned computers available for student use.

EXTRACURRICULARS

Activities: Student government. **Organizations:** 2 registered organizations, 2 honor societies.

ADMISSIONS

Selectivity Rating: 60 (of 100). **Freshman Academic Profile:** 100% from public high schools. TOEFL required of all international applicants, minimum TOEFL 480. **Basis for Candidate Selection:** *Important factors considered include:* character/personal qualities, interview. *Other factors considered include:* essays, extracurricular activities, recommendations, secondary school record, standardized test scores, talent/ability. **Freshman Admission Requirements:** High school diploma or GED is required. **Transfer Admission Requirements:** *Items required:* high school transcript, college transcript, essay, interview, statement of good standing from prior school. Minimum high school GPA of 2.0 required. Minimum college GPA of 2.0 required. Lowest grade transferable C. **General Admission Information:** Application fee $20. Regular application deadline July 10. Nonfall registration accepted. Neither credit nor placement offered for CEEB Advanced Placement tests.

COSTS AND FINANCIAL AID

Tuition $3,600. Room & board $3,600. Required fees $3,600. Average book expense $200. **Required Forms and Deadlines:** FAFSA and institution's own financial aid form. No deadline for regular filing. Priority filing deadline June 30. **Notification of Awards:** Applicants will be notified of awards on or about July 30. **Types of Aid:** *Need-based scholarships/grants:* Pell, SEOG. *Loans:* FFEL Subsidized Stafford, FFEL Unsubsidized Stafford, FFEL PLUS. **Student Employment:** Federal Work-Study Program available. Institutional employment available. Off-campus job opportunities are good. **Financial Aid Statistics:** 65% undergrads receive some form of aid. **Financial Aid Phone:** 404-627-2681.

BINGHAMTON UNIVERSITY (STATE UNIVERSITY OF NEW YORK)

PO Box 6000, Binghamton, NY 13902-6000
Phone: 607-777-2171 **E-mail:** admit@binghamton.edu **CEEB Code:** 2535
Fax: 607-777-4445 **Web:** www.binghamton.edu **ACT Code:** 2956

This public school was founded in 1946. It has an 887-acre campus.

STUDENTS AND FACULTY

Enrollment: 10,328. **Student Body:** Male 48%, female 52%, out-of-state 5%, international 3% (85 countries represented). **Ethnic Representation:** African American 6%, Asian 17%, Caucasian 55%, Hispanic 6%. **Retention and Graduation:** 91% freshmen return for sophomore year. 69% freshmen graduate within 4 years. 38% grads go on to further study within 1 year. 2% grads pursue business degrees. 7% grads pursue law degrees. 9% grads pursue medical degrees. **Faculty:** Student/faculty ratio 19:1. 495 full-time faculty, 93% hold PhDs. 90% faculty teach undergrads.

ACADEMICS

Degrees: Bachelor's, doctoral, master's, post-master's certificate. **Academic Requirements:** General education including some course work in arts/fine arts, English (including composition), humanities, mathematics, sciences (biological or physical), social science, physical education. **Classes:** 10-19 students in an average class. 20-29 students in an average lab/discussion section. **Majors with Highest Enrollment:** Business administration/management; English language and literature, general; psychology, general. **Disciplines with Highest Percentage of Degrees Awarded:** Social sciences and history 18%, business/marketing 16%, psychology 12%, biological life sciences 10%, English 9%. **Special Study Options:** Accelerated program, distance learning, double major, dual enrollment, English as a second language, student exchange program (domestic), honors program, independent study, internships, liberal arts/career combination, student-designed major, study abroad, teacher certification program.

FACILITIES

Housing: Coed, apartments for married students, apartments for single students, housing for disabled students, special-interest housing available. Extensive bus system, both school-operated and public transportation with free access. **Library Holdings:** 1,787,062 bound volumes. 8,630 periodicals. 1,815,514 microforms. 121,251 audiovisuals. **Special Academic Facilities/Equipment:** Art gallery, performing arts center, meteorological lab, atmospheric science research center, particle accelerator for ion implantation, nuclear accelerator, multiclimate greenhouse. **Computers:** School-owned computers available for student use.

EXTRACURRICULARS

Activities: Choral groups, concert band, dance, drama/theater, jazz band, literary magazine, music ensembles, musical theater, opera, pep band, radio station, student government, student newspaper, student-run film society, symphony orchestra, television station, yearbook. **Organizations:** 164 registered organizations, 20 honor societies, 12 religious organizations, 19 fraternities (10% men join), 12 sororities (10% women join). **Athletics (Intercollegiate):** *Men:* baseball, basketball, cross-country, diving, golf, indoor track, lacrosse, soccer, swimming, tennis, track & field, wrestling. *Women:* basketball, cross-country, diving, indoor track, lacrosse, soccer, softball, swimming, tennis, track & field, volleyball.

ADMISSIONS

Selectivity Rating: 92 (of 100). **Freshman Academic Profile:** Average high school GPA 3.6. 86% in top 25% of high school class, 99% in top 50% of high school class. 87% from public high schools. Average SAT I Math 637, SAT I Math middle 50% range 590-690. Average SAT I Verbal 599, SAT I Verbal middle 50% range 550-640. Average ACT 26, ACT middle 50% range 24-29. TOEFL required of all international applicants, minimum TOEFL 550. **Basis for Candidate Selection:** *Very important factors considered include:* secondary school record, standardized test scores. *Important factors considered include:* class rank, essays, extracurricular activities, minority status, talent/ability. *Other factors considered include:* alumni/ae relation, character/personal qualities, geographical residence, recommendations, state residency, volunteer work, work experience. **Freshman Admission Requirements:** High school diploma or GED is required. *Academic units required/recommended:* 16 total required; 4 English required, 3 math required, 4 math recommended, 2 science required, 3 science recommended, 3 foreign language required, 3 foreign language recommended, 2 social studies required, 3 history recommended. **Freshman Admission Statistics:** 18,315 applied, 42% accepted, 27% of those accepted enrolled. **Transfer Admission Requirements:** *Items required:* college transcript. Lowest grade transferable C. **General Admission Information:** Application fee $40. Priority application deadline January 15. Nonfall registration accepted. Admission may be deferred for a maximum of 1 year. Credit offered for CEEB Advanced Placement tests.

COSTS AND FINANCIAL AID

In-state tuition $3,400. Out-of-state tuition $8,300. Room & board $6,412. Required fees $1,317. Average book expense $800. **Required Forms and Deadlines:** FAFSA. Priority filing deadline March 1. **Notification of Awards:** Applicants will be notified of awards on a rolling basis beginning on or about March 15. **Types of Aid:** *Need-based scholarships/grants:* Pell, SEOG, state scholarships/grants, private scholarships, the school's own gift aid. *Loans:* Direct Subsidized Stafford, Direct Unsubsidized Stafford, Direct PLUS, Federal Perkins, Federal Nursing, college/university loans from institutional funds. **Student Employment:** Federal Work-Study Program available. Institutional employment available. Off-campus job opportunities are excellent. **Financial Aid Statistics:** 43% freshmen, 49% undergrads receive some form of aid. Average freshman grant $3,806. Average freshman loan $3,116. Average income from on-campus job $1,000. **Financial Aid Phone:** 607-777-2428.

BIOLA UNIVERSITY

13800 Biola Avenue, La Mirada, CA 90639
Phone: 562-903-4752 **E-mail:** admission@biola.edu **CEEB Code:** 4017
Fax: 562-903-4709 **Web:** www.biola.edu **ACT Code:** 172

This private school, which is affiliated with the Christian (Nondenominational) Church, was founded in 1908. It has a 95-acre campus.

STUDENTS AND FACULTY

Enrollment: 2,827. **Student Body:** Male 38%, female 62%, out-of-state 29%, international 5% (40 countries represented). **Ethnic Representation:** African American 4%, Asian 9%, Caucasian 78%, Hispanic 9%. **Retention and Graduation:** 85% freshmen return for sophomore year. 39% freshmen graduate within 4 years. **Faculty:** Student/faculty ratio 18:1. 172 full-time faculty. 100% faculty teach undergrads.

ACADEMICS

Degrees: Bachelor's, doctoral, first professional, master's. **Academic Requirements:** General education including some course work in arts/fine arts, English (including composition), foreign languages, history, humanities, mathematics, philosophy, sciences (biological or physical), social science, communication, physical education, biblical studies. **Disciplines with Highest Percentage of Degrees Awarded:** Other 37%, communications/communication technologies 7%, business/marketing 7%, psychology 7%, education 6%. **Special Study Options:** Accelerated program, cooperative (work-study) program, double major, English as a second language, student exchange program (domestic), honors program, independent study, internships, liberal arts/career combination, student-designed major, study abroad, teacher certification program.

FACILITIES

Housing: All-female, all-male, apartments for single students, housing for disabled students, flex-style dorms (separate floors and wings for specific genders), off-campus apartments, on-campus apartments. **Library Holdings:** 280,456 bound volumes. 13,123 periodicals. 509,583 microforms. 12,482 audiovisuals. **Special Academic Facilities/Equipment:** Art gallery, electron microscope, TV production facility, film editing facility, media center, writing center, student ministry union, and tutoring services. **Computers:** *Recommended operating system:* Mac. School-owned computers available for student use.

EXTRACURRICULARS

Activities: Choral groups, concert band, drama/theater, jazz band, music ensembles, radio station, student government, student newspaper, student-run film society, symphony orchestra, television station, yearbook. **Organizations:** 33 registered organizations, 2 honor societies. **Athletics (Intercollegiate):** *Men:* baseball, basketball, cross-country, soccer, swimming, track & field. *Women:* basketball, cross-country, soccer, softball, swimming, tennis, track & field, volleyball, water polo.

ADMISSIONS

Selectivity Rating: 81 (of 100). **Freshman Academic Profile:** Average high school GPA 3.6. 42% in top 10% of high school class, 76% in top 25% of high school class, 93% in top 50% of high school class. 60% from public high schools. Average SAT I Math 561, SAT I Math middle 50% range 510-630. Average SAT

I Verbal 556, SAT I Verbal middle 50% range 520-630. Average ACT 24, ACT middle 50% range 21-27. TOEFL required of all international applicants, minimum TOEFL 500. **Basis for Candidate Selection:** *Very important factors considered include:* essays, interview, recommendations, religious affiliation/commitment, secondary school record, standardized test scores. *Important factors considered include:* character/personal qualities. *Other factors considered include:* extracurricular activities, minority status, volunteer work, work experience. **Freshman Admission Requirements:** High school diploma or GED is required. *Academic units required/recommended:* 11 total required; 15 total recommended; 4 English required, 3 math required, 2 science required, 4 foreign language recommended, 2 social studies required. **Freshman Admission Statistics:** 1,818 applied, 51% accepted, 73% of those accepted enrolled. **Transfer Admission Requirements:** *Items required:* high school transcript, college transcript, essay, interview, statement of good standing from prior school. Minimum high school GPA of 3.0 required. Minimum college GPA of 2.5 required. Lowest grade transferable C. **General Admission Information:** Application fee $45. Regular application deadline March 1. Nonfall registration accepted. Admission may be deferred for a maximum of 2 years. Credit offered for CEEB Advanced Placement tests.

COSTS AND FINANCIAL AID

Tuition $19,564. Room & board $5,967. Required fees $0. Average book expense $648. **Required Forms and Deadlines:** FAFSA, institution's own financial aid form, state aid form and business/farm supplement. Financial aid filing deadline March 2. Priority filing deadline March 2. **Notification of Awards:** Applicants will be notified of awards on a rolling basis beginning on or about March 1. **Types of Aid:** *Need-based scholarships/grants:* Pell, SEOG, state scholarships/grants, private scholarships, the school's own gift aid. *Loans:* FFEL Subsidized Stafford, FFEL Unsubsidized Stafford, FFEL PLUS, Federal Perkins, Federal Nursing, college/university loans from institutional funds. **Student Employment:** Federal Work-Study Program available. Institutional employment available. Off-campus job opportunities are excellent. **Financial Aid Statistics:** 63% freshmen, 64% undergrads receive some form of aid. Average freshman grant $6,979. Average freshman loan $4,480. Average income from on-campus job $2,000. **Financial Aid Phone:** 562-903-4742.

BIRMINGHAM-SOUTHERN COLLEGE

900 Arkadelphia Road, Birmingham, AL 35254
Phone: 205-226-4698 **E-mail:** admissions@bsc.edu **CEEB Code:** 1064
Fax: 205-226-3074 **Web:** www.bsc.edu **ACT Code:** 12

This private school, which is affiliated with the Methodist Church, was founded in 1856. It has a 196-acre campus.

STUDENTS AND FACULTY

Enrollment: 1,316. **Student Body:** Male 42%, female 58%, out-of-state 26%. **Ethnic Representation:** African American 6%, Asian 2%, Caucasian 90%, Hispanic 1%. **Retention and Graduation:** 86% freshmen return for sophomore year. 67% freshmen graduate within 4 years. 65% grads go on to further study within 1 year. 2% grads pursue business degrees. 7% grads pursue law degrees. 10% grads pursue medical degrees. **Faculty:** Student/faculty ratio 12:1. 99 full-time faculty, 97% hold PhDs. 100% faculty teach undergrads.

ACADEMICS

Degrees: Bachelor's, master's. **Academic Requirements:** General education including some course work in arts/fine arts, computer literacy, English (including composition), foreign languages, history, humanities, mathematics, philosophy, sciences (biological or physical), social science, foundations curriculum. **Classes:** 10-19 students in an average class. 10-19 students in an average lab/discussion section. **Majors with Highest Enrollment:** Pre-law studies; health/medical preparatory programs; business administration/management. **Disciplines with Highest Percentage of Degrees Awarded:** Business/marketing 26%, interdisciplinary studies 13%, social sciences and history 12%, visual and performing arts 11%, education 8%. **Special Study Options:** Double major, dual enrollment, student exchange program (domestic), honors program, independent study, internships, liberal arts/career combination, student-designed major, study abroad, teacher certification program.

FACILITIES

Housing: All-female, all-male, apartments for married students, apartments for single students, housing for disabled students, fraternities and/or sororities. **Library Holdings:** 232,330 bound volumes. 949 periodicals. 34,552 microforms. 31,471 audiovisuals. **Special Academic Facilities/Equipment:** Theatre, planetarium, environmental center (hands-on, interactive museum for ecology education), ecosite (outdoor ecology education), ropes course for leadership training. **Computers:** School-owned computers available for student use.

EXTRACURRICULARS

Activities: Choral groups, dance, drama/theater, jazz band, literary magazine, musical theater, opera, pep band, student government, student newspaper, yearbook. **Organizations:** 70 registered organizations, 20 honor societies, 5 religious organizations, 6 fraternities (53% men join), 7 sororities (74% women join). **Athletics (Intercollegiate):** *Men:* baseball, basketball, cheerleading, cross-country, golf, soccer, tennis. *Women:* basketball, cheerleading, cross-country, golf, rifle, soccer, softball, tennis, volleyball.

ADMISSIONS

Selectivity Rating: 82 (of 100). **Freshman Academic Profile:** Average high school GPA 3.2. 38% in top 10% of high school class, 69% in top 25% of high school class, 89% in top 50% of high school class. 65% from public high schools. Average SAT I Math 588, SAT I Math middle 50% range 540-640. Average SAT I Verbal 598, SAT I Verbal middle 50% range 540-650. Average ACT 26, ACT middle 50% range 23-29. TOEFL required of all international applicants, minimum TOEFL 500. **Basis for Candidate Selection:** *Very important factors considered include:* essays, recommendations, secondary school record, standardized test scores. *Important factors considered include:* character/personal qualities. *Other factors considered include:* extracurricular activities, interview, state residency, talent/ability, volunteer work, work experience. **Freshman Admission Requirements:** High school diploma or GED is required. *Academic units required/recommended:* 16 total required; 4 English required, 4 math recommended, 4 science recommended, 2 foreign language recommended, 2 social studies recommended, 2 history recommended, 10 elective recommended. **Freshman Admission Statistics:** 1,040 applied, 90% accepted, 37% of those accepted enrolled. **Transfer Admission Requirements:** *Items required:* high school transcript, college transcript, essay, statement of good standing from prior school. Minimum college GPA of 2.0 required. Lowest grade transferable D. **General Admission Information:** Application fee $25. Priority application deadline January 15. Nonfall registration accepted. Admission may be deferred for a maximum of 1 year. Credit and/or placement offered for CEEB Advanced Placement tests.

COSTS AND FINANCIAL AID

Tuition $15,930. Room & board $5,652. Required fees $339. Average book expense $600. **Required Forms and Deadlines:** State aid form. Financial aid filing deadline May 1. Priority filing deadline March 1. **Notification of Awards:** Applicants will be notified of awards on a rolling basis beginning on or about February 1. **Types of Aid:** *Need-based scholarships/grants:* Pell, SEOG, state scholarships/grants, private scholarships, the school's own gift aid, United Negro College Fund. *Loans:* FFEL Subsidized Stafford, FFEL Unsubsidized Stafford, FFEL PLUS, Federal Perkins, college/university loans from institutional funds. **Student Employment:** Federal Work-Study Program available. Institutional employment available. Off-campus job opportunities are excellent. **Financial Aid Statistics:** 48% freshmen, 38% undergrads receive some form of aid. Average freshman grant $5,129. Average freshman loan $2,517. Average income from on-campus job $1,200. **Financial Aid Phone:** 205-226-4688.

BISHOP'S UNIVERSITY

Bishop's University, Lennoxville, QC J1M 1Z7
Phone: 819-822-9600 **E-mail:** admissio@ubishops.ca
Fax: 819-822-9661 **Web:** www.ubishops.ca

This public school was founded in 1843. It has a 550-acre campus.

STUDENTS AND FACULTY

Enrollment: 2,408. **Student Body:** Male 43%, female 57%. **Retention and Graduation:** 78% freshmen return for sophomore year. 57% freshmen graduate within 4 years. 50% grads go on to further study within 1 year. **Faculty:** Student/faculty ratio 12:1. 120 full-time faculty, 68% hold PhDs. 100% faculty teach undergrads.

ACADEMICS

Degrees: Bachelor's, certificate, master's. **Academic Requirements:** General education including some course work in English (including composition). **Classes:** 10-19 students in an average class. 10-19 students in an average lab/discussion section. **Majors with Highest Enrollment:** Biology/biological sciences, general; business administration/management; education, general. **Disciplines with Highest Percentage of Degrees Awarded:** Business/marketing 23%, social sciences and history 22%, education 13%, psychology

9%, computer and information sciences 8%. **Special Study Options:** Double major, English as a second language, student exchange program (domestic), honors program, independent study, liberal arts/career combination, student-designed major, study abroad, teacher certification program.

FACILITIES

Housing: Coed, all-female, housing for disabled students. **Library Holdings:** 315,048 bound volumes. 169,855 periodicals. 5,607 microforms. 5,797 audiovisuals. **Special Academic Facilities/Equipment:** Eastern Townships Research Centre, Cormier Economics Centre, Dobson-Lagasse Entrepreneurship Centre, Molson Fine Arts Building, art gallery. **Computers:** *Recommended operating system:* Windows NT. School-owned computers available for student use.

EXTRACURRICULARS

Activities: Choral groups, concert band, dance, drama/theater, jazz band, literary magazine, music ensembles, musical theater, radio station, student government, student newspaper, yearbook. **Organizations:** 60 registered organizations, 2 religious organizations, 3% men join fraternities, 3% women join sororities. **Athletics (Intercollegiate):** *Men:* basketball, football, golf, rugby, skiing (alpine). *Women:* basketball, rugby, skiing (alpine), soccer.

ADMISSIONS

Selectivity Rating: 60 (of 100). **Freshman Academic Profile:** 100% in top 50% of high school class. TOEFL required of all international applicants, minimum TOEFL 550. **Basis for Candidate Selection:** *Very important factors considered include:* secondary school record. *Important factors considered include:* standardized test scores. *Other factors considered include:* character/personal qualities, class rank, essays, extracurricular activities, recommendations, talent/ability, volunteer work. **Freshman Admission Requirements:** High school diploma or GED is required. **Transfer Admission Requirements:** *Items required:* college transcript. **General Admission Information:** Application fee $55. Priority application deadline March 1. Nonfall registration accepted. Admission may be deferred for a maximum of 1 year. Credit offered for CEEB Advanced Placement tests.

COSTS AND FINANCIAL AID

In-state tuition $1,668. Out-of-state tuition $3,438. Room & board $4,000. Required fees $525. Average book expense $625. **Required Forms and Deadlines:** state aid form. **Types of Aid:** *Loans:* Direct Subsidized Stafford, Direct Unsubsidized Stafford, FFEL Subsidized Stafford, FFEL Unsubsidized Stafford, state loans. **Student Employment:** Off-campus job opportunities are good. **Financial Aid Statistics:** Average freshman grant $2,000. **Financial Aid Phone:** 819-822-9600.

BISMARCK STATE COLLEGE

PO Box 5587, Attn: Admissions, Bismarck, ND 58506
Phone: 701-224-5429 **E-mail:** gabriel@gwmail.nodak.edu
Fax: 701-224-5643 **Web:** www.bismarckstate.com **ACT Code:** 3196

This public school was founded in 1939.

STUDENTS AND FACULTY

Ethnic Representation: Caucasian 97%, Native American 2%.

ACADEMICS

Degrees: Associate's, certificate, diploma, terminal, transfer. **Special Study Options:** Cooperative (work-study) program, distance learning, dual enrollment.

FACILITIES

Housing: All-female, all-male, apartments for married students.

EXTRACURRICULARS

Activities: Choral groups; drama/theater, jazz band, music ensembles, student government, student newspaper. **Organizations:** 1 honor society, 1 religious organization. **Athletics (Intercollegiate):** *Men:* baseball, basketball. *Women:* basketball, volleyball.

ADMISSIONS

Selectivity Rating: 63 (of 100). **Freshman Academic Profile:** Average ACT 20, ACT middle 50% range 17-22. TOEFL required of all international applicants, minimum TOEFL 525. **Freshman Admission Requirements:** High school diploma or GED is required. **Transfer Admission Requirements:** *Items required:* college transcript, statement of good standing from prior school. Lowest grade transferable D. **General Admission Information:** Application fee $25. Nonfall registration accepted.

COSTS AND FINANCIAL AID

In-state tuition $1,888. Average book expense $630. **Required Forms and Deadlines:** No deadline for regular filing. **Types of Aid:** *Need-based scholarships/grants:* Pell, SEOG, state scholarships/grants, private scholarships, the school's own gift aid. *Loans:* FFEL Subsidized Stafford, FFEL Unsubsidized Stafford, FFEL PLUS, Federal Perkins, state loans. **Financial Aid Phone:** 701-224-5494.

BLACK HILLS STATE UNIVERSITY

1200 University Ave. USB 9502, Spearfish, SD 57799-9502
Phone: 605-642-6343 **E-mail:** admissions@bhsu.edu **CEEB Code:** 6042
Fax: 605-642-6022 **Web:** www.bhsu.edu **ACT Code:** 3904

This public school was founded in 1883. It has a 123-acre campus.

STUDENTS AND FACULTY

Enrollment: 3,452. **Student Body:** Male 36%, female 64%, out-of-state 19%, international students represent 11 countries. **Ethnic Representation:** African American 1%, Asian 1%, Caucasian 91%, Hispanic 1%, Native American 3%. **Retention and Graduation:** 51% freshmen return for sophomore year. 9% freshmen graduate within 4 years. 20% grads go on to further study within 1 year. 2% grads pursue business degrees. 2% grads pursue law degrees. 2% grads pursue medical degrees. **Faculty:** Student/faculty ratio 21:1. 108 full-time faculty, 75% hold PhDs.

ACADEMICS

Degrees: Associate's, bachelor's, master's, post-bachelor's certificate. **Disciplines with Highest Percentage of Degrees Awarded:** Education 23%, business/marketing 22%, parks and recreation 8%, psychology 5%, English 5%. **Special Study Options:** Cross registration, distance learning, double major, dual enrollment, independent study, internships, study abroad, teacher certification program.

FACILITIES

Housing: Coed, all-female, all-male, apartments for married students, apartments for single students, housing for disabled students. **Library Holdings:** 209,738 bound volumes. 4,481 periodicals. 599,062 microforms. 23,901 audiovisuals. **Special Academic Facilities/Equipment:** Art galleries, museum collections, western historical studies library, center for Indian studies, center for advancement and study of tourism, small business institute, center of excellence for math and science education. **Computers:** School-owned computers available for student use.

EXTRACURRICULARS

Activities: Choral groups, dance, drama/theater, music ensembles, radio station, student government, student newspaper, television station. **Organizations:** 60 registered organizations, 5 honor societies, 3 religious organizations, 10 fraternities, 1 sorority. **Athletics (Intercollegiate):** *Men:* basketball, cross-country, football, indoor track, track & field. *Women:* basketball, cross-country, indoor track, track & field, volleyball.

ADMISSIONS

Selectivity Rating: 63 (of 100). **Freshman Academic Profile:** Average high school GPA 3.1. 9% in top 10% of high school class, 26% in top 25% of high school class, 58% in top 50% of high school class. Average ACT 21, ACT middle 50% range 18-23. TOEFL required of all international applicants, minimum TOEFL 520. **Basis for Candidate Selection:** *Very important factors considered include:* class rank, secondary school record, standardized test scores. *Other factors considered include:* character/personal qualities, extracurricular activities, talent/ability. **Freshman Admission Requirements:** High school diploma or GED is required. *Academic units required/recommended:* 14 total required; 4 English required, 3 math required, 3 science required, 3 science lab required, 3 social studies required. **Freshman Admission Statistics:** 1,299 applied, 99% accepted, 55% of those accepted enrolled. **Transfer Admission Requirements:** *Items required:* high school transcript, college transcript. Minimum high school GPA of 2.0 required. Minimum college GPA of 2.0 required. Lowest grade transferable C. **General Admission Information:** Application fee $20. Regular application deadline July 1. Nonfall registration accepted. Credit and/or placement offered for CEEB Advanced Placement tests.

COSTS AND FINANCIAL AID

In-state tuition $1,950. Out-of-state tuition $6,200. Room & board $3,127. Required fees $1,981. Average book expense $800. **Required Forms and Deadlines:** FAFSA. No deadline for regular filing. Priority filing deadline March 1. **Notification of Awards:** Applicants will be notified of awards on or about May 15. **Types of Aid:** *Need-based scholarships/grants:* Pell, SEOG, state scholarships/grants, private scholarships, the school's own gift aid. *Loans:* FFEL Subsidized Stafford, FFEL Unsubsidized Stafford, FFEL PLUS, Federal Perkins. **Student Employment:** Federal Work-Study Program available. Institutional employment available. Off-campus job opportunities are good. **Financial Aid Statistics:** Average income from on-campus job $1,700. **Financial Aid Phone:** 605-642-6254.

BLACKBURN COLLEGE

700 College Avenue, Carlinville, IL 62626
Phone: 217-854-3231 **CEEB Code:** 1065
Fax: 217-854-3713 **Web:** www.blackburn.edu **ACT Code:** 958

This private school, which is affiliated with the Presbyterian Church, was founded in 1837. It has an 80-acre campus.

STUDENTS AND FACULTY

Enrollment: 448. **Student Body:** Out-of-state 34%, international 5% (6 countries represented). **Ethnic Representation:** African American 10%, Asian 1%, Caucasian 87%, Hispanic 1%, Native American 1%. **Retention and Graduation:** 14% grads go on to further study within 1 year. 2% grads pursue business degrees. 1% grads pursue law degrees. 1% grads pursue medical degrees.

ACADEMICS

Degrees: Bachelor's. **Special Study Options:** Study abroad, Washington DC program, student-managed mandatory work program.

FACILITIES

Housing: Coed, apartments for single students. **Library Holdings:** 84,000 bound volumes. 283 periodicals. 84,668 microforms. **Special Academic Facilities/Equipment:** Electron microscope. **Computers:** *Recommended operating system:* Mac. School-owned computers available for student use.

EXTRACURRICULARS

Activities: Student government, student newspaper, yearbook. **Organizations:** 15 registered organizations, 2 honor societies, 1 religious organization. **Athletics (Intercollegiate):** *Men:* baseball, basketball, cross-country, football, golf, soccer, volleyball. *Women:* basketball, cross-country, softball, swimming, tennis, track & field, volleyball.

ADMISSIONS

Selectivity Rating: 76 (of 100). **Freshman Academic Profile:** 25% in top 10% of high school class, 55% in top 25% of high school class, 82% in top 50% of high school class. 85% from public high schools. Average ACT 21. TOEFL required of all international applicants, minimum TOEFL 500. **Freshman Admission Requirements:** High school diploma is required and GED is not accepted. *Academic units required/recommended:* 12 total recommended; 4 English recommended, 2 math recommended, 2 science recommended, 2 foreign language recommended, 2 social studies recommended. **Transfer Admission Requirements:** Minimum college GPA of 2.0 required. Lowest grade transferable C. **General Admission Information:** Regular application deadline rolling. Nonfall registration accepted. Credit and/or placement offered for CEEB Advanced Placement tests.

COSTS AND FINANCIAL AID

Tuition $7,795. Room & board $3,240. Average book expense $500. **Required Forms and Deadlines:** FAFSA. **Types of Aid:** *Need-based scholarships/grants:* state scholarships/grants. *Loans:* FFEL Subsidized Stafford, FFEL PLUS. **Student Employment:** Off-campus job opportunities are good. **Financial Aid Statistics:** Average freshman loan $1,050. **Financial Aid Phone:** 217-854-3231.

BLESSING-RIEMAN COLLEGE OF NURSING

$$

Broadway at 11th Street, PO Box 7005, Quincy, IL 62305-7005
Phone: 217-228-5520 **E-mail:** cmcgee@blessinghospital.com
Fax: 217-223-4661 **Web:** www.brcn.edu **ACT Code:** 956

This private school was founded in 1891. It has a 1-acre campus.

STUDENTS AND FACULTY

Enrollment: 153. **Student Body:** Male 6%, female 94%, out-of-state 23%. **Ethnic Representation:** African American 3%, Caucasian 80%, Hispanic 2%, Native American 1%. **Retention and Graduation:** 61% freshmen return for sophomore year. 40% freshmen graduate within 4 years. **Faculty:** Student/faculty ratio 9:1. 13 full-time faculty, 23% hold PhDs. 100% faculty teach undergrads.

ACADEMICS

Degrees: Bachelor's. **Academic Requirements:** General education including some course work in arts/fine arts, computer literacy, English (including composition), humanities, mathematics, philosophy, sciences (biological or physical), social science. **Classes:** 10-19 students in an average class. Under 10 students in an average lab/discussion section. **Disciplines with Highest Percentage of Degrees Awarded:** Health professions and related sciences 100%. **Special Study Options:** Double major.

FACILITIES

Housing: Apartments for single students, men's and women's dormitories available at Culver-Stockton College and Quincy University. **Computers:** *Recommended operating system:* Windows NT/2000. School-owned computers available for student use.

EXTRACURRICULARS

Activities: Student government. **Organizations:** 1 registered organization, 1 honor society.

ADMISSIONS

Selectivity Rating: 63 (of 100). **Freshman Academic Profile:** Average high school GPA 3.8. 20% in top 10% of high school class, 97% in top 25% of high school class, 100% in top 50% of high school class. 89% from public high schools. Average ACT 22, ACT middle 50% range 22-27. TOEFL required of all international applicants, minimum TOEFL 550. **Basis for Candidate Selection:** *Very important factors considered include:* class rank, secondary school record, standardized test scores. **Freshman Admission Requirements:** High school diploma or GED is required. *Academic units required/recommended:* 4 English required, 2 math required, 3 science required, 2 science lab required, 3 social studies required. **Freshman Admission Statistics:** 140 applied, 49% accepted, 49% of those accepted enrolled. **Transfer Admission Requirements:** *Items required:* college transcript, statement of good standing from prior school. Minimum college GPA of 2.0 required. Lowest grade transferable C. **General Admission Information:** Nonfall registration accepted.

COSTS AND FINANCIAL AID

Tuition $11,200. Room & board $4,975. Required fees $300. Average book expense $800. **Required Forms and Deadlines:** FAFSA. No deadline for regular filing. **Notification of Awards:** Applicants will be notified of awards on a rolling basis beginning on or about September 1. **Types of Aid:** *Need-based scholarships/grants:* Pell, state scholarships/grants, Federal Nursing. *Loans:* FFEL Subsidized Stafford, FFEL Unsubsidized Stafford, FFEL PLUS, Federal Nursing, college/university loans from institutional funds. **Student Employment:** Institutional employment available. Off-campus job opportunities are excellent. **Financial Aid Statistics:** 94% undergrads receive some form of aid. **Financial Aid Phone:** 217-228-5520.

BLOOMFIELD COLLEGE

1 Park Place, Bloomfield, NJ 07003
Phone: 973-748-9000 **E-mail:** admission@bloomfield.edu **CEEB Code:** 2044
Fax: 973-748-0916 **Web:** www.bloomfield.edu **ACT Code:** 2540

This private school, which is affiliated with the Presbyterian Church, was founded in 1868. It has a 12-acre campus.

STUDENTS AND FACULTY

Enrollment: 1,887. **Student Body:** Male 32%, female 68%, out-of-state 3%, international 2% (39 countries represented). **Ethnic Representation:** African American 52%, Asian 3%, Caucasian 17%, Hispanic 18%. **Retention and Graduation:** 72% freshmen return for sophomore year. 16% freshmen graduate within 4 years. 6% grads go on to further study within 1 year. **Faculty:** Student/faculty ratio 15:1. 62 full-time faculty, 77% hold PhDs. 100% faculty teach undergrads.

ACADEMICS

Degrees: Bachelor's, certificate. **Academic Requirements:** General education including some course work in arts/fine arts, computer literacy, English (including composition), history, humanities, mathematics, philosophy, sciences (biological or physical), social science. **Classes:** 10-19 students in an average class. 10-19 students in an average lab/discussion section. **Majors with Highest Enrollment:** Business administration/management; psychology, general; criminology. **Disciplines with Highest Percentage of Degrees Awarded:** Business/marketing 28%, psychology 13%, social sciences and history 12%, health professions and related sciences 12%, visual and performing arts 10%. **Special Study Options:** Accelerated program, cooperative (work-study) program, distance learning, double major, English as a second language, honors program, independent study, internships, liberal arts/career combination, student-designed major, study abroad, teacher certification program, weekend college.

FACILITIES

Housing: Coed, fraternities and/or sororities, theme housing. **Library Holdings:** 60,000 bound volumes. 375 periodicals. 59 microforms. 5,000 audiovisuals. **Special Academic Facilities/Equipment:** Westminster Theatre, art gallery, new library. **Computers:** *Recommended operating system:* Windows 95. School-owned computers available for student use.

EXTRACURRICULARS

Activities: Dance, drama/theater, literary magazine, musical theater, student government, student newspaper, student-run film society, yearbook. **Organizations:** 37 registered organizations, 3 honor societies, 1 religious organization, 5 fraternities (2% men join), 4 sororities (2% women join). **Athletics (Intercollegiate):** *Men:* baseball, basketball, cross-country, soccer. *Women:* basketball, soccer, softball, volleyball.

ADMISSIONS

Selectivity Rating: 68 (of 100). **Freshman Academic Profile:** Average high school GPA 2.6. 4% in top 10% of high school class, 21% in top 25% of high school class, 54% in top 50% of high school class. 65% from public high schools. Average SAT I Math 429, SAT I Math middle 50% range 390-460. Average SAT I Verbal 430, SAT I Verbal middle 50% range 390-460. TOEFL required of all international applicants, minimum TOEFL 550. **Basis for Candidate Selection:** *Very important factors considered include:* secondary school record, standardized test scores. *Important factors considered include:* essays, interview, recommendations. *Other factors considered include:* alumni/ae relation, character/personal qualities, class rank, extracurricular activities, talent/ability, volunteer work, work experience. **Freshman Admission Requirements:** High school diploma or GED is required. *Academic units required/recommended:* 14 total required;. **Freshman Admission Statistics:** 1,140 applied, 79% accepted, 43% of those accepted enrolled. **Transfer Admission Requirements:** *Items required:* college transcript. Minimum college GPA of 2.0 required. Lowest grade transferable C. **General Admission Information:** Application fee $35. Priority application deadline March 1. Regular application deadline August 1. Nonfall registration accepted. Admission may be deferred for a maximum of 2 years. Credit and/or placement offered for CEEB Advanced Placement tests.

COSTS AND FINANCIAL AID

Tuition $12,100. Room & board $5,850. Required fees $200. Average book expense $500. **Required Forms and Deadlines:** FAFSA and institution's own financial aid form. No deadline for regular filing. Priority filing deadline April 1. **Notification of Awards:** Applicants will be notified of awards on a rolling basis beginning on or about March 15. **Types of Aid:** *Need-based scholarships/grants:* Pell, SEOG, state scholarships/grants, private scholarships, the school's own gift aid. *Loans:* FFEL Subsidized Stafford, FFEL Unsubsidized Stafford, FFEL PLUS. **Student Employment:** Federal Work-Study Program available. Institutional employment available. Off-campus job opportunities are good. **Financial Aid Statistics:** 84% freshmen receive some form of aid. Average freshman grant $9,990. Average freshman loan $3,681. Average income from on-campus job $1,700. **Financial Aid Phone:** 973-748-9000.

See page 942.

BLOOMSBURG UNIVERSITY OF PENNSYLVANIA

104 Student Services Center, 400 East Second Street, Bloomsburg, PA 17815
Phone: 570-389-4316 **E-mail:** buadmiss@bloomu.edu **CEEB Code:** 2646
Fax: 570-389-4741 **Web:** www.bloomu.edu **ACT Code:** 3692

This public school was founded in 1839. It has a 282-acre campus.

STUDENTS AND FACULTY

Enrollment: 7,298. **Student Body:** Male 40%, female 60%, out-of-state 10%, (32 countries represented). **Ethnic Representation:** African American 4%, Asian 1%, Caucasian 93%, Hispanic 2%. **Retention and Graduation:** 79% freshmen return for sophomore year. 37% freshmen graduate within 4 years. 15% grads go on to further study within 1 year. **Faculty:** Student/faculty ratio 20:1. 350 full-time faculty, 81% hold PhDs.

ACADEMICS

Degrees: Associate's, bachelor's, master's, post-bachelor's certificate, terminal. **Academic Requirements:** General education including some course work in arts/fine arts, English (including composition), history, humanities, mathematics, philosophy, sciences (biological or physical), social science. **Classes:** 20-29 students in an average class. 10-19 students in an average lab/discussion section. **Majors with Highest Enrollment:** Business administration/management; elementary education and teaching; special education, general. **Disciplines with Highest Percentage of Degrees Awarded:** Education 27%, business/marketing 21%, social sciences and history 8%, English 8%, protective services/public administration 6%. **Special Study Options:** Cooperative (work-study) program, distance learning, double major, dual enrollment, honors program, independent study, internships, study abroad, teacher certification program.

FACILITIES

Housing: Coed, all-female, apartments for single students. **Library Holdings:** 430,815 bound volumes. 2,386 periodicals. 2,099,885 microforms. 7,961 audiovisuals. **Special Academic Facilities/Equipment:** Art gallery, language lab, TV studio, radio station. **Computers:** School-owned computers available for student use.

EXTRACURRICULARS

Activities: Choral groups, concert band, dance, drama/theater, jazz band, literary magazine, marching band, music ensembles, pep band, radio station, student government, student newspaper, symphony orchestra, television station, yearbook. **Organizations:** 208 registered organizations, 18 honor societies, 7 religious organizations, 11 fraternities (3% men join), 13 sororities (4% women join). **Athletics (Intercollegiate):** *Men:* baseball, basketball, cheerleading, cross-country, football, soccer, swimming, tennis, track & field, wrestling. *Women:* basketball, cheerleading, cross-country, field hockey, lacrosse, soccer, softball, swimming, tennis, track & field.

ADMISSIONS

Selectivity Rating: 69 (of 100). **Freshman Academic Profile:** Average high school GPA 3.0. 10% in top 10% of high school class, 35% in top 25% of high school class, 82% in top 50% of high school class. 91% from public high schools. Average SAT I Math 511, SAT I Math middle 50% range 460-560. Average SAT I Verbal 503, SAT I Verbal middle 50% range 460-550. TOEFL required of all international applicants, minimum TOEFL 500. **Basis for Candidate Selection:** *Very important factors considered include:* class rank, secondary school record, standardized test scores. *Important factors considered include:* recommendations. *Other factors considered include:* character/personal qualities, essays, extracurricular activities, geographical residence, interview, state residency, talent/ability, volunteer work, work experience. **Freshman Admission Requirements:** High school diploma or GED is required. *Academic units required/recommended:* 16 total required; 20 total recommended; 4 English required, 4 English recommended, 3 math required, 3 math recommended, 3 science required, 3 science recommended, 2 science lab required, 2 science lab recommended, 2 foreign language recommended, 2 social studies required, 2 social studies recommended, 2 history required, 2 history recommended. **Freshman Admission Statistics:** 6,888 applied, 69% accepted, 31% of those accepted enrolled. **Transfer Admission Requirements:** *Items required:* high school transcript, college transcript, standardized test scores. Minimum high school GPA of 3.0 required. Minimum college GPA of 2.0 required. Lowest grade transferable D. **General Admission Information:** Application fee $30. Priority application deadline December 1. Early decision application deadline November 15. Nonfall registration accepted. Admission may be deferred for a maximum of 2 years. Credit and/or placement offered for CEEB Advanced Placement tests.

COSTS AND FINANCIAL AID

In-state tuition $4,378. Out-of-state tuition $10,946. Room & board $4,776. Required fees $1,172. Average book expense $600. **Required Forms and Deadlines:** FAFSA and state aid form. Priority filing deadline March 15. **Notification of Awards:** Applicants will be notified of awards on a rolling basis beginning on or about April 1. **Types of Aid:** *Need-based scholarships/grants:* Pell, SEOG, state scholarships/grants, private scholarships, the school's own gift aid. *Loans:* FFEL Subsidized Stafford, FFEL Unsubsidized Stafford, FFEL PLUS, Federal Perkins, state loans, alternative loans. **Student Employment:** Federal Work-Study Program available. Institutional employment available. Off-campus job opportunities are fair. **Financial Aid Statistics:** 65% freshmen, 61% undergrads receive some form of aid. Average income from on-campus job $2,500. **Financial Aid Phone:** 570-389-4279.

BLUE MOUNTAIN COLLEGE

PO Box 160, Blue Mountain, MS 38610
Phone: 662-685-4771 **E-mail:** admissions@bmc.edu
Fax: 662-685-4776 **Web:** bmc.edu

This private school, which is affiliated with the Baptist Church, was founded in 1873. It has a 44-acre campus.

STUDENTS AND FACULTY

Enrollment: 389. **Student Body:** Male 17%, female 83%, out-of-state 11%. **Ethnic Representation:** African American 10%, Caucasian 89%, Native American 1%. **Retention and Graduation:** 71% freshmen return for sophomore year. 29% freshmen graduate within 4 years. 25% grads go on to further study within 1 year. 2% grads pursue business degrees. 1% grads pursue law degrees. 1% grads pursue medical degrees. **Faculty:** Student/faculty ratio 14:1. 21 full-time faculty, 57% hold PhDs. 100% faculty teach undergrads.

ACADEMICS

Degrees: Bachelor's, diploma. **Academic Requirements:** General education including some course work in arts/fine arts, computer literacy, English (including composition), history, mathematics, philosophy, sciences (biological or physical), social science. **Classes:** Under 10 students in an average class. Under 10 students in an average lab/discussion section. **Majors with Highest Enrollment:** Elementary education and teaching; Bible/biblical studies; psychology. **Disciplines with Highest Percentage of Degrees Awarded:** Education 60%, psychology 17%, philosophy/religion/theology 12%, biological life sciences 6%, business/marketing 3%. **Special Study Options:** Double major, honors program, teacher certification program.

FACILITIES

Housing: All-female, Campus-owned housing for men. **Library Holdings:** 61,297 bound volumes. 186 periodicals. 380 microforms. 4,554 audiovisuals. **Computers:** School-owned computers available for student use.

EXTRACURRICULARS

Activities: Choral groups, drama/theater, literary magazine, musical theater, student government, yearbook. **Organizations:** 28 registered organizations, 1 honor society, 1 religious organization. **Athletics (Intercollegiate):** *Men:* tennis. *Women:* basketball.

ADMISSIONS

Selectivity Rating: 63 (of 100). **Freshman Academic Profile:** Average high school GPA 3.1. 81% in top 50% of high school class. 79% from public high schools. Average ACT 20, ACT middle 50% range 17-24. TOEFL required of all international applicants, minimum TOEFL 500. **Basis for Candidate Selection:** *Important factors considered include:* class rank, secondary school record, standardized test scores. *Other factors considered include:* recommendations. **Freshman Admission Requirements:** High school diploma or GED is required. *Academic units required/recommended:* 15 total recommended; 4 English recommended, 3 math recommended, 3 science recommended, 2 science lab recommended, 2 foreign language recommended, 1 social studies recommended, 2 history recommended. **Freshman Admission Statistics:** 117 applied, 85% accepted, 59% of those accepted enrolled. **Transfer Admission Requirements:** *Items required:* college transcript, standardized test scores. Lowest grade transferable C. **General Admission Information:** Application fee $10. Nonfall registration accepted. Admission may be deferred.

COSTS AND FINANCIAL AID

Tuition $6,370. Room & board $3,120. Required fees $500. Average book expense $550. **Required Forms and Deadlines:** FAFSA and institution's own financial aid form. Financial aid filing deadline August 1. Priority filing deadline June 1. **Types of Aid:** *Need-based scholarships/grants:* Pell, SEOG, state scholarships/grants, private scholarships. *Loans:* FFEL Subsidized Stafford, FFEL Unsubsidized Stafford, FFEL PLUS, Federal Perkins. **Student Employment:** Federal Work-Study Program available. Institutional employment available. Off-campus job opportunities are good. **Financial Aid Statistics:** 86% freshmen, 88% undergrads receive some form of aid. Average freshman loan $2,326. Average income from on-campus job $1,400. **Financial Aid Phone:** 662-685-4771.

BLUEFIELD COLLEGE

3000 College Drive, Bluefield, VA 24605
Phone: 540-326-4214 **E-mail:** thavens@mail.bluefield.edu **CEEB Code:** 5063
Fax: 540-326-4288 **Web:** www.bluefield.edu **ACT Code:** 4340

This private school, which is affiliated with the Baptist Church, was founded in 1922.

STUDENTS AND FACULTY

Enrollment: 858. **Student Body:** Male 46%, female 54%, out-of-state 37%. **Ethnic Representation:** African American 14%, Asian 1%, Caucasian 83%, Native American 2%. **Retention and Graduation:** 65% freshmen return for sophomore year. 36% freshmen graduate within 4 years. 23% grads go on to further study within 1 year. 8% grads pursue business degrees. 3% grads pursue law degrees. 2% grads pursue medical degrees. **Faculty:** Student/faculty ratio 15:1. 32 full-time faculty, 53% hold PhDs. 100% faculty teach undergrads.

ACADEMICS

Degrees: Associate's, bachelor's. **Academic Requirements:** General education including some course work in arts/fine arts, computer literacy, English (including composition), history, mathematics, sciences (biological or physical), social science. **Classes:** Under 10 students in an average class. Under 10 students in an average lab/discussion section. **Majors with Highest Enrollment:** Criminal justice/law enforcement administration; business administration/management; Christian studies. **Disciplines with Highest Percentage of Degrees Awarded:** Business/marketing 55%, law/legal studies 15%, education 6%, philosophy/religion/theology 5%, interdisciplinary studies 5%. **Special Study Options:** Accelerated program, double major, dual enrollment, honors program, internships, student-designed major, study abroad, teacher certification program, weekend college.

FACILITIES

Housing: Coed, all-female, all-male. **Library Holdings:** 500,000 bound volumes. 195 periodicals. 0 microforms. 1,746 audiovisuals. **Special Academic Facilities/Equipment:** Art center. **Computers:** School-owned computers available for student use.

EXTRACURRICULARS

Activities: Choral groups, drama/theater, literary magazine, music ensembles, student government, student newspaper, yearbook. **Organizations:** 18 registered organizations, 7 honor societies, 6 religious organizations, 2 fraternities (10% men join), 2 sororities (11% women join). **Athletics (Intercollegiate):** *Men:* baseball, basketball, golf, soccer, tennis. *Women:* basketball, soccer, softball, tennis, volleyball.

ADMISSIONS

Selectivity Rating: 65 (of 100). **Freshman Academic Profile:** Average high school GPA 3.0. 5% in top 10% of high school class, 28% in top 25% of high school class, 64% in top 50% of high school class. 95% from public high schools. Average SAT I Math 453, SAT I Math middle 50% range 400-520. Average SAT I Verbal 471, SAT I Verbal middle 50% range 410-510. ACT middle 50% range 17-21. TOEFL required of all international applicants, minimum TOEFL 500. **Basis for Candidate Selection:** *Very important factors considered include:* character/personal qualities, secondary school record, standardized test scores. *Important factors considered include:* class rank, interview. *Other factors considered include:* alumni/ae relation, essays, extracurricular activities, recommendations, talent/ability, volunteer work, work experience. **Freshman Admission Requirements:** High school diploma or GED is required. *Academic units required/recommended:* 22 total required; 4 English required, 3 math required, 3 science required, 1 science lab required, 3 social studies required, 6 elective required. **Freshman Admission Statistics:** 514 applied, 74% accepted, 47% of those accepted enrolled. **Transfer Admission**

Requirements: *Items required:* college transcript. Minimum high school GPA of 2.0 required. Minimum college GPA of 2.0 required. Lowest grade transferable D. **General Admission Information:** Application fee $20. Nonfall registration accepted. Admission may be deferred.

COSTS AND FINANCIAL AID

Tuition $6,900. Room & board $4,890. Average book expense $900. **Required Forms and Deadlines:** FAFSA, institution's own financial aid form and state aid form. No deadline for regular filing. Priority filing deadline March 10. **Notification of Awards:** Applicants will be notified of awards on a rolling basis beginning on or about March 10. **Types of Aid:** *Loans:* FFEL Subsidized Stafford, FFEL PLUS. **Student Employment:** Federal Work-Study Program available. Off-campus job opportunities are good. **Financial Aid Statistics:** 63% freshmen, 72% undergrads receive some form of aid. Average freshman grant $3,716. Average freshman loan $2,282. Average income from on-campus job $700. **Financial Aid Phone:** 540-326-4215.

BLUEFIELD STATE COLLEGE

219 Rock Street, Bluefield, WV 24701
Phone: 304-327-4065 **E-mail:** bscadmit@bluefieldstate.edu **CEEB Code:** 5064
Fax: 304-325-7747 **Web:** www.bluefieldstate.edu **ACT Code:** 4514

This public school was founded in 1895. It has a 40-acre campus.

STUDENTS AND FACULTY

Enrollment: 2,831. **Student Body:** Male 39%, female 61%, out-of-state 5%, international 1% (15 countries represented). **Ethnic Representation:** African American 10%, Caucasian 89%, Hispanic 1%. **Retention and Graduation:** 76% freshmen return for sophomore year. 22% freshmen graduate within 4 years. 5% grads go on to further study within 1 year. 3% grads pursue business degrees. 1% grads pursue law degrees. 1% grads pursue medical degrees. **Faculty:** Student/faculty ratio 17:1. 82 full-time faculty, 37% hold PhDs. 100% faculty teach undergrads.

ACADEMICS

Degrees: Associate's, bachelor's, certificate, terminal, transfer. **Academic Requirements:** General education including some course work in computer literacy, English (including composition), humanities, mathematics, sciences (biological or physical), social science, PE activity. **Classes:** 10-19 students in an average class. 10-19 students in an average lab/discussion section. **Majors with Highest Enrollment:** Business administration/management; elementary education and teaching; nursing/registered nurse training (RN, ASN, BSN, MSN). **Disciplines with Highest Percentage of Degrees Awarded:** Engineering/engineering technology 19%, business/marketing 19%, education 14%, health professions and related sciences 14%, liberal arts/general studies 12%. **Special Study Options:** Distance learning, dual enrollment, honors program, internships, student-designed major, teacher certification program.

FACILITIES

Housing: Off-campus housing services provided, including referrals and resources. **Library Holdings:** 84,857 bound volumes. 2,453 periodicals. 706,413 microforms. 341 audiovisuals. **Computers:** School-owned computers available for student use.

EXTRACURRICULARS

Activities: Choral groups, student government, student newspaper, yearbook. **Organizations:** 28 registered organizations, 6 honor societies, 1 religious organization, 3 fraternities (5% men join), 4 sororities (10% women join). **Athletics (Intercollegiate):** *Men:* baseball, basketball, cross-country, golf, tennis. *Women:* basketball, cheerleading, cross-country, softball, tennis.

ADMISSIONS

Selectivity Rating: 69 (of 100). **Freshman Academic Profile:** Average high school GPA 3.2. 10% in top 10% of high school class, 27% in top 25% of high school class, 73% in top 50% of high school class. 98% from public high schools. Average ACT 18, ACT middle 50% range 21-16. TOEFL required of all international applicants, minimum TOEFL 550. **Basis for Candidate Selection:** *Important factors considered include:* secondary school record, standardized test scores. **Freshman Admission Requirements:** High school diploma or GED is required. *Academic units required/recommended:* 17 total required; 4 English required, 3 math required, 3 science required, 2 science lab required, 2 foreign language recommended, 3 social studies required, 1 history required, 1 elective required. **Freshman Admission Statistics:** 1,191 applied, 99% accepted, 51% of those accepted enrolled. **Transfer Admission Requirements:** *Items required:* college transcript. Lowest grade transferable D. **General Admission Information:** Nonfall registration accepted. Admission may be deferred. Credit and/or placement offered for CEEB Advanced Placement tests.

COSTS AND FINANCIAL AID

In-state tuition $2,598. Out-of-state tuition $6,296. Average book expense $800. **Required Forms and Deadlines:** FAFSA, institution's own financial aid form, and state aid form. No deadline for regular filing. Priority filing deadline March 1. **Notification of Awards:** Applicants will be notified of awards on a rolling basis beginning on or about June 1. **Types of Aid:** *Need-based scholarships/grants:* Pell, SEOG, state scholarships/grants, private scholarships, the school's own gift aid. *Loans:* Direct Subsidized Stafford, Direct Unsubsidized Stafford, Direct PLUS, Federal Perkins. **Student Employment:** Federal Work-Study Program available. Institutional employment available. Off-campus job opportunities are good. **Financial Aid Statistics:** 70% freshmen, 34% undergrads receive some form of aid. Average freshman grant $1,400. Average freshman loan $2,200. Average income from on-campus job $1,500. **Financial Aid Phone:** 304-327-4020..

BLUFFTON COLLEGE

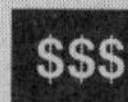

Office of Admissions, 280 West College Avenue, Bluffton, OH 45817
Phone: 419-358-3257 **E-mail:** admissions@bluffton.edu **CEEB Code:** 1067
Fax: 419-358-3232 **Web:** www.bluffton.edu **ACT Code:** 3238

This private school, which is affiliated with the Mennonite Church, was founded in 1899. It has a 65-acre campus.

STUDENTS AND FACULTY

Enrollment: 999. **Student Body:** Male 46%, female 54%, out-of-state 8%, international 1%. **Ethnic Representation:** African American 3%, Asian 1%, Caucasian 94%, Hispanic 1%. **Retention and Graduation:** 72% freshmen return for sophomore year. 51% freshmen graduate within 4 years. 9% grads go on to further study within 1 year. 1% grads pursue law degrees. 1% grads pursue medical degrees. **Faculty:** Student/faculty ratio 13:1. 64 full-time faculty, 71% hold PhDs. 100% faculty teach undergrads.

ACADEMICS

Degrees: Bachelor's, master's. **Academic Requirements:** General education including some course work in arts/fine arts, English (including composition), foreign languages, history, humanities, mathematics, sciences (biological or physical), social science. **Classes:** 10-19 students in an average class. 10-19 students in an average lab/discussion section. **Disciplines with Highest Percentage of Degrees Awarded:** Business/marketing 35%, education 26%, home economics and vocational home economics 6%, communications/communication technologies 4%, parks and recreation 4%. **Special Study Options:** Double major, English as a second language, student exchange program (domestic), honors program, internships, student-designed major, study abroad, teacher certification program, American Studies program (Washington, DC). Other term-away programs available.

FACILITIES

Housing: All-female, all-male. **Library Holdings:** 150,000 bound volumes. 1,000 periodicals. 97,000 microforms. 500 audiovisuals. **Special Academic Facilities/Equipment:** Mennonite historical library, peace arts center, nature preserve. **Computers:** School-owned computers available for student use.

EXTRACURRICULARS

Activities: Choral groups, concert band, dance, drama/theater, jazz band, literary magazine, music ensembles, musical theater, pep band, radio station, student government, student newspaper, yearbook. **Organizations:** 50 registered organizations, 19 honor societies, 10 religious organizations. **Athletics (Intercollegiate):** *Men:* baseball, basketball, cheerleading, cross-country, football, golf, indoor track, soccer, tennis, track & field. *Women:* basketball, cheerleading, cross-country, golf, indoor track, soccer, softball, tennis, track & field, volleyball.

ADMISSIONS

Selectivity Rating: 67 (of 100). **Freshman Academic Profile:** Average high school GPA 3.3. 19% in top 10% of high school class, 46% in top 25% of high school class, 79% in top 50% of high school class. 98% from public high schools. Average SAT I Math 531, SAT I Math middle 50% range 470-580. Average SAT I Verbal 539, SAT I Verbal middle 50% range 470-600. Average ACT 23, ACT middle 50% range 20-25. TOEFL required of all international applicants, minimum TOEFL 500. **Basis for Candidate Selection:** *Important factors considered include:* class rank, recommendations, secondary school record, standardized test scores. *Other factors considered include:* essays, interview. **Freshman Admission Requirements:** High school diploma is required and

GED is not accepted. *Academic units required/recommended:* 16 total recommended; 4 English recommended, 3 math recommended, 3 science recommended, 3 foreign language recommended, 3 social studies recommended. **Freshman Admission Statistics:** 733 applied, 86% accepted, 35% of those accepted enrolled. **Transfer Admission Requirements:** *Items required:* college transcript, standardized test scores, statement of good standing from prior school. Minimum college GPA of 2.0 required. Lowest grade transferable C. **General Admission Information:** Application fee $20. Regular application deadline May 31. Nonfall registration accepted. Admission may be deferred for a maximum of 2 years. Credit and/or placement offered for CEEB Advanced Placement tests.

COSTS AND FINANCIAL AID

Tuition $15,046. Room & board $5,268. Required fees $300. Average book expense $500. **Required Forms and Deadlines:** FAFSA. Financial aid filing deadline October 1. Priority filing deadline May 1. **Notification of Awards:** Applicants will be notified of awards on a rolling basis beginning on or about March 1. **Types of Aid:** *Need-based scholarships/grants:* Pell, SEOG, state scholarships/grants, private scholarships, the school's own gift aid. *Loans:* FFEL Subsidized Stafford, FFEL Unsubsidized Stafford, FFEL PLUS, Federal Perkins. **Student Employment:** Federal Work-Study Program available. Institutional employment available. Off-campus job opportunities are good. **Financial Aid Statistics:** 83% freshmen, 71% undergrads receive some form of aid. Average freshman grant $13,232. Average freshman loan $3,521. Average income from on-campus job $1,350. **Financial Aid Phone:** 800-488-3257.

See page 944.

BOISE STATE UNIVERSITY

1910 University Drive, Boise, ID 83725
Phone: 208-426-1156 **E-mail:** bsuinfo@boisestate.edu **CEEB Code:** 4018
Fax: 208-426-3765 **Web:** www.boisestate.edu **ACT Code:** 914

This public school was founded in 1932. It has a 110-acre campus.

STUDENTS AND FACULTY

Enrollment: 14,750. **Student Body:** Male 45%, female 55%, out-of-state 11%, international 1%. **Ethnic Representation:** African American 1%, Asian 2%, Caucasian 85%, Hispanic 5%, Native American 1%. **Retention and Graduation:** 61% freshmen return for sophomore year. 3% freshmen graduate within 4 years. **Faculty:** 95% faculty teach undergrads.

ACADEMICS

Degrees: Associate's, bachelor's, certificate, doctoral, master's.

FACILITIES

Housing: Coed, all-female, all-male, apartments for married students, apartments for single students, fraternities and/or sororities. **Library Holdings:** 433,000 bound volumes. 4,709 periodicals. 1,133,200 microforms. 55,240 audiovisuals. **Computers:** *Recommended operating system:* Mac. School-owned computers available for student use.

EXTRACURRICULARS

Activities: Choral groups, drama/theater, literary magazine, marching band, music ensembles, student government, student newspaper, student-run film society. **Organizations:** 4 fraternities (1% men join), 3 sororities (1% women join). **Athletics (Intercollegiate):** *Men:* basketball, cheerleading, cross-country, football, golf, indoor track, tennis, track & field, wrestling. *Women:* basketball, cheerleading, cross-country, golf, gymnastics, indoor track, soccer, tennis, track & field, volleyball.

ADMISSIONS

Selectivity Rating: 71 (of 100). **Freshman Academic Profile:** Average high school GPA 3.2. 98% from public high schools. SAT I Math middle 50% range 475-575. SAT I Verbal middle 50% range 450-550. Average ACT 21, ACT middle 50% range 18-24. TOEFL required of all international applicants, minimum TOEFL 500. **Freshman Admission Requirements:** High school diploma is required and GED is not accepted. *Academic units required/recommended:* 15 total required; 4 English required, 3 math required, 3 science required, 1 foreign language required, 2 social studies required, 1 elective required. **Freshman Admission Statistics:** 3,820 applied, 87% accepted, 63% of those accepted enrolled. **Transfer Admission Requirements:** Minimum college GPA of 2.0 required. **General Admission Information:** Application fee $20. Regular application deadline July 22. Nonfall registration accepted. Credit offered for CEEB Advanced Placement tests.

COSTS AND FINANCIAL AID

In-state tuition $2,294. Out-of-state tuition $8,174. Room & board $3,370. Average book expense $600. **Required Forms and Deadlines:** FAFSA. Financial aid filing deadline April 1. Priority filing deadline February 1. **Notification of Awards:** Applicants will be notified of awards on a rolling basis beginning on or about April 1. **Types of Aid:** *Need-based scholarships/grants:* Pell, SEOG, state scholarships/grants, private scholarships, the school's own gift aid. *Loans:* Direct Subsidized Stafford, Direct Unsubsidized Stafford, Direct PLUS, Federal Perkins, college/university loans from institutional funds. **Student Employment:** Federal Work-Study Program available. Institutional employment available. Off-campus job opportunities are excellent. **Financial Aid Phone:** 208-385-1664.

BORICUA COLLEGE

3755 Broadway, New York, NY 10032
Phone: 212-694-1000 **CEEB Code:** 2901
Fax: 212-694-1015

This private school was founded in 1973.

STUDENTS AND FACULTY

Enrollment: 1,072. **Ethnic Representation:** Hispanic 100%.

ACADEMICS

Degrees: Associate's, bachelor's. **Special Study Options:** Undergrads may take grad classes.

FACILITIES

Library Holdings: 128,727 bound volumes. 227 periodicals.

ADMISSIONS

Selectivity Rating: 60 (of 100). High school diploma is required and GED is not accepted. **Transfer Admission Requirements:** Lowest grade transferable C. **General Admission Information:** Regular application deadline January 15. Nonfall registration accepted.

COSTS AND FINANCIAL AID

Required fees $50. Average book expense $450. **Required Forms and Deadlines:** FAFSA. **Types of Aid:** *Loans:* FFEL Subsidized Stafford, FFEL PLUS. **Financial Aid Phone:** 212-694-1000.

BOROUGH OF MANHATTAN COMMUNITY COLLEGE

New York, NY 10007-1097
Phone: 212-220-1265 **E-mail:** ebarrios@bmcc.cuny.edu
Fax: 212-346-8110 **Web:** WWW.bmcc.cuny.edu

This public school was founded in 1964. It has a 5-acre campus.

STUDENTS AND FACULTY

Enrollment: 16,025. **Student Body:** Male 36%, female 64%, international 13%. **Ethnic Representation:** African American 42%, Asian 11%, Caucasian 12%, Hispanic 34%. **Retention and Graduation:** 40% grads go on to further study within 1 year. **Faculty:** Student/faculty ratio 21:1. 315 full-time faculty.

ACADEMICS

Degrees: Associate's, certificate, terminal, transfer. **Academic Requirements:** General education including some course work in English (including composition), mathematics, social science, fundamentals of speech communication. **Special Study Options:** Cooperative (work-study) program, distance learning, English as a second language, honors program, independent study, internships, study abroad, weekend college.

FACILITIES

Computers: *Recommended operating system:* Windows 95. School-owned computers available for student use.

EXTRACURRICULARS

Activities: Dance, drama/theater, musical theater, student government, student newspaper, yearbook.

ADMISSIONS

Selectivity Rating: 63 (of 100). High school diploma or GED is required. *Academic units required/recommended:* 16 total recommended; 4 English recommended, 3 math recommended, 2 science lab recommended, 2 foreign language recommended, 4 social studies recommended. **Freshman Admission Statistics:** 6,374 applied, 85% accepted, 60% of those accepted enrolled. **Transfer Admission Requirements:** *Items required:* college transcript. **General Admission Information:** Application fee $40.

COSTS AND FINANCIAL AID

In-state tuition $3,076. Out-of-state tuition $3,076. Required fees $80. Average book expense $350. **Types of Aid:** *Need-based scholarships/grants:* Pell, SEOG, state scholarships/grants, private scholarships, the school's own gift aid. *Loans:* FFEL Subsidized Stafford, FFEL Unsubsidized Stafford, FFEL PLUS, Federal Perkins, college/university loans from institutional funds. **Student Employment:** Federal Work-Study Program available. Institutional employment available. Off-campus job opportunities are good. **Financial Aid Phone:** 212-220-1430.

BOSTON ARCHITECTURAL CENTER

320 Newbury Street, Boston, MA 02115-2703
Phone: 617-585-0123 **E-mail:** admissions@the-bac.edu **CEEB Code:** 1168
Fax: 617-585-0121 **Web:** www.the-bac.edu

This private school was founded in 1889.

STUDENTS AND FACULTY

Enrollment: 365. **Student Body:** Male 78%, female 22%. **Ethnic Representation:** African American 2%, Asian 3%, Caucasian 43%, Hispanic 5%. **Faculty:** Student/faculty ratio 15:1. 100% faculty teach undergrads.

ACADEMICS

Degrees: Bachelor's, certificate, first professional, master's. **Academic Requirements:** General education including some course work in arts/fine arts, computer literacy, English (including composition), humanities, mathematics, sciences (biological or physical), social science. **Disciplines with Highest Percentage of Degrees Awarded:** Architecture 40%, other 14%. **Special Study Options:** Cross registration, distance learning, study abroad, concurrent academic and practice-based learning.

FACILITIES

Library Holdings: 25,000 bound volumes. 125 periodicals. **Special Academic Facilities/Equipment:** McCormick Gallery. **Computers:** School-owned computers available for student use.

EXTRACURRICULARS

Activities: Student newspaper. **Organizations:** 2 registered organizations.

ADMISSIONS

Selectivity Rating: 62 (of 100). **Freshman Academic Profile:** TOEFL required of all international applicants, minimum TOEFL 550. **Freshman Admission Requirements:** High school diploma or GED is required. **Freshman Admission Statistics:** 368 applied, 94% accepted, 32% of those accepted enrolled. **Transfer Admission Requirements:** *Items required:* high school transcript, college transcript. Lowest grade transferable C. **General Admission Information:** Application fee $50. Nonfall registration accepted. Admission may be deferred. Credit and/or placement offered for CEEB Advanced Placement tests.

COSTS AND FINANCIAL AID

Tuition $7,438. Required fees $150. Average book expense $1,105. **Required Forms and Deadlines:** FAFSA and institution's own financial aid form. Financial aid filing deadline March 31. Priority filing deadline March 31. **Notification of Awards:** Applicants will be notified of awards on a rolling basis beginning on or about April 30. **Types of Aid:** *Need-based scholarships/grants:* Pell, state scholarships/grants, private scholarships. *Loans:* FFEL Subsidized Stafford, FFEL Unsubsidized Stafford, FFEL PLUS, state loans. **Student Employment:** Off-campus job opportunities are excellent. **Financial Aid Statistics:** Average freshman grant $1,440. Average freshman loan $5,830. **Financial Aid Phone:** 617-585-0125.

BOSTON COLLEGE

140 Commonwealth Avenue, Devlin Hall 208, Chestnut Hill, MA 02467-3809
Phone: 617-552-3100 **E-mail:** ugadmis@bc.edu **CEEB Code:** 3083
Fax: 617-552-0798 **Web:** www.bc.edu **ACT Code:** 1788

This private school, which is affiliated with the Roman Catholic Church, was founded in 1863. It has a 240-acre campus.

STUDENTS AND FACULTY

Enrollment: 9,000. **Student Body:** Out-of-state 72%, international 1% (86 countries represented). **Ethnic Representation:** African American 5%, Asian 8%, Caucasian 75%, Hispanic 6%. **Retention and Graduation:** 95% freshmen return for sophomore year. 16% grads go on to further study within 1 year. 4% grads pursue business degrees. 5% grads pursue law degrees. 2% grads pursue medical degrees. **Faculty:** Student/faculty ratio 13:1. 645 full-time faculty, 98% hold PhDs. 100% faculty teach undergrads.

ACADEMICS

Degrees: Bachelor's, doctoral, first professional, master's, post-master's certificate. **Academic Requirements:** General education including some course work in arts/fine arts, history, mathematics, philosophy, sciences (biological or physical), social science, theology, cultural diversity, writing, and literature. **Classes:** 10-19 students in an average class. **Disciplines with Highest Percentage of Degrees Awarded:** Business/marketing 22%, social sciences and history 21%, communications/communication technologies 10%, English 10%, education 9%. **Special Study Options:** Accelerated program, cross registration, double major, English as a second language, student exchange program (domestic), honors program, independent study, internships, liberal arts/career combination, student-designed major, study abroad, teacher certification program.

FACILITIES

Housing: Coed, all-female, Greycliff Honors House, multicultural and intercultural floors, quiet floor, social justice floor, community living floor, leadership house. Also apartment-style housing and townhouse apartments. **Library Holdings:** 2,042,493 bound volumes. 21,296 periodicals. 3,443,937 microforms. 122,674 audiovisuals. **Special Academic Facilities/Equipment:** Art museum, theatre arts center, on-campus school for multihandicapped students, observatory, state-of-the-art science facilities. **Computers:** School-owned computers available for student use.

EXTRACURRICULARS

Activities: Choral groups, concert band, dance, drama/theater, jazz band, literary magazine, marching band, music ensembles, musical theater, pep band, radio station, student government, student newspaper, student-run film society, symphony orchestra, television station, yearbook. **Organizations:** 230 registered organizations, 11 religious organizations. **Athletics (Intercollegiate):** *Men:* baseball, basketball, cross-country, diving, fencing, football, golf, ice hockey, indoor track, lacrosse, sailing, skiing (alpine), soccer, swimming, tennis, track & field, water polo, wrestling. *Women:* basketball, crew, cross-country, diving, fencing, field hockey, golf, ice hockey, indoor track, lacrosse, sailing, skiing (alpine), soccer, softball, swimming, tennis, track & field, volleyball.

ADMISSIONS

Selectivity Rating: 96 (of 100). **Freshman Academic Profile:** 69% in top 10% of high school class, 93% in top 25% of high school class, 99% in top 50% of high school class. 61% from public high schools. SAT I Math middle 50% range 620-700. SAT I Verbal middle 50% range 600-690. TOEFL required of all international applicants, minimum TOEFL 600. **Basis for Candidate Selection:** *Very important factors considered include:* character/personal qualities, secondary school record, standardized test scores. *Important factors considered include:* alumni/ae relation, class rank, essays, extracurricular activities, minority status, recommendations, religious affiliation/commitment, talent/ability, volunteer work, work experience. **Freshman Admission Requirements:** High school diploma or GED is required. *Academic units required/recommended:* 20 total recommended; 4 English recommended, 4 math recommended, 4 science recommended, 4 science lab recommended, 4 foreign language recommended. **Freshman Admission Statistics:** 19,059 applied, 34% accepted, 33% of those accepted enrolled. **Transfer Admission Requirements:** *Items required:* high school transcript, college transcript, essay, standardized test scores, statement of good standing from prior school. Minimum college GPA of 3.0 required. Lowest grade transferable C. **General Admission Information:** Application fee $55. Regular application deadline January 2. Nonfall registration accepted. Admission may be deferred for a maximum of 2 years. Placement offered for CEEB Advanced Placement tests.

COSTS AND FINANCIAL AID

Tuition $24,050. Room & board $9,785. Required fees $420. Average book expense $600. **Required Forms and Deadlines:** FAFSA, CSS/Financial Aid PROFILE, noncustodial (divorced/separated) parent's statement, business/farm supplement, and parent and student tax returns and W-2 statements. Priority filing deadline February 1. **Notification of Awards:** Applicants will be notified of awards on or about April 15. **Types of Aid:** *Need-based scholarships/grants:* Pell, SEOG, state scholarships/grants, private scholarships, the school's own gift aid. *Loans:* FFEL Subsidized Stafford, FFEL Unsubsidized Stafford, FFEL PLUS, Federal Perkins, Federal Nursing, state loans. **Student Employment:** Federal Work-Study Program available. Institutional employment available. Off-campus job opportunities are good. **Financial Aid Statistics:** 90% freshmen, 42% undergrads receive some form of aid. Average freshman grant $13,934. Average freshman loan $3,459. Average income from on-campus job $1,400. **Financial Aid Phone:** 800-294-0294.

BOSTON CONSERVATORY

8 The Fenway, Boston, MA 02215
Phone: 617-912-9153 **E-mail:** admissions@bostonconservatory.edu **CEEB Code:** 3084
Fax: 617-536-3176 **Web:** www.bostonconservatory.edu **ACT Code:** 1790

This private school was founded in 1867.

STUDENTS AND FACULTY

Enrollment: 350. **Student Body:** Male 29%, female 71%, international 7% (26 countries represented). **Ethnic Representation:** African American 3%, Asian 6%, Caucasian 43%, Hispanic 5%, Native American 1%. **Retention and Graduation:** 68% freshmen return for sophomore year. **Faculty:** 100% faculty teach undergrads.

ACADEMICS

Degrees: Bachelor's, diploma, master's, post-bachelor's certificate, post-master's certificate. **Academic Requirements:** General education including some course work in English (including composition), history, social science, liberal arts core 5th and 6th semester; 9 credits of electives. **Special Study Options:** Cross registration, double major, English as a second language, independent study, teacher certification program.

FACILITIES

Housing: Coed, all-female, graduate house. **Library Holdings:** 40,000 bound volumes. 250 periodicals. 10,050 audiovisuals. **Computers:** *Recommended operating system:* Windows NT/2000. School-owned computers available for student use.

EXTRACURRICULARS

Activities: Literary magazine, student government, student newspaper. **Organizations:** 11 registered organizations, 1 honor society, 1 religious organization.

ADMISSIONS

Selectivity Rating: 74 (of 100). **Freshman Academic Profile:** 90% from public high schools. TOEFL required of all international applicants, **Basis for Candidate Selection:** *Very important factors considered include:* character/personal qualities, recommendations, talent/ability. *Important factors considered include:* class rank, essays, interview, secondary school record, standardized test scores. *Other factors considered include:* extracurricular activities. **Freshman Admission Requirements:** High school diploma or GED is required. *Academic units required/recommended:* 4 English required, 3 math required, 2 science required, 2 foreign language required, 2 social studies required, 2 history required. **Transfer Admission Requirements:** *Items required:* college transcript, essay. Minimum college GPA of 2.5 required. Lowest grade transferable C. **General Admission Information:** Application fee $60. Priority application deadline March 1. Nonfall registration accepted. Admission may be deferred for a maximum of 1 year. Credit offered for CEEB Advanced Placement tests.

COSTS AND FINANCIAL AID

Tuition $20,400. Room & board $7,370. Required fees $1,075. Average book expense $500. **Required Forms and Deadlines:** FAFSA and institution's own financial aid form. Financial aid filing deadline March 1. Priority filing deadline March 1. **Notification of Awards:** Applicants will be notified of awards on or about April 1. **Types of Aid:** *Need-based scholarships/grants:* Pell, SEOG, state scholarships/grants, the school's own gift aid. *Loans:* FFEL Subsidized Stafford, FFEL Unsubsidized Stafford, FFEL PLUS, college/university loans from institutional funds. **Student Employment:** Federal Work-Study Program available. Institutional employment available. Off-campus job opportunities are excellent. **Financial Aid Statistics:** 39% freshmen, 53% undergrads receive some form of aid. Average freshman grant $6,736. Average freshman loan $3,260. Average income from on-campus job $830. **Financial Aid Phone:** 617-912-9147.

BOSTON UNIVERSITY

121 Bay State Road, Boston, MA 02215
Phone: 617-353-2300 **E-mail:** admissions@bu.edu **CEEB Code:** 3087
Fax: 617-353-9695 **Web:** www.bu.edu **ACT Code:** 1794

This private school was founded in 1839. It has a 132-acre campus.

STUDENTS AND FACULTY

Enrollment: 17,860. **Student Body:** Male 40%, female 60%, out-of-state 76%, international 6% (101 countries represented). **Ethnic Representation:** African American 3%, Asian 13%, Caucasian 67%, Hispanic 5%. **Retention and Graduation:** 89% freshmen return for sophomore year. 62% freshmen graduate within 4 years. **Faculty:** Student/faculty ratio 14:1. 2,500 full-time faculty. 74% faculty teach undergrads.

ACADEMICS

Degrees: Bachelor's, doctoral, first professional, master's, post-master's certificate. **Academic Requirements:** General education including some course work in computer literacy, English (including composition), foreign languages, humanities, mathematics, sciences (biological or physical), social science. **Classes:** 10-19 students in an average class. 20-29 students in an average lab/discussion section. **Disciplines with Highest Percentage of Degrees Awarded:** Business/marketing 18%, social sciences and history 18%, communications/communication technologies 17%, psychology 8%, engineering/engineering technology 6%. **Special Study Options:** Accelerated program, cooperative (work-study) program, cross registration, double major, dual enrollment, English as a second language, honors program, independent study, internships, liberal arts/career combination, student-designed major, study abroad, teacher certification program, weekend college, field study in marine science at the Woods Hole Institute and in environmental/ecological science in Ecuador at the Biodiversity Station in the tropical rain forest; The Photonics Center.

FACILITIES

Housing: Coed, all-female, apartments for married students, apartments for single students, housing for disabled students, cooperative housing, specialty dorms/floors for groups of students with a common interest or academic major. **Library Holdings:** 2,244,486 bound volumes. 4,093,998 periodicals. 71,067 microforms. 29,389 audiovisuals. **Special Academic Facilities/Equipment:** center for computational science, center for advanced biotechnology, center for photonics research, art galleries, planetarium, commercial TV station, National Public Radio station, 20th-century archives, professional theatre and theatre company, center for remote sensing, Geddes Language Laboratory, culinary center, Metcalf Center for Science and Engineering, Tsai Performance Center, College of Communication multimedia lab, and speech, language, and hearing clinic. **Computers:** School-owned computers available for student use.

EXTRACURRICULARS

Activities: Choral groups, dance, drama/theater, literary magazine, marching band, opera, radio station, student government, student newspaper, student-run film society, symphony orchestra, yearbook. **Organizations:** 360 registered organizations, 10 honor societies, 23 religious organizations, 9 fraternities (3% men join), 10 sororities (5% women join). **Athletics (Intercollegiate):** *Men:* basketball, crew, cross-country, diving, golf, ice hockey, indoor track, soccer, swimming, tennis, track & field, wrestling. *Women:* basketball, crew, cross-country, diving, field hockey, golf, indoor track, lacrosse, soccer, softball, swimming, tennis, track & field.

ADMISSIONS

Selectivity Rating: 91 (of 100). **Freshman Academic Profile:** Average high school GPA 3.5. 56% in top 10% of high school class, 90% in top 25% of high school class, 100% in top 50% of high school class. 70% from public high schools. Average SAT I Math 650, SAT I Math middle 50% range 610-690. Average SAT I Verbal 634, SAT I Verbal middle 50% range 590-680. Average ACT 28, ACT middle 50% range 25-29. TOEFL required of all international applicants, minimum TOEFL 550. **Basis for Candidate Selection:** *Very important factors considered include:* secondary school record. *Important factors considered include:* class rank, essays, recommendations, standardized test scores. *Other factors considered include:* alumni/ae relation, character/personal qualities, extracurricular activities, interview, volunteer work, work experience. **Freshman Admission Requirements:** High school diploma or GED is required. *Academic units required/recommended:* 15 total required; 20 total recommended; 4 English required, 4 English recommended, 3 math required, 4 math recommended, 3 science required, 4 science recommended, 3 social studies required, 4 social studies recommended, 2 foreign language required, 4 foreign language recommended. **Freshman Admission Statistics:** 27,038 applied, 58% accepted, 29% of those accepted enrolled. **Transfer Admission Requirements:** *Items required:* high school transcript, college transcript, essay, standardized test scores, statement of good standing from prior school. Lowest grade transferable C. **General Admission Information:** Application fee $60. Early decision application deadline November 1. Regular application deadline January 1. Nonfall registration accepted. Admission may be deferred for a maximum of 1 year. Credit and/or placement offered for CEEB Advanced Placement tests.

COSTS AND FINANCIAL AID

Tuition $28,512. Room & board $9,288. Required fees $394. Average book expense $753. **Required Forms and Deadlines:** FAFSA, CSS/Financial Aid PROFILE, state aid form, noncustodial (divorced/separated) parent's statement, and business/farm supplement. Priority filing deadline February 15. **Notification of Awards:** Applicants will be notified of awards on a rolling basis beginning on or about March 22. **Types of Aid:** *Need-based scholarships/ grants:* Pell, SEOG, state scholarships/grants, private scholarships, the school's own gift aid. *Loans:* Direct Subsidized Stafford, Direct Unsubsidized Stafford, Direct PLUS, Federal Perkins, state loans. **Student Employment:** Federal Work-Study Program available. Institutional employment available. Off-campus job opportunities are excellent. **Financial Aid Statistics:** 52% freshmen, 46% undergrads receive some form of aid. Average freshman grant $17,494. Average freshman loan $3,644. Average income from on-campus job $1,425. **Financial Aid Phone:** 617-353-2965.

See page 946.

BOWDOIN COLLEGE

5000 College Station, Brunswick, ME 04011-8441
Phone: 207-725-3100 **E-mail:** admissions@bowdoin.edu **CEEB Code:** 3089
Fax: 207-725-3101 **Web:** www.bowdoin.edu **ACT Code:** 1636

This private school was founded in 1794. It has a 200-acre campus.

STUDENTS AND FACULTY

Enrollment: 1,657. **Student Body:** Male 49%, female 51%, out-of-state 85%, international 3% (27 countries represented). **Ethnic Representation:** African American 4%, Asian 9%, Caucasian 79%, Hispanic 4%, Native American 1%. **Retention and Graduation:** 95% freshmen return for sophomore year. 83% freshmen graduate within 4 years. 15% grads go on to further study within 1 year. 17% grads pursue business degrees. 22% grads pursue law degrees. 16% grads pursue medical degrees. **Faculty:** Student/faculty ratio 10:1. 151 full-time faculty, 94% hold PhDs. 100% faculty teach undergrads.

ACADEMICS

Degrees: Bachelor's. **Academic Requirements:** General education including some course work in arts/fine arts, humanities, mathematics, sciences (biological or physical), social science, non-Eurocentric studies. **Classes:** 10-19 students in an average class. 10-19 students in an average lab/discussion section. **Majors with Highest Enrollment:** Political science and government, general; biology/biological sciences, general; English language and literature, general. **Disciplines with Highest Percentage of Degrees Awarded:** Social sciences and history 38%, biological life sciences 13%, foreign languages and literature 9%, English 8%, visual and performing arts 5%. **Special Study Options:** Accelerated program, double major, student exchange program (domestic), independent study, liberal arts/career combination, student-designed major, study abroad, teacher certification program. 3-2 engineering degree programs with California Institute of Technology and Columbia University; 3-3 legal studies degree program with Columbia University Law School. Pass/Fail grading options are available.

FACILITIES

Housing: Coed; apartments for single students; college house system whereby students are assigned a house from the first year, combining social and academic experiences. **Library Holdings:** 948,879 bound volumes. 1,983 periodicals. 105,899 microforms. 20,214 audiovisuals. **Special Academic Facilities/Equipment:** Art museum, Arctic Museum, coastal marine biology and ornithology research facilities, experimental black box theater, new 600-seat theater, Baldwin Center for Learning and Teaching, outdoor leadership center, crafts center, 6 specialized libraries, Coleman Farm. **Computers:** School-owned computers available for student use.

EXTRACURRICULARS

Activities: Choral groups, concert band, dance, drama/theater, jazz band, literary magazine, music ensembles, musical theater, radio station, student government, student newspaper, student-run film society, symphony orchestra, television station, yearbook. **Organizations:** 96 registered organizations, 1 honor society, 6 religious organizations. **Athletics (Intercollegiate):** *Men:* baseball, basketball, cross-country, diving, football, golf, ice hockey, indoor track, lacrosse, sailing, skiing (alpine), skiing (Nordic), soccer, squash, swimming, tennis, track & field. *Women:* basketball, cross-country, diving, field hockey, golf, ice hockey, indoor track, lacrosse, sailing, skiing (alpine), skiing (Nordic), soccer, softball, squash, swimming, tennis, track & field, volleyball.

ADMISSIONS

Selectivity Rating: 96 (of 100). **Freshman Academic Profile:** 72% in top 10% of high school class, 94% in top 25% of high school class, 100% in top 50% of high school class. 53% from public high schools. Average SAT I Math 680, SAT I Math middle 50% range 640-720. Average SAT I Verbal 680, SAT I Verbal middle 50% range 640-730. TOEFL required of all international applicants, minimum TOEFL 600. **Basis for Candidate Selection:** *Very important factors considered include:* character/personal qualities, class rank, essays, minority status, recommendations, secondary school record. *Important factors considered include:* alumni/ae relation, extracurricular activities, geographical residence, talent/ability, volunteer work. *Other factors considered include:* interview, standardized test scores, work experience. **Freshman Admission Requirements:** High school diploma or equivalent is not required. *Academic units required/recommended:* 20 total recommended; 4 English recommended, 4 math recommended, 4 science recommended, 3 science lab recommended, 4 foreign language recommended, 4 social studies recommended. **Freshman Admission Statistics:** 4,505 applied, 25% accepted, 41% of those accepted enrolled. **Transfer Admission Requirements:** *Items required:* high school transcript, college transcript, essay, statement of good standing from prior school. Minimum college GPA of 3.0 required. Lowest grade transferable C. **General Admission Information:** Application fee $60. Early decision application deadline November 15. Regular application deadline January 1. Admission may be deferred for a maximum of 1 year. Credit and/or placement offered for CEEB Advanced Placement tests.

COSTS AND FINANCIAL AID

Tuition $28,070. Room & board $7,305. Required fees $615. Average book expense $850. **Required Forms and Deadlines:** FAFSA, institution's own financial aid form, CSS/Financial Aid PROFILE, noncustodial (divorced/ separated) parent's statement, and business/farm supplement. Financial aid filing deadline February 15. **Notification of Awards:** Applicants will be notified of awards on or about April 5. **Types of Aid:** *Need-based scholarships/ grants:* Pell, SEOG, state scholarships/grants, private scholarships, the school's own gift aid. *Loans:* FFEL Subsidized Stafford, FFEL Unsubsidized Stafford, FFEL PLUS, Federal Perkins, state loans, college/university loans from institutional funds. **Student Employment:** Federal Work-Study Program available. Institutional employment available. Off-campus job opportunities are fair. **Financial Aid Statistics:** 45% freshmen, 40% undergrads receive some form of aid. Average freshman grant $22,660. Average freshman loan $2,375. Average income from on-campus job $1,264. **Financial Aid Phone:** 207-725-3273.

BOWIE STATE UNIVERSITY

14000 Jericho Park Road, Henry Administration Building, Bowie, MD 20715
Phone: 301-860-3415 **E-mail:** schanaiwa@bowiestate.edu **CEEB Code:** 5401
Fax: 301-860-3438 **Web:** www.bowiestate.edu

This public school was founded in 1865. It has a 312-acre campus.

STUDENTS AND FACULTY

Enrollment: 3,673. **Student Body:** Male 38%, female 62%, out-of-state 7%, international 1% (48 countries represented). **Ethnic Representation:** African American 90%, Asian 1%, Caucasian 6%, Hispanic 1%. **Retention and Graduation:** 75% freshmen return for sophomore year. 14% freshmen graduate within 4 years. **Faculty:** Student/faculty ratio 18:1. 149 full-time faculty, 66% hold PhDs. 95% faculty teach undergrads.

ACADEMICS

Degrees: Bachelor's, certificate, doctoral, master's, post-bachelor's certificate. **Academic Requirements:** General education including some course work in arts/fine arts, computer literacy, English (including composition), history, humanities, mathematics, philosophy, sciences (biological or physical), social science, health and wellness, orientation to college. **Classes:** 20-29 students in an average class. **Majors with Highest Enrollment:** Computer science; psychology, general; business administration/management. **Disciplines with Highest Percentage of Degrees Awarded:** Business/marketing 25%, interdisciplinary studies 16%, social sciences and history 15%, psychology 10%, communications/communication technologies 9%. **Special Study Options:** Cooperative (work-study) program, cross registration, distance learning, double major, dual enrollment, student exchange program (domestic), honors program, independent study, internships, liberal arts/career combination, study abroad, teacher certification program, dual degree mathematics/engineering program.

FACILITIES

Housing: Coed, all-female, all-male, honors' residence, special-interest floors. **Library Holdings:** 409,036 bound volumes. 684 periodicals. 394,883 microforms. 4,475 audiovisuals. **Special Academic Facilities/Equipment:** Science and math labs, computer academy, art galleries. **Computers:** School-owned computers available for student use.

EXTRACURRICULARS

Activities: Choral groups, concert band, dance, drama/theater, jazz band, literary magazine, marching band, music ensembles, musical theater, pep band, radio station, student government, student newspaper, television station, yearbook. **Organizations:** 71 registered organizations, 17 honor societies, 2 religious organizations, 4 fraternities (1% men join), 4 sororities (2% women join). **Athletics (Intercollegiate):** *Men:* basketball, cross-country, football, track & field. *Women:* basketball, cross-country, softball, tennis, track & field, volleyball.

ADMISSIONS

Selectivity Rating: 63 (of 100). **Freshman Academic Profile:** Average high school GPA 3.1. Average SAT I Math 446, SAT I Math middle 50% range 400-490. Average SAT I Verbal 455, SAT I Verbal middle 50% range 410-490. TOEFL required of all international applicants, minimum TOEFL 500. **Basis for Candidate Selection:** *Very important factors considered include:* secondary school record, standardized test scores. *Other factors considered include:* alumni/ae relation, character/personal qualities, class rank, essays, extracurricular activities, geographical residence, interview, recommendations, state residency, talent/ability, volunteer work, work experience. **Freshman Admission Requirements:** High school diploma or GED is required. *Academic units required/recommended:* 4 English required, 3 math required, 3 science required, 2 foreign language required, 1 social studies required, 2 history required. **Freshman Admission Statistics:** 2,609 applied, 52% accepted, 42% of those accepted enrolled. **Transfer Admission Requirements:** *Items required:* college transcript. Minimum college GPA of 2.0 required. Lowest grade transferable C. **General Admission Information:** Application fee $40. Nonfall registration accepted. Admission may be deferred for a maximum of 1 year. Credit and/or placement offered for CEEB Advanced Placement tests.

COSTS AND FINANCIAL AID

In-state tuition $3,103. Out-of-state tuition $9,519. Room & board $5,673. Required fees $961. Average book expense $1,172. **Required Forms and Deadlines:** FAFSA and institution's own financial aid form. No deadline for regular filing. **Notification of Awards:** Applicants will be notified of awards on a rolling basis. **Types of Aid:** *Need-based scholarships/grants:* Pell, SEOG, state scholarships/grants, private scholarships, the school's own gift aid. *Loans:* FFEL Subsidized Stafford, FFEL Unsubsidized Stafford, FFEL PLUS, Federal Perkins. **Student Employment:** Federal Work-Study Program available. Institutional employment available. Off-campus job opportunities are good. **Financial Aid Statistics:** 63% freshmen, 58% undergrads receive some form of aid. **Financial Aid Phone:** 301-860-3540.

BOWLING GREEN STATE UNIVERSITY

110 McFall Center, Bowling Green, OH 43403
Phone: 419-372-2086 **E-mail:** admissions@bgnet.bgsu.edu **CEEB Code:** 1069
Fax: 419-372-6955 **Web:** www.bgsu.edu **ACT Code:** 3240

This public school was founded in 1910. It has a 1,250-acre campus.

STUDENTS AND FACULTY

Enrollment: 15,703. **Student Body:** Male 44%, female 56%, out-of-state 7%, international 1%. **Ethnic Representation:** African American 5%, Asian 1%, Caucasian 88%, Hispanic 2%. **Retention and Graduation:** 74% freshmen return for sophomore year. 24% freshmen graduate within 4 years. **Faculty:** Student/faculty ratio 19:1. 802 full-time faculty, 80% hold PhDs.

ACADEMICS

Degrees: Bachelor's, doctoral, master's, post-master's certificate. **Academic Requirements:** General education including some course work in English (including composition), humanities, mathematics, sciences (biological or physical), social science, multicultural perspective. **Classes:** 20-29 students in an average class. **Majors with Highest Enrollment:** Early childhood education and teaching; biology/biological sciences, general; psychology, general. **Disciplines with Highest Percentage of Degrees Awarded:** Education 24%, business/marketing 15%, visual and performing arts 9%, health professions and related sciences 8%, English 7%. **Special Study Options:** Accelerated program, cooperative (work-study) program, cross registration, distance learning, double major, dual enrollment, student exchange program (domestic), honors program, independent study, internships, liberal arts/career combination, student-designed major, study abroad, teacher certification program.

FACILITIES

Housing: Coed, fraternities and/or sororities, residential housing communities. **Library Holdings:** 2,416,042 bound volumes. 4,833 periodicals. 2,330,490 microforms. 718,734 audiovisuals. **Computers:** School-owned computers available for student use.

EXTRACURRICULARS

Activities: Choral groups, concert band, dance, drama/theater, jazz band, literary magazine, marching band, music ensembles, musical theater, radio station, student government, student newspaper, student-run film society, symphony orchestra, television station, yearbook. **Organizations:** 285 registered organizations, 20 honor societies, 19 fraternities (8% men join), 17 sororities (11% women join). **Athletics (Intercollegiate):** *Men:* baseball, basketball, cross-country, diving, football, golf, ice hockey, soccer, swimming, tennis, track & field. *Women:* basketball, cross-country, diving, golf, gymnastics, soccer, softball, swimming, tennis, track & field, volleyball.

ADMISSIONS

Selectivity Rating: 63 (of 100). **Freshman Academic Profile:** Average high school GPA 3.2. 10% in top 10% of high school class, 35% in top 25% of high school class, 65% in top 50% of high school class. Average SAT I Math 508, SAT I Math middle 50% range 450-560. Average SAT I Verbal 505, SAT I Verbal middle 50% range 460-560. Average ACT 22, ACT middle 50% range 19-24. TOEFL required of all international applicants, minimum TOEFL 500. **Basis for Candidate Selection:** *Very important factors considered include:* secondary school record, standardized test scores. *Important factors considered include:* recommendations, talent/ability. *Other factors considered include:* alumni/ae relation, character/personal qualities, class rank, essays, extracurricular activities, interview, minority status, volunteer work, work experience. **Freshman Admission Requirements:** High school diploma or GED is required. *Academic units required/recommended:* 16 total required; 4 English required, 3 math required, 3 science required, 2 science lab required, 2 foreign language required, 3 social studies required. **Freshman Admission Statistics:** 10,128 applied, 91% accepted, 39% of those accepted enrolled. **Transfer Admission Requirements:** Minimum high school GPA of 2.5 required. Minimum college GPA of 2.5 required. Lowest grade transferable C. **General Admission Information:** Application fee $35. Priority application deadline February 1. Regular application deadline July 15. Nonfall registration accepted. Admission may be deferred for a maximum of 1 year. Credit and/or placement offered for CEEB Advanced Placement tests.

COSTS AND FINANCIAL AID

In-state tuition $5,358. Out-of-state tuition $11,986. Room & board $6,490. Required fees $1,144. Average book expense $884. **Required Forms and Deadlines:** FAFSA. No deadline for regular filing. **Notification of Awards:** Applicants will be notified of awards on a rolling basis beginning on or about April 15. **Types of Aid:** *Need-based scholarships/grants:* Pell, SEOG, state scholarships/grants, private scholarships, the school's own gift aid. *Loans:* Direct Subsidized Stafford, Direct Unsubsidized Stafford, Direct PLUS, Federal Perkins, Federal Nursing, state loans, college/university loans from institutional funds. **Student Employment:** Federal Work-Study Program available. Institutional employment available. Off-campus job opportunities are good. **Financial Aid Statistics:** 59% freshmen, 54% undergrads receive some form of aid. **Financial Aid Phone:** 419-372-2651.

BRADLEY UNIVERSITY

1501 West Bradley Avenue, Peoria, IL 61625
Phone: 309-677-1000 **E-mail:** admissions@bradley.edu **CEEB Code:** 1070
Fax: 309-677-2797 **Web:** www.bradley.edu **ACT Code:** 960

This private school was founded in 1897. It has a 75-acre campus.

STUDENTS AND FACULTY

Enrollment: 5,190. **Student Body:** Male 45%, female 55%, out-of-state 14%, international 2% (26 countries represented). **Ethnic Representation:** African American 5%, Asian 2%, Caucasian 85%, Hispanic 2%. **Retention and Graduation:** 86% freshmen return for sophomore year. 17% grads go on to further study within 1 year. **Faculty:** Student/faculty ratio 14:1. 330 full-time faculty, 81% hold PhDs. 100% faculty teach undergrads.

ACADEMICS

Degrees: Bachelor's, master's. **Academic Requirements:** General education including some course work in arts/fine arts, computer literacy, English (including composition), history, humanities, mathematics, sciences (biological or physical), social science. **Classes:** 10-19 students in an average class. **Majors with Highest Enrollment:** Elementary education and teaching; psychology, general; actuarial science. **Disciplines with Highest Percentage of Degrees Awarded:** Business/marketing 21%, engineering/engineering technology 16%, communications/communication technologies 12%, education 10%, health professions and related sciences 9%. **Special Study Options:** Accelerated program, cooperative (work-study) program, distance learning, double major, honors program, independent study, internships, liberal arts/career combination, student-designed major, study abroad, teacher certification program.

FACILITIES

Housing: Coed, all-male, apartments for single students, fraternities and/or sororities. **Library Holdings:** 424,752 bound volumes. 1,996 periodicals. 806,754 microforms. 9,574 audiovisuals. **Special Academic Facilities/ Equipment:** Caterpillar Global Communication Center, two art galleries on campus. **Computers:** School-owned computers available for student use.

EXTRACURRICULARS

Activities: Choral groups, concert band, drama/theater, jazz band, literary magazine, music ensembles, musical theater, opera, pep band, radio station, student government, student newspaper, symphony orchestra, television station, yearbook. **Organizations:** 220 registered organizations, 31 honor societies, 7 religious organizations, 18 fraternities (34% men join), 12 sororities (33% women join). **Athletics (Intercollegiate):** *Men:* baseball, basketball, cross-country, golf, soccer, tennis. *Women:* basketball, cross-country, golf, indoor track, softball, tennis, track & field, volleyball.

ADMISSIONS

Selectivity Rating: 77 (of 100). **Freshman Academic Profile:** 33% in top 10% of high school class, 68% in top 25% of high school class, 93% in top 50% of high school class. 76% from public high schools. Average SAT I Math 610, SAT I Math middle 50% range 550-670. Average SAT I Verbal 590, SAT I Verbal middle 50% range 540-650. Average ACT 25, ACT middle 50% range 23-29. TOEFL required of all international applicants, minimum TOEFL 500. **Basis for Candidate Selection:** *Very important factors considered include:* secondary school record. *Important factors considered include:* class rank, standardized test scores. *Other factors considered include:* alumni/ae relation, character/personal qualities, essays, extracurricular activities, interview, minority status, recommendations, talent/ability, volunteer work, work experience. **Freshman Admission Requirements:** High school diploma or GED is required. *Academic units required/recommended:* 16 total required; 4 English required, 5 English recommended, 3 math required, 4 math recommended, 2 science required, 3 science recommended, 2 science lab required, 3 science lab recommended, 2 foreign language recommended, 2 social studies required, 3 social studies recommended, 2 history recommended. **Freshman Admission Statistics:** 5,506 applied, 67% accepted, 30% of those accepted enrolled. **Transfer Admission Requirements:** *Items required:* college transcript, statement of good standing from prior school. Minimum college GPA of 2.0 required. Lowest grade transferable C. **General Admission Information:** Application fee $35. Priority application deadline March 1. Regular application deadline rolling. Nonfall registration accepted. Admission may be deferred for a maximum of 1 year. Neither credit nor placement offered for CEEB Advanced Placement tests.

COSTS AND FINANCIAL AID

Average book expense $500. **Required Forms and Deadlines:** FAFSA. Priority filing deadline March 1. **Notification of Awards:** Applicants will be notified of awards on a rolling basis. **Types of Aid:** *Need-based scholarships/ grants:* Pell, SEOG, state scholarships/grants, private scholarships, the school's own gift aid. *Loans:* Direct Subsidized Stafford, Direct Unsubsidized Stafford, Direct PLUS, Federal Perkins, Federal Nursing, college/university loans from institutional funds. **Student Employment:** Federal Work-Study Program available. Institutional employment available. Off-campus job opportunities are good. **Financial Aid Statistics:** 63% freshmen, 71% undergrads receive some form of aid. Average freshman grant $9,279. Average freshman loan $3,671. **Financial Aid Phone:** 309-677-3089.

BRANDEIS UNIVERSITY

415 South St., MS003, Waltham, MA 02454
Phone: 781-736-3500 **E-mail:** sendinfo@brandeis.edu **CEEB Code:** 3092
Fax: 781-736-3536 **Web:** www.brandeis.edu **ACT Code:** 1802

This private school was founded in 1948. It has a 235-acre campus.

STUDENTS AND FACULTY

Enrollment: 3,057. **Student Body:** Male 44%, female 56%, out-of-state 75%, international 6% (54 countries represented). **Ethnic Representation:** African American 3%, Asian 10%, Caucasian 75%, Hispanic 3%. **Retention and Graduation:** 94% freshmen return for sophomore year. 80% freshmen graduate within 4 years. 23% grads go on to further study within 1 year. 2% grads pursue business degrees. 6% grads pursue law degrees. 4% grads pursue medical degrees. **Faculty:** Student/faculty ratio 8:1. 333 full-time faculty, 97% hold PhDs. 100% faculty teach undergrads.

ACADEMICS

Degrees: Bachelor's, diploma, doctoral, master's, post-bachelor's certificate. **Academic Requirements:** General education including some course work in arts/fine arts, foreign languages, humanities, sciences (biological or physical), social science, nonwestern and comparative studies, quantitative reasoning, physical education, writing intensive course, freshman-year course in humanistic inquiry. **Classes:** 10-19 students in an average class. **Majors with Highest Enrollment:** Biology/biological sciences, general; economics, general; political science and government, general. **Disciplines with Highest Percentage of Degrees Awarded:** Social sciences and history 44%, biological life sciences 15%, area and ethnic studies 10%, psychology 7%, English 6%. **Special Study Options:** Cross registration, double major, independent study, internships, student-designed major, study abroad, teacher certification program.

FACILITIES

Housing: Coed, apartments for single students, housing for disabled students. **Library Holdings:** 938,835 bound volumes. 4,956 periodicals. 914,322 microforms. 35,287 audiovisuals. **Special Academic Facilities/Equipment:** Art museum, multicultural library, intercultural center, theatre arts complex, language lab, American Jewish Historical Society headquarters, spatial orientation lab, research centers (on aging, basic medical sciences, complex systems, family/children's policy, health policy, mental retardation, public policy, and study of European Jewry), student leadership development room. **Computers:** School-owned computers available for student use.

EXTRACURRICULARS

Activities: Choral groups, concert band, dance, drama/theater, jazz band, literary magazine, music ensembles, musical theater, radio station, student government, student newspaper, student-run film society, symphony orchestra, television station, yearbook. **Organizations:** 184 registered organizations, 4 honor societies, 10 religious organizations. **Athletics (Intercollegiate):** *Men:* baseball, basketball, cross-country, diving, fencing, golf, indoor track, sailing, soccer, swimming, tennis, track & field. *Women:* basketball, cheerleading, cross-country, diving, fencing, indoor track, sailing, soccer, softball, swimming, tennis, track & field, volleyball.

ADMISSIONS

Selectivity Rating: 91 (of 100). **Freshman Academic Profile:** Average high school GPA 3.8. 62% in top 10% of high school class, 93% in top 25% of high school class, 100% in top 50% of high school class. 70% from public high schools. Average SAT I Math 670, SAT I Math middle 50% range 630-710. Average SAT I Verbal 660, SAT I Verbal middle 50% range 627-710. TOEFL required of all international applicants, minimum TOEFL 600. **Basis for Candidate Selection:** *Very important factors considered include:* class rank, secondary school record. *Important factors considered include:* character/ personal qualities, essays, extracurricular activities, recommendations, standardized test scores, talent/ability, volunteer work, work experience. *Other factors considered include:* alumni/ae relation, interview, minority status.

Freshman Admission Requirements: High school diploma or GED is required. *Academic units required/recommended:* 16 total recommended; 4 English recommended, 3 math recommended, 1 science recommended, 1 science lab recommended, 3 foreign language recommended, 1 history recommended, 4 elective recommended. **Freshman Admission Statistics:** 6,080 applied, 42% accepted, 33% of those accepted enrolled. **Transfer Admission Requirements:** *Items required:* high school transcript, college transcript, essay, standardized test scores, statement of good standing from prior school. Minimum college GPA of 3.0 required. Lowest grade transferable C-. **General Admission Information:** Application fee $55. Early decision application deadline January 1. Regular application deadline January 31. Nonfall registration accepted. Admission may be deferred for a maximum of 1 year. Credit and/or placement offered for CEEB Advanced Placement tests.

COSTS AND FINANCIAL AID

Tuition $27,345. Room & board $7,849. Required fees $820. Average book expense $700. **Required Forms and Deadlines:** FAFSA, CSS/Financial Aid PROFILE, noncustodial (divorced/separated) parent's statement, and business/farm supplement. No deadline for regular filing. Priority filing deadline January 31. **Notification of Awards:** Applicants will be notified of awards on or about April 1. **Types of Aid:** *Need-based scholarships/grants:* Pell, SEOG, state scholarships/grants, the school's own gift aid. *Loans:* Direct Subsidized Stafford, Direct Unsubsidized Stafford, Direct PLUS, Federal Perkins, state loans, college/university loans from institutional funds. **Student Employment:** Federal Work-Study Program available. Institutional employment available. Off-campus job opportunities are excellent. **Financial Aid Statistics:** 50% freshmen, 50% undergrads receive some form of aid. Average freshman grant $15,012. Average freshman loan $4,647. Average income from on-campus job $1,326. **Financial Aid Phone:** 781-736-3700.

BRANDON UNIVERSITY

270-18th Street, Brandon, MB R7A 6A9
Phone: 204-727-9784 **E-mail:** admission@brandonu.ca
Fax: 204-728-3221 **Web:** www.brandonu.ca

This public school was founded in 1899. It has a 3-acre campus.

STUDENTS AND FACULTY

Enrollment: 2,867. **Student Body:** Male 33%, female 67%, out-of-state 25%, international students represent 30 countries. **Retention and Graduation:** 65% freshmen return for sophomore year. 44% grads go on to further study within 1 year. **Faculty:** Student/faculty ratio 14:1. 199 full-time faculty. 100% faculty teach undergrads.

ACADEMICS

Degrees: Bachelor's, certificate, master's. **Academic Requirements:** General education including some course work in humanities, sciences (biological or physical), social science. **Classes:** Under 10 students in an average class. **Majors with Highest Enrollment:** Business administration/management; computer science; psychology, general. **Disciplines with Highest Percentage of Degrees Awarded:** Education 32%, liberal arts/general studies 31%, other 28%, health professions and related sciences 6%, business/marketing 3%. **Special Study Options:** Distance learning, double major, English as a second language, teacher certification program.

FACILITIES

Housing: Coed, all-female, all-male, housing for disabled students. **Library Holdings:** 1,000,000 bound volumes. **Special Academic Facilities/Equipment:** B.J. Hales Museum. **Computers:** School-owned computers available for student use.

EXTRACURRICULARS

Activities: Choral groups, concert band, drama/theater, jazz band, music ensembles, musical theater, opera, radio station, student government, student newspaper, symphony orchestra. **Athletics (Intercollegiate):** *Men:* basketball, ice hockey. *Women:* basketball.

ADMISSIONS

Selectivity Rating: 60 (of 100). **Freshman Academic Profile:** Average high school GPA 3.5. TOEFL required of all international applicants, minimum TOEFL 550. **Basis for Candidate Selection:** *Very important factors considered include:* secondary school record. **Freshman Admission Requirements:** High school diploma or GED is required. **Transfer Admission Requirements:** *Items required:* college transcript, statement of good standing from prior school. **General Admission Information:** Application fee $35. Nonfall registration accepted. Admission may be deferred.

COSTS AND FINANCIAL AID

In-state tuition $3,354. Out-of-state tuition $3,354. Room & board $4,415. Required fees $386. Average book expense $900. **Required Forms and Deadlines:** institution's own financial aid form. **Student Employment:** Off-campus job opportunities are good. **Financial Aid Phone:** 204-727-9737.

BRENAU UNIVERSITY WOMEN'S COLLEGE

One Centennial Circle, Gainesville, GA 30501
Phone: 770-534-6100 **E-mail:** wcadmissions@lib.brenau.edu **CEEB Code:** 5066
Fax: 770-538-4306 **Web:** www.brenau.edu **ACT Code:** 800

This private school was founded in 1878. It has a 56-acre campus.

STUDENTS AND FACULTY

Enrollment: 603. **Student Body:** Out-of-state 12%, international 5% (22 countries represented). **Ethnic Representation:** African American 11%, Asian 2%, Caucasian 76%, Hispanic 3%, Native American 1%. **Retention and Graduation:** 70% freshmen return for sophomore year. 32% freshmen graduate within 4 years. 6% grads pursue business degrees. 1% grads pursue law degrees. 1% grads pursue medical degrees. **Faculty:** Student/faculty ratio 8:1. 79 full-time faculty, 93% hold PhDs. 100% faculty teach undergrads.

ACADEMICS

Degrees: Bachelor's, master's. **Academic Requirements:** General education including some course work in arts/fine arts, computer literacy, English (including composition), foreign languages, history, humanities, mathematics, philosophy, sciences (biological or physical), social science, health. **Classes:** 10-19 students in an average class. 10-19 students in an average lab/discussion section. **Majors with Highest Enrollment:** Nursing/registered nurse training (RN, ASN, BSN, MSN); occupational therapy/therapist; mass communications/media studies. **Disciplines with Highest Percentage of Degrees Awarded:** Health professions and related sciences 38%, education 17%, visual and performing arts 9%, communications/communication technologies 8%, business/marketing 8%. **Special Study Options:** Cooperative (work-study) program, cross registration, distance learning, double major, honors program, independent study, internships, study abroad.

FACILITIES

Housing: All-female, apartments for single students, fraternities and/or sororities. **Library Holdings:** 61,059 bound volumes. 205 periodicals. 872 microforms. 2,104 audiovisuals. **Special Academic Facilities/Equipment:** Simmons Art Gallery, Wages House, Whitepath House, Natatorium Physical Fitness Center, Leo Castelli Art Gallery. **Computers:** *Recommended operating system:* Windows 95/98 or 2000. School-owned computers available for student use.

EXTRACURRICULARS

Activities: Choral groups, dance, drama/theater, literary magazine, music ensembles, musical theater, opera, radio station, student government, student newspaper, symphony orchestra, television station, yearbook. **Organizations:** 32 registered organizations, 12 honor societies, 2 religious organizations, 8 sororities (50% women join). **Athletics (Intercollegiate):** *Women:* cross-country, soccer, tennis, volleyball.

ADMISSIONS

Selectivity Rating: 73 (of 100). **Freshman Academic Profile:** Average high school GPA 3.4. 89% from public high schools. Average SAT I Math 495, SAT I Math middle 50% range 440-560. Average SAT I Verbal 524, SAT I Verbal middle 50% range 460-590. TOEFL required of all international applicants, minimum TOEFL 500. **Basis for Candidate Selection:** *Very important factors considered include:* secondary school record, standardized test scores. *Important factors considered include:* character/personal qualities, extracurricular activities, interview, talent/ability. *Other factors considered include:* class rank, essays, recommendations, volunteer work, work experience. **Freshman Admission Requirements:** High school diploma or GED is required. *Academic units required/recommended:* 4 English required, 4 English recommended, 3 math required, 3 math recommended, 2 science required, 2 science recommended, 2 science lab required, 2 science lab recommended, 2 foreign language recommended, 2 social studies required, 3 social studies recommended, 7 elective required, 9 elective recommended. **Freshman Admission Statistics:** 293 applied, 75% accepted, 55% of those accepted enrolled. **Transfer Admission Requirements:** *Items required:* college transcript, essay. Minimum college GPA of 2.5 required. Lowest grade transferable C. **General Admission Information:** Application fee $35. Nonfall registration accepted. Admission may be deferred for a maximum of 1 year. Credit and/or placement offered for CEEB Advanced Placement tests.

COSTS AND FINANCIAL AID

Tuition $13,440. Room & board $7,320. Required fees $0. Average book expense $750. **Required Forms and Deadlines:** FAFSA and state aid form. Priority filing deadline May 1. **Notification of Awards:** Applicants will be notified of awards on a rolling basis beginning on or about March 15. **Types of Aid:** *Need-based scholarships/grants:* Pell, SEOG, state scholarships/grants, private scholarships, the school's own gift aid. *Loans:* FFEL Subsidized Stafford, FFEL Unsubsidized Stafford, FFEL PLUS, Federal Perkins, state loans. **Student Employment:** Federal Work-Study Program available. Institutional employment available. Off-campus job opportunities are good. **Financial Aid Statistics:** 80% freshmen, 63% undergrads receive some form of aid. **Financial Aid Phone:** 770-534-6152.

BRESCIA UNIVERSITY

717 Frederica Street, Owensboro, KY 42301-3023
Phone: 270-686-4241 **E-mail:** admissions@brescia.edu **CEEB Code:** 1071
Fax: 270-686-4314 **Web:** www.brescia.edu **ACT Code:** 14980

This private school, which is affiliated with the Roman Catholic Church, was founded in 1950. It has a 9-acre campus.

STUDENTS AND FACULTY

Enrollment: 756. **Student Body:** Male 39%, female 61%, out-of-state 16%, international 4% (3 countries represented). **Ethnic Representation:** African American 4%, Asian 1%, Caucasian 94%, Hispanic 1%. **Retention and Graduation:** 67% freshmen return for sophomore year. 39% freshmen graduate within 4 years. **Faculty:** Student/faculty ratio 14:1. 41 full-time faculty, 73% hold PhDs. 100% faculty teach undergrads.

ACADEMICS

Degrees: Associate's, bachelor's, master's, post-bachelor's certificate. **Academic Requirements:** General education including some course work in arts/fine arts, computer literacy, English (including composition), foreign languages, history, mathematics, philosophy, sciences (biological or physical), social science, religious studies. **Classes:** 10-19 students in an average class. Under 10 students in an average lab/discussion section. **Majors with Highest Enrollment:** General studies; social sciences, general; business/commerce, general. **Disciplines with Highest Percentage of Degrees Awarded:** Business/marketing 33%, protective services/public administration 15%, education 14%, biological life sciences 9%, visual and performing arts 8%. **Special Study Options:** Cross registration, double major, dual enrollment, English as a second language, honors program, independent study, internships, liberal arts/career combination, student-designed major, study abroad, teacher certification program, weekend college.

FACILITIES

Housing: Coed, all-female, all-male, apartments for single students, shared apartment homes. **Library Holdings:** 83,222 bound volumes. 5,334 periodicals. 364,553 microforms. 6,580 audiovisuals. **Special Academic Facilities/Equipment:** Art gallery, computer labs, campus center, greenhouse, observatory, science building. **Computers:** *Recommended operating system:* Windows 95. School-owned computers available for student use.

EXTRACURRICULARS

Activities: Choral groups, drama/theater, literary magazine, music ensembles, student government, student newspaper. **Organizations:** 22 registered organizations, 2 honor societies, 2 religious organizations. **Athletics (Intercollegiate):** *Men:* baseball, basketball, golf, soccer. *Women:* basketball, golf, soccer, softball, tennis, volleyball.

ADMISSIONS

Selectivity Rating: 73 (of 100). **Freshman Academic Profile:** Average high school GPA 3.2. 23% in top 10% of high school class, 48% in top 25% of high school class, 71% in top 50% of high school class. 61% from public high schools. SAT I Math middle 50% range 540-560. SAT I Verbal middle 50% range 430-430. Average ACT 21, ACT middle 50% range 18-24. TOEFL required of all international applicants, minimum TOEFL 550. **Basis for Candidate Selection:** *Very important factors considered include:* class rank, interview, secondary school record, standardized test scores. *Important factors considered include:* character/personal qualities, essays, extracurricular activities, recommendations, talent/ability. *Other factors considered include:* volunteer work. **Freshman Admission Requirements:** High school diploma or GED is required. *Academic units required/recommended:* 17 total recommended; 4 English recommended, 3 math recommended, 2 science recommended, 2 foreign language recommended, 2 social studies recommended. **Freshman Admission Statistics:** 264 applied, 80% accepted, 56% of those accepted enrolled. **Transfer Admission Requirements:** *Items required:* high school transcript, college transcript, essay. Minimum high school GPA of 2.0 required. Minimum college GPA of 2.0 required. Lowest grade transferable C. **General Admission Information:** Application fee $25. Nonfall registration accepted. Admission may be deferred for a maximum of 1 year. Credit and/or placement offered for CEEB Advanced Placement tests.

COSTS AND FINANCIAL AID

Tuition $9,690. Room & board $4,380. Required fees $155. Average book expense $800. **Required Forms and Deadlines:** FAFSA. No deadline for regular filing. Priority filing deadline March 1. **Notification of Awards:** Applicants will be notified of awards on a rolling basis. **Types of Aid:** *Need-based scholarships/grants:* Pell, SEOG, state scholarships/grants, private scholarships, the school's own gift aid. *Loans:* FFEL Subsidized Stafford, FFEL Unsubsidized Stafford, FFEL PLUS, Federal Perkins, college/university loans from institutional funds. **Student Employment:** Federal Work-Study Program available. Institutional employment available. Off-campus job opportunities are excellent. **Financial Aid Statistics:** 84% freshmen, 79% undergrads receive some form of aid. Average freshman grant $5,441. Average freshman loan $2,625. Average income from on-campus job $1,236. **Financial Aid Phone:** 270-686-4290.

BREVARD COLLEGE

400 North Broad Street, Brevard, NC 28712-3306
Phone: 800-527-9090 **E-mail:** admissions@brevard.edu **CEEB Code:** 5067
Fax: 828-884-3790 **Web:** www.brevard.edu **ACT Code:** 3074

This private school, which is affiliated with the Methodist Church, was founded in 1853. It has a 120-acre campus.

STUDENTS AND FACULTY

Enrollment: 664. **Student Body:** Male 53%, female 47%, out-of-state 54%, international 2%. **Ethnic Representation:** African American 7%, Caucasian 89%, Hispanic 2%, Native American 1%. **Retention and Graduation:** 63% freshmen return for sophomore year. 18% freshmen graduate within 4 years. 20% grads go on to further study within 1 year. 2% grads pursue business degrees. 1% grads pursue law degrees. 3% grads pursue medical degrees. **Faculty:** Student/faculty ratio 10:1. 61 full-time faculty, 57% hold PhDs. 100% faculty teach undergrads.

ACADEMICS

Degrees: Associate's, bachelor's, transfer. **Academic Requirements:** General education including some course work in arts/fine arts, computer literacy, English (including composition), foreign languages, history, humanities, mathematics, philosophy, sciences (biological or physical), social science, environmental studies; physical education. **Classes:** Under 10 students in an average class. 10-19 students in an average lab/discussion section. **Majors with Highest Enrollment:** Parks, recreation and leisure studies; art/art studies, general; music/music and performing arts studies, general. **Disciplines with Highest Percentage of Degrees Awarded:** Interdisciplinary studies 24%, business/marketing 19%, visual and performing arts 19%, parks and recreation 18%, natural resources/environmental sciences 8%. **Special Study Options:** Double major, dual enrollment, English as a second language, honors program, independent study, internships, student-designed major, study abroad.

FACILITIES

Housing: Coed, all-female, all-male, coed upperclassperson dorm. **Library Holdings:** 42,275 bound volumes. 322 periodicals. 3,278 microforms. 3,742 audiovisuals. **Special Academic Facilities/Equipment:** Porter Center for Performing Arts; Sims Art Gallery; Morrison Playhouse. **Computers:** School-owned computers available for student use.

EXTRACURRICULARS

Activities: Choral groups, concert band, dance, drama/theater, jazz band, literary magazine, music ensembles, musical theater, opera, student government, student newspaper, symphony orchestra, yearbook. **Organizations:** 19 registered organizations, 1 honor society, 1 religious organization. **Athletics (Intercollegiate):** *Men:* baseball, basketball, cheerleading, cross-country, golf, soccer, track & field. *Women:* basketball, cheerleading, cross-country, soccer, softball, tennis, track & field, volleyball.

ADMISSIONS

Selectivity Rating: 63 (of 100). **Freshman Academic Profile:** Average high school GPA 2.9. 75% from public high schools. Average SAT I Math 459, SAT I Math middle 50% range 349-585. Average SAT I Verbal 480, SAT I Verbal middle 50% range 364-601. Average ACT 19. TOEFL required of all international applicants, minimum TOEFL 500. **Basis for Candidate Selection:** *Important factors considered include:* character/personal qualities, class rank, extracurricular activities, interview, secondary school record, standardized test scores, talent/ability, volunteer work. *Other factors considered include:* alumni/ae relation, essays, recommendations, work experience. **Freshman Admission Requirements:** High school diploma or GED is required. *Academic units required/recommended:* 22 total recommended; 4 English recommended, 3 math recommended, 3 science recommended, 1 science lab recommended, 2 foreign language recommended, 4 social studies recommended, 1 history recommended, 4 elective recommended. **Freshman Admission Statistics:** 518 applied, 87% accepted, 34% of those accepted enrolled. **Transfer Admission Requirements:** *Items required:* high school transcript, college transcript, essay, standardized test score, statement of good standing from prior school. Minimum college GPA of 2.0 required. Lowest grade transferable C-. **General Admission Information:** Application fee $30. Nonfall registration accepted. Admission may be deferred. Credit and/or placement offered for CEEB Advanced Placement tests.

COSTS AND FINANCIAL AID

Tuition $11,980. Room & board $5,400. Required fees $950. Average book expense $800. **Required Forms and Deadlines:** FAFSA and state aid form. No deadline for regular filing. Priority filing deadline April 15. **Notification of Awards:** Applicants will be notified of awards on a rolling basis beginning on or about February 15. **Types of Aid:** *Need-based scholarships/grants:* Pell, SEOG, state scholarships/grants, private scholarships, the school's own gift aid. *Loans:* FFEL Subsidized Stafford, FFEL Unsubsidized Stafford, FFEL PLUS, Federal Perkins. **Student Employment:** Federal Work-Study Program available. Institutional employment available. Off-campus job opportunities are fair. **Financial Aid Statistics:** 63% freshmen, 66% undergrads receive some form of aid. Average freshman grant $8,798. Average freshman loan $3,020. Average income from on-campus job $945. **Financial Aid Phone:** 828-884-8287.

See page 948.

BREWTON-PARKER COLLEGE

PO Box 2011, Mt. Vernon, GA 30445
Phone: 912-583-2241 **E-mail:** admissions@bpc.edu
Fax: 912-583-3598 **Web:** www.bpc.edu

This private school, which is affiliated with the Baptist Church, was founded in 1904.

STUDENTS AND FACULTY

Enrollment: 1,269. **Student Body:** Male 39%, female 61%, out-of-state 3%, international 3% (13 countries represented). **Ethnic Representation:** African American 19%, Asian 1%, Caucasian 70%, Hispanic 2%. **Retention and Graduation:** 52% freshmen return for sophomore year. 9% freshmen graduate within 4 years. **Faculty:** Student/faculty ratio 10:1. 51 full-time faculty, 68% hold PhDs. 100% faculty teach undergrads.

ACADEMICS

Degrees: Associate's, bachelor's. **Academic Requirements:** General education including some course work in arts/fine arts, computer literacy, English (including composition), foreign languages, history, humanities, mathematics, philosophy, sciences (biological or physical), social science. **Classes:** Under 10 students in an average class. **Majors with Highest Enrollment:** Business administration/management; education, general; psychology, general. **Disciplines with Highest Percentage of Degrees Awarded:** Business/marketing 32%, education 24%, psychology 10%, communications/communication technologies 3%, social sciences and history 3%. **Special Study Options:** Double major, dual enrollment, student exchange program (domestic), honors program, independent study, internships, teacher certification program, weekend college.

FACILITIES

Housing: All-female, all-male. **Library Holdings:** 70,352 bound volumes. 350 periodicals. 2,863 microforms. 5,567 audiovisuals. **Special Academic Facilities/Equipment:** Library. **Computers:** *Recommended operating system:* Windows 98, Windows XP, Windows 2000. School-owned computers available for student use.

EXTRACURRICULARS

Activities: Choral groups, concert band, drama/theater, jazz band, literary magazine, music ensembles, musical theater, student government, student newspaper, yearbook. **Organizations:** 24 registered organizations, 1 honor society, 5 religious organizations, 3 fraternities (24% men join), 3 sororities (26% women join). **Athletics (Intercollegiate):** *Men:* baseball, basketball, cheerleading, soccer. *Women:* basketball, cheerleading, soccer, softball, volleyball.

ADMISSIONS

Selectivity Rating: 75 (of 100). **Freshman Academic Profile:** Average high school GPA 2.9. 19% in top 10% of high school class, 20% in top 25% of high school class, 71% in top 50% of high school class. 80% from public high schools. Average SAT I Math 485, SAT I Math middle 50% range 540-420. Average SAT I Verbal 478, SAT I Verbal middle 50% range 540-420. Average ACT 18. **Basis for Candidate Selection:** *Very important factors considered include:* standardized test scores. *Important factors considered include:* secondary school record. *Other factors considered include:* character/personal qualities, class rank, extracurricular activities, interview, religious affiliation/commitment, talent/ability, volunteer work, work experience. **Freshman Admission Requirements:** High school diploma or GED is required. *Academic units required/recommended:* 13 total required; 4 English required, 3 math required, 3 science required, 2 foreign language required, 3 social studies required. **Freshman Admission Statistics:** 377 applied, 89% accepted, 84% of those accepted enrolled. **Transfer Admission Requirements:** *Items required:* high school transcript, college transcript. Minimum high school GPA of 2.0 required. Minimum college GPA of 2.0 required. Lowest grade transferable C. **General Admission Information:** Application fee $25. Nonfall registration accepted. Admission may be deferred for a maximum of 2 years.

COSTS AND FINANCIAL AID

Tuition $9,600. Room & board $4,900. Required fees $300. Average book expense $750. **Required Forms and Deadlines:** FAFSA, state aid form and Certification Statement. Priority filing deadline April 1. **Notification of Awards:** Applicants will be notified of awards on a rolling basis beginning on or about February 28. **Types of Aid:** *Need-based scholarships/grants:* Pell, SEOG, state scholarships/grants, private scholarships, the school's own gift aid, Georgia Baptist Funds. *Loans:* FFEL Subsidized Stafford, FFEL Unsubsidized Stafford, FFEL PLUS, Federal Perkins. **Student Employment:** Federal Work-Study Program available. Institutional employment available. Off-campus job opportunities are fair. **Financial Aid Statistics:** 79% freshmen, 83% undergrads receive some form of aid. Average freshman grant $7,617. Average freshman loan $2,126. Average income from on-campus job $1,235. **Financial Aid Phone:** 912-583-3215.

BRIAR CLIFF UNIVERSITY

Admissions Office, Box 2100, Sioux City, IA 51104-0100
Phone: 712-279-5200 **E-mail:** admissions@briarcliff.edu **CEEB Code:** 1846
Fax: 712-279-1632 **Web:** www.briarcliff.edu **ACT Code:** 1276

This private school, which is affiliated with the Roman Catholic Church, was founded in 1927. It has a 70-acre campus.

STUDENTS AND FACULTY

Enrollment: 973. **Student Body:** Male 41%, female 59%, out-of-state 31%, international students represent 3 countries. **Ethnic Representation:** African American 3%, Asian 1%, Caucasian 91%, Hispanic 4%, Native American 1%. **Retention and Graduation:** 70% freshmen return for sophomore year. 39% freshmen graduate within 4 years. 13% grads go on to further study within 1 year. 3% grads pursue business degrees. 5% grads pursue law degrees. 2% grads pursue medical degrees. **Faculty:** Student/faculty ratio 14:1. 47 full-time faculty, 59% hold PhDs. 100% faculty teach undergrads.

ACADEMICS

Degrees: Associate's, bachelor's, master's. **Academic Requirements:** General education including some course work in arts/fine arts, computer literacy, English (including composition), foreign languages, history, humanities, mathematics, philosophy, sciences (biological or physical), social science. **Majors with Highest Enrollment:** Business administration/management; education, general; nursing/registered nurse training (RN, ASN, BSN, MSN). **Disciplines with Highest Percentage of Degrees Awarded:** Business/marketing 31%, education 9%, protective services/public administration 9%, health professions and related sciences 9%, parks and recreation 8%. **Special Study Options:** Cross registration, double major, dual enrollment, independent study, internships, liberal arts/career combination, student-designed major, study abroad, teacher certification program, weekend college.

FACILITIES

Housing: Coed, all-female, all-male, apartments for single students. **Library Holdings:** 83,737 bound volumes. 6,366 periodicals. 21,464 microforms. 9,791 audiovisuals. **Special Academic Facilities/Equipment:** Mueller Library, Newman Flanagan Center. **Computers:** School-owned computers available for student use.

EXTRACURRICULARS

Activities: Choral groups, drama/theater, literary magazine, music ensembles, musical theater, opera, radio station, student government, student newspaper. **Organizations:** 25 registered organizations, 3 religious organizations. **Athletics (Intercollegiate):** *Men:* baseball, basketball, cross-country, football, golf, indoor track, soccer, wrestling. *Women:* basketball, cross-country, golf, indoor track, soccer, softball, volleyball.

ADMISSIONS

Selectivity Rating: 74 (of 100). **Freshman Academic Profile:** Average high school GPA 3.2. 11% in top 10% of high school class, 30% in top 25% of high school class, 57% in top 50% of high school class. Average ACT 22, ACT middle 50% range 18-24. TOEFL required of all international applicants, minimum TOEFL 500. **Basis for Candidate Selection:** *Very important factors considered include:* secondary school record. *Important factors considered include:* extracurricular activities, recommendations. *Other factors considered include:* alumni/ae relation, essays, interview, standardized test scores. **Freshman Admission Requirements:** High school diploma or GED is required. *Academic units required/recommended:* 16 total recommended; 4 English recommended, 3 math recommended, 3 science recommended, 2 foreign language recommended, 3 social studies recommended, 1 elective recommended. **Freshman Admission Statistics:** 1,080 applied, 81% accepted, 28% of those accepted enrolled. **Transfer Admission Requirements:** *Items required:* high school transcript, college transcript, statement of good standing from prior school. Minimum college GPA of 2.0 required. Lowest grade transferable D. **General Admission Information:** Application fee $20. Priority application deadline May 1. Nonfall registration accepted. Admission may be deferred for a maximum of 1 year. Credit offered for CEEB Advanced Placement tests.

COSTS AND FINANCIAL AID

Tuition $15,180. Room & board $5,238. Required fees $360. Average book expense $700. **Required Forms and Deadlines:** FAFSA. Priority filing deadline March 15. **Types of Aid:** *Need-based scholarships/grants:* Pell, SEOG, state scholarships/grants, private scholarships, the school's own gift aid. *Loans:* FFEL Subsidized Stafford, FFEL Unsubsidized Stafford, FFEL PLUS, Federal Perkins, state loans. **Student Employment:** Federal Work-Study Program available. Institutional employment available. Off-campus job opportunities are excellent. **Financial Aid Statistics:** 75% freshmen, 73% undergrads receive some form of aid. Average freshman grant $11,400. Average freshman loan $5,800. **Financial Aid Phone:** 712-279-5200.

BRIDGEWATER COLLEGE

402 East College Street, Bridgewater, VA 22812-1599
Phone: 540-828-5375 **E-mail:** admissions@bridgewater.edu **CEEB Code:** 5069
Fax: 540-828-5481 **Web:** www.bridgewater.edu **ACT Code:** 4342

This private school, which is affiliated with the Church of Brethren, was founded in 1880. It has a 190-acre campus.

STUDENTS AND FACULTY

Enrollment: 1,363. **Student Body:** Male 45%, female 55%, out-of-state 22%, international 1% (8 countries represented). **Ethnic Representation:** African American 8%, Asian 1%, Caucasian 89%, Hispanic 1%. **Retention and Graduation:** 81% freshmen return for sophomore year. 51% freshmen graduate within 4 years. **Faculty:** Student/faculty ratio 15:1. 82 full-time faculty, 78% hold PhDs. 100% faculty teach undergrads.

ACADEMICS

Degrees: Bachelor's. **Academic Requirements:** General education including some course work in arts/fine arts, English (including composition), foreign languages, history, humanities, mathematics, philosophy, sciences (biological or physical), social science. Personal development and the liberal arts must be completed by each entering student unless the student transfers 15 or more units to Bridgewater College. **Classes:** 10-19 students in an average class. 10-19 students in an average lab/discussion section. **Majors with Highest Enrollment:** Business administration/management; biology/biological sciences, general; psychology, general. **Disciplines with Highest Percentage of Degrees Awarded:** Business/marketing 21%, biological life sciences 16%, parks and recreation 12%, social sciences and history 11%, psychology 11%. **Special Study Options:** Double major, honors program, independent study, internships, liberal arts/career combination, study abroad, teacher certification program. Dual Degree Programs: 3-2 engineering program with George Washington University (BA/BA); 3-2 forestry program with Duke University (BA/MA); 3-4 veterinary medicine program with Virginia Tech (BA/DVM); 3-2 physical therapy program with George Washington University (BA/MPT); 3-4 physical therapy program with Shenandoah University (BA/DPT). Pre-professional programs in dentistry, engineering, law, medicine, pharmacy, physical therapy, and veterinary medicine.

FACILITIES

Housing: All-female, all-male, apartments for single students, housing for disabled students, housing for international students, honor housing. **Library Holdings:** 132,739 bound volumes. 659 periodicals. 412,460 microforms. 8,793 audiovisuals. **Special Academic Facilities/Equipment:** Museum of Shenandoah region and Brethren history. **Computers:** School-owned computers available for student use.

EXTRACURRICULARS

Activities: Choral groups, concert band, dance, drama/theater, jazz band, literary magazine, music ensembles, pep band, radio station, student government, student newspaper, television station, yearbook. **Organizations:** 68 registered organizations, 7 honor societies, 9 religious organizations. **Athletics (Intercollegiate):** *Men:* baseball, basketball, cross-country, equestrian, football, golf, indoor track, soccer, tennis, track & field. *Women:* basketball, cross-country, equestrian, field hockey, indoor track, lacrosse, soccer, softball, tennis, track & field, volleyball.

ADMISSIONS

Selectivity Rating: 72 (of 100). **Freshman Academic Profile:** Average high school GPA 3.2. 19% in top 10% of high school class, 41% in top 25% of high school class, 74% in top 50% of high school class. 87% from public high schools. Average SAT I Math 502, SAT I Math middle 50% range 440-560. Average SAT I Verbal 506, SAT I Verbal middle 50% range 440-560. Average ACT 21, ACT middle 50% range 18-25. TOEFL required of all international applicants, minimum TOEFL 500. **Basis for Candidate Selection:** *Very important factors considered include:* class rank, secondary school record, standardized test scores. *Important factors considered include:* character/personal qualities, essays, interview, recommendations. *Other factors considered include:* alumni/ae relation, extracurricular activities, geographical residence, minority status, religious affiliation/commitment, state residency, volunteer work, work experience. **Freshman Admission Requirements:** High school diploma or GED is required. *Academic units required/recommended:* 17 total required; 22 total recommended; 4 English required, 4 English recommended, 3 math required, 4 math recommended, 2 science required, 4 science recommended, 2 foreign language required, 3 foreign language recommended, 4 elective required, 4 elective recommended. **Freshman Admission Statistics:** 1,332 applied, 88% accepted, 35% of those accepted enrolled. **Transfer Admission Requirements:** *Items required:* high school transcript, college transcript, essay, standardized test score, statement of good standing from prior school. Minimum college GPA of 2.0 required. Lowest grade transferable C. **General Admission Information:** Application fee $30. Nonfall registration accepted. Admission may be deferred for a maximum of 1 year. Credit and/or placement offered for CEEB Advanced Placement tests.

COSTS AND FINANCIAL AID

Tuition $16,990. Room & board $8,160. Average book expense $860. **Required Forms and Deadlines:** FAFSA and state aid form. Priority filing deadline March 1. **Notification of Awards:** Applicants will be notified of awards on a rolling basis beginning on or about March 15. **Types of Aid:** *Need-based scholarships/grants:* Pell, SEOG, state scholarships/grants, private scholarships, the school's own gift aid. *Loans:* FFEL Subsidized Stafford, FFEL Unsubsidized Stafford, FFEL PLUS, Federal Perkins. **Student Employment:** Federal Work-Study Program available. Institutional employment available. Off-campus job opportunities are good. **Financial Aid Statistics:** 76% freshmen, 72% undergrads receive some form of aid. Average freshman grant $11,484. Average freshman loan $5,974. Average income from on-campus job $491. **Financial Aid Phone:** 540-828-5377.

BRIDGEWATER STATE COLLEGE

Gates House, Bridgewater, MA 02325
Phone: 508-531-1237 **E-mail:** admission@bridgew.edu **CEEB Code:** 3517
Fax: 508-531-1746 **Web:** www.bridgew.edu **ACT Code:** 1900

This public school was founded in 1840. It has a 235-acre campus.

STUDENTS AND FACULTY

Enrollment: 7,434. **Student Body:** Male 38%, female 62%, out-of-state 3%, international 2% (32 countries represented). **Ethnic Representation:** African American 4%, Asian 1%, Caucasian 84%, Hispanic 2%. **Retention and Graduation:** 74% freshmen return for sophomore year. 19% freshmen graduate within 4 years. 16% grads go on to further study within 1 year. 1% grads pursue business degrees. 2% grads pursue law degrees. **Faculty:** Student/faculty ratio 19:1. 252 full-time faculty, 90% hold PhDs. 100% faculty teach undergrads.

ACADEMICS

Degrees: Bachelor's, certificate, first professional certificate, master's, post-bachelor's certificate, post-master's certificate. **Academic Requirements:** General education including some course work in arts/fine arts, English (including composition), foreign languages, history, humanities, mathematics, philosophy, sciences (biological or physical), social science, communication, information resources. **Classes:** 20-29 students in an average class. 10-19 students in an average lab/discussion section. **Majors with Highest Enrollment:** Business administration/management; elementary education and teaching; psychology, general. **Disciplines with Highest Percentage of Degrees Awarded:** Business/marketing 15%, social sciences and history 15%, education 13%, psychology 12%, communications/communication technologies 8%. **Special Study Options:** Accelerated program, cross registration, distance learning, double major, dual enrollment, English as a second language, student exchange program (domestic), honors program, independent study, internships, study abroad, teacher certification program.

FACILITIES

Housing: Coed, all-female, apartments for single students, housing for disabled students, break housing for athletes, student teachers, international students. **Library Holdings:** 326,662 bound volumes. 1,100 periodicals. 756,874 microforms. 10,590 audiovisuals. **Special Academic Facilities/Equipment:** On-campus school, children's physical development clinic, human performance lab, TV studio, observatory, flight simulators, electron microscope, Moakley Technology Center. **Computers:** School-owned computers available for student use.

EXTRACURRICULARS

Activities: Choral groups, concert band, dance, drama/theater, jazz band, literary magazine, marching band, music ensembles, musical theater, radio station, student government, student newspaper, yearbook. **Organizations:** 74 registered organizations, 11 honor societies, 1 religious organization, 5 fraternities, 3 sororities. **Athletics (Intercollegiate):** *Men:* baseball, basketball, cross-country, football, soccer, swimming, tennis, track & field, wrestling. *Women:* basketball, cross-country, field hockey, lacrosse, soccer, softball, swimming, tennis, track & field, volleyball.

ADMISSIONS

Selectivity Rating: 78 (of 100). **Freshman Academic Profile:** Average high school GPA 2.9. 5% in top 10% of high school class, 26% in top 25% of high school class, 73% in top 50% of high school class. Average SAT I Math 501, SAT I Math middle 50% range 450-550. Average SAT I Verbal 508, SAT I Verbal middle 50% range 450-550. Average ACT 21, ACT middle 50% range 18-23. TOEFL required of all international applicants, minimum TOEFL 500. **Basis for Candidate Selection:** *Very important factors considered include:* essays, secondary school record, standardized test scores. *Important factors considered include:* extracurricular activities. *Other factors considered include:* alumni/ae relation, character/personal qualities, class rank, interview, minority status, recommendations, talent/ability, volunteer work, work experience. **Freshman Admission Requirements:** High school diploma or GED is required. *Academic units required/recommended:* 16 total required; 4 English required, 3 math required, 3 science required, 2 science lab required, 2 foreign language required, 1 social studies required, 1 history required, 2 elective required. **Freshman Admission Statistics:** 5,252 applied, 68% accepted, 36% of those accepted enrolled. **Transfer Admission Requirements:** *Items required:* college transcript, essay. Minimum college GPA of 2.0 required. Lowest grade transferable C-. **General Admission Information:** Application fee $25. Regular application deadline February 15. Nonfall registration accepted. Admission may be deferred for a maximum of 1 year. Credit and/or placement offered for CEEB Advanced Placement tests.

COSTS AND FINANCIAL AID

In-state tuition $910. Out-of-state tuition $7,050. Room & board $5,366. Required fees $2,825. Average book expense $600. **Required Forms and Deadlines:** FAFSA. No deadline for regular filing. Priority filing deadline March 1. **Notification of Awards:** Applicants will be notified of awards on a rolling basis. **Types of Aid:** *Need-based scholarships/grants:* Pell, SEOG, state scholarships/grants, private scholarships, the school's own gift aid. *Loans:* Direct Subsidized Stafford, Direct Unsubsidized Stafford, Direct PLUS, Federal Perkins, state loans. **Student Employment:** Federal Work-Study Program available. Institutional employment available. Off-campus job opportunities are good. **Financial Aid Statistics:** 45% freshmen, 39% undergrads receive some form of aid. Average freshman grant $2,877. Average freshman loan $2,678. Average income from on-campus job $4,000. **Financial Aid Phone:** 508-697-1341.

See page 950.

BRIGHAM YOUNG UNIVERSITY (HI)

55 - 220 Kulanui Street, A153 A.S.B., Laie Oahu, HI 96762
Phone: 808-293-3738 **E-mail:** admissions@byuh.edu
Fax: 808-293-3457 **Web:** www.byuh.edu **ACT Code:** 899

This private school, which is affiliated with the Church of Jesus Christ of Latter-day Saints, was founded in 1955. It has a 60-acre campus.

STUDENTS AND FACULTY

Enrollment: 2,529. **Student Body:** Male 45%, female 55%, out-of-state 71%, international 48%. **Ethnic Representation:** Asian 27%, Caucasian 65%, Hispanic 3%, Native American 1%. **Retention and Graduation:** 58% freshmen return for sophomore year. 11% freshmen graduate within 4 years. **Faculty:** Student/faculty ratio 17:1. 118 full-time faculty, 63% hold PhDs. 100% faculty teach undergrads.

ACADEMICS

Degrees: Bachelor's, post-bachelor's certificate. **Academic Requirements:** General education including some course work in arts/fine arts, English (including composition), history, humanities, mathematics, sciences (biological or physical), social science, religion classes. **Classes:** 10-19 students in an average class. 20-29 students in an average lab/discussion section. **Majors with Highest Enrollment:** International business; information science/studies; psychology, general. **Disciplines with Highest Percentage of Degrees Awarded:** Computer and information sciences 19%, business/marketing 18%, education 11%, parks and recreation 8%, area and ethnic studies 6%. **Special Study Options:** Accelerated program, cooperative (work-study) program, distance learning, English as a second language, student exchange program (domestic), honors program, independent study, internships, student-designed major, teacher certification program.

FACILITIES

Housing: All-female, all-male, apartments for married students. **Library Holdings:** 321,400 bound volumes. 11,325 periodicals. 948,000 microforms. 7,000 audiovisuals. **Special Academic Facilities/Equipment:** Museum of Natural History, media lab. **Computers:** School-owned computers available for student use.

EXTRACURRICULARS

Activities: Choral groups, concert band, dance, drama/theater, jazz band, literary magazine, music ensembles, pep band, student government, student newspaper, student-run film society. **Organizations:** 40 registered organizations, 2 honor societies, 1 religious organization, 1 sorority. **Athletics (Intercollegiate):** *Men:* basketball, cheerleading, cross-country, soccer, tennis, water polo. *Women:* cheerleading, cross-country, softball, tennis, volleyball.

ADMISSIONS

Selectivity Rating: 85 (of 100). **Freshman Academic Profile:** Average high school GPA 3.2. Average ACT 22, ACT middle 50% range 18-24. TOEFL required of all international applicants, minimum TOEFL 475. **Basis for Candidate Selection:** *Very important factors considered include:* character/personal qualities, extracurricular activities, geographical residence, interview, recommendations, religious affiliation/commitment, secondary school record, standardized test scores. *Important factors considered include:* class rank, essays. *Other factors considered include:* alumni/ae relation, talent/ability, volunteer work, work experience. **Freshman Admission Requirements:** High school diploma is required and GED is not accepted. *Academic units required/recommended:* 4 English recommended, 2 math recommended, 2 science recommended, 3 social studies recommended, 2 history recommended.

Freshman Admission Statistics: 2,549 applied, 17% accepted, 85% of those accepted enrolled. **Transfer Admission Requirements:** *Items required:* college transcript, essay, statement of good standing from prior school. Minimum high school GPA of 3.0 required. Minimum college GPA of 2.5 required. Lowest grade transferable C-. **General Admission Information:** Application fee $25. Regular application deadline February 15. Nonfall registration accepted. Credit offered for CEEB Advanced Placement tests.

COSTS AND FINANCIAL AID

Tuition $2,564. Room & board $4,790. Required fees $25. Average book expense $875. **Required Forms and Deadlines:** FAFSA. Financial aid filing deadline April 30. **Notification of Awards:** Applicants will be notified of awards on or about May 1. **Types of Aid:** *Need-based scholarships/grants:* Pell, private scholarships, the school's own gift aid. *Loans:* FFEL Subsidized Stafford, FFEL Unsubsidized Stafford, FFEL PLUS, college/university loans from institutional funds. **Student Employment:** Institutional employment available. Off-campus job opportunities are fair. **Financial Aid Statistics:** 76% freshmen, 75% undergrads receive some form of aid. Average freshman grant $1,003. Average freshman loan $1,927. Average income from on-campus job $4,500. **Financial Aid Phone:** 808-293-3730.

BRIGHAM YOUNG UNIVERSITY (UT)

A-153 ASB, Provo, UT 84602-1110
Phone: 801-422-2507 **E-mail:** admissions@byu.edu **CEEB Code:** 4019
Fax: 801-422-0005 **Web:** www.byu.edu **ACT Code:** 4266

This private school, which is affiliated with the Church of Jesus Christ of Latter-day Saints, was founded in 1875. It has a 556-acre campus.

STUDENTS AND FACULTY

Enrollment: 29,379. **Student Body:** Male 50%, female 50%, out-of-state 70%, international 3% (127 countries represented). **Ethnic Representation:** Asian 3%, Caucasian 91%, Hispanic 3%, Native American 1%. **Retention and Graduation:** 93% freshmen return for sophomore year. 22% freshmen graduate within 4 years. **Faculty:** Student/faculty ratio 18:1. 95% faculty teach undergrads.

ACADEMICS

Degrees: Bachelor's, doctoral, first professional, master's. **Academic Requirements:** General education including some course work in arts/fine arts, English (including composition), foreign languages, history, mathematics, sciences (biological or physical), social science, religion, education, health and human performance. **Classes:** 10-19 students in an average class. 20-29 students in an average lab/discussion section. **Majors with Highest Enrollment:** Business administration/management; accounting; teacher education and professional development, specific subject areas. **Disciplines with Highest Percentage of Degrees Awarded:** Education 13%, business/marketing 12%, social sciences and history 12%, interdisciplinary studies 8%, engineering/engineering technology 7%. **Special Study Options:** Accelerated program, cooperative (work-study) program, distance learning, double major, dual enrollment, English as a second language, external degree program, honors program, independent study, internships, study abroad, teacher certification program.

FACILITIES

Housing: All-female, all-male, apartments for married students, apartments for single students; language studies houses are available. **Library Holdings:** 2,511,155 bound volumes. 619,493 periodicals. 1,211,807 microforms. 56,353 audiovisuals. **Special Academic Facilities/Equipment:** Art, peoples/cultures, life science, and earth science museums; film studio; on-campus nursery school; language research center; dairy, poultry, and agricultural farms; seismography equipment; electron microscope. **Computers:** School-owned computers available for student use.

EXTRACURRICULARS

Activities: Choral groups, concert band, dance, drama/theater, jazz band, literary magazine, marching band, music ensembles, musical theater, opera, pep band, radio station, student government, student newspaper, student-run film society, symphony orchestra, television station. **Organizations:** 230 registered organizations, 2 honor societies, 23 religious organizations. **Athletics (Intercollegiate):** *Men:* baseball, basketball, cheerleading, cross-country, diving, football, golf, swimming, tennis, track & field, volleyball. *Women:* basketball, cheerleading, cross-country, diving, golf, gymnastics, soccer, swimming, tennis, track & field, volleyball.

ADMISSIONS

Selectivity Rating: 88 (of 100). **Freshman Academic Profile:** Average high school GPA 3.8. 54% in top 10% of high school class, 86% in top 25% of high school class, 99% in top 50% of high school class. SAT I Math middle 50% range 560-670. SAT I Verbal middle 50% range 540-650. Average ACT 27, ACT middle 50% range 25-30. TOEFL required of all international applicants, minimum TOEFL 500. **Basis for Candidate Selection:** *Very important factors considered include:* character/personal qualities, interview, religious affiliation/commitment, secondary school record, standardized test scores. *Important factors considered include:* essays, extracurricular activities, minority status, recommendations, volunteer work. *Other factors considered include:* talent/ability, work experience. **Freshman Admission Requirements:** High school diploma or GED is required. *Academic units required/recommended:* 4 English required, 4 English recommended, 3 math required, 4 math recommended, 2 science required, 3 science recommended, 2 science lab required, 3 science lab recommended, 2 foreign language required, 4 foreign language recommended, 2 history required. **Freshman Admission Statistics:** 7,329 applied, 73% accepted, 79% of those accepted enrolled. **Transfer Admission Requirements:** *Items required:* college transcript, essay, interview. Minimum college GPA of 3.0 required. Lowest grade transferable C-. **General Admission Information:** Application fee $25. Regular application deadline February 15. Nonfall registration accepted. Admission may be deferred for a maximum of 2 years. Credit and/or placement offered for CEEB Advanced Placement tests.

COSTS AND FINANCIAL AID

Tuition $3,150. Room & board $4,874. Average book expense $1,110. **Required Forms and Deadlines:** FAFSA and institution's own financial aid form. No deadline for regular filing. Priority filing deadline April 15. **Notification of Awards:** Applicants will be notified of awards on a rolling basis beginning on or about April 1. **Types of Aid:** *Need-based scholarships/grants:* Pell, state scholarships/grants, private scholarships, the school's own gift aid. *Loans:* FFEL Subsidized Stafford, FFEL Unsubsidized Stafford, FFEL PLUS, college/university loans from institutional funds. **Student Employment:** Federal Work-Study Program available. Institutional employment available. Off-campus job opportunities are good. **Financial Aid Statistics:** 5% freshmen, 31% undergrads receive some form of aid. Average freshman grant $2,803. Average freshman loan $1,082. Average income from on-campus job $5,720. **Financial Aid Phone:** 801-378-4104.

BROCK UNIVERSITY

500 Glenridge Avenue, St. Catharines, ON L2S 3A1
Phone: 905-688-5550 **E-mail:** admissns@brocku.ca
Fax: 905-988-5488 **Web:** www.brocku.ca

This public school was founded in 1964. It has a 400-acre campus.

STUDENTS AND FACULTY

Enrollment: 11,270. **Student Body:** Male 39%, female 61%. **Faculty:** Student/faculty ratio 23:1. 385 full-time faculty, 91% hold PhDs. 100% faculty teach undergrads.

ACADEMICS

Degrees: Bachelor's, certificate, doctoral, master's. **Academic Requirements:** General education including some course work in foreign languages, humanities, sciences (biological or physical), social science. **Majors with Highest Enrollment:** Geography; music/music and performing arts studies, general; political science and government, general. **Special Study Options:** Cooperative (work-study) program, distance learning, double major, English as a second language, student exchange program (domestic), honors program, independent study, internships, liberal arts/career combination, student-designed major, study abroad, teacher certification program.

FACILITIES

Housing: Coed, all-female, all-male, housing for disabled students, Village Residence (townhouses). **Library Holdings:** 880,635 bound volumes. 666,859 periodicals. 659,816 microforms. 24,498 audiovisuals. **Special Academic Facilities/Equipment:** Cool Climate Oenology & Viticulture Institute, Leo LeBlanc Rowing Center, map library, instructional resource centre.

EXTRACURRICULARS

Activities: Choral groups, concert band, drama/theater, literary magazine, music ensembles, musical theater, radio station, student government, student newspaper, student-run film society, yearbook. **Organizations:** 51 registered organizations, 5 religious organizations. **Athletics (Intercollegiate):** *Men:* baseball, basketball, cheerleading, crew, cross-country, fencing, golf, ice hockey, rugby, soccer, squash, swimming, tennis, wrestling. *Women:* basketball, cheerleading, crew, cross-country, fencing, ice hockey, rugby, soccer, swimming, volleyball, wrestling.

ADMISSIONS

Selectivity Rating: 60 (of 100). **Freshman Academic Profile:** TOEFL required of all international applicants, minimum TOEFL 550. **Basis for Candidate Selection:** *Very important factors considered include:* secondary school record. *Other factors considered include:* talent/ability. **Freshman Admission Requirements:** High school diploma or GED is required. **General Admission Information:** Regular application deadline June 1. Nonfall registration accepted. Neither credit nor placement offered for CEEB Advanced Placement tests.

COSTS AND FINANCIAL AID

In-state tuition $4,073. Out-of-state tuition $4,073. Room & board $5,510. Required fees $0. Average book expense $500. **Student Employment:** Federal Work-Study Program available. Institutional employment available. Off-campus job opportunities are excellent. **Financial Aid Phone:** 905-688-5550.

BROOKS INSTITUTE OF PHOTOGRAPHY

801 Alston Rd., Santa Barbara, CA 93108
Phone: 805-966-3888 **E-mail:** admissions@brooks.edu
Fax: 805-564-1475 **Web:** www.brooks.edu

This private school was founded in 1945.

STUDENTS AND FACULTY

Enrollment: 302. **Student Body:** Male 68%, female 32%, out-of-state 45%, international 28%. **Ethnic Representation:** African American 1%, Asian 3%, Caucasian 87%, Hispanic 5%. **Retention and Graduation:** 84% freshmen return for sophomore year.

ACADEMICS

Degrees: Associate's, bachelor's, certificate, master's. **Academic Requirements:** General education including some course work in English (including composition), humanities, mathematics, sciences (biological or physical), social science. **Special Study Options:** Double major, independent study, internships.

FACILITIES

Housing: Apartments for single students. **Library Holdings:** 6,500 bound volumes. 128 periodicals. 275 audiovisuals. **Special Academic Facilities/ Equipment:** Photographic memorabilia pre-1900 to present (equipment and imaging). **Computers:** *Recommended operating system:* Mac. School-owned computers available for student use.

EXTRACURRICULARS

Activities: Student government. **Organizations:** 1 honor society.

ADMISSIONS

Selectivity Rating: 60 (of 100). **Freshman Academic Profile:** Average high school GPA 3.0. TOEFL required of all international applicants, minimum TOEFL 500. **Freshman Admission Requirements: Transfer Admission Requirements:** *Items required:* high school transcript, essay. Minimum high school GPA of 3.0 required. Minimum college GPA of 2.0 required. Lowest grade transferable C. **General Admission Information:** Regular application deadline rolling. Nonfall registration accepted. Credit offered for CEEB Advanced Placement tests.

COSTS AND FINANCIAL AID

Tuition $15,000. Required fees $450. Average book expense $6,000. **Required Forms and Deadlines:** FAFSA and institution's own financial aid form. Priority filing deadline March 2. **Notification of Awards:** Applicants will be notified of awards on a rolling basis. **Types of Aid:** *Need-based scholarships/ grants:* Pell, SEOG, state scholarships/grants, private scholarships. *Loans:* FFEL Subsidized Stafford, FFEL Unsubsidized Stafford, FFEL PLUS, alternative loans. **Student Employment:** Federal Work-Study Program available. Institutional employment available. Off-campus job opportunities are good. **Financial Aid Statistics:** Average freshman grant $2,200. Average freshman loan $4,625. **Financial Aid Phone:** 805-966-3888.

BROOME COMMUNITY COLLEGE

Admissions Office, Box 1017, Binghamton, NY 13902
Phone: 607-778-5001 **E-mail:** fiorelli_a@sunybroome.edu **CEEB Code:** 2048
Fax: 607-778-5310 **Web:** www.sunybroome.edu

This public school was founded in 1946. It has a 223-acre campus.

STUDENTS AND FACULTY

Enrollment: 5,555. **Student Body:** Male 44%, female 56%, out-of-state 22%, international 2% (30 countries represented). **Ethnic Representation:** African American 1%, Asian 1%, Caucasian 97%. **Retention and Graduation:** 42% grads go on to further study within 1 year. **Faculty:** 100% faculty teach undergrads.

ACADEMICS

Degrees: Associate's, certificate. **Academic Requirements:** General education including some course work in English (including composition). **Special Study Options:** Cooperative (work-study) program, distance learning, double major, English as a second language, honors program, independent study, internships, liberal arts/career combination, student-designed major, study abroad, weekend college.

FACILITIES

Library Holdings: 66,963 bound volumes. 377 periodicals. 1,029 microforms. 1,029 audiovisuals. **Computers:** *Recommended operating system:* Windows 95.

EXTRACURRICULARS

Activities: Choral groups, concert band, drama/theater, jazz band, music ensembles, student government, student newspaper. **Organizations:** 50 registered organizations, 1 honor society, 2 religious organizations. **Athletics (Intercollegiate):** *Men:* baseball, basketball, cheerleading, cross-country, golf, ice hockey, lacrosse, soccer, tennis. *Women:* basketball, cheerleading, cross-country, soccer, softball, volleyball.

ADMISSIONS

Selectivity Rating: 63 (of 100). **Freshman Academic Profile:** Average high school GPA 3.0. 5% in top 10% of high school class, 9% in top 25% of high school class, 40% in top 50% of high school class. 95% from public high schools. TOEFL required of all international applicants, minimum TOEFL 400. **Freshman Admission Requirements:** High school diploma or GED is required. *Academic units required/recommended:* 22 total recommended; 4 English recommended, 3 math recommended, 3 science recommended, 2 science lab recommended, 2 foreign language recommended, 4 social studies recommended, 4 history recommended. **Freshman Admission Statistics:** 3,840 applied, 82% accepted, 49% of those accepted enrolled. **General Admission Information:** Nonfall registration accepted. Admission may be deferred for a maximum of 1 year. Neither credit nor placement offered for CEEB Advanced Placement tests.

COSTS AND FINANCIAL AID

In-state tuition $2,338. Out-of-state tuition $4,676. Required fees $170. Average book expense $600. **Financial Aid Phone:** 607-778-5028.

BROWN UNIVERSITY

Box 1876, 45 Prospect Street, Providence, RI 02912
Phone: 401-863-2378 **E-mail:** admission_undergraduate@brown.edu
CEEB Code: 3094 **Fax:** 401-863-9300 **Web:** www.brown.edu **ACT Code:** 3800

This private school was founded in 1764. It has a 140-acre campus.

STUDENTS AND FACULTY

Enrollment: 6,030. **Student Body:** Male 45%, female 55%, out-of-state 96%, international 6% (72 countries represented). **Ethnic Representation:** African American 6%, Asian 15%, Caucasian 53%, Hispanic 7%, Native American 1%. **Retention and Graduation:** 97% freshmen return for sophomore year. 83% freshmen graduate within 4 years. 35% grads go on to further study within 1 year. 1% grads pursue business degrees. 10% grads pursue law degrees. 9% grads pursue medical degrees. **Faculty:** Student/faculty ratio 8:1. 785 full-time faculty, 97% hold PhDs. 100% faculty teach undergrads.

ACADEMICS
Degrees: Bachelor's, doctoral, first professional, master's. **Academic Requirements:** No requirements in specific areas. **Majors with Highest Enrollment:** Biology/biological sciences, general; international relations and affairs; history, general. **Disciplines with Highest Percentage of Degrees Awarded:** Social sciences and history 43%, humanities 26%, biological life sciences 17%, physical sciences 14%. **Special Study Options:** Accelerated program, cross registration, double major, student exchange program (domestic), honors program, independent study, internships, student-designed major, study abroad, teacher certification program, 8-year medical program (AB or SCB plus MD), 5-year degree program (AB and SCB).

FACILITIES
Housing: Coed, all-female, fraternities and/or sororities, cooperative housing, language houses, international house, environmental studies house, social dormitories, cultural houses, and other special program housing. **Library Holdings:** 3,000,000 bound volumes. 17,000 periodicals. 1,000,000 microforms. 26,350 audiovisuals. **Special Academic Facilities/Equipment:** Art gallery, anthropology museum, language lab, information technology center, NASA Research Center, center for modern culture/media. **Computers:** School-owned computers available for student use.

EXTRACURRICULARS
Activities: Choral groups, concert band, dance, drama/theater, jazz band, literary magazine, marching band, music ensembles, musical theater, radio station, student government, student newspaper, student-run film society, symphony orchestra, television station, yearbook. **Organizations:** 240 registered organizations, 10 fraternities (15% men join), 3 sororities (5% women join). **Athletics (Intercollegiate):** *Men:* baseball, basketball, crew, cross-country, diving, fencing, football, golf, ice hockey, indoor track, lacrosse, soccer, squash, swimming, tennis, track & field, water polo, wrestling. *Women:* basketball, crew, cross-country, diving, equestrian, fencing, field hockey, golf, gymnastics, ice hockey, indoor track, lacrosse, skiing (alpine), soccer, softball, squash, swimming, tennis, track & field, volleyball, water polo.

ADMISSIONS
Selectivity Rating: 99 (of 100). **Freshman Academic Profile:** 87% in top 10% of high school class, 97% in top 25% of high school class, 100% in top 50% of high school class. 60% from public high schools. Average SAT I Math 700, SAT I Math middle 50% range 650-750. Average SAT I Verbal 690, SAT I Verbal middle 50% range 640-750. Average ACT 29, ACT middle 50% range 26-32. TOEFL required of all international applicants, minimum TOEFL 600. **Basis for Candidate Selection:** *Very important factors considered include:* character/personal qualities, secondary school record, talent/ability. *Important factors considered include:* class rank, essays, extracurricular activities, recommendations. *Other factors considered include:* alumni/ae relation, geographical residence, interview, minority status, standardized test scores, state residency, volunteer work, work experience. **Freshman Admission Requirements:** High school diploma is required and GED is not accepted. *Academic units required/recommended:* 16 total required; 19 total recommended; 4 English required, 4 English recommended, 3 math required, 4 math recommended, 3 science required, 4 science recommended, 2 science lab required, 3 science lab recommended, 3 foreign language required, 4 foreign language recommended, 2 history required, 2 history recommended, 1 elective required, 1 elective recommended. **Freshman Admission Statistics:** 14,612 applied, 17% accepted, 59% of those accepted enrolled. **Transfer Admission Requirements:** *Items required:* high school transcript, college transcript, essay, standardized test scores, statement of good standing from prior school. Lowest grade transferable C. **General Admission Information:** Application fee $70. Early decision application deadline November 1. Regular application deadline January 1. Admission may be deferred for a maximum of 1 year. Placement offered for CEEB Advanced Placement tests.

COSTS AND FINANCIAL AID
Tuition $27,856. Room & board $7,876. Required fees $851. Average book expense $960. **Required Forms and Deadlines:** FAFSA, CSS/Financial Aid PROFILE, noncustodial (divorced/separated) parent's statement, and business/farm supplement. Financial aid filing deadline February 1. **Notification of Awards:** Applicants will be notified of awards on or about April 1. **Types of Aid:** *Need-based scholarships/grants:* Pell, SEOG, state scholarships/grants, private scholarships, the school's own gift aid. *Loans:* Direct Subsidized Stafford, Direct Unsubsidized Stafford, Direct PLUS, Federal Perkins, state loans, college/university loans from institutional funds. **Student Employment:** Federal Work-Study Program available. Institutional employment available. Off-campus job opportunities are excellent. **Financial Aid Statistics:** 41% freshmen, 40% undergrads receive some form of aid. Average freshman grant $20,800. Average freshman loan $2,700. Average income from on-campus job $2,000. **Financial Aid Phone:** 401-863-2721.

BRYAN COLLEGE

PO Box 7000, Dayton, TN 37321-7000
Phone: 423-775-2041 **E-mail:** admiss@bryan.edu **CEEB Code:** 1908
Fax: 423-775-7199 **Web:** www.bryan.edu

STUDENTS AND FACULTY
Student Body: Out-of-state 72%.

ACADEMICS
Degrees: Associate's, bachelor's.

FACILITIES
Housing: Coed, all-female, all-male.

EXTRACURRICULARS
Organizations: 2 honor societies, 2 religious organizations. **Athletics (Intercollegiate):** *Men:* basketball, cheerleading, cross-country, soccer, tennis, volleyball. *Women:* basketball, cheerleading, cross-country, tennis, volleyball.

ADMISSIONS
Selectivity Rating: 63 (of 100). **Freshman Academic Profile:** TOEFL required of all international applicants, minimum TOEFL 500. **Freshman Admission Requirements: General Admission Information:** Regular application deadline July 31.

COSTS AND FINANCIAL AID
Room & board $3,950. Required fees $600. Average book expense $500. **Types of Aid:** *Need-based scholarships/grants:* Pell, SEOG, state scholarships/grants, private scholarships, the school's own gift aid. *Loans:* FFEL Subsidized Stafford, FFEL Unsubsidized Stafford, FFEL PLUS, Federal Perkins, college/university loans from institutional funds. **Student Employment:** Federal Work-Study Program available. **Financial Aid Statistics:** Average freshman grant $2,850. Average income from on-campus job $800.

BRYANT COLLEGE

1150 Douglas Pike, Smithfield, RI 02917
Phone: 401-232-6100 **E-mail:** admission@bryant.edu **CEEB Code:** 3095
Fax: 401-232-6741 **Web:** www.bryant.edu **ACT Code:** 3802

This private school was founded in 1863. It has a 392-acre campus.

STUDENTS AND FACULTY
Enrollment: 2,912. **Student Body:** Male 60%, female 40%, out-of-state 74%, international 4% (37 countries represented). **Ethnic Representation:** African American 3%, Asian 2%, Caucasian 86%, Hispanic 3%. **Retention and Graduation:** 84% freshmen return for sophomore year. 60% freshmen graduate within 4 years. 4% grads go on to further study within 1 year. 3% grads pursue business degrees. **Faculty:** Student/faculty ratio 16:1. 132 full-time faculty, 86% hold PhDs. 100% faculty teach undergrads.

ACADEMICS
Degrees: Bachelor's, master's, post-master's certificate. **Academic Requirements:** General education including some course work in computer literacy, English (including composition), history, humanities, mathematics, sciences (biological or physical), social science, accounting, economics, finance, management, marketing, business law, computer science. **Classes:** 30-39 students in an average class. 20-29 students in an average lab/discussion section. **Majors with Highest Enrollment:** Business administration/management; finance and financial management services; marketing/marketing management, general. **Disciplines with Highest Percentage of Degrees Awarded:** Business/marketing 79%, computer and information sciences 18%, communications/communication technologies 1%, social sciences and history 1%. **Special Study Options:** Double major, English as a second language, honors program, independent study, internships, study abroad, Beta Gamma Sigma business honor society, Omicron Delta Epsilon economic honor society, Lambda Pi Eta communication honor society.

FACILITIES
Housing: Coed, all-female, housing for disabled students. Some fraternities and sororities are housed in residence halls. **Library Holdings:** 4,100,000 bound volumes. 1,000 periodicals. 14,000 microforms. 908 audiovisuals. **Special Academic Facilities/Equipment:** George E. Bello Center for Information

and Technology, Koffler Technology Center, discovery lab, learning/language lab, Davis Classroom, John H. Chafee Center for International Business. **Computers:** *Recommended operating system:* Microsoft 98 or NT. School-owned computers available for student use.

EXTRACURRICULARS

Activities: Choral groups, dance, drama/theater, literary magazine, pep band, radio station, student government, student newspaper, yearbook. **Organizations:** 65 registered organizations, 3 honor societies, 2 religious organizations, 6 fraternities (8% men join), 3 sororities (8% women join). **Athletics (Intercollegiate):** *Men:* baseball, basketball, cross-country, football, golf, indoor track, lacrosse, soccer, tennis, track & field. *Women:* basketball, cross-country, field hockey, golf, indoor track, lacrosse, soccer, softball, tennis, track & field, volleyball.

ADMISSIONS

Selectivity Rating: 69 (of 100). **Freshman Academic Profile:** Average high school GPA 3.0. 9% in top 10% of high school class, 36% in top 25% of high school class, 80% in top 50% of high school class. 78% from public high schools. Average SAT I Math 557, SAT I Math middle 50% range 510-610. Average SAT I Verbal 522, SAT I Verbal middle 50% range 480-560. Average ACT 22, ACT middle 50% range 19-24. TOEFL required of all international applicants, minimum TOEFL 550. **Basis for Candidate Selection:** *Very important factors considered include:* class rank, essays, recommendations, secondary school record, standardized test scores. *Important factors considered include:* alumni/ae relation, character/personal qualities, extracurricular activities, interview, talent/ability. *Other factors considered include:* geographical residence, minority status, volunteer work, work experience. **Freshman Admission Requirements:** High school diploma or GED is required. *Academic units required/recommended:* 16 total required; 4 English required, 3 math required, 4 math recommended, 1 science required, 3 science recommended, 1 science lab required, 2 science lab recommended, 2 foreign language recommended. **Freshman Admission Statistics:** 2,811 applied, 74% accepted, 36% of those accepted enrolled. **Transfer Admission Requirements:** *Items required:* high school transcript, college transcript, essay. Minimum college GPA of 2.5 required. Lowest grade transferable C. **General Admission Information:** Application fee $50. Priority application deadline November 1. Early decision application deadline November 15. Regular application deadline February 15. Nonfall registration accepted. Admission may be deferred for a maximum of 2 years. Credit and/or placement offered for CEEB Advanced Placement tests.

COSTS AND FINANCIAL AID

Required Forms and Deadlines: FAFSA and institution's own financial aid form. Financial aid filing deadline February 15. Priority filing deadline February 15. **Notification of Awards:** Applicants will be notified of awards on or about March 24. **Types of Aid:** *Need-based scholarships/grants:* Pell, SEOG, state scholarships/grants, private scholarships, the school's own gift aid. *Loans:* Direct Subsidized Stafford, Direct Unsubsidized Stafford, FFEL PLUS, Federal Perkins. **Student Employment:** Federal Work-Study Program available. Institutional employment available. Off-campus job opportunities are fair. **Financial Aid Statistics:** 65% freshmen, 70% undergrads receive some form of aid. Average freshman grant $7,774. Average freshman loan $3,914. Average income from on-campus job $1,435. **Financial Aid Phone:** 401-232-6020.

See page 952.

BRYN ATHYN COLLEGE OF THE NEW CHURCH

Dee Smith-Johns - Box 717, Bryn Athyn, PA 19009
Phone: 215-938-2511 **E-mail:** dsjohns@newchurch.edu **CEEB Code:** 2002
Fax: 215-938-2658 **Web:** www.newchurch.edu

This private school, which is affiliated with the Swedenborgian Church, was founded in 1877. It has a 130-acre campus.

STUDENTS AND FACULTY

Enrollment: 132. **Student Body:** Male 47%, female 53%, out-of-state 21%, international 15% (13 countries represented). **Ethnic Representation:** African American 1%, Asian 5%, Caucasian 94%. **Retention and Graduation:** 60% freshmen return for sophomore year. 26% freshmen graduate within 4 years. 40% grads go on to further study within 1 year. **Faculty:** Student/faculty ratio 6:1. 18 full-time faculty, 77% hold PhDs. 100% faculty teach undergrads.

ACADEMICS

Degrees: Associate's, bachelor's, first professional, first professional certificate, master's. **Academic Requirements:** General education including some course work in arts/fine arts, English (including composition), foreign languages, history, mathematics, philosophy, sciences (biological or physical), social science, religion, physical education. **Classes:** Under 10 students in an average class. Under 10 students in an average lab/discussion section. **Majors with Highest Enrollment:** Multi/interdisciplinary studies; English language and literature, general; history, general. **Disciplines with Highest Percentage of Degrees Awarded:** Education 36%, interdisciplinary studies 29%, English 21%, biological life sciences 7%, social sciences and history 7%. **Special Study Options:** Cooperative (work-study) program, dual enrollment, English as a second language, independent study, internships, student-designed major, study abroad.

FACILITIES

Housing: All-female, all-male. **Library Holdings:** 97,561 bound volumes. 180 periodicals. 3,984 microforms. 559 audiovisuals. **Special Academic Facilities/Equipment:** Glencairn Museum, Swedenborg Library, Swedenborgiana Academy of the New Church Archives, John Pitcairn Archives. **Computers:** *Recommended operating system:* Windows 95. School-owned computers available for student use.

EXTRACURRICULARS

Activities: Choral groups, drama/theater, literary magazine, musical theater, student government, student newspaper. **Organizations:** 2 registered organizations, 1 religious organization. **Athletics (Intercollegiate):** *Men:* ice hockey, lacrosse, soccer. *Women:* lacrosse, volleyball.

ADMISSIONS

Selectivity Rating: 63 (of 100). **Freshman Academic Profile:** Average SAT I Math 555, SAT I Math middle 50% range 490-620. Average SAT I Verbal 551, SAT I Verbal middle 50% range 500-620. Average ACT 22. TOEFL required of all international applicants, minimum TOEFL 520. **Basis for Candidate Selection:** *Very important factors considered include:* character/personal qualities, essays, recommendations, religious affiliation/commitment, secondary school record, standardized test scores. *Other factors considered include:* alumni/ae relation, class rank, extracurricular activities, interview, talent/ability, volunteer work, work experience. **Freshman Admission Requirements:** High school diploma or GED is required. *Academic units required/recommended:* 15 total required; 4 English required, 3 math required, 3 science required, 2 foreign language required. **Freshman Admission Statistics:** 50 applied, 98% accepted, 82% of those accepted enrolled. **Transfer Admission Requirements:** *Items required:* college transcript, essay. Lowest grade transferable C-. **General Admission Information:** Application fee $30. Regular application deadline February 1. Nonfall registration accepted. Admission may be deferred for a maximum of 1 year. Credit offered for CEEB Advanced Placement tests.

COSTS AND FINANCIAL AID

Room & board $4,404. Average book expense $525. **Required Forms and Deadlines:** Institution's own financial aid form and most recent year tax return. No deadline for regular filing. Priority filing deadline June 1. **Notification of Awards:** Applicants will be notified of awards on a rolling basis beginning on or about June 1. **Types of Aid:** *Need-based scholarships/grants:* private scholarships, the school's own gift aid. **Student Employment:** Institutional employment available. Off-campus job opportunities are good. **Financial Aid Statistics:** 58% freshmen, 51% undergrads receive some form of aid. Average freshman grant $5,029. Average freshman loan $2,000. Average income from on-campus job $1,600. **Financial Aid Phone:** 215-938-2630.

BRYN MAWR COLLEGE

101 North Merion Avenue, Bryn Mawr, PA 19010-2899
Phone: 610-526-5152 **E-mail:** admissions@brynmawr.edu **CEEB Code:** 2049
Fax: 610-526-7471 **Web:** www.brynmawr.edu **ACT Code:** 3526

This private school was founded in 1885. It has a 135-acre campus.

STUDENTS AND FACULTY

Enrollment: 1,322. **Student Body:** Male 2%, female 98%, out-of-state 80%, international 8% (45 countries represented). **Ethnic Representation:** African American 4%, Asian 14%, Caucasian 66%, Hispanic 3%. **Retention and Graduation:** 92% freshmen return for sophomore year. 77% freshmen graduate within 4 years. 20% grads go on to further study within 1 year. 2% grads pursue business degrees. 4% grads pursue law degrees. 3% grads pursue medical degrees. **Faculty:** Student/faculty ratio 8:1. 150 full-time faculty, 97% hold PhDs. 100% faculty teach undergrads.

ACADEMICS

Degrees: Bachelor's, doctoral, master's, post-bachelor's certificate. **Academic Requirements:** General education including some course work in English (including composition), foreign languages, humanities, mathematics, sciences (biological or physical), social science, 2 semesters of physical education, 8-10 courses in major. **Classes:** 10-19 students in an average class. 20-29 students in an average lab/discussion section. **Majors with Highest Enrollment:** English language and literature, general; mathematics, general; biology/biological sciences, general. **Disciplines with Highest Percentage of Degrees Awarded:** Social sciences and history 32%, mathematics 11%, English 10%, biological life sciences 9%, physical sciences 9%. **Special Study Options:** Accelerated program, cross registration, double major, dual enrollment, student exchange program (domestic), independent study, internships, liberal arts/career combination, student-designed major, study abroad, teacher certification program, AB/BS and 3-2 engineering programs with University of Pennsylvania, joint grad program in geology with University of Pennsylvania (MA or PhD), growth and structure of cities with University of Pennsylvania.

FACILITIES

Housing: Coed, all-female, apartments for single students, cooperative housing. **Library Holdings:** 1,089,128 bound volumes. 1,827 periodicals. 49,960 microforms. 1,380 audiovisuals. **Special Academic Facilities/Equipment:** Museum of classical and Near Eastern archaeology, mineral collection, Child Study Institute, on-campus nursery school, Newfeld Collection of African Art, language learning center. **Computers:** School-owned computers available for student use.

EXTRACURRICULARS

Activities: Choral groups, dance, drama/theater, literary magazine, music ensembles, musical theater, radio station, student government, student newspaper, student-run film society, yearbook. **Organizations:** 100 registered organizations, 9 religious organizations. **Athletics (Intercollegiate):** *Women:* basketball, crew, cross-country, field hockey, lacrosse, soccer, swimming, tennis, track & field, volleyball.

ADMISSIONS

Selectivity Rating: 93 (of 100). **Freshman Academic Profile:** 57% in top 10% of high school class, 93% in top 25% of high school class, 100% in top 50% of high school class. 56% from public high schools. Average SAT I Math 638, SAT I Math middle 50% range 600-690. Average SAT I Verbal 672, SAT I Verbal middle 50% range 630-730. Average ACT 28, ACT middle 50% range 27-30. TOEFL required of all international applicants, minimum TOEFL 600. **Basis for Candidate Selection:** *Very important factors considered include:* essays, recommendations, secondary school record. *Important factors considered include:* character/personal qualities, extracurricular activities. *Other factors considered include:* class rank, interview, standardized test scores, talent/ability, volunteer work, work experience. **Freshman Admission Requirements:** High school diploma or GED is required. *Academic units required/recommended:* 16 total recommended; 4 English recommended, 3 math recommended, 2 science recommended, 1 science lab recommended, 3 foreign language recommended, 2 social studies recommended, 2 history recommended, 2 elective required. **Freshman Admission Statistics:** 1,743 applied, 50% accepted, 35% of those accepted enrolled. **Transfer Admission Requirements:** *Items required:* high school transcript, college transcript, essay, standardized test scores, statement of good standing from prior school. Lowest grade transferable C. **General Admission Information:** Application fee $50. Early decision application deadline November 15. Regular application deadline January 15. Admission may be deferred for a maximum of 1 year. Credit and/or placement offered for CEEB Advanced Placement tests.

COSTS AND FINANCIAL AID

Tuition $25,550. Room & board $8,970. Required fees $670. Average book expense $1,450. **Required Forms and Deadlines:** FAFSA, CSS/Financial Aid PROFILE, noncustodial (divorced/separated) parent's statement, and business/farm supplement. Financial aid filing deadline January 15. Priority filing deadline January 15. **Notification of Awards:** Applicants will be notified of awards on or about April 1. **Types of Aid:** *Need-based scholarships/grants:* Pell, SEOG, state scholarships/grants, the school's own gift aid. *Loans:* FFEL Subsidized Stafford, FFEL Unsubsidized Stafford, FFEL PLUS, Federal Perkins, college/university loans from institutional funds. **Student Employment:** Federal Work-Study Program available. Institutional employment available. Off-campus job opportunities are good. **Financial Aid Statistics:** 57% freshmen, 58% undergrads receive some form of aid. Average freshman grant $21,251. Average freshman loan $2,760. Average income from on-campus job $1,400. **Financial Aid Phone:** 610-526-5245.

BUCKNELL UNIVERSITY

 $$$   

Freas Hall, Bucknell University, Lewisburg, PA 17837
Phone: 570-577-1101 **E-mail:** admissions@bucknell.edu **CEEB Code:** 2050
Fax: 570-577-3538 **Web:** www.bucknell.edu **ACT Code:** 3528

This private school was founded in 1846. It has a 396-acre campus.

STUDENTS AND FACULTY

Enrollment: 3,440. **Student Body:** Male 51%, female 49%, out-of-state 68%, international 2% (34 countries represented). **Ethnic Representation:** African American 3%, Asian 6%, Caucasian 87%, Hispanic 2%, Native American 1%. **Retention and Graduation:** 95% freshmen return for sophomore year. 84% freshmen graduate within 4 years. 22% grads go on to further study within 1 year. 1% grads pursue business degrees. 3% grads pursue law degrees. 2% grads pursue medical degrees. **Faculty:** Student/faculty ratio 12:1. 293 full-time faculty, 95% hold PhDs. 100% faculty teach undergrads.

ACADEMICS

Degrees: Bachelor's, master's. **Academic Requirements:** General education including some course work in English (including composition), humanities, mathematics, sciences (biological or physical), social science. **Classes:** 10-19 students in an average class. 10-19 students in an average lab/discussion section. **Majors with Highest Enrollment:** Business administration/management; English language and literature, general; economics, general. **Disciplines with Highest Percentage of Degrees Awarded:** Social sciences and history 24%, business/marketing 17%, engineering/engineering technology 16%, biological life sciences 7%, English 7%. **Special Study Options:** Double major, dual enrollment, honors program, independent study, internships, liberal arts/career combination, student-designed major, study abroad, teacher certification program.

FACILITIES

Housing: Coed, all-female, apartments for single students, housing for disabled students, housing for international students, fraternities and/or sororities, special-interest houses, substance free, quiet floor. **Library Holdings:** 710,985 bound volumes. 4,775 periodicals. 64 microforms. 15,300 audiovisuals. **Special Academic Facilities/Equipment:** Art gallery, center for performing arts, poetry center, photography lab, observatory, 63-acre nature site, greenhouse, primate facility, gas chromatograph/mass spectrometer, electron microscope, herbarium, race/gender resource center, engineering structural test lab, nuclear magnetic resonance spectrometer, 18-hole golf course, conference center. **Computers:** School-owned computers available for student use.

EXTRACURRICULARS

Activities: Choral groups, concert band, dance, drama/theater, jazz band, literary magazine, music ensembles, opera, pep band, radio station, student government, student newspaper, student-run film society, symphony orchestra, yearbook. **Organizations:** 120 registered organizations, 23 honor societies, 9 religious organizations, 13 fraternities (41% men join), 7 sororities (45% women join). **Athletics (Intercollegiate):** *Men:* baseball, basketball, cross-country, diving, football, golf, indoor track, lacrosse, soccer, swimming, tennis, track & field, water polo. *Women:* basketball, crew, cross-country, diving, field hockey, golf, indoor track, lacrosse, soccer, softball, swimming, tennis, track & field, volleyball, water polo.

ADMISSIONS

Selectivity Rating: 91 (of 100). **Freshman Academic Profile:** 64% in top 10% of high school class, 94% in top 25% of high school class, 99% in top 50% of high school class. 76% from public high schools. Average SAT I Math 659, SAT I Math middle 50% range 620-700. Average SAT I Verbal 631, SAT I Verbal middle 50% range 590-670. TOEFL required of all international applicants, minimum TOEFL 550. **Basis for Candidate Selection:** *Very important factors considered include:* character/personal qualities, recommendations, secondary school record, standardized test scores, talent/ability. *Important factors considered include:* class rank, extracurricular activities, minority status, volunteer work. *Other factors considered include:* alumni/ae relation, essays, geographical residence, interview, work experience. **Freshman Admission Requirements:** High school diploma or GED is required. *Academic units required/recommended:* 16 total required; 20 total recommended; 4 English required, 4 English recommended, 3 math required, 4 math recommended, 2 science required, 3 science recommended, 2 foreign language required, 4 foreign language recommended, 2 social studies required, 2 history required, 1 elective required. **Freshman Admission Statistics:** 7,760 applied, 39% accepted, 30% of those accepted enrolled. **Transfer Admission Requirements:** *Items required:* high school transcript, college transcript, essay, standardized test scores, statement of good standing from prior school. Minimum college GPA of 2.5 required. Lowest grade transferable C. **General**

Admission Information: Application fee $60. Early decision application deadline November 15. Regular application deadline January 1. Admission may be deferred for a maximum of 2 years. Credit and/or placement offered for CEEB Advanced Placement tests.

COSTS AND FINANCIAL AID

Tuition $27,340. Room & board $6,052. Required fees $191. Average book expense $750. **Required Forms and Deadlines:** FAFSA, CSS/Financial Aid PROFILE, noncustodial (divorced/separated) parent's statement, and business/farm supplement. Financial aid filing deadline January 1. **Notification of Awards:** Applicants will be notified of awards on or about April 10. **Types of Aid:** *Need-based scholarships/grants:* Pell, SEOG, state scholarships/grants, private scholarships, the school's own gift aid. *Loans:* FFEL Subsidized Stafford, FFEL Unsubsidized Stafford, FFEL PLUS, Federal Perkins. **Student Employment:** Federal Work-Study Program available. Institutional employment available. Off-campus job opportunities are poor. **Financial Aid Statistics:** 55% freshmen, 48% undergrads receive some form of aid. Average freshman grant $19,629. Average freshman loan $3,937. Average income from on-campus job $1,500. **Financial Aid Phone:** 570-577-1331.

BUENA VISTA UNIVERSITY

610 West Fourth Street, Storm Lake, IA 50588-1798
Phone: 712-749-2235 **E-mail:** admissions@bvu.edu **CEEB Code:** 6047
Fax: 712-749-1459 **Web:** www.bvu.edu **ACT Code:** 1278

This private school, which is affiliated with the Presbyterian Church, was founded in 1891. It has a 60-acre campus.

STUDENTS AND FACULTY

Enrollment: 1,267. **Student Body:** Male 48%, female 52%, out-of-state 16%, international 1%. **Ethnic Representation:** African American 1%, Asian 1%, Caucasian 93%, Hispanic 1%. **Retention and Graduation:** 67% freshmen return for sophomore year. 42% freshmen graduate within 4 years. 15% grads go on to further study within 1 year. 4% grads pursue business degrees. 1% grads pursue law degrees. 2% grads pursue medical degrees. **Faculty:** Student/faculty ratio 16:1. 81 full-time faculty, 65% hold PhDs. 100% faculty teach undergrads.

ACADEMICS

Degrees: Bachelor's, master's. **Academic Requirements:** General education including some course work in English (including composition), mathematics, social science. **Classes:** 10-19 students in an average class. **Majors with Highest Enrollment:** Education, general; management science, general; biology/biological sciences, general. **Disciplines with Highest Percentage of Degrees Awarded:** Business/marketing 33%, education 24%, interdisciplinary studies 14%, psychology 9%, social sciences and history 6%. **Special Study Options:** Distance learning, double major, English as a second language, student exchange program (domestic), external degree program, honors program, independent study, internships, liberal arts/career combination, student-designed major, study abroad, teacher certification program, off-campus study and other semester-away programs available. Academic and cultural events series brings national and world leaders and performers to campus; students earn credits for attendance.

FACILITIES

Housing: Coed, all-female, all-male, apartments for single students. **Library Holdings:** 154,782 bound volumes. 705 periodicals. 40,657 microforms. 3,920 audiovisuals. **Special Academic Facilities/Equipment:** Art gallery, language lab, television station, radio station, satellite telecommunications system, computer labs/centers, electron microscope. **Computers:** *Recommended operating system:* Windows NT/2000. School-owned computers available for student use.

EXTRACURRICULARS

Activities: Choral groups, concert band, drama/theater, jazz band, literary magazine, marching band, music ensembles, musical theater, radio station, student government, student newspaper, symphony orchestra, television station. **Organizations:** 50 registered organizations, 5 honor societies, 3 religious organizations. **Athletics (Intercollegiate):** *Men:* baseball, basketball, cross-country, diving, football, indoor track, soccer, swimming, tennis, track & field, wrestling. *Women:* basketball, cheerleading, cross-country, diving, golf, indoor track, soccer, softball, swimming, tennis, track & field, volleyball.

ADMISSIONS

Selectivity Rating: 79 (of 100). **Freshman Academic Profile:** Average high school GPA 3.2. 20% in top 10% of high school class, 43% in top 25% of high school class, 75% in top 50% of high school class. 85% from public high schools. Average ACT 23, ACT middle 50% range 20-25. TOEFL required of all international applicants, minimum TOEFL 500. **Basis for Candidate Selection:** *Very important factors considered include:* standardized test scores. *Important factors considered include:* class rank, secondary school record. *Other factors considered include:* alumni/ae relation, character/personal qualities, essays, extracurricular activities, geographical residence, interview, minority status, recommendations, religious affiliation/commitment, state residency, talent/ability, volunteer work, work experience. **Freshman Admission Requirements:** High school diploma or GED is required. *Academic units required/recommended:* 15 total required; 4 English required, 4 math recommended, 2 science required, 4 science recommended, 2 foreign language recommended, 2 social studies required, 2 history recommended. **Freshman Admission Statistics:** 1,233 applied, 84% accepted, 35% of those accepted enrolled. **Transfer Admission Requirements:** *Items required:* high school transcript, college transcript, statement of good standing from prior school. Minimum college GPA of 2.0 required. Lowest grade transferable D. **General Admission Information:** Regular application deadline April 1. Nonfall registration accepted. Admission may be deferred for a maximum of 1 year. Credit and/or placement offered for CEEB Advanced Placement tests.

COSTS AND FINANCIAL AID

Tuition $18,738. Room & board $5,230. Required fees $0. Average book expense $500. **Required Forms and Deadlines:** FAFSA and institution's own financial aid form. Priority filing deadline June 1. **Notification of Awards:** Applicants will be notified of awards on or about February 20. **Types of Aid:** *Need-based scholarships/grants:* Pell, SEOG, state scholarships/grants, private scholarships, the school's own gift aid. *Loans:* Direct Subsidized Stafford, Direct Unsubsidized Stafford, Direct PLUS, FFEL Subsidized Stafford, FFEL Unsubsidized Stafford, FFEL PLUS, Federal Perkins, college/university loans from institutional funds. **Student Employment:** Federal Work-Study Program available. Institutional employment available. Off-campus job opportunities are excellent. **Financial Aid Statistics:** 92% freshmen, 92% undergrads receive some form of aid. Average freshman grant $13,969. Average freshman loan $3,274. Average income from on-campus job $1,038. **Financial Aid Phone:** 712-749-2164.

BURLINGTON COLLEGE

95 North Avenue, Burlington, VT 05401
Phone: 802-862-9616 **E-mail:** kcolline@burcol.edu **CEEB Code:** 3944
Fax: 802-660-4331 **Web:** www.burlingtoncollege.edu

This private school was founded in 1972. It has a 1-acre campus.

STUDENTS AND FACULTY

Enrollment: 280. **Student Body:** Male 37%, female 63%, out-of-state 39%. **Ethnic Representation:** African American 2%, Caucasian 49%, Hispanic 1%. **Retention and Graduation:** 34% grads go on to further study within 1 year. **Faculty:** Student/faculty ratio 8:1. 100% faculty teach undergrads.

ACADEMICS

Degrees: Associate's, bachelor's, certificate. **Academic Requirements:** General education including some course work in arts/fine arts, computer literacy, English (including composition), history, humanities, mathematics, sciences (biological or physical), social science. **Majors with Highest Enrollment:** Film/cinema studies; social sciences, general; area, ethnic, cultural, and gender studies. **Special Study Options:** Cooperative (work-study) program, cross registration, distance learning, double major, external degree program, independent study, internships, student-designed major.

FACILITIES

Housing: Apartments for single students, cooperative housing. **Library Holdings:** 5,700 bound volumes. 80 periodicals. 0 microforms. 1,050 audiovisuals. **Computers:** School-owned computers available for student use.

EXTRACURRICULARS

Activities: Literary magazine, student government, student newspaper.

ADMISSIONS

Selectivity Rating: 63 (of 100). **Freshman Academic Profile:** TOEFL required of all international applicants, minimum TOEFL 500. **Basis for Candidate Selection:** *Very important factors considered include:* essays, interview, secondary school record. *Important factors considered include:* character/personal qualities, recommendations, talent/ability. *Other factors considered include:* extracurricular activities, volunteer work, work experience. **Freshman Admission Requirements:** High school diploma or GED is required. *Academic units required/recommended:* 24 total recommended; 4 English recommended, 3 math recommended, 3 science recommended, 1 science lab recommended, 2 foreign language recommended, 3 social studies recommended, 2 history recommended, 4 elective recommended. **Freshman Admission Statistics:** 43 applied, 95% accepted, 68% of those accepted enrolled. **Transfer Admission Requirements:** *Items required:* college transcript, essay, interview. Lowest grade transferable C. **General Admission Information:** Application fee $35. Regular application deadline August 1. Priority application deadline June 3. Nonfall registration accepted. Admission may be deferred for a maximum of 1 year. Credit offered for CEEB Advanced Placement tests.

COSTS AND FINANCIAL AID

Tuition $12,250. Required fees $0. Average book expense $500. **Required Forms and Deadlines:** FAFSA. No deadline for regular filing. **Notification of Awards:** Applicants will be notified of awards on a rolling basis. **Types of Aid:** *Need-based scholarships/grants:* Pell, SEOG, state scholarships/grants, private scholarships, the school's own gift aid, work-study aid. *Loans:* FFEL Subsidized Stafford, FFEL Unsubsidized Stafford, FFEL PLUS, Federal Perkins, college/university loans from institutional funds. **Student Employment:** Federal Work-Study Program available. Off-campus job opportunities are excellent. **Financial Aid Statistics:** 60% freshmen, 72% undergrads receive some form of aid. **Financial Aid Phone:** 802-862-9616.

BUTLER UNIVERSITY

4600 Sunset Avenue, Indianapolis, IN 46208
Phone: 317-940-8100 **E-mail:** admission@butler.edu **CEEB Code:** 1073
Fax: 317-940-8150 **Web:** www.butler.edu **ACT Code:** 1180

This private school was founded in 1855. It has a 290-acre campus.

STUDENTS AND FACULTY

Enrollment: 3,512. **Student Body:** Male 37%, female 63%, out-of-state 40%, international 2%. **Ethnic Representation:** African American 4%, Asian 2%, Caucasian 82%, Hispanic 1%. **Retention and Graduation:** 84% freshmen return for sophomore year. 49% freshmen graduate within 4 years. 20% grads go on to further study within 1 year. 1% grads pursue business degrees. 2% grads pursue law degrees. 4% grads pursue medical degrees. **Faculty:** Student/faculty ratio 12:1. 255 full-time faculty, 83% hold PhDs. 97% faculty teach undergrads.

ACADEMICS

Degrees: Associate's, bachelor's, first professional, master's, post-bachelor's certificate. **Academic Requirements:** General education including some course work in arts/fine arts, English (including composition), humanities, mathematics, sciences (biological or physical), social science. **Classes:** 20-29 students in an average class. 20-29 students in an average lab/discussion section. **Majors with Highest Enrollment:** Pharmacy (PharmD, BS/BPharm); marketing/marketing management, general; elementary education and teaching. **Disciplines with Highest Percentage of Degrees Awarded:** Business/marketing 23%, health professions and related sciences 13%, education 12%, communications/communication technologies 12%, social sciences and history 9%. **Special Study Options:** Cooperative (work-study) program, cross registration, double major, dual enrollment, English as a second language, student exchange program (domestic), honors program, independent study, internships, student-designed major, study abroad, teacher certification program.

FACILITIES

Housing: Coed, all-female, fraternities and/or sororities, service-learning housing for women. **Library Holdings:** 308,689 bound volumes. 2,000 periodicals. 180,392 microforms. 13,091 audiovisuals. **Special Academic Facilities/Equipment:** Holcomb Observatory, Clowes Memorial Hall (performing arts theatre),WBTU (public TV station). **Computers:** School-owned computers available for student use.

EXTRACURRICULARS

Activities: Choral groups, concert band, dance, drama/theater, jazz band, literary magazine, marching band, music ensembles, opera, pep band, student government, student newspaper, symphony orchestra, television station, yearbook. **Organizations:** 100 registered organizations, 8 honor societies, 6 religious organizations, 8 fraternities (26% men join), 8 sororities (26% women join). **Athletics (Intercollegiate):** *Men:* baseball, basketball, cross-country, football, golf, lacrosse, soccer, swimming, tennis, track & field. *Women:* basketball, cross-country, golf, soccer, softball, swimming, tennis, track & field, volleyball.

ADMISSIONS

Selectivity Rating: 71 (of 100). **Freshman Academic Profile:** Average high school GPA 3.6. 43% in top 10% of high school class, 75% in top 25% of high school class, 95% in top 50% of high school class. 86% from public high schools. Average SAT I Math 588, SAT I Math middle 50% range 540-640. Average SAT I Verbal 571, SAT I Verbal middle 50% range 520-620. Average ACT 26, ACT middle 50% range 23-28. TOEFL required of all international applicants, minimum TOEFL 550. **Basis for Candidate Selection:** *Very important factors considered include:* class rank, essays, recommendations, secondary school record, standardized test scores. *Important factors considered include:* extracurricular activities. *Other factors considered include:* alumni/ae relation, character/personal qualities, interview, minority status, talent/ability, volunteer work, work experience. **Freshman Admission Requirements:** High school diploma or GED is required. *Academic units required/recommended:* 16 total required; 4 English required, 3 math required, 3 science required, 2 foreign language required, 2 history required, 2 elective required. **Freshman Admission Statistics:** 3,817 applied, 80% accepted, 31% of those accepted enrolled. **Transfer Admission Requirements:** *Items required:* high school transcript, college transcript, essay, standardized test scores. Minimum college GPA of 2.0 required. Lowest grade transferable C. **General Admission Information:** Application fee $25. Priority application deadline December 15. Regular application deadline August 15. Nonfall registration accepted. Admission may be deferred for a maximum of 1 year. Credit offered for CEEB Advanced Placement tests.

COSTS AND FINANCIAL AID

Tuition $19,990. Room & board $6,710. Required fees $200. Average book expense $750. **Required Forms and Deadlines:** FAFSA and institution's own financial aid form. Financial aid filing deadline October 1. Priority filing deadline March 1. **Notification of Awards:** Applicants will be notified of awards on a rolling basis beginning on or about March 15. **Types of Aid:** *Need-based scholarships/grants:* Pell, SEOG, state scholarships/grants, private scholarships, the school's own gift aid. *Loans:* FFEL Subsidized Stafford, FFEL Unsubsidized Stafford, FFEL PLUS, Federal Perkins. **Student Employment:** Federal Work-Study Program available. Institutional employment available. Off-campus job opportunities are excellent. **Financial Aid Statistics:** 64% freshmen, 62% undergrads receive some form of aid. Average freshman grant $9,000. Average freshman loan $5,000. Average income from on-campus job $1,200. **Financial Aid Phone:** 317-940-8200.

See page 954.

CABRINI COLLEGE

610 King of Prussia Road, Radnor, PA 19087-3698
Phone: 610-902-8552 **E-mail:** admit@cabrini.edu **CEEB Code:** 2071
Fax: 610-902-8508 **Web:** www.cabrini.edu **ACT Code:** 3532

This private school, which is affiliated with the Roman Catholic Church, was founded in 1957. It has a 112-acre campus.

STUDENTS AND FACULTY

Enrollment: 1,678. **Student Body:** Male 35%, female 65%, out-of-state 30%, international 1%. **Ethnic Representation:** African American 6%, Asian 2%, Caucasian 82%, Hispanic 2%. **Retention and Graduation:** 74% freshmen return for sophomore year. 47% freshmen graduate within 4 years. 20% grads go on to further study within 1 year. 3% grads pursue business degrees. 1% grads pursue law degrees. 1% grads pursue medical degrees. **Faculty:** Student/faculty ratio 15:1. 59 full-time faculty, 76% hold PhDs. 99% faculty teach undergrads.

ACADEMICS

Degrees: Bachelor's, certificate, master's, post-bachelor's certificate. **Academic Requirements:** General education including some course work in arts/fine arts, computer literacy, English (including composition), foreign languages, history, humanities, mathematics, philosophy, sciences (biological or physical), social science, junior seminar that includes a service learning component and 1 religion. **Classes:** 10-19 students in an average class. 10-19 students in an average lab/discussion section. **Majors with Highest Enrollment:** Business, management, marketing, and related support services; communications studies/speech communication and rhetoric; elementary education and teaching. **Disciplines with Highest Percentage of Degrees Awarded:** Business/marketing 34%, education 21%, communications/communication technologies 11%, social sciences and history 6%, parks and recreation 5%. **Special Study Options:** Accelerated program, cooperative (work-study) program, cross registration, distance learning, double major, honors program, independent study, internships, liberal arts/career combination, student-designed major, study abroad, teacher certification program.

FACILITIES

Housing: Coed, all-female, apartments for single students, housing for disabled students. **Library Holdings:** 82,865 bound volumes. 523 periodicals. 118,435 microforms. 1,164 audiovisuals. **Computers:** *Recommended operating system:* Windows NT/2000. School-owned computers available for student use.

EXTRACURRICULARS

Activities: Choral groups, dance, drama/theater, literary magazine, musical theater, radio station, student government, student newspaper, television station, yearbook. **Organizations:** 22 registered organizations, 13 honor societies, 1 religious organization. **Athletics (Intercollegiate):** *Men:* basketball, cross-country, golf, indoor track, lacrosse, soccer, tennis, track & field. *Women:* basketball, cross-country, field hockey, indoor track, lacrosse, soccer, softball, tennis, track & field, volleyball.

ADMISSIONS

Selectivity Rating: 74 (of 100). **Freshman Academic Profile:** Average high school GPA 3.0. 5% in top 10% of high school class, 19% in top 25% of high school class, 50% in top 50% of high school class. 55% from public high schools. Average SAT I Math 472, SAT I Math middle 50% range 420-510. Average SAT I Verbal 479, SAT I Verbal middle 50% range 440-520. TOEFL required of all international applicants, minimum TOEFL 500. **Basis for Candidate Selection:** *Very important factors considered include:* class rank, extracurricular activities, secondary school record, standardized test scores. *Important factors considered include:* character/personal qualities, volunteer work. *Other factors considered include:* essays, interview, recommendations, work experience. **Freshman Admission Requirements:** High school diploma or GED is required. *Academic units required/recommended:* 4 English required, 3 math required, 3 science required, 2 foreign language required, 3 social studies required, 2 elective required, 4 elective recommended. **Freshman Admission Statistics:** 1,832 applied, 85% accepted, 27% of those accepted enrolled. **Transfer Admission Requirements:** *Items required:* college transcript. Minimum high school GPA of 2.0 required. Minimum college GPA of 2.2 required. Lowest grade transferable C-. **General Admission Information:** Application fee $25. Nonfall registration accepted. Admission may be deferred for a maximum of 1 year. Credit offered for CEEB Advanced Placement tests.

COSTS AND FINANCIAL AID

Tuition $16,150. Room & board $7,560. Required fees $750. Average book expense $900. **Required Forms and Deadlines:** FAFSA. No deadline for regular filing. **Notification of Awards:** Applicants will be notified of awards on a rolling basis beginning on or about March 1. **Types of Aid:** *Need-based scholarships/grants:* Pell, SEOG, state scholarships/grants, private scholarships, the school's own gift aid. *Loans:* FFEL Subsidized Stafford, FFEL Unsubsidized Stafford, FFEL PLUS, Federal Perkins. **Student Employment:** Federal Work-Study Program available. Institutional employment available. Off-campus job opportunities are excellent. **Financial Aid Statistics:** 84% freshmen, 74% undergrads receive some form of aid. **Financial Aid Phone:** 610-902-8420.

CALDWELL COLLEGE

9 Ryerson Avenue, Caldwell, NJ 07006-6195
Phone: 973-618-3500 **E-mail:** admissions@caldwell.edu **CEEB Code:** 2072
Fax: 973-618-3600 **Web:** www.caldwell.edu **ACT Code:** 2542

This private school, which is affiliated with the Roman Catholic Church, was founded in 1939. It has an 80-acre campus.

STUDENTS AND FACULTY

Enrollment: 1,861. **Student Body:** Male 30%, female 70%, out-of-state 4%, international 4% (26 countries represented). **Ethnic Representation:** African American 17%, Asian 2%, Caucasian 67%, Hispanic 10%. **Retention and Graduation:** 70% freshmen return for sophomore year. 40% freshmen graduate within 4 years. **Faculty:** Student/faculty ratio 13:1. 76 full-time faculty, 80% hold PhDs. 100% faculty teach undergrads.

ACADEMICS

Degrees: Bachelor's, certificate, master's, post-master's certificate. **Academic Requirements:** General education including some course work in arts/fine arts, computer literacy, English (including composition), foreign languages, history, humanities, mathematics, philosophy, sciences (biological or physical), social science, religious studies. **Classes:** 10-19 students in an average class. 10-19 students in an average lab/discussion section. **Majors with Highest Enrollment:** Business administration/management; elementary education and teaching; psychology, general. **Disciplines with Highest Percentage of Degrees Awarded:** Business/marketing 31%, psychology 16%, education 10%, protective services/public administration 9%, social sciences and history 6%. **Special Study Options:** Accelerated program, distance learning, double major, English as a second language, external degree program, honors program, independent study, internships, liberal arts/career combination, student-designed major, study abroad, teacher certification program, weekend college.

FACILITIES

Housing: Coed. **Library Holdings:** 140,714 bound volumes. 428 periodicals. 3,300 microforms. 2,450 audiovisuals. **Special Academic Facilities/Equipment:** Art gallery, theatre, library with media center, TV studio, state-of-the-art technology building with interactive television classroom, new student center. **Computers:** School-owned computers available for student use.

EXTRACURRICULARS

Activities: Choral groups, drama/theater, jazz band, literary magazine, music ensembles, musical theater, radio station, student government, student newspaper, yearbook. **Organizations:** 20 registered organizations, 15 honor societies, 1 religious organization. **Athletics (Intercollegiate):** *Men:* baseball, basketball, golf, soccer, tennis. *Women:* basketball, golf, soccer, softball, tennis.

ADMISSIONS

Selectivity Rating: 73 (of 100). **Freshman Academic Profile:** Average high school GPA 2.8. 3% in top 10% of high school class, 15% in top 25% of high school class, 47% in top 50% of high school class. 67% from public high schools. Average SAT I Math 462, SAT I Math middle 50% range 410-510. Average SAT I Verbal 458, SAT I Verbal middle 50% range 410-510. TOEFL required of all international applicants, minimum TOEFL 500. **Basis for Candidate Selection:** *Very important factors considered include:* extracurricular activities, secondary school record. *Important factors considered include:* class rank, standardized test scores, talent/ability. *Other factors considered include:* alumni/ae relation, character/personal qualities, essays, interview, recommendations, volunteer work, work experience. **Freshman Admission Requirements:** High school diploma or GED is required. *Academic units required/recommended:* 16 total required; 4 English required, 2 math required, 2 science required, 1 science lab required, 2 foreign language required, 1 history required, 5 elective required. **Freshman Admission Statistics:** 1,240 applied, 78% accepted, 33% of those accepted enrolled. **Transfer Admission Requirements:** *Items required:* high school transcript, college transcript. Minimum college GPA of 2.0 required. Lowest grade transferable C. **General Admission Information:** Application fee $40. Nonfall registration accepted. Admission may be deferred. Credit and/or placement offered for CEEB Advanced Placement tests.

COSTS AND FINANCIAL AID

Tuition $16,000. Room & board $6,800. Required fees $100. Average book expense $800. **Required Forms and Deadlines:** FAFSA and institution's own financial aid form. No deadline for regular filing. Priority filing deadline April 15. **Notification of Awards:** Applicants will be notified of awards on a rolling basis beginning on or about March 1. **Types of Aid:** *Need-based scholarships/grants:* Pell, SEOG, state scholarships/grants, private scholarships, the school's own gift aid. *Loans:* FFEL Subsidized Stafford, FFEL Unsubsidized Stafford, FFEL PLUS, state loans, alternative loans, such as Key, TERL, Signature. **Student Employment:** Federal Work-Study Program available. Institutional employment available. Off-campus job opportunities are excellent. **Financial Aid Statistics:** 78% freshmen, 70% undergrads receive some form of aid. Average freshman grant $6,525. Average freshman loan $1,975. Average income from on-campus job $1,000. **Financial Aid Phone:** 973-618-3221.

See page 956.

CALIFORNIA BAPTIST UNIVERSITY

8432 Magnolia Avenue, Riverside, CA 92504
Phone: 909-343-4212 **E-mail:** admissions@calbaptist.edu **CEEB Code:** 4094
Fax: 909-343-4525 **Web:** www.calbaptist.edu **ACT Code:** 4094

This private school, which is affiliated with the Southern Baptist Church, was founded in 1950. It has an 82-acre campus.

STUDENTS AND FACULTY

Enrollment: 1,618. **Student Body:** Male 36%, female 64%, out-of-state 3%, international 1% (16 countries represented). **Ethnic Representation:** African American 7%, Asian 3%, Caucasian 61%, Hispanic 14%, Native American 2%. **Retention and Graduation:** 81% freshmen return for sophomore year. 59% freshmen graduate within 4 years. **Faculty:** Student/faculty ratio 19:1. 75 full-time faculty, 62% hold PhDs. 100% faculty teach undergrads.

ACADEMICS

Degrees: Bachelor's, master's. **Academic Requirements:** General education including some course work in arts/fine arts, English (including composition), history, humanities, mathematics, philosophy, sciences (biological or physical), social science. **Classes:** 10-19 students in an average class. 10-19 students in an average lab/discussion section. **Majors with Highest Enrollment:** Business administration/management; liberal arts and sciences, general studies and humanities; psychology, general. **Disciplines with Highest Percentage of Degrees Awarded:** Liberal arts/general studies 34%, psychology 13%, business/marketing 12%, computer and information sciences 9%, social sciences and history 8%. **Special Study Options:** Accelerated program, double major, student exchange program (domestic), independent study, internships, liberal arts/career combination, study abroad, teacher certification program, weekend college.

FACILITIES

Housing: All-female, all-male, apartments for married students, apartments for single students. **Library Holdings:** 97,615 bound volumes. 38 periodicals. 42,389 microforms. 4,271 audiovisuals. **Special Academic Facilities/ Equipment:** Metcalf Art Gallery, Annie Gabriel Library, Book of Life Auditorium. **Computers:** School-owned computers available for student use.

EXTRACURRICULARS

Activities: Choral groups, drama/theater, music ensembles, musical theater, pep band, student government, student newspaper, yearbook. **Organizations:** 14 registered organizations, 2 honor societies, 6 religious organizations. **Athletics (Intercollegiate):** *Men:* baseball, basketball, diving, soccer, swimming, volleyball, water polo. *Women:* basketball, diving, soccer, softball, swimming, volleyball, water polo.

ADMISSIONS

Selectivity Rating: 69 (of 100). **Freshman Academic Profile:** Average high school GPA 3.2. 87% from public high schools. Average SAT I Math 488, SAT I Math middle 50% range 420-540. Average SAT I Verbal 486, SAT I Verbal middle 50% range 420-540. Average ACT 21, ACT middle 50% range 19-24. TOEFL required of all international applicants, minimum TOEFL 520. **Basis for Candidate Selection:** *Very important factors considered include:* secondary school record, standardized test scores. *Important factors considered include:* character/personal qualities, essays, recommendations. *Other factors considered include:* class rank, extracurricular activities, interview, religious affiliation/commitment, talent/ability. **Freshman Admission Requirements:** High school diploma or GED is required. *Academic units required/recommended:* 15 total required; 19 total recommended; 4 English required, 3 math required, 4 math recommended, 2 science required, 3 science recommended, 1 science lab required, 2 science lab recommended, 2 foreign language required, 3 foreign language recommended, 2 social studies required, 2 history required. **Freshman Admission Statistics:** 571 applied, 83% accepted, 41% of those accepted enrolled. **Transfer Admission Requirements:** *Items required:* college transcript. Minimum high school GPA of 2.5 required. Minimum college GPA of 2.0 required. Lowest grade transferable C. **General Admission Information:** Application fee $45. Priority application deadline February 1. Regular application deadline August 18. Nonfall registration accepted. Admission may be deferred for a maximum of 1 year. Credit and/or placement offered for CEEB Advanced Placement tests.

COSTS AND FINANCIAL AID

Average book expense $1,072. **Required Forms and Deadlines:** FAFSA and state aid form. No deadline for regular filing. Priority filing deadline March 2. **Notification of Awards:** Applicants will be notified of awards on a rolling basis beginning on or about March 2. **Types of Aid:** *Need-based scholarships/grants:* Pell, SEOG, state scholarships/grants, private scholarships, the school's own gift aid. *Loans:* FFEL Subsidized Stafford, FFEL Unsubsidized Stafford, FFEL PLUS, Federal Perkins, alternative loans. **Student Employment:** Federal Work-Study Program available. Institutional employment available. Off-campus job opportunities are good. **Financial Aid Statistics:** 91% freshmen, 94% undergrads receive some form of aid. Average freshman grant $6,600. Average freshman loan $2,625. Average income from on-campus job $1,800. **Financial Aid Phone:** 909-343-4236.

CALIFORNIA COLLEGE OF ARTS AND CRAFTS

$$$

1111 Eighth Street, San Francisco, CA 94107
Phone: 415-703-9523 **E-mail:** enroll@ccac-art.edu **CEEB Code:** 4031
Fax: 415-703-9539 **Web:** www.ccac-art.edu **ACT Code:** 176

This private school was founded in 1907. It has a 4-acre campus.

STUDENTS AND FACULTY

Enrollment: 1,261. **Student Body:** Male 40%, female 60%, out-of-state 30%, international 6% (21 countries represented). **Ethnic Representation:** African American 2%, Asian 12%, Caucasian 63%, Hispanic 8%, Native American 1%. **Retention and Graduation:** 79% freshmen return for sophomore year. 16% freshmen graduate within 4 years. **Faculty:** Student/faculty ratio 9:1. 34 full-time faculty, 70% hold PhDs. 97% faculty teach undergrads.

ACADEMICS

Degrees: Bachelor's, master's. **Academic Requirements:** General education including some course work in arts/fine arts, English (including composition), history, humanities, mathematics, philosophy, sciences (biological or physical), social science, art history, seminar. **Classes:** 10-19 students in an average class. **Majors with Highest Enrollment:** Graphic design; drawing; painting. **Disciplines with Highest Percentage of Degrees Awarded:** Visual and performing arts 51%, trade and industry 37%, architecture 12%. **Special Study Options:** Cross registration, dual enrollment, student exchange program (domestic), independent study, internships, student-designed major, study abroad.

FACILITIES

Housing: Coed, apartments for single students. **Library Holdings:** 50,000 bound volumes. 300 periodicals. 10 microforms. 1,000 audiovisuals. **Special Academic Facilities/Equipment:** Oliver Art Center on the Oakland campus, Logan Galleries on the San Francisco campus. **Computers:** School-owned computers available for student use.

EXTRACURRICULARS

Activities: Student government, student newspaper. **Organizations:** 18 registered organizations, 1 honor society.

ADMISSIONS

Selectivity Rating: 76 (of 100). **Freshman Academic Profile:** Average high school GPA 3.1. 69% from public high schools. Average SAT I Math 531, SAT I Math middle 50% range 410-590. Average SAT I Verbal 546, SAT I Verbal middle 50% range 490-600. Average ACT 21, ACT middle 50% range 16-26. TOEFL required of all international applicants, minimum TOEFL 550. **Basis for Candidate Selection:** *Very important factors considered include:* essays, secondary school record, talent/ability. *Important factors considered include:* interview, recommendations. *Other factors considered include:* character/ personal qualities, extracurricular activities, standardized test scores, volunteer work, work experience. **Freshman Admission Requirements:** High school diploma or GED is required. **Freshman Admission Statistics:** 554 applied, 73% accepted, 38% of those accepted enrolled. **Transfer Admission Requirements:** *Items required:* college transcript, essay. Minimum college GPA of 2.0 required. Lowest grade transferable C. **General Admission Information:** Application fee $50. Priority application deadline February 15. Nonfall registration accepted. Admission may be deferred. Credit and/or placement offered for CEEB Advanced Placement tests.

COSTS AND FINANCIAL AID

Tuition $21,670. Room & board $6,776. Required fees $250. Average book expense $810. **Required Forms and Deadlines:** FAFSA and state aid form. No deadline for regular filing. Priority filing deadline February 15. **Notification of Awards:** Applicants will be notified of awards on a rolling basis beginning on or about April 1. **Types of Aid:** *Need-based scholarships/grants:* Pell, SEOG, state scholarships/grants, private scholarships, the school's own gift aid. *Loans:* Direct Subsidized Stafford, Direct Unsubsidized Stafford, Direct PLUS, FFEL Subsidized Stafford, FFEL Unsubsidized Stafford, FFEL PLUS, Federal Perkins. **Student Employment:** Federal Work-Study Program available. Institutional employment available. Off-campus job opportunities are good. **Financial Aid Statistics:** 57% freshmen, 65% undergrads receive some form of aid. Average freshman grant $9,801. Average freshman loan $2,764. Average income from on-campus job $1,500. **Financial Aid Phone:** 415-703-9528.

See page 958.

CALIFORNIA INSTITUTE OF TECHNOLOGY

1200 East California Boulevard, Mail Code 328-87, Pasadena, CA 91125
Phone: 626-395-6341 **E-mail:** ugadmissions@caltech.edu **CEEB Code:** 4034
Fax: 626-683-3026 **Web:** www.caltech.edu **ACT Code:** 182

This private school was founded in 1891. It has a 124-acre campus.

STUDENTS AND FACULTY

Enrollment: 939. **Student Body:** Out-of-state 64%, international 8%. **Ethnic Representation:** African American 1%, Asian 29%, Caucasian 61%, Hispanic 7%, Native American 1%. **Retention and Graduation:** 95% freshmen return for sophomore year. 72% freshmen graduate within 4 years. 53% grads go on to further study within 1 year. 1% grads pursue law degrees. 3% grads pursue medical degrees. **Faculty:** Student/faculty ratio 3:1. 292 full-time faculty, 97% hold PhDs. 100% faculty teach undergrads.

ACADEMICS

Degrees: Bachelor's, doctoral, master's. **Academic Requirements:** General education including some course work in humanities, mathematics, sciences (biological or physical), social science, physical education—3 terms. **Classes:** 10-19 students in an average class. 10-19 students in an average lab/discussion section. **Majors with Highest Enrollment:** Electrical, electronics, and communications engineering; biology/biological sciences, general; physics, general. **Disciplines with Highest Percentage of Degrees Awarded:** Engineering/engineering technology 47%, physical sciences 34%, biological life sciences 9%, mathematics 8%, social sciences and history 2%. **Special Study Options:** Cross registration, double major, English as a second language, student exchange program (domestic), independent study, liberal arts/career combination, student-designed major, study abroad. 3-2 engineering program with Bowdoin, Grinnell, Oberlin, Occidental, Pomona, Reed, Wesleyan, Whitman, Ohio Wesleyan, Mt. Holyoke, and Spelman.

FACILITIES

Housing: Coed, apartments for married students, apartments for single students, housing for disabled students, single-unit houses. **Library Holdings:** 3,165,000 bound volumes. 3,500 periodicals. **Special Academic Facilities/Equipment:** Jet propulsion laboratory, Palomar Observatory, seismological laboratory, Beckman Institute for Fundamental Research in Biology and Chemistry, Mead Chemistry Laboratory, Moore Laboratory. **Computers:** School-owned computers available for student use.

EXTRACURRICULARS

Activities: Choral groups, concert band, dance, drama/theater, jazz band, literary magazine, music ensembles, musical theater, pep band, student government, student newspaper, student-run film society, symphony orchestra, yearbook. **Organizations:** 85 registered organizations, 2 honor societies, 5 religious organizations. **Athletics (Intercollegiate):** *Men:* baseball, basketball, cheerleading, cross-country, diving, fencing, golf, soccer, swimming, tennis, track & field, water polo. *Women:* basketball, cheerleading, cross-country, diving, fencing, swimming, tennis, track & field, volleyball, water polo.

ADMISSIONS

Selectivity Rating: 99 (of 100). **Freshman Academic Profile:** 99% in top 10% of high school class, 100% in top 25% of high school class, 81% from public high schools. Average SAT I Math 774, SAT I Math middle 50% range 760-800. Average SAT I Verbal 736, SAT I Verbal middle 50% range 710-780. **Basis for Candidate Selection:** *Very important factors considered include:* character/personal qualities, essays, recommendations, secondary school record. *Other factors considered include:* class rank, extracurricular activities, minority status, standardized test scores, talent/ability, volunteer work, work experience. **Freshman Admission Requirements:** High school diploma or equivalent is not required. *Academic units required/recommended:* 15 total required; 3 English required, 4 English recommended, 4 math required, 2 science required, 1 science lab required, 1 social studies required, 1 history required. **Freshman Admission Statistics:** 2,615 applied, 21% accepted, 45% of those accepted enrolled. **Transfer Admission Requirements:** *Items required:* high school transcript, college transcript, essay. Minimum college GPA of 3.0 required. **General Admission Information:** Application fee $50. Regular application deadline January 1. Admission may be deferred for a maximum of 1 year. Neither credit nor placement offered for CEEB Advanced Placement tests.

COSTS AND FINANCIAL AID

Tuition $23,901. Room & board $7,560. Required fees $216. Average book expense $1,005. **Required Forms and Deadlines:** FAFSA, CSS/Financial Aid PROFILE, noncustodial (divorced/separated) parent's statement, business/farm supplement. (Noncustodial parent's statement and business/farm supplement forms are required only when applicable.) Financial aid filing deadline March 2. Priority filing deadline January 15. **Notification of Awards:** Applicants will be notified of awards on or about April 15. **Types of Aid:** *Need-based scholarships/grants:* Pell, SEOG, state scholarships/grants, private scholarships, the school's own gift aid, United Negro College Fund. *Loans:* Direct Subsidized Stafford, Direct Unsubsidized Stafford, Direct PLUS, Federal Perkins, college/university loans from institutional funds. **Student Employment:** Federal Work-Study Program available. Institutional employment available. Off-campus job opportunities are excellent. **Financial Aid Statistics:** 54% freshmen, 57% undergrads receive some form of aid. Average freshman grant $20,485. Average freshman loan $1,404. **Financial Aid Phone:** 626-395-6280.

CALIFORNIA INSTITUTE OF THE ARTS

24700 McBean Parkway, Valencia, CA 91355
Phone: 661-255-1050 **E-mail:** admiss@calarts.edu **CEEB Code:** 4049
Fax: 661-253-7710 **Web:** www.calarts.edu **ACT Code:** 121

This private school was founded in 1961. It has a 60-acre campus.

STUDENTS AND FACULTY

Enrollment: 787. **Student Body:** Male 59%, female 41%, out-of-state 55%, international 9%. **Ethnic Representation:** African American 7%, Asian 12%, Caucasian 69%, Hispanic 10%, Native American 2%. **Retention and Graduation:** 74% freshmen return for sophomore year. 49% freshmen graduate within 4 years. **Faculty:** Student/faculty ratio 6:1. 122 full-time faculty. 100% faculty teach undergrads.

ACADEMICS

Degrees: Bachelor's, certificate, master's, post-bachelor's certificate. **Academic Requirements:** General education including some course work in arts/fine arts, computer literacy, English (including composition), history, humanities, mathematics, philosophy, sciences (biological or physical), social science. **Classes:** Under 10 students in an average class. **Majors with Highest Enrollment:** Art/art studies, general; film/video and photographic arts; acting. **Disciplines with Highest Percentage of Degrees Awarded:** Visual and performing arts 100%. **Special Study Options:** Independent study, internships, student-designed major, study abroad.

FACILITIES

Housing: Coed, apartments for single students, housing for disabled students. **Library Holdings:** 95,973 bound volumes. 613 periodicals. 5,235 microforms. 147,930 audiovisuals. **Special Academic Facilities/Equipment:** 7 art galleries, TV studio, Walt Disney Theater, Roy Disney Music Hall, Sharon Disney Lund Dance Theater, Bisou Film Theater. **Computers:** School-owned computers available for student use.

EXTRACURRICULARS

Activities: Choral groups, dance, drama/theater, jazz band, literary magazine, music ensembles, opera, radio station, student government, student newspaper, student-run film society, symphony orchestra, television station. **Organizations:** 5 registered organizations.

ADMISSIONS

Selectivity Rating: 89 (of 100). **Freshman Academic Profile:** 25% in top 10% of high school class, TOEFL required of all international applicants, minimum TOEFL 550. **Basis for Candidate Selection:** *Very important factors considered include:* essays, talent/ability. *Important factors considered include:* extracurricular activities, interview, recommendations. *Other factors considered include:* character/personal qualities. **Freshman Admission Requirements:** High school diploma or GED is required. **Transfer Admission Requirements:** *Items required:* high school transcript, college transcript, essay. Lowest grade transferable C. **General Admission Information:** Application fee $60. Priority application deadline January 6. Nonfall registration accepted. Admission may be deferred for a maximum of 1 year. Credit offered for CEEB Advanced Placement tests.

COSTS AND FINANCIAL AID

Tuition $22,190. Room & board $6,850. Required fees $765. Average book expense $1,200. **Required Forms and Deadlines:** FAFSA. Priority filing deadline March 1. **Notification of Awards:** Applicants will be notified of awards on a rolling basis beginning on or about April 1. **Types of Aid:** *Need-based scholarships/grants:* Pell, SEOG, state scholarships/grants, private scholarships, the school's own gift aid. *Loans:* FFEL Subsidized Stafford, FFEL Unsubsidized Stafford, FFEL PLUS, Federal Perkins, college/university loans from institutional funds. **Student Employment:** Federal Work-Study Program available. Institutional employment available. Off-campus job opportunities are excellent. **Financial Aid Statistics:** 66% freshmen, 68% undergrads receive some form of aid. Average freshman grant $10,013. Average freshman loan $12,924. Average income from on-campus job $1,536. **Financial Aid Phone:** 661-253-7865.

CALIFORNIA LUTHERAN UNIVERSITY

60 West Olsen Road, 1350, Thousand Oaks, CA 91360
Phone: 805-493-3135 **E-mail:** cluadm@clunet.edu **CEEB Code:** 4088
Fax: 805-493-3114 **Web:** www.clunet.edu **ACT Code:** 183

This private school, which is affiliated with the Lutheran Church, was founded in 1959. It has a 290-acre campus.

STUDENTS AND FACULTY

Enrollment: 1,891. **Student Body:** Male 42%, female 58%, out-of-state 23%, international 2%. **Ethnic Representation:** African American 2%, Asian 5%, Caucasian 71%, Hispanic 14%, Native American 1%. **Retention and Graduation:** 80% freshmen return for sophomore year. 61% freshmen graduate within 4 years. 65% grads go on to further study within 1 year. **Faculty:** Student/faculty ratio 15:1. 119 full-time faculty, 89% hold PhDs. 100% faculty teach undergrads.

ACADEMICS

Degrees: Bachelor's, certificate, doctoral, master's, post-bachelor's certificate, post-master's certificate. **Academic Requirements:** General education including some course work in arts/fine arts, computer literacy, English (including composition), foreign languages, history, humanities, mathematics, philosophy, sciences (biological or physical), social science, religion. **Classes:** 10-19 students in an average class. 10-19 students in an average lab/discussion section. **Majors with Highest Enrollment:** Liberal arts and sciences/liberal studies; business administration/management; computer science. **Disciplines with Highest Percentage of Degrees Awarded:** Business/marketing 25%, computer and information sciences 14%, communications/communication technologies 12%, liberal arts/general studies 10%, social sciences and history 9%. **Special Study Options:** Accelerated program, cooperative (work-study) program, double major, dual enrollment, student exchange program (domestic), honors program, independent study, internships, student-designed major, study abroad, teacher certification program.

FACILITIES

Housing: Coed, housing for disabled students. **Library Holdings:** 139,476 bound volumes. 536 periodicals. 22,000 microforms. 1,457 audiovisuals. **Special Academic Facilities/Equipment:** On-campus preschool, hypermedia lab, multimedia center and program, film studio, Kwan Fong Art Gallery, Scandinavian Center, educational technology center. **Computers:** School-owned computers available for student use.

EXTRACURRICULARS

Activities: Choral groups, concert band, dance, drama/theater, jazz band, literary magazine, music ensembles, musical theater, pep band, radio station, student government, student newspaper, symphony orchestra, television station, yearbook. **Organizations:** 45 registered organizations, 11 honor societies, 3 religious organizations. **Athletics (Intercollegiate):** *Men:* baseball, basketball, cheerleading, cross-country, diving, football, golf, soccer, swimming, tennis, track & field, water polo. *Women:* basketball, cheerleading, cross-country, diving, soccer, softball, swimming, tennis, track & field, volleyball, water polo.

ADMISSIONS

Selectivity Rating: 63 (of 100). **Freshman Academic Profile:** Average high school GPA 3.6. 34% in top 10% of high school class, 64% in top 25% of high school class, 99% in top 50% of high school class. Average SAT I Math 554, SAT I Math middle 50% range 500-600. Average SAT I Verbal 545, SAT I Verbal middle 50% range 490-590. Average ACT 24, ACT middle 50% range 22-27. TOEFL required of all international applicants, minimum TOEFL 530. **Basis for Candidate Selection:** *Very important factors considered include:* recommendations, secondary school record, standardized test scores. *Important factors considered include:* essays, extracurricular activities, talent/ability. *Other factors considered include:* alumni/ae relation, character/personal qualities, class rank, geographical residence, interview, minority status, religious affiliation/commitment, state residency, volunteer work, work experience. **Freshman Admission Requirements:** High school diploma or GED is required. *Academic units required/recommended:* 4 English required, 3 math required, 2 science required, 2 foreign language required, 2 social studies required. **Freshman Admission Statistics:** 1,051 applied, 69% accepted, 46% of those accepted enrolled. **Transfer Admission Requirements:** *Items required:* college transcript, essay, statement of good standing from prior school. Minimum high school GPA of 2.8 required. Minimum college GPA of 2.8 required. Lowest grade transferable D-. **General Admission Information:** Application fee $45. Nonfall registration accepted. Admission may be deferred for a maximum of 1 year. Credit and/or placement offered for CEEB Advanced Placement tests.

COSTS AND FINANCIAL AID

Tuition $19,060. Room & board $6,920. Required fees $200. Average book expense $1,206. **Required Forms and Deadlines:** FAFSA and student request form. No deadline for regular filing. Priority filing deadline March 2. **Notification of Awards:** Applicants will be notified of awards on a rolling basis beginning on or about April 1. **Types of Aid:** *Need-based scholarships/grants:* Pell, SEOG, state scholarships/grants, private scholarships, the school's own gift aid. *Loans:* FFEL Subsidized Stafford, FFEL Unsubsidized Stafford, FFEL PLUS, Federal Perkins, opportunity loans from loan servicer. **Student Employment:** Federal Work-Study Program available. Institutional employment available. Off-campus job opportunities are good. **Financial Aid Statistics:** 64% freshmen, 65% undergrads receive some form of aid. Average freshman grant $14,375. Average freshman loan $2,625. Average income from on-campus job $1,200. **Financial Aid Phone:** 805-493-3115.

CALIFORNIA MARITIME ACADEMY OF CALIFORNIA STATE UNIVERSITY

200 Maritime Academy Drive, Vallejo, CA 94590
Phone: 707-654-1330 **E-mail:** admission@csum.edu
Fax: 707-654-1336 **Web:** www.csum.edu **ACT Code:** 184

This public school was founded in 1929. It has a 67-acre campus.

STUDENTS AND FACULTY

Enrollment: 606. **Student Body:** Out-of-state 13%, international 6%. **Ethnic Representation:** African American 4%, Asian 11%, Caucasian 60%, Hispanic 7%, Native American 1%. **Retention and Graduation:** 93% freshmen return for sophomore year. 45% freshmen graduate within 4 years. **Faculty:** Student/faculty ratio 15:1. 49 full-time faculty, 53% hold PhDs. 100% faculty teach undergrads.

ACADEMICS

Degrees: Bachelor's. **Academic Requirements:** General education including some course work in computer literacy, English (including composition), history, humanities, mathematics, sciences (biological or physical), social science, maritime-related courses. **Disciplines with Highest Percentage of Degrees Awarded:** Engineering/engineering technology 38%, marine transportation 32%, business/marketing 30%. **Special Study Options:** Cooperative (work-study) program, distance learning, double major, internships. All students participate in at least one 2-month training cruise around the Pacific Rim over the summer on the *Golden Bear*.

FACILITIES

Housing: Coed. **Library Holdings:** 27,361 bound volumes. 275 periodicals. 20,686 microforms. 314 audiovisuals. **Special Academic Facilities/Equipment:** Bookstore, library, gym, swimming pool. **Computers:** School-owned computers available for student use.

EXTRACURRICULARS

Activities: Student government. **Organizations:** 16 registered organizations. **Athletics (Intercollegiate):** *Men:* basketball, crew, golf, sailing, soccer, water polo. *Women:* crew, sailing, volleyball.

ADMISSIONS

Selectivity Rating: 69 (of 100). **Freshman Academic Profile:** Average high school GPA 3.1. 80% from public high schools. Average SAT I Math 519. Average SAT I Verbal 510. TOEFL required of all international applicants, minimum TOEFL 550. **Basis for Candidate Selection:** *Very important factors considered include:* secondary school record, standardized test scores. *Other factors considered include:* alumni/ae relation, character/personal qualities, essays, extracurricular activities, geographical residence, interview, recommendations, state residency, talent/ability, volunteer work, work experience. **Freshman Admission Requirements:** High school diploma or GED is required. *Academic units required/recommended:* 15 total required; 4 English required, 3 math required, 2 science required, 2 science lab required, 2 foreign language required, 1 social studies required, 1 history required, 1 elective required. **Freshman Admission Statistics:** 432 applied, 83% accepted, 44% of those accepted enrolled. **Transfer Admission Requirements:** *Items required:* college transcript, statement of good standing from prior school. Minimum high school GPA of 2.0 required. Minimum college

GPA of 2.0 required. Lowest grade transferable C. **General Admission Information:** Application fee $55. Priority application deadline November 30. Regular application deadline May 1.

COSTS AND FINANCIAL AID

In-state tuition $1,572. Out-of-state tuition $8,460. Room & board $6,750. Required fees $1,050. Average book expense $846. **Required Forms and Deadlines:** FAFSA. No deadline for regular filing. Priority filing deadline March 2. **Notification of Awards:** Applicants will be notified of awards on a rolling basis beginning on or about April 15. **Types of Aid:** *Need-based scholarships/grants:* Pell, SEOG, state scholarships/grants, private scholarships, the school's own gift aid. *Loans:* FFEL Subsidized Stafford, FFEL Unsubsidized Stafford, FFEL PLUS, Federal Perkins. **Student Employment:** Federal Work-Study Program available. Off-campus job opportunities are fair. **Financial Aid Statistics:** 66% freshmen, 76% undergrads receive some form of aid. Average freshman loan $8,042. Average income from on-campus job $750. **Financial Aid Phone:** 707-654-1275.

CALIFORNIA POLYTECHNIC STATE UNIVERSITY—SAN LUIS OBISPO

Admissions Office, Cal Poly, San Luis Obispo, CA 93407
Phone: 805-756-2311 **E-mail:** admissions@calpoly.edu **CEEB Code:** 4038
Fax: 805-756-5400 **Web:** www.calpoly.edu **ACT Code:** 188

This public school was founded in 1901. It has a 5,000-acre campus.

STUDENTS AND FACULTY

Enrollment: 17,401. **Student Body:** Male 56%, female 44%, out-of-state 6%, international 1%. **Ethnic Representation:** African American 1%, Asian 11%, Caucasian 62%, Hispanic 10%, Native American 1%. **Retention and Graduation:** 89% freshmen return for sophomore year. **Faculty:** Student/faculty ratio 19:1. 791 full-time faculty, 66% hold PhDs.

ACADEMICS

Degrees: Bachelor's, master's. **Academic Requirements:** General education including some course work in arts/fine arts, English (including composition), history, humanities, mathematics, philosophy, sciences (biological or physical), social science, technology. **Classes:** 20-29 students in an average class. 20-29 students in an average lab/discussion section. **Majors with Highest Enrollment:** Business administration/management; agricultural business and management, general; mechanical engineering. **Disciplines with Highest Percentage of Degrees Awarded:** Engineering/engineering technology 21%, business/marketing 15%, agriculture 14%, social sciences and history 7%, architecture 7%. **Special Study Options:** Cooperative (work-study) program, cross registration, distance learning, double major, dual enrollment, English as a second language, student exchange program (domestic), external degree program, honors program, independent study, internships, study abroad, teacher certification program.

FACILITIES

Housing: Coed, all-female, all-male, apartment-style housing. **Library Holdings:** 763,651 bound volumes. 5,529 periodicals. 2,091,226 microforms. 5,204 audiovisuals. **Computers:** School-owned computers available for student use.

EXTRACURRICULARS

Activities: Choral groups, concert band, dance, drama/theater, jazz band, literary magazine, marching band, music ensembles, musical theater, pep band, radio station, student government, student newspaper, television station. **Organizations:** 375 registered organizations, 25 fraternities (10% men join), 10 sororities (9% women join). **Athletics (Intercollegiate):** *Men:* baseball, basketball, football, soccer, swimming, wrestling. *Women:* basketball, cross-country, gymnastics, soccer, softball, swimming, tennis, track & field, volleyball.

ADMISSIONS

Selectivity Rating: 86 (of 100). **Freshman Academic Profile:** Average high school GPA 3.7. 44% in top 10% of high school class, 78% in top 25% of high school class, 95% in top 50% of high school class. 91% from public high schools. Average SAT I Math 569, SAT I Math middle 50% range 570-670. Average SAT I Verbal 532, SAT I Verbal middle 50% range 530-620. Average ACT 23, ACT middle 50% range 23-28. TOEFL required of all international applicants, minimum TOEFL 550. **Basis for Candidate Selection:** *Very important factors considered include:* secondary school record, standardized test scores. *Other factors considered include:* extracurricular activities, talent/ability, volunteer work, work experience. **Freshman Admission Requirements:** High school diploma or GED is required. *Academic units required/recommended:* 15 total required; 4 English required, 3 math required, 3 science required, 1 science lab required, 2 foreign language required. **Freshman Admission Statistics:** 19,739 applied, 39% accepted, 34% of those accepted enrolled. **Transfer Admission Requirements:** *Items required:* college transcript. Minimum college GPA of 2.0 required. Lowest grade transferable D. **General Admission Information:** Application fee $55. Early decision application deadline October 31. Regular application deadline November 30. Nonfall registration accepted. Credit offered for CEEB Advanced Placement tests.

COSTS AND FINANCIAL AID

In-state tuition $3,046. Out-of-state tuition $15,519. Room & board $7,119. Required fees $2,877. Average book expense $1,080. **Required Forms and Deadlines:** FAFSA and institution's own financial aid form. No deadline for regular filing. Priority filing deadline March 2. **Notification of Awards:** Applicants will be notified of awards on a rolling basis beginning on or about May 1. **Types of Aid:** *Need-based scholarships/grants:* Pell, SEOG, state scholarships/grants, private scholarships, the school's own gift aid. *Loans:* FFEL Subsidized Stafford, FFEL Unsubsidized Stafford, FFEL PLUS, Federal Perkins, college/university loans from institutional funds, alternative loans. **Student Employment:** Federal Work-Study Program available. Institutional employment available. Off-campus job opportunities are good. **Financial Aid Statistics:** 29% freshmen, 34% undergrads receive some form of aid. **Financial Aid Phone:** 805-756-2927.

CALIFORNIA STATE POLYTECHNIC UNIVERSITY—POMONA

3801 West Temple Avenue, Pomona, CA 91768
Phone: 909-468-5020 **E-mail:** cppadmit@csupomona.edu **CEEB Code:** 4082
Fax: 909-869-4529 **Web:** www.csupomona.edu **ACT Code:** 4048

This public school was founded in 1938. It has a 1,437-acre campus.

STUDENTS AND FACULTY

Enrollment: 17,580. **Student Body:** Male 57%, female 43%, out-of-state 2%, international 4% (55 countries represented). **Ethnic Representation:** African American 3%, Asian 35%, Caucasian 26%, Hispanic 25%. **Retention and Graduation:** 79% freshmen return for sophomore year. 9% freshmen graduate within 4 years. **Faculty:** Student/faculty ratio 20:1. 689 full-time faculty, 64% hold PhDs. 100% faculty teach undergrads.

ACADEMICS

Degrees: Bachelor's, master's. **Academic Requirements:** General education including some course work in arts/fine arts, computer literacy, English (including composition), foreign languages, history, humanities, mathematics, philosophy, sciences (biological or physical), social science. **Classes:** 20-29 students in an average class. 20-29 students in an average lab/discussion section. **Majors with Highest Enrollment:** Business administration/management; computer science; electrical, electronics, and communications engineering. **Disciplines with Highest Percentage of Degrees Awarded:** Business/marketing 33%, engineering/engineering technology 17%, social sciences and history 7%, liberal arts/general studies 7%, psychology 6%. **Special Study Options:** Cooperative (work-study) program, cross registration, double major, dual enrollment, English as a second language, student exchange program (domestic), external degree program, internships, study abroad, teacher certification program, Ocean Studies Institute, Desert Studies Consortium. Undergrads may take grad classes.

FACILITIES

Housing: Coed, apartments for single students, housing for disabled students. **Library Holdings:** 465,018 bound volumes. 6,017 periodicals. 2,483,407 microforms. 13,260 audiovisuals. **Special Academic Facilities/Equipment:** Center for hospitality management; art gallery; center for regenerative studies; citrus-packing house; meat-processing building; poultry plant; feed mill; beef, sheep, swine, Arabian horse units; horse show arena; and aerospace wind tunnel. **Computers:** School-owned computers available for student use.

EXTRACURRICULARS

Activities: Choral groups, concert band, drama/theater, jazz band, music ensembles, musical theater, opera, pep band, student government, student newspaper, symphony orchestra, television station, yearbook. **Organizations:** 230 registered organizations, 26 honor societies, 9 religious organizations, 12 fraternities (1% men join), 8 sororities (1% women join). **Athletics (Intercollegiate):** *Men:* baseball, basketball, cheerleading, cross-country, soccer, tennis, track & field. *Women:* basketball, cheerleading, cross-country, soccer, tennis, track & field, volleyball.

ADMISSIONS

Selectivity Rating: 72 (of 100). **Freshman Academic Profile:** Average high school GPA 3.3. 98% from public high schools. Average SAT I Math 516, SAT I Math middle 50% range 460-590. Average SAT I Verbal 484, SAT I Verbal middle 50% range 420-540. Average ACT 20, ACT middle 50% range 17-23. TOEFL required of all international applicants, minimum TOEFL 525. **Basis for Candidate Selection:** *Very important factors considered include:* secondary school record, standardized test scores. *Important factors considered include:* recommendations. **Freshman Admission Requirements:** High school diploma or GED is required. *Academic units required/recommended:* 15 total required; 15 total recommended; 4 English required, 4 English recommended, 3 math required, 3 math recommended, 2 science required, 2 science lab required, 2 foreign language required, 3 foreign language recommended, 2 history required, 1 elective required, 3 elective recommended. **Freshman Admission Statistics:** 12,021 applied, 35% accepted, 53% of those accepted enrolled. **Transfer Admission Requirements:** *Items required:* college transcript. Minimum high school GPA of 2.0 required. Minimum college GPA of 2.0 required. Lowest grade transferable C. **General Admission Information:** Application fee $55. Priority application deadline November 30. Regular application deadline April 1. Nonfall registration accepted. Credit and/or placement offered for CEEB Advanced Placement tests.

COSTS AND FINANCIAL AID

In-state tuition $0. Out-of-state tuition $7,380. Room & board $6,626. Required fees $1,772. Average book expense $846. **Required Forms and Deadlines:** FAFSA. No deadline for regular filing. Priority filing deadline March 2. **Notification of Awards:** Applicants will be notified of awards on a rolling basis beginning on or about April 1. **Types of Aid:** *Need-based scholarships/grants:* Pell, SEOG, state scholarships/grants, private scholarships, the school's own gift aid. *Loans:* FFEL Subsidized Stafford, FFEL Unsubsidized Stafford, FFEL PLUS, Federal Perkins, college/university loans from institutional funds. **Student Employment:** Federal Work-Study Program available. Institutional employment available. Off-campus job opportunities are good. **Financial Aid Statistics:** 57% freshmen, 52% undergrads receive some form of aid. Average freshman grant $3,250. Average freshman loan $2,500. Average income from on-campus job $2,400. **Financial Aid Phone:** 909-869-3700.

CALIFORNIA STATE UNIVERSITY—BAKERSFIELD

9001 Stockdale Highway, Bakersfield, CA 93311
Phone: 661-664-3036 **E-mail:** swatkin@csub.edu **CEEB Code:** 4110
Fax: 661-664-3389 **Web:** www.csub.edu

This public school was founded in 1970. It has a 375-acre campus.

STUDENTS AND FACULTY

Enrollment: 4,309. **Student Body:** Male 38%, female 62%, out-of-state 10%, international 2%. **Ethnic Representation:** African American 7%, Asian 8%, Caucasian 47%, Hispanic 28%, Native American 2%. **Retention and Graduation:** 20% grads go on to further study within 1 year. 10% grads pursue business degrees. **Faculty:** Student/faculty ratio 19:1.

ACADEMICS

Degrees: Bachelor's, master's. **Academic Requirements:** General education including some course work in arts/fine arts, computer literacy, English (including composition), foreign languages, history, humanities, mathematics, philosophy, sciences (biological or physical), social science. **Majors with Highest Enrollment:** Business, management, marketing, and related support services; liberal arts and sciences/liberal studies; psychology, general. **Special Study Options:** Accelerated program, cooperative (work-study) program, cross registration, distance learning, double major, dual enrollment, English as a second language, student exchange program (domestic), external degree program, honors program, independent study, internships, liberal arts/career combination, student-designed major, study abroad, teacher certification program.

FACILITIES

Housing: Coed, all-female. **Library Holdings:** 400,000 bound volumes. 82 periodicals. 946 microforms. 5,000 audiovisuals. **Special Academic Facilities/Equipment:** Todd Madigan Art Gallery, Frances Doré Theater, California Well Sample Repository, geotechnology training center, family business institute. **Computers:** School-owned computers available for student use.

EXTRACURRICULARS

Activities: Choral groups, concert band, drama/theater, jazz band, literary magazine, music ensembles, musical theater, opera, pep band, student government, student newspaper. **Organizations:** 71 registered organizations, 1 honor society, 2 religious organizations, 2 fraternities (1% men join), 2 sororities (1% women join). **Athletics (Intercollegiate):** *Men:* basketball, diving, golf, soccer, swimming, track & field, wrestling. *Women:* basketball, cross-country, diving, soccer, softball, swimming, tennis, track & field, volleyball, water polo.

ADMISSIONS

Selectivity Rating: 65 (of 100). **Freshman Academic Profile:** 100% in top 50% of high school class. 99% from public high schools. TOEFL required of all international applicants, minimum TOEFL 550. **Freshman Admission Requirements:** High school diploma or GED is required. *Academic units required/recommended:* 15 total required; 4 English required, 3 math required, 1 science required, 2 science lab required, 2 foreign language required, 2 history required, 1 elective required. **Transfer Admission Requirements:** *Items required:* college transcript. Minimum high school GPA of 2.0 required. Minimum college GPA of 2.0 required. Lowest grade transferable D. **General Admission Information:** Application fee $55. Nonfall registration accepted. Admission may be deferred. Credit and/or placement offered for CEEB Advanced Placement tests.

COSTS AND FINANCIAL AID

In-state tuition $1,506. Out-of-state tuition $7,380. Room & board $5,801. Required fees $1,957. Average book expense $650. **Required Forms and Deadlines:** FAFSA and state aid form. Financial aid filing deadline April 1. Priority filing deadline April 1. **Types of Aid:** *Need-based scholarships/grants:* Pell, SEOG, state scholarships/grants, private scholarships, the school's own gift aid, United Negro College Fund, Federal Nursing. *Loans:* Direct Subsidized Stafford, FFEL Subsidized Stafford, Federal Perkins, Federal Nursing, state loans, college/university loans from institutional funds. **Student Employment:** Federal Work-Study Program available. Institutional employment available. Off-campus job opportunities are good. **Financial Aid Statistics:** Average freshman grant $1,000. Average income from on-campus job $3,916. **Financial Aid Phone:** 661-664-3016.

CALIFORNIA STATE UNIVERSITY—CHICO

400 West First Street, Chico, CA 95929-0722
Phone: 530-898-4428 **E-mail:** info@csuchico.edu **CEEB Code:** 4048
Fax: 530-898-6456 **Web:** www.csuchico.edu **ACT Code:** 212

This public school was founded in 1887. It has a 130-acre campus.

STUDENTS AND FACULTY

Enrollment: 14,356. **Student Body:** Male 47%, female 53%, out-of-state 2%, international 3%. **Ethnic Representation:** African American 2%, Asian 5%, Caucasian 67%, Hispanic 10%, Native American 1%. **Retention and Graduation:** 80% freshmen return for sophomore year. 11% freshmen graduate within 4 years. **Faculty:** Student/faculty ratio 20:1. 615 full-time faculty, 85% hold PhDs. 100% faculty teach undergrads.

ACADEMICS

Degrees: Bachelor's, certificate, master's, post-bachelor's certificate, post-master's certificate. **Academic Requirements:** General education including some course work in arts/fine arts, computer literacy, English (including composition), history, humanities, mathematics, philosophy, sciences (biological or physical), social science. **Classes:** 20-29 students in an average class. 20-29 students in an average lab/discussion section. **Disciplines with Highest Percentage of Degrees Awarded:** Business/marketing 16%, social sciences and history 13%, liberal arts/general studies 13%, communications/communication technologies 7%, engineering/engineering technology 6%. **Special Study Options:** Cooperative (work-study) program, cross registration, distance learning, double major, dual enrollment, English as a second language, student exchange program (domestic), external degree program, honors program, independent study, internships, student-designed major, study abroad, teacher certification program.

FACILITIES

Housing: Coed, apartments for single students, housing for disabled students, housing for international students, fraternities and/or sororities, thematic housing for honors, engineering, minorities in engineering and science, business, math, and agriculture. **Library Holdings:** 942,322 bound volumes. 24,244 periodicals. 1,145,593 microforms. 23,608 audiovisuals. **Special Academic Facilities/Equipment:** Anthropology museum, center for intercultural studies, satellite communication dishes, biological field station, university farm, electron microscope. **Computers:** School-owned computers available for student use.

EXTRACURRICULARS

Activities: Choral groups, concert band, dance, drama/theater, jazz band, literary magazine, music ensembles, musical theater, opera, pep band, radio station, student government, student newspaper, student-run film society, symphony orchestra, yearbook. **Organizations:** 15 honor societies, 19 religious organizations, 22 fraternities (6% men join), 18 sororities (7% women join). **Athletics (Intercollegiate):** *Men:* baseball, basketball, cross-country, soccer, track & field, volleyball. *Women:* basketball, cross-country, soccer, softball, track & field, volleyball.

ADMISSIONS

Selectivity Rating: 69 (of 100). **Freshman Academic Profile:** Average high school GPA 3.2. 35% in top 10% of high school class, 76% in top 25% of high school class, 100% in top 50% of high school class. 39% from public high schools. Average SAT I Math 487, SAT I Math middle 50% range 470-580. Average SAT I Verbal 486, SAT I Verbal middle 50% range 460-560. Average ACT 20, ACT middle 50% range 18-24. TOEFL required of all international applicants, minimum TOEFL 500. **Basis for Candidate Selection:** *Very important factors considered include:* secondary school record, standardized test scores. *Important factors considered include:* state residency. **Freshman Admission Requirements:** High school diploma or GED is required. *Academic units required/recommended:* 15 total required; 4 English required, 3 math required, 2 science required, 2 science lab required, 2 foreign language required, 2 history required, 1 elective required. **Freshman Admission Statistics:** 8,502 applied, 78% accepted, 31% of those accepted enrolled. **Transfer Admission Requirements:** *Items required:* college transcript, statement of good standing from prior school. Minimum high school GPA of 2.0 required. Minimum college GPA of 2.0 required. Lowest grade transferable D. **General Admission Information:** Application fee $55. Priority application deadline November 30. Regular application deadline November 30. Nonfall registration accepted. Admission may be deferred for a maximum of 1 year. Credit and/or placement offered for CEEB Advanced Placement tests.

COSTS AND FINANCIAL AID

In-state tuition $1,572. Out-of-state tuition $10,032. Room & board $7,312. Required fees $703. Average book expense $1,132. **Required Forms and Deadlines:** FAFSA. No deadline for regular filing. Priority filing deadline March 2. **Notification of Awards:** Applicants will be notified of awards on a rolling basis beginning on or about February 15. **Types of Aid:** *Need-based scholarships/grants:* Pell, SEOG, state scholarships/grants, private scholarships, the school's own gift aid, United Negro College Fund. *Loans:* Direct Subsidized Stafford, Direct Unsubsidized Stafford, Direct PLUS, Federal Perkins, college/university loans from institutional funds. **Student Employment:** Federal Work-Study Program available. Institutional employment available. Off-campus job opportunities are fair. **Financial Aid Phone:** 530-898-6451.

CALIFORNIA STATE UNIVERSITY—DOMINGUEZ HILLS

100 East Victoria Street, Carson, CA 90747
Phone: 310-243-3600 **E-mail:** lwise@csudh.edu **CEEB Code:** 4098
Fax: 310-516-3609 **Web:** www.csudh.edu

This public school was founded in 1960. It has a 346-acre campus.

STUDENTS AND FACULTY

Enrollment: 4,809. **Student Body:** Male 33%, female 67%, out-of-state 1%, international 2%. **Ethnic Representation:** African American 29%, Asian 7%, Caucasian 22%, Hispanic 29%, Native American 1%. **Retention and Graduation:** 77% freshmen return for sophomore year.

ACADEMICS

Degrees: Bachelor's, certificate, master's, post-bachelor's certificate. **Academic Requirements:** General education including some course work in English (including composition), humanities, mathematics, sciences (biological or physical), social science. **Special Study Options:** Cooperative (work-study) program, cross registration, distance learning, double major, dual enrollment, external degree program, honors program, independent study, internships, study abroad, teacher certification program, weekend college.

FACILITIES

Housing: Apartments for married students, apartments for single students. **Library Holdings:** 411,000 bound volumes. 800 periodicals. 24,069 microforms. **Special Academic Facilities/Equipment:** University art gallery, Olympic Velodrome, university theater. **Computers:** *Recommended operating system:* Mac. School-owned computers available for student use.

EXTRACURRICULARS

Activities: Choral groups, concert band, dance, drama/theater, jazz band, music ensembles, student government, student newspaper, symphony orchestra. **Organizations:** 65 registered organizations, 6 honor societies, 3 religious organizations, 4 fraternities, 4 sororities. **Athletics (Intercollegiate):** *Men:* baseball, basketball, golf, soccer. *Women:* basketball, cross-country, soccer, softball, tennis, track & field, volleyball.

ADMISSIONS

Selectivity Rating: 66 (of 100). **Freshman Academic Profile:** 100% in top 50% of high school class. 84% from public high schools. TOEFL required of all international applicants, minimum TOEFL 550. **Basis for Candidate Selection:** *Very important factors considered include:* secondary school record, standardized test scores. *Other factors considered include:* class rank, extracurricular activities, interview, recommendations, talent/ability. **Freshman Admission Requirements:** *Academic units required/recommended:* 15 total required; 4 English required, 3 math required, 1 science required, 2 science lab required, 2 foreign language required, 2 history required, 1 elective required. **Freshman Admission Statistics:** 2,145 applied, 74% accepted, 35% of those accepted enrolled. **Transfer Admission Requirements:** *Items required:* college transcript. Minimum college GPA of 2.0 required. Lowest grade transferable C. **General Admission Information:** Application fee $55. Priority application deadline November 1. Regular application deadline June 1. Nonfall registration accepted. Credit offered for CEEB Advanced Placement tests.

COSTS AND FINANCIAL AID

In-state tuition $1,506. Out-of-state tuition $7,380. Room & board $5,801. Average book expense $630. **Required Forms and Deadlines:** FAFSA, institution's own financial aid form, and state aid form. **Notification of Awards:** Applicants will be notified of awards on or about April 19. **Types of Aid:** *Need-based scholarships/grants:* state scholarships/grants. *Loans:* FFEL Subsidized Stafford, FFEL PLUS. **Student Employment:** Federal Work-Study Program available. Institutional employment available. Off-campus job opportunities are good. **Financial Aid Statistics:** Average income from on-campus job $3,000. **Financial Aid Phone:** 310-243-3691.

CALIFORNIA STATE UNIVERSITY—FRESNO

5150 North Maple Ave. M/S JA 57, Fresno, CA 93740-8026
Phone: 559-278-2261 **E-mail:** vivian_franco@csufresno.edu **CEEB Code:** 4312
Fax: 559-278-4812 **Web:** www.csufresno.edu **ACT Code:** 266

This public school was founded in 1911. It has a 327-acre campus.

STUDENTS AND FACULTY

Enrollment: 17,338. **Student Body:** Male 43%, female 57%, out-of-state 1%, international 3%. **Ethnic Representation:** African American 5%, Asian 12%, Caucasian 38%, Hispanic 28%, Native American 1%. **Retention and Graduation:** 76% freshmen return for sophomore year. 11% freshmen graduate within 4 years. 5% grads go on to further study within 1 year. 4% grads pursue business degrees. 1% grads pursue law degrees. 1% grads pursue medical degrees. **Faculty:** Student/faculty ratio 18:1. 703 full-time faculty. 100% faculty teach undergrads.

ACADEMICS

Degrees: Bachelor's, certificate, doctoral, master's. **Academic Requirements:** General education including some course work in arts/fine arts, computer literacy, English (including composition), foreign languages, history, humanities, mathematics, philosophy, sciences (biological or physical), social science, speech, critical thinking, political science, behavioral/ environmental systems. **Classes:** 20-29 students in an average class. 20-29 students in an average lab/discussion section. **Majors with Highest Enrollment:** Business/commerce, general; liberal arts and sciences/liberal studies; health services/allied health, general. **Disciplines with Highest Percentage of Degrees Awarded:** Liberal arts/general studies 24%, business/marketing 16%, social sciences and history 7%, health professions and related sciences 7%, education 5%. **Special Study Options:** Accelerated program, cooperative (work-study) program, cross registration, distance learning, double major, dual enrollment, English as a second language, student exchange program (domestic), honors program, independent study, internships, student-designed major, study abroad, teacher certification program, academic remediation, advanced placement credit, learning disabilities services, marine science program.

FACILITIES

Housing: Coed, all-female, all-male, apartments for married students, apartments for single students, fraternities and/or sororities. **Library Holdings:** 977,198 bound volumes. 2,673 periodicals. 1,469,875 microforms. 73,369 audiovisuals. **Special Academic Facilities/Equipment:** Marine lab, Downing Planetarium. **Computers:** School-owned computers available for student use.

EXTRACURRICULARS

Activities: Choral groups, concert band, dance, drama/theater, jazz band, literary magazine, marching band, music ensembles, musical theater, pep band, radio station, student government, student newspaper, symphony orchestra, television station, yearbook. **Organizations:** 250 registered organizations, 21 honor societies, 11 religious organizations, 19 fraternities (3% men join), 13 sororities (3% women join). **Athletics (Intercollegiate):** *Men:* baseball, basketball, cheerleading, cross-country, football, golf, soccer, tennis, track & field, wrestling. *Women:* baseball, basketball, cheerleading, cross-country, diving, equestrian, soccer, softball, swimming, tennis, track & field, volleyball.

ADMISSIONS

Selectivity Rating: 69 (of 100). **Freshman Academic Profile:** Average high school GPA 3.3. 99% from public high schools. Average SAT I Math 485, SAT I Math middle 50% range 420-550. Average SAT I Verbal 465, SAT I Verbal middle 50% range 400-530. Average ACT 19, ACT middle 50% range 16-22. TOEFL required of all international applicants, minimum TOEFL 500. **Basis for Candidate Selection:** *Very important factors considered include:* secondary school record, standardized test scores. **Freshman Admission Requirements:** High school diploma or GED is required. *Academic units required/recommended:* 15 total required; 4 English required, 4 English recommended, 3 math required, 3 math recommended, 2 science required, 2 science lab required, 2 foreign language required, 2 foreign language recommended, 1 social studies recommended, 2 history required, 1 elective required, 3 elective recommended. **Freshman Admission Statistics:** 9,013 applied, 66% accepted, 34% of those accepted enrolled. **Transfer Admission Requirements:** *Items required:* college transcript. Minimum college GPA of 2.0 required. Lowest grade transferable D. **General Admission Information:** Application fee $55. Regular application deadline July 28. Nonfall registration accepted. Credit offered for CEEB Advanced Placement tests.

COSTS AND FINANCIAL AID

In-state tuition $1,796. Out-of-state tuition $8,564. Room & board $6,000. Required fees $0. Average book expense $405. **Required Forms and Deadlines:** FAFSA. Priority filing deadline March 2. **Notification of Awards:** Applicants will be notified of awards on a rolling basis beginning on or about April 1. **Types of Aid:** *Need-based scholarships/grants:* Pell, SEOG, state scholarships/grants, private scholarships, the school's own gift aid. *Loans:* Direct Subsidized Stafford, Direct Unsubsidized Stafford, Direct PLUS, FFEL Subsidized Stafford, FFEL Unsubsidized Stafford, FFEL PLUS, Federal Perkins, Federal Nursing, college/university loans from institutional funds. **Student Employment:** Federal Work-Study Program available. Institutional employment available. Off-campus job opportunities are good. **Financial Aid Statistics:** 54% freshmen, 62% undergrads receive some form of aid. Average freshman grant $3,781. Average freshman loan $2,264. Average income from on-campus job $2,090. **Financial Aid Phone:** 559-278-2182.

CALIFORNIA STATE UNIVERSITY—FULLERTON

800 North State College Boulevard, Fullerton, CA 92834-6900
Phone: 714-773-2370 **E-mail:** admissions@fullerton.edu **CEEB Code:** 4589
Fax: 714-278-2356 **Web:** www.fullerton.edu

This public school was founded in 1957. It has a 225-acre campus.

STUDENTS AND FACULTY

Enrollment: 25,261. **Student Body:** Male 40%, female 60%, out-of-state 1%, international 4% (78 countries represented). **Ethnic Representation:** African American 3%, Asian 25%, Caucasian 35%, Hispanic 25%, Native American 1%. **Retention and Graduation:** 80% freshmen return for sophomore year. 8% freshmen graduate within 4 years. **Faculty:** Student/faculty ratio 21:1. 754 full-time faculty, 84% hold PhDs.

ACADEMICS

Degrees: Bachelor's, master's.**Academic Requirements:** General education including some course work in arts/fine arts, English (including composition), history, humanities, mathematics, sciences (biological or physical), social science, oral and written communication. **Classes:** 20-29 students in an average class. 20-29 students in an average lab/discussion section. **Special Study Options:** Cooperative (work-study) program, double major, honors program, independent study, internships, student-designed major, study abroad.

FACILITIES

Housing: Apartments for single students, fraternities and/or sororities. **Computers:** School-owned computers available for student use.

EXTRACURRICULARS

Activities: Choral groups, concert band, dance, drama/theater, jazz band, music ensembles, musical theater, radio station, student government, student newspaper. **Organizations:** 3% men join fraternities, 3% women join sororities. **Athletics (Intercollegiate):** *Men:* baseball, basketball, cross-country, fencing, soccer, track & field, wrestling. *Women:* basketball, cross-country, fencing, gymnastics, soccer, softball, tennis, track & field, volleyball.

ADMISSIONS

Selectivity Rating: 63 (of 100). **Freshman Academic Profile:** Average high school GPA 3.2. 15% in top 10% of high school class, 45% in top 25% of high school class, 81% in top 50% of high school class. 82% from public high schools. Average SAT I Math 502, SAT I Math middle 50% range 440-560. Average SAT I Verbal 476, SAT I Verbal middle 50% range 420-530. Average ACT 20, ACT middle 50% range 17-23. TOEFL required of all international applicants, minimum TOEFL 500. **Basis for Candidate Selection:** *Very important factors considered include:* secondary school record, standardized test scores. *Other factors considered include:* state residency. **Freshman Admission Requirements:** High school diploma or GED is required. *Academic units required/recommended:* 2 science required, 2 science lab required, 2 history required, 1 elective required. **Freshman Admission Statistics:** 13,721 applied, 69% accepted, 30% of those accepted enrolled. **Transfer Admission Requirements:** *Items required:* college transcript, statement of good standing from prior school. Minimum college GPA of 2.0 required. Lowest grade transferable C. **General Admission Information:** Application fee $55. Priority application deadline March 15. Regular application deadline April 15. Nonfall registration accepted. Credit and/or placement offered for CEEB Advanced Placement tests.

COSTS AND FINANCIAL AID

Out-of-state tuition $5,904. Room & board $3,953. Required fees $1,881. Average book expense $1,080. **Required Forms and Deadlines:** FAFSA and state aid form. No deadline for regular filing. Priority filing deadline March 2. **Notification of Awards:** Applicants will be notified of awards on a rolling basis beginning on or about March 1. **Types of Aid:** *Need-based scholarships/grants:* Pell, SEOG, state scholarships/grants, private scholarships, the school's own gift aid. *Loans:* FFEL Subsidized Stafford, FFEL Unsubsidized Stafford, FFEL PLUS, Federal Perkins, college/university loans from institutional funds. **Student Employment:** Federal Work-Study Program available. Institutional employment available. Off-campus job opportunities are good. **Financial Aid Statistics:** 35% freshmen, 35% undergrads receive some form of aid. **Financial Aid Phone:** 714-278-3125.

CALIFORNIA STATE UNIVERSITY—HAYWARD

25800 Carlos Bee Blvd., Hayward, CA 94542-3035
Phone: 510-885-2624 **E-mail:** adminfo@csuhayward.edu **CEEB Code:** 4011
Fax: 510-885-4059 **Web:** www.csuhayward.edu **ACT Code:** 4011

This public school was founded in 1957. It has a 342-acre campus.

STUDENTS AND FACULTY

Enrollment: 9,337. **Student Body:** Male 36%, female 64%, out-of-state 1%, international 5% (86 countries represented). **Ethnic Representation:** African American 13%, Asian 28%, Caucasian 27%, Hispanic 13%, Native American 1%. **Faculty:** Student/faculty ratio 20:1. 359 full-time faculty, 82% hold PhDs. 85% faculty teach undergrads.

ACADEMICS

Degrees: Bachelor's, certificate, master's, post-bachelor's certificate, post-master's certificate. **Academic Requirements:** General education including some course work in arts/fine arts, computer literacy, English (including composition), history, humanities, mathematics, sciences (biological or physical), social science, critical thinking. **Classes:** 20-29 students in an average class. 10-19 students in an average lab/discussion section. **Disciplines with Highest Percentage of Degrees Awarded:** Business/marketing 30%, liberal arts/general studies 16%, social sciences and history 13%, psychology 5%, health professions and related sciences 5%. **Special Study Options:** Accelerated program, cooperative (work-study) program, cross registration, distance learning, double major, dual enrollment, English as a second language, student exchange program (domestic), honors program, independent study, internships, liberal arts/career combination, student-designed major, study abroad, teacher certification program, year-round operation with state-supported summer quarter, joint master's degree in marine science offered at Moss Landing Marine Lab, joint MFA in creative writing in summer, and overseas MBA programs in Hong Kong, Moscow, Singapore, and Vienna.

FACILITIES

Housing: Apartments for single students, private coeducational dormitory adjacent to campus. **Library Holdings:** 908,577 bound volumes. 2,210 periodicals. 803,844 microforms. 28,416 audiovisuals. **Special Academic Facilities/Equipment:** Anthropology museum, art gallery, scanning electron microscope facility, marine lab, ecological field station, geology summer camp. **Computers:** School-owned computers available for student use.

EXTRACURRICULARS

Activities: Choral groups, concert band, dance, drama/theater, jazz band, literary magazine, music ensembles, musical theater, opera, pep band, radio station, student government, student newspaper, symphony orchestra, television station. **Organizations:** 75 registered organizations, 3 honor societies, 2 religious organizations, 7 fraternities, 7 sororities. **Athletics (Intercollegiate):** *Men:* baseball, basketball, cross-country, golf, soccer. *Women:* basketball, cross-country, golf, soccer, softball, swimming, volleyball, water polo.

ADMISSIONS

Selectivity Rating: 69 (of 100). **Freshman Academic Profile:** Average high school GPA 3.1. 80% from public high schools. SAT I Math middle 50% range 380-590. SAT I Verbal middle 50% range 350-520. ACT middle 50% range 15-22. TOEFL required of all international applicants, minimum TOEFL 525. **Basis for Candidate Selection:** *Very important factors considered include:* secondary school record, standardized test scores. **Freshman Admission Requirements:** High school diploma or GED is required. *Academic units required/recommended:* 15 total required; 4 English required, 3 math required, 2 science required, 2 science lab required, 2 foreign language required, 2 history required, 1 elective required. **Freshman Admission Statistics:** 3,240 applied, 62% accepted, 35% of those accepted enrolled. **Transfer Admission Requirements:** *Items required:* college transcript. Minimum college GPA of 2.0 required. Lowest grade transferable D. **General Admission Information:** Application fee $55. Regular application deadline September 7. Nonfall registration accepted. Admission may be deferred. Credit and/or placement offered for CEEB Advanced Placement tests.

COSTS AND FINANCIAL AID

In-state tuition $1,428. Out-of-state tuition $8,808. Room & board $6,910. Required fees $1,761. Average book expense $864. **Required Forms and Deadlines:** FAFSA. No deadline for regular filing. Priority filing deadline March 2. **Notification of Awards:** Applicants will be notified of awards on a rolling basis beginning on or about April 5. **Types of Aid:** *Need-based scholarships/grants:* Pell, SEOG, state scholarships/grants, private scholarships, the school's own gift aid. *Loans:* FFEL Subsidized Stafford, FFEL Unsubsidized Stafford, FFEL PLUS, Federal Perkins. **Student Employment:** Federal Work-Study Program available. Institutional employment available. Off-campus job opportunities are excellent. **Financial Aid Statistics:** 40% freshmen, 43% undergrads receive some form of aid. Average freshman grant $4,624. Average freshman loan $2,513. **Financial Aid Phone:** 510-885-3616.

CALIFORNIA STATE UNIVERSITY—LONG BEACH

1250 Bellflower Boulevard, Long Beach, CA 90840
Phone: 562-985-4111 **E-mail:** eslb@csulb.edu **CEEB Code:** 4389
Fax: 562-985-8887 **Web:** www.csulb.edu

This public school was founded in 1949. It has a 322-acre campus.

STUDENTS AND FACULTY

Enrollment: 27,863. **Student Body:** Male 41%, female 59%, out-of-state 2%, international 5%. **Ethnic Representation:** African American 6%, Asian 23%, Caucasian 34%, Hispanic 24%, Native American 1%. **Retention and Graduation:** 80% freshmen return for sophomore year. 7% freshmen graduate within 4 years. **Faculty:** Student/faculty ratio 20:1. 1,051 full-time faculty, 80% hold PhDs. 100% faculty teach undergrads.

ACADEMICS

Degrees: Bachelor's, master's, post-bachelor's certificate. **Academic Requirements:** General education including some course work in arts/fine arts, English (including composition), history, humanities, mathematics, sciences (biological or physical), social science. **Classes:** 20-29 students in an average class. 20-29 students in an average lab/discussion section. **Majors with Highest Enrollment:** Management information systems, general; corrections and criminal justice; psychology, general. **Disciplines with Highest Percentage of Degrees Awarded:** Business/marketing 22%, visual and performing arts 10%, English 11%, social sciences and history 9%, psychology 9%. **Special Study Options:** Accelerated program, cross registration, distance learning, double major, dual enrollment, English as a second language, honors program, independent study, internships, student-designed major, study abroad, teacher certification program.

FACILITIES

Housing: Coed, housing for international students. **Library Holdings:** 1,469,715 bound volumes. 3,965 periodicals. 1,477,133 microforms. 29,679 audiovisuals. **Special Academic Facilities/Equipment:** Art and science museums, Japanese garden, special events arena with meeting facilities. **Computers:** School-owned computers available for student use.

EXTRACURRICULARS

Activities: Choral groups, concert band, dance, drama/theater, jazz band, literary magazine, music ensembles, musical theater, opera, radio station, student government, student newspaper, student-run film society, symphony orchestra, television station, yearbook. **Organizations:** 300 registered organizations, 25 honor societies, 20 religious organizations, 16 fraternities (4% men join), 15 sororities (4% women join). **Athletics (Intercollegiate):** *Men:* baseball, basketball, cross-country, golf, track & field, volleyball, water polo. *Women:* basketball, cross-country, golf, soccer, softball, tennis, track & field, volleyball, water polo.

ADMISSIONS

Selectivity Rating: 63 (of 100). **Freshman Academic Profile:** Average high school GPA 3.4. 82% from public high schools. Average SAT I Math 501, SAT I Math middle 50% range 460-580. Average SAT I Verbal 477, SAT I Verbal middle 50% range 430-550. ACT middle 50% range 17-24. TOEFL required of all international applicants, minimum TOEFL 525. **Basis for Candidate Selection:** *Very important factors considered include:* secondary school record, standardized test scores. **Freshman Admission Requirements:** High school diploma or GED is required. *Academic units required/recommended:* 15 total recommended; 4 English recommended, 3 math recommended, 1 science recommended, 1 science lab recommended, 2 foreign language recommended, 1 history recommended, 3 elective recommended. **Freshman Admission Statistics:** 21,953 applied, 52% accepted, 26% of those accepted enrolled. **Transfer Admission Requirements:** *Items required:* college transcript. Minimum college GPA of 2.0 required. Lowest grade transferable C. **General Admission Information:** Application fee $55. Regular application deadline November 30. Nonfall registration accepted. Credit offered for CEEB Advanced Placement tests.

COSTS AND FINANCIAL AID

In-state tuition $0. Out-of-state tuition $7,380. Room & board $5,800. Required fees $1,744. Average book expense $1,000. **Required Forms and Deadlines:** FAFSA. Priority filing deadline March 2. **Notification of Awards:** Applicants will be notified of awards on or about April 1. **Types of Aid:** *Need-based scholarships/grants:* Pell, SEOG, state scholarships/grants, private scholarships, the school's own gift aid. *Loans:* FFEL Subsidized Stafford, FFEL Unsubsidized Stafford, FFEL PLUS, Federal Perkins. **Student Employment:** Federal Work-Study Program available. Institutional employment available. Off-campus job opportunities are good. **Financial Aid Statistics:** 49% freshmen, 47% undergrads receive some form of aid. Average income from on-campus job $3,000. **Financial Aid Phone:** 562-985-8403.

CALIFORNIA STATE UNIVERSITY—LOS ANGELES

5151 State University Drive, Los Angeles, CA 90032
Phone: 323-343-3901 **E-mail:** admission@calstatela.edu **CEEB Code:** 4399
Fax: 323-343-6306 **Web:** www.calstatela.edu **ACT Code:** 320

This public school was founded in 1947. It has a 173-acre campus.

STUDENTS AND FACULTY

Enrollment: 13,898. **Student Body:** Male 39%, female 61%, out-of-state 4%, international 4%. **Ethnic Representation:** African American 8%, Asian 21%, Caucasian 11%, Hispanic 52%. **Faculty:** Student/faculty ratio 20:1. 598 full-time faculty.

ACADEMICS

Degrees: Bachelor's, master's. **Academic Requirements:** General education including some course work in arts/fine arts, English (including composition), foreign languages, history, humanities, mathematics, philosophy, sciences (biological or physical), social science. **Disciplines with Highest Percentage of Degrees Awarded:** Business/marketing 18%, home economics and vocational home economics 16%, protective services/public administration 12%, social sciences and history 8%, computer and information sciences 7%. **Special Study Options:** Accelerated program, cooperative (work-study) program, cross registration, double major, dual enrollment, English as a second language, student exchange program (domestic), honors program, independent study, internships, student-designed major, study abroad, teacher certification program.

FACILITIES

Housing: All-female, all-male, apartments for single students, housing for international students. Special-interest housing: first-year house, quiet house, ALCP, the Neighborhood, international house, National Student Exchange (NSE). **Library Holdings:** 1,706,206 bound volumes. 2,438 periodicals. 1,017,007 microforms. 4,309 audiovisuals. **Special Academic Facilities/ Equipment:** Baroque pipe organ, bilingual center, entrepreneurship and small business institutes, center for study of armament and disarmament, Van de Graaff accelerator. **Computers:** School-owned computers available for student use.

EXTRACURRICULARS

Activities: Choral groups, concert band, dance, drama/theater, jazz band, literary magazine, music ensembles, musical theater, opera, student government, student newspaper, symphony orchestra, television station. **Organizations:** 1 religious organization, 8 fraternities, 6 sororities. **Athletics (Intercollegiate):** *Men:* baseball, basketball, cross-country, soccer, tennis, track & field. *Women:* basketball, cross-country, soccer, tennis, track & field, volleyball.

ADMISSIONS

Selectivity Rating: 63 (of 100). **Freshman Academic Profile:** TOEFL required of all international applicants, minimum TOEFL 550. **Basis for Candidate Selection:** *Very important factors considered include:* secondary school record, standardized test scores. *Other factors considered include:* state residency. **Freshman Admission Requirements:** High school diploma or GED is required. *Academic units required/recommended:* 15 total required; 4 English required, 3 math required, 1 science required, 2 science lab required, 2 foreign language required, 2 history required, 1 elective required. **Transfer Admission Requirements:** *Items required:* college transcript. Minimum college GPA of 2.0 required. Lowest grade transferable C. **General Admission Information:** Application fee $55. Priority application deadline November 30. Regular application deadline June 15. Nonfall registration accepted. Credit and/ or placement offered for CEEB Advanced Placement tests.

COSTS AND FINANCIAL AID

In-state tuition $1,722. Out-of-state tuition $7,625. Room & board $2,923. Average book expense $846. **Required Forms and Deadlines:** FAFSA and verification/household size. No deadline for regular filing. Priority filing deadline March 1. **Notification of Awards:** Applicants will be notified of awards on a rolling basis. **Types of Aid:** *Need-based scholarships/grants:* Pell, SEOG, state scholarships/grants, private scholarships, the school's own gift aid, Federal Nursing, state work-study. *Loans:* Direct Subsidized Stafford, Direct Unsubsidized Stafford, Direct PLUS, Federal Perkins, Federal Nursing. **Student Employment:** Federal Work-Study Program available. Institutional employment available. Off-campus job opportunities are good. **Financial Aid Statistics:** 72% freshmen, 64% undergrads receive some form of aid. **Financial Aid Phone:** 213-343-1784.

CALIFORNIA STATE UNIVERSITY—NORTHRIDGE

PO Box 1286, Northridge, CA 91328-1286
Phone: 818-677-3773 **E-mail:** lorraine.newlon@csun.edu **CEEB Code:** 4707
Fax: 818-677-4665 **Web:** www.csun.edu **ACT Code:** 400

This public school was founded in 1956. It has a 350-acre campus.

STUDENTS AND FACULTY

Enrollment: 20,955. **Student Body:** Male 43%, female 57%, out-of-state 1%, international 3%. **Ethnic Representation:** African American 9%, Asian 16%, Caucasian 34%, Hispanic 24%, Native American 1%. **Retention and Graduation:** 78% freshmen return for sophomore year. 4% freshmen graduate within 4 years.

ACADEMICS

Degrees: Bachelor's, master's. **Special Study Options:** Accelerated program, English as a second language, honors program, student-designed major, study abroad.

FACILITIES

Housing: Coed, apartments for married students, apartments for single students, housing for international students, fraternities and/or sororities. **Library Holdings:** 1,207,345 bound volumes. 2,754 periodicals. 3,043,380 microforms. **Special Academic Facilities/Equipment:** Anthropology museum, art galleries, deafness center, urban archives, map library, cancer research/developmental biology center, planetarium, observatory. **Computers:** *Recommended operating system:* Mac. School-owned computers available for student use.

EXTRACURRICULARS

Activities: Choral groups, concert band, drama/theater, jazz band, literary magazine, marching band, music ensembles, musical theater, radio station, student government, student newspaper, yearbook. **Organizations:** 267 registered organizations, 18 honor societies, 13 religious organizations, 24 fraternities, 12 sororities. **Athletics (Intercollegiate):** *Men:* baseball, basketball, cross-country, diving, football, golf, indoor track, soccer, swimming, track & field, volleyball. *Women:* basketball, cross-country, diving, football, golf, indoor track, soccer, softball, swimming, tennis, track & field, volleyball.

ADMISSIONS

Selectivity Rating: 69 (of 100). **Freshman Academic Profile:** Average high school GPA 3.1. 33% in top 25% of high school class, 33% in top 50% of high school class. 81% from public high schools. TOEFL required of all international applicants, minimum TOEFL 500. **Basis for Candidate Selection:** *Very important factors considered include:* standardized test scores. **Freshman Admission Requirements:** High school diploma is required and GED is not accepted. *Academic units required/recommended:* 4 English required, 3 math required, 1 science required, 2 science lab required, 2 foreign language required, 2 history required, 1 elective required. **Freshman Admission Statistics:** 7,931 applied, 78% accepted, 38% of those accepted enrolled. **Transfer Admission Requirements:** Lowest grade transferable D. **General Admission Information:** Application fee $55. Nonfall registration accepted. Credit and/or placement offered for CEEB Advanced Placement tests.

COSTS AND FINANCIAL AID

In-state tuition $1,506. Out-of-state tuition $7,874. Room & board $5,801. Average book expense $648. **Required Forms and Deadlines:** institution's own financial aid form. **Types of Aid:** *Need-based scholarships/grants:* Pell, SEOG, state scholarships/grants, private scholarships, the school's own gift aid, Federal Nursing. *Loans:* FFEL Subsidized Stafford, FFEL Unsubsidized Stafford, FFEL PLUS, Federal Perkins, Federal Nursing, college/university loans from institutional funds. **Student Employment:** Federal Work-Study Program available. Institutional employment available. Off-campus job opportunities are good. **Financial Aid Statistics:** Average income from on-campus job $3,000. **Financial Aid Phone:** 818-677-3000.

CALIFORNIA STATE UNIVERSITY—SACRAMENTO

6000 J Street, Sacramento, CA 95819-6048
Phone: 916-278-3901 **E-mail:** admissions@csus.edu **CEEB Code:** 4671
Fax: 916-278-5603 **Web:** www.csus.edu

This public school was founded in 1947. It has a 282-acre campus.

STUDENTS AND FACULTY

Enrollment: 22,564. **Student Body:** Male 43%, female 57%, out-of-state 1%, international 2%. **Ethnic Representation:** African American 6%, Asian 19%, Caucasian 45%, Hispanic 14%, Native American 1%. **Retention and Graduation:** 76% freshmen return for sophomore year. **Faculty:** Student/ faculty ratio 21:1. 874 full-time faculty, 76% hold PhDs.

ACADEMICS

Degrees: Bachelor's, doctoral, master's. **Academic Requirements:** General education including some course work in arts/fine arts, English (including composition), foreign languages, history, humanities, mathematics, sciences (biological or physical), social science, personal development. **Classes:** 20-29 students in an average class. **Majors with Highest Enrollment:** Business administration/management; liberal arts and sciences/liberal studies; criminal justice/law enforcement administration. **Disciplines with Highest Percent-**

age of Degrees Awarded: Business/marketing 21%, protective services/public administration 11%, social sciences and history 10%, communications/communication technologies 8%, liberal arts/general studies 6%. **Special Study Options:** Accelerated program, cooperative (work-study) program, cross registration, distance learning, double major, dual enrollment, English as a second language, independent study, internships, student-designed major, study abroad, teacher certification program.

FACILITIES

Housing: Coed. **Library Holdings:** 967,418 bound volumes. 4,071 periodicals. 2,317,727 microforms. 135,074 audiovisuals.

EXTRACURRICULARS

Activities: Choral groups, concert band, dance, drama/theater, jazz band, literary magazine, marching band, music ensembles, musical theater, opera, pep band, radio station, student government, student newspaper, symphony orchestra, yearbook. **Organizations:** 7% men join fraternities, 5% women join sororities. **Athletics (Intercollegiate):** *Men:* baseball, basketball, cross-country, football, golf, soccer, tennis, track & field. *Women:* basketball, crew, cross-country, golf, gymnastics, soccer, softball, tennis, track & field, volleyball.

ADMISSIONS

Selectivity Rating: 71 (of 100). **Freshman Academic Profile:** Average high school GPA 3.2. Average SAT I Math 496, SAT I Math middle 50% range 430-560. Average SAT I Verbal 471, SAT I Verbal middle 50% range 410-530. Average ACT 20, ACT middle 50% range 16-22. TOEFL required of all international applicants, minimum TOEFL 510. **Basis for Candidate Selection:** *Very important factors considered include:* secondary school record, standardized test scores. *Important factors considered include:* state residency. *Other factors considered include:* extracurricular activities, geographical residence, interview, recommendations, talent/ability. **Freshman Admission Requirements:** High school diploma or GED is required. *Academic units required/recommended:* 15 total required; 4 English required, 3 math required, 1 science required, 2 science lab required, 2 foreign language required, 2 history required, 1 elective required. **Freshman Admission Statistics:** 10,400 applied, 51% accepted, 47% of those accepted enrolled. **Transfer Admission Requirements:** *Items required:* college transcript, statement of good standing from prior school. Minimum college GPA of 2.0 required. Lowest grade transferable D. **General Admission Information:** Application fee $55. Priority application deadline May 1. Regular application deadline May 1. Nonfall registration accepted. Admission may be deferred. Credit and/or placement offered for CEEB Advanced Placement tests.

COSTS AND FINANCIAL AID

In-state tuition $1,428. Out-of-state tuition $9,888. Room & board $6,163. Required fees $232. Average book expense $846. **Required Forms and Deadlines:** FAFSA. **Types of Aid:** *Need-based scholarships/grants:* Pell, SEOG, state scholarships/grants, private scholarships, Federal Nursing. *Loans:* Direct Subsidized Stafford, Direct Unsubsidized Stafford, Direct PLUS, Federal Perkins, Federal Nursing. **Student Employment:** Federal Work-Study Program available. Institutional employment available. Off-campus job opportunities are good. **Financial Aid Statistics:** 48% freshmen, 47% undergrads receive some form of aid. **Financial Aid Phone:** 916-278-6554.

CALIFORNIA STATE UNIVERSITY—SAN BERNARDINO

5500 University Parkway, San Bernardino, CA 92407-2397
Phone: 909-880-5188 **E-mail:** moreinfo@mail.csusb.edu **CEEB Code:** 4099
Fax: 909-880-7034 **Web:** www.csusb.edu **ACT Code:** 205

This public school was founded in 1965. It has a 430-acre campus.

STUDENTS AND FACULTY

Enrollment: 11,256. **Student Body:** Male 37%, female 63%, out-of-state 0%, international 3% (49 countries represented). **Ethnic Representation:** African American 12%, Asian 7%, Caucasian 38%, Hispanic 29%, Native American 1%. **Retention and Graduation:** 76% freshmen return for sophomore year. 12% freshmen graduate within 4 years. **Faculty:** Student/faculty ratio 20:1. 466 full-time faculty.

ACADEMICS

Degrees: Bachelor's, master's. **Academic Requirements:** General education including some course work in arts/fine arts, computer literacy, English (including composition), foreign languages, history, humanities, mathematics, philosophy, sciences (biological or physical), social science, kinesiology or physical education. **Classes:** 20-29 students in an average class. 20-29 students in an average lab/discussion section. **Majors with Highest Enrollment:** Business administration/management; liberal arts and sciences/liberal studies; psychology, general. **Disciplines with Highest Percentage of Degrees Awarded:** Business/marketing 24%, liberal arts/general studies 21%, social sciences and history 11%, psychology 10%, protective services/public administration 6%. **Special Study Options:** Cooperative (work-study) program, cross registration, distance learning, double major, dual enrollment, student exchange program (domestic), honors program, independent study, internships, study abroad, teacher certification program.

FACILITIES

Housing: Coed, apartments for single students. **Library Holdings:** 731,259 bound volumes. 2,028 periodicals. 643,292 microforms. 15,252 audiovisuals. **Special Academic Facilities/Equipment:** Simulation labs, electronic music studios, language lab, desert studies center. **Computers:** School-owned computers available for student use.

EXTRACURRICULARS

Activities: Choral groups, dance, drama/theater, jazz band, music ensembles, musical theater, radio station, student government, student newspaper, television station. **Organizations:** 3 religious organizations, 9 fraternities (6% men join), 6 sororities (3% women join). **Athletics (Intercollegiate):** *Men:* baseball, basketball, golf, soccer. *Women:* basketball, cross-country, soccer, softball, tennis, volleyball, water polo.

ADMISSIONS

Selectivity Rating: 63 (of 100). **Freshman Academic Profile:** Average high school GPA 3.1. 83% from public high schools. SAT I Math middle 50% range 390-510. SAT I Verbal middle 50% range 380-500. ACT middle 50% range 16-21. TOEFL required of all international applicants, minimum TOEFL 500. **Basis for Candidate Selection:** *Very important factors considered include:* recommendations, secondary school record, standardized test scores. *Important factors considered include:* state residency. **Freshman Admission Requirements:** High school diploma or GED is required. *Academic units required/recommended:* 15 total required; 4 English required, 3 math required, 2 science required, 2 science lab required, 2 foreign language required, 2 history required, 1 elective required. **Freshman Admission Statistics:** 3,592 applied, 95% accepted, 35% of those accepted enrolled. **Transfer Admission Requirements:** *Items required:* college transcript. Minimum college GPA of 2.0 required. Lowest grade transferable C. **General Admission Information:** Application fee $55. Nonfall registration accepted. Credit and/or placement offered for CEEB Advanced Placement tests.

COSTS AND FINANCIAL AID

In-state tuition $0. Out-of-state tuition $9,336. Room & board $4,956. Required fees $2,568. Average book expense $1,215. **Required Forms and Deadlines:** FAFSA and state aid form. **Notification of Awards:** Applicants will be notified of awards on or about May 1. **Types of Aid:** *Loans:* FFEL Subsidized Stafford, FFEL PLUS. **Student Employment:** Federal Work-Study Program available. Institutional employment available. Off-campus job opportunities are good. **Financial Aid Statistics:** Average income from on-campus job $4,100. **Financial Aid Phone:** 909-880-7800.

CALIFORNIA STATE UNIVERSITY—SAN MARCOS

333 S. Twin Oaks Valley Road, San Marcos, CA 92096-0001
Phone: 760-750-4848 **E-mail:** apply@csusm.edu **CEEB Code:** 5677
Fax: 760-750-3285 **Web:** www.csusm.edu

This public school was founded in 1989. It has a 300-acre campus.

STUDENTS AND FACULTY

Enrollment: 6,149. **Student Body:** Male 40%, female 60%, out-of-state 0%, international 2%. **Ethnic Representation:** African American 3%, Asian 10%, Caucasian 54%, Hispanic 18%, Native American 1%. **Retention and Graduation:** 70% freshmen return for sophomore year. 10% freshmen graduate within 4 years. **Faculty:** Student/faculty ratio 19:1. 189 full-time faculty, 95% hold PhDs. 100% faculty teach undergrads.

ACADEMICS

Degrees: Bachelor's, master's. **Academic Requirements:** General education including some course work in arts/fine arts, computer literacy, English (including composition), foreign languages, history, humanities, mathematics, sciences (biological or physical), social science, and U.S. history, Constitution, and American ideals requirement. 2,500-word all-university writing requirement. **Disciplines with Highest Percentage of Degrees Awarded:** Business/marketing 26%, liberal arts/general studies 26%, social sciences and history 18%, psychology 7%, communications/communication technologies 6%. **Special Study Options:** Cross registration, distance learning, double major, dual enrollment, English as a second language, independent study, internships, student-designed major, study abroad, teacher certification program, weekend college, Program for Adult College Education (PACE), Saturday classes, Air Force ROTC, extended studies, open university, special sessions, including winter.

FACILITIES

Housing: Housing scheduled to open fall 2003. **Library Holdings:** 179,439 bound volumes. 2,984 periodicals. 894,593 microforms. 7,576 audiovisuals. **Computers:** *Recommended operating system:* Mac. School-owned computers available for student use.

EXTRACURRICULARS

Activities: Choral groups, dance, drama/theater, music ensembles, student newspaper. **Organizations:** 39 registered organizations, 5 honor societies, 2 religious organizations, 2 fraternities, 2 sororities.

ADMISSIONS

Selectivity Rating: 60 (of 100). **Freshman Academic Profile:** Average high school GPA 3.2. SAT I Math middle 50% range 440-550. SAT I Verbal middle 50% range 430-540. TOEFL required of all international applicants, minimum TOEFL 550. **Basis for Candidate Selection:** *Very important factors considered include:* secondary school record, standardized test scores. **Freshman Admission Requirements:** High school diploma or GED is required. *Academic units required/recommended:* 15 total required; 4 English required, 3 math required, 2 science required, 2 science lab required, 2 foreign language required, 2 social studies required, 1 elective required. **Freshman Admission Statistics:** 4,314 applied, 67% accepted, 29% of those accepted enrolled. **Transfer Admission Requirements:** *Items required:* college transcript. Minimum college GPA of 2.0 required. Lowest grade transferable C. **General Admission Information:** Application fee $55. Regular application deadline November 30. Nonfall registration accepted. Credit and/or placement offered for CEEB Advanced Placement tests.

COSTS AND FINANCIAL AID

In-state tuition $0. Out-of-state tuition $7,473. Required fees $2,048. Average book expense $750. **Required Forms and Deadlines:** FAFSA. Priority filing deadline March 2. **Notification of Awards:** Applicants will be notified of awards on or about April 15. **Types of Aid:** *Need-based scholarships/grants:* Pell, SEOG, state scholarships/grants, private scholarships, the school's own gift aid. *Loans:* Direct Subsidized Stafford, Direct Unsubsidized Stafford, Direct PLUS, Federal Perkins, college/university loans from institutional funds. **Student Employment:** Federal Work-Study Program available. Institutional employment available. Off-campus job opportunities are good. **Financial Aid Statistics:** 39% freshmen, 45% undergrads receive some form of aid. Average income from on-campus job $6,850. **Financial Aid Phone:** 760-750-4850.

CALIFORNIA STATE UNIVERSITY—STANISLAUS

801 W. Monte Vista Avenue, Turlock, CA 95382
Phone: 209-667-3070 **E-mail:** outreach_help_desk@stan.csustan.edu
CEEB Code: 4713 **Fax:** 209-667-3788 **Web:** www.csustan.edu **ACT Code:** 435

This public school was founded in 1957. It has a 225-acre campus.

STUDENTS AND FACULTY

Enrollment: 5,624. **Student Body:** Male 33%, female 67%, out-of-state 1%, international 1% (24 countries represented). **Ethnic Representation:** African American 3%, Asian 9%, Caucasian 46%, Hispanic 25%, Native American 1%. **Retention and Graduation:** 81% freshmen return for sophomore year. 21% freshmen graduate within 4 years. **Faculty:** Student/faculty ratio 18:1. 262 full-time faculty, 83% hold PhDs.

ACADEMICS

Degrees: Bachelor's, master's, post-bachelor's certificate. **Academic Requirements:** General education including some course work in arts/fine arts, computer literacy, English (including composition), foreign languages, history, humanities, mathematics, philosophy, sciences (biological or physical), social science, public speaking, upper-division writing proficiency. **Classes:** 10-19 students in an average class. 10-19 students in an average lab/discussion section. **Majors with Highest Enrollment:** Liberal arts and sciences/liberal studies; business administration/management; psychology, general. **Disciplines with Highest Percentage of Degrees Awarded:** Liberal arts/general studies 32%, business/marketing 17%, social sciences and history 13%, psychology 7%, protective services/public administration 6%. **Special Study Options:** Accelerated program, cooperative (work-study) program, distance learning, double major, dual enrollment, English as a second language, student exchange program (domestic), external degree program, honors program, independent study, internships, liberal arts/career combination, student-designed major, study abroad, teacher certification program, weekend college.

FACILITIES

Housing: Coed, apartments for single students, housing available in summer months. **Library Holdings:** 347,651 bound volumes. 1,974 periodicals. 1,315,053 microforms. 4,302 audiovisuals. **Special Academic Facilities/Equipment:** Marine sciences station, laser lab, greenhouse, art gallery, mainstage theatre, recital hall, observatory, science building, art complex, distance learning studios, BioAg Eco building. **Computers:** School-owned computers available for student use.

EXTRACURRICULARS

Activities: Choral groups, concert band, dance, drama/theater, jazz band, marching band, music ensembles, musical theater, opera, pep band, radio station, student government, student newspaper, symphony orchestra. **Organizations:** 79 registered organizations, 1 honor society, 4 religious organizations, 5 fraternities (5% men join), 9 sororities (5% women join). **Athletics (Intercollegiate):** *Men:* baseball, basketball, cheerleading, cross-country, golf, indoor track, soccer, track & field. *Women:* basketball, cheerleading, cross-country, indoor track, soccer, softball, track & field, volleyball.

ADMISSIONS

Selectivity Rating: 71 (of 100). **Freshman Academic Profile:** Average high school GPA 3.3. 91% from public high schools. Average SAT I Math 480, SAT I Math middle 50% range 137-130. Average SAT I Verbal 480, SAT I Verbal middle 50% range 117-134. Average ACT 20, ACT middle 50% range 24-36. TOEFL required of all international applicants, minimum TOEFL 500. **Basis for Candidate Selection:** *Very important factors considered include:* secondary school record, standardized test scores. *Other factors considered include:* essays. **Freshman Admission Requirements:** High school diploma or GED is required. *Academic units required/recommended:* 15 total required; 4 English required, 3 math required, 2 science required, 2 science lab required, 2 foreign language required, 2 history required, 1 elective required. **Freshman Admission Statistics:** 1,875 applied, 68% accepted, 45% of those accepted enrolled. **Transfer Admission Requirements:** *Items required:* college transcript, statement of good standing from prior school. Minimum high school GPA of 3.0 required. Minimum college GPA of 2.0 required. Lowest grade transferable D-. **General Admission Information:** Application fee $55. Priority application deadline November 30. Early decision application deadline November 30. Regular application deadline May 31. Nonfall registration accepted. Admission may be deferred for a maximum of 1 year. Credit and/or placement offered for CEEB Advanced Placement tests.

COSTS AND FINANCIAL AID

In-state tuition $0. Out-of-state tuition $7,380. Room & board $7,020. Required fees $1,875. Average book expense $846. **Required Forms and Deadlines:** FAFSA and state aid form. Priority filing deadline March 2. **Notification of Awards:** Applicants will be notified of awards on a rolling basis beginning on or about March 15. **Types of Aid:** *Need-based scholarships/grants:* Pell, SEOG, state scholarships/grants, private scholarships, the school's own gift aid. *Loans:* FFEL Subsidized Stafford, FFEL Unsubsidized Stafford, FFEL PLUS, Federal Perkins, college/university loans from institutional funds. **Student Employment:** Federal Work-Study Program available. Institutional employment available. Off-campus job opportunities are good. **Financial Aid Statistics:** 62% freshmen, 62% undergrads receive some form of aid. Average income from on-campus job $1,200. **Financial Aid Phone:** 209-667-3336.

CALIFORNIA UNIVERSITY OF PENNSYLVANIA

250 University Avenue, California, PA 15419
Phone: 724-938-4404 **E-mail:** inquiry@cup.edu **CEEB Code:** 2647
Fax: 724-938-4564 **Web:** www.cup.edu **ACT Code:** 3694

This public school was founded in 1852. It has a 194-acre campus.

STUDENTS AND FACULTY

Enrollment: 5,027. **Student Body:** Male 48%, female 52%, out-of-state 4%, international 1% (18 countries represented). **Ethnic Representation:** African American 5%, Caucasian 81%. **Retention and Graduation:** 73% freshmen return for sophomore year. 16% freshmen graduate within 4 years. 21% grads go on to further study within 1 year. 3% grads pursue business degrees. 1% grads pursue law degrees. 1% grads pursue medical degrees. **Faculty:** Student/faculty ratio 20:1. 281 full-time faculty, 59% hold PhDs. 98% faculty teach undergrads.

ACADEMICS

Degrees: Associate's, bachelor's, certificate, master's, post-bachelor's certificate, terminal, transfer. **Academic Requirements:** General education including some course work in English (including composition), humanities, mathematics. **Classes:** 20-29 students in an average class. **Majors with Highest Enrollment:** Education, general; sociology; business administration/management. **Disciplines with Highest Percentage of Degrees Awarded:** Education 30%, business/marketing 12%, social sciences and history 7%, psychology 6%, communications/communication technologies 5%. **Special Study Options:** Accelerated program, cooperative (work-study) program, distance learning, double major, student exchange program (domestic), honors program, internships, study abroad, teacher certification program, weekend college. Undergrads may take grad classes.

FACILITIES

Housing: All-female, all-male, apartments for single students, fraternities and/or sororities. **Library Holdings:** 423,426 bound volumes. 1,022 periodicals. 1,421,092 microforms. 60,904 audiovisuals. **Special Academic Facilities/Equipment:** Art museum. **Computers:** *Recommended operating system:* Windows NT/2000. School-owned computers available for student use.

EXTRACURRICULARS

Activities: Choral groups, concert band, drama/theater, jazz band, literary magazine, marching band, music ensembles, musical theater, radio station, student government, student newspaper, television station, yearbook. **Organizations:** 7 honor societies, 1 religious organization, 9 fraternities (10% men join), 7 sororities (10% women join). **Athletics (Intercollegiate):** *Men:* baseball, basketball, football, rugby, soccer, track & field. *Women:* basketball, rugby, soccer, softball, tennis, track & field, volleyball.

ADMISSIONS

Selectivity Rating: 68 (of 100). **Freshman Academic Profile:** Average high school GPA 2.9. 3% in top 10% of high school class, 15% in top 25% of high school class, 43% in top 50% of high school class. Average SAT I Math 484, SAT I Math middle 50% range 430-550. Average SAT I Verbal 488, SAT I Verbal middle 50% range 440-540. TOEFL required of all international applicants, minimum TOEFL 450. **Basis for Candidate Selection:** *Very important factors considered include:* secondary school record. *Important factors considered include:* recommendations, standardized test scores. *Other factors considered include:* alumni/ae relation, extracurricular activities, interview, minority status, talent/ability. **Freshman Admission Requirements:** High school diploma or GED is required. *Academic units required/recommended:* 4 English recommended, 3 math recommended, 2 science recommended, 2 foreign language recommended, 3 social studies recommended, 1 history recommended. **Freshman Admission Statistics:** 2,804 applied, 76% accepted, 46% of those accepted enrolled. **Transfer Admission Requirements:** *Items required:* high school transcript, college transcript, statement of good standing from prior school. Minimum college GPA of 2.3 required. Lowest grade transferable C. **General Admission Information:** Application fee $25. Priority application deadline May 1. Nonfall registration accepted. Admission may be deferred. Credit offered for CEEB Advanced Placement tests.

COSTS AND FINANCIAL AID

In-state tuition $4,016. Out-of-state tuition $10,400. Room & board $5,134. Required fees $1,188. Average book expense $650. **Required Forms and Deadlines:** FAFSA and state aid form. **Types of Aid:** *Need-based scholarships/grants:* state scholarships/grants. *Loans:* FFEL Subsidized Stafford, FFEL PLUS. **Student Employment:** Federal Work-Study Program available. Institutional employment available. Off-campus job opportunities are fair. **Financial Aid Phone:** 724-938-4415.

CALUMET COLLEGE OF SAINT JOSEPH

2400 New York Avenue, Whiting, IN 46394
Phone: 219-473-4215 **E-mail:** admissions@ccsj.edu **CEEB Code:** 1776
Fax: 219-473-4259 **Web:** www.ccsj.edu **ACT Code:** 1245

This private school, which is affiliated with the Roman Catholic Church, was founded in 1951. It has a 256-acre campus.

STUDENTS AND FACULTY

Enrollment: 1,004. **Student Body:** Male 38%, female 62%, out-of-state 24%, international students represent 4 countries. **Ethnic Representation:** African American 28%, Asian 1%, Caucasian 48%, Hispanic 17%. **Retention and Graduation:** 75% freshmen return for sophomore year. 5% freshmen graduate within 4 years. **Faculty:** Student/faculty ratio 15:1. 21 full-time faculty, 85% hold PhDs. 100% faculty teach undergrads.

ACADEMICS

Degrees: Associate's, bachelor's, certificate, terminal, transfer. **Academic Requirements:** General education including some course work in arts/fine arts, computer literacy, English (including composition), history, humanities, mathematics, philosophy, sciences (biological or physical), social science. **Classes:** 10-19 students in an average class. 10-19 students in an average lab/discussion section. **Disciplines with Highest Percentage of Degrees Awarded:** Business/marketing 46%, health professions and related sciences 14%, social sciences and history 8%, law/legal studies 7%, psychology 5%. **Special Study Options:** Accelerated program, cooperative (work-study) program, distance learning, double major, English as a second language, independent study, internships, liberal arts/career combination, teacher certification program, weekend college.

FACILITIES

Library Holdings: 111,742 bound volumes. 530 periodicals. 3,838 microforms. 6,237 audiovisuals. **Special Academic Facilities/Equipment:** Art gallery, chapel.

EXTRACURRICULARS

Activities: Drama/theater, literary magazine, student government, student newspaper. **Organizations:** 8 registered organizations, 19 honor societies, 6 religious organizations, 1 sorority. **Athletics (Intercollegiate):** *Men:* basketball. *Women:* basketball, cheerleading.

ADMISSIONS

Selectivity Rating: 63 (of 100). **Freshman Academic Profile:** 13% in top 10% of high school class, 24% in top 25% of high school class, 59% in top 50% of high school class. 50% from public high schools. TOEFL required of all international applicants, minimum TOEFL 550. **Basis for Candidate Selection:** *Important factors considered include:* interview. *Other factors considered include:* character/personal qualities, class rank, essays, extracurricular activities, recommendations, secondary school record, standardized test scores. **Freshman Admission Requirements:** High school diploma or GED is required. *Academic units required/recommended:* 15 total recommended; 4 English recommended, 3 math recommended, 2 science recommended, 1 foreign language recommended, 2 social studies recommended, 1 history recommended, 2 elective recommended. **Freshman Admission Statistics:** 412 applied, 54% accepted, 37% of those accepted enrolled. **Transfer Admission Requirements:** *Items required:* college transcript, essay, interview, statement of good standing from prior school. Minimum college GPA of 2.0 required. Lowest grade transferable D. **General Admission Information:** Nonfall registration accepted.

COSTS AND FINANCIAL AID

Required fees $25. Average book expense $600. **Required Forms and Deadlines:** FAFSA and institution's own financial aid form. Priority filing deadline March 1. **Notification of Awards:** Applicants will be notified of awards on a rolling basis beginning on or about May 1. **Types of Aid:** *Need-based scholarships/grants:* Pell, SEOG, state scholarships/grants, private scholarships, the school's own gift aid. *Loans:* FFEL Subsidized Stafford, FFEL Unsubsidized Stafford, FFEL PLUS. **Student Employment:** Federal Work-Study Program available. Institutional employment available. Off-campus job opportunities are good. **Financial Aid Statistics:** Average income from on-campus job $1,500. **Financial Aid Phone:** 219-473-4296.

CALVIN COLLEGE

3201 Burton Street SE, Grand Rapids, MI 49546
Phone: 616-957-6106 **E-mail:** admissions@calvin.edu **CEEB Code:** 1095
Fax: 616-957-8513 **Web:** www.calvin.edu **ACT Code:** 1968

This private school was founded in 1876. It has a 370-acre campus.

STUDENTS AND FACULTY

Enrollment: 4,286. **Student Body:** Male 44%, female 56%, out-of-state 39%, international 8%. **Ethnic Representation:** African American 1%, Asian 2%, Caucasian 92%, Hispanic 1%. **Retention and Graduation:** 87% freshmen return for sophomore year. 57% freshmen graduate within 4 years. 20% grads go on to further study within 1 year. 4% grads pursue business degrees. 3% grads pursue law degrees. 3% grads pursue medical degrees. **Faculty:** Student/faculty ratio 15:1. 291 full-time faculty, 82% hold PhDs. 100% faculty teach undergrads.

ACADEMICS

Degrees: Bachelor's, master's, post-bachelor's certificate. **Academic Requirements:** General education including some course work in arts/fine arts, communications, computer literacy, cross-cultural study, English, foreign languages, history, humanities, mathematics, philosophy, physical education, religion and theology, sciences (biological or physical), social science. **Classes:** 20-29 students in an average class. 20-29 students in an average lab/discussion section. **Majors with Highest Enrollment:** Business administration/management; elementary education and teaching; English language and literature, general. **Disciplines with Highest Percentage of Degrees Awarded:** Business/marketing 13%, education 9%, social sciences and history 9%, biological life sciences 7%, health professions and related sciences 7%. **Special Study Options:** Double major, dual enrollment, honors program, independent study, internships, student-designed major, study abroad, teacher certification program, academically based service-learning, accelerated program.

FACILITIES

Housing: All-female, all-male, apartments for single students, Project Neighborhood houses. **Library Holdings:** 801,802 bound volumes. 2,658 periodicals. 784,893 microforms. 22,394 audiovisuals. **Special Academic Facilities/Equipment:** Art gallery, observatory, ecosystem preserve, electron microscope, seismograph lab. **Computers:** School-owned computers available for student use.

EXTRACURRICULARS

Activities: Choral groups, concert band, dance, drama/theater, jazz band, literary magazine, music ensembles, musical theater, pep band, radio station, student government, student newspaper, student-run film society, symphony orchestra, yearbook. **Organizations:** 52 registered organizations, 6 honor societies, 5 religious organizations. **Athletics (Intercollegiate):** *Men:* baseball, basketball, cross-country, golf, soccer, swimming, tennis, track & field. *Women:* basketball, cross-country, golf, soccer, softball, swimming, tennis, track & field, volleyball.

ADMISSIONS

Selectivity Rating: 78 (of 100). **Freshman Academic Profile:** Average high school GPA 3.5. 27% in top 10% of high school class, 52% in top 25% of high school class, 81% in top 50% of high school class. 42% from public high schools. Average SAT I Math 595, SAT I Math middle 50% range 530-660. Average SAT I Verbal 584, SAT I Verbal middle 50% range 520-640. Average ACT 26, ACT middle 50% range 22-28. TOEFL required of all international applicants, minimum TOEFL 550. **Basis for Candidate Selection:** *Very important factors considered include:* religious affiliation/commitment, secondary school record, standardized test scores. *Important factors considered include:* character/personal qualities, essays, extracurricular activities, recommendations. *Other factors considered include:* class rank, volunteer work, work experience. **Freshman Admission Requirements:** High school diploma or GED is required. *Academic units required/recommended:* 12 total required; 17 total recommended; 3 English required, 4 English recommended, 3 math required, 3 math recommended, 2 science required, 2 science recommended, 1 science lab recommended, 2 foreign language recommended, 2 social studies required, 3 social studies recommended, 3 elective required, 3 elective recommended. **Freshman Admission Statistics:** 1,862 applied, 98% accepted, 57% of those accepted enrolled. **Transfer Admission Requirements:** *Items required:* high school transcript, college transcript, essay, statement of good standing from prior school. Minimum college GPA of 2.5 required. Lowest grade transferable C. **General Admission Information:** Application fee $50. Regular application deadline August 15. Nonfall registration accepted. Admission may be deferred for a maximum of 1 year. Credit and/or placement offered for CEEB Advanced Placement tests.

COSTS AND FINANCIAL AID

Tuition $15,750. Room & board $5,485. Required fees $0. Average book expense $655. **Required Forms and Deadlines:** FAFSA and institution's own financial aid form. No deadline for regular filing. Priority filing deadline February 15. **Notification of Awards:** Applicants will be notified of awards on a rolling basis beginning on or about March 15. **Types of Aid:** *Need-based scholarships/grants:* Pell, SEOG, state scholarships/grants, private scholarships, the school's own gift aid. *Loans:* Direct Subsidized Stafford, Direct Unsubsidized Stafford, Direct PLUS, Federal Perkins, state loans, college/university loans from institutional funds, private alternative. **Student Employment:** Federal Work-Study Program available. Institutional employment available. Off-campus job opportunities are excellent. **Financial Aid Statistics:** 63% freshmen, 64% undergrads receive some form of aid. Average freshman grant $7,600. Average freshman loan $4,700. Average income from on-campus job $1,250. **Financial Aid Phone:** 616-957-6134.

CAMERON UNIVERSITY

2800 West Gore Boulevard, Lawton, OK 73505
Phone: 580-581-2230 **E-mail:** admiss@cua.cameron.edu **CEEB Code:** 6080
Fax: 580-581-5514 **Web:** www.cameron.edu **ACT Code:** 3386

This public school was founded in 1908. It has a 369-acre campus.

STUDENTS AND FACULTY

Enrollment: 4,822. **Student Body:** Male 42%, female 58%, out-of-state 5%, international 4% (34 countries represented). **Ethnic Representation:** African American 18%, Asian 3%, Caucasian 62%, Hispanic 8%, Native American 6%. **Retention and Graduation:** 43% freshmen return for sophomore year. 39% grads pursue business degrees. **Faculty:** Student/faculty ratio 12:1. 186 full-time faculty, 50% hold PhDs. 99% faculty teach undergrads.

ACADEMICS

Degrees: Associate's, bachelor's, master's. **Academic Requirements:** General education including some course work in computer literacy, English (including composition), history, humanities, mathematics, sciences (biological or physical), social science. **Classes:** 20-29 students in an average class. 10-19 students in an average lab/discussion section. **Majors with Highest Enrollment:** Business administration/management; elementary education and teaching; criminal justice/law enforcement administration. **Disciplines with Highest Percentage of Degrees Awarded:** Business/marketing 19%, social sciences and history 12%, protective services/public administration 10%, computer and information sciences 9%, education 8%. **Special Study Options:** Distance learning, double major, dual enrollment, honors program, internships, student-designed major. Undergrads may take grad classes. Evening and Saturday classes offered; extension study possible.

FACILITIES

Housing: All-female, all-male, quiet and wellness (nonsmoking) areas available. **Library Holdings:** 255,058 bound volumes. 1,897 periodicals. 496,172 microforms. 6,993 audiovisuals. **Special Academic Facilities/Equipment:** Satellite labs. **Computers:** School-owned computers available for student use.

EXTRACURRICULARS

Activities: Choral groups, concert band, dance, drama/theater, jazz band, literary magazine, music ensembles, musical theater, pep band, radio station, student government, student newspaper, symphony orchestra, television station, yearbook. **Organizations:** 57 registered organizations, 18 honor societies, 3 religious organizations, 2 fraternities (4% men join), 2 sororities (6% women join). **Athletics (Intercollegiate):** *Men:* baseball, basketball, golf, tennis. *Women:* basketball, softball, tennis, volleyball.

ADMISSIONS

Selectivity Rating: 64 (of 100). **Freshman Academic Profile:** 8% in top 10% of high school class, 29% in top 25% of high school class, 62% in top 50% of high school class. 96% from public high schools. Average ACT 20, ACT middle 50% range 17-22. TOEFL required of all international applicants, minimum TOEFL 500. **Basis for Candidate Selection:** *Important factors considered include:* class rank, secondary school record, standardized test scores, state residency. *Other factors considered include:* character/personal qualities, talent/ability. **Freshman Admission Requirements:** High school diploma or GED is required. *Academic units required/recommended:* 15 total required; 4 English required, 3 math required, 2 science required, 3 science recommended, 2 science lab required, 1 foreign language recommended, 2 social studies required, 2 history required, 2 elective required. **Freshman Admission Statistics:** 1,527 applied, 95% accepted, 64% of those accepted enrolled. **Transfer Admission Requirements:** *Items required:* college transcript. Minimum college GPA of 2.0 required. Lowest grade transferable D. **General Admission Information:** Application fee $15. Priority application deadline August 1. Nonfall registration accepted. Admission may be deferred for a maximum of 1 year. Credit and/or placement offered for CEEB Advanced Placement tests.

COSTS AND FINANCIAL AID

In-state tuition $2,370. Out-of-state tuition $5,700. Room & board $2,830. Required fees $120. Average book expense $1,000. **Required Forms and Deadlines:** FAFSA and institution's own financial aid form. Financial aid filing deadline June 15. **Notification of Awards:** Applicants will be notified of awards on a rolling basis beginning on or about July 1. **Types of Aid:** *Need-based scholarships/grants:* Pell, SEOG, state scholarships/grants, private scholarships, the school's own gift aid. *Loans:* FFEL Subsidized Stafford, FFEL Unsubsidized Stafford, FFEL PLUS. **Student Employment:** Federal Work-Study Program available. Institutional employment available. Off-campus job opportunities are good. **Financial Aid Statistics:** 47% freshmen, 47%

undergrads receive some form of aid. Average freshman grant $2,671. Average freshman loan $2,000. Average income from on-campus job $850. **Financial Aid Phone:** 580-581-2295.

CAMPBELL UNIVERSITY

PO Box 546, Buies Creek, NC 27506
Phone: 910-893-1320 **E-mail:** adm@mailcenter.campbell.edu **CEEB Code:** 5100
Fax: 910-893-1288 **Web:** www.campbell.edu **ACT Code:** 3076

This private school, which is affiliated with the Southern Baptist Church, was founded in 1887. It has an 850-acre campus.

STUDENTS AND FACULTY

Enrollment: 2,543. **Student Body:** Male 45%, female 55%, out-of-state 38%, international 3%. **Ethnic Representation:** African American 11%, Asian 1%, Caucasian 83%, Hispanic 2%, Native American 1%. **Retention and Graduation:** 87% freshmen return for sophomore year. 73% freshmen graduate within 4 years. 21% grads go on to further study within 1 year. 7% grads pursue business degrees. 4% grads pursue law degrees. **Faculty:** Student/faculty ratio 13:1. 202 full-time faculty, 75% hold PhDs. 100% faculty teach undergrads.

ACADEMICS

Degrees: Associate's, bachelor's, first professional, master's. **Academic Requirements:** General education including some course work in arts/fine arts, computer literacy, English (including composition), foreign languages, history, humanities, mathematics, sciences (biological or physical), social science. **Classes:** Under 10 students in an average class. **Majors with Highest Enrollment:** Pre-pharmacy studies; business administration/management; pre-law studies. **Disciplines with Highest Percentage of Degrees Awarded:** Business/marketing 41%, psychology 13%, social sciences and history 12%, health professions and related sciences 8%, communications/communication technologies 5%. **Special Study Options:** Accelerated program, cooperative (work-study) program, distance learning, double major, student exchange program (domestic), honors program, independent study, internships, liberal arts/career combination, study abroad, teacher certification program.

FACILITIES

Housing: All-female, all-male, apartments for married students, apartments for single students, housing for disabled students, graduate student apartments. All off-campus housing must be approved by the Residence Life Office. **Library Holdings:** 208,000 bound volumes. 9,211 periodicals. 858,520 microforms. 4,064 audiovisuals. **Special Academic Facilities/Equipment:** Taylor Bott-Rogers Fine Arts Building, Lundy-Fetterman School of Business museum and Exhibit Hall, School of Pharmacy Clinical Research Facility. **Computers:** School-owned computers available for student use.

EXTRACURRICULARS

Activities: Choral groups, concert band, drama/theater, jazz band, literary magazine, music ensembles, musical theater, pep band, radio station, student government, student newspaper, television station, yearbook. **Organizations:** 73 registered organizations, 14 honor societies, 20 religious organizations. **Athletics (Intercollegiate):** *Men:* baseball, basketball, cross-country, golf, soccer, tennis, track & field, wrestling. *Women:* basketball, cheerleading, cross-country, golf, soccer, softball, tennis, track & field, volleyball.

ADMISSIONS

Selectivity Rating: 74 (of 100). **Freshman Academic Profile:** Average high school GPA 3.0. 40% in top 10% of high school class, 52% in top 25% of high school class, 72% in top 50% of high school class. 90% from public high schools. Average SAT I Math 514. Average SAT I Verbal 546. TOEFL required of all international applicants, minimum TOEFL 500. **Basis for Candidate Selection:** *Very important factors considered include:* secondary school record, standardized test scores. *Important factors considered include:* character/personal qualities, class rank, interview. *Other factors considered include:* alumni/ae relation, essays, extracurricular activities, recommendations, talent/ability, volunteer work, work experience. **Freshman Admission Requirements:** High school diploma or GED is required. *Academic units required/recommended:* 4 English required, 3 math required, 2 science required, 1 science lab required, 2 foreign language required. **Freshman Admission Statistics:** 2,884 applied, 74% accepted, 39% of those accepted enrolled. **Transfer Admission Requirements:** *Items required:* high school transcript, college transcript, standardized test scores, statement of good standing from prior school. Minimum college GPA of 2.0 required. Lowest grade transferable C. **General Admission Information:** Application fee $25. Regular application deadline August 26. Nonfall registration accepted. Admission may be deferred for a maximum of 1 year. Credit and/or placement offered for CEEB Advanced Placement tests.

COSTS AND FINANCIAL AID

Tuition $13,270. Room & board $4,750. Required fees $281. Average book expense $850. **Required Forms and Deadlines:** FAFSA. No deadline for regular filing. Priority filing deadline March 15. **Notification of Awards:** Applicants will be notified of awards on a rolling basis beginning on or about April 15. **Types of Aid:** *Need-based scholarships/grants:* Pell, SEOG, state scholarships/grants, private scholarships, the school's own gift aid. *Loans:* FFEL Subsidized Stafford, FFEL Unsubsidized Stafford, FFEL PLUS, Federal Perkins, state loans, college/university loans from institutional funds. **Student Employment:** Federal Work-Study Program available. Institutional employment available. Off-campus job opportunities are good. **Financial Aid Statistics:** 76% freshmen, 59% undergrads receive some form of aid. Average freshman grant $10,403. Average freshman loan $3,094. Average income from on-campus job $600. **Financial Aid Phone:** 910-893-1310.

CAMPBELLSVILLE UNIVERSITY

1 University Drive, Campbellsville, KY 42718-2799
Phone: 270-789-5220 **E-mail:** admissions@campbellsville.edu **CEEB Code:** 1097
Fax: 270-789-5071 **Web:** www.campbellsville.edu **ACT Code:** 1500

This private school, which is affiliated with the Baptist Church, was founded in 1906. It has a 70-acre campus.

STUDENTS AND FACULTY

Enrollment: 1,655. **Student Body:** Male 43%, female 57%, out-of-state 8%, international 3%. **Ethnic Representation:** African American 6%, Caucasian 93%, Hispanic 1%. **Retention and Graduation:** 64% freshmen return for sophomore year. 22% freshmen graduate within 4 years. 20% grads go on to further study within 1 year. 15% grads pursue business degrees. 1% grads pursue law degrees. 1% grads pursue medical degrees. **Faculty:** Student/faculty ratio 17:1. 70 full-time faculty, 60% hold PhDs. 100% faculty teach undergrads.

ACADEMICS

Degrees: Associate's, bachelor's, master's. **Academic Requirements:** General education including some course work in arts/fine arts, computer literacy, English (including composition), foreign languages, history, humanities, mathematics, philosophy, sciences (biological or physical), social science. **Classes:** Under 10 students in an average class. **Majors with Highest Enrollment:** Business, management, marketing, and related support services; junior high/intermediate/middle school education and teaching; biology/biological sciences, general. **Disciplines with Highest Percentage of Degrees Awarded:** Business/marketing 31%, education 19%, social sciences and history 9%, philosophy/religion/theology 8%, communications/communication technologies 6%. **Special Study Options:** Cooperative (work-study) program, distance learning, double major, dual enrollment, English as a second language, honors program, independent study, internships, liberal arts/career combination, study abroad, teacher certification program.

FACILITIES

Housing: All-female, all-male, apartments for married students. **Library Holdings:** 162,492 bound volumes. 512 periodicals. 25,070 microforms. 15,993 audiovisuals. **Special Academic Facilities/Equipment:** Computer labs and technology lab. **Computers:** School-owned computers available for student use.

EXTRACURRICULARS

Activities: Choral groups, concert band, dance, drama/theater, jazz band, literary magazine, marching band, music ensembles, pep band, radio station, student government, student newspaper, television station, yearbook. **Organizations:** 49 registered organizations, 1 honor society, 7 religious organizations. **Athletics (Intercollegiate):** *Men:* baseball, basketball, cheerleading, cross-country, football, golf, soccer, tennis. *Women:* basketball, cheerleading, cross-country, golf, soccer, softball, tennis, volleyball.

ADMISSIONS

Selectivity Rating: 74 (of 100). **Freshman Academic Profile:** Average high school GPA 3.2. 22% in top 10% of high school class, 45% in top 25% of high school class, 71% in top 50% of high school class. 90% from public high schools. SAT I Math middle 50% range 440-500. SAT I Verbal middle 50% range 460-520. Average ACT 20, ACT middle 50% range 18-24. TOEFL required of all international applicants, minimum TOEFL 500. **Basis for Candidate Selection:** *Very important factors considered include:* secondary school record. *Important factors considered include:* character/personal qualities, class rank, interview, recommendations, standardized test scores. *Other factors considered include:* alumni/ae relation, essays, extracurricular activities, religious affiliation/

commitment, talent/ability, volunteer work, work experience. **Freshman Admission Requirements:** High school diploma or GED is required. *Academic units required/recommended:* 21 total recommended; 4 English recommended, 3 math recommended, 3 science recommended, 1 science lab recommended, 2 social studies recommended, 1 history recommended, 6 elective recommended. **Freshman Admission Statistics:** 973 applied, 78% accepted, 40% of those accepted enrolled. **Transfer Admission Requirements:** *Items required:* college transcript. Lowest grade transferable C. **General Admission Information:** Application fee $20. Priority application deadline April 15. Regular application deadline August 15. Nonfall registration accepted. Admission may be deferred for a maximum of 1 year. Credit and/or placement offered for CEEB Advanced Placement tests.

COSTS AND FINANCIAL AID

Tuition $11,160. Room & board $4,740. Required fees $180. Average book expense $800. **Required Forms and Deadlines:** FAFSA. No deadline for regular filing. **Notification of Awards:** Applicants will be notified of awards on a rolling basis beginning on or about February 15. **Types of Aid:** *Need-based scholarships/grants:* Pell, SEOG, state scholarships/grants, private scholarships, the school's own gift aid. *Loans:* FFEL Subsidized Stafford, FFEL Unsubsidized Stafford, FFEL PLUS, Federal Perkins, college/university loans from institutional funds. **Student Employment:** Federal Work-Study Program available. Institutional employment available. Off-campus job opportunities are good. **Financial Aid Statistics:** 75% freshmen, 76% undergrads receive some form of aid. Average freshman grant $7,019. Average freshman loan $2,500. Average income from on-campus job $1,500. **Financial Aid Phone:** 270-789-5013.

CANISIUS COLLEGE

2001 Main Street, Buffalo, NY 14208
Phone: 716-888-2200 **E-mail:** inquiry@canisius.edu **CEEB Code:** 2073
Fax: 716-888-3230 **Web:** www.canisius.edu **ACT Code:** 2690

This private school, which is affiliated with the Roman Catholic Church, was founded in 1870. It has a 32-acre campus.

STUDENTS AND FACULTY

Enrollment: 3,440. **Student Body:** Male 47%, female 53%, out-of-state 7%, international 3% (35 countries represented). **Ethnic Representation:** African American 7%, Asian 1%, Caucasian 82%, Hispanic 3%. **Retention and Graduation:** 82% freshmen return for sophomore year. 53% freshmen graduate within 4 years. 25% grads go on to further study within 1 year. 4% grads pursue business degrees. 5% grads pursue law degrees. 6% grads pursue medical degrees. **Faculty:** Student/faculty ratio 16:1. 209 full-time faculty, 94% hold PhDs. 98% faculty teach undergrads.

ACADEMICS

Degrees: Associate's, bachelor's, master's. **Academic Requirements:** General education including some course work in arts/fine arts, English (including composition), foreign languages, history, humanities, mathematics, philosophy, sciences (biological or physical), social science, religious studies requirement—9 credit hours. **Classes:** 20-29 students in an average class. 20-29 students in an average lab/discussion section. **Majors with Highest Enrollment:** Management science, general; biology/biological sciences, general; psychology, general. **Disciplines with Highest Percentage of Degrees Awarded:** Education 23%, social sciences and history 17%, psychology 13%, biological life sciences 11%, business/marketing 10%. **Special Study Options:** Cooperative (work-study) program, cross registration, double major, dual enrollment, English as a second language, honors program, independent study, internships, study abroad, teacher certification program, 4 + 1 BS/MBA or BS/DD.

FACILITIES

Housing: Coed, apartments for single students, housing for international students, honors student housing. All college-owned housing is handicapped accessible. **Library Holdings:** 328,278 bound volumes. 1,637 periodicals. 570,475 microforms. 7,710 audiovisuals. **Special Academic Facilities/Equipment:** TV studio, electron microscope, seismograph, language lab, digital lab, human performance lab, molecular biology and physics labs, mini-planetarium. **Computers:** School-owned computers available for student use.

EXTRACURRICULARS

Activities: Choral groups, concert band, dance, drama/theater, jazz band, literary magazine, music ensembles, musical theater, pep band, radio station, student government, student newspaper, television station, yearbook. **Organizations:** 102 registered organizations, 15 honor societies, 2 religious organizations, 1 fraternity (3% men join), 1 sorority (2% women join). **Athletics (Intercollegiate):** *Men:* baseball, basketball, cross-country, football, golf, ice hockey, indoor track, lacrosse, rifle, soccer, tennis, track & field. *Women:* basketball, cross-country, diving, indoor track, lacrosse, rifle, soccer, softball, swimming, tennis, track & field, volleyball.

ADMISSIONS

Selectivity Rating: 72 (of 100). **Freshman Academic Profile:** Average high school GPA 3.5. 24% in top 10% of high school class, 51% in top 25% of high school class, 84% in top 50% of high school class. 71% from public high schools. Average SAT I Math 555, SAT I Math middle 50% range 500-610. Average SAT I Verbal 542, SAT I Verbal middle 50% range 480-590. Average ACT 24, ACT middle 50% range 20-27. TOEFL required of all international applicants, minimum TOEFL 500. **Basis for Candidate Selection:** *Very important factors considered include:* class rank, secondary school record, standardized test scores. *Important factors considered include:* essays, interview, recommendations. *Other factors considered include:* alumni/ae relation, character/personal qualities, extracurricular activities, geographical residence, state residency, talent/ability, volunteer work, work experience. **Freshman Admission Requirements:** High school diploma or GED is required. *Academic units required/recommended:* 16 total required; 4 English required, 3 math required, 1 science required, 2 foreign language required, 2 social studies required, 4 elective required. **Freshman Admission Statistics:** 3,614 applied, 80% accepted, 29% of those accepted enrolled. **Transfer Admission Requirements:** *Items required:* high school transcript, college transcript. Minimum college GPA of 2.0 required. Lowest grade transferable C. **General Admission Information:** Application fee $25. Priority application deadline May 1. Regular application deadline August 15. Nonfall registration accepted. Admission may be deferred. Credit and/or placement offered for CEEB Advanced Placement tests.

COSTS AND FINANCIAL AID

Tuition $18,264. Room & board $7,540. Required fees $576. Average book expense $500. **Required Forms and Deadlines:** FAFSA, institution's own financial aid form, and state aid form. No deadline for regular filing. Priority filing deadline February 15. **Notification of Awards:** Applicants will be notified of awards on a rolling basis beginning on or about March 15. **Types of Aid:** *Need-based scholarships/grants:* Pell, SEOG, state scholarships/grants, private scholarships, the school's own gift aid. *Loans:* FFEL Subsidized Stafford, FFEL Unsubsidized Stafford, FFEL PLUS, Federal Perkins, college/university loans from institutional funds. **Student Employment:** Federal Work-Study Program available. Institutional employment available. Off-campus job opportunities are excellent. **Financial Aid Statistics:** 80% freshmen, 71% undergrads receive some form of aid. Average freshman grant $12,530. Average freshman loan $2,965. Average income from on-campus job $1,364. **Financial Aid Phone:** 716-888-2300.

CAPITAL UNIVERSITY

2199 East Main Street, Columbus, OH 43209
Phone: 614-236-6101 **E-mail:** admissions@capital.edu **CEEB Code:** 1099
Fax: 614-236-6926 **Web:** www.capital.edu **ACT Code:** 3242

This private school, which is affiliated with the Lutheran Church, was founded in 1830. It has a 48-acre campus.

STUDENTS AND FACULTY

Enrollment: 2,798. **Student Body:** Male 37%, female 63%, out-of-state 8%. **Ethnic Representation:** African American 18%, Asian 1%, Caucasian 77%, Hispanic 1%. **Retention and Graduation:** 79% freshmen return for sophomore year. 54% freshmen graduate within 4 years. 21% grads go on to further study within 1 year. 2% grads pursue business degrees. 5% grads pursue law degrees. 2% grads pursue medical degrees. **Faculty:** Student/faculty ratio 11:1. 182 full-time faculty, 70% hold PhDs. 100% faculty teach undergrads.

ACADEMICS

Degrees: Bachelor's, first professional, master's. **Academic Requirements:** General education including some course work in arts/fine arts, English (including composition), history, humanities, mathematics, sciences (biological or physical), social science, speech, cultural diversity, lifetime health, religion. **Classes:** 10-19 students in an average class. **Disciplines with Highest Percentage of Degrees Awarded:** Business/marketing 16%, social sciences and history 14%, interdisciplinary studies 14%, education 13%, protective services/public administration 10%. **Special Study Options:** Cross registration, double major, English as a second language, honors program, independent study, internships, student-designed major, study abroad, teacher certification program.

FACILITIES

Housing: Coed, apartments for single students. **Library Holdings:** 183,462 bound volumes. 8,528 periodicals. 144,880 microforms. 14,869 audiovisuals. **Special Academic Facilities/Equipment:** Art gallery, conservatory of music. **Computers:** School-owned computers available for student use.

EXTRACURRICULARS

Activities: Choral groups, concert band, dance, drama/theater, jazz band, literary magazine, music ensembles, musical theater, opera, pep band, radio station, student government, student newspaper, student-run film society, symphony orchestra, television station, yearbook. **Organizations:** 60 registered organizations, 16 honor societies, 5 religious organizations, 5 fraternities (15% men join), 5 sororities (20% women join). **Athletics (Intercollegiate):** *Men:* baseball, basketball, cheerleading, cross-country, football, golf, indoor track, soccer, tennis, wrestling. *Women:* basketball, cheerleading, cross-country, golf, indoor track, soccer, softball, tennis, volleyball.

ADMISSIONS

Selectivity Rating: 74 (of 100). **Freshman Academic Profile:** Average high school GPA 3.4. 24% in top 10% of high school class, 67% in top 25% of high school class, 88% in top 50% of high school class. 92% from public high schools. Average SAT I Math 536, SAT I Math middle 50% range 480-590. Average SAT I Verbal 541, SAT I Verbal middle 50% range 480-590. Average ACT 23, ACT middle 50% range 20-25. TOEFL required of all international applicants, minimum TOEFL 500. **Basis for Candidate Selection:** *Very important factors considered include:* extracurricular activities, secondary school record, standardized test scores. *Important factors considered include:* alumni/ae relation, character/personal qualities, class rank, minority status, recommendations, religious affiliation/commitment, talent/ability. *Other factors considered include:* geographical residence, interview, volunteer work, work experience. **Freshman Admission Requirements:** High school diploma or GED is required. *Academic units required/recommended:* 16 total required; 4 English required, 3 math required, 3 science required, 2 science lab required, 2 foreign language required, 2 social studies required, 1 history required. **Freshman Admission Statistics:** 2,221 applied, 81% accepted, 29% of those accepted enrolled. **Transfer Admission Requirements:** *Items required:* high school transcript, college transcript, statement of good standing from prior school. Minimum college GPA of 2.3 required. Lowest grade transferable C-. **General Admission Information:** Application fee $25. Priority application deadline April 1. Regular application deadline April 15. Nonfall registration accepted. Admission may be deferred for a maximum of 1 year. Credit and/or placement offered for CEEB Advanced Placement tests.

COSTS AND FINANCIAL AID

Tuition $18,990. Room & board $5,940. Required fees $0. Average book expense $910. **Required Forms and Deadlines:** FAFSA. No deadline for regular filing. Priority filing deadline February 28. **Notification of Awards:** Applicants will be notified of awards on a rolling basis beginning on or about March 15. **Types of Aid:** *Need-based scholarships/grants:* Pell, SEOG, state scholarships/grants, private scholarships, the school's own gift aid. *Loans:* FFEL Subsidized Stafford, FFEL Unsubsidized Stafford, FFEL PLUS, Federal Perkins, Federal Nursing, college/university loans from institutional funds. **Student Employment:** Federal Work-Study Program available. Institutional employment available. Off-campus job opportunities are excellent. **Financial Aid Statistics:** 92% freshmen, 79% undergrads receive some form of aid. Average freshman grant $7,850. Average freshman loan $2,500. Average income from on-campus job $841. **Financial Aid Phone:** 614-236-6511.

CAPITOL COLLEGE

11301 Springfield Road, Laurel, MD 20708
Phone: 800-950-1992 **E-mail:** admissions@capitol-college.edu **CEEB Code:** 5101
Fax: 301-953-1442 **Web:** www.capitol-college.edu

This private school was founded in 1964. It has a 52-acre campus.

STUDENTS AND FACULTY

Enrollment: 876. **Student Body:** Male 79%, female 21%, out-of-state 14%, international 2%. **Ethnic Representation:** African American 37%, Asian 7%, Caucasian 50%, Hispanic 3%. **Retention and Graduation:** 60% freshmen return for sophomore year. 5% freshmen graduate within 4 years. 10% grads go on to further study within 1 year. **Faculty:** Student/faculty ratio 12:1. 21 full-time faculty, 33% hold PhDs. 100% faculty teach undergrads.

ACADEMICS

Degrees: Associate's, bachelor's, certificate, master's, post-bachelor's certificate, transfer. **Academic Requirements:** General education including some course work in arts/fine arts, computer literacy, English (including composition), history, humanities, mathematics, sciences (biological or physical), social science. **Classes:** 10-19 students in an average class. Under 10 students in an average lab/discussion section. **Majors with Highest Enrollment:** Aerospace, aeronautical, and astronautical engineering; computer engineering, general; electrical, electronics, and communications engineering. **Disciplines with Highest Percentage of Degrees Awarded:** Engineering/engineering technology 69%, computer and information sciences 31%. **Special Study Options:** Cooperative (work-study) program, distance learning, double major, independent study, internships, weekend college.

FACILITIES

Housing: All-female, all-male, apartments for single students. **Library Holdings:** 9,260 bound volumes. 87 periodicals. 0 microforms. 118 audiovisuals. **Computers:** School-owned computers available for student use.

EXTRACURRICULARS

Activities: Dance, drama/theater, literary magazine, radio station, student government, student newspaper. **Organizations:** 10 registered organizations, 3 honor societies.

ADMISSIONS

Selectivity Rating: 66 (of 100). **Freshman Academic Profile:** Average high school GPA 2.9. 85% from public high schools. Average SAT I Math 470, SAT I Math middle 50% range 350-590. Average SAT I Verbal 460, SAT I Verbal middle 50% range 400-520. TOEFL required of all international applicants, minimum TOEFL 500. **Basis for Candidate Selection:** *Very important factors considered include:* secondary school record. *Important factors considered include:* essays, standardized test scores. *Other factors considered include:* alumni/ae relation, character/personal qualities, extracurricular activities, interview, recommendations, talent/ability, volunteer work, work experience. **Freshman Admission Requirements:** High school diploma or GED is required. *Academic units required/recommended:* 4 English required, 4 English recommended, 3 math required, 4 math recommended, 3 science required, 4 science recommended, 2 science lab required, 2 science lab recommended, 2 social studies recommended, 2 history recommended. **Freshman Admission Statistics:** 190 applied, 86% accepted, 21% of those accepted enrolled. **Transfer Admission Requirements:** *Items required:* college transcript, essay. Minimum college GPA of 2.0 required. Lowest grade transferable C. **General Admission Information:** Application fee $25. Priority application deadline March 1. Nonfall registration accepted. Admission may be deferred for a maximum of 1 year. Credit and/or placement offered for CEEB Advanced Placement tests.

COSTS AND FINANCIAL AID

Tuition $16,500. Room & board $3,710. Required fees $600. Average book expense $800. **Required Forms and Deadlines:** FAFSA and institution's own financial aid form. No deadline for regular filing. Priority filing deadline February 1. **Notification of Awards:** Applicants will be notified of awards on a rolling basis beginning on or about June 30. **Types of Aid:** *Need-based scholarships/grants:* Pell, SEOG, state scholarships/grants, private scholarships, the school's own gift aid. *Loans:* FFEL Subsidized Stafford, FFEL Unsubsidized Stafford, FFEL PLUS, Federal Perkins. **Student Employment:** Federal Work-Study Program available. Institutional employment available. Off-campus job opportunities are excellent. **Financial Aid Statistics:** 22% freshmen, 43% undergrads receive some form of aid. Average income from on-campus job $2,000. **Financial Aid Phone:** 301-369-2800.

CARDINAL STRITCH COLLEGE

6801 N. Yates Rd., Box 237, Milwaukee, WI 53217-3985
Phone: 414-410-4040 **E-mail:** admityou@stritch.edu **CEEB Code:** 1100
Fax: 414-410-4058 **Web:** www.stritch.edu **ACT Code:** 6755

This private school, which is affiliated with the Roman Catholic Church, was founded in 1937. It has a 40-acre campus.

STUDENTS AND FACULTY

Enrollment: 3,123. **Student Body:** Male 31%, female 69%, out-of-state 11%, international 1%. **Ethnic Representation:** African American 17%, Asian 2%, Caucasian 74%, Hispanic 3%. **Retention and Graduation:** 73% freshmen return for sophomore year. 19% freshmen graduate within 4 years. **Faculty:** Student/faculty ratio 18:1. 98 full-time faculty, 54% hold PhDs.

ACADEMICS

Degrees: Associate's, bachelor's, certificate, doctoral, master's, post-bachelor's certificate, terminal, transfer. **Academic Requirements:** General education including some course work in arts/fine arts, English (including composition), foreign languages, history, humanities, mathematics, philosophy, sciences (biological or physical), social science, religious studies. **Classes:** 10-19 students in an average class. 10-19 students in an average lab/discussion section. **Majors with Highest Enrollment:** Business administration/management; management information systems, general; education, general. **Disciplines with Highest Percentage of Degrees Awarded:** Business/marketing 80%, education 6%, visual and performing arts 3%, health professions and related sciences 3%, communications/communication technologies 2%. **Special Study Options:** Accelerated program, cooperative (work-study) program, distance learning, double major, dual enrollment, English as a second language, external degree program, honors program, independent study, internships, student-designed major, study abroad, teacher certification program, remedial/tutoring services, academic/career counseling center, employment/placement services.

FACILITIES

Housing: Coed. **Library Holdings:** 99,904 bound volumes. 688 periodicals. 173,216 microforms. 6,310 audiovisuals. **Special Academic Facilities/ Equipment:** Reading and learning center, children's center, art gallery. **Computers:** School-owned computers available for student use.

EXTRACURRICULARS

Activities: Choral groups, concert band, dance, drama/theater, jazz band, literary magazine, music ensembles, musical theater, pep band, radio station, student government, student newspaper, yearbook. **Organizations:** 6 honor societies, 1 religious organization. **Athletics (Intercollegiate):** *Men:* baseball, basketball, cross-country, soccer, volleyball. *Women:* basketball, cross-country, soccer, softball, volleyball.

ADMISSIONS

Selectivity Rating: 72 (of 100). **Freshman Academic Profile:** Average high school GPA 3.0. 14% in top 10% of high school class, 37% in top 25% of high school class, 66% in top 50% of high school class. Average ACT 22, ACT middle 50% range 19-24. TOEFL required of all international applicants, minimum TOEFL 550. **Basis for Candidate Selection:** *Very important factors considered include:* secondary school record, standardized test scores. *Important factors considered include:* character/personal qualities, essays, recommendations, talent/ability. *Other factors considered include:* class rank, extracurricular activities, interview, minority status, volunteer work, work experience. **Freshman Admission Requirements:** High school diploma or GED is required. *Academic units required/recommended:* 16 total required; 4 English required, 2 math required, 3 math recommended, 2 science required, 3 science recommended, 2 foreign language required, 1 social studies required, 1 history required, 4 elective required. **Freshman Admission Statistics:** 387 applied, 71% accepted, 50% of those accepted enrolled. **Transfer Admission Requirements:** *Items required:* college transcript. Minimum college GPA of 2.0 required. Lowest grade transferable C-. **General Admission Information:** Application fee $25. Priority application deadline April 1. Nonfall registration accepted. Admission may be deferred for a maximum of 1 year. Credit and/or placement offered for CEEB Advanced Placement tests.

COSTS AND FINANCIAL AID

Tuition $12,480. Room & board $4,840. Required fees $300. Average book expense $500. **Required Forms and Deadlines:** FAFSA and institution's own financial aid form. No deadline for regular filing. Priority filing deadline April 1. **Notification of Awards:** Applicants will be notified of awards on a rolling basis beginning on or about April 1. **Types of Aid:** *Need-based scholarships/grants:* Pell, SEOG, state scholarships/grants, private scholarships, the school's own gift aid. *Loans:* FFEL Subsidized Stafford, FFEL Unsubsidized Stafford, FFEL PLUS, Federal Perkins, state loans. **Student Employment:** Federal Work-Study Program available. Institutional employment available. Off-campus job opportunities are excellent. **Financial Aid Statistics:** 46% freshmen, 72% undergrads receive some form of aid. **Financial Aid Phone:** 414-410-4048.

CARLETON COLLEGE

100 South College Street, Northfield, MN 55057
Phone: 507-646-4190 **E-mail:** admissions@acs.carleton.edu **CEEB Code:** 6081
Fax: 507-646-4526 **Web:** www.carleton.edu **ACT Code:** 2092

This private school was founded in 1866. It has a 955-acre campus.

STUDENTS AND FACULTY

Enrollment: 1,932. **Student Body:** Male 48%, female 52%, out-of-state 77%, international 3%. **Ethnic Representation:** African American 4%, Asian 9%, Caucasian 82%, Hispanic 4%. **Retention and Graduation:** 96% freshmen return for sophomore year. 82% freshmen graduate within 4 years. 16% grads go on to further study within 1 year. 2% grads pursue law degrees. 1% grads pursue medical degrees. **Faculty:** Student/faculty ratio 9:1. 195 full-time faculty, 91% hold PhDs. 100% faculty teach undergrads.

ACADEMICS

Degrees: Bachelor's. **Academic Requirements:** General education including some course work in arts/fine arts, English (including composition), foreign languages, humanities, mathematics, sciences (biological or physical), social science, recognition and affirmation of difference requirement. **Classes:** 10-19 students in an average class. 10-19 students in an average lab/discussion section. **Majors with Highest Enrollment:** Political science and government, general; biology/biological sciences, general; social sciences, general. **Disciplines with Highest Percentage of Degrees Awarded:** Social sciences and history 26%, biological life sciences 13%, visual and performing arts 13%, physical sciences 12%, psychology 7%. **Special Study Options:** Accelerated program, cross registration, double major, dual enrollment, independent study, internships, student-designed major, study abroad, teacher certification program.

FACILITIES

Housing: Coed, apartments for single students, housing for disabled students, special-interest houses. **Library Holdings:** 662,871 bound volumes. 1,626 periodicals. 127,753 microforms. 778 audiovisuals. **Special Academic Facilities/Equipment:** Arboretum, greenhouse, observatory, scanning and transmission electron microscopes, refractor and reflector telescopes, nuclear magnetic resonance spectrometer, art gallery. **Computers:** School-owned computers available for student use.

EXTRACURRICULARS

Activities: Choral groups, concert band, dance, drama/theater, jazz band, literary magazine, music ensembles, musical theater, radio station, student government, student newspaper, student-run film society, symphony orchestra, yearbook. **Organizations:** 134 registered organizations, 3 honor societies, 9 religious organizations. **Athletics (Intercollegiate):** *Men:* baseball, basketball, cross-country, diving, football, golf, ice hockey, soccer, swimming, tennis, track & field. *Women:* basketball, cross-country, diving, golf, ice hockey, soccer, softball, swimming, tennis, track & field, volleyball.

ADMISSIONS

Selectivity Rating: 97 (of 100). **Freshman Academic Profile:** 70% in top 10% of high school class, 93% in top 25% of high school class, 99% in top 50% of high school class. 74% from public high schools. SAT I Math middle 50% range 640-720. SAT I Verbal middle 50% range 640-740. ACT middle 50% range 27-31. TOEFL required of all international applicants, minimum TOEFL 600. **Basis for Candidate Selection:** *Very important factors considered include:* secondary school record. *Important factors considered include:* character/personal qualities, class rank, essays, extracurricular activities, minority status, recommendations, standardized test scores, talent/ability, volunteer work, work experience. *Other factors considered include:* alumni/ae relation, geographical residence, interview, state residency. **Freshman Admission Requirements:** High school diploma or GED is required. *Academic units required/recommended:* 4 English recommended, 3 math recommended, 3 science recommended, 1 science lab recommended, 3 foreign language recommended. **Freshman Admission Statistics:** 4,170 applied, 35% accepted, 35% of those accepted enrolled. **Transfer Admission Requirements:** *Items required:* high school transcript, college transcript, essay, standardized test scores, statement of good standing from prior school. Minimum college GPA of 2.0 required. Lowest grade transferable C-. **General Admission Information:** Application fee $30. Early decision application deadline November 15. Regular application deadline January 15. Admission may be deferred for a maximum of 1 year. Credit and/or placement offered for CEEB Advanced Placement tests.

COSTS AND FINANCIAL AID

Tuition $26,745. Room & board $5,535. Required fees $165. Average book expense $1,200. **Required Forms and Deadlines:** FAFSA, CSS/Financial Aid PROFILE, noncustodial (divorced/separated) parent's statement and business/farm supplement. Financial aid filing deadline February 15. Priority filing deadline February 15. **Notification of Awards:** Applicants will be notified of awards on or about April 15. **Types of Aid:** *Need-based scholarships/grants:* Pell, SEOG, state scholarships/grants, private scholarships, the school's own gift aid. *Loans:* FFEL Subsidized Stafford, FFEL Unsubsidized Stafford, FFEL PLUS, Federal Perkins, state loans, college/university loans from institutional funds, Minnesota SELF Loan program. **Student Employment:** Federal Work-Study Program available. Institutional employment available. Off-campus job opportunities are good. **Financial Aid Statistics:** 55% freshmen, 54% undergrads receive some form of aid. Average freshman grant $17,184. Average freshman loan $2,781. Average income from on-campus job $0. **Financial Aid Phone:** 507-646-4138.

CARLOW COLLEGE

3333 Fifth Avenue, Pittsburgh, PA 15213-3165
Phone: 412-578-6059 **E-mail:** admissions@carlow.edu **CEEB Code:** 2421
Fax: 412-578-6668 **Web:** www.carlow.edu **ACT Code:** 3638

This private school, which is affiliated with the Roman Catholic Church, was founded in 1929. It has a 15-acre campus.

STUDENTS AND FACULTY

Enrollment: 1,745. **Student Body:** Male 5%, female 95%, out-of-state 4%, (24 countries represented). **Ethnic Representation:** African American 22%, Asian 1%, Caucasian 70%, Hispanic 1%. **Retention and Graduation:** 65% freshmen return for sophomore year. 43% freshmen graduate within 4 years. 18% grads go on to further study within 1 year. 2% grads pursue business degrees. 1% grads pursue law degrees. 4% grads pursue medical degrees. **Faculty:** Student/faculty ratio 14:1. 69 full-time faculty, 76% hold PhDs. 90% faculty teach undergrads.

ACADEMICS

Degrees: Bachelor's, master's, post-master's certificate. **Academic Requirements:** General education including some course work in arts/fine arts, English (including composition), history, humanities, mathematics, philosophy, sciences (biological or physical), social science. **Classes:** Under 10 students in an average class. Under 10 students in an average lab/discussion section. **Majors with Highest Enrollment:** Nursing; business administration/management; elementary education and teaching. **Disciplines with Highest Percentage of Degrees Awarded:** Health professions and related sciences 27%, education 23%, business/marketing 13%, communications/communication technologies 8%, computer and information sciences 6%. **Special Study Options:** Accelerated program, cooperative (work-study) program, cross registration, distance learning, double major, English as a second language, honors program, independent study, internships, liberal arts/career combination, student-designed major, study abroad, teacher certification program, weekend college. 3/2 programs with Carnegie Mellon for chemical engineering, environmental engineering, mechanical engineering. Other programs with Duquesne University in athletic training (2/2), environmental science and management (3/2), occupational therapy (2/3), physical therapy (3/3), and physician assistant (2/3).

FACILITIES

Housing: All-female. **Library Holdings:** 81,532 bound volumes. 382 periodicals. 11,556 microforms. 4,631 audiovisuals. **Special Academic Facilities/Equipment:** The A.J. Palumbo Hall of Science and Technology features research labs as well as a greenhouse, darkroom, biochamber, on-site reference library, and specially designed study and work zones on every floor to encourage team research. The building incorporates more than 1,000 outlets for Internet access. Also, on-campus preschool and elementary school, media center, and the Bayer Children's Science Learning Lab. **Computers:** School-owned computers available for student use.

EXTRACURRICULARS

Activities: Choral groups, drama/theater, literary magazine, student government, student newspaper, yearbook. **Organizations:** 28 registered organizations, 5 honor societies, 1 religious organization. **Athletics (Intercollegiate):** *Women:* basketball, soccer, softball, tennis, volleyball.

ADMISSIONS

Selectivity Rating: 69 (of 100). **Freshman Academic Profile:** Average high school GPA 3.2. 12% in top 10% of high school class, 32% in top 25% of high school class, 72% in top 50% of high school class. 84% from public high schools. Average SAT I Math 489, SAT I Math middle 50% range 430-550. Average SAT I Verbal 511, SAT I Verbal middle 50% range 450-570. Average ACT 21, ACT middle 50% range 18-24. TOEFL required of all international applicants, minimum TOEFL 500. **Basis for Candidate Selection:** *Very important factors considered include:* secondary school record. *Important factors considered include:* character/personal qualities, class rank, interview, standardized test scores. *Other factors considered include:* alumni/ae relation, essays, extracurricular activities, minority status, recommendations, talent/ability, volunteer work, work experience. **Freshman Admission Requirements:** High school diploma or GED is required. *Academic units required/recommended:* 18 total required; 4 English required, 3 math required, 3 science required, 4 elective required. **Freshman Admission Statistics:** 1,356 applied, 68% accepted, 27% of those accepted enrolled. **Transfer Admission Requirements:** *Items required:* college transcript. Minimum college GPA of 2.0 required. Lowest grade transferable C. **General Admission Information:** Application fee $20. Nonfall registration accepted. Admission may be deferred. Credit and/or placement offered for CEEB Advanced Placement tests.

COSTS AND FINANCIAL AID

Tuition $14,006. Room & board $5,710. Required fees $424. Average book expense $700. **Required Forms and Deadlines:** FAFSA. Priority filing deadline April 1. **Notification of Awards:** Applicants will be notified of awards on a rolling basis beginning on or about February 15. **Types of Aid:** *Need-based scholarships/grants:* Pell, SEOG, state scholarships/grants, private scholarships, the school's own gift aid. *Loans:* FFEL Subsidized Stafford, FFEL Unsubsidized Stafford, FFEL PLUS, Federal Perkins, Federal Nursing. **Student Employment:** Federal Work-Study Program available. Institutional employment available. Off-campus job opportunities are excellent. **Financial Aid Statistics:** 99% freshmen, 96% undergrads receive some form of aid. Average freshman grant $9,916. Average freshman loan $2,907. Average income from on-campus job $1,000. **Financial Aid Phone:** 412-578-6058.

CARNEGIE MELLON UNIVERSITY

5000 Forbes Avenue, Pittsburgh, PA 15213
Phone: 412-268-2082 **E-mail:** undergraduate-admissions@andrew.cmu.edu
CEEB Code: 2074 **Fax:** 412-268-7838 **Web:** www.cmu.edu **ACT Code:** 3534

This private school was founded in 1900. It has a 110-acre campus.

STUDENTS AND FACULTY

Enrollment: 5,475. **Student Body:** Male 61%, female 39%, out-of-state 76%, international 11% (100 countries represented). **Ethnic Representation:** African American 5%, Asian 26%, Caucasian 48%, Hispanic 5%, Native American 1%. **Retention and Graduation:** 96% freshmen return for sophomore year. 65% freshmen graduate within 4 years. **Faculty:** Student/faculty ratio 11:1. 747 full-time faculty.

ACADEMICS

Degrees: Bachelor's, doctoral, master's, post-master's certificate. **Classes:** 10-19 students in an average class. 20-29 students in an average lab/discussion section. **Majors with Highest Enrollment:** Computer science; computer engineering, general; business administration/management. **Disciplines with Highest Percentage of Degrees Awarded:** Engineering/engineering technology 25%, computer and information sciences 20%, visual and performing arts 14%, business/marketing 10%, social sciences and history 6%. **Special Study Options:** Accelerated program, cooperative (work-study) program, cross registration, double major, English as a second language, student exchange program (domestic), honors program, independent study, internships, liberal arts/career combination, student-designed major, study abroad, teacher certification program, weekend college.

FACILITIES

Housing: Coed, all-female, all-male, housing for disabled students, fraternities and/or sororities. **Library Holdings:** 999,798 bound volumes. 3,143 periodicals. 938,851 microforms. 221,743 audiovisuals. **Special Academic Facilities/Equipment:** Art galleries, theatres, on-campus school, botanical institute, extensive lab facilities and equipment. **Computers:** School-owned computers available for student use.

EXTRACURRICULARS

Activities: Choral groups, concert band, dance, drama/theater, jazz band, literary magazine, marching band, music ensembles, musical theater, opera, pep band, radio station, student government, student newspaper, student-run film society, symphony orchestra, yearbook. **Organizations:** 100 registered organizations, 13 fraternities (14% men join), 5 sororities (10% women join). **Athletics (Intercollegiate):** *Men:* basketball, cross-country, diving, football, golf, soccer, swimming, tennis, track & field. *Women:* basketball, cross-country, diving, soccer, swimming, tennis, track & field, volleyball.

ADMISSIONS

Selectivity Rating: 92 (of 100). **Freshman Academic Profile:** Average high school GPA 3.6. 72% in top 10% of high school class, 95% in top 25% of high school class, 100% in top 50% of high school class. Average SAT I Math 716, SAT I Math middle 50% range 680-770. Average SAT I Verbal 646, SAT I Verbal middle 50% range 590-700. Average ACT 29, ACT middle 50% range 27-32. TOEFL required of all international applicants, minimum TOEFL 600. **Basis for Candidate Selection:** *Very important factors considered include:* secondary school record, standardized test scores. *Important factors considered include:* alumni/ae relation, character/personal qualities, class rank, extracurricular activities, recommendations, talent/ability, volunteer work, work experience. *Other factors considered include:* essays, interview, minority status. **Freshman Admission Requirements:** High school diploma or GED is required. *Academic units required/recommended:* 4 English required, 4 English recommended, 4 math required, 4 math recommended, 3 science required, 3 science recommended, 3 science lab required, 3 science lab recommended, 2 foreign language required, 2 foreign language recommended, 1 social studies required, 1 social studies recommended, 2 history required, 2 history recommended, 3 elective required, 4 elective recommended. **Freshman Admission Statistics:** 14,271 applied, 38% accepted, 25% of those accepted enrolled. **Transfer Admission Requirements:** *Items required:* high school transcript, college transcript, essay, standardized test score, statement of good standing from prior school. Minimum college GPA of 2.5 required. Lowest grade transferable C. **General Admission Information:** Application fee $55. Early decision application deadline November 15. Regular application deadline January 1. Admission may be deferred for a maximum of 1 year. Credit offered for CEEB Advanced Placement tests.

COSTS AND FINANCIAL AID

Required Forms and Deadlines: FAFSA, institution's own financial aid form, parent and student federal tax returns, parent W-2 forms. Financial aid filing deadline May 1. Priority filing deadline February 15. **Notification of Awards:** Applicants will be notified of awards on a rolling basis. **Types of Aid:** *Need-based scholarships/grants:* Pell, SEOG, state scholarships/grants, private scholarships, the school's own gift aid. *Loans:* FFEL Subsidized Stafford, FFEL Unsubsidized Stafford, FFEL PLUS, Federal Perkins, Gate Student Loan. **Student Employment:** Federal Work-Study Program available. Institutional employment available. Off-campus job opportunities are good. **Financial Aid Statistics:** 54% freshmen, 49% undergrads receive some form of aid. Average freshman grant $19,902. Average freshman loan $4,021. **Financial Aid Phone:** 412-268-2068.

CARROLL COLLEGE (MT)

1601 North Benton Avenue, Helena, MT 59625
Phone: 406-447-4384 **E-mail:** enroll@carroll.edu **CEEB Code:** 4041
Fax: 406-447-4533 **Web:** www.carroll.edu **ACT Code:** 2408

This private school, which is affiliated with the Roman Catholic Church, was founded in 1909. It has a 63-acre campus.

STUDENTS AND FACULTY

Enrollment: 1,341. **Student Body:** Male 40%, female 60%, out-of-state 34%, international 1% (7 countries represented). **Ethnic Representation:** Asian 1%, Caucasian 87%, Hispanic 2%, Native American 1%. **Retention and Graduation:** 76% freshmen return for sophomore year. 40% freshmen graduate within 4 years. 22% grads go on to further study within 1 year. **Faculty:** Student/faculty ratio 13:1. 80 full-time faculty, 68% hold PhDs. 100% faculty teach undergrads.

ACADEMICS

Degrees: Associate's, bachelor's, transfer. **Academic Requirements:** General education including some course work in arts/fine arts, English (including composition), history, humanities, mathematics, philosophy, sciences (biological or physical), social science, theology, communications. **Classes:** 10-19 students in an average class. 10-19 students in an average lab/discussion section. **Majors with Highest Enrollment:** Business administration/management; nursing/registered nurse training (RN, ASN, BSN, MSN); biology/biological sciences, general. **Disciplines with Highest Percentage of Degrees Awarded:** Business/marketing 17%, social sciences and history 17%, education 9%, health professions and related sciences 9%, biological life sciences 8%. **Special Study Options:** Accelerated program, cooperative (work-study) program, double major, dual enrollment, English as a second language, student exchange program (domestic), honors program, independent study, internships, liberal arts/career combination, student-designed major, study abroad, teacher certification program.

FACILITIES

Housing: Coed, all-female, all-male, new apartment-style dorms. **Library Holdings:** 170,858 bound volumes. 588 periodicals. 6,450 microforms. 3,973 audiovisuals. **Special Academic Facilities/Equipment:** Arts lab, observatory, seismograph station, engineering lab. **Computers:** School-owned computers available for student use.

EXTRACURRICULARS

Activities: Choral groups, dance, drama/theater, music ensembles, pep band, radio station, student government, student newspaper, yearbook. **Organizations:** 34 registered organizations, 10 honor societies, 4 religious organizations. **Athletics (Intercollegiate):** *Men:* basketball, cheerleading, football, golf. *Women:* basketball, cheerleading, golf, soccer, volleyball.

ADMISSIONS

Selectivity Rating: 75 (of 100). **Freshman Academic Profile:** Average high school GPA 3.4. 24% in top 10% of high school class, 49% in top 25% of high school class, 79% in top 50% of high school class. 93% from public high schools. Average SAT I Math 543, SAT I Math middle 50% range 480-610. Average SAT I Verbal 545, SAT I Verbal middle 50% range 480-600. Average ACT 24, ACT middle 50% range 21-26. TOEFL required of all international applicants, minimum TOEFL 550. **Basis for Candidate Selection:** *Very important factors considered include:* secondary school record, standardized test scores. *Important factors considered include:* class rank, essays, recommendations. *Other factors considered include:* alumni/ae relation, character/personal qualities, extracurricular activities, interview, religious affiliation/commitment, talent/ability, volunteer work, work experience. **Freshman Admission Requirements:** High school diploma or GED is required. *Academic units required/recommended:* 16 total recommended; 4 English recommended, 3 math recommended, 2 science recommended, 1 science lab recommended, 2 foreign language recommended, 2 social studies recommended, 2 history recommended. **Freshman Admission Statistics:** 800 applied, 88% accepted, 40% of those accepted enrolled. **Transfer Admission Requirements:** *Items required:* college transcript, essay, statement of good standing from prior school. Minimum high school GPA of 2.5 required. Minimum college GPA of 2.5 required. Lowest grade transferable C. **General Admission Information:** Application fee $35. Priority application deadline March 1. Regular application deadline June 1. Nonfall registration accepted. Admission may be deferred. Credit and/or placement offered for CEEB Advanced Placement tests.

COSTS AND FINANCIAL AID

Tuition $13,728. Room & board $5,566. Required fees $200. Average book expense $600. **Required Forms and Deadlines:** FAFSA. No deadline for regular filing. Priority filing deadline March 1. **Notification of Awards:** Applicants will be notified of awards on a rolling basis beginning on or about March 1. **Types of Aid:** *Need-based scholarships/grants:* Pell, SEOG, state scholarships/grants, private scholarships, the school's own gift aid. *Loans:* FFEL Subsidized Stafford, FFEL Unsubsidized Stafford, FFEL PLUS, Federal Perkins, private. **Student Employment:** Federal Work-Study Program available. Institutional employment available. Off-campus job opportunities are good. **Financial Aid Statistics:** 67% freshmen, 66% undergrads receive some form of aid. Average freshman grant $7,582. Average freshman loan $5,304. **Financial Aid Phone:** 406-447-5425.

CARROLL COLLEGE (WI)

100 North East Avenue, Waukesha, WI 53186
Phone: 262-524-7220 **E-mail:** ccinfo@ccadmin.cc.edu **CEEB Code:** 1101
Fax: 262-951-3037 **Web:** www.cc.edu **ACT Code:** 4570

This private school, which is affiliated with the Presbyterian Church, was founded in 1846. It has a 52-acre campus.

STUDENTS AND FACULTY

Enrollment: 2,444. **Student Body:** Male 34%, female 66%, out-of-state 17%, international 2% (14 countries represented). **Ethnic Representation:** African American 3%, Asian 1%, Caucasian 92%, Hispanic 3%. **Retention and Graduation:** 80% freshmen return for sophomore year. 48% freshmen graduate within 4 years. 13% grads go on to further study within 1 year. **Faculty:** 100% faculty teach undergrads.

ACADEMICS

Degrees: Bachelor's, master's, post-bachelor's certificate. **Academic Requirements:** General education including some course work in arts/fine arts, computer literacy, English (including composition), humanities, mathematics, sciences (biological or physical), social science. **Special Study Options:** Double major, student exchange program (domestic), honors program, independent study, internships, student-designed major, study abroad, teacher certification program.

FACILITIES

Housing: Coed, all-female, apartments for married students, fraternities and/or sororities. **Library Holdings:** 195,578 bound volumes. 667 periodicals. 84 microforms. 671 audiovisuals. **Computers:** School-owned computers available for student use.

EXTRACURRICULARS

Activities: Choral groups, drama/theater, jazz band, literary magazine, music ensembles, musical theater, opera, radio station, student government, student newspaper, symphony orchestra, yearbook. **Organizations:** 56 registered organizations, 16 honor societies, 2 religious organizations, 3 fraternities (12% men join), 4 sororities (10% women join). **Athletics (Intercollegiate):** *Men:* baseball, basketball, cheerleading, cross-country, diving, football, golf, indoor track, soccer, swimming, tennis, track & field. *Women:* basketball, cheerleading, cross-country, diving, golf, indoor track, soccer, softball, swimming, tennis, track & field, volleyball.

ADMISSIONS

Selectivity Rating: 72 (of 100). **Freshman Academic Profile:** Average high school GPA 2.8. 22% in top 10% of high school class, 55% in top 25% of high school class, 78% in top 50% of high school class. 85% from public high schools. Average ACT 23, ACT middle 50% range 21-27. TOEFL required of all international applicants, minimum TOEFL 550. **Basis for Candidate Selection:** *Very important factors considered include:* class rank, secondary school record, standardized test scores. *Important factors considered include:* recommendations. *Other factors considered include:* alumni/ae relation, character/personal qualities, interview. **Freshman Admission Requirements:** High school diploma or GED is required. **Transfer Admission Requirements:** *Items required:* high school transcript, college transcript. Minimum high school GPA of 2.0 required. Minimum college GPA of 2.0 required. Lowest grade transferable C. **General Admission Information:** Regular application deadline rolling. Nonfall registration accepted. Admission may be deferred. Credit and/or placement offered for CEEB Advanced Placement tests.

COSTS AND FINANCIAL AID

Tuition $14,740. Room & board $4,600. Required fees $260. Average book expense $540. **Required Forms and Deadlines:** FAFSA. No deadline for regular filing. **Notification of Awards:** Applicants will be notified of awards on a rolling basis beginning on or about March 1. **Types of Aid:** *Need-based scholarships/grants:* Pell, SEOG, state scholarships/grants, the school's own gift aid. *Loans:* FFEL Subsidized Stafford, FFEL Unsubsidized Stafford, FFEL PLUS, Federal Perkins. **Student Employment:** Federal Work-Study Program available. Institutional employment available. Off-campus job opportunities are excellent. **Financial Aid Statistics:** Average freshman grant $8,350. Average income from on-campus job $793. **Financial Aid Phone:** 414-524-7296.

CARSON-NEWMAN COLLEGE

1646 Russell Avenue, Jefferson City, TN 37760
Phone: 865-471-3223 **E-mail:** sgray@.cn.edu **CEEB Code:** 1102
Fax: 865-471-3502 **Web:** www.cn.edu **ACT Code:** 3950

This private school, which is affiliated with the Baptist Church, was founded in 1851. It has a 90-acre campus.

STUDENTS AND FACULTY

Enrollment: 2,019. **Student Body:** Male 43%, female 57%, out-of-state 33%, international 2%. **Ethnic Representation:** African American 8%, Caucasian 91%. **Retention and Graduation:** 74% freshmen return for sophomore year. 25% grads go on to further study within 1 year. 1% grads pursue business degrees. 3% grads pursue law degrees. 2% grads pursue medical degrees. **Faculty:** Student/faculty ratio 13:1. 122 full-time faculty, 54% hold PhDs. 100% faculty teach undergrads.

ACADEMICS

Degrees: Associate's, bachelor's, master's. **Academic Requirements:** General education including some course work in arts/fine arts, computer literacy, English (including composition), foreign languages, history, humanities, mathematics, sciences (biological or physical), social science. Regardless of major, all students must complete a 51-semester-hour general education core for graduation, including 2 classes in religion. **Classes:** 10-19 students in an average class. 10-19 students in an average lab/discussion section. **Disciplines with Highest Percentage of Degrees Awarded:** Education 16%, business/marketing 15%, communications/communication technologies 9%, psychology 8%, philosophy/religion/theology 7%. **Special Study Options:** Cooperative (work-study) program, double major, dual enrollment, English as a second language, honors program, independent study, internships, student-designed major, study abroad, teacher certification program.

FACILITIES

Housing: All-female, all-male, apartments for married students, apartments for single students. **Library Holdings:** 300,000 bound volumes. 2,245 periodicals. 221,960 microforms. 15,000 audiovisuals. **Special Academic Facilities/Equipment:** Art galleries, Appalachian history museum, home management house, language lab. **Computers:** School-owned computers available for student use.

EXTRACURRICULARS

Activities: Choral groups, concert band, dance, drama/theater, jazz band, literary magazine, marching band, music ensembles, musical theater, pep band, student government, student newspaper, television station, yearbook. **Organizations:** 45 registered organizations, 10 honor societies, 5 religious organizations, 2 fraternities, 2 sororities. **Athletics (Intercollegiate):** *Men:* baseball, basketball, cheerleading, cross-country, football, golf, soccer, tennis, track & field, wrestling. *Women:* basketball, cheerleading, cross-country, soccer, softball, tennis, track & field, volleyball.

ADMISSIONS

Selectivity Rating: 70 (of 100). **Freshman Academic Profile:** Average high school GPA 3.3. 28% in top 10% of high school class, 49% in top 25% of high school class, 77% in top 50% of high school class. 87% from public high schools. Average ACT 23. TOEFL required of all international applicants, minimum TOEFL 550. **Basis for Candidate Selection:** *Very important factors considered include:* secondary school record, standardized test scores. *Important factors considered include:* class rank. *Other factors considered include:* alumni/ae relation, character/personal qualities, essays, extracurricular activities, interview, recommendations, religious affiliation/commitment, talent/ability, volunteer work, work experience. **Freshman Admission Requirements:** High school diploma or GED is required. *Academic units required/recommended:* 20 total required; 4 English required, 2 math required, 2 science required, 1 science lab required, 2 foreign language recommended, 1 social studies required, 1 history required, 4 elective required. **Freshman Admission Statistics:** 1,168 applied, 86% accepted, 43% of those accepted enrolled. **Transfer Admission Requirements:** *Items required:* college transcript. Minimum high school GPA of 2.0 required. Minimum college GPA of 2.0 required. Lowest grade transferable D. **General Admission Information:** Application fee $25. Priority application deadline April 1. Nonfall registration accepted. Admission may be deferred for a maximum of 2 years. Credit and/or placement offered for CEEB Advanced Placement tests.

COSTS AND FINANCIAL AID

Tuition $12,900. Room & board $5,000. Required fees $720. Average book expense $900. **Required Forms and Deadlines:** FAFSA and institution's own financial aid form. No deadline for regular filing. Priority filing deadline March 1. **Types of Aid:** *Need-based scholarships/grants:* Pell, SEOG, state scholarships/grants, private scholarships, the school's own gift aid. *Loans:* Direct Subsidized Stafford, Direct Unsubsidized Stafford, Direct PLUS, Federal Perkins, Federal Nursing. **Student Employment:** Federal Work-Study Program available. Institutional employment available. Off-campus job opportunities are good. **Financial Aid Statistics:** 74% freshmen, 70% undergrads receive some form of aid. Average freshman grant $4,100. Average freshman loan $2,625. Average income from on-campus job $900. **Financial Aid Phone:** 865-471-3414.

CARTHAGE COLLEGE

2001 Alford Park Drive, Kenosha, WI 53140-1994
Phone: 262-551-6000 **E-mail:** admissions@carthage.edu **CEEB Code:** 1103
Fax: 262-551-5762 **Web:** www.carthage.edu **ACT Code:** 4571

This private school, which is affiliated with the Lutheran Church, was founded in 1847. It has a 72-acre campus.

STUDENTS AND FACULTY

Enrollment: 2,388. **Student Body:** Male 41%, female 59%, out-of-state 50%, international 1% (9 countries represented). **Ethnic Representation:** African American 6%, Asian 1%, Caucasian 89%, Hispanic 4%, Native American 1%. **Retention and Graduation:** 73% freshmen return for sophomore year. 54% freshmen graduate within 4 years. 16% grads go on to further study within 1 year. 1% grads pursue business degrees. 2% grads pursue law degrees. 1% grads pursue medical degrees. **Faculty:** Student/faculty ratio 17:1. 113 full-time faculty, 82% hold PhDs. 100% faculty teach undergrads.

ACADEMICS

Degrees: Bachelor's, master's. **Academic Requirements:** General education including some course work in arts/fine arts, foreign languages, humanities, mathematics, sciences (biological or physical), social science. **Majors with Highest Enrollment:** Business administration/management; education, general; physical education teaching and coaching. **Disciplines with Highest Percentage of Degrees Awarded:** Business/marketing 26%, education 12%, other 12%, social sciences and history 8%, parks and recreation 6%. **Special Study Options:** Accelerated program, cooperative (work-study) program, cross registration, double major, honors program, independent study, internships, student-designed major, study abroad, teacher certification program, weekend college, master's in education.

FACILITIES

Housing: Coed, all-female, all-male, apartments for single students, fraternities and/or sororities. **Library Holdings:** 125,448 bound volumes. 425 periodicals. 7,149 microforms. 4,361 audiovisuals. **Special Academic Facilities/ Equipment:** Language lab, Civil War museum, science research lab. **Computers:** School-owned computers available for student use.

EXTRACURRICULARS

Activities: Choral groups, concert band, dance, drama/theater, jazz band, literary magazine, music ensembles, musical theater, pep band, radio station, student government, student newspaper, student-run film society, yearbook. **Organizations:** 85 registered organizations, 20 honor societies, 5 religious organizations, 8 fraternities (23% men join), 5 sororities (23% women join). **Athletics (Intercollegiate):** *Men:* baseball, basketball, cross-country, football, golf, indoor track, soccer, swimming, tennis, track & field. *Women:* basketball, cross-country, golf, indoor track, soccer, softball, swimming, tennis, track & field, volleyball, water polo.

ADMISSIONS

Selectivity Rating: 75 (of 100). **Freshman Academic Profile:** Average high school GPA 3.2. 15% in top 10% of high school class, 42% in top 25% of high school class, 71% in top 50% of high school class. Average SAT I Math 555, SAT I Math middle 50% range 500-630. Average SAT I Verbal 550, SAT I Verbal middle 50% range 500-600. Average ACT 23, ACT middle 50% range 19-26. TOEFL required of all international applicants, minimum TOEFL 500. **Basis for Candidate Selection:** *Very important factors considered include:* character/personal qualities, secondary school record, standardized test scores, talent/ability. *Important factors considered include:* class rank, extracurricular activities. *Other factors considered include:* alumni/ae relation, geographical residence, interview, minority status, recommendations, state residency, volunteer work, work experience. **Freshman Admission Requirements:** High school diploma or GED is required. *Academic units required/recommended:* 16 total required; 16 total recommended; 4 English required, 4 English recommended, 3 math required, 3 math recommended, 3 science required, 3 science recommended, 2 foreign language recommended, 3 social studies required, 3 social studies recommended, 3 elective required. **Freshman Admission Statistics:** 2,847 applied, 83% accepted, 26% of those accepted enrolled. **Transfer Admission Requirements:** *Items required:* college transcript. Minimum college GPA of 2.0 required. **General Admission Information:** Application fee $25. Priority application deadline December 8. Nonfall registration accepted. Credit and/or placement offered for CEEB Advanced Placement tests.

COSTS AND FINANCIAL AID

Tuition $19,150. Room & board $5,750. Required fees $0. Average book expense $600. **Required Forms and Deadlines:** FAFSA. **Types of Aid:** *Need-based scholarships/grants:* Pell, SEOG, state scholarships/grants, private scholarships, the school's own gift aid. *Loans:* FFEL Subsidized Stafford, FFEL Unsubsidized Stafford, FFEL PLUS, Federal Perkins, state loans, college/ university loans from institutional funds. **Student Employment:** Federal Work-Study Program available. Institutional employment available. Off-campus job opportunities are good. **Financial Aid Statistics:** Average freshman grant $7,851. Average freshman loan $3,553. Average income from on-campus job $1,000. **Financial Aid Phone:** 262-551-6001.

CASCADE COLLEGE

9101 East Burnside Street, Portland, OR 97216-1515
Phone: 503-257-1202 **E-mail:** admissions@cascade.edu
Fax: 503-257-1222 **Web:** www.cascade.edu

This private school, which is affiliated with the Church of Christ, was founded in 1993. It has a 13-acre campus.

STUDENTS AND FACULTY

Enrollment: 310. **Student Body:** Male 49%, female 51%, out-of-state 59%, international 4%. **Ethnic Representation:** African American 8%, Asian 3%, Caucasian 83%, Hispanic 4%, Native American 1%. **Retention and Graduation:** 3% grads go on to further study within 1 year. **Faculty:** Student/faculty ratio 17:1. 15 full-time faculty, 46% hold PhDs. 100% faculty teach undergrads.

ACADEMICS

Degrees: Bachelor's. **Academic Requirements:** General education including some course work in arts/fine arts, computer literacy, English (including composition), history, humanities, mathematics, philosophy, sciences (biological or physical), social science. All students are required to take Bible courses. **Classes:** 10-19 students in an average class. 20-29 students in an average lab/ discussion section. **Majors with Highest Enrollment:** Business administration/management; liberal arts and sciences/liberal studies; psychology, general. **Disciplines with Highest Percentage of Degrees Awarded:** Liberal arts/ general studies 26%, psychology 9%, philosophy/religion/theology 6%, business/ marketing 4%, natural resources/environmental sciences 1%. **Special Study Options:** Double major, independent study, internships, study abroad, teacher certification program.

FACILITIES

Housing: Coed, all-female, all-male. **Library Holdings:** 25,000 bound volumes. 110 periodicals. 62,045 microforms. 1,200 audiovisuals. **Computers:** School-owned computers available for student use.

EXTRACURRICULARS

Activities: Choral groups, concert band, drama/theater, jazz band, literary magazine, music ensembles, student government, yearbook. **Organizations:** 8 registered organizations, 2 honor societies. **Athletics (Intercollegiate):** *Men:* basketball, cross-country, soccer, track & field. *Women:* basketball, cross-country, soccer, track & field, volleyball.

ADMISSIONS

Selectivity Rating: 63 (of 100). **Freshman Academic Profile:** 85% from public high schools. SAT I Math middle 50% range 430-530. SAT I Verbal middle 50% range 450-560. Average ACT 21, ACT middle 50% range 17-23. TOEFL required of all international applicants, minimum TOEFL 500. **Freshman Admission Requirements:** High school diploma or GED is required. **Freshman Admission Statistics:** 247 applied, 100% accepted, 30% of those accepted enrolled. **Transfer Admission Requirements:** *Items required:* high school transcript, college transcript. Lowest grade transferable D. **General Admission Information:** Application fee $25. Nonfall registration accepted. Admission may be deferred for a maximum of 1 year. Credit offered for CEEB Advanced Placement tests.

COSTS AND FINANCIAL AID

Tuition $10,060. Room & board $5,530. Required fees $200. Average book expense $800. **Required Forms and Deadlines:** FAFSA and institution's own financial aid form. Financial aid filing deadline August 1. Priority filing deadline April 1. **Notification of Awards:** Applicants will be notified of awards on a rolling basis beginning on or about February 1. **Types of Aid:** *Need-based scholarships/grants:* Pell, SEOG, private scholarships, the school's own gift aid. *Loans:* FFEL Subsidized Stafford, FFEL Unsubsidized Stafford, FFEL PLUS, private loans. **Student Employment:** Federal Work-Study Program available. Institutional employment available. Off-campus job opportunities are excellent. **Financial Aid Statistics:** Average freshman grant $3,990. Average freshman loan $5,272. Average income from on-campus job $1,300. **Financial Aid Phone:** 503-257-1218.

CASE WESTERN RESERVE UNIVERSITY

103 Tomlinson Hall, 10900 Euclid Avenue, Cleveland, OH 44106-7055
Phone: 216-368-4450 **E-mail:** admission@po.cwru.edu **CEEB Code:** 1105
Fax: 216-368-5111 **Web:** www.cwru.edu **ACT Code:** 3244

This private school was founded in 1826. It has a 150-acre campus.

STUDENTS AND FACULTY

Enrollment: 3,457. **Student Body:** Male 61%, female 39%, out-of-state 40%, international 4% (89 countries represented). **Ethnic Representation:** African American 5%, Asian 15%, Caucasian 76%, Hispanic 2%. **Retention and Graduation:** 92% freshmen return for sophomore year. 35% grads go on to further study within 1 year. 2% grads pursue business degrees. 3% grads pursue law degrees. 9% grads pursue medical degrees. **Faculty:** Student/faculty ratio 8:1. 594 full-time faculty, 94% hold PhDs. 72% faculty teach undergrads.

ACADEMICS

Degrees: Bachelor's, doctoral, first professional, master's, post-bachelor's certificate. **Academic Requirements:** General education including some course work in English (including composition), humanities, mathematics, sciences (biological or physical), social science, global and cultural diversity. **Classes:** 10-19 students in an average class. 10-19 students in an average lab/ discussion section. **Majors with Highest Enrollment:** Business administration/management; biology/biological sciences, general; psychology, general. **Disciplines with Highest Percentage of Degrees Awarded:** Engineering/ engineering technology 30%, social sciences and history 12%, business/

marketing 10%, biological life sciences 9%, psychology 7%. **Special Study Options:** Accelerated program, cooperative (work-study) program, cross registration, double major, dual enrollment, English as a second language, honors program, independent study, internships, liberal arts/career combination, student-designed major, study abroad, teacher certification program, Washington Semester.

FACILITIES

Housing: Coed, all-male, fraternities and/or sororities, special housing for students in college scholars program. **Library Holdings:** 17,506 periodicals. 2,475,337 microforms. 49,889 audiovisuals. **Special Academic Facilities/ Equipment:** Art, natural history, and auto-aviation museums, historical society, botanical garden, biology field stations, observatory. **Computers:** School-owned computers available for student use.

EXTRACURRICULARS

Activities: Choral groups, concert band, dance, drama/theater, jazz band, literary magazine, marching band, music ensembles, musical theater, pep band, radio station, student government, student newspaper, student-run film society, symphony orchestra, yearbook. **Organizations:** 100 registered organizations, 4 honor societies, 4 religious organizations, 18 fraternities (36% men join), 5 sororities (15% women join). **Athletics (Intercollegiate):** *Men:* baseball, basketball, cross-country, fencing, football, golf, indoor track, soccer, swimming, tennis, track & field, wrestling. *Women:* basketball, cross-country, fencing, indoor track, soccer, softball, swimming, tennis, track & field, volleyball.

ADMISSIONS

Selectivity Rating: 86 (of 100). **Freshman Academic Profile:** 66% in top 10% of high school class, 92% in top 25% of high school class, 99% in top 50% of high school class. 70% from public high schools. SAT I Math middle 50% range 630-730. SAT I Verbal middle 50% range 590-710. ACT middle 50% range 26-31. TOEFL required of all international applicants, minimum TOEFL 550. **Basis for Candidate Selection:** *Very important factors considered include:* extracurricular activities, secondary school record, talent/ability, volunteer work, work experience. *Important factors considered include:* alumni/ae relation, character/personal qualities, class rank, essays, interview, minority status, recommendations, standardized test scores. **Freshman Admission Requirements:** High school diploma or GED is required. *Academic units required/recommended:* 16 total required; 4 English required, 3 math required, 4 math recommended, 3 science required, 1 science lab required, 2 science lab recommended, 2 foreign language required, 3 foreign language recommended, 3 social studies required, 4 social studies recommended. **Freshman Admission Statistics:** 4,428 applied, 78% accepted, 24% of those accepted enrolled. **Transfer Admission Requirements:** *Items required:* high school transcript, college transcript, essay, statement of good standing from prior school. Minimum college GPA of 3.0 required. Lowest grade transferable C. **General Admission Information:** Application fee $35. Early decision application deadline January 1. Regular application deadline February 1. Nonfall registration accepted. Admission may be deferred for a maximum of 1 year. Credit and/or placement offered for CEEB Advanced Placement tests.

COSTS AND FINANCIAL AID

Tuition $24,100. Room & board $7,660. Required fees $242. Average book expense $800. **Required Forms and Deadlines:** FAFSA, CSS/Financial Aid PROFILE, noncustodial (divorced/separated) parent's statement, business/farm supplement, and parent and student income tax returns and W-2 forms. Financial aid filing deadline April 15. Priority filing deadline February 1. **Notification of Awards:** Applicants will be notified of awards on a rolling basis beginning on or about March 15. **Types of Aid:** *Need-based scholarships/ grants:* Pell, SEOG, state scholarships/grants, private scholarships, the school's own gift aid. *Loans:* Direct Subsidized Stafford, Direct Unsubsidized Stafford, FFEL PLUS, Federal Perkins, Federal Nursing, state loans, college/university loans from institutional funds. **Student Employment:** Federal Work-Study Program available. Institutional employment available. Off-campus job opportunities are good. **Financial Aid Statistics:** 63% freshmen, 54% undergrads receive some form of aid. Average freshman grant $15,865. Average freshman loan $5,580. Average income from on-campus job $2,900. **Financial Aid Phone:** 216-368-4530.

See page 960.

CASTLETON STATE COLLEGE

Office of Admissions, Castleton, VT 05735
Phone: 802-468-1213 **E-mail:** info@castleton.edu **CEEB Code:** 3765
Fax: 802-468-1476 **Web:** www.castleton.edu **ACT Code:** 4314

This public school was founded in 1787. It has a 160-acre campus.

STUDENTS AND FACULTY

Enrollment: 1,643. **Student Body:** Male 40%, female 60%, out-of-state 35%. **Ethnic Representation:** Asian 1%, Caucasian 91%, Hispanic 1%. **Retention and Graduation:** 70% freshmen return for sophomore year. 34% freshmen graduate within 4 years. **Faculty:** Student/faculty ratio 13:1. 86 full-time faculty, 94% hold PhDs. 100% faculty teach undergrads.

ACADEMICS

Degrees: Associate's, bachelor's, master's, post-master's certificate. **Academic Requirements:** General education including some course work in arts/fine arts, computer literacy, English (including composition), history, humanities, mathematics, sciences (biological or physical), social science. **Classes:** 10-19 students in an average class. 10-19 students in an average lab/discussion section. **Majors with Highest Enrollment:** Business administration/management; mass communications/media studies; psychology, general. **Disciplines with Highest Percentage of Degrees Awarded:** Business/marketing 17%, education 16%, psychology 13%, social sciences and history 10%, protective services/public administration 9%. **Special Study Options:** Cooperative (work-study) program, double major, dual enrollment, honors program, independent study, internships, liberal arts/career combination, student-designed major, study abroad, teacher certification program. Special programs with other institutions lead to degrees in engineering and chemistry and to an MBA.

FACILITIES

Housing: Coed. **Library Holdings:** 157,075 bound volumes. 938 periodicals. 484,597 microforms. 2,922 audiovisuals. **Computers:** School-owned computers available for student use.

EXTRACURRICULARS

Activities: Choral groups, dance, drama/theater, jazz band, literary magazine, music ensembles, musical theater, radio station, student government, student newspaper, television station, yearbook. **Organizations:** 44 registered organizations, 7 honor societies, 2 religious organizations. **Athletics (Intercollegiate):** *Men:* baseball, basketball, cross-country, ice hockey, lacrosse, skiing (alpine), soccer, tennis. *Women:* basketball, cross-country, field hockey, ice hockey, lacrosse, skiing (alpine), soccer, softball, tennis.

ADMISSIONS

Selectivity Rating: 63 (of 100). **Freshman Academic Profile:** Average high school GPA 2.7. 4% in top 10% of high school class, 17% in top 25% of high school class, 50% in top 50% of high school class. Average SAT I Math 481, SAT I Math middle 50% range 410-520. Average SAT I Verbal 469, SAT I Verbal middle 50% range 430-530. Average ACT 20, ACT middle 50% range 17-24. TOEFL required of all international applicants, minimum TOEFL 500. **Basis for Candidate Selection:** *Very important factors considered include:* essays, secondary school record. *Important factors considered include:* extracurricular activities, recommendations, standardized test scores. *Other factors considered include:* alumni/ae relation, character/personal qualities, class rank, interview, talent/ability, volunteer work, work experience. **Freshman Admission Requirements:** High school diploma or GED is required. *Academic units required/recommended:* 14 total required; 16 total recommended; 4 English required, 4 English recommended, 3 math required, 3 math recommended, 2 science required, 2 science recommended, 2 science lab required, 2 science lab recommended, 2 foreign language recommended, 3 social studies required, 4 social studies recommended, 2 elective recommended. **Freshman Admission Statistics:** 1,199 applied, 85% accepted, 39% of those accepted enrolled. **Transfer Admission Requirements:** *Items required:* college transcript, essay, statement of good standing from prior school. Minimum college GPA of 2.0 required. Lowest grade transferable C. **General Admission Information:** Application fee $30. Nonfall registration accepted. Admission may be deferred for a maximum of 1 year. Credit and/or placement offered for CEEB Advanced Placement tests.

COSTS AND FINANCIAL AID

In-state tuition $4,624. Out-of-state tuition $10,836. Room & board $5,782. Required fees $880. Average book expense $800. **Required Forms and Deadlines:** FAFSA. No deadline for regular filing. Priority filing deadline March 15. **Notification of Awards:** Applicants will be notified of awards on a rolling basis beginning on or about February 15. **Types of Aid:** *Need-based scholarships/grants:* Pell, SEOG, state scholarships/grants, private scholarships, the school's own gift aid. *Loans:* FFEL Subsidized Stafford, FFEL Unsubsidized Stafford, FFEL PLUS, Federal Perkins, Federal Nursing, state loans. **Student Employment:** Federal Work-Study Program available. Institutional employment available. Off-campus job opportunities are good. **Financial Aid Statistics:** 69% freshmen, 67% undergrads receive some form of aid. Average freshman grant $3,284. Average freshman loan $2,630. Average income from on-campus job $1,200. **Financial Aid Phone:** 802-468-1286.

See page 962.

CATAWBA COLLEGE

2300 West Innes Street, Salisbury, NC 28144
Phone: 704-637-4402 **E-mail:** admission@catawba.edu **CEEB Code:** 5103
Fax: 704-637-4222 **Web:** www.catawba.edu **ACT Code:** 3080

This private school, which is affiliated with the United Church of Christ, was founded in 1851. It has a 276-acre campus.

STUDENTS AND FACULTY

Enrollment: 1,538. **Student Body:** Male 47%, female 53%, out-of-state 39%. **Ethnic Representation:** African American 18%, Caucasian 77%, Hispanic 1%. **Retention and Graduation:** 60% freshmen return for sophomore year. 47% freshmen graduate within 4 years. 13% grads go on to further study within 1 year. 4% grads pursue business degrees. 2% grads pursue law degrees. 1% grads pursue medical degrees. **Faculty:** Student/faculty ratio 15:1. 68 full-time faculty, 76% hold PhDs. 100% faculty teach undergrads.

ACADEMICS

Degrees: Bachelor's, master's, post-bachelor's certificate. **Academic Requirements:** General education including some course work in arts/fine arts, computer literacy, English (including composition), foreign languages, humanities, mathematics, sciences (biological or physical), social science. **Classes:** 10-19 students in an average class. 10-19 students in an average lab/ discussion section. **Majors with Highest Enrollment:** Acting; sports and fitness administration/management; business administration/management. **Disciplines with Highest Percentage of Degrees Awarded:** Business/ marketing 36%, education 11%, social sciences and history 11%, computer and information sciences 6%, communications/communication technologies 5%. **Special Study Options:** Cooperative (work-study) program, double major, dual enrollment, English as a second language, honors program, independent study, internships, student-designed major, study abroad, teacher certification program.

FACILITIES

Housing: Coed, all-female, all-male, substance-free housing. **Library Holdings:** 146,612 bound volumes. 461 periodicals. 576,857 microforms. 25,038 audiovisuals. **Special Academic Facilities/Equipment:** Ecology preserve (183 acres), wildlife preserve (300 acres). **Computers:** *Recommended operating system:* Windows 95. School-owned computers available for student use.

EXTRACURRICULARS

Activities: Choral groups, concert band, dance, drama/theater, jazz band, literary magazine, music ensembles, musical theater, pep band, student government, student newspaper, symphony orchestra, yearbook. **Organizations:** 38 registered organizations, 9 honor societies, 4 religious organizations. **Athletics (Intercollegiate):** *Men:* baseball, basketball, cross-country, football, golf, lacrosse, soccer, tennis. *Women:* basketball, cross-country, field hockey, golf, soccer, softball, swimming, tennis, volleyball.

ADMISSIONS

Selectivity Rating: 70 (of 100). **Freshman Academic Profile:** Average high school GPA 3.0. 7% in top 10% of high school class, 24% in top 25% of high school class, 54% in top 50% of high school class. Average SAT I Math 494, SAT I Math middle 50% range 420-585. Average SAT I Verbal 488, SAT I Verbal middle 50% range 423-583. Average ACT 20. TOEFL required of all international applicants, minimum TOEFL 525. **Basis for Candidate Selection:** *Very important factors considered include:* class rank, secondary school record, standardized test scores. *Important factors considered include:* character/personal qualities, essays, extracurricular activities, recommendations, talent/ability, volunteer work. *Other factors considered include:* alumni/ae relation, interview, minority status, work experience. **Freshman Admission Requirements:** High school diploma or GED is required. *Academic units required/recommended:* 16 total required; 4 English required, 4 English recommended, 2 math required, 3 math recommended, 2 science required, 3 science recommended, 3 science lab recommended, 2 foreign language recommended, 2 social studies required, 2 social studies recommended, 6 elective required. **Freshman Admission Statistics:** 1,179 applied, 78% accepted, 30% of those accepted enrolled. **Transfer Admission Requirements:** *Items required:* college transcript, statement of good standing from prior school. Lowest grade transferable C. **General Admission Information:** Application fee $25. Early decision application deadline December 1. Nonfall registration accepted. Admission may be deferred for a maximum of 1 year. Credit and/or placement offered for CEEB Advanced Placement tests.

COSTS AND FINANCIAL AID

Tuition $13,330. Room & board $4,980. Required fees $0. Average book expense $750. **Required Forms and Deadlines:** FAFSA. No deadline for regular filing. Priority filing deadline March 1. **Notification of Awards:** Applicants will be notified of awards on a rolling basis beginning on or about February 15. **Types of Aid:** *Need-based scholarships/grants:* Pell, SEOG, state scholarships/grants, private scholarships, the school's own gift aid. *Loans:* Direct Subsidized Stafford, Direct Unsubsidized Stafford, Direct PLUS, FFEL Subsidized Stafford, FFEL Unsubsidized Stafford, FFEL PLUS, Federal Perkins, college/university loans from institutional funds. **Student Employment:** Federal Work-Study Program available. Institutional employment available. Off-campus job opportunities are excellent. **Financial Aid Statistics:** 62% freshmen, 84% undergrads receive some form of aid. Average freshman grant $3,529. Average freshman loan $2,634. Average income from on-campus job $1,000. **Financial Aid Phone:** 704-637-4416.

THE CATHOLIC UNIVERSITY OF AMERICA

Washington DC, DC 20064
Phone: 202-319-5305 **E-mail:** cua-admissions@cua.edu **CEEB Code:** 5104
Fax: 202-319-6533 **Web:** www.cua.edu **ACT Code:** 654

This private school, which is affiliated with the Roman Catholic Church, was founded in 1887. It has a 144-acre campus.

STUDENTS AND FACULTY

Enrollment: 2,668. **Student Body:** Male 45%, female 55%, out-of-state 96%, international 2% (31 countries represented). **Ethnic Representation:** African American 6%, Asian 3%, Caucasian 79%, Hispanic 3%. **Retention and Graduation:** 85% freshmen return for sophomore year. 58% freshmen graduate within 4 years. 36% grads go on to further study within 1 year. 10% grads pursue law degrees. 3% grads pursue medical degrees. **Faculty:** Student/ faculty ratio 8:1. 359 full-time faculty, 91% hold PhDs. 74% faculty teach undergrads.

ACADEMICS

Degrees: Bachelor's, doctoral, first professional, master's. **Academic Requirements:** General education including some course work in English (including composition), foreign languages, humanities, mathematics, philosophy, social science, religion and religious education. **Classes:** 10-19 students in an average class. 10-19 students in an average lab/discussion section. **Disciplines with Highest Percentage of Degrees Awarded:** Social sciences and history 14%, engineering/engineering technology 11%, architecture 10%, visual and performing arts 9%, business/marketing 8%. **Special Study Options:** Accelerated program, cross registration, double major, dual enrollment, English as a second language, honors program, independent study, internships, study abroad, teacher certification program.

FACILITIES

Housing: Coed, all-female, all-male, apartments for single students, housing for disabled students, residential college. **Library Holdings:** 1,026,238 bound volumes. 11,200 periodicals. 1,654,037 microforms. 38,200 audiovisuals. **Special Academic Facilities/Equipment:** Anthropology and art museums, rare book collection, youth and development building, nuclear reactor, electron microscope, vitreous-state labs. **Computers:** School-owned computers available for student use.

EXTRACURRICULARS

Activities: Choral groups, dance, drama/theater, jazz band, literary magazine, music ensembles, musical theater, opera, pep band, radio station, student government, student newspaper, symphony orchestra, yearbook. **Organizations:** 84 registered organizations, 13 honor societies, 2 religious organizations, 2 fraternities (1% men join), 2 sororities (1% women join). **Athletics (Intercollegiate):** *Men:* baseball, basketball, cross-country, football, indoor track, lacrosse, soccer, swimming, tennis, track & field. *Women:* basketball, cross-country, field hockey, indoor track, lacrosse, soccer, softball, swimming, tennis, track & field, volleyball.

ADMISSIONS

Selectivity Rating: 86 (of 100). **Freshman Academic Profile:** Average high school GPA 3.4. 33% in top 10% of high school class, 62% in top 25% of high school class, 87% in top 50% of high school class. 39% from public high schools. SAT I Math middle 50% range 520-640. SAT I Verbal middle 50% range 530-640. ACT middle 50% range 21-28. TOEFL required of all international applicants, minimum TOEFL 550. **Basis for Candidate Selection:** *Very important factors considered include:* character/personal qualities, essays, recommendations, secondary school record, standardized test scores, volunteer work. *Important factors considered include:* extracurricular activities, interview, talent/ability. *Other factors considered include:* alumni/ae relation, class rank, minority status, work experience. **Freshman Admission Requirements:** High school diploma or GED is required. *Academic units required/recommended:* 17 total recommended; 4 English recommended, 3 math recommended, 3 science recommended, 1 science lab recommended, 2 foreign language recommended, 4 social studies recommended, 1 history recommended. **Freshman Admission Statistics:** 2,708 applied, 82% accepted, 32% of those accepted enrolled. **Transfer Admission Requirements:** *Items required:* high school transcript, college transcript, essay, standardized test scores. Minimum college GPA of 2.7 required. Lowest grade transferable C. **General Admission Information:** Application fee $55. Early decision application deadline December 1. Regular application deadline February 15. Nonfall registration accepted. Admission may be deferred for a maximum of 1 year. Credit and/or placement offered for CEEB Advanced Placement tests.

COSTS AND FINANCIAL AID

Tuition $22,200. Room & board $9,002. Required fees $1,050. Average book expense $925. **Required Forms and Deadlines:** FAFSA. Financial aid filing deadline February 1. Priority filing deadline January 15. **Notification of Awards:** Applicants will be notified of awards on a rolling basis beginning on or about April 1. **Types of Aid:** *Need-based scholarships/grants:* Pell, SEOG, state scholarships/grants, private scholarships, the school's own gift aid, Federal Nursing. *Loans:* FFEL Subsidized Stafford, FFEL Unsubsidized Stafford, FFEL PLUS, Federal Perkins, Federal Nursing. **Student Employment:** Federal Work-Study Program available. Institutional employment available. Off-campus job opportunities are excellent. **Financial Aid Statistics:** 78% freshmen, 78% undergrads receive some form of aid. Average freshman grant $13,573. Average freshman loan $3,460. **Financial Aid Phone:** 202-319-5307.

CAZENOVIA COLLEGE

13 Nickerson St., Cazenovia, NY 13035
Phone: 315-655-7208 **E-mail:** admission@cazenovia.edu **CEEB Code:** 2078
Fax: 315-655-4860 **Web:** www.cazenovia.edu

This private school was founded in 1824.

STUDENTS AND FACULTY

Enrollment: 1,004. **Student Body:** Male 26%, female 74%, out-of-state 11%, international students represent 2 countries. **Ethnic Representation:** African American 5%, Caucasian 79%, Hispanic 3%, Native American 1%. **Retention and Graduation:** 60% freshmen return for sophomore year. 16% freshmen graduate within 4 years. 65% grads go on to further study within 1 year. **Faculty:** Student/faculty ratio 11:1. 46 full-time faculty, 63% hold PhDs. 100% faculty teach undergrads.

ACADEMICS

Degrees: Associate's, bachelor's, terminal. **Academic Requirements:** General education including some course work in computer literacy, English (including composition), history, mathematics, social science. **Classes:** 10-19 students in an average class. **Majors with Highest Enrollment:** Design and visual communications, general; business, management, marketing, and related support services; human services, general. **Disciplines with Highest Percentage of Degrees Awarded:** Business/marketing 30%, protective services/public administration 27%, visual and performing arts 23%, liberal arts/general studies 17%, education 3%. **Special Study Options:** Honors program, independent study, internships, student-designed major, study abroad, teacher certification program, spring term for junior in London.

FACILITIES

Housing: Coed, all-female. **Library Holdings:** 61,694 bound volumes. 526 periodicals. 11,710 microforms. 1,630 audiovisuals. **Computers:** School-owned computers available for student use.

EXTRACURRICULARS

Activities: Choral groups, drama/theater, literary magazine, music ensembles, musical theater, radio station, student government, student newspaper, television station, yearbook. **Organizations:** 17 registered organizations, 1 honor society. **Athletics (Intercollegiate):** *Men:* baseball, basketball, crew, golf, lacrosse, soccer. *Women:* basketball, crew, lacrosse, soccer, softball, volleyball.

ADMISSIONS

Selectivity Rating: 63 (of 100). **Freshman Academic Profile:** Average high school GPA 2.8. 90% from public high schools. Average SAT I Math 447, SAT I Math middle 50% range 410-510. Average SAT I Verbal 455, SAT I Verbal middle 50% range 420-530. Average ACT 18, ACT middle 50% range 16-22. TOEFL required of all international applicants, minimum TOEFL 550. **Basis for Candidate Selection:** *Very important factors considered include:* character/personal qualities, extracurricular activities, interview, secondary school record. *Important factors considered include:* class rank, recommendations, standardized test scores, work experience. *Other factors considered include:* alumni/ae relation, essays, talent/ability, volunteer work. **Freshman Admission Requirements:** High school diploma or GED is required. *Academic units required/recommended:* 16 total recommended; 4 English recommended, 2 math recommended, 2 science recommended, 4 social studies recommended. **Freshman Admission Statistics:** 964 applied, 82% accepted, 33% of those accepted enrolled. **Transfer Admission Requirements:** *Items required:* high school transcript, college transcript. Minimum high school GPA of 2.0 required. Minimum college GPA of 2.0 required. Lowest grade transferable C. **General Admission Information:** Application fee $25. Priority application deadline July 2. Regular application deadline August 25. Nonfall registration accepted. Credit and/or placement offered for CEEB Advanced Placement tests.

COSTS AND FINANCIAL AID

Tuition $15,650. Room & board $6,700. Required fees $220. Average book expense $900. **Required Forms and Deadlines:** FAFSA. No deadline for regular filing. **Notification of Awards:** Applicants will be notified of awards on a rolling basis. **Types of Aid:** *Need-based scholarships/grants:* Pell, SEOG, state scholarships/grants, private scholarships, the school's own gift aid. *Loans:* Direct Subsidized Stafford, Direct Unsubsidized Stafford, Direct PLUS, FFEL Subsidized Stafford, FFEL PLUS, Federal Perkins, state loans. **Student Employment:** Federal Work-Study Program available. Institutional employment available. Off-campus job opportunities are good. **Financial Aid Statistics:** 89% freshmen, 68% undergrads receive some form of aid. Average freshman grant $6,000. Average freshman loan $3,000. Average income from on-campus job $367. **Financial Aid Phone:** 315-655-7208.

See page 964.

CEDAR CREST COLLEGE

100 College Drive, Allentown, PA 18104-6196
Phone: 610-740-3780 **E-mail:** cccadmis@cedarcrest.edu **CEEB Code:** 2079
Fax: 610-606-4647 **Web:** www.cedarcrest.edu **ACT Code:** 3536

This private school, which is affiliated with the United Church of Christ, was founded in 1867. It has an 84-acre campus.

STUDENTS AND FACULTY

Enrollment: 1,593. **Student Body:** Male 5%, female 95%, out-of-state 18%, international 1% (18 countries represented). **Ethnic Representation:** African American 5%, Asian 2%, Caucasian 85%, Hispanic 5%. **Retention and Graduation:** 83% freshmen return for sophomore year. 54% freshmen graduate within 4 years. 40% grads go on to further study within 1 year. 1% grads pursue business degrees. 1% grads pursue law degrees. 2% grads pursue medical degrees. **Faculty:** Student/faculty ratio 11:1. 69 full-time faculty, 75% hold PhDs. 100% faculty teach undergrads.

ACADEMICS

Degrees: Associate's, bachelor's, certificate, post-bachelor's certificate, terminal. **Academic Requirements:** General education including some course work in arts/fine arts, English (including composition), mathematics, sciences (biological or physical), philosophy, foreign languages, history, and social science. **Classes:** 10-19 students in an average class. 10-19 students in an average lab/discussion section. **Disciplines with Highest Percentage of Degrees Awarded:** Psychology 20%, health professions and related sciences 19%, business/marketing 15%, protective services/public administration 8%, computer and information sciences 6%. **Special Study Options:** Accelerated program, cross registration, distance learning, double major, dual enrollment, English as a second language, honors program, independent study, internships, student-designed major, study abroad, teacher certification program, weekend college.

FACILITIES

Housing: All-female, housing for disabled students. **Library Holdings:** 105,038 bound volumes. 676 periodicals. 12,941 microforms. 16,126 audiovisuals. **Special Academic Facilities/Equipment:** Art gallery, theatres, arboretum, genetic engineering labs, nutrition computer lab, radio station, sculpture garden, multimedia lecture hall, alumnae museum. **Computers:** *Recommended operating system:* Windows 95. School-owned computers available for student use.

EXTRACURRICULARS

Activities: Choral groups, dance, drama/theater, literary magazine, music ensembles, musical theater, radio station, student government, student newspaper, television station, yearbook. **Organizations:** 46 registered organizations, 11 honor societies, 3 religious organizations. **Athletics (Intercollegiate):** *Women:* basketball, cross-country, field hockey, lacrosse, soccer, softball, tennis, volleyball.

ADMISSIONS

Selectivity Rating: 69 (of 100). **Freshman Academic Profile:** Average high school GPA 3.2. 22% in top 10% of high school class, 54% in top 25% of high school class, 88% in top 50% of high school class. 95% from public high schools. Average SAT I Math 531, SAT I Math middle 50% range 460-590. Average SAT I Verbal 548, SAT I Verbal middle 50% range 480-610. Average ACT 24, ACT middle 50% range 21-28. TOEFL required of all international applicants, minimum TOEFL 500. **Basis for Candidate Selection:** *Very important factors considered include:* class rank, secondary school record, standardized test scores. *Important factors considered include:* character/personal qualities, essays, extracurricular activities, interview, recommendations, talent/ability. *Other factors considered include:* alumni/ae relation, volunteer work, work experience. **Freshman Admission Requirements:** High school diploma or GED is required. *Academic units required/recommended:* 16 total required; 3 total recommended; 4 English required, 3 math required, 2 science required, 2 science lab required, 2 foreign language required, 3 social studies required, 3 elective recommended. **Freshman Admission Statistics:** 1,083 applied, 76% accepted, 21% of those accepted enrolled. **Transfer Admission Requirements:** *Items required:* high school transcript, college transcript. Minimum college GPA of 2.0 required. Lowest grade transferable C. **General Admission Information:** Application fee $30. Nonfall registration accepted. Admission may be deferred for a maximum of 2 years. Credit and/or placement offered for CEEB Advanced Placement tests.

COSTS AND FINANCIAL AID

Tuition $18,680. Room & board $6,725. Required fees $0. Average book expense $500. **Required Forms and Deadlines:** FAFSA and institution's own financial aid form. No deadline for regular filing. **Notification of Awards:** Applicants will be notified of awards on a rolling basis beginning on or about November 1. **Types of Aid:** *Need-based scholarships/grants:* Pell, SEOG, state scholarships/grants, private scholarships, the school's own gift aid. *Loans:* FFEL Subsidized Stafford, FFEL Unsubsidized Stafford, FFEL PLUS, Federal Perkins, Federal Nursing, college/university loans from institutional funds. **Student Employment:** Federal Work-Study Program available. Institutional employment available. Off-campus job opportunities are excellent. **Financial Aid Statistics:** 89% freshmen, 86% undergrads receive some form of aid. Average freshman grant $13,985. Average freshman loan $3,272. Average income from on-campus job $1,100. **Financial Aid Phone:** 610-740-3785.

CEDARVILLE UNIVERSITY

251 N. Main Street, Cedarville, OH 45314
Phone: 937-766-7700 **E-mail:** admissions@cedarville.edu
Fax: 937-766-7575 **Web:** www.cedarville.edu **ACT Code:** 3245

This private school, which is affiliated with the Baptist Church, was founded in 1887. It has a 400-acre campus.

STUDENTS AND FACULTY

Enrollment: 2,986. **Student Body:** Male 46%, female 54%, out-of-state 65%, international 1% (3 countries represented). **Ethnic Representation:** African American 1%, Asian 1%, Caucasian 97%, Hispanic 1%. **Retention and Graduation:** 83% freshmen return for sophomore year. 56% freshmen graduate within 4 years. 9% grads go on to further study within 1 year. 1% grads pursue business degrees. 1% grads pursue law degrees. 1% grads pursue medical degrees. **Faculty:** Student/faculty ratio 16:1. 194 full-time faculty, 54% hold PhDs. 95% faculty teach undergrads.

ACADEMICS

Degrees: Bachelor's, certificate, master's. **Academic Requirements:** General education including some course work in arts/fine arts, English (including composition), history, humanities, mathematics, sciences (biological or physical), social science, biblical, PE. **Classes:** 10-19 students in an average class. 10-19 students in an average lab/discussion section. **Majors with Highest Enrollment:** Nursing/registered nurse training (RN, ASN, BSN, MSN); business administration/management; elementary education and teaching. **Disciplines with Highest Percentage of Degrees Awarded:** Education 18%, business/marketing 12%, philosophy/religion/theology 12%, communications/communication technologies 10%, health professions and related sciences 10%. **Special Study Options:** Accelerated program, distance learning, double major, dual enrollment, honors program, independent study, internships, study abroad, teacher certification program.

FACILITIES

Housing: All-female, all-male, apartments for married students. **Library Holdings:** 149,164 bound volumes. 4,932 periodicals. 21,382 microforms. 15,452 audiovisuals. **Computers:** *Recommended operating system:* Windows 95. School-owned computers available for student use.

EXTRACURRICULARS

Activities: Choral groups, concert band, drama/theater, music ensembles, musical theater, pep band, radio station, student government, student newspaper, yearbook. **Organizations:** 55 registered organizations. **Athletics (Intercollegiate):** *Men:* baseball, basketball, cheerleading, cross-country, golf, soccer, tennis, track & field. *Women:* basketball, cheerleading, cross-country, soccer, softball, tennis, track & field, volleyball.

ADMISSIONS

Selectivity Rating: 76 (of 100). **Freshman Academic Profile:** Average high school GPA 3.5. 31% in top 10% of high school class, 60% in top 25% of high school class, 88% in top 50% of high school class. 51% from public high schools. Average SAT I Math 581, SAT I Math middle 50% range 520-640. Average SAT I Verbal 583, SAT I Verbal middle 50% range 520-630. Average ACT 25, ACT middle 50% range 23-28. TOEFL required of all international applicants, minimum TOEFL 550. **Basis for Candidate Selection:** *Very important factors considered include:* character/personal qualities, essays, religious affiliation/commitment, secondary school record, standardized test scores. *Important factors considered include:* minority status, recommendations. *Other factors considered include:* alumni/ae relation, class rank, extracurricular activities, interview, talent/ability, volunteer work. **Freshman Admission Requirements:** High school diploma or GED is required. *Academic units required/recommended:* 15 total recommended; 4 English recommended, 3 math recommended, 3 science lab recommended, 2 foreign language recommended, 3 social studies recommended. **Freshman Admission Statistics:** 2,031 applied, 81% accepted, 47% of those accepted enrolled. **Transfer Admission Requirements:** *Items required:* high school transcript, college transcript, essay. Minimum college GPA of 3.0 required. Lowest grade transferable C-. **General Admission Information:** Application fee $30. Nonfall registration accepted. Admission may be deferred for a maximum of 1 year. Credit and/or placement offered for CEEB Advanced Placement tests.

COSTS AND FINANCIAL AID

Tuition $13,696. Room & board $5,010. Required fees $90. Average book expense $740. **Required Forms and Deadlines:** FAFSA and institution's own financial aid form. No deadline for regular filing. Priority filing deadline March 1. **Notification of Awards:** Applicants will be notified of awards on a rolling basis beginning on or about March 1. **Types of Aid:** *Need-based scholarships/grants:* Pell, SEOG, state scholarships/grants, private scholarships, the school's own gift aid. *Loans:* FFEL Subsidized Stafford, FFEL Unsubsidized Stafford, FFEL PLUS, Federal Perkins, Federal Nursing, state loans, college/university loans from institutional funds. **Student Employment:** Federal Work-Study Program available. Institutional employment available. Off-campus job opportunities are excellent. **Financial Aid Statistics:** 63% freshmen, 57% undergrads receive some form of aid. Average freshman grant $4,200. Average freshman loan $8,490. **Financial Aid Phone:** 937-766-7866.

CENTENARY COLLEGE (NJ)

400 Jefferson Street, Hackettstown, NJ 07840
Phone: 800-236-8679 **E-mail:** admissions@centenarycollege.edu **CEEB Code:** 2080
Fax: 908-852-3454 **Web:** www.centenarycollege.edu **ACT Code:** 2544

This private school, which is affiliated with the Methodist Church, was founded in 1867. It has a 42-acre campus.

STUDENTS AND FACULTY

Enrollment: 1,549. **Student Body:** Male 32%, female 68%, out-of-state 15%, international 4% (15 countries represented). **Ethnic Representation:** African American 3%, Asian 6%, Caucasian 58%, Hispanic 4%. **Retention and Graduation:** 71% freshmen return for sophomore year. 24% grads go on to further study within 1 year. 16% grads pursue business degrees. **Faculty:** Student/faculty ratio 15:1. 47 full-time faculty, 57% hold PhDs. 100% faculty teach undergrads.

ACADEMICS

Degrees: Associate's, bachelor's, master's, post-bachelor's certificate, terminal, transfer. **Academic Requirements:** General education including some course work in arts/fine arts, English (including composition), history, humanities, mathematics, sciences (biological or physical), social science. **Majors with Highest Enrollment:** Equestrian/equine studies; elementary education and teaching; business administration/management. **Disciplines with Highest Percentage of Degrees Awarded:** Business/marketing 42%, social sciences and history 16%, psychology 15%, English 10%, agriculture 6%. **Special Study Options:** Accelerated program, double major, English as a second language, honors program, independent study, internships, liberal arts/career combination, student-designed major, study abroad, teacher certification program.

FACILITIES

Housing: Coed, all-female. **Library Holdings:** 96,939 bound volumes. 211 periodicals. 21,472 microforms. 5,124 audiovisuals. **Special Academic Facilities/Equipment:** Art gallery, radio station WNTI 91.9FM, Equity-status theater, equestrian center. **Computers:** School-owned computers available for student use.

EXTRACURRICULARS

Activities: Choral groups, dance, drama/theater, literary magazine, radio station, student government, student newspaper, television station, yearbook. **Organizations:** 27 registered organizations, 2 honor societies, 2 fraternities (18% men join), 3 sororities (21% women join). **Athletics (Intercollegiate):** *Men:* baseball, basketball, cross-country, golf, lacrosse, soccer, wrestling. *Women:* basketball, cross-country, golf, lacrosse, soccer, softball, volleyball.

ADMISSIONS

Selectivity Rating: 63 (of 100). **Freshman Academic Profile:** Average high school GPA 2.5. 8% in top 10% of high school class, 22% in top 25% of high school class, 56% in top 50% of high school class. 85% from public high schools. Average SAT I Math 455, SAT I Math middle 50% range 400-500. Average SAT I Verbal 460, SAT I Verbal middle 50% range 400-510. Average ACT 19, ACT middle 50% range 17-21. TOEFL required of all international applicants, minimum TOEFL 450. **Basis for Candidate Selection:** *Very important factors considered include:* secondary school record, standardized test scores. *Important factors considered include:* alumni/ae relation, character/personal qualities, essays, extracurricular activities, talent/ability, volunteer work. *Other factors considered include:* class rank, interview, recommendations, work experience. **Freshman Admission Requirements:** High school diploma or GED is required. *Academic units required/recommended:* 16 total required; 4 English required, 3 math required, 4 math recommended, 2 science required, 4 science recommended, 2 science lab required, 2 foreign language recommended, 4 social studies recommended, 2 history required, 3 history recommended, 3 elective required. **Freshman Admission Statistics:** 737 applied, 73% accepted, 44% of those accepted enrolled. **Transfer Admission Requirements:** *Items required:* college transcript. Minimum college GPA of 1.8 required. Lowest grade transferable C-. **General Admission Information:** Application fee $30. Priority application deadline July 1. Nonfall registration accepted. Admission may be deferred. Credit offered for CEEB Advanced Placement tests.

COSTS AND FINANCIAL AID

Tuition $15,700. Room & board $6,850. Required fees $1,100. Average book expense $666. **Required Forms and Deadlines:** FAFSA and institution's own financial aid form. No deadline for regular filing. Priority filing deadline June 1. **Notification of Awards:** Applicants will be notified of awards on a rolling basis beginning on or about March 1. **Types of Aid:** *Need-based scholarships/grants:* Pell, SEOG, state scholarships/grants, the school's own gift aid. *Loans:* FFEL Subsidized Stafford, FFEL Unsubsidized Stafford, FFEL PLUS, Federal Perkins. **Student Employment:** Federal Work-Study Program available. Institutional employment available. Off-campus job opportunities are excellent. **Financial Aid Statistics:** 58% freshmen receive some form of aid. Average freshman grant $5,267. Average freshman loan $6,468. Average income from on-campus job $645. **Financial Aid Phone:** 908-852-1400.

CENTENARY COLLEGE OF LOUISIANA

PO Box 41188, Shreveport, LA 71134-1188
Phone: 318-869-5131 **E-mail:** admissions@centenary.edu **CEEB Code:** 6082
Fax: 318-869-5005 **Web:** www.centenary.edu **ACT Code:** 1576

This private school, which is affiliated with the Methodist Church, was founded in 1825. It has a 68-acre campus.

STUDENTS AND FACULTY

Enrollment: 897. **Student Body:** Male 39%, female 61%, out-of-state 39%, international 3% (18 countries represented). **Ethnic Representation:** African American 7%, Asian 2%, Caucasian 88%, Hispanic 2%, Native American 1%. **Retention and Graduation:** 69% freshmen return for sophomore year. 50% grads go on to further study within 1 year. **Faculty:** Student/faculty ratio 12:1. 73 full-time faculty, 91% hold PhDs. 100% faculty teach undergrads.

ACADEMICS

Degrees: Bachelor's, master's. **Academic Requirements:** General education including some course work in arts/fine arts, computer literacy, English (including composition), foreign languages, history, humanities, mathematics, sciences (biological or physical), social science, religion. **Classes:** 10-19 students in an average class. **Majors with Highest Enrollment:** Business administration/management; biology/biological sciences, general; communications, journalism, and related fields. **Disciplines with Highest Percentage of Degrees Awarded:** Business/marketing 17%, health professions and related sciences 12%, biological life sciences 10%, communications/communication technologies 8%, visual and performing arts 8%. **Special Study Options:** Cross registration, double major, dual enrollment, student exchange program (domestic), independent study, internships, liberal arts/career combination, student-designed major, study abroad, teacher certification program, Oak Ridge National Observatory semester 3-2 engineering program, 3-2 communication disorder program, and Washington semester.

FACILITIES

Housing: Coed, all-female, all-male, fraternities and/or sororities. **Library Holdings:** 325,671 bound volumes. 59,899 periodicals. 1,454 microforms. 5,945 audiovisuals. **Special Academic Facilities/Equipment:** Art museum, art center, art studios, theatre, performance and practice organs, piano lab, language lab, School of Music recording studio, science hall multimedia auditorium. **Computers:** School-owned computers available for student use.

EXTRACURRICULARS

Activities: Choral groups, concert band, dance, drama/theater, jazz band, literary magazine, music ensembles, musical theater, opera, pep band, radio station, student government, student newspaper, student-run film society, symphony orchestra, yearbook. **Organizations:** 3 religious organizations, 4 fraternities (12% men join), 2 sororities (18% women join). **Athletics (Intercollegiate):** *Men:* baseball, basketball, cross-country, golf, rifle, soccer, swimming, tennis. *Women:* basketball, cross-country, golf, gymnastics, rifle, soccer, softball, swimming, tennis, volleyball.

ADMISSIONS

Selectivity Rating: 76 (of 100). **Freshman Academic Profile:** 30% in top 10% of high school class, 60% in top 25% of high school class, 87% in top 50% of high school class. SAT I Math middle 50% range 550-650. SAT I Verbal middle 50% range 530-650. Average ACT 25, ACT middle 50% range 23-28. TOEFL required of all international applicants, minimum TOEFL 600. **Basis for Candidate Selection:** *Very important factors considered include:* secondary school record. *Important factors considered include:* alumni/ae relation, character/personal qualities, extracurricular activities, interview, standardized test scores, talent/ability, volunteer work. *Other factors considered include:* class rank, essays, geographical residence, minority status, recommendations, religious affiliation/commitment, work experience. **Freshman Admission Requirements:** High school diploma or GED is required. *Academic units required/recommended:* 15 total recommended; 4 English recommended, 3 math recommended, 3 science recommended, 2 science lab recommended, 2 foreign language recommended, 3 social studies recommended. **Freshman Admission Statistics:** 936 applied, 65% accepted, 45% of those accepted enrolled. **Transfer Admission Requirements:** *Items required:* high school transcript, college transcript. Minimum high school GPA of 2.0 required. Minimum college GPA of 2.0 required. Lowest grade transferable C. **General Admission Information:** Application fee $30. Priority application deadline February 15. Early decision application deadline December 1. Nonfall registration accepted. Admission may be deferred for a maximum of 1 year. Credit and/or placement offered for CEEB Advanced Placement tests.

COSTS AND FINANCIAL AID

Tuition $16,000. Room & board $5,550. Required fees $450. Average book expense $1,000. **Required Forms and Deadlines:** FAFSA and institution's own financial aid form. No deadline for regular filing. Priority filing deadline February 15. **Notification of Awards:** Applicants will be notified of awards on or about March 15. **Types of Aid:** *Need-based scholarships/grants:* Pell, SEOG, state scholarships/grants, private scholarships, the school's own gift aid. *Loans:* FFEL Subsidized Stafford, FFEL Unsubsidized Stafford, FFEL PLUS, Federal Perkins. **Student Employment:** Federal Work-Study Program available. Institutional employment available. Off-campus job opportunities are excellent. **Financial Aid Statistics:** 67% freshmen, 63% undergrads receive some form of aid. **Financial Aid Phone:** 318-869-5137.

CENTRAL COLLEGE

812 University Street, Pella, IA 50219-1999
Phone: 877-462-3687 **E-mail:** admission@central.edu **CEEB Code:** 6087
Fax: 641-628-5316 **Web:** www.central.edu **ACT Code:** 1284

This private school, which is affiliated with the Reformed Church, was founded in 1853. It has a 133-acre campus.

STUDENTS AND FACULTY

Enrollment: 1,659. **Student Body:** Male 43%, female 57%, out-of-state 17%, international 1%. **Ethnic Representation:** African American 1%, Asian 1%, Caucasian 96%, Hispanic 2%. **Retention and Graduation:** 82% freshmen return for sophomore year. 51% freshmen graduate within 4 years. 15% grads go on to further study within 1 year. 1% grads pursue business degrees. 1% grads pursue law degrees. 4% grads pursue medical degrees. **Faculty:** Student/faculty ratio 14:1. 89 full-time faculty, 79% hold PhDs. 100% faculty teach undergrads.

ACADEMICS

Degrees: Bachelor's. **Academic Requirements:** General education including some course work in arts/fine arts, English (including composition), foreign languages, history, humanities, mathematics, philosophy, sciences (biological or physical), social science, religion, nonwestern culture. **Majors with Highest Enrollment:** Business administration/management; education, general; kinesiology and exercise science. **Disciplines with Highest Percentage of Degrees Awarded:** Education 15%, business/marketing 14%, health professions and related sciences 11%, computer and information sciences 8%, social sciences and history 8%. **Special Study Options:** Double major, English as a second language, honors program, independent study, internships, liberal arts/career combination, student-designed major, study abroad, teacher certification program. Off-campus study: Washington, DC; Chicago Metro Program. Exploring Student Program encourages 2 years of multidisciplinary study before selecting a major.

FACILITIES

Housing: Coed, all-female, all-male, apartments for married students, apartments for single students, housing for international students, fraternities and/or sororities. **Library Holdings:** 220,526 bound volumes. 1,161 periodicals. 55,313 microforms. 13,160 audiovisuals. **Special Academic Facilities/Equipment:** Art gallery, center for communication and theatre, music center, language lab, glass-blowing studio. **Computers:** School-owned computers available for student use.

EXTRACURRICULARS

Activities: Choral groups, concert band, drama/theater, jazz band, literary magazine, music ensembles, musical theater, radio station, student government, student newspaper, symphony orchestra, yearbook. **Organizations:** 50 registered organizations, 4 religious organizations, 4 fraternities (15% men join), 2 sororities (7% women join). **Athletics (Intercollegiate):** *Men:* baseball, basketball, football, golf, soccer, tennis, track & field. *Women:* basketball, cross-country, golf, softball, tennis, track & field, volleyball.

ADMISSIONS

Selectivity Rating: 76 (of 100). **Freshman Academic Profile:** Average high school GPA 3.5. 27% in top 10% of high school class, 58% in top 25% of high school class, 85% in top 50% of high school class. 98% from public high schools. Average SAT I Math 575. Average SAT I Verbal 553. Average ACT 23. TOEFL required of all international applicants, minimum TOEFL 530. **Basis for Candidate Selection:** *Very important factors considered include:* secondary school record, standardized test scores. *Important factors considered include:* class rank, recommendations. *Other factors considered include:* character/personal qualities, essays, extracurricular activities, interview, volunteer work, work experience. **Freshman Admission Requirements:** High school diploma or GED is required. *Academic units required/recommended:* 18 total recommended; 4 English recommended, 3 math recommended, 2 science recommended, 2 science lab recommended, 2 foreign language recommended, 3 social studies recommended, 2 history recommended. **Freshman Admission Statistics:** 1,598 applied, 86% accepted, 31% of those accepted enrolled. **Transfer Admission Requirements:** *Items required:* high school transcript, college transcript, standardized test scores. Minimum college GPA of 2.0 required. Lowest grade transferable C-. **General Admission Information:** Application fee $25. Nonfall registration accepted. Admission may be deferred for a maximum of 1 year. Credit and/or placement offered for CEEB Advanced Placement tests.

COSTS AND FINANCIAL AID

Tuition $16,612. Room & board $5,796. Required fees $144. Average book expense $750. **Required Forms and Deadlines:** FAFSA. Priority filing deadline March 1. **Notification of Awards:** Applicants will be notified of awards on a rolling basis beginning on or about March 10. **Types of Aid:** *Need-based scholarships/grants:* Pell, SEOG, state scholarships/grants, private scholarships, the school's own gift aid. *Loans:* Direct Subsidized Stafford, Direct Unsubsidized Stafford, Direct PLUS, Federal Perkins, college/university loans from institutional funds. **Student Employment:** Federal Work-Study Program available. Institutional employment available. Off-campus job opportunities are excellent. **Financial Aid Statistics:** 84% freshmen, 83% undergrads receive some form of aid. Average freshman grant $11,404. Average freshman loan $3,548. Average income from on-campus job $1,089. **Financial Aid Phone:** 641-628-5268.

CENTRAL CONNECTICUT STATE UNIVERSITY

1615 Stanley Street, New Britain, CT 06050
Phone: 800-832-3200 **E-mail:** admissions@ccsu.edu **CEEB Code:** 3898
Fax: 862-832-2295 **Web:** www.ccsu.edu **ACT Code:** 596

This public school was founded in 1849. It has a 294-acre campus.

STUDENTS AND FACULTY

Enrollment: 9,794. **Student Body:** Male 49%, female 51%, out-of-state 4%, international 2%. **Ethnic Representation:** African American 7%, Asian 3%, Caucasian 77%, Hispanic 5%. **Retention and Graduation:** 74% freshmen return for sophomore year. 15% freshmen graduate within 4 years. 28% grads go on to further study within 1 year. 6% grads pursue business degrees. 1% grads pursue law degrees. **Faculty:** Student/faculty ratio 17:1. 400 full-time faculty, 75% hold PhDs. 100% faculty teach undergrads.

ACADEMICS

Degrees: Bachelor's, doctoral, master's, post-bachelor's certificate. **Academic Requirements:** General education including some course work in arts/fine arts, computer literacy, English (including composition), foreign languages, history, humanities, mathematics, philosophy, sciences (biological or physical), social science. **Classes:** 20-29 students in an average class. 10-19 students in an average lab/discussion section. **Majors with Highest Enrollment:** Accounting; teacher education, multiple levels; psychology, general. **Disciplines with Highest Percentage of Degrees Awarded:** Business/marketing 27%, social sciences and history 16%, psychology 9%, English 8%, engineering/engineering technology 7%. **Special Study Options:** Cooperative (work-study) program, cross registration, distance learning, double major, student exchange program (domestic), honors program, independent study, internships, student-designed major, study abroad, teacher certification program. Undergrads may take grad classes. Co-op programs: arts, business, computer science, education, humanities, natural science, social/behavioral science, technologies.

FACILITIES

Housing: Coed, all-female, all-male. **Library Holdings:** 639,257 bound volumes. 2,762 periodicals. 552,591 microforms. 5,669 audiovisuals. **Special Academic Facilities/Equipment:** Art gallery, language lab, childhood center, planetarium and space science center, center for economic education, TV studio. **Computers:** School-owned computers available for student use.

EXTRACURRICULARS

Activities: Choral groups, concert band, dance, drama/theater, jazz band, literary magazine, musical theater, radio station, student government, student newspaper, student-run film society, television station. **Organizations:** 100 registered organizations, 18 honor societies, 1% men join fraternities, 1% women join sororities. **Athletics (Intercollegiate):** *Men:* baseball, basketball, cross-country, football, golf, soccer, track & field. *Women:* cross-country, diving, golf, lacrosse, soccer, softball, swimming, track & field, volleyball.

ADMISSIONS

Selectivity Rating: 69 (of 100). **Freshman Academic Profile:** 5% in top 10% of high school class, 22% in top 25% of high school class, 61% in top 50% of high school class. Average SAT I Math 493, SAT I Math middle 50% range 440-530. Average SAT I Verbal 491, SAT I Verbal middle 50% range 440-540. TOEFL required of all international applicants, minimum TOEFL 500. **Basis for Candidate Selection:** *Very important factors considered include:* secondary school record. *Important factors considered include:* class rank, standardized test scores. *Other factors considered include:* essays, extracurricular activities, interview, minority status, recommendations, state residency, talent/ability. **Freshman Admission Requirements:** High school diploma or GED is required. *Academic units required/recommended:* 13 total required; 4 total recommended; 4 English required, 3 math required, 1 math recommended, 2 science required, 1 science lab required, 3 foreign language recommended, 2 social studies required, 1 history required. **Freshman Admission Statistics:** 5,123 applied, 61% accepted, 50% of those accepted enrolled. **Transfer Admission Requirements:** *Items required:* high school transcript, college transcript, statement of good standing from prior school. Minimum college GPA of 2.0 required. Lowest grade transferable C. **General Admission Information:** Application fee $40. Priority application deadline October 1. Regular application deadline May 1. Nonfall registration accepted. Credit offered for CEEB Advanced Placement tests.

COSTS AND FINANCIAL AID

In-state tuition $2,313. Out-of-state tuition $7,485. Room & board $6,280. Required fees $2,456. Average book expense $750. **Required Forms and Deadlines:** FAFSA. Financial aid filing deadline September 24. Priority filing deadline February 15. **Notification of Awards:** Applicants will be notified of awards on a rolling basis beginning on or about March 15. **Types of Aid:** *Need-based scholarships/grants:* Pell, SEOG, state scholarships/grants, the school's own gift aid. *Loans:* Direct Subsidized Stafford, Direct Unsubsidized Stafford, Direct PLUS, FFEL PLUS, Federal Perkins. **Student Employment:** Federal Work-Study Program available. Off-campus job opportunities are excellent. **Financial Aid Statistics:** 37% freshmen, 29% undergrads receive some form of aid. Average freshman grant $3,306. Average freshman loan $3,023. Average income from on-campus job $1,000. **Financial Aid Phone:** 860-832-2200.

CENTRAL METHODIST COLLEGE

411 CMC Square, Fayette, MO 65248
Phone: 660-248-6251 **E-mail:** admissions@cmc.edu **CEEB Code:** 6089
Fax: 660-248-1872 **Web:** www.cmc.edu **ACT Code:** 2270

This private school, which is affiliated with the Methodist Church, was founded in 1854. It has a 90-acre campus.

STUDENTS AND FACULTY

Enrollment: 1,295. **Student Body:** Male 42%, female 58%, out-of-state 3%, international 1% (15 countries represented). **Ethnic Representation:** African American 7%, Asian 1%, Caucasian 87%, Hispanic 1%. **Retention and Graduation:** 63% freshmen return for sophomore year. 16% freshmen graduate within 4 years. 15% grads go on to further study within 1 year. 5% grads pursue business degrees. 5% grads pursue law degrees. 4% grads pursue medical degrees. **Faculty:** Student/faculty ratio 14:1. 52 full-time faculty, 67% hold PhDs. 100% faculty teach undergrads.

ACADEMICS

Degrees: Associate's, bachelor's, master's. **Academic Requirements:** General education including some course work in computer literacy, English (including composition), history, humanities, mathematics, sciences (biological or physical), social science, human character formation, development and cultural diversity. **Classes:** 10-19 students in an average class. **Majors with Highest Enrollment:** Business administration/management; elementary education and teaching; early childhood education and teaching. **Disciplines with Highest Percentage of Degrees Awarded:** Education 46%, business/marketing 15%, psychology 6%, protective services/public administration 6%, biological life sciences 5%. **Special Study Options:** Accelerated program, distance learning, double major, dual enrollment, honors program, independent study, internships, liberal arts/career combination, student-designed major, study abroad, teacher certification program.

FACILITIES

Housing: Coed, all-female, all-male, apartments for married students, apartments for single students. **Library Holdings:** 97,793 bound volumes. 316 periodicals. 140,742 microforms. 3,709 audiovisuals. **Special Academic Facilities/Equipment:** 2 museums, telecommunity technology center, computer lab in residence halls. **Computers:** *Recommended operating system:* Windows 2000 Pro or greater. School-owned computers available for student use.

EXTRACURRICULARS

Activities: Choral groups, concert band, drama/theater, jazz band, literary magazine, marching band, music ensembles, musical theater, radio station, student government, student newspaper, symphony orchestra, television station. **Organizations:** 41 registered organizations, 13 honor societies, 2 religious organizations, 6 fraternities (25% men join), 4 sororities (30% women join). **Athletics (Intercollegiate):** *Men:* baseball, basketball, cheerleading, cross-country, football, golf, soccer, track & field. *Women:* basketball, cheerleading, cross-country, golf, soccer, softball, track & field, volleyball.

ADMISSIONS

Selectivity Rating: 66 (of 100). **Freshman Academic Profile:** Average high school GPA 3.0. 11% in top 10% of high school class, 33% in top 25% of high school class, 70% in top 50% of high school class. Average ACT 21, ACT middle 50% range 18-23. TOEFL required of all international applicants, minimum TOEFL 500. **Basis for Candidate Selection:** *Very important factors considered include:* class rank, extracurricular activities, secondary school record, standardized test scores. *Important factors considered include:* alumni/ae relation, character/personal qualities, minority status, religious affiliation/commitment, talent/ability, volunteer work, work experience. *Other factors considered include:* geographical residence, interview, recommendations, state residency. **Freshman Admission Requirements:** High school diploma or GED is required. *Academic units required/recommended:* 20 total recommended; 4 English recommended, 4 math recommended, 5 science recommended, 2 foreign language recommended, 3 social studies recommended. **Freshman Admission Statistics:** 1,059 applied, 76% accepted, 29% of those accepted enrolled. **Transfer Admission Requirements:** *Items required:* high school transcript, college transcript, standardized test scores, statement of good standing from prior school. Minimum college GPA of 2.0 required. Lowest grade transferable D. **General Admission Information:** Priority application deadline July 1. Regular application deadline August 1. Nonfall registration accepted. Admission may be deferred. Credit offered for CEEB Advanced Placement tests.

COSTS AND FINANCIAL AID

Tuition $12,420. Room & board $4,820. Required fees $210. Average book expense $650. **Required Forms and Deadlines:** FAFSA. Priority filing deadline March 15. **Notification of Awards:** Applicants will be notified of awards on a rolling basis beginning on or about March 1. **Types of Aid:** *Need-based scholarships/grants:* Pell, SEOG, state scholarships/grants, private scholarships, the school's own gift aid. *Loans:* FFEL Subsidized Stafford, FFEL Unsubsidized Stafford, FFEL PLUS, Federal Perkins, Federal Nursing. **Student Employment:** Federal Work-Study Program available. Off-campus job opportunities are good. **Financial Aid Statistics:** Average freshman grant $11,521. Average freshman loan $2,625. Average income from on-campus job $4,098. **Financial Aid Phone:** 660-248-6245.

CENTRAL MICHIGAN UNIVERSITY

105 Warriner Hall, Mount Pleasant, MI 48859
Phone: 989-774-3076 **E-mail:** cmuadmit@cmich.edu **CEEB Code:** 1106
Fax: 989-774-7267 **Web:** www.cmich.edu **ACT Code:** 1972

This public school was founded in 1892. It has an 854-acre campus.

STUDENTS AND FACULTY

Enrollment: 19,696. **Student Body:** Male 41%, female 59%, out-of-state 3%, international 1%. **Ethnic Representation:** African American 6%, Asian 1%, Caucasian 87%, Hispanic 2%, Native American 1%. **Retention and Graduation:** 17% freshmen graduate within 4 years. 11% grads go on to further study within 1 year. **Faculty:** Student/faculty ratio 22:1. 719 full-time faculty, 78% hold PhDs. 99% faculty teach undergrads.

ACADEMICS

Degrees: Bachelor's, doctoral, master's, post-bachelor's certificate. **Academic Requirements:** General education including some course work in arts/fine arts, English (including composition), humanities, mathematics, sciences (biological or physical), social science. **Classes:** 20-29 students in an average class. 20-29 students in an average lab/discussion section. **Majors with Highest Enrollment:** Business, management, marketing, and related support services; psychology, general; community organization and advocacy. **Disciplines with Highest Percentage of Degrees Awarded:** Business/marketing 31%, education 10%, social sciences and history 10%, parks and recreation 6%, English 6%. **Special Study Options:** Accelerated program, cooperative (work-study) program, distance learning, double major, dual enrollment, English as a second language, external degree program, honors program, independent study, internships, student-designed major, study abroad, teacher certification program. Undergrads may take grad classes. Co-op programs: technologies, vocational arts.

FACILITIES

Housing: Coed, all-female, all-male, apartments for married students, apartments for single students, housing for disabled students, fraternities and/or sororities. **Library Holdings:** 998,460 bound volumes. 4,634 periodicals. 1,281,501 microforms. 24,630 audiovisuals. **Special Academic Facilities/ Equipment:** Cultural and natural history center, language lab. **Computers:** *Recommended operating system:* Windows NT/2000. School-owned computers available for student use.

EXTRACURRICULARS

Activities: Choral groups, concert band, dance, drama/theater, jazz band, literary magazine, marching band, music ensembles, musical theater, pep band, radio station, student government, student newspaper, symphony orchestra, television station, yearbook. **Organizations:** 200 registered organizations, 34 honor societies, 10 religious organizations, 15 fraternities (7% men join), 16 sororities (8% women join). **Athletics (Intercollegiate):** *Men:* baseball, basketball, cross-country, football, indoor track, track & field, wrestling. *Women:* basketball, cross-country, field hockey, gymnastics, indoor track, soccer, softball, track & field, volleyball.

ADMISSIONS

Selectivity Rating: 70 (of 100). **Freshman Academic Profile:** Average high school GPA 3.4. 19% in top 10% of high school class, 48% in top 25% of high school class, 83% in top 50% of high school class. 95% from public high schools. SAT I Math middle 50% range 450-575. SAT I Verbal middle 50% range 475-600. Average ACT 22, ACT middle 50% range 20-25. TOEFL required of all international applicants, minimum TOEFL 550. **Basis for Candidate Selection:** *Very important factors considered include:* secondary school record. *Important factors considered include:* extracurricular activities, recommendations, standardized test scores. *Other factors considered include:* alumni/ae relation, class rank, essays, geographical residence, interview, state residency, talent/ability, volunteer work, work experience. **Freshman Admission Requirements:** High school diploma or GED is required. *Academic units required/recommended:* 19 total recommended; 4 English recommended, 4 math recommended, 3 science recommended, 2 foreign language recommended, 2 social studies recommended, 2 history recommended. **Freshman Admission Statistics:** 13,445 applied, 68% accepted, 40% of those accepted enrolled. **Transfer Admission Requirements:** *Items required:* college transcript, statement of good standing from prior school. Minimum college GPA of 2.7 required. Lowest grade transferable C. **General Admission Information:** Application fee $25. Priority application deadline April 1. Nonfall registration accepted. Admission may be deferred for a maximum of 1 year. Credit and/or placement offered for CEEB Advanced Placement tests.

COSTS AND FINANCIAL AID

In-state tuition $3,992. Out-of-state tuition $10,364. Room & board $5,524. Required fees $755. Average book expense $850. **Required Forms and Deadlines:** FAFSA. No deadline for regular filing. Priority filing deadline February 1. **Notification of Awards:** Applicants will be notified of awards on a rolling basis beginning on or about April 1. **Types of Aid:** *Need-based scholarships/grants:* Pell, SEOG, state scholarships/grants, private scholarships, the school's own gift aid. *Loans:* Direct Subsidized Stafford, Direct Unsubsidized Stafford, Direct PLUS, Federal Perkins, state loans, alternative loans. **Student Employment:** Federal Work-Study Program available. Institutional employment available. Off-campus job opportunities are good. **Financial Aid Statistics:** 53% freshmen, 51% undergrads receive some form of aid. Average freshman grant $1,400. Average income from on-campus job $1,000. **Financial Aid Phone:** 989-774-3674.

CENTRAL MISSOURI STATE UNIVERSITY

Office of Admissions, WDE 1401, Warrensburg, MO 64093
Phone: 660-543-4290 **E-mail:** admit@cmsuvmb.cmsu.edu **CEEB Code:** 6090
Fax: 660-543-8517 **Web:** www.cmsu.edu **ACT Code:** 2272

This public school was founded in 1871. It has a 1,561-acre campus.

STUDENTS AND FACULTY

Enrollment: 8,732. **Student Body:** Male 46%, female 54%, out-of-state 6%, international 4% (65 countries represented). **Ethnic Representation:** African American 5%, Asian 1%, Caucasian 88%, Hispanic 2%, Native American 1%. **Retention and Graduation:** 70% freshmen return for sophomore year. 16% freshmen graduate within 4 years. 16% grads go on to further study within 1 year. 15% grads pursue business degrees. **Faculty:** Student/faculty ratio 17:1. 425 full-time faculty, 76% hold PhDs. 95% faculty teach undergrads.

ACADEMICS

Degrees: Associate's, bachelor's, master's, post-bachelor's certificate, post-master's certificate. **Academic Requirements:** General education including some course work in arts/fine arts, computer literacy, English (including composition), history, humanities, mathematics, sciences (biological or physical), social science, multicultural education, speech, personal development, integrative studies. **Classes:** 20-29 students in an average class. Under 10 students in an average lab/discussion section. **Majors with Highest Enrollment:** Office management and supervision; education, general; criminal justice/ law enforcement administration. **Disciplines with Highest Percentage of Degrees Awarded:** Education 23%, business/marketing 15%, engineering/ engineering technology 9%, protective services/public administration 9%, visual and performing arts 6%. **Special Study Options:** Cooperative (work-study) program, cross registration, distance learning, double major, dual enrollment, English as a second language, honors program, internships, student-designed major, study abroad, teacher certification program, weekend college.

FACILITIES

Housing: Coed, all-female, apartments for married students, apartments for single students, housing for disabled students, housing for international students, fraternities and/or sororities, economy suites and townhouses. **Library Holdings:** 580,675 bound volumes. 3,606 periodicals. 1,576,341 microforms. 23,690 audiovisuals. **Special Academic Facilities/Equipment:** Art gallery, Nance Museum & Library of Antiquities, natural history museum, English language center, child development lab, speech and hearing lab, 260-acre farm, Missouri Safety Center, National Police Institute, driving/safety range, center for technology and business research, airport for aviation program. Extended campus at Lee's Summit, MO. KCMW-FM, KMOS-TV public broadcasting stations. **Computers:** School-owned computers available for student use.

EXTRACURRICULARS

Activities: Choral groups, concert band, dance, drama/theater, jazz band, literary magazine, marching band, music ensembles, musical theater, opera, pep band, radio station, student government, student newspaper, student-run film society, symphony orchestra, television station, yearbook. **Organizations:** 150 registered organizations, 24 honor societies, 9 religious organizations, 13 fraternities (19% men join), 9 sororities (13% women join). **Athletics (Intercollegiate):** *Men:* baseball, basketball, cross-country, football, golf, track & field, wrestling. *Women:* basketball, cross-country, soccer, softball, track & field, volleyball.

ADMISSIONS

Selectivity Rating: 73 (of 100). **Freshman Academic Profile:** 16% in top 10% of high school class, 40% in top 25% of high school class, 75% in top 50% of high school class. 91% from public high schools. Average ACT 22, ACT middle 50% range 19-24. TOEFL required of all international applicants, minimum TOEFL 500. **Basis for Candidate Selection:** *Very important factors considered include:* class rank, secondary school record, standardized test scores. *Other factors considered include:* alumni/ae relation, character/ personal qualities, extracurricular activities, recommendations, talent/ability. **Freshman Admission Requirements:** High school diploma or GED is required. *Academic units required/recommended:* 16 total required; 2 total recommended; 4 English required, 3 math required, 2 science required, 1 science lab required, 2 foreign language recommended, 3 social studies required, 3 elective required. **Freshman Admission Statistics:** 3,154 applied, 79% accepted, 54% of those accepted enrolled. **Transfer Admission Requirements:** *Items required:* college transcript. Minimum college GPA of 2.0 required. Lowest grade transferable D. **General Admission Information:** Application fee $25. Priority application deadline June 3. Regular application deadline August 20. Nonfall registration accepted. Admission may be deferred. Credit offered for CEEB Advanced Placement tests.

COSTS AND FINANCIAL AID

In-state tuition $3,450. Out-of-state tuition $6,900. Room & board $4,410. Required fees $60. Average book expense $450. **Required Forms and Deadlines:** FAFSA. No deadline for regular filing. Priority filing deadline March 3. **Notification of Awards:** Applicants will be notified of awards on a rolling basis. **Types of Aid:** *Need-based scholarships/grants:* Pell, SEOG, state scholarships/grants, private scholarships, the school's own gift aid. *Loans:* Direct Subsidized Stafford, Direct Unsubsidized Stafford, Direct PLUS, Federal Perkins, state loans. **Student Employment:** Federal Work-Study Program available. Institutional employment available. Off-campus job opportunities are excellent. **Financial Aid Statistics:** 49% freshmen, 57% undergrads receive some form of aid. Average freshman grant $5,093. Average freshman loan $2,189. Average income from on-campus job $1,800. **Financial Aid Phone:** 660-543-4040.

CENTRAL STATE UNIVERSITY

PO Box 1004, Wilberforce, OH 45384
Phone: 937-376-6348 **E-mail:** admissions@csu.ces.edu **CEEB Code:** 1107
Fax: 937-376-6648 **Web:** www.centralstate.edu **ACT Code:** 3246

This public school was founded in 1887. It has a 60-acre campus.

STUDENTS AND FACULTY

Enrollment: 1,426. **Student Body:** Male 45%, female 55%, out-of-state 22%, international 1%. **Ethnic Representation:** African American 89%, Caucasian 1%. **Retention and Graduation:** 58% freshmen return for sophomore year. 4% freshmen graduate within 4 years. 32% grads go on to further study within 1 year. 29% grads pursue business degrees. 7% grads pursue law degrees. **Faculty:** Student/faculty ratio 13:1. 77 full-time faculty, 62% hold PhDs.

ACADEMICS

Degrees: Bachelor's, master's, post-bachelor's certificate. **Academic Requirements:** General education including some course work in arts/fine arts, computer literacy, English (including composition), history, humanities, mathematics, sciences (biological or physical), social science. **Classes:** Under 10 students in an average class. **Majors with Highest Enrollment:** Business administration/management; early childhood education and teaching; biology/biological sciences, general. **Disciplines with Highest Percentage of Degrees Awarded:** Business/marketing 28%, education 20%, communications/communication technologies 13%, engineering/engineering technology 7%, social sciences and history 7%. **Special Study Options:** Cooperative (work-study) program, cross registration, double major, honors program, independent study, internships, study abroad, teacher certification program.

FACILITIES

Housing: All-female, all-male. **Library Holdings:** 188,144 bound volumes. 525 periodicals. 635,103 microforms. 500 audiovisuals. **Special Academic Facilities/Equipment:** National Afro-American museum and cultural center; C. J. McLin International Center for Water Resources Management; center for integrated manufacturing protocols; architecture and logistics laboratory; biology technique laboratory; electrochemistry research laboratory; Cosby Mass Communication Center; Paul Robeson Cultural & Performing Arts Center. **Computers:** *Recommended operating system:* Windows NT/2000. School-owned computers available for student use.

EXTRACURRICULARS

Activities: Choral groups, concert band, dance, drama/theater, jazz band, marching band, music ensembles, pep band, radio station, student government. **Organizations:** 30 registered organizations, 3 honor societies, 4 religious organizations, 1 fraternity (1% men join), 3 sororities (1% women join). **Athletics (Intercollegiate):** *Men:* basketball, cheerleading, cross-country, golf, track & field. *Women:* basketball, cheerleading, cross-country, golf, track & field, volleyball.

ADMISSIONS

Selectivity Rating: 71 (of 100). **Freshman Academic Profile:** Average high school GPA 2.3. 6% in top 10% of high school class, 14% in top 25% of high school class, 49% in top 50% of high school class. Average ACT 15, ACT middle 50% range 13-16. TOEFL required of all international applicants, minimum TOEFL 500. **Basis for Candidate Selection:** *Very important factors considered include:* secondary school record, standardized test scores. *Important factors considered include:* character/personal qualities, class rank, essays, geographical residence, state residency. *Other factors considered include:* extracurricular activities, interview, recommendations, talent/ability. **Freshman Admission Requirements:** High school diploma or GED is required. *Academic units required/recommended:* 16 total recommended; 4 English recommended, 3 math recommended, 3 science recommended, 2 foreign language recommended, 3 social studies recommended. **Freshman Admission Statistics:** 3,234 applied, 39% accepted, 30% of those accepted enrolled. **Transfer Admission Requirements:** *Items required:* college transcript, statement of good standing from prior school. Minimum high school GPA of 2.0 required. Minimum college GPA of 2.0 required. Lowest grade transferable C. **General Admission Information:** Application fee $20. Nonfall registration accepted. Admission may be deferred. Credit and/or placement offered for CEEB Advanced Placement tests.

COSTS AND FINANCIAL AID

In-state tuition $2,208. Out-of-state tuition $6,921. Room & board $5,727. Required fees $1,836. Average book expense $900. **Required Forms and Deadlines:** FAFSA and institution's own financial aid form. No deadline for regular filing. Priority filing deadline March 1. **Notification of Awards:** Applicants will be notified of awards on a rolling basis beginning on or about May 1. **Types of Aid:** *Need-based scholarships/grants:* Pell, SEOG, state scholarships/grants, private scholarships, the school's own gift aid, United Negro College Fund. *Loans:* Direct Subsidized Stafford, Direct Unsubsidized Stafford, Direct PLUS, college/university loans from institutional funds. **Student Employment:** Federal Work-Study Program available. Institutional employment available. Off-campus job opportunities are fair. **Financial Aid Statistics:** 76% freshmen, 74% undergrads receive some form of aid. Average freshman grant $4,747. Average freshman loan $6,371. **Financial Aid Phone:** 937-376-6579.

CENTRAL WASHINGTON UNIVERSITY

Admissions Office, 400 E. 8th Avenue, Ellensburg, WA 98926-7463
Phone: 509-963-1211 **E-mail:** cwuadmis@cwu.edu **CEEB Code:** 4044
Fax: 509-963-3022 **Web:** www.cwu.edu **ACT Code:** 4444

This public school was founded in 1891. It has a 350-acre campus.

STUDENTS AND FACULTY

Enrollment: 8,683. **Student Body:** Male 47%, female 53%, out-of-state 3%, international 1%. **Ethnic Representation:** African American 2%, Asian 5%, Caucasian 79%, Hispanic 6%, Native American 2%. **Retention and Graduation:** 75% freshmen return for sophomore year. 25% freshmen graduate within 4 years. **Faculty:** Student/faculty ratio 21:1. 335 full-time faculty, 86% hold PhDs. 99% faculty teach undergrads.

ACADEMICS

Degrees: Bachelor's, master's, post-bachelor's certificate. **Academic Requirements:** General education including some course work in arts/fine arts, computer literacy, English (including composition), foreign languages, history, humanities, mathematics, philosophy, sciences (biological or physical), social science. **Classes:** 20-29 students in an average class. Under 10 students in an average lab/discussion section. **Majors with Highest Enrollment:** Business administration/management; elementary education and teaching; criminal justice/safety studies. **Disciplines with Highest Percentage of Degrees Awarded:** Business/marketing 24%, education 20%, protective services/public administration 10%, social sciences and history 9%, engineering/engineering technology 4%. **Special Study Options:** Cooperative (work-study) program, distance learning, double major, dual enrollment, English as a second language, student exchange program (domestic), honors program, independent study, internships, student-designed major, study abroad, teacher certification program, weekend college.

FACILITIES

Housing: Coed, all-female, apartments for married students, apartments for single students. Housing for disabled students, international students, academic interests, upperclassmen, and 21 years and older. **Library Holdings:** 434,424 bound volumes. 1,469 periodicals. 1,148,136 microforms. 9,230 audiovisuals. **Computers:** School-owned computers available for student use.

EXTRACURRICULARS

Activities: Choral groups, concert band, dance, drama/theater, jazz band, literary magazine, marching band, music ensembles, musical theater, opera, pep band, radio station, student government, student newspaper, student-run film society, symphony orchestra. **Organizations:** 86 registered organizations, 9 honor societies, 12 religious organizations. **Athletics (Intercollegiate):** *Men:* baseball, basketball, cheerleading, cross-country, football, indoor track, swimming, track & field, wrestling. *Women:* basketball, cheerleading, cross-country, indoor track, soccer, softball, swimming, track & field, volleyball.

ADMISSIONS

Selectivity Rating: 80 (of 100). **Freshman Academic Profile:** Average high school GPA 3.2. 12% in top 10% of high school class, 37% in top 25% of high school class, 70% in top 50% of high school class. 94% from public high schools. Average SAT I Math 499, SAT I Math middle 50% range 440-550. Average SAT I Verbal 498, SAT I Verbal middle 50% range 440-550. Average ACT 21, ACT middle 50% range 18-23. TOEFL required of all international applicants, minimum TOEFL 525. **Basis for Candidate Selection:** *Very important factors considered include:* secondary school record. *Important factors considered include:* standardized test scores. *Other factors considered include:* character/personal qualities, essays, extracurricular activities, geographical residence, interview, recommendations, talent/ability, volunteer work, work experience. **Freshman Admission Requirements:** High school diploma or GED is required. *Academic units required/recommended:* 15 total required; 17 total recommended; 4 English required, 3 math required, 2 science required, 3 science recommended, 1 science lab required, 2 foreign language required, 3 foreign language recommended, 3 social studies required. **Freshman Admission Statistics:** 3,575 applied, 85% accepted, 44% of those accepted enrolled. **Transfer Admission Requirements:** *Items required:* college transcript, statement of good standing from prior school. Minimum college GPA of 2.5 required. Lowest grade transferable D-. **General Admission Information:** Application fee $35. Priority application deadline May 1. Nonfall registration accepted. Credit and/or placement offered for CEEB Advanced Placement tests.

COSTS AND FINANCIAL AID

In-state tuition $3,423. Out-of-state tuition $11,412. Room & board $5,410. Required fees $369. Average book expense $720. **Required Forms and Deadlines:** FAFSA. Priority filing deadline March 1. **Notification of Awards:** Applicants will be notified of awards on a rolling basis beginning on or about April 15. **Types of Aid:** *Need-based scholarships/grants:* Pell, SEOG, state scholarships/grants, private scholarships, the school's own gift aid. *Loans:* Direct Subsidized Stafford, Direct Unsubsidized Stafford, Direct PLUS, FFEL Subsidized Stafford, FFEL Unsubsidized Stafford, FFEL PLUS, Federal Perkins, state loans, college/university loans from institutional funds. **Student Employment:** Federal Work-Study Program available. Institutional employment available. Off-campus job opportunities are good. **Financial Aid Statistics:** 44% freshmen, 48% undergrads receive some form of aid. Average freshman grant $3,998. Average freshman loan $5,146. Average income from on-campus job $1,705. **Financial Aid Phone:** 509-963-1611.

CENTRE COLLEGE

600 West Walnut Street, Danville, KY 40422
Phone: 859-238-5350 **E-mail:** admissions@centre.edu **CEEB Code:** 1109
Fax: 859-238-5373 **Web:** www.centre.edu **ACT Code:** 1506

This private school, which is affiliated with the Presbyterian Church, was founded in 1819. It has a 115-acre campus.

STUDENTS AND FACULTY

Enrollment: 1,055. **Student Body:** Male 47%, female 53%, out-of-state 29%, international 1% (12 countries represented). **Ethnic Representation:** African American 2%, Asian 2%, Caucasian 95%. **Retention and Graduation:** 85% freshmen return for sophomore year. 74% freshmen graduate within 4 years. 41% grads go on to further study within 1 year. 3% grads pursue business degrees. 21% grads pursue law degrees. 13% grads pursue medical degrees. **Faculty:** Student/faculty ratio 11:1. 89 full-time faculty, 96% hold PhDs. 100% faculty teach undergrads.

ACADEMICS

Degrees: Bachelor's. **Academic Requirements:** General education including some course work in arts/fine arts, English (including composition), foreign languages, history, humanities, mathematics, philosophy, sciences (biological or physical), social science, religion, freshman studies seminar, health and human performance. **Classes:** 10-19 students in an average class. 10-19 students in an average lab/discussion section. **Majors with Highest Enrollment:** Economics, general; English language and literature, general; history, general. **Disciplines with Highest Percentage of Degrees Awarded:** Social sciences and history 35%, psychology 13%, English 13%, biological life sciences 11%, visual and performing arts 7%. **Special Study Options:** Cross registration, double major, honors program, independent study, internships, liberal arts/career combination, student-designed major, study abroad, teacher certification program.

FACILITIES

Housing: Coed, all-female, all-male, apartments for single students, housing for disabled students, fraternities and/or sororities. **Library Holdings:** 217,751 bound volumes. 750 periodicals. 52,512 microforms. 0 audiovisuals. **Special Academic Facilities/Equipment:** Arts center, physical science and math facility, electron microscope, visible and infrared mass spectroscopy equipment, visual arts center. **Computers:** School-owned computers available for student use.

EXTRACURRICULARS

Activities: Choral groups, concert band, dance, drama/theater, jazz band, literary magazine, music ensembles, musical theater, pep band, student government, student newspaper, student-run film society, yearbook. **Organizations:** 70 registered organizations, 12 honor societies, 6 religious organizations, 6 fraternities (55% men join), 4 sororities (59% women join). **Athletics (Intercollegiate):** *Men:* baseball, basketball, cheerleading, cross-country, diving, football, golf, soccer, swimming, tennis, track & field. *Women:* basketball, cheerleading, cross-country, diving, field hockey, golf, soccer, softball, swimming, tennis, track & field, volleyball.

ADMISSIONS

Selectivity Rating: 77 (of 100). **Freshman Academic Profile:** Average high school GPA 3.9. 55% in top 10% of high school class, 81% in top 25% of high school class, 99% in top 50% of high school class. 79% from public high schools. Average SAT I Math 603, SAT I Math middle 50% range 580-660. Average SAT I Verbal 619, SAT I Verbal middle 50% range 590-670. Average ACT 27, ACT middle 50% range 25-29. TOEFL required of all international applicants, minimum TOEFL 580. **Basis for Candidate Selection:** *Very important factors considered include:* class rank, secondary school record. *Important factors considered include:* essays, standardized test scores. *Other factors considered include:* alumni/ae relation, character/personal qualities, extracurricular activities, interview, recommendations, talent/ability. **Freshman Admission Requirements:** High school diploma or equivalent is not required. *Academic units required/recommended:* 13 total required; 4 English required, 4 math required, 2 science required, 3 science recommended, 2 science lab required, 2 foreign language required, 2 history required. **Freshman Admission Statistics:** 1,354 applied, 78% accepted, 28% of those accepted enrolled. **Transfer Admission Requirements:** *Items required:* high school transcript, college transcript, essay, standardized test scores, statement of good standing from prior school. Lowest grade transferable C-. **General Admission Information:** Application fee $40. Regular application deadline February 1. Admission may be deferred for a maximum of 1 year. Credit and/or placement offered for CEEB Advanced Placement tests.

COSTS AND FINANCIAL AID

Tuition $19,125. Room & board $6,475. Required fees $0. Average book expense $700. **Required Forms and Deadlines:** FAFSA and institution's own financial aid form. Financial aid filing deadline March 1. **Notification of Awards:** Applicants will be notified of awards on or about April 1. **Types of Aid:** *Need-based scholarships/grants:* Pell, SEOG, state scholarships/grants, private scholarships, the school's own gift aid. *Loans:* FFEL Subsidized Stafford, FFEL Unsubsidized Stafford, FFEL PLUS, Federal Perkins, college/university loans from institutional funds. **Student Employment:** Federal Work-Study Program available. Institutional employment available. Off-campus job opportunities are fair. **Financial Aid Statistics:** 70% freshmen, 66% undergrads receive some form of aid. Average freshman grant $12,406. Average freshman loan $2,600. **Financial Aid Phone:** 859-238-5365.

CHADRON STATE COLLEGE

1000 Main Street, Chadron, NE 69337
Phone: 308-432-6263 **E-mail:** inquire@csc.edu **CEEB Code:** 6466
Fax: 308-432-6229 **Web:** www.csc.edu **ACT Code:** 2466

This public school was founded in 1911. It has a 281-acre campus.

STUDENTS AND FACULTY

Enrollment: 2,392. **Student Body:** Male 42%, female 58%, out-of-state 26%, international 1% (10 countries represented). **Ethnic Representation:** African American 1%, Asian 1%, Caucasian 90%, Hispanic 2%, Native American 2%. **Retention and Graduation:** 78% freshmen return for sophomore year. 20% freshmen graduate within 4 years. 41% grads go on to further study within 1 year. 10% grads pursue business degrees. 3% grads pursue law degrees. 3% grads pursue medical degrees. **Faculty:** Student/faculty ratio 17:1. 102 full-time faculty, 65% hold PhDs. 100% faculty teach undergrads.

ACADEMICS

Degrees: Bachelor's, master's, post-master's certificate. **Academic Requirements:** General education including some course work in arts/fine arts, English (including composition), history, humanities, mathematics, philosophy, sciences (biological or physical), social science, ethics, communications, government, global studies, and physical education. **Classes:** 10-19 students in an average class. 10-19 students in an average lab/discussion section. **Majors with Highest Enrollment:** Elementary education and teaching; business administration/management; criminal justice/law enforcement administration. **Disciplines with Highest Percentage of Degrees Awarded:** Education 25%, business/marketing 25%, protective services/public administration 10%, biological life sciences 6%, health professions and related sciences 6%. **Special Study Options:** Accelerated program, cooperative (work-study) program, distance learning, double major, dual enrollment, honors program, independent study, internships, student-designed major, study abroad, teacher certification program.

FACILITIES

Housing: Coed, all-female, all-male, apartments for married students, apartments for single students. **Library Holdings:** 129,660 bound volumes. 112,500 periodicals. 325,063 microforms. 5,596 audiovisuals. **Special Academic Facilities/Equipment:** Planetarium, herbarium, geology museum, Mari Sandoz Center. **Computers:** School-owned computers available for student use.

EXTRACURRICULARS

Activities: Choral groups, concert band, dance, drama/theater, jazz band, music ensembles, musical theater, pep band, radio station, student government, student newspaper. **Organizations:** 60 registered organizations, 1 honor society, 4 religious organizations. **Athletics (Intercollegiate):** *Men:* basketball, football, indoor track, track & field, wrestling. *Women:* basketball, golf, indoor track, track & field, volleyball.

ADMISSIONS

Selectivity Rating: 78 (of 100). **Freshman Academic Profile:** Average high school GPA 3.2. 16% in top 10% of high school class, 40% in top 25% of high school class, 67% in top 50% of high school class. 83% from public high schools. Average SAT I Math 446, SAT I Math middle 50% range 460-550. Average SAT I Verbal 450, SAT I Verbal middle 50% range 400-580. Average ACT 21, ACT middle 50% range 18-25. TOEFL required of all international applicants, minimum TOEFL 550. **Basis for Candidate Selection:** *Important factors considered include:* alumni/ae relation, character/personal qualities, class rank, essays, extracurricular activities, recommendations, secondary school record, standardized test scores, talent/ability, volunteer work. **Freshman Admission Requirements:** High school diploma or GED is required. *Academic units required/recommended:* 12 total recommended; 4 English recommended, 3 math recommended, 2 science recommended, 2 science lab recommended, 3 social studies recommended. **Freshman Admission Statistics:** 754 applied, 100% accepted, 53% of those accepted enrolled. **Transfer Admission Requirements:** *Items required:* college transcript. Minimum college GPA of 2.0 required. Lowest grade transferable D. **General Admission Information:** Application fee $15. Nonfall registration accepted. Credit and/or placement offered for CEEB Advanced Placement tests.

COSTS AND FINANCIAL AID

In-state tuition $2,093. Out-of-state tuition $4,185. Room & board $3,638. Required fees $388. Average book expense $650. **Required Forms and Deadlines:** FAFSA and institution's own financial aid form. No deadline for regular filing. Priority filing deadline June 1. **Notification of Awards:** Applicants will be notified of awards on a rolling basis beginning on or about April 1. **Types of Aid:** *Need-based scholarships/grants:* Pell, SEOG, state scholarships/grants, the school's own gift aid. *Loans:* Direct Subsidized Stafford, Direct Unsubsidized Stafford, Direct PLUS, FFEL Subsidized Stafford, FFEL Unsubsidized Stafford, FFEL PLUS, Federal Perkins. **Student Employment:** Federal Work-Study Program available. Institutional employment available. Off-campus job opportunities are good. **Financial Aid Statistics:** 55% freshmen, 57% undergrads receive some form of aid. Average freshman grant $1,200. Average freshman loan $1,912. Average income from on-campus job $1,000. **Financial Aid Phone:** 308-432-6230.

CHAMINADE UNIVERSITY OF HONOLULU

3140 Waialae Avenue, Honolulu, HI 96816-1578
Phone: 808-735-4735 **E-mail:** admissions@chaminade.edu **CEEB Code:** 4105
Fax: 808-739-4647 **Web:** www.chaminade.edu **ACT Code:** 898

This private school, which is affiliated with the Roman Catholic Church, was founded in 1955. It has a 67-acre campus.

STUDENTS AND FACULTY

Enrollment: 2,213. **Student Body:** Male 39%, female 61%, out-of-state 59%, international 2%. **Ethnic Representation:** African American 13%, Asian 41%, Caucasian 35%, Hispanic 9%, Native American 1%. **Retention and Graduation:** 72% freshmen return for sophomore year. 30% freshmen graduate within 4 years. **Faculty:** Student/faculty ratio 16:1. 57 full-time faculty, 68% hold PhDs. 100% faculty teach undergrads.

ACADEMICS

Degrees: Associate's, bachelor's, master's, post-bachelor's certificate. **Academic Requirements:** General education including some course work in arts/fine arts, computer literacy, English (including composition), foreign languages, history, humanities, mathematics, philosophy, sciences (biological or physical), social science. **Classes:** 10-19 students in an average class. **Majors with Highest Enrollment:** Criminal justice/safety studies; psychology, general; business administration/management. **Disciplines with Highest Percentage of Degrees Awarded:** Protective services/public administration 22%, social sciences and history 18%, business/marketing 16%, psychology 15%, education 13%. **Special Study Options:** Accelerated program, cooperative (work-study) program, distance learning, double major, dual enrollment, English as a second language, student exchange program (domestic), independent study, internships, study abroad, teacher certification program.

FACILITIES

Housing: Coed, all-female, apartments for single students. **Library Holdings:** 78,000 bound volumes. 312 periodicals. 6,361 microforms. 566 audiovisuals. **Special Academic Facilities/Equipment:** Montessori school, language lab, writing lab. **Computers:** School-owned computers available for student use.

EXTRACURRICULARS

Activities: Choral groups, literary magazine, music ensembles, student government, student newspaper, yearbook. **Organizations:** 28 registered organizations, 4 honor societies, 4 religious organizations. **Athletics (Intercollegiate):** *Men:* basketball, cross-country, tennis, water polo. *Women:* cross-country, softball, tennis, volleyball.

ADMISSIONS

Selectivity Rating: 63 (of 100). **Freshman Academic Profile:** Average high school GPA 3.1. 15% in top 10% of high school class, 32% in top 25% of high school class, 63% in top 50% of high school class. Average SAT I Math 475, SAT I Math middle 50% range 420-510. Average SAT I Verbal 461, SAT I Verbal middle 50% range 400-500. Average ACT 20, ACT middle 50% range 16-20. TOEFL required of all international applicants, minimum TOEFL 450. **Basis for Candidate Selection:** *Very important factors considered include:* secondary school record, standardized test scores. *Important factors considered include:* character/personal qualities, essays, extracurricular activities, interview, talent/ability, volunteer work. *Other factors considered include:* recommendations, work experience. **Freshman Admission Requirements:** High school diploma or GED is required. *Academic units required/recommended:* 4 English required, 3 math required, 2 science required, 2 science lab recommended, 3 social studies required, 4 elective required. **Freshman Admission Statistics:** 1,140 applied, 65% accepted, 29% of those accepted enrolled. **Transfer Admission Requirements:** *Items required:* college transcript, essay, statement of good standing from prior school. Minimum college GPA of 2.0 required. Lowest grade transferable C. **General Admission Information:** Application fee $50. Priority application deadline May 1. Nonfall registration accepted. Admission may be deferred for a maximum of 1 year. Credit and/or placement offered for CEEB Advanced Placement tests.

COSTS AND FINANCIAL AID

Tuition $13,380. Room & board $7,380. Required fees $120. Average book expense $720. **Required Forms and Deadlines:** FAFSA and institution's own financial aid form. Priority filing deadline March 1. **Notification of Awards:** Applicants will be notified of awards on a rolling basis beginning on or about March 1. **Types of Aid:** *Need-based scholarships/grants:* Pell, SEOG, state scholarships/grants, private scholarships, the school's own gift aid. *Loans:* FFEL Subsidized Stafford, FFEL Unsubsidized Stafford, FFEL PLUS, Federal Perkins, CitiAssist loans, Sallie Mae's Signature Education Loan Program, alternative loans, U.S. Bank Gap Education loans. **Student Employment:**

Federal Work-Study Program available. Institutional employment available. Off-campus job opportunities are fair. **Financial Aid Statistics:** 76% freshmen, 63% undergrads receive some form of aid. Average freshman grant $6,306. Average freshman loan $7,475. **Financial Aid Phone:** 808-735-4780.

See page 966.

CHAMPLAIN COLLEGE

163 South Willard Street Box 670, PO Box 670, Burlington, VT 05402-0670
Phone: 802-860-2727 **E-mail:** admission@champlain.edu **CEEB Code:** 3291
Fax: 802-860-2767 **Web:** www.champlain.edu **ACT Code:** 3291

This private school was founded in 1878. It has a 19-acre campus.

STUDENTS AND FACULTY

Enrollment: 2,466. **Student Body:** Male 47%, female 53%, out-of-state 45%, international 2%. **Ethnic Representation:** African American 1%, Asian 2%, Caucasian 96%, Hispanic 1%, Native American 1%. **Retention and Graduation:** 75% freshmen return for sophomore year. 80% freshmen graduate within 4 years. 10% grads go on to further study within 1 year. 6% grads pursue business degrees. 1% grads pursue law degrees. **Faculty:** Student/faculty ratio 15:1. 78 full-time faculty, 32% hold PhDs. 100% faculty teach undergrads.

ACADEMICS

Degrees: Associate's, bachelor's, certificate, master's. **Academic Requirements:** General education including some course work in arts/fine arts, computer literacy, English (including composition), history, humanities, mathematics, philosophy, sciences (biological or physical), social science. **Classes:** 20-29 students in an average class. Under 10 students in an average lab/discussion section. **Majors with Highest Enrollment:** Business administration/management; computer/information technology services administration and management; elementary education and teaching. **Disciplines with Highest Percentage of Degrees Awarded:** Liberal arts/general studies 40%, business/marketing 36%, education 13%, computer and information sciences 11%. **Special Study Options:** Distance learning, double major, honors program, independent study, internships, liberal arts/career combination, study abroad, teacher certification program.

FACILITIES

Housing: Coed, all-female, all-male, housing for international students, wellness dorm, first-year seminar dorms. **Library Holdings:** 60,000 bound volumes. 270 periodicals. 19,200 microforms. 270 audiovisuals. **Computers:** School-owned computers available for student use.

EXTRACURRICULARS

Activities: Choral groups, dance, drama/theater, literary magazine, musical theater, student government, student newspaper. **Organizations:** 40 registered organizations, 1 religious organization.

ADMISSIONS

Selectivity Rating: 63 (of 100). **Freshman Academic Profile:** Average high school GPA 3.0. 15% in top 10% of high school class, 35% in top 25% of high school class, 85% in top 50% of high school class. 85% from public high schools. Average SAT I Math 500, SAT I Math middle 50% range 450-540. Average SAT I Verbal 500, SAT I Verbal middle 50% range 460-550. Average ACT 22, ACT middle 50% range 19-23. TOEFL required of all international applicants, minimum TOEFL 500. **Basis for Candidate Selection:** *Very important factors considered include:* secondary school record. *Important factors considered include:* class rank, essays, interview, recommendations, standardized test scores. *Other factors considered include:* character/personal qualities, extracurricular activities, talent/ability, volunteer work, work experience. **Freshman Admission Requirements:** High school diploma or GED is required. *Academic units required/recommended:* 20 total required; 4 English required, 3 math required, 4 math recommended, 3 science required, 4 science recommended, 2 science lab required, 3 science lab recommended, 2 foreign language required, 3 foreign language recommended, 4 history required, 4 elective required. **Freshman Admission Statistics:** 1,330 applied, 68% accepted, 45% of those accepted enrolled. **Transfer Admission Requirements:** *Items required:* high school transcript, college transcript, essay. Minimum college GPA of 2.0 required. Lowest grade transferable C. **General Admission Information:** Application fee $40. Priority application deadline January 15. Nonfall registration accepted. Admission may be deferred. Credit offered for CEEB Advanced Placement tests.

COSTS AND FINANCIAL AID

Tuition $12,195. Room & board $8,400. Required fees $100. Average book expense $600. **Required Forms and Deadlines:** FAFSA, institution's own financial aid form, state aid form, and noncustodial (divorced/separated) parent's statement. No deadline for regular filing. Priority filing deadline May 1. **Notification of Awards:** Applicants will be notified of awards on a rolling basis beginning on or about March 1. **Types of Aid:** *Need-based scholarships/grants:* Pell, state scholarships/grants, private scholarships, the school's own gift aid. *Loans:* Direct Subsidized Stafford, Direct Unsubsidized Stafford, Direct PLUS, Federal Perkins, state loans. **Student Employment:** Federal Work-Study Program available. Institutional employment available. Off-campus job opportunities are excellent. **Financial Aid Statistics:** 63% freshmen, 62% undergrads receive some form of aid. Average freshman grant $5,593. Average freshman loan $3,112. Average income from on-campus job $2,211. **Financial Aid Phone:** 802-860-2730.

See page 968.

CHAPMAN UNIVERSITY

One University Drive, Orange, CA 92866
Phone: 714-997-6711 **E-mail:** admit@chapman.edu **CEEB Code:** 4047
Fax: 714-997-6713 **Web:** www.chapman.edu **ACT Code:** 210

This private school, which is affiliated with the Disciples of Christ Church, was founded in 1861. It has a 100-acre campus.

STUDENTS AND FACULTY

Enrollment: 3,263. **Student Body:** Male 43%, female 57%, out-of-state 15%, international 3% (38 countries represented). **Ethnic Representation:** African American 2%, Asian 7%, Caucasian 67%, Hispanic 11%. **Retention and Graduation:** 84% freshmen return for sophomore year. 38% freshmen graduate within 4 years. **Faculty:** Student/faculty ratio 16:1. 222 full-time faculty, 81% hold PhDs. 100% faculty teach undergrads.

ACADEMICS

Degrees: Bachelor's, certificate, doctoral, first professional, master's, post-bachelor's certificate, post-master's certificate. **Academic Requirements:** General education including some course work in arts/fine arts, English (including composition), foreign languages, history, humanities, mathematics, philosophy, sciences (biological or physical), social science, cultural heritage/human diversity, junior-year writing proficiency examination (taken at completion of 60 semester credits). **Classes:** 10-19 students in an average class. 10-19 students in an average lab/discussion section. **Majors with Highest Enrollment:** Business administration/management; secondary education and teaching; cinematography and film/video production. **Disciplines with Highest Percentage of Degrees Awarded:** Visual and performing arts 24%, business/marketing 23%, social sciences and history 11%, communications/communication technologies 10%, psychology 6%. **Special Study Options:** Cooperative (work-study) program, double major, English as a second language, external degree program, honors program, independent study, internships, liberal arts/career combination, student-designed major, study abroad, teacher certification program.

FACILITIES

Housing: Coed, apartments for married students, apartments for single students, housing for disabled students, houses for families, houses for single students. **Library Holdings:** 188,682 bound volumes. 1,777 periodicals. 412,457 microforms. 6,334 audiovisuals. **Special Academic Facilities/Equipment:** Anderson Center for Economic Research, Leatherby Center for Entrepreneurship and Business Ethics, Schmid Center for International Business, law and organizational economics center, center for Cold War studies, Henley Social Science Research Laboratory, Guggenhiem Art Gallery, TV studio, film/TV lab, Waltmer Theatre, Beckman Information and Technology Hall, DeMille Hall film and TV production and digital editing studios. **Computers:** *Recommended operating system:* Windows NT/2000. School-owned computers available for student use.

EXTRACURRICULARS

Activities: Choral groups, dance, drama/theater, jazz band, literary magazine, music ensembles, musical theater, opera, pep band, radio station, student government, student newspaper, student-run film society, symphony orchestra, yearbook. **Organizations:** 66 registered organizations, 7 honor societies, 6 religious organizations, 5 fraternities (13% men join), 5 sororities (20% women join). **Athletics (Intercollegiate):** *Men:* baseball, basketball, cheerleading, crew, cross-country, football, golf, lacrosse, soccer, tennis, water polo. *Women:* basketball, cheerleading, crew, cross-country, golf, lacrosse, soccer, softball, swimming, tennis, track & field, volleyball, water polo.

ADMISSIONS

Selectivity Rating: 79 (of 100). **Freshman Academic Profile:** Average high school GPA 3.5. 37% in top 10% of high school class, 80% in top 25% of high school class, 100% in top 50% of high school class. 73% from public high schools. Average SAT I Math 597, SAT I Math middle 50% range 541-653. Average SAT I Verbal 585, SAT I Verbal middle 50% range 530-641. Average ACT 25, ACT middle 50% range 22-28. TOEFL required of all international applicants, minimum TOEFL 500. **Basis for Candidate Selection:** *Very important factors considered include:* essays, secondary school record. *Important factors considered include:* character/personal qualities, class rank, extracurricular activities, standardized test scores, volunteer work. *Other factors considered include:* alumni/ae relation, interview, minority status, recommendations, talent/ability, work experience. **Freshman Admission Requirements:** High school diploma or GED is required. *Academic units required/recommended:* 11 total required; 2 English required, 2 math required, 2 science required, 1 science lab required, 2 foreign language required, 3 social studies required. **Freshman Admission Statistics:** 2,728 applied, 60% accepted, 44% of those accepted enrolled. **Transfer Admission Requirements:** *Items required:* college transcript, essay. Minimum college GPA of 2.5 required. Lowest grade transferable D. **General Admission Information:** Application fee $50. Regular application deadline January 31. Nonfall registration accepted. Credit and/or placement offered for CEEB Advanced Placement tests.

COSTS AND FINANCIAL AID

Tuition $23,950. Room & board $8,528. Required fees $640. Average book expense $800. **Required Forms and Deadlines:** FAFSA. Financial aid filing deadline March 1. Priority filing deadline March 1. **Notification of Awards:** Applicants will be notified of awards on or about April 1. **Types of Aid:** *Need-based scholarships/grants:* Pell, SEOG, state scholarships/grants, private scholarships, the school's own gift aid. *Loans:* Direct Subsidized Stafford, Direct Unsubsidized Stafford, Direct PLUS, Federal Perkins. **Student Employment:** Federal Work-Study Program available. Institutional employment available. Off-campus job opportunities are excellent. **Financial Aid Statistics:** 62% freshmen, 64% undergrads receive some form of aid. Average freshman grant $18,013. Average freshman loan $3,276. Average income from on-campus job $1,500. **Financial Aid Phone:** 714-997-6741.

See page 970.

CHARLESTON SOUTHERN UNIVERSITY

Enrollment Services, PO Box 118087, Charleston, SC 29423
Phone: 843-863-7050 **E-mail:** enroll@csuniv.edu **CEEB Code:** 5079
Fax: 843-863-7070 **Web:** www.charlestonsouthern.edu **ACT Code:** 3833

This private school, which is affiliated with the Southern Baptist Church, was founded in 1964. It has a 300-acre campus.

STUDENTS AND FACULTY

Enrollment: 2,481. **Student Body:** Male 38%, female 62%, out-of-state 18%, international 2%. **Ethnic Representation:** African American 20%, Asian 1%, Caucasian 58%, Hispanic 1%. **Retention and Graduation:** 76% freshmen return for sophomore year. 17% freshmen graduate within 4 years. **Faculty:** Student/faculty ratio 20:1. 98 full-time faculty, 64% hold PhDs.

ACADEMICS

Degrees: Associate's, bachelor's, master's. **Academic Requirements:** General education including some course work in arts/fine arts, computer literacy, English (including composition), foreign languages, history, humanities, mathematics, sciences (biological or physical), social science. **Classes:** 20-29 students in an average class. 10-19 students in an average lab/discussion section. **Majors with Highest Enrollment:** Business administration/management; education. **Disciplines with Highest Percentage of Degrees Awarded:** Business/marketing 21%, education 16%, social sciences and history 12%, physical sciences 10%, psychology 7%. **Special Study Options:** Accelerated program, cooperative (work-study) program, cross registration, double major, dual enrollment, honors program, internships, study abroad, teacher certification program, evening division.

FACILITIES

Housing: All-female, all-male. **Library Holdings:** 163,738 bound volumes. 831 periodicals. 211,985 microforms. **Special Academic Facilities/Equipment:** Earthquake education center, computer labs with wireless Internet, nursing clinical lab, specialized music rehearsal modules, and advanced music keyboard technology. **Computers:** *Recommended operating system:* Windows 95. School-owned computers available for student use.

EXTRACURRICULARS

Activities: Choral groups, concert band, dance, drama/theater, jazz band, literary magazine, marching band, music ensembles, musical theater, pep band, student government, student newspaper, yearbook. **Organizations:** 24 registered organizations, 3 honor societies, 10% men join fraternities, 10% women join sororities. **Athletics (Intercollegiate):** *Men:* baseball, basketball, cross-country, football, golf, indoor track, tennis, track & field. *Women:* basketball, cross-country, golf, indoor track, soccer, softball, tennis, track & field, volleyball.

ADMISSIONS

Selectivity Rating: 72 (of 100). **Freshman Academic Profile:** Average high school GPA 3.1. 20% in top 10% of high school class, 52% in top 25% of high school class, 75% in top 50% of high school class. 80% from public high schools. Average SAT I Math 520, SAT I Math middle 50% range 490-650. Average SAT I Verbal 550, SAT I Verbal middle 50% range 490-580. Average ACT 21, ACT middle 50% range 20-24. TOEFL required of all international applicants, minimum TOEFL 550. **Basis for Candidate Selection:** *Very important factors considered include:* class rank, secondary school record, standardized test scores. *Other factors considered include:* character/personal qualities, essays, extracurricular activities, interview, recommendations, religious affiliation/commitment, talent/ability, work experience. **Freshman Admission Requirements:** High school diploma or GED is required. *Academic units required/recommended:* 16 total required; 4 English required, 3 math required, 4 math recommended, 3 science required, 2 foreign language recommended, 3 history required, 3 elective required. **Freshman Admission Statistics:** 2,028 applied, 77% accepted, 82% of those accepted enrolled. **Transfer Admission Requirements:** *Items required:* college transcript, statement of good standing from prior school. Minimum high school GPA of 2.0 required. Minimum college GPA of 2.0 required. Lowest grade transferable C. **General Admission Information:** Application fee $30. Nonfall registration accepted. Credit and/or placement offered for CEEB Advanced Placement tests.

COSTS AND FINANCIAL AID

Tuition $14,426. Room & board $5,544. Required fees $0. Average book expense $1,000. **Required Forms and Deadlines:** FAFSA. No deadline for regular filing. Priority filing deadline April 15. **Notification of Awards:** Applicants will be notified of awards on a rolling basis beginning on or about February 1. **Types of Aid:** *Need-based scholarships/grants:* Pell, SEOG, state scholarships/grants, private scholarships, the school's own gift aid. *Loans:* Direct Subsidized Stafford, Direct Unsubsidized Stafford, Direct PLUS, FFEL Subsidized Stafford, FFEL PLUS, Federal Perkins, state loans. **Student Employment:** Federal Work-Study Program available. Institutional employment available. Off-campus job opportunities are good. **Financial Aid Statistics:** 50% freshmen, 66% undergrads receive some form of aid. Average freshman grant $10,500. Average freshman loan $2,500. **Financial Aid Phone:** 800-947-7474.

CHARTER OAK STATE COLLEGE

55 Paul J. Manafort Drive, New Britain, CT 06053-2142
Phone: 860-832-3800 **E-mail:** info@charteroak.edu
Fax: 860-832-3800 **Web:** www.charteroak.edu

This public school was founded in 1973.

STUDENTS AND FACULTY

Enrollment: 1,561. **Student Body:** Male 45%, female 55%, out-of-state 33%, international students represent 4 countries. **Ethnic Representation:** African American 9%, Asian 2%, Caucasian 72%, Hispanic 5%, Native American 3%. **Retention and Graduation:** 43% grads go on to further study within 1 year. 21% grads pursue business degrees. 5% grads pursue law degrees.

ACADEMICS

Degrees: Associate's, bachelor's, transfer. **Academic Requirements:** General education including some course work in arts/fine arts, English (including composition), history, humanities, mathematics, philosophy, sciences (biological or physical), social science. **Classes:** 10-19 students in an average class. **Disciplines with Highest Percentage of Degrees Awarded:** Liberal arts/general studies 100%. **Special Study Options:** Distance learning, external degree program, independent study, liberal arts/career combination, student-designed major.

FACILITIES

Computers: School-owned computers available for student use.

ADMISSIONS

Selectivity Rating: 63 (of 100). High school diploma or equivalent is not required. **Transfer Admission Requirements:** *Items required:* college transcript. Lowest grade transferable D. **General Admission Information:** Application fee $45. Nonfall registration accepted. Admission may be deferred for a maximum of 1 year. Credit offered for CEEB Advanced Placement tests.

COSTS AND FINANCIAL AID

Required Forms and Deadlines: FAFSA, institution's own financial aid form, Contractual Consortium Agreement form and course approval form and if applicable. No deadline for regular filing. **Notification of Awards:** Applicants will be notified of awards on a rolling basis beginning on or about August 15. **Types of Aid:** *Need-based scholarships/grants:* Pell, state scholarships/grants, private scholarships, the school's own gift aid. *Loans:* FFEL Subsidized Stafford, FFEL Unsubsidized Stafford, FFEL PLUS. **Financial Aid Phone:** 860-832-3872.

CHATHAM COLLEGE

Woodland Road, Pittsburgh, PA 15232
Phone: 412-365-1290 **E-mail:** admissions@chatham.edu **CEEB Code:** 2081
Fax: 412-365-1609 **Web:** www.chatham.edu **ACT Code:** 3538

This private school was founded in 1869. It has a 32-acre campus.

STUDENTS AND FACULTY

Enrollment: 639. **Student Body:** Out-of-state 33%, international 4% (22 countries represented). **Ethnic Representation:** African American 15%, Asian 2%, Caucasian 78%, Hispanic 1%. **Retention and Graduation:** 65% freshmen return for sophomore year. 59% freshmen graduate within 4 years. 36% grads go on to further study within 1 year. 3% grads pursue law degrees. 6% grads pursue medical degrees. **Faculty:** Student/faculty ratio 12:1. 71 full-time faculty, 90% hold PhDs. 100% faculty teach undergrads.

ACADEMICS

Degrees: Bachelor's, doctoral, master's, post-bachelor's certificate. **Academic Requirements:** General education including some course work in computer literacy, English (including composition), history, humanities, mathematics, philosophy, sciences (biological or physical), social science. **Classes:** 10-19 students in an average class. **Majors with Highest Enrollment:** English language and literature, general; biology/biological sciences, general; psychology, general. **Disciplines with Highest Percentage of Degrees Awarded:** Biological life sciences 17%, psychology 17%, business/marketing 16%, visual and performing arts 9%, social sciences and history 9%. **Special Study Options:** Accelerated program, cooperative (work-study) program, cross registration, double major, dual enrollment, English as a second language, student exchange program (domestic), independent study, internships, liberal arts/career combination, student-designed major, study abroad, teacher certification program, 3-2 engineering with Carnegie Mellon University and other institutions, joint physics degree with Carnegie Mellon University, computer programming and software systems development certificates through Carnegie Technology Education (division of Carnegie Mellon University), and 3-2 master of environmental health with University of Pittsburgh.

FACILITIES

Housing: All-female, apartments for married students, apartments for single students, intercultural residence hall, community service wing within a larger residence hall. **Library Holdings:** 81,160 bound volumes. 368 periodicals. 7,748 microforms. 374 audiovisuals. **Special Academic Facilities/Equipment:** Arboretum, art gallery, media center, Eddy Theater, Purnell Theater, greenhouse. **Computers:** School-owned computers available for student use.

EXTRACURRICULARS

Activities: Choral groups, dance, drama/theater, literary magazine, music ensembles, musical theater, student government, student newspaper, yearbook. **Organizations:** 23 registered organizations, 9 honor societies, 2 religious organizations. **Athletics (Intercollegiate):** *Women:* basketball, ice hockey, soccer, softball, tennis, volleyball.

ADMISSIONS

Selectivity Rating: 67 (of 100). **Freshman Academic Profile:** Average high school GPA 3.3. 25% in top 10% of high school class, 42% in top 25% of high school class, 75% in top 50% of high school class. 96% from public high schools. Average SAT I Math 516, SAT I Math middle 50% range 470-570. Average SAT I Verbal 565, SAT I Verbal middle 50% range 500-630. Average ACT 22, ACT middle 50% range 19-25. TOEFL required of all international applicants, minimum TOEFL 550. **Basis for Candidate Selection:** *Very important factors considered include:* secondary school record. *Important factors considered include:* essays, standardized test scores. *Other factors considered include:* alumni/ae relation, character/personal qualities, class rank, extracurricular activities, interview, recommendations, talent/ability, volunteer work, work experience. **Freshman Admission Requirements:** High school diploma or GED is required. *Academic units required/recommended:* 12 total required; 16 total recommended; 4 English required, 4 English recommended, 2 math required, 3 math recommended, 2 science required, 3 science recommended, 2 social studies required, 2 social studies recommended, 2 history required, 3 history recommended. **Freshman Admission Statistics:** 376 applied, 73% accepted, 40% of those accepted enrolled. **Transfer Admission Requirements:** *Items required:* high school transcript, college transcript, essay. Minimum high school GPA of 2.0 required. Minimum college GPA of 2.0 required. Lowest grade transferable C. **General Admission Information:** Application fee $25. Priority application deadline March 15. Nonfall registration accepted. Admission may be deferred for a maximum of 1 year. Credit and/or placement offered for CEEB Advanced Placement tests.

COSTS AND FINANCIAL AID

Tuition $18,803. Room & board $6,496. Required fees $156. Average book expense $700. **Required Forms and Deadlines:** FAFSA. No deadline for regular filing. Priority filing deadline May 1. **Notification of Awards:** Applicants will be notified of awards on a rolling basis beginning on or about February 15. **Types of Aid:** *Need-based scholarships/grants:* Pell, SEOG, state scholarships/grants, private scholarships, the school's own gift aid. *Loans:* FFEL Subsidized Stafford, FFEL Unsubsidized Stafford, FFEL PLUS, Federal Perkins, alternative loans. **Student Employment:** Federal Work-Study Program available. Institutional employment available. Off-campus job opportunities are good. **Financial Aid Statistics:** 78% freshmen, 79% undergrads receive some form of aid. Average freshman grant $9,518. Average freshman loan $2,497. Average income from on-campus job $1,796. **Financial Aid Phone:** 412-365-1777.

CHESTNUT HILL COLLEGE

9601 Germantown Avenue, Philadelphia, PA 19118-2693
Phone: 215-248-7001 **E-mail:** chcapply@chc.edu **CEEB Code:** 2082
Fax: 215-248-7082 **Web:** www.chc.edu **ACT Code:** 3540

This private school, which is affiliated with the Roman Catholic Church, was founded in 1924. It has a 45-acre campus.

STUDENTS AND FACULTY

Enrollment: 846. **Student Body:** Male 11%, female 89%, out-of-state 10%, international 1%. **Ethnic Representation:** African American 43%, Asian 2%, Caucasian 47%, Hispanic 5%. **Retention and Graduation:** 71% freshmen return for sophomore year. 59% freshmen graduate within 4 years. 30% grads go on to further study within 1 year. 3% grads pursue business degrees. 2% grads pursue law degrees. 4% grads pursue medical degrees. **Faculty:** Student/faculty ratio 10:1. 56 full-time faculty, 80% hold PhDs. 67% faculty teach undergrads.

ACADEMICS

Degrees: Associate's, bachelor's, certificate, doctoral, master's, post-bachelor's certificate, post-master's certificate, transfer. **Academic Requirements:** General education including some course work in arts/fine arts, computer literacy, English (including composition), foreign languages, history, humanities, mathematics, sciences (biological or physical), social science. **Classes:** 10-19 students in an average class. Under 10 students in an average lab/discussion section. **Majors with Highest Enrollment:** Elementary education and teaching; psychology, general; business administration/management. **Disciplines with Highest Percentage of Degrees Awarded:** Business/marketing 24%, education 14%, social sciences and history 14%, psychology 10%, protective services/public administration 10%. **Special Study Options:** Cooperative (work-study) program, double major, dual enrollment, English as a second language, student exchange program (domestic), honors program, independent study, internships, student-designed major, study abroad, teacher certification program, weekend college. Undergrads may take grad classes. Post-baccalaureate certificates in education and technology, leadership, and technology. Post-baccalaureate business administration certificate program for graduates with degrees in fields other than business. Post-master's certificate programs in addictions counseling, child and adolescent therapy, marriage and family therapy, spiritual direction, applied spirituality. Co-op programs: arts, business, computer science, education, health professions. 2-2 double bachelor's program in biology or chemistry and medical technology with Thomas Jefferson University. Bachelor's/doctoral program with College of Podiatric Medicine of

Temple University. Five-year bachelor's/master's combination programs in counseling psychology, education, and computer information sciences/applied technology.

FACILITIES

Housing: All-female, all-male. **Library Holdings:** 122,753 bound volumes. 516 periodicals. 213,912 microforms. 4,804 audiovisuals. **Special Academic Facilities/Equipment:** Archival museum, rare book collection, Irish literature collection, observatory, planetarium. **Computers:** School-owned computers available for student use.

EXTRACURRICULARS

Activities: Choral groups, drama/theater, literary magazine, music ensembles, musical theater, opera, student government, student newspaper, symphony orchestra, yearbook. **Organizations:** 28 registered organizations, 5 honor societies, 1 religious organization. **Athletics (Intercollegiate):** *Men:* basketball, soccer, tennis. *Women:* basketball, field hockey, lacrosse, soccer, softball, tennis, volleyball.

ADMISSIONS

Selectivity Rating: 72 (of 100). **Freshman Academic Profile:** Average high school GPA 3.1. 30% in top 10% of high school class, 52% in top 25% of high school class, 70% in top 50% of high school class. 55% from public high schools. Average SAT I Math 461, SAT I Math middle 50% range 410-530. Average SAT I Verbal 484, SAT I Verbal middle 50% range 430-540. Average ACT 19, ACT middle 50% range 17-21. TOEFL required of all international applicants, minimum TOEFL 500. **Basis for Candidate Selection:** *Very important factors considered include:* essays, secondary school record. *Important factors considered include:* character/personal qualities, class rank, extracurricular activities, interview, recommendations, standardized test scores. *Other factors considered include:* alumni/ae relation, talent/ability, volunteer work, work experience. **Freshman Admission Requirements:** High school diploma or GED is required. *Academic units required/recommended:* 16 total recommended; 4 English recommended, 3 math recommended, 3 science recommended, 2 foreign language recommended, 4 social studies recommended. **Freshman Admission Statistics:** 536 applied, 69% accepted, 27% of those accepted enrolled. **Transfer Admission Requirements:** *Items required:* college transcript, essay. Minimum high school GPA of 2.0 required. Minimum college GPA of 2.0 required. Lowest grade transferable C. **General Admission Information:** Application fee $35. Priority application deadline January 20. Nonfall registration accepted. Admission may be deferred for a maximum of 1 year. Credit and/or placement offered for CEEB Advanced Placement tests.

COSTS AND FINANCIAL AID

Required Forms and Deadlines: FAFSA. No deadline for regular filing. Priority filing deadline April 15. **Notification of Awards:** Applicants will be notified of awards on a rolling basis beginning on or about March 1. **Types of Aid:** *Need-based scholarships/grants:* Pell, SEOG, state scholarships/grants, private scholarships, the school's own gift aid. *Loans:* FFEL Subsidized Stafford, FFEL Unsubsidized Stafford, FFEL PLUS, Federal Perkins. **Student Employment:** Federal Work-Study Program available. Institutional employment available. Off-campus job opportunities are excellent. **Financial Aid Statistics:** 89% freshmen, 86% undergrads receive some form of aid. Average freshman grant $13,900. Average freshman loan $2,625. Average income from on-campus job $1,500. **Financial Aid Phone:** 215-248-7182.

See page 972.

CHEYNEY UNIVERSITY OF PENNSYLVANIA

Cheyney and Creek Roads, Cheyney, PA 19319
Phone: 610-399-2275 **E-mail:** jbrown@cheyney.edu **CEEB Code:** 2648
Fax: 610-399-2099 **Web:** www.cheyney.edu

This public school was founded in 1837. It has a 275-acre campus.

STUDENTS AND FACULTY

Enrollment: 1,132. **Student Body:** Male 44%, female 56%, out-of-state 17%, international 1%. **Ethnic Representation:** African American 98%, Hispanic 1%. **Faculty:** Student/faculty ratio 18:1. 74 full-time faculty, 58% hold PhDs. 89% faculty teach undergrads.

ACADEMICS

Degrees: Bachelor's, master's, post-bachelor's certificate. **Academic Requirements:** General education including some course work in arts/fine arts, computer literacy, English (including composition), foreign languages, humanities, mathematics, sciences (biological or physical), social science. **Disciplines with Highest Percentage of Degrees Awarded:** Social sciences and history 30%, education 20%, business/marketing 20%, psychology 12%, communications/communication technologies 5%. **Special Study Options:** Cooperative (work-study) program, cross registration, distance learning, double major, independent study, internships, teacher certification program.

FACILITIES

Housing: Coed, all-female, all-male. **Library Holdings:** 85,533 bound volumes. 1,526 periodicals. 601,000 microforms. 1,379 audiovisuals. **Special Academic Facilities/Equipment:** Afro-American history/culture collection, planetarium, weather station, satellite communication network. **Computers:** School-owned computers available for student use.

EXTRACURRICULARS

Activities: Choral groups, dance, drama/theater, jazz band, marching band, music ensembles, radio station, student government, student newspaper, student-run film society, television station, yearbook. **Organizations:** 41 registered organizations, 12 honor societies, 4 fraternities (5% men join), 4 sororities (8% women join). **Athletics (Intercollegiate):** *Men:* basketball, cross-country, football, tennis, track & field, wrestling. *Women:* basketball, cross-country, tennis, track & field, volleyball.

ADMISSIONS

Selectivity Rating: 73 (of 100). **Freshman Academic Profile:** TOEFL required of all international applicants, minimum TOEFL 500. **Basis for Candidate Selection:** *Very important factors considered include:* recommendations, secondary school record. *Important factors considered include:* class rank, essays, extracurricular activities, interview, standardized test scores, state residency. *Other factors considered include:* minority status, talent/ability. **Freshman Admission Requirements:** High school diploma or GED is required. *Academic units required/recommended:* 13 total required; 4 English required, 3 math required, 2 science required, 2 foreign language required, 2 history required. **Freshman Admission Statistics:** 1,164 applied, 82% accepted, 31% of those accepted enrolled. **Transfer Admission Requirements:** *Items required:* college transcript, interview, statement of good standing from prior school. Minimum high school GPA of 1.6 required. Minimum college GPA of 2.0 required. Lowest grade transferable C. **General Admission Information:** Application fee $20. Priority application deadline June 15. Nonfall registration accepted. Admission may be deferred for a maximum of 1 year.

COSTS AND FINANCIAL AID

In-state tuition $3,792. Out-of-state tuition $9,480. Room & board $4,983. Required fees $655. Average book expense $675. **Required Forms and Deadlines:** FAFSA. Priority filing deadline May 1. **Notification of Awards:** Applicants will be notified of awards on a rolling basis beginning on or about April 1. **Types of Aid:** *Need-based scholarships/grants:* Pell, SEOG, state scholarships/grants, private scholarships, the school's own gift aid. *Loans:* FFEL Subsidized Stafford, FFEL Unsubsidized Stafford, FFEL PLUS, Federal Perkins. **Student Employment:** Federal Work-Study Program available. Institutional employment available. Off-campus job opportunities are good. **Financial Aid Statistics:** 84% freshmen, 80% undergrads receive some form of aid. **Financial Aid Phone:** 610-399-2302.

CHICAGO STATE UNIVERSITY

9501 South Street King Drive, ADM-200, Chicago, IL 60628
Phone: 773-995-2513 **E-mail:** ug-Admissions@csu.edu
Fax: 773-995-3820 **Web:** www.csu.edu **ACT Code:** 1694

This public school was founded in 1867. It has a 161-acre campus.

STUDENTS AND FACULTY

Enrollment: 4,979. **Student Body:** Male 26%, female 74%, out-of-state 2%. **Ethnic Representation:** African American 89%, Caucasian 3%, Hispanic 6%. **Faculty:** Student/faculty ratio 13:1. 322 full-time faculty.

ACADEMICS

Degrees: Bachelor's, master's. **Academic Requirements:** General education including some course work in English (including composition), foreign languages, humanities, mathematics, sciences (biological or physical), social science. **Classes:** 20-29 students in an average class. **Majors with Highest Enrollment:** Nursing/registered nurse training (RN, ASN, BSN, MSN); elementary education and teaching; liberal arts and sciences/liberal studies. **Disciplines with Highest Percentage of Degrees Awarded:** Liberal arts/ general studies 31%, education 13%, business/marketing 12%, health professions and related sciences 9%, psychology 7%. **Special Study Options:** Cooperative (work-study) program, distance learning, double major, English as a second language, honors program, independent study, internships, student-designed major, study abroad, teacher certification program, programs for mature adults (University Without Walls, individual curriculum, and Board of Governors degree program).

FACILITIES

Housing: Coed. **Library Holdings:** 482,110 bound volumes. 2,200 periodicals. 587,812 microforms. 7,905 audiovisuals. **Special Academic Facilities/ Equipment:** Art gallery, electron microscopes, greenhouse. **Computers:** School-owned computers available for student use.

EXTRACURRICULARS

Activities: Choral groups, concert band, dance, drama/theater, jazz band, literary magazine, music ensembles, radio station, student government, student newspaper, television station. **Organizations:** 47 registered organizations, 30 honor societies, 4 religious organizations, 4 fraternities, 4 sororities. **Athletics (Intercollegiate):** *Men:* baseball, basketball, cross-country, golf, indoor track, tennis, track & field. *Women:* basketball, cross-country, golf, indoor track, tennis, track & field, volleyball.

ADMISSIONS

Selectivity Rating: 63 (of 100). **Freshman Academic Profile:** Average high school GPA 2.6. 11% in top 10% of high school class, 29% in top 25% of high school class, 58% in top 50% of high school class. 80% from public high schools. Average ACT 18, ACT middle 50% range 16-19. TOEFL required of all international applicants, minimum TOEFL 500. **Basis for Candidate Selection:** *Very important factors considered include:* secondary school record, standardized test scores. **Freshman Admission Requirements:** High school diploma or GED is required. *Academic units required/recommended:* 15 total required; 4 English required, 3 math required, 3 science required, 3 social studies required, 2 elective required. **Freshman Admission Statistics:** 2,235 applied, 39% accepted, 54% of those accepted enrolled. **Transfer Admission Requirements:** *Items required:* college transcript. Minimum high school GPA of 2.0 required. Minimum college GPA of 2.0 required. Lowest grade transferable D. **General Admission Information:** Application fee $25. Priority application deadline July 15. Regular application deadline July 15. Nonfall registration accepted. Admission may be deferred. Credit and/or placement offered for CEEB Advanced Placement tests.

COSTS AND FINANCIAL AID

In-state tuition $3,762. Out-of-state tuition $8,448. Room & board $5,700. Required fees $1,060. Average book expense $1,400. **Required Forms and Deadlines:** FAFSA and institution's own financial aid form. No deadline for regular filing. **Notification of Awards:** Applicants will be notified of awards on a rolling basis beginning on or about March 1. **Types of Aid:** *Need-based scholarships/grants:* Pell, SEOG, state scholarships/grants, private scholarships, the school's own gift aid. *Loans:* FFEL Subsidized Stafford, FFEL Unsubsidized Stafford, FFEL PLUS, Federal Perkins. **Student Employment:** Federal Work-Study Program available. Institutional employment available. Off-campus job opportunities are good. **Financial Aid Statistics:** 85% freshmen, 87% undergrads receive some form of aid. Average freshman grant $6,555. Average freshman loan $2,625. Average income from on-campus job $2,000. **Financial Aid Phone:** 773-995-2304.

CHOWAN COLLEGE

PO Box 1848, Murfreesboro, NC 27855
Phone: 252-398-1236 **E-mail:** admissions@chowan.edu **CEEB Code:** 5107
Fax: 252-398-1190 **Web:** www.chowan.edu **ACT Code:** 3084

This private school, which is affiliated with the Baptist Church, was founded in 1848. It has a 300-acre campus.

STUDENTS AND FACULTY

Enrollment: 726. **Student Body:** Male 57%, female 43%, out-of-state 58%, international 2% (6 countries represented). **Ethnic Representation:** African American 25%, Asian 1%, Caucasian 71%, Hispanic 2%, Native American 1%. **Retention and Graduation:** 49% freshmen return for sophomore year. 5% grads go on to further study within 1 year. 1% grads pursue business degrees. 1% grads pursue law degrees. 1% grads pursue medical degrees. **Faculty:** Student/faculty ratio 12:1. 53 full-time faculty, 56% hold PhDs. 100% faculty teach undergrads.

ACADEMICS

Degrees: Associate's, bachelor's. **Academic Requirements:** General education including some course work in arts/fine arts, computer literacy, English (including composition), history, humanities, mathematics, philosophy, sciences (biological or physical), social science, religion, physical education. **Disciplines with Highest Percentage of Degrees Awarded:** Business/ marketing 30%, education 20%, computer and information sciences 15%, communications/communication technologies 10%, biological life sciences 10%. **Special Study Options:** Double major, dual enrollment, independent study, internships, study abroad, teacher certification program.

FACILITIES

Housing: Coed, all-female, all-male. **Library Holdings:** 101,682 bound volumes. 929 periodicals. 31,022 microforms. 3,714 audiovisuals. **Special Academic Facilities/Equipment:** Antiquities room in Whitaker Library, Ward Parlor in McDowell Columns Building, Green Hall Art Gallery, Daniel Hall Recital Hall. **Computers:** School-owned computers available for student use.

EXTRACURRICULARS

Activities: Choral groups, concert band, drama/theater, jazz band, marching band, music ensembles, musical theater, pep band, student government, student newspaper, yearbook. **Organizations:** 52 registered organizations, 5 honor societies, 2 religious organizations, 2 fraternities (12% men join), 2 sororities (13% women join). **Athletics (Intercollegiate):** *Men:* baseball, basketball, cheerleading, football, golf, soccer, tennis. *Women:* basketball, cheerleading, golf, soccer, softball, tennis, volleyball.

ADMISSIONS

Selectivity Rating: 63 (of 100). **Freshman Academic Profile:** Average high school GPA 2.7. 5% in top 10% of high school class, 19% in top 25% of high school class, 55% in top 50% of high school class. Average SAT I Math 451, SAT I Math middle 50% range 410-490. Average SAT I Verbal 458, SAT I Verbal middle 50% range 410-500. Average ACT 17, ACT middle 50% range 16-19. TOEFL required of all international applicants, minimum TOEFL 450. **Basis for Candidate Selection:** *Very important factors considered include:* secondary school record. *Important factors considered include:* character/ personal qualities, standardized test scores. *Other factors considered include:* class rank, essays, extracurricular activities, interview, recommendations, talent/ ability, volunteer work, work experience. **Freshman Admission Requirements:** High school diploma or GED is required. *Academic units required/ recommended:* 17 total required; 21 total recommended; 4 English required, 4 English recommended, 2 math required, 3 math recommended, 2 science required, 3 science recommended, 2 science lab required, 2 science lab recommended, 2 foreign language recommended, 2 social studies required, 3 social studies recommended, 7 elective required, 9 elective recommended. **Freshman Admission Statistics:** 1,297 applied, 90% accepted, 22% of those accepted enrolled. **Transfer Admission Requirements:** *Items required:* high school transcript, college transcript. Minimum college GPA of 2.0 required. Lowest grade transferable C. **General Admission Information:** Application fee $20. Priority application deadline July 1. Regular application deadline August 15. Nonfall registration accepted. Admission may be deferred for a maximum of 1 year. Credit offered for CEEB Advanced Placement tests.

COSTS AND FINANCIAL AID

Tuition $11,820. Room & board $4,780. Required fees $50. Average book expense $540. **Required Forms and Deadlines:** FAFSA. No deadline for regular filing. Priority filing deadline May 1. **Notification of Awards:** Applicants will be notified of awards on a rolling basis. **Types of Aid:** *Need-based scholarships/grants:* Pell, SEOG, state scholarships/grants, private scholarships, the school's own gift aid. *Loans:* Direct Subsidized Stafford, Direct Unsubsidized Stafford, Direct PLUS, FFEL Subsidized Stafford, FFEL Unsubsidized Stafford, FFEL PLUS, Federal Perkins. **Student Employment:** Federal Work-Study Program available. Institutional employment available. Off-campus job opportunities are good. **Financial Aid Statistics:** 84% freshmen, 84% undergrads receive some form of aid. Average freshman grant $4,500. Average freshman loan $2,500. Average income from on-campus job $700. **Financial Aid Phone:** 252-398-1229.

CHRISTENDOM COLLEGE

134 Christendom Drive, Front Royal, VA 22630
Phone: 540-636-2900 **E-mail:** admissions@christendom.edu **CEEB Code:** 5691
Fax: 540-636-1655 **Web:** www.christendom.edu **ACT Code:** 4339

This private school, which is affiliated with the Roman Catholic Church, was founded in 1977. It has a 100-acre campus.

STUDENTS AND FACULTY

Enrollment: 352. **Student Body:** Male 41%, female 59%, out-of-state 78%, international 3%. **Ethnic Representation:** Asian 2%, Caucasian 94%, Hispanic 4%. **Retention and Graduation:** 80% freshmen return for sophomore year.

74% freshmen graduate within 4 years. 25% grads go on to further study within 1 year. 5% grads pursue business degrees. 5% grads pursue law degrees. **Faculty:** Student/faculty ratio 12:1. 23 full-time faculty, 78% hold PhDs. 100% faculty teach undergrads.

ACADEMICS

Degrees: Associate's, bachelor's, master's. **Academic Requirements:** General education including some course work in English (including composition), foreign languages, history, humanities, mathematics, philosophy, sciences (biological or physical), social science, theology. **Classes:** 20-29 students in an average class. **Majors with Highest Enrollment:** History, general; philosophy; political science and government, general. **Disciplines with Highest Percentage of Degrees Awarded:** Social sciences and history 50%, philosophy/religion/theology 34%, English 12%, foreign languages and literature 4%. **Special Study Options:** Double major, honors program, independent study, internships, study abroad.

FACILITIES

Housing: All-female, all-male. **Library Holdings:** 64,265 bound volumes. 249 periodicals. 851 microforms. 1,302 audiovisuals. **Computers:** School-owned computers available for student use.

EXTRACURRICULARS

Activities: Choral groups, drama/theater, student government, student newspaper, yearbook. **Organizations:** 1 registered organization, 4 religious organizations. **Athletics (Intercollegiate):** *Men:* baseball, basketball, soccer. *Women:* basketball, soccer.

ADMISSIONS

Selectivity Rating: 60 (of 100). **Freshman Academic Profile:** Average high school GPA 3.5. 60% in top 10% of high school class, 86% in top 25% of high school class, 100% in top 50% of high school class. 20% from public high schools. Average SAT I Math 585, SAT I Math middle 50% range 540-640. Average SAT I Verbal 654, SAT I Verbal middle 50% range 600-700. Average ACT 25. TOEFL required of all international applicants, minimum TOEFL 550. **Basis for Candidate Selection:** *Very important factors considered include:* essays. *Important factors considered include:* character/personal qualities, recommendations, religious affiliation/commitment, secondary school record, standardized test scores. *Other factors considered include:* alumni/ae relation, class rank, extracurricular activities, interview, talent/ability, volunteer work, work experience. **Freshman Admission Requirements:** High school diploma or equivalent is not required. *Academic units required/recommended:* 14 total recommended; 4 English recommended, 2 math recommended, 2 science recommended, 2 foreign language recommended, 1 social studies recommended, 2 history recommended, 1 elective recommended. **Freshman Admission Statistics:** 220 applied, 77% accepted, 55% of those accepted enrolled. **Transfer Admission Requirements:** *Items required:* college transcript, essay. Minimum high school GPA of 2.0 required. Minimum college GPA of 2.8 required. Lowest grade transferable C. **General Admission Information:** Application fee $25. Priority application deadline March 1. Regular application deadline March 1. Nonfall registration accepted. Credit offered for CEEB Advanced Placement tests.

COSTS AND FINANCIAL AID

Tuition $11,750. Room & board $4,700. Required fees $250. Average book expense $450. **Required Forms and Deadlines:** Institution's own financial aid form. Priority filing deadline March 1. **Notification of Awards:** Applicants will be notified of awards on a rolling basis beginning on or about February 1. **Types of Aid:** *Need-based scholarships/grants:* private scholarships, the school's own gift aid. *Loans:* college/university loans from institutional funds. **Student Employment:** Institutional employment available. Off-campus job opportunities are good. **Financial Aid Statistics:** 45% freshmen, 51% undergrads receive some form of aid. Average freshman grant $5,275. Average freshman loan $3,685. Average income from on-campus job $1,780. **Financial Aid Phone:** 800-877-5456.

CHRISTIAN BROTHERS UNIVERSITY

Admissions, Box T-6, 650 East Parkway South, Memphis, TN 38104-5519
Phone: 901-321-3205 **E-mail:** admissions@cbu.edu **CEEB Code:** 1121
Fax: 901-321-3202 **Web:** www.cbu.edu **ACT Code:** 3952

This private school, which is affiliated with the Roman Catholic Church, was founded in 1871. It has a 75-acre campus.

STUDENTS AND FACULTY

Enrollment: 1,585. **Student Body:** Male 44%, female 56%, out-of-state 23%, international 3% (29 countries represented). **Ethnic Representation:** African American 32%, Asian 5%, Caucasian 58%, Hispanic 2%. **Retention and Graduation:** 76% freshmen return for sophomore year. **Faculty:** Student/faculty ratio 12:1. 109 full-time faculty, 84% hold PhDs. 100% faculty teach undergrads.

ACADEMICS

Degrees: Bachelor's, master's. **Academic Requirements:** General education including some course work in computer literacy, English (including composition), mathematics, sciences (biological or physical), social science, religious studies, and moral philosophy. **Classes:** 10-19 students in an average class. **Majors with Highest Enrollment:** Accounting; psychology, general; biology/biological sciences, general. **Disciplines with Highest Percentage of Degrees Awarded:** Business/marketing 41%, engineering/engineering technology 16%, psychology 16%, English 6%, education 5%. **Special Study Options:** Accelerated program, cross registration, double major, dual enrollment, honors program, internships, study abroad, teacher certification program.

FACILITIES

Housing: Coed, all-female, all-male, apartments for single students, housing for international students. **Library Holdings:** 150,000 bound volumes. 520 periodicals. 51,000 microforms. 1,100 audiovisuals. **Special Academic Facilities/Equipment:** Art exhibits, audiovisual lab, telecommunication and information systems center, engineering graphics lab, space center, Ghandi Institute for Nonviolence. **Computers:** *Recommended operating system:* Windows 95. School-owned computers available for student use.

EXTRACURRICULARS

Activities: Choral groups, drama/theater, literary magazine, music ensembles, student government, student newspaper, yearbook. **Organizations:** 33 registered organizations, 6 honor societies, 1 religious organization, 6 fraternities (24% men join), 5 sororities (20% women join). **Athletics (Intercollegiate):** *Men:* baseball, basketball, cross-country, golf, soccer, tennis. *Women:* basketball, cross-country, soccer, softball, tennis, volleyball.

ADMISSIONS

Selectivity Rating: 80 (of 100). **Freshman Academic Profile:** Average high school GPA 3.4. 31% in top 10% of high school class, 52% in top 25% of high school class, 79% in top 50% of high school class. 65% from public high schools. Average SAT I Math 566, SAT I Math middle 50% range 480-650. Average SAT I Verbal 538, SAT I Verbal middle 50% range 480-610. Average ACT 24, ACT middle 50% range 20-25. TOEFL required of all international applicants, minimum TOEFL 500. **Basis for Candidate Selection:** *Very important factors considered include:* secondary school record, standardized test scores. *Important factors considered include:* character/personal qualities, class rank. *Other factors considered include:* alumni/ae relation, essays, extracurricular activities, interview, recommendations, talent/ability, volunteer work, work experience. **Freshman Admission Requirements:** High school diploma or GED is required. *Academic units required/recommended:* 4 English recommended, 4 math recommended, 4 science recommended. **Freshman Admission Statistics:** 1,847 applied, 41% accepted, 31% of those accepted enrolled. **Transfer Admission Requirements:** *Items required:* college transcript, essay. Minimum college GPA of 2.5 required. Lowest grade transferable C. **General Admission Information:** Application fee $25. Priority application deadline January 1. Regular application deadline August 1. Nonfall registration accepted. Admission may be deferred for a maximum of 1 year. Credit and/or placement offered for CEEB Advanced Placement tests.

COSTS AND FINANCIAL AID

Tuition $15,790. Room & board $4,900. Required fees $450. Average book expense $600. **Required Forms and Deadlines:** FAFSA. No deadline for regular filing. Priority filing deadline April 1. **Notification of Awards:** Applicants will be notified of awards on a rolling basis. **Types of Aid:** *Need-based scholarships/grants:* Pell, SEOG, state scholarships/grants, private scholarships, the school's own gift aid, engineering scholarships. *Loans:* Direct Subsidized Stafford, FFEL Subsidized Stafford, Federal Perkins, state loans, college/university loans from institutional funds. **Student Employment:** Federal Work-Study Program available. Institutional employment available. Off-campus job opportunities are excellent. **Financial Aid Statistics:** 81% freshmen, 60% undergrads receive some form of aid. **Financial Aid Phone:** 901-321-3305.

See page 974.

CHRISTIAN HERITAGE COLLEGE

2100 Greenfield Dr., El Cajon, CA 92019-1157
Phone: 619-588-7747 **E-mail:** chcadm@adm.Christianheritage.edu
Fax: 619-440-0209 **Web:** www.Christianheritage.edu **ACT Code:** 211

This private school was founded in 1970. It has a 32-acre campus.

STUDENTS AND FACULTY

Enrollment: 617. **Student Body:** Male 40%, female 60%, out-of-state 13%, international 2% (14 countries represented). **Ethnic Representation:** African American 9%, Asian 3%, Caucasian 75%, Hispanic 11%. **Retention and Graduation:** 68% freshmen return for sophomore year. 18% freshmen graduate within 4 years. 25% grads go on to further study within 1 year. **Faculty:** 100% faculty teach undergrads.

ACADEMICS

Degrees: Bachelor's, certificate. **Academic Requirements:** General education including some course work in arts/fine arts, computer literacy, English (including composition), history, humanities, mathematics, philosophy, sciences (biological or physical), social science. **Special Study Options:** English as a second language, independent study, internships, student-designed major, study abroad, teacher certification program.

FACILITIES

Housing: All-female, all-male, apartments for single students. **Library Holdings:** 70,000 bound volumes. 75,500 periodicals. 81 microforms. 3,821 audiovisuals. **Computers:** *Recommended operating system:* Windows 95. School-owned computers available for student use.

EXTRACURRICULARS

Activities: Choral groups, music ensembles, student government, yearbook. **Organizations:** 12 registered organizations, 1 honor society. **Athletics (Intercollegiate):** *Men:* basketball, soccer. *Women:* basketball, cheerleading, soccer, volleyball.

ADMISSIONS

Selectivity Rating: 60 (of 100). **Freshman Academic Profile:** Average high school GPA 3.2. 7% in top 10% of high school class, 21% in top 25% of high school class, 45% in top 50% of high school class. 70% from public high schools. Average SAT I Math 475. Average SAT I Verbal 512. Average ACT 18. TOEFL required of all international applicants, minimum TOEFL 500. **Basis for Candidate Selection:** *Very important factors considered include:* essays, recommendations, religious affiliation/commitment, secondary school record, standardized test scores. *Important factors considered include:* class rank, extracurricular activities. *Other factors considered include:* character/personal qualities, interview, volunteer work. **Freshman Admission Requirements:** High school diploma or GED is required. *Academic units required/recommended:* 15 total recommended; 4 English recommended, 3 math recommended, 3 science recommended, 1 science lab recommended, 2 foreign language recommended, 3 history recommended. **Transfer Admission Requirements:** *Items required:* college transcript, essay, statement of good standing from prior school. Minimum high school GPA of 2.3 required. Minimum college GPA of 2.0 required. Lowest grade transferable C. **General Admission Information:** Application fee $25. Regular application deadline August 1. Nonfall registration accepted. Admission may be deferred for a maximum of 1 year. Credit and/or placement offered for CEEB Advanced Placement tests.

COSTS AND FINANCIAL AID

Tuition $10,240. Room & board $4,500. Average book expense $600. **Required Forms and Deadlines:** FAFSA and state aid form. Financial aid filing deadline September 1. Priority filing deadline March 2. **Notification of Awards:** Applicants will be notified of awards on a rolling basis beginning on or about April 1. **Types of Aid:** *Need-based scholarships/grants:* Pell, SEOG, state scholarships/grants, private scholarships, the school's own gift aid. *Loans:* Direct Subsidized Stafford, Direct Unsubsidized Stafford, Direct PLUS, Federal Perkins. **Student Employment:** Federal Work-Study Program available. Institutional employment available. Off-campus job opportunities are good. **Financial Aid Statistics:** Average freshman grant $3,000. Average freshman loan $2,500. Average income from on-campus job $1,750. **Financial Aid Phone:** 619-590-1786.

CHRISTOPHER NEWPORT UNIVERSITY

1 University Place, Newport News, VA 23608-2998
Phone: 757-594-7015 **E-mail:** admit@cnu.edu **CEEB Code:** 5128
Fax: 757-594-7333 **Web:** www.cnu.edu **ACT Code:** 4345

This public school was founded in 1960. It has a 150-acre campus.

STUDENTS AND FACULTY

Enrollment: 5,192. **Student Body:** Male 40%, female 60%, out-of-state 3%. **Ethnic Representation:** African American 1%, Asian 3%, Caucasian 92%, Hispanic 3%. **Retention and Graduation:** 81% freshmen return for sophomore year. 13% freshmen graduate within 4 years. **Faculty:** Student/faculty ratio 23:1. 185 full-time faculty, 83% hold PhDs. 100% faculty teach undergrads.

ACADEMICS

Degrees: Bachelor's, master's. **Academic Requirements:** General education including some course work in computer literacy, English (including composition), foreign languages, history, humanities, mathematics, philosophy, sciences (biological or physical), social science, physical education/health. **Classes:** 20-29 students in an average class. **Majors with Highest Enrollment:** Business administration/management; psychology, general; public administration. **Disciplines with Highest Percentage of Degrees Awarded:** Business/marketing 22%, psychology 12%, protective services/public administration 12%, social sciences and history 11%, English 10%. **Special Study Options:** Accelerated program, cooperative (work-study) program, cross registration, distance learning, double major, dual enrollment, honors program, independent study, internships, student-designed major, study abroad.

FACILITIES

Housing: Coed, apartments for single students. **Library Holdings:** 328,319 bound volumes. 1,695 periodicals. 765,028 microforms. 10,238 audiovisuals. **Special Academic Facilities/Equipment:** Falk Art Gallery, Japanese teahouse, greenhouse. **Computers:** School-owned computers available for student use.

EXTRACURRICULARS

Activities: Choral groups, concert band, dance, drama/theater, jazz band, literary magazine, music ensembles, musical theater, pep band, radio station, student government, student newspaper, symphony orchestra. **Organizations:** 60 registered organizations, 13 honor societies, 8 religious organizations, 5 fraternities (3% men join), 5 sororities (2% women join). **Athletics (Intercollegiate):** *Men:* baseball, basketball, cheerleading, cross-country, football, golf, indoor track, sailing, soccer, tennis, track & field. *Women:* basketball, cheerleading, cross-country, field hockey, indoor track, lacrosse, sailing, soccer, softball, tennis, track & field, volleyball.

ADMISSIONS

Selectivity Rating: 63 (of 100). **Freshman Academic Profile:** Average high school GPA 3.3. 13% in top 10% of high school class, 46% in top 25% of high school class, 88% in top 50% of high school class. Average SAT I Math 559, SAT I Math middle 50% range 520-600. Average SAT I Verbal 563, SAT I Verbal middle 50% range 520-600. Average ACT 22, ACT middle 50% range 20-24. TOEFL required of all international applicants, minimum TOEFL 530. **Basis for Candidate Selection:** *Very important factors considered include:* secondary school record, standardized test scores. *Important factors considered include:* class rank. *Other factors considered include:* essays, extracurricular activities, recommendations, volunteer work, work experience. **Freshman Admission Requirements:** High school diploma or GED is required. *Academic units required/recommended:* 23 total required; 4 English required, 4 math required, 1 math recommended, 3 science required, 2 foreign language required, 3 social studies required, 3 history required, 3 elective recommended. **Freshman Admission Statistics:** 5,097 applied, 48% accepted, 48% of those accepted enrolled. **Transfer Admission Requirements:** *Items required:* high school transcript, college transcript, statement of good standing from prior school. Minimum high school GPA of 3.0 required. Minimum college GPA of 3.5 required. Lowest grade transferable C. **General Admission Information:** Application fee $35. Priority application deadline December 1. Regular application deadline March 1. Nonfall registration accepted. Admission may be deferred for a maximum of 1 year. Credit and/or placement offered for CEEB Advanced Placement tests.

COSTS AND FINANCIAL AID

In-state tuition $2,558. Out-of-state tuition $9,140. Room & board $6,350. Required fees $1,474. Average book expense $736. **Required Forms and Deadlines:** FAFSA. No deadline for regular filing. Priority filing deadline March 1. **Notification of Awards:** Applicants will be notified of awards on a rolling basis beginning on or about February 17. **Types of Aid:** *Need-based scholarships/grants:* Pell, SEOG, state scholarships/grants, private scholarships, the school's own gift aid. *Loans:* FFEL Subsidized Stafford, FFEL Unsubsidized Stafford, FFEL PLUS. **Student Employment:** Federal Work-Study Program available. Institutional employment available. Off-campus job opportunities are excellent. **Financial Aid Statistics:** 60% freshmen, 61% undergrads receive some form of aid. Average freshman grant $2,798. Average freshman loan $2,625. Average income from on-campus job $1,987. **Financial Aid Phone:** 757-594-7170.

CIRCLEVILLE BIBLE COLLEGE

1476 Lancaster Pike, PO Box 458, Circleville, OH 43113-9487
Phone: 740-477-7701 **E-mail:** enroll@Biblecollege.edu
Fax: 740-477-7755 **Web:** www.Biblecollege.edu **ACT Code:** 3030

This private school was founded in 1948.

STUDENTS AND FACULTY

Enrollment: 307. **Student Body:** Male 53%, female 47%, out-of-state 24%. **Ethnic Representation:** African American 7%, Asian 1%, Caucasian 91%, Hispanic 1%, Native American 1%. **Retention and Graduation:** 58% freshmen return for sophomore year. **Faculty:** Student/faculty ratio 14:1. 10 full-time faculty, 40% hold PhDs.

ACADEMICS

Degrees: Bachelor's, terminal, transfer. **Academic Requirements:** General education including some course work in arts/fine arts, computer literacy, English (including composition), history, humanities, mathematics, philosophy, sciences (biological or physical), social science. **Classes:** 10-19 students in an average class. **Disciplines with Highest Percentage of Degrees Awarded:** Other 84%, psychology 9%, education 7%. **Special Study Options:** Double major, independent study, internships, liberal arts/career combination, student-designed major.

FACILITIES

Housing: All-female, all-male, apartments for married students, housing for international students. **Computers:** *Recommended operating system:* Windows NT/2000. School-owned computers available for student use.

EXTRACURRICULARS

Activities: Choral groups, drama/theater, music ensembles, student government, yearbook. **Athletics (Intercollegiate):** *Men:* baseball, basketball. *Women:* basketball, volleyball.

ADMISSIONS

Selectivity Rating: 63 (of 100). **Freshman Academic Profile:** 21% in top 10% of high school class, 24% in top 25% of high school class, 32% in top 50% of high school class. Average ACT 20, ACT middle 50% range 15-22. **Basis for Candidate Selection:** *Very important factors considered include:* class rank, recommendations, religious affiliation/commitment, secondary school record, standardized test scores. *Important factors considered include:* character/personal qualities, essays. **Freshman Admission Requirements:** High school diploma or GED is required. *Academic units required/recommended:* 15 total recommended; 4 English recommended, 3 math recommended, 3 science recommended, 2 foreign language recommended, 3 social studies recommended. **Freshman Admission Statistics:** 112 applied, 58% accepted, 74% of those accepted enrolled. **Transfer Admission Requirements:** *Items required:* high school transcript, college transcript, essay, standardized test score, statement of good standing from prior school. Minimum college GPA of 2.0 required. Lowest grade transferable C. **General Admission Information:** Application fee $25. Nonfall registration accepted. Admission may be deferred for a maximum of 1 year.

COSTS AND FINANCIAL AID

Tuition $7,944. Room & board $5,098. Required fees $852. Average book expense $500. **Required Forms and Deadlines:** FAFSA, institution's own financial aid form, and CSS/Financial Aid PROFILE. Priority filing deadline April 1. **Notification of Awards:** Applicants will be notified of awards on or about June 1. **Student Employment:** Federal Work-Study Program available. Off-campus job opportunities are excellent. **Financial Aid Statistics:** 97% freshmen, 98% undergrads receive some form of aid. **Financial Aid Phone:** 740-477-7749.

THE CITADEL, THE MILITARY COLLEGE OF SOUTH CAROLINA

171 Moultrie Street, Charleston, SC 29409
Phone: 843-953-5230 **E-mail:** admissions@citadel.edu
Fax: 843-953-7036 **Web:** www.citadel.edu **ACT Code:** 3838

This public school was founded in 1842. It has a 176-acre campus.

STUDENTS AND FACULTY

Enrollment: 2,099. **Student Body:** Male 92%, female 8%, out-of-state 53%, international 3% (28 countries represented). **Ethnic Representation:** African American 9%, Asian 3%, Caucasian 83%, Hispanic 5%. **Retention and Graduation:** 78% freshmen return for sophomore year. 56% freshmen graduate within 4 years. 27% grads go on to further study within 1 year. 6% grads pursue business degrees. 3% grads pursue law degrees. 1% grads pursue medical degrees. **Faculty:** Student/faculty ratio 15:1. 148 full-time faculty, 95% hold PhDs. 100% faculty teach undergrads.

ACADEMICS

Degrees: Bachelor's, master's, post-master's certificate. **Academic Requirements:** General education including some course work in English (including composition), foreign languages, history, mathematics, sciences (biological or physical), social science, ROTC. **Classes:** 20-29 students in an average class. 10-19 students in an average lab/discussion section. **Majors with Highest Enrollment:** Business administration/management; criminal justice/law enforcement administration; political science and government, general. **Disciplines with Highest Percentage of Degrees Awarded:** Business/marketing 39%, social sciences and history 15%, engineering/engineering technology 13%, education 8%, protective services/public administration 8%. **Special Study Options:** Cross registration, double major, English as a second language, honors program, independent study, internships, study abroad, teacher certification program.

FACILITIES

Housing: Coed. **Library Holdings:** 234,282 bound volumes. 1,336 periodicals. 1,177,586 microforms. 4,507 audiovisuals. **Special Academic Facilities/Equipment:** Archives and museum. **Computers:** School-owned computers available for student use.

EXTRACURRICULARS

Activities: Choral groups, concert band, drama/theater, literary magazine, marching band, music ensembles, pep band, student government, student newspaper, yearbook. **Organizations:** 61 registered organizations, 3 honor societies, 14 religious organizations. **Athletics (Intercollegiate):** *Men:* baseball, basketball, cross-country, football, golf, indoor track, soccer, tennis, track & field, wrestling. *Women:* cross-country, golf, indoor track, soccer, track & field, volleyball.

ADMISSIONS

Selectivity Rating: 74 (of 100). **Freshman Academic Profile:** Average high school GPA 3.2. 10% in top 10% of high school class, 30% in top 25% of high school class, 64% in top 50% of high school class. Average SAT I Math 544, SAT I Math middle 50% range 500-600. Average SAT I Verbal 528, SAT I Verbal middle 50% range 480-580. Average ACT 23, ACT middle 50% range 20-25. TOEFL required of all international applicants, minimum TOEFL 550. **Basis for Candidate Selection:** *Very important factors considered include:* secondary school record, standardized test scores. *Important factors considered include:* character/personal qualities, extracurricular activities, minority status, state residency, talent/ability. *Other factors considered include:* alumni/ae relation, class rank, geographical residence, interview, volunteer work. **Freshman Admission Requirements:** High school diploma or GED is required. *Academic units required/recommended:* 20 total required; 4 English required, 3 math required, 3 science required, 3 science lab required, 2 foreign language required, 2 social studies required, 1 history required, 4 elective required. **Freshman Admission Statistics:** 1,922 applied, 68% accepted, 40% of those accepted enrolled. **Transfer Admission Requirements:** *Items required:* high school transcript, college transcript, standardized test scores, statement of good standing from prior school. Minimum high school GPA of 2.0 required. Minimum college GPA of 2.0 required. Lowest grade transferable C. **General Admission Information:** Application fee $35. Credit and/or placement offered for CEEB Advanced Placement tests.

COSTS AND FINANCIAL AID

Required Forms and Deadlines: FAFSA. Financial aid filing deadline February 28. Priority filing deadline March 17. **Notification of Awards:** Applicants will be notified of awards on or about April 15. **Types of Aid:** *Need-*

based scholarships/grants: Pell, SEOG, state scholarships/grants, private scholarships, the school's own gift aid. *Loans:* Direct Subsidized Stafford, Direct Unsubsidized Stafford, Direct PLUS, Federal Perkins, college/university loans from institutional funds. **Student Employment:** Federal Work-Study Program available. **Financial Aid Statistics:** 53% freshmen, 45% undergrads receive some form of aid. **Financial Aid Phone:** 843-953-5187.

CLAFLIN UNIVERSITY

400 Magnolia Street, Orangeburg, SC 29115
Phone: 803-535-5339 **E-mail:** kboyd@clafl.claflin.edu
Fax: 803-535-5387 **Web:** www.clafin.edu

This private school, which is affiliated with the Methodist Church, was founded in 1866.

STUDENTS AND FACULTY

Enrollment: 1,546. **Student Body:** Male 32%, female 68%, out-of-state 0%, international 4% (8 countries represented). **Ethnic Representation:** African American 99%, Caucasian 1%. **Retention and Graduation:** 79% freshmen return for sophomore year. 46% freshmen graduate within 4 years. 20% grads go on to further study within 1 year. 5% grads pursue business degrees. 1% grads pursue law degrees. 2% grads pursue medical degrees. **Faculty:** 100% faculty teach undergrads.

ACADEMICS

Degrees: Bachelor's, master's. **Academic Requirements:** General education including some course work in arts/fine arts, computer literacy, English (including composition), foreign languages, history, humanities, mathematics, philosophy, sciences (biological or physical), social science. **Special Study Options:** Accelerated program, cross registration, double major, dual enrollment, English as a second language, honors program, independent study, internships, study abroad, teacher certification program, weekend college, 2-2 in engineering technology with South Carolina State University, 2-2 in medical technology with the Medical University of South Carolina.

FACILITIES

Housing: All-female, all-male. **Library Holdings:** 148,584 bound volumes. 334 periodicals. 51,707 microforms. 469 audiovisuals. **Special Academic Facilities/Equipment:** TV studio, NMR, Wilbur R. Gregg Collection. **Computers:** School-owned computers available for student use.

EXTRACURRICULARS

Activities: Concert band, dance, drama/theater, jazz band, literary magazine, music ensembles, radio station, student government, student newspaper, student-run film society, television station, yearbook. **Organizations:** 3 honor societies, 4 fraternities, 4 sororities (26% women join). **Athletics (Intercollegiate):** *Men:* baseball, basketball, track & field. *Women:* basketball, softball, track & field, volleyball.

ADMISSIONS

Selectivity Rating: 63 (of 100). **Freshman Academic Profile:** 30% in top 10% of high school class, 52% in top 25% of high school class, 79% in top 50% of high school class. 100% from public high schools. SAT I Math middle 50% range 370-485. SAT I Verbal middle 50% range 400-520. TOEFL required of all international applicants, minimum TOEFL 500. **Basis for Candidate Selection:** *Very important factors considered include:* character/personal qualities, recommendations, secondary school record, standardized test scores, talent/ability. *Important factors considered include:* alumni/ae relation, class rank, extracurricular activities. *Other factors considered include:* state residency, volunteer work, work experience. **Freshman Admission Requirements:** High school diploma or GED is required. *Academic units required/recommended:* 16 total required; 4 English required, 3 math required, 2 science required, 2 science lab required, 2 foreign language required, 2 social studies required, 3 elective required. **Freshman Admission Statistics:** 1,456 applied, 54% accepted, 35% of those accepted enrolled. **Transfer Admission Requirements:** *Items required:* high school transcript, college transcript, statement of good standing from prior school. Minimum high school GPA of 2.0 required. Minimum college GPA of 2.0 required. Lowest grade transferable C. **General Admission Information:** Application fee $20. Regular application deadline rolling. Nonfall registration accepted. Admission may be deferred for a maximum of 1 year. Credit offered for CEEB Advanced Placement tests.

COSTS AND FINANCIAL AID

Tuition $6,068. Room & board $3,314. Required fees $974. Average book expense $800. **Required Forms and Deadlines:** FAFSA and institution's own financial aid form. No deadline for regular filing. Priority filing deadline April 15. **Notification of Awards:** Applicants will be notified of awards on a rolling basis beginning on or about May 15. **Types of Aid:** *Need-based scholarships/grants:* Pell, SEOG, state scholarships/grants, private scholarships, the school's own gift aid, United Negro College Fund. *Loans:* Direct Subsidized Stafford, Direct Unsubsidized Stafford, Direct PLUS, FFEL PLUS, Federal Perkins. **Student Employment:** Federal Work-Study Program available. Institutional employment available. Off-campus job opportunities are good. **Financial Aid Statistics:** 95% freshmen, 92% undergrads receive some form of aid. Average freshman grant $4,994. Average freshman loan $2,625. **Financial Aid Phone:** 803-535-5331.

CLAREMONT MCKENNA COLLEGE

890 Columbia Avenue, Claremont, CA 91711
Phone: 909-621-8088 **E-mail:** admission@claremontmckenna.edu **CEEB Code:** 4054
Fax: 909-621-8516 **Web:** www.claremontmckenna.edu **ACT Code:** 224

This private school was founded in 1946. It has a 56-acre campus.

STUDENTS AND FACULTY

Enrollment: 1,024. **Student Body:** Out-of-state 51%, international 3%. **Ethnic Representation:** African American 4%, Asian 16%, Caucasian 64%, Hispanic 10%, Native American 1%. **Retention and Graduation:** 93% freshmen return for sophomore year. 81% freshmen graduate within 4 years. 45% grads go on to further study within 1 year. 25% grads pursue business degrees. 25% grads pursue law degrees. 10% grads pursue medical degrees. **Faculty:** Student/faculty ratio 8:1. 129 full-time faculty, 83% hold PhDs. 100% faculty teach undergrads.

ACADEMICS

Degrees: Bachelor's. **Academic Requirements:** General education including some course work in English (including composition), foreign languages, humanities, mathematics, sciences (biological or physical), social science, civilization course (questions of civilization), senior thesis (major research paper). **Majors with Highest Enrollment:** Economics, general; international relations and affairs; political science and government, general. **Disciplines with Highest Percentage of Degrees Awarded:** Social sciences and history 58%, interdisciplinary studies 9%, biological life sciences 8%, psychology 7%, English 7%. **Special Study Options:** Accelerated program, cooperative (work-study) program, cross registration, double major, student exchange program (domestic), honors program, independent study, internships, liberal arts/career combination, student-designed major, study abroad.

FACILITIES

Housing: Coed, apartments for single students, substance-free dormitory, living exchanges with other Claremont Colleges. **Library Holdings:** 1,971,686 bound volumes. 6,000 periodicals. 1,367,536 microforms. 606 audiovisuals. **Special Academic Facilities/Equipment:** Art galleries, athenaeum complex, centers for Black and Chicano studies, computer lab, leadership lab, science center. **Computers:** School-owned computers available for student use.

EXTRACURRICULARS

Activities: Choral groups, concert band, dance, drama/theater, jazz band, literary magazine, music ensembles, musical theater, pep band, radio station, student government, student newspaper, student-run film society, symphony orchestra, yearbook. **Organizations:** 73 registered organizations, 7 honor societies, 5 religious organizations. **Athletics (Intercollegiate):** *Men:* baseball, basketball, cross-country, diving, football, golf, soccer, swimming, tennis, track & field, water polo. *Women:* basketball, cross-country, diving, lacrosse, soccer, softball, swimming, tennis, track & field, volleyball, water polo.

ADMISSIONS

Selectivity Rating: 97 (of 100). **Freshman Academic Profile:** 82% in top 10% of high school class, 94% in top 25% of high school class, 100% in top 50% of high school class. 70% from public high schools. Average SAT I Math 700, SAT I Math middle 50% range 650-730. Average SAT I Verbal 690, SAT I Verbal middle 50% range 630-730. Average ACT 30, ACT middle 50% range 27-31. TOEFL required of all international applicants, minimum TOEFL 600. **Basis for Candidate Selection:** *Very important factors considered include:* character/personal qualities, essays, extracurricular activities, secondary school record, standardized test scores. *Important factors considered include:* recommendations, talent/ability. *Other factors considered include:* alumni/ae relation, class rank, geographical residence, interview, minority status, state residency, volunteer work, work experience. **Freshman Admission Requirements:** High school diploma or GED is required. *Academic units required/recommended:* 15 total required; 18 total recommended; 4 English required, 4

English recommended, 3 math required, 4 math recommended, 2 science required, 3 science recommended, 3 foreign language required, 3 foreign language recommended, 2 social studies required, 2 social studies recommended, 1 history required, 2 history recommended. **Freshman Admission Statistics:** 2,918 applied, 28% accepted, 31% of those accepted enrolled. **Transfer Admission Requirements:** *Items required:* high school transcript, college transcript, essay, standardized test scores, statement of good standing from prior school. Lowest grade transferable C. **General Admission Information:** Application fee $50. Early decision application deadline November 15. Regular application deadline January 2. Nonfall registration accepted. Admission may be deferred for a maximum of 1 year. Credit and/or placement offered for CEEB Advanced Placement tests.

COSTS AND FINANCIAL AID

Tuition $26,350. Room & board $8,740. Required fees $190. Average book expense $850. **Required Forms and Deadlines:** FAFSA and CSS/Financial Aid PROFILE. Financial aid filing deadline February 1. **Notification of Awards:** Applicants will be notified of awards on or about April 1. **Types of Aid:** *Need-based scholarships/grants:* Pell, SEOG, state scholarships/grants, private scholarships, the school's own gift aid. *Loans:* Direct Subsidized Stafford, Direct Unsubsidized Stafford, Direct PLUS, Federal Perkins, college/university loans from institutional funds. **Student Employment:** Federal Work-Study Program available. Institutional employment available. Off-campus job opportunities are excellent. **Financial Aid Statistics:** 57% freshmen, 56% undergrads receive some form of aid. Average freshman grant $25,250. Average freshman loan $3,500. **Financial Aid Phone:** 909-621-8356.

CLARION UNIVERSITY OF PENNSYLVANIA

Admissions Office, 840 Wood Street, Clarion, PA 16214
Phone: 814-393-2306 **E-mail:** admissions@clarion.edu **CEEB Code:** 2649
Fax: 814-393-2030 **Web:** www.clarion.edu **ACT Code:** 3698

This public school was founded in 1867. It has a 191-acre campus.

STUDENTS AND FACULTY

Enrollment: 6,003. **Student Body:** Male 39%, female 61%, out-of-state 5%, international 1% (29 countries represented). **Ethnic Representation:** African American 5%, Caucasian 94%, Hispanic 1%. **Retention and Graduation:** 72% freshmen return for sophomore year. 25% freshmen graduate within 4 years. 2% grads pursue business degrees. 1% grads pursue medical degrees. **Faculty:** Student/faculty ratio 18:1. 298 full-time faculty. 100% faculty teach undergrads.

ACADEMICS

Degrees: Associate's, bachelor's, master's, post-master's certificate. **Academic Requirements:** General education including some course work in arts/fine arts, computer literacy, English (including composition), humanities, mathematics, sciences (biological or physical), social science. **Disciplines with Highest Percentage of Degrees Awarded:** Education 30%, business/marketing 18%, social sciences and history 8%, health professions and related sciences 8%, communications/communication technologies 7%. **Special Study Options:** Accelerated program, distance learning, double major, student exchange program (domestic), honors program, internships, study abroad, teacher certification program.

FACILITIES

Housing: Coed, all-female, all-male. **Library Holdings:** 429,800 bound volumes. 750 periodicals. 1,576,759 microforms. 23,444 audiovisuals. **Special Academic Facilities/Equipment:** Planetarium, art gallery. **Computers:** School-owned computers available for student use.

EXTRACURRICULARS

Activities: Choral groups, concert band, dance, drama/theater, jazz band, marching band, music ensembles, musical theater, radio station, student government, student newspaper, television station, yearbook. **Organizations:** 130 registered organizations, 2 religious organizations, 10 fraternities (11% men join), 10 sororities (10% women join). **Athletics (Intercollegiate):** *Men:* baseball, basketball, cross-country, diving, football, golf, swimming, track & field, wrestling. *Women:* basketball, cross-country, diving, soccer, softball, swimming, tennis, track & field, volleyball.

ADMISSIONS

Selectivity Rating: 63 (of 100). **Freshman Academic Profile:** Average SAT I Math 470, SAT I Math middle 50% range 410-520. Average SAT I Verbal 480, SAT I Verbal middle 50% range 420-520. TOEFL required of all international applicants, minimum TOEFL 550. **Basis for Candidate Selection:** *Very important factors considered include:* secondary school record. *Important factors considered include:* class rank, standardized test scores. *Other factors considered include:* character/personal qualities, essays, extracurricular activities, minority status, recommendations, talent/ability. **Freshman Admission Requirements:** High school diploma or GED is required. *Academic units required/recommended:* 4 English required, 2 math required, 4 math recommended, 3 science required, 4 science recommended, 2 foreign language recommended, 4 social studies required. **Freshman Admission Statistics:** 3,424 applied, 81% accepted, 49% of those accepted enrolled. **Transfer Admission Requirements:** *Items required:* high school transcript, college transcript, statement of good standing from prior school. Minimum college GPA of 2.5 required. Lowest grade transferable C. **General Admission Information:** Application fee $30. Nonfall registration accepted. Admission may be deferred. Credit and/or placement offered for CEEB Advanced Placement tests.

COSTS AND FINANCIAL AID

In-state tuition $4,378. Out-of-state tuition $6,568. Room & board $4,344. Required fees $1,362. Average book expense $800. **Required Forms and Deadlines:** FAFSA. Financial aid filing deadline May 1. Priority filing deadline May 1. **Notification of Awards:** Applicants will be notified of awards on a rolling basis starting April 15. **Types of Aid:** *Need-based scholarships/grants:* Pell, SEOG, state scholarships/grants, private scholarships, the school's own gift aid, United Negro College Fund. *Loans:* FFEL Subsidized Stafford, FFEL Unsubsidized Stafford, FFEL PLUS, Federal Perkins. **Student Employment:** Federal Work-Study Program available. Institutional employment available. Off-campus job opportunities are good. **Financial Aid Statistics:** 63% freshmen, 64% undergrads receive some form of aid. Average income from on-campus job $1,375. **Financial Aid Phone:** 814-226-2315.

See page 976.

CLARK ATLANTA UNIVERSITY

223 James P. Brawley Drive at Fair Street, Atlanta, GA 30314
Phone: 404-880-8000 **E-mail:** admissions@panthernet.cau.edu **CEEB Code:** 5110
Fax: 404-880-6174 **Web:** www.cau.edu **ACT Code:** 804

This private school, which is affiliated with the Methodist Church, was founded in 1988. It has a 123-acre campus.

STUDENTS AND FACULTY

Enrollment: 3,864. **Student Body:** Male 29%, female 71%, out-of-state 60%, international students represent 25 countries. **Ethnic Representation:** African American 94%. **Retention and Graduation:** 71% freshmen return for sophomore year. **Faculty:** Student/faculty ratio 15:1. 319 full-time faculty, 77% hold PhDs.

ACADEMICS

Degrees: Bachelor's, doctoral, master's, post-master's certificate. **Academic Requirements:** General education including some course work in arts/fine arts, computer literacy, English (including composition), foreign languages, history, humanities, mathematics, philosophy, sciences (biological or physical), social science. **Disciplines with Highest Percentage of Degrees Awarded:** Business/marketing 25%, communications/communication technologies 15%, psychology 12%, protective services/public administration 9%, biological life sciences 7%. **Special Study Options:** Accelerated program, cooperative (work-study) program, cross registration, double major, dual enrollment, student exchange program (domestic), honors program, internships, study abroad, teacher certification program, weekend college, co-op programs in engineering.

FACILITIES

Housing: Coed, all-female, all-male, housing for disabled students, fraternities and/or sororities. **Library Holdings:** 750,000 bound volumes. **Special Academic Facilities/Equipment:** Language lab.

EXTRACURRICULARS

Activities: Choral groups, concert band, dance, drama/theater, jazz band, marching band, music ensembles, musical theater, pep band, radio station, student government, student newspaper, student-run film society, symphony orchestra, television station, yearbook. **Organizations:** 60 registered organizations, 12 honor societies, 4 fraternities, 4 sororities. **Athletics (Intercollegiate):** *Men:* baseball, basketball, cross-country, football, tennis, track & field, volleyball. *Women:* basketball, cheerleading, cross-country, tennis, track & field.

ADMISSIONS

Selectivity Rating: 66 (of 100). **Freshman Academic Profile:** Average high school GPA 2.8. Average SAT I Math 444. Average SAT I Verbal 466. Average ACT 19. TOEFL required of all international applicants, minimum TOEFL 500. **Basis for Candidate Selection:** *Very important factors considered include:* character/personal qualities, secondary school record, standardized test scores. *Important factors considered include:* alumni/ae relation, essays, extracurricular activities, minority status, recommendations, talent/ability. *Other factors considered include:* geographical residence, state residency, volunteer work, work experience. **Freshman Admission Requirements:** High school diploma or GED is required. *Academic units required/recommended:* 18 total recommended; 4 English recommended, 3 math recommended, 2 science recommended, 1 science lab recommended, 2 foreign language recommended, 3 social studies recommended, 3 elective recommended. **Freshman Admission Statistics:** 6,910 applied, 48% accepted, 28% of those accepted enrolled. **Transfer Admission Requirements:** *Items required:* college transcript, essay. Minimum high school GPA of 2.0 required. Minimum college GPA of 2.0 required. Lowest grade transferable C. **General Admission Information:** Application fee $35. Priority application deadline March 1. Early decision application deadline March 1. Regular application deadline July 1. Nonfall registration accepted. Admission may be deferred for a maximum of 1 year. Neither credit nor placement offered for CEEB Advanced Placement tests.

COSTS AND FINANCIAL AID

Tuition $12,862. Room & board $6,438. Required fees $550. Average book expense $1,000. **Required Forms and Deadlines:** FAFSA and institution's own financial aid form. Financial aid filing deadline April 1. Priority filing deadline February 15. **Notification of Awards:** Applicants will be notified of awards on a rolling basis beginning April 15. **Types of Aid:** *Need-based scholarships/grants:* Pell, SEOG, state scholarships/grants, private scholarships, the school's own gift aid, United Negro College Fund. *Loans:* FFEL Subsidized Stafford, FFEL Unsubsidized Stafford, FFEL PLUS, Federal Perkins, state loans. **Student Employment:** Federal Work-Study Program available. Institutional employment available. Off-campus job opportunities are fair. **Financial Aid Statistics:** 72% freshmen, 79% undergrads receive some form of aid. Average income from on-campus job $2,000. **Financial Aid Phone:** 404-880-8992.

CLARK UNIVERSITY

950 Main Street, Worcester, MA 01610
Phone: 508-793-7431 **E-mail:** admissions@clarku.edu **CEEB Code:** 3279
Fax: 508-793-8821 **Web:** www.clarku.edu **ACT Code:** 1808

This private school was founded in 1887. It has a 50-acre campus.

STUDENTS AND FACULTY

Enrollment: 2,167. **Student Body:** Male 39%, female 61%, out-of-state 62%, international 7% (57 countries represented). **Ethnic Representation:** African American 3%, Asian 4%, Caucasian 71%, Hispanic 3%. **Retention and Graduation:** 87% freshmen return for sophomore year. 64% freshmen graduate within 4 years. 31% grads go on to further study within 1 year. 4% grads pursue business degrees. 3% grads pursue law degrees. 1% grads pursue medical degrees. **Faculty:** Student/faculty ratio 10:1. 164 full-time faculty, 96% hold PhDs. 100% faculty teach undergrads.

ACADEMICS

Degrees: Bachelor's, doctoral, master's, post-bachelor's certificate, post-master's certificate. **Academic Requirements:** General education including some course work in arts/fine arts, English (including composition), foreign languages, history, humanities, mathematics, philosophy, sciences (biological or physical), social science. **Classes:** 10-19 students in an average class. 10-19 students in an average lab/discussion section. **Majors with Highest Enrollment:** Psychology, general; political science and government, general; visual and performing arts, general. **Disciplines with Highest Percentage of Degrees Awarded:** Social sciences and history 26%, psychology 17%, business/marketing 10%, biological life sciences 10%, communications/communication technologies 8%. **Special Study Options:** Cross registration, double major, English as a second language, independent study, internships, student-designed major, study abroad, teacher certification program.

FACILITIES

Housing: Coed, all-female, apartments for single students, housing for disabled students, housing for international students. **Library Holdings:** 289,658 bound volumes. 1,383 periodicals. 60,084 microforms. 1,007 audiovisuals. **Special Academic Facilities/Equipment:** Galleries, theatres, Robert H. Goddard Historical Exhibition, rare book room, craft center, music center, map library, arboretum, herbarium, extensive darkroom facilities, satellite dish for international program reception, electron microscope, nuclear magnetic resonance spectrometer. **Computers:** School-owned computers available for student use.

EXTRACURRICULARS

Activities: Choral groups, concert band, dance, drama/theater, jazz band, literary magazine, marching band, music ensembles, musical theater, pep band, radio station, student government, student newspaper, student-run film society, symphony orchestra, television station, yearbook. **Organizations:** 80 registered organizations, 6 honor societies, 7 religious organizations. **Athletics (Intercollegiate):** *Men:* baseball, basketball, crew, cross-country, diving, lacrosse, soccer, swimming, tennis. *Women:* basketball, crew, cross-country, diving, field hockey, soccer, softball, swimming, tennis, volleyball.

ADMISSIONS

Selectivity Rating: 82 (of 100). **Freshman Academic Profile:** Average high school GPA 3.4. 29% in top 10% of high school class, 67% in top 25% of high school class, 93% in top 50% of high school class. 71% from public high schools. Average SAT I Math 586, SAT I Math middle 50% range 540-640. Average SAT I Verbal 589, SAT I Verbal middle 50% range 540-650. Average ACT 25, ACT middle 50% range 22-27. TOEFL required of all international applicants, minimum TOEFL 550. **Basis for Candidate Selection:** *Very important factors considered include:* character/personal qualities, recommendations, secondary school record, standardized test scores. *Important factors considered include:* essays, extracurricular activities, talent/ability, volunteer work. *Other factors considered include:* alumni/ae relation, class rank, geographical residence, interview, minority status, work experience. **Freshman Admission Requirements:** High school diploma or GED is required. *Academic units required/recommended:* 16 total recommended; 4 English recommended, 3 math recommended, 3 science recommended, 2 science lab recommended, 2 foreign language recommended, 2 social studies recommended, 2 history recommended. **Freshman Admission Statistics:** 3,694 applied, 68% accepted, 23% of those accepted enrolled. **Transfer Admission Requirements:** *Items required:* high school transcript, college transcript, essay, standardized test scores, statement of good standing from prior school. Minimum college GPA of 2.8 required. Lowest grade transferable C. **General Admission Information:** Application fee $50. Early decision application deadline November 15. Regular application deadline February 1. Nonfall registration accepted. Admission may be deferred for a maximum of 1 year. Credit and/or placement offered for CEEB Advanced Placement tests.

COSTS AND FINANCIAL AID

Tuition $25,600. Room & board $4,950. Required fees $265. Average book expense $800. **Required Forms and Deadlines:** FAFSA and CSS/Financial Aid PROFILE. Priority filing deadline February 1. **Notification of Awards:** Applicants will be notified of awards on or about March 31. **Types of Aid:** *Need-based scholarships/grants:* Pell, SEOG, state scholarships/grants, the school's own gift aid. *Loans:* FFEL Subsidized Stafford, FFEL Unsubsidized Stafford, FFEL PLUS, Federal Perkins, state loans, college/university loans from institutional funds. **Student Employment:** Federal Work-Study Program available. Off-campus job opportunities are good. **Financial Aid Statistics:** 59% freshmen, 57% undergrads receive some form of aid. Average freshman grant $12,000. Average freshman loan $3,625. **Financial Aid Phone:** 508-793-7478.

CLARKE COLLEGE

1550 Clarke Drive, Dubuque, IA 52001-3198
Phone: 563-588-6316 **E-mail:** admissions@clarke.edu **CEEB Code:** 6099
Fax: 563-588-6789 **Web:** www.clarke.edu **ACT Code:** 1290

This private school, which is affiliated with the Roman Catholic Church, was founded in 1843. It has a 55-acre campus.

STUDENTS AND FACULTY

Enrollment: 998. **Student Body:** Male 31%, female 69%, out-of-state 38%, international 2% (10 countries represented). **Ethnic Representation:** African American 1%, Caucasian 97%, Hispanic 2%. **Retention and Graduation:** 78% freshmen return for sophomore year. 49% freshmen graduate within 4 years. 25% grads go on to further study within 1 year. 2% grads pursue business degrees. **Faculty:** Student/faculty ratio 10:1. 77 full-time faculty, 54% hold PhDs. 100% faculty teach undergrads.

ACADEMICS

Degrees: Associate's, bachelor's, master's, terminal. **Academic Requirements:** General education including some course work in arts/fine arts, computer literacy, English (including composition), foreign languages, history, humanities, mathematics, philosophy, sciences (biological or physical), social science. **Classes:** Under 10 students in an average class. 10-19 students in an average lab/discussion section. **Majors with Highest Enrollment:** Nursing/registered nurse training (RN, ASN, BSN, MSN); business administration/management; psychology, general. **Disciplines with Highest Percentage of Degrees Awarded:** Business/marketing 17%, education 15%, health professions and related sciences 15%, computer and information sciences 11%, psychology 10%. **Special Study Options:** Accelerated program, cooperative (work-study) program, cross registration, distance learning, double major, English as a second language, honors program, independent study, internships, liberal arts/career combination, student-designed major, study abroad, teacher certification program.

FACILITIES

Housing: Coed, all-female, all-male, apartments for single students. **Library Holdings:** 127,089 bound volumes. 897 periodicals. 11,015 microforms. 1,504 audiovisuals. **Special Academic Facilities/Equipment:** Art gallery; computer classrooms for math, biology, and computer science; computer-interfaced chemistry lab; human gross anatomy and nursing labs; electron microscope; music performance hall; foreign language lab; distance learning classroom. **Computers:** School-owned computers available for student use.

EXTRACURRICULARS

Activities: Choral groups, drama/theater, jazz band, literary magazine, music ensembles, musical theater, opera, pep band, student government, student newspaper, symphony orchestra, yearbook. **Organizations:** 48 registered organizations, 5 honor societies, 1 religious organization. **Athletics (Intercollegiate):** *Men:* baseball, basketball, cheerleading, cross-country, golf, soccer, tennis, volleyball. *Women:* basketball, cheerleading, cross-country, golf, soccer, softball, tennis, volleyball.

ADMISSIONS

Selectivity Rating: 75 (of 100). **Freshman Academic Profile:** Average high school GPA 3.3. 14% in top 10% of high school class, 36% in top 25% of high school class, 72% in top 50% of high school class. 81% from public high schools. Average SAT I Math 493, SAT I Math middle 50% range 425-555. Average SAT I Verbal 446, SAT I Verbal middle 50% range 410-505. Average ACT 22, ACT middle 50% range 19-24. TOEFL required of all international applicants, minimum TOEFL 525. **Basis for Candidate Selection:** *Very important factors considered include:* secondary school record, standardized test scores. *Important factors considered include:* class rank. *Other factors considered include:* extracurricular activities, interview, minority status, talent/ability, volunteer work. **Freshman Admission Requirements:** High school diploma or GED is required. *Academic units required/recommended:* 21 total required; 4 English required, 3 math required, 4 math recommended, 3 science required, 4 science recommended, 2 science lab required, 2 foreign language required, 3 social studies required, 4 elective required. **Freshman Admission Statistics:** 712 applied, 66% accepted, 38% of those accepted enrolled. **Transfer Admission Requirements:** *Items required:* high school transcript, college transcript, statement of good standing from prior school. Minimum college GPA of 2.0 required. Lowest grade transferable C. **General Admission Information:** Application fee $25. Nonfall registration accepted. Admission may be deferred for a maximum of 1 year. Credit and/or placement offered for CEEB Advanced Placement tests.

COSTS AND FINANCIAL AID

Tuition $15,715. Room & board $5,765. Required fees $475. Average book expense $600. **Required Forms and Deadlines:** FAFSA. No deadline for regular filing. Priority filing deadline April 15. **Types of Aid:** *Need-based scholarships/grants:* Pell, SEOG, state scholarships/grants, private scholarships, the school's own gift aid. *Loans:* FFEL Subsidized Stafford, FFEL Unsubsidized Stafford, FFEL PLUS, Federal Perkins, Federal Nursing, state loans, college/university loans from institutional funds. **Student Employment:** Federal Work-Study Program available. Institutional employment available. Off-campus job opportunities are excellent. **Financial Aid Statistics:** 81% freshmen, 80% undergrads receive some form of aid. Average freshman grant $10,538. Average freshman loan $2,918. Average income from on-campus job $1,422. **Financial Aid Phone:** 563-588-6327.

CLARKSON COLLEGE

101 South 42nd Street, Omaha, NE 68131
Phone: 402-552-3041 **E-mail:** admiss@clarksoncollege.edu **CEEB Code:** 6066
Fax: 402-552-6057 **Web:** www.clarksoncollege.edu **ACT Code:** 2436

This private school, which is affiliated with the Episcopal Church, was founded in 1888. It has a 29-acre campus.

STUDENTS AND FACULTY

Enrollment: 380. **Student Body:** Male 11%, female 89%, out-of-state 33%, international students represent 3 countries. **Ethnic Representation:** African American 5%, Asian 1%, Caucasian 90%, Hispanic 2%. **Retention and Graduation:** 20% grads go on to further study within 1 year. 10% grads pursue business degrees. 1% grads pursue law degrees. 1% grads pursue medical degrees. **Faculty:** Student/faculty ratio 20:1. 34 full-time faculty. 100% faculty teach undergrads.

ACADEMICS

Degrees: Associate's, bachelor's, master's, post-master's certificate. **Academic Requirements:** General education including some course work in computer literacy, English (including composition), humanities, mathematics, sciences (biological or physical), social science. **Special Study Options:** Accelerated program, cooperative (work-study) program, distance learning, double major, independent study, internships, study abroad.

FACILITIES

Housing: Coed, apartments for single students. **Library Holdings:** 8,152 bound volumes. 380 periodicals. 119 microforms. 617 audiovisuals. **Special Academic Facilities/Equipment:** Two hospitals next to campus. **Computers:** *Recommended operating system:* Windows 95. School-owned computers available for student use.

EXTRACURRICULARS

Activities: Student government. **Organizations:** 10 registered organizations, 4 honor societies.

ADMISSIONS

Selectivity Rating: 80 (of 100). **Freshman Academic Profile:** Average high school GPA 3.5. 10% in top 10% of high school class, 40% in top 25% of high school class, 90% in top 50% of high school class. Average ACT 21. TOEFL required of all international applicants, minimum TOEFL 600. **Basis for Candidate Selection:** *Very important factors considered include:* secondary school record. *Important factors considered include:* class rank. *Other factors considered include:* essays, recommendations, standardized test scores, work experience. **Freshman Admission Requirements:** High school diploma or GED is required. *Academic units required/recommended:* 3 English required, 4 English recommended, 2 math required, 4 math recommended, 2 science required, 4 science recommended, 1 science lab required, 2 science lab recommended, 2 social studies required, 4 social studies recommended. **Transfer Admission Requirements:** *Items required:* high school transcript, college transcript, essay. Minimum high school GPA of 2.0 required. Minimum college GPA of 2.5 required. Lowest grade transferable C-. **General Admission Information:** Application fee $15. Early decision application deadline March 1. Regular application deadline rolling. Nonfall registration accepted. Admission may be deferred for a maximum of 1 year. Credit and/or placement offered for CEEB Advanced Placement tests.

COSTS AND FINANCIAL AID

Tuition $8,970. Room & board $2,900. Required fees $192. Average book expense $600. **Required Forms and Deadlines:** FAFSA and institution's own financial aid form. No deadline for regular filing. Priority filing deadline April 1. **Notification of Awards:** Applicants will be notified of awards on a rolling basis beginning on or about April 1. **Types of Aid:** *Need-based scholarships/grants:* Pell, SEOG, state scholarships/grants, private scholarships, the school's own gift aid. *Loans:* FFEL Subsidized Stafford, FFEL Unsubsidized Stafford, FFEL PLUS, Federal Nursing. **Student Employment:** Federal Work-Study Program available. Institutional employment available. Off-campus job opportunities are excellent. **Financial Aid Phone:** 402-552-2749.

CLARKSON UNIVERSITY

Box 5605, Potsdam, NY 13699
Phone: 315-268-6479 **E-mail:** admission@clarkson.edu **CEEB Code:** 2084
Fax: 315-268-7647 **Web:** www.clarkson.edu

This private school was founded in 1896. It has a 640-acre campus.

STUDENTS AND FACULTY

Enrollment: 2,756. **Student Body:** Male 75%, female 25%, out-of-state 23%, international 3% (46 countries represented). **Ethnic Representation:** African American 2%, Asian 3%, Caucasian 93%, Hispanic 2%, Native American 1%. **Retention and Graduation:** 88% freshmen return for sophomore year. 56% freshmen graduate within 4 years. 15% grads go on to further study within 1 year. 4% grads pursue business degrees. **Faculty:** Student/faculty ratio 17:1. 168 full-time faculty, 80% hold PhDs. 95% faculty teach undergrads.

ACADEMICS

Degrees: Bachelor's, doctoral, master's. **Academic Requirements:** General education including some course work in computer literacy, humanities, mathematics, sciences (biological or physical), social science, engineering, management. **Classes:** 20-29 students in an average class. 20-29 students in an average lab class. **Majors with Highest Enrollment:** Mechanical engineering/mechanical technology/technician; multi/interdisciplinary studies; civil engineering technologies/technicians. **Disciplines with Highest Percentage of Degrees Awarded:** Engineering/engineering technology 48%, business/marketing 21%, interdisciplinary studies 11%, computer and information sciences 5%, biological life sciences 3%. **Special Study Options:** Accelerated program, cooperative (work-study) program, cross registration, distance learning, double major, dual enrollment, English as a second language, honors program, independent study, internships, liberal arts/career combination, student-designed major, study abroad.

FACILITIES

Housing: Coed, all-female, all-male, apartments for married students, apartments for single students, housing for disabled students, fraternities and/or sororities. **Library Holdings:** 272,204 bound volumes. 1,656 periodicals. 267,759 microforms. 2,004 audiovisuals. **Special Academic Facilities/Equipment:** CAMP (Center for Advanced Materials Processing): The center emphasizes development of scientific and technological expertise in the field of colloids and surfaces. CAMP is an interdisciplinary endeavor, bringing together participants from departments of science and engineering. **Computers:** *Recommended operating system:* Windows 95. School-owned computers available for student use.

EXTRACURRICULARS

Activities: Choral groups, drama/theater, jazz band, literary magazine, musical theater, pep band, radio station, student government, student newspaper, symphony orchestra, television station, yearbook. **Organizations:** 55 registered organizations, 9 honor societies, 10 fraternities (15% men join), 2 sororities (12% women join). **Athletics (Intercollegiate):** *Men:* baseball, basketball, skiing (cross-country), diving, golf, ice hockey, lacrosse, skiing (alpine), skiing (Nordic), soccer, swimming, tennis. *Women:* basketball, skiing (cross-country), diving, ice hockey, lacrosse, skiing (alpine), skiing (Nordic), soccer, swimming, tennis, volleyball.

ADMISSIONS

Selectivity Rating: 82 (of 100). **Freshman Academic Profile:** Average high school GPA 3.5. 36% in top 10% of high school class, 72% in top 25% of high school class, 95% in top 50% of high school class. 87% from public high schools. Average SAT I Math 621, SAT I Math middle 50% range 580-670. Average SAT I Verbal 570, SAT I Verbal middle 50% range 520-620. TOEFL required of all international applicants, minimum TOEFL 500. **Basis for Candidate Selection:** *Very important factors considered include:* interview, secondary school record. *Important factors considered include:* class rank, extracurricular activities, recommendations, standardized test scores, volunteer work. *Other factors considered include:* alumni/ae relation, character/personal qualities, essays, talent/ability, work experience. **Freshman Admission Requirements:** High school diploma or GED is required. *Academic units required/recommended:* 16 total required; 4 English required, 3 math required, 4 math recommended, 2 science required, 3 science recommended. **Freshman Admission Statistics:** 2,556 applied, 82% accepted, 35% of those accepted enrolled. **Transfer Admission Requirements:** *Items required:* college transcript. Minimum college GPA of 2.5 required. Lowest grade transferable C. **General Admission Information:** Application fee $30. Priority application deadline February 1. Early decision application deadline December 1. Regular application deadline March 15. Nonfall registration accepted. Admission may be deferred for a maximum of 1 year. Neither credit nor placement offered for CEEB Advanced Placement tests.

COSTS AND FINANCIAL AID

Tuition $23,100. Room & board $8,726. Required fees $400. Average book expense $900. **Required Forms and Deadlines:** FAFSA, institution's own financial aid form and state aid form. Priority filing deadline March 1. **Notification of Awards:** Applicants will be notified of awards on or about March 23. **Types of Aid:** *Need-based scholarships/grants:* Pell, SEOG, state scholarships/grants, private scholarships, the school's own gift aid, HEOP. *Loans:* Direct Subsidized Stafford, Direct Unsubsidized Stafford, Direct PLUS, Federal Perkins, college/university loans from institutional funds, Gate. **Student Employment:** Federal Work-Study Program available. Institutional employment available. Off-campus job opportunities are fair. **Financial Aid Statistics:** 80% freshmen, 81% undergrads receive some form of aid. Average freshman grant $10,662. Average freshman loan $5,388. Average income from on-campus job $1,000. **Financial Aid Phone:** 315-268-7699.

See page 978.

CLEARWATER CHRISTIAN COLLEGE

3400 Gulf-to-Bay Boulevard, Clearwater, FL 33759-4595
Phone: 727-726-1153 **E-mail:** admissions@clearwater.edu
Fax: 727-726-8597 **Web:** www.clearwater.edu

This private school was founded in 1966.

STUDENTS AND FACULTY

Enrollment: 641. **Student Body:** Male 44%, female 56%, out-of-state 50%, international 2%. **Ethnic Representation:** African American 1%, Asian 1%, Caucasian 94%, Hispanic 4%. **Retention and Graduation:** 34% freshmen graduate within 4 years. 19% grads go on to further study within 1 year. 2% grads pursue business degrees. 2% grads pursue law degrees. **Faculty:** Student/faculty ratio 18:1. 34 full-time faculty, 61% hold PhDs. 100% faculty teach undergrads.

ACADEMICS

Degrees: Associate's, bachelor's. **Academic Requirements:** General education including some course work in arts/fine arts, computer literacy, English (including composition), history, humanities, mathematics, philosophy, sciences (biological or physical), social science, Bible. **Disciplines with Highest Percentage of Degrees Awarded:** Education 31%, business/marketing 18%, psychology 14%, philosophy/religion/theology 13%, biological life sciences 9%. **Special Study Options:** Cooperative (work-study) program, double major, dual enrollment, honors program, internships, liberal arts/career combination, study abroad, teacher certification program.

FACILITIES

Housing: All-female, all-male. **Library Holdings:** 106,820 bound volumes. 506 periodicals. 197,774 microforms. 7,952 audiovisuals. **Computers:** *Recommended operating system:* Windows 2000. School-owned computers available for student use.

EXTRACURRICULARS

Activities: Choral groups, concert band, drama/theater, music ensembles, pep band, student government, yearbook. **Organizations:** 17 registered organizations, 1 honor society, 1 religious organization, 7 fraternities (100% men join), 7 sororities (100% women join). **Athletics (Intercollegiate):** *Men:* baseball, basketball, golf, soccer. *Women:* basketball, cheerleading, softball, volleyball.

ADMISSIONS

Selectivity Rating: 64 (of 100). **Freshman Academic Profile:** 40% from public high schools. Average SAT I Math 442. Average SAT I Verbal 433. Average ACT 22. TOEFL required of all international applicants, minimum TOEFL 500. **Basis for Candidate Selection:** *Very important factors considered include:* character/personal qualities, recommendations, secondary school record, standardized test scores. *Important factors considered include:* extracurricular activities, interview, talent/ability. *Other factors considered include:* alumni/ae relation, geographical residence, minority status, religious affiliation/commitment, state residency, volunteer work, work experience. **Freshman Admission Requirements:** High school diploma or GED is required. **Freshman Admission Statistics:** 306 applied, 67% accepted, 83% of those accepted enrolled. **Transfer Admission Requirements:** *Items required:* high school transcript, college transcript, essay, standardized test scores, statement of good standing from prior school. Minimum high school GPA of 2.0 required. Minimum college GPA of 2.0 required. Lowest grade transferable C-. **General Admission Information:** Application fee $35. Regular application deadline August 1. Neither credit nor placement offered for CEEB Advanced Placement tests.

COSTS AND FINANCIAL AID

Tuition $8,100. Room & board $3,850. Required fees $500. Average book expense $600. **Required Forms and Deadlines:** FAFSA, institution's own financial aid form and state aid form. Priority filing deadline April 5. **Notification of Awards:** Applicants will be notified of awards on a rolling basis. **Types of Aid:** *Need-based scholarships/grants:* Pell, SEOG, state scholarships/grants, private scholarships, the school's own gift aid. *Loans:* FFEL Subsidized Stafford, FFEL Unsubsidized Stafford, FFEL PLUS, state loans. **Student Employment:** Federal Work-Study Program available. Off-campus job opportunities are excellent. **Financial Aid Statistics:** 83% freshmen, 71% undergrads receive some form of aid. Average freshman loan $2,841. Average income from on-campus job $900. **Financial Aid Phone:** 727-726-1153.

CLEARY UNIVERSITY

3750 Cleary Drive, Howell, MI 48843
Phone: 517-548-3670 **E-mail:** cbono@cleary.edu **CEEB Code:** 1123
Fax: 517-582-7805 **Web:** www.cleary.edu **ACT Code:** 1974

This private school was founded in 1883. It has a 32-acre campus.

STUDENTS AND FACULTY

Enrollment: 594. **Student Body:** Male 41%, female 59%, out-of-state 1%. **Ethnic Representation:** African American 10%, Asian 1%, Caucasian 70%, Hispanic 2%, Native American 1%. **Faculty:** Student/faculty ratio 10:1. 11 full-time faculty, 54% hold PhDs. 100% faculty teach undergrads.

ACADEMICS

Degrees: Associate's, bachelor's, master's, terminal, transfer. **Academic Requirements:** General education including some course work in computer literacy, English (including composition), humanities, mathematics, philosophy, business law, finance, accounting, marketing, management, economics, business computer systems. **Classes:** Under 10 students in an average class. 10-19 students in an average lab class. **Majors with Highest Enrollment:** Business administration/management; management information systems, general; accounting. **Disciplines with Highest Percentage of Degrees Awarded:** Business/marketing 100%. **Special Study Options:** Accelerated program, cooperative (work-study) program, distance learning, dual enrollment, independent study, internships.

FACILITIES

Library Holdings: 4,500 bound volumes. 22 periodicals. 0 microforms. 100 audiovisuals. **Special Academic Facilities/Equipment:** Center for quality, quality resource collection, center for business ethics and leadership. **Computers:** *Recommended operating system:* Windows NT/2000 or XP. School-owned computers available for student use.

ADMISSIONS

Selectivity Rating: 76 (of 100). **Freshman Academic Profile:** Average high school GPA 3.0. 86% from public high schools. Average ACT 18. TOEFL required of all international applicants, minimum TOEFL 600. **Basis for Candidate Selection:** *Very important factors considered include:* secondary school record. *Important factors considered include:* interview, standardized test scores. *Other factors considered include:* essays, recommendations. **Freshman Admission Requirements:** High school diploma or GED is required. *Academic units required/recommended:* 24 total recommended; 4 English recommended, 2 math recommended, 2 science recommended, 2 social studies recommended, 2 history recommended, 12 elective recommended. **Transfer Admission Requirements:** *Items required:* high school transcript, college transcript, statement of good standing from prior school. Minimum high school GPA of 2.5 required. Minimum college GPA of 2.5 required. Lowest grade transferable D. **General Admission Information:** Application fee $25. Priority application deadline July 15. Regular application deadline August 15. Admission may be deferred for a maximum of 1 year. Credit and/or placement offered for CEEB Advanced Placement tests.

COSTS AND FINANCIAL AID

Tuition $11,040. **Required Forms and Deadlines:** FAFSA and institution's own financial aid form. Financial aid filing deadline June 15. Priority filing deadline March 15. **Notification of Awards:** Applicants will be notified of awards on a rolling basis. **Types of Aid:** *Need-based scholarships/grants:* Pell, SEOG, state scholarships/grants, private scholarships, the school's own gift aid. *Loans:* FFEL Subsidized Stafford, FFEL Unsubsidized Stafford, FFEL PLUS. **Student Employment:** Federal Work-Study Program available. Institutional employment available. Off-campus job opportunities are excellent. **Financial Aid Statistics:** 89% undergrads receive some form of aid. **Financial Aid Phone:** 517-548-3670.

CLEMSON UNIVERSITY

105 Sikes Hall, Box 345124, Clemson, SC 29634-5124
Phone: 864-656-2287 **E-mail:** cuadmissions@clemson.edu **CEEB Code:** 5111
Fax: 864-656-2464 **Web:** www.clemson.edu **ACT Code:** 3842

This public school was founded in 1889. It has a 1,400-acre campus.

STUDENTS AND FACULTY

Enrollment: 13,734. **Student Body:** Male 55%, female 45%, out-of-state 30%, international 1% (84 countries represented). **Ethnic Representation:** African American 7%, Asian 2%, Caucasian 85%, Hispanic 1%. **Retention and Graduation:** 90% freshmen return for sophomore year. 37% freshmen graduate within 4 years. 28% grads go on to further study within 1 year. 21% grads pursue business degrees. 5% grads pursue law degrees. 8% grads pursue medical degrees. **Faculty:** Student/faculty ratio 16:1. 964 full-time faculty, 87% hold PhDs. 95% faculty teach undergrads.

ACADEMICS

Degrees: Bachelor's, doctoral, master's. **Classes:** 20-29 students in an average class. 20-29 students in an average lab class. **Majors with Highest Enrollment:** Tourism and travel services management; business, management, marketing, and related support services; engineering, general. **Disciplines with Highest Percentage of Degrees Awarded:** Business/marketing 23%, engineering/engineering technology 15%, education 9%, social sciences and history 7%, health professions and related sciences 7%. **Special Study Options:** Cooperative (work-study) program, distance learning, double major, student exchange program (domestic), honors program, independent study, internships, study abroad, teacher certification program.

FACILITIES

Housing: Coed, all-female, all-male, apartments for married students, apartments for single students. **Library Holdings:** 1,126,413 bound volumes. 7,629 periodicals. 1,162,165 microforms. 117,769 audiovisuals. **Special Academic Facilities/Equipment:** South Carolina Botanical Gardens, Campbell Geology Museum, Brooks Center for the Performing Arts, Rudolph Lee Art Gallery, Garrison Livestock Arena, John C. Calhoun Home. **Computers:** *Recommended operating system:* Windows NT/2000. School-owned computers available for student use.

EXTRACURRICULARS

Activities: Choral groups, concert band, dance, drama/theater, jazz band, literary magazine, marching band, music ensembles, pep band, radio station, student government, student newspaper, television station, yearbook. **Organizations:** 265 registered organizations, 22 honor societies, 16 religious organizations, 25 fraternities (15% men join), 15 sororities (22% women join). **Athletics (Intercollegiate):** *Men:* baseball, basketball, cheerleading, cross-country, diving, football, golf, indoor track, soccer, swimming, tennis, track & field. *Women:* basketball, cheerleading, crew, cross-country, diving, indoor track, soccer, swimming, tennis, track & field, volleyball.

ADMISSIONS

Selectivity Rating: 83 (of 100). **Freshman Academic Profile:** 45% in top 10% of high school class, 80% in top 25% of high school class, 97% in top 50% of high school class. 89% from public high schools. Average SAT I Math 618, SAT I Math middle 50% range 560-650. Average SAT I Verbal 587, SAT I Verbal middle 50% range 530-630. Average ACT 26, ACT middle 50% range 23-28. TOEFL required of all international applicants, minimum TOEFL 550. **Basis for Candidate Selection:** *Very important factors considered include:* class rank, secondary school record, standardized test scores, state residency. *Important factors considered include:* alumni/ae relation. *Other factors considered include:* essays, geographical residence, recommendations, talent/ability. **Freshman Admission Requirements:** High school diploma or GED is required. *Academic units required/recommended:* 19 total required; 4 English required, 3 math required, 4 math recommended, 3 science required, 3 science lab required, 4 science lab recommended, 3 foreign language required, 3 social studies required, 1 history required, 2 elective required. **Freshman Admission Statistics:** 11,315 applied, 52% accepted, 42% of those accepted enrolled. **Transfer Admission Requirements:** *Items required:* college transcript. Minimum college GPA of 2.5 required. Lowest grade transferable C. **General Admission Information:** Application fee $40. Regular application deadline May 1. Nonfall registration accepted. Credit and/or placement offered for CEEB Advanced Placement tests.

COSTS AND FINANCIAL AID

In-state tuition $5,624. Out-of-state tuition $12,722. Room & board $4,454. Required fees $210. Average book expense $846. **Required Forms and Deadlines:** FAFSA. Priority filing deadline April 1. **Notification of Awards:**

Applicants will be notified of awards on a rolling basis beginning on or about April 1. **Types of Aid:** *Need-based scholarships/grants:* Pell, SEOG, state scholarships/grants, private scholarships, the school's own gift aid, Federal Nursing. *Loans:* FFEL Subsidized Stafford, FFEL Unsubsidized Stafford, FFEL PLUS, Federal Perkins, state loans, college/university loans from institutional funds. **Student Employment:** Federal Work-Study Program available. Institutional employment available. Off-campus job opportunities are good. **Financial Aid Statistics:** 38% freshmen, 36% undergrads receive some form of aid. Average freshman grant $4,357. Average freshman loan $3,673. Average income from on-campus job $1,325. **Financial Aid Phone:** 864-656-2280.

CLEVELAND INSTITUTE OF ART

11141 East Boulevard, Cleveland, OH 44106
Phone: 216-421-7418 **E-mail:** admiss@gate.cia.edu **CEEB Code:** 1152
Fax: 216-754-3634 **Web:** www.cia.edu **ACT Code:** 3243

This private school was founded in 1882. It has a 488-acre campus.

STUDENTS AND FACULTY

Enrollment: 525. **Student Body:** Male 52%, female 48%, out-of-state 20%, international 4%. **Ethnic Representation:** African American 5%, Asian 2%, Caucasian 91%, Hispanic 2%. **Retention and Graduation:** 80% freshmen return for sophomore year. 42% grads go on to further study within 1 year. **Faculty:** Student/faculty ratio 10:1. 43 full-time faculty, 76% hold PhDs. 100% faculty teach undergrads.

ACADEMICS

Degrees: Bachelor's. **Academic Requirements:** General education including some course work in arts/fine arts, computer literacy, English (including composition), history. There are various elective requirements for the liberal arts. **Classes:** 10-19 students in an average class. 10-19 students in an average lab class. **Disciplines with Highest Percentage of Degrees Awarded:** Visual and performing arts 100%. **Special Study Options:** Cross registration, student exchange program (domestic), independent study, internships, liberal arts/career combination, study abroad.

FACILITIES

Housing: Coed. **Library Holdings:** 42,000 bound volumes. 260 periodicals. 18,000 microforms. 120,000 audiovisuals. **Special Academic Facilities/ Equipment:** Cleveland Museum of Art, Cleveland Museum of Natural History, Cleveland Botanical Gardens, Crawford Auto Museum, Case Western Reserve University, Cleveland Institute of Music, Gund School of Law, Nottingham Spirk Design Firm, University Hospital, Mt. Sinai Hospital, Rainbow Babies Hospital. **Computers:** School-owned computers available for student use.

EXTRACURRICULARS

Activities: Student government, student newspaper. **Organizations:** 7 registered organizations.

ADMISSIONS

Selectivity Rating: 63 (of 100). **Freshman Academic Profile:** Average high school GPA 3.2. 15% in top 10% of high school class, 40% in top 25% of high school class, 75% in top 50% of high school class. Average SAT I Math 525, SAT I Math middle 50% range 480-610. Average SAT I Verbal 551, SAT I Verbal middle 50% range 510-610. Average ACT 21, ACT middle 50% range 20-26. TOEFL required of all international applicants, minimum TOEFL 525. **Basis for Candidate Selection:** *Very important factors considered include:* interview, recommendations, secondary school record, standardized test scores, talent/ability. *Important factors considered include:* character/personal qualities, essays. **Freshman Admission Requirements:** High school diploma or GED is required. **Freshman Admission Statistics:** 548 applied, 74% accepted, 43% of those accepted enrolled. **Transfer Admission Requirements:** *Items required:* college transcript, essay. Minimum high school GPA of 2.0 required. Minimum college GPA of 2.0 required. Lowest grade transferable C. **General Admission Information:** Application fee $30. Priority application deadline July 1. Admission may be deferred for a maximum of 1 year. Credit and/or placement offered for CEEB Advanced Placement tests.

COSTS AND FINANCIAL AID

Tuition $19,744. Room & board $6,426. Required fees $1,400. Average book expense $1,140. **Required Forms and Deadlines:** FAFSA and institution's own financial aid form. No deadline for regular filing. Priority filing deadline March 15. **Notification of Awards:** Applicants will be notified of awards on a rolling basis. **Types of Aid:** *Need-based scholarships/grants:* Pell, SEOG, state scholarships/grants, private scholarships, the school's own gift aid, academic merit scholarships/grants (institutional funds). *Loans:* FFEL Subsidized Stafford, FFEL Unsubsidized Stafford, FFEL PLUS, Federal Perkins. **Student Employment:** Federal Work-Study Program available. Off-campus job opportunities are excellent. **Financial Aid Statistics:** 68% freshmen, 77% undergrads receive some form of aid. **Financial Aid Phone:** 216-421-7424.

CLEVELAND INSTITUTE OF MUSIC

$$$

Admission Office, 11021 East Boulevard, Cleveland, OH 44106-1776
Phone: 216-795-3107 **E-mail:** cimadmission@po.cwru.edu **CEEB Code:** 1124
Fax: 216-791-1530 **Web:** www.cim.edu **ACT Code:** 3250

This private school was founded in 1920. It has a 500-acre campus.

STUDENTS AND FACULTY

Enrollment: 228. **Student Body:** Out-of-state 79%, international 11% (26 countries represented). **Ethnic Representation:** African American 1%, Asian 9%, Caucasian 87%, Hispanic 3%. **Retention and Graduation:** 87% freshmen return for sophomore year. 82% grads go on to further study within 1 year. **Faculty:** Student/faculty ratio 7:1. 31 full-time faculty, 29% hold PhDs. 100% faculty teach undergrads.

ACADEMICS

Degrees: Bachelor's, doctoral, master's. **Academic Requirements:** General education including some course work in arts/fine arts, English (including composition), foreign languages, 24 credit hours of liberal arts courses. **Disciplines with Highest Percentage of Degrees Awarded:** Visual and performing arts 100%. **Special Study Options:** Accelerated program, cross registration, distance learning, double major, dual enrollment, English as a second language, independent study, internships.

FACILITIES

Housing: Coed. **Library Holdings:** 47,000 bound volumes. 115 periodicals. 20,500 audiovisuals. **Computers:** School-owned computers available for student use.

EXTRACURRICULARS

Activities: Choral groups, music ensembles, student government, symphony orchestra.

ADMISSIONS

Selectivity Rating: 86 (of 100). **Freshman Academic Profile:** Average SAT I Math 590. Average SAT I Verbal 640. TOEFL required of all international applicants, minimum TOEFL 550. **Basis for Candidate Selection:** *Very important factors considered include:* talent/ability. *Important factors considered include:* character/personal qualities, class rank, essays, interview, recommendations, secondary school record, standardized test scores. *Other factors considered include:* extracurricular activities. **Freshman Admission Requirements:** High school diploma or GED is required. *Academic units required/recommended:* 16 total recommended; 4 English recommended, 3 math recommended, 3 science recommended, 3 foreign language recommended, 3 social studies recommended. **Freshman Admission Statistics:** 361 applied, 29% accepted, 51% of those accepted enrolled. **Transfer Admission Requirements:** *Items required:* high school transcript, college transcript, essay, standardized test scores, statement of good standing from prior school. Minimum high school GPA of 3.0 required. Minimum college GPA of 3.0 required. Lowest grade transferable C. **General Admission Information:** Application fee $70. Regular application deadline December 1. Admission may be deferred. Credit and/or placement offered for CEEB Advanced Placement tests.

COSTS AND FINANCIAL AID

Tuition $17,875. Room & board $5,590. Average book expense $750. **Required Forms and Deadlines:** FAFSA, institution's own financial aid form, and CSS/Financial Aid PROFILE. Financial aid filing deadline February 15. Priority filing deadline February 15. **Notification of Awards:** Applicants will be notified of awards on or about April 1. **Types of Aid:** *Need-based scholarships/grants:* Pell, SEOG, state scholarships/grants, private scholarships, the school's own gift aid. *Loans:* Direct Subsidized Stafford, Direct Unsubsidized Stafford, Direct PLUS, Federal Perkins. **Student Employment:** Federal Work-Study Program available. Off-campus job opportunities are good. **Financial Aid Statistics:** 60% freshmen, 65% undergrads receive some form of aid. Average freshman grant $7,690. Average freshman loan $4,558. Average income from on-campus job $1,000. **Financial Aid Phone:** 216-791-5000.

CLEVELAND STATE UNIVERSITY

East 24 and Euclid Avenue, Cleveland, OH 44115
Phone: 216-687-2100 **E-mail:** admissions@csuohio.edu **CEEB Code:** 3032
Fax: 216-687-9210 **Web:** www.csuohio.edu **ACT Code:** 1221

This public school was founded in 1964. It has an 82-acre campus.

STUDENTS AND FACULTY

Enrollment: 16,326. **Student Body:** Male 46%, female 54%, out-of-state 10%, international 1% (66 countries represented). **Ethnic Representation:** African American 20%, Asian 2%, Caucasian 58%, Hispanic 3%. **Retention and Graduation:** 64% freshmen return for sophomore year. 5% freshmen graduate within 4 years. **Faculty:** 95% faculty teach undergrads.

ACADEMICS

Degrees: Bachelor's, doctoral, first professional, master's. **Academic Requirements:** General education including some course work in arts/fine arts, English (including composition), history, humanities, mathematics, sciences (biological or physical), social science. **Special Study Options:** Accelerated program, cooperative (work-study) program, cross registration, distance learning, double major, dual enrollment, English as a second language, student exchange program (domestic), internships, student-designed major, study abroad, teacher certification program.

FACILITIES

Housing: Coed, fraternities and/or sororities. **Library Holdings:** 936,974 bound volumes. 5,050 periodicals. 660,867 microforms. 42,292 audiovisuals. **Computers:** *Recommended operating system:* Mac. School-owned computers available for student use.

EXTRACURRICULARS

Activities: Choral groups, concert band, dance, drama/theater, jazz band, literary magazine, music ensembles, opera, pep band, radio station, student government, student newspaper, symphony orchestra. **Organizations:** 115 registered organizations, 8 honor societies, 9 religious organizations, 7 fraternities, 6 sororities. **Athletics (Intercollegiate):** *Men:* baseball, basketball, fencing, golf, soccer, swimming, wrestling. *Women:* basketball, cross-country, fencing, indoor track, softball, swimming, tennis, track & field, volleyball.

ADMISSIONS

Selectivity Rating: 63 (of 100). **Freshman Academic Profile:** Average high school GPA 2.9. 7% in top 10% of high school class, 15% in top 25% of high school class, 29% in top 50% of high school class. Average SAT I Math 478. Average SAT I Verbal 483. Average ACT 19. TOEFL required of all international applicants, minimum TOEFL 525. **Basis for Candidate Selection:** *Very important factors considered include:* secondary school record. **Freshman Admission Requirements:** *Academic units required/recommended:* 18 total recommended; 4 English recommended, 3 math recommended, 3 science recommended, 1 science lab recommended, 2 foreign language required, 2 foreign language recommended, 3 social studies recommended, 3 elective recommended. **Freshman Admission Statistics:** 2,414 applied, 79% accepted, 55% of those accepted enrolled. **General Admission Information:** Application fee $25. Priority application deadline July 15. Nonfall registration accepted. Admission may be deferred for a maximum of 1 year. Credit and/or placement offered for CEEB Advanced Placement tests.

COSTS AND FINANCIAL AID

In-state tuition $1,872. Out-of-state tuition $3,744. Room & board $4,848. Required fees $72. Average book expense $600. **Student Employment:** Federal Work-Study Program available. Institutional employment available. Off-campus job opportunities are excellent. **Financial Aid Statistics:** Average income from on-campus job $3,000. **Financial Aid Phone:** 216-687-3764.

COASTAL CAROLINA UNIVERSITY

PO Box 261954, Conway, SC 29528-6054
Phone: 843-349-2026 **E-mail:** admissions@coastal.edu **CEEB Code:** 5837
Fax: 843-349-2127 **Web:** www.coastal.edu **ACT Code:** 5837

This public school was founded in 1954. It has a 240-acre campus.

STUDENTS AND FACULTY

Enrollment: 5,058. **Student Body:** Male 47%, female 53%, out-of-state 41%, international 3% (49 countries represented). **Ethnic Representation:** African American 9%, Asian 1%, Caucasian 87%, Hispanic 2%. **Retention and Graduation:** 71% freshmen return for sophomore year. 15% freshmen graduate within 4 years. **Faculty:** Student/faculty ratio 19:1. 200 full-time faculty, 80% hold PhDs. 100% faculty teach undergrads.

ACADEMICS

Degrees: Bachelor's, master's, post-bachelor's certificate. **Academic Requirements:** General education including some course work in computer literacy, English (including composition), foreign languages, history, humanities, mathematics, sciences (biological or physical), social science, behavioral science. **Classes:** 20-29 students in an average class. 20-29 students in an average lab class. **Majors with Highest Enrollment:** Business administration/management; marketing/marketing management, general; marine biology and biological oceanography. **Disciplines with Highest Percentage of Degrees Awarded:** Business/marketing 24%, education 17%, biological life sciences 16%, social sciences and history 12%, psychology 8%. **Special Study Options:** Accelerated program, cooperative (work-study) program, distance learning, double major, dual enrollment, honors program, independent study, internships, student-designed major, study abroad, teacher certification program.

FACILITIES

Housing: Coed, housing for disabled students. **Library Holdings:** 201,805 bound volumes. 958 periodicals. 93,171 microforms. 12,465 audiovisuals. **Computers:** *Recommended operating system:* WIN XP or 2000. School-owned computers available for student use.

EXTRACURRICULARS

Activities: Choral groups, concert band, dance, drama/theater, literary magazine, marching band, music ensembles, musical theater, pep band, student government, student newspaper. **Organizations:** 97 registered organizations, 19 honor societies, 3 religious organizations, 7 fraternities (12% men join), 6 sororities (7% women join). **Athletics (Intercollegiate):** *Men:* baseball, basketball, cheerleading, cross-country, football, golf, soccer, tennis, track & field. *Women:* basketball, cheerleading, cross-country, golf, soccer, softball, tennis, track & field, volleyball.

ADMISSIONS

Selectivity Rating: 71 (of 100). **Freshman Academic Profile:** Average high school GPA 3.3. 13% in top 10% of high school class, 44% in top 25% of high school class, 75% in top 50% of high school class. 95% from public high schools. Average SAT I Math 520, SAT I Math middle 50% range 480-570. Average SAT I Verbal 510, SAT I Verbal middle 50% range 460-550. Average ACT 22, ACT middle 50% range 20-24. TOEFL required of all international applicants, minimum TOEFL 500. **Basis for Candidate Selection:** *Very important factors considered include:* secondary school record, standardized test scores. *Important factors considered include:* class rank. *Other factors considered include:* alumni/ae relation, character/personal qualities, essays, extracurricular activities, geographical residence, interview, recommendations, state residency, talent/ability, work experience. **Freshman Admission Requirements:** High school diploma or GED is required. *Academic units required/recommended:* 20 total required; 4 English required, 3 math required, 4 math recommended, 3 science required, 3 science lab required, 2 foreign language required, 2 social studies required, 1 history required, 4 elective required. **Freshman Admission Statistics:** 3,599 applied, 72% accepted, 42% of those accepted enrolled. **Transfer Admission Requirements:** *Items required:* college transcript, statement of good standing from prior school. Minimum college GPA of 2.0 required. Lowest grade transferable C. **General Admission Information:** Application fee $35. Regular application deadline August 15. Nonfall registration accepted. Admission may be deferred for a maximum of 1 year. Credit and/or placement offered for CEEB Advanced Placement tests.

COSTS AND FINANCIAL AID

In-state tuition $4,430. Out-of-state tuition $11,840. Room & board $5,610. Required fees $0. Average book expense $363. **Required Forms and Deadlines:** FAFSA. Priority filing deadline April 1. **Notification of Awards:** Applicants will be notified of awards on a rolling basis beginning on or about March 1. **Types of Aid:** *Need-based scholarships/grants:* Pell, SEOG, state scholarships/grants, private scholarships, the school's own gift aid. *Loans:* FFEL Subsidized Stafford, FFEL Unsubsidized Stafford, FFEL PLUS, Federal Perkins, state loans. **Student Employment:** Federal Work-Study Program available. Institutional employment available. Off-campus job opportunities are excellent. **Financial Aid Statistics:** 61% freshmen, 62% undergrads receive some form of aid. Average freshman grant $2,906. Average income from on-campus job $2,560. **Financial Aid Phone:** 843-349-2313.

COE COLLEGE

1220 First Avenue NE, Cedar Rapids, IA 52402
Phone: 319-399-8500 **E-mail:** admission@coe.edu **CEEB Code:** 6101
Fax: 319-399-8816 **Web:** www.coe.edu **ACT Code:** 1294

This private school, which is affiliated with the Presbyterian Church, was founded in 1851. It has a 55-acre campus.

STUDENTS AND FACULTY

Enrollment: 1,300. **Student Body:** Male 43%, female 57%, out-of-state 34%, international 3% (15 countries represented). **Ethnic Representation:** African American 2%, Asian 1%, Caucasian 95%, Hispanic 1%. **Retention and Graduation:** 77% freshmen return for sophomore year. 59% freshmen graduate within 4 years. 26% grads go on to further study within 1 year. 2% grads pursue business degrees. 3% grads pursue law degrees. 2% grads pursue medical degrees. **Faculty:** Student/faculty ratio 12:1. 74 full-time faculty, 90% hold PhDs. 100% faculty teach undergrads.

ACADEMICS

Degrees: Bachelor's, master's. **Academic Requirements:** General education including some course work in arts/fine arts, English (including composition), humanities, sciences (biological or physical), social science, foreign culture requirement. **Classes:** 10-19 students in an average class. 10-19 students in an average lab class. **Majors with Highest Enrollment:** Business administration/ management; psychology, general; biology/biological sciences, general. **Disciplines with Highest Percentage of Degrees Awarded:** Business/ marketing 17%, education 12%, visual and performing arts 12%, social sciences and history 12%, psychology 9%. **Special Study Options:** Accelerated program, cross registration, double major, dual enrollment, English as a second language, student exchange program (domestic), honors program, independent study, internships, student-designed major, study abroad, teacher certification program, New York semester, co-op program in architecture, social service administration program with University of Chicago.

FACILITIES

Housing: Coed, all-female, all-male, apartments for single students, fraternities and/or sororities. **Library Holdings:** 213,270 bound volumes. 750 periodicals. 5,886 microforms. 8,653 audiovisuals. **Special Academic Facilities/ Equipment:** Ornithological museum, writing lab, theatre. **Computers:** School-owned computers available for student use..

EXTRACURRICULARS

Activities: Choral groups, concert band, drama/theater, jazz band, literary magazine, music ensembles, pep band, radio station, student government, student newspaper, symphony orchestra, yearbook. **Organizations:** 69 registered organizations, 14 honor societies, 2 religious organizations, 4 fraternities (27% men join), 3 sororities (21% women join). **Athletics (Intercollegiate):** *Men:* baseball, basketball, cross-country, diving, football, golf, indoor track, soccer, swimming, tennis, track & field, wrestling. *Women:* basketball, cheerleading, cross-country, diving, golf, indoor track, soccer, softball, swimming, tennis, track & field, volleyball.

ADMISSIONS

Selectivity Rating: 83 (of 100). **Freshman Academic Profile:** Average high school GPA 3.6. 30% in top 10% of high school class, 65% in top 25% of high school class, 92% in top 50% of high school class. 92% from public high schools. Average SAT I Math 572, SAT I Math middle 50% range 520-640. Average SAT I Verbal 577, SAT I Verbal middle 50% range 520-640. Average ACT 25, ACT middle 50% range 22-27. TOEFL required of all international applicants, minimum TOEFL 500. **Basis for Candidate Selection:** *Very important factors considered include:* secondary school record. *Important factors considered include:* class rank, essays, recommendations, standardized test scores. *Other factors considered include:* alumni/ae relation, character/personal qualities, extracurricular activities, interview, minority status, talent/ability, volunteer work. **Freshman Admission Requirements:** High school diploma or GED is required. *Academic units required/recommended:* 18 total recommended; 4 English recommended, 3 math recommended, 3 science recommended, 1 science lab recommended, 2 foreign language recommended, 3 social studies recommended, 2 elective recommended. **Freshman Admission Statistics:** 1,285 applied, 77% accepted, 30% of those accepted enrolled. **Transfer Admission Requirements:** *Items required:* high school transcript, college transcript. Minimum college GPA of 2.5 required. Lowest grade transferable C. **General Admission Information:** Priority application deadline December 15. Regular application deadline March 1. Nonfall registration accepted. Admission may be deferred for a maximum of 2 years. Credit and/or placement offered for CEEB Advanced Placement tests.

COSTS AND FINANCIAL AID

Tuition $20,280. Room & board $5,610. Required fees $260. Average book expense $600. **Required Forms and Deadlines:** FAFSA. Financial aid filing deadline April 30. Priority filing deadline March 1. **Notification of Awards:** Applicants will be notified of awards on a rolling basis beginning on or about March 1. **Types of Aid:** *Need-based scholarships/grants:* Pell, SEOG, state scholarships/grants, private scholarships, the school's own gift aid. *Loans:* Direct Subsidized Stafford, Direct Unsubsidized Stafford, Direct PLUS, Federal Perkins, college/university loans from institutional funds. **Student Employment:** Federal Work-Study Program available. Institutional employment available. Off-campus job opportunities are excellent. **Financial Aid Statistics:** 83% freshmen, 80% undergrads receive some form of aid. Average freshman grant $13,493. Average freshman loan $4,000. Average income from on-campus job $500. **Financial Aid Phone:** 319-399-8540.

COGSWELL POLYTECHNICAL COLLEGE

1175 Bordeaux Drive, Sunnyvale, CA 94089-1299
Phone: 408-541-0100 **E-mail:** admin@cogswell.edu **CEEB Code:** 1177
Fax: 408-747-0764 **Web:** www.cogswell.edu **ACT Code:** 1177

This private school was founded in 1887. It has a 5-acre campus.

STUDENTS AND FACULTY

Enrollment: 388. **Student Body:** Male 87%, female 13%, out-of-state 12%, international 2% (21 countries represented). **Ethnic Representation:** African American 3%, Asian 14%, Caucasian 58%, Hispanic 7%, Native American 1%. **Retention and Graduation:** 9% grads go on to further study within 1 year. 2% grads pursue business degrees. **Faculty:** Student/faculty ratio 9:1. 12 full-time faculty, 8% hold PhDs. 100% faculty teach undergrads.

ACADEMICS

Degrees: Bachelor's. **Academic Requirements:** General education including some course work in computer literacy, English (including composition), history, humanities, mathematics, sciences (biological or physical), social science. **Classes:** 10-19 students in an average class. **Majors with Highest Enrollment:** Engineering, general; fire services administration; visual and performing arts, general. **Disciplines with Highest Percentage of Degrees Awarded:** Visual and performing arts 68%, parks and recreation 22%, engineering/engineering technology 10%. **Special Study Options:** Distance learning, internships.

FACILITIES

Housing: Coed, apartments for single students. **Library Holdings:** 11,257 bound volumes. 102 periodicals. 43 microforms. 359 audiovisuals. **Computers:** School-owned computers available for student use.

EXTRACURRICULARS

Activities: Student government, student newspaper. **Organizations:** 1 registered organization.

ADMISSIONS

Selectivity Rating: 89 (of 100). **Freshman Academic Profile:** 80% in top 10% of high school class, 80% in top 25% of high school class, 80% in top 50% of high school class. 77% from public high schools. TOEFL required of all international applicants, minimum TOEFL 550. **Basis for Candidate Selection:** *Very important factors considered include:* essays, secondary school record. *Important factors considered include:* character/personal qualities, talent/ability. *Other factors considered include:* alumni/ae relation, class rank, extracurricular activities, interview, recommendations, volunteer work, work experience. **Freshman Admission Requirements:** High school diploma or GED is required. *Academic units required/recommended:* 3 English required, 3 math required, 1 science required. **Freshman Admission Statistics:** 30 applied, 100% accepted, 67% of those accepted enrolled. **Transfer Admission Requirements:** *Items required:* high school transcript, college transcript, essay, statement of good standing from prior school. Minimum high school GPA of 2.5 required. Minimum college GPA of 2.0 required. Lowest grade transferable C. **General Admission Information:** Application fee $50. Regular application deadline June 1. Nonfall registration accepted. Admission may be deferred for a maximum of 1 year. Credit and/or placement offered for CEEB Advanced Placement tests.

COSTS AND FINANCIAL AID

Tuition $11,280. Room & board $6,300. Required fees $40. Average book expense $846. **Required Forms and Deadlines:** FAFSA and institution's own financial aid form. No deadline for regular filing. Priority filing deadline March 2. **Notification of Awards:** Applicants will be notified of awards on a rolling basis beginning on or about April 30. **Types of Aid:** *Need-based scholarships/grants:* Pell, SEOG, state scholarships/grants, the school's own gift aid. *Loans:* FFEL Subsidized Stafford, FFEL Unsubsidized Stafford, FFEL PLUS, Federal Perkins, college/university loans from institutional funds. **Student Employment:** Federal Work-Study Program available. Off-campus job opportunities are excellent. **Financial Aid Statistics:** 47% freshmen, 42% undergrads receive some form of aid. **Financial Aid Phone:** 408-541-0100.

COKER COLLEGE

300 East College Avenue, Hartsville, SC 29550
Phone: 843-383-8050 **E-mail:** admissions@coker.edu **CEEB Code:** 5112
Fax: 843-383-8056 **Web:** www.coker.edu **ACT Code:** 3844

This private school was founded in 1908. It has a 15-acre campus.

STUDENTS AND FACULTY

Enrollment: 449. **Student Body:** Male 37%, female 63%, out-of-state 20%, international 3%. **Ethnic Representation:** African American 21%, Caucasian 77%, Hispanic 2%. **Retention and Graduation:** 63% freshmen return for sophomore year. 29% freshmen graduate within 4 years. **Faculty:** Student/faculty ratio 8:1. 55 full-time faculty, 80% hold PhDs. 100% faculty teach undergrads.

ACADEMICS

Degrees: Bachelor's. **Academic Requirements:** General education including some course work in arts/fine arts, English (including composition), foreign languages, history, humanities, mathematics, philosophy, sciences (biological or physical), social science, wellness/health class. **Classes:** 10-19 students in an average class. 10-19 students in an average lab class. **Majors with Highest Enrollment:** Education, general; business administration/management; visual and performing arts. **Disciplines with Highest Percentage of Degrees Awarded:** Education 16%, business/marketing 8%, visual and performing arts 7%, parks and recreation 6%, social sciences and history 4%. **Special Study Options:** Cooperative (work-study) program, cross registration, double major, dual enrollment, English as a second language, student exchange program (domestic), honors program, independent study, internships, liberal arts/career combination, student-designed major, study abroad, teacher certification program.

FACILITIES

Housing: Coed, housing for international students. **Library Holdings:** 64,888 bound volumes. 581 periodicals. 43,602 microforms. 3,717 audiovisuals. **Special Academic Facilities/Equipment:** Art gallery, state-of-the-art performing arts center, dark rooms, botanical gardens, graduate-level science equipment. **Computers:** School-owned computers available for student use.

EXTRACURRICULARS

Activities: Choral groups, dance, drama/theater, literary magazine, musical theater, student government, student newspaper. **Organizations:** 1 religious organization. **Athletics (Intercollegiate):** *Men:* baseball, basketball, cheerleading, cross-country, golf, soccer, tennis. *Women:* basketball, cheerleading, cross-country, soccer, softball, tennis, volleyball.

ADMISSIONS

Selectivity Rating: 70 (of 100). **Freshman Academic Profile:** Average high school GPA 3.3. 18% in top 10% of high school class, 46% in top 25% of high school class, 80% in top 50% of high school class. Average SAT I Math 493, SAT I Math middle 50% range 440-550. Average SAT I Verbal 498, SAT I Verbal middle 50% range 450-550. Average ACT 20, ACT middle 50% range 17-26. TOEFL required of all international applicants, minimum TOEFL 500. **Basis for Candidate Selection:** *Very important factors considered include:* extracurricular activities, interview, recommendations, secondary school record, talent/ability. *Important factors considered include:* alumni/ae relation, character/personal qualities, standardized test scores. *Other factors considered include:* class rank, essays, volunteer work, work experience. **Freshman Admission Requirements:** High school diploma or GED is required. *Academic units required/recommended:* 19 total required; 4 English required, 3 math required, 3 science recommended, 3 foreign language recommended, 2 social studies recommended, 1 history recommended, 3 elective recommended. **Freshman Admission Statistics:** 134 applied, 90% accepted, 100% of those accepted enrolled. **Transfer Admission Requirements:** *Items required:* college transcript, statement of good standing from prior school. Minimum college GPA of 2.0 required. Lowest grade transferable C. **General Admission Information:** Application fee $15. Nonfall registration accepted. Admission may be deferred for a maximum of 1 year. Credit and/or placement offered for CEEB Advanced Placement tests.

COSTS AND FINANCIAL AID

Tuition $15,240. Room & board $5,196. Required fees $470. Average book expense $1,000. **Required Forms and Deadlines:** FAFSA. Financial aid filing deadline June 1. Priority filing deadline April 1. **Notification of Awards:** Applicants will be notified of awards on a rolling basis beginning on or about December 15. **Types of Aid:** *Need-based scholarships/grants:* Pell, SEOG, state scholarships/grants, private scholarships, the school's own gift aid. *Loans:* FFEL Subsidized Stafford, FFEL Unsubsidized Stafford, FFEL PLUS, Federal Perkins. **Student Employment:** Federal Work-Study Program available. Institutional employment available. Off-campus job opportunities are good. **Financial Aid Statistics:** 86% freshmen, 81% undergrads receive some form of aid. Average freshman grant $12,494. Average freshman loan $5,261. Average income from on-campus job $1,072. **Financial Aid Phone:** 800-950-1908.

COLBY COLLEGE

4000 Mayflower Hill, Waterville, ME 04901-8840
E-mail: admissions@colby.edu **CEEB Code:** 3280
Fax: 207-872-3474 **Web:** www.colby.edu **ACT Code:** 1638

This private school was founded in 1813. It has a 714-acre campus.

STUDENTS AND FACULTY

Enrollment: 1,830. **Student Body:** Out-of-state 84%, international 6% (63 countries represented). **Ethnic Representation:** African American 3%, Asian 6%, Caucasian 89%, Hispanic 2%. **Retention and Graduation:** 92% freshmen return for sophomore year. 85% freshmen graduate within 4 years. 18% grads go on to further study within 1 year. 4% grads pursue law degrees. 2% grads pursue medical degrees. **Faculty:** Student/faculty ratio 11:1. 158 full-time faculty, 94% hold PhDs. 100% faculty teach undergrads.

ACADEMICS

Degrees: Bachelor's. **Academic Requirements:** General education including some course work in arts/fine arts, English (including composition), foreign languages, history, humanities, mathematics, sciences (biological or physical), social science. Students must meet both the diversity and wellness requirements. **Classes:** 10-19 students in an average class. 10-19 students in an average lab class. **Majors with Highest Enrollment:** English language and literature, general; biology/biological sciences, general; political science and government, general. **Disciplines with Highest Percentage of Degrees Awarded:** Social sciences and history 32%, biological life sciences 10%, area and ethnic studies 14%, English 9%, foreign language and litrature 8%. **Special Study Options:** Cross registration, double major, student exchange program (domestic), honors program, independent study, internships, student-designed major, study abroad, teacher certification program, summer research assistantships. Colby has coordinated 3-2 engineering programs with Dartmouth. Colby offers junior-year abroad programs in Ireland, England, France, Spain, Russia. Colby, Bates, and Bowdoin have established a study abroad consortium with centers in Quito, Ecuador; London; and Cape Town, South Africa.

FACILITIES

Housing: Coed, quiet halls, chemical-free halls, apartments for seniors only. **Library Holdings:** 350,000 bound volumes. 1,850 periodicals. 301,700 microforms. 20,645 audiovisuals. **Special Academic Facilities/Equipment:** 28,000-square-foot art museum, arboretum, electronic microscopes, greenhouse, astronomical observatory, writer's center, multicultural center, rare books and archives library, computer research classroom, language lab. **Computers:** School-owned computers available for student use.

EXTRACURRICULARS

Activities: Choral groups, concert band, dance, drama/theater, jazz band, literary magazine, music ensembles, musical theater, radio station, student government, student newspaper, student-run film society, symphony orchestra, yearbook. **Organizations:** 101 registered organizations, 9 honor societies, 6 religious organizations. **Athletics (Intercollegiate):** *Men:* baseball, basketball, crew, skiing (cross-country), cross-country, diving, football, golf, ice hockey, indoor track, lacrosse, skiing (alpine), skiing (Nordic), soccer, squash, swimming, tennis, track & field. *Women:* basketball, crew, skiing (cross-country), cross-country, diving, field hockey, golf, ice hockey, indoor track, lacrosse, skiing (alpine), skiing (Nordic), soccer, softball, squash, swimming, tennis, track & field, volleyball.

ADMISSIONS

Selectivity Rating: 96 (of 100). **Freshman Academic Profile:** 64% in top 10% of high school class, 90% in top 25% of high school class, 99% in top 50%

of high school class. 58% from public high schools. Average SAT I Math 670, SAT I Math middle 50% range 640-710. Average SAT I Verbal 660, SAT I Verbal middle 50% range 620-700. Average ACT 28, ACT middle 50% range 27-30. TOEFL required of all international applicants, minimum TOEFL 600. **Basis for Candidate Selection:** *Very important factors considered include:* character/personal qualities, secondary school record. *Important factors considered include:* class rank, essays, extracurricular activities, interview, minority status, recommendations, standardized test scores, talent/ability. *Other factors considered include:* alumni/ae relation, geographical residence, state residency, volunteer work, work experience. **Freshman Admission Requirements:** High school diploma or equivalent is not required. *Academic units required/recommended:* 16 total recommended; 4 English recommended, 3 math recommended, 2 science recommended, 2 science lab recommended, 3 foreign language recommended, 2 social studies recommended, 2 elective recommended. **Freshman Admission Statistics:** 3,873 applied, 33% accepted, 37% of those accepted enrolled. **Transfer Admission Requirements:** *Items required:* high school transcript, college transcript, essay, standardized test scores, statement of good standing from prior school. Minimum college GPA of 3.0 required. Lowest grade transferable C. **General Admission Information:** Application fee $55. Early decision application deadline November 15. Regular application deadline January 1. Nonfall registration accepted. Admission may be deferred for a maximum of 1 year. Credit and/or placement offered for CEEB Advanced Placement tests.

COSTS AND FINANCIAL AID

Average book expense $650. **Required Forms and Deadlines:** FAFSA and either institutional application or CSS/Financial Aid PROFILE and institutional supplement. Financial aid filing deadline February 1. **Notification of Awards:** Applicants will be notified of awards on or about April 1. **Types of Aid:** *Need-based scholarships/grants:* Pell, SEOG, state scholarships/grants, private scholarships, the school's own gift aid. *Loans:* Direct Subsidized Stafford, Direct Unsubsidized Stafford, Direct PLUS, FFEL Subsidized Stafford, FFEL Unsubsidized Stafford, FFEL PLUS, Federal Perkins, state loans, college/university loans from institutional funds, alternative loans. **Student Employment:** Federal Work-Study Program available. Institutional employment available. Off-campus job opportunities are fair. **Financial Aid Statistics:** 43% freshmen, 38% undergrads receive some form of aid. Average freshman grant $21,966. Average freshman loan $3,243. Average income from on-campus job $905. **Financial Aid Phone:** 207-872-3168.

COLBY-SAWYER COLLEGE

100 Main Street, New London, NH 03257
Phone: 603-526-3700 **E-mail:** csadmiss@colbysawyer.edu **CEEB Code:** 3281
Fax: 603-526-3452 **Web:** www.colby-sawyer.edu **ACT Code:** 2506

This private school was founded in 1837. It has a 200-acre campus.

STUDENTS AND FACULTY

Enrollment: 940. **Student Body:** Male 37%, female 63%, out-of-state 70%, international 2%. **Ethnic Representation:** Asian 1%, Caucasian 94%. **Retention and Graduation:** 83% freshmen return for sophomore year. 41% freshmen graduate within 4 years. **Faculty:** Student/faculty ratio 12:1. 49 full-time faculty, 77% hold PhDs. 100% faculty teach undergrads.

ACADEMICS

Degrees: Associate's, bachelor's, transfer. **Academic Requirements:** General education including some course work in arts/fine arts, computer literacy, English (including composition), history, humanities, mathematics, sciences (biological or physical), social science. **Classes:** 20-29 students in an average class. Under 10 students in an average lab class. **Majors with Highest Enrollment:** Business administration/management; psychology, general; fine/studio arts, general. **Disciplines with Highest Percentage of Degrees Awarded:** Business/marketing 18%, parks and recreation 16%, visual and performing arts 15%, psychology 15%, communications/communication technologies 9%. **Special Study Options:** Accelerated program, cross registration, double major, dual enrollment, English as a second language, student exchange program (domestic), honors program, independent study, internships, student-designed major, study abroad, teacher certification program.

FACILITIES

Housing: Coed, all-female, housing for disabled students, substance-free residence hall. **Library Holdings:** 90,305 bound volumes. 467 periodicals. 199,638 microforms. 3,512 audiovisuals. **Special Academic Facilities/Equipment:** Sawyer Fine Arts Center, Windy Hill School (preschool through grade 3). **Computers:** School-owned computers available for student use.

EXTRACURRICULARS

Activities: Choral groups, dance, drama/theater, literary magazine, musical theater, radio station, student government, student newspaper, yearbook. **Organizations:** 40 registered organizations, 3 honor societies, 1 religious organization. **Athletics (Intercollegiate):** *Men:* baseball, basketball, diving, equestrian, skiing (alpine), soccer, swimming, tennis, track & field. *Women:* basketball, diving, equestrian, lacrosse, skiing (alpine), soccer, swimming, tennis, track & field, volleyball.

ADMISSIONS

Selectivity Rating: 72 (of 100). **Freshman Academic Profile:** Average high school GPA 2.9. 69% from public high schools. Average SAT I Math 496, SAT I Math middle 50% range 450-550. Average SAT I Verbal 503, SAT I Verbal middle 50% range 450-540. Average ACT 19, ACT middle 50% range 17-21. TOEFL required of all international applicants, minimum TOEFL 500. **Basis for Candidate Selection:** *Very important factors considered include:* interview, secondary school record. *Important factors considered include:* character/personal qualities, essays, recommendations, standardized test scores. *Other factors considered include:* alumni/ae relation, class rank, extracurricular activities, geographical residence, volunteer work, work experience. **Freshman Admission Requirements:** High school diploma or GED is required. *Academic units required/recommended:* 15 total required; 4 English required, 3 math required, 2 science required, 2 science lab required, 2 foreign language required, 3 social studies required. **Freshman Admission Statistics:** 1,251 applied, 86% accepted, 25% of those accepted enrolled. **Transfer Admission Requirements:** *Items required:* high school transcript, college transcript, essay, standardized test scores, statement of good standing from prior school. Minimum high school GPA of 2.5 required. Minimum college GPA of 2.0 required. Lowest grade transferable C. **General Admission Information:** Application fee $40. Priority application deadline March 1. Nonfall registration accepted. Admission may be deferred for a maximum of 1 year. Credit and/or placement offered for CEEB Advanced Placement tests.

COSTS AND FINANCIAL AID

Tuition $20,130. Room & board $7,720. Required fees $0. Average book expense $700. **Required Forms and Deadlines:** FAFSA and institution's own financial aid form. Priority filing deadline March 1. **Notification of Awards:** Applicants will be notified of awards on or about March 25. **Types of Aid:** *Need-based scholarships/grants:* Pell, SEOG, state scholarships/grants, private scholarships, the school's own gift aid. *Loans:* FFEL Subsidized Stafford, FFEL Unsubsidized Stafford, FFEL PLUS, Federal Perkins, college/university loans from institutional funds. **Student Employment:** Federal Work-Study Program available. Institutional employment available. Off-campus job opportunities are good. **Financial Aid Statistics:** 75% freshmen, 61% undergrads receive some form of aid. Average freshman grant $8,254. Average freshman loan $2,625. **Financial Aid Phone:** 603-526-3717.

See page 980.

COLGATE UNIVERSITY

13 Oak Drive, Hamilton, NY 13346
Phone: 315-228-7401 **E-mail:** admission@mail.colgate.edu **CEEB Code:** 2086
Fax: 315-228-7544 **Web:** www.colgate.edu **ACT Code:** 2702

This private school was founded in 1819. It has a 515-acre campus.

STUDENTS AND FACULTY

Enrollment: 2,827. **Student Body:** Male 49%, female 51%, out-of-state 67%, international 5% (32 countries represented). **Ethnic Representation:** African American 4%, Asian 5%, Caucasian 85%, Hispanic 3%. **Retention and Graduation:** 94% freshmen return for sophomore year. 83% freshmen graduate within 4 years. 16% grads go on to further study within 1 year. 1% grads pursue business degrees. 25% grads pursue law degrees. 21% grads pursue medical degrees. **Faculty:** Student/faculty ratio 10:1. 242 full-time faculty, 94% hold PhDs. 100% faculty teach undergrads.

ACADEMICS

Degrees: Bachelor's, master's. **Academic Requirements:** General education including some course work in humanities, sciences (biological or physical), social science. **Classes:** 10-19 students in an average class. 10-19 students in an average lab class. **Majors with Highest Enrollment:** History, general; English language and literature, general; economics, general. **Disciplines with Highest Percentage of Degrees Awarded:** Social sciences and history 40%, English 10%, philosophy/religion/theology 7%, foreign languages and literature 8%, biological life sciences 6%. **Special Study Options:** Double major, honors program, independent study, internships, student-designed major, study abroad, teacher certification program.

FACILITIES

Housing: Coed, apartments for single students, housing for disabled students, fraternities and/or sororities, cooperative housing. Theme housing: peace studies, La Casa Pan Latina, Harlem Renaissance Center, French-Italian house, etc. **Library Holdings:** 1,110,309 bound volumes. 2,315 periodicals. 533,419 microforms. 8,805 audiovisuals. **Special Academic Facilities/Equipment:** Art gallery, anthropology museum, language lab, closed-circuit TV system, life sciences complex, geology/fossil collection, observatory, electron microscopes, laser lab, weather lab. **Computers:** School-owned computers available for student use.

EXTRACURRICULARS

Activities: Choral groups, concert band, dance, drama/theater, jazz band, literary magazine, music ensembles, pep band, radio station, student government, student newspaper, symphony orchestra, television station, yearbook. **Organizations:** 100 registered organizations, 4 honor societies, 6 religious organizations, 8 fraternities (35% men join), 4 sororities (32% women join). **Athletics (Intercollegiate):** *Men:* basketball, crew, cross-country, diving, football, golf, ice hockey, indoor track, lacrosse, soccer, swimming, tennis, track & field. *Women:* basketball, crew, cross-country, diving, field hockey, ice hockey, indoor track, lacrosse, soccer, softball, swimming, tennis, track & field, volleyball.

ADMISSIONS

Selectivity Rating: 95 (of 100). **Freshman Academic Profile:** Average high school GPA 3.6. 68% in top 10% of high school class, 92% in top 25% of high school class, 100% in top 50% of high school class. 70% from public high schools. Average SAT I Math 665, SAT I Math middle 50% range 630-710. Average SAT I Verbal 652, SAT I Verbal middle 50% range 610-700. Average ACT 29, ACT middle 50% range 27-31. TOEFL required of all international applicants, minimum TOEFL 600. **Basis for Candidate Selection:** *Very important factors considered include:* class rank, secondary school record. *Important factors considered include:* character/personal qualities, essays, extracurricular activities, recommendations, standardized test scores, talent/ability, volunteer work, work experience. *Other factors considered include:* alumni/ae relation, geographical residence, minority status. **Freshman Admission Requirements:** High school diploma or GED is required. *Academic units required/recommended:* 16 total required; 20 total recommended; 4 English required, 4 English recommended, 3 math required, 4 math recommended, 3 science required, 4 science recommended, 2 science lab required, 3 science lab recommended, 3 foreign language required, 4 foreign language recommended, 2 social studies required, 2 social studies recommended, 1 history required, 3 history recommended. **Freshman Admission Statistics:** 6,268 applied, 34% accepted, 35% of those accepted enrolled. **Transfer Admission Requirements:** *Items required:* high school transcript, college transcript, essay, standardized test score, statement of good standing from prior school, faculty recommendation, dean's report. Minimum college GPA of 3.0 required. Lowest grade transferable C. **General Admission Information:** Application fee $55. Early decision application deadline November 15. Regular application deadline January 15. Admission may be deferred for a maximum of 1 year. Credit and/or placement offered for CEEB Advanced Placement tests.

COSTS AND FINANCIAL AID

Tuition $26,845. Room & board $6,455. Required fees $180. Average book expense $620. **Required Forms and Deadlines:** FAFSA, CSS/Financial Aid PROFILE, noncustodial (divorced/separated) parent's statement, and business/farm supplement. Financial aid filing deadline February 1. Priority filing deadline February 1. **Notification of Awards:** Applicants will be notified of awards on or about April 1. **Types of Aid:** *Need-based scholarships/grants:* Pell, SEOG, state scholarships/grants, private scholarships, the school's own gift aid. *Loans:* FFEL Subsidized Stafford, FFEL Unsubsidized Stafford, FFEL PLUS, Federal Perkins. **Student Employment:** Federal Work-Study Program available. Institutional employment available. Off-campus job opportunities are good. **Financial Aid Statistics:** 49% freshmen, 45% undergrads receive some form of aid. Average freshman grant $25,261. Average freshman loan $2,625. Average income from on-campus job $1,600. **Financial Aid Phone:** 315-228-7431.

See page 982.

COLLEGE FOR CREATIVE STUDIES

$$$

201 East Kirby, Detroit, MI 48202-4304
Phone: 313-664-7425 **E-mail:** admissions@ccscad.edu
Fax: 313-872-2739 **Web:** www.ccscad.edu

This private school was founded in 1906. It has an 11-acre campus.

STUDENTS AND FACULTY

Enrollment: 1,152. **Student Body:** Male 59%, female 41%, out-of-state 16%, international 6%. **Ethnic Representation:** African American 7%, Asian 6%, Caucasian 69%, Hispanic 4%. **Retention and Graduation:** 69% freshmen return for sophomore year. 32% freshmen graduate within 4 years. **Faculty:** Student/faculty ratio 9:1. 44 full-time faculty. 100% faculty teach undergrads.

ACADEMICS

Degrees: Bachelor's. **Academic Requirements:** General education including some course work in arts/fine arts, English (including composition), history, humanities, philosophy, social science. **Disciplines with Highest Percentage of Degrees Awarded:** Visual and performing arts 100%. **Special Study Options:** Double major, independent study, internships, study abroad.

FACILITIES

Housing: Apartments for single students. **Special Academic Facilities/Equipment:** Top-of-the-line technology for design, animation, and audiovisual editing; wood and metal shops; hot glass studio; gallery; private studios. **Computers:** School-owned computers available for student use.

EXTRACURRICULARS

Activities: Student government.

ADMISSIONS

Selectivity Rating: 72 (of 100). **Freshman Academic Profile:** Average SAT I Math 516, SAT I Math middle 50% range 500-516. Average SAT I Verbal 511, SAT I Verbal middle 50% range 500-511. Average ACT 21, ACT middle 50% range 21-23. TOEFL required of all international applicants, minimum TOEFL 500. **Basis for Candidate Selection:** *Very important factors considered include:* secondary school record, talent/ability. *Important factors considered include:* essays. *Other factors considered include:* character/personal qualities, recommendations, standardized test scores. **Freshman Admission Requirements:** High school diploma or GED is required. *Academic units required/recommended:* 13 total recommended; 4 English recommended, 3 math recommended, 2 science recommended, 2 foreign language recommended, 2 social studies recommended. **Freshman Admission Statistics:** 405 applied, 79% accepted, 60% of those accepted enrolled. **Transfer Admission Requirements:** *Items required:* high school transcript, college transcript, essay. Minimum high school GPA of 2.5 required. Minimum college GPA of 2.0 required. Lowest grade transferable C. **General Admission Information:** Application fee $35. Priority application deadline March 1. Regular application deadline August 1. Nonfall registration accepted. Admission may be deferred for a maximum of 1 year. Credit offered for CEEB Advanced Placement tests.

COSTS AND FINANCIAL AID

Tuition $17,520. Room & board $5,500. Required fees $1,078. Average book expense $2,500. **Required Forms and Deadlines:** FAFSA. No deadline for regular filing. Priority filing deadline February 21. **Notification of Awards:** Applicants will be notified of awards on a rolling basis beginning on or about March 15. **Types of Aid:** *Need-based scholarships/grants:* Pell, SEOG, state scholarships/grants, private scholarships, the school's own gift aid. *Loans:* FFEL Subsidized Stafford, FFEL Unsubsidized Stafford, FFEL PLUS, alternative loan programs. **Student Employment:** Federal Work-Study Program available. Institutional employment available. Off-campus job opportunities are good. **Financial Aid Statistics:** Average freshman grant $3,000. Average freshman loan $2,625. Average income from on-campus job $1,000. **Financial Aid Phone:** 313-664-7495.

COLLEGE MISERICORDIA

301 Lake Street, Dallas, PA 18612
Phone: 570-674-6460 **E-mail:** admiss@misericordia.edu **CEEB Code:** 2087
Fax: 570-675-2441 **Web:** www.misericodia.edu **ACT Code:** 3539

This private school, which is affiliated with the Roman Catholic Church, was founded in 1924. It has a 100-acre campus.

STUDENTS AND FACULTY

Student Body: Out-of-state 24%. **Retention and Graduation:** 83% freshmen return for sophomore year. 43% freshmen graduate within 4 years. 15% grads go on to further study within 1 year. **Faculty:** Student/faculty ratio 14:1. 86 full-time faculty, 55% hold PhDs. 96% faculty teach undergrads.

ACADEMICS

Degrees: Bachelor's, master's. **Academic Requirements:** General education including some course work in arts/fine arts, computer literacy, English (including composition), history, humanities, mathematics, sciences (biological or physical), social science, religious studies. **Classes:** Under 10 students in an average class. 10-19 students in an average lab class. **Disciplines with Highest Percentage of Degrees Awarded:** Health professions and related sciences 54%, business/marketing 11%, education 8%, personal and miscellaneous services 7%, social sciences and history 5%. **Special Study Options:** Accelerated program, cooperative (work-study) program, cross registration, distance learning, double major, dual enrollment, student exchange program (domestic), honors program, independent study, internships, student-designed major, study abroad, teacher certification program, weekend college.

FACILITIES

Housing: Coed, wellness housing. **Library Holdings:** 72,836 bound volumes. 782 periodicals. 6,054 microforms. 2,240 audiovisuals. **Special Academic Facilities/Equipment:** On-campus nursery school and retirement center, art museum, and dance/aerobic studio. **Computers:** School-owned computers available for student use.

EXTRACURRICULARS

Activities: Choral groups, concert band, dance, drama/theater, jazz band, literary magazine, music ensembles, student government, student newspaper, symphony orchestra, yearbook. **Organizations:** 26 registered organizations, 1 honor society, 1 religious organization. **Athletics (Intercollegiate):** *Men:* baseball, basketball, cheerleading, cross-country, golf, lacrosse, soccer, swimming, track & field. *Women:* basketball, cheerleading, cross-country, field hockey, lacrosse, soccer, softball, swimming, track & field, volleyball.

ADMISSIONS

Selectivity Rating: 82 (of 100). **Freshman Academic Profile:** 40% from public high schools. Average SAT I Math 500, SAT I Math middle 50% range 350-630. Average SAT I Verbal 510, SAT I Verbal middle 50% range 510-610. Average ACT 23. TOEFL required of all international applicants, minimum TOEFL 500. **Basis for Candidate Selection:** *Very important factors considered include:* class rank, secondary school record. *Important factors considered include:* character/personal qualities, extracurricular activities, interview, recommendations, standardized test scores, volunteer work. *Other factors considered include:* essays, talent/ability. **Freshman Admission Requirements:** High school diploma or GED is required. *Academic units required/recommended:* 16 total required; 4 English required, 4 math required, 4 science required, 4 social studies required. **Freshman Admission Statistics:** 923 applied, 84% accepted, 75% of those accepted enrolled. **Transfer Admission Requirements:** *Items required:* college transcript. Minimum high school GPA of 2.0 required. Minimum college GPA of 2.0 required. Lowest grade transferable C. **General Admission Information:** Application fee $25. Nonfall registration accepted. Admission may be deferred for a maximum of 1 year. Credit and/or placement offered for CEEB Advanced Placement tests.

COSTS AND FINANCIAL AID

Tuition $15,800. Room & board $6,600. Required fees $853. Average book expense $600. **Required Forms and Deadlines:** FAFSA and institution's own financial aid form. No deadline for regular filing. Priority filing deadline March 1. **Notification of Awards:** Applicants will be notified of awards on a rolling basis beginning on or about March 1. **Types of Aid:** *Need-based scholarships/grants:* Pell, SEOG, state scholarships/grants, private scholarships, the school's own gift aid, Federal Nursing. *Loans:* FFEL Subsidized Stafford, FFEL Unsubsidized Stafford, FFEL PLUS, Federal Perkins, Federal Nursing, state loans. **Student Employment:** Federal Work-Study Program available. Institutional employment available. Off-campus job opportunities are excellent. **Financial Aid Statistics:** 85% freshmen, 64% undergrads receive some form of aid. Average freshman grant $5,137. Average freshman loan $2,683. Average income from on-campus job $1,000. **Financial Aid Phone:** 570-674-6280.

COLLEGE OF AERONAUTICS

LaGuardia Airport, 86-01 23rd Avenue, Flushing, NY 11369
Phone: 718-429-6600 **E-mail:** admissions@aero.edu **CEEB Code:** 2001
Fax: 718-779-2231 **Web:** www.aero.edu

This private school was founded in 1932. It has a 6-acre campus.

STUDENTS AND FACULTY

Enrollment: 1,316. **Student Body:** Male 91%, female 9%, out-of-state 1%. **Retention and Graduation:** 67% freshmen return for sophomore year. 8% freshmen graduate within 4 years. 5% grads pursue business degrees. **Faculty:** Student/faculty ratio 11:1. 56 full-time faculty, 33% hold PhDs.

ACADEMICS

Degrees: Associate's, bachelor's, certificate. **Academic Requirements:** General education including some course work in computer literacy, English (including composition), mathematics, sciences (biological or physical). **Classes:** 10-19 students in an average class. 10-19 students in an average lab class. **Majors with Highest Enrollment:** Business administration/management; electrical/electronics equipment installation and repair, general; airframe mechanics and aircraft maintenance technology/technician. **Disciplines with Highest Percentage of Degrees Awarded:** Trade and industry 70%, engineering/engineering technology 30%. **Special Study Options:** Cooperative (work-study) program, distance learning, internships.

FACILITIES

Library Holdings: 62,000 bound volumes. 400 periodicals. 0 microforms. 1,849 audiovisuals. **Computers:** *Recommended operating system:* Mac. School-owned computers available for student use.

EXTRACURRICULARS

Activities: Literary magazine, student government, student newspaper. **Organizations:** 5 registered organizations. **Athletics (Intercollegiate):** *Men:* basketball, softball, volleyball. *Women:* basketball, softball, volleyball.

ADMISSIONS

Selectivity Rating: 63 (of 100). **Freshman Academic Profile:** Average high school GPA 2.3. 5% in top 10% of high school class, 15% in top 25% of high school class, 57% in top 50% of high school class. Average SAT I Math 450, SAT I Math middle 50% range 400-460. Average SAT I Verbal 450, SAT I Verbal middle 50% range 350-420. TOEFL required of all international applicants, minimum TOEFL 500. **Basis for Candidate Selection:** *Very important factors considered include:* interview. *Other factors considered include:* alumni/ae relation, class rank, extracurricular activities, recommendations, secondary school record, talent/ability. **Freshman Admission Requirements:** High school diploma or GED is required. *Academic units required/recommended:* 4 English required, 4 English recommended, 3 math required, 4 math recommended, 3 science required, 4 science recommended, 1 science lab required, 4 foreign language recommended, 3 social studies required, 4 social studies recommended, 3 history required, 4 history recommended, 3 elective recommended. **Freshman Admission Statistics:** 544 applied, 80% accepted, 82% of those accepted enrolled. **Transfer Admission Requirements:** *Items required:* high school transcript, college transcript. Minimum high school GPA of 2.0 required. Minimum college GPA of 2.0 required. Lowest grade transferable C. **General Admission Information:** Application fee $35. Priority application deadline July 2. Regular application deadline rolling. Nonfall registration accepted. Admission may be deferred for a maximum of 2 years. Neither credit nor placement offered for CEEB Advanced Placement tests.

COSTS AND FINANCIAL AID

Tuition $10,330. Room & board $4,280. Required fees $400. Average book expense $1,050. **Required Forms and Deadlines:** FAFSA and state aid form. No deadline for regular filing. **Notification of Awards:** Applicants will be notified of awards on a rolling basis beginning on or about September 1. **Types of Aid:** *Need-based scholarships/grants:* Pell, SEOG, state scholarships/grants, private scholarships, the school's own gift aid. *Loans:* FFEL Subsidized Stafford, FFEL Unsubsidized Stafford, FFEL PLUS. **Student Employment:** Federal Work-Study Program available. Institutional employment available. Off-campus job opportunities are good. **Financial Aid Statistics:** 70% freshmen, 80% undergrads receive some form of aid. Average freshman grant $1,250. Average freshman loan $2,625. **Financial Aid Phone:** 718-429-6600.

COLLEGE OF CHARLESTON

66 George Street, Charleston, SC 29424
Phone: 843-953-5670 **E-mail:** admissions@cofc.edu **CEEB Code:** 5113
Fax: 843-953-6322 **Web:** www.cofc.edu **ACT Code:** 3846

This public school was founded in 1770. It has a 52-acre campus.

STUDENTS AND FACULTY

Enrollment: 10,044. **Student Body:** Male 37%, female 63%, out-of-state 35%, international 2%. **Ethnic Representation:** African American 9%, Asian 1%, Caucasian 87%, Hispanic 1%. **Retention and Graduation:** 82% freshmen return for sophomore year. 33% freshmen graduate within 4 years. 33% grads go on to further study within 1 year. 14% grads pursue business degrees. 12% grads pursue law degrees. 12% grads pursue medical degrees. **Faculty:** Student/faculty ratio 14:1. 463 full-time faculty, 84% hold PhDs.

ACADEMICS

Degrees: Bachelor's, master's, post-bachelor's certificate. **Academic Requirements:** General education including some course work in English (including composition), foreign languages, history, humanities, mathematics, sciences (biological or physical), social science. **Classes:** 20-29 students in an average class. 20-29 students in an average lab class. **Majors with Highest Enrollment:** Business administration/management; communications studies/speech communication and rhetoric; biology/biological sciences, general. **Disciplines with Highest Percentage of Degrees Awarded:** Business/marketing 18%, communications/communication technologies 15%, social sciences and history 15%, education 12%, psychology 10%. **Special Study Options:** Accelerated program, cooperative (work-study) program, cross registration, distance learning, double major, dual enrollment, English as a second language, student exchange program (domestic), honors program, independent study, internships, liberal arts/career combination, study abroad, teacher certification program, semester at sea.

FACILITIES

Housing: Coed, all-female, all-male, housing for disabled students, housing for international students, fraternities and/or sororities, restored old Charleston house, international house. **Library Holdings:** 499,370 bound volumes. 3,310 periodicals. 822,143 microforms. 5,902 audiovisuals. **Special Academic Facilities/Equipment:** Art gallery, broadcast museum, early childhood development center, African American history and culture institute, observatory, marine sciences station, sculpture facility, sailing marina, sports facilities. **Computers:** School-owned computers available for student use.

EXTRACURRICULARS

Activities: Choral groups, dance, drama/theater, jazz band, literary magazine, music ensembles, musical theater, pep band, radio station, student government, student newspaper, symphony orchestra, yearbook. **Organizations:** 115 registered organizations, 19 honor societies, 17 religious organizations, 12 fraternities (13% men join), 10 sororities (18% women join). **Athletics (Intercollegiate):** *Men:* baseball, basketball, cross-country, diving, golf, sailing, soccer, swimming, tennis. *Women:* basketball, cross-country, diving, equestrian, golf, sailing, soccer, softball, swimming, tennis, volleyball.

ADMISSIONS

Selectivity Rating: 82 (of 100). **Freshman Academic Profile:** Average high school GPA 3.6. 25% in top 10% of high school class, 58% in top 25% of high school class, 91% in top 50% of high school class. 83% from public high schools. Average SAT I Math 590, SAT I Math middle 50% range 550-630. Average SAT I Verbal 595, SAT I Verbal middle 50% range 550-640. Average ACT 24, ACT middle 50% range 22-26. TOEFL required of all international applicants, minimum TOEFL 550. **Basis for Candidate Selection:** *Very important factors considered include:* class rank, secondary school record, standardized test scores, state residency. *Important factors considered include:* essays, minority status, recommendations. *Other factors considered include:* character/personal qualities, extracurricular activities, geographical residence, talent/ability, volunteer work, work experience. **Freshman Admission Requirements:** High school diploma or GED is required. *Academic units required/recommended:* 20 total required; 4 English required, 3 math required, 4 math recommended, 3 science required, 4 science recommended, 3 science lab required, 2 foreign language required, 3 foreign language recommended, 3 social studies required, 2 history recommended, 4 elective required. **Freshman Admission Statistics:** 8,635 applied, 60% accepted, 39% of those accepted enrolled. **Transfer Admission Requirements:** *Items required:* college transcript. Minimum college GPA of 2.6 required. Lowest grade transferable C. **General Admission Information:** Application fee $35. Priority application deadline December 1. Regular application deadline April 1. Nonfall registration accepted. Admission may be deferred. Credit and/or placement offered for CEEB Advanced Placement tests.

COSTS AND FINANCIAL AID

In-state tuition $4,556. Out-of-state tuition $10,290. Room & board $5,661. Required fees $0. Average book expense $851. **Required Forms and Deadlines:** FAFSA. No deadline for regular filing. Priority filing deadline March 15. **Notification of Awards:** Applicants will be notified of awards on a rolling basis beginning on or about April 10. **Types of Aid:** *Need-based scholarships/grants:* Pell, SEOG, state scholarships/grants, private scholarships, the school's own gift aid. *Loans:* Direct Subsidized Stafford, Direct Unsubsidized Stafford, Direct PLUS, Federal Perkins. **Student Employment:** Federal Work-Study Program available. Institutional employment available. Off-campus job opportunities are good. **Financial Aid Statistics:** 36% freshmen, 34% undergrads receive some form of aid. Average freshman grant $1,500. Average freshman loan $2,625. Average income from on-campus job $1,935. **Financial Aid Phone:** 843-953-5540.

See page 984.

COLLEGE OF MOUNT SAINT JOSEPH

5701 Delhi Road, Cincinnati, OH 45233-1672
Phone: 513-244-4531 **E-mail:** peggy_minnich@mail.msj.edu **CEEB Code:** 1129
Fax: 513-244-4629 **Web:** www.msj.edu **ACT Code:** 3254

This private school, which is affiliated with the Roman Catholic Church, was founded in 1920. It has a 75-acre campus.

STUDENTS AND FACULTY

Enrollment: 1,842. **Student Body:** Male 31%, female 69%, out-of-state 12%, international 1% (13 countries represented). **Ethnic Representation:** African American 8%, Asian 1%, Caucasian 86%. **Retention and Graduation:** 75% freshmen return for sophomore year. 60% freshmen graduate within 4 years. 24% grads go on to further study within 1 year. **Faculty:** Student/faculty ratio 14:1. 119 full-time faculty, 57% hold PhDs. 99% faculty teach undergrads.

ACADEMICS

Degrees: Associate's, bachelor's, certificate, master's, post-bachelor's certificate, terminal. **Academic Requirements:** General education including some course work in arts/fine arts, computer literacy, English (including composition), foreign languages, history, humanities, mathematics, philosophy, sciences (biological or physical), social science, ethics, physical education. **Classes:** 10-19 students in an average class. 10-19 students in an average lab class. **Majors with Highest Enrollment:** Nursing/registered nurse training (RN, ASN, BSN, MSN); physical therapy/therapist; business administration/management. **Disciplines with Highest Percentage of Degrees Awarded:** Business/marketing 23%, health professions and related sciences 19%, visual and performing arts 13%, education 12%, social sciences and history 6%. **Special Study Options:** Accelerated program, cooperative (work-study) program, cross registration, distance learning, double major, English as a second language, honors program, independent study, internships, liberal arts/career combination, study abroad, teacher certification program, weekend college.

FACILITIES

Housing: Coed, apartments for single students. **Library Holdings:** 98,849 bound volumes. 429 periodicals. 376,991 microforms. 3,109 audiovisuals. **Special Academic Facilities/Equipment:** Art studio/gallery. **Computers:** *Recommended operating system:* Windows NT/2000. School-owned computers available for student use.

EXTRACURRICULARS

Activities: Choral groups, concert band, dance, drama/theater, jazz band, literary magazine, marching band, music ensembles, musical theater, pep band, student government, student newspaper, yearbook. **Organizations:** 36 registered organizations, 4 honor societies, 1 religious organization. **Athletics (Intercollegiate):** *Men:* baseball, basketball, cross-country, football, golf, soccer, tennis, wrestling. *Women:* basketball, cheerleading, cross-country, golf, soccer, softball, tennis, volleyball.

ADMISSIONS

Selectivity Rating: 73 (of 100). **Freshman Academic Profile:** Average high school GPA 3.2. 13% in top 10% of high school class, 38% in top 25% of high school class, 70% in top 50% of high school class. 64% from public high schools. Average SAT I Math 510, SAT I Math middle 50% range 440-580. Average SAT I Verbal 504, SAT I Verbal middle 50% range 440-550. Average ACT 21, ACT middle 50% range 18-23. TOEFL required of all international applicants, minimum TOEFL 500. **Basis for Candidate Selection:** *Very important factors considered include:* class rank, secondary school record, standardized test scores. *Other factors considered include:* alumni/ae relation, essays, extracurricular activities, recommendations, talent/ability. **Freshman Admission Requirements:** High school diploma or GED is required. *Academic units required/recommended:* 13 total required; 20 total recommended; 4 English required, 4 English recommended, 2 math required, 4 math recommended, 2 science required, 4 science recommended, 1 science lab required, 2 science lab recommended, 2 foreign language required, 4 foreign language recommended, 1 social studies required, 2 social studies recommended, 1 history required, 4 history recommended, 1 elective required, 4 elective recommended. **Freshman Admission Statistics:** 932 applied, 75% accepted, 50% of those accepted enrolled. **Transfer Admission Requirements:** *Items required:* high school transcript, college transcript. Minimum high school GPA of 2.3 required. Minimum college GPA of 2.0 required. Lowest grade transferable C. **General Admission Information:** Application fee $25. Priority application deadline April 1. Regular application deadline August 15. Nonfall registration accepted. Admission may be deferred for a maximum of 1 year. Credit and/or placement offered for CEEB Advanced Placement tests.

COSTS AND FINANCIAL AID

Tuition $14,200. Room & board $5,200. Required fees $90. Average book expense $600. **Required Forms and Deadlines:** FAFSA. No deadline for regular filing. Priority filing deadline March 1. **Notification of Awards:** Applicants will be notified of awards on a rolling basis beginning on or about February 15. **Types of Aid:** *Need-based scholarships/grants:* Pell, SEOG, state scholarships/grants, private scholarships, the school's own gift aid. *Loans:* FFEL Subsidized Stafford, FFEL Unsubsidized Stafford, FFEL PLUS, Federal Perkins, Federal Nursing, state loans. **Student Employment:** Federal Work-Study Program available. Institutional employment available. Off-campus job opportunities are excellent. **Financial Aid Statistics:** 70% freshmen, 65% undergrads receive some form of aid. Average freshman grant $6,955. Average freshman loan $4,975. **Financial Aid Phone:** 513-244-4418.

COLLEGE OF MOUNT SAINT VINCENT

6301 Riverdale Avenue, Riverdale, NY 10471
Phone: 718-405-3267 **E-mail:** admissns@mountsaintvincent.edu **CEEB Code:** 2088
Fax: 718-549-7945 **Web:** www.mountsaintvincent.edu

This private school, which is affiliated with the Roman Catholic Church, was founded in 1847. It has a 70-acre campus.

STUDENTS AND FACULTY

Enrollment: 1,205. **Student Body:** Male 23%, female 77%, out-of-state 7%, international 1%. **Ethnic Representation:** African American 17%, Asian 10%, Caucasian 36%, Hispanic 33%. **Retention and Graduation:** 75% freshmen return for sophomore year. 54% freshmen graduate within 4 years. 25% grads go on to further study within 1 year. 7% grads pursue business degrees. 3% grads pursue law degrees. 2% grads pursue medical degrees. **Faculty:** Student/faculty ratio 12:1. 69 full-time faculty, 89% hold PhDs. 100% faculty teach undergrads.

ACADEMICS

Degrees: Associate's, bachelor's, certificate, master's, post-master's certificate. **Academic Requirements:** General education including some course work in arts/fine arts, computer literacy, English (including composition), foreign languages, history, humanities, mathematics, philosophy, sciences (biological or physical), social science, world literature, 2 integrated courses. **Classes:** 10-19 students in an average class. 10-19 students in an average lab class. **Majors with Highest Enrollment:** Nursing/registered nurse training (RN, ASN, BSN, MSN); business administration/management; communications and media studies. **Disciplines with Highest Percentage of Degrees Awarded:** Health professions and related sciences 34%, business/marketing 14%, communications/communication technologies 12%, education 11%, social sciences and history 6%. **Special Study Options:** Accelerated program, cross registration, double major, honors program, independent study, internships, liberal arts/career combination, study abroad, teacher certification program.

FACILITIES

Housing: Coed, all-female, housing for disabled students. **Library Holdings:** 122,825 bound volumes. 727 periodicals. 9,852 microforms. 5,750 audiovisuals. **Special Academic Facilities/Equipment:** Nursing lab, language lab, TV studio, radio station, Elizabeth Seton Travelling Museum, electron microscope. **Computers:** School-owned computers available for student use.

EXTRACURRICULARS

Activities: Choral groups, dance, drama/theater, literary magazine, musical theater, radio station, student government, student newspaper, television station, yearbook. **Organizations:** 30 registered organizations, 15 honor societies, 1 religious organization. **Athletics (Intercollegiate):** *Men:* basketball, cross-country, lacrosse, soccer, tennis, volleyball. *Women:* basketball, cheerleading, cross-country, soccer, softball, swimming, tennis, track & field, volleyball.

ADMISSIONS

Selectivity Rating: 66 (of 100). **Freshman Academic Profile:** Average high school GPA 2.9. 15% in top 10% of high school class, 40% in top 25% of high school class, 73% in top 50% of high school class. Average SAT I Math 485, SAT I Math middle 50% range 430-530. Average SAT I Verbal 502, SAT I Verbal middle 50% range 450-540. TOEFL required of all international applicants, minimum TOEFL 500. **Basis for Candidate Selection:** *Very important factors considered include:* character/personal qualities, recommendations, secondary school record, standardized test scores. *Important factors considered include:* essays, extracurricular activities, interview. *Other factors considered include:* alumni/ae relation, class rank, volunteer work, work experience. **Freshman Admission Requirements:** High school diploma or GED is required. *Academic units required/recommended:* 16 total required; 20 total recommended; 4 English required, 2 math required, 3 math recommended, 2 science required, 3 science recommended, 2 foreign language required, 3 foreign language recommended, 3 social studies required, 4 social studies recommended, 3 elective required. **Freshman Admission Statistics:** 1,292 applied, 76% accepted, 34% of those accepted enrolled. **Transfer Admission Requirements:** *Items required:* college transcript, essay. Minimum college GPA of 2.0 required. Lowest grade transferable C. **General Admission Information:** Application fee $35. Early decision application deadline November 15. Nonfall registration accepted. Admission may be deferred for a maximum of 1 year. Credit and/or placement offered for CEEB Advanced Placement tests.

COSTS AND FINANCIAL AID

Tuition $17,880. Room & board $7,550. Required fees $360. Average book expense $800. **Required Forms and Deadlines:** FAFSA and state aid form. No deadline for regular filing. Priority filing deadline February 15. **Notification of Awards:** Applicants will be notified of awards on a rolling basis beginning on or about March 1. **Types of Aid:** *Need-based scholarships/grants:* Pell, SEOG, state scholarships/grants, private scholarships, the school's own gift aid. *Loans:* FFEL Subsidized Stafford, FFEL Unsubsidized Stafford, FFEL PLUS, Federal Perkins, Federal Nursing. **Student Employment:** Federal Work-Study Program available. Institutional employment available. Off-campus job opportunities are good. **Financial Aid Statistics:** 86% freshmen, 86% undergrads receive some form of aid. Average freshman grant $5,572. Average freshman loan $2,625. **Financial Aid Phone:** 718-405-3290.

THE COLLEGE OF NEW JERSEY

PO Box 7718, Ewing, NJ 08628-0718
Phone: 609-771-2131 **E-mail:** admiss@vm.tcnj.edu **CEEB Code:** 2519
Fax: 609-637-5174 **Web:** www.tcnj.edu **ACT Code:** 2614

This public school was founded in 1855. It has a 289-acre campus.

STUDENTS AND FACULTY

Enrollment: 5,961. **Student Body:** Male 41%, female 59%, out-of-state 5%, international students represent 17 countries. **Ethnic Representation:** African American 6%, Asian 5%, Caucasian 77%, Hispanic 6%. **Retention and Graduation:** 94% freshmen return for sophomore year. 54% freshmen graduate within 4 years. 25% grads go on to further study within 1 year. 7% grads pursue business degrees. 2% grads pursue law degrees. 1% grads pursue medical degrees. **Faculty:** Student/faculty ratio 13:1. 324 full-time faculty, 89% hold PhDs. 95% faculty teach undergrads.

ACADEMICS

Degrees: Bachelor's, master's, post-bachelor's certificate, post-master's certificate. **Academic Requirements:** General education including some course work in arts/fine arts, computer literacy, English (including composition), foreign languages, history, humanities, mathematics, philosophy, sciences (biological or physical), social science, 2-semester interdisciplinary core. **Classes:** 20-29 students in an average class. 20-29 students in an average lab class. **Majors with Highest Enrollment:** Elementary education and teaching; English language and literature, general; biology/biological sciences, general. **Disciplines with Highest Percentage of Degrees Awarded:** Education 30%, business/marketing 21%, English 11%, protective services/public administration 7%, biological life sciences 5%. **Special Study Options:** Double major, dual enrollment, student exchange program (domestic), honors program, independent study, internships, liberal arts/career combination, study abroad, teacher certification program.

FACILITIES

Housing: Coed, all-female, all-male, apartments for single students, housing for disabled students, housing for transfer students. **Library Holdings:** 550,000 bound volumes. 7,900 periodicals. 319,000 microforms. 4,000 audiovisuals. **Special Academic Facilities/Equipment:** Art gallery, observatory, scanning and transmission electron microscopes, concert hall. **Computers:** School-owned computers available for student use.

EXTRACURRICULARS

Activities: Choral groups, concert band, dance, drama/theater, jazz band, literary magazine, music ensembles, musical theater, opera, radio station, student government, student newspaper, symphony orchestra, television station, yearbook. **Organizations:** 186 registered organizations, 11 honor societies, 10 religious organizations, 13 fraternities (6% men join), 11 sororities (8% women join). **Athletics (Intercollegiate):** *Men:* baseball, basketball, cross-country, diving, football, golf, indoor track, soccer, swimming, tennis, track & field, wrestling. *Women:* basketball, cross-country, diving, field hockey, indoor track, lacrosse, soccer, softball, swimming, tennis, track & field.

ADMISSIONS

Selectivity Rating: 91 (of 100). **Freshman Academic Profile:** 61% in top 10% of high school class, 89% in top 25% of high school class, 98% in top 50% of high school class. 65% from public high schools. Average SAT I Math 630, SAT I Math middle 50% range 590-690. Average SAT I Verbal 610, SAT I Verbal middle 50% range 570-660. TOEFL required of all international applicants, minimum TOEFL 550. **Basis for Candidate Selection:** *Very important factors considered include:* class rank, secondary school record, standardized test scores. *Important factors considered include:* character/personal qualities, essays, talent/ability. *Other factors considered include:* extracurricular activities, minority status, recommendations. **Freshman Admission Requirements:** High school diploma or GED is required. *Academic units required/recommended:* 18 total required; 4 English required, 3 math required, 3 science required, 4 science recommended, 2 science lab required, 2 foreign language recommended, 2 social studies required, 3 social studies recommended. **Freshman Admission Statistics:** 6,323 applied, 48% accepted, 41% of those accepted enrolled. **Transfer Admission Requirements:** *Items required:* high school transcript, college transcript, essay, standardized test scores, statement of good standing from prior school. Minimum college GPA of 3.0 required. Lowest grade transferable C. **General Admission Information:** Application fee $50. Early decision application deadline November 15. Regular application deadline February 15. Nonfall registration accepted. Admission may be deferred for a maximum of 1 year. Credit and/or placement offered for CEEB Advanced Placement tests.

COSTS AND FINANCIAL AID

Out-of-state tuition $9,822. Room & board $7,416. Required fees $1,891. Average book expense $736. **Required Forms and Deadlines:** FAFSA. No deadline for regular filing. **Notification of Awards:** Applicants will be notified of awards on a rolling basis beginning on or about April 1. **Types of Aid:** *Need-based scholarships/grants:* Pell, SEOG, state scholarships/grants, private scholarships, the school's own gift aid, Federal Nursing. *Loans:* Direct Subsidized Stafford, Direct Unsubsidized Stafford, Direct PLUS, Federal Perkins, Federal Nursing, state loans. **Student Employment:** Federal Work-Study Program available. Institutional employment available. Off-campus job opportunities are good. **Financial Aid Statistics:** Average freshman grant $3,500. Average freshman loan $3,000. Average income from on-campus job $800. **Financial Aid Phone:** 609-771-2211.

See page 986.

THE COLLEGE OF NEW ROCHELLE

29 Castle Place, New Rochelle, NY 10805-2339
Phone: 914-654-5452 **E-mail:** admission@cnr.edu **CEEB Code:** 2089
Fax: 914-654-5464 **Web:** www.cnr.edu **ACT Code:** 2712

This private school, which is affiliated with the Roman Catholic Church, was founded in 1904. It has a 20-acre campus.

STUDENTS AND FACULTY

Enrollment: 951. **Student Body:** Male 5%, female 95%, out-of-state 11%, international students represent 6 countries. **Ethnic Representation:** African American 19%, Asian 2%, Caucasian 12%, Hispanic 8%. **Retention and Graduation:** 80% freshmen return for sophomore year. 24% freshmen graduate within 4 years. 15% grads go on to further study within 1 year. **Faculty:** Student/faculty ratio 10:1. 85 full-time faculty, 83% hold PhDs. 100% faculty teach undergrads.

ACADEMICS

Degrees: Bachelor's, master's, post-master's certificate. **Academic Requirements:** General education including some course work in arts/fine arts, English (including composition), foreign languages, history, humanities, mathematics, philosophy, sciences (biological or physical), social science. **Classes:** 20-29 students in an average class. 20-29 students in an average lab class. **Majors with Highest Enrollment:** Mass communications/media studies; nursing/registered nurse training (RN, ASN, BSN, MSN); psychology, general. **Disciplines with Highest Percentage of Degrees Awarded:** Health professions and related sciences 49%, psychology 16%, business/marketing 8%, English 7%, communications/communication technologies 5%. **Special Study Options:** Accelerated program, cooperative (work-study) program, cross registration, double major, student exchange program (domestic), honors program, independent study, internships, liberal arts/career combination, student-designed major, study abroad, teacher certification program.

FACILITIES

Housing: All-female. **Library Holdings:** 220,000 bound volumes. 1,400 periodicals. 3,417,044 microforms. 4,350 audiovisuals. **Special Academic Facilities/Equipment:** Art gallery, multimedia theatre/teleconference center, language lab, centers for media, computer studies, TV studio, learning center for women, learning center for nursing. **Computers:** School-owned computers available for student use.

EXTRACURRICULARS

Activities: Choral groups, dance, drama/theater, literary magazine, musical theater, student government, student newspaper, yearbook. **Organizations:** 26 registered organizations, 2 honor societies, 1 religious organization. **Athletics (Intercollegiate):** *Women:* basketball, softball, swimming, tennis, volleyball.

ADMISSIONS

Selectivity Rating: 67 (of 100). **Freshman Academic Profile:** Average high school GPA 2.8. 19% in top 10% of high school class, 38% in top 25% of high school class, 76% in top 50% of high school class. 76% from public high schools. Average SAT I Math 468, SAT I Math middle 50% range 420-500. Average SAT I Verbal 491, SAT I Verbal middle 50% range 440-530. Average ACT 19, ACT middle 50% range 15-20. TOEFL required of all international applicants, minimum TOEFL 550. **Basis for Candidate Selection:** *Very important factors considered include:* secondary school record. *Important factors considered include:* class rank, essays, standardized test scores. *Other factors considered include:* alumni/ae relation, character/personal qualities, extracurricular activities, interview, recommendations, talent/ability, volunteer work, work experience. **Freshman Admission Requirements:** High school diploma or GED is required. *Academic units required/recommended:* 16 total required; 4 English required, 4 English recommended, 3 math required, 3 math recommended, 3 science required, 3 science recommended, 2 science lab recommended, 2 foreign language recommended, 1 social studies required, 3 social studies recommended, 1 history required, 1 elective recommended. **Transfer Admission Requirements:** *Items required:* high school transcript, college transcript. Minimum high school GPA of 2.0 required. Lowest grade transferable C-. **General Admission Information:** Application fee $20. Priority application deadline March 30. Early decision application deadline November 1. Nonfall registration accepted. Admission may be deferred for a maximum of 1 year. Credit and/or placement offered for CEEB Advanced Placement tests.

COSTS AND FINANCIAL AID

Tuition $13,000. Room & board $6,850. Required fees $250. Average book expense $300. **Required Forms and Deadlines:** FAFSA and institution's own financial aid form. No deadline for regular filing. **Notification of Awards:** Applicants will be notified of awards on a rolling basis beginning on or about January 1. **Types of Aid:** *Need-based scholarships/grants:* Pell, SEOG, state scholarships/grants, private scholarships, the school's own gift aid. *Loans:* Direct Subsidized Stafford, Direct Unsubsidized Stafford, Direct PLUS, FFEL PLUS, Federal Perkins, Federal Nursing. **Student Employment:** Federal Work-Study Program available. Institutional employment available. Off-campus job opportunities are excellent. **Financial Aid Statistics:** 100% freshmen, 100% undergrads receive some form of aid. Average freshman grant $5,000. Average freshman loan $2,625. Average income from on-campus job $1,500. **Financial Aid Phone:** 914-654-5224.

See page 988.

COLLEGE OF NOTRE DAME OF MARYLAND

4701 North Charles Street, Baltimore, MD 21210
Phone: 410-532-5330 **E-mail:** admiss@ndm.edu **CEEB Code:** 5114
Fax: 410-532-6287 **Web:** www.ndm.edu **ACT Code:** 1727

This private school, which is affiliated with the Roman Catholic Church, was founded in 1896. It has a 58-acre campus.

STUDENTS AND FACULTY

Enrollment: 1,691. **Student Body:** Male 4%, female 96%, out-of-state 16%, international 2%. **Ethnic Representation:** African American 24%, Asian 3%, Caucasian 70%, Hispanic 2%. **Retention and Graduation:** 87% freshmen return for sophomore year. **Faculty:** Student/faculty ratio 13:1. 82 full-time faculty, 71% hold PhDs. 100% faculty teach undergrads.

ACADEMICS

Degrees: Bachelor's, master's, post-master's certificate. **Academic Requirements:** General education including some course work in arts/fine arts, English (including composition), foreign languages, history, mathematics, philosophy, sciences (biological or physical), social science, religious studies, physical education, and oral communication. **Classes:** 10-19 students in an average class. 10-19 students in an average lab class. **Majors with Highest Enrollment:** Business, management, marketing, and related support services; nursing/registered nurse training (RN, ASN, BSN, MSN); liberal arts and sciences/liberal studies. **Disciplines with Highest Percentage of Degrees Awarded:** Business/marketing 27%, interdisciplinary studies 13%, liberal arts/general studies 11%, health professions and related sciences 10%, computer and information sciences 7%. **Special Study Options:** Accelerated program, cross registration, double major, dual enrollment, English as a second language, student exchange program (domestic), honors program, independent study, internships, liberal arts/career combination, student-designed major, study abroad, teacher certification program, weekend college, Smart Start program for all new students to college that includes orientation programs and a first-semester seminar course for entering freshmen, career action plan for all students, and an academic consortium with 7 local colleges and universities.

FACILITIES

Housing: All-female. **Library Holdings:** 400,000 bound volumes. 1,800 periodicals. 27,000 audiovisuals. **Special Academic Facilities/Equipment:** Art gallery, photo labs, language labs, child care center, fitness center, television and radio studios, music practice labs, planetarium. **Computers:** School-owned computers available for student use.

EXTRACURRICULARS

Activities: Choral groups, dance, drama/theater, literary magazine, music ensembles, radio station, student government, student newspaper, yearbook. **Organizations:** 24 registered organizations, 7 honor societies. **Athletics (Intercollegiate):** *Women:* basketball, field hockey, lacrosse, soccer, swimming, tennis, volleyball.

ADMISSIONS

Selectivity Rating: 76 (of 100). **Freshman Academic Profile:** Average high school GPA 3.3. 26% in top 10% of high school class, 47% in top 25% of high school class, 77% in top 50% of high school class. 68% from public high schools. Average SAT I Math 520, SAT I Math middle 50% range 460-560. Average SAT I Verbal 535, SAT I Verbal middle 50% range 490-570. TOEFL required of all international applicants, minimum TOEFL 500. **Basis for Candidate Selection:** *Very important factors considered include:* essays, interview, recommendations, secondary school record, standardized test scores. *Important factors considered include:* extracurricular activities, talent/ability, volunteer work. *Other factors considered include:* alumni/ae relation, character/personal qualities, class rank, work experience. **Freshman Admission Requirements:** High school diploma or GED is required. *Academic units required/recommended:* 18 total required; 4 English required, 3 math required, 2 science required, 2 science lab required, 3 foreign language required, 2 history required, 4 elective required. **Freshman Admission Statistics:** 400 applied, 75% accepted, 51% of those accepted enrolled. **Transfer Admission Requirements:** *Items required:* college transcript, essay. Minimum college GPA of 2.5 required. Lowest grade transferable C. **General Admission Information:** Application fee $25. Priority application deadline February 15. Nonfall registration accepted. Admission may be deferred for a maximum of 1 year. Credit and/or placement offered for CEEB Advanced Placement tests.

COSTS AND FINANCIAL AID

Tuition $17,600. Room & board $7,400. Required fees $325. Average book expense $600. **Required Forms and Deadlines:** FAFSA and institution's own financial aid form. Priority filing deadline February 15. **Notification of Awards:** Applicants will be notified of awards on a rolling basis beginning on or about March 1. **Types of Aid:** *Need-based scholarships/grants:* Pell, SEOG, state scholarships/grants. *Loans:* Direct Subsidized Stafford, Direct Unsubsidized Stafford, Direct PLUS, Federal Perkins. **Student Employment:** Federal Work-Study Program available. Institutional employment available. Off-campus job opportunities are good. **Financial Aid Statistics:** 84% freshmen, 68% undergrads receive some form of aid. Average freshman loan $2,625. Average income from on-campus job $600. **Financial Aid Phone:** 410-532-5369.

See page 990.

COLLEGE OF ST. CATHERINE

2004 Randolph Avenue, Saint Paul, MN 55105
Phone: 651-690-8850 **E-mail:** admissions@stkate.edu **CEEB Code:** 6105
Fax: 651-690-8824 **Web:** www.stkate.edu **ACT Code:** 2096

This private school, which is affiliated with the Roman Catholic Church, was founded in 1905. It has a 110-acre campus.

STUDENTS AND FACULTY

Enrollment: 3,600. **Student Body:** Male 2%, female 98%, out-of-state 10%, international 2%. **Ethnic Representation:** African American 6%, Asian 5%, Caucasian 77%, Hispanic 2%, Native American 1%. **Retention and Graduation:** 76% freshmen return for sophomore year. 41% freshmen graduate within 4 years. 19% grads go on to further study within 1 year. 15% grads pursue business degrees. 7% grads pursue law degrees. 5% grads pursue medical degrees. **Faculty:** Student/faculty ratio 10:1. 184 full-time faculty, 73% hold PhDs. 100% faculty teach undergrads.

ACADEMICS

Degrees: Associate's, bachelor's, certificate, master's, post-bachelor's certificate. **Academic Requirements:** General education including some course work in arts/fine arts, computer literacy, English (including composition), foreign languages, history, mathematics, philosophy, sciences (biological or physical); 2 core classes: the reflective woman and global search for justice. **Classes:** 10-19 students in an average class. 10-19 students in an average lab class. **Disciplines with Highest Percentage of Degrees Awarded:** Health professions and related sciences 31%, education 18%, business/marketing 8%, English 7%, biological life sciences 5%. **Special Study Options:** Cooperative (work-study) program, cross registration, distance learning, double major, dual enrollment, student exchange program (domestic), honors program, independent study, internships, liberal arts/career combination, student-designed major, study abroad, teacher certification program, weekend college, cooperative program in fashion merchandising with Fashion Institute of Technology in New York City and Fashion Institute of Design in Los Angeles; exchange program with other Carondelet colleges; internship program includes over 500 sites in Twin Cities area.

FACILITIES

Housing: All-female, apartments for single students. **Library Holdings:** 263,495 bound volumes. 1,141 periodicals. 169,236 microforms. 13,627 audiovisuals. **Special Academic Facilities/Equipment:** Art gallery, theatre, recital hall, experimental psychology lab, language lab, observatory. **Computers:** School-owned computers available for student use.

EXTRACURRICULARS

Activities: Choral groups, concert band, dance, drama/theater, literary magazine, music ensembles, musical theater, student government, student newspaper, symphony orchestra. **Organizations:** 42 registered organizations, 24 honor societies, 5 religious organizations, 5 sororities. **Athletics (Intercollegiate):** *Women:* basketball, cross-country, diving, ice hockey, soccer, softball, swimming, tennis, track & field, volleyball.

ADMISSIONS

Selectivity Rating: 73 (of 100). **Freshman Academic Profile:** Average high school GPA 3.4. 26% in top 10% of high school class, 50% in top 25% of high school class, 82% in top 50% of high school class. 82% from public high schools. Average SAT I Math 572, SAT I Math middle 50% range 510-640. Average SAT I Verbal 542, SAT I Verbal middle 50% range 435-635. Average ACT 22, ACT middle 50% range 19-26. TOEFL required of all international applicants, minimum TOEFL 500. **Basis for Candidate Selection:** *Very important factors considered include:* secondary school record. *Important factors considered include:* class rank, essays, extracurricular activities, recommendations, standardized test scores. *Other factors considered include:* character/personal qualities, interview, minority status, talent/ability, volunteer work, work experience. **Freshman Admission Requirements:** High school diploma or GED is required. *Academic units required/recommended:* 19 total recommended; 4 English recommended, 3 math recommended, 2 science recommended, 4 foreign language recommended, 2 social studies recommended, 1 history recommended, 3 elective recommended. **Transfer Admission Requirements:** *Items required:* high school transcript, college transcript, statement of good standing from prior school. Minimum college GPA of 2.0 required. Lowest grade transferable C-. **General Admission Information:** Application fee $20. Priority application deadline August 15. Nonfall registration accepted. Admission may be deferred for a maximum of 1 year. Credit and/or placement offered for CEEB Advanced Placement tests.

COSTS AND FINANCIAL AID

Tuition $18,240. Room & board $5,170. Required fees $122. Average book expense $640. **Required Forms and Deadlines:** FAFSA and institution's own financial aid form. Priority filing deadline April 1. **Notification of Awards:** Applicants will be notified of awards on a rolling basis beginning on or about March 15. **Types of Aid:** *Need-based scholarships/grants:* Pell, SEOG, state scholarships/grants, private scholarships, the school's own gift aid. *Loans:* FFEL Subsidized Stafford, FFEL Unsubsidized Stafford, FFEL PLUS, Federal Perkins, Federal Nursing, state loans. **Student Employment:** Federal Work-Study Program available. Institutional employment available. Off-campus job opportunities are excellent. **Financial Aid Statistics:** 75% freshmen, 72% undergrads receive some form of aid. Average freshman grant $16,068. Average freshman loan $3,368. **Financial Aid Phone:** 651-690-6540.

COLLEGE OF SAINT ELIZABETH

Admissions Office, 2 Convent Road, Morristown, NJ 07960-6989
Phone: 973-290-4700 **E-mail:** apply@cse.edu **CEEB Code:** 2090
Fax: 973-290-4710 **Web:** www.cse.edu

This private school, which is affiliated with the Roman Catholic Church, was founded in 1899. It has a 200-acre campus.

STUDENTS AND FACULTY

Enrollment: 1,203. **Student Body:** Male 6%, female 94%, out-of-state 3%, international 3%. **Ethnic Representation:** African American 14%, Asian 5%, Caucasian 66%, Hispanic 13%. **Retention and Graduation:** 87% freshmen return for sophomore year. 60% freshmen graduate within 4 years. 21% grads go on to further study within 1 year. 6% grads pursue business degrees. 3% grads pursue medical degrees. **Faculty:** Student/faculty ratio 11:1. 58 full-time faculty, 79% hold PhDs. 83% faculty teach undergrads.

ACADEMICS

Degrees: Bachelor's, certificate, master's, post-bachelor's certificate, post-master's certificate. **Academic Requirements:** General education including some course work in arts/fine arts, English (including composition), foreign languages, history, humanities, mathematics, philosophy, sciences (biological or physical), social science, religious studies, fitness/wellness, and perspectives on an interdependent world. **Classes:** 10-19 students in an average class. 10-19 students in an average lab class. **Majors with Highest Enrollment:** Business administration/management; teacher education, multiple levels; psychology, general. **Disciplines with Highest Percentage of Degrees Awarded:** Business/marketing 39%, education 13%, psychology 9%, communications/communication technologies 7%, health professions and related sciences 5%. **Special Study Options:** Accelerated program, cross registration, distance learning, double major, dual enrollment, English as a second language, student exchange program (domestic), honors program, independent study, internships, student-designed major, study abroad, teacher certification program, weekend college.

FACILITIES

Housing: All-female. **Library Holdings:** 138,344 bound volumes. 718 periodicals. 120,741 microforms. 1,737 audiovisuals. **Computers:** *Recommended operating system:* Windows 98. School-owned computers available for student use.

EXTRACURRICULARS

Activities: Choral groups, drama/theater, literary magazine, music ensembles, student government, student newspaper, yearbook. **Organizations:** 28 registered organizations, 9 honor societies, 1 religious organization. **Athletics (Intercollegiate):** *Women:* basketball, equestrian, soccer, softball, swimming, tennis.

ADMISSIONS

Selectivity Rating: 72 (of 100). **Freshman Academic Profile:** Average high school GPA 3.0. 16% in top 10% of high school class, 32% in top 25% of high school class, 64% in top 50% of high school class. 68% from public high schools. Average SAT I Math 490, SAT I Math middle 50% range 410-510. Average SAT I Verbal 488, SAT I Verbal middle 50% range 410-520. TOEFL required of all international applicants, minimum TOEFL 500. **Basis for Candidate Selection:** *Very important factors considered include:* class rank, recommendations, secondary school record, standardized test scores. *Important factors considered include:* character/personal qualities. *Other factors considered include:* alumni/ae relation, essays, extracurricular activities, geographical residence, interview, talent/ability, volunteer work, work experience. **Freshman Admission Requirements:** High school diploma or GED is required. *Academic units required/recommended:* 16 total required; 16 total recommended; 3 English required, 4 English recommended, 2 math required, 3 math recommended, 1 science required, 2 science recommended, 2 foreign language required, 1 history required, 1 history recommended, 7 elective required. **Freshman Admission Statistics:** 445 applied, 81% accepted, 42% of those accepted enrolled. **Transfer Admission Requirements:** *Items required:* college transcript, essay, statement of good standing from prior school. Minimum college GPA of 2.0 required. Lowest grade transferable C. **General Admission Information:** Application fee $35. Priority application deadline March 1. Regular application deadline August 15. Nonfall registration accepted. Admission may be deferred for a maximum of 1 year. Credit and/or placement offered for CEEB Advanced Placement tests.

COSTS AND FINANCIAL AID

Average book expense $800. **Required Forms and Deadlines:** FAFSA. No deadline for regular filing. Priority filing deadline March 1. **Notification of Awards:** Applicants will be notified of awards on a rolling basis beginning on or about November 15. **Types of Aid:** *Need-based scholarships/grants:* Pell, SEOG, state scholarships/grants, private scholarships, the school's own gift aid. *Loans:* FFEL Subsidized Stafford, FFEL Unsubsidized Stafford, FFEL PLUS, Federal Perkins, state loans. **Student Employment:** Federal Work-Study Program available. Institutional employment available. Off-campus job opportunities are excellent. **Financial Aid Statistics:** 80% freshmen, 67% undergrads receive some form of aid. Average freshman grant $16,212. Average freshman loan $2,700. Average income from on-campus job $1,000. **Financial Aid Phone:** 973-290-4445.

COLLEGE OF ST. JOSEPH IN VERMONT

71 Clement Road, Rutland, VT 05701
Phone: 802-773-5900 **E-mail:** admissions@csj.edu **CEEB Code:** 3297
Fax: 802-773-5900 **Web:** www.csj.edu

This private school, which is affiliated with the Roman Catholic Church, was founded in 1956. It has a 90-acre campus.

STUDENTS AND FACULTY

Enrollment: 291. **Student Body:** Male 43%, female 57%, out-of-state 38%, international 1%. **Ethnic Representation:** African American 3%, Asian 1%, Caucasian 95%, Hispanic 1%. **Retention and Graduation:** 60% freshmen return for sophomore year. 33% freshmen graduate within 4 years. 5% grads go on to further study within 1 year. **Faculty:** Student/faculty ratio 11:1. 14 full-time faculty, 57% hold PhDs. 100% faculty teach undergrads.

ACADEMICS

Degrees: Associate's, bachelor's, diploma, master's, post-bachelor's certificate. **Academic Requirements:** General education including some course work in arts/fine arts, computer literacy, English (including composition), history, humanities, mathematics, sciences (biological or physical), social science. **Classes:** Under 10 students in an average class. **Majors with Highest Enrollment:** Psychology, general; elementary education and teaching; business administration/management. **Disciplines with Highest Percentage of Degrees Awarded:** Business/marketing 28%, education 11%, social sciences and history 6%, psychology 6%, communications/communication technologies 4%. **Special Study Options:** Accelerated program, double major, dual enrollment, independent study, internships, liberal arts/career combination, study abroad, teacher certification program.

FACILITIES

Housing: All-female, all-male. **Library Holdings:** 48,000 bound volumes. 281 periodicals. 16,000 microforms. 22,000 audiovisuals. **Special Academic Facilities/Equipment:** Theater and athletic center. **Computers:** *Recommended operating system:* Windows NT/2000. School-owned computers available for student use.

EXTRACURRICULARS

Activities: Choral groups, drama/theater, literary magazine, student government, student newspaper. **Organizations:** 20 registered organizations, 2 honor societies, 1 religious organization. **Athletics (Intercollegiate):** *Men:* basketball, soccer. *Women:* basketball, soccer, softball.

ADMISSIONS

Selectivity Rating: 70 (of 100). **Freshman Academic Profile:** 2% in top 10% of high school class, 21% in top 25% of high school class, 68% in top 50% of high school class. 50% from public high schools. Average SAT I Math 450, SAT I Math middle 50% range 390-520. Average SAT I Verbal 450, SAT I Verbal middle 50% range 420-530. TOEFL required of all international applicants, minimum TOEFL 500. **Basis for Candidate Selection:** *Very important factors considered include:* essays, secondary school record. *Important factors considered include:* extracurricular activities, interview, recommendations, standardized test scores. *Other factors considered include:* alumni/ae relation, character/personal qualities, class rank, talent/ability, volunteer work. **Freshman Admission Requirements:** High school diploma or GED is required. *Academic units required/recommended:* 16 total required; 4 English required, 3 math required, 2 science required, 2 foreign language recommended, 2 social studies required, 2 history required, 5 elective required. **Transfer Admission Requirements:** *Items required:* high school transcript, college transcript, essay. Minimum college GPA of 2.0 required. Lowest grade transferable C. **General Admission Information:** Application fee $25. Priority application deadline January 2. Nonfall registration accepted. Admission may be deferred for a maximum of 1 year. Credit and/or placement offered for CEEB Advanced Placement tests.

COSTS AND FINANCIAL AID

Tuition $12,000. Room & board $6,400. Required fees $200. Average book expense $600. **Required Forms and Deadlines:** FAFSA and institution's own financial aid form. No deadline for regular filing. **Notification of Awards:** Applicants will be notified of awards on a rolling basis beginning on or about March 15. **Types of Aid:** *Need-based scholarships/grants:* Pell, SEOG, state scholarships/grants, private scholarships, the school's own gift aid. *Loans:* FFEL Subsidized Stafford, FFEL Unsubsidized Stafford, FFEL PLUS, Federal Perkins. **Student Employment:** Federal Work-Study Program available. Institutional employment available. Off-campus job opportunities are good. **Financial Aid Statistics:** 77% freshmen, 83% undergrads receive some form of aid. Average freshman grant $6,857. Average freshman loan $2,798. **Financial Aid Phone:** 802-773-5900.

COLLEGE OF SAINT MARY

1901 South 72nd Street, Omaha, NE 68124
Phone: 402-399-2405 **E-mail:** enroll@csm.edu **CEEB Code:** 6106
Fax: 402-399-2412 **Web:** www.csm.edu **ACT Code:** 2440

This private school, which is affiliated with the Roman Catholic Church, was founded in 1923. It has a 25-acre campus.

STUDENTS AND FACULTY

Enrollment: 852. **Student Body:** Out-of-state 12%, international 1%. **Ethnic Representation:** African American 7%, Caucasian 89%, Hispanic 3%, Native American 1%. **Retention and Graduation:** 64% freshmen return for sophomore year. 30% freshmen graduate within 4 years. 16% grads go on to further study within 1 year. 2% grads pursue business degrees. 1% grads pursue law degrees. 1% grads pursue medical degrees. **Faculty:** Student/faculty ratio 14:1. 41 full-time faculty, 41% hold PhDs. 100% faculty teach undergrads.

ACADEMICS

Degrees: Associate's, bachelor's, certificate, post-bachelor's certificate, terminal, transfer. **Academic Requirements:** General education including some course work in arts/fine arts, computer literacy, English (including composition), history, mathematics, philosophy, sciences (biological or physical), social science. **Classes:** Under 10 students in an average class. Under 10 students in an average lab class. **Majors with Highest Enrollment:** Nursing/registered nurse training (RN, ASN, BSN, MSN); occupational therapy/therapist; business, management, marketing, and related support services. **Disciplines with Highest Percentage of Degrees Awarded:** Business/marketing 29%, health professions and related sciences 25%, computer and information sciences 12%, education 10%, law/legal studies 8%. **Special Study Options:** Accelerated program, cooperative (work-study) program, double major, independent study, internships, study abroad, teacher certification program, weekend college.

FACILITIES

Housing: All-female, housing for disabled students, women with children housing. **Library Holdings:** 63,088 bound volumes. 12,675 periodicals. 0 microforms. 1,371 audiovisuals. **Special Academic Facilities/Equipment:** Hillmer Art Gallery, Brigit Saint Brigit Theatre. **Computers:** School-owned computers available for student use.

EXTRACURRICULARS

Activities: Choral groups, drama/theater, student government, student newspaper. **Organizations:** 20 registered organizations, 2 honor societies, 2 religious organizations. **Athletics (Intercollegiate):** *Women:* basketball, cross-country, golf, soccer, softball, volleyball.

ADMISSIONS

Selectivity Rating: 67 (of 100). **Freshman Academic Profile:** Average high school GPA 3.3. 6% in top 10% of high school class, 33% in top 25% of high school class, 72% in top 50% of high school class. 74% from public high schools. Average ACT 21, ACT middle 50% range 19-23. TOEFL required of all international applicants, minimum TOEFL 550. **Basis for Candidate Selection:** *Very important factors considered include:* class rank, secondary school record, standardized test scores. *Other factors considered include:* alumni/ae relation, character/personal qualities, essays, extracurricular activities, recommendations, talent/ability, volunteer work. **Freshman Admission Requirements:** High school diploma or GED is required. *Academic units required/recommended:* 16 total required; 4 English required, 2 math required, 3 math recommended, 2 science required, 3 science recommended, 2 social studies required, 1 history recommended. **Freshman Admission Statistics:** 279 applied, 66% accepted, 52% of those accepted enrolled. **Transfer Admission Requirements:** *Items required:* high school transcript, college transcript. Minimum college GPA of 2.0 required. Lowest grade transferable C. **General Admission Information:** Application fee $25. Priority application deadline January 31. Nonfall registration accepted. Admission may be deferred for a maximum of 1 year. Credit offered for CEEB Advanced Placement tests.

COSTS AND FINANCIAL AID

Tuition $14,700. Room & board $5,100. Required fees $240. Average book expense $600. **Required Forms and Deadlines:** FAFSA. Financial aid filing deadline March 15. Priority filing deadline April 15. **Notification of Awards:** Applicants will be notified of awards on a rolling basis beginning on or about March 15. **Types of Aid:** *Need-based scholarships/grants:* Pell, SEOG, state scholarships/grants, private scholarships, the school's own gift aid. *Loans:* FFEL Subsidized Stafford, FFEL Unsubsidized Stafford, FFEL PLUS, Federal Perkins, Federal Nursing. **Student Employment:** Federal Work-Study Program available. Institutional employment available. Off-campus job opportunities are excellent. **Financial Aid Statistics:** 62% freshmen, 72% undergrads receive some form of aid. Average freshman grant $5,212. Average freshman loan $2,625. Average income from on-campus job $1,500. **Financial Aid Phone:** 402-399-2362.

THE COLLEGE OF SAINT ROSE

432 Western Avenue, Albany, NY 12203
Phone: 518-454-5150 **E-mail:** admit@mail.strose.edu
Fax: 518-454-2013 **Web:** www.strose.edu

This private school, which is affiliated with the Roman Catholic Church, was founded in 1920. It has a 25-acre campus.

STUDENTS AND FACULTY

Enrollment: 2,726. **Student Body:** Male 27%, female 73%, out-of-state 5%, international students represent 14 countries. **Ethnic Representation:** African American 3%, Asian 1%, Caucasian 85%, Hispanic 2%. **Retention and Graduation:** 87% freshmen return for sophomore year. 60% freshmen graduate within 4 years. 42% grads go on to further study within 1 year. **Faculty:** Student/faculty ratio 15:1. 147 full-time faculty, 75% hold PhDs. 96% faculty teach undergrads.

ACADEMICS

Degrees: Bachelor's, certificate, master's, post-bachelor's certificate, post-master's certificate. **Academic Requirements:** General education including some course work in arts/fine arts, computer literacy, English (including composition), foreign languages, history, humanities, mathematics, philosophy, sciences (biological or physical), social science. As part of the liberal education core, a writing requirement and a diversity requirement are required for all students. Students must also complete 2 credits in the area of wellness and physical education. **Classes:** 10-19 students in an average class. 10-19 students in an average lab class. **Disciplines with Highest Percentage of Degrees Awarded:** Education 43%, business/marketing 9%, communications/communication technologies 7%, psychology 7%, health professions and related sciences 7%. **Special Study Options:** Accelerated program, cross registration, double major, dual enrollment, student exchange program (domestic), independent study, internships, liberal arts/career combination, student-designed major, study abroad, teacher certification program.

FACILITIES

Housing: Coed, all-female, all-male, apartments for married students, apartments for single students; student rooms wired for computers and cable television services. **Library Holdings:** 200,987 bound volumes. 975 periodicals. 265,734 microforms. 1,089 audiovisuals. **Special Academic Facilities/Equipment:** The Picotte Hall Art Center houses the Saint Rose Art Gallery, the venue for student art shows and exhibits by acclaimed visiting artists, in addition to one of the largest screen printing facilities in the state of New York. The college's full-scale television studio is where communications students produce three 30-minute weekly television shows aired on Time Warner Cable. The music center features the Saints & Sinners Sound Studio, a 16-track professional recording studio, in addition to a music library. Athletic facilities include the college's new fitness center, competition-size pool, weight room, and regulation NCAA basketball court. The Hubbard Interfaith Sanctuary is home to campus ministry and hosts a variety of interfaith lectures, concerts, and poetry readings. With private meditation rooms and an indoor garden, this interreligious space provides a place to escape for a few minutes of quiet prayer. The Center for Cultural Diversity provides academic, social, and cultural support in an effort to enhance the quality of experiences for our diverse student population. **Computers:** School-owned computers available for student use.

EXTRACURRICULARS

Activities: Choral groups, drama/theater, jazz band, literary magazine, music ensembles, student government, student newspaper, yearbook. **Organizations:** 38 registered organizations, 6 honor societies, 1 religious organization. **Athletics (Intercollegiate):** *Men:* baseball, basketball, cross-country, golf, soccer, swimming. *Women:* basketball, cheerleading, cross-country, soccer, softball, swimming, volleyball.

ADMISSIONS

Selectivity Rating: 75 (of 100). **Freshman Academic Profile:** 14% in top 10% of high school class, 41% in top 25% of high school class, 76% in top 50% of high school class. 82% from public high schools. Average SAT I Math 533, SAT I Math middle 50% range 490-570. Average SAT I Verbal 542, SAT I Verbal middle 50% range 480-570. Average ACT 23, ACT middle 50% range 20-25. TOEFL required of all international applicants, minimum TOEFL 500. **Basis for Candidate Selection:** *Very important factors considered include:* secondary school record. *Important factors considered include:* character/personal qualities, class rank, recommendations, standardized test scores, talent/ability. *Other factors considered include:* alumni/ae relation, essays, extracurricular activities, geographical residence, interview, minority status, state residency, volunteer work, work experience. **Freshman Admission Requirements:** High school diploma or GED is required. *Academic units required/recommended:* 4 English required, 4 math required, 4 science required, 3 science lab required, 4 foreign language required, 4 social studies required, 4 history required. **Freshman Admission Statistics:** 1,606 applied, 75% accepted, 40% of those accepted enrolled. **Transfer Admission Requirements:** *Items required:* college transcript, essay. Minimum college GPA of 2.5 required. Lowest grade transferable C-. **General Admission Information:** Application fee $30. Priority application deadline February 1. Nonfall registration accepted. Admission may be deferred. Credit and/or placement offered for CEEB Advanced Placement tests.

COSTS AND FINANCIAL AID

Tuition $12,870. Room & board $6,550. Required fees $290. Average book expense $1,000. **Required Forms and Deadlines:** FAFSA and state aid form. Financial aid filing deadline October 1. Priority filing deadline March 1. **Notification of Awards:** Applicants will be notified of awards on a rolling basis beginning on or about March 15. **Types of Aid:** *Need-based scholarships/grants:* Pell, SEOG, state scholarships/grants, private scholarships, the school's own gift aid, and scholarships for talent, art, music, English, and Spanish. *Loans:* FFEL Subsidized Stafford, FFEL Unsubsidized Stafford, FFEL PLUS, Federal Perkins, Citibank CitiAssist loan, Educaid EXTRA Premier loans, Fleetbank Fleetfirst Education loan, First Marblehead Corporation Gate Family loan, Keybank Key alternative loan, Nellie Mae Excel Preferred Family Education loan. **Student Employment:** Federal Work-Study Program available. Institutional employment available. Off-campus job opportunities are excellent. **Financial Aid Statistics:** 83% freshmen, 80% undergrads receive some form of aid. Average freshman grant $5,084. Average freshman loan $3,190. Average income from on-campus job $800. **Financial Aid Phone:** 518-454-2013.

THE COLLEGE OF SAINT SCHOLASTICA

1200 Kenwood Avenue, Duluth, MN 55811-4199
Phone: 218-723-6046 **E-mail:** admissions@css.edu **CEEB Code:** 6107
Fax: 218-723-5991 **Web:** www.css.edu **ACT Code:** 2098

This private school, which is affiliated with the Roman Catholic Church, was founded in 1912. It has a 160-acre campus.

STUDENTS AND FACULTY

Enrollment: 1,981. **Student Body:** Male 30%, female 70%, out-of-state 11%, international 1%. **Ethnic Representation:** African American 1%, Asian 1%, Caucasian 90%, Hispanic 1%, Native American 2%. **Retention and Graduation:** 84% freshmen return for sophomore year. 49% freshmen graduate within 4 years. 40% grads go on to further study within 1 year. 1% grads pursue business degrees. 1% grads pursue law degrees. 1% grads pursue medical degrees. **Faculty:** Student/faculty ratio 13:1. 117 full-time faculty, 77% hold PhDs. 100% faculty teach undergrads.

ACADEMICS

Degrees: Bachelor's, master's, post-bachelor's certificate, post-master's certificate. **Academic Requirements:** General education including some course work in arts/fine arts, computer literacy, English (including composition), foreign languages, history, humanities, mathematics, philosophy, sciences (biological or physical), social science. **Classes:** 10-19 students in an average class. Under 10 students in an average lab class. **Majors with Highest Enrollment:** Nursing/registered nurse training (RN, ASN, BSN, MSN); business administration/management; educational/instructional media design. **Disciplines with Highest Percentage of Degrees Awarded:** Health professions and related sciences 35%, business/marketing 18%, education 8%, social sciences and history 7%, biological life sciences 6%. **Special Study Options:** Accelerated program, cross registration, distance learning, double major, dual enrollment, honors program, independent study, internships, liberal arts/career combination, student-designed major, study abroad, teacher certification program.

FACILITIES

Housing: Coed, apartments for single students, housing for disabled students, housing for international students, apartments for students with dependent children, quiet or study wings available. **Library Holdings:** 125,091 bound volumes. 1,135 periodicals. 1,795 microforms. 15,262 audiovisuals. **Computers:** School-owned computers available for student use.

EXTRACURRICULARS

Activities: Choral groups, concert band, dance, drama/theater, jazz band, literary magazine, music ensembles, pep band, student government, student newspaper, yearbook. **Organizations:** 52 registered organizations, 2 honor societies, 3 religious organizations. **Athletics (Intercollegiate):** *Men:* baseball, basketball, cross-country, ice hockey, soccer, tennis. *Women:* basketball, cross-country, soccer, softball, tennis, volleyball.

ADMISSIONS

Selectivity Rating: 72 (of 100). **Freshman Academic Profile:** Average high school GPA 3.5. 30% in top 10% of high school class, 60% in top 25% of high school class, 87% in top 50% of high school class. Average SAT I Math 572, SAT I Math middle 50% range 540-640. Average SAT I Verbal 585, SAT I Verbal middle 50% range 540-640. Average ACT 24, ACT middle 50% range 21-27. TOEFL required of all international applicants, minimum TOEFL 550. **Basis for Candidate Selection:** *Very important factors considered include:* secondary school record, standardized test scores. *Important factors considered include:* class rank. *Other factors considered include:* alumni/ae relation, character/personal qualities, essays, extracurricular activities, interview, recommendations, talent/ability, volunteer work, work experience. **Freshman Admission Requirements:** High school diploma or GED is required. *Academic units required/recommended:* 4 English recommended, 3 math recommended, 3 science recommended, 3 foreign language recommended, 2 social studies recommended, 2 history recommended. **Freshman Admission Statistics:** 1,055 applied, 88% accepted, 41% of those accepted enrolled. **Transfer Admission Requirements:** *Items required:* college transcript. Minimum college GPA of 2.0 required. Lowest grade transferable C. **General Admission Information:** Application fee $25. Priority application deadline June 1. Nonfall registration accepted. Admission may be deferred for a maximum of 1 year. Credit and/or placement offered for CEEB Advanced Placement tests.

COSTS AND FINANCIAL AID

Tuition $18,106. Room & board $5,406. Required fees $110. Average book expense $750. **Required Forms and Deadlines:** FAFSA and institution's own

financial aid form. No deadline for regular filing. Priority filing deadline March 15. **Notification of Awards:** Applicants will be notified of awards on a rolling basis beginning on or about March 1. **Types of Aid:** *Need-based scholarships/grants:* Pell, SEOG, state scholarships/grants, private scholarships, the school's own gift aid, Federal Nursing. *Loans:* FFEL Subsidized Stafford, FFEL Unsubsidized Stafford, FFEL PLUS, Federal Perkins, Federal Nursing, state loans, alternative loans. **Student Employment:** Federal Work-Study Program available. Institutional employment available. Off-campus job opportunities are good. **Financial Aid Statistics:** 85% freshmen, 84% undergrads receive some form of aid. Average freshman grant $6,342. Average freshman loan $2,278. Average income from on-campus job $1,782. **Financial Aid Phone:** 218-723-6047.

THE COLLEGE OF SAINT THOMAS MORE

3020 Lubbock, Fort Worth, TX 76109-2323
Phone: 817-923-8459 **E-mail:** more-info@cstm.edu
Fax: 817-924-3206 **Web:** www.cstm.edu

This private school, which is affiliated with the Roman Catholic Church, was founded in 1981.

STUDENTS AND FACULTY

Enrollment: 66. **Student Body:** Male 56%, female 44%, out-of-state 6%, international 2%. **Ethnic Representation:** African American 8%, Caucasian 38%, Hispanic 38%, Native American 8%. **Faculty:** Student/faculty ratio 4:1. 4 full-time faculty, 100% hold PhDs. 100% faculty teach undergrads.

ACADEMICS

Degrees: Bachelor's. **Academic Requirements:** General education including some course work in foreign languages, history, humanities, mathematics, philosophy, theology. **Special Study Options:** Foreign programs in Oxford, England; Rome; and Greece.

FACILITIES

Housing: All-female, all-male, apartments for married students, apartments for single students. **Library Holdings:** 11,798 bound volumes. 62 periodicals. 424 audiovisuals. **Computers:** *Recommended operating system:* Windows 95. School-owned computers available for student use.

EXTRACURRICULARS

Activities: Dance, student government, student-run film society. **Organizations:** 1 religious organization.

ADMISSIONS

Selectivity Rating: 63 (of 100). **Freshman Academic Profile:** 66% from public high schools. **Basis for Candidate Selection:** *Very important factors considered include:* character/personal qualities, essays, interview, recommendations, secondary school record, talent/ability. *Important factors considered include:* class rank, extracurricular activities, standardized test scores. *Other factors considered include:* religious affiliation/commitment, volunteer work, work experience. **Freshman Admission Requirements:** High school diploma or GED is required. *Academic units required/recommended:* 2 foreign language recommended. **Transfer Admission Requirements:** *Items required:* college transcript, essay, interview. Minimum high school GPA of 2.0 required. Minimum college GPA of 2.0 required. **General Admission Information:** Application fee $25. Priority application deadline December 1. Early decision application deadline December 1. Regular application deadline February 1. Nonfall registration accepted. Admission may be deferred for a maximum of 1 year.

COSTS AND FINANCIAL AID

Required fees $400. Average book expense $200. **Required Forms and Deadlines:** FAFSA. No deadline for regular filing. **Notification of Awards:** Applicants will be notified of awards on a rolling basis beginning on or about January 1. **Types of Aid:** *Need-based scholarships/grants:* state scholarships/grants, private scholarships, the school's own gift aid. *Loans:* Direct Subsidized Stafford, Direct Unsubsidized Stafford, Direct PLUS, FFEL Subsidized Stafford, FFEL Unsubsidized Stafford, FFEL PLUS. **Student Employment:** Institutional employment available. Off-campus job opportunities are excellent. **Financial Aid Statistics:** Average freshman grant $2,000. Average income from on-campus job $750. **Financial Aid Phone:** 817-923-8459.

COLLEGE OF SANTA FE

1600 St. Michaels Drive, Santa Fe, NM 87505-7634
Phone: 505-473-6133 **E-mail:** admissions@csf.edu **CEEB Code:** 4676
Fax: 505-473-6129 **Web:** www.csf.edu **ACT Code:** 2648

This private school was founded in 1874. It has a 100-acre campus.

STUDENTS AND FACULTY

Enrollment: 1,403. **Student Body:** Male 38%, female 62%, out-of-state 66%, international students represent 3 countries. **Ethnic Representation:** African American 2%, Asian 2%, Caucasian 60%, Hispanic 23%, Native American 3%. **Retention and Graduation:** 67% freshmen return for sophomore year. 26% freshmen graduate within 4 years. **Faculty:** Student/faculty ratio 8:1. 70 full-time faculty, 81% hold PhDs. 100% faculty teach undergrads.

ACADEMICS

Degrees: Associate's, bachelor's, master's, transfer. **Academic Requirements:** General education including some course work in arts/fine arts, English (including composition), humanities, mathematics, philosophy, sciences (biological or physical), social science. **Classes:** 10-19 students in an average class. 10-19 students in an average lab class. **Majors with Highest Enrollment:** Creative writing; drama and dramatics/theatre arts, general; film/cinema studies. **Disciplines with Highest Percentage of Degrees Awarded:** Visual and performing arts 28%, business/marketing 19%, computer and information sciences 16%, education 8%, psychology 6%. **Special Study Options:** Accelerated program, double major, student exchange program (domestic), independent study, internships, student-designed major, study abroad, teacher certification program.

FACILITIES

Housing: Coed, all-female, all-male, apartments for single students. **Library Holdings:** 128,982 bound volumes. 421 periodicals. 87,639 microforms. 10,082 audiovisuals. **Special Academic Facilities/Equipment:** Thaw Art History Library, Marion Center Photographic Library. **Computers:** School-owned computers available for student use.

EXTRACURRICULARS

Activities: Choral groups, dance, drama/theater, literary magazine, music ensembles, musical theater, student government, student newspaper. **Organizations:** 20 registered organizations, 1 honor society, 4 religious organizations. **Athletics (Intercollegiate):** *Men:* tennis. *Women:* tennis.

ADMISSIONS

Selectivity Rating: 84 (of 100). **Freshman Academic Profile:** Average high school GPA 3.2. 6% in top 10% of high school class, 25% in top 25% of high school class, 43% in top 50% of high school class. 68% from public high schools. Average SAT I Math 529, SAT I Math middle 50% range 480-580. Average SAT I Verbal 578, SAT I Verbal middle 50% range 520-640. Average ACT 23, ACT middle 50% range 21-25. TOEFL required of all international applicants, minimum TOEFL 550. **Basis for Candidate Selection:** *Very important factors considered include:* character/personal qualities, interview, secondary school record, talent/ability. *Important factors considered include:* class rank, essays, extracurricular activities, recommendations, standardized test scores, volunteer work. *Other factors considered include:* alumni/ae relation, geographical residence, minority status, state residency, work experience. **Freshman Admission Requirements:** High school diploma or GED is required. *Academic units required/recommended:* 18 total required; 22 total recommended; 4 English required, 4 English recommended, 2 math required, 3 math recommended, 2 science required, 3 science recommended, 2 science lab required, 2 science lab recommended, 2 foreign language recommended, 2 social studies required, 2 social studies recommended, 2 history recommended, 6 elective required. **Freshman Admission Statistics:** 489 applied, 83% accepted, 36% of those accepted enrolled. **Transfer Admission Requirements:** *Items required:* high school transcript, college transcript, essay. Lowest grade transferable C-. **General Admission Information:** Application fee $35. Priority application deadline March 15. Early decision application deadline November 15. Nonfall registration accepted. Admission may be deferred for a maximum of 1 year. Credit and/or placement offered for CEEB Advanced Placement tests.

COSTS AND FINANCIAL AID

Required fees $420. Average book expense $792. **Required Forms and Deadlines:** FAFSA and tax returns. No deadline for regular filing. Priority filing deadline March 15. **Notification of Awards:** Applicants will be notified of awards on a rolling basis beginning on or about March 1. **Types of Aid:** *Need-based scholarships/grants:* Pell, SEOG, state scholarships/grants, private scholarships, the school's own gift aid. *Loans:* FFEL Subsidized Stafford, FFEL

Unsubsidized Stafford, FFEL PLUS, Federal Perkins, state loans, college/university loans from institutional funds. **Student Employment:** Federal Work-Study Program available. Institutional employment available. Off-campus job opportunities are excellent. **Financial Aid Statistics:** 41% freshmen, 72% undergrads receive some form of aid. Average freshman grant $9,382. Average freshman loan $3,316. Average income from on-campus job $2,000. **Financial Aid Phone:** 505-473-6453.

COLLEGE OF THE ATLANTIC

105 Eden Street, Bar Harbor, ME 04609
Phone: 207-288-5015 **E-mail:** inquiry@ecology.coa.edu **CEEB Code:** 3305
Fax: 207-288-4126 **Web:** www.coa.edu **ACT Code:** 1637

This private school was founded in 1969. It has a 25-acre campus.

STUDENTS AND FACULTY

Enrollment: 278. **Student Body:** Male 36%, female 64%, out-of-state 60%, international 5% (9 countries represented). **Ethnic Representation:** Caucasian 23%. **Retention and Graduation:** 89% freshmen return for sophomore year. 53% freshmen graduate within 4 years. 25% grads go on to further study within 1 year. 1% grads pursue business degrees. 10% grads pursue law degrees. 2% grads pursue medical degrees. **Faculty:** Student/faculty ratio 10:1. 20 full-time faculty, 100% hold PhDs. 100% faculty teach undergrads.

ACADEMICS

Degrees: Bachelor's, master's. **Academic Requirements:** General education including some course work in arts/fine arts, English (including composition), history, humanities, mathematics, sciences (biological or physical). Human ecology core course required of all entering first-year students. Math and English competency required, or course completion. **Disciplines with Highest Percentage of Degrees Awarded:** Human ecology 100%. **Special Study Options:** Independent study, internships, liberal arts/career combination, student-designed major, study abroad, teacher certification program.

FACILITIES

Housing: Coed, housing for disabled students, housing for international students, substance-free housing. **Library Holdings:** 37,049 bound volumes. 469 periodicals. 37,000 microforms. 2,162 audiovisuals. **Special Academic Facilities/Equipment:** Natural history museum, pottery studio, greenhouse, geographical information systems lab. **Computers:** School-owned computers available for student use.

EXTRACURRICULARS

Activities: Choral groups, dance, drama/theater, jazz band, literary magazine, music ensembles, musical theater, student government, student newspaper, student-run film society. **Organizations:** 12 registered organizations. **Athletics (Intercollegiate):** *Men:* skiing (cross-country), sailing, soccer, volleyball. *Women:* skiing (cross-country), sailing, soccer, volleyball.

ADMISSIONS

Selectivity Rating: 85 (of 100). **Freshman Academic Profile:** 34% in top 10% of high school class, 73% in top 25% of high school class, 93% in top 50% of high school class. 67% from public high schools. Average SAT I Math 586, SAT I Math middle 50% range 550-640. Average SAT I Verbal 624, SAT I Verbal middle 50% range 570-670. Average ACT 28, ACT middle 50% range 25-29. TOEFL required of all international applicants, minimum TOEFL 550. **Basis for Candidate Selection:** *Very important factors considered include:* essays, extracurricular activities, interview, recommendations, secondary school record, volunteer work. *Important factors considered include:* character/personal qualities, talent/ability. *Other factors considered include:* alumni/ae relation, class rank, minority status, standardized test scores, work experience. **Freshman Admission Requirements:** High school diploma or GED is required. *Academic units required/recommended:* 15 total required; 19 total recommended; 4 English required, 4 math required, 2 science required, 3 science recommended, 2 science lab required, 2 foreign language recommended, 2 social studies required, 2 history recommended, 1 elective recommended. **Freshman Admission Statistics:** 282 applied, 71% accepted, 34% of those accepted enrolled. **Transfer Admission Requirements:** *Items required:* high school transcript, college transcript, essay. Minimum college GPA of 3.0 required. Lowest grade transferable C. **General Admission Information:** Application fee $45. Priority application deadline March 1. Early decision application deadline December 1. Regular application deadline March 1. Nonfall registration accepted. Admission may be deferred for a maximum of 1 year. Credit and/or placement offered for CEEB Advanced Placement tests.

COSTS AND FINANCIAL AID

Tuition $22,265. Room & board $6,087. Required fees $270. Average book expense $500. **Required Forms and Deadlines:** FAFSA, institution's own financial aid form, noncustodial (divorced/separated) parent's statement, and business/farm supplement. Financial aid filing deadline February 15. Priority filing deadline February 15. **Notification of Awards:** Applicants will be notified of awards on or about April 1. **Types of Aid:** *Need-based scholarships/grants:* Pell, SEOG, private scholarships, the school's own gift aid. *Loans:* Direct Subsidized Stafford, Direct Unsubsidized Stafford, Direct PLUS, Federal Perkins. **Student Employment:** Federal Work-Study Program available. Institutional employment available. Off-campus job opportunities are good. **Financial Aid Statistics:** 90% freshmen, 77% undergrads receive some form of aid. Average freshman grant $8,640. Average freshman loan $2,625. Average income from on-campus job $1,600. **Financial Aid Phone:** 207-288-5015.

COLLEGE OF THE HOLY CROSS

Admissions Office, 1 College Street, Worcester, MA 01610-2395
Phone: 508-793-2443 **E-mail:** admissions@holycross.edu **CEEB Code:** 3282
Fax: 508-793-3888 **Web:** www.holycross.edu **ACT Code:** 1810

This private school, which is affiliated with the Roman Catholic Church, was founded in 1843. It has a 174-acre campus.

STUDENTS AND FACULTY

Enrollment: 2,801. **Student Body:** Male 47%, female 53%, out-of-state 66%, international 1% (17 countries represented). **Ethnic Representation:** African American 3%, Asian 4%, Caucasian 79%, Hispanic 5%. **Retention and Graduation:** 96% freshmen return for sophomore year. 88% freshmen graduate within 4 years. 19% grads go on to further study within 1 year. 1% grads pursue business degrees. 8% grads pursue law degrees. 2% grads pursue medical degrees. **Faculty:** Student/faculty ratio 11:1. 236 full-time faculty, 94% hold PhDs. 100% faculty teach undergrads.

ACADEMICS

Degrees: Bachelor's. **Academic Requirements:** General education including some course work in arts/fine arts, foreign languages, history, mathematics, philosophy, sciences (biological or physical), social science, one course each in literature, studies in religion, and cross-cultural studies. **Classes:** 10-19 students in an average class. Under 10 students in an average lab class. **Majors with Highest Enrollment:** English language and literature, general; psychology, general; political science and government, general. **Disciplines with Highest Percentage of Degrees Awarded:** Social sciences and history 42%, English 17%, psychology 12%, biological life sciences 6%, foreign languages and literature 6%. **Special Study Options:** Accelerated program, cross registration, double major, dual enrollment, honors program, independent study, internships, liberal arts/career combination, student-designed major, study abroad, teacher certification program.

FACILITIES

Housing: Coed, housing for disabled students, on-campus suites for juniors and seniors, fit-for-life program house, apartment-style residence hall. **Library Holdings:** 584,883 bound volumes. 1,921 periodicals. 15,589 microforms. 24,933 audiovisuals. **Special Academic Facilities/Equipment:** Art gallery, concert hall, Taylor and Boody tracker organ, O'Callahan Science Library, multimedia resource center, wellness center, electron microscope, facilities for aquatic research. **Computers:** *Recommended operating system:* Windows XP, Windows 98, Mac 9, Mac X. School-owned computers available for student use.

EXTRACURRICULARS

Activities: Choral groups, dance, drama/theater, jazz band, literary magazine, marching band, music ensembles, musical theater, pep band, radio station, student government, student newspaper, yearbook. **Organizations:** 94 registered organizations, 15 honor societies. **Athletics (Intercollegiate):** *Men:* baseball, basketball, crew, cross-country, diving, football, golf, ice hockey, lacrosse, soccer, swimming, tennis, track & field. *Women:* basketball, crew, cross-country, diving, field hockey, golf, ice hockey, lacrosse, soccer, softball, swimming, tennis, track & field, volleyball.

ADMISSIONS

Selectivity Rating: 92 (of 100). **Freshman Academic Profile:** 59% in top 10% of high school class, 100% in top 50% of high school class. 42% from public high schools. Average SAT I Math 630, SAT I Math middle 50% range 590-670. Average SAT I Verbal 627, SAT I Verbal middle 50% range 570-650. TOEFL required of all international applicants, minimum TOEFL 550. **Basis for Candidate Selection:** *Very important factors considered include:* class rank, secondary school record, standardized test scores. *Important factors considered include:* alumni/ae relation, character/personal qualities, essays, extracurricular activities, interview, recommendations. *Other factors considered include:* geographical residence, minority status, talent/ability, volunteer work, work experience. **Freshman Admission Requirements:** High school diploma or GED is required. *Academic units required/recommended:* 20 total recommended; 4 English recommended, 4 math recommended, 4 science recommended, 3 foreign language recommended, 2 social studies recommended, 2 history recommended, 1 elective recommended. **Freshman Admission Statistics:** 4,884 applied, 43% accepted, 34% of those accepted enrolled. **Transfer Admission Requirements:** *Items required:* high school transcript, college transcript, essay, standardized test scores, statement of good standing from prior school. Minimum college GPA of 3.3 required. Lowest grade transferable C. **General Admission Information:** Application fee $50. Early decision application deadline December 15. Regular application deadline January 15. Nonfall registration accepted. Admission may be deferred for a maximum of 1 year. Credit and/or placement offered for CEEB Advanced Placement tests.

COSTS AND FINANCIAL AID

Tuition $27,560. Room & board $8,440. Required fees $451. Average book expense $400. **Required Forms and Deadlines:** FAFSA, CSS/Financial Aid PROFILE, noncustodial (divorced/separated) parent's statement, business/farm supplement, and parent and student federal tax returns. Financial aid filing deadline February 1. **Notification of Awards:** Applicants will be notified of awards on or about April 3. **Types of Aid:** *Need-based scholarships/grants:* Pell, SEOG, state scholarships/grants, private scholarships, the school's own gift aid. *Loans:* FFEL Subsidized Stafford, FFEL Unsubsidized Stafford, FFEL PLUS, Federal Perkins, MEFA. **Student Employment:** Federal Work-Study Program available. Institutional employment available. Off-campus job opportunities are good. **Financial Aid Statistics:** 53% freshmen, 50% undergrads receive some form of aid. Average freshman grant $13,433. Average freshman loan $3,904. Average income from on-campus job $601. **Financial Aid Phone:** 508-793-2265.

COLLEGE OF THE OZARKS

Office of Admissions, Point Lookout, MO 65726
Phone: 417-334-6411 **E-mail:** admiss4@cofo.edu **CEEB Code:** 6713
Fax: 417-335-2618 **Web:** www.cofo.edu **ACT Code:** 2364

This private school, which is affiliated with the Presbyterian Church, was founded in 1906. It has a 1,000-acre campus.

STUDENTS AND FACULTY

Enrollment: 1,348. **Student Body:** Male 43%, female 57%, out-of-state 33%, international 2%. **Ethnic Representation:** Caucasian 89%, Hispanic 1%, Native American 1%. **Retention and Graduation:** 94% freshmen return for sophomore year. 35% grads go on to further study within 1 year. 10% grads pursue business degrees. 1% grads pursue law degrees. 1% grads pursue medical degrees. **Faculty:** Student/faculty ratio 14:1. 73 full-time faculty, 63% hold PhDs. 100% faculty teach undergrads.

ACADEMICS

Degrees: Bachelor's. **Academic Requirements:** General education including some course work in arts/fine arts, English (including composition), history, humanities, mathematics, philosophy, sciences (biological or physical), social science. **Classes:** Under 10 students in an average class. 10-19 students in an average lab class. **Majors with Highest Enrollment:** Agricultural business and management, general; English/language arts teacher education; criminal justice/police science. **Disciplines with Highest Percentage of Degrees Awarded:** Business/marketing 19%, education 16%, psychology 10%, agriculture 9%, visual and performing arts 6%. **Special Study Options:** Accelerated program, double major, dual enrollment, honors program, independent study, internships, student-designed major, study abroad, teacher certification program.

FACILITIES

Housing: All-female, all-male. All full-time students must live in residence halls unless they meet one of the following criteria: 21 years of age or older, married, living with parents, or veteran of the armed forces. **Library Holdings:** 118,235 bound volumes. 503 periodicals. 30,604 microforms. 5,193 audiovisuals. **Special Academic Facilities/Equipment:** Ralph Foster Museum, Graham Clark Airport, Edwards Mill, Friendship House Restaurant, Fruitcake & Jelly Kitchen. **Computers:** *Recommended operating system:* Windows NT/2000. School-owned computers available for student use.

EXTRACURRICULARS

Activities: Choral groups, concert band, dance, drama/theater, jazz band, literary magazine, music ensembles, musical theater, pep band, radio station, student government, student newspaper, student-run film society, symphony orchestra, yearbook. **Organizations:** 46 registered organizations, 4 honor societies, 10 religious organizations. **Athletics (Intercollegiate):** *Men:* baseball, basketball, cheerleading. *Women:* basketball, cheerleading, volleyball.

ADMISSIONS

Selectivity Rating: 85 (of 100). **Freshman Academic Profile:** Average high school GPA 3.4. 11% in top 10% of high school class, 39% in top 25% of high school class, 82% in top 50% of high school class. Average ACT 22, ACT middle 50% range 17-26. TOEFL required of all international applicants, minimum TOEFL 550. **Basis for Candidate Selection:** *Very important factors considered include:* character/personal qualities, class rank, essays, extracurricular activities, interview, secondary school record. *Important factors considered include:* alumni/ae relation, recommendations, standardized test scores, talent/ability, volunteer work, work experience. *Other factors considered include:* geographical residence, minority status, religious affiliation/commitment, state residency. **Freshman Admission Requirements:** High school diploma or GED is required. *Academic units required/recommended:* 24 total recommended; 4 English recommended, 3 math recommended, 2 science recommended, 1 science lab recommended, 2 foreign language recommended, 3 social studies recommended. **Freshman Admission Statistics:** 2,417 applied, 12% accepted, 89% of those accepted enrolled. **Transfer Admission Requirements:** *Items required:* college transcript, essay, interview, statement of good standing from prior school. Minimum college GPA of 2.0 required. Lowest grade transferable C. **General Admission Information:** Priority application deadline February 15. Regular application deadline August 20. Nonfall registration accepted. Credit offered for CEEB Advanced Placement tests.

COSTS AND FINANCIAL AID

Tuition $0. Room & board $3,250. Required fees $250. Average book expense $600. **Required Forms and Deadlines:** FAFSA. Priority filing deadline March 15. **Notification of Awards:** Applicants will be notified of awards on or about July 1. **Types of Aid:** *Need-based scholarships/grants:* Pell, SEOG, state scholarships/grants, private scholarships, the school's own gift aid. **Student Employment:** Federal Work-Study Program available. Off-campus job opportunities are excellent. **Financial Aid Statistics:** 90% freshmen, 90% undergrads receive some form of aid. Average freshman grant $12,467. Average freshman loan $0. Average income from on-campus job $2,900. **Financial Aid Phone:** 417-334-6411.

COLLEGE OF THE SOUTHWEST

6610 Lovington Highway, Hobbs, NM 88240
Phone: 505-392-6561 **E-mail:** admissions@csw.edu **CEEB Code:** 4116
Fax: 505-392-6006 **Web:** www.csw.edu **ACT Code:** 2633

This private school was founded in 1962. It has a 162-acre campus.

STUDENTS AND FACULTY

Enrollment: 637. **Student Body:** Male 37%, female 63%, out-of-state 21%, international 1%. **Ethnic Representation:** African American 3%, Caucasian 71%, Hispanic 26%, Native American 1%. **Retention and Graduation:** 50% freshmen return for sophomore year. 19% freshmen graduate within 4 years. 30% grads go on to further study within 1 year. **Faculty:** Student/faculty ratio 11:1. 27 full-time faculty, 37% hold PhDs. 100% faculty teach undergrads.

ACADEMICS

Degrees: Bachelor's, master's. **Academic Requirements:** General education including some course work in arts/fine arts, computer literacy, English (including composition), history, humanities, mathematics, sciences (biological or physical), social science; must complete 6 semester hours of religion classes. **Classes:** Under 10 students in an average class. Under 10 students in an average lab class. **Majors with Highest Enrollment:** Elementary education and teaching; psychology, general; business administration/management. **Disciplines with Highest Percentage of Degrees Awarded:** Education 36%, psychology 20%, business/marketing 19%, liberal arts/general studies 9%, biological life sciences 3%. **Special Study Options:** Distance learning, teacher certification program.

FACILITIES

Housing: All-female, all-male. **Library Holdings:** 73,876 bound volumes. 302 periodicals. 21,515 microforms. 1,538 audiovisuals. **Computers:** School-owned computers available for student use.

EXTRACURRICULARS

Activities: Choral groups, drama/theater, literary magazine, student government, student newspaper, yearbook. **Organizations:** 2 honor societies, 1 religious organization. **Athletics (Intercollegiate):** *Men:* baseball, golf, soccer. *Women:* golf, soccer, volleyball.

ADMISSIONS

Selectivity Rating: 79 (of 100). **Freshman Academic Profile:** Average high school GPA 3.3. 2% in top 10% of high school class, 40% in top 25% of high school class, 86% in top 50% of high school class. Average SAT I Math 496, SAT I Math middle 50% range 400-610. Average SAT I Verbal 498, SAT I Verbal middle 50% range 450-580. Average ACT 20, ACT middle 50% range 17-23. TOEFL required of all international applicants, minimum TOEFL 550. **Basis for Candidate Selection:** *Very important factors considered include:* class rank, secondary school record, standardized test scores. *Important factors considered include:* extracurricular activities, interview, talent/ability. *Other factors considered include:* recommendations. **Freshman Admission Requirements:** High school diploma or GED is required. **Freshman Admission Statistics:** 102 applied, 49% accepted, 84% of those accepted enrolled. **Transfer Admission Requirements:** *Items required:* college transcript. Minimum college GPA of 2.0 required. Lowest grade transferable D. **General Admission Information:** Application fee $25. Regular application deadline August 20. Nonfall registration accepted. Credit offered for CEEB Advanced Placement tests.

COSTS AND FINANCIAL AID

Tuition $6,720. Room & board $4,900. Required fees $430. Average book expense $804. **Required Forms and Deadlines:** FAFSA and institution's own financial aid form. Financial aid filing deadline June 2. Priority filing deadline April 2. **Notification of Awards:** Applicants will be notified of awards on or about April 2. **Types of Aid:** *Need-based scholarships/grants:* Pell, SEOG, state scholarships/grants, private scholarships, the school's own gift aid. *Loans:* FFEL Subsidized Stafford, FFEL Unsubsidized Stafford, FFEL PLUS. **Student Employment:** Federal Work-Study Program available. Institutional employment available. Off-campus job opportunities are fair. **Financial Aid Statistics:** 97% freshmen, 98% undergrads receive some form of aid. Average freshman grant $6,636. Average freshman loan $1,634. Average income from on-campus job $1,405. **Financial Aid Phone:** 505-392-6561.

COLLEGE OF WILLIAM AND MARY

PO Box 8795, Williamsburg, VA 23187-8795
Phone: 757-221-4223 **E-mail:** admiss@wm.edu **CEEB Code:** 5115
Fax: 757-221-1242 **Web:** www.wm.edu **ACT Code:** 4344

This public school was founded in 1693. It has a 1,200-acre campus.

STUDENTS AND FACULTY

Enrollment: 5,694. **Student Body:** Male 44%, female 56%, out-of-state 34%, international 1% (73 countries represented). **Ethnic Representation:** African American 5%, Asian 7%, Caucasian 84%, Hispanic 3%. **Retention and Graduation:** 96% freshmen return for sophomore year. 31% grads go on to further study within 1 year. 5% grads pursue law degrees. 6% grads pursue medical degrees. **Faculty:** Student/faculty ratio 12:1. 567 full-time faculty, 91% hold PhDs. 63% faculty teach undergrads.

ACADEMICS

Degrees: Bachelor's, doctoral, first professional, master's. **Academic Requirements:** General education including some course work in arts/fine arts, computer literacy, English (including composition), foreign languages, history, humanities, mathematics, philosophy, sciences (biological or physical), social science. **Classes:** 10-19 students in an average class. **Majors with Highest Enrollment:** Business administration/management; English language and literature, general; psychology, general. **Disciplines with Highest Percentage of Degrees Awarded:** Social sciences and history 28%, business/marketing 16%, biological life sciences 9%, psychology 9%, English 9%. **Special Study Options:** Accelerated program, double major, dual enrollment, student exchange program (domestic), honors program, independent study, internships, student-designed major, study abroad, teacher certification program.

FACILITIES

Housing: Coed, all-female, all-male, fraternities and/or sororities. **Library Holdings:** 2,128,645 bound volumes. 11,313 periodicals. 2,346,524 microforms. 29,977 audiovisuals. **Special Academic Facilities/Equipment:** Art museum, language lab, greenhouse, herbarium, archaeological conservation lab, electron microscope, spectrometer, chromatograph, population ecology lab, marine sciences institute, rare books collection. **Computers:** School-owned computers available for student use.

EXTRACURRICULARS

Activities: Choral groups, concert band, dance, drama/theater, jazz band, literary magazine, music ensembles, musical theater, opera, pep band, radio station, student government, student newspaper, student-run film society, symphony orchestra, television station, yearbook. **Organizations:** 358 registered organizations, 28 honor societies, 28 religious organizations, 15 fraternities (31% men join), 12 sororities (33% women join). **Athletics (Intercollegiate):** *Men:* baseball, basketball, cheerleading, cross-country, diving, football, golf, gymnastics, soccer, swimming, tennis, track & field. *Women:* basketball, cheerleading, cross-country, diving, field hockey, golf, gymnastics, lacrosse, soccer, swimming, tennis, track & field, volleyball.

ADMISSIONS

Selectivity Rating: 94 (of 100). **Freshman Academic Profile:** 90% in top 10% of high school class, 99% in top 25% of high school class, 100% in top 50% of high school class. Average SAT I Math 666, SAT I Math middle 50% range 630-710. Average SAT I Verbal 669, SAT I Verbal middle 50% range 620-730. Average ACT 29, ACT middle 50% range 27-31. TOEFL required of all international applicants, minimum TOEFL 600. **Basis for Candidate Selection:** *Very important factors considered include:* secondary school record, state residency. *Important factors considered include:* alumni/ae relation, class rank, essays, extracurricular activities, standardized test scores. *Other factors considered include:* character/personal qualities, geographical residence, minority status, recommendations, talent/ability, volunteer work, work experience. **Freshman Admission Requirements:** High school diploma or equivalent is not required. *Academic units required/recommended:* 4 English recommended, 4 math recommended, 4 science recommended, 3 science lab recommended, 4 foreign language recommended, 4 social studies recommended. **Freshman Admission Statistics:** 8,917 applied, 35% accepted, 43% of those accepted enrolled. **Transfer Admission Requirements:** *Items required:* high school transcript, college transcript, essay, statement of good standing from prior school. Minimum college GPA of 3.0 required. Lowest grade transferable C-. **General Admission Information:** Application fee $40. Early decision application deadline November 1. Regular application deadline January 7. Nonfall registration accepted. Admission may be deferred for a maximum of 1 year. Credit and/or placement offered for CEEB Advanced Placement tests.

COSTS AND FINANCIAL AID

Required Forms and Deadlines: FAFSA, CSS/Financial Aid PROFILE and CSS/Financial Aid PROFILE (required of early decision applicants only). Financial aid filing deadline March 15. Priority filing deadline February 15. **Notification of Awards:** Applicants will be notified of awards on or about April 1. **Types of Aid:** *Need-based scholarships/grants:* Pell, SEOG, state scholarships/grants, private scholarships, the school's own gift aid. *Loans:* FFEL Subsidized Stafford, FFEL Unsubsidized Stafford, FFEL PLUS, Federal Perkins. **Student Employment:** Federal Work-Study Program available. Institutional employment available. Off-campus job opportunities are good. **Financial Aid Statistics:** 26% freshmen, 25% undergrads receive some form of aid. Average freshman grant $8,626. Average freshman loan $3,202. Average income from on-campus job $1,200. **Financial Aid Phone:** 757-221-2420.

THE COLLEGE OF WOOSTER

$$$

1189 Beall Ave., Wooster, OH 44691
Phone: 330-263-2322 **E-mail:** admissions@wooster.edu **CEEB Code:** 1134
Fax: 330-263-2621 **Web:** www.wooster.edu **ACT Code:** 3260

This private school was founded in 1866. It has a 240-acre campus.

STUDENTS AND FACULTY

Enrollment: 1,856. **Student Body:** Male 47%, female 53%, out-of-state 44%, international 7% (21 countries represented). **Ethnic Representation:** African American 5%, Asian 2%, Caucasian 88%, Hispanic 1%. **Retention and Graduation:** 86% freshmen return for sophomore year. 58% freshmen graduate within 4 years. 34% grads go on to further study within 1 year. 1% grads pursue business degrees. 4% grads pursue law degrees. 3% grads pursue medical degrees. **Faculty:** Student/faculty ratio 13:1. 133 full-time faculty, 95% hold PhDs. 100% faculty teach undergrads.

ACADEMICS

Degrees: Bachelor's. **Academic Requirements:** General education including some course work in arts/fine arts, English (including composition), foreign languages, global and cultural perspectives, history, humanities, mathematics, religous perspectives, sciences (biological or physical), social science. **Classes:** Under 10 students in an average class. 10-19 students in an average lab class. **Majors with Highest Enrollment:** History, general; English language and literature, general; communications studies/speech communication and rhetoric. **Disciplines with Highest Percentage of Degrees Awarded:** Social sciences and history 25%, communications/communication technologies 11%, English 11%, visual and performing arts 9%, biological life sciences 8%. **Special Study Options:** Double major, student exchange program (domestic), independent study, internships, student-designed major, study abroad, teacher certification program.

FACILITIES

Housing: Coed, all-female, all-male, fraternities and/or sororities, special housing for students participating in volunteer programs. **Library Holdings:** 581,518 bound volumes. 1,855 periodicals. 210,094 microforms. 12,416 audiovisuals. **Special Academic Facilities/Equipment:** Art museum, language lab, on-campus nursery school. **Computers:** School-owned computers available for student use.

EXTRACURRICULARS

Activities: Choral groups, concert band, dance, drama/theater, jazz band, literary magazine, marching band, music ensembles, musical theater, pep band, radio station, student government, student newspaper, student-run film society, symphony orchestra, yearbook. **Organizations:** 100 registered organizations, 13 honor societies, 10 religious organizations, 4 fraternities (7% men join), 6 sororities (8% women join). **Athletics (Intercollegiate):** *Men:* baseball, basketball, cross-country, diving, football, golf, indoor track, lacrosse, soccer, swimming, tennis, track & field. *Women:* basketball, cross-country, diving, field hockey, indoor track, lacrosse, soccer, softball, swimming, tennis, track & field, volleyball.

ADMISSIONS

Selectivity Rating: 80 (of 100). **Freshman Academic Profile:** Average high school GPA 3.5. 46% in top 10% of high school class, 71% in top 25% of high school class, 93% in top 50% of high school class. 73% from public high schools. Average SAT I Math 598, SAT I Math middle 50% range 550-650. Average SAT I Verbal 595, SAT I Verbal middle 50% range 550-650. Average ACT 26, ACT middle 50% range 23-29. TOEFL required of all international applicants, minimum TOEFL 550. **Basis for Candidate Selection:** *Very important factors considered include:* class rank, secondary school record. *Important factors considered include:* character/personal qualities, essays, recommendations, standardized test scores, talent/ability. *Other factors considered include:* alumni/ae relation, extracurricular activities, geographical residence, interview, minority status, state residency, volunteer work, work experience. **Freshman Admission Requirements:** High school diploma or GED is required. *Academic units required/recommended:* 4 English required, 3 math required, 4 math recommended, 3 science required, 4 science recommended, 2 foreign language required, 3 foreign language recommended, 3 social studies required, 4 social studies recommended, 2 elective required. **Freshman Admission Statistics:** 2,392 applied, 72% accepted, 30% of those accepted enrolled. **Transfer Admission Requirements:** *Items required:* high school transcript, college transcript, essay, standardized test scores, statement of good standing from prior school. Minimum college GPA of 2.5 required. Lowest grade transferable C. **General Admission Information:** Application fee $40. Early decision application deadline December 1. Regular application deadline February 15. Nonfall registration accepted. Admission may be deferred for a maximum of 1 year. Credit and/or placement offered for CEEB Advanced Placement tests.

COSTS AND FINANCIAL AID

Tuition $23,687. Room & board $5,960. Required fees $153. Average book expense $700. **Required Forms and Deadlines:** FAFSA, institution's own financial aid form, and CSS/Financial Aid PROFILE. No deadline for regular filing. Priority filing deadline February 15. **Notification of Awards:** Applicants will be notified of awards on or about April 1. **Types of Aid:** *Need-based scholarships/grants:* Pell, SEOG, state scholarships/grants, private scholarships, the school's own gift aid. *Loans:* Direct Subsidized Stafford, Direct Unsubsidized Stafford, Direct PLUS, Federal Perkins, college/university loans from institutional funds. **Student Employment:** Federal Work-Study Program available. Institutional employment available. Off-campus job opportunities are good. **Financial Aid Statistics:** 65% freshmen, 63% undergrads receive some form of aid. Average freshman grant $13,225. Average freshman loan $3,291. **Financial Aid Phone:** 800-877-3688.

COLLINS COLLEGE

1140 S. Priest Dr., Tempe, AZ 85281
Phone: 480-966-3000 **E-mail:** jen@alcollins.com
Fax: 480-966-2599 **Web:** www.collinscollege.edu/princeton/

STUDENTS AND FACULTY

Student Body: 20 countries represented. **Faculty:** Student/faculty ratio 24:1. 57 full-time faculty.

ACADEMICS

Degrees: Associate's, bachelor's, certificate. **Academic Requirements:** General education including some course work in arts/fine arts, computer literacy. **Special Study Options:** Honors program.

FACILITIES

Housing: Apartments for married students, apartments for single students. **Special Academic Facilities/Equipment:** Media studio, production center, library, student store, photo darkroom. **Computers:** School-owned computers available for student use.

ADMISSIONS

Selectivity Rating: 60 (of 100). **Basis for Candidate Selection:** *Factors considered include:* essays, secondary school record. **Freshman Admission Requirements:** High school diploma or GED is required. **Transfer Admission Requirements:** *Items required:* high school transcript, college transcript, essay. **General Admission Information:** Application fee $100. Nonfall registration accepted. Admission may be deferred.

COSTS AND FINANCIAL AID

Required fees $100. **Required Forms and Deadlines:** FAFSA. **Types of Aid:** *Need-based scholarships/grants:* Pell, SEOG. *Loans:* FFEL Subsidized Stafford, FFEL Unsubsidized Stafford, FFEL PLUS, Sallie Mae.

COLORADO CHRISTIAN UNIVERSITY

180 South Garrison Street, Lakewood, CO 80226
Phone: 303-963-3200 **E-mail:** admission@ccu.edu **CEEB Code:** 4659
Fax: 303-963-3201 **Web:** www.ccu.edu **ACT Code:** 523

This private school, which is affiliated with the Christian (Nondenominational) Church, was founded in 1914. It has a 26-acre campus.

STUDENTS AND FACULTY

Enrollment: 1,691. **Student Body:** Male 43%, female 57%, out-of-state 52%, international 1%. **Ethnic Representation:** African American 5%, Asian 1%, Caucasian 77%, Hispanic 6%, Native American 1%. **Retention and Graduation:** 66% freshmen return for sophomore year. 33% freshmen graduate within 4 years. **Faculty:** Student/faculty ratio 12:1. 56 full-time faculty. 100% faculty teach undergrads.

ACADEMICS

Degrees: Associate's, bachelor's, master's. **Academic Requirements:** General education including some course work in arts/fine arts, computer literacy, English (including composition), foreign languages, history, humanities, mathematics, philosophy, sciences (biological or physical), social science, 12 credits of biblical studies. **Classes:** 10-19 students in an average class. 10-19 students in an average lab class. **Majors with Highest Enrollment:** Management information systems, general; computer/information technology services administration and management; liberal arts and sciences/liberal studies. **Disciplines with Highest Percentage of Degrees Awarded:** Business/marketing 38%, computer and information sciences 36%, philosophy/religion/theology 6%, liberal arts/general studies 6%, psychology 3%. **Special Study Options:** Accelerated program, cooperative (work-study) program, distance learning, double major, honors program, independent study, internships, student-designed major, study abroad, teacher certification program, weekend college. Off-campus studies: American studies program (Washington DC); host university for Institute for Family Studies; China studies Program (various sites in China); Latin American studies program (Costa Rica); Los Angeles Film Studies Center; Middle East studies (Cairo, Egypt); Oxford honors program (University of Oxford, England); Russian studies program (various sites in Russia); Summer Institute of Journalism (Washington, DC).

FACILITIES

Housing: Coed, all-female, all-male, apartments for single students, housing for disabled students. **Special Academic Facilities/Equipment:** Music recording studio, electron microscope. **Computers:** School-owned computers available for student use.

EXTRACURRICULARS

Activities: Choral groups, concert band, drama/theater, jazz band, literary magazine, music ensembles, musical theater, student government, student newspaper, symphony orchestra. **Organizations:** 21 registered organizations, 3 honor societies, 14 religious organizations. **Athletics (Intercollegiate):** *Men:* basketball, cross-country, golf, soccer, tennis. *Women:* basketball, cross-country, soccer, tennis, volleyball.

ADMISSIONS

Selectivity Rating: 70 (of 100). **Freshman Academic Profile:** Average high school GPA 3.4. 22% in top 10% of high school class, 45% in top 25% of high school class, 76% in top 50% of high school class. Average SAT I Math 540, SAT I Math middle 50% range 490-580. Average SAT I Verbal 560, SAT I Verbal middle 50% range 520-600. Average ACT 24, ACT middle 50% range 20-26. TOEFL required of all international applicants, minimum TOEFL 500. **Basis for Candidate Selection:** *Very important factors considered include:* character/personal qualities, essays, religious affiliation/commitment, secondary school record, talent/ability, volunteer work. *Important factors considered include:* class rank, minority status, recommendations, standardized test scores. *Other factors considered include:* alumni/ae relation, extracurricular activities, interview, work experience. **Freshman Admission Requirements:** High school diploma or GED is required. *Academic units required/recommended:* 19 total recommended; 4 English recommended, 3 math recommended, 3 science recommended, 2 science lab recommended, 3 foreign language recommended, 1 social studies recommended, 2 history recommended. **Freshman Admission Statistics:** 896 applied, 58% accepted, 39% of those accepted enrolled. **Transfer Admission Requirements:** *Items required:* college transcript, essay, statement of good standing from prior school. Lowest grade transferable C. **General Admission Information:** Application fee $40. Priority application deadline March 1. Regular application deadline August 1. Nonfall registration accepted. Admission may be deferred for a maximum of 1 year. Credit and/or placement offered for CEEB Advanced Placement tests.

COSTS AND FINANCIAL AID

Tuition $15,040. Room & board $5,200. Required fees $0. Average book expense $1,000. **Required Forms and Deadlines:** FAFSA. No deadline for regular filing. Priority filing deadline March 15. **Notification of Awards:** Applicants will be notified of awards on a rolling basis beginning on or about April 1. **Types of Aid:** *Need-based scholarships/grants:* Pell, SEOG, private scholarships, the school's own gift aid. *Loans:* FFEL Subsidized Stafford, FFEL Unsubsidized Stafford, FFEL PLUS, Federal Perkins. **Student Employment:** Federal Work-Study Program available. Institutional employment available. Off-campus job opportunities are good. **Financial Aid Statistics:** 49% freshmen, 60% undergrads receive some form of aid. **Financial Aid Phone:** 303-963-3230.

COLORADO COLLEGE

14 East Cache la Poudre Street, Colorado Springs, CO 80903
Phone: 719-389-6344 **E-mail:** admission@coloradocollege.edu **CEEB Code:** 4072
Fax: 719-389-6816 **Web:** www.coloradocollege.edu **ACT Code:** 498

This private school was founded in 1874. It has a 90-acre campus.

STUDENTS AND FACULTY

Enrollment: 1,902. **Student Body:** Male 44%, female 56%, out-of-state 67%, international 3% (26 countries represented). **Ethnic Representation:** African American 2%, Asian 4%, Caucasian 79%, Hispanic 7%, Native American 1%. **Retention and Graduation:** 92% freshmen return for sophomore year. 77% freshmen graduate within 4 years. **Faculty:** Student/faculty ratio 9:1. 163 full-time faculty, 97% hold PhDs. 100% faculty teach undergrads.

ACADEMICS

Degrees: Bachelor's, master's. **Academic Requirements:** General education including some course work in foreign languages, humanities, sciences (biological or physical), social science. **Classes:** 10-19 students in an average class. **Majors with Highest Enrollment:** English language and literature, general; biology/biological sciences, general; economics, general. **Disciplines with Highest Percentage of Degrees Awarded:** Social sciences and history 32%, English 14%, biological life sciences 12%, physical sciences 10%, visual and performing arts 9%. **Special Study Options:** Double major, English as a second language, independent study, internships, liberal arts/career combination, student-designed major, study abroad, teacher certification program.

FACILITIES

Housing: Coed, all-female, all-male, apartments for single students, housing for international students, theme housing. **Library Holdings:** 535,657 bound volumes. 1,313 periodicals. 119,085 microforms. 21,419 audiovisuals. **Special Academic Facilities/Equipment:** Electronic music studio, telescope dome, multimedia computer laboratory, Balinese orchestras, Colorado Electronic Music Studio, observatory, extensive herbarium collection, 4 greenhouses, environmental science van equipped for field research, Fourier transform nuclear magnetic resonance spectrometer, 300-seat concert/lecture hall, photography darkrooms, 740-seat proscenium theatre, 100-seat experimental theatre, 4 dance studios, drama computer lab, petrographic microscopes, X-ray diffractometer, sedimentology lab, El Pomar Sports Center, metabolic equipment (COSMED Quark PFT Ergo), hydrostatic weighing equipment, cadaver study in sports science, scanning electron microscope, transmission electron microscope. **Computers:** School-owned computers available for student use.

EXTRACURRICULARS

Activities: Choral groups, concert band, dance, drama/theater, jazz band, literary magazine, music ensembles, radio station, student government, student newspaper, student-run film society, yearbook. **Organizations:** 92 registered organizations, 10 honor societies, 19 religious organizations, 3 fraternities (13% men join), 3 sororities (13% women join). **Athletics (Intercollegiate):** *Men:* basketball, cross-country, diving, football, ice hockey, lacrosse, soccer, swimming, tennis, track & field. *Women:* basketball, cross-country, diving, lacrosse, soccer, softball, swimming, tennis, track & field, volleyball.

ADMISSIONS

Selectivity Rating: 91 (of 100). **Freshman Academic Profile:** 42% in top 10% of high school class, 81% in top 25% of high school class, 96% in top 50% of high school class. 70% from public high schools. Average SAT I Math 625, SAT I Math middle 50% range 590-670. Average SAT I Verbal 622, SAT I Verbal middle 50% range 590-670. Average ACT 27, ACT middle 50% range 26-30. TOEFL required of all international applicants, minimum TOEFL 550. **Basis for Candidate Selection:** *Very important factors considered include:* secondary school record, standardized test scores. *Important factors considered include:* extracurricular activities, recommendations. *Other factors considered include:* alumni/ae relation, character/personal qualities, class rank, essays, geographical residence, interview, minority status, talent/ability, volunteer work, work experience. **Freshman Admission Requirements:** High school diploma or equivalent is not required. *Academic units required/recommended:* 16 total required; 18 total recommended. **Freshman Admission Statistics:** 3,411 applied, 53% accepted, 27% of those accepted enrolled. **Transfer Admission Requirements:** *Items required:* college transcript, essay, statement of good standing from prior school. Lowest grade transferable C. **General Admission Information:** Application fee $45. Regular application deadline January 15. Nonfall registration accepted. Admission may be deferred for a maximum of 1 year. Credit and/or placement offered for CEEB Advanced Placement tests.

COSTS AND FINANCIAL AID

Tuition $25,968. Room & board $6,480. Required fees $175. Average book expense $766. **Required Forms and Deadlines:** FAFSA, CSS/Financial Aid PROFILE, and noncustodial (divorced/separated) parent's statement. Financial aid filing deadline February 15. **Notification of Awards:** Applicants will be notified of awards on or about March 25. **Types of Aid:** *Need-based scholarships/grants:* Pell, SEOG, state scholarships/grants, private scholarships, the school's own gift aid. *Loans:* FFEL Subsidized Stafford, FFEL Unsubsidized Stafford, FFEL PLUS, Federal Perkins. **Student Employment:** Federal Work-Study Program available. Institutional employment available. Off-campus job opportunities are good. **Financial Aid Statistics:** 41% freshmen, 43% undergrads receive some form of aid. Average freshman grant $17,550. Average freshman loan $3,035. **Financial Aid Phone:** 719-389-6651.

COLORADO MOUNTAIN COLLEGE—ALPINE CAMPUS

Admissions Office, 1330 Bob Adams Drive, Steamboat Springs, CO 80487
Phone: 970-870-4417 **E-mail:** joinus@coloradomtn.edu **CEEB Code:** 4140
Fax: 970-947-8324 **ACT Code:** 499

This public school was founded in 1967.

STUDENTS AND FACULTY

Enrollment: 1,293. **Student Body:** Male 50%, female 50%. **Ethnic Representation:** African American 1%, Asian 1%, Caucasian 88%, Hispanic 3%, Native American 1%. **Faculty:** Student/faculty ratio 13:1. 18 full-time faculty, 16% hold PhDs. 100% faculty teach undergrads.

ACADEMICS

Degrees: Associate's, certificate, terminal, transfer. **Academic Requirements:** General education including some course work in arts/fine arts, computer literacy, English (including composition), humanities, mathematics, sciences (biological or physical), social science. **Special Study Options:** Distance learning, dual enrollment, honors program, independent study, internships, liberal arts/career combination, study abroad.

FACILITIES

Housing: Coed. **Computers:** School-owned computers available for student use.

EXTRACURRICULARS

Activities: Dance, drama/theater, student government. **Organizations:** 1 honor society. **Athletics (Intercollegiate):** *Men:* skiing (alpine), skiing (Nordic), soccer. *Women:* skiing (alpine), skiing (Nordic), soccer.

ADMISSIONS

Selectivity Rating: 63 (of 100). **Freshman Academic Profile:** TOEFL required of all international applicants, minimum TOEFL 500. **Basis for Candidate Selection:** *Other factors considered include:* class rank, secondary school record, standardized test scores. **Freshman Admission Requirements:** High school diploma or equivalent is not required. **Freshman Admission Statistics:** 374 applied, 100% accepted, 57% of those accepted enrolled. **Transfer Admission Requirements:** Lowest grade transferable C. **General Admission Information:** Nonfall registration accepted. Admission may be deferred for a maximum of 1 year. Credit offered for CEEB Advanced Placement tests.

COSTS AND FINANCIAL AID

In-state tuition $1,584. Out-of-state tuition $5,160. Room & board $5,000. Required fees $180. Average book expense $550. **Required Forms and Deadlines:** FAFSA. Priority filing deadline March 31. **Notification of Awards:** Applicants will be notified of awards on a rolling basis beginning on or about April 15. **Types of Aid:** *Need-based scholarships/grants:* Pell, SEOG, state scholarships/grants, private scholarships. *Loans:* FFEL Subsidized Stafford, FFEL Unsubsidized Stafford, FFEL PLUS. **Student Employment:** Federal Work-Study Program available. Institutional employment available. Off-campus job opportunities are excellent. **Financial Aid Phone:** 800-621-8559.

COLORADO MOUNTAIN COLLEGE—SPRING VALLEY

Admissions Office, 3000 County Rd. 114, Glenwood Springs, CO 81602
Phone: 970-947-8276 **E-mail:** joinus@coloradomtn.edu **CEEB Code:** 4112
Fax: 970-947-8324 **ACT Code:** 501

STUDENTS AND FACULTY

Enrollment: 827. **Student Body:** Male 40%, female 60%, out-of-state 15%. **Ethnic Representation:** Asian 1%, Caucasian 84%, Hispanic 4%, Native American 1%. **Faculty:** Student/faculty ratio 13:1. 24 full-time faculty, 25% hold PhDs. 100% faculty teach undergrads.

ACADEMICS

Degrees: Associate's, certificate, terminal, transfer. **Academic Requirements:** General education including some course work in arts/fine arts, computer literacy, humanities, mathematics, philosophy, sciences (biological or physical), social science. **Special Study Options:** Cooperative (work-study) program, distance learning, dual enrollment, internships, liberal arts/career combination, study abroad.

FACILITIES

Housing: Coed. **Special Academic Facilities/Equipment:** Vet tech farm, photo studio, graphic design lab.

EXTRACURRICULARS

Activities: Dance, drama/theater, student government. **Organizations:** 10 registered organizations, 1 honor society. **Athletics (Intercollegiate):** *Men:* skiing (alpine), skiing (Nordic), soccer. *Women:* skiing (alpine), skiing (Nordic), soccer.

ADMISSIONS

Selectivity Rating: 63 (of 100). **Freshman Academic Profile:** TOEFL required of all international applicants, minimum TOEFL 500. **Basis for Candidate Selection:** *Factors considered include:* class rank, secondary school record, standardized test scores. **Freshman Admission Requirements:** High school diploma or equivalent is not required. **Freshman Admission Statistics:** 557 applied, 100% accepted, 71% of those accepted enrolled. **Transfer Admission Requirements:** Lowest grade transferable C. **General Admission Information:** Nonfall registration accepted. Admission may be deferred for a maximum of 1 year. Credit offered for CEEB Advanced Placement tests.

COSTS AND FINANCIAL AID

In-state tuition $1,584. Out-of-state tuition $5,160. Room & board $5,000. Required fees $130. Average book expense $550. **Required Forms and Deadlines:** FAFSA. Priority filing deadline March 31. **Notification of Awards:** Applicants will be notified of awards on a rolling basis beginning on or about April 15. **Types of Aid:** *Need-based scholarships/grants:* Pell, SEOG, state scholarships/grants, private scholarships. *Loans:* FFEL Subsidized Stafford, FFEL Unsubsidized Stafford, FFEL PLUS. **Student Employment:** Federal Work-Study Program available. Institutional employment available. Off-campus job opportunities are excellent. **Financial Aid Phone:** 800-621-8559.

COLORADO MOUNTAIN COLLEGE—TIMBERLINE CAMPUS

Admissions Office, 901 South Hwy 24, Leadville, CO 80461
Phone: 719-486-4291 **E-mail:** joinus@coloradomtn.edu **CEEB Code:** 4113
Fax: 970-947-8324 **Web:** www.coloradomtn.edu **ACT Code:** 503

STUDENTS AND FACULTY

Enrollment: 1,090. **Student Body:** Male 48%, female 52%, out-of-state 30%. **Ethnic Representation:** Asian 1%, Caucasian 80%, Hispanic 15%. **Faculty:** Student/faculty ratio 13:1. 17 full-time faculty, 17% hold PhDs. 100% faculty teach undergrads.

ACADEMICS

Degrees: Associate's, certificate, terminal, transfer. **Academic Requirements:** General education including some course work in arts/fine arts, computer literacy, English (including composition), humanities, mathematics, sciences (biological or physical), social science. **Special Study Options:** Cooperative (work-study) program, distance learning, dual enrollment, internships, liberal arts/career combination, study abroad.

FACILITIES

Housing: Coed. **Special Academic Facilities/Equipment:** Greenhouse, Lab-Ski trails for labs. **Computers:** School-owned computers available for student use.

EXTRACURRICULARS

Athletics (Intercollegiate): *Men:* skiing (alpine), skiing (Nordic). *Women:* skiing (alpine), skiing (Nordic).

ADMISSIONS

Selectivity Rating: 63 (of 100). **Freshman Academic Profile:** TOEFL required of all international applicants. **Basis for Candidate Selection:** *Factors considered include:* class rank, secondary school record, standardized test scores. **Freshman Admission Requirements:** High school diploma or equivalent is not required. **Freshman Admission Statistics:** 202 applied, 100% accepted, 63% of those accepted enrolled. **Transfer Admission Requirements:** Lowest grade transferable C. **General Admission Information:** Nonfall registration accepted. Admission may be deferred for a maximum of 1 year. Credit offered for CEEB Advanced Placement tests.

COSTS AND FINANCIAL AID

In-state tuition $1,584. Out-of-state tuition $5,160. Room & board $5,000. Required fees $180. Average book expense $550. **Required Forms and Deadlines:** FAFSA. Priority filing deadline March 31. **Notification of Awards:** Applicants will be notified of awards on a rolling basis beginning on or about April 15. **Types of Aid:** *Need-based scholarships/grants:* Pell, SEOG, state scholarships/grants, private scholarships. *Loans:* FFEL Subsidized Stafford, FFEL Unsubsidized Stafford, FFEL PLUS. **Student Employment:** Federal Work-Study Program available. Institutional employment available. Off-campus job opportunities are good. **Financial Aid Phone:** 800-621-8559.

COLORADO SCHOOL OF MINES

Ben H. Parker Student Center, 1600 Maple Street, Golden, CO 80401
Phone: 303-273-3220 **E-mail:** admit@mines.edu **CEEB Code:** 4073
Fax: 303-273-3509 **Web:** www.mines.edu **ACT Code:** 500

This public school was founded in 1874. It has a 373-acre campus.

STUDENTS AND FACULTY

Enrollment: 2,504. **Student Body:** Male 76%, female 24%, out-of-state 21%, international 4% (62 countries represented). **Ethnic Representation:** African American 1%, Asian 6%, Caucasian 81%, Hispanic 7%, Native American 1%. **Retention and Graduation:** 30% freshmen graduate within 4 years. 14% grads go on to further study within 1 year. 2% grads pursue business degrees. 1% grads pursue law degrees. 1% grads pursue medical degrees. **Faculty:** Student/faculty ratio 12:1. 196 full-time faculty, 91% hold PhDs. 86% faculty teach undergrads.

ACADEMICS

Degrees: Bachelor's, doctoral, master's. **Academic Requirements:** General education including some course work in computer literacy, English (including composition), humanities, mathematics, sciences (biological or physical), social science. **Classes:** 10-19 students in an average class. 20-29 students in an average lab class. **Majors with Highest Enrollment:** Chemical engineering; mechanical engineering; mathematics, general. **Disciplines with Highest Percentage of Degrees Awarded:** Engineering/engineering technology 84%, computer and information sciences 7%, physical sciences 5%, business/marketing 3%, mathematics 1%. **Special Study Options:** Accelerated program, cooperative (work-study) program, double major, dual enrollment, English as a second language, honors program, independent study, internships, study abroad.

FACILITIES

Housing: Coed, all-male, apartments for married students, apartments for single students, fraternities and/or sororities. **Library Holdings:** 329,838 bound volumes. 1,910 periodicals. 260,038 microforms. 57 audiovisuals. **Special Academic Facilities/Equipment:** Geology museum, experimental mine, field camps, geophysical lab, energy research institute, other research institutes. **Computers:** *Recommended operating system:* UNIX. School-owned computers available for student use.

EXTRACURRICULARS

Activities: Choral groups, concert band, drama/theater, jazz band, literary magazine, marching band, music ensembles, musical theater, student government, student newspaper, symphony orchestra, yearbook. **Organizations:** 126 registered organizations, 7 honor societies, 5 religious organizations, 7 fraternities (20% men join), 4 sororities (20% women join). **Athletics (Intercollegiate):** *Men:* baseball, basketball, cross-country, diving, football, golf, soccer, swimming, tennis, track & field, wrestling. *Women:* basketball, cross-country, diving, golf, softball, swimming, track & field, volleyball.

ADMISSIONS

Selectivity Rating: 87 (of 100). **Freshman Academic Profile:** Average high school GPA 3.7. 47% in top 10% of high school class, 86% in top 25% of high school class, 100% in top 50% of high school class. 90% from public high schools. Average SAT I Math 650, SAT I Math middle 50% range 610-700. Average SAT I Verbal 590, SAT I Verbal middle 50% range 540-640. Average ACT 28, ACT middle 50% range 25-29. TOEFL required of all international applicants, minimum TOEFL 550. **Basis for Candidate Selection:** *Very important factors considered include:* class rank, secondary school record. *Important factors considered include:* standardized test scores. *Other factors considered include:* essays, extracurricular activities, interview, recommendations, talent/ability. **Freshman Admission Requirements:** High school diploma or GED is required. *Academic units required/recommended:* 16 total required; 4 English required, 4 math required, 3 science required, 3 science lab required, 2 foreign language recommended, 2 social studies required, 2 history recommended, 3 elective required. **Freshman Admission Statistics:** 2,720 applied, 67% accepted, 32% of those accepted enrolled. **Transfer Admission Requirements:** *Items required:* high school transcript, college transcript, statement of good standing from prior school. Minimum college GPA of 2.5 required. Lowest grade transferable C. **General Admission Information:** Application fee $45. Priority application deadline April 15. Regular application deadline June 1. Nonfall registration accepted. Admission may be deferred for a maximum of 1 year. Credit and/or placement offered for CEEB Advanced Placement tests.

COSTS AND FINANCIAL AID

In-state tuition $5,640. Out-of-state tuition $18,830. Room & board $6,100. Required fees $740. Average book expense $1,300. **Required Forms and Deadlines:** FAFSA. Priority filing deadline March 1. **Notification of Awards:** Applicants will be notified of awards on a rolling basis beginning on or about March 15. **Types of Aid:** *Need-based scholarships/grants:* Pell, SEOG, state scholarships/grants, private scholarships, the school's own gift aid. *Loans:* FFEL Subsidized Stafford, FFEL Unsubsidized Stafford, FFEL PLUS, Federal Perkins, college/university loans from institutional funds. **Student Employment:** Federal Work-Study Program available. Institutional employment available. Off-campus job opportunities are good. **Financial Aid Statistics:** 60% freshmen, 60% undergrads receive some form of aid. Average freshman grant $4,500. Average freshman loan $4,300. Average income from on-campus job $1,000. **Financial Aid Phone:** 303-273-3301.

COLORADO STATE UNIVERSITY

Spruce Hall, Fort Collins, CO 80523
Phone: 970-491-6909 **E-mail:** admissions@colostate.edu **CEEB Code:** 4075
Fax: 970-491-7799 **Web:** www.colostate.edu **ACT Code:** 504

This public school was founded in 1870. It has a 579-acre campus.

STUDENTS AND FACULTY

Enrollment: 21,677. **Student Body:** Male 49%, female 51%, out-of-state 20%, international 1%. **Ethnic Representation:** African American 2%, Asian 3%, Caucasian 85%, Hispanic 6%, Native American 1%. **Retention and Graduation:** 82% freshmen return for sophomore year. 31% freshmen graduate within 4 years. **Faculty:** Student/faculty ratio 17:1. 860 full-time faculty, 99% hold PhDs.

ACADEMICS

Degrees: Bachelor's, doctoral, first professional, master's. **Academic Requirements:** General education including some course work in arts/fine arts, English (including composition), humanities, mathematics, sciences (biological or physical), social science, health/wellness, critical thinking. **Classes:** 10-19 students in an average class. 20-29 students in an average lab class. **Majors with Highest Enrollment:** Business administration/management; kinesiology and exercise science; journalism. **Disciplines with Highest Percentage of Degrees Awarded:** Business/marketing 16%, engineering/engineering technology 10%, biological life sciences 8%, social sciences and history 8%, home economics and vocational home economics 8%. **Special Study Options:** Accelerated program, cooperative (work-study) program, distance learning, double major, dual enrollment, English as a second language, student exchange program (domestic), honors program, independent study, internships, liberal arts/career combination, study abroad, teacher certification program.

FACILITIES

Housing: Coed, apartments for married students, apartments for single students, housing for disabled students, housing for international students, fraternities and/or sororities. **Library Holdings:** 1,882,297 bound volumes. 20,712 periodicals. 2,520,216 microforms. 31,850 audiovisuals. **Special Academic Facilities/Equipment:** International poster collection, Gustafson Gallery of Historic Clothing, student recreation center, ropes course. **Computers:** School-owned computers available for student use.

EXTRACURRICULARS

Activities: Choral groups, concert band, dance, drama/theater, jazz band, literary magazine, marching band, music ensembles, musical theater, opera, pep band, radio station, student government, student newspaper, symphony orchestra, television station, yearbook. **Organizations:** 300 registered organizations, 43 honor societies, 23 religious organizations, 20 fraternities (8% men join), 15 sororities (8% women join). **Athletics (Intercollegiate):** *Men:* basketball, cross-country, football, golf, track & field. *Women:* basketball, cross-country, diving, golf, softball, swimming, tennis, track & field, volleyball.

ADMISSIONS

Selectivity Rating: 73 (of 100). **Freshman Academic Profile:** Average high school GPA 3.5. 22% in top 10% of high school class, 53% in top 25% of high school class, 90% in top 50% of high school class. Average SAT I Math 559, SAT I Math middle 50% range 500-610. Average SAT I Verbal 548, SAT I Verbal middle 50% range 500-600. Average ACT 24, ACT middle 50% range 22-26. TOEFL required of all international applicants, minimum TOEFL 525. **Basis for Candidate Selection:** *Very important factors considered include:* class rank, secondary school record, standardized test scores. *Important factors considered include:* essays, recommendations. *Other factors considered include:* alumni/ae relation, character/personal qualities, extracurricular activities, geographical residence, interview, minority status, state residency, talent/ability, volunteer work, work experience. **Freshman Admission Requirements:** High school diploma or GED is required. *Academic units required/recommended:* 15 total required; 18 total recommended; 4 English required, 3 math required, 4 math recommended, 2 science required, 3 science recommended, 1 science lab recommended, 2 foreign language required, 3 social studies required. **Freshman Admission Statistics:** 12,249 applied, 77% accepted, 40% of those accepted enrolled. **Transfer Admission Requirements:** *Items required:* college transcript. Minimum college GPA of 2.0 required. Lowest grade transferable C. **General Admission Information:** Application fee $30. Regular application deadline July 1. Nonfall registration accepted. Admission may be deferred. Credit and/or placement offered for CEEB Advanced Placement tests.

COSTS AND FINANCIAL AID

In-state tuition $2,655. Out-of-state tuition $11,925. Required fees $780. Average book expense $900. **Required Forms and Deadlines:** FAFSA. Priority filing deadline March 1. **Notification of Awards:** Applicants will be notified of awards on a rolling basis beginning on or about March 1. **Types of Aid:** *Need-based scholarships/grants:* Pell, SEOG, state scholarships/grants, private scholarships, the school's own gift aid. *Loans:* Direct Subsidized Stafford, Direct Unsubsidized Stafford, Direct PLUS, Federal Perkins, college/university loans from institutional funds, alternative loans. **Student Employment:** Federal Work-Study Program available. Institutional employment available. Off-campus job opportunities are good. **Financial Aid Statistics:** 39% freshmen, 39% undergrads receive some form of aid. **Financial Aid Phone:** 970-491-6321.

COLORADO TECHNICAL UNIVERSITY

4435 North Chestnut Street, Colorado Springs, CO 80907-3896
Phone: 719-598-0200 **E-mail:** cosadmissions@coloradotech.edu **CEEB Code:** 4133
Fax: 719-598-3740 **Web:** www.colotechu.edu **ACT Code:** 515

This proprietary school was founded in 1965. It has a 13-acre campus.

STUDENTS AND FACULTY

Enrollment: 1,297. **Student Body:** International 1%. **Ethnic Representation:** African American 8%, Asian 4%, Caucasian 73%, Hispanic 6%. **Retention and Graduation:** 15% grads go on to further study within 1 year. 10% grads pursue business degrees. **Faculty:** Student/faculty ratio 25:1. 31 full-time faculty, 51% hold PhDs. 100% faculty teach undergrads.

ACADEMICS

Degrees: Associate's, bachelor's, certificate, doctoral, master's, transfer. **Academic Requirements:** General education including some course work in computer literacy, mathematics, sciences (biological or physical). **Classes:** 10-19 students in an average class. **Majors with Highest Enrollment:** Information technology; management information systems, general; computer science. **Disciplines with Highest Percentage of Degrees Awarded:** Business/marketing 36%, computer and information sciences 34%, engineering/engineering technology 25%, communications/communication technologies 5%. **Special Study Options:** Accelerated program, double major, independent study, internships, weekend college, 16.5-month MS degree programs, and 2-year doctoral programs.

FACILITIES

Library Holdings: 28,000 bound volumes. 350 periodicals. 25,000 microforms. 500 audiovisuals. **Computers:** School-owned computers available for student use.

EXTRACURRICULARS

Activities: Student government. **Organizations:** 5 registered organizations, 1 honor society.

ADMISSIONS

Selectivity Rating: 76 (of 100). **Freshman Academic Profile:** Average SAT I Math 582. Average SAT I Verbal 498. Average ACT 24. TOEFL required of all international applicants, minimum TOEFL 550. **Basis for Candidate Selection:** *Factors considered include:* alumni/ae relation, character/personal qualities, class rank, interview, recommendations, secondary school record, standardized test scores, work experience. **Freshman Admission Requirements:** High school diploma or GED is required. *Academic units required/recommended:* 1 English required, 2 English recommended, 1 math required, 2 math recommended, 1 science required, 2 science recommended, 1 science lab required, 1 science lab recommended. **Transfer Admission Requirements:** *Items required:* high school transcript, college transcript, statement of good standing from prior school. Lowest grade transferable C. **General Admission Information:** Application fee $50. Regular application deadline October 2. Nonfall registration accepted. Credit and/or placement offered for CEEB Advanced Placement tests.

COSTS AND FINANCIAL AID

Required fees $171. Average book expense $1,000. **Required Forms and Deadlines:** FAFSA, institution's own financial aid form, and state aid form. No deadline for regular filing. **Notification of Awards:** Applicants will be notified of awards on a rolling basis beginning on or about February 1. **Types of Aid:** *Need-based scholarships/grants:* Pell, SEOG, state scholarships/grants. *Loans:* FFEL Subsidized Stafford, FFEL Unsubsidized Stafford, FFEL PLUS, Federal Perkins. **Student Employment:** Federal Work-Study Program available. Institutional employment available. Off-campus job opportunities are excellent. **Financial Aid Statistics:** Average freshman grant $3,500. Average freshman loan $758. **Financial Aid Phone:** 719-598-0200.

COLUMBIA COLLEGE (MO)

1001 Rogers St., Columbia, MO 65216
Phone: 573-875-7352 **E-mail:** admissions@email.ccis.edu **CEEB Code:** 6095
Fax: 573-875-7506 **Web:** www.ccis.edu **ACT Code:** 2276

This private school, which is affiliated with the Disciples of Christ Church, was founded in 1851. It has a 27-acre campus.

STUDENTS AND FACULTY

Enrollment: 855. **Student Body:** Male 43%, female 57%, out-of-state 5%, international 7% (30 countries represented). **Ethnic Representation:** African American 5%, Asian 1%, Caucasian 87%, Hispanic 2%, Native American 1%. **Retention and Graduation:** 61% freshmen return for sophomore year. 24% freshmen graduate within 4 years. **Faculty:** Student/faculty ratio 12:1. 51 full-time faculty, 90% hold PhDs. 100% faculty teach undergrads.

ACADEMICS

Degrees: Associate's, bachelor's, master's, terminal, transfer. **Academic Requirements:** General education including some course work in computer literacy, English (including composition), history, humanities, mathematics, sciences (biological or physical), social science. **Classes:** Under 10 students in an average class. 10-19 students in an average lab class. **Majors with Highest Enrollment:** Business administration/management; education, general; criminal justice/law enforcement administration. **Disciplines with Highest Percentage of Degrees Awarded:** Business/marketing 24%, liberal arts/general studies 24%, education 19%, visual and performing arts 9%, protective services/public administration 7%. **Special Study Options:** Accelerated program, cooperative (work-study) program, cross registration, distance learning, double major, dual enrollment, English as a second language, honors program, independent study, internships, student-designed major, study abroad, teacher certification program.

FACILITIES

Housing: Coed, all-female. **Library Holdings:** 62,331 bound volumes. 444 periodicals. 16,588 microforms. 3,152 audiovisuals. **Special Academic Facilities/Equipment:** Arts center, cultural arts center, Larson Gallery, Jane Froman Archive. **Computers:** *Recommended operating system:* Windows XP. School-owned computers available for student use.

EXTRACURRICULARS

Activities: Choral groups, literary magazine, pep band, student government, student newspaper. **Organizations:** 35 registered organizations, 9 honor societies. **Athletics (Intercollegiate):** *Men:* basketball, soccer. *Women:* basketball, softball, volleyball.

ADMISSIONS

Selectivity Rating: 63 (of 100). **Freshman Academic Profile:** Average high school GPA 3.1. 11% in top 10% of high school class, 31% in top 25% of high

school class, 61% in top 50% of high school class. 90% from public high schools. Average SAT I Math 270, SAT I Math middle 50% range 540-700. Average SAT I Verbal 570, SAT I Verbal middle 50% range 560-690. Average ACT 22, ACT middle 50% range 19-24. TOEFL required of all international applicants, minimum TOEFL 500. **Basis for Candidate Selection:** *Very important factors considered include:* class rank, secondary school record, standardized test scores. *Other factors considered include:* extracurricular activities, interview, recommendations. **Freshman Admission Requirements:** High school diploma or GED is required. *Academic units required/recommended:* 11 total required; 4 English required, 3 math required, 2 science required, 2 social studies required. **Freshman Admission Statistics:** 707 applied, 56% accepted, 42% of those accepted enrolled. **Transfer Admission Requirements:** *Items required:* college transcript. Minimum college GPA of 2.0 required. Lowest grade transferable C. **General Admission Information:** Application fee $25. Nonfall registration accepted. Admission may be deferred for a maximum of 1 year. Credit offered for CEEB Advanced Placement tests.

COSTS AND FINANCIAL AID

Tuition $10,506. Room & board $4,576. Required fees $0. Average book expense $800. **Required Forms and Deadlines:** FAFSA and institution's own financial aid form. No deadline for regular filing. Priority filing deadline March 15. **Notification of Awards:** Applicants will be notified of awards on a rolling basis. **Types of Aid:** *Need-based scholarships/grants:* Pell, SEOG, state scholarships/grants, private scholarships, the school's own gift aid. *Loans:* Direct Subsidized Stafford, Direct Unsubsidized Stafford, Direct PLUS, Federal Perkins, college/university loans from institutional funds. **Student Employment:** Federal Work-Study Program available. Institutional employment available. Off-campus job opportunities are excellent. **Financial Aid Statistics:** 56% freshmen, 52% undergrads receive some form of aid. Average freshman grant $4,797. Average freshman loan $2,584. Average income from on-campus job $1,811. **Financial Aid Phone:** 573-875-7361.

COLUMBIA COLLEGE (SC)

1301 Columbia College Drive, Columbia, SC 29203
Phone: 803-786-3871 **E-mail:** admissions@colacoll.edu **CEEB Code:** 5117
Fax: 803-786-3674 **Web:** www.colacoll.edu. **ACT Code:** 3850

This private school, which is affiliated with the Methodist Church, was founded in 1854. It has a 33-acre campus.

STUDENTS AND FACULTY

Enrollment: 1,242. **Student Body:** Male 0%, female 100%, out-of-state 4%, international students represent 4 countries. **Ethnic Representation:** African American 38%, Asian 1%, Caucasian 61%, Hispanic 1%. **Retention and Graduation:** 78% freshmen return for sophomore year. 15% grads go on to further study within 1 year. **Faculty:** 98% faculty teach undergrads.

ACADEMICS

Degrees: Bachelor's, master's. **Academic Requirements:** General education including some course work in arts/fine arts, English (including composition), foreign languages, history, humanities, mathematics, sciences (biological or physical), social science. **Special Study Options:** Cross registration, distance learning, double major, dual enrollment, honors program, independent study, internships, student-designed major, study abroad, teacher certification program.

FACILITIES

Housing: All-female, special programs: leadership, honors program. **Library Holdings:** 94,976 bound volumes. 645 periodicals. 12,027 microforms. 8,123 audiovisuals. **Special Academic Facilities/Equipment:** Language lab, alumnae hall, Barbara Bush Center for Science and Technology, Breed Leadership Center for Women. **Computers:** *Recommended operating system:* Windows 3x. School-owned computers available for student use.

EXTRACURRICULARS

Activities: Choral groups, dance, drama/theater, literary magazine, music ensembles, student government, student newspaper, yearbook. **Organizations:** 27 registered organizations, 10 honor societies. **Athletics (Intercollegiate):** *Women:* football, golf, tennis, volleyball.

ADMISSIONS

Selectivity Rating: 74 (of 100). **Freshman Academic Profile:** Average high school GPA 3.3. 27% in top 10% of high school class, 69% in top 25% of high school class, 88% in top 50% of high school class. Average SAT I Math 497, SAT I Math middle 50% range 480-550. Average SAT I Verbal 522, SAT I Verbal middle 50% range 490-580. Average ACT 23. TOEFL required of all international applicants, minimum TOEFL 550. **Basis for Candidate Selection:** *Very important factors considered include:* secondary school record, standardized test scores. *Important factors considered include:* recommendations, talent/ability. *Other factors considered include:* alumni/ae relation, character/personal qualities, class rank, essays, extracurricular activities, interview. **Freshman Admission Requirements:** High school diploma or GED is required. *Academic units required/recommended:* 4 English recommended, 3 math recommended, 3 science recommended, 2 foreign language recommended, 2 social studies recommended, 1 history recommended. **Freshman Admission Statistics:** 903 applied, 77% accepted, 39% of those accepted enrolled. **Transfer Admission Requirements:** *Items required:* college transcript, statement of good standing from prior school. Minimum college GPA of 2.0 required. **General Admission Information:** Application fee $20. Priority application deadline March 15. Regular application deadline August 10. Nonfall registration accepted. Admission may be deferred for a maximum of 1 year. Credit and/or placement offered for CEEB Advanced Placement tests.

COSTS AND FINANCIAL AID

Tuition $13,200. Room & board $4,500. Required fees $200. Average book expense $300. **Required Forms and Deadlines:** FAFSA. No deadline for regular filing. Priority filing deadline April 1. **Notification of Awards:** Applicants will be notified of awards on a rolling basis beginning on or about March 1. **Types of Aid:** *Need-based scholarships/grants:* Pell, SEOG, state scholarships/grants, private scholarships, the school's own gift aid. *Loans:* FFEL Subsidized Stafford, FFEL Unsubsidized Stafford, FFEL PLUS, Federal Perkins, state loans. **Student Employment:** Federal Work-Study Program available. Institutional employment available. Off-campus job opportunities are excellent. **Financial Aid Statistics:** Average freshman grant $8,360. Average freshman loan $3,755. Average income from on-campus job $700. **Financial Aid Phone:** 803-786-3612.

COLUMBIA COLLEGE CHICAGO

600 South Michigan Avenue, Chicago, IL 60605-1996
Phone: 312-344-7130 **E-mail:** admissions@colum.edu **CEEB Code:** 1135
Fax: 312-344-8024 **Web:** www.colum.edu **ACT Code:** 1002

This private school was founded in 1890.

STUDENTS AND FACULTY

Enrollment: 9,257. **Student Body:** Male 49%, female 51%, out-of-state 22%, international 3%. **Ethnic Representation:** African American 17%, Asian 4%, Caucasian 65%, Hispanic 10%, Native American 1%. **Retention and Graduation:** 9% grads go on to further study within 1 year. 1% grads pursue law degrees. 1% grads pursue medical degrees. **Faculty:** Student/faculty ratio 13:1. 269 full-time faculty. 100% faculty teach undergrads.

ACADEMICS

Degrees: Bachelor's, master's, post-bachelor's certificate. **Academic Requirements:** General education including some course work in arts/fine arts, computer literacy, English (including composition), history, humanities, mathematics, sciences (biological or physical), social science. **Classes:** 10-19 students in an average class. **Majors with Highest Enrollment:** Cinematography and film/video production; fine/studio arts, general; arts management. **Disciplines with Highest Percentage of Degrees Awarded:** Visual and performing arts 32%, liberal arts/general studies 25%, communications/ communication technologies 21%, business/marketing 17%, English 3%. **Special Study Options:** English as a second language, independent study, internships, liberal arts/career combination, student-designed major, study abroad, teacher certification program.

FACILITIES

Housing: Coed. **Library Holdings:** 219,952 bound volumes. 1,150 periodicals. **Special Academic Facilities/Equipment:** Art galleries, center for Black music research, contemporary photography museum, dance center.

EXTRACURRICULARS

Activities: Choral groups, dance, drama/theater, jazz band, literary magazine, music ensembles, musical theater, radio station, student government, student newspaper, television station. **Organizations:** 30 registered organizations.

ADMISSIONS

Selectivity Rating: 67 (of 100). **Freshman Academic Profile:** 38% in top 25% of high school class, 69% in top 50% of high school class. 82% from public high schools. Average ACT 20, ACT middle 50% range 17-23. TOEFL required of all international applicants, minimum TOEFL 500. **Basis for Candidate**

Selection: *Very important factors considered include:* essays. *Important factors considered include:* recommendations, talent/ability. *Other factors considered include:* character/personal qualities, class rank, extracurricular activities, interview, secondary school record, standardized test scores, volunteer work, work experience. **Freshman Admission Requirements:** High school diploma or GED is required. *Academic units required/recommended:* 4 English recommended, 2 math recommended, 3 science recommended, 3 social studies recommended, 3 history recommended. **Freshman Admission Statistics:** 3,199 applied, 90% accepted, 59% of those accepted enrolled. **Transfer Admission Requirements:** *Items required:* high school transcript, college transcript, essay. Lowest grade transferable C. **General Admission Information:** Application fee $25. Priority application deadline August 15. Nonfall registration accepted. Admission may be deferred for a maximum of 1 year. Credit and/or placement offered for CEEB Advanced Placement tests.

COSTS AND FINANCIAL AID

Tuition $13,714. Required fees $390. Average book expense $828. **Required Forms and Deadlines:** FAFSA and institution's own financial aid form. No deadline for regular filing. Priority filing deadline August 15. **Notification of Awards:** Applicants will be notified of awards on a rolling basis. **Types of Aid:** *Need-based scholarships/grants:* Pell, SEOG, state scholarships/grants, private scholarships, the school's own gift aid. *Loans:* Direct Subsidized Stafford, Direct Unsubsidized Stafford, Direct PLUS. **Student Employment:** Federal Work-Study Program available. Institutional employment available. Off-campus job opportunities are excellent. **Financial Aid Phone:** 312-663-1600.

COLUMBIA COLLEGE—HOLLYWOOD

18618 Oxnard St., Tarzana, CA 91356
Phone: 818-345-8414 **E-mail:** cchadfin@columbiacollege.edu **CEEB Code:** 7213
Fax: 818-345-9053 **Web:** www.columbiacollege.edu

STUDENTS AND FACULTY

Enrollment: 144. **Retention and Graduation:** 47% freshmen return for sophomore year. 36% freshmen graduate within 4 years. 5% grads go on to further study within 1 year. **Faculty:** 100% faculty teach undergrads.

ACADEMICS

Degrees: Associate's, bachelor's. **Academic Requirements:** General education including some course work in arts/fine arts, English (including composition), humanities, sciences (biological or physical), social science, film/television. **Special Study Options:** Accelerated program, double major, internships, liberal arts/career combination.

FACILITIES

Library Holdings: 6,200 bound volumes. 28 periodicals. 0 microforms. **Computers:** School-owned computers available for student use.

EXTRACURRICULARS

Activities: Student government, student newspaper.

ADMISSIONS

Selectivity Rating: 60 (of 100). **Freshman Academic Profile:** Average high school GPA 3.3. TOEFL required of all international applicants, minimum TOEFL 550. **Basis for Candidate Selection:** *Very important factors considered include:* essays, recommendations, secondary school record. *Other factors considered include:* character/personal qualities, extracurricular activities, interview, standardized test scores. **Freshman Admission Requirements:** High school diploma or GED is required. **Freshman Admission Statistics:** 32 applied, 88% accepted, 82% of those accepted enrolled. **Transfer Admission Requirements:** *Items required:* high school transcript, college transcript, essay. Minimum high school GPA of 2.0 required. Minimum college GPA of 2.0 required. Lowest grade transferable C. **General Admission Information:** Application fee $50. Nonfall registration accepted. Admission may be deferred for a maximum of 1 year. Neither credit nor placement offered for CEEB Advanced Placement tests.

COSTS AND FINANCIAL AID

Tuition $10,500. Required fees $225. Average book expense $400. **Required Forms and Deadlines:** FAFSA, institution's own financial aid form. **Notification of Awards:** Applicants will be notified of awards on a rolling basis. **Types of Aid:** *Need-based scholarships/grants:* Pell, SEOG, state scholarships/grants. *Loans:* FFEL Subsidized Stafford, FFEL Unsubsidized Stafford, FFEL PLUS. **Student Employment:** Federal Work-Study Program available. Off-campus job opportunities are excellent. **Financial Aid Statistics:** Average freshman grant $3,000. Average freshman loan $6,625. **Financial Aid Phone:** 818-345-8414.

COLUMBIA INTERNATIONAL UNIVERSITY

PO Box 3122, Columbia, SC 29230-3122
Phone: 803-754-4100 **E-mail:** yesciu@ciu.edu
Fax: 803-786-4041 **Web:** www.ciu.edu **ACT Code:** 5016

This private school was founded in 1923. It has a 400-acre campus.

STUDENTS AND FACULTY

Enrollment: 580. **Student Body:** Male 46%, female 54%, out-of-state 56%. **Retention and Graduation:** 77% freshmen return for sophomore year. 35% freshmen graduate within 4 years. **Faculty:** Student/faculty ratio 19:1. 19 full-time faculty, 57% hold PhDs. 100% faculty teach undergrads.

ACADEMICS

Degrees: Associate's, bachelor's, certificate, doctoral, first professional, master's, post-bachelor's certificate, terminal, transfer. **Academic Requirements:** General education including some course work in arts/fine arts, computer literacy, English (including composition), history, humanities, mathematics, philosophy, sciences (biological or physical), social science, . **Disciplines with Highest Percentage of Degrees Awarded:** Philosophy/religion/theology 91%, education 9%. **Special Study Options:** Cross registration, distance learning, double major, dual enrollment, English as a second language, independent study, internships, liberal arts/career combination, study abroad, cooperative studies with Midlands Technical College.

FACILITIES

Housing: All-female, all-male, apartments for single students, mobile home park for married students. **Library Holdings:** 108,427 bound volumes. 425 periodicals. 30,439 microforms. 5,080 audiovisuals. **Computers:** School-owned computers available for student use.

EXTRACURRICULARS

Activities: Choral groups, concert band, drama/theater, music ensembles, student government, symphony orchestra, yearbook. **Organizations:** 4 religious organizations.

ADMISSIONS

Selectivity Rating: 63 (of 100). **Freshman Academic Profile:** Average high school GPA 3.2. 18% in top 10% of high school class, 40% in top 25% of high school class, 66% in top 50% of high school class. TOEFL required of all international applicants, minimum TOEFL 525. **Basis for Candidate Selection:** *Very important factors considered include:* character/personal qualities, religious affiliation/commitment, secondary school record. *Important factors considered include:* essays, recommendations, standardized test scores, volunteer work. *Other factors considered include:* class rank, extracurricular activities, interview, talent/ability. **Freshman Admission Requirements:** High school diploma or GED is required. *Academic units required/recommended:* 2 math recommended, 1 science recommended, 2 foreign language recommended, 2 social studies recommended. **Freshman Admission Statistics:** 323 applied, 56% accepted, 62% of those accepted enrolled. **Transfer Admission Requirements:** *Items required:* college transcript, essay, statement of good standing from prior school. Minimum high school GPA of 2.0 required. Minimum college GPA of 2.0 required. Lowest grade transferable C. **General Admission Information:** Application fee $25. Priority application deadline May 1. Nonfall registration accepted. Admission may be deferred.

COSTS AND FINANCIAL AID

Tuition $8,980. Room & board $4,520. Required fees $160. Average book expense $800. **Required Forms and Deadlines:** FAFSA. No deadline for regular filing. Priority filing deadline March 1. **Notification of Awards:** Applicants will be notified of awards on a rolling basis. **Types of Aid:** *Need-based scholarships/grants:* Pell, SEOG, state scholarships/grants, private scholarships, the school's own gift aid. *Loans:* FFEL Subsidized Stafford, FFEL Unsubsidized Stafford, FFEL PLUS, college/university loans from institutional funds. **Student Employment:** Federal Work-Study Program available. Off-campus job opportunities are good. **Financial Aid Statistics:** Average freshman grant $3,900. Average freshman loan $7,625. Average income from on-campus job $1,200. **Financial Aid Phone:** 803-754-4100.

COLUMBIA UNION COLLEGE

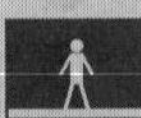  

7600 Flower Avenue, Takoma Park, MD 20912
Phone: 301-891-4080 **E-mail:** enroll@cuc.edu **CEEB Code:** 5890
Fax: 301-891-4230 **Web:** www.cuc.edu **ACT Code:** 1687

This private school, which is affiliated with the Seventh-Day Adventist Church, was founded in 1904. It has a 19-acre campus.

STUDENTS AND FACULTY

Enrollment: 1,154. **Student Body:** Male 37%, female 63%, out-of-state 43%, international 2% (47 countries represented). **Ethnic Representation:** African American 49%, Asian 8%, Caucasian 25%, Hispanic 9%. **Retention and Graduation:** 63% freshmen return for sophomore year. 13% freshmen graduate within 4 years. **Faculty:** Student/faculty ratio 13:1. 54 full-time faculty, 40% hold PhDs. 100% faculty teach undergrads.

ACADEMICS

Degrees: Associate's, bachelor's, master's. **Academic Requirements:** General education including some course work in computer literacy, English (including composition), history, humanities, mathematics, sciences (biological or physical), social science. **Classes:** Under 10 students in an average class. Under 10 students in an average lab class. **Majors with Highest Enrollment:** Business administration/management; nursing/registered nurse training (RN, ASN, BSN, MSN); counseling psychology. **Disciplines with Highest Percentage of Degrees Awarded:** Business/marketing 28%, computer and information sciences 21%, psychology 19%, health professions and related sciences 10%, communications/communication technologies 5%. **Special Study Options:** Accelerated program, cooperative (work-study) program, cross registration, distance learning, double major, dual enrollment, English as a second language, external degree program, independent study, internships, student-designed major, study abroad, teacher certification program. Co-op programs: business, biochemistry, communication/journalism, computer science, education, health professions. Other special programs: adult education and external degree programs.

FACILITIES

Housing: All-female, all-male, apartments for married students, apartments for single students. **Library Holdings:** 131,617 bound volumes. 5,350 periodicals. 7,500 audiovisuals. **Special Academic Facilities/Equipment:** Hospital adjacent to campus for students in health fields. **Computers:** School-owned computers available for student use.

EXTRACURRICULARS

Activities: Choral groups, concert band, jazz band, literary magazine, music ensembles, musical theater, radio station, student government, student newspaper, symphony orchestra, yearbook. **Organizations:** 5 honor societies. **Athletics (Intercollegiate):** *Men:* baseball, basketball, cross-country, gymnastics, soccer. *Women:* basketball, cross-country, gymnastics, soccer, softball.

ADMISSIONS

Selectivity Rating: 71 (of 100). **Freshman Academic Profile:** Average high school GPA 2.9. 40% from public high schools. Average SAT I Math 421, SAT I Math middle 50% range 360-500. Average SAT I Verbal 455, SAT I Verbal middle 50% range 380-530. Average ACT 19, ACT middle 50% range 16-25. TOEFL required of all international applicants, minimum TOEFL 550. **Basis for Candidate Selection:** *Very important factors considered include:* secondary school record. *Important factors considered include:* character/personal qualities, recommendations, religious affiliation/commitment, standardized test scores, talent/ability. *Other factors considered include:* essays, extracurricular activities, volunteer work, work experience. **Freshman Admission Requirements:** High school diploma or GED is required. *Academic units required/recommended:* 16 total required; 4 English required, 2 math required, 2 science required, 2 science lab required, 2 history required, 4 elective required. **Freshman Admission Statistics:** 739 applied, 63% accepted, 38% of those accepted enrolled. **Transfer Admission Requirements:** *Items required:* college transcript. Minimum college GPA of 2.0 required. Lowest grade transferable C. **General Admission Information:** Application fee $25. Admission may be deferred for a maximum of 1 year. Credit and/or placement offered for CEEB Advanced Placement tests.

COSTS AND FINANCIAL AID

Tuition $20,536. Room & board $5,043. Required fees $550. Average book expense $945. **Required Forms and Deadlines:** FAFSA, institution's own financial aid form, and state aid form. **Types of Aid:** *Need-based scholarships/grants:* state scholarships/grants. *Loans:* FFEL Subsidized Stafford, FFEL PLUS. **Student Employment:** Federal Work-Study Program available. Institutional employment available. Off-campus job opportunities are excellent. **Financial Aid Phone:** 301-891-4005.

COLUMBIA UNIVERSITY, COLUMBIA COLLEGE

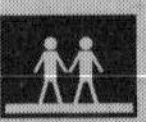   

212 Hamilton Hall MC 2807, 1130 Amsterdam Avenue, New York, NY 10027
Phone: 212-854-2522 **CEEB Code:** 2116
Fax: 212-854-1209 **Web:** www.college.columbia.edu/ **ACT Code:** 2717

This private school was founded in 1754. It has a 36-acre campus.

STUDENTS AND FACULTY

Enrollment: 4,109. **Student Body:** Out-of-state 75%, international 5%. **Ethnic Representation:** African American 9%, Asian 13%, Caucasian 55%, Hispanic 8%. **Retention and Graduation:** 99% freshmen return for sophomore year. 83% freshmen graduate within 4 years.

ACADEMICS

Degrees: Bachelor's. **Academic Requirements:** General education including some course work in English (including composition), foreign languages, humanities, sciences (biological or physical), western literature, philosophy, art, music, nonwestern cultures. **Classes:** 10-19 students in an average class. **Disciplines with Highest Percentage of Degrees Awarded:** Social sciences and history 34%, English 13%, visual and performing arts 8%, interdisciplinary studies 7%, psychology 6%. **Special Study Options:** Accelerated program, cross registration, double major, student exchange program (domestic), independent study, internships, liberal arts/career combination, student-designed major, study abroad, teacher certification program, combined plan 3-2 with engineering BS.

FACILITIES

Housing: Coed, apartments for married students, housing for disabled students, fraternities and/or sororities, special-interest housing; single-sex first-year floor available. **Library Holdings:** 7,200,000 bound volumes. **Special Academic Facilities/Equipment:** Art and architecture galleries, theatres. **Computers:** School-owned computers available for student use.

EXTRACURRICULARS

Activities: Choral groups, concert band, dance, drama/theater, jazz band, literary magazine, marching band, music ensembles, musical theater, opera, pep band, radio station, student government, student newspaper, student-run film society, symphony orchestra, television station, yearbook. **Organizations:** 109 registered organizations, 1 honor society, 22 religious organizations, 13 fraternities, 6 sororities. **Athletics (Intercollegiate):** *Men:* baseball, basketball, cheerleading, crew, cross-country, diving, fencing, football, golf, indoor track, soccer, swimming, tennis, track & field, wrestling. *Women:* basketball, cheerleading, cross-country, diving, fencing, field hockey, indoor track, lacrosse, soccer, softball, swimming, tennis, track & field, volleyball.

ADMISSIONS

Selectivity Rating: 99 (of 100). **Freshman Academic Profile:** Average high school GPA 3.8. 84% in top 10% of high school class, 95% in top 25% of high school class, 100% in top 50% of high school class. Average SAT I Math 693, SAT I Math middle 50% range 660-750. Average SAT I Verbal 701, SAT I Verbal middle 50% range 660-760. ACT middle 50% range 27-33. TOEFL required of all international applicants, minimum TOEFL 600. **Basis for Candidate Selection:** *Very important factors considered include:* character/personal qualities, class rank, essays, recommendations, secondary school record, standardized test scores. *Important factors considered include:* extracurricular activities, talent/ability. *Other factors considered include:* alumni/ae relation, geographical residence, interview, minority status. **Freshman Admission Requirements:** High school diploma or GED is required. *Academic units required/recommended:* 4 math recommended, 4 science recommended, 4 science lab recommended, 4 social studies recommended, 3 elective recommended. **Freshman Admission Statistics:** 14,129 applied, 12% accepted, 63% of those accepted enrolled. **Transfer Admission Requirements:** *Items required:* high school transcript, college transcript, essay, statement of good standing from prior school. Lowest grade transferable C. **General Admission Information:** Application fee $65. Early decision application deadline November 1. Regular application deadline January 1. Admission may be deferred for a maximum of 2 years. Credit and/or placement offered for CEEB Advanced Placement tests.

COSTS AND FINANCIAL AID

Required Forms and Deadlines: FAFSA, institution's own financial aid form, CSS/Financial Aid PROFILE, noncustodial (divorced/separated) parent's statement, business/farm supplement, and parent and student income tax returns. Financial aid filing deadline February 10. **Notification of Awards:** Applicants will be notified of awards on or about April 1. **Types of Aid:** *Need-based scholarships/grants:* Pell, SEOG, state scholarships/grants, private scholarships, the school's own gift aid. *Loans:* FFEL Subsidized Stafford, FFEL

Unsubsidized Stafford, FFEL PLUS, Federal Perkins, state loans, college/university loans from institutional funds, alternative loans. **Student Employment:** Federal Work-Study Program available. Institutional employment available. Off-campus job opportunities are excellent. **Financial Aid Statistics:** 44% freshmen, 41% undergrads receive some form of aid. Average freshman grant $18,662. Average freshman loan $2,445. **Financial Aid Phone:** 212-854-3711.

COLUMBUS COLLEGE OF ART & DESIGN

107 North Ninth Street, Columbus, OH 43215-3875
Phone: 614-222-3261 **E-mail:** admissions@ccad.edu **CEEB Code:** 1085
Fax: 614-232-8344 **Web:** www.ccad.edu **ACT Code:** 3281

This private school was founded in 1879. It has a 17-acre campus.

STUDENTS AND FACULTY

Enrollment: 1,507. **Student Body:** Male 43%, female 57%, out-of-state 28%, international 4% (29 countries represented). **Ethnic Representation:** African American 6%, Asian 4%, Caucasian 83%, Hispanic 2%. **Retention and Graduation:** 79% freshmen return for sophomore year. 32% freshmen graduate within 4 years. 12% grads go on to further study within 1 year. **Faculty:** Student/faculty ratio 15:1. 72 full-time faculty, 55% hold PhDs. 100% faculty teach undergrads.

ACADEMICS

Degrees: Bachelor's. **Academic Requirements:** General education including some course work in arts/fine arts, computer literacy, English (including composition), sciences (biological or physical), social science. **Special Study Options:** Cooperative (work-study) program, cross registration, internships, study abroad. Undergrads may take grad-level classes. Other special programs: evening classes for credit, Saturday school (ages 6-18).

FACILITIES

Housing: Coed. **Library Holdings:** 42,637 bound volumes. 251 periodicals. 14,172 microforms. 1,093 audiovisuals. **Special Academic Facilities/Equipment:** Student art exhibition hall, gallery, auditorium, recreation center. **Computers:** School-owned computers available for student use.

EXTRACURRICULARS

Activities: Literary magazine, student government, student newspaper. **Organizations:** 2 registered organizations, 1 religious organization.

ADMISSIONS

Selectivity Rating: 72 (of 100). **Freshman Academic Profile:** Average high school GPA 2.9. 10% in top 10% of high school class, 30% in top 25% of high school class, 61% in top 50% of high school class. Average SAT I Math 518, SAT I Math middle 50% range 433-550. Average SAT I Verbal 524, SAT I Verbal middle 50% range 433-580. Average ACT 21, ACT middle 50% range 18-23. TOEFL required of all international applicants, minimum TOEFL 500. **Basis for Candidate Selection:** *Very important factors considered include:* secondary school record, talent/ability. *Important factors considered include:* character/personal qualities, essays, interview, recommendations, standardized test scores. *Other factors considered include:* class rank, extracurricular activities. **Freshman Admission Requirements:** High school diploma or GED is required. *Academic units required/recommended:* 4 English recommended, 4 math recommended, 4 science recommended, 2 foreign language recommended. **Transfer Admission Requirements:** *Items required:* high school transcript, college transcript, essay. Minimum college GPA of 2.0 required. Lowest grade transferable C. **General Admission Information:** Application fee $25. Nonfall registration accepted. Admission may be deferred for a maximum of 1 year. Credit and/or placement offered for CEEB Advanced Placement tests.

COSTS AND FINANCIAL AID

Tuition $17,160. Room & board $6,300. Required fees $390. Average book expense $1,800. **Required Forms and Deadlines:** FAFSA. Priority filing deadline April 3. **Notification of Awards:** Applicants will be notified of awards on a rolling basis. **Types of Aid:** *Need-based scholarships/grants:* Pell, SEOG, state scholarships/grants, private scholarships, the school's own gift aid. *Loans:* FFEL Subsidized Stafford, FFEL Unsubsidized Stafford, FFEL PLUS, Federal Perkins, state loans. **Student Employment:** Federal Work-Study Program available. Institutional employment available. Off-campus job opportunities are excellent. **Financial Aid Statistics:** Average freshman grant $6,500. Average freshman loan $3,994. Average income from on-campus job $2,500. **Financial Aid Phone:** 614-222-3275.

See page 992.

COLUMBUS STATE UNIVERSITY

4225 University Avenue, Columbus, GA 31907-5645
Phone: 706-568-2035 **E-mail:** admissions@colstate.edu
Fax: 706-568-5091 **Web:** www.colstate.edu

This public school was founded in 1958. It has a 132-acre campus.

STUDENTS AND FACULTY

Enrollment: 5,319. **Student Body:** Male 39%, female 61%, international 1%. **Ethnic Representation:** African American 28%, Asian 2%, Caucasian 63%, Hispanic 3%. **Retention and Graduation:** 61% freshmen return for sophomore year. **Faculty:** Student/faculty ratio 18:1. 219 full-time faculty, 69% hold PhDs.

ACADEMICS

Degrees: Associate's, bachelor's, certificate, master's, post-bachelor's certificate, transfer. **Academic Requirements:** General education including some course work in arts/fine arts, computer literacy, English (including composition), history, humanities, mathematics, sciences (biological or physical), social science. **Majors with Highest Enrollment:** Computer science; curriculum and instruction; criminal justice/law enforcement administration. **Special Study Options:** Accelerated program, cooperative (work-study) program, distance learning, double major, dual enrollment, English as a second language, honors program, independent study, internships, study abroad, teacher certification program, weekend college.

FACILITIES

Housing: Coed, fraternities and/or sororities. **Special Academic Facilities/Equipment:** Fine arts and science halls. **Computers:** School-owned computers available for student use.

EXTRACURRICULARS

Activities: Choral groups, concert band, drama/theater, jazz band, music ensembles, musical theater, opera, student government, student newspaper. **Organizations:** 54 registered organizations, 13 honor societies, 2 religious organizations, 5 fraternities, 6 sororities. **Athletics (Intercollegiate):** *Men:* baseball, basketball, cheerleading, golf, tennis, track & field. *Women:* basketball, cheerleading, softball, tennis, track & field.

ADMISSIONS

Selectivity Rating: 60 (of 100). **Freshman Academic Profile:** Average high school GPA 3.0. Average SAT I Math 479. Average SAT I Verbal 494. Average ACT 19. TOEFL required of all international applicants, minimum TOEFL 550. **Basis for Candidate Selection:** *Very important factors considered include:* secondary school record, standardized test scores. *Other factors considered include:* class rank, extracurricular activities, geographical residence, recommendations, state residency, talent/ability. **Freshman Admission Requirements:** High school diploma or GED is required. *Academic units required/recommended:* 16 total required; 16 total recommended; 4 English required, 4 English recommended, 4 math required, 4 math recommended, 3 science required, 3 science recommended, 3 science lab required, 3 science lab recommended, 2 foreign language required, 2 foreign language recommended, 3 social studies required, 3 social studies recommended. **Transfer Admission Requirements:** *Items required:* college transcript. Minimum high school GPA of 2.0 required. Minimum college GPA of 2.0 required. Lowest grade transferable D. **General Admission Information:** Application fee $25. Priority application deadline July 3. Regular application deadline July 3. Nonfall registration accepted. Admission may be deferred for a maximum of 1 year. Credit offered for CEEB Advanced Placement tests.

COSTS AND FINANCIAL AID

In-state tuition $2,466. Out-of-state tuition $8,496. Room & board $5,620. Required fees $300. Average book expense $750. **Required Forms and Deadlines:** FAFSA and institution's own financial aid form. Priority filing deadline May 2. **Notification of Awards:** Applicants will be notified of awards on a rolling basis. **Types of Aid:** *Need-based scholarships/grants:* Pell, SEOG, state scholarships/grants, private scholarships, the school's own gift aid, United Negro College Fund. *Loans:* Direct Subsidized Stafford, Direct Unsubsidized Stafford, Direct PLUS, Federal Perkins, Federal Nursing, college/university loans from institutional funds. **Student Employment:** Federal Work-Study Program available. Institutional employment available. Off-campus job opportunities are good. **Financial Aid Statistics:** 49% freshmen, 69% undergrads receive some form of aid. **Financial Aid Phone:** 706-568-2036.

CONCORD COLLEGE—ATHENS

1000 Vermillion Street, PO Box 1000, Athens, WV 24712
Phone: 304-384-5248 **E-mail:** admissions@concord.edu **CEEB Code:** 5120
Fax: 304-384-9044 **Web:** www.concord.edu

This public school was founded in 1872. It has a 123-acre campus.

STUDENTS AND FACULTY

Enrollment: 3,055. **Student Body:** Male 43%, female 57%, out-of-state 11%, international students represent 29 countries. **Ethnic Representation:** African American 4%, Asian 2%, Caucasian 94%. **Retention and Graduation:** 64% freshmen return for sophomore year. 23% grads go on to further study within 1 year. 10% grads pursue business degrees. 2% grads pursue law degrees. 3% grads pursue medical degrees. **Faculty:** Student/faculty ratio 24:1. 84 full-time faculty, 69% hold PhDs.

ACADEMICS

Degrees: Associate's, bachelor's, terminal. **Academic Requirements:** General education including some course work in arts/fine arts, English (including composition), foreign languages, mathematics, sciences (biological or physical), social science, physical education. **Classes:** Under 10 students in an average class. 10-19 students in an average lab class. **Disciplines with Highest Percentage of Degrees Awarded:** Education 26%, business/marketing 15%, liberal arts/general studies 12%, social sciences and history 10%, biological life sciences 7%. **Special Study Options:** Cooperative (work-study) program, double major, dual enrollment, English as a second language, honors program, student-designed major, teacher certification program.

FACILITIES

Housing: Coed, all-female, all-male, apartments for married students, housing for disabled students, housing for international students. **Library Holdings:** 96,787 bound volumes. 552 periodicals. 268,451 microforms. 1,077 audiovisuals.

EXTRACURRICULARS

Activities: Choral groups, concert band, drama/theater, jazz band, pep band, radio station, student government, student newspaper, student-run film society, television station, yearbook. **Organizations:** 57 registered organizations, 1 honor society, 1 religious organization, 6 fraternities (15% men join), 4 sororities (20% women join). **Athletics (Intercollegiate):** *Men:* baseball, basketball, cheerleading, cross-country, football, golf, soccer, tennis, track & field. *Women:* basketball, cheerleading, cross-country, golf, soccer, softball, tennis, track & field, volleyball.

ADMISSIONS

Selectivity Rating: 63 (of 100). **Freshman Academic Profile:** Average high school GPA 3.6. 17% in top 10% of high school class, 38% in top 25% of high school class, 65% in top 50% of high school class. SAT I Math middle 50% range 410-560. SAT I Verbal middle 50% range 390-560. ACT middle 50% range 23-27. TOEFL required of all international applicants, minimum TOEFL 500. **Basis for Candidate Selection:** *Very important factors considered include:* secondary school record. *Important factors considered include:* class rank, extracurricular activities, standardized test scores. *Other factors considered include:* alumni/ae relation, character/personal qualities, essays, geographical residence, interview, minority status, recommendations, talent/ability, volunteer work, work experience. **Freshman Admission Requirements:** High school diploma or GED is required. *Academic units required/recommended:* 4 English required, 2 math required, 3 math recommended, 2 science required, 2 science lab required, 2 foreign language recommended, 2 social studies required, 1 history required, 6 elective required. **Freshman Admission Statistics:** 2,330 applied, 65% accepted, 42% of those accepted enrolled. **Transfer Admission Requirements:** *Items required:* college transcript. Minimum high school GPA of 2.0 required. Lowest grade transferable D. **General Admission Information:** Nonfall registration accepted. Admission may be deferred for a maximum of 1 year.

COSTS AND FINANCIAL AID

In-state tuition $2,724. Out-of-state tuition $6,116. Room & board $4,358. Required fees $0. Average book expense $650. **Required Forms and Deadlines:** FAFSA, institution's own financial aid form, and verification worksheet. Priority filing deadline March 1. **Notification of Awards:** Applicants will be notified of awards on a rolling basis beginning on or about March 1. **Types of Aid:** *Need-based scholarships/grants:* Pell, SEOG, state scholarships/grants, the school's own gift aid. *Loans:* FFEL Subsidized Stafford, FFEL Unsubsidized Stafford, FFEL PLUS, Federal Perkins. **Student Employment:** Federal Work-Study Program available. Institutional employment available. Off-campus job opportunities are excellent. **Financial Aid Statistics:** 87% freshmen, 82% undergrads receive some form of aid. Average freshman loan $2,396. Average income from on-campus job $823. **Financial Aid Phone:** 304-384-6069.

See page 994.

CONCORDIA COLLEGE (MOORHEAD, MN)

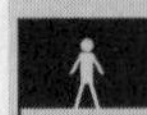

901 Eighth Street South, Moorhead, MN 56562
Phone: 218-299-3004 **E-mail:** admissions@cord.edu **CEEB Code:** 6113
Fax: 218-299-4720 **Web:** www.goconcordia.com **ACT Code:** 2104

This private school, which is affiliated with the Lutheran Church, was founded in 1891. It has a 120-acre campus.

STUDENTS AND FACULTY

Enrollment: 2,775. **Student Body:** Male 37%, female 63%, out-of-state 38%, international 6% (41 countries represented). **Ethnic Representation:** African American 1%, Asian 1%, Caucasian 96%, Hispanic 1%. **Retention and Graduation:** 80% freshmen return for sophomore year. 20% grads go on to further study within 1 year. 3% grads pursue business degrees. 4% grads pursue law degrees. 4% grads pursue medical degrees. **Faculty:** Student/faculty ratio 14:1. 180 full-time faculty, 73% hold PhDs. 100% faculty teach undergrads.

ACADEMICS

Degrees: Bachelor's. **Academic Requirements:** General education including some course work in arts/fine arts, English (including composition), foreign languages, history, humanities, mathematics, sciences (biological or physical), social science. **Classes:** 10-19 students in an average class. **Special Study Options:** Cooperative (work-study) program, double major, student exchange program (domestic), honors program, independent study, internships, liberal arts/career combination, study abroad, teacher certification program.

FACILITIES

Housing: Coed, all-female, all-male, apartments for single students, housing for disabled students; French, German, and Spanish language houses. **Library Holdings:** 333,236 bound volumes. 1,460 periodicals. **Special Academic Facilities/Equipment:** Cyrus M. Running Gallery. **Computers:** School-owned computers available for student use.

EXTRACURRICULARS

Activities: Choral groups, concert band, dance, drama/theater, jazz band, literary magazine, music ensembles, musical theater, pep band, radio station, student government, student newspaper, symphony orchestra, television station, yearbook. **Organizations:** 100 registered organizations, 22 honor societies, 12 religious organizations, 2 fraternities (4% men join), 2 sororities (4% women join). **Athletics (Intercollegiate):** *Men:* baseball, basketball, cheerleading, cross-country, football, golf, ice hockey, indoor track, soccer, tennis, track & field, wrestling. *Women:* basketball, cheerleading, cross-country, diving, golf, ice hockey, indoor track, soccer, softball, swimming, tennis, track & field, volleyball.

ADMISSIONS

Selectivity Rating: 75 (of 100). **Freshman Academic Profile:** 31% in top 10% of high school class, 62% in top 25% of high school class, 89% in top 50% of high school class. TOEFL required of all international applicants, minimum TOEFL 500. **Basis for Candidate Selection:** *Very important factors considered include:* secondary school record. *Important factors considered include:* class rank, recommendations. *Other factors considered include:* alumni/ae relation, character/personal qualities, extracurricular activities, minority status, standardized test scores, talent/ability, volunteer work. **Freshman Admission Requirements:** High school diploma or GED is required. *Academic units required/recommended:* 4 English recommended, 3 math recommended, 3 science recommended, 2 foreign language recommended, 3 social studies recommended. **Freshman Admission Statistics:** 2,613 applied, 84% accepted, 36% of those accepted enrolled. **Transfer Admission Requirements:** *Items required:* college transcript. Minimum college GPA of 2.0 required. Lowest grade transferable C-. **General Admission Information:** Application fee $20. Nonfall registration accepted. Admission may be deferred for a maximum of 1 year. Credit and/or placement offered for CEEB Advanced Placement tests.

COSTS AND FINANCIAL AID

Tuition $16,420. Room & board $4,540. Required fees $140. Average book expense $600. **Required Forms and Deadlines:** FAFSA and institution's own financial aid form. No deadline for regular filing. **Notification of Awards:** Applicants will be notified of awards on a rolling basis beginning on or about March 1. **Types of Aid:** *Need-based scholarships/grants:* Pell, SEOG, state scholarships/grants, private scholarships, the school's own gift aid. *Loans:* FFEL Subsidized Stafford, FFEL Unsubsidized Stafford, FFEL PLUS, Federal

Perkins, state loans, college/university loans from institutional funds. **Student Employment:** Federal Work-Study Program available. Institutional employment available. Off-campus job opportunities are excellent. **Financial Aid Statistics:** 71% freshmen, 71% undergrads receive some form of aid. **Financial Aid Phone:** 218-299-3010.

See page 996.

CONCORDIA COLLEGE (NY)

171 White Plains Road, Bronxville, NY 10708
Phone: 914-337-9300 **E-mail:** admission@concordia-ny.edu **CEEB Code:** 2096
Fax: 914-395-4636 **Web:** www.concordia-ny.edu **ACT Code:** 2722

This private school, which is affiliated with the Lutheran Church, was founded in 1881. It has a 33-acre campus.

STUDENTS AND FACULTY

Enrollment: 662. **Student Body:** Male 39%, female 61%, out-of-state 21%, international 9% (36 countries represented). **Ethnic Representation:** African American 10%, Asian 2%, Caucasian 74%, Hispanic 10%. **Retention and Graduation:** 76% freshmen return for sophomore year. 23% freshmen graduate within 4 years. 40% grads go on to further study within 1 year. 30% grads pursue business degrees. 2% grads pursue law degrees. 10% grads pursue medical degrees. **Faculty:** Student/faculty ratio 11:1. 34 full-time faculty, 61% hold PhDs. 100% faculty teach undergrads.

ACADEMICS

Degrees: Associate's, bachelor's. **Academic Requirements:** General education including some course work in arts/fine arts, computer literacy, English (including composition), foreign languages, history, humanities, mathematics, philosophy, sciences (biological or physical), social science, religion. **Classes:** 10-19 students in an average class. 10-19 students in an average lab class. **Majors with Highest Enrollment:** Business administration/management; education, general; social sciences, general. **Disciplines with Highest Percentage of Degrees Awarded:** Business/marketing 33%, education 22%, liberal arts/general studies 15%, social sciences and history 12%, biological life sciences 5%. **Special Study Options:** Accelerated program, cooperative (work-study) program, cross registration, distance learning, English as a second language, student exchange program (domestic), honors program, independent study, internships, student-designed major, study abroad.

FACILITIES

Housing: All-female, all-male. **Library Holdings:** 72,947 bound volumes. 467 periodicals. 20,850 microforms. 7,660 audiovisuals. **Special Academic Facilities/Equipment:** Art gallery, center for worship and performing arts, English language center, distance learning classroom. **Computers:** School-owned computers available for student use.

EXTRACURRICULARS

Activities: Choral groups, concert band, drama/theater, jazz band, literary magazine, music ensembles, musical theater, student government, student newspaper, yearbook. **Organizations:** 35 registered organizations, 1 honor society, 3 religious organizations, 2% men join fraternities, 2% women join sororities. **Athletics (Intercollegiate):** *Men:* baseball, basketball, soccer, tennis, volleyball. *Women:* basketball, soccer, softball, tennis, volleyball.

ADMISSIONS

Selectivity Rating: 75 (of 100). **Freshman Academic Profile:** Average high school GPA 2.7. 5% in top 10% of high school class, 14% in top 25% of high school class, 44% in top 50% of high school class. 60% from public high schools. Average SAT I Math 500, SAT I Math middle 50% range 430-530. Average SAT I Verbal 500, SAT I Verbal middle 50% range 420-540. Average ACT 23, ACT middle 50% range 18-24. TOEFL required of all international applicants, minimum TOEFL 550. **Basis for Candidate Selection:** *Very important factors considered include:* secondary school record. *Important factors considered include:* character/personal qualities, class rank, interview, standardized test scores. *Other factors considered include:* alumni/ae relation, essays, extracurricular activities, recommendations, religious affiliation/commitment, talent/ability, volunteer work, work experience. **Freshman Admission Requirements:** High school diploma or GED is required. *Academic units required/recommended:* 15 total required; 4 English required, 3 math required, 2 science required, 2 foreign language recommended, 2 social studies required. **Freshman Admission Statistics:** 515 applied, 22% of those accepted enrolled. **Transfer Admission Requirements:** *Items required:* high school transcript, college transcript, statement of good standing from prior school. Minimum high school GPA of 2.5 required. Minimum college GPA of 2.0 required. Lowest grade transferable C-. **General Admission Information:** Application fee $30. Priority application deadline March 15. Early decision application deadline November 15. Regular application deadline June 1. Nonfall registration accepted. Admission may be deferred for a maximum of 1 year. Credit and/or placement offered for CEEB Advanced Placement tests.

COSTS AND FINANCIAL AID

Tuition $15,550. Room & board $6,850. Required fees $0. Average book expense $750. **Required Forms and Deadlines:** FAFSA and state aid form. No deadline for regular filing. Priority filing deadline May 1. **Notification of Awards:** Applicants will be notified of awards on a rolling basis beginning on or about March 1. **Types of Aid:** *Need-based scholarships/grants:* Pell, SEOG, state scholarships/grants, private scholarships, the school's own gift aid. *Loans:* FFEL Subsidized Stafford, FFEL Unsubsidized Stafford, FFEL PLUS, college/university loans from institutional funds. **Student Employment:** Federal Work-Study Program available. Institutional employment available. Off-campus job opportunities are excellent. **Financial Aid Statistics:** Average freshman grant $8,180. Average freshman loan $2,625. Average income from on-campus job $2,000. **Financial Aid Phone:** 914-337-9300.

CONCORDIA COLLEGE (SAINT PAUL, MN)

275 North Syndicate Street, Saint Paul, MN 55104-5494
Phone: 612-641-8278 **E-mail:** admiss@luther.edu **CEEB Code:** 6114
Fax: 612-659-0207 **Web:** www.csp.edu **ACT Code:** 2106

This private school was founded in 1893. It has a 37-acre campus.

STUDENTS AND FACULTY

Enrollment: 1,027. **Student Body:** Out-of-state 15%. **Ethnic Representation:** African American 6%, Asian 5%, Caucasian 88%, Hispanic 1%. **Retention and Graduation:** 68% freshmen return for sophomore year. 2% grads go on to further study within 1 year. 1% grads pursue business degrees. 1% grads pursue medical degrees.

ACADEMICS

Degrees: Associate's, bachelor's, master's. **Special Study Options:** Student exchange program (domestic), study abroad. Undergrads may take grad-level classes.

FACILITIES

Housing: Coed, all-female, all-male, apartments for single students. **Library Holdings:** 116,275 bound volumes. 911 periodicals. 11,407 microforms. 6,000 audiovisuals. **Special Academic Facilities/Equipment:** Greenhouse, museum. **Computers:** School-owned computers available for student use.

EXTRACURRICULARS

Activities: Student government, student newspaper, yearbook. **Organizations:** 111 registered organizations.

ADMISSIONS

Selectivity Rating: 77 (of 100). **Freshman Academic Profile:** Average high school GPA 3.0. 77% from public high schools. Average ACT 21. TOEFL required of all international applicants, minimum TOEFL 500. **Freshman Admission Requirements:** High school diploma is required and GED is not accepted. *Academic units required/recommended:* 4 English required, 2 math required, 2 science required, 2 social studies required, 2 elective required. **Transfer Admission Requirements:** Minimum college GPA of 2.0 required. Lowest grade transferable D. **General Admission Information:** Early decision application deadline August 15. Regular application deadline August 15. Nonfall registration accepted. Credit and/or placement offered for CEEB Advanced Placement tests.

COSTS AND FINANCIAL AID

Tuition $12,658. Room & board $4,726. Average book expense $500. **Required Forms and Deadlines:** FAFSA and institution's own financial aid form. **Types of Aid:** *Need-based scholarships/grants:* Pell, SEOG, state scholarships/grants, private scholarships, the school's own gift aid. *Loans:* FFEL Subsidized Stafford, FFEL Unsubsidized Stafford, FFEL PLUS, Federal Perkins, state loans. **Student Employment:** Federal Work-Study Program available. Institutional employment available. Off-campus job opportunities are good. **Financial Aid Statistics:** Average freshman grant $6,980. Average freshman loan $3,100. **Financial Aid Phone:** 612-641-8209.

CONCORDIA UNIVERSITY (QC)

Office of Admissions, 1455 de Maisconneuve W., Montreal, QC H3G 1M8 Canada
Phone: 514-848-2668 **E-mail:** admreg@alcor.concordia.ca **CEEB Code:** 956
Fax: 514-848-2621 **Web:** www.concordia.ca

This public school was founded in 1974. It has a 135-acre campus.

STUDENTS AND FACULTY

Enrollment: 22,040. **Student Body:** Male 47%, female 53%, out-of-state 8%, international 5% (125 countries represented). **Retention and Graduation:** 86% freshmen return for sophomore year. **Faculty:** Student/faculty ratio 20:1. 696 full-time faculty, 91% hold PhDs. 98% faculty teach undergrads.

ACADEMICS

Degrees: Bachelor's, certificate, diploma, doctoral, master's, post-bachelor's certificate, post-master's certificate. **Academic Requirements:** All students must complete a general education 12-credit core within their program, which includes social sciences, humanities, sciences, and selected courses in commerce, engineering, and fine arts. **Classes:** 40-49 students in an average class. **Majors with Highest Enrollment:** Computer science; accounting; marketing/marketing management, general. **Disciplines with Highest Percentage of Degrees Awarded:** Business/marketing 31%, visual and performing arts 10%, social sciences and history 10%, liberal arts/general studies 10%, engineering/engineering technology 6%. **Special Study Options:** Accelerated program, cooperative (work-study) program, cross registration, distance learning, double major, English as a second language, student exchange program (domestic), honors program, independent study, internships, liberal arts/career combination, student-designed major, study abroad, teacher certification program.

FACILITIES

Housing: Coed, off-campus housing service. The service is an extensive databank listing that has vacant apartments and rooms and lists of people who are seeking roommates. This service is fully web-accessible: http://cug.concordia.ca/-housjob. **Library Holdings:** 1,728,000 bound volumes. 79,600 periodicals. 1,007,100 microforms. 38,000 audiovisuals. **Computers:** School-owned computers available for student use.

EXTRACURRICULARS

Activities: Choral groups, concert band, dance, drama/theater, jazz band, literary magazine, music ensembles, musical theater, radio station, student government, student newspaper, student-run film society, television station, yearbook. **Organizations:** 125 registered organizations, 12 honor societies, 8 religious organizations, 4 fraternities, 2 sororities. **Athletics (Intercollegiate):** *Men:* baseball, basketball, crew, cross-country, football, ice hockey, indoor track, rugby, skiing (alpine), soccer, swimming, track & field, volleyball, wrestling. *Women:* basketball, crew, cross-country, ice hockey, indoor track, rugby, skiing (alpine), soccer, swimming, track & field, volleyball, wrestling.

ADMISSIONS

Selectivity Rating: 63 (of 100). **Freshman Academic Profile:** Average high school GPA 2.8. 21% in top 10% of high school class, 49% in top 25% of high school class, 85% in top 50% of high school class. 92% from public high schools. Average SAT I Math 563, SAT I Math middle 50% range 430-590. Average SAT I Verbal 525, SAT I Verbal middle 50% range 430-580. TOEFL required of all international applicants, minimum TOEFL 550. **Basis for Candidate Selection:** *Very important factors considered include:* class rank, secondary school record. *Important factors considered include:* interview, standardized test scores, talent/ability, work experience. *Other factors considered include:* character/personal qualities, essays, extracurricular activities, recommendations. **Freshman Admission Requirements:** High school diploma is required and GED is not accepted. *Academic units required/recommended:* 4 English required, 4 English recommended, 4 math recommended, 4 science recommended. **Freshman Admission Statistics:** 13,064 applied, 65% accepted, 59% of those accepted enrolled. **Transfer Admission Requirements:** *Items required:* high school transcript, college transcript, statement of good standing from prior school. Minimum college GPA of 2.5 required. Lowest grade transferable D-. **General Admission Information:** Application fee $50. Priority application deadline February 1. Regular application deadline March 1. Nonfall registration accepted. Credit and/or placement offered for CEEB Advanced Placement tests.

COSTS AND FINANCIAL AID

In-state tuition $1,670. Out-of-state tuition $3,800. Room & board $4,970. Required fees $911. Average book expense $1,322. **Required Forms and Deadlines:** FAFSA, state aid form, and noncustodial (divorced/separated) parent's statement. Financial aid filing deadline June 1. Priority filing deadline March 1. **Notification of Awards:** Applicants will be notified of awards on a rolling basis beginning on or about July 1. **Types of Aid:** *Loans:* Direct Subsidized Stafford, Direct Unsubsidized Stafford, Direct PLUS. **Student Employment:** Off-campus job opportunities are excellent. **Financial Aid Statistics:** 52% undergrads receive some form of aid. Average freshman grant $1,500. **Financial Aid Phone:** 514-848-3507.

CONCORDIA UNIVERSITY AT AUSTIN

3400 I-35 N, Austin, TX 78705
Phone: 512-486-1106 **E-mail:** admissions@concordia.edu **CEEB Code:** 6127
Fax: 512-459-8517 **Web:** www.concordia.edu **ACT Code:** 4124

This private school, which is affiliated with the Lutheran Church, was founded in 1926. It has a 23-acre campus.

STUDENTS AND FACULTY

Enrollment: 785. **Student Body:** Male 45%, female 55%, out-of-state 10%, international 2% (14 countries represented). **Ethnic Representation:** African American 4%, Caucasian 77%, Hispanic 14%. **Retention and Graduation:** 57% freshmen return for sophomore year. 18% freshmen graduate within 4 years. 12% grads go on to further study within 1 year. 2% grads pursue business degrees. 1% grads pursue law degrees. **Faculty:** Student/faculty ratio 12:1. 37 full-time faculty, 72% hold PhDs. 100% faculty teach undergrads.

ACADEMICS

Degrees: Associate's, bachelor's, certificate, diploma, master's, post-bachelor's certificate. **Academic Requirements:** General education including some course work in arts/fine arts, computer literacy, English (including composition), foreign languages, history. **Classes:** 10-19 students in an average class. 10-19 students in an average lab class. **Disciplines with Highest Percentage of Degrees Awarded:** Business/marketing 42%, education 27%, communications/communication technologies 11%, psychology 7%, liberal arts/general studies 7%. **Special Study Options:** Accelerated program, cross registration, distance learning, double major, dual enrollment, English as a second language, external degree program, honors program, independent study, internships, liberal arts/career combination, study abroad, teacher certification program.

FACILITIES

Housing: Coed, all-female, all-male. **Library Holdings:** 50,323 bound volumes. 632 periodicals. 28,509 microforms. 1,683 audiovisuals. **Computers:** School-owned computers available for student use.

EXTRACURRICULARS

Activities: Choral groups, concert band, drama/theater, jazz band, literary magazine, music ensembles, musical theater, student government, television station, yearbook. **Organizations:** 20 registered organizations, 1 honor society, 5 religious organizations. **Athletics (Intercollegiate):** *Men:* baseball, basketball, golf, rugby, soccer, tennis. *Women:* basketball, golf, soccer, softball, tennis, volleyball.

ADMISSIONS

Selectivity Rating: 63 (of 100). **Freshman Academic Profile:** Average high school GPA 3.2. 7% in top 10% of high school class, 21% in top 25% of high school class, 52% in top 50% of high school class. 86% from public high schools. Average SAT I Math 493, SAT I Math middle 50% range 440-520. Average SAT I Verbal 482, SAT I Verbal middle 50% range 430-535. Average ACT 21, ACT middle 50% range 16-21. TOEFL required of all international applicants, minimum TOEFL 550. **Basis for Candidate Selection:** *Very important factors considered include:* secondary school record, standardized test scores. *Other factors considered include:* class rank, essays, recommendations. **Freshman Admission Requirements:** High school diploma or GED is required. *Academic units required/recommended:* 10 total recommended; 4 English recommended, 3 math recommended, 3 science recommended. **Freshman Admission Statistics:** 563 applied, 52% accepted, 50% of those accepted enrolled. **Transfer Admission Requirements:** *Items required:* college transcript. Minimum high school GPA of 2.5 required. Minimum college GPA of 2.0 required. Lowest grade transferable C. **General Admission Information:** Application fee $25. Nonfall registration accepted. Credit and/or placement offered for CEEB Advanced Placement tests.

COSTS AND FINANCIAL AID

Tuition $13,120. Room & board $5,750. Required fees $110. Average book expense $600. **Required Forms and Deadlines:** FAFSA and institution's own financial aid form. No deadline for regular filing. **Notification of Awards:** Applicants will be notified of awards on a rolling basis beginning on or about February 20. **Types of Aid:** *Need-based scholarships/grants:* Pell, SEOG, state scholarships/grants, private scholarships, the school's own gift aid. *Loans:* FFEL Subsidized Stafford, FFEL Unsubsidized Stafford, FFEL PLUS, state loans. **Student Employment:** Federal Work-Study Program available. Institutional employment available. Off-campus job opportunities are good. **Financial Aid Statistics:** 63% freshmen, 68% undergrads receive some form of aid. Average freshman grant $7,670. Average freshman loan $2,500. Average income from on-campus job $1,000. **Financial Aid Phone:** 800-854-4282.

CONCORDIA UNIVERSITY IRVINE

1530 Concordia West, Irvine, CA 92612-3299
Phone: 949-854-8002 **E-mail:** admission@cui.edu
Fax: 949-854-6894 **Web:** www.cui.edu **ACT Code:** 227

This private school, which is affiliated with the Lutheran Church, was founded in 1976. It has a 70-acre campus.

STUDENTS AND FACULTY

Enrollment: 1,289. **Student Body:** Male 33%, female 67%, out-of-state 15%, international 1% (17 countries represented). **Ethnic Representation:** African American 3%, Asian 5%, Caucasian 76%, Hispanic 11%, Native American 1%. **Retention and Graduation:** 76% freshmen return for sophomore year. 50% freshmen graduate within 4 years. 43% grads go on to further study within 1 year. **Faculty:** Student/faculty ratio 14:1. 72 full-time faculty, 66% hold PhDs. 100% faculty teach undergrads.

ACADEMICS

Degrees: Bachelor's, master's, post-bachelor's certificate. **Academic Requirements:** General education including some course work in arts/fine arts, computer literacy, English (including composition), foreign languages, history, humanities, mathematics, philosophy, sciences (biological or physical), social science, religion. **Classes:** 20-29 students in an average class. 20-29 students in an average lab class. **Majors with Highest Enrollment:** Business administration/management; education, general; religion/religious studies. **Disciplines with Highest Percentage of Degrees Awarded:** Education 20%, business/marketing 20%, social sciences and history 12%, philosophy/religion/theology 8%, communications/communication technologies 6%. **Special Study Options:** Accelerated program, cross registration, double major, English as a second language, student exchange program (domestic), honors program, internships, student-designed major, teacher certification program.

FACILITIES

Housing: All-female, all-male, housing for disabled students. **Library Holdings:** 94,250 bound volumes. 377 periodicals. 45,291 microforms. 2,079 audiovisuals. **Computers:** School-owned computers available for student use.

EXTRACURRICULARS

Activities: Choral groups, drama/theater, music ensembles, radio station, student government, student newspaper, student-run film society, yearbook. **Organizations:** 19 registered organizations, 6 religious organizations. **Athletics (Intercollegiate):** *Men:* baseball, basketball, cross-country, indoor track, soccer, track & field. *Women:* basketball, cross-country, indoor track, soccer, softball, track & field, volleyball.

ADMISSIONS

Selectivity Rating: 72 (of 100). **Freshman Academic Profile:** Average high school GPA 3.5. 23% in top 10% of high school class, 54% in top 25% of high school class, 87% in top 50% of high school class. Average SAT I Math 520, SAT I Math middle 50% range 460-580. Average SAT I Verbal 510, SAT I Verbal middle 50% range 460-560. Average ACT 22, ACT middle 50% range 19-24. TOEFL required of all international applicants, minimum TOEFL 525. **Basis for Candidate Selection:** *Very important factors considered include:* class rank, secondary school record, standardized test scores. *Important factors considered include:* character/personal qualities, recommendations, religious affiliation/commitment. *Other factors considered include:* alumni/ae relation, essays, extracurricular activities, interview, minority status, talent/ability, volunteer work, work experience. **Freshman Admission Requirements:** High school diploma or GED is required. *Academic units required/recommended:* 16 total required; 4 English required, 3 math required, 3 science required, 2 science lab required, 2 foreign language required, 2 social studies required, 4 social studies recommended. **Freshman Admission Statistics:** 878 applied, 70% accepted, 41% of those accepted enrolled. **Transfer Admission Requirements:** *Items required:* high school transcript, college transcript, statement of good standing from prior school. Minimum college GPA of 2.3 required. Lowest grade transferable C. **General Admission Information:** Application fee $50. Nonfall registration accepted. Admission may be deferred for a maximum of 1 year. Credit and/or placement offered for CEEB Advanced Placement tests.

COSTS AND FINANCIAL AID

Tuition $17,990. Room & board $6,430. Required fees $0. Average book expense $700. **Required Forms and Deadlines:** FAFSA and institution's own financial aid form. No deadline for regular filing. Priority filing deadline March 2. **Notification of Awards:** Applicants will be notified of awards on a rolling basis beginning on or about March 1. **Types of Aid:** *Need-based scholarships/grants:* Pell, SEOG, state scholarships/grants, private scholarships, the school's own gift aid. *Loans:* FFEL Subsidized Stafford, FFEL Unsubsidized Stafford, FFEL PLUS. **Student Employment:** Federal Work-Study Program available. Institutional employment available. Off-campus job opportunities are good. **Financial Aid Statistics:** 65% freshmen, 68% undergrads receive some form of aid. Average freshman grant $8,000. Average freshman loan $2,625. Average income from on-campus job $2,000. **Financial Aid Phone:** 949-854-8002.

CONCORDIA UNIVERSITY NEBRASKA

Concordia University, 800 North Columbia, Seward, NE 68434
Phone: 800-535-5494 **E-mail:** admiss@seaward.cune.edu **CEEB Code:** 6116
Fax: 402-643-4073 **Web:** www.cune.edu **ACT Code:** 2442

This private school, which is affiliated with the Lutheran Church, was founded in 1894. It has a 120-acre campus.

STUDENTS AND FACULTY

Enrollment: 1,087. **Student Body:** Out-of-state 64%, international 1%. **Ethnic Representation:** African American 1%, Asian 1%, Caucasian 96%, Hispanic 1%, Native American 1%. **Retention and Graduation:** 79% freshmen return for sophomore year. 30% freshmen graduate within 4 years.

ACADEMICS

Degrees: Bachelor's, master's. **Special Study Options:** Study abroad. Undergrads may take grad-level classes. Other special programs: correspondence and extension courses.

FACILITIES

Housing: Coed, all-female, all-male, apartments for married students. **Library Holdings:** 180,000 bound volumes. 650 periodicals. 11,000 microforms. 13,500 audiovisuals. **Special Academic Facilities/Equipment:** Art gallery, museum of natural history, audiovisual equipment, observatory. **Computers:** *Recommended operating system:* Mac. School-owned computers available for student use.

EXTRACURRICULARS

Organizations: 1 religious organization. **Athletics (Intercollegiate):** *Men:* baseball, basketball, cross-country, football, golf, soccer, tennis, track & field. *Women:* basketball, cross-country, golf, soccer, softball, tennis, track & field, volleyball.

ADMISSIONS

Selectivity Rating: 65 (of 100). **Freshman Academic Profile:** Average high school GPA 3.5. SAT I Math middle 50% range 460-610. SAT I Verbal middle 50% range 450-600. Average ACT 23, ACT middle 50% range 21-27. TOEFL required of all international applicants, minimum TOEFL 525. **Freshman Admission Requirements:** High school diploma is required and GED is not accepted. *Academic units required/recommended:* 16 total recommended; 4 English recommended, 3 math recommended, 2 science recommended, 2 foreign language recommended, 3 social studies recommended, 6 elective recommended. **Transfer Admission Requirements:** Minimum college GPA of 2.0 required. Lowest grade transferable C. **General Admission Information:** Application fee $15. Early decision application deadline March 1. Regular application deadline August 1. Nonfall registration accepted.

COSTS AND FINANCIAL AID

Tuition $11,310. Room & board $3,786. Required fees $200. Average book expense $550. **Required Forms and Deadlines:** FAFSA, institution's own financial aid form, and state aid form. **Types of Aid:** *Loans:* FFEL Subsidized Stafford, FFEL PLUS. **Student Employment:** Federal Work-Study Program available. Institutional employment available. Off-campus job opportunities are good. **Financial Aid Statistics:** Average income from on-campus job $750. **Financial Aid Phone:** 402-643-7270.

CONCORDIA UNIVERSITY RIVER FOREST

7400 Augusta Street, River Forest, IL 60305-1499
Phone: 708-209-3100 **E-mail:** crfadmis@curf.edu **CEEB Code:** 1140
Fax: 708-209-3473 **Web:** www.curf.edu **ACT Code:** 1004

This private school, which is affiliated with the Lutheran Church, was founded in 1864. It has a 40-acre campus.

STUDENTS AND FACULTY

Enrollment: 1,285. **Student Body:** Male 32%, female 68%, out-of-state 32%, international students represent 4 countries. **Ethnic Representation:** African American 7%, Asian 2%, Caucasian 62%, Hispanic 5%. **Retention and Graduation:** 63% freshmen return for sophomore year. 20% grads go on to further study within 1 year. 2% grads pursue business degrees. 1% grads pursue law degrees. 1% grads pursue medical degrees. **Faculty:** Student/faculty ratio 11:1. 75 full-time faculty, 70% hold PhDs. 90% faculty teach undergrads.

ACADEMICS

Degrees: Bachelor's, doctoral, master's, post-master's certificate. **Academic Requirements:** General education including some course work in arts/fine arts, computer literacy, English (including composition), foreign languages, history, humanities, mathematics, sciences (biological or physical), social science, ethics, theology, wellness, world studies. **Majors with Highest Enrollment:** Elementary education and teaching; nursing/registered nurse training (RN, ASN, BSN, MSN); business administration/management. **Disciplines with Highest Percentage of Degrees Awarded:** Education 32%, business/marketing 32%, health professions and related sciences 13%, social sciences and history 4%, psychology 4%. **Special Study Options:** Distance learning, double major, student exchange program (domestic), honors program, independent study, internships, study abroad, teacher certification program.

FACILITIES

Housing: Coed, housing for disabled students. **Library Holdings:** 171,510 bound volumes. 256 periodicals. 653,020 microforms. 6,010 audiovisuals. **Special Academic Facilities/Equipment:** Art museum, zoology exhibit, human performance lab, early childhood education lab school, TV studio, weather station. **Computers:** School-owned computers available for student use.

EXTRACURRICULARS

Activities: Choral groups, concert band, dance, drama/theater, jazz band, literary magazine, music ensembles, musical theater, pep band, student government, student newspaper, yearbook. **Organizations:** 15 registered organizations, 3 honor societies, 5 religious organizations. **Athletics (Intercollegiate):** *Men:* baseball, basketball, cheerleading, cross-country, football, golf, soccer, tennis, track & field. *Women:* basketball, cheerleading, cross-country, soccer, softball, tennis, track & field, volleyball.

ADMISSIONS

Selectivity Rating: 77 (of 100). **Freshman Academic Profile:** Average high school GPA 3.4. 20% in top 10% of high school class, 47% in top 25% of high school class, 76% in top 50% of high school class. 67% from public high schools. Average ACT 23, ACT middle 50% range 26-20. TOEFL required of all international applicants, minimum TOEFL 525. **Basis for Candidate Selection:** *Important factors considered include:* class rank, essays, recommendations, secondary school record, standardized test scores. **Freshman Admission Requirements:** High school diploma or GED is required. *Academic units required/recommended:* 15 total required; 3 English required, 4 English recommended, 1 math required, 2 math recommended, 2 science required, 4 science recommended, 2 foreign language recommended, 1 social studies required, 2 social studies recommended, 2 history recommended. **Freshman Admission Statistics:** 981 applied, 57% accepted, 43% of those accepted enrolled. **Transfer Admission Requirements:** *Items required:* college transcript, statement of good standing from prior school. Minimum high school GPA of 2.0 required. Minimum college GPA of 2.0 required. Lowest grade transferable C. **General Admission Information:** Nonfall registration accepted. Admission may be deferred for a maximum of 1 year. Credit offered for CEEB Advanced Placement tests.

COSTS AND FINANCIAL AID

Tuition $17,900. Room & board $5,400. Required fees $300. Average book expense $600. **Required Forms and Deadlines:** FAFSA and institution's own financial aid form. Financial aid filing deadline June 1. Priority filing deadline April 1. **Notification of Awards:** Applicants will be notified of awards on a rolling basis beginning on or about March 1. **Types of Aid:** *Need-based scholarships/grants:* Pell, SEOG, state scholarships/grants, private scholarships, the school's own gift aid. *Loans:* FFEL Subsidized Stafford, FFEL PLUS, Federal Perkins, college/university loans from institutional funds. **Student Employment:** Federal Work-Study Program available. Institutional employment available. Off-campus job opportunities are good. **Financial Aid Statistics:** 70% freshmen, 70% undergrads receive some form of aid. Average freshman grant $5,690. Average freshman loan $3,098. Average income from on-campus job $1,500. **Financial Aid Phone:** 708-209-3113.

See page 998.

CONCORDIA UNIVERSITY WISCONSIN

12800 North Lakeshore Drive, Mequon, WI 53097
Phone: 262-243-5700 **E-mail:** admission@cuw.edu **CEEB Code:** 1139
Fax: 262-243-4545 **Web:** www.cuw.edu **ACT Code:** 4574

This private school, which is affiliated with the Lutheran Church, was founded in 1881. It has a 155-acre campus.

STUDENTS AND FACULTY

Enrollment: 3,975. **Student Body:** Male 35%, female 65%, out-of-state 35%, international 1%. **Ethnic Representation:** African American 10%, Asian 1%, Caucasian 47%, Hispanic 2%, Native American 1%. **Retention and Graduation:** 78% freshmen return for sophomore year. **Faculty:** Student/faculty ratio 11:1. 93 full-time faculty, 60% hold PhDs.

ACADEMICS

Degrees: Associate's, bachelor's, master's. **Classes:** 10-19 students in an average class. 10-19 students in an average lab class. **Majors with Highest Enrollment:** Business/commerce, general; education, general; health services/allied health, general. **Disciplines with Highest Percentage of Degrees Awarded:** Business/marketing 46%, health professions and related sciences 15%, education 13%, law/legal studies 8%, communications/communication technologies 2%. **Special Study Options:** Accelerated program, cross registration, distance learning, double major, dual enrollment, English as a second language, student exchange program (domestic), independent study, internships, student-designed major, study abroad, teacher certification program, weekend college, cooperative programs with Cardinal Stritch, Marquette University, and Milwaukee Institute of Art and Design.

FACILITIES

Housing: All-female, all-male. **Computers:** School-owned computers available for student use.

EXTRACURRICULARS

Activities: Choral groups, concert band, drama/theater, jazz band, music ensembles, musical theater, radio station, student government, student newspaper. **Athletics (Intercollegiate):** *Men:* baseball, basketball, cross-country, football, soccer, tennis, track & field, volleyball, wrestling. *Women:* basketball, cross-country, soccer, softball, tennis, track & field, volleyball.

ADMISSIONS

Selectivity Rating: 74 (of 100). **Freshman Academic Profile:** Average high school GPA 3.2. 15% in top 10% of high school class, 35% in top 25% of high school class, 65% in top 50% of high school class. Average ACT 22, ACT middle 50% range 18-25. TOEFL required of all international applicants, minimum TOEFL 500. **Basis for Candidate Selection:** *Very important factors considered include:* secondary school record, standardized test scores. *Other factors considered include:* alumni/ae relation, class rank, essays, extracurricular activities, interview, minority status, recommendations, religious affiliation/commitment, talent/ability, volunteer work, work experience. **Freshman Admission Requirements:** High school diploma or GED is required. *Academic units required/recommended:* 16 total required; 3 English required, 4 English recommended, 2 math required, 3 math recommended, 2 science required, 2 foreign language recommended, 2 social studies required. **Freshman Admission Statistics:** 1,009 applied, 79% accepted, 37% of those accepted enrolled. **Transfer Admission Requirements:** *Items required:* college transcript, statement of good standing from prior school. Minimum college GPA of 2.0 required. Lowest grade transferable C. **General Admission Information:** Application fee $35. Priority application deadline May 1. Regular application deadline August 15. Nonfall registration accepted.

COSTS AND FINANCIAL AID

Tuition $15,515. Room & board $5,790. Required fees $60. Average book expense $750. **Required Forms and Deadlines:** FAFSA and institution's own financial aid form. Priority filing deadline May 1. **Notification of Awards:** Applicants will be notified of awards on a rolling basis beginning on or about

January 15. **Types of Aid:** *Need-based scholarships/grants:* Pell, SEOG, state scholarships/grants, private scholarships, the school's own gift aid. *Loans:* Direct Subsidized Stafford, Direct PLUS. **Student Employment:** Federal Work-Study Program available. Institutional employment available. Off-campus job opportunities are excellent. **Financial Aid Statistics:** 79% freshmen, 76% undergrads receive some form of aid. **Financial Aid Phone:** 262-243-4348.

CONNECTICUT COLLEGE

270 Mohegan Avenue, New London, CT 06320
Phone: 860-439-2200 **CEEB Code:** 3284
Fax: 860-439-4301 **Web:** www.connecticutcollege.edu **ACT Code:** 556

This private school was founded in 1911. It has a 750-acre campus.

STUDENTS AND FACULTY

Enrollment: 1,890. **Student Body:** Male 40%, female 60%, out-of-state 81%, international 7% (56 countries represented). **Ethnic Representation:** African American 3%, Asian 3%, Caucasian 82%, Hispanic 4%. **Retention and Graduation:** 88% freshmen return for sophomore year. 78% freshmen graduate within 4 years. 26% grads go on to further study within 1 year. 1% grads pursue business degrees. 6% grads pursue law degrees. 2% grads pursue medical degrees. **Faculty:** Student/faculty ratio 11:1. 149 full-time faculty, 89% hold PhDs. 100% faculty teach undergrads.

ACADEMICS

Degrees: Bachelor's, master's. **Academic Requirements:** General education including some course work in arts/fine arts, English (including composition), foreign languages, history, mathematics, philosophy, sciences (biological or physical), social science. **Classes:** 10-19 students in an average class. 10-19 students in an average lab class. **Majors with Highest Enrollment:** English language and literature, general; psychology, general; political science and government, general. **Disciplines with Highest Percentage of Degrees Awarded:** Social sciences and history 40%, biological life sciences 14%, visual and performing arts 9%, English 8%, foreign languages and literature 7%. **Special Study Options:** Accelerated program, cross registration, double major, student exchange program (domestic), independent study, internships, liberal arts/career combination, student-designed major, study abroad, teacher certification program. Joint programs: cross registration with the Coast Guard Academy, Trinity College, and Wesleyan University; liberal arts/career combination; 3-2 program with Washington University or Boston University for a 5-year BA/BS degree.

FACILITIES

Housing: Coed, housing for disabled students, cooperative housing, thematic, men's floors, women's floors. **Library Holdings:** 870,283 bound volumes. 2,279 periodicals. 153,545 microforms. 155,837 audiovisuals. **Special Academic Facilities/Equipment:** Art museum, children's school, language lab, 750-acre arboretum, botanic garden, greenhouse, environment control labs, transmission and scanning electron microscope, ion accelerator, refracting telescope, observatory. **Computers:** School-owned computers available for student use.

EXTRACURRICULARS

Activities: Choral groups, concert band, dance, drama/theater, literary magazine, music ensembles, musical theater, radio station, student government, student newspaper, student-run film society, symphony orchestra, yearbook. **Organizations:** 60 registered organizations, 6 religious organizations. **Athletics (Intercollegiate):** *Men:* basketball, crew, cross-country, diving, ice hockey, lacrosse, sailing, soccer, squash, swimming, tennis, track & field, water polo. *Women:* basketball, crew, cross-country, diving, field hockey, ice hockey, lacrosse, sailing, soccer, squash, swimming, tennis, track & field, volleyball, water polo.

ADMISSIONS

Selectivity Rating: 93 (of 100). **Freshman Academic Profile:** 50% in top 10% of high school class, 86% in top 25% of high school class, 98% in top 50% of high school class. 49% from public high schools. Average SAT I Math 640, SAT I Math middle 50% range 602-682. Average SAT I Verbal 640, SAT I Verbal middle 50% range 612-687. Average ACT 28. TOEFL required of all international applicants, minimum TOEFL 647. **Basis for Candidate Selection:** *Very important factors considered include:* character/personal qualities, essays, minority status, recommendations, secondary school record. *Important factors considered include:* alumni/ae relation, class rank, standardized test scores, talent/ability. *Other factors considered include:* geographical residence, interview, volunteer work, work experience. **Freshman Admission Requirements:** High school diploma or GED is required. *Academic units required/recommended:* 4 English recommended, 4 math recommended, 4 science recommended, 2 foreign language recommended, 2 social studies recommended, 3 history recommended, 3 elective recommended. **Freshman Admission Statistics:** 3,915 applied, 35% accepted, 36% of those accepted enrolled. **Transfer Admission Requirements:** *Items required:* high school transcript, college transcript, essay, statement of good standing from prior school. Minimum college GPA of 3.0 required. Lowest grade transferable C. **General Admission Information:** Application fee $55. Early decision application deadline November 15. Regular application deadline January 1. Nonfall registration accepted. Admission may be deferred for a maximum of 1 year. Credit and/or placement offered for CEEB Advanced Placement tests.

COSTS AND FINANCIAL AID

Required Forms and Deadlines: FAFSA, CSS/Financial Aid PROFILE, noncustodial (divorced/separated) parent's statement, business/farm supplement, federal tax returns; personal, partnership, and federal W-2 statements. Financial aid filing deadline January 15. **Notification of Awards:** Applicants will be notified of awards on or about April 1. **Types of Aid:** *Need-based scholarships/grants:* Pell, SEOG, state scholarships/grants, the school's own gift aid. *Loans:* FFEL Subsidized Stafford, FFEL Unsubsidized Stafford, FFEL PLUS, Federal Perkins. **Student Employment:** Federal Work-Study Program available. Institutional employment available. Off-campus job opportunities are good. **Financial Aid Statistics:** 41% freshmen, 44% undergrads receive some form of aid. Average freshman grant $21,509. Average freshman loan $2,708. Average income from on-campus job $1,100. **Financial Aid Phone:** 860-439-2058.

CONVERSE COLLEGE

580 East Main Street, Spartanburg, SC 29302
Phone: 864-596-9040 **E-mail:** admissions@converse.edu **CEEB Code:** 5121
Fax: 864-596-9225 **Web:** www.converse.edu **ACT Code:** 3852

This private school was founded in 1889. It has a 70-acre campus.

STUDENTS AND FACULTY

Enrollment: 687. **Student Body:** Out-of-state 24%, international 1%. **Ethnic Representation:** African American 8%, Asian 1%, Caucasian 83%, Hispanic 1%, Native American 1%. **Retention and Graduation:** 77% freshmen return for sophomore year. 46% freshmen graduate within 4 years. 20% grads go on to further study within 1 year. 4% grads pursue business degrees. 2% grads pursue law degrees. 2% grads pursue medical degrees. **Faculty:** Student/faculty ratio 13:1. 72 full-time faculty, 93% hold PhDs. 100% faculty teach undergrads.

ACADEMICS

Degrees: Bachelor's, master's, post-master's certificate. **Academic Requirements:** General education including some course work in arts/fine arts, computer literacy, English (including composition), foreign languages, history, humanities, mathematics, sciences (biological or physical), social science, ideas and cultures, public speaking. **Classes:** Under 10 students in an average class. Under 10 students in an average lab class. **Majors with Highest Enrollment:** Education, general; psychology, general; music/music and performing arts studies, general. **Disciplines with Highest Percentage of Degrees Awarded:** Visual and performing arts 24%, business/marketing 19%, education 17%, social sciences and history 8%, psychology 7%. **Special Study Options:** Cross registration, double major, English as a second language, honors program, independent study, internships, liberal arts/career combination, student-designed major, study abroad, teacher certification program. Undergrads may take grad-level classes.

FACILITIES

Housing: All-female. **Library Holdings:** 129,473 bound volumes. 717 periodicals. 68,703 microforms. 30,782 audiovisuals. **Special Academic Facilities/Equipment:** Language lab. **Computers:** *Recommended operating system:* Windows XP. School-owned computers available for student use.

EXTRACURRICULARS

Activities: Choral groups, concert band, dance, drama/theater, literary magazine, music ensembles, musical theater, opera, student government, student newspaper, symphony orchestra, yearbook. **Organizations:** 45 registered organizations, 14 honor societies, 4 religious organizations. **Athletics (Intercollegiate):** *Women:* basketball, cheerleading, equestrian, soccer, tennis, volleyball.

ADMISSIONS

Selectivity Rating: 82 (of 100). **Freshman Academic Profile:** Average high school GPA 3.5. 25% in top 10% of high school class, 58% in top 25% of high

school class, 87% in top 50% of high school class. 80% from public high schools. Average SAT I Math 520, SAT I Math middle 50% range 460-570. Average SAT I Verbal 558, SAT I Verbal middle 50% range 500-600. Average ACT 22, ACT middle 50% range 19-25. TOEFL required of all international applicants, minimum TOEFL 550. **Basis for Candidate Selection:** *Very important factors considered include:* class rank, secondary school record, standardized test scores. *Important factors considered include:* essays, interview, recommendations, talent/ability. *Other factors considered include:* alumni/ae relation, character/personal qualities, extracurricular activities, volunteer work, work experience. **Freshman Admission Requirements:** High school diploma or GED is required. *Academic units required/recommended:* 20 total required; 19 total recommended; 4 English required, 4 English recommended, 3 math required, 2 science required, 2 science recommended, 2 science lab required, 2 science lab recommended, 2 foreign language required, 2 foreign language recommended, 1 history required, 1 history recommended, 6 elective required, 6 elective recommended. **Freshman Admission Statistics:** 692 applied, 57% accepted, 31% of those accepted enrolled. **Transfer Admission Requirements:** *Items required:* college transcript, statement of good standing from prior school. Minimum high school GPA of 2.0 required. Minimum college GPA of 2.0 required. Lowest grade transferable C. **General Admission Information:** Application fee $35. Priority application deadline March 1. Early decision application deadline November 15. Regular application deadline August 1. Nonfall registration accepted. Credit offered for CEEB Advanced Placement tests.

COSTS AND FINANCIAL AID

Tuition $16,850. Room & board $5,140. Required fees $0. Average book expense $650. **Required Forms and Deadlines:** FAFSA. Priority filing deadline March 1. **Notification of Awards:** Applicants will be notified of awards on a rolling basis beginning on or about February 20. **Types of Aid:** *Need-based scholarships/grants:* Pell, SEOG, state scholarships/grants, private scholarships, the school's own gift aid. *Loans:* FFEL Subsidized Stafford, FFEL Unsubsidized Stafford, FFEL PLUS, Federal Perkins. **Student Employment:** Federal Work-Study Program available. Institutional employment available. Off-campus job opportunities are excellent. **Financial Aid Statistics:** 61% freshmen, 71% undergrads receive some form of aid. Average freshman grant $7,800. Average freshman loan $2,475. Average income from on-campus job $1,500. **Financial Aid Phone:** 864-596-9019.

COOPER UNION

30 Cooper Square, New York, NY 10003
Phone: 212-353-4120 **E-mail:** admissions@cooper.edu **CEEB Code:** 2097
Fax: 212-353-4342 **Web:** www.cooper.edu **ACT Code:** 2724

This private school was founded in 1859.

STUDENTS AND FACULTY

Enrollment: 870. **Student Body:** Male 66%, female 34%, out-of-state 39%, international 10%. **Ethnic Representation:** African American 6%, Asian 28%, Caucasian 57%, Hispanic 9%. **Retention and Graduation:** 92% freshmen return for sophomore year. 60% freshmen graduate within 4 years. 60% grads go on to further study within 1 year. 30% grads pursue business degrees. 6% grads pursue law degrees. 3% grads pursue medical degrees. **Faculty:** Student/faculty ratio 7:1. 53 full-time faculty, 75% hold PhDs. 100% faculty teach undergrads.

ACADEMICS

Degrees: Bachelor's, certificate, master's. **Academic Requirements:** General education including some course work in humanities. **Classes:** 10-19 students in an average class. **Disciplines with Highest Percentage of Degrees Awarded:** Engineering/engineering technology 56%, visual and performing arts 32%, architecture 12%. **Special Study Options:** Cross registration, student exchange program (domestic), independent study, internships, study abroad. All Cooper Union is indeed an honors program.

FACILITIES

Housing: Coed. **Library Holdings:** 97,000 bound volumes. 370 periodicals. 100,000 microforms. 0 audiovisuals. **Special Academic Facilities/Equipment:** Great Hall, Houghton Gallery, Brooks Lab. **Computers:** School-owned computers available for student use.

EXTRACURRICULARS

Activities: Drama/theater, jazz band, literary magazine, music ensembles, opera, student government, student newspaper, yearbook. **Organizations:** 65 registered organizations, 5 honor societies, 8 religious organizations, 2 fraternities (10% men join), 1 sorority (5% women join). **Athletics (Intercollegiate):** *Men:* basketball, golf, lacrosse, soccer, tennis, track & field, volleyball. *Women:* golf, tennis, volleyball.

ADMISSIONS

Selectivity Rating: 99 (of 100). **Freshman Academic Profile:** Average high school GPA 3.2. 80% in top 10% of high school class, 100% in top 25% of high school class, 65% from public high schools. Average SAT I Math 700, SAT I Math middle 50% range 670-740. Average SAT I Verbal 680, SAT I Verbal middle 50% range 600-720. TOEFL required of all international applicants, minimum TOEFL 600. **Basis for Candidate Selection:** *Very important factors considered include:* secondary school record, standardized test scores, talent/ability. *Important factors considered include:* essays. *Other factors considered include:* character/personal qualities, extracurricular activities, recommendations, volunteer work, work experience. **Freshman Admission Requirements:** High school diploma or GED is required. *Academic units required/recommended:* 16 total required; 18 total recommended; 4 English required, 1 math required, 1 science required, 1 social studies required, 1 history required, 8 elective required. **Freshman Admission Statistics:** 2,216 applied, 13% accepted, 64% of those accepted enrolled. **Transfer Admission Requirements:** *Items required:* high school transcript, college transcript, essay, standardized test scores, statement of good standing from prior school. Minimum college GPA of 3.0 required. Lowest grade transferable B. **General Admission Information:** Application fee $35. Early decision application deadline December 1. Regular application deadline January 1. Admission may be deferred for a maximum of 1 year. Credit and/or placement offered for CEEB Advanced Placement tests.

COSTS AND FINANCIAL AID

Tuition $0. Room & board $10,000. Required fees $500. Average book expense $1,350. **Required Forms and Deadlines:** FAFSA, CSS/Financial Aid PROFILE, and state aid form. Financial aid filing deadline May 1. Priority filing deadline April 15. **Notification of Awards:** Applicants will be notified of awards on or about June 1. **Types of Aid:** *Need-based scholarships/grants:* Pell, SEOG, state scholarships/grants, private scholarships, the school's own gift aid. *Loans:* FFEL Subsidized Stafford, FFEL Unsubsidized Stafford, FFEL PLUS, Federal Perkins, college/university loans from institutional funds. **Student Employment:** Federal Work-Study Program available. Institutional employment available. Off-campus job opportunities are excellent. **Financial Aid Statistics:** 100% freshmen, 100% undergrads receive some form of aid. Average freshman grant $12,247. Average freshman loan $2,519. **Financial Aid Phone:** 212-353-4130.

COPPIN STATE COLLEGE

2500 West North Avenue, Baltimore, MD 21216
Phone: 410-951-3600 **E-mail:** admissions@coppin.edu **CEEB Code:** 5122
Fax: 410-523-7351 **Web:** WWW.COPPIN.EDU **ACT Code:** 1688

This public school was founded in 1900. It has a 38-acre campus.

STUDENTS AND FACULTY

Enrollment: 3,273. **Student Body:** Male 24%, female 76%, out-of-state 9%, international 3%. **Ethnic Representation:** African American 98%, Caucasian 1%, Hispanic 1%. **Retention and Graduation:** 69% freshmen return for sophomore year. 6% freshmen graduate within 4 years. **Faculty:** Student/faculty ratio 22:1. 109 full-time faculty, 63% hold PhDs.

ACADEMICS

Degrees: Bachelor's, master's. **Academic Requirements:** General education including some course work in arts/fine arts, English (including composition), history, humanities, mathematics, philosophy, sciences (biological or physical), social science. **Majors with Highest Enrollment:** Psychology, general; management science, general; liberal arts and sciences/liberal studies. **Disciplines with Highest Percentage of Degrees Awarded:** Business/marketing 17%, psychology 17%, liberal arts/general studies 14%, social sciences and history 12%, law/legal studies 10%. **Special Study Options:** Accelerated program, cooperative (work-study) program, distance learning, double major, dual enrollment, external degree program, honors program, independent study, internships, liberal arts/career combination, teacher certification program, weekend college, and 3-2 programs in engineering, pharmacy, dentistry, physical therapy.

FACILITIES

Housing: Coed, housing for disabled students. **Special Academic Facilities/Equipment:** Language lab, school of special education, TV studio. **Computers:** *Recommended operating system:* Windows NT/2000. School-owned computers available for student use.

EXTRACURRICULARS

Activities: Choral groups, dance, drama/theater, music ensembles, student government, student newspaper, student-run film society, television station, yearbook. **Organizations:** 27 registered organizations, 1 honor society, 2 religious organizations, 4 fraternities (10% men join), 4 sororities (10% women join). **Athletics (Intercollegiate):** *Men:* baseball, basketball, cross-country, indoor track, tennis, track & field. *Women:* basketball, cheerleading, cross-country, indoor track, softball, tennis, track & field, volleyball.

ADMISSIONS

Selectivity Rating: 63 (of 100). **Freshman Academic Profile:** Average high school GPA 2.5. Average SAT I Math 415, SAT I Math middle 50% range 350-450. Average SAT I Verbal 436, SAT I Verbal middle 50% range 400-550. TOEFL required of all international applicants, minimum TOEFL 500. **Basis for Candidate Selection:** *Very important factors considered include:* secondary school record. *Important factors considered include:* recommendations, standardized test scores, talent/ability. *Other factors considered include:* alumni/ae relation, character/personal qualities, class rank, essays, extracurricular activities, geographical residence, interview, minority status, state residency, volunteer work, work experience. **Freshman Admission Requirements:** High school diploma or GED is required. *Academic units required/recommended:* 17 total required; 4 English required, 3 math required, 3 science required, 2 science lab required, 2 foreign language required, 3 social studies required. **Freshman Admission Statistics:** 4,306 applied, 35% accepted, 41% of those accepted enrolled. **Transfer Admission Requirements:** *Items required:* college transcript. Minimum high school GPA of 2.5 required. Minimum college GPA of 2.0 required. Lowest grade transferable C. **General Admission Information:** Application fee $35. Priority application deadline March 15. Regular application deadline July 15. Nonfall registration accepted. Admission may be deferred. Credit and/or placement offered for CEEB Advanced Placement tests.

COSTS AND FINANCIAL AID

In-state tuition $2,837. Out-of-state tuition $8,168. Room & board $5,659. Required fees $962. Average book expense $600. **Required Forms and Deadlines:** FAFSA and institution's own financial aid form. No deadline for regular filing. Priority filing deadline March 1. **Notification of Awards:** Applicants will be notified of awards on a rolling basis beginning on or about June 1. **Types of Aid:** *Need-based scholarships/grants:* Pell, SEOG, state scholarships/grants, private scholarships, the school's own gift aid, United Negro College Fund, Federal Nursing. *Loans:* Direct Subsidized Stafford, Direct Unsubsidized Stafford, Direct PLUS, FFEL PLUS, Federal Perkins, college/university loans from institutional funds, Sallie Mae's Signature loans, Key alternative loan. **Student Employment:** Federal Work-Study Program available. Institutional employment available. Off-campus job opportunities are excellent. **Financial Aid Statistics:** 73% freshmen, 72% undergrads receive some form of aid. Average freshman grant $5,567. Average freshman loan $2,522. **Financial Aid Phone:** 410-951-3636.

CORCORAN COLLEGE OF ART AND DESIGN

500 17th Street NW, Washington, DC 20006-4804
Phone: 202-639-1814 **E-mail:** admissions@corcoran.org **CEEB Code:** 5705
Fax: 202-639-1830 **Web:** www.corcoran.edu **ACT Code:** 671

This private school was founded in 1890. It has a 7-acre campus.

STUDENTS AND FACULTY

Enrollment: 372. **Student Body:** Male 33%, female 67%, out-of-state 84%, international students represent 20 countries. **Ethnic Representation:** African American 7%, Asian 13%, Caucasian 67%, Hispanic 8%. **Retention and Graduation:** 67% freshmen return for sophomore year. 37% freshmen graduate within 4 years. **Faculty:** Student/faculty ratio 8:1. 26 full-time faculty, 73% hold PhDs. 100% faculty teach undergrads.

ACADEMICS

Degrees: Associate's, bachelor's. **Academic Requirements:** General education including some course work in arts/fine arts, English (including composition), humanities, philosophy. **Majors with Highest Enrollment:** Fine/studio arts, general; graphic design; photography. **Disciplines with Highest Percentage of Degrees Awarded:** Visual and performing arts 100%. **Special Study Options:** Student exchange program (domestic), internships, study abroad.

FACILITIES

Housing: Corcoran-leased apartments and assistance in finding area housing. **Library Holdings:** 20,518 bound volumes. 130 periodicals. 0 microforms. 45,175 audiovisuals. **Special Academic Facilities/Equipment:** Art gallery, student exhibition spaces. **Computers:** *Recommended operating system:* Mac. School-owned computers available for student use.

EXTRACURRICULARS

Activities: Student government.

ADMISSIONS

Selectivity Rating: 65 (of 100). **Freshman Academic Profile:** Average high school GPA 3.1. 4% in top 10% of high school class, 8% in top 25% of high school class, 58% in top 50% of high school class. Average SAT I Math 514. Average SAT I Verbal 546, SAT I Verbal middle 50% range 500-550. Average ACT 20. TOEFL required of all international applicants, minimum TOEFL 550. **Basis for Candidate Selection:** *Very important factors considered include:* interview, secondary school record, talent/ability. *Important factors considered include:* alumni/ae relation, class rank, recommendations, standardized test scores. *Other factors considered include:* character/personal qualities, essays, extracurricular activities, volunteer work, work experience. **Freshman Admission Requirements:** High school diploma or GED is required. *Academic units required/recommended:* 4 English recommended. **Freshman Admission Statistics:** 198 applied, 62% accepted, 35% of those accepted enrolled. **Transfer Admission Requirements:** *Items required:* high school transcript, college transcript. Minimum high school GPA of 2.5 required. Minimum college GPA of 2.5 required. Lowest grade transferable C. **General Admission Information:** Application fee $30. Nonfall registration accepted. Admission may be deferred for a maximum of 1 year. Credit offered for CEEB Advanced Placement tests.

COSTS AND FINANCIAL AID

Tuition $16,970. Room & board $6,000. Required fees $30. Average book expense $2,000. **Required Forms and Deadlines:** FAFSA and institution's own financial aid form. No deadline for regular filing. **Notification of Awards:** Applicants will be notified of awards on a rolling basis beginning on or about March 15. **Types of Aid:** *Need-based scholarships/grants:* Pell, SEOG, state scholarships/grants, the school's own gift aid. *Loans:* FFEL Subsidized Stafford, FFEL Unsubsidized Stafford, FFEL PLUS, Federal Perkins, alternative loans (e.g., PLATO, Signature loans). **Student Employment:** Federal Work-Study Program available. Institutional employment available. Off-campus job opportunities are good. **Financial Aid Statistics:** 75% freshmen, 82% undergrads receive some form of aid. **Financial Aid Phone:** 202-639-1818.

See page 1000.

CORNELL COLLEGE

600 First Street West, Mount Vernon, IA 52314-1098
Phone: 319-895-4477 **E-mail:** admissions@cornellcollege.edu **CEEB Code:** 6119
Fax: 319-895-4451 **Web:** www.cornellcollege.edu **ACT Code:** 1296

This private school, which is affiliated with the Methodist Church, was founded in 1853. It has a 129-acre campus.

STUDENTS AND FACULTY

Enrollment: 1,001. **Student Body:** Male 40%, female 60%, out-of-state 68%, international 1% (5 countries represented). **Ethnic Representation:** African American 3%, Asian 1%, Caucasian 90%, Hispanic 2%, Native American 1%. **Retention and Graduation:** 76% freshmen return for sophomore year. 51% freshmen graduate within 4 years. 31% grads go on to further study within 1 year. 4% grads pursue business degrees. 9% grads pursue law degrees. 7% grads pursue medical degrees. **Faculty:** Student/faculty ratio 11:1. 82 full-time faculty, 82% hold PhDs. 100% faculty teach undergrads.

ACADEMICS

Degrees: Bachelor's. **Academic Requirements:** General education including some course work in arts/fine arts, English (including composition), foreign languages, humanities, mathematics, sciences (biological or physical), social science. **Classes:** 10-19 students in an average class. **Majors with Highest Enrollment:** Elementary education and teaching; psychology, general; economics, general. **Disciplines with Highest Percentage of Degrees Awarded:** Social sciences and history 20%, education 18%, biological life sciences 10%, psychology 8%, visual and performing arts 7%. **Special Study Options:** Double major, English as a second language, student exchange program (domestic), independent study, internships, student-designed major, study abroad, teacher certification program.

FACILITIES

Housing: Coed, all-female, all-male, apartments for single students. **Library Holdings:** 197,780 bound volumes. 1,236 periodicals. 235,000 microforms.

4,471 audiovisuals. **Special Academic Facilities/Equipment:** Geology center and museum, nuclear magnetic resonance machine in West Science Building. **Computers:** School-owned computers available for student use.

EXTRACURRICULARS

Activities: Choral groups, concert band, drama/theater, jazz band, literary magazine, music ensembles, musical theater, opera, pep band, radio station, student government, student newspaper, symphony orchestra, yearbook. **Organizations:** 81 registered organizations, 9 honor societies, 6 religious organizations, 7 fraternities (30% men join), 7 sororities (32% women join). **Athletics (Intercollegiate):** *Men:* baseball, basketball, cross-country, football, golf, indoor track, soccer, tennis, track & field, wrestling. *Women:* basketball, cross-country, golf, indoor track, soccer, softball, tennis, track & field, volleyball.

ADMISSIONS

Selectivity Rating: 80 (of 100). **Freshman Academic Profile:** Average high school GPA 3.5. 26% in top 10% of high school class, 59% in top 25% of high school class, 91% in top 50% of high school class. 93% from public high schools. Average SAT I Math 590, SAT I Math middle 50% range 540-640. Average SAT I Verbal 599, SAT I Verbal middle 50% range 540-660. Average ACT 26, ACT middle 50% range 23-28. TOEFL required of all international applicants, minimum TOEFL 500. **Basis for Candidate Selection:** *Very important factors considered include:* class rank, essays, recommendations, secondary school record, standardized test scores, talent/ability. *Important factors considered include:* character/personal qualities, extracurricular activities, interview, minority status, volunteer work, work experience. **Freshman Admission Requirements:** High school diploma or GED is required. *Academic units required/recommended:* 16 total recommended; 4 English recommended, 4 math recommended, 3 science recommended, 2 foreign language recommended, 3 social studies recommended. **Freshman Admission Statistics:** 1,625 applied, 62% accepted, 31% of those accepted enrolled. **Transfer Admission Requirements:** *Items required:* high school transcript, college transcript, essay, standardized test scores. Lowest grade transferable C. **General Admission Information:** Application fee $25. Priority application deadline March 1. Nonfall registration accepted. Admission may be deferred for a maximum of 1 year. Credit and/or placement offered for CEEB Advanced Placement tests.

COSTS AND FINANCIAL AID

Tuition $20,090. Room & board $5,600. Required fees $160. Average book expense $920. **Required Forms and Deadlines:** FAFSA, institution's own financial aid form, and noncustodial (divorced/separated) parent's statement. Priority filing deadline March 1. **Notification of Awards:** Applicants will be notified of awards on a rolling basis beginning on or about October 1. **Types of Aid:** *Need-based scholarships/grants:* Pell, SEOG, state scholarships/grants, private scholarships, the school's own gift aid. *Loans:* FFEL Subsidized Stafford, FFEL Unsubsidized Stafford, FFEL PLUS, Federal Perkins, college/university loans from institutional funds, McElroy loan, Sherman loan, United Methodist loan. **Student Employment:** Federal Work-Study Program available. Institutional employment available. Off-campus job opportunities are fair. **Financial Aid Statistics:** 83% freshmen, 80% undergrads receive some form of aid. Average freshman grant $19,120. Average freshman loan $3,745. **Financial Aid Phone:** 319-895-4216.

CORNELL UNIVERSITY

Undergraduate Admissions, 410 Thurston Avenue, Ithaca, NY 14850
Phone: 607-255-5241 **E-mail:** admissions@cornell.edu **CEEB Code:** 2098
Fax: 607-255-0659 **Web:** www.cornell.edu **ACT Code:** 2726

This private school was founded in 1865. It has a 745-acre campus.

STUDENTS AND FACULTY

Enrollment: 13,725. **Student Body:** Out-of-state 60%, international 7% (79 countries represented). **Ethnic Representation:** African American 5%, Asian 18%, Caucasian 66%, Hispanic 6%, Native American 1%. **Retention and Graduation:** 96% freshmen return for sophomore year. 82% freshmen graduate within 4 years. 32% grads go on to further study within 1 year. 2% grads pursue business degrees. 20% grads pursue law degrees. 19% grads pursue medical degrees. **Faculty:** Student/faculty ratio 9:1. 1,644 full-time faculty, 89% hold PhDs. 100% faculty teach undergrads.

ACADEMICS

Degrees: Bachelor's, doctoral, first professional, master's. **Academic Requirements:** General education including some course work in English (including composition), social science. **Classes:** 10-19 students in an average class. 10-19 students in an average lab class. **Majors with Highest Enrollment:** History, general; engineering, general; biology/biological sciences, general. **Disciplines with Highest Percentage of Degrees Awarded:** Engineering/engineering technology 18%, business/marketing 17%, social sciences and history 11%, biological life sciences 10%, agriculture 7%. **Special Study Options:** Accelerated program, cooperative (work-study) program, cross registration, distance learning, double major, English as a second language, student exchange program (domestic), honors program, independent study, internships, liberal arts/career combination, student-designed major, study abroad, teacher certification program, undergraduate research program.

FACILITIES

Housing: Coed, all-female, all-male, apartments for married students, apartments for single students, housing for disabled students, housing for international students, fraternities and/or sororities, cooperative housing, ecology house, JAM (Just about Music), language house, international living center, Ujamaa Residential College (third-world house), Risley Residential College (theater and expressive arts), multicultural living learning unit, Akwe:Kon (Native American and non-Native American), Latino living center, transfer center. **Library Holdings:** 6,797,144 bound volumes. 62,732 periodicals. 7,787,351 microforms. 388,894 audiovisuals. **Special Academic Facilities/Equipment:** Art museum, Africana studies/research center, theory center for supercomputing, ornithology laboratory, plantations. **Computers:** School-owned computers available for student use.

EXTRACURRICULARS

Activities: Choral groups, concert band, dance, drama/theater, jazz band, literary magazine, marching band, music ensembles, musical theater, pep band, radio station, student government, student newspaper, student-run film society, symphony orchestra, yearbook. **Organizations:** 600 registered organizations, 3 honor societies, 46 religious organizations, 44 fraternities (25% men join), 21 sororities (24% women join). **Athletics (Intercollegiate):** *Men:* baseball, basketball, crew, cross-country, diving, football, golf, ice hockey, lacrosse, soccer, squash, swimming, tennis, track & field, wrestling. *Women:* basketball, crew, cross-country, diving, equestrian, fencing, field hockey, gymnastics, ice hockey, lacrosse, soccer, softball, squash, swimming, tennis, track & field, volleyball.

ADMISSIONS

Selectivity Rating: 98 (of 100). **Freshman Academic Profile:** 83% in top 10% of high school class, 95% in top 25% of high school class, 100% in top 50% of high school class. Average SAT I Math 700, SAT I Math middle 50% range 660-750. Average SAT I Verbal 667, SAT I Verbal middle 50% range 620-720. Average ACT 27, ACT middle 50% range 25-30. TOEFL required of all international applicants, minimum TOEFL 550. **Basis for Candidate Selection:** *Very important factors considered include:* essays, extracurricular activities, recommendations, secondary school record, standardized test scores, talent/ability. *Important factors considered include:* class rank. *Other factors considered include:* alumni/ae relation, character/personal qualities, geographical residence, interview, minority status, state residency, volunteer work, work experience. **Freshman Admission Requirements:** High school diploma or equivalent is not required. *Academic units required/recommended:* 16 total required; 4 English required, 3 math required, 3 science recommended, 3 science lab recommended, 3 foreign language recommended, 3 social studies recommended, 3 history recommended. **Freshman Admission Statistics:** 21,502 applied, 29% accepted, 49% of those accepted enrolled. **Transfer Admission Requirements:** *Items required:* high school transcript, college transcript, standardized test scores. Lowest grade transferable C. **General Admission Information:** Application fee $65. Early decision application deadline November 10. Regular application deadline January 1. Nonfall registration accepted. Admission may be deferred for a maximum of 1 year. Credit and/or placement offered for CEEB Advanced Placement tests.

COSTS AND FINANCIAL AID

Tuition $27,270. Room & board $8,980. Required fees $124. Average book expense $620. **Required Forms and Deadlines:** FAFSA, CSS/Financial Aid PROFILE, noncustodial (divorced/separated) parent's statement, business/farm supplement, and prior year tax forms. Financial aid filing deadline February 11. **Notification of Awards:** Applicants will be notified of awards on or about April 1. **Types of Aid:** *Need-based scholarships/grants:* Pell, SEOG, state scholarships/grants, private scholarships, the school's own gift aid. *Loans:* Direct Subsidized Stafford, Direct Unsubsidized Stafford, Direct PLUS, FFEL Subsidized Stafford, FFEL Unsubsidized Stafford, FFEL PLUS, Federal Perkins, college/university loans from institutional funds, Key Bank alternative loan. **Student Employment:** Federal Work-Study Program available. Institutional employment available. Off-campus job opportunities are good. **Financial Aid Statistics:** 49% freshmen, 47% undergrads receive some form of aid. Average freshman grant $17,021. Average freshman loan $5,811. Average income from on-campus job $1,800. **Financial Aid Phone:** 607-255-5145.

CORNISH COLLEGE OF THE ARTS

710 East Roy, Seattle, WA 98102
Phone: 800-726-5016 **E-mail:** admissions@cornish.edu **CEEB Code:** 58
Fax: 206-720-1011 **Web:** www.cornish.edu **ACT Code:** 4801

This private school was founded in 1914. It has a 4-acre campus.

STUDENTS AND FACULTY

Enrollment: 649. **Student Body:** Male 39%, female 61%, out-of-state 35%, international 5% (6 countries represented). **Ethnic Representation:** African American 2%, Asian 5%, Caucasian 71%, Hispanic 4%, Native American 1%. **Retention and Graduation:** 72% freshmen return for sophomore year. 12% grads go on to further study within 1 year. **Faculty:** Student/faculty ratio 9:1. 48 full-time faculty, 47% hold PhDs. 100% faculty teach undergrads.

ACADEMICS

Degrees: Bachelor's. **Academic Requirements:** General education including some course work in arts/fine arts, English (including composition), history, humanities, sciences (biological or physical), social science. **Disciplines with Highest Percentage of Degrees Awarded:** Visual and performing arts 100%. **Special Study Options:** Independent study, internships.

FACILITIES

Library Holdings: 12,000 bound volumes. 3,000 periodicals. 613,019 microforms. 2,000 audiovisuals. **Special Academic Facilities/Equipment:** Art galleries, extensive art studio space, theatres, electronic music studio, dance studio, concert hall. **Computers:** *Recommended operating system:* Apple PowerBook G3. School-owned computers available for student use.

EXTRACURRICULARS

Activities: Choral groups, dance, drama/theater, jazz band, music ensembles, musical theater, opera, student government, student newspaper. **Organizations:** 1 registered organization, 6 honor societies.

ADMISSIONS

Selectivity Rating: 72 (of 100). **Freshman Academic Profile:** Average high school GPA 3.1. 75% from public high schools. TOEFL required of all international applicants, minimum TOEFL 525. **Basis for Candidate Selection:** *Very important factors considered include:* talent/ability. *Important factors considered include:* essays, secondary school record. *Other factors considered include:* extracurricular activities, recommendations, standardized test scores. **Freshman Admission Requirements:** High school diploma or GED is required. **Freshman Admission Statistics:** 569 applied, 79% accepted, 30% of those accepted enrolled. **Transfer Admission Requirements:** *Items required:* high school transcript, college transcript, essay, interview. Minimum high school GPA of 2.0 required. Minimum college GPA of 2.0 required. Lowest grade transferable C. **General Admission Information:** Application fee $35. Priority application deadline March 1. Regular application deadline August 15. Admission may be deferred for a maximum of 1 year. Credit offered for CEEB Advanced Placement tests.

COSTS AND FINANCIAL AID

Tuition $14,900. Required fees $200. Average book expense $1,600. **Required Forms and Deadlines:** FAFSA and institution's own financial aid form. Financial aid filing deadline March 1. Priority filing deadline February 1. **Notification of Awards:** Applicants will be notified of awards on or about May 15. **Types of Aid:** *Need-based scholarships/grants:* Pell, SEOG, state scholarships/grants, merit scholarships based on artistic merit and merit-with-need scholarships (both are institutional money). *Loans:* FFEL Subsidized Stafford, FFEL Unsubsidized Stafford, FFEL PLUS, Federal Perkins. **Student Employment:** Federal Work-Study Program available. Off-campus job opportunities are excellent. **Financial Aid Statistics:** 78% undergrads receive some form of aid. Average freshman grant $3,000. Average freshman loan $8,000. Average income from on-campus job $3,000. **Financial Aid Phone:** 206-726-5014.

COVENANT COLLEGE

14049 Scenic Highway, Lookout Mountain., GA 30750
Phone: 706-820-2398 **E-mail:** admissions@covenant.edu **CEEB Code:** 6124
Fax: 706-820-0893 **Web:** www.covenant.edu **ACT Code:** 3951

This private school was founded in 1955. It has a 300-acre campus.

STUDENTS AND FACULTY

Enrollment: 1,152. **Student Body:** Male 41%, female 59%, out-of-state 76%, international 1%. **Ethnic Representation:** African American 5%, Asian 1%, Caucasian 91%, Hispanic 2%. **Retention and Graduation:** 70% freshmen return for sophomore year. 50% freshmen graduate within 4 years. **Faculty:** Student/faculty ratio 14:1. 56 full-time faculty, 78% hold PhDs. 100% faculty teach undergrads.

ACADEMICS

Degrees: Associate's, bachelor's, master's, transfer. **Academic Requirements:** General education including some course work in computer literacy, English (including composition), foreign languages, history, humanities, mathematics, sciences (biological or physical), social science, religion. **Classes:** 10-19 students in an average class. Under 10 students in an average lab class. **Majors with Highest Enrollment:** History, general; English language and literature, general; sociology. **Disciplines with Highest Percentage of Degrees Awarded:** Social sciences and history 22%, philosophy/religion/theology 18%, education 14%, English 12%, business/marketing 8%. **Special Study Options:** Double major, dual enrollment, independent study, internships, student-designed major, study abroad, teacher certification program, dual-engineering degree with Georgia Tech; cooperative nursing program with Emory University and Chattanooga State; bridge program for Master of Science in Nursing with Vanderbilt University.

FACILITIES

Housing: All-female, all-male, apartments for single students, housing for disabled students. **Library Holdings:** 85,000 bound volumes. 475 periodicals. 4,800 microforms. 4,300 audiovisuals. **Computers:** *Recommended operating system:* Windows NT/2000. School-owned computers available for student use.

EXTRACURRICULARS

Activities: Choral groups, drama/theater, literary magazine, music ensembles, student government, student newspaper, student-run film society, symphony orchestra, yearbook. **Organizations:** 68 registered organizations, 2 honor societies, 10 religious organizations. **Athletics (Intercollegiate):** *Men:* basketball, cross-country, soccer. *Women:* basketball, cross-country, soccer, volleyball.

ADMISSIONS

Selectivity Rating: 74 (of 100). **Freshman Academic Profile:** Average high school GPA 3.6. 20% in top 10% of high school class, 52% in top 25% of high school class, 82% in top 50% of high school class. Average SAT I Math 567, SAT I Math middle 50% range 510-630. Average SAT I Verbal 596, SAT I Verbal middle 50% range 540-670. Average ACT 25, ACT middle 50% range 19-27. TOEFL required of all international applicants, minimum TOEFL 540. **Basis for Candidate Selection:** *Very important factors considered include:* religious affiliation/commitment, secondary school record, standardized test scores. *Important factors considered include:* character/personal qualities, essays, interview, recommendations. *Other factors considered include:* minority status. **Freshman Admission Requirements:** High school diploma or GED is required. *Academic units required/recommended:* 16 total recommended; 4 English recommended, 3 math recommended, 2 science recommended, 2 foreign language recommended, 2 social studies recommended, 3 elective recommended. **Freshman Admission Statistics:** 544 applied, 96% accepted, 43% of those accepted enrolled. **Transfer Admission Requirements:** *Items required:* high school transcript, college transcript, essay, interview, standardized test scores, statement of good standing from prior school. Minimum high school GPA of 2.5 required. Minimum college GPA of 2.0 required. Lowest grade transferable C-. **General Admission Information:** Application fee $25. Priority application deadline May 1. Nonfall registration accepted. Admission may be deferred. Credit offered for CEEB Advanced Placement tests.

COSTS AND FINANCIAL AID

Tuition $17,750. Room & board $5,260. Required fees $480. Average book expense $1,000. **Required Forms and Deadlines:** FAFSA, institution's own financial aid form, and state aid form. Financial aid filing deadline March 31. Priority filing deadline March 1. **Notification of Awards:** Applicants will be notified of awards on a rolling basis beginning on or about April 15. **Types of Aid:** *Need-based scholarships/grants:* Pell, SEOG, state scholarships/grants, private scholarships, the school's own gift aid. *Loans:* FFEL Subsidized

Stafford, FFEL Unsubsidized Stafford, FFEL PLUS, Federal Perkins, state loans. **Student Employment:** Federal Work-Study Program available. Institutional employment available. Off-campus job opportunities are fair. **Financial Aid Statistics:** 68% freshmen, 68% undergrads receive some form of aid. Average freshman grant $13,812. Average freshman loan $3,682. Average income from on-campus job $1,856. **Financial Aid Phone:** 706-419-1126.

CREIGHTON UNIVERSITY

2500 California Plaza, Omaha, NE 68178
Phone: 402-280-2703 **E-mail:** admissions@creighton.edu **CEEB Code:** 6121
Fax: 402-280-2685 **Web:** www.creighton.edu **ACT Code:** 2444

This private school, which is affiliated with the Roman Catholic Church, was founded in 1878. It has a 93-acre campus.

STUDENTS AND FACULTY

Enrollment: 3,607. **Student Body:** Male 40%, female 60%, out-of-state 50%, international 2%. **Ethnic Representation:** African American 3%, Asian 8%, Caucasian 85%, Hispanic 3%, Native American 1%. **Retention and Graduation:** 89% freshmen return for sophomore year. 52% freshmen graduate within 4 years. 31% grads go on to further study within 1 year. 2% grads pursue business degrees. 9% grads pursue law degrees. 11% grads pursue medical degrees. **Faculty:** Student/faculty ratio 14:1. 622 full-time faculty, 91% hold PhDs. 100% faculty teach undergrads.

ACADEMICS

Degrees: Associate's, bachelor's, certificate, doctoral, first professional, master's, post-master's certificate, transfer. **Academic Requirements:** General education including some course work in arts/fine arts, English (including composition), foreign languages, history, humanities, mathematics, philosophy, sciences (biological or physical), social science, theology, ethics. **Classes:** 10-19 students in an average class. 10-19 students in an average lab class. **Majors with Highest Enrollment:** Psychology, general; nursing/registered nurse training (RN, ASN, BSN, MSN); biology/biological sciences, general. **Disciplines with Highest Percentage of Degrees Awarded:** Business/marketing 21%, health professions and related sciences 21%, psychology 9%, biological life sciences 7%, communications/communication technologies 6%. **Special Study Options:** Accelerated program, cross registration, distance learning, double major, dual enrollment, English as a second language, student exchange program (domestic), honors program, independent study, internships, liberal arts/career combination, study abroad opportunities at 110 partner institutions in 40 countries, teacher certification program, 3-2 programming engineering with University of Detroit Mercy.

FACILITIES

Housing: Coed, all-female, apartments for married students, apartments for single students, housing for disabled students; residence halls co-ed by floor. **Library Holdings:** 437,950 bound volumes. 1,864 periodicals. 787,327 microforms. 7,318 audiovisuals. **Special Academic Facilities/Equipment:** Fine arts/performing center, health science and research complex, hospital.

EXTRACURRICULARS

Activities: Choral groups, concert band, dance, drama/theater, jazz band, literary magazine, music ensembles, musical theater, pep band, radio station, student government, student newspaper, symphony orchestra, television station, yearbook. **Organizations:** 155 registered organizations, 11 honor societies, 5 religious organizations, 5 fraternities (26% men join), 5 sororities (25% women join). **Athletics (Intercollegiate):** *Men:* baseball, basketball, cross-country, golf, soccer, tennis. *Women:* basketball, crew, cross-country, golf, soccer, softball, tennis, volleyball.

ADMISSIONS

Selectivity Rating: 74 (of 100). **Freshman Academic Profile:** Average high school GPA 3.7. 33% in top 10% of high school class, 64% in top 25% of high school class, 90% in top 50% of high school class. 64% from public high schools. Average SAT I Math 582, SAT I Math middle 50% range 520-640. Average SAT I Verbal 574, SAT I Verbal middle 50% range 530-620. Average ACT 26, ACT middle 50% range 23-28. TOEFL required of all international applicants, minimum TOEFL 550. **Basis for Candidate Selection:** *Very important factors considered include:* secondary school record. *Important factors considered include:* recommendations, standardized test scores. *Other factors considered include:* character/personal qualities, class rank, essays, extracurricular activities, minority status, talent/ability, volunteer work. **Freshman Admission Requirements:** High school diploma or GED is required. *Academic units required/recommended:* 16 total recommended; 4 English recommended, 3 math recommended, 2 science recommended, 2 foreign language recommended, 1 social studies recommended, 1 history recommended, 3 elective recommended. **Freshman Admission Statistics:** 2,605 applied, 90% accepted, 34% of those accepted enrolled. **Transfer Admission Requirements:** *Items required:* high school transcript, college transcript, essay. Minimum high school GPA of 2.8 required. Minimum college GPA of 2.5 required. Lowest grade transferable C. **General Admission Information:** Application fee $40. Priority application deadline January 1. Regular application deadline August 1. Nonfall registration accepted. Admission may be deferred for a maximum of 1 year. Credit offered for CEEB Advanced Placement tests.

COSTS AND FINANCIAL AID

Average book expense $900. **Required Forms and Deadlines:** FAFSA and institution's own financial aid form. No deadline for regular filing. Priority filing deadline April 1. **Notification of Awards:** Applicants will be notified of awards on a rolling basis beginning on or about March 15. **Types of Aid:** *Need-based scholarships/grants:* Pell, SEOG, state scholarships/grants, private scholarships, the school's own gift aid. *Loans:* FFEL Subsidized Stafford, FFEL Unsubsidized Stafford, FFEL PLUS, Federal Perkins, Federal Nursing, college/university loans from institutional funds. **Student Employment:** Federal Work-Study Program available. Institutional employment available. Off-campus job opportunities are excellent. **Financial Aid Statistics:** Average freshman grant $11,736. Average freshman loan $3,667. Average income from on-campus job $1,393. **Financial Aid Phone:** 402-280-2731.

CROWN COLLEGE

6425 County Road 30, St. Bonifacius, MN 55375-9001
Phone: 952-446-4142 **E-mail:** info@crown.edu
Fax: 952-446-4149 **Web:** www.crown.edu **ACT Code:** 2152

This private school, which is affiliated with the Christian & Missionary Alliance Church, was founded in 1916. It has a 193-acre campus.

STUDENTS AND FACULTY

Enrollment: 898. **Student Body:** Male 43%, female 57%, out-of-state 36%, international students represent 3 countries. **Ethnic Representation:** African American 2%, Asian 4%, Caucasian 88%, Hispanic 2%, Native American 1%. **Retention and Graduation:** 73% freshmen return for sophomore year. 30% freshmen graduate within 4 years. **Faculty:** Student/faculty ratio 14:1. 33 full-time faculty, 57% hold PhDs. 100% faculty teach undergrads.

ACADEMICS

Degrees: Associate's, bachelor's, certificate, master's. **Academic Requirements:** General education including some course work in computer literacy, English (including composition), history, humanities, sciences (biological or physical), Bible classes. **Classes:** 10-19 students in an average class. Under 10 students in an average lab class. **Majors with Highest Enrollment:** Business administration/management; elementary education and teaching; psychology, general. **Disciplines with Highest Percentage of Degrees Awarded:** Philosophy/religion/theology 32%, business/marketing 26%, education 20%, computer and information sciences 5%, liberal arts/general studies 4%. **Special Study Options:** Accelerated program, distance learning, double major, dual enrollment, English as a second language, honors program, independent study, internships, study abroad, teacher certification program, weekend college, 2-2 with nonaccredited Bible colleges.

FACILITIES

Housing: All-female, all-male, apartments for married students, housing for disabled students. **Library Holdings:** 78,000 bound volumes. 8,000 periodicals. 73,700 microforms. 2,400 audiovisuals. **Computers:** *Recommended operating system:* Windows 3x. School-owned computers available for student use.

EXTRACURRICULARS

Activities: Choral groups, concert band, drama/theater, jazz band, music ensembles, musical theater, pep band, student government, student newspaper, yearbook. **Organizations:** 13 registered organizations. **Athletics (Intercollegiate):** *Men:* baseball, basketball, cross-country, football, golf, soccer. *Women:* basketball, cross-country, golf, soccer, softball, volleyball.

ADMISSIONS

Selectivity Rating: 69 (of 100). **Freshman Academic Profile:** Average high school GPA 3.2. 9% in top 10% of high school class, 36% in top 25% of high school class, 63% in top 50% of high school class. Average SAT I Math 513, SAT I Math middle 50% range 450-560. Average SAT I Verbal 518, SAT I Verbal middle 50% range 440-570. Average ACT 22, ACT middle 50% range 19-25. TOEFL required of all international applicants, minimum TOEFL 450. **Basis**

for Candidate Selection: *Very important factors considered include:* essays, recommendations, religious affiliation/commitment, secondary school record, standardized test scores. *Important factors considered include:* class rank. *Other factors considered include:* character/personal qualities, interview, talent/ability, volunteer work, work experience. **Freshman Admission Requirements:** High school diploma or GED is required. *Academic units required/recommended:* 4 English recommended, 3 math recommended, 3 science recommended, 2 foreign language recommended, 3 social studies recommended. **Freshman Admission Statistics:** 408 applied, 75% accepted, 45% of those accepted enrolled. **Transfer Admission Requirements:** *Items required:* high school transcript, college transcript, essay. Minimum college GPA of 2.0 required. Lowest grade transferable C. **General Admission Information:** Application fee $35. Nonfall registration accepted. Admission may be deferred for a maximum of 1 year. Credit offered for CEEB Advanced Placement tests.

COSTS AND FINANCIAL AID

Tuition $11,236. Room & board $4,980. Required fees $746. Average book expense $800. **Required Forms and Deadlines:** FAFSA and institution's own financial aid form. Financial aid filing deadline August 1. Priority filing deadline May 1. **Notification of Awards:** Applicants will be notified of awards on a rolling basis beginning on or about April 1. **Types of Aid:** *Need-based scholarships/grants:* Pell, SEOG, state scholarships/grants, private scholarships, the school's own gift aid. *Loans:* FFEL Subsidized Stafford, FFEL Unsubsidized Stafford, FFEL PLUS, Federal Perkins, state loans, Bremer educational loans, U.S. Bank no-fee education loans, CitiAssist loans, Signature loans, GAP loans. **Student Employment:** Federal Work-Study Program available. Institutional employment available. Off-campus job opportunities are excellent. **Financial Aid Statistics:** 89% freshmen, 69% undergrads receive some form of aid. Average freshman grant $9,630. Average freshman loan $3,880. **Financial Aid Phone:** 952-446-4177.

CULVER-STOCKTON COLLEGE

One College Hill, Canton, MO 63435
Phone: 217-231-6331 **E-mail:** enrollment@culver.edu **CEEB Code:** 6123
Fax: 217-231-6618 **Web:** www.culver.edu **ACT Code:** 2290

This private school, which is affiliated with the Disciples of Christ Church, was founded in 1853. It has a 139-acre campus.

STUDENTS AND FACULTY

Enrollment: 828. **Student Body:** Male 43%, female 57%, out-of-state 44%, international 1% (7 countries represented). **Ethnic Representation:** African American 6%, Asian 1%, Caucasian 91%, Hispanic 2%. **Retention and Graduation:** 66% freshmen return for sophomore year. 37% freshmen graduate within 4 years. 10% grads go on to further study within 1 year. 1% grads pursue business degrees. 1% grads pursue law degrees. 1% grads pursue medical degrees. **Faculty:** Student/faculty ratio 12:1. 58 full-time faculty, 81% hold PhDs. 100% faculty teach undergrads.

ACADEMICS

Degrees: Bachelor's. **Academic Requirements:** General education including some course work in arts/fine arts, computer literacy, English (including composition), humanities, mathematics, sciences (biological or physical), social science, Christian heritage. **Classes:** 10-19 students in an average class. 10-19 students in an average lab class. **Majors with Highest Enrollment:** Nursing/registered nurse training (RN, ASN, BSN, MSN); business administration/management; elementary education and teaching. **Disciplines with Highest Percentage of Degrees Awarded:** Business/marketing 22%, education 21%, health professions and related sciences 14%, visual and performing arts 9%, psychology 9%. **Special Study Options:** Double major, dual enrollment, honors program, independent study, internships, liberal arts/career combination, student-designed major, study abroad, teacher certification program.

FACILITIES

Housing: Coed, all-female, all-male, fraternities and/or sororities. **Library Holdings:** 155,487 bound volumes. 777 periodicals. 5,117 microforms. 4,327 audiovisuals. **Special Academic Facilities/Equipment:** Art gallery, performing arts center. **Computers:** School-owned computers available for student use.

EXTRACURRICULARS

Activities: Choral groups, concert band, drama/theater, jazz band, literary magazine, music ensembles, radio station, student government, student newspaper. **Organizations:** 37 registered organizations, 8 honor societies, 2 religious organizations, 4 fraternities (43% men join), 2 sororities (75% women join). **Athletics (Intercollegiate):** *Men:* baseball, basketball, football, golf, soccer. *Women:* basketball, golf, soccer, softball, volleyball.

ADMISSIONS

Selectivity Rating: 71 (of 100). **Freshman Academic Profile:** Average high school GPA 3.2. 15% in top 10% of high school class, 33% in top 25% of high school class, 82% in top 50% of high school class. 90% from public high schools. Average ACT 22. TOEFL required of all international applicants, minimum TOEFL 500. **Basis for Candidate Selection:** *Very important factors considered include:* class rank, secondary school record, standardized test scores. *Other factors considered include:* alumni/ae relation, character/personal qualities, essays, extracurricular activities, interview, recommendations, talent/ability, volunteer work, work experience. **Freshman Admission Requirements:** High school diploma or GED is required. *Academic units required/recommended:* 15 total required; 4 English recommended, 2 math recommended, 2 science recommended, 3 social studies recommended. **Freshman Admission Statistics:** 943 applied, 77% accepted, 31% of those accepted enrolled. **Transfer Admission Requirements:** *Items required:* college transcript. Minimum college GPA of 2.0 required. Lowest grade transferable D. **General Admission Information:** Application fee $25. Nonfall registration accepted. Admission may be deferred for a maximum of 1 year. Credit and/or placement offered for CEEB Advanced Placement tests.

COSTS AND FINANCIAL AID

Tuition $11,800. Room & board $5,200. Required fees $0. Average book expense $600. **Required Forms and Deadlines:** FAFSA. Financial aid filing deadline June 15. **Notification of Awards:** Applicants will be notified of awards on a rolling basis beginning on or about February 15. **Types of Aid:** *Need-based scholarships/grants:* Pell, SEOG, state scholarships/grants, private scholarships, the school's own gift aid. *Loans:* Direct Subsidized Stafford, Direct Unsubsidized Stafford, Direct PLUS, Federal Perkins, Federal Nursing, state loans, college/university loans from institutional funds. **Student Employment:** Federal Work-Study Program available. Institutional employment available. Off-campus job opportunities are fair. **Financial Aid Statistics:** 82% freshmen, 83% undergrads receive some form of aid. Average freshman grant $15,575. Average freshman loan $3,329. Average income from on-campus job $772. **Financial Aid Phone:** 217-231-6306.

CUMBERLAND COLLEGE

6178 College Station Drive, Williamsburg, KY 40769
Phone: 606-539-4241 **E-mail:** admiss@cumberlandcollege.edu **CEEB Code:** 1145
Fax: 606-539-4303 **Web:** www.cumberlandcollege.edu **ACT Code:** 1510

This private school was founded in 1889. It has a 50-acre campus.

STUDENTS AND FACULTY

Enrollment: 1,588. **Student Body:** Male 47%, female 53%, out-of-state 41%, international 2% (18 countries represented). **Ethnic Representation:** African American 5%, Caucasian 93%, Hispanic 1%. **Retention and Graduation:** 63% freshmen return for sophomore year. 35% grads go on to further study within 1 year. 12% grads pursue business degrees. 2% grads pursue law degrees. 6% grads pursue medical degrees. **Faculty:** Student/faculty ratio 17:1. 90 full-time faculty, 64% hold PhDs. 100% faculty teach undergrads.

ACADEMICS

Degrees: Associate's, bachelor's, master's, terminal. **Academic Requirements:** General education including some course work in arts/fine arts, computer literacy, English (including composition), history, humanities, mathematics, philosophy, sciences (biological or physical), social science, religion. **Classes:** 10-19 students in an average class. Under 10 students in an average lab class. **Majors with Highest Enrollment:** Business administration/management; secondary education and teaching; biology/biological sciences, general. **Disciplines with Highest Percentage of Degrees Awarded:** Education 19%, business/marketing 16%, biological life sciences 10%, psychology 8%, protective services/public administration 8%. **Special Study Options:** Accelerated program, cooperative (work-study) program, distance learning, double major, honors program, independent study, internships, liberal arts/career combination, student-designed major, study abroad, teacher certification program.

FACILITIES

Housing: All-female, all-male. **Library Holdings:** 191,701 bound volumes. 3,655 periodicals. 777,233 microforms. 7,043 audiovisuals. **Special Academic Facilities/Equipment:** Natural science, history, and student art museums. **Computers:** School-owned computers available for student use.

EXTRACURRICULARS

Activities: Choral groups, concert band, dance, drama/theater, jazz band, marching band, music ensembles, musical theater, pep band, student government, student newspaper, television station. **Organizations:** 43 registered organizations, 11 honor societies, 18 religious organizations. **Athletics (Intercollegiate):** *Men:* baseball, basketball, cheerleading, cross-country, football, golf, soccer, swimming, tennis, track & field, wrestling. *Women:* basketball, cheerleading, cross-country, golf, soccer, softball, swimming, tennis, track & field, volleyball, wrestling.

ADMISSIONS

Selectivity Rating: 78 (of 100). **Freshman Academic Profile:** Average high school GPA 3.4. 19% in top 10% of high school class, 46% in top 25% of high school class, 77% in top 50% of high school class. 90% from public high schools. Average SAT I Math 532, SAT I Math middle 50% range 430-570. Average SAT I Verbal 515, SAT I Verbal middle 50% range 440-550. Average ACT 22, ACT middle 50% range 18-23. TOEFL required of all international applicants, minimum TOEFL 550. **Basis for Candidate Selection:** *Very important factors considered include:* essays, recommendations, secondary school record, standardized test scores. *Other factors considered include:* class rank, interview. **Freshman Admission Requirements:** High school diploma or GED is required. *Academic units required/recommended:* 4 English required, 4 English recommended, 3 math required, 3 math recommended, 2 science required, 3 science recommended, 1 social studies required, 2 social studies recommended. **Freshman Admission Statistics:** 1,147 applied, 67% accepted, 51% of those accepted enrolled. **Transfer Admission Requirements:** *Items required:* college transcript, essay, statement of good standing from prior school. Lowest grade transferable C. **General Admission Information:** Application fee $25. Nonfall registration accepted. Credit offered for CEEB Advanced Placement tests.

COSTS AND FINANCIAL AID

Tuition $11,098. Room & board $4,926. Required fees $360. Average book expense $800. **Required Forms and Deadlines:** FAFSA. Priority filing deadline March 1. **Notification of Awards:** Applicants will be notified of awards on or about April 1. **Types of Aid:** *Need-based scholarships/grants:* Pell, SEOG, state scholarships/grants, private scholarships, the school's own gift aid. *Loans:* Direct Subsidized Stafford, Direct Unsubsidized Stafford, Direct PLUS, FFEL Subsidized Stafford, FFEL Unsubsidized Stafford, FFEL PLUS, Federal Perkins, college/university loans from institutional funds. **Student Employment:** Federal Work-Study Program available. Institutional employment available. Off-campus job opportunities are fair. **Financial Aid Statistics:** 84% freshmen, 83% undergrads receive some form of aid. Average freshman grant $8,643. Average freshman loan $2,973. Average income from on-campus job $1,700. **Financial Aid Phone:** 800-532-0828.

See page 1002.

CUMBERLAND UNIVERSITY

One Cumberland Square, Lebanon, TN 37087-3554
Phone: 615-444-2562 **E-mail:** admissions@cumberland.edu **CEEB Code:** 1146
Fax: 615-444-2569 **Web:** www.cumberland.edu **ACT Code:** 3954

This private school was founded in 1842. It has a 40-acre campus.

STUDENTS AND FACULTY

Enrollment: 912. **Student Body:** Male 49%, female 51%, out-of-state 12%, international students represent 17 countries. **Ethnic Representation:** African American 13%, Asian 1%, Caucasian 79%, Hispanic 2%. **Retention and Graduation:** 63% freshmen return for sophomore year. 22% freshmen graduate within 4 years. 15% grads go on to further study within 1 year. 5% grads pursue business degrees. 2% grads pursue law degrees. 1% grads pursue medical degrees. **Faculty:** Student/faculty ratio 11:1. 73 full-time faculty, 39% hold PhDs. 98% faculty teach undergrads.

ACADEMICS

Degrees: Associate's, bachelor's, master's. **Academic Requirements:** General education including some course work in arts/fine arts, computer literacy, English (including composition), history, humanities, mathematics, sciences (biological or physical), social science. **Classes:** Under 10 students in an average class. **Majors with Highest Enrollment:** Business/commerce, general; elementary education and teaching; nursing/registered nurse training (RN, ASN, BSN, MSN). **Disciplines with Highest Percentage of Degrees Awarded:** Business/marketing 29%, education 20%, health professions and related sciences 13%, protective services/public administration 7%, liberal arts/general studies 6%. **Special Study Options:** Accelerated program, double major, honors program, teacher certification program.

FACILITIES

Housing: All-female, all-male, housing for disabled students. **Library Holdings:** 40,000 bound volumes. 400 periodicals. 1,000 audiovisuals. **Special Academic Facilities/Equipment:** Calvert Wild Game Collection. **Computers:** School-owned computers available for student use.

EXTRACURRICULARS

Activities: Choral groups, dance, drama/theater, jazz band, literary magazine, marching band, music ensembles, musical theater, pep band, radio station, student government, student newspaper, yearbook. **Organizations:** 25 registered organizations, 7 honor societies, 2 religious organizations, 3 fraternities (4% men join), 2 sororities (1% women join). **Athletics (Intercollegiate):** *Men:* baseball, basketball, cheerleading, cross-country, football, golf, soccer, tennis, wrestling. *Women:* basketball, cheerleading, cross-country, golf, soccer, softball, tennis, volleyball.

ADMISSIONS

Selectivity Rating: 63 (of 100). **Freshman Academic Profile:** Average high school GPA 3.1. 15% in top 10% of high school class, 38% in top 25% of high school class, 69% in top 50% of high school class. 80% from public high schools. SAT I Math middle 50% range 400-490. SAT I Verbal middle 50% range 400-490. Average ACT 20, ACT middle 50% range 17-22. TOEFL required of all international applicants, minimum TOEFL 500. **Basis for Candidate Selection:** *Very important factors considered include:* class rank, secondary school record, standardized test scores. *Important factors considered include:* essays. *Other factors considered include:* alumni/ae relation, recommendations. **Freshman Admission Requirements:** High school diploma or GED is required. *Academic units required/recommended:* 4 English recommended, 4 math recommended, 2 science recommended, 2 foreign language recommended, 2 social studies recommended. **Freshman Admission Statistics:** 475 applied, 73% accepted, 54% of those accepted enrolled. **Transfer Admission Requirements:** *Items required:* college transcript. Minimum college GPA of 2.0 required. Lowest grade transferable C. **General Admission Information:** Application fee $25. Priority application deadline March 1. Nonfall registration accepted. Admission may be deferred. Credit offered for CEEB Advanced Placement tests.

COSTS AND FINANCIAL AID

Tuition $8,000. Room & board $5,200. Required fees $250. Average book expense $800. **Required Forms and Deadlines:** FAFSA and institution's own financial aid form. Financial aid filing deadline May 1. Priority filing deadline February 15. **Notification of Awards:** Applicants will be notified of awards on or about May 1. **Types of Aid:** *Need-based scholarships/grants:* Pell, SEOG, state scholarships/grants, private scholarships, the school's own gift aid. *Loans:* FFEL Subsidized Stafford, FFEL Unsubsidized Stafford, FFEL PLUS, Federal Perkins, state loans. **Student Employment:** Federal Work-Study Program available. Institutional employment available. Off-campus job opportunities are excellent. **Financial Aid Statistics:** Average freshman grant $3,000. Average freshman loan $3,000. Average income from on-campus job $700. **Financial Aid Phone:** 615-444-2562.

CUNY—BARUCH COLLEGE

Undergraduate Admissions, One Bernard Baruch Way Box H0702, New York, NY 10010
Phone: 646-312-1400 **E-mail:** admissions@baruch.cuny.edu **CEEB Code:** 2034
Fax: 646-312-1362 **Web:** www.baruch.cuny.edu

This public school was founded in 1968.

STUDENTS AND FACULTY

Enrollment: 12,653. **Student Body:** Male 42%, female 58%, out-of-state 4%, international 9% (120 countries represented). **Ethnic Representation:** African American 18%, Asian 28%, Caucasian 33%, Hispanic 20%. **Retention and Graduation:** 88% freshmen return for sophomore year. 14% freshmen graduate within 4 years. **Faculty:** Student/faculty ratio 19:1. 408 full-time faculty, 94% hold PhDs. 95% faculty teach undergrads.

ACADEMICS

Degrees: Bachelor's, doctoral, master's, post-master's certificate. **Academic Requirements:** General education including some course work in arts/fine arts, computer literacy, English (including composition), foreign languages, history, humanities, mathematics, philosophy, sciences (biological or physical), social science, speech communications. **Classes:** 20-29 students in an average class. 100+ students in an average lab/discussion section. **Majors with Highest Enrollment:** Accounting; finance, general; computer and information sciences, general. **Disciplines with Highest Percentage of Degrees Awarded:**

Business/marketing 68%, computer and information sciences 22%, liberal arts/general studies 4%, psychology 3%, communications/communication technologies 2%. **Special Study Options:** Accelerated program, cross registration, distance learning, double major, English as a second language, student exchange program (domestic), honors program, independent study, internships, liberal arts/career combination, student-designed major, study abroad.

FACILITIES

Library Holdings: 297,959 bound volumes. 4,038 periodicals. 2,065,330 microforms. 1,044 audiovisuals. **Special Academic Facilities/Equipment:** Art gallery, Subotnik Financial Services Center, Wasserman Trading Floor. **Computers:** School-owned computers available for student use.

EXTRACURRICULARS

Activities: Choral groups, dance, drama/theater, literary magazine, musical theater, radio station, student government, student newspaper, yearbook. **Organizations:** 110 registered organizations, 9 honor societies, 5 religious organizations, 4 fraternities (1% men join), 4 sororities (1% women join). **Athletics (Intercollegiate):** *Men:* baseball, basketball, soccer, swimming, tennis, volleyball. *Women:* baseball, basketball, cheerleading, cross-country, softball, swimming, tennis, volleyball.

ADMISSIONS

Selectivity Rating: 66 (of 100). **Freshman Academic Profile:** Average SAT I Math 571, SAT I Math middle 50% range 520-620. Average SAT I Verbal 514, SAT I Verbal middle 50% range 460-560. TOEFL required of all international applicants, minimum TOEFL 620. **Basis for Candidate Selection:** *Very important factors considered include:* secondary school record, standardized test scores. *Important factors considered include:* essays, recommendations. *Other factors considered include:* alumni/ae relation, character/personal qualities, class rank, extracurricular activities, interview, talent/ability, work experience. **Freshman Admission Requirements:** High school diploma or GED is required. *Academic units required/recommended:* 16 total required; 4 English required, 3 math required, 4 math recommended, 2 science required, 2 science lab required, 2 foreign language required, 3 foreign language recommended, 4 social studies required, 1 elective recommended. **Freshman Admission Statistics:** 9,039 applied, 34% accepted, 54% of those accepted enrolled. **Transfer Admission Requirements:** *Items required:* high school transcript, college transcript, statement of good standing from prior school. Minimum high school GPA of 2.5 required. Minimum college GPA of 2.5 required. Lowest grade transferable C. **General Admission Information:** Application fee $40. Priority application deadline March 1. Early decision application deadline December 13. Regular application deadline April 1. Nonfall registration accepted. Credit and/or placement offered for CEEB Advanced Placement tests.

COSTS AND FINANCIAL AID

In-state tuition $3,800. Out-of-state tuition $7,400. Required fees $300. **Required Forms and Deadlines:** FAFSA and Baruch student employment forms. Financial aid filing deadline April 30. Priority filing deadline March 15. **Notification of Awards:** Applicants will be notified of awards on a rolling basis beginning on or about April 1. **Types of Aid:** *Need-based scholarships/grants:* Pell, SEOG, state scholarships/grants, private scholarships, the school's own gift aid, city merit scholarships. *Loans:* Direct Subsidized Stafford, Direct Unsubsidized Stafford, Direct PLUS, Federal Perkins. **Student Employment:** Federal Work-Study Program available. Institutional employment available. Off-campus job opportunities are excellent. **Financial Aid Statistics:** 91% freshmen, 86% undergrads receive some form of aid. Average freshman grant $3,410. Average freshman loan $1,200. Average income from on-campus job $3,000. **Financial Aid Phone:** 646-312-1360.

CUNY—BROOKLYN COLLEGE

2900 Bedford Avenue, Brooklyn, NY 11210
Phone: 718-951-5001 **E-mail:** adminqry@brooklyn.cuny.edu
Fax: 718-951-4506 **Web:** www.brooklyn.cuny.edu **ACT Code:** 20169

This public school was founded in 1930. It has a 26-acre campus.

STUDENTS AND FACULTY

Enrollment: 10,767. **Student Body:** Male 39%, female 61%, out-of-state 2%, international 5%. **Ethnic Representation:** African American 30%, Asian 10%, Caucasian 48%, Hispanic 11%. **Retention and Graduation:** 86% freshmen return for sophomore year. 15% freshmen graduate within 4 years. 21% grads go on to further study within 1 year. 8% grads pursue business degrees. 5% grads pursue law degrees. 2% grads pursue medical degrees. **Faculty:** Student/faculty ratio 16:1. 485 full-time faculty, 91% hold PhDs.

ACADEMICS

Degrees: Bachelor's, certificate, master's, post-bachelor's certificate, post-master's certificate. **Academic Requirements:** General education including some course work in arts/fine arts, computer literacy, English (including composition), foreign languages, history, humanities, mathematics, philosophy, sciences (biological or physical), social science; most of these areas are part of the core curriculum. **Classes:** 20-29 students in an average class. **Majors with Highest Enrollment:** Business administration/management; computer and information sciences, general; education, general. **Disciplines with Highest Percentage of Degrees Awarded:** Business/marketing 22%, education 15%, psychology 13%, computer and information sciences 11%, social sciences and history 10%. **Special Study Options:** Accelerated program, cooperative (work-study) program, cross registration, distance learning, double major, dual enrollment, English as a second language, student exchange program (domestic), honors program, independent study, internships, study abroad, teacher certification program, weekend college.

FACILITIES

Library Holdings: 1,305,602 bound volumes. 13,541 periodicals. 1,624,712 microforms. 21,731 audiovisuals. **Special Academic Facilities/Equipment:** Art museum, language lab, TV studios, speech clinic, research centers and institutes, particle accelerator. **Computers:** *Recommended operating system:* Windows 95. School-owned computers available for student use.

EXTRACURRICULARS

Activities: Choral groups, concert band, dance, drama/theater, literary magazine, music ensembles, musical theater, opera, radio station, student government, student newspaper, student-run film society, symphony orchestra, television station, yearbook. **Organizations:** 150 registered organizations, 1 honor society, 6 religious organizations, 5 fraternities (2% men join), 4 sororities (2% women join). **Athletics (Intercollegiate):** *Men:* basketball, cross-country, soccer, swimming, tennis, track & field, volleyball. *Women:* basketball, cross-country, softball, swimming, tennis, track & field, volleyball.

ADMISSIONS

Selectivity Rating: 60 (of 100). **Freshman Academic Profile:** Average high school GPA 3.0. 73% from public high schools. Average SAT I Math 523, SAT I Math middle 50% range 470-570. Average SAT I Verbal 497, SAT I Verbal middle 50% range 440-550. TOEFL required of all international applicants, minimum TOEFL 500. **Basis for Candidate Selection:** *Very important factors considered include:* secondary school record, standardized test scores. *Other factors considered include:* extracurricular activities, interview, recommendations, talent/ability. **Freshman Admission Requirements:** High school diploma or GED is required. *Academic units required/recommended:* 4 English recommended, 3 math recommended, 3 science recommended, 3 foreign language recommended, 4 social studies recommended, 4 elective recommended. **Freshman Admission Statistics:** 6,184 applied, 36% accepted, 55% of those accepted enrolled. **Transfer Admission Requirements:** *Items required:* high school transcript, college transcript, statement of good standing from prior school. Minimum high school GPA of 2.5 required. Minimum college GPA of 2.0 required. Lowest grade transferable C. **General Admission Information:** Application fee $40. Priority application deadline December 15. Nonfall registration accepted. Admission may be deferred. Credit offered for CEEB Advanced Placement tests.

COSTS AND FINANCIAL AID

In-state tuition $3,200. Out-of-state tuition $6,800. Room & board $4,200. Required fees $353. **Required Forms and Deadlines:** FAFSA and state aid form. No deadline for regular filing. Priority filing deadline April 1. **Notification of Awards:** Applicants will be notified of awards on a rolling basis beginning on or about June 1. **Types of Aid:** *Need-based scholarships/grants:* Pell, SEOG, state scholarships/grants, private scholarships, the school's own gift aid. *Loans:* Direct Subsidized Stafford, Direct Unsubsidized Stafford, Direct PLUS, Federal Perkins. **Student Employment:** Federal Work-Study Program available. Institutional employment available. Off-campus job opportunities are excellent. **Financial Aid Statistics:** 66% freshmen, 81% undergrads receive some form of aid. **Financial Aid Phone:** 718-951-5051.

CUNY—CITY COLLEGE

Convent Avenue at 138th Street, New York, NY 10031-9198
Phone: 212-650-6977 **E-mail:** admissions@ccny.cuny.edu **CEEB Code:** 2083
Fax: 212-650-6417 **Web:** www.ccny.cuny.edu

This public school was founded in 1847. It has a 34-acre campus.

STUDENTS AND FACULTY

Enrollment: 8,638. **Student Body:** Male 49%, female 51%, out-of-state 12%, international 7% (85 countries represented). **Ethnic Representation:** African American 34%, Asian 17%, Caucasian 12%, Hispanic 36%. **Retention and Graduation:** 78% freshmen return for sophomore year. 1% grads pursue medical degrees. **Faculty:** Student/faculty ratio 15:1. 483 full-time faculty, 89% hold PhDs. 100% faculty teach undergrads.

ACADEMICS

Degrees: Bachelor's, first professional certificate, master's. **Academic Requirements:** General education including some course work in arts/fine arts, computer literacy, English (including composition), foreign languages, history, humanities, mathematics, philosophy, sciences (biological or physical), social science. **Majors with Highest Enrollment:** Architecture (BArch, BA/BS, MArch, MA/MS, PhD); computer science; psychology, general. **Disciplines with Highest Percentage of Degrees Awarded:** Liberal arts/general studies 14%, psychology 12%, social sciences and history 11%, engineering/engineering technology 8%, architecture 8%. **Special Study Options:** Accelerated program, cooperative (work-study) program, cross registration, English as a second language, honors program, independent study, internships, study abroad, teacher certification program.

FACILITIES

Library Holdings: 1,397,720 bound volumes. 2,207 periodicals. 838,027 microforms. 19,506 audiovisuals. **Special Academic Facilities/Equipment:** Art museum, electron microscope, spectroscopy lab, planetarium, aquarium, weather station. **Computers:** School-owned computers available for student use.

EXTRACURRICULARS

Activities: Choral groups, dance, drama/theater, jazz band, literary magazine, radio station, student government, student newspaper, yearbook. **Organizations:** 85 registered organizations, 2 fraternities. **Athletics (Intercollegiate):** *Men:* basketball, indoor track, lacrosse, soccer, tennis, track & field, volleyball. *Women:* basketball, fencing, indoor track, soccer, tennis, track & field, volleyball.

ADMISSIONS

Selectivity Rating: 68 (of 100). **Freshman Academic Profile:** 85% from public high schools. Average SAT I Math 530, SAT I Math middle 50% range 450-600. Average SAT I Verbal 493, SAT I Verbal middle 50% range 410-560. TOEFL required of all international applicants, minimum TOEFL 500. **Basis for Candidate Selection:** *Very important factors considered include:* secondary school record. *Important factors considered include:* standardized test scores. *Other factors considered include:* essays. **Freshman Admission Requirements:** High school diploma or GED is required. *Academic units required/recommended:* 17 total required; 19 total recommended; 4 English required, 4 English recommended, 2 math required, 3 math recommended, 2 science required, 2 science recommended, 2 science lab required, 2 science lab recommended, 2 foreign language required, 3 foreign language recommended, 4 social studies required, 4 social studies recommended. **Freshman Admission Statistics:** 5,267 applied, 38% accepted, 53% of those accepted enrolled. **Transfer Admission Requirements:** *Items required:* college transcript. Minimum college GPA of 2.0 required. Lowest grade transferable C. **General Admission Information:** Application fee $40. Priority application deadline March 1. Nonfall registration accepted. Credit offered for CEEB Advanced Placement tests.

COSTS AND FINANCIAL AID

In-state tuition $3,200. Out-of-state tuition $6,800. Required fees $259. Average book expense $670. **Required Forms and Deadlines:** FAFSA. Priority filing deadline January 15. **Notification of Awards:** Applicants will be notified of awards on a rolling basis. **Types of Aid:** *Need-based scholarships/grants:* Pell, SEOG, state scholarships/grants, private scholarships. *Loans:* Direct Subsidized Stafford, Direct Unsubsidized Stafford, Direct PLUS, Federal Perkins, college/university loans from institutional funds. **Student Employment:** Federal Work-Study Program available. Institutional employment available. **Financial Aid Statistics:** 82% undergrads receive some form of aid. **Financial Aid Phone:** 212-650-5918.

CUNY—COLLEGE OF STATEN ISLAND

2800 Victory Boulevard, Staten Island, NY 10314
Phone: 718-982-2010 **E-mail:** recruitment@postbox.csi.cuny.edu **CEEB Code:** 2778
Fax: 718-982-2500 **Web:** www.csi.cuny.edu

This public school was founded in 1955. It has a 204-acre campus.

STUDENTS AND FACULTY

Enrollment: 10,616. **Student Body:** Male 41%, female 59%, out-of-state 0%, international 3% (116 countries represented). **Ethnic Representation:** African American 10%, Asian 9%, Caucasian 70%, Hispanic 11%. **Retention and Graduation:** 85% freshmen return for sophomore year. 16% freshmen graduate within 4 years. **Faculty:** Student/faculty ratio 18:1. 317 full-time faculty, 80% hold PhDs. 80% faculty teach undergrads.

ACADEMICS

Degrees: Associate's, bachelor's, master's, post-master's certificate. **Academic Requirements:** General education including some course work in arts/fine arts, English (including composition), foreign languages, history, mathematics, sciences (biological or physical), social science. **Classes:** 20-29 students in an average class. 10-19 students in an average lab/discussion section. **Majors with Highest Enrollment:** Business administration/management; educational, instructional, and curriculum supervision; psychology, general. **Disciplines with Highest Percentage of Degrees Awarded:** Business/marketing 31%, social sciences and history 13%, psychology 10%, liberal arts/general studies 10%, computer and information sciences 7%. **Special Study Options:** Cooperative (work-study) program, cross registration, distance learning, double major, English as a second language, honors program, independent study, internships, liberal arts/career combination, student-designed major, study abroad, teacher certification program, weekend college.

FACILITIES

Library Holdings: 212,554 bound volumes. 994 periodicals. 877,357 microforms. 14,500 audiovisuals. **Special Academic Facilities/Equipment:** astrophysical observatory, artificial intelligence lab. **Computers:** *Recommended operating system:* Windows 95. School-owned computers available for student use.

EXTRACURRICULARS

Activities: Dance, drama/theater, jazz band, literary magazine, radio station, student government, student newspaper, yearbook. **Organizations:** 41 registered organizations, 8 honor societies, 3 religious organizations. **Athletics (Intercollegiate):** *Men:* baseball, basketball, diving, soccer, swimming, tennis. *Women:* diving, softball, swimming, tennis, volleyball.

ADMISSIONS

Selectivity Rating: 63 (of 100). **Freshman Academic Profile:** Average SAT I Math 510, SAT I Math middle 50% range 460-560. Average SAT I Verbal 500, SAT I Verbal middle 50% range 450-550. TOEFL required of all international applicants, minimum TOEFL 550. **Basis for Candidate Selection:** *Very important factors considered include:* secondary school record, standardized test scores. **Freshman Admission Requirements:** High school diploma or GED is required. *Academic units required/recommended:* 16 total required; 16 total recommended; 4 English required, 4 English recommended, 3 math required, 3 math recommended, 2 science required, 2 science recommended, 2 foreign language required, 2 foreign language recommended, 4 social studies required, 4 social studies recommended. **Freshman Admission Statistics:** 3,897 applied, 89% accepted, 57% of those accepted enrolled. **Transfer Admission Requirements:** *Items required:* college transcript. Minimum high school GPA of 2.0 required. Minimum college GPA of 2.0 required. Lowest grade transferable C. **General Admission Information:** Application fee $40. Nonfall registration accepted. Admission may be deferred. Placement offered for CEEB Advanced Placement tests.

COSTS AND FINANCIAL AID

In-state tuition $3,200. Out-of-state tuition $6,800. Required fees $159. Average book expense $500. **Required Forms and Deadlines:** FAFSA and state aid form. No deadline for regular filing. **Notification of Awards:** Applicants will be notified of awards on a rolling basis beginning on or about August 1. **Types of Aid:** *Need-based scholarships/grants:* Pell, SEOG, state scholarships/grants, private scholarships, Federal Nursing. *Loans:* Direct Subsidized Stafford, Direct Unsubsidized Stafford, Direct PLUS, Federal Perkins. **Student Employment:** Federal Work-Study Program available. Institutional employment available. Off-campus job opportunities are good. **Financial Aid Statistics:** 52% freshmen, 50% undergrads receive some form of aid. Average freshman grant $6,625. Average freshman loan $8,800. **Financial Aid Phone:** 718-982-2030.

CUNY—HOSTOS COMMUNITY COLLEGE

120 East 149th Street, Room D210, Bronx, NY 10451
Phone: 718-518-4405 **E-mail:** admissions@hostos.cuny.edu
Fax: 718-518-6643 **Web:** www.hostos.cuny.edu

This public school was founded in 1968. It has an 8-acre campus.

STUDENTS AND FACULTY

Enrollment: 3,285. **Student Body:** Male 23%, female 77%, out-of-state 1%, international 4%. **Ethnic Representation:** African American 23%, Asian 3%, Caucasian 1%, Hispanic 68%. **Retention and Graduation:** 59% freshmen return for sophomore year. **Faculty:** Student/faculty ratio 14:1. 150 full-time faculty, 50% hold PhDs.

ACADEMICS

Degrees: Associate's, certificate, terminal. **Academic Requirements:** General education including some course work in English (including composition), humanities, mathematics. **Classes:** 20-29 students in an average class. **Majors with Highest Enrollment:** Nursing/registered nurse training (RN, ASN, BSN, MSN); early childhood education and teaching; liberal arts and sciences/liberal studies. **Special Study Options:** Distance learning, English as a second language, honors program, internships, study abroad.

FACILITIES

Library Holdings: 37,533 bound volumes. 312 periodicals. 30,137 microforms. 534 audiovisuals. **Special Academic Facilities/Equipment:** Art gallery. **Computers:** *Recommended operating system:* Windows NT/2000. School-owned computers available for student use.

EXTRACURRICULARS

Activities: Drama/theater, student government, student newspaper, television station. **Organizations:** 30 registered organizations.

ADMISSIONS

Selectivity Rating: 63 (of 100). **Freshman Academic Profile:** 95% from public high schools. **Freshman Admission Requirements:** High school diploma or GED is required. *Academic units required/recommended:* 16 total required; 4 English required, 3 math required, 2 science required, 2 foreign language required, 4 social studies required. **Transfer Admission Requirements:** *Items required:* high school transcript, college transcript. Minimum high school GPA of 2.0 required. Minimum college GPA of 2.0 required. Lowest grade transferable C. **General Admission Information:** Application fee $40. Regular application deadline August 15. Nonfall registration accepted. Admission may be deferred. Neither credit nor placement offered for CEEB Advanced Placement tests.

COSTS AND FINANCIAL AID

In-state tuition $2,500. Out-of-state tuition $3,076. Required fees $86. Average book expense $670. **Required Forms and Deadlines:** FAFSA, institution's own financial aid form, and state aid form. No deadline for regular filing. Priority filing deadline July 1. **Notification of Awards:** Applicants will be notified of awards on a rolling basis. **Types of Aid:** *Need-based scholarships/grants:* Pell, state scholarships/grants. **Student Employment:** Off-campus job opportunities are good. **Financial Aid Statistics:** 81% freshmen, 81% undergrads receive some form of aid.

CUNY—HUNTER COLLEGE

695 Park Avenue, New York, NY 10021
Phone: 212-772-4490 **E-mail:** admissions@hunter.cuny.edu **CEEB Code:** 2301
Fax: 212-650-3336 **Web:** www.hunter.cuny.edu

This public school was founded in 1870.

STUDENTS AND FACULTY

Enrollment: 15,494. **Student Body:** Male 30%, female 70%, out-of-state 2%, international 6%. **Ethnic Representation:** African American 20%, Asian 16%, Caucasian 41%, Hispanic 23%. **Retention and Graduation:** 80% freshmen return for sophomore year. 9% freshmen graduate within 4 years. **Faculty:** 573 full-time faculty, 79% hold PhDs.

ACADEMICS

Degrees: Bachelor's, first professional certificate, master's, post-master's certificate. **Academic Requirements:** General education including some course work in arts/fine arts, English (including composition), foreign languages, humanities, mathematics, sciences (biological or physical), social science. **Disciplines with Highest Percentage of Degrees Awarded:** Social sciences and history 25%, English 14%, psychology 10%, visual and performing arts 9%, health professions and related sciences 9%. **Special Study Options:** Accelerated program, cross registration, distance learning, double major, dual enrollment, student exchange program (domestic), honors program, internships, liberal arts/career combination, student-designed major, study abroad, teacher certification program.

FACILITIES

Housing: Coed. **Library Holdings:** 534,283 bound volumes. 2,160 periodicals. 1,167,566 microforms. 13,137 audiovisuals. **Special Academic Facilities/Equipment:** Art gallery, theatre, geology lab, on-campus elementary and secondary schools. **Computers:** School-owned computers available for student use.

EXTRACURRICULARS

Activities: Choral groups, concert band, dance, drama/theater, jazz band, literary magazine, music ensembles, musical theater, radio station, student government, student newspaper, student-run film society, symphony orchestra, television station, yearbook. **Organizations:** 130 registered organizations, 20 honor societies, 2 fraternities (1% men join), 2 sororities (1% women join). **Athletics (Intercollegiate):** *Men:* basketball, cross-country, fencing, indoor track, soccer, tennis, track & field, volleyball, wrestling. *Women:* basketball, cross-country, fencing, indoor track, softball, swimming, tennis, track & field, volleyball.

ADMISSIONS

Selectivity Rating: 79 (of 100). **Freshman Academic Profile:** 74% from public high schools. Average SAT I Math 531, SAT I Math middle 50% range 480-580. Average SAT I Verbal 517, SAT I Verbal middle 50% range 470-570. TOEFL required of all international applicants, minimum TOEFL 500. **Basis for Candidate Selection:** *Very important factors considered include:* secondary school record, standardized test scores. *Other factors considered include:* essays, recommendations. **Freshman Admission Requirements:** High school diploma or GED is required. *Academic units required/recommended:* 14 total required; 16 total recommended; 2 English required, 4 English recommended, 2 math required, 3 math recommended, 1 science required, 2 science recommended, 1 science lab required, 2 science lab recommended, 2 foreign language recommended, 4 social studies recommended, 1 elective recommended. **Freshman Admission Statistics:** 10,550 applied, 29% accepted, 49% of those accepted enrolled. **Transfer Admission Requirements:** *Items required:* college transcript. Minimum college GPA of 2.0 required. Lowest grade transferable C. **General Admission Information:** Application fee $50. Priority application deadline January 2. Nonfall registration accepted. Admission may be deferred. Credit and/or placement offered for CEEB Advanced Placement tests.

COSTS AND FINANCIAL AID

Out-of-state tuition $6,800. Required fees $300. Average book expense $692. **Required Forms and Deadlines:** FAFSA and state aid form. No deadline for regular filing. Priority filing deadline April 1. **Notification of Awards:** Applicants will be notified of awards on a rolling basis. **Types of Aid:** *Need-based scholarships/grants:* Pell, SEOG, state scholarships/grants, private scholarships, the school's own gift aid. *Loans:* Direct Subsidized Stafford, Direct Unsubsidized Stafford, Direct PLUS, Federal Perkins. **Student Employment:** Federal Work-Study Program available. Institutional employment available. Off-campus job opportunities are good. **Financial Aid Statistics:** 58% freshmen, 59% undergrads receive some form of aid. Average freshman grant $4,200. Average freshman loan $2,600. Average income from on-campus job $1,500. **Financial Aid Phone:** 212-772-4820.

CUNY—JOHN JAY COLLEGE OF CRIMINAL JUSTICE

899 Tenth Avenue, New York, NY 10019
Phone: 212-237-8000 **CEEB Code:** 2115
Fax: 212-237-8901 **Web:** www.cuny.edu

STUDENTS AND FACULTY

Enrollment: 9,772. **Student Body:** Out-of-state 4%, international students represent 25 countries.

ACADEMICS

Degrees: Associate's, bachelor's, master's. **Special Study Options:** Cooperative (work-study) program, student exchange program (domestic), study abroad. Undergrads may take grad-level classes. Off-campus study: Albany Internship Program. Co-op programs: Public service.

FACILITIES

Library Holdings: 197,715 bound volumes. 2,603 periodicals. 218,077 microforms. **Special Academic Facilities/Equipment:** Criminal justice center, center for violence/human survival, toxicology research/training center, fire science institute, institute for criminal justice ethics, institute for the study of genocide, and institute on alcohol/substance abuse. **Computers:** *Recommended operating system:* UNIX. School-owned computers available for student use.

EXTRACURRICULARS

Athletics (Intercollegiate): *Men:* softball. *Women:* basketball, cross-country, softball, tennis, volleyball.

ADMISSIONS

Selectivity Rating: 63 (of 100). **Freshman Academic Profile:** 63% from public high schools. TOEFL required of all international applicants, minimum TOEFL 500. **Freshman Admission Requirements:** High school diploma is required and GED is not accepted. *Academic units required/recommended:* 15 total recommended; 4 English recommended, 3 math recommended, 2 science recommended, 2 social studies recommended, 4 elective recommended. **Transfer Admission Requirements:** Minimum college GPA of 2.0 required. Lowest grade transferable C. **General Admission Information:** Early decision application deadline January 1. Regular application deadline rolling. Nonfall registration accepted. Credit offered for CEEB Advanced Placement tests.

COSTS AND FINANCIAL AID

In-state tuition $2,450. Out-of-state tuition $5,050. Required fees $100. Average book expense $500. **Required Forms and Deadlines:** FAFSA. **Types of Aid:** *Need-based scholarships/grants:* Pell, SEOG, state scholarships/grants, private scholarships, the school's own gift aid. *Loans:* FFEL Subsidized Stafford, FFEL Unsubsidized Stafford, FFEL PLUS, Federal Perkins, college/university loans from institutional funds. **Student Employment:** Federal Work-Study Program available. Institutional employment available. Off-campus job opportunities are good. **Financial Aid Statistics:** Average freshman grant $2,000. Average income from on-campus job $2,500. **Financial Aid Phone:** 212-237-8151.

CUNY—KINGSBOROUGH COMMUNITY COLLEGE

2001 Oriental Boulevard, Brooklyn, NY 11235
Phone: 718-368-4600 **E-mail:** info@kbcc.cuny.edu
Fax: 718-368-5356 **Web:** www.kbcc.cuny.edu

This public school was founded in 1963. It has a 72-acre campus.

STUDENTS AND FACULTY

Enrollment: 15,017. **Student Body:** Male 40%, female 60%, out-of-state 1%, international 5%. **Ethnic Representation:** African American 35%, Asian 9%, Caucasian 40%, Hispanic 15%. **Retention and Graduation:** 51% grads go on to further study within 1 year. **Faculty:** Student/faculty ratio 25:1. 233 full-time faculty, 75% hold PhDs.

ACADEMICS

Degrees: Associate's, certificate, terminal, transfer. **Academic Requirements:** General education including some course work in English (including composition). **Classes:** 20-29 students in an average class. **Majors with Highest Enrollment:** Liberal arts and sciences/liberal studies; business administration/management; biology/biological sciences, general. **Special Study Options:** Accelerated program, cross registration, dual enrollment, English as a second language, honors program, independent study, internships, My Turn Program for senior citizens, New Start Program for students academically dismissed from 4-year institutions.

FACILITIES

Library Holdings: 155,432 bound volumes. 471 periodicals. 10,000 microforms. 2,388 audiovisuals. **Computers:** School-owned computers available for student use.

EXTRACURRICULARS

Activities: Choral groups, concert band, dance, drama/theater, jazz band, literary magazine, music ensembles, musical theater, opera, radio station, student government, student newspaper, student-run film society, symphony orchestra, yearbook. **Athletics (Intercollegiate):** *Men:* baseball, basketball, soccer, tennis, track & field. *Women:* basketball, softball, tennis, track & field, volleyball.

ADMISSIONS

Selectivity Rating: 63 (of 100). **Freshman Academic Profile:** Average SAT I Math 399. Average SAT I Verbal 386. **Freshman Admission Requirements:** *Academic units required/recommended:* 16 total recommended; 4 English recommended, 3 math recommended, 2 science recommended, 2 foreign language recommended, 4 social studies recommended. **Freshman Admission Statistics:** 3,846 applied, 84% accepted, 61% of those accepted enrolled. **Transfer Admission Requirements:** *Items required:* college transcript. Lowest grade transferable C. **General Admission Information:** Application fee $40. Priority application deadline July 15. Regular application deadline August 15. Nonfall registration accepted.

COSTS AND FINANCIAL AID

In-state tuition $2,500. Out-of-state tuition $3,076. Required fees $280. Average book expense $692. **Financial Aid Phone:** 718-368-4644.

CUNY—LAGUARDIA COMMUNITY COLLEGE

31-10 Thompson Avenue M-147, Long Island City, NY 11101
Phone: 718-482-7206 **E-mail:** admissions@lagcc.cuny.edu
Fax: 718-603-2033 **Web:** www.lagcc.cuny.edu

This public school was founded in 1971.

STUDENTS AND FACULTY

Enrollment: 12,433. **Student Body:** Male 37%, female 63%, international 11% (147 countries represented). **Ethnic Representation:** African American 22%, Asian 15%, Caucasian 18%, Hispanic 44%. **Retention and Graduation:** 57% grads go on to further study within 1 year. **Faculty:** Student/faculty ratio 24:1. 231 full-time faculty, 45% hold PhDs. 100% faculty teach undergrads.

ACADEMICS

Degrees: Associate's, certificate. **Academic Requirements:** General education including some course work in English (including composition), history, humanities, sciences (biological or physical), social science. **Majors with Highest Enrollment:** Business administration/management; computer science; liberal arts and sciences, general studies and humanities. **Special Study Options:** Cooperative (work-study) program, dual enrollment, English as a second language, honors program, independent study, internships, study abroad.

FACILITIES

Library Holdings: 115,019 bound volumes. 797 periodicals. 583,009 microforms. 5,529 audiovisuals. **Special Academic Facilities/Equipment:** LaGuardia and Wagner Archives. **Computers:** School-owned computers available for student use.

EXTRACURRICULARS

Activities: Dance, drama/theater, literary magazine, music ensembles, radio station, student government, student newspaper, yearbook.

ADMISSIONS

Selectivity Rating: 63 (of 100). **Freshman Academic Profile:** 55% from public high schools. High school diploma or GED is required. *Academic units required/recommended:* 16 total required; 4 English required, 3 math required, 2 science required, 2 foreign language required, 4 social studies required. **Freshman Admission Statistics:** 4,194 applied, 87% accepted, 57% of those accepted enrolled. **Transfer Admission Requirements:** *Items required:* college transcript. **General Admission Information:** Application fee $40. Nonfall registration accepted. Admission may be deferred for a maximum of 1 year. Credit and/or placement offered for CEEB Advanced Placement tests. TOEFL required of all international applicants, minimum TOEFL 450.

COSTS AND FINANCIAL AID

In-state tuition $2,500. Out-of-state tuition $3,076. Required fees $272. Average book expense $692. **Types of Aid:** *Need-based scholarships/grants:* Pell, SEOG, state scholarships/grants, private scholarships, the school's own gift aid. *Loans:* FFEL Subsidized Stafford, FFEL Unsubsidized Stafford, FFEL PLUS, Federal Perkins, college/university loans from institutional funds. **Financial Aid Phone:** 718-482-7218.

CUNY—LEHMAN COLLEGE

250 Bedford Park Boulevard West, Bronx, NY 10468
Phone: 718-960-8000 **E-mail:** wilkes@alpha.lehman.cuny.edu **CEEB Code:** 2950
Fax: 718-960-8712 **Web:** www.lehman.cuny.edu

This public school was founded in 1968. It has a 38-acre campus.

STUDENTS AND FACULTY

Enrollment: 7,322. **Student Body:** Male 28%, female 72%, out-of-state 1%, international 2%. **Ethnic Representation:** African American 38%, Asian 4%, Caucasian 11%, Hispanic 47%. **Retention and Graduation:** 72% freshmen return for sophomore year. 8% freshmen graduate within 4 years. **Faculty:** Student/faculty ratio 15:1. 292 full-time faculty, 84% hold PhDs.

ACADEMICS

Degrees: Bachelor's, master's. **Majors with Highest Enrollment:** Nursing/registered nurse training (RN, ASN, BSN, MSN); accounting; psychology, general. **Disciplines with Highest Percentage of Degrees Awarded:** Social sciences and history 21%, health professions and related sciences 20%, business/marketing 16%, psychology 11%, protective services/public administration 8%. **Special Study Options:** Accelerated program, cooperative (work-study) program, cross registration, distance learning, double major, dual enrollment, student exchange program (domestic), honors program, independent study, internships, student-designed major, study abroad, teacher certification program, weekend college. Undergrads may take grad-level classes. Off-campus study: Washington, DC.

FACILITIES

Library Holdings: 510,597 bound volumes. 1,769 periodicals. 415,000 microforms. **Special Academic Facilities/Equipment:** Art gallery, concert hall, sports complex. **Computers:** *Recommended operating system:* Mac. School-owned computers available for student use.

EXTRACURRICULARS

Activities: Choral groups, concert band, dance, drama/theater, jazz band, literary magazine, music ensembles, musical theater, opera, radio station, student government, student newspaper, student-run film society, symphony orchestra, television station, yearbook. **Organizations:** 3 honor societies, 1 religious organization, 14 fraternity, 1 sorority. **Athletics (Intercollegiate):** *Men:* baseball, basketball, soccer, tennis, track & field, volleyball, wrestling. *Women:* baseball, basketball, cross-country, softball, tennis, track & field, volleyball.

ADMISSIONS

Selectivity Rating: 66 (of 100). **Freshman Academic Profile:** Average high school GPA 2.7. 61% from public high schools. Average SAT I Math 448, SAT I Math middle 50% range 410-500. Average SAT I Verbal 444, SAT I Verbal middle 50% range 410-520. TOEFL required of all international applicants, minimum TOEFL 500. **Basis for Candidate Selection:** *Very important factors considered include:* secondary school record. *Other factors considered include:* essays, interview, recommendations, standardized test scores. **Freshman Admission Requirements:** High school diploma or GED is required. *Academic units required/recommended:* 10 total required; 1 English required, 1 math required, 1 foreign language recommended, 3 social studies recommended. **Freshman Admission Statistics:** 3,882 applied, 32% accepted, 60% of those accepted enrolled. **Transfer Admission Requirements:** *Items required:* high school transcript, college transcript. Minimum college GPA of 2.0 required. Lowest grade transferable C. **General Admission Information:** Application fee $40. Priority application deadline February 15. Regular application deadline March 25. Nonfall registration accepted. Credit offered for CEEB Advanced Placement tests.

COSTS AND FINANCIAL AID

In-state tuition $3,200. Out-of-state tuition $6,800. Required fees $260. **Required Forms and Deadlines:** FAFSA and state aid form. **Types of Aid:** *Loans:* Direct Subsidized Stafford, Direct Unsubsidized Stafford, Direct PLUS, Federal Perkins. **Student Employment:** Federal Work-Study Program available. Institutional employment available. Off-campus job opportunities are excellent. **Financial Aid Statistics:** 89% freshmen, 89% undergrads receive some form of aid. **Financial Aid Phone:** 718-960-8545.

CUNY—MEDGAR EVERS COLLEGE

1650 Bedford Avenue, Brooklyn, NY 11225
Phone: 718-270-6023 **E-mail:** website@mec.cuny.edu
Fax: 718-270-6188 **Web:** www.mec.cuny.edu

This public school was founded in 1969.

STUDENTS AND FACULTY

Enrollment: 4,873. **Student Body:** Male 21%, female 79%, out-of-state 1%, international 6%. **Ethnic Representation:** African American 93%, Asian 1%, Caucasian 1%, Hispanic 5%. **Retention and Graduation:** 10% freshmen graduate within 4 years. **Faculty:** Student/faculty ratio 17:1. 127 full-time faculty. 100% faculty teach undergrads.

ACADEMICS

Degrees: Associate's, bachelor's, certificate. **Academic Requirements:** General education including some course work in arts/fine arts, computer literacy, English (including composition), foreign languages, history, mathematics, philosophy, sciences (biological or physical), social science. **Classes:** 20-29 students in an average class. 10-19 students in an average lab/discussion section. **Majors with Highest Enrollment:** Business administration/management; psychology, general; biology/biological sciences, general. **Disciplines with Highest Percentage of Degrees Awarded:** Business/marketing 27%, education 16%, health professions and related sciences 15%, psychology 13%, other 12%. **Special Study Options:** Distance learning, double major, English as a second language, honors program, independent study, internships, study abroad, weekend college.

FACILITIES

Library Holdings: 111,000 bound volumes. 467 periodicals. **Computers:** *Recommended operating system:* Windows NT/2000.

EXTRACURRICULARS

Activities: Choral groups, dance, drama/theater, radio station, student government, student newspaper, television station, yearbook. **Organizations:** 30 registered organizations, 3 honor societies, 3 religious organizations. **Athletics (Intercollegiate):** *Men:* basketball, cross-country, indoor track, soccer, track & field. *Women:* basketball, cross-country, indoor track, softball, track & field, volleyball.

ADMISSIONS

Selectivity Rating: 63 (of 100). **Freshman Academic Profile:** Average high school GPA 2.0. SAT I Math middle 50% range 288-415. SAT I Verbal middle 50% range 330-475. **Freshman Admission Requirements:** High school diploma or GED is required. *Academic units required/recommended:* 15 total recommended; 4 English recommended, 3 math recommended, 2 science recommended, 2 history recommended, 4 elective recommended. **Freshman Admission Statistics:** 1,679 applied, 80% accepted, 50% of those accepted enrolled. **Transfer Admission Requirements:** *Items required:* college transcript. Lowest grade transferable C. **General Admission Information:** Application fee $40. Regular application deadline rolling. Nonfall registration accepted. Admission may be deferred for a maximum of 1 year.

COSTS AND FINANCIAL AID

In-state tuition $3,200. Out-of-state tuition $6,800. Required fees $141. Average book expense $500. **Types of Aid:** *Need-based scholarships/grants:* Pell, SEOG, state scholarships/grants, private scholarships. *Loans:* Direct Subsidized Stafford, Direct PLUS, Federal Perkins. **Student Employment:** Federal Work-Study Program available. Off-campus job opportunities are excellent. **Financial Aid Statistics:** Average income from on-campus job $1,300. **Financial Aid Phone:** 718-270-6139.

CUNY—NEW YORK CITY COLLEGE OF TECHNOLOGY

300 Jay Street, NG17, Brooklyn, NY 11201
Phone: (718) 260-5500 **E-mail:** admissions@nyctc.cuny.edu **CEEB Code:** 2550
Fax: (718) 260-5504 **Web:** www.nyctc.cuny.edu **ACT Code:** 2950

This public school was founded in 1946. It has a 3-acre campus.

STUDENTS AND FACULTY

Enrollment: 11,699. **Student Body:** Male 49%, female 51%, out-of-state 1%, international 3% (108 countries represented). **Ethnic Representation:** African American 48%, Asian 13%, Caucasian 13%, Hispanic 27%. **Retention and Graduation:** 78% freshmen return for sophomore year. 13% freshmen graduate within 4 years. **Faculty:** Student/faculty ratio 25:1. 270 full-time faculty, 44% hold PhDs. 100% faculty teach undergrads.

ACADEMICS

Degrees: Associate's, bachelor's, certificate. **Academic Requirements:** General education including some course work in computer literacy, English (including composition), humanities, mathematics, sciences (biological or physical), social science. **Classes:** 20-29 students in an average class. 20-29 students in an average lab/discussion section. **Majors with Highest Enrollment:** Hotel/motel administration/management; computer systems analysis/analyst; public administration and services. **Disciplines with Highest Percentage of Degrees Awarded:** Business/marketing 41%, engineering/engineering technology 21%, protective services/public administration 18%, communications/communication technologies 9%, computer and information sciences 7%. **Special Study Options:** Cooperative (work-study) program, distance learning, dual enrollment, English as a second language, honors program, independent study, internships, student-designed major, study abroad, teacher certification program, weekend college.

FACILITIES

Library Holdings: 175,000 bound volumes. 700 periodicals. 87 microforms. 6,000 audiovisuals. **Computers:** School-owned computers available for student use.

EXTRACURRICULARS

Activities: Choral groups, musical theater, student government, student newspaper. **Organizations:** 2 fraternities, 2 sororities. **Athletics (Intercollegiate):** *Men:* basketball, tennis, track & field. *Women:* basketball, tennis, track & field.

ADMISSIONS

Selectivity Rating: 63 (of 100). **Freshman Academic Profile:** 90% from public high schools. Average SAT I Math 460, SAT I Math middle 50% range 430-510. Average SAT I Verbal 425, SAT I Verbal middle 50% range 410-503. TOEFL required of all international applicants, minimum TOEFL 500. **Basis for Candidate Selection:** *Important factors considered include:* secondary school record. *Other factors considered include:* class rank, recommendations, standardized test scores. **Freshman Admission Requirements:** High school diploma or GED is required. *Academic units required/recommended:* 9 total required; 2 English required, 1 math required, 1 science required. **Freshman Admission Statistics:** 5,833 applied, 84% accepted, 48% of those accepted enrolled. **Transfer Admission Requirements:** *Items required:* high school transcript, college transcript, statement of good standing from prior school. Minimum college GPA of 2.0 required. Lowest grade transferable C. **General Admission Information:** Application fee $40. Nonfall registration accepted. Admission may be deferred. Credit and/or placement offered for CEEB Advanced Placement tests.

COSTS AND FINANCIAL AID

In-state tuition $3,200. Out-of-state tuition $6,800. Room & board $0. Required fees $119. Average book expense $0. **Required Forms and Deadlines:** FAFSA. **Types of Aid:** *Need-based scholarships/grants:* Pell, SEOG, state scholarships/grants, Federal Nursing. *Loans:* Direct Subsidized Stafford, Direct Unsubsidized Stafford, Direct PLUS, Federal Perkins. **Student Employment:** Federal Work-Study Program available. Institutional employment available. Off-campus job opportunities are excellent. **Financial Aid Statistics:** 68% freshmen, 45% undergrads receive some form of aid. Average freshman grant $1,313. Average freshman loan $1,283. **Financial Aid Phone:** (718) 260-5702.

CUNY—QUEENS COLLEGE

65-30 Kissena Blvd., Flushing, NY 11367
Phone: 718-997-5000 **E-mail:** admissions@qc.edu **CEEB Code:** 2750
Fax: 718-997-5617 **Web:** www.qc.edu **ACT Code:** 20173

This public school was founded in 1937. It has a 76-acre campus.

STUDENTS AND FACULTY

Enrollment: 12,012. **Student Body:** Male 37%, female 63%, out-of-state 1%, international 5%. **Ethnic Representation:** African American 10%, Asian 20%, Caucasian 53%, Hispanic 16%. **Retention and Graduation:** 85% freshmen return for sophomore year. 22% freshmen graduate within 4 years. 25% grads go on to further study within 1 year. 1% grads pursue business degrees. 3% grads pursue law degrees. 1% grads pursue medical degrees. **Faculty:** Student/faculty ratio 17:1. 514 full-time faculty, 79% hold PhDs. 90% faculty teach undergrads.

ACADEMICS

Degrees: Bachelor's, master's, post-bachelor's certificate, post-master's certificate. **Academic Requirements:** General education including some course work in arts/fine arts, computer literacy, English (including composition), foreign languages, history, humanities, mathematics, philosophy, sciences (biological or physical), social science, pre-industrial and/or nonwestern civilizations. **Classes:** 20-29 students in an average class. **Majors with Highest Enrollment:** Accounting; computer science; psychology, general. **Disciplines with Highest Percentage of Degrees Awarded:** Social sciences and history 32%, business/marketing 12%, psychology 10%, education 9%, computer and information sciences 7%. **Special Study Options:** Accelerated program, cooperative (work-study) program, cross registration, distance learning, double major, dual enrollment, English as a second language, honors program, independent study, internships, liberal arts/career combination, student-designed major, study abroad, teacher certification program, weekend college, Albany semester, and New York City internship.

FACILITIES

Library Holdings: 763,322 bound volumes. 5,301 periodicals. 879,115 microforms. 32,648 audiovisuals. **Special Academic Facilities/Equipment:** Art museum; centers for Asian, Byzantine, Modern Greek, and Jewish Studies; Italian American institute; Art Center for the Biology of Natural Systems; Art Library; Louis Armstrong Archival Center; music library. **Computers:** School-owned computers available for student use.

EXTRACURRICULARS

Activities: Choral groups, concert band, dance, drama/theater, jazz band, literary magazine, music ensembles, musical theater, radio station, student government, student newspaper, student-run film society, symphony orchestra, television station, yearbook. **Organizations:** 138 registered organizations, 22 honor societies, 8 religious organizations, 3 fraternities (1% men join), 2 sororities (1% women join). **Athletics (Intercollegiate):** *Men:* baseball, basketball, cross-country, golf, indoor track, swimming, tennis, track & field, volleyball, water polo. *Women:* basketball, cross-country, equestrian, field hockey, indoor track, soccer, softball, swimming, tennis, track & field, volleyball, water polo.

ADMISSIONS

Selectivity Rating: 75 (of 100). **Freshman Academic Profile:** Average high school GPA 3.1. 67% from public high schools. Average SAT I Math 537, SAT I Math middle 50% range 480-590. Average SAT I Verbal 504, SAT I Verbal middle 50% range 440-550. TOEFL required of all international applicants, minimum TOEFL 500. **Basis for Candidate Selection:** *Very important factors considered include:* secondary school record. *Important factors considered include:* standardized test scores, talent/ability. *Other factors considered include:* essays, recommendations. **Freshman Admission Requirements:** High school diploma or GED is required. *Academic units required/recommended:* 16 total required; 18 total recommended; 4 English required, 4 English recommended, 3 math required, 4 math recommended, 2 science required, 3 science recommended, 2 science lab required, 3 foreign language required, 3 foreign language recommended, 4 social studies required, 4 social studies recommended. **Freshman Admission Statistics:** 6,280 applied, 41% accepted, 48% of those accepted enrolled. **Transfer Admission Requirements:** *Items required:* college transcript, statement of good standing from prior school. Minimum college GPA of 2.2 required. Lowest grade transferable C. **General Admission Information:** Application fee $40. Priority application deadline October 15. Nonfall registration accepted. Admission may be deferred. Credit offered for CEEB Advanced Placement tests.

COSTS AND FINANCIAL AID

In-state tuition $3,200. Out-of-state tuition $6,800. Required fees $203. **Required Forms and Deadlines:** FAFSA and state aid form. No deadline for regular filing. Priority filing deadline February 1. **Notification of Awards:** Applicants will be notified of awards on a rolling basis beginning on or about March 1. **Types of Aid:** *Need-based scholarships/grants:* Pell, SEOG, state scholarships/grants, private scholarships, the school's own gift aid. *Loans:* Direct Subsidized Stafford, Direct Unsubsidized Stafford, Direct PLUS, Federal Perkins. **Student Employment:** Federal Work-Study Program available. Institutional employment available. Off-campus job opportunities are good. **Financial Aid Statistics:** 83% freshmen, 61% undergrads receive some form of aid. Average freshman grant $3,500. Average freshman loan $2,500. Average income from on-campus job $700. **Financial Aid Phone:** 718-997-5101.

CUNY—YORK COLLEGE

94-20 Guy R Brewer Boulevard, Jamaica, NY 11451
Phone: 718-262-2165 **E-mail:** admissions@york.cuny.edu **CEEB Code:** 2992
Fax: 718-262-2601 **Web:** www.york.cuny.edu **ACT Code:** 20175

This public school was founded in 1968. It has a 50-acre campus.

STUDENTS AND FACULTY

Enrollment: 5,748. **Student Body:** Male 29%, female 71%, international 7% (113 countries represented). **Ethnic Representation:** African American 48%, Asian 8%, Caucasian 4%, Hispanic 15%. **Retention and Graduation:** 77% freshmen return for sophomore year. 9% freshmen graduate within 4 years. **Faculty:** Student/faculty ratio 15:1. 166 full-time faculty, 72% hold PhDs. 100% faculty teach undergrads.

ACADEMICS

Degrees: Bachelor's. **Academic Requirements:** General education including some course work in arts/fine arts, English (including composition), history, mathematics, philosophy, sciences (biological or physical), social science. **Majors with Highest Enrollment:** Business administration/management; psychology, general; social work. **Disciplines with Highest Percentage of Degrees Awarded:** Psychology 21%, business/marketing 20%, mathematics 12%, health professions and related sciences 10%, education 9%. **Special Study Options:** Cooperative (work-study) program, double major, dual enrollment, English as a second language, honors program, independent study, internships, teacher certification program. Co-op programs: business, computer science, health professions.

FACILITIES

Library Holdings: 178,047 bound volumes. 1,121 periodicals. 156,196 microforms. **Special Academic Facilities/Equipment:** Center for educational technology, state-of-the-art cardio-pneumo-simulator. **Computers:** *Recommended operating system:* Windows 95. School-owned computers available for student use.

EXTRACURRICULARS

Activities: Choral groups, drama/theater, jazz band, literary magazine, student government, student newspaper, student-run film society, television station, yearbook. **Organizations:** 50 registered organizations, 1 honor society, 2 religious organizations. **Athletics (Intercollegiate):** *Men:* basketball, cheerleading, cross-country, soccer, swimming, tennis, track & field, volleyball. *Women:* basketball, cheerleading, cross-country, softball, swimming, track & field, volleyball.

ADMISSIONS

Selectivity Rating: 63 (of 100). **Freshman Academic Profile:** 68% from public high schools. SAT I Math middle 50% range 390-470. SAT I Verbal middle 50% range 363-460. TOEFL required of all international applicants, minimum TOEFL 470. **Basis for Candidate Selection:** *Very important factors considered include:* secondary school record, standardized test scores. **Freshman Admission Requirements:** High school diploma or GED is required. *Academic units required/recommended:* 15 total required; 3 English required, 2 math required, 2 science recommended, 2 science lab recommended, 1 foreign language recommended, 1 social studies recommended, 2 history recommended, 10 elective required. **Freshman Admission Statistics:** 2,389 applied, 31% accepted, 80% of those accepted enrolled. **Transfer Admission Requirements:** *Items required:* high school transcript, college transcript, standardized test scores. Minimum high school GPA of 2.0 required. Minimum college GPA of 2.0 required. Lowest grade transferable C. **General Admission Information:** Application fee $40. Nonfall registration accepted. Admission may be deferred. Placement offered for CEEB Advanced Placement tests.

COSTS AND FINANCIAL AID

In-state tuition $3,200. Out-of-state tuition $6,800. Required fees $242. Average book expense $692. **Required Forms and Deadlines:** FAFSA and state aid form. No deadline for regular filing. **Notification of Awards:** Applicants will be notified of awards on a rolling basis beginning on or about March 1. **Types of Aid:** *Need-based scholarships/grants:* Pell, SEOG, state scholarships/grants, private scholarships. *Loans:* Direct Subsidized Stafford, Direct Unsubsidized Stafford, Direct PLUS, Federal Perkins, college/university loans from institutional funds. **Student Employment:** Federal Work-Study Program available. **Financial Aid Phone:** 718-262-2230.

CURRY COLLEGE

1071 Blue Hill Avenue, Milton, MA 02186
Phone: 617-333-2210 **E-mail:** curryadm@curry.edu **CEEB Code:** 3285
Fax: 617-333-2114 **Web:** www.curry.edu **ACT Code:** 1814

This private school was founded in 1879. It has a 132-acre campus.

STUDENTS AND FACULTY

Enrollment: 2,082. **Student Body:** Male 47%, female 53%, out-of-state 40%, international 1% (15 countries represented). **Ethnic Representation:** African American 4%, Asian 1%, Caucasian 48%, Hispanic 2%. **Retention and Graduation:** 68% freshmen return for sophomore year. 44% freshmen graduate within 4 years. 17% grads go on to further study within 1 year. 2% grads pursue business degrees. 1% grads pursue law degrees. **Faculty:** 100% faculty teach undergrads.

ACADEMICS

Degrees: Bachelor's, master's. **Academic Requirements:** General education including some course work in arts/fine arts, computer literacy, English (including composition), humanities, mathematics, philosophy, sciences (biological or physical), social science, communications. **Special Study Options:** Double major, honors program, independent study, internships, liberal arts/career combination, student-designed major, study abroad, teacher certification program, weekend college.

FACILITIES

Housing: Coed, all-female, housing for international students. **Library Holdings:** 90,000 bound volumes. 625 periodicals. 23,927 microforms. **Special Academic Facilities/Equipment:** On-campus preschool, nursing lab, psychology lab. **Computers:** *Recommended operating system:* Mac. School-owned computers available for student use.

EXTRACURRICULARS

Activities: Choral groups, dance, drama/theater, literary magazine, music ensembles, radio station, student government, student newspaper, television station, yearbook. **Organizations:** 1 honor society, 2 religious organizations. **Athletics (Intercollegiate):** *Men:* baseball, basketball, cheerleading, football, ice hockey, lacrosse, soccer, tennis. *Women:* basketball, cheerleading, cross-country, lacrosse, soccer, softball, tennis.

ADMISSIONS

Selectivity Rating: 68 (of 100). **Freshman Academic Profile:** Average high school GPA 2.3. 5% in top 10% of high school class, 22% in top 25% of high school class, 65% in top 50% of high school class. 76% from public high schools. Average SAT I Math 420. Average SAT I Verbal 440. TOEFL required of all international applicants, minimum TOEFL 500. **Basis for Candidate Selection:** *Important factors considered include:* class rank, recommendations, secondary school record. *Other factors considered include:* alumni/ae relation, character/personal qualities, essays, extracurricular activities, interview, standardized test scores, volunteer work, work experience. **Freshman Admission Requirements:** High school diploma or GED is required. *Academic units required/recommended:* 16 total required; 4 English required, 3 math required, 2 science required, 2 science lab required, 1 social studies required, 1 history required, 5 elective required. **Freshman Admission Statistics:** 1,296 applied, 82% accepted, 36% of those accepted enrolled. **Transfer Admission Requirements:** *Items required:* college transcript, essay. Minimum college GPA of 2.0 required. Lowest grade transferable C-. **General Admission Information:** Application fee $40. Priority application deadline April 1. Early decision application deadline December 1. Regular application deadline March 1. Nonfall registration accepted. Admission may be deferred for a maximum of 1 year. Credit and/or placement offered for CEEB Advanced Placement tests.

COSTS AND FINANCIAL AID

Tuition $17,160. Room & board $6,870. Required fees $755. Average book expense $700. **Required Forms and Deadlines:** FAFSA and institution's own

financial aid form. Priority filing deadline March 1. **Notification of Awards:** Applicants will be notified of awards on a rolling basis beginning on or about March 1. **Types of Aid:** *Need-based scholarships/grants:* Pell, SEOG, state scholarships/grants, private scholarships, the school's own gift aid. *Loans:* FFEL Subsidized Stafford, FFEL Unsubsidized Stafford, FFEL PLUS, Federal Perkins, state loans. **Student Employment:** Federal Work-Study Program available. Institutional employment available. Off-campus job opportunities are good. **Financial Aid Statistics:** 50% freshmen, 47% undergrads receive some form of aid. Average freshman grant $6,500. Average freshman loan $2,625. Average income from on-campus job $1,400. **Financial Aid Phone:** 617-333-2146.

DAEMEN COLLEGE

4380 Main Street, Amherst, NY 14226-3592
Phone: 716-839-8225 **E-mail:** admissions@daemen.edu **CEEB Code:** 2762
Fax: 716-839-8229 **Web:** www.daemen.edu **ACT Code:** 2874

This private school was founded in 1947. It has a 35-acre campus.

STUDENTS AND FACULTY

Enrollment: 1,887. **Student Body:** Male 23%, female 77%, out-of-state 4%, international 1% (10 countries represented). **Ethnic Representation:** African American 14%, Asian 2%, Caucasian 81%, Hispanic 2%, Native American 1%. **Retention and Graduation:** 71% freshmen return for sophomore year. 18% freshmen graduate within 4 years. 15% grads go on to further study within 1 year. 1% grads pursue business degrees. **Faculty:** Student/faculty ratio 16:1. 70 full-time faculty, 75% hold PhDs. 99% faculty teach undergrads.

ACADEMICS

Degrees: Bachelor's, certificate, first professional, master's, post-bachelor's certificate, post-master's certificate. **Academic Requirements:** General education including some course work in arts/fine arts, English (including composition), history, humanities, mathematics, philosophy, sciences (biological or physical), social science. **Classes:** 10-19 students in an average class. 10-19 students in an average lab class. **Majors with Highest Enrollment:** Nursing/registered nurse training (RN, ASN, BSN, MSN); physical therapy/therapist; physician assistant. **Disciplines with Highest Percentage of Degrees Awarded:** Health professions and related sciences 55%, education 16%, business/marketing 11%, biological life sciences 5%, psychology 4%. **Special Study Options:** Accelerated program, cooperative (work-study) program, cross registration, double major, dual enrollment, honors program, independent study, internships, student-designed major, study abroad, teacher certification program, weekend college, Washington semester; off-campus study with any of the 20 members of the Western New York Consortium. Dual degree (BS/MS) awarded at the completion of the program in physician assistant studies.

FACILITIES

Housing: Coed, apartments for single students, coed apartment-style residence halls; some apartments are handicapped accessible. **Library Holdings:** 128,029 bound volumes. 915 periodicals. 26,270 microforms. 14,029 audiovisuals. **Special Academic Facilities/Equipment:** Teaching resource center, Franette Goldman/Carolyn Greenfield Art Gallery, natural and health sciences research center, videoconferencing center. **Computers:** School-owned computers available for student use.

EXTRACURRICULARS

Activities: Choral groups, drama/theater, literary magazine, student government, student newspaper, yearbook. **Organizations:** 35 registered organizations, 8 honor societies, 2 fraternities (3% men join), 4 sororities (4% women join). **Athletics (Intercollegiate):** *Men:* basketball, cross-country, golf, soccer. *Women:* basketball, cross-country, soccer, volleyball.

ADMISSIONS

Selectivity Rating: 63 (of 100). **Freshman Academic Profile:** Average high school GPA 3.1. 7% in top 10% of high school class, 35% in top 25% of high school class, 74% in top 50% of high school class. Average SAT I Math 489, SAT I Math middle 50% range 430-540. Average SAT I Verbal 482, SAT I Verbal middle 50% range 430-530. Average ACT 20, ACT middle 50% range 18-22. TOEFL required of all international applicants, minimum TOEFL 500. **Basis for Candidate Selection:** *Very important factors considered include:* secondary school record, standardized test scores. *Important factors considered include:* alumni/ae relation, class rank, essays, extracurricular activities, interview, recommendations. *Other factors considered include:* character/personal qualities, talent/ability, volunteer work, work experience. **Freshman Admission Requirements:** High school diploma or GED is required. *Academic units required/recommended:* 16 total recommended; 4 English recommended, 4 math recommended, 4 science recommended, 1 science lab recommended, 4 social studies recommended, 4 history recommended. **Freshman Admission Statistics:** 1,755 applied, 74% accepted, 24% of those accepted enrolled. **Transfer Admission Requirements:** *Items required:* college transcript. Minimum college GPA of 2.0 required. Lowest grade transferable C. **General Admission Information:** Application fee $25. Nonfall registration accepted. Admission may be deferred for a maximum of 1 year. Credit offered for CEEB Advanced Placement tests.

COSTS AND FINANCIAL AID

Tuition $13,200. Room & board $6,400. Required fees $420. Average book expense $800. **Required Forms and Deadlines:** FAFSA and state aid form. No deadline for regular filing. Priority filing deadline March 15. **Notification of Awards:** Applicants will be notified of awards on a rolling basis beginning on or about February 15. **Types of Aid:** *Need-based scholarships/grants:* Pell, SEOG, state scholarships/grants, private scholarships, the school's own gift aid. *Loans:* FFEL Subsidized Stafford, FFEL Unsubsidized Stafford, FFEL PLUS, Federal Perkins, college/university loans from institutional funds, alternative loans. **Student Employment:** Federal Work-Study Program available. Institutional employment available. Off-campus job opportunities are excellent. **Financial Aid Statistics:** 92% freshmen, 85% undergrads receive some form of aid. Average freshman grant $6,651. Average freshman loan $3,163. Average income from on-campus job $796. **Financial Aid Phone:** 716-839-8254.

See page 1004.

DAKOTA STATE UNIVERSITY

820 North Washington Ave., Madison, SD 57042
Phone: 605-256-5139 **E-mail:** yourfuture@dsu.edu **CEEB Code:** 6247
Fax: 605-256-5020 **Web:** www.dsu.edu **ACT Code:** 3910

This public school was founded in 1881. It has a 20-acre campus.

STUDENTS AND FACULTY

Enrollment: 1,965. **Student Body:** Male 49%, female 51%, out-of-state 16%, international 1%. **Ethnic Representation:** African American 1%, Asian 1%, Caucasian 93%, Hispanic 1%, Native American 1%. **Retention and Graduation:** 65% freshmen return for sophomore year. 14% freshmen graduate within 4 years. 1% grads go on to further study within 1 year. 1% grads pursue business degrees. 1% grads pursue law degrees. **Faculty:** Student/faculty ratio 23:1. 77 full-time faculty, 59% hold PhDs.

ACADEMICS

Degrees: Associate's, bachelor's, certificate, master's. **Academic Requirements:** General education including some course work in arts/fine arts, computer literacy, English (including composition), humanities, mathematics, sciences (biological or physical), social science. **Classes:** 10-19 students in an average class. 10-19 students in an average lab class. **Majors with Highest Enrollment:** Computer science; elementary education and teaching. **Disciplines with Highest Percentage of Degrees Awarded:** Business/marketing 32%, education 30%, computer and information sciences 29%, biological life sciences 2%, parks and recreation 2%. **Special Study Options:** Cooperative (work-study) program, cross registration, distance learning, double major, dual enrollment, English as a second language, honors program, independent study, internships, student-designed major, study abroad, teacher certification program.

FACILITIES

Housing: Coed, all-female, all-male, apartment-style residence halls. **Library Holdings:** 98,156 bound volumes. 350 periodicals. 3,111 microforms. 2,435 audiovisuals. **Special Academic Facilities/Equipment:** Natural history museum. **Computers:** School-owned computers available for student use.

EXTRACURRICULARS

Activities: Choral groups, concert band, dance, drama/theater, jazz band, literary magazine, marching band, music ensembles, musical theater, pep band, student government, student newspaper, student-run film society, yearbook. **Organizations:** 30 registered organizations, 3 honor societies, 2 religious organizations. **Athletics (Intercollegiate):** *Men:* baseball, basketball, cheerleading, cross-country, football, golf, indoor track, track & field. *Women:* basketball, cheerleading, cross-country, golf, indoor track, softball, track & field, volleyball.

ADMISSIONS

Selectivity Rating: 64 (of 100). **Freshman Academic Profile:** Average ACT 22. TOEFL required of all international applicants, minimum TOEFL 550. **Basis for Candidate Selection:** *Very important factors considered include:*

standardized test scores. *Other factors considered include:* character/personal qualities, class rank, extracurricular activities, minority status, talent/ability, volunteer work, work experience. **Freshman Admission Requirements:** High school diploma or GED is required. *Academic units required/recommended:* 4 English required, 3 math required, 3 science required, 3 science lab required, 3 social studies required, 2 elective required. **Freshman Admission Statistics:** 584 applied, 86% accepted, 52% of those accepted enrolled. **Transfer Admission Requirements:** *Items required:* college transcript, essay. Minimum college GPA of 2.0 required. Lowest grade transferable C. **General Admission Information:** Application fee $20. Nonfall registration accepted. Admission may be deferred for a maximum of 1 year. Credit and/or placement offered for CEEB Advanced Placement tests.

COSTS AND FINANCIAL AID

Average book expense $600. **Required Forms and Deadlines:** FAFSA and institutional scholarship application form. No deadline for regular filing. Priority filing deadline March 1. **Notification of Awards:** Applicants will be notified of awards on a rolling basis beginning on or about April 20. **Types of Aid:** *Need-based scholarships/grants:* Pell, SEOG, state scholarships/grants, private scholarships, the school's own gift aid. *Loans:* FFEL Subsidized Stafford, FFEL Unsubsidized Stafford, FFEL PLUS, Federal Perkins, alternative loans. **Student Employment:** Federal Work-Study Program available. Institutional employment available. Off-campus job opportunities are good. **Financial Aid Statistics:** 66% freshmen, 65% undergrads receive some form of aid. **Financial Aid Phone:** 605-256-5152.

DAKOTA WESLEYAN UNIVERSITY

1200 West University Avenue, Mitchell, SD 57301-4398
Phone: 605-995-2650 **E-mail:** admissions@dwu.edu **CEEB Code:** 6155
Fax: 605-995-2699 **Web:** www.dwu.edu **ACT Code:** 3906

This private school, which is affiliated with the Methodist Church, was founded in 1885. It has a 40-acre campus.

STUDENTS AND FACULTY

Enrollment: 717. **Student Body:** Male 41%, female 59%, out-of-state 27%, international students represent 3 countries. **Ethnic Representation:** African American 5%, Asian 1%, Caucasian 87%, Hispanic 3%, Native American 4%. **Retention and Graduation:** 66% freshmen return for sophomore year. 38% freshmen graduate within 4 years. 6% grads go on to further study within 1 year. 1% grads pursue law degrees. 1% grads pursue medical degrees. **Faculty:** Student/faculty ratio 14:1. 42 full-time faculty, 61% hold PhDs. 100% faculty teach undergrads.

ACADEMICS

Degrees: Associate's, bachelor's, terminal. **Academic Requirements:** General education including some course work in arts/fine arts, computer literacy, English (including composition), history, humanities, mathematics, philosophy, sciences (biological or physical), social science, cultural awareness. **Classes:** 10-19 students in an average class. 10-19 students in an average lab class. **Majors with Highest Enrollment:** Business administration/management; elementary education and teaching; criminal justice/law enforcement administration. **Disciplines with Highest Percentage of Degrees Awarded:** Education 34%, business/marketing 20%, protective services/public administration 16%, biological life sciences 7%, parks and recreation 7%. **Special Study Options:** Distance learning, double major, dual enrollment, honors program, independent study, internships, liberal arts/career combination, student-designed major, study abroad, teacher certification program.

FACILITIES

Housing: Coed, all-female, all-male, Koka "honor housing" for upperclass women; Dakota "honor housing" for upperclass men. **Library Holdings:** 53,300 bound volumes. 404 periodicals. 75,500 microforms. 7,605 audiovisuals. **Special Academic Facilities/Equipment:** Friends of the Middle Border Museum and Grounds. **Computers:** School-owned computers available for student use.

EXTRACURRICULARS

Activities: Choral groups, drama/theater, literary magazine, music ensembles, student government, student newspaper, yearbook. **Organizations:** 5 registered organizations, 6 honor societies, 3 religious organizations. **Athletics (Intercollegiate):** *Men:* baseball, basketball, cheerleading, cross-country, football, golf, indoor track, track & field, wrestling. *Women:* basketball, cheerleading, cross-country, golf, indoor track, softball, track & field, volleyball.

ADMISSIONS

Selectivity Rating: 74 (of 100). **Freshman Academic Profile:** Average high school GPA 2.9. 11% in top 10% of high school class, 28% in top 25% of high school class, 70% in top 50% of high school class. 98% from public high schools. Average ACT 21, ACT middle 50% range 21-24. TOEFL required of all international applicants, minimum TOEFL 500. **Basis for Candidate Selection:** *Very important factors considered include:* class rank, secondary school record, standardized test scores. *Important factors considered include:* essays. *Other factors considered include:* recommendations. **Freshman Admission Requirements:** High school diploma or GED is required. *Academic units required/recommended:* 4 English recommended, 4 math recommended, 4 social studies recommended. **Freshman Admission Statistics:** 468 applied, 84% accepted, 38% of those accepted enrolled. **Transfer Admission Requirements:** *Items required:* college transcript. Minimum high school GPA of 2.0 required. Minimum college GPA of 2.0 required. Lowest grade transferable D-. **General Admission Information:** Application fee $25. Priority application deadline May 1. Regular application deadline August 25. Nonfall registration accepted. Credit and/or placement offered for CEEB Advanced Placement tests.

COSTS AND FINANCIAL AID

Tuition $12,998. Room & board $4,416. Required fees $400. Average book expense $800. **Required Forms and Deadlines:** FAFSA. No deadline for regular filing. Priority filing deadline April 1. **Notification of Awards:** Applicants will be notified of awards on a rolling basis beginning on or about March 1. **Types of Aid:** *Need-based scholarships/grants:* Pell, SEOG, private scholarships, the school's own gift aid, Federal Nursing, South Dakota Board of Nursing scholarships/loans. *Loans:* FFEL Subsidized Stafford, FFEL Unsubsidized Stafford, FFEL PLUS, Federal Perkins, Methodist loans, private alternative student loans. **Student Employment:** Federal Work-Study Program available. Institutional employment available. Off-campus job opportunities are good. **Financial Aid Statistics:** 97% freshmen, 99% undergrads receive some form of aid. Average freshman grant $4,442. Average freshman loan $3,293. **Financial Aid Phone:** 605-995-2656.

DALHOUSIE UNIVERSITY

Registrar Office, Halifax, NS B3H4H6
Phone: 902-494-2450 **E-mail:** admissions@dal.ca **CEEB Code:** 915
Fax: 902-494-1630 **Web:** www.dal.ca

This public school was founded in 1818. It has an 80-acre campus.

STUDENTS AND FACULTY

Enrollment: 10,432. **Student Body:** Male 44%, female 56%. **Retention and Graduation:** 74% freshmen return for sophomore year. 33% grads pursue law degrees. 33% grads pursue medical degrees. **Faculty:** Student/faculty ratio 14:1. 912 full-time faculty.

ACADEMICS

Degrees: Bachelor's, diploma, doctoral, first professional, master's. **Academic Requirements:** General education including some course work in arts/fine arts, foreign languages, humanities, mathematics, sciences (biological or physical), social science, writing course (not necessarily English). **Majors with Highest Enrollment:** Business/commerce, general; computer science; engineering, general. **Special Study Options:** Cooperative (work-study) program, distance learning, double major, dual enrollment, English as a second language, student exchange program (domestic), honors program, internships, liberal arts/career combination, study abroad.

FACILITIES

Housing: Coed, all-female, all-male, apartments for married students, apartments for single students, housing for international students, fraternities and/or sororities. Off-campus housing office offers help to students looking for their own accommodations. **Library Holdings:** 1,700,000 bound volumes. 8,306 periodicals. 421,897 microforms. 6,001 audiovisuals. **Special Academic Facilities/Equipment:** Art gallery, Dalplex (sports complex), Rebecca Cohn Arts Center. **Computers:** School-owned computers available for student use.

EXTRACURRICULARS

Activities: Choral groups, concert band, dance, drama/theater, jazz band, music ensembles, musical theater, radio station, student government, student newspaper, student-run film society, yearbook. **Organizations:** 200 registered organizations, 8 fraternities, 2 sororities. **Athletics (Intercollegiate):** *Men:* basketball, cross-country, diving, ice hockey, soccer, swimming, track & field, volleyball. *Women:* basketball, cross-country, diving, soccer, swimming, track & field, volleyball.

ADMISSIONS

Selectivity Rating: 60 (of 100). **Freshman Academic Profile:** Average high school GPA 3.0. TOEFL required of all international applicants, minimum TOEFL 580. **Basis for Candidate Selection:** *Very important factors considered include:* secondary school record. *Important factors considered include:* class rank, standardized test scores. *Other factors considered include:* recommendations. **Freshman Admission Requirements:** High school diploma is required and GED is not accepted. *Academic units required/recommended:* 22 total required; 27 total recommended; 3 English required, 3 English recommended, 3 math required, 3 math recommended, 1 science required, 3 science recommended, 1 foreign language recommended, 1 social studies recommended, 1 history recommended, 15 elective required, 15 elective recommended. **Freshman Admission Statistics:** 8,382 applied, 67% accepted. **Transfer Admission Requirements:** *Items required:* college transcript. **General Admission Information:** Application fee $40. Priority application deadline March 15. Regular application deadline June 1. Nonfall registration accepted. Admission may be deferred for a maximum of 1 year. Credit and/or placement offered for CEEB Advanced Placement tests.

COSTS AND FINANCIAL AID

In-state tuition $9,110. Out-of-state tuition $9,110. Room & board $3,769. Required fees $400. Average book expense $602. **Required Forms and Deadlines:** FAFSA, institution's own financial aid form, state aid form. No deadline for regular filing. **Notification of Awards:** Applicants will be notified of awards on a rolling basis. **Types of Aid:** *Need-based scholarships/grants:* the school's own gift aid. *Loans:* Direct Subsidized Stafford, Direct Unsubsidized Stafford, college/university loans from institutional funds. **Student Employment:** Off-campus job opportunities are good. **Financial Aid Phone:** 902-494-2302.

DALLAS BAPTIST UNIVERSITY

3000 Mountain Creek Parkway, Dallas, TX 75211-9299
Phone: 214-333-5360 **E-mail:** admiss@dbu.edu **CEEB Code:** 6159
Fax: 214-333-5447 **Web:** www.dbu.edu **ACT Code:** 4080

This private school was founded in 1898. It has a 293-acre campus.

STUDENTS AND FACULTY

Enrollment: 3,407. **Student Body:** Male 40%, female 60%, out-of-state 7%, international 6% (48 countries represented). **Ethnic Representation:** African American 22%, Asian 2%, Caucasian 54%, Hispanic 9%, Native American 3%. **Retention and Graduation:** 62% freshmen return for sophomore year. **Faculty:** Student/faculty ratio 18:1. 85 full-time faculty, 75% hold PhDs. 100% faculty teach undergrads.

ACADEMICS

Degrees: Associate's, bachelor's, master's, post-bachelor's certificate. **Academic Requirements:** General education including some course work in arts/fine arts, computer literacy, English (including composition), history, mathematics, sciences (biological or physical), social science, religion. **Classes:** 10-19 students in an average class. 20-29 students in an average lab class. **Majors with Highest Enrollment:** Business administration/management; general studies; psychology, general. **Disciplines with Highest Percentage of Degrees Awarded:** Business/marketing 44%, liberal arts/general studies 23%, visual and performing arts 7%, psychology 6%, philosophy/religion/theology 5%. **Special Study Options:** Accelerated program, distance learning, double major, dual enrollment, English as a second language, independent study, internships, study abroad, teacher certification program, weekend college.

FACILITIES

Housing: All-female, all-male, apartments for married students, apartments for single students, housing for disabled students. **Library Holdings:** 221,742 bound volumes. 626 periodicals. 494,012 microforms. 6,378 audiovisuals. **Special Academic Facilities/Equipment:** On-campus elementary school, Corrie Ten Boom Collection. **Computers:** *Recommended operating system:* Windows 3x. School-owned computers available for student use.

EXTRACURRICULARS

Activities: Choral groups, drama/theater, music ensembles, musical theater, opera, student government, yearbook. **Organizations:** 28 registered organizations, 4 honor societies, 3 religious organizations. **Athletics (Intercollegiate):** *Men:* baseball, cross-country, soccer, tennis, track & field, volleyball. *Women:* cross-country, soccer, tennis, track & field, volleyball.

ADMISSIONS

Selectivity Rating: 66 (of 100). **Freshman Academic Profile:** Average high school GPA 3.4. 13% in top 10% of high school class, 42% in top 25% of high school class, 77% in top 50% of high school class. 75% from public high schools. Average SAT I Math 522, SAT I Math middle 50% range 437-550. Average SAT I Verbal 541, SAT I Verbal middle 50% range 443-574. Average ACT 22, ACT middle 50% range 19-23. TOEFL required of all international applicants, minimum TOEFL 525. **Basis for Candidate Selection:** *Very important factors considered include:* class rank, essays, secondary school record, standardized test scores. *Important factors considered include:* religious affiliation/commitment. *Other factors considered include:* character/personal qualities, extracurricular activities, interview, recommendations, talent/ability, volunteer work, work experience. **Freshman Admission Requirements:** High school diploma or GED is required. *Academic units required/recommended:* 16 total recommended; 4 English recommended, 3 math recommended, 2 science recommended, 2 foreign language recommended, 3 social studies recommended, 2 history recommended. **Freshman Admission Statistics:** 678 applied, 62% accepted, 64% of those accepted enrolled. **Transfer Admission Requirements:** *Items required:* college transcript, essay. Minimum college GPA of 2.0 required. Lowest grade transferable C. **General Admission Information:** Application fee $25. Priority application deadline January 15. Nonfall registration accepted. Credit offered for CEEB Advanced Placement tests.

COSTS AND FINANCIAL AID

Tuition $10,350. Room & board $4,140. Required fees $0. Average book expense $900. **Required Forms and Deadlines:** FAFSA and institution's own financial aid form. Financial aid filing deadline May 1. Priority filing deadline March 15. **Notification of Awards:** Applicants will be notified of awards on a rolling basis. **Types of Aid:** *Need-based scholarships/grants:* Pell, SEOG, state scholarships/grants, private scholarships, the school's own gift aid. *Loans:* FFEL Subsidized Stafford, FFEL Unsubsidized Stafford, FFEL PLUS, Federal Perkins, state loans, college/university loans from institutional funds. **Student Employment:** Federal Work-Study Program available. Institutional employment available. Off-campus job opportunities are good. **Financial Aid Statistics:** 62% freshmen, 57% undergrads receive some form of aid. Average freshman grant $2,063. Average freshman loan $3,433. Average income from on-campus job $2,880. **Financial Aid Phone:** 214-333-5363.

DANA COLLEGE

2848 College Drive, Blair, NE 68008-1099
Phone: 402-426-7222 **E-mail:** admissions@acad2.dana.edu
Fax: 402-426-7386 **Web:** www.dana.edu **ACT Code:** 2446

This private school, which is affiliated with the Lutheran Church, was founded in 1884. It has a 150-acre campus.

STUDENTS AND FACULTY

Enrollment: 580. **Student Body:** Male 55%, female 45%, out-of-state 50%, international 1%. **Ethnic Representation:** African American 7%, Asian 3%, Caucasian 86%, Hispanic 3%, Native American 1%. **Retention and Graduation:** 65% freshmen return for sophomore year. 37% freshmen graduate within 4 years. 13% grads go on to further study within 1 year. 1% grads pursue business degrees. 1% grads pursue law degrees. 1% grads pursue medical degrees. **Faculty:** Student/faculty ratio 12:1. 49 full-time faculty, 48% hold PhDs. 100% faculty teach undergrads.

ACADEMICS

Degrees: Bachelor's. **Academic Requirements:** General education including some course work in arts/fine arts, English (including composition), foreign languages, history, mathematics, sciences (biological or physical), physical education, religion, communication. **Classes:** Under 10 students in an average class. **Disciplines with Highest Percentage of Degrees Awarded:** Education 29%, business/marketing 17%, protective services/public administration 16%, visual and performing arts 7%, biological life sciences 5%. **Special Study Options:** Accelerated program, cross registration, double major, dual enrollment, English as a second language, honors program, independent study, internships, liberal arts/career combination, student-designed major, study abroad, teacher certification program.

FACILITIES

Housing: Coed, all-female, apartments for married students, apartments for single students. **Library Holdings:** 197,080 bound volumes. 8,743 periodicals. 1,783 microforms. 3,757 audiovisuals. **Special Academic Facilities/Equipment:** Danish Archives. **Computers:** School-owned computers available for student use.

EXTRACURRICULARS

Activities: Choral groups, concert band, dance, drama/theater, jazz band, literary magazine, music ensembles, musical theater, radio station, student government, student newspaper, television station, yearbook. **Organizations:** 25 registered organizations, 3 honor societies, 2 religious organizations. **Athletics (Intercollegiate):** *Men:* baseball, basketball, cross-country, football, soccer, track & field, wrestling. *Women:* basketball, cheerleading, cross-country, soccer, softball, track & field, volleyball.

ADMISSIONS

Selectivity Rating: 72 (of 100). **Freshman Academic Profile:** Average high school GPA 3.3. 12% in top 10% of high school class, 36% in top 25% of high school class, 65% in top 50% of high school class. SAT I Math middle 50% range 400-500. SAT I Verbal middle 50% range 390-500. Average ACT 22, ACT middle 50% range 19-24. TOEFL required of all international applicants, minimum TOEFL 500. **Basis for Candidate Selection:** *Very important factors considered include:* secondary school record, standardized test scores. *Other factors considered include:* essays, extracurricular activities, interview, recommendations, volunteer work, work experience. **Freshman Admission Requirements:** High school diploma or GED is required. *Academic units required/recommended:* 16 total recommended; 4 English recommended, 3 math recommended, 3 science recommended, 2 science lab recommended, 2 foreign language recommended, 4 social studies recommended. **Freshman Admission Statistics:** 591 applied, 95% accepted, 25% of those accepted enrolled. **Transfer Admission Requirements:** *Items required:* college transcript. Minimum high school GPA of 2.0 required. Minimum college GPA of 2.0 required. Lowest grade transferable C. **General Admission Information:** Nonfall registration accepted. Admission may be deferred for a maximum of 2 years. Credit offered for CEEB Advanced Placement tests.

COSTS AND FINANCIAL AID

Tuition $14,200. Room & board $4,676. Required fees $550. Average book expense $600. **Required Forms and Deadlines:** FAFSA and institution's own financial aid form. No deadline for regular filing. Priority filing deadline April 1. **Notification of Awards:** Applicants will be notified of awards on a rolling basis beginning on or about March 1. **Types of Aid:** *Need-based scholarships/grants:* Pell, SEOG, state scholarships/grants, private scholarships, the school's own gift aid. *Loans:* FFEL Subsidized Stafford, FFEL Unsubsidized Stafford, FFEL PLUS, Federal Perkins. **Student Employment:** Federal Work-Study Program available. Off-campus job opportunities are excellent. **Financial Aid Statistics:** 86% freshmen, 81% undergrads receive some form of aid. Average freshman grant $11,964. Average freshman loan $4,209. **Financial Aid Phone:** 402-426-7226.

DANIEL WEBSTER COLLEGE

20 University Drive, Nashua, NH 03063-1300
Phone: 603-577-6600 **E-mail:** admissions@dwc.edu **CEEB Code:** 3648
Fax: 603-577-6001 **Web:** www.dwc.edu **ACT Code:** 2525

This private school was founded in 1965. It has a 50-acre campus.

STUDENTS AND FACULTY

Enrollment: 1,058. **Student Body:** Male 74%, female 26%, out-of-state 72%, international 1% (11 countries represented). **Ethnic Representation:** African American 2%, Asian 1%, Caucasian 65%, Hispanic 2%. **Retention and Graduation:** 64% freshmen return for sophomore year. 40% freshmen graduate within 4 years. 8% grads go on to further study within 1 year. **Faculty:** Student/faculty ratio 13:1. 34 full-time faculty, 47% hold PhDs. 100% faculty teach undergrads.

ACADEMICS

Degrees: Associate's, bachelor's. **Academic Requirements:** General education including some course work in computer literacy, English (including composition), humanities, mathematics, sciences (biological or physical), social science. **Classes:** 10-19 students in an average class. Under 10 students in an average lab class. **Majors with Highest Enrollment:** Business administration/ management; computer science; airline/commercial/professional pilot and flight crew. **Disciplines with Highest Percentage of Degrees Awarded:** Business/marketing 72%, trade and industry 18%, computer and information sciences 7%, parks and recreation 3%. **Special Study Options:** Accelerated program, cooperative (work-study) program, cross registration, double major, dual enrollment, independent study, internships, study abroad.

FACILITIES

Housing: Coed, all-female, all-male. **Library Holdings:** 34,195 bound volumes. 440 periodicals. 60,064 microforms. 1,439 audiovisuals. **Special Academic Facilities/Equipment:** Campus is adjacent to municipal airport; over 35 aircraft are available for flight training. Three flight simulators, aviation center. **Computers:** School-owned computers available for student use.

EXTRACURRICULARS

Activities: Choral groups, drama/theater, jazz band, musical theater, student government, student newspaper, student-run film society, yearbook. **Organizations:** 17 registered organizations, 2 honor societies, 1 religious organization. **Athletics (Intercollegiate):** *Men:* baseball, basketball, cross-country, lacrosse, soccer. *Women:* basketball, cross-country, soccer, softball, volleyball.

ADMISSIONS

Selectivity Rating: 70 (of 100). **Freshman Academic Profile:** Average high school GPA 3.1. 7% in top 10% of high school class, 21% in top 25% of high school class, 52% in top 50% of high school class. 83% from public high schools. Average SAT I Math 538, SAT I Math middle 50% range 480-610. Average SAT I Verbal 525, SAT I Verbal middle 50% range 470-570. Average ACT 21, ACT middle 50% range 19-24. TOEFL required of all international applicants, minimum TOEFL 520. **Basis for Candidate Selection:** *Very important factors considered include:* secondary school record. *Important factors considered include:* class rank, extracurricular activities, recommendations, standardized test scores. *Other factors considered include:* character/personal qualities, essays, interview, talent/ability, volunteer work, work experience. **Freshman Admission Requirements:** High school diploma or GED is required. *Academic units required/recommended:* 16 total required; 18 total recommended; 4 English required, 3 math required, 2 science required, 2 foreign language recommended, 1 social studies required, 2 history required, 2 elective required. **Freshman Admission Statistics:** 683 applied, 77% accepted, 32% of those accepted enrolled. **Transfer Admission Requirements:** *Items required:* high school transcript, college transcript. Minimum high school GPA of 2.0 required. Minimum college GPA of 2.0 required. Lowest grade transferable C. **General Admission Information:** Application fee $35. Nonfall registration accepted. Admission may be deferred for a maximum of 1 year. Credit and/or placement offered for CEEB Advanced Placement tests.

COSTS AND FINANCIAL AID

Tuition $18,500. Room & board $7,440. Required fees $700. Average book expense $750. **Required Forms and Deadlines:** FAFSA and institution's own financial aid form. Priority filing deadline March 1. **Notification of Awards:** Applicants will be notified of awards on a rolling basis beginning on or about March 15. **Types of Aid:** *Need-based scholarships/grants:* Pell, SEOG, state scholarships/grants, the school's own gift aid. *Loans:* Direct Subsidized Stafford, Direct Unsubsidized Stafford, Direct PLUS. **Student Employment:** Federal Work-Study Program available. Institutional employment available. Off-campus job opportunities are excellent. **Financial Aid Statistics:** 92% freshmen, 95% undergrads receive some form of aid. Average freshman grant $5,875. Average freshman loan $2,625. Average income from on-campus job $2,000. **Financial Aid Phone:** 603-577-6590.

DARTMOUTH COLLEGE

6016 McNutt Hall, Hanover, NH 03755
Phone: 603-646-2875 **E-mail:** admissions.office@dartmouth.edu **CEEB Code:** 3351
Fax: 603-646-1216 **Web:** www.dartmouth.edu

This private school was founded in 1769. It has a 265-acre campus.

STUDENTS AND FACULTY

Enrollment: 4,118. **Student Body:** Male 51%, female 49%, out-of-state 98%, international 4%. **Ethnic Representation:** African American 7%, Asian 12%, Caucasian 61%, Hispanic 7%, Native American 3%. **Retention and Graduation:** 97% freshmen return for sophomore year. 89% freshmen graduate within 4 years. **Faculty:** Student/faculty ratio 8:1. 446 full-time faculty, 95% hold PhDs. 100% faculty teach undergrads.

ACADEMICS

Degrees: Bachelor's, doctoral, first professional, master's. **Academic Requirements:** General education including some course work in arts/fine arts, English (including composition), foreign languages, humanities, mathematics, sciences (biological or physical), social science, one course in history, philosophy, or religion. **Classes:** 10-19 students in an average class. **Disciplines with Highest Percentage of Degrees Awarded:** Social sciences and history 33%, English 10%, biological life sciences 9%, psychology 7%, computer and information sciences 6%. **Special Study Options:** Double major, student exchange program (domestic), honors program, independent study, internships, student-designed major, study abroad, teacher certification program.

FACILITIES

Housing: Coed, apartments for married students, apartments for single students, housing for international students, fraternities and/or sororities, cooperative housing, academic affinity housing, faculty-in-residence programs, special-interest housing. **Library Holdings:** 5,009,690 bound volumes. 20,834 periodicals. 2,629,991 microforms. 727,233 audiovisuals. **Special Academic Facilities/Equipment:** Art museum; observatory; centers for performing arts, humanities, social science, science, ethics, and volunteer services. **Computers:** School-owned computers available for student use.

EXTRACURRICULARS

Activities: Choral groups, concert band, dance, drama/theater, jazz band, literary magazine, marching band, music ensembles, musical theater, opera, pep band, radio station, student government, student newspaper, student-run film society, symphony orchestra, television station, yearbook. **Organizations:** 250 registered organizations, 8 religious organizations, 14 fraternities (23% men join), 8 sororities (21% women join). **Athletics (Intercollegiate):** *Men:* baseball, basketball, crew, skiing (cross-country), cross-country, diving, equestrian, football, golf, ice hockey, indoor track, lacrosse, sailing, skiing (alpine), skiing (Nordic), soccer, squash, swimming, tennis, track & field. *Women:* basketball, crew, skiing (cross-country), cross-country, diving, equestrian, field hockey, golf, ice hockey, indoor track, lacrosse, sailing, skiing (alpine), skiing (Nordic), soccer, softball, squash, swimming, tennis, track & field, volleyball.

ADMISSIONS

Selectivity Rating: 99 (of 100). **Freshman Academic Profile:** 87% in top 10% of high school class, 100% in top 50% of high school class. 62% from public high schools. Average SAT I Math 713, SAT I Math middle 50% range 680-770. Average SAT I Verbal 702, SAT I Verbal middle 50% range 650-750. Average ACT 31, ACT middle 50% range 28-33. TOEFL required of all international applicants, minimum TOEFL 580. **Basis for Candidate Selection:** *Very important factors considered include:* character/personal qualities, class rank, essays, extracurricular activities, recommendations, secondary school record, standardized test scores. *Important factors considered include:* talent/ability. *Other factors considered include:* alumni/ae relation, geographical residence, interview, minority status, volunteer work, work experience. **Freshman Admission Requirements:** High school diploma or equivalent is not required. *Academic units required/recommended:* 4 English recommended, 4 math recommended, 4 science recommended, 3 foreign language recommended, 3 social studies recommended. **Freshman Admission Statistics:** 10,193 applied, 21% accepted, 51% of those accepted enrolled. **Transfer Admission Requirements:** *Items required:* high school transcript, college transcript, essay, standardized test scores, statement of good standing from prior school. Lowest grade transferable B. **General Admission Information:** Application fee $65. Early decision application deadline November 1. Regular application deadline January 1. Admission may be deferred for a maximum of 2 years. Credit and/or placement offered for CEEB Advanced Placement tests.

COSTS AND FINANCIAL AID

Tuition $26,400. Room & board $7,896. Required fees $162. Average book expense $810. **Required Forms and Deadlines:** FAFSA, CSS/Financial Aid PROFILE, noncustodial (divorced/separated) parent's statement, and business/farm supplement. Priority filing deadline February 1. **Notification of Awards:** Applicants will be notified of awards on or about April 15. **Types of Aid:** *Need-based scholarships/grants:* Pell, SEOG, state scholarships/grants, the school's own gift aid. *Loans:* FFEL Subsidized Stafford, FFEL Unsubsidized Stafford, FFEL PLUS, Federal Perkins, college/university loans from institutional funds. **Student Employment:** Federal Work-Study Program available. Institutional employment available. Off-campus job opportunities are excellent. **Financial Aid Statistics:** 51% freshmen, 47% undergrads receive some form of aid. Average freshman grant $22,900. Average freshman loan $2,050. **Financial Aid Phone:** 603-646-2451.

See page 1006.

DAVENPORT UNIVERSITY

4801 Oakman Boulevard, Dearborn, MI 48126-3799
Phone: 313-581-4400 **E-mail:** dbajsalloum@davenport.edu
Fax: 313-581-6822 **Web:** www.davenport.edu

This private school was founded in 1962. It has a 17-acre campus.

STUDENTS AND FACULTY

Enrollment: 5,382. **Student Body:** Male 25%, female 75%. **Ethnic Representation:** African American 50%, Asian 1%, Caucasian 37%, Hispanic 2%, Native American 1%. **Retention and Graduation:** 42% freshmen return for sophomore year. **Faculty:** Student/faculty ratio 22:1. 44 full-time faculty, 13% hold PhDs. 100% faculty teach undergrads.

ACADEMICS

Degrees: Associate's, bachelor's, master's. **Academic Requirements:** General education including some course work in computer literacy, English (including composition), mathematics, social science. **Classes:** 10-19 students in an average class. 10-19 students in an average lab class. **Disciplines with Highest Percentage of Degrees Awarded:** Business/marketing 91%, health professions and related sciences 9%. **Special Study Options:** Accelerated program, cooperative (work-study) program, distance learning, double major, dual enrollment, external degree program, independent study, internships, on-line (networking) classes.

FACILITIES

Housing: Off campus. **Library Holdings:** 43,060 bound volumes. 409 periodicals. 184 microforms. 536 audiovisuals. **Computers:** *Recommended operating system:* Windows 95. School-owned computers available for student use.

EXTRACURRICULARS

Activities: Student government, student newspaper. **Organizations:** 33 registered organizations. **Athletics (Intercollegiate):** *Men:* golf, softball. *Women:* golf, softball.

ADMISSIONS

Selectivity Rating: 63 (of 100). **Freshman Academic Profile:** 98% from public high schools. TOEFL required of all international applicants, minimum TOEFL 550. **Basis for Candidate Selection:** *Very important factors considered include:* secondary school record. *Important factors considered include:* interview. *Other factors considered include:* class rank, standardized test scores. **Freshman Admission Requirements:** High school diploma or GED is required. **Freshman Admission Statistics:** 1,006 applied, 100% accepted, 63% of those accepted enrolled. **Transfer Admission Requirements:** *Items required:* high school transcript. Lowest grade transferable C. **General Admission Information:** Application fee $20. Priority application deadline March 15. Regular application deadline September 19. Nonfall registration accepted. Admission may be deferred for a maximum of 1 year. Neither credit nor placement offered for CEEB Advanced Placement tests.

COSTS AND FINANCIAL AID

Tuition $6,984. Required fees $0. Average book expense $680. **Required Forms and Deadlines:** FAFSA and institution's own financial aid form. **Types of Aid:** *Need-based scholarships/grants:* Pell, state scholarships/grants. **Student Employment:** Federal Work-Study Program available. Institutional employment available. Off-campus job opportunities are good. **Financial Aid Statistics:** 87% freshmen, 89% undergrads receive some form of aid. Average freshman grant $12,280. **Financial Aid Phone:** 313-581-4400.

DAVIDSON COLLEGE

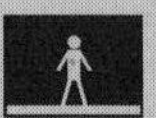

Box 7156, Davidson, NC 28035-7156
Phone: 704-894-2230 **E-mail:** admission@davidson.edu **CEEB Code:** 5150
Fax: 704-894-2016 **Web:** www.davidson.edu **ACT Code:** 3086

This private school, which is affiliated with the Presbyterian Church, was founded in 1837. It has a 450-acre campus.

STUDENTS AND FACULTY

Enrollment: 1,673. **Student Body:** Out-of-state 81%, international 3% (32 countries represented). **Ethnic Representation:** African American 5%, Asian 3%, Caucasian 87%, Hispanic 3%. **Retention and Graduation:** 96% freshmen return for sophomore year. 86% freshmen graduate within 4 years. 25% grads go on to further study within 1 year. **Faculty:** Student/faculty ratio 11:1. 154 full-time faculty, 97% hold PhDs. 100% faculty teach undergrads.

ACADEMICS

Degrees: Bachelor's. **Academic Requirements:** General education including some course work in arts/fine arts, English (including composition), foreign languages, history, mathematics, philosophy, sciences (biological or physical), social science, religion, cultural diversity. **Classes:** Under 10 students in an average class. 10-19 students in an average lab class. **Majors with Highest Enrollment:** English language and literature, general; biology/biological sciences, general; political science and government, general. **Disciplines with Highest Percentage of Degrees Awarded:** Social sciences and history 35%, English 15%, biological life sciences 14%, psychology 10%, foreign languages and literature 8%. **Special Study Options:** Cross registration, double major, student exchange program (domestic), honors program, independent study, student-designed major, study abroad, teacher certification program.

FACILITIES

Housing: Coed, all-female, all-male, apartments for single students. **Library Holdings:** 422,035 bound volumes. 2,767 periodicals. 475,798 microforms. 9,497 audiovisuals. **Special Academic Facilities/Equipment:** Art gallery, scanning electron microscopes, UV-visible spectrometer, laser systems, Baker Sports Complex, visual arts building. **Computers:** School-owned computers available for student use.

EXTRACURRICULARS

Activities: Choral groups, concert band, dance, drama/theater, jazz band, music ensembles, musical theater, opera, pep band, radio station, student government, student newspaper, symphony orchestra, yearbook. **Organizations:** 106 registered organizations, 15 honor societies, 10 religious organizations, 7 fraternities (48% men join). **Athletics (Intercollegiate):** *Men:* baseball, basketball, cross-country, diving, football, golf, soccer, swimming, tennis, track & field, wrestling. *Women:* basketball, cross-country, diving, field hockey, lacrosse, soccer, swimming, tennis, track & field, volleyball.

ADMISSIONS

Selectivity Rating: 99 (of 100). **Freshman Academic Profile:** 75% in top 10% of high school class, 93% in top 25% of high school class, 99% in top 50% of high school class. 48% from public high schools. Average SAT I Math 656, SAT I Math middle 50% range 615-700. Average SAT I Verbal 659, SAT I Verbal middle 50% range 620-710. Average ACT 28, ACT middle 50% range 26-31. TOEFL required of all international applicants, minimum TOEFL 600. **Basis for Candidate Selection:** *Very important factors considered include:* character/personal qualities, secondary school record, volunteer work. *Important factors considered include:* essays, extracurricular activities, recommendations, talent/ability. *Other factors considered include:* alumni/ae relation, class rank, geographical residence, minority status, standardized test scores, work experience. **Freshman Admission Requirements:** High school diploma is required and GED is not accepted. *Academic units required/recommended:* 16 total required; 4 English required, 3 math required, 4 math recommended, 2 science required, 4 science recommended, 2 foreign language required, 4 foreign language recommended. **Freshman Admission Statistics:** 3,363 applied, 35% accepted, 40% of those accepted enrolled. **Transfer Admission Requirements:** *Items required:* high school transcript, college transcript, essay, standardized test scores, statement of good standing from prior school. Minimum college GPA of 3.0 required. Lowest grade transferable C. **General Admission Information:** Application fee $50. Early decision application deadline November 15. Regular application deadline January 2. Admission may be deferred for a maximum of 1 year. Credit and/or placement offered for CEEB Advanced Placement tests.

COSTS AND FINANCIAL AID

Tuition $24,049. Room & board $7,094. Required fees $881. Average book expense $950. **Required Forms and Deadlines:** FAFSA, CSS/Financial Aid PROFILE, noncustodial (divorced/separated) parent's statement, and business/farm supplement. Financial aid filing deadline February 15. **Notification of Awards:** Applicants will be notified of awards on or about April 1. **Types of Aid:** *Need-based scholarships/grants:* Pell, SEOG, state scholarships/grants, private scholarships, the school's own gift aid, need-linked special talent scholarship. *Loans:* FFEL Subsidized Stafford, FFEL Unsubsidized Stafford, FFEL PLUS, Federal Perkins, alternative loans. **Student Employment:** Federal Work-Study Program available. Institutional employment available. Off-campus job opportunities are excellent. **Financial Aid Statistics:** 31% freshmen, 33% undergrads receive some form of aid. Average freshman grant $13,292. Average freshman loan $2,314. **Financial Aid Phone:** 704-894-2232.

See page 1008.

DAVIS & ELKINS COLLEGE

100 Campus Drive, Elkins, WV 26241
Phone: 304-637-1230 **E-mail:** admiss@dne.wvnet.edu **CEEB Code:** 5151
Fax: 304-637-1800 **Web:** www.dne.edu **ACT Code:** 4518

This private school, which is affiliated with the Presbyterian Church, was founded in 1904. It has a 170-acre campus.

STUDENTS AND FACULTY

Enrollment: 668. **Student Body:** Male 39%, female 61%, out-of-state 39%, international students represent 14 countries. **Ethnic Representation:** African American 2%, Asian 4%, Caucasian 93%, Hispanic 1%. **Retention and Graduation:** 64% freshmen return for sophomore year. 30% freshmen graduate within 4 years. 8% grads go on to further study within 1 year. **Faculty:** Student/faculty ratio 12:1. 56 full-time faculty. 100% faculty teach undergrads.

ACADEMICS

Degrees: Associate's, bachelor's. **Academic Requirements:** General education including some course work in arts/fine arts, computer literacy, English (including composition), history, humanities, mathematics, philosophy, sciences (biological or physical), social science. **Majors with Highest Enrollment:** Business administration/management; education, general; psychology, general. **Disciplines with Highest Percentage of Degrees Awarded:** Business/marketing 43%, social sciences and history 13%, psychology 13%, education 10%, biological life sciences 9%. **Special Study Options:** Accelerated program, cooperative (work-study) program, cross registration, double major, dual enrollment, English as a second language, honors program, independent study, internships, student-designed major, study abroad, teacher certification program.

FACILITIES

Housing: Coed, all-female, all-male, housing for disabled students, fraternities and/or sororities. **Library Holdings:** 194,641 bound volumes. 1,525 periodicals. 202,687 microforms. 12,540 audiovisuals. **Special Academic Facilities/Equipment:** Planetarium, Graceland Inn and Conference Center (19th century Victorian mansion now used as training center for the hospitality program), Darby Collection (Civil War collection), Comstock Collection, Pearl S. Buck Collection. **Computers:** School-owned computers available for student use.

EXTRACURRICULARS

Activities: Choral groups, concert band, drama/theater, jazz band, literary magazine, music ensembles, musical theater, radio station, student government, student newspaper, yearbook. **Organizations:** 37 registered organizations, 7 honor societies, 1 religious organization, 2 fraternities (16% men join), 1 sorority (16% women join). **Athletics (Intercollegiate):** *Men:* baseball, basketball, cross-country, golf, skiing (alpine), soccer, tennis. *Women:* basketball, cross-country, skiing (alpine), soccer, softball, tennis, volleyball.

ADMISSIONS

Selectivity Rating: 66 (of 100). **Freshman Academic Profile:** Average high school GPA 3.1. 8% in top 10% of high school class, 24% in top 25% of high school class, 63% in top 50% of high school class. 91% from public high schools. Average SAT I Math 500, SAT I Math middle 50% range 420-520. Average SAT I Verbal 500, SAT I Verbal middle 50% range 430-530. Average ACT 20, ACT middle 50% range 18-21. TOEFL required of all international applicants, minimum TOEFL 500. **Basis for Candidate Selection:** *Very important factors considered include:* secondary school record. *Important factors considered include:* character/personal qualities, class rank, interview, recommendations, standardized test scores. *Other factors considered include:* alumni/ae relation, essays, extracurricular activities, geographical residence, minority status, religious affiliation/commitment, state residency, talent/ability, volunteer work, work experience. **Freshman Admission Requirements:** High school diploma or GED is required. *Academic units required/recommended:* 14 total required; 15 total recommended; 4 English required, 3 math required, 3 science required, 1 science lab required, 1 foreign language required, 2 foreign language recommended, 3 social studies required. **Freshman Admission Statistics:** 421 applied, 83% accepted, 30% of those accepted enrolled. **Transfer Admission Requirements:** *Items required:* high school transcript, college transcript, standardized test scores. Minimum high school GPA of 2.0 required. Minimum college GPA of 2.0 required. Lowest grade transferable C. **General Admission Information:** Application fee $35. Nonfall registration accepted. Admission may be deferred for a maximum of 2 years. Credit and/or placement offered for CEEB Advanced Placement tests.

COSTS AND FINANCIAL AID

Tuition $13,700. Room & board $5,626. Required fees $420. Average book expense $750. **Required Forms and Deadlines:** FAFSA. No deadline for regular filing. Priority filing deadline March 1. **Notification of Awards:** Applicants will be notified of awards on a rolling basis beginning on or about March 15. **Types of Aid:** *Need-based scholarships/grants:* Pell, SEOG, state scholarships/grants, private scholarships, the school's own gift aid. *Loans:* FFEL Subsidized Stafford, FFEL Unsubsidized Stafford, FFEL PLUS, Federal Perkins, college/university loans from institutional funds. **Student Employment:** Federal Work-Study Program available. Institutional employment available. Off-campus job opportunities are fair. **Financial Aid Statistics:** 90% freshmen, 90% undergrads receive some form of aid. Average freshman grant $9,000. Average freshman loan $9,000. Average income from on-campus job $1,500. **Financial Aid Phone:** 304-637-1373.

DAWSON COMMUNITY COLLEGE

300 College Drive Box 421, Glendive, MT 59330
Phone: 406-377-3396 **E-mail:** wade@dawson.cc.mt.us
Fax: 406-377-8132 **Web:** www.dawson.cc.mt.us

STUDENTS AND FACULTY

Enrollment: 509. **Student Body:** Male 48%, female 52%, out-of-state 9%. **Ethnic Representation:** African American 1%, Caucasian 97%, Native American 1%. **Retention and Graduation:** 64% freshmen return for sophomore year.

ACADEMICS

Degrees: Associate's, certificate, terminal, transfer. **Academic Requirements:** General education including some course work in computer literacy, English (including composition), mathematics. **Special Study Options:** Independent study, internships.

FACILITIES

Housing: Coed. **Library Holdings:** 18,870 bound volumes. 1,221 periodicals. 1,112 audiovisuals.

EXTRACURRICULARS

Activities: Choral groups, drama/theater, jazz band, music ensembles, musical theater, pep band, student government.

ADMISSIONS

Selectivity Rating: 63 (of 100). High school diploma or GED is required. **Freshman Admission Statistics:** 294 applied, 100% accepted, 57% of those accepted enrolled. **Transfer Admission Requirements:** *Items required:* high school transcript, college transcript. Lowest grade transferable D. **General Admission Information:** Application fee $30. Regular application deadline rolling. Nonfall registration accepted. Admission may be deferred for a maximum of 1 year.

COSTS AND FINANCIAL AID

In-state tuition $1,442. Out-of-state tuition $4,816. Required fees $560. Average book expense $550. **Required Forms and Deadlines:** FAFSA. No deadline for regular filing. Priority filing deadline March 1. **Notification of Awards:** Applicants will be notified of awards on a rolling basis beginning on or about April 1. **Types of Aid:** *Need-based scholarships/grants:* Pell, SEOG, state scholarships/grants, private scholarships. *Loans:* FFEL Subsidized Stafford, FFEL Unsubsidized Stafford, FFEL PLUS, Federal Perkins. **Financial Aid Statistics:** 71% freshmen, 72% undergrads receive some form of aid.

DEACONESS COLLEGE OF NURSING

6150 Oakland Avenue, St. Louis, MO 63139
Phone: 314-768-3044 **E-mail:** lisa.grote@tenetstl.com
Fax: 314-768-5673 **Web:** www.deaconess.edu **ACT Code:** 2293

This proprietary school was founded in 1889.

STUDENTS AND FACULTY

Enrollment: 305. **Student Body:** Male 7%, female 93%, out-of-state 33%. **Ethnic Representation:** African American 19%, Asian 1%, Caucasian 78%, Hispanic 2%. **Retention and Graduation:** 72% freshmen return for sophomore year. 9% grads go on to further study within 1 year. 3% grads pursue business degrees. **Faculty:** 100% faculty teach undergrads.

ACADEMICS

Degrees: Associate's, bachelor's. **Academic Requirements:** General education including some course work in computer literacy, English (including composition), history, humanities, mathematics, philosophy, sciences (biological or physical), social science, nursing. **Special Study Options:** Cross registration, independent study.

FACILITIES

Housing: All-female, all-male. **Library Holdings:** 3,812 bound volumes. 223 periodicals. 0 microforms. 226 audiovisuals. **Computers:** *Recommended operating system:* Windows 95. School-owned computers available for student use.

EXTRACURRICULARS

Activities: Choral groups, music ensembles, student government, student newspaper, yearbook.

ADMISSIONS

Selectivity Rating: 63 (of 100). **Freshman Academic Profile:** Average high school GPA 2.8. 10% in top 10% of high school class, 45% in top 25% of high school class, 86% in top 50% of high school class. Average ACT 21, ACT middle 50% range 20-24. TOEFL required of all international applicants, minimum TOEFL 500. **Basis for Candidate Selection:** *Very important factors considered include:* class rank, secondary school record, standardized test scores. *Important factors considered include:* essays. *Other factors considered include:* alumni/ae relation, character/personal qualities, extracurricular activities, recommendations. **Freshman Admission Requirements:** High school diploma or GED is required. *Academic units required/recommended:* 4 English required, 3 math required, 3 science required. **Transfer Admission Requirements:** *Items required:* high school transcript, college transcript, essay, statement of good standing from prior school. Minimum high school GPA of 2.5 required. Minimum college GPA of 2.5 required. Lowest grade transferable C. **General Admission Information:** Application fee $30. Regular application deadline rolling. Nonfall registration accepted. Admission may be deferred.

COSTS AND FINANCIAL AID

Room & board $3,200. Average book expense $953. **Required Forms and Deadlines:** FAFSA and institution's own financial aid form. No deadline for regular filing. Priority filing deadline April 1. **Notification of Awards:** Applicants will be notified of awards on a rolling basis beginning on or about April 20. **Types of Aid:** *Need-based scholarships/grants:* Pell, SEOG, state scholarships/grants, private scholarships, the school's own gift aid. *Loans:* Direct Subsidized Stafford, Direct Unsubsidized Stafford, Direct PLUS, FFEL Subsidized Stafford, FFEL PLUS. **Student Employment:** Federal Work-Study Program available. Off-campus job opportunities are excellent. **Financial Aid Statistics:** Average income from on-campus job $2,535. **Financial Aid Phone:** 314-768-3044.

DEEP SPRINGS COLLEGE

Application Committee, H.C. 72, Box 45001, Deep Springs, California, via Dyer, NV 89010
Phone: 760-872-2000 **E-mail:** apcom@deepspring.edu **CEEB Code:** 4281
Fax: 760-872-4466 **Web:** www.deepsprings.edu

This private school was founded in 1917. It has a 30,000-acre campus.

STUDENTS AND FACULTY

Enrollment: 26. **Student Body:** Out-of-state 92%. **Retention and Graduation:** 100% freshmen return for sophomore year. 96% grads go on to further study within 1 year. 3% grads pursue business degrees. 11% grads pursue law degrees. 10% grads pursue medical degrees. **Faculty:** Student/faculty ratio 4:1. 3 full-time faculty, 100% hold PhDs. 100% faculty teach undergrads.

ACADEMICS

Degrees: Associate's. **Academic Requirements:** General education including some course work in English (including composition), public speaking (4 semesters). **Classes:** Under 10 students in an average class. **Disciplines with Highest Percentage of Degrees Awarded:** Liberal arts/general studies 100%. **Special Study Options:** Independent study, internships.

FACILITIES

Housing: All-male. **Library Holdings:** 22,000 bound volumes. 30 periodicals. 0 microforms. 0 audiovisuals. **Special Academic Facilities/Equipment:** Ranch, 300 cattle, 15 horses, organic farm; thousands of acres of wilderness surround the college. **Computers:** School-owned computers available for student use.

EXTRACURRICULARS

Activities: Literary magazine, student government, yearbook.

ADMISSIONS

Selectivity Rating: 99 (of 100). **Freshman Academic Profile:** Average high school GPA 3.9. 90% in top 10% of high school class, 90% in top 25% of high school class, 100% in top 50% of high school class. Average SAT I Math 715. Average SAT I Verbal 740. **Basis for Candidate Selection:** *Very important factors considered include:* character/personal qualities, essays, interview. *Important factors considered include:* class rank, extracurricular activities, secondary school record, volunteer work, work experience. *Other factors considered include:* minority status, recommendations, religious affiliation/commitment, standardized test scores, talent/ability. **Freshman Admission Requirements:** High school diploma or equivalent is not required. **Freshman**

Admission Statistics: 95 applied, 14% accepted, 100% of those accepted enrolled. **Transfer Admission Requirements:** *Items required:* high school transcript, college transcript, essay, interview, standardized test scores. **General Admission Information:** Regular application deadline November 15. Neither credit nor placement offered for CEEB Advanced Placement tests.

COSTS AND FINANCIAL AID

Tuition $0. Required fees $0. Average book expense $1,200. **Required Forms and Deadlines:** No deadline for regular filing. **Notification of Awards:** Applicants will be notified of awards on or about April 7. **Student Employment:** Off-campus job opportunities are poor. **Financial Aid Statistics:** Average freshman grant $52,000. Average freshman loan $0. Average income from on-campus job $0. **Financial Aid Phone:** 760-872-2000.

DEFIANCE COLLEGE

701 North Clinton Street, Defiance, OH 43512-1695
Phone: 419-783-2359 **E-mail:** admissions@defiance.edu **CEEB Code:** 1162
Fax: 419-783-2468 **Web:** www.defiance.edu **ACT Code:** 3264

This private school, which is affiliated with the United Church of Christ, was founded in 1850. It has a 150-acre campus.

STUDENTS AND FACULTY

Enrollment: 906. **Student Body:** Male 44%, female 56%, out-of-state 14%, international 1% (3 countries represented). **Ethnic Representation:** African American 4%, Caucasian 91%, Hispanic 3%. **Retention and Graduation:** 69% freshmen return for sophomore year. 7% grads go on to further study within 1 year. 1% grads pursue business degrees. 1% grads pursue law degrees. 1% grads pursue medical degrees. **Faculty:** Student/faculty ratio 13:1. 41 full-time faculty, 51% hold PhDs. 100% faculty teach undergrads.

ACADEMICS

Degrees: Associate's, bachelor's, master's. **Academic Requirements:** General education including some course work in arts/fine arts, computer literacy, English (including composition), history, humanities, mathematics, philosophy, sciences (biological or physical), social science. **Classes:** 10-19 students in an average class. 10-19 students in an average lab class. **Majors with Highest Enrollment:** Early childhood education and teaching; criminology; business administration/management. **Disciplines with Highest Percentage of Degrees Awarded:** Business/marketing 37%, education 29%, law/legal studies 7%, health professions and related sciences 6%, biological life sciences 5%. **Special Study Options:** Cooperative (work-study) program, distance learning, double major, dual enrollment, external degree program, honors program, independent study, internships, student-designed major, study abroad, teacher certification program, weekend college.

FACILITIES

Housing: All-female, all-male. **Library Holdings:** 100,121 bound volumes. 435 periodicals. 22,083 microforms. 0 audiovisuals. **Special Academic Facilities/Equipment:** Art gallery, media center, Eisenhower Archives Room, curriculum resource center, cultural arts center, Indian Wars Collection. **Computers:** *Recommended operating system:* Mac. School-owned computers available for student use.

EXTRACURRICULARS

Activities: Choral groups, drama/theater, literary magazine, musical theater, pep band, student government, student newspaper, yearbook. **Organizations:** 5 religious organizations, 2 fraternities (6% men join), 2 sororities (8% women join). **Athletics (Intercollegiate):** *Men:* baseball, basketball, cheerleading, cross-country, football, golf, indoor track, soccer, tennis, track & field. *Women:* basketball, cheerleading, cross-country, golf, indoor track, soccer, softball, tennis, track & field, volleyball.

ADMISSIONS

Selectivity Rating: 63 (of 100). **Freshman Academic Profile:** Average high school GPA 3.1. 13% in top 10% of high school class, 26% in top 25% of high school class, 5% in top 50% of high school class. Average SAT I Math 490, SAT I Math middle 50% range 450-570. Average SAT I Verbal 481, SAT I Verbal middle 50% range 420-580. Average ACT 21, ACT middle 50% range 19-24. TOEFL required of all international applicants, minimum TOEFL 500. **Basis for Candidate Selection:** *Very important factors considered include:* class rank, secondary school record, standardized test scores. *Important factors considered include:* essays, interview, recommendations. *Other factors considered include:* alumni/ae relation, character/personal qualities, extracurricular activities, volunteer work. **Freshman Admission Requirements:** High school diploma or GED is required. *Academic units required/recommended:* 15 total recommended; 4 English recommended, 3 math recommended, 3 science recommended, 2 science lab recommended, 2 foreign language recommended, 1 social studies recommended, 1 history recommended. **Freshman Admission Statistics:** 656 applied, 79% accepted, 41% of those accepted enrolled. **Transfer Admission Requirements:** *Items required:* high school transcript, college transcript, essay. Minimum college GPA of 2.0 required. Lowest grade transferable C. **General Admission Information:** Application fee $25. Regular application deadline August 25. Nonfall registration accepted. Admission may be deferred for a maximum of 1 year. Credit and/or placement offered for CEEB Advanced Placement tests.

COSTS AND FINANCIAL AID

Tuition $16,360. Room & board $5,700. Required fees $300. Average book expense $500. **Required Forms and Deadlines:** FAFSA. No deadline for regular filing. Priority filing deadline March 1. **Notification of Awards:** Applicants will be notified of awards on a rolling basis beginning on or about February 1. **Types of Aid:** *Need-based scholarships/grants:* Pell, SEOG, state scholarships/grants, private scholarships, the school's own gift aid. *Loans:* FFEL Subsidized Stafford, FFEL Unsubsidized Stafford, FFEL PLUS, Federal Perkins, alternative loans. **Student Employment:** Federal Work-Study Program available. Institutional employment available. Off-campus job opportunities are excellent. **Financial Aid Statistics:** 88% freshmen, 92% undergrads receive some form of aid. Average freshman grant $8,325. Average freshman loan $3,625. Average income from on-campus job $1,650. **Financial Aid Phone:** 419-783-2376.

DELAWARE STATE UNIVERSITY

1200 North Dupont Highway, Dover, DE 19901
Phone: 302-857-6361 **E-mail:** admissions@dsc.edu **CEEB Code:** 5153
Fax: 302-857-6362 **Web:** www.dsc.edu **ACT Code:** 630

This public school was founded in 1891. It has a 400-acre campus.

STUDENTS AND FACULTY

Enrollment: 3,149. **Student Body:** Male 43%, female 57%, out-of-state 44%, international students represent 30 countries. **Ethnic Representation:** African American 79%, Asian 1%, Caucasian 15%, Hispanic 2%. **Retention and Graduation:** 65% freshmen return for sophomore year. 16% freshmen graduate within 4 years. 15% grads go on to further study within 1 year. 8% grads pursue business degrees. 1% grads pursue law degrees. **Faculty:** Student/faculty ratio 13:1. 184 full-time faculty, 74% hold PhDs. 100% faculty teach undergrads.

ACADEMICS

Degrees: Bachelor's, master's. **Academic Requirements:** General education including some course work in arts/fine arts, English (including composition), foreign languages, history, humanities, mathematics, philosophy, sciences (biological or physical), social science, speech, fitness and health, university seminar. **Classes:** Under 10 students in an average class. **Disciplines with Highest Percentage of Degrees Awarded:** Business/marketing 29%, education 12%, communications/communication technologies 9%, social sciences and history 9%, protective services/public administration 9%. **Special Study Options:** Accelerated program, cooperative (work-study) program, distance learning, double major, English as a second language, student exchange program (domestic), honors program, independent study, internships, study abroad, teacher certification program, weekend college.

FACILITIES

Housing: Coed, all-female, all-male, apartments for single students. **Library Holdings:** 209,388 bound volumes. 12,953 microforms. 15,734 audiovisuals. **Special Academic Facilities/Equipment:** Art gallery, language lab, observatory, herbarium. **Computers:** School-owned computers available for student use.

EXTRACURRICULARS

Activities: Choral groups, concert band, dance, jazz band, marching band, music ensembles, pep band, radio station, student government, student newspaper, television station, yearbook. **Organizations:** 63 registered organizations, 9 honor societies, 3 religious organizations, 4 fraternities, 4 sororities. **Athletics (Intercollegiate):** *Men:* baseball, basketball, cross-country, football, tennis, track & field, wrestling. *Women:* basketball, cheerleading, cross-country, softball, tennis, track & field, volleyball.

ADMISSIONS

Selectivity Rating: 63 (of 100). **Freshman Academic Profile:** Average high school GPA 2.6. 4% in top 10% of high school class, 19% in top 25% of high

school class, 51% in top 50% of high school class. 80% from public high schools. SAT I Math middle 50% range 340-450. SAT I Verbal middle 50% range 350-460. TOEFL required of all international applicants, minimum TOEFL 500. **Basis for Candidate Selection:** *Very important factors considered include:* secondary school record. *Important factors considered include:* character/personal qualities, essays, recommendations, standardized test scores. *Other factors considered include:* alumni/ae relation, class rank, extracurricular activities, interview, state residency, talent/ability, volunteer work, work experience. **Freshman Admission Requirements:** High school diploma or GED is required. *Academic units required/recommended:* 16 total required; 4 English required, 3 math required, 3 science required, 2 social studies required, 4 elective required. **Freshman Admission Statistics:** 3,177 applied, 61% accepted, 42% of those accepted enrolled. **Transfer Admission Requirements:** *Items required:* high school transcript, college transcript, essay, interview, standardized test scores, statement of good standing from prior school. Minimum high school GPA of 2.0 required. Lowest grade transferable C. **General Admission Information:** Application fee $15. Regular application deadline April 1. Nonfall registration accepted. Admission may be deferred for a maximum of 1 year. Placement offered for CEEB Advanced Placement tests.

COSTS AND FINANCIAL AID

In-state tuition $3,096. Out-of-state tuition $7,088. Room & board $4,990. Required fees $600. Average book expense $1,000. **Required Forms and Deadlines:** FAFSA. Financial aid filing deadline April 1. Priority filing deadline February 15. **Notification of Awards:** Applicants will be notified of awards on a rolling basis beginning on or about March 30. **Types of Aid:** *Need-based scholarships/grants:* Pell, SEOG, state scholarships/grants, private scholarships, the school's own gift aid, Federal Nursing. *Loans:* FFEL Subsidized Stafford, FFEL Unsubsidized Stafford, FFEL PLUS, Federal Perkins, Signature loans (private). **Student Employment:** Federal Work-Study Program available. Institutional employment available. Off-campus job opportunities are good. **Financial Aid Statistics:** 79% freshmen, 72% undergrads receive some form of aid. Average freshman grant $5,519. Average freshman loan $3,990. Average income from on-campus job $1,500. **Financial Aid Phone:** 302-857-6250.

DELAWARE VALLEY COLLEGE

700 East Butler Avenue, Doylestown, PA 18901-2697
Phone: 215-489-2211 **E-mail:** ADMITME@devalcol.edu **CEEB Code:** 2510
Fax: 215-230-2968 **Web:** www.devalcol.edu **ACT Code:** 3551

This private school was founded in 1896. It has a 600-acre campus.

STUDENTS AND FACULTY

Enrollment: 1,925. **Student Body:** Male 48%, female 52%, out-of-state 29%. **Ethnic Representation:** African American 3%, Asian 1%, Caucasian 82%, Hispanic 1%. **Retention and Graduation:** 71% freshmen return for sophomore year. 38% freshmen graduate within 4 years. 10% grads go on to further study within 1 year. 31% grads pursue business degrees. 3% grads pursue law degrees. 7% grads pursue medical degrees. **Faculty:** Student/faculty ratio 14:1. 76 full-time faculty, 60% hold PhDs. 100% faculty teach undergrads.

ACADEMICS

Degrees: Associate's, bachelor's, certificate, master's, post-bachelor's certificate. **Academic Requirements:** General education including some course work in arts/fine arts, computer literacy, English (including composition), history, humanities, mathematics, philosophy, sciences (biological or physical), social science, macroeconomics, speech. **Classes:** Under 10 students in an average class. 10-19 students in an average lab class. **Majors with Highest Enrollment:** Business administration/management; animal sciences, general; equestrian/equine studies. **Disciplines with Highest Percentage of Degrees Awarded:** Agriculture 57%, business/marketing 19%, computer and information sciences 8%, biological life sciences 7%, protective services/public administration 4%. **Special Study Options:** Cooperative (work-study) program, cross registration, distance learning, double major, honors program, independent study, internships, liberal arts/career combination, study abroad, teacher certification program, weekend college.

FACILITIES

Housing: Coed, all-female, all-male. **Library Holdings:** 55,581 bound volumes. 727 periodicals. 152,632 microforms. **Special Academic Facilities/Equipment:** Dairy processing plant, greenhouse and nursery lab complex, small animal science labs, poultry diagnostic lab, arboretum, equine facilities, 500+-acre farm, tissue culture lab. **Computers:** *Recommended operating system:* Windows 95. School-owned computers available for student use.

EXTRACURRICULARS

Activities: Choral groups, concert band, drama/theater, literary magazine, radio station, student government, student newspaper, yearbook. **Organizations:** 38 registered organizations, 6 honor societies, 3 religious organizations, 5 fraternities (4% men join), 3 sororities (5% women join). **Athletics (Intercollegiate):** *Men:* baseball, basketball, cross-country, equestrian, football, golf, lacrosse, soccer, track & field, wrestling. *Women:* basketball, cheerleading, cross-country, equestrian, field hockey, golf, soccer, softball, track & field, volleyball.

ADMISSIONS

Selectivity Rating: 77 (of 100). **Freshman Academic Profile:** Average high school GPA 3.3. 11% in top 10% of high school class, 32% in top 25% of high school class, 63% in top 50% of high school class. Average SAT I Math 504, SAT I Math middle 50% range 455-555. Average SAT I Verbal 500, SAT I Verbal middle 50% range 455-545. Average ACT 22, ACT middle 50% range 20-23. TOEFL required of all international applicants, minimum TOEFL 500. **Basis for Candidate Selection:** *Very important factors considered include:* class rank, secondary school record, standardized test scores. *Important factors considered include:* minority status, recommendations. *Other factors considered include:* alumni/ae relation, essays, extracurricular activities, interview, talent/ability, volunteer work, work experience. **Freshman Admission Requirements:** High school diploma or GED is required. *Academic units required/recommended:* 15 total required; 3 English required, 2 math required, 2 science required, 1 science lab required, 2 social studies required, 6 elective required. **Freshman Admission Statistics:** 1,273 applied, 83% accepted, 39% of those accepted enrolled. **Transfer Admission Requirements:** *Items required:* high school transcript, college transcript, statement of good standing from prior school. Minimum high school GPA of 2.5 required. Minimum college GPA of 2.0 required. Lowest grade transferable C. **General Admission Information:** Application fee $35. Priority application deadline April 1. Nonfall registration accepted. Admission may be deferred for a maximum of 1 year. Credit and/or placement offered for CEEB Advanced Placement tests.

COSTS AND FINANCIAL AID

Required Forms and Deadlines: FAFSA. No deadline for regular filing. Priority filing deadline April 1. **Notification of Awards:** Applicants will be notified of awards on a rolling basis beginning on or about January 15. **Types of Aid:** *Need-based scholarships/grants:* Pell, SEOG, state scholarships/grants, private scholarships, the school's own gift aid. *Loans:* FFEL Subsidized Stafford, FFEL Unsubsidized Stafford, FFEL PLUS, Federal Perkins, state loans, alternative loans. **Student Employment:** Federal Work-Study Program available. Institutional employment available. Off-campus job opportunities are excellent. **Financial Aid Statistics:** 78% freshmen, 68% undergrads receive some form of aid. Average freshman grant $10,868. Average freshman loan $2,702. Average income from on-campus job $1,065. **Financial Aid Phone:** 215-489-2722.

DELTA STATE UNIVERSITY

Highway 8 West, Cleveland, MS 38733
Phone: 662-846-4018 **E-mail:** dheslep@deltastate.edu
Fax: 662-846-4683 **Web:** www.deltastate.edu **ACT Code:** 2190

This public school was founded in 1924. It has a 332-acre campus.

STUDENTS AND FACULTY

Enrollment: 3,219. **Student Body:** Male 39%, female 61%, out-of-state 8%, international students represent 3 countries. **Ethnic Representation:** African American 32%, Caucasian 67%. **Retention and Graduation:** 68% freshmen return for sophomore year. 18% freshmen graduate within 4 years. **Faculty:** 177 full-time faculty, 59% hold PhDs.

ACADEMICS

Degrees: Bachelor's, doctoral, master's, post-master's certificate. **Academic Requirements:** General education including some course work in arts/fine arts, English (including composition), history, mathematics, sciences (biological or physical), social science, psychology, physical education, speech communication. **Disciplines with Highest Percentage of Degrees Awarded:** Education 28%, business/marketing 23%, protective services/public administration 7%, health professions and related sciences 7%, biological life sciences 6%. **Special Study Options:** Cooperative (work-study) program, distance learning, double major, dual enrollment, honors program, independent study, internships, teacher certification program, weekend college.

FACILITIES

Housing: All-female, all-male, apartments for married students, apartments for students with dependent children. **Library Holdings:** 212,266 bound volumes. 4,546 periodicals. 733,383 microforms. 14,718 audiovisuals. **Special Academic Facilities/Equipment:** Art museum, performing arts center, natural history museum, language lab, airport facility with 12 airplanes, flight simulator, planetarium.

EXTRACURRICULARS

Activities: Choral groups, concert band, drama/theater, jazz band, literary magazine, marching band, music ensembles, musical theater, opera, student government, student newspaper, symphony orchestra, yearbook. **Organizations:** 46 registered organizations, 26 honor societies, 9 religious organizations, 6 fraternities (17% men join), 7 sororities (13% women join). **Athletics (Intercollegiate):** *Men:* baseball, basketball, diving, football, golf, swimming, tennis. *Women:* basketball, cross-country, diving, softball, swimming, tennis.

ADMISSIONS

Selectivity Rating: 63 (of 100). **Freshman Academic Profile:** 34% in top 25% of high school class, 63% in top 50% of high school class. Average ACT 20, ACT middle 50% range 18-23. TOEFL required of all international applicants, minimum TOEFL 525. **Basis for Candidate Selection:** *Very important factors considered include:* class rank, secondary school record, standardized test scores. *Other factors considered include:* interview, recommendations. **Freshman Admission Requirements:** High school diploma or GED is required. *Academic units required/recommended:* 16 total required; 4 English required, 3 math required, 3 science required, 2 science lab required, 1 foreign language required, 3 social studies required, 1 elective required. **Transfer Admission Requirements:** *Items required:* college transcript. Minimum college GPA of 2.0 required. Lowest grade transferable D. **General Admission Information:** Priority application deadline May 1. Regular application deadline August 1. Nonfall registration accepted. Admission may be deferred. Credit and/or placement offered for CEEB Advanced Placement tests.

COSTS AND FINANCIAL AID

Average book expense $500. **Required Forms and Deadlines:** FAFSA and institution's own financial aid form. No deadline for regular filing. Priority filing deadline April 1. **Notification of Awards:** Applicants will be notified of awards on a rolling basis beginning on or about May 1. **Types of Aid:** *Need-based scholarships/grants:* Pell, SEOG, private scholarships, the school's own gift aid. *Loans:* FFEL Subsidized Stafford, FFEL Unsubsidized Stafford, FFEL PLUS, Federal Perkins, college/university loans from institutional funds. **Student Employment:** Federal Work-Study Program available. Institutional employment available. Off-campus job opportunities are fair. **Financial Aid Statistics:** Average freshman grant $5,100. Average freshman loan $1,800. Average income from on-campus job $1,200. **Financial Aid Phone:** 662-846-4670.

DENISON UNIVERSITY

1 Southridge Road, Box H, Granville, OH 43023
Phone: 740-587-6276 **E-mail:** admissions@denison.edu **CEEB Code:** 1164
Fax: 740-587-6306 **Web:** www.denison.edu **ACT Code:** 3266

This private school was founded in 1831. It has a 1,200-acre campus.

STUDENTS AND FACULTY

Enrollment: 2,096. **Student Body:** Male 44%, female 56%, out-of-state 55%, international 5% (34 countries represented). **Ethnic Representation:** African American 5%, Asian 2%, Caucasian 88%, Hispanic 2%. **Retention and Graduation:** 86% freshmen return for sophomore year. 72% freshmen graduate within 4 years. 28% grads go on to further study within 1 year. 1% grads pursue business degrees. 6% grads pursue law degrees. 4% grads pursue medical degrees. **Faculty:** Student/faculty ratio 11:1. 183 full-time faculty, 96% hold PhDs. 100% faculty teach undergrads.

ACADEMICS

Degrees: Bachelor's. **Academic Requirements:** General education including some course work in arts/fine arts, English (including composition), foreign languages, history, humanities, philosophy, sciences (biological or physical), social science. **Classes:** 10-19 students in an average class. 10-19 students in an average lab class. **Majors with Highest Enrollment:** Communications studies/speech communication and rhetoric; economics, general; English language and literature, general. **Disciplines with Highest Percentage of Degrees Awarded:** Social sciences and history 27%, communications/communication technologies 14%, English 10%, psychology 9%, biological life sciences 8%. **Special Study Options:** Double major, honors program, independent study, internships, student-designed major, study abroad, teacher certification program.

FACILITIES

Housing: Coed, all-female, all-male, apartments for single students, suite-style. **Library Holdings:** 728,949 bound volumes. 1,195 periodicals. 105,598 microforms. 25,452 audiovisuals. **Special Academic Facilities/Equipment:** Burmese art collection, language lab, research station in 350-acre biological reserve, observatory, high resolution spectrometer lab, nuclear magnetic resonance spectrometer, planetarium, economics computer laboratories. **Computers:** School-owned computers available for student use.

EXTRACURRICULARS

Activities: Choral groups, concert band, dance, drama/theater, jazz band, literary magazine, music ensembles, musical theater, pep band, radio station, student government, student newspaper, student-run film society, symphony orchestra, television station, yearbook. **Organizations:** 156 registered organizations, 15 honor societies, 7 religious organizations, 8 fraternities (28% men join), 6 sororities (41% women join). **Athletics (Intercollegiate):** *Men:* baseball, basketball, cross-country, diving, football, golf, indoor track, lacrosse, soccer, swimming, tennis, track & field. *Women:* basketball, cross-country, diving, field hockey, indoor track, lacrosse, soccer, softball, swimming, tennis, track & field, volleyball.

ADMISSIONS

Selectivity Rating: 82 (of 100). **Freshman Academic Profile:** Average high school GPA 3.5. 48% in top 10% of high school class, 82% in top 25% of high school class, 89% in top 50% of high school class. 72% from public high schools. Average SAT I Math 615, SAT I Math middle 50% range 560-670. Average SAT I Verbal 602, SAT I Verbal middle 50% range 550-650. Average ACT 26, ACT middle 50% range 24-29. TOEFL required of all international applicants, minimum TOEFL 550. **Basis for Candidate Selection:** *Very important factors considered include:* class rank, essays, recommendations, secondary school record, standardized test scores. *Important factors considered include:* alumni/ae relation, character/personal qualities, extracurricular activities, interview, minority status, talent/ability. *Other factors considered include:* geographical residence, religious affiliation/commitment, state residency, volunteer work, work experience. **Freshman Admission Requirements:** High school diploma or GED is required. *Academic units required/recommended:* 19 total required; 4 English required, 4 math required, 4 science required, 3 foreign language required, 2 social studies required, 1 history required, 1 elective required. **Freshman Admission Statistics:** 3,289 applied, 61% accepted, 31% of those accepted enrolled. **Transfer Admission Requirements:** *Items required:* high school transcript, college transcript, essay, standardized test scores, statement of good standing from prior school. Minimum high school GPA of 2.7 required. Minimum college GPA of 2.7 required. Lowest grade transferable C-. **General Admission Information:** Application fee $40. Priority application deadline January 1. Early decision application deadline November 15. Regular application deadline February 1. Admission may be deferred for a maximum of 1 year. Credit and/or placement offered for CEEB Advanced Placement tests.

COSTS AND FINANCIAL AID

Tuition $23,680. Room & board $6,880. Required fees $560. Average book expense $600. **Required Forms and Deadlines:** FAFSA. No deadline for regular filing. Priority filing deadline February 15. **Notification of Awards:** Applicants will be notified of awards on a rolling basis beginning on or about April 1. **Types of Aid:** *Need-based scholarships/grants:* Pell, SEOG, state scholarships/grants, private scholarships, the school's own gift aid. *Loans:* Direct Subsidized Stafford, Direct Unsubsidized Stafford, Direct PLUS, Federal Perkins, college/university loans from institutional funds. **Student Employment:** Federal Work-Study Program available. Institutional employment available. Off-campus job opportunities are fair. **Financial Aid Statistics:** 50% freshmen, 48% undergrads receive some form of aid. Average freshman grant $12,180. Average freshman loan $4,625. Average income from on-campus job $2,100. **Financial Aid Phone:** 740-587-6279.

See page 1010.

DEPAUL UNIVERSITY

1 East Jackson Boulevard, Chicago, IL 60604-2287
Phone: 312-362-8300 **E-mail:** admitdpu@depaul.edu **CEEB Code:** 1165
Fax: 312-362-5749 **Web:** www.depaul.edu **ACT Code:** 1012

This private school, which is affiliated with the Roman Catholic Church, was founded in 1898. It has a 36-acre campus.

STUDENTS AND FACULTY

Enrollment: 15,343. **Student Body:** Male 46%, female 54%, out-of-state 11%, international 1% (85 countries represented). **Ethnic Representation:** African American 12%, Asian 10%, Caucasian 59%, Hispanic 13%. **Retention and Graduation:** 82% freshmen return for sophomore year. 43% freshmen graduate within 4 years. **Faculty:** Student/faculty ratio 19:1. 785 full-time faculty.

ACADEMICS

Degrees: Bachelor's, certificate, doctoral, first professional, master's, post-bachelor's certificate, post-master's certificate. **Academic Requirements:** General education including some course work in arts/fine arts, computer literacy, English (including composition), foreign languages, history, humanities, mathematics, philosophy, sciences (biological or physical), social science, experiential service learning, senior year capstone course. **Classes:** Under 10 students in an average class. **Majors with Highest Enrollment:** Computer science; communications studies/speech communication and rhetoric; accounting. **Disciplines with Highest Percentage of Degrees Awarded:** Business/marketing 31%, liberal arts/general studies 15%, computer and information sciences 14%, social sciences and history 9%, communications/communication technologies 7%. **Special Study Options:** Accelerated program, cooperative (work-study) program, distance learning, double major, English as a second language, honors program, independent study, internships, study abroad, teacher certification program, weekend college.

FACILITIES

Housing: Coed, apartments for single students, theme communities where groups of students who choose to live together in a house or apartment within Residence Life in order to further a particular theme. **Special Academic Facilities/Equipment:** McGowan Science Center, Merle Reskin Theatre, art gallery, environmental science building, Ray Meyer Fitness and Recreational Center, three-level student center (2002). **Computers:** School-owned computers available for student use.

EXTRACURRICULARS

Activities: Choral groups, concert band, dance, drama/theater, jazz band, music ensembles, musical theater, opera, pep band, student government, student newspaper, student-run film society, symphony orchestra. **Organizations:** 140 registered organizations, 2 honor societies, 11 religious organizations, 9 fraternities, 9 sororities. **Athletics (Intercollegiate):** *Men:* basketball, cross-country, golf, indoor track, soccer, tennis, track & field. *Women:* basketball, cross-country, indoor track, rifle, soccer, softball, tennis, track & field, volleyball.

ADMISSIONS

Selectivity Rating: 78 (of 100). **Freshman Academic Profile:** Average high school GPA 3.3. 16% in top 10% of high school class, 41% in top 25% of high school class, 75% in top 50% of high school class. 68% from public high schools. Average SAT I Math 552, SAT I Math middle 50% range 490-610. Average SAT I Verbal 564, SAT I Verbal middle 50% range 510-620. Average ACT 23, ACT middle 50% range 21-27. TOEFL required of all international applicants, minimum TOEFL 550. **Basis for Candidate Selection:** *Very important factors considered include:* character/personal qualities, secondary school record, volunteer work. *Important factors considered include:* class rank, extracurricular activities, minority status, recommendations, standardized test scores, work experience. *Other factors considered include:* alumni/ae relation, essays, geographical residence, interview, religious affiliation/commitment, state residency, talent/ability. **Freshman Admission Requirements:** High school diploma or GED is required. *Academic units required/recommended:* 16 total required; 4 English required, 2 math required, 2 science required, 2 science lab required, 2 social studies required, 4 elective required. **Freshman Admission Statistics:** 8,932 applied, 77% accepted, 33% of those accepted enrolled. **Transfer Admission Requirements:** *Items required:* college transcript, essay, statement of good standing from prior institution(s). Minimum high school GPA of 2.6 required. Minimum college GPA of 2.0 required. Lowest grade transferable C-. **General Admission Information:** Application fee $35. Priority application deadline February 1. Nonfall registration accepted. Admission may be deferred for a maximum of 1 year. Credit and/or placement offered for CEEB Advanced Placement tests.

COSTS AND FINANCIAL AID

Tuition $16,140. Room & board $6,960. Required fees $30. Average book expense $900. **Required Forms and Deadlines:** FAFSA. Financial aid filing deadline May 1. Priority filing deadline May 1. **Notification of Awards:** Applicants will be notified of awards on a rolling basis beginning on or about February 15. **Types of Aid:** *Need-based scholarships/grants:* Pell, SEOG, state scholarships/grants, private scholarships, the school's own gift aid. *Loans:* Direct Subsidized Stafford, Direct Unsubsidized Stafford, Direct PLUS, Federal Perkins. **Student Employment:** Federal Work-Study Program available. Institutional employment available. Off-campus job opportunities are excellent. **Financial Aid Statistics:** 60% freshmen, 63% undergrads receive some form of aid. Average income from on-campus job $2,250. **Financial Aid Phone:** 312-362-8091.

DEPAUW UNIVERSITY

101 E. Seminary, Greencastle, IN 46135
Phone: 765-658-4006 **E-mail:** admission@depauw.edu **CEEB Code:** 1166
Fax: 765-658-4007 **Web:** www.depauw.edu **ACT Code:** 1184

This private school, which is affiliated with the Methodist Church, was founded in 1837. It has a 175-acre campus.

STUDENTS AND FACULTY

Enrollment: 2,338. **Student Body:** Male 44%, female 56%, out-of-state 53%, international 1% (15 countries represented). **Ethnic Representation:** African American 5%, Asian 2%, Caucasian 88%, Hispanic 3%. **Retention and Graduation:** 91% freshmen return for sophomore year. 73% freshmen graduate within 4 years. 29% grads go on to further study within 1 year. 1% grads pursue business degrees. 8% grads pursue law degrees. 4% grads pursue medical degrees. **Faculty:** Student/faculty ratio 11:1. 195 full-time faculty, 93% hold PhDs. 100% faculty teach undergrads.

ACADEMICS

Degrees: Bachelor's. **Academic Requirements:** General education including some course work in arts/fine arts, English (including composition), foreign languages, history, humanities, mathematics, philosophy, sciences (biological or physical), social science. **Classes:** 10-19 students in an average class. **Majors with Highest Enrollment:** Communications studies/speech communication and rhetoric; creative writing; economics, general. **Disciplines with Highest Percentage of Degrees Awarded:** Social sciences and history 30%, communications/communication technologies 14%, English 14%, visual and performing arts 7%, computer and information sciences 6%. **Special Study Options:** Double major, dual enrollment, student exchange program (domestic), honors program, independent study, internships, student-designed major, study abroad, teacher certification program.

FACILITIES

Housing: Coed, apartments for single students, fraternities and/or sororities. **Library Holdings:** 283,735 bound volumes. 4,017 periodicals. 371,852 microforms. 15,659 audiovisuals. **Special Academic Facilities/Equipment:** Emison Art Center, center for contemporary media, performing arts center, anthropology museum, Shidzuo Iikudo Museum. **Computers:** School-owned computers available for student use.

EXTRACURRICULARS

Activities: Choral groups, concert band, dance, drama/theater, jazz band, literary magazine, music ensembles, musical theater, opera, pep band, radio station, student government, student newspaper, symphony orchestra, television station, yearbook. **Organizations:** 83 registered organizations, 11 honor societies, 9 religious organizations, 12 fraternities (77% men join), 10 sororities (69% women join). **Athletics (Intercollegiate):** *Men:* baseball, basketball, cross-country, diving, football, golf, indoor track, soccer, swimming, tennis, track & field. *Women:* basketball, cross-country, diving, field hockey, golf, indoor track, soccer, softball, swimming, tennis, track & field, volleyball.

ADMISSIONS

Selectivity Rating: 86 (of 100). **Freshman Academic Profile:** Average high school GPA 3.7. 56% in top 10% of high school class, 89% in top 25% of high school class, 99% in top 50% of high school class. 85% from public high schools. Average SAT I Math 620, SAT I Math middle 50% range 570-670. Average SAT I Verbal 610, SAT I Verbal middle 50% range 560-650. Average ACT 27, ACT middle 50% range 25-29. TOEFL required of all international applicants, minimum TOEFL 560. **Basis for Candidate Selection:** *Very important factors considered include:* class rank, essays, secondary school record, standardized test scores. *Important factors considered include:* alumni/ae relation, character/personal qualities, extracurricular activities, interview, minority status, recommendations, talent/ability, volunteer work. *Other factors considered include:* geographical residence, work experience. **Freshman Admission Requirements:** High school diploma or GED is required. *Academic units required/recommended:* 32 total recommended; 4 English recommended, 4 math recommended, 4 science recommended, 2 science lab recommended, 4 foreign language recommended, 4 social studies recommended, 3 history recommended, 10 elective recommended. **Freshman Admission Statistics:** 3,682 applied, 61% accepted, 30% of those accepted enrolled. **Transfer Admission Requirements:** *Items required:* high school transcript, college transcript, essay, standardized test scores, statement of good standing from prior school. Minimum college GPA of 3.0 required. Lowest grade transferable C. **General Admission Information:** Priority application deadline December 1. Early decision application deadline November 1. Regular application deadline February 1. Nonfall registration accepted. Admission may be deferred for a maximum of 1 year. Credit and/or placement offered for CEEB Advanced Placement tests.

COSTS AND FINANCIAL AID

Tuition $21,400. Room & board $6,800. Required fees $440. Average book expense $600. **Required Forms and Deadlines:** FAFSA and institution's own financial aid form. Financial aid filing deadline February 15. **Notification of Awards:** Applicants will be notified of awards on or about March 31. **Types of Aid:** *Need-based scholarships/grants:* Pell, SEOG, state scholarships/grants, private scholarships, the school's own gift aid. *Loans:* FFEL Subsidized Stafford, FFEL Unsubsidized Stafford, FFEL PLUS, Federal Perkins, college/university loans from institutional funds, alternative loans. **Student Employment:** Federal Work-Study Program available. Institutional employment available. Off-campus job opportunities are fair. **Financial Aid Statistics:** 53% freshmen, 51% undergrads receive some form of aid. Average freshman grant $17,150. Average freshman loan $2,917. Average income from on-campus job $434. **Financial Aid Phone:** 765-658-4030.

DESALES UNIVERSITY

2755 Station Avenue, Center Valley, PA 18034-9568
Phone: 610-282-4443 **E-mail:** admiss@desales.edu **CEEB Code:** 2021
Fax: 610-282-0131 **Web:** www.desales.edu

This private school, which is affiliated with the Roman Catholic Church, was founded in 1964. It has a 400-acre campus.

STUDENTS AND FACULTY

Enrollment: 2,179. **Student Body:** Male 43%, female 57%, out-of-state 17%. **Ethnic Representation:** African American 1%, Asian 1%, Caucasian 52%, Hispanic 1%. **Retention and Graduation:** 88% freshmen return for sophomore year. 53% freshmen graduate within 4 years. 11% grads go on to further study within 1 year. 1% grads pursue business degrees. 3% grads pursue medical degrees. **Faculty:** Student/faculty ratio 17:1. 89 full-time faculty, 76% hold PhDs. 100% faculty teach undergrads.

ACADEMICS

Degrees: Bachelor's, certificate, master's, post-bachelor's certificate, post-master's certificate. **Academic Requirements:** General education including some course work in arts/fine arts, computer literacy, English (including composition), foreign languages, history, humanities, mathematics, philosophy, sciences (biological or physical), social science, Catholic theology, foreign language or foreign culture. **Classes:** 10-19 students in an average class. 20-29 students in an average lab class. **Majors with Highest Enrollment:** Health professions and related sciences; business administration/management; visual and performing arts, general. **Disciplines with Highest Percentage of Degrees Awarded:** Business/marketing 34%, protective services/public administration 13%, health professions and related sciences 11%, visual and performing arts 9%, computer and information sciences 7%. **Special Study Options:** Accelerated program, cross registration, distance learning, double major, dual enrollment, honors program, independent study, internships, liberal arts/career combination, study abroad, teacher certification program, weekend college.

FACILITIES

Housing: Coed, all-female, all-male, cooperative housing. **Library Holdings:** 138,151 bound volumes. 538 periodicals. 399,884 microforms. 5,975 audiovisuals. **Computers:** School-owned computers available for student use.

EXTRACURRICULARS

Activities: Choral groups, dance, drama/theater, literary magazine, musical theater, radio station, student government, student newspaper, student-run film society, television station, yearbook. **Organizations:** 27 registered organizations, 10 honor societies, 1 religious organization. **Athletics (Intercollegiate):** *Men:* baseball, basketball, cross-country, golf, lacrosse, soccer, tennis, track & field. *Women:* basketball, cross-country, soccer, softball, tennis, track & field, volleyball.

ADMISSIONS

Selectivity Rating: 70 (of 100). **Freshman Academic Profile:** 20% in top 10% of high school class, 44% in top 25% of high school class, 80% in top 50% of high school class. 50% from public high schools. Average SAT I Math 534, SAT I Math middle 50% range 480-590. Average SAT I Verbal 536, SAT I Verbal middle 50% range 480-580. TOEFL required of all international applicants, minimum TOEFL 550. **Basis for Candidate Selection:** *Very important factors considered include:* secondary school record. *Important factors considered include:* character/personal qualities, class rank, extracurricular activities, recommendations, standardized test scores, talent/ability, volunteer work. *Other factors considered include:* essays, interview, work experience. **Freshman Admission Requirements:** High school diploma or GED is required. *Academic units required/recommended:* 20 total required; 24 total recommended; 4 English required, 4 English recommended, 3 math required, 4 math recommended, 2 science required, 4 science recommended, 2 science lab required, 4 science lab recommended, 2 foreign language required, 4 foreign language recommended, 2 social studies required, 2 social studies recommended, 1 history required, 2 history recommended, 6 elective required. **Freshman Admission Statistics:** 1,488 applied, 68% accepted, 31% of those accepted enrolled. **Transfer Admission Requirements:** *Items required:* high school transcript, college transcript. Minimum college GPA of 2.0 required. Lowest grade transferable C-. **General Admission Information:** Application fee $30. Priority application deadline December 1. Regular application deadline August 1. Admission may be deferred for a maximum of 1 year. Credit offered for CEEB Advanced Placement tests.

COSTS AND FINANCIAL AID

Tuition $17,000. Room & board $6,520. Required fees $340. Average book expense $800. **Required Forms and Deadlines:** FAFSA and institution's own financial aid form. Financial aid filing deadline May 1. Priority filing deadline February 1. **Notification of Awards:** Applicants will be notified of awards on a rolling basis beginning on or about February 15. **Types of Aid:** *Need-based scholarships/grants:* Pell, SEOG, state scholarships/grants, private scholarships, the school's own gift aid. *Loans:* FFEL Subsidized Stafford, FFEL Unsubsidized Stafford, FFEL PLUS, Federal Perkins, Federal Nursing. **Student Employment:** Federal Work-Study Program available. Institutional employment available. Off-campus job opportunities are good. **Financial Aid Statistics:** 65% undergrads receive some form of aid. Average freshman grant $6,630. Average freshman loan $2,318. Average income from on-campus job $640. **Financial Aid Phone:** 610-282-1100.

DEVRY COLLEGE OF TECHNOLOGY (NORTH BRUNSWICK, NJ)

630 US Highway One, N. Brunswick, NJ 08902-3362
Phone: 732-435-4850 **E-mail:** khillan@devry.com
Fax: 732-435-4850 **Web:** www.nj.devry.edu

This proprietary school was founded in 1969. It has a 15-acre campus.

STUDENTS AND FACULTY

Enrollment: 3,268. **Student Body:** Male 79%, female 21%, out-of-state 12%, international 1% (23 countries represented). **Ethnic Representation:** African American 25%, Asian 9%, Caucasian 42%, Hispanic 19%. **Retention and Graduation:** 45% freshmen return for sophomore year. **Faculty:** Student/faculty ratio 19:1. 78 full-time faculty.

ACADEMICS

Degrees: Associate's, bachelor's, diploma, terminal. **Academic Requirements:** General education including some course work in computer literacy, English (including composition), humanities, mathematics, sciences (biological or physical), social science. **Majors with Highest Enrollment:** Information science/studies; electrical, electronic, and communications engineering technology/technician. **Disciplines with Highest Percentage of Degrees Awarded:** Business/marketing 93%, engineering/engineering technology 7%. **Special Study Options:** Accelerated program, cooperative (work-study) program, weekend college.

FACILITIES

Library Holdings: 32,109 bound volumes. 210 periodicals. 0 microforms. 1,870 audiovisuals. **Computers:** School-owned computers available for student use.

EXTRACURRICULARS

Organizations: 12 registered organizations, 2 honor societies.

ADMISSIONS

Selectivity Rating: 63 (of 100). **Freshman Academic Profile:** TOEFL required of all international applicants, minimum TOEFL 500. **Basis for Candidate Selection:** *Very important factors considered include:* secondary school record, standardized test scores. *Other factors considered include:* interview. **Freshman Admission Requirements:** High school diploma or GED is required. **Transfer Admission Requirements:** *Items required:* college transcript, interview, statement of good standing from prior school. Minimum college GPA of 2.0 required. Lowest grade transferable C. **General Admission Information:** Application fee $50. Regular application deadline November 2. Nonfall registration accepted. Admission may be deferred for a maximum of 1 year. Credit offered for CEEB Advanced Placement tests.

COSTS AND FINANCIAL AID

Required fees $75. Average book expense $1,080. **Required Forms and Deadlines:** FAFSA. No deadline for regular filing. **Notification of Awards:** Applicants will be notified of awards on a rolling basis. **Types of Aid:** *Need-based scholarships/grants:* Pell, SEOG, state scholarships/grants, private scholarships. *Loans:* FFEL Subsidized Stafford, FFEL Unsubsidized Stafford, FFEL PLUS, Federal Perkins. **Student Employment:** Federal Work-Study Program available. Institutional employment available. Off-campus job opportunities are good. **Financial Aid Statistics:** 54% freshmen, 94% undergrads receive some form of aid. Average income from on-campus job $4,000.

See page 1012.

DEVRY INSTITUTE OF TECHNOLOGY (LONG ISLAND CITY, NY)

30-20 Thomson Avenue, Long Island City, NY 11101
Phone: 718-361-0004 **E-mail:** khillan@devry.com
Fax: 718-269-4288 **Web:** www.ny.devry.edu

This proprietary school was founded in 1998. It has a 4-acre campus.

STUDENTS AND FACULTY

Enrollment: 2,052. **Student Body:** Male 77%, female 23%, out-of-state 5%, international 3% (17 countries represented). **Ethnic Representation:** African American 24%, Asian 6%, Caucasian 8%, Hispanic 17%. **Retention and Graduation:** 36% freshmen return for sophomore year. **Faculty:** Student/faculty ratio 16:1. 60 full-time faculty.

ACADEMICS

Degrees: Associate's, bachelor's, terminal. **Academic Requirements:** General education including some course work in computer literacy, English (including composition), humanities, mathematics, sciences (biological or physical), social science. **Majors with Highest Enrollment:** Business/managerial operations; information science/studies; electrical, electronic, and communications engineering technology/technician. **Disciplines with Highest Percentage of Degrees Awarded:** Computer and information sciences 60%, business/marketing 25%, engineering/engineering technology 15%. **Special Study Options:** Accelerated program, cooperative (work-study) program, distance learning, weekend college.

FACILITIES

Library Holdings: 14,078 bound volumes. 62 periodicals. 0 microforms. 2,057 audiovisuals. **Computers:** School-owned computers available for student use.

EXTRACURRICULARS

Organizations: 4 registered organizations, 1 honor society.

ADMISSIONS

Selectivity Rating: 63 (of 100). **Freshman Academic Profile:** TOEFL required of all international applicants, minimum TOEFL 500. **Basis for Candidate Selection:** *Very important factors considered include:* secondary school record, standardized test scores. *Other factors considered include:* interview. **Freshman Admission Requirements:** High school diploma or GED is required. **Transfer Admission Requirements:** *Items required:* college transcript, interview, statement of good standing from prior school. Minimum college GPA of 2.0 required. Lowest grade transferable C. **General Admission Information:** Application fee $50. Priority application deadline November 2. Regular application deadline November 2. Nonfall registration accepted. Admission may be deferred for a maximum of 1 year. Credit offered for CEEB Advanced Placement tests.

COSTS AND FINANCIAL AID

Required fees $75. Average book expense $1,080. **Required Forms and Deadlines:** FAFSA and state aid form. No deadline for regular filing. **Notification of Awards:** Applicants will be notified of awards on a rolling basis. **Types of Aid:** *Need-based scholarships/grants:* Pell, SEOG, state scholarships/grants, private scholarships. *Loans:* FFEL Subsidized Stafford, FFEL Unsubsidized Stafford, FFEL PLUS, Federal Perkins. **Student Employment:** Federal Work-Study Program available. Off-campus job opportunities are good. **Financial Aid Statistics:** 69% freshmen, 79% undergrads receive some form of aid. Average income from on-campus job $5,994.

See page 1012.

DEVRY UNIVERSITY (ADDISON, IL)

1221 North Swift Road, Addision, IL 60101
Phone: 630-953-2000 **E-mail:** khillan@devry.com
Fax: 630-652-8207 **Web:** www.dpg.devry.edu

This proprietary school was founded in 1982. It has a 13-acre campus.

STUDENTS AND FACULTY

Enrollment: 3,028. **Student Body:** Male 77%, female 23%, out-of-state 6%, international 2% (23 countries represented). **Ethnic Representation:** African American 11%, Asian 16%, Caucasian 60%, Hispanic 10%. **Retention and Graduation:** 51% freshmen return for sophomore year. **Faculty:** Student/faculty ratio 19:1. 69 full-time faculty.

ACADEMICS

Degrees: Associate's, bachelor's, terminal. **Academic Requirements:** General education including some course work in computer literacy, English (including composition), humanities, mathematics, sciences (biological or physical), social science. **Majors with Highest Enrollment:** Information science/studies; electrical, electronic, and communications engineering technology/technician. **Disciplines with Highest Percentage of Degrees Awarded:** Business/marketing 62%, computer and information sciences 25%, engineering/engineering technology 13%. **Special Study Options:** Accelerated program, cooperative (work-study) program, distance learning, weekend college.

FACILITIES

Library Holdings: 18,500 bound volumes. 4,000 periodicals. 0 microforms. 1,000 audiovisuals. **Computers:** School-owned computers available for student use.

EXTRACURRICULARS

Activities: Student newspaper. **Organizations:** 11 registered organizations, 3 honor societies, 1 religious organization.

ADMISSIONS

Selectivity Rating: 63 (of 100). **Freshman Academic Profile:** TOEFL required of all international applicants, minimum TOEFL 500. **Basis for Candidate Selection:** *Very important factors considered include:* secondary school record, standardized test scores. *Other factors considered include:* interview. **Freshman Admission Requirements:** High school diploma or GED is required. **Transfer Admission Requirements:** *Items required:* college transcript, interview, statement of good standing from prior school. Minimum college GPA of 2.0 required. Lowest grade transferable C. **General Admission Information:** Application fee $50. Priority application deadline November 2. Regular application deadline November 2. Nonfall registration accepted. Admission may be deferred for a maximum of 1 year. Credit offered for CEEB Advanced Placement tests.

COSTS AND FINANCIAL AID

Required fees $75. Average book expense $1,080. **Required Forms and Deadlines:** FAFSA and state aid form. No deadline for regular filing. **Notification of Awards:** Applicants will be notified of awards on a rolling basis. **Types of Aid:** *Need-based scholarships/grants:* Pell, SEOG, state scholarships/grants, private scholarships. *Loans:* FFEL Subsidized Stafford, FFEL Unsubsidized Stafford, FFEL PLUS, Federal Perkins. **Student Employment:** Institutional employment available. Off-campus job opportunities are excellent. **Financial Aid Statistics:** 61% freshmen, 81% undergrads receive some form of aid. Average income from on-campus job $6,750. **Financial Aid Phone:** 630-953-1300.

See page 1012.

DEVRY UNIVERSITY (ALPHARETTA, GA)

2555 Northwinds Parkway, Alpharetta, GA 30004
Phone: 770-664-9520 **E-mail:** khillan@devry.com
Fax: 770-664-8824 **Web:** www.atl.devry.edu/alpharetta

This proprietary school was founded in 1997. It has a 15-acre campus.

STUDENTS AND FACULTY

Enrollment: 1,329. **Student Body:** Male 67%, female 33%, out-of-state 15%, international 3% (17 countries represented). **Ethnic Representation:** African American 35%, Asian 4%, Caucasian 36%, Hispanic 3%, Native American 1%. **Retention and Graduation:** 40% freshmen return for sophomore year. **Faculty:** Student/faculty ratio 16:1. 38 full-time faculty.

ACADEMICS

Degrees: Associate's, bachelor's, master's, post-bachelor's certificate, terminal. **Academic Requirements:** General education including some course work in computer literacy, English (including composition), humanities, mathematics, sciences (biological or physical), social science. **Majors with Highest Enrollment:** Business/managerial operations; information science/studies. **Disciplines with Highest Percentage of Degrees Awarded:** Business/marketing 60%, computer and information sciences 28%, engineering/engineering technology 11%. **Special Study Options:** Accelerated program, cooperative (work-study) program, distance learning, weekend college.

FACILITIES

Library Holdings: 11,500 bound volumes. 90 periodicals. 0 microforms. 350 audiovisuals. **Computers:** School-owned computers available for student use.

EXTRACURRICULARS

Activities: Student newspaper. **Organizations:** 12 registered organizations, 4 honor societies.

ADMISSIONS

Selectivity Rating: 63 (of 100). **Freshman Academic Profile:** TOEFL required of all international applicants, minimum TOEFL 500. **Basis for Candidate Selection:** *Very important factors considered include:* secondary school record, standardized test scores. *Other factors considered include:* interview. **Freshman Admission Requirements:** High school diploma or GED is required. **Transfer Admission Requirements:** *Items required:* college transcript, interview, statement of good standing from prior school. Minimum college GPA of 2.0 required. Lowest grade transferable C. **General Admission Information:** Application fee $50. Priority application deadline November 2. Regular application deadline November 2. Nonfall registration accepted. Admission may be deferred for a maximum of 1 year.

COSTS AND FINANCIAL AID

Required fees $75. Average book expense $1,080. **Required Forms and Deadlines:** FAFSA and state aid form. **Notification of Awards:** Applicants will be notified of awards on a rolling basis. **Types of Aid:** *Need-based scholarships/grants:* Pell, SEOG, state scholarships/grants, private scholarships. *Loans:* FFEL Subsidized Stafford, FFEL Unsubsidized Stafford, FFEL PLUS, Federal Perkins. **Student Employment:** Federal Work-Study Program available. Institutional employment available. Off-campus job opportunities are good. **Financial Aid Statistics:** 65% undergrads receive some form of aid. Average income from on-campus job $6,750.

See page 1012.

DEVRY UNIVERSITY (CHICAGO, IL)

3300 North Cambell Avenue, Chicago, IL 60618
Phone: 773-929-6550 **E-mail:** khillan@devry.com
Fax: 773-929-8093 **Web:** www.chi.devry.edu

This proprietary school was founded in 1931. It has a 16-acre campus.

STUDENTS AND FACULTY

Enrollment: 3,539. **Student Body:** Male 65%, female 35%, out-of-state 2%, international 2% (26 countries represented). **Ethnic Representation:** African American 35%, Asian 13%, Caucasian 24%, Hispanic 28%. **Retention and Graduation:** 46% freshmen return for sophomore year. **Faculty:** Student/faculty ratio 21:1. 74 full-time faculty.

ACADEMICS

Degrees: Associate's, bachelor's, terminal. **Academic Requirements:** General education including some course work in computer literacy, English (including composition), humanities, mathematics, sciences (biological or physical), social science. **Majors with Highest Enrollment:** Information science/studies; electrical, electronic, and communications engineering technology/technician. **Disciplines with Highest Percentage of Degrees Awarded:** Computer and information sciences 47%, business/marketing 34%, engineering/engineering technology 19%. **Special Study Options:** Accelerated program, cooperative (work-study) program, distance learning, English as a second language, weekend college.

FACILITIES

Library Holdings: 19,524 bound volumes. 34 periodicals. 0 microforms. 810 audiovisuals. **Computers:** School-owned computers available for student use.

EXTRACURRICULARS

Activities: Student government, student newspaper. **Organizations:** 16 registered organizations, 3 honor societies, 2 religious organizations.

ADMISSIONS

Selectivity Rating: 63 (of 100). **Freshman Academic Profile:** TOEFL required of all international applicants, minimum TOEFL 500. **Basis for Candidate Selection:** *Very important factors considered include:* secondary school record, standardized test scores. *Other factors considered include:* interview. **Freshman Admission Requirements:** High school diploma or GED is required. **Transfer Admission Requirements:** *Items required:* college transcript, interview, statement of good standing from prior school. Minimum college GPA of 2.0 required. Lowest grade transferable C. **General Admission Information:** Application fee $50. Priority application deadline November 2. Regular application deadline November 2. Nonfall registration accepted. Admission may be deferred for a maximum of 1 year. Credit offered for CEEB Advanced Placement tests.

COSTS AND FINANCIAL AID

Required fees $75. Average book expense $1,080. **Required Forms and Deadlines:** FAFSA and state aid form. **Notification of Awards:** Applicants will be notified of awards on a rolling basis. **Types of Aid:** *Need-based scholarships/grants:* Pell, SEOG, state scholarships/grants, private scholarships. *Loans:* FFEL Subsidized Stafford, FFEL Unsubsidized Stafford, FFEL PLUS, Federal Perkins. **Student Employment:** Federal Work-Study Program available. Institutional employment available. Off-campus job opportunities are fair. **Financial Aid Statistics:** 71% freshmen, 97% undergrads receive some form of aid. Average income from on-campus job $7,200.

See page 1012.

DEVRY UNIVERSITY (COLORADO SPRINGS, CO)

925 South Niagra Street, Denver, CO 80224
Phone: 303-329-3340 **E-mail:** rrodman@den.devry.edu
Fax: 303-329-0955 **Web:** www.cs.devry.edu

This proprietary school was founded in 2001. It has a 9-acre campus.

STUDENTS AND FACULTY

Enrollment: 221. **Student Body:** Male 74%, female 26%, out-of-state 6%. **Ethnic Representation:** African American 12%, Asian 2%, Caucasian 63%, Hispanic 10%, Native American 2%. **Retention and Graduation:** 23% freshmen return for sophomore year. **Faculty:** Student/faculty ratio 5:1. 11 full-time faculty.

ACADEMICS

Degrees: Associate's, bachelor's, master's, post-bachelor's certificate, terminal. **Academic Requirements:** General education including some course work in computer literacy, English (including composition), history, humanities, mathematics, social science. **Majors with Highest Enrollment:** Information science/studies; electrical, electronic, and communications engineering technology/technician. **Special Study Options:** Accelerated program, cooperative (work-study) program, distance learning, weekend college.

FACILITIES

Library Holdings: 430 bound volumes. 30 periodicals. 0 microforms. 100 audiovisuals.

EXTRACURRICULARS

Organizations: 1 registered organization.

ADMISSIONS

Selectivity Rating: 63 (of 100). **Freshman Academic Profile:** TOEFL required of all international applicants, minimum TOEFL 500. **Basis for Candidate Selection:** *Very important factors considered include:* secondary school record, standardized test scores. *Other factors considered include:* interview. **Freshman Admission Requirements:** High school diploma or GED is required. **Transfer Admission Requirements:** *Items required:* college transcript, interview, statement of good standing from prior school. Minimum high school GPA of 2.0 required. Lowest grade transferable C. **General Admission Information:** Application fee $50. Priority application deadline November 2. Regular application deadline November 2. Nonfall registration accepted. Admission may be deferred for a maximum of 1 year. Credit offered for CEEB Advanced Placement tests.

COSTS AND FINANCIAL AID

Required fees $90. Average book expense $1,100. **Required Forms and Deadlines:** FAFSA and state aid form. **Notification of Awards:** Applicants will be notified of awards on a rolling basis. **Types of Aid:** *Need-based scholarships/grants:* Pell, SEOG, state scholarships/grants, private scholarships. *Loans:* FFEL Subsidized Stafford, FFEL Unsubsidized Stafford, FFEL PLUS, Federal Perkins. **Student Employment:** Federal Work-Study Program available. Institutional employment available. Off-campus job opportunities are good. **Financial Aid Statistics:** 39% freshmen, 90% undergrads receive some form of aid. Average income from on-campus job $7,000.

See page 1012.

DEVRY UNIVERSITY (COLUMBUS, OH)

1350 Alum Creek Drive, Columbus, OH 43209-2705
Phone: 614-253-7291 **E-mail:** khillan@devry.com
Fax: 614-252-4108 **Web:** www.devrycols.edu

This proprietary school was founded in 1931. It has a 13-acre campus.

STUDENTS AND FACULTY

Enrollment: 3,493. **Student Body:** Male 76%, female 24%, out-of-state 12%, international 1% (3 countries represented). **Ethnic Representation:** African American 18%, Asian 3%, Caucasian 76%, Hispanic 2%. **Retention and Graduation:** 40% freshmen return for sophomore year. **Faculty:** Student/faculty ratio 22:1. 83 full-time faculty.

ACADEMICS

Degrees: Associate's, bachelor's, master's, post-bachelor's certificate, terminal. **Academic Requirements:** General education including some course work in computer literacy, English (including composition), humanities, mathematics, sciences (biological or physical), social science. **Majors with Highest Enrollment:** Information science/studies; electrical, electronic, and communications engineering technology/technician. **Disciplines with Highest Percentage of Degrees Awarded:** Computer and information sciences 54%, business/marketing 31%, engineering/engineering technology 15%. **Special Study Options:** Accelerated program, cooperative (work-study) program, distance learning, weekend college.

FACILITIES

Library Holdings: 30,000 bound volumes. 5,892 periodicals. 0 microforms. 1,050 audiovisuals. **Computers:** School-owned computers available for student use.

EXTRACURRICULARS

Activities: Student government, student newspaper. **Organizations:** 9 registered organizations, 2 honor societies.

ADMISSIONS

Selectivity Rating: 63 (of 100). **Freshman Academic Profile:** TOEFL required of all international applicants, minimum TOEFL 500. **Basis for Candidate Selection:** *Very important factors considered include:* secondary school record, standardized test scores. *Other factors considered include:* interview. **Freshman Admission Requirements:** High school diploma or GED is required. **Transfer Admission Requirements:** *Items required:* college transcript, interview, statement of good standing from prior school. Minimum college GPA of 2.0 required. Lowest grade transferable C. **General Admission Information:** Application fee $50. Priority application deadline November 2. Regular application deadline November 2. Nonfall registration accepted. Admission may be deferred for a maximum of 1 year. Credit offered for CEEB Advanced Placement tests.

COSTS AND FINANCIAL AID

Required fees $75. Average book expense $1,080. **Required Forms and Deadlines:** FAFSA. No deadline for regular filing. **Notification of Awards:** Applicants will be notified of awards on a rolling basis. **Types of Aid:** *Need-based scholarships/grants:* Pell, SEOG, state scholarships/grants, private scholarships. *Loans:* Direct Subsidized Stafford, Direct Unsubsidized Stafford, Direct PLUS, Federal Perkins, college/university loans from institutional funds. **Student Employment:** Federal Work-Study Program available. Institutional employment available. Off-campus job opportunities are excellent. **Financial Aid Statistics:** 71% freshmen receive some form of aid. Average income from on-campus job $12,000.

See page 1012.

DEVRY UNIVERSITY (CRYSTAL CITY, VA)

2341 Jefferson Davis Highway, Arlington, VA 22202
Phone: 866-338-7932 **E-mail:** cwargo@crys.devry.edu
Fax: 703-414-4040 **Web:** www.crys.devry.edu

This proprietary school was founded in 2001. It has a 2-acre campus.

STUDENTS AND FACULTY

Enrollment: 561. **Student Body:** Male 78%, female 22%, out-of-state 5%, international 2% (5 countries represented). **Ethnic Representation:** African American 58%, Asian 6%, Caucasian 18%, Hispanic 6%. **Faculty:** Student/faculty ratio 17:1. 20 full-time faculty.

ACADEMICS

Degrees: Associate's, bachelor's, master's, post-bachelor's certificate, terminal. **Academic Requirements:** General education including some course work in computer literacy, English (including composition), humanities, mathematics, sciences (biological or physical), social science. **Majors with Highest Enrollment:** Information science/studies; electrical, electronic, and communications engineering technology/technician. **Special Study Options:** Accelerated program, cooperative (work-study) program, distance learning, weekend college.

FACILITIES

Library Holdings: 7,800 bound volumes. 6,500 periodicals. 0 microforms. 210 audiovisuals. **Computers:** School-owned computers available for student use.

EXTRACURRICULARS

Organizations: 2 registered organizations.

ADMISSIONS

Selectivity Rating: 63 (of 100). **Freshman Academic Profile:** TOEFL required of all international applicants, minimum TOEFL 500. **Basis for Candidate Selection:** *Very important factors considered include:* secondary school record, standardized test scores. *Other factors considered include:* interview. **Freshman Admission Requirements:** High school diploma or GED is required. **Transfer Admission Requirements:** *Items required:* college transcript, interview, statement of good standing from prior school. Minimum college GPA of 2.0 required. Lowest grade transferable C. **General Admission Information:** Application fee $50. Priority application deadline November 2. Regular application deadline November 2. Nonfall registration accepted. Admission may be deferred for a maximum of 1 year. Credit offered for CEEB Advanced Placement tests.

COSTS AND FINANCIAL AID

Required fees $75. Average book expense $1,100. **Required Forms and Deadlines:** FAFSA. **Notification of Awards:** Applicants will be notified of awards on a rolling basis. **Types of Aid:** *Need-based scholarships/grants:* Pell, SEOG, private scholarships. *Loans:* FFEL Subsidized Stafford, FFEL Unsubsidized Stafford, FFEL PLUS, Federal Perkins. **Student Employment:** Federal Work-Study Program available. Institutional employment available. **Financial Aid Statistics:** 89% freshmen, 62% undergrads receive some form of aid. Average income from on-campus job $7,992.

See page 1012.

DEVRY UNIVERSITY (DECATUR, GA)

250 N. Arcadia Avenue, Decatur, GA 30030
Phone: 404-292-2645 **E-mail:** khillan@devry.com
Fax: 404-292-7011 **Web:** www.atl.devry.edu

This proprietary school was founded in 1969. It has a 15-acre campus.

STUDENTS AND FACULTY

Enrollment: 2,596. **Student Body:** Male 60%, female 40%, out-of-state 17%, international 2% (8 countries represented). **Ethnic Representation:** African American 80%, Asian 2%, Caucasian 8%, Hispanic 1%. **Retention and Graduation:** 41% freshmen return for sophomore year. **Faculty:** Student/faculty ratio 19:1. 63 full-time faculty.

ACADEMICS

Degrees: Associate's, bachelor's, master's, post-bachelor's certificate, terminal. **Academic Requirements:** General education including some course work in computer literacy, English (including composition), humanities, mathematics, sciences (biological or physical), social science. **Majors with Highest Enrollment:** Business/managerial operations; information science/studies. **Disciplines with Highest Percentage of Degrees Awarded:** Business/marketing 53%, computer and information sciences 39%, engineering/engineering technology 8%. **Special Study Options:** Accelerated program, cooperative (work-study) program, distance learning, weekend college.

FACILITIES

Library Holdings: 21,344 bound volumes. 91 periodicals. 21,024 microforms. 1,281 audiovisuals. **Computers:** School-owned computers available for student use.

EXTRACURRICULARS

Organizations: 10 registered organizations, 4 honor societies.

ADMISSIONS

Selectivity Rating: 63 (of 100). **Freshman Academic Profile:** TOEFL required of all international applicants, minimum TOEFL 500. **Basis for Candidate Selection:** *Very important factors considered include:* secondary school record, standardized test scores. *Other factors considered include:* interview. **Freshman Admission Requirements:** High school diploma or GED is required. **Transfer Admission Requirements:** *Items required:* college transcript, interview, statement of good standing from prior school. Minimum college GPA of 2.0 required. Lowest grade transferable C. **General Admission Information:** Application fee $50. Priority application deadline November 2. Regular application deadline November 2. Nonfall registration accepted. Admission may be deferred for a maximum of 1 year. Credit offered for CEEB Advanced Placement tests.

COSTS AND FINANCIAL AID

Required fees $75. Average book expense $1,080. **Required Forms and Deadlines:** FAFSA and state aid form. No deadline for regular filing. **Notification of Awards:** Applicants will be notified of awards on a rolling basis. **Types of Aid:** *Need-based scholarships/grants:* Pell, SEOG, state scholarships/grants, private scholarships. *Loans:* FFEL Subsidized Stafford, FFEL Unsubsidized Stafford, FFEL PLUS, Federal Perkins. **Student Employment:** Federal Work-Study Program available. Institutional employment available. Off-campus job opportunities are good. **Financial Aid Statistics:** 100% freshmen, 100% undergrads receive some form of aid. Average income from on-campus job $6,743.

See page 1012.

DEVRY UNIVERSITY (DENVER, CO)

925 South Niagra Street, Denver, CO 80224
Phone: 303-329-7221 **E-mail:** rrodman@devry.edu
Fax: 303-329-0955 **Web:** www.den.devry.edu

This proprietary school was founded in 2001.

STUDENTS AND FACULTY

Enrollment: 460. **Student Body:** Male 77%, female 23%, out-of-state 14%, international 2% (4 countries represented). **Ethnic Representation:** African American 11%, Asian 4%, Caucasian 54%, Hispanic 6%, Native American 1%. **Faculty:** Student/faculty ratio 7:1. 19 full-time faculty.

ACADEMICS

Degrees: Associate's, bachelor's, terminal. **Academic Requirements:** General education including some course work in computer literacy, English (including composition), humanities, mathematics, sciences (biological or physical), social science. **Majors with Highest Enrollment:** Business/managerial operations; information science/studies. **Special Study Options:** Accelerated program, cooperative (work-study) program, distance learning, weekend college.

FACILITIES

Library Holdings: 500 bound volumes. 50 periodicals. 0 microforms. 150 audiovisuals.

EXTRACURRICULARS

Activities: Student newspaper. **Organizations:** 3 registered organizations, 1 honor society.

ADMISSIONS

Selectivity Rating: 63 (of 100). **Freshman Academic Profile:** TOEFL required of all international applicants, minimum TOEFL 500. **Basis for Candidate Selection:** *Very important factors considered include:* secondary school record, standardized test scores. *Other factors considered include:* interview. **Freshman Admission Requirements:** High school diploma or GED is required. **Transfer Admission Requirements:** *Items required:* college transcript, interview, statement of good standing from prior school. Minimum college GPA of 2.0 required. Lowest grade transferable C. **General Admission Information:** Application fee $50. Priority application deadline November 2. Regular application deadline November 2. Nonfall registration accepted. Admission may be deferred for a maximum of 1 year. Credit offered for CEEB Advanced Placement tests.

COSTS AND FINANCIAL AID

Required fees $75. Average book expense $1,100. **Required Forms and Deadlines:** FAFSA and state aid form. **Notification of Awards:** Applicants will be notified of awards on a rolling basis. **Types of Aid:** *Need-based scholarships/grants:* Pell, SEOG, state scholarships/grants, private scholarships. *Loans:* FFEL Subsidized Stafford, FFEL Unsubsidized Stafford, FFEL PLUS, Federal Perkins. **Student Employment:** Federal Work-Study Program available. Institutional employment available. Off-campus job opportunities are good. **Financial Aid Statistics:** 41% freshmen, 87% undergrads receive some form of aid. Average income from on-campus job $7,000.

See page 1012.

DEVRY UNIVERSITY (FREMONT, CA)

6600 Dumbarton Circle, Fremont, CA 94555
Phone: 510-574-1100 **E-mail:** jadem@fre.devry.edu
Fax: 510-742-0866 **Web:** www.fre.devry.edu

This proprietary school was founded in 1998. It has a 17-acre campus.

STUDENTS AND FACULTY

Enrollment: 1,978. **Student Body:** Male 77%, female 23%, out-of-state 3%, international 2% (9 countries represented). **Ethnic Representation:** African American 5%, Asian 42%, Caucasian 26%, Hispanic 17%, Native American 6%. **Retention and Graduation:** 48% freshmen return for sophomore year. **Faculty:** Student/faculty ratio 23:1. 51 full-time faculty.

ACADEMICS

Degrees: Associate's, bachelor's, master's, post-bachelor's certificate, terminal. **Academic Requirements:** General education including some course work in computer literacy, English (including composition), humanities, mathematics, sciences (biological or physical), social science. **Majors with Highest Enrollment:** Information science/studies; electrical, electronic, and communications engineering technology/technician. **Disciplines with Highest Percentage of Degrees Awarded:** Business/marketing 50%, engineering/engineering technology 26%, computer and information sciences 24%. **Special Study Options:** Accelerated program, cooperative (work-study) program, distance learning, weekend college.

FACILITIES

Library Holdings: 40,000 bound volumes. 3,060 periodicals. 0 microforms. 2,000 audiovisuals. **Computers:** School-owned computers available for student use.

EXTRACURRICULARS

Activities: Student newspaper. **Organizations:** 12 registered organizations.

ADMISSIONS

Selectivity Rating: 63 (of 100). **Freshman Academic Profile:** TOEFL required of all international applicants, minimum TOEFL 500. **Basis for Candidate Selection:** *Very important factors considered include:* secondary school record, standardized test scores. *Other factors considered include:* interview. **Freshman Admission Requirements:** High school diploma or GED is required. **Transfer Admission Requirements:** *Items required:* college transcript, interview, statement of good standing from prior school. Minimum college GPA of 2.0 required. Lowest grade transferable C. **General Admission Information:** Application fee $50. Priority application deadline November 2. Regular application deadline November 2. Nonfall registration accepted. Admission may be deferred for a maximum of 1 year. Credit offered for CEEB Advanced Placement tests.

COSTS AND FINANCIAL AID

Required fees $75. Average book expense $1,080. **Required Forms and Deadlines:** FAFSA and state aid form. No deadline for regular filing. **Notification of Awards:** Applicants will be notified of awards on a rolling basis. **Types of Aid:** *Need-based scholarships/grants:* Pell, SEOG, state scholarships/grants, private scholarships. *Loans:* FFEL Subsidized Stafford, FFEL Unsubsidized Stafford, FFEL PLUS, Federal Perkins. **Student Employment:** Federal Work-Study Program available. Institutional employment available. Off-campus job opportunities are excellent. **Financial Aid Statistics:** 21% freshmen, 79% undergrads receive some form of aid. Average income from on-campus job $8,200.

See page 1012.

DEVRY UNIVERSITY (IRVING, TX)

4800 Regent Boulevard, Irving, TX 75063
Phone: 972-929-5777 **E-mail:** dmillan@dal.devry.edu
Fax: 972-929-2860 **Web:** www.dal.devry.edu

This proprietary school was founded in 1969. It has a 9-acre campus.

STUDENTS AND FACULTY

Enrollment: 2,984. **Student Body:** Male 72%, female 28%, out-of-state 7%, international 2% (5 countries represented). **Ethnic Representation:** African American 31%, Asian 7%, Caucasian 42%, Hispanic 19%. **Retention and Graduation:** 36% freshmen return for sophomore year. **Faculty:** Student/faculty ratio 16:1. 77 full-time faculty.

ACADEMICS

Degrees: Associate's, bachelor's, master's, post-bachelor's certificate, terminal. **Academic Requirements:** General education including some course work in computer literacy, English (including composition), humanities, mathematics, sciences (biological or physical), social science. **Majors with Highest Enrollment:** Information science/studies; electrical, electronic, and communications engineering technology/technician; computer systems networking and telecommunications. **Disciplines with Highest Percentage of Degrees Awarded:** Business/marketing 61%, computer and information sciences 28%, engineering/engineering technology 10%. **Special Study Options:** Accelerated program, cooperative (work-study) program, distance learning, weekend college.

FACILITIES

Library Holdings: 21,500 bound volumes. 6,365 periodicals. 0 microforms. 1,472 audiovisuals. **Computers:** School-owned computers available for student use.

EXTRACURRICULARS

Activities: Student newspaper. **Organizations:** 15 registered organizations.

ADMISSIONS

Selectivity Rating: 63 (of 100). **Freshman Academic Profile:** TOEFL required of all international applicants, minimum TOEFL 500. **Basis for Candidate Selection:** *Very important factors considered include:* secondary school record, standardized test scores. *Other factors considered include:* interview. **Freshman Admission Requirements:** High school diploma or GED is required. **Transfer Admission Requirements:** *Items required:* college transcript, interview, statement of good standing from prior school. Minimum college GPA of 2.0 required. Lowest grade transferable C. **General Admission Information:** Application fee $50. Priority application deadline November 2. Regular application deadline November 2. Nonfall registration accepted. Admission may be deferred for a maximum of 1 year. Credit offered for CEEB Advanced Placement tests.

COSTS AND FINANCIAL AID

Required fees $75. Average book expense $1,080. **Required Forms and Deadlines:** FAFSA. No deadline for regular filing. **Notification of Awards:** Applicants will be notified of awards on a rolling basis. **Types of Aid:** *Need-based scholarships/grants:* Pell, SEOG, private scholarships. *Loans:* FFEL Subsidized Stafford, FFEL Unsubsidized Stafford, FFEL PLUS, Federal Perkins. **Student Employment:** Federal Work-Study Program available. Institutional employment available. Off-campus job opportunities are good. **Financial Aid Statistics:** 69% freshmen, 92% undergrads receive some form of aid. Average income from on-campus job $6,800.

See page 1012.

DEVRY UNIVERSITY (KANSAS CITY, MO)

11224 Holmes Street, Kansas City, MO 64131
Phone: 816-941-2810 **E-mail:** khillan@devry.com
Fax: 816-941-0896 **Web:** www.kc.devry.edu

This proprietary school was founded in 1931. It has an 8-acre campus.

STUDENTS AND FACULTY

Enrollment: 2,374. **Student Body:** Male 76%, female 24%, out-of-state 42%, international 1% (8 countries represented). **Ethnic Representation:** African American 15%, Asian 3%, Caucasian 78%, Hispanic 3%, Native American 1%. **Retention and Graduation:** 51% freshmen return for sophomore year. **Faculty:** Student/faculty ratio 18:1. 69 full-time faculty.

ACADEMICS

Degrees: Associate's, bachelor's, master's, post-bachelor's certificate, terminal. **Academic Requirements:** General education including some course work in computer literacy, English (including composition), humanities, mathematics, sciences (biological or physical), social science. **Majors with Highest Enrollment:** Information science/studies; computer systems networking and telecommunications; electrical, electronic, and communications engineering technology/technician. **Disciplines with Highest Percentage of Degrees Awarded:** Business/marketing 55%, computer and information sciences 34%, engineering/engineering technology 11%. **Special Study Options:** Accelerated program, cooperative (work-study) program, distance learning, weekend college.

FACILITIES

Library Holdings: 15,000 bound volumes. 68 periodicals. 49 microforms. 457 audiovisuals. **Computers:** School-owned computers available for student use.

EXTRACURRICULARS

Activities: Student newspaper. **Organizations:** 8 registered organizations, 1 honor society.

ADMISSIONS

Selectivity Rating: 63 (of 100). **Freshman Academic Profile:** TOEFL required of all international applicants, minimum TOEFL 500. **Basis for Candidate Selection:** *Very important factors considered include:* secondary school record, standardized test scores. *Other factors considered include:* interview. **Freshman Admission Requirements:** High school diploma or GED is required. **Transfer Admission Requirements:** *Items required:* college transcript, interview, statement of good standing from prior school. Minimum college GPA of 2.0 required. Lowest grade transferable C. **General Admission Information:** Application fee $50. Priority application deadline November 2. Regular application deadline November 2. Nonfall registration accepted. Admission may be deferred for a maximum of 1 year. Credit offered for CEEB Advanced Placement tests.

COSTS AND FINANCIAL AID

Required fees $75. Average book expense $1,080. **Required Forms and Deadlines:** FAFSA. No deadline for regular filing. **Notification of Awards:** Applicants will be notified of awards on a rolling basis. **Types of Aid:** *Need-based scholarships/grants:* Pell, SEOG, state scholarships/grants, private scholarships. *Loans:* FFEL Subsidized Stafford, FFEL Unsubsidized Stafford, FFEL PLUS, Federal Perkins. **Student Employment:** Federal Work-Study Program available. Institutional employment available. Off-campus job opportunities are excellent. **Financial Aid Statistics:** 72% freshmen, 93% undergrads receive some form of aid. Average income from on-campus job $7,200.

See page 1012.

DEVRY UNIVERSITY (LONG BEACH, CA)

3880 Kilroy Airport Way, Long Beach, CA 90806
Phone: 562-427-4162 **E-mail:** rfrancis@admin.lb.devry.edu
Fax: 562-997-5371 **Web:** www.lb.devry.edu

This proprietary school was founded in 1994. It has a 25-acre campus.

STUDENTS AND FACULTY

Enrollment: 2,385. **Student Body:** Male 73%, female 27%, out-of-state 3%, international 2% (11 countries represented). **Ethnic Representation:** African American 13%, Asian 32%, Caucasian 18%, Hispanic 29%, Native American 1%. **Retention and Graduation:** 51% freshmen return for sophomore year. **Faculty:** Student/faculty ratio 18:1. 40 full-time faculty.

ACADEMICS

Degrees: Associate's, bachelor's, master's, post-bachelor's certificate, terminal. **Academic Requirements:** General education including some course work in computer literacy, English (including composition), humanities, mathematics, sciences (biological or physical), social science. **Majors with Highest Enrollment:** Business/managerial operations; information science/studies. **Disciplines with Highest Percentage of Degrees Awarded:** Business/marketing 61%, computer and information sciences 31%, engineering/engineering technology 7%. **Special Study Options:** Accelerated program, cooperative (work-study) program, distance learning, weekend college.

FACILITIES

Library Holdings: 15,500 bound volumes. 85 periodicals. 0 microforms. 2,000 audiovisuals. **Computers:** School-owned computers available for student use.

EXTRACURRICULARS

Activities: Radio station, student government. **Organizations:** 15 registered organizations, 5 honor societies.

ADMISSIONS

Selectivity Rating: 63 (of 100). **Freshman Academic Profile:** TOEFL required of all international applicants, minimum TOEFL 500. **Basis for Candidate Selection:** *Very important factors considered include:* secondary school record, standardized test scores. *Other factors considered include:* interview. **Freshman Admission Requirements:** High school diploma or GED is required. **Transfer Admission Requirements:** *Items required:* college transcript, interview, statement of good standing from prior school. Minimum college GPA of 2.0 required. Lowest grade transferable C. **General Admission Information:** Application fee $50. Priority application deadline November 2. Regular application deadline November 2. Nonfall registration accepted. Admission may be deferred for a maximum of 1 year. Credit offered for CEEB Advanced Placement tests.

COSTS AND FINANCIAL AID

Required fees $75. Average book expense $1,080. **Required Forms and Deadlines:** FAFSA and state aid form. No deadline for regular filing. **Notification of Awards:** Applicants will be notified of awards on a rolling basis. **Types of Aid:** *Need-based scholarships/grants:* Pell, SEOG, state scholarships/grants, private scholarships. *Loans:* FFEL Subsidized Stafford, FFEL Unsubsidized Stafford, FFEL PLUS, Federal Perkins, college/university loans from institutional funds. **Student Employment:** Federal Work-Study Program available. Off-campus job opportunities are good. **Financial Aid Statistics:** 35% freshmen, 90% undergrads receive some form of aid. Average income from on-campus job $6,743.

See page 1012.

DEVRY UNIVERSITY (ORLANDO, FL)

4000 Millenia Blvd., Orlando, FL 32839
Phone: 407-355-3131 **E-mail:** jwasmer@orl.devry.edu
Fax: 407-370-3198 **Web:** www.orl.devry.edu

This proprietary school was founded in 2000. It has an 11-acre campus.

STUDENTS AND FACULTY

Enrollment: 1,172. **Student Body:** Male 74%, female 26%, out-of-state 12%, international 4% (13 countries represented). **Ethnic Representation:** African American 26%, Asian 3%, Caucasian 32%, Hispanic 15%, Native American 1%. **Retention and Graduation:** 46% freshmen return for sophomore year. **Faculty:** Student/faculty ratio 18:1. 43 full-time faculty.

ACADEMICS

Degrees: Associate's, bachelor's, master's, post-bachelor's certificate, terminal. **Academic Requirements:** General education including some course work in computer literacy, English (including composition), humanities, mathematics, sciences (biological or physical), social science. **Majors with Highest Enrollment:** Information science/studies; computer systems networking and telecommunications; electrical, electronic, and communications engineering technology/technician. **Special Study Options:** Accelerated program, cooperative (work-study) program, distance learning, weekend college.

FACILITIES

Library Holdings: 11,000 bound volumes. 60 periodicals. 0 microforms. 130 audiovisuals. **Computers:** School-owned computers available for student use.

EXTRACURRICULARS

Activities: Student government, student newspaper. **Organizations:** 13 registered organizations, 2 honor societies.

ADMISSIONS

Selectivity Rating: 63 (of 100). **Freshman Academic Profile:** TOEFL required of all international applicants, minimum TOEFL 500. **Basis for Candidate Selection:** *Very important factors considered include:* secondary school record, standardized test scores. *Other factors considered include:* interview. **Freshman Admission Requirements:** High school diploma or GED is required. **Transfer Admission Requirements:** *Items required:* college transcript, interview, statement of good standing from prior school. Minimum college GPA of 2.0 required. Lowest grade transferable C. **General Admission Information:** Application fee $50. Priority application deadline November 2. Regular application deadline November 2. Nonfall registration accepted. Admission may be deferred for a maximum of 1 year. Credit offered for CEEB Advanced Placement tests.

COSTS AND FINANCIAL AID

Required fees $75. Average book expense $1,080. **Required Forms and Deadlines:** FAFSA and state aid form. No deadline for regular filing. **Notification of Awards:** Applicants will be notified of awards on a rolling basis. **Types of Aid:** *Need-based scholarships/grants:* Pell, SEOG, state scholarships/grants, private scholarships. *Loans:* FFEL Subsidized Stafford, FFEL Unsubsidized Stafford, FFEL PLUS, Federal Perkins. **Student Employment:** Federal Work-Study Program available. Institutional employment available. Off-campus job opportunities are fair. **Financial Aid Statistics:** 93% freshmen, 33% undergrads receive some form of aid. Average income from on-campus job $6,300.

See page 1012.

DEVRY UNIVERSITY (PHILADELPHIA, PA)

1140 Virginia Drive, Ft. Washington, PA 19034
Phone: 215-591-5745 **E-mail:** scohen@phi.devry.edu
Fax: 215-591-5745 **Web:** www.devry.edu/philadelphia

This proprietary school was founded in 2002. It has a 2-acre campus.

STUDENTS AND FACULTY

Enrollment: 322. **Student Body:** Male 84%, female 16%, out-of-state 20%. **Ethnic Representation:** African American 38%, Asian 7%, Caucasian 40%, Hispanic 7%. **Faculty:** Student/faculty ratio 11:1. 9 full-time faculty.

ACADEMICS

Degrees: Associate's, bachelor's, master's, post-bachelor's certificate, terminal. **Academic Requirements:** General education including some course work in computer literacy, English (including composition), humanities, mathematics, philosophy, sciences (biological or physical), social science. **Majors with Highest Enrollment:** Information science/studies; electrical, electronic, and communications engineering technology/technician. **Special Study Options:** Accelerated program, cooperative (work-study) program, distance learning, weekend college.

FACILITIES

Library Holdings: 12,755 bound volumes. 69 periodicals. 0 microforms. 427 audiovisuals. **Computers:** School-owned computers available for student use.

EXTRACURRICULARS

Organizations: 2 registered organizations.

ADMISSIONS

Selectivity Rating: 63 (of 100). **Freshman Academic Profile:** TOEFL required of all international applicants, minimum TOEFL 500. **Basis for Candidate Selection:** *Very important factors considered include:* secondary school record, standardized test scores. *Other factors considered include:* interview. **Freshman Admission Requirements:** High school diploma or GED is required. **Transfer Admission Requirements:** *Items required:* college transcript, interview, statement of good standing from prior school. Minimum college GPA of 2.0 required. Lowest grade transferable C. **General Admission Information:** Application fee $50. Priority application deadline November 2. Regular application deadline November 2. Nonfall registration accepted. Admission may be deferred for a maximum of 1 year. Credit offered for CEEB Advanced Placement tests.

COSTS AND FINANCIAL AID

Required fees $75. Average book expense $1,080. **Required Forms and Deadlines:** state aid form. **Notification of Awards:** Applicants will be notified of awards on a rolling basis. **Types of Aid:** *Need-based scholarships/grants:* Pell, SEOG, state scholarships/grants, private scholarships. *Loans:* FFEL Subsidized Stafford, FFEL Unsubsidized Stafford, FFEL PLUS, Federal Perkins. **Student Employment:** Institutional employment available. Off-campus job opportunities are good. **Financial Aid Statistics:** Average income from on-campus job $6,900.

See page 1012.

DEVRY UNIVERSITY (PHOENIX, AZ)

2149 West Dunlap, Phoenix, AZ 85021
Phone: 602-870-9201 **E-mail:** khillan@devry.com
Fax: 602-331-1494 **Web:** www.devry-phx.edu

This proprietary school was founded in 1967. It has a 12-acre campus.

STUDENTS AND FACULTY

Enrollment: 2,529. **Student Body:** Male 77%, female 23%, out-of-state 29%, international 1% (4 countries represented). **Ethnic Representation:** African American 6%, Asian 5%, Caucasian 67%, Hispanic 16%, Native American 5%. **Retention and Graduation:** 52% freshmen return for sophomore year. **Faculty:** Student/faculty ratio 25:1. 73 full-time faculty.

ACADEMICS

Degrees: Associate's, bachelor's, master's, post-bachelor's certificate, terminal. **Academic Requirements:** General education including some course work in computer literacy, history, humanities, mathematics, sciences (biological or physical), social science. **Majors with Highest Enrollment:** Information science/studies; electrical, electronic, and communications engineering technology/technician. **Disciplines with Highest Percentage of Degrees Awarded:** Computer and information sciences 57%, engineering/engineering technology 22%, business/marketing 20%. **Special Study Options:** Accelerated program, cooperative (work-study) program, distance learning.

FACILITIES

Library Holdings: 22,500 bound volumes. 7,230 periodicals. 1 microforms. 11 audiovisuals. **Computers:** School-owned computers available for student use.

EXTRACURRICULARS

Organizations: 17 registered organizations, 1 honor society.

ADMISSIONS

Selectivity Rating: 63 (of 100). **Freshman Academic Profile:** TOEFL required of all international applicants, minimum TOEFL 500. **Basis for Candidate Selection:** *Very important factors considered include:* secondary school record, standardized test scores. *Other factors considered include:* interview. **Freshman Admission Requirements:** High school diploma or GED is required. **Transfer Admission Requirements:** *Items required:* college transcript, interview, statement of good standing from prior school. Minimum college GPA of 2.0 required. Lowest grade transferable C. **General Admission Information:** Application fee $50. Priority application deadline November 2. Regular application deadline November 2. Nonfall registration accepted. Admission may be deferred for a maximum of 1 year. Credit offered for CEEB Advanced Placement tests.

COSTS AND FINANCIAL AID

Required fees $75. Average book expense $1,080. **Required Forms and Deadlines:** FAFSA and state aid form. No deadline for regular filing. **Notification of Awards:** Applicants will be notified of awards on a rolling basis. **Types of Aid:** *Need-based scholarships/grants:* Pell, SEOG, state scholarships/grants, private scholarships. *Loans:* FFEL Subsidized Stafford, FFEL Unsubsidized Stafford, FFEL PLUS, Federal Perkins. **Student Employment:** Off-campus job opportunities are excellent. **Financial Aid Statistics:** 37% freshmen, 68% undergrads receive some form of aid. Average income from on-campus job $6,800.

See page 1012.

DEVRY UNIVERSITY (POMONA, CA)

901 Corporate Center Drive, Pomona, CA 91768
Phone: 909-622-9800 **E-mail:** bchung@admin.pom.devry.edu
Fax: 909-623-3338 **Web:** www.pom.devry.edu

This proprietary school was founded in 1983. It has an 11-acre campus.

STUDENTS AND FACULTY

Enrollment: 2,998. **Student Body:** Male 75%, female 25%, out-of-state 2%, international 2% (19 countries represented). **Ethnic Representation:** African American 8%, Asian 33%, Caucasian 23%, Hispanic 34%, Native American 1%. **Retention and Graduation:** 49% freshmen return for sophomore year. **Faculty:** Student/faculty ratio 22:1. 49 full-time faculty.

ACADEMICS

Degrees: Associate's, bachelor's, master's, post-bachelor's certificate, terminal. **Academic Requirements:** General education including some course work in computer literacy, English (including composition), humanities, mathematics, sciences (biological or physical), social science. **Majors with Highest Enrollment:** Information science/studies; electrical, electronic, and communications engineering technology/technician. **Disciplines with Highest Percentage of Degrees Awarded:** Business/marketing 54%, computer and information sciences 34%, engineering/engineering technology 12%. **Special Study Options:** Accelerated program, cooperative (work-study) program, distance learning, weekend college.

FACILITIES

Library Holdings: 17,000 bound volumes. 77 periodicals. 0 microforms. 1,234 audiovisuals. **Computers:** School-owned computers available for student use.

EXTRACURRICULARS

Organizations: 15 registered organizations, 4 honor societies.

ADMISSIONS

Selectivity Rating: 63 (of 100). **Freshman Academic Profile:** TOEFL required of all international applicants, minimum TOEFL 500. **Basis for Candidate Selection:** *Very important factors considered include:* secondary school record, standardized test scores. *Important factors considered include:* interview. **Freshman Admission Requirements:** High school diploma or GED is required. **Transfer Admission Requirements:** *Items required:* college transcript, interview, statement of good standing from prior school. Minimum college GPA of 2.0 required. Lowest grade transferable C. **General Admission Information:** Application fee $50. Priority application deadline November 2. Regular application deadline November 2. Nonfall registration accepted. Admission may be deferred for a maximum of 1 year. Credit offered for CEEB Advanced Placement tests.

COSTS AND FINANCIAL AID

Required fees $75. Average book expense $1,080. **Required Forms and Deadlines:** FAFSA and state aid form. No deadline for regular filing. **Notification of Awards:** Applicants will be notified of awards on a rolling basis. **Types of Aid:** *Need-based scholarships/grants:* Pell, SEOG, state scholarships/grants, private scholarships. *Loans:* FFEL Subsidized Stafford, FFEL Unsubsidized Stafford, FFEL PLUS, Federal Perkins. **Student Employment:** Federal Work-Study Program available. Institutional employment available. Off-campus job opportunities are good. **Financial Aid Statistics:** 31% freshmen, 90% undergrads receive some form of aid. Average income from on-campus job $6,700.

See page 1012.

DEVRY UNIVERSITY (SEATTLE, WA)

3600 South 344th Way, Federal Way, WA 98001-2995
Phone: 253-943-2800 **E-mail:** kpuls@sea.devry.edu
Fax: 253-943-3290 **Web:** www.sea.devry.edu

This proprietary school was founded in 2001. It has a 12-acre campus.

STUDENTS AND FACULTY

Enrollment: 865. **Student Body:** Male 79%, female 21%, out-of-state 10%. **Ethnic Representation:** African American 11%, Asian 14%, Caucasian 63%, Hispanic 8%, Native American 2%. **Retention and Graduation:** 42% freshmen return for sophomore year. **Faculty:** Student/faculty ratio 24:1. 21 full-time faculty.

ACADEMICS

Degrees: Associate's, bachelor's, master's, post-bachelor's certificate, terminal. **Academic Requirements:** General education including some course work in computer literacy, English (including composition), history, humanities, mathematics, sciences (biological or physical), social science. **Majors with Highest Enrollment:** Information science/studies; computer systems networking and telecommunications; electrical, electronic, and communications engineering technology/technician. **Special Study Options:** Accelerated program, cooperative (work-study) program, distance learning, weekend college.

FACILITIES

Library Holdings: 6,021 bound volumes. 6,807 periodicals. 0 microforms. 61 audiovisuals. **Computers:** School-owned computers available for student use.

EXTRACURRICULARS

Activities: Student newspaper. **Organizations:** 20 registered organizations.

ADMISSIONS

Selectivity Rating: 63 (of 100). **Freshman Academic Profile:** TOEFL required of all international applicants, minimum TOEFL 500. **Basis for Candidate Selection:** *Very important factors considered include:* secondary school record, standardized test scores. *Other factors considered include:* interview. **Freshman Admission Requirements:** High school diploma or GED is required. **Transfer Admission Requirements:** *Items required:* college transcript, interview, statement of good standing from prior school. Minimum college GPA of 2.0 required. Lowest grade transferable C. **General Admission Information:** Application fee $50. Priority application deadline November 2. Regular application deadline November 2. Nonfall registration accepted. Admission may be deferred for a maximum of 1 year. Credit offered for CEEB Advanced Placement tests.

COSTS AND FINANCIAL AID

Required fees $90. Average book expense $1,100. **Required Forms and Deadlines:** FAFSA and state aid form. **Notification of Awards:** Applicants will be notified of awards on a rolling basis. **Types of Aid:** *Need-based scholarships/grants:* Pell, SEOG, private scholarships. *Loans:* FFEL Subsidized Stafford, FFEL Unsubsidized Stafford, FFEL PLUS, Federal Perkins. **Student Employment:** Federal Work-Study Program available. Institutional employment available. Off-campus job opportunities are good. **Financial Aid Statistics:** 73% freshmen, 79% undergrads receive some form of aid. Average income from on-campus job $7,000.

See page 1012.

DEVRY UNIVERSITY (TINLEY PARK, IL)

18624 West Creek Drive, Tinley Park, IL 60477
Phone: (708) 342-3100 **E-mail:** bjones@tp.devry.edu
Fax: (708) 342-3120 **Web:** www.tp.devry.edu

This proprietary school was founded in 2000. It has a 12-acre campus.

STUDENTS AND FACULTY

Enrollment: 1,701. **Student Body:** Male 73%, female 27%, out-of-state 8%, international 1% (9 countries represented). **Ethnic Representation:** African American 31%, Asian 2%, Caucasian 55%, Hispanic 8%. **Retention and Graduation:** 43% freshmen return for sophomore year. **Faculty:** Student/faculty ratio 17:1. 36 full-time faculty.

ACADEMICS

Degrees: Associate's, bachelor's, master's, post-bachelor's certificate. **Academic Requirements:** General education including some course work in computer literacy, English (including composition), humanities, mathematics, sciences (biological or physical), social science. **Majors with Highest Enrollment:** Information science/studies; electrical, electronic, and communications engineering technology/technician. **Special Study Options:** Accelerated program, cooperative (work-study) program, distance learning, weekend college.

FACILITIES

Library Holdings: 17,500 bound volumes. 82 periodicals. 0 microforms. 476 audiovisuals. **Computers:** School-owned computers available for student use.

EXTRACURRICULARS

Organizations: 8 registered organizations, 3 honor societies.

ADMISSIONS

Selectivity Rating: 63 (of 100). **Freshman Academic Profile:** TOEFL required of all international applicants, minimum TOEFL 500. **Basis for Candidate Selection:** *Very important factors considered include:* secondary school record, standardized test scores. *Other factors considered include:* interview. **Freshman Admission Requirements:** High school diploma or GED is required. **Transfer Admission Requirements:** *Items required:* college transcript, interview, statement of good standing from prior school. Minimum college GPA of 2.0 required. Lowest grade transferable C. **General Admission Information:** Application fee $50. Priority application deadline November 2. Regular application deadline November 2. Nonfall registration accepted. Admission may be deferred for a maximum of 1 year. Credit offered for CEEB Advanced Placement tests.

COSTS AND FINANCIAL AID

Required fees $75. Average book expense $1,100. **Required Forms and Deadlines:** FAFSA and state aid form. **Notification of Awards:** Applicants will be notified of awards on a rolling basis. **Types of Aid:** *Need-based scholarships/grants:* Pell, SEOG, state scholarships/grants, private scholarships. *Loans:* FFEL Subsidized Stafford, FFEL Unsubsidized Stafford, FFEL PLUS, Federal Perkins. **Student Employment:** Federal Work-Study Program available. Institutional employment available. Off-campus job opportunities are good. **Financial Aid Statistics:** 86% freshmen, 64% undergrads receive some form of aid. Average income from on-campus job $7,000.

See page 1012.

DEVRY UNIVERSITY (WEST HILLS, CA)

22801 Roscoe Boulevard, West Hills, CA 91304
Phone: 888-610-0800 **E-mail:** dbarba@focal.devry.edu
Fax: 818-713-8118 **Web:** www.wh.devry.edu

This proprietary school was founded in 1999. It has a 15-acre campus.

STUDENTS AND FACULTY

Enrollment: 1,306. **Student Body:** Male 76%, female 24%, out-of-state 3%, international 2% (13 countries represented). **Ethnic Representation:** African American 7%, Asian 31%, Caucasian 35%, Hispanic 22%, Native American 1%. **Retention and Graduation:** 46% freshmen return for sophomore year. **Faculty:** Student/faculty ratio 15:1. 19 full-time faculty.

ACADEMICS

Degrees: Associate's, bachelor's, master's, post-bachelor's certificate, terminal. **Academic Requirements:** General education including some course work in computer literacy, English (including composition), humanities, mathematics, sciences (biological or physical), social science. **Majors with Highest Enrollment:** Business/managerial operations; information science/studies. **Disciplines with Highest Percentage of Degrees Awarded:** Engineering/engineering technology 62%, business/marketing 34%, computer and information sciences 2%. **Special Study Options:** Accelerated program, cooperative (work-study) program, distance learning, weekend college.

FACILITIES

Library Holdings: 16,177 bound volumes. 130 periodicals. 0 microforms. 597 audiovisuals. **Computers:** School-owned computers available for student use.

EXTRACURRICULARS

Activities: Student government. **Organizations:** 10 registered organizations, 1 honor society.

ADMISSIONS

Selectivity Rating: 63 (of 100). **Freshman Academic Profile:** TOEFL required of all international applicants, minimum TOEFL 500. **Basis for Candidate Selection:** *Very important factors considered include:* secondary school record, standardized test scores. *Other factors considered include:* interview. **Freshman Admission Requirements:** High school diploma or GED is required. **Transfer Admission Requirements:** *Items required:* college transcript, interview, statement of good standing from prior school. Minimum college GPA of 2.0 required. Lowest grade transferable C. **General Admission Information:** Application fee $50. Priority application deadline November 2. Regular application deadline November 2. Nonfall registration accepted. Admission may be deferred for a maximum of 1 year. Credit offered for CEEB Advanced Placement tests.

COSTS AND FINANCIAL AID

Required fees $75. Average book expense $1,080. **Required Forms and Deadlines:** FAFSA and state aid form. No deadline for regular filing. **Notification of Awards:** Applicants will be notified of awards on a rolling basis. **Types of Aid:** *Need-based scholarships/grants:* Pell, SEOG, state scholarships/grants, private scholarships. *Loans:* FFEL Subsidized Stafford, FFEL Unsubsidized Stafford, Federal Perkins. **Student Employment:** Off-campus job opportunities are good. **Financial Aid Statistics:** 30% freshmen, 94% undergrads receive some form of aid. Average income from on-campus job $3,120.

See page 1012.

DICKINSON COLLEGE

PO Box 1773, Carlisle, PA 17013-2896
Phone: 717-245-1231 **E-mail:** admit@dickinson.edu **CEEB Code:** 2186
Fax: 717-245-1442 **Web:** www.dickinson.edu **ACT Code:** 3550

This private school was founded in 1783. It has a 116-acre campus.

STUDENTS AND FACULTY

Enrollment: 2,208. **Student Body:** Male 42%, female 58%, out-of-state 59%, international 1%. **Ethnic Representation:** African American 2%, Asian 2%, Caucasian 94%, Hispanic 2%. **Retention and Graduation:** 89% freshmen return for sophomore year. 75% freshmen graduate within 4 years. 17% grads go on to further study within 1 year. 1% grads pursue business degrees. 4% grads pursue law degrees. 2% grads pursue medical degrees. **Faculty:** Student/faculty ratio 12:1. 163 full-time faculty, 90% hold PhDs. 100% faculty teach undergrads.

ACADEMICS

Degrees: Bachelor's. **Academic Requirements:** General education including some course work in foreign languages, humanities, sciences (biological or physical), social science, freshman seminar, quantitative reasoning, U.S. diversity, writing-intensive course, community experience, physical education. **Classes:** 10-19 students in an average class. 20-29 students in an average lab class. **Majors with Highest Enrollment:** English language and literature, general; biology/biological sciences, general; political science and government, general. **Disciplines with Highest Percentage of Degrees Awarded:** Social sciences and history 23%, foreign languages and literature 15%, biological life sciences 11%, English 11%, psychology 8%. **Special Study Options:** Accelerated program, cross registration, double major, English as a second language, student exchange program (domestic), independent study, internships, liberal arts/career combination, student-designed major, study abroad, teacher certification program.

FACILITIES

Housing: Coed, apartments for single students, housing for disabled students, fraternities and/or sororities. Theme houses—foreign languages, arts, environmental, multicultural, etc. **Library Holdings:** 305,272 bound volumes. 6,163 periodicals. 176,399 microforms. 12,247 audiovisuals. **Special Academic Facilities/Equipment:** Art gallery, center for the arts, planetarium, observatory, scanning electron microscope. **Computers:** School-owned computers available for student use.

EXTRACURRICULARS

Activities: Choral groups, concert band, dance, drama/theater, jazz band, literary magazine, music ensembles, musical theater, radio station, student government, student newspaper, student-run film society, symphony orchestra, yearbook. **Organizations:** 120 registered organizations, 15 honor societies, 11 religious organizations, 8 fraternities (25% men join), 4 sororities (26% women join). **Athletics (Intercollegiate):** *Men:* baseball, basketball, cross-country, football, golf, indoor track, lacrosse, soccer, swimming, tennis, track & field. *Women:* basketball, cross-country, field hockey, golf, indoor track, lacrosse, soccer, softball, swimming, tennis, track & field, volleyball.

ADMISSIONS

Selectivity Rating: 82 (of 100). **Freshman Academic Profile:** 47% in top 10% of high school class, 79% in top 25% of high school class, 97% in top 50% of high school class. 62% from public high schools. Average SAT I Math 616, SAT I Math middle 50% range 570-650. Average SAT I Verbal 623, SAT I Verbal middle 50% range 580-670. Average ACT 26. TOEFL required of all international applicants, minimum TOEFL 550. **Basis for Candidate Selection:** *Very important factors considered include:* extracurricular activities, minority status, secondary school record, talent/ability, volunteer work. *Important factors considered include:* alumni/ae relation, class rank, recommendations, standardized test scores, work experience. *Other factors considered include:* character/personal qualities, essays, geographical residence, interview, state residency. **Freshman Admission Requirements:** High school diploma or GED is required. *Academic units required/recommended:* 16 total required; 4 English required, 3 math required, 3 science required, 2 science lab required, 2 foreign language required, 3 foreign language recommended, 2 social studies required, 2 elective required. **Freshman Admission Statistics:** 3,820 applied, 64% accepted, 25% of those accepted enrolled. **Transfer Admission Requirements:** *Items required:* high school transcript, college transcript, essay, statement of good standing from prior school. Minimum college GPA of 2.0 required. Lowest grade transferable C. **General Admission Information:** Application fee $40. Early decision application deadline November 15. Regular application deadline February 1. Nonfall registration accepted. Admission may be deferred for a maximum of 2 years. Credit and/or placement offered for CEEB Advanced Placement tests.

COSTS AND FINANCIAL AID

Average book expense $750. **Required Forms and Deadlines:** FAFSA, CSS/Financial Aid PROFILE, state aid form, noncustodial (divorced/separated) parent's statement, and business/farm supplement. Financial aid filing deadline November 15. Priority filing deadline November 15. **Notification of Awards:** Applicants will be notified of awards on or about December 15. **Types of Aid:** *Need-based scholarships/grants:* Pell, SEOG, state scholarships/grants, private scholarships, the school's own gift aid. *Loans:* FFEL Subsidized Stafford, FFEL Unsubsidized Stafford, FFEL PLUS, Federal Perkins, college/university loans from institutional funds. **Student Employment:** Federal Work-Study Program available. Institutional employment available. Off-campus job opportunities are good. **Financial Aid Statistics:** 55% freshmen, 59% undergrads receive some form of aid. Average freshman grant $14,557. Average freshman loan $3,401. Average income from on-campus job $1,167. **Financial Aid Phone:** 717-245-1308.

DICKINSON STATE UNIVERSITY

Office of Student Recruitment, Box 173, Dickinson, ND 58601-4896
Phone: 701-483-2175 **E-mail:** dsu.hawks@dsu.nodak.edu
Fax: 701-483-2409 **Web:** www.dickinsonstate.com **ACT Code:** 3210

This public school was founded in 1918. It has a 137-acre campus.

STUDENTS AND FACULTY

Enrollment: 2,326. **Student Body:** Male 44%, female 56%, out-of-state 24%, international 4% (26 countries represented). **Ethnic Representation:** African American 1%, Caucasian 84%, Hispanic 1%, Native American 2%. **Retention and Graduation:** 10% freshmen graduate within 4 years. **Faculty:** Student/faculty ratio 19:1. 73 full-time faculty, 56% hold PhDs. 100% faculty teach undergrads.

ACADEMICS

Degrees: Associate's, bachelor's, certificate, terminal, transfer. **Academic Requirements:** General education including some course work in arts/fine arts, computer literacy, English (including composition), history, humanities, mathematics, sciences (biological or physical), social science, freshman seminar, and physical education. **Classes:** 40-49 students in an average class. **Majors with Highest Enrollment:** Nursing/registered nurse training (RN, ASN, BSN, MSN); business administration/management; teacher education, multiple levels. **Disciplines with Highest Percentage of Degrees Awarded:** Business/marketing 25%, education 22%, liberal arts/general studies 15%, other 10%, health professions and related sciences 7%. **Special Study Options:** Accelerated program, distance learning, double major, dual enrollment, honors program, independent study, internships, liberal arts/career combination, student-designed major, study abroad, teacher certification program.

FACILITIES

Housing: Coed, all-female, all-male, apartments for married students, apartments for single students, housing for disabled students, apartments for upperclassmen, apartments for scholars. **Library Holdings:** 87,324 bound volumes. 5,450 periodicals. 8,850 microforms. 4,668 audiovisuals. **Special Academic Facilities/Equipment:** Art gallery, smart classrooms. **Computers:** School-owned computers available for student use.

EXTRACURRICULARS

Activities: Choral groups, concert band, dance, drama/theater, jazz band, literary magazine, marching band, music ensembles, musical theater, pep band, student government, student newspaper, student-run film society, yearbook. **Organizations:** 47 registered organizations, 7 honor societies, 6 religious organizations. **Athletics (Intercollegiate):** *Men:* baseball, basketball, cheerleading, cross-country, football, golf, indoor track, rodeo, track & field, wrestling. *Women:* basketball, cheerleading, cross-country, golf, indoor track, rodeo, softball, track & field, volleyball.

ADMISSIONS

Selectivity Rating: 70 (of 100). **Freshman Academic Profile:** Average high school GPA 3.1. 4% in top 10% of high school class, 15% in top 25% of high school class, 50% in top 50% of high school class. 98% from public high schools. SAT I Math middle 50% range 470-590. SAT I Verbal middle 50% range 430-530. Average ACT 21, ACT middle 50% range 18-23. TOEFL required of all international applicants, minimum TOEFL 525. **Freshman Admission Requirements:** High school diploma or GED is required. *Academic units required/recommended:* 13 total required; 4 English required, 3 math required, 3 science required. **Freshman Admission Statistics:** 625 applied, 100% accepted, 69% of those accepted enrolled. **Transfer Admission Requirements:** *Items required:* college transcript. Minimum college GPA of 2.0 required. Lowest grade transferable D. **General Admission Information:** Application fee $35. Nonfall registration accepted. Admission may be deferred. Neither credit nor placement offered for CEEB Advanced Placement tests.

COSTS AND FINANCIAL AID

In-state tuition $2,067. Out-of-state tuition $5,519. Room & board $3,032. Required fees $396. Average book expense $600. **Required Forms and Deadlines:** FAFSA. No deadline for regular filing. Priority filing deadline March 15. **Notification of Awards:** Applicants will be notified of awards on a rolling basis beginning on or about April 30. **Types of Aid:** *Need-based scholarships/grants:* Pell, SEOG, state scholarships/grants, private scholarships, the school's own gift aid. *Loans:* FFEL Subsidized Stafford, FFEL Unsubsidized Stafford, FFEL PLUS, Federal Perkins, Federal Nursing. **Student Employment:** Federal Work-Study Program available. Institutional employment available. Off-campus job opportunities are good. **Financial Aid Statistics:** Average freshman loan $2,625. Average income from on-campus job $1,304. **Financial Aid Phone:** 701-483-2371.

DILLARD UNIVERSITY

2601 Gentilly Boulevard, New Orleans, LA 70122
Phone: 504-816-4670 **E-mail:** admissions@dillard.edu **CEEB Code:** 6164
Fax: 504-816-4895 **Web:** www.dillard.edu **ACT Code:** 1578

This private school, which is affiliated with the United Church of Christ, was founded in 1869. It has a 48-acre campus.

STUDENTS AND FACULTY

Enrollment: 2,225. **Student Body:** Male 23%, female 77%, out-of-state 49%, international 1%. **Ethnic Representation:** African American 99%. **Retention and Graduation:** 78% freshmen return for sophomore year. 26% freshmen graduate within 4 years. 39% grads go on to further study within 1 year. 1% grads pursue business degrees. 1% grads pursue law degrees. 3% grads pursue medical degrees. **Faculty:** Student/faculty ratio 15:1. 143 full-time faculty, 69% hold PhDs. 100% faculty teach undergrads.

ACADEMICS

Degrees: Bachelor's, terminal. **Academic Requirements:** General education including some course work in arts/fine arts, computer literacy, English (including composition), foreign languages, history, humanities, mathematics, sciences (biological or physical), social science. **Classes:** 20-29 students in an average class. 10-19 students in an average lab class. **Disciplines with Highest Percentage of Degrees Awarded:** Health professions and related sciences 17%, business/marketing 15%, social sciences and history 15%, biological life sciences 11%, communications/communication technologies 9%. **Special Study Options:** Double major, dual enrollment, honors program, independent study, internships, liberal arts/career combination, study abroad.

FACILITIES

Housing: All-female, all-male, apartments for single students. **Library Holdings:** 104,615 bound volumes. 295 periodicals. 21,638 microforms. 426 audiovisuals. **Special Academic Facilities/Equipment:** Art gallery, language lab, communication studies facilities, electron microscope, observatory, outdoor challenge course. **Computers:** *Recommended operating system:* Mac. School-owned computers available for student use.

EXTRACURRICULARS

Activities: Choral groups, drama/theater, music ensembles, radio station, student government, student newspaper, yearbook. **Organizations:** 67 registered organizations, 6 honor societies, 3 religious organizations, 4 fraternities (4% men join), 4 sororities (11% women join). **Athletics (Intercollegiate):** *Men:* basketball, cross-country, tennis. *Women:* basketball, cross-country, tennis, volleyball.

ADMISSIONS

Selectivity Rating: 68 (of 100). **Freshman Academic Profile:** Average high school GPA 3.2. SAT I Math middle 50% range 400-510. SAT I Verbal middle 50% range 420-520. Average ACT 22, ACT middle 50% range 17-21. TOEFL required of all international applicants, minimum TOEFL 550. **Basis for Candidate Selection:** *Very important factors considered include:* essays, recommendations, secondary school record, standardized test scores. *Other factors considered include:* alumni/ae relation, class rank, extracurricular activities, interview. **Freshman Admission Requirements:** High school diploma or GED is required. *Academic units required/recommended:* 19 total required; 4 English required, 3 math required, 3 science required, 2 foreign language recommended, 3 social studies required, 6 elective required. **Freshman Admission Statistics:** 2,847 applied, 70% accepted, 32% of those accepted enrolled. **Transfer Admission Requirements:** *Items required:* college transcript, statement of good standing from prior school. Minimum college GPA of 2.0 required. Lowest grade transferable C. **General Admission Information:** Application fee $20. Regular application deadline July 1. Nonfall registration accepted. Credit and/or placement offered for CEEB Advanced Placement tests.

COSTS AND FINANCIAL AID

Tuition $10,094. Room & board $6,156. Required fees $665. Average book expense $1,000. **Required Forms and Deadlines:** FAFSA and institution's own financial aid form. Financial aid filing deadline May 1. Priority filing deadline March 1. **Notification of Awards:** Applicants will be notified of awards on a rolling basis beginning on or about March 1. **Types of Aid:** *Need-based scholarships/grants:* Pell, SEOG, state scholarships/grants, private scholarships, the school's own gift aid, United Negro College Fund, Federal Nursing. *Loans:* Direct Subsidized Stafford, Direct Unsubsidized Stafford, Direct PLUS, FFEL Subsidized Stafford, FFEL Unsubsidized Stafford, FFEL PLUS, Federal Perkins, Federal Nursing. **Student Employment:** Federal Work-Study Program available. Off-campus job opportunities are excellent. **Financial Aid Statistics:** 86% freshmen, 84% undergrads receive some form of aid. Average freshman grant $3,180. Average freshman loan $3,152. Average income from on-campus job $2,000. **Financial Aid Phone:** 504-816-4677.

DIVINE WORD COLLEGE

Office of Admissions, PO Box 380, Epworth, IA 52045
Phone: 563-876-3332 **E-mail:** dwm@mwci.net **CEEB Code:** 6174
Fax: 563-876-5515 **Web:** www.svd.org

STUDENTS AND FACULTY

Enrollment: 108. **Student Body:** Out-of-state 100%. **Faculty:** Student/faculty ratio 3:1. 16 full-time faculty, 37% hold PhDs.

ACADEMICS

Degrees: Associate's, bachelor's. **Academic Requirements:** General education including some course work in foreign languages, humanities, philosophy. **Classes:** Under 10 students in an average lab class. **Disciplines with Highest Percentage of Degrees Awarded:** Philosophy/religion/theology 17%. **Special Study Options:** English as a second language, liberal arts/career combination, study abroad.

FACILITIES

Housing: All-male. **Computers:** School-owned computers available for student use.

EXTRACURRICULARS

Activities: Student government. **Organizations:** 5 honor societies, 4 religious organizations. **Athletics (Intercollegiate):** *Men:* soccer.

ADMISSIONS

Selectivity Rating: 63 (of 100). **Basis for Candidate Selection:** *Very important factors considered include:* interview, recommendations, religious affiliation/commitment. *Other factors considered include:* standardized test scores. **Freshman Admission Requirements:** High school diploma or GED is required. **Freshman Admission Statistics:** 13 applied, 77% accepted, 80% of those accepted enrolled. **Transfer Admission Requirements:** *Items required:* college transcript, essay, interview. **General Admission Information:** Application fee $25. Regular application deadline July 1. Nonfall registration accepted.

COSTS AND FINANCIAL AID

Tuition $8,800. Room & board $2,000. Required fees $231. Average book expense $500. **Types of Aid:** *Loans:* FFEL Subsidized Stafford, FFEL PLUS.

DOANE COLLEGE

1014 Boswell Avenue, Crete, NE 68333
Phone: 402-826-8222 **E-mail:** admissions@doane.edu **CEEB Code:** 6165
Fax: 402-826-8600 **Web:** www.doane.edu **ACT Code:** 2448

This private school, which is affiliated with the United Church of Christ, was founded in 1872. It has a 300-acre campus.

STUDENTS AND FACULTY

Enrollment: 1,539. **Student Body:** Male 47%, female 53%, out-of-state 17%, international 1% (7 countries represented). **Ethnic Representation:** African American 2%, Asian 1%, Caucasian 94%, Hispanic 2%. **Retention and Graduation:** 83% freshmen return for sophomore year. 52% freshmen graduate within 4 years. 23% grads go on to further study within 1 year. **Faculty:** Student/faculty ratio 12:1. 72 full-time faculty, 62% hold PhDs. 100% faculty teach undergrads.

ACADEMICS

Degrees: Bachelor's, master's. **Academic Requirements:** General education including some course work in arts/fine arts, English (including composition), history, humanities, mathematics, sciences (biological or physical), social science. **Majors with Highest Enrollment:** Business administration/management; education, general; biology/biological sciences, general. **Disciplines with Highest Percentage of Degrees Awarded:** Business/marketing 47%, education 16%, biological life sciences 9%, communications/communication technologies 6%, social sciences and history 5%. **Special Study Options:** Double major, English as a second language, honors program, independent study, internships, student-designed major, study abroad, teacher certification program.

FACILITIES

Housing: Coed, all-female, all-male, special housing for leadership students. **Library Holdings:** 295,417 bound volumes. 3,500 periodicals. 6,256 microforms. 1,791 audiovisuals. **Special Academic Facilities/Equipment:** Art gallery, language lab, communication studies facilities, electron microscope, observatory, outdoor challenge course. **Computers:** School-owned computers available for student use.

EXTRACURRICULARS

Activities: Choral groups, concert band, dance, drama/theater, jazz band, literary magazine, marching band, music ensembles, pep band, radio station, student government, student newspaper, television station, yearbook. **Organizations:** 50 registered organizations, 8 honor societies, 2 religious organizations, 5 fraternities, 4 sororities. **Athletics (Intercollegiate):** *Men:* baseball, basketball, cross-country, football, golf, indoor track, soccer, tennis, track & field. *Women:* basketball, cross-country, golf, indoor track, soccer, softball, tennis, track & field, volleyball.

ADMISSIONS

Selectivity Rating: 71 (of 100). **Freshman Academic Profile:** Average high school GPA 3.5. Average ACT 23, ACT middle 50% range 21-26. TOEFL required of all international applicants, minimum TOEFL 550. **Basis for Candidate Selection:** *Very important factors considered include:* secondary school record, standardized test scores. *Important factors considered include:* alumni/ae relation, character/personal qualities, recommendations. *Other factors considered include:* class rank, essays, extracurricular activities, interview, minority status, talent/ability, volunteer work, work experience. **Freshman Admission Requirements:** High school diploma or GED is required. *Academic units required/recommended:* 4 English recommended, 3 math recommended, 4 science recommended, 3 social studies recommended. **Freshman Admission Statistics:** 1,043 applied, 85% accepted, 31% of those accepted enrolled. **Transfer Admission Requirements:** *Items required:* high school transcript, college transcript, standardized test scores, statement of good standing from prior school. Lowest grade transferable C. **General Admission Information:** Application fee $15. Nonfall registration accepted. Admission may be deferred. Credit offered for CEEB Advanced Placement tests.

COSTS AND FINANCIAL AID

Tuition $13,150. Room & board $4,130. Required fees $320. Average book expense $700. **Required Forms and Deadlines:** FAFSA and institution's own financial aid form. Priority filing deadline March 1. **Notification of Awards:** Applicants will be notified of awards on a rolling basis beginning on or about March 1. **Types of Aid:** *Need-based scholarships/grants:* Pell, SEOG, state scholarships/grants, private scholarships. *Loans:* FFEL Subsidized Stafford, FFEL Unsubsidized Stafford, FFEL PLUS, Federal Perkins. **Student Employment:** Federal Work-Study Program available. Institutional employment available. Off-campus job opportunities are good. **Financial Aid Statistics:** 83% freshmen, 76% undergrads receive some form of aid. **Financial Aid Phone:** 402-826-8260.

DOMINICAN COLLEGE OF BLAUVELT

470 Western Highway, Orangeburg, NY 10962
Phone: 845-359-7800 **E-mail:** admissions@dc.edu **CEEB Code:** 2190
Fax: 845-365-3150 **Web:** www.dc.edu **ACT Code:** 2730

This private school, which is affiliated with the Roman Catholic Church, was founded in 1952. It has a 50-acre campus.

STUDENTS AND FACULTY

Enrollment: 1,515. **Student Body:** Male 32%, female 68%, out-of-state 18%. **Ethnic Representation:** African American 15%, Asian 5%, Caucasian 60%, Hispanic 11%. **Retention and Graduation:** 67% freshmen return for sophomore year. 33% freshmen graduate within 4 years. 18% grads go on to further study within 1 year. **Faculty:** Student/faculty ratio 12:1. 62 full-time faculty, 46% hold PhDs. 95% faculty teach undergrads.

ACADEMICS

Degrees: Associate's, bachelor's, master's. **Academic Requirements:** General education including some course work in computer literacy, English (including composition), foreign languages, history, humanities, mathematics, sciences (biological or physical), speech. **Classes:** 10-19 students in an average class. **Majors with Highest Enrollment:** Nursing/registered nurse training (RN, ASN, BSN, MSN); occupational therapy/therapist; business administration/management. **Disciplines with Highest Percentage of Degrees Awarded:** Health professions and related sciences 41%, business/marketing 20%, social sciences and history 10%, computer and information sciences 9%, education 6%. **Special Study Options:** Accelerated program, cross registration, distance learning, dual enrollment, honors program, independent study, internships, teacher certification program, weekend college.

FACILITIES

Housing: Coed. **Library Holdings:** 102,329 bound volumes. 639 periodicals. 12,621 microforms. 216 audiovisuals. **Computers:** *Recommended operating system:* Windows NT/2000. School-owned computers available for student use.

EXTRACURRICULARS

Activities: Choral groups, drama/theater, literary magazine, musical theater, student government, student newspaper, yearbook. **Organizations:** 16 registered organizations, 4 honor societies. **Athletics (Intercollegiate):** *Men:* baseball, basketball, cheerleading, cross-country, golf, soccer. *Women:* basketball, cheerleading, cross-country, soccer, softball, volleyball.

ADMISSIONS

Selectivity Rating: 64 (of 100). **Freshman Academic Profile:** Average high school GPA 2.9. 73% from public high schools. Average SAT I Math 441, SAT I Math middle 50% range 370-510. Average SAT I Verbal 442, SAT I Verbal middle 50% range 380-490. TOEFL required of all international applicants, minimum TOEFL 550. **Basis for Candidate Selection:** *Very important factors considered include:* character/personal qualities, interview, secondary school record, standardized test scores. *Important factors considered include:* extracurricular activities, recommendations. *Other factors considered include:* alumni/ae relation, essays, talent/ability, volunteer work, work experience. **Freshman Admission Requirements:** High school diploma or GED is required. *Academic units required/recommended:* 8 total recommended; 2 English recommended, 2 math recommended, 2 science recommended, 2 foreign language recommended. **Transfer Admission Requirements:** *Items required:* college transcript. Minimum high school GPA of 2.0 required.

Minimum college GPA of 2.0 required. Lowest grade transferable C. **General Admission Information:** Application fee $35. Regular application deadline February 15. Nonfall registration accepted. Admission may be deferred for a maximum of 1 year. Placement offered for CEEB Advanced Placement tests.

COSTS AND FINANCIAL AID

Tuition $15,000. Room & board $7,770. Required fees $650. Average book expense $1,800. **Required Forms and Deadlines:** FAFSA, institution's own financial aid form, state aid form. No deadline for regular filing. Priority filing deadline February 15. **Notification of Awards:** Applicants will be notified of awards on a rolling basis. **Types of Aid:** *Need-based scholarships/grants:* Pell, SEOG, state scholarships/grants, private scholarships, the school's own gift aid, Federal Nursing. *Loans:* Direct Subsidized Stafford, Direct Unsubsidized Stafford, Direct PLUS, FFEL Subsidized Stafford, FFEL Unsubsidized Stafford, FFEL PLUS, Federal Perkins, Federal Nursing. **Student Employment:** Federal Work-Study Program available. Off-campus job opportunities are good. **Financial Aid Statistics:** 84% freshmen, 82% undergrads receive some form of aid. Average freshman grant $5,626. Average freshman loan $2,439. **Financial Aid Phone:** 845-359-7800.

DOMINICAN UNIVERSITY (IL)

7900 West Division, River Forest, IL 60305
Phone: 708-524-6800 **E-mail:** domadmis@dom.edu **CEEB Code:** 1667
Fax: 708-524-5990 **Web:** www.dom.edu **ACT Code:** 1126

This private school, which is affiliated with the Roman Catholic Church, was founded in 1901. It has a 30-acre campus.

STUDENTS AND FACULTY

Enrollment: 1,170. **Student Body:** Male 31%, female 69%, out-of-state 8%, international 2%. **Ethnic Representation:** African American 5%, Asian 2%, Caucasian 72%, Hispanic 17%. **Retention and Graduation:** 79% freshmen return for sophomore year. 53% freshmen graduate within 4 years. 15% grads go on to further study within 1 year. **Faculty:** Student/faculty ratio 13:1. 89 full-time faculty, 88% hold PhDs. 100% faculty teach undergrads.

ACADEMICS

Degrees: Bachelor's, certificate, master's, post-bachelor's certificate, post-master's certificate. **Academic Requirements:** General education including some course work in arts/fine arts, computer literacy, English (including composition), foreign languages, history, humanities, mathematics, philosophy, sciences (biological or physical), social science, theology. **Classes:** Under 10 students in an average class. 10-19 students in an average lab class. **Majors with Highest Enrollment:** Business administration/management; psychology, general; English language and literature, general. **Disciplines with Highest Percentage of Degrees Awarded:** Business/marketing 31%, social sciences and history 13%, psychology 10%, computer and information sciences 6%, communications/communication technologies 6%. **Special Study Options:** Accelerated program, cross registration, distance learning, double major, dual enrollment, English as a second language, honors program, independent study, internships, liberal arts/career combination, study abroad, teacher certification program.

FACILITIES

Housing: Coed, coed by floor. **Library Holdings:** 280,475 bound volumes. 1,388 periodicals. 46,534 microforms. 5,757 audiovisuals. **Special Academic Facilities/Equipment:** Art gallery, technology center, language lab, recital hall. **Computers:** School-owned computers available for student use.

EXTRACURRICULARS

Activities: Choral groups, drama/theater, literary magazine, musical theater, student government, student newspaper. **Organizations:** 30 registered organizations, 14 honor societies, 2 religious organizations. **Athletics (Intercollegiate):** *Men:* baseball, basketball, cross-country, soccer, tennis. *Women:* basketball, cross-country, soccer, softball, tennis, volleyball.

ADMISSIONS

Selectivity Rating: 73 (of 100). **Freshman Academic Profile:** Average high school GPA 3.5. 18% in top 10% of high school class, 50% in top 25% of high school class, 86% in top 50% of high school class. 59% from public high schools. Average ACT 23, ACT middle 50% range 20-25. TOEFL required of all international applicants, minimum TOEFL 550. **Basis for Candidate Selection:** *Very important factors considered include:* class rank, secondary school record, standardized test scores. *Important factors considered include:* character/personal qualities, essays, interview, recommendations. *Other factors considered include:* alumni/ae relation, extracurricular activities, geographical residence, state residency, talent/ability, volunteer work, work experience. **Freshman Admission Requirements:** High school diploma or GED is required. *Academic units required/recommended:* 16 total required; 4 English required, 3 math recommended, 2 science recommended, 2 science lab recommended, 2 foreign language recommended, 1 social studies recommended, 2 history recommended, 2 elective required. **Freshman Admission Statistics:** 513 applied, 81% accepted, 46% of those accepted enrolled. **Transfer Admission Requirements:** *Items required:* college transcript, essay, statement of good standing from prior school. Minimum high school GPA of 2.5 required. Minimum college GPA of 2.5 required. Lowest grade transferable D. **General Admission Information:** Application fee $20. Priority application deadline July 1. Nonfall registration accepted. Admission may be deferred. Credit offered for CEEB Advanced Placement tests.

COSTS AND FINANCIAL AID

Tuition $17,850. Room & board $5,400. Required fees $100. Average book expense $750. **Required Forms and Deadlines:** FAFSA. No deadline for regular filing. Priority filing deadline June 1. **Notification of Awards:** Applicants will be notified of awards on a rolling basis beginning on or about February 15. **Types of Aid:** *Need-based scholarships/grants:* Pell, SEOG, state scholarships/grants, private scholarships, the school's own gift aid. *Loans:* FFEL Subsidized Stafford, FFEL Unsubsidized Stafford, FFEL PLUS, Federal Perkins. **Student Employment:** Federal Work-Study Program available. Institutional employment available. Off-campus job opportunities are excellent. **Financial Aid Statistics:** 71% freshmen, 68% undergrads receive some form of aid. Average freshman grant $10,000. Average freshman loan $2,625. Average income from on-campus job $1,500. **Financial Aid Phone:** 708-524-6809.

DOMINICAN UNIVERSITY OF CALIFORNIA

Office of Admissions, 50 Acacia Avenue, San Rafael, CA 94901-2298
Phone: 415-485-3204 **E-mail:** enroll@dominican.edu **CEEB Code:** 4284
Fax: 415-485-3214 **Web:** www.dominican.edu

This private school, which is affiliated with the Roman Catholic Church, was founded in 1890. It has an 80-acre campus.

STUDENTS AND FACULTY

Enrollment: 984. **Student Body:** Male 19%, female 81%, out-of-state 3%, international 3% (22 countries represented). **Ethnic Representation:** African American 7%, Asian 12%, Caucasian 63%, Hispanic 9%, Native American 1%. **Retention and Graduation:** 76% freshmen return for sophomore year. 23% freshmen graduate within 4 years. 1% grads pursue medical degrees. **Faculty:** Student/faculty ratio 12:1. 43 full-time faculty, 60% hold PhDs. 74% faculty teach undergrads.

ACADEMICS

Degrees: Bachelor's, master's, post-bachelor's certificate. **Academic Requirements:** General education including some course work in arts/fine arts, English (including composition), history, humanities, mathematics, philosophy, sciences (biological or physical), social science. **Classes:** 10-19 students in an average class. 10-19 students in an average lab class. **Majors with Highest Enrollment:** Nursing/registered nurse training (RN, ASN, BSN, MSN); business administration/management; teacher education, multiple levels. **Disciplines with Highest Percentage of Degrees Awarded:** Health professions and related sciences 34%, business/marketing 19%, psychology 16%, liberal arts/general studies 10%, English 8%. **Special Study Options:** Accelerated program, cross registration, double major, English as a second language, student exchange program (domestic), honors program, independent study, internships, liberal arts/career combination, student-designed major, study abroad, teacher certification program.

FACILITIES

Housing: Coed, housing for disabled students. **Library Holdings:** 97,914 bound volumes. 425 periodicals. 2,624 microforms. 947 audiovisuals. **Special Academic Facilities/Equipment:** Art gallery, natural history museum. **Computers:** *Recommended operating system:* Windows 98/NT. School-owned computers available for student use.

EXTRACURRICULARS

Activities: Choral groups, literary magazine, music ensembles, student government, student newspaper, yearbook. **Organizations:** 10 registered organizations, 4 honor societies, 1 religious organization. **Athletics (Intercollegiate):** *Men:* basketball, soccer, tennis. *Women:* basketball, soccer, softball, tennis, volleyball.

ADMISSIONS

Selectivity Rating: 69 (of 100). **Freshman Academic Profile:** Average high school GPA 3.3. 9% in top 10% of high school class, 50% in top 25% of high

school class, 74% in top 50% of high school class. 56% from public high schools. Average SAT I Math 480. Average SAT I Verbal 508. TOEFL required of all international applicants, minimum TOEFL 550. **Basis for Candidate Selection:** *Very important factors considered include:* character/personal qualities, essays, recommendations, secondary school record, standardized test scores. *Important factors considered include:* class rank, extracurricular activities, interview, minority status, talent/ability, volunteer work. *Other factors considered include:* alumni/ae relation, work experience. **Freshman Admission Requirements:** High school diploma or GED is required. *Academic units required/recommended:* 4 English required, 2 math required, 2 science required, 1 science lab required, 2 foreign language required, 1 history required. **Transfer Admission Requirements:** *Items required:* college transcript, essay. Minimum college GPA of 2.0 required. Lowest grade transferable D-. **General Admission Information:** Application fee $40. Priority application deadline February 1. Nonfall registration accepted. Admission may be deferred. Placement offered for CEEB Advanced Placement tests.

COSTS AND FINANCIAL AID

Tuition $20,320. Room & board $9,060. Required fees $350. Average book expense $810. **Required Forms and Deadlines:** FAFSA and institution's own financial aid form. No deadline for regular filing. Priority filing deadline March 2. **Notification of Awards:** Applicants will be notified of awards on a rolling basis beginning on or about December 15. **Types of Aid:** *Need-based scholarships/grants:* Pell, SEOG, state scholarships/grants, private scholarships, the school's own gift aid. *Loans:* FFEL Subsidized Stafford, FFEL Unsubsidized Stafford, FFEL PLUS, Federal Perkins, Federal Nursing, college/university loans from institutional funds. **Student Employment:** Federal Work-Study Program available. Institutional employment available. Off-campus job opportunities are fair. **Financial Aid Statistics:** 65% freshmen, 63% undergrads receive some form of aid. Average freshman grant $11,291. Average freshman loan $2,859. Average income from on-campus job $2,297. **Financial Aid Phone:** 415-485-3221.

DORDT COLLEGE

498 4th Avenue, Northeast, Sioux Center, IA 51250
Phone: 712-722-6080 **E-mail:** admissions@dordt.edu **CEEB Code:** 6171
Fax: 712-722-1967 **Web:** www.dordt.edu **ACT Code:** 1301

This private school was founded in 1955. It has a 65-acre campus.

STUDENTS AND FACULTY

Enrollment: 1,347. **Student Body:** Male 45%, female 55%, out-of-state 58%, international 12% (12 countries represented). **Ethnic Representation:** African American 1%, Asian 1%, Caucasian 98%. **Retention and Graduation:** 84% freshmen return for sophomore year. 59% freshmen graduate within 4 years. 15% grads go on to further study within 1 year. 4% grads pursue business degrees. 1% grads pursue law degrees. 1% grads pursue medical degrees. **Faculty:** Student/faculty ratio 15:1. 80 full-time faculty, 85% hold PhDs. 100% faculty teach undergrads.

ACADEMICS

Degrees: Associate's, bachelor's, master's, terminal. **Academic Requirements:** General education including some course work in arts/fine arts, English (including composition), history, humanities, mathematics, philosophy, sciences (biological or physical), social science. **Classes:** 10-19 students in an average class. 10-19 students in an average lab/discussion section. **Disciplines with Highest Percentage of Degrees Awarded:** Education 25%, business/marketing 16%, agriculture 8%, engineering/engineering technology 7%, social sciences and history 7%. **Special Study Options:** Distance learning, double major, English as a second language, independent study, internships, liberal arts/career combination, student-designed major, study abroad, teacher certification program.

FACILITIES

Housing: All-female, all-male, apartments for married students, apartments for single students, housing for disabled students. **Library Holdings:** 170,000 bound volumes. 6,597 periodicals. 121,622 microforms. 1,989 audiovisuals. **Special Academic Facilities/Equipment:** Language lab, access to observatories. **Computers:** *Recommended operating system:* Windows NT/2000. School-owned computers available for student use.

EXTRACURRICULARS

Activities: Choral groups, concert band, dance, drama/theater, jazz band, literary magazine, music ensembles, musical theater, opera, pep band, radio station, student government, student newspaper, student-run film society, symphony orchestra, yearbook. **Organizations:** 40 registered organizations, 4 religious organizations. **Athletics (Intercollegiate):** *Men:* baseball, basketball, skiing (cross-country), golf, ice hockey, indoor track, soccer, tennis, track & field. *Women:* basketball, skiing (cross-country), indoor track, soccer, softball, tennis, track & field, volleyball.

ADMISSIONS

Selectivity Rating: 76 (of 100). **Freshman Academic Profile:** Average high school GPA 3.4. 17% in top 10% of high school class, 36% in top 25% of high school class, 62% in top 50% of high school class. 40% from public high schools. Average SAT I Math 580, SAT I Math middle 50% range 480-660. Average SAT I Verbal 580, SAT I Verbal middle 50% range 490-640. Average ACT 24, ACT middle 50% range 21-27. TOEFL required of all international applicants, minimum TOEFL 550. **Basis for Candidate Selection:** *Very important factors considered include:* religious affiliation/commitment, secondary school record, standardized test scores. *Other factors considered include:* character/personal qualities, class rank, extracurricular activities, talent/ability. **Freshman Admission Requirements:** High school diploma or GED is required. *Academic units required/recommended:* 17 total required; 25 total recommended; 3 English required, 4 English recommended, 2 math required, 3 math recommended, 2 science required, 4 science recommended, 2 foreign language required, 3 foreign language recommended, 1 social studies recommended, 2 history required, 6 elective required. **Freshman Admission Statistics:** 740 applied, 93% accepted, 55% of those accepted enrolled. **Transfer Admission Requirements:** *Items required:* high school transcript, college transcript, standardized test scores. Minimum college GPA of 2.0 required. Lowest grade transferable C. **General Admission Information:** Application fee $25. Nonfall registration accepted. Credit offered for CEEB Advanced Placement tests.

COSTS AND FINANCIAL AID

Average book expense $650. **Required Forms and Deadlines:** FAFSA and institution's own financial aid form. Priority filing deadline April 1. **Notification of Awards:** Applicants will be notified of awards on a rolling basis beginning on or about March 15. **Types of Aid:** *Need-based scholarships/grants:* Pell, SEOG, state scholarships/grants, private scholarships, the school's own gift aid. *Loans:* Direct Subsidized Stafford, Direct Unsubsidized Stafford, Direct PLUS, Federal Perkins, college/university loans from institutional funds. **Student Employment:** Federal Work-Study Program available. Institutional employment available. Off-campus job opportunities are good. **Financial Aid Statistics:** 80% freshmen, 79% undergrads receive some form of aid. Average freshman grant $6,000. Average freshman loan $4,782. Average income from on-campus job $1,300. **Financial Aid Phone:** 712-722-6087.

DOWLING COLLEGE

Idle Hour Boulevard, Oakdale, NY 11769-1999
Phone: 800-369-5464 **E-mail:** admissions@dowling.edu **CEEB Code:** 2011
Fax: 631-563-3827 **Web:** www.dowling.edu **ACT Code:** 2665

This private school was founded in 1959. It has a 51-acre campus.

STUDENTS AND FACULTY

Enrollment: 3,046. **Student Body:** Male 39%, female 61%, out-of-state 15%, international 1% (47 countries represented). **Ethnic Representation:** African American 10%, Asian 3%, Caucasian 61%, Hispanic 11%. **Retention and Graduation:** 67% freshmen return for sophomore year. 25% freshmen graduate within 4 years. **Faculty:** Student/faculty ratio 17:1. 120 full-time faculty, 75% hold PhDs.

ACADEMICS

Degrees: Bachelor's, doctoral, master's, post-bachelor's certificate, post-master's certificate. **Academic Requirements:** General education including some course work in arts/fine arts, English (including composition), history, humanities, mathematics, philosophy, sciences (biological or physical), social science. **Classes:** 10-19 students in an average class. 10-19 students in an average lab/discussion section. **Majors with Highest Enrollment:** Business administration/management; special education, general; elementary education and teaching. **Disciplines with Highest Percentage of Degrees Awarded:** Business/marketing 33%, education 29%, liberal arts/general studies 9%, computer and information sciences 8%, social sciences and history 8%. **Special Study Options:** Accelerated program, cooperative (work-study) program, double major, English as a second language, honors program, independent study, internships, liberal arts/career combination, teacher certification program, weekend college.

FACILITIES

Housing: Coed. **Library Holdings:** 121,561 bound volumes. 8,489 periodicals. 590,000 microforms. 2,362 audiovisuals. **Special Academic Facilities/Equipment:** Art gallery, cultural study center, media center, human factors lab, meteorology lab. **Computers:** *Recommended operating system:* Windows 95. School-owned computers available for student use.

EXTRACURRICULARS

Activities: Choral groups, concert band, dance, drama/theater, jazz band, literary magazine, music ensembles, radio station, student government, student newspaper, symphony orchestra, yearbook. **Organizations:** 1 honor society, 1 religious organization. **Athletics (Intercollegiate):** *Men:* baseball, basketball, crew, golf, lacrosse, soccer, tennis. *Women:* basketball, crew, cross-country, equestrian, softball, tennis, volleyball.

ADMISSIONS

Selectivity Rating: 63 (of 100). **Freshman Academic Profile:** Average high school GPA 2.6. 5% in top 10% of high school class, 23% in top 25% of high school class, 53% in top 50% of high school class. Average SAT I Math 459, SAT I Math middle 50% range 398-520. Average SAT I Verbal 448, SAT I Verbal middle 50% range 380-520. **Basis for Candidate Selection:** *Very important factors considered include:* secondary school record. *Important factors considered include:* class rank. *Other factors considered include:* alumni/ae relation, character/personal qualities, extracurricular activities, interview, recommendations, standardized test scores, talent/ability. **Freshman Admission Requirements:** High school diploma or GED is required. *Academic units required/recommended:* 16 total recommended; 4 English recommended, 3 math recommended, 2 science recommended, 3 social studies recommended. **Freshman Admission Statistics:** 2,104 applied, 93% accepted, 24% of those accepted enrolled. **Transfer Admission Requirements:** *Items required:* college transcript. Minimum college GPA of 2.0 required. Lowest grade transferable D. **General Admission Information:** Application fee $25. Nonfall registration accepted. Credit and/or placement offered for CEEB Advanced Placement tests.

COSTS AND FINANCIAL AID

Tuition $13,890. Required fees $810. Average book expense $750. **Required Forms and Deadlines:** FAFSA, institution's own financial aid form, and state aid form. No deadline for regular filing. Priority filing deadline June 1. **Notification of Awards:** Applicants will be notified of awards on a rolling basis beginning on or about March 15. **Types of Aid:** *Need-based scholarships/grants:* Pell, SEOG, state scholarships/grants, private scholarships, the school's own gift aid. *Loans:* Direct Subsidized Stafford, Direct Unsubsidized Stafford, Direct PLUS, Federal Perkins. **Student Employment:** Federal Work-Study Program available. Institutional employment available. Off-campus job opportunities are excellent. **Financial Aid Statistics:** 79% freshmen, 72% undergrads receive some form of aid. Average freshman grant $3,100. Average freshman loan $2,625. **Financial Aid Phone:** 631-244-3030.

DRAKE UNIVERSITY

2507 University Avenue, Des Moines, IA 50311-4505
Phone: 515-271-3181 **E-mail:** admission@drake.edu **CEEB Code:** 6168
Fax: 515-271-2831 **Web:** www.choose.drake.edu **ACT Code:** 1302

This private school was founded in 1881. It has a 120-acre campus.

STUDENTS AND FACULTY

Enrollment: 3,603. **Student Body:** Male 40%, female 60%, out-of-state 61%, international 5% (55 countries represented). **Ethnic Representation:** African American 3%, Asian 3%, Caucasian 89%, Hispanic 2%. **Retention and Graduation:** 83% freshmen return for sophomore year. 50% freshmen graduate within 4 years. 22% grads go on to further study within 1 year. 5% grads pursue business degrees. 5% grads pursue law degrees. 3% grads pursue medical degrees. **Faculty:** Student/faculty ratio 13:1. 244 full-time faculty, 93% hold PhDs. 100% faculty teach undergrads.

ACADEMICS

Degrees: Bachelor's, doctoral, first professional, master's, post-bachelor's certificate. **Academic Requirements:** General education including some course work in arts/fine arts, computer literacy, English (including composition), history, humanities, mathematics, philosophy, sciences (biological or physical). **Classes:** 10-19 students in an average class. 10-19 students in an average lab/discussion section. **Majors with Highest Enrollment:** Pharmacy (PharmD, BS/BPharm); advertising; biology/biological sciences, general. **Disciplines with Highest Percentage of Degrees Awarded:** Business/marketing 30%, communications/communication technologies 16%, visual and performing arts 11%, social sciences and history 11%, education 9%. **Special Study Options:** Accelerated program, cooperative (work-study) program, cross registration, distance learning, double major, English as a second language, student exchange program (domestic), honors program, independent study, internships, liberal arts/career combination, student-designed major, study abroad, teacher certification program.

FACILITIES

Housing: Coed, apartments for married students, apartments for single students, fraternities and/or sororities, houses. **Library Holdings:** 472,110 bound volumes. 2,000 periodicals. 848,010 microforms. 858 audiovisuals. **Special Academic Facilities/Equipment:** Language lab, observatory, media service center, Anderson Art Gallery. **Computers:** School-owned computers available for student use.

EXTRACURRICULARS

Activities: Choral groups, concert band, dance, drama/theater, jazz band, literary magazine, marching band, music ensembles, musical theater, pep band, radio station, student government, student newspaper, student-run film society, symphony orchestra, television station. **Organizations:** 150 registered organizations, 25 honor societies, 13 religious organizations, 9 fraternities (11% men join), 7 sororities (11% women join). **Athletics (Intercollegiate):** *Men:* basketball, cheerleading, cross-country, football, golf, indoor track, soccer, tennis, track & field. *Women:* basketball, cheerleading, crew, cross-country, indoor track, soccer, softball, tennis, track & field, volleyball.

ADMISSIONS

Selectivity Rating: 79 (of 100). **Freshman Academic Profile:** Average high school GPA 3.6. 37% in top 10% of high school class, 69% in top 25% of high school class, 92% in top 50% of high school class. 85% from public high schools. Average SAT I Math 584, SAT I Math middle 50% range 510-640. Average SAT I Verbal 570, SAT I Verbal middle 50% range 490-620. Average ACT 25, ACT middle 50% range 22-28. TOEFL required of all international applicants, minimum TOEFL 530. **Basis for Candidate Selection:** *Very important factors considered include:* secondary school record. *Important factors considered include:* class rank, extracurricular activities, recommendations, standardized test scores. *Other factors considered include:* character/personal qualities, essays, interview, talent/ability, volunteer work, work experience. **Freshman Admission Requirements:** High school diploma or GED is required. *Academic units required/recommended:* 16 total recommended; 4 English recommended, 3 math recommended, 2 science recommended, 2 foreign language recommended, 4 social studies recommended. **Freshman Admission Statistics:** 2,543 applied, 86% accepted, 35% of those accepted enrolled. **Transfer Admission Requirements:** *Items required:* college transcript. Minimum college GPA of 2.0 required. Lowest grade transferable C. **General Admission Information:** Application fee $25. Priority application deadline March 3. Nonfall registration accepted. Admission may be deferred for a maximum of 1 year. Credit and/or placement offered for CEEB Advanced Placement tests.

COSTS AND FINANCIAL AID

Tuition $18,190. Room & board $5,490. Required fees $320. Average book expense $700. **Required Forms and Deadlines:** FAFSA. Priority filing deadline March 3. **Notification of Awards:** Applicants will be notified of awards on a rolling basis beginning on or about March 3. **Types of Aid:** *Need-based scholarships/grants:* Pell, SEOG, state scholarships/grants, private scholarships, the school's own gift aid. *Loans:* FFEL Subsidized Stafford, FFEL Unsubsidized Stafford, FFEL PLUS, Federal Perkins, college/university loans from institutional funds, Federal Health Professional Loans. **Student Employment:** Federal Work-Study Program available. Institutional employment available. Off-campus job opportunities are excellent. **Financial Aid Statistics:** 60% freshmen, 60% undergrads receive some form of aid. Average freshman grant $11,236. Average freshman loan $4,276. Average income from on-campus job $1,175. **Financial Aid Phone:** 515-271-2905.

See page 1014.

DREW UNIVERSITY

  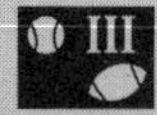 

Office of College Admission, Madison, NJ 07940-1493
Phone: 973-408-3739 **E-mail:** cadm@drew.edu **CEEB Code:** 2193
Fax: 973-408-3068 **Web:** www.drew.edu **ACT Code:** 2550

This private school, which is affiliated with the Methodist Church, was founded in 1868. It has a 186-acre campus.

STUDENTS AND FACULTY

Enrollment: 1,558. **Student Body:** Male 39%, female 61%, out-of-state 41%, international 1%. **Ethnic Representation:** African American 4%, Asian 6%, Caucasian 63%, Hispanic 5%. **Retention and Graduation:** 81% freshmen return for sophomore year. 19% grads go on to further study within 1 year. 2% grads pursue law degrees. 3% grads pursue medical degrees. **Faculty:** Student/faculty ratio 12:1. 121 full-time faculty, 96% hold PhDs. 100% faculty teach undergrads.

ACADEMICS

Degrees: Bachelor's, doctoral, first professional, master's, post-bachelor's certificate. **Academic Requirements:** General education including some course work in arts/fine arts, computer literacy, English (including composition), foreign languages, history, humanities, philosophy, sciences (biological or physical), social science. **Classes:** 10-19 students in an average class. 10-19 students in an average lab/discussion section. **Majors with Highest Enrollment:** English language and literature, general; psychology, general; political science and government, general. **Disciplines with Highest Percentage of Degrees Awarded:** Social sciences and history 34%, psychology 13%, visual and performing arts 10%, English 10%, foreign languages and literature 9%. **Special Study Options:** Accelerated program, cross registration, double major, student exchange program (domestic), independent study, internships, student-designed major, study abroad, teacher certification program. Joint-degree programs: 7-year dual degree BA/MD program with University of Medicine and Dentistry of New Jersey and 5-year dual degree (BA/BS or BEng) programs in engineering and technologies with Columbia University, Stevens Institute of Technology, and Washington University.

FACILITIES

Housing: Coed, housing for disabled students, housing for international students, cooperative housing. **Library Holdings:** 491,489 bound volumes. 2,589 periodicals. 370,197 microforms. 328 audiovisuals. **Special Academic Facilities/Equipment:** Art gallery, photography gallery, multimedia language lab, child development center, research greenhouse, arboretum, observatory, laser holography lab, nuclear magnetic resonator, electron microscope, optical and radio telescopes, computer graphics laboratory, New Jersey Shakespeare Festival (professional acting company). **Computers:** *Recommended operating system:* Windows 98/XP. School-owned computers available for student use.

EXTRACURRICULARS

Activities: Choral groups, dance, drama/theater, jazz band, literary magazine, music ensembles, pep band, radio station, student government, student newspaper, student-run film society, symphony orchestra, television station, yearbook. **Organizations:** 80 registered organizations, 12 honor societies, 9 religious organizations. **Athletics (Intercollegiate):** *Men:* baseball, basketball, cross-country, equestrian, fencing, lacrosse, soccer, swimming, tennis. *Women:* basketball, cross-country, equestrian, fencing, field hockey, lacrosse, soccer, softball, swimming, tennis.

ADMISSIONS

Selectivity Rating: 89 (of 100). **Freshman Academic Profile:** 33% in top 10% of high school class, 71% in top 25% of high school class, 92% in top 50% of high school class. 65% from public high schools. Average SAT I Math 590, SAT I Math middle 50% range 540-640. Average SAT I Verbal 620, SAT I Verbal middle 50% range 560-670. TOEFL required of all international applicants, minimum TOEFL 550. **Basis for Candidate Selection:** *Very important factors considered include:* secondary school record. *Important factors considered include:* class rank, standardized test scores. *Other factors considered include:* alumni/ae relation, character/personal qualities, essays, extracurricular activities, interview, minority status, recommendations, talent/ability, volunteer work, work experience. **Freshman Admission Requirements:** High school diploma or equivalent is not required. *Academic units required/recommended:* 4 English recommended, 3 math recommended, 2 science recommended, 2 foreign language recommended, 2 social studies recommended, 2 history recommended, 3 elective recommended. **Freshman Admission Statistics:** 2,587 applied, 72% accepted, 21% of those accepted enrolled. **Transfer Admission Requirements:** *Items required:* high school transcript, college transcript, essay, statement of good standing from prior school. Lowest grade transferable C. **General Admission Information:** Application fee $40. Early decision application deadline December 1. Regular application deadline February 15. Nonfall registration accepted. Admission may be deferred for a maximum of 1 year. Credit and/or placement offered for CEEB Advanced Placement tests.

COSTS AND FINANCIAL AID

Tuition $25,800. Room & board $7,288. Required fees $546. Average book expense $956. **Required Forms and Deadlines:** FAFSA and CSS/Financial Aid PROFILE. Financial aid filing deadline February 15. **Notification of Awards:** Applicants will be notified of awards on or about March 31. **Types of Aid:** *Need-based scholarships/grants:* Pell, SEOG, state scholarships/grants, private scholarships, the school's own gift aid. *Loans:* FFEL Subsidized Stafford, FFEL Unsubsidized Stafford, FFEL PLUS, Federal Perkins, state loans. **Student Employment:** Federal Work-Study Program available. Institutional employment available. Off-campus job opportunities are excellent. **Financial Aid Statistics:** 48% undergrads receive some form of aid. Average freshman grant $13,986. Average freshman loan $3,490. Average income from on-campus job $1,080. **Financial Aid Phone:** 973-408-3112.

DREXEL UNIVERSITY

3141 Chestnut Street, Main 212, Philadelphia, PA 19104-2875
Phone: 215-895-2400 **E-mail:** admissions@drexel.edu **CEEB Code:** 2194
Fax: 215-895-5939 **Web:** www.drexel.edu **ACT Code:** 3556

This private school was founded in 1891. It has a 38-acre campus.

STUDENTS AND FACULTY

Enrollment: 11,584. **Student Body:** Male 61%, female 39%, out-of-state 36%, international 5%. **Ethnic Representation:** African American 10%, Asian 15%, Caucasian 63%, Hispanic 2%. **Retention and Graduation:** 82% freshmen return for sophomore year. 13% freshmen graduate within 4 years. 13% grads go on to further study within 1 year. 2% grads pursue business degrees. 2% grads pursue law degrees. 2% grads pursue medical degrees. **Faculty:** Student/faculty ratio 14:1. 683 full-time faculty. 100% faculty teach undergrads.

ACADEMICS

Degrees: Associate's, bachelor's, certificate, doctoral, first professional, master's, post-bachelor's certificate, post-master's certificate. **Academic Requirements:** General education including some course work in computer literacy, English (including composition), history, humanities, mathematics, sciences (biological or physical). **Classes:** 10-19 students in an average class. 20-29 students in an average lab/discussion section. **Majors with Highest Enrollment:** Computer science; electrical, electronics, and communications engineering; mechanical engineering. **Disciplines with Highest Percentage of Degrees Awarded:** Business/marketing 29%, engineering/engineering technology 23%, computer and information sciences 13%, health professions and related sciences 9%, visual and performing arts 8%. **Special Study Options:** Accelerated program, cooperative (work-study) program, distance learning, double major, English as a second language, honors program, independent study, internships, study abroad, teacher certification program. 3-3 programs in engineering with Lincoln University, Indiana University of Pennsylvania, Eastern Mennonite College.

FACILITIES

Housing: Coed, housing for disabled students, housing for international students, fraternities and/or sororities; freshmen required to live on campus unless living with parents. **Library Holdings:** 443,597 bound volumes. 1,461 periodicals. 212,500 microforms. 8,076 audiovisuals. **Special Academic Facilities/Equipment:** Art museum, theatre, audiovisual center, TV studio, recreational center, center for automation technology, engineering center. **Computers:** School-owned computers available for student use.

EXTRACURRICULARS

Activities: Choral groups, concert band, dance, drama/theater, jazz band, literary magazine, music ensembles, musical theater, pep band, radio station, student government, student newspaper, student-run film society, television station, yearbook. **Organizations:** 100 registered organizations, 19 honor societies, 10 religious organizations, 16 fraternities (12% men join), 6 sororities (8% women join). **Athletics (Intercollegiate):** *Men:* baseball, basketball, crew, diving, golf, lacrosse, soccer, swimming, tennis, wrestling. *Women:* basketball, crew, diving, field hockey, lacrosse, soccer, softball, swimming, tennis, volleyball.

ADMISSIONS

Selectivity Rating: 79 (of 100). **Freshman Academic Profile:** Average high school GPA 3.3. 23% in top 10% of high school class, 55% in top 25% of high school class, 88% in top 50% of high school class. 70% from public high schools.

Average SAT I Math 600, SAT I Math middle 50% range 550-660. Average SAT I Verbal 570, SAT I Verbal middle 50% range 520-620. TOEFL required of all international applicants, minimum TOEFL 550. **Basis for Candidate Selection:** *Very important factors considered include:* class rank, essays, secondary school record, standardized test scores. *Important factors considered include:* character/personal qualities, extracurricular activities, interview, recommendations, talent/ability. *Other factors considered include:* alumni/ae relation, minority status, volunteer work, work experience. **Freshman Admission Requirements:** High school diploma or GED is required. *Academic units required/recommended:* 3 math required, 1 science required, 1 science lab required, 1 foreign language recommended. **Freshman Admission Statistics:** 11,981 applied, 61% accepted, 29% of those accepted enrolled. **Transfer Admission Requirements:** *Items required:* college transcript. Minimum college GPA of 2.5 required. Lowest grade transferable C. **General Admission Information:** Application fee $75. Regular application deadline March 1. Nonfall registration accepted. Admission may be deferred for a maximum of 1 year. Credit and/or placement offered for CEEB Advanced Placement tests.

COSTS AND FINANCIAL AID

Tuition $17,393. Room & board $9,090. Required fees $1,020. Average book expense $650. **Required Forms and Deadlines:** FAFSA. Priority filing deadline February 15. **Notification of Awards:** Applicants will be notified of awards on a rolling basis beginning on or about April 1. **Types of Aid:** *Need-based scholarships/grants:* Pell, SEOG, state scholarships/grants, private scholarships, the school's own gift aid, United Negro College Fund. *Loans:* FFEL Subsidized Stafford, FFEL Unsubsidized Stafford, FFEL PLUS, Federal Perkins, college/university loans from institutional funds. **Student Employment:** Federal Work-Study Program available. Institutional employment available. Off-campus job opportunities are excellent. **Financial Aid Statistics:** 73% freshmen, 69% undergrads receive some form of aid. **Financial Aid Phone:** 215-895-2535.

DRURY UNIVERSITY

900 North Benton Avenue, Springfield, MO 65802
Phone: 417-873-7205 **E-mail:** druryad@drury.edu **CEEB Code:** 6169
Fax: 417-866-3873 **Web:** www.drury.edu **ACT Code:** 2292

This private school was founded in 1873. It has an 80-acre campus.

STUDENTS AND FACULTY

Enrollment: 1,494. **Student Body:** Male 44%, female 56%, out-of-state 20%, international 6% (36 countries represented). **Ethnic Representation:** African American 1%, Asian 1%, Caucasian 96%, Hispanic 1%, Native American 1%. **Retention and Graduation:** 83% freshmen return for sophomore year. 41% freshmen graduate within 4 years. 29% grads go on to further study within 1 year. 7% grads pursue business degrees. 5% grads pursue law degrees. 10% grads pursue medical degrees. **Faculty:** Student/faculty ratio 11:1. 116 full-time faculty, 92% hold PhDs. 100% faculty teach undergrads.

ACADEMICS

Degrees: Bachelor's, master's. **Academic Requirements:** General education including some course work in arts/fine arts, computer literacy, English (including composition), foreign languages, history, humanities, mathematics, philosophy, sciences (biological or physical), health and wellness. **Classes:** 10-19 students in an average class. 10-19 students in an average lab/discussion section. **Majors with Highest Enrollment:** Biology/biological sciences, general; business administration/management; education, general. **Disciplines with Highest Percentage of Degrees Awarded:** Business/marketing 18%, communications/communication technologies 13%, biological life sciences 12%, visual and performing arts 9%, social sciences and history 9%. **Special Study Options:** Accelerated program, cooperative (work-study) program, distance learning, double major, dual enrollment, English as a second language, honors program, independent study, internships, liberal arts/career combination, student-designed major, study abroad, teacher certification program, Biosphere 2; Drury Center in Volos, Greece.

FACILITIES

Housing: Coed, all-female, all-male, apartments for married students, apartments for single students, housing for disabled students, fraternities and/or sororities. **Library Holdings:** 177,794 bound volumes. 868 periodicals. 119,683 microforms. 60,098 audiovisuals. **Special Academic Facilities/Equipment:** New science center, greenhouse, TV studio, radio station, art gallery, teleconference facility, language lab, electronic music lab, laser lab. **Computers:** School-owned computers available for student use.

EXTRACURRICULARS

Activities: Choral groups, concert band, dance, drama/theater, jazz band, literary magazine, music ensembles, musical theater, opera, pep band, radio station, student government, student newspaper, student-run film society, symphony orchestra, television station, yearbook. **Organizations:** 60 registered organizations, 13 honor societies, 6 religious organizations, 4 fraternities (39% men join), 4 sororities (42% women join). **Athletics (Intercollegiate):** *Men:* basketball, cheerleading, cross-country, diving, golf, soccer, swimming, tennis. *Women:* basketball, cheerleading, cross-country, diving, golf, soccer, swimming, tennis, volleyball.

ADMISSIONS

Selectivity Rating: 78 (of 100). **Freshman Academic Profile:** Average high school GPA 3.6. 29% in top 10% of high school class, 63% in top 25% of high school class, 90% in top 50% of high school class. 83% from public high schools. Average SAT I Math 557, SAT I Math middle 50% range 490-610. Average SAT I Verbal 562, SAT I Verbal middle 50% range 490-610. Average ACT 25, ACT middle 50% range 22-28. TOEFL required of all international applicants, minimum TOEFL 550. **Basis for Candidate Selection:** *Very important factors considered include:* secondary school record, standardized test scores. *Important factors considered include:* character/personal qualities, class rank, essays, recommendations. *Other factors considered include:* alumni/ae relation, extracurricular activities, geographical residence, interview, minority status, talent/ability, volunteer work, work experience. **Freshman Admission Requirements:** High school diploma or GED is required. *Academic units required/recommended:* 12 total required; 12 total recommended; 4 English required, 4 English recommended, 3 math required, 4 math recommended, 3 science required, 3 science recommended, 2 foreign language required, 2 foreign language recommended, 3 social studies required, 3 social studies recommended. **Freshman Admission Statistics:** 1,078 applied, 83% accepted, 42% of those accepted enrolled. **Transfer Admission Requirements:** *Items required:* high school transcript, college transcript, essay. Minimum college GPA of 2.0 required. Lowest grade transferable C. **General Admission Information:** Application fee $25. Regular application deadline March 15. Nonfall registration accepted. Admission may be deferred for a maximum of 1 year. Credit and/or placement offered for CEEB Advanced Placement tests.

COSTS AND FINANCIAL AID

Tuition $12,995. Room & board $4,885. Required fees $219. Average book expense $1,000. **Required Forms and Deadlines:** FAFSA and institution's own financial aid form. No deadline for regular filing. Priority filing deadline March 15. **Notification of Awards:** Applicants will be notified of awards on a rolling basis beginning on or about March 30. **Types of Aid:** *Need-based scholarships/grants:* Pell, SEOG, state scholarships/grants, private scholarships, the school's own gift aid. *Loans:* FFEL Subsidized Stafford, FFEL Unsubsidized Stafford, FFEL PLUS, Federal Perkins. **Student Employment:** Federal Work-Study Program available. Institutional employment available. Off-campus job opportunities are excellent. **Financial Aid Statistics:** 80% freshmen, 91% undergrads receive some form of aid. Average freshman grant $6,045. Average freshman loan $2,625. Average income from on-campus job $2,000. **Financial Aid Phone:** 417-873-7319.

DUKE UNIVERSITY

2138 Campus Drive, Durham, NC 27708
Phone: 919-684-3214 **E-mail:** undergrad-admissions@duke.edu **CEEB Code:** 5156
Fax: 919-681-8941 **Web:** www.duke.edu **ACT Code:** 3088

This private school, which is affiliated with the Methodist Church, was founded in 1838. It has an 8,500-acre campus.

STUDENTS AND FACULTY

Enrollment: 6,071. **Student Body:** Male 52%, female 48%, out-of-state 85%, international 4%. **Ethnic Representation:** African American 11%, Asian 12%, Caucasian 64%, Hispanic 6%. **Retention and Graduation:** 96% freshmen return for sophomore year. 86% freshmen graduate within 4 years. 38% grads go on to further study within 1 year. 1% grads pursue business degrees. 11% grads pursue law degrees. 12% grads pursue medical degrees. **Faculty:** Student/faculty ratio 11:1. 901 full-time faculty, 90% hold PhDs.

ACADEMICS

Degrees: Bachelor's, certificate, doctoral, first professional, master's, post-bachelor's certificate. **Academic Requirements:** General education including some course work in English (including composition), foreign languages, sciences (biological or physical), social science, arts and literature, civilizations, social sciences, natural sciences, and mathematics. **Classes:** 10-19 students in an average class. 10-19 students in an average lab/discussion section. **Majors with Highest Enrollment:** Psychology, general; economics, general; biology/biological sciences, general. **Disciplines with Highest Percentage of Degrees Awarded:** Social sciences and history 31%, engineering/engineering technology 13%, biological life sciences 13%, protective services/public administration 10%, psychology 9%. **Special Study Options:** Accelerated program, cross registration, distance learning, double major, student exchange program (domestic), honors program, independent study, internships, student-designed major, study abroad, teacher certification program. Undergrads may take grad-level classes. Off-campus study: New York Arts Program. Other special programs: Semester and summer programs in ecology, geology, oceanography, physiology, and zoology at marine laboratory in Beaufort, North Carolina.

FACILITIES

Housing: Coed, all-female, all-male, apartments for single students, fraternities and/or sororities, theme houses. **Library Holdings:** 5,149,772 bound volumes. 28,274 periodicals. 3,938,458 microforms. 472,618 audiovisuals. **Special Academic Facilities/Equipment:** Art museum, language lab, university forest, primate center, phytotron, electron laser, nuclear magnetic resonance machine, nuclear lab.

EXTRACURRICULARS

Activities: Choral groups, concert band, dance, drama/theater, jazz band, literary magazine, marching band, music ensembles, musical theater, opera, pep band, radio station, student government, student newspaper, student-run film society, symphony orchestra, television station, yearbook. **Organizations:** 200 registered organizations, 10 honor societies, 25 religious organizations, 19 fraternities (29% men join), 12 sororities (42% women join). **Athletics (Intercollegiate):** *Men:* baseball, basketball, cross-country, diving, fencing, football, golf, indoor track, lacrosse, soccer, swimming, tennis, track & field, volleyball, wrestling. *Women:* basketball, crew, cross-country, diving, fencing, field hockey, golf, indoor track, lacrosse, soccer, swimming, tennis, track & field, volleyball.

ADMISSIONS

Selectivity Rating: 99 (of 100). **Freshman Academic Profile:** Average high school GPA 3.9. 86% in top 10% of high school class, 98% in top 25% of high school class, 100% in top 50% of high school class. 66% from public high schools. SAT I Math middle 50% range 670-760. SAT I Verbal middle 50% range 650-740. Average ACT 30, ACT middle 50% range 29-33. **Basis for Candidate Selection:** *Very important factors considered include:* recommendations, secondary school record, standardized test scores, talent/ability. *Important factors considered include:* character/personal qualities, class rank, essays, extracurricular activities. *Other factors considered include:* alumni/ae relation, interview, minority status, state residency, volunteer work, work experience. **Freshman Admission Requirements:** High school diploma is required and GED is not accepted. *Academic units required/recommended:* 20 total recommended; 4 English recommended, 3 math recommended, 3 science recommended, 3 foreign language recommended, 3 social studies recommended. **Freshman Admission Statistics:** 13,976 applied, 26% accepted, 44% of those accepted enrolled. **Transfer Admission Requirements:** *Items required:* high school transcript, college transcript, essay, standardized test scores. Lowest grade transferable C. **General Admission Information:** Application fee $65. Early decision application deadline November 1. Regular application deadline January 2. Admission may be deferred for a maximum of 1 year. Credit and/or placement offered for CEEB Advanced Placement tests.

COSTS AND FINANCIAL AID

Tuition $27,050. Room & board $7,921. Required fees $794. Average book expense $875. **Required Forms and Deadlines:** FAFSA, CSS/Financial Aid PROFILE, noncustodial (divorced/separated) parent's statement, business/farm supplement, and parent and student income tax returns. Financial aid filing deadline February 1. **Notification of Awards:** Applicants will be notified of awards on or about April 1. **Types of Aid:** *Need-based scholarships/grants:* Pell, SEOG, state scholarships/grants, private scholarships, the school's own gift aid, ROTC. *Loans:* FFEL Subsidized Stafford, FFEL Unsubsidized Stafford, FFEL PLUS, Federal Perkins, college/university loans from institutional funds, private loans. **Student Employment:** Federal Work-Study Program available. Institutional employment available. Off-campus job opportunities are good. **Financial Aid Statistics:** 39% freshmen, 36% undergrads receive some form of aid. Average freshman grant $7,190. Average freshman loan $3,522. Average income from on-campus job $1,400. **Financial Aid Phone:** 919-684-6225.

DUQUESNE UNIVERSITY

600 Forbes Avenue, Pittsburgh, PA 15282
Phone: 412-396-5000 **E-mail:** admissions@duq.edu **CEEB Code:** 2196
Fax: 412-396-5644 **Web:** www.duq.edu **ACT Code:** 3560

This private school, which is affiliated with the Roman Catholic Church, was founded in 1878. It has a 43-acre campus.

STUDENTS AND FACULTY

Enrollment: 5,404. **Student Body:** Male 42%, female 58%, out-of-state 18%, international 3% (83 countries represented). **Ethnic Representation:** African American 4%, Asian 1%, Caucasian 84%, Hispanic 2%. **Retention and Graduation:** 85% freshmen return for sophomore year. 25% grads go on to further study within 1 year. 38% grads pursue business degrees. 10% grads pursue law degrees. 5% grads pursue medical degrees. **Faculty:** Student/faculty ratio 14:1. 410 full-time faculty.

ACADEMICS

Degrees: Bachelor's, doctoral, first professional, master's, post-bachelor's certificate, post-master's certificate. **Academic Requirements:** General education including some course work in arts/fine arts, computer literacy, English (including composition), foreign languages, history, humanities, mathematics, philosophy, sciences (biological or physical), social science, theology. **Classes:** 20-29 students in an average class. 20-29 students in an average lab/discussion section. **Majors with Highest Enrollment:** Marketing/marketing management, general; information technology; psychology, general. **Disciplines with Highest Percentage of Degrees Awarded:** Business/marketing 30%, health professions and related sciences 16%, education 13%, liberal arts/general studies 8%, communications/communication technologies 7%. **Special Study Options:** Accelerated program, cross registration, distance learning, double major, dual enrollment, English as a second language, student exchange program (domestic), honors program, independent study, internships, liberal arts/career combination, student-designed major, study abroad, teacher certification program, weekend college.

FACILITIES

Housing: Coed, housing for disabled students, single-sex wings, sorority and fraternity wings. **Library Holdings:** 333,603 bound volumes. 5,359 periodicals. 421,026 microforms. 31,966 audiovisuals. **Special Academic Facilities/Equipment:** Center for study in existential phenomenological psychology, electron microscope, Kurzweil 250 digital keyboard, music career center, and family institute. **Computers:** School-owned computers available for student use.

EXTRACURRICULARS

Activities: Choral groups, concert band, dance, drama/theater, jazz band, literary magazine, marching band, music ensembles, musical theater, opera, pep band, radio station, student government, student newspaper, symphony orchestra, television station, yearbook. **Organizations:** 134 registered organizations, 22 honor societies, 6 religious organizations, 8 fraternities (14% men join), 8 sororities (14% women join). **Athletics (Intercollegiate):** *Men:* baseball, basketball, cross-country, football, golf, rifle, soccer, swimming, tennis, track & field, wrestling. *Women:* basketball, crew, cross-country, indoor track, lacrosse, rifle, soccer, swimming, tennis, track & field, volleyball.

ADMISSIONS

Selectivity Rating: 76 (of 100). **Freshman Academic Profile:** Average high school GPA 3.4. 22% in top 10% of high school class, 43% in top 25% of high school class, 71% in top 50% of high school class. 79% from public high schools. Average SAT I Math 540, SAT I Math middle 50% range 490-590. Average SAT I Verbal 539, SAT I Verbal middle 50% range 490-590. Average ACT 24, ACT middle 50% range 23-25. **Basis for Candidate Selection:** *Very important factors considered include:* secondary school record. *Important factors considered include:* character/personal qualities, essays, extracurricular activities, recommendations, standardized test scores, talent/ability. *Other factors considered include:* alumni/ae relation, class rank, interview, volunteer work, work experience. **Freshman Admission Requirements:** High school diploma or GED is required. *Academic units required/recommended:* 16 total recommended; 4 English recommended, 2 math recommended, 2 science recommended, 2 foreign language recommended, 2 social studies recommended. **Freshman Admission Statistics:** 3,139 applied, 96% accepted, 39% of those accepted enrolled. **Transfer Admission Requirements:** *Items required:* high school transcript, college transcript, statement of good standing from prior school. Minimum college GPA of 2.5 required. Lowest grade transferable C. **General Admission Information:** Application fee $50. Priority application deadline November 1. Early decision application deadline

November 1. Regular application deadline July 1. Nonfall registration accepted. Admission may be deferred for a maximum of 1 year. Credit and/or placement offered for CEEB Advanced Placement tests.

COSTS AND FINANCIAL AID

Tuition $16,049. Room & board $6,764. Required fees $1,429. Average book expense $550. **Required Forms and Deadlines:** FAFSA and institution's own financial aid form. Financial aid filing deadline May 1. **Notification of Awards:** Applicants will be notified of awards on a rolling basis beginning on or about March 15. **Types of Aid:** *Need-based scholarships/grants:* Pell, SEOG, state scholarships/grants, private scholarships, the school's own gift aid. *Loans:* FFEL Subsidized Stafford, FFEL Unsubsidized Stafford, FFEL PLUS, Federal Perkins, Federal Nursing, college/university loans from institutional funds, health profession loans. **Student Employment:** Federal Work-Study Program available. Institutional employment available. Off-campus job opportunities are excellent. **Financial Aid Statistics:** 66% freshmen, 62% undergrads receive some form of aid. Average freshman grant $7,629. Average freshman loan $2,449. **Financial Aid Phone:** 412-396-6607.

D'YOUVILLE COLLEGE

One D'Youville Square, 320 Porter Avenue, Buffalo, NY 14201
Phone: 716-881-7600 **E-mail:** admiss@dyc.edu **CEEB Code:** 2197
Fax: 716-881-7790 **Web:** www.dyc.edu **ACT Code:** 2732

This private school was founded in 1908. It has a 7-acre campus.

STUDENTS AND FACULTY

Enrollment: 908. **Student Body:** Male 27%, female 73%, out-of-state 6%, international 13% (55 countries represented). **Ethnic Representation:** African American 17%, Asian 2%, Caucasian 70%, Hispanic 6%, Native American 2%. **Retention and Graduation:** 72% freshmen return for sophomore year. 8% freshmen graduate within 4 years. **Faculty:** Student/faculty ratio 14:1. 105 full-time faculty, 60% hold PhDs.

ACADEMICS

Degrees: Bachelor's, doctoral, master's, post-bachelor's certificate, post-master's certificate. **Academic Requirements:** General education including some course work in arts/fine arts, computer literacy, English (including composition), foreign languages, history, humanities, mathematics, philosophy, sciences (biological or physical), social science. **Classes:** 10-19 students in an average class. 10-19 students in an average lab/discussion section. **Majors with Highest Enrollment:** Nursing/registered nurse training (RN, ASN, BSN, MSN); education, general; physician assistant. **Disciplines with Highest Percentage of Degrees Awarded:** Health professions and related sciences 70%, business/marketing 7%, home economics and vocational home economics 7%, education 6%, biological life sciences 2%. **Special Study Options:** Cross registration, distance learning, double major, dual enrollment, student exchange program (domestic), independent study, internships, study abroad, teacher certification program, weekend college.

FACILITIES

Housing: Coed, housing for disabled students. **Library Holdings:** 95,995 bound volumes. 1,235 periodicals. 181,884 microforms. 3,280 audiovisuals. **Special Academic Facilities/Equipment:** Kavinoky Theatre (professional theatre). **Computers:** School-owned computers available for student use.

EXTRACURRICULARS

Activities: Choral groups, drama/theater, student government, student newspaper, yearbook. **Organizations:** 25 registered organizations, 1 honor society, 1 religious organization. **Athletics (Intercollegiate):** *Men:* baseball, basketball, golf, soccer, volleyball. *Women:* basketball, golf, soccer, softball, volleyball.

ADMISSIONS

Selectivity Rating: 76 (of 100). **Freshman Academic Profile:** Average high school GPA 2.9. 10% in top 10% of high school class, 41% in top 25% of high school class, 80% in top 50% of high school class. Average SAT I Math 488, SAT I Math middle 50% range 420-520. Average SAT I Verbal 475, SAT I Verbal middle 50% range 430-520. Average ACT 23, ACT middle 50% range 21-25. TOEFL required of all international applicants, minimum TOEFL 500. **Basis for Candidate Selection:** *Very important factors considered include:* secondary school record, standardized test scores. *Important factors considered include:* class rank. *Other factors considered include:* alumni/ae relation, character/personal qualities, extracurricular activities, interview, recommendations, talent/ability, volunteer work, work experience. **Freshman Admission Requirements:** High school diploma or GED is required. *Academic units required/recommended:* 16 total recommended; 4 English recommended, 3 math recommended, 3 science recommended, 3 foreign language recommended, 3 social studies recommended. **Freshman Admission Statistics:** 820 applied, 89% accepted, 18% of those accepted enrolled. **Transfer Admission Requirements:** *Items required:* college transcript. Minimum college GPA of 2.0 required. Lowest grade transferable C. **General Admission Information:** Application fee $25. Nonfall registration accepted. Admission may be deferred for a maximum of 1 year. Credit offered for CEEB Advanced Placement tests.

COSTS AND FINANCIAL AID

Average book expense $680. **Required Forms and Deadlines:** FAFSA, institution's own financial aid form and state aid form. No deadline for regular filing. Priority filing deadline March 1. **Notification of Awards:** Applicants will be notified of awards on a rolling basis beginning on or about April 15. **Types of Aid:** *Need-based scholarships/grants:* Pell, SEOG, state scholarships/grants, private scholarships, the school's own gift aid, Federal Nursing. *Loans:* FFEL Subsidized Stafford, FFEL Unsubsidized Stafford, FFEL PLUS, Federal Perkins, Federal Nursing, college/university loans from institutional funds. **Student Employment:** Federal Work-Study Program available. Institutional employment available. Off-campus job opportunities are good. **Financial Aid Statistics:** 65% freshmen, 75% undergrads receive some form of aid. Average freshman grant $4,500. Average freshman loan $3,500. Average income from on-campus job $2,000. **Financial Aid Phone:** 716-881-7691.

See page 1016.

EARLHAM COLLEGE

Earlham College Admissions, Drawer #192, Richmond, IN 47374
Phone: 765-983-1600 **E-mail:** admission@earlham.edu **CEEB Code:** 1195
Fax: 765-983-1560 **Web:** www.earlham.edu **ACT Code:** 1186

This private school, which is affiliated with the Quaker Church, was founded in 1847. It has an 800-acre campus.

STUDENTS AND FACULTY

Enrollment: 1,080. **Student Body:** Male 44%, female 56%, out-of-state 68%, international 5% (35 countries represented). **Ethnic Representation:** African American 9%, Asian 3%, Caucasian 83%, Hispanic 3%. **Retention and Graduation:** 85% freshmen return for sophomore year. 62% freshmen graduate within 4 years. 20% grads go on to further study within 1 year. 6% grads pursue business degrees. 10% grads pursue law degrees. 20% grads pursue medical degrees. **Faculty:** Student/faculty ratio 11:1. 92 full-time faculty, 97% hold PhDs. 100% faculty teach undergrads.

ACADEMICS

Degrees: Bachelor's, first professional, master's. **Academic Requirements:** General education including some course work in arts/fine arts, computer literacy, English (including composition), foreign languages, history, humanities, mathematics, philosophy, sciences (biological or physical), social science, other: multicultural and intercultural perspectives; athletics, wellness, and physical education. Computer literacy and mathematics are core components of natural science requirement. **Classes:** 10-19 students in an average class. 20-29 students in an average lab/discussion section. **Majors with Highest Enrollment:** History, general; biology/biological sciences, general; psychology, general. **Disciplines with Highest Percentage of Degrees Awarded:** Social sciences and history 14%, interdisciplinary studies 12%, biological life sciences 11%, visual and performing arts 10%, psychology 9%. **Special Study Options:** Accelerated program, cross registration, double major, English as a second language, independent study, internships, student-designed major, study abroad, teacher certification program.

FACILITIES

Housing: Coed, housing for disabled students, cooperative housing, single-sex halls in some coed dorms. **Library Holdings:** 392,100 bound volumes. 1,660 periodicals. 235,400 microforms. 52,997 audiovisuals. **Special Academic Facilities/Equipment:** Living history and natural history museums, cultural centers, language labs, greenhouse, observatory, planetarium. **Computers:** School-owned computers available for student use.

EXTRACURRICULARS

Activities: Choral groups, dance, drama/theater, jazz band, literary magazine, music ensembles, musical theater, radio station, student government, student newspaper, student-run film society, symphony orchestra, yearbook. **Organizations:** 68 registered organizations, 1 honor society, 9 religious organizations. **Athletics (Intercollegiate):** *Men:* baseball, basketball, cross-country, football, soccer, tennis, track & field. *Women:* basketball, cross-country, field hockey, lacrosse, soccer, tennis, track & field, volleyball.

ADMISSIONS

Selectivity Rating: 80 (of 100). **Freshman Academic Profile:** Average high school GPA 3.4. 28% in top 10% of high school class, 56% in top 25% of high school class, 84% in top 50% of high school class. 65% from public high schools. Average SAT I Math 590, SAT I Math middle 50% range 530-650. Average SAT I Verbal 620, SAT I Verbal middle 50% range 550-690. Average ACT 26, ACT middle 50% range 23-29. TOEFL required of all international applicants, minimum TOEFL 550. **Basis for Candidate Selection:** *Very important factors considered include:* character/personal qualities, essays, minority status, recommendations, secondary school record. *Important factors considered include:* extracurricular activities, interview, standardized test scores, talent/ability, volunteer work. *Other factors considered include:* alumni/ae relation, class rank, geographical residence, religious affiliation/commitment, state residency, work experience. **Freshman Admission Requirements:** High school diploma or GED is required. *Academic units required/recommended:* 15 total required; 24 total recommended; 4 English required, 4 English recommended, 3 math required, 4 math recommended, 2 science required, 3 science recommended, 2 foreign language required, 3 foreign language recommended, 1 social studies required, 1 social studies recommended, 1 history required, 1 history recommended, 2 elective required, 8 elective recommended. **Freshman Admission Statistics:** 1,269 applied, 78% accepted, 29% of those accepted enrolled. **Transfer Admission Requirements:** *Items required:* high school transcript, college transcript, essay, standardized test scores, statement of good standing from prior school. Minimum high school GPA of 3.0 required. Minimum college GPA of 2.3 required. Lowest grade transferable C. **General Admission Information:** Application fee $30. Early decision application deadline December 1. Regular application deadline February 15. Nonfall registration accepted. Admission may be deferred for a maximum of 1 year. Credit offered for CEEB Advanced Placement tests.

COSTS AND FINANCIAL AID

Tuition $22,800. Room & board $5,138. Required fees $608. Average book expense $550. **Required Forms and Deadlines:** FAFSA and institution's own financial aid form. Priority filing deadline March 1. **Notification of Awards:** Applicants will be notified of awards on a rolling basis beginning on or about March 30. **Types of Aid:** *Need-based scholarships/grants:* Pell, SEOG, state scholarships/grants, private scholarships, the school's own gift aid. *Loans:* Direct Subsidized Stafford, Direct Unsubsidized Stafford, Direct PLUS, Federal Perkins, college/university loans from institutional funds. **Student Employment:** Federal Work-Study Program available. Institutional employment available. Off-campus job opportunities are good. **Financial Aid Statistics:** 65% freshmen, 65% undergrads receive some form of aid. Average freshman grant $12,651. Average freshman loan $3,168. Average income from on-campus job $812. **Financial Aid Phone:** 765-983-1217.

See page 1018.

EAST CAROLINA UNIVERSITY

Office of Undergraduate Admissions, 106 Whichard Building, Greenville, NC 27858-4353
Phone: 252-328-6640 **E-mail:** admis@mail.ecu.edu **CEEB Code:** 5180
Fax: 252-328-6945 **Web:** www.ecu.edu **ACT Code:** 3094

This public school was founded in 1907. It has a 1,000-acre campus.

STUDENTS AND FACULTY

Enrollment: 16,225. **Student Body:** Male 42%, female 58%, out-of-state 15%, international students represent 50 countries. **Ethnic Representation:** African American 14%, Asian 2%, Caucasian 80%, Hispanic 2%, Native American 1%. **Retention and Graduation:** 77% freshmen return for sophomore year. 26% freshmen graduate within 4 years. **Faculty:** Student/faculty ratio 18:1. 952 full-time faculty, 68% hold PhDs. 86% faculty teach undergrads.

ACADEMICS

Degrees: Bachelor's, doctoral, first professional, master's, post-master's certificate. **Academic Requirements:** General education including some course work in arts/fine arts, English (including composition), humanities, mathematics, sciences (biological or physical), social science, health and exercise & sport science. **Classes:** 20-29 students in an average class. 10-19 students in an average lab/discussion section. **Majors with Highest Enrollment:** Elementary education and teaching; engineering-related technologies/technicians; fine/studio arts, general. **Disciplines with Highest Percentage of Degrees Awarded:** Business/marketing 19%, health professions and related sciences 15%, education 14%, communications/communication technologies 8%, social sciences and history 7%. **Special Study Options:** Accelerated program, cooperative (work-study) program, distance learning, double major, dual enrollment, student exchange program (domestic), honors program, independent study, internships, student-designed major, study abroad, teacher certification program.

FACILITIES

Housing: Coed, all-female, all-male, fraternities and/or sororities, first-year students floor, leadership hall, extended quiet-study-hours floor, substance-free hall, nonsmoking floor, academic-year residence halls. **Library Holdings:** 1,294,045 bound volumes. 4,453 periodicals. 1,940,208 microforms. 27,816 audiovisuals. **Special Academic Facilities/Equipment:** Wellington B. Gray Gallery, Museum Without Walls, Ledonia Wright Cultural Center, A.J. Fletcher Recital Hall, Hendrix Theatre, Jenkins Fine Arts Center, McGinnis Theatre, and Mendenhall Student Center. **Computers:** School-owned computers available for student use.

EXTRACURRICULARS

Activities: Choral groups, concert band, dance, drama/theater, jazz band, literary magazine, marching band, music ensembles, musical theater, opera, pep band, radio station, student government, student newspaper, student-run film society, symphony orchestra. **Organizations:** 237 registered organizations, 15 honor societies, 24 religious organizations, 15 fraternities (10% men join), 13 sororities (7% women join). **Athletics (Intercollegiate):** *Men:* baseball, basketball, cross-country, diving, football, golf, soccer, swimming, tennis, track & field. *Women:* basketball, cross-country, diving, golf, soccer, softball, swimming, tennis, track & field, volleyball.

ADMISSIONS

Selectivity Rating: 66 (of 100). **Freshman Academic Profile:** Average high school GPA 3.3. 13% in top 10% of high school class, 40% in top 25% of high school class, 83% in top 50% of high school class. 90% from public high schools. Average SAT I Math 524, SAT I Math middle 50% range 480-570. Average SAT I Verbal 512, SAT I Verbal middle 50% range 470-550. Average ACT 21, ACT middle 50% range 18-23. TOEFL required of all international applicants, minimum TOEFL 550. **Basis for Candidate Selection:** *Very important factors considered include:* class rank, secondary school record, standardized test scores. *Other factors considered include:* alumni/ae relation, character/personal qualities, extracurricular activities, geographical residence, recommendations, state residency, talent/ability. **Freshman Admission Requirements:** High school diploma or GED is required. *Academic units required/recommended:* 20 total required; 4 English required, 3 math required, 3 science required, 1 science lab required, 2 foreign language recommended, 2 social studies required. **Freshman Admission Statistics:** 11,333 applied, 77% accepted, 41% of those accepted enrolled. **Transfer Admission Requirements:** *Items required:* high school transcript, college transcript. Minimum college GPA of 2.0 required. Lowest grade transferable C. **General Admission Information:** Application fee $45. Regular application deadline March 15. Nonfall registration accepted. Admission may be deferred. Credit and/or placement offered for CEEB Advanced Placement tests.

COSTS AND FINANCIAL AID

In-state tuition $1,819. Out-of-state tuition $11,475. Room & board $5,090. Required fees $1,161. Average book expense $750. **Required Forms and Deadlines:** FAFSA. No deadline for regular filing. Priority filing deadline April 15. **Notification of Awards:** Applicants will be notified of awards on a rolling basis beginning on or about March 15. **Types of Aid:** *Need-based scholarships/grants:* Pell, SEOG, state scholarships/grants, private scholarships, the school's own gift aid. *Loans:* FFEL Subsidized Stafford, FFEL Unsubsidized Stafford, FFEL PLUS, Federal Perkins, Federal Nursing. **Student Employment:** Federal Work-Study Program available. Institutional employment available. Off-campus job opportunities are good. **Financial Aid Statistics:** 38% freshmen, 32% undergrads receive some form of aid. **Financial Aid Phone:** 252-328-6610.

EAST CENTRAL UNIVERSITY

Office of Admissions, Ada, OK 74820-6899
Phone: 580-332-8000 **E-mail:** tesarry@mailclerk.ecok.edu **CEEB Code:** 6186
Fax: 580-436-5495 **Web:** www.ecok.edu **ACT Code:** 3394

This public school was founded in 1909. It has a 130-acre campus.

STUDENTS AND FACULTY

Enrollment: 3,786. **Student Body:** Out-of-state 3%, international 1%. **Ethnic Representation:** African American 3%, Caucasian 88%, Hispanic 1%, Native American 8%. **Retention and Graduation:** 62% freshmen return for sophomore year. 12% grads go on to further study within 1 year. 1% grads pursue law degrees. 1% grads pursue medical degrees.

ACADEMICS

Degrees: Associate's, master's. **Special Study Options:** Student exchange program (domestic). Undergrads may take grad-level classes.

FACILITIES

Housing: Coed, all-female, all-male, apartments for married students, apartments for single students, fraternities and/or sororities. **Library Holdings:** 203,301 bound volumes. 1,300 periodicals. 293,094 microforms. **Computers:** *Recommended operating system:* Mac.

EXTRACURRICULARS

Organizations: 8 religious organizations, 4 fraternities (9% men join), 3 sororities (10% women join). **Athletics (Intercollegiate):** *Men:* baseball, basketball, cheerleading, cross-country, football, golf, softball, tennis, track & field. *Women:* basketball, cheerleading, cross-country, softball, tennis.

ADMISSIONS

Selectivity Rating: 66 (of 100). **Freshman Academic Profile:** 15% in top 10% of high school class, 41% in top 25% of high school class, 77% in top 50% of high school class. 99% from public high schools. Average ACT 21. TOEFL required of all international applicants, minimum TOEFL 500. **Freshman Admission Requirements:** High school diploma is required and GED is not accepted. *Academic units required/recommended:* 4 English required, 3 math required, 2 science required, 2 history required. **Transfer Admission Requirements:** Minimum college GPA of 2.0 required. Lowest grade transferable D. **General Admission Information:** Early decision application deadline May 1. Regular application deadline August 21. Nonfall registration accepted.

COSTS AND FINANCIAL AID

In-state tuition $1,106. Out-of-state tuition $3,323. Room & board $2,200. Required fees $28. Average book expense $400. **Required Forms and Deadlines:** FAFSA and institution's own financial aid form. **Types of Aid:** *Need-based scholarships/grants:* Pell, SEOG, state scholarships/grants, private scholarships, the school's own gift aid. *Loans:* FFEL Subsidized Stafford, FFEL Unsubsidized Stafford, FFEL PLUS, Federal Perkins, college/university loans from institutional funds. **Student Employment:** Federal Work-Study Program available. Institutional employment available. Off-campus job opportunities are good. **Financial Aid Statistics:** Average income from on-campus job $3,200. **Financial Aid Phone:** 580-332-8000.

EAST STROUDSBURG UNIVERSITY OF PENNSYLVANIA

200 Prospect Street, East Stroudsburg, PA 18301-2999
Phone: 570-422-3542 **E-mail:** undergrads@po-box.esu.edu **CEEB Code:** 2650
Fax: 570-422-3933 **Web:** www.esu.edu **ACT Code:** 3700

This public school was founded in 1893. It has a 184-acre campus.

STUDENTS AND FACULTY

Enrollment: 5,150. **Student Body:** Male 43%, female 57%, out-of-state 19%, international 1%. **Ethnic Representation:** African American 4%, Asian 1%, Caucasian 91%, Hispanic 3%. **Retention and Graduation:** 73% freshmen return for sophomore year. 23% freshmen graduate within 4 years. **Faculty:** Student/faculty ratio 19:1. 246 full-time faculty, 76% hold PhDs. 100% faculty teach undergrads.

ACADEMICS

Degrees: Associate's, bachelor's, master's. **Academic Requirements:** General education including some course work in arts/fine arts, English (including composition), humanities, mathematics, sciences (biological or physical), social science. **Classes:** 20-29 students in an average class. 10-19 students in an average lab/discussion section. **Disciplines with Highest Percentage of Degrees Awarded:** Education 29%, social sciences and history 13%, business/marketing 12%, biological life sciences 10%, parks and recreation 8%. **Special Study Options:** Accelerated program, distance learning, double major, dual enrollment, student exchange program (domestic), honors program, independent study, internships, student-designed major, study abroad, teacher certification program.

FACILITIES

Housing: Coed, all-female, all-male, apartments for single students, housing for international students, fraternities and/or sororities. **Library Holdings:** 449,107 bound volumes. 1,175 periodicals. 1,364,859 microforms. 12,289 audiovisuals. **Special Academic Facilities/Equipment:** Natural history museum, human performance lab, TV production studios, 52-acre student-owned/operated recreation area and wildlife sanctuary, observatory, electron microscopes. **Computers:** School-owned computers available for student use.

EXTRACURRICULARS

Activities: Choral groups, concert band, dance, drama/theater, jazz band, literary magazine, music ensembles, musical theater, pep band, radio station, student government, student newspaper, yearbook. **Organizations:** 100 registered organizations, 14 honor societies, 7 fraternities (4% men join), 7 sororities (5% women join). **Athletics (Intercollegiate):** *Men:* baseball, basketball, cross-country, football, indoor track, soccer, tennis, track & field, volleyball, wrestling. *Women:* basketball, cross-country, field hockey, indoor track, lacrosse, soccer, softball, swimming, tennis, track & field, volleyball.

ADMISSIONS

Selectivity Rating: 63 (of 100). **Freshman Academic Profile:** 4% in top 10% of high school class, 18% in top 25% of high school class, 56% in top 50% of high school class. 90% from public high schools. Average SAT I Math 440, SAT I Math middle 50% range 440-520. Average SAT I Verbal 430, SAT I Verbal middle 50% range 430-520. TOEFL required of all international applicants, minimum TOEFL 500. **Basis for Candidate Selection:** *Very important factors considered include:* secondary school record. *Important factors considered include:* class rank, standardized test scores. *Other factors considered include:* alumni/ae relation, character/personal qualities, essays, extracurricular activities, geographical residence, recommendations, state residency, talent/ability, volunteer work, work experience. **Freshman Admission Requirements:** High school diploma or GED is required. *Academic units required/recommended:* 4 English recommended, 4 math recommended, 3 science recommended, 2 science lab recommended, 2 foreign language recommended, 3 social studies recommended. **Freshman Admission Statistics:** 3,805 applied, 79% accepted, 38% of those accepted enrolled. **Transfer Admission Requirements:** *Items required:* high school transcript, college transcript. Minimum college GPA of 2.0 required. **General Admission Information:** Application fee $25. Priority application deadline March 1. Regular application deadline April 1. Nonfall registration accepted. Credit and/or placement offered for CEEB Advanced Placement tests.

COSTS AND FINANCIAL AID

In-state tuition $4,378. Out-of-state tuition $10,946. Room & board $4,290. Required fees $1,024. Average book expense $900. **Required Forms and Deadlines:** FAFSA. Financial aid filing deadline May 1. Priority filing deadline March 1. **Notification of Awards:** Applicants will be notified of awards on or about April 1. **Types of Aid:** *Need-based scholarships/grants:* Pell, SEOG, state scholarships/grants, private scholarships, the school's own gift aid. *Loans:* FFEL Subsidized Stafford, FFEL Unsubsidized Stafford, FFEL PLUS, Federal Perkins, alternative loans. **Student Employment:** Federal Work-Study Program available. Institutional employment available. Off-campus job opportunities are good. **Financial Aid Statistics:** 51% freshmen, 54% undergrads receive some form of aid. Average income from on-campus job $1,140. **Financial Aid Phone:** 570-422-3340.

EAST TENNESSEE STATE UNIVERSITY

Box 70731, Johnson City, TN 37614-0731
Phone: 423-439-4213 **E-mail:** go2etsu@mail.etsu.edu **CEEB Code:** 1198
Fax: 423-439-4630 **Web:** www.etsu.edu **ACT Code:** 3958

This public school was founded in 1911. It has a 366-acre campus.

STUDENTS AND FACULTY

Enrollment: 9,336. **Student Body:** Male 43%, female 57%, out-of-state 9%, international 1% (64 countries represented). **Ethnic Representation:** African American 4%, Asian 1%, Caucasian 92%, Hispanic 1%. **Retention and Graduation:** 66% freshmen return for sophomore year. 13% freshmen graduate within 4 years. **Faculty:** Student/faculty ratio 18:1. 464 full-time faculty, 69% hold PhDs.

ACADEMICS

Degrees: Associate's, bachelor's, doctoral, first professional, master's, post-bachelor's certificate, post-master's certificate, terminal. **Academic Requirements:** General education including some course work in arts/fine arts, computer literacy, English (including composition), history, humanities, mathematics, philosophy, sciences (biological or physical), social science. **Classes:** 20-29 students in an average class. 20-29 students in an average lab/discussion section. **Majors with Highest Enrollment:** Nursing/registered nurse training (RN, ASN, BSN, MSN); engineering technology, general; general studies. **Disciplines with Highest Percentage of Degrees Awarded:** Business/marketing 17%, health professions and related sciences 11%, engineering/engineering technology 8%, protective services/public administration 7%, home economics and vocational home economics 7%. **Special Study Options:** Accelerated program, cooperative (work-study) program, distance learning, double major, dual enrollment, student exchange program (domestic), honors program, independent study, internships, study abroad, teacher certification program.

FACILITIES

Housing: All-female, all-male, apartments for married students, apartments for single students, housing for disabled students, fraternities and/or sororities. **Library Holdings:** 1,120,171 bound volumes. 3,711 periodicals. 1,652,836 microforms. 20,265 audiovisuals. **Special Academic Facilities/Equipment:** Regional history museum, art gallery, archives of Appalachia, planetarium. **Computers:** School-owned computers available for student use.

EXTRACURRICULARS

Activities: Choral groups, concert band, drama/theater, jazz band, literary magazine, marching band, music ensembles, pep band, radio station, student government, student newspaper, television station. **Organizations:** 215 registered organizations, 19 honor societies, 13 religious organizations, 9 fraternities (5% men join), 6 sororities (5% women join). **Athletics (Intercollegiate):** *Men:* baseball, basketball, cheerleading, cross-country, football, golf, indoor track, tennis, track & field. *Women:* basketball, cheerleading, cross-country, golf, indoor track, soccer, softball, tennis, track & field, volleyball.

ADMISSIONS

Selectivity Rating: 70 (of 100). **Freshman Academic Profile:** Average high school GPA 3.2. 13% in top 10% of high school class, 32% in top 25% of high school class, 63% in top 50% of high school class. 90% from public high schools. Average SAT I Math 509, SAT I Math middle 50% range 440-570. Average SAT I Verbal 506, SAT I Verbal middle 50% range 450-560. Average ACT 22, ACT middle 50% range 19-24. TOEFL required of all international applicants, minimum TOEFL 500. **Basis for Candidate Selection:** *Very important factors considered include:* secondary school record, standardized test scores. *Important factors considered include:* character/personal qualities. *Other factors considered include:* minority status. **Freshman Admission Requirements:** High school diploma or GED is required. *Academic units required/recommended:* 14 total required; 16 total recommended; 4 English required, 3 math required, 4 math recommended, 2 science required, 3 science recommended, 1 science lab required, 2 foreign language required, 1 social studies required, 1 history required. **Freshman Admission Statistics:** 3,532 applied, 83% accepted, 52% of those accepted enrolled. **Transfer Admission Requirements:** *Items required:* college transcript. Minimum college GPA of 2.0 required. Lowest grade transferable D. **General Admission Information:** Application fee $15. Priority application deadline July 1. Nonfall registration accepted. Credit and/or placement offered for CEEB Advanced Placement tests.

COSTS AND FINANCIAL AID

In-state tuition $2,748. Out-of-state tuition $9,706. Room & board $4,390. Required fees $563. Average book expense $900. **Required Forms and Deadlines:** FAFSA. No deadline for regular filing. Priority filing deadline April 15. **Notification of Awards:** Applicants will be notified of awards on a rolling basis beginning on or about April 30. **Types of Aid:** *Need-based scholarships/grants:* Pell, SEOG, state scholarships/grants, private scholarships, the school's own gift aid, Federal Nursing. *Loans:* FFEL Subsidized Stafford, FFEL Unsubsidized Stafford, FFEL PLUS, Federal Perkins, state loans, college/university loans from institutional funds. **Student Employment:** Federal Work-Study Program available. Institutional employment available. Off-campus job opportunities are good. **Financial Aid Statistics:** 27% freshmen, 50% undergrads receive some form of aid. Average freshman grant $3,093. Average freshman loan $6,418. Average income from on-campus job $1,404. **Financial Aid Phone:** 423-439-4300.

EAST TEXAS BAPTIST UNIVERSITY

1209 North Grove, Marshall, TX 75670-1498
Phone: 903-923-2000 **E-mail:** admissions@etbu.edu **CEEB Code:** 6187
Fax: 903-923-2001 **Web:** www.etbu.edu **ACT Code:** 4086

This private school, which is affiliated with the Baptist Church, was founded in 1912. It has a 200-acre campus.

STUDENTS AND FACULTY

Enrollment: 1,496. **Student Body:** Male 46%, female 54%, out-of-state 10%, international 2% (18 countries represented). **Ethnic Representation:** African American 14%, Caucasian 81%, Hispanic 4%, Native American 1%. **Retention and Graduation:** 59% freshmen return for sophomore year. 21% freshmen graduate within 4 years. **Faculty:** Student/faculty ratio 15:1. 78 full-time faculty, 70% hold PhDs. 100% faculty teach undergrads.

ACADEMICS

Degrees: Associate's, bachelor's. **Academic Requirements:** General education including some course work in arts/fine arts, computer literacy, English (including composition), history, humanities, mathematics, sciences (biological or physical), social science, physical activity. **Classes:** 10-19 students in an average class. 10-19 students in an average lab/discussion section. **Majors with Highest Enrollment:** Elementary education and teaching; Christian studies; nursing/registered nurse training (RN, ASN, BSN, MSN). **Disciplines with Highest Percentage of Degrees Awarded:** Education 26%, philosophy/religion/theology 17%, business/marketing 16%, social sciences and history 9%, health professions and related sciences 9%. **Special Study Options:** Accelerated program, double major, dual enrollment, English as a second language, external degree program, honors program, independent study, internships, study abroad, teacher certification program.

FACILITIES

Housing: All-female, all-male, apartments for married students, apartments for single students, housing for disabled students, fraternities and/or sororities, Houses for families adjacent to campus. **Computers:** *Recommended operating system:* other. School-owned computers available for student use.

EXTRACURRICULARS

Activities: Choral groups, concert band, drama/theater, jazz band, literary magazine, marching band, music ensembles, musical theater, opera, student government, student newspaper, yearbook. **Organizations:** 35 registered organizations, 3 honor societies, 3 religious organizations, 2 fraternities (2% men join), 2 sororities (2% women join). **Athletics (Intercollegiate):** *Men:* baseball, basketball, cheerleading, cross-country, football, soccer. *Women:* basketball, cheerleading, cross-country, soccer, softball, volleyball.

ADMISSIONS

Selectivity Rating: 77 (of 100). **Freshman Academic Profile:** 15% in top 10% of high school class, 45% in top 25% of high school class, 81% in top 50% of high school class. 90% from public high schools. Average ACT 21, ACT middle 50% range 18-24. TOEFL required of all international applicants, minimum TOEFL 500. **Basis for Candidate Selection:** *Very important factors considered include:* class rank, essays, secondary school record, standardized test scores. *Other factors considered include:* character/personal qualities. **Freshman Admission Requirements:** High school diploma or GED is required. *Academic units required/recommended:* 22 total required; 4 English required, 3 math required, 2 science required, 2 social studies required, 1 elective required. **Freshman Admission Statistics:** 714 applied, 74% accepted, 65% of those accepted enrolled. **Transfer Admission Requirements:** *Items required:* college transcript, essay, statement of good standing from prior school. Minimum college GPA of 2.0 required. Lowest grade transferable D. **General Admission Information:** Application fee $25. Regular application deadline August 15. Nonfall registration accepted. Admission may be deferred for a maximum of 1 year. Credit and/or placement offered for CEEB Advanced Placement tests.

COSTS AND FINANCIAL AID

Required Forms and Deadlines: FAFSA and institution's own financial aid form. Priority filing deadline June 1. **Notification of Awards:** Applicants will be notified of awards on a rolling basis beginning on or about January 15. **Types of Aid:** *Need-based scholarships/grants:* Pell, SEOG, state scholarships/grants, the school's own gift aid. *Loans:* FFEL Subsidized Stafford, FFEL Unsubsidized Stafford, FFEL PLUS, Federal Perkins, state loans. **Student Employment:** Federal Work-Study Program available. Institutional employment available. Off-campus job opportunities are good. **Financial Aid Statistics:** 80% freshmen, 69% undergrads receive some form of aid. Average freshman grant $5,301. Average freshman loan $2,639. Average income from on-campus job $1,248. **Financial Aid Phone:** 903-923-2138.

EASTERN COLLEGE

1300 Eagle Road, St. Davids, PA 19087-3696
Phone: 610-341-5967 **E-mail:** ugadm@eastern.edu **CEEB Code:** 2220
Fax: 610-341-1723 **Web:** www.eastern.edu **ACT Code:** 3562

This private school, which is affiliated with the American Baptist Church, was founded in 1952. It has a 107-acre campus.

STUDENTS AND FACULTY

Enrollment: 2,039. **Student Body:** Male 34%, female 66%, out-of-state 52%, international 2% (21 countries represented). **Ethnic Representation:** African American 14%, Asian 1%, Caucasian 77%, Hispanic 4%. **Retention and Graduation:** 72% freshmen return for sophomore year. 39% freshmen graduate within 4 years. 19% grads go on to further study within 1 year. 4% grads pursue business degrees. 4% grads pursue law degrees. **Faculty:** Student/faculty ratio 15:1. 79 full-time faculty, 78% hold PhDs.

ACADEMICS

Degrees: Associate's, bachelor's, master's, transfer. **Academic Requirements:** General education including some course work in English (including composition), foreign languages, history, humanities, philosophy, sciences (biological or physical), social science, biblical and theological studies. **Disciplines with Highest Percentage of Degrees Awarded:** Business/marketing 49%, education 9%, communications/communication technologies 6%, health professions and related sciences 6%, philosophy/religion/theology 5%. **Special Study Options:** Accelerated program, cross registration, distance learning, double major, honors program, independent study, internships, liberal arts/career combination, student-designed major, study abroad, teacher certification program, American studies program (Washington, DC), Argonne science semester (Illinois), Au Sable Institute of Environmental Studies program (Michigan), and Oregon extension program.

FACILITIES

Housing: Coed, apartments for single students. **Library Holdings:** 155,000 bound volumes. 975 periodicals. 739,228 microforms. 14,074 audiovisuals. **Special Academic Facilities/Equipment:** Planetarium. **Computers:** *Recommended operating system:* Windows 95. School-owned computers available for student use.

EXTRACURRICULARS

Activities: Choral groups, concert band, dance, drama/theater, jazz band, literary magazine, music ensembles, musical theater, pep band, student government, student newspaper, yearbook. **Organizations:** 75 registered organizations, 10 honor societies, 20 religious organizations. **Athletics (Intercollegiate):** *Men:* baseball, basketball, lacrosse, soccer, tennis. *Women:* basketball, field hockey, lacrosse, soccer, softball, tennis, volleyball.

ADMISSIONS

Selectivity Rating: 76 (of 100). **Freshman Academic Profile:** Average high school GPA 3.3. 19% in top 10% of high school class, 47% in top 25% of high school class, 79% in top 50% of high school class. 75% from public high schools. Average SAT I Math 533, SAT I Math middle 50% range 480-590. Average SAT I Verbal 552, SAT I Verbal middle 50% range 490-610. Average ACT 25, ACT middle 50% range 21-27. TOEFL required of all international applicants, minimum TOEFL 500. **Basis for Candidate Selection:** *Very important factors considered include:* class rank, secondary school record. *Important factors considered include:* standardized test scores, talent/ability. *Other factors considered include:* alumni/ae relation, character/personal qualities, essays, extracurricular activities, geographical residence, interview, minority status, recommendations, religious affiliation/commitment, state residency, volunteer work, work experience. **Freshman Admission Requirements:** High school diploma or GED is required. *Academic units required/recommended:* 15 total required; 15 total recommended. **Freshman Admission Statistics:** 1,045 applied, 79% accepted, 49% of those accepted enrolled. **Transfer Admission Requirements:** *Items required:* high school transcript, college transcript, essay, statement of good standing from prior school. Minimum high school GPA of 2.0 required. Minimum college GPA of 2.0 required. Lowest grade transferable C. **General Admission Information:** Application fee $25. Nonfall registration accepted. Admission may be deferred for a maximum of 1 year. Credit and/or placement offered for CEEB Advanced Placement tests.

COSTS AND FINANCIAL AID

Tuition $15,150. Room & board $6,490. Required fees $40. Average book expense $700. **Required Forms and Deadlines:** No deadline for regular filing. **Notification of Awards:** Applicants will be notified of awards on a rolling basis. **Student Employment:** Federal Work-Study Program available. Institutional employment available. Off-campus job opportunities are good. **Financial Aid Statistics:** Average freshman loan $2,625. Average income from on-campus job $1,200. **Financial Aid Phone:** 610-341-5842.

EASTERN CONNECTICUT STATE UNIVERSITY

83 Windham Street, Willimantic, CT 06226
Phone: 860-465-5286 **E-mail:** admissions@easternct.edu **CEEB Code:** 3966
Fax: 860-465-5280 **Web:** www.easternct.edu

This public school was founded in 1889. It has a 179-acre campus.

STUDENTS AND FACULTY

Enrollment: 4,869. **Student Body:** Male 42%, female 58%, out-of-state 6%, international 2% (26 countries represented). **Ethnic Representation:** African American 7%, Asian 1%, Caucasian 85%, Hispanic 4%, Native American 1%. **Retention and Graduation:** 76% freshmen return for sophomore year. 18% freshmen graduate within 4 years. 29% grads go on to further study within 1 year. **Faculty:** Student/faculty ratio 17:1. 178 full-time faculty, 89% hold PhDs. 75% faculty teach undergrads.

ACADEMICS

Degrees: Associate's, bachelor's, master's. **Academic Requirements:** General education including some course work in computer literacy, English (including composition), foreign languages, humanities, mathematics, sciences (biological or physical), social science. **Classes:** 20-29 students in an average class. Under 10 students in an average lab/discussion section. **Disciplines with Highest Percentage of Degrees Awarded:** Psychology 19%, social sciences and history 15%, liberal arts/general studies 13%, business/marketing 11%, communications/communication technologies 8%. **Special Study Options:** Accelerated program, cooperative (work-study) program, cross registration, distance learning, double major, dual enrollment, student exchange program (domestic), honors program, independent study, internships, student-designed major, study abroad, teacher certification program, weekend college.

FACILITIES

Housing: Coed, all-female, apartments for single students. **Library Holdings:** 234,319 bound volumes. 2,068 periodicals. 60,373 microforms. 3,657 audiovisuals. **Special Academic Facilities/Equipment:** Art gallery, electron microscope, planetarium with teaching facilities, center for Connecticut studies, media center with TV studio.

EXTRACURRICULARS

Activities: Choral groups, concert band, dance, drama/theater, literary magazine, music ensembles, musical theater, radio station, student government, student newspaper, television station, yearbook. **Organizations:** 60 registered organizations, 10 honor societies. **Athletics (Intercollegiate):** *Men:* baseball, basketball, cross-country, lacrosse, soccer, track & field. *Women:* basketball, cross-country, lacrosse, soccer, softball, track & field, volleyball.

ADMISSIONS

Selectivity Rating: 63 (of 100). **Freshman Academic Profile:** 4% in top 10% of high school class, 24% in top 25% of high school class, 65% in top 50% of high school class. Average SAT I Math 506, SAT I Math middle 50% range 460-550. Average SAT I Verbal 511, SAT I Verbal middle 50% range 470-550. TOEFL required of all international applicants, minimum TOEFL 550. **Basis for Candidate Selection:** *Very important factors considered include:* class rank, standardized test scores. *Important factors considered include:* interview, recommendations, secondary school record. *Other factors considered include:* character/personal qualities, essays, extracurricular activities, geographical residence, state residency, talent/ability, volunteer work, work experience. **Freshman Admission Requirements:** High school diploma or GED is required. *Academic units required/recommended:* 4 English required, 3 math required, 2 science required, 1 science lab required, 2 foreign language required, 2 social studies required, 3 history required. **Freshman Admission Statistics:** 3,057 applied, 60% accepted, 45% of those accepted enrolled. **Transfer Admission Requirements:** *Items required:* high school transcript, college transcript. Minimum college GPA of 2.0 required. Lowest grade transferable C-. **General Admission Information:** Application fee $40. Regular application deadline May 1. Nonfall registration accepted. Admission may be deferred for a maximum of 1 year. Credit and/or placement offered for CEEB Advanced Placement tests.

COSTS AND FINANCIAL AID

In-state tuition $2,648. Out-of-state tuition $8,570. Required fees $2,773. **Required Forms and Deadlines:** FAFSA and institution's own financial aid form. Priority filing deadline March 15. **Notification of Awards:** Applicants will be notified of awards on a rolling basis beginning on or about February 15.

Types of Aid: *Need-based scholarships/grants:* Pell, SEOG. *Loans:* FFEL Subsidized Stafford, FFEL Unsubsidized Stafford, FFEL PLUS, Federal Perkins. **Student Employment:** Federal Work-Study Program available. Institutional employment available. Off-campus job opportunities are good. **Financial Aid Statistics:** 56% freshmen, 70% undergrads receive some form of aid. Average income from on-campus job $1,800. **Financial Aid Phone:** 860-465-5205.

EASTERN ILLINOIS UNIVERSITY

600 Lincoln Avenue, Charleston, IL 61920
Phone: 217-581-2223 **E-mail:** admissns@www.eiu.edu **CEEB Code:** 1199
Fax: 217-581-7060 **Web:** www.eiu.edu **ACT Code:** 1016

This public school was founded in 1895. It has a 320-acre campus.

STUDENTS AND FACULTY

Enrollment: 9,528. **Student Body:** Male 43%, female 57%, out-of-state 2%, international 1% (29 countries represented). **Ethnic Representation:** African American 7%, Asian 1%, Caucasian 87%, Hispanic 2%. **Retention and Graduation:** 31% freshmen graduate within 4 years. 1% grads pursue law degrees. **Faculty:** Student/faculty ratio 16:1. 585 full-time faculty, 73% hold PhDs. 99% faculty teach undergrads.

ACADEMICS

Degrees: Bachelor's, master's, post-bachelor's certificate, post-master's certificate. **Academic Requirements:** General education including some course work in arts/fine arts, English (including composition), foreign languages, humanities, sciences (biological or physical). **Classes:** 20-29 students in an average class. **Majors with Highest Enrollment:** Business administration/management; elementary education and teaching; English language and literature, general. **Disciplines with Highest Percentage of Degrees Awarded:** Education 19%, other 18%, business/marketing 15%, English 8%, social sciences and history 7%. **Special Study Options:** Double major, English as a second language, honors program, independent study, internships, study abroad, teacher certification program.

FACILITIES

Housing: Coed, all-female, all-male, apartments for married students, apartments for single students, housing for disabled students, housing for international students, fraternities and/or sororities. **Library Holdings:** 955,245 bound volumes. 3,510 periodicals. 1,282,865 microforms. 33,460 audiovisuals. **Special Academic Facilities/Equipment:** Arts center, electron microscope. **Computers:** School-owned computers available for student use.

EXTRACURRICULARS

Activities: Choral groups, concert band, dance, drama/theater, jazz band, literary magazine, marching band, music ensembles, musical theater, pep band, radio station, student government, student newspaper, symphony orchestra, television station, yearbook. **Organizations:** 155 registered organizations, 18 honor societies, 10 religious organizations, 13 fraternities (17% men join), 13 sororities (15% women join). **Athletics (Intercollegiate):** *Men:* baseball, basketball, cross-country, football, golf, soccer, swimming, tennis, track & field, wrestling. *Women:* basketball, cross-country, golf, rugby, soccer, softball, swimming, tennis, track & field, volleyball.

ADMISSIONS

Selectivity Rating: 72 (of 100). **Freshman Academic Profile:** 8% in top 10% of high school class, 27% in top 25% of high school class, 65% in top 50% of high school class. Average ACT 22, ACT middle 50% range 20-23. TOEFL required of all international applicants, minimum TOEFL 500. **Basis for Candidate Selection:** *Very important factors considered include:* class rank, standardized test scores. *Other factors considered include:* essays, recommendations. **Freshman Admission Requirements:** High school diploma or GED is required. *Academic units required/recommended:* 15 total required; 4 English required, 3 math required, 3 science required, 3 science lab required, 3 social studies required, 2 elective required. **Freshman Admission Statistics:** 7,544 applied, 78% accepted, 34% of those accepted enrolled. **Transfer Admission Requirements:** *Items required:* high school transcript, college transcript, standardized test scores. Minimum college GPA of 2.0 required. Lowest grade transferable D. **General Admission Information:** Application fee $30. Nonfall registration accepted. Credit offered for CEEB Advanced Placement tests.

COSTS AND FINANCIAL AID

Out-of-state tuition $9,761. Room & board $6,000. Required fees $1,394. Average book expense $120. **Required Forms and Deadlines:** FAFSA. No deadline for regular filing. Priority filing deadline April 15. **Notification of Awards:** Applicants will be notified of awards on a rolling basis beginning on or about May 1. **Types of Aid:** *Need-based scholarships/grants:* Pell, SEOG, state scholarships/grants, the school's own gift aid. *Loans:* Direct Subsidized Stafford, Direct Unsubsidized Stafford, Direct PLUS, Federal Perkins. **Student Employment:** Federal Work-Study Program available. Institutional employment available. Off-campus job opportunities are fair. **Financial Aid Statistics:** 47% freshmen, 50% undergrads receive some form of aid. Average income from on-campus job $1,500. **Financial Aid Phone:** 217-581-3713.

EASTERN KENTUCKY UNIVERSITY

Coates Box 2A, Richmond, KY 40475
Phone: 859-622-2106 **E-mail:** stephen.byrn@eku.edu **CEEB Code:** 1200
Fax: 606-622-8024 **Web:** www.eku.edu **ACT Code:** 1512

This public school was founded in 1906. It has a 628-acre campus.

STUDENTS AND FACULTY

Enrollment: 12,867. **Student Body:** Male 40%, female 60%, out-of-state 5%. **Ethnic Representation:** African American 4%, Asian 1%, Caucasian 89%, Hispanic 1%. **Retention and Graduation:** 65% freshmen return for sophomore year. 9% freshmen graduate within 4 years. 24% grads go on to further study within 1 year. **Faculty:** Student/faculty ratio 16:1.

ACADEMICS

Degrees: Associate's, bachelor's, certificate, master's, post-bachelor's certificate, post-master's certificate. **Academic Requirements:** General education including some course work in arts/fine arts, computer literacy, English (including composition), foreign languages, history, humanities, mathematics, sciences (biological or physical), social science. **Classes:** Under 10 students in an average class. **Majors with Highest Enrollment:** Criminal justice/police science; nursing/registered nurse training (RN, ASN, BSN, MSN); elementary education and teaching. **Disciplines with Highest Percentage of Degrees Awarded:** Education 16%, protective services/public administration 15%, health professions and related sciences 15%, business/marketing 8%, social sciences and history 8%. **Special Study Options:** Cooperative (work-study) program, distance learning, double major, English as a second language, honors program, independent study, internships, teacher certification program.

FACILITIES

Housing: Coed, all-female, all-male, apartments for married students, apartments for single students, housing for disabled students, housing for international students, fraternities and/or sororities. **Library Holdings:** 768,300 bound volumes. 3,128 periodicals. 1,281,814 microforms. 13,580 audiovisuals. **Special Academic Facilities/Equipment:** Planetarium, model lab school. **Computers:** School-owned computers available for student use.

EXTRACURRICULARS

Activities: Choral groups, concert band, dance, drama/theater, jazz band, literary magazine, marching band, music ensembles, musical theater, opera, pep band, radio station, student government, student newspaper, symphony orchestra, television station, yearbook. **Organizations:** 147 registered organizations, 30 honor societies, 7 religious organizations, 11 fraternities (3% men join), 8 sororities (4% women join). **Athletics (Intercollegiate):** *Men:* baseball, basketball, cheerleading, cross-country, football, golf, tennis. *Women:* basketball, cheerleading, cross-country, golf, softball, tennis, volleyball.

ADMISSIONS

Selectivity Rating: 74 (of 100). **Freshman Academic Profile:** 92% from public high schools. Average ACT 19. TOEFL required of all international applicants, minimum TOEFL 500. **Basis for Candidate Selection:** *Very important factors considered include:* secondary school record, standardized test scores. *Important factors considered include:* class rank, state residency. *Other factors considered include:* alumni/ae relation, talent/ability. **Freshman Admission Requirements:** High school diploma or GED is required. *Academic units required/recommended:* 22 total required; 4 English required, 3 math required, 3 science required, 1 science lab required, 3 social studies required, 1 history required, 7 elective required. **Freshman Admission Statistics:** 5,003 applied, 79% accepted, 60% of those accepted enrolled. **Transfer Admission Requirements:** *Items required:* college transcript. Minimum high school GPA of 2.0 required. Minimum college GPA of 2.0 required. Lowest grade transferable D. **General Admission Information:** Application fee $25. Regular application deadline August 1. Nonfall registration accepted. Admission may be deferred. Credit and/or placement offered for CEEB Advanced Placement tests.

COSTS AND FINANCIAL AID

In-state tuition $2,928. Out-of-state tuition $8,040. Room & board $3,803. Required fees $0. Average book expense $800. **Required Forms and Deadlines:** FAFSA. Priority filing deadline April 15. **Notification of Awards:** Applicants will be notified of awards on a rolling basis beginning on or about April 15. **Types of Aid:** *Need-based scholarships/grants:* Pell, SEOG, state scholarships/grants, private scholarships, the school's own gift aid. *Loans:* FFEL Subsidized Stafford, FFEL Unsubsidized Stafford, FFEL PLUS, Federal Perkins, state loans, college/university loans from institutional funds. **Student Employment:** Federal Work-Study Program available. Institutional employment available. Off-campus job opportunities are good. **Financial Aid Statistics:** 54% freshmen, 53% undergrads receive some form of aid. Average income from on-campus job $1,800. **Financial Aid Phone:** 606-622-2361.

EASTERN MENNONITE UNIVERSITY

$$$

1200 Park Rd., Harrisonburg, VA 22802
Phone: 540-432-4118 **E-mail:** admiss@emu.edu **CEEB Code:** 5181
Fax: 540-432-4444 **Web:** www.emu.edu **ACT Code:** 3708

This private school, which is affiliated with the Mennonite Church, was founded in 1917. It has a 93-acre campus.

STUDENTS AND FACULTY

Enrollment: 996. **Student Body:** Male 40%, female 60%, out-of-state 57%, international 4% (20 countries represented). **Ethnic Representation:** African American 6%, Asian 2%, Caucasian 89%, Hispanic 1%. **Retention and Graduation:** 82% freshmen return for sophomore year. 47% freshmen graduate within 4 years. 10% grads go on to further study within 1 year. 1% grads pursue business degrees. 1% grads pursue law degrees. 4% grads pursue medical degrees. **Faculty:** Student/faculty ratio 14:1. 98 full-time faculty, 72% hold PhDs. 98% faculty teach undergrads.

ACADEMICS

Degrees: Associate's, bachelor's, certificate, first professional, master's, post-bachelor's certificate, terminal. **Academic Requirements:** General education including some course work in arts/fine arts, English (including composition), history, humanities, mathematics, sciences (biological or physical), social science, physical education, Bible, speech, cross-cultural understanding. **Classes:** 10-19 students in an average class. 10-19 students in an average lab/discussion section. **Majors with Highest Enrollment:** Nursing/registered nurse training (RN, ASN, BSN, MSN); business administration/management; biology/biological sciences, general. **Disciplines with Highest Percentage of Degrees Awarded:** Business/marketing 29%, health professions and related sciences 13%, education 10%, biological life sciences 9%, liberal arts/general studies 8%. **Special Study Options:** Distance learning, double major, dual enrollment, English as a second language, honors program, independent study, internships, liberal arts/career combination, study abroad, teacher certification program.

FACILITIES

Housing: Coed, all-female, all-male, apartments for married students, apartments for single students, intentional communities. **Library Holdings:** 156,268 bound volumes. 1,287 periodicals. 82,281 microforms. 3,002 audiovisuals. **Special Academic Facilities/Equipment:** Natural history museum, planetarium, observatory. **Computers:** School-owned computers available for student use.

EXTRACURRICULARS

Activities: Choral groups, dance, drama/theater, jazz band, literary magazine, music ensembles, musical theater, pep band, radio station, student government, student newspaper, symphony orchestra, yearbook. **Organizations:** 35 registered organizations, 2 honor societies, 3 religious organizations. **Athletics (Intercollegiate):** *Men:* baseball, basketball, cross-country, soccer, tennis, track & field, volleyball. *Women:* basketball, cross-country, field hockey, soccer, softball, tennis, track & field, volleyball.

ADMISSIONS

Selectivity Rating: 73 (of 100). **Freshman Academic Profile:** Average high school GPA 3.4. 64% from public high schools. Average SAT I Math 540, SAT I Math middle 50% range 470-620. Average SAT I Verbal 550, SAT I Verbal middle 50% range 480-610. Average ACT 22, ACT middle 50% range 19-27. TOEFL required of all international applicants, minimum TOEFL 550. **Basis for Candidate Selection:** *Very important factors considered include:* secondary school record, standardized test scores. *Important factors considered include:* recommendations, religious affiliation/commitment. *Other factors considered include:* character/personal qualities. **Freshman Admission Requirements:** High school diploma or GED is required. *Academic units required/recommended:* 21 total recommended; 4 English recommended, 3 math recommended, 3 science recommended, 3 science lab recommended, 2 foreign language recommended, 3 social studies recommended, 6 elective recommended. **Freshman Admission Statistics:** 676 applied, 77% accepted, 41% of those accepted enrolled. **Transfer Admission Requirements:** *Items required:* high school transcript, college transcript. Minimum college GPA of 2.0 required. Lowest grade transferable C-. **General Admission Information:** Application fee $25. Priority application deadline February 1. Regular application deadline August 1. Nonfall registration accepted. Admission may be deferred for a maximum of 2 years. Credit and/or placement offered for CEEB Advanced Placement tests.

COSTS AND FINANCIAL AID

Tuition $16,324. Room & board $5,350. Required fees $46. Average book expense $700. **Required Forms and Deadlines:** FAFSA and state aid form. Priority filing deadline March 15. **Notification of Awards:** Applicants will be notified of awards on a rolling basis beginning on or about March 1. **Types of Aid:** *Need-based scholarships/grants:* Pell, SEOG, state scholarships/grants, private scholarships, the school's own gift aid. *Loans:* FFEL Subsidized Stafford, FFEL Unsubsidized Stafford, FFEL PLUS, Federal Perkins, Federal Nursing, state loans. **Student Employment:** Federal Work-Study Program available. Institutional employment available. Off-campus job opportunities are excellent. **Financial Aid Statistics:** 78% freshmen, 68% undergrads receive some form of aid. Average freshman grant $9,720. Average freshman loan $5,060. Average income from on-campus job $2,150. **Financial Aid Phone:** 540-432-4137.

EASTERN MICHIGAN UNIVERSITY

Eastern Michigan University, 400 Pierce Hall, Ypsilanti, MI 48197
Phone: 734-487-3060 **E-mail:** admissions@emich.edu **CEEB Code:** 1201
Fax: 734-487-1484 **Web:** www.emich.edu **ACT Code:** 1990

This public school was founded in 1849. It has a 460-acre campus.

STUDENTS AND FACULTY

Enrollment: 18,757. **Student Body:** Male 39%, female 61%, out-of-state 7%, international 2% (74 countries represented). **Ethnic Representation:** African American 17%, Asian 2%, Caucasian 73%, Hispanic 2%, Native American 1%. **Retention and Graduation:** 70% freshmen return for sophomore year. 10% freshmen graduate within 4 years. **Faculty:** Student/faculty ratio 19:1. 759 full-time faculty, 75% hold PhDs. 100% faculty teach undergrads.

ACADEMICS

Degrees: Bachelor's, doctoral, master's, post-master's certificate. **Academic Requirements:** General education including some course work in arts/fine arts, computer literacy, English (including composition), history, humanities, mathematics, philosophy, sciences (biological or physical), social science, physical education, and health education. **Classes:** 20-29 students in an average class. 10-19 students in an average lab/discussion section. **Majors with Highest Enrollment:** Elementary education and teaching; multi/interdisciplinary studies; psychology, general. **Disciplines with Highest Percentage of Degrees Awarded:** Education 23%, business/marketing 20%, social sciences and history 10%, health professions and related sciences 7%, psychology 5%. **Special Study Options:** Accelerated program, cooperative (work-study) program, distance learning, double major, dual enrollment, English as a second language, honors program, independent study, internships, student-designed major, study abroad, teacher certification program, weekend college.

FACILITIES

Housing: Coed, all-female, apartments for married students, apartments for single students, housing for disabled students, housing for international students, house rental, 1 sorority house. **Library Holdings:** 658,648 bound volumes. 4,457 periodicals. 973,380 microforms. 11,524 audiovisuals. **Special Academic Facilities/Equipment:** Intermedia art gallery, paint research center, Sherzer Observatory, Bruce T. Halle Library, terrestial and aquatics ecology research facility, Coatings Research Institute, the new John W. Porter Building housing the College of Education, and the new Marshall Building housing the College of Health and Human Services. **Computers:** School-owned computers available for student use.

EXTRACURRICULARS

Activities: Choral groups, concert band, dance, drama/theater, jazz band, literary magazine, marching band, music ensembles, musical theater, pep band, radio station, student government, student newspaper, student-run film society, symphony orchestra, television station. **Organizations:** 134 registered organizations, 9 honor societies, 13 religious organizations, 13 fraternities (4% men join), 13 sororities (4% women join). **Athletics (Intercollegiate):** *Men:* baseball, basketball, cross-country, diving, football, golf, indoor track, swimming, track & field, wrestling. *Women:* basketball, crew, cross-country, diving, golf, gymnastics, indoor track, soccer, softball, swimming, tennis, track & field, volleyball.

ADMISSIONS

Selectivity Rating: 74 (of 100). **Freshman Academic Profile:** Average high school GPA 3.0. 12% in top 10% of high school class, 32% in top 25% of high school class, 63% in top 50% of high school class. 90% from public high schools. Average SAT I Math 516, SAT I Math middle 50% range 450-590. Average SAT I Verbal 509, SAT I Verbal middle 50% range 450-580. Average ACT 20, ACT middle 50% range 18-23. TOEFL required of all international applicants, minimum TOEFL 500. **Basis for Candidate Selection:** *Very important factors considered include:* secondary school record, standardized test scores. *Important factors considered include:* character/personal qualities. *Other factors considered include:* extracurricular activities, interview, recommendations, talent/ability, volunteer work. **Freshman Admission Requirements:** High school diploma or GED is required. *Academic units required/recommended:* 16 total recommended; 4 English recommended, 3 math recommended, 2 science recommended, 1 science lab recommended, 2 foreign language recommended, 2 social studies recommended, 1 history recommended. **Freshman Admission Statistics:** 8,947 applied, 75% accepted, 41% of those accepted enrolled. **Transfer Admission Requirements:** *Items required:* college transcript. Minimum college GPA of 2.0 required. Lowest grade transferable C. **General Admission Information:** Application fee $25. Priority application deadline February 15. Regular application deadline June 30. Nonfall registration accepted. Admission may be deferred for a maximum of 1 year. Credit and/or placement offered for CEEB Advanced Placement tests.

COSTS AND FINANCIAL AID

In-state tuition $4,047. Out-of-state tuition $12,780. Room & board $5,597. Required fees $980. Average book expense $900. **Required Forms and Deadlines:** FAFSA. No deadline for regular filing. Priority filing deadline March 15. **Notification of Awards:** Applicants will be notified of awards on a rolling basis beginning on or about March 2. **Types of Aid:** *Need-based scholarships/grants:* Pell, SEOG, state scholarships/grants, private scholarships, the school's own gift aid, Nursing Disadvantaged Student Grant. *Loans:* FFEL Subsidized Stafford, FFEL Unsubsidized Stafford, FFEL PLUS, Federal Perkins, state loans, college/university loans from institutional funds. **Student Employment:** Federal Work-Study Program available. Institutional employment available. Off-campus job opportunities are excellent. **Financial Aid Statistics:** 39% freshmen, 48% undergrads receive some form of aid. Average freshman grant $2,050. Average freshman loan $2,625. Average income from on-campus job $4,300. **Financial Aid Phone:** 734-487-0455.

EASTERN NAZARENE COLLEGE

23 East Elm Avenue, Quincy, MA 02170-2999
Phone: 617-745-3000 **E-mail:** admissions@enc.edu **CEEB Code:** 3365
Fax: 617-745-3490 **Web:** www.enc.edu

This private school, which is affiliated with the Nazarene Church, was founded in 1918. It has a 19-acre campus.

STUDENTS AND FACULTY

Enrollment: 2,500. **Student Body:** Male 50%, female 50%, out-of-state 58%. **Retention and Graduation:** 22% grads go on to further study within 1 year. 2% grads pursue business degrees. 1% grads pursue law degrees. 2% grads pursue medical degrees. **Faculty:** Student/faculty ratio 15:1.

ACADEMICS

Degrees: Associate's, bachelor's, diploma, first professional certificate, master's. **Academic Requirements:** General education including some course work in arts/fine arts, English (including composition), history, sciences (biological or physical), social science. **Majors with Highest Enrollment:** Communications studies/speech communication and rhetoric; biology/biological sciences, general; business administration/management. **Special Study Options:** Accelerated program, cooperative (work-study) program, double major, honors program, independent study, internships, study abroad, teacher certification program.

FACILITIES

Housing: All-female, all-male, apartments for married students, housing for disabled students, men's and women's suites. **Library Holdings:** 117,540 bound volumes. 466 periodicals. **Computers:** School-owned computers available for student use.

EXTRACURRICULARS

Activities: Choral groups, drama/theater, music ensembles, musical theater, radio station, student government, student newspaper, yearbook. **Organizations:** 1 religious organization. **Athletics (Intercollegiate):** *Men:* baseball, basketball, cross-country, soccer, tennis. *Women:* basketball, cross-country, soccer, softball, tennis, volleyball.

ADMISSIONS

Selectivity Rating: 73 (of 100). **Freshman Academic Profile:** Average high school GPA 3.1. 17% in top 10% of high school class, 40% in top 25% of high school class, 64% in top 50% of high school class. Average SAT I Math 480. Average SAT I Verbal 480. TOEFL required of all international applicants, minimum TOEFL 600. **Basis for Candidate Selection:** *Very important factors considered include:* essays, interview, recommendations, secondary school record, standardized test scores. *Other factors considered include:* character/personal qualities, class rank, extracurricular activities, religious affiliation/commitment, talent/ability, volunteer work, work experience. **Freshman Admission Requirements:** High school diploma or GED is required. *Academic units required/recommended:* 16 total required; 4 English required, 2 math required, 4 math recommended, 1 science required, 4 science recommended, 2 foreign language required, 4 foreign language recommended, 1 social studies required, 2 social studies recommended, 1 history required, 2 history recommended. **Transfer Admission Requirements:** *Items required:* high school transcript, college transcript, essay, interview, standardized test scores. Minimum high school GPA of 2.0 required. Minimum college GPA of 2.0 required. Lowest grade transferable C. **General Admission Information:** Application fee $25. Nonfall registration accepted.

COSTS AND FINANCIAL AID

Tuition $14,850. Room & board $5,215. Required fees $515. Average book expense $500. **Required Forms and Deadlines:** FAFSA and institution's own financial aid form. No deadline for regular filing. **Notification of Awards:** Applicants will be notified of awards on a rolling basis. **Types of Aid:** *Need-based scholarships/grants:* Pell, SEOG, state scholarships/grants, private scholarships, the school's own gift aid, church scholarships. *Loans:* FFEL Subsidized Stafford, FFEL Unsubsidized Stafford, FFEL PLUS, Federal Perkins, state loans. **Student Employment:** Federal Work-Study Program available. **Financial Aid Statistics:** 88% freshmen, 90% undergrads receive some form of aid. Average freshman loan $4,353. Average income from on-campus job $3,000. **Financial Aid Phone:** 617-745-3869.

EASTERN NEW MEXICO UNIVERSITY

Station #7, ENMU, Portales, NM 88130
Phone: 505-562-2178 **E-mail:** admissions@enmu.edu **CEEB Code:** 4299
Fax: 505-562-2118 **Web:** www.enmu.edu **ACT Code:** 2636

This public school was founded in 1934. It has a 400-acre campus.

STUDENTS AND FACULTY

Enrollment: 3,000. **Student Body:** Male 42%, female 58%, out-of-state 17%, international 1% (19 countries represented). **Ethnic Representation:** African American 6%, Asian 1%, Caucasian 57%, Hispanic 30%, Native American 3%. **Retention and Graduation:** 58% freshmen return for sophomore year. 1% freshmen graduate within 4 years. **Faculty:** Student/faculty ratio 17:1. 135 full-time faculty, 80% hold PhDs. 100% faculty teach undergrads.

ACADEMICS

Degrees: Associate's, bachelor's, master's, terminal, transfer. **Academic Requirements:** General education including some course work in arts/fine arts, English (including composition), humanities, mathematics, sciences (biological or physical), social science, physical well-being. **Majors with Highest Enrollment:** Elementary education and teaching; biology/biological sciences, general; psychology, general. **Disciplines with Highest Percentage of Degrees Awarded:** Education 23%, business/marketing 14%, social sciences and history 10%, liberal arts/general studies 9%, psychology 6%. **Special Study Options:** Accelerated program, cooperative (work-study) program, distance learning, double major, dual enrollment, student exchange program (domestic), honors program, independent study, internships, student-designed major, study abroad, teacher certification program.

FACILITIES

Housing: Coed, all-female, apartments for married students, apartments for single students, housing for disabled students, fraternities and/or sororities;

doubles, private rooms, and suites available. **Library Holdings:** 240,163 bound volumes. 1,903 periodicals. 755,873 microforms. 24,005 audiovisuals. **Special Academic Facilities/Equipment:** Natural history and historical museums, theatre, child development center, audiovisual center, electron microscopes, laser. **Computers:** *Recommended operating system:* Windows 98 or Windows NT. School-owned computers available for student use.

EXTRACURRICULARS

Activities: Choral groups, concert band, dance, drama/theater, jazz band, literary magazine, marching band, music ensembles, musical theater, pep band, radio station, student government, student newspaper, student-run film society, symphony orchestra, television station, yearbook. **Organizations:** 3 honor societies, 5 fraternities, 2 sororities. **Athletics (Intercollegiate):** *Men:* baseball, basketball, cross-country, football, rodeo, track & field. *Women:* basketball, cross-country, rodeo, softball, tennis, track & field, volleyball.

ADMISSIONS

Selectivity Rating: 66 (of 100). **Freshman Academic Profile:** Average high school GPA 3.1. SAT I Math middle 50% range 410-540. SAT I Verbal middle 50% range 400-520. Average ACT 18, ACT middle 50% range 16-21. TOEFL required of all international applicants, minimum TOEFL 500. **Basis for Candidate Selection:** *Very important factors considered include:* secondary school record, standardized test scores. *Other factors considered include:* extracurricular activities, interview, recommendations, talent/ability. **Freshman Admission Requirements:** High school diploma or GED is required. *Academic units required/recommended:* 14 total recommended; 4 English recommended, 3 math recommended, 4 science recommended, 1 foreign language recommended, 2 social studies recommended. **Freshman Admission Statistics:** 2,195 applied, 70% accepted, 34% of those accepted enrolled. **Transfer Admission Requirements:** *Items required:* college transcript, statement of good standing from prior school. Minimum college GPA of 2.0 required. Lowest grade transferable D. **General Admission Information:** Priority application deadline August 1. Nonfall registration accepted. Admission may be deferred. Credit and/or placement offered for CEEB Advanced Placement tests.

COSTS AND FINANCIAL AID

In-state tuition $1,752. Out-of-state tuition $6,510. Room & board $3,104. Required fees $66. Average book expense $66. **Required Forms and Deadlines:** FAFSA. Financial aid filing deadline March 30. Priority filing deadline March 1. **Notification of Awards:** Applicants will be notified of awards on a rolling basis beginning on or about April 15. **Types of Aid:** *Need-based scholarships/grants:* Pell, SEOG, state scholarships/grants, the school's own gift aid. *Loans:* FFEL Subsidized Stafford, FFEL Unsubsidized Stafford, FFEL PLUS, Federal Perkins. **Student Employment:** Federal Work-Study Program available. Institutional employment available. Off-campus job opportunities are fair. **Financial Aid Statistics:** 72% freshmen, 73% undergrads receive some form of aid. **Financial Aid Phone:** 505-562-2194.

EASTERN OREGON UNIVERSITY

One University Boulevard, LaGrande, OR 97850
Phone: 541-962-3393 **E-mail:** admissions@eou.edu **CEEB Code:** 4300
Fax: 541-962-3418 **Web:** www.eou.edu **ACT Code:** 3460

This public school was founded in 1929. It has a 121-acre campus.

STUDENTS AND FACULTY

Enrollment: 3,075. **Student Body:** Male 42%, female 58%, out-of-state 28%, international 3%. **Ethnic Representation:** African American 1%, Asian 3%, Caucasian 85%, Hispanic 3%, Native American 2%. **Retention and Graduation:** 68% freshmen return for sophomore year. 21% freshmen graduate within 4 years. **Faculty:** Student/faculty ratio 15:1. 91 full-time faculty, 83% hold PhDs. 100% faculty teach undergrads.

ACADEMICS

Degrees: Associate's, bachelor's, master's, post-bachelor's certificate, terminal, transfer. **Academic Requirements:** General education including some course work in arts/fine arts, computer literacy, English (including composition), foreign languages, humanities, mathematics, sciences (biological or physical), social science, writing intensive. **Classes:** 20-29 students in an average class. 20-29 students in an average lab/discussion section. **Disciplines with Highest Percentage of Degrees Awarded:** Liberal arts/general studies 24%, interdisciplinary studies 24%, business/marketing 19%, social sciences and history 8%, education 7%. **Special Study Options:** Cooperative (work-study) program, cross registration, distance learning, double major, dual enrollment, English as a second language, student exchange program (domestic), external degree program, honors program, independent study, internships, liberal arts/career combination, student-designed major, study abroad, teacher certification program, weekend college.

FACILITIES

Housing: Coed, all-female, all-male, apartments for married students. **Library Holdings:** 329,942 bound volumes. 998 periodicals. 205,724 microforms. 35,556 audiovisuals. **Special Academic Facilities/Equipment:** Art gallery, archaeological museum, Indian education institute, on-campus elementary school. **Computers:** School-owned computers available for student use.

EXTRACURRICULARS

Activities: Choral groups, concert band, dance, drama/theater, jazz band, literary magazine, music ensembles, musical theater, radio station, student government, student newspaper, symphony orchestra, television station. **Organizations:** 60 registered organizations, 2 honor societies, 4 religious organizations. **Athletics (Intercollegiate):** *Men:* baseball, basketball, cheerleading, cross-country, football, indoor track, rodeo, track & field. *Women:* basketball, cheerleading, cross-country, indoor track, rodeo, soccer, softball, track & field, volleyball.

ADMISSIONS

Selectivity Rating: 66 (of 100). **Freshman Academic Profile:** Average high school GPA 3.3. 14% in top 10% of high school class, 36% in top 25% of high school class, 73% in top 50% of high school class. 98% from public high schools. Average SAT I Math 485, SAT I Math middle 50% range 430-540. Average SAT I Verbal 495, SAT I Verbal middle 50% range 450-550. Average ACT 20, ACT middle 50% range 17-22. TOEFL required of all international applicants, minimum TOEFL 500. **Basis for Candidate Selection:** *Very important factors considered include:* secondary school record. *Important factors considered include:* essays, recommendations, talent/ability. *Other factors considered include:* class rank, extracurricular activities, geographical residence, minority status, standardized test scores, volunteer work, work experience. **Freshman Admission Requirements:** High school diploma or GED is required. *Academic units required/recommended:* 14 total required; 4 English required, 3 math required, 2 science required, 1 science lab recommended, 2 foreign language required, 3 social studies required. **Freshman Admission Statistics:** 765 applied, 93% accepted, 59% of those accepted enrolled. **Transfer Admission Requirements:** *Items required:* college transcript. Minimum college GPA of 2.2 required. Lowest grade transferable D-. **General Admission Information:** Application fee $50. Regular application deadline September 27. Nonfall registration accepted. Admission may be deferred for a maximum of 1 year. Credit offered for CEEB Advanced Placement tests.

COSTS AND FINANCIAL AID

In-state tuition $3,057. Out-of-state tuition $3,057. Room & board $5,775. Required fees $1,248. Average book expense $1,017. **Required Forms and Deadlines:** FAFSA. No deadline for regular filing. Priority filing deadline March 1. **Notification of Awards:** Applicants will be notified of awards on a rolling basis beginning on or about April 1. **Types of Aid:** *Need-based scholarships/grants:* Pell, SEOG, state scholarships/grants, private scholarships, the school's own gift aid. *Loans:* Direct Subsidized Stafford, Direct Unsubsidized Stafford, Direct PLUS, FFEL Subsidized Stafford, FFEL Unsubsidized Stafford, FFEL PLUS, Federal Perkins. **Student Employment:** Federal Work-Study Program available. Institutional employment available. Off-campus job opportunities are good. **Financial Aid Statistics:** 56% freshmen, 62% undergrads receive some form of aid. Average freshman loan $6,763. **Financial Aid Phone:** 541-962-3550.

EASTERN WASHINGTON UNIVERSITY

526 Fifth Street, MS 148, Cheney, WA 99004
Phone: 509-359-2397 **E-mail:** admissions@mail.ewu.edu **CEEB Code:** 4301
Fax: 509-359-6692 **Web:** www.ewu.edu **ACT Code:** 4454

This public school was founded in 1882. It has a 335-acre campus.

STUDENTS AND FACULTY

Enrollment: 8,798. **Student Body:** Male 42%, female 58%, international 2%. **Ethnic Representation:** African American 2%, Asian 3%, Caucasian 78%, Hispanic 4%, Native American 2%. **Retention and Graduation:** 74% freshmen return for sophomore year. 16% freshmen graduate within 4 years. **Faculty:** Student/faculty ratio 23:1. 356 full-time faculty, 60% hold PhDs. 100% faculty teach undergrads.

ACADEMICS

Degrees: Bachelor's, doctoral, master's. **Academic Requirements:** General education including some course work in arts/fine arts, computer literacy,

English (including composition), history, humanities, mathematics, philosophy, sciences (biological or physical), social science, cultural/gender diversity, international studies, and senior capstone. **Classes:** 20-29 students in an average class. **Disciplines with Highest Percentage of Degrees Awarded:** Business/marketing 19%, education 17%, social sciences and history 9%, psychology 7%, communications/communication technologies 6%. **Special Study Options:** Cooperative (work-study) program, distance learning, double major, English as a second language, honors program, independent study, internships, student-designed major, study abroad, teacher certification program, weekend college, nursing consortium.

FACILITIES

Housing: Coed, all-female, all-male, apartments for married students, housing for disabled students, apartments for students with children. **Library Holdings:** 852,186 bound volumes. 6,429 periodicals. 1,419,725 microforms. 31,832 audiovisuals. **Special Academic Facilities/Equipment:** Anthropology museum, on-campus elementary school, education lab, primate research center, marine biology lab, ecological studies lab, wildlife refuge, planetarium. **Computers:** School-owned computers available for student use.

EXTRACURRICULARS

Activities: Choral groups, concert band, dance, drama/theater, jazz band, literary magazine, marching band, music ensembles, musical theater, opera, pep band, radio station, student government, student newspaper, symphony orchestra, television station. **Organizations:** 90 registered organizations, 14 honor societies, 10 religious organizations, 5 fraternities, 5 sororities. **Athletics (Intercollegiate):** *Men:* basketball, cross-country, football, golf, indoor track, tennis, track & field. *Women:* basketball, cross-country, golf, indoor track, soccer, tennis, track & field, volleyball.

ADMISSIONS

Selectivity Rating: 63 (of 100). **Freshman Academic Profile:** Average high school GPA 3.3. 12% in top 10% of high school class, 27% in top 25% of high school class, 48% in top 50% of high school class. 95% from public high schools. Average SAT I Math 502, SAT I Math middle 50% range 450-560. Average SAT I Verbal 502, SAT I Verbal middle 50% range 450-550. Average ACT 21, ACT middle 50% range 19-24. TOEFL required of all international applicants, minimum TOEFL 525. **Basis for Candidate Selection:** *Very important factors considered include:* secondary school record, standardized test scores. *Other factors considered include:* character/personal qualities, essays, extracurricular activities, interview, recommendations, talent/ability, volunteer work, work experience. **Freshman Admission Requirements:** High school diploma or GED is required. *Academic units required/recommended:* 15 total required; 4 English required, 3 math required, 2 science required, 1 science lab required, 2 foreign language required, 3 social studies required, 1 elective required. **Freshman Admission Statistics:** 3,578 applied, 81% accepted, 45% of those accepted enrolled. **Transfer Admission Requirements:** *Items required:* college transcript. Minimum high school GPA of 2.0 required. Minimum college GPA of 2.0 required. Lowest grade transferable D-. **General Admission Information:** Application fee $35. Nonfall registration accepted. Admission may be deferred for a maximum of 1 year. Credit and/or placement offered for CEEB Advanced Placement tests.

COSTS AND FINANCIAL AID

In-state tuition $3,357. Out-of-state tuition $11,634. Room & board $5,025. Required fees $225. Average book expense $750. **Required Forms and Deadlines:** FAFSA. Priority filing deadline February 15. **Notification of Awards:** Applicants will be notified of awards on or about April 1. **Types of Aid:** *Need-based scholarships/grants:* Pell, SEOG, state scholarships/grants, private scholarships, the school's own gift aid, Trio/Gearup. *Loans:* FFEL Subsidized Stafford, FFEL Unsubsidized Stafford, FFEL PLUS, Federal Perkins, Scholarships for disadvantaged students. **Student Employment:** Federal Work-Study Program available. Institutional employment available. Off-campus job opportunities are excellent. **Financial Aid Statistics:** 53% freshmen, 60% undergrads receive some form of aid. Average freshman grant $3,454. Average freshman loan $1,698. Average income from on-campus job $2,457. **Financial Aid Phone:** 509-359-2314.

EASTMAN SCHOOL OF MUSIC, UNIVERSITY OF ROCHESTER

$$$

26 Gibbs Street, Rochester, NY 14604-2599
Phone: 716-274-1060 **E-mail:** esmadmit@mail.rochester.edu **CEEB Code:** 2224
Fax: 716-232-8601 **Web:** www.rochester.edu/Eastman **ACT Code:** 2980

This private school was founded in 1921. It has a 5-acre campus.

STUDENTS AND FACULTY

Enrollment: 503. **Student Body:** Male 45%, female 55%, out-of-state 83%, international 11% (42 countries represented). **Ethnic Representation:** African American 3%, Asian 7%, Caucasian 80%, Hispanic 2%. **Retention and Graduation:** 89% freshmen return for sophomore year. 72% freshmen graduate within 4 years. 72% grads go on to further study within 1 year. 3% grads pursue business degrees. 2% grads pursue law degrees. 2% grads pursue medical degrees. **Faculty:** 100% faculty teach undergrads.

ACADEMICS

Degrees: Bachelor's, certificate, diploma, doctoral, master's. **Academic Requirements:** General education including some course work in arts/fine arts, history, humanities. **Special Study Options:** Cooperative (work-study) program, double major, English as a second language, independent study, internships, liberal arts/career combination, study abroad, teacher certification program.

FACILITIES

Housing: Coed, all-female, all-male, housing for disabled students, fraternities and/or sororities. **Library Holdings:** 185,758 bound volumes. 620 periodicals. 15,868 microforms. 66,564 audiovisuals. **Computers:** *Recommended operating system:* Mac. School-owned computers available for student use.

EXTRACURRICULARS

Activities: Choral groups, concert band, dance, jazz band, literary magazine, music ensembles, musical theater, opera, radio station, student government, student newspaper, student-run film society, symphony orchestra. **Organizations:** 8 registered organizations, 3 honor societies, 2 religious organizations, 2 fraternities (16% men join), 1 sorority (15% women join).

ADMISSIONS

Selectivity Rating: 97 (of 100). **Freshman Academic Profile:** Average high school GPA 3.3. 80% from public high schools. Average SAT I Math 650, SAT I Math middle 50% range 510-650. Average SAT I Verbal 600, SAT I Verbal middle 50% range 500-650. ACT middle 50% range 22-28. TOEFL required of all international applicants, minimum TOEFL 500. **Basis for Candidate Selection:** *Very important factors considered include:* talent/ability. *Important factors considered include:* class rank, interview, recommendations, secondary school record, standardized test scores. *Other factors considered include:* alumni/ae relation, character/personal qualities, essays, minority status. **Freshman Admission Requirements:** High school diploma or GED is required. *Academic units required/recommended:* 16 total recommended; 4 English recommended. **Freshman Admission Statistics:** 899 applied, 29% accepted, 47% of those accepted enrolled. **Transfer Admission Requirements:** *Items required:* high school transcript, college transcript, statement of good standing from prior school. Minimum college GPA of 2.0 required. Lowest grade transferable C. **General Admission Information:** Application fee $50. Priority application deadline January 1. Regular application deadline January 1. Nonfall registration accepted. Admission may be deferred for a maximum of 1 year. Placement offered for CEEB Advanced Placement tests.

COSTS AND FINANCIAL AID

Tuition $20,320. Room & board $7,512. Required fees $484. Average book expense $600. **Required Forms and Deadlines:** FAFSA, institution's own financial aid form, and CSS/Financial Aid PROFILE. No deadline for regular filing. Priority filing deadline February 1. **Notification of Awards:** Applicants will be notified of awards on or about April 15. **Types of Aid:** *Need-based scholarships/grants:* Pell, SEOG, state scholarships/grants, private scholarships, the school's own gift aid. *Loans:* Direct Subsidized Stafford, Direct Unsubsidized Stafford, Direct PLUS, Federal Perkins, college/university loans from institutional funds. **Student Employment:** Federal Work-Study Program available. Institutional employment available. Off-campus job opportunities are good. **Financial Aid Statistics:** 70% freshmen, 59% undergrads receive some form of aid. Average freshman grant $10,000. Average freshman loan $2,625. Average income from on-campus job $300. **Financial Aid Phone:** 716-274-1070.

EAST-WEST UNIVERSITY

816 South Michigan Avenue, Chicago, IL 60605
Phone: 312-939-0111 **E-mail:** admissions@eastwest.edu
Fax: 312-939-0083 **Web:** www.eastwest.edu

This private school was founded in 1980.

STUDENTS AND FACULTY

Enrollment: 1,113. **Student Body:** Male 35%, female 65%, international 14%. **Ethnic Representation:** African American 82%, Asian 2%, Caucasian 3%, Hispanic 13%. **Retention and Graduation:** 60% freshmen return for sophomore year. 8% freshmen graduate within 4 years. **Faculty:** Student/faculty ratio 20:1. 14 full-time faculty, 71% hold PhDs.

ACADEMICS

Degrees: Associate's, bachelor's. **Academic Requirements:** General education including some course work in arts/fine arts, computer literacy, English (including composition), foreign languages, history, humanities, mathematics, philosophy, sciences (biological or physical), social science. **Majors with Highest Enrollment:** Computer and information sciences, general; liberal arts and sciences, general studies and humanities; business administration/management. **Disciplines with Highest Percentage of Degrees Awarded:** Computer and information sciences 3%, business/marketing 2%, liberal arts/general studies 2%, English 2%, engineering/engineering technology 1%. **Special Study Options:** Cooperative (work-study) program, double major, independent study, internships.

FACILITIES

Library Holdings: 26,450 bound volumes. 1,547 periodicals. 2,410 microforms. 1,941 audiovisuals. **Computers:** School-owned computers available for student use.

EXTRACURRICULARS

Activities: Drama/theater, student government, student newspaper. **Athletics (Intercollegiate):** *Men:* basketball.

ADMISSIONS

Selectivity Rating: 63 (of 100). **Freshman Academic Profile:** 80% from public high schools. **Basis for Candidate Selection:** *Very important factors considered include:* state residency. *Other factors considered include:* character/personal qualities, essays, extracurricular activities, interview, recommendations, secondary school record, work experience. **Freshman Admission Requirements:** High school diploma or GED is required. **Freshman Admission Statistics:** 947 applied, 90% accepted, 90% of those accepted enrolled. **Transfer Admission Requirements:** *Items required:* high school transcript, college transcript, interview, statement of good standing from prior school. Lowest grade transferable C. **General Admission Information:** Application fee $30. Nonfall registration accepted. Admission may be deferred for a maximum of 1 year.

COSTS AND FINANCIAL AID

Tuition $9,900. Required fees $495. Average book expense $600. **Types of Aid:** *Need-based scholarships/grants:* Pell, SEOG, state scholarships/grants, private scholarships, the school's own gift aid. *Loans:* Direct Subsidized Stafford, Direct Unsubsidized Stafford, FFEL Subsidized Stafford, FFEL PLUS. **Student Employment:** Federal Work-Study Program available. **Financial Aid Statistics:** Average freshman grant $9,220. Average freshman loan $2,625. **Financial Aid Phone:** 312-939-0111.

ECKERD COLLEGE

4200 54th Avenue South, St. Petersburg, FL 33711
Phone: 727-864-8331 **E-mail:** admissions@eckerd.edu **CEEB Code:** 5223
Fax: 727-866-2304 **Web:** www.eckerd.edu **ACT Code:** 731

This private school, which is affiliated with the Presbyterian Church, was founded in 1958. It has a 267-acre campus.

STUDENTS AND FACULTY

Enrollment: 1,608. **Student Body:** Male 46%, female 54%, out-of-state 70%, international 6% (49 countries represented). **Ethnic Representation:** African American 3%, Asian 2%, Caucasian 83%, Hispanic 5%. **Retention and Graduation:** 75% freshmen return for sophomore year. 57% freshmen graduate within 4 years. 14% grads go on to further study within 1 year. 19% grads pursue business degrees. 6% grads pursue law degrees. 4% grads pursue medical degrees. **Faculty:** Student/faculty ratio 14:1. 97 full-time faculty, 91% hold PhDs. 100% faculty teach undergrads.

ACADEMICS

Degrees: Bachelor's. **Academic Requirements:** General education including some course work in arts/fine arts, computer literacy, foreign languages, history, humanities, mathematics, philosophy, sciences (biological or physical), social science, writing competency, oral competency, technology competency. **Classes:** 20-29 students in an average class. **Majors with Highest Enrollment:** Business administration/management; marine biology and biological oceanography; psychology, general. **Disciplines with Highest Percentage of Degrees Awarded:** Business/marketing 18%, biological life sciences 18%, social sciences and history 15%, psychology 14%, natural resources/environmental sciences 9%. **Special Study Options:** Accelerated program, cooperative (work-study) program, cross registration, double major, English as a second language, student exchange program (domestic), honors program, independent study, internships, liberal arts/career combination, student-designed major, study abroad, winter-term exchange with other 4-1-4 colleges. 3-2 engineering program with Columbia University, Washington University (MO), University of Miami, and Auburn University.

FACILITIES

Housing: Coed, all-female, all-male, apartments for single students, housing for disabled students, suite-style dorms. **Library Holdings:** 113,850 bound volumes. 3,009 periodicals. 14,606 microforms. 1,941 audiovisuals. **Special Academic Facilities/Equipment:** Language lab, oral communications lab, marine science center, marine mammal necropsy lab. **Computers:** *Recommended operating system:* Macintosh, UNIX, and Windows 95. School-owned computers available for student use.

EXTRACURRICULARS

Activities: Choral groups, drama/theater, literary magazine, music ensembles, radio station, student government, student newspaper, student-run film society, television station, yearbook. **Organizations:** 56 registered organizations, 7 honor societies, 6 religious organizations. **Athletics (Intercollegiate):** *Men:* baseball, basketball, golf, sailing, soccer, swimming, tennis, volleyball. *Women:* basketball, cheerleading, cross-country, sailing, soccer, softball, swimming, tennis, volleyball.

ADMISSIONS

Selectivity Rating: 79 (of 100). **Freshman Academic Profile:** Average high school GPA 3.2. 16% in top 10% of high school class, 29% in top 25% of high school class, 81% in top 50% of high school class. 80% from public high schools. Average SAT I Math 564, SAT I Math middle 50% range 500-620. Average SAT I Verbal 564, SAT I Verbal middle 50% range 510-620. Average ACT 25, ACT middle 50% range 20-26. TOEFL required of all international applicants, minimum TOEFL 550. **Basis for Candidate Selection:** *Very important factors considered include:* character/personal qualities, extracurricular activities, secondary school record. *Important factors considered include:* essays, interview, recommendations, standardized test scores, talent/ability, volunteer work, work experience. *Other factors considered include:* class rank. **Freshman Admission Requirements:** High school diploma or GED is required. *Academic units required/recommended:* 18 total required; 22 total recommended; 4 English required, 3 math required, 4 math recommended, 3 science required, 4 science recommended, 2 science lab required, 3 science lab recommended, 2 foreign language required, 3 foreign language recommended, 2 social studies required, 1 history required, 2 history recommended, 3 elective required, 3 elective recommended. **Freshman Admission Statistics:** 1,943 applied, 79% accepted, 29% of those accepted enrolled. **Transfer Admission Requirements:** *Items required:* college transcript, essay. Minimum college GPA of 2.5 required. Lowest grade transferable C. **General Admission Information:** Application fee $25. Priority application deadline February 15. Nonfall registration accepted. Admission may be deferred for a maximum of 1 year. Credit and/or placement offered for CEEB Advanced Placement tests.

COSTS AND FINANCIAL AID

Tuition $21,262. Room & board $5,688. Required fees $226. Average book expense $946. **Required Forms and Deadlines:** FAFSA. Priority filing deadline April 1. **Notification of Awards:** Applicants will be notified of awards on a rolling basis beginning on or about February 1. **Types of Aid:** *Need-based scholarships/grants:* Pell, SEOG, state scholarships/grants, private scholarships, the school's own gift aid. *Loans:* FFEL Subsidized Stafford, FFEL Unsubsidized Stafford, FFEL PLUS, Federal Perkins, college/university loans from institutional funds. **Student Employment:** Federal Work-Study Program available. Institutional employment available. Off-campus job opportunities are excellent. **Financial Aid Statistics:** 60% freshmen, 57% undergrads receive some form of aid. Average freshman grant $11,000. Average freshman loan $3,500. Average income from on-campus job $1,200. **Financial Aid Phone:** 727-864-8334.

EDGEWOOD COLLEGE

1000 Edgewood College Drive, Madison, WI 53711-1997
Phone: 608-663-2294 **E-mail:** admissions@edgewood.edu **CEEB Code:** 1202
Fax: 608-663-3291 **Web:** www.edgewood.edu **ACT Code:** 4582

This private school, which is affiliated with the Roman Catholic Church, was founded in 1927. It has a 55-acre campus.

STUDENTS AND FACULTY

Enrollment: 1,731. **Student Body:** Male 27%, female 73%, out-of-state 4%, international 2% (21 countries represented). **Ethnic Representation:** African American 2%, Asian 1%, Caucasian 61%, Hispanic 2%. **Retention and Graduation:** 73% freshmen return for sophomore year. 26% freshmen graduate within 4 years. 16% grads go on to further study within 1 year. 4% grads pursue business degrees. 2% grads pursue law degrees. 1% grads pursue medical degrees. **Faculty:** Student/faculty ratio 13:1. 86 full-time faculty, 75% hold PhDs. 100% faculty teach undergrads.

ACADEMICS

Degrees: Associate's, bachelor's, doctoral, master's. **Academic Requirements:** General education including some course work in arts/fine arts, computer literacy, English (including composition), foreign languages, history, humanities, mathematics, philosophy, sciences (biological or physical), social science. **Classes:** 10-19 students in an average class. **Majors with Highest Enrollment:** Nursing/registered nurse training (RN, ASN, BSN, MSN); business administration/management; education, general. **Disciplines with Highest Percentage of Degrees Awarded:** Business/marketing 20%, education 17%, health professions and related sciences 16%, psychology 10%, visual and performing arts 6%. **Special Study Options:** Accelerated program, cross registration, distance learning, double major, dual enrollment, honors program, independent study, internships, liberal arts/career combination, student-designed major, study abroad, teacher certification program, weekend college.

FACILITIES

Housing: Coed, all-female, apartments for single students, housing for disabled students, student leadership house. **Library Holdings:** 90,253 bound volumes. 447 periodicals. 96,072 microforms. 4,359 audiovisuals. **Special Academic Facilities/Equipment:** DeRicci Art Gallery, Science Exploration Center. **Computers:** School-owned computers available for student use.

EXTRACURRICULARS

Activities: Choral groups, concert band, drama/theater, jazz band, literary magazine, music ensembles, musical theater, pep band, student government, student newspaper, symphony orchestra. **Organizations:** 30 registered organizations, 4 honor societies, 1 religious organization. **Athletics (Intercollegiate):** *Men:* baseball, basketball, cross-country, golf, soccer. *Women:* basketball, cross-country, golf, soccer, softball, tennis, volleyball.

ADMISSIONS

Selectivity Rating: 74 (of 100). **Freshman Academic Profile:** Average high school GPA 3.2. 13% in top 10% of high school class, 38% in top 25% of high school class, 75% in top 50% of high school class. 87% from public high schools. Average SAT I Math 550, SAT I Math middle 50% range 520-640. Average SAT I Verbal 490, SAT I Verbal middle 50% range 440-560. Average ACT 22, ACT middle 50% range 20-25. TOEFL required of all international applicants, minimum TOEFL 525. **Basis for Candidate Selection:** *Very important factors considered include:* class rank, secondary school record, standardized test scores. *Important factors considered include:* interview, talent/ability. *Other factors considered include:* alumni/ae relation, character/personal qualities, essays, extracurricular activities, geographical residence, minority status, recommendations, volunteer work. **Freshman Admission Requirements:** High school diploma or GED is required. *Academic units required/recommended:* 16 total required; 4 English required, 2 math required, 2 science required, 1 science lab required, 2 social studies required, 1 history required. **Freshman Admission Statistics:** 984 applied, 79% accepted, 35% of those accepted enrolled. **Transfer Admission Requirements:** *Items required:* high school transcript, college transcript. Minimum high school GPA of 2.0 required. Minimum college GPA of 2.0 required. Lowest grade transferable C. **General Admission Information:** Application fee $25. Priority application deadline August 1. Nonfall registration accepted. Admission may be deferred for a maximum of 1 year. Credit and/or placement offered for CEEB Advanced Placement tests.

COSTS AND FINANCIAL AID

Tuition $13,300. Room & board $5,005. Required fees $0. Average book expense $750. **Required Forms and Deadlines:** FAFSA and institution's own financial aid form. No deadline for regular filing. **Notification of Awards:** Applicants will be notified of awards on or about March 15. **Types of Aid:** *Need-based scholarships/grants:* SEOG, state scholarships/grants, private scholarships, the school's own gift aid. *Loans:* FFEL Subsidized Stafford, FFEL Unsubsidized Stafford, FFEL PLUS, Federal Perkins, college/university loans from institutional funds. **Student Employment:** Federal Work-Study Program available. Institutional employment available. Off-campus job opportunities are good. **Financial Aid Statistics:** 73% freshmen, 67% undergrads receive some form of aid. Average freshman grant $8,245. Average freshman loan $2,625. Average income from on-campus job $1,600. **Financial Aid Phone:** 608-663-2206.

EDINBORO UNIVERSITY OF PENNSYLVANIA

Biggers House, Edinboro, PA 16444
Phone: 814-732-2761 **E-mail:** eup_admissions@edinboro.edu **CEEB Code:** 2651
Fax: 814-732-2420 **Web:** www.edinboro.edu **ACT Code:** 3702

This public school was founded in 1857. It has a 585-acre campus.

STUDENTS AND FACULTY

Enrollment: 6,922. **Student Body:** Male 43%, female 57%, out-of-state 11%, international 3%. **Ethnic Representation:** African American 6%, Asian 1%, Caucasian 92%, Hispanic 1%. **Retention and Graduation:** 71% freshmen return for sophomore year. 19% freshmen graduate within 4 years. **Faculty:** Student/faculty ratio 18:1. 378 full-time faculty, 50% hold PhDs. 98% faculty teach undergrads.

ACADEMICS

Degrees: Associate's, bachelor's, master's, post-bachelor's certificate, post-master's certificate. **Academic Requirements:** General education including some course work in arts/fine arts, computer literacy, English (including composition), history, humanities, mathematics, philosophy, sciences (biological or physical), social science. **Classes:** 20-29 students in an average class. **Majors with Highest Enrollment:** Business administration/management; elementary education and teaching; fine/studio arts, general. **Disciplines with Highest Percentage of Degrees Awarded:** Education 15%, visual and performing arts 15%, protective services/public administration 11%, health professions and related sciences 9%, communications/communication technologies 8%. **Special Study Options:** Distance learning, double major, honors program, independent study, internships, liberal arts/career combination, student-designed major, study abroad, teacher certification program.

FACILITIES

Housing: Coed, housing for disabled students, housing for international students; areas are reserved for nonsmokers, graduate/nontraditional age students, students who prefer a quiet living environment, honors students, and floors by academic major are also available. **Library Holdings:** 468,175 bound volumes. 1,653 periodicals. 1,372,659 microforms. 27,819 audiovisuals. **Special Academic Facilities/Equipment:** Planetarium, solar observatory, Governor George Leader Speech and Hearing Center, and Miller Laborary School. **Computers:** School-owned computers available for student use.

EXTRACURRICULARS

Activities: Choral groups, dance, drama/theater, literary magazine, marching band, pep band, radio station, student government, student newspaper, student-run film society, television station. **Organizations:** 89 registered organizations, 10 honor societies, 4 religious organizations, 10 fraternities (7% men join), 8 sororities (7% women join). **Athletics (Intercollegiate):** *Men:* baseball, basketball, cross-country, football, indoor track, swimming, tennis, track & field, wrestling. *Women:* basketball, cross-country, indoor track, soccer, softball, swimming, tennis, track & field, volleyball.

ADMISSIONS

Selectivity Rating: 66 (of 100). **Freshman Academic Profile:** 5% in top 10% of high school class, 19% in top 25% of high school class, 51% in top 50% of high school class. Average SAT I Math 468, SAT I Math middle 50% range 410-520. Average SAT I Verbal 478, SAT I Verbal middle 50% range 420-520. Average ACT 19, ACT middle 50% range 16-22. TOEFL required of all international applicants, minimum TOEFL 500. **Basis for Candidate Selection:** *Very important factors considered include:* class rank, secondary school record, standardized test scores. *Important factors considered include:* extracurricular activities, minority status, state residency. *Other factors considered include:* alumni/ae relation, character/personal qualities, essays, geographical residence, interview, recommendations, talent/ability, volunteer work, work experience. **Freshman Admission Requirements:** High school diploma or GED is required. *Academic units required/recommended:* 17 total recommended; 4 English recommended, 3 math recommended, 3 science recommended, 2 foreign language recommended, 3 social studies recommended, 4 elective recommended. **Freshman Admission Statistics:** 3,856 applied, 76% accepted, 49% of those accepted enrolled. **Transfer Admission Requirements:** *Items required:* high school transcript, college transcript, statement of good standing from prior school. Minimum college GPA of 1.5 required. Lowest grade transferable C. **General Admission Information:** Application fee $25. Priority application deadline April 1. Nonfall registration accepted. Admission may be deferred for a maximum of 1 year. Credit and/or placement offered for CEEB Advanced Placement tests.

COSTS AND FINANCIAL AID

In-state tuition $4,378. Out-of-state tuition $6,568. Room & board $4,884. Required fees $1,086. Average book expense $700. **Required Forms and Deadlines:** FAFSA. Financial aid filing deadline May 1. Priority filing deadline March 15. **Notification of Awards:** Applicants will be notified of awards on a rolling basis beginning on or about March 31. **Types of Aid:** *Need-based scholarships/grants:* Pell, SEOG, state scholarships/grants, private scholarships, the school's own gift aid. *Loans:* FFEL Subsidized Stafford, FFEL Unsubsidized Stafford, FFEL PLUS, Federal Perkins, Federal Nursing, alternative loans. **Student Employment:** Federal Work-Study Program available. Institutional employment available. Off-campus job opportunities are good. **Financial Aid Statistics:** Average freshman grant $1,213. Average freshman loan $2,297. Average income from on-campus job $1,400. **Financial Aid Phone:** 888-611-2680.

ELIZABETH CITY STATE UNIVERSITY

1704 Weeksville Road, Elizabeth City, NC 27909
Phone: 252-335-3305 **E-mail:** admissions@mail.ecsu.edu **CEEB Code:** 5629
Fax: 252-335-3537 **Web:** www.ecsu.edu **ACT Code:** 3095

This public school was founded in 1891. It has a 114-acre campus.

STUDENTS AND FACULTY

Enrollment: 2,133. **Student Body:** Male 37%, female 63%, out-of-state 12%. **Ethnic Representation:** African American 77%, Caucasian 22%, Hispanic 1%. **Retention and Graduation:** 39% freshmen graduate within 4 years. 20% grads go on to further study within 1 year. **Faculty:** Student/faculty ratio 12:1. 114 full-time faculty, 70% hold PhDs.

ACADEMICS

Degrees: Bachelor's, master's. **Academic Requirements:** General education including some course work in arts/fine arts, computer literacy, English (including composition), history, mathematics, sciences (biological or physical). **Classes:** Under 10 students in an average class. **Disciplines with Highest Percentage of Degrees Awarded:** Protective services/public administration 23%, business/marketing 22%, education 12%, social sciences and history 9%, biological life sciences 8%. **Special Study Options:** Cooperative (work-study) program, distance learning, double major, honors program, independent study, internships, liberal arts/career combination, teacher certification program, weekend college.

FACILITIES

Housing: Coed, all-female, all-male, apartments for single students, college-leased housing available. **Library Holdings:** 184,684 bound volumes. 1,845 periodicals. 500,890 microforms. 1,672 audiovisuals. **Special Academic Facilities/Equipment:** Lab school, planetarium, science complex, music engineering station. **Computers:** School-owned computers available for student use.

EXTRACURRICULARS

Activities: Choral groups, concert band, dance, drama/theater, jazz band, literary magazine, marching band, music ensembles, musical theater, pep band, radio station, student government, student newspaper, symphony orchestra, television station, yearbook. **Organizations:** 46 registered organizations, 3 honor societies, 4 religious organizations, 4 fraternities (10% men join), 4 sororities (10% women join). **Athletics (Intercollegiate):** *Men:* baseball, basketball, cheerleading, cross-country, football, golf, softball, tennis, track & field, volleyball. *Women:* baseball, basketball, cheerleading, cross-country, golf, softball, tennis, track & field, volleyball.

ADMISSIONS

Selectivity Rating: 63 (of 100). **Freshman Academic Profile:** Average high school GPA 2.7. 5% in top 10% of high school class, 21% in top 25% of high school class, 64% in top 50% of high school class. 99% from public high schools. Average SAT I Math 415, SAT I Math middle 50% range 360-450. Average SAT I Verbal 422, SAT I Verbal middle 50% range 360-450. TOEFL required of all international applicants, minimum TOEFL 550. **Basis for Candidate Selection:** *Very important factors considered include:* character/personal qualities, geographical residence, secondary school record, standardized test scores, state residency. *Important factors considered include:* class rank, minority status, talent/ability. *Other factors considered include:* alumni/ae relation, essays, extracurricular activities, interview, recommendations, religious affiliation/commitment, work experience. **Freshman Admission Requirements:** High school diploma or GED is required. *Academic units required/recommended:* 20 total required; 4 English required, 3 math required, 3 science required, 2 foreign language recommended, 1 social studies required, 1 history required, 8 elective required. **Freshman Admission Statistics:** 1,262 applied, 77% accepted, 48% of those accepted enrolled. **Transfer Admission Requirements:** *Items required:* high school transcript, college transcript, statement of good standing from prior school. Minimum high school GPA of 2.0 required. Minimum college GPA of 2.0 required. Lowest grade transferable C. **General Admission Information:** Application fee $30. Priority application deadline May 1. Regular application deadline August 1. Nonfall registration accepted. Admission may be deferred for a maximum of 1 year. Credit and/or placement offered for CEEB Advanced Placement tests.

COSTS AND FINANCIAL AID

Required Forms and Deadlines: FAFSA and institution's own financial aid form. **Notification of Awards:** Applicants will be notified of awards on or about April 1. **Types of Aid:** *Need-based scholarships/grants:* Pell, SEOG, state scholarships/grants, private scholarships, the school's own gift aid. *Loans:* FFEL Subsidized Stafford, FFEL Unsubsidized Stafford, FFEL PLUS, Federal Perkins, college/university loans from institutional funds. **Student Employment:** Federal Work-Study Program available. Off-campus job opportunities are fair. **Financial Aid Statistics:** Average freshman grant $3,000. Average income from on-campus job $643. **Financial Aid Phone:** 919-335-3283.

ELIZABETHTOWN COLLEGE

Leffler House, One Alpha Drive, Elizabethtown, PA 17022
Phone: 717-361-1400 **E-mail:** admissions@etown.edu **CEEB Code:** 2225
Fax: 717-361-1365 **Web:** www.etown.edu **ACT Code:** 3568

This private school, which is affiliated with the Church of Brethren, was founded in 1899. It has a 193-acre campus.

STUDENTS AND FACULTY

Enrollment: 1,891. **Student Body:** Male 36%, female 64%, out-of-state 26%, international 3% (17 countries represented). **Ethnic Representation:** African American 2%, Asian 2%, Caucasian 95%, Hispanic 1%. **Retention and Graduation:** 84% freshmen return for sophomore year. 62% freshmen graduate within 4 years. 20% grads go on to further study within 1 year. **Faculty:** Student/faculty ratio 13:1. 112 full-time faculty, 83% hold PhDs. 100% faculty teach undergrads.

ACADEMICS

Degrees: Associate's, bachelor's, certificate, diploma, master's, post-bachelor's certificate. **Academic Requirements:** General education including some course work in arts/fine arts, English (including composition), history, humanities, mathematics, philosophy, sciences (biological or physical), social science, foreign cultures and international studies, physical well-being. **Classes:** 10-19 students in an average class. 10-19 students in an average lab/discussion section. **Majors with Highest Enrollment:** Business administration/management; communications, journalism, and related fields; biology/biological sciences, general. **Disciplines with Highest Percentage of Degrees Awarded:** Business/marketing 24%, education 16%, health professions and related sciences 12%, communications/communication technologies 10%, protective services/public administration 6%. **Special Study Options:** Accelerated program, cooperative (work-study) program, distance learning, double major, dual enrollment, English as a second language, student exchange program (domestic), honors program, independent study, internships, liberal arts/career combination, study abroad, teacher certification program. 2+2, 3+3, and 4+2 (part time doctorate) programs with Thomas Jefferson University in nursing, physical therapy, laboratory sciences, diagnostic imaging. 3+2 in engineering with Pennsylvania State University. 3+2 with Duke University in Forestry. 3+3 in physical therapy with Widener University and University of Maryland, Baltimore County. 3+1 in Invasive Cardiovascular Technology with Lancaster Institute for Health Education. Articulation agreements with Lehigh University, Rutgers University, Loyola College (MD), and Pennsylvania State University—Harrisburg to satisfy 150-hour requirement in accounting.

FACILITIES

Housing: Coed, all-female, apartments for single students, housing for international students, off-campus houses for student service-learning groups. **Library Holdings:** 143,302 bound volumes. 1,090 periodicals. 15,659 microforms. 31,195 audiovisuals. **Special Academic Facilities/Equipment:** Art gallery, meetinghouse/center for Anabaptist and Pietist studies, chapel/performance center, Fourier transform multinuclear NMR spectrometer, blood gas analyzer, scanning densitometer, PCR machine, radiometer/data logger, automated ion analyzer, computerized language lab. **Computers:** School-owned computers available for student use.

EXTRACURRICULARS

Activities: Choral groups, concert band, dance, drama/theater, jazz band, literary magazine, music ensembles, musical theater, pep band, radio station, student government, student newspaper, student-run film society, symphony orchestra, television station, yearbook. **Organizations:** 80 registered organizations, 16 honor societies, 6 religious organizations. **Athletics (Intercollegiate):** *Men:* baseball, basketball, cheerleading, cross-country, diving, golf, indoor track, lacrosse, soccer, swimming, tennis, track & field, wrestling. *Women:* basketball, cross-country, diving, field hockey, indoor track, lacrosse, soccer, softball, swimming, tennis, track & field, volleyball.

ADMISSIONS

Selectivity Rating: 77 (of 100). **Freshman Academic Profile:** 29% in top 10% of high school class, 64% in top 25% of high school class, 91% in top 50% of high school class. 80% from public high schools. SAT I Math middle 50% range 500-610. SAT I Verbal middle 50% range 500-600. ACT middle 50% range 21-27. TOEFL required of all international applicants, minimum TOEFL 525. **Basis for Candidate Selection:** *Very important factors considered include:* secondary school record. *Important factors considered include:* class rank, interview, minority status, recommendations, standardized test scores, volunteer work. *Other factors considered include:* alumni/ae relation, character/personal qualities, essays, extracurricular activities, geographical residence, religious affiliation/commitment, state residency, talent/ability, work experience. **Freshman Admission Requirements:** High school diploma or GED is required. *Academic units required/recommended:* 15 total required; 20 total recommended; 4 English required, 4 English recommended, 3 math required, 4 math recommended, 2 science required, 4 science recommended, 2 science lab required, 2 science lab recommended, 2 foreign language recommended, 2 social studies required, 2 social studies recommended, 2 history required, 2 history recommended, 2 elective recommended. **Freshman Admission Statistics:** 2,509 applied, 68% accepted, 27% of those accepted enrolled. **Transfer Admission Requirements:** *Items required:* high school transcript, college transcript, essay, standardized test scores. Minimum college GPA of 2.5 required. Lowest grade transferable C. **General Admission Information:** Application fee $20. Nonfall registration accepted. Admission may be deferred for a maximum of 1 year. Credit and/or placement offered for CEEB Advanced Placement tests.

COSTS AND FINANCIAL AID

Tuition $20,200. Room & board $5,800. Required fees $0. Average book expense $600. **Required Forms and Deadlines:** FAFSA, institution's own financial aid form, and federal tax records. Priority filing deadline March 15. **Notification of Awards:** Applicants will be notified of awards on a rolling basis beginning on or about February 15. **Types of Aid:** *Need-based scholarships/grants:* Pell, SEOG, state scholarships/grants, private scholarships, the school's own gift aid. *Loans:* FFEL Subsidized Stafford, FFEL Unsubsidized Stafford, FFEL PLUS, Federal Perkins, state loans. **Student Employment:** Federal Work-Study Program available. Institutional employment available. Off-campus job opportunities are good. **Financial Aid Statistics:** 74% freshmen, 73% undergrads receive some form of aid. **Financial Aid Phone:** 717-361-1404.

ELMHURST COLLEGE

190 Prospect Avenue, Elmhurst, IL 60126
Phone: 630-617-3400 **E-mail:** admit@elmhurst.edu **CEEB Code:** 1204
Fax: 630-617-5501 **Web:** www.elmhurst.edu **ACT Code:** 1020

This private school, which is affiliated with the United Church of Christ, was founded in 1871. It has a 38-acre campus.

STUDENTS AND FACULTY

Enrollment: 2,410. **Student Body:** Male 36%, female 64%, out-of-state 8%, international 1% (20 countries represented). **Ethnic Representation:** African American 7%, Asian 2%, Caucasian 78%, Hispanic 5%. **Retention and Graduation:** 86% freshmen return for sophomore year. 52% freshmen graduate within 4 years. 15% grads go on to further study within 1 year. 25% grads pursue business degrees. 7% grads pursue law degrees. 3% grads pursue medical degrees. **Faculty:** Student/faculty ratio 13:1. 107 full-time faculty, 92% hold PhDs. 100% faculty teach undergrads.

ACADEMICS

Degrees: Bachelor's, master's. **Academic Requirements:** General education including some course work in arts/fine arts, English (including composition), foreign languages, history, humanities, philosophy, sciences (biological or physical), social science, Judeo-Christian heritage. **Classes:** 10-19 students in an average class. Under 10 students in an average lab/discussion section. **Disciplines with Highest Percentage of Degrees Awarded:** Business/marketing 32%, education 17%, health professions and related sciences 8%, computer and information sciences 7%, psychology 7%. **Special Study Options:** Accelerated program, cooperative (work-study) program, double major, dual enrollment, honors program, independent study, internships, study abroad, teacher certification program.

FACILITIES

Housing: Coed. **Library Holdings:** 211,151 bound volumes. 2,000 periodicals. 17,822 microforms. 6,531 audiovisuals. **Special Academic Facilities/Equipment:** Language lab, recording studio, computer science/technology center, 4 electron microscopes, accelerator laboratory. **Computers:** School-owned computers available for student use.

EXTRACURRICULARS

Activities: Choral groups, concert band, drama/theater, jazz band, literary magazine, music ensembles, musical theater, radio station, student government, student newspaper, yearbook. **Organizations:** 74 registered organizations, 15 honor societies, 2 religious organizations, 5 fraternities (3% men join), 7 sororities (12% women join). **Athletics (Intercollegiate):** *Men:* baseball, basketball, cheerleading, cross-country, football, golf, tennis, track & field, wrestling. *Women:* basketball, cheerleading, cross-country, golf, soccer, softball, tennis, track & field, volleyball.

ADMISSIONS

Selectivity Rating: 72 (of 100). **Freshman Academic Profile:** Average high school GPA 3.3. 16% in top 10% of high school class, 42% in top 25% of high school class, 78% in top 50% of high school class. 92% from public high schools. Average ACT 22, ACT middle 50% range 20-25. TOEFL required of all international applicants, minimum TOEFL 520. **Basis for Candidate Selection:** *Very important factors considered include:* class rank, interview, secondary school record. *Important factors considered include:* essays, extracurricular activities, standardized test scores. *Other factors considered include:* alumni/ae relation, character/personal qualities, minority status, recommendations, talent/ability, volunteer work, work experience. **Freshman Admission Requirements:** High school diploma or GED is required. *Academic units required/recommended:* 16 total required; 18 total recommended; 4 English required, 4 English recommended, 2 math required, 3 math recommended, 2 science required, 3 science recommended, 2 science lab required, 3 science lab recommended, 1 foreign language required, 2 foreign language recommended, 2 social studies required, 3 social studies recommended, 1 history required, 2 history recommended, 4 elective required. **Freshman Admission Statistics:** 1,210 applied, 77% accepted, 35% of those accepted enrolled. **Transfer Admission Requirements:** *Items required:* college transcript, statement of good standing from prior school. Minimum college GPA of 2.6 required. Lowest grade transferable C. **General Admission Information:** Application fee $25. Regular application deadline May 15. Nonfall registration accepted. Admission may be deferred for a maximum of 2 years. Credit offered for CEEB Advanced Placement tests.

COSTS AND FINANCIAL AID

Tuition $17,500. Room & board $5,790. Required fees $0. Average book expense $600. **Required Forms and Deadlines:** FAFSA and institution's own financial aid form. No deadline for regular filing. Priority filing deadline April 15. **Notification of Awards:** Applicants will be notified of awards on or about February 10. **Types of Aid:** *Need-based scholarships/grants:* Pell, SEOG, state scholarships/grants, private scholarships, the school's own gift aid. *Loans:* Direct Subsidized Stafford, Direct Unsubsidized Stafford, Direct PLUS, Federal Perkins, college/university loans from institutional funds. **Student Employment:** Federal Work-Study Program available. Institutional employment available. Off-campus job opportunities are good. **Financial Aid Statistics:** 77% freshmen, 64% undergrads receive some form of aid. Average freshman grant $10,733. Average freshman loan $4,190. Average income from on-campus job $960. **Financial Aid Phone:** 630-617-3075.

ELMIRA COLLEGE

One Park Place, Elmira, NY 14901
Phone: 607-735-1724 **E-mail:** admissions@elmira.edu **CEEB Code:** 2226
Fax: 607-735-1718 **Web:** www.elmira.edu **ACT Code:** 2736

This private school was founded in 1855. It has a 42-acre campus.

STUDENTS AND FACULTY

Enrollment: 1,547. **Student Body:** Male 29%, female 71%, out-of-state 51%, international 4% (23 countries represented). **Ethnic Representation:** African American 2%, Asian 1%, Caucasian 85%, Hispanic 1%. **Retention and Graduation:** 81% freshmen return for sophomore year. 55% freshmen graduate within 4 years. 45% grads go on to further study within 1 year. 9% grads pursue business degrees. 2% grads pursue law degrees. 1% grads pursue medical degrees. **Faculty:** Student/faculty ratio 12:1. 80 full-time faculty, 100% hold PhDs. 100% faculty teach undergrads.

ACADEMICS

Degrees: Bachelor's, master's. **Academic Requirements:** General education including some course work in arts/fine arts, computer literacy, English (including composition), humanities, mathematics, sciences (biological or physical), social science. **Classes:** Under 10 students in an average class. 10-19 students in an average lab/discussion section. **Majors with Highest Enrollment:** Business administration/management; elementary education and teaching; psychology, general. **Disciplines with Highest Percentage of Degrees Awarded:** Education 28%, psychology 14%, business/marketing 13%, health professions and related sciences 12%, protective services/public administration 8%. **Special Study Options:** Accelerated program, double major, English as a second language, student exchange program (domestic), independent study, internships, liberal arts/career combination, student-designed major, study abroad, teacher certification program.

FACILITIES

Housing: Coed, all-female, apartments for single students. **Library Holdings:** 389,036 bound volumes. 1,755 periodicals. 1,320,000 microforms. 46,000 audiovisuals. **Special Academic Facilities/Equipment:** Center for Mark Twain studies, American studies center. **Computers:** School-owned computers available for student use.

EXTRACURRICULARS

Activities: Choral groups, concert band, dance, drama/theater, literary magazine, music ensembles, musical theater, pep band, radio station, student government, student newspaper, yearbook. **Organizations:** 74 registered organizations, 13 honor societies, 2 religious organizations. **Athletics (Intercollegiate):** *Men:* basketball, golf, ice hockey, lacrosse, soccer, tennis. *Women:* basketball, cheerleading, field hockey, golf, ice hockey, lacrosse, soccer, softball, tennis, volleyball.

ADMISSIONS

Selectivity Rating: 80 (of 100). **Freshman Academic Profile:** Average high school GPA 3.5. 24% in top 10% of high school class, 49% in top 25% of high school class, 83% in top 50% of high school class. 70% from public high schools. Average SAT I Math 560, SAT I Math middle 50% range 520-600. Average SAT I Verbal 560, SAT I Verbal middle 50% range 510-610. Average ACT 25, ACT middle 50% range 23-28. TOEFL required of all international applicants, minimum TOEFL 500. **Basis for Candidate Selection:** *Very important factors considered include:* character/personal qualities, class rank, secondary school record. *Important factors considered include:* essays, extracurricular activities, recommendations, standardized test scores. *Other factors considered include:* alumni/ae relation, geographical residence, interview, minority status, talent/ability, volunteer work, work experience. **Freshman Admission Requirements:** High school diploma or GED is required. *Academic units required/recommended:* 16 total required; 4 English required, 3 math required, 3 science required, 2 science lab required, 2 foreign language recommended, 3 social studies required, 1 history required, 2 elective required. **Freshman Admission Statistics:** 1,786 applied, 74% accepted, 26% of those accepted enrolled. **Transfer Admission Requirements:** *Items required:* college transcript, essay. Minimum college GPA of 2.0 required. Lowest grade transferable C-. **General Admission Information:** Application fee $50. Priority application deadline March 15. Early decision application deadline November 15. Regular application deadline rolling. Nonfall registration accepted. Admission may be deferred for a maximum of 1 year. Credit and/or placement offered for CEEB Advanced Placement tests.

COSTS AND FINANCIAL AID

Tuition $25,040. Room & board $8,080. Required fees $700. Average book expense $450. **Required Forms and Deadlines:** FAFSA, state aid form if applicable (New York, Vermont, and Rhode Island). No deadline for regular filing. Priority filing deadline February 1. **Notification of Awards:** Applicants will be notified of awards on a rolling basis beginning on or about February 1. **Types of Aid:** *Need-based scholarships/grants:* Pell, SEOG, state scholarships/grants, private scholarships, the school's own gift aid. *Loans:* FFEL Subsidized Stafford, FFEL Unsubsidized Stafford, FFEL PLUS, Federal Perkins, college/university loans from institutional funds, GATE student loan, alternative loans. **Student Employment:** Federal Work-Study Program available. Institutional employment available. Off-campus job opportunities are good. **Financial Aid Statistics:** 83% freshmen, 77% undergrads receive some form of aid. Average freshman grant $15,159. Average freshman loan $5,765. Average income from on-campus job $1,000. **Financial Aid Phone:** 607-735-1728.

ELMS COLLEGE

291 Springfield St., Chicopee, MA 01013
Phone: 413-592-3189 **E-mail:** admissions@elms.edu **CEEB Code:** 3283
Fax: 413-594-2781 **Web:** www.elms.edu **ACT Code:** 1812

This private school, which is affiliated with the Roman Catholic Church, was founded in 1928. It has a 32-acre campus.

STUDENTS AND FACULTY

Enrollment: 685. **Student Body:** Male 19%, female 81%, out-of-state 17%, international students represent 10 countries. **Ethnic Representation:** African American 4%, Asian 2%, Caucasian 76%, Hispanic 4%. **Retention and Graduation:** 62% freshmen return for sophomore year. 48% freshmen graduate within 4 years. **Faculty:** Student/faculty ratio 12:1. 44 full-time faculty, 75% hold PhDs. 100% faculty teach undergrads.

ACADEMICS

Degrees: Associate's, bachelor's, certificate, master's, terminal. **Academic Requirements:** General education including some course work in arts/fine arts, computer literacy, English (including composition), foreign languages, history, humanities, mathematics, philosophy, sciences (biological or physical), social science, community service. **Classes:** Under 10 students in an average class. **Majors with Highest Enrollment:** Education, general; social work; nursing/registered nurse training (RN, ASN, BSN, MSN). **Disciplines with Highest Percentage of Degrees Awarded:** Health professions and related sciences 25%, business/marketing 19%, social sciences and history 12%, psychology 10%, education 7%. **Special Study Options:** Cross registration, distance learning, double major, English as a second language, student exchange program (domestic), honors program, independent study, internships, liberal arts/career combination, study abroad, teacher certification program, weekend college.

FACILITIES

Housing: Coed, all-female. **Library Holdings:** 111,379 bound volumes. 529 periodicals. 3,334 microforms. 2,948 audiovisuals. **Special Academic Facilities/Equipment:** Art gallery, rare book gallery with Edward Bellamy Collection of rare manuscripts. **Computers:** *Recommended operating system:* Windows 3x. School-owned computers available for student use.

EXTRACURRICULARS

Activities: Choral groups, dance, drama/theater, literary magazine, radio station, student government, student newspaper, yearbook. **Organizations:** 25 registered organizations, 6 honor societies, 1 religious organization. **Athletics (Intercollegiate):** *Men:* basketball, cross-country, golf, soccer, swimming, volleyball. *Women:* basketball, cross-country, equestrian, field hockey, lacrosse, soccer, softball, swimming, volleyball.

ADMISSIONS

Selectivity Rating: 67 (of 100). **Freshman Academic Profile:** Average high school GPA 2.8. 13% in top 10% of high school class, 40% in top 25% of high school class, 67% in top 50% of high school class. 86% from public high schools. Average SAT I Math 477, SAT I Math middle 50% range 430-640. Average SAT I Verbal 490, SAT I Verbal middle 50% range 430-530. TOEFL required of all international applicants, minimum TOEFL 450. **Basis for Candidate Selection:** *Very important factors considered include:* alumni/ae relation, essays, secondary school record. *Important factors considered include:* character/personal qualities, class rank, extracurricular activities, interview, recommendations, standardized test scores, volunteer work. *Other factors considered include:* talent/ability, work experience. **Freshman Admission Requirements:** High school diploma or GED is required. *Academic units required/recommended:* 12 total required; 20 total recommended; 4 English required, 4 English recommended, 2 math required, 4 math recommended, 2 science required, 4 science recommended, 2 science lab required, 2 science lab recommended, 2 foreign language required, 4 foreign language recommended, 1 social studies required, 2 social studies recommended, 1 history required, 2 history recommended. **Freshman Admission Statistics:** 384 applied, 90% accepted, 41% of those accepted enrolled. **Transfer Admission Requirements:** *Items required:* high school transcript, college transcript, essay, interview. Minimum high school GPA of 2.0 required. Minimum college GPA of 2.0 required. Lowest grade transferable C. **General Admission Information:** Application fee $30. Priority application deadline March 1. Nonfall registration accepted. Admission may be deferred for a maximum of 1 year. Credit and/or placement offered for CEEB Advanced Placement tests.

COSTS AND FINANCIAL AID

Tuition $16,490. Room & board $6,490. Required fees $670. Average book expense $600. **Required Forms and Deadlines:** FAFSA, institution's own financial aid form, and state aid form. No deadline for regular filing. Priority filing deadline March 1. **Notification of Awards:** Applicants will be notified of awards on a rolling basis beginning on or about February 15. **Types of Aid:** *Need-based scholarships/grants:* Pell, SEOG, state scholarships/grants, private scholarships, the school's own gift aid. *Loans:* FFEL Subsidized Stafford, FFEL Unsubsidized Stafford, FFEL PLUS, Federal Perkins, state loans, alternative loan sources. **Student Employment:** Federal Work-Study Program available. Institutional employment available. Off-campus job opportunities are good. **Financial Aid Statistics:** 82% freshmen, 85% undergrads receive some form of aid. **Financial Aid Phone:** 413-594-2761.

ELON UNIVERSITY

2700 Campus Box, Elon, NC 27244
Phone: 336-278-3566 **E-mail:** admissions@elon.edu **CEEB Code:** 5183
Fax: 336-278-7699 **Web:** www.elon.edu **ACT Code:** 3096

This private school, which is affiliated with the United Church of Christ, was founded in 1889. It has a 502-acre campus.

STUDENTS AND FACULTY

Enrollment: 3,900. **Student Body:** Male 39%, female 61%, out-of-state 72%, international 2% (41 countries represented). **Ethnic Representation:** African American 6%, Asian 1%, Caucasian 88%, Hispanic 1%. **Retention and Graduation:** 84% freshmen return for sophomore year. 59% freshmen graduate within 4 years. 16% grads go on to further study within 1 year. 2% grads pursue business degrees. 3% grads pursue law degrees. 2% grads pursue medical degrees. **Faculty:** Student/faculty ratio 15:1. 235 full-time faculty, 83% hold PhDs. 100% faculty teach undergrads.

ACADEMICS

Degrees: Bachelor's, doctoral, master's. **Academic Requirements:** General education including some course work in English (including composition), humanities, mathematics, sciences (biological or physical), social science. **Classes:** 20-29 students in an average class. 20-29 students in an average lab/discussion section. **Majors with Highest Enrollment:** Business administration/management; mass communications/media studies; education, general. **Disciplines with Highest Percentage of Degrees Awarded:** Business/marketing 24%, communications/communication technologies 19%, education 11%, social sciences and history 10%, parks and recreation 8%. **Special Study Options:** Accelerated program, cross registration, double major, English as a second language, student exchange program (domestic), honors program, independent study, internships, liberal arts/career combination, student-designed major, study abroad, teacher certification program.

FACILITIES

Housing: Coed, all-female, all-male, apartments for single students, housing for international students, fraternities and/or sororities. **Library Holdings:** 214,979 bound volumes. 1,214 periodicals. 850,466 microforms. 12,164 audiovisuals. **Special Academic Facilities/Equipment:** Resource center, fine arts center with recital hall, theatre, television studios, music rooms, campus center, athletic center, art gallery. **Computers:** School-owned computers available for student use.

EXTRACURRICULARS

Activities: Choral groups, concert band, dance, drama/theater, jazz band, literary magazine, marching band, music ensembles, musical theater, pep band, radio station, student government, student newspaper, student-run film society, symphony orchestra, television station, yearbook. **Organizations:** 140 registered organizations, 22 honor societies, 9 religious organizations, 8 fraternities (29% men join), 10 sororities (39% women join). **Athletics (Intercollegiate):** *Men:* baseball, basketball, cheerleading, cross-country, football, soccer, tennis. *Women:* basketball, cheerleading, cross-country, golf, indoor track, soccer, softball, tennis, track & field, volleyball.

ADMISSIONS

Selectivity Rating: 74 (of 100). **Freshman Academic Profile:** Average high school GPA 3.6. 22% in top 10% of high school class, 56% in top 25% of high school class, 92% in top 50% of high school class. 79% from public high schools. Average SAT I Math 578, SAT I Math middle 50% range 530-620. Average SAT I Verbal 567, SAT I Verbal middle 50% range 520-610. Average ACT 25. TOEFL required of all international applicants, minimum TOEFL 500. **Basis for Candidate Selection:** *Very important factors considered include:* secondary school record, standardized test scores. *Important factors considered include:* class rank, essays. *Other factors considered include:* alumni/ae relation, character/personal qualities, extracurricular activities, minority status, recommendations, talent/ability, volunteer work, work experience. **Freshman Admission Requirements:** High school diploma or GED is required. *Academic units required/recommended:* 4 English required, 3 math required, 4 math recommended, 2 science required, 3 science recommended, 1 science lab required, 1 science lab recommended, 2 foreign language required, 2 social studies required, 2 social studies recommended, 1 history required, 1 history recommended. **Freshman Admission Statistics:** 6,504 applied, 50% accepted, 37% of those accepted enrolled. **Transfer Admission Requirements:** *Items required:* high school transcript, college transcript, standardized test scores, statement of good standing from prior school. Minimum high school GPA of 2.3 required. Minimum college GPA of 2.5 required. Lowest grade transferable C-. **General Admission Information:** Application fee $35. Priority application deadline January 10. Early decision application deadline November 15. Admission may be deferred for a maximum of 1 year. Credit and/or placement offered for CEEB Advanced Placement tests.

COSTS AND FINANCIAL AID

Tuition $15,280. Room & board $5,090. Required fees $225. Average book expense $800. **Required Forms and Deadlines:** FAFSA, institution's own financial aid form, and CSS/Financial Aid PROFILE. Priority filing deadline February 15. **Notification of Awards:** Applicants will be notified of awards on a rolling basis beginning on or about March 30. **Types of Aid:** *Need-based scholarships/grants:* Pell, SEOG, state scholarships/grants, private scholarships, the school's own gift aid. *Loans:* FFEL Subsidized Stafford, FFEL Unsubsidized Stafford, FFEL PLUS, Federal Perkins, state loans, college/university loans from institutional funds, privately funded alternative loans. **Student Employment:** Federal Work-Study Program available. Institutional employment available. Off-campus job opportunities are excellent. **Financial Aid Statistics:** 37% freshmen, 36% undergrads receive some form of aid. Average freshman grant $4,296. Average freshman loan $2,167. Average income from on-campus job $1,500. **Financial Aid Phone:** 800-334-8448.

EMBRY RIDDLE AERONAUTICAL UNIVERSITY (AZ)

3200 Willow Creek Road, Prescott, AZ 86301-3720
Phone: 928-777-6600 **E-mail:** pradmit@erau.edu **CEEB Code:** 4305
Fax: 928-777-6606 **Web:** www.embryriddle.edu **ACT Code:** 725

This private school was founded in 1926. It has a 565-acre campus.

STUDENTS AND FACULTY

Enrollment: 1,671. **Student Body:** Male 85%, female 15%, out-of-state 77%, international 9%. **Ethnic Representation:** African American 2%, Asian 7%, Caucasian 83%, Hispanic 6%, Native American 1%. **Retention and Graduation:** 69% freshmen return for sophomore year. 27% freshmen graduate within 4 years. **Faculty:** Student/faculty ratio 17:1. 84 full-time faculty, 57% hold PhDs. 100% faculty teach undergrads.

ACADEMICS

Degrees: Bachelor's, master's. **Academic Requirements:** General education including some course work in computer literacy, English (including composition), humanities, mathematics, sciences (biological or physical), social science. **Classes:** 20-29 students in an average class. 10-19 students in an average lab/discussion section. **Majors with Highest Enrollment:** Aerospace, aeronautical and astronautical engineering; aeronautics/aviation/aerospace science and technology, general; airline/commercial/professional pilot and flight crew. **Disciplines with Highest Percentage of Degrees Awarded:** Trade and industry 62%, engineering/engineering technology 36%, computer and information sciences 2%. **Special Study Options:** Cooperative (work-study) program, distance learning, double major, dual enrollment, English as a second language, independent study, internships, study abroad.

FACILITIES

Housing: Coed, apartments for single students. **Library Holdings:** 28,264 bound volumes. 629 periodicals. 188,740 microforms. 2,518 audiovisuals. **Special Academic Facilities/Equipment:** Fully equipped aircraft, training simulators, airway science simulation lab, wind tunnel. **Computers:** School-owned computers available for student use.

EXTRACURRICULARS

Activities: Jazz band, literary magazine, radio station, student government, student newspaper, television station. **Organizations:** 63 registered organizations, 3 honor societies, 3 religious organizations, 4 fraternities (11% men join), 1 sorority (16% women join). **Athletics (Intercollegiate):** *Men:* wrestling. *Women:* volleyball.

ADMISSIONS

Selectivity Rating: 71 (of 100). **Freshman Academic Profile:** Average high school GPA 3.4. 15% in top 10% of high school class, 40% in top 25% of high school class, 82% in top 50% of high school class. Average SAT I Math 554, SAT I Math middle 50% range 500-630. Average SAT I Verbal 519, SAT I Verbal middle 50% range 460-580. Average ACT 23, ACT middle 50% range 21-26. TOEFL required of all international applicants, minimum TOEFL 500. **Basis for Candidate Selection:** *Very important factors considered include:* secondary school record. *Important factors considered include:* class rank, essays, extracurricular activities, interview, standardized test scores. *Other factors considered include:* alumni/ae relation, character/personal qualities, recommendations, talent/ability, volunteer work, work experience. **Freshman Admission Requirements:** High school diploma or GED is required. *Academic units required/recommended:* 12 total required; 4 English required, 4 English recommended, 3 math required, 4 math recommended, 2 science required, 3 science recommended, 1 science lab required, 2 science lab recommended, 2 foreign language recommended, 3 social studies required, 3 social studies recommended. **Freshman Admission Statistics:** 1,389 applied, 78% accepted, 29% of those accepted enrolled. **Transfer Admission Requirements:** *Items required:* high school transcript, college transcript. Minimum high school GPA of 2.5 required. Minimum college GPA of 2.0 required. Lowest grade transferable D. **General Admission Information:** Application fee $30. Priority application deadline March 1. Early decision application deadline December 1. Nonfall registration accepted. Admission may be deferred for a maximum of 1 year. Credit and/or placement offered for CEEB Advanced Placement tests.

COSTS AND FINANCIAL AID

Tuition $19,300. Room & board $5,808. Required fees $630. Average book expense $900. **Required Forms and Deadlines:** FAFSA. No deadline for regular filing. Priority filing deadline April 15. **Notification of Awards:** Applicants will be notified of awards on a rolling basis beginning on or about February 1. **Types of Aid:** *Need-based scholarships/grants:* Pell, SEOG, state scholarships/grants, private scholarships, the school's own gift aid. *Loans:* Direct Subsidized Stafford, Direct Unsubsidized Stafford, Direct PLUS. **Student Employment:** Federal Work-Study Program available. Institutional employment available. Off-campus job opportunities are fair. **Financial Aid Statistics:** 64% freshmen, 65% undergrads receive some form of aid. Average freshman grant $3,526. Average freshman loan $3,253. **Financial Aid Phone:** 928-708-3765.

EMBRY RIDDLE AERONAUTICAL UNIVERSITY (FL)

600 South Clyde Morris Boulevard, Daytona Beach, FL 32114-3900
Phone: 386-226-6100 **E-mail:** dbadmit@erau.edu **CEEB Code:** 5190
Fax: 386-226-7070 **Web:** www.embryriddle.edu **ACT Code:** 725

This private school was founded in 1926. It has a 178-acre campus.

STUDENTS AND FACULTY

Enrollment: 4,485. **Student Body:** Male 82%, female 18%, out-of-state 69%, international 16%. **Ethnic Representation:** African American 6%, Asian 4%, Caucasian 81%, Hispanic 6%, Native American 1%. **Retention and Graduation:** 80% freshmen return for sophomore year. 19% freshmen graduate within 4 years. 5% grads go on to further study within 1 year. **Faculty:** Student/faculty ratio 19:1. 203 full-time faculty, 61% hold PhDs. 100% faculty teach undergrads.

ACADEMICS

Degrees: Associate's, bachelor's, master's. **Academic Requirements:** General education including some course work in computer literacy, English (including composition), humanities, mathematics, sciences (biological or physical), social science. **Classes:** 20-29 students in an average class. 10-19 students in an average lab/discussion section. **Majors with Highest Enrollment:** Business/managerial operations; aerospace, aeronautical and astronautical engineering; airline/commercial/professional pilot and flight crew. **Disciplines with Highest Percentage of Degrees Awarded:** Trade and industry 54%, engineering/engineering technology 28%, business/marketing 10%, computer and information sciences 3%, psychology 3%. **Special Study Options:** Cooperative (work-study) program, distance learning, double major, dual enrollment, English as a second language, independent study, internships, study abroad.

FACILITIES

Housing: Coed, apartments for single students, housing for disabled students, special units in regular, coed dorms. **Library Holdings:** 138,327 bound volumes. 741 periodicals. 295,619 microforms. 7,030 audiovisuals. **Special Academic Facilities/Equipment:** Fully equipped aircraft, training simulators, airway science simulation lab, wind tunnel. **Computers:** School-owned computers available for student use.

EXTRACURRICULARS

Activities: Choral groups, dance, drama/theater, pep band, radio station, student government, student newspaper, yearbook. **Organizations:** 113 registered organizations, 6 honor societies, 6 religious organizations, 12 fraternities (9% men join), 4 sororities (6% women join). **Athletics (Intercollegiate):** *Men:* baseball, basketball, cross-country, golf, soccer, tennis. *Women:* cross-country, soccer, tennis, volleyball.

ADMISSIONS

Selectivity Rating: 69 (of 100). **Freshman Academic Profile:** Average high school GPA 3.3. 19% in top 10% of high school class, 48% in top 25% of high school class, 81% in top 50% of high school class. Average SAT I Math 572, SAT I Math middle 50% range 520-630. Average SAT I Verbal 543, SAT I Verbal middle 50% range 490-600. Average ACT 24, ACT middle 50% range 21-27. TOEFL required of all international applicants, minimum TOEFL 500. **Basis for Candidate Selection:** *Very important factors considered include:* class rank, recommendations, secondary school record, standardized test scores. *Important factors considered include:* essays. *Other factors considered include:* alumni/ae relation, character/personal qualities, extracurricular activities, interview, talent/ability, volunteer work, work experience. **Freshman Admission Requirements:** High school diploma or GED is required. *Academic units required/recommended:* 15 total required; 18 total recommended; 4 English required, 4 English recommended, 2 math required, 3 math recommended, 2 science required, 3 science recommended, 2 science lab required, 3 science lab recommended, 2 foreign language recommended, 3 social studies required, 3 social studies recommended, 1 history required, 2 history recommended, 3 elective required, 3 elective recommended. **Freshman Admission Statistics:** 2,858 applied, 78% accepted, 39% of those accepted enrolled. **Transfer Admission Requirements:** *Items required:* college transcript, essay. Minimum high school GPA of 2.0 required. Minimum college GPA of 2.0 required. Lowest grade transferable D. **General Admission Information:** Application fee $30. Priority application deadline March 1. Early decision application deadline December 1. Regular application deadline July 1. Nonfall registration accepted. Admission may be deferred for a maximum of 1 year. Credit and/or placement offered for CEEB Advanced Placement tests.

COSTS AND FINANCIAL AID

Tuition $21,289. Room & board $6,370. Required fees $660. Average book expense $900. **Required Forms and Deadlines:** FAFSA. No deadline for regular filing. Priority filing deadline April 15. **Notification of Awards:** Applicants will be notified of awards on a rolling basis beginning on or about February 1. **Types of Aid:** *Need-based scholarships/grants:* Pell, SEOG, state scholarships/grants, private scholarships, the school's own gift aid. *Loans:* Direct Subsidized Stafford, Direct Unsubsidized Stafford, Direct PLUS, Federal Perkins, college/university loans from institutional funds. **Student Employment:** Federal Work-Study Program available. Institutional employment available. Off-campus job opportunities are excellent. **Financial Aid Statistics:** 67% freshmen, 55% undergrads receive some form of aid. Average freshman grant $3,865. Average freshman loan $3,067. **Financial Aid Phone:** 800-943-6279.

See page 1020.

EMERSON COLLEGE

120 Boylston Street, Boston, MA 02116-4624
Phone: 617-824-8600 **E-mail:** admission@emerson.edu **CEEB Code:** 3367
Fax: 617-824-8609 **Web:** www.emerson.edu **ACT Code:** 1820

This private school was founded in 1880.

STUDENTS AND FACULTY

Enrollment: 3,518. **Student Body:** Male 38%, female 62%, out-of-state 65%, international 4% (62 countries represented). **Ethnic Representation:** African American 2%, Asian 3%, Caucasian 90%, Hispanic 5%. **Retention and Graduation:** 84% freshmen return for sophomore year. 66% freshmen graduate within 4 years. 4% grads go on to further study within 1 year. **Faculty:** Student/faculty ratio 15:1. 128 full-time faculty, 71% hold PhDs. 97% faculty teach undergrads.

ACADEMICS

Degrees: Bachelor's, master's. **Academic Requirements:** General education including some course work in arts/fine arts, English (including composition), foreign languages, history, humanities, mathematics, philosophy, sciences (biological or physical), social science. **Classes:** 10-19 students in an average class. 10-19 students in an average lab/discussion section. **Majors with Highest Enrollment:** Visual and performing arts, general; cinematography and film/video production; communications, journalism, and related fields. **Disciplines with Highest Percentage of Degrees Awarded:** Visual and performing arts 57%, communications/communication technologies 19%, English 15%, business/marketing 8%, education 1%. **Special Study Options:** Cross registration, double major, honors program, independent study, internships, liberal arts/career combination, student-designed major, study abroad, teacher certification program.

FACILITIES

Housing: Coed, learning/living clusters (e.g. writers' block and digital culture floors). **Library Holdings:** 141,715 bound volumes. 679 periodicals. 11,056 microforms. 8,597 audiovisuals. **Special Academic Facilities/Equipment:** New 11-story Tufte Performance & Production Center housing TV studios and performing arts facilities; 2 on-campus radio stations; 1,200-seat Emerson Majestic Theatre; digital production labs and Avid composers; 7 clinics/programs for observing speech and hearing therapy; Internet kiosks across campus; and a new multistory college center and residence hall is in the design stage. **Computers:** School-owned computers available for student use.

EXTRACURRICULARS

Activities: Dance, drama/theater, literary magazine, musical theater, radio station, student government, student newspaper, student-run film society, television station, yearbook. **Organizations:** 52 registered organizations, 4 honor societies, 3 religious organizations, 5 fraternities (5% men join), 4 sororities (4% women join). **Athletics (Intercollegiate):** *Men:* baseball, basketball, lacrosse, soccer, tennis. *Women:* basketball, cross-country, lacrosse, soccer, softball, tennis, volleyball.

ADMISSIONS

Selectivity Rating: 82 (of 100). **Freshman Academic Profile:** Average high school GPA 3.5. 29% in top 10% of high school class, 71% in top 25% of high school class, 98% in top 50% of high school class. 76% from public high schools. Average SAT I Math 584, SAT I Math middle 50% range 540-630. Average SAT I Verbal 619, SAT I Verbal middle 50% range 570-660. Average ACT 27, ACT middle 50% range 24-28. TOEFL required of all international applicants, minimum TOEFL 550. **Basis for Candidate Selection:** *Very important factors considered include:* secondary school record, standardized test scores. *Important factors considered include:* character/personal qualities, essays, extracurricular activities, recommendations, talent/ability. *Other factors considered include:* alumni/ae relation, class rank, interview, minority status, volunteer work, work experience. **Freshman Admission Requirements:** High school diploma or GED is required. *Academic units required/recommended:* 16 total required; 20 total recommended; 4 English required, 4 English recommended, 3 math required, 3 math recommended, 3 science required, 3 science recommended, 3 foreign language required, 3 foreign language recommended, 3 social studies required, 3 social studies recommended, 4 elective recommended. **Freshman Admission Statistics:** 3,805 applied, 52% accepted, 33% of those accepted enrolled. **Transfer Admission Requirements:** *Items required:* high school transcript, college transcript, essay. Minimum college GPA of 3.0 required. Lowest grade transferable C. **General Admission Information:** Application fee $55. Regular application deadline February 1. Nonfall registration accepted. Admission may be deferred for a maximum of 1 year. Credit and/or placement offered for CEEB Advanced Placement tests.

COSTS AND FINANCIAL AID

Tuition $21,120. Room & board $9,542. Required fees $504. Average book expense $680. **Required Forms and Deadlines:** FAFSA, institution's own financial aid form, CSS/Financial Aid PROFILE, noncustodial (divorced/separated) parent's statement, business/farm supplement, and tax returns. Priority filing deadline March 1. **Notification of Awards:** Applicants will be notified of awards on or about April 1. **Types of Aid:** *Need-based scholarships/grants:* Pell, SEOG, state scholarships/grants, private scholarships, the school's own gift aid. *Loans:* FFEL Subsidized Stafford, FFEL Unsubsidized Stafford, FFEL PLUS, Federal Perkins, state loans. **Student Employment:** Federal Work-Study Program available. Institutional employment available. Off-campus job opportunities are excellent. **Financial Aid Statistics:** 70% freshmen, 61% undergrads receive some form of aid. Average freshman grant $13,000. Average freshman loan $3,000. Average income from on-campus job $2,000. **Financial Aid Phone:** 617-824-8655.

See page 1022.

EMILY CARR INSTITUTE OF ART AND DESIGN

1399 Johnston Street, Granville Island, Vancouver, BC V6H 3R9
Phone: 604-844-3897 **E-mail:** admissions@eciad.bc.ca
Fax: 604-844-3089

This public school was founded in 1925. It has an 80-acre campus.

STUDENTS AND FACULTY

Enrollment: 1,293. **Student Body:** Male 37%, female 63%, out-of-state 32%. **Retention and Graduation:** 20% grads go on to further study within 1 year. **Faculty:** Student/faculty ratio 22:1. 60 full-time faculty, 30% hold PhDs. 100% faculty teach undergrads.

ACADEMICS

Degrees: Bachelor's, post-bachelor's certificate. **Academic Requirements:** General education including some course work in arts/fine arts, computer literacy, English (including composition), humanities, social science, art history and theory. **Classes:** 10-19 students in an average class. 10-19 students in an average lab/discussion section. **Majors with Highest Enrollment:** Visual and performing arts, general; design and visual communications, general; animation, interactive technology, video graphics, and special effects. **Disciplines with Highest Percentage of Degrees Awarded:** Visual and performing arts 56%, communications/communication technologies 19%. **Special Study Options:** Cooperative (work-study) program, cross registration, distance learning, student exchange program (domestic), independent study, internships, liberal arts/career combination, student-designed major, study abroad.

FACILITIES

Housing: Off-campus housing assistance. **Library Holdings:** 21,000 bound volumes. 25,000 periodicals. 118,000 microforms. 2,500 audiovisuals. **Special Academic Facilities/Equipment:** 2 galleries, center for art and technology. **Computers:** School-owned computers available for student use.

EXTRACURRICULARS

Activities: Radio station, student government, student newspaper, student-run film society, yearbook. **Organizations:** 12 registered organizations.

ADMISSIONS

Selectivity Rating: 60 (of 100). **Freshman Academic Profile:** Average high school GPA 3.2. 15% in top 10% of high school class, 35% in top 25% of high school class, 95% in top 50% of high school class. 35% from public high schools. TOEFL required of all international applicants, minimum TOEFL 570. **Basis for Candidate Selection:** *Very important factors considered include:* secondary school record, talent/ability. *Important factors considered include:* essays. **Transfer Admission Requirements:** *Items required:* college transcript, essay. **General Admission Information:** Application fee $30. Early decision application deadline November 1. Regular application deadline March 1. Nonfall registration accepted. Admission may be deferred for a maximum of 1 year. Credit and/or placement offered for CEEB Advanced Placement tests.

COSTS AND FINANCIAL AID

Required fees $90. Average book expense $1,500. **Types of Aid:** *Need-based scholarships/grants:* Pell, SEOG, state scholarships/grants, private scholarships, the school's own gift aid. *Loans:* FFEL Subsidized Stafford, FFEL Unsubsidized Stafford, FFEL PLUS, Federal Perkins, college/university loans from institutional funds. **Student Employment:** Institutional employment available. Off-campus job opportunities are good. **Financial Aid Statistics:** Average freshman grant $2,000. Average freshman loan $6,000. Average income from on-campus job $1,200. **Financial Aid Phone:** 604-844-3844.

EMMANUEL COLLEGE (GA)

PO Box 129, Franklin Springs, GA 30639-0129
Phone: 706-245-7226 **E-mail:** admissions@emmanuelcollege.edu **CEEB Code:** 5184
Fax: 706-245-4424 **Web:** www.emmanuelcollege.edu

This private school, which is affiliated with the Pentecostal Church, was founded in 1919. It has a 150-acre campus.

STUDENTS AND FACULTY

Enrollment: 768. **Student Body:** Male 45%, female 55%, out-of-state 23%, international 1% (10 countries represented). **Ethnic Representation:** African American 16%, Asian 2%, Caucasian 82%, Native American 1%. **Retention and Graduation:** 65% freshmen return for sophomore year. 28% freshmen graduate within 4 years. **Faculty:** Student/faculty ratio 15:1. 43 full-time faculty, 58% hold PhDs. 100% faculty teach undergrads.

ACADEMICS

Degrees: Associate's, bachelor's, terminal, transfer. **Academic Requirements:** General education including some course work in computer literacy, English (including composition), history, humanities, mathematics, philosophy, sciences (biological or physical), social science, Bible survey. **Classes:** 10-19 students in an average class. **Majors with Highest Enrollment:** Elementary education and teaching; theological studies and religious vocations; psychology, general. **Disciplines with Highest Percentage of Degrees Awarded:** Education 26%, philosophy/religion/theology 18%, business/marketing 11%, psychology 10%, parks and recreation 10%. **Special Study Options:** Double major, dual enrollment, independent study, internships, teacher certification program.

FACILITIES

Housing: All-female, all-male, apartments for married students. **Library Holdings:** 44,966 bound volumes. 187 periodicals. 4,491 microforms. 3,092 audiovisuals. **Computers:** School-owned computers available for student use.

EXTRACURRICULARS

Activities: Choral groups, drama/theater, jazz band, literary magazine, music ensembles, musical theater, student government, student newspaper, yearbook. **Organizations:** 25 registered organizations, 3 honor societies, 15 religious organizations. **Athletics (Intercollegiate):** *Men:* baseball, basketball, soccer, tennis. *Women:* basketball, soccer, softball, tennis.

ADMISSIONS

Selectivity Rating: 63 (of 100). **Freshman Academic Profile:** 85% from public high schools. TOEFL required of all international applicants, minimum TOEFL 550. **Basis for Candidate Selection:** *Very important factors considered include:* secondary school record, standardized test scores. *Other factors considered include:* recommendations. **Freshman Admission Requirements:** High school diploma or GED is required. **Freshman Admission Statistics:** 1,304 applied, 40% accepted, 37% of those accepted enrolled. **Transfer Admission Requirements:** *Items required:* college transcript, standardized test scores. Lowest grade transferable D. **General Admission Information:** Application fee $25. Regular application deadline August 1. Nonfall registration accepted. Credit offered for CEEB Advanced Placement tests.

COSTS AND FINANCIAL AID

Tuition $8,232. Room & board $3,934. Required fees $220. Average book expense $600. **Required Forms and Deadlines:** FAFSA, institution's own financial aid form, and state aid form. Priority filing deadline May 15. **Notification of Awards:** Applicants will be notified of awards on a rolling basis beginning on or about March 15. **Types of Aid:** *Need-based scholarships/grants:* Pell, SEOG, state scholarships/grants. *Loans:* FFEL Subsidized Stafford, FFEL Unsubsidized Stafford, FFEL PLUS. **Student Employment:** Federal Work-Study Program available. Institutional employment available. Off-campus job opportunities are good. **Financial Aid Statistics:** 76% freshmen, 73% undergrads receive some form of aid. Average freshman grant $8,817. Average freshman loan $2,407. **Financial Aid Phone:** 706-245-7226.

EMMANUEL COLLEGE (MA)

400 The Fenway, Boston, MA 02115
Phone: 617-735-9715 **E-mail:** enroll@emmanuel.edu **CEEB Code:** 3368
Fax: 617-735-9801 **Web:** www.emmanuel.edu **ACT Code:** 1822

This private school, which is affiliated with the Roman Catholic Church, was founded in 1919. It has a 16-acre campus.

STUDENTS AND FACULTY

Enrollment: 847. **Student Body:** Out-of-state 36%, international 9%. **Ethnic Representation:** African American 10%, Asian 4%, Caucasian 64%, Hispanic 6%. **Retention and Graduation:** 79% freshmen return for sophomore year. 51% freshmen graduate within 4 years. **Faculty:** Student/faculty ratio 14:1. 47 full-time faculty, 82% hold PhDs. 100% faculty teach undergrads.

ACADEMICS

Degrees: Bachelor's, master's. **Academic Requirements:** General education including some course work in arts/fine arts, computer literacy, English (including composition), foreign languages, history, humanities, mathematics, philosophy, sciences (biological or physical), social science. **Classes:** 10-19 students in an average class. **Majors with Highest Enrollment:** Education, general; psychology, general; economics, general. **Disciplines with Highest Percentage of Degrees Awarded:** Interdisciplinary studies 14%, education 13%, business/marketing 13%, social sciences and history 12%, psychology 11%. **Special Study Options:** Accelerated program, cross registration, double major, English as a second language, student exchange program (domestic), honors program, independent study, internships, student-designed major, study abroad, teacher certification program, weekend college.

FACILITIES

Housing: Coed, all-female, all-male; upperclassmen housing. **Library Holdings:** 98,513 bound volumes. 876 periodicals. 1,970 microforms. 515 audiovisuals. **Special Academic Facilities/Equipment:** Art gallery, academic resource center, language lab, science center, computer lab. **Computers:** School-owned computers available for student use.

EXTRACURRICULARS

Activities: Choral groups, dance, drama/theater, literary magazine, music ensembles, musical theater, student government, student newspaper, symphony orchestra, yearbook. **Organizations:** 8 registered organizations. **Athletics (Intercollegiate):** *Men:* basketball, cross-country, soccer, track & field, volleyball. *Women:* basketball, cross-country, field hockey, soccer, softball, tennis, track & field, volleyball.

ADMISSIONS

Selectivity Rating: 65 (of 100). **Freshman Academic Profile:** Average high school GPA 3.2. 13% in top 10% of high school class, 43% in top 25% of high school class, 73% in top 50% of high school class. 73% from public high schools. Average SAT I Math 500, SAT I Math middle 50% range 450-570. Average SAT I Verbal 530, SAT I Verbal middle 50% range 470-580. Average ACT 23, ACT middle 50% range 20-21. TOEFL required of all international applicants, minimum TOEFL 500. **Basis for Candidate Selection:** *Very important factors considered include:* secondary school record. *Important factors considered include:* essays, interview, recommendations, standardized test scores. *Other factors considered include:* alumni/ae relation, character/personal qualities, class rank, extracurricular activities, talent/ability, volunteer work, work experience. **Freshman Admission Requirements:** High school diploma or GED is required. *Academic units required/recommended:* 16 total required; 4 English required, 3 math required, 2 science required, 2 science lab required, 2 foreign language required, 2 social studies required. **Freshman Admission Statistics:** 1,463 applied, 70% accepted. **Transfer Admission Requirements:** *Items required:* high school transcript, college transcript, essay, statement of good standing from prior school. Minimum college GPA of 2.0 required. Lowest grade transferable C. **General Admission Information:** Application fee $40. Priority application deadline February 15. Early decision application deadline November 1. Nonfall registration accepted. Admission may be deferred for a maximum of 1 year. Credit and/or placement offered for CEEB Advanced Placement tests.

COSTS AND FINANCIAL AID

Tuition $17,800. Room & board $8,000. Required fees $300. Average book expense $750. **Required Forms and Deadlines:** FAFSA, institution's own financial aid form, and federal tax returns. Priority filing deadline April 1. **Notification of Awards:** Applicants will be notified of awards on a rolling basis beginning on or about March 15. **Types of Aid:** *Need-based scholarships/grants:* Pell, SEOG, state scholarships/grants, private scholarships, the school's own gift aid. *Loans:* Direct Subsidized Stafford, Direct Unsubsidized Stafford,

Direct PLUS, Federal Perkins, state loans, MEFA, Nellie Mae Student EXCEL, Signature, CitiAssist, TERI. **Student Employment:** Federal Work-Study Program available. Institutional employment available. Off-campus job opportunities are excellent. **Financial Aid Statistics:** 81% freshmen, 80% undergrads receive some form of aid. Average freshman grant $10,714. Average freshman loan $5,018. Average income from on-campus job $1,500. **Financial Aid Phone:** 617-735-9725.

EMORY AND HENRY COLLEGE

PO Box 947, Emory, VA 24327
Phone: 800-848-5493 **E-mail:** ehadmiss@ehc.edu **CEEB Code:** 5185
Fax: 276-944-6935 **Web:** www.ehc.edu **ACT Code:** 4350

This private school, which is affiliated with the Methodist Church, was founded in 1836. It has a 165-acre campus.

STUDENTS AND FACULTY

Enrollment: 989. **Student Body:** Male 48%, female 52%, out-of-state 26%, international 1% (6 countries represented). **Ethnic Representation:** African American 4%, Asian 1%, Caucasian 95%. **Retention and Graduation:** 73% freshmen return for sophomore year. 47% freshmen graduate within 4 years. 20% grads go on to further study within 1 year. 2% grads pursue business degrees. 3% grads pursue law degrees. 6% grads pursue medical degrees. **Faculty:** Student/faculty ratio 14:1. 62 full-time faculty, 85% hold PhDs. 100% faculty teach undergrads.

ACADEMICS

Degrees: Bachelor's, master's. **Academic Requirements:** General education including some course work in computer literacy, English (including composition), humanities, sciences (biological or physical), social science. **Classes:** Under 10 students in an average class. Under 10 students in an average lab/discussion section. **Disciplines with Highest Percentage of Degrees Awarded:** Social sciences and history 23%, business/marketing 16%, communications/communication technologies 10%, parks and recreation 8%, interdisciplinary studies 8%. **Special Study Options:** Distance learning, double major, dual enrollment, honors program, independent study, internships, student-designed major, study abroad, teacher certification program.

FACILITIES

Housing: All-female, all-male. **Library Holdings:** 313,338 bound volumes. 12,000 periodicals. 31,821 microforms. 6,169 audiovisuals. **Special Academic Facilities/Equipment:** Language lab, capillary gas chromatograph, DNA vertical slab gel electrophoretic equipment, infrared spectrophotometer. **Computers:** School-owned computers available for student use.

EXTRACURRICULARS

Activities: Choral groups, drama/theater, literary magazine, music ensembles, pep band, radio station, student government, student newspaper, yearbook. **Organizations:** 53 registered organizations, 7 honor societies, 4 religious organizations, 7 fraternities (11% men join), 6 sororities (14% women join). **Athletics (Intercollegiate):** *Men:* baseball, basketball, cross-country, football, golf, soccer, tennis. *Women:* basketball, cross-country, soccer, softball, tennis, volleyball.

ADMISSIONS

Selectivity Rating: 68 (of 100). **Freshman Academic Profile:** Average high school GPA 3.4. 26% in top 10% of high school class, 53% in top 25% of high school class, 88% in top 50% of high school class. 92% from public high schools. SAT I Math middle 50% range 420-570. SAT I Verbal middle 50% range 468-578. Average ACT 23, ACT middle 50% range 19-25. TOEFL required of all international applicants, minimum TOEFL 550. **Basis for Candidate Selection:** *Very important factors considered include:* essays, secondary school record, standardized test scores. *Important factors considered include:* character/personal qualities, class rank, extracurricular activities, interview, recommendations, talent/ability, volunteer work, work experience. *Other factors considered include:* alumni/ae relation, geographical residence, minority status, religious affiliation/commitment, state residency. **Freshman Admission Requirements:** High school diploma or GED is required. *Academic units required/recommended:* 18 total required; 22 total recommended; 4 English required, 4 English recommended, 3 math required, 3 math recommended, 2 science required, 2 science recommended, 2 science lab required, 2 science lab recommended, 2 foreign language required, 2 foreign language recommended, 2 social studies required, 2 social studies recommended, 2 history required, 2 history recommended, 1 elective required, 1 elective recommended. **Freshman Admission Statistics:** 1,127 applied, 78% accepted, 31% of those accepted enrolled. **Transfer Admission Requirements:** *Items required:* college transcript, essay, statement of good standing from prior school. Minimum college GPA of 2.0 required. Lowest grade transferable C. **General Admission Information:** Application fee $30. Priority application deadline February 15. Early decision application deadline December 1. Nonfall registration accepted. Admission may be deferred for a maximum of 1 year. Credit and/or placement offered for CEEB Advanced Placement tests.

COSTS AND FINANCIAL AID

Tuition $12,950. Room & board $5,322. Required fees $200. Average book expense $700. **Required Forms and Deadlines:** FAFSA, institution's own financial aid form, and state aid form. Financial aid filing deadline July 31. Priority filing deadline April 1. **Notification of Awards:** Applicants will be notified of awards on a rolling basis beginning on or about March 1. **Types of Aid:** *Need-based scholarships/grants:* Pell, SEOG, state scholarships/grants, private scholarships, the school's own gift aid. *Loans:* Direct Subsidized Stafford, Direct Unsubsidized Stafford, Direct PLUS, Federal Perkins. **Student Employment:** Federal Work-Study Program available. Off-campus job opportunities are fair. **Financial Aid Statistics:** 76% freshmen, 73% undergrads receive some form of aid. **Financial Aid Phone:** 540-944-6115.

EMORY UNIVERSITY

Boisfeuillet Jones Center, Atlanta, GA 30322
Phone: 404-727-6036 **E-mail:** admiss@emory.edu **CEEB Code:** 5187
Fax: 404-727-4303 **Web:** www.emory.edu **ACT Code:** 810

This private school, which is affiliated with the Methodist Church, was founded in 1836. It has a 631-acre campus.

STUDENTS AND FACULTY

Enrollment: 6,285. **Student Body:** Male 44%, female 56%, out-of-state 72%, international 4%. **Ethnic Representation:** African American 10%, Asian 15%, Caucasian 65%, Hispanic 3%. **Retention and Graduation:** 94% freshmen return for sophomore year. 83% freshmen graduate within 4 years. 63% grads go on to further study within 1 year. 14% grads pursue business degrees. 17% grads pursue law degrees. 16% grads pursue medical degrees. **Faculty:** Student/faculty ratio 6:1. 1,282 full-time faculty, 99% hold PhDs. 90% faculty teach undergrads.

ACADEMICS

Degrees: Associate's, bachelor's, certificate, doctoral, first professional, master's. **Academic Requirements:** General education including some course work in English (including composition), foreign languages, history, humanities, mathematics, sciences (biological or physical), social science, physical education, and historical, cultural, and international perspectives. Students have to take 1 course on the history of politics, society, or culture in the United States providing a perspective on American diversity. **Classes:** 10-19 students in an average class. Under 10 students in an average lab/discussion section. **Majors with Highest Enrollment:** Psychology, general; economics, general; political science and government, general. **Disciplines with Highest Percentage of Degrees Awarded:** Social sciences and history 31%, business/marketing 16%, psychology 12%, biological life sciences 11%, English 6%. **Special Study Options:** Accelerated program, cross registration, double major, student exchange program (domestic), honors program, independent study, internships, study abroad, teacher certification program. Undergrads may take grad-level courses. Off-campus study: Washington, DC.

FACILITIES

Housing: Coed, all-female, apartments for married students, apartments for single students, housing for disabled students, housing for international students, fraternities and/or sororities. **Library Holdings:** 2,790,060 bound volumes. 28,158 periodicals. 4,253,790 microforms. 38,814 audiovisuals. **Special Academic Facilities/Equipment:** Carlos Museum of Art, U.S. Centers for Disease Control, Carter Presidential Center, Yerkes Primate Center.

EXTRACURRICULARS

Activities: Choral groups, dance, drama/theater, jazz band, literary magazine, music ensembles, musical theater, radio station, student government, student newspaper, student-run film society, television station. **Organizations:** 220 registered organizations, 22 honor societies, 25 religious organizations, 14 fraternities (30% men join), 10 sororities (30% women join). **Athletics (Intercollegiate):** *Men:* baseball, basketball, cross-country, diving, golf, soccer, swimming, tennis, track & field. *Women:* basketball, cross-country, diving, soccer, softball, swimming, tennis, track & field, volleyball.

ADMISSIONS

Selectivity Rating: 93 (of 100). **Freshman Academic Profile:** Average high school GPA 3.8. 90% in top 10% of high school class, 99% in top 25% of high school class, 100% in top 50% of high school class. 65% from public high schools. SAT I Math middle 50% range 660-740. SAT I Verbal middle 50% range 640-720. ACT middle 50% range 29-33. **Basis for Candidate Selection:** *Very important factors considered include:* recommendations, secondary school record. *Important factors considered include:* alumni/ae relation, character/personal qualities, essays, extracurricular activities, geographical residence, minority status, standardized test scores, state residency, talent/ability, volunteer work, work experience. *Other factors considered include:* class rank. **Freshman Admission Requirements:** High school diploma is required and GED is not accepted. *Academic units required/recommended:* 16 total required; 4 English required, 3 math required, 2 science required, 2 science lab required, 2 foreign language required, 2 social studies required, 2 history required, 3 elective required. **Freshman Admission Statistics:** 9,789 applied, 42% accepted, 32% of those accepted enrolled. **Transfer Admission Requirements:** *Items required:* college transcript, essay, statement of good standing from prior school. Minimum high school GPA of 3.0 required. Minimum college GPA of 3.0 required. Lowest grade transferable C. **General Admission Information:** Application fee $40. Early decision application deadline November 1. Regular application deadline January 15. Admission may be deferred for a maximum of 1 year. Credit and/or placement offered for CEEB Advanced Placement tests.

COSTS AND FINANCIAL AID

Tuition $26,600. Room & board $9,198. Required fees $332. Average book expense $700. **Required Forms and Deadlines:** FAFSA and CSS/Financial Aid PROFILE. Financial aid filing deadline April 1. Priority filing deadline February 15. **Notification of Awards:** Applicants will be notified of awards on or about April 15. **Types of Aid:** *Need-based scholarships/grants:* Pell, SEOG, state scholarships/grants, private scholarships, the school's own gift aid. *Loans:* FFEL Subsidized Stafford, FFEL Unsubsidized Stafford, FFEL PLUS, Federal Perkins, Federal Nursing, state loans, college/university loans from institutional funds. **Student Employment:** Federal Work-Study Program available. Institutional employment available. Off-campus job opportunities are excellent. **Financial Aid Statistics:** 36% freshmen, 37% undergrads receive some form of aid. Average freshman grant $20,208. Average freshman loan $3,478. Average income from on-campus job $963. **Financial Aid Phone:** 404-727-6039.

See page 1024.

EMPORIA STATE UNIVERSITY

1200 Commercial, Emporia, KS 66801-5087
Phone: 620-341-5465 **E-mail:** goto@esumail.emporia.edu **CEEB Code:** 6335
Fax: 620-341-5599 **Web:** www.emporia.edu **ACT Code:** 1430

This public school was founded in 1863. It has a 207-acre campus.

STUDENTS AND FACULTY

Enrollment: 4,393. **Student Body:** Male 39%, female 61%, out-of-state 7%, international 2%. **Ethnic Representation:** African American 4%, Asian 1%, Caucasian 88%, Hispanic 4%, Native American 1%. **Retention and Graduation:** 70% freshmen return for sophomore year. 22% freshmen graduate within 4 years. 17% grads go on to further study within 1 year. 15% grads pursue business degrees. 3% grads pursue law degrees. 1% grads pursue medical degrees. **Faculty:** Student/faculty ratio 19:1. 246 full-time faculty, 75% hold PhDs.

ACADEMICS

Degrees: Bachelor's, certificate, doctoral, master's, post-bachelor's certificate, post-master's certificate. **Academic Requirements:** General education including some course work in arts/fine arts, computer literacy, English (including composition), history, humanities, mathematics, sciences (biological or physical), social science, speech, cultural diversity, applied science, physical education. **Classes:** 20-29 students in an average class. 20-29 students in an average lab/discussion section. **Majors with Highest Enrollment:** Business administration/management; elementary education and teaching; sociology. **Disciplines with Highest Percentage of Degrees Awarded:** Education 29%, business/marketing 22%, social sciences and history 10%, health professions and related sciences 7%, visual and performing arts 6%. **Special Study Options:** Distance learning, double major, dual enrollment, English as a second language, honors program, independent study, internships, study abroad, teacher certification program, continuing education courses, evening courses, interdisciplinary or interdepartmental course of study, learning assistance program, pass-fail grading option, student exchange program, summer sessions, tutorial programs, trio programs, service members opportunity college. Undergrads may take grad-level classes, except 800-level.

FACILITIES

Housing: Coed, apartments for married students, apartments for single students, housing for disabled students, housing for international students, fraternities and/or sororities. **Library Holdings:** 558,565 bound volumes. 1,416 periodicals. 1,172,916 microforms. 7,649 audiovisuals. **Special Academic Facilities/Equipment:** Art gallery, geology and natural history museums, Great Plains Study Center, planetarium. **Computers:** *Recommended operating system:* Windows NT/2000. School-owned computers available for student use.

EXTRACURRICULARS

Activities: Choral groups, concert band, dance, drama/theater, jazz band, literary magazine, marching band, music ensembles, musical theater, opera, pep band, student government, student newspaper, student-run film society, symphony orchestra, yearbook. **Organizations:** 113 registered organizations, 15 honor societies, 12 religious organizations, 6 fraternities (12% men join), 3 sororities (7% women join). **Athletics (Intercollegiate):** *Men:* baseball, basketball, cheerleading, cross-country, football, indoor track, tennis, track & field. *Women:* basketball, cheerleading, cross-country, indoor track, soccer, softball, tennis, track & field, volleyball.

ADMISSIONS

Selectivity Rating: 76 (of 100). **Freshman Academic Profile:** 97% from public high schools. Average ACT 22, ACT middle 50% range 19-25. TOEFL required of all international applicants, minimum TOEFL 450. **Basis for Candidate Selection:** *Very important factors considered include:* class rank, secondary school record, standardized test scores. *Important factors considered include:* talent/ability. *Other factors considered include:* essays, extracurricular activities. **Freshman Admission Requirements:** High school diploma or GED is required. *Academic units required/recommended:* 4 English required, 4 English recommended, 3 math required, 3 math recommended, 3 science required, 3 science recommended, 3 social studies required, 3 social studies recommended. **Freshman Admission Statistics:** 1,367 applied, 71% accepted, 82% of those accepted enrolled. **Transfer Admission Requirements:** *Items required:* college transcript, statement of good standing from prior school. Minimum college GPA of 2.0 required. Lowest grade transferable D. **General Admission Information:** Application fee $25. Nonfall registration accepted. Admission may be deferred for a maximum of 1 year. Credit and/or placement offered for CEEB Advanced Placement tests.

COSTS AND FINANCIAL AID

In-state tuition $1,896. Out-of-state tuition $7,188. Room & board $4,046. Required fees $558. Average book expense $720. **Required Forms and Deadlines:** FAFSA and state aid form. No deadline for regular filing. Priority filing deadline March 15. **Notification of Awards:** Applicants will be notified of awards on a rolling basis beginning on or about February 2. **Types of Aid:** *Need-based scholarships/grants:* Pell, SEOG, state scholarships/grants, private scholarships, the school's own gift aid, Jones Foundation grants. *Loans:* FFEL Subsidized Stafford, FFEL Unsubsidized Stafford, FFEL PLUS, Federal Perkins, college/university loans from institutional funds, Alaska loans, alternative loans. **Student Employment:** Federal Work-Study Program available. Institutional employment available. Off-campus job opportunities are excellent. **Financial Aid Statistics:** 32% freshmen, 54% undergrads receive some form of aid. Average freshman grant $2,137. Average freshman loan $1,833. Average income from on-campus job $2,185. **Financial Aid Phone:** 620-341-5457.

ENDICOTT COLLEGE

376 Hale Street, Beverly, MA 01915
Phone: 978-921-1000 **E-mail:** admissio@endicott.edu **CEEB Code:** 3369
Fax: 978-232-2520 **Web:** www.endicott.edu **ACT Code:** 1824

This private school was founded in 1939. It has a 235-acre campus.

STUDENTS AND FACULTY

Enrollment: 1,574. **Student Body:** Male 34%, female 66%, out-of-state 53%, international 8%. **Ethnic Representation:** African American 1%, Asian 1%, Caucasian 89%, Hispanic 2%. **Retention and Graduation:** 78% freshmen return for sophomore year. 37% freshmen graduate within 4 years. 19% grads go on to further study within 1 year. **Faculty:** Student/faculty ratio 14:1. 53 full-time faculty, 54% hold PhDs. 100% faculty teach undergrads.

ACADEMICS

Degrees: Associate's, bachelor's, master's, terminal. **Academic Requirements:** General education including some course work in English (including composition), humanities, mathematics, sciences (biological or physical), social science. **Classes:** 10-19 students in an average class. Under 10 students in an average lab/discussion section. **Majors with Highest Enrollment:** Business administration/management; communications and media studies; liberal arts and sciences/liberal studies. **Disciplines with Highest Percentage of Degrees Awarded:** Business/marketing 31%, visual and performing arts 22%, communications/communication technologies 12%, parks and recreation 9%, psychology 6%. **Special Study Options:** Accelerated program, cross registration, distance learning, English as a second language, honors program, independent study, internships, student-designed major, study abroad, teacher certification program.

FACILITIES

Housing: Coed, all-female, apartments for single students, housing for disabled students, suite-type, modular, substance-free. **Library Holdings:** 121,000 bound volumes. 3,500 periodicals. 23,500 microforms. 475 audiovisuals. **Special Academic Facilities/Equipment:** Endicott Archives Museum. **Computers:** School-owned computers available for student use.

EXTRACURRICULARS

Activities: Choral groups, dance, drama/theater, literary magazine, radio station, student government, student newspaper, television station, yearbook. **Organizations:** 27 registered organizations, 3 honor societies, 1 religious organization. **Athletics (Intercollegiate):** *Men:* baseball, basketball, cross-country, equestrian, football, golf, lacrosse, soccer, tennis, volleyball. *Women:* basketball, cross-country, equestrian, field hockey, golf, lacrosse, soccer, softball, tennis, volleyball.

ADMISSIONS

Selectivity Rating: 63 (of 100). **Freshman Academic Profile:** 12% in top 10% of high school class, 40% in top 25% of high school class, 76% in top 50% of high school class. Average SAT I Math 524, SAT I Math middle 50% range 580-570. Average SAT I Verbal 519, SAT I Verbal middle 50% range 480-560. ACT middle 50% range 19-23. TOEFL required of all international applicants, minimum TOEFL 525. **Basis for Candidate Selection:** *Very important factors considered include:* character/personal qualities, secondary school record. *Important factors considered include:* alumni/ae relation, class rank, essays, extracurricular activities, geographical residence, standardized test scores, talent/ability, volunteer work, work experience. *Other factors considered include:* interview, minority status, recommendations, state residency. **Freshman Admission Requirements:** High school diploma or GED is required. *Academic units required/recommended:* 16 total recommended; 4 English recommended, 3 math recommended, 2 science recommended, 2 social studies recommended, 1 history recommended, 4 elective recommended. **Freshman Admission Statistics:** 2,245 applied, 57% accepted, 38% of those accepted enrolled. **Transfer Admission Requirements:** *Items required:* high school transcript, college transcript, essay, standardized test scores. Minimum high school GPA of 2.5 required. Minimum college GPA of 2.5 required. Lowest grade transferable C. **General Admission Information:** Application fee $40. Priority application deadline March 15. Nonfall registration accepted. Admission may be deferred for a maximum of 2 years. Credit offered for CEEB Advanced Placement tests.

COSTS AND FINANCIAL AID

Tuition $15,810. Room & board $8,364. Required fees $650. Average book expense $600. **Required Forms and Deadlines:** FAFSA, institution's own financial aid form, and noncustodial (divorced/separated) parent's statement. No deadline for regular filing. Priority filing deadline March 15. **Notification of Awards:** Applicants will be notified of awards on a rolling basis beginning on or about March 15. **Types of Aid:** *Need-based scholarships/grants:* Pell, SEOG, state scholarships/grants, private scholarships, the school's own gift aid. *Loans:* FFEL Subsidized Stafford, FFEL Unsubsidized Stafford, FFEL PLUS, Federal Perkins, state loans, college/university loans from institutional funds. **Student Employment:** Federal Work-Study Program available. Institutional employment available. Off-campus job opportunities are good. **Financial Aid Statistics:** 69% freshmen, 62% undergrads receive some form of aid. Average freshman grant $5,096. Average freshman loan $3,625. **Financial Aid Phone:** 978-232-2060.

ERIE COMMUNITY COLLEGE—CITY CAMPUS

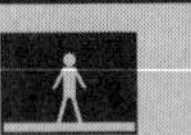

121 Ellicott Street, Buffalo, NY 14203-2698
Phone: 716-851-1155 **E-mail:** hannen@ecc.edu
Fax: 716-851-1129 **Web:** www.ecc.edu **ACT Code:** 2742

This public school was founded in 1971.

STUDENTS AND FACULTY

Enrollment: 2,155. **Student Body:** Male 37%, female 63%, international students represent 7 countries. **Ethnic Representation:** African American 39%, Asian 2%, Caucasian 48%, Hispanic 9%, Native American 2%. **Retention and Graduation:** 41% grads go on to further study within 1 year. **Faculty:** Student/faculty ratio 16:1. 101 full-time faculty. 100% faculty teach undergrads.

ACADEMICS

Degrees: Associate's, certificate, terminal, transfer. **Academic Requirements:** General education including some course work in computer literacy, English (including composition), humanities, mathematics, sciences (biological or physical), social science. **Special Study Options:** Cooperative (work-study) program, cross registration, distance learning, double major, English as a second language, student exchange program (domestic), honors program, independent study, internships, liberal arts/career combination, student-designed major, study abroad, teacher certification program, weekend college, dual-admission with 4-year institution.

FACILITIES

Housing: An up-to-date listing of housing options in the local area is available from the campus dean of students office. **Library Holdings:** 25,831 bound volumes. 266 periodicals. 23,389 microforms. 2,365 audiovisuals. **Computers:** School-owned computers available for student use.

EXTRACURRICULARS

Activities: Choral groups, dance, music ensembles, student government, student newspaper, yearbook. **Organizations:** 34 registered organizations, 3 honor societies, 1 religious organization. **Athletics (Intercollegiate):** *Men:* baseball, basketball, cross-country, diving, golf, ice hockey, soccer, swimming, track & field. *Women:* basketball, cross-country, diving, golf, soccer, softball, swimming, track & field.

ADMISSIONS

Selectivity Rating: 60 (of 100). **Freshman Academic Profile:** TOEFL required of all international applicants. **Basis for Candidate Selection:** *Factors considered include:* class rank, secondary school record, standardized test scores. **Freshman Admission Requirements:** High school diploma or GED is required. **Transfer Admission Requirements:** *Items required:* college transcript, standardized test scores. Lowest grade transferable C. **General Admission Information:** Priority application deadline August 12. Nonfall registration accepted. Credit and/or placement offered for CEEB Advanced Placement tests.

COSTS AND FINANCIAL AID

In-state tuition $4,950. Out-of-state tuition $4,950. Required fees $100. **Required Forms and Deadlines:** FAFSA, institution's own financial aid form, and state aid form. No deadline for regular filing. Priority filing deadline April 30. **Notification of Awards:** Applicants will be notified of awards on a rolling basis beginning on or about May 1. **Types of Aid:** *Need-based scholarships/grants:* Pell, SEOG, state scholarships/grants, ECC Foundation. *Loans:* FFEL Subsidized Stafford, FFEL Unsubsidized Stafford, FFEL PLUS. **Student Employment:** Federal Work-Study Program available. Off-campus job opportunities are excellent. **Financial Aid Phone:** 716-851-1177.

ERIE COMMUNITY COLLEGE—NORTH CAMPUS

6205 Main Street, Williamsville, NY 14221-7095
Phone: 716-851-1455 **E-mail:** smith-br@ecc.edu
Fax: 716-851-1429 **Web:** www.ecc.edu **ACT Code:** 2740

This public school was founded in 1946. It has a 120-acre campus.

STUDENTS AND FACULTY

Enrollment: 4,877. **Student Body:** Male 49%, female 51%, international 1% (17 countries represented). **Ethnic Representation:** African American 10%, Asian 2%, Caucasian 86%, Hispanic 2%. **Retention and Graduation:** 37%

grads go on to further study within 1 year. **Faculty:** Student/faculty ratio 19:1. 169 full-time faculty. 100% faculty teach undergrads.

ACADEMICS

Degrees: Associate's, certificate, terminal, transfer. **Academic Requirements:** General education including some course work in computer literacy, English (including composition), humanities, mathematics, sciences (biological or physical), social science. **Special Study Options:** Cooperative (work-study) program, cross registration, distance learning, double major, English as a second language, student exchange program (domestic), honors program, independent study, internships, liberal arts/career combination, student-designed major, study abroad, teacher certification program, weekend college, dual admissions with 4-year institutions, bilingual education.

FACILITIES

Library Holdings: 71,217 bound volumes. 390 periodicals. 47,134 microforms. 7,026 audiovisuals. **Computers:** School-owned computers available for student use.

EXTRACURRICULARS

Activities: Dance, drama/theater, jazz band, literary magazine, music ensembles, musical theater, radio station, student government, student newspaper, yearbook. **Organizations:** 29 registered organizations, 3 honor societies, 1 religious organization. **Athletics (Intercollegiate):** *Men:* baseball, basketball, cross-country, diving, golf, ice hockey, soccer, swimming, track & field. *Women:* basketball, cross-country, diving, golf, soccer, softball, swimming, track & field.

ADMISSIONS

Selectivity Rating: 60 (of 100). **Freshman Academic Profile:** TOEFL required of all international applicants. **Basis for Candidate Selection:** *Factors considered include:* class rank, secondary school record, standardized test scores. **Freshman Admission Requirements:** High school diploma or GED is required. **Transfer Admission Requirements:** *Items required:* college transcript, standardized test scores. Lowest grade transferable C. **General Admission Information:** Priority application deadline August 12. Nonfall registration accepted. Credit and/or placement offered for CEEB Advanced Placement tests.

COSTS AND FINANCIAL AID

In-state tuition $4,950. Out-of-state tuition $4,950. Required fees $100. **Required Forms and Deadlines:** FAFSA, institution's own financial aid form, and state aid form. No deadline for regular filing. Priority filing deadline April 30. **Notification of Awards:** Applicants will be notified of awards on a rolling basis beginning on or about June 15. **Types of Aid:** *Need-based scholarships/grants:* Pell, SEOG, state scholarships/grants, ECC Foundation. *Loans:* FFEL Subsidized Stafford, FFEL Unsubsidized Stafford, FFEL PLUS. **Student Employment:** Federal Work-Study Program available. Off-campus job opportunities are excellent. **Financial Aid Phone:** 716-851-1477.

ERIE COMMUNITY COLLEGE—SOUTH CAMPUS

4041 Southwestern Boulevard, Orchard Park, NY 14127-2199
Phone: 716-851-1655 **E-mail:** rosinskip@ecc.edu
Fax: 716-851-1629 **Web:** www.ecc.edu. **ACT Code:** 2741

This public school was founded in 1974.

STUDENTS AND FACULTY

Enrollment: 3,167. **Student Body:** Male 55%, female 45%. **Ethnic Representation:** African American 2%, Asian 1%, Caucasian 96%, Hispanic 1%, Native American 1%. **Retention and Graduation:** 37% grads go on to further study within 1 year. **Faculty:** Student/faculty ratio 17:1. 111 full-time faculty. 100% faculty teach undergrads.

ACADEMICS

Degrees: Associate's, certificate, terminal, transfer. **Academic Requirements:** General education including some course work in computer literacy, English (including composition), humanities, mathematics, sciences (biological or physical), social science. **Special Study Options:** Cooperative (work-study) program, cross registration, distance learning, double major, English as a second language, student exchange program (domestic), honors program, independent study, internships, liberal arts/career combination, student-designed major, study abroad, teacher certification program, weekend college, dual admissions with 4-year institutions.

FACILITIES

Housing: An up-to-date listing of housing options in the local area is available from the campus dean of students office. **Library Holdings:** 53,207 bound volumes. 365 periodicals. 20,571 microforms. 1,956 audiovisuals. **Computers:** School-owned computers available for student use.

EXTRACURRICULARS

Activities: Choral groups, dance, drama/theater, literary magazine, music ensembles, radio station, student government, student newspaper, yearbook. **Organizations:** 18 registered organizations, 2 honor societies, 1 religious organization. **Athletics (Intercollegiate):** *Men:* baseball, basketball, cross-country, diving, golf, ice hockey, soccer, swimming, track & field. *Women:* basketball, cross-country, diving, golf, soccer, softball, swimming, track & field.

ADMISSIONS

Selectivity Rating: 60 (of 100). **Freshman Academic Profile:** TOEFL required of all international applicants. **Basis for Candidate Selection:** *Factors considered include:* class rank, secondary school record, standardized test scores. **Freshman Admission Requirements:** High school diploma or GED is required. **Transfer Admission Requirements:** *Items required:* college transcript, standardized test scores. Lowest grade transferable C. **General Admission Information:** Priority application deadline August 12. Nonfall registration accepted. Credit and/or placement offered for CEEB Advanced Placement tests.

COSTS AND FINANCIAL AID

In-state tuition $4,950. Out-of-state tuition $4,950. Required fees $100. **Required Forms and Deadlines:** FAFSA, institution's own financial aid form, and state aid form. No deadline for regular filing. Priority filing deadline April 30. **Notification of Awards:** Applicants will be notified of awards on a rolling basis beginning on or about June 15. **Types of Aid:** *Need-based scholarships/grants:* Pell, SEOG, state scholarships/grants, ECC Foundation. *Loans:* FFEL Subsidized Stafford, FFEL Unsubsidized Stafford, FFEL PLUS. **Student Employment:** Federal Work-Study Program available. Off-campus job opportunities are excellent. **Financial Aid Phone:** 716-851-1677.

ERSKINE COLLEGE

Erskine College, 2 Washington Street, Due West, SC 29639
Phone: 864-379-8838 **E-mail:** admissions@erskine.edu
Fax: 864-379-2167 **Web:** www.erskine.edu

This private school, which is affiliated with the Presbyterian Church, was founded in 1839. It has an 85-acre campus.

STUDENTS AND FACULTY

Enrollment: 594. **Student Body:** Male 40%, female 60%, out-of-state 23%, international 1% (5 countries represented). **Ethnic Representation:** African American 5%, Asian 1%, Caucasian 93%, Hispanic 1%. **Retention and Graduation:** 76% freshmen return for sophomore year. 66% freshmen graduate within 4 years. 36% grads go on to further study within 1 year. 1% grads pursue business degrees. 2% grads pursue law degrees. 2% grads pursue medical degrees. **Faculty:** Student/faculty ratio 12:1. 40 full-time faculty, 97% hold PhDs. 100% faculty teach undergrads.

ACADEMICS

Degrees: Bachelor's. **Academic Requirements:** General education including some course work in arts/fine arts, computer literacy, English (including composition), foreign languages, history, humanities, mathematics, sciences (biological or physical). **Classes:** Under 10 students in an average class. 10-19 students in an average lab/discussion section. **Majors with Highest Enrollment:** Business administration/management; biology/biological sciences, general; psychology, general. **Disciplines with Highest Percentage of Degrees Awarded:** Education 22%, business/marketing 15%, biological life sciences 14%, psychology 11%, philosophy/religion/theology 8%. **Special Study Options:** Cross registration, double major, dual enrollment, independent study, internships, study abroad, teacher certification program.

FACILITIES

Housing: All-female, all-male. **Library Holdings:** 352,292 bound volumes. 683 periodicals. 59,414 microforms. 1,582 audiovisuals. **Special Academic Facilities/Equipment:** Bowie Arts Center. **Computers:** School-owned computers available for student use.

EXTRACURRICULARS

Activities: Choral groups, concert band, dance, drama/theater, jazz band, literary magazine, music ensembles, musical theater, pep band, radio station, student government, student newspaper, television station, yearbook. **Organizations:** 45 registered organizations, 6 honor societies, 7 religious organizations, 3 fraternities (15% men join), 4 sororities (23% women join). **Athletics (Intercollegiate):** *Men:* baseball, basketball, cross-country, soccer, tennis. *Women:* basketball, cross-country, soccer, softball, tennis.

ADMISSIONS

Selectivity Rating: 83 (of 100). **Freshman Academic Profile:** 36% in top 10% of high school class, 90% in top 50% of high school class. 85% from public high schools. Average SAT I Math 566, SAT I Math middle 50% range 510-630. Average SAT I Verbal 559, SAT I Verbal middle 50% range 490-620. Average ACT 23, ACT middle 50% range 20-25. TOEFL required of all international applicants, minimum TOEFL 550. **Basis for Candidate Selection:** *Very important factors considered include:* alumni/ae relation, recommendations, secondary school record, standardized test scores. *Other factors considered include:* character/personal qualities, class rank, essays, extracurricular activities, interview, talent/ability, volunteer work, work experience. **Freshman Admission Requirements:** High school diploma or GED is required. *Academic units required/recommended:* 14 total required; 4 English required, 2 math required, 4 math recommended, 3 science recommended, 2 science lab recommended, 2 foreign language recommended, 2 social studies recommended. **Freshman Admission Statistics:** 848 applied, 69% accepted, 28% of those accepted enrolled. **Transfer Admission Requirements:** *Items required:* college transcript, statement of good standing from prior school. Minimum college GPA of 2.0 required. Lowest grade transferable C. **General Admission Information:** Application fee $15. Nonfall registration accepted. Credit and/or placement offered for CEEB Advanced Placement tests.

COSTS AND FINANCIAL AID

Tuition $15,700. Room & board $5,506. Required fees $1,015. Average book expense $800. **Required Forms and Deadlines:** FAFSA and institution's own financial aid form. No deadline for regular filing. Priority filing deadline May 1. **Notification of Awards:** Applicants will be notified of awards on a rolling basis beginning on or about December 15. **Types of Aid:** *Need-based scholarships/grants:* Pell, SEOG, state scholarships/grants, private scholarships, the school's own gift aid. *Loans:* FFEL Subsidized Stafford, FFEL Unsubsidized Stafford, FFEL PLUS, Federal Perkins, college/university loans from institutional funds. **Student Employment:** Federal Work-Study Program available. Institutional employment available. Off-campus job opportunities are fair. **Financial Aid Statistics:** 81% freshmen, 81% undergrads receive some form of aid. Average freshman loan $2,625. **Financial Aid Phone:** 864-379-8832.

EUGENE LANG COLLEGE/NEW SCHOOL UNIVERSITY

65 West 11th Street, Office of Admission, New York, NY 10011
Phone: 212-229-5665 **E-mail:** Lang@newschool.edu **CEEB Code:** 2521
Fax: 212-229-5166 **Web:** www.lang.edu/admissions.cfm **ACT Code:** 9384

This private school was founded in 1985. It has a 5-acre campus.

STUDENTS AND FACULTY

Enrollment: 637. **Student Body:** Male 32%, female 68%, out-of-state 57%, international 3%. **Ethnic Representation:** African American 5%, Asian 4%, Caucasian 55%, Hispanic 4%. **Retention and Graduation:** 65% freshmen return for sophomore year. 50% grads go on to further study within 1 year. 2% grads pursue business degrees. 12% grads pursue law degrees. **Faculty:** Student/faculty ratio 11:1. 48 full-time faculty. 100% faculty teach undergrads.

ACADEMICS

Degrees: Bachelor's. **Academic Requirements:** General education including some course work in arts/fine arts, English (including composition), humanities, sciences (biological or physical), social science. **Classes:** 10-19 students in an average class. **Majors with Highest Enrollment:** Creative writing; area, ethnic, cultural, and gender studies; social sciences, general. **Disciplines with Highest Percentage of Degrees Awarded:** Liberal arts/general studies 100%. **Special Study Options:** Accelerated program, cross registration, distance learning, student exchange program (domestic), independent study, internships, student-designed major, study abroad.

FACILITIES

Housing: Coed, apartments for single students, housing for disabled students. **Library Holdings:** 4,137,530 bound volumes. 22,150 periodicals. 4,656,806 microforms. 48,379 audiovisuals. **Special Academic Facilities/Equipment:** Art gallery, photography gallery, extensive collections of contemporary art. **Computers:** School-owned computers available for student use.

EXTRACURRICULARS

Activities: Choral groups, drama/theater, literary magazine, student government. **Organizations:** 7 registered organizations, 9 honor societies, 1 religious organization.

ADMISSIONS

Selectivity Rating: 77 (of 100). **Freshman Academic Profile:** Average high school GPA 3.2. 18% in top 10% of high school class, 50% in top 25% of high school class, 87% in top 50% of high school class. 64% from public high schools. Average SAT I Math 570, SAT I Math middle 50% range 510-610. Average SAT I Verbal 610, SAT I Verbal middle 50% range 580-690. Average ACT 27, ACT middle 50% range 21-27. TOEFL required of all international applicants, minimum TOEFL 550. **Basis for Candidate Selection:** *Very important factors considered include:* essays, recommendations, secondary school record. *Important factors considered include:* character/personal qualities, interview, standardized test scores, talent/ability, volunteer work. *Other factors considered include:* alumni/ae relation, class rank, extracurricular activities, geographical residence, minority status, work experience. **Freshman Admission Requirements:** High school diploma or GED is required. *Academic units required/recommended:* 16 total required; 18 total recommended; 4 English required, 3 math recommended, 3 science recommended, 2 foreign language recommended, 3 social studies recommended, 2 history recommended. **Freshman Admission Statistics:** 696 applied, 67% accepted, 37% of those accepted enrolled. **Transfer Admission Requirements:** *Items required:* high school transcript, college transcript, essay, interview, standardized test scores. Lowest grade transferable C. **General Admission Information:** Application fee $40. Early decision application deadline November 15. Regular application deadline February 1. Nonfall registration accepted. Admission may be deferred for a maximum of 1 year. Credit offered for CEEB Advanced Placement tests.

COSTS AND FINANCIAL AID

Tuition $22,500. Room & board $9,896. Required fees $490. Average book expense $918. **Required Forms and Deadlines:** FAFSA and state aid form. No deadline for regular filing. Priority filing deadline March 1. **Notification of Awards:** Applicants will be notified of awards on a rolling basis beginning on or about March 1. **Types of Aid:** *Need-based scholarships/grants:* Pell, SEOG, state scholarships/grants, private scholarships, the school's own gift aid. *Loans:* FFEL Subsidized Stafford, FFEL Unsubsidized Stafford, FFEL PLUS, Federal Perkins, college/university loans from institutional funds. **Student Employment:** Federal Work-Study Program available. Institutional employment available. Off-campus job opportunities are good. **Financial Aid Statistics:** 69% freshmen, 64% undergrads receive some form of aid. Average freshman grant $10,906. Average freshman loan $3,125. Average income from on-campus job $2,000. **Financial Aid Phone:** 212-229-8930.

See page 1026.

EUREKA COLLEGE

300 East College Avenue, Eureka, IL 61530
Phone: 309-467-6350 **E-mail:** admissions@eureka.edu **CEEB Code:** 1206
Fax: 309-467-4574 **Web:** www.eureka.edu **ACT Code:** 1022

This private school, which is affiliated with the Disciples of Christ Church, was founded in 1855. It has a 112-acre campus.

STUDENTS AND FACULTY

Enrollment: 516. **Student Body:** Male 44%, female 56%, out-of-state 10%, international 1%. **Ethnic Representation:** African American 9%, Asian 1%, Caucasian 89%, Hispanic 1%. **Retention and Graduation:** 80% freshmen return for sophomore year. 24% grads go on to further study within 1 year. 2% grads pursue business degrees. 6% grads pursue law degrees. 3% grads pursue medical degrees. **Faculty:** Student/faculty ratio 13:1. 42 full-time faculty, 83% hold PhDs. 100% faculty teach undergrads.

ACADEMICS

Degrees: Bachelor's, diploma. **Academic Requirements:** General education including some course work in arts/fine arts, English (including composition), foreign languages, history, humanities, mathematics, philosophy, sciences (biological or physical), social science. **Majors with Highest Enrollment:** Business administration/management; elementary education and teaching; psychology, general. **Disciplines with Highest Percentage of Degrees Awarded:** Business/marketing 21%, education 20%, social sciences and history 9%, biological life sciences 8%, communications/communication technologies 7%. **Special Study Options:** Cooperative (work-study) program, double major, English as a second language, student exchange program (domestic), honors program, independent study, internships, liberal arts/career combination, student-designed major, study abroad, teacher certification program.

FACILITIES

Housing: Coed, all-female, all-male, housing for disabled students, fraternities and/or sororities. **Library Holdings:** 90,000 bound volumes. 500 periodicals. **Special Academic Facilities/Equipment:** Ronald Reagan Museum, electron microscope, Peace Garden. **Computers:** School-owned computers available for student use.

EXTRACURRICULARS

Activities: Choral groups, drama/theater, literary magazine, student government, student newspaper, yearbook. **Organizations:** 41 registered organizations, 15 honor societies, 4 religious organizations, 3 fraternities (46% men join), 3 sororities (43% women join). **Athletics (Intercollegiate):** *Men:* baseball, basketball, cross-country, diving, football, golf, swimming, tennis, track & field. *Women:* basketball, cross-country, diving, golf, softball, swimming, tennis, track & field, volleyball.

ADMISSIONS

Selectivity Rating: 77 (of 100). **Freshman Academic Profile:** Average high school GPA 3.1. 17% in top 10% of high school class, 44% in top 25% of high school class, 79% in top 50% of high school class. 87% from public high schools. Average ACT 24, ACT middle 50% range 18-24. TOEFL required of all international applicants, minimum TOEFL 550. **Basis for Candidate Selection:** *Very important factors considered include:* class rank, secondary school record, standardized test scores. *Important factors considered include:* recommendations. *Other factors considered include:* character/personal qualities, extracurricular activities, interview, talent/ability, volunteer work, work experience. **Freshman Admission Requirements:** High school diploma or GED is required. *Academic units required/recommended:* 14 total recommended; 4 English recommended, 3 math recommended, 3 science recommended, 2 foreign language recommended, 3 social studies recommended, 2 history recommended. **Freshman Admission Statistics:** 635 applied, 75% accepted, 31% of those accepted enrolled. **Transfer Admission Requirements:** *Items required:* college transcript, statement of good standing from prior school. Minimum high school GPA of 2.0 required. Minimum college GPA of 2.0 required. Lowest grade transferable C. **General Admission Information:** Application fee $25. Nonfall registration accepted. Admission may be deferred for a maximum of 1 year. Credit offered for CEEB Advanced Placement tests.

COSTS AND FINANCIAL AID

Tuition $18,300. Room & board $5,890. Required fees $300. Average book expense $600. **Required Forms and Deadlines:** FAFSA and state aid form. **Notification of Awards:** Applicants will be notified of awards on or about February 15. **Types of Aid:** *Need-based scholarships/grants:* Pell, SEOG, state scholarships/grants, private scholarships, the school's own gift aid. *Loans:* FFEL Subsidized Stafford, FFEL Unsubsidized Stafford, FFEL PLUS, Federal Perkins, state loans, college/university loans from institutional funds. **Student Employment:** Federal Work-Study Program available. Institutional employment available. Off-campus job opportunities are fair. **Financial Aid Statistics:** Average freshman grant $2,650. Average freshman loan $2,430. Average income from on-campus job $1,000. **Financial Aid Phone:** 309-467-6310.

EVANGEL UNIVERSITY

111 North Glenstone, Springfield, MO 65802
Phone: 417-865-2811 **E-mail:** admissions@evangel.edu **CEEB Code:** 6198
Fax: 417-520-0545 **Web:** www.evangel.edu **ACT Code:** 2296

This private school was founded in 1955. It has an 80-acre campus.

STUDENTS AND FACULTY

Enrollment: 1,616. **Student Body:** Male 44%, female 56%, out-of-state 60%, international 1% (13 countries represented). **Ethnic Representation:** African American 3%, Asian 1%, Caucasian 96%. **Retention and Graduation:** 77% freshmen return for sophomore year. **Faculty:** 100% faculty teach undergrads.

ACADEMICS

Degrees: Associate's, bachelor's, master's. **Academic Requirements:** General education including some course work in arts/fine arts, computer literacy, English (including composition), history, humanities, mathematics, sciences (biological or physical), social science, Bible, physical education. **Special Study Options:** Cooperative (work-study) program, double major, dual enrollment, independent study, internships, teacher certification program.

FACILITIES

Housing: Coed, all-female, all-male, apartments for married students. **Library Holdings:** 112,000 bound volumes. 1,628 periodicals. 434,574 microforms. **Computers:** *Recommended operating system:* Windows 95. School-owned computers available for student use.

EXTRACURRICULARS

Activities: Choral groups, concert band, drama/theater, music ensembles, pep band, radio station, student government, student newspaper, television station, yearbook. **Organizations:** 14 registered organizations, 10 honor societies, 3 religious organizations. **Athletics (Intercollegiate):** *Men:* baseball, basketball, cheerleading, cross-country, football, golf, indoor track, track & field. *Women:* basketball, cheerleading, cross-country, golf, indoor track, softball, track & field, volleyball.

ADMISSIONS

Selectivity Rating: 63 (of 100). **Freshman Academic Profile:** 76% from public high schools. Average ACT 23. TOEFL required of all international applicants, minimum TOEFL 490. **Basis for Candidate Selection:** *Very important factors considered include:* class rank, recommendations, religious affiliation/commitment, secondary school record, standardized test scores. *Important factors considered include:* character/personal qualities. **Freshman Admission Requirements:** High school diploma or GED is required. *Academic units required/recommended:* 14 total recommended; 3 English recommended, 2 math recommended, 1 science recommended, 1 science lab recommended, 2 foreign language recommended, 2 social studies recommended, 3 elective recommended. **Freshman Admission Statistics:** 736 applied, 88% accepted, 63% of those accepted enrolled. **Transfer Admission Requirements:** *Items required:* college transcript, statement of good standing from prior school. Minimum college GPA of 2.0 required. Lowest grade transferable C. **General Admission Information:** Application fee $25. Early decision application deadline October 1. Regular application deadline August 15. Nonfall registration accepted. Admission may be deferred for a maximum of 1 year. Credit offered for CEEB Advanced Placement tests.

COSTS AND FINANCIAL AID

Tuition $8,390. Room & board $3,440. Required fees $420. Average book expense $750. **Required Forms and Deadlines:** FAFSA. No deadline for regular filing. **Notification of Awards:** Applicants will be notified of awards on a rolling basis beginning on or about April 1. **Types of Aid:** *Need-based scholarships/grants:* Pell, SEOG, private scholarships. *Loans:* Direct Subsidized Stafford, Direct Unsubsidized Stafford, Direct PLUS, FFEL Subsidized Stafford, FFEL Unsubsidized Stafford, FFEL PLUS, Federal Perkins, college/university loans from institutional funds. **Student Employment:** Federal Work-Study Program available. Institutional employment available. Off-campus job opportunities are excellent. **Financial Aid Phone:** 417-865-2811.

THE EVERGREEN STATE COLLEGE

Office of Admissions, Olympia, WA 98505
Phone: 360-867-6170 **E-mail:** admissions@evergreen.edu **CEEB Code:** 4292
Fax: 360-867-6576 **Web:** www.evergreen.edu **ACT Code:** 4457

This public school was founded in 1967. It has a 1,000-acre campus.

STUDENTS AND FACULTY

Enrollment: 4,081. **Student Body:** Male 44%, female 56%, out-of-state 23%. **Ethnic Representation:** African American 5%, Asian 4%, Caucasian 69%, Hispanic 4%, Native American 5%. **Retention and Graduation:** 72% freshmen return for sophomore year. 38% freshmen graduate within 4 years. 17% grads go on to further study within 1 year. 3% grads pursue business degrees. 2% grads pursue law degrees. 1% grads pursue medical degrees. **Faculty:** Student/faculty ratio 22:1. 161 full-time faculty, 83% hold PhDs. 100% faculty teach undergrads.

ACADEMICS

Degrees: Bachelor's, master's. **Academic Requirements:** Evergreen State College does not have distribution requirements for specific course work; however, students are expected to work toward the "expectations of an Evergreen graduate," which include a range of interdisciplinary study and student-learning outcomes. **Disciplines with Highest Percentage of Degrees Awarded:** Liberal arts/general studies 100%. **Special Study Options:** Cooperative (work-study) program, double major, independent study, internships, student-designed major, study abroad.

FACILITIES

Housing: Coed, apartments for married students, apartments for single students, housing for disabled students, housing for international students. **Library Holdings:** 476,386 bound volumes. 7,682 periodicals. 490,122 microforms. 90,396 audiovisuals. **Special Academic Facilities/Equipment:**

Longhouse Cultural Center, 4 computer music labs, 3 digital studio production studios, 4 analog audio recording studio/control room clusters, digital still-imaging lab, multimedia lab, 3 nonlinear video-editing suites, 4 linear analog video-editing suites, color and black and white photography labs, animation stand, 2 digital animation suites, film mixing studio with 5 editing suites, 2 flatbed film edit rooms, 3 audio/visual classrooms, 5 audio/visual lecture halls, media loan equipment checkout facility, academic sailing fleet (two 40 wooden sailboats), organic farm, scanning electron microscope, gas chromatography mass spectrometer, FTNMR, FTIR, scientific computing laboratory, printmaking studio, ceramics studio, academic wood and metal shops, weaving studio, fine metal studio, 2 art galleries. **Computers:** School-owned computers available for student use.

EXTRACURRICULARS

Activities: Choral groups, dance, drama/theater, literary magazine, music ensembles, radio station, student newspaper, student-run film society. **Organizations:** 55 registered organizations, 6 religious organizations. **Athletics (Intercollegiate):** *Men:* basketball, cross-country, soccer, swimming. *Women:* basketball, cross-country, soccer, swimming, volleyball.

ADMISSIONS

Selectivity Rating: 78 (of 100). **Freshman Academic Profile:** Average high school GPA 3.1. 14% in top 10% of high school class, 32% in top 25% of high school class, 67% in top 50% of high school class. Average SAT I Math 536, SAT I Math middle 50% range 480-590. Average SAT I Verbal 583, SAT I Verbal middle 50% range 520-650. Average ACT 23, ACT middle 50% range 20-26. TOEFL required of all international applicants, minimum TOEFL 600. **Basis for Candidate Selection:** *Very important factors considered include:* secondary school record, standardized test scores. *Important factors considered include:* essays, state residency. *Other factors considered include:* extracurricular activities, recommendations, talent/ability, volunteer work, work experience. **Freshman Admission Requirements:** High school diploma or GED is required. *Academic units required/recommended:* 16 total required; 4 English required, 3 math required, 2 science required, 1 science lab required, 2 foreign language required, 3 social studies required, 1 elective required. **Freshman Admission Statistics:** 1,399 applied, 94% accepted, 37% of those accepted enrolled. **Transfer Admission Requirements:** *Items required:* college transcript. Minimum college GPA of 2.0 required. Lowest grade transferable C. **General Admission Information:** Application fee $36. Priority application deadline March 1. Nonfall registration accepted. Credit offered for CEEB Advanced Placement tests.

COSTS AND FINANCIAL AID

In-state tuition $3,441. Out-of-state tuition $12,264. Room & board $5,610. Required fees $149. Average book expense $780. **Required Forms and Deadlines:** FAFSA and institution's own financial aid form. Financial aid filing deadline March 15. Priority filing deadline February 15. **Notification of Awards:** Applicants will be notified of awards on a rolling basis beginning on or about April 15. **Types of Aid:** *Need-based scholarships/grants:* Pell, SEOG, state scholarships/grants, private scholarships, the school's own gift aid. *Loans:* FFEL Subsidized Stafford, FFEL Unsubsidized Stafford, FFEL PLUS, Federal Perkins, college/university loans from institutional funds. **Student Employment:** Federal Work-Study Program available. Institutional employment available. Off-campus job opportunities are good. **Financial Aid Statistics:** 36% freshmen, 52% undergrads receive some form of aid. Average freshman grant $3,463. Average freshman loan $3,586. Average income from on-campus job $1,500. **Financial Aid Phone:** 360-867-6205.

See page 1028.

EXCELSIOR COLLEGE

7 Columbia Circle, Albany, NY 12203-5159
Phone: 518-464-8500 **E-mail:** admissions@excelsior.edu **CEEB Code:** 759
Fax: 518-464-8777 **Web:** www.excelsior.edu **ACT Code:** 20214

This private school was founded in 1970.

STUDENTS AND FACULTY

Enrollment: 20,105. **Student Body:** Out-of-state 87%, international 1% (47 countries represented). **Ethnic Representation:** African American 14%, Asian 8%, Caucasian 68%, Hispanic 6%, Native American 1%.

ACADEMICS

Degrees: Associate's, bachelor's, master's, post-bachelor's certificate. **Academic Requirements:** General education including some course work in English (including composition), mathematics. **Majors with Highest Enrollment:** Nursing/registered nurse training (RN, ASN, BSN, MSN); business/commerce, general; liberal arts and sciences, general studies and humanities. **Disciplines with Highest Percentage of Degrees Awarded:** Liberal arts/general studies 81%, business/marketing 11%, health professions and related sciences 4%, computer and information sciences 2%, engineering/engineering technology 1%. **Special Study Options:** Accelerated program, distance learning, external degree program, independent study.

FACILITIES

Computers: School-owned computers available for student use.

ADMISSIONS

Selectivity Rating: 60 (of 100). High school diploma or GED is required. **Transfer Admission Requirements:** Lowest grade transferable D. **General Admission Information:** Application fee $40. Nonfall registration accepted.

COSTS AND FINANCIAL AID

Tuition $945. **Required Forms and Deadlines:** Institution's own financial aid form. No deadline for regular filing. **Notification of Awards:** Applicants will be notified of awards on a rolling basis beginning on or about August 1. **Types of Aid:** *Need-based scholarships/grants:* private scholarships. **Financial Aid Phone:** 518-464-8500.

FAIRFIELD UNIVERSITY

1073 North Benson Road, Fairfield, CT 06824-5195
Phone: 203-254-4100 **E-mail:** admis@mail.fairfield.edu **CEEB Code:** 3390
Fax: 203-254-4199 **Web:** www.fairfield.edu **ACT Code:** 560

This private school, which is affiliated with the Roman Catholic-Jesuit Church, was founded in 1942. It has a 200-acre campus.

STUDENTS AND FACULTY

Enrollment: 4,073. **Student Body:** Male 44%, female 56%, out-of-state 76%, international 1% (43 countries represented). **Ethnic Representation:** African American 2%, Asian 3%, Caucasian 90%, Hispanic 5%. **Retention and Graduation:** 90% freshmen return for sophomore year. 73% freshmen graduate within 4 years. 18% grads go on to further study within 1 year. 3% grads pursue business degrees. 5% grads pursue law degrees. 5% grads pursue medical degrees. **Faculty:** Student/faculty ratio 13:1. 223 full-time faculty, 93% hold PhDs. 100% faculty teach undergrads.

ACADEMICS

Degrees: Associate's, bachelor's, master's, post-master's certificate. **Academic Requirements:** General education including some course work in arts/fine arts, English (including composition), foreign languages, history, mathematics, philosophy, sciences (biological or physical), social science, religious studies, diversity core. **Classes:** 20-29 students in an average class. 10-19 students in an average lab/discussion section. **Disciplines with Highest Percentage of Degrees Awarded:** Business/marketing 33%, social sciences and history 18%, English 11%, communications/communication technologies 9%, psychology 7%. **Special Study Options:** Double major, student exchange program (Washington, DC), honors program, independent study, internships, student-designed major, study abroad, teacher certification program.

FACILITIES

Housing: Coed, apartments for single students, wellness floor (substance-free). **Library Holdings:** 219,893 bound volumes. 1,790 periodicals. 800,922 microforms. 9,924 audiovisuals. **Special Academic Facilities/Equipment:** Center for the arts, media center, TV studio, language labs, computer center for teacher education. **Computers:** School-owned computers available for student use.

EXTRACURRICULARS

Activities: Choral groups, concert band, drama/theater, jazz band, literary magazine, music ensembles, pep band, radio station, student government, student newspaper, symphony orchestra, television station, yearbook. **Organizations:** 90 registered organizations, 16 honor societies, 1 religious organization. **Athletics (Intercollegiate):** *Men:* baseball, basketball, cross-country, diving, football, golf, ice hockey, lacrosse, skiing (alpine), soccer, swimming, tennis, track & field, volleyball. *Women:* basketball, crew, cross-country, diving, field hockey, golf, lacrosse, skiing (alpine), soccer, softball, swimming, tennis, track & field, volleyball.

ADMISSIONS

Selectivity Rating: 80 (of 100). **Freshman Academic Profile:** Average high school GPA 3.6. 33% in top 10% of high school class, 70% in top 25% of high school class, 97% in top 50% of high school class. Average SAT I Math 610, SAT I Math middle 50% range 570-650. Average SAT I Verbal 585, SAT I Verbal middle 50% range 540-630. Average ACT 28. TOEFL required of all international applicants, minimum TOEFL 550. **Basis for Candidate Selection:** *Very important factors considered include:* secondary school record, standardized test scores. *Important factors considered include:* class rank, essays, extracurricular activities, recommendations. *Other factors considered include:* alumni/ae relation, character/personal qualities, geographical residence, interview, minority status, talent/ability, volunteer work, work experience. **Freshman Admission Requirements:** High school diploma is required and GED is not accepted. *Academic units required/recommended:* 15 total required; 18 total recommended; 4 English required, 4 English recommended, 3 math required, 4 math recommended, 3 science required, 4 science recommended, 2 science lab required, 2 science lab recommended, 2 foreign language required, 4 foreign language recommended, 3 history required, 4 history recommended, 1 elective required. **Freshman Admission Statistics:** 6,974 applied, 50% accepted, 24% of those accepted enrolled. **Transfer Admission Requirements:** *Items required:* high school transcript, college transcript, essay, standardized test scores. Minimum college GPA of 2.5 required. Lowest grade transferable C. **General Admission Information:** Application fee $55. Early decision application deadline November 15. Regular application deadline February 1. Admission may be deferred for a maximum of 1 year. Credit offered for CEEB Advanced Placement tests.

COSTS AND FINANCIAL AID

Tuition $24,100. Room & board $8,560. Required fees $455. Average book expense $800. **Required Forms and Deadlines:** FAFSA and CSS/Financial Aid PROFILE. Financial aid filing deadline February 15. Priority filing deadline February 15. **Notification of Awards:** Applicants will be notified of awards on or about April 5. **Types of Aid:** *Need-based scholarships/grants:* Pell, SEOG, state scholarships/grants, private scholarships, the school's own gift aid. *Loans:* FFEL Subsidized Stafford, FFEL Unsubsidized Stafford, FFEL PLUS, Federal Perkins, Federal Nursing, state loans, alternative loans from lenders. **Student Employment:** Federal Work-Study Program available. Institutional employment available. Off-campus job opportunities are good. **Financial Aid Statistics:** 52% freshmen, 52% undergrads receive some form of aid. Average freshman grant $11,683. Average freshman loan $3,556. Average income from on-campus job $900. **Financial Aid Phone:** 203-254-4125.

See page 1030.

FAIRLEIGH DICKINSON UNIVERSITY, COLLEGE AT FLORHAM

285 Madison Avenue, Madison, NJ 07940
Phone: 973-443-8900 **E-mail:** globaleducation@fdu.edu
Fax: 973-443-8088 **Web:** www.fdu.edu

This private school has a 186-acre campus.

STUDENTS AND FACULTY

Enrollment: 2,578. **Student Body:** Male 46%, female 54%, out-of-state 15%, international 2%. **Ethnic Representation:** African American 6%, Asian 3%, Caucasian 74%, Hispanic 8%. **Retention and Graduation:** 76% freshmen return for sophomore year. 30% freshmen graduate within 4 years. **Faculty:** Student/faculty ratio 17:1. 111 full-time faculty. 100% faculty teach undergrads.

ACADEMICS

Degrees: Associate's, bachelor's, master's, post-bachelor's certificate, post-master's certificate, terminal. **Academic Requirements:** General education including some course work in arts/fine arts, computer literacy, English (including composition), foreign languages, humanities, mathematics, sciences (biological or physical), social science. **Classes:** 10-19 students in an average class. 10-19 students in an average lab/discussion section. **Disciplines with Highest Percentage of Degrees Awarded:** Business/marketing 27%, liberal arts/general studies 16%, psychology 11%, communications/communication technologies 6%, biological life sciences 6%. **Special Study Options:** Accelerated program, cooperative (work-study) program, distance learning, double major, English as a second language, honors program, independent study, internships, liberal arts/career combination, study abroad, teacher certification program, weekend college.

FACILITIES

Housing: Coed, housing for disabled students, fraternities and/or sororities. **Library Holdings:** 163,266 bound volumes. 661 periodicals. 107,856 microforms. 681 audiovisuals. **Computers:** School-owned computers available for student use.

EXTRACURRICULARS

Activities: Drama/theater, literary magazine, musical theater, pep band, radio station, student government, student newspaper, yearbook. **Organizations:** 60 registered organizations, 11 honor societies, 3 religious organizations, 4 fraternities (10% men join), 4 sororities (15% women join). **Athletics (Intercollegiate):** *Men:* baseball, basketball, cross-country, football, golf, lacrosse, soccer, swimming, tennis. *Women:* basketball, cheerleading, cross-country, field hockey, lacrosse, soccer, softball, swimming, tennis, volleyball.

ADMISSIONS

Selectivity Rating: 63 (of 100). **Freshman Academic Profile:** 7% in top 10% of high school class, 25% in top 25% of high school class, 59% in top 50% of high school class. SAT I Math middle 50% range 470-560. SAT I Verbal middle 50% range 460-560. TOEFL required of all international applicants, minimum TOEFL 500. **Basis for Candidate Selection:** *Very important factors considered include:* recommendations, secondary school record, standardized test scores. *Important factors considered include:* character/personal qualities, class rank, interview. *Other factors considered include:* alumni/ae relation, extracurricular activities, talent/ability. **Freshman Admission Requirements:** High school diploma or GED is required. *Academic units required/recommended:* 17 total required; 4 English required, 3 math required, 2 science required, 3 science recommended, 2 foreign language required, 2 history required, 4 elective required. **Transfer Admission Requirements:** *Items required:* college transcript, statement of good standing from prior school. Minimum college GPA of 2.5 required. Lowest grade transferable C. **General Admission Information:** Application fee $40. Priority application deadline January 15. Regular application deadline March 1. Nonfall registration accepted. Admission may be deferred for a maximum of 1 year. Credit and/or placement offered for CEEB Advanced Placement tests.

COSTS AND FINANCIAL AID

Tuition $18,654. Room & board $7,904. Required fees $420. Average book expense $672. **Student Employment:** Federal Work-Study Program available. Institutional employment available. Off-campus job opportunities are good. **Financial Aid Phone:** 973-443-8700.

FAIRLEIGH DICKINSON UNIVERSITY, METROPOLITAN CAMPUS

1000 River Road, Teaneck, NJ 07666-1966
Phone: 800-338-8803 **E-mail:** globaleducation@fdu.edu **CEEB Code:** 2255
Fax: 201-692-2560 **Web:** www.fdu.edu

This private school was founded in 1942. It has a 177-acre campus.

STUDENTS AND FACULTY

Enrollment: 4,587. **Student Body:** Male 43%, female 57%, out-of-state 11%, international 6%. **Ethnic Representation:** African American 23%, Asian 6%, Caucasian 39%, Hispanic 16%. **Retention and Graduation:** 68% freshmen return for sophomore year. 25% freshmen graduate within 4 years. **Faculty:** Student/faculty ratio 15:1. 165 full-time faculty.

ACADEMICS

Degrees: Associate's, bachelor's, certificate, doctoral, master's, post-bachelor's certificate, post-master's certificate, terminal. **Academic Requirements:** General education including some course work in arts/fine arts, computer literacy, English (including composition), humanities, mathematics, philosophy, sciences (biological or physical), social science. **Classes:** 10-19 students in an average class. 10-19 students in an average lab/discussion section. **Disciplines with Highest Percentage of Degrees Awarded:** Business/marketing 27%, liberal arts/general studies 16%, psychology 11%, communications/communication technologies 6%, biological life sciences 6%. **Special Study Options:** Accelerated program, cooperative (work-study) program, cross registration, distance learning, double major, English as a second language, honors program, independent study, internships, liberal arts/career combination, student-designed major, study abroad, teacher certification program, weekend college.

FACILITIES

Housing: Coed, all-female, all-male, housing for disabled students. **Library Holdings:** 287,755 bound volumes. 1,093 periodicals. 230,196 microforms. 1,052 audiovisuals. **Computers:** *Recommended operating system:* Mac. School-owned computers available for student use.

EXTRACURRICULARS

Activities: Choral groups, dance, drama/theater, literary magazine, radio station, student government, student newspaper, television station. **Organiza-**

tions: 90 registered organizations, 2 honor societies, 10 fraternities (1% men join), 8 sororities (1% women join). **Athletics (Intercollegiate):** *Men:* basketball, cross-country, fencing, tennis, track & field, volleyball.

ADMISSIONS

Selectivity Rating: 63 (of 100). **Freshman Academic Profile:** 10% in top 10% of high school class, 30% in top 25% of high school class, 62% in top 50% of high school class. SAT I Math middle 50% range 430-540. SAT I Verbal middle 50% range 420-530. TOEFL required of all international applicants, minimum TOEFL 500. **Basis for Candidate Selection:** *Very important factors considered include:* recommendations, secondary school record, standardized test scores. *Important factors considered include:* character/personal qualities, class rank, interview. *Other factors considered include:* alumni/ae relation, extracurricular activities, talent/ability. **Freshman Admission Requirements:** High school diploma or GED is required. *Academic units required/recommended:* 17 total required; 4 English required, 3 math required, 2 science required, 3 science recommended, 2 foreign language required, 2 history required, 4 elective required. **Transfer Admission Requirements:** *Items required:* college transcript, statement of good standing from prior school. Minimum college GPA of 2.5 required. Lowest grade transferable C. **General Admission Information:** Application fee $40. Priority application deadline January 15. Regular application deadline March 1. Nonfall registration accepted. Admission may be deferred for a maximum of 1 year. Credit offered for CEEB Advanced Placement tests.

COSTS AND FINANCIAL AID

Tuition $18,654. Room & board $7,904. Required fees $420. Average book expense $672. **Student Employment:** Federal Work-Study Program available. Institutional employment available. Off-campus job opportunities are fair. **Financial Aid Statistics:** Average income from on-campus job $1,100. **Financial Aid Phone:** 973-443-8700.

FAIRMONT STATE COLLEGE

1201 Locust Avenue, Fairmont, WV 26554
Phone: 304-367-4141 **E-mail:** admit@mail.fscwv.edu **CEEB Code:** 5211
Fax: 304-367-4789 **Web:** www.fscwv.edu **ACT Code:** 4520

This public school was founded in 1865. It has an 89-acre campus.

STUDENTS AND FACULTY

Enrollment: 6,496. **Student Body:** Male 44%, female 56%, out-of-state 6%, international 1%. **Ethnic Representation:** African American 3%, Caucasian 95%, Hispanic 1%. **Retention and Graduation:** 71% freshmen return for sophomore year. 14% freshmen graduate within 4 years. 22% grads go on to further study within 1 year. 1% grads pursue business degrees. 1% grads pursue law degrees. 1% grads pursue medical degrees. **Faculty:** Student/faculty ratio 17:1. 201 full-time faculty, 45% hold PhDs. 100% faculty teach undergrads.

ACADEMICS

Degrees: Associate's, bachelor's, certificate, terminal, transfer. **Academic Requirements:** General education including some course work in arts/fine arts, English (including composition), foreign languages, history, humanities, mathematics, philosophy, sciences (biological or physical), social science. **Classes:** 10-19 students in an average class. 10-19 students in an average lab/discussion section. **Disciplines with Highest Percentage of Degrees Awarded:** Business/marketing 24%, education 21%, protective services/public administration 12%, engineering/engineering technology 11%, psychology 9%. **Special Study Options:** Double major, dual enrollment, English as a second language, honors program, teacher certification program, weekend college.

FACILITIES

Housing: All-female, all-male. **Library Holdings:** 276,722 bound volumes. 883 periodicals. 27,211 microforms. 2,066 audiovisuals. **Special Academic Facilities/Equipment:** On-campus one-room schoolhouse. **Computers:** *Recommended operating system:* Windows 95. School-owned computers available for student use.

EXTRACURRICULARS

Activities: Choral groups, concert band, dance, drama/theater, jazz band, literary magazine, marching band, music ensembles, musical theater, opera, pep band, student government, student newspaper, student-run film society, symphony orchestra, yearbook. **Organizations:** 47 registered organizations, 16 honor societies, 4 religious organizations, 4 fraternities (1% men join), 4 sororities (2% women join). **Athletics (Intercollegiate):** *Men:* baseball, basketball, cross-country, football, golf, swimming, tennis. *Women:* basketball, cheerleading, cross-country, golf, softball, swimming, tennis, volleyball.

ADMISSIONS

Selectivity Rating: 63 (of 100). **Freshman Academic Profile:** Average high school GPA 2.6. 12% in top 10% of high school class, 25% in top 25% of high school class, 66% in top 50% of high school class. 95% from public high schools. Average ACT 19, ACT middle 50% range 16-21. TOEFL required of all international applicants, minimum TOEFL 500. **Basis for Candidate Selection:** *Important factors considered include:* class rank, extracurricular activities, secondary school record, standardized test scores. **Freshman Admission Requirements:** High school diploma or GED is required. *Academic units required/recommended:* 24 total required; 4 English required, 2 math required, 2 science required, 2 science lab required, 2 foreign language recommended, 2 social studies required, 1 history required, 11 elective required. **Freshman Admission Statistics:** 2,158 applied, 100% accepted, 54% of those accepted enrolled. **Transfer Admission Requirements:** *Items required:* college transcript, statement of good standing from prior school. Minimum college GPA of 2.0 required. Lowest grade transferable D. **General Admission Information:** Regular application deadline June 15. Nonfall registration accepted. Admission may be deferred. Credit and/or placement offered for CEEB Advanced Placement tests.

COSTS AND FINANCIAL AID

In-state tuition $2,316. Out-of-state tuition $5,396. Room & board $4,084. Required fees $100. Average book expense $500. **Required Forms and Deadlines:** FAFSA. Priority filing deadline March 1. **Notification of Awards:** Applicants will be notified of awards on a rolling basis beginning on or about April 15. **Types of Aid:** *Need-based scholarships/grants:* Pell, SEOG, state scholarships/grants, private scholarships, the school's own gift aid. *Loans:* Direct Subsidized Stafford, Direct Unsubsidized Stafford, Direct PLUS, Federal Perkins. **Student Employment:** Federal Work-Study Program available. Institutional employment available. Off-campus job opportunities are fair. **Financial Aid Statistics:** 41% freshmen, 46% undergrads receive some form of aid. Average freshman grant $2,500. Average freshman loan $2,625. Average income from on-campus job $800. **Financial Aid Phone:** 304-367-4213.

FASHION INSTITUTE OF TECHNOLOGY

Seventh Avenue at 27th Street, New York, NY 10001
Phone: 212-760-7675 **E-mail:** fitinfo@fitsuny.edu
Web: www.fitnyc.suny.edu

This public school was founded in 1944.

STUDENTS AND FACULTY

Student Body: Out-of-state 17%.

FACILITIES

Housing: Coed, all-female, all-male, apartments for single students.

EXTRACURRICULARS

Activities: Literary magazine, radio station, student government, student newspaper, yearbook. **Organizations:** 70 registered organizations, 7 honor societies, 1 religious organization.

ADMISSIONS

Selectivity Rating: 71 (of 100). **Freshman Academic Profile:** 11% in top 10% of high school class, 32% in top 25% of high school class, 68% in top 50% of high school class. Minimum TOEFL 550. **General Admission Information:** Regular application deadline January 15.

COSTS AND FINANCIAL AID

In-state tuition $2,500. Out-of-state tuition $5,950. Room & board $5,600. Required fees $210. Average book expense $1,200. **Required Forms and Deadlines:** FAFSA, institution's own financial aid form, and state aid form. **Types of Aid:** *Loans:* FFEL Subsidized Stafford, FFEL PLUS. **Student Employment:** Federal Work-Study Program available. **Financial Aid Statistics:** Average freshman loan $2,359. Average income from on-campus job $1,400.

FAULKNER UNIVERSITY

5345 Atlanta Highway, Montgomery, AL 36109-3398
Phone: 334-386-7200 **E-mail:** admissions@faulkner.edu **CEEB Code:** 1034
Fax: 334-386-7137 **Web:** www.faulkner.edu **ACT Code:** 3

This private school, which is affiliated with the Church of Christ, was founded in 1942. It has a 78-acre campus.

STUDENTS AND FACULTY

Enrollment: 2,280. **Student Body:** Male 38%, female 62%, out-of-state 10%, international students represent 5 countries. **Ethnic Representation:** African American 41%, Caucasian 56%, Hispanic 1%. **Retention and Graduation:** 13% freshmen graduate within 4 years. **Faculty:** Student/faculty ratio 22:1. 62 full-time faculty, 67% hold PhDs.

ACADEMICS

Degrees: Associate's, bachelor's, certificate, diploma, first professional, master's. **Academic Requirements:** General education including some course work in arts/fine arts, computer literacy, English (including composition), foreign languages, history, humanities, mathematics, sciences (biological or physical), social science. **Majors with Highest Enrollment:** Business administration/management; management information systems, general; pre-law studies. **Disciplines with Highest Percentage of Degrees Awarded:** Business/marketing 79%, law/legal studies 10%, psychology 4%, education 3%, computer and information sciences 1%. **Special Study Options:** Accelerated program, cross registration, distance learning, dual enrollment, honors program, independent study, internships, teacher certification program, weekend college.

FACILITIES

Housing: All-female, all-male, apartments for single students. **Library Holdings:** 118,039 bound volumes. 1,183 periodicals. 98,987 microforms. 730 audiovisuals. **Computers:** School-owned computers available for student use.

EXTRACURRICULARS

Activities: Choral groups, drama/theater, music ensembles, musical theater, student government, student newspaper, yearbook. **Organizations:** 12 registered organizations, 1 honor society, 1 religious organization, 4 fraternities, 4 sororities. **Athletics (Intercollegiate):** *Men:* baseball, basketball, cheerleading, cross-country track. *Women:* cheerleading, cross-country, softball, volleyball.

ADMISSIONS

Selectivity Rating: 72 (of 100). **Freshman Academic Profile:** Average ACT 21. TOEFL required of all international applicants, minimum TOEFL 450. **Basis for Candidate Selection:** *Very important factors considered include:* character/personal qualities, class rank, extracurricular activities, interview, recommendations, secondary school record, standardized test scores. *Important factors considered include:* alumni/ae relation, essays, religious affiliation/commitment, talent/ability. *Other factors considered include:* volunteer work, work experience. **Freshman Admission Requirements:** High school diploma or GED is required. *Academic units required/recommended:* 15 total required; 15 total recommended; 12 elective recommended. **Freshman Admission Statistics:** 538 applied, 73% accepted, 42% of those accepted enrolled. **Transfer Admission Requirements:** *Items required:* high school transcript, college transcript, standardized test scores. Lowest grade transferable C. **General Admission Information:** Application fee $10. Priority application deadline March 15. Nonfall registration accepted. Admission may be deferred for a maximum of 1 year. Placement offered for CEEB Advanced Placement tests.

COSTS AND FINANCIAL AID

Tuition $9,300. Room & board $4,600. Required fees $35. Average book expense $900. **Required Forms and Deadlines:** FAFSA, institution's own financial aid form, and state aid form. No deadline for regular filing. Priority filing deadline May 2. **Types of Aid:** *Need-based scholarships/grants:* Pell, SEOG, state scholarships/grants, private scholarships, the school's own gift aid. *Loans:* FFEL Subsidized Stafford, FFEL Unsubsidized Stafford, FFEL PLUS, Federal Perkins. **Student Employment:** Federal Work-Study Program available. Institutional employment available. Off-campus job opportunities are good. **Financial Aid Statistics:** 80% freshmen, 81% undergrads receive some form of aid. Average freshman grant $2,000. Average freshman loan $2,000. Average income from on-campus job $1,200. **Financial Aid Phone:** 334-386-7195.

FAYETTEVILLE STATE UNIVERSITY

Newbold Station, Fayetteville, NC 28301
Phone: 910-672-1371 **E-mail:** admissions@.uncfsu.edu **CEEB Code:** 5212
Fax: 910-672-1414 **Web:** www.uncfsu.edu **ACT Code:** 3098

This public school was founded in 1867. It has a 136-acre campus.

STUDENTS AND FACULTY

Enrollment: 3,807. **Student Body:** Male 37%, female 63%, out-of-state 11%. **Ethnic Representation:** African American 80%, Asian 1%, Caucasian 14%, Hispanic 4%, Native American 1%. **Retention and Graduation:** 74% freshmen return for sophomore year. 14% freshmen graduate within 4 years. 11% grads go on to further study within 1 year. 1% grads pursue business degrees. **Faculty:** Student/faculty ratio 20:1. 202 full-time faculty, 70% hold PhDs. 100% faculty teach undergrads.

ACADEMICS

Degrees: Bachelor's, doctoral, master's. **Academic Requirements:** General education including some course work in arts/fine arts, English (including composition), humanities, mathematics, sciences (biological or physical), social science. **Classes:** 20-29 students in an average class. 20-29 students in an average lab/discussion section. **Majors with Highest Enrollment:** Business administration/management; elementary education and teaching; criminal justice/police science. **Special Study Options:** Cooperative (work-study) program, distance learning, double major, honors program, independent study, internships, liberal arts/career combination, study abroad, teacher certification program, weekend college.

FACILITIES

Housing: All-female, all-male, apartments for married students, apartments for single students, housing for disabled students. **Library Holdings:** 206,370 bound volumes. 3,016 periodicals. 823,603 microforms. 4,194 audiovisuals. **Special Academic Facilities/Equipment:** Planetarium; observatory; distance learning center; science labs; health, physical education, and recreation complex; art gallery. **Computers:** *Recommended operating system:* Windows 95. School-owned computers available for student use.

EXTRACURRICULARS

Activities: Choral groups, concert band, dance, drama/theater, jazz band, marching band, music ensembles, musical theater, opera, pep band, radio station, student government, student newspaper, student-run film society, television station, yearbook. **Organizations:** 56 registered organizations, 7 honor societies, 3 religious organizations, 4 fraternities (5% men join), 4 sororities (5% women join). **Athletics (Intercollegiate):** *Men:* basketball, cheerleading, cross-country, football, golf. *Women:* basketball, cheerleading, cross-country, softball, tennis, volleyball.

ADMISSIONS

Selectivity Rating: 64 (of 100). **Freshman Academic Profile:** Average high school GPA 2.8. 12% in top 10% of high school class, 14% in top 25% of high school class, 48% in top 50% of high school class. Average SAT I Math 437, SAT I Math middle 50% range 360-470. Average SAT I Verbal 438, SAT I Verbal middle 50% range 380-470. **Basis for Candidate Selection:** *Important factors considered include:* character/personal qualities, class rank, extracurricular activities, secondary school record, standardized test scores, talent/ability. **Freshman Admission Requirements:** High school diploma is required and GED is not accepted. *Academic units required/recommended:* 18 total required; 4 English required, 3 math required, 3 science required, 2 foreign language recommended, 1 social studies required, 1 history required, 6 elective required. **Freshman Admission Statistics:** 1,570 applied, 85% accepted, 58% of those accepted enrolled. **Transfer Admission Requirements:** *Items required:* college transcript, statement of good standing from prior school. Lowest grade transferable C. **General Admission Information:** Application fee $25. Regular application deadline August 15. Nonfall registration accepted. Credit and/or placement offered for CEEB Advanced Placement tests.

COSTS AND FINANCIAL AID

In-state tuition $1,258. Out-of-state tuition $10,173. Room & board $3,820. Required fees $437. Average book expense $160. **Required Forms and Deadlines:** FAFSA and institution's own financial aid form. **Notification of Awards:** Applicants will be notified of awards on or about July 15. **Types of Aid:** *Need-based scholarships/grants:* Pell, SEOG, state scholarships/grants, private scholarships, the school's own gift aid. *Loans:* Direct Subsidized Stafford, Direct Unsubsidized Stafford, Direct PLUS, FFEL Subsidized Stafford, FFEL Unsubsidized Stafford, FFEL PLUS, Federal Perkins, Federal Nursing, state loans. **Student Employment:** Federal Work-Study Program available. Off-campus job opportunities are excellent. **Financial Aid Phone:** 910-672-1325.

FELICIAN COLLEGE

262 South Main Street, Lodi, NJ 07644
Phone: 201-559-6131 **E-mail:** admissions@inet.felician.edu **CEEB Code:** 2321
Fax: 201-559-6138 **Web:** www.felician.edu **ACT Code:** 2559

This private school, which is affiliated with the Roman Catholic Church, was founded in 1942. It has a 27-acre campus.

STUDENTS AND FACULTY

Enrollment: 1,618. **Student Body:** Male 24%, female 76%, out-of-state 2%, international 2%. **Ethnic Representation:** African American 14%, Asian 5%, Caucasian 58%, Hispanic 16%. **Retention and Graduation:** 92% freshmen return for sophomore year. 20% grads go on to further study within 1 year. 12% grads pursue business degrees. 10% grads pursue law degrees. 5% grads pursue medical degrees. **Faculty:** Student/faculty ratio 15:1. 72 full-time faculty, 48% hold PhDs. 100% faculty teach undergrads.

ACADEMICS

Degrees: Associate's, bachelor's, certificate, master's, post-bachelor's certificate, post-master's certificate, terminal, transfer. **Academic Requirements:** General education including some course work in arts/fine arts, computer literacy, English (including composition), humanities, mathematics, philosophy, sciences (biological or physical), social science. **Classes:** 10-19 students in an average class. **Majors with Highest Enrollment:** Nursing/registered nurse training (RN, ASN, BSN, MSN); business administration/management; psychology, general. **Disciplines with Highest Percentage of Degrees Awarded:** Education 20%, English 20%, psychology 15%, social sciences and history 10%, health professions and related sciences 10%. **Special Study Options:** Accelerated program, cooperative (work-study) program, cross registration, distance learning, double major, dual enrollment, English as a second language, honors program, independent study, internships, liberal arts/career combination, student-designed major, study abroad, teacher certification program, weekend college, post-baccalaureate certification in elementary and secondary education.

FACILITIES

Housing: Coed, all-female, all-male, housing for disabled students. **Library Holdings:** 109,273 bound volumes. 766 periodicals. 74,437 microforms. 4,000 audiovisuals. **Special Academic Facilities/Equipment:** On-campus elementary school for exceptional children. **Computers:** *Recommended operating system:* Windows 95. School-owned computers available for student use.

EXTRACURRICULARS

Activities: Choral groups, drama/theater, literary magazine, student government. **Organizations:** 25 registered organizations, 2 honor societies, 3 religious organizations, 13 fraternity, 2 sororities (20% women join). **Athletics (Intercollegiate):** *Men:* baseball, basketball, cheerleading, cross-country, soccer, track & field. *Women:* basketball, cheerleading, cross-country, soccer, softball, track & field.

ADMISSIONS

Selectivity Rating: 63 (of 100). **Freshman Academic Profile:** Average high school GPA 2.8. 9% in top 10% of high school class, 34% in top 25% of high school class, 50% in top 50% of high school class. 70% from public high schools. Average SAT I Math 448, SAT I Math middle 50% range 360-490. Average SAT I Verbal 453. **Basis for Candidate Selection:** *Very important factors considered include:* secondary school record, standardized test scores. *Other factors considered include:* alumni/ae relation, character/personal qualities, class rank, essays, extracurricular activities, interview, minority status, recommendations, work experience. **Freshman Admission Requirements:** High school diploma or GED is required. *Academic units required/recommended:* 16 total recommended; 4 English recommended, 3 math recommended, 2 science recommended, 2 foreign language recommended, 2 social studies recommended, 6 elective recommended. **Freshman Admission Statistics:** 947 applied, 63% accepted, 73% of those accepted enrolled. **Transfer Admission Requirements:** *Items required:* college transcript, essay. Minimum high school GPA of 2.0 required. Minimum college GPA of 2.5 required. Lowest grade transferable C. **General Admission Information:** Application fee $30. Nonfall registration accepted. Credit and/or placement offered for CEEB Advanced Placement tests.

COSTS AND FINANCIAL AID

Tuition $11,460. Room & board $6,250. Required fees $475. Average book expense $600. **Required Forms and Deadlines:** FAFSA. No deadline for regular filing. Priority filing deadline June 2. **Notification of Awards:** Applicants will be notified of awards on a rolling basis beginning on or about April 2. **Types of Aid:** *Need-based scholarships/grants:* Pell, SEOG, state scholarships/grants, private scholarships, the school's own gift aid, United Negro College Fund, Federal Nursing. *Loans:* Direct Subsidized Stafford, Direct Unsubsidized Stafford, Direct PLUS, FFEL Subsidized Stafford, FFEL Unsubsidized Stafford, FFEL PLUS, state loans. **Student Employment:** Federal Work-Study Program available. Off-campus job opportunities are good. **Financial Aid Statistics:** 47% freshmen, 57% undergrads receive some form of aid. Average freshman grant $3,000. Average freshman loan $2,000. **Financial Aid Phone:** 201-559-6010.

See page 1032.

FERRIS STATE UNIVERSITY

1201 South State Street, Center for Student Services, Big Rapids, MI 49307
Phone: 231-591-2100 **E-mail:** admissions@ferris.edu **CEEB Code:** 1222
Fax: 231-591-3944 **Web:** www.ferris.edu **ACT Code:** 1994

This public school was founded in 1884. It has a 600-acre campus.

STUDENTS AND FACULTY

Enrollment: 10,176. **Student Body:** Male 54%, female 46%, out-of-state 6%, international 2%. **Ethnic Representation:** African American 9%, Asian 2%, Caucasian 81%, Hispanic 1%, Native American 1%. **Retention and Graduation:** 64% freshmen return for sophomore year. 9% grads go on to further study within 1 year. **Faculty:** Student/faculty ratio 16:1. 465 full-time faculty, 42% hold PhDs. 100% faculty teach undergrads.

ACADEMICS

Degrees: Associate's, bachelor's, certificate, doctoral, first professional, master's, post-bachelor's certificate, post-master's certificate, terminal, transfer. **Academic Requirements:** General education including some course work in arts/fine arts, computer literacy, English (including composition), foreign languages, humanities, mathematics, sciences (biological or physical), social science, communications (speech). **Majors with Highest Enrollment:** Business administration/management; secondary education and teaching; criminal justice/police science. **Disciplines with Highest Percentage of Degrees Awarded:** Business/marketing 30%, health professions and related sciences 18%, engineering/engineering technology 15%, protective services/public administration 10%, visual and performing arts 8%. **Special Study Options:** Accelerated program, cooperative (work-study) program, distance learning, double major, dual enrollment, English as a second language, honors program, independent study, internships, liberal arts/career combination, student-designed major, study abroad, teacher certification program, weekend college.

FACILITIES

Housing: Coed, apartments for married students, apartments for single students, housing for disabled students, housing for international students, honors floors in selected residences. **Library Holdings:** 276,134 bound volumes. 3,955 periodicals. 35,597 microforms. 72,786 audiovisuals. **Special Academic Facilities/Equipment:** Rankin Art Gallery, student recreation center, wildlife museum, Jim Crowe Museum. **Computers:** *Recommended operating system:* Windows NT/2000. School-owned computers available for student use.

EXTRACURRICULARS

Activities: Choral groups, concert band, dance, drama/theater, jazz band, literary magazine, music ensembles, musical theater, pep band, radio station, student government, student newspaper, symphony orchestra, television station. **Organizations:** 200 registered organizations, 4 honor societies, 14 religious organizations, 15 fraternities (8% men join), 9 sororities (5% women join). **Athletics (Intercollegiate):** *Men:* baseball, basketball, cheerleading, cross-country, football, golf, ice hockey, rugby, tennis, track & field. *Women:* basketball, cheerleading, cross-country, golf, soccer, softball, tennis, track & field, volleyball.

ADMISSIONS

Selectivity Rating: 63 (of 100). **Freshman Academic Profile:** Average high school GPA 3.1. 90% from public high schools. Average ACT 20, ACT middle 50% range 17-22. TOEFL required of all international applicants, minimum TOEFL 500. **Basis for Candidate Selection:** *Very important factors considered include:* secondary school record, standardized test scores. *Other factors considered include:* alumni/ae relation, character/personal qualities, extracurricular activities, geographical residence, interview, minority status, recommendations, state residency, talent/ability. **Freshman Admission Requirements:** High school diploma or GED is required. *Academic units required/recommended:* 19 total recommended; 4 English recommended, 4 math recommended, 3 science recommended, 2 foreign language recommended, 3 social studies recommended. **Freshman Admission Statistics:** 7,388 applied, 46% accepted, 65% of those accepted enrolled. **Transfer Admission Requirements:** *Items required:* high school transcript, college transcript, statement of good standing from prior school. Minimum college GPA of 2.0 required. Lowest grade transferable C. **General Admission Information:** Application fee $30. Nonfall registration accepted. Admission may be deferred. Credit and/or placement offered for CEEB Advanced Placement tests.

COSTS AND FINANCIAL AID

In-state tuition $5,500. Out-of-state tuition $11,166. Room & board $5,968. Required fees $0. Average book expense $884. **Required Forms and Deadlines:** FAFSA. No deadline for regular filing. Priority filing deadline April 3. **Notification of Awards:** Applicants will be notified of awards on a rolling basis beginning on or about April 14. **Types of Aid:** *Need-based scholarships/grants:* Pell, SEOG, state scholarships/grants, private scholarships, the school's own gift aid. *Loans:* Direct Subsidized Stafford, Direct Unsubsidized Stafford, Direct PLUS, Federal Perkins, Federal Nursing, state loans, college/university loans from institutional funds. **Student Employment:** Federal Work-Study Program available. Institutional employment available. Off-campus job opportunities are good. **Financial Aid Statistics:** 80% freshmen, 55% undergrads receive some form of aid. Average freshman grant $4,050. Average freshman loan $2,100. Average income from on-campus job $1,950. **Financial Aid Phone:** 800-940-4243.

FERRUM COLLEGE

PO Box 1000, Ferrum, VA 24088
Phone: 540-365-4290 **E-mail:** admissions@ferrum.edu **CEEB Code:** 5213
Fax: 540-365-4366 **Web:** www.ferrum.edu **ACT Code:** 4352

This private school, which is affiliated with the Methodist Church, was founded in 1913. It has a 700-acre campus.

STUDENTS AND FACULTY

Enrollment: 951. **Student Body:** Male 60%, female 40%, out-of-state 18%, international 1% (6 countries represented). **Ethnic Representation:** African American 18%, Asian 1%, Caucasian 71%, Hispanic 1%. **Retention and Graduation:** 55% freshmen return for sophomore year. 20% freshmen graduate within 4 years. **Faculty:** Student/faculty ratio 13:1. 68 full-time faculty, 64% hold PhDs. 100% faculty teach undergrads.

ACADEMICS

Degrees: Bachelor's. **Academic Requirements:** General education including some course work in arts/fine arts, computer literacy, English (including composition), foreign languages, history, humanities, mathematics, philosophy, sciences (biological or physical), social science, religion. **Classes:** 10-19 students in an average class. 20-29 students in an average lab/discussion section. **Majors with Highest Enrollment:** Business administration/management; environmental science; criminal justice/safety studies. **Disciplines with Highest Percentage of Degrees Awarded:** Business/marketing 24%, protective services/public administration 16%; biological life sciences 9%, education 8%, social sciences and history 5%. **Special Study Options:** Cooperative (work-study) program, double major, dual enrollment, honors program, independent study, internships, student-designed major, study abroad, teacher certification program.

FACILITIES

Housing: Coed, all-female, all-male, apartments for married students, apartments for single students. **Library Holdings:** 123,500 bound volumes. 7,739 periodicals. 7,953 microforms. 1,610 audiovisuals. **Special Academic Facilities/Equipment:** Blue Ridge Institute and Farm Museum. **Computers:** *Recommended operating system:* Windows NT/2000. School-owned computers available for student use.

EXTRACURRICULARS

Activities: Choral groups, dance, drama/theater, jazz band, literary magazine, music ensembles, musical theater, radio station, student government, student newspaper. **Organizations:** 60 registered organizations, 6 honor societies, 2 religious organizations. **Athletics (Intercollegiate):** *Men:* baseball, basketball, cheerleading, cross-country, football, golf, soccer, tennis. *Women:* basketball, cheerleading, cross-country, lacrosse, soccer, softball, tennis, volleyball.

ADMISSIONS

Selectivity Rating: 65 (of 100). **Freshman Academic Profile:** Average high school GPA 2.6. 6% in top 10% of high school class, 19% in top 25% of high school class, 46% in top 50% of high school class. 85% from public high schools. Average SAT I Math 447, SAT I Math middle 50% range 400-545. Average SAT I Verbal 452, SAT I Verbal middle 50% range 390-540. TOEFL required of all international applicants, minimum TOEFL 550. **Basis for Candidate Selection:** *Very important factors considered include:* secondary school record. *Important factors considered include:* character/personal qualities, extracurricular activities, recommendations, standardized test scores, talent/ability. *Other factors considered include:* class rank, interview, volunteer work, work experience. **Freshman Admission Requirements:** High school diploma or GED is required. *Academic units required/recommended:* 4 English recommended, 3 math recommended, 2 science recommended, 1 science lab recommended, 2 foreign language recommended, 3 social studies recommended, 2 elective recommended. **Freshman Admission Statistics:** 1,111 applied, 72% accepted, 37% of those accepted enrolled. **Transfer Admission Requirements:** *Items required:* college transcript. Minimum college GPA of 2.0 required. Lowest grade transferable C. **General Admission Information:** Application fee $25. Priority application deadline March 1. Nonfall registration accepted. Admission may be deferred for a maximum of 1 year. Credit and/or placement offered for CEEB Advanced Placement tests.

COSTS AND FINANCIAL AID

Tuition $14,390. Room & board $5,600. Required fees $25. Average book expense $600. **Required Forms and Deadlines:** FAFSA and state aid form. Priority filing deadline March 1. **Notification of Awards:** Applicants will be notified of awards on a rolling basis beginning on or about March 1. **Types of Aid:** *Need-based scholarships/grants:* Pell, SEOG, state scholarships/grants, private scholarships, the school's own gift aid. *Loans:* FFEL Subsidized Stafford, FFEL Unsubsidized Stafford, FFEL PLUS, Federal Perkins, college/university loans from institutional funds. **Student Employment:** Federal Work-Study Program available. Institutional employment available. Off-campus job opportunities are fair. **Financial Aid Statistics:** 74% freshmen, 76% undergrads receive some form of aid. Average freshman grant $6,900. Average freshman loan $3,383. Average income from on-campus job $2,000. **Financial Aid Phone:** 540-365-4282.

FISK UNIVERSITY

1000 17th Avenue North, Nashville, TN 37208-3051
Phone: 615-329-8666 **E-mail:** admissions@fisk.edu **CEEB Code:** 1224
Fax: 615-329-8774 **Web:** www.fisk.edu **ACT Code:** 3960

This private school was founded in 1866. It has a 40-acre campus.

STUDENTS AND FACULTY

Enrollment: 812. **Student Body:** Male 28%, female 72%, out-of-state 71%, international 2% (5 countries represented). **Ethnic Representation:** African American 100%. **Retention and Graduation:** 88% freshmen return for sophomore year. 48% freshmen graduate within 4 years. 25% grads go on to further study within 1 year. 10% grads pursue business degrees. 10% grads pursue law degrees. 20% grads pursue medical degrees. **Faculty:** Student/faculty ratio 11:1. 63 full-time faculty, 69% hold PhDs. 100% faculty teach undergrads.

ACADEMICS

Degrees: Bachelor's, master's. **Academic Requirements:** General education including some course work in arts/fine arts, English (including composition), foreign languages, humanities, mathematics, sciences (biological or physical), social science, African American heritage. **Disciplines with Highest Percentage of Degrees Awarded:** Psychology 27%, business/marketing 21%, biological life sciences 17%, social sciences and history 15%, English 9%. **Special Study Options:** Cooperative (work-study) program, cross registration, student exchange program (domestic), honors program, independent study, internships, student-designed major, study abroad, teacher certification program.

FACILITIES

Housing: All-female, all-male, apartments for married students, fraternities and/or sororities. **Library Holdings:** 210,000 bound volumes. 700 periodicals. 6,200 microforms. **Special Academic Facilities/Equipment:** Speech and language labs. **Computers:** School-owned computers available for student use.

EXTRACURRICULARS

Activities: Choral groups, dance, drama/theater, jazz band, literary magazine, music ensembles, radio station. **Organizations:** 9 honor societies, 5 religious organizations, 4 fraternities, 4 sororities. **Athletics (Intercollegiate):** *Men:* baseball, basketball, cross-country, tennis, track & field. *Women:* basketball, cross-country, tennis, track & field, volleyball.

ADMISSIONS

Selectivity Rating: 76 (of 100). **Freshman Academic Profile:** Average high school GPA 3.0. 35% in top 10% of high school class, 48% in top 25% of high school class, 73% in top 50% of high school class. 85% from public high schools. Average SAT I Math 441, SAT I Math middle 50% range 365-540. Average SAT I Verbal 448, SAT I Verbal middle 50% range 395-545. Average ACT 19, ACT middle 50% range 17-22. TOEFL required of all international applicants, minimum TOEFL 500. **Basis for Candidate Selection:** *Very important factors considered include:* class rank. *Important factors considered include:* alumni/ae relation, character/personal qualities, essays, extracurricular activities, recommendations, secondary school record. *Other factors considered include:* standardized test scores, talent/ability. **Freshman Admission Requirements:** High school diploma or GED is required. *Academic units required/recommended:* 3 math recommended, 3 science recommended, 2 foreign language recommended. **Freshman Admission Statistics:** 683 applied, 97% accepted, 37% of those accepted enrolled. **Transfer Admission Requirements:** *Items required:* high school transcript, college transcript. Minimum high school GPA of 3.0 required. Minimum college GPA of 2.0 required. Lowest grade transferable C. **General Admission Information:** Application fee $25. Regular application deadline June 15. Nonfall registration accepted. Admission may be deferred for a maximum of 2 years. Credit offered for CEEB Advanced Placement tests.

COSTS AND FINANCIAL AID

Tuition $8,480. Room & board $4,930. Required fees $290. Average book expense $800. **Types of Aid:** *Need-based scholarships/grants:* Pell, SEOG, state scholarships/grants, the school's own gift aid, United Negro College Fund. *Loans:* Direct Subsidized Stafford, Direct Unsubsidized Stafford, Direct PLUS, Federal Perkins. **Student Employment:** Federal Work-Study Program available. Off-campus job opportunities are good. **Financial Aid Statistics:** 90% freshmen, 90% undergrads receive some form of aid. Average freshman grant $2,200. Average freshman loan $6,700. Average income from on-campus job $1,100. **Financial Aid Phone:** 615-329-8735.

FITCHBURG STATE COLLEGE

160 Pearl Street, Fitchburg, MA 01420-2697
Phone: 978-665-3144 **E-mail:** admissions@fsc.edu **CEEB Code:** 3518
Fax: 978-665-4540 **Web:** www.fsc.edu **ACT Code:** 1902

This public school was founded in 1894. It has a 47-acre campus.

STUDENTS AND FACULTY

Enrollment: 3,342. **Student Body:** Male 42%, female 58%, out-of-state 5%, international 1%. **Ethnic Representation:** African American 4%, Asian 2%, Caucasian 82%, Hispanic 4%. **Retention and Graduation:** 70% freshmen return for sophomore year. 10% grads go on to further study within 1 year. 3% grads pursue business degrees. **Faculty:** Student/faculty ratio 13:1. 183 full-time faculty, 87% hold PhDs. 100% faculty teach undergrads.

ACADEMICS

Degrees: Bachelor's, certificate, master's, post-bachelor's certificate, post-master's certificate. **Academic Requirements:** General education including some course work in arts/fine arts, computer literacy, English (including composition), history, humanities, mathematics, philosophy, sciences (biological or physical), social science. **Majors with Highest Enrollment:** Business administration/management; communications studies/speech communication and rhetoric; education, general. **Disciplines with Highest Percentage of Degrees Awarded:** Communications/communication technologies 15%, business/marketing 15%, education 14%, health professions and related sciences 14%, social sciences and history 11%. **Special Study Options:** Accelerated program, cross registration, distance learning, double major, dual enrollment, honors program, independent study, internships, liberal arts/career combination, student-designed major, study abroad, teacher certification program.

FACILITIES

Housing: Coed, apartments for single students, housing for disabled students. **Library Holdings:** 229,505 bound volumes. 1,665 periodicals. 476,000 microforms. 2,159 audiovisuals. **Special Academic Facilities/Equipment:** Art gallery, graphics center, on-campus teacher education school, 120-acre conservation area. **Computers:** School-owned computers available for student use.

EXTRACURRICULARS

Activities: Choral groups, concert band, dance, drama/theater, jazz band, literary magazine, radio station, student government, student newspaper, yearbook. **Organizations:** 66 registered organizations, 7 honor societies, 1 religious organization, 3 fraternities (1% men join), 3 sororities (2% women join). **Athletics (Intercollegiate):** *Men:* baseball, basketball, cross-country, football, ice hockey, indoor track, soccer, track & field. *Women:* basketball, cross-country, field hockey, ice hockey, indoor track, soccer, softball, track & field, volleyball.

ADMISSIONS

Selectivity Rating: 63 (of 100). **Freshman Academic Profile:** Average high school GPA 3.0. 85% from public high schools. Average SAT I Math 500, SAT I Math middle 50% range 440-550. Average SAT I Verbal 500, SAT I Verbal middle 50% range 450-540. TOEFL required of all international applicants, minimum TOEFL 550. **Basis for Candidate Selection:** *Very important factors considered include:* secondary school record. *Important factors considered include:* essays, standardized test scores. *Other factors considered include:* alumni/ae relation, extracurricular activities, recommendations, talent/ability, volunteer work, work experience. **Freshman Admission Requirements:** High school diploma or GED is required. *Academic units required/recommended:* 16 total required; 4 English required, 3 math required, 4 math recommended, 3 science required, 2 science lab required, 2 foreign language required, 1 social studies required, 1 history required, 2 elective required. **Freshman Admission Statistics:** 3,057 applied, 54% accepted, 32% of those accepted enrolled. **Transfer Admission Requirements:** *Items required:* college transcript, essay. Minimum college GPA of 2.0 required. Lowest grade transferable C. **General Admission Information:** Application fee $10. Priority application deadline April 1. Nonfall registration accepted. Admission may be deferred for a maximum of 1 year. Credit offered for CEEB Advanced Placement tests.

COSTS AND FINANCIAL AID

In-state tuition $970. Out-of-state tuition $7,050. Room & board $5,120. Required fees $2,718. Average book expense $600. **Required Forms and Deadlines:** FAFSA. Financial aid filing deadline March 1. **Types of Aid:** *Need-based scholarships/grants:* Pell, SEOG, state scholarships/grants, private scholarships, the school's own gift aid. *Loans:* Direct Subsidized Stafford, Direct Unsubsidized Stafford, Direct PLUS, Federal Perkins, Federal Nursing, state loans. **Student Employment:** Federal Work-Study Program available. Institutional employment available. Off-campus job opportunities are good. **Financial Aid Phone:** 978-665-3156.

FIVE TOWNS COLLEGE

Five Towns College, 305 North Service Road, Dix Hills, NY 11746
Phone: 631-424-7000 **E-mail:** admissions@ftc.edu **CEEB Code:** 3142
Fax: 631-424-7008 **Web:** www.fivetowns.edu

This private school was founded in 1972. It has a 35-acre campus.

STUDENTS AND FACULTY

Enrollment: 1,026. **Student Body:** Male 67%, female 33%, out-of-state 5%. **Ethnic Representation:** African American 20%, Asian 2%, Caucasian 63%, Hispanic 14%. **Retention and Graduation:** 74% freshmen return for sophomore year. **Faculty:** Student/faculty ratio 13:1. 41 full-time faculty, 48% hold PhDs. 100% faculty teach undergrads.

ACADEMICS

Degrees: Associate's, bachelor's, master's. **Academic Requirements:** General education including some course work in computer literacy, English (including composition), humanities, social science. **Disciplines with Highest Percentage of Degrees Awarded:** Business/marketing 63%, visual and performing arts 30%, education 7%. **Special Study Options:** Cross registration, distance learning, dual enrollment, honors program, independent study, internships, liberal arts/career combination, teacher certification program.

FACILITIES

Housing: Coed. **Library Holdings:** 32,000 bound volumes. 549 periodicals. 35 microforms. 9,600 audiovisuals. **Computers:** School-owned computers available for student use.

EXTRACURRICULARS

Activities: Choral groups, concert band, dance, drama/theater, jazz band, music ensembles, musical theater, opera, radio station, student government, student newspaper, symphony orchestra, television station, yearbook. **Organizations:** 1 honor society.

ADMISSIONS

Selectivity Rating: 63 (of 100). **Freshman Academic Profile:** 80% from public high schools. Average SAT I Math 460. Average SAT I Verbal 465.

Average ACT 19. TOEFL required of all international applicants, minimum TOEFL 500. **Basis for Candidate Selection:** *Very important factors considered include:* character/personal qualities, secondary school record, standardized test scores, talent/ability. *Important factors considered include:* class rank, essays, extracurricular activities, interview, recommendations. *Other factors considered include:* volunteer work, work experience. **Freshman Admission Requirements:** High school diploma or GED is required. *Academic units required/recommended:* 4 English recommended, 3 math recommended, 2 science recommended, 2 foreign language recommended, 3 social studies recommended. **Freshman Admission Statistics:** 990 applied, 85% accepted, 48% of those accepted enrolled. **Transfer Admission Requirements:** *Items required:* high school transcript, college transcript, essay. Minimum high school GPA of 2.0 required. Minimum college GPA of 2.0 required. Lowest grade transferable C. **General Admission Information:** Application fee $25. Nonfall registration accepted. Admission may be deferred. Placement offered for CEEB Advanced Placement tests.

COSTS AND FINANCIAL AID

Tuition $11,400. Room & board $7,200. Required fees $400. Average book expense $750. **Required Forms and Deadlines:** FAFSA, institution's own financial aid form, and state aid form. No deadline for regular filing. **Notification of Awards:** Applicants will be notified of awards on a rolling basis beginning on or about March 31. **Types of Aid:** *Need-based scholarships/grants:* Pell, SEOG, state scholarships/grants, private scholarships, the school's own gift aid. *Loans:* Direct Subsidized Stafford, Direct Unsubsidized Stafford, Direct PLUS. **Student Employment:** Federal Work-Study Program available. Institutional employment available. Off-campus job opportunities are good. **Financial Aid Statistics:** 78% freshmen, 78% undergrads receive some form of aid. Average freshman grant $2,000. Average freshman loan $2,625. Average income from on-campus job $3,500. **Financial Aid Phone:** 631-424-7000.

See page 1034.

FLAGLER COLLEGE

74 King Street, PO Box 1027, St. Augustine, FL 32085-1027
Phone: 800-304-4208 **E-mail:** admiss@flagler.edu **CEEB Code:** 5235
Fax: 904-826-0094 **Web:** www.flagler.edu **ACT Code:** 772

This private school was founded in 1968. It has a 38-acre campus.

STUDENTS AND FACULTY

Enrollment: 1,830. **Student Body:** Male 37%, female 63%, out-of-state 31%, international 3% (22 countries represented). **Ethnic Representation:** African American 1%, Asian 1%, Caucasian 94%, Hispanic 3%. **Retention and Graduation:** 70% freshmen return for sophomore year. 45% freshmen graduate within 4 years. 20% grads go on to further study within 1 year. 4% grads pursue business degrees. 2% grads pursue law degrees. **Faculty:** Student/faculty ratio 20:1. 62 full-time faculty, 64% hold PhDs. 100% faculty teach undergrads.

ACADEMICS

Degrees: Bachelor's. **Academic Requirements:** General education including some course work in arts/fine arts, computer literacy, English (including composition), history, humanities, mathematics, philosophy, sciences (biological or physical), social science. **Classes:** 20-29 students in an average class. **Disciplines with Highest Percentage of Degrees Awarded:** Education 27%, business/marketing 21%, visual and performing arts 13%, communications/communication technologies 12%, psychology 8%. **Special Study Options:** Double major, student exchange program (domestic), internships, study abroad, teacher certification program.

FACILITIES

Housing: All-female, all-male. **Library Holdings:** 82 bound volumes. 458 periodicals. 70,020 microforms. 2,880 audiovisuals. **Special Academic Facilities/Equipment:** Museum/theatre, learning disabilities clinic for student teachers. **Computers:** School-owned computers available for student use.

EXTRACURRICULARS

Activities: Choral groups, drama/theater, literary magazine, radio station, student government, student newspaper. **Organizations:** 23 registered organizations, 5 honor societies, 2 religious organizations. **Athletics (Intercollegiate):** *Men:* baseball, basketball, cross-country, golf, soccer, tennis. *Women:* basketball, cross-country, golf, soccer, tennis, volleyball.

ADMISSIONS

Selectivity Rating: 78 (of 100). **Freshman Academic Profile:** Average high school GPA 3.0. 21% in top 10% of high school class, 59% in top 25% of high school class, 96% in top 50% of high school class. 79% from public high schools. Average SAT I Math 543, SAT I Math middle 50% range 500-580. Average SAT I Verbal 559, SAT I Verbal middle 50% range 550-600. Average ACT 23, ACT middle 50% range 21-25. TOEFL required of all international applicants, minimum TOEFL 550. **Basis for Candidate Selection:** *Very important factors considered include:* character/personal qualities, secondary school record, standardized test scores. *Important factors considered include:* alumni/ae relation, class rank, essays, geographical residence, interview, state residency. *Other factors considered include:* extracurricular activities, recommendations, talent/ability, volunteer work, work experience. **Freshman Admission Requirements:** High school diploma or GED is required. *Academic units required/recommended:* 16 total required; 21 total recommended; 4 English required, 3 math required, 2 science required, 3 science recommended, 1 science lab required, 2 science lab recommended, 2 foreign language recommended, 3 social studies required, 4 social studies recommended, 2 history required, 3 history recommended, 1 elective required, 2 elective recommended. **Freshman Admission Statistics:** 1,757 applied, 28% accepted, 82% of those accepted enrolled. **Transfer Admission Requirements:** *Items required:* college transcript, essay, standardized test scores, statement of good standing from prior school. Minimum high school GPA of 2.5 required. Minimum college GPA of 2.0 required. Lowest grade transferable C. **General Admission Information:** Application fee $20. Priority application deadline January 15. Early decision application deadline December 1. Regular application deadline March 1. Nonfall registration accepted. Admission may be deferred for a maximum of 1 year. Credit and/or placement offered for CEEB Advanced Placement tests.

COSTS AND FINANCIAL AID

Tuition $6,320. Room & board $3,910. Required fees $0. Average book expense $700. **Required Forms and Deadlines:** FAFSA, institution's own financial aid form, and state aid form. Priority filing deadline May 1. **Notification of Awards:** Applicants will be notified of awards on a rolling basis beginning on or about March 1. **Student Employment:** Federal Work-Study Program available. Institutional employment available. Off-campus job opportunities are good. **Financial Aid Statistics:** 37% freshmen, 36% undergrads receive some form of aid. **Financial Aid Phone:** 904-829-6481.

FLORIDA A&M UNIVERSITY

Suite G-9, Foote-Hilyer Administration Center, Tallahassee, FL 32307
Phone: 850-599-3796 **E-mail:** adm@famu.edu **CEEB Code:** 5215
Fax: 850-561-2428 **Web:** www.famu.edu **ACT Code:** 726

This public school was founded in 1887. It has a 419-acre campus.

STUDENTS AND FACULTY

Enrollment: 10,803. **Student Body:** Male 43%, female 57%, out-of-state 21%, international 1%. **Ethnic Representation:** African American 96%, Caucasian 3%, Hispanic 1%. **Retention and Graduation:** 25% grads go on to further study within 1 year. **Faculty:** Student/faculty ratio 20:1. 558 full-time faculty, 77% hold PhDs.

ACADEMICS

Degrees: Associate's, bachelor's, doctoral, first professional, master's. **Academic Requirements:** General education including some course work in computer literacy, English (including composition), foreign languages, history, humanities, mathematics, sciences (biological or physical), social science. **Disciplines with Highest Percentage of Degrees Awarded:** Business/marketing 19%, health professions and related sciences 14%, education 11%, engineering/engineering technology 8%, protective services/public administration 8%. **Special Study Options:** Accelerated program, cooperative (work-study) program, distance learning, double major, dual enrollment, honors program, independent study, internships, study abroad, teacher certification program, weekend college.

FACILITIES

Housing: Coed, all-female, all-male, apartments for married students. **Library Holdings:** 484,801 bound volumes. 7,672 periodicals. 156,018 microforms. 73,957 audiovisuals. **Special Academic Facilities/Equipment:** Black Archives and Resource Center, Coleman Memorial Library, Foster Tanner Music/Art Building. **Computers:** *Recommended operating system:* Windows 95. School-owned computers available for student use.

EXTRACURRICULARS

Activities: Choral groups, concert band, dance, drama/theater, jazz band, marching band, music ensembles, pep band, radio station, student government, student newspaper, symphony orchestra, television station, yearbook.

Organizations: 9 registered organizations, 16 honor societies, 11 religious organizations, 4 fraternities, 4 sororities. **Athletics (Intercollegiate):** *Men:* baseball, basketball, cross-country, football, golf, swimming, tennis, track & field. *Women:* basketball, cross-country, golf, softball, swimming, tennis, track & field, volleyball.

ADMISSIONS

Selectivity Rating: 80 (of 100). **Freshman Academic Profile:** Average high school GPA 3.2. 85% from public high schools. SAT I Math middle 50% range 450-560. SAT I Verbal middle 50% range 450-550. Average ACT 20, ACT middle 50% range 18-22. TOEFL required of all international applicants, minimum TOEFL 500. **Basis for Candidate Selection:** *Very important factors considered include:* secondary school record, standardized test scores. *Other factors considered include:* alumni/ae relation, character/personal qualities, essays, extracurricular activities, geographical residence, minority status, recommendations, state residency, talent/ability, volunteer work, work experience. **Freshman Admission Requirements:** High school diploma or GED is required. *Academic units required/recommended:* 19 total required; 19 total recommended; 4 English required, 4 English recommended, 3 math required, 3 math recommended, 3 science required, 3 science recommended, 1 science lab required, 2 foreign language required, 2 foreign language recommended, 3 social studies required, 3 social studies recommended, 4 elective required, 4 elective recommended. **Freshman Admission Statistics:** 4,819 applied, 78% accepted, 51% of those accepted enrolled. **Transfer Admission Requirements:** *Items required:* college transcript. Minimum high school GPA of 2.0 required. Minimum college GPA of 2.0 required. Lowest grade transferable C. **General Admission Information:** Application fee $20. Regular application deadline May 9. Nonfall registration accepted. Admission may be deferred. Credit offered for CEEB Advanced Placement tests.

COSTS AND FINANCIAL AID

In-state tuition $1,777. Out-of-state tuition $7,368. Room & board $3,896. Required fees $129. Average book expense $600. **Required Forms and Deadlines:** FAFSA. Financial aid filing deadline June 30. Priority filing deadline March 1. **Notification of Awards:** Applicants will be notified of awards on a rolling basis beginning on or about March 1. **Types of Aid:** *Need-based scholarships/grants:* Pell, SEOG, state scholarships/grants, private scholarships, the school's own gift aid, United Negro College Fund, Federal Nursing. *Loans:* Direct Subsidized Stafford, Direct Unsubsidized Stafford, Direct PLUS, Federal Perkins. **Student Employment:** Federal Work-Study Program available. Off-campus job opportunities are good. **Financial Aid Statistics:** 75% freshmen, 78% undergrads receive some form of aid. Average freshman grant $3,031. Average income from on-campus job $900. **Financial Aid Phone:** 850-599-3730.

FLORIDA ATLANTIC UNIVERSITY

777 Glades Road, PO Box 3091, Boca Raton, FL 33431-0991
Phone: 561-297-3040 **E-mail:** admisweb@fau.edu **CEEB Code:** 5229
Fax: 561-297-2758 **Web:** www.fau.edu **ACT Code:** 729

This public school was founded in 1961. It has an 860-acre campus.

STUDENTS AND FACULTY

Enrollment: 18,757. **Student Body:** Male 39%, female 61%, out-of-state 9%, international 5%. **Ethnic Representation:** African American 18%, Asian 5%, Caucasian 64%, Hispanic 13%. **Retention and Graduation:** 69% freshmen return for sophomore year. 18% freshmen graduate within 4 years. **Faculty:** Student/faculty ratio 15:1. 681 full-time faculty, 89% hold PhDs. 85% faculty teach undergrads.

ACADEMICS

Degrees: Associate's, bachelor's, doctoral, master's, post-master's certificate. **Academic Requirements:** General education including some course work in arts/fine arts, English (including composition), foreign languages, history, humanities, mathematics, sciences (biological or physical), social science. **Classes:** 20-29 students in an average class. 20-29 students in an average lab/discussion section. **Disciplines with Highest Percentage of Degrees Awarded:** Business/marketing 25%, education 12%, social sciences and history 8%, English 8%, psychology 7%. **Special Study Options:** Accelerated program, cooperative (work-study) program, cross registration, distance learning, double major, dual enrollment, English as a second language, student exchange program (domestic), honors program, independent study, internships, liberal arts/career combination, study abroad, teacher certification program, weekend college.

FACILITIES

Housing: Coed, all-female, all-male, apartments for single students. **Library Holdings:** 850,727 bound volumes. 3,927 periodicals. 2,747,115 microforms. 10,211 audiovisuals. **Special Academic Facilities/Equipment:** Art gallery, on-campus elementary school, robotics lab, marine research facilities. **Computers:** *Recommended operating system:* Windows 95. School-owned computers available for student use.

EXTRACURRICULARS

Activities: Choral groups, dance, drama/theater, jazz band, music ensembles, musical theater, opera, radio station, student government, student newspaper. **Organizations:** 150 registered organizations, 11 honor societies, 6 religious organizations, 9 fraternities (2% men join), 4 sororities (2% women join). **Athletics (Intercollegiate):** *Men:* baseball, basketball, cheerleading, cross-country, diving, golf, soccer, swimming, tennis. *Women:* basketball, cheerleading, cross-country, diving, golf, soccer, softball, swimming, tennis, track & field, volleyball.

ADMISSIONS

Selectivity Rating: 68 (of 100). **Freshman Academic Profile:** Average high school GPA 3.4. Average SAT I Math 530, SAT I Math middle 50% range 470-570. Average SAT I Verbal 520, SAT I Verbal middle 50% range 460-560. Average ACT 21, ACT middle 50% range 19-24. TOEFL required of all international applicants, minimum TOEFL 550. **Basis for Candidate Selection:** *Very important factors considered include:* secondary school record, standardized test scores. *Important factors considered include:* recommendations, talent/ability. *Other factors considered include:* class rank, extracurricular activities, minority status. **Freshman Admission Requirements:** High school diploma or GED is required. *Academic units required/recommended:* 19 total required; 4 English required, 3 math required, 3 science required, 2 science lab required, 2 foreign language required, 3 social studies required, 4 elective required. **Freshman Admission Statistics:** 6,289 applied, 71% accepted, 50% of those accepted enrolled. **Transfer Admission Requirements:** *Items required:* college transcript, statement of good standing from prior school. Minimum college GPA of 2.0 required. Lowest grade transferable D. **General Admission Information:** Application fee $20. Regular application deadline June 1. Nonfall registration accepted. Admission may be deferred for a maximum of 1 year. Credit offered for CEEB Advanced Placement tests.

COSTS AND FINANCIAL AID

In-state tuition $2,699. Out-of-state tuition $10,586. Room & board $6,134. Average book expense $636. **Required Forms and Deadlines:** FAFSA and financial aid transcript. Priority filing deadline March 1. **Notification of Awards:** Applicants will be notified of awards on a rolling basis beginning on or about May 1. **Types of Aid:** *Need-based scholarships/grants:* Pell, SEOG, private scholarships, the school's own gift aid, Federal Nursing. *Loans:* FFEL Subsidized Stafford, FFEL Unsubsidized Stafford, FFEL PLUS, Federal Perkins, Federal Nursing, state loans, college/university loans from institutional funds. **Student Employment:** Federal Work-Study Program available. Institutional employment available. Off-campus job opportunities are excellent. **Financial Aid Statistics:** Average freshman grant $8,000. Average freshman loan $3,560. Average income from on-campus job $1,500. **Financial Aid Phone:** 561-297-3530.

FLORIDA INSTITUTE OF TECHNOLOGY

150 West University Boulevard, Melbourne, FL 32901-6975
Phone: 321-674-8030 **E-mail:** admissions@fit.edu **CEEB Code:** 5080
Fax: 321-723-9468 **Web:** www.fit.edu **ACT Code:** 716

This private school was founded in 1958. It has a 130-acre campus.

STUDENTS AND FACULTY

Enrollment: 2,168. **Student Body:** Male 71%, female 29%, out-of-state 44%, international 22% (103 countries represented). **Ethnic Representation:** African American 5%, Asian 4%, Caucasian 73%, Hispanic 7%. **Retention and Graduation:** 74% freshmen return for sophomore year. 35% freshmen graduate within 4 years. 24% grads go on to further study within 1 year. 6% grads pursue business degrees. 1% grads pursue law degrees. 5% grads pursue medical degrees. **Faculty:** Student/faculty ratio 12:1. 181 full-time faculty, 86% hold PhDs. 95% faculty teach undergrads.

ACADEMICS

Degrees: Bachelor's, doctoral, master's, post-master's certificate. **Academic Requirements:** General education including some course work in computer literacy, English (including composition), humanities, mathematics, sciences (biological or physical), social science. **Classes:** 10-19 students in an average class. 10-19 students in an average lab/discussion section. **Majors with Highest**

Enrollment: Computer science; computer engineering, general; aviation/airway management and operations. **Disciplines with Highest Percentage of Degrees Awarded:** Engineering/engineering technology 40%, trade and industry 16%, biological life sciences 13%, computer and information sciences 8%, physical sciences 8%. **Special Study Options:** Accelerated program, cooperative (work-study) program, distance learning, double major, dual enrollment, English as a second language, internships, liberal arts/career combination, study abroad, teacher certification program; dual degrees in computer engineering/electrical engineering, chemical engineering/chemistry, molecular/marine biology.

FACILITIES

Housing: Coed, all-female, all-male, apartments for single students, housing for disabled students, fraternities and/or sororities. **Library Holdings:** 163,407 bound volumes. 3,347 periodicals. 303,775 microforms. 4,968 audiovisuals. **Special Academic Facilities/Equipment:** Medical genetics lab, research vessel, observatory, wind and hurricane impacts research lab, aquaculture lab, center for airport management. **Computers:** School-owned computers available for student use.

EXTRACURRICULARS

Activities: Choral groups, dance, drama/theater, literary magazine, pep band, radio station, student government, student newspaper, television station, yearbook. **Organizations:** 103 registered organizations, 9 honor societies, 3 religious organizations, 7 fraternities (15% men join), 3 sororities (11% women join). **Athletics (Intercollegiate):** *Men:* baseball, basketball, crew, cross-country, soccer. *Women:* basketball, crew, cross-country, softball, volleyball.

ADMISSIONS

Selectivity Rating: 77 (of 100). **Freshman Academic Profile:** Average high school GPA 3.6. 27% in top 10% of high school class, 60% in top 25% of high school class, 88% in top 50% of high school class. 80% from public high schools. Average SAT I Math 600, SAT I Math middle 50% range 550-650. Average SAT I Verbal 555, SAT I Verbal middle 50% range 500-610. Average ACT 25, ACT middle 50% range 22-27. TOEFL required of all international applicants, minimum TOEFL 550. **Basis for Candidate Selection:** *Very important factors considered include:* secondary school record. *Important factors considered include:* class rank, standardized test scores. *Other factors considered include:* character/personal qualities, essays, recommendations, work experience. **Freshman Admission Requirements:** High school diploma or GED is required. *Academic units required/recommended:* 12 total required; 4 English required, 4 math required, 3 science required, 4 science recommended. **Freshman Admission Statistics:** 1,982 applied, 84% accepted, 31% of those accepted enrolled. **Transfer Admission Requirements:** *Items required:* high school transcript, college transcript. Minimum high school GPA of 2.8 required. Minimum college GPA of 2.5 required. Lowest grade transferable C. **General Admission Information:** Application fee $40. Nonfall registration accepted. Admission may be deferred for a maximum of 2 years. Credit and/or placement offered for CEEB Advanced Placement tests.

COSTS AND FINANCIAL AID

Tuition $20,900. Room & board $5,800. Required fees $0. Average book expense $1,000. **Required Forms and Deadlines:** FAFSA and state aid form. No deadline for regular filing. Priority filing deadline March 15. **Notification of Awards:** Applicants will be notified of awards on a rolling basis beginning on or about March 1. **Types of Aid:** *Need-based scholarships/grants:* Pell, SEOG, state scholarships/grants, private scholarships, the school's own gift aid. *Loans:* FFEL Subsidized Stafford, FFEL Unsubsidized Stafford, FFEL PLUS, Federal Perkins, state loans, college/university loans from institutional funds. **Student Employment:** Federal Work-Study Program available. Off-campus job opportunities are excellent. **Financial Aid Statistics:** 71% freshmen, 61% undergrads receive some form of aid. Average freshman grant $16,924. Average freshman loan $3,498. Average income from on-campus job $4,200. **Financial Aid Phone:** 321-674-8070.

FLORIDA INTERNATIONAL UNIVERSITY

University Park, PC 140, Miami, FL 33199
Phone: 305-348-2363 **E-mail:** admiss@fiu.edu **CEEB Code:** 5206
Fax: 305-348-3648 **Web:** www.fiu.edu **ACT Code:** 776

This public school was founded in 1965. It has a 573-acre campus.

STUDENTS AND FACULTY

Enrollment: 27,153. **Student Body:** Male 44%, female 56%, out-of-state 15%, international 7% (144 countries represented). **Ethnic Representation:** African American 15%, Asian 4%, Caucasian 20%, Hispanic 60%. **Retention and Graduation:** 85% freshmen return for sophomore year. 37% grads go on to further study within 1 year. 11% grads pursue business degrees. 4% grads pursue law degrees. 3% grads pursue medical degrees. **Faculty:** Student/faculty ratio 17:1. 714 full-time faculty, 81% hold PhDs.

ACADEMICS

Degrees: Bachelor's, doctoral, first professional, master's, post-bachelor's certificate. **Academic Requirements:** General education including some course work in computer literacy, English (including composition), foreign languages, humanities, mathematics, sciences (biological or physical), social science. **Classes:** 20-29 students in an average class. 20-29 students in an average lab/discussion section. **Majors with Highest Enrollment:** Accounting; elementary education and teaching; psychology, general. **Disciplines with Highest Percentage of Degrees Awarded:** Business/marketing 35%, education 9%, psychology 8%, health professions and related sciences 8%, protective services/public administration 7%. **Special Study Options:** Distance learning, double major, dual enrollment, student exchange program (domestic), honors program, independent study, internships, study abroad, teacher certification program, weekend college.

FACILITIES

Housing: Coed, apartments for married students, apartments for single students. **Library Holdings:** 765,285 bound volumes. 14,978 periodicals. 3,275,278 microforms. 121,173 audiovisuals. **Special Academic Facilities/Equipment:** Art gallery, consumer affairs institute, center for economic studies, women's studies center, robotics lab. **Computers:** School-owned computers available for student use.

EXTRACURRICULARS

Activities: Drama/theater, jazz band, marching band, music ensembles, musical theater, radio station, student government, student newspaper, yearbook. **Organizations:** 190 registered organizations, 40 honor societies, 2 religious organizations, 13 fraternities (14% men join), 10 sororities (14% women join). **Athletics (Intercollegiate):** *Men:* baseball, basketball, cross-country, football, soccer, track & field. *Women:* basketball, cross-country, golf, soccer, softball, tennis, track & field, volleyball.

ADMISSIONS

Selectivity Rating: 71 (of 100). **Freshman Academic Profile:** Average high school GPA 3.4. 42% in top 10% of high school class, 89% in top 25% of high school class, 99% in top 50% of high school class. 52% from public high schools. Average SAT I Math 533, SAT I Math middle 50% range 480-570. Average SAT I Verbal 528, SAT I Verbal middle 50% range 480-570. Average ACT 22, ACT middle 50% range 20-24. TOEFL required of all international applicants, minimum TOEFL 500. **Basis for Candidate Selection:** *Very important factors considered include:* character/personal qualities, class rank, extracurricular activities, geographical residence, secondary school record, standardized test scores, state residency, talent/ability. *Other factors considered include:* interview, recommendations. **Freshman Admission Requirements:** High school diploma or GED is required. *Academic units required/recommended:* 19 total required; 4 English required, 3 math required, 3 science required, 2 science lab required, 2 foreign language required, 3 social studies required, 4 elective required. **Freshman Admission Statistics:** 11,307 applied, 64% accepted, 44% of those accepted enrolled. **Transfer Admission Requirements:** *Items required:* college transcript. Minimum high school GPA of 3.0 required. Minimum college GPA of 2.0 required. Lowest grade transferable D. **General Admission Information:** Application fee $20. Priority application deadline February 15. Nonfall registration accepted. Admission may be deferred for a maximum of 1 year. Credit offered for CEEB Advanced Placement tests.

COSTS AND FINANCIAL AID

In-state tuition $2,696. Out-of-state tuition $12,162. Room & board $7,180. Required fees $185. Average book expense $1,080. **Required Forms and Deadlines:** FAFSA. No deadline for regular filing. Priority filing deadline March 1. **Notification of Awards:** Applicants will be notified of awards on a rolling basis beginning on or about April 15. **Types of Aid:** *Need-based scholarships/grants:* Pell, SEOG, state scholarships/grants, private scholarships, the school's own gift aid. *Loans:* FFEL Subsidized Stafford, FFEL Unsubsidized Stafford, FFEL PLUS, Federal Perkins, college/university loans from institutional funds. **Student Employment:** Federal Work-Study Program available. Institutional employment available. Off-campus job opportunities are good. **Financial Aid Statistics:** 48% freshmen, 48% undergrads receive some form of aid. Average freshman grant $2,329. Average freshman loan $2,354. **Financial Aid Phone:** 305-348-1500.

FLORIDA MEMORIAL COLLEGE

15800 NW 42nd Avenue, Miami, FL 33054
Phone: 800-822-1362 **E-mail:** pmartin@fmc.edu **CEEB Code:** 5217
Fax: 305-625-4141 **Web:** www.fmc.edu **ACT Code:** 730

This private school, which is affiliated with the Baptist Church, was founded in 1879.

STUDENTS AND FACULTY

Enrollment: 1,488. **Student Body:** Out-of-state 20%. **Ethnic Representation:** African American 89%, Caucasian 1%, Hispanic 10%.

ACADEMICS

Degrees: Bachelor's. **Special Study Options:** Cooperative (work-study) program, student exchange program (domestic), study abroad, co-op program in business.

FACILITIES

Housing: Coed, all-female, all-male, fraternities and/or sororities. **Special Academic Facilities/Equipment:** Reading and study skills labs. **Computers:** *Recommended operating system:* Mac.

EXTRACURRICULARS

Organizations: 1 honor society, 1 religious organization, 4 fraternities, 4 sororities. **Athletics (Intercollegiate):** *Men:* baseball, basketball, cross-country, soccer, softball, track & field, volleyball. *Women:* basketball, softball, volleyball.

ADMISSIONS

Selectivity Rating: 63 (of 100). **Freshman Academic Profile:** 100% from public high schools. **Freshman Admission Requirements:** High school diploma is required and GED is not accepted. *Academic units required/recommended:* 15 total recommended; 4 English recommended, 4 math recommended, 3 science recommended, 2 foreign language recommended, 2 social studies recommended. **Transfer Admission Requirements:** Lowest grade transferable C. **General Admission Information:** Early decision application deadline April 1. Regular application deadline July 1. Nonfall registration accepted.

COSTS AND FINANCIAL AID

Tuition $5,420. Room & board $2,428. Required fees $1,030. Average book expense $550. **Required Forms and Deadlines:** FAFSA. **Types of Aid:** *Need-based scholarships/grants:* United Negro College Fund. *Loans:* FFEL Subsidized Stafford, FFEL PLUS. **Student Employment:** Federal Work-Study Program available. Off-campus job opportunities are excellent. **Financial Aid Statistics:** Average income from on-campus job $1,000. **Financial Aid Phone:** 305-626-3745.

FLORIDA METROPOLITAN UNIVERSITY

2401 North Harbor City Boulevard, Melbourne, FL 32935
Phone: 321-253-2929 **E-mail:** tkumar@cci.edu
Fax: 321-255-2017 **Web:** www.fmu.edu

STUDENTS AND FACULTY

Enrollment: 544. **Student Body:** Male 32%, female 68%. **Faculty:** 13 full-time faculty, 30% hold PhDs. 90% faculty teach undergrads.

ACADEMICS

Degrees: Associate's, bachelor's, master's. **Academic Requirements:** General education including some course work in English (including composition), mathematics, strategies for success, critical thinking. **Special Study Options:** Accelerated program, distance learning, internships, weekend college.

FACILITIES

Computers: School-owned computers available for student use.

EXTRACURRICULARS

Activities: Student newspaper.

ADMISSIONS

Selectivity Rating: 63 (of 100). **Freshman Academic Profile:** TOEFL required of all international applicants, minimum TOEFL 450. **Basis for Candidate Selection:** *Very important factors considered include:* interview, secondary school record. *Important factors considered include:* standardized test scores. *Other factors considered include:* alumni/ae relation, character/personal qualities, essays, recommendations, talent/ability. **Freshman Admission Requirements:** High school diploma or GED is required. **Freshman Admission Statistics:** 241 applied, 60% accepted. **Transfer Admission Requirements:** *Items required:* high school transcript, college transcript, interview, standardized test scores. Lowest grade transferable C. **General Admission Information:** Application fee $50. Nonfall registration accepted.

COSTS AND FINANCIAL AID

Types of Aid: *Need-based scholarships/grants:* Pell, SEOG, state scholarships/grants, private scholarships, the school's own gift aid, company tuition reimbursement. *Loans:* FFEL Subsidized Stafford, FFEL Unsubsidized Stafford, FFEL PLUS, Federal Perkins, Federal Nursing, state loans, college/university loans from institutional funds, Sallie Mae. **Student Employment:** Federal Work-Study Program available. Off-campus job opportunities are good. **Financial Aid Phone:** 321-253-2929.

FLORIDA SOUTHERN COLLEGE

111 Lake Hollingworth Drive, Lakeland, FL 33801
Phone: 863-680-4131 **E-mail:** fscadm@flsouthern.edu **CEEB Code:** 5218
Fax: 863-680-4120 **Web:** www.flsouthern.edu **ACT Code:** 732

This private school, which is affiliated with the Methodist Church, was founded in 1885. It has a 100-acre campus.

STUDENTS AND FACULTY

Enrollment: 1,881. **Student Body:** Male 39%, female 61%, out-of-state 23%, international 4% (37 countries represented). **Ethnic Representation:** African American 6%, Asian 1%, Caucasian 87%, Hispanic 5%. **Retention and Graduation:** 72% freshmen return for sophomore year. 48% freshmen graduate within 4 years. 14% grads go on to further study within 1 year. 2% grads pursue law degrees. 3% grads pursue medical degrees. **Faculty:** Student/faculty ratio 17:1. 109 full-time faculty, 82% hold PhDs. 100% faculty teach undergrads.

ACADEMICS

Degrees: Bachelor's, master's. **Academic Requirements:** General education including some course work in arts/fine arts, English (including composition), history, humanities, mathematics, philosophy, sciences (biological or physical), social science. **Classes:** 10-19 students in an average class. **Majors with Highest Enrollment:** Marketing/marketing management, general; elementary education and teaching; biology/biological sciences, general. **Disciplines with Highest Percentage of Degrees Awarded:** Business/marketing 36%, education 17%, communications/communication technologies 7%, health professions and related sciences 7%, biological life sciences 6%. **Special Study Options:** Double major, honors program, independent study, internships, study abroad, teacher certification program.

FACILITIES

Housing: All-female, all-male, fraternities and/or sororities. **Library Holdings:** 172,803 bound volumes. 939 periodicals. 448,221 microforms. 11,490 audiovisuals. **Special Academic Facilities/Equipment:** Art gallery, visitors' center, preschool lab, radio and TV studios. **Computers:** School-owned computers available for student use.

EXTRACURRICULARS

Activities: Choral groups, concert band, drama/theater, jazz band, literary magazine, music ensembles, musical theater, opera, pep band, student government, student newspaper, yearbook. **Organizations:** 95 registered organizations, 16 honor societies, 9 religious organizations, 5 fraternities (15% men join), 5 sororities (16% women join). **Athletics (Intercollegiate):** *Men:* baseball, basketball, cross-country, golf, soccer, tennis. *Women:* basketball, cross-country, golf, soccer, softball, tennis, volleyball.

ADMISSIONS

Selectivity Rating: 79 (of 100). **Freshman Academic Profile:** Average high school GPA 3.4. 18% in top 10% of high school class, 42% in top 25% of high school class, 73% in top 50% of high school class. 83% from public high schools. Average SAT I Math 516, SAT I Math middle 50% range 460-560. Average SAT I Verbal 517, SAT I Verbal middle 50% range 470-570. Average ACT 22, ACT middle 50% range 20-25. TOEFL required of all international applicants, minimum TOEFL 550. **Basis for Candidate Selection:** *Very important factors considered include:* secondary school record, standardized test scores. *Important factors considered include:* character/personal qualities, extracurricular activities, recommendations. *Other factors considered include:* class rank, essays, interview, talent/ability. **Freshman Admission Requirements:** High school diploma or GED is required. *Academic units required/recommended:* 4 English required, 3 math required, 3 science required, 2 foreign language recommended, 3 social studies required, 3 history required. **Freshman Admission Statistics:** 1,668 applied, 78% accepted, 38% of those accepted enrolled. **Transfer Admission Requirements:** *Items required:* college transcript, essay, statement of good standing from prior school. Minimum college GPA of 2.5 required. Lowest grade transferable D. **General Admission Information:** Application fee $35. Priority application deadline April 1. Nonfall registration accepted. Admission may be deferred for a maximum of 1 year. Credit offered for CEEB Advanced Placement tests.

COSTS AND FINANCIAL AID

Tuition $14,778. Room & board $5,700. Required fees $300. Average book expense $800. **Required Forms and Deadlines:** FAFSA and institution's own financial aid form. Financial aid filing deadline August 1. Priority filing deadline April 1. **Notification of Awards:** Applicants will be notified of awards on a rolling basis beginning on or about March 15. **Types of Aid:** *Need-based scholarships/grants:* Pell, SEOG, state scholarships/grants, private scholarships, the school's own gift aid. *Loans:* Direct Subsidized Stafford, Direct Unsubsidized Stafford, Direct PLUS, FFEL Subsidized Stafford, Federal Perkins. **Student Employment:** Federal Work-Study Program available. Institutional employment available. Off-campus job opportunities are good. **Financial Aid Statistics:** 78% freshmen, 79% undergrads receive some form of aid. Average freshman grant $8,500. Average freshman loan $3,500. Average income from on-campus job $1,400. **Financial Aid Phone:** 863-680-4140.

FLORIDA STATE UNIVERSITY

2249 University Center, Tallahassee, FL 32306-2400
Phone: 850-644-6200 **E-mail:** admissions@admin.fsu.edu **CEEB Code:** 5219
Fax: 850-644-0197 **Web:** www.fsu.edu **ACT Code:** 734

This public school was founded in 1851. It has a 463-acre campus.

STUDENTS AND FACULTY

Enrollment: 29,195. **Student Body:** Male 44%, female 56%, out-of-state 15%, international 1% (135 countries represented). **Ethnic Representation:** African American 12%, Asian 3%, Caucasian 74%, Hispanic 9%. **Retention and Graduation:** 87% freshmen return for sophomore year. 40% freshmen graduate within 4 years. 35% grads go on to further study within 1 year. **Faculty:** Student/faculty ratio 23:1. 1,124 full-time faculty, 91% hold PhDs. 95% faculty teach undergrads.

ACADEMICS

Degrees: Associate's, bachelor's, certificate, doctoral, first professional, master's, post-bachelor's certificate, post-master's certificate, transfer. **Academic Requirements:** General education including some course work in arts/fine arts, English (including composition), history, humanities, mathematics, sciences (biological or physical), social science. **Classes:** 20-29 students in an average class. **Majors with Highest Enrollment:** Finance, general; criminal justice/safety studies; communications studies/speech communication and rhetoric. **Disciplines with Highest Percentage of Degrees Awarded:** Business/marketing 23%, social sciences and history 15%, education 8%, protective services/public administration 7%, communications/communication technologies 6%. **Special Study Options:** Accelerated program, cooperative (work-study) program, cross registration, distance learning, double major, dual enrollment, English as a second language, honors program, independent study, internships, study abroad, teacher certification program.

FACILITIES

Housing: Coed, all-female, apartments for married students, apartments for single students, housing for disabled students, fraternities and/or sororities. On-campus: honors residences, living learning communities. Off-campus: cooperative housing through Southern Scholarship Foundation, private residence halls. **Library Holdings:** 2,488,398 bound volumes. 19,309 periodicals. 6,795,647 microforms. **Special Academic Facilities/Equipment:** Art gallery, museum, developmental research school, marine lab, oceanographic institute, tandem Van de Graaff accelerator, national high magnetic-field lab. **Computers:** School-owned computers available for student use.

EXTRACURRICULARS

Activities: Choral groups, concert band, dance, drama/theater, jazz band, literary magazine, marching band, music ensembles, musical theater, opera, pep band, radio station, student government, student newspaper, student-run film society, symphony orchestra, television station, yearbook. **Organizations:** 267 registered organizations, 13 honor societies, 23 religious organizations, 25 fraternities (14% men join), 22 sororities (13% women join). **Athletics (Intercollegiate):** *Men:* baseball, basketball, cheerleading, cross-country, diving, football, golf, swimming, tennis, track & field. *Women:* basketball, cheerleading, cross-country, diving, golf, soccer, softball, swimming, tennis, track & field, volleyball.

ADMISSIONS

Selectivity Rating: 84 (of 100). **Freshman Academic Profile:** Average high school GPA 3.8. 58% in top 10% of high school class, 85% in top 25% of high school class, 100% in top 50% of high school class. 89% from public high schools. Average SAT I Math 577, SAT I Math middle 50% range 520-620. Average SAT I Verbal 569, SAT I Verbal middle 50% range 520-620. Average ACT 24, ACT middle 50% range 22-26. TOEFL required of all international applicants, minimum TOEFL 550. **Basis for Candidate Selection:** *Very important factors considered include:* secondary school record. *Important factors considered include:* class rank, standardized test scores, state residency, talent/ability. *Other factors considered include:* alumni/ae relation, character/personal qualities, essays, extracurricular activities, recommendations, volunteer work, work experience. **Freshman Admission Requirements:** High school diploma or GED is required. *Academic units required/recommended:* 19 total required; 4 English required, 4 English recommended, 3 math required, 4 math recommended, 3 science required, 4 science recommended, 2 science lab required, 2 science lab recommended, 2 foreign language required, 2 foreign language recommended, 4 elective required, 4 elective recommended. **Freshman Admission Statistics:** 21,046 applied, 70% accepted, 43% of those accepted enrolled. **Transfer Admission Requirements:** *Items required:* college transcript. Minimum college GPA of 2.5 required. Lowest grade transferable D-. **General Admission Information:** Application fee $20. Priority application deadline December 31. Regular application deadline March 1. Nonfall registration accepted. Credit and/or placement offered for CEEB Advanced Placement tests.

COSTS AND FINANCIAL AID

In-state tuition $1,984. Out-of-state tuition $11,528. Room & board $5,740. Required fees $701. Average book expense $702. **Required Forms and Deadlines:** FAFSA. Priority filing deadline February 15. **Notification of Awards:** Applicants will be notified of awards on a rolling basis beginning on or about March 15. **Types of Aid:** *Need-based scholarships/grants:* Pell, SEOG, state scholarships/grants, private scholarships, the school's own gift aid. *Loans:* FFEL Subsidized Stafford, FFEL Unsubsidized Stafford, FFEL PLUS, Federal Perkins. **Student Employment:** Federal Work-Study Program available. Institutional employment available. Off-campus job opportunities are excellent. **Financial Aid Statistics:** 38% freshmen, 42% undergrads receive some form of aid. Average freshman grant $4,033. Average freshman loan $2,511. **Financial Aid Phone:** 850-644-5871.

FONTBONNE UNIVERSITY

6800 Wydown Boulevard, St. Louis, MO 63105
Phone: 314-889-1478 **E-mail:** fcadmis@fontbonne.edu **CEEB Code:** 6216
Fax: 314-889-1451 **Web:** www.fontbonne.edu **ACT Code:** 2298

This private school, which is affiliated with the Roman Catholic Church, was founded in 1917. It has an 11-acre campus.

STUDENTS AND FACULTY

Enrollment: 1,611. **Student Body:** Male 24%, female 76%, international students represent 10 countries. **Ethnic Representation:** African American 25%, Asian 1%, Caucasian 72%, Hispanic 1%, Native American 1%. **Retention and Graduation:** 68% freshmen return for sophomore year. 46% freshmen graduate within 4 years. 10% grads go on to further study within 1 year. 5% grads pursue business degrees. 2% grads pursue law degrees. **Faculty:** Student/faculty ratio 12:1. 60 full-time faculty, 65% hold PhDs. 85% faculty teach undergrads.

ACADEMICS

Degrees: Bachelor's, certificate, master's, post-bachelor's certificate. **Academic Requirements:** General education including some course work in arts/fine arts, computer literacy, English (including composition), history, humanities, mathematics, philosophy, sciences (biological or physical), social science. **Classes:** 10-19 students in an average class. 10-19 students in an average lab/discussion section. **Disciplines with Highest Percentage of Degrees Awarded:** Business/marketing 54%, education 16%, home economics and vocational home economics 5%, English 5%, health professions and related sciences 4%. **Special Study Options:** Accelerated program, cooperative (work-study) program, cross registration, distance learning, double major, English as a second language, student exchange program (domestic), honors program, independent study, internships, liberal arts/career combination, student-designed major, study abroad, teacher certification program.

FACILITIES

Housing: Coed, apartments for single students. **Library Holdings:** 109,411 bound volumes. 333 periodicals. 0 microforms. 14,983 audiovisuals. **Special Academic Facilities/Equipment:** Art museum. **Computers:** *Recommended operating system:* Windows 95. School-owned computers available for student use.

EXTRACURRICULARS

Activities: Choral groups, drama/theater, literary magazine, music ensembles, student government, student newspaper. **Organizations:** 34 registered organizations, 8 honor societies, 4 religious organizations, 9 fraternities. **Athletics (Intercollegiate):** *Men:* baseball, basketball, cross-country, golf, soccer, tennis. *Women:* basketball, cross-country, golf, soccer, softball, tennis, volleyball.

ADMISSIONS

Selectivity Rating: 71 (of 100). **Freshman Academic Profile:** Average high school GPA 3.4. 20% in top 10% of high school class, 44% in top 25% of high school class, 76% in top 50% of high school class. 49% from public high schools. Average ACT 22, ACT middle 50% range 21-26. TOEFL required of all international applicants, minimum TOEFL 500. **Basis for Candidate Selection:** *Very important factors considered include:* character/personal qualities, secondary school record. *Important factors considered include:* alumni/ae relation, extracurricular activities, interview, standardized test scores, talent/ability, volunteer work. *Other factors considered include:* class rank, essays, recommendations, work experience. **Freshman Admission Requirements:** High school diploma or GED is required. *Academic units required/recommended:* 16 total required; 4 English required, 3 math required, 3 science required, 1 science lab required, 3 social studies required, 3 elective required. **Freshman Admission Statistics:** 474 applied, 81% accepted, 49% of those accepted enrolled. **Transfer Admission Requirements:** *Items required:* college transcript, essay. Minimum college GPA of 2.0 required. Lowest grade transferable D. **General Admission Information:** Application fee $25. Priority application deadline May 2. Regular application deadline August 2. Nonfall registration accepted. Admission may be deferred for a maximum of 1 year. Credit and/or placement offered for CEEB Advanced Placement tests.

COSTS AND FINANCIAL AID

Tuition $13,415. Room & board $6,535. Required fees $300. Average book expense $300. **Required Forms and Deadlines:** FAFSA and institution's own financial aid form. Financial aid filing deadline July 1. Priority filing deadline April 1. **Notification of Awards:** Applicants will be notified of awards on a rolling basis. **Types of Aid:** *Need-based scholarships/grants:* Pell, SEOG, state scholarships/grants, private scholarships, the school's own gift aid. *Loans:* Direct Subsidized Stafford, Direct Unsubsidized Stafford, Direct PLUS, Federal Perkins, state loans, college/university loans from institutional funds. **Student Employment:** Federal Work-Study Program available. Institutional employment available. Off-campus job opportunities are excellent. **Financial Aid Statistics:** 63% freshmen, 63% undergrads receive some form of aid. Average freshman grant $4,400. Average freshman loan $2,450. Average income from on-campus job $1,600. **Financial Aid Phone:** 314-889-1414.

FORDHAM UNIVERSITY

441 East Fordham Road, Thebaud Hall, New York, NY 10458
Phone: 718-817-4000 **E-mail:** enroll@fordham.edu **CEEB Code:** 2259
Fax: 718-367-9404 **Web:** www.fordham.edu **ACT Code:** 2748

This private school, which is affiliated with the Roman Catholic Church, was founded in 1841. It has an 85-acre campus.

STUDENTS AND FACULTY

Enrollment: 7,228. **Student Body:** Male 41%, female 59%, out-of-state 39%, international 1% (38 countries represented). **Ethnic Representation:** African American 6%, Asian 6%, Caucasian 60%, Hispanic 11%. **Retention and Graduation:** 88% freshmen return for sophomore year. 71% freshmen graduate within 4 years. 20% grads go on to further study within 1 year. 3% grads pursue business degrees. 6% grads pursue law degrees. 2% grads pursue medical degrees. **Faculty:** Student/faculty ratio 11:1. 601 full-time faculty, 93% hold PhDs. 77% faculty teach undergrads.

ACADEMICS

Degrees: Bachelor's, doctoral, first professional, master's, post-master's certificate. **Academic Requirements:** General education including some course work in arts/fine arts, English (including composition), foreign languages, history, humanities, mathematics, philosophy, sciences (biological or physical), social science, religion. **Classes:** 10-19 students in an average class. 10-19 students in an average lab/discussion section. **Disciplines with Highest Percentage of Degrees Awarded:** Social sciences and history 24%, business/marketing 22%, communications/communication technologies 11%, psychology 9%, English 8%. **Special Study Options:** Double major, English as a second language, student exchange program (domestic), honors program, independent study, internships, student-designed major, study abroad, teacher certification program, Globe Program in international business, 3-2 engineering cooperative with Columbia University or Case Western Reserve.

FACILITIES

Housing: Coed, residential college. **Library Holdings:** 1,848,397 bound volumes. 16,224 periodicals. 3,056,558 microforms. 16,777 audiovisuals. **Computers:** School-owned computers available for student use.

EXTRACURRICULARS

Activities: Choral groups, concert band, dance, drama/theater, literary magazine, marching band, music ensembles, musical theater, pep band, radio station, student government, student newspaper, student-run film society, yearbook. **Organizations:** 130 registered organizations, 12 honor societies, 1 religious organization. **Athletics (Intercollegiate):** *Men:* baseball, basketball, cheerleading, crew, cross-country, diving, equestrian, football, golf, ice hockey, indoor track, lacrosse, rugby, sailing, soccer, squash, swimming, tennis, track & field, volleyball, water polo. *Women:* basketball, cheerleading, crew, cross-country, diving, equestrian, indoor track, lacrosse, rugby, sailing, soccer, softball, swimming, tennis, track & field, volleyball.

ADMISSIONS

Selectivity Rating: 83 (of 100). **Freshman Academic Profile:** Average high school GPA 3.6. 30% in top 10% of high school class, 68% in top 25% of high school class, 94% in top 50% of high school class. 40% from public high schools. Average SAT I Math 606, SAT I Math middle 50% range 530-630. Average SAT I Verbal 606, SAT I Verbal middle 50% range 530-630. Average ACT 26, ACT middle 50% range 23-27. TOEFL required of all international applicants, minimum TOEFL 550. **Basis for Candidate Selection:** *Very important factors considered include:* class rank, secondary school record, standardized test scores. *Important factors considered include:* alumni/ae relation, character/personal qualities, essays, extracurricular activities, interview, recommendations, talent/ability. *Other factors considered include:* geographical residence, minority status, volunteer work, work experience. **Freshman Admission Requirements:** High school diploma or GED is required. *Academic units required/recommended:* 22 total required; 25 total recommended; 4 English required, 4 English recommended, 3 math required, 4 math recommended, 3 science required, 4 science recommended, 2 foreign language required, 3 foreign language recommended, 2 social studies required, 3 social studies recommended, 6 elective required, 6 elective recommended. **Freshman Admission Statistics:** 11,380 applied, 57% accepted, 27% of those accepted enrolled. **Transfer Admission Requirements:** *Items required:* high school transcript, college transcript, essay, statement of good standing from prior school. Minimum college GPA of 3.0 required. Lowest grade transferable C. **General Admission Information:** Application fee $50. Priority application deadline February 1. Regular application deadline February 1. Nonfall registration accepted. Credit and/or placement offered for CEEB Advanced Placement tests.

COSTS AND FINANCIAL AID

Tuition $21,210. Room & board $8,745. Required fees $460. Average book expense $660. **Required Forms and Deadlines:** FAFSA, CSS/Financial Aid PROFILE, state aid form, noncustodial (divorced/separated) parent's statement, and business/farm supplement. Priority filing deadline February 1. **Notification of Awards:** Applicants will be notified of awards on or about April 1. **Types of Aid:** *Need-based scholarships/grants:* Pell, SEOG, state scholarships/grants. *Loans:* FFEL Subsidized Stafford, FFEL Unsubsidized Stafford, FFEL PLUS, Federal Perkins. **Student Employment:** Federal Work-Study Program available. Off-campus job opportunities are excellent. **Financial Aid Statistics:** 73% freshmen, 73% undergrads receive some form of aid. Average income from on-campus job $1,200. **Financial Aid Phone:** 718-817-3800.

FORT HAYS STATE UNIVERSITY

600 Park Street, Hays, KS 67601-4099
Phone: 785-628-5666 **E-mail:** tigers@fhsu.edu **CEEB Code:** 6218
Fax: 785-628-4187 **Web:** www.fhsu.edu **ACT Code:** 1408

This public school was founded in 1902. It has a 4,160-acre campus.

STUDENTS AND FACULTY

Enrollment: 5,570. **Student Body:** Male 45%, female 55%, out-of-state 9%, international 9%. **Ethnic Representation:** African American 1%, Asian 1%, Caucasian 87%, Hispanic 2%, Native American 1%. **Retention and Graduation:** 71% freshmen return for sophomore year. 21% freshmen graduate within 4 years. 20% grads go on to further study within 1 year. **Faculty:** Student/faculty ratio 17:1. 256 full-time faculty, 78% hold PhDs. 92% faculty teach undergrads.

ACADEMICS

Degrees: Associate's, bachelor's, certificate, first professional, master's, terminal. **Academic Requirements:** General education including some course work in arts/fine arts, computer literacy, English (including composition), humanities, mathematics, sciences (biological or physical), social science. **Majors with Highest Enrollment:** Business administration/management; elementary education and teaching; health and physical education, general. **Disciplines with Highest Percentage of Degrees Awarded:** Health professions and related sciences 19%, business/marketing 16%, education 11%, communications/communication technologies 7%, visual and performing arts 5%. **Special Study Options:** Accelerated program, distance learning, double major, dual enrollment, English as a second language, student exchange program (domestic), external degree program, independent study, internships, liberal arts/career combination, student-designed major, study abroad, teacher certification program.

FACILITIES

Housing: Coed, all-female, apartments for married students, apartments for single students, housing for disabled students, fraternities and/or sororities. **Library Holdings:** 624,637 bound volumes. 1,689 periodicals. 404,433 microforms. **Special Academic Facilities/Equipment:** Paleontology, natural history, visual arts and media center, farm, NMR gas analyzer, telescope (HG). **Computers:** School-owned computers available for student use.

EXTRACURRICULARS

Activities: Choral groups, concert band, drama/theater, jazz band, literary magazine, marching band, music ensembles, musical theater, opera, pep band, radio station, student government, student newspaper, symphony orchestra, television station, yearbook. **Organizations:** 103 registered organizations, 20 honor societies, 12 religious organizations, 3 fraternities (3% men join), 3 sororities (3% women join). **Athletics (Intercollegiate):** *Men:* baseball, basketball, cheerleading, cross-country, football, golf, indoor track, track & field, wrestling. *Women:* basketball, cheerleading, cross-country, indoor track, softball, tennis, track & field, volleyball.

ADMISSIONS

Selectivity Rating: 67 (of 100). **Freshman Academic Profile:** Average high school GPA 3.3. 95% from public high schools. Average ACT 22. TOEFL required of all international applicants, minimum TOEFL 500. **Basis for Candidate Selection:** *Factors considered include:* class rank, secondary school record, standardized test scores. **Freshman Admission Requirements:** High school diploma or GED is required. *Academic units required/recommended:* 4 English recommended, 3 math recommended, 3 science recommended, 1 science lab recommended, 1 foreign language recommended, 2 social studies recommended, 1 history recommended. **Freshman Admission Statistics:** 1,468 applied, 93% accepted, 61% of those accepted enrolled. **Transfer Admission Requirements:** *Items required:* college transcript. Minimum college GPA of 2.0 required. Lowest grade transferable D. **General Admission Information:** Application fee $25. Nonfall registration accepted. Admission may be deferred. Credit offered for CEEB Advanced Placement tests.

COSTS AND FINANCIAL AID

In-state tuition $1,851. Out-of-state tuition $7,011. Room & board $4,843. Required fees $477. Average book expense $1,000. **Required Forms and Deadlines:** FAFSA, state aid form, and application for admission. No deadline for regular filing. Priority filing deadline March 15. **Notification of Awards:** Applicants will be notified of awards on a rolling basis beginning on or about April 1. **Types of Aid:** *Need-based scholarships/grants:* Pell, SEOG, state scholarships/grants, private scholarships, Kansas Comprehensive Grant. *Loans:* FFEL Subsidized Stafford, FFEL Unsubsidized Stafford, FFEL PLUS, Federal Perkins, college/university loans from institutional funds. **Student Employment:** Federal Work-Study Program available. Institutional employment available. Off-campus job opportunities are good. **Financial Aid Statistics:** 75% freshmen, 78% undergrads receive some form of aid. Average freshman grant $2,946. Average freshman loan $4,619. Average income from on-campus job $2,000. **Financial Aid Phone:** 800-628-3478.

FORT LEWIS COLLEGE

1000 Rim Drive, Durango, CO 81301
Phone: 970-247-7184 **E-mail:** admisson@fortlewis.edu **CEEB Code:** 4310
Fax: 970-247-7179 **Web:** www.fortlewis.edu **ACT Code:** 510

This public school was founded in 1911. It has a 362-acre campus.

STUDENTS AND FACULTY

Enrollment: 4,347. **Student Body:** Male 53%, female 47%, out-of-state 34%, international 1% (19 countries represented). **Ethnic Representation:** African American 1%, Asian 1%, Caucasian 71%, Hispanic 5%, Native American 17%. **Retention and Graduation:** 53% freshmen return for sophomore year. 11% freshmen graduate within 4 years. 18% grads go on to further study within 1 year. 15% grads pursue business degrees. 1% grads pursue law degrees. 1% grads pursue medical degrees. **Faculty:** Student/faculty ratio 19:1. 172 full-time faculty, 80% hold PhDs. 100% faculty teach undergrads.

ACADEMICS

Degrees: Bachelor's. **Academic Requirements:** General education including some course work in computer literacy, English (including composition), sciences (biological or physical), social science, physical education. **Classes:** 10-19 students in an average class. 10-19 students in an average lab/discussion section. **Majors with Highest Enrollment:** Business administration/management; multi/interdisciplinary studies; psychology, general. **Disciplines with Highest Percentage of Degrees Awarded:** Business/marketing 23%, social sciences and history 14%, English 9%, psychology 8%, interdisciplinary studies 8%. **Special Study Options:** Accelerated program, cooperative (work-study) program, distance learning, double major, dual enrollment, English as a second language, student exchange program (domestic), honors program, independent study, internships, liberal arts/career combination, student-designed major, study abroad, teacher certification program.

FACILITIES

Housing: Coed, apartments for married students, apartments for single students. Early application for housing advised. Freshmen required to live on campus. **Library Holdings:** 184,860 bound volumes. 743 periodicals. 339,467 microforms. 4,334 audiovisuals. **Special Academic Facilities/Equipment:** Center of Southwest Studies, archaeological dig site, chemistry hall, student life center, community concert hall, nuclear magnetic resonance spectrometer, separations and spectroscopy lab, mass spectrometer facilities, tissue culture facility, atomic force microscope. **Computers:** School-owned computers available for student use.

EXTRACURRICULARS

Activities: Choral groups, concert band, drama/theater, jazz band, literary magazine, music ensembles, radio station, student government, student newspaper, student-run film society, symphony orchestra. **Organizations:** 60 registered organizations, 14 honor societies, 2 religious organizations. **Athletics (Intercollegiate):** *Men:* basketball, cross-country, football, golf, soccer. *Women:* basketball, cross-country, soccer, softball, volleyball.

ADMISSIONS

Selectivity Rating: 63 (of 100). **Freshman Academic Profile:** Average high school GPA 3.0. 7% in top 10% of high school class, 21% in top 25% of high school class, 50% in top 50% of high school class. 95% from public high schools. Average SAT I Math 500, SAT I Math middle 50% range 430-560. Average SAT I Verbal 500, SAT I Verbal middle 50% range 450-550. Average ACT 20, ACT middle 50% range 17-23. TOEFL required of all international applicants, minimum TOEFL 500. **Basis for Candidate Selection:** *Very important factors considered include:* class rank, secondary school record, standardized test scores. *Other factors considered include:* essays, extracurricular activities, interview, recommendations. **Freshman Admission Requirements:** High school diploma or GED is required. *Academic units required/recommended:* 15 total recommended; 4 English recommended, 4 math recommended, 2 science recommended, 2 social studies recommended. **Freshman Admission Statistics:** 3,350 applied, 80% accepted, 40% of those accepted enrolled. **Transfer Admission Requirements:** *Items required:* college transcript. Minimum college GPA of 2.0 required. Lowest grade transferable C-. **General Admission Information:** Application fee $20. Regular application deadline

August 1. Nonfall registration accepted. Credit and/or placement offered for CEEB Advanced Placement tests.

COSTS AND FINANCIAL AID

In-state tuition $1,902. Out-of-state tuition $9,600. Room & board $5,446. Required fees $730. Average book expense $750. **Required Forms and Deadlines:** FAFSA. No deadline for regular filing. Priority filing deadline February 15. **Notification of Awards:** Applicants will be notified of awards on a rolling basis beginning on or about April 1. **Types of Aid:** *Need-based scholarships/grants:* Pell, SEOG, state scholarships/grants, private scholarships, the school's own gift aid. *Loans:* FFEL Subsidized Stafford, FFEL Unsubsidized Stafford, FFEL PLUS, Federal Perkins, college/university loans from institutional funds. **Student Employment:** Federal Work-Study Program available. Institutional employment available. Off-campus job opportunities are good. **Financial Aid Statistics:** 42% freshmen, 54% undergrads receive some form of aid. Average freshman grant $3,910. Average freshman loan $3,021. Average income from on-campus job $1,700. **Financial Aid Phone:** 970-247-7142.

FORT VALLEY STATE UNIVERSITY

1005 State University Drive, Fort Valley, GA 31030
Phone: 912-825-6307 **CEEB Code:** 5220
Fax: 912-825-6394 **Web:** www.fvsc.peachnet.edu **ACT Code:** 814

This public school was founded in 1902. It has a 630-acre campus.

STUDENTS AND FACULTY

Enrollment: 2,218. **Student Body:** Male 43%, female 57%, out-of-state 6%, international 1%. **Ethnic Representation:** African American 95%, Caucasian 3%, Hispanic 1%, Native American 1%. **Retention and Graduation:** 67% freshmen return for sophomore year. 9% freshmen graduate within 4 years. 46% grads go on to further study within 1 year. 7% grads pursue business degrees. 1% grads pursue law degrees. 7% grads pursue medical degrees.

ACADEMICS

Degrees: Associate's, bachelor's, master's. **Special Study Options:** Cooperative (work-study) program, distance learning, dual enrollment, honors program, internships, study abroad. Undergrads may take grad-level classes. Co-op programs: fisheries biology and wildlife conservation. Other special programs: credit for study tours, summer institutes, and work experiences.

FACILITIES

Housing: Coed, all-female, all-male, apartments for single students. **Library Holdings:** 190,062 bound volumes. 1,213 periodicals. **Special Academic Facilities/Equipment:** Experimental agricultural plots cover most of campus.

EXTRACURRICULARS

Activities: Concert band, dance, jazz band, marching band, radio station, student government, student newspaper, television station, yearbook. **Organizations:** 7 honor societies, 2 religious organizations, 4 fraternities, 4 sororities. **Athletics (Intercollegiate):** *Men:* baseball, basketball, football, golf, soccer, tennis. *Women:* basketball, tennis, track & field, volleyball.

ADMISSIONS

Selectivity Rating: 63 (of 100). **Basis for Candidate Selection:** *Very important factors considered include:* secondary school record, standardized test scores. *Important factors considered include:* minority status. *Other factors considered include:* alumni/ae relation, character/personal qualities, class rank, essays, recommendations, state residency. **Freshman Admission Requirements:** High school diploma is required and GED is not accepted. *Academic units required/recommended:* 21 total required; 4 English required, 3 math required, 3 science required, 2 foreign language required, 3 social studies required, 6 elective required. **Transfer Admission Requirements:** Minimum college GPA of 2.0 required. Lowest grade transferable C-. **General Admission Information:** Application fee $20. Regular application deadline September 5. Nonfall registration accepted. Credit and/or placement offered for CEEB Advanced Placement tests.

COSTS AND FINANCIAL AID

In-state tuition $2,468. Out-of-state tuition $4,132. Room & board $3,830. Required fees $232. Average book expense $800. **Required Forms and Deadlines:** FAFSA. **Types of Aid:** *Need-based scholarships/grants:* Pell, SEOG, state scholarships/grants, private scholarships. *Loans:* FFEL Subsidized Stafford, FFEL PLUS. **Student Employment:** Institutional employment available. Off-campus job opportunities are good. **Financial Aid Phone:** 912-825-6363.

FRAMINGHAM STATE COLLEGE

PO Box 9101, 100 State Street, Framingham, MA 01701
Phone: 508-626-4500 **E-mail:** admiss@frc.mass.edu **CEEB Code:** 3519
Fax: 508-626-4017 **Web:** www.framingham.edu **ACT Code:** 1904

This public school was founded in 1839. It has a 73-acre campus.

STUDENTS AND FACULTY

Enrollment: 4,052. **Student Body:** Male 35%, female 65%, out-of-state 8%, international 2%. **Ethnic Representation:** African American 4%, Asian 3%, Caucasian 84%, Hispanic 3%. **Retention and Graduation:** 68% freshmen return for sophomore year. 20% freshmen graduate within 4 years. 15% grads go on to further study within 1 year. 25% grads pursue business degrees. 1% grads pursue law degrees. 1% grads pursue medical degrees. **Faculty:** Student/faculty ratio 15:1. 161 full-time faculty, 80% hold PhDs. 100% faculty teach undergrads.

ACADEMICS

Degrees: Bachelor's, master's, post-bachelor's certificate. **Academic Requirements:** General education including some course work in arts/fine arts, English (including composition), foreign languages, history, humanities, mathematics, sciences (biological or physical), social science. **Classes:** 30-39 students in an average class. 10-19 students in an average lab/discussion section. **Majors with Highest Enrollment:** Business administration/management; elementary education and teaching; psychology. **Disciplines with Highest Percentage of Degrees Awarded:** Social sciences and history 18%, business/marketing 15%, education 12%, communications/communication technologies 11%, psychology 11%. **Special Study Options:** Cross registration, distance learning, double major, student exchange program (domestic), honors program, independent study, internships, liberal arts/career combination, study abroad, teacher certification program.

FACILITIES

Housing: Coed, all-female. **Library Holdings:** 165,219 bound volumes. 409 periodicals. 658,878 microforms. 3,313 audiovisuals. **Special Academic Facilities/Equipment:** Christa Corrigan McAuliffe Challenger Center, art gallery, language lab, greenhouse, planetarium. **Computers:** School-owned computers available for student use.

EXTRACURRICULARS

Activities: Choral groups, drama/theater, literary magazine, radio station, student government, student newspaper, yearbook. **Organizations:** 35 registered organizations, 8 honor societies, 3 religious organizations. **Athletics (Intercollegiate):** *Men:* baseball, basketball, cross-country, football, ice hockey, soccer. *Women:* basketball, cross-country, field hockey, soccer, softball, volleyball.

ADMISSIONS

Selectivity Rating: 64 (of 100). **Freshman Academic Profile:** Average high school GPA 3.0. 6% in top 10% of high school class, 27% in top 25% of high school class, 71% in top 50% of high school class. 75% from public high schools. Average SAT I Math 513, SAT I Math middle 50% range 470-570. Average SAT I Verbal 528, SAT I Verbal middle 50% range 470-580. TOEFL required of all international applicants, minimum TOEFL 550. **Basis for Candidate Selection:** *Very important factors considered include:* secondary school record. *Important factors considered include:* class rank, extracurricular activities, recommendations, standardized test scores, talent/ability. *Other factors considered include:* alumni/ae relation, character/personal qualities, essays, geographical residence, minority status, state residency, volunteer work, work experience. **Freshman Admission Requirements:** High school diploma or GED is required. *Academic units required/recommended:* 16 total required; 20 total recommended; 4 English required, 4 English recommended, 3 math required, 4 math recommended, 3 science required, 4 science recommended, 2 science lab required, 4 science lab recommended, 2 foreign language required, 4 foreign language recommended, 1 social studies required, 1 social studies recommended, 1 history required, 2 history recommended, 2 elective required. **Freshman Admission Statistics:** 3,994 applied, 59% accepted, 31% of those accepted enrolled. **Transfer Admission Requirements:** *Items required:* high school transcript, college transcript, essay. Minimum high school GPA of 2.5 required. Minimum college GPA of 2.5 required. Lowest grade transferable C-. **General Admission Information:** Application fee $25. Priority application deadline March 1. Regular application deadline May 15. Nonfall registration accepted. Admission may be deferred for a maximum of 1 year. Credit and/or placement offered for CEEB Advanced Placement tests.

COSTS AND FINANCIAL AID

In-state tuition $970. Out-of-state tuition $7,050. Room & board $4,651. Required fees $2,364. Average book expense $600. **Required Forms and**

Deadlines: FAFSA. No deadline for regular filing. Priority filing deadline March 1. **Notification of Awards:** Applicants will be notified of awards on a rolling basis beginning on or about April 15. **Types of Aid:** *Need-based scholarships/grants:* Pell, SEOG, state scholarships/grants, private scholarships, the school's own gift aid. *Loans:* FFEL Subsidized Stafford, FFEL Unsubsidized Stafford, FFEL PLUS, Federal Perkins, state loans, college/university loans from institutional funds. **Student Employment:** Federal Work-Study Program available. Institutional employment available. Off-campus job opportunities are excellent. **Financial Aid Statistics:** 38% freshmen, 34% undergrads receive some form of aid. Average freshman grant $3,025. Average freshman loan $2,625. Average income from on-campus job $1,000. **Financial Aid Phone:** 508-626-4534.

FRANCIS MARION UNIVERSITY

Office of Admissions, PO Box 100547, Florence, SC 29501-0547
Phone: 843-661-1231 **E-mail:** admissions@fmarion.edu **CEEB Code:** 5442
Fax: 843-661-4635 **Web:** www.fmarion.edu **ACT Code:** 3856

This public school was founded in 1970. It has a 300-acre campus.

STUDENTS AND FACULTY

Enrollment: 2,966. **Student Body:** Male 39%, female 61%, out-of-state 6%, international 2%. **Ethnic Representation:** African American 33%, Asian 1%, Caucasian 62%, Hispanic 1%, Native American 1%. **Retention and Graduation:** 69% freshmen return for sophomore year. 19% freshmen graduate within 4 years. **Faculty:** Student/faculty ratio 15:1. 159 full-time faculty, 83% hold PhDs. 100% faculty teach undergrads.

ACADEMICS

Degrees: Bachelor's, master's. **Academic Requirements:** General education including some course work in arts/fine arts, computer literacy, English (including composition), foreign languages, history, humanities, mathematics, philosophy, sciences (biological or physical), social science. **Classes:** 20-29 students in an average class. **Majors with Highest Enrollment:** Business administration/management; elementary education and teaching; biology/biological sciences, general. **Disciplines with Highest Percentage of Degrees Awarded:** Business/marketing 30%, social sciences and history 15%, education 13%, biological life sciences 13%, psychology 7%. **Special Study Options:** Accelerated program, cooperative (work-study) program, cross registration, distance learning, double major, dual enrollment, honors program, independent study, internships, study abroad, teacher certification program.

FACILITIES

Housing: All-female, all-male, apartments for single students, housing for disabled students. **Library Holdings:** 321,202 bound volumes. 1,704 periodicals. 489,953 microforms. 36,166 audiovisuals. **Special Academic Facilities/Equipment:** Media center, planetarium, observatory. **Computers:** *Recommended operating system:* Windows 95. School-owned computers available for student use.

EXTRACURRICULARS

Activities: Choral groups, drama/theater, jazz band, literary magazine, music ensembles, pep band, student government, student newspaper, television station. **Organizations:** 60 registered organizations, 12 honor societies, 5 religious organizations, 7 fraternities (4% men join), 7 sororities (6% women join). **Athletics (Intercollegiate):** *Men:* baseball, basketball, cheerleading, cross-country, golf, soccer, tennis, track & field. *Women:* basketball, cheerleading, cross-country, soccer, softball, tennis, track & field, volleyball.

ADMISSIONS

Selectivity Rating: 65 (of 100). **Freshman Academic Profile:** Average high school GPA 3.3. 14% in top 10% of high school class, 36% in top 25% of high school class, 66% in top 50% of high school class. 87% from public high schools. Average SAT I Math 475, SAT I Math middle 50% range 430-530. Average SAT I Verbal 477, SAT I Verbal middle 50% range 430-515. Average ACT 19. TOEFL required of all international applicants, minimum TOEFL 500. **Basis for Candidate Selection:** *Very important factors considered include:* secondary school record, standardized test scores. *Other factors considered include:* recommendations. **Freshman Admission Requirements:** High school diploma or GED is required. *Academic units required/recommended:* 20 total required; 4 English required, 3 math required, 4 math recommended, 3 science required, 4 science recommended, 3 science lab required, 2 foreign language required, 2 social studies required, 1 history required, 4 elective required. **Freshman Admission Statistics:** 1,939 applied, 76% accepted, 51% of those accepted enrolled. **Transfer Admission Requirements:** *Items required:* high school transcript, college transcript. Minimum high school GPA of 2.0 required. Minimum college GPA of 2.0 required. Lowest grade transferable C. **General Admission Information:** Application fee $30. Nonfall registration accepted. Admission may be deferred. Credit offered for CEEB Advanced Placement tests.

COSTS AND FINANCIAL AID

In-state tuition $4,190. Out-of-state tuition $8,380. Room & board $4,082. Required fees $150. Average book expense $760. **Required Forms and Deadlines:** FAFSA and institution's own financial aid form. Priority filing deadline March 1. **Notification of Awards:** Applicants will be notified of awards on a rolling basis beginning on or about April 15. **Types of Aid:** *Need-based scholarships/grants:* Pell, SEOG, state scholarships/grants, private scholarships, the school's own gift aid. *Loans:* FFEL Subsidized Stafford, FFEL Unsubsidized Stafford, FFEL PLUS, Federal Perkins. **Student Employment:** Federal Work-Study Program available. Institutional employment available. Off-campus job opportunities are excellent. **Financial Aid Statistics:** Average income from on-campus job $1,222. **Financial Aid Phone:** 843-661-1190.

THE FRANCISCAN UNIVERSITY

400 North Bluff Boulevard, PO Box 2967, Clinton, IA 52733-2967
Phone: 563-242-4153 **E-mail:** admissns@clare.edu **CEEB Code:** 6418
Fax: 563-243-6102 **Web:** www.clare.edu **ACT Code:** 1342

This private school, which is affiliated with the Roman Catholic Church, was founded in 1918. It has a 25-acre campus.

STUDENTS AND FACULTY

Enrollment: 458. **Student Body:** Male 43%, female 57%, out-of-state 40%, international 3% (10 countries represented). **Ethnic Representation:** African American 6%, Asian 1%, Caucasian 89%, Hispanic 3%. **Retention and Graduation:** 58% freshmen return for sophomore year. 21% freshmen graduate within 4 years. 25% grads go on to further study within 1 year. **Faculty:** Student/faculty ratio 12:1. 27 full-time faculty, 48% hold PhDs. 100% faculty teach undergrads.

ACADEMICS

Degrees: Associate's, bachelor's, transfer. **Academic Requirements:** General education including some course work in arts/fine arts, computer literacy, English (including composition), history, humanities, mathematics, philosophy, sciences (biological or physical), social science, speech. Competencies required in computer, mathematics, writing & speech, critical thinking, and applied ethics. Required courses from six general education outcome areas and courses. **Classes:** 10-19 students in an average class. Under 10 students in an average lab/discussion section. **Majors with Highest Enrollment:** Education, general; liberal arts and sciences, general studies and humanities; social sciences, general. **Disciplines with Highest Percentage of Degrees Awarded:** Education 29%, liberal arts/general studies 22%, social sciences and history 18%, business/marketing 13%, accounting 9%. **Special Study Options:** Double major, English as a second language, honors program, independent study, internships, student-designed major, study abroad, teacher certification program, Advanced Placement program, summer school.

FACILITIES

Housing: Coed. **Library Holdings:** 91,923 bound volumes. 623 periodicals. 73,536 microforms. 2,796 audiovisuals. **Special Academic Facilities/Equipment:** On-campus preschool, indoor swimming pool, multipurpose educational center. **Computers:** *Recommended operating system:* Windows NT/2000. School-owned computers available for student use.

EXTRACURRICULARS

Activities: Choral groups, music ensembles, student government, student newspaper. **Organizations:** 20 registered organizations, 2 honor societies. **Athletics (Intercollegiate):** *Men:* baseball, basketball, cross-country, golf, soccer, track & field. *Women:* basketball, cross-country, soccer, softball, track & field, volleyball.

ADMISSIONS

Selectivity Rating: 67 (of 100). **Freshman Academic Profile:** Average high school GPA 3.0. 10% in top 10% of high school class, 33% in top 25% of high school class, 62% in top 50% of high school class. 89% from public high schools. SAT I Math middle 50% range 360-400. SAT I Verbal middle 50% range 390-480. Average ACT 20, ACT middle 50% range 17-21. TOEFL required of all international applicants, minimum TOEFL 430. **Basis for Candidate Selection:** *Very important factors considered include:* class rank, secondary school record, standardized test scores. *Other factors considered include:* recommendations. **Freshman Admission Requirements:** High school diploma or GED is required. *Academic units required/recommended:* 18 total recommended; 4 English recommended, 3 math recommended, 3 science recommended, 2 science lab recommended, 2 foreign language recommended, 3 social studies recommended, 3 history recommended. **Freshman Admission Statistics:** 224 applied, 76% accepted, 28% of those accepted enrolled. **Transfer Admission Requirements:** *Items required:* college transcript, statement of good standing from prior school. Minimum high school GPA of 2.0 required. Minimum college GPA of 2.0 required. Lowest grade transferable C. **General Admission Information:** Application fee $20. Regular application deadline August 15. Nonfall registration accepted. Admission may be deferred for a maximum of 1 year. Credit and/or placement offered for CEEB Advanced Placement tests.

COSTS AND FINANCIAL AID

Tuition $13,800. Room & board $5,000. Required fees $250. Average book expense $600. **Required Forms and Deadlines:** FAFSA. Financial aid filing deadline August 1. Priority filing deadline April 1. **Notification of Awards:** Applicants will be notified of awards on a rolling basis beginning on or about March 15. **Types of Aid:** *Need-based scholarships/grants:* Pell, SEOG, state scholarships/grants, private scholarships, the school's own gift aid. *Loans:* FFEL Subsidized Stafford, FFEL Unsubsidized Stafford, FFEL PLUS, Federal Perkins, private Loan Company. **Student Employment:** Federal Work-Study Program available. Institutional employment available. Off-campus job opportunities are good. **Financial Aid Statistics:** 94% freshmen, 88% undergrads receive some form of aid. **Financial Aid Phone:** 563-242-4023.

FRANCISCAN UNIVERSITY OF STEUBENVILLE

1235 University Boulevard., Steubenville, OH 43952-1763
Phone: 740-283-6226 **E-mail:** admissions@franciscan.edu **CEEB Code:** 1133
Fax: 740-284-5456 **Web:** www.franciscan.edu **ACT Code:** 3258

This private school, which is affiliated with the Roman Catholic Church, was founded in 1946. It has a 124-acre campus.

STUDENTS AND FACULTY

Enrollment: 1,799. **Student Body:** Male 40%, female 60%, out-of-state 79%, international 2% (20 countries represented). **Ethnic Representation:** African American 1%, Asian 2%, Caucasian 86%, Hispanic 5%. **Retention and Graduation:** 81% freshmen return for sophomore year. 64% freshmen graduate within 4 years. 19% grads go on to further study within 1 year. 2% grads pursue business degrees. 2% grads pursue law degrees. 2% grads pursue medical degrees. **Faculty:** Student/faculty ratio 14:1. 102 full-time faculty, 70% hold PhDs. 91% faculty teach undergrads.

ACADEMICS

Degrees: Associate's, bachelor's, master's, terminal. **Academic Requirements:** General education including some course work in English (including composition), foreign languages, history, humanities, philosophy, sciences (biological or physical), social science, theology. **Classes:** 10-19 students in an average class. 10-19 students in an average lab/discussion section. **Majors with Highest Enrollment:** Business administration/management; education leadership and administration, general; theology/theological studies. **Disciplines with Highest Percentage of Degrees Awarded:** Philosophy/religion/theology 33%, education 12%, business/marketing 9%, health professions and related sciences 9%, social sciences and history 8%. **Special Study Options:** Accelerated program, distance learning, double major, honors program, independent study, internships, liberal arts/career combination, study abroad, teacher certification program.

FACILITIES

Housing: All-female, all-male. Household groups of 10-20 students in residence halls may develop distinctive environment for their group within the context of Christian and Franciscan perspective. **Library Holdings:** 231,176 bound volumes. 578 periodicals. 256,000 microforms. 1,260 audiovisuals. **Special Academic Facilities/Equipment:** Art gallery. **Computers:** School-owned computers available for student use.

EXTRACURRICULARS

Activities: Choral groups, drama/theater, literary magazine, music ensembles, radio station, student government, student newspaper, yearbook. **Organizations:** 31 registered organizations, 3 honor societies, 6 religious organizations, 20 fraternities, 1 sorority.

ADMISSIONS

Selectivity Rating: 76 (of 100). **Freshman Academic Profile:** Average high school GPA 3.4. 27% in top 10% of high school class, 51% in top 25% of high school class, 80% in top 50% of high school class. 45% from public high schools. Average SAT I Math 557, SAT I Math middle 50% range 500-610. Average SAT I Verbal 578, SAT I Verbal middle 50% range 520-620. Average ACT 24. TOEFL required of all international applicants, minimum TOEFL 550. **Basis for Candidate Selection:** *Very important factors considered include:* character/personal qualities, essays, interview, secondary school record, standardized test scores. *Important factors considered include:* extracurricular activities, talent/ability. *Other factors considered include:* recommendations. **Freshman Admission Requirements:** High school diploma or GED is required. *Academic units required/recommended:* 15 total required; 4 English recommended, 3 math recommended, 3 science recommended, 3 foreign language recommended. **Freshman Admission Statistics:** 765 applied, 89% accepted, 53% of those accepted enrolled. **Transfer Admission Requirements:** *Items required:* high school transcript, college transcript, essay. Minimum high school GPA of 2.4 required. Minimum college GPA of 2.0 required. Lowest grade transferable C. **General Admission Information:** Application fee $20. Regular application deadline May 1. Nonfall registration accepted. Admission may be deferred. Credit and/or placement offered for CEEB Advanced Placement tests.

COSTS AND FINANCIAL AID

Average book expense $800. **Required Forms and Deadlines:** FAFSA and institution's own financial aid form. No deadline for regular filing. Priority filing deadline April 15. **Notification of Awards:** Applicants will be notified of awards on a rolling basis beginning on or about March 1. **Types of Aid:** *Need-based scholarships/grants:* Pell, SEOG, state scholarships/grants, private scholarships, the school's own gift aid. *Loans:* FFEL Subsidized Stafford, FFEL Unsubsidized Stafford, FFEL PLUS, Federal Perkins, alternative loans. **Student Employment:** Federal Work-Study Program available. Institutional employment available. Off-campus job opportunities are fair. **Financial Aid Statistics:** 69% freshmen, 85% undergrads receive some form of aid. Average freshman grant $4,819. Average freshman loan $4,011. Average income from on-campus job $1,729. **Financial Aid Phone:** 740-283-6211.

FRANKLIN & MARSHALL COLLEGE

PO Box 3003, Lancaster, PA 17604
Phone: 717-291-3953 **E-mail:** admission@fandm.edu **CEEB Code:** 2261
Fax: 717-291-4389 **Web:** www.fandm.edu **ACT Code:** 3574

This private school was founded in 1787. It has a 125-acre campus.

STUDENTS AND FACULTY

Enrollment: 1,926. **Student Body:** Male 52%, female 48%, out-of-state 65%, international 7%. **Ethnic Representation:** African American 3%, Asian 4%, Caucasian 87%, Hispanic 2%. **Retention and Graduation:** 90% freshmen return for sophomore year. 79% freshmen graduate within 4 years. 25% grads go on to further study within 1 year. 1% grads pursue business degrees. 10% grads pursue law degrees. 4% grads pursue medical degrees. **Faculty:** Student/faculty ratio 11:1. 162 full-time faculty, 97% hold PhDs. 100% faculty teach undergrads.

ACADEMICS

Degrees: Bachelor's. **Academic Requirements:** General education including some course work in arts/fine arts, foreign languages, humanities, sciences (biological or physical), social science. **Classes:** 20-29 students in an average class. 10-19 students in an average lab/discussion section. **Majors with Highest Enrollment:** Business administration/management; English language and literature, general; political science and government, general. **Disciplines with Highest Percentage of Degrees Awarded:** Social sciences and history 28%, business/marketing 17%, biological life sciences 16%, English 9%, foreign languages and literature 6%. **Special Study Options:** Accelerated program, cross registration, double major, dual enrollment, student exchange program (domestic), honors program, independent study, internships, liberal arts/career combination, student-designed major, study abroad, teacher certification program.

FACILITIES

Housing: Coed, all-female, all-male, apartments for single students, housing for disabled students, housing for international students, arts house, French house, community outreach house. **Library Holdings:** 435,771 bound volumes. 2,090 periodicals. 511,661 microforms. 11,649 audiovisuals. **Special Academic Facilities/Equipment:** Art gallery associated with natural history museums, bronze casting foundry, retail sales complex, psychology and language labs, TV and radio stations, observatory/planetarium. **Computers:** *Recommended operating system:* Mac. School-owned computers available for student use.

EXTRACURRICULARS

Activities: Choral groups, concert band, dance, drama/theater, jazz band, literary magazine, music ensembles, musical theater, radio station, student government, student newspaper, symphony orchestra, television station, yearbook. **Organizations:** 120 registered organizations, 13 honor societies, 8 religious organizations. **Athletics (Intercollegiate):** *Men:* baseball, basketball, cross-country, football, golf, indoor track, lacrosse, soccer, squash, swimming, tennis, track & field, wrestling. *Women:* basketball, cross-country, field hockey, golf, indoor track, lacrosse, soccer, softball, squash, swimming, tennis, track & field, volleyball.

ADMISSIONS

Selectivity Rating: 89 (of 100). **Freshman Academic Profile:** 46% in top 10% of high school class, 63% in top 25% of high school class, 92% in top 50% of high school class. 55% from public high schools. Average SAT I Math 633, SAT I Math middle 50% range 590-680. Average SAT I Verbal 615, SAT I Verbal middle 50% range 570-660. TOEFL required of all international applicants, minimum TOEFL 600. **Basis for Candidate Selection:** *Very important factors considered include:* character/personal qualities, class rank, secondary school record. *Important factors considered include:* essays, extracurricular activities, interview, minority status, recommendations, standardized test scores, talent/ability, volunteer work. *Other factors considered include:* alumni/ae relation, geographical residence, work experience. **Freshman Admission Requirements:** High school diploma or GED is required. *Academic units required/recommended:* 4 English required, 3 math required, 4 math recommended, 2 science required, 3 science recommended, 2 science lab required, 3 science lab recommended, 2 foreign language required, 4 foreign language recommended, 1 social studies required, 3 social studies recommended, 2 history required, 3 history recommended. **Freshman Admission Statistics:** 3,425 applied, 62% accepted, 25% of those accepted enrolled. **Transfer Admission Requirements:** *Items required:* high school transcript, college transcript, essay, interview, standardized test scores, statement of good standing from prior school. Lowest grade transferable C-. **General Admission Information:** Application fee $50. Early decision application deadline November 15. Regular application deadline February 1. Nonfall registration accepted. Admission may be deferred for a maximum of 1 year. Credit and/or placement offered for CEEB Advanced Placement tests.

COSTS AND FINANCIAL AID

Tuition $27,230. Room & board $6,580. Required fees $50. Average book expense $650. **Required Forms and Deadlines:** FAFSA, CSS/Financial Aid PROFILE, state aid form, noncustodial (divorced/separated) parent's statement, business/farm supplement, and 2000 federal taxes and W-2s. Financial aid filing deadline February 1. Priority filing deadline February 1. **Notification of Awards:** Applicants will be notified of awards on or about April 1. **Types of Aid:** *Need-based scholarships/grants:* Pell, SEOG, state scholarships/grants, private scholarships, the school's own gift aid. *Loans:* FFEL Subsidized Stafford, FFEL Unsubsidized Stafford, FFEL PLUS, Federal Perkins, college/university loans from institutional funds. **Student Employment:** Federal Work-Study Program available. Institutional employment available. Off-campus job opportunities are excellent. **Financial Aid Statistics:** 43% freshmen, 45% undergrads receive some form of aid. Average freshman grant $15,913. Average freshman loan $3,879. Average income from on-campus job $1,350. **Financial Aid Phone:** 717-291-3991.

FRANKLIN COLLEGE

501 E. Monroe Street, Franklin, IN 46142-2598
Phone: 317-738-8062 **E-mail:** admissions@franklincollege.edu **CEEB Code:** 1228
Fax: 317-738-8274 **Web:** www.franklincollege.edu **ACT Code:** 1194

This private school, which is affiliated with the American Baptist Church, was founded in 1834. It has a 74-acre campus.

STUDENTS AND FACULTY

Enrollment: 1,048. **Student Body:** Male 44%, female 56%, out-of-state 6%, international 1% (7 countries represented). **Ethnic Representation:** African American 3%, Caucasian 94%, Hispanic 1%. **Retention and Graduation:** 76% freshmen return for sophomore year. 48% freshmen graduate within 4 years. 19% grads go on to further study within 1 year. 3% grads pursue law degrees. 4% grads pursue medical degrees. **Faculty:** Student/faculty ratio 14:1. 59 full-time faculty, 89% hold PhDs. 100% faculty teach undergrads.

ACADEMICS

Degrees: Bachelor's. **Academic Requirements:** General education including some course work in arts/fine arts, English (including composition), history, humanities, mathematics, sciences (biological or physical), social science, leadership. **Classes:** 20-29 students in an average class. **Majors with Highest Enrollment:** Business/commerce, general; journalism; elementary education and teaching. **Disciplines with Highest Percentage of Degrees Awarded:** Education 21%, social sciences and history 19%, communications/communication technologies 16%, business/marketing 16%, biological life sciences 6%. **Special Study Options:** Cooperative (work-study) program, cross registration, double major, student exchange program (domestic), independent study, internships, study abroad, teacher certification program.

FACILITIES

Housing: Coed, all-female, all-male, housing for disabled students, fraternities and/or sororities. **Library Holdings:** 122,605 bound volumes. 484 periodicals. 285,893 microforms. 7,388 audiovisuals. **Special Academic Facilities/Equipment:** Pulliam School of Journalism, Dietz Center for Professional Development, leadership center. **Computers:** School-owned computers available for student use.

EXTRACURRICULARS

Activities: Choral groups, dance, drama/theater, literary magazine, musical theater, radio station, student government, student newspaper, television station, yearbook. **Organizations:** 62 registered organizations, 13 honor societies, 2 religious organizations, 5 fraternities (39% men join), 4 sororities (44% women join). **Athletics (Intercollegiate):** *Men:* baseball, basketball, cross-country, football, golf, soccer, tennis, track & field. *Women:* basketball, cross-country, golf, soccer, softball, tennis, track & field, volleyball.

ADMISSIONS

Selectivity Rating: 74 (of 100). **Freshman Academic Profile:** Average high school GPA 3.2. 22% in top 10% of high school class, 85% in top 50% of high school class. Average SAT I Math 533, SAT I Math middle 50% range 470-580. Average SAT I Verbal 528, SAT I Verbal middle 50% range 460-590. Average ACT 22, ACT middle 50% range 19-25. TOEFL required of all international applicants, minimum TOEFL 550. **Basis for Candidate Selection:** *Very important factors considered include:* class rank, geographical residence, minority status, secondary school record. *Important factors considered include:* alumni/ae relation, character/personal qualities, essays, extracurricular activities, interview, recommendations, religious affiliation/commitment, standardized test scores, state residency, talent/ability, volunteer work. *Other factors considered include:* work experience. **Freshman Admission Requirements:** High school diploma or GED is required. *Academic units required/recommended:* 4 English recommended, 3 math recommended, 1 science recommended, 2 foreign language recommended, 3 social studies recommended. **Freshman Admission Statistics:** 713 applied, 85% accepted, 50% of those accepted enrolled. **Transfer Admission Requirements:** *Items required:* high school transcript, college transcript, essay, standardized test scores, statement of good standing from prior school. Minimum college GPA of 2.0 required. Lowest grade transferable C-. **General Admission Information:** Application fee $30. Priority application deadline May 1. Nonfall registration accepted. Admission may be deferred for a maximum of 1 year. Credit offered for CEEB Advanced Placement tests.

COSTS AND FINANCIAL AID

Tuition $15,500. Room & board $5,060. Required fees $135. Average book expense $700. **Required Forms and Deadlines:** FAFSA and institution's own financial aid form. Financial aid filing deadline March 1. Priority filing deadline March 1. **Notification of Awards:** Applicants will be notified of awards on or about April 1. **Types of Aid:** *Need-based scholarships/grants:* Pell, SEOG, state scholarships/grants, private scholarships, the school's own gift aid. *Loans:* FFEL Subsidized Stafford, FFEL Unsubsidized Stafford, FFEL PLUS, Federal Perkins, college/university loans from institutional funds. **Student Employment:** Federal Work-Study Program available. Institutional employment available. Off-campus job opportunities are excellent. **Financial Aid Statistics:** 72% freshmen, 75% undergrads receive some form of aid. Average freshman grant $12,656. Average freshman loan $3,105. Average income from on-campus job $950. **Financial Aid Phone:** 317-738-8075.

FRANKLIN PIERCE COLLEGE

College Road, Box 60, Rindge, NH 03461-0060
Phone: 603-899-4050 **E-mail:** admissions@fpc.edu **CEEB Code:** 3395
Fax: 603-889-4394 **Web:** www.fpc.edu **ACT Code:** 2509

This private school was founded in 1962. It has a 1,200-acre campus.

STUDENTS AND FACULTY

Enrollment: 1,574. **Student Body:** Male 51%, female 49%, out-of-state 84%, international 2%. **Ethnic Representation:** African American 3%, Asian 1%,

Caucasian 83%, Hispanic 3%. **Retention and Graduation:** 58% freshmen return for sophomore year. 21% grads go on to further study within 1 year. 7% grads pursue business degrees. 3% grads pursue law degrees. 1% grads pursue medical degrees. **Faculty:** Student/faculty ratio 18:1. 61 full-time faculty, 68% hold PhDs. 100% faculty teach undergrads.

ACADEMICS

Degrees: Bachelor's. **Academic Requirements:** General education including some course work in arts/fine arts, English (including composition), history, humanities, mathematics, sciences (biological or physical), social science. **Classes:** 10-19 students in an average class. 20-29 students in an average lab/discussion section. **Majors with Highest Enrollment:** Communications and media studies; education, general; criminal justice/safety studies. **Disciplines with Highest Percentage of Degrees Awarded:** Business/marketing 18%, visual and performing arts 17%, communications/communication technologies 16%, social sciences and history 12%, parks and recreation 7%. **Special Study Options:** Cooperative (work-study) program, distance learning, double major, dual enrollment, English as a second language, student exchange program (domestic), honors program, independent study, internships, liberal arts/career combination, student-designed major, study abroad, teacher certification program, Walk Across Europe Program, Washington semester.

FACILITIES

Housing: Coed, apartments for single students, housing for disabled students, condominiums (townhouses). **Library Holdings:** 110,210 bound volumes. 267 periodicals. 26,111 microforms. 10,589 audiovisuals. **Special Academic Facilities/Equipment:** Thoreau Art Gallery, Flynt Center, Fitzwater Communications Center, dance studio, pottery kiln, glass-blowing studio, TV station, radio station, Grimshaw-Gudewicz Activities Center. **Computers:** *Recommended operating system:* Windows NT/2000. School-owned computers available for student use.

EXTRACURRICULARS

Activities: Choral groups, dance, drama/theater, literary magazine, music ensembles, musical theater, radio station, student government, student newspaper, television station, yearbook. **Organizations:** 38 registered organizations, 8 honor societies, 3 religious organizations. **Athletics (Intercollegiate):** *Men:* baseball, basketball, crew, cross-country, golf, ice hockey, lacrosse, soccer, tennis. *Women:* basketball, cheerleading, crew, cross-country, field hockey, golf, lacrosse, soccer, softball, tennis, volleyball.

ADMISSIONS

Selectivity Rating: 69 (of 100). **Freshman Academic Profile:** Average high school GPA 2.8. 89% from public high schools. Average SAT I Math 493, SAT I Math middle 50% range 440-545. Average SAT I Verbal 506, SAT I Verbal middle 50% range 450-550. TOEFL required of all international applicants, minimum TOEFL 500. **Basis for Candidate Selection:** *Very important factors considered include:* character/personal qualities, recommendations, secondary school record. *Important factors considered include:* class rank, essays, extracurricular activities, volunteer work. *Other factors considered include:* interview, standardized test scores, talent/ability, work experience. **Freshman Admission Requirements:** High school diploma or GED is required. *Academic units required/recommended:* 16 total required; 4 English required, 3 math required, 2 science required, 2 science lab required, 3 social studies required, 4 elective required. **Freshman Admission Statistics:** 3,570 applied, 78% accepted, 20% of those accepted enrolled. **Transfer Admission Requirements:** *Items required:* college transcript, essay. Minimum college GPA of 2.0 required. Lowest grade transferable C-. **General Admission Information:** Regular application deadline rolling. Nonfall registration accepted. Admission may be deferred for a maximum of 1 year. Credit and/or placement offered for CEEB Advanced Placement tests.

COSTS AND FINANCIAL AID

Tuition $20,790. Room & board $7,250. Required fees $590. Average book expense $786. **Required Forms and Deadlines:** FAFSA. No deadline for regular filing. **Notification of Awards:** Applicants will be notified of awards on a rolling basis beginning on or about February 15. **Types of Aid:** *Need-based scholarships/grants:* Pell, SEOG, state scholarships/grants, private scholarships, the school's own gift aid. *Loans:* FFEL Subsidized Stafford, FFEL Unsubsidized Stafford, FFEL PLUS, Federal Perkins, state loans. **Student Employment:** Federal Work-Study Program available. Institutional employment available. Off-campus job opportunities are good. **Financial Aid Statistics:** 68% freshmen, 75% undergrads receive some form of aid. Average freshman grant $10,449. Average freshman loan $3,455. Average income from on-campus job $1,500. **Financial Aid Phone:** 603-899-4180.

See page 1036.

FRANKLIN UNIVERSITY

201 South Grant Avenue, Columbus, OH 43215-5399
Phone: 614-797-4700 **E-mail:** info@franklin.edu **CEEB Code:** 1229
Fax: 614-224-8027 **Web:** www.franklin.edu **ACT Code:** 3275

This private school was founded in 1902. It has a 14-acre campus.

STUDENTS AND FACULTY

Enrollment: 4,863. **Student Body:** Male 46%, female 54%, out-of-state 16%, international 8%. **Ethnic Representation:** African American 18%, Asian 3%, Caucasian 73%, Hispanic 2%, Native American 1%. **Retention and Graduation:** 55% freshmen return for sophomore year. **Faculty:** Student/faculty ratio 17:1. 36 full-time faculty, 38% hold PhDs.

ACADEMICS

Degrees: Associate's, bachelor's, master's. **Academic Requirements:** General education including some course work in computer literacy, English (including composition), history, humanities, mathematics, sciences (biological or physical), social science, speech. **Classes:** 10-19 students in an average class. **Majors with Highest Enrollment:** Business administration/management; accounting; computer and information sciences, general. **Disciplines with Highest Percentage of Degrees Awarded:** Business/marketing 71%, computer and information sciences 14%, health professions and related sciences 8%, interdisciplinary studies 5%, communications/communication technologies 2%. **Special Study Options:** Accelerated program, cooperative (work-study) program, cross registration, distance learning, dual enrollment, English as a second language, independent study, internships, student-designed major, study abroad.

FACILITIES

Library Holdings: 73,702 bound volumes. 432 periodicals. 176,600 microforms. 220 audiovisuals. **Computers:** *Recommended operating system:* Windows 95. School-owned computers available for student use.

EXTRACURRICULARS

Organizations: 6 registered organizations.

ADMISSIONS

Selectivity Rating: 72 (of 100). **Freshman Academic Profile:** TOEFL required of all international applicants, minimum TOEFL 430. **Freshman Admission Requirements:** High school diploma or GED is required. *Academic units required/recommended:* 3 math recommended. **Freshman Admission Statistics:** 251 applied, 100% accepted, 28% of those accepted enrolled. **Transfer Admission Requirements:** *Items required:* college transcript. Lowest grade transferable C-. **General Admission Information:** Nonfall registration accepted. Admission may be deferred. Credit and/or placement offered for CEEB Advanced Placement tests.

COSTS AND FINANCIAL AID

Tuition $6,324. Required fees $0. Average book expense $0. **Required Forms and Deadlines:** FAFSA and institution's own financial aid form. No deadline for regular filing. Priority filing deadline June 15. **Notification of Awards:** Applicants will be notified of awards on a rolling basis. **Types of Aid:** *Need-based scholarships/grants:* Pell, SEOG, state scholarships/grants, private scholarships, the school's own gift aid. *Loans:* FFEL Subsidized Stafford, FFEL Unsubsidized Stafford, FFEL PLUS, college/university loans from institutional funds. **Student Employment:** Federal Work-Study Program available. Institutional employment available. Off-campus job opportunities are good. **Financial Aid Statistics:** 38% freshmen, 42% undergrads receive some form of aid. **Financial Aid Phone:** 614-797-4700.

FREED-HARDEMAN UNIVERSITY

158 East Main Street, Henderson, TN 38340
Phone: 731-989-6651 **E-mail:** admissions@fhu.edu **CEEB Code:** 1230
Fax: 731-989-6047 **Web:** www.fhu.edu **ACT Code:** 3962

This private school, which is affiliated with the Church of Christ, was founded in 1869. It has a 122-acre campus.

STUDENTS AND FACULTY

Enrollment: 1,444. **Student Body:** Male 47%, female 53%, out-of-state 51%, international 2%. **Ethnic Representation:** African American 5%, Caucasian

93%, Hispanic 1%. **Retention and Graduation:** 76% freshmen return for sophomore year. 33% freshmen graduate within 4 years. **Faculty:** Student/faculty ratio 16:1. 94 full-time faculty, 75% hold PhDs. 97% faculty teach undergrads.

ACADEMICS

Degrees: Bachelor's, master's, post-bachelor's certificate. **Academic Requirements:** General education including some course work in arts/fine arts, computer literacy, English (including composition), history, humanities, mathematics, sciences (biological or physical), social science, Bible. Each full-time student is required to take a Bible course, and students must take a values class before graduation. **Classes:** 20-29 students in an average class. 20-29 students in an average lab/discussion section. **Majors with Highest Enrollment:** Liberal arts and sciences, general studies and humanities; biology/biological sciences, general; Bible/biblical studies. **Disciplines with Highest Percentage of Degrees Awarded:** Business/marketing 22%, interdisciplinary studies 17%, philosophy/religion/theology 11%, communications/communication technologies 6%, psychology 6%. **Special Study Options:** Accelerated program, cooperative (work-study) program, cross registration, distance learning, double major, dual enrollment, honors college, independent study, internships, liberal arts/career combination, student-designed major, study abroad in Belgium, teacher certification program, 3-2 engineering.

FACILITIES

Housing: All-female, all-male; some student teacher housing is available. **Library Holdings:** 154,689 bound volumes. 1,715 periodicals. 255,909 microforms. 42,735 audiovisuals. **Special Academic Facilities/Equipment:** Child development lab, nursery school, Cancer Research Institute of West Tennessee. **Computers:** School-owned computers available for student use.

EXTRACURRICULARS

Activities: Choral groups, concert band, drama/theater, jazz band, music ensembles, musical theater, pep band, radio station, student government, student newspaper, television station, yearbook. **Organizations:** 52 registered organizations, 4 honor societies, 5 religious organizations. **Athletics (Intercollegiate):** *Men:* baseball, basketball, cross-country, golf, soccer, tennis. *Women:* basketball, cheerleading, cross-country, golf, soccer, softball, tennis, volleyball.

ADMISSIONS

Selectivity Rating: 68 (of 100). **Freshman Academic Profile:** Average high school GPA 3.4. 29% in top 10% of high school class, 52% in top 25% of high school class, 79% in top 50% of high school class. 84% from public high schools. Average ACT 23, ACT middle 50% range 20-26. **Basis for Candidate Selection:** *Very important factors considered include:* secondary school record, standardized test scores. *Other factors considered include:* alumni/ae relation, character/personal qualities, extracurricular activities, minority status, recommendations, religious affiliation/commitment, volunteer work, work experience. **Freshman Admission Requirements:** High school diploma or GED is required. *Academic units required/recommended:* 20 total recommended; 4 English recommended, 2 math recommended, 2 science recommended, 2 social studies recommended, 10 elective recommended. **Freshman Admission Statistics:** 836 applied, 100% accepted. **Transfer Admission Requirements:** *Items required:* college transcript. Lowest grade transferable D. **General Admission Information:** Nonfall registration accepted. Admission may be deferred for a maximum of 2 years. Credit and/or placement offered for CEEB Advanced Placement tests.

COSTS AND FINANCIAL AID

Average book expense $1,100. **Required Forms and Deadlines:** FAFSA. No deadline for regular filing. Priority filing deadline April 1. **Notification of Awards:** Applicants will be notified of awards on a rolling basis beginning on or about March 1. **Types of Aid:** *Need-based scholarships/grants:* Pell, SEOG, state scholarships/grants, private scholarships, the school's own gift aid. *Loans:* FFEL Subsidized Stafford, FFEL Unsubsidized Stafford, FFEL PLUS, Federal Perkins, alternative loan programs. **Student Employment:** Federal Work-Study Program available. Institutional employment available. Off-campus job opportunities are fair. **Financial Aid Statistics:** 73% undergrads receive some form of aid. **Financial Aid Phone:** 731-989-6662.

FRESNO PACIFIC UNIVERSITY

1717 South Chestnut Avenue, Fresno, CA 93702
Phone: 559-453-2039 **E-mail:** ugadmis@fresno.edu
Fax: 559-453-2007 **Web:** www.fresno.edu

This private school, which is affiliated with the Mennonite Church, was founded in 1944. It has a 42-acre campus.

STUDENTS AND FACULTY

Enrollment: 884. **Student Body:** Male 33%, female 67%, out-of-state 3%, international 4%. **Ethnic Representation:** African American 4%, Asian 5%, Caucasian 67%, Hispanic 18%, Native American 2%. **Retention and Graduation:** 82% freshmen return for sophomore year. 49% freshmen graduate within 4 years. **Faculty:** Student/faculty ratio 15:1. 76 full-time faculty, 25% hold PhDs.

ACADEMICS

Degrees: Associate's, bachelor's, master's. **Academic Requirements:** General education including some course work in arts/fine arts, English (including composition), foreign languages, history, humanities, mathematics, philosophy, sciences (biological or physical), social science, biblical and religious studies. **Disciplines with Highest Percentage of Degrees Awarded:** Business/marketing 43%, education 35%, philosophy/religion/theology 5%, English 4%, psychology 3%. **Special Study Options:** Accelerated program, cooperative (work-study) program, cross registration, distance learning, double major, English as a second language, independent study, internships, liberal arts/career combination, student-designed major, study abroad, teacher certification program.

FACILITIES

Housing: All-female, all-male, apartments for single students. **Library Holdings:** 148,000 bound volumes. 2,000 periodicals. 250,000 microforms. 6,000 audiovisuals. **Special Academic Facilities/Equipment:** English language training institute. **Computers:** School-owned computers available for student use.

EXTRACURRICULARS

Activities: Choral groups, dance, drama/theater, jazz band, music ensembles, pep band, student government, student newspaper, yearbook. **Organizations:** 36 registered organizations, 1 honor society, 11 religious organizations. **Athletics (Intercollegiate):** *Men:* basketball, cross-country, soccer, track & field. *Women:* basketball, cross-country, soccer, track & field, volleyball.

ADMISSIONS

Selectivity Rating: 79 (of 100). **Freshman Academic Profile:** Average high school GPA 3.5. Average SAT I Math 515. Average SAT I Verbal 516. Average ACT 22. TOEFL required of all international applicants, minimum TOEFL 500. **Basis for Candidate Selection:** *Very important factors considered include:* secondary school record, standardized test scores. *Important factors considered include:* class rank, essays, recommendations. **Freshman Admission Requirements:** High school diploma or GED is required. *Academic units required/recommended:* 13 total required; 4 English required, 3 math required, 1 science required, 1 science lab required, 2 foreign language required, 2 social studies required. **Freshman Admission Statistics:** 418 applied, 81% accepted, 50% of those accepted enrolled. **Transfer Admission Requirements:** *Items required:* high school transcript, college transcript, essay. Minimum college GPA of 2.4 required. Lowest grade transferable C. **General Admission Information:** Application fee $30. Priority application deadline March 2. Regular application deadline July 31. Nonfall registration accepted. Admission may be deferred. Credit offered for CEEB Advanced Placement tests.

COSTS AND FINANCIAL AID

Tuition $13,950. Room & board $4,530. Required fees $298. Average book expense $810. **Required Forms and Deadlines:** FAFSA and institution's own financial aid form. No deadline for regular filing. Priority filing deadline March 2. **Notification of Awards:** Applicants will be notified of awards on or about February 1. **Types of Aid:** *Need-based scholarships/grants:* Pell, SEOG, state scholarships/grants, private scholarships, the school's own gift aid. *Loans:* FFEL Subsidized Stafford, FFEL Unsubsidized Stafford, FFEL PLUS, Federal Perkins, college/university loans from institutional funds. **Student Employment:** Federal Work-Study Program available. Off-campus job opportunities are good. **Financial Aid Statistics:** 84% freshmen, 81% undergrads receive some form of aid. Average freshman loan $2,516. Average income from on-campus job $2,000. **Financial Aid Phone:** 559-453-2041.

FRIENDS UNIVERSITY

2100 University Street., Wichita, KS 67213
Phone: 316-295-5100 **E-mail:** learn@friends.edu
Fax: 316-295-5101 **Web:** www.friends.edu **ACT Code:** 1918

This private school, which is affiliated with the Quaker Church, was founded in 1898. It has a 45-acre campus.

STUDENTS AND FACULTY

Enrollment: 2,614. **Student Body:** Male 50%, female 50%, out-of-state 13%, international students represent 20 countries. **Retention and Graduation:** 63% freshmen return for sophomore year. 33% grads go on to further study within 1 year. **Faculty:** Student/faculty ratio 10:1. 72 full-time faculty, 43% hold PhDs. 95% faculty teach undergrads.

ACADEMICS

Degrees: Bachelor's, master's, terminal, transfer. **Academic Requirements:** General education including some course work in arts/fine arts, computer literacy, English (including composition), history, humanities, mathematics, sciences (biological or physical), religion. **Special Study Options:** Cooperative (work-study) program, cross registration, double major, dual enrollment, external degree program, honors program, independent study, internships, student-designed major, study abroad, teacher certification program, degree completion program for working adults.

FACILITIES

Housing: All-female, all-male, apartments for married students, apartments for single students, university-owned houses. **Library Holdings:** 106,000 bound volumes. 3,200 periodicals. 21,981 microforms. 5,980 audiovisuals.

EXTRACURRICULARS

Activities: Choral groups, concert band, dance, drama/theater, jazz band, literary magazine, music ensembles, musical theater, pep band, student government, symphony orchestra, yearbook. **Organizations:** 32 registered organizations, 4 honor societies, 3 religious organizations, 2 fraternities, 1 sorority. **Athletics (Intercollegiate):** *Men:* baseball, basketball, cheerleading, cross-country, football, golf, soccer, tennis, track & field. *Women:* basketball, cheerleading, cross-country, soccer, softball, tennis, track & field, volleyball.

ADMISSIONS

Selectivity Rating: 81 (of 100). **Freshman Academic Profile:** Average high school GPA 3.4. ACT middle 50% range 17-26. TOEFL required of all international applicants, minimum TOEFL 500. **Basis for Candidate Selection:** *Very important factors considered include:* secondary school record, standardized test scores. *Important factors considered include:* interview, recommendations. *Other factors considered include:* alumni/ae relation, extracurricular activities, minority status, religious affiliation/commitment, talent/ability. **Freshman Admission Requirements:** High school diploma or GED is required. *Academic units required/recommended:* 3 math recommended, 3 science recommended. **Freshman Admission Statistics:** 668 applied, 93% accepted. **Transfer Admission Requirements:** *Items required:* college transcript, statement of good standing from prior school. Minimum college GPA of 2.0 required. Lowest grade transferable C. **General Admission Information:** Application fee $15. Nonfall registration accepted. Credit and/or placement offered for CEEB Advanced Placement tests.

COSTS AND FINANCIAL AID

Tuition $11,050. Room & board $3,420. Required fees $90. Average book expense $750. **Required Forms and Deadlines:** FAFSA and institution's own financial aid form. Priority filing deadline April 1. **Types of Aid:** *Need-based scholarships/grants:* Pell, SEOG, private scholarships. *Loans:* Direct Subsidized Stafford, Direct Unsubsidized Stafford, Direct PLUS, Federal Perkins. **Student Employment:** Federal Work-Study Program available. Institutional employment available. Off-campus job opportunities are excellent. **Financial Aid Phone:** 316-295-5200.

FROSTBURG STATE UNIVERSITY

FSU, 101 Braddock Road, Frostburg, MD 21532
Phone: 301-687-4201 **E-mail:** fsuadmissions@frostburg.edu **CEEB Code:** 5402
Fax: 301-687-7074 **Web:** www.frostburg.edu **ACT Code:** 1714

This public school was founded in 1898. It has a 260-acre campus.

STUDENTS AND FACULTY

Enrollment: 4,544. **Student Body:** Male 48%, female 52%, out-of-state 12%, international students represent 26 countries. **Ethnic Representation:** African American 13%, Asian 2%, Caucasian 81%, Hispanic 2%. **Retention and Graduation:** 76% freshmen return for sophomore year. 21% freshmen graduate within 4 years. **Faculty:** Student/faculty ratio 18:1. 248 full-time faculty, 79% hold PhDs. 95% faculty teach undergrads.

ACADEMICS

Degrees: Bachelor's, certificate, master's, post-bachelor's certificate, post-master's certificate. **Academic Requirements:** General education including some course work in arts/fine arts, English (including composition), history, humanities, mathematics, sciences (biological or physical), social science, personal wellness. **Classes:** 20-29 students in an average class. Under 10 students in an average lab/discussion section. **Majors with Highest Enrollment:** Elementary education and teaching; early childhood education and teaching; business administration/management. **Disciplines with Highest Percentage of Degrees Awarded:** Education 17%, business/marketing 16%, social sciences and history 15%, psychology 8%, visual and performing arts 7%. **Special Study Options:** Accelerated program, cross registration, distance learning, double major, dual enrollment, honors program, independent study, internships, liberal arts/career combination, study abroad, teacher certification program, weekend college, learning communities, dual degree program.

FACILITIES

Housing: Coed, all-female, all-male; special-interest housing: leadership hall, honors housing, community service. **Library Holdings:** 261,712 bound volumes. 2,430 periodicals. 293,802 microforms. 32,224 audiovisuals. **Special Academic Facilities/Equipment:** Art gallery, planetarium, electron microscope. **Computers:** School-owned computers available for student use.

EXTRACURRICULARS

Activities: Choral groups, concert band, dance, drama/theater, jazz band, literary magazine, marching band, music ensembles, musical theater, radio station, student government, student newspaper, symphony orchestra, television station. **Organizations:** 95 registered organizations, 17 honor societies, 6 religious organizations, 5 fraternities (10% men join), 5 sororities (10% women join). **Athletics (Intercollegiate):** *Men:* baseball, basketball, cross-country, diving, football, indoor track, soccer, swimming, tennis, track & field. *Women:* basketball, cross-country, diving, field hockey, indoor track, lacrosse, soccer, softball, swimming, tennis, track & field, volleyball.

ADMISSIONS

Selectivity Rating: 63 (of 100). **Freshman Academic Profile:** Average high school GPA 3.1. 14% in top 10% of high school class, 36% in top 25% of high school class, 70% in top 50% of high school class. SAT I Math middle 50% range 460-560. SAT I Verbal middle 50% range 460-550. TOEFL required of all international applicants, minimum TOEFL 560. **Basis for Candidate Selection:** *Very important factors considered include:* secondary school record, standardized test scores. *Important factors considered include:* interview, recommendations. *Other factors considered include:* alumni/ae relation, character/personal qualities, extracurricular activities, talent/ability. **Freshman Admission Requirements:** High school diploma or GED is required. *Academic units required/recommended:* 15 total required; 4 English required, 3 math required, 3 science required, 2 science lab required, 2 foreign language required, 3 social studies required. **Freshman Admission Statistics:** 3,765 applied, 70% accepted, 38% of those accepted enrolled. **Transfer Admission Requirements:** *Items required:* college transcript. Minimum college GPA of 2.0 required. Lowest grade transferable C. **General Admission Information:** Application fee $30. Priority application deadline June 1. Nonfall registration accepted. Credit and/or placement offered for CEEB Advanced Placement tests.

COSTS AND FINANCIAL AID

In-state tuition $4,158. Out-of-state tuition $10,806. Room & board $5,616. Required fees $1,026. Average book expense $750. **Required Forms and Deadlines:** FAFSA. Priority filing deadline March 1. **Notification of Awards:** Applicants will be notified of awards on a rolling basis beginning on or about March 15. **Types of Aid:** *Need-based scholarships/grants:* Pell, SEOG, state scholarships/grants, private scholarships, the school's own gift aid. *Loans:* Direct

Subsidized Stafford, Direct Unsubsidized Stafford, Direct PLUS, Federal Perkins, college/university loans from institutional funds. **Student Employment:** Federal Work-Study Program available. Institutional employment available. Off-campus job opportunities are poor. **Financial Aid Statistics:** 46% freshmen, 50% undergrads receive some form of aid. Average freshman grant $3,800. Average freshman loan $3,000. Average income from on-campus job $895. **Financial Aid Phone:** 301-687-4301.

FURMAN UNIVERSITY

3300 Poinsett Highway, Greenville, SC 29613
Phone: 864-294-2034 **E-mail:** admissions@furman.edu **CEEB Code:** 5222
Fax: 864-294-3127 **Web:** www.furman.edu **ACT Code:** 3858

This private school was founded in 1826. It has a 750-acre campus.

STUDENTS AND FACULTY

Enrollment: 2,772. **Student Body:** Male 44%, female 56%, out-of-state 68%, international 1% (28 countries represented). **Ethnic Representation:** African American 6%, Asian 1%, Caucasian 89%, Hispanic 1%. **Retention and Graduation:** 91% freshmen return for sophomore year. 74% freshmen graduate within 4 years. 36% grads go on to further study within 1 year. 2% grads pursue business degrees. 6% grads pursue law degrees. 5% grads pursue medical degrees. **Faculty:** Student/faculty ratio 11:1. 211 full-time faculty, 97% hold PhDs. 100% faculty teach undergrads.

ACADEMICS

Degrees: Bachelor's, master's, post-bachelor's certificate. **Academic Requirements:** General education including some course work in arts/fine arts, English (including composition), foreign languages, history, humanities, mathematics, philosophy, sciences (biological or physical), social science, Asian and African courses that emphasize major dimensions of experience from the nonwestern two-thirds of humanity. **Classes:** 20-29 students in an average class. **Majors with Highest Enrollment:** Political science and government, general; business administration/management; history, general. **Disciplines with Highest Percentage of Degrees Awarded:** Social sciences and history 26%, business/marketing 13%, biological life sciences 8%, education 6%, visual and performing arts 6%. **Special Study Options:** Double major, independent study, internships, student-designed major, study abroad, teacher certification program.

FACILITIES

Housing: Coed, all-female, all-male, apartments for single students, housing for international students, lakeside cottages, language houses for students focusing on a specific language, eco-cottage (an environmentally responsible cottage). **Library Holdings:** 453,211 bound volumes. 2,052 periodicals. 811,000 microforms. 5,644 audiovisuals. **Special Academic Facilities/Equipment:** Visual arts gallery and teaching facility, language lab, astronomical lab, center for engaged learning, and center for collaborative learning and communication. **Computers:** School-owned computers available for student use.

EXTRACURRICULARS

Activities: Choral groups, concert band, dance, drama/theater, jazz band, literary magazine, marching band, music ensembles, musical theater, opera, pep band, radio station, student government, student newspaper, symphony orchestra, television station, yearbook. **Organizations:** 152 registered organizations, 29 honor societies, 17 religious organizations, 8 fraternities (30% men join), 7 sororities (35% women join). **Athletics (Intercollegiate):** *Men:* baseball, basketball, cheerleading, cross-country, football, golf, soccer, tennis, track & field. *Women:* basketball, cheerleading, cross-country, golf, indoor track, soccer, softball, tennis, track & field, volleyball.

ADMISSIONS

Selectivity Rating: 84 (of 100). **Freshman Academic Profile:** Average high school GPA 3.9. 61% in top 10% of high school class, 81% in top 25% of high school class, 99% in top 50% of high school class. 68% from public high schools. SAT I Math middle 50% range 590-680. SAT I Verbal middle 50% range 590-690. ACT middle 50% range 24-29. TOEFL required of all international applicants, minimum TOEFL 570. **Basis for Candidate Selection:** *Very important factors considered include:* secondary school record. *Important factors considered include:* character/personal qualities, class rank, essays, extracurricular activities, standardized test scores. *Other factors considered include:* alumni/ae relation, minority status, recommendations, talent/ability, volunteer work, work experience. **Freshman Admission Requirements:** High school diploma or GED is required. *Academic units required/recommended:* 14 total required; 18 total recommended; 4 English required, 4 English recommended, 3 math required, 4 math recommended, 2 science required, 3 science recommended, 2 science lab required, 3 science lab recommended, 2 foreign language required, 3 foreign language recommended, 3 social studies required, 4 social studies recommended. **Freshman Admission Statistics:** 3,866 applied, 58% accepted, 33% of those accepted enrolled. **Transfer Admission Requirements:** *Items required:* high school transcript, college transcript, essay, standardized test scores, statement of good standing from prior school. Minimum college GPA of 3.0 required. Lowest grade transferable C. **General Admission Information:** Application fee $40. Early decision application deadline November 15. Regular application deadline January 15. Credit offered for CEEB Advanced Placement tests.

COSTS AND FINANCIAL AID

Required Forms and Deadlines: FAFSA, institution's own financial aid form, and South Carolina residents must complete required state forms for South Carolina (when noted). Financial aid filing deadline January 15. **Notification of Awards:** Applicants will be notified of awards on or about March 5. **Types of Aid:** *Need-based scholarships/grants:* Pell, SEOG, state scholarships/grants, private scholarships, the school's own gift aid. *Loans:* FFEL Subsidized Stafford, FFEL Unsubsidized Stafford, FFEL PLUS, Federal Perkins, state loans, donor-sponsored loans for study abroad. **Student Employment:** Federal Work-Study Program available. Institutional employment available. Off-campus job opportunities are excellent. **Financial Aid Statistics:** 48% freshmen, 42% undergrads receive some form of aid. Average freshman grant $13,350. Average freshman loan $3,750. Average income from on-campus job $1,200. **Financial Aid Phone:** 864-294-2204.

GALLAUDET UNIVERSITY

800 Florida Avenue, NE, Washington DC, DC 20002
Phone: 202-651-5750 **E-mail:** admissions@gallaudet.edu **CEEB Code:** 5240
Fax: 202-651-5744 **Web:** www.gallaudet.edu **ACT Code:** 662

This private school was founded in 1864. It has a 99-acre campus.

STUDENTS AND FACULTY

Enrollment: 1,194. **Student Body:** Male 47%, female 53%, out-of-state 97%, international 14%. **Ethnic Representation:** African American 12%, Asian 5%, Caucasian 71%, Hispanic 8%, Native American 1%. **Retention and Graduation:** 69% freshmen return for sophomore year. 4% freshmen graduate within 4 years. 49% grads go on to further study within 1 year. **Faculty:** Student/faculty ratio 8:1. 240 full-time faculty, 50% hold PhDs.

ACADEMICS

Degrees: Bachelor's, certificate, doctoral, master's, post-master's certificate. **Academic Requirements:** General education including some course work in English (including composition), foreign languages, humanities, mathematics, sciences (biological or physical), social science. **Classes:** Under 10 students in an average class. Under 10 students in an average lab/discussion section. **Majors with Highest Enrollment:** Psychology, general; communications, journalism, and related fields; biology/biological sciences, general. **Disciplines with Highest Percentage of Degrees Awarded:** Visual and performing arts 14%, business/marketing 13%, education 9%, computer and information sciences 8%, area and ethnic studies 7%. **Special Study Options:** Accelerated program, cooperative (work-study) program, cross registration, double major, dual enrollment, English as a second language, student exchange program (domestic), honors program, independent study, internships, student-designed major, study abroad, teacher certification program.

FACILITIES

Housing: Coed, apartments for married students, housing for disabled students, apartments for students with children. All dorms are equipped for deaf and hard-of-hearing students. **Library Holdings:** 239,433 bound volumes. 1,784 periodicals. 623,982 microforms. 7,282 audiovisuals. **Special Academic Facilities/Equipment:** Demonstration elementary school and model secondary school for the deaf, TV/film studio, national information center, international center for the deaf, and Braille equipment for deaf/blind students. **Computers:** School-owned computers available for student use.

EXTRACURRICULARS

Activities: Dance, drama/theater, literary magazine, student government, student newspaper, student-run film society, television station, yearbook. **Organizations:** 29 registered organizations, 1 honor society, 1 religious organization, 5 fraternities (13% men join), 3 sororities (14% women join). **Athletics (Intercollegiate):** *Men:* baseball, basketball, cross-country, diving, football, soccer, swimming, tennis, track & field, wrestling. *Women:* basketball, cross-country, diving, soccer, softball, swimming, tennis, track & field, volleyball.

ADMISSIONS

Selectivity Rating: 84 (of 100). **Freshman Academic Profile: Basis for Candidate Selection:** *Very important factors considered include:* recommendations, secondary school record, standardized test scores. *Important factors considered include:* character/personal qualities, essays, extracurricular activities, talent/ability. *Other factors considered include:* class rank, volunteer work, work experience. **Freshman Admission Requirements:** High school diploma or GED is required. *Academic units required/recommended:* 16 total recommended; 4 English recommended, 4 math recommended, 4 science recommended, 2 science lab recommended, 4 social studies recommended, 4 history recommended. **Freshman Admission Statistics:** 601 applied, 71% accepted, 57% of those accepted enrolled. **Transfer Admission Requirements:** *Items required:* college transcript, essay, statement of good standing from prior school. Minimum college GPA of 2.0 required. Lowest grade transferable C. **General Admission Information:** Application fee $35. Priority application deadline May 1. Regular application deadline August 15. Nonfall registration accepted. Admission may be deferred for a maximum of 1 year. Credit and/or placement offered for CEEB Advanced Placement tests.

COSTS AND FINANCIAL AID

Tuition $9,000. Room & board $8,030. Required fees $580. Average book expense $742. **Required Forms and Deadlines:** FAFSA and institution's own financial aid form. No deadline for regular filing. Priority filing deadline June 15. **Notification of Awards:** Applicants will be notified of awards on a rolling basis beginning on or about April 15. **Types of Aid:** *Need-based scholarships/grants:* Pell, SEOG, state scholarships/grants, private scholarships, the school's own gift aid. *Loans:* FFEL Subsidized Stafford, FFEL Unsubsidized Stafford, FFEL PLUS, Federal Perkins. **Student Employment:** Federal Work-Study Program available. Institutional employment available. Off-campus job opportunities are good. **Financial Aid Statistics:** 70% freshmen, 67% undergrads receive some form of aid. **Financial Aid Phone:** 202-651-5290.

GANNON UNIVERSITY

University Square, Erie, PA 16541
Phone: 814-871-7240 **E-mail:** admissions@gannon.edu **CEEB Code:** 2270
Fax: 814-871-5803 **Web:** www.gannon.edu **ACT Code:** 3576

This private school, which is affiliated with the Roman Catholic Church, was founded in 1925. It has a 13-acre campus.

STUDENTS AND FACULTY

Enrollment: 2,470. **Student Body:** Male 41%, female 59%, out-of-state 18%, international 3%. **Ethnic Representation:** African American 3%, Asian 1%, Caucasian 95%, Hispanic 1%. **Retention and Graduation:** 79% freshmen return for sophomore year. 24% grads go on to further study within 1 year. 9% grads pursue business degrees. 2% grads pursue law degrees. 4% grads pursue medical degrees. **Faculty:** Student/faculty ratio 13:1. 170 full-time faculty, 55% hold PhDs. 95% faculty teach undergrads.

ACADEMICS

Degrees: Associate's, bachelor's, certificate, doctoral, master's, terminal, transfer. **Academic Requirements:** General education including some course work in arts/fine arts, English (including composition), foreign languages, humanities, philosophy, sciences (biological or physical). **Classes:** 10-19 students in an average class. 10-19 students in an average lab/discussion section. **Disciplines with Highest Percentage of Degrees Awarded:** Health professions and related sciences 26%, business/marketing 14%, biological life sciences 12%, education 9%, engineering/engineering technology 7%. **Special Study Options:** Accelerated program, cooperative (work-study) program, cross registration, distance learning, double major, dual enrollment, English as a second language, external degree program, honors program, independent study, internships, liberal arts/career combination, study abroad, teacher certification program, weekend college.

FACILITIES

Housing: Coed, apartments for single students, fraternities and/or sororities. **Library Holdings:** 257,670 bound volumes. 2,962 periodicals. 460,392 microforms. 2,274 audiovisuals. **Special Academic Facilities/Equipment:** Laser and spectrographic labs, metallurgy institute, computer-integrated manufacturing facilities, Schuster Art Gallery, Schuster Theatres. **Computers:** *Recommended operating system:* Windows 95. School-owned computers available for student use.

EXTRACURRICULARS

Activities: Choral groups, dance, drama/theater, literary magazine, music ensembles, musical theater, pep band, radio station, student government, student newspaper, yearbook. **Organizations:** 70 registered organizations, 10 honor societies, 2 religious organizations, 6 fraternities (18% men join), 5 sororities (16% women join). **Athletics (Intercollegiate):** *Men:* baseball, basketball, cross-country, diving, football, golf, soccer, swimming, tennis, water polo, wrestling. *Women:* basketball, cross-country, diving, golf, lacrosse, soccer, softball, swimming, tennis, volleyball, water polo.

ADMISSIONS

Selectivity Rating: 73 (of 100). **Freshman Academic Profile:** Average high school GPA 3.2. 9% in top 10% of high school class, 35% in top 25% of high school class, 66% in top 50% of high school class. 80% from public high schools. Average SAT I Math 519, SAT I Math middle 50% range 460-560. Average SAT I Verbal 524, SAT I Verbal middle 50% range 470-570. Average ACT 21, ACT middle 50% range 19-25. TOEFL required of all international applicants, minimum TOEFL 500. **Basis for Candidate Selection:** *Very important factors considered include:* class rank, secondary school record, standardized test scores. *Important factors considered include:* character/personal qualities, essays, interview, recommendations. *Other factors considered include:* alumni/ae relation, extracurricular activities, volunteer work, work experience. **Freshman Admission Requirements:** High school diploma or GED is required. *Academic units required/recommended:* 16 total required; 4 English required, 4 math required, 2 science required. **Freshman Admission Statistics:** 1,980 applied, 90% accepted, 32% of those accepted enrolled. **Transfer Admission Requirements:** *Items required:* college transcript. Minimum high school GPA of 2.0 required. Minimum college GPA of 2.0 required. Lowest grade transferable C. **General Admission Information:** Application fee $25. Nonfall registration accepted. Admission may be deferred. Credit and/or placement offered for CEEB Advanced Placement tests.

COSTS AND FINANCIAL AID

Tuition $14,490. Room & board $5,850. Required fees $442. Average book expense $750. **Required Forms and Deadlines:** FAFSA and institution's own financial aid form. Financial aid filing deadline May 1. Priority filing deadline March 15. **Notification of Awards:** Applicants will be notified of awards on a rolling basis beginning on or about October 30. **Types of Aid:** *Need-based scholarships/grants:* Pell, SEOG, state scholarships/grants, private scholarships, the school's own gift aid. *Loans:* Direct Subsidized Stafford, Direct Unsubsidized Stafford, Direct PLUS, FFEL Subsidized Stafford, FFEL Unsubsidized Stafford, FFEL PLUS, Federal Perkins, Federal Nursing, deferred payment. **Student Employment:** Federal Work-Study Program available. Institutional employment available. Off-campus job opportunities are excellent. **Financial Aid Statistics:** 64% freshmen, 80% undergrads receive some form of aid. Average freshman grant $5,300. Average freshman loan $2,500. Average income from on-campus job $1,400. **Financial Aid Phone:** 814-871-7337.

GARDNER-WEBB UNIVERSITY

PO Box 817, Boiling Springs, NC 28017
Phone: 704-406-4498 **E-mail:** admissions@gardner-webb.edu **CEEB Code:** 5242
Fax: 704-406-4488 **Web:** www.gardner-webb.edu **ACT Code:** 3102

This private school, which is affiliated with the Baptist Church, was founded in 1905. It has a 250-acre campus.

STUDENTS AND FACULTY

Enrollment: 2,648. **Student Body:** Male 35%, female 65%, out-of-state 28%. **Ethnic Representation:** African American 13%, Asian 1%, Caucasian 83%, Hispanic 1%. **Retention and Graduation:** 65% freshmen return for sophomore year. 81% freshmen graduate within 4 years. 30% grads go on to further study within 1 year. 20% grads pursue business degrees. 1% grads pursue law degrees. 2% grads pursue medical degrees. **Faculty:** Student/faculty ratio 15:1. 123 full-time faculty, 78% hold PhDs. 100% faculty teach undergrads.

ACADEMICS

Degrees: Associate's, bachelor's, doctoral, first professional, master's. **Academic Requirements:** General education including some course work in arts/fine arts, computer literacy, English (including composition), foreign languages, history, mathematics, philosophy, sciences (biological or physical), social science. **Classes:** 30-39 students in an average class. 30-39 students in an average lab/discussion section. **Majors with Highest Enrollment:** Nursing/registered nurse training (RN, ASN, BSN, MSN); business administration/management; political science and government, general. **Disciplines with Highest Percentage of Degrees Awarded:** Business/marketing 36%, social sciences and history 21%, health professions and related sciences 12%, psychology 4%, philosophy/religion/theology 3%. **Special Study Options:** Cooperative (work-study) program, double major, dual enrollment, honors program, internships, study abroad, teacher certification program.

FACILITIES

Housing: All-female, all-male, apartments for single students, housing for disabled students, housing for honor students. **Library Holdings:** 200,333 bound volumes. 885 periodicals. 528,980 microforms. 8,587 audiovisuals. **Special Academic Facilities/Equipment:** Williams Observatory, Millennium Playhouse. **Computers:** School-owned computers available for student use.

EXTRACURRICULARS

Activities: Choral groups, concert band, drama/theater, jazz band, literary magazine, music ensembles, musical theater, pep band, radio station, student government, student newspaper, symphony orchestra, television station, yearbook. **Organizations:** 30 registered organizations, 8 honor societies, 3 religious organizations. **Athletics (Intercollegiate):** *Men:* baseball, basketball, cheerleading, cross-country, football, golf, soccer, tennis, track & field, wrestling. *Women:* basketball, cheerleading, cross-country, golf, soccer, softball, swimming, tennis, track & field, volleyball.

ADMISSIONS

Selectivity Rating: 80 (of 100). **Freshman Academic Profile:** Average high school GPA 3.4. 23% in top 10% of high school class, 50% in top 25% of high school class, 80% in top 50% of high school class. 80% from public high schools. Average SAT I Math 515, SAT I Math middle 50% range 450-570. Average SAT I Verbal 525, SAT I Verbal middle 50% range 450-570. Average ACT 22, ACT middle 50% range 18-24. TOEFL required of all international applicants, minimum TOEFL 500. **Basis for Candidate Selection:** *Very important factors considered include:* secondary school record. *Important factors considered include:* class rank, interview, recommendations, standardized test scores. *Other factors considered include:* essays, extracurricular activities, talent/ability, volunteer work. **Freshman Admission Requirements:** High school diploma or GED is required. *Academic units required/recommended:* 4 English required, 4 English recommended, 2 math required, 2 math recommended, 2 science required, 2 science recommended, 2 foreign language required, 2 foreign language recommended, 2 social studies required, 2 social studies recommended, 1 history required, 1 history recommended. **Freshman Admission Statistics:** 1,805 applied, 76% accepted, 30% of those accepted enrolled. **Transfer Admission Requirements:** *Items required:* college transcript, statement of good standing from prior school. Minimum college GPA of 2.0 required. Lowest grade transferable C. **General Admission Information:** Application fee $25. Nonfall registration accepted. Admission may be deferred. Credit and/or placement offered for CEEB Advanced Placement tests.

COSTS AND FINANCIAL AID

Tuition $13,220. Room & board $2,540. Required fees $2,440. Average book expense $275. **Required Forms and Deadlines:** FAFSA. No deadline for regular filing. **Notification of Awards:** Applicants will be notified of awards on or about March 15. **Types of Aid:** *Need-based scholarships/grants:* Pell, SEOG, state scholarships/grants, private scholarships. *Loans:* Direct Subsidized Stafford, Direct Unsubsidized Stafford, Direct PLUS, FFEL Subsidized Stafford, FFEL PLUS, Federal Perkins. **Student Employment:** Federal Work-Study Program available. Institutional employment available. Off-campus job opportunities are good. **Financial Aid Statistics:** 74% freshmen, 67% undergrads receive some form of aid. **Financial Aid Phone:** 800-253-6472.

GENEVA COLLEGE

3200 College Avenue, Beaver Falls, PA 15010
Phone: 724-847-6500 **E-mail:** admissions@geneva.edu **CEEB Code:** 2273
Fax: 724-847-6776 **Web:** www.geneva.edu **ACT Code:** 33578

This private school, which is affiliated with the Presbyterian Church, was founded in 1848. It has a 55-acre campus.

STUDENTS AND FACULTY

Enrollment: 1,763. **Student Body:** Male 44%, female 56%, out-of-state 26%, international 1% (18 countries represented). **Ethnic Representation:** African American 5%, Caucasian 93%, Hispanic 1%. **Retention and Graduation:** 76% freshmen return for sophomore year. 44% freshmen graduate within 4 years. 14% grads go on to further study within 1 year. 1% grads pursue business degrees. 1% grads pursue law degrees. 4% grads pursue medical degrees. **Faculty:** Student/faculty ratio 17:1. 74 full-time faculty, 77% hold PhDs. 100% faculty teach undergrads.

ACADEMICS

Degrees: Associate's, bachelor's, master's. **Academic Requirements:** General education including some course work in arts/fine arts, English (including composition), humanities, sciences (biological or physical), social science. **Majors with Highest Enrollment:** Business/commerce, general; elementary education and teaching; biology/biological sciences, general. **Disciplines with Highest Percentage of Degrees Awarded:** Business/marketing 38%, philosophy/religion/theology 15%, education 8%, protective services/public administration 6%, engineering/engineering technology 4%. **Special Study Options:** Accelerated program, cooperative (work-study) program, cross registration, double major, dual enrollment, honors program, independent study, internships, student-designed major, study abroad, teacher certification program.

FACILITIES

Housing: All-female, all-male, apartments for married students, small houses. **Library Holdings:** 165,442 bound volumes. 937 periodicals. 187,632 microforms. 24,393 audiovisuals. **Special Academic Facilities/Equipment:** Center for technology development. **Computers:** School-owned computers available for student use.

EXTRACURRICULARS

Activities: Choral groups, concert band, dance, drama/theater, jazz band, literary magazine, marching band, music ensembles, pep band, radio station, student government, student newspaper, yearbook. **Organizations:** 50 registered organizations, 2 honor societies, 12 religious organizations. **Athletics (Intercollegiate):** *Men:* baseball, basketball, cross-country, football, indoor track, soccer, track & field. *Women:* basketball, cheerleading, cross-country, indoor track, soccer, softball, tennis, track & field, volleyball.

ADMISSIONS

Selectivity Rating: 69 (of 100). **Freshman Academic Profile:** Average high school GPA 3.2. 12% in top 10% of high school class, 22% in top 25% of high school class, 27% in top 50% of high school class. 90% from public high schools. Average SAT I Math 529, SAT I Math middle 50% range 470-530. Average SAT I Verbal 540, SAT I Verbal middle 50% range 480-540. Average ACT 22, ACT middle 50% range 19-25. TOEFL required of all international applicants, minimum TOEFL 480. **Basis for Candidate Selection:** *Very important factors considered include:* essays, recommendations, secondary school record, standardized test scores. *Other factors considered include:* alumni/ae relation, character/personal qualities, class rank, extracurricular activities, interview, minority status. **Freshman Admission Requirements:** High school diploma or GED is required. *Academic units required/recommended:* 16 total required; 4 English required, 2 math required, 1 science required, 2 foreign language required, 3 social studies required, 4 elective required. **Freshman Admission Statistics:** 1,058 applied, 81% accepted, 43% of those accepted enrolled. **Transfer Admission Requirements:** *Items required:* college transcript, essay, statement of good standing from prior school. Minimum college GPA of 2.0 required. Lowest grade transferable D. **General Admission Information:** Application fee $25. Nonfall registration accepted. Admission may be deferred for a maximum of 3 years. Credit and/or placement offered for CEEB Advanced Placement tests.

COSTS AND FINANCIAL AID

Tuition $14,270. Room & board $6,130. Required fees $490. Average book expense $700. **Required Forms and Deadlines:** FAFSA. Priority filing deadline March 15. **Notification of Awards:** Applicants will be notified of awards on a rolling basis beginning on or about March 1. **Types of Aid:** *Need-based scholarships/grants:* Pell, SEOG, state scholarships/grants, private scholarships, the school's own gift aid, FSEOG. *Loans:* FFEL Subsidized Stafford, FFEL Unsubsidized Stafford, FFEL PLUS, Federal Perkins. **Student Employment:** Federal Work-Study Program available. Institutional employment available. Off-campus job opportunities are fair. **Financial Aid Statistics:** 80% freshmen, 83% undergrads receive some form of aid. Average freshman grant $5,000. Average freshman loan $3,600. Average income from on-campus job $1,000. **Financial Aid Phone:** 724-847-6530.

GEORGE FOX UNIVERSITY

414 N. Meridian, Newberg, OR 97132
Phone: 503-554-2240 **E-mail:** admissions@georgefox.edu **CEEB Code:** 4325
Fax: 503-554-3110 **Web:** www.georgefox.edu **ACT Code:** 3462

This private school, which is affiliated with the Quaker Church, was founded in 1891. It has a 75-acre campus.

STUDENTS AND FACULTY

Enrollment: 1,709. **Student Body:** Male 41%, female 59%, out-of-state 37%, international 3%. **Ethnic Representation:** African American 1%, Asian 2%, Caucasian 93%, Hispanic 3%, Native American 1%. **Retention and Graduation:** 83% freshmen return for sophomore year. 49% freshmen graduate within 4 years. **Faculty:** Student/faculty ratio 14:1. 119 full-time faculty, 68% hold PhDs. 79% faculty teach undergrads.

ACADEMICS

Degrees: Bachelor's, diploma, doctoral, first professional, master's. **Academic Requirements:** General education including some course work in arts/fine arts, English (including composition), history, humanities, mathematics, sciences (biological or physical), social science, Bible/religion, globalization. **Classes:** 20-29 students in an average class. **Disciplines with Highest Percentage of Degrees Awarded:** Business/marketing 50%, education 8%, psychology 5%, philosophy/religion/theology 5%, communications/communication technologies 4%. **Special Study Options:** Accelerated program, cooperative (work-study) program, cross registration, double major, dual enrollment, English as a second language, student exchange program (domestic), external degree program, honors program, independent study, internships, liberal arts/career combination, student-designed major, study abroad, teacher certification program. Undergrads may take grad-level classes. Off-campus study: Washington, DC; Los Angeles Film Institute (California); Fashion Institute of Merchandising and Design, Au Sable Environmental Studies Institute (Michigan). Co-op programs: engineering.

FACILITIES

Housing: All-female, all-male, apartments for married students, apartments for single students, 16 university-owned houses for upper-class students. **Library Holdings:** 123,734 bound volumes. 1,323 periodicals. 207,180 microforms. 2,687 audiovisuals. **Special Academic Facilities/Equipment:** Quaker museum, language lab, electron microscope. **Computers:** School-owned computers available for student use.

EXTRACURRICULARS

Activities: Choral groups, concert band, dance, drama/theater, jazz band, literary magazine, music ensembles, musical theater, pep band, radio station, student government, student newspaper, symphony orchestra, television station, yearbook. **Organizations:** 25 registered organizations, 4 honor societies, 3 religious organizations. **Athletics (Intercollegiate):** *Men:* baseball, basketball, cross-country, soccer, tennis, track & field. *Women:* basketball, cross-country, soccer, softball, tennis, track & field, volleyball.

ADMISSIONS

Selectivity Rating: 67 (of 100). **Freshman Academic Profile:** Average high school GPA 3.6. 31% in top 10% of high school class, 62% in top 25% of high school class, 88% in top 50% of high school class. 80% from public high schools. Average SAT I Math 566, SAT I Math middle 50% range 500-620. Average SAT I Verbal 577, SAT I Verbal middle 50% range 510-640. Average ACT 25, ACT middle 50% range 23-27. TOEFL required of all international applicants, minimum TOEFL 550. **Basis for Candidate Selection:** *Very important factors considered include:* secondary school record, standardized test scores. *Important factors considered include:* character/personal qualities, essays, extracurricular activities, interview, minority status, recommendations, religious affiliation/commitment, talent/ability. *Other factors considered include:* alumni/ae relation, geographical residence, state residency, volunteer work, work experience. **Freshman Admission Requirements:** High school diploma or GED is required. *Academic units required/recommended:* 16 total recommended; 4 English recommended, 2 math recommended, 2 science recommended, 2 foreign language recommended, 2 social studies recommended, 3 elective recommended. **Freshman Admission Statistics:** 852 applied, 90% accepted, 48% of those accepted enrolled. **Transfer Admission Requirements:** *Items required:* college transcript, essay, statement of good standing from prior school. Minimum college GPA of 2.3 required. Lowest grade transferable C. **General Admission Information:** Application fee $40. Priority application deadline February 1. Regular application deadline June 1. Nonfall registration accepted. Admission may be deferred for a maximum of 2 years. Credit and/or placement offered for CEEB Advanced Placement tests.

COSTS AND FINANCIAL AID

Tuition $18,000. Room & board $5,770. Required fees $325. Average book expense $600. **Required Forms and Deadlines:** FAFSA and state aid form. Financial aid filing deadline June 15. Priority filing deadline February 1. **Notification of Awards:** Applicants will be notified of awards on a rolling basis beginning on or about February 1. **Types of Aid:** *Need-based scholarships/grants:* Pell, SEOG, state scholarships/grants, private scholarships, the school's own gift aid. *Loans:* Direct Subsidized Stafford, Direct Unsubsidized Stafford, Direct PLUS, FFEL Subsidized Stafford, FFEL Unsubsidized Stafford, FFEL PLUS, Federal Perkins. **Student Employment:** Federal Work-Study Program available. Institutional employment available. Off-campus job opportunities are excellent. **Financial Aid Statistics:** 78% freshmen, 76% undergrads receive some form of aid. Average freshman grant $10,870. Average freshman loan $2,572. **Financial Aid Phone:** 503-554-2230.

GEORGE MASON UNIVERSITY

Undergraduate Admissions Office, 4400 Univ. Drive MSN 3A4, Fairfax, VA 22030-4444
Phone: 703-993-2400 **E-mail:** admissions@gmu.edu **CEEB Code:** 5827
Fax: 703-993-2392 **Web:** www.gmu.edu **ACT Code:** 4357

This public school was founded in 1957. It has a 667-acre campus.

STUDENTS AND FACULTY

Enrollment: 15,802. **Student Body:** Male 44%, female 56%, out-of-state 10%, international 4%. **Ethnic Representation:** African American 10%, Asian 17%, Caucasian 65%, Hispanic 8%. **Retention and Graduation:** 79% freshmen return for sophomore year. 26% freshmen graduate within 4 years. **Faculty:** Student/faculty ratio 16:1. 847 full-time faculty, 84% hold PhDs. 82% faculty teach undergrads.

ACADEMICS

Degrees: Bachelor's, doctoral, first professional, master's, post-bachelor's certificate. **Academic Requirements:** General education including some course work in arts/fine arts, computer literacy, English (including composition), foreign languages, history, humanities, mathematics, philosophy, sciences (biological or physical), social science. **Classes:** 20-29 students in an average class. 10-19 students in an average lab/discussion section. **Majors with Highest Enrollment:** Business, management, marketing, and related support services; political science and government, general; computer science. **Disciplines with Highest Percentage of Degrees Awarded:** Business/marketing 23%, social sciences and history 13%, interdisciplinary studies 9%, communications/communication technologies 8%, psychology 8%. **Special Study Options:** Accelerated program, cooperative (work-study) program, cross registration, distance learning, double major, dual enrollment, English as a second language, student exchange program (domestic), external degree program, honors program, independent study, internships, liberal arts/career combination, student-designed major, study abroad, teacher certification program.

FACILITIES

Housing: Coed, all-female, all-male, apartments for single students, housing for disabled students. **Library Holdings:** 1,311,854 bound volumes. 11,533 periodicals. 2,566,724 microforms. 24,771 audiovisuals. **Special Academic Facilities/Equipment:** Arts center, science/technology building, television studio. **Computers:** School-owned computers available for student use.

EXTRACURRICULARS

Activities: Choral groups, concert band, dance, drama/theater, jazz band, literary magazine, music ensembles, musical theater, opera, pep band, radio station, student government, student newspaper, student-run film society, symphony orchestra, television station, yearbook. **Organizations:** 255 registered organizations, 18 fraternities (3% men join), 10 sororities (3% women join). **Athletics (Intercollegiate):** *Men:* baseball, basketball, cross-country, diving, golf, indoor track, rifle, soccer, swimming, tennis, track & field, volleyball, wrestling. *Women:* basketball, cross-country, diving, indoor track, lacrosse, rifle, soccer, softball, swimming, tennis, track & field, volleyball.

ADMISSIONS

Selectivity Rating: 85 (of 100). **Freshman Academic Profile:** Average high school GPA 3.2. Average SAT I Math 542, SAT I Math middle 50% range 490-590. Average SAT I Verbal 534, SAT I Verbal middle 50% range 480-580. ACT middle 50% range 19-23. TOEFL required of all international applicants, minimum TOEFL 570. **Basis for Candidate Selection:** *Very important factors considered include:* secondary school record. *Important factors considered include:* character/personal qualities, essays, recommendations, standardized test scores, talent/ability. *Other factors considered include:* alumni/ae relation, class rank, extracurricular activities, geographical residence, interview, minority status, state residency, volunteer work, work experience. **Freshman Admission Requirements:** High school diploma or GED is required. *Academic units required/recommended:* 18 total required; 24 total recommended; 4 English required, 4 English recommended, 3 math required, 4 math recommended, 3 science required, 4 science recommended, 3 science lab required, 4 science lab recommended, 2 foreign language required, 3 foreign language recommended, 3 social studies required, 4 social studies recommended, 3 elective required, 5 elective recommended. **Freshman Admission Statistics:** 8,106 applied, 68% accepted, 39% of those accepted enrolled. **Transfer Admission Requirements:** *Items required:* college transcript. Minimum college GPA of 2.0 required. Lowest grade transferable C. **General Admission Information:** Application fee $35. Regular application deadline February 1. Nonfall registration accepted. Admission may be deferred for a maximum of 1 year. Credit and/or placement offered for CEEB Advanced Placement tests.

COSTS AND FINANCIAL AID

In-state tuition $2,376. Out-of-state tuition $11,220. Room & board $5,400. Required fees $1,416. Average book expense $750. **Required Forms and Deadlines:** FAFSA. Priority filing deadline March 1. **Notification of Awards:** Applicants will be notified of awards on a rolling basis beginning on or about April 1. **Types of Aid:** *Need-based scholarships/grants:* Pell, SEOG, state scholarships/grants, private scholarships, the school's own gift aid. *Loans:* Direct Subsidized Stafford, Direct Unsubsidized Stafford, Direct PLUS, Federal Perkins. **Student Employment:** Federal Work-Study Program available. Institutional employment available. Off-campus job opportunities are excellent. **Financial Aid Statistics:** 37% freshmen, 40% undergrads receive some form of aid. Average freshman grant $3,756. Average freshman loan $6,222. Average income from on-campus job $9,000. **Financial Aid Phone:** 703-993-2353.

THE GEORGE WASHINGTON UNIVERSITY

2121 I Street NW, Suite 201, Washington, DC 20052
Phone: 202-994-6040 **E-mail:** gwadm@gwu.edu **CEEB Code:** 5246
Fax: 202-994-0325 **Web:** www.gwu.edu **ACT Code:** 664

This private school was founded in 1821. It has a 45-acre campus.

STUDENTS AND FACULTY

Enrollment: 10,063. **Student Body:** Male 44%, female 56%, out-of-state 94%, international 5% (101 country represented). **Ethnic Representation:** African American 6%, Asian 11%, Caucasian 68%, Hispanic 5%. **Retention and Graduation:** 92% freshmen return for sophomore year. 66% freshmen graduate within 4 years. 19% grads go on to further study within 1 year. 2% grads pursue business degrees. 6% grads pursue law degrees. 4% grads pursue medical degrees. **Faculty:** Student/faculty ratio 14:1. 787 full-time faculty, 90% hold PhDs. 67% faculty teach undergrads.

ACADEMICS

Degrees: Associate's, bachelor's, certificate, doctoral, first professional, master's, post-bachelor's certificate, post-master's certificate. **Academic Requirements:** General education including some course work in English (including composition), humanities, mathematics, sciences (biological or physical), social science. **Classes:** 10-19 students in an average class. 20-29 students in an average lab/discussion section. **Disciplines with Highest Percentage of Degrees Awarded:** Social sciences and history 32%, business/marketing 16%, psychology 8%, English 7%, engineering/engineering technology 4%. **Special Study Options:** Accelerated program, cooperative (work-study) program, cross registration, distance learning, double major, dual enrollment, English as a second language, honors program, independent study, internships, liberal arts/career combination, student-designed major, study abroad.

FACILITIES

Housing: Coed, all-female, apartments for single students, fraternities and/or sororities. We accommodate disabled students. **Library Holdings:** 1,984,094 bound volumes. 15,365 periodicals. 2,615,141 microforms. 171,397 audiovisuals. **Special Academic Facilities/Equipment:** Art gallery, language lab, word processing center. **Computers:** School-owned computers available for student use.

EXTRACURRICULARS

Activities: Choral groups, concert band, dance, drama/theater, jazz band, literary magazine, marching band, music ensembles, musical theater, pep band, radio station, student government, student newspaper, student-run film society, television station, yearbook. **Organizations:** 220 registered organizations, 3 honor societies, 5 religious organizations, 12 fraternities (14% men join), 9 sororities (11% women join). **Athletics (Intercollegiate):** *Men:* baseball, basketball, crew, cross-country, diving, fencing, golf, rugby, soccer, squash, swimming, tennis, water polo. *Women:* basketball, crew, cross-country, fencing, gymnastics, soccer, swimming, tennis, volleyball.

ADMISSIONS

Selectivity Rating: 91 (of 100). **Freshman Academic Profile:** 46% in top 10% of high school class, 83% in top 25% of high school class, 99% in top 50% of high school class. 70% from public high schools. Average SAT I Math 620, SAT I Math middle 50% range 580-670. Average SAT I Verbal 620, SAT I Verbal middle 50% range 570-660. Average ACT 26, ACT middle 50% range 24-29. TOEFL required of all international applicants, minimum TOEFL 550. **Basis for Candidate Selection:** *Very important factors considered include:* secondary school record. *Important factors considered include:* class rank, essays, extracurricular activities, interview, recommendations, standardized test scores, talent/ability, volunteer work. *Other factors considered include:* alumni/ae relation, character/personal qualities, geographical residence, minority status, work experience. **Freshman Admission Requirements:** High school diploma is required and GED is not accepted. *Academic units required/recommended:* 4 English required, 4 English recommended, 2 math required, 4 math recommended, 2 science required, 4 science recommended, 1 science lab required, 2 foreign language required, 4 foreign language recommended, 2 social studies required, 4 social studies recommended. **Freshman Admission Statistics:** 15,960 applied, 48% accepted, 33% of those accepted enrolled. **Transfer Admission Requirements:** *Items required:* high school transcript, college transcript, essay, standardized test scores. Lowest grade transferable C-. **General Admission Information:** Application fee $60. Priority application deadline December 1. Early decision application deadline December 1. Regular application deadline January 15. Nonfall registration accepted. Admission may be deferred for a maximum of 1 year. Credit and/or placement offered for CEEB Advanced Placement tests.

COSTS AND FINANCIAL AID

Tuition $27,790. Room & board $9,110. Required fees $30. Average book expense $850. **Required Forms and Deadlines:** FAFSA and CSS/Financial Aid PROFILE. Priority filing deadline January 31. **Notification of Awards:** Applicants will be notified of awards on or about March 20. **Types of Aid:** *Need-based scholarships/grants:* Pell, SEOG, state scholarships/grants, the school's own gift aid. *Loans:* FFEL Subsidized Stafford, FFEL Unsubsidized Stafford, FFEL PLUS, Federal Perkins. **Student Employment:** Federal Work-Study Program available. Institutional employment available. Off-campus job opportunities are excellent. **Financial Aid Statistics:** 41% freshmen, 38% undergrads receive some form of aid. Average freshman grant $11,800. Average freshman loan $3,000. Average income from on-campus job $3,160. **Financial Aid Phone:** 202-994-6620.

GEORGETOWN COLLEGE

400 East College Street, Georgetown, KY 40324
Phone: 502-863-8009 **E-mail:** admissions@georgetowncollege.edu **CEEB Code:** 1249
Fax: 502-868-7733 **Web:** www.georgetowncollege.edu **ACT Code:** 1514

This private school, which is affiliated with the Baptist Church, was founded in 1787. It has a 104-acre campus.

STUDENTS AND FACULTY

Enrollment: 1,290. **Student Body:** Male 43%, female 57%, out-of-state 18%, international 2% (13 countries represented). **Ethnic Representation:** African American 3%, Caucasian 97%. **Retention and Graduation:** 78% freshmen return for sophomore year. 40% freshmen graduate within 4 years. 55% grads go on to further study within 1 year. 5% grads pursue business degrees. 20% grads pursue law degrees. 20% grads pursue medical degrees. **Faculty:** Student/faculty ratio 12:1. 92 full-time faculty, 91% hold PhDs. 100% faculty teach undergrads.

ACADEMICS

Degrees: Bachelor's, master's. **Academic Requirements:** General education including some course work in arts/fine arts, computer literacy, English (including composition), foreign languages, history, humanities, mathematics, philosophy, sciences (biological or physical), social science. **Classes:** 20-29 students in an average class. **Majors with Highest Enrollment:** Biology/biological sciences, general; psychology, general; elementary education and teaching. **Disciplines with Highest Percentage of Degrees Awarded:** Business/marketing 21%, visual and performing arts 18%, psychology 15%, biological life sciences 13%, education 8%. **Special Study Options:** Cooperative (work-study) program, double major, dual enrollment, honors program, independent study, internships, liberal arts/career combination, student-designed major, study abroad, teacher certification program.

FACILITIES

Housing: All-female, all-male, fraternities and/or sororities, apartments for upperclassmen. **Library Holdings:** 152,531 bound volumes. 733 periodicals. 177,421 microforms. 4,064 audiovisuals. **Computers:** School-owned computers available for student use.

EXTRACURRICULARS

Activities: Choral groups, concert band, dance, drama/theater, literary magazine, music ensembles, pep band, radio station, student government, student newspaper, yearbook. **Organizations:** 110 registered organizations, 18 honor societies, 8 religious organizations, 5 fraternities (28% men join), 4 sororities (40% women join). **Athletics (Intercollegiate):** *Men:* baseball, basketball, cross-country, football, golf, soccer, tennis. *Women:* basketball, cheerleading, cross-country, golf, soccer, tennis, volleyball.

ADMISSIONS

Selectivity Rating: 76 (of 100). **Freshman Academic Profile:** Average high school GPA 3.5. 32% in top 10% of high school class, 64% in top 25% of high school class, 91% in top 50% of high school class. 87% from public high schools. Average SAT I Math 540, SAT I Math middle 50% range 480-610. Average SAT I Verbal 540, SAT I Verbal middle 50% range 470-610. Average ACT 24, ACT middle 50% range 21-26. TOEFL required of all international applicants, minimum TOEFL 520. **Basis for Candidate Selection:** *Very important factors considered include:* essays, secondary school record. *Important factors considered include:* character/personal qualities, class rank, extracurricular activities, recommendations, standardized test scores, talent/ability. *Other factors considered include:* alumni/ae relation, geographical residence, interview, minority status, religious affiliation/commitment, state residency, volunteer work. **Freshman Admission Requirements:** High school diploma or GED is required. *Academic units required/recommended:* 20 total recommended; 4 English recommended, 3 math recommended, 3 science recommended, 2 foreign language recommended, 2 social studies recommended. **Freshman Admission Statistics:** 810 applied, 93% accepted, 43% of those accepted enrolled. **Transfer Admission Requirements:** *Items required:* high school transcript, college transcript, essay, statement of good standing from prior school. Minimum high school GPA of 2.5 required. Minimum college GPA of 2.5 required. Lowest grade transferable C. **General Admission Information:** Application fee $30. Early decision application deadline November 15. Nonfall registration accepted. Admission may be deferred for a maximum of 1 year. Credit and/or placement offered for CEEB Advanced Placement tests.

COSTS AND FINANCIAL AID

Tuition $15,260. Room & board $5,180. Required fees $680. Average book expense $650. **Required Forms and Deadlines:** FAFSA. No deadline for regular filing. Priority filing deadline February 15. **Notification of Awards:** Applicants will be notified of awards on a rolling basis beginning on or about March 15. **Types of Aid:** *Need-based scholarships/grants:* Pell, SEOG, state scholarships/grants, private scholarships, the school's own gift aid. *Loans:* FFEL Subsidized Stafford, FFEL Unsubsidized Stafford, FFEL PLUS, Federal Perkins, college/university loans from institutional funds. **Student Employment:** Federal Work-Study Program available. Institutional employment available. Off-campus job opportunities are good. **Financial Aid Statistics:** 67% freshmen, 64% undergrads receive some form of aid. Average freshman grant $10,581. Average freshman loan $2,629. Average income from on-campus job $1,100. **Financial Aid Phone:** 502-863-8027.

GEORGETOWN UNIVERSITY

37th and P Streets, NW, Washington, DC 20057
Phone: 202-687-3600 **E-mail:** @georgetown.edu **CEEB Code:** 5244
Fax: 202-687-5084 **Web:** www.georgetown.edu **ACT Code:** 668

This private school, which is affiliated with the Roman Catholic Church, was founded in 1789. It has a 110-acre campus.

STUDENTS AND FACULTY

Enrollment: 6,332. **Student Body:** Male 47%, female 53%, out-of-state 98%, international 4%. **Ethnic Representation:** African American 7%, Asian 10%, Caucasian 74%, Hispanic 5%. **Retention and Graduation:** 97% freshmen return for sophomore year. 89% freshmen graduate within 4 years. 24% grads go on to further study within 1 year. 3% grads pursue business degrees. 9% grads pursue law degrees. 4% grads pursue medical degrees. **Faculty:** Student/faculty ratio 11:1. 639 full-time faculty, 93% hold PhDs. 100% faculty teach undergrads.

ACADEMICS

Degrees: Bachelor's, certificate, doctoral, first professional, master's. **Academic Requirements:** General education including some course work in English (including composition), philosophy, social science, theology. **Classes:** 10-19 students in an average class. 10-19 students in an average lab/discussion section. **Majors with Highest Enrollment:** Finance, general; English language and literature, general; international relations and affairs. **Disciplines with Highest Percentage of Degrees Awarded:** Social sciences and history 36%, business/marketing 21%, English 11%, foreign languages and literature 8%, psychology 6%. **Special Study Options:** Cross registration, double major, English as a second language, honors program, independent study, internships, student-designed major, study abroad.

FACILITIES

Housing: Coed, apartments for single students, housing for disabled students. Freshmen and sophomores are required to live on campus. **Library Holdings:** 2,234,338 bound volumes. 21,901 periodicals. 3,598,609 microforms. 15,730 audiovisuals. **Special Academic Facilities/Equipment:** Language lab, seismological observatory. **Computers:** School-owned computers available for student use.

EXTRACURRICULARS

Activities: Choral groups, concert band, dance, drama/theater, jazz band, literary magazine, music ensembles, musical theater, pep band, radio station, student government, student newspaper, student-run film society, symphony orchestra, television station, yearbook. **Organizations:** 133 registered organizations, 14 honor societies, 17 religious organizations. **Athletics (Intercollegiate):** *Men:* baseball, basketball, crew, cross-country, diving, football, golf, indoor track, lacrosse, sailing, soccer, swimming, tennis, track & field. *Women:* basketball, crew, cross-country, diving, field hockey, indoor track, lacrosse, sailing, soccer, swimming, tennis, track & field, volleyball.

ADMISSIONS

Selectivity Rating: 99 (of 100). **Freshman Academic Profile:** 80% in top 10% of high school class, 94% in top 25% of high school class, 99% in top 50% of high school class. 46% from public high schools. SAT I Math middle 50% range 640-730. SAT I Verbal middle 50% range 640-730. ACT middle 50% range 27-32. TOEFL required of all international applicants, minimum TOEFL 550. **Basis for Candidate Selection:** *Very important factors considered include:* character/personal qualities, class rank, essays, recommendations, secondary school record, standardized test scores, talent/ability. *Important factors considered include:* extracurricular activities, interview, volunteer work. *Other factors considered include:* alumni/ae relation, geographical residence, minority status, state residency, work experience. **Freshman Admission Requirements:** High school diploma or GED is required. *Academic units required/recommended:* 4 English required, 4 English recommended, 2 math required, 4 math recommended, 2 science required, 4 science recommended, 1 science lab recommended, 2 foreign language required, 4 foreign language recommended, 2 social studies required, 4 social studies recommended. **Freshman Admission Statistics:** 15,536 applied, 21% accepted, 46% of those accepted enrolled. **Transfer Admission Requirements:** *Items required:* high school transcript, college transcript, essay, standardized test scores, statement of good standing from prior school. Minimum college GPA of 3.0 required. Lowest grade transferable C. **General Admission Information:** Application fee $60. Regular application deadline January 10. Admission may be deferred for a maximum of 1 year. Credit and/or placement offered for CEEB Advanced Placement tests.

COSTS AND FINANCIAL AID

Tuition $26,544. Room & board $9,692. Required fees $309. Average book expense $940. **Required Forms and Deadlines:** FAFSA, CSS/Financial Aid PROFILE, state aid form, noncustodial (divorced/separated) parent's statement, and business/farm supplement. Priority filing deadline February 1. **Notification of Awards:** Applicants will be notified of awards on or about April 1. **Types of Aid:** *Need-based scholarships/grants:* Pell, SEOG, state scholarships/grants, private scholarships, the school's own gift aid, ROTC. *Loans:* FFEL Subsidized Stafford, FFEL Unsubsidized Stafford, FFEL PLUS, Federal Perkins, Federal Nursing. **Student Employment:** Federal Work-Study Program available. Institutional employment available. Off-campus job opportunities are excellent. **Financial Aid Statistics:** 41% freshmen, 41% undergrads receive some form of aid. Average freshman grant $16,300. Average freshman loan $2,250. Average income from on-campus job $3,745. **Financial Aid Phone:** 202-687-4547.

GEORGIA COLLEGE & STATE UNIVERSITY

Campus Box 23, Milledgeville, GA 31061
Phone: 478-445-5004 **E-mail:** gcsu@mail.gcsu.edu **CEEB Code:** 5252
Fax: 478-445-1914 **Web:** www.gcsu.edu **ACT Code:** 828

This public school was founded in 1889. It has a 696-acre campus.

STUDENTS AND FACULTY

Enrollment: 4,444. **Student Body:** Male 39%, female 61%, international 2%. **Ethnic Representation:** African American 12%, Asian 1%, Caucasian 85%, Hispanic 1%. **Retention and Graduation:** 77% freshmen return for sophomore year. 11% freshmen graduate within 4 years. **Faculty:** Student/faculty ratio 14:1. 271 full-time faculty, 76% hold PhDs. 100% faculty teach undergrads.

ACADEMICS

Degrees: Bachelor's, master's, post-master's certificate. **Academic Requirements:** General education including some course work in arts/fine arts, English (including composition), foreign languages, history, humanities, mathematics, sciences (biological or physical), social science. **Classes:** 20-29 students in an average class. 20-29 students in an average lab/discussion section. **Disciplines with Highest Percentage of Degrees Awarded:** Education 36%, business/marketing 26%, health professions and related sciences 10%, protective services/public administration 7%, psychology 5%. **Special Study Options:** Accelerated program, distance learning, double major, English as a second language, external degree program, honors program, independent study, internships, student-designed major, study abroad, teacher certification program.

FACILITIES

Housing: Coed, all-female, all-male, apartments for single students. **Library Holdings:** 156,738 bound volumes. 1,080 periodicals. 637,557 microforms. 4,586 audiovisuals. **Special Academic Facilities/Equipment:** Education archives museum, old governor's mansion. **Computers:** School-owned computers available for student use.

EXTRACURRICULARS

Activities: Choral groups, concert band, dance, drama/theater, jazz band, literary magazine, music ensembles, musical theater, pep band, radio station, student government, student newspaper, television station. **Organizations:** 85 registered organizations, 10 honor societies, 7 religious organizations, 6 fraternities, 7 sororities. **Athletics (Intercollegiate):** *Men:* baseball, basketball, cheerleading, cross-country, golf, tennis. *Women:* basketball, cheerleading, cross-country, softball, tennis.

ADMISSIONS

Selectivity Rating: 63 (of 100). **Freshman Academic Profile:** Average high school GPA 3.1. Average SAT I Math 527, SAT I Math middle 50% range 490-565. Average SAT I Verbal 534, SAT I Verbal middle 50% range 490-570. Average ACT 22, ACT middle 50% range 20-23. TOEFL required of all international applicants, minimum TOEFL 500. **Basis for Candidate Selection:** *Very important factors considered include:* secondary school record, standardized test scores. **Freshman Admission Requirements:** High school diploma or GED is required. *Academic units required/recommended:* 16 total required; 4 English required, 4 math required, 3 science required, 2 science lab required, 2 foreign language required, 3 social studies required. **Freshman Admission Statistics:** 2,700 applied, 68% accepted, 50% of those accepted enrolled. **Transfer Admission Requirements:** *Items required:* college transcript, statement of good standing from prior school. Minimum high school GPA of 2.0 required. Minimum college GPA of 2.0 required. Lowest grade transferable D. **General Admission Information:** Application fee $25. Regular application deadline July 15. Nonfall registration accepted. Admission may be deferred for a maximum of 1 year. Credit offered for CEEB Advanced Placement tests.

COSTS AND FINANCIAL AID

In-state tuition $1,808. Out-of-state tuition $7,232. Room & board $4,170. Required fees $406. Average book expense $600. **Required Forms and Deadlines:** FAFSA and institution's own financial aid form. No deadline for regular filing. Priority filing deadline March 1. **Notification of Awards:** Applicants will be notified of awards on a rolling basis beginning on or about April 1. **Types of Aid:** *Need-based scholarships/grants:* Pell, SEOG, state scholarships/grants, the school's own gift aid. *Loans:* Direct Subsidized Stafford, Direct Unsubsidized Stafford, Direct PLUS, Federal Perkins, state loans, college/university loans from institutional funds. **Student Employment:** Federal Work-Study Program available. Institutional employment available. Off-campus job opportunities are good. **Financial Aid Statistics:** 61% freshmen, 36% undergrads receive some form of aid. **Financial Aid Phone:** 478-445-5149.

GEORGIA INSTITUTE OF TECHNOLOGY

Office of Undergrad Admission, 219 Uncle Heine Way, Atlanta, GA 30332-0320
Phone: 404-894-4154 **E-mail:** admission@gatech.edu **CEEB Code:** 5248
Fax: 404-894-9511 **Web:** www.gatech.edu **ACT Code:** 818

This public school was founded in 1885. It has a 330-acre campus.

STUDENTS AND FACULTY

Enrollment: 11,043. **Student Body:** Male 71%, female 29%, out-of-state 32%, international 4%. **Ethnic Representation:** African American 8%, Asian 15%, Caucasian 74%, Hispanic 3%. **Retention and Graduation:** 90% freshmen return for sophomore year. 20% grads go on to further study within 1 year. **Faculty:** Student/faculty ratio 13:1. 748 full-time faculty, 94% hold PhDs. 100% faculty teach undergrads.

ACADEMICS

Degrees: Bachelor's, doctoral, master's. **Academic Requirements:** General education including some course work in computer literacy, English (including composition), history, humanities, mathematics, sciences (biological or physical), social science. **Classes:** 20-29 students in an average class. 10-19 students in an average lab/discussion section. **Majors with Highest Enrollment:** Mechanical engineering; electrical, electronics, and communications engineering; computer science. **Disciplines with Highest Percentage of Degrees Awarded:** Engineering/engineering technology 63%, business/marketing 13%, computer and information sciences 10%, social sciences and history 3%, physical sciences 3%. **Special Study Options:** Accelerated program, cooperative (work-study) program, cross registration, distance learning, double major, dual enrollment, English as a second language, honors program, independent study, internships, student-designed major, study abroad, teacher certification program, dual degree program (3-2) with approximately 90 liberal arts colleges and universities, Regents Engineering Transfer Program (RETP) with 11 Georgia colleges. Georgia Tech Regional Engineering Program (GTREP) offers undergraduate and graduate engineering degrees in collaboration with Armstrong Atlantic State University, Georgia Southern University, and Savannah State University.

FACILITIES

Housing: Coed, all-female, all-male, apartments for married students, apartments for single students, housing for disabled students, fraternities and/or sororities. **Library Holdings:** 4,233,606 microforms. 15,254 audiovisuals. **Special Academic Facilities/Equipment:** Advanced technology development center, research institute, oceanography institute, nuclear research center, nuclear reactor, electron microscope. **Computers:** *Recommended operating system:* Dictated by computer ownership requirements. School-owned computers available for student use.

EXTRACURRICULARS

Activities: Choral groups, concert band, dance, drama/theater, jazz band, literary magazine, marching band, music ensembles, musical theater, opera, pep band, radio station, student government, student newspaper, symphony orchestra, television station, yearbook. **Organizations:** 300 registered organizations, 26 honor societies, 26 religious organizations, 32 fraternities (29% men join), 9 sororities (20% women join). **Athletics (Intercollegiate):** *Men:* baseball, basketball, cross-country, football, golf, indoor track, swimming, tennis, track & field. *Women:* basketball, cross-country, indoor track, softball, swimming, tennis, track & field, volleyball.

ADMISSIONS

Selectivity Rating: 92 (of 100). **Freshman Academic Profile:** Average high school GPA 3.7. 82% from public high schools. Average SAT I Math 689, SAT I Math middle 50% range 650-730. Average SAT I Verbal 642, SAT I Verbal middle 50% range 600-690. TOEFL required of all international applicants, minimum TOEFL 600. **Basis for Candidate Selection:** *Very important factors considered include:* secondary school record. *Important factors considered include:* essays, extracurricular activities, standardized test scores, volunteer work, work experience. *Other factors considered include:* alumni/ae relation, state residency, talent/ability. **Freshman Admission Requirements:** High school diploma or GED is required. *Academic units required/recommended:* 20 total required; 4 English required, 4 math required, 3 science required, 4 science recommended, 2 science lab required, 2 foreign language required, 3 social studies required, 4 elective required. **Freshman Admission Statistics:** 9,476 applied, 54% accepted, 43% of those accepted enrolled. **Transfer Admission Requirements:** *Items required:* college transcript. Lowest grade transferable C. **General Admission Information:** Application fee $50. Regular application deadline January 15. Nonfall registration accepted. Credit and/or placement offered for CEEB Advanced Placement tests.

COSTS AND FINANCIAL AID

In-state tuition $2,780. Out-of-state tuition $13,160. Room & board $5,922. Required fees $826. Average book expense $1,278. **Required Forms and Deadlines:** FAFSA and institution's own financial aid form. Priority filing deadline March 1. **Notification of Awards:** Applicants will be notified of awards on or about April 1. **Types of Aid:** *Need-based scholarships/grants:* Pell, SEOG, state scholarships/grants, private scholarships, the school's own gift aid. *Loans:* FFEL Subsidized Stafford, FFEL Unsubsidized Stafford, FFEL PLUS, Federal Perkins, college/university loans from institutional funds, CitiAssist alternative loan. **Student Employment:** Federal Work-Study Program available. Institutional employment available. Off-campus job opportunities are excellent. **Financial Aid Statistics:** 31% freshmen, 20% undergrads receive some form of aid. Average freshman grant $9,876. Average freshman loan $3,395. Average income from on-campus job $3,587. **Financial Aid Phone:** 404-894-4160.

GEORGIA SOUTHERN UNIVERSITY

PO Box 8024, Statesboro, GA 30460
Phone: 912-681-5391 **E-mail:** admissions@gasou.edu **CEEB Code:** 5253
Fax: 912-486-7240 **Web:** www.gasou.edu **ACT Code:** 830

This public school was founded in 1906. It has a 634-acre campus.

STUDENTS AND FACULTY

Enrollment: 13,354. **Student Body:** Male 49%, female 51%, out-of-state 4%, international 1% (77 countries represented). **Ethnic Representation:** African American 26%, Asian 1%, Caucasian 72%, Hispanic 1%. **Retention and Graduation:** 77% freshmen return for sophomore year. 12% freshmen graduate within 4 years. **Faculty:** Student/faculty ratio 19:1. 612 full-time faculty, 76% hold PhDs. 83% faculty teach undergrads.

ACADEMICS

Degrees: Bachelor's, doctoral, master's, post-master's certificate. **Academic Requirements:** General education including some course work in arts/fine arts, computer literacy, English (including composition), history, humanities, mathematics, sciences (biological or physical), social science, physical activity, healthful living. **Classes:** 20-29 students in an average class. 20-29 students in an average lab/discussion section. **Majors with Highest Enrollment:** Nursing/registered nurse training (RN, ASN, BSN, MSN); business administration/management; biology/biological sciences, general. **Disciplines with Highest Percentage of Degrees Awarded:** Business/marketing 28%, education 15%, parks and recreation 9%, communications/communication technologies 6%, home economics and vocational home economics 6%. **Special Study Options:** Accelerated program, cooperative (work-study) program, cross registration, distance learning, double major, dual enrollment, English as a second language, honors program, independent study, internships, study abroad, teacher certification program, weekend college.

FACILITIES

Housing: Coed, all-female, all-male, apartments for single students, housing for disabled students, housing for international students, fraternities and/or sororities. **Library Holdings:** 532,722 bound volumes. 3,470 periodicals. 837,493 microforms. 29,522 audiovisuals. **Special Academic Facilities/Equipment:** Art galleries, teaching museum, raptor and wildlife center, broadcasting studios, institute of arthropodology and parasitology, planetarium, botanical garden, radio station. **Computers:** School-owned computers available for student use.

EXTRACURRICULARS

Activities: Choral groups, concert band, dance, drama/theater, jazz band, literary magazine, marching band, music ensembles, musical theater, opera, pep band, radio station, student government, student newspaper, student-run film society, symphony orchestra. **Organizations:** 152 registered organizations, 14 honor societies, 17 religious organizations, 14 fraternities (10% men join), 7 sororities (11% women join). **Athletics (Intercollegiate):** *Men:* baseball, basketball, cheerleading, football, golf, soccer, tennis. *Women:* basketball, cheerleading, cross-country, diving, soccer, softball, swimming, tennis, track & field, volleyball.

ADMISSIONS

Selectivity Rating: 65 (of 100). **Freshman Academic Profile:** Average high school GPA 3.0. 90% from public high schools. Average SAT I Math 525, SAT I Math middle 50% range 480-570. Average SAT I Verbal 523, SAT I Verbal middle 50% range 480-560. Average ACT 21, ACT middle 50% range 19-23. TOEFL required of all international applicants, minimum TOEFL 500. **Basis for Candidate Selection:** *Very important factors considered include:* secondary school record, standardized test scores. **Freshman Admission Requirements:** High school diploma is required and GED is not accepted. *Academic units required/recommended:* 16 total required; 4 English required, 4 math required, 3 science required, 2 science lab required, 2 foreign language required, 3 social studies required. **Freshman Admission Statistics:** 8,181 applied, 55% accepted, 58% of those accepted enrolled. **Transfer Admission Requirements:** *Items required:* college transcript. Minimum high school GPA of 2.0 required. Minimum college GPA of 2.0 required. Lowest grade transferable D. **General Admission Information:** Application fee $20. Regular application deadline August 1. Nonfall registration accepted. Admission may be deferred. Credit and/or placement offered for CEEB Advanced Placement tests.

COSTS AND FINANCIAL AID

In-state tuition $2,010. Out-of-state tuition $8,040. Room & board $4,620. Required fees $684. Average book expense $968. **Required Forms and Deadlines:** FAFSA. Priority filing deadline March 31. **Notification of Awards:** Applicants will be notified of awards on or about April 15. **Types of Aid:** *Need-based scholarships/grants:* Pell, SEOG, state scholarships/grants, private scholarships, the school's own gift aid, Hope Scholarships. *Loans:* Direct Subsidized Stafford, Direct Unsubsidized Stafford, Direct PLUS, Federal Perkins, service-cancelable state direct student loans, external alternative loans. **Student Employment:** Federal Work-Study Program available. Institutional employment available. Off-campus job opportunities are good. **Financial Aid Statistics:** 42% freshmen, 47% undergrads receive some form of aid. Average freshman grant $3,820. Average freshman loan $3,406. Average income from on-campus job $1,217. **Financial Aid Phone:** 912-681-5413.

GEORGIA SOUTHWESTERN STATE UNIVERSITY

800 Wheately Street, Americus, GA 31709-4693
Phone: 912-928-1273 **E-mail:** gswapps@canes.gsw.edu **CEEB Code:** 5250
Fax: 912-931-2983 **Web:** www.gsw.edu **ACT Code:** 824

This public school was founded in 1906. It has a 250-acre campus.

STUDENTS AND FACULTY

Enrollment: 2,101. **Student Body:** Male 36%, female 64%, out-of-state 2%, international 2% (33 countries represented). **Ethnic Representation:** African American 28%, Asian 1%, Caucasian 70%, Hispanic 1%. **Retention and Graduation:** 71% freshmen return for sophomore year. **Faculty:** Student/faculty ratio 14:1. 110 full-time faculty, 75% hold PhDs. 100% faculty teach undergrads.

ACADEMICS

Degrees: Associate's, bachelor's, master's, post-master's certificate. **Academic Requirements:** General education including some course work in English (including composition), humanities, mathematics, sciences (biological or physical), social science. **Classes:** 20-29 students in an average class. **Majors with Highest Enrollment:** Elementary education and teaching; psychology, general; business administration/management. **Disciplines with Highest Percentage of Degrees Awarded:** Business/marketing 33%, education 25%, psychology 14%, social sciences and history 8%, physical sciences 6%. **Special Study Options:** Accelerated program, cooperative (work-study) program, distance learning, double major, dual enrollment, English as a second language, honors program, independent study, internships, study abroad, teacher certification program. Undergrads may take grad-level classes. Associate degree program in trade and industry with South Georgia Technical College in Americus and Albany Area Technical College in Albany, Georgia. 3-2 program in engineering with Georgia Institute of Technology.

FACILITIES

Housing: Coed, all-female, all-male, housing for disabled students, housing for international students, fraternities and/or sororities. **Library Holdings:** 190,000 bound volumes. 140,575 periodicals. 589,953 microforms. 1,849 audiovisuals. **Special Academic Facilities/Equipment:** Museum, observatory, electron microscope. **Computers:** School-owned computers available for student use.

EXTRACURRICULARS

Activities: Choral groups, concert band, dance, drama/theater, jazz band, literary magazine, marching band, music ensembles, musical theater, student government, student newspaper, symphony orchestra, television station, yearbook. **Organizations:** 12 honor societies, 5 religious organizations, 7 fraternities (17% men join), 7 sororities (10% women join). **Athletics (Intercollegiate):** *Men:* baseball, basketball, tennis. *Women:* basketball, softball, tennis, volleyball.

ADMISSIONS

Selectivity Rating: 74 (of 100). **Freshman Academic Profile:** Average high school GPA 3.1. 15% in top 10% of high school class, 44% in top 25% of high school class, 71% in top 50% of high school class. Average SAT I Math 488, SAT I Math middle 50% range 450-550. Average SAT I Verbal 499, SAT I Verbal middle 50% range 450-550. Average ACT 20, ACT middle 50% range 18-21. TOEFL required of all international applicants, minimum TOEFL 523. **Basis for Candidate Selection:** *Very important factors considered include:* secondary school record, standardized test scores. *Important factors considered include:* class rank. *Other factors considered include:* essays, extracurricular activities, interview, recommendations, talent/ability. **Freshman Admission Requirements:** High school diploma or GED is required. *Academic units required/recommended:* 18 total required; 4 English required, 4 math required, 3 science required, 2 science lab required, 2 foreign language required, 1 social studies required, 2 history required, 2 elective required. **Freshman Admission Statistics:** 1,026 applied, 79% accepted, 44% of those accepted enrolled. **Transfer Admission Requirements:** *Items required:* college transcript. Minimum college GPA of 2.0 required. Lowest grade transferable D. **General Admission Information:** Application fee $20. Early decision application deadline December 15. Regular application deadline December 26. Nonfall registration accepted. Admission may be deferred for a maximum of 1 year. Credit and/or placement offered for CEEB Advanced Placement tests.

COSTS AND FINANCIAL AID

Room & board $3,130. Required fees $480. **Required Forms and Deadlines:** FAFSA, institution's own financial aid form, and state aid form. **Types of Aid:** *Need-based scholarships/grants:* state scholarships/grants. *Loans:* FFEL Subsidized Stafford, FFEL PLUS. **Student Employment:** Federal Work-Study Program available. Institutional employment available. Off-campus job opportunities are good. **Financial Aid Phone:** 912-928-1378.

GEORGIA STATE UNIVERSITY

PO Box 4009, Atlanta, GA 30302-4009
Phone: 404-651-2365 **CEEB Code:** 5251
Fax: 404-651-4811 **Web:** www.gsu.edu **ACT Code:** 826

This public school was founded in 1913. It has a 57-acre campus.

STUDENTS AND FACULTY

Enrollment: 19,681. **Student Body:** Male 39%, female 61%, out-of-state 1%, international 5% (117 countries represented). **Ethnic Representation:** African American 31%, Asian 10%, Caucasian 44%, Hispanic 3%. **Retention and Graduation:** 82% freshmen return for sophomore year. 14% freshmen graduate within 4 years. **Faculty:** Student/faculty ratio 24:1. 998 full-time faculty, 85% hold PhDs. 59% faculty teach undergrads.

ACADEMICS

Degrees: Bachelor's, certificate, doctoral, first professional, master's, post-master's certificate. **Academic Requirements:** General education including some course work in computer literacy, English (including composition), foreign languages, mathematics, sciences (biological or physical). **Classes:** 20-29 students in an average class. **Disciplines with Highest Percentage of Degrees Awarded:** Business/marketing 30%, social sciences and history 11%, computer and information sciences 10%, visual and performing arts 9%, psychology 7%. **Special Study Options:** Accelerated program, cooperative (work-study) program, cross registration, distance learning, double major, dual enrollment, English as a second language, honors program, independent study, internships, liberal arts/career combination, student-designed major, study abroad, teacher certification program.

FACILITIES

Housing: Coed, housing for disabled students. **Library Holdings:** 1,309,321 bound volumes. 8,929 periodicals. 1,656,839 microforms. 18,396 audiovisuals. **Special Academic Facilities/Equipment:** Art gallery, language lab, on-campus daycare center for education majors, economic forecasting center, small business development center, instructional technology center. **Computers:** School-owned computers available for student use.

EXTRACURRICULARS

Activities: Choral groups, concert band, dance, drama/theater, jazz band, literary magazine, marching band, music ensembles, musical theater, pep band, radio station, student government, student newspaper, student-run film society, symphony orchestra, television station, yearbook. **Organizations:** 160 registered organizations, 17 honor societies, 8 religious organizations, 8 fraternities (2% men join), 11 sororities (3% women join). **Athletics (Intercollegiate):** *Men:* baseball, basketball, cross-country, golf, soccer, tennis. *Women:* basketball, cross-country, golf, soccer, softball, tennis, track & field, volleyball.

ADMISSIONS

Selectivity Rating: 60 (of 100). **Freshman Academic Profile:** Average high school GPA 3.3. Average SAT I Math 521, SAT I Math middle 50% range 490-590. Average SAT I Verbal 525, SAT I Verbal middle 50% range 480-580. Average ACT 22, ACT middle 50% range 19-23. TOEFL required of all international applicants, minimum TOEFL 525. **Basis for Candidate Selection:** *Very important factors considered include:* secondary school record, standardized test scores, state residency. *Other factors considered include:* alumni/ae relation, character/personal qualities, extracurricular activities, geographical residence, interview, minority status, recommendations, talent/ability, volunteer work, work experience. **Freshman Admission Requirements:** High school diploma is required and GED is not accepted. *Academic units required/recommended:* 16 total required; 16 total recommended; 4 English required, 4 English recommended, 4 math required, 4 math recommended, 3 science required, 3 science recommended, 2 science lab required, 2 science lab recommended, 2 foreign language required, 2 foreign language recommended, 1 social studies required, 1 social studies recommended, 2 history required, 2 history recommended. **Freshman Admission Statistics:** 9,654 applied, 57% accepted, 45% of those accepted enrolled. **Transfer Admission Requirements:** *Items required:* college transcript. Minimum college GPA of 2.3 required. Lowest grade transferable D. **General Admission Information:** Application fee $25. Priority application deadline February 1. Regular application deadline April 1. Nonfall registration accepted. Admission may be deferred for a maximum of 1 year. Credit offered for CEEB Advanced Placement tests.

COSTS AND FINANCIAL AID

In-state tuition $2,322. Out-of-state tuition $9,288. Room & board $7,948. Required fees $456. Average book expense $1,000. **Required Forms and Deadlines:** FAFSA. Priority filing deadline April 1. **Notification of Awards:** Applicants will be notified of awards on a rolling basis beginning on or about May 1. **Types of Aid:** *Need-based scholarships/grants:* Pell, SEOG, state scholarships/grants, private scholarships, the school's own gift aid. *Loans:* Direct Subsidized Stafford, Direct Unsubsidized Stafford, Direct PLUS, Federal Perkins, state loans, college/university loans from institutional funds. **Student Employment:** Federal Work-Study Program available. Institutional employment available. Off-campus job opportunities are excellent. **Financial Aid Statistics:** 84% freshmen, 65% undergrads receive some form of aid. Average freshman grant $2,605. Average freshman loan $3,025. **Financial Aid Phone:** 404-651-2227.

GEORGIAN COURT COLLEGE

900 Lakewood Avenue, Lakewood, NJ 08701-2697
Phone: 732-364-2200 **E-mail:** admissions@georgian.edu **CEEB Code:** 2274
Fax: 732-364-4442 **Web:** www.georgian.edu **ACT Code:** 2562

This private school, which is affiliated with the Roman Catholic Church, was founded in 1908. It has a 155-acre campus.

STUDENTS AND FACULTY

Enrollment: 1,885. **Student Body:** Male 9%, female 91%, out-of-state 1%, international 1% (13 countries represented). **Ethnic Representation:** African American 6%, Asian 2%, Caucasian 82%, Hispanic 5%. **Retention and Graduation:** 73% freshmen return for sophomore year. 38% freshmen graduate within 4 years. 19% grads go on to further study within 1 year. 23% grads pursue business degrees. 1% grads pursue law degrees. 1% grads pursue medical degrees. **Faculty:** Student/faculty ratio 14:1. 87 full-time faculty, 78% hold PhDs. 81% faculty teach undergrads.

ACADEMICS

Degrees: Bachelor's, certificate, master's, post-bachelor's certificate, post-master's certificate. **Academic Requirements:** General education including some course work in arts/fine arts, English (including composition), foreign languages, history, humanities, philosophy, sciences (biological or physical), social science. **Classes:** 10-19 students in an average class. **Majors with Highest Enrollment:** Business administration/management; English language and literature, general; psychology, general. **Disciplines with Highest Percentage of Degrees Awarded:** Business/marketing 20%, education 19%, psychology 16%, English 10%, liberal arts/general studies 8%. **Special Study Options:** Distance learning, double major, English as a second language, honors program, independent study, internships, liberal arts/career combination, study abroad, teacher certification program. Undergrads may take grad-level classes. Co-op programs: arts, business, health professions, natural science, social/behavioral science.

FACILITIES

Housing: All-female. **Library Holdings:** 136,760 bound volumes. 1,068 periodicals. 669,032 microforms. 2,188 audiovisuals. **Special Academic Facilities/Equipment:** Art gallery, arboretum, NASA Educator Resource Center. **Computers:** School-owned computers available for student use.

EXTRACURRICULARS

Activities: Choral groups, concert band, jazz band, literary magazine, music ensembles, student government, student newspaper, yearbook. **Organizations:** 36 registered organizations, 13 honor societies, 1 religious organization. **Athletics (Intercollegiate):** *Women:* basketball, cross-country, soccer, softball, tennis, volleyball.

ADMISSIONS

Selectivity Rating: 63 (of 100). **Freshman Academic Profile:** Average high school GPA 3.2. 9% in top 10% of high school class, 34% in top 25% of high school class, 73% in top 50% of high school class. 81% from public high schools. Average SAT I Math 465, SAT I Math middle 50% range 413-520. Average SAT I Verbal 465, SAT I Verbal middle 50% range 410-528. TOEFL required of all international applicants, minimum TOEFL 550. **Basis for Candidate Selection:** *Important factors considered include:* interview, secondary school record, standardized test scores. *Other factors considered include:* alumni/ae relation, class rank, essays, extracurricular activities, recommendations, talent/ability. **Freshman Admission Requirements:** High school diploma or GED is required. *Academic units required/recommended:* 16 total required; 4 English required, 2 math required, 1 science required, 1 science lab required, 2 foreign language required, 1 history required, 6 elective required. **Freshman Admission Statistics:** 489 applied, 79% accepted, 48% of those accepted enrolled. **Transfer Admission Requirements:** *Items required:* high school transcript, college transcript, statement of good standing from prior school. Minimum college GPA of 2.0 required. Lowest grade transferable C. **General Admission Information:** Application fee $40. Priority application deadline November 15. Regular application deadline August 1. Nonfall registration accepted. Credit and/or placement offered for CEEB Advanced Placement tests.

COSTS AND FINANCIAL AID

Tuition $14,455. Room & board $5,600. Required fees $400. Average book expense $600. **Required Forms and Deadlines:** FAFSA and institution's own financial aid form. Financial aid filing deadline October 1. Priority filing deadline March 1. **Notification of Awards:** Applicants will be notified of awards on a rolling basis. **Types of Aid:** *Need-based scholarships/grants:* Pell, SEOG, state scholarships/grants, private scholarships, the school's own gift aid. *Loans:* FFEL Subsidized Stafford, FFEL Unsubsidized Stafford, FFEL PLUS, Federal Perkins, state loans. **Student Employment:** Federal Work-Study Program available. Institutional employment available. Off-campus job opportunities are good. **Financial Aid Phone:** 732-364-2200.

See page 1038.

GETTYSBURG COLLEGE

Admissions Office, Eisenhower House, Gettysburg, PA 17325-1484
Phone: 717-337-6100 **E-mail:** admiss@gettysburg.edu **CEEB Code:** 2275
Fax: 717-337-6145 **Web:** www.gettysburg.edu **ACT Code:** 3580

This private school, which is affiliated with the Lutheran Church, was founded in 1832. It has a 200-acre campus.

STUDENTS AND FACULTY

Enrollment: 2,377. **Student Body:** Male 50%, female 50%, out-of-state 72%, international 2%. **Ethnic Representation:** African American 3%, Asian 1%, Caucasian 94%, Hispanic 1%. **Retention and Graduation:** 91% freshmen return for sophomore year. 73% freshmen graduate within 4 years. 35% grads go on to further study within 1 year. **Faculty:** Student/faculty ratio 11:1. 180 full-time faculty, 92% hold PhDs. 100% faculty teach undergrads.

ACADEMICS

Degrees: Bachelor's. **Academic Requirements:** General education including some course work in arts/fine arts, English (including composition), foreign languages, humanities, sciences (biological or physical), social science, nonwestern culture, quantitative reasoning. **Classes:** 10-19 students in an average class. **Majors with Highest Enrollment:** Psychology, general; sociology; business administration/management. **Disciplines with Highest Percentage of Degrees Awarded:** Social sciences and history 24%, business/marketing 20%, psychology 8%, English 8%, biological life sciences 8%. **Special Study Options:** Double major, student exchange program (domestic), independent study, internships, liberal arts/career combination, student-designed major, study abroad, teacher certification program.

FACILITIES

Housing: Coed, all-female, housing for international students, fraternities and/or sororities, special-interest and theme housing. **Library Holdings:** 351,848 bound volumes. 4,778 periodicals. 62,303 microforms. 21,752 audiovisuals. **Special Academic Facilities/Equipment:** Art gallery, language lab, child study lab, fine and performing arts facilities, planetarium and observatory, electron microscopes, NMR spectrometer, greenhouse, digital classrooms, wireless network, plasma physics labs, new science center. **Computers:** *Recommended operating system:* Windows NT/2000.

EXTRACURRICULARS

Activities: Choral groups, concert band, dance, drama/theater, jazz band, literary magazine, marching band, music ensembles, musical theater, radio station, student government, student newspaper, student-run film society, symphony orchestra, television station, yearbook. **Organizations:** 100 registered organizations, 17 honor societies, 6 religious organizations, 10 fraternities (44% men join), 5 sororities (26% women join). **Athletics (Intercollegiate):** *Men:* baseball, basketball, cross-country, football, golf, indoor track, lacrosse, soccer, swimming, tennis, track & field, wrestling. *Women:* basketball, cross-country, field hockey, golf, indoor track, lacrosse, soccer, softball, swimming, tennis, track & field, volleyball.

ADMISSIONS

Selectivity Rating: 87 (of 100). **Freshman Academic Profile:** 62% in top 10% of high school class, 80% in top 25% of high school class, 99% in top 50% of high school class. 70% from public high schools. SAT I Math middle 50% range 590-660. SAT I Verbal middle 50% range 580-650. Average ACT 26. TOEFL required of all international applicants, minimum TOEFL 570. **Basis for Candidate Selection:** *Very important factors considered include:* class rank, recommendations, secondary school record. *Important factors considered include:* character/personal qualities, essays, extracurricular activities, interview, standardized test scores, talent/ability, volunteer work. *Other factors considered include:* alumni/ae relation, geographical residence, minority status, work experience. **Freshman Admission Requirements:** High school diploma or GED is required. *Academic units required/recommended:* 4 English required, 4 English recommended, 3 math required, 4 math recommended, 3 science required, 4 science recommended, 3 science lab required, 4 science lab recommended, 3 foreign language required, 4 foreign language recommended, 3 social studies required, 4 social studies recommended, 3 history required, 4 history recommended. **Freshman Admission Statistics:** 4,573 applied, 50% accepted, 30% of those accepted enrolled. **Transfer Admission Requirements:** *Items required:* high school transcript, college transcript, essay, standardized test scores, statement of good standing from prior school. Minimum college GPA of 2.5 required. Lowest grade transferable C. **General Admission Information:** Application fee $45. Priority application deadline February 15. Early decision application deadline November 15. Nonfall registration accepted. Admission may be deferred for a maximum of 1 year. Credit and/or placement offered for CEEB Advanced Placement tests.

COSTS AND FINANCIAL AID

Tuition $25,630. Room & board $6,322. Required fees $118. Average book expense $500. **Required Forms and Deadlines:** FAFSA, CSS/Financial Aid PROFILE, noncustodial (divorced/separated) parent's statement, and business/farm supplement. Financial aid filing deadline March 15. Priority filing deadline February 15. **Notification of Awards:** Applicants will be notified of awards on or about March 30. **Types of Aid:** *Need-based scholarships/grants:* Pell, SEOG, state scholarships/grants, private scholarships, the school's own gift aid. *Loans:* FFEL Subsidized Stafford, FFEL Unsubsidized Stafford, FFEL PLUS, Federal Perkins, college/university loans from institutional funds. **Student Employment:** Federal Work-Study Program available. Institutional employment available. Off-campus job opportunities are good. **Financial Aid Statistics:** 53% freshmen, 56% undergrads receive some form of aid. Average freshman grant $27,775. Average freshman loan $3,500. Average income from on-campus job $1,500. **Financial Aid Phone:** 717-337-6611.

GLENVILLE STATE COLLEGE

200 High Street, Glenville, WV 26351
Phone: 304-462-4117 **E-mail:** visitor@glenville.edu
Fax: 304-462-8619 **Web:** www.glenville.edu **ACT Code:** 4522

This public school was founded in 1872.

STUDENTS AND FACULTY

Enrollment: 2,198. **Student Body:** Male 41%, female 59%. **Ethnic Representation:** African American 3%, Asian 3%, Caucasian 94%, Native American 1%. **Retention and Graduation:** 59% freshmen return for sophomore year. **Faculty:** Student/faculty ratio 15:1. 74 full-time faculty, 35% hold PhDs. 100% faculty teach undergrads.

ACADEMICS

Degrees: Associate's, bachelor's. **Classes:** 10-19 students in an average class. **Special Study Options:** Accelerated program, cooperative (work-study) program, distance learning, double major, English as a second language, honors program, internships, student-designed major, teacher certification program.

FACILITIES

Housing: All-female, all-male, apartments for married students, apartments for single students, housing for disabled students. **Library Holdings:** 115,892 bound volumes. 1,853 periodicals. 558,094 microforms. 20,145 audiovisuals.

EXTRACURRICULARS

Activities: Choral groups, concert band, drama/theater, jazz band, marching band, music ensembles, musical theater, student government, student newspaper, yearbook. **Organizations:** 30 registered organizations, 14 honor societies, 6 religious organizations. **Athletics (Intercollegiate):** *Men:* basketball, cross-country, football, golf, track & field. *Women:* basketball, cross-country, track & field, volleyball.

ADMISSIONS

Selectivity Rating: 62 (of 100). **Freshman Academic Profile:** Average SAT I Math 413. Average SAT I Verbal 405. Average ACT 20. TOEFL required of all international applicants, minimum TOEFL 550. **Basis for Candidate Selection:** *Very important factors considered include:* secondary school record, standardized test scores. *Other factors considered include:* class rank, recommendations. **Freshman Admission Requirements:** High school diploma or GED is required. *Academic units required/recommended:* 21 total required; 4 English required, 2 math required, 2 science required, 2 science lab required, 3 social studies required. **Freshman Admission Statistics:** 1,132 applied, 100% accepted, 41% of those accepted enrolled. **Transfer Admission Requirements:** *Items required:* college transcript. Minimum college GPA of 2.0 required. Lowest grade transferable C. **General Admission Information:** Application fee $10. Regular application deadline August 1. Nonfall registration accepted. Admission may be deferred for a maximum of 1 year. Credit offered for CEEB Advanced Placement tests.

COSTS AND FINANCIAL AID

Room & board $3,480. Average book expense $350. **Required Forms and Deadlines:** FAFSA. Priority filing deadline March 1. **Notification of Awards:** Applicants will be notified of awards on a rolling basis beginning on or about April 1. **Types of Aid:** *Need-based scholarships/grants:* Pell, SEOG, state scholarships/grants, private scholarships, the school's own gift aid. *Loans:* Direct Subsidized Stafford, Direct Unsubsidized Stafford, Direct PLUS, Federal Perkins. **Student Employment:** Federal Work-Study Program available. Off-campus job opportunities are fair. **Financial Aid Statistics:** 75% freshmen, 70% undergrads receive some form of aid. Average freshman loan $1,330. Average income from on-campus job $900. **Financial Aid Phone:** 304-462-4103.

GODDARD COLLEGE

123 Pitkin Road, Plainfield, VT 05667
Phone: 802-454-8311 **E-mail:** admissions@goddard.edu **CEEB Code:** 3416
Fax: 802-454-1029 **Web:** www.goddard.edu **ACT Code:** 4300

This private school was founded in 1938. It has a 250-acre campus.

STUDENTS AND FACULTY

Enrollment: 319. **Student Body:** Out-of-state 87%, international 2% (2 countries represented). **Ethnic Representation:** African American 3%, Asian 2%, Caucasian 87%, Hispanic 2%, Native American 1%. **Retention and Graduation:** 73% freshmen return for sophomore year. 8% freshmen graduate within 4 years. 5% grads go on to further study within 1 year. **Faculty:** Student/faculty ratio 11:1. 14 full-time faculty. 100% faculty teach undergrads.

ACADEMICS

Degrees: Bachelor's, master's. **Academic Requirements:** Students must have breadth and depth to their study as well as to be able to show competency in several areas according to our degree criteria. **Classes:** Under 10 students in an average class. **Majors with Highest Enrollment:** Liberal arts and sciences/liberal studies; education, general; psychology, general. **Disciplines with Highest Percentage of Degrees Awarded:** Liberal arts/general studies 51%, English 7%, health professions and related sciences 2%. **Special Study Options:** Cooperative (work-study) program, distance learning, double major, student exchange program (domestic), external degree program, independent study, internships, student-designed major, study abroad, teacher certification program.

FACILITIES

Housing: Coed, all-male, cooperative housing, student-designated theme dorms. **Library Holdings:** 70,000 bound volumes. 1,930 periodicals. 845,997 microforms. 170 audiovisuals. **Special Academic Facilities/Equipment:** Photography lab, radio station. **Computers:** School-owned computers available for student use.

EXTRACURRICULARS

Activities: Dance, drama/theater, jazz band, literary magazine, music ensembles, radio station, student government, student newspaper.

ADMISSIONS

Selectivity Rating: 73 (of 100). **Freshman Academic Profile:** Average high school GPA 2.5. 7% in top 10% of high school class, 27% in top 25% of high school class, 68% in top 50% of high school class. 93% from public high schools. Average SAT I Math 541, SAT I Math middle 50% range 480-590. Average SAT I Verbal 609, SAT I Verbal middle 50% range 550-680. ACT middle 50% range 19-27. TOEFL required of all international applicants, minimum TOEFL 550. **Basis for Candidate Selection:** *Very important factors considered include:* character/personal qualities, essays, interview. *Important factors considered include:* talent/ability, volunteer work, work experience. *Other factors considered include:* class rank, extracurricular activities, recommendations, secondary school record, standardized test scores. **Freshman Admission Requirements:** High school diploma or GED is required. **Freshman Admission Statistics:** 128 applied, 93% accepted, 40% of those accepted enrolled. **Transfer Admission Requirements:** *Items required:* high school transcript, college transcript, essay, interview. Lowest grade transferable C-. **General Admission Information:** Application fee $40. Nonfall registration accepted. Admission may be deferred for a maximum of 1 year. Credit offered for CEEB Advanced Placement tests.

COSTS AND FINANCIAL AID

Tuition $17,840. Room & board $2,964. Required fees $252. Average book expense $508. **Required Forms and Deadlines:** FAFSA. No deadline for regular filing. Priority filing deadline March 1. **Notification of Awards:** Applicants will be notified of awards on a rolling basis. **Types of Aid:** *Need-based scholarships/grants:* Pell, SEOG, state scholarships/grants, private scholarships, the school's own gift aid. *Loans:* FFEL Subsidized Stafford, FFEL Unsubsidized Stafford, FFEL PLUS, Federal Perkins, college/university loans from institutional funds. **Student Employment:** Federal Work-Study Program available. Off-campus job opportunities are fair. **Financial Aid Statistics:** 90% freshmen, 88% undergrads receive some form of aid. Average freshman grant $2,000. Average freshman loan $6,189. **Financial Aid Phone:** 802-454-8311.

GOLDEN GATE UNIVERSITY

536 Mission Street, San Francisco, CA 94105
Phone: 415-442-7800 **E-mail:** info@ggu.edu **CEEB Code:** 4329
Fax: 415-442-7807 **Web:** www.ggu.edu **ACT Code:** 278

This private school was founded in 1901.

STUDENTS AND FACULTY

Enrollment: 1,015. **Student Body:** Male 40%, female 60%, out-of-state 5%, international 14% (61 countries represented). **Ethnic Representation:** African American 14%, Asian 14%, Caucasian 49%, Hispanic 11%. **Retention and Graduation:** 26% freshmen graduate within 4 years. 15% grads go on to further study within 1 year. 30% grads pursue business degrees. **Faculty:** Student/faculty ratio 17:1. 95 full-time faculty, 97% hold PhDs. 100% faculty teach undergrads.

ACADEMICS

Degrees: Bachelor's, certificate, doctoral, first professional, master's, post-bachelor's certificate, post-master's certificate. **Academic Requirements:** General education including some course work in arts/fine arts, computer literacy, English (including composition), history, humanities, mathematics, philosophy, sciences (biological or physical), social science. **Classes:** 20-29 students in an average class. **Disciplines with Highest Percentage of Degrees Awarded:** Business/marketing 87%, computer and information sciences 9%, social sciences and history 1%, psychology 1%, liberal arts/general studies 1%. **Special Study Options:** Accelerated program, cooperative (work-study) program, distance learning, dual enrollment, English as a second language, internships, weekend college.

FACILITIES

Library Holdings: 120,000 bound volumes. 5,169 periodicals. 35,000 microforms. 500 audiovisuals. **Computers:** School-owned computers available for student use.

EXTRACURRICULARS

Activities: Student government, student newspaper. **Organizations:** 16 registered organizations, 5 honor societies.

ADMISSIONS

Selectivity Rating: 60 (of 100). **Freshman Academic Profile:** Average high school GPA 2.7. TOEFL required of all international applicants, minimum TOEFL 525. **Basis for Candidate Selection:** *Very important factors considered include:* secondary school record. *Other factors considered include:* class rank, essays, minority status, recommendations, standardized test scores, volunteer work, work experience. **Freshman Admission Requirements:** High school diploma or GED is required. *Academic units required/recommended:* 14 total recommended; 4 English recommended, 3 math recommended, 2 science recommended, 1 science lab recommended, 2 foreign language recommended, 1 social studies recommended, 1 history recommended. **Transfer Admission Requirements:** *Items required:* college transcript. Minimum college GPA of 2.0 required. Lowest grade transferable C-. **General Admission Information:** Application fee $55. Priority application deadline July 1. Nonfall registration accepted. Admission may be deferred for a maximum of 1 year. Credit offered for CEEB Advanced Placement tests.

COSTS AND FINANCIAL AID

Tuition $9,192. Required fees $0. Average book expense $1,000. **Student Employment:** Federal Work-Study Program available. Institutional employment available. Off-campus job opportunities are good. **Financial Aid Statistics:** Average freshman grant $5,233. Average freshman loan $7,048. Average income from on-campus job $2,480. **Financial Aid Phone:** 415-442-7270.

GOLDEY-BEACOM COLLEGE

4701 Limestone Road, Wilmington, DE 19808
Phone: 302-998-8814 **E-mail:** gbc@goldey.gbc.edu **CEEB Code:** 5255
Fax: 302-996-5408 **Web:** www.goldey.gbc.edu

This private school was founded in 1886. It has a 27-acre campus.

STUDENTS AND FACULTY

Enrollment: 894. **Student Body:** Male 52%, female 48%, out-of-state 50%, international 4% (60 countries represented). **Ethnic Representation:** African American 7%, Asian 2%, Caucasian 77%, Hispanic 2%. **Retention and Graduation:** 5% grads go on to further study within 1 year. 4% grads pursue business degrees. 1% grads pursue law degrees.

ACADEMICS

Degrees: Associate's, bachelor's, master's. **Academic Requirements:** General education including some course work in computer literacy, English (including composition), humanities, mathematics, philosophy, social science. **Special Study Options:** Accelerated program, cooperative (work-study) program, independent study, internships.

FACILITIES

Housing: Apartments for single students, fraternities and/or sororities.

EXTRACURRICULARS

Activities: Drama/theater, student government, student newspaper. **Organizations:** 4 religious organizations. **Athletics (Intercollegiate):** *Men:* soccer, softball. *Women:* softball.

ADMISSIONS

Selectivity Rating: 63 (of 100). **Freshman Academic Profile:** Average high school GPA 2.7. 12% in top 10% of high school class, 27% in top 25% of high school class, 81% in top 50% of high school class. 90% from public high schools. Average SAT I Math 490, SAT I Math middle 50% range 440-593. Average SAT I Verbal 473, SAT I Verbal middle 50% range 400-512. TOEFL required of all international applicants, minimum TOEFL 500. **Basis for Candidate Selection:** *Very important factors considered include:* secondary school record, standardized test scores. *Important factors considered include:* class rank, recommendations. *Other factors considered include:* character/personal qualities, interview. **Freshman Admission Requirements:** High school diploma or GED is required. *Academic units required/recommended:* 16 total required; 16 total recommended; 4 English required, 4 English recommended, 3 math required, 3 math recommended, 3 science required, 3 science recommended. **Freshman Admission Statistics:** 689 applied, 77% accepted, 56% of those accepted enrolled. **Transfer Admission Requirements:** *Items required:* high school transcript, college transcript. Minimum high school GPA of 2.0 required. Minimum college GPA of 2.0 required. **General Admission Information:** Application fee $30. Priority application deadline May 15. Regular application deadline August 15. Nonfall registration accepted. Admission may be deferred for a maximum of 1 year. Credit and/or placement offered for CEEB Advanced Placement tests.

COSTS AND FINANCIAL AID

Tuition $7,200. Room & board $3,290. Required fees $120. Average book expense $700. **Types of Aid:** *Need-based scholarships/grants:* Pell, SEOG, state scholarships/grants, private scholarships, the school's own gift aid. *Loans:* FFEL Subsidized Stafford, FFEL Unsubsidized Stafford, FFEL PLUS, Federal Perkins, state loans, college/university loans from institutional funds. **Student Employment:** Federal Work-Study Program available. Off-campus job opportunities are excellent. **Financial Aid Statistics:** Average freshman grant $1,250. **Financial Aid Phone:** 302-998-8814.

GONZAGA UNIVERSITY

502 E. Boone Avenue, Spokane, WA 99258
Phone: 509-323-6572 **E-mail:** ballinger@gu.gonzaga.edu **CEEB Code:** 4330
Fax: 509-324-5780 **Web:** www.gonzaga.edu **ACT Code:** 4458

This private school, which is affiliated with the Roman Catholic Church, was founded in 1887. It has a 108-acre campus.

STUDENTS AND FACULTY

Enrollment: 3,814. **Student Body:** Male 46%, female 54%, out-of-state 47%, international 2% (42 countries represented). **Ethnic Representation:** African American 1%, Asian 6%, Caucasian 81%, Hispanic 3%, Native American 1%. **Retention and Graduation:** 91% freshmen return for sophomore year. 62% freshmen graduate within 4 years. **Faculty:** Student/faculty ratio 13:1. 291 full-time faculty, 83% hold PhDs. 100% faculty teach undergrads.

ACADEMICS

Degrees: Bachelor's, doctoral, first professional, master's, post-master's certificate. **Academic Requirements:** General education including some course work in English (including composition), humanities, mathematics, philosophy, sciences (biological or physical). **Classes:** 20-29 students in an average class. 10-19 students in an average lab/discussion section. **Majors with Highest Enrollment:** Biology/biological sciences, general; political science and government, general; business/commerce, general. **Disciplines with Highest Percentage of Degrees Awarded:** Business/marketing 23%, social sciences and history 16%, engineering/engineering technology 9%, psychology 7%, education 6%. **Special Study Options:** Accelerated program, double major, English as a second language, student exchange program (domestic), honors program, internships, study abroad, teacher certification program, weekend college.

FACILITIES

Housing: Coed, all-female, all-male, apartments for married students, apartments for single students. **Library Holdings:** 228,622 bound volumes. 1,435 periodicals. 562,255 microforms. **Special Academic Facilities/ Equipment:** Art center, museum, language lab, TV production center, educational center, two electron microscopes. **Computers:** School-owned computers available for student use.

EXTRACURRICULARS

Activities: Choral groups, concert band, dance, drama/theater, jazz band, literary magazine, music ensembles, radio station, student government, student newspaper, symphony orchestra, television station, yearbook. **Organizations:** 71 registered organizations, 10 honor societies, 4 religious organizations. **Athletics (Intercollegiate):** *Men:* baseball, basketball, cheerleading, crew, cross-country, golf, soccer, tennis, track & field. *Women:* basketball, cheerleading, crew, cross-country, golf, soccer, tennis, track & field, volleyball.

ADMISSIONS

Selectivity Rating: 80 (of 100). **Freshman Academic Profile:** Average high school GPA 3.6. 37% in top 10% of high school class, 74% in top 25% of high school class, 95% in top 50% of high school class. 65% from public high schools. Average SAT I Math 593, SAT I Math middle 50% range 540-640. Average SAT I Verbal 578, SAT I Verbal middle 50% range 530-620. Average ACT 26, ACT middle 50% range 24-28. TOEFL required of all international applicants, minimum TOEFL 550. **Basis for Candidate Selection:** *Very important factors considered include:* character/personal qualities, secondary school record. *Important factors considered include:* extracurricular activities, recommendations, standardized test scores, talent/ability. *Other factors considered include:* alumni/ae relation, class rank, essays, interview, minority status, volunteer work, work experience. **Freshman Admission Requirements:** High school diploma or GED is required. *Academic units required/ recommended:* 4 total required; 4 total recommended; 3 English required, 4 English recommended, 1 math required, 4 math recommended, 1 science required, 4 science recommended, 1 science lab required, 4 science lab recommended, 2 foreign language required, 4 foreign language recommended, 1 social studies required, 1 history required, 3 history recommended, 6 elective required. **Freshman Admission Statistics:** 3,339 applied, 76% accepted, 36% of those accepted enrolled. **Transfer Admission Requirements:** *Items required:* college transcript, essay. Minimum college GPA of 2.7 required. Lowest grade transferable C. **General Admission Information:** Application fee $40. Priority application deadline February 1. Regular application deadline February 1. Nonfall registration accepted. Admission may be deferred for a maximum of 1 year. Credit and/or placement offered for CEEB Advanced Placement tests.

COSTS AND FINANCIAL AID

Tuition $20,510. Room & board $5,960. Required fees $175. Average book expense $750. **Required Forms and Deadlines:** FAFSA. Priority filing deadline February 1. **Notification of Awards:** Applicants will be notified of awards on a rolling basis beginning on or about March 1. **Types of Aid:** *Need-based scholarships/grants:* Pell, SEOG, state scholarships/grants, private scholarships, the school's own gift aid, United Negro College Fund, Federal Nursing. *Loans:* FFEL Subsidized Stafford, FFEL Unsubsidized Stafford, FFEL PLUS, Federal Perkins, Federal Nursing, state loans, college/university loans from institutional funds, private educational loans. **Student Employment:** Federal Work-Study Program available. Institutional employment available. Off-campus job opportunities are good. **Financial Aid Statistics:** 63% freshmen, 63% undergrads receive some form of aid. **Financial Aid Phone:** 800-793-1716.

See page 1040.

GORDON COLLEGE

255 Grapevine Road, Wenham, MA 01984-1899
Phone: 978-927-2300 **E-mail:** admissions@hope.gordon.edu **CEEB Code:** 3417
Fax: 978-524-3722 **Web:** www.gordon.edu **ACT Code:** 1838

This private school, which is affiliated with the Protestant Church, was founded in 1889. It has a 500-acre campus.

STUDENTS AND FACULTY

Enrollment: 1,631. **Student Body:** Male 34%, female 66%, out-of-state 71%, international 2% (25 countries represented). **Ethnic Representation:** African American 1%, Asian 2%, Caucasian 93%, Hispanic 2%. **Retention and Graduation:** 87% freshmen return for sophomore year. 52% freshmen graduate within 4 years. 19% grads go on to further study within 1 year. **Faculty:** Student/faculty ratio 15:1. 92 full-time faculty, 73% hold PhDs. 100% faculty teach undergrads.

ACADEMICS

Degrees: Bachelor's, master's. **Academic Requirements:** General education including some course work in arts/fine arts, English (including composition), foreign languages, history, humanities, philosophy, sciences (biological or physical), social science, Old Testament and New Testament courses. Students may also choose the option of taking a computer/math course or a second science course. Also first-year Christianity, character, and culture class is required. **Classes:** 10-19 students in an average class. 10-19 students in an average lab/discussion section. **Majors with Highest Enrollment:** Bible/ biblical studies; visual and performing arts, general; junior high/intermediate/ middle school education and teaching. **Disciplines with Highest Percentage of Degrees Awarded:** Philosophy/religion/theology 14%, education 11%, visual and performing arts 9%, social sciences and history 9%, communications/ communication technologies 8%. **Special Study Options:** Cooperative (work-study) program, cross registration, double major, student exchange program (domestic), honors program, independent study, internships, liberal arts/career combination, student-designed major, study abroad, teacher certification program. Off-campus study: Gordon-at-Oxford University, England; marine biology semester in Philippines; Italian sSemester in Orvieto, Italy; Oregon extension; LaVida Wilderness expedition; Boston urban semester. Co-op programs: arts, business, computer science, education, engineering, health professions, humanities, natural science, social/behavioral science.

FACILITIES

Housing: Coed, all-female, all-male, apartments for single students, housing for disabled students, housing for international students, international hall, mentoring hall, theme houses. Also,Gordon's dorms are coed by floors and/or wings. Men and women do not live together or share facilities. **Library Holdings:** 142,688 bound volumes. 8,555 periodicals. 31,285 microforms. 10,266 audiovisuals. **Special Academic Facilities/Equipment:** Human performance lab, psychology lab complex, electron microscope, gene sequencer, papers of British statesman/reformer William Wilberforce at East-West Institute, center for student leadership, center for Christian studies. **Computers:** School-owned computers available for student use.

EXTRACURRICULARS

Activities: Choral groups, concert band, drama/theater, jazz band, literary magazine, music ensembles, musical theater, pep band, student government, student newspaper, symphony orchestra, yearbook. **Organizations:** 35 registered organizations, 17 honor societies, 15 religious organizations. **Athletics (Intercollegiate):** *Men:* baseball, basketball, cross-country, lacrosse, soccer, swimming, tennis. *Women:* basketball, cheerleading, cross-country, field hockey, lacrosse, soccer, softball, swimming, tennis, volleyball.

ADMISSIONS

Selectivity Rating: 74 (of 100). **Freshman Academic Profile:** Average high school GPA 3.6. 34% in top 10% of high school class, 76% in top 25% of high school class, 95% in top 50% of high school class. 70% from public high schools. Average SAT I Math 592, SAT I Math middle 50% range 540-650. Average SAT I Verbal 610, SAT I Verbal middle 50% range 580-640. Average ACT 26. TOEFL required of all international applicants, minimum TOEFL 550. **Basis for Candidate Selection:** *Very important factors considered include:* character/personal qualities, essays, interview, recommendations, religious affiliation/commitment, secondary school record, standardized test scores. *Important factors considered include:* class rank. *Other factors considered include:* alumni/ae relation, extracurricular activities, minority status, talent/ ability, volunteer work, work experience. **Freshman Admission Requirements:** High school diploma or GED is required. *Academic units required/ recommended:* 20 total required; 25 total recommended; 4 English required, 4 English recommended, 2 math required, 3 math recommended, 2 science required, 3 science recommended, 1 science lab required, 3 science lab recommended, 2 foreign language required, 4 foreign language recommended, 2 social studies required, 3 social studies recommended, 5 elective required, 5 elective recommended. **Freshman Admission Statistics:** 1,100 applied, 74% accepted, 49% of those accepted enrolled. **Transfer Admission Requirements:** *Items required:* college transcript, essay, interview, statement of good standing from prior school. Minimum college GPA of 2.0 required. Lowest grade transferable C. **General Admission Information:** Application fee $40. Priority application deadline December 1. Early decision application deadline December 1. Nonfall registration accepted. Admission may be deferred for a maximum of 1 year. Credit offered for CEEB Advanced Placement tests.

COSTS AND FINANCIAL AID

Average book expense $800. **Required Forms and Deadlines:** FAFSA, CSS/ Financial Aid PROFILE, and state aid form. Financial aid filing deadline March 1. **Notification of Awards:** Applicants will be notified of awards on a rolling basis beginning on or about April 15. **Types of Aid:** *Need-based scholarships/grants:* Pell, SEOG, state scholarships/grants, private scholarships, the school's own gift aid. *Loans:* FFEL Subsidized Stafford, FFEL Unsubsidized Stafford, FFEL PLUS, Federal Perkins, state loans, college/ university loans from institutional funds. **Student Employment:** Federal Work-Study Program available. Institutional employment available. Off-campus job opportunities are excellent. **Financial Aid Statistics:** 64% freshmen, 68% undergrads receive some form of aid. Average freshman grant $13,497. Average freshman loan $2,902. Average income from on-campus job $1,300. **Financial Aid Phone:** 978-927-2300.

GOSHEN COLLEGE

1700 South Main Street, Goshen, IN 46526-4794
Phone: 574-535-7535 **E-mail:** admissions@goshen.edu **CEEB Code:** 1251
Fax: 574-535-7609 **Web:** www.goshen.edu. **ACT Code:** 1196

This private school, which is affiliated with the Mennonite Church, was founded in 1894. It has a 135-acre campus.

STUDENTS AND FACULTY

Enrollment: 871. **Student Body:** Male 37%, female 63%, out-of-state 55%, international 10% (28 countries represented). **Ethnic Representation:** African American 3%, Asian 1%, Caucasian 91%, Hispanic 5%. **Retention and Graduation:** 82% freshmen return for sophomore year. 43% freshmen graduate within 4 years. 20% grads go on to further study within 1 year. 2% grads pursue business degrees. 1% grads pursue law degrees. 4% grads pursue medical degrees. **Faculty:** Student/faculty ratio 9:1. 73 full-time faculty, 58% hold PhDs. 100% faculty teach undergrads.

ACADEMICS

Degrees: Bachelor's, certificate. **Academic Requirements:** General education including some course work in arts/fine arts, English (including composition), foreign languages, history, humanities, mathematics, philosophy, sciences (biological or physical), social science, Bible and religion, international education. **Classes:** 10-19 students in an average class. 10-19 students in an average lab/discussion section. **Majors with Highest Enrollment:** Nursing/ registered nurse training (RN, ASN, BSN, MSN); communications and media studies; elementary education and teaching. **Disciplines with Highest Percentage of Degrees Awarded:** Business/marketing 18%, computer and information sciences 9%, visual and performing arts 9%, interdisciplinary studies 9%, education 8%. **Special Study Options:** Cross registration, double major, dual enrollment, honors program, independent study, internships, liberal arts/career combination, student-designed major, study abroad, teacher certification program, adult degree completion program (1 evening per week, concentrated study).

FACILITIES

Housing: Coed, all-female, all-male, apartments for married students, apartments for single students, housing for disabled students. **Library Holdings:** 127,028 bound volumes. 3,050 periodicals. 178,314 microforms. 3,250 audiovisuals. **Special Academic Facilities/Equipment:** X-ray precision lab, lab kindergarten, historical library. **Computers:** School-owned computers available for student use.

EXTRACURRICULARS

Activities: Choral groups, drama/theater, music ensembles, musical theater, opera, radio station, student government, student newspaper, symphony orchestra, yearbook. **Organizations:** 21 registered organizations, 4 religious organizations. **Athletics (Intercollegiate):** *Men:* baseball, basketball, cross-country, golf, indoor track, soccer, tennis, track & field. *Women:* basketball, cross-country, indoor track, soccer, softball, tennis, track & field, volleyball.

ADMISSIONS

Selectivity Rating: 77 (of 100). **Freshman Academic Profile:** Average high school GPA 3.4. 26% in top 10% of high school class, 46% in top 25% of high school class, 67% in top 50% of high school class. 75% from public high schools. Average SAT I Math 578, SAT I Math middle 50% range 490-660. Average SAT I Verbal 588, SAT I Verbal middle 50% range 520-660. ACT middle 50% range 22-28. TOEFL required of all international applicants, minimum TOEFL 550. **Basis for Candidate Selection:** *Very important factors considered include:* recommendations, secondary school record, standardized test scores. *Important factors considered include:* character/personal qualities, class rank, interview. *Other factors considered include:* alumni/ae relation, essays, extracurricular activities, talent/ability, volunteer work, work experience. **Freshman Admission Requirements:** High school diploma or GED is required. *Academic units required/recommended:* 12 total required; 16 total recommended; 4 English required, 4 English recommended, 2 math required, 3 math recommended, 2 science required, 3 science recommended, 2 foreign language required, 2 foreign language recommended, 2 social studies required, 2 social studies recommended, 2 history required, 2 history recommended. **Freshman Admission Statistics:** 681 applied, 53% accepted, 38% of those accepted enrolled. **Transfer Admission Requirements:** *Items required:* high school transcript, college transcript. Minimum high school GPA of 2.0 required. Minimum college GPA of 2.0 required. Lowest grade transferable C. **General Admission Information:** Application fee $25. Priority application deadline February 15. Regular application deadline August 15. Nonfall registration accepted. Admission may be deferred for a maximum of 1 year. Credit and/or placement offered for CEEB Advanced Placement tests.

COSTS AND FINANCIAL AID

Tuition $14,700. Room & board $5,450. Required fees $300. Average book expense $700. **Required Forms and Deadlines:** FAFSA, institution's own financial aid form, and business/farm supplement. No deadline for regular filing. Priority filing deadline February 15. **Notification of Awards:** Applicants will be notified of awards on a rolling basis beginning on or about March 15. **Types of Aid:** *Need-based scholarships/grants:* Pell, SEOG, state scholarships/ grants, private scholarships, the school's own gift aid. *Loans:* Direct Subsidized Stafford, Direct Unsubsidized Stafford, Direct PLUS, Federal Perkins, Federal Nursing, college/university loans from institutional funds. **Student Employment:** Federal Work-Study Program available. Institutional employment available. Off-campus job opportunities are good. **Financial Aid Statistics:** 70% freshmen, 63% undergrads receive some form of aid. Average freshman grant $10,234. Average freshman loan $3,821. Average income from on-campus job $932. **Financial Aid Phone:** 574-535-7525.

GOUCHER COLLEGE

1021 Dulaney Valley Road, Baltimore, MD 21204-2794
Phone: 410-337-6100 **E-mail:** admission@goucher.edu **CEEB Code:** 5257
Fax: 410-337-6354 **Web:** www.goucher.edu **ACT Code:** 1696

This private school was founded in 1885. It has a 287-acre campus.

STUDENTS AND FACULTY

Enrollment: 1,270. **Student Body:** Male 30%, female 70%, out-of-state 62%, international 2%. **Ethnic Representation:** African American 6%, Asian 3%, Caucasian 62%, Hispanic 2%, Native American 1%. **Retention and Graduation:** 80% freshmen return for sophomore year. 60% freshmen graduate within 4 years. 4% grads pursue law degrees. 4% grads pursue medical degrees. **Faculty:** Student/faculty ratio 10:1. 96 full-time faculty, 87% hold PhDs. 100% faculty teach undergrads.

ACADEMICS

Degrees: Bachelor's, master's, post-bachelor's certificate. **Academic Requirements:** General education including some course work in arts/fine arts, computer literacy, English (including composition), foreign languages, humanities, mathematics, sciences (biological or physical), social science. **Classes:** 10-19 students in an average class. **Disciplines with Highest Percentage of Degrees Awarded:** Social sciences and history 17%, visual and performing arts 15%, education 12%, psychology 11%, English 10%. **Special Study Options:** Cross registration, distance learning, double major, dual enrollment, honors program, independent study, internships, student-designed major, study abroad, teacher certification program.

FACILITIES

Housing: Coed, all-female, all-male, apartments for single students, housing for disabled students, housing for international students, wellness dorm. **Library Holdings:** 303,364 bound volumes. 1,098 periodicals. 24,800 microforms. 5,691 audiovisuals. **Special Academic Facilities/Equipment:** Rosenberg Gallery, Mildred Dunock Theatre, Nations Bank Technology Center, Thorman International Center, Todd Dance Studio, Pilate's Studio, NMR facility, scientific visualization lab, Kraushaar Auditorium, sports and recreation center. **Computers:** School-owned computers available for student use.

EXTRACURRICULARS

Activities: Choral groups, dance, drama/theater, jazz band, literary magazine, music ensembles, opera, radio station, student government, student newspaper, student-run film society, television station, yearbook. **Organizations:** 38 registered organizations, 1 honor society, 3 religious organizations. **Athletics (Intercollegiate):** *Men:* basketball, cross-country, equestrian, lacrosse, soccer, swimming, tennis. *Women:* basketball, cross-country, equestrian, field hockey, lacrosse, soccer, swimming, tennis, volleyball.

ADMISSIONS

Selectivity Rating: 80 (of 100). **Freshman Academic Profile:** Average high school GPA 3.2. 19% in top 10% of high school class, 63% in top 25% of high school class, 75% in top 50% of high school class. 66% from public high schools. Average SAT I Math 575, SAT I Math middle 50% range 520-640. Average SAT I Verbal 605, SAT I Verbal middle 50% range 540-650. Average ACT 26, ACT middle 50% range 22-28. TOEFL required of all international applicants, minimum TOEFL 550. **Basis for Candidate Selection:** *Very important factors considered include:* recommendations, secondary school record. *Important factors considered include:* essays, extracurricular activities, standardized test scores, talent/ability. *Other factors considered include:* alumni/ae relation, character/personal qualities, class rank, interview, volunteer work, work experience. **Freshman Admission Requirements:** High school diploma is required and GED is not accepted. *Academic units required/recommended:* 16 total required; 4 English required, 3 math required, 2 science required, 2 science lab required, 2 foreign language required, 2 social studies required, 3 social studies recommended. **Freshman Admission Statistics:** 2,596 applied, 68% accepted, 21% of those accepted enrolled. **Transfer Admission Requirements:** *Items required:* college transcript, essay. Minimum college GPA of 2.5 required. Lowest grade transferable C. **General Admission Information:** Application fee $40. Early decision application deadline November 15. Regular application deadline February 1. Nonfall registration accepted. Admission may be deferred for a maximum of 1 year. Credit and/or placement offered for CEEB Advanced Placement tests.

COSTS AND FINANCIAL AID

Average book expense $800. **Required Forms and Deadlines:** FAFSA and CSS/Financial Aid PROFILE. Financial aid filing deadline February 15. Priority filing deadline February 15. **Notification of Awards:** Applicants will be notified of awards on or about April 1. **Types of Aid:** *Need-based scholarships/grants:* Pell, SEOG, state scholarships/grants, private scholarships, the school's own gift aid. *Loans:* Direct Subsidized Stafford, Direct Unsubsidized Stafford, Federal Perkins, state loans, college/university loans from institutional funds. **Student Employment:** Federal Work-Study Program available. Institutional employment available. Off-campus job opportunities are good. **Financial Aid Statistics:** 69% freshmen, 57% undergrads receive some form of aid. Average freshman grant $13,500. Average freshman loan $3,500. Average income from on-campus job $1,200. **Financial Aid Phone:** 410-337-6141.

See page 1042.

GOVERNORS STATE UNIVERSITY

1 University Parkway, University Park, IL 60466
Phone: 708-534-4490 **E-mail:** gsunow@govst.edu
Fax: 708-534-1640 **Web:** www.govst.edu

This public school was founded in 1969. It has a 720-acre campus.

STUDENTS AND FACULTY

Enrollment: 2,980. **Student Body:** Male 31%, female 69%, out-of-state 3%, international 1% (17 countries represented). **Ethnic Representation:** African American 29%, Asian 2%, Caucasian 60%, Hispanic 6%. **Retention and Graduation:** 38% grads go on to further study within 1 year. 16% grads pursue business degrees. 1% grads pursue law degrees. **Faculty:** Student/faculty ratio 16:1. 172 full-time faculty, 77% hold PhDs. 90% faculty teach undergrads.

ACADEMICS

Degrees: Bachelor's, master's. **Academic Requirements:** General education including some course work in arts/fine arts, English (including composition), humanities, mathematics, sciences (biological or physical), social science. **Majors with Highest Enrollment:** Communications and media studies; elementary education and teaching; business administration/management. **Disciplines with Highest Percentage of Degrees Awarded:** Education 19%, business/marketing 15%, liberal arts/general studies 14%, health professions and related sciences 13%, computer and information sciences 7%. **Special Study Options:** Cross registration, distance learning, dual enrollment, external degree program, independent study, internships, student-designed major, study abroad, teacher certification program.

FACILITIES

Library Holdings: 288,000 bound volumes. 1,100 periodicals. 762,000 microforms. 77,000 audiovisuals. **Special Academic Facilities/Equipment:** Manilow Sculpture Park. **Computers:** *Recommended operating system:* Windows 95. School-owned computers available for student use.

EXTRACURRICULARS

Activities: Drama/theater, literary magazine, student government, student newspaper. **Organizations:** 7 honor societies.

ADMISSIONS

Selectivity Rating: 63 (of 100). **Transfer Admission Requirements:** *Items required:* college transcript, statement of good standing from prior school. Minimum college GPA of 2.0 required. Lowest grade transferable C.

COSTS AND FINANCIAL AID

Out-of-state tuition $7,776. Required fees $320. **Types of Aid:** *Need-based scholarships/grants:* Pell, SEOG, state scholarships/grants, private scholarships, the school's own gift aid, Federal Nursing. *Loans:* Direct Subsidized Stafford, Federal Perkins, Federal Nursing, state loans, college/university loans from institutional funds. **Financial Aid Phone:** 708-534-4480.

GRACE COLLEGE AND SEMINARY

200 Seminary Drive, Winona Lake, IN 46590
Phone: 800-544-7223 **E-mail:** enroll@grace.edu **CEEB Code:** 1252
Fax: 574-372-5114 **Web:** www.grace.edu **ACT Code:** 1198

This private school was founded in 1948. It has a 150-acre campus.

STUDENTS AND FACULTY

Enrollment: 968. **Student Body:** Male 41%, female 59%, out-of-state 49%, international 2% (8 countries represented). **Ethnic Representation:** African American 5%, Caucasian 93%, Hispanic 1%. **Retention and Graduation:** 80% freshmen return for sophomore year. 6% freshmen graduate within 4 years. 24% grads go on to further study within 1 year. 1% grads pursue business degrees. 1% grads pursue law degrees. 5% grads pursue medical degrees. **Faculty:** Student/faculty ratio 19:1. 42 full-time faculty, 66% hold PhDs. 100% faculty teach undergrads.

ACADEMICS

Degrees: Associate's, bachelor's, master's. **Academic Requirements:** General education including some course work in arts/fine arts, English (including composition), history, humanities, mathematics, philosophy, sciences (biological or physical), Bible. **Classes:** 10-19 students in an average class. 10-19 students in an average lab/discussion section. **Disciplines with Highest Percentage of Degrees Awarded:** Education 19%, business/marketing 18%, visual and performing arts 7%, psychology 7%, communications/communication technologies 5%. **Special Study Options:** Distance learning, double major, English as a second language, internships, study abroad, teacher certification program.

FACILITIES

Housing: All-female, all-male. **Library Holdings:** 142,865 bound volumes. 12,500 periodicals. 22,885 microforms. 3,583 audiovisuals. **Special Academic Facilities/Equipment:** Westminster Museum. **Computers:** *Recommended operating system:* Windows 95. School-owned computers available for student use.

EXTRACURRICULARS

Activities: Choral groups, concert band, drama/theater, music ensembles, pep band, student government, student newspaper, television station, yearbook. **Organizations:** 9 registered organizations, 1 honor society, 8 religious organizations. **Athletics (Intercollegiate):** *Men:* baseball, basketball, crew, cross-country, golf, soccer, tennis, track & field. *Women:* basketball, crew, cross-country, soccer, softball, tennis, track & field, volleyball.

ADMISSIONS

Selectivity Rating: 76 (of 100). **Freshman Academic Profile:** Average high school GPA 3.4. 17% in top 10% of high school class, 43% in top 25% of high school class, 79% in top 50% of high school class. 65% from public high schools. Average SAT I Math 530, SAT I Math middle 50% range 480-590. Average SAT I Verbal 530, SAT I Verbal middle 50% range 470-590. Average ACT 23, ACT middle 50% range 20-25. TOEFL required of all international applicants, minimum TOEFL 500. **Basis for Candidate Selection:** *Very important factors considered include:* character/personal qualities, class rank, recommendations, religious affiliation/commitment, secondary school record. *Important factors considered include:* extracurricular activities, minority status, standardized test scores, talent/ability. *Other factors considered include:* essays, interview, volunteer work. **Freshman Admission Requirements:** High school diploma or GED is required. *Academic units required/recommended:* 14 total recommended; 4 English recommended, 2 math recommended, 2 science recommended, 1 science lab recommended, 2 foreign language recommended, 2 social studies recommended, 1 history recommended. **Freshman Admission Statistics:** 597 applied, 88% accepted, 41% of those accepted enrolled. **Transfer Admission Requirements:** *Items required:* high school transcript, college transcript, essay. Minimum college GPA of 2.0 required. Lowest grade transferable C-. **General Admission Information:** Application fee $20. Priority application deadline June 1. Regular application deadline August 1. Nonfall registration accepted. Admission may be deferred for a maximum of 1 year. Credit offered for CEEB Advanced Placement tests.

COSTS AND FINANCIAL AID

Tuition $11,440. Room & board $5,008. Required fees $320. Average book expense $500. **Required Forms and Deadlines:** FAFSA. No deadline for regular filing. Priority filing deadline March 1. **Types of Aid:** *Need-based scholarships/grants:* Pell, SEOG, state scholarships/grants, private scholarships, the school's own gift aid. *Loans:* FFEL Subsidized Stafford, FFEL Unsubsidized Stafford, FFEL PLUS, Federal Perkins. **Student Employment:** Federal Work-Study Program available. Institutional employment available. Off-campus job opportunities are excellent. **Financial Aid Statistics:** 65% freshmen, 79% undergrads receive some form of aid. Average freshman grant $4,500. Average freshman loan $4,600. Average income from on-campus job $1,300. **Financial Aid Phone:** 574-372-5245.

GRACELAND UNIVERSITY

Graceland University, 1 University Place, Lamoni, IA 50140
Phone: 641-784-5196 **E-mail:** admissions@graceland.edu **CEEB Code:** 6249
Fax: 641-784-5480 **Web:** www.graceland.edu **ACT Code:** 1314

This private school was founded in 1895. It has a 169-acre campus.

STUDENTS AND FACULTY

Enrollment: 2,066. **Student Body:** Male 32%, female 68%, out-of-state 68%, international 5%. **Ethnic Representation:** African American 3%, Asian 2%, Caucasian 82%, Hispanic 3%, Native American 1%. **Retention and Graduation:** 63% freshmen return for sophomore year. 27% freshmen graduate within 4 years. **Faculty:** Student/faculty ratio 16:1. 90 full-time faculty, 57% hold PhDs.

ACADEMICS

Degrees: Bachelor's, master's, post-master's certificate. **Academic Requirements:** General education including some course work in arts/fine arts, computer literacy, English (including composition), foreign languages, history, humanities, mathematics, philosophy, sciences (biological or physical), social science. **Classes:** Under 10 students in an average class. 20-29 students in an average lab/discussion section. **Disciplines with Highest Percentage of Degrees Awarded:** Health professions and related sciences 28%, business/marketing 21%, education 17%, liberal arts/general studies 10%, biological life sciences 4%. **Special Study Options:** Accelerated program (for nursing only), distance learning, double major, dual enrollment, English as a second language, external degree program, honors program, independent study, internships, liberal arts/career combination, student-designed major, study abroad, teacher certification program.

FACILITIES

Housing: All-female, all-male, apartments for married students. Students required to live on campus through their sophomore year unless married or living with relatives. **Library Holdings:** 143,523 bound volumes. 5,545 periodicals. 122,424 microforms. 3,500 audiovisuals. **Special Academic Facilities/Equipment:** Electron microscope, cyber cafe. **Computers:** School-owned computers available for student use.

EXTRACURRICULARS

Activities: Choral groups, concert band, drama/theater, jazz band, marching band, music ensembles, musical theater, pep band, student government, student newspaper, symphony orchestra, yearbook. **Organizations:** 50 registered organizations, 1 religious organization. **Athletics (Intercollegiate):** *Men:* baseball, basketball, cross-country, football, golf, indoor track, soccer, tennis, track & field, volleyball. *Women:* basketball, cross-country, golf, indoor track, soccer, softball, tennis, track & field, volleyball.

ADMISSIONS

Selectivity Rating: 76 (of 100). **Freshman Academic Profile:** Average high school GPA 3.2. 20% in top 10% of high school class, 41% in top 25% of high school class, 74% in top 50% of high school class. Average SAT I Math 524, SAT I Math middle 50% range 450-590. Average SAT I Verbal 495, SAT I Verbal middle 50% range 410-610. Average ACT 22, ACT middle 50% range 19-25. TOEFL required of all international applicants, minimum TOEFL 450. **Basis for Candidate Selection:** *Very important factors considered include:* class rank, secondary school record, standardized test scores. *Important factors considered include:* character/personal qualities, extracurricular activities, interview, talent/ability. *Other factors considered include:* minority status, recommendations. **Freshman Admission Requirements:** High school diploma or GED is required. *Academic units required/recommended:* 16 total recommended; 3 English recommended, 2 math recommended, 2 science recommended, 2 foreign language recommended, 2 social studies recommended. **Freshman Admission Statistics:** 1,135 applied, 69% accepted, 53% of those accepted enrolled. **Transfer Admission Requirements:** *Items required:* high school transcript, college transcript. Minimum high school GPA of 2.0 required. Minimum college GPA of 2.0 required. Lowest grade transferable D. **General Admission Information:** Application fee $30. Priority application deadline May 1. Nonfall registration accepted. Admission may be deferred. Credit and/or placement offered for CEEB Advanced Placement tests.

COSTS AND FINANCIAL AID

Tuition $13,750. Room & board $4,530. Required fees $150. Average book expense $900. **Required Forms and Deadlines:** FAFSA. No deadline for regular filing. Priority filing deadline March 1. **Notification of Awards:** Applicants will be notified of awards on a rolling basis beginning on or about February 1. **Types of Aid:** *Need-based scholarships/grants:* Pell, SEOG, state scholarships/grants, private scholarships, the school's own gift aid. *Loans:* Direct Subsidized Stafford, Direct Unsubsidized Stafford, Direct PLUS, Federal Perkins, college/university loans from institutional funds. **Student Employment:** Federal Work-Study Program available. Institutional employment available. Off-campus job opportunities are poor. **Financial Aid Statistics:** 76% freshmen, 59% undergrads receive some form of aid. Average freshman grant $8,778. Average freshman loan $3,633. Average income from on-campus job $864. **Financial Aid Phone:** 641-784-5136.

GRAMBLING STATE UNIVERSITY

100 Main Street, Grambling, LA 71245
Phone: 318-247-3811 **E-mail:** bingamann@medgar.gram.edu **CEEB Code:** 6250
Fax: 318-274-3292 **Web:** www.gram.edu **ACT Code:** 1582

This public school was founded in 1901. It has a 340-acre campus.

STUDENTS AND FACULTY

Enrollment: 4,052. **Student Body:** Male 43%, female 57%, out-of-state 34%, international 1% (21 countries represented). **Ethnic Representation:** African American 97%, Caucasian 2%, Hispanic 1%. **Retention and Graduation:** 71% freshmen return for sophomore year. 10% freshmen graduate within 4 years. 33% grads go on to further study within 1 year.

ACADEMICS

Degrees: Associate's, bachelor's, doctoral, master's. **Academic Requirements:** General education including some course work in arts/fine arts, computer literacy, English (including composition), history, humanities, mathematics, sciences (biological or physical), social science. **Special Study Options:** Accelerated program, cooperative (work-study) program, distance learning, double major, student exchange program (domestic), honors program, independent study, internships, study abroad, teacher certification program.

FACILITIES

Housing: All-female, all-male, fraternities and/or sororities, graduate dorm. **Library Holdings:** 305,288 bound volumes. 95,320 periodicals. 121,737 microforms. 5,608 audiovisuals. **Special Academic Facilities/Equipment:** Audiovisual and TV center, lab schools. **Computers:** *Recommended operating system:* Mac.

EXTRACURRICULARS

Activities: Choral groups, dance, drama/theater, jazz band, marching band, music ensembles, radio station, student government, student newspaper, television station, yearbook. **Organizations:** 50 registered organizations, 11 honor societies, 3 religious organizations, 4 fraternities (2% men join), 5 sororities (7% women join).

ADMISSIONS

Selectivity Rating: 69 (of 100). **Freshman Academic Profile:** Average ACT 16. **Basis for Candidate Selection:** *Very important factors considered include:* standardized test scores. *Other factors considered include:* alumni/ae relation, extracurricular activities, recommendations, talent/ability. **Freshman Admission Requirements:** High school diploma or GED is required. *Academic units required/recommended:* 23 total required; 4 English required, 3 math required, 3 science required, 3 social studies required, 8 elective required. **Freshman Admission Statistics:** 2,661 applied, 58% accepted, 58% of those accepted enrolled. **Transfer Admission Requirements:** *Items required:* college transcript, statement of good standing from prior school. Minimum high school GPA of 2.0 required. Minimum college GPA of 2.0 required. Lowest grade transferable C. **General Admission Information:** Application fee $20. Early decision application deadline April 15. Regular application deadline August 1. Nonfall registration accepted. Admission may be deferred.

COSTS AND FINANCIAL AID

In-state tuition $2,208. Out-of-state tuition $7,358. Room & board $2,636. Required fees $60. Average book expense $600. **Required Forms and Deadlines:** FAFSA, institution's own financial aid form, and state aid form. **Notification of Awards:** Applicants will be notified of awards on or about April 15. **Types of Aid:** *Need-based scholarships/grants:* state scholarships/ grants. *Loans:* FFEL Subsidized Stafford, FFEL PLUS. **Student Employment:** Federal Work-Study Program available. Off-campus job opportunities are good. **Financial Aid Phone:** 318-274-7878.

GRAND CANYON UNIVERSITY

PO Box 11097, 3300 W Camelback Road, Phoenix, AZ 85061-0197
Phone: 602-589-2855 **E-mail:** admissions@grand-canyon.edu **CEEB Code:** 4331
Fax: 602-589-2580 **Web:** www.grand-canyon.edu **ACT Code:** 92

This private school was founded in 1949. It has a 90-acre campus.

STUDENTS AND FACULTY

Enrollment: 1,609. **Student Body:** Male 36%, female 64%, out-of-state 19%, international 3%. **Ethnic Representation:** African American 3%, Asian 2%, Caucasian 57%, Hispanic 7%, Native American 1%. **Retention and Graduation:** 76% freshmen return for sophomore year. 32% freshmen graduate within 4 years. **Faculty:** Student/faculty ratio 16:1. 97 full-time faculty, 57% hold PhDs. 100% faculty teach undergrads.

ACADEMICS

Degrees: Bachelor's, diploma, master's. **Academic Requirements:** General education including some course work in arts/fine arts, English (including composition), history, humanities, mathematics, sciences (biological or physical). **Classes:** Under 10 students in an average class. 10-19 students in an average lab/discussion section. **Disciplines with Highest Percentage of Degrees Awarded:** Business/marketing 25%, health professions and related sciences 18%, education 17%, biological life sciences 13%, social sciences and history 6%. **Special Study Options:** Accelerated program, cooperative (work-study) program, distance learning, double major, dual enrollment, English as a second language, student exchange program (domestic), honors program, independent study, internships, study abroad, teacher certification program.

FACILITIES

Housing: All-female, all-male, apartments for married students, apartments for single students. **Library Holdings:** 75,905 bound volumes. 1,174 periodicals. 82,561 microforms. 404 audiovisuals. **Special Academic Facilities/Equipment:** Art gallery, dynamical systems laboratory. **Computers:** *Recommended operating system:* Windows 95. School-owned computers available for student use.

EXTRACURRICULARS

Activities: Choral groups, concert band, drama/theater, jazz band, literary magazine, music ensembles, musical theater, opera, student government, student newspaper. **Organizations:** 20 registered organizations, 3 honor societies, 4 religious organizations. **Athletics (Intercollegiate):** *Men:* baseball, basketball, golf, soccer. *Women:* basketball, soccer, tennis, volleyball.

ADMISSIONS

Selectivity Rating: 71 (of 100). **Freshman Academic Profile:** 29% in top 10% of high school class, 54% in top 25% of high school class, 78% in top 50% of high school class. Average SAT I Math 518. Average SAT I Verbal 528. Average ACT 23. TOEFL required of all international applicants, minimum TOEFL 500. **Basis for Candidate Selection:** *Very important factors considered include:* secondary school record, standardized test scores. *Important factors considered include:* class rank. *Other factors considered include:* character/personal qualities, essays, extracurricular activities, interview, recommendations, talent/ability. **Freshman Admission Requirements:** High school diploma or GED is required. *Academic units required/recommended:* 4 English required, 4 English recommended, 3 math required, 3 math recommended, 2 science required, 2 science recommended, 2 science lab required, 2 science lab recommended, 2 social studies required, 2 social studies recommended. **Freshman Admission Statistics:** 823 applied, 69% accepted, 44% of those accepted enrolled. **Transfer Admission Requirements:** *Items required:* college transcript. Minimum college GPA of 2.0 required. Lowest grade transferable C. **General Admission Information:** Application fee $50. Nonfall registration accepted. Credit offered for CEEB Advanced Placement tests.

COSTS AND FINANCIAL AID

Tuition $13,750. Room & board $4,800. Required fees $0. Average book expense $780. **Required Forms and Deadlines:** FAFSA. No deadline for regular filing. **Notification of Awards:** Applicants will be notified of awards on a rolling basis beginning on or about March 15. **Types of Aid:** *Need-based scholarships/grants:* Pell, SEOG, state scholarships/grants, private scholarships, the school's own gift aid, Bureau of Indian Affairs grant. *Loans:* FFEL Subsidized Stafford, FFEL Unsubsidized Stafford, FFEL PLUS, Federal Perkins, state loans, alternative loans. **Student Employment:** Federal Work-Study Program available. Institutional employment available. Off-campus job opportunities are excellent. **Financial Aid Statistics:** 64% freshmen, 63% undergrads receive some form of aid. Average freshman grant $3,158. Average freshman loan $2,859. Average income from on-campus job $1,500. **Financial Aid Phone:** 602-589-2885.

GRAND RAPIDS BAPTIST SEMINARY

1001 East Beltline NE, Grand Rapids, MI 49525-5897
Phone: 800-697-1133 **E-mail:** grbs@cornerstone.edu
Fax: 616-222-1400 **Web:** www.grbs.edu

This private school, which is affiliated with the Baptist Church, was founded in 1941. It has a 132-acre campus.

STUDENTS AND FACULTY

Enrollment: 1,120. **Student Body:** Out-of-state 21%.

ACADEMICS

Degrees: Associate's, bachelor's, doctoral, master's.

FACILITIES

Housing: Coed, all-female, all-male.

EXTRACURRICULARS

Activities: Student government, student newspaper, yearbook. **Organizations:** 25 registered organizations.

ADMISSIONS

Selectivity Rating: 63 (of 100). **Freshman Academic Profile:** 18% in top 10% of high school class, 38% in top 25% of high school class, 71% in top 50% of high school class. TOEFL required of all international applicants, minimum TOEFL 500. **General Admission Information:** Regular application deadline August 15.

COSTS AND FINANCIAL AID

Tuition $6,648. Room & board $7,020. Required fees $270. Average book expense $700. **Types of Aid:** *Loans:* FFEL Subsidized Stafford, FFEL PLUS. **Student Employment:** Federal Work-Study Program available. **Financial Aid Statistics:** Average income from on-campus job $1,200.

GRAND VALLEY STATE UNIVERSITY

1 Campus Drive, Allendale, MI 49401
Phone: 616-331-5000 **E-mail:** go2gvsu@gvsu.edu **CEEB Code:** 1258
Fax: 616-331-2000 **Web:** www.gvsu.edu **ACT Code:** 2005

This public school was founded in 1960. It has an 897-acre campus.

STUDENTS AND FACULTY

Enrollment: 16,875. **Student Body:** Male 40%, female 60%, out-of-state 4%, international 1% (39 countries represented). **Ethnic Representation:** African

American 5%, Asian 2%, Caucasian 90%, Hispanic 2%, Native American 1%. **Retention and Graduation:** 78% freshmen return for sophomore year. 17% freshmen graduate within 4 years. 35% grads go on to further study within 1 year. **Faculty:** Student/faculty ratio 22:1. 763 full-time faculty, 67% hold PhDs. 90% faculty teach undergrads.

ACADEMICS

Degrees: Bachelor's, master's, post-bachelor's certificate, post-master's certificate. **Academic Requirements:** General education including some course work in arts/fine arts, English (including composition), history, humanities, mathematics, philosophy, sciences (biological or physical), social science. **Classes:** 20-29 students in an average class. 20-29 students in an average lab/discussion section. **Disciplines with Highest Percentage of Degrees Awarded:** Business/marketing 21%, health professions and related sciences 14%, English 9%, protective services/public administration 8%, education 6%. **Special Study Options:** Cooperative (work-study) program, distance learning, double major, honors program, independent study, internships, liberal arts/career combination, student-designed major, study abroad, teacher certification program. Undergrads may take grad-level classes. Co-op programs: education, engineering, health professions. Off-campus study: Washington, DC.

FACILITIES

Housing: Coed, apartments for married students, apartments for single students, honors college building, specialty housing in languages and engineering. **Library Holdings:** 627,000 bound volumes. 3,690 periodicals. 600,000 microforms. 0 audiovisuals. **Special Academic Facilities/Equipment:** 2 Great Lakes research vessels, audiovisual center, performance/recital hall, pipe organ, physical therapy/human performance lab. **Computers:** School-owned computers available for student use.

EXTRACURRICULARS

Activities: Choral groups, concert band, dance, drama/theater, jazz band, marching band, music ensembles, musical theater, pep band, radio station, student government, student newspaper, student-run film society, symphony orchestra, television station. **Organizations:** 136 registered organizations, 14 honor societies, 10 fraternities (3% men join), 11 sororities (2% women join). **Athletics (Intercollegiate):** *Men:* baseball, basketball, cross-country, diving, football, golf, swimming, tennis, track & field. *Women:* basketball, cross-country, diving, golf, soccer, softball, swimming, tennis, track & field, volleyball.

ADMISSIONS

Selectivity Rating: 71 (of 100). **Freshman Academic Profile:** Average high school GPA 3.4. 15% in top 10% of high school class, 42% in top 25% of high school class, 81% in top 50% of high school class. 85% from public high schools. Average ACT 23, ACT middle 50% range 21-25. TOEFL required of all international applicants, minimum TOEFL 550. **Basis for Candidate Selection:** *Very important factors considered include:* class rank, secondary school record, standardized test scores. *Other factors considered include:* essays, extracurricular activities, geographical residence, interview, minority status, recommendations, state residency, talent/ability, volunteer work, work experience. **Freshman Admission Requirements:** High school diploma or GED is required. *Academic units required/recommended:* 20 total required; 4 English required, 3 math required, 4 math recommended, 3 science required, 2 foreign language recommended, 3 social studies required, 7 elective required. **Freshman Admission Statistics:** 10,167 applied, 71% accepted, 40% of those accepted enrolled. **Transfer Admission Requirements:** *Items required:* college transcript. Minimum college GPA of 2.0 required. Lowest grade transferable D. **General Admission Information:** Application fee $20. Priority application deadline February 1. Regular application deadline July 31. Nonfall registration accepted. Credit and/or placement offered for CEEB Advanced Placement tests.

COSTS AND FINANCIAL AID

In-state tuition $5,056. Out-of-state tuition $10,936. Room & board $5,656. Required fees $0. Average book expense $800. **Required Forms and Deadlines:** FAFSA. No deadline for regular filing. Priority filing deadline February 15. **Notification of Awards:** Applicants will be notified of awards on a rolling basis. **Types of Aid:** *Need-based scholarships/grants:* Pell, SEOG, state scholarships/grants, private scholarships, the school's own gift aid, Federal Nursing. *Loans:* Direct Subsidized Stafford, Direct Unsubsidized Stafford, Direct PLUS, Federal Perkins, Federal Nursing, state loans, college/university loans from institutional funds. **Student Employment:** Federal Work-Study Program available. Institutional employment available. Off-campus job opportunities are good. **Financial Aid Statistics:** 63% freshmen, 56% undergrads receive some form of aid. Average freshman loan $3,525. Average income from on-campus job $1,500. **Financial Aid Phone:** 616-331-3234.

See page 1044.

GRAND VIEW COLLEGE

1200 Grandview Avenue, Des Moines, IA 50316-1599
Phone: 515-263-2810 **E-mail:** admiss@gvc.edu **CEEB Code:** 6251
Fax: 515-263-2974 **Web:** www.gvc.edu **ACT Code:** 1316

This private school, which is affiliated with the Lutheran Church, was founded in 1896. It has a 35-acre campus.

STUDENTS AND FACULTY

Enrollment: 1,546. **Student Body:** Male 32%, female 68%, out-of-state 5%, international 2% (16 countries represented). **Ethnic Representation:** African American 3%, Asian 1%, Caucasian 63%, Hispanic 1%, Native American 1%. **Retention and Graduation:** 64% freshmen return for sophomore year. 23% freshmen graduate within 4 years. **Faculty:** Student/faculty ratio 13:1. 73 full-time faculty, 57% hold PhDs. 100% faculty teach undergrads.

ACADEMICS

Degrees: Associate's, bachelor's, certificate, terminal, transfer. **Academic Requirements:** General education including some course work in arts/fine arts, computer literacy, English (including composition), history, humanities, mathematics, sciences (biological or physical), social science. **Classes:** 10-19 students in an average class. 10-19 students in an average lab/discussion section. **Majors with Highest Enrollment:** Nursing/registered nurse training (RN, ASN, BSN, MSN); business administration/management; education, general. **Disciplines with Highest Percentage of Degrees Awarded:** Business/marketing 20%, health professions and related sciences 18%, protective services/public administration 15%, education 14%, liberal arts/general studies 8%. **Special Study Options:** Accelerated program, cooperative (work-study) program, cross registration, distance learning, double major, dual enrollment, honors program, independent study, internships, liberal arts/career combination, student-designed major, study abroad, teacher certification program, weekend college.

FACILITIES

Housing: Coed, apartments for single students, college-owned campus houses. **Library Holdings:** 103,468 bound volumes. 3,412 periodicals. 185,607 microforms. 6,360 audiovisuals. **Special Academic Facilities/Equipment:** Danish American Archives. **Computers:** School-owned computers available for student use.

EXTRACURRICULARS

Activities: Choral groups, drama/theater, music ensembles, radio station, student government, student newspaper, television station. **Organizations:** 28 registered organizations, 1 religious organization. **Athletics (Intercollegiate):** *Men:* baseball, basketball, soccer. *Women:* basketball, soccer, softball, volleyball.

ADMISSIONS

Selectivity Rating: 63 (of 100). **Freshman Academic Profile:** Average high school GPA 3.0. 13% in top 10% of high school class, 30% in top 25% of high school class, 62% in top 50% of high school class. SAT I Math middle 50% range 420-610. SAT I Verbal middle 50% range 370-690. Average ACT 20, ACT middle 50% range 18-22. TOEFL required of all international applicants, minimum TOEFL 550. **Basis for Candidate Selection:** *Very important factors considered include:* character/personal qualities, class rank, secondary school record. *Important factors considered include:* standardized test scores. *Other factors considered include:* alumni/ae relation, extracurricular activities, talent/ability. **Freshman Admission Requirements:** High school diploma or GED is required. *Academic units required/recommended:* 15 total recommended; 4 English recommended, 3 math recommended, 3 science recommended, 2 foreign language recommended, 3 social studies recommended. **Freshman Admission Statistics:** 421 applied, 94% accepted, 51% of those accepted enrolled. **Transfer Admission Requirements:** *Items required:* college transcript. Minimum college GPA of 2.0 required. Lowest grade transferable D. **General Admission Information:** Regular application deadline August 15. Nonfall registration accepted. Admission may be deferred. Credit and/or placement offered for CEEB Advanced Placement tests.

COSTS AND FINANCIAL AID

Tuition $13,914. Room & board $4,798. Required fees $280. Average book expense $600. **Required Forms and Deadlines:** FAFSA. No deadline for regular filing. Priority filing deadline March 1. **Notification of Awards:** Applicants will be notified of awards on a rolling basis beginning on or about March 1. **Types of Aid:** *Need-based scholarships/grants:* Pell, SEOG, state scholarships/grants, private scholarships, the school's own gift aid. *Loans:* FFEL Subsidized Stafford, FFEL Unsubsidized Stafford, FFEL PLUS, Federal Perkins. **Student Employment:** Federal Work-Study Program available. Institutional employment available. Off-campus job opportunities are excellent.

Financial Aid Statistics: 88% freshmen, 84% undergrads receive some form of aid. Average freshman grant $8,877. Average income from on-campus job $1,500. **Financial Aid Phone:** 515-263-2820.

GRATZ COLLEGE

7605 Old York Road, Melrose Park, PA 19027
Phone: 215-635-7300 **E-mail:** admissions@gratz.edu
Fax: 215-635-7320 **Web:** www.gratzcollege.edu

This private school, which is affiliated with the Jewish faith, was founded in 1895. It has a 28-acre campus.

STUDENTS AND FACULTY

Enrollment: 16. **Student Body:** Male 13%, female 88%, out-of-state 25%, international students represent 4 countries. **Ethnic Representation:** Asian 6%, Caucasian 94%. **Retention and Graduation:** 88% freshmen return for sophomore year. **Faculty:** Student/faculty ratio 12:1. 8 full-time faculty, 100% hold PhDs. 100% faculty teach undergrads.

ACADEMICS

Degrees: Bachelor's, master's, post-bachelor's certificate. **Academic Requirements:** General education including some course work in Jewish studies and Hebrew language. **Classes:** Under 10 students in an average class. Under 10 students in an average lab/discussion section. **Disciplines with Highest Percentage of Degrees Awarded:** Jewish studies 100%. **Special Study Options:** Cross registration, double major, dual enrollment, independent study, internships, liberal arts/career combination, study abroad, teacher certification program. Joint programs with area colleges and universities are offered only at the master's level.

FACILITIES

Library Holdings: 100,000 bound volumes. 200 periodicals. 100 microforms. 4,600 audiovisuals. **Computers:** School-owned computers available for student use.

EXTRACURRICULARS

Activities: Choral groups, music ensembles.

ADMISSIONS

Selectivity Rating: 60 (of 100). **Freshman Academic Profile:** Average high school GPA 3.5. TOEFL required of all international applicants, minimum TOEFL 450. **Basis for Candidate Selection:** *Very important factors considered include:* character/personal qualities, essays, recommendations, religious affiliation/commitment, talent/ability. *Important factors considered include:* interview, secondary school record, volunteer work. *Other factors considered include:* alumni/ae relation, class rank, extracurricular activities, minority status, standardized test scores, work experience. **Freshman Admission Requirements:** High school diploma or GED is required. *Academic units required/recommended:* 18 total required; 23 total recommended; 3 English required, 4 English recommended, 2 math required, 2 math recommended, 2 science required, 2 science recommended, 1 science lab required, 1 science lab recommended, 2 foreign language required, 4 foreign language recommended, 3 social studies required, 4 social studies recommended, 3 history required, 4 history recommended, 2 elective required, 2 elective recommended. **Transfer Admission Requirements:** *Items required:* high school transcript, college transcript, essay. Lowest grade transferable C. **General Admission Information:** Application fee $50. Nonfall registration accepted. Admission may be deferred for a maximum of 2 years. Neither credit nor placement offered for CEEB Advanced Placement tests.

COSTS AND FINANCIAL AID

Tuition $8,190. Required fees $400. Average book expense $550. **Required Forms and Deadlines:** FAFSA and institution's own financial aid form. No deadline for regular filing. **Notification of Awards:** Applicants will be notified of awards on a rolling basis. **Types of Aid:** *Need-based scholarships/grants:* Pell, private scholarships. *Loans:* FFEL Subsidized Stafford, FFEL Unsubsidized Stafford, FFEL PLUS. **Student Employment:** Institutional employment available. Off-campus job opportunities are good. **Financial Aid Phone:** 215-635-7300.

GREEN MOUNTAIN COLLEGE

One College Circle, Poultney, VT 05764-1199
Phone: 802-287-8208 **E-mail:** admiss@greenmtn.edu **CEEB Code:** 3418
Fax: 802-287-8099 **Web:** www.greenmtn.edu **ACT Code:** 4302

This private school, which is affiliated with the Methodist Church, was founded in 1834. It has a 155-acre campus.

STUDENTS AND FACULTY

Enrollment: 661. **Student Body:** Male 53%, female 47%, out-of-state 91%, international 4% (18 countries represented). **Ethnic Representation:** African American 2%, Caucasian 69%, Hispanic 3%, Native American 1%. **Retention and Graduation:** 56% freshmen return for sophomore year. 35% freshmen graduate within 4 years. 6% grads go on to further study within 1 year. 3% grads pursue business degrees. 3% grads pursue law degrees. **Faculty:** Student/faculty ratio 14:1. 37 full-time faculty, 86% hold PhDs. 100% faculty teach undergrads.

ACADEMICS

Degrees: Bachelor's, certificate. **Academic Requirements:** General education including some course work in English (including composition), history, humanities, mathematics, philosophy, sciences (biological or physical), social science, health and well-being. **Classes:** 20-29 students in an average class. **Majors with Highest Enrollment:** Business administration/management; environmental studies; parks, recreation and leisure studies. **Disciplines with Highest Percentage of Degrees Awarded:** Business/marketing 18%, parks and recreation 15%, natural resources/environmental sciences 14%, education 12%, psychology 9%. **Special Study Options:** Cooperative (work-study) program, double major, honors program, independent study, internships, liberal arts/career combination, student-designed major, study abroad, teacher certification program.

FACILITIES

Housing: Coed, housing for disabled students, substance-free theme. **Library Holdings:** 62,000 bound volumes. 230 periodicals. 4,650 microforms. 4,350 audiovisuals. **Special Academic Facilities/Equipment:** Welsh Heritage Collection, rare books room. **Computers:** School-owned computers available for student use.

EXTRACURRICULARS

Activities: Choral groups, concert band, drama/theater, jazz band, literary magazine, music ensembles, student government, student newspaper, yearbook. **Organizations:** 30 registered organizations, 2 honor societies, 2 religious organizations. **Athletics (Intercollegiate):** *Men:* basketball, cross-country, golf, lacrosse, skiing (alpine), soccer, tennis. *Women:* basketball, cross-country, golf, skiing (alpine), soccer, softball, tennis, volleyball.

ADMISSIONS

Selectivity Rating: 67 (of 100). **Freshman Academic Profile:** Average high school GPA 2.6. 84% from public high schools. Average SAT I Math 412, SAT I Math middle 50% range 410-540. Average SAT I Verbal 470, SAT I Verbal middle 50% range 430-570. Average ACT 21, ACT middle 50% range 18-26. TOEFL required of all international applicants, minimum TOEFL 500. **Basis for Candidate Selection:** *Very important factors considered include:* character/personal qualities, secondary school record. *Important factors considered include:* extracurricular activities, standardized test scores, talent/ability, volunteer work. *Other factors considered include:* essays, interview, minority status, recommendations, work experience. **Freshman Admission Requirements:** High school diploma or GED is required. *Academic units required/recommended:* 18 total required; 4 English required, 3 math required, 2 science required, 2 foreign language recommended, 1 social studies required, 2 history required, 6 elective required. **Freshman Admission Statistics:** 938 applied, 71% accepted, 27% of those accepted enrolled. **Transfer Admission Requirements:** *Items required:* high school transcript, college transcript, essay, statement of good standing from prior school. Minimum college GPA of 2.0 required. Lowest grade transferable C-. **General Admission Information:** Application fee $30. Priority application deadline April 1. Nonfall registration accepted. Admission may be deferred for a maximum of 1 year. Credit and/or placement offered for CEEB Advanced Placement tests.

COSTS AND FINANCIAL AID

Tuition $18,750. Room & board $5,980. Required fees $420. Average book expense $600. **Required Forms and Deadlines:** FAFSA. No deadline for regular filing. Priority filing deadline February 15. **Notification of Awards:** Applicants will be notified of awards on a rolling basis beginning on or about March 15. **Types of Aid:** *Need-based scholarships/grants:* Pell, SEOG, state scholarships/grants, private scholarships, the school's own gift aid. *Loans:* FFEL Subsidized Stafford, FFEL Unsubsidized Stafford, FFEL PLUS, Federal

Perkins, state loans, alternative loans. **Student Employment:** Federal Work-Study Program available. Institutional employment available. Off-campus job opportunities are excellent. **Financial Aid Statistics:** 75% freshmen, 71% undergrads receive some form of aid. Average freshman grant $9,245. Average freshman loan $2,424. Average income from on-campus job $1,300. **Financial Aid Phone:** 802-287-8210.

GREENSBORO COLLEGE

815 West Market Street, Greensboro, NC 27401-1875
Phone: 800-346-8226 **E-mail:** admissions@gborocollege.edu **CEEB Code:** 5260
Fax: 336-378-0154 **Web:** www.gborocollege.edu **ACT Code:** 3104

This private school, which is affiliated with the Methodist Church, was founded in 1838. It has a 40-acre campus.

STUDENTS AND FACULTY

Enrollment: 1,208. **Student Body:** Male 46%, female 54%, out-of-state 29%, international 1% (18 countries represented). **Ethnic Representation:** African American 16%, Asian 1%, Caucasian 81%, Hispanic 2%. **Retention and Graduation:** 65% freshmen return for sophomore year. 27% freshmen graduate within 4 years. 17% grads go on to further study within 1 year. 2% grads pursue business degrees. 1% grads pursue law degrees. 4% grads pursue medical degrees. **Faculty:** Student/faculty ratio 14:1. 56 full-time faculty, 80% hold PhDs. 100% faculty teach undergrads.

ACADEMICS

Degrees: Bachelor's, certificate, master's, post-bachelor's certificate. **Academic Requirements:** General education including some course work in arts/fine arts, computer literacy, English (including composition), foreign languages, history, humanities, mathematics, sciences (biological or physical), social science, religion, physical education. **Classes:** 10-19 students in an average class. 20-29 students in an average lab/discussion section. **Majors with Highest Enrollment:** Business/managerial economics; education, general; health and physical education, general. **Disciplines with Highest Percentage of Degrees Awarded:** Business/marketing 22%, social sciences and history 15%, education 14%, biological life sciences 10%, parks and recreation 9%. **Special Study Options:** Accelerated program, cross registration, double major, dual enrollment, English as a second language, honors program, independent study, internships, liberal arts/career combination, student-designed major, study abroad, teacher certification program, weekend college, academic development program.

FACILITIES

Housing: Coed, all-female, all-male, community service housing. **Library Holdings:** 108,350 bound volumes. 290 periodicals. 2,970 microforms. 2,686 audiovisuals. **Special Academic Facilities/Equipment:** Art gallery, historical museum, language lab, computer labs. **Computers:** School-owned computers available for student use.

EXTRACURRICULARS

Activities: Choral groups, dance, drama/theater, jazz band, literary magazine, marching band, music ensembles, musical theater, opera, pep band, student government, student newspaper, yearbook. **Organizations:** 43 registered organizations, 11 honor societies, 4 religious organizations, 1 fraternity (1% men join). **Athletics (Intercollegiate):** *Men:* baseball, basketball, cross-country, football, golf, lacrosse, soccer, tennis. *Women:* basketball, cheerleading, cross-country, lacrosse, soccer, softball, swimming, tennis, volleyball.

ADMISSIONS

Selectivity Rating: 63 (of 100). **Freshman Academic Profile:** Average high school GPA 2.9. 5% in top 10% of high school class, 15% in top 25% of high school class, 35% in top 50% of high school class. Average SAT I Math 480, SAT I Math middle 50% range 420-540. Average SAT I Verbal 471, SAT I Verbal middle 50% range 410-530. Average ACT 19, ACT middle 50% range 17-21. TOEFL required of all international applicants, minimum TOEFL 550. **Basis for Candidate Selection:** *Very important factors considered include:* class rank, essays, extracurricular activities, secondary school record. *Important factors considered include:* alumni/ae relation, character/personal qualities, interview, recommendations, standardized test scores, talent/ability. *Other factors considered include:* religious affiliation/commitment, volunteer work, work experience. **Freshman Admission Requirements:** High school diploma or GED is required. *Academic units required/recommended:* 4 English recommended, 3 math recommended, 2 science recommended, 1 science lab recommended, 2 foreign language recommended, 2 history recommended. **Freshman Admission Statistics:** 806 applied, 77% accepted, 39% of those accepted enrolled. **Transfer Admission Requirements:** *Items required:* college transcript, essay. Lowest grade transferable C. **General Admission Information:** Application fee $35. Priority application deadline December 15. Nonfall registration accepted. Admission may be deferred for a maximum of 1 year. Credit and/or placement offered for CEEB Advanced Placement tests.

COSTS AND FINANCIAL AID

Tuition $14,450. Room & board $5,760. Required fees $200. Average book expense $800. **Required Forms and Deadlines:** FAFSA, institution's own financial aid form, and state aid form. No deadline for regular filing. Priority filing deadline April 15. **Notification of Awards:** Applicants will be notified of awards on a rolling basis beginning on or about February 15. **Types of Aid:** *Need-based scholarships/grants:* Pell, SEOG, state scholarships/grants, private scholarships, the school's own gift aid. *Loans:* FFEL Subsidized Stafford, FFEL Unsubsidized Stafford, FFEL PLUS, Federal Perkins, college/university loans from institutional funds. **Student Employment:** Federal Work-Study Program available. Institutional employment available. Off-campus job opportunities are excellent. **Financial Aid Statistics:** 83% freshmen, 61% undergrads receive some form of aid. Average freshman grant $7,039. Average freshman loan $4,807. Average income from on-campus job $1,000. **Financial Aid Phone:** 800-346-8226.

See page 1046.

GREENVILLE COLLEGE

315 East College Avenue, Greenville, IL 62246-0159
Phone: 618-664-4401 **E-mail:** admissions@greenville.edu **CEEB Code:** 1256
Fax: 618-664-9841 **Web:** www.greenville.edu **ACT Code:** 1032

This private school was founded in 1892. It has a 40-acre campus.

STUDENTS AND FACULTY

Enrollment: 1,134. **Student Body:** Male 49%, female 51%, out-of-state 33%, international 1% (15 countries represented). **Ethnic Representation:** African American 7%, Asian 1%, Caucasian 87%, Hispanic 2%, Native American 1%. **Retention and Graduation:** 75% freshmen return for sophomore year. 35% freshmen graduate within 4 years. 17% grads go on to further study within 1 year. 8% grads pursue business degrees. 1% grads pursue law degrees. 2% grads pursue medical degrees. **Faculty:** Student/faculty ratio 16:1. 56 full-time faculty, 60% hold PhDs. 100% faculty teach undergrads.

ACADEMICS

Degrees: Bachelor's, master's. **Academic Requirements:** General education including some course work in arts/fine arts, English (including composition), history, humanities, mathematics, philosophy, sciences (biological or physical), social science. **Classes:** 10-19 students in an average class. **Disciplines with Highest Percentage of Degrees Awarded:** Business/marketing 46%, education 16%, communications/communication technologies 7%, social sciences and history 5%, philosophy/religion/theology 5%. **Special Study Options:** Accelerated program, cooperative (work-study) program, cross registration, double major, external degree program, honors program, independent study, internships, student-designed major, study abroad, teacher certification program, Au Sable Institute of Environmental Studies program (Michigan), Hollywood film semester (California), Washington semester.

FACILITIES

Housing: All-female, all-male, All single students not living at home must live in college approved housing. **Library Holdings:** 128,918 bound volumes. 1,990 periodicals. 11,935 microforms. 4,506 audiovisuals. **Special Academic Facilities/Equipment:** Sculpture museum, sports training annex. **Computers:** *Recommended operating system:* Windows 95. School-owned computers available for student use.

EXTRACURRICULARS

Activities: Choral groups, concert band, drama/theater, jazz band, music ensembles, musical theater, pep band, radio station, student government, student newspaper, yearbook. **Organizations:** 40 registered organizations, 4 honor societies, 2 religious organizations. **Athletics (Intercollegiate):** *Men:* baseball, basketball, cross-country, football, indoor track, soccer, tennis, track & field. *Women:* basketball, cross-country, indoor track, soccer, softball, tennis, track & field, volleyball.

ADMISSIONS

Selectivity Rating: 73 (of 100). **Freshman Academic Profile:** Average high school GPA 3.3. 20% in top 10% of high school class, 46% in top 25% of high school class, 72% in top 50% of high school class. 89% from public high schools. Average ACT 22, ACT middle 50% range 19-26. TOEFL required of all international applicants, minimum TOEFL 500. **Basis for Candidate**

Selection: *Very important factors considered include:* character/personal qualities, class rank, secondary school record, standardized test scores. *Important factors considered include:* recommendations. *Other factors considered include:* essays, extracurricular activities, interview, minority status, religious affiliation/commitment, talent/ability. **Freshman Admission Requirements:** High school diploma or GED is required. *Academic units required/recommended:* 16 total required; 4 English required, 2 math required, 2 science required, 1 science lab required, 2 foreign language required, 1 history required, 6 elective required. **Freshman Admission Statistics:** 523 applied, 97% accepted, 51% of those accepted enrolled. **Transfer Admission Requirements:** *Items required:* college transcript, essay. Minimum college GPA of 2.0 required. Lowest grade transferable C. **General Admission Information:** Application fee $25. Regular application deadline August 15. Nonfall registration accepted. Admission may be deferred for a maximum of 1 year. Credit and/or placement offered for CEEB Advanced Placement tests.

COSTS AND FINANCIAL AID

Tuition $12,954. Room & board $4,994. Required fees $10. Average book expense $600. **Required Forms and Deadlines:** FAFSA. No deadline for regular filing. **Types of Aid:** *Need-based scholarships/grants:* Pell, SEOG, state scholarships/grants, private scholarships, the school's own gift aid. *Loans:* Direct Subsidized Stafford, Direct Unsubsidized Stafford, Direct PLUS, college/university loans from institutional funds. **Student Employment:** Federal Work-Study Program available. Institutional employment available. Off-campus job opportunities are fair. **Financial Aid Statistics:** 81% freshmen, 83% undergrads receive some form of aid. Average freshman grant $11,469. Average freshman loan $3,561. Average income from on-campus job $900. **Financial Aid Phone:** 618-664-7111.

GRINNELL COLLEGE

1103 Park Street, 2nd Floor, Grinnell, IA 50112
Phone: 641-269-3600 **E-mail:** askgrin@grinnell.edu **CEEB Code:** 6252
Fax: 641-269-4800 **Web:** www.grinnell.edu **ACT Code:** 1318

This private school was founded in 1846. It has a 120-acre campus.

STUDENTS AND FACULTY

Enrollment: 1,485. **Student Body:** Male 45%, female 55%, out-of-state 85%, international 10% (52 countries represented). **Ethnic Representation:** African American 4%, Asian 5%, Caucasian 76%, Hispanic 4%, Native American 1%. **Retention and Graduation:** 91% freshmen return for sophomore year. 76% freshmen graduate within 4 years. 30% grads go on to further study within 1 year. 1% grads pursue business degrees. 5% grads pursue law degrees. 5% grads pursue medical degrees. **Faculty:** Student/faculty ratio 10:1. 137 full-time faculty, 96% hold PhDs. 100% faculty teach undergrads.

ACADEMICS

Degrees: Bachelor's. **Academic Requirements:** General education including first-semester tutorial focusing on writing. **Classes:** 10-19 students in an average class. 10-19 students in an average lab/discussion section. **Majors with Highest Enrollment:** English language and literature, general; biology/biological sciences, general; anthropology. **Disciplines with Highest Percentage of Degrees Awarded:** Social sciences and history 32%, biological life sciences 11%, visual and performing arts 10%, foreign languages and literature 10%, physical sciences 8%. **Special Study Options:** Accelerated program, double major, student exchange program (domestic), independent study, internships, liberal arts/career combination, student-designed major, study abroad, teacher certification program.

FACILITIES

Housing: Coed, cooperative housing. **Library Holdings:** 1,020,921 bound volumes. 3,470 periodicals. 384,389 microforms. 28,368 audiovisuals. **Special Academic Facilities/Equipment:** Art galleries, language lab, nuclear magnetic resonance spectrometer, electron microscope, 24-inch reflecting telescope, 365-acre environmental research area. **Computers:** School-owned computers available for student use.

EXTRACURRICULARS

Activities: Choral groups, concert band, dance, drama/theater, jazz band, literary magazine, music ensembles, musical theater, radio station, student government, student newspaper, student-run film society, symphony orchestra, yearbook. **Organizations:** 140 registered organizations, 2 honor societies, 6 religious organizations. **Athletics (Intercollegiate):** *Men:* baseball, basketball, cross-country, diving, football, golf, indoor track, soccer, swimming, tennis, track & field. *Women:* basketball, cross-country, diving, golf, indoor track, soccer, softball, swimming, tennis, track & field, volleyball.

ADMISSIONS

Selectivity Rating: 92 (of 100). **Freshman Academic Profile:** 59% in top 10% of high school class, 91% in top 25% of high school class, 99% in top 50% of high school class. 78% from public high schools. Average SAT I Math 663, SAT I Math middle 50% range 620-710. Average SAT I Verbal 676, SAT I Verbal middle 50% range 630-730. Average ACT 29, ACT middle 50% range 28-31. TOEFL required of all international applicants, minimum TOEFL 550. **Basis for Candidate Selection:** *Very important factors considered include:* character/personal qualities, class rank, essays, extracurricular activities, recommendations, secondary school record, standardized test scores, talent/ability. *Important factors considered include:* interview. *Other factors considered include:* alumni/ae relation, minority status, volunteer work, work experience. **Freshman Admission Requirements:** High school diploma or GED is required. *Academic units required/recommended:* 17 total recommended; 4 English recommended, 4 math recommended, 3 science recommended, 3 science lab recommended, 3 foreign language recommended, 3 social studies recommended. **Freshman Admission Statistics:** 2,067 applied, 65% accepted, 28% of those accepted enrolled. **Transfer Admission Requirements:** *Items required:* high school transcript, college transcript, essay, standardized test scores, statement of good standing from prior school. Lowest grade transferable C. **General Admission Information:** Application fee $30. Early decision application deadline November 20. Regular application deadline January 20. Admission may be deferred for a maximum of 1 year. Credit offered for CEEB Advanced Placement tests.

COSTS AND FINANCIAL AID

Tuition $22,960. Room & board $6,330. Required fees $570. Average book expense $400. **Required Forms and Deadlines:** FAFSA, institution's own financial aid form, and noncustodial (divorced/separated) parent's statement. Financial aid filing deadline February 1. Priority filing deadline February 1. **Notification of Awards:** Applicants will be notified of awards on or about April 1. **Types of Aid:** *Need-based scholarships/grants:* Pell, SEOG, state scholarships/grants, private scholarships, the school's own gift aid. *Loans:* FFEL Subsidized Stafford, FFEL Unsubsidized Stafford, FFEL PLUS, Federal Perkins, college/university loans from institutional funds. **Student Employment:** Federal Work-Study Program available. Institutional employment available. Off-campus job opportunities are fair. **Financial Aid Statistics:** 58% freshmen, 58% undergrads receive some form of aid. Average freshman grant $12,927. Average freshman loan $4,211. Average income from on-campus job $1,500. **Financial Aid Phone:** 641-269-3250.

GROVE CITY COLLEGE

100 Campus Drive, Grove City, PA 16127-2104
Phone: 724-458-2100 **E-mail:** admissions@gcc.edu **CEEB Code:** 2277
Fax: 724-458-3395 **Web:** www.gcc.edu **ACT Code:** 3582

This private school, which is affiliated with the Presbyterian Church, was founded in 1876. It has a 150-acre campus.

STUDENTS AND FACULTY

Enrollment: 2,288. **Student Body:** Male 49%, female 51%, out-of-state 46%, international 1% (22 countries represented). **Ethnic Representation:** Asian 1%, Caucasian 98%. **Retention and Graduation:** 90% freshmen return for sophomore year. 74% freshmen graduate within 4 years. 18% grads go on to further study within 1 year. 2% grads pursue business degrees. 1% grads pursue law degrees. 2% grads pursue medical degrees. **Faculty:** Student/faculty ratio 19:1. 122 full-time faculty, 76% hold PhDs. 100% faculty teach undergrads.

ACADEMICS

Degrees: Bachelor's. **Academic Requirements:** General education including some course work in foreign languages, history, humanities, mathematics, sciences (biological or physical), social science. **Classes:** 20-29 students in an average class. 10-19 students in an average lab/discussion section. **Majors with Highest Enrollment:** Business administration/management; elementary education and teaching; English/language arts teacher education. **Disciplines with Highest Percentage of Degrees Awarded:** Business/marketing 24%, education 17%, biological life sciences 11%, social sciences and history 10%, other 7%. **Special Study Options:** Double major, student exchange program (domestic), internships, student-designed major, study abroad, teacher certification program.

FACILITIES

Housing: All-female, all-male. **Library Holdings:** 140,000 bound volumes. 550 periodicals. 263,000 microforms. 0 audiovisuals. **Special Academic Facilities/Equipment:** Fine arts center, language lab, on-campus preschool, technological learning center. **Computers:** *Recommended operating system:* Windows NT/2000. School-owned computers available for student use.

EXTRACURRICULARS

Activities: Choral groups, concert band, dance, drama/theater, jazz band, literary magazine, marching band, music ensembles, musical theater, opera, pep band, radio station, student government, student newspaper, symphony orchestra, yearbook. **Organizations:** 123 registered organizations, 19 honor societies, 22 religious organizations, 10 fraternities (9% men join), 8 sororities (12% women join). **Athletics (Intercollegiate):** *Men:* baseball, basketball, cross-country, diving, football, golf, soccer, swimming, tennis, track & field, water polo. *Women:* basketball, cheerleading, cross-country, diving, golf, soccer, softball, swimming, tennis, track & field, volleyball, water polo.

ADMISSIONS

Selectivity Rating: 91 (of 100). **Freshman Academic Profile:** Average high school GPA 3.7. 60% in top 10% of high school class, 87% in top 25% of high school class, 98% in top 50% of high school class. 88% from public high schools. Average SAT I Math 639, SAT I Math middle 50% range 574-690. Average SAT I Verbal 633, SAT I Verbal middle 50% range 570-692. Average ACT 28, ACT middle 50% range 24-30. TOEFL required of all international applicants, minimum TOEFL 550. **Basis for Candidate Selection:** *Very important factors considered include:* character/personal qualities, interview, secondary school record. *Important factors considered include:* essays, extracurricular activities, recommendations, standardized test scores, talent/ability. *Other factors considered include:* alumni/ae relation, class rank, geographical residence, minority status, religious affiliation/commitment, state residency, volunteer work, work experience. **Freshman Admission Requirements:** High school diploma or GED is required. *Academic units required/recommended:* 16 total recommended; 4 English recommended, 3 math recommended, 3 science recommended, 3 foreign language recommended, 2 social studies recommended, 1 history recommended. **Freshman Admission Statistics:** 2,001 applied, 47% accepted, 62% of those accepted enrolled. **Transfer Admission Requirements:** *Items required:* high school transcript, college transcript, essay, standardized test scores, statement of good standing from prior school. Minimum college GPA of 2.0 required. Lowest grade transferable C. **General Admission Information:** Application fee $35. Priority application deadline November 15. Early decision application deadline November 15. Regular application deadline February 15. Nonfall registration accepted. Admission may be deferred for a maximum of 1 year. Credit offered for CEEB Advanced Placement tests.

COSTS AND FINANCIAL AID

Tuition $8,776. Room & board $4,626. Required fees $0. Average book expense $900. **Required Forms and Deadlines:** Institution's own financial aid form. Financial aid filing deadline April 15. Priority filing deadline April 15. **Notification of Awards:** Applicants will be notified of awards on a rolling basis beginning on or about March 15. **Types of Aid:** *Need-based scholarships/grants:* private scholarships, the school's own gift aid. *Loans:* College loan program funded by PNC Bank. **Student Employment:** Institutional employment available. Off-campus job opportunities are good. **Financial Aid Statistics:** 62% freshmen, 37% undergrads receive some form of aid. Average freshman grant $4,623. Average freshman loan $6,055. Average income from on-campus job $1,100. **Financial Aid Phone:** 724-458-3300.

GUILFORD COLLEGE

5800 West Friendly Avenue, Greensboro, NC 27410
Phone: 336-316-2100 **E-mail:** admission@guilford.edu **CEEB Code:** 5261
Fax: 336-316-2954 **Web:** www.guilford.edu **ACT Code:** 3106

This private school, which is affiliated with the Quaker Church, was founded in 1837. It has a 340-acre campus.

STUDENTS AND FACULTY

Enrollment: 1,801. **Student Body:** Male 42%, female 58%, out-of-state 39%, international 2% (21 countries represented). **Ethnic Representation:** African American 16%, Asian 1%, Caucasian 70%, Hispanic 2%, Native American 1%. **Retention and Graduation:** 75% freshmen return for sophomore year. 51% freshmen graduate within 4 years. 12% grads go on to further study within 1 year. 2% grads pursue business degrees. 2% grads pursue law degrees. 3% grads pursue medical degrees. **Faculty:** Student/faculty ratio 15:1. 74 full-time faculty, 79% hold PhDs. 100% faculty teach undergrads.

ACADEMICS

Degrees: Bachelor's, certificate. **Academic Requirements:** General education including some course work in arts/fine arts; English (including composition); foreign languages; humanities; sciences (biological or physical); social science; first-year experience; historical perspectives; interdisciplinary capstone course; exploration courses in intercultural studies, social justice/environmental responsibility, and diversity in the United States; breadth course in business and policy studies. **Classes:** 10-19 students in an average class. 20-29 students in an average lab/discussion section. **Majors with Highest Enrollment:** Business administration/management; English language and literature, general; psychology, general. **Disciplines with Highest Percentage of Degrees Awarded:** Social sciences and history 19%, business/marketing 15%, psychology 12%, protective services/public administration 7%, English 7%. **Special Study Options:** Accelerated program, cross registration, double major, honors program, independent study, internships, student-designed major, study abroad, teacher certification program, biosphere.

FACILITIES

Housing: Coed, all-female, all-male, apartments for single students, cooperative housing, special-interest housing. **Library Holdings:** 157,054 bound volumes. 829 periodicals. 21,238 microforms. 10,151 audiovisuals. **Special Academic Facilities/Equipment:** Friends Historical Collection, Frank Family Science Center, art gallery, language lab, research-grade observatory and planetarium. **Computers:** School-owned computers available for student use.

EXTRACURRICULARS

Activities: Choral groups, dance, drama/theater, jazz band, literary magazine, music ensembles, radio station, student government, student newspaper, student-run film society, yearbook. **Organizations:** 41 registered organizations, 1 honor society, 5 religious organizations. **Athletics (Intercollegiate):** *Men:* baseball, basketball, football, golf, lacrosse, soccer. *Women:* basketball, lacrosse, soccer, tennis, volleyball.

ADMISSIONS

Selectivity Rating: 74 (of 100). **Freshman Academic Profile:** Average high school GPA 3.0. 14% in top 10% of high school class, 37% in top 25% of high school class, 77% in top 50% of high school class. 67% from public high schools. Average SAT I Math 550, SAT I Math middle 50% range 490-620. Average SAT I Verbal 570, SAT I Verbal middle 50% range 500-640. Average ACT 25, ACT middle 50% range 20-27. TOEFL required of all international applicants, minimum TOEFL 550. **Basis for Candidate Selection:** *Very important factors considered include:* character/personal qualities, essays, secondary school record. *Important factors considered include:* alumni/ae relation, interview, recommendations, standardized test scores, talent/ability, volunteer work, work experience. *Other factors considered include:* class rank, extracurricular activities, geographical residence, minority status, state residency. **Freshman Admission Requirements:** High school diploma or GED is required. *Academic units required/recommended:* 18 total required; 4 English required, 3 math required, 4 math recommended, 2 science required, 2 science lab required, 2 foreign language required, 2 social studies required, 1 history required, 2 elective required. **Freshman Admission Statistics:** 1,211 applied, 83% accepted, 31% of those accepted enrolled. **Transfer Admission Requirements:** *Items required:* high school transcript, college transcript, essay, standardized test scores, statement of good standing from prior school. Minimum college GPA of 2.5 required. Lowest grade transferable C. **General Admission Information:** Application fee $25. Priority application deadline January 15. Early decision application deadline November 15. Regular application deadline February 15. Nonfall registration accepted. Admission may be deferred for a maximum of 1 year. Credit and/or placement offered for CEEB Advanced Placement tests.

COSTS AND FINANCIAL AID

Tuition $17,200. Room & board $5,610. Required fees $445. Average book expense $700. **Required Forms and Deadlines:** FAFSA, noncustodial (divorced/separated) parent's statement, and business/farm supplement. Priority filing deadline March 1. **Notification of Awards:** Applicants will be notified of awards on a rolling basis beginning on or about February 15. **Types of Aid:** *Need-based scholarships/grants:* Pell, SEOG, state scholarships/grants, private scholarships, the school's own gift aid. *Loans:* FFEL Subsidized Stafford, FFEL Unsubsidized Stafford, FFEL PLUS, Federal Perkins, college/university loans from institutional funds. **Student Employment:** Federal Work-Study Program available. Institutional employment available. Off-campus job opportunities are good. **Financial Aid Statistics:** 59% freshmen, 39% undergrads receive some form of aid. Average freshman grant $10,240. Average freshman loan $4,725. Average income from on-campus job $816. **Financial Aid Phone:** 336-316-2354.

GUSTAVUS ADOLPHUS COLLEGE

800 West College Avenue, Saint Peter, MN 56082
Phone: 507-933-7676 **E-mail:** admission@gustavus.edu **CEEB Code:** 6253
Fax: 507-933-7474 **Web:** www.gustavus.edu **ACT Code:** 2112

This private school, which is affiliated with the Lutheran Church, was founded in 1862. It has a 340-acre campus.

STUDENTS AND FACULTY

Enrollment: 2,536. **Student Body:** Male 42%, female 58%, out-of-state 18%, international 1% (17 countries represented). **Ethnic Representation:** African American 1%, Asian 3%, Caucasian 95%, Hispanic 1%. **Retention and Graduation:** 87% freshmen return for sophomore year. 80% freshmen graduate within 4 years. 35% grads go on to further study within 1 year. 9% grads pursue business degrees. 6% grads pursue law degrees. 4% grads pursue medical degrees. **Faculty:** Student/faculty ratio 13:1. 178 full-time faculty, 84% hold PhDs. 100% faculty teach undergrads.

ACADEMICS

Degrees: Bachelor's. **Academic Requirements:** General education including some course work in arts/fine arts, English (including composition), humanities, mathematics, sciences (biological or physical), social science, religion, meaning and value, the use of language and the historical process, personal fitness, foreign cultures. **Classes:** 10-19 students in an average class. 10-19 students in an average lab/discussion section. **Majors with Highest Enrollment:** Communications studies/speech communication and rhetoric; biology/biological sciences, general; psychology, general. **Disciplines with Highest Percentage of Degrees Awarded:** Social sciences and history 18%, business/marketing 12%, biological life sciences 8%, visual and performing arts 8%, education 7%. **Special Study Options:** Cross registration, double major, dual enrollment, student exchange program (domestic), honors program, independent study, internships, liberal arts/career combination, student-designed major, study abroad, teacher certification program.

FACILITIES

Housing: Coed, apartments for single students, theme or honors houses. **Library Holdings:** 281,761 bound volumes. 2,010 periodicals. 35,046 microforms. 16,063 audiovisuals. **Special Academic Facilities/Equipment:** Art gallery, mineral museum, electron microscopes, arboretum, 14-inch computer-guided Celestron telescope, artificial intelligence laboratory, materials science laboratory, 300MHz NMR spectrometer, 5-section greenhouse. **Computers:** School-owned computers available for student use.

EXTRACURRICULARS

Activities: Choral groups, concert band, dance, drama/theater, jazz band, literary magazine, music ensembles, musical theater, pep band, radio station, student government, student newspaper, symphony orchestra, yearbook. **Organizations:** 120 registered organizations, 14 honor societies, 12 religious organizations, 7 fraternities (27% men join), 5 sororities (22% women join). **Athletics (Intercollegiate):** *Men:* baseball, basketball, skiing (cross-country), cross-country, football, golf, ice hockey, indoor track, skiing (Nordic), soccer, swimming, tennis, track & field. *Women:* basketball, skiing (cross-country), cross-country, golf, gymnastics, ice hockey, indoor track, skiing (Nordic), soccer, softball, swimming, tennis, track & field, volleyball.

ADMISSIONS

Selectivity Rating: 84 (of 100). **Freshman Academic Profile:** Average high school GPA 3.6. 36% in top 10% of high school class, 69% in top 25% of high school class, 94% in top 50% of high school class. 92% from public high schools. Average SAT I Math 620, SAT I Math middle 50% range 540-670. Average SAT I Verbal 610, SAT I Verbal middle 50% range 550-660. Average ACT 26, ACT middle 50% range 23-28. TOEFL required of all international applicants, minimum TOEFL 550. **Basis for Candidate Selection:** *Very important factors considered include:* essays, secondary school record, standardized test scores. *Important factors considered include:* character/personal qualities, class rank, extracurricular activities, interview, recommendations, religious affiliation/commitment, talent/ability. *Other factors considered include:* alumni/ae relation, geographical residence, minority status, volunteer work, work experience. **Freshman Admission Requirements:** High school diploma or GED is required. *Academic units required/recommended:* 17 total required; 22 total recommended; 4 English required, 4 English recommended, 3 math required, 4 math recommended, 2 science required, 3 science recommended, 2 science lab required, 3 science lab recommended, 2 foreign language required, 3 foreign language recommended, 2 social studies required, 2 social studies recommended, 2 history required, 2 history recommended, 2 elective recommended. **Freshman Admission Statistics:** 2,203 applied, 77% accepted, 39% of those accepted enrolled. **Transfer Admission Requirements:** *Items required:* high school transcript, college transcript, essay, standardized test scores, statement of good standing from prior school. Minimum college GPA of 2.4 required. Lowest grade transferable C. **General Admission Information:** Application fee $25. Priority application deadline February 15. Early decision application deadline November 15. Regular application deadline April 1. Nonfall registration accepted. Admission may be deferred for a maximum of 1 year. Credit and/or placement offered for CEEB Advanced Placement tests.

COSTS AND FINANCIAL AID

Tuition $18,970. Room & board $4,927. Required fees $380. Average book expense $700. **Required Forms and Deadlines:** FAFSA, institution's own financial aid form, CSS/Financial Aid PROFILE. Students who want to receive an award by March 1 must file the PROFILE. Financial aid filing deadline June 15. Priority filing deadline April 15. **Notification of Awards:** Applicants will be notified of awards on a rolling basis beginning on or about March 1. **Types of Aid:** *Need-based scholarships/grants:* Pell, SEOG, state scholarships/grants, private scholarships, the school's own gift aid. *Loans:* Direct Subsidized Stafford, Direct Unsubsidized Stafford, Direct PLUS, Federal Perkins, state loans, college/university loans from institutional funds, alternative loans from private lenders. **Student Employment:** Federal Work-Study Program available. Institutional employment available. Off-campus job opportunities are good. **Financial Aid Statistics:** 65% freshmen, 65% undergrads receive some form of aid. Average freshman grant $6,500. Average freshman loan $4,500. Average income from on-campus job $1,800. **Financial Aid Phone:** 507-933-7527.

GWYNEDD-MERCY COLLEGE

PO Box 901, Sumneytown Pike, Gwynedd Valley, PA 19437-0901
Phone: 215-641-5510 **E-mail:** admissions@gmc.edu **CEEB Code:** 2278
Fax: 215-641-5556 **Web:** www.gmc.edu

This private school, which is affiliated with the Roman Catholic Church, was founded in 1948. It has a 160-acre campus.

STUDENTS AND FACULTY

Enrollment: 1,766. **Student Body:** Male 30%, female 70%, out-of-state 4%, international 2% (44 countries represented). **Ethnic Representation:** African American 7%, Asian 3%, Caucasian 88%, Hispanic 2%. **Retention and Graduation:** 92% freshmen return for sophomore year. **Faculty:** Student/faculty ratio 17:1. 74 full-time faculty, 35% hold PhDs. 94% faculty teach undergrads.

ACADEMICS

Degrees: Associate's, bachelor's, certificate, master's, post-bachelor's certificate, post-master's certificate. **Academic Requirements:** General education including some course work in arts/fine arts, English (including composition), foreign languages, history, humanities, mathematics, philosophy, sciences (biological or physical), social science. **Classes:** 10-19 students in an average class. 10-19 students in an average lab/discussion section. **Majors with Highest Enrollment:** Nursing/registered nurse training (RN, ASN, BSN, MSN); computer and information sciences, general; education, general. **Disciplines with Highest Percentage of Degrees Awarded:** Health professions and related sciences 43%, education 21%, business/marketing 16%, psychology 4%, social sciences and history 3%. **Special Study Options:** Accelerated program, cooperative (work-study) program, cross registration, double major, English as a second language, honors program, independent study, internships, liberal arts/career combination, teacher certification program, weekend college.

FACILITIES

Housing: Coed. **Library Holdings:** 94,322 bound volumes. 786 periodicals. 14,570 microforms. 52,989 audiovisuals. **Special Academic Facilities/Equipment:** Keiss Hall (health and science center), television production room and small theater, computer labs. **Computers:** School-owned computers available for student use.

EXTRACURRICULARS

Activities: Choral groups, dance, drama/theater, literary magazine, student government, student newspaper, yearbook. **Organizations:** 20 registered organizations, 10 honor societies, 1 religious organization. **Athletics (Intercollegiate):** *Men:* baseball, basketball, cross-country, golf, indoor track, soccer, tennis, track & field. *Women:* basketball, cross-country, field hockey, indoor track, lacrosse, soccer, softball, tennis, track & field, volleyball.

ADMISSIONS

Selectivity Rating: 71 (of 100). **Freshman Academic Profile:** 7% in top 10% of high school class, 31% in top 25% of high school class, 67% in top 50% of high school class. 57% from public high schools. Average SAT I Math 490, SAT I Math middle 50% range 520-430. Average SAT I Verbal 490, SAT I Verbal middle 50% range 530-450. TOEFL required of all international applicants, minimum TOEFL 500. **Basis for Candidate Selection:** *Important factors considered include:* character/personal qualities, class rank, interview, recommendations, secondary school record, standardized test scores, talent/ability. *Other factors considered include:* essays, extracurricular activities, volunteer work, work experience. **Freshman Admission Requirements:** High school diploma or GED is required. *Academic units required/recommended:* 4 English required, 3 math required, 3 science required, 2 foreign language required, 1 history required, 3 elective required. **Freshman Admission Statistics:** 446 applied, 36% accepted, 154% of those accepted enrolled. **Transfer Admission Requirements:** *Items required:* high school transcript, college transcript, standardized test scores. Minimum high school GPA of 2.0 required. Minimum college GPA of 2.0 required. Lowest grade transferable C. **General Admission Information:** Application fee $25. Nonfall registration accepted. Admission may be deferred for a maximum of 1 year. Credit and/or placement offered for CEEB Advanced Placement tests.

COSTS AND FINANCIAL AID

Tuition $15,600. Room & board $7,000. Required fees $275. Average book expense $400. **Required Forms and Deadlines:** FAFSA and institution's own financial aid form. Priority filing deadline March 15. **Notification of Awards:** Applicants will be notified of awards on a rolling basis beginning on or about March 15. **Types of Aid:** *Need-based scholarships/grants:* Pell, SEOG, state scholarships/grants, private scholarships, the school's own gift aid, Federal Nursing and. *Loans:* FFEL Subsidized Stafford, FFEL Unsubsidized Stafford, FFEL PLUS, Federal Perkins, Federal Nursing. **Student Employment:** Federal Work-Study Program available. Institutional employment available. Off-campus job opportunities are excellent. **Financial Aid Statistics:** 84% freshmen, 71% undergrads receive some form of aid. Average freshman grant $11,048. Average freshman loan $3,625. Average income from on-campus job $900. **Financial Aid Phone:** 215-641-5570.

HAMILTON COLLEGE

198 College Hill Road, Clinton, NY 13323
Phone: 315-859-4421 **E-mail:** admission@hamilton.edu **CEEB Code:** 2286
Fax: 315-859-4457 **Web:** www.hamilton.edu **ACT Code:** 2754

This private school was founded in 1812. It has a 1,250-acre campus.

STUDENTS AND FACULTY

Enrollment: 1,851. **Student Body:** Out-of-state 58%, international 3% (31 country represented). **Ethnic Representation:** African American 4%, Asian 5%, Caucasian 87%, Hispanic 4%, Native American 1%. **Retention and Graduation:** 93% freshmen return for sophomore year. 79% freshmen graduate within 4 years. 42% grads go on to further study within 1 year. 13% grads pursue business degrees. 22% grads pursue law degrees. 9% grads pursue medical degrees. **Faculty:** Student/faculty ratio 10:1. 179 full-time faculty, 93% hold PhDs. 100% faculty teach undergrads.

ACADEMICS

Degrees: Bachelor's. **Academic Requirements:** The Hamilton plan for liberal education provides highly motivated students with both the freedom and the responsibility to make educational choices that emphasize breadth and depth. Unique to this plan are two distinct capstone requirements—one prior to declaration of an area of concentration (the sophomore program) and one at the conclusion of the concentration (the senior program). As part of the new Hamilton plan for liberal education, the faculty has significantly strengthened the general education sequence by: (a) replacing distribution requirements with a series of recommended goals; (b) instituting special first- and second-year seminars; (c) reaffirming the centrality of the three-course writing-intensive program; (d) reinvigorating the advising system; and (e) establishing a multidisciplinary seminar program at the end of the sophomore year that culminates in an integrative project with public presentations. **Classes:** 10-19 students in an average class. 10-19 students in an average lab/discussion section. **Majors with Highest Enrollment:** Psychology, general; economics, general; political science and government, general. **Disciplines with Highest Percentage of Degrees Awarded:** Social sciences and history 38%, visual and performing arts 8%, psychology 8%, foreign languages and literature 9%, English 7%. **Special Study Options:** Accelerated program, cross registration, double major, English as a second language, independent study, internships, student-designed major, study abroad. 3-2 program in engineering with Columbia University, Rensselaer Polytechnic Institute, and Washington University (St. Louis). 3-3 program in law with Columbia University.

FACILITIES

Housing: Coed, apartments for married students, apartments for single students, housing for disabled students. **Library Holdings:** 558,808 bound volumes. 2,560 periodicals. 435,977 microforms. 55,327 audiovisuals. **Special Academic Facilities/Equipment:** Art gallery, language lab, fitness center, observatory, 2 electron microscopes, Arthur Levitt Public Affairs Center. **Computers:** School-owned computers available for student use.

EXTRACURRICULARS

Activities: Choral groups, concert band, dance, drama/theater, jazz band, literary magazine, music ensembles, musical theater, pep band, radio station, student government, student newspaper, student-run film society, symphony orchestra, yearbook. **Organizations:** 80 registered organizations, 3 honor societies, 3 religious organizations, 7 fraternities (34% men join), 3 sororities (20% women join). **Athletics (Intercollegiate):** *Men:* baseball, basketball, crew, cross-country, diving, football, golf, ice hockey, indoor track, lacrosse, soccer, squash, swimming, tennis, track & field. *Women:* basketball, crew, cross-country, diving, field hockey, ice hockey, indoor track, lacrosse, soccer, softball, squash, swimming, tennis, track & field, volleyball.

ADMISSIONS

Selectivity Rating: 92 (of 100). **Freshman Academic Profile:** 60% in top 10% of high school class, 87% in top 25% of high school class, 100% in top 50% of high school class. 63% from public high schools. SAT I Math middle 50% range 610-700. SAT I Verbal middle 50% range 600-700. TOEFL required of all international applicants, minimum TOEFL 600. **Basis for Candidate Selection:** *Very important factors considered include:* class rank, recommendations, secondary school record. *Important factors considered include:* alumni/ae relation, character/personal qualities, essays, extracurricular activities, interview, minority status, standardized test scores. *Other factors considered include:* talent/ability. **Freshman Admission Requirements:** High school diploma or equivalent is not required. *Academic units required/recommended:* 16 total recommended; 4 English recommended, 3 math recommended, 3 science recommended, 3 foreign language recommended, 3 social studies recommended. **Freshman Admission Statistics:** 4,565 applied, 35% accepted, 31% of those accepted enrolled. **Transfer Admission Requirements:** *Items required:* high school transcript, college transcript, essay, standardized test scores. Minimum college GPA of 3.0 required. Lowest grade transferable C. **General Admission Information:** Application fee $50. Early decision application deadline November 15. Regular application deadline January 15. Nonfall registration accepted. Admission may be deferred. Credit and/or placement offered for CEEB Advanced Placement tests.

COSTS AND FINANCIAL AID

Tuition $28,610. Room & board $7,040. Required fees $150. **Required Forms and Deadlines:** FAFSA, institution's own financial aid form, CSS/Financial Aid PROFILE, state aid form, noncustodial (divorced/separated) parent's statement, business/farm supplement, and parent and student federal taxes. Priority filing deadline February 1. **Notification of Awards:** Applicants will be notified of awards on or about April 1. **Types of Aid:** *Need-based scholarships/grants:* Pell, SEOG, state scholarships/grants, private scholarships, the school's own gift aid. *Loans:* FFEL Subsidized Stafford, FFEL Unsubsidized Stafford, FFEL PLUS, Federal Perkins, college/university loans from institutional funds. **Student Employment:** Federal Work-Study Program available. Institutional employment available. Off-campus job opportunities are fair. **Financial Aid Statistics:** 51% freshmen, 54% undergrads receive some form of aid. Average freshman grant $21,520. Average freshman loan $2,531. Average income from on-campus job $1,600. **Financial Aid Phone:** 800-859-4413.

HAMLINE UNIVERSITY

1536 Hewitt Avenue, MS-C1930, Saint Paul, MN 55104
Phone: 651-523-2207 **E-mail:** CLA-admis@hamline.edu **CEEB Code:** 6265
Fax: 651-523-2458 **Web:** www.hamline.edu **ACT Code:** 2114

This private school, which is affiliated with the Methodist Church, was founded in 1854. It has a 50-acre campus.

STUDENTS AND FACULTY

Enrollment: 1,918. **Student Body:** Male 36%, female 64%, out-of-state 23%, international 3% (35 countries represented). **Ethnic Representation:** African American 4%, Asian 6%, Caucasian 85%, Hispanic 2%, Native American 1%. **Retention and Graduation:** 83% freshmen return for sophomore year. 69% freshmen graduate within 4 years. 26% grads go on to further study within 1 year. 4% grads pursue business degrees. 8% grads pursue law degrees. 1% grads pursue medical degrees. **Faculty:** Student/faculty ratio 13:1. 174 full-time faculty, 88% hold PhDs. 100% faculty teach undergrads.

ACADEMICS

Degrees: Bachelor's, certificate, doctoral, first professional, first professional certificate, master's, post-bachelor's certificate, post-master's certificate. **Academic Requirements:** General education including some course work in arts/fine arts, computer literacy, English (including composition), humanities, sciences (biological or physical), social science. **Classes:** 10-19 students in an average class. **Majors with Highest Enrollment:** Business administration/ management; psychology, general; English language and literature, general. **Disciplines with Highest Percentage of Degrees Awarded:** Social sciences and history 23%, psychology 13%, business/marketing 9%, English 8%, communications/communication technologies 6%. **Special Study Options:** Cross registration, double major, English as a second language, student exchange program (domestic), honors program, independent study, internships, student-designed major, study abroad, teacher certification program. Undergrads may take grad-level classes. Off-campus study: Washington, DC; United Nations; arts program in New York. Co-op programs: engineering, occupational therapy. Other special programs: center for global environmental education, comprehensive regional assistant center, center for literacy and learning, center for women in government, Upper Midwest Women's History Center, Crossroads Center.

FACILITIES

Housing: Coed, apartments for married students, apartments for single students, fraternities and/or sororities. **Library Holdings:** 292,178 bound volumes. 3,858 periodicals. 931,602 microforms. 2,642 audiovisuals. **Special Academic Facilities/Equipment:** Computer resource center, language lab, theatre, music hall, art gallery, science center. **Computers:** *Recommended operating system:* Windows NT/2000. School-owned computers available for student use.

EXTRACURRICULARS

Activities: Choral groups, concert band, dance, drama/theater, jazz band, literary magazine, music ensembles, musical theater, radio station, student government, student newspaper, student-run film society, yearbook. **Organizations:** 85 registered organizations, 11 honor societies, 9 religious organizations, 12 fraternity, 2 sororities (5% women join). **Athletics (Intercollegiate):** *Men:* baseball, basketball, cross-country, diving, football, ice hockey, indoor track, soccer, swimming, tennis, track & field. *Women:* basketball, cross-country, diving, gymnastics, ice hockey, indoor track, soccer, softball, swimming, tennis, track & field, volleyball.

ADMISSIONS

Selectivity Rating: 82 (of 100). **Freshman Academic Profile:** Average high school GPA 3.5. 28% in top 10% of high school class, 57% in top 25% of high school class, 90% in top 50% of high school class. 81% from public high schools. Average ACT 24, ACT middle 50% range 21-28. TOEFL required of all international applicants, minimum TOEFL 550. **Basis for Candidate Selection:** *Very important factors considered include:* class rank, secondary school record. *Important factors considered include:* essays, extracurricular activities, interview, recommendations, standardized test scores, talent/ability. *Other factors considered include:* alumni/ae relation, character/personal qualities, minority status, volunteer work, work experience. **Freshman Admission Requirements:** High school diploma is required and GED is not accepted. *Academic units required/recommended:* 20 total recommended; 4 English recommended, 3 math recommended, 3 science recommended, 2 foreign language recommended, 2 social studies recommended, 2 history recommended, 4 elective recommended. **Freshman Admission Statistics:** 1,619 applied, 79% accepted, 33% of those accepted enrolled. **Transfer Admission Requirements:** *Items required:* college transcript. Minimum college GPA of 2.0 required. Lowest grade transferable C. **General Admission Information:** Priority application deadline December 1. Early decision application deadline December 1. Regular application deadline rolling. Credit and/or placement offered for CEEB Advanced Placement tests.

COSTS AND FINANCIAL AID

Tuition $17,670. Room & board $5,971. Required fees $250. Average book expense $1,200. **Required Forms and Deadlines:** FAFSA and institution's own financial aid form. No deadline for regular filing. Priority filing deadline May 2. **Notification of Awards:** Applicants will be notified of awards on a rolling basis beginning on or about March 15. **Types of Aid:** *Need-based scholarships/grants:* Pell, SEOG, state scholarships/grants, private scholarships, the school's own gift aid. *Loans:* Direct Subsidized Stafford, Direct Unsubsidized Stafford, Direct PLUS, FFEL Subsidized Stafford, FFEL Unsubsidized Stafford, FFEL PLUS, Federal Perkins, state loans. **Student Employment:** Federal Work-Study Program available. Institutional employment available. Off-campus job opportunities are excellent. **Financial Aid Statistics:** 76% freshmen, 70% undergrads receive some form of aid. Average freshman grant $16,703. Average freshman loan $2,232. Average income from on-campus job $3,000. **Financial Aid Phone:** 651-523-2280.

HAMPDEN-SYDNEY COLLEGE

PO Box 667, Hampden-Sydney, VA 23943
Phone: 434-223-6120 **E-mail:** hsapp@hsc.edu **CEEB Code:** 5291
Fax: 434-223-6346 **Web:** www.hsc.edu **ACT Code:** 4356

This private school, which is affiliated with the Presbyterian Church, was founded in 1776. It has a 660-acre campus.

STUDENTS AND FACULTY

Enrollment: 1,026. **Student Body:** Out-of-state 37%, international students represent 3 countries. **Ethnic Representation:** African American 4%, Asian 1%, Caucasian 88%, Hispanic 1%. **Retention and Graduation:** 79% freshmen return for sophomore year. 50% freshmen graduate within 4 years. **Faculty:** Student/faculty ratio 10:1. 79 full-time faculty, 81% hold PhDs. 100% faculty teach undergrads.

ACADEMICS

Degrees: Bachelor's. **Academic Requirements:** General education including some course work in arts/fine arts, English (including composition), foreign languages, history, humanities, mathematics, philosophy, sciences (biological or physical), social science. **Classes:** 10-19 students in an average class. **Majors with Highest Enrollment:** Economics, general; history, general; political science and government, general. **Disciplines with Highest Percentage of Degrees Awarded:** Social sciences and history 63%, biological life sciences 9%, philosophy/religion/theology 7%, English 6%, psychology 5%. **Special Study Options:** Accelerated program, cross registration, double major, student exchange program (domestic), honors program, independent study, internships, study abroad.

FACILITIES

Housing: All-male, apartments for married students, apartments for single students, fraternities and/or sororities. **Library Holdings:** 224,172 bound volumes. 823 periodicals. 45,312 microforms. 4,312 audiovisuals. **Special Academic Facilities/Equipment:** History museum, language lab, international communications center, observatory. **Computers:** *Recommended operating system:* Windows NT/2000. School-owned computers available for student use.

EXTRACURRICULARS

Activities: Choral groups, drama/theater, literary magazine, music ensembles, pep band, radio station, student government, student newspaper, yearbook. **Organizations:** 26 registered organizations, 14 honor societies, 2 religious organizations, 11 fraternities (37% men join). **Athletics (Intercollegiate):** *Men:* baseball, basketball, cross-country, football, golf, lacrosse, soccer, tennis.

ADMISSIONS

Selectivity Rating: 78 (of 100). **Freshman Academic Profile:** Average high school GPA 3.1. 13% in top 10% of high school class, 32% in top 25% of high school class, 69% in top 50% of high school class. 62% from public high schools. Average SAT I Math 562, SAT I Math middle 50% range 510-610. Average SAT I Verbal 561, SAT I Verbal middle 50% range 500-620. Average ACT 22, ACT middle 50% range 20-25. TOEFL required of all international applicants, minimum TOEFL 570. **Basis for Candidate Selection:** *Very important factors considered include:* character/personal qualities, essays, recommendations, secondary school record, standardized test scores. *Important factors considered include:* class rank, extracurricular activities. *Other factors considered include:* alumni/ae relation, interview, minority status, talent/ability, volunteer work, work experience. **Freshman Admission Requirements:** High school diploma or GED is required. *Academic units required/recommended:* 16 total required; 4 English required, 3 math required, 4 math recommended, 2 science required, 3 science recommended, 1 science lab required, 2 foreign language required, 3 foreign language recommended, 1 social studies required, 3 elective required. **Freshman Admission Statistics:** 925 applied, 77% accepted, 46% of those accepted enrolled. **Transfer Admission Requirements:** *Items required:* high school transcript, college transcript, essay, standardized test scores, statement of good standing from prior school. Minimum high school GPA of 2.5 required. Minimum college GPA of 2.5 required. Lowest grade transferable C. **General Admission Information:** Application fee $30. Early decision application deadline November 15. Regular application deadline March 1. Nonfall registration accepted. Credit and/or placement offered for CEEB Advanced Placement tests.

COSTS AND FINANCIAL AID

Tuition $17,858. Room & board $6,386. Required fees $627. Average book expense $800. **Required Forms and Deadlines:** FAFSA, CSS/Financial Aid PROFILE, and state aid form. Financial aid filing deadline May 1. Priority filing deadline March 1. **Notification of Awards:** Applicants will be notified of awards on or about March 1. **Types of Aid:** *Need-based scholarships/grants:*

Pell, SEOG, state scholarships/grants, private scholarships, the school's own gift aid. *Loans:* FFEL Subsidized Stafford, FFEL Unsubsidized Stafford, FFEL PLUS, Federal Perkins, college/university loans from institutional funds, private loans. **Student Employment:** Federal Work-Study Program available. Institutional employment available. Off-campus job opportunities are fair. **Financial Aid Statistics:** 50% freshmen, 46% undergrads receive some form of aid. Average freshman grant $11,589. Average freshman loan $3,294. Average income from on-campus job $900. **Financial Aid Phone:** 434-223-6119.

HAMPSHIRE COLLEGE

Admissions Office, 893 West Street, Amherst, MA 01002
Phone: 413-559-5471 **E-mail:** admissions@hampshire.edu **CEEB Code:** 3447
Fax: 413-559-5631 **Web:** www.hampshire.edu **ACT Code:** 1842

This private school was founded in 1965. It has an 800-acre campus.

STUDENTS AND FACULTY

Enrollment: 1,267. **Student Body:** Out-of-state 81%, international 3%. **Ethnic Representation:** African American 3%, Asian 4%, Caucasian 79%, Hispanic 5%. **Retention and Graduation:** 83% freshmen return for sophomore year. 40% freshmen graduate within 4 years. **Faculty:** Student/faculty ratio 11:1. 103 full-time faculty, 89% hold PhDs. 100% faculty teach undergrads.

ACADEMICS

Degrees: Bachelor's. **Academic Requirements:** General education including some course work in arts/fine arts, humanities, sciences (biological or physical), social science, humanities, arts and cultural studies, interdisciplinary arts, cognitive science. **Classes:** 10-19 students in an average class. **Special Study Options:** Accelerated program, cross registration, double major, student exchange program (domestic), independent study, internships, student-designed major, study abroad.

FACILITIES

Housing: Coed, apartments for single students, housing for disabled students. **Library Holdings:** 124,710 bound volumes. 731 periodicals. 4,534 microforms. 8,727 audiovisuals. **Special Academic Facilities/Equipment:** Performing and visual arts center, bioshelter (integrated greenhouse/aquaculture facility), farm center, electronic music and TV production studios, extensive film and photography facilities, multimedia center. **Computers:** School-owned computers available for student use.

EXTRACURRICULARS

Activities: Choral groups, dance, drama/theater, literary magazine, student newspaper, student-run film society, television station. **Organizations:** 80 registered organizations. **Athletics (Intercollegiate):** *Men:* baseball, basketball, fencing, soccer. *Women:* basketball, fencing, soccer.

ADMISSIONS

Selectivity Rating: 83 (of 100). **Freshman Academic Profile:** Average high school GPA 3.4. 23% in top 10% of high school class, 58% in top 25% of high school class, 95% in top 50% of high school class. 65% from public high schools. Average SAT I Math 597, SAT I Math middle 50% range 540-660. Average SAT I Verbal 648, SAT I Verbal middle 50% range 600-700. ACT middle 50% range 25-29. TOEFL required of all international applicants, minimum TOEFL 577. **Basis for Candidate Selection:** *Very important factors considered include:* essays, recommendations, secondary school record. *Important factors considered include:* character/personal qualities, extracurricular activities, talent/ability. *Other factors considered include:* alumni/ae relation, class rank, interview, minority status, standardized test scores, volunteer work, work experience. **Freshman Admission Requirements:** High school diploma or equivalent is not required. *Academic units required/recommended:* 19 total recommended; 4 English recommended, 4 math recommended, 4 science recommended, 2 science lab recommended, 3 foreign language recommended, 2 social studies recommended, 2 history recommended. **Freshman Admission Statistics:** 2,094 applied, 51% accepted, 29% of those accepted enrolled. **Transfer Admission Requirements:** *Items required:* high school transcript, college transcript, essay. **General Admission Information:** Application fee $50. Early decision application deadline November 15. Regular application deadline February 1. Nonfall registration accepted. Admission may be deferred for a maximum of 1 year. Credit and/or placement offered for CEEB Advanced Placement tests.

COSTS AND FINANCIAL AID

Tuition $27,354. Room & board $7,294. Required fees $516. Average book expense $400. **Required Forms and Deadlines:** FAFSA, institution's own financial aid form, CSS/Financial Aid PROFILE, and noncustodial (divorced/separated) parent's statement. Financial aid filing deadline February 1. Priority filing deadline February 1. **Notification of Awards:** Applicants will be notified of awards on a rolling basis beginning on or about April 1. **Types of Aid:** *Need-based scholarships/grants:* Pell, SEOG, state scholarships/grants, private scholarships, the school's own gift aid. *Loans:* Direct Subsidized Stafford, Direct Unsubsidized Stafford, FFEL PLUS, Federal Perkins. **Student Employment:** Federal Work-Study Program available. Institutional employment available. Off-campus job opportunities are fair. **Financial Aid Statistics:** 53% freshmen, 52% undergrads receive some form of aid. Average freshman grant $14,900. Average freshman loan $2,625. **Financial Aid Phone:** 413-559-5484.

See page 1048.

HAMPTON UNIVERSITY

Office of Admissions, Hampton University, Hampton, VA 23668
Phone: 757-727-5328 **E-mail:** admit@hamptonu.edu **CEEB Code:** 5292
Fax: 757-727-5095 **Web:** www.hamptonu.edu **ACT Code:** 4358

This private school was founded in 1868. It has a 285-acre campus.

STUDENTS AND FACULTY

Enrollment: 4,981. **Student Body:** Male 39%, female 61%, out-of-state 69%, international students represent 33 countries. **Ethnic Representation:** African American 96%, Caucasian 3%. **Retention and Graduation:** 85% freshmen return for sophomore year. 39% freshmen graduate within 4 years. 40% grads go on to further study within 1 year. 5% grads pursue business degrees. 5% grads pursue law degrees. 10% grads pursue medical degrees. **Faculty:** Student/faculty ratio 16:1. 284 full-time faculty. 100% faculty teach undergrads.

ACADEMICS

Degrees: Associate's, bachelor's, certificate, doctoral, first professional, master's, post-master's certificate. **Academic Requirements:** General education including some course work in arts/fine arts, computer literacy, English (including composition), foreign languages, history, humanities, mathematics, sciences (biological or physical), social science. **Classes:** Under 10 students in an average class. 10-19 students in an average lab/discussion section. **Majors with Highest Enrollment:** Business administration/management; biology/biological sciences, general; psychology, general. **Disciplines with Highest Percentage of Degrees Awarded:** Business/marketing 25%, biological life sciences 11%, psychology 11%, social sciences and history 10%, communications/communication technologies 8%. **Special Study Options:** Accelerated program, cooperative (work-study) program, cross registration, distance learning, double major, dual enrollment, honors program, independent study, internships, study abroad, teacher certification program. Undergrads may take grad-level programs. Co-op programs: arts, business, education, engineering, social/behavioral science, pre-college, Army ROTC, Navy ROTC. Member of Tidewater Consortium.

FACILITIES

Housing: Coed, all-female, all-male, housing for international students. **Library Holdings:** 336,092 bound volumes. 1,414 periodicals. 711,759 microforms. 1,649 audiovisuals. **Special Academic Facilities/Equipment:** African, Native American, and Oceanic museums; gallery. New Student Center. **Computers:** *Recommended operating system:* Windows NT/2000. School-owned computers available for student use.

EXTRACURRICULARS

Activities: Choral groups, concert band, dance, drama/theater, jazz band, marching band, music ensembles, musical theater, opera, pep band, radio station, student government, student newspaper, symphony orchestra, television station, yearbook. **Organizations:** 85 registered organizations, 16 honor societies, 3 religious organizations, 6 fraternities (5% men join), 3 sororities (4% women join). **Athletics (Intercollegiate):** *Men:* basketball, cross-country, football, golf, indoor track, sailing, tennis, track & field. *Women:* basketball, cross-country, golf, indoor track, sailing, softball, tennis, track & field, volleyball.

ADMISSIONS

Selectivity Rating: 79 (of 100). **Freshman Academic Profile:** Average high school GPA 3.0. 20% in top 10% of high school class, 45% in top 25% of high school class, 90% in top 50% of high school class. 90% from public high schools. Average SAT I Math 516, SAT I Math middle 50% range 480-580. Average SAT I Verbal 526, SAT I Verbal middle 50% range 490-590. Average ACT 20, ACT middle 50% range 20-24. TOEFL required of all international applicants, minimum TOEFL 550. **Basis for Candidate Selection:** *Very important factors considered include:* character/personal qualities, essays, secondary school record, standardized test scores. *Important factors considered include:* class rank, recommendations. *Other factors considered include:* alumni/ae relation, extracurricular activities, talent/ability, volunteer work. **Freshman Admission**

Requirements: High school diploma or GED is required. *Academic units required/recommended:* 17 total required; 4 English required, 3 math required, 2 science required, 2 science lab required, 2 foreign language recommended, 2 social studies required, 6 elective required. **Freshman Admission Statistics:** 5,696 applied, 62% accepted, 30% of those accepted enrolled. **Transfer Admission Requirements:** *Items required:* college transcript, essay, statement of good standing from prior school. Minimum college GPA of 2.3 required. Lowest grade transferable C. **General Admission Information:** Application fee $25. Priority application deadline March 1. Nonfall registration accepted. Admission may be deferred for a maximum of 1 year. Credit and/or placement offered for CEEB Advanced Placement tests.

COSTS AND FINANCIAL AID

Tuition $10,990. Room & board $5,828. Required fees $1,262. Average book expense $730. **Required Forms and Deadlines:** FAFSA. Priority filing deadline March 1. **Notification of Awards:** Applicants will be notified of awards on a rolling basis beginning on or about April 1. **Types of Aid:** *Need-based scholarships/grants:* Pell, SEOG, state scholarships/grants, private scholarships, the school's own gift aid, Federal Nursing. *Loans:* Direct Subsidized Stafford, Direct Unsubsidized Stafford, Direct PLUS, Federal Perkins, alternative loans. **Student Employment:** Federal Work-Study Program available. Off-campus job opportunities are excellent. **Financial Aid Statistics:** 56% freshmen, 58% undergrads receive some form of aid. Average freshman grant $2,885. Average freshman loan $2,254. **Financial Aid Phone:** 800-624-3341.

HANNIBAL-LAGRANGE COLLEGE

2800 Palmyra Road, Hannibal, MO 63401
Phone: 573-221-3113 **E-mail:** admissio@hlg.edu
Fax: 573-221-6594 **Web:** www.hlg.edu **ACT Code:** 2320

This private school, which is affiliated with the Southern Baptist Church, was founded in 1858. It has a 110-acre campus.

STUDENTS AND FACULTY

Enrollment: 1,117. **Student Body:** Male 39%, female 61%, out-of-state 17%, international 1% (7 countries represented). **Ethnic Representation:** African American 2%, Caucasian 95%, Hispanic 1%. **Retention and Graduation:** 66% freshmen return for sophomore year. 50% freshmen graduate within 4 years. 13% grads go on to further study within 1 year. 10% grads pursue business degrees. **Faculty:** Student/faculty ratio 13:1. 51 full-time faculty, 39% hold PhDs. 100% faculty teach undergrads.

ACADEMICS

Degrees: Associate's, bachelor's, terminal. **Academic Requirements:** General education including some course work in arts/fine arts, English (including composition), foreign languages, history, humanities, mathematics, sciences (biological or physical), social science, Bible. **Classes:** Under 10 students in an average class. Under 10 students in an average lab/discussion section. **Majors with Highest Enrollment:** Business administration/management; education, general; criminal justice/law enforcement administration. **Disciplines with Highest Percentage of Degrees Awarded:** Education 28%, business/marketing 26%, protective services/public administration 8%, philosophy/religion/theology 7%, social sciences and history 6%. **Special Study Options:** Accelerated program, double major, dual enrollment, honors program, independent study, internships, student-designed major, study abroad, teacher certification program, weekend college.

FACILITIES

Housing: All-female, all-male, apartments for single students. **Library Holdings:** 90,640 bound volumes. 507 periodicals. 21,005 microforms. 7,255 audiovisuals. **Special Academic Facilities/Equipment:** L. A. Foster Library, T. M. Matthews Science Building, Mary Wiehe Science Building, Partee Technology Center, Fewell Center, Muir Hall. **Computers:** School-owned computers available for student use.

EXTRACURRICULARS

Activities: Choral groups, concert band, drama/theater, jazz band, music ensembles, musical theater, student government, student newspaper, yearbook. **Organizations:** 5 registered organizations, 1 honor society, 4 religious organizations. **Athletics (Intercollegiate):** *Men:* baseball, basketball, cheerleading, cross-country, golf, soccer. *Women:* basketball, cheerleading, cross-country, soccer, softball, volleyball.

ADMISSIONS

Selectivity Rating: 63 (of 100). **Freshman Academic Profile:** Average high school GPA 3.0. 15% in top 10% of high school class, 36% in top 25% of high school class, 74% in top 50% of high school class. 98% from public high schools. SAT I Math middle 50% range 510-640, SAT I Verbal middle 50% range 520-560. Average ACT 22, ACT middle 50% range 19-25. TOEFL required of all international applicants, minimum TOEFL 520. **Basis for Candidate Selection:** *Very important factors considered include:* standardized test scores. *Other factors considered include:* class rank, recommendations, secondary school record. **Freshman Admission Requirements:** High school diploma or GED is required. **Freshman Admission Statistics:** 362 applied, 97% accepted, 74% of those accepted enrolled. **Transfer Admission Requirements:** *Items required:* college transcript, standardized test scores, statement of good standing from prior school. Minimum college GPA of 2.0 required. Lowest grade transferable D. **General Admission Information:** Application fee $25. Regular application deadline August 26. Nonfall registration accepted. Admission may be deferred for a maximum of 4 years. Neither credit nor placement offered for CEEB Advanced Placement tests.

COSTS AND FINANCIAL AID

Tuition $9,660. Room & board $3,710. Required fees $300. Average book expense $800. **Required Forms and Deadlines:** FAFSA. Financial aid filing deadline July 1. **Notification of Awards:** Applicants will be notified of awards on a rolling basis. **Types of Aid:** *Need-based scholarships/grants:* Pell, SEOG, state scholarships/grants, private scholarships. *Loans:* FFEL Subsidized Stafford, FFEL Unsubsidized Stafford, FFEL PLUS, Federal Perkins, state loans, college/university loans from institutional funds. **Student Employment:** Federal Work-Study Program available. Institutional employment available. Off-campus job opportunities are good. **Financial Aid Statistics:** 76% freshmen, 68% undergrads receive some form of aid. Average freshman grant $3,500. Average income from on-campus job $1,100. **Financial Aid Phone:** 573-221-3675.

HANOVER COLLEGE

PO Box 108, Hanover, IN 47243
Phone: 812-866-7021 **E-mail:** info@hanover.edu **CEEB Code:** 1290
Fax: 812-866-7098 **Web:** www.hanover.edu **ACT Code:** 1200

This private school, which is affiliated with the Presbyterian Church, was founded in 1827. It has a 650-acre campus.

STUDENTS AND FACULTY

Enrollment: 1,050. **Student Body:** Male 46%, female 54%, out-of-state 30%, international 4% (18 countries represented). **Ethnic Representation:** African American 1%, Asian 3%, Caucasian 91%, Hispanic 1%. **Retention and Graduation:** 75% freshmen return for sophomore year. 67% freshmen graduate within 4 years. 31% grads go on to further study within 1 year. 1% grads pursue business degrees. 8% grads pursue law degrees. 4% grads pursue medical degrees. **Faculty:** Student/faculty ratio 11:1. 92 full-time faculty, 92% hold PhDs. 100% faculty teach undergrads.

ACADEMICS

Degrees: Bachelor's. **Academic Requirements:** General education including some course work in arts/fine arts, English (including composition), foreign languages, history, humanities, mathematics, philosophy, sciences (biological or physical), social science, physical education, theology, communication. **Classes:** 10-19 students in an average class. **Majors with Highest Enrollment:** Business administration/management; sociology; chemistry, general. **Disciplines with Highest Percentage of Degrees Awarded:** Social sciences and history 24%, business/marketing 13%, physical sciences 10%, education 9%, biological life sciences 8%. **Special Study Options:** Cross registration, double major, dual enrollment, independent study, internships, study abroad, teacher certification program.

FACILITIES

Housing: Coed, all-female, all-male, apartments for single students, fraternities and/or sororities, theme housing. **Library Holdings:** 224,478 bound volumes. 1,035 periodicals. 44,770 microforms. 5,080 audiovisuals. **Special Academic Facilities/Equipment:** Geological museum, electronic language lab, observatory. **Computers:** School-owned computers available for student use.

EXTRACURRICULARS

Activities: Choral groups, concert band, drama/theater, jazz band, literary magazine, music ensembles, musical theater, pep band, student government, student newspaper, television station, yearbook. **Organizations:** 36 registered organizations, 5 honor societies, 5 religious organizations, 4 fraternities (33% men join), 4 sororities (47% women join). **Athletics (Intercollegiate):** *Men:* baseball, basketball, cross-country, football, golf, soccer, tennis, track & field. *Women:* basketball, cross-country, field hockey, golf, soccer, softball, tennis, track & field, volleyball.

ADMISSIONS

Selectivity Rating: 79 (of 100). **Freshman Academic Profile:** 38% in top 10% of high school class, 72% in top 25% of high school class, 95% in top 50% of high school class. 85% from public high schools. Average SAT I Math 576, SAT I Math middle 50% range 520-630. Average SAT I Verbal 559, SAT I Verbal middle 50% range 500-620. Average ACT 24, ACT middle 50% range 21-27. TOEFL required of all international applicants, minimum TOEFL 550. **Basis for Candidate Selection:** *Very important factors considered include:* class rank, secondary school record. *Important factors considered include:* character/personal qualities, essays, standardized test scores, talent/ability. *Other factors considered include:* alumni/ae relation, extracurricular activities, geographical residence, interview, minority status, recommendations, state residency, volunteer work, work experience. **Freshman Admission Requirements:** High school diploma is required and GED is not accepted. *Academic units required/recommended:* 4 English required, 3 math required, 4 math recommended, 3 science required, 3 science recommended, 2 science lab required, 2 foreign language required, 4 foreign language recommended, 2 social studies required, 2 history required. **Freshman Admission Statistics:** 1,227 applied, 76% accepted, 30% of those accepted enrolled. **Transfer Admission Requirements:** *Items required:* high school transcript, college transcript, essay. Lowest grade transferable C-. **General Admission Information:** Application fee $30. Priority application deadline March 1. Regular application deadline March 1. Nonfall registration accepted. Admission may be deferred for a maximum of 1 year. Credit and/or placement offered for CEEB Advanced Placement tests.

COSTS AND FINANCIAL AID

Average book expense $800. **Required Forms and Deadlines:** FAFSA. Priority filing deadline March 10. **Notification of Awards:** Applicants will be notified of awards on a rolling basis beginning on or about March 10. **Types of Aid:** *Need-based scholarships/grants:* Pell, state scholarships/grants, private scholarships, the school's own gift aid. *Loans:* FFEL Subsidized Stafford, FFEL Unsubsidized Stafford, FFEL PLUS, college/university loans from institutional funds. **Student Employment:** Institutional employment available. Off-campus job opportunities are fair. **Financial Aid Statistics:** 61% freshmen, 58% undergrads receive some form of aid. Average freshman grant $12,313. Average freshman loan $3,113. Average income from on-campus job $875. **Financial Aid Phone:** 812-866-7030.

HARDING UNIVERSITY

PO Box 12255, Searcy, AR 72149
Phone: 501-279-4407 **E-mail:** admissions@harding.edu **CEEB Code:** 10311
Fax: 501-279-4865 **Web:** www.harding.edu **ACT Code:** 124

This private school, which is affiliated with the Church of Christ, was founded in 1924. It has a 200-acre campus.

STUDENTS AND FACULTY

Enrollment: 4,089. **Student Body:** Male 45%, female 55%, out-of-state 69%, international 6% (45 countries represented). **Ethnic Representation:** African American 4%, Caucasian 92%, Hispanic 1%, Native American 1%. **Retention and Graduation:** 78% freshmen return for sophomore year. 31% freshmen graduate within 4 years. 30% grads go on to further study within 1 year. 5% grads pursue business degrees. 1% grads pursue law degrees. 2% grads pursue medical degrees. **Faculty:** Student/faculty ratio 19:1. 202 full-time faculty, 65% hold PhDs. 100% faculty teach undergrads.

ACADEMICS

Degrees: Bachelor's, master's. **Academic Requirements:** General education including some course work in arts/fine arts, English (including composition), history, humanities, mathematics, philosophy, sciences (biological or physical), social science, Bible and religion. **Classes:** Under 10 students in an average class. **Majors with Highest Enrollment:** Bible/biblical studies; marketing/marketing management, general; business administration/management. **Disciplines with Highest Percentage of Degrees Awarded:** Business/marketing 21%, education 12%, health professions and related sciences 10%, philosophy/religion/theology 8%, computer and information sciences 6%. **Special Study Options:** Accelerated program, cooperative (work-study) program, distance learning, double major, dual enrollment, English as a second language, honors program, independent study, internships, liberal arts/career combination, study abroad, teacher certification program.

FACILITIES

Housing: All-female, all-male, apartments for married students, apartments for single students, approved off-campus housing. **Library Holdings:** 243,052 bound volumes. 5,972 periodicals. 240,165 microforms. 8,649 audiovisuals. **Special Academic Facilities/Equipment:** On-campus academy (prep school grades K-12). **Computers:** School-owned computers available for student use.

EXTRACURRICULARS

Activities: Choral groups, concert band, drama/theater, jazz band, marching band, music ensembles, musical theater, pep band, radio station, student government, student newspaper, symphony orchestra, television station, yearbook. **Organizations:** 52 registered organizations, 4 honor societies, 5 religious organizations, 14 fraternities (48% men join), 12 sororities (46% women join). **Athletics (Intercollegiate):** *Men:* baseball, basketball, cheerleading, cross-country, football, golf, soccer, tennis, track & field. *Women:* basketball, cheerleading, cross-country, soccer, tennis, track & field, volleyball.

ADMISSIONS

Selectivity Rating: 81 (of 100). **Freshman Academic Profile:** Average high school GPA 3.3. 35% in top 10% of high school class, 62% in top 25% of high school class, 90% in top 50% of high school class. 89% from public high schools. Average SAT I Math 557, SAT I Math middle 50% range 480-620. Average SAT I Verbal 566, SAT I Verbal middle 50% range 500-620. Average ACT 24, ACT middle 50% range 21-28. TOEFL required of all international applicants, minimum TOEFL 500. **Basis for Candidate Selection:** *Very important factors considered include:* character/personal qualities, interview, recommendations, secondary school record, standardized test scores. *Important factors considered include:* class rank, talent/ability. *Other factors considered include:* alumni/ae relation, essays, extracurricular activities. **Freshman Admission Requirements:** High school diploma is required and GED is not accepted. *Academic units required/recommended:* 15 total required; 20 total recommended; 4 English required, 4 English recommended, 3 math required, 4 math recommended, 2 science required, 4 science recommended, 2 foreign language recommended, 3 social studies required, 4 social studies recommended, 3 elective required, 2 elective recommended. **Freshman Admission Statistics:** 1,712 applied, 78% accepted, 78% of those accepted enrolled. **Transfer Admission Requirements:** *Items required:* college transcript, essay, statement of good standing from prior school. Lowest grade transferable C. **General Admission Information:** Application fee $25. Regular application deadline July 1. Nonfall registration accepted. Admission may be deferred for a maximum of 1 year. Credit and/or placement offered for CEEB Advanced Placement tests.

COSTS AND FINANCIAL AID

Tuition $9,180. Room & board $4,650. Required fees $350. Average book expense $1,200. **Required Forms and Deadlines:** FAFSA and institution's own financial aid form. No deadline for regular filing. Priority filing deadline April 1. **Notification of Awards:** Applicants will be notified of awards on a rolling basis beginning on or about February 15. **Types of Aid:** *Need-based scholarships/grants:* Pell, SEOG, state scholarships/grants, private scholarships, the school's own gift aid, Federal Nursing, Stephens Scholars Program for African-American students. *Loans:* FFEL Subsidized Stafford, FFEL Unsubsidized Stafford, FFEL PLUS, Federal Perkins, Federal Nursing, state loans, college/university loans from institutional funds. **Student Employment:** Federal Work-Study Program available. Institutional employment available. Off-campus job opportunities are good. **Financial Aid Statistics:** 55% freshmen, 57% undergrads receive some form of aid. Average freshman grant $8,687. Average freshman loan $3,892. Average income from on-campus job $800. **Financial Aid Phone:** 501-279-4257.

HARDIN-SIMMONS UNIVERSITY

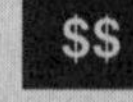

2200 Hickory Street, Abilene, TX 79698
Phone: 915-670-1206 **E-mail:** enroll@hsutx.edu **CEEB Code:** 6268
Fax: 915-671-1527 **Web:** www.hsutx.edu **ACT Code:** 4096

This private school, which is affiliated with the Southern Baptist Church, was founded in 1891. It has a 40-acre campus.

STUDENTS AND FACULTY

Enrollment: 1,914. **Student Body:** Male 46%, female 54%, out-of-state 4%, (8 countries represented). **Ethnic Representation:** African American 4%, Asian 1%, Caucasian 85%, Hispanic 7%. **Retention and Graduation:** 63% freshmen return for sophomore year. 24% freshmen graduate within 4 years. **Faculty:** Student/faculty ratio 14:1. 127 full-time faculty, 72% hold PhDs. 92% faculty teach undergrads.

ACADEMICS

Degrees: Bachelor's, first professional, master's. **Academic Requirements:** General education including some course work in arts/fine arts, computer literacy, English (including composition), history, humanities, mathematics, sciences (biological or physical), social science. **Classes:** 10-19 students in an average class. 10-19 students in an average lab/discussion section. **Disciplines with Highest Percentage of Degrees Awarded:** Education 22%, business/marketing 17%, biological life sciences 8%, protective services/public administration 8%, parks and recreation 8%. **Special Study Options:** Accelerated program, cross registration, distance learning, double major, dual enrollment, independent study, internships, liberal arts/career combination, study abroad, teacher certification program.

FACILITIES

Housing: All-female, all-male, apartments for married students, apartments for single students, housing for disabled students, single and duplex housing with priority given to families. **Library Holdings:** 400,000 bound volumes. 920 periodicals. 20,526 microforms. 16,390 audiovisuals. **Special Academic Facilities/Equipment:** Art center, observatory with 14-inch telescope. **Computers:** School-owned computers available for student use.

EXTRACURRICULARS

Activities: Choral groups, concert band, drama/theater, literary magazine, marching band, music ensembles, opera, student government, student newspaper, symphony orchestra, yearbook. **Organizations:** 55 registered organizations, 11 honor societies, 1 religious organization, 5 fraternities (10% men join), 5 sororities (10% women join). **Athletics (Intercollegiate):** *Men:* baseball, basketball, cheerleading, football, golf, soccer, tennis. *Women:* basketball, cheerleading, golf, soccer, tennis, volleyball.

ADMISSIONS

Selectivity Rating: 70 (of 100). **Freshman Academic Profile:** 19% in top 10% of high school class, 44% in top 25% of high school class, 80% in top 50% of high school class. 91% from public high schools. Average SAT I Math 510, SAT I Math middle 50% range 460-570. Average SAT I Verbal 508, SAT I Verbal middle 50% range 450-570. Average ACT 22, ACT middle 50% range 19-25. TOEFL required of all international applicants, minimum TOEFL 550. **Basis for Candidate Selection:** *Very important factors considered include:* class rank, secondary school record, standardized test scores. *Important factors considered include:* alumni/ae relation, character/personal qualities, talent/ability. *Other factors considered include:* essays, recommendations, religious affiliation/commitment. **Freshman Admission Requirements:** High school diploma or GED is required. *Academic units required/recommended:* 16 total required; 3 English required, 2 math required, 2 science required, 2 social studies required, 7 elective required. **Freshman Admission Statistics:** 1,139 applied, 52% accepted, 76% of those accepted enrolled. **Transfer Admission Requirements:** *Items required:* college transcript. Minimum college GPA of 2.0 required. Lowest grade transferable C. **General Admission Information:** Application fee $25. Priority application deadline August 2. Nonfall registration accepted. Admission may be deferred for a maximum of 1 year. Neither credit nor placement offered for CEEB Advanced Placement tests.

COSTS AND FINANCIAL AID

Tuition $11,400. Room & board $3,699. Required fees $776. Average book expense $750. **Required Forms and Deadlines:** FAFSA. No deadline for regular filing. Priority filing deadline March 15. **Notification of Awards:** Applicants will be notified of awards on a rolling basis beginning on or about January 1. **Types of Aid:** *Need-based scholarships/grants:* Pell, SEOG, state scholarships/grants, private scholarships, the school's own gift aid. *Loans:* FFEL Subsidized Stafford, FFEL Unsubsidized Stafford, FFEL PLUS, Federal Perkins, state loans. **Student Employment:** Federal Work-Study Program available. Institutional employment available. Off-campus job opportunities are good. **Financial Aid Statistics:** 65% freshmen, 64% undergrads receive some form of aid. Average freshman grant $4,358. Average freshman loan $4,302. Average income from on-campus job $2,094. **Financial Aid Phone:** 915-670-1331.

HARRINGTON INSTITUTE OF INTERIOR DESIGN

The Fine Arts Building, 410 S. Michigan Ave., Chicago, IL 60605-1496
Phone: 877-939-4975 **E-mail:** hiid@interiordesign.edu
Fax: 312-697-8032 **Web:** www.interiordesign.edu **ACT Code:** 6641

This proprietary school was founded in 1931.

STUDENTS AND FACULTY

Enrollment: 512. **Student Body:** Male 13%, female 87%. **Faculty:** Student/faculty ratio 17:1.

ACADEMICS

Degrees: Associate's, bachelor's, certificate, diploma. **Academic Requirements:** General education including some course work in arts/fine arts, computer literacy, English (including composition), history, humanities, sciences (biological or physical), social science. **Special Study Options:** Accelerated program, internships, study abroad.

FACILITIES

Library Holdings: 22,000 bound volumes. 92 periodicals. 23,000 microforms. **Computers:** School-owned computers available for student use.

EXTRACURRICULARS

Activities: Student government.

ADMISSIONS

Selectivity Rating: 63 (of 100). **Freshman Academic Profile:** TOEFL required of all international applicants, minimum TOEFL 500. **Basis for Candidate Selection:** *Very important factors considered include:* interview. *Important factors considered include:* character/personal qualities, talent/ability. *Other factors considered include:* class rank, essays, extracurricular activities, geographical residence, recommendations, secondary school record, standardized test scores, volunteer work, work experience. **Freshman Admission Requirements:** High school diploma or GED is required. **Freshman Admission Statistics:** 568 applied, 90% accepted, 7% of those accepted enrolled. **Transfer Admission Requirements:** *Items required:* college transcript, interview. Lowest grade transferable C. **General Admission Information:** Application fee $60. Nonfall registration accepted.

COSTS AND FINANCIAL AID

Room & board $4,000. Required fees $300. Average book expense $900. **Required Forms and Deadlines:** FAFSA. **Types of Aid:** *Need-based scholarships/grants:* Pell, SEOG. *Loans:* FFEL Subsidized Stafford, FFEL Unsubsidized Stafford, FFEL PLUS. **Student Employment:** Off-campus job opportunities are excellent. **Financial Aid Phone:** 877-939-4975.

HARRIS-STOWE STATE COLLEGE

3026 Laclede Avenue, St. Louis, MO 63103
Phone: 314-340-3366 **CEEB Code:** 6269
Fax: 314-340-3322 **ACT Code:** 2302

This public school was founded in 1857.

STUDENTS AND FACULTY

Enrollment: 1,723. **Student Body:** Out-of-state 1%.

ACADEMICS

Degrees: Bachelor's. **Special Study Options:** Undergrads may take grad-level classes.

FACILITIES

Library Holdings: 60,000 bound volumes. **Special Academic Facilities/Equipment:** Education resource center, urban education specialist/multicultural education collection, juvenile literature collection, audiovisual lab.

EXTRACURRICULARS

Organizations: 1 honor society, 2 religious organizations. **Athletics (Intercollegiate):** *Men:* baseball, basketball, soccer, track & field, volleyball. *Women:* basketball, track & field, volleyball.

ADMISSIONS

Selectivity Rating: 63 (of 100). High school diploma is required and GED is not accepted. **Transfer Admission Requirements:** Lowest grade transferable C. **General Admission Information:** Regular application deadline rolling. Nonfall registration accepted. Credit and/or placement offered for CEEB Advanced Placement tests.

COSTS AND FINANCIAL AID

In-state tuition $1,992. Out-of-state tuition $3,924. Required fees $15. Average book expense $750. **Required Forms and Deadlines:** FAFSA and institution's own financial aid form. **Types of Aid:** *Loans:* FFEL Subsidized Stafford, FFEL PLUS. **Student Employment:** Institutional employment available. **Financial Aid Phone:** 314-340-3500.

HARTWICK COLLEGE

PO Box 4020, Oneonta, NY 13820-4020
Phone: 607-431-4000 **E-mail:** admissions@hartwick.edu **CEEB Code:** 2288
Fax: 607-431-4102 **Web:** www.hartwick.edu

This private school was founded in 1797. It has a 425-acre campus.

STUDENTS AND FACULTY

Enrollment: 1,397. **Student Body:** Male 43%, female 57%, out-of-state 64%, international 4% (34 countries represented). **Ethnic Representation:** African American 5%, Asian 1%, Caucasian 68%, Hispanic 3%, Native American 1%. **Retention and Graduation:** 77% freshmen return for sophomore year. 48% freshmen graduate within 4 years. 16% grads go on to further study within 1 year. **Faculty:** Student/faculty ratio 11:1. 108 full-time faculty, 77% hold PhDs. 100% faculty teach undergrads.

ACADEMICS

Degrees: Bachelor's. **Academic Requirements:** General education including some course work in English (including composition), humanities, mathematics, sciences (biological or physical), social science. **Classes:** 10-19 students in an average class. 10-19 students in an average lab/discussion section. **Majors with Highest Enrollment:** Business administration/management; psychology, general; biology/biological sciences, general. **Disciplines with Highest Percentage of Degrees Awarded:** Business/marketing 21%, social sciences and history 19%, psychology 12%, visual and performing arts 11%, English 8%. **Special Study Options:** Accelerated program, double major, student exchange program (domestic), honors program, independent study, internships, student-designed major, study abroad, teacher certification program.

FACILITIES

Housing: Coed, apartments for single students, fraternities and/or sororities. Housing at Pine Lake environmental campus (lodge and cabins) also available. Special-interest housing available. **Library Holdings:** 353,776 bound volumes. 571 periodicals. 8,291 microforms. 1,838 audiovisuals. **Special Academic Facilities/Equipment:** Art and history museums, Indian artifact collection, environmental center, observatory, electron microscope, tissue culture lab, spectrophotometers. **Computers:** *Recommended operating system:* Windows 95. School-owned computers available for student use.

EXTRACURRICULARS

Activities: Choral groups, dance, drama/theater, jazz band, literary magazine, music ensembles, musical theater, radio station, student government, student newspaper, television station, yearbook. **Organizations:** 60 registered organizations, 30 honor societies, 3 religious organizations, 5 fraternities (15% men join), 4 sororities (17% women join). **Athletics (Intercollegiate):** *Men:* baseball, basketball, cross-country, diving, football, golf, indoor track, lacrosse, soccer, swimming, tennis, track & field. *Women:* basketball, cross-country, diving, equestrian, field hockey, indoor track, lacrosse, soccer, softball, swimming, tennis, track & field, volleyball, water polo.

ADMISSIONS

Selectivity Rating: 68 (of 100). **Freshman Academic Profile:** 22% in top 10% of high school class, 41% in top 25% of high school class, 78% in top 50% of high school class. Average SAT I Math 567, SAT I Math middle 50% range 510-620. Average SAT I Verbal 565, SAT I Verbal middle 50% range 520-610. TOEFL required of all international applicants, minimum TOEFL 550. **Basis for Candidate Selection:** *Very important factors considered include:* class rank, secondary school record. *Important factors considered include:* essays, extracurricular activities, recommendations. *Other factors considered include:* alumni/ae relation, character/personal qualities, geographical residence, interview, minority status, standardized test scores, state residency, talent/ability, volunteer work, work experience. **Freshman Admission Requirements:** High school diploma or GED is required. *Academic units required/recommended:* 19 total recommended; 4 English recommended, 3 math recommended, 3 science recommended, 2 science lab recommended, 3 foreign language recommended, 2 social studies recommended, 2 history recommended. **Freshman Admission Statistics:** 1,853 applied, 89% accepted, 23% of those accepted enrolled. **Transfer Admission Requirements:** *Items required:* high school transcript, college transcript, essay, statement of good standing from prior school. Minimum college GPA of 2.0 required. Lowest grade transferable C. **General Admission Information:** Application fee $35. Regular application deadline February 15. Nonfall registration accepted. Admission may be deferred for a maximum of 1 year. Credit offered for CEEB Advanced Placement tests.

COSTS AND FINANCIAL AID

Tuition $26,215. Room & board $7,050. Required fees $400. Average book expense $700. **Required Forms and Deadlines:** FAFSA, institution's own financial aid form, and state aid form. Financial aid filing deadline February 1. **Notification of Awards:** Applicants will be notified of awards on or about March 15. **Types of Aid:** *Need-based scholarships/grants:* Pell, SEOG, state scholarships/grants, private scholarships, the school's own gift aid. *Loans:* FFEL Subsidized Stafford, FFEL Unsubsidized Stafford, FFEL PLUS, Federal Perkins, Federal Nursing, alternative loans. **Student Employment:** Federal Work-Study Program available. Institutional employment available. Off-campus job opportunities are good. **Financial Aid Statistics:** 69% freshmen, 71% undergrads receive some form of aid. **Financial Aid Phone:** 607-431-4130.

See page 1050.

HARVARD COLLEGE

Byerly Hall, 8 Garden Street, Cambridge, MA 02318
Phone: 617-495-1551 **E-mail:** college@fas.harvard.edu **CEEB Code:** 3434
Fax: 617-495-8821 **Web:** www.fas.harvard.edu **ACT Code:** 1840

This private school was founded in 1636. It has a 380-acre campus.

STUDENTS AND FACULTY

Enrollment: 6,649. **Student Body:** Male 53%, female 47%, out-of-state 84%, international 7%. **Ethnic Representation:** African American 9%, Asian 19%, Caucasian 46%, Hispanic 8%, Native American 1%. **Retention and Graduation:** 96% freshmen return for sophomore year. 83% freshmen graduate within 4 years. 25% grads go on to further study within 1 year. 13% grads pursue business degrees. 15% grads pursue law degrees. 20% grads pursue medical degrees. **Faculty:** Student/faculty ratio 8:1. 775 full-time faculty, 100% hold PhDs. 100% faculty teach undergrads.

ACADEMICS

Degrees: Associate's, bachelor's, doctoral, master's. **Academic Requirements:** General education including some course work in arts/fine arts, English (including composition), foreign languages, history, humanities, mathematics, philosophy, sciences (biological or physical), social science. **Classes:** Under 10 students in an average class. Under 10 students in an average lab/discussion section. **Majors with Highest Enrollment:** Psychology, general; economics, general; political science and government, general. **Disciplines with Highest Percentage of Degrees Awarded:** Social sciences and history 40%, biological life sciences 13%, English 9%, psychology 6%, interdisciplinary studies 6%. **Special Study Options:** Accelerated program, cross registration, double major, honors program, independent study, internships, student-designed major, study abroad, teacher certification program.

FACILITIES

Housing: Coed, apartments for married students, apartments for single students, housing for disabled students. **Library Holdings:** 14,000,000 bound volumes. 1,200 periodicals. 270,000 microforms. 0 audiovisuals. **Special Academic Facilities/Equipment:** Museums (university arts museums, museums of cultural history, many others), language labs, observatory, many science and research laboratories and facilities, new state-of-the-art computer science facility. **Computers:** School-owned computers available for student use.

EXTRACURRICULARS

Activities: Choral groups, concert band, dance, drama/theater, jazz band, literary magazine, marching band, music ensembles, musical theater, opera, pep band, radio station, student government, student newspaper, student-run film society, symphony orchestra, television station, yearbook. **Organizations:** 260 registered organizations, 1 honor society. **Athletics (Intercollegiate):** *Men:* baseball, basketball, cheerleading, crew, skiing (cross-country), cross-country, diving, equestrian, fencing, football, golf, gymnastics, ice hockey, indoor track, lacrosse, rugby, sailing, skiing (alpine), skiing (Nordic), soccer, squash, swimming, tennis, track & field, volleyball, water polo, wrestling. *Women:* basketball, cheerleading, crew, skiing (cross-country), cross-country, diving, equestrian, fencing, field hockey, golf, gymnastics, ice hockey, indoor track, lacrosse, rugby, sailing, skiing (alpine), skiing (Nordic), soccer, softball, squash, swimming, tennis, track & field, volleyball, water polo.

ADMISSIONS

Selectivity Rating: 99 (of 100). **Freshman Academic Profile:** 90% in top 10% of high school class, 98% in top 25% of high school class, 100% in top 50% of high school class. 65% from public high schools. SAT I Math middle 50% range 700-790. SAT I Verbal middle 50% range 700-800. ACT middle 50% range 30-34. **Basis for Candidate Selection:** *Very important factors considered include:* character/personal qualities, extracurricular activities, recommendations, secondary school record, talent/ability. *Important factors considered include:* class rank, essays, interview, standardized test scores. *Other* *factors considered include:* alumni/ae relation, geographical residence, minority status, volunteer work, work experience. **Freshman Admission Requirements:** High school diploma or equivalent is not required. *Academic units required/recommended:* 19 total recommended; 4 English recommended, 4 math recommended, 4 science recommended, 4 foreign language recommended. **Freshman Admission Statistics:** 19,609 applied, 11% accepted, 79% of those accepted enrolled. **Transfer Admission Requirements:** *Items required:* college transcript, essay, standardized test scores. Lowest grade transferable C-. **General Admission Information:** Application fee $60. Priority application deadline December 15. Regular application deadline January 1. Admission may be deferred for a maximum of 1 year. Credit and/or placement offered for CEEB Advanced Placement tests.

COSTS AND FINANCIAL AID

Tuition $24,630. Room & board $8,502. Required fees $2,818. Average book expense $1,000. **Required Forms and Deadlines:** FAFSA, CSS/Financial Aid PROFILE, noncustodial (divorced/separated) parent's statement, business/farm supplement, and tax returns. No deadline for regular filing. Priority filing deadline February 1. **Notification of Awards:** Applicants will be notified of awards on or about April 1. **Types of Aid:** *Need-based scholarships/grants:* Pell, SEOG, state scholarships/grants, private scholarships, the school's own gift aid. *Loans:* Direct Subsidized Stafford, Direct Unsubsidized Stafford, Direct PLUS, Federal Perkins, state loans, college/university loans from institutional funds. **Student Employment:** Federal Work-Study Program available. Institutional employment available. Off-campus job opportunities are excellent. **Financial Aid Statistics:** 48% freshmen, 48% undergrads receive some form of aid. Average freshman grant $19,200. Average freshman loan $1,500. Average income from on-campus job $1,650. **Financial Aid Phone:** 617-495-1581.

HARVEY MUDD COLLEGE

301 East 12th Street, Claremont, CA 91711-5990
Phone: 909-621-8011 **E-mail:** admission@hmc.edu **CEEB Code:** 4341
Fax: 909-621-8360 **Web:** www.hmc.edu

This private school was founded in 1955. It has a 33-acre campus.

STUDENTS AND FACULTY

Enrollment: 703. **Student Body:** Out-of-state 59%, international 3%. **Ethnic Representation:** Asian 19%, Caucasian 63%, Hispanic 5%, Native American 1%. **Retention and Graduation:** 94% freshmen return for sophomore year. 73% freshmen graduate within 4 years. 47% grads go on to further study within 1 year. 1% grads pursue business degrees. 2% grads pursue law degrees. 2% grads pursue medical degrees. **Faculty:** Student/faculty ratio 9:1. 80 full-time faculty, 100% hold PhDs. 100% faculty teach undergrads.

ACADEMICS

Degrees: Bachelor's. **Academic Requirements:** General education including some course work in arts/fine arts, computer literacy, English (including composition), history, humanities, mathematics, philosophy, sciences (biological or physical), social science, integrative experience looking at the relationship between technology and society. **Classes:** 10-19 students in an average class. 20-29 students in an average lab/discussion section. **Majors with Highest Enrollment:** Computer science; engineering, general; physics, general. **Disciplines with Highest Percentage of Degrees Awarded:** Engineering/engineering technology 33%, physical sciences 21%, computer and information sciences 18%, mathematics 14%. **Special Study Options:** Cross registration, double major, dual enrollment.

FACILITIES

Housing: Coed, apartments for married students, apartments for single students. Housing exchange program with Pomona College, Pitzer College, Scripps College, and Claremont McKenna College. **Library Holdings:** 2,232,086 bound volumes. 5,959 periodicals. 1,448,719 microforms. 16,524 audiovisuals. **Computers:** School-owned computers available for student use.

EXTRACURRICULARS

Activities: Choral groups, concert band, dance, drama/theater, jazz band, literary magazine, music ensembles, musical theater, pep band, radio station, student government, student newspaper, student-run film society, symphony orchestra, television station, yearbook. **Organizations:** 90 registered organizations, 4 honor societies, 5 religious organizations. **Athletics (Intercollegiate):** *Men:* baseball, basketball, cross-country, diving, football, golf, soccer, swimming, tennis, track & field, water polo. *Women:* basketball, cross-country, diving, lacrosse, soccer, softball, swimming, tennis, track & field, volleyball, water polo.

ADMISSIONS

Selectivity Rating: 94 (of 100). **Freshman Academic Profile:** Average high school GPA 3.8. 83% in top 10% of high school class, 96% in top 25% of high school class, 100% in top 50% of high school class. Average SAT I Math 750, SAT I Math middle 50% range 720-790. Average SAT I Verbal 700, SAT I Verbal middle 50% range 650-750. TOEFL required of all international applicants, minimum TOEFL 600. **Basis for Candidate Selection:** *Very important factors considered include:* character/personal qualities, class rank, essays, recommendations, secondary school record, standardized test scores. *Important factors considered include:* alumni/ae relation, interview. *Other factors considered include:* extracurricular activities, geographical residence, minority status, talent/ability, volunteer work, work experience. **Freshman Admission Requirements:** High school diploma or GED is required. *Academic units required/recommended:* 4 English required, 4 math required, 3 science required, 3 science lab required, 2 foreign language recommended, 1 social studies recommended, 1 history recommended. **Freshman Admission Statistics:** 1,669 applied, 37% accepted, 30% of those accepted enrolled. **Transfer Admission Requirements:** *Items required:* high school transcript, college transcript, essay, standardized test scores, statement of good standing from prior school. Minimum college GPA of 3.0 required. Lowest grade transferable C-. **General Admission Information:** Application fee $50. Early decision application deadline November 15. Regular application deadline January 15. Admission may be deferred for a maximum of 1 year. Placement offered for CEEB Advanced Placement tests.

COSTS AND FINANCIAL AID

Tuition $26,425. Room & board $8,971. Required fees $612. Average book expense $800. **Required Forms and Deadlines:** FAFSA, CSS/Financial Aid PROFILE, state aid form, noncustodial (divorced/separated) parent's statement, and business/farm supplement. Financial aid filing deadline February 1. Priority filing deadline February 1. **Notification of Awards:** Applicants will be notified of awards on a rolling basis beginning on or about April 1. **Types of Aid:** *Need-based scholarships/grants:* Pell, SEOG, state scholarships/grants, private scholarships, the school's own gift aid. *Loans:* FFEL Subsidized Stafford, FFEL Unsubsidized Stafford, FFEL PLUS, Federal Perkins, college/university loans from institutional funds. **Student Employment:** Federal Work-Study Program available. Institutional employment available. Off-campus job opportunities are fair. **Financial Aid Statistics:** 58% freshmen, 57% undergrads receive some form of aid. Average freshman grant $12,141. Average freshman loan $3,103. Average income from on-campus job $1,779. **Financial Aid Phone:** 909-621-8055.

HASTINGS COLLEGE

Hastings College, 800 Turner Avenue, Hastings, NE 68901
Phone: 402-461-7403 **E-mail:** admissions@hastings.edu **CEEB Code:** 6270
Fax: 402-461-7490 **Web:** www.hastings.edu **ACT Code:** 2456

This private school, which is affiliated with the Presbyterian Church, was founded in 1882. It has a 104-acre campus.

STUDENTS AND FACULTY

Enrollment: 1,033. **Student Body:** Male 48%, female 52%, out-of-state 22%, international 1%. **Ethnic Representation:** African American 1%, Asian 1%, Caucasian 95%, Hispanic 2%. **Retention and Graduation:** 75% freshmen return for sophomore year. 52% freshmen graduate within 4 years. 18% grads go on to further study within 1 year. 1% grads pursue business degrees. 2% grads pursue law degrees. 1% grads pursue medical degrees. **Faculty:** Student/faculty ratio 13:1. 74 full-time faculty, 74% hold PhDs. 100% faculty teach undergrads.

ACADEMICS

Degrees: Bachelor's, master's. **Academic Requirements:** General education including some course work in arts/fine arts, computer literacy, English (including composition), foreign languages, history, humanities, mathematics, philosophy, sciences (biological or physical), social science, health/wellness, physical education, speech. **Classes:** 10-19 students in an average class. Under 10 students in an average lab/discussion section. **Majors with Highest Enrollment:** Business administration/management; mass communications/media studies; education, general. **Disciplines with Highest Percentage of Degrees Awarded:** Education 19%, business/marketing 16%, social sciences and history 10%, communications/communication technologies 9%, health professions and related sciences 8%. **Special Study Options:** Double major, English as a second language, student exchange program (domestic), independent study, internships, student-designed major, study abroad, teacher certification program.

FACILITIES

Housing: Coed, all-female, all-male, honors housing. **Library Holdings:** 93,750 bound volumes. 580 periodicals. 113,010 microforms. 1,200 audiovisuals. **Special Academic Facilities/Equipment:** Center for communication arts, glass-blowing studio, observatory, art gallery. **Computers:** School-owned computers available for student use.

EXTRACURRICULARS

Activities: Choral groups, concert band, drama/theater, jazz band, literary magazine, marching band, music ensembles, musical theater, radio station, student government, student newspaper, symphony orchestra, television station, yearbook. **Organizations:** 75 registered organizations, 12 honor societies, 13 religious organizations, 4 fraternities (16% men join), 4 sororities (32% women join). **Athletics (Intercollegiate):** *Men:* baseball, basketball, cross-country, football, golf, indoor track, soccer, tennis, track & field. *Women:* basketball, cross-country, golf, indoor track, soccer, softball, tennis, track & field, volleyball.

ADMISSIONS

Selectivity Rating: 79 (of 100). **Freshman Academic Profile:** 20% in top 10% of high school class, 35% in top 25% of high school class, 75% in top 50% of high school class. 90% from public high schools. Average SAT I Math 490, SAT I Math middle 50% range 490-590. Average SAT I Verbal 460, SAT I Verbal middle 50% range 460-600. Average ACT 23, ACT middle 50% range 20-26. TOEFL required of all international applicants, minimum TOEFL 600. **Basis for Candidate Selection:** *Very important factors considered include:* character/personal qualities, secondary school record. *Important factors considered include:* class rank, interview, recommendations, standardized test scores, talent/ability. *Other factors considered include:* alumni/ae relation, essays, extracurricular activities, geographical residence, minority status, religious affiliation/commitment, state residency, volunteer work. **Freshman Admission Requirements:** High school diploma or GED is required. *Academic units required/recommended:* 4 English required, 4 English recommended, 4 math required, 4 science required, 1 science lab required, 1 science lab recommended, 1 foreign language required, 2 foreign language recommended, 4 social studies required, 4 history required. **Freshman Admission Statistics:** 1,173 applied, 85% accepted, 33% of those accepted enrolled. **Transfer Admission Requirements:** *Items required:* high school transcript, college transcript, statement of good standing from prior school. Minimum college GPA of 2.3 required. Lowest grade transferable C. **General Admission Information:** Application fee $20. Priority application deadline March 1. Regular application deadline August 1. Nonfall registration accepted. Credit and/or placement offered for CEEB Advanced Placement tests.

COSTS AND FINANCIAL AID

Average book expense $650. **Required Forms and Deadlines:** FAFSA and institution's own financial aid form. Financial aid filing deadline September 1. Priority filing deadline May 1. **Notification of Awards:** Applicants will be notified of awards on a rolling basis beginning on or about February 15. **Types of Aid:** *Need-based scholarships/grants:* Pell, SEOG, state scholarships/grants, private scholarships, the school's own gift aid. *Loans:* FFEL Subsidized Stafford, FFEL Unsubsidized Stafford, FFEL PLUS, Federal Perkins. **Student Employment:** Federal Work-Study Program available. Institutional employment available. Off-campus job opportunities are good. **Financial Aid Statistics:** 70% freshmen, 69% undergrads receive some form of aid. Average freshman grant $5,978. Average freshman loan $3,383. Average income from on-campus job $600. **Financial Aid Phone:** 402-461-7455.

HAVERFORD COLLEGE

370 Lancaster Avenue, Haverford, PA 19041
Phone: 610-896-1350 **E-mail:** admitme@haverford.edu **CEEB Code:** 2289
Fax: 610-896-1338 **Web:** www.haverford.edu **ACT Code:** 3409

This private school was founded in 1833. It has a 200-acre campus.

STUDENTS AND FACULTY

Enrollment: 1,105. **Student Body:** Out-of-state 80%, international 3% (38 countries represented). **Ethnic Representation:** African American 5%, Asian 15%, Caucasian 72%, Hispanic 7%, Native American 1%. **Retention and Graduation:** 96% freshmen return for sophomore year. 86% freshmen graduate within 4 years. 41% grads go on to further study within 1 year. 2% grads pursue law degrees. 4% grads pursue medical degrees. **Faculty:** Student/faculty ratio 8:1. 105 full-time faculty, 100% hold PhDs. 100% faculty teach undergrads.

ACADEMICS

Degrees: Bachelor's. **Academic Requirements:** General education including some course work in English (including composition), foreign languages, humanities, mathematics, sciences (biological or physical), social science. **Classes:** 10-19 students in an average class. Under 10 students in an average lab/discussion section. **Majors with Highest Enrollment:** History, general; biology/biological sciences, general; political science and government, general. **Disciplines with Highest Percentage of Degrees Awarded:** Social sciences and history 33%, biological life sciences 12%, philosophy/religion/theology 11%, physical sciences 10%, English 10%. **Special Study Options:** Accelerated program, cross registration, double major, student exchange program (domestic), independent study, internships, liberal arts/career combination, student-designed major, study abroad, teacher certification program.

FACILITIES

Housing: Coed, all-female, all-male, apartments for single students, housing for disabled students, theme houses. **Library Holdings:** 497,784 bound volumes. 2,461 periodicals. 88,828 microforms. 10,716 audiovisuals. **Special Academic Facilities/Equipment:** Art gallery, center for cross-cultural study of religion, arboretum, observatory, foundry. **Computers:** School-owned computers available for student use.

EXTRACURRICULARS

Activities: Choral groups, dance, drama/theater, literary magazine, music ensembles, musical theater, radio station, student government, student newspaper, yearbook. **Organizations:** 50 registered organizations, 1 honor society, 6 religious organizations. **Athletics (Intercollegiate):** *Men:* baseball, basketball, cross-country, fencing, indoor track, lacrosse, soccer, squash, tennis, track & field. *Women:* basketball, cross-country, fencing, field hockey, indoor track, lacrosse, soccer, softball, squash, tennis, track & field, volleyball.

ADMISSIONS

Selectivity Rating: 98 (of 100). **Freshman Academic Profile:** 80% in top 10% of high school class, 94% in top 25% of high school class, 100% in top 50% of high school class. 58% from public high schools. SAT I Math middle 50% range 640-720. SAT I Verbal middle 50% range 640-740. **Basis for Candidate Selection:** *Very important factors considered include:* character/personal qualities, recommendations, secondary school record, standardized test scores. *Important factors considered include:* class rank, essays, extracurricular activities, volunteer work. *Other factors considered include:* alumni/ae relation, geographical residence, interview, minority status, talent/ability, work experience. **Freshman Admission Requirements:** High school diploma or GED is required. *Academic units required/recommended:* 12 total required; 4 English required, 3 math required, 4 math recommended, 1 science required, 2 science recommended, 1 science lab required, 3 foreign language required, 1 social studies required. **Freshman Admission Statistics:** 2,598 applied, 32% accepted, 37% of those accepted enrolled. **Transfer Admission Requirements:** *Items required:* high school transcript, college transcript, essay, statement of good standing from prior school. Minimum college GPA of 3.0 required. Lowest grade transferable C. **General Admission Information:** Application fee $50. Early decision application deadline November 15. Regular application deadline January 15. Admission may be deferred for a maximum of 1 year. Credit and/or placement offered for CEEB Advanced Placement tests.

COSTS AND FINANCIAL AID

Required Forms and Deadlines: FAFSA, CSS/Financial Aid PROFILE, state aid form, noncustodial (divorced/separated) parent's statement, and business/farm supplement. Financial aid filing deadline January 31. **Notification of Awards:** Applicants will be notified of awards on or about April 15. **Types of Aid:** *Need-based scholarships/grants:* Pell, SEOG, state scholarships/grants, private scholarships, the school's own gift aid. *Loans:* FFEL Subsidized Stafford, FFEL Unsubsidized Stafford, FFEL PLUS, Federal Perkins. **Student Employment:** Federal Work-Study Program available. Institutional employment available. Off-campus job opportunities are good. **Financial Aid Statistics:** 42% freshmen, 44% undergrads receive some form of aid. Average freshman grant $22,706. Average freshman loan $3,459. **Financial Aid Phone:** 610-896-1350.

See page 1052.

HAWAII PACIFIC UNIVERSITY

1164 Bishop Street, Honolulu, HI 96813
Phone: 808-544-0238 **E-mail:** admissions@hpu.edu **CEEB Code:** 4352
Fax: 808-544-1136 **Web:** www.hpu.edu **ACT Code:** 4352

This private school was founded in 1965. It has a 135-acre campus.

STUDENTS AND FACULTY

Enrollment: 6,899. **Student Body:** Male 46%, female 54%, out-of-state 23%, international 14% (105 countries represented). **Ethnic Representation:**

African American 10%, Asian 36%, Caucasian 41%, Hispanic 7%, Native American 1%. **Retention and Graduation:** 59% freshmen return for sophomore year. 24% freshmen graduate within 4 years. 70% grads go on to further study within 1 year. 45% grads pursue business degrees. 5% grads pursue law degrees. 3% grads pursue medical degrees. **Faculty:** Student/faculty ratio 18:1. 213 full-time faculty, 75% hold PhDs.

ACADEMICS

Degrees: Associate's, bachelor's, certificate, master's, post-bachelor's certificate. **Academic Requirements:** General education including some course work in computer literacy, English (including composition), history, humanities, mathematics, sciences (biological or physical), social science, geography, economics, communications. **Classes:** 20-29 students in an average class. **Majors with Highest Enrollment:** Nursing/registered nurse training (RN, ASN, BSN, MSN); business, management, marketing, and related support services; management information systems, general. **Disciplines with Highest Percentage of Degrees Awarded:** Business/marketing 50%, health professions and related sciences 16%, protective services/public administration 7%, computer and information sciences 6%, communications/communication technologies 5%. **Special Study Options:** Accelerated program, cooperative (work-study) program, distance learning, double major, dual enrollment, English as a second language, honors program, independent study, internships, liberal arts/career combination, student-designed major, study abroad, weekend college.

FACILITIES

Housing: Coed, all-female, apartments for married students, apartments for single students, apartment search and referral service. **Library Holdings:** 160,000 bound volumes. 11,000 periodicals. 325,863 microforms. 8,500 audiovisuals. **Special Academic Facilities/Equipment:** Hawaii Pacific University Art Gallery. **Computers:** *Recommended operating system:* Windows 95. School-owned computers available for student use.

EXTRACURRICULARS

Activities: Choral groups, dance, drama/theater, literary magazine, music ensembles, musical theater, pep band, student government, student newspaper, student-run film society. **Organizations:** 75 registered organizations, 15 honor societies, 4 religious organizations. **Athletics (Intercollegiate):** *Men:* baseball, basketball, cheerleading, cross-country, tennis. *Women:* cheerleading, cross-country, softball, tennis, volleyball.

ADMISSIONS

Selectivity Rating: 72 (of 100). **Freshman Academic Profile:** Average high school GPA 3.1. 18% in top 10% of high school class, 41% in top 25% of high school class, 72% in top 50% of high school class. 60% from public high schools. Average SAT I Math 504, SAT I Math middle 50% range 440-570. Average SAT I Verbal 488, SAT I Verbal middle 50% range 430-550. Average ACT 22, ACT middle 50% range 19-24. TOEFL required of all international applicants, minimum TOEFL 550. **Basis for Candidate Selection:** *Very important factors considered include:* secondary school record, talent/ability. *Important factors considered include:* extracurricular activities, interview, standardized test scores, work experience. *Other factors considered include:* character/personal qualities, class rank, essays, recommendations, volunteer work. **Freshman Admission Requirements:** High school diploma or GED is required. *Academic units required/recommended:* 14 total recommended; 4 English recommended, 3 math recommended, 2 science recommended, 1 foreign language recommended, 4 history recommended. **Freshman Admission Statistics:** 2,839 applied, 76% accepted, 27% of those accepted enrolled. **Transfer Admission Requirements:** *Items required:* college transcript. Minimum college GPA of 2.0 required. Lowest grade transferable C. **General Admission Information:** Application fee $50. Priority application deadline March 1. Nonfall registration accepted. Admission may be deferred for a maximum of 2 years. Credit and/or placement offered for CEEB Advanced Placement tests.

COSTS AND FINANCIAL AID

Tuition $9,850. Room & board $8,530. Required fees $0. Average book expense $1,455. **Required Forms and Deadlines:** FAFSA and institution's own financial aid form. No deadline for regular filing. Priority filing deadline March 1. **Notification of Awards:** Applicants will be notified of awards on a rolling basis. **Types of Aid:** *Need-based scholarships/grants:* Pell, SEOG, state scholarships/ grants, the school's own gift aid, Federal Nursing. *Loans:* FFEL Subsidized Stafford, FFEL Unsubsidized Stafford, FFEL PLUS, Federal Perkins, Federal Nursing. **Student Employment:** Federal Work-Study Program available. Institutional employment available. Off-campus job opportunities are excellent. **Financial Aid Statistics:** 42% freshmen, 37% undergrads receive some form of aid. Average freshman grant $3,666. Average freshman loan $3,616. Average income from on-campus job $3,600. **Financial Aid Phone:** 808-544-0253.

See page 1054.

HEIDELBERG COLLEGE

$$$

310 East Market Street, Tiffin, OH 44883

Phone: 419-448-2330 **E-mail:** adminfo@heidelberg.edu **CEEB Code:** 1292

Fax: 419-448-2124 **Web:** www.heidelberg.edu **ACT Code:** 3278

This private school, which is affiliated with the United Church of Christ, was founded in 1850. It has a 110-acre campus.

STUDENTS AND FACULTY

Enrollment: 1,382. **Student Body:** Male 48%, female 52%, out-of-state 12%, international 1%. **Ethnic Representation:** African American 3%, Caucasian 95%, Hispanic 1%. **Retention and Graduation:** 80% freshmen return for sophomore year. 48% freshmen graduate within 4 years. 18% grads go on to further study within 1 year. 1% grads pursue business degrees. 2% grads pursue law degrees. 5% grads pursue medical degrees. **Faculty:** Student/faculty ratio 13:1. 74 full-time faculty, 75% hold PhDs. 100% faculty teach undergrads.

ACADEMICS

Degrees: Bachelor's, master's. **Academic Requirements:** General education including some course work in arts/fine arts, computer literacy, English (including composition), foreign languages, history, humanities, mathematics, philosophy, sciences (biological or physical), social science. **Classes:** Under 10 students in an average class. Under 10 students in an average lab/discussion section. **Disciplines with Highest Percentage of Degrees Awarded:** Business/marketing 25%, education 16%, parks and recreation 10%, biological life sciences 7%, social sciences and history 6%. **Special Study Options:** Accelerated program, cooperative (work-study) program, cross registration, double major, dual enrollment, English as a second language, student exchange program (domestic), honors program, independent study, internships, liberal arts/career combination, student-designed major, study abroad, teacher certification program, weekend college.

FACILITIES

Housing: Coed, all-female, all-male, housing for disabled students, Undergraduate special housing by major. **Library Holdings:** 260,055 bound volumes. 829 periodicals. 108,640 microforms. 8,300 audiovisuals. **Special Academic Facilities/Equipment:** Forest research lots, infant studies lab, water quality lab. **Computers:** School-owned computers available for student use.

EXTRACURRICULARS

Activities: Choral groups, concert band, dance, drama/theater, jazz band, literary magazine, marching band, music ensembles, musical theater, opera, pep band, radio station, student government, student newspaper, symphony orchestra, television station, yearbook. **Organizations:** 85 registered organizations, 1 honor society, 3 fraternities, 4 sororities. **Athletics (Intercollegiate):** *Men:* baseball, basketball, cheerleading, cross-country, football, golf, indoor track, soccer, tennis, track & field, wrestling. *Women:* basketball, cheerleading, cross-country, golf, indoor track, soccer, softball, tennis, track & field, volleyball.

ADMISSIONS

Selectivity Rating: 63 (of 100). **Freshman Academic Profile:** Average high school GPA 3.2. 20% in top 10% of high school class, 47% in top 25% of high school class, 78% in top 50% of high school class. 61% from public high schools. Average SAT I Math 540, SAT I Math middle 50% range 490-580. Average SAT I Verbal 511, SAT I Verbal middle 50% range 470-590. Average ACT 22, ACT middle 50% range 20-25. TOEFL required of all international applicants, minimum TOEFL 520. **Basis for Candidate Selection:** *Very important factors considered include:* secondary school record. *Important factors considered include:* character/personal qualities, class rank, standardized test scores. *Other factors considered include:* alumni/ae relation, essays, extracurricular activities, geographical residence, interview, minority status, recommendations, religious affiliation/commitment, talent/ability, volunteer work, work experience. **Freshman Admission Requirements:** High school diploma or GED is required. *Academic units required/recommended:* 16 total required; 21 total recommended; 4 English required, 3 math required, 4 math recommended, 2 science required, 3 science recommended, 2 foreign language recommended, 3 social studies required, 4 social studies recommended, 4 elective required, 4 elective recommended. **Freshman Admission Statistics:** 1,590 applied, 87% accepted, 46% of those accepted enrolled. **Transfer Admission Requirements:** *Items required:* high school transcript, college transcript, standardized test scores, statement of good standing from prior school. Minimum high school GPA of 2.0 required. Minimum college GPA of 2.0 required. Lowest grade transferable C. **General Admission Information:** Application fee $25. Priority application deadline January 1. Early decision application deadline September 30. Regular application deadline August 1. Nonfall registration accepted. Admission may be deferred for a maximum of 1 year. Credit and/or placement offered for CEEB Advanced Placement tests.

COSTS AND FINANCIAL AID

Tuition $16,998. Room & board $5,474. Required fees $270. Average book expense $530. **Required Forms and Deadlines:** FAFSA. Financial aid filing deadline August 1. Priority filing deadline March 1. **Notification of Awards:** Applicants will be notified of awards on a rolling basis beginning on or about March 15. **Types of Aid:** *Need-based scholarships/grants:* Pell, SEOG, state scholarships/grants, private scholarships, the school's own gift aid. *Loans:* FFEL Subsidized Stafford, FFEL Unsubsidized Stafford, FFEL PLUS, Federal Perkins. **Student Employment:** Federal Work-Study Program available. Institutional employment available. Off-campus job opportunities are excellent. **Financial Aid Statistics:** 90% freshmen, 85% undergrads receive some form of aid. Average freshman grant $8,200. Average freshman loan $2,625. Average income from on-campus job $1,000. **Financial Aid Phone:** 419-448-2293.

HELLENIC COLLEGE

50 Goddard Avenue, Brookline, MA 02146
Phone: 617-731-3500 **E-mail:** admissions@hchc.edu
Fax: 617-232-7819 **Web:** www.hellenic.edu **ACT Code:** 1843

This private school, which is affiliated with the Greek Orthodox Church, was founded in 1937. It has a 52-acre campus.

STUDENTS AND FACULTY

Enrollment: 64. **Student Body:** Male 64%, female 36%, out-of-state 82%, international 42% (12 countries represented). **Ethnic Representation:** Caucasian 97%, Hispanic 3%. **Retention and Graduation:** 64% freshmen return for sophomore year. 50% grads go on to further study within 1 year. **Faculty:** 50% faculty teach undergrads.

ACADEMICS

Degrees: Bachelor's, master's. **Academic Requirements:** General education including some course work in English (including composition), foreign languages, history, humanities, mathematics, philosophy, sciences (biological or physical), social science.

FACILITIES

Housing: Coed, apartments for married students. **Library Holdings:** 103,899 bound volumes. 770 periodicals. 490 microforms. 1,297 audiovisuals. **Computers:** *Recommended operating system:* Windows 95. School-owned computers available for student use.

EXTRACURRICULARS

Activities: Choral groups, student government, yearbook. **Athletics (Intercollegiate):** *Women:* basketball, tennis.

ADMISSIONS

Selectivity Rating: 63 (of 100). **Freshman Academic Profile:** Average high school GPA 2.9. 100% from public high schools. Average SAT I Math 445. Average SAT I Verbal 485. TOEFL required of all international applicants, minimum TOEFL 500. **Basis for Candidate Selection:** *Very important factors considered include:* essays, recommendations, secondary school record, standardized test scores. *Important factors considered include:* class rank. *Other factors considered include:* alumni/ae relation, character/personal qualities, extracurricular activities, interview. **Freshman Admission Requirements:** High school diploma or GED is required. *Academic units required/recommended:* 14 total required; 4 English required, 2 math required, 2 science required, 2 foreign language required, 2 social studies required, 2 history required. **Freshman Admission Statistics:** 35 applied, 63% accepted, 64% of those accepted enrolled. **Transfer Admission Requirements:** *Items required:* college transcript, essay. Minimum high school GPA of 2.0 required. Minimum college GPA of 2.0 required. Lowest grade transferable C+. **General Admission Information:** Application fee $35. Regular application deadline rolling. Nonfall registration accepted. Admission may be deferred. Credit offered for CEEB Advanced Placement tests.

COSTS AND FINANCIAL AID

Tuition $7,600. Room & board $5,900. Required fees $525. Average book expense $500. **Required Forms and Deadlines:** FAFSA and institution's own financial aid form. Financial aid filing deadline May 1. Priority filing deadline May 1. **Notification of Awards:** Applicants will be notified of awards on a rolling basis beginning on or about June 1. **Types of Aid:** *Need-based scholarships/grants:* Pell, SEOG, state scholarships/grants, private scholarships, the school's own gift aid. *Loans:* FFEL Subsidized Stafford, FFEL Unsubsidized Stafford, FFEL PLUS. **Student Employment:** Federal Work-Study Program available. Institutional employment available. Off-campus job opportunities are good. **Financial Aid Statistics:** Average freshman grant $2,000. Average freshman loan $6,625. Average income from on-campus job $1,500. **Financial Aid Phone:** 617-731-3500.

HENDERSON STATE UNIVERSITY

1100 Henderson Street, HSU Box 7560, Arkadelphia, AR 71999-0001
Phone: 870-230-5028 **E-mail:** hardwrv@hsu.edu **CEEB Code:** 6272
Fax: 870-230-5066 **Web:** www.hsu.edu **ACT Code:** 126

This public school was founded in 1890. It has a 157-acre campus.

STUDENTS AND FACULTY

Enrollment: 3,130. **Student Body:** Male 44%, female 56%, out-of-state 10%, international 4% (22 countries represented). **Ethnic Representation:** African American 15%, Caucasian 82%, Hispanic 1%, Native American 1%. **Retention and Graduation:** 65% freshmen return for sophomore year. 12% freshmen graduate within 4 years. **Faculty:** Student/faculty ratio 16:1. 160 full-time faculty, 68% hold PhDs. 98% faculty teach undergrads.

ACADEMICS

Degrees: Associate's, bachelor's, master's. **Academic Requirements:** General education including some course work in arts/fine arts, English (including composition), history, humanities, mathematics, sciences (biological or physical), social science. Must complete a nonwestern course in order to graduate. **Classes:** Under 10 students in an average class. 20-29 students in an average lab/discussion section. **Majors with Highest Enrollment:** Business administration/management; elementary education and teaching; biology/biological sciences, general. **Disciplines with Highest Percentage of Degrees Awarded:** Education 26%, business/marketing 22%, social sciences and history 6%, health professions and related sciences 6%, biological life sciences 5%. **Special Study Options:** Cross registration, distance learning, honors program, internships, liberal arts/career combination, teacher certification program.

FACILITIES

Housing: Coed, all-female, all-male, housing for international students, honors dorm, on-campus apartments leased by outside firm, floor in dorm dedicated to ACE program students, international student housing. **Library Holdings:** 262,572 bound volumes. 1,516 periodicals. 212,722 microforms. 18,717 audiovisuals. **Special Academic Facilities/Equipment:** Closed-circuit TV studio, planetarium. **Computers:** School-owned computers available for student use.

EXTRACURRICULARS

Activities: Choral groups, concert band, dance, drama/theater, jazz band, literary magazine, marching band, music ensembles, radio station, student government, student newspaper, symphony orchestra, television station, yearbook. **Organizations:** 85 registered organizations, 8 fraternities, 8 sororities. **Athletics (Intercollegiate):** *Men:* baseball, basketball, football, golf, swimming. *Women:* basketball, cross-country, softball, swimming, tennis, volleyball.

ADMISSIONS

Selectivity Rating: 64 (of 100). **Freshman Academic Profile:** Average high school GPA 3.3. 16% in top 10% of high school class, 45% in top 25% of high school class, 87% in top 50% of high school class. Average SAT I Math 519, SAT I Math middle 50% range 470-550. Average SAT I Verbal 508, SAT I Verbal middle 50% range 450-560. Average ACT 22, ACT middle 50% range 19-25. TOEFL required of all international applicants, minimum TOEFL 500. **Basis for Candidate Selection:** *Very important factors considered include:* secondary school record, standardized test scores. *Other factors considered include:* character/personal qualities, class rank, essays, interview, recommendations. **Freshman Admission Requirements:** High school diploma or GED is required. *Academic units required/recommended:* 20 total required; 4 English required, 4 English recommended, 2 math required, 4 math recommended, 2 science required, 3 science recommended, 2 foreign language recommended, 2 social studies required, 2 social studies recommended, 1 history required, 2 history recommended, 3 elective recommended. **Freshman Admission Statistics:** 2,048 applied, 75% accepted, 30% of those accepted enrolled. **Transfer Admission Requirements:** *Items required:* college transcript. Lowest grade transferable C. **General Admission Information:** Regular application deadline July 15. Nonfall registration accepted. Admission may be deferred for a maximum of 1 year. Neither credit nor placement offered for CEEB Advanced Placement tests.

COSTS AND FINANCIAL AID

In-state tuition $2,520. Out-of-state tuition $5,040. Room & board $3,272. Required fees $275. Average book expense $800. **Required Forms and**

Deadlines: FAFSA. Financial aid filing deadline June 1. Priority filing deadline June 1. **Notification of Awards:** Applicants will be notified of awards on a rolling basis beginning on or about March 1. **Types of Aid:** *Need-based scholarships/grants:* Pell, SEOG, state scholarships/grants, private scholarships, the school's own gift aid. *Loans:* Direct Subsidized Stafford, Direct Unsubsidized Stafford, Direct PLUS, FFEL Subsidized Stafford, FFEL Unsubsidized Stafford, FFEL PLUS, Federal Perkins. **Student Employment:** Federal Work-Study Program available. Off-campus job opportunities are good. **Financial Aid Statistics:** 28% freshmen, 28% undergrads receive some form of aid. **Financial Aid Phone:** 870-230-5148.

HENDRIX COLLEGE

1600 Washington Avenue, Conway, AR 72032
Phone: 501-450-1362 **E-mail:** adm@hendrix.edu **CEEB Code:** 6273
Fax: 501-450-3843 **Web:** www.hendrix.edu **ACT Code:** 128

This private school, which is affiliated with the Methodist Church, was founded in 1876. It has a 160-acre campus.

STUDENTS AND FACULTY

Enrollment: 1,082. **Student Body:** Male 45%, female 55%, out-of-state 34%, international 1% (10 countries represented). **Ethnic Representation:** African American 4%, Asian 3%, Caucasian 74%, Hispanic 2%, Native American 1%. **Retention and Graduation:** 86% freshmen return for sophomore year. 61% freshmen graduate within 4 years. 46% grads go on to further study within 1 year. 3% grads pursue business degrees. 6% grads pursue law degrees. 12% grads pursue medical degrees. **Faculty:** Student/faculty ratio 12:1. 81 full-time faculty, 98% hold PhDs. 100% faculty teach undergrads.

ACADEMICS

Degrees: Bachelor's, master's. **Academic Requirements:** General education including some course work in arts/fine arts, English (including composition), foreign languages, history, humanities, mathematics, philosophy, sciences (biological or physical), social science. All freshmen are required to take "Journeys," a course that is global in its perspective and interdisciplinary in its approach. The course takes the concept of journeys as its touchstone and explores how different cultures and different peoples have made sense of their own life journeys. **Classes:** 10-19 students in an average class. 10-19 students in an average lab/discussion section. **Majors with Highest Enrollment:** Business/managerial economics; biology/biological sciences, general; psychology, general. **Disciplines with Highest Percentage of Degrees Awarded:** Social sciences and history 20%, biological life sciences 16%, psychology 16%, physical sciences 9%, interdisciplinary studies 9%. **Special Study Options:** Cooperative (work-study) program, double major, student exchange program (domestic), independent study, internships, student-designed major, study abroad, teacher certification program, Hendrix-in-Oxford, Hendrix-in-London, programs with Austria and Japan, Washington semester with American University.

FACILITIES

Housing: Coed, all-female, all-male, apartments for single students, housing for disabled students, coeducational foreign language house (Spanish, German, French in alternating years), suite-style small houses. **Library Holdings:** 211,374 bound volumes. 746 periodicals. 179,460 microforms. 3,769 audiovisuals. **Special Academic Facilities/Equipment:** Psychology lab, Wilbur A. Mills Library. **Computers:** School-owned computers available for student use.

EXTRACURRICULARS

Activities: Choral groups, concert band, dance, drama/theater, jazz band, literary magazine, music ensembles, musical theater, opera, pep band, radio station, student government, student newspaper, student-run film society, symphony orchestra, yearbook. **Organizations:** 72 registered organizations, 5 honor societies, 8 religious organizations. **Athletics (Intercollegiate):** *Men:* baseball, basketball, cheerleading, cross-country, diving, golf, soccer, swimming, tennis, track & field. *Women:* basketball, cheerleading, cross-country, diving, golf, soccer, softball, swimming, tennis, track & field, volleyball.

ADMISSIONS

Selectivity Rating: 83 (of 100). **Freshman Academic Profile:** Average high school GPA 3.7. 42% in top 10% of high school class, 76% in top 25% of high school class, 94% in top 50% of high school class. Average SAT I Math 610, SAT I Math middle 50% range 550-670. Average SAT I Verbal 630, SAT I Verbal middle 50% range 570-690. Average ACT 27, ACT middle 50% range 25-31. TOEFL required of all international applicants, minimum TOEFL 550. **Basis for Candidate Selection:** *Very important factors considered include:* essays, secondary school record, standardized test scores. *Important factors considered include:* character/personal qualities, class rank, extracurricular activities, interview, recommendations. *Other factors considered include:* minority status, talent/ability, volunteer work. **Freshman Admission Requirements:** High school diploma or GED is required. *Academic units required/recommended:* 14 total recommended; 4 English recommended, 3 math recommended, 2 science recommended, 2 foreign language recommended, 3 social studies recommended. **Freshman Admission Statistics:** 1,071 applied, 83% accepted, 35% of those accepted enrolled. **Transfer Admission Requirements:** *Items required:* college transcript, essay, statement of good standing from prior school. Minimum college GPA of 2.5 required. Lowest grade transferable C. **General Admission Information:** Application fee $40. Priority application deadline February 1. Nonfall registration accepted. Admission may be deferred for a maximum of 1 year. Credit and/or placement offered for CEEB Advanced Placement tests.

COSTS AND FINANCIAL AID

Tuition $14,900. Room & board $5,090. Required fees $0. Average book expense $700. **Required Forms and Deadlines:** FAFSA, institution's own financial aid form, and state aid form. Priority filing deadline February 15. **Notification of Awards:** Applicants will be notified of awards on a rolling basis beginning on or about March 1. **Types of Aid:** *Need-based scholarships/grants:* Pell, SEOG, state scholarships/grants, private scholarships, the school's own gift aid. *Loans:* FFEL Subsidized Stafford, FFEL Unsubsidized Stafford, FFEL PLUS, Federal Perkins, Methodist loan. **Student Employment:** Federal Work-Study Program available. Institutional employment available. Off-campus job opportunities are excellent. **Financial Aid Statistics:** 52% freshmen, 50% undergrads receive some form of aid. Average freshman grant $10,209. Average freshman loan $3,500. Average income from on-campus job $1,473. **Financial Aid Phone:** 501-450-1368.

HENRY COGSWELL COLLEGE

$$

3022 Colby Avenue, Everett, WA 98021
Phone: 425-258-3351 **E-mail:** admissions@henrycogswell.edu
Fax: 425-257-0405 **Web:** www.henrycogswell.edu

STUDENTS AND FACULTY

Enrollment: 249. **Student Body:** Male 83%, female 17%, international 1%. **Ethnic Representation:** African American 2%, Asian 11%, Caucasian 77%, Hispanic 2%, Native American 1%. **Retention and Graduation:** 95% freshmen return for sophomore year. **Faculty:** Student/faculty ratio 17:1. 8 full-time faculty, 75% hold PhDs.

ACADEMICS

Degrees: Bachelor's. **Academic Requirements:** General education including some course work in English (including composition), humanities, mathematics, sciences (biological or physical), social science. **Classes:** Under 10 students in an average class. **Disciplines with Highest Percentage of Degrees Awarded:** Engineering/engineering technology 60%, visual and performing arts 26%, computer and information sciences 7%, business/marketing 7%. **Special Study Options:** Accelerated program, cooperative (work-study) program, double major, independent study.

FACILITIES

Library Holdings: 9,423 bound volumes. 60 periodicals. 0 microforms. 53 audiovisuals.

EXTRACURRICULARS

Activities: Student government.

ADMISSIONS

Selectivity Rating: 63 (of 100). **Freshman Academic Profile:** Average high school GPA 3.3. SAT I Math middle 50% range 500-560. SAT I Verbal middle 50% range 500-590. **Basis for Candidate Selection:** *Very important factors considered include:* essays, secondary school record, standardized test scores. *Important factors considered include:* character/personal qualities, extracurricular activities, interview, recommendations, talent/ability. **Freshman Admission Requirements:** High school diploma or GED is required. *Academic units required/recommended:* 13 total required; 4 English required, 3 math required, 3 science required, 3 social studies required. **Freshman Admission Statistics:** 44 applied, 82% accepted, 53% of those accepted enrolled. **Transfer Admission Requirements:** *Items required:* college transcript, essay. Minimum college GPA of 2.0 required. Lowest grade transferable C. **General Admission Information:** Application fee $50. Admission may be deferred for a maximum of 1 year.

COSTS AND FINANCIAL AID

Tuition $14,400. Average book expense $656. **Required Forms and Deadlines:** FAFSA and institution's own financial aid form. No deadline for regular filing. Priority filing deadline March 1. **Notification of Awards:** Applicants will be notified of awards on a rolling basis beginning on or about January 1. **Types of Aid:** *Need-based scholarships/grants:* Pell, SEOG, state scholarships/grants, the school's own gift aid. *Loans:* FFEL Subsidized Stafford, FFEL Unsubsidized Stafford, FFEL PLUS. **Financial Aid Statistics:** 38% freshmen, 62% undergrads receive some form of aid.

HERITAGE COLLEGE

3240 Fort Road, Toppenish, WA 98948
Phone: 509-865-8508 **E-mail:** espindola_b@heritage.edu **CEEB Code:** 3777
Fax: 509-865-8508 **Web:** www.heritage.edu

This private school was founded in 1982. It has a 19-acre campus.

STUDENTS AND FACULTY

Student Body: Out-of-state 1%. **Faculty:** Student/faculty ratio 14:1. 39 full-time faculty, 38% hold PhDs. 68% faculty teach undergrads.

ACADEMICS

Degrees: Associate's, bachelor's, certificate, first professional, first professional certificate, master's, post-bachelor's certificate, post-master's certificate, terminal, transfer. **Academic Requirements:** General education including some course work in arts/fine arts, computer literacy, English (including composition), foreign languages, history, humanities, mathematics, philosophy, sciences (biological or physical), social science. **Special Study Options:** Double major, English as a second language, honors program, independent study, internships, liberal arts/career combination, teacher certification program.

FACILITIES

Computers: School-owned computers available for student use.

EXTRACURRICULARS

Activities: Student government. **Organizations:** 5 registered organizations.

ADMISSIONS

Selectivity Rating: 63 (of 100). **Freshman Academic Profile:** TOEFL required of all international applicants, minimum TOEFL 500. **Freshman Admission Requirements: General Admission Information:** Neither credit nor placement offered for CEEB Advanced Placement tests.

COSTS AND FINANCIAL AID

Average book expense $600. **Types of Aid:** *Loans:* FFEL Subsidized Stafford, FFEL PLUS. **Student Employment:** Federal Work-Study Program available. Off-campus job opportunities are fair. **Financial Aid Statistics:** Average freshman grant $3,694. Average freshman loan $1,627. Average income from on-campus job $1,028. **Financial Aid Phone:** 509-865-8504.

HERKIMER COUNTY COMMUNITY COLLEGE

Admissions Office, Reservoir Road, Herkimer, NY 13350
Phone: 315-866-0300 **E-mail:** hubbardpg@hccc.suny.edu
Fax: 315-866-7253 **Web:** www.hccc.ntcnet.com

This public school was founded in 1966. It has a 268-acre campus.

STUDENTS AND FACULTY

Enrollment: 2,448. **Student Body:** Male 46%, female 54%, out-of-state 3%, international 2%. **Ethnic Representation:** African American 3%, Asian 1%, Caucasian 94%, Hispanic 2%, Native American 1%. **Faculty:** Student/faculty ratio 28:1. 76 full-time faculty. 100% faculty teach undergrads.

ACADEMICS

Degrees: Associate's, certificate, terminal, transfer. **Academic Requirements:** General education including some course work in arts/fine arts, computer literacy, English (including composition), foreign languages, history, humanities, mathematics, philosophy, sciences (biological or physical), social science. **Special Study Options:** Distance learning, honors program, independent study.

FACILITIES

Housing: Apartments for single students, housing for disabled students, housing for international students. **Library Holdings:** 63,261 periodicals. 12,633 microforms. 5,322 audiovisuals. **Special Academic Facilities/ Equipment:** Radio station, cable TV public access station, professional education center, Cogar Gallery.

EXTRACURRICULARS

Activities: Dance, drama/theater, literary magazine, radio station, student government, student newspaper, television station. **Organizations:** 37 registered organizations, 1 honor society, 1 religious organization. **Athletics (Intercollegiate):** *Men:* baseball, basketball, cross-country, golf, lacrosse, soccer, swimming, tennis, track & field, volleyball. *Women:* basketball, cross-country, field hockey, golf, soccer, softball, swimming, tennis, track & field, volleyball.

ADMISSIONS

Selectivity Rating: 63 (of 100). **Freshman Academic Profile:** Average SAT I Math 450, SAT I Math middle 50% range 390-510. Average SAT I Verbal 450, SAT I Verbal middle 50% range 400-500. Average ACT 19, ACT middle 50% range 16-21. **Freshman Admission Requirements:** High school diploma or GED is required. **Freshman Admission Statistics:** 2,106 applied, 100% accepted, 46% of those accepted enrolled. **Transfer Admission Requirements:** *Items required:* high school transcript. Lowest grade transferable C. **General Admission Information:** Nonfall registration accepted. Admission may be deferred for a maximum of 1 year.

COSTS AND FINANCIAL AID

Required Forms and Deadlines: FAFSA and state aid form. No deadline for regular filing. Priority filing deadline April 1. **Notification of Awards:** Applicants will be notified of awards on a rolling basis. **Types of Aid:** *Need-based scholarships/grants:* Pell, SEOG, state scholarships/grants. *Loans:* Direct Subsidized Stafford, Direct Unsubsidized Stafford, Direct PLUS, Federal Perkins. **Student Employment:** Federal Work-Study Program available. Institutional employment available. Off-campus job opportunities are fair. **Financial Aid Statistics:** 72% freshmen, 72% undergrads receive some form of aid. Average freshman grant $1,500. Average freshman loan $2,000. **Financial Aid Phone:** 315-866-0300.

HIGH POINT UNIVERSITY

University Station 3598, High Point, NC 27262-3598
Phone: 336-841-9216 **E-mail:** admiss@highpoint.edu **CEEB Code:** 5293
Fax: 336-888-6382 **Web:** www.highpoint.edu **ACT Code:** 3108

This private school, which is affiliated with the Methodist Church, was founded in 1924. It has an 80-acre campus.

STUDENTS AND FACULTY

Enrollment: 2,559. **Student Body:** Male 38%, female 62%, out-of-state 55%, international 4% (41 countries represented). **Ethnic Representation:** African American 22%, Asian 1%, Caucasian 72%, Hispanic 2%. **Retention and Graduation:** 76% freshmen return for sophomore year. 44% freshmen graduate within 4 years. 17% grads go on to further study within 1 year. 2% grads pursue business degrees. 2% grads pursue law degrees. 2% grads pursue medical degrees. **Faculty:** Student/faculty ratio 16:1. 121 full-time faculty, 73% hold PhDs. 100% faculty teach undergrads.

ACADEMICS

Degrees: Bachelor's, master's, post-bachelor's certificate. **Academic Requirements:** General education including some course work in arts/fine arts, computer literacy, English (including composition), foreign languages, history, humanities, mathematics, philosophy, sciences (biological or physical), social science. **Classes:** 10-19 students in an average class. **Majors with Highest Enrollment:** Business administration/management; industrial and organizational psychology; biology/biological sciences, general. **Disciplines with Highest Percentage of Degrees Awarded:** Business/marketing 38%, computer and information sciences 18%, parks and recreation 9%, education 8%, psychology 6%. **Special Study Options:** Accelerated program, cooperative (work-study) program, cross registration, double major, dual enrollment, English as a second language. Joint degree programs in environmental science, forestry, and medical technology.

FACILITIES

Housing: Coed, all-female, all-male, apartments for married students, apartments for single students, housing for disabled students, fraternities and/or sororities, cooperative housing. **Library Holdings:** 205,000 bound volumes. 30,000 periodicals. 87,000 microforms. 15,000 audiovisuals. **Special Academic Facilities/Equipment:** Sechrest Gallery. **Computers:** *Recommended operating system:* Windows 2000, Windows XP, MAC X. School-owned computers available for student use.

EXTRACURRICULARS

Activities: Choral groups, concert band, dance, drama/theater, literary magazine, music ensembles, musical theater, pep band, radio station, student government, student newspaper, television station, yearbook. **Organizations:** 50 registered organizations, 4 honor societies, 6 religious organizations, 4 fraternities (33% men join), 5 sororities (33% women join). **Athletics (Intercollegiate):** *Men:* baseball, basketball, cheerleading, cross-country, golf, indoor track, soccer, tennis, track & field. *Women:* basketball, cheerleading, cross-country, golf, indoor track, soccer, tennis, track & field, volleyball.

ADMISSIONS

Selectivity Rating: 63 (of 100). **Freshman Academic Profile:** Average high school GPA 2.8. 15% in top 10% of high school class, 46% in top 25% of high school class, 71% in top 50% of high school class. 86% from public high schools. Average SAT I Math 514, SAT I Math middle 50% range 460-560. Average SAT I Verbal 506, SAT I Verbal middle 50% range 450-560. TOEFL required of all international applicants, minimum TOEFL 500. **Basis for Candidate Selection:** *Very important factors considered include:* secondary school record, standardized test scores. *Important factors considered include:* character/personal qualities. *Other factors considered include:* class rank, essays, extracurricular activities, interview, recommendations, volunteer work. **Freshman Admission Requirements:** High school diploma or GED is required. *Academic units required/recommended:* 14 total required; 4 English required, 3 math required, 2 science required, 2 science lab required, 2 foreign language recommended, 2 social studies required, 2 history required, 1 elective required, 2 elective recommended. **Freshman Admission Statistics:** 1,617 applied, 87% accepted, 35% of those accepted enrolled. **Transfer Admission Requirements:** *Items required:* college transcript, statement of good standing from prior school. Minimum college GPA of 2.0 required. Lowest grade transferable C. **General Admission Information:** Application fee $25. Priority application deadline June 30. Regular application deadline August 15. Nonfall registration accepted. Admission may be deferred for a maximum of 1 year. Credit and/or placement offered for CEEB Advanced Placement tests.

COSTS AND FINANCIAL AID

Tuition $13,370. Room & board $6,610. Required fees $1,340. Average book expense $1,000. **Required Forms and Deadlines:** FAFSA and state aid form. No deadline for regular filing. Priority filing deadline March 1. **Notification of Awards:** Applicants will be notified of awards on a rolling basis beginning on or about February 15. **Types of Aid:** *Need-based scholarships/grants:* Pell, SEOG, state scholarships/grants, private scholarships, the school's own gift aid. *Loans:* Direct Subsidized Stafford, Direct Unsubsidized Stafford, Direct PLUS, FFEL Subsidized Stafford, FFEL Unsubsidized Stafford, FFEL PLUS, Federal Perkins. **Student Employment:** Federal Work-Study Program available. Institutional employment available. Off-campus job opportunities are excellent. **Financial Aid Statistics:** 90% freshmen, 68% undergrads receive some form of aid. Average freshman grant $8,802. Average freshman loan $2,625. Average income from on-campus job $850. **Financial Aid Phone:** 336-841-9128.

HILBERT COLLEGE

5200 South Park Avenue, Hamburg, NY 14075-1597
Phone: 716-649-7900 **E-mail:** admissions@hilbert.edu **CEEB Code:** 2334
Fax: 716-649-0702 **Web:** www.hilbert.edu **ACT Code:** 2759

This private school was founded in 1957. It has a 40-acre campus.

STUDENTS AND FACULTY

Enrollment: 964. **Student Body:** Male 35%, female 65%, out-of-state 1%. **Ethnic Representation:** African American 4%, Caucasian 89%, Hispanic 2%, Native American 1%. **Retention and Graduation:** 66% freshmen return for sophomore year. 31% freshmen graduate within 4 years. 12% grads go on to further study within 1 year. 5% grads pursue business degrees. 2% grads pursue law degrees. **Faculty:** Student/faculty ratio 13:1. 36 full-time faculty, 61% hold PhDs. 100% faculty teach undergrads.

ACADEMICS

Degrees: Associate's, bachelor's, certificate, terminal. **Academic Requirements:** General education including some course work in computer literacy, English (including composition), history, humanities, mathematics, philosophy, sciences (biological or physical), social science. **Classes:** 10-19 students in an average class. Under 10 students in an average lab/discussion section. **Majors with Highest Enrollment:** Business administration/management; legal assistant/paralegal; criminal justice/law enforcement administration. **Disciplines with Highest Percentage of Degrees Awarded:** Protective services/public administration 44%, business/marketing 22%, health professions and related sciences 10%, law/legal studies 8%, English 7%. **Special Study Options:** Cross registration, distance learning, dual enrollment, honors program, independent study, internships.

FACILITIES

Housing: Coed, apartments for single students. **Library Holdings:** 40,127 bound volumes. 4,845 periodicals. 21,589 microforms. 940 audiovisuals. **Computers:** School-owned computers available for student use.

EXTRACURRICULARS

Activities: Choral groups, literary magazine, student government, student newspaper. **Organizations:** 18 registered organizations, 2 honor societies. **Athletics (Intercollegiate):** *Men:* baseball, basketball, golf, soccer, volleyball. *Women:* basketball, cross-country, golf, lacrosse, soccer, softball, volleyball.

ADMISSIONS

Selectivity Rating: 63 (of 100). **Freshman Academic Profile:** Average high school GPA 2.3. 4% in top 10% of high school class, 17% in top 25% of high school class, 52% in top 50% of high school class. 88% from public high schools. Average SAT I Math 451, SAT I Math middle 50% range 410-540. Average SAT I Verbal 457, SAT I Verbal middle 50% range 410-520. Average ACT 19, ACT middle 50% range 18-21. TOEFL required of all international applicants, minimum TOEFL 500. **Basis for Candidate Selection:** *Very important factors considered include:* secondary school record. *Important factors considered include:* recommendations. *Other factors considered include:* character/personal qualities, class rank, essays, extracurricular activities, interview, standardized test scores, talent/ability, volunteer work, work experience. **Freshman Admission Requirements:** High school diploma or GED is required. *Academic units required/recommended:* 18 total required; 19 total recommended; 4 English required, 4 English recommended, 2 math required, 3 math recommended, 2 science required, 3 science recommended, 1 science lab required, 1 foreign language recommended, 2 social studies required, 3 social studies recommended, 2 history required, 4 elective required. **Freshman Admission Statistics:** 303 applied, 88% accepted, 44% of those accepted enrolled. **Transfer Admission Requirements:** *Items required:* high school transcript, college transcript. Minimum high school GPA of 1.0 required. Minimum college GPA of 1.0 required. Lowest grade transferable D. **General Admission Information:** Application fee $20. Priority application deadline June 30. Regular application deadline September 1. Nonfall registration accepted. Admission may be deferred for a maximum of 1 year. Credit offered for CEEB Advanced Placement tests.

COSTS AND FINANCIAL AID

Tuition $13,000. Room & board $5,388. Required fees $500. Average book expense $800. **Required Forms and Deadlines:** FAFSA and state aid form. No deadline for regular filing. Priority filing deadline February 28. **Notification of Awards:** Applicants will be notified of awards on a rolling basis beginning on or about March 15. **Types of Aid:** *Need-based scholarships/grants:* Pell, SEOG, state scholarships/grants, private scholarships, the school's own gift aid. *Loans:* FFEL Subsidized Stafford, FFEL Unsubsidized Stafford, FFEL PLUS, Federal Perkins. **Student Employment:** Federal Work-Study Program available. Off-campus job opportunities are excellent. **Financial Aid Statistics:** 87% freshmen, 87% undergrads receive some form of aid. Average freshman grant $6,357. Average freshman loan $4,794. Average income from on-campus job $1,179. **Financial Aid Phone:** 716-649-7900.

See page 1056.

HILLSDALE COLLEGE

33 East College Street, Hillsdale, MI 49242
Phone: 517-607-2327 **E-mail:** admissions@hillsdale.edu **CEEB Code:** 1295
Fax: 517-607-2223 **Web:** www.hillsdale.edu **ACT Code:** 2010

This private school was founded in 1844. It has a 200-acre campus.

STUDENTS AND FACULTY

Enrollment: 1,215. **Student Body:** Male 46%, female 54%, out-of-state 51%, international 3%. **Retention and Graduation:** 83% freshmen return for sophomore year. 52% freshmen graduate within 4 years. 31% grads go on to further study within 1 year. 11% grads pursue business degrees. 6% grads pursue law degrees. 4% grads pursue medical degrees. **Faculty:** Student/faculty ratio 11:1. 89 full-time faculty, 96% hold PhDs. 100% faculty teach undergrads.

ACADEMICS

Degrees: Bachelor's. **Academic Requirements:** General education including some course work in arts/fine arts, English (including composition), foreign languages, history, humanities, mathematics, sciences (biological or physical), social science, two 1-credit week-long Center for Constructive Alternatives seminars. **Classes:** Under 10 students in an average class. **Disciplines with Highest Percentage of Degrees Awarded:** Business/marketing 28%, social sciences and history 17%, education 9%, biological life sciences 9%, interdisciplinary studies 9%. **Special Study Options:** Double major, dual enrollment, honors program, independent study, internships, study abroad, teacher certification program.

FACILITIES

Housing: All-female, all-male, apartments for single students, fraternities and/or sororities. **Library Holdings:** 205,000 bound volumes. 1,625 periodicals. 6,400 microforms. 7,950 audiovisuals. **Special Academic Facilities/Equipment:** Early childhood education lab, media center, K-8 private academy. **Computers:** *Recommended operating system:* Windows NT/2000. School-owned computers available for student use.

EXTRACURRICULARS

Activities: Choral groups, concert band, drama/theater, jazz band, literary magazine, music ensembles, musical theater, pep band, student government, student newspaper, symphony orchestra, yearbook. **Organizations:** 50 registered organizations, 4 religious organizations, 4 fraternities (35% men join), 4 sororities (45% women join). **Athletics (Intercollegiate):** *Men:* baseball, basketball, cheerleading, cross-country, football, golf, indoor track, track & field. *Women:* basketball, cheerleading, cross-country, diving, indoor track, softball, swimming, tennis, track & field, volleyball.

ADMISSIONS

Selectivity Rating: 84 (of 100). **Freshman Academic Profile:** Average high school GPA 3.6. 38% in top 10% of high school class, 76% in top 25% of high school class, 99% in top 50% of high school class. 65% from public high schools. Average SAT I Math 610, SAT I Math middle 50% range 520-690. Average SAT I Verbal 590, SAT I Verbal middle 50% range 580-720. Average ACT 26, ACT middle 50% range 24-29. TOEFL required of all international applicants, minimum TOEFL 510. **Basis for Candidate Selection:** *Very important factors considered include:* character/personal qualities, secondary school record, standardized test scores. *Important factors considered include:* class rank, essays, extracurricular activities, interview, recommendations, volunteer work, work experience. *Other factors considered include:* alumni/ae relation, talent/ability. **Freshman Admission Requirements:** High school diploma or GED is required. *Academic units required/recommended:* 15 total recommended; 4 English recommended, 3 math recommended, 3 science recommended, 1 science lab recommended, 2 foreign language recommended, 1 social studies recommended, 2 history recommended. **Freshman Admission Statistics:** 1,070 applied, 82% accepted, 49% of those accepted enrolled. **Transfer Admission Requirements:** *Items required:* high school transcript, college transcript, essay, standardized test scores, statement of good standing from prior school. Minimum college GPA of 3.0 required. Lowest grade transferable C. **General Admission Information:** Application fee $15. Priority application deadline July 1. Nonfall registration accepted. Admission may be deferred for a maximum of 1 year. Credit and/or placement offered for CEEB Advanced Placement tests.

COSTS AND FINANCIAL AID

Tuition $13,600. Room & board $5,700. Required fees $240. Average book expense $700. **Required Forms and Deadlines:** FAFSA and institution's own financial aid form. No deadline for regular filing. Priority filing deadline March 1. **Notification of Awards:** Applicants will be notified of awards on a rolling basis beginning on or about February 15. **Types of Aid:** *Need-based scholarships/grants:* state scholarships/grants, private scholarships, the school's own gift aid. *Loans:* college/university loans from institutional funds. **Student Employment:** Institutional employment available. Off-campus job opportunities are good. **Financial Aid Statistics:** 67% freshmen, 67% undergrads receive some form of aid. Average freshman grant $6,500. Average freshman loan $2,800. Average income from on-campus job $1,000. **Financial Aid Phone:** 517-437-7341.

See page 1058.

HIRAM COLLEGE

PO Box 96, Hiram, OH 44234
Phone: 800-362-5280 **E-mail:** admission@hiram.edu **CEEB Code:** 1297
Fax: 330-569-5944 **Web:** www.hiram.edu **ACT Code:** 3280

This private school, which is affiliated with the Disciples of Christ Church, was founded in 1850. It has a 110-acre campus.

STUDENTS AND FACULTY

Enrollment: 1,134. **Student Body:** Male 41%, female 59%, out-of-state 17%, international 3%. **Ethnic Representation:** African American 10%, Asian 1%, Caucasian 86%, Hispanic 2%. **Retention and Graduation:** 78% freshmen return for sophomore year. 62% freshmen graduate within 4 years. 36% grads go on to further study within 1 year. 1% grads pursue business degrees. 3% grads pursue law degrees. 2% grads pursue medical degrees. **Faculty:** Student/faculty ratio 11:1. 73 full-time faculty, 95% hold PhDs. 100% faculty teach undergrads.

ACADEMICS

Degrees: Bachelor's. **Academic Requirements:** General education including some course work in arts/fine arts, humanities, sciences (biological or physical), social science. **Classes:** 10-19 students in an average class. Under 10 students in an average lab/discussion section. **Majors with Highest Enrollment:** Business/commerce, general; education, general; biology/biological sciences, general. **Disciplines with Highest Percentage of Degrees Awarded:** Business/marketing 11%, social sciences and history 10%, communications/communication technologies 8%, education 7%, computer and information sciences 7%. **Special Study Options:** Accelerated program, double major, dual enrollment, English as a second language, independent study, internships, liberal arts/career combination, student-designed major, study abroad, teacher certification program, weekend college.

FACILITIES

Housing: Coed, all-female, all-male, housing for international students. **Library Holdings:** 213,735 bound volumes. 693 periodicals. 112,453 microforms. 5,514 audiovisuals. **Special Academic Facilities/Equipment:** Psychology lab, language lab, international center, center for literature and medicine, fitness center, health center, observatory, electron microscope, 2 field stations for study and research. **Computers:** *Recommended operating system:* Windows NT. School-owned computers available for student use.

EXTRACURRICULARS

Activities: Choral groups, concert band, dance, drama/theater, jazz band, literary magazine, music ensembles, musical theater, opera, pep band, radio station, student government, student newspaper, television station, yearbook. **Organizations:** 55 registered organizations, 7 honor societies, 6 religious organizations, 3 fraternities, 3 sororities. **Athletics (Intercollegiate):** *Men:* baseball, basketball, cheerleading, cross-country, diving, football, golf, indoor track, soccer, swimming, tennis, track & field. *Women:* basketball, cheerleading, cross-country, diving, indoor track, soccer, softball, swimming, tennis, track & field, volleyball.

ADMISSIONS

Selectivity Rating: 80 (of 100). **Freshman Academic Profile:** Average high school GPA 3.4. 32% in top 10% of high school class, 53% in top 25% of high school class, 85% in top 50% of high school class. 86% from public high schools. Average SAT I Math 566, SAT I Math middle 50% range 480-620. Average SAT I Verbal 573, SAT I Verbal middle 50% range 510-630. Average ACT 24, ACT middle 50% range 21-27. TOEFL required of all international applicants, minimum TOEFL 550. **Basis for Candidate Selection:** *Very important factors considered include:* secondary school record. *Important factors considered include:* character/personal qualities, class rank, essays, interview, recommendations, standardized test scores. *Other factors considered include:* alumni/ae relation, extracurricular activities, geographical residence, minority status, talent/ability, volunteer work, work experience. **Freshman Admission Requirements:** High school diploma or GED is required. *Academic units required/recommended:* 18 total required; 21 total recommended; 4 English required, 3 math required, 4 math recommended, 3 science required, 2 science lab required, 2 foreign language recommended, 3 social studies required, 1 history required, 2 elective required. **Freshman Admission Statistics:** 1,294 applied, 69% accepted, 26% of those accepted enrolled. **Transfer Admission Requirements:** *Items required:* high school transcript, college transcript, essay, statement of good standing from prior school. Minimum college GPA of 2.7 required. Lowest grade transferable C. **General Admission Information:** Application fee $35. Priority application deadline February 1. Early decision application deadline December 1. Regular application deadline February 1. Nonfall registration accepted. Admission may be deferred for a maximum of 1 year. Credit and/or placement offered for CEEB Advanced Placement tests.

COSTS AND FINANCIAL AID

Tuition $19,650. Room & board $7,100. Required fees $694. Average book expense $600. **Required Forms and Deadlines:** FAFSA. Priority filing

deadline March 1. **Notification of Awards:** Applicants will be notified of awards on a rolling basis beginning on or about February 15. **Types of Aid:** *Need-based scholarships/grants:* Pell, SEOG, state scholarships/grants, private scholarships, the school's own gift aid. *Loans:* FFEL Subsidized Stafford, FFEL Unsubsidized Stafford, FFEL PLUS, Federal Perkins, college/university loans from institutional funds. **Student Employment:** Federal Work-Study Program available. Institutional employment available. Off-campus job opportunities are good. **Financial Aid Statistics:** 83% freshmen, 83% undergrads receive some form of aid. Average freshman grant $10,998. Average freshman loan $5,176. Average income from on-campus job $500. **Financial Aid Phone:** 330-569-5107.

See page 1060.

HOBART AND WILLIAM SMITH COLLEGES

629 South Main Street, Geneva, NY 14456
Phone: 315-781-3472 **E-mail:** admissions@hws.edu **CEEB Code:** 2294
Fax: 315-781-3471 **Web:** www.hws.edu **ACT Code:** 2758

This private school was founded in 1822. It has a 170-acre campus.

STUDENTS AND FACULTY

Enrollment: 1,893. **Student Body:** Male 45%, female 55%, out-of-state 50%, international 2% (19 countries represented). **Ethnic Representation:** African American 4%, Asian 2%, Caucasian 88%, Hispanic 4%. **Retention and Graduation:** 85% freshmen return for sophomore year. 67% freshmen graduate within 4 years. 25% grads go on to further study within 1 year. 10% grads pursue business degrees. 7% grads pursue law degrees. 4% grads pursue medical degrees. **Faculty:** Student/faculty ratio 11:1. 157 full-time faculty, 92% hold PhDs. 100% faculty teach undergrads.

ACADEMICS

Degrees: Bachelor's. **Academic Requirements:** General education including some course work in arts/fine arts, humanities, mathematics, sciences (biological or physical), social science. **Classes:** 10-19 students in an average class. **Majors with Highest Enrollment:** History, general; English language and literature, general; economics, general. **Disciplines with Highest Percentage of Degrees Awarded:** Social sciences and history 30%, English 12%, psychology 11%, biological life sciences 7%, visual and performing arts 7%. **Special Study Options:** Accelerated program, cross registration, double major, dual enrollment, English as a second language, student exchange program (domestic), honors program, independent study, internships, student-designed major, study abroad, teacher certification program.

FACILITIES

Housing: Coed, all-female, all-male, apartments for single students, housing for international students, fraternities and/or sororities, cooperative housing, upperclass townhouses, theme houses, honors houses. **Library Holdings:** 370,770 bound volumes. 1,153 periodicals. 77,258 microforms. 8,712 audiovisuals. **Special Academic Facilities/Equipment:** Houghton Gallery, HWS Explorer (research vessel), 100-acre nature preserve, Melly Academic Center, Rosenberg Science Center. **Computers:** *Recommended operating system:* Windows 98, Windows NT/2000, Windows 2000/XP Pro. School-owned computers available for student use.

EXTRACURRICULARS

Activities: Choral groups, dance, drama/theater, literary magazine, music ensembles, radio station, student government, student newspaper, student-run film society, symphony orchestra, yearbook. **Organizations:** 60 registered organizations, 12 honor societies, 4 religious organizations, 5 fraternities (17% men join). **Athletics (Intercollegiate):** *Men:* basketball, crew, cross-country, football, golf, ice hockey, lacrosse, sailing, soccer, squash, tennis. *Women:* basketball, crew, cross-country, diving, field hockey, lacrosse, sailing, soccer, squash, swimming, tennis.

ADMISSIONS

Selectivity Rating: 86 (of 100). **Freshman Academic Profile:** Average high school GPA 3.3. 31% in top 10% of high school class, 60% in top 25% of high school class, 93% in top 50% of high school class. 65% from public high schools. Average SAT I Math 600, SAT I Math middle 50% range 540-630. Average SAT I Verbal 550, SAT I Verbal middle 50% range 540-620. TOEFL required of all international applicants, minimum TOEFL 550. **Basis for Candidate Selection:** *Very important factors considered include:* essays, secondary school record. *Important factors considered include:* character/personal qualities, class rank, extracurricular activities, recommendations, standardized test scores, volunteer work, work experience. *Other factors considered include:* alumni/ae relation, geographical residence, interview, minority status, talent/ability. **Freshman Admission Requirements:** High school diploma or GED is required. *Academic units required/recommended:* 19 total required; 19 total recommended; 4 English required, 4 English recommended, 3 math required, 3 math recommended, 3 science required, 3 science recommended, 2 science lab required, 2 science lab recommended, 3 foreign language required, 3 foreign language recommended, 2 social studies required, 2 social studies recommended, 2 history required, 2 history recommended, 4 elective recommended. **Freshman Admission Statistics:** 3,108 applied, 66% accepted, 26% of those accepted enrolled. **Transfer Admission Requirements:** *Items required:* high school transcript, college transcript, essay, standardized test scores. Minimum college GPA of 2.5 required. Lowest grade transferable C. **General Admission Information:** Application fee $45. Early decision application deadline November 15. Regular application deadline February 1. Admission may be deferred for a maximum of 2 years. Credit offered for CEEB Advanced Placement tests.

COSTS AND FINANCIAL AID

Tuition $26,818. Room & board $7,230. Required fees $530. Average book expense $850. **Required Forms and Deadlines:** FAFSA, CSS/Financial Aid PROFILE, state aid form, noncustodial (divorced/separated) parent's statement, business/farm supplement, and parent's and student's tax return. Financial aid filing deadline February 15. Priority filing deadline February 15. **Notification of Awards:** Applicants will be notified of awards on or about April 1. **Types of Aid:** *Need-based scholarships/grants:* Pell, SEOG, state scholarships/grants, private scholarships, the school's own gift aid. *Loans:* FFEL Subsidized Stafford, FFEL Unsubsidized Stafford, FFEL PLUS, Federal Perkins. **Student Employment:** Federal Work-Study Program available. Institutional employment available. Off-campus job opportunities are fair. **Financial Aid Statistics:** 62% freshmen, 64% undergrads receive some form of aid. Average freshman grant $17,918. Average freshman loan $3,420. Average income from on-campus job $575. **Financial Aid Phone:** 315-781-3315.

See page 1062.

HOFSTRA UNIVERSITY

Admissions Center, Bernon Hall, Hempstead, NY 11549
Phone: 516-463-6700 **E-mail:** admitme@hofstra.edu **CEEB Code:** 2295
Fax: 516-463-5100 **Web:** www.hofstra.edu **ACT Code:** 2760

This private school was founded in 1935. It has a 240-acre campus.

STUDENTS AND FACULTY

Enrollment: 9,469. **Student Body:** Male 46%, female 54%, out-of-state 22%, international 2% (67 countries represented). **Ethnic Representation:** African American 9%, Asian 5%, Caucasian 62%, Hispanic 7%. **Retention and Graduation:** 74% freshmen return for sophomore year. 37% freshmen graduate within 4 years. **Faculty:** Student/faculty ratio 15:1. 507 full-time faculty, 91% hold PhDs. 79% faculty teach undergrads.

ACADEMICS

Degrees: Bachelor's, doctoral, first professional, master's, post-bachelor's certificate, post-master's certificate. **Academic Requirements:** General education including some course work in English (including composition), foreign languages, humanities, mathematics, sciences (biological or physical), social science. **Classes:** 10-19 students in an average class. **Majors with Highest Enrollment:** Psychology, general; marketing/marketing management, general; business administration/management. **Disciplines with Highest Percentage of Degrees Awarded:** Business/marketing 29%, communications/communication technologies 12%, psychology 12%, social sciences and history 9%, education 8%. **Special Study Options:** Accelerated program, double major, dual enrollment, English as a second language, honors program, independent study, internships, liberal arts/career combination, student-designed major, study abroad, teacher certification program, weekend college.

FACILITIES

Housing: Coed, all-female, apartments for married students, apartments for single students, housing for disabled students, housing for international students, honors housing, and nonsmoking and quiet-hour floors. **Library Holdings:** 1,600,000 bound volumes. 7,017 periodicals. 3,450,000 microforms. 7,016 audiovisuals. **Special Academic Facilities/Equipment:** Museum, arboretum, bird sanctuary, writing center, career center, student computing services, Hofstra Cultural Center, language laboratory, McGraw-Hill Companies Business Technology Laboratory, Diane Lindner-Goldberg Child Care Institute. **Computers:** School-owned computers available for student use.

EXTRACURRICULARS

Activities: Choral groups, concert band, dance, drama/theater, jazz band, literary magazine, music ensembles, musical theater, opera, pep band, radio station, student government, student newspaper, student-run film society, symphony orchestra, television station, yearbook. **Organizations:** 155 registered organizations, 30 honor societies, 4 religious organizations, 21 fraternities (6% men join), 15 sororities (7% women join). **Athletics (Intercollegiate):** *Men:* baseball, basketball, cheerleading, cross-country, football, golf, lacrosse, soccer, tennis, wrestling. *Women:* basketball, cheerleading, cross-country, field hockey, golf, lacrosse, soccer, softball, tennis, volleyball.

ADMISSIONS

Selectivity Rating: 76 (of 100). **Freshman Academic Profile:** Average high school GPA 2.9. 16% in top 10% of high school class, 41% in top 25% of high school class, 77% in top 50% of high school class. Average SAT I Math 570, SAT I Math middle 50% range 520-610. Average SAT I Verbal 559, SAT I Verbal middle 50% range 510-600. Average ACT 25, ACT middle 50% range 23-27. TOEFL required of all international applicants, minimum TOEFL 550. **Basis for Candidate Selection:** *Very important factors considered include:* class rank, recommendations, secondary school record, standardized test scores. *Important factors considered include:* character/personal qualities, essays, extracurricular activities, interview, talent/ability. *Other factors considered include:* volunteer work, work experience. **Freshman Admission Requirements:** High school diploma or GED is required. *Academic units required/recommended:* 16 total required; 4 English required, 2 math required, 3 math recommended, 1 science required, 3 science recommended, 1 science lab required, 2 foreign language required, 3 social studies required, 4 social studies recommended, 4 elective required. **Freshman Admission Statistics:** 11,741 applied, 72% accepted, 21% of those accepted enrolled. **Transfer Admission Requirements:** *Items required:* college transcript. Lowest grade transferable C-. **General Admission Information:** Application fee $40. Nonfall registration accepted. Admission may be deferred for a maximum of 1 year. Credit and/or placement offered for CEEB Advanced Placement tests.

COSTS AND FINANCIAL AID

Tuition $15,740. Room & board $8,450. Required fees $802. Average book expense $760. **Required Forms and Deadlines:** FAFSA and state aid form. Priority filing deadline February 15. **Notification of Awards:** Applicants will be notified of awards on a rolling basis beginning on or about March 1. **Types of Aid:** *Need-based scholarships/grants:* Pell, SEOG, state scholarships/grants, private scholarships, the school's own gift aid. *Loans:* FFEL Subsidized Stafford, FFEL Unsubsidized Stafford, FFEL PLUS, Federal Perkins, college/university loans from institutional funds. **Student Employment:** Federal Work-Study Program available. Institutional employment available. Off-campus job opportunities are excellent. **Financial Aid Statistics:** 58% freshmen, 58% undergrads receive some form of aid. Average freshman grant $6,935. Average freshman loan $3,026. Average income from on-campus job $2,000. **Financial Aid Phone:** 516-463-6680.

HOLLINS UNIVERSITY

PO Box 9707, Roanoke, VA 24020-1707
Phone: 540-362-6401 **E-mail:** huadm@hollins.edu **CEEB Code:** 5294
Fax: 540-362-6218 **Web:** www.hollins.edu **ACT Code:** 4360

This private school was founded in 1842. It has a 475-acre campus.

STUDENTS AND FACULTY

Enrollment: 847. **Student Body:** Out-of-state 48%, international 3% (12 countries represented). **Ethnic Representation:** African American 7%, Asian 1%, Caucasian 83%, Hispanic 2%, Native American 1%. **Retention and Graduation:** 79% freshmen return for sophomore year. 65% freshmen graduate within 4 years. 22% grads go on to further study within 1 year. 1% grads pursue law degrees. 1% grads pursue medical degrees. **Faculty:** Student/faculty ratio 9:1. 75 full-time faculty, 96% hold PhDs. 100% faculty teach undergrads.

ACADEMICS

Degrees: Bachelor's, master's, post-master's certificate. **Academic Requirements:** General education including some course work in arts/fine arts, computer literacy, foreign languages, mathematics, sciences (biological or physical), writing, and oral communication. **Classes:** 10-19 students in an average class. Under 10 students in an average lab/discussion section. **Majors with Highest Enrollment:** Creative writing; psychology, general; fine/studio arts, general. **Disciplines with Highest Percentage of Degrees Awarded:** Social sciences and history 21%, visual and performing arts 16%, English 13%, foreign languages and literature 10%, psychology 8%. **Special Study Options:** Accelerated program, cross registration, double major, student exchange program (domestic), independent study, internships, student-designed major, study abroad, teacher certification program.

FACILITIES

Housing: All-female, apartments for single students, housing for international students. Theme houses: language, academic, community service, special-interest, and international. **Library Holdings:** 163,896 bound volumes. 12,749 periodicals. 110,050 microforms. 3,867 audiovisuals. **Special Academic Facilities/Equipment:** Athletic complex, a writing center, language labs, campuswide computer network, sophisticated scientific equipment and instrumentation, and a new state-of-the-art library. **Computers:** School-owned computers available for student use.

EXTRACURRICULARS

Activities: Choral groups, dance, drama/theater, literary magazine, student government, student newspaper, student-run film society, yearbook. **Organizations:** 35 registered organizations, 12 honor societies, 1 religious organization. **Athletics (Intercollegiate):** *Women:* basketball, equestrian, field hockey, lacrosse, soccer, swimming, tennis, volleyball.

ADMISSIONS

Selectivity Rating: 79 (of 100). **Freshman Academic Profile:** Average high school GPA 3.4. 30% in top 10% of high school class, 58% in top 25% of high school class, 89% in top 50% of high school class. 74% from public high schools. Average SAT I Math 550, SAT I Math middle 50% range 490-610. Average SAT I Verbal 595, SAT I Verbal middle 50% range 530-660. Average ACT 24, ACT middle 50% range 21-28. TOEFL required of all international applicants, minimum TOEFL 550. **Basis for Candidate Selection:** *Very important factors considered include:* recommendations, secondary school record, standardized test scores. *Important factors considered include:* class rank, essays, extracurricular activities, talent/ability. *Other factors considered include:* alumni/ae relation, character/personal qualities, interview, volunteer work, work experience. **Freshman Admission Requirements:** High school diploma or GED is required. *Academic units required/recommended:* 16 total required; 4 English recommended, 3 math recommended, 3 science recommended, 3 foreign language recommended, 3 social studies recommended. **Freshman Admission Statistics:** 686 applied, 80% accepted, 37% of those accepted enrolled. **Transfer Admission Requirements:** *Items required:* high school transcript, college transcript, essay. Minimum college GPA of 2.5 required. Lowest grade transferable C. **General Admission Information:** Application fee $35. Priority application deadline February 15. Early decision application deadline December 1. Nonfall registration accepted. Admission may be deferred for a maximum of 1 year. Credit and/or placement offered for CEEB Advanced Placement tests.

COSTS AND FINANCIAL AID

Tuition $18,200. Room & board $6,875. Required fees $250. Average book expense $600. **Required Forms and Deadlines:** FAFSA and state aid form. Financial aid filing deadline March 1. Priority filing deadline February 15. **Notification of Awards:** Applicants will be notified of awards on a rolling basis beginning on or about March 15. **Types of Aid:** *Need-based scholarships/grants:* Pell, SEOG, state scholarships/grants, private scholarships, the school's own gift aid, United Negro College Fund. *Loans:* Direct Subsidized Stafford, Direct Unsubsidized Stafford, Direct PLUS, Federal Perkins, state loans, Sallie Mae, OneChoice, Gate, Plato. **Student Employment:** Federal Work-Study Program available. Institutional employment available. Off-campus job opportunities are good. **Financial Aid Statistics:** 65% freshmen, 59% undergrads receive some form of aid. Average freshman grant $9,041. Average freshman loan $3,979. **Financial Aid Phone:** 540-362-6332.

HOLY FAMILY COLLEGE

Grant and Frankford Avenues, Philadephia, PA 19114-2094
Phone: 215-637-3050 **E-mail:** undergrad@hfc.edu gradstudy@hfc.edu **CEEB Code:** 2297
Fax: 215-281-1022 **Web:** www.hfc.edu **ACT Code:** 3592

This private school, which is affiliated with the Roman Catholic Church, was founded in 1954. It has a 46-acre campus.

STUDENTS AND FACULTY

Enrollment: 1,781. **Student Body:** Male 26%, female 74%, out-of-state 11%, international students represent 4 countries. **Ethnic Representation:** African American 3%, Asian 3%, Caucasian 84%, Hispanic 2%. **Retention and Graduation:** 77% freshmen return for sophomore year. 52% freshmen graduate within 4 years. 16% grads go on to further study within 1 year. 2% grads pursue business degrees. 2% grads pursue law degrees. 2% grads pursue medical degrees. **Faculty:** Student/faculty ratio 11:1. 87 full-time faculty, 64% hold PhDs. 100% faculty teach undergrads.

ACADEMICS

Degrees: Associate's, bachelor's, certificate, master's, post-bachelor's certificate. **Academic Requirements:** General education including some course work in arts/fine arts, English (including composition), foreign languages, history, humanities, mathematics, philosophy, sciences (biological or physical), social science, senior ethics. **Classes:** 10-19 students in an average class. **Majors with Highest Enrollment:** Nursing/registered nurse training (RN, ASN, BSN, MSN); elementary education and teaching; accounting. **Disciplines with Highest Percentage of Degrees Awarded:** Education 35%, business/marketing 23%, health professions and related sciences 13%, protective services/public administration 8%, psychology 5%. **Special Study Options:** Accelerated program, cooperative (work-study) program, double major, dual enrollment, independent study, internships, study abroad, teacher certification program.

FACILITIES

Housing: Housing available for some athletes. **Library Holdings:** 126,780 bound volumes. 742 periodicals. 3,337 microforms. 1,875 audiovisuals. **Special Academic Facilities/Equipment:** On-campus nursery school, language lab. **Computers:** School-owned computers available for student use.

EXTRACURRICULARS

Activities: Drama/theater, literary magazine, student government, student newspaper, yearbook. **Organizations:** 10 registered organizations, 14 honor societies, 1 religious organization. **Athletics (Intercollegiate):** *Men:* basketball, golf, soccer. *Women:* basketball, cross-country, soccer, softball.

ADMISSIONS

Selectivity Rating: 63 (of 100). **Freshman Academic Profile:** Average high school GPA 3.0. 11% in top 10% of high school class, 33% in top 25% of high school class, 73% in top 50% of high school class. 33% from public high schools. Average SAT I Math 448, SAT I Math middle 50% range 410-520. Average SAT I Verbal 469, SAT I Verbal middle 50% range 430-510. TOEFL required of all international applicants, minimum TOEFL 550. **Basis for Candidate Selection:** *Very important factors considered include:* class rank, interview, secondary school record. *Important factors considered include:* alumni/ae relation, character/personal qualities, essays, standardized test scores. *Other factors considered include:* extracurricular activities, recommendations, talent/ability, volunteer work, work experience. **Freshman Admission Requirements:** High school diploma or GED is required. *Academic units required/recommended:* 14 total required; 16 total recommended; 4 English required, 3 math required, 2 science required, 2 foreign language recommended, 2 history required, 3 elective required. **Freshman Admission Statistics:** 573 applied, 77% accepted, 52% of those accepted enrolled. **Transfer Admission Requirements:** *Items required:* high school transcript, college transcript, essay, statement of good standing from prior school. Minimum college GPA of 2.5 required. Lowest grade transferable C. **General Admission Information:** Application fee $25. Admission may be deferred for a maximum of 1 year. Neither credit nor placement offered for CEEB Advanced Placement tests.

COSTS AND FINANCIAL AID

Tuition $13,990. Required fees $500. **Required Forms and Deadlines:** FAFSA and institution's own financial aid form. No deadline for regular filing. Priority filing deadline March 1. **Notification of Awards:** Applicants will be notified of awards on a rolling basis beginning on or about April 1. **Types of Aid:** *Need-based scholarships/grants:* Pell, SEOG, state scholarships/grants, private scholarships, the school's own gift aid. *Loans:* FFEL Subsidized Stafford, FFEL Unsubsidized Stafford, FFEL PLUS, Federal Perkins, Federal Nursing, college/university loans from institutional funds. **Student Employment:** Federal Work-Study Program available. Institutional employment available. Off-campus job opportunities are excellent. **Financial Aid Statistics:** 78% freshmen receive some form of aid. **Financial Aid Phone:** 215-637-5538.

HOLY NAMES COLLEGE

3500 Mountain Boulevard, Oakland, CA 94619-1699
Phone: 510-436-1351 **E-mail:** admissions@hnc.edu **CEEB Code:** 4059
Fax: 510-436-1325 **Web:** www.hnc.edu **ACT Code:** 230

This private school, which is affiliated with the Roman Catholic Church, was founded in 1868. It has a 60-acre campus.

STUDENTS AND FACULTY

Enrollment: 532. **Student Body:** Male 23%, female 77%, out-of-state 4%, international 3% (15 countries represented). **Ethnic Representation:** African American 34%, Asian 7%, Caucasian 27%, Hispanic 17%, Native American 1%. **Retention and Graduation:** 61% freshmen return for sophomore year. 17% freshmen graduate within 4 years. **Faculty:** Student/faculty ratio 12:1. 36 full-time faculty, 91% hold PhDs. 63% faculty teach undergrads.

ACADEMICS

Degrees: Bachelor's, master's, post-bachelor's certificate. **Academic Requirements:** General education including some course work in arts/fine arts, computer literacy, English (including composition), foreign languages, history, humanities, mathematics, philosophy, sciences (biological or physical), social science, oral communication. Philosophy is a choice among the breadth requirements. **Classes:** 10-19 students in an average class. 10-19 students in an average lab/discussion section. **Majors with Highest Enrollment:** Business administration/management; nursing/registered nurse training (RN, ASN, BSN, MSN); psychology, general. **Disciplines with Highest Percentage of Degrees Awarded:** Health professions and related sciences 48%, business/marketing 14%, philosophy/religion/theology 9%, psychology 8%, liberal arts/general studies 8%. **Special Study Options:** Accelerated program, cross registration, distance learning, double major, English as a second language, student exchange program (domestic), independent study, internships, liberal arts/career combination, student-designed major, study abroad, teacher certification program, weekend college, academic remediating, independent study, learning disabled services, off-campus study.

FACILITIES

Housing: Coed, single-sex floor and wings. **Library Holdings:** 116,031 bound volumes. 200 periodicals. 50,931 microforms. 4,378 audiovisuals. **Special Academic Facilities/Equipment:** Valley Center for the Performing Arts and J. D. Kennedy Arts Center Gallery. **Computers:** School-owned computers available for student use.

EXTRACURRICULARS

Activities: Choral groups, drama/theater, music ensembles, student government, symphony orchestra. **Organizations:** 16 registered organizations, 11 honor societies, 1 religious organization. **Athletics (Intercollegiate):** *Men:* basketball, cross-country, golf, soccer. *Women:* basketball, cross-country, soccer, volleyball.

ADMISSIONS

Selectivity Rating: 63 (of 100). **Freshman Academic Profile:** Average high school GPA 3.1. 11% in top 10% of high school class, 37% in top 25% of high school class, 69% in top 50% of high school class. 75% from public high schools. Average SAT I Math 474, SAT I Math middle 50% range 420-530. Average SAT I Verbal 453, SAT I Verbal middle 50% range 400-520. Average ACT 19, ACT middle 50% range 16-24. TOEFL required of all international applicants, minimum TOEFL 490. **Basis for Candidate Selection:** *Very important factors considered include:* secondary school record. *Important factors considered include:* essays, recommendations, standardized test scores. *Other factors considered include:* alumni/ae relation, character/personal qualities, class rank, extracurricular activities, interview, talent/ability, volunteer work, work experience. **Freshman Admission Requirements:** High school diploma or GED is required. *Academic units required/recommended:* 15 total required; 4 English required, 3 math required, 1 science required, 1 science lab required, 2 foreign language required, 3 foreign language recommended, 1 history required, 4 elective required. **Freshman Admission Statistics:** 216 applied, 69% accepted, 44% of those accepted enrolled. **Transfer Admission Requirements:** *Items required:* college transcript, essay, statement of good standing from prior school. Minimum college GPA of 2.2 required. Lowest grade transferable C-. **General Admission Information:** Application fee $35. Priority application deadline March 3. Regular application deadline August 2. Nonfall registration accepted. Admission may be deferred for a maximum of 1 year. Credit and/or placement offered for CEEB Advanced Placement tests.

COSTS AND FINANCIAL AID

Tuition $19,970. Room & board $7,800. Required fees $210. Average book expense $946. **Required Forms and Deadlines:** FAFSA, institution's own financial aid form, and state aid form. No deadline for regular filing. Priority filing deadline March 2. **Notification of Awards:** Applicants will be notified of awards on a rolling basis beginning on or about October 1. **Types of Aid:** *Need-based scholarships/grants:* Pell, SEOG, state scholarships/grants, private scholarships, the school's own gift aid, Federal Nursing. *Loans:* FFEL Subsidized Stafford, FFEL Unsubsidized Stafford, FFEL PLUS, Federal Perkins. **Student Employment:** Federal Work-Study Program available. Institutional employment available. Off-campus job opportunities are good. **Financial Aid Statistics:** 67% freshmen, 64% undergrads receive some form of aid. Average freshman grant $13,500. Average freshman loan $2,625. Average income from on-campus job $1,500. **Financial Aid Phone:** 510-436-1327.

HOOD COLLEGE

401 Rosemont Avenue, Fredrick, MD 21701
Phone: 301-696-3400 **E-mail:** admissions@hood.edu **CEEB Code:** 5296
Fax: 301-696-3819 **Web:** www.hood.edu **ACT Code:** 1702

This private school was founded in 1893. It has a 50-acre campus.

STUDENTS AND FACULTY

Enrollment: 820. **Student Body:** Male 12%, female 88%, out-of-state 24%, international 5% (24 countries represented). **Ethnic Representation:** African American 14%, Asian 3%, Caucasian 69%, Hispanic 3%. **Retention and Graduation:** 80% freshmen return for sophomore year. 60% freshmen graduate within 4 years. 39% grads go on to further study within 1 year. 2% grads pursue business degrees. 2% grads pursue law degrees. **Faculty:** Student/faculty ratio 9:1. 75 full-time faculty, 96% hold PhDs. 100% faculty teach undergrads.

ACADEMICS

Degrees: Bachelor's, master's, post-bachelor's certificate. **Academic Requirements:** General education including some course work in arts/fine arts, computer literacy, English (including composition), foreign languages, history, humanities, mathematics, philosophy, sciences (biological or physical), social science, interdisciplinary. **Classes:** 10-19 students in an average class. 10-19 students in an average lab/discussion section. **Majors with Highest Enrollment:** Business administration/management; psychology, general; biology/biological sciences, general. **Disciplines with Highest Percentage of Degrees Awarded:** Psychology 16%, biological life sciences 14%, social sciences and history 13%, education 12%, business/marketing 11%. **Special Study Options:** Accelerated program, distance learning, double major, dual enrollment, student exchange program (domestic), honors program, independent study, internships, liberal arts/career combination, student-designed major, study abroad, teacher certification program.

FACILITIES

Housing: Housing for disabled students. **Library Holdings:** 182,786 bound volumes. 1,057 periodicals. 688,015 microforms. 3,864 audiovisuals. **Special Academic Facilities/Equipment:** Art gallery, child development lab, language lab, observatory, science labs. **Computers:** *Recommended operating system:* Windows 20/XP Professional. School-owned computers available for student use.

EXTRACURRICULARS

Activities: Choral groups, dance, drama/theater, literary magazine, music ensembles, musical theater, student government, student newspaper, yearbook. **Organizations:** 58 registered organizations, 14 honor societies, 3 religious organizations. **Athletics (Intercollegiate):** *Women:* basketball, field hockey, lacrosse, soccer, softball, swimming, tennis, volleyball.

ADMISSIONS

Selectivity Rating: 76 (of 100). **Freshman Academic Profile:** Average high school GPA 3.2. 31% in top 10% of high school class, 67% in top 25% of high school class, 91% in top 50% of high school class. 81% from public high schools. Average SAT I Math 531, SAT I Math middle 50% range 473-590. Average SAT I Verbal 552, SAT I Verbal middle 50% range 493-620. Average ACT 21, ACT middle 50% range 18-24. TOEFL required of all international applicants, minimum TOEFL 530. **Basis for Candidate Selection:** *Very important factors considered include:* class rank, secondary school record, standardized test scores. *Important factors considered include:* character/personal qualities, essays, extracurricular activities, interview, recommendations, talent/ability. *Other factors considered include:* alumni/ae relation, minority status, volunteer work, work experience. **Freshman Admission Requirements:** High school diploma or GED is required. *Academic units required/recommended:* 16 total required; 4 English required, 3 math required, 3 science required, 2 foreign language required, 1 social studies required, 2 history required, 1 elective required. **Freshman Admission Statistics:** 530 applied, 78% accepted, 43% of those accepted enrolled. **Transfer Admission Requirements:** *Items required:* college transcript, essay, interview. Minimum college GPA of 2.5 required. Lowest grade transferable C-. **General Admission Information:** Application fee $35. Priority application deadline December 1. Regular application deadline February 1. Nonfall registration accepted. Admission may be deferred for a maximum of 1 year. Credit and/or placement offered for CEEB Advanced Placement tests.

COSTS AND FINANCIAL AID

Tuition $19,360. Room & board $7,300. Required fees $335. Average book expense $800. **Required Forms and Deadlines:** FAFSA and state aid form. No deadline for regular filing. Priority filing deadline February 15. **Notification of Awards:** Applicants will be notified of awards on a rolling basis beginning on or about March 1. **Types of Aid:** *Need-based scholarships/grants:* Pell, SEOG, state scholarships/grants, private scholarships, the school's own gift aid. *Loans:* Direct Subsidized Stafford, Direct Unsubsidized Stafford, Direct PLUS, FFEL Subsidized Stafford, FFEL Unsubsidized Stafford, FFEL PLUS, Federal Perkins. **Student Employment:** Federal Work-Study Program available. Institutional employment available. Off-campus job opportunities are good. **Financial Aid Statistics:** 75% freshmen, 73% undergrads receive some form of aid. Average freshman grant $15,747. Average freshman loan $3,955. **Financial Aid Phone:** 301-696-3411.

HOPE COLLEGE

69 East 10th, PO Box 9000, Holland, MI 49422-9000
Phone: 616-395-7850 **E-mail:** admissions@hope.edu **CEEB Code:** 1301
Fax: 616-395-7130 **Web:** www.hope.edu **ACT Code:** 2012

This private school was founded in 1862. It has a 45-acre campus.

STUDENTS AND FACULTY

Enrollment: 3,035. **Student Body:** Male 39%, female 61%, out-of-state 23%, international 1% (36 countries represented). **Ethnic Representation:** African American 1%, Asian 2%, Caucasian 94%, Hispanic 2%. **Retention and Graduation:** 88% freshmen return for sophomore year. 68% freshmen graduate within 4 years. 20% grads go on to further study within 1 year. 1% grads pursue law degrees. 2% grads pursue medical degrees. **Faculty:** Student/faculty ratio 13:1. 200 full-time faculty, 84% hold PhDs. 94% faculty teach undergrads.

ACADEMICS

Degrees: Bachelor's. **Academic Requirements:** General education including some course work in arts/fine arts, English (including composition), foreign languages, history, humanities, mathematics, philosophy, sciences (biological or physical), social science. **Classes:** 10-19 students in an average class. 10-19 students in an average lab/discussion section. **Majors with Highest Enrollment:** Business administration/management; English language and literature, general; biology/biological sciences, general. **Disciplines with Highest Percentage of Degrees Awarded:** Business/marketing 13%, English 13%, social sciences and history 11%, psychology 10%, education 8%. **Special Study Options:** Double major, dual enrollment, independent study, internships, liberal arts/career combination, student-designed major, study abroad, teacher certification program.

FACILITIES

Housing: Coed, all-female, all-male, apartments for married students, apartments for single students, fraternities and/or sororities, cottages/houses on or near campus. **Library Holdings:** 343,865 bound volumes. 2,250 periodicals. 362,820 microforms. 11,970 audiovisuals. **Special Academic Facilities/Equipment:** Art gallery, particle accelerator, computational chemistry lab, electron microscopes, spectrometers, ultracentrifuge. **Computers:** School-owned computers available for student use.

EXTRACURRICULARS

Activities: Choral groups, concert band, dance, drama/theater, jazz band, literary magazine, music ensembles, musical theater, pep band, radio station, student government, student newspaper, symphony orchestra, television station, yearbook. **Organizations:** 67 registered organizations, 22 honor societies, 4 religious organizations, 6 fraternities (6% men join), 7 sororities (15% women join). **Athletics (Intercollegiate):** *Men:* baseball, basketball, cheerleading, cross-country, diving, football, golf, soccer, swimming, tennis, track & field. *Women:* basketball, cheerleading, cross-country, diving, golf, soccer, softball, swimming, tennis, track & field, volleyball.

ADMISSIONS

Selectivity Rating: 75 (of 100). **Freshman Academic Profile:** Average high school GPA 3.7. 32% in top 10% of high school class, 58% in top 25% of high school class, 91% in top 50% of high school class. 91% from public high schools. Average SAT I Math 596, SAT I Math middle 50% range 540-650. Average SAT I Verbal 585, SAT I Verbal middle 50% range 540-630. Average ACT 25, ACT middle 50% range 22-28. TOEFL required of all international applicants, minimum TOEFL 550. **Basis for Candidate Selection:** *Very important factors considered include:* secondary school record, standardized test scores. *Important factors considered include:* class rank. *Other factors considered include:* alumni/ae relation, character/personal qualities, essays, extracurricular activities, interview, recommendations, talent/ability, volunteer work, work experience. **Freshman Admission Requirements:** High school diploma or GED is required. *Academic units required/recommended:* 20 total recommended; 4 English required, 4 English recommended, 2 math required, 3 math recommended, 1 science required, 3 science recommended, 1 science lab required, 2 science lab recommended, 2 foreign language required, 2 foreign language recommended, 2 social studies required, 2 social studies recommended, 1 history required, 1 history recommended, 5 elective required, 5 elective recommended. **Freshman Admission Statistics:** 1,885 applied, 90% accepted, 42% of those accepted enrolled. **Transfer Admission Requirements:** *Items required:* high school transcript, college transcript, essay, standardized test scores. Minimum college GPA of 2.0 required. Lowest grade transferable C. **General Admission Information:** Application fee $25. Nonfall registration accepted. Admission may be deferred for a maximum of 1 year. Credit offered for CEEB Advanced Placement tests.

COSTS AND FINANCIAL AID

Tuition $18,158. Room & board $5,688. Required fees $110. Average book expense $640. **Required Forms and Deadlines:** FAFSA and institution's own financial aid form. No deadline for regular filing. Priority filing deadline February 15. **Notification of Awards:** Applicants will be notified of awards on a rolling basis beginning on or about March 1. **Types of Aid:** *Need-based scholarships/grants:* Pell, SEOG, state scholarships/grants, private scholarships, the school's own gift aid. *Loans:* Direct Subsidized Stafford, Direct Unsubsidized Stafford, Direct PLUS, Federal Perkins, state loans. **Student Employment:** Federal Work-Study Program available. Institutional employment available. Off-campus job opportunities are excellent. **Financial Aid Statistics:** 66% freshmen, 61% undergrads receive some form of aid. Average freshman grant $12,012. Average freshman loan $3,495. Average income from on-campus job $1,500. **Financial Aid Phone:** 616-395-7765.

HOPE INTERNATIONAL UNIVERSITY

2500 East Nutwood Avenue, Fullerton, CA 92831-3199
Phone: 800-762-1294 **E-mail:** admission@hiu.edu
Fax: 714-526-0231 **Web:** www.hiu.edu **ACT Code:** 356

This private school was founded in 1928. It has a 26-acre campus.

STUDENTS AND FACULTY

Enrollment: 822. **Student Body:** Out-of-state 44%. **Retention and Graduation:** 64% freshmen return for sophomore year. 35% grads go on to further study within 1 year. 5% grads pursue business degrees. **Faculty:** Student/faculty ratio 13:1. 36 full-time faculty, 36% hold PhDs.

ACADEMICS

Degrees: Associate's, bachelor's, master's. **Academic Requirements:** General education including some course work in English (including composition), history, humanities, mathematics, sciences (biological or physical), social science. **Majors with Highest Enrollment:** Youth ministry; psychology, general; teacher education, multiple levels. **Special Study Options:** Distance learning, double major, independent study, internships, liberal arts/career combination, study abroad, teacher certification program.

FACILITIES

Housing: Coed.

EXTRACURRICULARS

Activities: Choral groups, drama/theater, jazz band, music ensembles, student government, student newspaper, yearbook. **Athletics (Intercollegiate):** *Men:* basketball, soccer, tennis, volleyball. *Women:* basketball, soccer, softball, tennis, volleyball.

ADMISSIONS

Selectivity Rating: 63 (of 100). **Freshman Academic Profile:** 28% in top 25% of high school class. Average SAT I Math 519. Average SAT I Verbal 518. Average ACT 22. TOEFL required of all international applicants, minimum TOEFL 525. **General Admission Information:** Regular application deadline July 1. Credit and/or placement offered for CEEB Advanced Placement tests.

COSTS AND FINANCIAL AID

Room & board $3,584. Required fees $785. Average book expense $600. **Required Forms and Deadlines:** FAFSA, institution's own financial aid form, and state aid form. **Types of Aid:** *Need-based scholarships/grants:* Pell, SEOG, state scholarships/grants, private scholarships, the school's own gift aid. *Loans:* FFEL Subsidized Stafford, FFEL Unsubsidized Stafford, FFEL PLUS, Federal Perkins, state loans, college/university loans from institutional funds. **Student Employment:** Federal Work-Study Program available. Off-campus job opportunities are excellent. **Financial Aid Statistics:** Average freshman grant $2,207. Average freshman loan $2,099. Average income from on-campus job $2,000.

HOUGHTON COLLEGE

PO Box 128, Houghton, NY 14744
Phone: 800-777-2556 **E-mail:** admissions@houghton.edu **CEEB Code:** 2299
Fax: 716-567-9522 **Web:** www.houghton.edu **ACT Code:** 2766

This private school was founded in 1883. It has a 1,300-acre campus.

STUDENTS AND FACULTY

Enrollment: 1,380. **Student Body:** Male 37%, female 63%, out-of-state 38%, international 4% (27 countries represented). **Ethnic Representation:** African American 1%, Asian 1%, Caucasian 96%, Hispanic 1%. **Retention and Graduation:** 82% freshmen return for sophomore year. 48% freshmen graduate within 4 years. 25% grads go on to further study within 1 year. 4% grads pursue business degrees. 5% grads pursue law degrees. 6% grads pursue medical degrees. **Faculty:** Student/faculty ratio 14:1. 82 full-time faculty, 80% hold PhDs. 100% faculty teach undergrads.

ACADEMICS

Degrees: Associate's, bachelor's. **Academic Requirements:** General education including some course work in arts/fine arts, English (including composition), foreign languages, history, mathematics, philosophy, sciences (biological or physical), social science, Bible and theology, communication, library research. **Classes:** 10-19 students in an average class. 10-19 students in an average lab/discussion section. **Disciplines with Highest Percentage of Degrees Awarded:** Business/marketing 34%, education 11%, biological life sciences 10%, visual and performing arts 9%, English 8%. **Special Study Options:** Cross registration, double major, student exchange program (domestic), honors program, independent study, internships, study abroad, teacher certification program.

FACILITIES

Housing: All-female, all-male, apartments for single students, housing for international students. **Library Holdings:** 223,880 bound volumes. 3,656 periodicals. 28,586 microforms. 1,944 audiovisuals. **Special Academic Facilities/Equipment:** Electron microscope, art gallery, greenhouse. **Computers:** *Recommended operating system:* Windows 95. School-owned computers available for student use.

EXTRACURRICULARS

Activities: Choral groups, concert band, drama/theater, jazz band, literary magazine, music ensembles, musical theater, opera, radio station, student government, student newspaper, symphony orchestra, television station, yearbook. **Organizations:** 40 registered organizations, 2 honor societies, 9 religious organizations. **Athletics (Intercollegiate):** *Men:* basketball, cheerleading, cross-country, indoor track, soccer, track & field. *Women:* basketball, cheerleading, cross-country, field hockey, indoor track, soccer, track & field, volleyball.

ADMISSIONS

Selectivity Rating: 74 (of 100). **Freshman Academic Profile:** Average high school GPA 3.2. 30% in top 10% of high school class, 62% in top 25% of high school class, 89% in top 50% of high school class. 70% from public high schools. Average SAT I Math 579, SAT I Math middle 50% range 520-630. Average SAT I Verbal 597, SAT I Verbal middle 50% range 540-650. Average ACT 25, ACT middle 50% range 21-27. TOEFL required of all international applicants, minimum TOEFL 550. **Basis for Candidate Selection:** *Very important factors considered include:* character/personal qualities, class rank, religious affiliation/commitment, secondary school record. *Important factors considered include:* essays, recommendations, standardized test scores. *Other factors considered include:* alumni/ae relation, extracurricular activities, interview, minority status, talent/ability, volunteer work, work experience. **Freshman Admission Requirements:** High school diploma or GED is required. *Academic units required/recommended:* 16 total recommended; 4 English recommended, 3 math recommended, 2 science recommended, 2 science lab recommended, 2 foreign language recommended, 1 social studies recommended, 2 history recommended. **Freshman Admission Statistics:** 1,160 applied, 88% accepted, 35% of those accepted enrolled. **Transfer Admission Requirements:** *Items required:* college transcript, essay. Minimum high school GPA of 2.5 required. Minimum college GPA of 2.5 required. Lowest grade transferable C-. **General Admission Information:** Application fee $25. Nonfall registration accepted. Admission may be deferred for a maximum of 1 year. Credit and/or placement offered for CEEB Advanced Placement tests.

COSTS AND FINANCIAL AID

Tuition $15,180. Room & board $5,400. Required fees $0. Average book expense $750. **Required Forms and Deadlines:** FAFSA and institution's own financial aid form. No deadline for regular filing. Priority filing deadline March

1. **Notification of Awards:** Applicants will be notified of awards on a rolling basis beginning on or about March 15. **Types of Aid:** *Need-based scholarships/grants:* Pell, SEOG, state scholarships/grants, private scholarships, the school's own gift aid. *Loans:* FFEL Subsidized Stafford, FFEL Unsubsidized Stafford, FFEL PLUS, Federal Perkins, college/university loans from institutional funds, private alternative loans. **Student Employment:** Federal Work-Study Program available. Institutional employment available. Off-campus job opportunities are fair. **Financial Aid Statistics:** 78% freshmen, 79% undergrads receive some form of aid. Average freshman grant $7,164. Average freshman loan $6,711. Average income from on-campus job $1,200. **Financial Aid Phone:** 716-567-9328.

HOUSTON BAPTIST UNIVERSITY

7502 Fondren Road, Houston, TX 77074
Phone: 281-649-3211 **E-mail:** unadm@hbu.edu **CEEB Code:** 6282
Fax: 281-649-3217 **Web:** www.hbu.edu **ACT Code:** 4101

This private school, which is affiliated with the Southern Baptist Church, was founded in 1960. It has a 100-acre campus.

STUDENTS AND FACULTY

Enrollment: 1,941. **Student Body:** Male 30%, female 70%, out-of-state 2%, international 5%. **Ethnic Representation:** African American 21%, Asian 14%, Caucasian 48%, Hispanic 16%, Native American 1%. **Retention and Graduation:** 77% freshmen return for sophomore year. 21% freshmen graduate within 4 years. **Faculty:** Student/faculty ratio 16:1. 110 full-time faculty, 74% hold PhDs.

ACADEMICS

Degrees: Associate's, bachelor's, master's. **Academic Requirements:** General education including some course work in arts/fine arts, computer literacy, English (including composition), history, humanities, mathematics, sciences (biological or physical), social science. **Classes:** 20-29 students in an average class. Under 10 students in an average lab/discussion section. **Disciplines with Highest Percentage of Degrees Awarded:** Business/marketing 23%, education 12%, psychology 12%, biological life sciences 10%, social sciences and history 10%. **Special Study Options:** Distance learning, double major, dual enrollment, English as a second language, honors program, independent study, internships, study abroad, teacher certification program.

FACILITIES

Housing: All-female, all-male, apartments for single students. **Library Holdings:** 161,035 bound volumes. 26,447 periodicals. 100,224 microforms. 9,328 audiovisuals. **Special Academic Facilities/Equipment:** Museum of architecture/decorative arts, language lab, research center. **Computers:** School-owned computers available for student use.

EXTRACURRICULARS

Activities: Choral groups, concert band, jazz band, music ensembles, opera, pep band, student government, student newspaper, yearbook. **Organizations:** 1 honor society, 3 fraternities (13% men join), 3 sororities (6% women join). **Athletics (Intercollegiate):** *Men:* baseball, basketball. *Women:* basketball, softball, volleyball.

ADMISSIONS

Selectivity Rating: 68 (of 100). **Freshman Academic Profile:** 32% in top 25% of high school class, 58% in top 50% of high school class. Average SAT I Math 522, SAT I Math middle 50% range 470-610. Average SAT I Verbal 510, SAT I Verbal middle 50% range 480-590. Average ACT 22. TOEFL required of all international applicants, minimum TOEFL 600. **Basis for Candidate Selection:** *Very important factors considered include:* essays, recommendations, standardized test scores. *Important factors considered include:* class rank, extracurricular activities, geographical residence, religious affiliation/commitment, secondary school record, talent/ability, volunteer work. *Other factors considered include:* alumni/ae relation, character/personal qualities, interview. **Freshman Admission Requirements:** High school diploma or GED is required. *Academic units required/recommended:* 16 total recommended; 4 English recommended, 3 math recommended, 3 science recommended, 1 science lab recommended, 2 foreign language recommended, 2 social studies recommended, 1 history recommended. **Freshman Admission Statistics:** 724 applied, 67% accepted, 52% of those accepted enrolled. **Transfer Admission Requirements:** *Items required:* college transcript, essay, statement of good standing from prior school. Lowest grade transferable C. **General Admission Information:** Application fee $25. Nonfall registration accepted. Admission may be deferred. Credit offered for CEEB Advanced Placement tests.

COSTS AND FINANCIAL AID

Tuition $4,608. Room & board $2,300. **Required Forms and Deadlines:** FAFSA and institution's own financial aid form. Financial aid filing deadline April 15. Priority filing deadline March 1. **Notification of Awards:** Applicants will be notified of awards on a rolling basis beginning on or about April 15. **Types of Aid:** *Need-based scholarships/grants:* Pell, SEOG, state scholarships/grants, private scholarships, the school's own gift aid. *Loans:* FFEL Subsidized Stafford, FFEL Unsubsidized Stafford, FFEL PLUS. **Student Employment:** Institutional employment available. Off-campus job opportunities are excellent. **Financial Aid Statistics:** 50% freshmen, 39% undergrads receive some form of aid. **Financial Aid Phone:** 713-995-3204.

HOWARD PAYNE UNIVERSITY

Howard Payne Station, Brownwood, TX 76801
Phone: 915-649-8027 **E-mail:** enroll@hputx.edu
Fax: 915-649-8901 **Web:** www.hputx.edu **ACT Code:** 4102

This private school, which is affiliated with the Baptist Church, was founded in 1889. It has a 30-acre campus.

STUDENTS AND FACULTY

Enrollment: 1,412. **Student Body:** Male 52%, female 48%, out-of-state 2%, international students represent 6 countries. **Ethnic Representation:** African American 7%, Asian 2%, Caucasian 76%, Hispanic 12%. **Retention and Graduation:** 54% freshmen return for sophomore year. 26% freshmen graduate within 4 years. 15% grads go on to further study within 1 year. 2% grads pursue business degrees. 2% grads pursue law degrees. 2% grads pursue medical degrees. **Faculty:** Student/faculty ratio 13:1. 73 full-time faculty, 60% hold PhDs. 100% faculty teach undergrads.

ACADEMICS

Degrees: Associate's, bachelor's, certificate. **Academic Requirements:** General education including some course work in arts/fine arts, computer literacy, English (including composition), mathematics, sciences (biological or physical), social science. **Classes:** Under 10 students in an average class. **Majors with Highest Enrollment:** Education, general; Bible/biblical studies; business administration/management. **Disciplines with Highest Percentage of Degrees Awarded:** Business/marketing 17%, education 15%, philosophy/religion/theology 14%, social sciences and history 7%, psychology 7%. **Special Study Options:** Accelerated program, cooperative (work-study) program, distance learning, double major, dual enrollment, English as a second language, honors program, independent study, internships, liberal arts/career combination, study abroad, teacher certification program.

FACILITIES

Housing: All-female, all-male, apartments for single students. **Library Holdings:** 78,825 bound volumes. 1,017 periodicals. 279,911 microforms. 6,800 audiovisuals. **Special Academic Facilities/Equipment:** Douglas MacArther Academy of Freedom and Museum. **Computers:** School-owned computers available for student use.

EXTRACURRICULARS

Activities: Choral groups, concert band, drama/theater, jazz band, literary magazine, marching band, music ensembles, musical theater, opera, radio station, student government, student newspaper, yearbook. **Organizations:** 32 registered organizations, 3 honor societies, 4 religious organizations, 3 fraternities (11% men join), 5 sororities (11% women join). **Athletics (Intercollegiate):** *Men:* baseball, basketball, cheerleading, cross-country, football, golf, tennis, track & field. *Women:* basketball, cheerleading, cross-country, golf, softball, tennis, track & field, volleyball.

ADMISSIONS

Selectivity Rating: 63 (of 100). **Freshman Academic Profile:** Average high school GPA 3.2. 17% in top 10% of high school class, 41% in top 25% of high school class, 72% in top 50% of high school class. 86% from public high schools. Average SAT I Math 505, SAT I Math middle 50% range 410-601. Average SAT I Verbal 509, SAT I Verbal middle 50% range 400-625. Average ACT 21, ACT middle 50% range 17-27. TOEFL required of all international applicants, minimum TOEFL 500. **Basis for Candidate Selection:** *Very important factors considered include:* secondary school record, standardized test scores. *Important factors considered include:* interview, recommendations. *Other factors considered include:* character/personal qualities, class rank, work experience. **Freshman Admission Requirements:** High school diploma or GED is required. *Academic units required/recommended:* 15 total required; 22 total recommended; 4 English recommended, 3 math recommended, 2 science recommended, 1 science lab recommended, 3 social studies recommended, 10 elective recommended. **Freshman Admission Statistics:** 895 applied, 65% accepted, 60% of those accepted enrolled. **Transfer Admission Requirements:** *Items required:* college transcript. Minimum college GPA of 2.0 required. Lowest grade transferable D. **General Admission Information:** Application fee $25. Priority application deadline August 15. Regular application deadline August 31. Nonfall registration accepted. Admission may be deferred for a maximum of 1 year. Credit and/or placement offered for CEEB Advanced Placement tests.

COSTS AND FINANCIAL AID

Tuition $9,700. Room & board $3,834. Required fees $800. Average book expense $800. **Required Forms and Deadlines:** FAFSA and institution's own financial aid form. No deadline for regular filing. Priority filing deadline April 1. **Notification of Awards:** Applicants will be notified of awards on a rolling basis beginning on or about March 1. **Types of Aid:** *Need-based scholarships/grants:* Pell, SEOG, state scholarships/grants, private scholarships, the school's own gift aid. *Loans:* FFEL Subsidized Stafford, FFEL Unsubsidized Stafford, FFEL PLUS, Federal Perkins, state loans. **Student Employment:** Federal Work-Study Program available. Institutional employment available. Off-campus job opportunities are good. **Financial Aid Phone:** 915-649-8015.

HOWARD UNIVERSITY

2400 Sixth Street, NW, Washington, DC 20059
Phone: 202-806-2700 **E-mail:** admission@howard.edu **CEEB Code:** 5297
Fax: 202-806-4465 **Web:** www.howard.edu **ACT Code:** 4102

This private school was founded in 1867. It has an 89-acre campus.

STUDENTS AND FACULTY

Enrollment: 6,099. **Student Body:** Male 37%, female 63%, out-of-state 90%, international 2% (102 countries represented). **Ethnic Representation:** African American 80%, Asian 1%, Hispanic 1%. **Retention and Graduation:** 84% freshmen return for sophomore year. 24% freshmen graduate within 4 years. 57% grads go on to further study within 1 year. 15% grads pursue business degrees. 12% grads pursue law degrees. 12% grads pursue medical degrees. **Faculty:** Student/faculty ratio 7:1. 1,089 full-time faculty, 78% hold PhDs.

ACADEMICS

Degrees: Bachelor's, doctoral, master's. **Academic Requirements:** General education including some course work in English (including composition), foreign languages, mathematics, philosophy, physical education, African-American cluster. **Classes:** Under 10 students in an average class. Under 10 students in an average lab/discussion section. **Disciplines with Highest Percentage of Degrees Awarded:** Health professions and related sciences 20%, business/marketing 17%, biological life sciences 8%, communications/communication technologies 7%, engineering/engineering technology 5%. **Special Study Options:** Accelerated program, cooperative (work-study) program, distance learning, double major, English as a second language, student exchange program (domestic), honors program, independent study, internships, study abroad, tutorial program, advanced placement, continuing education.

FACILITIES

Housing: Coed, all-female, all-male, apartments for married students, apartments for single students. **Library Holdings:** 2,372,112 bound volumes. 14,368 periodicals. 3,606,759 microforms. **Special Academic Facilities/Equipment:** 3 art galleries, language labs, hospital, research center with comprehensive collection on Africa and persons of African descent. **Computers:** School-owned computers available for student use.

EXTRACURRICULARS

Activities: Choral groups, concert band, dance, drama/theater, jazz band, literary magazine, marching band, music ensembles, musical theater, opera, pep band, radio station, student government, student newspaper, student-run film society, symphony orchestra, television station, yearbook. **Organizations:** 150 registered organizations, 15 honor societies, 3 religious organizations, 4 fraternities, 4 sororities. **Athletics (Intercollegiate):** *Men:* baseball, basketball, cheerleading, cross-country, diving, football, soccer, softball, swimming, tennis, track & field, wrestling. *Women:* basketball, cheerleading, cross-country, diving, lacrosse, soccer, swimming, tennis, track & field, volleyball.

ADMISSIONS

Selectivity Rating: 80 (of 100). **Freshman Academic Profile:** 80% from public high schools. Average SAT I Math 517, SAT I Math middle 50% range 420-670. Average SAT I Verbal 533, SAT I Verbal middle 50% range 450-670. ACT middle 50% range 17-28. TOEFL required of all international applicants, minimum TOEFL 500. **Basis for Candidate Selection:** *Very important factors considered include:* class rank, secondary school record, standardized test scores. *Important factors considered include:* character/personal qualities, recommendations. *Other factors considered include:* alumni/ae relation, essays, extracurricular activities, talent/ability, volunteer work, work experience. **Freshman Admission Requirements:** High school diploma or GED is required. *Academic units required/recommended:* 4 English required, 2 math required, 2 science required, 2 foreign language required, 2 social studies required. **Freshman Admission Statistics:** 6,664 applied, 56% accepted, 27% of those accepted enrolled. **Transfer Admission Requirements:** *Items required:* college transcript, statement of good standing from prior school. Minimum college GPA of 2.5 required. Lowest grade transferable C. **General Admission Information:** Application fee $45. Priority application deadline November 30. Early decision application deadline November 30. Regular application deadline April 1. Nonfall registration accepted. Admission may be deferred for a maximum of 6 years. Credit and/or placement offered for CEEB Advanced Placement tests.

COSTS AND FINANCIAL AID

Tuition $8,750. Room & board $5,250. Required fees $405. Average book expense $800. **Required Forms and Deadlines:** FAFSA and institution's own financial aid form. Financial aid filing deadline April 1. **Notification of Awards:** Applicants will be notified of awards on a rolling basis. **Types of Aid:** *Need-based scholarships/grants:* Pell, SEOG, private scholarships, the school's own gift aid, Federal Nursing. *Loans:* FFEL Subsidized Stafford, FFEL PLUS, Federal Perkins, Federal Nursing, college/university loans from institutional funds. **Student Employment:** Federal Work-Study Program available. Institutional employment available. Off-campus job opportunities are excellent. **Financial Aid Statistics:** 68% freshmen, 68% undergrads receive some form of aid. Average freshman grant $4,475. Average freshman loan $9,457. Average income from on-campus job $3,500. **Financial Aid Phone:** 202-806-2800.

HUMBOLDT STATE UNIVERSITY

1 Harpst Street, Arcata, CA 95521-8299
Phone: 707-826-4402 **E-mail:** hsuinfo@humboldt.edu **CEEB Code:** 4345
Fax: 707-826-6194 **Web:** www.humboldt.edu

This public school was founded in 1913. It has a 161-acre campus.

STUDENTS AND FACULTY

Enrollment: 6,418. **Student Body:** Male 45%, female 55%, out-of-state 4%, (21 countries represented). **Ethnic Representation:** African American 3%, Asian 3%, Caucasian 66%, Hispanic 8%, Native American 3%. **Retention and Graduation:** 76% freshmen return for sophomore year. 8% freshmen graduate within 4 years. **Faculty:** Student/faculty ratio 16:1. 308 full-time faculty, 98% hold PhDs. 100% faculty teach undergrads.

ACADEMICS

Degrees: Bachelor's, certificate, diploma, master's. **Academic Requirements:** General education including some course work in English (including composition), history, humanities, mathematics. **Classes:** 20-29 students in an average class. 10-19 students in an average lab/discussion section. **Majors with Highest Enrollment:** Art/art studies, general; biology/biological sciences, general; liberal arts and sciences/liberal studies. **Disciplines with Highest Percentage of Degrees Awarded:** Interdisciplinary studies 19%, social sciences and history 14%, natural resources/environmental sciences 10%, biological life sciences 9%, visual and performing arts 9%. **Special Study Options:** Cooperative (work-study) program, cross registration, distance learning, double major, dual enrollment, English as a second language, student exchange program (domestic), honors program, independent study, internships, student-designed major, study abroad, teacher certification program.

FACILITIES

Housing: Coed, apartments for single students, fraternities and/or sororities, themed residence halls. **Library Holdings:** 570,552 bound volumes. 2,782 periodicals. 600,254 microforms. 18,562 audiovisuals. **Special Academic Facilities/Equipment:** Art and geology museums, marine research lab, fish hatchery, wildlife game pen, observatory, First Street Gallery. **Computers:** School-owned computers available for student use.

EXTRACURRICULARS

Activities: Choral groups, concert band, dance, drama/theater, jazz band, literary magazine, marching band, music ensembles, musical theater, radio station, student government, student newspaper, student-run film society. **Organizations:** 160 registered organizations, 6 honor societies, 2 fraternities, 4 sororities. **Athletics (Intercollegiate):** *Men:* basketball, cross-country, soccer, track & field. *Women:* basketball, cross-country, soccer, softball, track & field, volleyball.

ADMISSIONS

Selectivity Rating: 63 (of 100). **Freshman Academic Profile:** Average high school GPA 3.2. 79% from public high schools. Average SAT I Math 521, SAT I Math middle 50% range 460-590. Average SAT I Verbal 530, SAT I Verbal middle 50% range 470-570. Average ACT 22, ACT middle 50% range 20-25. TOEFL required of all international applicants, minimum TOEFL 550. **Basis for Candidate Selection:** *Very important factors considered include:* secondary school record, standardized test scores. *Other factors considered include:* character/personal qualities, essays, extracurricular activities, interview, minority status, recommendations, talent/ability, volunteer work. **Freshman Admission Requirements:** High school diploma or GED is required. *Academic units required/recommended:* 15 total required; 4 English required, 3 math required, 1 science required, 1 science lab required, 2 foreign language required, 1 history required, 3 elective required. **Freshman Admission Statistics:** 3,833 applied, 74% accepted, 26% of those accepted enrolled. **Transfer Admission Requirements:** *Items required:* college transcript. Minimum college GPA of 2.0 required. Lowest grade transferable D-. **General Admission Information:** Application fee $55. Nonfall registration accepted. Admission may be deferred. Credit and/or placement offered for CEEB Advanced Placement tests.

COSTS AND FINANCIAL AID

In-state tuition $0. Out-of-state tuition $5,904. Room & board $6,690. Required fees $1,892. Average book expense $1,030. **Required Forms and Deadlines:** FAFSA. No deadline for regular filing. Priority filing deadline March 2. **Notification of Awards:** Applicants will be notified of awards on a rolling basis beginning on or about March 10. **Types of Aid:** *Need-based scholarships/grants:* Pell, SEOG, state scholarships/grants, private scholarships. *Loans:* Direct Subsidized Stafford, Direct Unsubsidized Stafford, Direct PLUS, Federal Perkins. **Student Employment:** Federal Work-Study Program available. Institutional employment available. Off-campus job opportunities are fair. **Financial Aid Statistics:** 49% freshmen, 53% undergrads receive some form of aid. Average freshman grant $4,100. Average freshman loan $3,106. **Financial Aid Phone:** 707-826-4321.

HUNTINGDON COLLEGE

1500 East Fairview Avenue, Montgomery, AL 36106-2148
Phone: 334-833-4497 **E-mail:** admiss@huntingdon.edu **CEEB Code:** 1303
Fax: 334-833-4347 **Web:** www.huntingdon.edu **ACT Code:** 180

This private school, which is affiliated with the Methodist Church, was founded in 1854. It has a 58-acre campus.

STUDENTS AND FACULTY

Enrollment: 615. **Student Body:** Male 35%, female 65%, out-of-state 19%, international 4%. **Ethnic Representation:** African American 8%, Asian 1%, Caucasian 89%, Native American 1%. **Retention and Graduation:** 80% freshmen return for sophomore year. 34% freshmen graduate within 4 years. 40% grads go on to further study within 1 year. 10% grads pursue business degrees. 15% grads pursue law degrees. 6% grads pursue medical degrees. **Faculty:** Student/faculty ratio 12:1. 41 full-time faculty, 90% hold PhDs. 100% faculty teach undergrads.

ACADEMICS

Degrees: Associate's, bachelor's. **Academic Requirements:** General education including some course work in arts/fine arts, computer literacy, English (including composition), foreign languages, history, humanities, mathematics, philosophy, sciences (biological or physical), social science. Our core curriculum includes a topic-centered interdisciplinary liberal arts symposium (4 courses, 3 hours each) and distribution requirements that allow students a great deal of freedom of choice. **Classes:** Under 10 students in an average class. **Majors with Highest Enrollment:** Marketing/marketing management, general; biology/biological sciences, general; kinesiology and exercise science. **Disciplines with Highest Percentage of Degrees Awarded:** Business/marketing 19%, parks and recreation 11%, visual and performing arts 10%, social sciences and history 9%, communications/communication technologies 8%. **Special Study Options:** Cross registration, double major, honors program, independent study, internships, liberal arts/career combination, student-designed major, study abroad, teacher certification program, evening college, dual degree program in engineering with Auburn University. Member of the Sepphoris Consortium, allowing students to participate in archaeological expeditions in the Holy Land. Member of the Dauphin Island Sea Laboratory.

FACILITIES

Housing: Coed, housing for disabled students. **Library Holdings:** 105,604 bound volumes. 465 periodicals. 52,945 microforms. 1,894 audiovisuals. **Special Academic Facilities/Equipment:** Art gallery, "smart" classrooms in each academic building (equipped with large touch-screen computers, 20 laptops with wireless Internet connection, and capability to project via document cameras, slides, VCR, and other images), theater/performance center, excellent chemistry equipment in Bellingrath Hall (science building), individual studios available for art students in upper-level classes, Dungeon Theatre (proscenium house seating), Top Stage (outdoor stage), Ligon Chapel in Flowers Hall, Smith Music Building, Delchamps Student Center, excellent outdoor athletic facilities, United Methodist archives. **Computers:** *Recommended operating system:* Windows 95. School-owned computers available for student use.

EXTRACURRICULARS

Activities: Choral groups, concert band, dance, drama/theater, jazz band, literary magazine, music ensembles, musical theater, opera, student government, student newspaper, yearbook. **Organizations:** 50 registered organizations, 14 honor societies, 4 religious organizations, 2 fraternities (26% men join), 3 sororities (25% women join). **Athletics (Intercollegiate):** *Men:* baseball, basketball, cross-country, golf, soccer, tennis. *Women:* basketball, cross-country, soccer, softball, tennis, volleyball.

ADMISSIONS

Selectivity Rating: 72 (of 100). **Freshman Academic Profile:** Average high school GPA 3.4. 49% in top 10% of high school class, 73% in top 25% of high school class, 93% in top 50% of high school class. 75% from public high schools. Average SAT I Math 570, SAT I Math middle 50% range 520-610. Average SAT I Verbal 580, SAT I Verbal middle 50% range 480-610. Average ACT 24, ACT middle 50% range 21-27. TOEFL required of all international applicants, minimum TOEFL 500. **Basis for Candidate Selection:** *Very important factors considered include:* secondary school record, standardized test scores. *Important factors considered include:* essays. *Other factors considered include:* alumni/ae relation, character/personal qualities, class rank, extracurricular activities, interview, minority status, recommendations, talent/ability, volunteer work, work experience. **Freshman Admission Requirements:** High school diploma or GED is required. *Academic units required/recommended:* 15 total recommended; 4 English recommended, 3 math recommended, 2 science recommended, 2 science lab recommended, 2 foreign language recommended, 2 social studies recommended, 2 history recommended. **Freshman Admission Statistics:** 579 applied, 82% accepted, 32% of those accepted enrolled. **Transfer Admission Requirements:** *Items required:* high school transcript, college transcript, standardized test scores. Minimum high school GPA of 2.2 required. Minimum college GPA of 2.2 required. Lowest grade transferable C. **General Admission Information:** Application fee $25. Priority application deadline May 1. Nonfall registration accepted. Admission may be deferred for a maximum of 1 year. Credit and/or placement offered for CEEB Advanced Placement tests.

COSTS AND FINANCIAL AID

Tuition $11,960. Room & board $5,820. Required fees $1,150. Average book expense $700. **Required Forms and Deadlines:** FAFSA, institution's own financial aid form, and state aid form. Priority filing deadline April 15. **Notification of Awards:** Applicants will be notified of awards on or about March 1. **Types of Aid:** *Need-based scholarships/grants:* Pell, SEOG, state scholarships/grants, private scholarships, the school's own gift aid. *Loans:* FFEL Subsidized Stafford, FFEL Unsubsidized Stafford, FFEL PLUS, Federal Perkins, college/university loans from institutional funds, nonparent co-signed loans. **Student Employment:** Federal Work-Study Program available. Institutional employment available. Off-campus job opportunities are excellent. **Financial Aid Statistics:** 62% freshmen, 65% undergrads receive some form of aid. Average freshman grant $8,161. Average freshman loan $3,974. Average income from on-campus job $2,500. **Financial Aid Phone:** 334-833-4428.

HUNTINGTON COLLEGE

2303 College Avenue, Huntington, IN 46750
Phone: 260-359-4000 **E-mail:** admissions@huntington.edu **CEEB Code:** 1304
Fax: 260-358-3699 **Web:** www.huntington.edu **ACT Code:** 1202

This private school, which is affiliated with the Protestant Church, was founded in 1897. It has a 170-acre campus.

STUDENTS AND FACULTY

Enrollment: 868. **Student Body:** Male 42%, female 58%, out-of-state 44%, international 2%. **Ethnic Representation:** African American 1%, Caucasian

98%, Hispanic 1%. **Retention and Graduation:** 75% freshmen return for sophomore year. 45% freshmen graduate within 4 years. **Faculty:** Student/faculty ratio 16:1. 56 full-time faculty, 80% hold PhDs. 97% faculty teach undergrads.

ACADEMICS

Degrees: Associate's, bachelor's, diploma, master's, post-bachelor's certificate. **Academic Requirements:** General education including some course work in arts/fine arts, English (including composition), foreign languages, history, humanities, mathematics, philosophy, sciences (biological or physical), social science, Bible and religion. **Classes:** 10-19 students in an average class. 10-19 students in an average lab/discussion section. **Majors with Highest Enrollment:** Business/managerial economics; elementary education and teaching; theological and ministerial studies. **Disciplines with Highest Percentage of Degrees Awarded:** Education 23%, business/marketing 22%, physical sciences 14%, visual and performing arts 10%, social sciences and history 7%. **Special Study Options:** Accelerated program, cross registration, double major, dual enrollment, English as a second language, independent study, internships, study abroad, teacher certification program.

FACILITIES

Housing: All-female, all-male, apartments for married students, apartments for single students. Single undergraduates must live in resident halls or with parents. **Library Holdings:** 164,874 bound volumes. 315 periodicals. 17,681 microforms. 4,323 audiovisuals. **Special Academic Facilities/Equipment:** Thornhill Nature Preserve. **Computers:** School-owned computers available for student use.

EXTRACURRICULARS

Activities: Choral groups, concert band, drama/theater, jazz band, literary magazine, music ensembles, musical theater, pep band, radio station, student government, student newspaper, symphony orchestra, television station, yearbook. **Organizations:** 14 registered organizations, 5 honor societies, 4 religious organizations, 1 sorority. **Athletics (Intercollegiate):** *Men:* baseball, basketball, cheerleading, cross-country, golf, indoor track, soccer, tennis, track & field. *Women:* basketball, cheerleading, cross-country, golf, indoor track, soccer, softball, tennis, track & field, volleyball.

ADMISSIONS

Selectivity Rating: 76 (of 100). **Freshman Academic Profile:** Average high school GPA 3.6. 30% in top 10% of high school class, 57% in top 25% of high school class, 81% in top 50% of high school class. 88% from public high schools. Average SAT I Math 525, SAT I Math middle 50% range 430-620. Average SAT I Verbal 520, SAT I Verbal middle 50% range 420-650. Average ACT 23, ACT middle 50% range 19-29. TOEFL required of all international applicants, minimum TOEFL 550. **Basis for Candidate Selection:** *Very important factors considered include:* secondary school record, standardized test scores. *Important factors considered include:* class rank, essays, religious affiliation/commitment. *Other factors considered include:* alumni/ae relation, character/personal qualities, extracurricular activities, geographical residence, interview, minority status, recommendations, state residency, talent/ability, volunteer work, work experience. **Freshman Admission Requirements:** High school diploma or GED is required. *Academic units required/recommended:* 4 English required, 3 math required, 3 science required, 2 science lab required, 2 foreign language required, 2 social studies required, 2 history required. **Freshman Admission Statistics:** 713 applied, 98% accepted, 34% of those accepted enrolled. **Transfer Admission Requirements:** *Items required:* high school transcript, college transcript, essay. Minimum high school GPA of 2.3 required. Minimum college GPA of 2.0 required. Lowest grade transferable C. **General Admission Information:** Application fee $20. Priority application deadline March 2. Regular application deadline August 2. Nonfall registration accepted. Admission may be deferred for a maximum of 2 years. Credit and/or placement offered for CEEB Advanced Placement tests.

COSTS AND FINANCIAL AID

Average book expense $700. **Required Forms and Deadlines:** FAFSA. No deadline for regular filing. Priority filing deadline March 1. **Notification of Awards:** Applicants will be notified of awards on a rolling basis beginning on or about March 1. **Types of Aid:** *Need-based scholarships/grants:* Pell, SEOG, state scholarships/grants, private scholarships, the school's own gift aid. *Loans:* FFEL Subsidized Stafford, FFEL Unsubsidized Stafford, FFEL PLUS, Federal Perkins. **Student Employment:** Federal Work-Study Program available. Institutional employment available. Off-campus job opportunities are good. **Financial Aid Statistics:** 73% freshmen, 63% undergrads receive some form of aid. Average freshman grant $4,294. Average freshman loan $3,225. Average income from on-campus job $1,200. **Financial Aid Phone:** 260-359-4015.

HURON UNIVERSITY

333 9th Street, SW, Huron, SD 57350
Phone: 605-352-8721 **E-mail:** admissions@huron.edu **CEEB Code:** 6279
Fax: 605-352-7421 **Web:** www.huron.edu **ACT Code:** 3912

This public school was founded in 1883. It has a 15-acre campus.

STUDENTS AND FACULTY

Enrollment: 544. **Student Body:** Male 50%, female 50%, out-of-state 53%, international students represent 10 countries. **Ethnic Representation:** African American 11%, Asian 1%, Caucasian 79%, Hispanic 6%, Native American 3%. **Retention and Graduation:** 47% freshmen return for sophomore year. 20% grads go on to further study within 1 year. 20% grads pursue business degrees. 1% grads pursue law degrees. **Faculty:** Student/faculty ratio 12:1. 18 full-time faculty, 27% hold PhDs. 100% faculty teach undergrads.

ACADEMICS

Degrees: Associate's, bachelor's, master's. **Academic Requirements:** General education including some course work in arts/fine arts, computer literacy, English (including composition), history, humanities, mathematics, philosophy, sciences (biological or physical). **Classes:** 10-19 students in an average class. 10-19 students in an average lab/discussion section. **Disciplines with Highest Percentage of Degrees Awarded:** Business/marketing 23%, education 13%, protective services/public administration 8%, parks and recreation 4%, computer and information sciences 2%. **Special Study Options:** Accelerated program, cooperative (work-study) program, double major, independent study, internships, study abroad, teacher certification program.

FACILITIES

Housing: All-female, all-male, apartments for single students. **Library Holdings:** 65,000 bound volumes. 200,000 periodicals. **Computers:** School-owned computers available for student use.

EXTRACURRICULARS

Activities: Concert band, dance, jazz band, marching band, pep band, student government, student newspaper. **Organizations:** 10 registered organizations, 8 honor societies, 3 religious organizations, 15 fraternity. **Athletics (Intercollegiate):** *Men:* baseball, basketball, cheerleading, cross-country, football, indoor track, soccer, track & field, wrestling. *Women:* basketball, cheerleading, cross-country, indoor track, soccer, softball, track & field, volleyball.

ADMISSIONS

Selectivity Rating: 64 (of 100). **Freshman Academic Profile:** 20% in top 10% of high school class, 40% in top 25% of high school class, 90% in top 50% of high school class. Average ACT 22. TOEFL required of all international applicants, minimum TOEFL 575. **Basis for Candidate Selection:** *Very important factors considered include:* secondary school record. *Important factors considered include:* character/personal qualities, class rank, extracurricular activities, interview, recommendations, standardized test scores, talent/ability. *Other factors considered include:* alumni/ae relation, essays, minority status, state residency, volunteer work, work experience. **Freshman Admission Requirements:** High school diploma or GED is required. *Academic units required/recommended:* 27 total recommended; 4 English recommended, 4 math recommended, 4 science recommended, 2 science lab recommended, 1 foreign language recommended, 4 social studies recommended, 4 history recommended, 2 elective recommended. **Freshman Admission Statistics:** 400 applied, 94% accepted, 65% of those accepted enrolled. **Transfer Admission Requirements:** *Items required:* high school transcript, college transcript. Minimum high school GPA of 2.0 required. Minimum college GPA of 2.0 required. Lowest grade transferable C. **General Admission Information:** Application fee $35. Nonfall registration accepted. Admission may be deferred. Credit and/or placement offered for CEEB Advanced Placement tests.

COSTS AND FINANCIAL AID

Room & board $2,850. Required fees $250. Average book expense $1,000. **Required Forms and Deadlines:** FAFSA. No deadline for regular filing. **Types of Aid:** *Need-based scholarships/grants:* Pell, SEOG, the school's own gift aid. *Loans:* FFEL Subsidized Stafford, FFEL Unsubsidized Stafford, FFEL PLUS, Federal Perkins, alternative loans, South Dakota State Board of Nursing. **Student Employment:** Federal Work-Study Program available. Institutional employment available. Off-campus job opportunities are good. **Financial Aid Statistics:** 83% freshmen, 88% undergrads receive some form of aid. Average freshman grant $1,800. Average freshman loan $1,807. Average income from on-campus job $1,800. **Financial Aid Phone:** 605-352-8721.

HUSSON COLLEGE

One College Circle, Bangor, ME 04401
Phone: 207-941-7100 **E-mail:** admit@husson.edu **CEEB Code:** 3440
Fax: 207-941-7935 **Web:** www.husson.edu **ACT Code:** 1646

This private school was founded in 1898. It has a 170-acre campus.

STUDENTS AND FACULTY

Enrollment: 1,609. **Student Body:** Male 37%, female 63%, out-of-state 14%, international 3% (15 countries represented). **Ethnic Representation:** African American 1%, Asian 2%, Caucasian 95%, Hispanic 1%, Native American 1%. **Retention and Graduation:** 67% freshmen return for sophomore year. 3% grads go on to further study within 1 year. 2% grads pursue business degrees. 1% grads pursue law degrees. **Faculty:** Student/faculty ratio 19:1. 46 full-time faculty, 63% hold PhDs. 100% faculty teach undergrads.

ACADEMICS

Degrees: Associate's, bachelor's, master's, post-master's certificate. **Academic Requirements:** General education including some course work in arts/fine arts, computer literacy, English (including composition), humanities, mathematics, sciences (biological or physical), social science. **Classes:** 10-19 students in an average class. Under 10 students in an average lab/discussion section. **Majors with Highest Enrollment:** Nursing/registered nurse training (RN, ASN, BSN, MSN); business administration/management; computer systems analysis/analyst. **Disciplines with Highest Percentage of Degrees Awarded:** Business/marketing 59%, health professions and related sciences 19%, computer and information sciences 10%, social sciences and history 4%, psychology 3%. **Special Study Options:** Cooperative (work-study) program, distance learning, English as a second language, independent study, internships, liberal arts/career combination, student-designed major, teacher certification program, weekend college.

FACILITIES

Housing: Coed, fraternities and/or sororities. **Library Holdings:** 36,294 bound volumes. 500 periodicals. 12,838 microforms. 220 audiovisuals. **Computers:** School-owned computers available for student use.

EXTRACURRICULARS

Activities: Drama/theater, literary magazine, radio station, student government, student newspaper, yearbook. **Organizations:** 26 registered organizations, 1 religious organization, 4 fraternities (2% men join), 3 sororities (4% women join). **Athletics (Intercollegiate):** *Men:* baseball, basketball, cross-country, football, golf, soccer. *Women:* basketball, cross-country, field hockey, golf, soccer, softball, swimming, volleyball.

ADMISSIONS

Selectivity Rating: 64 (of 100). **Freshman Academic Profile:** Average high school GPA 3.1. 8% in top 10% of high school class, 24% in top 25% of high school class, 65% in top 50% of high school class. 92% from public high schools. Average SAT I Math 464, SAT I Math middle 50% range 490-490. Average SAT I Verbal 456, SAT I Verbal middle 50% range 400-500. Average ACT 24, ACT middle 50% range 17-26. TOEFL required of all international applicants, minimum TOEFL 500. **Basis for Candidate Selection:** *Very important factors considered include:* interview, recommendations, secondary school record. *Important factors considered include:* character/personal qualities, class rank, essays, extracurricular activities, standardized test scores. *Other factors considered include:* alumni/ae relation, volunteer work, work experience. **Freshman Admission Requirements:** High school diploma or GED is required. *Academic units required/recommended:* 16 total recommended; 4 English recommended, 3 math recommended, 3 science recommended, 2 science lab recommended, 1 social studies recommended, 1 history recommended. **Freshman Admission Statistics:** 500 applied, 99% accepted, 43% of those accepted enrolled. **Transfer Admission Requirements:** *Items required:* high school transcript, college transcript, essay. Minimum college GPA of 2.0 required. Lowest grade transferable C. **General Admission Information:** Application fee $25. Priority application deadline April 1. Nonfall registration accepted. Admission may be deferred for a maximum of 1 year. Credit and/or placement offered for CEEB Advanced Placement tests.

COSTS AND FINANCIAL AID

Tuition $9,840. Room & board $5,350. Required fees $150. Average book expense $900. **Required Forms and Deadlines:** FAFSA. No deadline for regular filing. Priority filing deadline April 15. **Notification of Awards:** Applicants will be notified of awards on a rolling basis beginning on or about March 1. **Types of Aid:** *Need-based scholarships/grants:* Pell, SEOG, state scholarships/grants, private scholarships, the school's own gift aid. *Loans:* FFEL Subsidized Stafford, FFEL Unsubsidized Stafford, FFEL PLUS, Federal Perkins, state loans. **Student Employment:** Federal Work-Study Program available. Institutional employment available. Off-campus job opportunities are excellent. **Financial Aid Statistics:** 50% freshmen, 58% undergrads receive some form of aid. Average freshman grant $8,366. Average freshman loan $2,625. Average income from on-campus job $1,300. **Financial Aid Phone:** 207-941-7156.

HUSTON-TILLOTSON COLLEGE

900 Chicon Street, Austin, TX 78702-2795
Phone: 512-505-3028 **E-mail:** thshakir@htc.edu **CEEB Code:** 6280
Fax: 512-505-3192 **Web:** www.htc.edu **ACT Code:** 4104

This private school was founded in 1875. It has a 35-acre campus.

STUDENTS AND FACULTY

Enrollment: 554. **Student Body:** Male 50%, female 50%, out-of-state 7%, intenational 6% (international students represent 13 countries). **Ethnic Representation:** African American 88%, Caucasian 3%, Asian 1%, Hispanic 8%. **Retention and Graduation:** 54% freshmen return for sophomore year. 9% freshmen graduate within 4 years. **Faculty:** Student/faculty ratio 12:1. 36 full-time faculty, 61% hold PhDs. 100% faculty teach undergrads.

ACADEMICS

Degrees: Bachelor's. **Academic Requirements:** General education including some course work in arts/fine arts, computer literacy, English (including composition), foreign languages, history, humanities, mathematics, philosophy, sciences (biological or physical), social science. **Majors with Highest Enrollment:** Business/commerce, general; computer and information sciences, general; education, general. **Disciplines with Highest Percentage of Degrees Awarded:** Business/marketing 33%, social sciences and history 12%, computer and information sciences 11%, education 8%, psychology 7%. **Special Study Options:** Cross registration, distance learning, double major, dual enrollment, external degree program, honors program, independent study, internships, study abroad, teacher certification program.

FACILITIES

Housing: All-female, all-male. **Library Holdings:** 70,542 bound volumes. 349 periodicals. 68,340 microforms. 8,585 audiovisuals. **Computers:** School-owned computers available for student use.

EXTRACURRICULARS

Activities: Choral groups, literary magazine, music ensembles, student government, student newspaper, yearbook. **Organizations:** 20 registered organizations, 5 honor societies, 5 religious organizations. 4% of men are in fraternities. 5% of women are in sororities. **Athletics (Intercollegiate):** *Men:* baseball, basketball, soccer, track & field. *Women:* basketball, track & field, volleyball.

ADMISSIONS

Selectivity Rating: 63 (of 100). **Freshman Academic Profile:** Average high school GPA 3.0. 3% in top 10% of high school class, 17% in top 25% of high school class, 40% in top 50% of high school class. Average SAT I Math 381, SAT I Math middle 50% range 350-440. Average SAT I Verbal 389, SAT I Verbal middle 50% range 360-410. Average ACT 16, ACT middle 50% range 15-17. TOEFL required of all international applicants, minimum TOEFL 500. **Basis for Candidate Selection:** *Important factors considered include:* class rank, essays, secondary school record, standardized test scores. *Other factors considered include:* character/personal qualities, extracurricular activities, talent/ability. **Freshman Admission Requirements:** High school diploma or GED is required. *Academic units required/recommended:* 22 total required; 4 English required, 3 math required, 2 science required, 2 science lab required, 2 foreign language recommended, 2 social studies required, 1 elective required. **Freshman Admission Statistics:** 326 applied, 93% accepted, 44% of those accepted enrolled. **Transfer Admission Requirements:** *Items required:* college transcript, essay. Minimum college GPA of 2.5 required. Lowest grade transferable C. **General Admission Information:** Application fee $25. Regular application deadline rolling. Priority application deadline March 1. Nonfall registration accepted. Admission may be deferred. Credit and/or placement offered for CEEB Advanced Placement tests.

COSTS AND FINANCIAL AID

Tuition $7,020. Room & board $5,027. Required fees $1,216. Average book expense $645. **Types of Aid:** *Need-based scholarships/grants:* Pell, SEOG, state scholarships/grants, private scholarships, the school's own gift aid, United Negro College Fund. *Loans:* FFEL Subsidized Stafford, FFEL Unsubsidized Stafford, FFEL PLUS. **Student Employment:** Federal Work-Study Program available. Off-campus job opportunities are good. **Financial Aid Phone:** 512-505-3030.

IDAHO STATE UNIVERSITY

Admissions Office, Campus Box 8270, Pocatello, ID 83209-8270
Phone: 208-282-2475 **E-mail:** info@isu.edu **CEEB Code:** 4355
Fax: 208-282-4231 **Web:** www.isu.edu **ACT Code:** 918

This public school was founded in 1901. It has a 972-acre campus.

STUDENTS AND FACULTY

Enrollment: 11,330. **Student Body:** Male 45%, female 55%, out-of-state 4%, international 2% (56 countries represented). **Ethnic Representation:** African American 1%, Asian 1%, Caucasian 90%, Hispanic 4%, Native American 2%. **Retention and Graduation:** 64% freshmen return for sophomore year. **Faculty:** Student/faculty ratio 17:1. 538 full-time faculty, 60% hold PhDs.

ACADEMICS

Degrees: Associate's, bachelor's, certificate, diploma, doctoral, first professional, master's, post-bachelor's certificate, post-master's certificate. **Academic Requirements:** General education including some course work in arts/fine arts, English (including composition), foreign languages, humanities, mathematics, philosophy, sciences (biological or physical). **Classes:** Under 10 students in an average class. **Majors with Highest Enrollment:** Elementary education and teaching; biology/biological sciences, general; social work. **Disciplines with Highest Percentage of Degrees Awarded:** Education 21%, business/marketing 16%, health professions and related sciences 14%, biological life sciences 12%, social sciences and history 6%. **Special Study Options:** Cross registration, distance learning, double major, English as a second language, student exchange program (domestic), external degree program, honors program, independent study, internships, student-designed major, study abroad, teacher certification program.

FACILITIES

Housing: Coed, all-female, all-male, apartments for married students, apartments for single students, housing for disabled students, fraternities and/or sororities. **Library Holdings:** 682,984 bound volumes. 2,121 periodicals. 1,933,536 microforms. 701 audiovisuals. **Special Academic Facilities/ Equipment:** Museum of natural history, Idaho Accelerator Center. **Computers:** *Recommended operating system:* Windows 95. School-owned computers available for student use.

EXTRACURRICULARS

Activities: Choral groups, concert band, dance, drama/theater, marching band, musical theater, pep band, radio station, student government, student newspaper, symphony orchestra, television station, yearbook. **Organizations:** 140 registered organizations, 11 honor societies, 8 religious organizations, 3 fraternities (1% men join), 3 sororities (1% women join). **Athletics (Intercollegiate):** *Men:* basketball, cross-country, football, golf, tennis, track & field. *Women:* basketball, cross-country, golf, soccer, tennis, track & field, volleyball.

ADMISSIONS

Selectivity Rating: 66 (of 100). **Freshman Academic Profile:** 3% in top 10% of high school class, 13% in top 25% of high school class, 38% in top 50% of high school class. Average ACT 21. TOEFL required of all international applicants, minimum TOEFL 500. **Basis for Candidate Selection:** *Very important factors considered include:* secondary school record. *Important factors considered include:* standardized test scores. *Other factors considered include:* alumni/ae relation, character/personal qualities, class rank, recommendations, talent/ability. **Freshman Admission Requirements:** High school diploma or GED is required. *Academic units required/recommended:* 4 English required, 3 math required, 3 science required, 1 science lab required, 1 foreign language required, 2 social studies required. **Transfer Admission Requirements:** *Items required:* college transcript. Minimum college GPA of 2.0 required. Lowest grade transferable D. **General Admission Information:** Application fee $30. Priority application deadline March 1. Regular application deadline August 1. Nonfall registration accepted. Admission may be deferred. Credit offered for CEEB Advanced Placement tests.

COSTS AND FINANCIAL AID

Out-of-state tuition $6,240. Room & board $4,410. Required fees $3,686. Average book expense $700. **Required Forms and Deadlines:** FAFSA. Financial aid filing deadline June 30. Priority filing deadline March 15. **Notification of Awards:** Applicants will be notified of awards on or about May 1. **Types of Aid:** *Need-based scholarships/grants:* Pell, SEOG, state scholarships/grants, private scholarships. *Loans:* Direct Subsidized Stafford, Direct Unsubsidized Stafford, Direct PLUS, Federal Perkins. **Student Employment:** Federal Work-Study Program available. Institutional employment available. Off-campus job opportunities are good. **Financial Aid Statistics:** 57% freshmen, 46% undergrads receive some form of aid. **Financial Aid Phone:** 208-282-2756.

ILLINOIS COLLEGE

1101 West College, Jacksonville, IL 62650
Phone: 217-245-3030 **E-mail:** admissions@hilltop.ic.edu **CEEB Code:** 1315
Fax: 217-245-3034 **Web:** www.ic.edu **ACT Code:** 1034

This private school, which is affiliated with the Presbyterian Church, was founded in 1829. It has a 62-acre campus.

STUDENTS AND FACULTY

Enrollment: 937. **Student Body:** Male 45%, female 55%, out-of-state 5%, international 1%. **Ethnic Representation:** African American 3%, Caucasian 95%, Hispanic 1%, Native American 1%. **Retention and Graduation:** 70% freshmen return for sophomore year. 41% freshmen graduate within 4 years. 22% grads go on to further study within 1 year. 2% grads pursue business degrees. 5% grads pursue law degrees. 4% grads pursue medical degrees. **Faculty:** Student/faculty ratio 14:1. 55 full-time faculty, 80% hold PhDs. 100% faculty teach undergrads.

ACADEMICS

Degrees: Bachelor's. **Academic Requirements:** General education including some course work in arts/fine arts, English (including composition), history, humanities, mathematics, sciences (biological or physical), social science, speech. **Classes:** 10-19 students in an average class. 10-19 students in an average lab/discussion section. **Disciplines with Highest Percentage of Degrees Awarded:** Education 19%, business/marketing 19%, biological life sciences 11%, social sciences and history 9%, English 8%. **Special Study Options:** Cross registration, double major, dual enrollment, independent study, internships, liberal arts/career combination, student-designed major, study abroad, teacher certification program.

FACILITIES

Housing: Coed, all-female, all-male. **Library Holdings:** 145,500 bound volumes. 620 periodicals. 127 microforms. 3,000 audiovisuals. **Special Academic Facilities/Equipment:** Art gallery, language lab. **Computers:** School-owned computers available for student use.

EXTRACURRICULARS

Activities: Choral groups, concert band, drama/theater, literary magazine, music ensembles, pep band, student government, student newspaper, television station, yearbook. **Organizations:** 72 registered organizations, 12 honor societies, 3 religious organizations, 4 fraternities (20% men join), 3 sororities (18% women join). **Athletics (Intercollegiate):** *Men:* baseball, basketball, cross-country, football, golf, indoor track, soccer, tennis, track & field, wrestling. *Women:* basketball, cheerleading, cross-country, golf, indoor track, soccer, softball, tennis, track & field, volleyball.

ADMISSIONS

Selectivity Rating: 81 (of 100). **Freshman Academic Profile:** Average high school GPA 3.5. 15% in top 10% of high school class, 47% in top 25% of high school class, 76% in top 50% of high school class. 80% from public high schools. Average SAT I Math 567, SAT I Math middle 50% range 520-610. Average SAT I Verbal 565, SAT I Verbal middle 50% range 510-630. Average ACT 23, ACT middle 50% range 20-25. TOEFL required of all international applicants, minimum TOEFL 550. **Basis for Candidate Selection:** *Very important factors considered include:* class rank, secondary school record. *Important factors considered include:* character/personal qualities, recommendations, standardized test scores. *Other factors considered include:* essays, extracurricular activities, geographical residence, interview, minority status. **Freshman Admission Requirements:** High school diploma or GED is required. *Academic units required/recommended:* 15 total required; 3 English required, 4 English recommended, 3 math required, 7 elective required. **Freshman Admission Statistics:** 970 applied, 74% accepted, 33% of those accepted enrolled. **Transfer Admission Requirements:** *Items required:* high school transcript, college transcript, standardized test scores. Minimum college GPA of 2.0 required. Lowest grade transferable C. **General Admission Information:** Application fee $10. Priority application deadline June 1. Nonfall registration accepted. Admission may be deferred for a maximum of 1 year. Credit and/or placement offered for CEEB Advanced Placement tests.

COSTS AND FINANCIAL AID

Tuition $10,735. Room & board $4,725. Average book expense $600. **Required Forms and Deadlines:** FAFSA. Priority filing deadline March 15. **Notification of Awards:** Applicants will be notified of awards on a rolling basis beginning on or about March 15. **Types of Aid:** *Need-based scholarships/ grants:* Pell, SEOG, state scholarships/grants, private scholarships, the school's own gift aid. *Loans:* FFEL Subsidized Stafford, FFEL Unsubsidized Stafford, FFEL PLUS, Federal Perkins. **Student Employment:** Federal Work-Study

Program available. Institutional employment available. Off-campus job opportunities are good. **Financial Aid Statistics:** 79% freshmen, 74% undergrads receive some form of aid. Average freshman grant $5,372. Average freshman loan $3,204. Average income from on-campus job $800. **Financial Aid Phone:** 217-245-3035.

THE ILLINOIS INSTITUTE OF ART SCHAUMBURG

1000 Plaza Drive, Suite 100, Schaumburg, IL 60173-4990
Phone: 847-619-3450
Fax: 847-619-3064 **ACT Code:** 6863

This private school was founded in 1918.

STUDENTS AND FACULTY

Ethnic Representation: African American 3%, Asian 10%, Caucasian 80%, Hispanic 7%. **Faculty:** Student/faculty ratio 20:1. 30 full-time faculty, 16% hold PhDs. 100% faculty teach undergrads.

ACADEMICS

Degrees: Bachelor's, certificate. **Academic Requirements:** General education including some course work in arts/fine arts, computer literacy, humanities, mathematics, philosophy, sciences (biological or physical), social science. **Disciplines with Highest Percentage of Degrees Awarded:** Other 47%.

FACILITIES

Housing: Apartments for single students. **Library Holdings:** 5,500 bound volumes. 150 periodicals. 225 audiovisuals. **Computers:** School-owned computers available for student use.

EXTRACURRICULARS

Activities: Student newspaper. **Organizations:** 5 registered organizations.

ADMISSIONS

Selectivity Rating: 60 (of 100). **Freshman Academic Profile:** TOEFL required of all international applicants. **Basis for Candidate Selection:** *Very important factors considered include:* class rank. *Important factors considered include:* alumni/ae relation, recommendations. *Other factors considered include:* extracurricular activities, minority status, secondary school record, standardized test scores, talent/ability, work experience. **Freshman Admission Requirements:** High school diploma or GED is required. **Freshman Admission Statistics:** 300 applied. **Transfer Admission Requirements:** *Items required:* college transcript, essay. Lowest grade transferable C. **General Admission Information:** Application fee $50. Nonfall registration accepted. Admission may be deferred for a maximum of 3 years. Credit and/or placement offered for CEEB Advanced Placement tests.

COSTS AND FINANCIAL AID

Average book expense $75. **Required Forms and Deadlines:** FAFSA. No deadline for regular filing. **Notification of Awards:** Applicants will be notified of awards on a rolling basis beginning on or about January 1. **Types of Aid:** *Need-based scholarships/grants:* Pell, SEOG, the school's own gift aid. *Loans:* Direct Subsidized Stafford, Direct Unsubsidized Stafford, Direct PLUS. **Student Employment:** Institutional employment available. Off-campus job opportunities are excellent. **Financial Aid Statistics:** Average freshman loan $2,625. **Financial Aid Phone:** 847-619-3450.

ILLINOIS INSTITUTE OF TECHNOLOGY

10 West 33rd Street, Chicago, IL 60616
Phone: 312-567-3025 **E-mail:** admission@iit.edu **CEEB Code:** 1318
Fax: 312-567-6939 **Web:** www.iit.edu **ACT Code:** 1040

This private school was founded in 1892. It has a 120-acre campus.

STUDENTS AND FACULTY

Enrollment: 1,905. **Student Body:** Male 76%, female 24%, out-of-state 46%, international 16%. **Ethnic Representation:** African American 7%, Asian 20%, Caucasian 57%, Hispanic 10%. **Retention and Graduation:** 85% freshmen return for sophomore year. 34% freshmen graduate within 4 years. 55% grads go on to further study within 1 year. **Faculty:** Student/faculty ratio 12:1. 339 full-time faculty, 97% hold PhDs. 74% faculty teach undergrads.

ACADEMICS

Degrees: Bachelor's, certificate, doctoral, first professional, master's, post-bachelor's certificate. **Academic Requirements:** General education including some course work in computer literacy, English (including composition), humanities, mathematics, sciences (biological or physical), social science. **Classes:** 10-19 students in an average class. 10-19 students in an average lab/discussion section. **Majors with Highest Enrollment:** Architecture (BArch, BA/BS, MArch, MA/MS, PhD); computer science; electrical, electronics, and communications engineering. **Disciplines with Highest Percentage of Degrees Awarded:** Education 65%, computer and information sciences 14%, architecture 13%, engineering/engineering technology 2%, biological life sciences 2%. **Special Study Options:** Accelerated program, cooperative (work-study) program, distance learning, double major, student exchange program (domestic), honors program, internships, study abroad, teacher certification program.

FACILITIES

Housing: Coed, all-female, all-male, apartments for married students, apartments for single students, fraternities and/or sororities, law house. **Library Holdings:** 854,771 bound volumes. 773 periodicals. 184,326 microforms. 52,368 audiovisuals. **Special Academic Facilities/Equipment:** Environment chamber, wind tunnel, extrusion press, railroad simulator, model railroad, electron microscope. **Computers:** School-owned computers available for student use.

EXTRACURRICULARS

Activities: Choral groups, concert band, dance, drama/theater, jazz band, music ensembles, musical theater, radio station, student government, student newspaper, student-run film society. **Organizations:** 80 registered organizations, 2 honor societies, 8 religious organizations, 7 fraternities (19% men join), 3 sororities (10% women join). **Athletics (Intercollegiate):** *Men:* baseball, basketball, cross-country, diving, soccer, swimming. *Women:* basketball, cross-country, diving, soccer, swimming, volleyball.

ADMISSIONS

Selectivity Rating: 84 (of 100). **Freshman Academic Profile:** Average high school GPA 3.6. 40% in top 10% of high school class, 74% in top 25% of high school class, 94% in top 50% of high school class. 71% from public high schools. Average SAT I Math 681, SAT I Math middle 50% range 630-730. Average SAT I Verbal 602, SAT I Verbal middle 50% range 550-650. Average ACT 28, ACT middle 50% range 25-31. TOEFL required of all international applicants, minimum TOEFL 550. **Basis for Candidate Selection:** *Very important factors considered include:* secondary school record, standardized test scores. *Important factors considered include:* character/personal qualities, class rank, essays, recommendations. *Other factors considered include:* alumni/ae relation, extracurricular activities, interview, talent/ability, volunteer work, work experience. **Freshman Admission Requirements:** High school diploma is required and GED is not accepted. *Academic units required/recommended:* 4 English required, 4 math required, 4 math recommended, 3 science required, 2 science lab required, 2 social studies required. **Freshman Admission Statistics:** 2,309 applied, 67% accepted, 24% of those accepted enrolled. **Transfer Admission Requirements:** *Items required:* college transcript, essay, statement of good standing from prior school. Minimum college GPA of 3.0 required. Lowest grade transferable C. **General Admission Information:** Application fee $40. Nonfall registration accepted. Admission may be deferred for a maximum of 2 years. Credit and/or placement offered for CEEB Advanced Placement tests.

COSTS AND FINANCIAL AID

Tuition $19,775. Room & board $6,282. Required fees $556. Average book expense $1,000. **Required Forms and Deadlines:** FAFSA. Priority filing deadline April 15. **Notification of Awards:** Applicants will be notified of awards on a rolling basis beginning on or about March 1. **Types of Aid:** *Need-based scholarships/grants:* Pell, SEOG, state scholarships/grants, private scholarships, the school's own gift aid. *Loans:* FFEL Subsidized Stafford, FFEL Unsubsidized Stafford, FFEL PLUS, Federal Perkins, college/university loans from institutional funds. **Student Employment:** Federal Work-Study Program available. Institutional employment available. Off-campus job opportunities are excellent. **Financial Aid Statistics:** 63% freshmen, 54% undergrads receive some form of aid. Average freshman grant $14,695. Average freshman loan $7,534. Average income from on-campus job $1,702. **Financial Aid Phone:** 312-567-3025.

See page 1064.

ILLINOIS STATE UNIVERSITY

Admissions Office, Campus Box 2200, Normal, IL 61790-2200
Phone: 309-438-2181 **E-mail:** ugradadm@ilstu.edu **CEEB Code:** 1319
Fax: 309-438-3932 **Web:** www.ilstu.edu **ACT Code:** 1042

This public school was founded in 1857. It has an 850-acre campus.

STUDENTS AND FACULTY

Enrollment: 18,353. **Student Body:** Male 42%, female 58%, out-of-state 1%, international 1% (60 countries represented). **Ethnic Representation:** African American 6%, Asian 1%, Caucasian 90%, Hispanic 3%. **Retention and Graduation:** 80% freshmen return for sophomore year. 28% freshmen graduate within 4 years. **Faculty:** Student/faculty ratio 19:1. 847 full-time faculty, 83% hold PhDs. 93% faculty teach undergrads.

ACADEMICS

Degrees: Bachelor's, doctoral, master's, post-bachelor's certificate, post-master's certificate. **Academic Requirements:** General education including some course work in arts/fine arts, computer literacy, English (including composition), history, humanities, mathematics, philosophy, sciences (biological or physical), social science. **Classes:** 20-29 students in an average class. 20-29 students in an average lab/discussion section. **Majors with Highest Enrollment:** Business administration/management; special education, general; elementary education and teaching. **Disciplines with Highest Percentage of Degrees Awarded:** Education 23%, business/marketing 18%, social sciences and history 10%, communications/communication technologies 6%, protective services/public administration 6%. **Special Study Options:** Accelerated program, cooperative (work-study) program, distance learning, double major, dual enrollment, English as a second language, student exchange program (domestic), honors program, independent study, internships, student-designed major, study abroad, teacher certification program.

FACILITIES

Housing: Coed, all-female, apartments for married students, apartments for single students, housing for disabled students, housing for international students, fraternities and/or sororities. **Library Holdings:** 1,532,901 bound volumes. 4,873 periodicals. 2,122,235 microforms. 60,824 audiovisuals. **Special Academic Facilities/Equipment:** Art gallery, cultural museums, on-campus elementary and secondary schools, greenhouse, farm, planetarium. **Computers:** School-owned computers available for student use.

EXTRACURRICULARS

Activities: Choral groups, concert band, dance, drama/theater, jazz band, literary magazine, marching band, music ensembles, musical theater, pep band, radio station, student government, student newspaper, student-run film society, symphony orchestra, television station. **Organizations:** 270 registered organizations, 21 honor societies, 22 religious organizations, 21 fraternities (9% men join), 17 sororities (15% women join). **Athletics (Intercollegiate):** *Men:* baseball, basketball, cheerleading, cross-country, football, golf, indoor track, tennis, track & field. *Women:* basketball, cheerleading, cross-country, diving, golf, gymnastics, indoor track, soccer, softball, swimming, tennis, track & field, volleyball.

ADMISSIONS

Selectivity Rating: 71 (of 100). **Freshman Academic Profile:** 11% in top 10% of high school class, 39% in top 25% of high school class, 85% in top 50% of high school class. 89% from public high schools. Average ACT 23, ACT middle 50% range 20-25. TOEFL required of all international applicants, minimum TOEFL 550. **Basis for Candidate Selection:** *Important factors considered include:* class rank, secondary school record, standardized test scores. *Other factors considered include:* essays, extracurricular activities, talent/ability. **Freshman Admission Requirements:** High school diploma or GED is required. *Academic units required/recommended:* 15 total required; 4 English required, 3 math required, 2 science required, 2 science lab required, 2 foreign language required, 2 social studies required, 2 elective required. **Freshman Admission Statistics:** 9,070 applied, 81% accepted, 42% of those accepted enrolled. **Transfer Admission Requirements:** *Items required:* college transcript. Minimum college GPA of 2.0 required. Lowest grade transferable D. **General Admission Information:** Application fee $30. Priority application deadline December 31. Regular application deadline March 1. Nonfall registration accepted. Credit and/or placement offered for CEEB Advanced Placement tests.

COSTS AND FINANCIAL AID

In-state tuition $3,639. Out-of-state tuition $7,830. Room & board $5,062. Required fees $1,397. Average book expense $686. **Required Forms and Deadlines:** FAFSA. Priority filing deadline March 1. **Notification of Awards:** Applicants will be notified of awards on a rolling basis beginning on or about April 1. **Types of Aid:** *Need-based scholarships/grants:* Pell, SEOG, state scholarships/grants, private scholarships, the school's own gift aid, Federal Nursing. *Loans:* Direct Subsidized Stafford, Direct Unsubsidized Stafford, Direct PLUS, FFEL Subsidized Stafford, FFEL Unsubsidized Stafford, FFEL PLUS, Federal Perkins, Federal Nursing. **Student Employment:** Federal Work-Study Program available. Institutional employment available. Off-campus job opportunities are excellent. **Financial Aid Statistics:** 39% freshmen, 45% undergrads receive some form of aid. Average freshman grant $5,102. Average freshman loan $4,179. Average income from on-campus job $2,416. **Financial Aid Phone:** 309-438-2231.

ILLINOIS WESLEYAN UNIVERSITY

PO Box 2900, Bloomington, IL 61702-2900
Phone: 309-556-3031 **E-mail:** iwuadmit@titan.iwu.edu **CEEB Code:** 1320
Fax: 309-556-3411 **Web:** www.iwu.edu **ACT Code:** 1044

This private school, which is affiliated with the Methodist Church, was founded in 1850. It has a 79-acre campus.

STUDENTS AND FACULTY

Enrollment: 2,107. **Student Body:** Male 43%, female 57%, out-of-state 11%, international 2% (22 countries represented). **Ethnic Representation:** African American 3%, Asian 3%, Caucasian 88%, Hispanic 2%. **Retention and Graduation:** 76% freshmen graduate within 4 years. 28% grads go on to further study within 1 year. 2% grads pursue business degrees. 4% grads pursue law degrees. 3% grads pursue medical degrees. **Faculty:** Student/faculty ratio 12:1. 162 full-time faculty, 93% hold PhDs. 100% faculty teach undergrads.

ACADEMICS

Degrees: Bachelor's. **Academic Requirements:** General education including some course work in arts/fine arts, English (including composition), foreign languages, history, humanities, mathematics, philosophy, sciences (biological or physical), social science. Each student is required to take a gateway colloquia, which are small, discussion-oriented classes designed to develop students' proficiency in writing academic and public discourse. **Classes:** 10-19 students in an average class. 10-19 students in an average lab/discussion section. **Majors with Highest Enrollment:** Business administration/management; biology/biological sciences, general; music performance, general. **Disciplines with Highest Percentage of Degrees Awarded:** Business/marketing 25%, social sciences and history 18%, biological life sciences 10%, visual and performing arts 10%, psychology 6%. **Special Study Options:** Cooperative (work-study) program, double major, student exchange program (domestic), independent study, internships, student-designed major, study abroad, teacher certification program.

FACILITIES

Housing: Coed, housing for international students, fraternities and/or sororities. **Library Holdings:** 307,861 bound volumes. 14,264 periodicals. 16,434 microforms. 13,833 audiovisuals. **Special Academic Facilities/Equipment:** Observatory, computerized music lab, graphic design studio. **Computers:** School-owned computers available for student use.

EXTRACURRICULARS

Activities: Choral groups, concert band, dance, drama/theater, jazz band, literary magazine, music ensembles, musical theater, opera, pep band, radio station, student government, student newspaper, student-run film society, symphony orchestra, television station, yearbook. **Organizations:** 106 registered organizations, 40 honor societies, 8 religious organizations, 6 fraternities (30% men join), 5 sororities (41% women join). **Athletics (Intercollegiate):** *Men:* baseball, basketball, cheerleading, cross-country, diving, football, golf, indoor track, soccer, swimming, tennis, track & field. *Women:* basketball, cheerleading, cross-country, diving, golf, indoor track, soccer, softball, swimming, tennis, track & field, volleyball.

ADMISSIONS

Selectivity Rating: 91 (of 100). **Freshman Academic Profile:** 47% in top 10% of high school class, 83% in top 25% of high school class, 100% in top 50% of high school class. 82% from public high schools. Average SAT I Math 625, SAT I Math middle 50% range 590-690. Average SAT I Verbal 635, SAT I Verbal middle 50% range 580-670. Average ACT 28, ACT middle 50% range 26-30. TOEFL required of all international applicants, minimum TOEFL 550. **Basis for Candidate Selection:** *Very important factors considered include:* secondary school record. *Important factors considered include:* character/personal qualities, class rank, essays, recommendations, standardized test scores, talent/ability. *Other factors considered include:* alumni/ae relation, extracurricular activities, geographical residence, interview, minority status, volunteer work, work experience. **Freshman Admission Requirements:** High school diploma or GED is required. *Academic units required/recommended:* 4 English recommended, 3 math recommended, 3 science recommended, 2 science lab recommended, 3 foreign language recommended, 2 social studies recommended. **Freshman Admission Statistics:** 3,116 applied, 48% accepted, 39% of those accepted enrolled. **Transfer Admission Requirements:** *Items required:* high school transcript, college transcript, essay, standardized test scores. Minimum high school GPA of 2.0 required. Minimum college GPA of 2.0 required. Lowest grade transferable C-. **General Admission Information:** Priority application deadline November 1. Regular application deadline February 15. Nonfall registration accepted. Admission may be deferred for a maximum of 1 year. Credit and/or placement offered for CEEB Advanced Placement tests.

COSTS AND FINANCIAL AID

Tuition $24,390. Room & board $5,840. Required fees $150. Average book expense $650. **Required Forms and Deadlines:** FAFSA, institution's own financial aid form, CSS/Financial Aid PROFILE, business/farm supplement. Financial aid filing deadline March 1. **Notification of Awards:** Applicants will be notified of awards on a rolling basis beginning on or about January 1. **Types of Aid:** *Need-based scholarships/grants:* Pell, SEOG, state scholarships/grants, private scholarships, the school's own gift aid. *Loans:* FFEL Subsidized Stafford, FFEL Unsubsidized Stafford, FFEL PLUS, Federal Perkins, Federal Nursing, college/university loans from institutional funds. **Student Employment:** Federal Work-Study Program available. Institutional employment available. Off-campus job opportunities are good. **Financial Aid Statistics:** 56% freshmen, 54% undergrads receive some form of aid. Average freshman grant $11,835. Average freshman loan $2,816. Average income from on-campus job $1,531. **Financial Aid Phone:** 309-556-3096.

IMMACULATA UNIVERSITY

1145 King Road, PO Box 642, Immaculata, PA 19345-0642
Phone: 610-647-4400 **E-mail:** admiss@immaculata.edu **CEEB Code:** 2320
Fax: 610-640-0836 **Web:** www.immaculata.edu **ACT Code:** 3596

This private school, which is affiliated with the Roman Catholic Church, was founded in 1920. It has a 400-acre campus.

STUDENTS AND FACULTY

Enrollment: 2,768. **Student Body:** Male 17%, female 83%, out-of-state 18%, international 1% (27 countries represented). **Ethnic Representation:** African American 9%, Asian 2%, Caucasian 86%, Hispanic 2%. **Retention and Graduation:** 81% freshmen return for sophomore year. 84% freshmen graduate within 4 years. 21% grads go on to further study within 1 year. 8% grads pursue business degrees. 4% grads pursue law degrees. 4% grads pursue medical degrees. **Faculty:** Student/faculty ratio 13:1. 74 full-time faculty, 67% hold PhDs. 100% faculty teach undergrads.

ACADEMICS

Degrees: Associate's, bachelor's, doctoral, master's. **Academic Requirements:** General education including some course work in computer literacy, English (including composition), foreign languages, history, humanities, mathematics, philosophy, sciences (biological or physical), social science, theology. **Classes:** 10-19 students in an average class. **Disciplines with Highest Percentage of Degrees Awarded:** Health professions and related sciences 39%, business/marketing 31%, psychology 15%, biological life sciences 3%, computer and information sciences 2%. **Special Study Options:** Double major, honors program, independent study, internships, liberal arts/career combination, study abroad, teacher certification program.

FACILITIES

Housing: All-female, housing for disabled students. **Library Holdings:** 132,560 bound volumes. 755 periodicals. 1,354 microforms. 1,800 audiovisuals. **Special Academic Facilities/Equipment:** On-campus early childhood school, annual art show on-campus. **Computers:** School-owned computers available for student use.

EXTRACURRICULARS

Activities: Choral groups, dance, drama/theater, literary magazine, music ensembles, musical theater, student government, student newspaper, symphony orchestra, yearbook. **Organizations:** 28 registered organizations, 14 honor societies, 1 religious organization. **Athletics (Intercollegiate):** *Women:* basketball, cross-country, field hockey, lacrosse, soccer, softball, tennis, volleyball.

ADMISSIONS

Selectivity Rating: 66 (of 100). **Freshman Academic Profile:** Average high school GPA 3.1. 7% in top 10% of high school class, 27% in top 25% of high school class, 49% in top 50% of high school class. 60% from public high schools. Average SAT I Math 460, SAT I Math middle 50% range 400-530. Average SAT I Verbal 502, SAT I Verbal middle 50% range 430-560. TOEFL required of all international applicants, minimum TOEFL 550. **Basis for Candidate Selection:** *Very important factors considered include:* recommendations, secondary school record. *Important factors considered include:* character/personal qualities, class rank, essays, extracurricular activities, interview, standardized test scores, volunteer work. *Other factors considered include:* alumni/ae relation, talent/ability, work experience. **Freshman Admission Requirements:** High school diploma or GED is required. *Academic units required/recommended:* 16 total required; 4 English required, 2 math required, 2 science required, 1 science lab required, 2 foreign language required, 2 social studies required, 4 elective required. **Freshman Admission Statistics:** 356 applied, 89% accepted, 35% of those accepted enrolled. **Transfer Admission Requirements:** *Items required:* high school transcript, college transcript, standardized test scores, statement of good standing from prior school. Minimum college GPA of 2.0 required. Lowest grade transferable C. **General Admission Information:** Application fee $25. Priority application deadline May 15. Regular application deadline August 15. Nonfall registration accepted. Admission may be deferred for a maximum of 1 year. Credit and/or placement offered for CEEB Advanced Placement tests.

COSTS AND FINANCIAL AID

Tuition $14,900. Room & board $7,600. Required fees $300. Average book expense $1,050. **Required Forms and Deadlines:** FAFSA and institution's own financial aid form. Financial aid filing deadline April 15. Priority filing deadline April 15. **Notification of Awards:** Applicants will be notified of awards on a rolling basis beginning on or about January 1. **Types of Aid:** *Need-based scholarships/grants:* Pell, SEOG, state scholarships/grants, private scholarships, the school's own gift aid, United Negro College Fund. *Loans:* FFEL Subsidized Stafford, FFEL Unsubsidized Stafford, FFEL PLUS, Federal Perkins. **Student Employment:** Federal Work-Study Program available. Institutional employment available. Off-campus job opportunities are good. **Financial Aid Statistics:** 91% freshmen, 67% undergrads receive some form of aid. Average freshman grant $9,000. Average freshman loan $2,625. Average income from on-campus job $750. **Financial Aid Phone:** 610-647-4400.

INDIANA INSTITUTE OF TECHNOLOGY

1600 East Washington Boulevard, Fort Wayne, IN 46803
Phone: 260-422-5561 **E-mail:** admissions@indtech.edu **CEEB Code:** 1805
Fax: 260-422-7696 **Web:** www.indtech.edu **ACT Code:** 1208

This private school was founded in 1930. It has a 57-acre campus.

STUDENTS AND FACULTY

Enrollment: 2,696. **Student Body:** Male 45%, female 55%, out-of-state 16%, international 1% (14 countries represented). **Ethnic Representation:** African American 16%, Asian 1%, Caucasian 53%, Hispanic 2%, Native American 1%. **Faculty:** Student/faculty ratio 22:1. 39 full-time faculty, 38% hold PhDs. 100% faculty teach undergrads.

ACADEMICS

Degrees: Associate's, bachelor's, master's. **Academic Requirements:** General education including some course work in computer literacy, English (including composition), humanities, mathematics, social science. **Classes:** 10-19 students in an average class. **Majors with Highest Enrollment:** Business administration/management; electrical, electronics, and communications engineering; engineering. **Disciplines with Highest Percentage of Degrees Awarded:** Business/marketing 78%, engineering/engineering technology 18%, computer and information sciences 2%, parks and recreation 2%. **Special Study Options:** Accelerated program, cooperative (work-study) program, distance learning, double major, English as a second language, external degree program, independent study, internships, student-designed major.

FACILITIES

Housing: Coed, apartments for single students, fraternities and/or sororities. **Library Holdings:** 33,000 bound volumes. 160 periodicals. 1,000 microforms. 150 audiovisuals. **Computers:** School-owned computers available for student use.

EXTRACURRICULARS

Activities: Dance, pep band, student government. **Organizations:** 14 registered organizations, 1 honor society, 3 fraternities (15% men join), 1 sorority (5% women join). **Athletics (Intercollegiate):** *Men:* baseball, basketball, soccer. *Women:* basketball, soccer, softball.

ADMISSIONS

Selectivity Rating: 71 (of 100). **Freshman Academic Profile:** 8% in top 10% of high school class, 27% in top 25% of high school class, 57% in top 50% of high school class. 80% from public high schools. Average SAT I Math 495. Average SAT I Verbal 477. Average ACT 22. TOEFL required of all international applicants, minimum TOEFL 500. **Basis for Candidate Selection:** *Very important factors considered include:* alumni/ae relation, secondary school record. *Important factors considered include:* class rank, interview, minority status, standardized test scores. *Other factors considered include:* character/personal qualities, essays, extracurricular activities, recommendations, talent/ability, volunteer work, work experience. **Freshman Admission Requirements:** High school diploma or GED is required. *Academic units required/recommended:* 4 English required, 4 English recommended, 3 math required, 4 math recommended, 2 science required, 3 science recommended. **Freshman Admission Statistics:** 2,589 applied, 49% accepted. **Transfer Admission Requirements:** *Items required:* college transcript. Minimum college GPA of 2.0 required. Lowest grade transferable C. **General Admission Information:** Application fee $50. Regular application deadline September 1. Nonfall registration accepted. Admission may be deferred for a maximum of 2 years. Credit and/or placement offered for CEEB Advanced Placement tests.

COSTS AND FINANCIAL AID

Tuition $14,848. Room & board $5,246. **Required Forms and Deadlines:** FAFSA and institution's own financial aid form. No deadline for regular filing. **Notification of Awards:** Applicants will be notified of awards on a rolling basis beginning on or about February 2. **Types of Aid:** *Need-based scholarships/grants:* Pell, SEOG, state scholarships/grants, private scholarships, the school's own gift aid, United Negro College Fund. *Loans:* FFEL Subsidized Stafford, FFEL Unsubsidized Stafford, FFEL PLUS, Federal Perkins. **Student Employment:** Federal Work-Study Program available. Institutional employment available. Off-campus job opportunities are good. **Financial Aid Statistics:** 83% freshmen, 87% undergrads receive some form of aid. **Financial Aid Phone:** 800-937-2448.

INDIANA STATE UNIVERSITY

Office of Admissions, Tirey Hall, Terre Haute, IN 47809
Phone: 812-237-2121 **E-mail:** admisu@amber.indstate.edu **CEEB Code:** 1322
Fax: 812-237-8023 **Web:** www.indstate.edu **ACT Code:** 1206

This public school was founded in 1865. It has a 92-acre campus.

STUDENTS AND FACULTY

Enrollment: 9,997. **Student Body:** Male 48%, female 52%, out-of-state 8%, international 2%. **Ethnic Representation:** African American 11%, Asian 1%, Caucasian 84%, Hispanic 1%. **Retention and Graduation:** 70% freshmen return for sophomore year. 21% freshmen graduate within 4 years. **Faculty:** Student/faculty ratio 18:1. 536 full-time faculty. 90% faculty teach undergrads.

ACADEMICS

Degrees: Associate's, bachelor's, doctoral, first professional, master's, terminal, transfer. **Academic Requirements:** General education including some course work in arts/fine arts, computer literacy, English (including composition), foreign languages, history, mathematics, sciences (biological or physical), social science, physical education. **Classes:** Under 10 students in an average class. **Disciplines with Highest Percentage of Degrees Awarded:** Education 20%, business/marketing 18%, engineering/engineering technology 10%, social sciences and history 10%, communications/communication technologies 5%. **Special Study Options:** Accelerated program, cooperative (work-study) program, distance learning, double major, English as a second language, honors program, independent study, internships, study abroad, teacher certification program.

FACILITIES

Housing: Coed, all-female, all-male, apartments for married students, apartments for single students, fraternities and/or sororities, special housing for freshmen, and apartments for students with dependent children. **Special Academic Facilities/Equipment:** Music hall, art gallery, civic center, museum, on-campus school, audiovisual center, observatory.

EXTRACURRICULARS

Activities: Choral groups, concert band, dance, drama/theater, jazz band, literary magazine, marching band, music ensembles, musical theater, pep band, radio station, student government, student newspaper, student-run film society, symphony orchestra, yearbook. **Organizations:** 300 registered organizations, 40 honor societies, 23 fraternities, 14 sororities. **Athletics (Intercollegiate):** *Men:* baseball, basketball, cross-country, football, tennis, track & field. *Women:* basketball, cross-country, softball, tennis, track & field, volleyball.

ADMISSIONS

Selectivity Rating: 63 (of 100). **Freshman Academic Profile:** Average high school GPA 2.9. 7% in top 10% of high school class, 24% in top 25% of high school class, 59% in top 50% of high school class. 90% from public high schools. Average SAT I Math 468, SAT I Math middle 50% range 410-520. Average SAT I Verbal 471, SAT I Verbal middle 50% range 420-520. Average ACT 19, ACT middle 50% range 17-22. TOEFL required of all international applicants, minimum TOEFL 500. **Basis for Candidate Selection:** *Very important factors considered include:* class rank, secondary school record. *Important factors considered include:* essays, recommendations, standardized test scores. *Other factors considered include:* character/personal qualities, extracurricular activities, interview, talent/ability. **Freshman Admission Requirements:** High school diploma or GED is required. *Academic units required/recommended:* 40 total recommended; 8 English recommended, 7 math recommended, 6 science recommended, 6 science lab recommended, 2 foreign language recommended, 4 social studies recommended, 2 history recommended, 3 elective recommended. **Freshman Admission Statistics:** 5,542 applied, 83% accepted, 47% of those accepted enrolled. **Transfer Admission Requirements:** *Items required:* college transcript. Minimum college GPA of 2.0 required. Lowest grade transferable C. **General Admission Information:** Application fee $25. Priority application deadline August 1. Regular application deadline August 15. Nonfall registration accepted. Admission may be deferred for a maximum of 1 year. Credit offered for CEEB Advanced Placement tests.

COSTS AND FINANCIAL AID

In-state tuition $4,116. Out-of-state tuition $10,276. Room & board $4,604. Required fees $100. Average book expense $750. **Required Forms and Deadlines:** FAFSA. No deadline for regular filing. Priority filing deadline March 1. **Notification of Awards:** Applicants will be notified of awards on a rolling basis beginning on or about April 15. **Types of Aid:** *Need-based scholarships/grants:* Pell, SEOG, state scholarships/grants, private scholarships, the school's own gift aid. *Loans:* Direct Subsidized Stafford, Direct Unsubsidized Stafford, Direct PLUS, FFEL Subsidized Stafford, FFEL Unsubsidized Stafford, FFEL PLUS, Federal Perkins. **Student Employment:** Federal Work-Study Program available. Institutional employment available. Off-campus job opportunities are excellent. **Financial Aid Statistics:** 50% freshmen, 48% undergrads receive some form of aid. **Financial Aid Phone:** 812-237-2215.

INDIANA UNIVERSITY—BLOOMINGTON

300 North Jordan Avenue, Bloomington, IN 47405-1106
Phone: 812-855-0661 **E-mail:** iuadmit@indiana.edu **CEEB Code:** 1324
Fax: 812-855-5102 **Web:** www.indiana.edu **ACT Code:** 1210

This public school was founded in 1820. It has a 1,878-acre campus.

STUDENTS AND FACULTY

Enrollment: 30,157. **Student Body:** Male 47%, female 53%, out-of-state 28%, international 4%. **Ethnic Representation:** African American 4%, Asian 3%, Caucasian 90%, Hispanic 2%. **Retention and Graduation:** 87% freshmen return for sophomore year. 40% freshmen graduate within 4 years. **Faculty:** Student/faculty ratio 20:1. 1,655 full-time faculty, 78% hold PhDs.

ACADEMICS

Degrees: Associate's, bachelor's, certificate, diploma, doctoral, first professional, master's, post-bachelor's certificate. **Academic Requirements:** General education including some course work in arts/fine arts, English (including composition), humanities, mathematics, sciences (biological or physical), social science. **Classes:** 20-29 students in an average class. 20-29 students in an average lab/discussion section. **Majors with Highest Enrollment:** Business administration/management; elementary education and teaching; biological and biomedical sciences. **Disciplines with Highest Percentage of Degrees Awarded:** Business/marketing 23%, education 16%, communications/communication technologies 8%, protective services/public administration 8%, visual and performing arts 7%. **Special Study Options:** Accelerated program, cooperative (work-study) program, distance learning, double major, dual enrollment, English as a second language, external degree program, honors program, independent study, internships, liberal arts/career combination, student-designed major, study abroad, teacher certification program.

FACILITIES

Housing: Coed, all-female, all-male, apartments for married students, apartments for single students, housing for disabled students, housing for international students, fraternities and/or sororities, cooperative housing, apartments for students with dependent children, residential language houses, living/learning centers, wellness center, African-American living/learning centers, honor college floors, first-year academic interest group housing, suites for 2 or 3 students. **Library Holdings:** 6,384,711 bound volumes. 64,027 periodicals. 4,520,143 microforms. 545,061 audiovisuals. **Special Academic Facilities/Equipment:** Art gallery; radio station; natural history museum; TV station; art museum; Mathers Museum of World Cultures; Kirkwood Observatory; Hilltop Garden and Nature Center; arboretum; student recreational sports and aquatic center; auditorium; Beck Chapel; golf-driving range; musical arts center; health, physical education and recreation facilities (HPER); indoor swimming; outdoor swimming; Wildermuth Intramural Center (in HPER complex); cyclotron; Lilly Library; and more than 70 research centers. **Computers:** School-owned computers available for student use.

EXTRACURRICULARS

Activities: Choral groups, concert band, dance, drama/theater, jazz band, literary magazine, marching band, music ensembles, musical theater, opera, pep band, radio station, student government, student newspaper, symphony orchestra, television station, yearbook. **Organizations:** 331 registered organizations, 25 fraternities (17% men join), 19 sororities (15% women join). **Athletics (Intercollegiate):** *Men:* baseball, basketball, cheerleading, cross-country, diving, football, golf, soccer, swimming, tennis, track & field, wrestling. *Women:* basketball, cheerleading, crew, cross-country, diving, golf, soccer, softball, swimming, tennis, track & field, volleyball, water polo.

ADMISSIONS

Selectivity Rating: 75 (of 100). **Freshman Academic Profile:** 22% in top 10% of high school class, 52% in top 25% of high school class, 90% in top 50% of high school class. Average SAT I Math 554, SAT I Math middle 50% range 490-610. Average SAT I Verbal 542, SAT I Verbal middle 50% range 490-600. Average ACT 24, ACT middle 50% range 22-27. TOEFL required of all international applicants, minimum TOEFL 550. **Basis for Candidate Selection:** *Very important factors considered include:* class rank, secondary school record. *Other factors considered include:* alumni/ae relation, character/personal qualities, essays, extracurricular activities, interview, minority status, recommendations, standardized test scores, state residency, talent/ability. **Freshman Admission Requirements:** High school diploma or GED is required. *Academic units required/recommended:* 14 total required; 19 total recommended; 4 English required, 4 English recommended, 3 math required, 4 math recommended, 1 science required, 3 science recommended, 1 science lab required, 3 foreign language recommended, 2 social studies required, 3 social studies recommended, 4 elective required. **Freshman Admission Statistics:** 20,228 applied, 83% accepted, 41% of those accepted enrolled. **Transfer Admission Requirements:** *Items required:* high school transcript, college transcript. Minimum college GPA of 2.0 required. Lowest grade transferable C. **General Admission Information:** Application fee $40. Priority application deadline February 1. Nonfall registration accepted. Admission may be deferred for a maximum of 1 year. Credit and/or placement offered for CEEB Advanced Placement tests.

COSTS AND FINANCIAL AID

In-state tuition $4,196. Out-of-state tuition $13,930. Room & board $5,978. Required fees $539. Average book expense $736. **Required Forms and Deadlines:** FAFSA. Priority filing deadline March 1. **Notification of Awards:** Applicants will be notified of awards on a rolling basis beginning on or about May 1. **Types of Aid:** *Need-based scholarships/grants:* Pell, SEOG, state scholarships/grants, private scholarships, the school's own gift aid. *Loans:* Direct Subsidized Stafford, Direct Unsubsidized Stafford, Direct PLUS, Federal Perkins, Federal Nursing, college/university loans from institutional funds. **Student Employment:** Federal Work-Study Program available. Institutional employment available. Off-campus job opportunities are excellent. **Financial Aid Statistics:** 37% freshmen, 34% undergrads receive some form of aid. Average freshman grant $4,001. Average freshman loan $2,367. **Financial Aid Phone:** 812-855-0321.

INDIANA UNIVERSITY EAST

2325 Chester Boulevard, WZ 116, Richmond, IN 47374-1289
Phone: 765-973-8208 **E-mail:** eaadmit@indiana.edu
Fax: 765-973-8288 **Web:** www.indiana.edu

This public school was founded in 1971. It has a 194-acre campus.

STUDENTS AND FACULTY

Enrollment: 2,405. **Student Body:** Male 29%, female 71%, out-of-state 5%. **Ethnic Representation:** African American 4%, Asian 1%, Caucasian 90%, Hispanic 1%, Native American 1%. **Retention and Graduation:** 56% freshmen return for sophomore year. 4% freshmen graduate within 4 years. **Faculty:** Student/faculty ratio 15:1. 69 full-time faculty, 59% hold PhDs.

ACADEMICS

Degrees: Associate's, bachelor's, post-bachelor's certificate. **Academic Requirements:** General education including some course work in computer literacy, English (including composition), humanities, sciences (biological or physical), social science. **Classes:** 10-19 students in an average class. 10-19 students in an average lab/discussion section. **Majors with Highest Enrollment:** Nursing/registered nurse training (RN, ASN, BSN, MSN); business administration/management; elementary education and teaching. **Disciplines with Highest Percentage of Degrees Awarded:** Education 27%, health professions and related sciences 21%, liberal arts/general studies 20%, business/marketing 13%, protective services/public administration 6%. **Special Study Options:** Cooperative (work-study) program, cross registration, distance learning, double major, dual enrollment, external degree program, independent study, internships, teacher certification program, weekend college, statewide technology program with Purdue University.

FACILITIES

Library Holdings: 65,884 bound volumes. 436 periodicals. 52,383 microforms. 9,798 audiovisuals.

EXTRACURRICULARS

Activities: Drama/theater, student government, student newspaper, television station. **Organizations:** 30 registered organizations, 3 honor societies, 1 religious organization, 22 fraternity, 1 sorority. **Athletics (Intercollegiate):** *Men:* basketball, golf. *Women:* basketball, cheerleading, golf.

ADMISSIONS

Selectivity Rating: 64 (of 100). **Freshman Academic Profile:** 2% in top 10% of high school class, 16% in top 25% of high school class, 45% in top 50% of high school class. Average SAT I Math 445, SAT I Math middle 50% range 390-500. Average SAT I Verbal 462, SAT I Verbal middle 50% range 400-510. Average ACT 19, ACT middle 50% range 17-21. **Basis for Candidate Selection:** *Very important factors considered include:* secondary school record, standardized test scores. *Important factors considered include:* class rank. **Freshman Admission Requirements:** High school diploma or GED is required. *Academic units required/recommended:* 15 total required; 16 total recommended; 4 English required, 4 English recommended, 2 math required, 3 math recommended, 1 science required, 1 science recommended, 1 science lab required, 1 science lab recommended, 2 foreign language required, 2 foreign language recommended, 2 social studies required, 2 social studies recommended, 4 elective recommended. **Freshman Admission Statistics:** 546 applied, 79% accepted. **Transfer Admission Requirements:** *Items required:* college transcript. Minimum college GPA of 2.0 required. Lowest grade transferable C. **General Admission Information:** Application fee $25. Nonfall registration accepted. Admission may be deferred.

COSTS AND FINANCIAL AID

In-state tuition $3,221. Out-of-state tuition $8,250. Required fees $194. **Required Forms and Deadlines:** FAFSA and institution's own financial aid form. Priority filing deadline March 1. **Notification of Awards:** Applicants will be notified of awards on a rolling basis beginning on or about May 1. **Types of Aid:** *Need-based scholarships/grants:* Pell, SEOG, state scholarships/grants, private scholarships, the school's own gift aid. *Loans:* FFEL Subsidized Stafford, FFEL Unsubsidized Stafford, FFEL PLUS, Federal Perkins, Federal Nursing, college/university loans from institutional funds. **Student Employment:** Federal Work-Study Program available. Institutional employment available. Off-campus job opportunities are good. **Financial Aid Statistics:** 64% freshmen, 67% undergrads receive some form of aid. Average freshman grant $2,578. Average freshman loan $2,966. **Financial Aid Phone:** 765-973-8206.

INDIANA UNIVERSITY—KOKOMO

Office of Admissions, PO Box 9003, KC 230A, Kokomo, IN 46904-9003
Phone: 765-455-9217 **E-mail:** iuadmis@iuk.edu **CEEB Code:** 1337
Fax: 765-455-9537 **Web:** www.indiana.edu **ACT Code:** 1219

This public school was founded in 1945. It has a 51-acre campus.

STUDENTS AND FACULTY

Enrollment: 2,519. **Student Body:** Male 30%, female 70%, out-of-state 1%. **Ethnic Representation:** African American 3%, Asian 1%, Caucasian 92%, Hispanic 2%. **Retention and Graduation:** 53% freshmen return for sophomore year. 3% freshmen graduate within 4 years. **Faculty:** Student/faculty ratio 16:1. 70 full-time faculty, 65% hold PhDs.

ACADEMICS

Degrees: Associate's, bachelor's, certificate, master's, post-bachelor's certificate. **Academic Requirements:** General education including some course work in computer literacy, English (including composition), mathematics, public speaking. **Classes:** 20-29 students in an average class. 10-19 students in an average lab/discussion section. **Majors with Highest Enrollment:** Nursing/registered nurse training (RN, ASN, BSN, MSN); elementary education and teaching; business administration/management. **Disciplines with Highest Percentage of Degrees Awarded:** Education 21%, liberal arts/general studies 20%, business/marketing 18%, health professions and related sciences 16%, protective services/public administration 8%. **Special Study Options:** Accelerated program, cross registration, distance learning, double major, dual enrollment, external degree program, honors program, independent study, internships, study abroad, teacher certification program, Project Success program.

FACILITIES

Library Holdings: 133,962 bound volumes. 1,598 periodicals. 439,799 microforms. 5,287 audiovisuals. **Special Academic Facilities/Equipment:** Observatory, art gallery. **Computers:** School-owned computers available for student use.

EXTRACURRICULARS

Activities: Choral groups, drama/theater, student government, student newspaper. **Organizations:** 16 registered organizations, 6 honor societies, 7 religious organizations.

ADMISSIONS

Selectivity Rating: 63 (of 100). **Freshman Academic Profile:** 5% in top 10% of high school class, 23% in top 25% of high school class, 55% in top 50% of high school class. Average SAT I Math 465, SAT I Math middle 50% range 410-520. Average SAT I Verbal 479, SAT I Verbal middle 50% range 430-540. Average ACT 19, ACT middle 50% range 17-21. TOEFL required of all international applicants, minimum TOEFL 550. **Basis for Candidate Selection:** *Very important factors considered include:* secondary school record. *Important factors considered include:* standardized test scores. *Other factors considered include:* recommendations. **Freshman Admission Requirements:** High school diploma or GED is required. *Academic units required/recommended:* 14 total required; 14 total recommended; 4 English required, 4 English recommended, 3 math required, 3 math recommended, 1 science required, 1 science recommended, 2 foreign language recommended, 2 social studies required, 2 social studies recommended, 2 history recommended. **Freshman Admission Statistics:** 699 applied, 87% accepted, 85% of those accepted enrolled. **Transfer Admission Requirements:** *Items required:* college transcript. Minimum college GPA of 2.0 required. Lowest grade transferable C. **General Admission Information:** Application fee $30. Priority application deadline August 3. Nonfall registration accepted. Admission may be deferred. Credit and/or placement offered for CEEB Advanced Placement tests.

COSTS AND FINANCIAL AID

In-state tuition $3,221. Out-of-state tuition $8,520. Required fees $201. **Required Forms and Deadlines:** FAFSA and institution's own financial aid form. Priority filing deadline March 1. **Notification of Awards:** Applicants will be notified of awards on a rolling basis beginning on or about May 1. **Types of Aid:** *Need-based scholarships/grants:* Pell, SEOG, state scholarships/grants, private scholarships, the school's own gift aid. *Loans:* FFEL Subsidized Stafford, FFEL Unsubsidized Stafford, FFEL PLUS, Federal Perkins, Federal Nursing, college/university loans from institutional funds. **Student Employment:** Federal Work-Study Program available. Institutional employment available. Off-campus job opportunities are excellent. **Financial Aid Statistics:** 37% freshmen, 39% undergrads receive some form of aid. Average freshman grant $2,362. Average freshman loan $2,619. **Financial Aid Phone:** 765-455-9216.

INDIANA UNIVERSITY NORTHWEST

3400 Broadway, Hawthorn 100, Gary, IN 46408-1197
Phone: 219-980-6991 **E-mail:** pkeshei@iun.edu
Fax: 219-981-4219 **Web:** www.indiana.edu

This public school was founded in 1948. It has a 38-acre campus.

STUDENTS AND FACULTY

Enrollment: 4,027. **Student Body:** Male 30%, female 70%, out-of-state 1%. **Ethnic Representation:** African American 24%, Asian 1%, Caucasian 61%, Hispanic 11%. **Retention and Graduation:** 60% freshmen return for sophomore year. 8% freshmen graduate within 4 years. **Faculty:** Student/faculty ratio 14:1. 137 full-time faculty, 62% hold PhDs.

ACADEMICS

Degrees: Associate's, bachelor's, certificate, master's, post-bachelor's certificate. **Academic Requirements:** General education including some course work in computer literacy, English (including composition), foreign languages, humanities, mathematics, sciences (biological or physical), social science. **Classes:** Under 10 students in an average class. Under 10 students in an average lab/discussion section. **Majors with Highest Enrollment:** Business administration/management; nursing/registered nurse training (RN, ASN, BSN, MSN); criminal justice/safety studies. **Disciplines with Highest Percentage of Degrees Awarded:** Business/marketing 22%, liberal arts/general studies 15%, health professions and related sciences 14%, education 11%, protective services/public administration 11%. **Special Study Options:** Accelerated program, cooperative (work-study) program, distance learning, double major, dual enrollment, external degree program, honors program, independent study, internships, student-designed major, study abroad, teacher certification program, weekend college, off-campus study (Washington semester).

FACILITIES

Library Holdings: 241,735 bound volumes. 1,628 periodicals. 340,519 microforms. 1,212 audiovisuals. **Computers:** School-owned computers available for student use.

EXTRACURRICULARS

Activities: Choral groups, drama/theater, literary magazine, student government, student newspaper. **Organizations:** 60 registered organizations, 4 honor societies, 2 religious organizations, 2 fraternities, 3 sororities. **Athletics (Intercollegiate):** *Men:* baseball, basketball, golf. *Women:* basketball, volleyball.

ADMISSIONS

Selectivity Rating: 65 (of 100). **Freshman Academic Profile:** 8% in top 10% of high school class, 22% in top 25% of high school class, 50% in top 50% of high school class. Average SAT I Math 429, SAT I Math middle 50% range 360-490. Average SAT I Verbal 451, SAT I Verbal middle 50% range 390-500. Average ACT 20, ACT middle 50% range 17-23. TOEFL required of all international applicants, minimum TOEFL 550. **Basis for Candidate Selection:** *Very important factors considered include:* class rank, secondary school record. *Important factors considered include:* standardized test scores. *Other factors considered include:* recommendations. **Freshman Admission Requirements:** High school diploma or GED is required. *Academic units required/recommended:* 16 total required; 4 English required, 3 math required, 1 science required, 2 foreign language recommended, 2 social studies required, 4 elective required. **Freshman Admission Statistics:** 1,135 applied, 79% accepted, 74% of those accepted enrolled. **Transfer Admission Requirements:** *Items required:* high school transcript, college transcript. Lowest grade transferable C. **General Admission Information:** Application fee $25. Priority application deadline August 1. Nonfall registration accepted. Admission may be deferred. Credit offered for CEEB Advanced Placement tests.

COSTS AND FINANCIAL AID

In-state tuition $3,221. Out-of-state tuition $8,520. Required fees $226. **Required Forms and Deadlines:** FAFSA and institution's own financial aid form. No deadline for regular filing. Priority filing deadline March 1. **Notification of Awards:** Applicants will be notified of awards on a rolling basis beginning on or about May 1. **Types of Aid:** *Need-based scholarships/grants:* Pell, SEOG, state scholarships/grants, private scholarships, the school's own gift aid. *Loans:* FFEL Subsidized Stafford, FFEL Unsubsidized Stafford, FFEL PLUS, Federal Perkins, Federal Nursing, college/university loans from institutional funds. **Student Employment:** Federal Work-Study Program available. Off-campus job opportunities are good. **Financial Aid Statistics:** 38% freshmen, 44% undergrads receive some form of aid. Average freshman grant $2,544. Average freshman loan $2,658. **Financial Aid Phone:** 219-980-6778.

INDIANA UNIVERSITY OF PENNSYLVANIA

117 Sutton Hall, Indiana, PA 15705
Phone: 724-357-2210 **E-mail:** admissions-inquiry@iup.edu **CEEB Code:** 2652
Fax: 724-357-6281 **Web:** www.iup.edu **ACT Code:** 3704

This public school was founded in 1875. It has a 342-acre campus.

STUDENTS AND FACULTY

Enrollment: 11,834. **Student Body:** Male 44%, female 56%, out-of-state 3%, international 2% (71 country represented). **Ethnic Representation:** African

American 6%, Asian 1%, Caucasian 91%, Hispanic 1%. **Retention and Graduation:** 76% freshmen return for sophomore year. 25% freshmen graduate within 4 years. 19% grads go on to further study within 1 year. 1% grads pursue business degrees. 3% grads pursue law degrees. 2% grads pursue medical degrees. **Faculty:** Student/faculty ratio 17:1. 636 full-time faculty, 92% hold PhDs. 100% faculty teach undergrads.

ACADEMICS

Degrees: Associate's, bachelor's, certificate, doctoral, master's, post-bachelor's certificate, post-master's certificate. **Academic Requirements:** General education including some course work in arts/fine arts, computer literacy, English (including composition), history, humanities, mathematics, philosophy, sciences (biological or physical), social science, liberal studies. **Classes:** 20-29 students in an average class. **Majors with Highest Enrollment:** Communications studies/speech communication and rhetoric; elementary education and teaching; criminology. **Disciplines with Highest Percentage of Degrees Awarded:** Education 24%, business/marketing 21%, social sciences and history 15%, communications/communication technologies 9%, psychology 4%. **Special Study Options:** Accelerated program, cooperative (work-study) program, distance learning, double major, English as a second language, student exchange program (domestic), honors program, independent study, internships, study abroad, teacher certification program, weekend college.

FACILITIES

Housing: Coed, all-female, all-male, apartments for single students, fraternities and/or sororities, substance-free, honors college. **Library Holdings:** 570,735 bound volumes. 2,626 periodicals. 2,364,916 microforms. 109,308 audiovisuals. **Special Academic Facilities/Equipment:** Art museum, natural history museum, on-campus elementary school, lodge, farm, cogeneration plant, ski slope, sailing base. **Computers:** School-owned computers available for student use.

EXTRACURRICULARS

Activities: Choral groups, concert band, dance, drama/theater, jazz band, marching band, music ensembles, musical theater, opera, pep band, radio station, student government, student newspaper, symphony orchestra, television station. **Organizations:** 200 registered organizations, 21 honor societies, 19 fraternities (10% men join), 14 sororities (11% women join). **Athletics (Intercollegiate):** *Men:* baseball, basketball, cross-country, diving, football, golf, swimming, track & field. *Women:* basketball, cross-country, diving, field hockey, lacrosse, soccer, softball, swimming, tennis, track & field, volleyball.

ADMISSIONS

Selectivity Rating: 78 (of 100). **Freshman Academic Profile:** 17% in top 10% of high school class, 44% in top 25% of high school class, 77% in top 50% of high school class. 95% from public high schools. Average SAT I Math 528, SAT I Math middle 50% range 480-570. Average SAT I Verbal 534, SAT I Verbal middle 50% range 480-580. TOEFL required of all international applicants, minimum TOEFL 500. **Basis for Candidate Selection:** *Very important factors considered include:* secondary school record, talent/ability. *Important factors considered include:* class rank, standardized test scores. *Other factors considered include:* alumni/ae relation, character/personal qualities, essays, extracurricular activities, geographical residence, interview, recommendations, state residency, volunteer work, work experience. **Freshman Admission Requirements:** High school diploma or GED is required. *Academic units required/recommended:* 16 total recommended; 4 English recommended, 3 math recommended, 3 science recommended, 2 foreign language recommended, 2 social studies recommended, 1 history recommended, 1 elective recommended. **Freshman Admission Statistics:** 8,005 applied, 54% accepted, 64% of those accepted enrolled. **Transfer Admission Requirements:** *Items required:* high school transcript, college transcript. Minimum college GPA of 2.0 required. Lowest grade transferable C. **General Admission Information:** Application fee $30. Priority application deadline December 31. Nonfall registration accepted. Admission may be deferred for a maximum of 1 year. Credit offered for CEEB Advanced Placement tests.

COSTS AND FINANCIAL AID

In-state tuition $4,378. Out-of-state tuition $10,946. Room & board $4,524. Required fees $1,163. Average book expense $800. **Required Forms and Deadlines:** FAFSA. Financial aid filing deadline April 15. **Notification of Awards:** Applicants will be notified of awards on a rolling basis beginning on or about April 15. **Types of Aid:** *Need-based scholarships/grants:* Pell, SEOG, state scholarships/grants, private scholarships, the school's own gift aid. *Loans:* FFEL Subsidized Stafford, FFEL Unsubsidized Stafford, FFEL PLUS, Federal Perkins, private alternative loans. **Student Employment:** Federal Work-Study Program available. Institutional employment available. Off-campus job opportunities are fair. **Financial Aid Statistics:** 64% freshmen, 64% undergrads receive some form of aid. Average freshman grant $3,682. Average freshman loan $2,573. Average income from on-campus job $1,500. **Financial Aid Phone:** 724-357-2218.

INDIANA UNIVERSITY—PURDUE UNIVERSITY FORT WAYNE

2101 East Coliseum Boulevard, Fort Wayne, IN 46805-1499
Phone: 260-481-6812 **E-mail:** ipfwadms@ipfw.edu **CEEB Code:** 1336
Fax: 260-481-6880 **Web:** www.ipfw.edu **ACT Code:** 1217

This public school was founded in 1917. It has a 565-acre campus.

STUDENTS AND FACULTY

Enrollment: 10,880. **Student Body:** Male 42%, female 58%, out-of-state 5%, international 1% (71 country represented). **Ethnic Representation:** African American 5%, Asian 2%, Caucasian 88%, Hispanic 2%. **Retention and Graduation:** 60% freshmen return for sophomore year. **Faculty:** Student/faculty ratio 19:1. 329 full-time faculty, 82% hold PhDs. 99% faculty teach undergrads.

ACADEMICS

Degrees: Associate's, bachelor's, certificate, master's, post-bachelor's certificate, post-master's certificate, terminal, transfer. **Academic Requirements:** General education including some course work in arts/fine arts, English (including composition), humanities, mathematics, sciences (biological or physical), social science. **Classes:** 20-29 students in an average class. 20-29 students in an average lab/discussion section. **Majors with Highest Enrollment:** Nursing/registered nurse training (RN, ASN, BSN, MSN); business/commerce, general; elementary education and teaching. **Disciplines with Highest Percentage of Degrees Awarded:** Education 19%, business/marketing 17%, liberal arts/general studies 14%, engineering/engineering technology 8%, communications/communication technologies 5%. **Special Study Options:** Cooperative (work-study) program, distance learning, double major, English as a second language, student exchange program (domestic), honors program, independent study, internships, liberal arts/career combination, student-designed major, study abroad, teacher certification program, weekend college.

FACILITIES

Housing: Coed dorms expected opening fall 2004. **Library Holdings:** 479,992 bound volumes. 10,964 periodicals. 536,519 microforms. 1,000 audiovisuals. **Special Academic Facilities/Equipment:** Williams Theatre, recital hall, anthropology and geology exhibits, art gallery. **Computers:** School-owned computers available for student use.

EXTRACURRICULARS

Activities: Choral groups, concert band, dance, drama/theater, jazz band, literary magazine, music ensembles, musical theater, opera, pep band, student government, student newspaper, symphony orchestra, television station. **Organizations:** 65 registered organizations, 7 honor societies, 3 religious organizations, 2 fraternities (1% men join), 3 sororities (1% women join). **Athletics (Intercollegiate):** *Men:* baseball, basketball, cross-country, soccer, tennis, track & field, volleyball. *Women:* basketball, cross-country, soccer, softball, tennis, track & field, volleyball.

ADMISSIONS

Selectivity Rating: 63 (of 100). **Freshman Academic Profile:** Average high school GPA 2.6. 7% in top 10% of high school class, 24% in top 25% of high school class, 57% in top 50% of high school class. 84% from public high schools. Average SAT I Math 486, SAT I Math middle 50% range 430-550. Average SAT I Verbal 481, SAT I Verbal middle 50% range 420-540. Average ACT 21, ACT middle 50% range 17-23. TOEFL required of all international applicants, minimum TOEFL 550. **Basis for Candidate Selection:** *Very important factors considered include:* class rank, secondary school record, standardized test scores. *Other factors considered include:* recommendations, state residency. **Freshman Admission Requirements:** High school diploma or GED is required. *Academic units required/recommended:* 10 total required; 4 English required, 3 math required, 1 science required, 3 science recommended, 1 science lab recommended, 1 foreign language required, 3 foreign language recommended, 1 social studies required, 3 social studies recommended. **Freshman Admission Statistics:** 2,471 applied, 97% accepted, 71% of those accepted enrolled. **Transfer Admission Requirements:** *Items required:* high school transcript, college transcript. Minimum college GPA of 2.0 required. Lowest grade transferable C-. **General Admission Information:** Application fee $30. Priority application deadline March 1. Regular application deadline August 1. Nonfall registration accepted. Credit and/or placement offered for CEEB Advanced Placement tests.

COSTS AND FINANCIAL AID

In-state tuition $3,100. Out-of-state tuition $7,728. Required fees $384. Average book expense $800. **Required Forms and Deadlines:** FAFSA. Priority filing deadline March 1. **Notification of Awards:** Applicants will be notified of awards on or about April 30. **Types of Aid:** *Need-based scholarships/grants:* Pell, SEOG, state scholarships/grants, private scholarships, Federal Nursing. *Loans:* FFEL Subsidized Stafford, FFEL Unsubsidized Stafford, FFEL PLUS, Federal Perkins, Federal Nursing. **Student Employment:** Federal Work-Study Program available. Institutional employment available. Off-campus job opportunities are excellent. **Financial Aid Statistics:** 51% freshmen, 67% undergrads receive some form of aid. Average freshman grant $3,900. Average freshman loan $2,500. Average income from on-campus job $1,200. **Financial Aid Phone:** 260-481-6820.

INDIANA UNIVERSITY—PURDUE UNIVERSITY INDIANAPOLIS

425 N. University Blvd., Cavanaugh Hall, Room 129, Indianapolis, IN 46202-5143
Phone: 317-274-4591 **E-mail:** apply@iupui.edu
Fax: 317-278-1862 **Web:** www.indiana.edu **ACT Code:** 1214

This public school was founded in 1969. It has a 511-acre campus.

STUDENTS AND FACULTY

Enrollment: 30,157. **Student Body:** Male 47%, female 53%, out-of-state 3%, international 1%. **Ethnic Representation:** African American 11%, Asian 2%, Caucasian 85%, Hispanic 2%. **Retention and Graduation:** 62% freshmen return for sophomore year. 5% freshmen graduate within 4 years. **Faculty:** Student/faculty ratio 19:1. 1,787 full-time faculty, 84% hold PhDs.

ACADEMICS

Degrees: Associate's, bachelor's, certificate, doctoral, first professional, master's, post-bachelor's certificate. **Academic Requirements:** General education including some course work in English (including composition), humanities, mathematics, sciences (biological or physical), social science. **Classes:** 20-29 students in an average class. Under 10 students in an average lab/discussion section. **Majors with Highest Enrollment:** Business administration/management; nursing/registered nurse training (RN, ASN, BSN, MSN); elementary education and teaching. **Disciplines with Highest Percentage of Degrees Awarded:** Health professions and related sciences 24%, business/marketing 20%, liberal arts/general studies 15%, education 14%, protective services/public administration 9%. **Special Study Options:** Cooperative (work-study) program, cross registration, distance learning, double major, dual enrollment, English as a second language, external degree program, honors program, independent study, internships, study abroad, teacher certification program, weekend college.

FACILITIES

Housing: Coed, apartments for married students, housing for international students. **Library Holdings:** 1,307,346 bound volumes. 14,798 periodicals. 2,346,208 microforms. 430,127 audiovisuals. **Computers:** School-owned computers available for student use.

EXTRACURRICULARS

Activities: Choral groups, dance, drama/theater, jazz band, literary magazine, music ensembles, opera, pep band, student government, student newspaper. **Organizations:** 126 registered organizations, 9 honor societies, 10 religious organizations, 2 fraternities (1% men join), 1 sorority (1% women join). **Athletics (Intercollegiate):** *Men:* baseball, basketball, cross-country, diving, golf, soccer, swimming, tennis. *Women:* basketball, cross-country, diving, soccer, softball, swimming, tennis, volleyball.

ADMISSIONS

Selectivity Rating: 63 (of 100). **Freshman Academic Profile:** 8% in top 10% of high school class, 27% in top 25% of high school class, 63% in top 50% of high school class. Average SAT I Math 489, SAT I Math middle 50% range 430-540. Average SAT I Verbal 492, SAT I Verbal middle 50% range 430-550. Average ACT 20, ACT middle 50% range 17-23. TOEFL required of all international applicants, minimum TOEFL 550. **Basis for Candidate Selection:** *Very important factors considered include:* class rank, secondary school record, standardized test scores. *Other factors considered include:* character/personal qualities, essays, geographical residence, interview, recommendations, state residency, talent/ability, volunteer work, work experience. **Freshman Admission Requirements:** High school diploma or GED is required. *Academic units required/recommended:* 14 total required; 16 total recommended; 4 English required, 4 English recommended, 3 math required, 3 math recommended, 1 science required, 1 science recommended, 1 science lab required, 1 science lab recommended, 2 foreign language recommended, 2 social studies required, 2 social studies recommended, 4 elective required, 4 elective recommended. **Freshman Admission Statistics:** 6,060 applied, 73% accepted, 68% of those accepted enrolled. **Transfer Admission Requirements:** *Items required:* college transcript, statement of good standing from prior school. Minimum college GPA of 2.0 required. Lowest grade transferable C. **General Admission Information:** Application fee $35. Priority application deadline June 1. Nonfall registration accepted. Admission may be deferred for a maximum of 1 year. Credit and/or placement offered for CEEB Advanced Placement tests.

COSTS AND FINANCIAL AID

In-state tuition $3,839. Out-of-state tuition $11,940. Room & board $5,302. Required fees $333. Average book expense $768. **Required Forms and Deadlines:** FAFSA. No deadline for regular filing. Priority filing deadline March 1. **Notification of Awards:** Applicants will be notified of awards on a rolling basis beginning on or about April 1. **Types of Aid:** *Need-based scholarships/grants:* Pell, SEOG, state scholarships/grants, private scholarships, the school's own gift aid. *Loans:* FFEL Subsidized Stafford, FFEL Unsubsidized Stafford, FFEL PLUS, Federal Perkins, Federal Nursing, college/university loans from institutional funds. **Student Employment:** Federal Work-Study Program available. Institutional employment available. Off-campus job opportunities are good. **Financial Aid Statistics:** 51% freshmen, 51% undergrads receive some form of aid. Average freshman grant $2,889. Average freshman loan $2,987. **Financial Aid Phone:** 317-274-4162.

INDIANA UNIVERSITY SOUTH BEND

1700 Mishawaka Avenue, PO Box 7111, A169, South Bend, IN 46634-7111
Phone: 219-237-4400 **E-mail:** admissions@iusb.edu **CEEB Code:** 1339
Fax: 219-237-4834 **Web:** www.indiana.edu

This public school was founded in 1922. It has an 80-acre campus.

STUDENTS AND FACULTY

Enrollment: 6,070. **Student Body:** Male 36%, female 64%, out-of-state 3%, international 2%. **Ethnic Representation:** African American 7%, Asian 1%, Caucasian 88%, Hispanic 3%, Native American 1%. **Retention and Graduation:** 64% freshmen return for sophomore year. 8% freshmen graduate within 4 years. **Faculty:** Student/faculty ratio 14:1. 239 full-time faculty, 60% hold PhDs.

ACADEMICS

Degrees: Associate's, bachelor's, certificate, diploma, master's, post-bachelor's certificate. **Academic Requirements:** General education including some course work in arts/fine arts, computer literacy, English (including composition), humanities, mathematics, sciences (biological or physical), social science. **Classes:** 10-19 students in an average class. Under 10 students in an average lab/discussion section. **Majors with Highest Enrollment:** Elementary education and teaching; business administration/management; nursing/registered nurse training (RN, ASN, BSN, MSN). **Disciplines with Highest Percentage of Degrees Awarded:** Education 24%, business/marketing 19%, liberal arts/general studies 13%, health professions and related sciences 10%, protective services/public administration 9%. **Special Study Options:** Accelerated program, cross registration, distance learning, double major, English as a second language, external degree program, honors program, internships, liberal arts/career combination, study abroad, teacher certification program, weekend college. Joint program in electrical and mechanical engineering or computer technology with Purdue University on Indiana University South Bend Campus. Northern Indiana Consortium for Education (NICE)—Indiana University South Bend is one of 6 member institutions sharing library resources, faculty expertise, and academic strengths resulting in broadened course opportunities to students.

FACILITIES

Housing: Housing for international students. **Library Holdings:** 288,750 bound volumes. 1,968 periodicals. 437,348 microforms. 29,869 audiovisuals.

EXTRACURRICULARS

Activities: Choral groups, drama/theater, jazz band, literary magazine, music ensembles, musical theater, opera, pep band, student government, student newspaper, student-run film society, symphony orchestra. **Organizations:** 30 registered organizations. **Athletics (Intercollegiate):** *Men:* basketball. *Women:* basketball, cheerleading.

ADMISSIONS

Selectivity Rating: 63 (of 100). **Freshman Academic Profile:** 7% in top 10% of high school class, 22% in top 25% of high school class, 57% in top 50% of high school class. Average SAT I Math 475, SAT I Math middle 50% range 420-530. Average SAT I Verbal 486, SAT I Verbal middle 50% range 430-540. Average ACT 20, ACT middle 50% range 16-23. TOEFL required of all international applicants, minimum TOEFL 550. **Basis for Candidate Selection:** *Very important factors considered include:* secondary school record. *Important factors considered include:* class rank. *Other factors considered include:* extracurricular activities, interview, recommendations, standardized test scores, state residency. **Freshman Admission Requirements:** High school diploma or GED is required. *Academic units required/recommended:* 13 total required; 4 English required, 3 math required, 1 science required, 2 foreign language recommended, 2 social studies required. **Freshman Admission Statistics:** 1,600 applied, 88% accepted, 73% of those accepted enrolled. **Transfer Admission Requirements:** *Items required:* college transcript. Minimum college GPA of 2.0 required. Lowest grade transferable C. **General Admission Information:** Application fee $40. Priority application deadline July 1. Nonfall registration accepted. Admission may be deferred. Neither credit nor placement offered for CEEB Advanced Placement tests.

COSTS AND FINANCIAL AID

In-state tuition $3,278. Out-of-state tuition $9,147. Required fees $237. **Required Forms and Deadlines:** FAFSA and institution's own financial aid form. Priority filing deadline March 1. **Notification of Awards:** Applicants will be notified of awards on a rolling basis beginning on or about May 1. **Types of Aid:** *Need-based scholarships/grants:* Pell, SEOG, state scholarships/grants, private scholarships, the school's own gift aid. *Loans:* Direct Subsidized Stafford, Direct Unsubsidized Stafford, Direct PLUS, Federal Perkins, Federal Nursing, college/university loans from institutional funds. **Student Employment:** Federal Work-Study Program available. Off-campus job opportunities are good. **Financial Aid Statistics:** 45% freshmen, 46% undergrads receive some form of aid. Average freshman grant $2,367. Average freshman loan $2,591. **Financial Aid Phone:** 219-237-4357.

INDIANA UNIVERSITY SOUTHEAST

4201 Grant Line Road, UC-100, New Albany, IN 47150
Phone: 812-941-2212 **E-mail:** admissions@ius.edu **CEEB Code:** 1314
Fax: 812-941-2595 **Web:** www.indiana.edu **ACT Code:** 1229

This public school was founded in 1941. It has a 177-acre campus.

STUDENTS AND FACULTY

Enrollment: 5,668. **Student Body:** Male 37%, female 63%, out-of-state 15%. **Ethnic Representation:** African American 2%, Caucasian 92%. **Retention and Graduation:** 64% freshmen return for sophomore year. 7% freshmen graduate within 4 years. **Faculty:** Student/faculty ratio 17:1. 161 full-time faculty, 72% hold PhDs.

ACADEMICS

Degrees: Associate's, bachelor's, certificate, master's, post-bachelor's certificate. **Academic Requirements:** General education including some course work in computer literacy, English (including composition), humanities, mathematics, sciences (biological or physical), social science. **Classes:** 20-29 students in an average class. 10-19 students in an average lab/discussion section. **Majors with Highest Enrollment:** Business administration/management; elementary education and teaching; general studies. **Disciplines with Highest Percentage of Degrees Awarded:** Education 26%, business/marketing 20%, liberal arts/general studies 15%, health professions and related sciences 12%, psychology 6%. **Special Study Options:** Accelerated program, cross registration, double major, dual enrollment, external degree program, independent study, internships, study abroad, teacher certification program, weekend college.

FACILITIES

Library Holdings: 207,815 bound volumes. 1,041 periodicals. 348,192 microforms. 7,489 audiovisuals. **Special Academic Facilities/Equipment:** Paul W. Ogle Center, concert hall, theatre, recital hall, Japanese Cultural Center, Ronald L. Barr Art Gallery. **Computers:** School-owned computers available for student use.

EXTRACURRICULARS

Activities: Choral groups, concert band, drama/theater, literary magazine, music ensembles, student government, student newspaper, symphony orchestra. **Organizations:** 76 registered organizations, 1 religious organization, 2 fraternities (3% men join), 4 sororities (3% women join). **Athletics (Intercollegiate):** *Men:* baseball, basketball, cross-country, tennis. *Women:* basketball, cross-country, softball, tennis, volleyball.

ADMISSIONS

Selectivity Rating: 63 (of 100). **Freshman Academic Profile:** 8% in top 10% of high school class, 28% in top 25% of high school class, 61% in top 50% of high school class. Average SAT I Math 468, SAT I Math middle 50% range 420-520. Average SAT I Verbal 480, SAT I Verbal middle 50% range 430-530. Average ACT 20, ACT middle 50% range 18-23. TOEFL required of all international applicants, minimum TOEFL 550. **Basis for Candidate Selection:** *Very important factors considered include:* secondary school record. *Important factors considered include:* standardized test scores. *Other factors considered include:* interview, recommendations, state residency. **Freshman Admission Requirements:** High school diploma or GED is required. *Academic units required/recommended:* 14 total required; 4 English required, 3 math required, 1 science required, 1 science lab required, 2 foreign language recommended, 2 social studies required, 4 elective required. **Freshman Admission Statistics:** 1,352 applied, 87% accepted, 78% of those accepted enrolled. **Transfer Admission Requirements:** *Items required:* college transcript. Minimum college GPA of 2.0 required. Lowest grade transferable C. **General Admission Information:** Application fee $30. Priority application deadline July 15. Nonfall registration accepted. Admission may be deferred. Credit offered for CEEB Advanced Placement tests.

COSTS AND FINANCIAL AID

In-state tuition $3,221. Out-of-state tuition $8,520. Required fees $238. **Required Forms and Deadlines:** FAFSA and institution's own financial aid form. Priority filing deadline March 1. **Notification of Awards:** Applicants will be notified of awards on a rolling basis beginning on or about May 1. **Types of Aid:** *Need-based scholarships/grants:* Pell, SEOG, state scholarships/grants, private scholarships, the school's own gift aid. *Loans:* FFEL Subsidized Stafford, FFEL Unsubsidized Stafford, FFEL PLUS, Federal Perkins, Federal Nursing, college/university loans from institutional funds. **Student Employment:** Federal Work-Study Program available. Institutional employment available. Off-campus job opportunities are excellent. **Financial Aid Statistics:** 42% freshmen, 43% undergrads receive some form of aid. Average freshman grant $2,652. Average freshman loan $2,491. **Financial Aid Phone:** 812-941-2246.

INDIANA WESLEYAN UNIVERSITY

4201 South Washington Street, Marion, IN 46953-4999
Phone: 800-332-6901 **E-mail:** admissions@indwes.edu **CEEB Code:** 1446
Fax: 317-677-2333 **Web:** www.indwes.edu **ACT Code:** 1226

This private school was founded in 1920. It has a 75-acre campus.

STUDENTS AND FACULTY

Enrollment: 6,210. **Student Body:** Male 37%, female 63%, out-of-state 43%, international 1% (14 countries represented). **Ethnic Representation:** African American 11%, Asian 1%, Caucasian 84%, Hispanic 1%, Native American 1%. **Retention and Graduation:** 90% freshmen return for sophomore year. **Faculty:** Student/faculty ratio 17:1. 106 full-time faculty, 50% hold PhDs. 98% faculty teach undergrads.

ACADEMICS

Degrees: Associate's, bachelor's, master's. **Academic Requirements:** General education including some course work in arts/fine arts, English (including composition), foreign languages, history, humanities, mathematics, philosophy, sciences (biological or physical). **Classes:** 10-19 students in an average class. 10-19 students in an average lab/discussion section. **Majors with Highest Enrollment:** Business administration/management; elementary education and teaching; social sciences, general. **Disciplines with Highest Percentage of Degrees Awarded:** Business/marketing 55%, health professions and related sciences 19%, education 5%, philosophy/religion/theology 5%, psychology 2%. **Special Study Options:** Distance learning, honors program, independent study, liberal arts/career combination, teacher certification program.

FACILITIES

Housing: All-female, all-male, apartments for single students, specially designed townhouses and dorm spaces are available. The housing types listed are specific to the main campus in Marion, Indiana, for traditional students. The ages reflect this same population (Indiana Wesleyan University has 5 campuses). **Library Holdings:** 111,647 bound volumes. 10,195 periodicals. 185,593 microforms. 9,220 audiovisuals. **Special Academic Facilities/Equipment:** Lee Howard Art Collection (European artists), Lewis Jackson Library, Tom & Joanne Phillippe Performing Arts Center, bronze statues from Israel, Williams Chapel (medieval replica), Burns Hall of Science and Nursing, Luckey Recreation and Wellness Center, John Maxwell Business Center. **Computers:** School-owned computers available for student use.

EXTRACURRICULARS

Activities: Choral groups, concert band, drama/theater, jazz band, music ensembles, musical theater, opera, pep band, radio station, student government, student newspaper, student-run film society, symphony orchestra, television station, yearbook. **Athletics (Intercollegiate):** *Men:* baseball, basketball, cheerleading, cross-country, golf, indoor track, soccer, tennis, track & field. *Women:* basketball, cheerleading, cross-country, indoor track, soccer, softball, tennis, track & field, volleyball.

ADMISSIONS

Selectivity Rating: 83 (of 100). **Freshman Academic Profile:** Average high school GPA 3.5. 31% in top 10% of high school class, 59% in top 25% of high school class, 83% in top 50% of high school class. Average SAT I Math 542, SAT I Math middle 50% range 480-600. Average SAT I Verbal 539, SAT I Verbal middle 50% range 480-600. Average ACT 24, ACT middle 50% range 22-27. TOEFL required of all international applicants, minimum TOEFL 550. **Basis for Candidate Selection:** *Very important factors considered include:* secondary school record, standardized test scores. *Important factors considered include:* recommendations. *Other factors considered include:* class rank, essays. **Freshman Admission Requirements:** High school diploma or GED is required. *Academic units required/recommended:* 10 total required. **Freshman Admission Statistics:** 2,577 applied, 90% accepted, 45% of those accepted enrolled. **Transfer Admission Requirements:** *Items required:* college transcript, statement of good standing from prior school. Minimum college GPA of 2.0 required. Lowest grade transferable C. **General Admission Information:** Application fee $25. Priority application deadline January 2. Regular application deadline July 1. Nonfall registration accepted. Credit offered for CEEB Advanced Placement tests.

COSTS AND FINANCIAL AID

Tuition $13,496. Room & board $5,158. Required fees $0. Average book expense $800. **Required Forms and Deadlines:** FAFSA and institution's own financial aid form. **Types of Aid:** *Need-based scholarships/grants:* Pell, SEOG, state scholarships/grants, private scholarships, the school's own gift aid. *Loans:* FFEL Subsidized Stafford, FFEL Unsubsidized Stafford, FFEL PLUS, Federal Perkins, Federal Nursing, college/university loans from institutional funds. **Student Employment:** Federal Work-Study Program available. Institutional employment available. Off-campus job opportunities are good. **Financial Aid Phone:** 765-677-2116.

INTERNATIONAL ACADEMY OF DESIGN & TECHNOLOGY—TAMPA

5225 Memorial Highway, Tampa, FL 33634
Phone: 813-881-0007 **E-mail:** leads@academy.edu
Fax: 813-881-0008 **Web:** www.academy.edu

This proprietary school was founded in 1984. It has a 10-acre campus.

STUDENTS AND FACULTY

Enrollment: 2,043. **Student Body:** Male 47%, female 53%, out-of-state 24%, international 3% (17 countries represented). **Ethnic Representation:** African American 13%, Asian 3%, Caucasian 65%, Hispanic 17%, Native American 1%. **Retention and Graduation:** 72% freshmen return for sophomore year. 21% freshmen graduate within 4 years. 18% grads go on to further study within 1 year. **Faculty:** Student/faculty ratio 16:1. 20 full-time faculty, 25% hold PhDs. 100% faculty teach undergrads.

ACADEMICS

Degrees: Associate's, bachelor's. **Academic Requirements:** General education including some course work in arts/fine arts, computer literacy, English (including composition), humanities, mathematics, social science. **Majors with Highest Enrollment:** Design and visual communications, general; fashion/apparel design; interior design. **Disciplines with Highest Percentage of Degrees Awarded:** Visual and performing arts 84%, business/marketing 16%. **Special Study Options:** Accelerated program, distance learning, independent study, internships, study abroad.

FACILITIES

Housing: Apartments for married students, apartments for single students through outside agency. **Library Holdings:** 8,233 bound volumes. 3 periodicals. 0 microforms. 665 audiovisuals. **Computers:** School-owned computers available for student use.

EXTRACURRICULARS

Organizations: 1 registered organization.

ADMISSIONS

Selectivity Rating: 63 (of 100). **Freshman Academic Profile: Basis for Candidate Selection:** *Very important factors considered include:* interview. *Other factors considered include:* character/personal qualities, talent/ability, work experience. **Freshman Admission Requirements:** High school diploma or GED is required. **Freshman Admission Statistics:** 467 applied, 71% accepted, 69% of those accepted enrolled. **Transfer Admission Requirements:** *Items required:* college transcript, interview. Lowest grade transferable C. **General Admission Information:** Application fee $100. Nonfall registration accepted. Admission may be deferred. Neither credit nor placement offered for CEEB Advanced Placement tests.

COSTS AND FINANCIAL AID

Required fees $150. Average book expense $1,300. **Required Forms and Deadlines:** FAFSA. No deadline for regular filing. **Types of Aid:** *Need-based scholarships/grants:* Pell, SEOG, state scholarships/grants, private scholarships, the school's own gift aid. *Loans:* FFEL Subsidized Stafford, FFEL Unsubsidized Stafford, FFEL PLUS, private loans via lenders. **Student Employment:** Federal Work-Study Program available. Off-campus job opportunities are excellent. **Financial Aid Phone:** 813-881-0007.

IONA COLLEGE

715 North Avenue, New Rochelle, NY 10801
Phone: 914-633-2502 **E-mail:** icad@iona.edu **CEEB Code:** 2324
Fax: 914-633-2642 **Web:** www.iona.edu **ACT Code:** 2770

This private school, which is affiliated with the Roman Catholic Church, was founded in 1940. It has a 35-acre campus.

STUDENTS AND FACULTY

Enrollment: 3,464. **Student Body:** Male 48%, female 52%, out-of-state 16%, international students represent 32 countries. **Ethnic Representation:** African American 9%, Asian 2%, Caucasian 63%, Hispanic 11%. **Retention and Graduation:** 76% freshmen return for sophomore year. 39% freshmen graduate within 4 years. 26% grads go on to further study within 1 year. 10% grads pursue business degrees. **Faculty:** Student/faculty ratio 15:1. 173 full-time faculty, 83% hold PhDs. 100% faculty teach undergrads.

ACADEMICS

Degrees: Bachelor's, certificate, master's, post-master's certificate. **Academic Requirements:** General education including some course work in computer literacy, English (including composition), foreign languages, history, humanities, mathematics, philosophy, sciences (biological or physical), social science. **Classes:** 10-19 students in an average class. 10-19 students in an average lab/discussion section. **Majors with Highest Enrollment:** Finance, general; business, management, marketing, and related support services; mass communications/media studies. **Disciplines with Highest Percentage of Degrees Awarded:** Business/marketing 29%, communications/communication technologies 15%, computer and information sciences 10%, social sciences and history 9%, protective services/public administration 9%. **Special Study Options:** Accelerated program, distance learning, double major, dual enrollment, honors program, independent study, internships, study abroad, teacher certification program, weekend college.

FACILITIES

Housing: Coed, apartments for single students. **Library Holdings:** 270,731 bound volumes. 738 periodicals. 487,817 microforms. 3,022 audiovisuals. **Special Academic Facilities/Equipment:** Community arts center, Irish and rare book collection. **Computers:** *Recommended operating system:* Windows 95. School-owned computers available for student use.

EXTRACURRICULARS

Activities: Choral groups, dance, drama/theater, literary magazine, musical theater, pep band, radio station, student government, student newspaper, television station, yearbook. **Organizations:** 47 registered organizations, 20 honor societies, 1 religious organization, 8 fraternities, 7 sororities. **Athletics (Intercollegiate):** *Men:* baseball, basketball, crew, cross-country, diving, football, golf, ice hockey, indoor track, soccer, swimming, tennis, track & field, water polo. *Women:* basketball, cheerleading, crew, cross-country, diving, indoor track, soccer, softball, swimming, tennis, track & field, volleyball, water polo.

ADMISSIONS

Selectivity Rating: 63 (of 100). **Freshman Academic Profile:** Average high school GPA 2.8. Average SAT I Math 507, SAT I Math middle 50% range 490-590. Average SAT I Verbal 504, SAT I Verbal middle 50% range 500-590. Average ACT 21. TOEFL required of all international applicants, minimum TOEFL 550. **Basis for Candidate Selection:** *Very important factors considered include:* secondary school record, standardized test scores. *Important factors considered include:* character/personal qualities, class rank, essays, extracurricular activities, interview, recommendations. *Other factors considered include:* alumni/ae relation, geographical residence, talent/ability, volunteer work. **Freshman Admission Requirements:** High school diploma or GED is required. *Academic units required/recommended:* 16 total required;

17 total recommended; 4 English required, 4 English recommended, 3 math required, 3 math recommended, 1 science required, 3 science recommended, 1 science lab required, 2 science lab recommended, 2 foreign language required, 2 foreign language recommended, 1 social studies required, 1 social studies recommended, 1 history required, 1 history recommended, 4 elective required, 3 elective recommended. **Freshman Admission Statistics:** 3,318 applied, 69% accepted, 35% of those accepted enrolled. **Transfer Admission Requirements:** *Items required:* high school transcript, college transcript, standardized test scores. Minimum high school GPA of 2.5 required. Minimum college GPA of 2.5 required. Lowest grade transferable C. **General Admission Information:** Application fee $40. Priority application deadline March 15. Nonfall registration accepted. Admission may be deferred for a maximum of 1 year. Credit and/or placement offered for CEEB Advanced Placement tests.

COSTS AND FINANCIAL AID

Tuition $17,326. Room & board $9,700. Required fees $540. Average book expense $700. **Required Forms and Deadlines:** FAFSA, institution's own financial aid form, and state aid form. No deadline for regular filing. **Notification of Awards:** Applicants will be notified of awards on a rolling basis beginning on or about December 20. **Types of Aid:** *Need-based scholarships/grants:* Pell, SEOG, state scholarships/grants, private scholarships, the school's own gift aid. *Loans:* FFEL Subsidized Stafford, FFEL Unsubsidized Stafford, FFEL PLUS, Federal Perkins, alternative loans. **Student Employment:** Federal Work-Study Program available. Institutional employment available. Off-campus job opportunities are good. **Financial Aid Statistics:** 75% freshmen, 70% undergrads receive some form of aid. Average freshman grant $6,998. Average freshman loan $7,246. Average income from on-campus job $1,146. **Financial Aid Phone:** 914-633-2497.

IOWA STATE UNIVERSITY OF SCIENCE AND TECHNOLOGY

100 Alumni Hall, Ames, IA 50011-2011
Phone: 515-294-5836 **E-mail:** admissions@iastate.edu **CEEB Code:** 6306
Fax: 515-294-2592 **Web:** www.iastate.edu **ACT Code:** 1320

This public school was founded in 1858. It has a 1,788-acre campus.

STUDENTS AND FACULTY

Enrollment: 22,999. **Student Body:** Male 56%, female 44%, out-of-state 19%, international 4% (117 countries represented). **Ethnic Representation:** African American 3%, Asian 3%, Caucasian 87%, Hispanic 2%. **Retention and Graduation:** 83% freshmen return for sophomore year. 28% freshmen graduate within 4 years. 16% grads go on to further study within 1 year. 8% grads pursue business degrees. 7% grads pursue law degrees. 14% grads pursue medical degrees. **Faculty:** Student/faculty ratio 16:1. 1,399 full-time faculty, 92% hold PhDs. 86% faculty teach undergrads.

ACADEMICS

Degrees: Bachelor's, doctoral, first professional, master's, post-master's certificate. **Academic Requirements:** General education including some course work in English (including composition), humanities, mathematics, sciences (biological or physical), social science, diversity, international perspectives, use of library. **Classes:** 20-29 students in an average class. 20-29 students in an average lab/discussion section. **Majors with Highest Enrollment:** Management information systems, general; elementary education and teaching; mechanical engineering. **Disciplines with Highest Percentage of Degrees Awarded:** Business/marketing 20%, engineering/engineering technology 17%, agriculture 10%, education 8%, biological life sciences 6%. **Special Study Options:** Accelerated program, cooperative (work-study) program, cross registration, distance learning, double major, dual enrollment, English as a second language, student exchange program (domestic), external degree program, honors program, independent study, internships, liberal arts/career combination, student-designed major, study abroad, teacher certification program, weekend college.

FACILITIES

Housing: Coed, all-female, all-male, apartments for married students, apartments for single students, housing for disabled students, housing for international students, fraternities and/or sororities, learning communities, family housing; quiet, nonsmoking, or alcohol-free floors; graduate/adult undergraduate housing. **Library Holdings:** 2,348,646 bound volumes. 29,681 periodicals. 3,380,573 microforms. 58,055 audiovisuals. **Special Academic Facilities/Equipment:** Brunnier Art Museum, Farm House Museum, observatory, numerous institutes, research centers, College of Design Gallery. **Computers:** School-owned computers available for student use.

EXTRACURRICULARS

Activities: Choral groups, concert band, dance, drama/theater, jazz band, literary magazine, marching band, music ensembles, musical theater, opera, pep band, radio station, student government, student newspaper, student-run film society, symphony orchestra, television station. **Organizations:** 542 registered organizations, 34 honor societies, 36 religious organizations, 31 fraternities (13% men join), 18 sororities (12% women join). **Athletics (Intercollegiate):** *Men:* basketball, cross-country, football, golf, indoor track, track & field, wrestling. *Women:* basketball, cross-country, golf, gymnastics, indoor track, soccer, softball, swimming, tennis, track & field, volleyball.

ADMISSIONS

Selectivity Rating: 76 (of 100). **Freshman Academic Profile:** Average high school GPA 3.5. 25% in top 10% of high school class, 58% in top 25% of high school class, 93% in top 50% of high school class. 93% from public high schools. Average SAT I Math 620, SAT I Math middle 50% range 550-670. Average SAT I Verbal 590, SAT I Verbal middle 50% range 510-650. Average ACT 24, ACT middle 50% range 22-27. TOEFL required of all international applicants, minimum TOEFL 500. **Basis for Candidate Selection:** *Very important factors considered include:* class rank, secondary school record, standardized test scores. *Other factors considered include:* character/personal qualities, essays, extracurricular activities, geographical residence, interview, recommendations, state residency, talent/ability, volunteer work, work experience. **Freshman Admission Requirements:** High school diploma or GED is required. *Academic units required/recommended:* 4 English required, 3 math required, 3 science required, 2 science lab required, 2 foreign language recommended, 2 social studies required, 3 social studies recommended. **Freshman Admission Statistics:** 10,370 applied, 89% accepted, 46% of those accepted enrolled. **Transfer Admission Requirements:** *Items required:* college transcript, statement of good standing from prior school. Minimum college GPA of 2.0 required. Lowest grade transferable D-. **General Admission Information:** Application fee $30. Regular application deadline August 1. Nonfall registration accepted. Admission may be deferred for a maximum of 1 year. Credit and/or placement offered for CEEB Advanced Placement tests.

COSTS AND FINANCIAL AID

In-state tuition $4,342. Out-of-state tuition $13,684. Room & board $5,020. Required fees $686. Average book expense $754. **Required Forms and Deadlines:** FAFSA. No deadline for regular filing. Priority filing deadline March 1. **Notification of Awards:** Applicants will be notified of awards on a rolling basis beginning on or about April 1. **Types of Aid:** *Need-based scholarships/grants:* Pell, SEOG, state scholarships/grants, private scholarships, the school's own gift aid. *Loans:* Direct Subsidized Stafford, Direct Unsubsidized Stafford, Direct PLUS, Federal Perkins, state loans, college/university loans from institutional funds, private alternative loans. **Student Employment:** Federal Work-Study Program available. Institutional employment available. Off-campus job opportunities are excellent. **Financial Aid Statistics:** 57% freshmen, 46% undergrads receive some form of aid. Average freshman grant $4,260. Average freshman loan $5,923. Average income from on-campus job $1,849. **Financial Aid Phone:** 515-294-2223.

IOWA WESLEYAN COLLEGE

601 North Main Street, Mt. Pleasant, IA 52641
Phone: 319-385-6231 **E-mail:** admitrwl@iwc.edu **CEEB Code:** 6308
Fax: 319-385-6296 **Web:** www.iwc.edu **ACT Code:** 1324

This private school, which is affiliated with the Methodist Church, was founded in 1842. It has a 60-acre campus.

STUDENTS AND FACULTY

Enrollment: 785. **Student Body:** Male 39%, female 61%, out-of-state 22%, international 3% (11 country represented). **Ethnic Representation:** African American 6%, Asian 1%, Caucasian 91%, Hispanic 2%. **Retention and Graduation:** 55% freshmen return for sophomore year. 23% freshmen graduate within 4 years. 2% grads go on to further study within 1 year. 1% grads pursue business degrees. 1% grads pursue medical degrees. **Faculty:** Student/faculty ratio 12:1. 44 full-time faculty, 38% hold PhDs. 100% faculty teach undergrads.

ACADEMICS

Degrees: Bachelor's. **Academic Requirements:** General education including some course work in arts/fine arts, computer literacy, English (including composition), history, humanities, mathematics, philosophy, sciences (biological or physical), social science. **Classes:** Under 10 students in an average class. **Disciplines with Highest Percentage of Degrees Awarded:** Education

28%, business/marketing 22%, other 21%, psychology 7%, biological life sciences 6%. **Special Study Options:** Cooperative (work-study) program, cross registration, distance learning, double major, dual enrollment, English as a second language, student exchange program (domestic), independent study, internships, liberal arts/career combination, student-designed major, study abroad, teacher certification program.

FACILITIES

Housing: All-female, all-male, housing for international students. **Library Holdings:** 106,816 bound volumes. 431 periodicals. 26,757 microforms. 3,492 audiovisuals. **Special Academic Facilities/Equipment:** Art gallery, biological environment chamber. **Computers:** School-owned computers available for student use.

EXTRACURRICULARS

Activities: Choral groups, concert band, jazz band, literary magazine, music ensembles, pep band, radio station, student government, student newspaper, symphony orchestra, yearbook. **Organizations:** 42 registered organizations, 2 religious organizations, 1 fraternity (3% men join), 2 sororities (12% women join). **Athletics (Intercollegiate):** *Men:* baseball, basketball, cross-country, football, golf, soccer, track & field. *Women:* basketball, cross-country, golf, soccer, softball, track & field, volleyball.

ADMISSIONS

Selectivity Rating: 65 (of 100). **Freshman Academic Profile:** Average high school GPA 2.9. 9% in top 10% of high school class, 18% in top 25% of high school class, 45% in top 50% of high school class. 96% from public high schools. Average ACT 18. TOEFL required of all international applicants, minimum TOEFL 500. **Basis for Candidate Selection:** *Very important factors considered include:* alumni/ae relation, secondary school record, volunteer work, work experience. *Important factors considered include:* class rank, extracurricular activities, geographical residence, standardized test scores, talent/ability. *Other factors considered include:* character/personal qualities, essays, recommendations, religious affiliation/commitment, state residency. **Freshman Admission Requirements:** High school diploma or GED is required. *Academic units required/recommended:* 16 total recommended; 4 English recommended, 3 math recommended, 2 science recommended, 2 science lab recommended, 3 social studies recommended, 4 elective recommended. **Freshman Admission Statistics:** 408 applied, 85% accepted, 33% of those accepted enrolled. **Transfer Admission Requirements:** *Items required:* college transcript. Minimum high school GPA of 2.0 required. Minimum college GPA of 2.0 required. Lowest grade transferable D. **General Admission Information:** Application fee $15. Priority application deadline May 1. Early decision application deadline May 1. Regular application deadline August 15. Nonfall registration accepted. Admission may be deferred for a maximum of 1 year. Credit and/or placement offered for CEEB Advanced Placement tests.

COSTS AND FINANCIAL AID

Tuition $13,200. Room & board $4,250. Average book expense $735. **Required Forms and Deadlines:** FAFSA. No deadline for regular filing. Priority filing deadline April 1. **Notification of Awards:** Applicants will be notified of awards on a rolling basis beginning on or about March 1. **Types of Aid:** *Need-based scholarships/grants:* Pell, SEOG, state scholarships/grants, private scholarships, the school's own gift aid. *Loans:* FFEL Subsidized Stafford, FFEL Unsubsidized Stafford, FFEL PLUS, Federal Perkins, alternative loans. **Student Employment:** Federal Work-Study Program available. Institutional employment available. Off-campus job opportunities are good. **Financial Aid Statistics:** 89% freshmen, 87% undergrads receive some form of aid. Average freshman grant $12,500. Average freshman loan $2,625. Average income from on-campus job $500. **Financial Aid Phone:** 319-385-6242.

ITHACA COLLEGE

100 Job Hall, Ithaca, NY 14850-7020
Phone: 607-274-3124 **E-mail:** admission@ithaca.edu **CEEB Code:** 2325
Fax: 607-274-1900 **Web:** www.ithaca.edu **ACT Code:** 2772

This private school was founded in 1892. It has a 757-acre campus.

STUDENTS AND FACULTY

Enrollment: 6,190. **Student Body:** Male 43%, female 57%, out-of-state 51%, international 3% (76 countries represented). **Ethnic Representation:** African American 2%, Asian 3%, Caucasian 91%, Hispanic 3%. **Retention and Graduation:** 87% freshmen return for sophomore year. 64% freshmen graduate within 4 years. 33% grads go on to further study within 1 year. 1% grads pursue business degrees. 1% grads pursue law degrees. 1% grads pursue medical degrees. **Faculty:** Student/faculty ratio 12:1. 440 full-time faculty, 88% hold PhDs. 99% faculty teach undergrads.

ACADEMICS

Degrees: Bachelor's, certificate, master's. **Classes:** 10-19 students in an average class. **Majors with Highest Enrollment:** Mass communications/media studies; music/music and performing arts studies, general; business administration/management. **Disciplines with Highest Percentage of Degrees Awarded:** Communications/communication technologies 21%, visual and performing arts 16%, education 10%, health professions and related sciences 10%, business/marketing 9%. **Special Study Options:** Accelerated program, cross registration, double major, dual enrollment, honors program, independent study, internships, liberal arts/career combination, student-designed major, study abroad, teacher certification program. Off-campus study: London Center (London, England); Los Angeles Program; Washington, DC, semester.

FACILITIES

Housing: Coed; all-female; apartments for single students; housing for disabled students; housing for international students; fraternities and/or sororities; first-year-students-only; quiet residence hall; music, honor, fraternity housing; smoke-free buildings and floors; coed-by-floor buildings; substance-free building; honors floor; several freshman seminar groups housed together; H.O.M.E. (Housing Offering a Multicultural Experience) program. **Library Holdings:** 246,545 bound volumes. 2,305 periodicals. 305,164 microforms. 25,547 audiovisuals. **Special Academic Facilities/Equipment:** Art gallery, radio and TV stations, digital technology throughout communications building, observatory, wellness clinic, fitness center, trading room, speech and hearing handicapped clinic, physical therapy clinic, performing arts centers (music and theater), music recording facility. **Computers:** School-owned computers available for student use.

EXTRACURRICULARS

Activities: Choral groups, concert band, dance, drama/theater, jazz band, literary magazine, music ensembles, musical theater, opera, pep band, radio station, student government, student newspaper, student-run film society, symphony orchestra, television station, yearbook. **Organizations:** 140 registered organizations, 25 honor societies, 13 religious organizations, 2% men join fraternities, 2% women join sororities. **Athletics (Intercollegiate):** *Men:* baseball, basketball, crew, cross-country, diving, football, lacrosse, soccer, swimming, tennis, track & field, wrestling. *Women:* basketball, crew, cross-country, diving, field hockey, gymnastics, lacrosse, soccer, softball, swimming, tennis, track & field, volleyball.

ADMISSIONS

Selectivity Rating: 83 (of 100). **Freshman Academic Profile:** 36% in top 10% of high school class, 76% in top 25% of high school class, 98% in top 50% of high school class. 85% from public high schools. Average SAT I Math 595, SAT I Math middle 50% range 550-640. Average SAT I Verbal 587, SAT I Verbal middle 50% range 540-630. TOEFL required of all international applicants, minimum TOEFL 550. **Basis for Candidate Selection:** *Very important factors considered include:* secondary school record, standardized test scores. *Important factors considered include:* character/personal qualities, class rank, essays, extracurricular activities, interview, recommendations, talent/ability. *Other factors considered include:* alumni/ae relation, volunteer work, work experience. **Freshman Admission Requirements:** High school diploma or GED is required. *Academic units required/recommended:* 16 total required; 4 English required, 3 math required, 3 science required, 2 foreign language required, 3 social studies required, 1 elective required. **Freshman Admission Statistics:** 11,305 applied, 56% accepted, 24% of those accepted enrolled. **Transfer Admission Requirements:** *Items required:* high school transcript, college transcript, essay, statement of good standing from prior school. Minimum college GPA of 2.8 required. Lowest grade transferable C-. **General Admission Information:** Application fee $55. Priority application deadline March 1. Early decision application deadline November 1. Nonfall registration accepted. Admission may be deferred for a maximum of 1 year. Credit and/or placement offered for CEEB Advanced Placement tests.

COSTS AND FINANCIAL AID

Tuition $21,102. Room & board $8,960. Required fees $0. Average book expense $876. **Required Forms and Deadlines:** FAFSA and CSS PROFILE required of early decision applicants; deadline November 1. Priority filing deadline February 1. **Notification of Awards:** Applicants will be notified of awards on a rolling basis beginning on or about February 15. **Types of Aid:** *Need-based scholarships/grants:* Pell, SEOG, state scholarships/grants, private scholarships, the school's own gift aid. *Loans:* FFEL Subsidized Stafford, FFEL Unsubsidized Stafford, FFEL PLUS, Federal Perkins, college/university loans from institutional funds. **Student Employment:** Federal Work-Study Program available. Institutional employment available. Off-campus job opportunities are good. **Financial Aid Statistics:** 71% freshmen, 68% undergrads receive some form of aid. Average freshman grant $13,111. Average freshman loan $3,868. **Financial Aid Phone:** 607-274-3131.

See page 1066.

JACKSON STATE UNIVERSITY

1400 J. R. Lynch Street, PO Box 17330, Jackson, MS 39217
Phone: 601-979-2100 **E-mail:** schatman@ccaix.jsums.edu **CEEB Code:** 1341
Fax: 601-979-3445 **ACT Code:** 2204

This public school was founded in 1877. It has a 128-acre campus.

STUDENTS AND FACULTY

Enrollment: 5,471. **Student Body:** Male 39%, female 61%, out-of-state 18%, international 1%. **Ethnic Representation:** African American 99%, Caucasian 1%. **Retention and Graduation:** 69% freshmen return for sophomore year. 11% freshmen graduate within 4 years. 13% grads go on to further study within 1 year. 6% grads pursue law degrees. 7% grads pursue medical degrees. **Faculty:** Student/faculty ratio 16:1. 335 full-time faculty, 75% hold PhDs.

ACADEMICS

Degrees: Bachelor's, doctoral, master's, post-master's certificate. **Academic Requirements:** General education including some course work in arts/fine arts, computer literacy, English (including composition), foreign languages, history, humanities, mathematics, philosophy, sciences (biological or physical), social science. **Disciplines with Highest Percentage of Degrees Awarded:** Business/marketing 21%, education 18%, protective services/public administration 16%, biological life sciences 11%, computer and information sciences 6%. **Special Study Options:** Cooperative (work-study) program, distance learning, double major, honors program, internships, study abroad, teacher certification program. Undergrads may take grad-level classes. Off-campus programs: research semester at Lawrence Berkeley Lab. Co-op programs: business, computer science, natural science.

FACILITIES

Housing: Coed, all-female, all-male. **Library Holdings:** 387,492 bound volumes. 3,185 periodicals. 840,697 microforms. 0 audiovisuals. **Special Academic Facilities/Equipment:** Research center. **Computers:** School-owned computers available for student use.

EXTRACURRICULARS

Activities: Choral groups, dance, literary magazine, marching band, pep band, radio station, student government, student newspaper, television station, yearbook. **Organizations:** 120 registered organizations, 9 honor societies, 4 religious organizations, 4 fraternities, 4 sororities. **Athletics (Intercollegiate):** *Men:* baseball, basketball, cross-country, football, golf, indoor track, tennis, track & field, volleyball. *Women:* basketball, cross-country, golf, indoor track, softball, tennis, track & field, volleyball.

ADMISSIONS

Selectivity Rating: 68 (of 100). **Freshman Academic Profile:** Average high school GPA 2.9. 5% in top 10% of high school class, 41% in top 25% of high school class, 76% in top 50% of high school class. 85% from public high schools. Average ACT 17. TOEFL required of all international applicants, minimum TOEFL 525. **Basis for Candidate Selection:** *Important factors considered include:* class rank, extracurricular activities, secondary school record, standardized test scores, talent/ability. *Other factors considered include:* essays, geographical residence, interview, recommendations, state residency. **Freshman Admission Requirements:** High school diploma or GED is required. *Academic units required/recommended:* 15 total required; 4 English required, 3 math required, 3 science required, 3 social studies required, 2 elective required. **Freshman Admission Statistics:** 4,659 applied, 46% accepted, 57% of those accepted enrolled. **Transfer Admission Requirements:** *Items required:* high school transcript, college transcript. Minimum college GPA of 2.0 required. Lowest grade transferable C. **General Admission Information:** Priority application deadline August 15. Nonfall registration accepted.

COSTS AND FINANCIAL AID

In-state tuition $2,788. Out-of-state tuition $6,414. Room & board $3,698. Required fees $50. Average book expense $1,000. **Required Forms and Deadlines:** institution's own financial aid form. **Types of Aid:** *Need-based scholarships/grants:* Pell, SEOG, state scholarships/grants, private scholarships, the school's own gift aid. *Loans:* FFEL Subsidized Stafford, FFEL Unsubsidized Stafford, FFEL PLUS, Federal Perkins, college/university loans from institutional funds. **Student Employment:** Federal Work-Study Program available. Institutional employment available. Off-campus job opportunities are good. **Financial Aid Statistics:** Average income from on-campus job $2,200. **Financial Aid Phone:** 601-979-2227.

JACKSONVILLE STATE UNIVERSITY

700 Pelham Road North, Jacksonville, AL 36265
Phone: 256-782-5400 **E-mail:** lbedford@jsucc.jsu.edu
Fax: 256-782-5121 **Web:** www.jsu.edu **ACT Code:** 20

This public school was founded in 1883. It has a 360-acre campus.

STUDENTS AND FACULTY

Enrollment: 7,324. **Student Body:** Male 42%, female 58%, out-of-state 16%, international 1% (73 countries represented). **Ethnic Representation:** African American 21%, Asian 1%, Caucasian 75%, Hispanic 1%, Native American 1%. **Retention and Graduation:** 60% freshmen return for sophomore year. **Faculty:** Student/faculty ratio 20:1. 289 full-time faculty, 62% hold PhDs. 100% faculty teach undergrads.

ACADEMICS

Degrees: Bachelor's, master's, post-master's certificate. **Academic Requirements:** General education including some course work in arts/fine arts, computer literacy, English (including composition), history, humanities, mathematics, sciences (biological or physical), social science. **Classes:** 20-29 students in an average class. **Disciplines with Highest Percentage of Degrees Awarded:** Education 24%, business/marketing 15%, protective services/public administration 15%, social sciences and history 7%, health professions and related sciences 7%. **Special Study Options:** Accelerated program, cooperative (work-study) program, distance learning, double major, dual enrollment, honors program, independent study, internships, teacher certification program.

FACILITIES

Housing: Coed, all-female, all-male, apartments for married students, apartments for single students, housing for international students, fraternities and/or sororities, apartments for students with dependent children. **Library Holdings:** 420,583 bound volumes. 1,695 periodicals. 1,273,105 microforms. 32,875 audiovisuals. **Computers:** School-owned computers available for student use.

EXTRACURRICULARS

Activities: Choral groups, concert band, dance, drama/theater, jazz band, marching band, music ensembles, musical theater, pep band, radio station, student government, student newspaper, symphony orchestra, yearbook. **Organizations:** 100 registered organizations, 8 religious organizations, 11 fraternities (10% men join), 9 sororities (10% women join). **Athletics (Intercollegiate):** *Men:* baseball, basketball, cheerleading, football, golf, rifle, tennis. *Women:* basketball, cheerleading, cross-country, golf, rifle, soccer, softball, tennis, track & field, volleyball.

ADMISSIONS

Selectivity Rating: 66 (of 100). **Freshman Academic Profile:** Average ACT 20, ACT middle 50% range 18-23. TOEFL required of all international applicants, minimum TOEFL 500. **Basis for Candidate Selection:** *Very important factors considered include:* secondary school record, standardized test scores. **Freshman Admission Requirements:** High school diploma or GED is required. *Academic units required/recommended:* 15 total required; 3 English required, 4 elective required. **Freshman Admission Statistics:** 2,600 applied, 43% accepted, 100% of those accepted enrolled. **Transfer Admission Requirements:** *Items required:* college transcript. Lowest grade transferable D. **General Admission Information:** Application fee $20. Nonfall registration accepted. Admission may be deferred for a maximum of 4 years. Credit and/or placement offered for CEEB Advanced Placement tests.

COSTS AND FINANCIAL AID

In-state tuition $3,240. Out-of-state tuition $6,480. Room & board $2,876. Required fees $100. Average book expense $900. **Required Forms and Deadlines:** FAFSA and institution's own financial aid form. No deadline for regular filing. Priority filing deadline March 15. **Notification of Awards:** Applicants will be notified of awards on a rolling basis beginning on or about May 15. **Types of Aid:** *Need-based scholarships/grants:* Pell, SEOG, state scholarships/grants, private scholarships, Federal Nursing. *Loans:* Direct Subsidized Stafford, Direct Unsubsidized Stafford, Direct PLUS, college/university loans from institutional funds. **Student Employment:** Federal Work-Study Program available. Institutional employment available. Off-campus job opportunities are fair. **Financial Aid Phone:** 256-782-5006.

JACKSONVILLE UNIVERSITY

$$$

Office of Admissions, 2800 University Boulevard North, Jacksonville, FL 32211
Phone: 904-256-7000 **E-mail:** admissions@ju.edu **CEEB Code:** 5331
Fax: 904-256-7012 **Web:** www.ju.edu **ACT Code:** 740

This private school was founded in 1934. It has a 260-acre campus.

STUDENTS AND FACULTY

Enrollment: 2,171. **Student Body:** Male 50%, female 50%, out-of-state 40%, international 3%. **Ethnic Representation:** African American 18%, Asian 2%, Caucasian 66%, Hispanic 4%. **Retention and Graduation:** 71% freshmen return for sophomore year. 31% freshmen graduate within 4 years. **Faculty:** Student/faculty ratio 14:1. 116 full-time faculty, 74% hold PhDs. 100% faculty teach undergrads.

ACADEMICS

Degrees: Bachelor's, master's. **Academic Requirements:** General education including some course work in arts/fine arts, computer literacy, English (including composition), foreign languages, history, humanities, mathematics, philosophy, sciences (biological or physical), social science. **Classes:** 10-19 students in an average class. **Majors with Highest Enrollment:** Aviation/ airway management and operations; business administration/management; nursing/registered nurse training (RN, ASN, BSN, MSN). **Disciplines with Highest Percentage of Degrees Awarded:** Business/marketing 31%, health professions and related sciences 12%, computer and information sciences 8%, communications/communication technologies 8%, visual and performing arts 6%. **Special Study Options:** Accelerated program, cooperative (work-study) program, distance learning, double major, dual enrollment, honors program, independent study, internships, liberal arts/career combination, student-designed major, study abroad, teacher certification program.

FACILITIES

Housing: Coed, all-female, all-male, apartments for single students. **Library Holdings:** 374,016 bound volumes. 686 periodicals. 312,297 microforms. 32,887 audiovisuals. **Special Academic Facilities/Equipment:** Art museum, dance pavilion, concert hall, on-campus preschool. **Computers:** *Recommended operating system:* Windows 95. School-owned computers available for student use.

EXTRACURRICULARS

Activities: Choral groups, concert band, dance, drama/theater, jazz band, literary magazine, music ensembles, pep band, radio station, student government, student newspaper, symphony orchestra, television station, yearbook. **Organizations:** 50 registered organizations, 8 honor societies, 1 religious organization, 18% men join fraternities, 13% women join sororities. **Athletics (Intercollegiate):** *Men:* baseball, basketball, cross-country, football, golf, soccer, tennis. *Women:* basketball, crew, cross-country, golf, indoor track, soccer, softball, tennis, track & field, volleyball.

ADMISSIONS

Selectivity Rating: 74 (of 100). **Freshman Academic Profile:** Average high school GPA 3.2. 21% in top 10% of high school class, 47% in top 25% of high school class, 79% in top 50% of high school class. Average SAT I Math 533, SAT I Math middle 50% range 480-590. Average SAT I Verbal 524, SAT I Verbal middle 50% range 460-580. Average ACT 22, ACT middle 50% range 19-25. TOEFL required of all international applicants, minimum TOEFL 550. **Basis for Candidate Selection:** *Very important factors considered include:* secondary school record. *Important factors considered include:* essays, recommendations, standardized test scores. *Other factors considered include:* alumni/ae relation, character/personal qualities, class rank, extracurricular activities, interview, talent/ability, volunteer work, work experience. **Freshman Admission Requirements:** High school diploma or GED is required. *Academic units required/recommended:* 14 total required; 16 total recommended; 4 English required, 3 math required, 4 math recommended, 2 science required, 2 science lab required, 2 foreign language required, 3 foreign language recommended, 3 social studies required. **Freshman Admission Statistics:** 1,553 applied, 73% accepted, 35% of those accepted enrolled. **Transfer Admission Requirements:** *Items required:* college transcript, essay, statement of good standing from prior school. Minimum college GPA of 2.0 required. Lowest grade transferable C. **General Admission Information:** Application fee $30. Nonfall registration accepted. Admission may be deferred for a maximum of 1 year. Credit and/or placement offered for CEEB Advanced Placement tests.

COSTS AND FINANCIAL AID

Tuition $16,540. Room & board $5,900. Required fees $240. Average book expense $600. **Required Forms and Deadlines:** FAFSA and institution's own financial aid form. No deadline for regular filing. Priority filing deadline January 15. **Notification of Awards:** Applicants will be notified of awards on a rolling basis beginning on or about October 15. **Types of Aid:** *Need-based scholarships/grants:* Pell, SEOG, state scholarships/grants, private scholarships, the school's own gift aid, Navy ROTC. *Loans:* FFEL Subsidized Stafford, FFEL Unsubsidized Stafford, FFEL PLUS, Federal Perkins, college/university loans from institutional funds, private alternative loans. **Student Employment:** Federal Work-Study Program available. Institutional employment available. Off-campus job opportunities are excellent. **Financial Aid Statistics:** 63% freshmen, 65% undergrads receive some form of aid. **Financial Aid Phone:** 904-256-7060.

JAMES MADISON UNIVERSITY

Undergraduate Admission, Sonner Hall MSC 0101, Harrisonburg, VA 22807
Phone: 540-568-5681 **E-mail:** gotojmu@jmu.edu **CEEB Code:** 5392
Fax: 540-568-3332 **Web:** www.jmu.edu **ACT Code:** 4370

This public school was founded in 1908. It has a 495-acre campus.

STUDENTS AND FACULTY

Enrollment: 14,828. **Student Body:** Male 41%, female 59%, out-of-state 29%, international 1% (60 countries represented). **Ethnic Representation:** African American 4%, Asian 5%, Caucasian 86%, Hispanic 2%. **Retention and Graduation:** 92% freshmen return for sophomore year. 60% freshmen graduate within 4 years. 17% grads go on to further study within 1 year. **Faculty:** Student/faculty ratio 17:1. 704 full-time faculty, 83% hold PhDs. 100% faculty teach undergrads.

ACADEMICS

Degrees: Bachelor's, doctoral, master's, post-master's certificate. **Academic Requirements:** General education including some course work in arts/fine arts, computer literacy, English (including composition), history, humanities, mathematics, philosophy, sciences (biological or physical), social science, speech communication, critical thinking, wellness, U.S. history/government. **Classes:** 20-29 students in an average class. 20-29 students in an average lab/discussion section. **Majors with Highest Enrollment:** Marketing/marketing management, general; psychology, general; community health services/liaison/ counseling. **Disciplines with Highest Percentage of Degrees Awarded:** Business/marketing 19%, social sciences and history 12%, computer and information sciences 9%, health professions and related sciences 9%, communications/communication technologies 8%. **Special Study Options:** Accelerated program, distance learning, double major, honors program, independent study, internships, study abroad, teacher certification program.

FACILITIES

Housing: Coed, apartments for single students, fraternities and/or sororities, theme housing for international living. Students must apply. **Library Holdings:** 744,041 bound volumes. 3,367 periodicals. 1,120,585 microforms. 28,465 audiovisuals. **Special Academic Facilities/Equipment:** Language lab, development center, TV/film center, music and fine arts buildings, herbarium, university farm, planetarium. **Computers:** *Recommended operating system:* Windows 95, 2000 or XP. School-owned computers available for student use.

EXTRACURRICULARS

Activities: Choral groups, concert band, dance, drama/theater, jazz band, literary magazine, marching band, music ensembles, musical theater, opera, pep band, radio station, student government, student newspaper, symphony orchestra, yearbook. **Organizations:** 272 registered organizations, 21 honor societies, 19 religious organizations, 15 fraternities (11% men join), 11 sororities (13% women join). **Athletics (Intercollegiate):** *Men:* baseball, basketball, cheerleading, cross-country, diving, football, golf, gymnastics, soccer, swimming, tennis, track & field, wrestling. *Women:* basketball, cheerleading, cross-country, diving, fencing, field hockey, golf, gymnastics, lacrosse, soccer, softball, swimming, tennis, track & field, volleyball.

ADMISSIONS

Selectivity Rating: 84 (of 100). **Freshman Academic Profile:** Average high school GPA 3.6. 30% in top 10% of high school class, 80% in top 25% of high school class, 99% in top 50% of high school class. 95% from public high schools. Average SAT I Math 587, SAT I Math middle 50% range 540-630. Average SAT I Verbal 578, SAT I Verbal middle 50% range 540-620. TOEFL required of all international applicants, minimum TOEFL 570. **Basis for Candidate Selection:** *Very important factors considered include:* class rank, secondary school record, standardized test scores. *Important factors considered include:* essays, extracurricular activities. *Other factors considered include:* alumni/ae relation, character/personal qualities, geographical residence, minority status, recommendations, state residency, talent/ability, volunteer work, work experience. **Freshman Admission Requirements:** High school diploma or GED is required. *Academic units required/recommended:* 14 total required; 22 total recommended; 4 English required, 4 English recommended, 3 math required, 4 math recommended, 3 science required, 4 science recommended, 2 science lab required, 3 science lab recommended, 3 foreign language recommended, 1 social studies required, 2 social studies recommended, 1 history required, 2 history recommended. **Freshman Admission Statistics:** 15,639 applied, 58% accepted, 36% of those accepted enrolled. **Transfer Admission Requirements:** *Items required:* high school transcript, college transcript, essay. Minimum college GPA of 2.0 required. Lowest grade transferable C. **General Admission Information:** Application fee $40. Priority application deadline November 1. Regular application deadline January 15. Admission may be deferred for a maximum of 1 year. Credit offered for CEEB Advanced Placement tests.

COSTS AND FINANCIAL AID

In-state tuition $4,094. Out-of-state tuition $10,606. Room & board $5,458. Required fees $0. Average book expense $750. **Required Forms and Deadlines:** FAFSA. Priority filing deadline March 1. **Notification of Awards:** Applicants will be notified of awards on a rolling basis beginning on or about April 1. **Types of Aid:** *Need-based scholarships/grants:* Pell, SEOG, state scholarships/grants, private scholarships. *Loans:* FFEL Subsidized Stafford, FFEL Unsubsidized Stafford, FFEL PLUS, Federal Perkins. **Student Employment:** Federal Work-Study Program available. Institutional employment available. Off-campus job opportunities are excellent. **Financial Aid Statistics:** 34% freshmen, 27% undergrads receive some form of aid. Average freshman grant $3,437. Average freshman loan $2,959. Average income from on-campus job $1,614. **Financial Aid Phone:** 540-568-7820.

JAMESTOWN COLLEGE

6081 College Lane, Jamestown, ND 58405-0001
Phone: 701-252-3467 **E-mail:** admissions@jc.edu
Fax: 701-253-4318 **Web:** www.jc.edu **ACT Code:** 3200

This private school, which is affiliated with the Presbyterian Church, was founded in 1884. It has a 107-acre campus.

STUDENTS AND FACULTY

Enrollment: 1,185. **Student Body:** Male 44%, female 56%, out-of-state 38%, international 3%. **Ethnic Representation:** African American 1%, Asian 1%, Caucasian 95%, Hispanic 2%, Native American 1%. **Retention and Graduation:** 75% freshmen return for sophomore year. 30% freshmen graduate within 4 years. 10% grads go on to further study within 1 year. 1% grads pursue business degrees. 1% grads pursue law degrees. 2% grads pursue medical degrees. **Faculty:** Student/faculty ratio 17:1. 56 full-time faculty, 50% hold PhDs. 100% faculty teach undergrads.

ACADEMICS

Degrees: Bachelor's. **Academic Requirements:** General education including some course work in arts/fine arts, computer literacy, English (including composition), foreign languages, history, mathematics, philosophy, sciences (biological or physical), social science. **Classes:** 20-29 students in an average class. 20-29 students in an average lab/discussion section. **Majors with Highest Enrollment:** Nursing/registered nurse training (RN, ASN, BSN, MSN); business administration/management; elementary education and teaching. **Disciplines with Highest Percentage of Degrees Awarded:** Business/marketing 24%, education 22%, health professions and related sciences 14%, computer and information sciences 7%, protective services/public administration 7%. **Special Study Options:** Cooperative (work-study) program, double major, dual enrollment, student exchange program (domestic), honors program, independent study, internships, student-designed major, study abroad, teacher certification program.

FACILITIES

Housing: Coed, apartments for single students, housing for disabled students, houses. **Library Holdings:** 128,915 bound volumes. 675 periodicals. 12,745 microforms. 5,219 audiovisuals. **Computers:** School-owned computers available for student use.

EXTRACURRICULARS

Activities: Choral groups, concert band, drama/theater, jazz band, literary magazine, music ensembles, musical theater, pep band, student government, student newspaper, yearbook. **Organizations:** 35 registered organizations, 5 religious organizations. **Athletics (Intercollegiate):** *Men:* baseball, basketball, cross-country, football, golf, indoor track, track & field, wrestling. *Women:* basketball, cross-country, golf, indoor track, soccer, softball, track & field, volleyball.

ADMISSIONS

Selectivity Rating: 70 (of 100). **Freshman Academic Profile:** Average high school GPA 3.3. 13% in top 10% of high school class, 36% in top 25% of high school class, 63% in top 50% of high school class. Average ACT 22, ACT middle 50% range 19-26. TOEFL required of all international applicants, minimum TOEFL 525. **Basis for Candidate Selection:** *Very important factors considered include:* secondary school record. *Important factors considered include:* class rank, standardized test scores. *Other factors considered include:* alumni/ae relation, character/personal qualities, extracurricular activities, interview, recommendations, talent/ability, volunteer work, work experience. **Freshman Admission Requirements:** High school diploma or GED is required. *Academic units required/recommended:* 15 total recommended; 4 English recommended, 3 math recommended, 3 science recommended, 2 foreign language recommended, 2 social studies recommended, 1 history recommended. **Freshman Admission Statistics:** 1,094 applied, 99% accepted, 27% of those accepted enrolled. **Transfer Admission Requirements:** *Items required:* college transcript. Minimum high school GPA of 2.5 required. Minimum college GPA of 2.0 required. Lowest grade transferable C. **General Admission Information:** Application fee $20. Nonfall registration accepted. Admission may be deferred for a maximum of 1 year. Credit offered for CEEB Advanced Placement tests.

COSTS AND FINANCIAL AID

Tuition $8,750. Room & board $3,850. Required fees $0. Average book expense $1,000. **Required Forms and Deadlines:** FAFSA. No deadline for regular filing. **Notification of Awards:** Applicants will be notified of awards on a rolling basis. **Types of Aid:** *Need-based scholarships/grants:* Pell, SEOG, state scholarships/grants, private scholarships, the school's own gift aid. *Loans:* FFEL Subsidized Stafford, FFEL Unsubsidized Stafford, FFEL PLUS, Federal Perkins, Federal Nursing, state loans, college/university loans from institutional funds, alternative loans (private). **Student Employment:** Federal Work-Study Program available. Institutional employment available. Off-campus job opportunities are good. **Financial Aid Statistics:** 88% freshmen, 89% undergrads receive some form of aid. Average freshman grant $4,787. Average freshman loan $3,836. Average income from on-campus job $832. **Financial Aid Phone:** 701-252-3467.

JARVIS CHRISTIAN COLLEGE

PO Box 1470, Hawkins, TX 75765-1470
Phone: 903-769-5730 **E-mail:** colemana@jarvis.edu
Fax: 903-769-4842 **Web:** www.jarvis.edu **ACT Code:** 4110

This private school, which is affiliated with the Disciples of Christ Church, was founded in 1913.

STUDENTS AND FACULTY

Enrollment: 519. **Student Body:** Male 43%, female 57%, out-of-state 9%. **Ethnic Representation:** African American 99%, Caucasian 1%. **Retention and Graduation:** 50% freshmen return for sophomore year. 13% freshmen graduate within 4 years. 23% grads go on to further study within 1 year. 6% grads pursue business degrees. 3% grads pursue law degrees. **Faculty:** Student/faculty ratio 14:1. 39 full-time faculty, 51% hold PhDs. 100% faculty teach undergrads.

ACADEMICS

Degrees: Bachelor's. **Academic Requirements:** General education including some course work in arts/fine arts, computer literacy, English (including composition), foreign languages, history, humanities, mathematics, sciences (biological or physical), social science. **Classes:** 10-19 students in an average class. 20-29 students in an average lab/discussion section. **Disciplines with Highest Percentage of Degrees Awarded:** Business/marketing 32%, social sciences and history 20%, education 19%, computer and information sciences 11%, biological life sciences 11%. **Special Study Options:** Cooperative (work-study) program, cross registration, distance learning, double major, dual enrollment, honors program, internships, liberal arts/career combination, student-designed major, teacher certification program.

FACILITIES

Housing: All-female, all-male, apartments for married students, apartments for single students. **Library Holdings:** 78,498 bound volumes. 400 periodicals. 6,000 microforms. 100 audiovisuals. **Computers:** *Recommended operating system:* Windows 95. School-owned computers available for student use.

EXTRACURRICULARS

Activities: Choral groups, drama/theater, music ensembles, student government, yearbook. **Organizations:** 33 registered organizations, 3 honor societies, 5 religious organizations, 4 fraternities (10% men join), 4 sororities (5% women join). **Athletics (Intercollegiate):** *Men:* baseball, basketball, soccer, track & field, volleyball. *Women:* basketball, cheerleading, track & field, volleyball.

ADMISSIONS

Selectivity Rating: 65 (of 100). **Freshman Academic Profile:** Average high school GPA 2.8. 7% in top 10% of high school class, 18% in top 25% of high school class, 24% in top 50% of high school class. 99% from public high schools. Average SAT I Math 375. Average SAT I Verbal 375. Average ACT 15. TOEFL required of all international applicants, minimum TOEFL 500. **Basis for Candidate Selection:** *Important factors considered include:* secondary school record, standardized test scores. *Other factors considered include:* extracurricular activities. **Freshman Admission Requirements:** High school diploma or GED is required. *Academic units required/recommended:* 16 total required; 16 total recommended; 3 English required, 3 English recommended, 2 math required, 2 math recommended, 1 science required, 1 science recommended, 3 social studies required, 3 social studies recommended, 7 elective required, 7 elective recommended. **Freshman Admission Statistics:** 161 applied, 67% accepted. **Transfer Admission Requirements:** *Items required:* high school transcript, college transcript, standardized test scores. Lowest grade transferable F. **General Admission Information:** Application fee $25. Priority application deadline May 1. Nonfall registration accepted. Admission may be deferred for a maximum of 1 year. Neither credit nor placement offered for CEEB Advanced Placement tests.

COSTS AND FINANCIAL AID

Tuition $5,200. Room & board $3,485. Required fees $350. Average book expense $600. **Required Forms and Deadlines:** FAFSA. No deadline for regular filing. Priority filing deadline April 15. **Notification of Awards:** Applicants will be notified of awards on a rolling basis beginning on or about May 1. **Types of Aid:** *Need-based scholarships/grants:* Pell, SEOG, state scholarships/grants, private scholarships, the school's own gift aid, United Negro College Fund. *Loans:* FFEL Subsidized Stafford, FFEL Unsubsidized Stafford, FFEL PLUS, Federal Perkins, UNCF Institutional. **Student Employment:** Federal Work-Study Program available. Off-campus job opportunities are fair. **Financial Aid Statistics:** 87% freshmen, 95% undergrads receive some form of aid. Average freshman grant $6,715. Average freshman loan $2,265. Average income from on-campus job $1,729.

JAZZ & CONTEMPORARY MUSIC PROGRAM/ NEW SCHOOL UNIVERSITY

$$$

55 W 13th Street, New York, NY 10011
Phone: 212-229-5896 **E-mail:** jazzadm@newschool.edu
Fax: 212-229-8936 **Web:** www.newschool.edu/jazz/

STUDENTS AND FACULTY

Enrollment: 271. **Student Body:** Male 81%, female 19%, out-of-state 59%, international 18%. **Ethnic Representation:** African American 12%, Asian 1%, Caucasian 43%, Hispanic 10%. **Retention and Graduation:** 81% freshmen return for sophomore year. **Faculty:** Student/faculty ratio 4:1. 3 full-time faculty.

ACADEMICS

Degrees: Associate's, bachelor's, certificate, master's. **Academic Requirements:** General education including some course work in arts/fine arts, computer literacy, English (including composition), humanities, social science. **Classes:** Under 10 students in an average class. **Disciplines with Highest Percentage of Degrees Awarded:** Visual and performing arts 100%. **Special Study Options:** Accelerated program, cooperative (work-study) program, cross registration, distance learning, dual enrollment, English as a second language, student exchange program (domestic), honors program, independent study, internships, liberal arts/career combination, student-designed major, study abroad, teacher certification program.

FACILITIES

Housing: Coed, housing for disabled students. **Library Holdings:** 4,137,530 bound volumes. 22,150 periodicals. 4,656,806 microforms. 48,379 audiovisuals.

EXTRACURRICULARS

Activities: Choral groups, concert band, music ensembles, opera, symphony orchestra.

ADMISSIONS

Selectivity Rating: 60 (of 100). **Freshman Academic Profile:** Average high school GPA 2.9. SAT I Math middle 50% range 470-600. SAT I Verbal middle 50% range 480-600. **Basis for Candidate Selection:** *Very important factors considered include:* talent/ability. *Important factors considered include:* secondary school record. *Other factors considered include:* essays, extracurricular activities, recommendations. **Freshman Admission Requirements:** High school diploma or GED is required. **Freshman Admission Statistics:** 139 applied, 76% accepted, 49% of those accepted enrolled. **Transfer Admission Requirements:** *Items required:* college transcript, essay, interview. Lowest grade transferable C. **General Admission Information:** Application fee $40. Nonfall registration accepted. Admission may be deferred.

COSTS AND FINANCIAL AID

Tuition $21,670. Required fees $490. Average book expense $2,062. **Required Forms and Deadlines:** FAFSA and state aid form. No deadline for regular filing. Priority filing deadline March 1. **Notification of Awards:** Applicants will be notified of awards on a rolling basis beginning on or about March 1. **Types of Aid:** *Need-based scholarships/grants:* Pell, SEOG, state scholarships/grants, private scholarships, the school's own gift aid. *Loans:* FFEL Subsidized Stafford, FFEL Unsubsidized Stafford, FFEL PLUS, Federal Perkins, college/university loans from institutional funds. **Financial Aid Statistics:** 28% freshmen, 50% undergrads receive some form of aid.

JOHN BROWN UNIVERSITY

2000 West University Street, Siloam Springs, AR 72761
Phone: 800-634-6969 **E-mail:** jbuinfo@jbu.edu **CEEB Code:** 6321
Fax: 501-524-4196 **Web:** www.jbu.edu **ACT Code:** 130

This private school was founded in 1919. It has a 200-acre campus.

STUDENTS AND FACULTY

Enrollment: 1,393. **Student Body:** Male 46%, female 54%, out-of-state 65%, international 9%. **Ethnic Representation:** African American 1%, Asian 1%, Caucasian 95%, Hispanic 2%, Native American 1%. **Retention and Graduation:** 80% freshmen return for sophomore year. 29% freshmen graduate within 4 years. 19% grads go on to further study within 1 year. 10% grads pursue business degrees. 2% grads pursue law degrees. 2% grads pursue medical degrees. **Faculty:** 100% faculty teach undergrads.

ACADEMICS

Degrees: Associate's, bachelor's, master's, transfer. **Academic Requirements:** General education including some course work in arts/fine arts, computer literacy, history, humanities, mathematics, sciences (biological or physical), social science, biblical studies. **Special Study Options:** English as a second language, external degree program, honors program, independent study, internships, student-designed major, study abroad, teacher certification program.

FACILITIES

Housing: Coed, all-female, all-male, apartments for married students, apartments for single students. **Library Holdings:** 93,190 bound volumes. 1,580 periodicals. 49,725 microforms. 8,310 audiovisuals. **Special Academic Facilities/Equipment:** Wellness assessment center, human anatomy lab, TV studio. **Computers:** *Recommended operating system:* Mac.

EXTRACURRICULARS

Activities: Choral groups, drama/theater, music ensembles, opera, pep band, radio station, student government, student newspaper, television station, yearbook. **Organizations:** 20 registered organizations, 4 honor societies, 2 religious organizations. **Athletics (Intercollegiate):** *Men:* basketball, cross-country, diving, soccer, swimming, tennis, track & field, volleyball. *Women:* basketball, cross-country, diving, swimming, tennis, track & field, volleyball.

ADMISSIONS

Selectivity Rating: 77 (of 100). **Freshman Academic Profile:** Average high school GPA 3.6. 31% in top 10% of high school class, 61% in top 25% of high school class, 89% in top 50% of high school class. 65% from public high schools. Average SAT I Math 544, SAT I Math middle 50% range 500-640. Average SAT I Verbal 552, SAT I Verbal middle 50% range 490-710. Average ACT 24, ACT middle 50% range 22-28. TOEFL required of all international applicants, minimum TOEFL 550. **Basis for Candidate Selection:** *Very important factors considered include:* character/personal qualities, essays, secondary school record, standardized test scores. *Important factors considered include:* extracurricular activities, interview, recommendations. *Other factors considered include:* alumni/ae relation, class rank, religious affiliation/commitment, talent/

ability, volunteer work, work experience. **Freshman Admission Requirements:** High school diploma or GED is required. *Academic units required/recommended:* 4 English required, 4 English recommended, 4 math required, 4 math recommended, 3 science required, 4 science recommended, 2 science lab required, 3 science lab recommended, 1 foreign language recommended, 1 social studies required, 1 social studies recommended, 1 history required, 1 history recommended. **Freshman Admission Statistics:** 556 applied, 54% accepted, 88% of those accepted enrolled. **Transfer Admission Requirements:** *Items required:* college transcript, essay, statement of good standing from prior school. Minimum college GPA of 2.0 required. Lowest grade transferable C. **General Admission Information:** Application fee $25. Priority application deadline May 1. Regular application deadline rolling. Nonfall registration accepted. Admission may be deferred for a maximum of 1 year. Neither credit nor placement offered for CEEB Advanced Placement tests.

COSTS AND FINANCIAL AID

Tuition $9,482. Room & board $4,478. Required fees $320. Average book expense $550. **Required Forms and Deadlines:** FAFSA. Priority filing deadline March 1. **Notification of Awards:** Applicants will be notified of awards on or about March 1. **Types of Aid:** *Need-based scholarships/grants:* Pell, SEOG, state scholarships/grants, private scholarships, the school's own gift aid. *Loans:* FFEL Subsidized Stafford, FFEL Unsubsidized Stafford, FFEL PLUS, Federal Perkins, state loans, alternative loans. **Student Employment:** Federal Work-Study Program available. Institutional employment available. Off-campus job opportunities are good. **Financial Aid Statistics:** 64% freshmen, 55% undergrads receive some form of aid. Average freshman grant $1,700. Average freshman loan $2,788. Average income from on-campus job $1,200. **Financial Aid Phone:** 800-634-6969.

JOHN CARROLL UNIVERSITY

20700 North Park Boulevard, University Heights, OH 44118-4581
Phone: 216-397-4294 **E-mail:** admission@jcu.edu **CEEB Code:** 1342
Fax: 216-397-3098 **Web:** www.jcu.edu **ACT Code:** 3282

This private school, which is affiliated with the Roman Catholic Church, was founded in 1886. It has a 60-acre campus.

STUDENTS AND FACULTY

Enrollment: 3,527. **Student Body:** Male 47%, female 53%, out-of-state 27%. **Ethnic Representation:** African American 4%, Asian 3%, Caucasian 90%, Hispanic 2%. **Retention and Graduation:** 88% freshmen return for sophomore year. 60% freshmen graduate within 4 years. 36% grads go on to further study within 1 year. 1% grads pursue business degrees. 5% grads pursue law degrees. 3% grads pursue medical degrees. **Faculty:** Student/faculty ratio 14:1. 234 full-time faculty, 85% hold PhDs. 99% faculty teach undergrads.

ACADEMICS

Degrees: Bachelor's, master's. **Academic Requirements:** General education including some course work in English (including composition), foreign languages, history, humanities, mathematics, philosophy, sciences (biological or physical), social science. **Classes:** 20-29 students in an average class. **Disciplines with Highest Percentage of Degrees Awarded:** Business/marketing 27%, social sciences and history 14%, communications/communication technologies 10%, education 9%, biological life sciences 9%. **Special Study Options:** Accelerated program, cooperative (work-study) program, cross registration, double major, dual enrollment, student exchange program (domestic), independent study, internships, liberal arts/career combination, student-designed major, study abroad, teacher certification program. Undergrads may take grad-level classes. Co-op programs: all majors.

FACILITIES

Housing: Coed, all-female, all-male, apartments for single students. **Library Holdings:** 607,256 bound volumes. 1,860 periodicals. 680,005 microforms. 8,228 audiovisuals. **Special Academic Facilities/Equipment:** International studies center, closed-circuit TV studio, broadcast archives. **Computers:** School-owned computers available for student use.

EXTRACURRICULARS

Activities: Choral groups, concert band, dance, drama/theater, jazz band, literary magazine, music ensembles, musical theater, pep band, radio station, student government, student newspaper, television station, yearbook. **Organizations:** 68 registered organizations, 9 honor societies, 3 religious organizations, 12 fraternities (22% men join), 7 sororities (27% women join). **Athletics (Intercollegiate):** *Men:* baseball, basketball, crew, cross-country, diving, football, golf, ice hockey, indoor track, lacrosse, rugby, sailing, skiing (alpine), soccer, swimming, tennis, track & field, wrestling. *Women:* basketball, cheerleading, crew, cross-country, diving, golf, indoor track, rugby, sailing, skiing (alpine), soccer, softball, swimming, tennis, track & field, volleyball.

ADMISSIONS

Selectivity Rating: 81 (of 100). **Freshman Academic Profile:** Average high school GPA 3.3. 31% in top 10% of high school class, 56% in top 25% of high school class, 88% in top 50% of high school class. 55% from public high schools. Average SAT I Math 574, SAT I Math middle 50% range 510-630. Average SAT I Verbal 566, SAT I Verbal middle 50% range 510-620. Average ACT 23, ACT middle 50% range 21-26. TOEFL required of all international applicants, minimum TOEFL 550. **Basis for Candidate Selection:** *Very important factors considered include:* secondary school record, standardized test scores. *Important factors considered include:* character/personal qualities, essays, extracurricular activities, interview, recommendations. *Other factors considered include:* alumni/ae relation, class rank, geographical residence, minority status, talent/ability, volunteer work, work experience. **Freshman Admission Requirements:** High school diploma or GED is required. *Academic units required/recommended:* 16 total required; 21 total recommended; 4 English required, 4 English recommended, 3 math required, 4 math recommended, 2 science required, 3 science recommended, 2 science lab required, 3 science lab recommended, 2 foreign language required, 3 foreign language recommended, 1 social studies required, 1 social studies recommended, 1 history required, 3 history recommended, 3 elective required, 3 elective recommended. **Freshman Admission Statistics:** 2,612 applied, 88% accepted, 36% of those accepted enrolled. **Transfer Admission Requirements:** *Items required:* college transcript. Minimum college GPA of 2.0 required. **General Admission Information:** Application fee $25. Regular application deadline February 1. Nonfall registration accepted. Admission may be deferred for a maximum of 1 year. Credit and/or placement offered for CEEB Advanced Placement tests.

COSTS AND FINANCIAL AID

Tuition $16,334. Room & board $6,128. Required fees $50. Average book expense $800. **Required Forms and Deadlines:** FAFSA. Priority filing deadline March 1. **Notification of Awards:** Applicants will be notified of awards on a rolling basis beginning on or about March 1. **Types of Aid:** *Need-based scholarships/grants:* Pell, SEOG, state scholarships/grants, private scholarships, the school's own gift aid. *Loans:* FFEL Subsidized Stafford, FFEL Unsubsidized Stafford, FFEL PLUS, Federal Perkins, college/university loans from institutional funds. **Student Employment:** Federal Work-Study Program available. Institutional employment available. Off-campus job opportunities are good. **Financial Aid Statistics:** 72% freshmen, 65% undergrads receive some form of aid. Average freshman grant $7,400. Average freshman loan $3,150. Average income from on-campus job $1,200. **Financial Aid Phone:** 216-397-4248.

See page 1068.

JOHN F. KENNEDY UNIVERSITY

12 Altarinda Road, Orinda, CA 94563
Phone: 925-258-2213 **E-mail:** proginfo@jfku.edu **CEEB Code:** 4365
Fax: 925-254-6964 **Web:** www.jfku.edu **ACT Code:** 291

This private school was founded in 1964. It has a 10-acre campus.

STUDENTS AND FACULTY

Enrollment: 196. **Student Body:** Male 19%, female 81%. **Ethnic Representation:** African American 12%, Asian 4%, Caucasian 66%, Hispanic 8%, Native American 3%. **Faculty:** Student/faculty ratio 12:1. 33 full-time faculty, 60% hold PhDs.

ACADEMICS

Degrees: Bachelor's, certificate, doctoral, first professional, master's. **Academic Requirements:** General education including some course work in English (including composition), humanities, mathematics, sciences (biological or physical), social science. **Classes:** 10-19 students in an average class. **Disciplines with Highest Percentage of Degrees Awarded:** Liberal arts/general studies 64%, business/marketing 22%, psychology 9%. **Special Study Options:** Independent study, internships, student-designed major, weekend college.

FACILITIES

Library Holdings: 91,170 bound volumes. 811 periodicals. 39,000 microforms. 1,854 audiovisuals. **Computers:** School-owned computers available for student use.

EXTRACURRICULARS

Activities: Student government, student newspaper.

ADMISSIONS

Selectivity Rating: 60 (of 100). **Freshman Academic Profile:** TOEFL required of all international applicants, minimum TOEFL 550. **Transfer Admission Requirements:** *Items required:* high school transcript, college transcript, essay, interview, statement of good standing from prior school. **General Admission Information:** Application fee $50. Admission may be deferred for a maximum of 1 year. Credit offered for CEEB Advanced Placement tests.

COSTS AND FINANCIAL AID

Tuition $8,568. Required fees $27. Average book expense $0. **Required Forms and Deadlines:** FAFSA. No deadline for regular filing. **Types of Aid:** *Need-based scholarships/grants:* Pell, SEOG, state scholarships/grants, private scholarships, the school's own gift aid. *Loans:* FFEL Subsidized Stafford, FFEL Unsubsidized Stafford, FFEL PLUS, Federal Perkins, college/university loans from institutional funds. **Student Employment:** Off-campus job opportunities are fair. **Financial Aid Statistics:** 59% undergrads receive some form of aid. Average freshman loan $2,625. **Financial Aid Phone:** 925-258-2385.

JOHNS HOPKINS UNIVERSITY

3400 North Charles Street/140 Garland, Baltimore, MD 21218
Phone: 410-516-8171 **E-mail:** gotojhu@jhu.edu **CEEB Code:** 5332
Fax: 410-516-6025 **Web:** www.jhu.edu

This private school was founded in 1876. It has a 140-acre campus.

STUDENTS AND FACULTY

Enrollment: 5,523. **Student Body:** Male 52%, female 48%, out-of-state 78%, international 6%. **Ethnic Representation:** African American 6%, Asian 18%, Caucasian 72%, Hispanic 4%. **Retention and Graduation:** 94% freshmen return for sophomore year. 81% freshmen graduate within 4 years. **Faculty:** Student/faculty ratio 8:1.

ACADEMICS

Degrees: Bachelor's, doctoral, first professional, master's, post-bachelor's certificate, post-master's certificate. **Academic Requirements:** General education including some course work in humanities, mathematics, sciences (biological or physical), social science. **Classes:** Under 10 students in an average class. 10-19 students in an average lab/discussion section. **Majors with Highest Enrollment:** Biomedical/medical engineering; biology/biological sciences, general; international relations and affairs. **Disciplines with Highest Percentage of Degrees Awarded:** Social sciences and history 20%, health professions and related sciences 18%, engineering/engineering technology 16%, biological life sciences 11%, visual and performing arts 6%. **Special Study Options:** Cross registration, double major, independent study, internships, student-designed major, study abroad.

FACILITIES

Housing: Coed, fraternities and/or sororities, substance-free floors, vacation housing floors. **Library Holdings:** 3,509,413 bound volumes. 30,023 periodicals. 4,224,868 microforms. 299,605 audiovisuals. **Special Academic Facilities/Equipment:** Baltimore Museum of Art on campus, art gallery, electron microscope, space telescope institute, 4 major research centers, undergraduate physics lab. **Computers:** School-owned computers available for student use.

EXTRACURRICULARS

Activities: Choral groups, concert band, dance, drama/theater, jazz band, literary magazine, music ensembles, musical theater, pep band, radio station, student government, student newspaper, student-run film society, symphony orchestra, yearbook. **Organizations:** 163 registered organizations, 17 honor societies, 10 religious organizations, 11 fraternities (18% men join), 7 sororities (19% women join). **Athletics (Intercollegiate):** *Men:* baseball, basketball, crew, cross-country, diving, fencing, football, lacrosse, soccer, swimming, tennis, track & field, water polo, wrestling. *Women:* basketball, crew, cross-country, diving, fencing, field hockey, lacrosse, soccer, swimming, tennis, track & field, volleyball.

ADMISSIONS

Selectivity Rating: 99 (of 100). **Freshman Academic Profile:** Average high school GPA 3.7. 72% in top 10% of high school class, 94% in top 25% of high school class, 100% in top 50% of high school class. 59% from public high schools. Average SAT I Math 703, SAT I Math middle 50% range 660-760. Average SAT I Verbal 671, SAT I Verbal middle 50% range 620-730. Average ACT 29, ACT middle 50% range 27-31. TOEFL required of all international applicants, minimum TOEFL 200. **Basis for Candidate Selection:** *Very important factors considered include:* character/personal qualities, essays, recommendations, secondary school record. *Important factors considered include:* class rank, extracurricular activities, standardized test scores, talent/ability, volunteer work. *Other factors considered include:* alumni/ae relation, geographical residence, interview, minority status, state residency, work experience. **Freshman Admission Requirements:** High school diploma or equivalent is not required. *Academic units required/recommended:* 20 total recommended; 4 English required, 3 math required, 4 math recommended, 3 science required, 2 foreign language recommended, 3 social studies required. **Freshman Admission Statistics:** 8,915 applied, 35% accepted, 36% of those accepted enrolled. **Transfer Admission Requirements:** *Items required:* high school transcript, college transcript, essay. Lowest grade transferable C. **General Admission Information:** Application fee $60. Early decision application deadline November 15. Regular application deadline January 1. Admission may be deferred for a maximum of 2 years. Credit and/or placement offered for CEEB Advanced Placement tests.

COSTS AND FINANCIAL AID

Required Forms and Deadlines: FAFSA, institution's own financial aid form, noncustodial (divorced/separated) parent's statement, business/farm supplement, and prior and current year federal tax returns. Financial aid filing deadline February 15. Priority filing deadline February 1. **Notification of Awards:** Applicants will be notified of awards on or about April 1. **Types of Aid:** *Need-based scholarships/grants:* Pell, SEOG, state scholarships/grants, private scholarships, the school's own gift aid. *Loans:* Direct Subsidized Stafford, Direct Unsubsidized Stafford, FFEL PLUS, Federal Perkins, college/university loans from institutional funds. **Student Employment:** Federal Work-Study Program available. Institutional employment available. Off-campus job opportunities are excellent. **Financial Aid Statistics:** 43% freshmen, 40% undergrads receive some form of aid. Average freshman grant $21,375. Average freshman loan $2,529. Average income from on-campus job $2,000. **Financial Aid Phone:** 410-516-8028.

JOHNSON & WALES UNIVERSITY—CHARLESTON

701 East Bay Street, Charleston, SC 29403
Phone: 843-727-3000 **E-mail:** admissions@jwu.edu
Fax: 843-763-0318 **Web:** www.jwu.edu

This private school was founded in 1914. It has a 47-acre campus.

STUDENTS AND FACULTY

Enrollment: 1,497. **Student Body:** Male 54%, female 46%, international 1%. **Ethnic Representation:** African American 9%, Asian 1%, Caucasian 87%, Hispanic 1%, Native American 1%. **Faculty:** Student/faculty ratio 29:1. 45 full-time faculty, 8% hold PhDs. 100% faculty teach undergrads.

ACADEMICS

Degrees: Associate's, bachelor's, terminal, transfer. **Academic Requirements:** General education including some course work in English (including composition), mathematics, sciences (biological or physical), professional development. **Special Study Options:** Accelerated program, cooperative (work-study) program, honors program, independent study, internships, study abroad.

FACILITIES

Housing: Coed, apartments for single students.

EXTRACURRICULARS

Activities: Choral groups, drama/theater, literary magazine, student government, yearbook.

ADMISSIONS

Selectivity Rating: 60 (of 100). **Freshman Academic Profile:** 96% from public high schools. TOEFL required of all international applicants, minimum TOEFL 550. **Basis for Candidate Selection:** *Very important factors considered include:* secondary school record. *Other factors considered include:* class rank, extracurricular activities, interview, recommendations, standardized test scores. **Freshman Admission Requirements:** High school diploma or GED is required. *Academic units required/recommended:* 10 total recommended; 4 English recommended, 3 math recommended, 2 science recommended, 1 social studies recommended. **Transfer Admission Requirements:**

Items required: high school transcript, college transcript. Minimum high school GPA of 2.0 required. Minimum college GPA of 2.0 required. Lowest grade transferable C. **General Admission Information:** Nonfall registration accepted. Admission may be deferred for a maximum of 1 year.

COSTS AND FINANCIAL AID

Tuition $15,222. Room & board $4,860. Required fees $750. Average book expense $750. **Required Forms and Deadlines:** FAFSA. No deadline for regular filing. **Notification of Awards:** Applicants will be notified of awards on a rolling basis beginning on or about March 1. **Types of Aid:** *Need-based scholarships/grants:* Pell, SEOG, state scholarships/grants, the school's own gift aid. *Loans:* FFEL Subsidized Stafford, FFEL Unsubsidized Stafford, FFEL PLUS, Federal Perkins, college/university loans from institutional funds. **Student Employment:** Federal Work-Study Program available. Off-campus job opportunities are good. **Financial Aid Statistics:** 78% freshmen, 69% undergrads receive some form of aid. **Financial Aid Phone:** 800-342-5598.

See page 1070.

JOHNSON & WALES UNIVERSITY—DENVER

7150 Montview Boulevard, Denver, CO 80220
Phone: 303-256-9300 **E-mail:** admissions@jwu.edu
Fax: 303-256-9333 **Web:** www.jwu.edu

This private school was founded in 1914. It has a 13-acre campus.

STUDENTS AND FACULTY

Enrollment: 963. **Student Body:** Male 57%, female 43%. **Faculty:** Student/faculty ratio 18:1. 31 full-time faculty. 100% faculty teach undergrads.

ACADEMICS

Degrees: Associate's, bachelor's. **Academic Requirements:** General education including some course work in computer literacy, English (including composition), foreign languages, history, humanities, mathematics, philosophy, sciences (biological or physical), social science, leadership, service learning. **Majors with Highest Enrollment:** Business administration/management; hotel/motel administration/management; restaurant/food services management. **Special Study Options:** Accelerated program, cooperative (work-study) program, English as a second language, honors program, internships, liberal arts/career combination, study abroad, externships/practicums.

FACILITIES

Housing: Coed. **Computers:** School-owned computers available for student use.

ADMISSIONS

Selectivity Rating: 60 (of 100). **Freshman Academic Profile:** TOEFL required of all international applicants, minimum TOEFL 550. **Basis for Candidate Selection:** *Very important factors considered include:* secondary school record. *Other factors considered include:* class rank, extracurricular activities, interview, recommendations, standardized test scores. **Freshman Admission Requirements:** High school diploma or GED is required. *Academic units required/recommended:* 10 total recommended; 4 English recommended, 3 math recommended, 1 science recommended, 2 social studies recommended. **Transfer Admission Requirements:** *Items required:* high school transcript, college transcript. Minimum high school GPA of 2.0 required. Minimum college GPA of 2.0 required. **General Admission Information:** Nonfall registration accepted. Admission may be deferred for a maximum of 1 year.

COSTS AND FINANCIAL AID

Tuition $15,438. Room & board $7,602. Required fees $750. Average book expense $750. **Required Forms and Deadlines:** FAFSA. No deadline for regular filing. **Notification of Awards:** Applicants will be notified of awards on a rolling basis beginning on or about March 1. **Types of Aid:** *Need-based scholarships/grants:* Pell, SEOG, state scholarships/grants, the school's own gift aid. *Loans:* FFEL Subsidized Stafford, FFEL Unsubsidized Stafford, FFEL PLUS, Federal Perkins, college/university loans from institutional funds. **Student Employment:** Federal Work-Study Program available. Off-campus job opportunities are good. **Financial Aid Statistics:** 76% freshmen, 70% undergrads receive some form of aid. **Financial Aid Phone:** 800-342-5598.

See page 1070.

JOHNSON & WALES UNIVERSITY—NORFOLK

$$$

2428 Almeda Avenue, Suite 316, Norfolk, VA 23513
Phone: 757-853-3508 **E-mail:** admissions@jwu.edu
Fax: 757-857-4869 **Web:** www.jwu.edu

STUDENTS AND FACULTY

Enrollment: 709. **Student Body:** Male 52%, female 48%. **Ethnic Representation:** African American 33%, Asian 2%, Caucasian 59%, Hispanic 5%, Native American 1%. **Faculty:** Student/faculty ratio 26:1. 19 full-time faculty.

ACADEMICS

Degrees: Associate's, certificate. **Academic Requirements:** General education including some course work in English (including composition), humanities, mathematics, sciences (biological or physical), culinary arts, food service management. **Special Study Options:** Accelerated program, cooperative (work-study) program, internships.

FACILITIES

Housing: Coed, apartments for single students.

EXTRACURRICULARS

Activities: Choral groups, student newspaper, yearbook.

ADMISSIONS

Selectivity Rating: 63 (of 100). **Freshman Academic Profile:** 3% in top 10% of high school class, 11% in top 25% of high school class, 39% in top 50% of high school class. SAT I Math middle 50% range 370-480. SAT I Verbal middle 50% range 400-530. **Basis for Candidate Selection:** *Very important factors considered include:* secondary school record. *Other factors considered include:* class rank, extracurricular activities, interview, recommendations, standardized test scores. **Freshman Admission Requirements:** High school diploma or GED is required. *Academic units required/recommended:* 10 total recommended; 4 English recommended, 3 math recommended, 2 science recommended, 1 social studies recommended. **Freshman Admission Statistics:** 553 applied, 80% accepted. **Transfer Admission Requirements:** *Items required:* high school transcript, college transcript. Lowest grade transferable C. **General Admission Information:** Regular application deadline rolling. Nonfall registration accepted. Admission may be deferred for a maximum of 1 year.

COSTS AND FINANCIAL AID

Tuition $18,444. Room & board $6,621. Required fees $750. Average book expense $750. **Required Forms and Deadlines:** FAFSA. No deadline for regular filing. **Notification of Awards:** Applicants will be notified of awards on a rolling basis beginning on or about March 1. **Types of Aid:** *Need-based scholarships/grants:* Pell, SEOG, state scholarships/grants, the school's own gift aid. *Loans:* FFEL Subsidized Stafford, FFEL Unsubsidized Stafford, FFEL PLUS, Federal Perkins, college/university loans from institutional funds. **Financial Aid Statistics:** 83% freshmen, 80% undergrads receive some form of aid.

See page 1070.

JOHNSON & WALES UNIVERSITY—NORTH MIAMI

$$$

1701 NE 127th Street, North Miami, FL 33181
Phone: 305-892-7600 **E-mail:** admissions@jwu.edu
Fax: 305-892-7020 **Web:** www.jwu.edu

STUDENTS AND FACULTY

Enrollment: 2,146. **Student Body:** Male 46%, female 54%, international 7%. **Ethnic Representation:** African American 37%, Asian 2%, Caucasian 38%, Hispanic 24%. **Faculty:** Student/faculty ratio 25:1. 52 full-time faculty.

ACADEMICS

Degrees: Associate's, bachelor's, terminal, transfer. **Academic Requirements:** General education including some course work in English (including composition), mathematics. **Special Study Options:** Cooperative (work-study) program, English as a second language.

FACILITIES

Library Holdings: 5,856 bound volumes. 133 periodicals. 0 microforms. 452 audiovisuals. **Computers:** *Recommended operating system:* Windows NT/2000.

ADMISSIONS

Selectivity Rating: 60 (of 100). **Basis for Candidate Selection:** *Very important factors considered include:* secondary school record. *Other factors considered include:* class rank, extracurricular activities, interview, recommendations, standardized test scores. **Freshman Admission Requirements:** High school diploma or GED is required. *Academic units required/recommended:* 10 total recommended; 4 English recommended, 3 math recommended, 2 science recommended, 1 social studies recommended. **Transfer Admission Requirements:** *Items required:* high school transcript, college transcript. Lowest grade transferable C. **General Admission Information:** Nonfall registration accepted. Admission may be deferred for a maximum of 1 year.

COSTS AND FINANCIAL AID

Tuition $15,438. Required fees $750. Average book expense $750. **Required Forms and Deadlines:** FAFSA. No deadline for regular filing. **Notification of Awards:** Applicants will be notified of awards on a rolling basis beginning on or about March 1. **Types of Aid:** *Need-based scholarships/grants:* Pell, SEOG, state scholarships/grants, the school's own gift aid. *Loans:* FFEL Subsidized Stafford, FFEL Unsubsidized Stafford, FFEL PLUS, Federal Perkins, college/university loans from institutional funds. **Student Employment:** Federal Work-Study Program available. Institutional employment available. **Financial Aid Statistics:** 79% freshmen, 76% undergrads receive some form of aid.

See page 1070.

JOHNSON & WALES UNIVERSITY—PROVIDENCE

8 Abbott Park Place, Providence, RI 02903-3703
Phone: 401-598-2310 **E-mail:** admissions@jwu.edu
Fax: 401-598-2948 **Web:** www.jwu.edu **ACT Code:** 3804

This private school was founded in 1914. It has a 50-acre campus.

STUDENTS AND FACULTY

Enrollment: 9,071. **Student Body:** Male 50%, female 50%, international 4%. **Ethnic Representation:** African American 13%, Asian 3%, Caucasian 77%, Hispanic 6%. **Retention and Graduation:** 28% grads go on to further study within 1 year. 27% grads pursue business degrees. **Faculty:** Student/faculty ratio 30:1. 281 full-time faculty. 100% faculty teach undergrads.

ACADEMICS

Degrees: Associate's, bachelor's, doctoral, master's. **Academic Requirements:** General education including some course work in computer literacy, English (including composition), foreign languages, history, humanities, mathematics, philosophy, sciences (biological or physical), social science. **Special Study Options:** Accelerated program, cooperative (work-study) program, double major, English as a second language, honors program, independent study, internships, liberal arts/career combination, study abroad, teacher certification program, weekend college, externships/practicums.

FACILITIES

Housing: Coed, housing for international students, wellness housing. **Library Holdings:** 85,523 bound volumes. 771 periodicals. 346,949 microforms. 2,531 audiovisuals. **Special Academic Facilities/Equipment:** Culinary archives and museum. **Computers:** School-owned computers available for student use.

EXTRACURRICULARS

Activities: Choral groups, dance, drama/theater, student government, student newspaper, yearbook. **Organizations:** 80 registered organizations, 2 honor societies, 1 religious organization, 9 fraternities, 12 sororities. **Athletics (Intercollegiate):** *Men:* baseball, basketball, cheerleading, cross-country, equestrian, golf, ice hockey, soccer, tennis, volleyball, wrestling. *Women:* basketball, cheerleading, cross-country, equestrian, golf, ice hockey, soccer, softball, tennis, volleyball.

ADMISSIONS

Selectivity Rating: 60 (of 100). **Freshman Academic Profile:** 90% from public high schools. TOEFL required of all international applicants, minimum TOEFL 550. **Basis for Candidate Selection:** *Very important factors considered include:* secondary school record. *Important factors considered include:* class rank. *Other factors considered include:* extracurricular activities, interview, recommendations, standardized test scores, volunteer work, work experience. **Freshman Admission Requirements:** High school diploma or GED is required. *Academic units required/recommended:* 10 total recommended; 4 English recommended, 3 math recommended, 1 science recommended, 2 social studies recommended. **Transfer Admission Requirements:** *Items required:* high school transcript, college transcript. Lowest grade transferable C. **General Admission Information:** Nonfall registration accepted. Admission may be deferred for a maximum of 1 year. Neither credit nor placement offered for CEEB Advanced Placement tests.

COSTS AND FINANCIAL AID

Tuition $18,444. Room & board $6,777. Required fees $750. Average book expense $750. **Required Forms and Deadlines:** FAFSA. No deadline for regular filing. **Notification of Awards:** Applicants will be notified of awards on a rolling basis beginning on or about March 1. **Types of Aid:** *Need-based scholarships/grants:* Pell, SEOG, state scholarships/grants, the school's own gift aid. *Loans:* FFEL Subsidized Stafford, FFEL Unsubsidized Stafford, FFEL PLUS, Federal Perkins, college/university loans from institutional funds. **Student Employment:** Federal Work-Study Program available. Institutional employment available. Off-campus job opportunities are excellent. **Financial Aid Statistics:** 75% freshmen, 61% undergrads receive some form of aid. **Financial Aid Phone:** 800-342-5598.

See page 1070.

JOHNSON BIBLE COLLEGE

7900 Johnson Drive, Knoxville, TN 37998
Phone: 800-827-2122 **E-mail:** jbc@jbc.edu **CEEB Code:** 1345
Fax: 865-251-2336 **Web:** www.jbc.edu

This private school, which is affiliated with the Christian (Nondenominational) Church, was founded in 1893. It has a 350-acre campus.

STUDENTS AND FACULTY

Enrollment: 1,414. **Student Body:** Male 50%, female 50%, out-of-state 73%, international 1%. **Ethnic Representation:** African American 3%, Asian 1%, Caucasian 95%, Hispanic 1%. **Retention and Graduation:** 77% freshmen return for sophomore year. 26% freshmen graduate within 4 years. **Faculty:** Student/faculty ratio 17:1. 24 full-time faculty, 50% hold PhDs. 99% faculty teach undergrads.

ACADEMICS

Degrees: Associate's, bachelor's, certificate, master's. **Academic Requirements:** General education including some course work in English (including composition), history, mathematics, sciences (biological or physical). **Classes:** 50-99 students in an average class. Under 10 students in an average lab/discussion section. **Disciplines with Highest Percentage of Degrees Awarded:** Philosophy/religion/theology 87%, education 13%. **Special Study Options:** Accelerated program, cooperative (work-study) program, distance learning, English as a second language, honors program, independent study, internships, teacher certification program.

FACILITIES

Housing: All-female, all-male, apartments for married students. **Library Holdings:** 101,086 bound volumes. 402 periodicals. 15,332 microforms. 12,334 audiovisuals.

EXTRACURRICULARS

Activities: Music ensembles, radio station, student government, yearbook. **Organizations:** 3 honor societies, 3 religious organizations. **Athletics (Intercollegiate):** *Men:* baseball, basketball, cheerleading, soccer. *Women:* basketball, cheerleading, volleyball.

ADMISSIONS

Selectivity Rating: 69 (of 100). **Freshman Academic Profile:** Average high school GPA 3.2. 17% in top 10% of high school class, 42% in top 25% of high school class, 68% in top 50% of high school class. Average SAT I Math 499, SAT I Math middle 50% range 430-550. Average SAT I Verbal 520, SAT I Verbal middle 50% range 460-580. Average ACT 22, ACT middle 50% range 19-25. TOEFL required of all international applicants, minimum TOEFL 500. **Basis for Candidate Selection:** *Very important factors considered include:* character/personal qualities, class rank, recommendations, religious affiliation/commitment, secondary school record, standardized test scores. *Important factors considered include:* interview. *Other factors considered include:* alumni/ae relation, essays. **Freshman Admission Requirements:** High school diploma or GED is required. *Academic units required/recommended:* 16 total required. **Freshman Admission Statistics:** 198 applied, 91% accepted, 100% of those accepted enrolled. **Transfer Admission Requirements:** *Items required:* high school transcript, college transcript, essay, statement of good standing from prior school. Lowest grade transferable C. **General Admission Information:** Application fee $35. Regular application deadline August 1. Nonfall registration accepted. Admission may be deferred for a maximum of 1 year.

COSTS AND FINANCIAL AID

Tuition $9,560. Room & board $3,710. Required fees $610. Average book expense $800. **Required Forms and Deadlines:** FAFSA and institution's own financial aid form. No deadline for regular filing. **Notification of Awards:** Applicants will be notified of awards on or about April 30. **Types of Aid:** *Need-based scholarships/grants:* Pell, SEOG, state scholarships/grants, private scholarships, the school's own gift aid. *Loans:* FFEL Subsidized Stafford, FFEL Unsubsidized Stafford, FFEL PLUS. **Student Employment:** Federal Work-Study Program available. Off-campus job opportunities are good. **Financial Aid Statistics:** 97% freshmen, 94% undergrads receive some form of aid.

JOHNSON C. SMITH UNIVERSITY

100 Beatties Ford Road, Charlotte, NC 28216-5398
Phone: 704-378-1011 **CEEB Code:** 5333
Fax: 704-378-1242 **Web:** www.jcsu.edu **ACT Code:** 3112

This private school was founded in 1867. It has a 105-acre campus.

STUDENTS AND FACULTY

Enrollment: 1,283. **Student Body:** Out-of-state 72%. **Ethnic Representation:** African American 98%, Caucasian 1%, Native American 1%. **Retention and Graduation:** 20% grads go on to further study within 1 year. 5% grads pursue business degrees. 2% grads pursue law degrees. 3% grads pursue medical degrees.

ACADEMICS

Degrees: Bachelor's. **Special Study Options:** Cooperative (work-study) program, study abroad. Co-op programs: arts, business, computer science, education, health professions, humanities.

FACILITIES

Housing: Coed. **Library Holdings:** 115,226 bound volumes. 800 periodicals. 24,069 microforms. **Special Academic Facilities/Equipment:** Language lab, honors college, banking and finance center. **Computers:** *Recommended operating system:* Mac. School-owned computers available for student use.

EXTRACURRICULARS

Activities: Student newspaper, yearbook. **Organizations:** 45 registered organizations, 9 honor societies, 4 religious organizations, 4 fraternities (20% men join), 4 sororities (25% women join). **Athletics (Intercollegiate):** *Women:* basketball, indoor track, softball, track & field, volleyball.

ADMISSIONS

Selectivity Rating: 64 (of 100). **Freshman Academic Profile:** 6% in top 10% of high school class, 14% in top 25% of high school class, 76% in top 50% of high school class. **Freshman Admission Requirements:** High school diploma is required and GED is not accepted. *Academic units required/recommended:* 16 total required; 4 English required, 2 math required, 2 science required, 2 social studies required, 7 elective required. **Transfer Admission Requirements:** Minimum college GPA of 2.0 required. Lowest grade transferable C. **General Admission Information:** Early decision application deadline April 15. Regular application deadline rolling. Nonfall registration accepted. Credit and/or placement offered for CEEB Advanced Placement tests.

COSTS AND FINANCIAL AID

Tuition $8,126. Room & board $3,846. Required fees $100. Average book expense $755. **Required Forms and Deadlines:** FAFSA and state aid form. **Notification of Awards:** Applicants will be notified of awards on or about April 16. **Types of Aid:** *Need-based scholarships/grants:* state scholarships/grants, United Negro College Fund. *Loans:* FFEL Subsidized Stafford, FFEL PLUS. **Student Employment:** Federal Work-Study Program available. Institutional employment available. Off-campus job opportunities are fair. **Financial Aid Statistics:** Average income from on-campus job $2,000. **Financial Aid Phone:** 704-378-1034.

JOHNSON STATE COLLEGE

337 College Hill, Johnson, VT 05656-9408
Phone: 802-635-1219 **E-mail:** jscapply@badger.jsc.vsc.edu **CEEB Code:** 3766
Fax: 802-635-1230 **Web:** www.johnsonstatecollege.edu **ACT Code:** 4316

This public school was founded in 1828. It has a 350-acre campus.

STUDENTS AND FACULTY

Enrollment: 1,361. **Student Body:** Male 43%, female 57%, out-of-state 39%, international 1%. **Ethnic Representation:** Caucasian 74%, Hispanic 1%, Native American 2%. **Retention and Graduation:** 62% freshmen return for sophomore year. 20% freshmen graduate within 4 years. **Faculty:** Student/faculty ratio 16:1. 62 full-time faculty, 90% hold PhDs. 100% faculty teach undergrads.

ACADEMICS

Degrees: Associate's, bachelor's, master's, terminal. **Academic Requirements:** General education including some course work in arts/fine arts, English (including composition), history, humanities, mathematics, sciences (biological or physical), social science. **Majors with Highest Enrollment:** Environmental science; elementary education and teaching; tourism and travel services management. **Disciplines with Highest Percentage of Degrees Awarded:** Business/marketing 18%, social sciences and history 13%, education 11%, psychology 11%, liberal arts/general studies 10%. **Special Study Options:** Cross registration, double major, dual enrollment, student exchange program (domestic), external degree program, honors program, internships, study abroad, teacher certification program.

FACILITIES

Housing: Coed, apartments for students who have 60 credits and a 3.0 average. **Library Holdings:** 100,053 bound volumes. 522 periodicals. 180,158 microforms. 7,200 audiovisuals. **Special Academic Facilities/Equipment:** Art gallery, visual arts center, child development center, human performance lab, 1,000-acre nature preserve, snowboard terrain park, dance studio. **Computers:** *Recommended operating system:* Windows NT/2000. School-owned computers available for student use.

EXTRACURRICULARS

Activities: Choral groups, concert band, dance, drama/theater, jazz band, literary magazine, music ensembles, radio station, student government, student newspaper, yearbook. **Organizations:** 40 registered organizations, 1 honor society, 1 religious organization. **Athletics (Intercollegiate):** *Men:* basketball, cross-country, lacrosse, soccer, tennis. *Women:* basketball, cross-country, soccer, softball, tennis.

ADMISSIONS

Selectivity Rating: 69 (of 100). **Freshman Academic Profile:** 6% in top 10% of high school class, 24% in top 25% of high school class, 52% in top 50% of high school class. Average SAT I Math 490, SAT I Math middle 50% range 430-530. Average SAT I Verbal 500, SAT I Verbal middle 50% range 430-550. TOEFL required of all international applicants, minimum TOEFL 500. **Basis for Candidate Selection:** *Very important factors considered include:* secondary school record, standardized test scores. *Important factors considered include:* class rank, essays, recommendations. *Other factors considered include:* character/personal qualities, extracurricular activities, interview, talent/ability, volunteer work, work experience. **Freshman Admission Requirements:** High school diploma or GED is required. *Academic units required/recommended:* 9 total required; 15 total recommended; 4 English required, 3 math required, 4 math recommended, 2 science required, 3 science recommended, 1 science lab required, 2 science lab recommended, 2 foreign language recommended, 2 social studies recommended, 2 history recommended. **Freshman Admission Statistics:** 870 applied, 78% accepted, 35% of those accepted enrolled. **Transfer Admission Requirements:** *Items required:* college transcript, essay. Minimum college GPA of 2.0 required. Lowest grade transferable C-. **General Admission Information:** Application fee $30. Priority application deadline March 1. Nonfall registration accepted. Admission may be deferred for a maximum of 1 year. Credit and/or placement offered for CEEB Advanced Placement tests.

COSTS AND FINANCIAL AID

In-state tuition $4,624. Out-of-state tuition $10,836. Room & board $5,782. Required fees $880. Average book expense $600. **Required Forms and Deadlines:** FAFSA. Priority filing deadline March 3. **Notification of Awards:** Applicants will be notified of awards on a rolling basis beginning on or about April 1. **Types of Aid:** *Need-based scholarships/grants:* Pell, SEOG, state scholarships/grants, private scholarships, the school's own gift aid. *Loans:* Direct Subsidized Stafford, Direct Unsubsidized Stafford, Direct PLUS, Federal

Perkins. **Student Employment:** Federal Work-Study Program available. Institutional employment available. Off-campus job opportunities are good. **Financial Aid Statistics:** 66% freshmen, 65% undergrads receive some form of aid. **Financial Aid Phone:** 802-635-2356.

JUDSON COLLEGE (AL)

PO Box 120, Marion, AL 36756
Phone: 334-683-5110 **E-mail:** admissions@future.judson.edu **CEEB Code:** 1349
Fax: 334-683-5158 **Web:** www.judson.edu **ACT Code:** 22

This private school, which is affiliated with the Baptist Church, was founded in 1838. It has an 80-acre campus.

STUDENTS AND FACULTY

Enrollment: 363. **Student Body:** Male 4%, female 96%, out-of-state 16%, international 1%. **Ethnic Representation:** African American 13%, Asian 1%, Caucasian 85%, Native American 1%. **Retention and Graduation:** 70% freshmen return for sophomore year. 47% freshmen graduate within 4 years. 18% grads go on to further study within 1 year. 4% grads pursue business degrees. 4% grads pursue law degrees. 2% grads pursue medical degrees. **Faculty:** Student/faculty ratio 11:1. 27 full-time faculty, 70% hold PhDs. 100% faculty teach undergrads.

ACADEMICS

Degrees: Bachelor's. **Academic Requirements:** General education including some course work in computer literacy, English (including composition), history, humanities, mathematics, sciences (biological or physical), social science, religion, women's studies, health/activity. **Classes:** Under 10 students in an average class. Under 10 students in an average lab/discussion section. **Majors with Highest Enrollment:** Business/commerce, general; education, general; psychology, general. **Disciplines with Highest Percentage of Degrees Awarded:** Psychology 18%, business/marketing 16%, education 12%, English 12%, biological life sciences 10%. **Special Study Options:** Accelerated program, cross registration, distance learning, double major, dual enrollment, honors program, independent study, internships, liberal arts/career combination, student-designed major, study abroad, teacher certification program.

FACILITIES

Housing: All-female. **Library Holdings:** 70,746 bound volumes. 5,287 periodicals. 2,035 microforms. 7,359 audiovisuals. **Special Academic Facilities/Equipment:** Alabama Women's Hall of Fame. **Computers:** *Recommended operating system:* Windows NT/2000. School-owned computers available for student use.

EXTRACURRICULARS

Activities: Choral groups, dance, drama/theater, literary magazine, music ensembles, student government, student newspaper, yearbook. **Organizations:** 30 registered organizations, 9 honor societies, 1 religious organization. **Athletics (Intercollegiate):** *Women:* basketball, equestrian, softball, tennis, volleyball.

ADMISSIONS

Selectivity Rating: 69 (of 100). **Freshman Academic Profile:** Average high school GPA 3.2. 24% in top 10% of high school class, 55% in top 25% of high school class, 86% in top 50% of high school class. 90% from public high schools. SAT I Math middle 50% range 430-550. SAT I Verbal middle 50% range 500-590. Average ACT 22, ACT middle 50% range 19-24. TOEFL required of all international applicants, minimum TOEFL 500. **Basis for Candidate Selection:** *Very important factors considered include:* interview, secondary school record, standardized test scores. *Important factors considered include:* alumni/ae relation, character/personal qualities, class rank, extracurricular activities, recommendations, religious affiliation/commitment, talent/ability. *Other factors considered include:* essays. **Freshman Admission Requirements:** High school diploma or GED is required. *Academic units required/recommended:* 16 total required; 4 English required, 4 English recommended, 2 math required, 4 math recommended, 2 science required, 4 science recommended, 2 foreign language recommended, 3 social studies required, 4 social studies recommended, 2 history recommended, 5 elective required. **Freshman Admission Statistics:** 290 applied, 81% accepted, 42% of those accepted enrolled. **Transfer Admission Requirements:** *Items required:* college transcript, interview, statement of good standing from prior school. Minimum high school GPA of 2.0 required. Minimum college GPA of 2.0 required. Lowest grade transferable C-. **General Admission Information:** Application fee $25. Nonfall registration accepted. Credit and/or placement offered for CEEB Advanced Placement tests.

COSTS AND FINANCIAL AID

Tuition $8,150. Room & board $5,380. Required fees $470. Average book expense $700. **Required Forms and Deadlines:** FAFSA, institution's own financial aid form, and state aid form. No deadline for regular filing. Priority filing deadline March 1. **Notification of Awards:** Applicants will be notified of awards on a rolling basis beginning on or about January 15. **Types of Aid:** *Need-based scholarships/grants:* Pell, SEOG, state scholarships/grants, private scholarships, the school's own gift aid. *Loans:* FFEL Subsidized Stafford, FFEL Unsubsidized Stafford, FFEL PLUS, Federal Perkins, college/university loans from institutional funds. **Student Employment:** Federal Work-Study Program available. Institutional employment available. Off-campus job opportunities are poor. **Financial Aid Statistics:** 72% freshmen, 75% undergrads receive some form of aid. Average freshman grant $5,630. Average freshman loan $2,500. Average income from on-campus job $746. **Financial Aid Phone:** 334-683-5157.

JUDSON COLLEGE (IL)

1151 North State Street, Elgin, IL 60123
Phone: 847-628-2510 **E-mail:** admission@judsoncollege.edu
Fax: 847-695-0216 **Web:** www.judsoncollege.edu

This private school, which is affiliated with the Baptist Church, was founded in 1963.

STUDENTS AND FACULTY

Enrollment: 1,167. **Student Body:** Male 44%, female 56%, out-of-state 25%, international 2%. **Ethnic Representation:** African American 4%, Asian 1%, Caucasian 69%, Hispanic 5%. **Retention and Graduation:** 78% freshmen return for sophomore year. 39% freshmen graduate within 4 years. **Faculty:** Student/faculty ratio 15:1. 43 full-time faculty, 60% hold PhDs.

ACADEMICS

Degrees: Bachelor's, master's. **Academic Requirements:** General education including some course work in arts/fine arts, computer literacy, English (including composition), history, humanities, mathematics, sciences (biological or physical), social science, Bible. **Classes:** 10-19 students in an average class. **Special Study Options:** Distance learning, double major.

FACILITIES

Housing: All-female, all-male, apartments for married students. **Library Holdings:** 104,331 bound volumes. 450 periodicals. 20,000 microforms. 12,500 audiovisuals.

EXTRACURRICULARS

Activities: Choral groups, concert band, drama/theater, jazz band, music ensembles, student government, student newspaper, yearbook. **Organizations:** 30 registered organizations, 1 religious organization. **Athletics (Intercollegiate):** *Men:* baseball, basketball, cross-country, soccer, softball, tennis. *Women:* basketball, cross-country, soccer, softball, tennis, volleyball.

ADMISSIONS

Selectivity Rating: 73 (of 100). **Freshman Academic Profile:** Average high school GPA 3.3. 7% in top 10% of high school class, 35% in top 25% of high school class, 59% in top 50% of high school class. SAT I Math middle 50% range 473-580. SAT I Verbal middle 50% range 483-560. Average ACT 22, ACT middle 50% range 20-25. TOEFL required of all international applicants, minimum TOEFL 550. **Basis for Candidate Selection:** *Very important factors considered include:* secondary school record, standardized test scores. *Other factors considered include:* character/personal qualities, class rank, extracurricular activities, recommendations, talent/ability. **Freshman Admission Requirements:** High school diploma or GED is required. *Academic units required/recommended:* 8 total recommended; 4 English recommended, 3 math recommended, 2 science recommended, 2 science lab recommended, 2 social studies recommended. **Freshman Admission Statistics:** 534 applied, 71% accepted, 45% of those accepted enrolled. **Transfer Admission Requirements:** *Items required:* college transcript. Lowest grade transferable C. **General Admission Information:** Application fee $30. Priority application deadline August 15. Nonfall registration accepted.

COSTS AND FINANCIAL AID

Tuition $13,872. Room & board $5,570. Required fees $550. Average book expense $680. **Required Forms and Deadlines:** FAFSA. No deadline for regular filing. **Notification of Awards:** Applicants will be notified of awards on a rolling basis beginning on or about January 1. **Types of Aid:** *Need-based scholarships/grants:* Pell, SEOG, state scholarships/grants, private scholarships, the school's own gift aid. *Loans:* Direct Subsidized Stafford, Direct

Unsubsidized Stafford, Direct PLUS, Federal Perkins. **Student Employment:** Federal Work-Study Program available. **Financial Aid Statistics:** 82% freshmen, 68% undergrads receive some form of aid. Average freshman grant $1,900. Average freshman loan $2,961. Average income from on-campus job $1,200.

THE JUILLIARD SCHOOL

60 Lincoln Center Plaza, New York, NY 10023-6588
Phone: 212-799-5000 **E-mail:** mgray@juilliard.edu **CEEB Code:** 2340
Fax: 212-724-0263 **Web:** www.juilliard.edu

This private school was founded in 1905.

STUDENTS AND FACULTY

Enrollment: 488. **Student Body:** Male 49%, female 51%, out-of-state 78%, international 23% (24 countries represented). **Ethnic Representation:** African American 13%, Asian 17%, Caucasian 61%, Hispanic 8%. **Retention and Graduation:** 95% freshmen return for sophomore year. 63% freshmen graduate within 4 years. **Faculty:** Student/faculty ratio 4:1. 120 full-time faculty.

ACADEMICS

Degrees: Bachelor's, diploma, doctoral, master's, post-bachelor's certificate, post-master's certificate, transfer. **Academic Requirements:** General education including some course work in arts/fine arts, foreign languages, humanities. **Classes:** Under 10 students in an average class. 10-19 students in an average lab/discussion section. **Disciplines with Highest Percentage of Degrees Awarded:** Visual and performing arts 100%. **Special Study Options:** Accelerated program, cross registration, double major, student exchange program (domestic), honors program, study abroad. Eligible Juilliard students can enroll in courses at Barnard and Columbia Colleges to fulfill their liberal arts elective requirement.

FACILITIES

Housing: Coed, apartments for married students, apartments for single students, single-sex floor, quiet floor, graduate floor, nonsmoking floors available. **Library Holdings:** 80,793 bound volumes. 220 periodicals. 153 microforms. 21,862 audiovisuals. **Special Academic Facilities/Equipment:** 5 theatres, 15 two-story studios, 35 private teaching studios, 106 practice rooms, organ studios, concert and production spaces.

EXTRACURRICULARS

Activities: Choral groups, dance, drama/theater, music ensembles, opera, student newspaper, symphony orchestra. **Organizations:** 5 registered organizations.

ADMISSIONS

Selectivity Rating: 99 (of 100). **Freshman Academic Profile:** TOEFL required of all international applicants, minimum TOEFL 550. **Basis for Candidate Selection:** *Very important factors considered include:* talent/ability. *Important factors considered include:* character/personal qualities, essays, secondary school record. *Other factors considered include:* extracurricular activities, minority status, recommendations. **Freshman Admission Requirements:** High school diploma or GED is required. **Freshman Admission Statistics:** 1,806 applied, 8% accepted, 83% of those accepted enrolled. **Transfer Admission Requirements:** *Items required:* high school transcript, college transcript, essay. Lowest grade transferable C. **General Admission Information:** Application fee $100. Regular application deadline December 1. Neither credit nor placement offered for CEEB Advanced Placement tests.

COSTS AND FINANCIAL AID

Tuition $19,700. Room & board $7,850. Required fees $600. Average book expense $3,100. **Required Forms and Deadlines:** FAFSA, institution's own financial aid form, state aid form, and tax returns. Financial aid filing deadline March 1. Priority filing deadline March 1. **Notification of Awards:** Applicants will be notified of awards on or about April 1. **Types of Aid:** *Need-based scholarships/grants:* Pell, SEOG, state scholarships/grants, private scholarships, the school's own gift aid. *Loans:* Direct Subsidized Stafford, Direct Unsubsidized Stafford, Direct PLUS, Federal Perkins, college/university loans from institutional funds. **Student Employment:** Federal Work-Study Program available. Institutional employment available. Off-campus job opportunities are excellent. **Financial Aid Statistics:** 67% freshmen, 75% undergrads receive some form of aid. Average freshman grant $15,166. Average freshman loan $2,676. Average income from on-campus job $1,500. **Financial Aid Phone:** 212-799-5000.

JUNIATA COLLEGE

1700 Moore Street, Huntingdon, PA 16652
Phone: 814-641-3420 **E-mail:** info@juniata.edu **CEEB Code:** 2341
Fax: 814-641-3100 **Web:** www.juniata.edu **ACT Code:** 3600

This private school, which is affiliated with the Church of Brethren, was founded in 1876. It has an 800-acre campus.

STUDENTS AND FACULTY

Enrollment: 1,345. **Student Body:** Male 42%, female 58%, out-of-state 24%, international 3% (27 countries represented). **Ethnic Representation:** African American 1%, Asian 1%, Caucasian 97%, Hispanic 1%. **Retention and Graduation:** 86% freshmen return for sophomore year. 67% freshmen graduate within 4 years. 35% grads go on to further study within 1 year. 2% grads pursue business degrees. 3% grads pursue law degrees. 7% grads pursue medical degrees. **Faculty:** Student/faculty ratio 13:1. 89 full-time faculty, 94% hold PhDs. 100% faculty teach undergrads.

ACADEMICS

Degrees: Bachelor's. **Academic Requirements:** General education including some course work in arts/fine arts, computer literacy, English (including composition), humanities, mathematics, sciences (biological or physical), social science, international studies. **Classes:** 10-19 students in an average class. 20-29 students in an average lab/discussion section. **Majors with Highest Enrollment:** Business administration/management; education, general; biology/biological sciences, general. **Disciplines with Highest Percentage of Degrees Awarded:** Business/marketing 16%, biological life sciences 16%, education 10%, social sciences and history 8%, computer and information sciences 7%. **Special Study Options:** Accelerated program, distance learning, double major, English as a second language, student exchange program (domestic), honors program, independent study, internships, student-designed major, study abroad, teacher certification program, Philadelphia urban semester, marine science semester, Washington semester, cooperative degree programs (3-1, 3-2, etc.).

FACILITIES

Housing: Coed, all-female, apartments for single students, housing for international students, special-interest housing, substance-free housing. **Library Holdings:** 255,000 bound volumes. 1,000 periodicals. 200 microforms. 1,500 audiovisuals. **Special Academic Facilities/Equipment:** Environmental studies field station, Juniata Museum of Art, early childhood development center, ceramics studio and Anagama kiln, nature preserve and peace chapel, observatory, electron microscopes, nuclear magnetic resonance spectrometers, human interaction lab. **Computers:** *Recommended operating system:* Windows XP Professional. School-owned computers available for student use.

EXTRACURRICULARS

Activities: Choral groups, concert band, dance, drama/theater, jazz band, literary magazine, music ensembles, musical theater, pep band, radio station, student government, student newspaper, symphony orchestra, yearbook. **Organizations:** 90 registered organizations, 10 honor societies, 5 religious organizations. **Athletics (Intercollegiate):** *Men:* baseball, basketball, cross-country, football, indoor track, soccer, tennis, track & field, volleyball. *Women:* basketball, cross-country, field hockey, indoor track, soccer, softball, swimming, tennis, track & field, volleyball.

ADMISSIONS

Selectivity Rating: 75 (of 100). **Freshman Academic Profile:** Average high school GPA 3.7. 36% in top 10% of high school class, 71% in top 25% of high school class, 98% in top 50% of high school class. 89% from public high schools. Average SAT I Math 583, SAT I Math middle 50% range 530-640. Average SAT I Verbal 574, SAT I Verbal middle 50% range 520-620. TOEFL required of all international applicants, minimum TOEFL 550. **Basis for Candidate Selection:** *Very important factors considered include:* character/personal qualities, essays, extracurricular activities, recommendations, secondary school record, standardized test scores. *Important factors considered include:* alumni/ae relation, interview, talent/ability, volunteer work. *Other factors considered include:* class rank, minority status, work experience. **Freshman Admission Requirements:** High school diploma or GED is required. *Academic units required/recommended:* 16 total required; 4 English required, 3 math required, 3 science required, 2 science lab required, 2 foreign language required, 1 social studies required, 3 history required. **Freshman Admission Statistics:** 1,346 applied, 79% accepted, 35% of those accepted enrolled. **Transfer Admission Requirements:** *Items required:* high school transcript, college transcript, essay. Minimum college GPA of 2.5 required. Lowest grade transferable C-. **General Admission Information:** Application fee $30. Priority application deadline November 15. Early decision application deadline November 15. Regular application deadline March 15. Nonfall registration accepted. Admission may be deferred for a maximum of 1 year. Credit and/or placement offered for CEEB Advanced Placement tests.

COSTS AND FINANCIAL AID

Tuition $22,240. Room & board $6,290. Required fees $520. Average book expense $450. **Required Forms and Deadlines:** FAFSA and CSS/Financial Aid PROFILE. Priority filing deadline March 1. **Notification of Awards:** Applicants will be notified of awards on a rolling basis beginning on or about December 1. **Types of Aid:** *Need-based scholarships/grants:* Pell, SEOG, state scholarships/grants, private scholarships, the school's own gift aid. *Loans:* FFEL Subsidized Stafford, FFEL Unsubsidized Stafford, FFEL PLUS, Federal Perkins. **Student Employment:** Federal Work-Study Program available. Institutional employment available. Off-campus job opportunities are fair. **Financial Aid Statistics:** 77% freshmen, 77% undergrads receive some form of aid. Average freshman grant $14,651. Average freshman loan $2,965. Average income from on-campus job $757. **Financial Aid Phone:** 814-641-3142.

KALAMAZOO COLLEGE

1200 Academy Street, Kalamazoo, MI 49006
Phone: 616-337-7166 **E-mail:** admission@kzoo.edu **CEEB Code:** 1365
Fax: 269-337-7390 **Web:** www.kzoo.edu **ACT Code:** 2018

This private school was founded in 1833. It has a 60-acre campus.

STUDENTS AND FACULTY

Enrollment: 1,265. **Student Body:** Out-of-state 21%, international students represent 20 countries. **Ethnic Representation:** African American 2%, Asian 5%, Caucasian 83%, Hispanic 2%. **Retention and Graduation:** 86% freshmen return for sophomore year. 66% freshmen graduate within 4 years. **Faculty:** Student/faculty ratio 12:1. 103 full-time faculty, 86% hold PhDs. 100% faculty teach undergrads.

ACADEMICS

Degrees: Bachelor's. **Academic Requirements:** General education including some course work in arts/fine arts, computer literacy, English (including composition), foreign languages, mathematics, philosophy, sciences (biological or physical), social science. **Classes:** 20-29 students in an average class. 20-29 students in an average lab/discussion section. **Majors with Highest Enrollment:** Business/commerce, general; biology/biological sciences, general; psychology, general. **Disciplines with Highest Percentage of Degrees Awarded:** Social sciences and history 19%, business/marketing 14%, English 11%, psychology 10%, visual and performing arts 8%. **Special Study Options:** Cross registration, double major, dual enrollment, student exchange program (domestic), independent study, internships, study abroad, teacher certification program.

FACILITIES

Housing: Coed; themed housing: Asian house, wellness house, African-American house, nonviolent student organization house, women's resource center. **Library Holdings:** 342,939 bound volumes. 1,495 periodicals. 23,862 microforms. 6,967 audiovisuals. **Special Academic Facilities/Equipment:** Science center. **Computers:** School-owned computers available for student use.

EXTRACURRICULARS

Activities: Choral groups, concert band, dance, drama/theater, jazz band, literary magazine, music ensembles, musical theater, pep band, radio station, student government, student newspaper, symphony orchestra, yearbook. **Organizations:** 50 registered organizations, 3 honor societies, 3 religious organizations. **Athletics (Intercollegiate):** *Men:* baseball, basketball, cross-country, diving, football, golf, soccer, swimming, tennis. *Women:* basketball, cross-country, diving, golf, soccer, softball, swimming, tennis, volleyball.

ADMISSIONS

Selectivity Rating: 82 (of 100). **Freshman Academic Profile:** Average high school GPA 3.6. 42% in top 10% of high school class, 74% in top 25% of high school class, 95% in top 50% of high school class. 85% from public high schools. Average SAT I Math 630, SAT I Math middle 50% range 580-690. Average SAT I Verbal 631, SAT I Verbal middle 50% range 590-680. Average ACT 28, ACT middle 50% range 26-30. TOEFL required of all international applicants, minimum TOEFL 550. **Basis for Candidate Selection:** *Very important factors considered include:* extracurricular activities, secondary school record, standardized test scores, talent/ability. *Important factors considered include:* character/personal qualities, class rank, essays, recommendations, volunteer work, work experience. *Other factors considered include:* alumni/ae relation, geographical residence, interview, minority status, state residency. **Freshman Admission Requirements:** High school diploma or GED is required. *Academic units required/recommended:* 17 total required; 4 English recommended, 3 math recommended, 3 science recommended, 3 foreign language recommended, 2 social studies recommended, 2 history recommended. **Freshman Admission Statistics:** 1,411 applied, 73% accepted, 33% of those accepted enrolled. **Transfer Admission Requirements:** *Items required:* high school transcript, college transcript, essay, interview, standardized test scores, statement of good standing from prior school. Minimum college GPA of 3.0 required. Lowest grade transferable C. **General Admission Information:** Application fee $45. Priority application deadline February 15. Early decision application deadline November 15. Regular application deadline February 15. Admission may be deferred for a maximum of 1 year. Credit and/or placement offered for CEEB Advanced Placement tests.

COSTS AND FINANCIAL AID

Required Forms and Deadlines: FAFSA and institution's own financial aid form. No deadline for regular filing. Priority filing deadline February 15. **Notification of Awards:** Applicants will be notified of awards on or about March 21. **Types of Aid:** *Need-based scholarships/grants:* Pell, SEOG, state scholarships/grants, private scholarships, the school's own gift aid. *Loans:* Direct Subsidized Stafford, Direct Unsubsidized Stafford, Direct PLUS, Federal Perkins, state loans. **Student Employment:** Federal Work-Study Program available. Institutional employment available. Off-campus job opportunities are good. **Financial Aid Statistics:** 58% freshmen, 50% undergrads receive some form of aid. Average freshman grant $12,510. Average freshman loan $4,230. **Financial Aid Phone:** 269-337-7192.

KANSAS CITY ART INSTITUTE

$$$

4415 Warwick Boulevard, Kansas City, MO 64111-1762
Phone: 816-474-5225 **E-mail:** admiss@kcai.edu **CEEB Code:** 6330
Fax: 816-802-3309 **Web:** www.kcai.edu **ACT Code:** 2277

This private school was founded in 1885. It has a 15-acre campus.

STUDENTS AND FACULTY

Enrollment: 548. **Student Body:** Male 46%, female 54%, out-of-state 84%, international 2%. **Ethnic Representation:** African American 3%, Asian 1%, Caucasian 82%, Hispanic 6%, Native American 2%. **Retention and Graduation:** 82% freshmen return for sophomore year. 46% freshmen graduate within 4 years. 40% grads go on to further study within 1 year. **Faculty:** Student/faculty ratio 9:1. 44 full-time faculty, 86% hold PhDs. 100% faculty teach undergrads.

ACADEMICS

Degrees: Bachelor's. **Academic Requirements:** General education including some course work in arts/fine arts. **Classes:** 10-19 students in an average class. **Majors with Highest Enrollment:** Design and visual communications, general; film/video and photographic arts; painting. **Special Study Options:** Cooperative (work-study) program, cross registration, double major, English as a second language, student exchange program (domestic), independent study, internships, study abroad.

FACILITIES

Housing: Coed, apartments for single students. **Library Holdings:** 30,000 bound volumes. 125 periodicals. **Special Academic Facilities/Equipment:** H&R Block Artspace, student art gallery. **Computers:** School-owned computers available for student use.

EXTRACURRICULARS

Activities: Student government.

ADMISSIONS

Selectivity Rating: 77 (of 100). **Freshman Academic Profile:** Average high school GPA 3.3. 7% in top 10% of high school class, 30% in top 25% of high school class, 57% in top 50% of high school class. 80% from public high schools. Average SAT I Math 540, SAT I Math middle 50% range 470-610. Average SAT I Verbal 559, SAT I Verbal middle 50% range 490-620. Average ACT 23, ACT middle 50% range 20-25. TOEFL required of all international applicants, minimum TOEFL 550. **Basis for Candidate Selection:** *Very important factors considered include:* character/personal qualities, essays, interview, recommendations, secondary school record, standardized test scores, talent/ability. *Other factors considered include:* extracurricular activities, volunteer work, work experience. **Freshman Admission Requirements:** High school diploma or GED is required. *Academic units required/recommended:* 20 total recommended; 4 English recommended, 3 math recommended, 3 science recommended, 3 social studies recommended, 3 elective recommended. **Freshman Admission Statistics:** 441 applied, 79% accepted, 34% of those accepted enrolled. **Transfer Admission Requirements:** *Items required:* high school transcript, college transcript, essay, statement of good standing from prior school. Minimum high school GPA of 2.5 required. Minimum college GPA of 2.5 required. Lowest grade transferable C. **General Admission Information:** Application fee $25. Priority application deadline January 15. Nonfall registration accepted. Admission may be deferred for a maximum of 1 year. Credit offered for CEEB Advanced Placement tests.

COSTS AND FINANCIAL AID

Tuition $19,274. Room & board $6,540. Required fees $1,036. Average book expense $2,500. **Required Forms and Deadlines:** FAFSA and institution's own financial aid form. Financial aid filing deadline August 1. Priority filing deadline March 15. **Notification of Awards:** Applicants will be notified of awards on a rolling basis beginning on or about March 31. **Types of Aid:** *Need-based scholarships/grants:* Pell, SEOG, state scholarships/grants, the school's own gift aid. *Loans:* FFEL Subsidized Stafford, FFEL Unsubsidized Stafford, FFEL PLUS, Federal Perkins, alternative loans. **Student Employment:** Federal Work-Study Program available. Institutional employment available. Off-campus job opportunities are good. **Financial Aid Statistics:** 74% freshmen, 73% undergrads receive some form of aid. Average freshman grant $8,000. Average freshman loan $2,525. Average income from on-campus job $1,000. **Financial Aid Phone:** 816-802-3300.

See page 1072.

KANSAS STATE UNIVERSITY

119 Anderson Hall, Manhattan, KS 66506
Phone: 785-532-6250 **E-mail:** kstate@ksu.edu **CEEB Code:** 6334
Fax: 785-532-6393 **Web:** www.ksu.edu **ACT Code:** 1428

This public school was founded in 1863. It has a 668-acre campus.

STUDENTS AND FACULTY

Enrollment: 19,048. **Student Body:** Male 52%, female 48%, out-of-state 9%, international 1%. **Ethnic Representation:** African American 3%, Asian 1%, Caucasian 90%, Hispanic 2%, Native American 1%. **Retention and Graduation:** 79% freshmen return for sophomore year. 22% freshmen graduate within 4 years. 17% grads go on to further study within 1 year. **Faculty:** Student/faculty ratio 20:1. 882 full-time faculty, 85% hold PhDs. 74% faculty teach undergrads.

ACADEMICS

Degrees: Associate's, bachelor's, doctoral, first professional, master's. **Academic Requirements:** General education including some course work in arts/fine arts, English (including composition), history, humanities, mathematics, social science. **Classes:** 10-19 students in an average class. **Disciplines with Highest Percentage of Degrees Awarded:** Business/marketing 21%, agriculture 12%, engineering/engineering technology 11%, education 10%, social sciences and history 10%. **Special Study Options:** Accelerated program, cooperative (work-study) program, distance learning, double major, English as a second language, student exchange program (domestic), honors program, independent study, internships, study abroad, teacher certification program, minors.

FACILITIES

Housing: Coed, all-female, all-male, apartments for married students, apartments for single students, fraternities and/or sororities, cooperative housing. **Library Holdings:** 1,547,943 bound volumes. 13,483 periodicals. 2,504,048 microforms. 4,258 audiovisuals. **Special Academic Facilities/Equipment:** South Asian area study center, education communications center, center for cancer research, planetarium, nuclear reactor/accelerator, Beach Art Museum. **Computers:** *Recommended operating system:* UNIX. School-owned computers available for student use.

EXTRACURRICULARS

Activities: Choral groups, concert band, dance, drama/theater, jazz band, marching band, music ensembles, musical theater, pep band, radio station, student government, student newspaper, symphony orchestra, yearbook. **Organizations:** 350 registered organizations, 78 honor societies, 1 religious organization, 28 fraternities (20% men join), 15 sororities (20% women join). **Athletics (Intercollegiate):** *Men:* baseball, basketball, cheerleading, cross-country, football, golf, indoor track, track & field. *Women:* basketball, cheerleading, crew, cross-country, equestrian, golf, indoor track, tennis, track & field, volleyball.

ADMISSIONS

Selectivity Rating: 82 (of 100). **Freshman Academic Profile:** 59% in top 25% of high school class, 90% in top 50% of high school class. 90% from public high schools. Average ACT 24, ACT middle 50% range 19-25. TOEFL required of all international applicants, minimum TOEFL 550. **Basis for Candidate Selection:** *Very important factors considered include:* class rank, secondary school record, standardized test scores. *Other factors considered include:* recommendations. **Freshman Admission Requirements:** High school diploma or GED is required. *Academic units required/recommended:* 14 total required; 4 English required, 3 math required, 3 science required, 3 social studies required. **Freshman Admission Statistics:** 8,212 applied, 58% accepted, 74% of those accepted enrolled. **Transfer Admission Requirements:** *Items required:* college transcript, statement of good standing from prior school. Minimum college GPA of 2.0 required. Lowest grade transferable D. **General Admission Information:** Application fee $25. Nonfall registration accepted. Credit and/or placement offered for CEEB Advanced Placement tests.

COSTS AND FINANCIAL AID

In-state tuition $2,918. Out-of-state tuition $10,178. Room & board $4,500. Required fees $526. Average book expense $1,000. **Required Forms and Deadlines:** FAFSA. No deadline for regular filing. Priority filing deadline March 1. **Notification of Awards:** Applicants will be notified of awards on a rolling basis beginning on or about April 15. **Types of Aid:** *Need-based scholarships/grants:* Pell, SEOG, state scholarships/grants. *Loans:* Direct Subsidized Stafford, Direct Unsubsidized Stafford, Direct PLUS, Federal Perkins, college/university loans from institutional funds. **Student Employment:** Federal Work-Study Program available. Institutional employment available. Off-campus job opportunities are good. **Financial Aid Statistics:** 55% freshmen, 56% undergrads receive some form of aid. Average freshman grant $2,000. Average freshman loan $1,098. Average income from on-campus job $1,704. **Financial Aid Phone:** 785-532-6420.

KANSAS WESLEYAN UNIVERSITY

100 East Claflin, Salina, KS 67401-6196
Phone: 785-827-5541 **E-mail:** admissions@kwu.edu
Fax: 785-827-0927 **Web:** www.kwu.edu

This private school, which is affiliated with the Methodist Church, was founded in 1886. It has a 10-acre campus.

STUDENTS AND FACULTY

Enrollment: 684. **Student Body:** Male 40%, female 60%, out-of-state 39%, international 5% (4 countries represented). **Ethnic Representation:** African American 8%, Asian 1%, Caucasian 86%, Hispanic 4%, Native American 1%. **Faculty:** 100% faculty teach undergrads.

ACADEMICS

Degrees: Associate's, bachelor's, master's, terminal. **Academic Requirements:** General education including some course work in arts/fine arts, computer literacy, English (including composition), foreign languages, history, humanities, mathematics, philosophy, sciences (biological or physical), social science. **Special Study Options:** Cooperative (work-study) program, cross registration, distance learning, double major, dual enrollment, English as a second language, student exchange program (domestic), independent study, internships, liberal arts/career combination, student-designed major, study abroad, teacher certification program.

FACILITIES

Housing: Coed, all-female, all-male, apartments for married students, apartments for single students. **Library Holdings:** 177,000 bound volumes. 370 periodicals. 100,000 microforms. 1,055 audiovisuals. **Computers:** School-owned computers available for student use.

EXTRACURRICULARS

Activities: Choral groups, concert band, dance, drama/theater, jazz band, music ensembles, musical theater, pep band, student government, student newspaper, yearbook. **Organizations:** 15 registered organizations, 7 honor societies, 1 religious organization, 1% men join fraternities, 1% women join sororities. **Athletics (Intercollegiate):** *Men:* baseball, basketball, cheerleading, cross-country, football, golf, indoor track, soccer, track & field. *Women:* basketball, cheerleading, cross-country, golf, indoor track, soccer, softball, track & field, volleyball.

ADMISSIONS

Selectivity Rating: 69 (of 100). **Freshman Academic Profile:** Average high school GPA 3.2. 16% in top 10% of high school class, 27% in top 25% of high school class, 88% in top 50% of high school class. 97% from public high schools. Average SAT I Math 550. Average SAT I Verbal 650. Average ACT 22. TOEFL required of all international applicants, minimum TOEFL 500. **Basis for Candidate Selection:** *Very important factors considered include:* secondary school record, standardized test scores. *Important factors considered include:* class rank. *Other factors considered include:* essays, recommendations. **Freshman Admission Requirements:** High school diploma or GED is required. *Academic units required/recommended:* 4 total recommended; 2 English recommended, 3 math recommended, 2 science recommended, 2 science lab recommended, 2 foreign language recommended, 1 social studies recommended, 4 history recommended. **Freshman Admission Statistics:** 774 applied, 70% accepted, 21% of those accepted enrolled. **Transfer Admission Requirements:** *Items required:* college transcript. Minimum high school GPA of 2.5 required. Minimum college GPA of 2.0 required. Lowest grade transferable D. **General Admission Information:** Application fee $15. Priority application deadline March 15. Regular application deadline rolling. Nonfall registration accepted. Credit and/or placement offered for CEEB Advanced Placement tests.

COSTS AND FINANCIAL AID

Tuition $11,000. Room & board $4,000. Average book expense $400. **Required Forms and Deadlines:** FAFSA, institution's own financial aid form. Financial aid filing deadline August 15. Priority filing deadline March 15. **Notification of Awards:** Applicants will be notified of awards on a rolling basis beginning on or about March 15. **Types of Aid:** *Need-based scholarships/grants:* Pell, SEOG, state scholarships/grants, private scholarships, the school's own gift aid. *Loans:* Direct Subsidized Stafford, Direct Unsubsidized Stafford, Direct PLUS, FFEL Subsidized Stafford, FFEL Unsubsidized Stafford, FFEL PLUS, Federal Perkins, Federal Nursing, college/university loans from institutional funds. **Student Employment:** Federal Work-Study Program available. Institutional employment available. Off-campus job opportunities are excellent. **Financial Aid Statistics:** 71% freshmen, 86% undergrads receive some form of aid. Average freshman grant $11,095. Average freshman loan $4,670. Average income from on-campus job $500. **Financial Aid Phone:** 785-827-5541.

KEAN UNIVERSITY

PO Box 411, Union, NJ 07083-0411
Phone: 908-737-7100 **E-mail:** admitme@kean.edu **CEEB Code:** 2517
Fax: 908-737-7105 **Web:** www.kean.edu **ACT Code:** 2582

This public school was founded in 1855. It has a 150-acre campus.

STUDENTS AND FACULTY

Enrollment: 9,970. **Student Body:** Male 36%, female 64%, out-of-state 5%, international 3%. **Ethnic Representation:** African American 21%, Asian 6%, Caucasian 49%, Hispanic 20%. **Retention and Graduation:** 79% freshmen return for sophomore year. **Faculty:** Student/faculty ratio 21:1. 372 full-time faculty, 84% hold PhDs. 100% faculty teach undergrads.

ACADEMICS

Degrees: Bachelor's, master's, post-bachelor's certificate, post-master's certificate. **Academic Requirements:** General education including some course work in arts/fine arts, computer literacy, English (including composition), history, humanities, mathematics, sciences (biological or physical), social science. **Classes:** 20-29 students in an average class. 10-19 students in an average lab/discussion section. **Majors with Highest Enrollment:** Management science, general; elementary education and teaching; psychology, general. **Disciplines with Highest Percentage of Degrees Awarded:** Business/marketing 23%, education 20%, protective services/public administration 9%, social sciences and history 8%, psychology 8%. **Special Study Options:** Accelerated program, cooperative (work-study) program, distance learning, double major, dual enrollment, English as a second language, student exchange program (domestic), honors program, independent study, internships, liberal arts/career combination, study abroad, teacher certification program, weekend college.

FACILITIES

Housing: Coed, apartments for single students. **Library Holdings:** 270,000 bound volumes. 11,164 periodicals. **Special Academic Facilities/Equipment:** Holocaust resource center. **Computers:** School-owned computers available for student use.

EXTRACURRICULARS

Activities: Choral groups, dance, drama/theater, jazz band, literary magazine, music ensembles, musical theater, radio station, student government, student newspaper, yearbook. **Organizations:** 130 registered organizations, 22 honor societies, 3 religious organizations, 13 fraternities (2% men join), 17 sororities (3% women join). **Athletics (Intercollegiate):** *Men:* baseball, basketball, cross-country, football, lacrosse, soccer, track & field. *Women:* basketball, cheerleading, cross-country, field hockey, indoor track, lacrosse, soccer, softball, swimming, tennis, track & field, volleyball.

ADMISSIONS

Selectivity Rating: 63 (of 100). **Freshman Academic Profile:** 6% in top 10% of high school class, 23% in top 25% of high school class, 57% in top 50% of high school class. Average SAT I Math 510, SAT I Math middle 50% range 400-510. Average SAT I Verbal 500, SAT I Verbal middle 50% range 400-500. **Basis for Candidate Selection:** *Very important factors considered include:* secondary school record, standardized test scores, talent/ability. *Important factors considered include:* recommendations. *Other factors considered include:* alumni/ae relation, character/personal qualities, essays, extracurricular activities, interview, minority status, volunteer work, work experience. **Freshman Admission Requirements:** High school diploma or GED is required. *Academic units required/recommended:* 16 total required; 4 English required, 3 math required, 2 science required, 2 foreign language recommended, 2 social studies required, 5 elective required. **Freshman Admission Statistics:** 5,081 applied, 52% accepted, 53% of those accepted enrolled. **Transfer Admission Requirements:** *Items required:* high school transcript, college transcript, essay, statement of good standing from prior school. Minimum college GPA of 2.0 required. Lowest grade transferable C. **General Admission Information:** Application fee $35. Priority application deadline March 1. Regular application deadline June 15. Nonfall registration accepted. Credit and/or placement offered for CEEB Advanced Placement tests.

COSTS AND FINANCIAL AID

Average book expense $935. **Required Forms and Deadlines:** FAFSA. Priority filing deadline March 15. **Notification of Awards:** Applicants will be notified of awards on a rolling basis beginning on or about April 15. **Types of Aid:** *Need-based scholarships/grants:* Pell, SEOG, state scholarships/grants, private scholarships, the school's own gift aid. *Loans:* Direct Subsidized Stafford, Direct Unsubsidized Stafford, Direct PLUS, FFEL Subsidized Stafford, FFEL Unsubsidized Stafford, FFEL PLUS, Federal Perkins, college/university loans from institutional funds. **Student Employment:** Federal Work-Study Program available. Institutional employment available. Off-campus job opportunities are excellent. **Financial Aid Statistics:** 54% freshmen, 48% undergrads receive some form of aid. **Financial Aid Phone:** 908-737-3190.

See page 1074.

KEENE STATE COLLEGE

229 Main Street, Keene, NH 03435-2604
Phone: 603-358-2276 **E-mail:** admissions@keene.edu **CEEB Code:** 3472
Fax: 603-358-2767 **Web:** www.keene.edu **ACT Code:** 2510

This public school was founded in 1909. It has a 160-acre campus.

STUDENTS AND FACULTY

Enrollment: 4,690. **Student Body:** Male 42%, female 58%, out-of-state 46%, international students represent 29 countries. **Ethnic Representation:** Asian 1%, Caucasian 95%, Hispanic 1%. **Retention and Graduation:** 78% freshmen return for sophomore year. 10% grads go on to further study within 1 year. 1% grads pursue business degrees. **Faculty:** Student/faculty ratio 17:1. 187 full-time faculty, 81% hold PhDs. 100% faculty teach undergrads.

ACADEMICS

Degrees: Associate's, bachelor's, certificate, master's, post-bachelor's certificate, post-master's certificate, terminal, transfer. **Academic Requirements:** General education including some course work in arts/fine arts, English (including composition), history, humanities, mathematics, sciences (biological or physical), social science. **Classes:** 10-19 students in an average class. **Majors with Highest Enrollment:** Communications and media studies; elementary education and teaching; psychology, general. **Disciplines with Highest Percentage of Degrees Awarded:** Social sciences and history 16%, visual and performing arts 15%, communications/communication technologies 14%, psychology 13%, business/marketing 11%. **Special Study Options:** Cooperative (work-study) program, double major, English as a second language, student exchange program (domestic), honors program, independent study, internships, student-designed major, study abroad, teacher certification program.

FACILITIES

Housing: Coed, all-female, apartments for married students, apartments for single students, housing for disabled students, fraternities and/or sororities, special-interest housing, such as the environmental house. **Special Academic Facilities/Equipment:** Art gallery, theatre arts and film production facilities, Holocaust resource center, learning resource center, safety center, early childhood development center, 400-acre nature preserve. **Computers:** School-owned computers available for student use.

EXTRACURRICULARS

Activities: Choral groups, concert band, dance, drama/theater, literary magazine, music ensembles, radio station, student government, student newspaper, student-run film society, television station, yearbook. **Organizations:** 66 registered organizations, 15 honor societies, 4 religious organizations, 6 fraternities (5% men join), 6 sororities (5% women join). **Athletics (Intercollegiate):** *Men:* baseball, basketball, cheerleading, cross-country, diving, indoor track, lacrosse, soccer, swimming, track & field, volleyball. *Women:* basketball, cheerleading, cross-country, diving, field hockey, indoor track, lacrosse, soccer, softball, swimming, track & field, volleyball.

ADMISSIONS

Selectivity Rating: 70 (of 100). **Freshman Academic Profile:** Average high school GPA 2.9. 4% in top 10% of high school class, 19% in top 25% of high school class, 57% in top 50% of high school class. Average SAT I Math 488, SAT I Math middle 50% range 440-530. Average SAT I Verbal 499, SAT I Verbal middle 50% range 450-550. ACT middle 50% range 17-22. TOEFL required of all international applicants, minimum TOEFL 500. **Basis for Candidate Selection:** *Very important factors considered include:* secondary school record. *Important factors considered include:* class rank, essays, interview, recommendations, standardized test scores. *Other factors considered include:* alumni/ae relation, extracurricular activities, talent/ability, volunteer work, work experience. **Freshman Admission Requirements:** High school diploma or GED is required. *Academic units required/recommended:* 4 English required, 3 math required, 3 science required, 1 science lab required, 4 social studies required. **Transfer Admission Requirements:** *Items required:* high school transcript, college transcript, essay. Minimum college GPA of 2.0 required. Lowest grade transferable C. **General Admission Information:** Application fee $25. Regular application deadline April 1. Nonfall registration accepted. Admission may be deferred for a maximum of 1 year. Credit offered for CEEB Advanced Placement tests.

COSTS AND FINANCIAL AID

In-state tuition $4,450. Out-of-state tuition $10,110. Room & board $5,430. Required fees $1,682. Average book expense $600. **Required Forms and Deadlines:** FAFSA. Financial aid filing deadline March 1. **Notification of Awards:** Applicants will be notified of awards on a rolling basis. **Types of Aid:** *Need-based scholarships/grants:* Pell, SEOG, state scholarships/grants, private scholarships, the school's own gift aid. *Loans:* FFEL Subsidized Stafford, FFEL Unsubsidized Stafford, FFEL PLUS, Federal Perkins, college/university loans from institutional funds. **Student Employment:** Federal Work-Study Program available. Institutional employment available. Off-campus job opportunities are fair. **Financial Aid Statistics:** 55% freshmen, 52% undergrads receive some form of aid. Average freshman grant $4,012. Average freshman loan $3,010. **Financial Aid Phone:** 603-358-2280.

KENDALL COLLEGE

2408 Orrington Avenue, Evanston, IL 60201-2899
Phone: 847-866-1304 **E-mail:** admissions@kendall.edu
Fax: 847-733-7450 **Web:** www.kendall.edu **ACT Code:** 1703

This private school, which is affiliated with the Methodist Church, was founded in 1934. It has a 1-acre campus.

STUDENTS AND FACULTY

Enrollment: 622. **Student Body:** Male 47%, female 53%, out-of-state 15%, international 2%. **Ethnic Representation:** African American 14%, Asian 4%, Caucasian 75%, Hispanic 5%, Native American 1%. **Retention and Graduation:** 38% freshmen return for sophomore year. 38% freshmen graduate within 4 years. 30% grads go on to further study within 1 year. **Faculty:** Student/faculty ratio 15:1. 100% faculty teach undergrads.

ACADEMICS

Degrees: Associate's, bachelor's, certificate, terminal. **Academic Requirements:** General education including some course work in computer literacy, English (including composition), humanities, mathematics, philosophy, sciences (biological or physical), social science. **Disciplines with Highest Percentage of Degrees Awarded:** Business/marketing 35%, education 6%, social sciences and history 6%, liberal arts/general studies 6%. **Special Study Options:** Accelerated program, cooperative (work-study) program, distance learning, double major, independent study, internships, liberal arts/career combination, student-designed major, study abroad, teacher certification program.

FACILITIES

Housing: Coed. **Library Holdings:** 39,000 bound volumes. 200 periodicals. 200 microforms. 500 audiovisuals. **Special Academic Facilities/Equipment:** Mitchell Museum (Native American collection). **Computers:** *Recommended operating system:* Windows NT/2000. School-owned computers available for student use.

EXTRACURRICULARS

Activities: Student government, student newspaper. **Organizations:** 9 registered organizations, 2 honor societies, 1 religious organization. **Athletics (Intercollegiate):** *Men:* basketball, soccer, volleyball. *Women:* basketball, volleyball.

ADMISSIONS

Selectivity Rating: 63 (of 100). **Freshman Academic Profile:** 15% in top 10% of high school class, 15% in top 25% of high school class, 76% in top 50% of high school class. 85% from public high schools. Average SAT I Math 480. Average SAT I Verbal 510. Average ACT 23. TOEFL required of all international applicants, minimum TOEFL 500. **Basis for Candidate Selection:** *Important factors considered include:* secondary school record. *Other factors considered include:* character/personal qualities, class rank, essays, extracurricular activities, interview, recommendations, standardized test scores, talent/ability, volunteer work, work experience. **Freshman Admission Requirements:** High school diploma or GED is required. **Freshman Admission Statistics:** 109 applied, 83% accepted, 62% of those accepted enrolled. **Transfer Admission Requirements:** *Items required:* college transcript, essay, statement of good standing from prior school. Minimum college GPA of 2.0 required. Lowest grade transferable C. **General Admission Information:** Application fee $30. Nonfall registration accepted. Admission may be deferred for a maximum of 2 years. Credit and/or placement offered for CEEB Advanced Placement tests.

COSTS AND FINANCIAL AID

Tuition $13,500. Room & board $5,008. Required fees $330. Average book expense $200. **Types of Aid:** *Need-based scholarships/grants:* Pell, SEOG, state scholarships/grants, the school's own gift aid. *Loans:* FFEL Subsidized Stafford, FFEL Unsubsidized Stafford, FFEL PLUS, Federal Perkins, college/university loans from institutional funds. **Student Employment:** Federal Work-Study Program available. Institutional employment available. Off-campus job opportunities are excellent. **Financial Aid Statistics:** Average freshman grant $4,840. Average income from on-campus job $1,500.

KENDALL COLLEGE OF ART AND DESIGN

17 Fountain Street NW, Grand Rapids, MI 49503-3002
Phone: 616-451-2787 **E-mail:** packarda@kcad.edu **CEEB Code:** 1983
Fax: 616-831-9689 **Web:** www.kcad.edu **ACT Code:** 1983

This public school was founded in 1928.

STUDENTS AND FACULTY

Enrollment: 1,520. **Student Body:** Male 48%, female 52%, out-of-state 8%, international students represent 15 countries. **Retention and Graduation:** 67% freshmen return for sophomore year. 7% grads go on to further study within 1 year. **Faculty:** 100% faculty teach undergrads.

ACADEMICS

Degrees: Bachelor's, master's. **Academic Requirements:** General education including some course work in arts/fine arts, English (including composition), history, humanities, mathematics, sciences (biological or physical), social science. **Special Study Options:** Cooperative (work-study) program, double major, dual enrollment, independent study, internships, liberal arts/career combination, study abroad, teacher certification program.

FACILITIES

Computers: School-owned computers available for student use.

EXTRACURRICULARS

Organizations: 5 registered organizations, 3 religious organizations.

ADMISSIONS

Selectivity Rating: 75 (of 100). **Freshman Academic Profile:** Average high school GPA 2.8. 5% in top 10% of high school class, 15% in top 25% of high

school class, 57% in top 50% of high school class. Average SAT I Math 456. Average SAT I Verbal 495. Average ACT 20. TOEFL required of all international applicants, minimum TOEFL 500. **Basis for Candidate Selection:** *Very important factors considered include:* talent/ability. *Important factors considered include:* character/personal qualities, essays, interview, secondary school record, standardized test scores. *Other factors considered include:* alumni/ae relation, class rank, extracurricular activities, recommendations, volunteer work, work experience. **Freshman Admission Requirements:** High school diploma or GED is required. **Transfer Admission Requirements:** *Items required:* high school transcript, college transcript, essay. Lowest grade transferable C. **General Admission Information:** Application fee $35. Regular application deadline rolling. Nonfall registration accepted. Admission may be deferred. Credit offered for CEEB Advanced Placement tests.

COSTS AND FINANCIAL AID

Required fees $355. Average book expense $1,850. **Required Forms and Deadlines:** FAFSA. **Notification of Awards:** Applicants will be notified of awards on a rolling basis. **Types of Aid:** *Need-based scholarships/grants:* Pell, SEOG, state scholarships/grants, private scholarships. *Loans:* FFEL Subsidized Stafford, FFEL Unsubsidized Stafford, FFEL PLUS, Federal Perkins. **Student Employment:** Federal Work-Study Program available. Off-campus job opportunities are good. **Financial Aid Statistics:** Average freshman grant $5,000. Average freshman loan $2,625. Average income from on-campus job $1,625. **Financial Aid Phone:** 616-451-2787.

KENNESAW STATE UNIVERSITY

1000 Chastain Road, Box 0115, Kennesaw, GA 30144-5591
Phone: 770-423-6000 **E-mail:** ksuadmit@.kennesaw.edu **CEEB Code:** 5359
Fax: 770-423-6541 **Web:** www.kennesaw.edu **ACT Code:** 833

This public school was founded in 1963. It has a 185-acre campus.

STUDENTS AND FACULTY

Enrollment: 11,980. **Student Body:** Male 38%, female 62%, international 3%. **Ethnic Representation:** African American 9%, Asian 3%, Caucasian 86%, Hispanic 2%. **Retention and Graduation:** 71% freshmen return for sophomore year. 4% freshmen graduate within 4 years. **Faculty:** Student/faculty ratio 27:1. 382 full-time faculty, 75% hold PhDs. 100% faculty teach undergrads.

ACADEMICS

Degrees: Bachelor's, master's. **Academic Requirements:** General education including some course work in arts/fine arts, computer literacy, English (including composition), foreign languages, history, humanities, mathematics, philosophy, sciences (biological or physical), social science. **Classes:** 20-29 students in an average class. 20-29 students in an average lab/discussion section. **Majors with Highest Enrollment:** Nursing/registered nurse training (RN, ASN, BSN, MSN); business administration/management; early childhood education and teaching. **Disciplines with Highest Percentage of Degrees Awarded:** Business/marketing 28%, education 20%, computer and information sciences 11%, visual and performing arts 6%, social sciences and history 6%. **Special Study Options:** Cooperative (work-study) program, distance learning, double major, English as a second language, honors program, independent study, internships, teacher certification program, weekend college.

FACILITIES

Housing: Apartments for single students. **Library Holdings:** 407,810 bound volumes. 4,580 periodicals. 1,618,303 microforms. 10,500 audiovisuals. **Special Academic Facilities/Equipment:** Center for excellence in teaching and learning. **Computers:** *Recommended operating system:* Windows 95. School-owned computers available for student use.

EXTRACURRICULARS

Activities: Choral groups, concert band, dance, drama/theater, jazz band, literary magazine, music ensembles, musical theater, student government, student newspaper, symphony orchestra. **Organizations:** 50 registered organizations, 8 religious organizations, 2 fraternities, 5 sororities. **Athletics (Intercollegiate):** *Men:* baseball, basketball, cross-country, golf. *Women:* basketball, cheerleading, cross-country, soccer, softball, tennis.

ADMISSIONS

Selectivity Rating: 66 (of 100). **Freshman Academic Profile:** Average high school GPA 3.1. 90% from public high schools. Average SAT I Math 541, SAT I Math middle 50% range 460-550. Average SAT I Verbal 548, SAT I Verbal middle 50% range 470-568. ACT middle 50% range 19-23. TOEFL required of all international applicants, minimum TOEFL 550. **Basis for Candidate Selection:** *Very important factors considered include:* secondary school record, standardized test scores. **Freshman Admission Requirements:** High school diploma or GED is required. *Academic units required/recommended:* 18 total required; 4 English required, 4 math required, 3 science required, 2 science lab required, 2 foreign language required, 3 social studies required, 2 elective required. **Freshman Admission Statistics:** 3,461 applied, 80% accepted, 67% of those accepted enrolled. **Transfer Admission Requirements:** *Items required:* college transcript. Minimum high school GPA of 2.0 required. Minimum college GPA of 2.0 required. Lowest grade transferable D. **General Admission Information:** Application fee $40. Priority application deadline July 8. Regular application deadline July 15. Nonfall registration accepted. Admission may be deferred for a maximum of 1 year. Credit offered for CEEB Advanced Placement tests.

COSTS AND FINANCIAL AID

In-state tuition $2,350. Out-of-state tuition $7,990. Required fees $478. Average book expense $812. **Required Forms and Deadlines:** FAFSA. No deadline for regular filing. Priority filing deadline April 1. **Notification of Awards:** Applicants will be notified of awards on or about May 1. **Types of Aid:** *Need-based scholarships/grants:* Pell, SEOG, state scholarships/grants, private scholarships, the school's own gift aid. *Loans:* FFEL Subsidized Stafford, FFEL Unsubsidized Stafford, FFEL PLUS, Federal Perkins, state loans, college/university loans from institutional funds. **Student Employment:** Federal Work-Study Program available. Institutional employment available. Off-campus job opportunities are good. **Financial Aid Statistics:** 41% freshmen, 40% undergrads receive some form of aid. Average freshman grant $2,175. Average freshman loan $2,200. Average income from on-campus job $2,000. **Financial Aid Phone:** 770-423-6074.

KENT STATE UNIVERSITY

PO Box 5190, Kent, OH 44242-0001
Phone: 330-672-2444 **E-mail:** kentadm@admissions.kent.edu **CEEB Code:** 1367
Fax: 330-672-2499 **Web:** www.kent.edu **ACT Code:** 3284

This public school was founded in 1910. It has a 1,200-acre campus.

STUDENTS AND FACULTY

Enrollment: 18,813. **Student Body:** Male 41%, female 59%, out-of-state 7%, international 1% (83 countries represented). **Ethnic Representation:** African American 8%, Asian 1%, Caucasian 88%, Hispanic 1%. **Retention and Graduation:** 72% freshmen return for sophomore year. 16% freshmen graduate within 4 years. **Faculty:** Student/faculty ratio 20:1. 801 full-time faculty, 81% hold PhDs.

ACADEMICS

Degrees: Associate's, bachelor's, certificate, doctoral, master's, post-bachelor's certificate, post-master's certificate, terminal, transfer. **Academic Requirements:** General education including some course work in arts/fine arts, computer literacy, English (including composition), foreign languages, history, humanities, mathematics, philosophy, sciences (biological or physical), social science, diversity, and writing intensive. **Classes:** 20-29 students in an average class. **Majors with Highest Enrollment:** Psychology, general; criminal justice/safety studies; early childhood education and teaching. **Disciplines with Highest Percentage of Degrees Awarded:** Business/marketing 22%, education 18%, health professions and related sciences 7%, social sciences and history 5%, protective services/public administration 5%. **Special Study Options:** Accelerated program, cooperative (work-study) program, cross registration, distance learning, double major, dual enrollment, English as a second language, student exchange program (domestic), external degree program, honors program, independent study, internships, liberal arts/career combination, student-designed major, study abroad, teacher certification program, weekend college.

FACILITIES

Housing: Coed, all-female, all-male, apartments for married students, apartments for single students, fraternities and/or sororities, learning communities. **Library Holdings:** 1,120,598 bound volumes. 8,771 periodicals. 1,268,118 microforms. 27,447 audiovisuals. **Special Academic Facilities/Equipment:** Fashion museum, herbarium, liquid crystal institute, planetarium, airport. **Computers:** School-owned computers available for student use.

EXTRACURRICULARS

Activities: Choral groups, concert band, dance, drama/theater, jazz band, marching band, music ensembles, musical theater, opera, pep band, radio station, student government, student newspaper, student-run film society, television station. **Organizations:** 205 registered organizations, 21 honor societies, 21 religious organizations, 18 fraternities (4% men join), 9 sororities

(4% women join). **Athletics (Intercollegiate):** *Men:* baseball, basketball, cheerleading, cross-country, football, golf, indoor track, track & field, wrestling. *Women:* basketball, cheerleading, cross-country, field hockey, football, golf, gymnastics, indoor track, soccer, softball, track & field, volleyball.

ADMISSIONS

Selectivity Rating: 65 (of 100). **Freshman Academic Profile:** Average high school GPA 3.1. 11% in top 10% of high school class, 32% in top 25% of high school class, 70% in top 50% of high school class. Average SAT I Math 515, SAT I Math middle 50% range 460-570. Average SAT I Verbal 513, SAT I Verbal middle 50% range 450-570. Average ACT 21, ACT middle 50% range 19-24. TOEFL required of all international applicants, minimum TOEFL 525. **Basis for Candidate Selection:** *Very important factors considered include:* secondary school record. *Important factors considered include:* standardized test scores. *Other factors considered include:* class rank. **Freshman Admission Requirements:** High school diploma or GED is required. *Academic units required/recommended:* 16 total recommended; 4 English recommended, 3 math recommended, 3 science recommended, 2 science lab recommended, 2 foreign language recommended, 3 social studies recommended. **Freshman Admission Statistics:** 10,056 applied, 90% accepted, 41% of those accepted enrolled. **Transfer Admission Requirements:** *Items required:* college transcript. Minimum college GPA of 2.0 required. Lowest grade transferable C. **General Admission Information:** Application fee $30. Regular application deadline May 1. Nonfall registration accepted. Credit and/or placement offered for CEEB Advanced Placement tests.

COSTS AND FINANCIAL AID

In-state tuition $6,374. Out-of-state tuition $12,330. Room & board $5,570. Average book expense $960. **Required Forms and Deadlines:** FAFSA and University Scholarship Application Form. Priority filing deadline March 1. **Notification of Awards:** Applicants will be notified of awards on or about March 15. **Types of Aid:** *Need-based scholarships/grants:* Pell, SEOG, state scholarships/grants, private scholarships, the school's own gift aid. *Loans:* Direct Subsidized Stafford, Direct Unsubsidized Stafford, Direct PLUS, Federal Perkins, Federal Nursing, state loans, college/university loans from institutional funds, alternative loans. **Student Employment:** Federal Work-Study Program available. Institutional employment available. Off-campus job opportunities are good. **Financial Aid Statistics:** 67% freshmen, 57% undergrads receive some form of aid. **Financial Aid Phone:** 330-672-2972.

KENTUCKY CHRISTIAN COLLEGE

100 Academic Parkway, Grayson, KY 41143
Phone: 606-474-3266 **E-mail:** sdeakins@email.kcc.edu
Fax: 606-474-3155 **Web:** www.kcc.edu

This private school was founded in 1919. It has a 121-acre campus.

STUDENTS AND FACULTY

Enrollment: 569. **Student Body:** Male 45%, female 55%, out-of-state 65%, international 5%. **Ethnic Representation:** African American 1%, Caucasian 98%. **Retention and Graduation:** 65% freshmen return for sophomore year. 25% freshmen graduate within 4 years. **Faculty:** Student/faculty ratio 16:1. 30 full-time faculty, 90% hold PhDs. 100% faculty teach undergrads.

ACADEMICS

Degrees: Associate's, bachelor's, master's. **Academic Requirements:** General education including some course work in computer literacy, English (including composition), history, mathematics, sciences (biological or physical). **Classes:** Under 10 students in an average class. 20-29 students in an average lab/discussion section. **Disciplines with Highest Percentage of Degrees Awarded:** Philosophy/religion/theology 39%, education 35%, business/marketing 12%, other 7%, psychology 6%. **Special Study Options:** Accelerated program, cooperative (work-study) program, double major, independent study, internships, teacher certification program, learning disabilities studies and off-campus studies.

FACILITIES

Housing: All-female, all-male, apartments for married students, honors housing. **Library Holdings:** 101,873 bound volumes. 2,050 periodicals. 1,669 audiovisuals.

EXTRACURRICULARS

Activities: Choral groups, drama/theater, jazz band, music ensembles, musical theater, pep band, student government, student newspaper, yearbook. **Athletics (Intercollegiate):** *Men:* basketball, cheerleading, cross-country, soccer, tennis. *Women:* basketball, cheerleading, cross-country, tennis, volleyball.

ADMISSIONS

Selectivity Rating: 71 (of 100). **Freshman Academic Profile:** Average high school GPA 3.2. 10% in top 10% of high school class, 27% in top 25% of high school class, 52% in top 50% of high school class. Average SAT I Math 495, SAT I Math middle 50% range 430-560. Average SAT I Verbal 520, SAT I Verbal middle 50% range 430-580. Average ACT 20, ACT middle 50% range 18-24. TOEFL required of all international applicants, minimum TOEFL 500. **Basis for Candidate Selection:** *Very important factors considered include:* character/personal qualities, religious affiliation/commitment, secondary school record, standardized test scores. *Important factors considered include:* essays. *Other factors considered include:* class rank, recommendations. **Freshman Admission Requirements:** High school diploma or GED is required. **Freshman Admission Statistics:** 268 applied, 90% accepted, 62% of those accepted enrolled. **Transfer Admission Requirements:** *Items required:* high school transcript, college transcript, essay, standardized test scores. Minimum college GPA of 2.0 required. Lowest grade transferable C. **General Admission Information:** Application fee $25. Nonfall registration accepted. Admission may be deferred for a maximum of 1 year.

COSTS AND FINANCIAL AID

Tuition $7,360. Room & board $4,070. Required fees $0. Average book expense $750. **Required Forms and Deadlines:** FAFSA and institution's own financial aid form. No deadline for regular filing. Priority filing deadline April 1. **Notification of Awards:** Applicants will be notified of awards on a rolling basis beginning on or about May 1. **Types of Aid:** *Need-based scholarships/grants:* Pell, SEOG, state scholarships/grants, private scholarships, the school's own gift aid. *Loans:* FFEL Subsidized Stafford, FFEL Unsubsidized Stafford, FFEL PLUS, Federal Perkins. **Student Employment:** Federal Work-Study Program available. Institutional employment available. Off-campus job opportunities are good. **Financial Aid Statistics:** 66% freshmen, 71% undergrads receive some form of aid.

KENTUCKY STATE UNIVERSITY

400 East Main Street, 3rd Floor, Frankfort, KY 40601
Phone: 502-597-6813 **E-mail:** jburrell@gwmail.kysu.edu **CEEB Code:** 1368
Fax: 502-597-6239 **Web:** www.kysu.edu **ACT Code:** 1516

This public school was founded in 1886. It has a 308-acre campus.

STUDENTS AND FACULTY

Enrollment: 2,129. **Student Body:** Male 44%, female 56%, out-of-state 35%, international 1%. **Ethnic Representation:** African American 64%, Asian 1%, Caucasian 32%, Hispanic 1%. **Retention and Graduation:** 59% freshmen return for sophomore year. 12% freshmen graduate within 4 years. **Faculty:** Student/faculty ratio 17:1. 114 full-time faculty. 98% faculty teach undergrads.

ACADEMICS

Degrees: Associate's, bachelor's, master's, terminal, transfer. **Academic Requirements:** General education including some course work in arts/fine arts, English (including composition), foreign languages, history, humanities, mathematics, sciences (biological or physical), social science. **Classes:** 10-19 students in an average class. 10-19 students in an average lab/discussion section. **Disciplines with Highest Percentage of Degrees Awarded:** Business/marketing 22%, education 19%, protective services/public administration 17%, biological life sciences 9%, home economics and vocational home economics 8%. **Special Study Options:** Cooperative (work-study) program, distance learning, double major, English as a second language, honors program, independent study, internships, study abroad, teacher certification program.

FACILITIES

Housing: All-female, all-male, housing for international students. **Library Holdings:** 296,631 bound volumes. 1,097 periodicals. 320,739 microforms. 3,025 audiovisuals. **Special Academic Facilities/Equipment:** Art gallery, school for early childhood education, nutrition lab, agriculture research building, research farm, fish hatchery, electron microscope. **Computers:** *Recommended operating system:* Windows 95. School-owned computers available for student use.

EXTRACURRICULARS

Activities: Choral groups, concert band, dance, drama/theater, jazz band, marching band, music ensembles, musical theater, opera, pep band, student government, student newspaper, symphony orchestra, yearbook. **Organizations:** 40 registered organizations, 1 honor society, 2 religious organizations, 5 fraternities, 4 sororities. **Athletics (Intercollegiate):** *Men:* baseball, basketball, cheerleading, cross-country, football, golf, indoor track, tennis, track & field. *Women:* basketball, cheerleading, cross-country, indoor track, softball, tennis, track & field, volleyball.

ADMISSIONS

Selectivity Rating: 69 (of 100). **Freshman Academic Profile:** Average high school GPA 2.7. Average ACT 18. TOEFL required of all international applicants, minimum TOEFL 525. **Basis for Candidate Selection:** *Very important factors considered include:* secondary school record, standardized test scores. *Other factors considered include:* alumni/ae relation, extracurricular activities, geographical residence, recommendations. **Freshman Admission Requirements:** High school diploma or GED is required. *Academic units required/recommended:* 21 total required; 4 English required, 3 math required, 2 science required, 2 foreign language recommended, 1 social studies required, 1 history required. **Transfer Admission Requirements:** *Items required:* college transcript. Lowest grade transferable C. **General Admission Information:** Application fee $15. Nonfall registration accepted. Credit and/or placement offered for CEEB Advanced Placement tests.

COSTS AND FINANCIAL AID

In-state tuition $2,100. Out-of-state tuition $6,302. Room & board $3,740. Required fees $340. Average book expense $350. **Required Forms and Deadlines:** FAFSA and institution's own financial aid form. Financial aid filing deadline May 31. Priority filing deadline April 15. **Notification of Awards:** Applicants will be notified of awards on or about July 1. **Types of Aid:** *Need-based scholarships/grants:* Pell, SEOG, state scholarships/grants, private scholarships, the school's own gift aid, United Negro College Fund. *Loans:* Direct Subsidized Stafford, Direct Unsubsidized Stafford, Direct PLUS, FFEL Subsidized Stafford, FFEL Unsubsidized Stafford, FFEL PLUS, Federal Perkins, state loans. **Student Employment:** Federal Work-Study Program available. Institutional employment available. Off-campus job opportunities are good. **Financial Aid Statistics:** 68% freshmen, 56% undergrads receive some form of aid. Average freshman grant $3,714. Average freshman loan $2,500. Average income from on-campus job $1,000. **Financial Aid Phone:** 502-597-5960.

KENTUCKY WESLEYAN COLLEGE

3000 Frederica Street, PO Box 1039, Owensboro, KY 42302
Phone: 270-852-3120 **E-mail:** admission@kwc.edu **CEEB Code:** 1369
Fax: 270-926-3196 **Web:** www.kwc.edu **ACT Code:** 1518

This private school, which is affiliated with the Methodist Church, was founded in 1858. It has a 52-acre campus.

STUDENTS AND FACULTY

Enrollment: 636. **Student Body:** Male 50%, female 50%, out-of-state 29%, international 1% (4 countries represented). **Ethnic Representation:** African American 7%, Caucasian 86%, Hispanic 1%. **Retention and Graduation:** 58% freshmen return for sophomore year. 27% freshmen graduate within 4 years. 41% grads go on to further study within 1 year. 10% grads pursue business degrees. 5% grads pursue law degrees. 9% grads pursue medical degrees. **Faculty:** Student/faculty ratio 12:1. 39 full-time faculty, 84% hold PhDs. 100% faculty teach undergrads.

ACADEMICS

Degrees: Associate's, bachelor's, terminal. **Academic Requirements:** General education including some course work in interdisciplinary requirement and multicultural requirement. **Majors with Highest Enrollment:** Business administration/management; communications studies/speech communication and rhetoric; psychology, general. **Disciplines with Highest Percentage of Degrees Awarded:** Business/marketing 19%, education 15%, communications/communication technologies 9%, computer and information sciences 7%, biological life sciences 6%. **Special Study Options:** Double major, independent study, internships, study abroad, teacher certification program.

FACILITIES

Housing: Coed, all-female, all-male, fraternities and/or sororities. **Library Holdings:** 85,085 bound volumes. 315 periodicals. 68,195 microforms. 3,308 audiovisuals. **Special Academic Facilities/Equipment:** FM radio station. **Computers:** *Recommended operating system:* Windows NT/2000. School-owned computers available for student use.

EXTRACURRICULARS

Activities: Choral groups, drama/theater, literary magazine, pep band, radio station, student government, student newspaper, yearbook. **Organizations:** 40 registered organizations, 6 honor societies, 6 religious organizations, 3 fraternities (8% men join), 2 sororities (11% women join). **Athletics (Intercollegiate):** *Men:* baseball, basketball, cheerleading, football, golf, soccer. *Women:* basketball, cheerleading, golf, soccer, softball, tennis, volleyball.

ADMISSIONS

Selectivity Rating: 76 (of 100). **Freshman Academic Profile:** Average high school GPA 3.2. 20% in top 10% of high school class, 40% in top 25% of high school class, 71% in top 50% of high school class. 84% from public high schools. SAT I Math middle 50% range 470-560. SAT I Verbal middle 50% range 423-570. Average ACT 22, ACT middle 50% range 19-24. TOEFL required of all international applicants, minimum TOEFL 500. **Basis for Candidate Selection:** *Very important factors considered include:* secondary school record. *Important factors considered include:* character/personal qualities, class rank, extracurricular activities, standardized test scores, talent/ability. *Other factors considered include:* alumni/ae relation, essays, interview, minority status, recommendations, volunteer work, work experience. **Freshman Admission Requirements:** High school diploma or GED is required. *Academic units required/recommended:* 13 total required; 4 English required, 3 math required, 3 science required, 2 foreign language recommended, 3 social studies required. **Freshman Admission Statistics:** 696 applied, 75% accepted, 35% of those accepted enrolled. **Transfer Admission Requirements:** *Items required:* college transcript. Minimum college GPA of 2.0 required. Lowest grade transferable C. **General Admission Information:** Application fee $20. Priority application deadline June 1. Regular application deadline August 21. Nonfall registration accepted. Admission may be deferred for a maximum of 1 year. Credit and/or placement offered for CEEB Advanced Placement tests.

COSTS AND FINANCIAL AID

Tuition $11,100. Room & board $5,160. Required fees $300. Average book expense $900. **Required Forms and Deadlines:** FAFSA and institution's own financial aid form. No deadline for regular filing. Priority filing deadline March 15. **Notification of Awards:** Applicants will be notified of awards on a rolling basis beginning on or about March 15. **Types of Aid:** *Need-based scholarships/grants:* Pell, SEOG, state scholarships/grants, private scholarships, the school's own gift aid. *Loans:* FFEL Subsidized Stafford, FFEL Unsubsidized Stafford, FFEL PLUS, Federal Perkins, alternative education loans. **Student Employment:** Federal Work-Study Program available. Off-campus job opportunities are excellent. **Financial Aid Statistics:** 83% freshmen, 81% undergrads receive some form of aid. **Financial Aid Phone:** 270-852-3120.

KENYON COLLEGE

Admissions Office, Ransom Hall, Gambier, OH 43022-9623
Phone: 740-427-5776 **E-mail:** admissions@kenyon.edu **CEEB Code:** 1370
Fax: 740-427-5770 **Web:** www.kenyon.edu **ACT Code:** 3286

This private school was founded in 1824. It has a 1,000-acre campus.

STUDENTS AND FACULTY

Enrollment: 1,576. **Student Body:** Male 46%, female 54%, out-of-state 80%, international 3% (26 countries represented). **Ethnic Representation:** African American 4%, Asian 3%, Caucasian 87%, Hispanic 2%. **Retention and Graduation:** 89% freshmen return for sophomore year. 80% freshmen graduate within 4 years. 25% grads go on to further study within 1 year. 13% grads pursue business degrees. 17% grads pursue law degrees. 12% grads pursue medical degrees. **Faculty:** Student/faculty ratio 9:1. 144 full-time faculty, 95% hold PhDs. 100% faculty teach undergrads.

ACADEMICS

Degrees: Bachelor's. **Academic Requirements:** General education including some course work in arts/fine arts, foreign languages, humanities, sciences (biological or physical), social science, quantitative reasoning requirement (not necessarily a mathematics course), interdisciplinary. **Classes:** 10-19 students in an average class. **Majors with Highest Enrollment:** History, general; English language and literature, general; political science and government, general. **Disciplines with Highest Percentage of Degrees Awarded:** Social sciences and history 39%, English 19%, visual and performing arts 10%, psychology 8%, foreign languages and literature 7%. **Special Study Options:** Accelerated program, double major, student exchange program (domestic), honors program, independent study, internships, liberal arts/career combination, student-designed major, study abroad.

FACILITIES

Housing: Coed, all-female, apartments for single students. Housing is guaranteed for all students. All housing is smoke free. There are substance-free, wellness, and community service/social group halls. **Library Holdings:** 364,492 bound volumes. 5,300 periodicals. 138,841 microforms. 171,230 audiovisuals. **Special Academic Facilities/Equipment:** Olin Art Gallery, Bolton Theatre, greenhouse, Olin/Chalmers Library, Hill Theatre, center for environmental studies, Rosse Hall (music department), Peirce Hall, Art Barn. New science facilities have just been completed, and a $60 million athletic facility is under construction. **Computers:** School-owned computers available for student use.

EXTRACURRICULARS

Activities: Choral groups, concert band, dance, drama/theater, jazz band, literary magazine, music ensembles, musical theater, opera, pep band, radio station, student government, student newspaper, student-run film society, symphony orchestra, yearbook. **Organizations:** 178 registered organizations, 4 honor societies, 7 religious organizations, 8 fraternities (34% men join), 4 sororities (10% women join). **Athletics (Intercollegiate):** *Men:* baseball, basketball, diving, football, golf, indoor track, lacrosse, soccer, swimming, tennis, track & field. *Women:* basketball, diving, field hockey, indoor track, lacrosse, soccer, softball, swimming, tennis, track & field, volleyball.

ADMISSIONS

Selectivity Rating: 92 (of 100). **Freshman Academic Profile:** Average high school GPA 3.7. 51% in top 10% of high school class, 80% in top 25% of high school class, 97% in top 50% of high school class. 53% from public high schools. Average SAT I Math 649, SAT I Math middle 50% range 610-690. Average SAT I Verbal 671, SAT I Verbal middle 50% range 620-720. Average ACT 30, ACT middle 50% range 27-32. TOEFL required of all international applicants, minimum TOEFL 570. **Basis for Candidate Selection:** *Very important factors considered include:* character/personal qualities, class rank, recommendations, secondary school record. *Important factors considered include:* essays, extracurricular activities, interview, standardized test scores, talent/ability. *Other factors considered include:* alumni/ae relation, geographical residence, minority status, state residency, volunteer work, work experience. **Freshman Admission Requirements:** High school diploma or GED is required. *Academic units required/recommended:* 18 total required; 23 total recommended; 4 English required, 4 English recommended, 3 math required, 4 math recommended, 3 science required, 4 science recommended, 2 science lab required, 3 science lab recommended, 3 foreign language required, 4 foreign language recommended, 2 social studies required, 3 social studies recommended, 3 elective required, 4 elective recommended. **Freshman Admission Statistics:** 2,838 applied, 52% accepted, 30% of those accepted enrolled. **Transfer Admission Requirements:** *Items required:* high school transcript, college transcript, essay, standardized test scores, statement of good standing from prior school. Minimum college GPA of 3.0 required. Lowest grade transferable C. **General Admission Information:** Application fee $45. Early decision application deadline December 1. Regular application deadline February 1. Admission may be deferred for a maximum of 1 year. Credit offered for CEEB Advanced Placement tests.

COSTS AND FINANCIAL AID

Tuition $26,800. Room & board $4,580. Required fees $750. Average book expense $950. **Required Forms and Deadlines:** FAFSA, CSS/Financial Aid PROFILE, noncustodial (divorced/separated) parent's statement, and completed tax returns. Financial aid filing deadline February 15. Priority filing deadline February 15. **Notification of Awards:** Applicants will be notified of awards on or about April 1. **Types of Aid:** *Need-based scholarships/grants:* Pell, SEOG, state scholarships/grants, private scholarships, the school's own gift aid. *Loans:* FFEL Subsidized Stafford, FFEL Unsubsidized Stafford, FFEL PLUS, Federal Perkins, college/university loans from institutional funds. **Student Employment:** Federal Work-Study Program available. Institutional employment available. Off-campus job opportunities are fair. **Financial Aid Statistics:** 39% freshmen, 43% undergrads receive some form of aid. Average freshman grant $22,835. Average freshman loan $3,577. Average income from on-campus job $961. **Financial Aid Phone:** 740-427-5430.

See page 1076.

KETTERING UNIVERSITY

1700 West Third Ave., Flint, MI 48504
Phone: 810-762-7865 **E-mail:** admissions@kettering.edu **CEEB Code:** 1246
Fax: 810-762-9837 **Web:** www.kettering.edu **ACT Code:** 1998

This private school was founded in 1919. It has a 54-acre campus.

STUDENTS AND FACULTY

Enrollment: 2,487. **Student Body:** Out-of-state 36%, international 2% (18 countries represented). **Ethnic Representation:** African American 7%, Asian 5%, Caucasian 77%, Hispanic 2%. **Retention and Graduation:** 81% freshmen return for sophomore year. 1% freshmen graduate within 4 years. 41% grads go on to further study within 1 year. 18% grads pursue business degrees. 3% grads pursue law degrees. **Faculty:** Student/faculty ratio 9:1. 140 full-time faculty, 90% hold PhDs. 100% faculty teach undergrads.

ACADEMICS

Degrees: Bachelor's, master's. **Academic Requirements:** General education including some course work in computer literacy, English (including composition), history, humanities, mathematics, sciences (biological or physical), social science, written and oral communication. **Classes:** 20-29 students in an average class. 10-19 students in an average lab/discussion section. **Majors with Highest Enrollment:** Computer engineering, general; electrical, electronics, and communications engineering; mechanical engineering. **Disciplines with Highest Percentage of Degrees Awarded:** Engineering/engineering technology 87%, computer and information sciences 5%, business/marketing 5%, physical sciences 2%, mathematics 1%. **Special Study Options:** Accelerated program, cooperative (work-study) program, distance learning, double major, independent study, study abroad. Co-op is required of all undergraduate students and typically begins in the first year. Each 24-week semester is divided into 11 weeks of classes and 12 to 13 weeks of paid professional co-op experience in industry. Students co-op with employers in 43 states and several countries. Income from co-op is a major resource for Kettering students whose total co-op income over their 4.5-year program typically ranges between $40,000 and $65,000. In addition to study abroad, some Kettering students also gain experience in foreign locations for their co-op employer.

FACILITIES

Housing: Coed, apartments for single students, fraternities and/or sororities. **Library Holdings:** 115,000 bound volumes. 1,200 periodicals. 35,000 microforms. 778 audiovisuals. **Special Academic Facilities/Equipment:** Art museum, Scharschburg Industrial History Museum. Kettering is renown for the variety and quality of its laboratories for student use and teaching. Labs are required in nearly all science and engineering courses. Of special note are the Ford Design Simulation Studio; the GM/PACE e-Design and e-Manufacturing Studio; the computer integrated manufacturing (CIM), polymer processing, and mechatronics labs; the Lubrizol Engine Test Center; SAE Project Vehicle facilities; the environmental scanning electron microscopy lab; the Connie and Jim John Recreation Center; and Kettering Park (outdoor recreation). **Computers:** *Recommended operating system:* Windows NT/2000. School-owned computers available for student use.

EXTRACURRICULARS

Activities: Choral groups, drama/theater, jazz band, literary magazine, music ensembles, radio station, student government, student newspaper, yearbook. **Organizations:** 40 registered organizations, 11 honor societies, 2 religious organizations, 14 fraternities (45% men join), 6 sororities (47% women join).

ADMISSIONS

Selectivity Rating: 87 (of 100). **Freshman Academic Profile:** Average high school GPA 3.6. 35% in top 10% of high school class, 67% in top 25% of high school class, 94% in top 50% of high school class. 90% from public high schools. Average SAT I Math 639, SAT I Math middle 50% range 590-690. Average SAT I Verbal 590, SAT I Verbal middle 50% range 540-640. Average ACT 26, ACT middle 50% range 24-28. TOEFL required of all international applicants, minimum TOEFL 550. **Basis for Candidate Selection:** *Very important factors considered include:* class rank, secondary school record, standardized test scores. *Important factors considered include:* character/personal qualities, extracurricular activities, talent/ability, work experience. *Other factors considered include:* interview, minority status, recommendations, volunteer work. **Freshman Admission Requirements:** High school diploma is required and GED is not accepted. *Academic units required/recommended:* 18 total required; 22 total recommended; 3 English required, 4 English recommended, 4 math required, 4 math recommended, 2 science required, 4 science recommended, 2 science lab required, 4 science lab recommended, 2 foreign language recommended, 4 social studies recommended, 4 elective recommended. **Freshman Admission Statistics:** 2,596 applied, 56% accepted, 30% of those accepted enrolled. **Transfer Admission Requirements:** *Items required:* college transcript. Minimum college GPA of 3.0 required. Lowest grade transferable C. **General Admission Information:** Application fee $35. Nonfall registration accepted. Admission may be deferred for a maximum of 1 year. Credit offered for CEEB Advanced Placement tests.

COSTS AND FINANCIAL AID

Tuition $20,224. Room & board $4,336. Required fees $365. Average book expense $800. **Required Forms and Deadlines:** FAFSA and institution's own financial aid form. No deadline for regular filing. Priority filing deadline February 14. **Notification of Awards:** Applicants will be notified of awards on a rolling basis beginning on or about February 15. **Types of Aid:** *Need-based scholarships/grants:* Pell, SEOG, state scholarships/grants, private scholarships, the school's own gift aid. *Co-op resource:* While income from required professional co-op experience is not financial aid, it is a substantial resource earned by all Kettering students. *Loans:* Direct Subsidized Stafford, Direct Unsubsidized Stafford, Direct PLUS, state loans, alternative loans. **Student Employment:** Federal Work-Study Program available. Institutional employment available. Off-campus job opportunities are excellent. **Financial Aid**

Statistics: 78% freshmen, 67% undergrads receive some form of aid. Average freshman grant $10,521. Average freshman loan $2,664. Average income from on-campus job $1,000. **Financial Aid Phone:** 810-762-7859.

See page 1078.

KEUKA COLLEGE

Office of Admissions, Keuka Park, NY 14478-0098
Phone: 315-279-5254 **E-mail:** admissions@mail.keuka.edu **CEEB Code:** 2744
Fax: 315-536-5386 **Web:** www.keuka.edu **ACT Code:** 2782

This private school, which is affiliated with the American Baptist Church, was founded in 1890. It has a 203-acre campus.

STUDENTS AND FACULTY

Enrollment: 1,128. **Student Body:** Male 30%, female 70%, out-of-state 6%, international students represent 4 countries. **Ethnic Representation:** African American 4%, Asian 1%, Caucasian 91%, Hispanic 1%. **Retention and Graduation:** 70% freshmen return for sophomore year. 22% freshmen graduate within 4 years. **Faculty:** Student/faculty ratio 18:1. 52 full-time faculty, 59% hold PhDs. 100% faculty teach undergrads.

ACADEMICS

Degrees: Bachelor's, master's, terminal. **Academic Requirements:** General education including some course work in arts/fine arts, computer literacy, English (including composition), history, humanities, mathematics, philosophy, sciences (biological or physical), social science, integrative studies-institutional courses, physical activity, political science. **Classes:** 10-19 students in an average class. 10-19 students in an average lab/discussion section. **Majors with Highest Enrollment:** Education, general; nonprofit/public/organizational management; occupational therapy/therapist. **Disciplines with Highest Percentage of Degrees Awarded:** Health professions and related sciences 42%, education 22%, business/marketing 12%, protective services/public administration 7%, social sciences and history 5%. **Special Study Options:** Accelerated program, cooperative (work-study) program, cross registration, double major, dual enrollment, independent study, internships, student-designed major, study abroad, teacher certification program.

FACILITIES

Housing: Coed, all-female, all-male, housing for disabled students, cooperative housing. **Library Holdings:** 83,882 bound volumes. 357 periodicals. 4,063 microforms. 3,005 audiovisuals. **Special Academic Facilities/Equipment:** Bird museum, Lightner Gallery. **Computers:** *Recommended operating system:* Windows NT/2000. School-owned computers available for student use.

EXTRACURRICULARS

Activities: Choral groups, dance, drama/theater, literary magazine, musical theater, radio station, student government, student newspaper, student-run film society, yearbook. **Organizations:** 32 registered organizations, 7 honor societies, 2 religious organizations. **Athletics (Intercollegiate):** *Men:* baseball, basketball, lacrosse, soccer. *Women:* basketball, soccer, softball, swimming, volleyball.

ADMISSIONS

Selectivity Rating: 70 (of 100). **Freshman Academic Profile:** Average high school GPA 3.0. 7% in top 10% of high school class, 24% in top 25% of high school class, 60% in top 50% of high school class. 96% from public high schools. Average SAT I Math 475, SAT I Math middle 50% range 430-520. Average SAT I Verbal 478, SAT I Verbal middle 50% range 420-535. Average ACT 21, ACT middle 50% range 19-23. TOEFL required of all international applicants, minimum TOEFL 500. **Basis for Candidate Selection:** *Very important factors considered include:* secondary school record. *Important factors considered include:* character/personal qualities, class rank, essays, extracurricular activities, recommendations, standardized test scores. *Other factors considered include:* alumni/ae relation, interview, minority status, religious affiliation/commitment, talent/ability, volunteer work, work experience. **Freshman Admission Requirements:** High school diploma or GED is required. *Academic units required/recommended:* 18 total recommended; 4 English recommended, 3 math recommended, 3 science recommended, 2 science lab recommended, 3 foreign language recommended, 3 social studies recommended, 2 history recommended. **Freshman Admission Statistics:** 685 applied, 79% accepted, 36% of those accepted enrolled. **Transfer Admission Requirements:** *Items required:* college transcript, essay. Minimum college GPA of 2.0 required. Lowest grade transferable C. **General Admission Information:** Application fee $30. Early decision application deadline December 1. Nonfall registration accepted. Admission may be deferred for a maximum of 1 year. Credit and/or placement offered for CEEB Advanced Placement tests.

COSTS AND FINANCIAL AID

Tuition $15,800. Room & board $7,600. Required fees $250. Average book expense $800. **Required Forms and Deadlines:** FAFSA and institution's own financial aid form. No deadline for regular filing. **Notification of Awards:** Applicants will be notified of awards on a rolling basis beginning on or about December 1. **Types of Aid:** *Need-based scholarships/grants:* Pell, SEOG, state scholarships/grants, the school's own gift aid. *Loans:* FFEL Subsidized Stafford, FFEL Unsubsidized Stafford, FFEL PLUS, Federal Perkins. **Student Employment:** Federal Work-Study Program available. Institutional employment available. Off-campus job opportunities are fair. **Financial Aid Statistics:** 89% freshmen, 92% undergrads receive some form of aid. Average freshman grant $10,355. Average freshman loan $3,400. Average income from on-campus job $11,945. **Financial Aid Phone:** 315-279-5232.

KING COLLEGE (TN)

1350 King College Road, Bristol, TN 37620-2699
Phone: 423-652-4861 **E-mail:** admissions@king.edu **CEEB Code:** 1371
Fax: 423-652-4727 **Web:** www.king.edu **ACT Code:** 3970

This private school, which is affiliated with the Presbyterian Church, was founded in 1867. It has a 195-acre campus.

STUDENTS AND FACULTY

Enrollment: 688. **Student Body:** Male 39%, female 61%, out-of-state 42%, international 9%. **Ethnic Representation:** African American 2%, Asian 1%, Caucasian 93%, Hispanic 1%. **Retention and Graduation:** 69% freshmen return for sophomore year. 54% freshmen graduate within 4 years. 38% grads go on to further study within 1 year. 4% grads pursue business degrees. 4% grads pursue law degrees. 3% grads pursue medical degrees. **Faculty:** Student/faculty ratio 11:1. 45 full-time faculty, 75% hold PhDs. 100% faculty teach undergrads.

ACADEMICS

Degrees: Bachelor's, master's. **Academic Requirements:** General education including some course work in arts/fine arts, computer literacy, English (including composition), foreign languages, history, humanities, mathematics, philosophy, sciences (biological or physical), social science, Bible and religion. **Classes:** Under 10 students in an average class. 10-19 students in an average lab/discussion section. **Majors with Highest Enrollment:** Business administration/management; history, general; biology/biological sciences, general. **Disciplines with Highest Percentage of Degrees Awarded:** Social sciences and history 22%, business/marketing 20%, English 13%, health professions and related sciences 12%, biological life sciences 9%. **Special Study Options:** Double major, dual enrollment, English as a second language, independent study, internships, liberal arts/career combination, study abroad, teacher certification program. Co-op programs: arts, business, education, humanities, social/behavioral science. American studies program (Washington, DC) and Los Angeles film studies.

FACILITIES

Housing: All-female, all-male, apartments for married students, housing for disabled students. **Library Holdings:** 80,888 bound volumes. 1,539 periodicals. 33,051 microforms. 5,074 audiovisuals. **Special Academic Facilities/Equipment:** Electron microscope, observatory with 2 reflecting telescopes, solar telescope. **Computers:** *Recommended operating system:* Mac. School-owned computers available for student use.

EXTRACURRICULARS

Activities: Choral groups, dance, drama/theater, literary magazine, music ensembles, musical theater, student government, student newspaper, student-run film society, yearbook. **Organizations:** 37 registered organizations, 5 honor societies, 9 religious organizations. **Athletics (Intercollegiate):** *Men:* baseball, basketball, cheerleading, golf, soccer, tennis. *Women:* basketball, cheerleading, soccer, tennis, volleyball.

ADMISSIONS

Selectivity Rating: 75 (of 100). **Freshman Academic Profile:** Average high school GPA 3.5. 26% in top 10% of high school class, 53% in top 25% of high school class, 87% in top 50% of high school class. 76% from public high schools. Average SAT I Math 536, SAT I Math middle 50% range 480-600. Average SAT I Verbal 566, SAT I Verbal middle 50% range 490-590. Average ACT 23, ACT middle 50% range 20-25. **Basis for Candidate Selection:** *Very important factors considered include:* secondary school record, standardized test scores. *Important factors considered include:* essays. **Freshman Admission Requirements:** High school diploma or GED is required. *Academic units required/recommended:* 16 total required; 4 English required, 3 math required,

1 science required, 1 science lab required, 2 foreign language required, 1 social studies required, 1 history required, 4 elective required. **Freshman Admission Statistics:** 694 applied, 60% accepted, 33% of those accepted enrolled. **Transfer Admission Requirements:** *Items required:* college transcript, essay, statement of good standing from prior school. Minimum high school GPA of 2.4 required. Minimum college GPA of 2.0 required. Lowest grade transferable C. **General Admission Information:** Application fee $20. Nonfall registration accepted. Admission may be deferred for a maximum of 2 years. Credit and/or placement offered for CEEB Advanced Placement tests.

COSTS AND FINANCIAL AID

Tuition $13,980. Room & board $4,960. Required fees $1,054. Average book expense $600. **Required Forms and Deadlines:** FAFSA. No deadline for regular filing. Priority filing deadline March 1. **Notification of Awards:** Applicants will be notified of awards on a rolling basis beginning on or about March 15. **Types of Aid:** *Need-based scholarships/grants:* Pell, SEOG, state scholarships/grants, private scholarships, the school's own gift aid. *Loans:* FFEL Subsidized Stafford, FFEL Unsubsidized Stafford, FFEL PLUS, Federal Perkins, state loans, college/university loans from institutional funds. **Student Employment:** Federal Work-Study Program available. Institutional employment available. Off-campus job opportunities are fair. **Financial Aid Statistics:** 76% freshmen, 69% undergrads receive some form of aid. Average freshman grant $7,800. Average freshman loan $4,125. Average income from on-campus job $1,300. **Financial Aid Phone:** 423-652-4725.

KING'S COLLEGE (PA)

133 North River Street, Wilkes-Barre, PA 18711
Phone: 570-208-5858 **E-mail:** admissions@kings.edu **CEEB Code:** 2353
Fax: 570-208-5971 **Web:** www.kings.edu **ACT Code:** 3604

This private school, which is affiliated with the Roman Catholic Church, was founded in 1946. It has a 48-acre campus.

STUDENTS AND FACULTY

Enrollment: 2,039. **Student Body:** Male 47%, female 53%, out-of-state 24%, international students represent 6 countries. **Ethnic Representation:** African American 2%, Asian 1%, Caucasian 89%, Hispanic 1%. **Retention and Graduation:** 82% freshmen return for sophomore year. 66% freshmen graduate within 4 years. 10% grads go on to further study within 1 year. 1% grads pursue business degrees. 1% grads pursue law degrees. 3% grads pursue medical degrees. **Faculty:** Student/faculty ratio 13:1. 114 full-time faculty, 80% hold PhDs. 100% faculty teach undergrads.

ACADEMICS

Degrees: Associate's, bachelor's, master's. **Academic Requirements:** General education including some course work in arts/fine arts, computer literacy, English (including composition), foreign languages, history, humanities, mathematics, philosophy, sciences (biological or physical), social science, theology. **Classes:** 10-19 students in an average class. 10-19 students in an average lab/discussion section. **Majors with Highest Enrollment:** Business administration/management; elementary education and teaching; criminal justice/law enforcement administration. **Disciplines with Highest Percentage of Degrees Awarded:** Business/marketing 27%, health professions and related sciences 14%, education 11%, protective services/public administration 8%, communications/communication technologies 7%. **Special Study Options:** Accelerated program, cross registration, distance learning, double major, dual enrollment, English as a second language, honors program, independent study, internships, student-designed major, study abroad, teacher certification program, weekend college.

FACILITIES

Housing: All-female, all-male, apartments for single students. **Library Holdings:** 166,395 bound volumes. 791 periodicals. 562,271 microforms. 2,478 audiovisuals. **Special Academic Facilities/Equipment:** Electron microscope, rooftop greenhouse, molecular biology lab, computer graphics lab. **Computers:** *Recommended operating system:* Windows 95/98/2000. School-owned computers available for student use.

EXTRACURRICULARS

Activities: Choral groups, dance, drama/theater, literary magazine, music ensembles, pep band, radio station, student government, student newspaper, yearbook. **Organizations:** 50 registered organizations, 15 honor societies, 2 religious organizations. **Athletics (Intercollegiate):** *Men:* baseball, basketball, cheerleading, cross-country, football, golf, lacrosse, soccer, swimming, tennis, wrestling. *Women:* basketball, cheerleading, cross-country, field hockey, lacrosse, soccer, softball, swimming, tennis, volleyball.

ADMISSIONS

Selectivity Rating: 77 (of 100). **Freshman Academic Profile:** Average high school GPA 3.2. 18% in top 10% of high school class, 43% in top 25% of high school class, 76% in top 50% of high school class. 70% from public high schools. Average SAT I Math 515, SAT I Math middle 50% range 460-570. Average SAT I Verbal 512, SAT I Verbal middle 50% range 460-560. TOEFL required of all international applicants, minimum TOEFL 525. **Basis for Candidate Selection:** *Very important factors considered include:* extracurricular activities, secondary school record, standardized test scores, talent/ability. *Important factors considered include:* alumni/ae relation, character/personal qualities, class rank, essays, interview, minority status, recommendations, volunteer work. **Freshman Admission Requirements:** High school diploma or GED is required. *Academic units required/recommended:* 16 total required; 22 total recommended; 4 English required, 4 English recommended, 3 math required, 4 math recommended, 3 science required, 4 science recommended, 2 science lab required, 2 science lab recommended, 2 foreign language required, 4 foreign language recommended, 3 social studies required, 3 social studies recommended, 1 history required, 1 history recommended, 2 elective recommended. **Freshman Admission Statistics:** 1,543 applied, 78% accepted, 34% of those accepted enrolled. **Transfer Admission Requirements:** *Items required:* high school transcript, college transcript, essay, standardized test scores. Minimum high school GPA of 2.5 required. Minimum college GPA of 2.0 required. Lowest grade transferable C. **General Admission Information:** Application fee $30. Priority application deadline April 1. Nonfall registration accepted. Admission may be deferred for a maximum of 1 year. Neither credit nor placement offered for CEEB Advanced Placement tests.

COSTS AND FINANCIAL AID

Tuition $17,390. Room & board $7,550. Required fees $760. Average book expense $850. **Required Forms and Deadlines:** FAFSA and institution's own financial aid form. No deadline for regular filing. Priority filing deadline February 15. **Notification of Awards:** Applicants will be notified of awards on a rolling basis beginning on or about March 1. **Types of Aid:** *Need-based scholarships/grants:* Pell, SEOG, state scholarships/grants, private scholarships, the school's own gift aid. *Loans:* FFEL Subsidized Stafford, FFEL Unsubsidized Stafford, FFEL PLUS, Federal Perkins, private loans. **Student Employment:** Federal Work-Study Program available. Institutional employment available. Off-campus job opportunities are good. **Financial Aid Statistics:** 85% freshmen, 79% undergrads receive some form of aid. Average freshman grant $10,317. Average freshman loan $3,522. Average income from on-campus job $1,600. **Financial Aid Phone:** 570-208-5868.

KNOX COLLEGE

Campus Box 148, Galesburg, IL 61401
Phone: 309-341-7100 **E-mail:** admission@knox.edu **CEEB Code:** 1372
Fax: 309-341-7070 **Web:** www.knox.edu **ACT Code:** 1052

This private school was founded in 1837. It has an 82-acre campus.

STUDENTS AND FACULTY

Enrollment: 1,121. **Student Body:** Male 47%, female 53%, out-of-state 44%, international 8% (32 countries represented). **Ethnic Representation:** African American 5%, Asian 5%, Caucasian 78%, Hispanic 4%, Native American 1%. **Retention and Graduation:** 87% freshmen return for sophomore year. 60% freshmen graduate within 4 years. 31% grads go on to further study within 1 year. 1% grads pursue business degrees. 3% grads pursue law degrees. 5% grads pursue medical degrees. **Faculty:** Student/faculty ratio 12:1. 90 full-time faculty, 93% hold PhDs. 100% faculty teach undergrads.

ACADEMICS

Degrees: Bachelor's. **Academic Requirements:** General education including some course work in arts/fine arts, foreign languages, humanities, mathematics, sciences (biological or physical), social science. Students are required to complete credits in the college's preceptorial program in the first year. Students also complete a total of 3 writing-intensive courses, coursework focused on diversity, a speaking-intensive course, and a experiential learning experience. **Classes:** 10-19 students in an average class. 10-19 students in an average lab/discussion section. **Majors with Highest Enrollment:** Psychology, general; economics, general; biology/biological sciences, general. **Disciplines with Highest Percentage of Degrees Awarded:** Social sciences and history 26%, biological life sciences 11%, visual and performing arts 10%, education 9%, psychology 8%. **Special Study Options:** Double major, dual enrollment, honors program, independent study, internships, liberal arts/career combination, student-designed major, study abroad, teacher certification program.

FACILITIES

Housing: Coed, all-female, all-male, apartments for single students, fraternities and/or sororities. Coed, men's, and women's residence halls consist of bedrooms arranged around a common living area that houses 5 to 18 students. **Library Holdings:** 185,923 bound volumes. 1,037 periodicals. 96,952 microforms. 6,336 audiovisuals. **Special Academic Facilities/Equipment:** Anthropology, art, and field museums; theatre with revolving stage and computerized lighting; ceramics, sculpture, painting, and printmaking studios; 760-acre biological field station; environmental climate chambers; electron microscope. **Computers:** School-owned computers available for student use.

EXTRACURRICULARS

Activities: Choral groups, concert band, dance, drama/theater, jazz band, literary magazine, music ensembles, radio station, student government, student newspaper, symphony orchestra, yearbook. **Organizations:** 102 registered organizations, 8 honor societies, 6 religious organizations, 5 fraternities (30% men join), 2 sororities (10% women join). **Athletics (Intercollegiate):** *Men:* baseball, basketball, cross-country, football, golf, indoor track, soccer, swimming, tennis, track & field, wrestling. *Women:* basketball, cross-country, golf, indoor track, soccer, softball, swimming, tennis, track & field, volleyball.

ADMISSIONS

Selectivity Rating: 81 (of 100). **Freshman Academic Profile:** 33% in top 10% of high school class, 67% in top 25% of high school class, 94% in top 50% of high school class. 88% from public high schools. SAT I Math middle 50% range 550-660. SAT I Verbal middle 50% range 550-680. ACT middle 50% range 23-29. TOEFL required of all international applicants, minimum TOEFL 550. **Basis for Candidate Selection:** *Very important factors considered include:* secondary school record. *Important factors considered include:* class rank, essays, recommendations. *Other factors considered include:* alumni/ae relation, character/personal qualities, extracurricular activities, interview, minority status, standardized test scores, talent/ability, volunteer work. **Freshman Admission Requirements:** High school diploma or GED is required. *Academic units required/recommended:* 15 total required; 18 total recommended; 4 English recommended, 4 math recommended, 3 science recommended, 2 science lab recommended, 3 foreign language recommended, 2 social studies recommended, 2 history recommended. **Freshman Admission Statistics:** 1,542 applied, 72% accepted, 27% of those accepted enrolled. **Transfer Admission Requirements:** *Items required:* high school transcript, college transcript, essay. Minimum college GPA of 2.7 required. Lowest grade transferable C. **General Admission Information:** Application fee $35. Regular application deadline February 1. Nonfall registration accepted. Admission may be deferred for a maximum of 1 year. Credit and/or placement offered for CEEB Advanced Placement tests.

COSTS AND FINANCIAL AID

Tuition $24,105. Room & board $5,925. Required fees $264. Average book expense $600. **Required Forms and Deadlines:** FAFSA and institution's own financial aid form. No deadline for regular filing. Priority filing deadline March 1. **Notification of Awards:** Applicants will be notified of awards on a rolling basis beginning on or about March 15. **Types of Aid:** *Need-based scholarships/grants:* Pell, SEOG, state scholarships/grants, private scholarships, the school's own gift aid. *Loans:* Direct Subsidized Stafford, Direct Unsubsidized Stafford, Direct PLUS, Federal Perkins, college/university loans from institutional funds. **Student Employment:** Federal Work-Study Program available. Institutional employment available. Off-campus job opportunities are fair. **Financial Aid Statistics:** 71% freshmen, 75% undergrads receive some form of aid. Average freshman grant $20,531. Average freshman loan $4,306. Average income from on-campus job $773. **Financial Aid Phone:** 309-341-7149.

KNOXVILLE COLLEGE

901 College Street, Knoxville, TN 37921
Phone: 800-743-5669 **CEEB Code:** 1373
Fax: 615-524-6583 **ACT Code:** 3972

This private school, which is affiliated with the Presbyterian Church, was founded in 1875. It has a 39-acre campus.

STUDENTS AND FACULTY

Enrollment: 1,177. **Student Body:** Out-of-state 72%. **Ethnic Representation:** African American 100%.

ACADEMICS

Degrees: Associate's, bachelor's. **Special Study Options:** Cooperative (work-study) program; economics, engineering, food and lodging administration, and philosophy with the University of Tennessee; teaching training program.

FACILITIES

Housing: Coed. **Library Holdings:** 85,563 bound volumes. 166 periodicals. 5,687 microforms. **Special Academic Facilities/Equipment:** Language lab. **Computers:** *Recommended operating system:* Mac. School-owned computers available for student use.

EXTRACURRICULARS

Organizations: 5 honor societies, 2 religious organizations, 5 fraternities (16% men join), 5 sororities (18% women join). **Athletics (Intercollegiate):** *Women:* basketball, tennis, track & field, volleyball.

ADMISSIONS

Selectivity Rating: 63 (of 100). **Freshman Academic Profile:** 90% from public high schools. **Freshman Admission Requirements:** High school diploma or GED is required. *Academic units required/recommended:* 15 total required; 4 English required, 2 math required, 3 math recommended, 2 science required, 2 social studies required, 4 elective required. **Transfer Admission Requirements:** Minimum college GPA of 2.0 required. Lowest grade transferable C. **General Admission Information:** Regular application deadline July 1. Nonfall registration accepted. Credit offered for CEEB Advanced Placement tests.

COSTS AND FINANCIAL AID

Tuition $5,400. Room & board $3,450. Required fees $420. Average book expense $600. **Required Forms and Deadlines:** FAFSA, institution's own financial aid form, and state aid form. **Types of Aid:** *Need-based scholarships/grants:* Pell, SEOG, state scholarships/grants, private scholarships, the school's own gift aid, United Negro College Fund. *Loans:* FFEL Subsidized Stafford, FFEL Unsubsidized Stafford, FFEL PLUS, Federal Perkins, college/university loans from institutional funds. **Student Employment:** Federal Work-Study Program available. Institutional employment available. Off-campus job opportunities are fair. **Financial Aid Statistics:** Average freshman grant $1,650. **Financial Aid Phone:** 615-524-6525.

KUTZTOWN UNIVERSITY OF PENNSYLVANIA

Admission Office, PO Box 730, Kutztown, PA 19530-0730
Phone: 610-683-4060 **E-mail:** admission@kutztown.edu **CEEB Code:** 2653
Fax: 610-683-1375 **Web:** www.kutztown.edu **ACT Code:** 3706

This public school was founded in 1866. It has a 326-acre campus.

STUDENTS AND FACULTY

Enrollment: 7,591. **Student Body:** Male 39%, female 61%, out-of-state 8%, international 1%. **Ethnic Representation:** African American 5%, Asian 1%, Caucasian 90%, Hispanic 3%. **Retention and Graduation:** 77% freshmen return for sophomore year. 17% freshmen graduate within 4 years. 13% grads go on to further study within 1 year. 10% grads pursue business degrees. 3% grads pursue law degrees. 5% grads pursue medical degrees. **Faculty:** Student/faculty ratio 21:1. 358 full-time faculty, 77% hold PhDs. 99% faculty teach undergrads.

ACADEMICS

Degrees: Bachelor's, master's. **Academic Requirements:** General education including some course work in arts/fine arts, computer literacy, English (including composition), foreign languages, history, humanities, mathematics, sciences (biological or physical), social science. **Classes:** 20-29 students in an average class. 20-29 students in an average lab/discussion section. **Majors with Highest Enrollment:** Special education, general; English language and literature, general; psychology, general. **Disciplines with Highest Percentage of Degrees Awarded:** Education 21%, business/marketing 16%, visual and performing arts 14%, psychology 10%, social sciences and history 8%. **Special Study Options:** Cross registration, distance learning, double major, dual enrollment, honors program, independent study, internships, liberal arts/career combination, student-designed major, study abroad, teacher certification program.

FACILITIES

Housing: Coed, all-female, apartments for single students, cooperative housing. **Library Holdings:** 497,752 bound volumes. 5,573 periodicals. 1,307,315 microforms. 15,981 audiovisuals. **Special Academic Facilities/Equipment:** Art gallery, German cultural heritage center, early childhood learning center, cartography lab, observatory, planetarium, daycare center. **Computers:** *Recommended operating system:* Windows 95. School-owned computers available for student use.

EXTRACURRICULARS

Activities: Choral groups, concert band, dance, drama/theater, jazz band, literary magazine, marching band, music ensembles, musical theater, radio station, student government, student newspaper, television station, yearbook. **Organizations:** 131 registered organizations, 9 honor societies, 3 religious organizations, 5 fraternities (4% men join), 6 sororities (4% women join). **Athletics (Intercollegiate):** *Men:* baseball, basketball, cross-country, football, indoor track, soccer, swimming, tennis, track & field, wrestling. *Women:* basketball, cheerleading, cross-country, field hockey, golf, indoor track, soccer, softball, swimming, tennis, track & field, volleyball.

ADMISSIONS

Selectivity Rating: 66 (of 100). **Freshman Academic Profile:** 5% in top 10% of high school class, 18% in top 25% of high school class, 54% in top 50% of high school class. Average SAT I Math 491, SAT I Math middle 50% range 440-540. Average SAT I Verbal 495, SAT I Verbal middle 50% range 450-540. TOEFL required of all international applicants, minimum TOEFL 500. **Basis for Candidate Selection:** *Very important factors considered include:* class rank, secondary school record, standardized test scores. *Other factors considered include:* character/personal qualities, essays, extracurricular activities, geographical residence, interview, minority status, recommendations, state residency, talent/ability, volunteer work, work experience. **Freshman Admission Requirements:** High school diploma or GED is required. *Academic units required/recommended:* 16 total recommended; 4 English recommended, 3 math recommended, 3 science recommended, 2 foreign language recommended, 4 social studies recommended. **Freshman Admission Statistics:** 6,688 applied, 66% accepted, 41% of those accepted enrolled. **Transfer Admission Requirements:** *Items required:* high school transcript, college transcript, statement of good standing from prior school. Minimum high school GPA of 2.0 required. Minimum college GPA of 2.0 required. Lowest grade transferable C. **General Admission Information:** Application fee $30. Priority application deadline January 1. Nonfall registration accepted. Admission may be deferred for a maximum of 1 year. Credit and/or placement offered for CEEB Advanced Placement tests.

COSTS AND FINANCIAL AID

In-state tuition $4,378. Out-of-state tuition $10,946. Room & board $4,682. Required fees $1,099. Average book expense $1,000. **Required Forms and Deadlines:** FAFSA. No deadline for regular filing. Priority filing deadline February 15. **Notification of Awards:** Applicants will be notified of awards on a rolling basis beginning on or about March 30. **Types of Aid:** *Need-based scholarships/grants:* Pell, SEOG, state scholarships/grants, private scholarships, the school's own gift aid. *Loans:* FFEL Subsidized Stafford, FFEL Unsubsidized Stafford, FFEL PLUS, Federal Perkins. **Student Employment:** Federal Work-Study Program available. Institutional employment available. Off-campus job opportunities are excellent. **Financial Aid Statistics:** 55% freshmen, 51% undergrads receive some form of aid. Average freshman grant $3,816. Average freshman loan $2,350. Average income from on-campus job $1,002. **Financial Aid Phone:** 610-683-4077.

LA SIERRA UNIVERSITY

4700 Pierce Street, Riverside, CA 92515-8247
Phone: 909-785-2176 **E-mail:** ivy@lasierra.edu **CEEB Code:** 4380
Fax: 909-785-2447 **Web:** www.lasierra.edu **ACT Code:** 4380

This private school, which is affiliated with the Seventh-Day Adventist Church, was founded in 1922. It has a 147-acre campus.

STUDENTS AND FACULTY

Enrollment: 1,169. **Student Body:** Male 46%, female 54%, out-of-state 15%, international 8% (59 countries represented). **Ethnic Representation:** African American 6%, Asian 25%, Caucasian 45%, Hispanic 18%, Native American 1%. **Retention and Graduation:** 55% freshmen return for sophomore year. **Faculty:** 100% faculty teach undergrads.

ACADEMICS

Degrees: Bachelor's, doctoral, master's, post-master's certificate, terminal, transfer. **Academic Requirements:** General education including some course work in arts/fine arts, foreign languages, humanities, mathematics, philosophy, sciences (biological or physical), social science, religion, health and fitness. **Special Study Options:** Accelerated program, cooperative (work-study) program, double major, dual enrollment, English as a second language, honors program, internships, student-designed major, study abroad, teacher certification program.

FACILITIES

Housing: All-female, all-male, apartments for married students, apartments for single students, honors residence hall. **Library Holdings:** 238,369 bound volumes. 1,585 periodicals. 353,000 microforms. 15,279 audiovisuals. **Special Academic Facilities/Equipment:** Art gallery, natural history museum, arboretum, observatory. **Computers:** *Recommended operating system:* Mac. School-owned computers available for student use.

EXTRACURRICULARS

Activities: Choral groups, concert band, drama/theater, jazz band, literary magazine, music ensembles, student government, student newspaper, symphony orchestra, yearbook. **Organizations:** 30 registered organizations, 5 religious organizations. **Athletics (Intercollegiate):** *Men:* football, tennis, volleyball. *Women:* basketball, football, gymnastics, volleyball.

ADMISSIONS

Selectivity Rating: 70 (of 100). **Freshman Academic Profile:** Average high school GPA 3.3. 14% in top 10% of high school class, 34% in top 25% of high school class, 68% in top 50% of high school class. 38% from public high schools. Average SAT I Math 509, SAT I Math middle 50% range 430-600. Average SAT I Verbal 500, SAT I Verbal middle 50% range 430-570. Average ACT 20, ACT middle 50% range 17-24. TOEFL required of all international applicants, minimum TOEFL 550. **Basis for Candidate Selection:** *Very important factors considered include:* recommendations, secondary school record. *Important factors considered include:* character/personal qualities, religious affiliation/commitment. *Other factors considered include:* essays, interview. **Freshman Admission Requirements:** High school diploma or GED is required. *Academic units required/recommended:* 18 total recommended; 4 English recommended, 3 math recommended, 3 science recommended, 3 science lab recommended, 2 foreign language recommended, 1 social studies recommended, 1 history recommended. **Transfer Admission Requirements:** *Items required:* high school transcript, college transcript, statement of good standing from prior school. Minimum college GPA of 2.0 required. Lowest grade transferable D. **General Admission Information:** Application fee $30. Priority application deadline August 15. Early decision application deadline August 15. Nonfall registration accepted. Credit offered for CEEB Advanced Placement tests.

COSTS AND FINANCIAL AID

Room & board $2,496. Average book expense $900. **Required Forms and Deadlines:** FAFSA, institution's own financial aid form, and state aid form. No deadline for regular filing. Priority filing deadline May 1. **Notification of Awards:** Applicants will be notified of awards on a rolling basis beginning on or about July 15. **Types of Aid:** *Need-based scholarships/grants:* Pell, SEOG, private scholarships, the school's own gift aid. *Loans:* FFEL Subsidized Stafford, FFEL Unsubsidized Stafford, Federal Perkins. **Student Employment:** Federal Work-Study Program available. Institutional employment available. Off-campus job opportunities are good. **Financial Aid Statistics:** 74% freshmen, 69% undergrads receive some form of aid. **Financial Aid Phone:** 909-785-2175.

LABORATORY INSTITUTE OF MERCHANDISING

12 East 53rd Street, New York, NY 10022
Phone: 212-752-1530 **E-mail:** admissions@limcollege.edu **CEEB Code:** 2380
Fax: 212-421-4341 **Web:** www.limcollege.edu **ACT Code:** 4807

This private school was founded in 1939.

STUDENTS AND FACULTY

Enrollment: 405. **Student Body:** Out-of-state 49%, international 2% (8 countries represented). **Ethnic Representation:** African American 9%, Asian 6%, Caucasian 69%, Hispanic 16%. **Faculty:** Student/faculty ratio 8:1. 9 full-time faculty, 11% hold PhDs. 100% faculty teach undergrads.

ACADEMICS

Degrees: Associate's, bachelor's. **Academic Requirements:** General education including some course work in computer literacy, English (including composition), humanities, mathematics. **Disciplines with Highest Percentage of Degrees Awarded:** Fashion merchandising 80%, business/marketing 20%. **Special Study Options:** Cooperative (work-study) program; internships; 3-credit trip in winter/summer to France, England, Germany, Spain, Italy, or China.

FACILITIES

Housing: Cooperative housing. **Library Holdings:** 11,550 bound volumes. 100 periodicals. 0 microforms. 462 audiovisuals. **Computers:** School-owned computers available for student use.

EXTRACURRICULARS

Activities: Student government, student-run film society, yearbook. **Organizations:** 6 registered organizations, 1 honor society.

ADMISSIONS

Selectivity Rating: 68 (of 100). **Freshman Academic Profile:** 2% in top 10% of high school class, 14% in top 25% of high school class, 32% in top 50% of high school class. 76% from public high schools. Average SAT I Math 444, SAT I Math middle 50% range 410-470. Average SAT I Verbal 465, SAT I Verbal middle 50% range 420-500. ACT middle 50% range 16-21. TOEFL required of all international applicants, minimum TOEFL 550. **Basis for Candidate Selection:** *Very important factors considered include:* interview, secondary school record. *Important factors considered include:* character/personal qualities, class rank, essays, standardized test scores. *Other factors considered include:* extracurricular activities, recommendations, talent/ability, volunteer work, work experience. **Freshman Admission Requirements:** High school diploma or GED is required. **Freshman Admission Statistics:** 302 applied, 62% accepted, 49% of those accepted enrolled. **Transfer Admission Requirements:** *Items required:* high school transcript, college transcript, essay, interview. Lowest grade transferable C. **General Admission Information:** Application fee $40. Nonfall registration accepted. Admission may be deferred. Credit and/or placement offered for CEEB Advanced Placement tests.

COSTS AND FINANCIAL AID

Tuition $14,000. Required fees $150. Average book expense $600. **Required Forms and Deadlines:** FAFSA and institution's own financial aid form. No deadline for regular filing. **Notification of Awards:** Applicants will be notified of awards on a rolling basis beginning on or about February 15. **Types of Aid:** *Need-based scholarships/grants:* Pell, SEOG, state scholarships/grants, the school's own gift aid. *Loans:* Direct Subsidized Stafford, Direct Unsubsidized Stafford, Direct PLUS. **Student Employment:** Federal Work-Study Program available. Institutional employment available. Off-campus job opportunities are excellent. **Financial Aid Statistics:** 80% freshmen, 83% undergrads receive some form of aid. Average freshman grant $4,500. Average freshman loan $4,000. Average income from on-campus job $500. **Financial Aid Phone:** 212-752-1530.

See page 1080.

LAFAYETTE COLLEGE

$$$

118 Markle Hall, Easton, PA 18042
Phone: 610-330-5100 **E-mail:** admissions@lafayette.edu **CEEB Code:** 2361
Fax: 610-330-5355 **Web:** www.lafayette.edu

This private school, which is affiliated with the Presbyterian Church, was founded in 1826. It has a 340-acre campus.

STUDENTS AND FACULTY

Enrollment: 2,300. **Student Body:** Male 51%, female 49%, out-of-state 70%, international 5% (46 countries represented). **Ethnic Representation:** African American 5%, Asian 2%, Caucasian 91%, Hispanic 2%. **Retention and Graduation:** 95% freshmen return for sophomore year. 80% freshmen graduate within 4 years. 29% grads go on to further study within 1 year. 5% grads pursue business degrees. 7% grads pursue law degrees. 3% grads pursue medical degrees. **Faculty:** Student/faculty ratio 11:1. 184 full-time faculty, 100% hold PhDs. 100% faculty teach undergrads.

ACADEMICS

Degrees: Bachelor's. **Academic Requirements:** General education including some course work in English (including composition), foreign languages, humanities, mathematics, sciences (biological or physical), social science. **Classes:** 10-19 students in an average class. 10-19 students in an average lab/discussion section. **Disciplines with Highest Percentage of Degrees Awarded:** Social sciences and history 38%, engineering/engineering technology 17%, biological life sciences 11%, English 10%, psychology 8%. **Special Study Options:** Accelerated program, cooperative (work-study) program, cross registration, distance learning, double major, honors program, internships, liberal arts/career combination, student-designed major, study abroad.

FACILITIES

Housing: Coed, all-female, all-male, apartments for married students, apartments for single students, housing for disabled students, housing for international students, fraternities and/or sororities, cooperative housing. **Library Holdings:** 526,000 bound volumes. 1,937 periodicals. 0 microforms. 956 audiovisuals. **Special Academic Facilities/Equipment:** Art and geological museums, center for the arts, engineering labs, INSTRON materials testing machine, electron microscopes, transform nuclear magnetic resonance spectrometer, computerized gas chromatograph/mass spectrometer. **Computers:** School-owned computers available for student use.

EXTRACURRICULARS

Activities: Choral groups, dance, drama/theater, jazz band, literary magazine, music ensembles, musical theater, pep band, radio station, student government, student newspaper, student-run film society, symphony orchestra, yearbook. **Organizations:** 250 registered organizations, 14 honor societies, 7 religious organizations, 7 fraternities (26% men join), 6 sororities (45% women join). **Athletics (Intercollegiate):** *Men:* baseball, basketball, cheerleading, crew, cross-country, diving, equestrian, fencing, football, golf, gymnastics, ice hockey, indoor track, lacrosse, soccer, softball, swimming, tennis, track & field, volleyball, wrestling. *Women:* basketball, cheerleading, crew, cross-country, diving, equestrian, fencing, field hockey, golf, gymnastics, indoor track, softball, swimming, tennis, track & field, volleyball.

ADMISSIONS

Selectivity Rating: 86 (of 100). **Freshman Academic Profile:** Average high school GPA 3.8. 59% in top 10% of high school class, 89% in top 25% of high school class, 100% in top 50% of high school class. 68% from public high schools. Average SAT I Math 665, SAT I Math middle 50% range 610-700. Average SAT I Verbal 620, SAT I Verbal middle 50% range 560-650. Average ACT 28, ACT middle 50% range 25-29. TOEFL required of all international applicants, minimum TOEFL 550. **Basis for Candidate Selection:** *Very important factors considered include:* secondary school record. *Important factors considered include:* alumni/ae relation, character/personal qualities, class rank, essays, extracurricular activities, minority status, recommendations, standardized test scores, talent/ability, volunteer work. *Other factors considered include:* geographical residence, interview, work experience. **Freshman Admission Requirements:** High school diploma or equivalent is not required. *Academic units required/recommended:* 16 total recommended; 4 English recommended, 3 math recommended, 2 science recommended, 2 science lab recommended, 2 foreign language recommended, 5 elective recommended. **Freshman Admission Statistics:** 5,504 applied, 36% accepted, 30% of those accepted enrolled. **Transfer Admission Requirements:** *Items required:* high school transcript, college transcript, essay. Minimum college GPA of 3.0 required. Lowest grade transferable C. **General Admission Information:** Application fee $50. Priority application deadline January 1. Early decision application deadline February 15. Regular application deadline January 1. Nonfall registration accepted. Admission may be deferred for a maximum of 1 year. Credit and/or placement offered for CEEB Advanced Placement tests.

COSTS AND FINANCIAL AID

Tuition $25,884. Room & board $8,069. Required fees $98. Average book expense $600. **Required Forms and Deadlines:** FAFSA, CSS/Financial Aid PROFILE, noncustodial (divorced/separated) parent's statement, and business/farm supplement. Financial aid filing deadline February 1. Priority filing deadline February 1. **Notification of Awards:** Applicants will be notified of awards on or about April 1. **Types of Aid:** *Need-based scholarships/grants:* Pell, SEOG, state scholarships/grants, private scholarships. *Loans:* FFEL Subsidized Stafford, FFEL Unsubsidized Stafford, FFEL PLUS, Federal Perkins, state loans, college/university loans from institutional funds, HELP loans to parents. **Student Employment:** Federal Work-Study Program available. Institutional employment available. Off-campus job opportunities are good. **Financial Aid Statistics:** 57% freshmen, 54% undergrads receive some form of aid. Average freshman grant $20,552. Average freshman loan $3,500. Average income from on-campus job $1,000. **Financial Aid Phone:** 610-330-5055.

LAGRANGE COLLEGE

Office of Admission, 601 Broad Street, LaGrange, GA 30240
Phone: 706-880-8005 **E-mail:** lgcadmis@lagrange.edu **CEEB Code:** 5362
Fax: 706-880-8010 **Web:** www.lagrange.edu **ACT Code:** 834

This private school, which is affiliated with the Methodist Church, was founded in 1831. It has a 120-acre campus.

STUDENTS AND FACULTY

Enrollment: 967. **Student Body:** Male 37%, female 63%, out-of-state 11%, international 1% (12 countries represented). **Ethnic Representation:** African American 16%, Asian 1%, Caucasian 81%, Hispanic 1%, Native American 1%. **Retention and Graduation:** 72% freshmen return for sophomore year. 35% freshmen graduate within 4 years. 20% grads go on to further study within 1 year. **Faculty:** Student/faculty ratio 10:1. 63 full-time faculty, 79% hold PhDs. 100% faculty teach undergrads.

ACADEMICS

Degrees: Associate's, bachelor's, master's, terminal. **Academic Requirements:** General education including some course work in arts/fine arts, computer literacy, English (including composition), foreign languages, history, humanities, mathematics, sciences (biological or physical), social science, religion. **Classes:** Under 10 students in an average class. Under 10 students in an average lab/discussion section. **Majors with Highest Enrollment:** Business administration/management; elementary education and teaching; social work. **Disciplines with Highest Percentage of Degrees Awarded:** Business/ marketing 30%, protective services/public administration 12%, education 10%, visual and performing arts 8%, psychology 7%. **Special Study Options:** Double major, dual enrollment, independent study, internships, liberal arts/ career combination, study abroad, teacher certification program.

FACILITIES

Housing: Coed, all-female, all-male. **Library Holdings:** 108,389 bound volumes. 527 periodicals. 171,946 microforms. 3,650 audiovisuals. **Special Academic Facilities/Equipment:** Art center, center for the performing arts, language lab. **Computers:** School-owned computers available for student use.

EXTRACURRICULARS

Activities: Choral groups, dance, drama/theater, literary magazine, music ensembles, musical theater, student government, student newspaper, yearbook. **Organizations:** 32 registered organizations, 12 honor societies, 4 religious organizations, 2 fraternities (22% men join), 3 sororities (25% women join). **Athletics (Intercollegiate):** *Men:* baseball, basketball, cross-country, golf, soccer, swimming, tennis. *Women:* basketball, cheerleading, cross-country, soccer, softball, swimming, tennis, volleyball.

ADMISSIONS

Selectivity Rating: 71 (of 100). **Freshman Academic Profile:** Average high school GPA 3.2. 20% in top 10% of high school class, 48% in top 25% of high school class, 78% in top 50% of high school class. Average SAT I Math 500, SAT I Math middle 50% range 440-560. Average SAT I Verbal 520, SAT I Verbal middle 50% range 460-580. Average ACT 21, ACT middle 50% range 18-23. TOEFL required of all international applicants, minimum TOEFL 500. **Basis for Candidate Selection:** *Very important factors considered include:* character/personal qualities, secondary school record, standardized test scores. *Important factors considered include:* interview, recommendations. *Other factors considered include:* alumni/ae relation, class rank, essays, extracurricular activities, geographical residence, talent/ability, volunteer work. **Freshman Admission Requirements:** High school diploma or GED is required. *Academic units required/recommended:* 12 total required; 16 total recommended; 4 English required, 4 English recommended, 4 math required, 4 math recommended, 2 science required, 3 science recommended, 2 foreign language recommended, 3 social studies required, 3 social studies recommended. **Freshman Admission Statistics:** 751 applied, 61% accepted, 51% of those accepted enrolled. **Transfer Admission Requirements:** *Items required:* college transcript, essay. Minimum college GPA of 2.0 required. Lowest grade transferable C. **General Admission Information:** Application fee $20. Nonfall registration accepted. Admission may be deferred. Credit and/or placement offered for CEEB Advanced Placement tests.

COSTS AND FINANCIAL AID

Tuition $13,226. Room & board $5,494. Required fees $0. Average book expense $750. **Required Forms and Deadlines:** FAFSA, institution's own financial aid form, and state aid form. Financial aid filing deadline March 1. **Notification of Awards:** Applicants will be notified of awards on a rolling basis. **Types of Aid:** *Need-based scholarships/grants:* Pell, SEOG, state scholarships/grants, private scholarships, the school's own gift aid. *Loans:* FFEL Subsidized Stafford, FFEL Unsubsidized Stafford, FFEL PLUS, Federal Perkins. **Student Employment:** Federal Work-Study Program available. Institutional employment available. Off-campus job opportunities are excellent. **Financial Aid Statistics:** 69% freshmen, 66% undergrads receive some form of aid. Average freshman grant $13,465. Average freshman loan $2,520. Average income from on-campus job $604. **Financial Aid Phone:** 706-880-8229.

LAKE ERIE COLLEGE

 $$$  

391 West Washington Street, Painesville, OH 44077-3389
Phone: 800-639-7879 **E-mail:** lecadmit@lakeerie.edu **CEEB Code:** 1391
Fax: 440-352-3533 **Web:** www.lakeerie.edu **ACT Code:** 3288

This private school was founded in 1856. It has a 48-acre campus.

STUDENTS AND FACULTY

Enrollment: 509. **Student Body:** Male 26%, female 74%, out-of-state 11%, international students represent 6 countries. **Ethnic Representation:** African American 4%, Asian 1%, Caucasian 94%, Hispanic 2%. **Retention and Graduation:** 63% freshmen return for sophomore year. 24% freshmen graduate within 4 years. 22% grads go on to further study within 1 year. 5% grads pursue business degrees. 5% grads pursue law degrees. 2% grads pursue medical degrees. **Faculty:** Student/faculty ratio 12:1. 29 full-time faculty, 79% hold PhDs. 100% faculty teach undergrads.

ACADEMICS

Degrees: Bachelor's, certificate, master's, post-bachelor's certificate. **Academic Requirements:** General education including some course work in arts/fine arts, computer literacy, English (including composition), foreign languages, history, humanities, mathematics, philosophy, sciences (biological or physical), social science, intercultural. **Classes:** 10-19 students in an average class. **Disciplines with Highest Percentage of Degrees Awarded:** Business/ marketing 40%, education 12%, agriculture 10%, biological life sciences 7%, psychology 6%. **Special Study Options:** Cross registration, distance learning, double major, independent study, internships, student-designed major, study abroad, teacher certification program, weekend college.

FACILITIES

Housing: Coed, all-female, all-male. **Library Holdings:** 72,455 bound volumes. 1,720 periodicals. 10,349 microforms. 2,402 audiovisuals. **Special Academic Facilities/Equipment:** Indian museum. **Computers:** School-owned computers available for student use.

EXTRACURRICULARS

Activities: Choral groups, dance, drama/theater, radio station, student government. **Organizations:** 15 registered organizations, 2 honor societies, 6 religious organizations. **Athletics (Intercollegiate):** *Men:* basketball, cross-country, equestrian, golf, soccer, tennis. *Women:* basketball, cheerleading, equestrian, soccer, softball, tennis, volleyball.

ADMISSIONS

Selectivity Rating: 69 (of 100). **Freshman Academic Profile:** Average high school GPA 3.0. 15% in top 10% of high school class, 36% in top 25% of high school class, 60% in top 50% of high school class. 80% from public high schools. Average SAT I Math 460, SAT I Math middle 50% range 410-530. Average SAT I Verbal 500, SAT I Verbal middle 50% range 410-540. Average ACT 22, ACT middle 50% range 18-24. TOEFL required of all international applicants, minimum TOEFL 550. **Basis for Candidate Selection:** *Very important factors considered include:* secondary school record. *Important factors considered include:* interview, standardized test scores. *Other factors considered include:* alumni/ae relation, character/personal qualities, class rank, essays, extracurricular activities, geographical residence, minority status, recommendations, religious affiliation/commitment, state residency, talent/ability, volunteer work, work experience. **Freshman Admission Requirements:** High school diploma or GED is required. *Academic units required/recommended:* 4 English required, 4 English recommended, 3 math required, 3 math recommended, 3 science required, 3 science recommended, 2 science lab required, 2 science lab recommended, 2 foreign language required, 2 foreign language recommended, 3 social studies required, 3 social studies recommended. **Freshman Admission Statistics:** 336 applied, 87% accepted, 35% of those accepted enrolled. **Transfer Admission Requirements:** *Items required:* high school transcript, college transcript. Minimum college GPA of 2.0 required. Lowest grade transferable C. **General Admission Information:** Application fee $25. Nonfall registration accepted. Admission may be deferred for a maximum of 1 year. Credit and/or placement offered for CEEB Advanced Placement tests.

COSTS AND FINANCIAL AID

Tuition $15,140. Room & board $5,420. Required fees $892. Average book expense $530. **Required Forms and Deadlines:** FAFSA. No deadline for regular filing. **Notification of Awards:** Applicants will be notified of awards on a rolling basis beginning on or about January 20. **Types of Aid:** *Need-based scholarships/grants:* Pell, SEOG, state scholarships/grants, private scholarships, the school's own gift aid. *Loans:* FFEL Subsidized Stafford, FFEL Unsubsidized Stafford, FFEL PLUS, Federal Perkins, payment plans. **Student Employment:** Federal Work-Study Program available. Institutional employment available. Off-campus job opportunities are excellent. **Financial Aid Statistics:** Average freshman grant $5,800. Average freshman loan $2,650. Average income from on-campus job $1,200. **Financial Aid Phone:** 440-639-7815.

LAKE FOREST COLLEGE

555 North Sheridan Road, Lake Forest, IL 60045
Phone: 847-735-5000 **E-mail:** admissions@lakeforest.edu **CEEB Code:** 1392
Fax: 847-735-6271 **Web:** www.lakeforest.edu **ACT Code:** 1054

This private school, which is affiliated with the Presbyterian Church, was founded in 1857. It has a 107-acre campus.

STUDENTS AND FACULTY

Enrollment: 1,319. **Student Body:** Male 41%, female 59%, out-of-state 52%, international 8% (42 countries represented). **Ethnic Representation:** African American 6%, Asian 5%, Caucasian 85%, Hispanic 3%. **Retention and Graduation:** 79% freshmen return for sophomore year. 58% freshmen graduate within 4 years. 34% grads go on to further study within 1 year. 6% grads pursue business degrees. 7% grads pursue law degrees. 5% grads pursue medical degrees. **Faculty:** Student/faculty ratio 13:1. 87 full-time faculty, 96% hold PhDs. 100% faculty teach undergrads.

ACADEMICS

Degrees: Bachelor's, master's. **Academic Requirements:** General education including some course work in English (including composition), humanities, mathematics, sciences (biological or physical), social science. **Classes:** 10-19 students in an average class. 10-19 students in an average lab/discussion section. **Majors with Highest Enrollment:** Business/commerce, general; psychology, general; communications studies/speech communication and rhetoric. **Disciplines with Highest Percentage of Degrees Awarded:** Social sciences and history 22%, communications/communication technologies 10%, business/marketing 10%, psychology 8%, English 8%. **Special Study Options:** Cross registration, double major, honors program, independent study, internships, liberal arts/career combination, student-designed major, study abroad, teacher certification program.

FACILITIES

Housing: Coed, all-female, all-male, housing for disabled students, housing for international students. **Library Holdings:** 231,145 bound volumes. 886 periodicals. 103,822 microforms. 12,125 audiovisuals. **Special Academic Facilities/Equipment:** Art gallery, language labs, electron microscope, computer molecular modeling equipment, fiber optic wired network, high-resolution FT-IR, NMR spectrometer, neutron howitzer, music/recording studio with synthesizers, 11 public access computer labs. **Computers:** School-owned computers available for student use.

EXTRACURRICULARS

Activities: Choral groups, dance, drama/theater, jazz band, literary magazine, music ensembles, musical theater, pep band, radio station, student government, student newspaper, student-run film society, television station, yearbook. **Organizations:** 72 registered organizations, 11 honor societies, 11 religious organizations, 3 fraternities (19% men join), 4 sororities (27% women join). **Athletics (Intercollegiate):** *Men:* basketball, cross-country, diving, football, ice hockey, soccer, swimming, tennis. *Women:* basketball, cross-country, diving, ice hockey, soccer, softball, swimming, tennis, volleyball.

ADMISSIONS

Selectivity Rating: 79 (of 100). **Freshman Academic Profile:** Average high school GPA 3.4. 25% in top 10% of high school class, 53% in top 25% of high school class, 80% in top 50% of high school class. 65% from public high schools. Average SAT I Math 573, SAT I Math middle 50% range 510-620. Average SAT I Verbal 570, SAT I Verbal middle 50% range 520-620. Average ACT 25, ACT middle 50% range 23-28. TOEFL required of all international applicants, minimum TOEFL 550. **Basis for Candidate Selection:** *Very important factors considered include:* secondary school record. *Important factors considered include:* essays, extracurricular activities. *Other factors considered include:* alumni/ae relation, character/personal qualities, class rank, geographical residence, interview, recommendations, standardized test scores, talent/ability, volunteer work, work experience. **Freshman Admission Requirements:** High school diploma or GED is required. *Academic units required/recommended:* 16 total required; 19 total recommended; 4 English required, 4 English recommended, 3 math required, 4 math recommended, 2 science required, 3 science recommended, 2 science lab required, 3 science lab recommended, 2 foreign language required, 4 foreign language recommended, 1 social studies required, 2 social studies recommended, 1 history required, 2 history recommended, 3 elective required. **Freshman Admission Statistics:** 1,666 applied, 66% accepted, 33% of those accepted enrolled. **Transfer Admission Requirements:** *Items required:* high school transcript, college transcript. Minimum college GPA of 2.0 required. Lowest grade transferable C-. **General Admission Information:** Application fee $40. Priority application deadline March 1. Early decision application deadline January 1. Regular application deadline July 1. Nonfall registration accepted. Admission may be deferred for a maximum of 1 year. Credit and/or placement offered for CEEB Advanced Placement tests.

COSTS AND FINANCIAL AID

Tuition $22,976. Room & board $5,764. Required fees $310. Average book expense $600. **Required Forms and Deadlines:** FAFSA, CSS/Financial Aid PROFILE, and federal income tax return. Priority filing deadline March 1. **Notification of Awards:** Applicants will be notified of awards on a rolling basis beginning on or about March 15. **Types of Aid:** *Need-based scholarships/grants:* Pell, SEOG, state scholarships/grants, private scholarships, the school's own gift aid. *Loans:* Direct Subsidized Stafford, Direct Unsubsidized Stafford, Direct PLUS, Federal Perkins, college/university loans from institutional funds. **Student Employment:** Federal Work-Study Program available. Institutional employment available. Off-campus job opportunities are good. **Financial Aid Statistics:** 70% freshmen, 70% undergrads receive some form of aid. Average freshman grant $17,496. Average freshman loan $3,599. Average income from on-campus job $1,600. **Financial Aid Phone:** 847-735-5103.

See page 1082.

LAKE SUPERIOR STATE UNIVERSITY

650 W. Easterday Avenue, Sault Saint Marie, MI 49783-1699
Phone: 906-635-2231 **E-mail:** admissions@gw.lssu.edu **CEEB Code:** 1421
Fax: 906-635-6669 **Web:** www.lssu.edu **ACT Code:** 2031

This public school was founded in 1946. It has a 121-acre campus.

STUDENTS AND FACULTY

Enrollment: 3,186. **Student Body:** Male 48%, female 52%, out-of-state 5%, international 13%. **Ethnic Representation:** African American 2%, Asian 1%, Caucasian 87%, Hispanic 1%, Native American 9%. **Retention and Graduation:** 68% freshmen return for sophomore year. 20% freshmen graduate within 4 years. 8% grads go on to further study within 1 year. **Faculty:** Student/faculty ratio 18:1. 121 full-time faculty, 52% hold PhDs.

ACADEMICS

Degrees: Associate's, bachelor's, certificate, master's. **Academic Requirements:** General education including some course work in computer literacy, English (including composition), humanities, mathematics, sciences (biological or physical), social science, critical thinking, oral communication, aesthetics, ethics, cultural diversity. **Classes:** 20-29 students in an average class. 10-19 students in an average lab/discussion section. **Disciplines with Highest Percentage of Degrees Awarded:** Business/marketing 22%, protective services/public administration 19%, health professions and related sciences 12%, engineering/engineering technology 8%, education 8%. **Special Study Options:** Cooperative (work-study) program, cross registration, distance learning, double major, honors program, independent study, internships, student-designed major, teacher certification program, weekend college.

FACILITIES

Housing: Coed, all-female, all-male, apartments for married students, apartments for single students, fraternities and/or sororities, mobile home lots for student-owned mobile homes. **Library Holdings:** 152,689 bound volumes. 873 periodicals. 97,222 microforms. **Special Academic Facilities/Equipment:** Natural science, Michigan history, and Great Lakes shipping museums; planetarium; industrial robots; atomic absorption/flame emission spectrophotometer. **Computers:** *Recommended operating system:* Mac. School-owned computers available for student use.

EXTRACURRICULARS

Activities: Choral groups, concert band, drama/theater, jazz band, literary magazine, music ensembles, pep band, radio station, student government, student newspaper, symphony orchestra. **Organizations:** 50 registered organizations, 5 fraternities, 4 sororities. **Athletics (Intercollegiate):** *Men:* basketball, cross-country, golf, ice hockey, indoor track, tennis, track & field, volleyball. *Women:* basketball, cross-country, softball, tennis, volleyball.

ADMISSIONS

Selectivity Rating: 63 (of 100). **Freshman Academic Profile:** Average high school GPA 3.0. 11% in top 10% of high school class, 33% in top 25% of high school class, 60% in top 50% of high school class. 95% from public high schools. Average ACT 21, ACT middle 50% range 18-24. TOEFL required of all international applicants, minimum TOEFL 550. **Basis for Candidate Selection:** *Very important factors considered include:* secondary school record, standardized test scores. *Other factors considered include:* class rank, geographical residence, interview, recommendations. **Freshman Admission**

Requirements: High school diploma or GED is required. *Academic units required/recommended:* 18 total recommended; 4 English recommended, 3 math recommended, 3 science recommended, 3 science lab recommended, 2 foreign language recommended, 2 social studies recommended, 1 history recommended. **Freshman Admission Statistics:** 1,396 applied, 66% accepted, 62% of those accepted enrolled. **Transfer Admission Requirements:** *Items required:* college transcript. Minimum college GPA of 2.0 required. Lowest grade transferable D. **General Admission Information:** Application fee $20. Regular application deadline August 15. Nonfall registration accepted. Admission may be deferred for a maximum of 1 year. Credit offered for CEEB Advanced Placement tests.

COSTS AND FINANCIAL AID

In-state tuition $4,128. Out-of-state tuition $8,106. Room & board $5,281. Required fees $206. Average book expense $700. **Required Forms and Deadlines:** FAFSA. No deadline for regular filing. Priority filing deadline February 21. **Notification of Awards:** Applicants will be notified of awards on a rolling basis beginning on or about November 1. **Types of Aid:** *Need-based scholarships/grants:* Pell, SEOG, state scholarships/grants, private scholarships, the school's own gift aid, Federal Nursing, third party payments. *Loans:* Direct Subsidized Stafford, Direct Unsubsidized Stafford, Direct PLUS, Federal Perkins, Federal Nursing, state loans. **Student Employment:** Federal Work-Study Program available. Institutional employment available. Off-campus job opportunities are good. **Financial Aid Statistics:** 85% freshmen, 79% undergrads receive some form of aid. Average freshman grant $1,700. Average income from on-campus job $1,400. **Financial Aid Phone:** 906-635-2678.

LAKEHEAD UNIVERSITY

955 Oliver Road, Thunder Bay, ON P7B 5E1
Phone: 807-343-8500 **E-mail:** liaison@lakeheadu.ca
Fax: 807-343-8156 **Web:** www.lakeheadu.ca

This public school was founded in 1965. It has a 345-acre campus.

STUDENTS AND FACULTY

Enrollment: 5,854. **Student Body:** Male 43%, female 57%. **Retention and Graduation:** 80% freshmen return for sophomore year. **Faculty:** Student/faculty ratio 19:1. 240 full-time faculty, 80% hold PhDs. 100% faculty teach undergrads.

ACADEMICS

Degrees: Bachelor's, certificate, diploma, doctoral, master's. **Classes:** 20-29 students in an average class. **Majors with Highest Enrollment:** Engineering, general; forestry, general; business administration/management. **Disciplines with Highest Percentage of Degrees Awarded:** Other 96%. **Special Study Options:** Cooperative (work-study) program, distance learning, double major, student exchange program (domestic), honors program, study abroad, teacher certification program.

FACILITIES

Housing: Coed, all-female. **Library Holdings:** 725,396 bound volumes. 2,200 periodicals. 373,926 microforms. 260 audiovisuals. **Computers:** School-owned computers available for student use.

EXTRACURRICULARS

Activities: Student government, student newspaper. **Athletics (Intercollegiate):** *Men:* basketball, crew, cross-country, ice hockey, rugby, skiing (Nordic), track & field, volleyball, wrestling. *Women:* basketball, crew, cross-country, rugby, skiing (Nordic), track & field, volleyball, wrestling.

ADMISSIONS

Selectivity Rating: 60 (of 100). **Freshman Academic Profile:** 70% from public high schools. TOEFL required of all international applicants, minimum TOEFL 550. **Basis for Candidate Selection:** *Important factors considered include:* secondary school record. **Freshman Admission Requirements:** High school diploma is required and GED is not accepted. **General Admission Information:** Application fee $85. Regular application deadline September 18. Nonfall registration accepted. Neither credit nor placement offered for CEEB Advanced Placement tests.

COSTS AND FINANCIAL AID

In-state tuition $3,550. Out-of-state tuition $3,550. Room & board $4,917. Required fees $364. Average book expense $700. **Required Forms and Deadlines:** Financial aid filing deadline January 1. **Student Employment:** Federal Work-Study Program available. Off-campus job opportunities are fair. **Financial Aid Phone:** 807-343-8206.

LAKELAND COLLEGE

PO Box 359, Sheboygan, WI 53082-0359
Phone: 920-565-2111 **E-mail:** admissions@lakeland.edu **CEEB Code:** 1393
Fax: 920-565-1206 **Web:** www.lakeland.edu **ACT Code:** 4592

This private school, which is affiliated with the United Church of Christ, was founded in 1862. It has a 145-acre campus.

STUDENTS AND FACULTY

Enrollment: 3,328. **Student Body:** Male 39%, female 61%, out-of-state 23%, international 3%. **Ethnic Representation:** African American 5%, Asian 2%, Caucasian 88%, Hispanic 1%, Native American 1%. **Retention and Graduation:** 23% freshmen graduate within 4 years. 17% grads go on to further study within 1 year. 8% grads pursue business degrees. 2% grads pursue law degrees. 2% grads pursue medical degrees. **Faculty:** Student/faculty ratio 15:1. 42 full-time faculty, 57% hold PhDs. 42% faculty teach undergrads.

ACADEMICS

Degrees: Bachelor's, master's. **Academic Requirements:** General education including some course work in arts/fine arts. **Disciplines with Highest Percentage of Degrees Awarded:** Business/marketing 71%, computer and information sciences 12%, education 9%, psychology 2%, biological life sciences 1%. **Special Study Options:** Double major, dual enrollment, English as a second language, honors program, independent study, internships, study abroad, teacher certification program.

FACILITIES

Housing: Coed, all-female, all-male, apartments for single students, housing for disabled students, apartments for honors students, cultural suites available. **Library Holdings:** 116,171 bound volumes. 298 periodicals. 31,971 microforms. 587 audiovisuals. **Special Academic Facilities/Equipment:** Museum of college history. **Computers:** School-owned computers available for student use.

EXTRACURRICULARS

Activities: Choral groups, concert band, drama/theater, jazz band, music ensembles, pep band, student government, student newspaper, television station, yearbook. **Organizations:** 30 registered organizations, 3 fraternities, 3 sororities. **Athletics (Intercollegiate):** *Men:* baseball, basketball, cross-country, football, golf, ice hockey, skiing (alpine), skiing (Nordic), soccer, softball, tennis, volleyball, wrestling. *Women:* basketball, cross-country, golf, skiing (alpine), soccer, softball, tennis, volleyball.

ADMISSIONS

Selectivity Rating: 69 (of 100). **Freshman Academic Profile:** Average high school GPA 2.5. 9% in top 10% of high school class, 27% in top 25% of high school class, 53% in top 50% of high school class. 95% from public high schools. Average ACT 20, ACT middle 50% range 13-23. TOEFL required of all international applicants, minimum TOEFL 500. **Basis for Candidate Selection:** *Very important factors considered include:* class rank, extracurricular activities, secondary school record, standardized test scores. *Important factors considered include:* alumni/ae relation, interview, minority status, talent/ability. *Other factors considered include:* essays, recommendations. **Freshman Admission Requirements:** High school diploma or GED is required. *Academic units required/recommended:* 4 English recommended, 2 math recommended, 4 science recommended, 2 foreign language recommended, 1 social studies recommended. **Freshman Admission Statistics:** 580 applied, 74% accepted, 42% of those accepted enrolled. **Transfer Admission Requirements:** *Items required:* college transcript. Minimum college GPA of 2.0 required. Lowest grade transferable C. **General Admission Information:** Application fee $20. Regular application deadline August 1. Nonfall registration accepted. Admission may be deferred for a maximum of 1 year. Credit and/or placement offered for CEEB Advanced Placement tests.

COSTS AND FINANCIAL AID

Tuition $11,980. Room & board $4,860. Required fees $500. Average book expense $500. **Required Forms and Deadlines:** FAFSA and institution's own financial aid form. Financial aid filing deadline August 1. Priority filing deadline May 1. **Notification of Awards:** Applicants will be notified of awards on a rolling basis beginning on or about March 1. **Types of Aid:** *Need-based scholarships/grants:* Pell, SEOG, state scholarships/grants, private scholarships, the school's own gift aid. *Loans:* FFEL Subsidized Stafford, FFEL Unsubsidized Stafford, FFEL PLUS, Federal Perkins, college/university loans from institutional funds. **Student Employment:** Federal Work-Study Program available. Institutional employment available. Off-campus job opportunities are good. **Financial Aid Statistics:** 91% freshmen, 68% undergrads receive some form of aid. Average income from on-campus job $1,250. **Financial Aid Phone:** 920-565-1297.

LAMAR UNIVERSITY

PO Box 10009, Beaumont, TX 77710
Phone: 409-880-8888 **E-mail:** admissions@hal.lamar.edu **CEEB Code:** 6360
Fax: 409-880-8463 **Web:** www.lamar.edu **ACT Code:** 4114

This public school was founded in 1923. It has a 200-acre campus.

STUDENTS AND FACULTY

Enrollment: 9,551. **Student Body:** Male 45%, female 55%, out-of-state 1%, international 1%. **Ethnic Representation:** African American 21%, Asian 3%, Caucasian 71%, Hispanic 4%, Native American 1%.

ACADEMICS

Degrees: Bachelor's, doctoral, master's. **Academic Requirements:** General education including some course work in arts/fine arts, computer literacy, English (including composition), history, humanities, mathematics, philosophy, sciences (biological or physical), social science. **Special Study Options:** Cooperative (work-study) program, distance learning, double major, dual enrollment, English as a second language, honors program, internships, study abroad, teacher certification program. Texas Academy for Leadership in the Humanities is a 2-year residential, early admission program for gifted high school students. Students are selected during the sophomore year of high school and enter the university at the end of their junior year.

FACILITIES

Housing: Coed, all-female, all-male, apartments for single students, fraternities and/or sororities. **Library Holdings:** 1,000,000 bound volumes. 2,800 periodicals. 222,975 microforms. **Special Academic Facilities/Equipment:** Museum. **Computers:** *Recommended operating system:* Mac. School-owned computers available for student use.

EXTRACURRICULARS

Activities: Student government, student newspaper. **Organizations:** 145 registered organizations, 11 fraternities (5% men join), 8 sororities (5% women join). **Athletics (Intercollegiate):** *Men:* baseball, basketball, cross-country, golf, tennis, track & field. *Women:* basketball, cross-country, golf, tennis, track & field, volleyball.

ADMISSIONS

Selectivity Rating: 63 (of 100). **Freshman Academic Profile:** 10% in top 10% of high school class, 27% in top 25% of high school class, 90% in top 50% of high school class. 96% from public high schools. Average SAT I Math 459. Average SAT I Verbal 413. Average ACT 20. TOEFL required of all international applicants, minimum TOEFL 500. **Freshman Admission Requirements:** High school diploma is required and GED is not accepted. *Academic units required/recommended:* 16 total recommended; 4 English recommended, 3 math recommended, 2 science recommended, 2 social studies recommended, 2 elective recommended. **Transfer Admission Requirements:** Minimum college GPA of 2.0 required. Lowest grade transferable D. **General Admission Information:** Regular application deadline August 1. Nonfall registration accepted. Credit and/or placement offered for CEEB Advanced Placement tests.

COSTS AND FINANCIAL AID

In-state tuition $864. Out-of-state tuition $5,976. Room & board $3,040. Required fees $840. Average book expense $587. **Required Forms and Deadlines:** FAFSA, institution's own financial aid form, and state aid form. **Types of Aid:** *Loans:* FFEL Subsidized Stafford, FFEL PLUS. **Student Employment:** Federal Work-Study Program available. Institutional employment available. Off-campus job opportunities are good. **Financial Aid Statistics:** Average freshman loan $1,943. Average income from on-campus job $1,200. **Financial Aid Phone:** 409-880-8454.

LAMBUTH UNIVERSITY

705 Lambuth Boulevard, Jackson, TN 38301-5296
Phone: 731-425-3223 **E-mail:** admit@lambuth.edu **CEEB Code:** 1394
Fax: 731-425-3496 **Web:** www.lambuth.edu **ACT Code:** 3974

This private school, which is affiliated with the Methodist Church, was founded in 1843. It has a 50-acre campus.

STUDENTS AND FACULTY

Enrollment: 888. **Student Body:** Male 44%, female 56%, out-of-state 21%, international 3% (20 countries represented). **Ethnic Representation:** African American 18%, Caucasian 79%, Hispanic 2%. **Retention and Graduation:** 61% freshmen return for sophomore year. 24% freshmen graduate within 4 years. 25% grads go on to further study within 1 year. 6% grads pursue business degrees. 5% grads pursue law degrees. 1% grads pursue medical degrees. **Faculty:** Student/faculty ratio 14:1. 52 full-time faculty, 76% hold PhDs. 100% faculty teach undergrads.

ACADEMICS

Degrees: Bachelor's. **Academic Requirements:** General education including some course work in arts/fine arts, computer literacy, English (including composition), history, humanities, mathematics, sciences (biological or physical), social science. **Classes:** 10-19 students in an average class. 20-29 students in an average lab/discussion section. **Majors with Highest Enrollment:** Business/commerce, general; teacher education and professional development, specific subject areas; social sciences. **Disciplines with Highest Percentage of Degrees Awarded:** Business/marketing 22%, education 17%, social sciences and history 10%, psychology 9%, biological life sciences 8%. **Special Study Options:** Accelerated program, cross registration, double major, English as a second language, honors program, independent study, internships, liberal arts/career combination, student-designed major, study abroad, teacher certification program.

FACILITIES

Housing: Coed, all-female, all-male, apartments for single students, housing for disabled students, fraternities and/or sororities. **Library Holdings:** 177,792 bound volumes. 56,927 periodicals. 175,328 microforms. 1,044 audiovisuals. **Special Academic Facilities/Equipment:** Learning enrichment center, interior design lab, planetarium, biological field station, curriculum lab, log cabin museum. **Computers:** School-owned computers available for student use.

EXTRACURRICULARS

Activities: Choral groups, concert band, dance, drama/theater, jazz band, literary magazine, music ensembles, musical theater, pep band, radio station, student government, student newspaper, yearbook. **Organizations:** 30 registered organizations, 6 honor societies, 3 religious organizations, 3 fraternities (30% men join), 4 sororities (29% women join). **Athletics (Intercollegiate):** *Men:* baseball, basketball, cheerleading, cross-country, football, golf, soccer, tennis. *Women:* basketball, cheerleading, cross-country, soccer, softball, tennis, volleyball.

ADMISSIONS

Selectivity Rating: 78 (of 100). **Freshman Academic Profile:** Average high school GPA 3.3. 24% in top 10% of high school class, 49% in top 25% of high school class, 82% in top 50% of high school class. 82% from public high schools. Average SAT I Math 500, SAT I Math middle 50% range 430-560. Average SAT I Verbal 500, SAT I Verbal middle 50% range 430-570. Average ACT 23, ACT middle 50% range 19-25. TOEFL required of all international applicants, minimum TOEFL 425. **Basis for Candidate Selection:** *Very important factors considered include:* secondary school record, standardized test scores. *Other factors considered include:* class rank, essays, extracurricular activities, recommendations. **Freshman Admission Requirements:** High school diploma or GED is required. *Academic units required/recommended:* 4 English recommended, 4 math recommended, 3 science recommended, 2 science lab recommended, 2 foreign language recommended, 2 social studies recommended, 2 history recommended. **Freshman Admission Statistics:** 768 applied, 71% accepted, 36% of those accepted enrolled. **Transfer Admission Requirements:** *Items required:* college transcript, statement of good standing from prior school. Minimum high school GPA of 2.0 required. Minimum college GPA of 2.0 required. Lowest grade transferable D. **General Admission Information:** Application fee $25. Nonfall registration accepted. Admission may be deferred. Credit and/or placement offered for CEEB Advanced Placement tests.

COSTS AND FINANCIAL AID

Tuition $10,350. Room & board $4,930. Required fees $150. Average book expense $800. **Required Forms and Deadlines:** FAFSA, institution's own financial aid form, and admission application. No deadline for regular filing. Priority filing deadline February 1. **Notification of Awards:** Applicants will be notified of awards on a rolling basis beginning on or about December 15. **Types of Aid:** *Need-based scholarships/grants:* Pell, SEOG, state scholarships/grants, private scholarships, the school's own gift aid. *Loans:* FFEL Subsidized Stafford, FFEL Unsubsidized Stafford, FFEL PLUS, Federal Perkins. **Student Employment:** Federal Work-Study Program available. Institutional employment available. Off-campus job opportunities are excellent. **Financial Aid Statistics:** 70% freshmen, 64% undergrads receive some form of aid. Average freshman grant $5,200. Average freshman loan $2,231. Average income from on-campus job $1,000. **Financial Aid Phone:** 901-425-3332.

LANCASTER BIBLE COLLEGE

PO Box 83403, 901 Eden Rd., Lancaster, PA 17608
Phone: 717-560-8271 **E-mail:** admissions@lbc.edu **CEEB Code:** 2388
Fax: 717-560-8213 **Web:** www.lbc.edu **ACT Code:** 3707

This private school was founded in 1933. It has a 100-acre campus.

STUDENTS AND FACULTY

Enrollment: 757. **Student Body:** Male 45%, female 55%, out-of-state 29%, international 1%. **Ethnic Representation:** African American 3%, Asian 1%, Caucasian 94%, Hispanic 1%, Native American 1%. **Retention and Graduation:** 70% freshmen return for sophomore year. 22% freshmen graduate within 4 years. **Faculty:** Student/faculty ratio 15:1. 29 full-time faculty, 72% hold PhDs. 100% faculty teach undergrads.

ACADEMICS

Degrees: Associate's, bachelor's, certificate, master's, post-bachelor's certificate. **Academic Requirements:** General education including some course work in arts/fine arts, English (including composition), history, humanities, mathematics, philosophy, sciences (biological or physical), social science. **Classes:** Under 10 students in an average class. 10-19 students in an average lab/discussion section. **Majors with Highest Enrollment:** Elementary education and teaching; Bible/biblical studies. **Disciplines with Highest Percentage of Degrees Awarded:** Philosophy/religion/theology 92%, education 8%. **Special Study Options:** Accelerated program, double major, independent study, internships, study abroad, teacher certification program.

FACILITIES

Housing: All-female, all-male. **Library Holdings:** 122,993 bound volumes. 5,539 periodicals. 27,846 microforms. 4,385 audiovisuals. **Computers:** School-owned computers available for student use.

EXTRACURRICULARS

Activities: Choral groups, concert band, drama/theater, music ensembles, student government, student newspaper, yearbook. **Organizations:** 20 registered organizations. **Athletics (Intercollegiate):** *Men:* baseball, basketball, soccer, volleyball. *Women:* basketball, cheerleading, lacrosse, soccer, volleyball.

ADMISSIONS

Selectivity Rating: 69 (of 100). **Freshman Academic Profile:** Average high school GPA 3.3. 15% in top 10% of high school class, 32% in top 25% of high school class, 65% in top 50% of high school class. Average SAT I Math 480, SAT I Math middle 50% range 410-530. Average SAT I Verbal 520, SAT I Verbal middle 50% range 470-570. Average ACT 20, ACT middle 50% range 19-22. TOEFL required of all international applicants, minimum TOEFL 550. **Basis for Candidate Selection:** *Very important factors considered include:* character/personal qualities, essays, recommendations, religious affiliation/commitment, secondary school record, standardized test scores. *Other factors considered include:* class rank. **Freshman Admission Requirements:** High school diploma or GED is required. **Freshman Admission Statistics:** 235 applied, 80% accepted, 70% of those accepted enrolled. **Transfer Admission Requirements:** *Items required:* high school transcript, college transcript, essay, standardized test scores, statement of good standing from prior school. Minimum high school GPA of 2.0 required. Minimum college GPA of 2.0 required. Lowest grade transferable C. **General Admission Information:** Application fee $25. Priority application deadline August 1. Nonfall registration accepted. Admission may be deferred for a maximum of 1 year.

COSTS AND FINANCIAL AID

Tuition $10,560. Room & board $5,010. Required fees $215. Average book expense $700. **Required Forms and Deadlines:** FAFSA, institution's own financial aid form, and state aid form. No deadline for regular filing. Priority filing deadline May 2. **Notification of Awards:** Applicants will be notified of awards on a rolling basis beginning on or about March 15. **Types of Aid:** *Need-based scholarships/grants:* Pell, SEOG, state scholarships/grants, private scholarships, the school's own gift aid, office of vocational rehabilitation blindness, visual services awards. *Loans:* FFEL Subsidized Stafford, FFEL Unsubsidized Stafford, FFEL PLUS, Federal Perkins, alternative loans. **Student Employment:** Federal Work-Study Program available. Institutional employment available. Off-campus job opportunities are excellent. **Financial Aid Statistics:** 77% freshmen, 73% undergrads receive some form of aid. Average freshman grant $3,005. Average freshman loan $5,227. Average income from on-campus job $1,400. **Financial Aid Phone:** 717-560-8254.

LANDER UNIVERSITY

320 Stanley Avenue, Greenwood, SC 29649
Phone: 864-388-8307 **E-mail:** admissions@lander.edu **CEEB Code:** 5363
Fax: 864-388-8125 **Web:** www.lander.edu **ACT Code:** 3860

This public school was founded in 1872. It has a 100-acre campus.

STUDENTS AND FACULTY

Enrollment: 2,613. **Student Body:** Male 38%, female 62%, out-of-state 6%, international 2% (22 countries represented). **Ethnic Representation:** African American 20%, Caucasian 78%, Hispanic 1%. **Retention and Graduation:** 67% freshmen return for sophomore year. 31% freshmen graduate within 4 years. **Faculty:** Student/faculty ratio 17:1. 114 full-time faculty, 79% hold PhDs. 98% faculty teach undergrads.

ACADEMICS

Degrees: Bachelor's, certificate, master's. **Academic Requirements:** General education including some course work in arts/fine arts, English (including composition), foreign languages, history, humanities, mathematics, sciences (biological or physical), social science. **Classes:** 20-29 students in an average class. **Majors with Highest Enrollment:** Business administration/management; elementary education and teaching; early childhood education and teaching. **Disciplines with Highest Percentage of Degrees Awarded:** Business/marketing 28%, education 16%, social sciences and history 12%, psychology 11%, health professions and related sciences 9%. **Special Study Options:** Cooperative (work-study) program, distance learning, double major, dual enrollment, honors program, independent study, internships, student-designed major, study abroad, teacher certification program, nursing (RN to BSN completion) program courses now offered on the web, MBA from Clemson University offered on campus, MEd counseling/school administration and MEd elementary education, Master of Art in Teaching from Clemson University offered on campus, dual degree in engineering offered in conjunction with Clemson University.

FACILITIES

Housing: Coed, all-female, apartments for single students. **Library Holdings:** 170,091 bound volumes. 692 periodicals. 141,945 microforms. 2,170 audiovisuals. **Special Academic Facilities/Equipment:** Art gallery, continuing education center, media center, electronic piano instruction facility, amphitheater. **Computers:** *Recommended operating system:* Windows NT/2000. School-owned computers available for student use.

EXTRACURRICULARS

Activities: Choral groups, concert band, dance, drama/theater, jazz band, literary magazine, music ensembles, student government, student newspaper. **Organizations:** 65 registered organizations, 7 honor societies, 7 religious organizations, 6 fraternities (11% men join), 6 sororities (12% women join). **Athletics (Intercollegiate):** *Men:* baseball, basketball, soccer, tennis. *Women:* basketball, cross-country, soccer, softball, volleyball.

ADMISSIONS

Selectivity Rating: 73 (of 100). **Freshman Academic Profile:** Average high school GPA 3.5. 8% in top 10% of high school class, 34% in top 25% of high school class, 77% in top 50% of high school class. Average SAT I Math 492, SAT I Math middle 50% range 440-540. Average SAT I Verbal 484, SAT I Verbal middle 50% range 430-530. Average ACT 20, ACT middle 50% range 18-23. TOEFL required of all international applicants, minimum TOEFL 550. **Basis for Candidate Selection:** *Very important factors considered include:* class rank, secondary school record, standardized test scores. *Other factors considered include:* alumni/ae relation, character/personal qualities, essays, extracurricular activities, interview, recommendations, talent/ability, volunteer work, work experience. **Freshman Admission Requirements:** High school diploma or GED is required. *Academic units required/recommended:* 20 total required; 20 total recommended; 4 English required, 4 English recommended, 3 math required, 3 math recommended, 3 science required, 3 science recommended, 3 science lab required, 3 science lab recommended, 2 foreign language required, 2 foreign language recommended, 2 social studies required, 2 social studies recommended, 1 history required, 1 history recommended, 4 elective required, 4 elective recommended. **Freshman Admission Statistics:** 1,603 applied, 81% accepted, 41% of those accepted enrolled. **Transfer Admission Requirements:** *Items required:* college transcript, statement of good standing from prior school. Minimum college GPA of 2.0 required. Lowest grade transferable C. **General Admission Information:** Application fee $25. Regular application deadline August 4. Nonfall registration accepted. Admission may be deferred. Credit and/or placement offered for CEEB Advanced Placement tests.

COSTS AND FINANCIAL AID

In-state tuition $4,704. Out-of-state tuition $9,648. Room & board $4,548. Required fees $100. Average book expense $824. **Required Forms and Deadlines:** FAFSA. No deadline for regular filing. Priority filing deadline April 15. **Notification of Awards:** Applicants will be notified of awards on or about June 1. **Types of Aid:** *Need-based scholarships/grants:* Pell, SEOG, state scholarships/grants, the school's own gift aid, Federal Nursing. *Loans:* FFEL Subsidized Stafford, FFEL Unsubsidized Stafford, FFEL PLUS, Federal Perkins, state loans. **Student Employment:** Federal Work-Study Program available. Institutional employment available. Off-campus job opportunities are good. **Financial Aid Statistics:** 48% freshmen, 54% undergrads receive some form of aid. Average freshman grant $4,430. Average freshman loan $2,030. Average income from on-campus job $1,350. **Financial Aid Phone:** 864-388-8340.

LANE COLLEGE

545 Lane Avenue, Jackson, TN 38301
Phone: 731-426-7532 **E-mail:** admissions@lanecollege.edu
Fax: 731-426-7559 **Web:** www.lanecollege.edu **ACT Code:** 3976

This private school, which is affiliated with the Methodist Church, was founded in 1882. It has a 25-acre campus.

STUDENTS AND FACULTY

Enrollment: 813. **Student Body:** Male 49%, female 51%, out-of-state 41%. **Ethnic Representation:** African American 100%. **Retention and Graduation:** 63% freshmen return for sophomore year. 20% freshmen graduate within 4 years. 52% grads go on to further study within 1 year. 2% grads pursue business degrees. 3% grads pursue law degrees. 5% grads pursue medical degrees. **Faculty:** Student/faculty ratio 18:1. 45 full-time faculty, 71% hold PhDs. 100% faculty teach undergrads.

ACADEMICS

Degrees: Bachelor's. **Academic Requirements:** General education including some course work in arts/fine arts, computer literacy, English (including composition), foreign languages, history, mathematics, sciences (biological or physical), social science, religion. **Classes:** 20-29 students in an average class. **Majors with Highest Enrollment:** Computer science; biology/biological sciences, general; criminal justice/law enforcement administration. **Disciplines with Highest Percentage of Degrees Awarded:** Interdisciplinary studies 18%, protective services/public administration 17%, social sciences and history 15%, biological life sciences 14%, computer and information sciences 10%. **Special Study Options:** Accelerated program, internships, study abroad, teacher certification program.

FACILITIES

Housing: All-female, all-male. **Library Holdings:** 196,759 bound volumes. 612 periodicals. 53,125 microforms. 1,874 audiovisuals. **Special Academic Facilities/Equipment:** Student center annex, recreational center. **Computers:** School-owned computers available for student use.

EXTRACURRICULARS

Activities: Choral groups, concert band, dance, drama/theater, marching band, music ensembles, pep band, student government, student newspaper, yearbook. **Organizations:** 21 registered organizations, 6 honor societies, 4 religious organizations, 2 fraternities (1% men join), 4 sororities (5% women join). **Athletics (Intercollegiate):** *Men:* baseball, basketball, cross-country, football, track & field. *Women:* basketball, cross-country, softball, track & field, volleyball.

ADMISSIONS

Selectivity Rating: 73 (of 100). **Freshman Academic Profile:** Average high school GPA 2.5. 28% in top 10% of high school class, 53% in top 25% of high school class, 65% in top 50% of high school class. 96% from public high schools. Average ACT 15, ACT middle 50% range 14-17. TOEFL required of all international applicants, minimum TOEFL 339. **Basis for Candidate Selection:** *Very important factors considered include:* character/personal qualities, recommendations, secondary school record. *Important factors considered include:* extracurricular activities, standardized test scores, talent/ability. *Other factors considered include:* alumni/ae relation, class rank, interview. **Freshman Admission Requirements:** High school diploma or GED is required. *Academic units required/recommended:* 16 total required; 4 English required, 2 math required, 2 science required, 1 science lab required, 2 foreign language recommended, 2 social studies required, 2 history required. **Freshman Admission Statistics:** 2,188 applied, 36% accepted, 38% of those accepted enrolled. **Transfer Admission Requirements:** *Items required:* college transcript, standardized test scores, statement of good standing from prior school. Minimum college GPA of 2.0 required. Lowest grade transferable C. **General Admission Information:** Priority application deadline July 1. Early decision application deadline August 1. Regular application deadline August 1. Nonfall registration accepted. Admission may be deferred. Credit offered for CEEB Advanced Placement tests.

COSTS AND FINANCIAL AID

Tuition $6,020. Room & board $4,080. Required fees $550. Average book expense $550. **Required Forms and Deadlines:** FAFSA. No deadline for regular filing. Priority filing deadline April 1. **Notification of Awards:** Applicants will be notified of awards on a rolling basis beginning on or about March 31. **Types of Aid:** *Need-based scholarships/grants:* Pell, SEOG, state scholarships/grants, private scholarships, the school's own gift aid, United Negro College Fund. *Loans:* Direct Subsidized Stafford, Direct Unsubsidized Stafford, Direct PLUS. **Student Employment:** Federal Work-Study Program available. Off-campus job opportunities are excellent. **Financial Aid Statistics:** 93% freshmen, 94% undergrads receive some form of aid. Average freshman grant $8,631. Average freshman loan $2,424. **Financial Aid Phone:** 731-426-7535.

LANGSTON UNIVERSITY

PO Box 728, Langston, OK 73050
Phone: 405-466-2231 **E-mail:** admission@speedy.lunet.edu **CEEB Code:** 6361
Fax: 405-466-3381 **Web:** www.lunet.edu **ACT Code:** 3400

This public school was founded in 1897. It has a 40-acre campus.

STUDENTS AND FACULTY

Enrollment: 3,864. **Student Body:** Out-of-state 20%, international 4%. **Ethnic Representation:** African American 54%, Asian 1%, Caucasian 44%, Hispanic 1%.

ACADEMICS

Degrees: Associate's, bachelor's, master's.

FACILITIES

Housing: Coed, all-female, all-male, apartments for married students. **Library Holdings:** 160,000 bound volumes. 680 periodicals. 3,175 microforms. **Computers:** *Recommended operating system:* Mac. School-owned computers available for student use.

EXTRACURRICULARS

Organizations: 9 honor societies, 3 religious organizations, 4 fraternities (10% men join), 4 sororities (15% women join). **Athletics (Intercollegiate):** *Men:* basketball, cheerleading, cross-country, football, track & field. *Women:* basketball, cheerleading, cross-country, track & field.

ADMISSIONS

Selectivity Rating: 63 (of 100). **Freshman Academic Profile:** 90% from public high schools. **Freshman Admission Requirements:** High school diploma is required and GED is not accepted. *Academic units required/recommended:* 11 total required; 4 English required, 3 math required, 2 science required, 2 history required. **Transfer Admission Requirements:** Minimum college GPA of 2.0 required. Lowest grade transferable D. **General Admission Information:** Regular application deadline August 1.

COSTS AND FINANCIAL AID

In-state tuition $4,700. Out-of-state tuition $7,000. Room & board $2,944. Required fees $1,057. Average book expense $450. **Required Forms and Deadlines:** FAFSA and institution's own financial aid form. **Notification of Awards:** Applicants will be notified of awards on or about July 15. **Types of Aid:** *Need-based scholarships/grants:* Pell, SEOG, state scholarships/grants, private scholarships, the school's own gift aid. *Loans:* FFEL Subsidized Stafford, FFEL Unsubsidized Stafford, FFEL PLUS, Federal Perkins, college/university loans from institutional funds. **Student Employment:** Institutional employment available. Off-campus job opportunities are poor. **Financial Aid Statistics:** Average freshman grant $1,313. Average freshman loan $932. **Financial Aid Phone:** 405-466-3282.

LAROCHE COLLEGE

9000 Babcock Boulevard, Pittsburgh, PA 15237
Phone: 412-536-1271 **E-mail:** admsns@laroche.edu **CEEB Code:** 2379
Fax: 412-536-1048 **Web:** www.laroche.edu **ACT Code:** 3607

This private school, which is affiliated with the Roman Catholic Church, was founded in 1963. It has an 80-acre campus.

STUDENTS AND FACULTY

Enrollment: 1,760. **Student Body:** Male 37%, female 63%, out-of-state 5%, international 18%. **Ethnic Representation:** African American 4%, Asian 1%, Caucasian 94%, Hispanic 1%. **Retention and Graduation:** 73% freshmen return for sophomore year. 38% freshmen graduate within 4 years. **Faculty:** Student/faculty ratio 14:1. 66 full-time faculty, 80% hold PhDs. 100% faculty teach undergrads.

ACADEMICS

Degrees: Associate's, bachelor's, certificate, master's, terminal. **Academic Requirements:** General education including some course work in arts/fine arts, computer literacy, English (including composition), foreign languages, history, humanities, mathematics, philosophy, sciences (biological or physical), social science. **Classes:** 10-19 students in an average class. 10-19 students in an average lab/discussion section. **Majors with Highest Enrollment:** Business administration/management; design and visual communications, general; elementary education and teaching. **Disciplines with Highest Percentage of Degrees Awarded:** Business/marketing 21%, visual and performing arts 15%, education 11%, psychology 10%, communications/communication technologies 9%. **Special Study Options:** Accelerated program, cross registration, distance learning, double major, English as a second language, honors program, independent study, internships, study abroad, teacher certification program.

FACILITIES

Housing: Coed. **Library Holdings:** 90,241 bound volumes. 601 periodicals. 30,000 microforms. 988 audiovisuals. **Special Academic Facilities/Equipment:** Cantellopes Art Gallery; new college center extension has state-of-the-art smart classrooms. **Computers:** School-owned computers available for student use.

EXTRACURRICULARS

Activities: Choral groups, dance, drama/theater, literary magazine, musical theater, radio station, student government, student newspaper. **Organizations:** 31 registered organizations, 4 honor societies, 1 religious organization. **Athletics (Intercollegiate):** *Men:* baseball, basketball, cross-country, golf, soccer. *Women:* basketball, cheerleading, cross-country, soccer, softball, tennis, volleyball.

ADMISSIONS

Selectivity Rating: 63 (of 100). **Freshman Academic Profile:** Average high school GPA 2.7. 2% in top 10% of high school class, 15% in top 25% of high school class, 44% in top 50% of high school class. 79% from public high schools. Average SAT I Math 460, SAT I Math middle 50% range 400-510. Average SAT I Verbal 520, SAT I Verbal middle 50% range 420-520. ACT middle 50% range 16-21. TOEFL required of all international applicants, minimum TOEFL 550. **Basis for Candidate Selection:** *Very important factors considered include:* character/personal qualities, essays, interview, recommendations, secondary school record, standardized test scores. *Important factors considered include:* extracurricular activities, talent/ability. *Other factors considered include:* volunteer work, work experience. **Freshman Admission Requirements:** High school diploma or GED is required. *Academic units required/recommended:* 15 total required; 22 total recommended; 3 English required, 4 English recommended, 3 math required, 4 math recommended, 3 science required, 4 science recommended, 2 foreign language recommended, 3 social studies required, 4 social studies recommended, 3 history required, 4 history recommended. **Freshman Admission Statistics:** 637 applied, 77% accepted, 60% of those accepted enrolled. **Transfer Admission Requirements:** *Items required:* college transcript. Minimum college GPA of 2.0 required. Lowest grade transferable C. **General Admission Information:** Application fee $35. Priority application deadline May 1. Regular application deadline August 26. Nonfall registration accepted. Admission may be deferred for a maximum of 1 year. Credit and/or placement offered for CEEB Advanced Placement tests.

COSTS AND FINANCIAL AID

Tuition $12,790. Room & board $6,474. Required fees $400. Average book expense $800. **Required Forms and Deadlines:** FAFSA, institution's own financial aid form, and state aid form. Financial aid filing deadline May 1. Priority filing deadline March 1. **Notification of Awards:** Applicants will be notified of awards on a rolling basis beginning on or about March 1. **Types of Aid:** *Need-based scholarships/grants:* Pell, SEOG, state scholarships/grants, private scholarships, the school's own gift aid. *Loans:* FFEL Subsidized Stafford, FFEL Unsubsidized Stafford, FFEL PLUS, Federal Perkins, state loans. **Student Employment:** Federal Work-Study Program available. Off-campus job opportunities are excellent. **Financial Aid Statistics:** 62% freshmen, 56% undergrads receive some form of aid. Average freshman grant $6,800. Average freshman loan $2,625. **Financial Aid Phone:** 412-536-1120.

LASALLE UNIVERSITY

 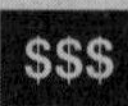  

1900 West Olney Avenue, Philadelphia, PA 19141-1199
Phone: 215-951-1500 **E-mail:** admiss@lasalle.edu **CEEB Code:** 2363
Fax: 215-951-1656 **Web:** www.lasalle.edu **ACT Code:** 3608

This private school, which is affiliated with the Roman Catholic Church, was founded in 1863. It has a 120-acre campus.

STUDENTS AND FACULTY

Enrollment: 4,080. **Student Body:** Male 43%, female 57%, out-of-state 30%, international 1% (16 countries represented). **Ethnic Representation:** African American 11%, Asian 2%, Caucasian 77%, Hispanic 6%. **Retention and Graduation:** 87% freshmen return for sophomore year. 56% freshmen graduate within 4 years. 20% grads go on to further study within 1 year. 3% grads pursue business degrees. 5% grads pursue law degrees. 3% grads pursue medical degrees. **Faculty:** Student/faculty ratio 17:1. 197 full-time faculty, 80% hold PhDs. 100% faculty teach undergrads.

ACADEMICS

Degrees: Associate's, bachelor's, doctoral, master's. **Academic Requirements:** General education including some course work in arts/fine arts, computer literacy, English (including composition), foreign languages, history, humanities, mathematics, philosophy, sciences (biological or physical), social science, religion. **Classes:** 20-29 students in an average class. Under 10 students in an average lab/discussion section. **Majors with Highest Enrollment:** Communications, journalism, and related fields; education, general; biology/biological sciences, general. **Disciplines with Highest Percentage of Degrees Awarded:** Business/marketing 27%, communications/communication technologies 12%, education 9%, health professions and related sciences 8%, other 7%. **Special Study Options:** Accelerated program, cooperative (work-study) program, cross registration, double major, dual enrollment, student exchange program (domestic), honors program, independent study, internships, student-designed major, study abroad, teacher certification program, 2+2 with Thomas Jefferson University.

FACILITIES

Housing: Coed, apartments for single students, fraternities and/or sororities. **Library Holdings:** 421,953 bound volumes. 1,721 periodicals. 333,857 microforms. 21,253 audiovisuals. **Special Academic Facilities/Equipment:** Art museum, Japanese tea house, language lab, child development center, urban studies center. **Computers:** *Recommended operating system:* Windows NT/2000.

EXTRACURRICULARS

Activities: Choral groups, concert band, drama/theater, jazz band, literary magazine, music ensembles, musical theater, pep band, radio station, student government, student newspaper, student-run film society, television station, yearbook. **Organizations:** 90 registered organizations, 10 honor societies, 4 religious organizations, 6 fraternities (10% men join), 5 sororities (10% women join). **Athletics (Intercollegiate):** *Men:* baseball, basketball, cheerleading, crew, cross-country, diving, football, golf, soccer, swimming, tennis, track & field, wrestling. *Women:* basketball, cheerleading, crew, cross-country, diving, field hockey, golf, lacrosse, soccer, softball, swimming, tennis, track & field, volleyball.

ADMISSIONS

Selectivity Rating: 81 (of 100). **Freshman Academic Profile:** Average high school GPA 3.1. 25% in top 10% of high school class, 55% in top 25% of high school class, 86% in top 50% of high school class. 35% from public high schools. Average SAT I Math 542, SAT I Math middle 50% range 490-590. Average SAT I Verbal 549, SAT I Verbal middle 50% range 490-600. Average ACT 26, ACT middle 50% range 22-26. TOEFL required of all international applicants, minimum TOEFL 500. **Basis for Candidate Selection:** *Very important factors considered include:* secondary school record. *Important factors considered include:* class rank, essays, standardized test scores. *Other factors considered include:* alumni/ae relation, character/personal qualities, extracurricular activities, interview, recommendations, talent/ability, volunteer work, work experience. **Freshman Admission Requirements:** High school diploma or GED is required. *Academic units required/recommended:* 16 total required; 4 English required, 3 math required, 1 science required, 1 science lab required, 2 foreign language required, 1 history required, 5 elective required. **Freshman Admission Statistics:** 4,261 applied, 77% accepted, 26% of those accepted enrolled. **Transfer Admission Requirements:** *Items required:* high school transcript, college transcript, essay, standardized test scores, statement of good standing from prior school. Minimum college GPA of 2.5 required. Lowest grade transferable C. **General Admission Information:** Application fee $35. Priority application deadline March 1. Regular application deadline April 1. Nonfall registration accepted. Admission may be deferred. Neither credit nor placement offered for CEEB Advanced Placement tests.

COSTS AND FINANCIAL AID

Tuition $21,270. Room & board $7,810. Required fees $150. Average book expense $500. **Required Forms and Deadlines:** FAFSA. Priority filing deadline February 15. **Notification of Awards:** Applicants will be notified of awards on a rolling basis beginning on or about November 15. **Types of Aid:** *Need-based scholarships/grants:* Pell, SEOG, state scholarships/grants, private scholarships, the school's own gift aid. *Loans:* FFEL Subsidized Stafford, FFEL Unsubsidized Stafford, FFEL PLUS, Federal Perkins. **Student Employment:** Federal Work-Study Program available. Institutional employment available. Off-campus job opportunities are good. **Financial Aid Statistics:** 78% freshmen, 75% undergrads receive some form of aid. Average freshman grant $12,293. Average freshman loan $2,799. **Financial Aid Phone:** 215-951-1070.

LASELL COLLEGE

Office of Admissions, 1844 Commonwealth Avenue, Newton, MA 02466
Phone: 617-243-2225 **E-mail:** info@lasell.edu **CEEB Code:** 3481
Fax: 617-796-4343 **Web:** www.lasell.edu **ACT Code:** 1848

This private school was founded in 1851. It has a 50-acre campus.

STUDENTS AND FACULTY

Enrollment: 841. **Student Body:** Male 24%, female 76%, out-of-state 50%, international 3%. **Ethnic Representation:** African American 12%, Asian 4%, Caucasian 74%, Hispanic 6%. **Retention and Graduation:** 73% freshmen return for sophomore year. 18% grads go on to further study within 1 year. 5% grads pursue business degrees. **Faculty:** Student/faculty ratio 10:1. 45 full-time faculty, 40% hold PhDs. 100% faculty teach undergrads.

ACADEMICS

Degrees: Associate's, bachelor's. **Academic Requirements:** General education including some course work in computer literacy, English (including composition), foreign languages, history, humanities, mathematics, sciences (biological or physical), social science. **Classes:** 10-19 students in an average class. Under 10 students in an average lab/discussion section. **Disciplines with Highest Percentage of Degrees Awarded:** Business/marketing 49%, health professions and related sciences 21%, education 17%, social sciences and history 11%, psychology 1%. **Special Study Options:** Cooperative (work-study) program, double major, English as a second language, honors program, independent study, internships, liberal arts/career combination, study abroad.

FACILITIES

Housing: Coed, all-female, special-interest (human services). Some houses alcohol free. All houses smoke free. **Library Holdings:** 55,302 bound volumes. 478 periodicals. 45,089 microforms. 1,594 audiovisuals. **Special Academic Facilities/Equipment:** Center for public service, Yamawaki Art/Cultural Center. **Computers:** *Recommended operating system:* Windows 95. School-owned computers available for student use.

EXTRACURRICULARS

Activities: Choral groups, dance, drama/theater, student government, student newspaper, yearbook. **Organizations:** 20 registered organizations, 1 honor society, 1 religious organization. **Athletics (Intercollegiate):** *Men:* basketball, cross-country, lacrosse, soccer, volleyball. *Women:* basketball, cross-country, field hockey, lacrosse, soccer, softball, volleyball.

ADMISSIONS

Selectivity Rating: 63 (of 100). **Freshman Academic Profile:** Average high school GPA 2.4. 6% in top 10% of high school class, 32% in top 25% of high school class, 79% in top 50% of high school class. 90% from public high schools. Average SAT I Math 445, SAT I Math middle 50% range 400-490. Average SAT I Verbal 460, SAT I Verbal middle 50% range 410-500. Average ACT 18. TOEFL required of all international applicants, minimum TOEFL 500. **Basis for Candidate Selection:** *Very important factors considered include:* recommendations, secondary school record. *Important factors considered include:* class rank, extracurricular activities, interview, standardized test scores. *Other factors considered include:* alumni/ae relation, character/personal qualities, essays, talent/ability, volunteer work, work experience. **Freshman Admission Requirements:** High school diploma or GED is required. *Academic units required/recommended:* 16 total recommended; 4 English recommended, 3 math recommended, 3 science recommended, 2 science lab recommended, 2 foreign language recommended, 4 social studies recommended. **Freshman Admission Statistics:** 1,801 applied, 79% accepted, 21% of those accepted enrolled. **Transfer Admission Requirements:** *Items required:* high school transcript, college transcript, standardized test scores, statement of good standing from prior school. Minimum high school GPA of 2.0 required. Minimum college GPA of 2.3 required. Lowest grade transferable C. **General Admission Information:** Application fee $25. Priority application deadline April 1. Nonfall registration accepted. Admission may be deferred for a maximum of 1 year. Credit offered for CEEB Advanced Placement tests.

COSTS AND FINANCIAL AID

Tuition $14,700. Room & board $7,700. Required fees $800. Average book expense $600. **Required Forms and Deadlines:** FAFSA and institution's own financial aid form. No deadline for regular filing. Priority filing deadline April 1. **Notification of Awards:** Applicants will be notified of awards on a rolling basis beginning on or about February 15. **Types of Aid:** *Need-based scholarships/grants:* Pell, SEOG, state scholarships/grants, private scholarships, the school's own gift aid. *Loans:* FFEL Subsidized Stafford, FFEL Unsubsidized Stafford, FFEL PLUS, Federal Perkins, state loans. **Student Employment:** Federal Work-Study Program available. Institutional employment available. Off-campus job opportunities are excellent. **Financial Aid Statistics:** 84% freshmen, 88% undergrads receive some form of aid. Average freshman grant $5,500. Average freshman loan $2,625. Average income from on-campus job $700. **Financial Aid Phone:** 617-243-2227.

LAURA AND ALVIN SIEGAL COLLEGE OF JUDAIC STUDIES

26500 Shaker Boulevard, Beachwood, OH 44122-7116
Phone: 216-464-4050 **E-mail:** admissions@siegalcollege.edu
Fax: 216-464-5827 **Web:** www.siegalcollege.edu

This private school, which is affiliated with the Jewish Church, was founded in 1963.

STUDENTS AND FACULTY

Enrollment: 15. **Ethnic Representation:** Caucasian 100%. **Retention and Graduation:** 100% freshmen return for sophomore year. **Faculty:** Student/faculty ratio 8:1. 12 full-time faculty, 83% hold PhDs. 80% faculty teach undergrads.

ACADEMICS

Degrees: Bachelor's, master's. **Academic Requirements:** General education including some course work in arts/fine arts, English (including composition), foreign languages, history, humanities, sciences (biological or physical). **Special Study Options:** Distance learning, double major, independent study, internships.

FACILITIES

Library Holdings: 30,000 bound volumes. 50 periodicals. 0 microforms. 15 audiovisuals. **Computers:** School-owned computers available for student use.

EXTRACURRICULARS

Organizations: 1 registered organization.

ADMISSIONS

Selectivity Rating: 63 (of 100). **Basis for Candidate Selection:** *Important factors considered include:* essays, interview, recommendations. *Other factors considered include:* character/personal qualities, secondary school record, standardized test scores. **Freshman Admission Requirements:** High school diploma or GED is required. **Freshman Admission Statistics:** 5 applied, 60% accepted, 100% of those accepted enrolled. **Transfer Admission Requirements:** *Items required:* college transcript, essay, interview. Minimum college GPA of 2.7 required. Lowest grade transferable C. **General Admission Information:** Application fee $50. Nonfall registration accepted. Admission may be deferred for a maximum of 1 year.

COSTS AND FINANCIAL AID

Tuition $9,750. Required fees $25. Average book expense $300. **Required Forms and Deadlines:** Institution's own financial aid form. No deadline for regular filing. **Notification of Awards:** Applicants will be notified of awards on a rolling basis beginning on or about September 2. **Types of Aid:** *Need-based scholarships/grants:* the school's own gift aid. **Student Employment:** Off-campus job opportunities are good. **Financial Aid Phone:** 216-464-4050.

LAURENTIAN UNIVERSITY

Ramsey Lake Road, Sudbury, ON P3E 2C6
Phone: 705-675-4843 **E-mail:** admissions@laurentian.ca
Fax: 705-675-4891 **Web:** www.laurentian.ca

This public school was founded in 1960. It has a 750-acre campus.

STUDENTS AND FACULTY

Enrollment: 5,657. **Student Body:** Male 34%, female 66%. **Faculty:** Student/faculty ratio 13:1. 286 full-time faculty, 80% hold PhDs.

ACADEMICS

Degrees: Bachelor's, certificate, diploma, first professional, master's. **Majors with Highest Enrollment:** Business/commerce, general; environmental science; kinesiotherapy/kinesiotherapist. **Special Study Options:** Cooperative (work-study) program, distance learning, double major, English as a second language, honors program, internships, study abroad, teacher certification program.

FACILITIES

Housing: Coed, apartments for married students, apartments for single students. **Library Holdings:** 454,801 bound volumes. 207,526 periodicals. 384,879 microforms. 80,358 audiovisuals.

EXTRACURRICULARS

Activities: Drama/theater, radio station, student newspaper. **Athletics (Intercollegiate):** *Men:* basketball, skiing (Nordic), soccer, swimming. *Women:* basketball, cross-country, skiing (Nordic), soccer, swimming.

ADMISSIONS

Selectivity Rating: 60 (of 100). **Freshman Academic Profile:** TOEFL required of all international applicants, minimum TOEFL 550.

COSTS AND FINANCIAL AID

Financial Aid Phone: 705-673-6578.

LAWRENCE TECHNOLOGICAL UNIVERSITY

21000 West Ten Mile Rd., Southfield, MI 48075-1058
Phone: 248-204-3160 **E-mail:** admissions@ltu.edu **CEEB Code:** 1399
Fax: 248-204-3188 **Web:** www.ltu.edu **ACT Code:** 2020

This private school was founded in 1932. It has a 115-acre campus.

STUDENTS AND FACULTY

Enrollment: 2,806. **Student Body:** Male 74%, female 26%, international 1%. **Ethnic Representation:** African American 12%, Asian 6%, Caucasian 57%, Hispanic 1%, Native American 1%. **Retention and Graduation:** 71% freshmen return for sophomore year. **Faculty:** Student/faculty ratio 13:1. 103 full-time faculty, 77% hold PhDs. 100% faculty teach undergrads.

ACADEMICS

Degrees: Associate's, bachelor's, doctoral, master's. **Academic Requirements:** General education including some course work in computer literacy, English (including composition), history, humanities, mathematics, sciences (biological or physical), social science. **Classes:** 10-19 students in an average class. 10-19 students in an average lab/discussion section. **Majors with Highest Enrollment:** Architecture (BArch, BA/BS, MArch, MA/MS, PhD); computer and information sciences, general; mechanical engineering. **Disciplines with Highest Percentage of Degrees Awarded:** Engineering/engineering technology 60%, architecture 24%, other 9%, computer and information sciences 4%, communications/communication technologies 1%. **Special Study Options:** Cooperative (work-study) program, cross registration, distance learning, double major, dual enrollment, English as a second language, independent study, internships, liberal arts/career combination, study abroad.

FACILITIES

Housing: Apartments for married students, apartments for single students, fraternities and/or sororities. **Library Holdings:** 110,250 bound volumes. 700 periodicals. 28,000 microforms. 420 audiovisuals. **Computers:** *Recommended operating system:* LINUX, Windows NT, Windows 2000, UNIX. School-owned computers available for student use.

EXTRACURRICULARS

Activities: Literary magazine, music ensembles, student government, student newspaper. **Organizations:** 38 registered organizations, 6 honor societies, 4 religious organizations, 5 fraternities (4% men join), 3 sororities (6% women join).

ADMISSIONS

Selectivity Rating: 74 (of 100). **Freshman Academic Profile:** Average high school GPA 3.1. 30% in top 10% of high school class, 67% in top 25% of high school class, 84% in top 50% of high school class. 65% from public high schools. Average ACT 23, ACT middle 50% range 19-26. TOEFL required of all international applicants, minimum TOEFL 550. **Basis for Candidate Selection:** *Very important factors considered include:* secondary school record, standardized test scores. *Other factors considered include:* essays, interview, recommendations. **Freshman Admission Requirements:** High school diploma or GED is required. *Academic units required/recommended:* 12 total required; 4 English required, 3 math required, 2 science required, 3 social studies required. **Freshman Admission Statistics:** 1,208 applied, 84% accepted, 42% of those accepted enrolled. **Transfer Admission Requirements:** *Items required:* high school transcript, college transcript, statement of good standing from prior school. Minimum high school GPA of 2.5 required. Minimum college GPA of 2.0 required. Lowest grade transferable C. **General Admission Information:** Application fee $30. Priority application deadline August 15. Nonfall registration accepted. Admission may be deferred for a maximum of 1 year. Credit and/or placement offered for CEEB Advanced Placement tests.

COSTS AND FINANCIAL AID

Tuition $13,050. Room & board $4,840. Required fees $240. Average book expense $1,069. **Required Forms and Deadlines:** FAFSA and state aid form. No deadline for regular filing. Priority filing deadline April 1. **Notification of Awards:** Applicants will be notified of awards on a rolling basis. **Types of Aid:** *Need-based scholarships/grants:* Pell, SEOG, state scholarships/grants, private scholarships, the school's own gift aid. *Loans:* FFEL Subsidized Stafford, FFEL Unsubsidized Stafford, FFEL PLUS, Federal Perkins, state loans, college/university loans from institutional funds, private alternative loans. **Student Employment:** Federal Work-Study Program available. Institutional employment available. Off-campus job opportunities are excellent. **Financial Aid Statistics:** Average freshman grant $4,800. Average freshman loan $2,500. Average income from on-campus job $2,625. **Financial Aid Phone:** 248-204-2120.

See page 1084.

LAWRENCE UNIVERSITY

PO Box 599, Appleton, WI 54912-0599
Phone: 920-832-6500 **E-mail:** excel@lawrence.edu **CEEB Code:** 1398
Fax: 920-832-6782 **Web:** www.lawrence.edu **ACT Code:** 4596

This private school was founded in 1847. It has an 84-acre campus.

STUDENTS AND FACULTY

Enrollment: 1,392. **Student Body:** Male 47%, female 53%, out-of-state 59%, international 10%. **Ethnic Representation:** African American 2%, Asian 2%, Caucasian 78%, Hispanic 3%, Native American 1%. **Retention and Graduation:** 93% freshmen return for sophomore year. 62% freshmen graduate within 4 years. 30% grads go on to further study within 1 year. 5% grads pursue business degrees. 15% grads pursue law degrees. 12% grads pursue medical degrees. **Faculty:** Student/faculty ratio 11:1. 137 full-time faculty, 90% hold PhDs. 100% faculty teach undergrads.

ACADEMICS

Degrees: Bachelor's. **Academic Requirements:** General education including some course work in arts/fine arts, English (including composition), foreign languages, history, humanities, mathematics, philosophy, sciences (biological or physical), social science. **Classes:** 10-19 students in an average class. **Majors with Highest Enrollment:** Biology/biological sciences, general; psychology, general; music performance, general. **Disciplines with Highest Percentage of Degrees Awarded:** Visual and performing arts 28%, social sciences and history 18%, interdisciplinary studies 10%, biological life sciences 9%, psychology 8%. **Special Study Options:** Double major, English as a second language, honors program, independent study, internships, student-designed major, study abroad, teacher certification program.

FACILITIES

Housing: Coed, all-female, apartments for married students, housing for international students, fraternities and/or sororities. All single students are required to live in university residence halls for 4 years. **Library Holdings:** 376,814 bound volumes. 1,500 periodicals. 104,000 microforms. 21,000 audiovisuals. **Special Academic Facilities/Equipment:** Art galleries, anthropology collection, 425-acre estate on Lake Michigan hosting retreats and seminars for students, electron microscope, laser physics lab, physics/computational graphics lab, nuclear magnetic resonance spectrometer. **Computers:** School-owned computers available for student use.

EXTRACURRICULARS

Activities: Choral groups, concert band, drama/theater, jazz band, literary magazine, music ensembles, musical theater, opera, pep band, radio station, student government, student newspaper, student-run film society, symphony orchestra, yearbook. **Organizations:** 120 registered organizations, 7 honor societies, 4 religious organizations, 5 fraternities (30% men join), 3 sororities (15% women join). **Athletics (Intercollegiate):** *Men:* baseball, basketball, cross-country, diving, fencing, football, golf, ice hockey, indoor track, soccer, swimming, tennis, track & field, wrestling. *Women:* basketball, cross-country, diving, fencing, golf, indoor track, soccer, softball, swimming, tennis, track & field, volleyball.

ADMISSIONS

Selectivity Rating: 86 (of 100). **Freshman Academic Profile:** Average high school GPA 3.5. 36% in top 10% of high school class, 73% in top 25% of high school class, 94% in top 50% of high school class. 81% from public high schools. Average SAT I Math 625, SAT I Math middle 50% range 560-670. Average SAT I Verbal 620, SAT I Verbal middle 50% range 560-690. Average ACT 27, ACT middle 50% range 24-30. TOEFL required of all international applicants, minimum TOEFL 575. **Basis for Candidate Selection:** *Very important factors considered include:* secondary school record. *Important factors considered include:* alumni/ae relation, class rank, essays, minority status, recommendations, standardized test scores, talent/ability. *Other factors considered include:* character/personal qualities, extracurricular activities, interview, volunteer work, work experience. **Freshman Admission Requirements:** High school diploma is required and GED is not accepted. *Academic units required/recommended:* 4 English recommended, 3 math recommended, 3 science recommended, 3 foreign language recommended, 2 social studies recommended, 2 history recommended. **Freshman Admission Statistics:** 1,812 applied, 68% accepted, 29% of those accepted enrolled. **Transfer Admission Requirements:** *Items required:* college transcript, essay, standardized test scores. Minimum college GPA of 2.7 required. Lowest grade transferable C. **General Admission Information:** Application fee $30. Early decision application deadline November 15. Regular application deadline January 15. Admission may be deferred for a maximum of 1 year. Credit and/or placement offered for CEEB Advanced Placement tests.

COSTS AND FINANCIAL AID

Tuition $23,487. Room & board $5,337. Required fees $180. Average book expense $555. **Required Forms and Deadlines:** FAFSA and institution's own financial aid form. Financial aid filing deadline March 15. Priority filing deadline March 1. **Notification of Awards:** Applicants will be notified of awards on or about April 15. **Types of Aid:** *Need-based scholarships/grants:* Pell, SEOG, state scholarships/grants, private scholarships, the school's own gift aid. *Loans:* Direct Subsidized Stafford, Direct Unsubsidized Stafford, Direct PLUS, Federal Perkins. **Student Employment:** Federal Work-Study Program available. Institutional employment available. Off-campus job opportunities are excellent. **Financial Aid Statistics:** 69% freshmen, 70% undergrads receive some form of aid. Average freshman grant $13,332. Average freshman loan $2,113. **Financial Aid Phone:** 920-832-6583.

LE MOYNE COLLEGE

1419 Salt Springs Rd., Syracuse, NY 13214-1399
Phone: 315-445-4300 **E-mail:** admission@lemoyne.edu **CEEB Code:** 2366
Fax: 315-445-4711 **Web:** www.lemoyne.edu **ACT Code:** 2790

This private school, which is affiliated with the Roman Catholic Church, was founded in 1946. It has a 151-acre campus.

STUDENTS AND FACULTY

Enrollment: 2,485. **Student Body:** Male 41%, female 59%, out-of-state 6%, international 1% (4 countries represented). **Ethnic Representation:** African American 4%, Asian 2%, Caucasian 84%, Hispanic 4%, Native American 1%. **Retention and Graduation:** 83% freshmen return for sophomore year. 71% freshmen graduate within 4 years. 24% grads go on to further study within 1 year. 1% grads pursue business degrees. 4% grads pursue law degrees. 2% grads pursue medical degrees. **Faculty:** Student/faculty ratio 13:1. 146 full-time faculty, 91% hold PhDs. 100% faculty teach undergrads.

ACADEMICS

Degrees: Bachelor's, master's, post-bachelor's certificate. **Academic Requirements:** General education including some course work in English (including composition), foreign languages, history, humanities, mathematics, philosophy, sciences (biological or physical), social science, religious studies. **Classes:** 20-29 students in an average class. 10-19 students in an average lab/discussion section. **Majors with Highest Enrollment:** Business administration/management; psychology, general; English language and literature, general. **Disciplines with Highest Percentage of Degrees Awarded:** Business/marketing 35%, psychology 21%, social sciences and history 20%, English 10%, biological life sciences 8%. **Special Study Options:** Accelerated program, double major, honors program, independent study, internships, study abroad, teacher certification program, physician assistant program leading to physician assistant certification.

FACILITIES

Housing: Coed, all-female, all-male, apartments for single students, housing for disabled students, living/learning communities. **Library Holdings:** 159,159 bound volumes. 1,448 periodicals. 557,198 microforms. 10,129 audiovisuals. **Special Academic Facilities/Equipment:** Art gallery, audiovisual center, electron microscopes, and academic support center. **Computers:** School-owned computers available for student use.

EXTRACURRICULARS

Activities: Choral groups, concert band, dance, drama/theater, jazz band, literary magazine, music ensembles, musical theater, pep band, radio station, student government, student newspaper, yearbook. **Organizations:** 70 registered organizations, 14 honor societies, 9 religious organizations. **Athletics (Intercollegiate):** *Men:* baseball, basketball, cross-country, diving, golf, lacrosse, soccer, swimming, tennis. *Women:* basketball, cross-country, diving, lacrosse, soccer, softball, swimming, tennis, volleyball.

ADMISSIONS

Selectivity Rating: 77 (of 100). **Freshman Academic Profile:** Average high school GPA 3.3. 22% in top 10% of high school class, 53% in top 25% of high school class, 89% in top 50% of high school class. 76% from public high schools. Average SAT I Math 560, SAT I Math middle 50% range 510-600. Average SAT I Verbal 550, SAT I Verbal middle 50% range 490-600. Average ACT 23, ACT middle 50% range 20-26. TOEFL required of all international applicants, minimum TOEFL 550. **Basis for Candidate Selection:** *Very important factors considered include:* class rank, secondary school record, standardized test scores. *Important factors considered include:* essays, extracurricular activities, interview, recommendations, talent/ability, work experience. *Other factors considered include:* alumni/ae relation, character/personal qualities, geographical residence, minority status, state residency, volunteer work. **Freshman Admission Requirements:** High school diploma or GED is required. *Academic units required/recommended:* 16 total required; 4 English required, 3 math required, 4 math recommended, 3 science required, 4 science recommended, 3 science lab recommended, 3 foreign language required, 3 social studies required, 4 social studies recommended. **Freshman Admission Statistics:** 2,667 applied, 74% accepted, 28% of those accepted enrolled. **Transfer Admission Requirements:** *Items required:* high school transcript, college transcript, essay, statement of good standing from prior school. Minimum college GPA of 2.6 required. Lowest grade transferable C-. **General Admission Information:** Application fee $35. Priority application deadline March 1. Early decision application deadline December 1. Nonfall registration accepted. Admission may be deferred for a maximum of 1 year. Credit and/or placement offered for CEEB Advanced Placement tests.

COSTS AND FINANCIAL AID

Tuition $17,410. Room & board $7,250. Required fees $500. Average book expense $550. **Required Forms and Deadlines:** FAFSA, institution's own financial aid form, and state aid form. Priority filing deadline February 1. **Notification of Awards:** Applicants will be notified of awards on or about March 15. **Types of Aid:** *Need-based scholarships/grants:* Pell, SEOG, state scholarships/grants, private scholarships, the school's own gift aid. *Loans:* FFEL Subsidized Stafford, FFEL Unsubsidized Stafford, FFEL PLUS, Federal Perkins. **Student Employment:** Federal Work-Study Program available. Institutional employment available. Off-campus job opportunities are excellent. **Financial Aid Statistics:** 81% freshmen, 79% undergrads receive some form of aid. Average freshman grant $11,573. Average freshman loan $3,356. Average income from on-campus job $1,125. **Financial Aid Phone:** 315-445-4400.

LEBANON VALLEY COLLEGE

101 North College Avenue, Anville, PA 17003-6100
Phone: 717-867-6181 **E-mail:** admission@lvc.edu **CEEB Code:** 2364
Fax: 717-867-6026 **Web:** www.lvc.edu **ACT Code:** 3610

This private school, which is affiliated with the Methodist Church, was founded in 1866. It has a 200-acre campus.

STUDENTS AND FACULTY

Enrollment: 1,879. **Student Body:** Male 41%, female 59%, international 0%. **Ethnic Representation:** African American 1%, Asian 1%, Caucasian 93%, Hispanic 2%. **Retention and Graduation:** 85% freshmen return for sophomore year. 64% freshmen graduate within 4 years. 10% grads go on to further study within 1 year. 1% grads pursue business degrees. 1% grads pursue law degrees. 1% grads pursue medical degrees. **Faculty:** Student/faculty ratio 14:1. 95 full-time faculty, 87% hold PhDs. 100% faculty teach undergrads.

ACADEMICS

Degrees: Associate's, bachelor's, certificate, master's, post-bachelor's certificate, terminal. **Academic Requirements:** General education including some course work in arts/fine arts, English (including composition), foreign languages, history, humanities, mathematics, philosophy, sciences (biological or physical), social science. **Classes:** 10-19 students in an average class. 10-19 students in an average lab/discussion section. **Majors with Highest Enrollment:** Business administration/management; education, general; psychology, general. **Disciplines with Highest Percentage of Degrees Awarded:** Business/marketing 26%, education 24%, social sciences and history 10%, visual and performing arts 10%, psychology 9%. **Special Study Options:** Cross registration, double major, dual enrollment, independent study, internships, student-designed major, study abroad, teacher certification program.

FACILITIES

Housing: Coed, all-female, all-male, apartments for single students, housing for disabled students, fraternities and/or sororities, interest housing, suite-style living, substance-free and clean-air halls. **Library Holdings:** 168,709 bound volumes. 800 periodicals. 11,756 microforms. 7,205 audiovisuals. **Special Academic Facilities/Equipment:** Electric pianos, sound recording studio, electron microscope, scanning electron microscope, Fourier transform infrared spectrometer, atomic absorption spectrophotometer, nuclear magnetic resonance spectrometer. **Computers:** *Recommended operating system:* Mac. School-owned computers available for student use.

EXTRACURRICULARS

Activities: Choral groups, concert band, drama/theater, jazz band, literary magazine, marching band, music ensembles, radio station, student government, student newspaper, symphony orchestra, yearbook. **Organizations:** 76 registered organizations, 6 honor societies, 9 religious organizations, 4 fraternities (16% men join), 3 sororities (12% women join). **Athletics (Intercollegiate):** *Men:* baseball, basketball, cross-country, football, golf, indoor hockey, soccer, swimming, tennis, track & field. *Women:* basketball, cross-country, field hockey, soccer, softball, swimming, tennis, track & field, volleyball.

ADMISSIONS

Selectivity Rating: 77 (of 100). **Freshman Academic Profile:** 29% in top 10% of high school class, 67% in top 25% of high school class, 93% in top 50% of high school class. 95% from public high schools. Average SAT I Math 547, SAT I Math middle 50% range 500-620. Average SAT I Verbal 547, SAT I Verbal middle 50% range 490-600. ACT middle 50% range 19-25. TOEFL required of all international applicants, minimum TOEFL 550. **Basis for Candidate Selection:** *Very important factors considered include:* class rank, secondary school record. *Important factors considered include:* character/personal qualities, extracurricular activities, interview, standardized test scores, talent/ability. *Other factors considered include:* alumni/ae relation, essays, geographical residence, minority status, recommendations, state residency, volunteer work, work experience. **Freshman Admission Requirements:** High school diploma or GED is required. *Academic units required/recommended:* 16 total required; 4 English required, 2 math required, 3 math recommended, 1 science required, 3 science recommended, 2 science lab recommended, 2 foreign language required, 3 foreign language recommended, 1 social studies required. **Freshman Admission Statistics:** 1,802 applied, 77% accepted, 31% of those accepted enrolled. **Transfer Admission Requirements:** *Items required:* high school transcript, college transcript, statement of good standing from prior school. Minimum college GPA of 2.0 required. Lowest grade transferable C-. **General Admission Information:** Application fee $25. Nonfall registration accepted. Credit offered for CEEB Advanced Placement tests.

COSTS AND FINANCIAL AID

Tuition $19,210. Room & board $5,890. Required fees $600. Average book expense $700. **Required Forms and Deadlines:** FAFSA and institution's own financial aid form. Priority filing deadline March 1. **Notification of Awards:** Applicants will be notified of awards on a rolling basis beginning on or about March 1. **Types of Aid:** *Need-based scholarships/grants:* Pell, SEOG, state scholarships/grants, private scholarships, the school's own gift aid. *Loans:* FFEL Subsidized Stafford, FFEL Unsubsidized Stafford, FFEL PLUS, Federal Perkins. **Student Employment:** Federal Work-Study Program available. Institutional employment available. Off-campus job opportunities are good. **Financial Aid Statistics:** 80% freshmen, 76% undergrads receive some form of aid. Average income from on-campus job $588. **Financial Aid Phone:** 866-582-4236.

LEE UNIVERSITY

PO Box 3450, Cleveland, TN 37320-3450
Phone: 423-614-8500 **E-mail:** admissions@leeuniversity.edu
Fax: 423-614-8533 **Web:** www.leeuniversity.edu **ACT Code:** 3978

This private school, which is affiliated with the Church of God, was founded in 1918. It has a 47-acre campus.

STUDENTS AND FACULTY

Enrollment: 3,487. **Student Body:** Male 43%, female 57%, out-of-state 63%, international 3%. **Ethnic Representation:** African American 3%, Asian 1%, Caucasian 86%, Hispanic 3%, Native American 1%. **Retention and Graduation:** 50% freshmen return for sophomore year. 24% freshmen graduate within 4 years. 20% grads go on to further study within 1 year. **Faculty:** Student/faculty ratio 18:1. 136 full-time faculty, 62% hold PhDs. 100% faculty teach undergrads.

ACADEMICS

Degrees: Bachelor's, master's. **Academic Requirements:** General education including some course work in arts/fine arts, computer literacy, English (including composition), foreign languages, history, humanities, mathematics, sciences (biological or physical), social science, religion. **Classes:** 10-19 students in an average class. 10-19 students in an average lab/discussion section. **Disciplines with Highest Percentage of Degrees Awarded:** Education 20%, philosophy/religion/theology 20%, business/marketing 12%, communications/communication technologies 11%, social sciences and history 10%. **Special Study Options:** Distance learning, double major, dual enrollment, English as a second language, student exchange program (domestic), external degree program, honors program, independent study, internships, liberal arts/career combination, study abroad, teacher certification program.

FACILITIES

Housing: All-female, all-male, apartments for married students, apartments for single students. Lee University leases apartments and houses for students. **Library Holdings:** 167,435 bound volumes. 1,444 periodicals. 53,700 microforms. 14,335 audiovisuals. **Computers:** School-owned computers available for student use.

EXTRACURRICULARS

Activities: Choral groups, concert band, drama/theater, jazz band, literary magazine, music ensembles, musical theater, opera, pep band, student government, student newspaper, symphony orchestra, yearbook. **Organizations:** 56 registered organizations, 8 honor societies, 10 religious organizations. **Athletics (Intercollegiate):** *Men:* baseball, basketball, cross-country, golf, soccer, tennis. *Women:* basketball, cross-country, soccer, softball, tennis, volleyball.

ADMISSIONS

Selectivity Rating: 85 (of 100). **Freshman Academic Profile:** 78% from public high schools. Average SAT I Math 535, SAT I Math middle 50% range 440-600. Average SAT I Verbal 515, SAT I Verbal middle 50% range 460-600. Average ACT 22, ACT middle 50% range 19-26. TOEFL required of all international applicants, minimum TOEFL 450. **Basis for Candidate Selection:** *Very important factors considered include:* class rank, secondary school record, standardized test scores. *Important factors considered include:* character/personal qualities. *Other factors considered include:* alumni/ae relation, extracurricular activities, interview, minority status, recommendations, religious affiliation/commitment, talent/ability. **Freshman Admission Requirements:** High school diploma or GED is required. *Academic units required/recommended:* 13 total required; 14 total recommended; 4 English required, 4 English recommended, 3 math required, 3 math recommended, 2 science required, 2 science recommended, 1 foreign language required, 1 foreign language recommended, 2 social studies required, 2 social studies recommended, 1 history required, 1 history recommended. **Freshman Admission Statistics:** 1,254 applied, 58% accepted, 99% of those accepted enrolled. **Transfer Admission Requirements:** *Items required:* high school transcript, college transcript, standardized test scores. Minimum high school GPA of 2.0 required. Minimum college GPA of 2.0 required. Lowest grade transferable D. **General Admission Information:** Application fee $25. Regular application deadline September 1. Nonfall registration accepted. Admission may be deferred. Credit and/or placement offered for CEEB Advanced Placement tests.

COSTS AND FINANCIAL AID

Tuition $8,520. Room & board $4,950. Required fees $210. Average book expense $700. **Required Forms and Deadlines:** FAFSA and institution's own financial aid form. No deadline for regular filing. Priority filing deadline April 15. **Notification of Awards:** Applicants will be notified of awards on a rolling basis beginning on or about February 1. **Types of Aid:** *Need-based scholarships/grants:* Pell, SEOG, state scholarships/grants, private scholarships, the school's own gift aid. *Loans:* FFEL Subsidized Stafford, FFEL Unsubsidized Stafford, FFEL PLUS, Federal Perkins, college/university loans from institutional funds. **Student Employment:** Federal Work-Study Program available. Institutional employment available. Off-campus job opportunities are excellent. **Financial Aid Statistics:** 50% freshmen, 60% undergrads receive some form of aid. Average freshman grant $1,561. Average freshman loan $2,692. **Financial Aid Phone:** 423-614-8300.

LEES-MCRAE COLLEGE

Admissions Office, PO Box 128, Banner Elk, NC 28604
Phone: 828-898-8723 **E-mail:** admissions@lmc.edu **CEEB Code:** 5364
Fax: 828-898-8707 **Web:** www.lmc.edu **ACT Code:** 3116

This private school, which is affiliated with the Presbyterian Church, was founded in 1900. It has a 400-acre campus.

STUDENTS AND FACULTY

Enrollment: 792. **Student Body:** Male 43%, female 57%, out-of-state 35%, international 4%. **Ethnic Representation:** African American 6%, Asian 1%, Caucasian 91%, Hispanic 1%. **Retention and Graduation:** 59% freshmen return for sophomore year. 17% freshmen graduate within 4 years. **Faculty:** Student/faculty ratio 14:1. 69 full-time faculty, 71% hold PhDs. 100% faculty teach undergrads.

ACADEMICS

Degrees: Bachelor's. **Academic Requirements:** General education including some course work in arts/fine arts, computer literacy, English (including composition), history, humanities, mathematics, sciences (biological or physical), 1 unit of introduction to the Bible. **Classes:** Under 10 students in an average class. 10-19 students in an average lab/discussion section. **Majors with Highest Enrollment:** Criminal justice/law enforcement administration; business administration/management; elementary education and teaching. **Disciplines with Highest Percentage of Degrees Awarded:** Education 29%, business/marketing 17%, biological life sciences 13%, protective services/public administration 13%, psychology 10%. **Special Study Options:** Double major, English as a second language, honors program, independent study, internships, student-designed major, study abroad, teacher certification program, 3-2 program in environmental science/forestry with Duke University.

FACILITIES

Housing: Coed, all-female, all-male, substance-free. **Library Holdings:** 96,628 bound volumes. 343 periodicals. 256,447 microforms. 2,326 audiovisuals. **Special Academic Facilities/Equipment:** Curriculum center for teacher education. **Computers:** *Recommended operating system:* Windows NT/2000. School-owned computers available for student use.

EXTRACURRICULARS

Activities: Choral groups, dance, drama/theater, music ensembles, musical theater, student government, student newspaper, yearbook. **Organizations:** 17 registered organizations, 3 honor societies, 4 religious organizations. **Athletics (Intercollegiate):** *Men:* basketball, cheerleading, cross-country, golf, lacrosse, skiing (alpine), soccer, tennis, track & field. *Women:* basketball, cheerleading, cross-country, lacrosse, skiing (alpine), soccer, softball, tennis, track & field, volleyball.

ADMISSIONS

Selectivity Rating: 73 (of 100). **Freshman Academic Profile:** Average high school GPA 3.0. 7% in top 10% of high school class, 19% in top 25% of high school class, 54% in top 50% of high school class. Average SAT I Math 480, SAT I Math middle 50% range 420-520. Average SAT I Verbal 480, SAT I Verbal middle 50% range 420-530. Average ACT 20, ACT middle 50% range 17-21. TOEFL required of all international applicants, minimum TOEFL 500. **Basis for Candidate Selection:** *Very important factors considered include:* secondary school record, standardized test scores. *Other factors considered include:* alumni/ae relation, character/personal qualities, class rank, essays, extracurricular activities, interview, recommendations, talent/ability, volunteer work, work experience. **Freshman Admission Requirements:** High school diploma or GED is required. *Academic units required/recommended:* 18 total required; 4 English recommended, 3 math recommended, 2 science recommended, 1 science lab recommended, 2 foreign language recommended, 2 social studies recommended, 1 history recommended, 6 elective recommended. **Transfer Admission Requirements:** *Items required:* college transcript, statement of good standing from prior school. Minimum college GPA of 2.0 required. Lowest grade transferable C. **General Admission Information:** Application fee $15. Priority application deadline June 1. Nonfall registration accepted. Admission may be deferred for a maximum of 1 year. Credit and/or placement offered for CEEB Advanced Placement tests.

COSTS AND FINANCIAL AID

Tuition $12,292. Room & board $4,664. Required fees $150. Average book expense $760. **Required Forms and Deadlines:** FAFSA. No deadline for regular filing. Priority filing deadline March 15. **Notification of Awards:** Applicants will be notified of awards on a rolling basis beginning on or about March 1. **Types of Aid:** *Need-based scholarships/grants:* Pell, SEOG, state scholarships/grants, private scholarships, the school's own gift aid, Federal Nursing. *Loans:* FFEL Subsidized Stafford, FFEL Unsubsidized Stafford, FFEL PLUS, Federal Perkins, Federal Nursing, state loans. **Student Employment:** Federal Work-Study Program available. Institutional employment available. Off-campus job opportunities are excellent. **Financial Aid Statistics:** 60% freshmen, 64% undergrads receive some form of aid. Average freshman grant $7,143. Average freshman loan $3,795. Average income from on-campus job $1,071. **Financial Aid Phone:** 828-898-8793.

LEHIGH UNIVERSITY

27 Memorial Drive West, Bethlehem, PA 18015
Phone: 610-758-3100 **E-mail:** admissions@lehigh.edu **CEEB Code:** 2365
Fax: 610-758-4361 **Web:** www.lehigh.edu **ACT Code:** 3612

This private school was founded in 1865. It has a 1,600-acre campus.

STUDENTS AND FACULTY

Enrollment: 4,706. **Student Body:** Male 60%, female 40%, international 3%. **Ethnic Representation:** African American 3%, Asian 6%, Caucasian 78%, Hispanic 3%. **Retention and Graduation:** 92% freshmen return for sophomore year. 69% freshmen graduate within 4 years. 23% grads go on to further study within 1 year. 3% grads pursue business degrees. 7% grads pursue law degrees. 9% grads pursue medical degrees. **Faculty:** Student/faculty ratio 11:1. 406 full-time faculty, 99% hold PhDs. 100% faculty teach undergrads.

ACADEMICS

Degrees: Bachelor's, doctoral, master's. **Academic Requirements:** General education including some course work in computer literacy, English (including composition), humanities, mathematics, sciences (biological or physical), social science. **Disciplines with Highest Percentage of Degrees Awarded:** Other 30%, engineering/engineering technology 28%, social sciences and history 7%, computer and information sciences 6%, biological life sciences 5%. **Special Study Options:** Accelerated program, cooperative (work-study) program, cross registration, distance learning, double major, dual enrollment, English as a second language, student exchange program (domestic), external degree program, honors program, independent study, internships, study abroad, teacher certification program.

FACILITIES

Housing: Coed, apartments for married students, apartments for single students, housing for international students, fraternities and/or sororities. **Special Academic Facilities/Equipment:** Art museum, Zoellner Arts Center, electron optical labs, civil engineering lab, particle accelerator, electron optical labs. **Computers:** School-owned computers available for student use.

EXTRACURRICULARS

Activities: Choral groups, concert band, dance, drama/theater, jazz band, literary magazine, marching band, music ensembles, musical theater, pep band, radio station, student government, student newspaper, student-run film society, symphony orchestra, yearbook. **Organizations:** 130 registered organizations,

18 honor societies, 7 religious organizations, 27 fraternities (33% men join), 8 sororities (43% women join). **Athletics (Intercollegiate):** *Men:* baseball, basketball, cross-country, diving, football, golf, lacrosse, rifle, soccer, swimming, tennis, track & field, wrestling. *Women:* basketball, cross-country, diving, field hockey, lacrosse, rifle, soccer, softball, swimming, tennis, track & field, volleyball.

ADMISSIONS

Selectivity Rating: 88 (of 100). **Freshman Academic Profile:** 55% in top 10% of high school class, 88% in top 25% of high school class, 99% in top 50% of high school class. 69% from public high schools. Average SAT I Math 659, SAT I Math middle 50% range 620-710. Average SAT I Verbal 615, SAT I Verbal middle 50% range 570-660. TOEFL required of all international applicants, minimum TOEFL 570. **Basis for Candidate Selection:** *Very important factors considered include:* secondary school record. *Important factors considered include:* character/personal qualities, essays, extracurricular activities, recommendations, standardized test scores, talent/ability, volunteer work. *Other factors considered include:* alumni/ae relation, class rank, geographical residence, minority status, state residency, work experience. **Freshman Admission Requirements:** High school diploma or equivalent is not required. *Academic units required/recommended:* 16 total required; 4 English required, 3 math required, 2 science required, 2 foreign language required, 2 social studies required, 3 elective required. **Freshman Admission Statistics:** 8,254 applied, 46% accepted, 30% of those accepted enrolled. **Transfer Admission Requirements:** *Items required:* high school transcript, college transcript, essay, statement of good standing from prior school. Minimum college GPA of 3.0 required. Lowest grade transferable C. **General Admission Information:** Application fee $50. Early decision application deadline November 15. Regular application deadline January 1. Nonfall registration accepted. Admission may be deferred for a maximum of 1 year. Credit and/or placement offered for CEEB Advanced Placement tests.

COSTS AND FINANCIAL AID

Tuition $25,980. Room & board $7,530. Required fees $200. **Required Forms and Deadlines:** FAFSA, CSS/Financial Aid PROFILE, noncustodial (divorced/separated) parent's statement, and business/farm supplement. **Notification of Awards:** Applicants will be notified of awards on or about March 30. **Types of Aid:** *Need-based scholarships/grants:* UNCF, Pell, SEOG, state scholarships/grants, private scholarships, the school's own gift aid. *Loans:* FFEL Subsidized Stafford, FFEL Unsubsidized Stafford, FFEL PLUS, Federal Perkins, college/university loans from institutional funds, alternate private education loans. **Student Employment:** Federal Work-Study Program available. Institutional employment available. Off-campus job opportunities are fair. **Financial Aid Statistics:** 43% freshmen, 46% undergrads receive some form of aid. Average freshman grant $13,676. Average freshman loan $4,424. Average income from on-campus job $1,000. **Financial Aid Phone:** 610-758-3181.

LEMOYNE-OWEN COLLEGE

807 Walker Avenue, Memphis, TN 38126
Phone: 800-737-7778 **E-mail:** admission@loc.edu **CEEB Code:** 1403
Fax: 901-942-6233 **Web:** www.loc.edu **ACT Code:** 3980

This private school was founded in 1862. It has a 15-acre campus.

STUDENTS AND FACULTY

Enrollment: 1,440. **Student Body:** Male 50%, female 50%, out-of-state 3%, international 1%. **Ethnic Representation:** African American 99%. **Retention and Graduation:** 38% freshmen graduate within 4 years. **Faculty:** Student/faculty ratio 12:1. 54 full-time faculty, 79% hold PhDs. 100% faculty teach undergrads.

ACADEMICS

Degrees: Bachelor's, post-bachelor's certificate. **Academic Requirements:** General education including some course work in arts/fine arts, computer literacy, English (including composition), foreign languages, history, humanities, mathematics, sciences (biological or physical), social science. **Classes:** 20-29 students in an average class. **Majors with Highest Enrollment:** Business administration/management; biology/biological sciences, general; education, general. **Disciplines with Highest Percentage of Degrees Awarded:** Business/marketing 49%, social sciences and history 25%, computer and information sciences 7%, biological life sciences 6%, interdisciplinary studies 3%. **Special Study Options:** Cross registration, double major, honors program, independent study, internships, student-designed major, study abroad, teacher certification program. Undergrads may take grad-level courses.

FACILITIES

Housing: Coed, all-female, all-male. **Library Holdings:** 90,231 bound volumes. 216 periodicals. **Special Academic Facilities/Equipment:** Museum/gallery, language lab. **Computers:** School-owned computers available for student use.

EXTRACURRICULARS

Activities: Choral groups, drama/theater, jazz band, music ensembles, student government, student newspaper, yearbook. **Organizations:** 5 honor societies, 6 religious organizations, 4 fraternities (35% men join), 3 sororities (55% women join). **Athletics (Intercollegiate):** *Men:* baseball, basketball, cross-country, tennis. *Women:* basketball, cross-country, softball, tennis, volleyball.

ADMISSIONS

Selectivity Rating: 63 (of 100). **Freshman Academic Profile:** 95% from public high schools. Average ACT 16. TOEFL required of all international applicants, minimum TOEFL 475. **Freshman Admission Requirements:** High school diploma or GED is required. *Academic units required/recommended:* 20 total required. **Transfer Admission Requirements:** Minimum college GPA of 2.0 required. Lowest grade transferable C. **General Admission Information:** Regular application deadline June 15. Nonfall registration accepted. Credit and/or placement offered for CEEB Advanced Placement tests.

COSTS AND FINANCIAL AID

Tuition $8,250. Room & board $4,620. Required fees $200. Average book expense $700. **Required Forms and Deadlines:** FAFSA. **Types of Aid:** *Need-based scholarships/grants:* United Negro College Fund. *Loans:* FFEL Subsidized Stafford, FFEL PLUS. **Student Employment:** Federal Work-Study Program available. Off-campus job opportunities are excellent. **Financial Aid Phone:** 901-942-7313.

LENOIR-RHYNE COLLEGE

Admissions Office, LRC Box 7227, Hickory, NC 28603
Phone: 828-328-7300 **E-mail:** admission@lrc.edu **CEEB Code:** 5365
Fax: 828-328-7378 **Web:** www.lrc.edu **ACT Code:** 2941

This private school, which is affiliated with the Lutheran Church, was founded in 1891. It has a 100-acre campus.

STUDENTS AND FACULTY

Enrollment: 1,358. **Student Body:** Male 36%, female 64%, out-of-state 29%. **Ethnic Representation:** African American 7%, Asian 1%, Caucasian 91%, Hispanic 1%. **Retention and Graduation:** 80% freshmen return for sophomore year. 10% grads go on to further study within 1 year. 5% grads pursue business degrees. 4% grads pursue law degrees. 4% grads pursue medical degrees. **Faculty:** Student/faculty ratio 12:1. 107 full-time faculty. 100% faculty teach undergrads.

ACADEMICS

Degrees: Bachelor's, certificate, master's. **Academic Requirements:** General education including some course work in arts/fine arts, computer literacy, English (including composition), foreign languages, history, humanities, mathematics, philosophy, sciences (biological or physical), social science, religion, healthful living. **Special Study Options:** Accelerated program, double major, dual enrollment, English as a second language, honors program, independent study, internships, student-designed major, study abroad, teacher certification program.

FACILITIES

Housing: Coed, all-female, all-male, housing for disabled students, fraternities and/or sororities, honors, hearing impaired. **Library Holdings:** 141,781 bound volumes. 5,059 periodicals. 436,307 microforms. 37,613 audiovisuals. **Special Academic Facilities/Equipment:** Language lab. **Computers:** School-owned computers available for student use.

EXTRACURRICULARS

Activities: Choral groups, concert band, dance, drama/theater, jazz band, music ensembles, musical theater, pep band, radio station, student government, student newspaper, television station, yearbook. **Organizations:** 54 registered organizations, 10 honor societies, 6 religious organizations, 4 fraternities (23% men join), 4 sororities (27% women join). **Athletics (Intercollegiate):** *Men:* baseball, basketball, cheerleading, cross-country, football, golf, soccer. *Women:* basketball, cheerleading, cross-country, golf, soccer, softball, volleyball.

ADMISSIONS

Selectivity Rating: 65 (of 100). **Freshman Academic Profile:** Average high school GPA 3.5. 18% in top 10% of high school class, 50% in top 25% of high

school class, 82% in top 50% of high school class. 90% from public high schools. Average SAT I Math 519, SAT I Math middle 50% range 470-580. Average SAT I Verbal 517, SAT I Verbal middle 50% range 460-570. Average ACT 22, ACT middle 50% range 17-24. TOEFL required of all international applicants, minimum TOEFL 500. **Basis for Candidate Selection:** *Very important factors considered include:* secondary school record, standardized test scores. *Important factors considered include:* class rank, interview. *Other factors considered include:* character/personal qualities, essays, extracurricular activities, recommendations, volunteer work, work experience. **Freshman Admission Requirements:** High school diploma or GED is required. *Academic units required/recommended:* 4 English required, 3 math required, 1 science required, 1 science lab required, 2 foreign language required, 1 social studies required, 1 history required. **Freshman Admission Statistics:** 915 applied, 85% accepted, 35% of those accepted enrolled. **Transfer Admission Requirements:** *Items required:* college transcript, statement of good standing from prior school. Minimum college GPA of 2.5 required. Lowest grade transferable C. **General Admission Information:** Application fee $25. Nonfall registration accepted. Admission may be deferred for a maximum of 1 year. Credit offered for CEEB Advanced Placement tests.

COSTS AND FINANCIAL AID

Tuition $12,870. Room & board $4,920. Required fees $486. Average book expense $700. **Required Forms and Deadlines:** FAFSA, institution's own financial aid form, and state aid form. Priority filing deadline March 1. **Notification of Awards:** Applicants will be notified of awards on a rolling basis. **Types of Aid:** *Need-based scholarships/grants:* Pell, SEOG, state scholarships/grants, the school's own gift aid. *Loans:* Direct Subsidized Stafford, Direct Unsubsidized Stafford, Direct PLUS, Federal Perkins. **Student Employment:** Federal Work-Study Program available. Institutional employment available. Off-campus job opportunities are excellent. **Financial Aid Statistics:** Average freshman grant $7,500. Average freshman loan $7,000. Average income from on-campus job $1,000. **Financial Aid Phone:** 828-328-7304.

LESLEY COLLEGE

Lesley College Office of Admissions, 29 Everett Street, Cambridge, MA 02138
Phone: 617-349-8800 **E-mail:** ugadm@mail.lesley.edu **CEEB Code:** 3483
Fax: 617-349-8810 **Web:** www.lesley.edu/lc **ACT Code:** 1850

This private school was founded in 1909. It has a 5-acre campus.

STUDENTS AND FACULTY

Enrollment: 1,065. **Student Body:** Male 21%, female 79%, out-of-state 38%, international 3% (16 countries represented). **Ethnic Representation:** African American 10%, Asian 6%, Caucasian 75%, Hispanic 6%. **Retention and Graduation:** 80% freshmen return for sophomore year. 41% freshmen graduate within 4 years. 20% grads go on to further study within 1 year. 15% grads pursue business degrees. 10% grads pursue law degrees. **Faculty:** Student/faculty ratio 13:1. 30 full-time faculty, 76% hold PhDs. 100% faculty teach undergrads.

ACADEMICS

Degrees: Associate's, bachelor's, certificate, diploma, doctoral, master's, post-bachelor's certificate, post-master's certificate, terminal. **Academic Requirements:** General education including some course work in arts/fine arts, computer literacy, English (including composition), history, humanities, mathematics, philosophy, sciences (biological or physical), social science, multicultural perspectives. **Classes:** 10-19 students in an average class. **Majors with Highest Enrollment:** Elementary education and teaching; early childhood education and teaching; counseling psychology. **Disciplines with Highest Percentage of Degrees Awarded:** Education 48%, psychology 25%, liberal arts/general studies 10%, business/marketing 9%, health professions and related sciences 4%. **Special Study Options:** Accelerated program, cross registration, distance learning, double major, English as a second language, student exchange program (domestic), honors program, independent study, internships, liberal arts/career combination, study abroad, teacher certification program.

FACILITIES

Housing: All-female, special housing for nontraditional-age students. **Library Holdings:** 98,271 bound volumes. 739 periodicals. 785,000 microforms. 47,312 audiovisuals. **Special Academic Facilities/Equipment:** Kresge Center for Teaching Resources and Educational Software Collection, art gallery. **Computers:** School-owned computers available for student use.

EXTRACURRICULARS

Activities: Choral groups, dance, drama/theater, literary magazine, student government, student newspaper, yearbook. **Organizations:** 25 registered organizations, 2 honor societies, 2 religious organizations. **Athletics (Intercollegiate):** *Women:* basketball, crew, soccer, softball, volleyball.

ADMISSIONS

Selectivity Rating: 71 (of 100). **Freshman Academic Profile:** Average high school GPA 2.9. 15% in top 10% of high school class, 48% in top 25% of high school class, 77% in top 50% of high school class. 76% from public high schools. Average SAT I Math 500, SAT I Math middle 50% range 410-530. Average SAT I Verbal 510, SAT I Verbal middle 50% range 440-580. TOEFL required of all international applicants, minimum TOEFL 500. **Basis for Candidate Selection:** *Very important factors considered include:* secondary school record. *Important factors considered include:* character/personal qualities, class rank, interview, recommendations, standardized test scores, volunteer work. *Other factors considered include:* alumni/ae relation, essays, extracurricular activities, geographical residence, minority status, talent/ability, work experience. **Freshman Admission Requirements:** High school diploma or GED is required. *Academic units required/recommended:* 18 total required; 20 total recommended; 4 English required, 4 English recommended, 3 math required, 3 math recommended, 2 science required, 3 science recommended, 1 science lab required, 2 science lab recommended, 2 foreign language recommended, 1 social studies required, 2 social studies recommended, 1 history required, 2 history recommended, 7 elective required. **Freshman Admission Statistics:** 345 applied, 84% accepted, 41% of those accepted enrolled. **Transfer Admission Requirements:** *Items required:* high school transcript, college transcript, essay. Minimum college GPA of 2.5 required. Lowest grade transferable C-. **General Admission Information:** Application fee $35. Priority application deadline March 15. Nonfall registration accepted. Admission may be deferred for a maximum of 1 year. Credit and/or placement offered for CEEB Advanced Placement tests.

COSTS AND FINANCIAL AID

Tuition $19,525. Room & board $8,800. Required fees $175. Average book expense $700. **Required Forms and Deadlines:** FAFSA and institution's own financial aid form. Priority filing deadline February 1. **Notification of Awards:** Applicants will be notified of awards on a rolling basis beginning on or about March 15. **Types of Aid:** *Need-based scholarships/grants:* Pell, SEOG, state scholarships/grants, private scholarships, the school's own gift aid. *Loans:* FFEL Subsidized Stafford, FFEL Unsubsidized Stafford, FFEL PLUS, Federal Perkins, state loans. **Student Employment:** Federal Work-Study Program available. Institutional employment available. Off-campus job opportunities are excellent. **Financial Aid Statistics:** 97% freshmen, 66% undergrads receive some form of aid. Average freshman grant $12,491. Average freshman loan $4,520. Average income from on-campus job $1,196. **Financial Aid Phone:** 617-349-8710.

See page 1086.

LETOURNEAU UNIVERSITY

PO Box 7001, Longview, TX 75607
Phone: 903-233-3400 **E-mail:** admissions@letu.edu **CEEB Code:** 6365
Fax: 903-233-3411 **Web:** www.letu.edu **ACT Code:** 4120

This private school was founded in 1946. It has a 162-acre campus.

STUDENTS AND FACULTY

Enrollment: 2,921. **Student Body:** Male 48%, female 52%, out-of-state 52%, international 1%. **Ethnic Representation:** African American 18%, Asian 1%, Caucasian 72%, Hispanic 6%. **Retention and Graduation:** 77% freshmen return for sophomore year. 15% freshmen graduate within 4 years. **Faculty:** Student/faculty ratio 16:1. 62 full-time faculty, 72% hold PhDs.

ACADEMICS

Degrees: Associate's, bachelor's, master's. **Academic Requirements:** General education including some course work in English (including composition), history, humanities, mathematics, sciences (biological or physical), social science, Bible. **Classes:** 10-19 students in an average class. 10-19 students in an average lab/discussion section. **Majors with Highest Enrollment:** Business administration/management; engineering, general; aviation/airway management and operations. **Disciplines with Highest Percentage of Degrees Awarded:** Engineering/engineering technology 47%, business/marketing 19%, education 9%, biological life sciences 7%, computer and information sciences 4%. **Special Study Options:** Cooperative (work-study) program, distance learning, double major, honors program, independent study, internships, study abroad, teacher certification program, weekend college.

FACILITIES

Housing: All-female, all-male, apartments for married students, apartments for single students, housing for disabled students, residential societies available.

Library Holdings: 84,779 bound volumes. 383 periodicals. 50,481 microforms. 3,144 audiovisuals. **Special Academic Facilities/Equipment:** Longview Citizens Resource Center, R.G. LeTourneau Memorial Museum.

EXTRACURRICULARS

Activities: Choral groups, drama/theater, jazz band, music ensembles, student government, student newspaper, yearbook. **Organizations:** 32 registered organizations, 4 honor societies, 4 religious organizations. **Athletics (Intercollegiate):** *Men:* baseball, basketball, cross-country, golf, soccer, tennis. *Women:* basketball, cross-country, golf, soccer, softball, tennis, volleyball.

ADMISSIONS

Selectivity Rating: 78 (of 100). **Freshman Academic Profile:** Average high school GPA 3.5. 26% in top 10% of high school class, 53% in top 25% of high school class, 83% in top 50% of high school class. SAT I Math middle 50% range 530-650. SAT I Verbal middle 50% range 510-630. ACT middle 50% range 22-28. TOEFL required of all international applicants, minimum TOEFL 500. **Basis for Candidate Selection:** *Very important factors considered include:* standardized test scores. *Important factors considered include:* character/personal qualities, class rank, essays, religious affiliation/commitment, secondary school record. *Other factors considered include:* alumni/ae relation, extracurricular activities, interview, recommendations, talent/ability, volunteer work, work experience. **Freshman Admission Requirements:** High school diploma or GED is required. *Academic units required/recommended:* 16 total required; 4 English required, 3 math required, 3 science required, 3 science lab required, 1 foreign language recommended, 2 social studies required, 1 history required, 2 elective recommended. **Freshman Admission Statistics:** 698 applied, 93% accepted, 38% of those accepted enrolled. **Transfer Admission Requirements:** *Items required:* college transcript, essay, statement of good standing from prior school. Minimum college GPA of 2.0 required. Lowest grade transferable C. **General Admission Information:** Application fee $25. Priority application deadline December 31. Regular application deadline August 1. Nonfall registration accepted. Admission may be deferred for a maximum of 2 years. Credit and/or placement offered for CEEB Advanced Placement tests.

COSTS AND FINANCIAL AID

Tuition $14,010. Room & board $5,820. Required fees $180. Average book expense $1,040. **Required Forms and Deadlines:** FAFSA. No deadline for regular filing. Priority filing deadline February 15. **Notification of Awards:** Applicants will be notified of awards on a rolling basis beginning on or about March 1. **Types of Aid:** *Need-based scholarships/grants:* Pell, SEOG, state scholarships/grants, private scholarships, the school's own gift aid. *Loans:* FFEL Subsidized Stafford, FFEL Unsubsidized Stafford, FFEL PLUS, Federal Perkins. **Student Employment:** Federal Work-Study Program available. Institutional employment available. Off-campus job opportunities are excellent. **Financial Aid Statistics:** 69% freshmen, 72% undergrads receive some form of aid. **Financial Aid Phone:** 903-233-3430.

LEWIS & CLARK COLLEGE

 $$$  

0615 SW Palatine Hill Road, Portland, OR 97219-7899
Phone: 503-768-7040 **E-mail:** admissions@lclark.edu **CEEB Code:** 4384
Fax: 503-768-7055 **Web:** www.lclark.edu **ACT Code:** 3464

This private school was founded in 1867. It has a 134-acre campus.

STUDENTS AND FACULTY

Enrollment: 1,763. **Student Body:** Male 40%, female 60%, out-of-state 87%, international 5% (44 countries represented). **Ethnic Representation:** African American 2%, Asian 6%, Caucasian 67%, Hispanic 3%, Native American 1%. **Retention and Graduation:** 83% freshmen return for sophomore year. 54% freshmen graduate within 4 years. 23% grads go on to further study within 1 year. 1% grads pursue business degrees. 2% grads pursue law degrees. 2% grads pursue medical degrees. **Faculty:** Student/faculty ratio 12:1. 191 full-time faculty, 91% hold PhDs. 100% faculty teach undergrads.

ACADEMICS

Degrees: Bachelor's, first professional, master's, post-bachelor's certificate. **Academic Requirements:** General education including some course work in arts/fine arts, foreign languages, humanities, mathematics, sciences (biological or physical), first-year course, 2 semesters of international studies. **Classes:** 10-19 students in an average class. 10-19 students in an average lab/discussion section. **Majors with Highest Enrollment:** English language and literature, general; biology/biological sciences, general; psychology, general. **Disciplines with Highest Percentage of Degrees Awarded:** Social sciences and history 26%, foreign languages and literature 11%, English 11%, psychology 10%, biological life sciences 9%. **Special Study Options:** Accelerated program, cross registration, double major, dual enrollment, English as a second language, honors program, independent study, internships, student-designed major, study abroad.

FACILITIES

Housing: Coed, all-female, theme floors. **Library Holdings:** 227,609 bound volumes. 7,477 periodicals. 1,997,645 microforms. 11,586 audiovisuals. **Special Academic Facilities/Equipment:** Art gallery, observatory, world music room, 85 Rank Casavant organ, newly renovated greenhouse. **Computers:** School-owned computers available for student use.

EXTRACURRICULARS

Activities: Choral groups, concert band, dance, drama/theater, jazz band, literary magazine, music ensembles, musical theater, radio station, student government, student newspaper, symphony orchestra, television station, yearbook. **Organizations:** 75 registered organizations, 5 honor societies, 10 religious organizations. **Athletics (Intercollegiate):** *Men:* baseball, basketball, crew, cross-country, football, golf, swimming, tennis, track & field. *Women:* basketball, crew, cross-country, golf, softball, swimming, tennis, track & field, volleyball.

ADMISSIONS

Selectivity Rating: 85 (of 100). **Freshman Academic Profile:** Average high school GPA 3.6. 36% in top 10% of high school class, 73% in top 25% of high school class, 96% in top 50% of high school class. 66% from public high schools. SAT I Math middle 50% range 580-670. SAT I Verbal middle 50% range 600-690. ACT middle 50% range 25-29. TOEFL required of all international applicants, minimum TOEFL 550. **Basis for Candidate Selection:** *Very important factors considered include:* alumni/ae relation, minority status, secondary school record. *Important factors considered include:* character/personal qualities, class rank, essays, extracurricular activities, interview, recommendations, standardized test scores, talent/ability, volunteer work. *Other factors considered include:* geographical residence, state residency, work experience. **Freshman Admission Requirements:** High school diploma or GED is required. *Academic units required/recommended:* 18 total recommended; 4 English recommended, 3 math recommended, 3 science recommended, 2 science lab recommended, 2 foreign language recommended, 3 social studies recommended, 1 fine arts recommended. **Freshman Admission Statistics:** 3,223 applied, 68% accepted, 23% of those accepted enrolled. **Transfer Admission Requirements:** *Items required:* high school transcript, college transcript, essay. Minimum high school GPA of 2.0 required. Minimum college GPA of 2.0 required. Lowest grade transferable C. **General Admission Information:** Application fee $45. Priority application deadline February 1. Regular application deadline February 1. Nonfall registration accepted. Admission may be deferred for a maximum of 1 year. Credit and/or placement offered for CEEB Advanced Placement tests.

COSTS AND FINANCIAL AID

Tuition $23,730. Room & board $6,630. Average book expense $800. **Required Forms and Deadlines:** FAFSA. Financial aid filing deadline March 1. Priority filing deadline March 1. **Notification of Awards:** Applicants will be notified of awards on or about April 1. **Types of Aid:** *Need-based scholarships/grants:* Pell, SEOG, state scholarships/grants, private scholarships, the school's own gift aid. *Loans:* FFEL Subsidized Stafford, FFEL Unsubsidized Stafford, FFEL PLUS, Federal Perkins. **Student Employment:** Federal Work-Study Program available. Institutional employment available. Off-campus job opportunities are fair. **Financial Aid Statistics:** 55% freshmen, 54% undergrads receive some form of aid. Average income from on-campus job $1,500. **Financial Aid Phone:** 503-768-7090.

LEWIS UNIVERSITY

One University Parkway, Box 297, Romeoville, IL 60446-2200
Phone: 815-836-5250 **E-mail:** admissions@lewisu.edu **CEEB Code:** 1404
Fax: 815-836-5002 **Web:** www.lewisu.edu **ACT Code:** 1058

This private school, which is affiliated with the Roman Catholic Church, was founded in 1932. It has a 330-acre campus.

STUDENTS AND FACULTY

Enrollment: 3,194. **Student Body:** Male 44%, female 56%, out-of-state 3%, international 4% (31 country represented). **Ethnic Representation:** African American 16%, Asian 2%, Caucasian 72%, Hispanic 8%. **Retention and Graduation:** 74% freshmen return for sophomore year. **Faculty:** Student/faculty ratio 17:1. 98% faculty teach undergrads.

ACADEMICS

Degrees: Associate's, bachelor's, certificate, master's, post-bachelor's certificate, terminal, transfer. **Academic Requirements:** General education including some course work in arts/fine arts, English (including composition), history, humanities, mathematics, philosophy, sciences (biological or physical), social science, university-identified mission-related courses. **Classes:** 10-19 students in an average class. 10-19 students in an average lab/discussion section. **Majors with Highest Enrollment:** Nursing/registered nurse training (RN, ASN, BSN, MSN); business administration/management; criminal justice/police science. **Disciplines with Highest Percentage of Degrees Awarded:** Business/marketing 27%, health professions and related sciences 24%, protective services/public administration 15%, trade and industry 7%, education 5%. **Special Study Options:** Accelerated program, distance learning, double major, dual enrollment, English as a second language, honors program, independent study, internships, liberal arts/career combination, student-designed major, study abroad, teacher certification program.

FACILITIES

Housing: Coed, housing for disabled students. **Library Holdings:** 149,870 bound volumes. 1,990 periodicals. 147,132 microforms. 2,281 audiovisuals. **Special Academic Facilities/Equipment:** Campus is located immediately adjacent to the Lewis University Airport and contains an aviation complex that includes a Boeing 737 located on campus for use by students studying aviation maintenance. Special collections on campus include: curriculum collection, Eva White Memorial Aviation Collection, library of American civilization (ultrafiche), library of English literature (ultrafiche), ERIC fiche, government documents, and canal and regional history collection/I&M Canal Archives (one of the largest collections of documents, photographs, and artifacts pertaining to the canal era in the United States). **Computers:** School-owned computers available for student use.

EXTRACURRICULARS

Activities: Choral groups, concert band, dance, drama/theater, jazz band, literary magazine, music ensembles, pep band, radio station, student government, student newspaper, symphony orchestra, television station, yearbook. **Organizations:** 45 registered organizations, 10 honor societies, 7 religious organizations, 9 fraternities, 5 sororities. **Athletics (Intercollegiate):** *Men:* baseball, basketball, cheerleading, cross-country, golf, indoor track, soccer, swimming, tennis, track & field, volleyball. *Women:* basketball, cheerleading, cross-country, golf, indoor track, soccer, softball, swimming, tennis, track & field, volleyball.

ADMISSIONS

Selectivity Rating: 63 (of 100). **Freshman Academic Profile:** Average high school GPA 3.0. 10% in top 10% of high school class, 27% in top 25% of high school class, 59% in top 50% of high school class. SAT I Math middle 50% range 460-590. SAT I Verbal middle 50% range 430-580. ACT middle 50% range 19-24. TOEFL required of all international applicants, minimum TOEFL 500. **Basis for Candidate Selection:** *Very important factors considered include:* secondary school record, standardized test scores. *Important factors considered include:* class rank. *Other factors considered include:* alumni/ae relation, character/personal qualities, essays, extracurricular activities, interview, recommendations, religious affiliation/commitment, talent/ability, volunteer work, work experience. **Freshman Admission Requirements:** High school diploma or GED is required. *Academic units required/recommended:* 18 total required; 3 English required, 4 English recommended, 3 math recommended, 2 science recommended, 1 science lab recommended, 2 foreign language recommended, 2 social studies recommended, 1 history recommended, 4 elective recommended. **Freshman Admission Statistics:** 1,208 applied, 68% accepted, 46% of those accepted enrolled. **Transfer Admission Requirements:** *Items required:* college transcript. Minimum college GPA of 2.0 required. Lowest grade transferable D. **General Admission Information:** Application fee $35. Priority application deadline April 15. Nonfall registration accepted. Admission may be deferred for a maximum of 2 years. Credit and/or placement offered for CEEB Advanced Placement tests.

COSTS AND FINANCIAL AID

Tuition $15,250. Room & board $3,625. Required fees $0. Average book expense $500. **Required Forms and Deadlines:** FAFSA. No deadline for regular filing. Priority filing deadline May 1. **Notification of Awards:** Applicants will be notified of awards on a rolling basis beginning on or about February 1. **Types of Aid:** *Need-based scholarships/grants:* Pell, SEOG, state scholarships/grants, private scholarships, the school's own gift aid, Federal Nursing. *Loans:* FFEL Subsidized Stafford, FFEL Unsubsidized Stafford, FFEL PLUS, Federal Perkins. **Student Employment:** Federal Work-Study Program available. Institutional employment available. Off-campus job opportunities are good. **Financial Aid Statistics:** 72% freshmen, 66% undergrads receive some form of aid. Average freshman grant $14,078. Average freshman loan $2,356. Average income from on-campus job $1,200. **Financial Aid Phone:** 815-836-5263.

See page 1088.

LEWIS-CLARK STATE COLLEGE

500 Eighth Avenue, Lewiston, ID 83501
Phone: 208-792-2210 **E-mail:** admissions@lcsc.edu **CEEB Code:** 4385
Fax: 208-792-2876 **Web:** www.lcsc.edu **ACT Code:** 920

This public school was founded in 1893. It has a 44-acre campus.

STUDENTS AND FACULTY

Enrollment: 3,108. **Student Body:** Male 40%, female 60%, out-of-state 14%, international 2%. **Ethnic Representation:** Asian 1%, Caucasian 86%, Hispanic 2%, Native American 5%. **Retention and Graduation:** 59% freshmen return for sophomore year. 7% grads go on to further study within 1 year. **Faculty:** Student/faculty ratio 16:1. 134 full-time faculty, 70% hold PhDs. 100% faculty teach undergrads.

ACADEMICS

Degrees: Associate's, bachelor's, certificate. **Academic Requirements:** General education including some course work in arts/fine arts, English (including composition), humanities, mathematics, sciences (biological or physical), social science, communication. **Classes:** Under 10 students in an average class. 20-29 students in an average lab/discussion section. **Majors with Highest Enrollment:** Elementary education and teaching; nursing/registered nurse training (RN, ASN, BSN, MSN); business administration/management. **Disciplines with Highest Percentage of Degrees Awarded:** Education 20%, business/marketing 20%, protective services/public administration 20%, health professions and related sciences 11%, parks and recreation 6%. **Special Study Options:** Accelerated program, cooperative (work-study) program, distance learning, double major, dual enrollment, English as a second language, independent study, internships, liberal arts/career combination, student-designed major, study abroad, teacher certification program, weekend college.

FACILITIES

Housing: Coed, apartments for married students, apartments for single students. **Library Holdings:** 139,499 bound volumes. 1,612 periodicals. 155,600 microforms. 6,957 audiovisuals. **Special Academic Facilities/Equipment:** Museum/art gallery, educational technology center. **Computers:** *Recommended operating system:* Windows NT/2000. School-owned computers available for student use.

EXTRACURRICULARS

Activities: Choral groups, dance, drama/theater, jazz band, literary magazine, music ensembles, radio station, student government, student newspaper, student-run film society, television station. **Organizations:** 37 registered organizations, 1 honor society, 3 religious organizations. **Athletics (Intercollegiate):** *Men:* baseball, basketball, cross-country, golf, tennis. *Women:* basketball, cross-country, golf, tennis, volleyball.

ADMISSIONS

Selectivity Rating: 63 (of 100). **Freshman Academic Profile:** Average high school GPA 3.0. 4% in top 10% of high school class, 17% in top 25% of high school class, 48% in top 50% of high school class. 99% from public high schools. Average SAT I Math 483. Average SAT I Verbal 482. Average ACT 20. TOEFL required of all international applicants, minimum TOEFL 500. **Basis for Candidate Selection:** *Very important factors considered include:* secondary school record, standardized test scores. **Freshman Admission Requirements:** High school diploma or GED is required. *Academic units required/recommended:* 15 total required; 15 total recommended; 4 English required, 3 math required, 3 science required, 1 foreign language recommended, 2 social studies required, 1 elective required. **Freshman Admission Statistics:** 1,023 applied, 59% accepted, 80% of those accepted enrolled. **Transfer Admission Requirements:** *Items required:* college transcript. Minimum high school GPA of 2.0 required. Minimum college GPA of 2.0 required. Lowest grade transferable D. **General Admission Information:** Application fee $30. Priority application deadline March 1. Nonfall registration accepted. Admission may be deferred for a maximum of 1 year. Credit and/or placement offered for CEEB Advanced Placement tests.

COSTS AND FINANCIAL AID

Average book expense $750. **Required Forms and Deadlines:** FAFSA. Priority filing deadline March 1. **Notification of Awards:** Applicants will be notified of awards on a rolling basis beginning on or about April 15. **Types of Aid:** *Need-based scholarships/grants:* Pell, SEOG, state scholarships/grants, private scholarships, the school's own gift aid. *Loans:* FFEL Subsidized Stafford, FFEL Unsubsidized Stafford, FFEL PLUS, Federal Perkins, Federal Nursing. **Student Employment:** Federal Work-Study Program available. Institutional employment available. Off-campus job opportunities are good. **Financial Aid Statistics:** 68% freshmen, 62% undergrads receive some form of aid. **Financial Aid Phone:** 208-792-2224.

LEXINGTON COLLEGE

310 South Peoria Street, Suite 512, Chicago, IL 60607
Phone: 312-226-6294 **E-mail:** admissio@lexcollege.org
Fax: 312-226-6405 **Web:** www.lexcollege.org

This private school is affiliated with the Roman Catholic Church.

STUDENTS AND FACULTY

Enrollment: 40. **Student Body:** International 10%. **Ethnic Representation:** African American 81%, Caucasian 8%, Hispanic 11%. **Faculty:** Student/faculty ratio 5:1.

ACADEMICS

Degrees: Associate's. **Academic Requirements:** General education including some course work in arts/fine arts, computer literacy, English (including composition), humanities, mathematics, social science. **Special Study Options:** Double major, independent study.

ADMISSIONS

Selectivity Rating: 62 (of 100). **Freshman Admission Statistics:** 54 applied, 93% accepted, 40% of those accepted enrolled. **General Admission Information:** Application fee $25. Nonfall registration accepted. Credit offered for CEEB Advanced Placement tests.

COSTS AND FINANCIAL AID

Tuition $9,100. Required fees $700. Average book expense $750. **Student Employment:** Off-campus job opportunities are excellent. **Financial Aid Phone:** 312-226-6294.

LIBERTY UNIVERSITY

1971 University Boulevard, Lynchburg, VA 24502
Phone: 434-582-5985 **E-mail:** admissions@liberty.edu **CEEB Code:** 5385
Fax: 800-542-2311 **Web:** www.liberty.edu **ACT Code:** 4364

This private school, which is affiliated with the Baptist Church, was founded in 1971. It has a 160-acre campus.

STUDENTS AND FACULTY

Enrollment: 6,448. **Student Body:** Male 49%, female 51%, out-of-state 59%, international 3%. **Ethnic Representation:** African American 11%, Asian 2%, Caucasian 81%, Hispanic 3%, Native American 1%. **Retention and Graduation:** 76% freshmen return for sophomore year. 21% freshmen graduate within 4 years. 10% grads go on to further study within 1 year. 1% grads pursue business degrees. 1% grads pursue law degrees. 1% grads pursue medical degrees. **Faculty:** Student/faculty ratio 24:1. 181 full-time faculty, 62% hold PhDs. 99% faculty teach undergrads.

ACADEMICS

Degrees: Associate's, bachelor's, doctoral, first professional, master's, post-master's certificate, terminal. **Academic Requirements:** General education including some course work in computer literacy, English (including composition), history, humanities, mathematics, philosophy, sciences (biological or physical), social science, Bible, theology, apologetics. **Classes:** 20-29 students in an average class. 20-29 students in an average lab/discussion section. **Disciplines with Highest Percentage of Degrees Awarded:** Philosophy/religion/theology 16%, psychology 14%, business/marketing 13%, communications/communication technologies 12%, interdisciplinary studies 12%. **Special Study Options:** Accelerated program, distance learning, double major, dual enrollment, English as a second language, external degree program, honors program, independent study, internships, student-designed major, study abroad, teacher certification program.

FACILITIES

Housing: All-female, all-male, housing for disabled students. **Library Holdings:** 192,985 bound volumes. 9,072 periodicals. 95,329 microforms. 5,027 audiovisuals. **Special Academic Facilities/Equipment:** Displays from the museum of life and earth history are located in the library. **Computers:** *Recommended operating system:* Windows NT/2000. School-owned computers available for student use.

EXTRACURRICULARS

Activities: Choral groups, concert band, drama/theater, marching band, music ensembles, musical theater, opera, pep band, radio station, student government, student newspaper, television station, yearbook. **Organizations:** 25 registered organizations, 7 honor societies. **Athletics (Intercollegiate):** *Men:* baseball, basketball, cheerleading, cross-country, football, golf, indoor track, soccer, tennis, track & field. *Women:* basketball, cheerleading, cross-country, indoor track, soccer, softball, tennis, track & field, volleyball.

ADMISSIONS

Selectivity Rating: 63 (of 100). **Freshman Academic Profile:** Average high school GPA 3.1. Average SAT I Math 494, SAT I Math middle 50% range 430-550. Average SAT I Verbal 509, SAT I Verbal middle 50% range 440-570. Average ACT 21, ACT middle 50% range 18-24. TOEFL required of all international applicants, minimum TOEFL 500. **Basis for Candidate Selection:** *Very important factors considered include:* character/personal qualities, essays, extracurricular activities, religious affiliation/commitment, secondary school record, standardized test scores. *Important factors considered include:* recommendations. *Other factors considered include:* class rank, interview, volunteer work, work experience. **Freshman Admission Requirements:** High school diploma or GED is required. *Academic units required/recommended:* 17 total recommended; 4 English recommended, 3 math recommended, 2 science recommended, 2 science lab recommended, 2 foreign language recommended, 2 social studies recommended, 2 elective recommended. **Freshman Admission Statistics:** 5,734 applied, 92% accepted, 30% of those accepted enrolled. **Transfer Admission Requirements:** *Items required:* high school transcript, college transcript, essay, statement of good standing from prior school. Minimum high school GPA of 2.0 required. Minimum college GPA of 2.0 required. Lowest grade transferable C. **General Admission Information:** Application fee $35. Priority application deadline May 1. Nonfall registration accepted. Admission may be deferred for a maximum of 1 year. Credit and/or placement offered for CEEB Advanced Placement tests.

COSTS AND FINANCIAL AID

Tuition $11,520. Room & board $5,200. Required fees $500. Average book expense $800. **Required Forms and Deadlines:** FAFSA and state aid form. Priority filing deadline April 15. **Notification of Awards:** Applicants will be notified of awards on a rolling basis beginning on or about May 1. **Types of Aid:** *Need-based scholarships/grants:* Pell, SEOG, state scholarships/grants, private scholarships, the school's own gift aid. *Loans:* Direct Subsidized Stafford, Direct Unsubsidized Stafford, Direct PLUS, FFEL Subsidized Stafford, FFEL Unsubsidized Stafford, FFEL PLUS. **Student Employment:** Federal Work-Study Program available. Institutional employment available. Off-campus job opportunities are good. **Financial Aid Statistics:** 77% freshmen, 71% undergrads receive some form of aid. **Financial Aid Phone:** 434-582-2270.

LIFE PACIFIC COLLEGE (FORMERLY LIFE BIBLE COLLEGE)

1100 Covina Blvd., San Dimas, CA 91773
Phone: 909-599-5433 **E-mail:** adm@lifeBible.edu
Fax: 909-599-6690 **Web:** www.lifepacific.edu **ACT Code:** 489

This private school, which is affiliated with the Protestant Church, was founded in 1923. It has a 9-acre campus.

STUDENTS AND FACULTY

Enrollment: 386. **Student Body:** Male 46%, female 54%, out-of-state 47%, international 1%. **Ethnic Representation:** African American 4%, Asian 6%, Caucasian 72%, Hispanic 14%, Native American 2%. **Retention and Graduation:** 47% freshmen return for sophomore year. 21% freshmen graduate within 4 years. **Faculty:** Student/faculty ratio 16:1. 16 full-time faculty, 18% hold PhDs. 100% faculty teach undergrads.

ACADEMICS

Degrees: Associate's, bachelor's. **Academic Requirements:** General education including some course work in English (including composition), foreign languages, history, mathematics, philosophy, sciences (biological or physical), social science, theology, Bible, ministry. **Classes:** Under 10 students in an average class. 20-29 students in an average lab/discussion section. **Disciplines with Highest Percentage of Degrees Awarded:** Philosophy/religion/theology 100%. **Special Study Options:** Cooperative (work-study) program, distance learning, external degree program, independent study, internships.

FACILITIES

Housing: All-female, all-male. **Library Holdings:** 38,084 bound volumes. 244 periodicals. 516 microforms. 1,104 audiovisuals. **Computers:** School-owned computers available for student use.

EXTRACURRICULARS

Activities: Choral groups, dance, drama/theater, music ensembles, musical theater, student government, student newspaper, yearbook. **Athletics (Intercollegiate):** *Men:* basketball. *Women:* volleyball.

ADMISSIONS

Selectivity Rating: 63 (of 100). **Freshman Academic Profile:** Average high school GPA 2.9. 5% in top 10% of high school class, 22% in top 25% of high school class, 50% in top 50% of high school class. SAT I Math middle 50% range 480-587. SAT I Verbal middle 50% range 552-630. ACT middle 50% range 19-23. TOEFL required of all international applicants, minimum TOEFL 550. **Basis for Candidate Selection:** *Very important factors considered include:* character/personal qualities, essays, recommendations, religious affiliation/commitment, secondary school record, standardized test scores. *Other factors considered include:* talent/ability. **Freshman Admission Requirements:** High school diploma or GED is required. **Freshman Admission Statistics:** 100 applied, 57% accepted, 82% of those accepted enrolled. **Transfer Admission Requirements:** *Items required:* high school transcript, college transcript, essay, statement of good standing from prior school. Minimum college GPA of 2.0 required. Lowest grade transferable C. **General Admission Information:** Application fee $35. Regular application deadline July 1. Nonfall registration accepted. Admission may be deferred for a maximum of 1 year. Credit offered for CEEB Advanced Placement tests.

COSTS AND FINANCIAL AID

Tuition $6,450. Room & board $3,600. Required fees $250. Average book expense $700. **Required Forms and Deadlines:** FAFSA. Priority filing deadline July 1. **Notification of Awards:** Applicants will be notified of awards on a rolling basis beginning on or about March 15. **Types of Aid:** *Need-based scholarships/grants:* Pell, SEOG, state scholarships/grants, private scholarships. *Loans:* FFEL Subsidized Stafford, FFEL Unsubsidized Stafford, FFEL PLUS. **Student Employment:** Federal Work-Study Program available. Institutional employment available. Off-campus job opportunities are good. **Financial Aid Statistics:** 64% freshmen, 62% undergrads receive some form of aid. Average freshman grant $3,418. Average freshman loan $2,625. Average income from on-campus job $3,840. **Financial Aid Phone:** 909-599-5433.

LIFE UNIVERSITY

1269 Barclay Circle, Marietta, GA 30060-2903
Phone: 770-426-2884 **E-mail:** admission@life.edu
Fax: 770-426-9886 **Web:** www.life.edu **ACT Code:** 845

This private school was founded in 1974.

STUDENTS AND FACULTY

Enrollment: 823. **Student Body:** Male 63%, female 37%, international students represent 321 countries. **Ethnic Representation:** African American 46%, Asian 2%, Caucasian 40%, Hispanic 3%. **Faculty:** 100% faculty teach undergrads.

ACADEMICS

Degrees: Associate's, bachelor's, certificate, first professional, master's, transfer. **Academic Requirements:** General education including some course work in arts/fine arts, computer literacy, English (including composition), foreign languages, history, humanities, mathematics, philosophy, sciences (biological or physical), social science. **Special Study Options:** Accelerated program, cooperative (work-study) program, cross registration, double major, dual enrollment, English as a second language, honors program, internships, liberal arts/career combination.

FACILITIES

Housing: Apartments for married students, apartments for single students, off-campus living. **Library Holdings:** 42,496 bound volumes. 1,301 periodicals. 6,000 microforms. 6,132 audiovisuals. **Special Academic Facilities/Equipment:** Wellness center.

EXTRACURRICULARS

Activities: Choral groups, dance, drama/theater, jazz band, music ensembles, pep band, student government, student newspaper, yearbook. **Organizations:** 50 registered organizations, 1 honor society, 5 religious organizations, 1 sorority. **Athletics (Intercollegiate):** *Men:* basketball, cheerleading, cross-country, golf, ice hockey, rugby, soccer, track & field. *Women:* basketball, cheerleading, cross-country, golf, track & field.

ADMISSIONS

Selectivity Rating: 60 (of 100). **Freshman Academic Profile:** TOEFL required of all international applicants, minimum TOEFL 500. **Basis for Candidate Selection:** *Important factors considered include:* secondary school record, standardized test scores. *Other factors considered include:* character/personal qualities, class rank, extracurricular activities. **Freshman Admission Requirements:** High school diploma or GED is required. **Transfer Admission Requirements:** *Items required:* college transcript. Minimum high school GPA of 2.0 required. Minimum college GPA of 2.0 required. **General Admission Information:** Nonfall registration accepted. Admission may be deferred. Credit and/or placement offered for CEEB Advanced Placement tests.

COSTS AND FINANCIAL AID

Required Forms and Deadlines: FAFSA and institution's own financial aid form. No deadline for regular filing. Priority filing deadline March 1. **Notification of Awards:** Applicants will be notified of awards on a rolling basis beginning on or about June 1. **Types of Aid:** *Need-based scholarships/grants:* Pell, SEOG, state scholarships/grants, private scholarships, the school's own gift aid. *Loans:* FFEL Subsidized Stafford, FFEL Unsubsidized Stafford, FFEL PLUS, Federal Perkins.

LIMESTONE COLLEGE

1115 College Drive, Gaffey, SC 29340
Phone: 800-345-3792 **E-mail:** admiss@saint.limestone.edu **CEEB Code:** 5366
Fax: 864-487-8706 **Web:** www.limestone.edu **ACT Code:** 3862

This private school was founded in 1845. It has a 116-acre campus.

STUDENTS AND FACULTY

Enrollment: 1,784. **Student Body:** Male 42%, female 58%, out-of-state 20%, international students represent 5 countries. **Ethnic Representation:** African American 29%, Asian 1%, Caucasian 66%, Hispanic 1%. **Retention and Graduation:** 62% freshmen return for sophomore year. 6% freshmen graduate within 4 years. **Faculty:** 100% faculty teach undergrads.

ACADEMICS

Degrees: Associate's, bachelor's. **Academic Requirements:** General education including some course work in arts/fine arts, computer literacy, English (including composition), foreign languages, history, humanities, mathematics, philosophy, sciences (biological or physical), social science. **Special Study Options:** Accelerated program, distance learning, double major, English as a second language, honors program, independent study, internships, liberal arts/career combination, student-designed major, teacher certification program.

FACILITIES

Housing: All-female, all-male, fraternities and/or sororities. **Library Holdings:** 34,763 bound volumes. 250 periodicals. 2,289 microforms. 2,357 audiovisuals. **Computers:** *Recommended operating system:* Windows 95. School-owned computers available for student use.

EXTRACURRICULARS

Activities: Choral groups, concert band, drama/theater, jazz band, literary magazine, music ensembles, student government, yearbook. **Organizations:** 17 registered organizations, 1 honor society, 2 religious organizations, 2 sororities (16% women join). **Athletics (Intercollegiate):** *Men:* baseball, basketball, golf, lacrosse, soccer, tennis. *Women:* basketball, cheerleading, lacrosse, soccer, softball, tennis, volleyball.

ADMISSIONS

Selectivity Rating: 63 (of 100). **Freshman Academic Profile:** Average high school GPA 2.9. 8% in top 10% of high school class, 15% in top 25% of high school class, 50% in top 50% of high school class. 95% from public high schools. Average SAT I Math 446. Average SAT I Verbal 480. Average ACT 18. TOEFL required of all international applicants, minimum TOEFL 500. **Basis for Candidate Selection:** *Very important factors considered include:* secondary school record, standardized test scores, talent/ability. *Important factors considered include:* character/personal qualities, interview, recommendations. *Other factors considered include:* alumni/ae relation, class rank, essays, extracurricular activities, work experience. **Freshman Admission Requirements:** High school diploma or GED is required. *Academic units required/recommended:* 15 total recommended; 4 English recommended, 3 math recommended, 3 science recommended, 2 science lab recommended, 3 foreign language recommended. **Freshman Admission Statistics:** 1,344 applied, 80% accepted, 21% of those accepted enrolled. **Transfer Admission Requirements:** *Items required:* college transcript, statement of good standing from prior school. Minimum high school GPA of 2.0 required. Minimum college GPA of 2.0 required. Lowest grade transferable C. **General Admission**

Information: Application fee $25. Regular application deadline rolling. Nonfall registration accepted. Admission may be deferred. Credit offered for CEEB Advanced Placement tests.

COSTS AND FINANCIAL AID

Average book expense $1,000. **Required Forms and Deadlines:** FAFSA and institution's own financial aid form. Financial aid filing deadline June 30. Priority filing deadline March 31. **Notification of Awards:** Applicants will be notified of awards on a rolling basis beginning on or about January 15. **Types of Aid:** *Need-based scholarships/grants:* Pell, SEOG, state scholarships/grants, private scholarships, the school's own gift aid. *Loans:* FFEL Subsidized Stafford, FFEL Unsubsidized Stafford, FFEL PLUS, Federal Perkins. **Student Employment:** Federal Work-Study Program available. Institutional employment available. Off-campus job opportunities are good. **Financial Aid Statistics:** 92% freshmen, 89% undergrads receive some form of aid. Average freshman grant $4,744. Average freshman loan $4,838. Average income from on-campus job $745. **Financial Aid Phone:** 800-765-7151.

LINCOLN MEMORIAL UNIVERSITY

Cumberland Gap Parkway, Harrogate, TN 37752
Phone: 423-869-6280 **E-mail:** admissions@inetlmu.lmunet.edu **CEEB Code:** 1408
Fax: 423-869-6250 **Web:** www.lmunet.edu **ACT Code:** 3982

This private school was founded in 1897. It has a 1,000-acre campus.

STUDENTS AND FACULTY

Enrollment: 875. **Student Body:** Male 33%, female 67%, out-of-state 54%, international 5% (14 countries represented). **Ethnic Representation:** African American 4%, Caucasian 96%. **Retention and Graduation:** 54% freshmen return for sophomore year. 37% freshmen graduate within 4 years. **Faculty:** Student/faculty ratio 9:1. 86 full-time faculty, 54% hold PhDs. 74% faculty teach undergrads.

ACADEMICS

Degrees: Associate's, bachelor's, master's, post-bachelor's certificate, post-master's certificate. **Academic Requirements:** General education including some course work in arts/fine arts, computer literacy, English (including composition), history, humanities, mathematics, sciences (biological or physical), social science. **Classes:** Under 10 students in an average class. Under 10 students in an average lab/discussion section. **Disciplines with Highest Percentage of Degrees Awarded:** Education 26%, business/marketing 24%, parks and recreation 10%, social sciences and history 8%, physical sciences 5%. **Special Study Options:** Accelerated program, double major, English as a second language, honors program, independent study, internships, teacher certification program.

FACILITIES

Housing: Coed, all-female, all-male, apartments for married students, apartments for single students. **Library Holdings:** 191,864 bound volumes. 6,000 periodicals. 71,824 microforms. 254 audiovisuals. **Special Academic Facilities/Equipment:** Civil War museum, including Abraham Lincoln memorabilia collection of over 6,000 books, paintings, and manuscripts. **Computers:** School-owned computers available for student use.

EXTRACURRICULARS

Activities: Choral groups, drama/theater, literary magazine, radio station, student government, student newspaper, television station, yearbook. **Organizations:** 26 registered organizations, 5 honor societies, 3 religious organizations, 3 fraternities (5% men join), 3 sororities (10% women join). **Athletics (Intercollegiate):** *Men:* baseball, basketball, cross-country, golf, soccer, tennis. *Women:* basketball, cross-country, golf, soccer, softball, tennis, volleyball.

ADMISSIONS

Selectivity Rating: 75 (of 100). **Freshman Academic Profile:** Average high school GPA 2.8. 36% in top 10% of high school class, 58% in top 25% of high school class, 94% in top 50% of high school class. 90% from public high schools. Average ACT 23, ACT middle 50% range 18-24. TOEFL required of all international applicants, minimum TOEFL 500. **Basis for Candidate Selection:** *Very important factors considered include:* secondary school record, standardized test scores. *Important factors considered include:* alumni/ae relation, character/personal qualities. *Other factors considered include:* class rank, interview, minority status, recommendations, volunteer work. **Freshman Admission Requirements:** High school diploma or GED is required. *Academic units required/recommended:* 10 total required; 22 total recommended; 4 English required, 4 English recommended, 2 math required, 3 math recommended, 2 science required, 2 science recommended, 2 science lab recommended, 2 foreign language recommended, 1 social studies required, 2 social studies recommended, 1 history required, 1 history recommended, 7 elective recommended. **Freshman Admission Statistics:** 806 applied, 84% accepted, 21% of those accepted enrolled. **Transfer Admission Requirements:** *Items required:* high school transcript, college transcript, standardized test scores. Minimum college GPA of 2.0 required. Lowest grade transferable C. **General Admission Information:** Application fee $25. Priority application deadline March 1. Nonfall registration accepted. Credit offered for CEEB Advanced Placement tests.

COSTS AND FINANCIAL AID

Tuition $9,600. Room & board $3,900. Average book expense $550. **Required Forms and Deadlines:** FAFSA. No deadline for regular filing. Priority filing deadline April 1. **Notification of Awards:** Applicants will be notified of awards on a rolling basis beginning on or about April 15. **Types of Aid:** *Need-based scholarships/grants:* Pell, SEOG, state scholarships/grants, private scholarships, the school's own gift aid. *Loans:* FFEL Subsidized Stafford, FFEL Unsubsidized Stafford, FFEL PLUS, Federal Perkins. **Student Employment:** Federal Work-Study Program available. Off-campus job opportunities are fair. **Financial Aid Statistics:** 69% freshmen, 69% undergrads receive some form of aid. Average freshman grant $7,201. Average freshman loan $2,625. Average income from on-campus job $1,500. **Financial Aid Phone:** 423-869-6336.

LINCOLN UNIVERSITY (MO)

Admissions Office, PO Box 29, JeffersonCity, MO 65102-0029
Phone: 573-681-5599 **E-mail:** enroll@lincolnu.edu
Fax: 573-681-5889 **Web:** www.lincolnu.edu **ACT Code:** 6366

This public school was founded in 1866. It has a 155-acre campus.

STUDENTS AND FACULTY

Enrollment: 2,881. **Student Body:** Male 39%, female 61%, out-of-state 10%, international 5%. **Ethnic Representation:** African American 41%, Asian 1%, Caucasian 56%, Hispanic 1%, Native American 1%. **Retention and Graduation:** 46% freshmen return for sophomore year. 9% freshmen graduate within 4 years. **Faculty:** Student/faculty ratio 18:1. 119 full-time faculty, 52% hold PhDs. 98% faculty teach undergrads.

ACADEMICS

Degrees: Associate's, bachelor's, master's. **Academic Requirements:** General education including some course work in arts/fine arts, computer literacy, English (including composition), foreign languages, history, humanities, mathematics, philosophy, sciences (biological or physical), social science, cultural diversity, and lifetime wellness. **Classes:** 20-29 students in an average class. 10-19 students in an average lab/discussion section. **Majors with Highest Enrollment:** Business administration/management; computer and information sciences, general; elementary education and teaching. **Disciplines with Highest Percentage of Degrees Awarded:** Business/marketing 22%, education 21%, social sciences and history 17%, computer and information sciences 16%, liberal arts/general studies 5%. **Special Study Options:** Accelerated program, cooperative (work-study) program, double major, dual enrollment, student exchange program (domestic), honors program, internships, liberal arts/career combination, teacher certification program, senior citizen program.

FACILITIES

Housing: All-female, all-male; housing for international students, honor students. **Library Holdings:** 165,956 bound volumes. 837 periodicals. 91,582 microforms. 6,519 audiovisuals. **Special Academic Facilities/Equipment:** World Wide Web access, large computer lab, distance learning capabilities, TV and radio station for student use, student accessible multimedia equipment. **Computers:** *Recommended operating system:* Windows 98. School-owned computers available for student use.

EXTRACURRICULARS

Activities: Choral groups, concert band, dance, drama/theater, jazz band, marching band, music ensembles, pep band, radio station, student government, student newspaper, television station, yearbook. **Organizations:** 18 registered organizations, 4 honor societies, 3 religious organizations, 4 fraternities (2% men join), 4 sororities (2% women join). **Athletics (Intercollegiate):** *Men:* baseball, basketball, cross-country, football, golf, track & field. *Women:* basketball, cheerleading, cross-country, softball, tennis, track & field.

ADMISSIONS

Selectivity Rating: 63 (of 100). **Freshman Academic Profile:** 10% in top 10% of high school class, 23% in top 25% of high school class, 46% in top 50% of high school class. 92% from public high schools. Average ACT 17. TOEFL required of all international applicants, minimum TOEFL 500. **Basis for Candidate Selection:** *Very important factors considered include:* class rank, recommendations, secondary school record, standardized test scores. *Important factors considered include:* alumni/ae relation, character/personal qualities. **Freshman Admission Requirements:** High school diploma or GED is required. *Academic units required/recommended:* 4 English required, 3 math required, 2 science required, 1 foreign language recommended, 3 social studies required, 3 elective required. **Freshman Admission Statistics:** 594 applied, 91% accepted, 87% of those accepted enrolled. **Transfer Admission Requirements:** *Items required:* college transcript, statement of good standing from prior school. Minimum college GPA of 2.0 required. Lowest grade transferable C. **General Admission Information:** Application fee $17. Priority application deadline July 15. Regular application deadline August 1. Nonfall registration accepted. Credit and/or placement offered for CEEB Advanced Placement tests.

COSTS AND FINANCIAL AID

In-state tuition $3,540. Out-of-state tuition $7,080. Room & board $3,790. Required fees $428. Average book expense $800. **Required Forms and Deadlines:** FAFSA. No deadline for regular filing. Priority filing deadline March 1. **Notification of Awards:** Applicants will be notified of awards on a rolling basis beginning on or about February 1. **Types of Aid:** *Need-based scholarships/grants:* Pell, SEOG, state scholarships/grants, private scholarships, the school's own gift aid, Federal Nursing. *Loans:* FFEL Subsidized Stafford, FFEL Unsubsidized Stafford, FFEL PLUS. **Student Employment:** Federal Work-Study Program available. Institutional employment available. Off-campus job opportunities are good. **Financial Aid Statistics:** 42% freshmen, 53% undergrads receive some form of aid. Average freshman grant $5,300. Average freshman loan $2,625. Average income from on-campus job $1,200. **Financial Aid Phone:** 314-681-6156.

LINCOLN UNIVERSITY (PA)

Lincoln Hall, Lincoln University, PA 19352-0999
Phone: 610-932-8300 **E-mail:** admiss@lu.lincoln.edu **CEEB Code:** 2367
Fax: 610-932-1209 **Web:** www.lincoln.edu **ACT Code:** 3614

This public school was founded in 1854. It has a 422-acre campus.

STUDENTS AND FACULTY

Enrollment: 1,438. **Student Body:** Male 40%, female 60%, out-of-state 47%, international 5%. **Ethnic Representation:** African American 98%, Caucasian 1%. **Retention and Graduation:** 64% freshmen return for sophomore year. 22% freshmen graduate within 4 years. 10% grads pursue business degrees. 1% grads pursue law degrees. 1% grads pursue medical degrees. **Faculty:** Student/faculty ratio 14:1. 108 full-time faculty, 67% hold PhDs. 94% faculty teach undergrads.

ACADEMICS

Degrees: Bachelor's, certificate, master's. **Classes:** 20-29 students in an average class. Under 10 students in an average lab/discussion section. **Majors with Highest Enrollment:** Business administration/management; computer science; biology/biological sciences, general. **Disciplines with Highest Percentage of Degrees Awarded:** Business/marketing 17%, education 14%, social sciences and history 13%, protective services/public administration 11%, physical sciences 11%. **Special Study Options:** Accelerated program, cooperative (work-study) program, double major, dual enrollment, student exchange program (domestic), honors program, internships, liberal arts/career combination, study abroad, teacher certification program. Joint programs in communications and journalism with Temple University. 2-2 in advanced science/engineering with Drexel University, Pennsylvania State University, University of Pittsburgh, Lafayette University, and New Jersey Institute of Technology.

FACILITIES

Housing: Coed, all-female, all-male. **Library Holdings:** 185,197 bound volumes. 540 periodicals. 210,009 microforms. 2,630 audiovisuals. **Special Academic Facilities/Equipment:** African museum, fine arts center, hall for life sciences, learning resource center. **Computers:** *Recommended operating system:* Windows 95. School-owned computers available for student use.

EXTRACURRICULARS

Activities: Choral groups, concert band, dance, drama/theater, jazz band, music ensembles, radio station, student government, student newspaper, television station, yearbook. **Organizations:** 15 registered organizations, 4 honor societies, 4 fraternities (3% men join), 4 sororities (10% women join). **Athletics (Intercollegiate):** *Men:* baseball, basketball, cross-country, indoor track, soccer, tennis, track & field. *Women:* basketball, cross-country, indoor track, soccer, tennis, track & field, volleyball.

ADMISSIONS

Selectivity Rating: 74 (of 100). **Freshman Academic Profile:** Average high school GPA 2.7. Average SAT I Math 410. Average SAT I Verbal 422. Average ACT 14. **Basis for Candidate Selection:** *Very important factors considered include:* secondary school record. *Important factors considered include:* extracurricular activities, standardized test scores, talent/ability. *Other factors considered include:* alumni/ae relation, class rank, essays, interview, recommendations. **Freshman Admission Requirements:** High school diploma or GED is required. *Academic units required/recommended:* 21 total required; 4 English required, 3 math required, 3 science required, 2 foreign language recommended, 3 social studies required, 5 elective required. **Freshman Admission Statistics:** 1,763 applied, 28% accepted, 99% of those accepted enrolled. **Transfer Admission Requirements:** *Items required:* high school transcript, college transcript, statement of good standing from prior school. Minimum college GPA of 2.0 required. Lowest grade transferable C. **General Admission Information:** Application fee $20. Nonfall registration accepted. Placement offered for CEEB Advanced Placement tests.

COSTS AND FINANCIAL AID

In-state tuition $4,032. Out-of-state tuition $6,862. Room & board $5,332. Required fees $2,068. Average book expense $350. **Required Forms and Deadlines:** FAFSA, state aid form, and noncustodial (divorced/separated) parent's statement. Priority filing deadline March 15. **Notification of Awards:** Applicants will be notified of awards on a rolling basis beginning on or about May 2. **Types of Aid:** *Need-based scholarships/grants:* Pell, SEOG, state scholarships/grants, private scholarships, the school's own gift aid. *Loans:* FFEL Subsidized Stafford, FFEL Unsubsidized Stafford, FFEL PLUS, Federal Perkins. **Student Employment:** Federal Work-Study Program available. Institutional employment available. Off-campus job opportunities are poor. **Financial Aid Statistics:** 81% freshmen, 39% undergrads receive some form of aid. Average freshman loan $2,000. **Financial Aid Phone:** 610-932-8300.

See page 1090.

LINDENWOOD COLLEGE

209 South Kingshighway, St. Charles, MO 63301-1695
Phone: 314-949-4949 **E-mail:** admissions@lc.lindenwood.edu **CEEB Code:** 6367
Fax: 314-949-4910 **Web:** www.lindenwood.edu **ACT Code:** 2324

This private school, which is affiliated with the Presbyterian Church, was founded in 1827. It has a 172-acre campus.

STUDENTS AND FACULTY

Enrollment: 2,891. **Student Body:** Out-of-state 15%, international 1% (17 countries represented). **Ethnic Representation:** African American 8%, Asian 1%, Caucasian 88%, Hispanic 1%, Native American 1%. **Retention and Graduation:** 20% grads go on to further study within 1 year. 10% grads pursue business degrees. 1% grads pursue law degrees. 1% grads pursue medical degrees.

ACADEMICS

Degrees: Bachelor's. **Special Study Options:** Cooperative (work-study) program, evening programs. Undergrads may take grad-level classes. Co-op programs: business, computer science. Other special programs: College for Individualized Education (primarily for adults and other nontraditional students) offers degree programs at regional centers.

FACILITIES

Housing: Coed, all-female, all-male, apartments for married students. **Library Holdings:** 132,131 bound volumes. 447 periodicals. 32,300 microforms. **Special Academic Facilities/Equipment:** Archival museum. **Computers:** *Recommended operating system:* Mac. School-owned computers available for student use.

EXTRACURRICULARS

Activities: Radio station, student government, student newspaper, yearbook. **Organizations:** 20 registered organizations, 3 honor societies, 2 religious organizations, 3 fraternities (13% men join), 1 sorority (11% women join). **Athletics (Intercollegiate):** *Men:* baseball, basketball, cheerleading, cross-country, golf, indoor track, soccer, softball, track & field, volleyball, wrestling. *Women:* basketball, cheerleading, cross-country, golf, indoor track, soccer, softball, track & field, volleyball.

ADMISSIONS

Selectivity Rating: 63 (of 100). **Freshman Academic Profile:** 53% in top 10% of high school class, 79% in top 25% of high school class, 98% in top 50% of high school class. 75% from public high schools. Average SAT I Math 477.

Average SAT I Verbal 480. Average ACT 23. TOEFL required of all international applicants, minimum TOEFL 500. **Freshman Admission Requirements:** High school diploma is required and GED is not accepted. *Academic units required/recommended:* 4 English recommended, 3 math recommended, 3 science recommended, 2 foreign language recommended, 2 social studies recommended, 2 history recommended. **Transfer Admission Requirements:** Minimum college GPA of 2.0 required. Lowest grade transferable D. **General Admission Information:** Regular application deadline August 1. Nonfall registration accepted. Credit and/or placement offered for CEEB Advanced Placement tests.

COSTS AND FINANCIAL AID

Room & board $5,000. Required fees $200. Average book expense $1,050. **Required Forms and Deadlines:** FAFSA. **Types of Aid:** *Need-based scholarships/grants:* Pell, SEOG, state scholarships/grants, private scholarships, the school's own gift aid, United Negro College Fund. *Loans:* FFEL Subsidized Stafford, FFEL Unsubsidized Stafford, FFEL PLUS, Federal Perkins, college/university loans from institutional funds. **Student Employment:** Federal Work-Study Program available. Institutional employment available. Off-campus job opportunities are good. **Financial Aid Statistics:** Average freshman grant $6,544. Average freshman loan $2,000. Average income from on-campus job $1,500. **Financial Aid Phone:** 314-949-4923.

LINDSEY WILSON COLLEGE

210 Lindsey Wilson Street, Columbia, KY 42728
Phone: 800-264-0138 **E-mail:** admissions@lindsey.edu **CEEB Code:** 1409
Fax: 270-384-8591 **Web:** www.lindsey.edu **ACT Code:** 1522

This private school, which is affiliated with the Methodist Church, was founded in 1903. It has a 43-acre campus.

STUDENTS AND FACULTY

Enrollment: 1,451. **Student Body:** Male 36%, female 64%, out-of-state 6%, international 4%. **Ethnic Representation:** African American 8%, Asian 1%, Caucasian 87%, Hispanic 2%. **Retention and Graduation:** 49% freshmen return for sophomore year. **Faculty:** Student/faculty ratio 21:1.

ACADEMICS

Degrees: Associate's, bachelor's, master's. **Academic Requirements:** General education including some course work in arts/fine arts, English (including composition), humanities, mathematics, sciences (biological or physical). **Majors with Highest Enrollment:** Biology/biological sciences, general; elementary education and teaching; social sciences, general. **Special Study Options:** Cooperative (work-study) program, English as a second language, internships, study abroad.

FACILITIES

Housing: All-female, all-male, apartments for single students. **Library Holdings:** 62,164 bound volumes. 1,350 periodicals. 227,812 microforms. **Computers:** School-owned computers available for student use.

EXTRACURRICULARS

Activities: Choral groups, literary magazine, student government, student newspaper, yearbook. **Organizations:** 28 registered organizations. **Athletics (Intercollegiate):** *Men:* baseball, basketball, cross-country, golf, soccer, tennis, track & field. *Women:* basketball, cross-country, golf, soccer, softball, tennis, track & field, volleyball.

ADMISSIONS

Selectivity Rating: 63 (of 100). **Freshman Academic Profile:** Average ACT 19. TOEFL required of all international applicants, minimum TOEFL 490. **Freshman Admission Requirements:** High school diploma or GED is required. **Freshman Admission Statistics:** 1,335 applied, 57% accepted, 55% of those accepted enrolled. **Transfer Admission Requirements:** *Items required:* college transcript, standardized test scores, statement of good standing from prior school. Lowest grade transferable D. **General Admission Information:** Nonfall registration accepted. Placement offered for CEEB Advanced Placement tests.

COSTS AND FINANCIAL AID

Tuition $12,456. Room & board $5,484. Required fees $146. Average book expense $350. **Required Forms and Deadlines:** FAFSA, institution's own financial aid form, and state aid form. **Types of Aid:** *Need-based scholarships/grants:* Pell, SEOG, state scholarships/grants, private scholarships, the school's own gift aid. *Loans:* FFEL Subsidized Stafford, FFEL PLUS, Federal Perkins, college/university loans from institutional funds. **Student Employment:** Federal Work-Study Program available. Institutional employment available. Off-campus job opportunities are good. **Financial Aid Statistics:** Average freshman grant $7,192. Average freshman loan $2,625. **Financial Aid Phone:** 270-384-8022.

LINFIELD COLLEGE

900 South East Baker Street, McMinnville, OR 97128-6894
Phone: 503-883-2213 **E-mail:** admissions@linfield.edu **CEEB Code:** 4387
Fax: 503-883-2472 **Web:** www.linfield.edu **ACT Code:** 3466

This private school, which is affiliated with the American Baptist Church, was founded in 1849. It has a 193-acre campus.

STUDENTS AND FACULTY

Enrollment: 1,627. **Student Body:** Male 44%, female 56%, out-of-state 44%, international 2% (16 countries represented). **Ethnic Representation:** African American 2%, Asian 6%, Caucasian 81%, Hispanic 2%, Native American 1%. **Retention and Graduation:** 81% freshmen return for sophomore year. 60% freshmen graduate within 4 years. 22% grads go on to further study within 1 year. 2% grads pursue business degrees. 2% grads pursue law degrees. 2% grads pursue medical degrees. **Faculty:** Student/faculty ratio 12:1. 101 full-time faculty, 97% hold PhDs. 100% faculty teach undergrads.

ACADEMICS

Degrees: Bachelor's. **Academic Requirements:** General education including some course work in arts/fine arts, English (including composition), foreign languages, history, humanities, mathematics, philosophy, sciences (biological or physical), social science, diversity. **Classes:** 10-19 students in an average class. **Majors with Highest Enrollment:** Business administration/management; elementary education and teaching; mathematics, general. **Disciplines with Highest Percentage of Degrees Awarded:** Business/marketing 22%, social sciences and history 13%, education 10%, parks and recreation 9%, communications/communication technologies 7%. **Special Study Options:** Cross registration, distance learning, double major, English as a second language, external degree program, independent study, internships, liberal arts/career combination, student-designed major, study abroad, teacher certification program, off-campus study, learning support services, unique January term courses.

FACILITIES

Housing: Coed, all-female, all-male, apartments for single students, housing for disabled students, fraternities and/or sororities. **Library Holdings:** 162,892 bound volumes. 1,296 periodicals. 16,680 microforms. 19,549 audiovisuals. **Special Academic Facilities/Equipment:** Art gallery, anthropology museum, environmental field station, research institute, electron microscope, scanning auger microprobe spectrometer. **Computers:** School-owned computers available for student use.

EXTRACURRICULARS

Activities: Choral groups, concert band, dance, drama/theater, jazz band, literary magazine, music ensembles, musical theater, opera, pep band, radio station, student government, student newspaper, symphony orchestra, yearbook. **Organizations:** 70 registered organizations, 12 honor societies, 4 religious organizations, 4 fraternities (22% men join), 4 sororities (28% women join). **Athletics (Intercollegiate):** *Men:* baseball, basketball, cheerleading, cross-country, football, golf, soccer, swimming, tennis, track & field. *Women:* basketball, cheerleading, cross-country, golf, lacrosse, soccer, softball, swimming, tennis, track & field, volleyball.

ADMISSIONS

Selectivity Rating: 76 (of 100). **Freshman Academic Profile:** Average high school GPA 3.5. 30% in top 10% of high school class, 55% in top 25% of high school class, 87% in top 50% of high school class. 74% from public high schools. Average SAT I Math 550, SAT I Math middle 50% range 490-600. Average SAT I Verbal 560, SAT I Verbal middle 50% range 480-590. Average ACT 23, ACT middle 50% range 20-26. **Basis for Candidate Selection:** *Very important factors considered include:* secondary school record, standardized test scores. *Important factors considered include:* class rank, essays, recommendations. *Other factors considered include:* alumni/ae relation, character/personal qualities, extracurricular activities, geographical residence, minority status, talent/ability, volunteer work, work experience. **Freshman Admission Requirements:** High school diploma or GED is required. *Academic units required/recommended:* 17 total recommended; 4 English recommended, 4 math recommended, 3 science recommended, 2 foreign language recommended, 2 social studies recommended, 2 history recommended. **Freshman Admission Statistics:** 1,651 applied, 80% accepted, 33% of those accepted enrolled. **Transfer Admission Requirements:** *Items required:* college transcript, essay. Minimum college GPA of 2.0 required. Lowest grade transferable C. **General Admission Information:** Application fee $40. Priority application deadline February 15. Nonfall registration accepted. Admission may be deferred for a maximum of 1 year. Credit offered for CEEB Advanced Placement tests.

COSTS AND FINANCIAL AID

Tuition $20,160. Room & board $6,553. Required fees $170. Average book expense $600. **Required Forms and Deadlines:** FAFSA. Priority filing deadline February 1. **Notification of Awards:** Applicants will be notified of awards on or about April 1. **Types of Aid:** *Need-based scholarships/grants:* Pell, SEOG, state scholarships/grants, private scholarships, the school's own gift aid. *Loans:* FFEL Subsidized Stafford, FFEL Unsubsidized Stafford, FFEL PLUS, Federal Perkins, college/university loans from institutional funds, private loans from multiple lenders. **Student Employment:** Federal Work-Study Program available. Institutional employment available. Off-campus job opportunities are good. **Financial Aid Statistics:** 66% freshmen, 69% undergrads receive some form of aid. Average freshman grant $5,985. Average freshman loan $3,333. Average income from on-campus job $915. **Financial Aid Phone:** 503-434-2225.

LIPSCOMB UNIVERSITY

3901 Granny White Pike, Nashville, TN 37204-3951
Phone: 615-269-1776 **E-mail:** admissions@lipscomb.edu **CEEB Code:** 1161
Fax: 615-269-1804 **Web:** www.lipscomb.edu **ACT Code:** 3956

This private school was founded in 1891. It has a 65-acre campus.

STUDENTS AND FACULTY

Enrollment: 2,317. **Student Body:** Male 44%, female 56%, out-of-state 34%, international 1% (43 countries represented). **Ethnic Representation:** African American 4%, Asian 1%, Caucasian 88%. **Retention and Graduation:** 79% freshmen return for sophomore year. 29% freshmen graduate within 4 years. **Faculty:** 100% faculty teach undergrads.

ACADEMICS

Degrees: Bachelor's, first professional, master's. **Special Study Options:** Accelerated program, double major, dual enrollment, honors program, independent study, internships, student-designed major.

FACILITIES

Housing: All-female, all-male. **Library Holdings:** 150,512 bound volumes. 38,685 periodicals. 26,018 microforms. **Special Academic Facilities/ Equipment:** On-campus elementary, middle, and secondary schools. **Computers:** *Recommended operating system:* Windows 95. School-owned computers available for student use.

EXTRACURRICULARS

Activities: Radio station, student government, student newspaper, television station, yearbook. **Organizations:** 65 registered organizations, 5 honor societies, 7 fraternities (16% men join), 7 sororities (19% women join). **Athletics (Intercollegiate):** *Men:* baseball, basketball, cross-country, golf, soccer, tennis, track & field. *Women:* basketball, cheerleading, cross-country, softball, tennis.

ADMISSIONS

Selectivity Rating: 63 (of 100). **Freshman Academic Profile:** Average high school GPA 3.3. 26% in top 10% of high school class, 53% in top 25% of high school class, 78% in top 50% of high school class. 75% from public high schools. Average SAT I Math 475, SAT I Math middle 50% range 480-610. Average SAT I Verbal 554, SAT I Verbal middle 50% range 500-610. Average ACT 24, ACT middle 50% range 20-27. TOEFL required of all international applicants, minimum TOEFL 500. **Basis for Candidate Selection:** *Very important factors considered include:* character/personal qualities, class rank, recommendations, secondary school record, standardized test scores. *Other factors considered include:* alumni/ae relation, essays, extracurricular activities, minority status, religious affiliation/commitment, talent/ability. **Freshman Admission Requirements:** High school diploma or GED is required. *Academic units required/recommended:* 14 total required; 4 English required, 2 math required, 2 science required, 2 science lab recommended, 2 foreign language required, 2 history required, 2 elective required. **Freshman Admission Statistics:** 1,594 applied, 93% accepted, 41% of those accepted enrolled. **Transfer Admission Requirements:** *Items required:* college transcript. Minimum high school GPA of 2.3 required. Minimum college GPA of 2.0 required. Lowest grade transferable C. **General Admission Information:** Application fee $55. Priority application deadline November 15. Regular application deadline August 15. Nonfall registration accepted. Credit and/or placement offered for CEEB Advanced Placement tests.

COSTS AND FINANCIAL AID

Tuition $8,470. Room & board $3,910. Required fees $244. Average book expense $200. **Required Forms and Deadlines:** FAFSA. **Notification of Awards:** Applicants will be notified of awards on or about March 1. **Types of Aid:** *Need-based scholarships/grants:* Pell, SEOG, state scholarships/grants, private scholarships, the school's own gift aid. *Loans:* FFEL Subsidized Stafford, FFEL PLUS, Federal Perkins, state loans, college/university loans from institutional funds. **Student Employment:** Federal Work-Study Program available. Institutional employment available. Off-campus job opportunities are excellent. **Financial Aid Statistics:** Average freshman grant $6,200. Average freshman loan $2,848. Average income from on-campus job $810. **Financial Aid Phone:** 615-269-1791.

LOCK HAVEN UNIVERSITY OF PENNSYLVANIA

Lock Haven University, Akeley Hall, Lock Haven, PA 17745
Phone: 570-893-2027 **E-mail:** admissions@lhup.edu **CEEB Code:** 2654
Fax: 570-893-2201 **Web:** www.lhup.edu **ACT Code:** 3708

This public school was founded in 1870. It has a 165-acre campus.

STUDENTS AND FACULTY

Enrollment: 4,394. **Student Body:** Male 40%, female 60%, out-of-state 8%, international 2% (25 countries represented). **Ethnic Representation:** African American 3%, Asian 1%, Caucasian 94%, Hispanic 1%. **Retention and Graduation:** 70% freshmen return for sophomore year. 23% freshmen graduate within 4 years. **Faculty:** Student/faculty ratio 18:1. 214 full-time faculty, 57% hold PhDs. 99% faculty teach undergrads.

ACADEMICS

Degrees: Associate's, bachelor's, certificate, master's, terminal. **Academic Requirements:** General education including some course work in arts/fine arts, computer literacy, English (including composition), foreign languages, history, humanities, mathematics, philosophy, sciences (biological or physical), social science. **Classes:** 20-29 students in an average class. 20-29 students in an average lab/discussion section. **Majors with Highest Enrollment:** Elementary education and teaching; health professions and related sciences; health and physical education/fitness. **Disciplines with Highest Percentage of Degrees Awarded:** Education 23%, parks and recreation 21%, health professions and related sciences 11%, business/marketing 7%, social sciences and history 7%. **Special Study Options:** Cooperative (work-study) program, distance learning, double major, honors program, independent study, internships, student-designed major, study abroad, teacher certification program.

FACILITIES

Housing: Coed, all-female, apartments for single students. **Library Holdings:** 370,967 bound volumes. 1,117 periodicals. 772,071 microforms. **Special Academic Facilities/Equipment:** Planetarium, Sloan Art Gallery, library archives. **Computers:** School-owned computers available for student use.

EXTRACURRICULARS

Activities: Choral groups, concert band, dance, drama/theater, jazz band, marching band, music ensembles, radio station, student government, student newspaper, television station. **Organizations:** 82 registered organizations, 14 honor societies, 5 religious organizations, 7 fraternities (4% men join), 4 sororities (3% women join). **Athletics (Intercollegiate):** *Men:* baseball, basketball, cheerleading, cross-country, football, indoor track, soccer, track & field, wrestling. *Women:* basketball, cheerleading, cross-country, field hockey, indoor track, lacrosse, soccer, softball, swimming, track & field, volleyball.

ADMISSIONS

Selectivity Rating: 76 (of 100). **Freshman Academic Profile:** Average high school GPA 3.1. 8% in top 10% of high school class, 27% in top 25% of high school class, 65% in top 50% of high school class. Average SAT I Math 482, SAT I Math middle 50% range 430-530. Average SAT I Verbal 485, SAT I Verbal middle 50% range 430-530. TOEFL required of all international applicants, minimum TOEFL 550. **Basis for Candidate Selection:** *Very important factors considered include:* character/personal qualities, class rank, secondary school record, talent/ability. *Important factors considered include:* standardized test scores. *Other factors considered include:* essays, extracurricular activities, interview, recommendations, volunteer work, work experience. **Freshman Admission Requirements:** High school diploma or GED is required. *Academic units required/recommended:* 16 total required; 17 total recommended; 4 English required, 3 math required, 4 math recommended, 3 science required, 4 science recommended, 2 science lab required, 3 science lab recommended, 2 foreign language recommended, 2 social studies required, 2 social studies recommended, 2 history required, 2 history recommended.

Freshman Admission Statistics: 3,577 applied, 83% accepted, 36% of those accepted enrolled. **Transfer Admission Requirements:** *Items required:* college transcript, statement of good standing from prior school. Minimum college GPA of 2.0 required. Lowest grade transferable C. **General Admission Information:** Application fee $25. Priority application deadline March 1. Nonfall registration accepted. Admission may be deferred for a maximum of 1 year. Credit and/or placement offered for CEEB Advanced Placement tests.

COSTS AND FINANCIAL AID

In-state tuition $4,378. Out-of-state tuition $8,946. Room & board $4,742. Required fees $1,228. Average book expense $900. **Required Forms and Deadlines:** FAFSA and institution's own financial aid form. No deadline for regular filing. Priority filing deadline March 15. **Notification of Awards:** Applicants will be notified of awards on a rolling basis beginning on or about March 1. **Types of Aid:** *Need-based scholarships/grants:* Pell, SEOG, state scholarships/grants, the school's own gift aid. *Loans:* FFEL Subsidized Stafford, FFEL Unsubsidized Stafford, FFEL PLUS, Federal Perkins. **Student Employment:** Federal Work-Study Program available. Institutional employment available. Off-campus job opportunities are good. **Financial Aid Statistics:** 89% freshmen, 75% undergrads receive some form of aid. Average freshman grant $2,350. Average freshman loan $2,800. Average income from on-campus job $1,200. **Financial Aid Phone:** 877-405-3057.

See page 1092.

LOMA LINDA UNIVERSITY

Office of Admissions, Loma Linda, CA 92350
Phone: 909-824-4599
Fax: 909-824-4291 **Web:** www.llu.edu

This private school is affiliated with the Seventh-Day Adventist Church.

STUDENTS AND FACULTY

Enrollment: 1,255. **Student Body:** International students represent 80 countries.

ACADEMICS

Degrees: Associate's, bachelor's, certificate, doctoral, master's, post-bachelor's certificate. **Academic Requirements:** General education including some course work in sciences (biological or physical). **Special Study Options:** Distance learning.

FACILITIES

Housing: Coed, all-female, all-male, apartments for single students. **Computers:** *Recommended operating system:* Mac.

EXTRACURRICULARS

Activities: Student government, student newspaper, yearbook. **Organizations:** 1 honor society, 1 religious organization.

ADMISSIONS

Selectivity Rating: 60 (of 100). **Basis for Candidate Selection:** *Very important factors considered include:* character/personal qualities, essays, interview, recommendations, religious affiliation/commitment. *Important factors considered include:* talent/ability, volunteer work, work experience. *Other factors considered include:* alumni/ae relation, extracurricular activities. **Freshman Admission Requirements:** High school diploma or GED is required. **Transfer Admission Requirements:** *Items required:* high school transcript, college transcript, essay, interview. Minimum college GPA of 2.0 required. Lowest grade transferable 2. **General Admission Information:** Application fee $50. Regular application deadline rolling. Admission may be deferred for a maximum of 1 year.

COSTS AND FINANCIAL AID

Tuition $13,650. Room & board $1,890. Average book expense $975. **Types of Aid:** *Loans:* FFEL Subsidized Stafford, FFEL PLUS. **Financial Aid Phone:** 909-824-4509.

LONG ISLAND UNIVERSITY—BROOKLYN

One University Plaza, Brooklyn, NY 11201
Phone: 800-548-7526 **CEEB Code:** 2369
Fax: 718-797-2399 **Web:** www.liunet.edu

This private school was founded in 1926. It has a 10-acre campus.

STUDENTS AND FACULTY

Enrollment: 4,193. **Student Body:** Out-of-state 7%, international 3% (30 countries represented). **Ethnic Representation:** African American 48%, Asian 11%, Caucasian 22%, Hispanic 19%. **Retention and Graduation:** 15% grads go on to further study within 1 year.

ACADEMICS

Degrees: Associate's, bachelor's, doctoral, master's. **Special Study Options:** Cooperative (work-study) program. Undergrads may take grad-level classes. Co-op programs: arts, business, computer science, technologies. Off-campus study: United Nations.

FACILITIES

Housing: Coed, all-female, all-male, apartments for single students. **Library Holdings:** 250,000 bound volumes. 1,265 periodicals. 40,500 microforms. **Special Academic Facilities/Equipment:** Language lab, instructional resources center. **Computers:** *Recommended operating system:* Mac. School-owned computers available for student use.

EXTRACURRICULARS

Organizations: 3 fraternities, 3 sororities. **Athletics (Intercollegiate):** *Men:* basketball, cross-country, softball, tennis, track & field. *Women:* basketball, cross-country, softball, tennis, track & field.

ADMISSIONS

Selectivity Rating: 63 (of 100). **Freshman Academic Profile:** 82% from public high schools. TOEFL required of all international applicants, minimum TOEFL 550. **Freshman Admission Requirements:** High school diploma is required and GED is not accepted. *Academic units required/recommended:* 16 total required; 4 English required, 2 math required, 1 science required, 2 foreign language required, 3 social studies required, 4 elective required. **Transfer Admission Requirements:** Minimum college GPA of 2.0 required. Lowest grade transferable C. **General Admission Information:** Regular application deadline rolling. Nonfall registration accepted. Credit and/or placement offered for CEEB Advanced Placement tests.

COSTS AND FINANCIAL AID

Room & board $7,620. Average book expense $700. **Required Forms and Deadlines:** FAFSA, institution's own financial aid form, and state aid form. **Types of Aid:** *Need-based scholarships/grants:* Pell, SEOG, state scholarships/grants, private scholarships, the school's own gift aid. *Loans:* FFEL Subsidized Stafford, FFEL Unsubsidized Stafford, FFEL PLUS, Federal Perkins, college/university loans from institutional funds. **Student Employment:** Federal Work-Study Program available. Institutional employment available. Off-campus job opportunities are good. **Financial Aid Statistics:** Average freshman grant $7,000. **Financial Aid Phone:** 718-488-1037.

LONG ISLAND UNIVERSITY—C.W. POST

720 Northern Boulevard, Brookville, NY 11548
Phone: 516-299-2900 **E-mail:** enroll@cwpost.liu.edu **CEEB Code:** 2070
Fax: 516-299-2137 **Web:** www.liu.edu

This private school was founded in 1954. It has a 308-acre campus.

STUDENTS AND FACULTY

Enrollment: 5,748. **Student Body:** Male 43%, female 57%, out-of-state 6%, international 2%. **Ethnic Representation:** African American 7%, Asian 2%, Caucasian 50%, Hispanic 7%, Native American 1%. **Faculty:** 100% faculty teach undergrads.

ACADEMICS

Degrees: Associate's, bachelor's, certificate, doctoral, master's. **Academic Requirements:** General education including some course work in arts/fine arts, computer literacy, English (including composition), foreign languages, history, humanities, mathematics, philosophy, sciences (biological or physical), social science. **Special Study Options:** Accelerated program, cooperative (work-study) program, cross registration, double major, English as a second language, honors program, independent study, internships, liberal arts/career combination, student-designed major, study abroad, teacher certification program, weekend college.

FACILITIES

Housing: Coed. **Library Holdings:** 859,212 bound volumes. 11,446 periodicals. 770,573 microforms. 34,530 audiovisuals. **Special Academic Facilities/Equipment:** Art museum, performing arts center, concert theatre, television equipment, video production facility, 3 electron microscopes. **Computers:** *Recommended operating system:* Windows 95. School-owned computers available for student use.

EXTRACURRICULARS

Activities: Choral groups, concert band, dance, drama/theater, jazz band, literary magazine, music ensembles, musical theater, radio station, student government, student newspaper, symphony orchestra, television station, yearbook. **Organizations:** 104 registered organizations, 19 honor societies, 5 fraternities (1% men join), 4 sororities (1% women join). **Athletics (Intercollegiate):** *Men:* baseball, basketball, cross-country, football, lacrosse, soccer, track & field. *Women:* basketball, cheerleading, cross-country, field hockey, soccer, softball, tennis, track & field, volleyball.

ADMISSIONS

Selectivity Rating: 79 (of 100). **Freshman Academic Profile:** Average high school GPA 3.0. 10% in top 10% of high school class, 26% in top 25% of high school class, 61% in top 50% of high school class. 80% from public high schools. Average SAT I Math 518, SAT I Math middle 50% range 500-600. Average SAT I Verbal 517, SAT I Verbal middle 50% range 500-550. TOEFL required of all international applicants, minimum TOEFL 500. **Basis for Candidate Selection:** *Very important factors considered include:* secondary school record. *Important factors considered include:* class rank, interview, recommendations, standardized test scores. *Other factors considered include:* alumni/ae relation, character/personal qualities, essays, extracurricular activities, talent/ability, volunteer work, work experience. **Freshman Admission Requirements:** High school diploma or GED is required. *Academic units required/recommended:* 16 total required; 24 total recommended; 4 English required, 4 English recommended, 2 math required, 4 math recommended, 2 science required, 4 science recommended, 2 science lab required, 4 science lab recommended, 2 foreign language required, 4 foreign language recommended, 3 social studies required, 4 social studies recommended, 1 elective required. **Freshman Admission Statistics:** 3,315 applied, 85% accepted, 26% of those accepted enrolled. **Transfer Admission Requirements:** *Items required:* college transcript, statement of good standing from prior school. Minimum high school GPA of 2.0 required. Minimum college GPA of 2.0 required. Lowest grade transferable C. **General Admission Information:** Application fee $30. Regular application deadline rolling. Nonfall registration accepted. Admission may be deferred. Credit offered for CEEB Advanced Placement tests.

COSTS AND FINANCIAL AID

Average book expense $600. **Required Forms and Deadlines:** FAFSA, CSS/Financial Aid PROFILE, and state aid form. Financial aid filing deadline May 15. Priority filing deadline February 1. **Notification of Awards:** Applicants will be notified of awards on a rolling basis beginning on or about March 1. **Types of Aid:** *Need-based scholarships/grants:* Pell, SEOG, state scholarships/grants, private scholarships, the school's own gift aid. *Loans:* Direct Subsidized Stafford, Direct Unsubsidized Stafford, Direct PLUS, Federal Perkins, college/university loans from institutional funds. **Student Employment:** Federal Work-Study Program available. Institutional employment available. Off-campus job opportunities are good. **Financial Aid Statistics:** 88% freshmen, 62% undergrads receive some form of aid. Average freshman grant $4,400. Average freshman loan $4,125. Average income from on-campus job $600. **Financial Aid Phone:** 516-299-2338.

LONGWOOD UNIVERSITY

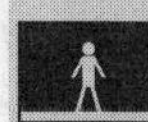

Admissions Office, 201 High Street, Farmville, VA 23909
Phone: 434-395-2060 **E-mail:** admit@longwood.edu **CEEB Code:** 5368
Fax: 434-395-2332 **Web:** www.longwood.edu **ACT Code:** 4366

This public school was founded in 1839. It has a 160-acre campus.

STUDENTS AND FACULTY

Enrollment: 3,640. **Student Body:** Male 34%, female 66%, out-of-state 10%, international students represent 20 countries. **Ethnic Representation:** African American 8%, Asian 2%, Caucasian 87%, Hispanic 2%. **Retention and Graduation:** 82% freshmen return for sophomore year. 39% freshmen graduate within 4 years. 15% grads go on to further study within 1 year. **Faculty:** Student/faculty ratio 20:1. 171 full-time faculty, 80% hold PhDs. 100% faculty teach undergrads.

ACADEMICS

Degrees: Bachelor's, master's. **Academic Requirements:** General education including some course work in arts/fine arts, English (including composition), foreign languages, history, humanities, mathematics, sciences (biological or physical), social science, literature, physical activity, ethics, issues of citizen leadership. **Classes:** 20-29 students in an average class. 20-29 students in an average lab/discussion section. **Majors with Highest Enrollment:** Business administration/management; elementary education and teaching; psychology, general. **Disciplines with Highest Percentage of Degrees Awarded:** Business/marketing 25%, education 20%, social sciences and history 13%, psychology 7%, health professions and related sciences 6%. **Special Study Options:** Accelerated program, cross registration, distance learning, double major, dual enrollment, honors program, independent study, internships, liberal arts/career combination, study abroad, teacher certification program.

FACILITIES

Housing: Coed, all-female, apartments for single students, housing for disabled students, fraternities and/or sororities. **Library Holdings:** 242,056 bound volumes. 2,505 periodicals. 679,788 microforms. 31,587 audiovisuals. **Special Academic Facilities/Equipment:** Longwood Center for the Visual Arts. **Computers:** School-owned computers available for student use.

EXTRACURRICULARS

Activities: Choral groups, concert band, dance, drama/theater, jazz band, literary magazine, music ensembles, musical theater, radio station, student government, student newspaper, yearbook. **Organizations:** 125 registered organizations, 4 honor societies, 9 religious organizations, 8 fraternities (18% men join), 12 sororities (20% women join). **Athletics (Intercollegiate):** *Men:* baseball, basketball, cheerleading, golf, soccer, tennis. *Women:* basketball, cheerleading, field hockey, golf, lacrosse, soccer, softball, tennis.

ADMISSIONS

Selectivity Rating: 67 (of 100). **Freshman Academic Profile:** Average high school GPA 3.2. 9% in top 10% of high school class, 38% in top 25% of high school class, 85% in top 50% of high school class. 92% from public high schools. Average SAT I Math 530, SAT I Math middle 50% range 500-560. Average SAT I Verbal 550, SAT I Verbal middle 50% range 500-570. **Basis for Candidate Selection:** *Very important factors considered include:* secondary school record, standardized test scores. *Important factors considered include:* essays. *Other factors considered include:* alumni/ae relation, character/personal qualities, class rank, extracurricular activities, geographical residence, minority status, recommendations, state residency, talent/ability, volunteer work, work experience. **Freshman Admission Requirements:** High school diploma or GED is required. *Academic units required/recommended:* 18 total required; 23 total recommended; 4 English required, 3 math required, 4 math recommended, 3 science required, 4 science recommended, 2 science lab required, 2 foreign language required, 3 foreign language recommended, 1 social studies recommended, 3 history required, 3 elective required, 4 elective recommended. **Freshman Admission Statistics:** 3,223 applied, 67% accepted, 41% of those accepted enrolled. **Transfer Admission Requirements:** *Items required:* high school transcript, college transcript, essay. Minimum college GPA of 2.5 required. Lowest grade transferable C. **General Admission Information:** Application fee $40. Priority application deadline March 1. Regular application deadline March 1. Nonfall registration accepted. Admission may be deferred for a maximum of 1 year.

COSTS AND FINANCIAL AID

In-state tuition $2,148. Out-of-state tuition $8,074. Room & board $5,070. Required fees $2,513. Average book expense $700. **Required Forms and Deadlines:** FAFSA. Priority filing deadline March 1. **Notification of Awards:** Applicants will be notified of awards on a rolling basis beginning on or about April 1. **Types of Aid:** *Need-based scholarships/grants:* Pell, SEOG, state scholarships/grants, private scholarships, the school's own gift aid. *Loans:* FFEL Subsidized Stafford, FFEL Unsubsidized Stafford, FFEL PLUS, Federal Perkins, college/university loans from institutional funds. **Student Employment:** Federal Work-Study Program available. Institutional employment available. Off-campus job opportunities are fair. **Financial Aid Statistics:** 44% freshmen, 39% undergrads receive some form of aid. Average income from on-campus job $1,320. **Financial Aid Phone:** 800-281-4677.

LORAS COLLEGE

1450 Alta Vista, Dubuque, IA 52004-0178
Phone: 800-245-6727 **E-mail:** adms@loras.edu **CEEB Code:** 6370
Fax: 563-588-7119 **Web:** www.loras.edu **ACT Code:** 1328

This private school, which is affiliated with the Roman Catholic Church, was founded in 1839. It has a 60-acre campus.

STUDENTS AND FACULTY

Enrollment: 1,614. **Student Body:** Male 49%, female 51%, out-of-state 44%, international 1%. **Ethnic Representation:** African American 1%, Caucasian 92%, Hispanic 2%. **Retention and Graduation:** 77% freshmen return for sophomore year. 53% freshmen graduate within 4 years. 15% grads go on to further study within 1 year. 3% grads pursue law degrees. 2% grads pursue medical degrees. **Faculty:** Student/faculty ratio 12:1. 118 full-time faculty, 83% hold PhDs. 100% faculty teach undergrads.

ACADEMICS

Degrees: Associate's, bachelor's, master's. **Academic Requirements:** General education including some course work in arts/fine arts, computer literacy, English (including composition), history, humanities, mathematics, philosophy, sciences (biological or physical), social science. **Classes:** 10-19 students in an average class. **Majors with Highest Enrollment:** Elementary education and teaching; secondary education and teaching; business administration/ management. **Disciplines with Highest Percentage of Degrees Awarded:** Business/marketing 29%, education 17%, social sciences and history 13%, communications/communication technologies 7%, parks and recreation 7%. **Special Study Options:** Cooperative (work-study) program, cross registration, double major, dual enrollment, English as a second language, honors program, independent study, internships, liberal arts/career combination, student-designed major, study abroad, teacher certification program. Undergrads may take graduate-level classes if certain qualifications are met.

FACILITIES

Housing: Coed, all-female, all-male, apartments for single students. **Library Holdings:** 290,517 bound volumes. 912 periodicals. 76,936 microforms. 1,676 audiovisuals. **Special Academic Facilities/Equipment:** Language lab, television studio, observatory, and planetarium. **Computers:** *Recommended operating system:* Windows NT/2000. School-owned computers available for student use.

EXTRACURRICULARS

Activities: Choral groups, concert band, drama/theater, jazz band, music ensembles, musical theater, radio station, student government, student newspaper, television station, yearbook. **Organizations:** 46 registered organizations, 7 honor societies, 3 religious organizations, 3 fraternities (3% men join), 2 sororities (2% women join). **Athletics (Intercollegiate):** *Men:* baseball, basketball, cross-country, diving, football, golf, indoor track, soccer, swimming, tennis, track & field, wrestling. *Women:* basketball, cross-country, diving, golf, indoor track, soccer, softball, swimming, tennis, track & field, volleyball.

ADMISSIONS

Selectivity Rating: 77 (of 100). **Freshman Academic Profile:** Average high school GPA 3.2. 11% in top 10% of high school class, 30% in top 25% of high school class, 62% in top 50% of high school class. 57% from public high schools. Average SAT I Math 534, SAT I Math middle 50% range 510-560. Average SAT I Verbal 518, SAT I Verbal middle 50% range 450-570. Average ACT 22, ACT middle 50% range 19-25. TOEFL required of all international applicants, minimum TOEFL 550. **Basis for Candidate Selection:** *Very important factors considered include:* secondary school record, standardized test scores. *Important factors considered include:* alumni/ae relation, character/personal qualities, class rank, interview, minority status, religious affiliation/commitment. *Other factors considered include:* essays, extracurricular activities, geographical residence, recommendations, state residency, talent/ability, volunteer work, work experience. **Freshman Admission Requirements:** High school diploma or GED is required. *Academic units required/recommended:* 13 total recommended; 4 English recommended, 3 math recommended, 4 science recommended, 2 elective recommended. **Freshman Admission Statistics:** 1,374 applied, 80% accepted, 34% of those accepted enrolled. **Transfer Admission Requirements:** *Items required:* high school transcript, college transcript, standardized test scores. Minimum high school GPA of 2.5 required. Minimum college GPA of 2.0 required. Lowest grade transferable C. **General Admission Information:** Application fee $25. Nonfall registration accepted. Admission may be deferred for a maximum of 1 year. Credit offered for CEEB Advanced Placement tests.

COSTS AND FINANCIAL AID

Tuition $16,860. Room & board $5,895. Required fees $1,089. Average book expense $800. **Required Forms and Deadlines:** FAFSA. No deadline for regular filing. Priority filing deadline April 15. **Notification of Awards:** Applicants will be notified of awards on a rolling basis beginning on or about March 1. **Types of Aid:** *Need-based scholarships/grants:* Pell, SEOG, state scholarships/grants, private scholarships, the school's own gift aid. *Loans:* FFEL Subsidized Stafford, FFEL Unsubsidized Stafford, FFEL PLUS, Federal Perkins, college/university loans from institutional funds. **Student Employment:** Federal Work-Study Program available. Institutional employment available. Off-campus job opportunities are good. **Financial Aid Statistics:** 74% freshmen, 77% undergrads receive some form of aid. Average freshman grant $5,669. Average freshman loan $4,385. Average income from on-campus job $1,500. **Financial Aid Phone:** 563-588-7136.

LOUISIANA COLLEGE

1140 College Drive, PO Box 560, Pineville, LA 71359-0560
Phone: 318-487-7259 **E-mail:** admissions@lacollege.edu **CEEB Code:** 6371
Fax: 318-487-7550 **Web:** www.lacollege.edu **ACT Code:** 1586

This private school, which is affiliated with the Baptist Church, was founded in 1906. It has an 81-acre campus.

STUDENTS AND FACULTY

Enrollment: 1,161. **Student Body:** Male 42%, female 58%, out-of-state 7%, international 1%. **Ethnic Representation:** African American 8%, Asian 1%, Caucasian 89%, Hispanic 1%, Native American 1%. **Retention and Graduation:** 64% freshmen return for sophomore year. 21% freshmen graduate within 4 years. **Faculty:** Student/faculty ratio 16:1. 74 full-time faculty, 63% hold PhDs. 100% faculty teach undergrads.

ACADEMICS

Degrees: Bachelor's. **Academic Requirements:** General education including some course work in arts/fine arts, computer literacy, English (including composition), foreign languages, history, humanities, mathematics, philosophy, sciences (biological or physical), social science, religion, health and physical education, oral communication. **Classes:** 10-19 students in an average class. **Majors with Highest Enrollment:** Elementary education and teaching; biology/biological sciences, general; psychology, general. **Disciplines with Highest Percentage of Degrees Awarded:** Education 15%, health professions and related sciences 11%, business/marketing 10%, biological life sciences 10%, social sciences and history 9%. **Special Study Options:** Double major, honors program, independent study, internships, student-designed major, study abroad, teacher certification program.

FACILITIES

Housing: All-female, all-male, apartments for married students, apartments for single students. **Library Holdings:** 134,454 bound volumes. 432 periodicals. 108,456 microforms. 3,000 audiovisuals. **Special Academic Facilities/ Equipment:** Art gallery, radio station, performing arts center, theater. **Computers:** School-owned computers available for student use.

EXTRACURRICULARS

Activities: Choral groups, concert band, drama/theater, jazz band, literary magazine, music ensembles, musical theater, opera, pep band, radio station, student government, student newspaper, yearbook. **Organizations:** 60 registered organizations, 13 honor societies, 8 religious organizations, 4 fraternities (20% men join), 3 sororities (35% women join). **Athletics (Intercollegiate):** *Men:* baseball, basketball, cheerleading, football, golf, soccer. *Women:* basketball, cheerleading, cross-country, soccer, softball, tennis.

ADMISSIONS

Selectivity Rating: 71 (of 100). **Freshman Academic Profile:** Average high school GPA 3.4. 23% in top 10% of high school class, 47% in top 25% of high school class, 78% in top 50% of high school class. 82% from public high schools. SAT I Math middle 50% range 450-570. SAT I Verbal middle 50% range 450-640. Average ACT 23, ACT middle 50% range 21-25. TOEFL required of all international applicants, minimum TOEFL 550. **Basis for Candidate Selection:** *Very important factors considered include:* class rank, secondary school record, standardized test scores. *Important factors considered include:* extracurricular activities. *Other factors considered include:* interview, volunteer work. **Freshman Admission Requirements:** High school diploma or GED is required. *Academic units required/recommended:* 17 total required; 4 English required, 3 math required, 3 science required, 1 foreign language recommended, 3 social studies required. **Freshman Admission Statistics:** 664 applied, 77% accepted, 48% of those accepted enrolled. **Transfer Admission Requirements:** *Items required:* college transcript, statement of good standing from prior school. Minimum college GPA of 2.0 required. Lowest grade transferable D. **General Admission Information:** Application fee $25.

Priority application deadline August 15. Nonfall registration accepted. Admission may be deferred for a maximum of 1 year. Credit and/or placement offered for CEEB Advanced Placement tests.

COSTS AND FINANCIAL AID

Tuition $8,200. Room & board $3,486. Required fees $800. Average book expense $750. **Required Forms and Deadlines:** FAFSA and institution's own financial aid form. No deadline for regular filing. Priority filing deadline March 31. **Notification of Awards:** Applicants will be notified of awards on a rolling basis. **Types of Aid:** *Need-based scholarships/grants:* Pell, SEOG, state scholarships/grants, private scholarships, the school's own gift aid. *Loans:* FFEL Subsidized Stafford, FFEL Unsubsidized Stafford, FFEL PLUS, college/university loans from institutional funds. **Student Employment:** Federal Work-Study Program available. Institutional employment available. Off-campus job opportunities are excellent. **Financial Aid Statistics:** 65% freshmen, 65% undergrads receive some form of aid. Average freshman loan $9,007. Average income from on-campus job $400. **Financial Aid Phone:** 318-487-7386.

LOUISIANA STATE UNIVERSITY—BATON ROUGE

110 Thomas Boyd Hall, Baton Rouge, LA 70803
Phone: 225-578-1175 **E-mail:** admissions@lsu.edu **CEEB Code:** 6373
Fax: 225-578-4433 **Web:** www.lsu.edu **ACT Code:** 1590

This public school was founded in 1860. It has a 2,000-acre campus.

STUDENTS AND FACULTY

Enrollment: 26,518. **Student Body:** Male 47%, female 53%, out-of-state 8%, international 3% (123 countries represented). **Ethnic Representation:** African American 10%, Asian 4%, Caucasian 82%, Hispanic 2%. **Retention and Graduation:** 83% freshmen return for sophomore year. 22% freshmen graduate within 4 years. **Faculty:** Student/faculty ratio 21:1. 1,299 full-time faculty, 80% hold PhDs. 61% faculty teach undergrads.

ACADEMICS

Degrees: Bachelor's, doctoral, first professional, master's, post-master's certificate. **Academic Requirements:** General education including some course work in arts/fine arts, computer literacy, English (including composition), foreign languages, history, humanities, mathematics, sciences (biological or physical), social science. **Classes:** 10-19 students in an average class. 10-19 students in an average lab/discussion section. **Majors with Highest Enrollment:** Management information systems and services; marketing/marketing management, general; general studies. **Disciplines with Highest Percentage of Degrees Awarded:** Business/marketing 26%, engineering/engineering technology 12%, education 10%, biological life sciences 7%, social sciences and history 6%. **Special Study Options:** Accelerated program, cooperative (work-study) program, cross registration, distance learning, double major, dual enrollment, English as a second language, student exchange program (domestic), honors program, independent study, internships, liberal arts/career combination, student-designed major, study abroad, teacher certification program.

FACILITIES

Housing: Coed, all-female, all-male, apartments for married students, apartments for single students, housing for disabled students, fraternities and/or sororities. **Library Holdings:** 1,369,607 bound volumes. 18,344 periodicals. 5,237,168 microforms. 22,336 audiovisuals. **Special Academic Facilities/Equipment:** Art museum, natural science museum, rural life museum, lichen/bryophyte mycological and vascular plant herbarium. **Computers:** School-owned computers available for student use.

EXTRACURRICULARS

Activities: Choral groups, concert band, dance, drama/theater, jazz band, literary magazine, marching band, music ensembles, musical theater, opera, pep band, radio station, student government, student newspaper, symphony orchestra, television station, yearbook. **Organizations:** 311 registered organizations, 39 honor societies, 21 religious organizations, 23 fraternities (12% men join), 15 sororities (16% women join). **Athletics (Intercollegiate):** *Men:* baseball, basketball, cheerleading, cross-country, diving, football, golf, indoor track, swimming, tennis, track & field. *Women:* basketball, cheerleading, cross-country, diving, golf, gymnastics, indoor track, soccer, softball, swimming, tennis, track & field, volleyball.

ADMISSIONS

Selectivity Rating: 63 (of 100). **Freshman Academic Profile:** Average high school GPA 3.4. 26% in top 10% of high school class, 55% in top 25% of high school class, 84% in top 50% of high school class. Average ACT 24, ACT middle 50% range 21-26. TOEFL required of all international applicants, minimum TOEFL 500. **Basis for Candidate Selection:** *Very important factors considered include:* secondary school record, standardized test scores. *Important factors considered include:* class rank. *Other factors considered include:* character/personal qualities, essays, extracurricular activities, recommendations, talent/ability. **Freshman Admission Requirements:** High school diploma or GED is required. *Academic units required/recommended:* 18 total required; 4 English required, 3 math required, 3 science required, 2 foreign language required, 3 social studies required, 2 elective required. **Freshman Admission Statistics:** 10,536 applied, 79% accepted, 64% of those accepted enrolled. **Transfer Admission Requirements:** *Items required:* college transcript, statement of good standing from prior school. Minimum high school GPA of 2.5 required. Minimum college GPA of 2.5 required. Lowest grade transferable D. **General Admission Information:** Application fee $25. Priority application deadline December 1. Regular application deadline April 1. Nonfall registration accepted. Credit offered for CEEB Advanced Placement tests.

COSTS AND FINANCIAL AID

In-state tuition $2,551. Out-of-state tuition $7,851. Room & board $4,546. Required fees $917. Average book expense $1,000. **Required Forms and Deadlines:** FAFSA. Priority filing deadline April 1. **Notification of Awards:** Applicants will be notified of awards on a rolling basis beginning on or about March 1. **Types of Aid:** *Need-based scholarships/grants:* Pell, SEOG, state scholarships/grants, private scholarships, the school's own gift aid. *Loans:* FFEL Subsidized Stafford, FFEL Unsubsidized Stafford, FFEL PLUS, Federal Perkins. **Student Employment:** Federal Work-Study Program available. Institutional employment available. Off-campus job opportunities are excellent. **Financial Aid Statistics:** 43% freshmen, 42% undergrads receive some form of aid. Average freshman grant $3,960. Average freshman loan $4,000. Average income from on-campus job $2,000. **Financial Aid Phone:** 225-578-3103.

LOUISIANA STATE UNIVERSITY—SHREVEPORT

One University Place, Shreveport, LA 71115-2399
Phone: 318-797-5061 **E-mail:** admissions@pilot.lsus.edu **CEEB Code:** 6355
Fax: 318-797-5286 **Web:** www.lsus.edu **ACT Code:** 1593

This public school was founded in 1965. It has a 200-acre campus.

STUDENTS AND FACULTY

Enrollment: 3,542. **Student Body:** Male 38%, female 62%, out-of-state 2%. **Ethnic Representation:** African American 21%, Asian 2%, Caucasian 66%, Hispanic 2%, Native American 1%. **Retention and Graduation:** 59% freshmen return for sophomore year. **Faculty:** Student/faculty ratio 16:1. 161 full-time faculty, 70% hold PhDs. 100% faculty teach undergrads.

ACADEMICS

Degrees: Bachelor's, master's, post-master's certificate. **Academic Requirements:** General education including some course work in arts/fine arts, English (including composition), humanities, mathematics, sciences (biological or physical), social science. **Classes:** 20-29 students in an average class. **Majors with Highest Enrollment:** Business administration/management; elementary education and teaching; general studies. **Disciplines with Highest Percentage of Degrees Awarded:** Business/marketing 28%, education 17%, liberal arts/general studies 16%, psychology 9%, biological life sciences 7%. **Special Study Options:** Cooperative (work-study) program, study abroad, teacher certification program. Undergrads may take grad-level courses and evening courses.

FACILITIES

Housing: Apartments for married students, apartments for single students. **Library Holdings:** 279,821 bound volumes. 1,190 periodicals. 364,744 microforms. 1,914 audiovisuals. **Special Academic Facilities/Equipment:** Art center, life science museum, pioneer heritage center. **Computers:** School-owned computers available for student use.

EXTRACURRICULARS

Activities: Student government, student newspaper. **Organizations:** 52 registered organizations, 4 honor societies, 3 religious organizations, 5 fraternities (1% men join), 3 sororities (1% women join). **Athletics (Intercollegiate):** *Men:* baseball.

ADMISSIONS

Selectivity Rating: 66 (of 100). **Freshman Academic Profile:** Average high school GPA 3.2. 90% from public high schools. Average ACT 21, ACT middle 50% range 18-23. TOEFL required of all international applicants, minimum TOEFL 500. **Basis for Candidate Selection:** *Other factors considered* *include:* secondary school record, standardized test scores. **Freshman Admission Requirements:** High school diploma or GED is required. *Academic units required/recommended:* 4 English recommended, 3 math recommended, 3 science recommended, 3 social studies recommended. **Freshman Admission Statistics:** 790 applied, 100% accepted, 63% of those accepted enrolled. **Transfer Admission Requirements:** *Items required:* college transcript. Minimum college GPA of 2.0 required. Lowest grade transferable D. **General Admission Information:** Application fee $10. Regular application deadline August 1. Nonfall registration accepted. Credit offered for CEEB Advanced Placement tests.

COSTS AND FINANCIAL AID

In-state tuition $2,568. Out-of-state tuition $6,898. Required fees $250. **Required Forms and Deadlines:** FAFSA and institution's own financial aid form. **Types of Aid:** *Need-based scholarships/grants:* state scholarships/grants. *Loans:* FFEL Subsidized Stafford, FFEL PLUS. **Student Employment:** Federal Work-Study Program available. Institutional employment available. Off-campus job opportunities are good. **Financial Aid Statistics:** Average income from on-campus job $2,000. **Financial Aid Phone:** 318-797-5363.

LOUISIANA TECH UNIVERSITY

PO Box 3178, Ruston, LA 71272
Phone: 318-257-3036 **E-mail:** bulldog@latech.edu
Fax: 318-257-2499 **Web:** www.latech.edu **ACT Code:** 1588

This public school was founded in 1894. It has a 247-acre campus.

STUDENTS AND FACULTY

Enrollment: 9,375. **Student Body:** Male 52%, female 48%, out-of-state 12%, international 2% (61 countries represented). **Ethnic Representation:** African American 16%, Asian 1%, Caucasian 77%, Hispanic 2%, Native American 1%. **Retention and Graduation:** 72% freshmen return for sophomore year. 32% grads go on to further study within 1 year. **Faculty:** Student/faculty ratio 23:1. 389 full-time faculty, 80% hold PhDs. 100% faculty teach undergrads.

ACADEMICS

Degrees: Associate's, bachelor's, doctoral, first professional certificate, master's, terminal. **Academic Requirements:** General education including some course work in arts/fine arts, computer literacy, English (including composition), humanities, mathematics, sciences (biological or physical), social science. **Classes:** 20-29 students in an average class. **Disciplines with Highest Percentage of Degrees Awarded:** Business/marketing 22%, engineering/engineering technology 15%, liberal arts/general studies 12%, education 8%, home economics and vocational home economics 6%. **Special Study Options:** Cooperative (work-study) program, cross registration, distance learning, double major, dual enrollment, English as a second language, honors program, independent study, internships, study abroad, teacher certification program.

FACILITIES

Housing: All-female, all-male, apartments for married students, housing for disabled students, housing for international students. **Library Holdings:** 3,319 bound volumes. 2,469 periodicals. 1,891,666 microforms. 14,532 audiovisuals. **Special Academic Facilities/Equipment:** Art gallery, natural history museum, on-campus elementary school, arboretum, planetarium, center for rehabilitation science and biomedical engineering, institute for microengineering, water resources center. **Computers:** *Recommended operating system:* Mac. School-owned computers available for student use.

EXTRACURRICULARS

Activities: Choral groups, concert band, dance, drama/theater, jazz band, marching band, music ensembles, musical theater, pep band, radio station, student government, yearbook. **Organizations:** 121 registered organizations, 17 honor societies, 11 religious organizations, 12 fraternities (7% men join), 8 sororities (11% women join). **Athletics (Intercollegiate):** *Men:* baseball, basketball, cross-country, football, golf, track & field. *Women:* basketball, cross-country, softball, tennis, track & field, volleyball.

ADMISSIONS

Selectivity Rating: 71 (of 100). **Freshman Academic Profile:** Average high school GPA 3.3. 18% in top 10% of high school class, 43% in top 25% of high school class, 74% in top 50% of high school class. Average ACT 22, ACT middle 50% range 19-24. TOEFL required of all international applicants, minimum TOEFL 500. **Basis for Candidate Selection:** *Very important factors considered include:* class rank, secondary school record, standardized test scores. *Important factors considered include:* talent/ability. *Other factors considered include:* alumni/ae relation, extracurricular activities, minority status, recommendations. **Freshman Admission Requirements:** High school diploma or GED is required. *Academic units required/recommended:* 4 English required, 3 math required, 3 science required, 3 social studies required, 5 elective required. **Freshman Admission Statistics:** 3,607 applied, 92% accepted, 62% of those accepted enrolled. **Transfer Admission Requirements:** *Items required:* college transcript, statement of good standing from prior school. Minimum college GPA of 2.0 required. Lowest grade transferable D. **General Admission Information:** Application fee $20. Regular application deadline July 31. Nonfall registration accepted. Credit and/or placement offered for CEEB Advanced Placement tests.

COSTS AND FINANCIAL AID

In-state tuition $3,038. Out-of-state tuition $7,943. Room & board $3,345. Required fees $300. Average book expense $750. **Required Forms and Deadlines:** FAFSA and institution's own financial aid form. **Notification of Awards:** Applicants will be notified of awards on a rolling basis beginning on or about April 18. **Types of Aid:** *Need-based scholarships/grants:* Pell, SEOG, state scholarships/grants, private scholarships, the school's own gift aid. *Loans:* FFEL Subsidized Stafford, FFEL Unsubsidized Stafford, FFEL PLUS, Federal Perkins, state loans. **Student Employment:** Federal Work-Study Program available. Institutional employment available. Off-campus job opportunities are good. **Financial Aid Statistics:** 48% freshmen, 38% undergrads receive some form of aid. Average freshman grant $3,417. Average freshman loan $1,767. **Financial Aid Phone:** 318-257-2641.

LOURDES COLLEGE

6832 Convent Road, Sylvania, OH 43560-2898
Phone: 419-885-5291 **E-mail:** lcadmits@lourdes.edu **CEEB Code:** 1427
Fax: 419-882-3987 **Web:** www.lourdes.edu **ACT Code:** 3598

This private school, which is affiliated with the Roman Catholic Church, was founded in 1958. It has an 89-acre campus.

STUDENTS AND FACULTY

Enrollment: 1,272. **Student Body:** Male 19%, female 81%, international students represent 11 country. **Ethnic Representation:** African American 12%, Caucasian 68%, Hispanic 2%, Native American 1%. **Retention and Graduation:** 63% freshmen return for sophomore year. 3% freshmen graduate within 4 years. 33% grads go on to further study within 1 year. 16% grads pursue business degrees. 5% grads pursue law degrees. 7% grads pursue medical degrees. **Faculty:** Student/faculty ratio 14:1. 61 full-time faculty, 27% hold PhDs. 100% faculty teach undergrads.

ACADEMICS

Degrees: Associate's, bachelor's, certificate, master's, terminal, transfer. **Academic Requirements:** General education including some course work in arts/fine arts, computer literacy, English (including composition), history, humanities, mathematics, philosophy, sciences (biological or physical), social science. **Classes:** 10-19 students in an average class. **Majors with Highest Enrollment:** Nursing/registered nurse training (RN, ASN, BSN, MSN); business administration/management; corrections and criminal justice. **Disciplines with Highest Percentage of Degrees Awarded:** Business/marketing 29%, health professions and related sciences 20%, interdisciplinary studies 12%, education 9%, protective services/public administration 9%. **Special Study Options:** Accelerated program, cooperative (work-study) program, double major, dual enrollment, independent study, internships, liberal arts/career combination, student-designed major, teacher certification program, weekend college.

FACILITIES

Library Holdings: 57,730 bound volumes. 448 periodicals. 10,187 microforms. 1,571 audiovisuals. **Special Academic Facilities/Equipment:** Planetarium, nature lab. **Computers:** School-owned computers available for student use.

EXTRACURRICULARS

Activities: Choral groups, literary magazine, student government, student newspaper. **Organizations:** 19 registered organizations, 6 honor societies, 2 religious organizations.

ADMISSIONS

Selectivity Rating: 70 (of 100). **Freshman Academic Profile:** Average high school GPA 2.9. 11% in top 10% of high school class, 30% in top 25% of high school class, 56% in top 50% of high school class. Average ACT 23, ACT middle 50% range 19-23. TOEFL required of all international applicants, minimum TOEFL 500. **Basis for Candidate Selection:** *Very important factors considered include:* secondary school record, standardized test scores. *Important factors considered include:* essays, interview, recommendations.

Other factors considered include: character/personal qualities, class rank, talent/ability. **Freshman Admission Requirements:** High school diploma or GED is required. *Academic units required/recommended:* 12 total required; 14 total recommended; 4 English required, 4 English recommended, 3 math required, 3 math recommended, 2 science recommended, 3 history recommended. **Freshman Admission Statistics:** 356 applied, 27% accepted, 100% of those accepted enrolled. **Transfer Admission Requirements:** *Items required:* college transcript. Minimum college GPA of 2.0 required. Lowest grade transferable C. **General Admission Information:** Application fee $25. Nonfall registration accepted. Admission may be deferred for a maximum of 4 years. Credit and/or placement offered for CEEB Advanced Placement tests.

COSTS AND FINANCIAL AID

Tuition $13,700. Required fees $900. **Required Forms and Deadlines:** FAFSA and institution's own financial aid form. No deadline for regular filing. Priority filing deadline March 1. **Notification of Awards:** Applicants will be notified of awards on a rolling basis beginning on or about March 1. **Types of Aid:** *Need-based scholarships/grants:* Pell, SEOG, state scholarships/grants, private scholarships, the school's own gift aid. *Loans:* FFEL Subsidized Stafford, FFEL Unsubsidized Stafford, FFEL PLUS, Federal Perkins, state loans, college/university loans from institutional funds. **Student Employment:** Federal Work-Study Program available. Institutional employment available. Off-campus job opportunities are excellent. **Financial Aid Statistics:** 81% freshmen, 83% undergrads receive some form of aid. Average freshman grant $6,252. Average freshman loan $4,744. Average income from on-campus job $1,869. **Financial Aid Phone:** 419-885-3211.

LOYOLA COLLEGE IN MARYLAND

 $$$   

4501 North Charles Street, Baltimore, MD 21210
Phone: 410-617-5012 **CEEB Code:** 5370
Fax: 410-617-2176 **Web:** www.loyola.edu

This private school, which is affiliated with the Roman Catholic Church, was founded in 1852. It has an 89-acre campus.

STUDENTS AND FACULTY

Enrollment: 3,488. **Student Body:** Male 42%, female 58%, out-of-state 79%, international students represent 18 countries. **Ethnic Representation:** African American 5%, Asian 2%, Caucasian 90%, Hispanic 2%. **Retention and Graduation:** 91% freshmen return for sophomore year. 73% freshmen graduate within 4 years. **Faculty:** Student/faculty ratio 12:1. 272 full-time faculty, 86% hold PhDs.

ACADEMICS

Degrees: Bachelor's, doctoral, master's, post-master's certificate. **Academic Requirements:** General education including some course work in arts/fine arts, English (including composition), foreign languages, history, humanities, mathematics, philosophy, sciences (biological or physical), social science. **Classes:** 20-29 students in an average class. **Majors with Highest Enrollment:** Business administration/management; communications studies/speech communication and rhetoric; psychology, general. **Disciplines with Highest Percentage of Degrees Awarded:** Business/marketing 35%, social sciences and history 13%, communications/communication technologies 11%, English 7%, biological life sciences 6%. **Special Study Options:** Accelerated program, cross registration, double major, honors program, independent study, internships, study abroad, teacher certification program.

FACILITIES

Housing: Coed, apartments for single students. **Library Holdings:** 293,639 bound volumes. 2,126 periodicals. 312,725 microforms. 38,878 audiovisuals. **Special Academic Facilities/Equipment:** Art gallery, advanced biology lab, humanities building, speech pathology lab and audiology center.

EXTRACURRICULARS

Activities: Choral groups, dance, drama/theater, jazz band, literary magazine, music ensembles, musical theater, pep band, student government, student newspaper, radio station, yearbook. **Organizations:** 6 religious organizations. **Athletics (Intercollegiate):** *Men:* basketball, crew, cross-country, diving, golf, lacrosse, soccer, swimming, tennis. *Women:* basketball, crew, cross-country, diving, lacrosse, soccer, swimming, tennis, volleyball.

ADMISSIONS

Selectivity Rating: 83 (of 100). **Freshman Academic Profile:** Average high school GPA 3.0. 35% in top 10% of high school class, 76% in top 25% of high school class, 97% in top 50% of high school class. SAT I Math middle 50% range 570-650. SAT I Verbal middle 50% range 560-640. TOEFL required of all international applicants, minimum TOEFL 550. **Basis for Candidate Selection:** *Very important factors considered include:* secondary school record. *Important factors considered include:* standardized test scores. *Other factors considered include:* alumni/ae relation, character/personal qualities, class rank, essays, extracurricular activities, minority status, recommendations, talent/ability, volunteer work, work experience. **Freshman Admission Requirements:** High school diploma or GED is required. *Academic units required/recommended:* 16 total required; 19 total recommended; 4 English required, 4 English recommended, 3 math required, 4 math recommended, 3 science required, 4 science recommended, 3 foreign language required, 4 foreign language recommended, 2 history required, 3 history recommended. **Freshman Admission Statistics:** 6,368 applied, 61% accepted, 23% of those accepted enrolled. **Transfer Admission Requirements:** *Items required:* high school transcript, college transcript, essay, standardized test scores, statement of good standing from prior school. Minimum college GPA of 2.7 required. Lowest grade transferable C. **General Admission Information:** Application fee $30. Priority application deadline January 15. Regular application deadline January 15. Admission may be deferred for a maximum of 1 year. Credit offered for CEEB Advanced Placement tests.

COSTS AND FINANCIAL AID

Tuition $20,973. Room & board $7,400. Required fees $570. Average book expense $740. **Required Forms and Deadlines:** FAFSA, CSS/Financial Aid PROFILE, noncustodial (divorced/separated) parent's statement, and business/farm supplement. Financial aid filing deadline February 10. **Notification of Awards:** Applicants will be notified of awards on or about April 5. **Types of Aid:** *Need-based scholarships/grants:* Pell, SEOG, state scholarships/grants, private scholarships, the school's own gift aid. *Loans:* Direct Subsidized Stafford, Direct Unsubsidized Stafford, FFEL PLUS, Federal Perkins, college/university loans from institutional funds. **Student Employment:** Federal Work-Study Program available. Institutional employment available. Off-campus job opportunities are good. **Financial Aid Statistics:** 44% freshmen, 45% undergrads receive some form of aid. **Financial Aid Phone:** 410-617-2576.

LOYOLA MARYMOUNT UNIVERSITY

 $$$  

One LMU Drive, Los Angeles, CA 90045
Phone: 310-338-2750 **E-mail:** admissions@lmu.edu **CEEB Code:** 4403
Fax: 310-338-2797 **Web:** www.lmu.edu **ACT Code:** 326

This private school, which is affiliated with the Roman Catholic Church, was founded in 1911. It has a 128-acre campus.

STUDENTS AND FACULTY

Enrollment: 5,358. **Student Body:** Male 42%, female 58%, out-of-state 22%, international 2%. **Ethnic Representation:** African American 6%, Asian 11%, Caucasian 52%, Hispanic 19%, Native American 1%. **Retention and Graduation:** 96% freshmen return for sophomore year. 57% freshmen graduate within 4 years. **Faculty:** Student/faculty ratio 13:1. 405 full-time faculty, 87% hold PhDs. 100% faculty teach undergrads.

ACADEMICS

Degrees: Bachelor's, first professional, first professional certificate, master's, post-bachelor's certificate, post-master's certificate. **Academic Requirements:** General education including some course work in English (including composition), history, mathematics, philosophy, sciences (biological or physical), social science, American cultures, communication or critical thinking, critical and creative arts, literature, and theological studies. **Classes:** 20-29 students in an average class. 10-19 students in an average lab/discussion section. **Majors with Highest Enrollment:** Business administration/management; communications, journalism, and related fields; psychology, general. **Disciplines with Highest Percentage of Degrees Awarded:** Business/marketing 30%, visual and performing arts 16%, social sciences and history 9%, psychology 9%, communications/communication technologies 7%. **Special Study Options:** Cross registration, double major, dual enrollment, honors program, independent study, internships, liberal arts/career combination, student-designed major, study abroad, teacher certification program, Encore program for adult students.

FACILITIES

Housing: Coed, all-female, all-male, apartments for single students. **Library Holdings:** 661,498 bound volumes. 10,249 periodicals. 145,553 microforms. 19,743 audiovisuals. **Special Academic Facilities/Equipment:** Art gallery, theater, TV production labs, computer graphics lab. **Computers:** School-owned computers available for student use.

EXTRACURRICULARS

Activities: Choral groups, dance, drama/theater, literary magazine, music ensembles, musical theater, radio station, student government, student newspaper, student-run film society, yearbook. **Organizations:** 120 registered organizations, 12 honor societies, 2 religious organizations, 4 fraternities (7% men join), 3 sororities (7% women join). **Athletics (Intercollegiate):** *Men:* baseball, basketball, crew, cross-country, golf, soccer, tennis, water polo. *Women:* basketball, crew, cross-country, soccer, softball, swimming, tennis, volleyball, water polo.

ADMISSIONS

Selectivity Rating: 74 (of 100). **Freshman Academic Profile:** Average high school GPA 3.4. 30% in top 10% of high school class, 95% in top 25% of high school class, 99% in top 50% of high school class. Average SAT I Math 581, SAT I Math middle 50% range 530-620. Average SAT I Verbal 573, SAT I Verbal middle 50% range 510-610. TOEFL required of all international applicants, minimum TOEFL 550. **Basis for Candidate Selection:** *Very important factors considered include:* secondary school record. *Important factors considered include:* class rank, standardized test scores, talent/ability. *Other factors considered include:* alumni/ae relation, character/personal qualities, essays, extracurricular activities, geographical residence, interview, recommendations, volunteer work, work experience. **Freshman Admission Requirements:** High school diploma or GED is required. *Academic units required/recommended:* 16 total recommended; 4 English recommended, 3 math recommended, 2 science recommended, 2 science lab recommended, 3 foreign language recommended, 3 social studies recommended, 1 elective recommended. **Freshman Admission Statistics:** 7,959 applied, 56% accepted, 27% of those accepted enrolled. **Transfer Admission Requirements:** *Items required:* college transcript, statement of good standing from prior school. Minimum college GPA of 2.8 required. Lowest grade transferable C. **General Admission Information:** Application fee $45. Priority application deadline February 1. Nonfall registration accepted. Admission may be deferred for a maximum of 1 year. Credit and/or placement offered for CEEB Advanced Placement tests.

COSTS AND FINANCIAL AID

Tuition $20,342. Room & board $7,800. Required fees $612. Average book expense $810. **Required Forms and Deadlines:** FAFSA, CSS/Financial Aid PROFILE, and state aid form. No deadline for regular filing. Priority filing deadline February 15. **Notification of Awards:** Applicants will be notified of awards on a rolling basis beginning on or about April 10. **Types of Aid:** *Need-based scholarships/grants:* Pell, SEOG, state scholarships/grants, private scholarships, the school's own gift aid. *Loans:* FFEL Subsidized Stafford, FFEL Unsubsidized Stafford, FFEL PLUS, Federal Perkins, college/university loans from institutional funds. **Student Employment:** Federal Work-Study Program available. Institutional employment available. Off-campus job opportunities are excellent. **Financial Aid Phone:** 310-338-2753.

LOYOLA UNIVERSITY NEW ORLEANS

$$$

6363 St. Charles Avenue, Box 18, New Orleans, LA 70118
Phone: 504-865-3240 **E-mail:** admit@loyno.edu **CEEB Code:** 6374
Fax: 504-865-3383 **Web:** www.loyno.edu **ACT Code:** 1592

This private school, which is affiliated with the Roman Catholic Church, was founded in 1912. It has a 26-acre campus.

STUDENTS AND FACULTY

Enrollment: 3,772. **Student Body:** Male 36%, female 64%, out-of-state 50%, international 4%. **Ethnic Representation:** African American 11%, Asian 4%, Caucasian 68%, Hispanic 10%. **Retention and Graduation:** 82% freshmen return for sophomore year. 14% grads go on to further study within 1 year. 12% grads pursue business degrees. 14% grads pursue law degrees. 7% grads pursue medical degrees. **Faculty:** Student/faculty ratio 13:1. 277 full-time faculty, 90% hold PhDs. 90% faculty teach undergrads.

ACADEMICS

Degrees: Bachelor's, first professional, master's, post-bachelor's certificate. **Academic Requirements:** General education including some course work in arts/fine arts, English (including composition), foreign languages, history, humanities, mathematics, philosophy, sciences (biological or physical), social science, religious studies. **Classes:** 10-19 students in an average class. 10-19 students in an average lab/discussion section. **Majors with Highest Enrollment:** Marketing/marketing management, general; communications studies/speech communication and rhetoric; psychology, general. **Disciplines with Highest Percentage of Degrees Awarded:** Business/marketing 19%, communications/communication technologies 14%, social sciences and history 10%, visual and performing arts 9%, health professions and related sciences 9%. **Special Study Options:** Accelerated program, cross registration, distance learning, double major, dual enrollment, English as a second language, student exchange program (domestic), external degree program, honors program, independent study, internships, liberal arts/career combination, student-designed major, study abroad, teacher certification program, weekend college, 3-2 engineering program with Tulane University.

FACILITIES

Housing: Coed, all-female, apartments for single students, housing for disabled students, honors floor. Chaplains live in each hall to provide spiritual/counseling assistance. **Library Holdings:** 401,548 bound volumes. 4,948 periodicals. 1,304,300 microforms. 15,484 audiovisuals. **Special Academic Facilities/Equipment:** Art gallery, electron microscope, humanities lab with Perseus Project and TLG, TV and radio production studios, multimedia classrooms, 24-hour microcomputer labs, computer science lab, graphics lab, visual arts lab, ad club/communications lab, RATHE Business Computer Lab, audio recording studio, multimedia training center. **Computers:** *Recommended operating system:* Windows XP. School-owned computers available for student use.

EXTRACURRICULARS

Activities: Choral groups, concert band, dance, drama/theater, jazz band, literary magazine, music ensembles, musical theater, radio station, student government, student newspaper, symphony orchestra, yearbook. **Organizations:** 120 registered organizations, 16 honor societies, 12 religious organizations, 6 fraternities (16% men join), 6 sororities (19% women join). **Athletics (Intercollegiate):** *Men:* baseball, basketball, cross-country, swimming, track & field. *Women:* basketball, cross-country, soccer, swimming, track & field, volleyball.

ADMISSIONS

Selectivity Rating: 77 (of 100). **Freshman Academic Profile:** Average high school GPA 3.8. 28% in top 10% of high school class, 59% in top 25% of high school class, 88% in top 50% of high school class. 38% from public high schools. Average SAT I Math 605, SAT I Math middle 50% range 520-620. Average SAT I Verbal 629, SAT I Verbal middle 50% range 540-650. Average ACT 27, ACT middle 50% range 23-28. TOEFL required of all international applicants, minimum TOEFL 550. **Basis for Candidate Selection:** *Very important factors considered include:* secondary school record, standardized test scores. *Important factors considered include:* character/personal qualities, essays, extracurricular activities, interview, recommendations, talent/ability, volunteer work, work experience. *Other factors considered include:* alumni/ae relation, class rank. **Freshman Admission Requirements:** High school diploma or GED is required. *Academic units required/recommended:* 10 total required; 15 total recommended; 4 English required, 4 English recommended, 2 math required, 3 math recommended, 2 science required, 3 science recommended, 2 foreign language recommended, 2 social studies required, 3 social studies recommended. **Freshman Admission Statistics:** 3,603 applied, 68% accepted, 36% of those accepted enrolled. **Transfer Admission Requirements:** *Items required:* college transcript, essay. Minimum college GPA of 2.3 required. Lowest grade transferable C. **General Admission Information:** Application fee $20. Priority application deadline December 1. Regular application deadline January 15. Nonfall registration accepted. Admission may be deferred for a maximum of 1 year. Credit and/or placement offered for CEEB Advanced Placement tests.

COSTS AND FINANCIAL AID

Tuition $19,450. Room & board $7,660. Required fees $656. Average book expense $1,000. **Required Forms and Deadlines:** FAFSA. Financial aid filing deadline May 1. Priority filing deadline February 15. **Notification of Awards:** Applicants will be notified of awards on a rolling basis beginning on or about March 1. **Types of Aid:** *Need-based scholarships/grants:* Pell, SEOG, private scholarships, the school's own gift aid. *Loans:* FFEL Subsidized Stafford, FFEL Unsubsidized Stafford, FFEL PLUS, Federal Perkins. **Student Employment:** Federal Work-Study Program available. Institutional employment available. Off-campus job opportunities are good. **Financial Aid Statistics:** 57% freshmen, 53% undergrads receive some form of aid. Average freshman grant $16,591. Average freshman loan $2,696. **Financial Aid Phone:** 504-865-3231.

See page 1094.

LOYOLA UNIVERSITY OF CHICAGO

820 North Michigan Avenue, Chicago, IL 60611
Phone: 312-915-6500 **E-mail:** admission@luc.edu **CEEB Code:** 1412
Fax: 312-915-7216 **Web:** www.luc.edu

This private school, which is affiliated with the Roman Catholic-Jesuit Church, was founded in 1870. It has a 105-acre campus.

STUDENTS AND FACULTY

Enrollment: 7,533. **Student Body:** Male 34%, female 66%, out-of-state 32%, international 2%. **Ethnic Representation:** African American 9%, Asian 11%, Caucasian 58%, Hispanic 10%. **Retention and Graduation:** 84% freshmen return for sophomore year. 53% freshmen graduate within 4 years. **Faculty:** Student/faculty ratio 13:1. 940 full-time faculty, 97% hold PhDs.

ACADEMICS

Degrees: Bachelor's, certificate, doctoral, first professional, master's, post-bachelor's certificate, post-master's certificate. **Academic Requirements:** General education including some course work in English (including composition), humanities, mathematics, philosophy. **Classes:** 20-29 students in an average class. Under 10 students in an average lab/discussion section. **Majors with Highest Enrollment:** Biology/biological sciences, general; psychology, general; business administration/management. **Disciplines with Highest Percentage of Degrees Awarded:** Business/marketing 21%, social sciences and history 14%, biological life sciences 11%, psychology 11%, communications/communication technologies 7%. **Special Study Options:** Accelerated program, double major, English as a second language, honors program, independent study, internships, student-designed major, study abroad, teacher certification program. Mundelein College offers part-time evening programs leading to bachelor's degrees. Study abroad in Italy and Mexico.

FACILITIES

Housing: Coed, all-female, apartments for single students, fraternities and/or sororities. **Library Holdings:** 1,108,157 bound volumes. 68,886 periodicals. 1,742,052 microforms. 35,090 audiovisuals. **Special Academic Facilities/ Equipment:** Renaissance art gallery, seismograph station. **Computers:** *Recommended operating system:* Windows NT/2000. School-owned computers available for student use.

EXTRACURRICULARS

Activities: Choral groups, drama/theater, jazz band, literary magazine, music ensembles, musical theater, radio station, student government, student newspaper. **Organizations:** 145 registered organizations, 1 honor society, 1 religious organization, 6 fraternities (7% men join), 5 sororities (5% women join). **Athletics (Intercollegiate):** *Men:* basketball, cross-country, golf, soccer, softball, track & field, volleyball. *Women:* basketball, cross-country, soccer, softball, track & field, volleyball.

ADMISSIONS

Selectivity Rating: 73 (of 100). **Freshman Academic Profile:** 29% in top 10% of high school class, 63% in top 25% of high school class, 92% in top 50% of high school class. 57% from public high schools. Average SAT I Math 574, SAT I Math middle 50% range 520-640. Average SAT I Verbal 574, SAT I Verbal middle 50% range 520-630. Average ACT 25, ACT middle 50% range 22-27. TOEFL required of all international applicants, minimum TOEFL 550. **Basis for Candidate Selection:** *Very important factors considered include:* class rank, secondary school record, standardized test scores. *Important factors considered include:* character/personal qualities, essays, recommendations. *Other factors considered include:* alumni/ae relation, extracurricular activities, geographical residence, interview, minority status, state residency, talent/ability, volunteer work, work experience. **Freshman Admission Requirements:** High school diploma or GED is required. *Academic units required/recommended:* 15 total required; 18 total recommended; 4 English required, 4 English recommended, 2 math required, 4 math recommended, 1 science required, 2 science recommended, 2 foreign language required, 3 foreign language recommended, 1 social studies required, 3 social studies recommended. **Freshman Admission Statistics:** 8,759 applied, 84% accepted, 22% of those accepted enrolled. **Transfer Admission Requirements:** *Items required:* college transcript. Minimum college GPA of 2.5 required. Lowest grade transferable C. **General Admission Information:** Application fee $25. Priority application deadline February 1. Regular application deadline April 1. Nonfall registration accepted. Admission may be deferred for a maximum of 1 year. Credit and/or placement offered for CEEB Advanced Placement tests.

COSTS AND FINANCIAL AID

Tuition $20,544. Room & board $7,900. Required fees $510. Average book expense $800. **Required Forms and Deadlines:** FAFSA. No deadline for regular filing. Priority filing deadline March 1. **Notification of Awards:** Applicants will be notified of awards on a rolling basis beginning on or about February 15. **Types of Aid:** *Need-based scholarships/grants:* Pell, SEOG, state scholarships/grants, private scholarships, the school's own gift aid. *Loans:* FFEL Subsidized Stafford, FFEL Unsubsidized Stafford, FFEL PLUS, Federal Perkins, Federal Nursing. **Student Employment:** Federal Work-Study Program available. Institutional employment available. Off-campus job opportunities are excellent. **Financial Aid Statistics:** 71% freshmen, 68% undergrads receive some form of aid. Average freshman grant $19,520. Average freshman loan $3,958. Average income from on-campus job $2,000. **Financial Aid Phone:** 773-508-3155.

See page 1096.

LUBBOCK CHRISTIAN UNIVERSITY

5601 19th Street, Lubbock, TX 79407
Phone: 800-720-7151 **E-mail:** admissions@lcu.edu **CEEB Code:** 6378
Fax: 806-720-7162 **Web:** www.lcu.edu **ACT Code:** 4123

This private school, which is affiliated with the Church of Christ, was founded in 1957. It has a 120-acre campus.

STUDENTS AND FACULTY

Enrollment: 1,686. **Student Body:** Male 43%, female 57%, out-of-state 12%, international 1%. **Ethnic Representation:** African American 6%, Asian 1%, Caucasian 80%, Hispanic 13%. **Retention and Graduation:** 64% freshmen return for sophomore year. 17% freshmen graduate within 4 years. **Faculty:** Student/faculty ratio 16:1. 74 full-time faculty, 51% hold PhDs. 100% faculty teach undergrads.

ACADEMICS

Degrees: Associate's, bachelor's, master's, terminal. **Academic Requirements:** General education including some course work in arts/fine arts, computer literacy, English (including composition), history, humanities, mathematics, sciences (biological or physical), social science. **Classes:** 10-19 students in an average class. 10-19 students in an average lab/discussion section. **Majors with Highest Enrollment:** Elementary education and teaching; small business administration/ management; humanities/humanistic studies. **Disciplines with Highest Percentage of Degrees Awarded:** Business/marketing 30%, education 18%, philosophy/religion/theology 8%, protective services/public administration 7%, liberal arts/general studies 6%. **Special Study Options:** Accelerated program, distance learning, double major, dual enrollment, honors program, internships, liberal arts/career combination, student-designed major, study abroad, teacher certification program, academic remediation, learning disabilities services. Undergrads may take graduate courses.

FACILITIES

Housing: All-female, all-male, apartments for married students, apartments for single students. **Library Holdings:** 108,000 bound volumes. 556 periodicals. **Computers:** *Recommended operating system:* Windows NT/2000. School-owned computers available for student use.

EXTRACURRICULARS

Activities: Choral groups, drama/theater, jazz band, music ensembles, student government, student newspaper, yearbook. **Athletics (Intercollegiate):** *Men:* baseball, basketball, cheerleading. *Women:* basketball, cheerleading, volleyball.

ADMISSIONS

Selectivity Rating: 63 (of 100). **Freshman Academic Profile:** Average high school GPA 3.3. 16% in top 10% of high school class, 37% in top 25% of high school class, 70% in top 50% of high school class. Average SAT I Math 508, SAT I Math middle 50% range 440-570. Average SAT I Verbal 508, SAT I Verbal middle 50% range 440-570. Average ACT 21, ACT middle 50% range 18-23. TOEFL required of all international applicants, minimum TOEFL 500. **Basis for Candidate Selection:** *Very important factors considered include:* character/ personal qualities, standardized test scores, talent/ability. *Important factors considered include:* alumni/ae relation, class rank. *Other factors considered include:* essays, extracurricular activities, interview, minority status, recommendations, secondary school record, volunteer work, work experience. **Freshman Admission Requirements:** High school diploma or GED is required. *Academic units required/recommended:* 19 total recommended; 4 English recommended, 3 math recommended, 3 science recommended, 2 science lab recommended, 2 foreign language recommended, 2 social studies recommended, 3 history recommended. **Freshman Admission Statistics:** 748 applied, 71% accepted, 55% of those accepted enrolled. **Transfer Admission Requirements:** *Items required:* college transcript. Lowest grade transferable C. **General Admission**

Information: Application fee $20. Priority application deadline June 15. Regular application deadline August 1. Nonfall registration accepted. Credit and/or placement offered for CEEB Advanced Placement tests.

COSTS AND FINANCIAL AID

Required Forms and Deadlines: FAFSA and institution's own financial aid form. No deadline for regular filing. Priority filing deadline June 1. **Notification of Awards:** Applicants will be notified of awards on a rolling basis beginning on or about March 1. **Types of Aid:** *Need-based scholarships/grants:* Pell, SEOG, state scholarships/grants, private scholarships, the school's own gift aid. *Loans:* FFEL Subsidized Stafford, FFEL Unsubsidized Stafford, FFEL PLUS, Federal Perkins. **Student Employment:** Federal Work-Study Program available. Off-campus job opportunities are excellent. **Financial Aid Statistics:** 82% freshmen, 67% undergrads receive some form of aid. **Financial Aid Phone:** 806-720-7180.

LUTHER COLLEGE

700 College Drive, Decorah, IA 52101-1042
Phone: 563-387-1287 **E-mail:** admissions@luther.edu **CEEB Code:** 6375
Fax: 563-387-2159 **Web:** www.luther.edu **ACT Code:** 1330

This private school, which is affiliated with the Lutheran Church, was founded in 1861. It has an 800-acre campus.

STUDENTS AND FACULTY

Enrollment: 2,572. **Student Body:** Male 40%, female 60%, out-of-state 61%, international 6% (41 countries represented). **Ethnic Representation:** African American 1%, Asian 1%, Caucasian 92%, Hispanic 1%. **Retention and Graduation:** 87% freshmen return for sophomore year. 66% freshmen graduate within 4 years. 22% grads go on to further study within 1 year. 4% grads pursue business degrees. 2% grads pursue law degrees. 4% grads pursue medical degrees. **Faculty:** Student/faculty ratio 13:1. 175 full-time faculty, 80% hold PhDs. 100% faculty teach undergrads.

ACADEMICS

Degrees: Bachelor's. **Academic Requirements:** General education including some course work in arts/fine arts, English (including composition), foreign languages, history, humanities, mathematics, philosophy, sciences (biological or physical), social science, religion. **Classes:** 20-29 students in an average class. 10-19 students in an average lab/discussion section. **Majors with Highest Enrollment:** Education, general; biology/biological sciences, general; psychology, general. **Disciplines with Highest Percentage of Degrees Awarded:** Business/marketing 14%, biological life sciences 14%, education 12%, visual and performing arts 12%, social sciences and history 10%. **Special Study Options:** Double major, dual enrollment, honors program, independent study, internships, student-designed major, study abroad, teacher certification program.

FACILITIES

Housing: Coed; apartments for married students; apartments for single students; housing for disabled students; language houses: French, German, Spanish. **Library Holdings:** 336,605 bound volumes. 1,600 periodicals. 25,000 microforms. 7,000 audiovisuals. **Special Academic Facilities/Equipment:** Natural history museum, Norwegian-American museum, 5 art galleries, planetarium, live animal center, archaeological research center, computer music lab, 2 electron microscopes. **Computers:** School-owned computers available for student use.

EXTRACURRICULARS

Activities: Choral groups, concert band, dance, drama/theater, jazz band, literary magazine, music ensembles, musical theater, pep band, radio station, student government, student newspaper, student-run film society, symphony orchestra, yearbook. **Organizations:** 116 registered organizations, 10 honor societies, 5 religious organizations, 2 fraternities (7% men join), 3 sororities (9% women join). **Athletics (Intercollegiate):** *Men:* baseball, basketball, cheerleading, cross-country, diving, football, golf, indoor track, rugby, soccer, swimming, tennis, track & field, wrestling. *Women:* basketball, cheerleading, cross-country, diving, golf, indoor track, soccer, softball, swimming, tennis, track & field, volleyball.

ADMISSIONS

Selectivity Rating: 81 (of 100). **Freshman Academic Profile:** Average high school GPA 3.6. 31% in top 10% of high school class, 61% in top 25% of high school class, 88% in top 50% of high school class. 90% from public high schools. Average SAT I Math 608, SAT I Math middle 50% range 550-680. Average SAT I Verbal 596, SAT I Verbal middle 50% range 530-660. Average ACT 26, ACT middle 50% range 23-28. TOEFL required of all international applicants, minimum TOEFL 550. **Basis for Candidate Selection:** *Very important factors considered include:* class rank, recommendations, secondary school record, standardized test scores. *Important factors considered include:* character/personal qualities, essays, extracurricular activities, minority status, talent/ability, volunteer work. *Other factors considered include:* alumni/ae relation, geographical residence, interview, religious affiliation/commitment. **Freshman Admission Requirements:** High school diploma or GED is required. *Academic units required/recommended:* 14 total recommended; 4 English recommended, 3 math recommended, 2 science recommended, 1 science lab recommended, 2 foreign language recommended, 3 social studies recommended. **Freshman Admission Statistics:** 1,953 applied, 78% accepted, 40% of those accepted enrolled. **Transfer Admission Requirements:** *Items required:* high school transcript, college transcript, essay, standardized test scores. Minimum college GPA of 2.5 required. Lowest grade transferable C. **General Admission Information:** Application fee $25. Nonfall registration accepted. Admission may be deferred for a maximum of 1 year. Credit and/or placement offered for CEEB Advanced Placement tests.

COSTS AND FINANCIAL AID

Tuition $20,310. Room & board $4,040. Required fees $0. Average book expense $710. **Required Forms and Deadlines:** FAFSA and institution's own financial aid form. No deadline for regular filing. Priority filing deadline February 15. **Notification of Awards:** Applicants will be notified of awards on a rolling basis beginning on or about March 15. **Types of Aid:** *Need-based scholarships/grants:* Pell, SEOG, state scholarships/grants, private scholarships, the school's own gift aid. *Loans:* Direct Subsidized Stafford, Direct Unsubsidized Stafford, Direct PLUS, Federal Perkins, college/university loans from institutional funds. **Student Employment:** Federal Work-Study Program available. Institutional employment available. Off-campus job opportunities are good. **Financial Aid Statistics:** 66% freshmen, 64% undergrads receive some form of aid. Average freshman grant $11,785. Average freshman loan $3,601. Average income from on-campus job $319. **Financial Aid Phone:** 563-387-1018.

LYCOMING COLLEGE

700 College Place, Williamsport, PA 17701
Phone: 570-321-4026 **E-mail:** admissions@lycoming.edu **CEEB Code:** 2372
Fax: 570-321-4317 **Web:** www.lycoming.edu **ACT Code:** 3622

This private school, which is affiliated with the Methodist Church, was founded in 1812. It has a 35-acre campus.

STUDENTS AND FACULTY

Enrollment: 1,418. **Student Body:** Male 46%, female 54%, out of state 23%, international 1% (9 countries represented). **Ethnic Representation:** African American 2%, Caucasian 97%. **Retention and Graduation:** 81% freshmen return for sophomore year. 65% freshmen graduate within 4 years. 20% grads go on to further study within 1 year. 1% grads pursue business degrees. 1% grads pursue law degrees. 6% grads pursue medical degrees. **Faculty:** Student/faculty ratio 13:1. 88 full-time faculty, 86% hold PhDs. 100% faculty teach undergrads.

ACADEMICS

Degrees: Bachelor's. **Academic Requirements:** General education including some course work in arts/fine arts, English (including composition), foreign languages, history, humanities, mathematics, philosophy, sciences (biological or physical), social science. Students are required to complete a cultural diversity course and the writing across the curriculum program, which consists of 3 writing-intensive courses. **Classes:** 10-19 students in an average class. 10-19 students in an average lab/discussion section. **Majors with Highest Enrollment:** Business administration/management; biology/biological sciences, general; psychology, general. **Disciplines with Highest Percentage of Degrees Awarded:** Business/marketing 20%, psychology 18%, biological life sciences 16%, social sciences and history 9%, visual and performing arts 7%. **Special Study Options:** Accelerated program, cross registration, double major, honors program, independent study, internships, liberal arts/career combination, student-designed major, study abroad, teacher certification program.

FACILITIES

Housing: Coed, all-female, apartments for single students, housing for international students, fraternities and/or sororities, substance-free housing, study-intensive housing, Creative Arts Society housing. **Library Holdings:** 180,000 bound volumes. 950 periodicals. **Special Academic Facilities/Equipment:** Language lab, tissue culture lab, TV studio, planetarium, videoconferencing. **Computers:** *Recommended operating system:* Windows NT/ 2000. School-owned computers available for student use.

EXTRACURRICULARS

Activities: Choral groups, concert band, dance, drama/theater, literary magazine, music ensembles, musical theater, pep band, radio station, student government, student newspaper, student-run film society, symphony orchestra, television station, yearbook. **Organizations:** 70 registered organizations, 19 honor societies, 2 religious organizations, 5 fraternities (17% men join), 4 sororities (21% women join). **Athletics (Intercollegiate):** *Men:* basketball, cross-country, football, golf, lacrosse, soccer, swimming, tennis, track & field, wrestling. *Women:* basketball, cross-country, lacrosse, soccer, softball, swimming, tennis, track & field, volleyball.

ADMISSIONS

Selectivity Rating: 77 (of 100). **Freshman Academic Profile:** Average high school GPA 3.2. 22% in top 10% of high school class, 50% in top 25% of high school class, 79% in top 50% of high school class. Average SAT I Math 540, SAT I Math middle 50% range 480-590. Average SAT I Verbal 540, SAT I Verbal middle 50% range 490-600. Average ACT 22, ACT middle 50% range 21-24. TOEFL required of all international applicants, minimum TOEFL 500. **Basis for Candidate Selection:** *Very important factors considered include:* secondary school record. *Important factors considered include:* character/ personal qualities, class rank, interview, standardized test scores. *Other factors considered include:* alumni/ae relation, essays, extracurricular activities, recommendations, talent/ability, volunteer work, work experience. **Freshman Admission Requirements:** High school diploma or GED is required. *Academic units required/recommended:* 16 total required; 4 English required, 3 math required, 4 math recommended, 2 science required, 3 science recommended, 2 science lab required, 3 science lab recommended, 2 foreign language required, 3 foreign language recommended, 3 social studies required, 4 social studies recommended, 2 elective required. **Freshman Admission Statistics:** 1,553 applied, 79% accepted, 30% of those accepted enrolled. **Transfer Admission Requirements:** *Items required:* college transcript, statement of good standing from prior school. Minimum college GPA of 2.0 required. Lowest grade transferable C. **General Admission Information:** Application fee $35. Priority application deadline April 1. Regular application deadline July 1. Nonfall registration accepted. Admission may be deferred for a maximum of 1 year. Credit offered for CEEB Advanced Placement tests.

COSTS AND FINANCIAL AID

Required Forms and Deadlines: FAFSA and institution's own financial aid form. Financial aid filing deadline May 1. Priority filing deadline April 15. **Notification of Awards:** Applicants will be notified of awards on a rolling basis beginning on or about March 15. **Types of Aid:** *Need-based scholarships/ grants:* Pell, SEOG, state scholarships/grants, private scholarships, the school's own gift aid. *Loans:* Direct Subsidized Stafford, Direct Unsubsidized Stafford, Direct PLUS, FFEL Subsidized Stafford, FFEL Unsubsidized Stafford, FFEL PLUS, Federal Perkins, state loans. **Student Employment:** Federal Work-Study Program available. Off-campus job opportunities are good. **Financial Aid Statistics:** 81% freshmen, 82% undergrads receive some form of aid. Average freshman grant $9,400. Average freshman loan $3,200. Average income from on-campus job $600. **Financial Aid Phone:** 570-321-4040.

LYME ACADEMY OF FINE ARTS

84 Lyme Street, Old Lyme, CT 06371
Phone: 860-434-5232 **E-mail:** admissions@lymeacademy.edu
Fax: 860-434-8725 **Web:** www.lymeacademy.edu

This private school was founded in 1976. It has a 4-acre campus.

STUDENTS AND FACULTY

Enrollment: 171. **Student Body:** Male 36%, female 64%, out-of-state 32%. **Ethnic Representation:** African American 2%, Asian 2%, Caucasian 94%, Hispanic 2%. **Retention and Graduation:** 46% freshmen return for sophomore year. 20% freshmen graduate within 4 years. 21% grads go on to further study within 1 year. 7% grads pursue medical degrees. **Faculty:** Student/faculty ratio 2:1. 9 full-time faculty, 44% hold PhDs. 100% faculty teach undergrads.

ACADEMICS

Degrees: Bachelor's. **Academic Requirements:** General education including some course work in arts/fine arts, English (including composition), humanities, mathematics, social science. **Classes:** 10-19 students in an average class. **Disciplines with Highest Percentage of Degrees Awarded:** Visual and performing arts 100%. **Special Study Options:** Independent study.

FACILITIES

Library Holdings: 8,805 bound volumes. 60 periodicals. 0 microforms. 135 audiovisuals. **Special Academic Facilities/Equipment:** Sill House Gallery. **Computers:** School-owned computers available for student use.

EXTRACURRICULARS

Activities: Student government, student newspaper.

ADMISSIONS

Selectivity Rating: 63 (of 100). **Freshman Academic Profile:** Average high school GPA 3.2. 12% in top 25% of high school class. 60% from public high schools. Average SAT I Math 501. Average SAT I Verbal 585. TOEFL required of all international applicants, minimum TOEFL 550. **Basis for Candidate Selection:** *Very important factors considered include:* interview, talent/ability. *Important factors considered include:* character/personal qualities, essays, recommendations. *Other factors considered include:* class rank, extracurricular activities, secondary school record, standardized test scores, volunteer work, work experience. **Freshman Admission Requirements:** High school diploma or GED is required. **Freshman Admission Statistics:** 32 applied, 97% accepted, 58% of those accepted enrolled. **Transfer Admission Requirements:** *Items required:* college transcript, essay, interview. Lowest grade transferable C. **General Admission Information:** Application fee $35. Admission may be deferred for a maximum of 1 year.

COSTS AND FINANCIAL AID

Tuition $12,200. Required fees $100. Average book expense $800. **Required Forms and Deadlines:** FAFSA, institution's own financial aid form, CSS/ Financial Aid PROFILE, and copies of previous year's tax forms and W-2s. Financial aid filing deadline March 15. Priority filing deadline February 15. **Notification of Awards:** Applicants will be notified of awards on a rolling basis beginning on or about April 15. **Types of Aid:** *Need-based scholarships/ grants:* Pell, SEOG, state scholarships/grants, private scholarships, the school's own gift aid. *Loans:* FFEL Subsidized Stafford, FFEL Unsubsidized Stafford, FFEL PLUS, state loans. **Student Employment:** Federal Work-Study Program available. Institutional employment available. Off-campus job opportunities are excellent. **Financial Aid Statistics:** 100% freshmen, 60% undergrads receive some form of aid. **Financial Aid Phone:** 860-434-5232.

LYNCHBURG COLLEGE

1501 Lakeside Drive, Lynchburg, VA 24501
Phone: 804-544-8300 **E-mail:** admissions@lynchburg.edu **CEEB Code:** 5372
Fax: 804-544-8653 **Web:** www.lynchburg.edu

This private school was founded in 1903. It has a 214-acre campus.

STUDENTS AND FACULTY

Enrollment: 1,652. **Student Body:** Male 36%, female 64%, out-of-state 42%, international 2% (12 countries represented). **Ethnic Representation:** African American 11%, Asian 1%, Caucasian 86%, Hispanic 2%. **Retention and Graduation:** 73% freshmen return for sophomore year. 43% freshmen graduate within 4 years. 22% grads go on to further study within 1 year. 5% grads pursue business degrees. 1% grads pursue law degrees. 1% grads pursue medical degrees.

ACADEMICS

Degrees: Bachelor's, master's. **Special Study Options:** Honors program, internships, study abroad. Undergrads may take grad-level classes. Foreign exchange program abroad in Japan (Joshi Seigakun College) and South Korea (Kijeon Women's College, Han Nam University), also China, England, France, and Spain.

FACILITIES

Housing: Coed, apartments for single students. **Library Holdings:** 287,601 bound volumes. 636 periodicals. 12,909 microforms. 9,360 audiovisuals. **Special Academic Facilities/Equipment:** Art gallery, language labs, technical assistance center for preschool and handicapped children, arboretum, herbarium, greenhouse, center for advanced engineering, writing center, math lab. **Computers:** *Recommended operating system:* Mac. School-owned computers available for student use.

EXTRACURRICULARS

Activities: Choral groups, dance, drama/theater, literary magazine, music ensembles, student government, student newspaper, yearbook. **Organizations:** 71 registered organizations, 13 honor societies, 5 religious organizations, 5 fraternities (23% men join), 5 sororities (10% women join). **Athletics (Intercollegiate):** *Men:* baseball, basketball, cheerleading, cross-country, equestrian, golf, lacrosse, soccer, tennis, track & field. *Women:* basketball, cheerleading, cross-country, equestrian, field hockey, lacrosse, soccer, softball, tennis, track & field, volleyball.

ADMISSIONS

Selectivity Rating: 68 (of 100). **Freshman Academic Profile:** Average high school GPA 3.1. 12% in top 10% of high school class, 41% in top 25% of high school class, 80% in top 50% of high school class. 78% from public high schools. Average SAT I Math 503. Average SAT I Verbal 506. TOEFL required of all international applicants, minimum TOEFL 525. **Freshman Admission Requirements:** High school diploma or GED is required. *Academic units required/recommended:* 16 total required; 20 total recommended; 4 English required, 4 English recommended, 3 math required, 3 math recommended, 3 science required, 3 science recommended, 2 science lab required, 2 science lab recommended, 2 foreign language required, 2 foreign language recommended, 4 social studies required, 4 social studies recommended, 4 elective recommended. **Freshman Admission Statistics:** 1,937 applied, 76% accepted, 30% of those accepted enrolled. **Transfer Admission Requirements:** *Items required:* college transcript, essay. Minimum college GPA of 2.0 required. Lowest grade transferable C-. **General Admission Information:** Application fee $30. Early decision application deadline November 15. Regular application deadline rolling. Nonfall registration accepted. Credit offered for CEEB Advanced Placement tests.

COSTS AND FINANCIAL AID

Tuition $17,120. Room & board $4,400. Required fees $125. **Required Forms and Deadlines:** FAFSA and state aid form. No deadline for regular filing. Priority filing deadline March 1. **Notification of Awards:** Applicants will be notified of awards on a rolling basis beginning on or about March 15. **Types of Aid:** *Need-based scholarships/grants:* Pell, SEOG, state scholarships/grants, the school's own gift aid. *Loans:* FFEL Subsidized Stafford, FFEL Unsubsidized Stafford, FFEL PLUS, Federal Perkins. **Student Employment:** Federal Work-Study Program available. Institutional employment available. Off-campus job opportunities are fair. **Financial Aid Statistics:** 70% freshmen, 68% undergrads receive some form of aid. Average freshman grant $12,681. Average freshman loan $3,105. Average income from on-campus job $925. **Financial Aid Phone:** 804-544-8228.

LYNDON STATE COLLEGE

1001 College Road, PO Box 919, Lyndonville, VT 05851
Phone: 802-626-6413 **E-mail:** admissions@lyndonstate.edu **CEEB Code:** 3767
Fax: 802-626-6335 **Web:** www.lsc.vsc.edu **ACT Code:** 4318

This public school was founded in 1911. It has a 175-acre campus.

STUDENTS AND FACULTY

Enrollment: 1,280. **Student Body:** Male 47%, female 53%, out-of-state 44%. **Ethnic Representation:** Caucasian 57%. **Retention and Graduation:** 67% freshmen return for sophomore year. 24% freshmen graduate within 4 years. 10% grads go on to further study within 1 year. **Faculty:** Student/faculty ratio 17:1. 56 full-time faculty, 96% hold PhDs. 100% faculty teach undergrads.

ACADEMICS

Degrees: Associate's, bachelor's, certificate, master's. **Academic Requirements:** General education including some course work in arts/fine arts, computer literacy, English (including composition), humanities, mathematics, sciences (biological or physical), social science. **Classes:** 10-19 students in an average class. Under 10 students in an average lab/discussion section. **Disciplines with Highest Percentage of Degrees Awarded:** Psychology 16%, business/marketing 13%, parks and recreation 13%, liberal arts/general studies 13%, education 11%. **Special Study Options:** Accelerated program, cooperative (work-study) program, double major, dual enrollment, student exchange program (domestic), independent study, internships, liberal arts/career combination, student-designed major, study abroad, teacher certification program.

FACILITIES

Housing: Coed, all-female, housing for disabled students, Substance free dorms. **Library Holdings:** 101,872 bound volumes. 16,468 periodicals. 13,532 microforms. 4,883 audiovisuals. **Special Academic Facilities/Equipment:** Museum of college history, weather satellite lab, television studio, radio station, science labs (geology, chemistry, physics), GIS/GPS lab.

EXTRACURRICULARS

Activities: Choral groups, dance, drama/theater, literary magazine, musical theater, radio station, student government, student newspaper, television station. **Organizations:** 26 registered organizations, 1 honor society, 1 religious organization. **Athletics (Intercollegiate):** *Men:* baseball, basketball, cross-country, soccer, tennis. *Women:* basketball, cross-country, soccer, softball, tennis.

ADMISSIONS

Selectivity Rating: 66 (of 100). **Freshman Academic Profile:** Average high school GPA 2.5. 12% in top 10% of high school class, 22% in top 25% of high school class, 69% in top 50% of high school class. Average SAT I Math 475, SAT I Math middle 50% range 400-480. Average SAT I Verbal 475, SAT I Verbal middle 50% range 430-530. Average ACT 21. TOEFL required of all international applicants, minimum TOEFL 500. **Basis for Candidate Selection:** *Very important factors considered include:* secondary school record. *Important factors considered include:* character/personal qualities, class rank, interview, recommendations, talent/ability. *Other factors considered include:* alumni/ae relation, essays, extracurricular activities, standardized test scores, volunteer work, work experience. **Freshman Admission Requirements:** High school diploma or GED is required. *Academic units required/recommended:* 14 total recommended; 4 English required, 3 math required, 4 math recommended, 2 science required, 3 science recommended, 2 science lab required, 2 foreign language recommended, 2 social studies required, 2 history required. **Freshman Admission Statistics:** 757 applied, 97% accepted, 49% of those accepted enrolled. **Transfer Admission Requirements:** *Items required:* college transcript, statement of good standing from prior school. Minimum college GPA of 2.0 required. Lowest grade transferable C-. **General Admission Information:** Application fee $30. Priority application deadline May 1. Nonfall registration accepted. Admission may be deferred for a maximum of 1 year. Credit and/or placement offered for CEEB Advanced Placement tests.

COSTS AND FINANCIAL AID

In-state tuition $4,404. Out-of-state tuition $10,320. Room & board $5,520. Required fees $998. Average book expense $600. **Required Forms and Deadlines:** FAFSA. Priority filing deadline February 13. **Notification of Awards:** Applicants will be notified of awards on a rolling basis beginning on or about April 1. **Types of Aid:** *Need-based scholarships/grants:* Pell, SEOG, state scholarships/grants, private scholarships, the school's own gift aid. *Loans:* Direct Subsidized Stafford, Direct Unsubsidized Stafford, Direct PLUS, Federal Perkins, state loans. **Student Employment:** Federal Work-Study Program available. Institutional employment available. Off-campus job opportunities are good. **Financial Aid Statistics:** 78% freshmen, 74% undergrads receive some form of aid. Average income from on-campus job $700. **Financial Aid Phone:** 802-626-6218.

See page 1098.

LYNN UNIVERSITY

3601 North Military Trail, Boca Raton, FL 33431-5598
Phone: 561-237-7900 **E-mail:** admission@lynn.edu **CEEB Code:** 5437
Fax: 561-237-7100 **Web:** www.lynn.edu **ACT Code:** 706

This private school was founded in 1962. It has a 123-acre campus.

STUDENTS AND FACULTY

Enrollment: 1,821. **Student Body:** Male 48%, female 52%, out-of-state 45%, international 18% (70 countries represented). **Ethnic Representation:** African American 7%, Asian 1%, Caucasian 60%, Hispanic 7%. **Retention and Graduation:** 53% freshmen return for sophomore year. 15% grads go on to further study within 1 year. **Faculty:** Student/faculty ratio 14:1. 68 full-time faculty, 61% hold PhDs. 81% faculty teach undergrads.

ACADEMICS

Degrees: Associate's, bachelor's, certificate, doctoral, master's. **Academic Requirements:** General education including course work in arts/fine arts, computer literacy, English (including composition), humanities, mathematics, sciences (biological or physical), social science, speech, international relations/political science. **Classes:** 10-19 students in an average class. Under 10 students in an average lab/discussion section. **Majors with Highest Enrollment:** Business administration/management; hospitality administration/management, general. **Disciplines with Highest Percentage of Degrees Awarded:** Business/marketing 40%, communications/communication technologies 10%, education 8%, health professions and related sciences 8%, visual and performing arts 7%. **Special Study Options:** Distance learning, double major, English as a second language, honors program, independent study, internships, study abroad, teacher certification program.

FACILITIES

Housing: Coed, all-female, housing for disabled students. **Library Holdings:** 79,670 bound volumes. 750 periodicals. 108,720 microforms. 1,760 audiovisuals. **Computers:** *Recommended operating system:* Windows 95. School-owned computers available for student use.

EXTRACURRICULARS

Activities: Choral groups, dance, drama/theater, literary magazine, music ensembles, radio station, student government, student newspaper, symphony orchestra, yearbook. **Organizations:** 25 registered organizations, 2 religious organizations, 4 fraternities (2% men join), 2 sororities (2% women join). **Athletics (Intercollegiate):** *Men:* baseball, basketball, crew, cross-country, golf, soccer, tennis. *Women:* basketball, crew, cross-country, golf, soccer, softball, tennis.

ADMISSIONS

Selectivity Rating: 66 (of 100). **Freshman Academic Profile:** Average high school GPA 2.6. 10% in top 10% of high school class, 24% in top 25% of high school class, 54% in top 50% of high school class. Average SAT I Math 482, SAT I Math middle 50% range 420-520. Average SAT I Verbal 471, SAT I Verbal middle 50% range 410-510. Average ACT 21, ACT middle 50% range 16-22. TOEFL required of all international applicants, minimum TOEFL 500. **Basis for Candidate Selection:** *Very important factors considered include:* secondary school record. *Important factors considered include:* recommendations, standardized test scores. *Other factors considered include:* alumni/ae relation, character/personal qualities, essays, extracurricular activities, interview, minority status, talent/ability, volunteer work, work experience. **Freshman Admission Requirements:** High school diploma or GED is required. *Academic units required/recommended:* 20 total recommended; 4 English recommended, 3 math recommended, 3 science recommended, 1 foreign language recommended, 2 social studies recommended, 2 history recommended, 5 elective recommended. **Freshman Admission Statistics:** 401 applied, 346% accepted, 28% of those accepted enrolled. **Transfer Admission Requirements:** *Items required:* college transcript, essay, statement of good standing from prior school. Minimum college GPA of 2.0 required. Lowest grade transferable C. **General Admission Information:** Application fee $25. Nonfall registration accepted. Admission may be deferred for a maximum of 1 year. Neither credit nor placement offered for CEEB Advanced Placement tests.

COSTS AND FINANCIAL AID

Tuition $21,000. Room & board $7,650. Required fees $750. Average book expense $800. **Required Forms and Deadlines:** FAFSA and institution's own financial aid form. No deadline for regular filing. Priority filing deadline March 1. **Notification of Awards:** Applicants will be notified of awards on a rolling basis beginning on or about February 15. **Types of Aid:** *Need-based scholarships/grants:* Pell, SEOG, state scholarships/grants, private scholarships, the school's own gift aid. *Loans:* Direct Subsidized Stafford, Direct Unsubsidized Stafford, Direct PLUS, FFEL Subsidized Stafford, FFEL Unsubsidized Stafford, FFEL PLUS, Federal Perkins, college/university loans from institutional funds. **Student Employment:** Federal Work-Study Program available. Institutional employment available. Off-campus job opportunities are excellent. **Financial Aid Statistics:** 31% freshmen, 29% undergrads receive some form of aid. Average freshman grant $9,479. Average freshman loan $2,713. Average income from on-campus job $1,200. **Financial Aid Phone:** 561-237-7807.

See page 1100.

LYON COLLEGE

PO Box 2317, Batesville, AR 72503-2317
Phone: 870-698-4250 **E-mail:** admissions@lyon.edu **CEEB Code:** 1088
Fax: 870-793-1791 **Web:** www.lyon.edu **ACT Code:** 112

This private school, which is affiliated with the Presbyterian Church, was founded in 1872. It has a 136-acre campus.

STUDENTS AND FACULTY

Enrollment: 538. **Student Body:** Male 46%, female 54%, out-of-state 14%, international 6% (15 countries represented). **Ethnic Representation:** African American 3%, Asian 2%, Caucasian 92%, Hispanic 1%, Native American 1%. **Retention and Graduation:** 76% freshmen return for sophomore year. 47% freshmen graduate within 4 years. 28% grads go on to further study within 1 year. 1% grads pursue business degrees. 2% grads pursue law degrees. 2% grads pursue medical degrees. **Faculty:** Student/faculty ratio 11:1. 43 full-time faculty, 86% hold PhDs. 100% faculty teach undergrads.

ACADEMICS

Degrees: Bachelor's. **Academic Requirements:** General education including some course work in arts/fine arts, English (including composition), foreign languages, history, humanities, mathematics, philosophy, sciences (biological or physical), social science, physical education. **Classes:** 10-19 students in an average class. 10-19 students in an average lab/discussion section. **Majors with Highest Enrollment:** Biology/biological sciences, general; psychology, general; business administration/management. **Disciplines with Highest Percentage of Degrees Awarded:** Biological life sciences 20%, psychology 20%, social sciences and history 17%, business/marketing 12%, English 11%. **Special Study Options:** Accelerated program, cross registration, double major, dual enrollment, independent study, internships, student-designed major, study abroad, teacher certification program.

FACILITIES

Housing: All-female, all-male, limited college-owned off-campus housing. **Library Holdings:** 172,738 bound volumes. 854 periodicals. 2,921 microforms. 6,103 audiovisuals. **Special Academic Facilities/Equipment:** Ozark Regional Studies Center. **Computers:** School-owned computers available for student use.

EXTRACURRICULARS

Activities: Choral groups, drama/theater, jazz band, literary magazine, music ensembles, student government, student newspaper, student-run film society, yearbook. **Organizations:** 40 registered organizations, 9 honor societies, 9 religious organizations, 3 fraternities (13% men join), 2 sororities (27% women join). **Athletics (Intercollegiate):** *Men:* baseball, basketball, cross-country, golf, soccer, tennis. *Women:* basketball, cross-country, golf, soccer, tennis, volleyball.

ADMISSIONS

Selectivity Rating: 87 (of 100). **Freshman Academic Profile:** Average high school GPA 3.5. 32% in top 10% of high school class, 59% in top 25% of high school class, 90% in top 50% of high school class. Average SAT I Math 560, SAT I Math middle 50% range 500-630. Average SAT I Verbal 580, SAT I Verbal middle 50% range 520-620. Average ACT 25, ACT middle 50% range 23-27. TOEFL required of all international applicants, minimum TOEFL 550. **Basis for Candidate Selection:** *Very important factors considered include:* class rank, essays, secondary school record, standardized test scores. *Important factors considered include:* character/personal qualities, extracurricular activities. *Other factors considered include:* recommendations, talent/ability, volunteer work. **Freshman Admission Requirements:** High school diploma or GED is required. *Academic units required/recommended:* 16 total required; 18 total recommended; 4 English required, 4 English recommended, 3 math required, 4 math recommended, 3 science required, 4 science recommended, 2 science lab required, 2 science lab recommended, 2 foreign language required, 2 foreign language recommended, 1 social studies required, 1 social studies recommended, 2 history required, 2 history recommended, 1 elective required, 1 elective recommended. **Freshman Admission Statistics:** 409 applied, 74% accepted, 37% of those accepted enrolled. **Transfer Admission Requirements:** *Items required:* college transcript, essay, statement of good standing from prior school. Minimum college GPA of 2.8 required. Lowest grade transferable C. **General Admission Information:** Application fee $25. Priority application deadline January 15. Nonfall registration accepted. Admission may be deferred for a maximum of 1 year. Credit and/or placement offered for CEEB Advanced Placement tests.

COSTS AND FINANCIAL AID

Required Forms and Deadlines: FAFSA. No deadline for regular filing. Priority filing deadline March 15. **Notification of Awards:** Applicants will be notified of awards on a rolling basis beginning on or about March 1. **Types of Aid:** *Need-based scholarships/grants:* Pell, SEOG, state scholarships/grants, private scholarships, the school's own gift aid. *Loans:* FFEL Subsidized Stafford, FFEL Unsubsidized Stafford, FFEL PLUS, Federal Perkins. **Student Employment:** Federal Work-Study Program available. Institutional employment available. Off-campus job opportunities are fair. **Financial Aid Statistics:** 62% freshmen, 63% undergrads receive some form of aid. Average freshman grant $9,371. Average freshman loan $2,625. Average income from on-campus job $1,193. **Financial Aid Phone:** 870-698-4257.

MACALESTER COLLEGE

1600 Grand Avenue, St. Paul, MN 55105
Phone: 651-696-6357 **E-mail:** admissions@macalester.edu **CEEB Code:** 6390
Fax: 651-696-6724 **Web:** www.macalester.edu **ACT Code:** 2122

This private school, which is affiliated with the Presbyterian Church, was founded in 1874. It has a 53-acre campus. Paul.

STUDENTS AND FACULTY

Enrollment: 1,840. **Student Body:** Male 42%, female 58%, out-of-state 72%, international 14% (77 countries represented). **Ethnic Representation:** African American 4%, Asian 6%, Caucasian 85%, Hispanic 3%, Native American 1%. **Retention and Graduation:** 93% freshmen return for sophomore year. 77% freshmen graduate within 4 years. 60% grads go on to further study within 1 year. 1% grads pursue business degrees. 3% grads pursue law degrees. 2% grads pursue medical degrees. **Faculty:** Student/faculty ratio 10:1. 150 full-time faculty, 93% hold PhDs. 100% faculty teach undergrads.

ACADEMICS

Degrees: Bachelor's. **Academic Requirements:** General education including some course work in arts/fine arts, foreign languages, humanities, mathematics, sciences (biological or physical), social science, domestic diversity, international diversity. **Classes:** 10-19 students in an average class. 10-19 students in an average lab/discussion section. **Majors with Highest Enrollment:** Biology/biological sciences, general; psychology, general; economics, general. **Disciplines with Highest Percentage of Degrees Awarded:** Social sciences and history 35%, biological life sciences 9%, psychology 8%, visual and performing arts 7%, communications/communication technologies 6%. **Special Study Options:** Cross registration, double major, dual enrollment, honors program, independent study, internships, student-designed major, study abroad, teacher certification program, Combined bachelors/graduate programs: BA/Master's in Architecture with Washington University, St. Louis, Missouri; BA/BS in Engineering with Washington University, St. Louis or the University of Minnesota; BA/BS in Nursing with Rush University in Chicago, Illinois.

FACILITIES

Housing: Coed, apartments for single students, cooperative housing, language houses. **Library Holdings:** 407,321 bound volumes. 2,119 periodicals. 72,539 microforms. 9,288 audiovisuals. **Special Academic Facilities/Equipment:** Humanities learning center, econometrics lab, cartography lab, 250-acre nature preserve, observatory and planetarium, two electron microscopes, nuclear magnetic resonance spectrometer, laser spectroscopy lab, X-ray diffractometer, International Center, Center for Scholarship and Teaching. **Computers:** School-owned computers available for student use.

EXTRACURRICULARS

Activities: Choral groups, concert band, dance, drama/theater, jazz band, literary magazine, music ensembles, radio station, student government, student newspaper, symphony orchestra. **Organizations:** 70 registered organizations, 14 honor societies, 7 religious organizations. **Athletics (Intercollegiate):** *Men:* baseball, basketball, skiing (cross-country), cross-country, diving, football, golf, indoor track, skiing (Nordic), soccer, swimming, tennis, track & field. *Women:* basketball, skiing (cross-country), cross-country, diving, golf, indoor track, skiing (Nordic), soccer, softball, swimming, tennis, track & field, volleyball, water polo.

ADMISSIONS

Selectivity Rating: 96 (of 100). **Freshman Academic Profile:** 71% in top 10% of high school class, 96% in top 25% of high school class, 100% in top 50% of high school class. 66% from public high schools. Average SAT I Math 668, SAT I Math middle 50% range 620-710. Average SAT I Verbal 681, SAT I Verbal middle 50% range 630-730. Average ACT 29, ACT middle 50% range 27-31. TOEFL required of all international applicants, minimum TOEFL 570. **Basis for Candidate Selection:** *Very important factors considered include:* secondary school record. *Important factors considered include:* character/personal qualities, essays, extracurricular activities, recommendations, standardized test scores. *Other factors considered include:* alumni/ae relation, class rank, interview, minority status, talent/ability, volunteer work, work experience. **Freshman Admission Requirements:** High school diploma or equivalent is not required. *Academic units required/recommended:* 4 English recommended, 3 math recommended, 3 science recommended, 3 science lab recommended, 3 foreign language recommended, 3 social studies recommended. **Freshman Admission Statistics:** 3,713 applied, 44% accepted, 27% of those accepted enrolled. **Transfer Admission Requirements:** *Items required:* high school transcript, college transcript, essay, standardized test score, statement of good standing from prior school. Lowest grade transferable C-. **General Admission Information:** Application fee $40. Early decision application deadline November 15. Regular application deadline January 15. Admission may be deferred for a maximum of 1 year. Credit and/or placement offered for CEEB Advanced Placement tests.

COSTS AND FINANCIAL AID

Tuition $24,902. Room & board $6,874. Required fees $168. Average book expense $750. **Required Forms and Deadlines:** FAFSA, CSS/Financial Aid PROFILE, noncustodial (divorced/separated) parent's statement and business/farm supplement. Financial aid filing deadline April 15. Priority filing deadline February 7. **Notification of Awards:** Applicants will be notified of awards on or about April 1. **Types of Aid:** *Need-based scholarships/grants:* Pell, SEOG, state scholarships/grants, private scholarships, the school's own gift aid. *Loans:* FFEL Subsidized Stafford, FFEL Unsubsidized Stafford, FFEL PLUS, Federal Perkins, state loans. **Student Employment:** Federal Work-Study Program available. Institutional employment available. Off-campus job opportunities are excellent. **Financial Aid Statistics:** 77% freshmen, 69% undergrads receive some form of aid. Average freshman grant $15,564. Average freshman loan $3,113. Average income from on-campus job $1,429. **Financial Aid Phone:** 651-696-6214.

MACMURRAY COLLEGE

447 East College, Jacksonville, IL 62650
Phone: 217-479-7056 **E-mail:** admiss@mac.edu **CEEB Code:** 1435
Fax: 217-291-0702 **Web:** www.mac.edu **ACT Code:** 1068

This private school, which is affiliated with the Methodist Church, was founded in 1846. It has a 60-acre campus.

STUDENTS AND FACULTY

Enrollment: 633. **Student Body:** Male 42%, female 58%, out-of-state 15%, international 2% (5 countries represented). **Ethnic Representation:** African American 11%, Caucasian 83%, Hispanic 5%. **Retention and Graduation:** 57% freshmen return for sophomore year. 38% freshmen graduate within 4 years. 10% grads go on to further study within 1 year. 1% grads pursue law degrees. 1% grads pursue medical degrees. **Faculty:** Student/faculty ratio 13:1. 46 full-time faculty, 71% hold PhDs. 100% faculty teach undergrads.

ACADEMICS

Degrees: Associate's, bachelor's. **Academic Requirements:** General education including some course work in arts/fine arts, English (including composition), history, humanities, mathematics, philosophy, sciences (biological or physical), social science. **Classes:** 10-19 students in an average class. 10-19 students in an average lab/discussion section. **Disciplines with Highest Percentage of Degrees Awarded:** Education 31%, protective services/public administration 13%, business/marketing 12%, social sciences and history 9%, psychology 8%. **Special Study Options:** Cross registration, double major, independent study, internships, liberal arts/career combination, study abroad, teacher certification program.

FACILITIES

Housing: Coed, all-female, all-male, apartments for single students, housing for disabled students, housing for international students. **Library Holdings:** 935,000 bound volumes. 235 periodicals. 24,600 microforms. 936 audiovisuals. **Special Academic Facilities/Equipment:** Art gallery, language lab. **Computers:** *Recommended operating system:* Windows NT/2000. School-owned computers available for student use.

EXTRACURRICULARS

Activities: Choral groups, dance, drama/theater, music ensembles, student government, student newspaper, yearbook. **Organizations:** 37 registered organizations, 2 honor societies, 1 religious organization, 2 fraternities (18% men join), 1 sorority (10% women join). **Athletics (Intercollegiate):** *Men:* baseball, basketball, cheerleading, cross-country, diving, football, golf, soccer, swimming, tennis, water polo, wrestling. *Women:* basketball, cheerleading, cross-country, diving, golf, soccer, softball, swimming, tennis, volleyball, water polo.

ADMISSIONS

Selectivity Rating: 66 (of 100). **Freshman Academic Profile:** Average high school GPA 3.6. 12% in top 10% of high school class, 27% in top 25% of high school class, 88% in top 50% of high school class. 75% from public high schools. Average SAT I Math 474, SAT I Math middle 50% range 460-540. Average SAT I Verbal 447, SAT I Verbal middle 50% range 480-540. Average ACT 20, ACT middle 50% range 20-25. TOEFL required of all international applicants, minimum TOEFL 550. **Basis for Candidate Selection:** *Very important factors considered include:* secondary school record, standardized test scores. *Important factors considered include:* character/personal qualities, class rank, extracurricular activities. *Other factors considered include:* essays, interview, recommendations, volunteer work, work experience. **Freshman Admission Requirements:** High school diploma or GED is required. *Academic units required/recommended:* 13 total recommended; 4 English recommended, 3 math recommended, 2 science recommended, 2 science lab recommended, 2 foreign language recommended, 2 social studies recommended. **Freshman Admission Statistics:** 1,340 applied, 56% accepted, 21% of those accepted enrolled. **Transfer Admission Requirements:** *Items required:* college transcript. Minimum college GPA of 2.0 required. Lowest grade transferable D. **General Admission Information:** Priority application deadline May 1. Nonfall registration accepted. Admission may be deferred for a maximum of 1 year. Credit and/or placement offered for CEEB Advanced Placement tests.

COSTS AND FINANCIAL AID

Tuition $14,500. Room & board $5,183. Required fees $0. Average book expense $800. **Required Forms and Deadlines:** FAFSA. No deadline for regular filing. **Notification of Awards:** Applicants will be notified of awards on a rolling basis beginning on or about March 1. **Types of Aid:** *Need-based scholarships/grants:* Pell, SEOG, state scholarships/grants, private scholarships, the school's own gift aid. *Loans:* FFEL Subsidized Stafford, FFEL Unsubsidized Stafford, FFEL PLUS, Federal Perkins. **Student Employment:** Federal Work-Study Program available. Institutional employment available. Off-campus job opportunities are good. **Financial Aid Statistics:** 100% freshmen, 99% undergrads receive some form of aid. Average freshman grant $3,166. Average freshman loan $3,637. Average income from on-campus job $945. **Financial Aid Phone:** 217-479-7041.

MADONNA UNIVERSITY

36600 Schoolcraft Road, Livonia, MI 48150-1173
Phone: 734-432-5339 **E-mail:** muinfo@smtp.munet.edu **CEEB Code:** 1437
Fax: 734-432-5393 **Web:** www.munet.edu **ACT Code:** 2022

This private school, which is affiliated with the Roman Catholic Church, was founded in 1947. It has a 49-acre campus.

STUDENTS AND FACULTY

Enrollment: 3,307. **Student Body:** Male 22%, female 78%, out-of-state 3%, (40 countries represented). **Ethnic Representation:** African American 11%, Asian 2%, Caucasian 76%, Hispanic 4%, Native American 1%. **Retention and Graduation:** 68% freshmen return for sophomore year. 18% freshmen graduate within 4 years. 48% grads go on to further study within 1 year. **Faculty:** 100% faculty teach undergrads.

ACADEMICS

Degrees: Associate's, bachelor's, master's. **Academic Requirements:** General education including some course work in arts/fine arts, computer literacy, English (including composition), history, humanities, mathematics, philosophy, sciences (biological or physical), social science, religious studies. **Special Study Options:** Cooperative (work-study) program, cross registration, distance learning, double major, dual enrollment, English as a second language, honors program, independent study, internships, liberal arts/career combination, student-designed major, study abroad, teacher certification program, credit for experiential learning.

FACILITIES

Housing: All-female, all-male, housing for disabled students, housing for international students. **Library Holdings:** 142,551 bound volumes. 3,100 periodicals. 450,000 microforms. 117,983 audiovisuals. **Special Academic Facilities/Equipment:** Paraprofessional training institute, psycho-educational center. **Computers:** School-owned computers available for student use.

EXTRACURRICULARS

Activities: Choral groups, literary magazine, music ensembles, student government, student newspaper, television station. **Organizations:** 18 registered organizations, 8 honor societies, 1 religious organization. **Athletics (Intercollegiate):** *Men:* baseball, basketball, soccer. *Women:* basketball, soccer, softball, volleyball.

ADMISSIONS

Selectivity Rating: 68 (of 100). **Freshman Academic Profile:** Average high school GPA 3.3. 22% in top 10% of high school class, 47% in top 25% of high school class, 89% in top 50% of high school class. ACT middle 50% range 17-22. TOEFL required of all international applicants, minimum TOEFL 540. **Basis for Candidate Selection:** *Very important factors considered include:* secondary school record. *Important factors considered include:* character/personal qualities, class rank, essays, interview, standardized test scores. *Other factors considered include:* alumni/ae relation, extracurricular activities, recommendations, religious affiliation/commitment, talent/ability, volunteer work, work experience. **Freshman Admission Requirements:** High school diploma or GED is required. *Academic units required/recommended:* 19 total required; 3 English required, 2 math required, 2 science required, 2 foreign language recommended, 3 social studies required. **Freshman Admission Statistics:** 440 applied, 289% accepted, 26% of those accepted enrolled. **Transfer Admission Requirements:** *Items required:* high school transcript, college transcript. Minimum high school GPA of 2.0 required. Minimum college GPA of 2.0 required. Lowest grade transferable C. **General Admission Information:** Priority application deadline March 1. Regular application deadline rolling. Nonfall registration accepted. Admission may be deferred. Neither credit nor placement offered for CEEB Advanced Placement tests.

COSTS AND FINANCIAL AID

Tuition $6,610. Room & board $4,676. Required fees $100. Average book expense $580. **Required Forms and Deadlines:** FAFSA. Financial aid filing deadline August 30. Priority filing deadline March 30. **Notification of Awards:** Applicants will be notified of awards on a rolling basis beginning on or about March 1. **Types of Aid:** *Need-based scholarships/grants:* Pell, SEOG, state scholarships/grants, private scholarships, the school's own gift aid. *Loans:* Direct Subsidized Stafford, Direct Unsubsidized Stafford, Direct PLUS, Federal Perkins. **Student Employment:** Federal Work-Study Program available. Institutional employment available. Off-campus job opportunities are good. **Financial Aid Statistics:** Average freshman grant $3,000. Average income from on-campus job $1,200. **Financial Aid Phone:** 734-432-5663.

MAHARISHI UNIVERSITY OF MANAGEMENT

1000 North Fourth Street, Fairfield, IA 52557
Phone: 641-472-7000 **E-mail:** admissions@mum.edu
Fax: 641-472-1179 **Web:** www.mum.edu **ACT Code:** 1317

This private school was founded in 1971. It has a 242-acre campus.

STUDENTS AND FACULTY

Enrollment: 185. **Student Body:** Male 49%, female 51%, out-of-state 48%, international 23%. **Ethnic Representation:** African American 2%, Asian 4%, Caucasian 90%, Hispanic 4%. **Retention and Graduation:** 66% freshmen return for sophomore year. 32% freshmen graduate within 4 years. 42% grads go on to further study within 1 year. **Faculty:** Student/faculty ratio 8:1. 51 full-time faculty, 70% hold PhDs.

ACADEMICS

Degrees: Associate's, bachelor's, certificate, doctoral, master's. **Academic Requirements:** General education including some course work in arts/fine arts, computer literacy, English (including composition), foreign languages, humanities, mathematics, sciences (biological or physical). All new students take a foundation course, "the science of creative intelligence." All entering undergraduates take a special series of courses called "natural law seminars," which span the full range of human knowledge, from the arts to the sciences to the humanities. Courses are on a block system, each block being two to four weeks long. **Classes:** Under 10 students in an average class. **Disciplines with Highest Percentage of Degrees Awarded:** Business/marketing 31%, visual and performing arts 24%, mathematics 12%, computer and information sciences 10%, education 5%. **Special Study Options:** Double major, student exchange program (domestic), honors program, independent study, internships, study abroad, teacher certification program.

FACILITIES

Housing: All-female, all-male, apartments for married students, apartments for single students, housing for disabled students, apartments for students with dependent children, "quiet" dorms. **Library Holdings:** 113,580 bound volumes. 868 periodicals. 59,851 microforms. 21,850 audiovisuals. **Special Academic Facilities/Equipment:** Art gallery, scanning electron microscope, real-time cell-imaging computer system, DNA synthesizer, rock-climbing wall. **Computers:** School-owned computers available for student use.

EXTRACURRICULARS

Activities: Choral groups, dance, drama/theater, music ensembles, musical theater, radio station, student government, student newspaper, yearbook. **Organizations:** 25 registered organizations, 3 honor societies, 1 religious organization. **Athletics (Intercollegiate):** *Men:* golf. *Women:* golf.

ADMISSIONS

Selectivity Rating: 73 (of 100). **Freshman Academic Profile:** Average high school GPA 3.5. Average SAT I Math 530, SAT I Math middle 50% range 460-

608. Average SAT I Verbal 554, SAT I Verbal middle 50% range 500-610. Average ACT 26, ACT middle 50% range 22-26. TOEFL required of all international applicants, minimum TOEFL 550. **Basis for Candidate Selection:** *Very important factors considered include:* character/personal qualities, essays, interview, recommendations. *Important factors considered include:* extracurricular activities, secondary school record, standardized test scores, volunteer work. *Other factors considered include:* alumni/ae relation, class rank, state residency, talent/ability, work experience. **Freshman Admission Requirements:** High school diploma or GED is required. *Academic units required/recommended:* 15 total recommended; 4 English recommended, 3 math recommended, 3 science recommended, 2 foreign language recommended, 3 social studies recommended. **Freshman Admission Statistics:** 71 applied, 63% accepted, 82% of those accepted enrolled. **Transfer Admission Requirements:** *Items required:* high school transcript, college transcript, essay, interview. Minimum high school GPA of 2.5 required. Minimum college GPA of 2.5 required. Lowest grade transferable C. **General Admission Information:** Application fee $25. Nonfall registration accepted. Admission may be deferred. Credit offered for CEEB Advanced Placement tests.

COSTS AND FINANCIAL AID

Tuition $23,600. Room & board $5,200. Required fees $450. Average book expense $800. **Required Forms and Deadlines:** FAFSA. No deadline for regular filing. Priority filing deadline April 15. **Notification of Awards:** Applicants will be notified of awards on a rolling basis beginning on or about March 1. **Types of Aid:** *Need-based scholarships/grants:* Pell, state scholarships/grants, private scholarships, the school's own gift aid, Federal Work Study, Veterans, Benefits, University Trustees' Scholarship. *Loans:* Direct Subsidized Stafford, FFEL Subsidized Stafford, Federal Perkins, state loans, college/university loans from institutional funds. **Student Employment:** Federal Work-Study Program available. Off-campus job opportunities are good. **Financial Aid Statistics:** 97% freshmen, 96% undergrads receive some form of aid. Average freshman grant $11,268. Average freshman loan $7,000. Average income from on-campus job $1,020. **Financial Aid Phone:** 641-472-1156.

MAINE COLLEGE OF ART

97 Spring Street, Portland, ME 04101
Phone: 207-775-3052 **E-mail:** admissions@meca.edu **CEEB Code:** 3701
Fax: 207-772-5069 **Web:** www.meca.edu **ACT Code:** 6908

This private school was founded in 1882.

STUDENTS AND FACULTY

Enrollment: 430. **Student Body:** Male 39%, female 61%, out-of-state 44%, international 1% (4 countries represented). **Ethnic Representation:** African American 1%, Hispanic 1%, Asian 1%, Caucasian 72%. **Retention and Graduation:** 61% freshmen return for sophomore year. **Faculty:** Student/faculty ratio 10:1. 32 full-time faculty, 93% hold PhDs. 100% faculty teach undergrads.

ACADEMICS

Degrees: Bachelor's, master's. **Academic Requirements:** General education including some course work in arts/fine arts, English (including composition), humanities, mathematics, sciences (biological or physical), social science. **Disciplines with Highest Percentage of Degrees Awarded:** Visual and performing arts 100%. **Special Study Options:** Cross registration, double major, student exchange program (domestic), independent study, internships, liberal arts/career combination, student-designed major, study abroad, teacher certification program, mobility program with 36 AICAD (Associated Independent Colleges of Art and Design) institutions in USA and Canada, cross-registration program with 4 other colleges and universities in the greater Portland area, exchange program with Hanoi Fine Arts College in Vietnam, and BFA credit available through Provincetown, Maine, Fine Arts Work Center.

FACILITIES

Housing: Coed, apartments for single students, cooperative housing. **Library Holdings:** 20,000 bound volumes. 100 periodicals. 150 audiovisuals. **Special Academic Facilities/Equipment:** Institute of Contemporary Art, June Fitzpatrick Gallery, ArtMart (art supply store). **Computers:** *Recommended operating system:* Mac. School-owned computers available for student use.

EXTRACURRICULARS

Activities: Student government, student newspaper, student-run film society.

ADMISSIONS

Selectivity Rating: 80 (of 100). **Freshman Academic Profile:** 11% in top 10% of high school class, 35% in top 25% of high school class, 83% in top 50% of high school class. Average SAT I Math 485, SAT I Math middle 50% range 450-540. Average SAT I Verbal 533, SAT I Verbal middle 50% range 475-590. ACT middle 50% range 23-26. TOEFL required of all international applicants, minimum TOEFL 500. **Basis for Candidate Selection:** *Very important factors considered include:* essays, interview, recommendations, secondary school record. *Important factors considered include:* character/personal qualities, class rank. *Other factors considered include:* alumni/ae relation, extracurricular activities, standardized test scores, talent/ability, volunteer work, work experience. **Freshman Admission Requirements:** High school diploma or GED is required. *Academic units required/recommended:* 16 total recommended; 4 English recommended, 3 math recommended, 2 science recommended, 2 foreign language recommended, 2 social studies recommended. **Freshman Admission Statistics:** 296 applied, 90% accepted, 36% of those accepted enrolled. **Transfer Admission Requirements:** *Items required:* high school transcript, college transcript, essay, statement of good standing from prior school. Minimum high school GPA of 2.0 required. Minimum college GPA of 2.0 required. Lowest grade transferable C. **General Admission Information:** Application fee $40. Priority application deadline March 1. Nonfall registration accepted. Admission may be deferred for a maximum of 1 year. Credit and/or placement offered for CEEB Advanced Placement tests.

COSTS AND FINANCIAL AID

Tuition $19,400. Room & board $7,140. Required fees $478. Average book expense $1,714. **Required Forms and Deadlines:** FAFSA. Financial aid filing deadline April 1. Priority filing deadline March 1. **Notification of Awards:** Applicants will be notified of awards on a rolling basis. **Student Employment:** Federal Work-Study Program available. Institutional employment available. Off-campus job opportunities are excellent. **Financial Aid Statistics:** 84% freshmen, 95% undergrads receive some form of aid. Average freshman grant $7,439. Average freshman loan $5,603. **Financial Aid Phone:** 207-775-3052.

See page 1102.

MAINE MARITIME ACADEMY

66 Pleasant Street, Castine, ME 04420
Phone: 207-326-2206 **E-mail:** admissions@mma.edu **CEEB Code:** 3505
Fax: 207-326-2515 **Web:** www.mainemaritime.edu **ACT Code:** 1648

This public school was founded in 1941. It has a 35-acre campus.

STUDENTS AND FACULTY

Enrollment: 635. **Student Body:** Out-of-state 39%, international students represent 10 countries. **Retention and Graduation:** 75% freshmen return for sophomore year. 2% grads go on to further study within 1 year. 1% grads pursue law degrees. **Faculty:** Student/faculty ratio 10:1. 55 full-time faculty. 100% faculty teach undergrads.

ACADEMICS

Degrees: Associate's, bachelor's, master's. **Academic Requirements:** General education including some course work in computer literacy, English (including composition), humanities, mathematics, sciences (biological or physical). **Special Study Options:** Cooperative (work-study) program, internships, Annual Training Cruises.

FACILITIES

Housing: Coed, apartments for single students. **Library Holdings:** 100,000 bound volumes. 900 periodicals. **Computers:** *Recommended operating system:* Windows 95.

EXTRACURRICULARS

Activities: Concert band, drama/theater, jazz band, marching band, student government, yearbook. **Organizations:** 28 registered organizations. **Athletics (Intercollegiate):** *Men:* basketball, cross-country, football, golf, lacrosse, sailing, soccer. *Women:* basketball, cross-country, golf, sailing, soccer, softball.

ADMISSIONS

Selectivity Rating: 72 (of 100). **Freshman Academic Profile:** 28% in top 10% of high school class, 48% in top 25% of high school class, 74% in top 50% of high school class. Average SAT I Math 523. Average SAT I Verbal 499. TOEFL required of all international applicants, minimum TOEFL 550. **Basis for Candidate Selection:** *Very important factors considered include:* character/personal qualities, secondary school record. *Important factors considered include:* interview. *Other factors considered include:* alumni/ae relation, class rank, extracurricular activities, recommendations, talent/ability, volunteer work, work experience. **Freshman Admission Requirements:** High school diploma or GED is required. *Academic units required/recommended:* 4 English required, 3 math required, 3 math recommended, 2 science required, 3 science recommended, 2 science lab required, 3 science lab recommended, 2 foreign language recommended. **Freshman Admission Statistics:** 613 applied, 76% accepted, 49% of those accepted enrolled. **Transfer Admission Requirements:** *Items required:* high school transcript, college transcript, standardized test score, statement of good standing from prior school. Minimum college GPA of 2.0 required. Lowest grade transferable C. **General Admission Information:** Application fee $15. Early decision application deadline December 20. Regular application deadline July 1. Nonfall registration accepted. Admission may be deferred for a maximum of 1 year. Credit offered for CEEB Advanced Placement tests.

COSTS AND FINANCIAL AID

In-state tuition $4,739. Out-of-state tuition $8,774. Room & board $5,227. Required fees $715. Average book expense $700. **Types of Aid:** *Loans:* FFEL Subsidized Stafford, FFEL PLUS. **Student Employment:** Federal Work-Study Program available. Institutional employment available. Off-campus job opportunities are fair. **Financial Aid Statistics:** Average income from on-campus job $1,200. **Financial Aid Phone:** 207-326-2339.

MALONE COLLEGE

515 25th Street NW, Canton, OH 44709
Phone: 330-471-8145 **E-mail:** admissions@malone.edu **CEEB Code:** 1439
Fax: 330-471-8149 **Web:** www.malone.edu **ACT Code:** 3289

This private school was founded in 1892. It has a 78-acre campus.

STUDENTS AND FACULTY

Enrollment: 1,878. **Student Body:** Male 40%, female 60%, out-of-state 10%, international 1% (9 countries represented). **Ethnic Representation:** African American 5%, Caucasian 93%, Hispanic 1%. **Retention and Graduation:** 70% freshmen return for sophomore year. 36% freshmen graduate within 4 years. 31% grads go on to further study within 1 year. 13% grads pursue business degrees. 1% grads pursue law degrees. 1% grads pursue medical degrees. **Faculty:** Student/faculty ratio 14:1. 100 full-time faculty, 65% hold PhDs. 97% faculty teach undergrads.

ACADEMICS

Degrees: Bachelor's, master's. **Academic Requirements:** General education including some course work in arts/fine arts, English (including composition), history, humanities, mathematics, philosophy, sciences (biological or physical), social science, biblical lit/theology, communication skills, personal finance, physical education. **Classes:** 10-19 students in an average class. Under 10 students in an average lab/discussion section. **Majors with Highest Enrollment:** Nursing/registered nurse training (RN, ASN, BSN, MSN); business administration/management. **Disciplines with Highest Percentage of Degrees Awarded:** Business/marketing 47%, education 18%, health professions and related sciences 9%, communications/communication technologies 6%, social sciences and history 3%. **Special Study Options:** Accelerated program, cooperative (work-study) program, cross registration, distance learning, double major, dual enrollment, student exchange program (domestic), honors program, independent study, internships, student-designed major, study abroad, teacher certification program, weekend college, 2 degree-completion programs for adults (nursing and management).

FACILITIES

Housing: All-female, all-male. **Library Holdings:** 158,974 bound volumes. 1,517 periodicals. 601,487 microforms. 9,693 audiovisuals. **Special Academic Facilities/Equipment:** Child development center. **Computers:** *Recommended operating system:* Windows NT/2000/XP. School-owned computers available for student use.

EXTRACURRICULARS

Activities: Choral groups, concert band, drama/theater, jazz band, literary magazine, marching band, music ensembles, musical theater, pep band, radio station, student government, student newspaper, yearbook. **Organizations:** 45 registered organizations, 7 honor societies, 12 religious organizations. **Athletics (Intercollegiate):** *Men:* baseball, basketball, cheerleading, cross-country, football, golf, indoor track, soccer, tennis, track & field. *Women:* basketball, cheerleading, cross-country, golf, indoor track, soccer, softball, tennis, track & field, volleyball.

ADMISSIONS

Selectivity Rating: 63 (of 100). **Freshman Academic Profile:** Average high school GPA 3.3. 22% in top 10% of high school class, 47% in top 25% of high school class, 79% in top 50% of high school class. 82% from public high schools. Average SAT I Math 540, SAT I Math middle 50% range 470-610. Average SAT I Verbal 540, SAT I Verbal middle 50% range 490-600. Average ACT 23, ACT middle 50% range 20-26. TOEFL required of all international applicants, minimum TOEFL 500. **Basis for Candidate Selection:** *Very important factors considered include:* character/personal qualities, secondary school record, standardized test scores. *Important factors considered include:* class rank, essays, recommendations, religious affiliation/commitment, talent/ability. *Other factors considered include:* alumni/ae relation, extracurricular activities, interview, minority status, volunteer work. **Freshman Admission Requirements:** High school diploma or GED is required. *Academic units required/recommended:* 18 total required; 4 English required, 3 math required, 3 science required, 1 science lab required, 2 foreign language required, 2 social studies required, 1 history required, 2 elective required. **Freshman Admission Statistics:** 896 applied, 91% accepted, 44% of those accepted enrolled. **Transfer Admission Requirements:** *Items required:* high school transcript, college transcript, essay, statement of good standing from prior school. Minimum college GPA of 2.0 required. Lowest grade transferable C. **General Admission Information:** Application fee $20. Regular application deadline July 1. Nonfall registration accepted. Admission may be deferred for a maximum of 2 years. Credit and/or placement offered for CEEB Advanced Placement tests.

COSTS AND FINANCIAL AID

Tuition $13,910. Room & board $5,630. Required fees $240. Average book expense $500. **Required Forms and Deadlines:** FAFSA and Verification worksheet and tax forms if chosen for verification. Financial aid filing deadline July 31. Priority filing deadline March 1. **Notification of Awards:** Applicants will be notified of awards on a rolling basis beginning on or about March 1. **Types of Aid:** *Need-based scholarships/grants:* Pell, SEOG, state scholarships/grants, private scholarships, the school's own gift aid. *Loans:* FFEL Subsidized Stafford, FFEL Unsubsidized Stafford, FFEL PLUS, Federal Perkins, state loans, college/university loans from institutional funds, private loans. **Student Employment:** Federal Work-Study Program available. Institutional employment available. Off-campus job opportunities are excellent. **Financial Aid Statistics:** 82% freshmen, 68% undergrads receive some form of aid. Average freshman grant $8,107. Average freshman loan $3,958. Average income from on-campus job $1,695. **Financial Aid Phone:** 330-471-8159.

MANCHESTER COLLEGE

604 College Avenue, N. Manchester, IN 46962
Phone: 260-982-5055 **E-mail:** admitinfo@manchester.edu **CEEB Code:** 1440
Fax: 260-982-5239 **Web:** www.manchester.edu **ACT Code:** 1222

This private school, which is affiliated with the Church of Brethren, was founded in 1889. It has a 124-acre campus.

STUDENTS AND FACULTY

Enrollment: 1,127. **Student Body:** Male 43%, female 57%, out-of-state 12%, international 6% (29 countries represented). **Ethnic Representation:** African American 4%, Asian 1%, Caucasian 93%, Hispanic 3%. **Retention and Graduation:** 73% freshmen return for sophomore year. 38% freshmen graduate within 4 years. 25% grads go on to further study within 1 year. 11% grads pursue business degrees. 1% grads pursue law degrees. 2% grads pursue medical degrees. **Faculty:** Student/faculty ratio 14:1. 67 full-time faculty, 79% hold PhDs. 100% faculty teach undergrads.

ACADEMICS

Degrees: Associate's, bachelor's, master's. **Academic Requirements:** General education including some course work in arts/fine arts, English (including composition), history, humanities, mathematics, philosophy, sciences (biological or physical), social science. **Classes:** 20-29 students in an average class. **Majors with Highest Enrollment:** Education, general; psychology, general; accounting and business/management. **Disciplines with Highest Percentage of Degrees Awarded:** Business/marketing 26%, education 22%, social sciences and history 12%, psychology 8%, health professions and related sciences 7%. **Special Study Options:** Double major, dual enrollment, student exchange program (domestic), honors program, independent study, internships, liberal arts/career combination, student-designed major, study abroad, teacher certification program.

FACILITIES

Housing: Coed, all-female, apartments for married students, apartments for single students, housing for disabled students. **Library Holdings:** 172,822 bound volumes. 733 periodicals. 22,975 microforms. 5,188 audiovisuals. **Special Academic Facilities/Equipment:** Language lab, observatory, environmental center and labs. **Computers:** School-owned computers available for student use.

EXTRACURRICULARS

Activities: Choral groups, concert band, dance, drama/theater, jazz band, literary magazine, music ensembles, musical theater, pep band, radio station, student government, student newspaper, symphony orchestra, yearbook. **Organizations:** 38 registered organizations, 3 honor societies, 5 religious organizations. **Athletics (Intercollegiate):** *Men:* baseball, basketball, cheerleading, cross-country, football, golf, soccer, tennis, track & field, wrestling. *Women:* basketball, cheerleading, cross-country, golf, soccer, softball, tennis, track & field, volleyball.

ADMISSIONS

Selectivity Rating: 73 (of 100). **Freshman Academic Profile:** 18% in top 10% of high school class, 46% in top 25% of high school class, 79% in top 50% of high school class. 98% from public high schools. Average SAT I Math 502, SAT I Math middle 50% range 430-560. Average SAT I Verbal 497, SAT I Verbal middle 50% range 430-550. Average ACT 22, ACT middle 50% range 19-25. TOEFL required of all international applicants, minimum TOEFL 550. **Basis for Candidate Selection:** *Very important factors considered include:* secondary school record. *Important factors considered include:* recommendations, standardized test scores. *Other factors considered include:* alumni/ae relation, character/personal qualities, class rank, interview, religious affiliation/commitment, talent/ability. **Freshman Admission Requirements:** High school diploma or GED is required. *Academic units required/recommended:* 14 total required; 17 total recommended; 4 English required, 4 English recommended, 2 math required, 3 math recommended, 2 science required, 3 science recommended, 2 science lab required, 3 science lab recommended, 2 foreign language required, 2 foreign language recommended, 2 social studies required, 2 social studies recommended, 1 history required, 2 history recommended, 1 elective required, 2 elective recommended. **Freshman Admission Statistics:** 1,061 applied, 83% accepted, 35% of those accepted enrolled. **Transfer Admission Requirements:** *Items required:* high school transcript, college transcript, standardized test score, statement of good standing from prior school. Lowest grade transferable C. **General Admission Information:** Application fee $20. Nonfall registration accepted. Admission may be deferred for a maximum of 1 year. Credit and/or placement offered for CEEB Advanced Placement tests.

COSTS AND FINANCIAL AID

Tuition $16,940. Room & board $6,340. Required fees $100. Average book expense $550. **Required Forms and Deadlines:** FAFSA. No deadline for regular filing. **Notification of Awards:** Applicants will be notified of awards on a rolling basis beginning on or about February 15. **Types of Aid:** *Need-based scholarships/grants:* Pell, SEOG, state scholarships/grants, private scholarships, the school's own gift aid. *Loans:* FFEL Subsidized Stafford, FFEL Unsubsidized Stafford, FFEL PLUS, Federal Perkins. **Student Employment:** Federal Work-Study Program available. Institutional employment available. Off-campus job opportunities are fair. **Financial Aid Statistics:** 83% freshmen, 80% undergrads receive some form of aid. Average freshman grant $12,953. Average income from on-campus job $1,000. **Financial Aid Phone:** 800-852-3648.

MANHATTAN COLLEGE

Manhattan College Parkway, Riverdale, NY 10471
Phone: 718-862-7200 **E-mail:** admit@manhattan.edu **CEEB Code:** 2395
Fax: 718-862-8019 **Web:** www.manhattan.edu

This private school, which is affiliated with the Roman Catholic Church, was founded in 1853. It has a 50-acre campus.

STUDENTS AND FACULTY

Enrollment: 2,651. **Student Body:** Male 53%, female 47%, out-of-state 17%, international 1%. **Ethnic Representation:** African American 5%, Asian 5%, Caucasian 70%, Hispanic 13%. **Retention and Graduation:** 82% freshmen return for sophomore year. 56% freshmen graduate within 4 years. 15% grads go on to further study within 1 year. 4% grads pursue business degrees. 2% grads pursue law degrees. 4% grads pursue medical degrees. **Faculty:** Student/faculty ratio 13:1. 100% faculty teach undergrads.

ACADEMICS

Degrees: Bachelor's, master's. **Academic Requirements:** General education including some course work in arts/fine arts, computer literacy, English (including composition), foreign languages, history, humanities, mathematics, philosophy, sciences (biological or physical). **Disciplines with Highest Percentage of Degrees Awarded:** Business/marketing 31%, education 19%, engineering/engineering technology 15%, computer and information sciences 8%, social sciences and history 6%. **Special Study Options:** Cooperative (work-study) program, cross registration, double major, student exchange program (domestic), honors program, independent study, internships, liberal arts/career combination, student-designed major, study abroad, teacher certification program.

FACILITIES

Housing: Coed. **Library Holdings:** 193,100 bound volumes. 1,527 periodicals. 383,480 microforms. 3,680 audiovisuals. **Special Academic Facilities/Equipment:** Research and learning center, plant morphogenesis lab, nuclear reactor.

EXTRACURRICULARS

Activities: Choral groups, concert band, dance, drama/theater, jazz band, literary magazine, music ensembles, musical theater, radio station, student government, student newspaper, television station, yearbook. **Organizations:** 70 registered organizations, 30 honor societies, 5 fraternities (8% men join), 3 sororities (7% women join). **Athletics (Intercollegiate):** *Men:* baseball, basketball, crew, cross-country, golf, indoor track, lacrosse, soccer, tennis, track & field. *Women:* basketball, crew, cross-country, indoor track, lacrosse, soccer, softball, swimming, tennis, track & field, volleyball.

ADMISSIONS

Selectivity Rating: 75 (of 100). **Freshman Academic Profile:** Average high school GPA 3.4. 60% from public high schools. Average SAT I Math 551, SAT I Math middle 50% range 640-490. Average SAT I Verbal 539, SAT I Verbal middle 50% range 620-490. TOEFL required of all international applicants, minimum TOEFL 520. **Basis for Candidate Selection:** *Very important factors considered include:* secondary school record, standardized test scores. *Important factors considered include:* class rank, essays, extracurricular activities, interview, recommendations. *Other factors considered include:* alumni/ae relation, character/personal qualities, talent/ability, volunteer work, work experience. **Freshman Admission Requirements:** High school diploma or GED is required. *Academic units required/recommended:* 16 total required; 17 total recommended; 4 English required, 4 English recommended, 3 math required, 4 math recommended, 2 science required, 3 science recommended, 2 foreign language required, 3 foreign language recommended, 3 social studies required, 3 social studies recommended, 2 elective required. **Transfer Admission Requirements:** *Items required:* college transcript. Minimum college GPA of 2.5 required. Lowest grade transferable C. **General Admission Information:** Application fee $40. Priority application deadline March 1. Early decision application deadline December 1. Nonfall registration accepted. Admission may be deferred for a maximum of 1 year. Credit and/or placement offered for CEEB Advanced Placement tests.

COSTS AND FINANCIAL AID

Tuition $17,800. Room & board $8,100. Required fees $1,200. Average book expense $250. **Required Forms and Deadlines:** FAFSA. No deadline for regular filing. Priority filing deadline March 1. **Notification of Awards:** Applicants will be notified of awards on a rolling basis beginning on or about February 15. **Types of Aid:** *Need-based scholarships/grants:* Pell, SEOG, the school's own gift aid. *Loans:* Direct Subsidized Stafford, Direct Unsubsidized Stafford, Direct PLUS. **Student Employment:** Federal Work-Study Program available. Institutional employment available. Off-campus job opportunities are excellent. **Financial Aid Statistics:** 67% freshmen, 65% undergrads receive some form of aid. Average freshman grant $4,000. Average freshman loan $2,625. Average income from on-campus job $1,000. **Financial Aid Phone:** 718-862-7300.

MANHATTAN SCHOOL OF MUSIC

120 Claremont Avenue, New York, NY 10027
Phone: 212-749-2802 **E-mail:** admission@msmnyc.edu **CEEB Code:** 2396
Fax: 212-749-3025 **Web:** www.msmnyc.edu **ACT Code:** 2809

This private school was founded in 1917. It has a 1-acre campus.

STUDENTS AND FACULTY

Enrollment: 400. **Student Body:** Male 54%, female 47%, out-of-state 78%, international 31% (40 countries represented). **Ethnic Representation:** African American 6%, Asian 15%, Caucasian 66%, Hispanic 6%, Native American 1%. **Retention and Graduation:** 82% freshmen return for sophomore year. 50% grads go on to further study within 1 year. 1% grads pursue business degrees. 1% grads pursue law degrees. 1% grads pursue medical degrees. **Faculty:** 100% faculty teach undergrads.

ACADEMICS

Degrees: Bachelor's, diploma, doctoral, master's, post-bachelor's certificate, post-master's certificate. **Academic Requirements:** General education including some course work in arts/fine arts, history, humanities. **Special Study Options:** Cross registration, English as a second language, study abroad.

FACILITIES

Housing: Coed. **Library Holdings:** 39,684 bound volumes. 134 periodicals. 0 microforms. 25,074 audiovisuals. **Special Academic Facilities/Equipment:** Electronic music studios, electronic piano lab, recording studio, practice rooms, 1,000-seat auditorium, 3 recital halls. **Computers:** *Recommended operating system:* Windows 95. School-owned computers available for student use.

EXTRACURRICULARS

Activities: Choral groups, jazz band, music ensembles, musical theater, opera, student government, student newspaper, symphony orchestra. **Organizations:** 7 registered organizations.

ADMISSIONS

Selectivity Rating: 76 (of 100). **Freshman Academic Profile:** 75% from public high schools. TOEFL required of all international applicants, minimum TOEFL 500. **Basis for Candidate Selection:** *Very important factors considered include:* secondary school record, talent/ability. *Important factors considered include:* character/personal qualities, essays, extracurricular activities, recommendations, standardized test scores. *Other factors considered include:* alumni/ae relation, class rank, geographical residence, interview, minority status, state residency, volunteer work, work experience. **Freshman Admission Requirements:** High school diploma or GED is required. *Academic units required/recommended:* 2 English required, 4 English recommended, 2 math required, 3 math recommended, 2 science required, 3 science recommended, 4 foreign language recommended, 3 social studies required, 4 social studies recommended, 3 history required, 4 history recommended. **Freshman Admission Statistics:** 582 applied, 40% accepted, 38% of those accepted enrolled. **Transfer Admission Requirements:** *Items required:* college transcript, essay, interview. Minimum high school GPA of 3.0 required. Minimum college GPA of 3.0 required. Lowest grade transferable C. **General Admission Information:** Application fee $90. Priority application deadline December 15. Regular application deadline April 1. Credit offered for CEEB Advanced Placement tests.

COSTS AND FINANCIAL AID

Tuition $21,100. Room & board $11,400. Required fees $400. Average book expense $800. **Required Forms and Deadlines:** FAFSA, institution's own financial aid form, CSS/Financial Aid PROFILE and noncustodial (divorced/separated) parent's statement. Financial aid filing deadline April 15. Priority filing deadline March 1. **Notification of Awards:** Applicants will be notified of awards on a rolling basis. **Types of Aid:** *Need-based scholarships/grants:* Pell, SEOG, state scholarships/grants, the school's own gift aid. *Loans:* FFEL Subsidized Stafford, FFEL Unsubsidized Stafford, FFEL PLUS. **Student Employment:** Federal Work-Study Program available. Institutional employment available. Off-campus job opportunities are excellent. **Financial Aid Statistics:** 90% freshmen, 65% undergrads receive some form of aid. Average freshman grant $6,000. Average freshman loan $2,625. Average income from on-campus job $500. **Financial Aid Phone:** 212-749-2802.

MANHATTANVILLE COLLEGE

2900 Purchase Street, Admissions Office, Purchase, NY 10577
Phone: 914-323-5124 **E-mail:** admissions@mville.edu **CEEB Code:** 2397
Fax: 914-694-1732 **Web:** www.mville.edu **ACT Code:** 2800

This private school was founded in 1841. It has a 100-acre campus.

STUDENTS AND FACULTY

Enrollment: 1,618. **Student Body:** Male 32%, female 68%, out-of-state 31%, international 7%. **Ethnic Representation:** African American 7%, Asian 3%, Caucasian 65%, Hispanic 14%. **Retention and Graduation:** 80% freshmen return for sophomore year. 43% freshmen graduate within 4 years. 29% grads go on to further study within 1 year. 1% grads pursue business degrees. 2% grads pursue law degrees. 3% grads pursue medical degrees. **Faculty:** Student/faculty ratio 12:1. 82 full-time faculty, 95% hold PhDs. 100% faculty teach undergrads.

ACADEMICS

Degrees: Bachelor's, master's. **Academic Requirements:** General education including some course work in arts/fine arts, English (including composition), foreign languages, humanities, sciences (biological or physical), social science, preceptorial, library and information skills, and English writing competency. **Classes:** 10-19 students in an average class. **Majors with Highest Enrollment:** Psychology, general; business administration/management; sociology. **Disciplines with Highest Percentage of Degrees Awarded:** Business/marketing 22%, social sciences and history 21%, visual and performing arts 18%, psychology 17%, English 6%. **Special Study Options:** Accelerated program, cross registration, distance learning, double major, English as a second language, student exchange program (domestic), honors program, independent study, internships, student-designed major, study abroad, teacher certification program.

FACILITIES

Housing: Coed. **Library Holdings:** 281,949 bound volumes. 13,697 periodicals. 531,469 microforms. 3,921 audiovisuals. **Special Academic Facilities/Equipment:** Art gallery, art and music studios, English Language Institute, two electron microscopes, library. **Computers:** *Recommended operating system:* Windows 95. School-owned computers available for student use.

EXTRACURRICULARS

Activities: Choral groups, concert band, dance, drama/theater, jazz band, literary magazine, music ensembles, musical theater, pep band, radio station, student government, student newspaper, student-run film society, symphony orchestra, yearbook. **Organizations:** 40 registered organizations, 2 honor societies, 3 religious organizations. **Athletics (Intercollegiate):** *Men:* baseball, basketball, cheerleading, golf, ice hockey, lacrosse, soccer, swimming, tennis. *Women:* basketball, cheerleading, field hockey, ice hockey, lacrosse, soccer, softball, swimming, tennis, volleyball.

ADMISSIONS

Selectivity Rating: 77 (of 100). **Freshman Academic Profile:** Average high school GPA 3.0. Average SAT I Math 530, SAT I Math middle 50% range 470-560. Average SAT I Verbal 530, SAT I Verbal middle 50% range 480-590. Average ACT 24, ACT middle 50% range 22-26. TOEFL required of all international applicants, minimum TOEFL 550. **Basis for Candidate Selection:** *Very important factors considered include:* secondary school record, standardized test scores. *Important factors considered include:* essays, extracurricular activities, interview, recommendations. *Other factors considered include:* alumni/ae relation, character/personal qualities, geographical residence, talent/ability, volunteer work, work experience. **Freshman Admission Requirements:** High school diploma or GED is required. *Academic units required/recommended:* 16 total required; 4 English required, 3 math required, 2 science required, 2 social studies required, 5 elective required. **Freshman Admission Statistics:** 2,330 applied, 55% accepted, 32% of those accepted enrolled. **Transfer Admission Requirements:** *Items required:* college transcript, statement of good standing from prior school. Minimum college GPA of 2.5 required. Lowest grade transferable C. **General Admission Information:** Application fee $50. Priority application deadline March 1. Early decision application deadline December 1. Regular application deadline March 1. Nonfall registration accepted. Admission may be deferred for a maximum of 1 year. Credit and/or placement offered for CEEB Advanced Placement tests.

COSTS AND FINANCIAL AID

Tuition $22,150. Room & board $9,380. Required fees $890. Average book expense $800. **Required Forms and Deadlines:** FAFSA and state aid form. No deadline for regular filing. Priority filing deadline April 15. **Notification of Awards:** Applicants will be notified of awards on a rolling basis. **Types of Aid:** *Need-based scholarships/grants:* Pell, SEOG, state scholarships/grants, private scholarships, the school's own gift aid. *Loans:* FFEL Subsidized Stafford, FFEL Unsubsidized Stafford, FFEL PLUS, Federal Perkins. **Student Employment:** Federal Work-Study Program available. Institutional employment available. Off-campus job opportunities are excellent. **Financial Aid Statistics:** 61% freshmen, 65% undergrads receive some form of aid. Average freshman grant $15,372. Average freshman loan $3,071. Average income from on-campus job $1,200. **Financial Aid Phone:** 914-323-5357.

MANNES COLLEGE OF MUSIC

150 West 85th Street, New York, NY 10024
Phone: 212-580-0210 **E-mail:** mannesadmissions@newschool.edu **CEEB Code:** 2398
Fax: 212-580-1738 **Web:** www.mannes.edu

This private school was founded in 1916. It has a 1-acre campus.

STUDENTS AND FACULTY

Enrollment: 172. **Student Body:** Male 40%, female 60%, out-of-state 36%, international 31% (26 countries represented). **Ethnic Representation:** African American 7%, Asian 8%, Caucasian 47%, Hispanic 5%, Native American 1%. **Retention and Graduation:** 90% freshmen return for sophomore year. **Faculty:** Student/faculty ratio 4:1. 6 full-time faculty.

ACADEMICS

Degrees: Bachelor's, diploma, first professional, master's. **Academic Requirements:** General education including some course work in arts/fine arts, English (including composition), humanities. **Classes:** Under 10 students in an average class. **Disciplines with Highest Percentage of Degrees Awarded:** Visual and performing arts 100%. **Special Study Options:** Cross registration, double major, English as a second language.

FACILITIES

Housing: Coed, housing for disabled students. **Library Holdings:** 4,137,530 bound volumes. 22,150 periodicals. 4,656,806 microforms. 48,379 audiovisuals. **Computers:** School-owned computers available for student use.

EXTRACURRICULARS

Activities: Choral groups, music ensembles, opera, symphony orchestra.

ADMISSIONS

Selectivity Rating: 76 (of 100). **Freshman Academic Profile:** 55% from public high schools. TOEFL required of all international applicants, minimum TOEFL 550. **Basis for Candidate Selection:** *Very important factors considered include:* talent/ability. *Important factors considered include:* recommendations, secondary school record. *Other factors considered include:* character/personal qualities, class rank, essays, extracurricular activities. **Freshman Admission Requirements:** High school diploma or GED is required. *Academic units required/recommended:* 4 English required, 2 math required, 2 science required, 2 science lab required, 2 foreign language recommended, 4 social studies required. **Freshman Admission Statistics:** 355 applied, 32% accepted, 32% of those accepted enrolled. **Transfer Admission Requirements:** *Items required:* high school transcript, college transcript, essay. Minimum college GPA of 2.0 required. Lowest grade transferable C. **General Admission Information:** Application fee $100. Priority application deadline November 15. Regular application deadline December 15. Nonfall registration accepted. Admission may be deferred for a maximum of 1 year. Credit and/or placement offered for CEEB Advanced Placement tests.

COSTS AND FINANCIAL AID

Tuition $20,700. Room & board $9,896. Required fees $500. Average book expense $2,062. **Required Forms and Deadlines:** FAFSA and state aid form. No deadline for regular filing. Priority filing deadline March 1. **Notification of Awards:** Applicants will be notified of awards on a rolling basis beginning on or about March 1. **Types of Aid:** *Need-based scholarships/grants:* Pell, SEOG, state scholarships/grants, private scholarships, the school's own gift aid. *Loans:* FFEL Subsidized Stafford, FFEL Unsubsidized Stafford, FFEL PLUS, Federal Perkins, college/university loans from institutional funds. **Student Employment:** Federal Work-Study Program available. Off-campus job opportunities are good. **Financial Aid Statistics:** 33% freshmen, 41% undergrads receive some form of aid. Average freshman grant $6,000. Average freshman loan $5,200. Average income from on-campus job $1,500. **Financial Aid Phone:** 212-580-0210.

See page 1101.

MANSFIELD UNIVERSITY OF PENNSYLVANIA

Office of Admissions, Alumni Hall, Mansfield, PA 16933
Phone: 570-662-4243 **E-mail:** admissions@mansfield.edu **CEEB Code:** 2655
Fax: 570-662-4121 **Web:** www.mansfild.edu **ACT Code:** 3710

This public school was founded in 1857. It has a 174-acre campus.

STUDENTS AND FACULTY

Enrollment: 3,057. **Student Body:** Male 39%, female 61%, out-of-state 22%, international 1%. **Ethnic Representation:** African American 3%, Asian 1%, Caucasian 94%, Hispanic 1%, Native American 1%. **Retention and Graduation:** 68% freshmen return for sophomore year. 31% freshmen graduate within 4 years. 14% grads go on to further study within 1 year. 1% grads pursue business degrees. 1% grads pursue law degrees. 1% grads pursue medical degrees. **Faculty:** Student/faculty ratio 18:1. 155 full-time faculty, 66% hold PhDs. 100% faculty teach undergrads.

ACADEMICS

Degrees: Associate's, bachelor's, certificate, master's, post-bachelor's certificate, terminal, transfer. **Academic Requirements:** General education including some course work in arts/fine arts, English (including composition), foreign languages, history, humanities, mathematics, philosophy, sciences (biological or physical), social science. **Classes:** 20-29 students in an average class. 10-19 students in an average lab/discussion section. **Majors with Highest Enrollment:** Education, general; music teacher education; criminal justice/law enforcement administration. **Disciplines with Highest Percentage of Degrees Awarded:** Education 17%, protective services/public administration 17%, business/marketing 13%, communications/communication technologies 9%, social sciences and history 7%. **Special Study Options:** Cooperative (work-study) program, distance learning, double major, dual enrollment, student exchange program (domestic), honors program, independent study, internships, liberal arts/career combination, student-designed major, study abroad, teacher certification program, Off-campus study opportunities possible.

FACILITIES

Housing: Coed, all-female, fraternities and/or sororities. **Library Holdings:** 242,441 bound volumes. 1,148 periodicals. 806,719 microforms. 26,831 audiovisuals. **Special Academic Facilities/Equipment:** Science museum, two art galleries, animal collection, planetarium, solar collector. **Computers:** School-owned computers available for student use.

EXTRACURRICULARS

Activities: Choral groups, concert band, drama/theater, jazz band, literary magazine, marching band, music ensembles, musical theater, radio station, student government, student newspaper, symphony orchestra, television station. **Organizations:** 100 registered organizations, 10 honor societies, 4 religious organizations, 6 fraternities (5% men join), 4 sororities (5% women join). **Athletics (Intercollegiate):** *Men:* baseball, basketball, cross-country, football, track & field. *Women:* basketball, cheerleading, cross-country, diving, field hockey, soccer, softball, swimming, track & field.

ADMISSIONS

Selectivity Rating: 68 (of 100). **Freshman Academic Profile:** Average high school GPA 3.2. 8% in top 10% of high school class, 26% in top 25% of high school class, 61% in top 50% of high school class. Average SAT I Math 485, SAT I Math middle 50% range 430-530. Average SAT I Verbal 494, SAT I Verbal middle 50% range 440-540. Average ACT 20. TOEFL required of all international applicants, minimum TOEFL 550. **Basis for Candidate Selection:** *Very important factors considered include:* class rank, secondary school record, standardized test scores, talent/ability. *Important factors considered include:* interview. *Other factors considered include:* alumni/ae relation, character/personal qualities, essays, extracurricular activities, minority status, recommendations, volunteer work, work experience. **Freshman Admission Requirements:** High school diploma or GED is required. *Academic units required/recommended:* 21 total required; 23 total recommended; 4 English required, 3 math required, 2 science required, 3 science recommended, 2 science lab required, 2 foreign language recommended, 4 social studies required, 6 elective required. **Freshman Admission Statistics:** 2,094 applied, 78% accepted, 41% of those accepted enrolled. **Transfer Admission Requirements:** *Items required:* college transcript. Minimum college GPA of 2.0 required. Lowest grade transferable D. **General Admission Information:** Application fee $25. Nonfall registration accepted. Admission may be deferred for a maximum of 1 year. Credit offered for CEEB Advanced Placement tests.

COSTS AND FINANCIAL AID

In-state tuition $4,378. Out-of-state tuition $10,946. Room & board $5,006. Required fees $1,246. Average book expense $800. **Required Forms and Deadlines:** FAFSA and institution's own financial aid form. No deadline for regular filing. Priority filing deadline March 15. **Notification of Awards:** Applicants will be notified of awards on a rolling basis beginning on or about April 1. **Types of Aid:** *Need-based scholarships/grants:* Pell, SEOG, state scholarships/grants, private scholarships, the school's own gift aid. *Loans:* FFEL Subsidized Stafford, FFEL Unsubsidized Stafford, FFEL PLUS, Federal Perkins, alternative loans. **Student Employment:** Federal Work-Study Program available. Institutional employment available. Off-campus job opportunities are fair. **Financial Aid Statistics:** 48% freshmen, 43% undergrads receive some form of aid. Average freshman grant $1,725. Average freshman loan $2,625. Average income from on-campus job $1,236. **Financial Aid Phone:** 570-662-4878.

MARIAN COLLEGE (IN)

3200 Cold Spring Road, Indianapolis, IN 46222
Phone: 317-955-6300 **E-mail:** admit@marian.edu **CEEB Code:** 1442
Fax: 317-955-6401 **Web:** www.marian.edu **ACT Code:** 1224

This private school, which is affiliated with the Roman Catholic Church, was founded in 1937. It has a 114-acre campus.

STUDENTS AND FACULTY

Enrollment: 1,412. **Student Body:** Male 31%, female 69%, out-of-state 8%, international 2%. **Ethnic Representation:** African American 18%, Asian 1%,

Caucasian 67%, Hispanic 2%, Native American 1%. **Retention and Graduation:** 71% freshmen return for sophomore year. 5% grads go on to further study within 1 year. 2% grads pursue business degrees. 2% grads pursue law degrees. 1% grads pursue medical degrees. **Faculty:** Student/faculty ratio 12:1. 65 full-time faculty, 55% hold PhDs. 100% faculty teach undergrads.

ACADEMICS

Degrees: Associate's, bachelor's, certificate, master's. **Academic Requirements:** General education including some course work in arts/fine arts, English (including composition), foreign languages, history, humanities, mathematics, philosophy, sciences (biological or physical), social science. **Classes:** Under 10 students in an average class. Under 10 students in an average lab/discussion section. **Majors with Highest Enrollment:** Nursing/registered nurse training (RN, ASN, BSN, MSN); business administration/management; education, general. **Disciplines with Highest Percentage of Degrees Awarded:** Business/marketing 21%, education 15%, health professions and related sciences 14%, parks and recreation 9%, biological life sciences 6%. **Special Study Options:** Accelerated program, cross registration, double major, dual enrollment, honors program, independent study, internships, liberal arts/career combination, study abroad, teacher certification program, mentor leadership training.

FACILITIES

Housing: Coed, all-female, all-male, apartments for single students, housing for disabled students. **Library Holdings:** 150,000 bound volumes. 550 periodicals.

EXTRACURRICULARS

Activities: Choral groups, dance, drama/theater, jazz band, literary magazine, music ensembles, musical theater, pep band, student government, student newspaper, television station. **Organizations:** 40 registered organizations, 2 honor societies, 2 religious organizations. **Athletics (Intercollegiate):** *Men:* baseball, basketball, cheerleading, cross-country, golf, indoor track, soccer, tennis, track & field, volleyball. *Women:* basketball, cheerleading, cross-country, golf, indoor track, soccer, softball, tennis, track & field, volleyball.

ADMISSIONS

Selectivity Rating: 76 (of 100). **Freshman Academic Profile:** Average high school GPA 3.1. 11% in top 10% of high school class, 29% in top 25% of high school class, 61% in top 50% of high school class. 75% from public high schools. Average SAT I Math 497, SAT I Math middle 50% range 420-550. Average SAT I Verbal 508, SAT I Verbal middle 50% range 440-540. ACT middle 50% range 17-23. TOEFL required of all international applicants, minimum TOEFL 550. **Basis for Candidate Selection:** *Very important factors considered include:* class rank, secondary school record, standardized test scores. *Other factors considered include:* alumni/ae relation, character/personal qualities, essays, extracurricular activities, geographical residence, interview, recommendations, state residency, talent/ability, volunteer work, work experience. **Freshman Admission Requirements:** High school diploma or GED is required. *Academic units required/recommended:* 20 total required; 20 total recommended; 4 English required, 4 English recommended, 2 math required, 3 math recommended, 1 science required, 3 science recommended, 2 foreign language required, 2 foreign language recommended, 1 social studies required, 2 social studies recommended, 1 history required, 2 history recommended, 9 elective required, 4 elective recommended. **Freshman Admission Statistics:** 836 applied, 76% accepted, 40% of those accepted enrolled. **Transfer Admission Requirements:** *Items required:* college transcript, statement of good standing from prior school. Minimum high school GPA of 2.0 required. Minimum college GPA of 2.0 required. Lowest grade transferable C. **General Admission Information:** Application fee $20. Priority application deadline June 1. Nonfall registration accepted. Credit and/or placement offered for CEEB Advanced Placement tests.

COSTS AND FINANCIAL AID

Tuition $16,800. Room & board $5,700. Required fees $580. Average book expense $700. **Required Forms and Deadlines:** FAFSA, institution's own financial aid form and state aid form. Priority filing deadline March 1. **Notification of Awards:** Applicants will be notified of awards on a rolling basis beginning on or about April 1. **Types of Aid:** *Need-based scholarships/grants:* Pell, state scholarships/grants, private scholarships, the school's own gift aid. *Loans:* Direct Subsidized Stafford, Direct Unsubsidized Stafford, Direct PLUS, FFEL Subsidized Stafford, FFEL PLUS, Federal Perkins, state loans. **Student Employment:** Federal Work-Study Program available. Institutional employment available. Off-campus job opportunities are excellent. **Financial Aid Statistics:** 83% freshmen, 81% undergrads receive some form of aid. Average freshman grant $14,322. Average freshman loan $2,970. Average income from on-campus job $500. **Financial Aid Phone:** 317-929-0234.

MARIAN COLLEGE OF FOND DU LAC

$$

45 South National Avenue, Fond du Lac, WI 54935
Phone: 920-923-7650 **E-mail:** admissions@mariancollege.edu **CEEB Code:** 1443
Fax: 920-923-8755 **Web:** www.mariancollege.edu **ACT Code:** 4606

This private school, which is affiliated with the Roman Catholic Church, was founded in 1936. It has a 97-acre campus.

STUDENTS AND FACULTY

Enrollment: 1,745. **Student Body:** Male 29%, female 71%, out-of-state 7%, international 2% (11 country represented). **Ethnic Representation:** African American 5%, Asian 1%, Caucasian 90%, Hispanic 1%, Native American 1%. **Retention and Graduation:** 71% freshmen return for sophomore year. 27% freshmen graduate within 4 years. 10% grads go on to further study within 1 year. **Faculty:** Student/faculty ratio 14:1. 73 full-time faculty, 60% hold PhDs. 100% faculty teach undergrads.

ACADEMICS

Degrees: Bachelor's, master's. **Academic Requirements:** General education including some course work in arts/fine arts, English (including composition), foreign languages, history, humanities, mathematics, philosophy, sciences (biological or physical), social science, theology. **Classes:** Under 10 students in an average class. Under 10 students in an average lab/discussion section. **Majors with Highest Enrollment:** Teacher education and professional development, specific levels and methods; nursing/registered nurse training (RN, ASN, BSN, MSN); business administration/management. **Disciplines with Highest Percentage of Degrees Awarded:** Business/marketing 37%, health professions and related sciences 18%, protective services/public administration 15%, education 8%, parks and recreation 5%. **Special Study Options:** Accelerated program, cooperative (work-study) program, distance learning, double major, dual enrollment, English as a second language, honors program, independent study, internships, liberal arts/career combination, student-designed major, study abroad, teacher certification program.

FACILITIES

Housing: Coed, apartments for single students, housing for disabled students, fraternities and/or sororities, townhouses, penthouses, suites. **Library Holdings:** 1,708 bound volumes. 698 periodicals. 14,057 microforms. 397 audiovisuals. **Special Academic Facilities/Equipment:** On-campus child-care center, electron microscope. **Computers:** School-owned computers available for student use.

EXTRACURRICULARS

Activities: Choral groups, concert band, drama/theater, jazz band, literary magazine, music ensembles, pep band, student government, student newspaper, symphony orchestra. **Organizations:** 25 registered organizations, 7 honor societies, 1 religious organization, 2 fraternities (10% men join), 3 sororities (8% women join). **Athletics (Intercollegiate):** *Men:* baseball, basketball, golf, ice hockey, soccer, tennis. *Women:* basketball, golf, soccer, softball, tennis, volleyball.

ADMISSIONS

Selectivity Rating: 69 (of 100). **Freshman Academic Profile:** Average high school GPA 2.8. 8% in top 10% of high school class, 29% in top 25% of high school class, 56% in top 50% of high school class. 83% from public high schools. Average ACT 20, ACT middle 50% range 17-22. TOEFL required of all international applicants, minimum TOEFL 525. **Basis for Candidate Selection:** *Very important factors considered include:* class rank, secondary school record, standardized test scores. *Important factors considered include:* character/personal qualities, interview. *Other factors considered include:* alumni/ae relation, essays, extracurricular activities, recommendations, talent/ability, volunteer work, work experience. **Freshman Admission Requirements:** High school diploma or GED is required. *Academic units required/recommended:* 17 total required; 4 English required, 2 math required, 3 math recommended, 1 science required, 2 science recommended, 1 science lab required, 2 foreign language recommended, 1 social studies required. **Freshman Admission Statistics:** 767 applied, 83% accepted, 39% of those accepted enrolled. **Transfer Admission Requirements:** *Items required:* high school transcript, college transcript. Minimum high school GPA of 2.0 required. Minimum college GPA of 2.0 required. Lowest grade transferable C. **General Admission Information:** Application fee $20. Priority application deadline April 1. Nonfall registration accepted. Admission may be deferred. Credit and/or placement offered for CEEB Advanced Placement tests.

COSTS AND FINANCIAL AID

Tuition $13,880. Room & board $4,800. Required fees $315. Average book expense $700. **Required Forms and Deadlines:** FAFSA and institution's own

financial aid form. Priority filing deadline March 1. **Notification of Awards:** Applicants will be notified of awards on a rolling basis beginning on or about March 1. **Types of Aid:** *Need-based scholarships/grants:* Pell, SEOG, state scholarships/grants, private scholarships, the school's own gift aid. *Loans:* FFEL Subsidized Stafford, FFEL Unsubsidized Stafford, FFEL PLUS, Federal Perkins, Federal Nursing. **Student Employment:** Federal Work-Study Program available. Institutional employment available. Off-campus job opportunities are good. **Financial Aid Statistics:** 84% freshmen, 77% undergrads receive some form of aid. Average freshman grant $7,700. Average freshman loan $3,900. Average income from on-campus job $1,100. **Financial Aid Phone:** 920-923-7614.

MARIETTA COLLEGE

215 Fifth Street, Marietta, OH 45750
Phone: 740-376-4643 **E-mail:** admit@marietta.edu **CEEB Code:** 1444
Fax: 740-376-8888 **Web:** www.marietta.edu **ACT Code:** 3290

This private school was founded in 1835. It has a 120-acre campus.

STUDENTS AND FACULTY

Enrollment: 1,118. **Student Body:** Male 50%, female 50%, out-of-state 50%, international 5% (10 countries represented). **Ethnic Representation:** African American 2%, Asian 1%, Caucasian 89%, Hispanic 1%. **Retention and Graduation:** 69% freshmen return for sophomore year. 39% freshmen graduate within 4 years. 23% grads go on to further study within 1 year. 2% grads pursue business degrees. 3% grads pursue law degrees. 2% grads pursue medical degrees. **Faculty:** Student/faculty ratio 12:1. 78 full-time faculty, 85% hold PhDs. 100% faculty teach undergrads.

ACADEMICS

Degrees: Associate's, bachelor's, master's. **Academic Requirements:** General education including some course work in arts/fine arts, computer literacy, English (including composition), history, humanities, mathematics, philosophy, sciences (biological or physical), social science. **Classes:** 10-19 students in an average class. 10-19 students in an average lab/discussion section. **Disciplines with Highest Percentage of Degrees Awarded:** Business/marketing 35%, parks and recreation 10%, social sciences and history 9%, education 8%, communications/communication technologies 7%. **Special Study Options:** Double major, English as a second language, honors program, independent study, internships, liberal arts/career combination, student-designed major, study abroad, teacher certification program.

FACILITIES

Housing: Coed, all female, all male, apartments for single students, housing for disabled students, housing for international students, fraternities and/or sororities, theme housing. **Library Holdings:** 155,700 bound volumes. 1,160 periodicals. 127,800 microforms. 5,600 audiovisuals. **Special Academic Facilities/Equipment:** Mass media building, fine arts center, natural science field camp, observatory, special collections in library. **Computers:** School-owned computers available for student use.

EXTRACURRICULARS

Activities: Choral groups, concert band, dance, drama/theater, jazz band, literary magazine, music ensembles, musical theater, pep band, radio station, student government, student newspaper, television station, yearbook. **Organizations:** 65 registered organizations, 15 honor societies, 2 religious organizations, 4 fraternities (20% men join), 3 sororities (30% women join). **Athletics (Intercollegiate):** *Men:* baseball, basketball, crew, cross-country, football, indoor track, lacrosse, soccer, tennis, track & field. *Women:* basketball, crew, cross-country, indoor track, soccer, softball, tennis, track & field, volleyball.

ADMISSIONS

Selectivity Rating: 75 (of 100). **Freshman Academic Profile:** Average high school GPA 3.3. 24% in top 10% of high school class, 50% in top 25% of high school class, 75% in top 50% of high school class. 82% from public high schools. Average SAT I Math 539, SAT I Math middle 50% range 480-590. Average SAT I Verbal 542, SAT I Verbal middle 50% range 480-600. Average ACT 23, ACT middle 50% range 20-27. TOEFL required of all international applicants, minimum TOEFL 550. **Basis for Candidate Selection:** *Very important factors considered include:* secondary school record. *Important factors considered include:* character/personal qualities, class rank, essays, extracurricular activities, interview, recommendations, standardized test scores. *Other factors considered include:* alumni/ae relation, minority status, talent/ability, volunteer work, work experience. **Freshman Admission Requirements:** High school diploma or GED is required. *Academic units required/recommended:* 16 total required; 4 English required, 3 math required, 3 science required, 2 science lab required, 2 foreign language required, 2 foreign language recommended, 1 social studies required, 1 history required, 3 history recommended. **Freshman Admission Statistics:** 1,056 applied, 94% accepted, 28% of those accepted enrolled. **Transfer Admission Requirements:** *Items required:* college transcript, essay, statement of good standing from prior school. Minimum college GPA of 2.3 required. Lowest grade transferable C. **General Admission Information:** Application fee $25. Priority application deadline March 1. Regular application deadline rolling. Nonfall registration accepted. Admission may be deferred for a maximum of 1 year. Credit and/or placement offered for CEEB Advanced Placement tests.

COSTS AND FINANCIAL AID

Tuition $18,838. Room & board $5,504. Required fees $238. Average book expense $575. **Required Forms and Deadlines:** FAFSA and institution's own financial aid form. Priority filing deadline March 1. **Notification of Awards:** Applicants will be notified of awards on a rolling basis beginning on or about March 15. **Types of Aid:** *Need-based scholarships/grants:* Pell, SEOG, state scholarships/grants, private scholarships, the school's own gift aid. *Loans:* Direct Subsidized Stafford, Direct Unsubsidized Stafford, Direct PLUS, FFEL Subsidized Stafford, FFEL Unsubsidized Stafford, FFEL PLUS, Federal Perkins. **Student Employment:** Federal Work-Study Program available. Institutional employment available. Off-campus job opportunities are good. **Financial Aid Statistics:** 77% freshmen, 74% undergrads receive some form of aid. Average freshman grant $9,075. Average freshman loan $2,625. Average income from on-campus job $1,000. **Financial Aid Phone:** 800-331-2709.

MARIST COLLEGE

3399 North Road, Poughkeepsie, NY 12601-1387
Phone: 845-575-3226 **E-mail:** admissions@marist.edu **CEEB Code:** 2400
Fax: 845-575-3215 **Web:** www.marist.edu **ACT Code:** 2804

This private school was founded in 1929. It has a 150-acre campus.

STUDENTS AND FACULTY

Enrollment: 4,866. **Student Body:** Male 42%, female 58%, out-of-state 45%, (17 countries represented). **Ethnic Representation:** African American 3%, Asian 1%, Caucasian 79%, Hispanic 6%. **Retention and Graduation:** 92% freshmen return for sophomore year. 59% freshmen graduate within 4 years. 24% grads go on to further study within 1 year. 3% grads pursue business degrees. 3% grads pursue law degrees. 1% grads pursue medical degrees. **Faculty:** Student/faculty ratio 16:1. 182 full-time faculty, 79% hold PhDs. 96% faculty teach undergrads.

ACADEMICS

Degrees: Bachelor's, master's, post-bachelor's certificate. **Academic Requirements:** General education including some course work in arts/fine arts, computer literacy, English (including composition), history, humanities, mathematics, philosophy, sciences (biological or physical), social science. **Classes:** 20-29 students in an average class. 10-19 students in an average lab/discussion section. **Disciplines with Highest Percentage of Degrees Awarded:** Communications/communication technologies 19%, business/marketing 17%, protective services/public administration 13%, education 12%, computer and information sciences 8%. **Special Study Options:** Accelerated program, cooperative (work-study) program, cross registration, distance learning, evening division double major, honors program, independent study, internships, liberal arts/career combination, student-designed major, study abroad, teacher certification program, weekend college. Undergrads may take grad-level classes. Cooperative education in arts, business, computer science, education, humanities, natural science, social/behavioral science, technologies. Off-campus study: Washington, DC.

FACILITIES

Housing: Coed, apartments for single students, garden apartments, town houses, suites. **Library Holdings:** 167,033 bound volumes. 10,702 periodicals. 233,136 microforms. 4,438 audiovisuals. **Special Academic Facilities/Equipment:** Art gallery, language lab, estuarine and environmental studies lab, public opinion institute, audiovisual/TV center, communications center, high-tech classroom, digital state of the art library. **Computers:** *Recommended operating system:* Windows 95. School-owned computers available for student use.

EXTRACURRICULARS

Activities: Choral groups, concert band, dance, drama/theater, jazz band, literary magazine, marching band, music ensembles, musical theater, pep band, radio station, student government, student newspaper, student-run film society, television station, yearbook. **Organizations:** 70 registered organizations, 8 honor societies, 2 religious organizations, 3 fraternities (3% men join), 2 sororities (5% women join). **Athletics (Intercollegiate):** *Men:* baseball, basketball, crew, cross-country, diving, football, ice hockey, lacrosse, rugby, soccer, swimming, tennis, track & field, volleyball. *Women:* basketball, crew, cross-country, diving, lacrosse, rugby, soccer, softball, swimming, tennis, track & field, volleyball, water polo.

ADMISSIONS

Selectivity Rating: 85 (of 100). **Freshman Academic Profile:** Average high school GPA 3.2. 19% in top 10% of high school class, 62% in top 25% of high school class, 99% in top 50% of high school class. 78% from public high schools. Average SAT I Math 582, SAT I Math middle 50% range 560-660. Average SAT I Verbal 574, SAT I Verbal middle 50% range 550-650. Average ACT 25, ACT middle 50% range 24-25. TOEFL required of all international applicants, minimum TOEFL 550. **Basis for Candidate Selection:** *Very important factors considered include:* class rank, recommendations, secondary school record, standardized test scores. *Important factors considered include:* character/personal qualities, essays, extracurricular activities, minority status, talent/ability, volunteer work, work experience. *Other factors considered include:* alumni/ae relation. **Freshman Admission Requirements:** High school diploma or GED is required. *Academic units required/recommended:* 17 total required; 4 English required, 3 math required, 4 math recommended, 3 science required, 4 science recommended, 2 science lab required, 3 science lab recommended, 2 foreign language recommended, 2 social studies required, 1 history required, 2 elective required. **Freshman Admission Statistics:** 6,204 applied, 54% accepted, 29% of those accepted enrolled. **Transfer Admission Requirements:** *Items required:* high school transcript, college transcript, essay, statement of good standing from prior school. Minimum college GPA of 2.8 required. Lowest grade transferable C. **General Admission Information:** Application fee $40. Regular application deadline February 15. Nonfall registration accepted. Admission may be deferred for a maximum of 1 year. Credit and/or placement offered for CEEB Advanced Placement tests.

COSTS AND FINANCIAL AID

Tuition $17,444. Room & board $8,332. Required fees $438. Average book expense $850. **Required Forms and Deadlines:** FAFSA and institution's own financial aid form. Financial aid filing deadline February 15. Priority filing deadline February 15. **Notification of Awards:** Applicants will be notified of awards on a rolling basis beginning on or about March 15. **Types of Aid:** *Need-based scholarships/grants:* Pell, SEOG, state scholarships/grants, private scholarships, the school's own gift aid. *Loans:* FFEL Subsidized Stafford, FFEL Unsubsidized Stafford, FFEL PLUS, Federal Perkins. **Student Employment:** Federal Work-Study Program available. Institutional employment available. Off-campus job opportunities are excellent. **Financial Aid Statistics:** 79% freshmen, 76% undergrads receive some form of aid. Average freshman grant $7,378. Average freshman loan $3,958. Average income from on-campus job $1,200. **Financial Aid Phone:** 845-575-3230.

MARLBORO COLLEGE

PO Box A, South Road, Marlboro, VT 05344-0300
Phone: 802-258-9236 **E-mail:** admissions@marlboro.edu **CEEB Code:** 3509
Fax: 802-451-7555 **Web:** www.marlboro.edu **ACT Code:** 4304

This private school was founded in 1947. It has a 350-acre campus.

STUDENTS AND FACULTY

Enrollment: 290. **Student Body:** Male 41%, female 59%, out-of-state 82%, international 2% (6 countries represented). **Ethnic Representation:** African American 1%, Asian 1%, Caucasian 87%, Hispanic 2%, Native American 1%. **Retention and Graduation:** 78% freshmen return for sophomore year. 31% freshmen graduate within 4 years. 33% grads go on to further study within 1 year. **Faculty:** Student/faculty ratio 7:1. 33 full-time faculty, 81% hold PhDs. 100% faculty teach undergrads.

ACADEMICS

Degrees: Bachelor's, master's. **Academic Requirements:** General education including some course work in English (including composition), clear writing requirement, plan of concentration. **Disciplines with Highest Percentage of Degrees Awarded:** Visual and performing arts 30%, social sciences and history 28%, biological life sciences 11%, psychology 8%, English 8%. **Special Study Options:** Accelerated program, cross registration, double major, dual enrollment, independent study, internships, student-designed major, study abroad, World Studies Program.

FACILITIES

Housing: Coed, all-female, apartments for married students, cabins and cottages are available. **Library Holdings:** 52,000 bound volumes. 171 periodicals. 5,100 microforms. 750 audiovisuals. **Special Academic Facilities/ Equipment:** Art gallery, theatre, dance studio, observatory, darkroom, art studio. **Computers:** *Recommended operating system:* Windows 95. School-owned computers available for student use.

EXTRACURRICULARS

Activities: Choral groups, dance, drama/theater, jazz band, literary magazine, music ensembles, student government, student newspaper, student-run film society. **Organizations:** 25 registered organizations. **Athletics (Intercollegiate):** *Men:* soccer. *Women:* soccer.

ADMISSIONS

Selectivity Rating: 82 (of 100). **Freshman Academic Profile:** Average high school GPA 3.2. 31% in top 10% of high school class, 51% in top 25% of high school class, 79% in top 50% of high school class. 65% from public high schools. Average SAT I Math 580, SAT I Math middle 50% range 500-620. Average SAT I Verbal 610, SAT I Verbal middle 50% range 580-680. TOEFL required of all international applicants, minimum TOEFL 550. **Basis for Candidate Selection:** *Very important factors considered include:* interview, secondary school record. *Important factors considered include:* character/personal qualities, class rank, essays, extracurricular activities, recommendations, standardized test scores, talent/ability, volunteer work. *Other factors considered include:* alumni/ae relation, geographical residence, work experience. **Freshman Admission Requirements:** High school diploma or GED is required. *Academic units required/recommended:* 4 English required, 4 English recommended, 3 math recommended, 3 science recommended, 3 foreign language recommended, 3 social studies recommended, 3 history recommended. **Freshman Admission Statistics:** 308 applied, 80% accepted, 40% of those accepted enrolled. **Transfer Admission Requirements:** *Items required:* high school transcript, college transcript, essay, interview, standardized test scores. Minimum college GPA of 2.0 required. Lowest grade transferable C. **General Admission Information:** Application fee $50. Priority application deadline March 1. Early decision application deadline November 15. Regular application deadline March 1. Nonfall registration accepted. Admission may be deferred for a maximum of 1 year. Credit offered for CEEB Advanced Placement tests.

COSTS AND FINANCIAL AID

Tuition $18,800. Room & board $6,750. Required fees $760. Average book expense $600. **Required Forms and Deadlines:** FAFSA, CSS/Financial Aid PROFILE and noncustodial (divorced/separated) parent's statement. Financial aid filing deadline March 1. Priority filing deadline February 15. **Notification of Awards:** Applicants will be notified of awards on a rolling basis beginning on or about April 1. **Types of Aid:** *Need-based scholarships/grants:* Pell, SEOG, state scholarships/grants, private scholarships, the school's own gift aid. *Loans:* FFEL Subsidized Stafford, FFEL Unsubsidized Stafford, FFEL PLUS, college/university loans from institutional funds. **Student Employment:** Federal Work-Study Program available. Institutional employment available. Off-campus job opportunities are fair. **Financial Aid Statistics:** 82% freshmen, 76% undergrads receive some form of aid. Average freshman grant $12,007. Average freshman loan $2,619. Average income from on-campus job $1,866. **Financial Aid Phone:** 802-257-4333.

See page 1106.

MARQUETTE UNIVERSITY

PO Box 1881, Milwaukee, WI 53201-1881
Phone: 414-288-7302 **E-mail:** Admissions@Marquette.edu **CEEB Code:** 1448
Fax: 414-288-3764 **Web:** www.Marquette.edu **ACT Code:** 4610

This private school, which is affiliated with the Roman Catholic Church, was founded in 1881. It has an 80-acre campus.

STUDENTS AND FACULTY

Enrollment: 7,644. **Student Body:** Male 44%, female 56%, out-of-state 53%, international 2% (80 countries represented). **Ethnic Representation:** African American 5%, Asian 5%, Caucasian 86%, Hispanic 4%. **Retention and Graduation:** 87% freshmen return for sophomore year. 57% freshmen graduate within 4 years. 28% grads go on to further study within 1 year. **Faculty:** Student/faculty ratio 15:1. 617 full-time faculty, 81% hold PhDs.

ACADEMICS

Degrees: Associate's, bachelor's, doctoral, first professional, master's, post-bachelor's certificate, post-master's certificate. **Academic Requirements:**

General education including some course work in arts/fine arts, English (including composition), foreign languages, history, humanities, mathematics, philosophy, sciences (biological or physical), social science, theology. **Classes:** 10-19 students in an average class. 10-19 students in an average lab/discussion section. **Majors with Highest Enrollment:** Nursing/registered nurse training (RN, ASN, BSN, MSN); business administration/management; biomedical sciences, general. **Disciplines with Highest Percentage of Degrees Awarded:** Business/marketing 22%, communications/communication technologies 16%, health professions and related sciences 15%, engineering/engineering technology 11%, social sciences and history 8%. **Special Study Options:** Cooperative (work-study) program, cross registration, double major, dual enrollment, English as a second language, honors program, internships, study abroad, teacher certification program, weekend college.

FACILITIES

Housing: Coed, all-female, all-male, apartments for married students, apartments for single students, housing for disabled students, housing for international students, fraternities and/or sororities. **Library Holdings:** 1,120,694 bound volumes. 5,894 periodicals. 575,652 microforms. 9,332 audiovisuals. **Special Academic Facilities/Equipment:** Haggerty Museum of Art, Helfaer Theatre, broadcast facilities, dental school/clinic. **Computers:** School-owned computers available for student use.

EXTRACURRICULARS

Activities: Choral groups, concert band, dance, drama/theater, jazz band, literary magazine, music ensembles, pep band, radio station, student government, student newspaper, student-run film society, symphony orchestra, television station, yearbook. **Organizations:** 156 registered organizations, 9 honor societies, 8 religious organizations, 10 fraternities (7% men join), 9 sororities (8% women join). **Athletics (Intercollegiate):** *Men:* basketball, cross-country, golf, indoor track, soccer, tennis, track & field. *Women:* basketball, cross-country, indoor track, soccer, tennis, track & field, volleyball.

ADMISSIONS

Selectivity Rating: 78 (of 100). **Freshman Academic Profile:** 20% in top 10% of high school class, 40% in top 25% of high school class, 94% in top 50% of high school class. 55% from public high schools. Average SAT I Math 590, SAT I Math middle 50% range 530-650. Average SAT I Verbal 560, SAT I Verbal middle 50% range 520-640. Average ACT 25, ACT middle 50% range 23-28. TOEFL required of all international applicants, minimum TOEFL 525. **Basis for Candidate Selection:** *Very important factors considered include:* secondary school record, standardized test scores. *Important factors considered include:* class rank. *Other factors considered include:* alumni/ae relation, character/personal qualities, essays, extracurricular activities, geographical residence, interview, minority status, recommendations, religious affiliation/commitment, state residency, talent/ability, volunteer work, work experience. **Freshman Admission Requirements:** High school diploma or GED is required. *Academic units required/recommended:* 16 total recommended; 4 English recommended, 3 math recommended, 3 science recommended, 2 science lab recommended, 2 foreign language recommended, 2 social studies recommended, 2 history recommended, 3 elective recommended. **Freshman Admission Statistics:** 7,593 applied, 82% accepted, 30% of those accepted enrolled. **Transfer Admission Requirements:** *Items required:* high school transcript, college transcript, statement of good standing from prior school. Minimum college GPA of 2.0 required. Lowest grade transferable C. **General Admission Information:** Application fee $30. Priority application deadline February 1. Nonfall registration accepted. Admission may be deferred for a maximum of 1 year. Credit and/or placement offered for CEEB Advanced Placement tests.

COSTS AND FINANCIAL AID

Tuition $20,350. Room & board $7,036. Required fees $374. Average book expense $900. **Required Forms and Deadlines:** FAFSA and Admission Application for Marquette University Ignatius Scholarship. Financial aid filing deadline March 1. Priority filing deadline March 1. **Notification of Awards:** Applicants will be notified of awards on a rolling basis beginning on or about March 21. **Types of Aid:** *Need-based scholarships/grants:* Pell, SEOG, state scholarships/grants, private scholarships, the school's own gift aid, Federal Nursing, Marquette merit-based scholarships. *Loans:* Direct Subsidized Stafford, Direct Unsubsidized Stafford, Direct PLUS, Federal Perkins, Federal Nursing, state loans, college/university loans from institutional funds, alternative educational loans. **Student Employment:** Federal Work-Study Program available. Institutional employment available. Off-campus job opportunities are excellent. **Financial Aid Statistics:** 65% freshmen, 60% undergrads receive some form of aid. Average freshman grant $11,640. Average freshman loan $4,385. Average income from on-campus job $1,900. **Financial Aid Phone:** 414-288-7390.

MARS HILL COLLEGE

$$

PO Box 370, Mars Hill, NC 28754
Phone: 828-689-1201 **E-mail:** admissions@mhc.edu **CEEB Code:** 5395
Fax: 828-689-1473 **Web:** www.mhc.edu **ACT Code:** 3124

This private school, which is affiliated with the Baptist Church, was founded in 1856. It has a 180-acre campus.

STUDENTS AND FACULTY

Enrollment: 1,224. **Student Body:** Male 43%, female 57%, out-of-state 40%, international 3% (20 countries represented). **Ethnic Representation:** African American 7%, Caucasian 91%, Hispanic 1%, Native American 1%. **Retention and Graduation:** 71% freshmen return for sophomore year. 23% grads go on to further study within 1 year. 5% grads pursue business degrees. 4% grads pursue law degrees. 4% grads pursue medical degrees. **Faculty:** Student/faculty ratio 12:1. 78 full-time faculty, 62% hold PhDs. 100% faculty teach undergrads.

ACADEMICS

Degrees: Bachelor's. **Disciplines with Highest Percentage of Degrees Awarded:** Education 31%, business/marketing 14%, social sciences and history 9%, protective services/public administration 8%, communications/communication technologies 7%. **Special Study Options:** Accelerated program, cooperative (work-study) program, distance learning, double major, dual enrollment, English as a second language, honors program, independent study, internships, liberal arts/career combination, study abroad, teacher certification program.

FACILITIES

Housing: Coed, all-female, all-male, apartments for married students, apartments for single students. **Library Holdings:** 90,000 bound volumes. 750 periodicals. 70,000 microforms. **Special Academic Facilities/Equipment:** Language lab, Appalachian artifacts museum, rural life museum. **Computers:** School-owned computers available for student use.

EXTRACURRICULARS

Activities: Choral groups, concert band, drama/theater, jazz band, literary magazine, marching band, music ensembles, musical theater, pep band, radio station, student government, student newspaper, yearbook. **Organizations:** 40 registered organizations, 9 honor societies, 5 religious organizations, 6 fraternities (10% men join), 5 sororities (12% women join). **Athletics (Intercollegiate):** *Men:* baseball, basketball, cheerleading, cross-country, football, golf, lacrosse, soccer, tennis, track & field. *Women:* basketball, cheerleading, cross-country, soccer, softball, tennis, track & field, volleyball.

ADMISSIONS

Selectivity Rating: 65 (of 100). **Freshman Academic Profile:** Average high school GPA 3.2. 74% in top 10% of high school class, 63% in top 25% of high school class, 55% in top 50% of high school class. 70% from public high schools. Average SAT I Math 450, SAT I Math middle 50% range 430-550. Average SAT I Verbal 450, SAT I Verbal middle 50% range 450-550. Average ACT 19. TOEFL required of all international applicants, minimum TOEFL 500. **Basis for Candidate Selection:** *Very important factors considered include:* secondary school record, standardized test scores. *Important factors considered include:* character/personal qualities, class rank, extracurricular activities. *Other factors considered include:* alumni/ae relation, interview, recommendations, religious affiliation/commitment, talent/ability, volunteer work, work experience. **Freshman Admission Requirements:** High school diploma or GED is required. *Academic units required/recommended:* 18 total required; 4 English required, 3 math required, 2 science required, 1 science lab required, 2 foreign language recommended, 2 social studies required, 2 history required. **Freshman Admission Statistics:** 963 applied, 90% accepted, 40% of those accepted enrolled. **Transfer Admission Requirements:** *Items required:* college transcript, statement of good standing from prior school. Minimum high school GPA of 2.0 required. Minimum college GPA of 2.0 required. Lowest grade transferable C. **General Admission Information:** Application fee $25. Nonfall registration accepted.

COSTS AND FINANCIAL AID

Tuition $12,000. Room & board $4,500. Required fees $800. Average book expense $600. **Required Forms and Deadlines:** FAFSA and state aid form. **Types of Aid:** *Need-based scholarships/grants:* state scholarships/grants. *Loans:* FFEL Subsidized Stafford, FFEL PLUS. **Student Employment:** Federal Work-Study Program available. Institutional employment available. Off-campus job opportunities are good. **Financial Aid Statistics:** Average freshman grant $5,000. Average income from on-campus job $1,000. **Financial Aid Phone:** 828-689-1123.

MARSHALL UNIVERSITY

One John Marshall Drive, Huntington, WV 25755
Phone: 304-696-3160 **E-mail:** admissions@marshall.edu **CEEB Code:** 5396
Fax: 304-696-3135 **Web:** www.marshall.edu **ACT Code:** 4526

This public school was founded in 1837. It has a 70-acre campus.

STUDENTS AND FACULTY

Enrollment: 9,823. **Student Body:** Male 45%, female 55%, out-of-state 17%, international 1%. **Ethnic Representation:** African American 4%, Asian 1%, Caucasian 87%, Native American 1%. **Retention and Graduation:** 73% freshmen return for sophomore year. 27% grads go on to further study within 1 year. **Faculty:** Student/faculty ratio 20:1. 451 full-time faculty, 77% hold PhDs.

ACADEMICS

Degrees: Associate's, bachelor's, certificate, doctoral, first professional, master's, post-master's certificate. **Academic Requirements:** General education including some course work in arts/fine arts, computer literacy, English (including composition), humanities, mathematics, sciences (biological or physical), social science. **Classes:** 20-29 students in an average class. **Majors with Highest Enrollment:** Counselor education/school counseling and guidance services; biology/biological sciences, general; secondary education and teaching. **Disciplines with Highest Percentage of Degrees Awarded:** Business/marketing 24%, education 20%, liberal arts/general studies 14%, health professions and related sciences 7%, psychology 6%. **Special Study Options:** Accelerated program, cooperative (work-study) program, cross registration, distance learning, double major, English as a second language, student exchange program (domestic), honors program, independent study, internships, study abroad, teacher certification program.

FACILITIES

Housing: Coed, all-female, all-male, apartments for married students, housing for disabled students, fraternities and/or sororities. **Library Holdings:** 423,946 bound volumes. 2,189 periodicals. 960,933 microforms. 24,412 audiovisuals. **Special Academic Facilities/Equipment:** Art gallery, audiovisual center, language lab, superconducting nuclear magnetic resonance spectrometer. **Computers:** *Recommended operating system:* Windows 98. School-owned computers available for student use.

EXTRACURRICULARS

Activities: Choral groups, concert band, dance, drama/theater, jazz band, literary magazine, marching band, music ensembles, musical theater, opera, pep band, radio station, student government, student newspaper, symphony orchestra, television station, yearbook. **Organizations:** 100 registered organizations, 11 honor societies, 10 religious organizations, 12 fraternities, 7 sororities. **Athletics (Intercollegiate):** *Men:* baseball, basketball, cross-country, football, golf, soccer, track & field. *Women:* basketball, cross-country, golf, soccer, softball, swimming, tennis, track & field, volleyball.

ADMISSIONS

Selectivity Rating: 60 (of 100). **Freshman Academic Profile:** Average high school GPA 3.3. ACT middle 50% range 19-24. TOEFL required of all international applicants, minimum TOEFL 500. **Basis for Candidate Selection:** *Very important factors considered include:* secondary school record, standardized test scores. **Freshman Admission Requirements:** High school diploma or GED is required. *Academic units required/recommended:* 11 total required; 2 total recommended; 4 English required, 2 math required, 2 science required, 2 science lab required, 2 foreign language recommended, 3 social studies required. **Freshman Admission Statistics:** 2,339 applied, 94% accepted, 86% of those accepted enrolled. **Transfer Admission Requirements:** *Items required:* college transcript. Minimum college GPA of 2.0 required. Lowest grade transferable D. **General Admission Information:** Application fee $25. Nonfall registration accepted. Admission may be deferred for a maximum of 1 year. Credit offered for CEEB Advanced Placement tests.

COSTS AND FINANCIAL AID

In-state tuition $2,468. Out-of-state tuition $7,470. Room & board $5,380. Required fees $516. Average book expense $800. **Required Forms and Deadlines:** FAFSA and state aid form. Priority filing deadline March 1. **Notification of Awards:** Applicants will be notified of awards on a rolling basis beginning on or about May 1. **Types of Aid:** *Need-based scholarships/grants:* Pell, SEOG, state scholarships/grants, private scholarships, the school's own gift aid. *Loans:* Direct Subsidized Stafford, Direct Unsubsidized Stafford, Direct PLUS, Federal Perkins. **Student Employment:** Federal Work-Study Program available. Institutional employment available. Off-campus job opportunities are fair. **Financial Aid Statistics:** 59% freshmen, 52% undergrads receive some form of aid. Average freshman grant $3,261. Average freshman loan $2,320. Average income from on-campus job $2,110. **Financial Aid Phone:** 304-696-3162.

MARTIN LUTHER COLLEGE

1995 Luther Court, New Ulm, MN 56073-3965
Phone: 507-354-8221 **E-mail:** seboldja-fac@mlc-wels.edu **CEEB Code:** 6435
Fax: 507-354-8225 **Web:** www.mlc-wels.edu **ACT Code:** 2127

This private school, which is affiliated with the Lutheran Church, was founded in 1995. It has a 50-acre campus.

STUDENTS AND FACULTY

Enrollment: 811. **Student Body:** Male 52%, female 48%, out-of-state 80%, international 1% (5 countries represented). **Ethnic Representation:** African American 1%, Asian 1%, Caucasian 98%, Hispanic 1%. **Retention and Graduation:** 80% freshmen return for sophomore year. 52% freshmen graduate within 4 years. 2% grads go on to further study within 1 year. **Faculty:** 85% faculty teach undergrads.

ACADEMICS

Degrees: Bachelor's. **Academic Requirements:** General education including some course work in arts/fine arts, computer literacy, English (including composition), history, mathematics, sciences (biological or physical), social science. **Special Study Options:** Double major, English as a second language.

FACILITIES

Housing: All-female, all-male. **Library Holdings:** 117,465 bound volumes. 583 periodicals. 65 microforms. 2,774 audiovisuals. **Special Academic Facilities/Equipment:** Organ facilities for music students. **Computers:** *Recommended operating system:* Windows 95. School-owned computers available for student use.

EXTRACURRICULARS

Activities: Choral groups, concert band, drama/theater, musical theater, student government, student newspaper, yearbook. **Athletics (Intercollegiate):** *Men:* baseball, basketball, cross-country, football, golf, soccer, tennis, track & field, wrestling. *Women:* basketball, cross-country, soccer, softball, tennis, track & field, volleyball.

ADMISSIONS

Selectivity Rating: 76 (of 100). **Freshman Academic Profile:** Average high school GPA 3.3. 17% in top 10% of high school class, 38% in top 25% of high school class, 67% in top 50% of high school class. 13% from public high schools. Average ACT 24, ACT middle 50% range 21-27. TOEFL required of all international applicants, minimum TOEFL 500. **Basis for Candidate Selection:** *Very important factors considered include:* character/personal qualities, recommendations, religious affiliation/commitment, secondary school record. *Important factors considered include:* class rank, interview, standardized test scores, talent/ability. *Other factors considered include:* extracurricular activities, volunteer work, work experience. **Freshman Admission Requirements:** High school diploma or GED is required. *Academic units required/recommended:* 12 total required; 4 English required, 2 math required, 3 math recommended, 2 science required, 3 science recommended, 2 science lab required, 2 social studies required, 2 elective required. **Freshman Admission Statistics:** 274 applied, 89% accepted, 82% of those accepted enrolled. **Transfer Admission Requirements:** *Items required:* high school transcript, college transcript, statement of good standing from prior school. Minimum high school GPA of 2.0 required. Minimum college GPA of 2.0 required. Lowest grade transferable C-. **General Admission Information:** Application fee $25. Regular application deadline May 1. Nonfall registration accepted. Admission may be deferred. Credit and/or placement offered for CEEB Advanced Placement tests.

COSTS AND FINANCIAL AID

Tuition $4,130. Room & board $2,285. Required fees $490. Average book expense $670. **Required Forms and Deadlines:** FAFSA and institution's own financial aid form. No deadline for regular filing. Priority filing deadline May 1. **Notification of Awards:** Applicants will be notified of awards on a rolling basis beginning on or about March 1. **Types of Aid:** *Need-based scholarships/grants:* Pell, SEOG, state scholarships/grants, private scholarships, the school's own gift aid. *Loans:* FFEL Subsidized Stafford, FFEL Unsubsidized Stafford, FFEL PLUS, Federal Perkins, state loans, college/university loans from institutional funds. **Student Employment:** Federal Work-Study Program available. Institutional employment available. Off-campus job opportunities are good. **Financial Aid Statistics:** Average freshman grant $1,995. Average freshman loan $2,175. Average income from on-campus job $950. **Financial Aid Phone:** 507-354-8221.

MARY BALDWIN COLLEGE

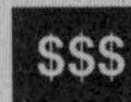

PO Box 1500, Staunton, VA 24402
Phone: 540-887-7019 **E-mail:** admit@mbc.edu **CEEB Code:** 5397
Fax: 540-887-7279 **Web:** www.mbc.edu **ACT Code:** 4374

This private school, which is affiliated with the Presbyterian Church, was founded in 1842. It has a 54-acre campus.

STUDENTS AND FACULTY

Enrollment: 1,514. **Student Body:** Male 5%, female 95%, out-of-state 25%, international 2% (9 countries represented). **Ethnic Representation:** African American 20%, Asian 2%, Caucasian 74%, Hispanic 3%. **Retention and Graduation:** 69% freshmen return for sophomore year. 46% freshmen graduate within 4 years. 24% grads go on to further study within 1 year. 4% grads pursue business degrees. 4% grads pursue law degrees. 3% grads pursue medical degrees. **Faculty:** Student/faculty ratio 11:1. 75 full-time faculty, 86% hold PhDs. 100% faculty teach undergrads.

ACADEMICS

Degrees: Bachelor's, certificate, master's. **Academic Requirements:** General education including some course work in arts/fine arts, computer literacy, English (including composition), history, humanities, mathematics, philosophy, sciences (biological or physical), social science, women's studies, physical education, writing emphasis, oral communication, international education. **Classes:** 10-19 students in an average class. 10-19 students in an average lab/discussion section. **Majors with Highest Enrollment:** Business administration/management; psychology, general; sociology. **Disciplines with Highest Percentage of Degrees Awarded:** Social sciences and history 23%, business/marketing 19%, psychology 14%, visual and performing arts 9%, communications/communication technologies 7%. **Special Study Options:** Accelerated program, cross registration, distance learning, double major, dual enrollment, English as a second language, student exchange program (domestic), external degree program, honors program, independent study, internships, liberal arts/career combination, student-designed major, study abroad, teacher certification program, summer exchange program with Doshisha Women's College in Kyoto, Japan.

FACILITIES

Housing: All-female, apartments for single students, housing for international students. Special-interest (club) housing focuses on students, honors, leadership, and community services available. **Library Holdings:** 168,900 bound volumes. 8,000 periodicals. 64,100 microforms. 9,250 audiovisuals. **Special Academic Facilities/Equipment:** Audiovisual center, TV studio, communications lab, electron microscope, gas chromatoscope, greenhouse. **Computers:** School-owned computers available for student use.

EXTRACURRICULARS

Activities: Choral groups, dance, drama/theater, literary magazine, marching band, music ensembles, musical theater, radio station, student government, student newspaper, student-run film society, television station, yearbook. **Organizations:** 34 registered organizations, 9 honor societies, 4 religious organizations. **Athletics (Intercollegiate):** *Women:* basketball, skiing (cross-country), field hockey, soccer, softball, swimming, tennis, volleyball.

ADMISSIONS

Selectivity Rating: 76 (of 100). **Freshman Academic Profile:** Average high school GPA 3.3. 16% in top 10% of high school class, 53% in top 25% of high school class, 80% in top 50% of high school class. 75% from public high schools. Average SAT I Math 513, SAT I Math middle 50% range 450-580. Average SAT I Verbal 543, SAT I Verbal middle 50% range 480-590. Average ACT 22, ACT middle 50% range 18-25. TOEFL required of all international applicants, minimum TOEFL 500. **Basis for Candidate Selection:** *Very important factors considered include:* secondary school record, standardized test scores. *Important factors considered include:* character/personal qualities, extracurricular activities, interview. *Other factors considered include:* alumni/ae relation, class rank, essays, recommendations, talent/ability, volunteer work, work experience. **Freshman Admission Requirements:** High school diploma or GED is required. *Academic units required/recommended:* 4 English required, 3 math required, 2 science required, 1 science lab required, 2 foreign language required, 3 foreign language recommended, 3 social studies required, 2 elective recommended. **Freshman Admission Statistics:** 1,292 applied, 78% accepted, 26% of those accepted enrolled. **Transfer Admission Requirements:** *Items required:* high school transcript, college transcript, statement of good standing from prior school. Minimum college GPA of 2.0 required. Lowest grade transferable C-. **General Admission Information:** Application fee $25. Early decision application deadline November 15. Nonfall registration accepted. Admission may be deferred. Credit offered for CEEB Advanced Placement tests.

COSTS AND FINANCIAL AID

Tuition $19,234. Room & board $5,525. Required fees $175. Average book expense $700. **Required Forms and Deadlines:** FAFSA and state aid form. Priority filing deadline May 15. **Notification of Awards:** Applicants will be notified of awards on a rolling basis beginning on or about January 1. **Types of Aid:** *Need-based scholarships/grants:* Pell, SEOG, state scholarships/grants, private scholarships, the school's own gift aid. *Loans:* FFEL Subsidized Stafford, FFEL Unsubsidized Stafford, FFEL PLUS, Federal Perkins, private alternative loans. **Student Employment:** Federal Work-Study Program available. Institutional employment available. Off-campus job opportunities are excellent. **Financial Aid Statistics:** 76% freshmen, 75% undergrads receive some form of aid. Average freshman grant $8,400. Average freshman loan $3,496. Average income from on-campus job $1,356. **Financial Aid Phone:** 540-887-7022.

MARY WASHINGTON COLLEGE

1301 College Avenue, Fredericksburg, VA 22401
Phone: 540-654-2000 **E-mail:** admit@mwc.edu **CEEB Code:** 5398
Fax: 540-654-1857 **Web:** www.mwc.edu **ACT Code:** 4414

This public school was founded in 1908. It has a 176-acre campus.

STUDENTS AND FACULTY

Enrollment: 4,275. **Student Body:** Male 32%, female 68%, out-of-state 35%, international students represent 11 countries. **Ethnic Representation:** African American 4%, Asian 4%, Caucasian 88%, Hispanic 3%. **Retention and Graduation:** 88% freshmen return for sophomore year. 62% freshmen graduate within 4 years. 25% grads go on to further study within 1 year. 4% grads pursue business degrees. 6% grads pursue law degrees. 2% grads pursue medical degrees. **Faculty:** Student/faculty ratio 17:1. 205 full-time faculty, 85% hold PhDs. 100% faculty teach undergrads.

ACADEMICS

Degrees: Bachelor's, master's. **Academic Requirements:** General education including some course work in arts/fine arts, computer literacy, English (including composition), foreign languages, history, humanities, mathematics, sciences (biological or physical), social science. **Classes:** 20-29 students in an average class. 20-29 students in an average lab/discussion section. **Majors with Highest Enrollment:** Business administration/management; English language and literature, general; psychology, general. **Disciplines with Highest Percentage of Degrees Awarded:** Social sciences and history 20%, business/marketing 15%, liberal arts/general studies 12%, psychology 11%, biological life sciences 9%. **Special Study Options:** Double major, independent study, internships, student-designed major, study abroad, teacher certification program.

FACILITIES

Housing: Coed, all-female, all-male, apartments for single students, housing for disabled students. **Library Holdings:** 355,478 bound volumes. 2,419 periodicals. 559,809 microforms. 1,079 audiovisuals. **Special Academic Facilities/Equipment:** Galleries, center for historic preservation, language labs. **Computers:** School-owned computers available for student use.

EXTRACURRICULARS

Activities: Choral groups, concert band, dance, drama/theater, jazz band, literary magazine, music ensembles, musical theater, radio station, student government, student newspaper, student-run film society, symphony orchestra, yearbook. **Organizations:** 96 registered organizations, 21 honor societies, 20 religious organizations. **Athletics (Intercollegiate):** *Men:* baseball, basketball, crew, cross-country, equestrian, indoor track, lacrosse, soccer, swimming, tennis, track & field. *Women:* basketball, crew, cross-country, equestrian, field hockey, indoor track, lacrosse, soccer, softball, swimming, tennis, track & field, volleyball.

ADMISSIONS

Selectivity Rating: 91 (of 100). **Freshman Academic Profile:** Average high school GPA 3.7. 40% in top 10% of high school class, 85% in top 25% of high school class, 99% in top 50% of high school class. 76% from public high schools. Average SAT I Math 595, SAT I Math middle 50% range 560-640. Average SAT I Verbal 613, SAT I Verbal middle 50% range 570-660. Average ACT 27, ACT middle 50% range 24-29. TOEFL required of all international applicants, minimum TOEFL 550. **Basis for Candidate Selection:** *Very important factors considered include:* secondary school record. *Important factors considered include:* class rank, essays, standardized test scores. *Other factors considered include:* alumni/ae relation, character/personal qualities, extracurricular activities, geographical residence, minority status, recommendations, state residency, talent/ability, volunteer work, work experience. **Freshman Admission Requirements:** High school diploma or GED is required. *Academic units required/recommended:* 4 English required, 4 English recommended, 3 math required, 4 math recommended, 3 science required, 4 science recommended, 3 science lab required, 4 science lab recommended, 2 foreign language required, 4 foreign language recommended, 2 social studies required, 2 social studies recommended, 1 history required, 2 history recommended. **Transfer Admission Requirements:** *Items required:* high school transcript, college transcript, essay, standardized test score, statement of good standing from prior school. Minimum college GPA of 3.0 required. Lowest grade transferable C. **General Admission Information:** Application fee $35. Priority application deadline January 15. Regular application deadline February 1. Nonfall registration accepted. Admission may be deferred for a maximum of 1 year. Credit offered for CEEB Advanced Placement tests.

COSTS AND FINANCIAL AID

In-state tuition $4,089. Out-of-state tuition $11,122. Room & board $5,318. Average book expense $800. **Required Forms and Deadlines:** FAFSA. Priority filing deadline March 1. **Notification of Awards:** Applicants will be notified of awards on or about April 15. **Types of Aid:** *Need-based scholarships/grants:* Pell, SEOG, state scholarships/grants, private scholarships, the school's own gift aid. *Loans:* FFEL Subsidized Stafford, FFEL Unsubsidized Stafford, FFEL PLUS, Federal Perkins. **Student Employment:** Federal Work-Study Program available. Institutional employment available. Off-campus job opportunities are excellent. **Financial Aid Statistics:** 44% freshmen, 39% undergrads receive some form of aid. Average freshman grant $2,753. Average freshman loan $1,894. Average income from on-campus job $1,500. **Financial Aid Phone:** 800-468-5614.

MARYGROVE COLLEGE

8425 West McNichols R, Detroit, MI 48221-2599
Phone: 313-927-1240 **E-mail:** info@marygrove.edu **CEEB Code:** 1452
Fax: 313-927-1345 **Web:** www.marygrove.edu **ACT Code:** 2024

This private school, which is affiliated with the Roman Catholic Church, was founded in 1905. It has a 50-acre campus.

STUDENTS AND FACULTY

Enrollment: 866. **Student Body:** Male 18%, female 82%, out-of-state 2%, international 2%. **Ethnic Representation:** African American 78%, Caucasian 6%, Hispanic 1%. **Retention and Graduation:** 71% freshmen return for sophomore year. 3% freshmen graduate within 4 years. 30% grads go on to further study within 1 year. **Faculty:** Student/faculty ratio 15:1. 71 full-time faculty, 66% hold PhDs. 100% faculty teach undergrads.

ACADEMICS

Degrees: Associate's, bachelor's, certificate, master's, post-bachelor's certificate. **Academic Requirements:** General education including some course work in arts/fine arts, English (including composition), history, humanities, mathematics, philosophy, sciences (biological or physical), social science. **Classes:** Under 10 students in an average class. **Majors with Highest Enrollment:** Business/commerce, general; computer and information sciences, general; social work. **Disciplines with Highest Percentage of Degrees Awarded:** Social sciences and history 23%, computer and information sciences 11%, business/marketing 10%, English 10%, mathematics 8%. **Special Study Options:** Cooperative (work-study) program, distance learning, double major, honors program, independent study, student-designed major, study abroad, teacher certification program.

FACILITIES

Housing: Coed. **Library Holdings:** 76,292 bound volumes. 487 periodicals. 65,650 microforms. 2,132 audiovisuals. **Special Academic Facilities/Equipment:** conference center, chapel, theatre, art gallery. **Computers:** School-owned computers available for student use.

EXTRACURRICULARS

Activities: Choral groups, music ensembles. **Organizations:** 17 registered organizations, 6 honor societies.

ADMISSIONS

Selectivity Rating: 71 (of 100). **Freshman Academic Profile:** Average high school GPA 2.7. 10% in top 10% of high school class, 75% in top 25% of high school class, 100% in top 50% of high school class. 80% from public high schools. Average ACT 17, ACT middle 50% range 15-20. TOEFL required of all international applicants, minimum TOEFL 520. **Basis for Candidate Selection:** *Important factors considered include:* character/personal qualities, interview, secondary school record, standardized test scores, talent/ability. *Other factors considered include:* extracurricular activities, recommendations, volunteer work, work experience. **Freshman Admission Requirements:** High school diploma or GED is required. *Academic units required/recommended:* 25 total recommended; 8 English recommended, 4 math recommended, 1 science recommended, 1 foreign language recommended, 4 social studies recommended, 5 history recommended. **Freshman Admission Statistics:** 256 applied, 25% accepted, 62% of those accepted enrolled. **Transfer Admission Requirements:** *Items required:* college transcript, statement of good standing from prior school. Minimum college GPA of 2.7 required. Lowest grade transferable C. **General Admission Information:** Application fee $25. Priority application deadline August 15. Regular application deadline August 15. Nonfall registration accepted. Admission may be deferred for a maximum of 1 year. Credit and/or placement offered for CEEB Advanced Placement tests.

COSTS AND FINANCIAL AID

Tuition $11,500. Room & board $5,800. Required fees $250. Average book expense $1,180. **Required Forms and Deadlines:** FAFSA and institution's own financial aid form. No deadline for regular filing. Priority filing deadline March 15. **Notification of Awards:** Applicants will be notified of awards on a rolling basis beginning on or about May 1. **Types of Aid:** *Need-based scholarships/grants:* Pell, state scholarships/grants, private scholarships. *Loans:* Direct Subsidized Stafford, Direct Unsubsidized Stafford, Direct PLUS, FFEL Subsidized Stafford, FFEL Unsubsidized Stafford, FFEL PLUS, Federal Perkins, state loans. **Student Employment:** Federal Work-Study Program available. Off-campus job opportunities are good. **Financial Aid Statistics:** Average freshman grant $7,200. Average freshman loan $2,000. Average income from on-campus job $2,700. **Financial Aid Phone:** 313-927-1200.

MARYLAND INSTITUTE COLLEGE OF ART

1300 Mount Royal Avenue, Baltimore, MD 21217
Phone: 410-225-2222 **E-mail:** admissions@mica.edu **CEEB Code:** 5399
Fax: 410-225-2337 **Web:** www.mica.edu **ACT Code:** 1710

This private school was founded in 1826. It has a 12-acre campus.

STUDENTS AND FACULTY

Enrollment: 1,201. **Student Body:** Male 38%, female 62%, out-of-state 76%, international 5%. **Ethnic Representation:** African American 4%, Asian 8%, Caucasian 72%, Hispanic 4%. **Retention and Graduation:** 86% freshmen return for sophomore year. 61% freshmen graduate within 4 years. 20% grads go on to further study within 1 year. **Faculty:** Student/faculty ratio 10:1. 101 full-time faculty, 72% hold PhDs. 86% faculty teach undergrads.

ACADEMICS

Degrees: Bachelor's, master's, post-bachelor's certificate. **Academic Requirements:** General education including some course work in arts/fine arts, English (including composition), history, humanities, sciences (biological or physical), social science. **Classes:** 10-19 students in an average class. **Majors with Highest Enrollment:** Intermedia/multimedia; painting; graphic design. **Disciplines with Highest Percentage of Degrees Awarded:** Visual and performing arts 94%, education 6%. **Special Study Options:** Accelerated program, cross registration, distance learning, double major, dual enrollment, student exchange program (domestic), independent study, internships, student-designed major, study abroad, teacher certification program. Cooperative exchange programs with Johns Hopkins University, Goucher College, The Peabody Conservatory of Music, University of Baltimore, Loyola College, Notre Dame College, University of Maryland Baltimore County, Morgan State University, Baltimore Hebrew College, and Towson University.

FACILITIES

Housing: Coed, apartments for married students, apartments for single students, housing for disabled students, housing for international students. **Library Holdings:** 53,000 bound volumes. 305 periodicals. 0 microforms. 4,600 audiovisuals. **Special Academic Facilities/Equipment:** There are seven art galleries open to the public year-round featuring work by MICA faculty, students, and nationally/internationally known artists; a nature library; and an extensive slide library containing over 200,000 slides. **Computers:** *Recommended operating system:* Mac. School-owned computers available for student use.

EXTRACURRICULARS

Activities: Literary magazine, student government, student newspaper, student-run film society. **Organizations:** 25 registered organizations, 1 religious organization.

ADMISSIONS

Selectivity Rating: 84 (of 100). **Freshman Academic Profile:** Average high school GPA 3.5. 28% in top 10% of high school class, 50% in top 25% of high school class, 86% in top 50% of high school class. 86% from public high schools. Average SAT I Math 560, SAT I Math middle 50% range 500-610. Average SAT I Verbal 580, SAT I Verbal middle 50% range 520-640. TOEFL required of all international applicants, minimum TOEFL 550. **Basis for Candidate Selection:** *Very important factors considered include:* secondary school record, talent/ability. *Important factors considered include:* class rank, essays, extracurricular activities, interview, standardized test scores. *Other factors considered include:* alumni/ae relation, character/personal qualities, minority status, recommendations, volunteer work. **Freshman Admission Requirements:** High school diploma or GED is required. *Academic units required/ recommended:* 24 total required; 24 total recommended; 4 English required, 4 English recommended, 2 math required, 3 math recommended, 2 science required, 3 science recommended, 1 science lab required, 1 science lab recommended, 4 social studies required, 4 social studies recommended, 3 history required, 4 history recommended, 6 elective required. **Freshman Admission Statistics:** 1,917 applied, 43% accepted, 34% of those accepted enrolled. **Transfer Admission Requirements:** *Items required:* high school transcript, college transcript, essay. Minimum college GPA of 2.8 required. Lowest grade transferable C. **General Admission Information:** Application fee $50. Priority application deadline January 15. Early decision application deadline November 15. Regular application deadline March 1. Nonfall registration accepted. Admission may be deferred for a maximum of 1 year. Credit and/or placement offered for CEEB Advanced Placement tests.

COSTS AND FINANCIAL AID

Tuition $19,800. Room & board $6,540. Required fees $250. Average book expense $1,400. **Required Forms and Deadlines:** FAFSA and institution's own financial aid form. Financial aid filing deadline March 1. **Notification of Awards:** Applicants will be notified of awards on or about April 15. **Types of Aid:** *Need-based scholarships/grants:* Pell, SEOG, state scholarships/grants, private scholarships, the school's own gift aid. *Loans:* FFEL Subsidized Stafford, FFEL Unsubsidized Stafford, FFEL PLUS, Federal Perkins. **Student Employment:** Federal Work-Study Program available. Institutional employment available. Off-campus job opportunities are excellent. **Financial Aid Statistics:** Average freshman grant $4,900. Average freshman loan $2,625. Average income from on-campus job $1,100. **Financial Aid Phone:** 410-225-2285.

MARYLHURST UNIVERSITY

PO Box 261, Marylhurst, OR 97036
Phone: 503-699-6268 **E-mail:** admissions@marylhurst.edu **CEEB Code:** 440
Fax: 503-636-9526 **Web:** www.marylhurst.edu **ACT Code:** 3470

This private school, which is affiliated with the Roman Catholic Church, was founded in 1893. It has a 68-acre campus.

STUDENTS AND FACULTY

Enrollment: 672. **Student Body:** Male 22%, female 78%, out-of-state 2%. **Retention and Graduation:** 50% freshmen return for sophomore year. 17% freshmen graduate within 4 years. **Faculty:** Student/faculty ratio 7:1. 31 full-time faculty, 54% hold PhDs. 100% faculty teach undergrads.

ACADEMICS

Degrees: Bachelor's, certificate, master's. **Academic Requirements:** General education including some course work in arts/fine arts, computer literacy, English (including composition), history, humanities, mathematics, philosophy, sciences (biological or physical), social science, interdisciplinary and integrated learning. **Classes:** Under 10 students in an average class. **Disciplines with Highest Percentage of Degrees Awarded:** Communications/communication technologies 25%, business/marketing 21%, visual and performing arts 15%, liberal arts/general studies 15%, interdisciplinary studies 10%. **Special Study Options:** Cross registration, distance learning, double major, dual enrollment, English as a second language, independent study, internships, student-designed major, study abroad, weekend college, Online BS (Business Administration and Organizational Communication) and MBA programs.

FACILITIES

Housing: Temporary housing. **Library Holdings:** 93,418 bound volumes. 564 periodicals. 216 microforms. 2,492 audiovisuals. **Special Academic Facilities/ Equipment:** "Art Gym," Streff Gallery. **Computers:** School-owned computers available for student use.

EXTRACURRICULARS

Activities: Choral groups, literary magazine, music ensembles, symphony orchestra. **Organizations:** 2 registered organizations, 1 religious organization.

ADMISSIONS

Selectivity Rating: 63 (of 100). **Freshman Academic Profile:** 90% from public high schools. TOEFL required of all international applicants, minimum TOEFL 550. **Freshman Admission Requirements:** High school diploma or GED is required. **Freshman Admission Statistics:** applied. **Transfer Admission Requirements:** *Items required:* high school transcript, college transcript. Lowest grade transferable C-. **General Admission Information:** Application fee $20. Nonfall registration accepted. Admission may be deferred for a maximum of 1 year. Credit and/or placement offered for CEEB Advanced Placement tests.

COSTS AND FINANCIAL AID

Tuition $12,690. Room & board $25. Required fees $270. Average book expense $900. **Required Forms and Deadlines:** FAFSA and institution's own financial aid form. No deadline for regular filing. **Notification of Awards:** Applicants will be notified of awards on a rolling basis beginning on or about April 15. **Types of Aid:** *Need-based scholarships/grants:* Pell, SEOG, state scholarships/grants, private scholarships, the school's own gift aid. *Loans:* FFEL Subsidized Stafford, FFEL Unsubsidized Stafford, FFEL PLUS, Federal Perkins. **Student Employment:** Federal Work-Study Program available. Institutional employment available. Off-campus job opportunities are fair. **Financial Aid Statistics:** 61% freshmen, 76% undergrads receive some form of aid. Average freshman grant $6,000. Average freshman loan $4,000. Average income from on-campus job $3,000. **Financial Aid Phone:** 503-699-6253.

MARYMOUNT COLLEGE OF FORDHAM UNIVERSITY

$$$

100 Marymount Avenue, Tarrytown, NY 10591-3798
Phone: 914-323-8295 **E-mail:** admiss@mmc.marymt.edu **CEEB Code:** 2406
Fax: 914-332-7442 **Web:** www.marymt.edu **ACT Code:** 2810

This private school, which is affiliated with the Roman Catholic Church, was founded in 1907. It has a 25-acre campus.

STUDENTS AND FACULTY

Enrollment: 1,061. **Student Body:** Male 3%, female 97%, out-of-state 21%, international 4% (16 countries represented). **Ethnic Representation:** African American 16%, Asian 3%, Caucasian 42%, Hispanic 14%. **Retention and Graduation:** 62% freshmen return for sophomore year. 62% freshmen graduate within 4 years. 25% grads go on to further study within 1 year. 2% grads pursue business degrees. 3% grads pursue law degrees. 2% grads pursue medical degrees. **Faculty:** Student/faculty ratio 12:1. 58 full-time faculty, 86% hold PhDs. 100% faculty teach undergrads.

ACADEMICS

Degrees: Associate's, bachelor's, transfer. **Academic Requirements:** General education including some course work in arts/fine arts, computer literacy, English (including composition), foreign languages, history, mathematics, philosophy, sciences (biological or physical), social science, theology/religious studies. **Classes:** 10-19 students in an average class. 10-19 students in an average lab/discussion section. **Majors with Highest Enrollment:** Business/ commerce, general; elementary education and teaching; psychology, general. **Disciplines with Highest Percentage of Degrees Awarded:** Business/ marketing 25%, education 17%, psychology 10%, visual and performing arts 8%, biological life sciences 7%. **Special Study Options:** Cross registration, distance learning, double major, English as a second language, student exchange program (domestic), honors program, independent study, internships, liberal arts/career combination, student-designed major, study abroad, teacher certification program, weekend college.

FACILITIES

Housing: All-female. **Library Holdings:** 2,492,212 bound volumes. 16,224 periodicals. 3,056,558 microforms. 17,756 audiovisuals. **Special Academic Facilities/Equipment:** Multimedia language and learning lab, CAD lab. **Computers:** *Recommended operating system:* Windows 95. School-owned computers available for student use.

EXTRACURRICULARS

Activities: Choral groups, dance, drama/theater, literary magazine, music ensembles, musical theater, student government, student newspaper, television station, yearbook. **Organizations:** 30 registered organizations, 3 honor societies, 1 religious organization. **Athletics (Intercollegiate):** *Women:* basketball, equestrian, softball, swimming, volleyball.

ADMISSIONS

Selectivity Rating: 65 (of 100). **Freshman Academic Profile:** Average high school GPA 2.8. 6% in top 10% of high school class, 26% in top 25% of high school class, 60% in top 50% of high school class. 79% from public high schools. Average SAT I Math 447, SAT I Math middle 50% range 430-520. Average SAT I Verbal 484, SAT I Verbal middle 50% range 450-552. ACT middle 50% range 18-24. TOEFL required of all international applicants, minimum TOEFL 500. **Basis for Candidate Selection:** *Very important factors considered include:* essays, secondary school record, standardized test scores. *Important factors considered include:* character/personal qualities, extracurricular activities, interview, volunteer work. *Other factors considered include:* alumni/ae relation, class rank, recommendations, talent/ability. **Freshman Admission Requirements:** High school diploma or GED is required. *Academic units required/recommended:* 16 total recommended; 4 English recommended, 3 math recommended, 3 science recommended, 2 science lab recommended, 3 foreign language recommended, 3 social studies recommended, 3 history recommended, 2 elective recommended. **Freshman Admission Statistics:** 1,446 applied, 82% accepted, 22% of those accepted enrolled. **Transfer Admission Requirements:** *Items required:* college transcript, essay. Minimum high school GPA of 2.0 required. Minimum college GPA of 2.0 required. Lowest grade transferable C. **General Admission Information:** Application fee $30. Priority application deadline February 1. Nonfall registration accepted. Admission may be deferred for a maximum of 1 year. Credit and/or placement offered for CEEB Advanced Placement tests.

COSTS AND FINANCIAL AID

Tuition $15,300. Room & board $8,100. Required fees $450. Average book expense $840. **Required Forms and Deadlines:** FAFSA, state aid form and Special circumstances forms. No deadline for regular filing. Priority filing deadline March 15. **Notification of Awards:** Applicants will be notified of awards on a rolling basis beginning on or about March 15. **Types of Aid:** *Need-based scholarships/grants:* Pell, SEOG, state scholarships/grants, private scholarships, the school's own gift aid. *Loans:* Direct Subsidized Stafford, Direct Unsubsidized Stafford, Direct PLUS, FFEL Subsidized Stafford, FFEL Unsubsidized Stafford, FFEL PLUS, Federal Perkins, alternative loans. **Student Employment:** Federal Work-Study Program available. Institutional employment available. Off-campus job opportunities are excellent. **Financial Aid Statistics:** 81% freshmen, 66% undergrads receive some form of aid. Average freshman grant $15,085. Average freshman loan $4,079. Average income from on-campus job $1,200. **Financial Aid Phone:** 914-332-8345.

MARYMOUNT MANHATTAN COLLEGE

221 East 71st Street, New York, NY 10021
Phone: 212-517-0430 **E-mail:** admissions@mmm.edu **CEEB Code:** 2405
Fax: 212-517-0465 **Web:** www.marymount.mmm.edu **ACT Code:** 2810

This private school was founded in 1936. It has a 1-acre campus.

STUDENTS AND FACULTY

Enrollment: 2,497. **Student Body:** Male 21%, female 79%, out-of-state 35%, international 5% (60 countries represented). **Ethnic Representation:** African American 23%, Asian 5%, Caucasian 54%, Hispanic 17%. **Retention and Graduation:** 73% freshmen return for sophomore year. 45% grads go on to further study within 1 year. 17% grads pursue business degrees. 10% grads pursue law degrees. 10% grads pursue medical degrees. **Faculty:** Student/faculty ratio 18:1. 65 full-time faculty, 63% hold PhDs. 100% faculty teach undergrads.

ACADEMICS

Degrees: Bachelor's, certificate. **Academic Requirements:** General education including some course work in arts/fine arts, English (including composition), humanities, mathematics, sciences (biological or physical), social science. **Classes:** 10-19 students in an average class. **Disciplines with Highest Percentage of Degrees Awarded:** Visual and performing arts 30%, business/marketing 23%, communications/communication technologies 14%, social sciences and history 12%, psychology 9%. **Special Study Options:** Accelerated program, distance learning, double major, dual enrollment, English as a second language, student exchange program (domestic), honors program, independent study, study abroad, teacher certification program.

FACILITIES

Housing: Coed. **Library Holdings:** 100,535 bound volumes. 600 periodicals. 150 microforms. 3,500 audiovisuals. **Special Academic Facilities/Equipment:** Gallery, communications and learning center, theatre, media center, college skills center, mathematics lab, Samuel Freeman science center, communication arts multimedia suite. **Computers:** School-owned computers available for student use.

EXTRACURRICULARS

Activities: Choral groups, dance, drama/theater, literary magazine, musical theater, opera, radio station, student government, student newspaper, yearbook. **Organizations:** 30 registered organizations, 5 honor societies.

ADMISSIONS

Selectivity Rating: 70 (of 100). **Freshman Academic Profile:** Average high school GPA 3.4. 25% in top 10% of high school class, 75% in top 25% of high school class, 89% in top 50% of high school class. 70% from public high schools. Average SAT I Math 510, SAT I Math middle 50% range 400-550. Average SAT I Verbal 540, SAT I Verbal middle 50% range 430-600. Average ACT 25. TOEFL required of all international applicants, minimum TOEFL 500. **Basis for Candidate Selection:** *Very important factors considered include:* secondary school record. *Important factors considered include:* character/personal qualities, class rank, extracurricular activities, geographical residence, interview, recommendations, standardized test scores, talent/ability. *Other factors considered include:* alumni/ae relation, essays, volunteer work, work experience. **Freshman Admission Requirements:** High school diploma or GED is required. *Academic units required/recommended:* 16 total required; 4 English required, 3 math required, 1 science required, 3 science recommended, 1 science lab required, 3 foreign language recommended, 3 social studies required, 4 elective required. **Freshman Admission Statistics:** 1,643 applied, 65% accepted, 45% of those accepted enrolled. **Transfer Admission Requirements:** *Items required:* high school transcript, college transcript, statement of good standing from prior school. Minimum college GPA of 2.0 required. Lowest grade transferable C-. **General Admission Information:** Application fee $50. Priority application deadline March 15. Early decision application deadline November 1. Nonfall registration accepted. Admission may be deferred for a maximum of 1 year. Credit and/or placement offered for CEEB Advanced Placement tests.

COSTS AND FINANCIAL AID

Tuition $14,200. Room & board $8,500. Required fees $495. Average book expense $600. **Required Forms and Deadlines:** FAFSA and state aid form. Priority filing deadline February 15. **Notification of Awards:** Applicants will be notified of awards on a rolling basis beginning on or about March 15. **Types of Aid:** *Need-based scholarships/grants:* Pell, SEOG, state scholarships/grants, private scholarships, the school's own gift aid. *Loans:* FFEL Subsidized Stafford, FFEL Unsubsidized Stafford, FFEL PLUS. **Student Employment:** Federal Work-Study Program available. Institutional employment available. Off-campus job opportunities are excellent. **Financial Aid Statistics:** 51% freshmen, 65% undergrads receive some form of aid. Average freshman grant $3,500. Average freshman loan $2,611. Average income from on-campus job $2,000. **Financial Aid Phone:** 212-517-0480.

MARYMOUNT UNIVERSITY

2807 North Glebe Road, Arlington, VA 22207
Phone: 703-284-1500 **E-mail:** admissions@marymount.edu **CEEB Code:** 5405
Fax: 703-522-0349 **Web:** www.marymount.edu **ACT Code:** 4378

This private school, which is affiliated with the Roman Catholic Church, was founded in 1950. It has a 21-acre campus.

STUDENTS AND FACULTY

Enrollment: 2,145. **Student Body:** Male 27%, female 73%, out-of-state 44%, international 11%. **Ethnic Representation:** African American 18%, Asian 9%, Caucasian 50%, Hispanic 10%. **Retention and Graduation:** 74% freshmen return for sophomore year. 50% freshmen graduate within 4 years. **Faculty:** Student/faculty ratio 13:1. 128 full-time faculty, 84% hold PhDs. 83% faculty teach undergrads.

ACADEMICS

Degrees: Associate's, bachelor's, certificate, master's, post-bachelor's certificate, post-master's certificate, terminal. **Academic Requirements:** General education including some course work in English (including composition), history, humanities, mathematics, philosophy, sciences (biological or physical), social science. **Classes:** 10-19 students in an average class. Under 10 students in an average lab/discussion section. **Majors with Highest Enrollment:** Psychology, general; interior design; nursing/registered nurse training (RN, ASN, BSN, MSN). **Disciplines with Highest Percentage of Degrees Awarded:** Business/marketing 19%, visual and performing arts 15%, computer and information sciences 12%, social sciences and history 11%, liberal arts/general studies 10%. **Special Study Options:** Cross registration, double major,

English as a second language, independent study, internships, student-designed major, study abroad, teacher certification program.

FACILITIES

Housing: Coed, all-female, all-male, coed dorms with separate floors for men and women. **Library Holdings:** 187,097 bound volumes. 1,048 periodicals. 315,786 microforms. 908 audiovisuals. **Special Academic Facilities/ Equipment:** Art gallery, learning resource center, audiovisual center and studio, computer labs, virology research lab. **Computers:** School-owned computers available for student use.

EXTRACURRICULARS

Activities: Choral groups, dance, drama/theater, literary magazine, student government, student newspaper, yearbook. **Organizations:** 25 registered organizations, 8 honor societies, 1 religious organization. **Athletics (Intercollegiate):** *Men:* basketball, golf, lacrosse, soccer, swimming. *Women:* basketball, lacrosse, soccer, swimming, volleyball.

ADMISSIONS

Selectivity Rating: 67 (of 100). **Freshman Academic Profile:** Average high school GPA 3.0. 6% in top 10% of high school class, 28% in top 25% of high school class, 64% in top 50% of high school class. 64% from public high schools. Average SAT I Math 496, SAT I Math middle 50% range 430-540. Average SAT I Verbal 499, SAT I Verbal middle 50% range 440-550. Average ACT 20, ACT middle 50% range 16-24. TOEFL required of all international applicants, minimum TOEFL 500. **Basis for Candidate Selection:** *Very important factors considered include:* secondary school record, standardized test scores. *Important factors considered include:* class rank, extracurricular activities, recommendations, talent/ability, volunteer work, work experience. *Other factors considered include:* alumni/ae relation, character/personal qualities, essays, interview. **Freshman Admission Requirements:** High school diploma or GED is required. *Academic units required/recommended:* 15 total required; 4 English recommended, 3 math recommended, 2 science recommended, 3 foreign language recommended, 3 social studies recommended. **Freshman Admission Statistics:** 1,461 applied, 87% accepted, 29% of those accepted enrolled. **Transfer Admission Requirements:** *Items required:* college transcript. Minimum high school GPA of 2.5 required. Minimum college GPA of 2.0 required. Lowest grade transferable C. **General Admission Information:** Application fee $35. Priority application deadline May 1. Nonfall registration accepted. Admission may be deferred for a maximum of 1 year. Credit offered for CEEB Advanced Placement tests.

COSTS AND FINANCIAL AID

Tuition $15,600. Room & board $6,920. Required fees $132. Average book expense $500. **Required Forms and Deadlines:** FAFSA and state aid form. No deadline for regular filing. Priority filing deadline March 1. **Notification of Awards:** Applicants will be notified of awards on a rolling basis beginning on or about March 15. **Types of Aid:** *Need-based scholarships/grants:* Pell, SEOG, state scholarships/grants, private scholarships, the school's own gift aid, Federal Nursing. *Loans:* Direct Subsidized Stafford, Direct Unsubsidized Stafford, FFEL PLUS, Federal Perkins. **Student Employment:** Federal Work-Study Program available. Institutional employment available. Off-campus job opportunities are good. **Financial Aid Statistics:** 64% freshmen, 58% undergrads receive some form of aid. Average freshman grant $10,008. Average freshman loan $6,859. Average income from on-campus job $2,400. **Financial Aid Phone:** 703-284-1530.

MARYVILLE COLLEGE

502 East Lamar Alexander Parkway, Maryville, TN 37804-5907
Phone: 865-981-8092 **E-mail:** admissions@maryvillecollege.edu **CEEB Code:** 1454
Fax: 865-981-8005 **Web:** www.maryvillecollege.edu **ACT Code:** 3988

This private school, which is affiliated with the Presbyterian Church, was founded in 1819. It has a 370-acre campus.

STUDENTS AND FACULTY

Enrollment: 1,020. **Student Body:** Male 41%, female 59%, out-of-state 23%, international 3% (22 countries represented). **Ethnic Representation:** African American 7%, Asian 1%, Caucasian 89%, Hispanic 1%, Native American 1%. **Retention and Graduation:** 67% freshmen return for sophomore year. 52% freshmen graduate within 4 years. 45% grads go on to further study within 1 year. 8% grads pursue business degrees. 6% grads pursue law degrees. 6% grads pursue medical degrees. **Faculty:** Student/faculty ratio 12:1. 64 full-time faculty, 92% hold PhDs. 100% faculty teach undergrads.

ACADEMICS

Degrees: Bachelor's. **Academic Requirements:** General education including some course work in arts/fine arts, computer literacy, English (including composition), foreign languages, history, humanities, mathematics, philosophy, sciences (biological or physical), social science, interdisciplinary courses, seminars, religion. **Classes:** 10-19 students in an average class. 10-19 students in an average lab/discussion section. **Majors with Highest Enrollment:** Education, general; business administration/management; biology/biological sciences, general. **Disciplines with Highest Percentage of Degrees Awarded:** Business/marketing 22%, education 19%, social sciences and history 12%, computer and information sciences 8%, biological life sciences 8%. **Special Study Options:** Double major, English as a second language, honors program, independent study, internships, liberal arts/career combination, student-designed major, study abroad, teacher certification program.

FACILITIES

Housing: Coed, all-female, all-male, apartments for single students, housing for disabled students, special-interest housing. **Library Holdings:** 103,912 bound volumes. 7,190 microforms. 703 audiovisuals. **Special Academic Facilities/Equipment:** Art gallery, theatre, greenhouse. **Computers:** School-owned computers available for student use.

EXTRACURRICULARS

Activities: Choral groups, concert band, dance, drama/theater, jazz band, literary magazine, music ensembles, musical theater, radio station, student government, student newspaper, symphony orchestra, yearbook. **Organizations:** 39 registered organizations, 15 honor societies, 7 religious organizations. **Athletics (Intercollegiate):** *Men:* baseball, basketball, cross-country, equestrian, football, soccer, tennis. *Women:* basketball, cross-country, equestrian, soccer, softball, tennis, volleyball.

ADMISSIONS

Selectivity Rating: 71 (of 100). **Freshman Academic Profile:** Average high school GPA 3.5. 31% in top 10% of high school class, 63% in top 25% of high school class, 90% in top 50% of high school class. 90% from public high schools. Average SAT I Math 536, SAT I Math middle 50% range 480-590. Average SAT I Verbal 532, SAT I Verbal middle 50% range 470-590. Average ACT 24, ACT middle 50% range 21-27. TOEFL required of all international applicants, minimum TOEFL 525. **Basis for Candidate Selection:** *Very important factors considered include:* class rank, secondary school record. *Important factors considered include:* character/personal qualities, essays, interview, recommendations, standardized test scores. *Other factors considered include:* extracurricular activities, talent/ability, volunteer work. **Freshman Admission Requirements:** High school diploma or GED is required. *Academic units required/recommended:* 15 total required; 4 English required, 3 math required, 2 science required, 1 science lab required, 2 foreign language required, 2 social studies required, 1 history recommended, 1 elective required. **Freshman Admission Statistics:** 1,456 applied, 80% accepted, 21% of those accepted enrolled. **Transfer Admission Requirements:** *Items required:* college transcript, statement of good standing from prior school. Minimum high school GPA of 2.5 required. Minimum college GPA of 2.0 required. Lowest grade transferable C. **General Admission Information:** Application fee $25. Early decision application deadline November 15. Regular application deadline March 1. Nonfall registration accepted. Admission may be deferred for a maximum of 1 year. Credit and/or placement offered for CEEB Advanced Placement tests.

COSTS AND FINANCIAL AID

Tuition $16,985. Room & board $5,650. Required fees $475. Average book expense $600. **Required Forms and Deadlines:** FAFSA. No deadline for regular filing. Priority filing deadline March 1. **Notification of Awards:** Applicants will be notified of awards on a rolling basis. **Types of Aid:** *Need-based scholarships/grants:* Pell, SEOG, state scholarships/grants, private scholarships, the school's own gift aid. *Loans:* FFEL Subsidized Stafford, FFEL Unsubsidized Stafford, FFEL PLUS, Federal Perkins, state loans, college/university loans from institutional funds. **Student Employment:** Federal Work-Study Program available. Institutional employment available. Off-campus job opportunities are good. **Financial Aid Statistics:** 83% freshmen, 77% undergrads receive some form of aid. Average freshman grant $11,482. Average freshman loan $4,373. Average income from on-campus job $1,200. **Financial Aid Phone:** 865-981-8100.

MARYVILLE UNIVERSITY OF SAINT LOUIS

13550 Conway Road, St. Louis, MO 63141-7299
Phone: 314-529-9350 **E-mail:** admissions@maryville.edu **CEEB Code:** 6399
Fax: 314-529-9927 **Web:** www.maryville.edu **ACT Code:** 2326

This private school was founded in 1872. It has a 130-acre campus.

STUDENTS AND FACULTY

Enrollment: 2,710. **Student Body:** Male 26%, female 74%, out-of-state 8%, international 2% (38 countries represented). **Ethnic Representation:** African American 6%, Asian 1%, Caucasian 68%, Hispanic 1%. **Retention and Graduation:** 79% freshmen return for sophomore year. **Faculty:** Student/faculty ratio 13:1. 87 full-time faculty, 88% hold PhDs. 100% faculty teach undergrads.

ACADEMICS

Degrees: Bachelor's, master's. **Academic Requirements:** General education including some course work in arts/fine arts, English (including composition), humanities, mathematics, sciences (biological or physical), social science, multicultural studies. **Classes:** 10-19 students in an average class. Under 10 students in an average lab/discussion section. **Majors with Highest Enrollment:** Physical therapy/therapist; business administration/management; management information systems, general. **Disciplines with Highest Percentage of Degrees Awarded:** Business/marketing 40%, health professions and related sciences 26%, psychology 11%, education 5%, visual and performing arts 5%. **Special Study Options:** Accelerated program, cooperative (work-study) program, cross registration, distance learning, double major, dual enrollment, English as a second language, honors program, independent study, internships, liberal arts/career combination, student-designed major, study abroad, teacher certification program, weekend college, Prior Learning Assessment Program.

FACILITIES

Housing: Coed, apartments for single students. **Library Holdings:** 205,512 bound volumes. 787 periodicals. 487,824 microforms. 10,933 audiovisuals. **Special Academic Facilities/Equipment:** University Center, art galleries, auditorium, chapel, observatory, teaching lab, clinical labs, art and design labs, videoconferencing facility with downlinking and electronic multimedia capability for presentations. **Computers:** *Recommended operating system:* Windows 95, 98, NT,2000, XP. School-owned computers available for student use.

EXTRACURRICULARS

Activities: Choral groups, dance, drama/theater, literary magazine, music ensembles, student government, student newspaper. **Organizations:** 30 registered organizations, 8 honor societies, 4 religious organizations. **Athletics (Intercollegiate):** *Men:* baseball, basketball, cheerleading, cross-country, golf, soccer, tennis. *Women:* basketball, cheerleading, cross-country, soccer, softball, tennis, volleyball.

ADMISSIONS

Selectivity Rating: 73 (of 100). **Freshman Academic Profile:** Average high school GPA 3.2. 21% in top 10% of high school class, 44% in top 25% of high school class, 71% in top 50% of high school class. 77% from public high schools. Average ACT 23, ACT middle 50% range 20-25. TOEFL required of all international applicants, minimum TOEFL 500. **Basis for Candidate Selection:** *Very important factors considered include:* class rank, secondary school record, standardized test scores. *Important factors considered include:* recommendations. *Other factors considered include:* character/personal qualities, essays, extracurricular activities, interview, minority status, talent/ability, volunteer work. **Freshman Admission Requirements:** High school diploma or GED is required. *Academic units required/recommended:* 22 total required; 4 English required, 3 math required, 2 science required, 3 foreign language recommended, 2 social studies required, 8 elective required. **Freshman Admission Statistics:** 1,007 applied, 76% accepted, 40% of those accepted enrolled. **Transfer Admission Requirements:** *Items required:* college transcript. Minimum high school GPA of 2.5 required. Minimum college GPA of 2.0 required. Lowest grade transferable C-. **General Admission Information:** Application fee $25. Regular application deadline August 15. Nonfall registration accepted. Admission may be deferred for a maximum of 1 year. Credit offered for CEEB Advanced Placement tests.

COSTS AND FINANCIAL AID

Required Forms and Deadlines: FAFSA and institution's own financial aid form. No deadline for regular filing. Priority filing deadline April 1. **Notification of Awards:** Applicants will be notified of awards on a rolling basis. **Types of Aid:** *Need-based scholarships/grants:* Pell, SEOG, state scholarships/grants, private scholarships, the school's own gift aid. *Loans:* Direct Subsidized Stafford, Direct Unsubsidized Stafford, Direct PLUS, Federal Perkins, Sallie Mae Signature, Keybank, TERI, Norwest, CitiAssist. **Student Employment:** Federal Work-Study Program available. Institutional employment available. Off-campus job opportunities are good. **Financial Aid Statistics:** 69% freshmen, 68% undergrads receive some form of aid. **Financial Aid Phone:** 314-529-9360.

MARYWOOD UNIVERSITY

2300 Adams Avenue, Scranton, PA 18509-1598
Phone: 570-348-6234 **E-mail:** ugadm@ac.marywood.edu **CEEB Code:** 2407
Fax: 570-961-4763 **Web:** www.marywood.edu **ACT Code:** 3626

This private school, which is affiliated with the Roman Catholic Church, was founded in 1915. It has a 115-acre campus.

STUDENTS AND FACULTY

Enrollment: 1,750. **Student Body:** Male 27%, female 73%, out-of-state 21%, international 1%. **Ethnic Representation:** African American 1%, Asian 1%, Caucasian 91%, Hispanic 2%. **Retention and Graduation:** 78% freshmen return for sophomore year. 41% freshmen graduate within 4 years. 23% grads go on to further study within 1 year. 3% grads pursue business degrees. 2% grads pursue law degrees. **Faculty:** Student/faculty ratio 12:1. 135 full-time faculty, 82% hold PhDs. 70% faculty teach undergrads.

ACADEMICS

Degrees: Associate's, bachelor's, certificate, doctoral, master's, post-bachelor's certificate, post-master's certificate, terminal. **Academic Requirements:** General education including some course work in arts/fine arts, English (including composition), foreign languages, history, humanities, mathematics, philosophy, sciences (biological or physical), social science, speech, phys. ed., ethics/religious studies. **Classes:** 10-19 students in an average class. **Majors with Highest Enrollment:** Business administration/management; visual and performing arts, general; elementary education and teaching. **Disciplines with Highest Percentage of Degrees Awarded:** Education 23%, health professions and related sciences 20%, visual and performing arts 12%, business/marketing 9%, psychology 7%. **Special Study Options:** Accelerated program, cross registration, distance learning, double major, dual enrollment, English as a second language, honors program, independent study, internships, student-designed major, study abroad, teacher certification program.

FACILITIES

Housing: Coed, all-female, all-male, apartments for single students, housing for disabled students, housing for international students, Special-interest Housing. **Library Holdings:** 217,286 bound volumes. 881 periodicals. 346,552 microforms. 44,318 audiovisuals. **Special Academic Facilities/Equipment:** Mahady Gallery, Suraci Gallery, Performing Arts Center, O'Neill Center for Healthy Families, Insalaco Studio Arts Center, Marywood University Arboretum, curriculum lab, electronic learning labs, broadcast studios, instructional media lab, interactive video lab, computerized editing facility, center for natural and health sciences, psycho-physiology experimental lab, psychology/education research lab, science multimedia lab, language lab, center for justice and peace, on-campus preschool and day care, video teleconferencing lab. **Computers:** School-owned computers available for student use.

EXTRACURRICULARS

Activities: Choral groups, dance, drama/theater, jazz band, literary magazine, music ensembles, musical theater, radio station, student government, student newspaper, television station. **Organizations:** 58 registered organizations, 23 honor societies, 1 religious organization, 1 fraternity (2% men join), 1 sorority (2% women join). **Athletics (Intercollegiate):** *Men:* baseball, basketball, cross-country, soccer, tennis. *Women:* basketball, cross-country, field hockey, soccer, softball, tennis, volleyball.

ADMISSIONS

Selectivity Rating: 74 (of 100). **Freshman Academic Profile:** Average high school GPA 3.3. 15% in top 10% of high school class, 40% in top 25% of high school class, 76% in top 50% of high school class. Average SAT I Math 506, SAT I Math middle 50% range 445-555. Average SAT I Verbal 525, SAT I Verbal middle 50% range 470-570. Average ACT 21, ACT middle 50% range 18-24. TOEFL required of all international applicants, minimum TOEFL 500. **Basis for Candidate Selection:** *Very important factors considered include:* character/personal qualities, class rank, secondary school record, standardized test scores. *Important factors considered include:* interview, talent/ability. *Other factors considered include:* essays, extracurricular activities, recommendations, volunteer work. **Freshman Admission Requirements:** High school diploma or GED is required. *Academic units required/recommended:* 16 total required;

4 English required, 2 math required, 1 science required, 1 science lab required, 3 social studies required, 6 elective required. **Freshman Admission Statistics:** 1,307 applied, 77% accepted, 36% of those accepted enrolled. **Transfer Admission Requirements:** *Items required:* high school transcript, college transcript. Minimum college GPA of 2.5 required. Lowest grade transferable C. **General Admission Information:** Application fee $25. Nonfall registration accepted. Admission may be deferred for a maximum of 1 year. Credit and/or placement offered for CEEB Advanced Placement tests.

COSTS AND FINANCIAL AID

Tuition $18,560. Room & board $8,134. Required fees $740. Average book expense $700. **Required Forms and Deadlines:** FAFSA and institution's own financial aid form. No deadline for regular filing. **Notification of Awards:** Applicants will be notified of awards on a rolling basis beginning on or about February 15. **Types of Aid:** *Need-based scholarships/grants:* Pell, SEOG, state scholarships/grants, private scholarships, the school's own gift aid. *Loans:* FFEL Subsidized Stafford, FFEL Unsubsidized Stafford, FFEL PLUS, Federal Perkins, state loans, alternative loan programs. **Student Employment:** Federal Work-Study Program available. Institutional employment available. Off-campus job opportunities are good. **Financial Aid Statistics:** 95% freshmen, 85% undergrads receive some form of aid. Average freshman grant $12,920. Average freshman loan $2,977. **Financial Aid Phone:** 570-348-6225.

MASSACHUSETTS COLLEGE OF ART

621 Huntington Avenue, Boston, MA 02115
Phone: 617-879-7222 **E-mail:** admissions@massart.edu **CEEB Code:** 3516
Fax: 617-879-7250 **Web:** www.massart.edu **ACT Code:** 1846

This public school was founded in 1873. It has a 5-acre campus.

STUDENTS AND FACULTY

Enrollment: 1,984. **Student Body:** Male 34%, female 66%, out-of-state 23%, international 4%. **Ethnic Representation:** African American 3%, Asian 5%, Caucasian 78%, Hispanic 5%. **Retention and Graduation:** 84% freshmen return for sophomore year. 21% freshmen graduate within 4 years. 10% grads go on to further study within 1 year. **Faculty:** Student/faculty ratio 13:1. 74 full-time faculty, 74% hold PhDs. 100% faculty teach undergrads.

ACADEMICS

Degrees: Bachelor's, certificate, master's, post-bachelor's certificate. **Academic Requirements:** General education including some course work in English (including composition), history, humanities, mathematics, sciences (biological or physical), social science, liberal arts, studio foundation, studio electives. **Classes:** 10-19 students in an average class. **Disciplines with Highest Percentage of Degrees Awarded:** Fine art 92%, education 8%. **Special Study Options:** Cross registration, double major, student exchange program (domestic), independent study, internships, liberal arts/career combination, student-designed major, study abroad.

FACILITIES

Housing: Coed, off-campus housing assistance from school. **Library Holdings:** 231,586 bound volumes. 757 periodicals. 8,700 microforms. 125,000 audiovisuals. **Special Academic Facilities/Equipment:** Seven art galleries, foundry, glass furnaces, ceramic kiln, video and film studios, performance spaces, Polaroid 20x24 camera, individual studio spaces, design research unit. **Computers:** *Recommended operating system:* Mac. School-owned computers available for student use.

EXTRACURRICULARS

Activities: Drama/theater, music ensembles, musical theater, radio station, student government, student newspaper, student-run film society. **Organizations:** 30 registered organizations, 1 honor society, 3 religious organizations.

ADMISSIONS

Selectivity Rating: 76 (of 100). **Freshman Academic Profile:** Average high school GPA 3.2. 13% in top 10% of high school class, 41% in top 25% of high school class, 89% in top 50% of high school class. Average SAT I Math 513, SAT I Math middle 50% range 475-570. Average SAT I Verbal 549, SAT I Verbal middle 50% range 515-605. TOEFL required of all international applicants, minimum TOEFL 530. **Basis for Candidate Selection:** *Very important factors considered include:* essays, secondary school record, talent/ability. *Important factors considered include:* standardized test scores, state residency. *Other factors considered include:* character/personal qualities, class rank, extracurricular activities, minority status, recommendations, volunteer work, work experience. **Freshman Admission Requirements:** High school diploma or GED is required. *Academic units required/recommended:* 16 total required; 4 English required, 3 math required, 3 science required, 2 science lab required, 2 foreign language required, 2 social studies required, 2 history required, 2 elective required. **Freshman Admission Statistics:** 1,114 applied, 49% accepted, 40% of those accepted enrolled. **Transfer Admission Requirements:** *Items required:* college transcript, essay, statement of good standing from prior school. Minimum high school GPA of 3.0 required. Minimum college GPA of 2.5 required. Lowest grade transferable C. **General Admission Information:** Application fee $65. Early decision application deadline December 1. Regular application deadline February 15. Admission may be deferred for a maximum of 1 year. Credit and/or placement offered for CEEB Advanced Placement tests.

COSTS AND FINANCIAL AID

In-state tuition $1,030. Out-of-state tuition $10,240. Room & board $9,800. Required fees $3,938. Average book expense $2,000. **Required Forms and Deadlines:** FAFSA. Priority filing deadline March 15. **Notification of Awards:** Applicants will be notified of awards on or about March 15. **Types of Aid:** *Need-based scholarships/grants:* Pell, SEOG, state scholarships/grants, private scholarships, the school's own gift aid. *Loans:* Direct Subsidized Stafford, Direct Unsubsidized Stafford, Direct PLUS, FFEL Subsidized Stafford, FFEL Unsubsidized Stafford, FFEL PLUS, Federal Perkins, state loans, college/university loans from institutional funds, alternative loans (credit Based). **Student Employment:** Federal Work-Study Program available. Institutional employment available. Off-campus job opportunities are good. **Financial Aid Statistics:** 66% freshmen, 64% undergrads receive some form of aid. Average freshman loan $2,600. Average income from on-campus job $800. **Financial Aid Phone:** 617-232-1555.

MASSACHUSETTS COLLEGE OF LIBERAL ARTS

375 Church Street, North Adams, MA 01247
Phone: 413-662-5410 **E-mail:** admissions@mcla.edu **CEEB Code:** 3521
Fax: 413-662-5179 **Web:** www.mcla.edu **ACT Code:** 1908

This public school was founded in 1894. It has a 75-acre campus.

STUDENTS AND FACULTY

Enrollment: 1,392. **Student Body:** Male 39%, female 61%, out-of-state 16%, international students represent 5 countries. **Ethnic Representation:** African American 5%, Asian 1%, Caucasian 90%, Hispanic 2%, Native American 1%. **Retention and Graduation:** 72% freshmen return for sophomore year, 17% freshmen graduate within 4 years. 7% grads go on to further study within 1 year. **Faculty:** Student/faculty ratio 13:1. 84 full-time faculty, 72% hold PhDs. 100% faculty teach undergrads.

ACADEMICS

Degrees: Bachelor's, master's, post-bachelor's certificate. **Academic Requirements:** General education including some course work in arts/fine arts, computer literacy, English (including composition), history, humanities, mathematics, philosophy, sciences (biological or physical), social science, cross-cultural studies. **Classes:** 10-19 students in an average class. Under 10 students in an average lab/discussion section. **Disciplines with Highest Percentage of Degrees Awarded:** Social sciences and history 24%, business/marketing 21%, English 16%, psychology 15%, computer and information sciences 6%. **Special Study Options:** Cross registration, distance learning, double major, dual enrollment, student exchange program (domestic), honors program, independent study, internships, liberal arts/career combination, student-designed major, study abroad, teacher certification program.

FACILITIES

Housing: Coed, apartments for single students, housing for disabled students. **Library Holdings:** 167,225 bound volumes. 583 periodicals. 313,298 microforms. 6,645 audiovisuals. **Special Academic Facilities/Equipment:** On-campus day care, cable TV and radio facilities. **Computers:** *Recommended operating system:* Windows 95. School-owned computers available for student use.

EXTRACURRICULARS

Activities: Choral groups, concert band, drama/theater, jazz band, literary magazine, music ensembles, radio station, student government, student newspaper, television station, yearbook. **Organizations:** 47 registered organizations, 8 honor societies, 2 religious organizations, 2 fraternities (5% men join), 5 sororities (10% women join). **Athletics (Intercollegiate):** *Men:* baseball, basketball, cross-country, golf, ice hockey, soccer. *Women:* basketball, cross-country, soccer, softball, tennis, volleyball.

ADMISSIONS

Selectivity Rating: 63 (of 100). **Freshman Academic Profile:** Average high school GPA 2.9. 80% from public high schools. Average SAT I Math 522, SAT I Math middle 50% range 460-570. Average SAT I Verbal 535, SAT I Verbal middle 50% range 473-590. TOEFL required of all international applicants, minimum TOEFL 550. **Basis for Candidate Selection:** *Very important factors considered include:* secondary school record. *Important factors considered include:* character/personal qualities, standardized test scores. *Other factors considered include:* class rank, essays, extracurricular activities, interview, recommendations, talent/ability, volunteer work, work experience. **Freshman Admission Requirements:** High school diploma or GED is required. *Academic units required/recommended:* 16 total required; 4 English required, 3 math required, 3 science required, 2 foreign language required, 2 social studies required, 2 elective required. **Freshman Admission Statistics:** 1,019 applied, 70% accepted, 31% of those accepted enrolled. **Transfer Admission Requirements:** *Items required:* college transcript. Lowest grade transferable D. **General Admission Information:** Application fee $10. Nonfall registration accepted. Admission may be deferred for a maximum of 1 year. Credit offered for CEEB Advanced Placement tests.

COSTS AND FINANCIAL AID

In-state tuition $1,090. Out-of-state tuition $7,050. Room & board $4,290. Required fees $2,267. Average book expense $600. **Required Forms and Deadlines:** FAFSA and institution's own financial aid form. Priority filing deadline April 1. **Notification of Awards:** Applicants will be notified of awards on or about April 15. **Types of Aid:** *Need-based scholarships/grants:* Pell, SEOG, state scholarships/grants, private scholarships, the school's own gift aid. *Loans:* FFEL Subsidized Stafford, FFEL Unsubsidized Stafford, FFEL PLUS, Federal Perkins, state loans. **Student Employment:** Federal Work-Study Program available. Institutional employment available. Off-campus job opportunities are fair. **Financial Aid Statistics:** 70% freshmen, 64% undergrads receive some form of aid. Average freshman grant $3,778. Average freshman loan $3,081. Average income from on-campus job $3,950. **Financial Aid Phone:** 413-662-5219.

MASSACHUSETTS COLLEGE OF PHARMACY & HEALTH SCIENCE

Office of Admission, 179 Longwood Avenue, Boston, MA 02115
Phone: 617-732-2850 **E-mail:** admissions @ mcp.edu **CEEB Code:** 3512
Fax: 617-732-2118 **Web:** www.mcp.edu **ACT Code:** 1860

This private school was founded in 1823. It has a 3-acre campus.

STUDENTS AND FACULTY

Enrollment: 1,114. **Student Body:** Male 29%, female 71%, out-of-state 31%, international 1% (32 countries represented). **Ethnic Representation:** African American 6%, Asian 35%, Caucasian 47%, Hispanic 2%. **Retention and Graduation:** 77% freshmen return for sophomore year. 1% grads pursue business degrees. 1% grads pursue law degrees. 5% grads pursue medical degrees. **Faculty:** Student/faculty ratio 14:1. 124 full-time faculty, 99% hold PhDs. 100% faculty teach undergrads.

ACADEMICS

Degrees: Associate's, bachelor's, certificate, doctoral, first professional, master's. **Academic Requirements:** General education including some course work in English (including composition), mathematics, sciences (biological or physical), social science. **Classes:** Under 10 students in an average class. 50-99 students in an average lab/discussion section. **Majors with Highest Enrollment:** Pharmacy (PharmD, BS/BPharm); health professions and related sciences; physician assistant. **Disciplines with Highest Percentage of Degrees Awarded:** Health professions and related sciences 100%. **Special Study Options:** Cross registration, distance learning, double major, English as a second language, independent study, internships, liberal arts/career combination, undergrads may take grad-level courses.

FACILITIES

Housing: Coed. **Library Holdings:** 40,000 bound volumes. 700 periodicals. 0 microforms. 750 audiovisuals. **Special Academic Facilities/Equipment:** MFA and Gardner museum next door. **Computers:** School-owned computers available for student use.

EXTRACURRICULARS

Activities: Choral groups, drama/theater, student government, student newspaper, yearbook. **Organizations:** 25 registered organizations, 2 honor societies, 2 religious organizations, 8 fraternities (25% men join), 8 sororities (11% women join).

ADMISSIONS

Selectivity Rating: 63 (of 100). **Freshman Academic Profile:** Average high school GPA 3.3. 27% in top 10% of high school class, 60% in top 25% of high school class, 89% in top 50% of high school class. Average SAT I Math 550, SAT I Math middle 50% range 490-590. Average SAT I Verbal 490, SAT I Verbal middle 50% range 410-530. TOEFL required of all international applicants, minimum TOEFL 550. **Basis for Candidate Selection:** *Very important factors considered include:* essays, interview, secondary school record, standardized test scores. *Important factors considered include:* character/personal qualities, class rank. *Other factors considered include:* extracurricular activities, recommendations, talent/ability, volunteer work, work experience. **Freshman Admission Requirements:** High school diploma or GED is required. *Academic units required/recommended:* 16 total required; 18 total recommended; 4 English required, 4 English recommended, 3 math required, 4 math recommended, 2 science required, 3 science recommended, 2 science lab required, 3 science lab recommended, 1 history required, 1 history recommended, 6 elective required, 6 elective recommended. **Freshman Admission Statistics:** 548 applied, 76% accepted, 50% of those accepted enrolled. **Transfer Admission Requirements:** *Items required:* college transcript, essay, interview, standardized test scores. Minimum college GPA of 2.5 required. Lowest grade transferable C. **General Admission Information:** Application fee $70. Priority application deadline December 1. Early decision application deadline November 1. Regular application deadline March 1. Admission may be deferred for a maximum of 1 year. Credit and/or placement offered for CEEB Advanced Placement tests.

COSTS AND FINANCIAL AID

Tuition $18,000. Room & board $9,580. Required fees $550. Average book expense $450. **Required Forms and Deadlines:** FAFSA. Financial aid filing deadline March 15. Priority filing deadline March 15. **Notification of Awards:** Applicants will be notified of awards on a rolling basis beginning on or about February 1. **Types of Aid:** *Need-based scholarships/grants:* Pell, SEOG, state scholarships/grants, private scholarships, the school's own gift aid. *Loans:* FFEL Subsidized Stafford, FFEL Unsubsidized Stafford, FFEL PLUS, Federal Perkins, state loans, Health Professions Student Loans. **Student Employment:** Federal Work-Study Program available. Institutional employment available. Off-campus job opportunities are good. **Financial Aid Statistics:** 78% freshmen, 90% undergrads receive some form of aid. Average freshman grant $15,485. Average freshman loan $4,855. **Financial Aid Phone:** 800-225-2864.

MASSACHUSETTS INSTITUTE OF TECHNOLOGY

MIT Admissions Office Room 3-108, 77 Massachusetts Avenue, Cambridge, MA 02139
Phone: 617-253-4791 **CEEB Code:** 3514
Fax: 617-258-8304 **Web:** web.mit.edu **ACT Code:** 1858

This private school was founded in 1861. It has a 154-acre campus.

STUDENTS AND FACULTY

Enrollment: 4,178. **Student Body:** Male 59%, female 41%, out-of-state 91%, international 8% (108 countries represented). **Ethnic Representation:** African American 7%, Asian 30%, Caucasian 38%, Hispanic 13%, Native American 2%. **Retention and Graduation:** 98% freshmen return for sophomore year. 82% freshmen graduate within 4 years. 37% grads go on to further study within 1 year. 1% grads pursue business degrees. 1% grads pursue law degrees. 2% grads pursue medical degrees. **Faculty:** Student/faculty ratio 6:1. 1344 full-time faculty, 90% hold PhDs. 100% faculty teach undergrads.

ACADEMICS

Degrees: Bachelor's, doctoral, master's. **Academic Requirements:** General education including some course work in arts/fine arts, humanities, mathematics, sciences (biological or physical), social science, physical education requirement, communications requirement, lab requirement, restricted electives in science and technology requirement. **Classes:** Under 10 students in an average class. Under 10 students in an average lab/discussion section. **Majors with Highest Enrollment:** Business administration/management; computer science; electrical, electronics, and communications engineering. **Disciplines with Highest Percentage of Degrees Awarded:** Engineering/engineering technology 43%, computer and information sciences 14%, biological life sciences 10%, business/marketing 9%, physical sciences 7%. **Special Study Options:** Cooperative (work-study) program, cross registration, double major, English as a second language, internships, study abroad.

FACILITIES

Housing: Coed, all-female, apartments for married students, apartments for single students, housing for disabled students, fraternities and/or sororities, independent living group housing, apartments for students with dependent children. **Library Holdings:** 2,667,215 bound volumes. 22,358 periodicals. 2,357,872 microforms. 603,605 audiovisuals. **Special Academic Facilities/ Equipment:** Burndy Library/Dibner Institute, List Visual Arts Center, MIT Museum. Laboratories include the following: Artificial Intelligence Laboratory, Laboratory for Computer Science, Laboratory for Energy and the Environment, Laboratory for Information and Decision Systems, Laboratory for Manufacturing and Productivity, Laboratory for Nuclear Science, Lincoln Laboratory, Francis Bitter Magnet Laboratory, Media Laboratory, Microsystems Technology Laboratories. **Computers:** School-owned computers available for student use.

EXTRACURRICULARS

Activities: Choral groups, concert band, dance, drama/theater, jazz band, literary magazine, marching band, music ensembles, musical theater, opera, radio station, student government, student newspaper, student-run film society, symphony orchestra, television station, yearbook. **Organizations:** 315 registered organizations, 12 honor societies, 27 fraternities (26% men join), 5 sororities (8% women join). **Athletics (Intercollegiate):** *Men:* baseball, basketball, crew, skiing (cross-country), cross-country, diving, fencing, football, golf, gymnastics, indoor track, lacrosse, rifle, sailing, skiing (alpine), skiing (Nordic), soccer, squash, swimming, tennis, track & field, volleyball, water polo, wrestling. *Women:* basketball, crew, cross-country, diving, fencing, field hockey, gymnastics, ice hockey, indoor track, lacrosse, rifle, skiing (alpine), skiing (Nordic), softball, swimming, tennis, track & field, volleyball.

ADMISSIONS

Selectivity Rating: 99 (of 100). **Freshman Academic Profile:** 99% in top 10% of high school class, 100% in top 25% of high school class, 100% in top 50% of high school class. 68% from public high schools. Average SAT I Math 757, SAT I Math middle 50% range 740-800. Average SAT I Verbal 712, SAT I Verbal middle 50% range 680-760. Average ACT 31, ACT middle 50% range 30-34. TOEFL required of all international applicants, minimum TOEFL 577. **Basis for Candidate Selection:** *Very important factors considered include:* secondary school record. *Important factors considered include:* character/ personal qualities, class rank, extracurricular activities, recommendations, standardized test scores, talent/ability. *Other factors considered include:* alumni/ ae relation, essays, interview, minority status, volunteer work, work experience. **Freshman Admission Requirements:** High school diploma or equivalent is not required. *Academic units required/recommended:* 4 English recommended, 4 math recommended, 4 science recommended, 2 foreign language recommended, 1 social studies recommended, 1 history recommended. **Freshman Admission Statistics:** 10,664 applied, 16% accepted, 57% of those accepted enrolled. **Transfer Admission Requirements:** *Items required:* high school transcript, college transcript, essay, standardized test score, statement of good standing from prior school. Lowest grade transferable C. **General Admission Information:** Application fee $65. Regular application deadline January 1. Admission may be deferred for a maximum of 1 year. Credit and/or placement offered for CEEB Advanced Placement tests.

COSTS AND FINANCIAL AID

Tuition $28,030. Room & board $7,830. Required fees $1,100. **Required Forms and Deadlines:** FAFSA, CSS/Financial Aid PROFILE, noncustodial (divorced/separated) parent's statement, business/farm supplement, Parent's complete federal income tax returns from prior year and including all schedules and W-2s. Financial aid filing deadline February 1. **Notification of Awards:** Applicants will be notified of awards on or about March 15. **Types of Aid:** *Need-based scholarships/grants:* Pell, SEOG, state scholarships/grants, private scholarships, the school's own gift aid. *Loans:* Direct Subsidized Stafford, Direct Unsubsidized Stafford, Direct PLUS, Federal Perkins, college/university loans from institutional funds. **Student Employment:** Federal Work-Study Program available. Institutional employment available. Off-campus job opportunities are excellent. **Financial Aid Statistics:** 57% freshmen, 57% undergrads receive some form of aid. Average freshman grant $17,267. Average freshman loan $4,638. Average income from on-campus job $2,010. **Financial Aid Phone:** 617-253-4971.

MASSACHUSETTS MARITIME ACADEMY

101 Academy Drive, Buzzards Bay, MA 02532
Phone: 800-544-3411 **E-mail:** admissions@mma.mass.edu
Fax: 508-830-5077 **Web:** www.mma.mass.edu

This public school was founded in 1891. It has a 55-acre campus.

STUDENTS AND FACULTY

Enrollment: 904. **Student Body:** Male 87%, female 13%, out-of-state 21%, international students represent 6 countries. **Retention and Graduation:** 30% grads go on to further study within 1 year. 15% grads pursue business degrees. 4% grads pursue law degrees. 1% grads pursue medical degrees. **Faculty:** Student/faculty ratio 12:1. 100% faculty teach undergrads.

ACADEMICS

Degrees: Bachelor's, first professional certificate. **Academic Requirements:** General education including some course work in computer literacy, English (including composition), history, humanities, mathematics, sciences (biological or physical). **Majors with Highest Enrollment:** Ocean engineering; environmental science; environmental/environmental health engineering. **Special Study Options:** Cooperative (work-study) program, double major, internships, Semester-at-Sea.

FACILITIES

Housing: Coed. **Special Academic Facilities/Equipment:** Maritime Ship Model Museum, Training Ship Enterprise. **Computers:** *Recommended operating system:* Windows 95. School-owned computers available for student use.

EXTRACURRICULARS

Activities: Drama/theater, jazz band, marching band, music ensembles, student government, student newspaper, yearbook. **Organizations:** 12 registered organizations, 1 honor society, 1 religious organization. **Athletics (Intercollegiate):** *Men:* baseball, crew, cross-country, football, lacrosse, rifle, rugby, sailing, soccer. *Women:* crew, cross-country, rifle, rugby, sailing, softball, volleyball.

ADMISSIONS

Selectivity Rating: 63 (of 100). **Freshman Academic Profile:** Average high school GPA 2.8. 65% from public high schools. Average SAT I Math 550. Average SAT I Verbal 500. Average ACT 21. TOEFL required of all international applicants, minimum TOEFL 500. **Basis for Candidate Selection:** *Very important factors considered include:* secondary school record, standardized test scores. *Important factors considered include:* character/personal qualities, essays. *Other factors considered include:* alumni/ae relation, extracurricular activities, interview, recommendations, talent/ability, volunteer work, work experience. **Freshman Admission Requirements:** High school diploma or GED is required. *Academic units required/recommended:* 16 total required; 4 English required, 3 math required, 3 science required, 2 science lab required, 2 foreign language required, 2 history required, 2 elective required. **Freshman Admission Statistics:** 808 applied, 60% accepted, 56% of those accepted enrolled. **General Admission Information:** Application fee $40. Admission may be deferred for a maximum of 1 year. Credit and/or placement offered for CEEB Advanced Placement tests.

COSTS AND FINANCIAL AID

In-state tuition $9,165. Out-of-state tuition $19,500. Room & board $5,500. Required fees $2,600. Average book expense $700. **Required Forms and Deadlines:** FAFSA and institution's own financial aid form. No deadline for regular filing. Priority filing deadline April 30. **Notification of Awards:** Applicants will be notified of awards on a rolling basis beginning on or about March 1. **Types of Aid:** *Need-based scholarships/grants:* Pell, SEOG, state scholarships/grants, private scholarships, the school's own gift aid. *Loans:* Direct Subsidized Stafford, Direct Unsubsidized Stafford, Direct PLUS. **Student Employment:** Federal Work-Study Program available. Off-campus job opportunities are good. **Financial Aid Statistics:** 67% freshmen, 44% undergrads receive some form of aid. Average income from on-campus job $650. **Financial Aid Phone:** 508-830-5087.

MASTER'S COLLEGE AND SEMINARY

$$$

21726 Placerita Canyon Road, Santa Clarita, CA 91321
Phone: 661-259-3540 **E-mail:** enrollment@masters.edu **CEEB Code:** 4411
Fax: 805-288-1037 **Web:** www.masters.edu **ACT Code:** 303

This private school was founded in 1927. It has a 103-acre campus.

STUDENTS AND FACULTY

Enrollment: 1,129. **Student Body:** Male 49%, female 51%, out-of-state 28%, international 3% (19 countries represented). **Ethnic Representation:** African American 3%, Asian 3%, Caucasian 86%, Hispanic 7%, Native American 1%. **Retention and Graduation:** 86% freshmen return for sophomore year. 45% freshmen graduate within 4 years. 27% grads go on to further study within 1 year. 4% grads pursue business degrees. 2% grads pursue law degrees. 1% grads pursue medical degrees. **Faculty:** Student/faculty ratio 14:1. 69 full-time faculty, 65% hold PhDs. 100% faculty teach undergrads.

ACADEMICS

Degrees: Bachelor's, certificate, doctoral, first professional, first professional certificate, master's. **Academic Requirements:** General education including some course work in arts/fine arts, computer literacy, English (including composition), history, humanities, mathematics, philosophy, sciences (biological or physical), social science, biblical studies. **Classes:** Under 10 students in an average class. **Majors with Highest Enrollment:** Business administration/management; elementary education and teaching; Bible/biblical studies. **Disciplines with Highest Percentage of Degrees Awarded:** Philosophy/religion/theology 33%, business/marketing 17%, communications/communication technologies 10%, education 8%, liberal arts/general studies 7%. **Special Study Options:** Double major, independent study, internships, study abroad, teacher certification program.

FACILITIES

Housing: All-female, all-male, housing for international students. **Library Holdings:** 211,895 bound volumes. 1,288 periodicals. 105,129 microforms. 7,001 audiovisuals. **Computers:** *Recommended operating system:* Windows XP Pro. School-owned computers available for student use.

EXTRACURRICULARS

Activities: Choral groups, concert band, music ensembles, student government. **Organizations:** 14 registered organizations, 1 honor society, 10 religious organizations. **Athletics (Intercollegiate):** *Men:* baseball, basketball, cross-country, golf, soccer. *Women:* basketball, cross-country, soccer, softball, volleyball.

ADMISSIONS

Selectivity Rating: 78 (of 100). **Freshman Academic Profile:** Average high school GPA 3.6. 25% in top 10% of high school class, 52% in top 25% of high school class, 81% in top 50% of high school class. 70% from public high schools. Average SAT I Math 555, SAT I Math middle 50% range 490-620. Average SAT I Verbal 560, SAT I Verbal middle 50% range 500-620. Average ACT 24, ACT middle 50% range 21-26. TOEFL required of all international applicants, minimum TOEFL 525. **Basis for Candidate Selection:** *Very important factors considered include:* character/personal qualities, essays, interview, recommendations, religious affiliation/commitment, secondary school record, standardized test scores. *Other factors considered include:* alumni/ae relation, extracurricular activities, talent/ability. **Freshman Admission Requirements:** High school diploma or GED is required. *Academic units required/recommended:* 4 English required, 3 math required, 2 science required, 2 science recommended, 2 social studies required, 1 history recommended, 3 elective required. **Freshman Admission Statistics:** 429 applied, 84% accepted, 51% of those accepted enrolled. **Transfer Admission Requirements:** *Items required:* high school transcript, college transcript, essay, interview, statement of good standing from prior school. Minimum high school GPA of 2.5 required. Minimum college GPA of 2.0 required. Lowest grade transferable C. **General Admission Information:** Application fee $35. Priority application deadline November 17. Regular application deadline March 2. Nonfall registration accepted. Admission may be deferred for a maximum of 1 year. Credit and/or placement offered for CEEB Advanced Placement tests.

COSTS AND FINANCIAL AID

Tuition $16,420. Room & board $5,780. Required fees $200. Average book expense $1,224. **Required Forms and Deadlines:** FAFSA, institution's own financial aid form and state aid form. No deadline for regular filing. Priority filing deadline March 2. **Notification of Awards:** Applicants will be notified of awards on a rolling basis beginning on or about February 18. **Types of Aid:** *Need-based scholarships/grants:* Pell, SEOG, state scholarships/grants, private scholarships, the school's own gift aid. *Loans:* FFEL Subsidized Stafford, FFEL Unsubsidized Stafford, FFEL PLUS, Federal Perkins. **Student Employment:** Federal Work-Study Program available. Institutional employment available. Off-campus job opportunities are excellent. **Financial Aid Statistics:** 68% freshmen, 61% undergrads receive some form of aid. Average freshman grant $9,040. Average freshman loan $1,795. Average income from on-campus job $0. **Financial Aid Phone:** 800-568-6248.

MAYVILLE STATE UNIVERSITY

330 Third Street Northeast, Mayville, ND 58257-1299
Phone: 701-788-4842 **E-mail:** admit@mail.masu.nodak.edu **CEEB Code:** 6478
Fax: 701-788-4748 **Web:** www.mayvillestate.edu **ACT Code:** 3212

This public school was founded in 1889. It has a 55-acre campus.

STUDENTS AND FACULTY

Enrollment: 746. **Student Body:** Male 44%, female 56%, out-of-state 23%, international 3% (4 countries represented). **Ethnic Representation:** African American 2%, Asian 1%, Caucasian 95%, Hispanic 1%, Native American 2%. **Retention and Graduation:** 53% freshmen return for sophomore year. 18% freshmen graduate within 4 years. 6% grads go on to further study within 1 year. 3% grads pursue business degrees. 1% grads pursue law degrees. 1% grads pursue medical degrees. **Faculty:** Student/faculty ratio 14:1. 36 full-time faculty, 47% hold PhDs. 100% faculty teach undergrads.

ACADEMICS

Degrees: Bachelor's, transfer. **Academic Requirements:** General education including some course work in arts/fine arts, computer literacy, English (including composition), humanities, mathematics, sciences (biological or physical), social science. **Classes:** 10-19 students in an average class. **Majors with Highest Enrollment:** Business administration/management; computer science; elementary education and teaching. **Disciplines with Highest Percentage of Degrees Awarded:** Education 54%, business/marketing 30%, computer and information sciences 6%, biological life sciences 4%, parks and recreation 2%. **Special Study Options:** Accelerated program, cooperative (work-study) program, distance learning, double major, dual enrollment, internships, student-designed major, teacher certification program.

FACILITIES

Housing: All-female, all-male, apartments for married students, apartments for single students. **Library Holdings:** 71,595 bound volumes. 599 periodicals. 12,530 microforms. 20,679 audiovisuals. **Special Academic Facilities/Equipment:** Art gallery available in the Campus Center. **Computers:** *Recommended operating system:* Windows NT/2000. School-owned computers available for student use.

EXTRACURRICULARS

Activities: Choral groups, drama/theater, musical theater, student government, yearbook. **Organizations:** 17 registered organizations, 1 honor society, 2 religious organizations. **Athletics (Intercollegiate):** *Men:* baseball, basketball, football. *Women:* basketball, softball, volleyball.

ADMISSIONS

Selectivity Rating: 65 (of 100). **Freshman Academic Profile:** 32% in top 25% of high school class, 75% in top 50% of high school class. 97% from public high schools. Average ACT 19, ACT middle 50% range 17-22. TOEFL required of all international applicants, minimum TOEFL 525. **Basis for Candidate Selection:** *Very important factors considered include:* secondary school record. *Important factors considered include:* standardized test scores. *Other factors considered include:* character/personal qualities, interview. **Freshman Admission Requirements:** High school diploma or GED is required. *Academic units required/recommended:* 17 total required; 4 English required, 3 math required, 3 science required, 3 science lab required, 2 foreign language recommended, 3 social studies required. **Freshman Admission Statistics:** 197 applied, 99% accepted, 72% of those accepted enrolled. **Transfer Admission Requirements:** *Items required:* college transcript, statement of good standing from prior school. Minimum college GPA of 2.0 required. Lowest grade transferable D. **General Admission Information:** Application fee $35. Nonfall registration accepted. Admission may be deferred. Credit and/or placement offered for CEEB Advanced Placement tests.

COSTS AND FINANCIAL AID

Required Forms and Deadlines: FAFSA. Priority filing deadline April 15. **Notification of Awards:** Applicants will be notified of awards on a rolling basis beginning on or about May 1. **Types of Aid:** *Need-based scholarships/grants:* Pell, SEOG, state scholarships/grants, private scholarships, the school's own gift aid. *Loans:* FFEL Subsidized Stafford, FFEL Unsubsidized Stafford, FFEL PLUS, Federal Perkins. **Student Employment:** Federal Work-Study Program available. Institutional employment available. Off-campus job opportunities are good. **Financial Aid Statistics:** 60% freshmen, 70% undergrads receive some form of aid. Average freshman grant $3,014. Average freshman loan $2,568. Average income from on-campus job $1,200. **Financial Aid Phone:** 701-788-4767.

MCDANIEL COLLEGE

2 College Hill, Westminster, MD 21157
Phone: 410-857-2230 **E-mail:** admissio@mcdaniel.edu **CEEB Code:** 5898
Fax: 410-857-2757 **Web:** www.mcdaniel.edu **ACT Code:** 1756

This private school was founded in 1867. It has a 160-acre campus.

STUDENTS AND FACULTY

Enrollment: 1,695. **Student Body:** Male 42%, female 58%, out-of-state 28%, international 3% (16 countries represented). **Ethnic Representation:** African American 10%, Asian 1%, Caucasian 82%, Hispanic 1%. **Retention and Graduation:** 85% freshmen return for sophomore year. 61% freshmen graduate within 4 years. **Faculty:** Student/faculty ratio 12:1. 93 full-time faculty, 95% hold PhDs. 100% faculty teach undergrads.

ACADEMICS

Degrees: Bachelor's, master's. **Academic Requirements:** General education including some course work in arts/fine arts, English (including composition), foreign languages, history, humanities, mathematics, sciences (biological or physical), social science. **Classes:** 10-19 students in an average class. 20-29 students in an average lab/discussion section. **Majors with Highest Enrollment:** Business administration/management; communications studies/speech communication and rhetoric; sociology. **Disciplines with Highest Percentage of Degrees Awarded:** Social sciences and history 19%, business/marketing 15%, communications/communication technologies 12%, biological life sciences 8%. **Special Study Options:** Accelerated program, cross registration, double major, dual enrollment, honors program, independent study, internships, liberal arts/career combination, student-designed major, study abroad, teacher certification program.

FACILITIES

Housing: Coed, all-female, all-male, apartments for married students, apartments for single students, housing for disabled students. **Library Holdings:** 629,965 bound volumes. 3,500 periodicals. 1,427,000 microforms. 11,125 audiovisuals. **Special Academic Facilities/Equipment:** Art gallery, computer graphics and physiology labs, electron microscope, math spectrometer. **Computers:** School-owned computers available for student use.

EXTRACURRICULARS

Activities: Choral groups, concert band, drama/theater, jazz band, music ensembles, musical theater, radio station, student government, student newspaper, television station, yearbook. **Organizations:** 136 registered organizations, 22 honor societies, 5 religious organizations, 6 fraternities (17% men join), 4 sororities (13% women join). **Athletics (Intercollegiate):** *Men:* baseball, basketball, cross-country, football, golf, indoor track, lacrosse, soccer, swimming, tennis, track & field, volleyball, wrestling. *Women:* basketball, cross-country, field hockey, golf, indoor track, lacrosse, soccer, softball, swimming, tennis, track & field, volleyball.

ADMISSIONS

Selectivity Rating: 83 (of 100). **Freshman Academic Profile:** Average high school GPA 3.4. 31% in top 10% of high school class, 58% in top 25% of high school class, 89% in top 50% of high school class. Average SAT I Math 556, SAT I Math middle 50% range 510-610. Average SAT I Verbal 554, SAT I Verbal middle 50% range 500-590. TOEFL required of all international applicants, minimum TOEFL 550. **Basis for Candidate Selection:** *Very important factors considered include:* secondary school record. *Important factors considered include:* class rank, essays, interview, minority status, standardized test scores. *Other factors considered include:* extracurricular activities, recommendations, talent/ability, volunteer work, work experience. **Freshman Admission Requirements:** High school diploma or GED is required. *Academic units required/recommended:* 19 total required; 24 total recommended; 4 English required, 3 math required, 4 math recommended, 3 science required, 4 science recommended, 2 science lab required, 3 foreign language required, 4 foreign language recommended, 2 social studies required, 3 social studies recommended, 2 history required, 3 history recommended. **Freshman Admission Statistics:** 2,271 applied, 72% accepted, 27% of those accepted enrolled. **Transfer Admission Requirements:** *Items required:* college transcript, essay. Minimum high school GPA of 2.5 required. Minimum college GPA of 2.5 required. Lowest grade transferable C. **General Admission Information:** Application fee $50. Priority application deadline December 1. Regular application deadline February 1. Nonfall registration accepted. Admission may be deferred for a maximum of 1 year. Credit and/or placement offered for CEEB Advanced Placement tests.

COSTS AND FINANCIAL AID

Tuition $21,760. Room & board $5,280. Required fees $0. Average book expense $600. **Required Forms and Deadlines:** FAFSA, institution's own financial aid form and copies of parent and student federal tax returns. Priority filing deadline March 1. **Notification of Awards:** Applicants will be notified of awards on a rolling basis beginning on or about March 1. **Types of Aid:** *Need-based scholarships/grants:* Pell, SEOG, state scholarships/grants, private scholarships, the school's own gift aid. *Loans:* FFEL Subsidized Stafford, FFEL Unsubsidized Stafford, FFEL PLUS, Federal Perkins. **Student Employment:** Federal Work-Study Program available. Institutional employment available. Off-campus job opportunities are good. **Financial Aid Statistics:** 70% freshmen, 63% undergrads receive some form of aid. Average freshman grant $7,641. Average freshman loan $3,892. **Financial Aid Phone:** 410-857-2233.

MCGILL UNIVERSITY

845 Sherbrooke Street West, Montreal, QC H3A 2T5
Phone: 514-398-3910 **E-mail:** admissions@mcgill.ca **CEEB Code:** 935
Fax: 514-398-8939 **Web:** www.mcgill.ca

This public school was founded in 1821. It has an 80-acre campus.

STUDENTS AND FACULTY

Enrollment: 22,915. **Student Body:** Male 40%, female 60%, out-of-state 29%, international 13% (150 countries represented). **Faculty:** Student/faculty ratio 15:1. 1,534 full-time faculty, 94% hold PhDs. 100% faculty teach undergrads.

ACADEMICS

Degrees: Bachelor's, certificate, diploma, doctoral, first professional, master's. **Classes:** 100+ students in an average class. 20-29 students in an average lab/discussion section. **Majors with Highest Enrollment:** Mechanical engineering; English language and literature/letters; psychology, general. **Disciplines with Highest Percentage of Degrees Awarded:** Social sciences and history 15%, business/marketing 14%, biological life sciences 12%, engineering/engineering technology 11%, education 7%. **Special Study Options:** Double major, English as a second language, student exchange program (domestic), honors program, internships, student-designed major, study abroad, teacher certification program.

FACILITIES

Housing: Coed, all-female, apartments for single students, cooperative housing. A number of renovated homes in McGill vicinity with shared kitchens and common areas are available. Residence space is limited and available on a lottery basis to eligible first-year students. **Library Holdings:** 4,029,960 bound volumes. 22,513 periodicals. 1,623,988 microforms. 571,768 audiovisuals. **Special Academic Facilities/Equipment:** Ecomuseum, entomological, physics, and Canadiana museums, arboretum, herbarium, nature conservation and research center, tropical research institute, radiation lab with synchrocyclotron. **Computers:** School-owned computers available for student use.

EXTRACURRICULARS

Activities: Choral groups, concert band, dance, drama/theater, jazz band, literary magazine, music ensembles, musical theater, opera, radio station, student government, student newspaper, student-run film society, symphony orchestra, television station, yearbook. **Organizations:** 172 registered organizations, 10 religious organizations, 12 fraternities, 4 sororities. **Athletics (Intercollegiate):** *Men:* baseball, basketball, cheerleading, crew, skiing (cross-country), cross-country, fencing, football, golf, ice hockey, lacrosse, rugby, sailing, skiing (alpine), skiing (Nordic), soccer, squash, swimming, tennis, track & field, volleyball, wrestling. *Women:* basketball, cheerleading, crew, skiing (cross-country), cross-country, fencing, field hockey, golf, ice hockey, lacrosse, rugby, sailing, skiing (alpine), skiing (Nordic), soccer, squash, swimming, tennis, track & field, volleyball, wrestling.

ADMISSIONS

Selectivity Rating: 95 (of 100). **Freshman Academic Profile:** Average high school GPA 3.5. 90% in top 10% of high school class, 100% in top 25% of high school class, TOEFL required of all international applicants, minimum TOEFL 577. **Basis for Candidate Selection:** *Very important factors considered include:* secondary school record, standardized test scores. *Important factors considered include:* class rank. *Other factors considered include:* recommendations. **Freshman Admission Requirements:** High school diploma is required and GED is not accepted. **Freshman Admission Statistics:** 16,952 applied, 55% accepted, 47% of those accepted enrolled. **Transfer Admission Requirements:** *Items required:* high school transcript, college transcript. **General Admission Information:** Application fee $60. Regular application deadline January 15. Admission may be deferred for a maximum of 1 year. Credit and/or placement offered for CEEB Advanced Placement tests.

COSTS AND FINANCIAL AID

In-state tuition $1,668. Out-of-state tuition $3,438. Room & board $7,500. Required fees $1,200. Average book expense $1,000. **Required Forms and Deadlines:** FAFSA, institution's own financial aid form and C. **Notification of Awards:** Applicants will be notified of awards on a rolling basis. **Student Employment:** Institutional employment available. Off-campus job opportunities are fair. **Financial Aid Statistics:** Average freshman grant $3,000. Average freshman loan $2,625. **Financial Aid Phone:** 514-398-6013.

See page 1108.

MCKENDREE COLLEGE

701 College Road, Lebanon, IL 62254
Phone: 618-537-6831 **E-mail:** inquiry@mckendree.edu **CEEB Code:** 1456
Fax: 618-537-6496 **Web:** www.mckendree.edu **ACT Code:** 1076

This private school, which is affiliated with the Methodist Church, was founded in 1828. It has a 100-acre campus.

STUDENTS AND FACULTY

Enrollment: 2,107. **Student Body:** Male 38%, female 62%, out-of-state 31%, international 2% (12 countries represented). **Ethnic Representation:** African American 10%, Asian 1%, Caucasian 86%, Hispanic 1%. **Retention and Graduation:** 78% freshmen return for sophomore year. 28% freshmen graduate within 4 years. 14% grads go on to further study within 1 year. 6% grads pursue business degrees. 3% grads pursue law degrees. 1% grads pursue medical degrees. **Faculty:** Student/faculty ratio 17:1. 66 full-time faculty, 86% hold PhDs. 100% faculty teach undergrads.

ACADEMICS

Degrees: Bachelor's. **Academic Requirements:** General education including some course work in arts/fine arts, computer literacy, English (including composition), history, humanities, mathematics, philosophy, sciences (biological or physical), social science. **Classes:** 10-19 students in an average class. 10-19 students in an average lab/discussion section. **Disciplines with Highest Percentage of Degrees Awarded:** Business/marketing 29%, health professions and related sciences 20%, education 12%, computer and information sciences 10%, social sciences and history 10%. **Special Study Options:** Accelerated program, double major, honors program, independent study, internships, student-designed major, study abroad, teacher certification program, evening programs in accounting, business administration, organizational communication, 3-2 occupational therapy program with Washington University.

FACILITIES

Housing: Coed, all-female, apartments for single students. **Library Holdings:** 140,000 bound volumes. 45,000 periodicals. 40,000 microforms. 22,000 audiovisuals. **Computers:** School-owned computers available for student use.

EXTRACURRICULARS

Activities: Choral groups, concert band, dance, drama/theater, jazz band, literary magazine, marching band, music ensembles, musical theater, pep band, student government, student newspaper, yearbook. **Organizations:** 59 registered organizations, 9 honor societies, 2 religious organizations, 4 fraternities (8% men join), 3 sororities (6% women join). **Athletics (Intercollegiate):** *Men:* baseball, basketball, cheerleading, cross-country, football, golf, indoor track, soccer, tennis, track & field. *Women:* basketball, cheerleading, cross-country, golf, indoor track, soccer, softball, tennis, track & field, volleyball.

ADMISSIONS

Selectivity Rating: 70 (of 100). **Freshman Academic Profile:** Average high school GPA 3.6. 25% in top 10% of high school class, 55% in top 25% of high school class, 85% in top 50% of high school class. 90% from public high schools. Average ACT 24, ACT middle 50% range 20-26. TOEFL required of all international applicants, minimum TOEFL 520. **Basis for Candidate Selection:** *Very important factors considered include:* class rank, secondary school record, standardized test scores. *Important factors considered include:* alumni/ae relation, character/personal qualities, extracurricular activities, interview, recommendations, talent/ability, volunteer work, work experience. *Other factors considered include:* essays. **Freshman Admission Requirements:** High school diploma or GED is required. *Academic units required/recommended:* 13 total recommended; 4 English recommended, 3 math recommended, 3 science recommended, 2 social studies recommended, 1 history recommended. **Freshman Admission Statistics:** 1,156 applied, 68% accepted, 41% of those accepted enrolled. **Transfer Admission Requirements:** *Items required:* high school transcript, college transcript, statement of good standing from prior school. Minimum college GPA of 2.2 required. Lowest grade transferable C. **General Admission Information:** Priority application deadline August 1. Nonfall registration accepted. Admission may be deferred for a maximum of 6 years. Credit and/or placement offered for CEEB Advanced Placement tests.

COSTS AND FINANCIAL AID

Tuition $14,200. Room & board $5,070. Required fees $0. Average book expense $900. **Required Forms and Deadlines:** FAFSA and institution's own financial aid form. No deadline for regular filing. Priority filing deadline June 1. **Notification of Awards:** Applicants will be notified of awards on a rolling basis. **Types of Aid:** *Need-based scholarships/grants:* Pell, SEOG, state scholarships/grants. *Loans:* Direct Subsidized Stafford, Direct Unsubsidized Stafford, Direct PLUS, FFEL Subsidized Stafford, FFEL Unsubsidized Stafford, FFEL PLUS, Federal Perkins, college/university loans from institutional funds. **Student Employment:** Federal Work-Study Program available. Institutional employment available. Off-campus job opportunities are good. **Financial Aid Statistics:** 73% freshmen, 71% undergrads receive some form of aid. Average freshman grant $9,862. Average freshman loan $2,022. Average income from on-campus job $910. **Financial Aid Phone:** 618-537-4729.

MCMURRY UNIVERSITY

S. 14th and Sayles Boulevard, Abilene, TX 79697
Phone: 915-793-4700 **E-mail:** admissions@mcm.edu **CEEB Code:** 6402
Fax: 915-793-4718 **Web:** www.mcm.edu **ACT Code:** 4130

This private school, which is affiliated with the Methodist Church, was founded in 1923. It has a 50-acre campus.

STUDENTS AND FACULTY

Enrollment: 1,418. **Student Body:** Male 49%, female 51%, out-of-state 3%, international 1% (8 countries represented). **Ethnic Representation:** African American 8%, Asian 1%, Caucasian 76%, Hispanic 12%, Native American 1%. **Retention and Graduation:** 70% freshmen return for sophomore year. 15% grads go on to further study within 1 year. 1% grads pursue medical degrees. **Faculty:** Student/faculty ratio 14:1. 76 full-time faculty, 73% hold PhDs. 100% faculty teach undergrads.

ACADEMICS

Degrees: Bachelor's. **Academic Requirements:** General education including some course work in arts/fine arts, computer literacy, English (including composition), foreign languages, history, humanities, mathematics, philosophy, sciences (biological or physical), social science, religion, health fitness. **Classes:** 20-29 students in an average class. 10-19 students in an average lab/discussion section. **Disciplines with Highest Percentage of Degrees Awarded:** Education 32%, business/marketing 24%, biological life sciences 9%, social sciences and history 6%, visual and performing arts 5%. **Special Study Options:** Accelerated program, cross registration, double major, dual enrollment, honors program, independent study, internships, liberal arts/career combination, study abroad, teacher certification program, engineering with Texas Tech University.

FACILITIES

Housing: Coed, all-female, all-male, apartments for single students. **Library Holdings:** 115,704 bound volumes. 698 periodicals. 4,367 microforms. 9,341 audiovisuals. **Computers:** School-owned computers available for student use.

EXTRACURRICULARS

Activities: Choral groups, concert band, drama/theater, jazz band, literary magazine, marching band, music ensembles, musical theater, student government, student newspaper, yearbook. **Organizations:** 45 registered organizations, 13 honor societies, 2 religious organizations, 7 fraternities (29% men join), 6 sororities (20% women join). **Athletics (Intercollegiate):** *Men:* baseball, basketball, cross-country, diving, football, golf, indoor track, swimming, tennis, track & field. *Women:* basketball, cross-country, diving, golf, indoor track, swimming, tennis, track & field, volleyball.

ADMISSIONS

Selectivity Rating: 81 (of 100). **Freshman Academic Profile:** Average high school GPA 3.4. 15% in top 10% of high school class, 37% in top 25% of high school class, 72% in top 50% of high school class. 98% from public high schools. Average SAT I Math 504, SAT I Math middle 50% range 460-570. Average SAT I Verbal 490, SAT I Verbal middle 50% range 440-550. Average ACT 21, ACT middle 50% range 18-23. TOEFL required of all international applicants, minimum TOEFL 550. **Basis for Candidate Selection:** *Very important factors considered include:* class rank, secondary school record, standardized test scores. *Important factors considered include:* character/personal qualities, talent/ability. *Other factors considered include:* alumni/ae relation, essays, extracurricular activities, geographical residence, interview, recommendations, religious affiliation/commitment, state residency, volunteer work, work experience. **Freshman Admission Requirements:** High school diploma or GED is required. *Academic units required/recommended:* 14 total required; 16 total recommended; 4 English required, 3 math required, 4 math recommended, 2 science required, 3 science recommended, 2 foreign language required, 3 social studies required. **Freshman Admission Statistics:** 911 applied, 70% accepted, 51% of those accepted enrolled. **Transfer Admission Requirements:** *Items required:* college transcript. Minimum high school GPA of 2.0 required. Minimum college GPA of 2.0 required. Lowest grade transferable C. **General Admission Information:** Application fee $20. Priority application deadline August 15. Nonfall registration accepted. Admission may be deferred for a maximum of 1 year. Credit and/or placement offered for CEEB Advanced Placement tests.

COSTS AND FINANCIAL AID

Required Forms and Deadlines: FAFSA and institution's own financial aid form. Priority filing deadline March 15. **Notification of Awards:** Applicants will be notified of awards on a rolling basis beginning on or about March 15. **Types of Aid:** *Need-based scholarships/grants:* Pell, SEOG, state scholarships/ grants, private scholarships, the school's own gift aid. *Loans:* FFEL Subsidized Stafford, FFEL Unsubsidized Stafford, FFEL PLUS, Federal Perkins, state loans. **Student Employment:** Federal Work-Study Program available. Institutional employment available. Off-campus job opportunities are excellent. **Financial Aid Statistics:** 76% freshmen, 77% undergrads receive some form of aid. Average freshman grant $8,567. Average freshman loan $5,521. Average income from on-campus job $611. **Financial Aid Phone:** 915-793-4713.

MCNEESE STATE UNIVERSITY

PO Box 92495, Lake Charles, LA 70609-2495
Phone: 318-475-5146 **CEEB Code:** 6403
Fax: 318-475-5189 **Web:** www.mcneese.edu **ACT Code:** 1594

This public school was founded in 1939. It has a 171-acre campus.

STUDENTS AND FACULTY

Enrollment: 7,045. **Student Body:** Male 42%, female 58%, out-of-state 5%, international 1%. **Ethnic Representation:** African American 17%, Asian 1%, Caucasian 81%, Hispanic 1%, Native American 1%. **Retention and Graduation:** 64% freshmen return for sophomore year. 7% freshmen graduate within 4 years. 5% grads go on to further study within 1 year. **Faculty:** 100% faculty teach undergrads.

ACADEMICS

Degrees: Associate's, bachelor's, master's. **Academic Requirements:** General education including some course work in arts/fine arts, computer literacy, English (including composition), history, mathematics, sciences (biological or physical), social science. **Special Study Options:** Cooperative (work-study) program, double major, internships, teacher certification program.

FACILITIES

Housing: Coed, all-female, all-male, apartments for married students, apartments for single students, fraternities and/or sororities. **Library Holdings:** 429,093 bound volumes. 1,641 periodicals. 1,259,840 microforms. **Special Academic Facilities/Equipment:** Vertebrate Museum, art gallery, planetarium. **Computers:** *Recommended operating system:* Mac.

EXTRACURRICULARS

Activities: Choral groups, concert band, dance, drama/theater, jazz band, marching band, music ensembles, pep band, student government, student newspaper, yearbook. **Organizations:** 5 honor societies, 3 religious organizations, 8 fraternities (5% men join), 6 sororities (5% women join). **Athletics (Intercollegiate):** *Men:* basketball, cross-country, softball, tennis, track & field, volleyball.

ADMISSIONS

Selectivity Rating: 65 (of 100). **Freshman Academic Profile:** Average ACT 19, ACT middle 50% range 16-22. TOEFL required of all international applicants, minimum TOEFL 450. **Freshman Admission Requirements:** High school diploma or GED is required. **Freshman Admission Statistics:** 2,516 applied, 99% accepted, 62% of those accepted enrolled. **Transfer Admission Requirements:** Minimum college GPA of 2.0 required. Lowest grade transferable C. **General Admission Information:** Application fee $10. Early decision application deadline April 1. Regular application deadline August 1. Nonfall registration accepted. Credit and/or placement offered for CEEB Advanced Placement tests.

COSTS AND FINANCIAL AID

In-state tuition $2,006. Out-of-state tuition $6,446. Room & board $2,310. Average book expense $660. **Required Forms and Deadlines:** FAFSA, institution's own financial aid form and state aid form. **Types of Aid:** *Need-based scholarships/grants:* Pell, SEOG, state scholarships/grants, private scholarships, the school's own gift aid. *Loans:* FFEL Subsidized Stafford, FFEL Unsubsidized Stafford, FFEL PLUS, Federal Perkins, state loans, college/ university loans from institutional funds. **Student Employment:** Federal Work-Study Program available. Institutional employment available. Off-campus job opportunities are good. **Financial Aid Statistics:** Average freshman grant $1,541. Average income from on-campus job $1,220. **Financial Aid Phone:** 318-475-5065.

MCPHERSON COLLEGE

PO Box 1402, 1600 E. Euclid, McPherson, KS 67460
Phone: 316-241-0731 **E-mail:** admiss@mcpherson.edu **CEEB Code:** 6404
Fax: 316-241-8443 **Web:** www.mcpherson.edu **ACT Code:** 1440

This private school, which is affiliated with the Church of Brethren, was founded in 1887. It has a 23-acre campus.

STUDENTS AND FACULTY

Enrollment: 463. **Student Body:** Male 49%, female 51%, out-of-state 54%, international 2%. **Ethnic Representation:** African American 6%, Asian 1%, Caucasian 83%, Hispanic 5%, Native American 2%. **Retention and Graduation:** 45% freshmen return for sophomore year. 30% freshmen graduate within 4 years. 9% grads go on to further study within 1 year. 9% grads pursue medical degrees. **Faculty:** Student/faculty ratio 11:1. 38 full-time faculty, 65% hold PhDs.

ACADEMICS

Degrees: Associate's, bachelor's, certificate. **Academic Requirements:** General education including some course work in arts/fine arts, computer literacy, English (including composition), history, humanities, mathematics, philosophy, sciences (biological or physical), social science. **Classes:** Under 10 students in an average class. Under 10 students in an average lab/discussion section. **Disciplines with Highest Percentage of Degrees Awarded:** Social sciences and history 18%, education 17%, business/marketing 14%, visual and performing arts 11%, biological life sciences 9%. **Special Study Options:** Cross registration, double major, independent study, internships, student-designed major, study abroad, teacher certification program.

FACILITIES

Housing: Coed, all-male, apartments for married students, apartments for single students, housing for disabled students. **Library Holdings:** 90,535 bound volumes. 308 periodicals. 59,549 microforms. 4,484 audiovisuals. **Special Academic Facilities/Equipment:** Natural history museum. **Computers:** *Recommended operating system:* Mac. School-owned computers available for student use.

EXTRACURRICULARS

Activities: Choral groups, concert band, drama/theater, music ensembles, musical theater, pep band, student government, student newspaper, yearbook. **Athletics (Intercollegiate):** *Women:* basketball, cross-country, golf, tennis, track & field, volleyball.

ADMISSIONS

Selectivity Rating: 63 (of 100). **Freshman Academic Profile:** Average high school GPA 3.2. 7% in top 10% of high school class, 37% in top 25% of high school class, 65% in top 50% of high school class. 99% from public high schools. SAT I Math middle 50% range 420-500. SAT I Verbal middle 50% range 390-510. ACT middle 50% range 18-23. TOEFL required of all international applicants, minimum TOEFL 500. **Basis for Candidate Selection:** *Very important factors considered include:* secondary school record, standardized test scores. *Other factors considered include:* alumni/ae relation, character/personal qualities, class rank, extracurricular activities, interview, recommendations, talent/ability, volunteer work, work experience. **Freshman Admission Requirements:** High school diploma or GED is required. **Freshman Admission Statistics:** 702 applied, 69% accepted, 28% of those accepted enrolled. **Transfer Admission Requirements:** *Items required:* high school transcript, college transcript, statement of good standing from prior school. Minimum high school GPA of 2.0 required. Minimum college GPA of 2.0 required. Lowest grade transferable C. **General Admission Information:** Application fee $25. Priority application deadline March 1. Nonfall registration accepted. Admission may be deferred. Credit offered for CEEB Advanced Placement tests.

COSTS AND FINANCIAL AID

Tuition $12,500. Room & board $4,990. Required fees $220. Average book expense $700. **Required Forms and Deadlines:** FAFSA and state aid form. No deadline for regular filing. Priority filing deadline March 1. **Notification of Awards:** Applicants will be notified of awards on a rolling basis beginning on or about March 15. **Types of Aid:** *Need-based scholarships/grants:* Pell, SEOG, state scholarships/grants, private scholarships, the school's own gift aid. *Loans:* FFEL Subsidized Stafford, FFEL Unsubsidized Stafford, FFEL PLUS, Federal Perkins. **Student Employment:** Federal Work-Study Program available. Institutional employment available. Off-campus job opportunities are good. **Financial Aid Statistics:** 85% freshmen, 81% undergrads receive some form of aid. Average income from on-campus job $400. **Financial Aid Phone:** 316-241-0731.

MEDAILLE COLLEGE

18 Agassiz Circle, Buffalo, NY 14214
Phone: 716-884-3281 **E-mail:** jmatheny@medaille.edu **CEEB Code:** 2422
Fax: 716-884-0291 **Web:** www.medaille.edu **ACT Code:** 2822

This private school was founded in 1937. It has a 13-acre campus.

STUDENTS AND FACULTY

Enrollment: 1,630. **Student Body:** Male 32%, female 68%, out-of-state 0%, international 11%. **Ethnic Representation:** African American 16%, Asian 1%, Caucasian 73%, Hispanic 3%, Native American 1%. **Retention and Graduation:** 24% grads go on to further study within 1 year. 5% grads pursue business degrees. 1% grads pursue law degrees. 1% grads pursue medical degrees. **Faculty:** Student/faculty ratio 15:1. 63 full-time faculty, 60% hold PhDs. 100% faculty teach undergrads.

ACADEMICS

Degrees: Associate's, bachelor's, certificate, master's. **Academic Requirements:** General education including some course work in arts/fine arts, computer literacy, English (including composition), history, humanities, mathematics, sciences (biological or physical), social science. **Classes:** 10-19 students in an average class. 10-19 students in an average lab/discussion section. **Majors with Highest Enrollment:** Business administration/management; animal sciences; elementary education and teaching. **Disciplines with Highest Percentage of Degrees Awarded:** Education 56%, business/marketing 26%, protective services/public administration 4%, liberal arts/general studies 4%, computer and information sciences 3%. **Special Study Options:** Accelerated program, cooperative (work-study) program, cross registration, double major, honors program, independent study, internships, liberal arts/career combination, student-designed major, teacher certification program, weekend college, Module system for full-time evening studies.

FACILITIES

Housing: Coed, all-female, all-male, apartments for married students, apartments for single students. **Library Holdings:** 55,225 bound volumes. 209 periodicals. 208 microforms. 3,563 audiovisuals. **Special Academic Facilities/Equipment:** Veterinary technology labs, New Media Institute, Children's Literature Collection. **Computers:** School-owned computers available for student use.

EXTRACURRICULARS

Activities: Drama/theater, literary magazine, musical theater, radio station, student government, student newspaper, student-run film society, television station, yearbook. **Organizations:** 18 registered organizations, 1 honor society, 1 religious organization. **Athletics (Intercollegiate):** *Men:* baseball, basketball, cheerleading, lacrosse, soccer, volleyball. *Women:* basketball, cheerleading, cross-country, lacrosse, soccer, softball, volleyball.

ADMISSIONS

Selectivity Rating: 65 (of 100). **Freshman Academic Profile:** Average high school GPA 2.8. 14% in top 10% of high school class, 45% in top 25% of high school class, 75% in top 50% of high school class. 85% from public high schools. Average SAT I Math 480, SAT I Math middle 50% range 410-510. Average SAT I Verbal 490, SAT I Verbal middle 50% range 420-520. Average ACT 16, ACT middle 50% range 15-19. TOEFL required of all international applicants, minimum TOEFL 550. **Basis for Candidate Selection:** *Very important factors considered include:* interview, secondary school record, standardized test scores. *Important factors considered include:* essays, extracurricular activities, recommendations. *Other factors considered include:* alumni/ae relation, character/personal qualities, class rank, talent/ability, volunteer work, work experience. **Freshman Admission Requirements:** High school diploma or GED is required. *Academic units required/recommended:* 12 total required; 20 total recommended; 4 English required, 4 English recommended, 2 math required, 3 math recommended, 2 science required, 3 science recommended, 2 science lab recommended, 2 foreign language recommended, 4 social studies required, 4 social studies recommended, 2 history recommended. **Freshman Admission Statistics:** 655 applied, 66% accepted, 58% of those accepted enrolled. **Transfer Admission Requirements:** *Items required:* high school transcript, college transcript, essay. Minimum high school GPA of 2.0 required. Minimum college GPA of 2.0 required. Lowest grade transferable C. **General Admission Information:** Application fee $25. Priority application deadline August 1. Nonfall registration accepted. Admission may be deferred for a maximum of 1 year. Credit and/or placement offered for CEEB Advanced Placement tests.

COSTS AND FINANCIAL AID

Tuition $12,720. Room & board $5,950. Required fees $310. Average book expense $900. **Required Forms and Deadlines:** FAFSA, institution's own financial aid form and state aid form. No deadline for regular filing. Priority filing deadline April 15. **Notification of Awards:** Applicants will be notified of awards on a rolling basis beginning on or about May 1. **Types of Aid:** *Need-based scholarships/grants:* Pell, SEOG, state scholarships/grants, private scholarships, the school's own gift aid. *Loans:* FFEL Subsidized Stafford, FFEL Unsubsidized Stafford, FFEL PLUS. **Student Employment:** Federal Work-Study Program available. Institutional employment available. Off-campus job opportunities are good. **Financial Aid Statistics:** 84% freshmen, 80% undergrads receive some form of aid. Average freshman grant $9,000. Average freshman loan $3,500. Average income from on-campus job $1,500. **Financial Aid Phone:** 716-884-3281.

MEDCENTER ONE COLLEGE OF NURSING

512 North 7th Street, Bismarck, ND 58501
Phone: 701-323-6271 **E-mail:** msmith@mohs.org
Fax: 701-323-6967 **Web:** www.medcenterone.com/nursing/nursing.htm **ACT Code:** 3197

This private school was founded in 1988.

STUDENTS AND FACULTY

Enrollment: 99. **Student Body:** Out-of-state 2%. **Ethnic Representation:** Caucasian 97%, Hispanic 1%, Native American 2%. **Faculty:** Student/faculty ratio 7:1. 11 full-time faculty. 100% faculty teach undergrads.

ACADEMICS

Degrees: Bachelor's. **Academic Requirements:** General education including some course work in computer literacy, English (including composition), humanities, mathematics, sciences (biological or physical), social science. **Classes:** 40-49 students in an average class. 10-19 students in an average lab/discussion section. **Disciplines with Highest Percentage of Degrees Awarded:** Health professions and related sciences 100%. **Special Study Options:** Independent study, internships.

FACILITIES

Housing: Coed. **Library Holdings:** 26,700 bound volumes. 312 periodicals. 49 microforms. 1,424 audiovisuals. **Special Academic Facilities/Equipment:** Alumni Corner. **Computers:** School-owned computers available for student use.

EXTRACURRICULARS

Activities: Student government. **Organizations:** 1 honor society.

ADMISSIONS

Selectivity Rating: 63 (of 100). **Freshman Academic Profile:** TOEFL required of all international applicants, minimum TOEFL 525. **Freshman Admission Requirements:** High school diploma or GED is required. **Transfer Admission Requirements:** *Items required:* high school transcript, college transcript, essay, interview. Minimum college GPA of 2.5 required. Lowest grade transferable C. **General Admission Information:** Application fee $40.

COSTS AND FINANCIAL AID

Tuition $3,486. Required fees $500. Average book expense $1,089. **Required Forms and Deadlines:** FAFSA and institution's own financial aid form. No deadline for regular filing. Priority filing deadline April 15. **Notification of Awards:** Applicants will be notified of awards on a rolling basis beginning on or about June 1. **Types of Aid:** *Need-based scholarships/grants:* Pell, SEOG, state scholarships/grants, private scholarships, the school's own gift aid. *Loans:* FFEL Subsidized Stafford, FFEL Unsubsidized Stafford, FFEL PLUS, Federal Perkins, Federal Nursing. **Student Employment:** Federal Work-Study Program available. Off-campus job opportunities are excellent. **Financial Aid Statistics:** 65% undergrads receive some form of aid. **Financial Aid Phone:** 701-323-6270.

MEDICAL COLLEGE OF GEORGIA

Kelly Building-Administration, Room 170, Augusta, GA 30912
Phone: 706-721-2725 **E-mail:** underadm@mail.mcg.edu
Fax: 706-721-7279 **Web:** www.mcg.edu

This public school was founded in 1828. It has a 100-acre campus.

STUDENTS AND FACULTY
Enrollment: 716. **Student Body:** Male 13%, female 87%, out-of-state 11%. **Ethnic Representation:** African American 15%, Asian 2%, Caucasian 80%, Hispanic 1%. **Faculty:** Student/faculty ratio 0:1. 590 full-time faculty, 87% hold PhDs.

ACADEMICS
Degrees: Bachelor's, doctoral, first professional, master's, post-bachelor's certificate. **Disciplines with Highest Percentage of Degrees Awarded:** Health professions and related sciences 100%. **Special Study Options:** Distance learning, internships.

FACILITIES
Housing: Coed, apartments for married students, apartments for single students. **Library Holdings:** 164,154 bound volumes. 1,232 periodicals. 3,460 audiovisuals. **Computers:** School-owned computers available for student use.

EXTRACURRICULARS
Activities: Student government, student newspaper. **Organizations:** 1 religious organization.

ADMISSIONS
Selectivity Rating: 63 (of 100). **Freshman Academic Profile:** TOEFL required of all international applicants, minimum TOEFL 550. **Freshman Admission Requirements: Transfer Admission Requirements:** *Items required:* college transcript, essay, standardized test score, statement of good standing from prior school. Minimum college GPA of 2.3 required. Lowest grade transferable C. **General Admission Information:** Application fee $30.

COSTS AND FINANCIAL AID
In-state tuition $2,632. Out-of-state tuition $10,528. Room & board $1,302. Required fees $451. Average book expense $800. **Required Forms and Deadlines:** FAFSA, institution's own financial aid form and Financial Aid Transcript (for mid-year transfers). Priority filing deadline March 31. **Notification of Awards:** Applicants will be notified of awards on a rolling basis beginning on or about April 30. **Types of Aid:** *Need-based scholarships/grants:* Pell, SEOG, state scholarships/grants, private scholarships, the school's own gift aid. *Loans:* FFEL Subsidized Stafford, FFEL Unsubsidized Stafford, FFEL PLUS, Federal Perkins, Federal Nursing, state loans, college/university loans from institutional funds. **Student Employment:** Federal Work-Study Program available. **Financial Aid Statistics:** 68% undergrads receive some form of aid. **Financial Aid Phone:** 706-721-4901.

MEDICAL UNIVERSITY OF SOUTH CAROLINA

PO Box 250203, Charleston, SC 29425
Phone: 843-792-3281 **E-mail:** menzelj@musc.edu
Fax: 843-792-3764 **Web:** www.musc.edu **ACT Code:** 6440

This public school was founded in 1824. It has a 61-acre campus.

STUDENTS AND FACULTY
Enrollment: 352. **Student Body:** Male 20%, female 80%, out-of-state 15%. **Ethnic Representation:** African American 14%, Asian 2%, Caucasian 78%, Hispanic 1%, Native American 1%. **Faculty:** Student/faculty ratio 13:1. 1054 full-time faculty, 89% hold PhDs. 14% faculty teach undergrads.

ACADEMICS
Degrees: Bachelor's, doctoral, first professional, master's, post-bachelor's certificate. **Academic Requirements:** General education including some course work in varies with academic program. **Classes:** Under 10 students in an average class. **Majors with Highest Enrollment:** Health/health care administration/management; physician assistant; nursing/registered nurse training (RN, ASN, BSN, MSN). **Disciplines with Highest Percentage of Degrees Awarded:** Health professions and related sciences 100%. **Special Study Options:** Cross registration, distance learning.

FACILITIES
Housing: No on-campus housing available. **Library Holdings:** 219,864 bound volumes. 2,899 periodicals. 3,088 microforms. 6,470 audiovisuals. **Special Academic Facilities/Equipment:** Dental Museum, Medical Museum, Pharmacy Museum. **Computers:** School-owned computers available for student use.

EXTRACURRICULARS
Activities: Choral groups, literary magazine, student government, student-run film society. **Organizations:** 4 honor societies.

ADMISSIONS
Selectivity Rating: 63 (of 100). **Freshman Academic Profile:** TOEFL required of all international applicants, minimum TOEFL 600. **Freshman Admission Requirements: Transfer Admission Requirements:** *Items required:* high school transcript, college transcript, essay. Lowest grade transferable C.

COSTS AND FINANCIAL AID
In-state tuition $6,230. Out-of-state tuition $17,227. Required fees $245. Average book expense $0. **Required Forms and Deadlines:** FAFSA and institution's own financial aid form. **Types of Aid:** *Need-based scholarships/grants:* Pell, SEOG, state scholarships/grants, private scholarships, the school's own gift aid, Federal Nursing. *Loans:* FFEL Subsidized Stafford, FFEL Unsubsidized Stafford, FFEL PLUS, Federal Perkins, Federal Nursing. **Student Employment:** Federal Work-Study Program available. Institutional employment available. Off-campus job opportunities are excellent. **Financial Aid Statistics:** 70% undergrads receive some form of aid. **Financial Aid Phone:** 843-792-2536.

MEMPHIS COLLEGE OF ART

Overton Park, 1930 Poplar Avenue, Memphis, TN 38104-2764
Phone: 800-727-1088 **E-mail:** info@mca.edu **CEEB Code:** 1511
Fax: 901-726-9371 **Web:** www.mca.edu **ACT Code:** 3991

This private school was founded in 1936. It has a 340-acre campus.

STUDENTS AND FACULTY
Enrollment: 225. **Student Body:** Male 52%, female 48%, out-of-state 40%, international 4% (7 countries represented). **Ethnic Representation:** African American 16%, Asian 1%, Caucasian 82%, Hispanic 1%. **Retention and Graduation:** 54% freshmen return for sophomore year. 20% grads go on to further study within 1 year. 20% grads pursue business degrees.

ACADEMICS
Degrees: Bachelor's, master's. **Special Study Options:** Double major, student exchange program (domestic), independent study, internships, New York Studies Program. Arts Exchange possible with other AICAD schools.

FACILITIES
Housing: Coed, all-female, all-male, apartments for single students. **Library Holdings:** 14,500 bound volumes. 102 periodicals. **Special Academic Facilities/Equipment:** Art museum, numerous galleries for student exhibition, computer writing lab. **Computers:** *Recommended operating system:* Mac. School-owned computers available for student use.

EXTRACURRICULARS
Activities: Student government, student newspaper. **Organizations:** 14 honor societies, 3 religious organizations.

ADMISSIONS
Selectivity Rating: 73 (of 100). **Freshman Academic Profile:** Average high school GPA 2.5. 85% from public high schools. Average SAT I Math 480. Average SAT I Verbal 510, SAT I Verbal middle 50% range 450-580. Average ACT 19. TOEFL required of all international applicants, minimum TOEFL 500. **Freshman Admission Requirements:** High school diploma is required and GED is not accepted. **Transfer Admission Requirements:** Lowest grade transferable C. **General Admission Information:** Application fee $25. Early decision application deadline June 15. Regular application deadline rolling. Nonfall registration accepted. Admission may be deferred. Credit and/or placement offered for CEEB Advanced Placement tests.

COSTS AND FINANCIAL AID
Tuition $11,450. Room & board $4,500. Required fees $50. Average book expense $1,000. **Required Forms and Deadlines:** FAFSA and institution's own financial aid form. **Types of Aid:** *Loans:* FFEL Subsidized Stafford, FFEL PLUS. **Student Employment:** Federal Work-Study Program available. Institutional employment available. Off-campus job opportunities are good.

Financial Aid Statistics: Average income from on-campus job $800. **Financial Aid Phone:** 901-726-4085.

MENLO COLLEGE

1000 El Camino Real, Atherton, CA 94027
Phone: 650-688-3753 **E-mail:** admissions@menlo.edu **CEEB Code:** 4483
Fax: 650-617-2395 **Web:** www.menlo.edu **ACT Code:** 330

This private school was founded in 1927. It has a 45-acre campus.

STUDENTS AND FACULTY

Enrollment: 626. **Student Body:** Male 55%, female 45%, out-of-state 17%, international 7% (17 countries represented). **Ethnic Representation:** African American 9%, Asian 17%, Caucasian 39%, Hispanic 9%, Native American 1%. **Retention and Graduation:** 61% freshmen return for sophomore year. 28% freshmen graduate within 4 years. **Faculty:** Student/faculty ratio 16:1. 21 full-time faculty, 66% hold PhDs. 100% faculty teach undergrads.

ACADEMICS

Degrees: Bachelor's. **Academic Requirements:** General education including some course work in computer literacy, English (including composition), foreign languages, humanities, sciences (biological or physical), economics. **Classes:** 10-19 students in an average class. 20-29 students in an average lab/discussion section. **Disciplines with Highest Percentage of Degrees Awarded:** Business/marketing 64%, liberal arts/general studies 17%, communications/communication technologies 10%, computer and information sciences 4%, biological life sciences 1%. **Special Study Options:** Accelerated program, double major, dual enrollment, English as a second language, honors program, independent study, internships, student-designed major, study abroad, Advanced Placement credit, learning disability services.

FACILITIES

Housing: Coed, all-male. **Library Holdings:** 67,769 bound volumes. 249 periodicals. 276 microforms. 588 audiovisuals. **Computers:** School-owned computers available for student use.

EXTRACURRICULARS

Activities: Radio station, student government, student newspaper, television station. **Organizations:** 20 registered organizations, 1 honor society. **Athletics (Intercollegiate):** *Men:* baseball, basketball, cross-country, football, golf, soccer, tennis, track & field. *Women:* basketball, cross-country, golf, soccer, softball, tennis, track & field, volleyball.

ADMISSIONS

Selectivity Rating: 69 (of 100). **Freshman Academic Profile:** Average high school GPA 3.0. 5% in top 10% of high school class, 27% in top 25% of high school class, 63% in top 50% of high school class. SAT I Math middle 50% range 430-540. SAT I Verbal middle 50% range 430-550. ACT middle 50% range 17-24. TOEFL required of all international applicants, minimum TOEFL 550. **Basis for Candidate Selection:** *Very important factors considered include:* essays, recommendations, secondary school record, standardized test scores. *Important factors considered include:* extracurricular activities. *Other factors considered include:* alumni/ae relation, class rank, interview, volunteer work, work experience. **Freshman Admission Requirements:** High school diploma or GED is required. *Academic units required/recommended:* 24 total recommended; 4 English recommended, 3 math recommended, 3 science recommended, 1 science lab recommended, 2 foreign language recommended, 3 social studies recommended. **Freshman Admission Statistics:** 404 applied, 79% accepted, 30% of those accepted enrolled. **Transfer Admission Requirements:** *Items required:* college transcript, essay. Minimum high school GPA of 2.5 required. Minimum college GPA of 2.5 required. Lowest grade transferable C. **General Admission Information:** Application fee $40. Priority application deadline February 1. Early decision application deadline December 1. Nonfall registration accepted. Admission may be deferred for a maximum of 1 year. Credit offered for CEEB Advanced Placement tests.

COSTS AND FINANCIAL AID

Tuition $16,800. Room & board $6,800. Required fees $300. Average book expense $648. **Required Forms and Deadlines:** FAFSA, institution's own financial aid form and state aid form. Financial aid filing deadline August 1. Priority filing deadline March 2. **Notification of Awards:** Applicants will be notified of awards on a rolling basis. **Types of Aid:** *Need-based scholarships/grants:* Pell, SEOG, state scholarships/grants, the school's own gift aid. *Loans:* Direct Subsidized Stafford, Direct Unsubsidized Stafford, Direct PLUS. **Student Employment:** Federal Work-Study Program available. Institutional employment available. Off-campus job opportunities are excellent. **Financial Aid Statistics:** 53% freshmen, 55% undergrads receive some form of aid. Average freshman grant $4,718. Average freshman loan $3,785. Average income from on-campus job $2,000. **Financial Aid Phone:** 650-688-3880.

MERCER UNIVERSITY—ATLANTA

3001 Mercer University Drive, Atlanta, GA 30341

This private school is affiliated with the Baptist Church.

STUDENTS AND FACULTY

Enrollment: 235. **Student Body:** Out-of-state 5%.

EXTRACURRICULARS

Organizations: 7 honor societies, 4 religious organizations.

ADMISSIONS

Selectivity Rating: 63 (of 100). **Freshman Academic Profile:** TOEFL required of all international applicants, minimum TOEFL 500. **Freshman Admission Requirements: General Admission Information:** Regular application deadline rolling.

COSTS AND FINANCIAL AID

Tuition $14,706. Average book expense $200. **Types of Aid:** *Need-based scholarships/grants:* Pell, SEOG, state scholarships/grants, private scholarships, the school's own gift aid. *Loans:* FFEL Subsidized Stafford, FFEL Unsubsidized Stafford, FFEL PLUS, Federal Perkins, state loans, college/university loans from institutional funds. **Student Employment:** Federal Work-Study Program available.

MERCER UNIVERSITY—MACON

Admissions Office, 1400 Coleman Avenue, Macon, GA 31207-0001
Phone: 478-301-2650 **E-mail:** admissions@mercer.edu **CEEB Code:** 5409
Fax: 478-301-2828 **Web:** www.mercer.edu **ACT Code:** 838

This private school, which is affiliated with the Baptist Church, was founded in 1833. It has a 150-acre campus.

STUDENTS AND FACULTY

Enrollment: 4,673. **Student Body:** Male 33%, female 67%, out-of-state 18%, international 1%. **Ethnic Representation:** African American 18%, Asian 6%, Caucasian 72%, Hispanic 2%. **Retention and Graduation:** 74% freshmen return for sophomore year. 35% freshmen graduate within 4 years. 45% grads go on to further study within 1 year. **Faculty:** Student/faculty ratio 14:1. 330 full-time faculty, 85% hold PhDs.

ACADEMICS

Degrees: Bachelor's, doctoral, first professional, first professional certificate, master's, post-bachelor's certificate, post-master's certificate. **Academic Requirements:** General education including some course work in arts/fine arts, computer literacy, English (including composition), foreign languages, history, humanities, mathematics, philosophy, sciences (biological or physical), social science, religion/Christianity. **Classes:** 20-29 students in an average class. 10-19 students in an average lab/discussion section. **Majors with Highest Enrollment:** Drama and dramatics/theatre arts, general; finance, general; biology/biological sciences, general. **Disciplines with Highest Percentage of Degrees Awarded:** Business/marketing 25%, engineering/engineering technology 15%, social sciences and history 14%, visual and performing arts 10%, English 7%. **Special Study Options:** Accelerated program, cooperative (work-study) program, cross registration, double major, dual enrollment, honors program, independent study, internships, liberal arts/career combination, student-designed major, study abroad, teacher certification program, Great Books program.

FACILITIES

Housing: Coed, all-female, all-male, apartments for married students, apartments for single students, housing for disabled students, housing for international students, fraternities and/or sororities, apartments for students with dependent children. **Library Holdings:** 391,800 bound volumes. 5,729 periodicals. 3,223,373 microforms. 59,733 audiovisuals. **Computers:** *Recommended operating system:* Windows 95. School-owned computers available for student use.

EXTRACURRICULARS

Activities: Choral groups, concert band, dance, drama/theater, jazz band, literary magazine, music ensembles, opera, pep band, student government, student newspaper, student-run film society. **Organizations:** 110 registered organizations, 18 honor societies, 8 religious organizations, 10 fraternities (30% men join), 7 sororities (27% women join). **Athletics (Intercollegiate):** *Men:* baseball, basketball, cross-country, golf, rifle, soccer, tennis. *Women:* basketball, cross-country, golf, rifle, soccer, softball, tennis, volleyball.

ADMISSIONS

Selectivity Rating: 76 (of 100). **Freshman Academic Profile:** Average high school GPA 3.6. 44% in top 10% of high school class, 71% in top 25% of high school class, 89% in top 50% of high school class. Average SAT I Math 580, SAT I Math middle 50% range 530-640. Average SAT I Verbal 578, SAT I Verbal middle 50% range 530-630. Average ACT 25, ACT middle 50% range 22-28. TOEFL required of all international applicants, minimum TOEFL 550. **Basis for Candidate Selection:** *Very important factors considered include:* character/personal qualities, secondary school record, standardized test scores. *Important factors considered include:* extracurricular activities, talent/ability, volunteer work. *Other factors considered include:* alumni/ae relation, interview, recommendations. **Freshman Admission Requirements:** High school diploma or GED is required. *Academic units required/recommended:* 16 total required; 4 English required, 4 math required, 3 science required, 2 science lab required, 2 foreign language required, 1 social studies required, 2 history required. **Freshman Admission Statistics:** 2,697 applied, 85% accepted, 27% of those accepted enrolled. **Transfer Admission Requirements:** *Items required:* college transcript, statement of good standing from prior school. Minimum high school GPA of 2.5 required. Minimum college GPA of 2.5 required. Lowest grade transferable C. **General Admission Information:** Application fee $50. Priority application deadline March 1. Early decision application deadline December 1. Regular application deadline June 1. Nonfall registration accepted. Admission may be deferred for a maximum of 1 year. Credit and/or placement offered for CEEB Advanced Placement tests.

COSTS AND FINANCIAL AID

Tuition $19,728. Room & board $6,420. Required fees $0. Average book expense $650. **Required Forms and Deadlines:** FAFSA, institution's own financial aid form and state aid form. No deadline for regular filing. Priority filing deadline April 1. **Notification of Awards:** Applicants will be notified of awards on a rolling basis beginning on or about March 15. **Types of Aid:** *Need-based scholarships/grants:* Pell, SEOG, state scholarships/grants, the school's own gift aid, Federal Nursing. *Loans:* Direct Subsidized Stafford, Direct Unsubsidized Stafford, Direct PLUS, Federal Perkins, Federal Nursing, college/university loans from institutional funds. **Student Employment:** Federal Work-Study Program available. Institutional employment available. Off-campus job opportunities are excellent. **Financial Aid Statistics:** 68% freshmen, 68% undergrads receive some form of aid. Average income from on-campus job $2,100. **Financial Aid Phone:** 478-301-2670.

See page 1110.

internships, liberal arts/career combination, student-designed major, study abroad, teacher certification program, weekend college.

FACILITIES

Housing: Coed. **Library Holdings:** 200,000 bound volumes. 1,300 periodicals. 15,000 audiovisuals. **Computers:** School-owned computers available for student use.

EXTRACURRICULARS

Activities: Choral groups, drama/theater, radio station, student government, student newspaper, student-run film society. **Organizations:** 31 registered organizations, 1 honor society, 4 religious organizations. **Athletics (Intercollegiate):** *Men:* baseball, basketball, cross-country, golf, indoor track, soccer. *Women:* basketball, cross-country, indoor track, soccer, softball, tennis, volleyball.

ADMISSIONS

Selectivity Rating: 65 (of 100). **Freshman Academic Profile:** 6% in top 10% of high school class, 24% in top 25% of high school class, 51% in top 50% of high school class. 75% from public high schools. **Basis for Candidate Selection:** *Very important factors considered include:* secondary school record. *Important factors considered include:* essays, interview, recommendations, standardized test scores. *Other factors considered include:* alumni/ae relation, character/personal qualities, class rank, minority status, talent/ability. **Freshman Admission Requirements:** High school diploma or GED is required. *Academic units required/recommended:* 15 total recommended; 4 English recommended, 3 math recommended, 2 science recommended, 2 foreign language recommended, 4 social studies recommended. **Freshman Admission Statistics:** 2,282 applied, 47% accepted, 79% of those accepted enrolled. **Transfer Admission Requirements:** *Items required:* college transcript, interview. Minimum college GPA of 3.0 required. Lowest grade transferable C. **General Admission Information:** Application fee $35. Nonfall registration accepted. Credit offered for CEEB Advanced Placement tests.

COSTS AND FINANCIAL AID

Tuition $10,000. Room & board $8,000. Required fees $0. Average book expense $1,000. **Required Forms and Deadlines:** FAFSA. Financial aid filing deadline August 15. Priority filing deadline May 1. **Notification of Awards:** Applicants will be notified of awards on a rolling basis beginning on or about April 1. **Types of Aid:** *Need-based scholarships/grants:* Pell, SEOG, state scholarships/grants, private scholarships, the school's own gift aid. *Loans:* FFEL Subsidized Stafford, FFEL Unsubsidized Stafford, FFEL PLUS, college/university loans from institutional funds. **Student Employment:** Federal Work-Study Program available. Institutional employment available. Off-campus job opportunities are good. **Financial Aid Statistics:** 71% freshmen, 78% undergrads receive some form of aid. Average freshman grant $4,959. Average freshman loan $2,015. Average income from on-campus job $5,342. **Financial Aid Phone:** 914-693-7600.

See page 1112.

MERCY COLLEGE

555 Broadway, Dobbs Ferry, NY 10522
Phone: 914-674-7324 **E-mail:** admission@mercy.edu **CEEB Code:** 2409
Fax: 914-674-7382 **Web:** www.mercy.edu **ACT Code:** 2814

This private school was founded in 1950. It has a 60-acre campus.

STUDENTS AND FACULTY

Enrollment: 6,982. **Student Body:** Male 29%, female 71%, out-of-state 4%, international 2%. **Ethnic Representation:** African American 33%, Asian 3%, Caucasian 28%, Hispanic 37%. **Retention and Graduation:** 52% freshmen return for sophomore year. 33% grads go on to further study within 1 year. **Faculty:** Student/faculty ratio 15:1. 225 full-time faculty, 77% hold PhDs.

ACADEMICS

Degrees: Associate's, bachelor's, certificate, master's. **Academic Requirements:** General education including some course work in arts/fine arts, computer literacy, English (including composition), foreign languages, history, humanities, mathematics, philosophy, sciences (biological or physical), social science. **Classes:** 10-19 students in an average class. 10-19 students in an average lab/discussion section. **Majors with Highest Enrollment:** Business administration/management; liberal arts and sciences/liberal studies; psychology, general. **Special Study Options:** Accelerated program, cooperative (work-study) program, cross registration, distance learning, double major, dual enrollment, English as a second language, honors program, independent study,

MERCYHURST COLLEGE

Admissions, 501 E. 38th Street, Erie, PA 16546
Phone: 800-825-1926 **E-mail:** admug@mercyhurst.edu **CEEB Code:** 2410
Fax: 814-824-2071 **Web:** www.mercyhurst.edu **ACT Code:** 3629

This private school, which is affiliated with the Roman Catholic Church, was founded in 1926. It has an 88-acre campus.

STUDENTS AND FACULTY

Enrollment: 2,832. **Student Body:** Male 43%, female 57%, out-of-state 43%, international 3%. **Ethnic Representation:** African American 4%, Asian 1%, Caucasian 94%, Hispanic 1%. **Retention and Graduation:** 80% freshmen return for sophomore year. 48% freshmen graduate within 4 years. 16% grads go on to further study within 1 year. 3% grads pursue business degrees. 2% grads pursue law degrees. 2% grads pursue medical degrees. **Faculty:** Student/faculty ratio 17:1. 117 full-time faculty, 52% hold PhDs. 100% faculty teach undergrads.

ACADEMICS

Degrees: Associate's, bachelor's, diploma, master's, post-bachelor's certificate, terminal, transfer. **Academic Requirements:** General education including some course work in arts/fine arts, computer literacy, English (including composition), foreign languages, history, mathematics, philosophy, sciences (biological or physical), social science, religious studies. **Classes:** Under 10 students in an average class. **Disciplines with Highest Percentage of

Degrees Awarded: Business/marketing 33%, education 19%, social sciences and history 10%, visual and performing arts 7%, protective services/public administration 6%. **Special Study Options:** Accelerated program, cooperative (work-study) program, cross registration, double major, student exchange program (domestic), honors program, independent study, internships, liberal arts/career combination, student-designed major, study abroad, teacher certification program, weekend college. Off-campus study in Washington, DC. Undergrads may take grad-level classes.

FACILITIES

Housing: All-female, all-male, apartments for married students, apartments for single students. **Library Holdings:** 123,467 bound volumes. 849 periodicals. 61,493 microforms. 8,051 audiovisuals. **Special Academic Facilities/ Equipment:** Art gallery, college-owned restaurant for hotel/restaurant management department, observatory, archaeology lab. **Computers:** School-owned computers available for student use.

EXTRACURRICULARS

Activities: Choral groups, concert band, dance, drama/theater, literary magazine, music ensembles, opera, pep band, radio station, student government, student newspaper, symphony orchestra, television station, yearbook. **Organizations:** 11 honor societies, 2 religious organizations. **Athletics (Intercollegiate):** *Men:* baseball, basketball, crew, football, golf, ice hockey, lacrosse, soccer, tennis, volleyball. *Women:* basketball, cheerleading, crew, cross-country, field hockey, golf, ice hockey, lacrosse, soccer, softball, tennis, volleyball.

ADMISSIONS

Selectivity Rating: 77 (of 100). **Freshman Academic Profile:** Average high school GPA 3.2. 18% in top 10% of high school class, 45% in top 25% of high school class, 78% in top 50% of high school class. 78% from public high schools. Average SAT I Math 532, SAT I Math middle 50% range 480-580. Average SAT I Verbal 549, SAT I Verbal middle 50% range 490-580. Average ACT 23, ACT middle 50% range 20-25. TOEFL required of all international applicants, minimum TOEFL 550. **Basis for Candidate Selection:** *Very important factors considered include:* class rank, secondary school record. *Important factors considered include:* character/personal qualities, standardized test scores, talent/ability, volunteer work, work experience. *Other factors considered include:* alumni/ae relation, essays, extracurricular activities, geographical residence, interview, minority status, religious affiliation/commitment, state residency. **Freshman Admission Requirements:** High school diploma or GED is required. *Academic units required/recommended:* 16 total recommended; 4 English recommended, 3 math recommended, 3 science recommended, 1 science lab recommended, 2 foreign language recommended, 1 social studies recommended, 2 history recommended. **Freshman Admission Statistics:** 1,852 applied, 79% accepted, 37% of those accepted enrolled. **Transfer Admission Requirements:** *Items required:* high school transcript, college transcript, standardized test scores. Minimum high school GPA of 2.5 required. Minimum college GPA of 2.2 required. Lowest grade transferable C. **General Admission Information:** Application fee $30. Priority application deadline March 15. Nonfall registration accepted. Admission may be deferred for a maximum of 1 year. Credit and/or placement offered for CEEB Advanced Placement tests.

COSTS AND FINANCIAL AID

Tuition $13,190. Room & board $5,364. Required fees $900. Average book expense $750. **Required Forms and Deadlines:** FAFSA and institution's own financial aid form. Financial aid filing deadline August 1. Priority filing deadline May 1. **Notification of Awards:** Applicants will be notified of awards on a rolling basis beginning on or about March 1. **Types of Aid:** *Need-based scholarships/grants:* Pell, SEOG, state scholarships/grants, private scholarships, the school's own gift aid. *Loans:* FFEL Subsidized Stafford, FFEL Unsubsidized Stafford, FFEL PLUS, Federal Perkins. **Student Employment:** Federal Work-Study Program available. Institutional employment available. Off-campus job opportunities are good. **Financial Aid Statistics:** 72% freshmen, 65% undergrads receive some form of aid. Average freshman grant $4,530. Average freshman loan $2,387. Average income from on-campus job $750. **Financial Aid Phone:** 814-824-2288.

MEREDITH COLLEGE

3800 Hillsborough Street, Raleigh, NC 27607
Phone: 919-760-8581 **E-mail:** admissions@meredith.edu **CEEB Code:** 5410
Fax: 919-760-2348 **Web:** www.meredith.edu **ACT Code:** 3126

This private school was founded in 1891. It has a 225-acre campus.

STUDENTS AND FACULTY

Enrollment: 2,175. **Student Body:** Out-of-state 8%. **Retention and Graduation:** 77% freshmen return for sophomore year. 57% freshmen graduate within 4 years. 16% grads go on to further study within 1 year. 2% grads pursue business degrees. 2% grads pursue law degrees. 1% grads pursue medical degrees. **Faculty:** Student/faculty ratio 10:1. 139 full-time faculty, 83% hold PhDs. 99% faculty teach undergrads.

ACADEMICS

Degrees: Bachelor's, master's, post-bachelor's certificate. **Academic Requirements:** General education including some course work in arts/fine arts, English (including composition), foreign languages, history, humanities, mathematics, sciences (biological or physical), social science, religion. **Classes:** 10-19 students in an average class. 10-19 students in an average lab/discussion section. **Majors with Highest Enrollment:** Business administration/ management; child development; psychology, general. **Disciplines with Highest Percentage of Degrees Awarded:** Business/marketing 22%, visual and performing arts 15%, psychology 9%, home economics and vocational home economics 9%, social sciences and history 7%. **Special Study Options:** Accelerated program, cooperative (work-study) program, cross registration, double major, dual enrollment, student exchange program (domestic), honors program, independent study, internships, student-designed major, study abroad, teacher certification program, Capital City Semester. Semester programs at American University, Drew University, Marymount Manhattan.

FACILITIES

Housing: All-female. **Library Holdings:** 116,974 bound volumes. 2,680 periodicals. 64,302 microforms. 12,085 audiovisuals. **Special Academic Facilities/Equipment:** Art gallery, amphitheater, child-care lab, learning center, fitness center, autism lab, astronomy observation deck. **Computers:** School-owned computers available for student use.

EXTRACURRICULARS

Activities: Choral groups, dance, drama/theater, literary magazine, music ensembles, musical theater, student government, student newspaper, yearbook. **Organizations:** 95 registered organizations, 21 honor societies, 5 religious organizations. **Athletics (Intercollegiate):** *Women:* basketball, soccer, softball, tennis, volleyball.

ADMISSIONS

Selectivity Rating: 69 (of 100). **Freshman Academic Profile:** Average high school GPA 3.0. 22% in top 10% of high school class, 57% in top 25% of high school class, 90% in top 50% of high school class. 86% from public high schools. SAT I Math middle 50% range 470-570. SAT I Verbal middle 50% range 480-560. ACT middle 50% range 18-24. TOEFL required of all international applicants, minimum TOEFL 500. **Basis for Candidate Selection:** *Very important factors considered include:* class rank, secondary school record. *Important factors considered include:* character/personal qualities, recommendations, standardized test scores. *Other factors considered include:* alumni/ae relation, essays, extracurricular activities, interview, talent/ability, volunteer work, work experience. **Freshman Admission Requirements:** High school diploma is required and GED is not accepted. *Academic units required/ recommended:* 16 total required; 4 English required, 3 math required, 3 science required, 2 foreign language required, 1 elective recommended. **Freshman Admission Statistics:** 1,039 applied, 86% accepted, 44% of those accepted enrolled. **Transfer Admission Requirements:** *Items required:* high school transcript, college transcript, statement of good standing from prior school. Minimum college GPA of 2.0 required. Lowest grade transferable C. **General Admission Information:** Application fee $35. Priority application deadline February 15. Early decision application deadline October 15. Nonfall registration accepted. Admission may be deferred for a maximum of 1 year. Credit offered for CEEB Advanced Placement tests.

COSTS AND FINANCIAL AID

Tuition $18,065. Room & board $5,000. **Required Forms and Deadlines:** FAFSA, institution's own financial aid form and CSS/Financial Aid PROFILE required of Early Decision financial aid applicants. Priority filing deadline February 15. **Notification of Awards:** Applicants will be notified of awards on a rolling basis beginning on or about March 1. **Types of Aid:** *Need-based scholarships/grants:* Pell, SEOG, state scholarships/grants, private scholarships, the school's own gift aid. *Loans:* FFEL Subsidized Stafford, FFEL

Unsubsidized Stafford, FFEL PLUS, Federal Perkins. **Student Employment:** Federal Work-Study Program available. Institutional employment available. Off-campus job opportunities are excellent. **Financial Aid Statistics:** 51% freshmen, 47% undergrads receive some form of aid. Average freshman grant $9,514. Average freshman loan $2,182. Average income from on-campus job $918. **Financial Aid Phone:** 919-760-8565.

MERRIMACK COLLEGE

Office of Admission, Austin Hall, North Andover, MA 01845
Phone: 978-837-5100 **E-mail:** admission@merrimack.edu **CEEB Code:** 3525
Fax: 978-837-5133 **Web:** www.merrimack.edu

This private school, which is affiliated with the Roman Catholic Church, was founded in 1947. It has a 220-acre campus.

STUDENTS AND FACULTY

Enrollment: 2,501. **Student Body:** Male 47%, female 53%, out-of-state 20%, international 1% (28 countries represented). **Ethnic Representation:** African American 1%, Asian 1%, Caucasian 30%, Hispanic 2%. **Retention and Graduation:** 81% freshmen return for sophomore year. 39% freshmen graduate within 4 years. 23% grads go on to further study within 1 year. 19% grads pursue business degrees. 4% grads pursue law degrees. 1% grads pursue medical degrees. **Faculty:** Student/faculty ratio 13:1. 144 full-time faculty, 78% hold PhDs. 100% faculty teach undergrads.

ACADEMICS

Degrees: Associate's, bachelor's, master's. **Academic Requirements:** General education including some course work in arts/fine arts, English (including composition), history, humanities, mathematics, sciences (biological or physical), social science, religious studies, first year seminar. **Classes:** 10-19 students in an average class. Under 10 students in an average lab/discussion section. **Majors with Highest Enrollment:** Business administration/ management; psychology, general; communications studies/speech communication and rhetoric. **Disciplines with Highest Percentage of Degrees Awarded:** Business/marketing 41%, psychology 15%, social sciences and history 10%, communications/communication technologies 6%, engineering/ engineering technology 4%. **Special Study Options:** Cooperative (work-study) program, cross registration, double major, English as a second language, honors program, internships, liberal arts/career combination, student-designed major, study abroad, five-year combined BA/BS program, continuing education program, center for corporate education. ESL available through the American Language Academy (ALA) with offices on the college campus.

FACILITIES

Housing: Coed, apartments for single students, housing for disabled students, housing for international students, townhouses for single students. **Library Holdings:** 118,083 bound volumes. 1,069 periodicals. 11,100 microforms. 1,970 audiovisuals. **Special Academic Facilities/Equipment:** Observatory, National Microscale Chemistry Institute, American Language Academy, Urban Institute, New Freshmen Residence Halls, Rogers Center for the Arts. **Computers:** *Recommended operating system:* Windows NT/2000. School-owned computers available for student use.

EXTRACURRICULARS

Activities: Choral groups, drama/theater, literary magazine, music ensembles, musical theater, pep band, student government, student newspaper, student-run film society, television station, yearbook. **Organizations:** 48 registered organizations, 3 honor societies, 5 religious organizations, 3 fraternities (5% men join), 3 sororities (8% women join). **Athletics (Intercollegiate):** *Men:* baseball, basketball, cross-country, football, ice hockey, lacrosse, soccer, tennis. *Women:* basketball, cross-country, field hockey, lacrosse, soccer, softball, tennis, volleyball.

ADMISSIONS

Selectivity Rating: 77 (of 100). **Freshman Academic Profile:** Average high school GPA 3.1. 15% in top 10% of high school class, 41% in top 25% of high school class, 83% in top 50% of high school class. 72% from public high schools. Average SAT I Math 530, SAT I Math middle 50% range 520-620. Average SAT I Verbal 522, SAT I Verbal middle 50% range 510-610. Average ACT 23. TOEFL required of all international applicants, minimum TOEFL 600. **Basis for Candidate Selection:** *Very important factors considered include:* secondary school record, standardized test scores. *Important factors considered include:* character/personal qualities, class rank, essays, extracurricular activities, interview, recommendations. *Other factors considered include:* alumni/ae relation, geographical residence, state residency, talent/ability, volunteer work, work experience. **Freshman Admission Requirements:** High school diploma or GED is required. *Academic units required/recommended:* 16 total required; 21 total recommended; 4 English required, 4 English recommended, 3 math required, 4 math recommended, 2 science required, 3 science recommended, 2 science lab required, 3 science lab recommended, 2 foreign language recommended, 2 social studies required, 2 social studies recommended, 1 history required, 1 history recommended, 2 elective required, 2 elective recommended. **Freshman Admission Statistics:** 3,243 applied, 67% accepted, 26% of those accepted enrolled. **Transfer Admission Requirements:** *Items required:* college transcript, essay. Minimum high school GPA of 3.0 required. Minimum college GPA of 2.5 required. Lowest grade transferable C. **General Admission Information:** Application fee $50. Regular application deadline February 15. Nonfall registration accepted. Admission may be deferred for a maximum of 1 year. Credit and/or placement offered for CEEB Advanced Placement tests.

COSTS AND FINANCIAL AID

Tuition $18,800. Room & board $8,410. Required fees $200. Average book expense $700. **Required Forms and Deadlines:** FAFSA, CSS/Financial Aid PROFILE, noncustodial (divorced/separated) parent's statement and business/ farm supplement. Financial aid filing deadline February 15. **Notification of Awards:** Applicants will be notified of awards on a rolling basis beginning on or about March 1. **Types of Aid:** *Need-based scholarships/grants:* Pell, SEOG, state scholarships/grants, private scholarships, the school's own gift aid. *Loans:* Direct Subsidized Stafford, Direct Unsubsidized Stafford, Direct PLUS, Federal Perkins, state loans, college/university loans from institutional funds, alternative loans. **Student Employment:** Federal Work-Study Program available. Institutional employment available. Off-campus job opportunities are good. **Financial Aid Statistics:** 76% freshmen, 77% undergrads receive some form of aid. Average freshman grant $8,500. Average freshman loan $4,125. Average income from on-campus job $1,500. **Financial Aid Phone:** 978-837-5186.

MESA STATE COLLEGE

PO Box 2647, Grand Junction, CO 81502-2647
Phone: 970-248-1875 **E-mail:** admissions@mesastate.edu **CEEB Code:** 4484
Fax: 970-248-1973 **Web:** www.mesastate.edu **ACT Code:** 518

This public school was founded in 1925. It has a 57-acre campus.

STUDENTS AND FACULTY

Enrollment: 4,926. **Student Body:** Male 44%, female 56%, out-of-state 9%, international 1%. **Ethnic Representation:** African American 1%, Asian 1%, Caucasian 87%, Hispanic 7%, Native American 1%. **Retention and Graduation:** 61% freshmen return for sophomore year. 9% freshmen graduate within 4 years. 5% grads go on to further study within 1 year. **Faculty:** 100% faculty teach undergrads.

ACADEMICS

Degrees: Associate's, bachelor's, certificate, master's. **Academic Requirements:** General education including some course work in arts/fine arts, English (including composition), foreign languages, humanities, mathematics, sciences (biological or physical), social science. **Special Study Options:** Cooperative (work-study) program, distance learning, double major, student exchange program (domestic), external degree program, honors program, independent study, internships, teacher certification program, weekend college.

FACILITIES

Housing: Coed, apartments for single students. **Library Holdings:** 329,681 bound volumes. 1,010 periodicals. 803,012 microforms. 25,578 audiovisuals. **Special Academic Facilities/Equipment:** Art gallery, experimental farm, early childhood education center, electron microscopes, television studio. **Computers:** *Recommended operating system:* Windows 95. School-owned computers available for student use.

EXTRACURRICULARS

Activities: Choral groups, dance, drama/theater, jazz band, literary magazine, music ensembles, musical theater, pep band, radio station, student government, student newspaper, symphony orchestra, television station. **Organizations:** 50 registered organizations, 10 honor societies, 4 religious organizations. **Athletics (Intercollegiate):** *Men:* baseball, basketball, football, tennis. *Women:* basketball, skiing (cross-country), golf, soccer, softball, tennis, volleyball.

ADMISSIONS

Selectivity Rating: 77 (of 100). **Freshman Academic Profile:** Average high school GPA 3.1. 18% in top 10% of high school class, 32% in top 25% of high school class, 70% in top 50% of high school class. 98% from public high schools.

Average SAT I Math 483, SAT I Math middle 50% range 430-560. Average SAT I Verbal 486, SAT I Verbal middle 50% range 430-550. Average ACT 21, ACT middle 50% range 18-25. TOEFL required of all international applicants, minimum TOEFL 525. **Basis for Candidate Selection:** *Very important factors considered include:* class rank, recommendations, secondary school record, standardized test scores. *Other factors considered include:* character/personal qualities, essays, extracurricular activities, geographical residence, interview, state residency, volunteer work. **Freshman Admission Requirements:** High school diploma or GED is required. *Academic units required/recommended:* 14 total recommended; 1 science lab recommended. **Freshman Admission Statistics:** 1,940 applied, 94% accepted, 57% of those accepted enrolled. **Transfer Admission Requirements:** *Items required:* college transcript, statement of good standing from prior school. Minimum college GPA of 2.0 required. Lowest grade transferable C. **General Admission Information:** Application fee $30. Priority application deadline March 1. Regular application deadline August 15. Nonfall registration accepted. Admission may be deferred for a maximum of 1 year. Credit and/or placement offered for CEEB Advanced Placement tests.

COSTS AND FINANCIAL AID

In-state tuition $1,576. Out-of-state tuition $5,966. Room & board $5,048. Required fees $546. Average book expense $690. **Required Forms and Deadlines:** FAFSA. Priority filing deadline March 1. **Notification of Awards:** Applicants will be notified of awards on a rolling basis beginning on or about April 15. **Types of Aid:** *Need-based scholarships/grants:* Pell, SEOG, state scholarships/grants, private scholarships, the school's own gift aid. *Loans:* FFEL Subsidized Stafford, FFEL Unsubsidized Stafford, FFEL PLUS, Federal Perkins. **Student Employment:** Federal Work-Study Program available. Institutional employment available. Off-campus job opportunities are good. **Financial Aid Statistics:** 68% freshmen, 51% undergrads receive some form of aid. Average freshman grant $1,900. Average freshman loan $3,700. Average income from on-campus job $1,000. **Financial Aid Phone:** 970-248-1396.

MESSIAH COLLEGE

One College Avenue, Grantham, PA 17027
Phone: 717-691-6000 **E-mail:** admiss@messiah.edu **CEEB Code:** 2411
Fax: 717-796-5374 **Web:** www.messiah.edu **ACT Code:** 3630

This private school was founded in 1909. It has a 400-acre campus.

STUDENTS AND FACULTY

Enrollment: 2,895. **Student Body:** Male 38%, female 62%, out-of-state 48%, international 2% (34 countries represented). **Ethnic Representation:** African American 3%, Asian 1%, Caucasian 93%, Hispanic 2%. **Retention and Graduation:** 85% freshmen return for sophomore year. 67% freshmen graduate within 4 years. 8% grads go on to further study within 1 year. 1% grads pursue business degrees. **Faculty:** Student/faculty ratio 13:1. 166 full-time faculty, 72% hold PhDs. 100% faculty teach undergrads.

ACADEMICS

Degrees: Bachelor's. **Academic Requirements:** General education including some course work in arts/fine arts, English (including composition), foreign languages, history, humanities, mathematics, philosophy, sciences (biological or physical), social science, Bible. **Classes:** 20-29 students in an average class. 20-29 students in an average lab/discussion section. **Majors with Highest Enrollment:** Nursing/registered nurse training (RN, ASN, BSN, MSN); elementary education and teaching; engineering, general. **Disciplines with Highest Percentage of Degrees Awarded:** Education 15%, business/marketing 13%, social sciences and history 10%, health professions and related sciences 7%, philosophy/religion/theology 6%. **Special Study Options:** Accelerated program, double major, English as a second language, student exchange program (domestic), honors program, independent study, internships, student-designed major, study abroad, teacher certification program, pass/fail option.

FACILITIES

Housing: Coed, all-female, all-male, apartments for single students, housing for disabled students, housing for international students. **Library Holdings:** 258,097 bound volumes. 1,327 periodicals. 114,029 microforms. 14,141 audiovisuals. **Special Academic Facilities/Equipment:** Boyer Center for Advanced Studies, Brethren in Christ Archives, Oakes Museum of Natural History. **Computers:** *Recommended operating system:* Windows 95. School-owned computers available for student use.

EXTRACURRICULARS

Activities: Choral groups, concert band, dance, drama/theater, jazz band, literary magazine, music ensembles, musical theater, pep band, radio station, student government, student newspaper, student-run film society, symphony orchestra, yearbook. **Organizations:** 35 registered organizations, 2 honor societies, 7 religious organizations. **Athletics (Intercollegiate):** *Men:* baseball, basketball, cross-country, golf, indoor track, lacrosse, soccer, tennis, track & field, wrestling. *Women:* basketball, cross-country, field hockey, indoor track, lacrosse, soccer, softball, tennis, track & field, volleyball.

ADMISSIONS

Selectivity Rating: 76 (of 100). **Freshman Academic Profile:** Average high school GPA 3.8. 35% in top 10% of high school class, 69% in top 25% of high school class, 92% in top 50% of high school class. 76% from public high schools. Average SAT I Math 585, SAT I Math middle 50% range 530-640. Average SAT I Verbal 587, SAT I Verbal middle 50% range 540-640. Average ACT 25, ACT middle 50% range 23-28. TOEFL required of all international applicants, minimum TOEFL 550. **Basis for Candidate Selection:** *Very important factors considered include:* character/personal qualities, class rank, extracurricular activities, recommendations, religious affiliation/commitment, secondary school record, standardized test scores, talent/ability. *Important factors considered include:* essays, volunteer work. *Other factors considered include:* alumni/ae relation, interview, minority status, work experience. **Freshman Admission Requirements:** High school diploma or GED is required. *Academic units required/recommended:* 16 total required; 21 total recommended; 4 English required, 4 English recommended, 2 math required, 3 math recommended, 2 science required, 3 science recommended, 2 science lab required, 3 science lab recommended, 2 foreign language required, 3 foreign language recommended, 2 social studies required, 2 social studies recommended, 2 history recommended, 4 elective required, 4 elective recommended. **Freshman Admission Statistics:** 2,300 applied, 77% accepted, 43% of those accepted enrolled. **Transfer Admission Requirements:** *Items required:* college transcript, essay, statement of good standing from prior school. Minimum college GPA of 2.5 required. Lowest grade transferable C. **General Admission Information:** Application fee $30. Priority application deadline May 1. Early decision application deadline October 15. Nonfall registration accepted. Admission may be deferred for a maximum of 2 years. Credit offered for CEEB Advanced Placement tests.

COSTS AND FINANCIAL AID

Tuition $17,730. Room & board $6,130. Required fees $406. Average book expense $740. **Required Forms and Deadlines:** FAFSA. No deadline for regular filing. Priority filing deadline April 1. **Notification of Awards:** Applicants will be notified of awards on a rolling basis beginning on or about March 15. **Types of Aid:** *Need-based scholarships/grants:* Pell, SEOG, state scholarships/grants, private scholarships, the school's own gift aid. *Loans:* Direct Subsidized Stafford, Direct Unsubsidized Stafford, Direct PLUS, Federal Perkins, Federal Nursing. **Student Employment:** Federal Work-Study Program available. Institutional employment available. Off-campus job opportunities are good. **Financial Aid Statistics:** 72% freshmen, 71% undergrads receive some form of aid. Average freshman grant $8,497. Average freshman loan $7,294. Average income from on-campus job $2,466. **Financial Aid Phone:** 717-691-6007.

See page 1114.

METHODIST COLLEGE

5400 Ramsey Street, Fayetteville, NC 28311
Phone: 910-630-7027 **E-mail:** rlowe@methodist.edu **CEEB Code:** 5426
Fax: 910-630-7285 **Web:** www.methodist.edu **ACT Code:** 3127

This proprietary school, which is affiliated with the Methodist Church, was founded in 1956. It has a 600-acre campus.

STUDENTS AND FACULTY

Enrollment: 2,161. **Student Body:** Male 57%, female 43%, out-of-state 46%, international 2% (20 countries represented). **Ethnic Representation:** African American 23%, Asian 2%, Caucasian 68%, Hispanic 6%, Native American 1%. **Retention and Graduation:** 68% freshmen return for sophomore year. 20% freshmen graduate within 4 years. 32% grads go on to further study within 1 year. 12% grads pursue business degrees. 1% grads pursue law degrees. 7% grads pursue medical degrees. **Faculty:** Student/faculty ratio 15:1. 100 full-time faculty, 64% hold PhDs. 100% faculty teach undergrads.

ACADEMICS

Degrees: Associate's, bachelor's, master's, terminal, transfer. **Academic Requirements:** General education including some course work in arts/fine arts, computer literacy, English (including composition), foreign languages, history, humanities, mathematics, philosophy, sciences (biological or physical), social science, library competency (completed via coursework in freshman seminar course required of freshmen). **Classes:** Under 10 students in an average class. Under 10 students in an average lab/discussion section. **Majors with Highest Enrollment:** Business administration/management; secondary education and teaching; biology/biological sciences, general. **Disciplines with Highest Percentage of Degrees Awarded:** Business/marketing 45%, social sciences and history 11%, parks and recreation 11%, protective services/public administration 8%, education 6%. **Special Study Options:** Cooperative (work-study) program, distance learning, double major, English as a second language, honors program, independent study, internships, liberal arts/career combination, student-designed major, study abroad, teacher certification program, weekend college.

FACILITIES

Housing: Coed, all-female, all-male, apartments for single students, health and wellness hall, first-year experience hall. **Library Holdings:** 86,259 bound volumes. 571 periodicals. 62,814 microforms. 13,208 audiovisuals. **Special Academic Facilities/Equipment:** Art gallery, Nature Trail, 18-hole golf course with practice facilities for PGM students, Academic Development Center. **Computers:** School-owned computers available for student use.

EXTRACURRICULARS

Activities: Choral groups, concert band, dance, drama/theater, jazz band, literary magazine, music ensembles, musical theater, opera, pep band, student government, student newspaper, yearbook. **Organizations:** 72 registered organizations, 15 honor societies, 8 religious organizations, 2 fraternities (2% men join), 3 sororities (2% women join). **Athletics (Intercollegiate):** *Men:* baseball, basketball, cheerleading, cross-country, football, golf, soccer, tennis, track & field. *Women:* basketball, cheerleading, cross-country, golf, lacrosse, soccer, softball, tennis, track & field, volleyball.

ADMISSIONS

Selectivity Rating: 68 (of 100). **Freshman Academic Profile:** Average high school GPA 3.1. 11% in top 10% of high school class, 33% in top 25% of high school class, 67% in top 50% of high school class. 88% from public high schools. Average SAT I Math 501, SAT I Math middle 50% range 450-550. Average SAT I Verbal 489, SAT I Verbal middle 50% range 440-530. Average ACT 19, ACT middle 50% range 17-22. TOEFL required of all international applicants, minimum TOEFL 500. **Basis for Candidate Selection:** *Very important factors considered include:* secondary school record, standardized test scores. *Important factors considered include:* class rank, interview. *Other factors considered include:* alumni/ae relation, character/personal qualities, essays, extracurricular activities, recommendations, talent/ability. **Freshman Admission Requirements:** High school diploma or GED is required. *Academic units required/recommended:* 18 total required; 22 total recommended; 4 English required, 4 English recommended, 2 math required, 3 math recommended, 2 science required, 3 science recommended, 1 science lab required, 1 science lab recommended, 2 foreign language recommended, 2 social studies required, 2 social studies recommended, 2 history required, 3 history recommended, 6 elective required. **Freshman Admission Statistics:** 1,906 applied, 84% accepted, 29% of those accepted enrolled. **Transfer Admission Requirements:** *Items required:* high school transcript, college transcript, statement of good standing from prior school. Minimum college GPA of 2.0 required. Lowest grade transferable C. **General Admission Information:** Application fee $25. Nonfall registration accepted. Admission may be deferred for a maximum of 1 year. Credit and/or placement offered for CEEB Advanced Placement tests.

COSTS AND FINANCIAL AID

Tuition $12,600. Room & board $5,330. Required fees $126. Average book expense $800. **Required Forms and Deadlines:** FAFSA. No deadline for regular filing. **Notification of Awards:** Applicants will be notified of awards on a rolling basis beginning on or about March 1. **Types of Aid:** *Need-based scholarships/grants:* Pell, SEOG, state scholarships/grants, private scholarships, the school's own gift aid. *Loans:* FFEL Subsidized Stafford, FFEL Unsubsidized Stafford, FFEL PLUS, Federal Perkins. **Student Employment:** Federal Work-Study Program available. Institutional employment available. Off-campus job opportunities are good. **Financial Aid Statistics:** 48% freshmen, 55% undergrads receive some form of aid. Average freshman grant $12,591. Average freshman loan $2,625. Average income from on-campus job $1,000. **Financial Aid Phone:** 910-630-7189.

METROPOLITAN COLLEGE OF NEW YORK (FORMERLY AUDREY COHEN COLLEGE)

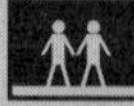

75 Varick Street, New York, NY 10013
Phone: 212-343-1234 **E-mail:** admissions@metropolitan.edu **CEEB Code:** 4802
Fax: 212-343-8470 **Web:** www.metropolitan.edu

This private school was founded in 1964.

STUDENTS AND FACULTY

Enrollment: 4,093. **Student Body:** Male 42%, female 58%, out-of-state 10%, (12 countries represented). **Ethnic Representation:** African American 74%, Asian 1%, Caucasian 4%, Hispanic 13%. **Retention and Graduation:** 72% freshmen return for sophomore year. 60% grads go on to further study within 1 year. 24% grads pursue business degrees. 15% grads pursue law degrees. **Faculty:** Student/faculty ratio 17:1. 26 full-time faculty. 85% faculty teach undergrads.

ACADEMICS

Degrees: Associate's, bachelor's, certificate, master's, transfer. **Academic Requirements:** General education including some course work in computer literacy, English (including composition), humanities, mathematics, philosophy, sciences (biological or physical), social science. **Classes:** 10-19 students in an average class. **Disciplines with Highest Percentage of Degrees Awarded:** Human service degree 75%, business/marketing 25%. **Special Study Options:** Accelerated program, cooperative (work-study) program, internships, weekend college.

FACILITIES

Library Holdings: 26,800 bound volumes. 3,414 periodicals. 263 microforms. 0 audiovisuals. **Computers:** *Recommended operating system:* Windows 95. School-owned computers available for student use.

EXTRACURRICULARS

Activities: Literary magazine, radio station, student government, student newspaper, yearbook. **Organizations:** 10 registered organizations.

ADMISSIONS

Selectivity Rating: 70 (of 100). **Freshman Academic Profile:** 70% from public high schools. TOEFL required of all international applicants, minimum TOEFL 550. **Basis for Candidate Selection:** *Very important factors considered include:* interview. *Important factors considered include:* extracurricular activities, talent/ability, volunteer work, work experience. *Other factors considered include:* character/personal qualities, recommendations. **Freshman Admission Requirements:** High school diploma or GED is required. **Freshman Admission Statistics:** 399 applied, 78% accepted, 62% of those accepted enrolled. **Transfer Admission Requirements:** *Items required:* high school transcript, essay, interview. Lowest grade transferable C. **General Admission Information:** Application fee $30. Early decision application deadline May 2. Nonfall registration accepted. Admission may be deferred for a maximum of 1 year. Neither credit nor placement offered for CEEB Advanced Placement tests.

COSTS AND FINANCIAL AID

Tuition $15,750. Required fees $400. Average book expense $1,500. **Required Forms and Deadlines:** FAFSA, state aid form, and noncustodial (divorced/separated) parent's statement. No deadline for regular filing. **Notification of Awards:** Applicants will be notified of awards on a rolling basis. **Types of Aid:** *Need-based scholarships/grants:* Pell, SEOG, state scholarships/grants, private scholarships, the school's own gift aid. *Loans:* FFEL Subsidized Stafford, FFEL Unsubsidized Stafford, FFEL PLUS, signature loan. **Student Employment:** Federal Work-Study Program available. Off-campus job opportunities are good. **Financial Aid Statistics:** 65% freshmen, 68% undergrads receive some form of aid. **Financial Aid Phone:** 212-343-1234.

See page 1116.

METROPOLITAN STATE COLLEGE OF DENVER

Campus Box 16, PO Box 173362, Denver, CO 80217-3362
Phone: 303-556-3058 **E-mail:** tolandva@mscd.edu **CEEB Code:** 4505
Fax: 303-556-6345 **Web:** www.mscd.edu **ACT Code:** 5190

This public school was founded in 1963. It has a 175-acre campus.

STUDENTS AND FACULTY

Enrollment: 18,445. **Student Body:** Male 43%, female 57%, out-of-state 1%, international 1%. **Ethnic Representation:** African American 6%, Asian 4%, Caucasian 71%, Hispanic 13%, Native American 1%. **Retention and Graduation:** 62% freshmen return for sophomore year. 4% freshmen graduate within 4 years. 23% grads go on to further study within 1 year. 2% grads pursue business degrees. 2% grads pursue law degrees. 1% grads pursue medical degrees. **Faculty:** Student/faculty ratio 21:1. 446 full-time faculty. 100% faculty teach undergrads.

ACADEMICS

Degrees: Bachelor's. **Academic Requirements:** General education including some course work in English (including composition), history, humanities, mathematics, sciences (biological or physical), social science. **Classes:** 20-29 students in an average class. 10-19 students in an average lab/discussion section. **Majors with Highest Enrollment:** Management information systems, general; behavioral sciences; criminal justice/safety studies. **Disciplines with Highest Percentage of Degrees Awarded:** Business/marketing 24%, social sciences and history 15%, protective services/public administration 11%, English 10%, psychology 6%. **Special Study Options:** Cooperative (work-study) program, cross registration, distance learning, double major, external degree program, honors program, independent study, internships, student-designed major, study abroad, teacher certification program, weekend college.

FACILITIES

Library Holdings: 692,677 bound volumes. 4,150 periodicals. 1,053,419 microforms. 16,975 audiovisuals. **Special Academic Facilities/Equipment:** Art gallery, child care center, flight simulators, historic brewery building, on-campus lab school, world indoor airport. **Computers:** School-owned computers available for student use.

EXTRACURRICULARS

Activities: Choral groups, dance, drama/theater, jazz band, literary magazine, music ensembles, student government, student newspaper. **Organizations:** 100 registered organizations, 9 honor societies, 10 religious organizations. **Athletics (Intercollegiate):** *Men:* baseball, basketball, diving, soccer, swimming. *Women:* basketball, diving, soccer, swimming, volleyball.

ADMISSIONS

Selectivity Rating: 63 (of 100). **Freshman Academic Profile:** Average high school GPA 2.8. 5% in top 10% of high school class, 19% in top 25% of high school class, 49% in top 50% of high school class. 96% from public high schools. Average SAT I Math 474, SAT I Math middle 50% range 420-520. Average SAT I Verbal 483, SAT I Verbal middle 50% range 420-540. Average ACT 19, ACT middle 50% range 16-21. TOEFL required of all international applicants, minimum TOEFL 500. **Basis for Candidate Selection:** *Important factors considered include:* secondary school record, standardized test scores. *Other factors considered include:* character/personal qualities, class rank, essays, recommendations. **Freshman Admission Requirements:** High school diploma or GED is required. **Freshman Admission Statistics:** 4,034 applied, 86% accepted, 65% of those accepted enrolled. **Transfer Admission Requirements:** *Items required:* college transcript. Lowest grade transferable C. **General Admission Information:** Application fee $25. Priority application deadline August 1. Regular application deadline August 26. Nonfall registration accepted. Admission may be deferred for a maximum of 1 year. Credit and/or placement offered for CEEB Advanced Placement tests.

COSTS AND FINANCIAL AID

In-state tuition $2,123. Out-of-state tuition $8,767. Required fees $1,452. Average book expense $1,100. **Required Forms and Deadlines:** FAFSA. No deadline for regular filing. **Notification of Awards:** Applicants will be notified of awards on a rolling basis beginning on or about April 1. **Types of Aid:** *Need-based scholarships/grants:* Pell, SEOG, state scholarships/grants, private scholarships, the school's own gift aid. *Loans:* FFEL Subsidized Stafford, FFEL Unsubsidized Stafford, FFEL PLUS, Federal Perkins. **Student Employment:** Federal Work-Study Program available. Institutional employment available. Off-campus job opportunities are excellent. **Financial Aid Statistics:** 26% freshmen, 38% undergrads receive some form of aid. Average income from on-campus job $2,000. **Financial Aid Phone:** 303-575-5880.

MIAMI UNIVERSITY

301 South Campus Avenue Building, Oxford, OH 45056
Phone: 513-529-2531 **E-mail:** admission@muohio.edu **CEEB Code:** 1463
Fax: 513-529-1550 **Web:** www.muohio.edu **ACT Code:** 3294

This public school was founded in 1809. It has a 2,000-acre campus.

STUDENTS AND FACULTY

Enrollment: 15,384. **Student Body:** Male 46%, female 54%, out-of-state 27%, international 1% (76 countries represented). **Ethnic Representation:** African American 4%, Asian 2%, Caucasian 89%, Hispanic 2%, Native American 1%. **Retention and Graduation:** 90% freshmen return for sophomore year. 62% freshmen graduate within 4 years. 52% grads go on to further study within 1 year. 1% grads pursue business degrees. 7% grads pursue law degrees. 8% grads pursue medical degrees. **Faculty:** Student/faculty ratio 17:1. 807 full-time faculty, 86% hold PhDs. 100% faculty teach undergrads.

ACADEMICS

Degrees: Associate's, bachelor's, doctoral, master's, post-master's certificate, terminal, transfer. **Academic Requirements:** General education including some course work in arts/fine arts, English (including composition), foreign languages, history, humanities, mathematics, philosophy, sciences (biological or physical), social science. **Classes:** 20-29 students in an average class. 20-29 students in an average lab/discussion section. **Disciplines with Highest Percentage of Degrees Awarded:** Business/marketing 35%, education 12%, social sciences and history 9%, biological life sciences 7%, psychology 6%. **Special Study Options:** Cooperative (work-study) program, cross registration, double major, student exchange program (domestic), honors program, independent study, internships, liberal arts/career combination, student-designed major, study abroad, teacher certification program.

FACILITIES

Housing: Coed, all-female, all-male, apartments for married students, housing for disabled students, housing for international students, fraternities and/or sororities, All first-year students live in first-year halls. Special arrangements include sorority suites in residence halls and an international hall. **Library Holdings:** 2,697,078 bound volumes. 14,089 periodicals. 2,992,366 microforms. 143,868 audiovisuals. **Special Academic Facilities/Equipment:** Geology, art, anthropology, and zoology museums; performing arts center; herbarium; environmental research center; 400-acre nature preserve; electron microscope center. **Computers:** *Recommended operating system:* Windows 95. School-owned computers available for student use.

EXTRACURRICULARS

Activities: Choral groups, concert band, dance, drama/theater, jazz band, literary magazine, marching band, music ensembles, musical theater, pep band, radio station, student government, student newspaper, student-run film society, symphony orchestra, television station, yearbook. **Organizations:** 350 registered organizations, 34 honor societies, 20 religious organizations, 28 fraternities (24% men join), 20 sororities (27% women join). **Athletics (Intercollegiate):** *Men:* baseball, basketball, cross-country, diving, football, golf, ice hockey, swimming, track & field. *Women:* basketball, cross-country, diving, field hockey, soccer, softball, swimming, tennis, track & field, volleyball.

ADMISSIONS

Selectivity Rating: 86 (of 100). **Freshman Academic Profile:** Average high school GPA 3.6. 36% in top 10% of high school class, 77% in top 25% of high school class, 97% in top 50% of high school class. Average SAT I Math 610, SAT I Math middle 50% range 580-660. Average SAT I Verbal 590, SAT I Verbal middle 50% range 550-640. Average ACT 26, ACT middle 50% range 24-29. TOEFL required of all international applicants, minimum TOEFL 530. **Basis for Candidate Selection:** *Very important factors considered include:* class rank, secondary school record, standardized test scores. *Important factors considered include:* essays, recommendations. *Other factors considered include:* alumni/ae relation, character/personal qualities, extracurricular activities, minority status, talent/ability, volunteer work, work experience. **Freshman Admission Requirements:** High school diploma or GED is required. *Academic units required/recommended:* 16 total recommended; 4 English recommended, 3 math recommended, 3 science recommended, 2 foreign language recommended, 3 social studies recommended. **Freshman Admission Statistics:** 12,204 applied, 77% accepted, 38% of those accepted enrolled. **Transfer Admission Requirements:** *Items required:* high school transcript, college transcript, essay. Minimum college GPA of 2.0 required. Lowest grade transferable C. **General Admission Information:** Application fee $45. Early decision application deadline November 1. Regular application deadline January 31. Nonfall registration accepted. Credit offered for CEEB Advanced Placement tests.

COSTS AND FINANCIAL AID

In-state tuition $6,386. Out-of-state tuition $15,110. Room & board $6,240. Required fees $1,214. Average book expense $803. **Required Forms and Deadlines:** FAFSA. No deadline for regular filing. Priority filing deadline February 15. **Notification of Awards:** Applicants will be notified of awards on a rolling basis beginning on or about March 31. **Types of Aid:** *Need-based scholarships/grants:* Pell, SEOG, state scholarships/grants, private scholarships, the school's own gift aid. *Loans:* Direct Subsidized Stafford, Direct Unsubsidized Stafford, Direct PLUS, Federal Perkins, Federal Nursing, college/university loans from institutional funds, Bank alternative loans. **Student Employment:** Federal Work-Study Program available. Institutional employment available. Off-campus job opportunities are good. **Financial Aid Statistics:** 34% freshmen, 31% undergrads receive some form of aid. **Financial Aid Phone:** 513-529-8734.

MICHIGAN STATE UNIVERSITY

250 Administration Building, East Lansing, MI 48824-1046
Phone: 517-355-8332 **E-mail:** admis@msu.edu **CEEB Code:** 1465
Fax: 517-353-1647 **Web:** www.msu.edu **ACT Code:** 2032

This public school was founded in 1855. It has a 5,200-acre campus.

STUDENTS AND FACULTY

Enrollment: 35,197. **Student Body:** Male 47%, female 53%, out-of-state 6%, international 2% (100 countries represented). **Ethnic Representation:** African American 9%, Asian 5%, Caucasian 82%, Hispanic 3%, Native American 1%. **Retention and Graduation:** 89% freshmen return for sophomore year. **Faculty:** Student/faculty ratio 18:1. 2,349 full-time faculty, 94% hold PhDs.

ACADEMICS

Degrees: Bachelor's, certificate, doctoral, first professional, master's, post-master's certificate. **Academic Requirements:** General education including some course work in English (including composition), humanities, mathematics, sciences (biological or physical), social science. **Classes:** 20-29 students in an average class. 20-29 students in an average lab/discussion section. **Majors with Highest Enrollment:** Marketing/marketing management, general; psychology, general; advertising. **Disciplines with Highest Percentage of Degrees Awarded:** Business/marketing 16%, communications/communication technologies 13%, social sciences and history 11%, engineering/engineering technology 9%, agriculture 7%. **Special Study Options:** Accelerated program, cooperative (work-study) program, distance learning, double major, dual enrollment, English as a second language, student exchange program (domestic), external degree program, honors program, independent study, internships, liberal arts/career combination, student-designed major, study abroad, teacher certification program.

FACILITIES

Housing: Coed, all-female, apartments for married students, apartments for single students, housing for disabled students, fraternities and/or sororities, cooperative housing. **Library Holdings:** 4,420,208 bound volumes. 29,470 periodicals. 5,556,525 microforms. 290,206 audiovisuals. **Special Academic Facilities/Equipment:** Art, natural history, Michigan history, and anthropology museums, art center, on-campus preschool and elementary school, biological station, experimental farms, botanical garden, planetarium, two superconducting cyclotrons, observatory.

EXTRACURRICULARS

Activities: Choral groups, concert band, dance, drama/theater, jazz band, marching band, music ensembles, musical theater, opera, pep band, radio station, student government, student newspaper, student-run film society, symphony orchestra, television station, yearbook. **Athletics (Intercollegiate):** *Men:* baseball, basketball, cheerleading, cross-country, diving, football, golf, ice hockey, indoor track, soccer, swimming, tennis, track & field, wrestling. *Women:* basketball, cheerleading, crew, cross-country, diving, field hockey, golf, gymnastics, indoor track, soccer, softball, swimming, tennis, track & field, volleyball.

ADMISSIONS

Selectivity Rating: 74 (of 100). **Freshman Academic Profile:** Average high school GPA 3.6. 26% in top 10% of high school class, 66% in top 25% of high school class, 95% in top 50% of high school class. Average SAT I Math 579, SAT I Math middle 50% range 520-640. Average SAT I Verbal 552, SAT I Verbal middle 50% range 490-610. Average ACT 24, ACT middle 50% range 22-27. TOEFL required of all international applicants, minimum TOEFL 550. **Basis for Candidate Selection:** *Very important factors considered include:* secondary school record. *Important factors considered include:* standardized test scores. *Other factors considered include:* alumni/ae relation, class rank, essays, extracurricular activities, geographical residence, minority status, recommendations, talent/ability, volunteer work, work experience. **Freshman Admission Requirements:** High school diploma or GED is required. *Academic units required/recommended:* 14 total required; 4 English required, 3 math required, 2 science required, 2 foreign language required, 3 social studies required. **Freshman Admission Statistics:** 25,210 applied, 67% accepted, 41% of those accepted enrolled. **Transfer Admission Requirements:** *Items required:* college transcript, statement of good standing from prior school. Minimum college GPA of 2.0 required. **General Admission Information:** Application fee $35. Regular application deadline August 1. Nonfall registration accepted. Admission may be deferred for a maximum of 1 year. Credit and/or placement offered for CEEB Advanced Placement tests.

COSTS AND FINANCIAL AID

In-state tuition $6,015. Out-of-state tuition $14,970. Room & board $4,932. Required fees $708. Average book expense $790. **Required Forms and Deadlines:** FAFSA and institution's own financial aid form. Financial aid filing deadline June 30. Priority filing deadline February 21. **Notification of Awards:** Applicants will be notified of awards on a rolling basis beginning on or about March 15. **Types of Aid:** *Need-based scholarships/grants:* Pell, SEOG, state scholarships/grants, private scholarships, the school's own gift aid. *Loans:* Direct Subsidized Stafford, Direct Unsubsidized Stafford, Direct PLUS, Federal Perkins, state loans, college/university loans from institutional funds. **Student Employment:** Federal Work-Study Program available. Institutional employment available. Off-campus job opportunities are excellent. **Financial Aid Statistics:** 54% freshmen, 40% undergrads receive some form of aid. **Financial Aid Phone:** 517-353-5940.

MICHIGAN TECHNOLOGICAL UNIVERSITY

1400 Townsend Drive, Houghton, MI 49931
Phone: 906-487-2335 **E-mail:** mtu4u@mtu.edu **CEEB Code:** 1464
Fax: 906-487-2125 **Web:** www.mtu.edu **ACT Code:** 2030

This public school was founded in 1885. It has a 240-acre campus.

STUDENTS AND FACULTY

Enrollment: 5,915. **Student Body:** Male 76%, female 24%, out-of-state 19%, international 6% (80 countries represented). **Ethnic Representation:** African American 3%, Asian 1%, Caucasian 90%, Hispanic 1%, Native American 1%. **Retention and Graduation:** 78% freshmen return for sophomore year. 29% freshmen graduate within 4 years. 30% grads go on to further study within 1 year. 10% grads pursue business degrees. **Faculty:** Student/faculty ratio 11:1. 377 full-time faculty, 88% hold PhDs. 100% faculty teach undergrads.

ACADEMICS

Degrees: Associate's, bachelor's, certificate, doctoral, master's, terminal. **Academic Requirements:** General education including some course work in computer literacy, English (including composition), humanities, mathematics, sciences (biological or physical), social science, physical education. **Classes:** 20-29 students in an average class. 10-19 students in an average lab/discussion section. **Majors with Highest Enrollment:** Civil engineering, general; electrical, electronics, and communications engineering; mechanical engineering. **Disciplines with Highest Percentage of Degrees Awarded:** Engineering/engineering technology 68%, business/marketing 9%, biological life sciences 6%, computer and information sciences 5%, natural resources/environmental sciences 3%. **Special Study Options:** Cooperative (work-study) program, distance learning, double major, dual enrollment, English as a second language, student exchange program (domestic), internships, liberal arts/career combination, student-designed major, study abroad, teacher certification program. Dual enrollment available with Northwestern Michigan College, Delta College, Gogebic Community College, Adrian College, Albion College, Augsburg College (MN), College of St. Scholastica (MN), Mount Senario College, Lansing Community College, Olivet College, Northland College, and University of Wisconsin-Superior.

FACILITIES

Housing: Coed, apartments for married students, apartments for single students, housing for international students, fraternities and/or sororities. **Library Holdings:** 820,414 bound volumes. 10,369 periodicals. 535,707 microforms. 4,529 audiovisuals. **Special Academic Facilities/Equipment:** Mineralogical museum, 4,700-acre research forest, scanning electron microscope, PUMA robots, x-ray fluorescence spectrometer, process simulation and control center, Rozsa Center for the Performing Arts, cleanrooms, MEMS Fabrication Facility, environmental scanning electron microscope, transmission electron microscope, radio-frequency plasma-assisted deposition chamber, electron lithography equipment. **Computers:** School-owned computers available for student use.

EXTRACURRICULARS

Activities: Choral groups, concert band, dance, drama/theater, jazz band, literary magazine, music ensembles, musical theater, opera, pep band, radio station, student government, student newspaper, student-run film society, symphony orchestra, yearbook. **Organizations:** 158 registered organizations, 8 honor societies, 16 religious organizations, 14 fraternities (9% men join), 8 sororities (16% women join). **Athletics (Intercollegiate):** *Men:* basketball, skiing (cross-country), cross-country, football, ice hockey, tennis, track & field. *Women:* basketball, skiing (cross-country), cross-country, tennis, track & field, volleyball.

ADMISSIONS

Selectivity Rating: 82 (of 100). **Freshman Academic Profile:** Average high school GPA 3.5. 31% in top 10% of high school class, 60% in top 25% of high school class, 89% in top 50% of high school class. Average SAT I Math 624, SAT I Math middle 50% range 570-690. Average SAT I Verbal 570, SAT I Verbal middle 50% range 510-640. Average ACT 25, ACT middle 50% range 23-28. TOEFL required of all international applicants, minimum TOEFL 500. **Basis for Candidate Selection:** *Very important factors considered include:* class rank, secondary school record, standardized test scores. *Other factors considered include:* alumni/ae relation, character/personal qualities, essays, extracurricular activities, interview, recommendations, talent/ability, volunteer work, work experience. **Freshman Admission Requirements:** High school diploma or GED is required. *Academic units required/recommended:* 15 total required; 3 English required, 4 English recommended, 3 math required, 4 math recommended, 2 science required, 3 science recommended, 1 foreign language recommended, 1 social studies recommended, 1 history recommended, 1 elective recommended. **Freshman Admission Statistics:** 2,957 applied, 92% accepted, 44% of those accepted enrolled. **Transfer Admission Requirements:** *Items required:* college transcript, statement of good standing from prior school. Minimum college GPA of 2.0 required. Lowest grade transferable C. **General Admission Information:** Application fee $30. Nonfall registration accepted. Admission may be deferred. Credit and/or placement offered for CEEB Advanced Placement tests.

COSTS AND FINANCIAL AID

In-state tuition $5,782. Out-of-state tuition $14,152. Room & board $5,465. Required fees $673. Average book expense $900. **Required Forms and Deadlines:** FAFSA. No deadline for regular filing. Priority filing deadline February 21. **Notification of Awards:** Applicants will be notified of awards on a rolling basis beginning on or about February 28. **Types of Aid:** *Need-based scholarships/grants:* Pell, SEOG, state scholarships/grants, private scholarships, the school's own gift aid. *Loans:* Direct Subsidized Stafford, Direct Unsubsidized Stafford, Direct PLUS, Federal Perkins, state loans, college/university loans from institutional funds, external private loans. **Student Employment:** Federal Work-Study Program available. Institutional employment available. Off-campus job opportunities are good. **Financial Aid Statistics:** 47% freshmen, 42% undergrads receive some form of aid. Average freshman grant $5,303. Average freshman loan $4,906. Average income from on-campus job $1,429. **Financial Aid Phone:** 906-487-2622.

MIDAMERICA NAZARENE UNIVERSITY

2030 College Way, Olathe, KS 66062
Phone: 913-791-3380 **E-mail:** admissions@mnu.edu **CEEB Code:** 6437
Fax: 913-791-3481 **Web:** www.mnu.edu **ACT Code:** 1445

This private school, which is affiliated with the Nazarene Church, was founded in 1966. It has a 105-acre campus.

STUDENTS AND FACULTY

Enrollment: 1,372. **Student Body:** Male 48%, female 52%, out-of-state 39%, international 1% (8 countries represented). **Ethnic Representation:** African American 7%, Asian 1%, Caucasian 77%, Hispanic 2%, Native American 1%. **Retention and Graduation:** 66% freshmen return for sophomore year. 26% freshmen graduate within 4 years. **Faculty:** Student/faculty ratio 18:1. 73 full-time faculty, 46% hold PhDs. 100% faculty teach undergrads.

ACADEMICS

Degrees: Associate's, bachelor's, master's. **Academic Requirements:** General education including some course work in arts/fine arts, computer literacy, English (including composition), foreign languages, history, humanities, mathematics, philosophy, sciences (biological or physical), social science. **Classes:** Under 10 students in an average class. Under 10 students in an average lab/discussion section. **Majors with Highest Enrollment:** Business administration/management; elementary education and teaching; psychology, general. **Disciplines with Highest Percentage of Degrees Awarded:** Business/marketing 44%, education 11%, computer and information sciences 10%, health professions and related sciences 10%, philosophy/religion/theology 7%. **Special Study Options:** Accelerated program, cross registration, distance learning, double major, dual enrollment, independent study, internships, study abroad, teacher certification program.

FACILITIES

Housing: All-female, all-male, apartments for single students, housing for disabled students. **Library Holdings:** 428,450 bound volumes. 225 periodicals. 299,000 microforms. 7,391 audiovisuals. **Computers:** School-owned computers available for student use.

EXTRACURRICULARS

Activities: Choral groups, concert band, drama/theater, jazz band, music ensembles, pep band, radio station, student government, student newspaper, television station, yearbook. **Organizations:** 28 registered organizations, 6 honor societies, 4 religious organizations. **Athletics (Intercollegiate):** *Men:* baseball, basketball, cheerleading, cross-country, football, indoor track, soccer, track & field. *Women:* basketball, cheerleading, cross-country, indoor track, soccer, softball, track & field, volleyball.

ADMISSIONS

Selectivity Rating: 69 (of 100). **Freshman Academic Profile:** Average high school GPA 3.4. 27% in top 10% of high school class, 45% in top 25% of high school class, 67% in top 50% of high school class. 93% from public high schools. Average SAT I Math 517, SAT I Math middle 50% range 440-610. Average SAT I Verbal 522, SAT I Verbal middle 50% range 455-610. Average ACT 23, ACT middle 50% range 19-26. TOEFL required of all international applicants, minimum TOEFL 500. **Basis for Candidate Selection:** *Very important factors considered include:* standardized test scores. *Important factors considered include:* secondary school record. *Other factors considered include:* character/personal qualities, recommendations. **Freshman Admission Requirements:** High school diploma or GED is required. *Academic units required/recommended:* 14 total recommended; 4 English recommended, 3 math recommended, 3 science recommended, 1 foreign language recommended, 3 social studies recommended. **Freshman Admission Statistics:** 651 applied, 46% accepted, 96% of those accepted enrolled. **Transfer Admission Requirements:** *Items required:* college transcript. Minimum college GPA of 2.0 required. Lowest grade transferable D. **General Admission Information:** Application fee $15. Regular application deadline August 1. Admission may be deferred for a maximum of 2 years. Credit offered for CEEB Advanced Placement tests.

COSTS AND FINANCIAL AID

Tuition $11,270. Room & board $5,886. Required fees $1,010. Average book expense $600. **Required Forms and Deadlines:** FAFSA and institution's own financial aid form. Priority filing deadline March 1. **Notification of Awards:** Applicants will be notified of awards on a rolling basis. **Types of Aid:** *Need-based scholarships/grants:* Pell, SEOG, state scholarships/grants, private scholarships, the school's own gift aid. *Loans:* FFEL Subsidized Stafford, FFEL Unsubsidized Stafford, FFEL PLUS, Federal Perkins, Federal Nursing. **Student Employment:** Federal Work-Study Program available. Institutional employment available. Off-campus job opportunities are excellent. **Financial Aid Statistics:** 81% freshmen, 70% undergrads receive some form of aid. **Financial Aid Phone:** 913-791-3298.

MIDDLE TENNESSEE STATE UNIVERSITY

Office of Admissions, Murfreesboro, TN 37132
Phone: 800-433-6878 **E-mail:** admissions@mtsu.edu **CEEB Code:** 1466
Fax: 615-898-5478 **Web:** www.mtsu.edu

This public school was founded in 1911. It has a 500-acre campus.

STUDENTS AND FACULTY

Enrollment: 15,890. **Student Body:** Out-of-state 5%, international 2%. **Ethnic Representation:** African American 10%, Asian 2%, Caucasian 86%, Hispanic 1%, Native American 1%. **Retention and Graduation:** 75% freshmen return for sophomore year. **Faculty:** 90% faculty teach undergrads.

ACADEMICS

Special Study Options: Study abroad.

FACILITIES

Housing: Coed, all-female, all-male. **Special Academic Facilities/Equipment:** On-campus nursery school, kindergarten, elementary school, radio/TV/photography mobile production lab, state-of-the-art recording studios.

EXTRACURRICULARS

Activities: Radio station, student government, student newspaper, television station, yearbook. **Organizations:** 155 registered organizations, 1 honor society, 1 religious organization, 14 fraternities (1% men join), 10 sororities (1% women join). **Athletics (Intercollegiate):** *Men:* basketball, cross-country, tennis, track & field, volleyball. *Women:* basketball, cross-country, tennis, track & field, volleyball.

ADMISSIONS

Selectivity Rating: 78 (of 100). **Freshman Academic Profile:** Average high school GPA 3.0. 17% in top 10% of high school class, 51% in top 25% of high school class, 64% in top 50% of high school class. Average ACT 22. TOEFL required of all international applicants, minimum TOEFL 525. **Freshman Admission Requirements: General Admission Information:** Regular application deadline July 1. Credit offered for CEEB Advanced Placement tests.

COSTS AND FINANCIAL AID

In-state tuition $1,906. Out-of-state tuition $6,732. Room & board $3,030. Required fees $154. Average book expense $600. **Required Forms and Deadlines:** FAFSA and institution's own financial aid form. **Types of Aid:** *Need-based scholarships/grants:* Pell, SEOG, state scholarships/grants, private scholarships, the school's own gift aid. *Loans:* FFEL Subsidized Stafford, FFEL Unsubsidized Stafford, FFEL PLUS, Federal Perkins, college/university loans from institutional funds. **Student Employment:** Federal Work-Study Program available. Off-campus job opportunities are good. **Financial Aid Statistics:** Average freshman grant $1,400. Average freshman loan $2,625. Average income from on-campus job $2,720. **Financial Aid Phone:** 615-898-2830.

MIDDLEBURY COLLEGE

The Emma Willard House, Middlebury, VT 05753-6002
Phone: 802-443-3000 **E-mail:** admissions@middlebury.edu **CEEB Code:** 3526
Fax: 802-443-2056 **Web:** www.middlebury.edu **ACT Code:** 4306

This private school was founded in 1800. It has a 350-acre campus.

STUDENTS AND FACULTY

Enrollment: 2,297. **Student Body:** Male 49%, female 51%, out-of-state 94%, international 8% (71 country represented). **Ethnic Representation:** African American 3%, Asian 8%, Caucasian 76%, Hispanic 6%, Native American 1%. **Retention and Graduation:** 96% freshmen return for sophomore year. 82% freshmen graduate within 4 years. **Faculty:** Student/faculty ratio 11:1. 217 full-time faculty, 94% hold PhDs. 100% faculty teach undergrads.

ACADEMICS

Degrees: Bachelor's, doctoral, master's. **Academic Requirements:** General education including some course work in arts/fine arts, English (including composition), foreign languages, history, philosophy, sciences (biological or physical), social science, 2 noncredit courses. **Classes:** 10-19 students in an average class. 10-19 students in an average lab/discussion section. **Majors with Highest Enrollment:** Economics, general; psychology, general; English language and literature, general. **Disciplines with Highest Percentage of Degrees Awarded:** Social sciences and history 26%, English 13%, interdisciplinary studies 10%, area and ethnic studies 9%, psychology 9%. **Special Study Options:** Accelerated program, double major, student exchange program (domestic), honors program, independent study, internships, student-designed major, study abroad, teacher certification program, Williams College-Mystic Seaport Program in American Maritime Studies, Oxford University summer Program, independent scholar programs with Berea College and Swarthmore College, 3-year international major.

FACILITIES

Housing: Coed, apartments for single students, housing for disabled students, Multicultural house, environmental house, foreign language house, 6 co-ed social houses. **Library Holdings:** 950,000 bound volumes. 2,694 periodicals. 360,094 microforms. 31,059 audiovisuals. **Special Academic Facilities/Equipment:** Art museum, theatres, language lab, observatory, electron microscope, mountain campus, private ski area, golf course. **Computers:** *Recommended operating system:* Windows NT/2000. School-owned computers available for student use.

EXTRACURRICULARS

Activities: Choral groups, dance, drama/theater, jazz band, literary magazine, music ensembles, musical theater, opera, radio station, student government, student newspaper, student-run film society, symphony orchestra, yearbook. **Organizations:** 100 registered organizations. **Athletics (Intercollegiate):** *Men:* baseball, basketball, skiing (cross-country), cross-country, diving, football, golf, ice hockey, indoor track, lacrosse, skiing (alpine), skiing (Nordic), soccer, swimming, tennis, track & field. *Women:* basketball, skiing (cross-country), cross-country, diving, field hockey, golf, ice hockey, indoor track, lacrosse, skiing (alpine), skiing (Nordic), soccer, softball, squash, swimming, tennis, track & field, volleyball.

ADMISSIONS

Selectivity Rating: 98 (of 100). **Freshman Academic Profile:** 74% in top 10% of high school class, 92% in top 25% of high school class, 99% in top 50% of high school class. Average SAT I Math 700, SAT I Math middle 50% range 670-740. Average SAT I Verbal 700, SAT I Verbal middle 50% range 680-750. Average ACT 30, ACT middle 50% range 29-32. **Basis for Candidate Selection:** *Very important factors considered include:* character/personal qualities, secondary school record. *Important factors considered include:* class rank, essays, extracurricular activities, recommendations, standardized test scores, talent/ability. *Other factors considered include:* alumni/ae relation, geographical residence, interview, minority status, volunteer work, work experience. **Freshman Admission Requirements:** High school diploma or equivalent is not required. *Academic units required/recommended:* 4 English recommended, 4 math recommended, 4 science recommended, 4 science lab recommended, 4 foreign language recommended, 3 social studies recommended. **Freshman Admission Statistics:** 4,599 applied, 31% accepted, 41% of those accepted enrolled. **Transfer Admission Requirements:** *Items required:* high school transcript, college transcript, essay, standardized test score, statement of good standing from prior school. Minimum college GPA of 3.0 required. Lowest grade transferable C. **General Admission Information:** Application fee $55. Early decision application deadline November 15. Regular application deadline December 15. Nonfall registration accepted. Admission may be deferred. Credit and/or placement offered for CEEB Advanced Placement tests.

COSTS AND FINANCIAL AID

Average book expense $750. **Required Forms and Deadlines:** FAFSA, institution's own financial aid form, CSS/Financial Aid PROFILE and Federal income tax return (or statement of nonfiling). Financial aid filing deadline December 31. Priority filing deadline November 15. **Notification of Awards:** Applicants will be notified of awards on or about April 1. **Types of Aid:** *Need-based scholarships/grants:* Pell, SEOG, state scholarships/grants, private scholarships, the school's own gift aid. *Loans:* Direct Subsidized Stafford, Direct Unsubsidized Stafford, Direct PLUS, Federal Perkins, college/university loans from institutional funds. **Student Employment:** Federal Work-Study Program available. Institutional employment available. Off-campus job opportunities are good. **Financial Aid Statistics:** 37% freshmen, 36% undergrads receive some form of aid. Average freshman grant $20,161. Average freshman loan $5,377. **Financial Aid Phone:** 802-443-5158.

MIDLAND LUTHERAN COLLEGE

900 North Clarkson, Fremont, NE 68025
Phone: 402-721-5487 **E-mail:** admissions@admin.mlc.edu
Fax: 402-721-0250 **Web:** www.mlc.edu

This private school, which is affiliated with the Lutheran Church, was founded in 1883.

STUDENTS AND FACULTY

Enrollment: 1,033. **Student Body:** Male 42%, female 58%, out-of-state 24%, international 1% (3 countries represented). **Ethnic Representation:** African American 4%, Caucasian 95%, Hispanic 1%. **Retention and Graduation:** 84% freshmen return for sophomore year. 45% freshmen graduate within 4 years. 19% grads go on to further study within 1 year. 2% grads pursue law degrees. 1% grads pursue medical degrees. **Faculty:** 90% faculty teach undergrads.

ACADEMICS

Degrees: Associate's, bachelor's, transfer. **Academic Requirements:** General education including some course work in arts/fine arts, computer literacy, English (including composition), foreign languages, history, humanities, mathematics, philosophy, sciences (biological or physical), social science. **Special Study Options:** Cooperative (work-study) program, double major, independent study, internships, student-designed major.

FACILITIES

Housing: Coed, apartments for single students. **Library Holdings:** 110,000 bound volumes. 900 periodicals. 1,750 microforms. 1,400 audiovisuals.

EXTRACURRICULARS

Organizations: 4 fraternities (20% men join), 4 sororities (20% women join). **Athletics (Intercollegiate):** *Men:* baseball, basketball, cross-country, football, golf, gymnastics, soccer, tennis, track & field, volleyball. *Women:* basketball, cross-country, golf, gymnastics, soccer, softball, tennis, track & field, volleyball.

ADMISSIONS

Selectivity Rating: 72 (of 100). **Freshman Academic Profile:** Average high school GPA 3.1. 18% in top 10% of high school class, 48% in top 25% of high school class, 81% in top 50% of high school class. 98% from public high schools. Average ACT 22, ACT middle 50% range 18-25. TOEFL required of all international applicants, minimum TOEFL 500. **Freshman Admission Requirements:** High school diploma or GED is required. *Academic units required/recommended:* 3 English required, 4 English recommended, 2 math required, 3 math recommended, 2 science recommended, 1 science lab recommended, 2 foreign language recommended, 2 social studies recommended, 10 elective recommended. **Freshman Admission Statistics:** 775 applied, 93% accepted, 44% of those accepted enrolled. **Transfer Admission Requirements:** *Items required:* high school transcript, standardized test score, statement of good standing from prior school. **General Admission Information:** Application fee $20. Regular application deadline September 1.

COSTS AND FINANCIAL AID

Tuition $12,800. Room & board $3,450. Average book expense $500. **Types of Aid:** *Need-based scholarships/grants:* Pell, SEOG, state scholarships/grants, private scholarships, the school's own gift aid. *Loans:* FFEL Subsidized Stafford, FFEL Unsubsidized Stafford, FFEL PLUS, Federal Perkins, college/university loans from institutional funds. **Student Employment:** Federal Work-Study Program available. Off-campus job opportunities are good. **Financial Aid Statistics:** Average freshman grant $3,884. Average freshman loan $3,600. Average income from on-campus job $800. **Financial Aid Phone:** 402-721-5480.

MIDWAY COLLEGE

512 East Stephen Street., Midway, KY 40347-1120
Phone: 859-846-5346 **E-mail:** admissions@midway.edu **CEEB Code:** 1975
Fax: 859-846-5823 **Web:** www.midway.edu **ACT Code:** 1528

This private school, which is affiliated with the Disciples of Christ Church, was founded in 1847. It has a 105-acre campus.

STUDENTS AND FACULTY

Enrollment: 1,042. **Student Body:** Male 14%, female 86%, out-of-state 11%, international 1%. **Ethnic Representation:** African American 7%, Caucasian 91%. **Retention and Graduation:** 30% freshmen return for sophomore year. 15% freshmen graduate within 4 years. **Faculty:** Student/faculty ratio 14:1. 35 full-time faculty, 57% hold PhDs. 100% faculty teach undergrads.

ACADEMICS

Degrees: Associate's, bachelor's. **Academic Requirements:** General education including some course work in computer literacy, English (including composition), history, humanities, mathematics, sciences (biological or physical), social science. **Classes:** Under 10 students in an average class. Under 10 students in an average lab/discussion section. **Majors with Highest Enrollment:** Nursing/registered nurse training (RN, ASN, BSN, MSN); business administration/management; equestrian/equine studies. **Disciplines with Highest Percentage of Degrees Awarded:** Business/marketing 78%, agriculture 8%, computer and information sciences 4%, biological life sciences 3%, psychology 2%. **Special Study Options:** Accelerated program, distance learning, double major, honors program, independent study, internships, liberal arts/career combination, study abroad, teacher certification program, weekend college.

FACILITIES

Housing: All-female. **Library Holdings:** 96,236 bound volumes. 250 periodicals. 58,217 microforms. 9,213 audiovisuals. **Computers:** *Recommended operating system:* Windows 95. School-owned computers available for student use.

EXTRACURRICULARS

Activities: Choral groups, concert band, literary magazine, music ensembles, student government, student newspaper, yearbook. **Organizations:** 21 registered organizations, 1 honor society, 3 religious organizations. **Athletics (Intercollegiate):** *Women:* basketball, equestrian, soccer, softball, tennis, volleyball.

ADMISSIONS

Selectivity Rating: 63 (of 100). **Freshman Academic Profile:** Average high school GPA 3.0. 11% in top 10% of high school class, 31% in top 25% of high school class, 66% in top 50% of high school class. Average SAT I Math 474, SAT I Math middle 50% range 400-500. Average SAT I Verbal 493, SAT I Verbal middle 50% range 440-530. Average ACT 20, ACT middle 50% range 18-22. TOEFL required of all international applicants, minimum TOEFL 500. **Basis for Candidate Selection:** *Very important factors considered include:* secondary school record, standardized test scores. *Important factors considered include:* alumni/ae relation. *Other factors considered include:* character/personal qualities, class rank, essays, extracurricular activities, interview, recommendations, talent/ability, volunteer work, work experience. **Freshman Admission Requirements:** High school diploma or GED is required. *Academic units required/recommended:* 15 total required; 4 English required, 3 math recommended, 2 science recommended, 1 foreign language recommended, 1 social studies recommended. **Freshman Admission Statistics:** 375 applied, 74% accepted, 40% of those accepted enrolled. **Transfer Admission Requirements:** *Items required:* high school transcript, college transcript. Minimum high school GPA of 2.0 required. Minimum college GPA of 2.0 required. Lowest grade transferable C. **General Admission Information:** Application fee $15. Priority application deadline April 1. Nonfall registration accepted. Admission may be deferred. Credit and/or placement offered for CEEB Advanced Placement tests.

COSTS AND FINANCIAL AID

Tuition $10,800. Room & board $5,540. Required fees $150. Average book expense $800. **Required Forms and Deadlines:** FAFSA and institution's own financial aid form. Financial aid filing deadline August 1. Priority filing deadline April 1. **Notification of Awards:** Applicants will be notified of awards on a rolling basis. **Types of Aid:** *Need-based scholarships/grants:* Pell, SEOG, state scholarships/grants, private scholarships. *Loans:* FFEL Subsidized Stafford, FFEL Unsubsidized Stafford, FFEL PLUS, Federal Perkins, college/university loans from institutional funds. **Student Employment:** Federal Work-Study Program available. Institutional employment available. Off-campus job opportunities are good. **Financial Aid Statistics:** 78% freshmen, 69% undergrads receive some form of aid. **Financial Aid Phone:** 859-846-5410.

MIDWESTERN STATE UNIVERSITY

3410 Taft Blvd., Wichita Falls, TX 76308-2099
Phone: 940-397-4334 **E-mail:** admissions@mwsu.edu **CEEB Code:** 6408
Fax: 940-397-4672 **Web:** www.mwsu.edu **ACT Code:** 4132

This public school was founded in 1922. It has a 179-acre campus.

STUDENTS AND FACULTY

Enrollment: 5,515. **Student Body:** Male 44%, female 56%, out-of-state 5%, international 5% (52 countries represented). **Ethnic Representation:** African American 10%, Asian 3%, Caucasian 77%, Hispanic 10%, Native American 1%. **Retention and Graduation:** 63% freshmen return for sophomore year. 15% freshmen graduate within 4 years. **Faculty:** Student/faculty ratio 20:1. 193 full-time faculty, 71% hold PhDs. 96% faculty teach undergrads.

ACADEMICS

Degrees: Associate's, bachelor's, master's. **Academic Requirements:** General education including some course work in arts/fine arts, computer literacy, English (including composition), foreign languages, history, humanities, mathematics, sciences (biological or physical), social science, speech communications, political science, kinesiology, lab sciences. **Classes:** 20-29 students in an average class. 20-29 students in an average lab/discussion section. **Majors with Highest Enrollment:** Nursing/registered nurse training (RN, ASN, BSN, MSN); accounting; criminal justice/safety studies. **Disciplines with Highest Percentage of Degrees Awarded:** Business/marketing 25%, interdisciplinary studies 22%, health professions and related sciences 12%, social sciences and history 7%, protective services/public administration 6%. **Special Study Options:** Cross registration, distance learning, double major, dual enrollment, English as a second language, honors program, independent study, internships, study abroad, teacher certification program.

FACILITIES

Housing: Coed, all-female, all-male, apartments for married students, apartments for single students, fraternities and/or sororities, housing for honor students. **Library Holdings:** 385,715 bound volumes. 1,695 periodicals. 22,149 microforms. 13,142 audiovisuals. **Special Academic Facilities/Equipment:** Language lab, technology lab, video lab, planetarium. **Computers:** School-owned computers available for student use.

EXTRACURRICULARS

Activities: Choral groups, concert band, drama/theater, jazz band, marching band, music ensembles, student government, student newspaper, symphony orchestra, television station, yearbook. **Organizations:** 113 registered organizations, 22 honor societies, 12 religious organizations, 7 fraternities, 7 sororities. **Athletics (Intercollegiate):** *Men:* basketball, football, soccer, tennis. *Women:* basketball, soccer, softball, tennis, volleyball.

ADMISSIONS

Selectivity Rating: 70 (of 100). **Freshman Academic Profile:** Average high school GPA 3.2. 5% in top 10% of high school class, 22% in top 25% of high school class, 59% in top 50% of high school class. Average SAT I Math 490, SAT I Math middle 50% range 430-540. Average SAT I Verbal 488, SAT I Verbal middle 50% range 430-530. Average ACT 20, ACT middle 50% range 18-22. TOEFL required of all international applicants, minimum TOEFL 500. **Basis for Candidate Selection:** *Other factors considered include:* class rank, geographical residence, secondary school record, standardized test scores, state residency, work experience. **Freshman Admission Requirements:** High school diploma or GED is required. *Academic units required/recommended:* 4 English required, 3 math required, 2 science required, 6 elective required. **Freshman Admission Statistics:** 2,196 applied, 68% accepted, 51% of those accepted enrolled. **Transfer Admission Requirements:** Minimum college GPA of 2.0 required. Lowest grade transferable D. **General Admission Information:** Nonfall registration accepted. Admission may be deferred for a maximum of 1 year. Credit and/or placement offered for CEEB Advanced Placement tests.

COSTS AND FINANCIAL AID

In-state tuition $1,320. Out-of-state tuition $7,860. Room & board $4,434. Required fees $1,750. Average book expense $1,099. **Required Forms and Deadlines:** FAFSA and institution's own financial aid form. **Types of Aid:** *Need-based scholarships/grants:* Pell, SEOG, state scholarships/grants, private scholarships, the school's own gift aid. *Loans:* FFEL Subsidized Stafford, FFEL Unsubsidized Stafford, FFEL PLUS, Federal Perkins, state loans, college/university loans from institutional funds. **Student Employment:** Federal Work-Study Program available. Institutional employment available. Off-campus job opportunities are good. **Financial Aid Statistics:** Average income from on-campus job $2,000. **Financial Aid Phone:** 940-689-4214.

MILES COLLEGE

PO Box 3800, Birmingham, AL 35208
Phone: 205-929-1661 **E-mail:** adm@mail.miles.edu
Fax: 205-929-1668 **Web:** www.miles.edu

This private school, which is affiliated with the Episcopal Church, was founded in 1905. It has a 37-acre campus.

STUDENTS AND FACULTY

Enrollment: 1,453. **Student Body:** Male 43%, female 57%. **Ethnic Representation:** African American 100%. **Retention and Graduation:** 43% freshmen graduate within 4 years. **Faculty:** Student/faculty ratio 20:1. 59 full-time faculty.

ACADEMICS

Degrees: Bachelor's. **Academic Requirements:** General education including some course work in English (including composition), history, humanities, mathematics, sciences (biological or physical), social science, speech. **Special Study Options:** Cooperative (work-study) program, honors program, teacher certification program, weekend college.

FACILITIES

Housing: All-female, all-male. **Library Holdings:** 100,000 bound volumes. 950 periodicals. 250 microforms. 384 audiovisuals.

EXTRACURRICULARS

Activities: Choral groups, marching band, student government, student newspaper. **Organizations:** 8 honor societies, 1 religious organization. **Athletics (Intercollegiate):** *Men:* baseball, basketball, cheerleading, football, tennis, track & field. *Women:* basketball, cheerleading, softball, tennis, track & field, volleyball.

ADMISSIONS

Selectivity Rating: 72 (of 100). **Freshman Academic Profile:** 15% in top 10% of high school class, 31% in top 25% of high school class, 48% in top 50% of high school class. TOEFL required of all international applicants, minimum TOEFL 450. **Freshman Admission Requirements: General Admission Information:** Regular application deadline July 1.

COSTS AND FINANCIAL AID

Tuition $4,280. Room & board $2,950. Required fees $350. Average book expense $600. **Types of Aid:** *Loans:* FFEL Subsidized Stafford, FFEL PLUS. **Student Employment:** Federal Work-Study Program available. **Financial Aid Statistics:** Average income from on-campus job $1,000.

MILES COMMUNITY COLLEGE

2715 Dickinson St., Miles City, MT 59301
Phone: 406-233-3513 **E-mail:** larsonm@po.mcc.cc.mt.us
Fax: 406-233-3599 **Web:** www.mcc.cc.mt.us **ACT Code:** 2421

This public school was founded in 1939.

STUDENTS AND FACULTY

Enrollment: 568. **Student Body:** Male 38%, female 62%, out-of-state 2%, international students represent 5 countries. **Ethnic Representation:** Asian 1%, Caucasian 94%, Hispanic 1%, Native American 3%. **Retention and Graduation:** 47% freshmen return for sophomore year. 63% grads go on to further study within 1 year. **Faculty:** 100% faculty teach undergrads.

ACADEMICS

Degrees: Associate's, certificate, transfer. **Academic Requirements:** General education including some course work in arts/fine arts, English (including composition), history, humanities, mathematics, sciences (biological or physical), social science. **Special Study Options:** Cooperative (work-study) program, cross registration, distance learning, dual enrollment, English as a second language, independent study, internships, liberal arts/career combination, student-designed major.

FACILITIES

Housing: Coed, apartments for single students. **Library Holdings:** 19,227 bound volumes. 182 periodicals. 0 microforms. 950 audiovisuals. **Computers:** School-owned computers available for student use.

EXTRACURRICULARS

Activities: Choral groups, drama/theater, literary magazine, music ensembles, pep band, student government, student newspaper, yearbook. **Organizations:** 3 registered organizations, 2 honor societies, 1 religious organization. **Athletics (Intercollegiate):** *Men:* baseball, golf, rodeo, soccer. *Women:* baseball, golf, rodeo, soccer.

ADMISSIONS

Selectivity Rating: 63 (of 100). **Freshman Academic Profile:** Average high school GPA 2.7. 10% in top 10% of high school class, 10% in top 25% of high school class, 70% in top 50% of high school class. 83% from public high schools. TOEFL required of all international applicants, minimum TOEFL 500. **Freshman Admission Requirements:** High school diploma or GED is required. **Freshman Admission Statistics:** 199 applied, 100% accepted, 76% of those accepted enrolled. **Transfer Admission Requirements:** *Items required:* high school transcript, college transcript, standardized test scores. Lowest grade transferable C. **General Admission Information:** Application fee $30. Nonfall registration accepted. Admission may be deferred for a maximum of 2 years. Credit offered for CEEB Advanced Placement tests.

COSTS AND FINANCIAL AID

In-state tuition $1,440. Out-of-state tuition $4,200. Room & board $3,500. Required fees $672. Average book expense $600. **Required Forms and Deadlines:** FAFSA. Financial aid filing deadline May 1. Priority filing deadline March 1. **Notification of Awards:** Applicants will be notified of awards on a rolling basis beginning on or about April 15. **Types of Aid:** *Need-based scholarships/grants:* Pell, SEOG, state scholarships/grants, private scholarships, the school's own gift aid. *Loans:* FFEL Subsidized Stafford, FFEL Unsubsidized Stafford, FFEL PLUS, Federal Perkins. **Student Employment:** Federal Work-Study Program available. Institutional employment available. Off-campus job opportunities are good. **Financial Aid Statistics:** 93% freshmen, 87% undergrads receive some form of aid. Average freshman grant $4,000. Average freshman loan $2,500. Average income from on-campus job $1,200. **Financial Aid Phone:** 406-233-3525.

MILLERSVILLE UNIVERSITY OF PENNSYLVANIA

PO Box 1002, Millersville, PA 17551-0302
Phone: 717-872-3371 **E-mail:** admissions@millersville.edu **CEEB Code:** 2656
Fax: 717-871-2147 **Web:** www.millersville.edu **ACT Code:** 3712

This public school was founded in 1855. It has a 220-acre campus.

STUDENTS AND FACULTY

Enrollment: 6,646. **Student Body:** Male 42%, female 58%, out-of-state 4%, international 1% (48 countries represented). **Ethnic Representation:** African American 6%, Asian 2%, Caucasian 90%, Hispanic 2%. **Retention and Graduation:** 84% freshmen return for sophomore year. 33% freshmen graduate within 4 years. 20% grads go on to further study within 1 year. **Faculty:** Student/faculty ratio 18:1. 295 full-time faculty, 92% hold PhDs. 100% faculty teach undergrads.

ACADEMICS

Degrees: Associate's, bachelor's, master's, post-bachelor's certificate, post-master's certificate. **Academic Requirements:** General education including some course work in English (including composition), humanities, mathematics, sciences (biological or physical), social science, health & physical education, fundamentals of speech. **Classes:** 20-29 students in an average class. 20-29 students in an average lab/discussion section. **Majors with Highest Enrollment:** Business administration/management; elementary education and teaching; psychology, general. **Disciplines with Highest Percentage of Degrees Awarded:** Education 22%, social sciences and history 13%, business/marketing 11%, psychology 10%, engineering/engineering technology 7%. **Special Study Options:** Accelerated program, cooperative (work-study) program, cross registration, distance learning, double major, dual enrollment, honors program, independent study, internships, study abroad, teacher certification program.

FACILITIES

Housing: Coed, all-female, center for service learning & leadership, freshmen residence hall. **Library Holdings:** 499,986 bound volumes. 5,776 periodicals. 567,917 microforms. 30,459 audiovisuals. **Special Academic Facilities/Equipment:** Art galleries, early childhood education lab school, language lab, extensive inventory of scientific and technological instrumentation. **Computers:** School-owned computers available for student use.

EXTRACURRICULARS

Activities: Choral groups, concert band, dance, drama/theater, jazz band, literary magazine, marching band, music ensembles, musical theater, pep band, radio station, student government, student newspaper, symphony orchestra, television station, yearbook. **Organizations:** 102 registered organizations, 5 honor societies, 9 religious organizations, 9 fraternities (6% men join), 8 sororities (6% women join). **Athletics (Intercollegiate):** *Men:* baseball, basketball, cross-country, football, golf, soccer, tennis, track & field, wrestling. *Women:* basketball, cheerleading, cross-country, field hockey, lacrosse, soccer, softball, swimming, tennis, track & field, volleyball.

ADMISSIONS

Selectivity Rating: 80 (of 100). **Freshman Academic Profile:** 13% in top 10% of high school class, 41% in top 25% of high school class, 85% in top 50% of high school class. Average SAT I Math 530, SAT I Math middle 50% range 480-590. Average SAT I Verbal 522, SAT I Verbal middle 50% range 470-570. TOEFL required of all international applicants, minimum TOEFL 500. **Basis for Candidate Selection:** *Very important factors considered include:* class rank, secondary school record, standardized test scores. *Other factors considered include:* alumni/ae relation, character/personal qualities, extracurricular activities, geographical residence, interview, recommendations, state residency, talent/ability, volunteer work. **Freshman Admission Requirements:** High school diploma or GED is required. *Academic units required/recommended:* 15 total required; 21 total recommended; 4 English required, 3 math required, 3 science required, 1 science lab required, 2 foreign language recommended, 3 social studies required, 2 history required, 4 elective recommended. **Freshman Admission Statistics:** 6,019 applied, 63% accepted, 34% of those accepted enrolled. **Transfer Admission Requirements:** *Items required:* high school transcript, college transcript. Minimum high school GPA of 2.0 required. Minimum college GPA of 2.0 required. Lowest grade transferable C. **General Admission Information:** Application fee $30. Priority application deadline January 1. Nonfall registration accepted. Admission may be deferred. Credit and/or placement offered for CEEB Advanced Placement tests.

COSTS AND FINANCIAL AID

In-state tuition $4,378. Out-of-state tuition $10,946. Room & board $5,310. Required fees $1,169. Average book expense $700. **Required Forms and Deadlines:** FAFSA. Financial aid filing deadline March 15. **Notification of Awards:** Applicants will be notified of awards on a rolling basis beginning on or about April 1. **Types of Aid:** *Need-based scholarships/grants:* Pell, SEOG, state scholarships/grants, private scholarships, the school's own gift aid, SICO Scholarship. *Loans:* FFEL Subsidized Stafford, FFEL Unsubsidized Stafford, FFEL PLUS, Federal Perkins, college/university loans from institutional funds. **Student Employment:** Federal Work-Study Program available. Institutional employment available. Off-campus job opportunities are excellent. **Financial Aid Statistics:** 49% freshmen, 47% undergrads receive some form of aid. Average freshman grant $2,393. Average freshman loan $2,066. Average income from on-campus job $1,202. **Financial Aid Phone:** 717-872-3026.

MILLIGAN COLLEGE

PO Box 210, Milligan Coll, TN 37682
Phone: 423-461-8730 **E-mail:** admissions@milligan.edu **CEEB Code:** 1469
Fax: 423-461-8982 **Web:** www.milligan.edu **ACT Code:** 3996

This private school was founded in 1866. It has a 145-acre campus.

STUDENTS AND FACULTY

Enrollment: 757. **Student Body:** Male 41%, female 59%, out-of-state 57%, international 2% (4 countries represented). **Ethnic Representation:** African American 2%, Asian 1%, Caucasian 97%, Hispanic 1%. **Retention and Graduation:** 72% freshmen return for sophomore year. **Faculty:** Student/faculty ratio 11:1. 66 full-time faculty, 69% hold PhDs. 93% faculty teach undergrads.

ACADEMICS

Degrees: Bachelor's, master's. **Academic Requirements:** General education including some course work in arts/fine arts, computer literacy, English (including composition), history, humanities, mathematics, philosophy, sciences (biological or physical), social science. **Classes:** 10-19 students in an average class. Under 10 students in an average lab/discussion section. **Majors with Highest Enrollment:** Business administration/management; mass communications/media studies; education, general. **Disciplines with Highest Percentage of Degrees Awarded:** Business/marketing 40%, communications/communication technologies 13%, education 10%, philosophy/religion/theology 8%, biological life sciences 5%. **Special Study Options:** Cross registration, double major, independent study, internships, study abroad, teacher certification program.

FACILITIES

Housing: All-female, all-male, apartments for married students, apartments for single students. **Library Holdings:** 125,504 bound volumes. 493 periodicals. 472,614 microforms. 3,335 audiovisuals. **Computers:** *Recommended operating system:* Windows 95. School-owned computers available for student use.

EXTRACURRICULARS

Activities: Choral groups, concert band, drama/theater, jazz band, literary magazine, music ensembles, musical theater, pep band, radio station, student government, student newspaper, symphony orchestra, yearbook. **Organizations:** 24 registered organizations, 5 honor societies, 5 religious organizations. **Athletics (Intercollegiate):** *Men:* baseball, basketball, cross-country, golf, soccer, tennis. *Women:* basketball, cross-country, soccer, softball, tennis, volleyball.

ADMISSIONS

Selectivity Rating: 78 (of 100). **Freshman Academic Profile:** Average high school GPA 3.4. 80% from public high schools. Average SAT I Math 534, SAT I Math middle 50% range 480-580. Average SAT I Verbal 535, SAT I Verbal middle 50% range 480-590. Average ACT 23, ACT middle 50% range 20-25. TOEFL required of all international applicants, minimum TOEFL 550. **Basis for Candidate Selection:** *Very important factors considered include:* character/personal qualities, essays, religious affiliation/commitment, secondary school record, standardized test scores. *Important factors considered include:* class rank, extracurricular activities, recommendations. *Other factors considered include:* alumni/ae relation, interview, minority status, talent/ability, volunteer work, work experience. **Freshman Admission Requirements:** High school diploma or GED is required. *Academic units required/recommended:* 17 total recommended; 4 English recommended, 3 math recommended, 3 science recommended, 2 foreign language recommended, 2 social studies recommended, 3 history recommended. **Freshman Admission Statistics:** 617 applied, 88% accepted, 31% of those accepted enrolled. **Transfer Admission Requirements:** *Items required:* college transcript, essay. Minimum college GPA of 2.0 required. Lowest grade transferable C-. **General Admission Information:** Application fee $30. Priority application deadline April 1.

Regular application deadline August 1. Nonfall registration accepted. Admission may be deferred for a maximum of 1 year. Credit and/or placement offered for CEEB Advanced Placement tests.

COSTS AND FINANCIAL AID

Tuition $13,880. Room & board $4,370. Required fees $460. Average book expense $700. **Required Forms and Deadlines:** FAFSA and institution's own financial aid form. Financial aid filing deadline March 1. **Notification of Awards:** Applicants will be notified of awards on a rolling basis beginning on or about March 1. **Types of Aid:** *Need-based scholarships/grants:* Pell, SEOG, state scholarships/grants, private scholarships, the school's own gift aid, Grants for Nursing students. *Loans:* FFEL Subsidized Stafford, FFEL Unsubsidized Stafford, FFEL PLUS, Federal Perkins, college/university loans from institutional funds, nursing grants. **Student Employment:** Federal Work-Study Program available. Institutional employment available. Off-campus job opportunities are excellent. **Financial Aid Statistics:** 80% freshmen, 85% undergrads receive some form of aid. Average freshman grant $11,505. Average freshman loan $2,753. **Financial Aid Phone:** 800-447-4880.

MILLIKIN UNIVERSITY

1184 West Main Street, Decatur, IL 62522-2084
Phone: 217-424-6210 **E-mail:** admis@mail.millikin.edu **CEEB Code:** 1470
Fax: 217-425-4669 **Web:** www.millikin.edu **ACT Code:** 1080

This private school, which is affiliated with the Presbyterian Church, was founded in 1901. It has a 70-acre campus.

STUDENTS AND FACULTY

Enrollment: 2,468. **Student Body:** Male 44%, female 56%, out-of-state 16%, international 1%. **Ethnic Representation:** African American 6%, Asian 1%, Caucasian 85%, Hispanic 3%. **Retention and Graduation:** 83% freshmen return for sophomore year. **Faculty:** Student/faculty ratio 13:1. 152 full-time faculty, 83% hold PhDs. 100% faculty teach undergrads.

ACADEMICS

Degrees: Bachelor's, master's. **Academic Requirements:** General education including some course work in arts/fine arts, English (including composition), mathematics, sciences (biological or physical). Required courses depend on the particular track student is enrolled in: second language, semiotic systems, or cultures and societies. **Disciplines with Highest Percentage of Degrees Awarded:** Business/marketing 23%, visual and performing arts 21%, education 17%, health professions and related sciences 7%, communications/communication technologies 6%. **Special Study Options:** Double major, student exchange program (domestic), honors program, independent study, internships, student-designed major, study abroad, teacher certification program.

FACILITIES

Housing: Coed, all-female, all-male, apartments for married students, apartments for single students, housing for disabled students, fraternities and/or sororities. **Library Holdings:** 199,660 bound volumes. 927 periodicals. 21,032 microforms. 9,017 audiovisuals. **Special Academic Facilities/Equipment:** Art galleries, art museum, fitness/wellness center, recording studio, indoor sports center. **Computers:** School-owned computers available for student use.

EXTRACURRICULARS

Activities: Choral groups, concert band, dance, drama/theater, jazz band, literary magazine, music ensembles, musical theater, opera, radio station, student government, student newspaper, symphony orchestra, yearbook. **Organizations:** 91 registered organizations, 9 honor societies, 1 religious organization, 5 fraternities (10% men join), 3 sororities (12% women join). **Athletics (Intercollegiate):** *Men:* baseball, basketball, cross-country, football, golf, soccer, swimming, tennis, track & field, wrestling. *Women:* basketball, cross-country, golf, soccer, softball, swimming, tennis, track & field, volleyball.

ADMISSIONS

Selectivity Rating: 69 (of 100). **Freshman Academic Profile:** 17% in top 10% of high school class, 45% in top 25% of high school class, 79% in top 50% of high school class. 91% from public high schools. Average SAT I Math 541, SAT I Math middle 50% range 460-620. Average SAT I Verbal 538, SAT I Verbal middle 50% range 460-600. Average ACT 24, ACT middle 50% range 21-27. TOEFL required of all international applicants, minimum TOEFL 550. **Basis for Candidate Selection:** *Very important factors considered include:* secondary school record. *Important factors considered include:* class rank, interview, recommendations, standardized test scores. *Other factors considered include:* alumni/ae relation, character/personal qualities, extracurricular activities, minority status, talent/ability, volunteer work, work experience. **Freshman Admission Requirements:** High school diploma or GED is required. *Academic units required/recommended:* 16 total recommended; 4 English recommended, 3 math recommended, 3 science recommended, 2 foreign language recommended, 2 social studies recommended, 2 history recommended. **Freshman Admission Statistics:** 2,753 applied, 78% accepted, 30% of those accepted enrolled. **Transfer Admission Requirements:** *Items required:* college transcript. Minimum college GPA of 2.0 required. Lowest grade transferable D. **General Admission Information:** Nonfall registration accepted. Admission may be deferred for a maximum of 1 year. Credit and/or placement offered for CEEB Advanced Placement tests.

COSTS AND FINANCIAL AID

Tuition $17,084. Room & board $5,594. Required fees $200. Average book expense $800. **Required Forms and Deadlines:** FAFSA. Financial aid filing deadline June 1. Priority filing deadline April 15. **Notification of Awards:** Applicants will be notified of awards on a rolling basis beginning on or about February 15. **Types of Aid:** *Need-based scholarships/grants:* Pell, SEOG, state scholarships/grants, private scholarships, the school's own gift aid. *Loans:* FFEL Subsidized Stafford, FFEL Unsubsidized Stafford, FFEL PLUS, Federal Perkins. **Student Employment:** Federal Work-Study Program available. Institutional employment available. Off-campus job opportunities are good. **Financial Aid Statistics:** 86% freshmen, 73% undergrads receive some form of aid. **Financial Aid Phone:** 217-424-6343.

MILLS COLLEGE

5000 MacArthur Boulevard, Oakland, CA 94613
Phone: 510-430-2135 **E-mail:** admission@mills.edu **CEEB Code:** 4485
Fax: 510-430-3314 **Web:** www.mills.edu **ACT Code:** 4485

This private school was founded in 1852. It has a 135-acre campus.

STUDENTS AND FACULTY

Enrollment: 727. **Student Body:** Out-of-state 20%. **Ethnic Representation:** African American 7%, Asian 8%, Caucasian 58%, Hispanic 7%, Native American 1%. **Retention and Graduation:** 77% freshmen return for sophomore year. 56% freshmen graduate within 4 years. 20% grads go on to further study within 1 year. **Faculty:** Student/faculty ratio 9:1. 89 full-time faculty, 105% hold PhDs. 100% faculty teach undergrads.

ACADEMICS

Degrees: Bachelor's, doctoral, master's, post-bachelor's certificate. **Academic Requirements:** General education including some course work in arts/fine arts, English (including composition), humanities, mathematics, sciences (biological or physical), social science, multicultural course, two interdisciplinary courses. **Disciplines with Highest Percentage of Degrees Awarded:** Interdisciplinary studies 18%, social sciences and history 12%, visual and performing arts 11%, biological life sciences 10%, psychology 9%. **Special Study Options:** Cross registration, double major, student exchange program (domestic), independent study, internships, student-designed major, study abroad, teacher certification program, Network Program for working women who wish to earn their BA in the evening.

FACILITIES

Housing: All-female, apartments for single students, cooperative housing. **Library Holdings:** 220,947 bound volumes. 816 periodicals. 27,658 microforms. 5,981 audiovisuals. **Special Academic Facilities/Equipment:** Art Museum, center for contemporary music, on-campus elementary school, botanical gardens. **Computers:** School-owned computers available for student use.

EXTRACURRICULARS

Activities: Choral groups, dance, drama/theater, literary magazine, music ensembles, student government, student newspaper, yearbook. **Organizations:** 30 registered organizations, 2 honor societies. **Athletics (Intercollegiate):** *Women:* basketball, crew, cross-country, soccer, swimming, tennis, volleyball.

ADMISSIONS

Selectivity Rating: 75 (of 100). **Freshman Academic Profile:** Average high school GPA 3.5. 35% in top 10% of high school class, 64% in top 25% of high school class, 96% in top 50% of high school class. 85% from public high schools. SAT I Math middle 50% range 490-590. SAT I Verbal middle 50% range 540-670. Average ACT 25. TOEFL required of all international applicants, minimum TOEFL 550. **Basis for Candidate Selection:** *Very important factors considered include:* essays, recommendations, secondary school record, standardized test scores. *Important factors considered include:* class rank. *Other factors considered include:* character/personal qualities, extracurricular activities, interview, minority status, talent/ability, volunteer work, work experience. **Freshman Admission Requirements:** High school diploma or GED is required. *Academic units* *required/recommended:* 4 English required, 3 math required, 4 math recommended, 2 science required, 4 science recommended, 2 science lab required, 4 science lab recommended, 2 foreign language required, 4 foreign language recommended, 2 social studies required, 4 social studies recommended. **Freshman Admission Statistics:** 461 applied, 78% accepted, 33% of those accepted enrolled. **Transfer Admission Requirements:** *Items required:* high school transcript, college transcript, essay. Minimum college GPA of 3.0 required. Lowest grade transferable D. **General Admission Information:** Application fee $40. Regular application deadline February 15. Nonfall registration accepted. Admission may be deferred for a maximum of 1 year. Credit and/or placement offered for CEEB Advanced Placement tests.

COSTS AND FINANCIAL AID

Tuition $17,250. Room & board $7,296. Required fees $1,012. Average book expense $740. **Required Forms and Deadlines:** FAFSA, institution's own financial aid form, state aid form and noncustodial (divorced/separated) parent's statement. Financial aid filing deadline February 15. Priority filing deadline March 2. **Notification of Awards:** Applicants will be notified of awards on or about April 15. **Types of Aid:** *Need-based scholarships/grants:* Pell, SEOG, state scholarships/grants, private scholarships, the school's own gift aid. *Loans:* FFEL Subsidized Stafford, FFEL Unsubsidized Stafford, FFEL PLUS, Federal Perkins, state loans, college/university loans from institutional funds. **Student Employment:** Federal Work-Study Program available. Institutional employment available. Off-campus job opportunities are excellent. **Financial Aid Statistics:** 83% freshmen, 75% undergrads receive some form of aid. Average income from on-campus job $1,800. **Financial Aid Phone:** 510-430-2000.

MILLSAPS COLLEGE

1701 North State Street, Jackson, MS 39210
Phone: 601-974-1050 **E-mail:** admissions@millsaps.edu **CEEB Code:** 1471
Fax: 601-974-1059 **Web:** www.millsaps.edu **ACT Code:** 2212

This private school, which is affiliated with the Methodist Church, was founded in 1890. It has a 100-acre campus.

STUDENTS AND FACULTY

Enrollment: 1,158. **Student Body:** Male 45%, female 55%, out-of-state 50%, international 1% (8 countries represented). **Ethnic Representation:** African American 11%, Asian 3%, Caucasian 83%, Hispanic 1%, Native American 1%. **Retention and Graduation:** 81% freshmen return for sophomore year. 60% freshmen graduate within 4 years. 35% grads go on to further study within 1 year. 24% grads pursue business degrees. 26% grads pursue law degrees. 15% grads pursue medical degrees. **Faculty:** Student/faculty ratio 13:1. 93 full-time faculty, 92% hold PhDs. 100% faculty teach undergrads.

ACADEMICS

Degrees: Bachelor's, master's. **Academic Requirements:** General education including some course work in arts/fine arts, English (including composition), history, humanities, mathematics, sciences (biological or physical), social science. **Classes:** 10-19 students in an average class. 20-29 students in an average lab/discussion section. **Majors with Highest Enrollment:** Business administration/management; biology/biological sciences, general; English language and literature, general. **Disciplines with Highest Percentage of Degrees Awarded:** Business/marketing 30%, social sciences and history 16%, biological life sciences 10%, psychology 9%, English 9%. **Special Study Options:** Cooperative (work-study) program, double major, honors program, independent study, internships, study abroad, teacher certification program.

FACILITIES

Housing: Coed, all-female, fraternities and/or sororities. **Library Holdings:** 136,937 bound volumes. 576 periodicals. 83,969 microforms. 7,936 audiovisuals. **Special Academic Facilities/Equipment:** Lewis Art Gallery, James Observatory. **Computers:** School-owned computers available for student use.

EXTRACURRICULARS

Activities: Choral groups, drama/theater, literary magazine, student government, student newspaper, yearbook. **Organizations:** 56 registered organizations, 25 honor societies, 8 religious organizations, 6 fraternities (50% men join), 6 sororities (50% women join). **Athletics (Intercollegiate):** *Men:* baseball, basketball, cross-country, football, golf, soccer, tennis. *Women:* basketball, cross-country, golf, soccer, softball, tennis, volleyball.

ADMISSIONS

Selectivity Rating: 81 (of 100). **Freshman Academic Profile:** Average high school GPA 3.5. 39% in top 10% of high school class, 68% in top 25% of high school class, 89% in top 50% of high school class. 61% from public high schools. Average SAT I Math 590, SAT I Math middle 50% range 530-650. Average SAT I Verbal 590, SAT I Verbal middle 50% range 550-640. Average ACT 25, ACT middle 50% range 23-29. TOEFL required of all international applicants, minimum TOEFL 550. **Basis for Candidate Selection:** *Very important factors considered include:* character/personal qualities, secondary school record, standardized test scores. *Important factors considered include:* class rank, essays, extracurricular activities, interview, recommendations, talent/ability, volunteer work, work experience. **Freshman Admission Requirements:** High school diploma or GED is required. *Academic units required/recommended:* 14 total required; 20 total recommended; 4 English required, 4 English recommended, 3 math required, 4 math recommended, 3 science required, 4 science recommended, 1 science lab required, 1 science lab recommended, 2 foreign language recommended, 2 social studies required, 2 social studies recommended, 2 history required, 2 history recommended, 2 elective recommended. **Freshman Admission Statistics:** 913 applied, 87% accepted, 31% of those accepted enrolled. **Transfer Admission Requirements:** *Items required:* high school transcript, college transcript, essay. Minimum college GPA of 2.8 required. Lowest grade transferable C. **General Admission Information:** Application fee $25. Priority application deadline February 1. Regular application deadline June 1. Nonfall registration accepted. Admission may be deferred for a maximum of 1 year. Credit and/or placement offered for CEEB Advanced Placement tests.

COSTS AND FINANCIAL AID

Tuition $17,346. Room & board $6,768. Required fees $1,068. Average book expense $800. **Required Forms and Deadlines:** FAFSA, institution's own financial aid form and state aid form. No deadline for regular filing. Priority filing deadline March 1. **Notification of Awards:** Applicants will be notified of awards on a rolling basis beginning on or about March 15. **Types of Aid:** *Need-based scholarships/grants:* Pell, SEOG, state scholarships/grants, private scholarships, the school's own gift aid. *Loans:* FFEL Subsidized Stafford, FFEL Unsubsidized Stafford, FFEL PLUS, Federal Perkins, college/university loans from institutional funds. **Student Employment:** Federal Work-Study Program available. Institutional employment available. Off-campus job opportunities are good. **Financial Aid Statistics:** 51% freshmen, 55% undergrads receive some form of aid. Average freshman grant $12,880. Average freshman loan $3,111. **Financial Aid Phone:** 601-974-1220.

MILWAUKEE INSTITUTE OF ART AND DESIGN

273 East Erie Street, Milwaukee, WI 53202
Phone: 414-291-8070 **E-mail:** admissions@miad.edu **CEEB Code:** 1506
Fax: 414-291-8077 **Web:** www.miad.edu **ACT Code:** 4701

This private school was founded in 1974. It has a 2-acre campus.

STUDENTS AND FACULTY

Enrollment: 634. **Student Body:** Male 49%, female 51%, out-of-state 28%, international 2% (3 countries represented). **Ethnic Representation:** African American 3%, Asian 4%, Caucasian 86%, Hispanic 6%, Native American 1%. **Retention and Graduation:** 74% freshmen return for sophomore year. 36% freshmen graduate within 4 years. 6% grads go on to further study within 1 year. **Faculty:** Student/faculty ratio 16:1. 36 full-time faculty, 80% hold PhDs. 100% faculty teach undergrads.

ACADEMICS

Degrees: Bachelor's. **Academic Requirements:** General education including some course work in arts/fine arts, computer literacy, English (including composition), humanities, sciences (biological or physical), social science. **Classes:** 10-19 students in an average class. **Disciplines with Highest Percentage of Degrees Awarded:** Visual and performing arts 100%. **Special Study Options:** Double major, student exchange program (domestic), internships, study abroad.

FACILITIES

Housing: Coed. **Library Holdings:** 26,000 bound volumes. 88 periodicals. 0 microforms. 536 audiovisuals. **Special Academic Facilities/Equipment:** Eisner Museum of Advertising & Design, Brook Stevens Gallery of Industrial Design, Frederick Layton Gallery. **Computers:** School-owned computers available for student use.

EXTRACURRICULARS

Activities: Literary magazine, student government. **Organizations:** 12 registered organizations, 2 honor societies, 1 religious organization.

ADMISSIONS

Selectivity Rating: 71 (of 100). **Freshman Academic Profile:** Average high school GPA 3.0. 9% in top 10% of high school class, 30% in top 25% of high

school class, 65% in top 50% of high school class. TOEFL required of all international applicants, minimum TOEFL 550. **Basis for Candidate Selection:** *Very important factors considered include:* character/personal qualities, essays, interview, secondary school record, talent/ability. *Other factors considered include:* extracurricular activities, recommendations, standardized test scores, volunteer work, work experience. **Freshman Admission Requirements:** High school diploma or GED is required. **Freshman Admission Statistics:** 336 applied, 84% accepted, 51% of those accepted enrolled. **Transfer Admission Requirements:** *Items required:* essay, interview. Lowest grade transferable C. **General Admission Information:** Application fee $25. Priority application deadline March 1. Nonfall registration accepted. Admission may be deferred for a maximum of 2 years. Credit and/or placement offered for CEEB Advanced Placement tests.

COSTS AND FINANCIAL AID

Tuition $19,900. Room & board $6,538. Required fees $130. Average book expense $1,650. **Required Forms and Deadlines:** FAFSA. No deadline for regular filing. Priority filing deadline March 1. **Notification of Awards:** Applicants will be notified of awards on a rolling basis beginning on or about April 1. **Types of Aid:** *Need-based scholarships/grants:* Pell, SEOG, state scholarships/grants, private scholarships, the school's own gift aid. *Loans:* Direct Subsidized Stafford, Direct Unsubsidized Stafford, Direct PLUS. **Student Employment:** Federal Work-Study Program available. Institutional employment available. Off-campus job opportunities are good. **Financial Aid Statistics:** 88% freshmen, 86% undergrads receive some form of aid. Average freshman grant $7,500. Average freshman loan $5,000. Average income from on-campus job $1,002. **Financial Aid Phone:** 414-291-3272.

MILWAUKEE SCHOOL OF ENGINEERING

1025 North Broadway, Milwaukee, WI 53202-3109
Phone: 414-277-6763 **E-mail:** explore@msoe.edu **CEEB Code:** 1476
Fax: 414-277-7475 **Web:** www.msoe.edu **ACT Code:** 4616

This private school was founded in 1903. It has a 13-acre campus.

STUDENTS AND FACULTY

Enrollment: 2,272. **Student Body:** Male 84%, female 16%, out-of-state 21%, international 3%. **Ethnic Representation:** African American 3%, Asian 3%, Caucasian 91%, Hispanic 2%. **Retention and Graduation:** 71% freshmen return for sophomore year. 39% freshmen graduate within 4 years. 6% grads go on to further study within 1 year. 16% grads pursue business degrees. 1% grads pursue law degrees. 1% grads pursue medical degrees. **Faculty:** Student/faculty ratio 11:1. 120 full-time faculty, 58% hold PhDs. 100% faculty teach undergrads.

ACADEMICS

Degrees: Bachelor's, master's. **Academic Requirements:** General education including some course work in computer literacy, English (including composition), humanities, mathematics, sciences (biological or physical), social science. **Classes:** 20-29 students in an average class. 10-19 students in an average lab/discussion section. **Majors with Highest Enrollment:** Architectural engineering; electrical, electronics, and communications engineering; mechanical engineering. **Disciplines with Highest Percentage of Degrees Awarded:** Engineering/engineering technology 75%, business/marketing 22%, health professions and related sciences 2%, communications/communication technologies 1%. **Special Study Options:** Cooperative (work-study) program, distance learning, double major, dual enrollment, English as a second language, independent study, internships, liberal arts/career combination, study abroad, BS in business and in electrical engineering with Fachhochschule Lubeck in Germany. Students may apply to study at Czech Technical University, Prague, Czech Republic.

FACILITIES

Housing: Coed, housing for disabled students, fraternities and/or sororities. **Library Holdings:** 56,044 bound volumes. 416 periodicals. 75,854 microforms. 852 audiovisuals. **Special Academic Facilities/Equipment:** School of Business, industrial robot, CAD/CAM system, fluid power institute, rapid prototyping center, applied technology center and the bio-molecular modeling lab. **Computers:** School-owned computers available for student use.

EXTRACURRICULARS

Activities: Jazz band, literary magazine, music ensembles, pep band, radio station, student government, student newspaper, student-run film society. **Organizations:** 49 registered organizations, 7 honor societies, 4 religious organizations, 3 fraternities (6% men join), 3 sororities (7% women join). **Athletics (Intercollegiate):** *Men:* baseball, basketball, cheerleading, cross-country, golf, ice hockey, indoor track, soccer, tennis, track & field, volleyball, wrestling. *Women:* basketball, cheerleading, cross-country, golf, indoor track, soccer, softball, tennis, track & field, volleyball.

ADMISSIONS

Selectivity Rating: 76 (of 100). **Freshman Academic Profile:** Average high school GPA 3.5. 29% in top 10% of high school class, 60% in top 25% of high school class, 92% in top 50% of high school class. 88% from public high schools. Average SAT I Math 625, SAT I Math middle 50% range 580-670. Average SAT I Verbal 570, SAT I Verbal middle 50% range 510-630. Average ACT 26, ACT middle 50% range 23-28. TOEFL required of all international applicants, minimum TOEFL 550. **Basis for Candidate Selection:** *Very important factors considered include:* secondary school record, standardized test scores. *Other factors considered include:* extracurricular activities, interview, recommendations, talent/ability. **Freshman Admission Requirements:** High school diploma or GED is required. *Academic units required/recommended:* 13 total required; 15 total recommended; 4 English required, 4 English recommended, 4 math required, 4 math recommended, 2 science required, 4 science recommended, 1 social studies required, 1 social studies recommended, 1 history required, 1 history recommended, 1 elective required, 1 elective recommended. **Freshman Admission Statistics:** 1,749 applied, 72% accepted, 40% of those accepted enrolled. **Transfer Admission Requirements:** *Items required:* college transcript, statement of good standing from prior school. Minimum high school GPA of 2.5 required. Minimum college GPA of 2.5 required. Lowest grade transferable C. **General Admission Information:** Application fee $25. Priority application deadline February 1. Nonfall registration accepted. Admission may be deferred for a maximum of 1 year. Placement offered for CEEB Advanced Placement tests.

COSTS AND FINANCIAL AID

Tuition $23,034. Room & board $5,445. Required fees $0. Average book expense $2,500. **Required Forms and Deadlines:** FAFSA. No deadline for regular filing. Priority filing deadline March 15. **Notification of Awards:** Applicants will be notified of awards on a rolling basis beginning on or about March 1. **Types of Aid:** *Need-based scholarships/grants:* Pell, SEOG, state scholarships/grants, private scholarships, the school's own gift aid. *Loans:* FFEL Subsidized Stafford, FFEL Unsubsidized Stafford, FFEL PLUS, Federal Perkins, college/university loans from institutional funds, alternative. **Student Employment:** Federal Work-Study Program available. Institutional employment available. Off-campus job opportunities are excellent. **Financial Aid Statistics:** 83% freshmen, 80% undergrads receive some form of aid. Average freshman grant $11,500. Average freshman loan $4,147. Average income from on-campus job $2,000. **Financial Aid Phone:** 800-778-7223.

See page 1118.

MINNEAPOLIS COLLEGE OF ART AND DESIGN

2501 Stevens Avenue, Minneapolis, MN 55404
Phone: 612-874-3760 **E-mail:** admissions@mn.mcad.edu **CEEB Code:** 6411
Fax: 612-874-3701 **Web:** www.mcad.edu **ACT Code:** 2130

This private school was founded in 1886. It has a 3-acre campus.

STUDENTS AND FACULTY

Enrollment: 606. **Student Body:** Male 57%, female 43%, out-of-state 33%, international students represent 10 countries. **Ethnic Representation:** African American 2%, Asian 4%, Caucasian 74%, Hispanic 2%, Native American 1%. **Retention and Graduation:** 76% freshmen return for sophomore year. 35% freshmen graduate within 4 years. 10% grads go on to further study within 1 year. **Faculty:** Student/faculty ratio 11:1. 36 full-time faculty, 13% hold PhDs. 100% faculty teach undergrads.

ACADEMICS

Degrees: Bachelor's, master's, post-bachelor's certificate. **Academic Requirements:** General education including some course work in arts/fine arts, computer literacy, English (including composition), history, humanities. **Classes:** 10-19 students in an average class. **Disciplines with Highest Percentage of Degrees Awarded:** Visual and performing arts 100%. **Special Study Options:** Cooperative (work-study) program, cross registration, distance learning, English as a second language, student exchange program (domestic), independent study, internships, study abroad. Off-campus study: Arts Program in New York. Co-op programs: Arts.

FACILITIES

Housing: Coed, apartments for married students, apartments for single students. **Library Holdings:** 49,605 bound volumes. 183 periodicals. 0 microforms. 139,058 audiovisuals. **Special Academic Facilities/Equipment:** Art gallery. **Computers:** School-owned computers available for student use.

EXTRACURRICULARS

Activities: Student government, student-run film society.

ADMISSIONS

Selectivity Rating: 76 (of 100). **Freshman Academic Profile:** Average high school GPA 3.0. 89% from public high schools. Average SAT I Math 500. Average SAT I Verbal 549. Average ACT 23. TOEFL required of all international applicants, minimum TOEFL 550. **Basis for Candidate Selection:** *Very important factors considered include:* secondary school record, talent/ability. *Important factors considered include:* character/personal qualities, class rank, essays, recommendations, standardized test scores. *Other factors considered include:* extracurricular activities, interview, volunteer work, work experience. **Freshman Admission Requirements:** High school diploma or GED is required. *Academic units required/recommended:* 4 English recommended, 4 social studies recommended, 4 history recommended. **Freshman Admission Statistics:** 222 applied, 73% accepted, 75% of those accepted enrolled. **Transfer Admission Requirements:** *Items required:* high school transcript, college transcript, essay. Minimum high school GPA of 2.5 required. Minimum college GPA of 2.5 required. Lowest grade transferable C-. **General Admission Information:** Application fee $35. Priority application deadline February 15. Regular application deadline August 1. Nonfall registration accepted. Admission may be deferred for a maximum of 2 years. Credit offered for CEEB Advanced Placement tests.

COSTS AND FINANCIAL AID

Tuition $21,300. Room & board $5,300. Required fees $344. Average book expense $1,750. **Required Forms and Deadlines:** FAFSA. No deadline for regular filing. Priority filing deadline March 15. **Notification of Awards:** Applicants will be notified of awards on a rolling basis beginning on or about March 1. **Types of Aid:** *Need-based scholarships/grants:* Pell, SEOG, state scholarships/grants, private scholarships, the school's own gift aid. *Loans:* FFEL Subsidized Stafford, FFEL Unsubsidized Stafford, FFEL PLUS, Federal Perkins, state loans. **Student Employment:** Federal Work-Study Program available. Institutional employment available. Off-campus job opportunities are good. **Financial Aid Statistics:** 80% freshmen, 80% undergrads receive some form of aid. Average freshman grant $6,440. Average freshman loan $3,984. Average income from on-campus job $1,656. **Financial Aid Phone:** 612-874-3782.

See page 1120.

MINNESOTA STATE UNIVERSITY—MANKATO

Minnesota State University, Mankato TC122, Mankato, MN 56001
Phone: 507-389-1822 **E-mail:** admissions@mnsu.edu **CEEB Code:** 6677
Fax: 507-389-1511 **Web:** www.mnsu.edu **ACT Code:** 2126

This public school was founded in 1868. It has a 354-acre campus.

STUDENTS AND FACULTY

Enrollment: 12,087. **Student Body:** Male 48%, female 52%, out-of-state 12%, international 4% (69 countries represented). **Ethnic Representation:** African American 1%, Asian 1%, Caucasian 62%, Hispanic 1%. **Retention and Graduation:** 79% freshmen return for sophomore year. 20% freshmen graduate within 4 years. 8% grads go on to further study within 1 year. **Faculty:** Student/faculty ratio 24:1. 452 full-time faculty, 80% hold PhDs. 96% faculty teach undergrads.

ACADEMICS

Degrees: Associate's, bachelor's, master's, post-master's certificate. **Academic Requirements:** General education including some course work in arts/fine arts, English (including composition), history, mathematics, sciences (biological or physical), social science, health and human performance. **Classes:** 20-29 students in an average class. 20-29 students in an average lab/discussion section. **Majors with Highest Enrollment:** Nursing/registered nurse training (RN, ASN, BSN, MSN); elementary education and teaching; computer and information sciences, general. **Disciplines with Highest Percentage of Degrees Awarded:** Business/marketing 21%, education 15%, protective services/public administration 10%, health professions and related sciences 8%, engineering/engineering technology 7%. **Special Study Options:** Cross registration, distance learning, double major, dual enrollment, English as a second language, student exchange program (domestic), honors program, independent study, internships, student-designed major, study abroad, teacher certification program.

FACILITIES

Housing: Coed, special rooms for disabled students. **Library Holdings:** 468,567 bound volumes. 3,275 periodicals. 256,198 microforms. 31,078 audiovisuals. **Special Academic Facilities/Equipment:** Art gallery, daycare facilities, astronomy observatories, black box theatre. **Computers:** School-owned computers available for student use.

EXTRACURRICULARS

Activities: Choral groups, concert band, dance, drama/theater, jazz band, literary magazine, music ensembles, musical theater, pep band, radio station, student government, student newspaper, symphony orchestra. **Organizations:** 140 registered organizations, 12 honor societies, 13 religious organizations, 7 fraternities (1% men join), 4 sororities (1% women join). **Athletics (Intercollegiate):** *Men:* baseball, basketball, cross-country, diving, football, golf, ice hockey, swimming, tennis, track & field, wrestling. *Women:* basketball, cross-country, diving, golf, ice hockey, soccer, softball, swimming, tennis, track & field, volleyball.

ADMISSIONS

Selectivity Rating: 68 (of 100). **Freshman Academic Profile:** 8% in top 10% of high school class, 27% in top 25% of high school class, 70% in top 50% of high school class. Average ACT 21, ACT middle 50% range 19-23. TOEFL required of all international applicants, minimum TOEFL 500. **Basis for Candidate Selection:** *Very important factors considered include:* class rank, secondary school record, standardized test scores. *Other factors considered include:* recommendations. **Freshman Admission Requirements:** High school diploma or GED is required. *Academic units required/recommended:* 16 total required; 4 English required, 3 math required, 3 science required, 3 science lab required, 2 foreign language required, 2 social studies required, 1 history required. **Freshman Admission Statistics:** 4,877 applied, 89% accepted, 48% of those accepted enrolled. **Transfer Admission Requirements:** *Items required:* college transcript, statement of good standing from prior school. Minimum college GPA of 2.0 required. Lowest grade transferable C. **General Admission Information:** Application fee $20. Priority application deadline April 20. Nonfall registration accepted. Admission may be deferred.

COSTS AND FINANCIAL AID

In-state tuition $3,310. Out-of-state tuition $7,020. Room & board $4,018. Required fees $671. Average book expense $750. **Required Forms and Deadlines:** FAFSA. Priority filing deadline March 15. **Notification of Awards:** Applicants will be notified of awards on a rolling basis beginning on or about March 15. **Types of Aid:** *Need-based scholarships/grants:* Pell, SEOG, state scholarships/grants, private scholarships, the school's own gift aid. *Loans:* FFEL Subsidized Stafford, FFEL Unsubsidized Stafford, FFEL PLUS, Federal Perkins, state loans, Self Loans. **Student Employment:** Federal Work-Study Program available. Institutional employment available. Off-campus job opportunities are excellent. **Financial Aid Statistics:** 51% freshmen, 51% undergrads receive some form of aid. Average freshman grant $5,438. Average freshman loan $2,939. **Financial Aid Phone:** 507-389-1185.

MINNESOTA STATE UNIVERSITY—MOORHEAD

Owens Hall, Moorhead, MN 56563
Phone: 218-236-2161 **E-mail:** dragon@mnstate.edu **CEEB Code:** 6678
Fax: 218-291-4374 **Web:** www.mnstate.edu **ACT Code:** 2134

This public school was founded in 1887. It has a 104-acre campus.

STUDENTS AND FACULTY

Enrollment: 7,044. **Student Body:** Male 38%, female 62%, out-of-state 44%, international 1%. **Ethnic Representation:** African American 1%, Asian 1%, Caucasian 81%, Hispanic 1%, Native American 1%. **Retention and Graduation:** 71% freshmen return for sophomore year. **Faculty:** Student/faculty ratio 18:1. 280 full-time faculty, 77% hold PhDs.

ACADEMICS

Degrees: Associate's, bachelor's, master's, post-master's certificate. **Academic Requirements:** General education including some course work in English (including composition), humanities, mathematics, sciences (biological or physical), social science. **Classes:** 20-29 students in an average class. 10-19 students in an average lab/discussion section. **Disciplines with Highest Percentage of Degrees Awarded:** Education 27%, business/marketing 17%, protective services/public administration 10%, communications/communication technologies 7%, visual and performing arts 6%. **Special Study Options:** Cross registration, distance learning, double major, dual enrollment, student exchange program (domestic), external degree program, honors program, independent study, internships, student-designed major, study abroad, teacher certification program.

FACILITIES

Housing: Coed, all-female, all-male, housing for disabled students, fraternities and/or sororities. **Library Holdings:** 515,843 bound volumes. 1,426 periodicals. 744,994 microforms. 7,191 audiovisuals. **Special Academic Facilities/ Equipment:** Art and biology museums, on-campus preschool, planetarium, regional science center, center for business. **Computers:** School-owned computers available for student use.

EXTRACURRICULARS

Activities: Choral groups, concert band, dance, drama/theater, jazz band, literary magazine, music ensembles, musical theater, radio station, student government, student newspaper, symphony orchestra, television station. **Organizations:** 98 registered organizations, 6 honor societies, 6 religious organizations, 2 fraternities (3% men join), 3 sororities (2% women join). **Athletics (Intercollegiate):** *Men:* basketball, cross-country, football, indoor track, track & field, wrestling. *Women:* basketball, cross-country, golf, indoor track, soccer, softball, tennis, track & field, volleyball.

ADMISSIONS

Selectivity Rating: 70 (of 100). **Freshman Academic Profile:** 10% in top 10% of high school class, 31% in top 25% of high school class, 67% in top 50% of high school class. 98% from public high schools. Average ACT 22, ACT middle 50% range 18-24. TOEFL required of all international applicants, minimum TOEFL 500. **Basis for Candidate Selection:** *Very important factors considered include:* class rank, secondary school record, standardized test scores. **Freshman Admission Requirements:** High school diploma or GED is required. *Academic units required/recommended:* 15 total required; 4 English required, 3 math required, 3 science required, 1 science lab required, 2 foreign language required, 3 social studies required. **Freshman Admission Statistics:** 2,165 applied, 87% accepted, 64% of those accepted enrolled. **Transfer Admission Requirements:** *Items required:* college transcript. Minimum high school GPA of 2.0 required. Minimum college GPA of 2.0 required. Lowest grade transferable D. **General Admission Information:** Application fee $20. Regular application deadline August 7. Nonfall registration accepted. Admission may be deferred. Credit and/or placement offered for CEEB Advanced Placement tests.

COSTS AND FINANCIAL AID

In-state tuition $2,874. Out-of-state tuition $6,444. Room & board $3,706. Required fees $510. Average book expense $700. **Required Forms and Deadlines:** FAFSA. No deadline for regular filing. Priority filing deadline March 1. **Notification of Awards:** Applicants will be notified of awards on a rolling basis beginning on or about June 15. **Types of Aid:** *Need-based scholarships/grants:* Pell, SEOG, state scholarships/grants, the school's own gift aid. *Loans:* Direct Subsidized Stafford, Direct Unsubsidized Stafford, Direct PLUS, Federal Perkins, state loans. **Student Employment:** Federal Work-Study Program available. Institutional employment available. Off-campus job opportunities are excellent. **Financial Aid Statistics:** 55% freshmen, 51% undergrads receive some form of aid. Average freshman grant $1,323. Average freshman loan $2,227. Average income from on-campus job $1,550. **Financial Aid Phone:** 218-236-2251.

MINOT STATE UNIVERSITY—BOTTINEAU

105 Simrall Blvd., Bottineau, ND 58318
Phone: 800-542-6866 **E-mail:** groszk@misu.nodak.edu
Fax: 701-288-5499 **Web:** www.misu-b.nodak.edu **ACT Code:** 2304

This public school was founded in 1907. It has a 36-acre campus.

STUDENTS AND FACULTY

Enrollment: 450. **Student Body:** Male 48%, female 52%, out-of-state 14%, international 4%. **Ethnic Representation:** African American 1%, Caucasian 89%, Hispanic 1%, Native American 9%. **Retention and Graduation:** 65% freshmen return for sophomore year. 50% grads go on to further study within 1 year. **Faculty:** Student/faculty ratio 11:1. 26 full-time faculty, 7% hold PhDs. 100% faculty teach undergrads.

ACADEMICS

Degrees: Associate's, certificate, diploma, terminal, transfer. **Academic Requirements:** General education including some course work in arts/fine arts, computer literacy, English (including composition), history, humanities, mathematics, sciences (biological or physical), social science. **Special Study Options:** Cooperative (work-study) program, distance learning, double major, dual enrollment, independent study.

FACILITIES

Housing: Coed, all-female, all-male. **Library Holdings:** 25,607 bound volumes. 246 periodicals. 21,836 microforms. 850 audiovisuals. **Computers:** School-owned computers available for student use.

EXTRACURRICULARS

Activities: Choral groups, concert band, dance, drama/theater, jazz band, music ensembles, pep band, student government, student newspaper. **Organizations:** 6 registered organizations. **Athletics (Intercollegiate):** *Men:* baseball, basketball, cheerleading, ice hockey. *Women:* basketball, cheerleading, volleyball.

ADMISSIONS

Selectivity Rating: 63 (of 100). High school diploma or GED is required. **Freshman Admission Statistics:** 238 applied, 100% accepted, 73% of those accepted enrolled. **Transfer Admission Requirements:** *Items required:* college transcript. **General Admission Information:** Application fee $25. Nonfall registration accepted. Admission may be deferred. Neither credit nor placement offered for CEEB Advanced Placement tests.

COSTS AND FINANCIAL AID

In-state tuition $1,632. Out-of-state tuition $4,357. Room & board $2,816. Required fees $326. Average book expense $600. **Required Forms and Deadlines:** FAFSA. No deadline for regular filing. Priority filing deadline April 15. **Notification of Awards:** Applicants will be notified of awards on a rolling basis. **Types of Aid:** *Need-based scholarships/grants:* Pell, SEOG, state scholarships/grants, private scholarships, the school's own gift aid. *Loans:* FFEL Subsidized Stafford, FFEL Unsubsidized Stafford, FFEL PLUS, Federal Perkins. **Student Employment:** Federal Work-Study Program available. Institutional employment available. Off-campus job opportunities are fair. **Financial Aid Statistics:** Average freshman grant $2,000. Average freshman loan $2,600. **Financial Aid Phone:** 701-228-5437.

MINOT STATE UNIVERSITY—MINOT

500 University Ave W, Minot, ND 58707
Phone: 701-858-3350 **E-mail:** msu@minotstateu.edu **CEEB Code:** 2994
Fax: 701-858-3386 **Web:** www.minotstateu.edu **ACT Code:** 3214

This public school was founded in 1913. It has a 103-acre campus.

STUDENTS AND FACULTY

Enrollment: 3,425. **Student Body:** Male 37%, female 63%, out-of-state 8%, international 5% (18 countries represented). **Ethnic Representation:** African American 3%, Asian 1%, Caucasian 90%, Hispanic 2%, Native American 5%. **Retention and Graduation:** 70% freshmen return for sophomore year. 12% grads go on to further study within 1 year. **Faculty:** Student/faculty ratio 16:1. 164 full-time faculty, 50% hold PhDs. 100% faculty teach undergrads.

ACADEMICS

Degrees: Associate's, bachelor's, certificate, master's, post-master's certificate. **Academic Requirements:** General education including some course work in English (including composition), history, humanities, mathematics, sciences (biological or physical), social science, wellness/personal development. **Classes:** 10-19 students in an average class. Under 10 students in an average lab/ discussion section. **Majors with Highest Enrollment:** Business administration/management; elementary education and teaching; criminal justice/safety studies. **Disciplines with Highest Percentage of Degrees Awarded:** Education 24%, business/marketing 24%, protective services/public administration 15%, health professions and related sciences 13%, psychology 6%. **Special Study Options:** Accelerated program, cooperative (work-study) program, distance learning, double major, dual enrollment, external degree program, honors program, independent study, internships, student-designed major, study abroad, teacher certification program.

FACILITIES

Housing: Coed, all-female, all-male, apartments for married students, apartments for single students, housing for disabled students. **Library Holdings:** 350,407 bound volumes. 805 periodicals. 680,052 microforms. 11,073 audiovisuals. **Special Academic Facilities/Equipment:** Art galleries, natural history museum, North Dakota Center for Persons with Disabilities, Native American Collection, Observatory. **Computers:** School-owned computers available for student use.

EXTRACURRICULARS

Activities: Choral groups, concert band, drama/theater, jazz band, literary magazine, marching band, music ensembles, musical theater, opera, pep band, radio station, student government, student newspaper, symphony orchestra, television station, yearbook. **Organizations:** 59 registered organizations, 5 honor societies, 5 religious organizations. **Athletics (Intercollegiate):** *Men:* baseball, basketball, cross-country, football, golf, indoor track, track & field. *Women:* basketball, cheerleading, cross-country, golf, indoor track, softball, track & field, volleyball.

ADMISSIONS

Selectivity Rating: 67 (of 100). **Freshman Academic Profile:** Average high school GPA 3.1. 98% from public high schools. Average ACT 21, ACT middle 50% range 18-23. TOEFL required of all international applicants, minimum TOEFL 525. **Basis for Candidate Selection:** *Very important factors considered include:* secondary school record, standardized test scores. **Freshman Admission Requirements:** High school diploma or GED is required. *Academic units required/recommended:* 4 English required, 3 math required, 3 science required, 3 science lab required, 2 foreign language recommended, 3 social studies required. **Freshman Admission Statistics:** 743 applied, 86% accepted, 89% of those accepted enrolled. **Transfer Admission Requirements:** *Items required:* college transcript. Minimum college GPA of 2.0 required. Lowest grade transferable D. **General Admission Information:** Application fee $35. Priority application deadline April 1. Nonfall registration accepted. Admission may be deferred. Credit and/or placement offered for CEEB Advanced Placement tests.

COSTS AND FINANCIAL AID

In-state tuition $2,244. Out-of-state tuition $5,991. Room & board $3,000. Required fees $310. Average book expense $700. **Required Forms and Deadlines:** FAFSA and institution's own financial aid form. No deadline for regular filing. Priority filing deadline April 15. **Notification of Awards:** Applicants will be notified of awards on a rolling basis beginning on or about June 1. **Types of Aid:** *Need-based scholarships/grants:* Pell, SEOG, state scholarships/grants, private scholarships, the school's own gift aid, Federal Nursing. *Loans:* FFEL Subsidized Stafford, FFEL Unsubsidized Stafford, FFEL PLUS, Federal Perkins, Federal Nursing. **Student Employment:** Federal Work-Study Program available. Institutional employment available. Off-campus job opportunities are excellent. **Financial Aid Statistics:** 63% freshmen, 67% undergrads receive some form of aid. Average freshman loan $2,275. **Financial Aid Phone:** 701-858-3375.

MISSISSIPPI COLLEGE

Box 4026, Clinton, MS 39058
Phone: 601-925-3800 **E-mail:** enrollment-services@mc.edu **CEEB Code:** 1477
Fax: 601-925-3950 **Web:** www.mc.edu **ACT Code:** 2214

This private school, which is affiliated with the Southern Baptist Church, was founded in 1826. It has a 320-acre campus.

STUDENTS AND FACULTY

Enrollment: 2,269. **Student Body:** Male 40%, female 60%, out-of-state 16%, international students represent 9 countries. **Ethnic Representation:** African American 13%, Asian 1%, Caucasian 85%. **Retention and Graduation:** 70% freshmen return for sophomore year. 46% freshmen graduate within 4 years. **Faculty:** Student/faculty ratio 15:1. 155 full-time faculty, 72% hold PhDs. 88% faculty teach undergrads.

ACADEMICS

Degrees: Bachelor's, first professional, master's, post-bachelor's certificate. **Academic Requirements:** General education including some course work in arts/fine arts, computer literacy, English (including composition), history, mathematics, sciences (biological or physical), social science, Bible, physical education, and foreign language (if in BA degree program). **Classes:** Under 10 students in an average class. **Majors with Highest Enrollment:** Accounting and finance; nursing/registered nurse training (RN, ASN, BSN, MSN); elementary education and teaching. **Disciplines with Highest Percentage of Degrees Awarded:** Business/marketing 20%, education 16%, health professions and related sciences 14%, psychology 6%, communications/communication technologies 5%. **Special Study Options:** Double major, dual enrollment, honors program, independent study, internships, study abroad, teacher certification program, academic remediation, Advanced Placement credit, Work-Study program, learning disabilities services.

FACILITIES

Housing: All-female, all-male, apartments for married students, housing for disabled students. **Library Holdings:** 273,868 bound volumes. 760 periodicals. 281,224 microforms. 13,450 audiovisuals. **Computers:** School-owned computers available for student use.

EXTRACURRICULARS

Activities: Choral groups, concert band, drama/theater, jazz band, literary magazine, marching band, music ensembles, musical theater, opera, radio station, student government, student newspaper, yearbook. **Organizations:** 22 registered organizations, 15 honor societies, 1 religious organization. **Athletics (Intercollegiate):** *Men:* baseball, basketball, cross-country, football, soccer, tennis, track & field. *Women:* basketball, cross-country, soccer, softball, tennis, track & field.

ADMISSIONS

Selectivity Rating: 76 (of 100). **Freshman Academic Profile:** Average high school GPA 3.1. Average ACT 24, ACT middle 50% range 21-27. TOEFL required of all international applicants, minimum TOEFL 550. **Basis for Candidate Selection:** *Very important factors considered include:* secondary school record, standardized test scores. *Important factors considered include:* character/personal qualities, essays, extracurricular activities. *Other factors considered include:* alumni/ae relation, class rank, interview, recommendations, talent/ability, volunteer work, work experience. **Freshman Admission Requirements:** High school diploma or GED is required. *Academic units required/recommended:* 22 total recommended; 4 English recommended, 3 math recommended, 3 science recommended, 1 science lab recommended, 1 foreign language recommended, 3 social studies recommended, 1 history recommended, 5 elective recommended. **Freshman Admission Statistics:** 1,145 applied, 68% accepted, 53% of those accepted enrolled. **Transfer Admission Requirements:** *Items required:* college transcript, essay, statement of good standing from prior school. Minimum college GPA of 2.0 required. Lowest grade transferable C. **General Admission Information:** Application fee $25. Priority application deadline August 1. Early decision application deadline December 1. Regular application deadline August 15. Nonfall registration accepted. Admission may be deferred for a maximum of 1 year. Credit offered for CEEB Advanced Placement tests.

COSTS AND FINANCIAL AID

Tuition $10,830. Room & board $4,962. Required fees $610. Average book expense $1,000. **Required Forms and Deadlines:** FAFSA, institution's own financial aid form and state aid form. No deadline for regular filing. Priority filing deadline March 1. **Notification of Awards:** Applicants will be notified of awards on a rolling basis beginning on or about March 1. **Types of Aid:** *Need-based scholarships/grants:* Pell, SEOG, state scholarships/grants, private scholarships. *Loans:* FFEL Subsidized Stafford, FFEL Unsubsidized Stafford, FFEL PLUS, Federal Perkins, Federal Nursing, college/university loans from institutional funds. **Student Employment:** Federal Work-Study Program available. Institutional employment available. Off-campus job opportunities are excellent. **Financial Aid Statistics:** 54% freshmen, 53% undergrads receive some form of aid. Average freshman grant $7,432. Average freshman loan $2,800. Average income from on-campus job $1,800. **Financial Aid Phone:** 601-925-3212.

MISSISSIPPI STATE UNIVERSITY

PO Box 6305, Mississippi State, MS 39762
Phone: 662-325-2224 **E-mail:** admit@admissions.msstate.edu **CEEB Code:** 1480
Fax: 662-325-7360 **Web:** www.msstate.edu **ACT Code:** 2220

This public school was founded in 1878. It has a 4,200-acre campus.

STUDENTS AND FACULTY

Enrollment: 13,373. **Student Body:** Male 53%, female 47%, out-of-state 18%, international 1% (65 countries represented). **Ethnic Representation:** African American 19%, Asian 1%, Caucasian 79%, Hispanic 1%. **Retention and Graduation:** 81% freshmen return for sophomore year. 25% freshmen graduate within 4 years. **Faculty:** Student/faculty ratio 16:1. 971 full-time faculty, 88% hold PhDs.

ACADEMICS

Degrees: Bachelor's, doctoral, first professional, master's, post-master's certificate. **Academic Requirements:** General education including some course work in arts/fine arts, computer literacy, English (including composition), history, humanities, mathematics, sciences (biological or physical), social science, speech/public speaking, junior/senior level writing. **Classes:** 20-29 students in an average class. Under 10 students in an average lab/discussion section. **Majors with Highest Enrollment:** Elementary education and teaching; business administration/management; marketing/marketing management, general. **Disciplines with Highest Percentage of Degrees Awarded:** Business/marketing 27%, education 22%, engineering/engineering technology 13%, agriculture 6%, communications/communication technologies 4%. **Special Study Options:** Accelerated program, cooperative (work-study) program, distance learning, double major, dual enrollment, English as a second language, student exchange program (domestic), honors program, independent study, internships, liberal arts/career combination, student-designed major, study abroad, teacher certification program.

FACILITIES

Housing: Coed, all-female, all-male, apartments for married students, apartments for single students, housing for disabled students, housing for international students, fraternities and/or sororities, honors housing, special housing for first-year students and graduate students. **Library Holdings:** 2,026,894 bound volumes. 17,722 periodicals. 2,867,364 microforms. 18,679 audiovisuals. **Special Academic Facilities/Equipment:** Art gallery, earth science museum, music museum, 78,000-acre experimental forest, institute of archaeology, flight research lab, planetarium. **Computers:** School-owned computers available for student use.

EXTRACURRICULARS

Activities: Choral groups, concert band, dance, drama/theater, jazz band, literary magazine, marching band, music ensembles, musical theater, pep band, radio station, student government, student newspaper, symphony orchestra, television station, yearbook. **Organizations:** 300 registered organizations, 40 honor societies, 27 religious organizations, 18 fraternities (17% men join), 12 sororities (18% women join). **Athletics (Intercollegiate):** *Men:* baseball, basketball, football, golf, tennis, track & field. *Women:* basketball, cross-country, golf, soccer, softball, tennis, track & field, volleyball.

ADMISSIONS

Selectivity Rating: 79 (of 100). **Freshman Academic Profile:** Average high school GPA 3.3. 28% in top 10% of high school class, 56% in top 25% of high school class, 82% in top 50% of high school class. Average ACT 24, ACT middle 50% range 20-27. TOEFL required of all international applicants, minimum TOEFL 525. **Basis for Candidate Selection:** *Very important factors considered include:* class rank, secondary school record, standardized test scores. *Other factors considered include:* alumni/ae relation, recommendations, talent/ability. **Freshman Admission Requirements:** High school diploma or GED is required. *Academic units required/recommended:* 16 total required; 21 total recommended; 4 English required, 4 English recommended, 3 math required, 4 math recommended, 3 science required, 4 science recommended, 2 science lab required, 2 science lab recommended, 1 foreign language required, 2 foreign language recommended, 1 social studies required, 2 social studies recommended, 2 history required, 2 history recommended, 1 elective required, 2 elective recommended. **Freshman Admission Statistics:** 5,000 applied, 74% accepted, 48% of those accepted enrolled. **Transfer Admission Requirements:** *Items required:* high school transcript, college transcript, standardized test score, statement of good standing from prior school. Minimum high school GPA of 2.0 required. Minimum college GPA of 2.0 required. Lowest grade transferable D. **General Admission Information:** Application fee $25. Regular application deadline May 2. Nonfall registration accepted. Admission may be deferred. Credit offered for CEEB Advanced Placement tests.

COSTS AND FINANCIAL AID

In-state tuition $3,874. Out-of-state tuition $8,780. Room & board $5,269. Required fees $0. Average book expense $750. **Required Forms and Deadlines:** FAFSA and State grant/scholarship application. Financial aid filing deadline April 1. **Notification of Awards:** Applicants will be notified of awards on a rolling basis beginning on or about February 15. **Types of Aid:** *Need-based scholarships/grants:* Pell, SEOG, state scholarships/grants, private scholarships, the school's own gift aid. *Loans:* FFEL Subsidized Stafford, FFEL Unsubsidized Stafford, FFEL PLUS, Federal Perkins, state loans, college/university loans from institutional funds. **Student Employment:** Federal Work-Study Program available. Institutional employment available. Off-campus job opportunities are good. **Financial Aid Statistics:** 61% freshmen, 57% undergrads receive some form of aid. **Financial Aid Phone:** 662-325-2450.

MISSISSIPPI UNIVERSITY FOR WOMEN

West Box 1613, Columbus, MS 39701
Phone: 662-329-7106 **E-mail:** admissions@muw.edu **CEEB Code:** 1481
Fax: 662-241-7481 **Web:** www.muw.edu **ACT Code:** 2222

This public school was founded in 1884. It has a 104-acre campus.

STUDENTS AND FACULTY

Enrollment: 3,314. **Student Body:** Male 19%, female 81%, out-of-state 9%, international 2% (36 countries represented). **Ethnic Representation:** African American 29%, Caucasian 70%, Hispanic 1%. **Retention and Graduation:** 64% freshmen return for sophomore year. 21% freshmen graduate within 4 years. **Faculty:** 86% faculty teach undergrads.

ACADEMICS

Degrees: Associate's, bachelor's, master's. **Academic Requirements:** General education including some course work in arts/fine arts, computer literacy, English (including composition), history, humanities, mathematics, sciences (biological or physical), social science. **Special Study Options:** Accelerated program, cooperative (work-study) program, cross registration, distance learning, double major, English as a second language, honors program, internships, study abroad, teacher certification program, weekend college.

FACILITIES

Housing: All-female, all-male, apartments for single students with children. **Library Holdings:** 198,909 bound volumes. 1,641 periodicals. 602,113 microforms. 164 audiovisuals. **Special Academic Facilities/Equipment:** Museum/gallery, university archives, language lab, TV studio, residential high school for gifted students, elementary school, speech and hearing center. **Computers:** School-owned computers available for student use.

EXTRACURRICULARS

Activities: Choral groups, dance, drama/theater, literary magazine, music ensembles, radio station, student government, student newspaper, television station, yearbook. **Organizations:** 78 registered organizations, 17 honor societies, 3 religious organizations, 2 fraternities (6% men join), 17 sororities (15% women join). **Athletics (Intercollegiate):** *Women:* basketball, cheerleading, softball, tennis, volleyball.

ADMISSIONS

Selectivity Rating: 79 (of 100). **Freshman Academic Profile:** Average high school GPA 3.2. 79% in top 10% of high school class, 68% in top 25% of high school class, 92% in top 50% of high school class. 65% from public high schools. Average ACT 24, ACT middle 50% range 21-27. TOEFL required of all international applicants, minimum TOEFL 525. **Basis for Candidate Selection:** *Very important factors considered include:* class rank, secondary school record, standardized test scores. *Other factors considered include:* alumni/ae relation, character/personal qualities, extracurricular activities, recommendations, talent/ability. **Freshman Admission Requirements:** High school diploma or GED is required. *Academic units required/recommended:* 16 total required; 20 total recommended; 4 English required, 3 math required, 4 math recommended, 3 science required, 2 science lab required, 1 foreign language recommended, 3 social studies required, 2 elective required. **Freshman Admission Statistics:** 855 applied, 78% accepted, 64% of those accepted enrolled. **Transfer Admission Requirements:** *Items required:* college transcript. Minimum college GPA of 2.0 required. Lowest grade transferable 1. **General Admission Information:** Application fee $0. Nonfall registration accepted. Admission may be deferred. Credit offered for CEEB Advanced Placement tests.

COSTS AND FINANCIAL AID

In-state tuition $2,556. Out-of-state tuition $5,546. Room & board $2,557. Average book expense $600. **Required Forms and Deadlines:** Priority filing deadline April 1. **Notification of Awards:** Applicants will be notified of awards on a rolling basis beginning on or about April 15. **Types of Aid:** *Need-based scholarships/grants:* Pell, SEOG, state scholarships/grants, private scholarships, the school's own gift aid, Federal Nursing. *Loans:* FFEL Subsidized Stafford, FFEL Unsubsidized Stafford, FFEL PLUS, Federal Perkins. **Student Employment:** Federal Work-Study Program available. Institutional employment available. Off-campus job opportunities are fair. **Financial Aid Statistics:** 60% freshmen, 50% undergrads receive some form of aid. Average freshman grant $946. Average freshman loan $1,129. Average income from on-campus job $1,185. **Financial Aid Phone:** 662-329-7114.

MISSISSIPPI VALLEY STATE UNIVERSITY

14000 Highway 82 West, Itta Bena, MS 38941-1400
Phone: 662-254-3344 **E-mail:** leewilson@mvsu.edu **CEEB Code:** 1482
Fax: 662-254-3655 **Web:** www.mvsu.edu **ACT Code:** 2224

This public school was founded in 1950. It has a 450-acre campus.

STUDENTS AND FACULTY

Enrollment: 3,014. **Student Body:** Male 30%, female 70%, out-of-state 6%, international students represent 3 countries. **Ethnic Representation:** African American 96%, Caucasian 3%. **Retention and Graduation:** 31% grads go on to further study within 1 year. 1% grads pursue business degrees. 2% grads pursue law degrees. 3% grads pursue medical degrees. **Faculty:** Student/faculty ratio 23:1. 106 full-time faculty, 62% hold PhDs.

ACADEMICS

Degrees: Bachelor's, master's. **Academic Requirements:** General education including some course work in arts/fine arts, English (including composition), mathematics, sciences (biological or physical), social science, health education, physical education, speech, general psychology. **Classes:** 100+ students in an average class. 20-29 students in an average lab/discussion section. **Majors with Highest Enrollment:** Business, management, marketing, and related support services; elementary education and teaching; criminal justice/safety studies. **Disciplines with Highest Percentage of Degrees Awarded:** Protective services/public administration 21%, computer and information sciences 16%, social sciences and history 16%, business/marketing 15%, biological life sciences 9%. **Special Study Options:** Cooperative (work-study) program, double major, honors program, internships, teacher certification program. Co-op programs: business, computer science, natural science, social/behavioral science.

FACILITIES

Housing: All-female, all-male, apartments for married students. **Library Holdings:** 130,918 bound volumes. 599 periodicals. 355,603 microforms. 3,525 audiovisuals. **Computers:** School-owned computers available for student use.

EXTRACURRICULARS

Activities: Choral groups, concert band, drama/theater, marching band, radio station, student government, student newspaper, yearbook. **Organizations:** 35 registered organizations, 19 honor societies, 6 religious organizations, 5 fraternities, 4 sororities. **Athletics (Intercollegiate):** *Men:* basketball, cross-country, track & field, volleyball. *Women:* basketball, cross-country, track & field, volleyball.

ADMISSIONS

Selectivity Rating: 63 (of 100). **Freshman Academic Profile:** Average high school GPA 2.7. 10% in top 10% of high school class, 23% in top 25% of high school class, 75% in top 50% of high school class. 96% from public high schools. ACT middle 50% range 14-19. TOEFL required of all international applicants, minimum TOEFL 525. **Freshman Admission Requirements:** High school diploma or GED is required. *Academic units required/recommended:* 16 total required; 17 total recommended; 4 English required, 3 math required, 3 science required, 2 science lab required, 1 foreign language recommended, 3 social studies required, 2 elective required. **Freshman Admission Statistics:** 3,783 applied, 19% accepted, 38% of those accepted enrolled. **Transfer Admission Requirements:** *Items required:* college transcript. Minimum college GPA of 2.0 required. Lowest grade transferable C. **General Admission Information:** Nonfall registration accepted.

COSTS AND FINANCIAL AID

In-state tuition $3,410. Out-of-state tuition $7,965. Room & board $3,374. Required fees $0. Average book expense $700. **Required Forms and Deadlines:** FAFSA and institution's own financial aid form. Priority filing deadline April 1. **Notification of Awards:** Applicants will be notified of awards on or about July 15. **Types of Aid:** *Need-based scholarships/grants:* Pell, SEOG, state scholarships/grants, private scholarships, the school's own gift aid. *Loans:* Direct Unsubsidized Stafford, Direct PLUS. **Student Employment:** Institutional employment available. Off-campus job opportunities are poor. **Financial Aid Statistics:** 85% freshmen, 84% undergrads receive some form of aid. Average freshman loan $1,753. **Financial Aid Phone:** 601-254-3335.

MISSOURI BAPTIST COLLEGE

One College Park Drive, St. Louis, MO 63141-8660
Phone: 314-434-1115 **E-mail:** admissions@mobap.edu **CEEB Code:** 2258
Fax: 314-434-7596 **Web:** www.mobap.edu **ACT Code:** 2323

This private school, which is affiliated with the Southern Baptist Church, was founded in 1964. It has a 65-acre campus.

STUDENTS AND FACULTY

Enrollment: 2,574. **Student Body:** Male 37%, female 63%, out-of-state 11%, international 2%. **Ethnic Representation:** African American 6%, Caucasian 91%, Hispanic 2%. **Retention and Graduation:** 61% freshmen return for sophomore year. 29% freshmen graduate within 4 years. **Faculty:** Student/faculty ratio 16:1. 37 full-time faculty, 59% hold PhDs. 100% faculty teach undergrads.

ACADEMICS

Degrees: Associate's, bachelor's, certificate, master's, post-bachelor's certificate, terminal. **Academic Requirements:** General education including some course work in arts/fine arts, computer literacy, English (including composition), foreign languages, history, humanities, mathematics, philosophy, sciences (biological or physical), social science, Old and New Testament history, World Literary Types, World Citizen (general education capstone), and healthy, physical education. U.S. history is required of all education students. Foreign language is required for the Bachelor of Arts degree. Two courses in philosophy are required for all students majoring in religion and religious education. **Classes:** 10-19 students in an average class. 10-19 students in an average lab/discussion section. **Disciplines with Highest Percentage of Degrees Awarded:** Education 27%, business/marketing 18%, philosophy/religion/theology 11%, parks and recreation 6%, psychology 5%. **Special Study Options:** Accelerated program, cross registration, distance learning, double major, dual enrollment, independent study, internships, liberal arts/career combination, student-designed major, study abroad, teacher certification program.

FACILITIES

Housing: All-female, all-male. **Library Holdings:** 90,387 bound volumes. 610 periodicals. 45,216 microforms. 4,181 audiovisuals. **Computers:** School-owned computers available for student use.

EXTRACURRICULARS

Activities: Choral groups, concert band, drama/theater, jazz band, literary magazine, music ensembles, musical theater, opera, student government, student newspaper. **Organizations:** 13 registered organizations, 5 honor societies, 4 religious organizations. **Athletics (Intercollegiate):** *Men:* baseball, basketball, cross-country, golf, soccer, track & field. *Women:* cheerleading, cross-country, soccer, softball, track & field, volleyball.

ADMISSIONS

Selectivity Rating: 77 (of 100). **Freshman Academic Profile:** Average high school GPA 3.1. 12% in top 10% of high school class, 43% in top 25% of high school class, 67% in top 50% of high school class. 74% from public high schools. Average SAT I Math 511. Average SAT I Verbal 495. Average ACT 22. TOEFL required of all international applicants, minimum TOEFL 500. **Basis for Candidate Selection:** *Very important factors considered include:* character/personal qualities, class rank, recommendations, secondary school record, standardized test scores. *Important factors considered include:* interview, religious affiliation/commitment, talent/ability. *Other factors considered include:* alumni/ae relation, extracurricular activities. **Freshman Admission Requirements:** High school diploma or GED is required. *Academic units required/recommended:* 22 total required; 4 English required, 3 math required, 2 science required, 1 science lab required, 2 foreign language recommended, 2 social studies required, 1 history required, 3 elective required. **Freshman Admission Statistics:** 370 applied, 75% accepted, 62% of those accepted enrolled. **Transfer Admission Requirements:** *Items required:* high school transcript, college transcript, statement of good standing from prior school. Minimum college GPA of 2.0 required. Lowest grade transferable D. **General Admission Information:** Application fee $25. Priority application deadline January 31. Nonfall registration accepted. Admission may be deferred for a maximum of 1 year. Credit and/or placement offered for CEEB Advanced Placement tests.

COSTS AND FINANCIAL AID

Tuition $10,290. Room & board $5,080. Required fees $392. Average book expense $1,500. **Required Forms and Deadlines:** FAFSA and institution's own financial aid form. Financial aid filing deadline November 15. Priority filing deadline April 1. **Notification of Awards:** Applicants will be notified of awards on a rolling basis beginning on or about April 15. **Types of Aid:** *Need-based scholarships/grants:* Pell, SEOG, state scholarships/grants, private scholarships, the school's own gift aid. *Loans:* FFEL Subsidized Stafford, FFEL Unsubsidized Stafford, FFEL PLUS, state loans, college/university loans from institutional funds. **Student Employment:** Federal Work-Study Program available. Institutional employment available. Off-campus job opportunities are good. **Financial Aid Statistics:** 88% undergrads receive some form of aid. Average freshman grant $6,463. Average freshman loan $3,754. Average income from on-campus job $1,779. **Financial Aid Phone:** 314-392-2368.

MISSOURI SOUTHERN STATE COLLEGE

3950 E. Newman Road, Joplin, MO 64801-1595
Phone: 417-625-9378 **E-mail:** admissions@mail.mssc.edu **CEEB Code:** 6322
Fax: 417-659-4429 **Web:** www.mssc.edu **ACT Code:** 2304

This public school was founded in 1937. It has a 365-acre campus.

STUDENTS AND FACULTY

Enrollment: 5,823. **Student Body:** Male 41%, female 59%, out-of-state 13%, international 2%. **Ethnic Representation:** African American 3%, Asian 1%, Caucasian 91%, Hispanic 2%, Native American 3%. **Retention and Gradua-**

tion: 64% freshmen return for sophomore year. 12% freshmen graduate within 4 years. **Faculty:** Student/faculty ratio 18:1. 202 full-time faculty, 62% hold PhDs. 100% faculty teach undergrads.

ACADEMICS

Degrees: Associate's, bachelor's, certificate. **Academic Requirements:** General education including some course work in arts/fine arts, computer literacy, English (including composition), foreign languages, history, humanities, mathematics, philosophy, sciences (biological or physical), social science, international studies, physical education, communication. **Classes:** 20-29 students in an average class. Under 10 students in an average lab/discussion section. **Majors with Highest Enrollment:** Business administration/management; education, general; criminal justice/law enforcement administration. **Disciplines with Highest Percentage of Degrees Awarded:** Business/marketing 29%, education 18%, protective services/public administration 9%, social sciences and history 6%, liberal arts/general studies 6%. **Special Study Options:** Accelerated program, cooperative (work-study) program, distance learning, double major, dual enrollment, English as a second language, student exchange program (domestic), honors program, independent study, internships, liberal arts/career combination, study abroad, teacher certification program, weekend college.

FACILITIES

Housing: Coed, all-female, all-male, apartments for single students, housing for disabled students. **Library Holdings:** 157,362 bound volumes. 1,574 periodicals. 736,120 microforms. 10,417 audiovisuals. **Special Academic Facilities/Equipment:** Art museum, biology pond, forensics laboratory, child development center. **Computers:** *Recommended operating system:* Windows 95. School-owned computers available for student use.

EXTRACURRICULARS

Activities: Choral groups, concert band, dance, drama/theater, jazz band, literary magazine, marching band, music ensembles, musical theater, pep band, radio station, student government, student newspaper, student-run film society, symphony orchestra, television station. **Organizations:** 81 registered organizations, 13 honor societies, 8 religious organizations, 2 fraternities (1% men join), 2 sororities (1% women join). **Athletics (Intercollegiate):** *Men:* baseball, basketball, cheerleading, cross-country, football, golf, soccer, track & field. *Women:* basketball, cheerleading, cross-country, soccer, softball, tennis, track & field, volleyball.

ADMISSIONS

Selectivity Rating: 66 (of 100). **Freshman Academic Profile:** 15% in top 10% of high school class, 36% in top 25% of high school class, 72% in top 50% of high school class. 98% from public high schools. Average ACT 22, ACT middle 50% range 19-24. TOEFL required of all international applicants, minimum TOEFL 535. **Basis for Candidate Selection:** *Very important factors considered include:* class rank, secondary school record, standardized test scores. *Other factors considered include:* recommendations. **Freshman Admission Requirements:** High school diploma or GED is required. *Academic units required/recommended:* 16 total recommended; 4 English recommended, 3 math recommended, 2 science recommended, 1 science lab recommended, 2 foreign language recommended, 3 social studies recommended, 3 elective recommended. **Freshman Admission Statistics:** 1,809 applied, 74% accepted, 54% of those accepted enrolled. **Transfer Admission Requirements:** *Items required:* college transcript. Minimum college GPA of 2.0 required. Lowest grade transferable D. **General Admission Information:** Application fee $15. Priority application deadline August 3. Nonfall registration accepted. Admission may be deferred for a maximum of 1 year. Credit and/or placement offered for CEEB Advanced Placement tests.

COSTS AND FINANCIAL AID

In-state tuition $3,720. Out-of-state tuition $7,440. Room & board $4,000. Required fees $166. Average book expense $500. **Required Forms and Deadlines:** FAFSA. Priority filing deadline February 15. **Notification of Awards:** Applicants will be notified of awards on a rolling basis beginning on or about February 15. **Types of Aid:** *Need-based scholarships/grants:* Pell, SEOG, state scholarships/grants, private scholarships. *Loans:* Direct Subsidized Stafford, Direct Unsubsidized Stafford, Direct PLUS, Federal Perkins, state loans. **Student Employment:** Federal Work-Study Program available. Institutional employment available. Off-campus job opportunities are excellent. **Financial Aid Statistics:** 80% freshmen, 86% undergrads receive some form of aid. Average freshman grant $3,911. Average freshman loan $1,743. Average income from on-campus job $1,710. **Financial Aid Phone:** 417-625-9325.

MISSOURI VALLEY COLLEGE

500 East College Street, Marshall, MO 65340
Phone: 660-831-4114 **E-mail:** admissions@moval.edu
Fax: 660-831-4233 **Web:** www.moval.edu **ACT Code:** 2330

This private school, which is affiliated with the Presbyterian Church, was founded in 1889. It has a 150-acre campus.

STUDENTS AND FACULTY

Enrollment: 1,600. **Student Body:** Male 56%, female 44%, out-of-state 29%, international 6%. **Ethnic Representation:** African American 13%, Asian 4%, Caucasian 77%, Hispanic 5%, Native American 1%. **Retention and Graduation:** 49% freshmen return for sophomore year. 12% freshmen graduate within 4 years. **Faculty:** Student/faculty ratio 17:1. 68 full-time faculty, 38% hold PhDs. 100% faculty teach undergrads.

ACADEMICS

Degrees: Associate's, bachelor's. **Academic Requirements:** General education including some course work in arts/fine arts, computer literacy, English (including composition), history, humanities, mathematics, sciences (biological or physical), social science, 3 hours of religion. **Classes:** 20-29 students in an average class. 30-39 students in an average lab/discussion section. **Majors with Highest Enrollment:** Business administration/management; elementary education and teaching; criminal justice/law enforcement administration. **Disciplines with Highest Percentage of Degrees Awarded:** Education 19%, business/marketing 13%, other 13%, protective services/public administration 11%, psychology 8%. **Special Study Options:** Double major, dual enrollment, internships, teacher certification program.

FACILITIES

Housing: All-female, all-male, apartments for married students, apartments for single students, fraternities and/or sororities. **Library Holdings:** 61,907 bound volumes. 391 periodicals. 25,463 microforms. 1,399 audiovisuals. **Computers:** School-owned computers available for student use.

EXTRACURRICULARS

Activities: Choral groups, dance, drama/theater, literary magazine, music ensembles, musical theater, pep band, radio station, student government, student newspaper, television station, yearbook. **Organizations:** 28 registered organizations, 8 honor societies, 7 religious organizations, 25% men join fraternities, 25% women join sororities. **Athletics (Intercollegiate):** *Men:* baseball, basketball, cheerleading, cross-country, football, golf, indoor track, rodeo, soccer, track & field, volleyball, wrestling. *Women:* basketball, cheerleading, cross-country, golf, indoor track, rodeo, soccer, softball, track & field, volleyball, wrestling.

ADMISSIONS

Selectivity Rating: 63 (of 100). **Freshman Academic Profile:** Average high school GPA 2.9. 4% in top 10% of high school class, 38% in top 25% of high school class, 54% in top 50% of high school class. Average SAT I Math 420. Average SAT I Verbal 420. Average ACT 19. TOEFL required of all international applicants, minimum TOEFL 450. **Basis for Candidate Selection:** *Very important factors considered include:* character/personal qualities, interview. *Important factors considered include:* extracurricular activities, talent/ability, volunteer work. *Other factors considered include:* alumni/ae relation, class rank, recommendations, secondary school record, standardized test scores, work experience. **Freshman Admission Requirements:** High school diploma or GED is required. *Academic units required/recommended:* 4 English recommended, 3 math recommended, 2 science recommended, 1 science lab recommended, 2 social studies recommended, 2 history recommended, 3 elective recommended. **Transfer Admission Requirements:** *Items required:* high school transcript, college transcript, standardized test scores. Minimum high school GPA of 2.0 required. Minimum college GPA of 2.0 required. Lowest grade transferable C. **General Admission Information:** Application fee $10. Priority application deadline March 1. Regular application deadline September 1. Nonfall registration accepted.

COSTS AND FINANCIAL AID

Tuition $12,600. Room & board $5,000. Required fees $500. Average book expense $1,300. **Required Forms and Deadlines:** FAFSA and state aid form. Priority filing deadline March 1. **Notification of Awards:** Applicants will be notified of awards on a rolling basis. **Types of Aid:** *Need-based scholarships/grants:* Pell, SEOG, state scholarships/grants, private scholarships, the school's own gift aid. *Loans:* FFEL Subsidized Stafford, FFEL Unsubsidized Stafford, FFEL PLUS, Federal Perkins. **Student Employment:** Federal Work-Study Program available. Institutional employment available. Off-campus job opportunities are excellent. **Financial Aid Statistics:** 95% freshmen, 96% undergrads receive some form of aid. **Financial Aid Phone:** 660-831-4176.

MISSOURI WESTERN STATE COLLEGE

4525 Downs Drive, Saint Joseph, MO 64507
Phone: 816-271-4266 **E-mail:** admissn@mwsc.edu
Fax: 816-271-5833 **Web:** www.mwsc.edu **ACT Code:** 2344

This public school was founded in 1969. It has a 740-acre campus.

STUDENTS AND FACULTY

Enrollment: 5,197. **Student Body:** Male 39%, female 61%, out-of-state 9%, international students represent 5 countries. **Ethnic Representation:** African American 11%, Asian 1%, Caucasian 86%, Hispanic 2%, Native American 1%. **Retention and Graduation:** 59% freshmen return for sophomore year. 13% freshmen graduate within 4 years. 20% grads go on to further study within 1 year. 6% grads pursue business degrees. 1% grads pursue law degrees. 2% grads pursue medical degrees. **Faculty:** Student/faculty ratio 18:1. 186 full-time faculty, 75% hold PhDs. 100% faculty teach undergrads.

ACADEMICS

Degrees: Associate's, bachelor's, certificate, terminal, transfer. **Academic Requirements:** General education including some course work in English (including composition), humanities, mathematics, sciences (biological or physical), social science, oral communications, physical health. **Classes:** 20-29 students in an average class. 20-29 students in an average lab/discussion section. **Majors with Highest Enrollment:** Business administration/management; nursing/registered nurse training (RN, ASN, BSN, MSN); criminal justice/law enforcement administration. **Disciplines with Highest Percentage of Degrees Awarded:** Business/marketing 26%, protective services/public administration 14%, parks and recreation 11%, education 9%, health professions and related sciences 7%. **Special Study Options:** Distance learning, double major, dual enrollment, honors program, internships, liberal arts/career combination, teacher certification program, weekend college.

FACILITIES

Housing: Coed, apartments for single students, fraternities and/or sororities. **Library Holdings:** 151,450 bound volumes. 1,504 periodicals. 111,544 microforms. 16,024 audiovisuals. **Special Academic Facilities/Equipment:** Multimedia classroom building, planetarium. **Computers:** School-owned computers available for student use.

EXTRACURRICULARS

Activities: Choral groups, concert band, dance, drama/theater, jazz band, marching band, music ensembles, pep band, student government, student newspaper, yearbook. **Organizations:** 64 registered organizations, 5 honor societies, 7 religious organizations, 5 fraternities (10% men join), 6 sororities (10% women join). **Athletics (Intercollegiate):** *Men:* baseball, basketball, football, golf. *Women:* basketball, golf, softball, tennis, volleyball.

ADMISSIONS

Selectivity Rating: 64 (of 100). **Freshman Academic Profile:** 7% in top 10% of high school class, 28% in top 25% of high school class, 61% in top 50% of high school class. 95% from public high schools. Average ACT 19, ACT middle 50% range 16-22. TOEFL required of all international applicants, minimum TOEFL 500. **Freshman Admission Requirements:** High school diploma or GED is required. *Academic units required/recommended:* 16 total required; 4 English required, 3 math required, 2 science required, 1 science lab required, 2 foreign language recommended, 3 social studies required, 3 elective required. **Freshman Admission Statistics:** 2,789 applied, 100% accepted, 44% of those accepted enrolled. **Transfer Admission Requirements:** *Items required:* college transcript. Lowest grade transferable D. **General Admission Information:** Application fee $15. Priority application deadline July 30. Regular application deadline August 15. Nonfall registration accepted. Credit offered for CEEB Advanced Placement tests.

COSTS AND FINANCIAL AID

In-state tuition $3,768. Out-of-state tuition $7,074. Room & board $3,804. Required fees $296. Average book expense $700. **Required Forms and Deadlines:** FAFSA and institution's own financial aid form. No deadline for regular filing. Priority filing deadline March 1. **Notification of Awards:** Applicants will be notified of awards on a rolling basis beginning on or about March 2. **Types of Aid:** *Need-based scholarships/grants:* Pell, SEOG, state scholarships/grants, private scholarships, the school's own gift aid. *Loans:* FFEL Subsidized Stafford, FFEL Unsubsidized Stafford, FFEL PLUS, Federal Perkins. **Student Employment:** Federal Work-Study Program available. Institutional employment available. Off-campus job opportunities are good. **Financial Aid Statistics:** 56% freshmen, 55% undergrads receive some form of aid. Average freshman grant $2,000. Average freshman loan $2,700. Average income from on-campus job $1,400. **Financial Aid Phone:** 816-271-4361.

MITCHELL COLLEGE

$$$

437 Pequot Avenue, New London, CT 06320
Phone: 800-443-2811 **E-mail:** admissions@mitchell.edu **CEEB Code:** 3528
Fax: 860-444-1209 **Web:** www.mitchell.edu **ACT Code:** 572

This private school was founded in 1938. It has a 65-acre campus.

STUDENTS AND FACULTY

Enrollment: 555. **Student Body:** Male 48%, female 52%, out-of-state 36%, international 1%. **Ethnic Representation:** African American 12%, Caucasian 70%, Hispanic 3%, Native American 5%. **Retention and Graduation:** 95% grads go on to further study within 1 year. **Faculty:** Student/faculty ratio 12:1. 26 full-time faculty, 46% hold PhDs. 100% faculty teach undergrads.

ACADEMICS

Degrees: Associate's, bachelor's. **Academic Requirements:** General education including some course work in computer literacy, English (including composition), history, mathematics, sciences (biological or physical), social science, public speaking. **Majors with Highest Enrollment:** Early childhood education and teaching; human development and family studies, general; liberal arts and sciences/liberal studies. **Disciplines with Highest Percentage of Degrees Awarded:** Liberal arts/general studies 61%, social sciences and history 39%. **Special Study Options:** Dual enrollment, English as a second language, internships.

FACILITIES

Housing: Coed, housing for disabled students, 4 residence halls are Victorian and Colonial houses located on the waterfront and 1 is reserved specifically for upperclassmen enrolled in the human development major. Three other residence halls are of traditional design. **Library Holdings:** 42,000 bound volumes. 90 periodicals. 38,928 microforms. 50 audiovisuals. **Special Academic Facilities/Equipment:** Private dock w/fleet of sailboats, 2 private beaches, 26 acres of woods. **Computers:** *Recommended operating system:* Windows NT/2000. School-owned computers available for student use.

EXTRACURRICULARS

Activities: Choral groups, dance, drama/theater, literary magazine, student government, student newspaper, yearbook. **Organizations:** 30 registered organizations, 2 honor societies, 2 religious organizations. **Athletics (Intercollegiate):** *Men:* baseball, basketball, cross-country, golf, lacrosse, soccer, tennis. *Women:* basketball, cross-country, golf, soccer, softball, tennis, volleyball.

ADMISSIONS

Selectivity Rating: 63 (of 100). **Freshman Academic Profile:** Average high school GPA 2.7. 3% in top 10% of high school class, 15% in top 25% of high school class, 35% in top 50% of high school class. 85% from public high schools. Average SAT I Math 440. Average SAT I Verbal 470. Average ACT 22. TOEFL required of all international applicants, minimum TOEFL 500. **Basis for Candidate Selection:** *Very important factors considered include:* interview, recommendations, secondary school record. *Important factors considered include:* character/personal qualities, essays, extracurricular activities, standardized test scores, talent/ability. *Other factors considered include:* alumni/ae relation, class rank, volunteer work, work experience. **Freshman Admission Requirements:** High school diploma or GED is required. **Transfer Admission Requirements:** *Items required:* high school transcript, college transcript, essay, standardized test scores. Lowest grade transferable C-. **General Admission Information:** Application fee $30. Priority application deadline April 1. Early decision application deadline November 15. Nonfall registration accepted. Admission may be deferred for a maximum of 1 year. Credit and/or placement offered for CEEB Advanced Placement tests.

COSTS AND FINANCIAL AID

Tuition $16,380. Room & board $7,875. Required fees $850. Average book expense $800. **Required Forms and Deadlines:** FAFSA and institution's own financial aid form. No deadline for regular filing. Priority filing deadline March 1. **Notification of Awards:** Applicants will be notified of awards on a rolling basis beginning on or about March 1. **Types of Aid:** *Need-based scholarships/grants:* Pell, SEOG, state scholarships/grants, private scholarships, the school's own gift aid. *Loans:* FFEL Subsidized Stafford, FFEL Unsubsidized Stafford, Plato. **Student Employment:** Federal Work-Study Program available. Institutional employment available. Off-campus job opportunities are excellent. **Financial Aid Statistics:** Average freshman grant $5,000. Average freshman loan $2,800. Average income from on-campus job $1,000. **Financial Aid Phone:** 800-443-2811.

MOHAWK VALLEY COMMUNITY COLLEGE

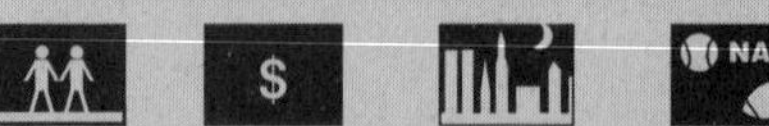

1101 Sherman Drive, Utica, NY 13501-5394
Phone: 315-792-5354 **E-mail:** admissions@mvcc.edu
Fax: 315-792-5527 **Web:** www.mvcc.edu

This public school was founded in 1946.

STUDENTS AND FACULTY

Enrollment: 5,225. **Student Body:** Male 45%, female 55%, out-of-state 2%, international 2%. **Ethnic Representation:** African American 5%, Asian 1%, Caucasian 88%, Hispanic 2%, Native American 1%. **Retention and Graduation:** 8% grads go on to further study within 1 year. 9% grads pursue business degrees. **Faculty:** Student/faculty ratio 999:1. 134 full-time faculty, 16% hold PhDs. 100% faculty teach undergrads.

ACADEMICS

Degrees: Associate's, terminal, transfer. **Academic Requirements:** General education including some course work in English (including composition), humanities, mathematics, sciences (biological or physical), social science. **Classes:** 10-19 students in an average class. 10-19 students in an average lab/discussion section. **Special Study Options:** Cross registration, distance learning, double major, English as a second language, honors program, independent study, internships, liberal arts/career combination, student-designed major.

FACILITIES

Housing: Coed, housing for disabled students, housing for international students. **Library Holdings:** 89,741 bound volumes. 639 periodicals. 9,269 microforms. 8,302 audiovisuals. **Computers:** School-owned computers available for student use.

EXTRACURRICULARS

Activities: Choral groups, concert band, drama/theater, jazz band, music ensembles, musical theater, radio station, student government, student newspaper, yearbook. **Organizations:** 45 registered organizations, 2 honor societies, 4 fraternities. **Athletics (Intercollegiate):** *Men:* baseball, basketball, skiing (cross-country), cross-country, golf, ice hockey, lacrosse, soccer, tennis, track & field. *Women:* basketball, skiing (cross-country), cross-country, golf, soccer, softball, tennis, track & field, volleyball.

ADMISSIONS

Selectivity Rating: 63 (of 100). **Freshman Academic Profile:** 3% in top 10% of high school class, 15% in top 25% of high school class, 40% in top 50% of high school class. **Basis for Candidate Selection:** *Very important factors considered include:* secondary school record. *Other factors considered include:* recommendations. **Freshman Admission Requirements:** High school diploma or equivalent is not required. *Academic units required/recommended:* 13 total recommended; 4 English recommended, 2 math recommended, 1 science recommended, 1 science lab recommended, 1 foreign language recommended, 2 social studies recommended, 1 history recommended. **Freshman Admission Statistics:** 2,851 applied, 91% accepted, 52% of those accepted enrolled. **Transfer Admission Requirements:** *Items required:* college transcript. Lowest grade transferable C. **General Admission Information:** Nonfall registration accepted. Admission may be deferred.

COSTS AND FINANCIAL AID

In-state tuition $2,500. Out-of-state tuition $3,750. Room & board $4,696. Required fees $100. Average book expense $800. **Required Forms and Deadlines:** FAFSA and institution's own financial aid form. No deadline for regular filing. **Notification of Awards:** Applicants will be notified of awards on a rolling basis beginning on or about March 1. **Types of Aid:** *Need-based scholarships/grants:* Pell, SEOG, state scholarships/grants. *Loans:* Direct Subsidized Stafford, Direct Unsubsidized Stafford, Direct PLUS, Federal Perkins. **Student Employment:** Federal Work-Study Program available. Institutional employment available. Off-campus job opportunities are fair. **Financial Aid Statistics:** Average freshman grant $1,875. Average freshman loan $2,625. **Financial Aid Phone:** 315-792-5415.

MOLLOY COLLEGE

1000 Hempstead Avenue, Rockville Centre, NY 11570
Phone: 516-678-5000 **E-mail:** admissions@molloy.edu **CEEB Code:** 2415
Fax: 516-256-2247 **Web:** www.molloy.edu **ACT Code:** 2820

This private school, which is affiliated with the Roman Catholic Church, was founded in 1955. It has a 30-acre campus.

STUDENTS AND FACULTY

Enrollment: 2,211. **Student Body:** Male 22%, female 78%, international 1%. **Ethnic Representation:** African American 19%, Asian 4%, Caucasian 63%, Hispanic 8%. **Faculty:** Student/faculty ratio 11:1. 129 full-time faculty, 54% hold PhDs. 100% faculty teach undergrads.

ACADEMICS

Degrees: Associate's, bachelor's, certificate, master's, post-master's certificate. **Academic Requirements:** General education including some course work in arts/fine arts, English (including composition), foreign languages, humanities, mathematics, philosophy, sciences (biological or physical), social science. **Majors with Highest Enrollment:** Nursing/registered nurse training (RN, ASN, BSN, MSN); education, general; psychology, general. **Disciplines with Highest Percentage of Degrees Awarded:** Health professions and related sciences 47%, psychology 12%, communications/communication technologies 7%, business/marketing 7%, protective services/public administration 7%. **Special Study Options:** Accelerated program, cooperative (work-study) program, cross registration, double major, English as a second language, honors program, independent study, internships, study abroad, teacher certification program.

FACILITIES

Library Holdings: 135,000 bound volumes. 750 periodicals. 13,850 microforms. 9,675 audiovisuals. **Special Academic Facilities/Equipment:** Professional Repertory Theatre Company in residence, dance studio, institute of cross-cultural and cross-ethnic studies, institute of gerontology, cablevision studio. **Computers:** School-owned computers available for student use.

EXTRACURRICULARS

Activities: Choral groups, jazz band, literary magazine, music ensembles, student government, student newspaper, yearbook. **Organizations:** 21 registered organizations, 17 honor societies, 1 religious organization. **Athletics (Intercollegiate):** *Men:* baseball, basketball, cross-country, equestrian, lacrosse, soccer, tennis. *Women:* basketball, cheerleading, cross-country, equestrian, soccer, softball, tennis, volleyball.

ADMISSIONS

Selectivity Rating: 66 (of 100). **Freshman Academic Profile:** Average high school GPA 2.7. 9% in top 10% of high school class, 60% in top 25% of high school class, 79% in top 50% of high school class. 71% from public high schools. Average SAT I Math 509, SAT I Math middle 50% range 440-580. Average SAT I Verbal 501, SAT I Verbal middle 50% range 450-540. TOEFL required of all international applicants, minimum TOEFL 500. **Basis for Candidate Selection:** *Very important factors considered include:* secondary school record, standardized test scores. *Important factors considered include:* class rank, extracurricular activities, interview. *Other factors considered include:* alumni/ae relation, character/personal qualities, essays, recommendations, talent/ability, volunteer work, work experience. **Freshman Admission Requirements:** High school diploma or GED is required. *Academic units required/recommended:* 16 total required; 4 English required, 2 math required, 2 science required, 2 foreign language required, 3 social studies required. **Freshman Admission Statistics:** 661 applied, 77% accepted, 51% of those accepted enrolled. **Transfer Admission Requirements:** *Items required:* college transcript, essay, statement of good standing from prior school. Minimum college GPA of 2.0 required. Lowest grade transferable C. **General Admission Information:** Application fee $30. Nonfall registration accepted. Admission may be deferred for a maximum of 1 year. Credit offered for CEEB Advanced Placement tests.

COSTS AND FINANCIAL AID

Tuition $13,940. Required fees $670. Average book expense $700. **Required Forms and Deadlines:** FAFSA, institution's own financial aid form and state aid form. **Notification of Awards:** Applicants will be notified of awards on a rolling basis beginning on or about March 1. **Types of Aid:** *Need-based scholarships/grants:* Pell, SEOG, state scholarships/grants, private scholarships, the school's own gift aid, Federal Nursing. *Loans:* Direct Subsidized Stafford, Direct Unsubsidized Stafford, Direct PLUS, FFEL Subsidized Stafford, FFEL Unsubsidized Stafford, FFEL PLUS, Federal Perkins, Federal Nursing. **Student Employment:** Federal Work-Study Program available. Off-campus job opportunities are excellent. **Financial Aid Phone:** 516-678-5000.

See page 1122.

MONMOUTH COLLEGE

700 East Broadway, Monmouth, IL 61462
Phone: 309-457-2131 **E-mail:** admit@monm.edu **CEEB Code:** 1484
Fax: 309-457-2141 **Web:** www.monm.edu **ACT Code:** 1084

This private school, which is affiliated with the Presbyterian Church, was founded in 1853. It has a 40-acre campus.

STUDENTS AND FACULTY

Enrollment: 1,089. **Student Body:** Male 47%, female 53%, out-of-state 6%, international 2% (23 countries represented). **Ethnic Representation:** African American 4%, Asian 1%, Caucasian 92%, Hispanic 3%. **Retention and Graduation:** 80% freshmen return for sophomore year. 50% freshmen graduate within 4 years. 25% grads go on to further study within 1 year. **Faculty:** Student/faculty ratio 14:1. 68 full-time faculty, 83% hold PhDs. 100% faculty teach undergrads.

ACADEMICS

Degrees: Bachelor's. **Academic Requirements:** General education including some course work in arts/fine arts, English (including composition), foreign languages, history, humanities, sciences (biological or physical), social science, freshman seminar and senior ideas and issues. **Classes:** 10-19 students in an average class. 10-19 students in an average lab/discussion section. **Majors with Highest Enrollment:** Business administration/management; education, general; English language and literature, general. **Disciplines with Highest Percentage of Degrees Awarded:** Education 30%, business/marketing 26%, English 13%, social sciences and history 9%, biological life sciences 3%. **Special Study Options:** Double major, honors program, independent study, internships, liberal arts/career combination, student-designed major, study abroad, teacher certification program.

FACILITIES

Housing: Coed, all-female, all-male, housing for international students, fraternities and/or sororities, theme housing, substance-free floors. **Library Holdings:** 176,470 bound volumes. 514 periodicals. 228,943 microforms. 3,975 audiovisuals. **Special Academic Facilities/Equipment:** Shields Art Collection, Wackerle Career and Leadership Center. **Computers:** *Recommended operating system:* Windows NT/2000. School-owned computers available for student use.

EXTRACURRICULARS

Activities: Choral groups, concert band, dance, drama/theater, jazz band, literary magazine, music ensembles, musical theater, radio station, student government, student newspaper, student-run film society, television station. **Organizations:** 60 registered organizations, 9 honor societies, 5 religious organizations, 3 fraternities (24% men join), 3 sororities (25% women join). **Athletics (Intercollegiate):** *Men:* baseball, basketball, cheerleading, cross-country, football, golf, indoor track, soccer, tennis, track & field. *Women:* basketball, cheerleading, cross-country, golf, indoor track, soccer, softball, tennis, track & field, volleyball.

ADMISSIONS

Selectivity Rating: 76 (of 100). **Freshman Academic Profile:** Average high school GPA 3.3. 15% in top 10% of high school class, 41% in top 25% of high school class, 73% in top 50% of high school class. 80% from public high schools. SAT I Math middle 50% range 0-0. SAT I Verbal middle 50% range 0-0. Average ACT 23, ACT middle 50% range 20-26. TOEFL required of all international applicants, minimum TOEFL 550. **Basis for Candidate Selection:** *Very important factors considered include:* class rank, secondary school record, standardized test scores. *Important factors considered include:* recommendations. *Other factors considered include:* character/personal qualities, essays, extracurricular activities, interview, talent/ability, volunteer work, work experience. **Freshman Admission Requirements:** High school diploma or GED is required. *Academic units required/recommended:* 14 total required; 20 total recommended; 4 English required, 3 math required, 4 math recommended, 2 science required, 4 science recommended, 1 science lab required, 2 science lab recommended, 3 foreign language recommended, 1 social studies required, 3 social studies recommended, 2 history required. **Freshman Admission Statistics:** 1,372 applied, 75% accepted, 29% of those accepted enrolled. **Transfer Admission Requirements:** *Items required:* college transcript, statement of good standing from prior school. Minimum college GPA of 2.3 required. Lowest grade transferable C-. **General Admission Information:** Nonfall registration accepted. Admission may be deferred for a maximum of 1 year. Credit and/or placement offered for CEEB Advanced Placement tests.

COSTS AND FINANCIAL AID

Tuition $18,600. Room & board $5,000. Required fees $0. Average book expense $650. **Required Forms and Deadlines:** FAFSA. No deadline for regular filing. Priority filing deadline April 15. **Notification of Awards:** Applicants will be notified of awards on a rolling basis beginning on or about March 1. **Types of Aid:** *Need-based scholarships/grants:* Pell, SEOG, state scholarships/grants, private scholarships, the school's own gift aid. *Loans:* FFEL Subsidized Stafford, FFEL Unsubsidized Stafford, FFEL PLUS, Federal Perkins. **Student Employment:** Federal Work-Study Program available. Institutional employment available. Off-campus job opportunities are good. **Financial Aid Statistics:** 79% freshmen, 75% undergrads receive some form of aid. Average freshman grant $11,207. Average freshman loan $3,732. Average income from on-campus job $1,293. **Financial Aid Phone:** 309-457-2129.

MONMOUTH UNIVERSITY

Admission, Monmouth University, 400 Cedar Avenue, West Long Branch, NJ 07764-1898
Phone: 732-571-3456 **E-mail:** admission@monmouth.edu **CEEB Code:** 2416
Fax: 732-263-5166 **Web:** www.monmouth.edu **ACT Code:** 2571

This private school was founded in 1933. It has a 153-acre campus.

STUDENTS AND FACULTY

Enrollment: 4,323. **Student Body:** Male 42%, female 58%, out-of-state 7%. **Ethnic Representation:** African American 5%, Asian 2%, Caucasian 79%, Hispanic 4%. **Retention and Graduation:** 73% freshmen return for sophomore year. 33% freshmen graduate within 4 years. **Faculty:** Student/faculty ratio 18:1. 229 full-time faculty, 72% hold PhDs. 85% faculty teach undergrads.

ACADEMICS

Degrees: Associate's, bachelor's, certificate, master's, post-bachelor's certificate, post-master's certificate. **Academic Requirements:** General education including some course work in arts/fine arts, computer literacy, English (including composition), history, humanities, mathematics, sciences (biological or physical), social science, experiential education requirement. **Classes:** 10-19 students in an average class. **Disciplines with Highest Percentage of Degrees Awarded:** Business/marketing 31%, education 16%, communications/communication technologies 16%, protective services/public administration 9%, psychology 7%. **Special Study Options:** Accelerated program, cooperative (work-study) program, cross registration, distance learning, double major, dual enrollment, honors program, independent study, internships, liberal arts/career combination, student-designed major, study abroad, teacher certification program, clinical lab science program in collaboration with University of Medicine and Dentistry of New Jersey, Air Force ROTC at Rutgers University. Affiliated with Washington Center providing semester and summer internships and shorter symposia. Monmouth Medical Scholars Program allows four incoming freshmen to complete undergraduate degree at Monmouth—including 9-credit clinical requirement at Monmouth Medical Center—and commence medical studies at MCP Hahnemann School of Medicine. Study abroad in London at Regent's College.

FACILITIES

Housing: Coed, apartments for single students. **Library Holdings:** 253,100 bound volumes. 11,900 periodicals. **Special Academic Facilities/Equipment:** Art museum, instructional media center, on-campus lab school for special education students. **Computers:** School-owned computers available for student use.

EXTRACURRICULARS

Activities: Choral groups, concert band, drama/theater, jazz band, literary magazine, music ensembles, musical theater, pep band, radio station, student government, student newspaper, television station, yearbook. **Organizations:** 73 registered organizations, 19 honor societies, 8 fraternities (9% men join), 6 sororities (11% women join). **Athletics (Intercollegiate):** *Men:* baseball, basketball, cross-country, football, golf, indoor track, soccer, tennis, track & field. *Women:* basketball, cross-country, field hockey, golf, indoor track, lacrosse, soccer, softball, tennis, track & field.

ADMISSIONS

Selectivity Rating: 63 (of 100). **Freshman Academic Profile:** Average high school GPA 3.0. 8% in top 10% of high school class, 26% in top 25% of high school class, 63% in top 50% of high school class. Average SAT I Math 523, SAT I Math middle 50% range 480-560. Average SAT I Verbal 512, SAT I Verbal middle 50% range 470-550. ACT middle 50% range 18-22. TOEFL required of all international applicants, minimum TOEFL 525. **Basis for Candidate Selection:** *Very important factors considered include:* secondary school record, standardized test scores. *Important factors considered include:* extracurricular activities, interview. *Other factors considered include:* alumni/ae relation, character/personal qualities, class rank, essays, recommendations, volunteer work, work experience. **Freshman Admission Requirements:** High school diploma or GED is required. *Academic units required/recommended:* 16 total required; 4 English required, 3 math required, 2 science required, 1 science lab required, 2 foreign language recommended, 2 social studies recommended, 2 history required, 5 elective required. **Freshman Admission Statistics:** 5,201 applied, 74% accepted, 25% of those accepted enrolled. **Transfer Admission Requirements:** *Items required:* college transcript. Minimum college GPA of 2.0 required. Lowest grade transferable C. **General Admission Information:** Application fee $35. Priority application deadline December 15. Early decision application deadline December 1. Regular application deadline March 1. Nonfall registration accepted. Admission may be deferred for a maximum of 1 year. Credit and/or placement offered for CEEB Advanced Placement tests.

COSTS AND FINANCIAL AID

Tuition $17,332. Room & board $7,240. Required fees $568. Average book expense $600. **Required Forms and Deadlines:** FAFSA. No deadline for regular filing. **Notification of Awards:** Applicants will be notified of awards on a rolling basis beginning on or about February 1. **Types of Aid:** *Need-based scholarships/grants:* Pell, SEOG, state scholarships/grants, private scholarships, the school's own gift aid. *Loans:* Direct Subsidized Stafford, Direct Unsubsidized Stafford, Direct PLUS, Federal Perkins, state loans. **Student Employment:** Federal Work-Study Program available. Institutional employment available. Off-campus job opportunities are good. **Financial Aid Statistics:** 68% freshmen, 65% undergrads receive some form of aid. Average freshman grant $7,376. **Financial Aid Phone:** 732-571-3463.

MONTANA STATE UNIVERSITY COLLEGE OF TECHNOLOGY—GREAT FALLS

PO Box 6010, Great Falls, MT 59406
Phone: 406-771-4300 **E-mail:** information@msugf.edu **CEEB Code:** 4482
Fax: 406-771-4317 **Web:** www.msugf.edu **ACT Code:** 2432

This public school was founded in 1969. It has a 20-acre campus.

STUDENTS AND FACULTY

Enrollment: 1,377. **Student Body:** Male 29%, female 71%, out-of-state 1%. **Ethnic Representation:** African American 2%, Asian 1%, Caucasian 82%, Hispanic 2%, Native American 6%. **Faculty:** Student/faculty ratio 15:1. 40 full-time faculty. 100% faculty teach undergrads.

ACADEMICS

Degrees: Associate's, certificate, transfer. **Academic Requirements:** General education including some course work in computer literacy, English (including composition), mathematics, sciences (biological or physical). **Majors with Highest Enrollment:** Licensed practical nurse training ; computer and information sciences, general; general studies. **Special Study Options:** Cooperative (work-study) program, distance learning, double major, dual enrollment, independent study, internships.

FACILITIES

Computers: School-owned computers available for student use.

EXTRACURRICULARS

Activities: Student government, student newspaper. **Organizations:** 3 registered organizations, 1 honor society.

ADMISSIONS

Selectivity Rating: 63 (of 100). **Freshman Academic Profile:** TOEFL required of all international applicants, minimum TOEFL 500. **Freshman Admission Requirements:** High school diploma or GED is required. **Freshman Admission Statistics:** 408 applied, 99% accepted, 92% of those accepted enrolled. **Transfer Admission Requirements:** *Items required:* high school transcript, college transcript. Lowest grade transferable C. **General Admission Information:** Application fee $30. Credit offered for CEEB Advanced Placement tests.

COSTS AND FINANCIAL AID

Average book expense $500. **Required Forms and Deadlines:** FAFSA. **Types of Aid:** *Need-based scholarships/grants:* Pell, private scholarships. *Loans:* Direct Subsidized Stafford, Direct Unsubsidized Stafford, Direct PLUS, FFEL Subsidized Stafford, FFEL Unsubsidized Stafford, FFEL PLUS. **Student Employment:** Federal Work-Study Program available. Institutional employment available. Off-campus job opportunities are fair. **Financial Aid Statistics:** 78% freshmen, 77% undergrads receive some form of aid. Average freshman grant $3,209. Average freshman loan $1,940. **Financial Aid Phone:** 406-771-4434.

MONTANA STATE UNIVERSITY—BILLINGS

1500 University Drive, Billings, MT 59101
Phone: 406-657-2158 **E-mail:** keverett@msubillings.edu **CEEB Code:** 4298
Fax: 406-657-2051 **Web:** www.msubillings.edu **ACT Code:** 2416

This public school was founded in 1927. It has a 92-acre campus.

STUDENTS AND FACULTY

Enrollment: 3,949. **Student Body:** Male 37%, female 63%, out-of-state 7%, international 1% (17 countries represented). **Ethnic Representation:** African American 1%, Asian 1%, Caucasian 84%, Hispanic 3%, Native American 7%. **Retention and Graduation:** 53% freshmen return for sophomore year. 9% freshmen graduate within 4 years. 7% grads go on to further study within 1 year. 13% grads pursue business degrees. **Faculty:** Student/faculty ratio 21:1. 148 full-time faculty, 72% hold PhDs. 100% faculty teach undergrads.

ACADEMICS

Degrees: Associate's, bachelor's, certificate, master's, post-bachelor's certificate, post-master's certificate, terminal, transfer. **Academic Requirements:** General education including some course work in arts/fine arts, English (including composition), history, humanities, mathematics, philosophy, sciences (biological or physical), social science, cultural diversity. **Classes:** 20-29 students in an average class. 10-19 students in an average lab/discussion section. **Majors with Highest Enrollment:** Business administration/management; elementary education and teaching; liberal arts and sciences/liberal studies. **Disciplines with Highest Percentage of Degrees Awarded:** Education 27%, business/marketing 26%, liberal arts/general studies 13%, communications/communication technologies 7%, psychology 7%. **Special Study Options:** Accelerated program, cooperative (work-study) program, cross registration, distance learning, double major, English as a second language, external degree program, honors program, independent study, internships, student-designed major, study abroad, teacher certification program, weekend college, online degrees and extensive online course offerings.

FACILITIES

Housing: Coed, all-female, all-male, apartments for married students, housing for disabled students, apartments for students with dependent children. **Library Holdings:** 488,004 bound volumes. 3,276 periodicals. 850,000 microforms. 2,125 audiovisuals. **Special Academic Facilities/Equipment:** Montana Center for Disabilities, business enterprise, small business institute, urban institute, public radio, applied economic research, biological station, Northern Plains Studies Center, Montana Business Connections, information commons, academic support center, advising center, TRIO programs, SOS programs. **Computers:** School-owned computers available for student use.

EXTRACURRICULARS

Activities: Choral groups, concert band, drama/theater, jazz band, literary magazine, music ensembles, pep band, radio station, student government, student newspaper, symphony orchestra. **Organizations:** 53 registered organizations, 10 honor societies, 4 religious organizations. **Athletics (Intercollegiate):** *Men:* basketball, cross-country, golf, soccer, tennis. *Women:* basketball, cross-country, golf, soccer, softball, tennis, volleyball.

ADMISSIONS

Selectivity Rating: 63 (of 100). **Freshman Academic Profile:** Average high school GPA 3.0. 9% in top 10% of high school class, 25% in top 25% of high school class, 53% in top 50% of high school class. 96% from public high schools. Average SAT I Math 490, SAT I Math middle 50% range 420-580. Average SAT I Verbal 493, SAT I Verbal middle 50% range 450-560. Average ACT 21, ACT middle 50% range 18-23. TOEFL required of all international applicants, minimum TOEFL 525. **Basis for Candidate Selection:** *Very important factors considered include:* class rank, secondary school record, standardized test scores. *Other factors considered include:* character/personal qualities. **Freshman Admission Requirements:** High school diploma or GED is required. *Academic units required/recommended:* 14 total required; 4 English required, 3 math required, 2 science required, 2 science lab required, 3 social studies required. **Freshman Admission Statistics:** 1,052 applied, 99% accepted, 75% of those accepted enrolled. **Transfer Admission Requirements:** *Items required:* college transcript, statement of good standing from prior school. Minimum college GPA of 2.0 required. Lowest grade transferable C. **General Admission Information:** Application fee $30. Priority application deadline March 3. Regular application deadline July 3. Nonfall registration accepted. Credit and/or placement offered for CEEB Advanced Placement tests.

COSTS AND FINANCIAL AID

In-state tuition $3,973. Out-of-state tuition $10,555. Required fees $30. Average book expense $800. **Required Forms and Deadlines:** FAFSA and institution's own financial aid form. No deadline for regular filing. Priority filing deadline March 1. **Notification of Awards:** Applicants will be notified of awards on a rolling basis. **Types of Aid:** *Need-based scholarships/grants:* Pell, SEOG, state scholarships/grants, private scholarships, the school's own gift aid, Montana State University-Billings Foundation. *Loans:* FFEL Subsidized Stafford, FFEL Unsubsidized Stafford, FFEL PLUS, Federal Perkins, college/university loans from institutional funds. **Student Employment:** Federal Work-Study Program available. Institutional employment available. Off-campus job opportunities are excellent. **Financial Aid Statistics:** 66% freshmen, 66% undergrads receive some form of aid. Average freshman grant $3,237. Average freshman loan $2,102. Average income from on-campus job $1,800. **Financial Aid Phone:** 406-657-2188.

MONTANA STATE UNIVERSITY—BOZEMAN

New Student Services, PO Box 172190, Bozeman, MT 59717-2190
Phone: 406-994-2452 **E-mail:** admissions@montana.edu **CEEB Code:** 4488
Fax: 406-994-1923 **Web:** www.montana.edu **ACT Code:** 2420

This public school was founded in 1893. It has a 1,170-acre campus.

STUDENTS AND FACULTY

Enrollment: 10,676. **Student Body:** Male 54%, female 46%, out-of-state 29%, international 1%. **Ethnic Representation:** Asian 1%, Caucasian 90%, Hispanic 1%, Native American 2%. **Retention and Graduation:** 71% freshmen return for sophomore year. 14% freshmen graduate within 4 years. 13% grads go on to further study within 1 year. **Faculty:** Student/faculty ratio 20:1. 587 full-time faculty, 81% hold PhDs. 95% faculty teach undergrads.

ACADEMICS

Degrees: Bachelor's, certificate, doctoral, master's. **Academic Requirements:** General education including some course work in arts/fine arts, English (including composition), humanities, mathematics, sciences (biological or physical), social science. **Classes:** 10-19 students in an average class. 10-19 students in an average lab/discussion section. **Majors with Highest Enrollment:** Business administration/management; education, general; biology/biological sciences, general. **Disciplines with Highest Percentage of Degrees Awarded:** Engineering/engineering technology 17%, business/marketing 11%, education 10%, biological life sciences 8%, visual and performing arts 7%. **Special Study Options:** Distance learning, double major, English as a second language, student exchange program (domestic), honors program, independent study, internships, student-designed major, study abroad, teacher certification program.

FACILITIES

Housing: Coed, all-female, all-male, apartments for married students, apartments for single students, housing for international students, fraternities and/or sororities, cooperative housing, nonsmoking, students over traditional age, wellness floors. **Library Holdings:** 4,492 periodicals. 2,107,544 microforms. 4,822 audiovisuals. **Special Academic Facilities/Equipment:** Paleontology and history museums, water resources and planetarium, wind tunnel, electron microscopes, telecommunications center, ag bio-science center. **Computers:** School-owned computers available for student use.

EXTRACURRICULARS

Activities: Choral groups, concert band, dance, drama/theater, jazz band, marching band, music ensembles, musical theater, pep band, radio station, student government, student newspaper, student-run film society, television station. **Organizations:** 140 registered organizations, 18 honor societies, 11 religious organizations, 8 fraternities (3% men join), 4 sororities (2% women join). **Athletics (Intercollegiate):** *Men:* basketball, cheerleading, cross-country, football, indoor track, rodeo, tennis, track & field. *Women:* basketball, cheerleading, skiing (cross-country), cross-country, golf, indoor track, rodeo, skiing (alpine), skiing (Nordic), tennis, track & field, volleyball.

ADMISSIONS

Selectivity Rating: 71 (of 100). **Freshman Academic Profile:** Average high school GPA 3.3. 17% in top 10% of high school class, 41% in top 25% of high school class, 73% in top 50% of high school class. Average SAT I Math 556, SAT I Math middle 50% range 500-620. Average SAT I Verbal 542, SAT I Verbal middle 50% range 480-600. Average ACT 23, ACT middle 50% range 20-26. TOEFL required of all international applicants, minimum TOEFL 525. **Basis for Candidate Selection:** *Very important factors considered include:* class rank, secondary school record, standardized test scores. **Freshman Admission Requirements:** High school diploma or GED is required. *Academic units required/recommended:* 14 total required; 4 English required, 3 math required, 2 science required, 2 science lab required, 3 social studies required. **Freshman Admission Statistics:** 4,072 applied, 85% accepted, 61% of those accepted enrolled. **Transfer Admission Requirements:** *Items required:* college transcript, statement of good standing from prior school. Minimum college GPA of 2.0 required. Lowest grade transferable D-. **General Admission Information:** Application fee $30. Nonfall registration accepted. Admission may be deferred for a maximum of 1 year. Credit offered for CEEB Advanced Placement tests.

COSTS AND FINANCIAL AID

In-state tuition $3,807. Out-of-state tuition $11,444. Room & board $5,120. Average book expense $850. **Required Forms and Deadlines:** FAFSA. No deadline for regular filing. Priority filing deadline March 1. **Notification of Awards:** Applicants will be notified of awards on a rolling basis beginning on or about April 1. **Types of Aid:** *Need-based scholarships/grants:* Pell, SEOG, state scholarships/grants, private scholarships, the school's own gift aid, Federal Nursing. *Loans:* Direct Subsidized Stafford, Direct Unsubsidized Stafford, Direct PLUS, Federal Perkins, Federal Nursing, college/university loans from institutional funds, Freeborn Loans. **Student Employment:** Federal Work-Study Program available. Institutional employment available. Off-campus job opportunities are good. **Financial Aid Statistics:** 47% freshmen, 50% undergrads receive some form of aid. Average freshman grant $1,274. Average freshman loan $2,291. Average income from on-campus job $1,800. **Financial Aid Phone:** 406-994-2845.

MONTANA STATE UNIVERSITY—NORTHERN

PO Box 7751, Havre, MT 59501
Phone: 406-265-3704 **E-mail:** msunadmit@msun.edu **CEEB Code:** 4538
Fax: 406-265-3777 **Web:** www.msun.edu **ACT Code:** 2424

This public school was founded in 1929. It has a 105-acre campus.

STUDENTS AND FACULTY

Enrollment: 1,367. **Student Body:** Male 48%, female 52%, out-of-state 4%. **Ethnic Representation:** African American 1%, Asian 1%, Caucasian 77%, Hispanic 1%, Native American 10%. **Retention and Graduation:** 4% grads go on to further study within 1 year.

ACADEMICS

Degrees: Associate's, bachelor's, certificate, master's. **Academic Requirements:** General education including some course work in computer literacy, English (including composition), mathematics, sciences (biological or physical). **Special Study Options:** Cooperative (work-study) program, distance learning, double major, honors program, independent study, teacher certification program. Co-op programs: agriculture, business, computer science, humanities, natural science, social/behavioral science, vocational arts.

FACILITIES

Housing: Coed, apartments for married students, apartments for single students. **Library Holdings:** 110,000 bound volumes. 800 periodicals. 380,000 microforms. **Computers:** *Recommended operating system:* Mac. School-owned computers available for student use.

EXTRACURRICULARS

Activities: Music ensembles, radio station, student government, student newspaper, yearbook. **Organizations:** 50 registered organizations, 12 honor societies, 18 religious organizations. **Athletics (Intercollegiate):** *Men:* basketball, cheerleading, swimming, wrestling. *Women:* basketball, cheerleading, swimming, volleyball.

ADMISSIONS

Selectivity Rating: 62 (of 100). **Freshman Academic Profile:** 98% from public high schools. minimum TOEFL 500. **Basis for Candidate Selection:** *Important factors considered include:* class rank, secondary school record, standardized test scores. *Other factors considered include:* state residency. **Freshman Admission Requirements:** High school diploma or GED is required. *Academic units required/recommended:* 14 total required; 4 English required, 3 math required, 2 science required, 3 social studies required, 2 elective required. **Freshman Admission Statistics:** 629 applied, 100% accepted, 38% of those accepted enrolled. **Transfer Admission Requirements:** *Items required:* high school transcript, college transcript. Minimum college GPA of 2.0 required. Lowest grade transferable C. **General Admission Information:** Application fee $30. Nonfall registration accepted. Credit and/or placement offered for CEEB Advanced Placement tests.

COSTS AND FINANCIAL AID

In-state tuition $2,692. Out-of-state tuition $8,078. Room & board $3,800. Required fees $2,692. Average book expense $800. **Required Forms and Deadlines:** FAFSA. **Types of Aid:** *Need-based scholarships/grants:* state scholarships/grants. *Loans:* FFEL Subsidized Stafford, FFEL PLUS. **Student Employment:** Federal Work-Study Program available. Institutional employment available. Off-campus job opportunities are fair. **Financial Aid Statistics:** Average income from on-campus job $2,250. **Financial Aid Phone:** 406-265-3787.

MONTANA TECH OF THE UNIVERSITY OF MONTANA

1300 West Park Street, Butte, MT 59701
Phone: 406-496-4178 **E-mail:** admissions@mtech.edu **CEEB Code:** 4487
Fax: 406-496-4710 **Web:** www.mtech.edu **ACT Code:** 24180

This public school was founded in 1893. It has a 56-acre campus.

STUDENTS AND FACULTY

Enrollment: 2,065. **Student Body:** Male 56%, female 44%, out-of-state 11%, international 2% (13 countries represented). **Ethnic Representation:** Asian 1%, Caucasian 87%, Hispanic 1%, Native American 2%. **Retention and Graduation:** 64% freshmen return for sophomore year. 14% grads go on to further study within 1 year. **Faculty:** Student/faculty ratio 16:1. 106 full-time faculty, 42% hold PhDs. 100% faculty teach undergrads.

ACADEMICS

Degrees: Associate's, bachelor's, certificate, master's, post-bachelor's certificate. **Academic Requirements:** General education including some course work in computer literacy, English (including composition), humanities, mathematics, sciences (biological or physical), social science, communications. **Classes:** Under 10 students in an average class. 10-19 students in an average lab/discussion section. **Majors with Highest Enrollment:** Business administration/management; engineering, general; petroleum engineering. **Disciplines with Highest Percentage of Degrees Awarded:** Engineering/engineering technology 56%, business/marketing 13%, health professions and related sciences 12%, computer and information sciences 5%, biological life sciences 4%. **Special Study Options:** Cooperative (work-study) program, cross registration, distance learning, double major, dual enrollment, independent study, internships, student-designed major, teacher certification program.

FACILITIES

Housing: Coed, apartments for married students, apartments for single students, housing for disabled students, apartments for families. **Library Holdings:** 58,101 bound volumes. 394 periodicals. 368,000 microforms. 3,894 audiovisuals. **Special Academic Facilities/Equipment:** Mineral Museum, World Museum of Mining. **Computers:** School-owned computers available for student use.

EXTRACURRICULARS

Activities: Choral groups, music ensembles, pep band, radio station, student government, student newspaper, symphony orchestra. **Organizations:** 33 registered organizations, 2 honor societies, 2 religious organizations. **Athletics (Intercollegiate):** *Men:* basketball, football, golf. *Women:* basketball, golf, volleyball.

ADMISSIONS

Selectivity Rating: 74 (of 100). **Freshman Academic Profile:** Average high school GPA 3.2. 15% in top 10% of high school class, 36% in top 25% of high school class, 67% in top 50% of high school class. Average SAT I Math 539, SAT I Math middle 50% range 480-610. Average SAT I Verbal 530, SAT I Verbal middle 50% range 480-590. Average ACT 22, ACT middle 50% range 19-25. TOEFL required of all international applicants, minimum TOEFL 525. **Basis for Candidate Selection:** *Important factors considered include:* class rank, secondary school record, standardized test scores. **Freshman Admission Requirements:** High school diploma or GED is required. *Academic units required/recommended:* 14 total required; 4 English required, 4 English recommended, 3 math required, 4 math recommended, 2 science required, 4 science recommended, 2 science lab recommended, 2 foreign language recommended, 3 social studies required. **Freshman Admission Statistics:** 395 applied, 97% accepted, 100% of those accepted enrolled. **Transfer Admission Requirements:** *Items required:* college transcript. Minimum college GPA of 2.0 required. Lowest grade transferable C. **General Admission Information:** Application fee $30. Priority application deadline March 1. Nonfall registration accepted. Admission may be deferred for a maximum of 1 year. Credit and/or placement offered for CEEB Advanced Placement tests.

COSTS AND FINANCIAL AID

In-state tuition $3,350. Out-of-state tuition $8,060. Room & board $4,980. Required fees $1,000. Average book expense $700. **Required Forms and Deadlines:** FAFSA. No deadline for regular filing. Priority filing deadline March 1. **Notification of Awards:** Applicants will be notified of awards on a rolling basis beginning on or about April 1. **Types of Aid:** *Need-based scholarships/grants:* Pell, SEOG, state scholarships/grants, private scholarships, the school's own gift aid. *Loans:* FFEL Subsidized Stafford, FFEL Unsubsidized Stafford, FFEL PLUS, Federal Perkins, college/university loans from institutional funds. **Student Employment:** Federal Work-Study Program available. Institutional employment available. Off-campus job opportunities are good. **Financial Aid Statistics:** 67% freshmen, 69% undergrads receive some form of aid. Average freshman grant $1,000. Average freshman loan $2,000. Average income from on-campus job $4,200. **Financial Aid Phone:** 406-496-4212.

MONTCLAIR STATE UNIVERSITY

One Normal Avenue, Upper Montclair, NJ 07043-1624
Phone: 973-655-5116 **E-mail:** undergraduate.admissions@montclair.edu
CEEB Code: 2520 **Fax:** 973-655-7700 **Web:** www.montclair.edu/admissions

This public school was founded in 1908. It has a 200-acre campus.

STUDENTS AND FACULTY

Enrollment: 10,939. **Student Body:** Male 38%, female 62%, out-of-state 2%, international 5% (85 countries represented). **Ethnic Representation:** African American 11%, Asian 5%, Caucasian 61%, Hispanic 16%. **Retention and Graduation:** 84% freshmen return for sophomore year. 16% freshmen graduate within 4 years. **Faculty:** Student/faculty ratio 17:1. 434 full-time faculty, 91% hold PhDs. 100% faculty teach undergrads.

ACADEMICS

Degrees: Bachelor's, doctoral, master's, post-bachelor's certificate, post-master's certificate. **Academic Requirements:** General education including some course work in arts/fine arts, computer literacy, English (including composition), foreign languages, history, humanities, mathematics, philosophy, sciences (biological or physical), social science. **Classes:** Under 10 students in an average lab/discussion section. **Disciplines with Highest Percentage of Degrees Awarded:** Business/marketing 21%, social sciences and history 15%, psychology 11%, visual and performing arts 8%, English 8%. **Special Study Options:** Cooperative (work-study) program, double major, English as a second language, honors program, independent study, internships, study abroad, teacher certification program, Arts, business, computer science, health professions, home economics, humanities, natural science, social/behavioral science, technologies, service learning.

FACILITIES

Housing: Coed, all-female, all-male, apartments for single students, housing for international students. **Library Holdings:** 368,830 bound volumes. 2,195 periodicals. 1,211,357 microforms. 47,826 audiovisuals. **Special Academic Facilities/Equipment:** The Dumont Television Center, Yogi Berra Museum and Stadium, Floyd Hall Arena. **Computers:** School-owned computers available for student use.

EXTRACURRICULARS

Activities: Choral groups, concert band, dance, drama/theater, literary magazine, marching band, music ensembles, radio station, student government, student newspaper, yearbook. **Organizations:** 99 registered organizations, 26 honor societies, 7 religious organizations, 15 fraternities, 19 sororities. **Athletics (Intercollegiate):** *Men:* baseball, basketball, cheerleading, cross-country, diving, football, golf, lacrosse, soccer, swimming, tennis, track & field, wrestling. *Women:* basketball, cheerleading, cross-country, diving, field hockey, golf, lacrosse, soccer, softball, swimming, tennis, track & field, volleyball.

ADMISSIONS

Selectivity Rating: 76 (of 100). **Freshman Academic Profile:** 17% in top 10% of high school class, 46% in top 25% of high school class, 81% in top 50% of high school class. 85% from public high schools. SAT I Math middle 50% range 460-570. SAT I Verbal middle 50% range 450-550. TOEFL required of all international applicants, minimum TOEFL 500. **Basis for Candidate Selection:** *Very important factors considered include:* secondary school record.

Important factors considered include: class rank, extracurricular activities, standardized test scores, talent/ability. *Other factors considered include:* alumni/ae relation, essays, minority status, recommendations, state residency. **Freshman Admission Requirements:** High school diploma or GED is required. *Academic units required/recommended:* 16 total required; 4 English required, 3 math required, 2 science required, 2 science lab required, 2 foreign language required, 2 social studies required, 3 elective required. **Freshman Admission Statistics:** 7,615 applied, 53% accepted, 38% of those accepted enrolled. **Transfer Admission Requirements:** *Items required:* college transcript, statement of good standing from prior school. Minimum college GPA of 2.0 required. Lowest grade transferable C. **General Admission Information:** Application fee $40. Regular application deadline March 1. Nonfall registration accepted. Admission may be deferred for a maximum of 1 year. Credit and/or placement offered for CEEB Advanced Placement tests.

COSTS AND FINANCIAL AID

Required Forms and Deadlines: FAFSA. No deadline for regular filing. Priority filing deadline March 1. **Notification of Awards:** Applicants will be notified of awards on a rolling basis beginning on or about April 1. **Types of Aid:** *Need-based scholarships/grants:* Pell, SEOG, state scholarships/grants, private scholarships, the school's own gift aid. *Loans:* FFEL Subsidized Stafford, FFEL Unsubsidized Stafford, FFEL PLUS, Federal Perkins, state loans, college/university loans from institutional funds. **Student Employment:** Federal Work-Study Program available. Institutional employment available. Off-campus job opportunities are good. **Financial Aid Statistics:** 54% freshmen, 46% undergrads receive some form of aid. **Financial Aid Phone:** 973-655-4461.

MONTREAT COLLEGE

310 Gaither Circle, Montreat, NC 28757-9987
Phone: 828-669-8011 **E-mail:** admissions@montreat.edu **CEEB Code:** 5423
Fax: 828-669-0120 **Web:** www.montreat.edu **ACT Code:** 5423

This private school, which is affiliated with the Presbyterian Church, was founded in 1916. It has a 96-acre campus.

STUDENTS AND FACULTY

Enrollment: 1,116. **Student Body:** Male 42%, female 58%, out-of-state 32%. **Ethnic Representation:** African American 12%, Asian 1%, Caucasian 86%, Hispanic 1%. **Retention and Graduation:** 68% freshmen return for sophomore year. 27% grads pursue business degrees. 6% grads pursue law degrees. 3% grads pursue medical degrees. **Faculty:** Student/faculty ratio 12:1. 33 full-time faculty. 94% faculty teach undergrads.

ACADEMICS

Degrees: Associate's, bachelor's, master's. **Academic Requirements:** General education including some course work in English (including composition), history, humanities, mathematics, philosophy, sciences (biological or physical), Bible and religion (old and new testaments). **Special Study Options:** Cooperative (work-study) program, double major, dual enrollment, honors program, independent study, internships, student-designed major, study abroad, teacher certification program, American Studies Program (Washington, DC), L.A. Film Studies Center (Los Angeles, CA).

FACILITIES

Housing: All-female, all-male. **Library Holdings:** 67,378 bound volumes. 426 periodicals. **Special Academic Facilities/Equipment:** Hamilton Art Gallery, Chapel of the Prodigal. **Computers:** School-owned computers available for student use.

EXTRACURRICULARS

Activities: Choral groups, drama/theater, literary magazine, music ensembles, student government, student newspaper, yearbook. **Organizations:** 11 registered organizations, 2 honor societies, 2 religious organizations. **Athletics (Intercollegiate):** *Men:* baseball, basketball, cross-country, golf, soccer, tennis. *Women:* basketball, cross-country, soccer, softball, tennis, volleyball.

ADMISSIONS

Selectivity Rating: 77 (of 100). **Freshman Academic Profile:** Average high school GPA 2.7. 83% from public high schools. Average SAT I Math 520. Average SAT I Verbal 520. Average ACT 24. TOEFL required of all international applicants, minimum TOEFL 500. **Basis for Candidate Selection:** *Very important factors considered include:* recommendations, secondary school record, standardized test scores. *Important factors considered include:* character/personal qualities, class rank, essays. *Other factors considered include:* alumni/ae relation, extracurricular activities, interview, minority status, talent/ability, volunteer work, work experience. **Freshman Admission Requirements:** High school diploma or GED is required. *Academic units required/recommended:* 14 total required; 4 English required, 3 math required, 3 science required, 1 foreign language required, 3 social studies required, 3 history required. **Freshman Admission Statistics:** 382 applied, 80% accepted, 54% of those accepted enrolled. **Transfer Admission Requirements:** *Items required:* college transcript. Minimum college GPA of 2.0 required. Lowest grade transferable C. **General Admission Information:** Application fee $15. Priority application deadline May 1. Regular application deadline August 20. Nonfall registration accepted. Admission may be deferred for a maximum of 6 years. Credit and/or placement offered for CEEB Advanced Placement tests.

COSTS AND FINANCIAL AID

Room & board $4,614. Average book expense $600. **Required Forms and Deadlines:** FAFSA, institution's own financial aid form and state aid form. No deadline for regular filing. Priority filing deadline March 1. **Notification of Awards:** Applicants will be notified of awards on a rolling basis beginning on or about March 1. **Types of Aid:** *Need-based scholarships/grants:* Pell, SEOG, state scholarships/grants, private scholarships, the school's own gift aid. *Loans:* FFEL Subsidized Stafford, FFEL Unsubsidized Stafford, FFEL PLUS, Federal Perkins. **Student Employment:** Federal Work-Study Program available. Institutional employment available. Off-campus job opportunities are excellent. **Financial Aid Statistics:** 57% freshmen, 66% undergrads receive some form of aid. Average freshman grant $4,203. Average freshman loan $2,856. Average income from on-campus job $1,377. **Financial Aid Phone:** 800-545-4656.

MONTSERRAT COLLEGE OF ART

23 Essex Street, Box 26, Beverly, MA 01915
Phone: 978-921-4242 **E-mail:** admiss@montserrat.edu **CEEB Code:** 9101
Fax: 978-921-4241 **Web:** www.montserrat.edu **ACT Code:** 1847

This private school was founded in 1970. It has a 12-acre campus.

STUDENTS AND FACULTY

Enrollment: 412. **Student Body:** Male 40%, female 60%, out-of-state 50%, international 1%. **Ethnic Representation:** African American 1%, Asian 2%, Caucasian 78%, Hispanic 1%, Native American 1%. **Retention and Graduation:** 76% freshmen return for sophomore year. 45% freshmen graduate within 4 years. **Faculty:** Student/faculty ratio 11:1. 21 full-time faculty, 19% hold PhDs. 100% faculty teach undergrads.

ACADEMICS

Degrees: Bachelor's, diploma. **Academic Requirements:** General education including some course work in arts/fine arts, computer literacy, English (including composition), history, humanities, sciences (biological or physical), art history. **Classes:** 10-19 students in an average class. **Disciplines with Highest Percentage of Degrees Awarded:** Visual and performing arts 63%. **Special Study Options:** Cross registration, dual enrollment, student exchange program (domestic), independent study, internships, study abroad, teacher certification program.

FACILITIES

Housing: Housing for disabled students, apartment-style coed buildings with single-sex apartments. **Library Holdings:** 12,134 bound volumes. 78 periodicals. 0 microforms. 50,031 audiovisuals. **Computers:** School-owned computers available for student use.

EXTRACURRICULARS

Activities: Literary magazine, music ensembles, radio station, student government, student newspaper.

ADMISSIONS

Selectivity Rating: 63 (of 100). **Freshman Academic Profile:** Average high school GPA 2.7. SAT I Math middle 50% range 410-540. SAT I Verbal middle 50% range 450-570. TOEFL required of all international applicants, minimum TOEFL 550. **Basis for Candidate Selection:** *Very important factors considered include:* essays, secondary school record, talent/ability. *Important factors considered include:* character/personal qualities, interview, recommendations. *Other factors considered include:* class rank, extracurricular activities, standardized test scores. **Freshman Admission Requirements:** High school diploma or GED is required. *Academic units required/recommended:* 4 English recommended, 2 social studies recommended, 2 history recommended. **Freshman Admission Statistics:** 377 applied, 81% accepted, 38% of those accepted enrolled. **Transfer Admission Requirements:** *Items required:* college transcript, essay. Minimum college GPA of 2.2 required. Lowest grade transferable C. **General Admission Information:** Application fee $40. Priority application deadline March 1. Nonfall registration accepted. Admission may be deferred for a maximum of 1 year. Credit offered for CEEB Advanced Placement tests.

COSTS AND FINANCIAL AID

Tuition $16,100. Room & board $4,640. Required fees $510. Average book expense $825. **Required Forms and Deadlines:** FAFSA. Financial aid filing deadline July 1. Priority filing deadline March 2. **Notification of Awards:** Applicants will be notified of awards on a rolling basis beginning on or about April 1. **Types of Aid:** *Need-based scholarships/grants:* Pell, SEOG, state scholarships/grants, private scholarships, the school's own gift aid. *Loans:* FFEL Subsidized Stafford, FFEL Unsubsidized Stafford, FFEL PLUS, state loans. **Student Employment:** Federal Work-Study Program available. Institutional employment available. Off-campus job opportunities are good. **Financial Aid Statistics:** 70% freshmen, 61% undergrads receive some form of aid. **Financial Aid Phone:** 978-921-4242.

MOORE COLLEGE OF ART & DESIGN

20th Street and The Parkway, Philadelphia, PA 19103-1179
Phone: 215-965-4014 **E-mail:** admiss@moore.edu **CEEB Code:** 2417
Fax: 215-568-3547 **Web:** www.moore.edu **ACT Code:** 2417

This private school was founded in 1848.

STUDENTS AND FACULTY

Enrollment: 495. **Student Body:** Out-of-state 59%, international 3% (8 countries represented). **Ethnic Representation:** African American 9%, Asian 4%, Caucasian 82%, Hispanic 5%, Native American 1%. **Retention and Graduation:** 79% freshmen return for sophomore year. 42% freshmen graduate within 4 years. 15% grads go on to further study within 1 year. **Faculty:** Student/faculty ratio 8:1. 40 full-time faculty, 80% hold PhDs. 100% faculty teach undergrads.

ACADEMICS

Degrees: Bachelor's, certificate. **Academic Requirements:** General education including some course work in arts/fine arts, English (including composition), history, humanities, social science. **Disciplines with Highest Percentage of Degrees Awarded:** Visual and performing arts 100%. **Special Study Options:** Double major, independent study, internships, teacher certification program.

FACILITIES

Housing: All-female, apartments for single students. **Library Holdings:** 33,114 bound volumes. 181 periodicals. 0 microforms. 722 audiovisuals. **Special Academic Facilities/Equipment:** Paley and Leavy Galleries. **Computers:** *Recommended operating system:* Mac. School-owned computers available for student use.

EXTRACURRICULARS

Activities: Literary magazine, student government, yearbook. **Organizations:** 4 registered organizations.

ADMISSIONS

Selectivity Rating: 73 (of 100). **Freshman Academic Profile:** Average high school GPA 3.2. 72% from public high schools. Average SAT I Verbal 550. TOEFL required of all international applicants, minimum TOEFL 500. **Basis for Candidate Selection:** *Very important factors considered include:* interview, recommendations, talent/ability. *Important factors considered include:* character/personal qualities, extracurricular activities, standardized test scores, work experience. *Other factors considered include:* volunteer work. **Freshman Admission Requirements:** High school diploma or GED is required. **Freshman Admission Statistics:** 319 applied, 59% accepted, 47% of those accepted enrolled. **Transfer Admission Requirements:** *Items required:* college transcript. Minimum college GPA of 2.5 required. Lowest grade transferable C. **General Admission Information:** Application fee $35. Priority application deadline April 1. Early decision application deadline November 1. Regular application deadline August 15. Nonfall registration accepted. Admission may be deferred for a maximum of 1 year. Credit offered for CEEB Advanced Placement tests.

COSTS AND FINANCIAL AID

Tuition $15,475. Room & board $6,100. Required fees $500. Average book expense $1,000. **Required Forms and Deadlines:** FAFSA. No deadline for regular filing. Priority filing deadline March 1. **Notification of Awards:** Applicants will be notified of awards on a rolling basis beginning on or about March 15. **Types of Aid:** *Need-based scholarships/grants:* Pell, SEOG, state scholarships/grants, private scholarships, the school's own gift aid. *Loans:* FFEL Subsidized Stafford, FFEL Unsubsidized Stafford, FFEL PLUS, Federal Perkins, alternative loans. **Student Employment:** Federal Work-Study Program available. Institutional employment available. Off-campus job opportunities are excellent. **Financial Aid Statistics:** 78% freshmen, 87% undergrads receive some form of aid. Average freshman grant $4,776. Average freshman loan $2,625. **Financial Aid Phone:** 215-568-4515.

MORAVIAN COLLEGE

1200 Main Street, Bethlehem, PA 18018
Phone: 610-861-1320 **E-mail:** admissions@moravian.edu **CEEB Code:** 2418
Fax: 610-625-7930 **Web:** www.moravian.edu **ACT Code:** 2418

This private school, which is affiliated with the Moravian Church, was founded in 1742. It has a 60-acre campus.

STUDENTS AND FACULTY

Enrollment: 1,824. **Student Body:** Male 39%, female 61%, out-of-state 39%, international 2% (21 countries represented). **Ethnic Representation:** African American 2%, Asian 1%, Caucasian 93%, Hispanic 4%. **Retention and Graduation:** 85% freshmen return for sophomore year. 68% freshmen graduate within 4 years. 20% grads go on to further study within 1 year. 3% grads pursue business degrees. 3% grads pursue law degrees. 3% grads pursue medical degrees. **Faculty:** Student/faculty ratio 12:1. 97 full-time faculty, 77% hold PhDs. 100% faculty teach undergrads.

ACADEMICS

Degrees: Bachelor's, first professional, master's, post-bachelor's certificate. **Academic Requirements:** General education including some course work in arts/fine arts, English (including composition), foreign languages, history, humanities, mathematics, philosophy, sciences (biological or physical), social science. **Classes:** 10-19 students in an average class. Under 10 students in an average lab/discussion section. **Majors with Highest Enrollment:** Psychology, general; business administration/management; fine/studio arts, general. **Disciplines with Highest Percentage of Degrees Awarded:** Social sciences and history 24%, business/marketing 16%, psychology 16%, visual and performing arts 13%, education 9%. **Special Study Options:** Cross registration, double major, honors program, independent study, internships, liberal arts/career combination, student-designed major, study abroad, teacher certification program.

FACILITIES

Housing: Coed, all-female, all-male, apartments for single students, fraternities and/or sororities, special-interest housing, wellness (substance free) floors. **Library Holdings:** 256,352 bound volumes. 1,318 periodicals. 11,414 microforms. 1,950 audiovisuals. **Special Academic Facilities/Equipment:** Art gallery, music and art center, language lab, greenhouse, student art studios. **Computers:** School-owned computers available for student use.

EXTRACURRICULARS

Activities: Choral groups, concert band, dance, drama/theater, jazz band, literary magazine, marching band, music ensembles, student government, student newspaper, yearbook. **Organizations:** 75 registered organizations, 15 honor societies, 5 religious organizations, 2 fraternities (14% men join), 4 sororities (22% women join). **Athletics (Intercollegiate):** *Men:* baseball, basketball, cross-country, football, golf, indoor track, lacrosse, soccer, tennis, track & field. *Women:* basketball, cross-country, field hockey, indoor track, lacrosse, soccer, softball, tennis, track & field, volleyball.

ADMISSIONS

Selectivity Rating: 78 (of 100). **Freshman Academic Profile:** 25% in top 10% of high school class, 56% in top 25% of high school class, 85% in top 50% of high school class. Average SAT I Math 556, SAT I Math middle 50% range 500-610. Average SAT I Verbal 553, SAT I Verbal middle 50% range 490-610. TOEFL required of all international applicants, minimum TOEFL 550. **Basis for Candidate Selection:** *Very important factors considered include:* character/personal qualities, class rank, secondary school record. *Important factors considered include:* essays, extracurricular activities, recommendations, standardized test scores. *Other factors considered include:* alumni/ae relation, geographical residence, interview, minority status, talent/ability, volunteer work, work experience. **Freshman Admission Requirements:** High school diploma or GED is required. *Academic units required/recommended:* 15 total required; 17 total recommended; 4 English required, 3 math required, 4 math recommended, 2 science required, 2 science lab required, 2 foreign language required, 3 foreign language recommended, 4 social studies required. **Freshman Admission Statistics:** 1,509 applied, 77% accepted, 32% of those accepted enrolled. **Transfer Admission Requirements:** *Items required:* high school transcript, college transcript, essay, standardized test score, statement of good standing from prior school. Minimum college GPA of 2.5 required. Lowest grade transferable C. **General Admission Information:** Application fee $30. Priority application deadline March 1. Early decision application deadline February 1. Regular application deadline March 1. Nonfall registration accepted. Admission may be deferred for a maximum of 1 year. Credit and/or placement offered for CEEB Advanced Placement tests.

COSTS AND FINANCIAL AID

Tuition $21,663. Room & board $7,095. Required fees $365. Average book expense $700. **Required Forms and Deadlines:** FAFSA, CSS/Financial Aid PROFILE, state aid form, noncustodial (divorced/separated) parent's statement, business/farm supplement and Copies of parent and student w-2's and 1040's. Financial aid filing deadline March 15. Priority filing deadline February 15. **Notification of Awards:** Applicants will be notified of awards on a rolling basis beginning on or about April 1. **Types of Aid:** *Need-based scholarships/grants:* Pell, SEOG, state scholarships/grants, private scholarships, the school's own gift aid. *Loans:* FFEL Subsidized Stafford, FFEL Unsubsidized Stafford, FFEL PLUS, Federal Perkins, state loans. **Student Employment:** Federal Work-Study Program available. Institutional employment available. Off-campus job opportunities are good. **Financial Aid Statistics:** 74% freshmen, 78% undergrads receive some form of aid. Average freshman grant $11,536. Average freshman loan $3,265. Average income from on-campus job $870. **Financial Aid Phone:** 610-861-1330.

MOREHEAD STATE UNIVERSITY

HM 301, Morehead, KY 40351
Phone: 606-783-2000 **E-mail:** admissions@morehead-st.edu
Fax: 606-783-5038 **Web:** www.moreheadstate.edu **ACT Code:** 1530

This public school was founded in 1922.

STUDENTS AND FACULTY

Enrollment: 7,705. **Student Body:** Male 40%, female 60%, out-of-state 17%, international 1%. **Ethnic Representation:** African American 4%, Caucasian 95%, Hispanic 1%. **Retention and Graduation:** 65% freshmen return for sophomore year. **Faculty:** Student/faculty ratio 18:1. 353 full-time faculty, 64% hold PhDs.

ACADEMICS

Degrees: Associate's, bachelor's, master's, post-master's certificate. **Academic Requirements:** General education including some course work in arts/fine arts, computer literacy, English (including composition), history, humanities, mathematics, sciences (biological or physical), social science. **Majors with Highest Enrollment:** Elementary education and teaching; general studies; biology/biological sciences, general. **Disciplines with Highest Percentage of Degrees Awarded:** Education 22%, business/marketing 20%, liberal arts/general studies 8%, social sciences and history 7%, communications/communication technologies 6%. **Special Study Options:** Accelerated program, cooperative (work-study) program, distance learning, double major, dual enrollment, student exchange program (domestic), honors program, independent study, internships, student-designed major, study abroad, teacher certification program, weekend college.

FACILITIES

Housing: Coed, all-female, all-male, apartments for married students, apartments for single students, housing for disabled students, housing for international students, fraternities and/or sororities. **Library Holdings:** 333,518 bound volumes. 2,627 periodicals. 781,060 microforms. 18,808 audiovisuals. **Special Academic Facilities/Equipment:** Kentucky Folk Art Center. **Computers:** School-owned computers available for student use.

EXTRACURRICULARS

Activities: Choral groups, concert band, dance, drama/theater, jazz band, marching band, music ensembles, musical theater, pep band, radio station, student government, student newspaper, television station, yearbook. **Organizations:** 86 registered organizations, 18 honor societies, 7 religious organizations, 12 fraternities, 10 sororities. **Athletics (Intercollegiate):** *Men:* baseball, basketball, cross-country, football, golf, rifle, tennis, track & field. *Women:* basketball, cross-country, indoor track, rifle, soccer, softball, tennis, track & field, volleyball.

ADMISSIONS

Selectivity Rating: 67 (of 100). **Freshman Academic Profile:** Average high school GPA 3.0. 10% in top 10% of high school class, 30% in top 25% of high school class, 65% in top 50% of high school class. Average ACT 20, ACT middle 50% range 17-22. TOEFL required of all international applicants, minimum TOEFL 500. **Basis for Candidate Selection:** *Very important factors considered include:* alumni/ae relation, geographical residence, minority status, secondary school record, standardized test scores, state residency. *Important factors considered include:* character/personal qualities, talent/ability. *Other factors considered include:* class rank, interview, recommendations, volunteer work, work experience. **Freshman Admission Requirements:** High school diploma or GED is required. *Academic units required/recommended:* 20 total required; 4 English required, 3 math required, 2 science required, 2 foreign language recommended, 2 social studies required. **Freshman Admission Statistics:** 5,122 applied, 72% accepted, 42% of those accepted enrolled. **Transfer Admission Requirements:** *Items required:* college transcript, statement of good standing from prior school. Minimum high school GPA of 2.0 required. Minimum college GPA of 2.0 required. Lowest grade transferable C. **General Admission Information:** Nonfall registration accepted. Admission may be deferred. Credit and/or placement offered for CEEB Advanced Placement tests.

COSTS AND FINANCIAL AID

In-state tuition $2,710. Out-of-state tuition $7,204. Room & board $3,800. Required fees $0. Average book expense $600. **Required Forms and Deadlines:** FAFSA and institution's own financial aid form. No deadline for regular filing. Priority filing deadline March 15. **Notification of Awards:** Applicants will be notified of awards on a rolling basis. **Types of Aid:** *Need-based scholarships/grants:* Pell, SEOG, state scholarships/grants, private scholarships, the school's own gift aid. *Loans:* Direct Subsidized Stafford, Direct Unsubsidized Stafford, Direct PLUS, Federal Perkins, college/university loans from institutional funds. **Student Employment:** Federal Work-Study Program available. Institutional employment available. Off-campus job opportunities are fair. **Financial Aid Statistics:** 66% freshmen, 67% undergrads receive some form of aid. **Financial Aid Phone:** 606-783-2011.

MOREHOUSE COLLEGE

830 Westview Drive, SW, Atlanta, GA 30314
Phone: 404-215-2632 **E-mail:** admissions@morehouse.edu **CEEB Code:** 5415
Fax: 404-524-5635 **Web:** www.morehouse.edu **ACT Code:** 792

This private school was founded in 1867. It has a 61-acre campus.

STUDENTS AND FACULTY

Enrollment: 2,738. **Student Body:** Out-of-state 66%, international 4%. **Ethnic Representation:** African American 98%. **Retention and Graduation:** 25% grads go on to further study within 1 year. 10% grads pursue business degrees. 5% grads pursue law degrees. 14% grads pursue medical degrees. **Faculty:** Student/faculty ratio 15:1. 158 full-time faculty, 81% hold PhDs. 100% faculty teach undergrads.

ACADEMICS

Degrees: Bachelor's. **Academic Requirements:** General education including some course work in arts/fine arts, English (including composition), foreign languages, history, humanities, mathematics, philosophy, sciences (biological or physical), social science. **Majors with Highest Enrollment:** Business administration/management; computer science; biology/biological sciences, general. **Disciplines with Highest Percentage of Degrees Awarded:** Business/marketing 33%, biological life sciences 9%, other 9%, psychology 9%, mathematics 6%. **Special Study Options:** Cooperative (work-study) program, cross registration, double major, dual enrollment, student exchange program (domestic), honors program, internships, study abroad, dual degree program in engineering and architecture with other institutions.

FACILITIES

Housing: All-male, apartments for single students. **Library Holdings:** 444,366 bound volumes. 1,427 periodicals. 851,268 microforms. 10,656 audiovisuals. **Special Academic Facilities/Equipment:** Three chapels, a meditation room, and an arena that was built by and used for the Olympic games in 1996. **Computers:** *Recommended operating system:* Windows 95. School-owned computers available for student use.

EXTRACURRICULARS

Activities: Choral groups, concert band, drama/theater, jazz band, literary magazine, marching band, music ensembles, pep band, student government, student newspaper, yearbook. **Organizations:** 34 registered organizations, 7 honor societies, 4 religious organizations, 6 fraternities (7% men join). **Athletics (Intercollegiate):** *Men:* basketball, cross-country, football, track & field.

ADMISSIONS

Selectivity Rating: 86 (of 100). **Freshman Academic Profile:** Average high school GPA 3.3. 21% in top 10% of high school class, 44% in top 25% of high school class, 77% in top 50% of high school class. 80% from public high schools. Average SAT I Math 540, SAT I Math middle 50% range 480-600. Average SAT I Verbal 535, SAT I Verbal middle 50% range 480-590. Average ACT 22, ACT middle 50% range 19-24. TOEFL required of all international applicants, minimum TOEFL 500. **Basis for Candidate Selection:** *Very important factors considered include:* standardized test scores. *Important factors considered include:* class rank, essays, recommendations, secondary school record. *Other factors considered include:* alumni/ae relation, character/personal qualities, extracurricular activities, geographical residence, interview, minority status, talent/ability, volunteer work. **Freshman Admission Requirements:** High school diploma or GED is required. *Academic units required/recommended:* 4 English required, 3 math required, 2 science required, 2 foreign language required, 2 social studies required. **Freshman Admission Statistics:** 2,394 applied, 64% accepted, 45% of those accepted enrolled. **Transfer Admission Requirements:** *Items required:* college transcript, essay, standardized test score, statement of good standing from prior school. Minimum college GPA of 2.5 required. Lowest grade transferable C. **General Admission Information:** Application fee $45. Early decision application deadline October 15. Regular application deadline February 15. Admission may be deferred for a maximum of 2 years.

COSTS AND FINANCIAL AID

Tuition $11,332. Room & board $8,172. Required fees $2,428. Average book expense $750. **Required Forms and Deadlines:** FAFSA, institution's own financial aid form and CSS/Financial Aid PROFILE. Financial aid filing deadline April 1. **Notification of Awards:** Applicants will be notified of awards on or about May 1. **Types of Aid:** *Need-based scholarships/grants:* Pell, SEOG, state scholarships/grants, private scholarships, the school's own gift aid, United Negro College Fund. *Loans:* Direct Subsidized Stafford, Direct Unsubsidized Stafford, Direct PLUS, Federal Perkins, state loans. **Student Employment:** Federal Work-Study Program available. Institutional employment available. Off-campus job opportunities are good. **Financial Aid Statistics:** Average income from on-campus job $1,500. **Financial Aid Phone:** 404-681-2800.

MORGAN STATE UNIVERSITY

1700 East Cold Spring Lane, Baltimore, MD 21251
Phone: 800-332-6674 **E-mail:** tjenness@moac.morgan.edu **CEEB Code:** 5416
Fax: 410-319-3684 **Web:** www.morgan.edu **ACT Code:** 1722

This public school was founded in 1867. It has a 122-acre campus.

STUDENTS AND FACULTY

Enrollment: 5,356. **Student Body:** Out-of-state 40%, international 2%. **Ethnic Representation:** African American 94%, Asian 2%, Caucasian 2%, Hispanic 1%, Native American 1%. **Retention and Graduation:** 76% freshmen return for sophomore year.

ACADEMICS

Degrees: Bachelor's, doctoral, master's. **Special Study Options:** Cooperative (work-study) program, business, education, engineering, social/behavioral science.

FACILITIES

Housing: Coed, all-female, all-male, apartments for single students. **Library Holdings:** 500,000 bound volumes. 2,003 periodicals. 297,913 microforms. **Special Academic Facilities/Equipment:** African-American collection, new science complex and school of engineering. **Computers:** *Recommended operating system:* Mac.

EXTRACURRICULARS

Activities: Radio station, student government, student newspaper, television station, yearbook. **Organizations:** 250 registered organizations, 1 religious organization, 4 fraternities, 4 sororities. **Athletics (Intercollegiate):** *Men:* basketball, cross-country, football, tennis, track & field, volleyball. *Women:* basketball, cross-country, tennis, track & field, volleyball.

ADMISSIONS

Selectivity Rating: 71 (of 100). **Freshman Academic Profile:** 20% in top 10% of high school class, 80% in top 25% of high school class, 96% in top 50% of high school class. TOEFL required of all international applicants, minimum TOEFL 550. **Freshman Admission Requirements:** High school diploma is required and GED is not accepted. *Academic units required/recommended:* 20 total recommended; 4 English recommended, 3 math recommended, 3 science recommended, 2 foreign language recommended, 3 social studies recommended, 2 history recommended. **Transfer Admission Requirements:** Minimum college GPA of 2.0 required. Lowest grade transferable C. **General Admission Information:** Early decision application deadline April 15. Regular application deadline April 15. Nonfall registration accepted. Credit offered for CEEB Advanced Placement tests.

COSTS AND FINANCIAL AID

In-state tuition $1,853. Out-of-state tuition $4,405. Room & board $5,296. Required fees $762. Average book expense $1,500. **Required Forms and Deadlines:** FAFSA, institution's own financial aid form and state aid form. **Types of Aid:** *Need-based scholarships/grants:* state scholarships/grants, United Negro College Fund. *Loans:* FFEL Subsidized Stafford, FFEL PLUS. **Student Employment:** Federal Work-Study Program available. Institutional employment available. Off-campus job opportunities are good. **Financial Aid Phone:** 410-319-3170.

MORNINGSIDE COLLEGE

1501 Morningside Avenue, Sioux City, IA 51106-1751
Phone: 712-274-5111 **E-mail:** mscadm@morningside.edu **CEEB Code:** 6415
Fax: 712-274-5101 **Web:** www.morningside.edu **ACT Code:** 1338

This private school, which is affiliated with the Methodist Church, was founded in 1894. It has a 41-acre campus.

STUDENTS AND FACULTY

Enrollment: 915. **Student Body:** Male 43%, female 57%, out-of-state 31%, international 2% (6 countries represented). **Ethnic Representation:** African American 3%, Asian 1%, Caucasian 83%, Hispanic 5%. **Retention and Graduation:** 69% freshmen return for sophomore year. 38% freshmen graduate within 4 years. 12% grads go on to further study within 1 year. 1% grads pursue business degrees. 1% grads pursue law degrees. 2% grads pursue medical degrees. **Faculty:** Student/faculty ratio 12:1. 67 full-time faculty, 80% hold PhDs. 100% faculty teach undergrads.

ACADEMICS

Degrees: Bachelor's, master's. **Academic Requirements:** General education including some course work in arts/fine arts, English (including composition), foreign languages, history, humanities, mathematics, philosophy, sciences (biological or physical), social science. **Classes:** 10-19 students in an average class. 10-19 students in an average lab/discussion section. **Disciplines with Highest Percentage of Degrees Awarded:** Education 25%, business/marketing 22%, visual and performing arts 12%, health professions and related sciences 8%, biological life sciences 5%. **Special Study Options:** Double major, dual enrollment, English as a second language, honors program, independent study, internships, liberal arts/career combination, student-designed major, study abroad, teacher certification program, engineering, health professions.

FACILITIES

Housing: Coed, apartments for married students, apartments for single students. **Library Holdings:** 114,250 bound volumes. 571 periodicals. 279,305 microforms. 5,372 audiovisuals. **Special Academic Facilities/Equipment:** media-enhanced "smart classroom," highspeed campus Internet connection, art gallery. **Computers:** *Recommended operating system:* Windows XP. School-owned computers available for student use.

EXTRACURRICULARS

Activities: Choral groups, dance, drama/theater, jazz band, literary magazine, music ensembles, radio station, student government, student newspaper, television station, yearbook. **Organizations:** 45 registered organizations, 15 honor societies, 10 religious organizations, 2 fraternities (13% men join), 2 sororities (8% women join). **Athletics (Intercollegiate):** *Men:* baseball, basketball, cross-country, football, golf, indoor track, soccer, track & field. *Women:* basketball, cross-country, golf, indoor track, soccer, softball, track & field, volleyball.

ADMISSIONS

Selectivity Rating: 72 (of 100). **Freshman Academic Profile:** Average high school GPA 3.3. 12% in top 10% of high school class, 37% in top 25% of high school class, 69% in top 50% of high school class. 95% from public high schools. Average SAT I Math 486, SAT I Math middle 50% range 430-570. Average SAT I Verbal 487, SAT I Verbal middle 50% range 430-570. Average ACT 22, ACT middle 50% range 19-25. TOEFL required of all international applicants, minimum TOEFL 425. **Basis for Candidate Selection:** *Very important factors considered include:* class rank, recommendations, secondary school record, standardized test scores. *Important factors considered include:*

extracurricular activities, interview, talent/ability. *Other factors considered include:* essays. **Freshman Admission Requirements:** High school diploma or GED is required. *Academic units required/recommended:* 10 total recommended; 3 English recommended, 2 math recommended, 2 science recommended, 3 social studies recommended. **Freshman Admission Statistics:** 1,130 applied, 73% accepted, 30% of those accepted enrolled. **Transfer Admission Requirements:** *Items required:* high school transcript, college transcript, statement of good standing from prior school. Minimum college GPA of 2.0 required. Lowest grade transferable D. **General Admission Information:** Application fee $25. Priority application deadline August 15. Nonfall registration accepted. Admission may be deferred. Credit and/or placement offered for CEEB Advanced Placement tests.

COSTS AND FINANCIAL AID

Tuition $14,570. Room & board $5,120. Required fees $890. Average book expense $800. **Required Forms and Deadlines:** FAFSA. No deadline for regular filing. Priority filing deadline March 1. **Notification of Awards:** Applicants will be notified of awards on a rolling basis beginning on or about March 31. **Types of Aid:** *Need-based scholarships/grants:* Pell, SEOG, state scholarships/grants, private scholarships, the school's own gift aid. *Loans:* FFEL Subsidized Stafford, FFEL Unsubsidized Stafford, FFEL PLUS, Federal Perkins, state loans, college/university loans from institutional funds. **Student Employment:** Federal Work-Study Program available. Institutional employment available. Off-campus job opportunities are excellent. **Financial Aid Statistics:** 90% freshmen, 90% undergrads receive some form of aid. Average freshman grant $10,545. Average freshman loan $3,255. Average income from on-campus job $1,309. **Financial Aid Phone:** 712-274-5159.

MORRIS BROWN COLLEGE

643 Martin Luther King Jr. Drive NW, Atlanta, GA 30314
Phone: 404-739-1560 **E-mail:** admission@morrisbrown.edu **CEEB Code:** 5417
Fax: 404-739-1565 **Web:** www.morrisbrown.edu **ACT Code:** 844

This private school was founded in 1881. It has a 18-acre campus.

STUDENTS AND FACULTY

Enrollment: 2,501. **Student Body:** Male 43%, female 57%, out-of-state 35%, international 2%. **Ethnic Representation:** African American 98%. **Retention and Graduation:** 75% freshmen return for sophomore year. 15% freshmen graduate within 4 years. **Faculty:** Student/faculty ratio 18:1. 105 full-time faculty, 64% hold PhDs. 100% faculty teach undergrads.

ACADEMICS

Degrees: Bachelor's. **Academic Requirements:** General education including some course work in arts/fine arts, computer literacy, English (including composition), foreign languages, history, humanities, mathematics, sciences (biological or physical), social science. **Classes:** 20-29 students in an average class. Under 10 students in an average lab/discussion section. **Majors with Highest Enrollment:** Business administration/management; biology/biological sciences, general; mass communications/media studies. **Disciplines with Highest Percentage of Degrees Awarded:** Business/marketing 31%, education 14%, social sciences and history 8%, psychology 7%, communications/communication technologies 6%. **Special Study Options:** Accelerated program, cross registration, honors program, independent study, internships, liberal arts/career combination, study abroad, teacher certification program.

FACILITIES

Housing: Coed, all-female, all-male. **Library Holdings:** 358,505 bound volumes. 354 periodicals. 788,365 microforms. 4,506 audiovisuals. **Special Academic Facilities/Equipment:** Art gallery, language lab, electron microscope. **Computers:** School-owned computers available for student use.

EXTRACURRICULARS

Activities: Choral groups, concert band, dance, drama/theater, jazz band, marching band, music ensembles, opera, student government, student newspaper, yearbook. **Organizations:** 23 registered organizations, 1 honor society, 1 religious organization, 4 fraternities (3% men join), 5 sororities (3% women join). **Athletics (Intercollegiate):** *Men:* baseball, basketball, cheerleading, cross-country, football, golf, tennis, track & field. *Women:* basketball, cheerleading, cross-country, golf, softball, tennis, track & field, volleyball.

ADMISSIONS

Selectivity Rating: 63 (of 100). **Freshman Academic Profile:** Average high school GPA 2.6. Average SAT I Math 396, SAT I Math middle 50% range 360-440. Average SAT I Verbal 400, SAT I Verbal middle 50% range 370-450. Average ACT 16, ACT middle 50% range 15-18. TOEFL required of all international applicants, minimum TOEFL 500. **Basis for Candidate Selection:** *Very important factors considered include:* character/personal qualities, geographical residence, secondary school record, standardized test scores, state residency. *Important factors considered include:* alumni/ae relation, class rank, recommendations, talent/ability. *Other factors considered include:* essays, extracurricular activities, interview, religious affiliation/commitment, volunteer work, work experience. **Freshman Admission Requirements:** High school diploma or GED is required. *Academic units required/recommended:* 12 total required; 2 total recommended; 3 English required, 3 math required, 3 science required, 2 foreign language recommended, 2 social studies required, 1 history required. **Freshman Admission Statistics:** 2,639 applied, 43% accepted, 40% of those accepted enrolled. **Transfer Admission Requirements:** *Items required:* college transcript, essay, statement of good standing from prior school. Minimum high school GPA of 2.0 required. Minimum college GPA of 2.0 required. Lowest grade transferable C. **General Admission Information:** Application fee $30. Priority application deadline May 1. Regular application deadline July 15. Nonfall registration accepted. Admission may be deferred.

COSTS AND FINANCIAL AID

Tuition $8,368. Room & board $5,262. Required fees $3,415. Average book expense $800. **Required Forms and Deadlines:** FAFSA. No deadline for regular filing. **Notification of Awards:** Applicants will be notified of awards on or about June 1. **Types of Aid:** *Need-based scholarships/grants:* Pell, SEOG, state scholarships/grants, private scholarships, the school's own gift aid, United Negro College Fund. *Loans:* Direct Subsidized Stafford, Direct Unsubsidized Stafford, Direct PLUS, FFEL Subsidized Stafford, FFEL Unsubsidized Stafford, FFEL PLUS, Federal Perkins, college/university loans from institutional funds. **Student Employment:** Federal Work-Study Program available. Institutional employment available. Off-campus job opportunities are excellent. **Financial Aid Statistics:** 96% freshmen, 93% undergrads receive some form of aid. **Financial Aid Phone:** 404-739-1050.

MORRIS COLLEGE

100 West College Street, Sumter, SC 29150
Phone: 803-934-3225 **E-mail:** gscriven@morris.edu **CEEB Code:** 5418
Fax: 803-773-8241 **Web:** www.morris.edu **ACT Code:** 3868

This private school, which is affiliated with the Baptist Church, was founded in 1908. It has a 34-acre campus.

STUDENTS AND FACULTY

Enrollment: 1,049. **Student Body:** Male 37%, female 63%, out-of-state 13%. **Ethnic Representation:** African American 100%. **Retention and Graduation:** 60% freshmen return for sophomore year. 18% freshmen graduate within 4 years. 6% grads go on to further study within 1 year. 1% grads pursue business degrees. 1% grads pursue law degrees. 2% grads pursue medical degrees. **Faculty:** Student/faculty ratio 19:1. 49 full-time faculty, 61% hold PhDs. 100% faculty teach undergrads.

ACADEMICS

Degrees: Bachelor's. **Academic Requirements:** General education including some course work in arts/fine arts, computer literacy, English (including composition), foreign languages, history, humanities, mathematics, philosophy, sciences (biological or physical), social science, speech. **Classes:** 20-29 students in an average class. 20-29 students in an average lab/discussion section. **Majors with Highest Enrollment:** Business administration/management; business/managerial operations; criminal justice/law enforcement administration. **Disciplines with Highest Percentage of Degrees Awarded:** Business/marketing 33%, social sciences and history 14%, protective services/public administration 11%, health professions and related sciences 8%, biological life sciences 7%. **Special Study Options:** Accelerated program, cooperative (work-study) program, double major, honors program, internships, teacher certification program, advanced degree program for adults 25 and older with 60 earned credit hours.

FACILITIES

Housing: All-female, all-male. **Library Holdings:** 101,296 bound volumes. 395 periodicals. 190,678 microforms. 3,734 audiovisuals. **Computers:** School-owned computers available for student use.

EXTRACURRICULARS

Activities: Choral groups, drama/theater, literary magazine, pep band, radio station, student government, student newspaper, yearbook. **Organizations:** 58 registered organizations, 4 honor societies, 2 religious organizations, 4 fraternities (3% men join), 4 sororities (8% women join). **Athletics (Intercolle-**

giate): *Men:* baseball, basketball, cheerleading, cross-country, golf, tennis, track & field. *Women:* basketball, cheerleading, cross-country, softball, tennis, track & field, volleyball.

ADMISSIONS

Selectivity Rating: 63 (of 100). **Freshman Academic Profile:** Average high school GPA 2.4. 3% in top 10% of high school class, 16% in top 25% of high school class, 32% in top 50% of high school class. 98% from public high schools. Average SAT I Math 371, SAT I Math middle 50% range 330-410. Average SAT I Verbal 366, SAT I Verbal middle 50% range 320-420. TOEFL required of all international applicants, minimum TOEFL 500. **Basis for Candidate Selection:** *Very important factors considered include:* secondary school record. *Other factors considered include:* class rank, standardized test scores. **Freshman Admission Requirements:** High school diploma or GED is required. *Academic units required/recommended:* 24 total required; 4 English required, 4 math required, 3 science required, 1 foreign language required, 2 foreign language recommended, 2 social studies required, 1 history required, 7 elective required. **Freshman Admission Statistics:** 1,210 applied, 92% accepted, 26% of those accepted enrolled. **Transfer Admission Requirements:** *Items required:* high school transcript, college transcript, statement of good standing from prior school. Minimum college GPA of 2.0 required. Lowest grade transferable C. **General Admission Information:** Application fee $10. Priority application deadline April 30. Regular application deadline June 30. Nonfall registration accepted. Admission may be deferred. Credit offered for CEEB Advanced Placement tests.

COSTS AND FINANCIAL AID

Tuition $6,783. Room & board $3,410. Required fees $210. Average book expense $1,000. **Required Forms and Deadlines:** FAFSA and institution's own financial aid form. No deadline for regular filing. Priority filing deadline March 30. **Notification of Awards:** Applicants will be notified of awards on a rolling basis beginning on or about June 2. **Types of Aid:** *Need-based scholarships/grants:* Pell, SEOG, state scholarships/grants, private scholarships, the school's own gift aid, United Negro College Fund. *Loans:* Direct Subsidized Stafford, Direct Unsubsidized Stafford, Direct PLUS, Federal Perkins. **Student Employment:** Federal Work-Study Program available. Off-campus job opportunities are good. **Financial Aid Statistics:** 99% freshmen, 98% undergrads receive some form of aid. Average freshman grant $5,990. Average freshman loan $2,625. Average income from on-campus job $0. **Financial Aid Phone:** 803-934-3238.

MOUNT ALLISON UNIVERSITY

65 York Street, Sackville, NB E4L 1E4
Phone: 506-364-2269 **E-mail:** admissions@mta.ca
Fax: 506-364-2272 **Web:** www.mta.ca

This public school was founded in 1839. It has a 25-acre campus.

STUDENTS AND FACULTY

Enrollment: 2,554. **Student Body:** Male 38%, female 62%, out-of-state 66%, international students represent 40 countries. **Retention and Graduation:** 82% freshmen return for sophomore year. 43% freshmen graduate within 4 years. **Faculty:** Student/faculty ratio 18:1. 124 full-time faculty. 100% faculty teach undergrads.

ACADEMICS

Degrees: Bachelor's, master's. **Academic Requirements:** General education including some course work in arts/fine arts, humanities, sciences (biological or physical), social science. **Classes:** Under 10 students in an average class. **Majors with Highest Enrollment:** Business/commerce, general; biology/biological sciences, general; psychology, general. **Disciplines with Highest Percentage of Degrees Awarded:** Business/marketing 20%, social sciences and history 16%, interdisciplinary studies 11%, biological life sciences 9%, psychology 7%. **Special Study Options:** Distance learning, double major, English as a second language, student exchange program (domestic), honors program, internships, student-designed major, study abroad.

FACILITIES

Housing: Coed, all-female, housing for disabled students, language immersion housing. **Library Holdings:** 450,000 bound volumes. 1,200 periodicals. **Special Academic Facilities/Equipment:** Art gallery.

EXTRACURRICULARS

Activities: Choral groups, concert band, dance, drama/theater, jazz band, literary magazine, music ensembles, musical theater, opera, pep band, radio station, student government, student newspaper, student-run film society, symphony orchestra, yearbook. **Organizations:** 106 registered organizations. **Athletics (Intercollegiate):** *Men:* basketball, football, rugby, soccer, swimming. *Women:* basketball, rugby, soccer, swimming, volleyball.

ADMISSIONS

Selectivity Rating: 60 (of 100). **Freshman Academic Profile:** Average high school GPA 3.0. 25% in top 10% of high school class, 50% in top 25% of high school class, 95% in top 50% of high school class. TOEFL required of all international applicants, minimum TOEFL 550. **Basis for Candidate Selection:** *Very important factors considered include:* character/personal qualities, extracurricular activities, interview, secondary school record. *Important factors considered include:* class rank, recommendations, talent/ability, volunteer work. *Other factors considered include:* essays, standardized test scores, work experience. **Freshman Admission Requirements:** High school diploma or GED is required. **Freshman Admission Statistics:** 2,084 applied. **Transfer Admission Requirements:** *Items required:* high school transcript, college transcript, essay, statement of good standing from prior school. **General Admission Information:** Application fee $27. Priority application deadline March 15. Regular application deadline April 1. Nonfall registration accepted. Admission may be deferred.

COSTS AND FINANCIAL AID

In-state tuition $4,390. Out-of-state tuition $4,390. Room & board $4,200. Required fees $116. Average book expense $1,200. **Required Forms and Deadlines:** institution's own financial aid form and state aid form. No deadline for regular filing. **Notification of Awards:** Applicants will be notified of awards on a rolling basis. **Types of Aid:** *Need-based scholarships/grants:* private scholarships, the school's own gift aid. *Loans:* state, college/university loans from institutional funds. **Student Employment:** Off-campus job opportunities are good. **Financial Aid Phone:** 506-364-2269.

MOUNT ALOYSIUS COLLEGE

7373 Admiral Peary Highway, Cresson, PA 16630
Phone: 814-886-6383 **E-mail:** admissions@mtaloy.edu **CEEB Code:** 2420
Fax: 814-886-6441 **Web:** www.mtaloy.edu **ACT Code:** 3635

This private school, which is affiliated with the Roman Catholic Church, was founded in 1939. It has a 125-acre campus.

STUDENTS AND FACULTY

Enrollment: 1,221. **Student Body:** Male 27%, female 73%, out-of-state 9%, international 2%. **Ethnic Representation:** African American 1%, Caucasian 79%. **Retention and Graduation:** 73% freshmen return for sophomore year. 22% grads go on to further study within 1 year. **Faculty:** Student/faculty ratio 13:1. 53 full-time faculty, 28% hold PhDs. 100% faculty teach undergrads.

ACADEMICS

Degrees: Associate's, bachelor's, diploma, terminal, transfer. **Academic Requirements:** General education including some course work in computer literacy, English (including composition), humanities, mathematics, philosophy, sciences (biological or physical), social science. **Classes:** 10-19 students in an average class. 10-19 students in an average lab/discussion section. **Disciplines with Highest Percentage of Degrees Awarded:** Health professions and related sciences 55%, protective services/public administration 25%, interdisciplinary studies 20%. **Special Study Options:** Cross registration, distance learning, independent study, internships, student-designed major, weekend college.

FACILITIES

Housing: All-female, all-male, housing for disabled students, residence hall rooms for hearing-impaired students. **Library Holdings:** 65,000 bound volumes. 3,398 periodicals. 3,400 microforms. 3,400 audiovisuals. **Computers:** *Recommended operating system:* Windows 98. School-owned computers available for student use.

EXTRACURRICULARS

Activities: Choral groups, drama/theater, music ensembles, musical theater, student government, student newspaper, yearbook. **Organizations:** 16 registered organizations, 2 honor societies, 1 religious organization. **Athletics (Intercollegiate):** *Men:* basketball, golf, soccer. *Women:* basketball, soccer, volleyball.

ADMISSIONS

Selectivity Rating: 63 (of 100). **Freshman Academic Profile:** Average high school GPA 2.0. 5% in top 10% of high school class, 21% in top 25% of high school class, 47% in top 50% of high school class. 85% from public high schools.

Average SAT I Math 440. Average SAT I Verbal 430. TOEFL required of all international applicants, minimum TOEFL 500. **Basis for Candidate Selection:** *Very important factors considered include:* interview, secondary school record, standardized test scores. *Important factors considered include:* character/personal qualities, essays, extracurricular activities, recommendations. *Other factors considered include:* alumni/ae relation, class rank, talent/ability, volunteer work, work experience. **Freshman Admission Requirements:** High school diploma or GED is required. *Academic units required/recommended:* 18 total recommended; 4 English recommended, 3 math recommended, 3 science recommended, 3 social studies recommended, 5 elective recommended. **Freshman Admission Statistics:** 811 applied, 53% accepted, 38% of those accepted enrolled. **Transfer Admission Requirements:** *Items required:* college transcript. Minimum high school GPA of 2.0 required. Minimum college GPA of 2.0 required. Lowest grade transferable C. **General Admission Information:** Application fee $25. Priority application deadline March 15. Nonfall registration accepted. Admission may be deferred for a maximum of 1 year. Credit and/or placement offered for CEEB Advanced Placement tests.

COSTS AND FINANCIAL AID

Tuition $9,800. Room & board $4,640. Required fees $100. Average book expense $750. **Required Forms and Deadlines:** FAFSA and state aid form. Financial aid filing deadline May 1. Priority filing deadline February 15. **Notification of Awards:** Applicants will be notified of awards on a rolling basis beginning on or about March 15. **Types of Aid:** *Need-based scholarships/grants:* Pell, SEOG, the school's own gift aid. *Loans:* FFEL Subsidized Stafford, FFEL Unsubsidized Stafford, FFEL PLUS, Federal Perkins, Federal Nursing. **Student Employment:** Federal Work-Study Program available. Institutional employment available. Off-campus job opportunities are poor. **Financial Aid Statistics:** 98% freshmen, 97% undergrads receive some form of aid. Average freshman grant $5,400. Average freshman loan $2,625. Average income from on-campus job $0. **Financial Aid Phone:** 814-886-6357.

MOUNT HOLYOKE COLLEGE

50 College Street, South Hadley, MA 01075
Phone: 413-538-2023 **E-mail:** admission@mtholyoke.edu **CEEB Code:** 3529
Fax: 413-538-2409 **Web:** www.mtholyoke.edu **ACT Code:** 1866

This private school was founded in 1837. It has an 800-acre campus.

STUDENTS AND FACULTY

Enrollment: 2,191. **Student Body:** Male 0%, female 100%, out-of-state 65%, international 15%. **Ethnic Representation:** African American 5%, Asian 12%, Caucasian 67%, Hispanic 5%, Native American 1%. **Retention and Graduation:** 93% freshmen return for sophomore year. 76% freshmen graduate within 4 years. 27% grads go on to further study within 1 year. 6% grads pursue business degrees. 12% grads pursue law degrees. 11% grads pursue medical degrees. **Faculty:** Student/faculty ratio 10:1. 206 full-time faculty, 94% hold PhDs. 100% faculty teach undergrads.

ACADEMICS

Degrees: Bachelor's, master's, post-bachelor's certificate. **Academic Requirements:** General education including some course work in foreign languages, humanities, sciences (biological or physical), social science, physical education, multicultural perspectives. **Classes:** 10-19 students in an average class. 10-19 students in an average lab/discussion section. **Majors with Highest Enrollment:** English language and literature, general; biology/biological sciences, general; psychology, general. **Disciplines with Highest Percentage of Degrees Awarded:** Social sciences and history 30%, biological life sciences 12%, visual and performing arts 10%, English 10%, psychology 9%. **Special Study Options:** Cooperative (work-study) program, cross registration, double major, student exchange program (domestic), independent study, internships, liberal arts/career combination, student-designed major, study abroad, teacher certification program, community-based learning courses.

FACILITIES

Housing: All-female, apartments for single students, special housing accommodations are available by need. **Library Holdings:** 670,304 bound volumes. 1,537 periodicals. 23,628 microforms. 3,443 audiovisuals. **Special Academic Facilities/Equipment:** Art and historical museums, bronze-casting foundry, child study center, audiovisual center, language learning center, greenhouse, Japanese meditation garden, equestrian center, observatory, linear accelerator, electron microscope, refracting telescope, nuclear magnetic resonance equipment. **Computers:** School-owned computers available for student use.

EXTRACURRICULARS

Activities: Choral groups, dance, drama/theater, jazz band, literary magazine, music ensembles, musical theater, radio station, student government, student newspaper, student-run film society, symphony orchestra, yearbook. **Organizations:** 139 registered organizations, 3 honor societies, 9 religious organizations. **Athletics (Intercollegiate):** *Women:* basketball, crew, cross-country, diving, equestrian, field hockey, golf, indoor track, lacrosse, soccer, softball, squash, swimming, tennis, track & field, volleyball.

ADMISSIONS

Selectivity Rating: 87 (of 100). **Freshman Academic Profile:** Average high school GPA 3.7. 52% in top 10% of high school class, 84% in top 25% of high school class, 98% in top 50% of high school class. 66% from public high schools. Average SAT I Math 627, SAT I Math middle 50% range 580-670. Average SAT I Verbal 651, SAT I Verbal middle 50% range 608-700. Average ACT 28, ACT middle 50% range 26-30. TOEFL required of all international applicants, minimum TOEFL 600. **Basis for Candidate Selection:** *Very important factors considered include:* class rank, essays, recommendations, secondary school record. *Important factors considered include:* character/personal qualities, extracurricular activities, interview, talent/ability, volunteer work, work experience. *Other factors considered include:* alumni/ae relation, geographical residence, minority status, standardized test scores. **Freshman Admission Requirements:** High school diploma or GED is required. *Academic units required/recommended:* 4 English recommended, 3 math recommended, 3 science recommended, 3 science lab recommended, 3 foreign language recommended, 3 history recommended, 1 elective recommended. **Freshman Admission Statistics:** 2,936 applied, 52% accepted, 38% of those accepted enrolled. **Transfer Admission Requirements:** *Items required:* high school transcript, college transcript, essay, statement of good standing from prior school. Minimum college GPA of 3.0 required. Lowest grade transferable C-. **General Admission Information:** Application fee $55. Early decision application deadline November 15. Regular application deadline January 15. Nonfall registration accepted. Admission may be deferred. Credit and/or placement offered for CEEB Advanced Placement tests.

COSTS AND FINANCIAL AID

Required Forms and Deadlines: FAFSA, CSS/Financial Aid PROFILE, noncustodial (divorced/separated) parent's statement, business/farm supplement and federal income tax returns and W-2 forms of parents and student. Financial aid filing deadline February 1. Priority filing deadline February 1. **Notification of Awards:** Applicants will be notified of awards on or about March 25. **Types of Aid:** *Need-based scholarships/grants:* Pell, SEOG, state scholarships/grants, private scholarships, the school's own gift aid. *Loans:* Direct Subsidized Stafford, Direct Unsubsidized Stafford, Direct PLUS, Federal Perkins, state loans, college/university loans from institutional funds. **Student Employment:** Federal Work-Study Program available. Institutional employment available. Off-campus job opportunities are excellent. **Financial Aid Statistics:** 65% freshmen, 67% undergrads receive some form of aid. Average freshman grant $21,087. Average freshman loan $2,700. Average income from on-campus job $1,034. **Financial Aid Phone:** 413-538-2291.

MOUNT IDA COLLEGE

777 Dedham Street, Newton, MA 02159
Phone: 617-928-4535 **E-mail:** admissions@mountida.edu
Fax: 617-928-4507 **Web:** www.mountida.edu

This private school was founded in 1899.

STUDENTS AND FACULTY

Enrollment: 2,009. **Student Body:** Out-of-state 25%, international 11% (46 countries represented). **Ethnic Representation:** African American 16%, Asian 9%, Caucasian 64%, Hispanic 5%, Native American 5%. **Retention and Graduation:** 65% freshmen return for sophomore year. **Faculty:** 100% faculty teach undergrads.

FACILITIES

Housing: Coed, apartments for single students.

EXTRACURRICULARS

Activities: Literary magazine, radio station, student government, student newspaper, yearbook. **Organizations:** 20 registered organizations, 1 honor society, 2 religious organizations, 2% men join fraternities, 2% women join sororities.

ADMISSIONS

Selectivity Rating: 63 (of 100). **Freshman Academic Profile:** TOEFL required of all international applicants, minimum TOEFL 425. **Freshman Admission Requirements: General Admission Information:** Early decision application deadline rolling. Regular application deadline rolling. Nonfall registration accepted.

COSTS AND FINANCIAL AID

Room & board $8,460. Average book expense $350. **Types of Aid:** *Loans:* FFEL Subsidized Stafford, FFEL PLUS. **Student Employment:** Federal Work-Study Program available. Off-campus job opportunities are excellent. **Financial Aid Statistics:** Average freshman grant $6,500. Average freshman loan $6,000. Average income from on-campus job $1,500. **Financial Aid Phone:** 617-928-4518.

MOUNT MARTY COLLEGE

1105 West Eighth Street, Yankton, SD 57078-3724
Phone: 605-668-1545 **E-mail:** mmcadmit@mtmc.edu **CEEB Code:** 6416
Fax: 605-668-1607 **Web:** www.mtmc.edu **ACT Code:** 3914

This private school, which is affiliated with the Roman Catholic Church, was founded in 1936. It has an 80-acre campus.

STUDENTS AND FACULTY

Enrollment: 1,030. **Student Body:** Male 32%, female 68%, out-of-state 22%, international students represent 8 countries. **Ethnic Representation:** African American 2%, Caucasian 95%, Hispanic 1%, Native American 1%. **Retention and Graduation:** 72% freshmen return for sophomore year. 35% freshmen graduate within 4 years. **Faculty:** Student/faculty ratio 13:1. 42 full-time faculty, 40% hold PhDs. 97% faculty teach undergrads.

ACADEMICS

Degrees: Associate's, bachelor's, certificate, master's. **Academic Requirements:** General education including some course work in arts/fine arts, computer literacy, English (including composition), history, humanities, mathematics, philosophy, sciences (biological or physical), social science, religious studies. **Classes:** 10-19 students in an average class. Under 10 students in an average lab/discussion section. **Majors with Highest Enrollment:** Nursing/registered nurse training (RN, ASN, BSN, MSN); business administration/management; education, general. **Disciplines with Highest Percentage of Degrees Awarded:** Business/marketing 28%, education 23%, health professions and related sciences 17%, liberal arts/general studies 8%, psychology 6%. **Special Study Options:** Accelerated program, double major, honors program, independent study, internships, liberal arts/career combination, student-designed major, teacher certification program.

FACILITIES

Housing: All-female, all-male, housing for disabled students, cooperative housing. **Library Holdings:** 79,167 bound volumes. 439 periodicals. 11,838 microforms. 8,537 audiovisuals. **Special Academic Facilities/Equipment:** Bede Art Gallery, Laddie E. Cimpl Athletic Arena, Marian Auditorium Theatre. **Computers:** *Recommended operating system:* Windows NT/2000. School-owned computers available for student use.

EXTRACURRICULARS

Activities: Choral groups, concert band, dance, drama/theater, jazz band, literary magazine, music ensembles, musical theater, pep band, student government, student newspaper. **Organizations:** 40 registered organizations, 7 honor societies, 4 religious organizations. **Athletics (Intercollegiate):** *Men:* baseball, basketball, cheerleading, cross-country, golf, indoor track, soccer, track & field. *Women:* basketball, cheerleading, cross-country, golf, indoor track, softball, track & field, volleyball.

ADMISSIONS

Selectivity Rating: 82 (of 100). **Freshman Academic Profile:** Average high school GPA 3.3. 15% in top 10% of high school class, 35% in top 25% of high school class, 69% in top 50% of high school class. 87% from public high schools. Average ACT 21, ACT middle 50% range 19-24. TOEFL required of all international applicants, minimum TOEFL 500. **Basis for Candidate Selection:** *Very important factors considered include:* secondary school record, standardized test scores. *Other factors considered include:* alumni/ae relation, character/personal qualities, class rank, extracurricular activities, interview, recommendations, talent/ability, volunteer work, work experience. **Freshman Admission Requirements:** High school diploma or GED is required. **Freshman Admission Statistics:** 315 applied, 90% accepted, 42% of those accepted enrolled. **Transfer Admission Requirements:** *Items required:* high school transcript, college transcript. Minimum high school GPA of 2.0 required. Minimum college GPA of 2.0 required. Lowest grade transferable C. **General Admission Information:** Application fee $35. Priority application deadline February 1. Regular application deadline August 30. Nonfall registration accepted. Credit and/or placement offered for CEEB Advanced Placement tests.

COSTS AND FINANCIAL AID

Tuition $11,580. Room & board $4,600. Required fees $1,080. Average book expense $600. **Required Forms and Deadlines:** FAFSA and institution's own financial aid form. Priority filing deadline March 1. **Notification of Awards:** Applicants will be notified of awards on a rolling basis beginning on or about March 15. **Types of Aid:** *Need-based scholarships/grants:* Pell, SEOG, state scholarships/grants, private scholarships, the school's own gift aid. *Loans:* FFEL Subsidized Stafford, FFEL Unsubsidized Stafford, FFEL PLUS, Federal Perkins, Federal Nursing. **Student Employment:** Federal Work-Study Program available. Institutional employment available. Off-campus job opportunities are good. **Financial Aid Statistics:** 88% freshmen, 87% undergrads receive some form of aid. Average freshman grant $4,833. Average freshman loan $3,500. Average income from on-campus job $800. **Financial Aid Phone:** 605-668-1589.

MOUNT MARY COLLEGE

2900 North Menomonee River Parkway, Milwaukee, WI 53222
Phone: 414-256-1219 **E-mail:** admiss@mtmary.edu **CEEB Code:** 1490
Fax: 414-256-0180 **Web:** www.mtmary.edu **ACT Code:** 4620

This private school, which is affiliated with the Roman Catholic Church, was founded in 1913. It has an 80-acre campus.

STUDENTS AND FACULTY

Enrollment: 1,223. **Student Body:** Male 5%, female 95%, out-of-state 5%, international students represent 8 countries. **Ethnic Representation:** African American 16%, Asian 4%, Caucasian 73%, Hispanic 4%, Native American 1%. **Retention and Graduation:** 58% freshmen return for sophomore year. 36% freshmen graduate within 4 years. 15% grads go on to further study within 1 year. 1% grads pursue business degrees. **Faculty:** Student/faculty ratio 9:1. 68 full-time faculty, 58% hold PhDs. 98% faculty teach undergrads.

ACADEMICS

Degrees: Bachelor's, master's, post-bachelor's certificate. **Academic Requirements:** General education including some course work in arts/fine arts, English (including composition), history, humanities, philosophy, sciences (biological or physical), social science. **Classes:** Under 10 students in an average class. 10-19 students in an average lab/discussion section. **Majors with Highest Enrollment:** Business administration/management; fashion/apparel design; interior design. **Disciplines with Highest Percentage of Degrees Awarded:** Health professions and related sciences 30%, visual and performing arts 18%, business/marketing 15%, home economics and vocational home economics 9%, social sciences and history 7%. **Special Study Options:** Accelerated program, distance learning, double major, dual enrollment, honors program, independent study, internships, liberal arts/career combination, student-designed major, study abroad, teacher certification program.

FACILITIES

Housing: All-female. **Library Holdings:** 113,006 bound volumes. 500 periodicals. 4,000 microforms. 9,832 audiovisuals. **Special Academic Facilities/Equipment:** Hagerty Library, Marian Art Gallery, Walter & Olive Stiemke Memorial Hall & Conference Center. **Computers:** School-owned computers available for student use.

EXTRACURRICULARS

Activities: Choral groups, dance, drama/theater, music ensembles, student government, student newspaper. **Organizations:** 32 registered organizations, 8 honor societies, 1 religious organization. **Athletics (Intercollegiate):** *Women:* soccer, softball, tennis, volleyball.

ADMISSIONS

Selectivity Rating: 76 (of 100). **Freshman Academic Profile:** Average high school GPA 3.1. 14% in top 10% of high school class, 30% in top 25% of high school class, 71% in top 50% of high school class. 78% from public high schools. SAT I Math middle 50% range 563-523. SAT I Verbal middle 50% range 540-650. Average ACT 21, ACT middle 50% range 18-23. TOEFL required of all international applicants, minimum TOEFL 500. **Basis for Candidate Selection:** *Very important factors considered include:* secondary school record, standardized test scores. *Important factors considered include:* character/personal qualities, class rank, talent/ability. *Other factors considered include:*

alumni/ae relation, essays, extracurricular activities, interview, recommendations, volunteer work. **Freshman Admission Requirements:** High school diploma or GED is required. *Academic units required/recommended:* 16 total required; 16 total recommended; 4 English required, 4 English recommended, 2 math required, 3 math recommended, 2 science required, 2 science recommended, 2 science lab required, 2 science lab recommended, 2 foreign language required, 2 foreign language recommended, 2 social studies required, 2 social studies recommended, 2 history required, 2 history recommended, 2 elective required. **Freshman Admission Statistics:** 435 applied, 56% accepted, 49% of those accepted enrolled. **Transfer Admission Requirements:** *Items required:* high school transcript, college transcript, statement of good standing from prior school. Minimum high school GPA of 2.5 required. Minimum college GPA of 2.0 required. Lowest grade transferable C. **General Admission Information:** Application fee $25. Nonfall registration accepted. Admission may be deferred for a maximum of 1 year. Credit offered for CEEB Advanced Placement tests.

COSTS AND FINANCIAL AID

Tuition $14,000. Room & board $4,900. Required fees $170. Average book expense $800. **Required Forms and Deadlines:** FAFSA. No deadline for regular filing. Priority filing deadline March 1. **Notification of Awards:** Applicants will be notified of awards on a rolling basis beginning on or about January 1. **Types of Aid:** *Need-based scholarships/grants:* Pell, SEOG, state scholarships/grants, private scholarships, the school's own gift aid. *Loans:* FFEL Subsidized Stafford, FFEL Unsubsidized Stafford, FFEL PLUS, Federal Perkins. **Student Employment:** Federal Work-Study Program available. Institutional employment available. Off-campus job opportunities are excellent. **Financial Aid Statistics:** 84% freshmen, 68% undergrads receive some form of aid. Average freshman grant $6,084. Average freshman loan $2,973. Average income from on-campus job $1,150. **Financial Aid Phone:** 414-258-4810.

MOUNT MERCY COLLEGE

1330 Elmhurst Drive Northeast, Cedar Rapids, IA 52402-4797
Phone: 319-368-6460 **E-mail:** admission@mmc.mtmercy.edu **CEEB Code:** 6417
Fax: 319-363-5270 **Web:** www.mtmercy.edu **ACT Code:** 1340

This private school, which is affiliated with the Roman Catholic Church, was founded in 1928. It has a 40-acre campus.

STUDENTS AND FACULTY

Enrollment: 1,414. **Student Body:** Male 32%, female 68%, out-of-state 7%. **Ethnic Representation:** African American 2%, Asian 1%, Caucasian 88%, Hispanic 1%. **Retention and Graduation:** 74% freshmen return for sophomore year. 50% freshmen graduate within 4 years. 9% grads go on to further study within 1 year. 2% grads pursue business degrees. 1% grads pursue law degrees. **Faculty:** Student/faculty ratio 14:1. 68 full-time faculty, 72% hold PhDs. 100% faculty teach undergrads.

ACADEMICS

Degrees: Bachelor's. **Academic Requirements:** General education including some course work in arts/fine arts, English (including composition), history, humanities, mathematics, philosophy, sciences (biological or physical), social science, religious studies. **Classes:** 10-19 students in an average class. **Majors with Highest Enrollment:** Nursing/registered nurse training (RN, ASN, BSN, MSN); business administration/management; education, general. **Disciplines with Highest Percentage of Degrees Awarded:** Business/marketing 33%, education 14%, health professions and related sciences 13%, computer and information sciences 7%, protective services/public administration 7%. **Special Study Options:** Accelerated program, cooperative (work-study) program, cross registration, double major, honors program, independent study, internships, liberal arts/career combination, student-designed major, study abroad, teacher certification program, weekend college.

FACILITIES

Housing: Coed, apartments for single students. **Library Holdings:** 118,500 bound volumes. 715 periodicals. 1,800 microforms. 5,000 audiovisuals. **Computers:** School-owned computers available for student use.

EXTRACURRICULARS

Activities: Choral groups, drama/theater, literary magazine, pep band, student government, student newspaper. **Organizations:** 35 registered organizations, 16 honor societies, 7 religious organizations. **Athletics (Intercollegiate):** *Men:* baseball, basketball, cross-country, golf, soccer, track & field. *Women:* basketball, cross-country, golf, soccer, softball, track & field, volleyball.

ADMISSIONS

Selectivity Rating: 72 (of 100). **Freshman Academic Profile:** Average high school GPA 3.4. 20% in top 10% of high school class, 51% in top 25% of high school class, 77% in top 50% of high school class. 83% from public high schools. Average ACT 22, ACT middle 50% range 20-26. TOEFL required of all international applicants, minimum TOEFL 550. **Basis for Candidate Selection:** *Very important factors considered include:* class rank, secondary school record, standardized test scores. *Important factors considered include:* essays, extracurricular activities, recommendations. *Other factors considered include:* character/personal qualities, interview, talent/ability, volunteer work. **Freshman Admission Requirements:** High school diploma or GED is required. *Academic units required/recommended:* 17 total recommended; 4 English recommended, 4 math recommended, 3 science recommended, 2 foreign language recommended, 2 social studies recommended, 2 history recommended. **Freshman Admission Statistics:** 471 applied, 84% accepted, 41% of those accepted enrolled. **Transfer Admission Requirements:** *Items required:* college transcript, statement of good standing from prior school. Minimum college GPA of 2.5 required. Lowest grade transferable D. **General Admission Information:** Application fee $20. Regular application deadline August 30. Nonfall registration accepted. Admission may be deferred for a maximum of 1 year. Credit and/or placement offered for CEEB Advanced Placement tests.

COSTS AND FINANCIAL AID

Required Forms and Deadlines: FAFSA. Priority filing deadline March 1. **Notification of Awards:** Applicants will be notified of awards on a rolling basis beginning on or about March 15. **Types of Aid:** *Need-based scholarships/grants:* Pell, SEOG, state scholarships/grants, the school's own gift aid. *Loans:* Direct Subsidized Stafford, Direct Unsubsidized Stafford, Direct PLUS, Federal Perkins, Federal Nursing, state loans, college/university loans from institutional funds. **Student Employment:** Federal Work-Study Program available. Institutional employment available. Off-campus job opportunities are excellent. **Financial Aid Statistics:** 86% freshmen, 88% undergrads receive some form of aid. Average freshman loan $2,185. **Financial Aid Phone:** 319-368-6467.

See page 1124.

MOUNT OLIVE COLLEGE

634 Henderson Street, Mount Olive, NC 28365
Phone: 919-658-7164 **E-mail:** admissions@moc.edu **CEEB Code:** 5435
Fax: 919-658-7180 **Web:** www.mountolivecollege.edu **ACT Code:** 3131

This private school, which is affiliated with the Baptist Church, was founded in 1951. It has a 138-acre campus.

STUDENTS AND FACULTY

Enrollment: 2,213. **Student Body:** Male 46%, female 54%, out-of-state 8%. **Retention and Graduation:** 20% grads go on to further study within 1 year. **Faculty:** Student/faculty ratio 18:1. 44 full-time faculty, 70% hold PhDs. 100% faculty teach undergrads.

ACADEMICS

Degrees: Associate's, bachelor's, terminal, transfer. **Academic Requirements:** General education including some course work in arts/fine arts, computer literacy, English (including composition), history, humanities, mathematics, philosophy, sciences (biological or physical), social science. **Classes:** Under 10 students in an average class. Under 10 students in an average lab/discussion section. **Disciplines with Highest Percentage of Degrees Awarded:** Business/marketing 69%, protective services/public administration 16%, parks and recreation 4%, biological life sciences 2%, psychology 2%. **Special Study Options:** Accelerated program, cooperative (work-study) program, double major, dual enrollment, external degree program, honors program, independent study, internships, liberal arts/career combination, teacher certification program.

FACILITIES

Housing: All-female, all-male, apartments for single students. **Library Holdings:** 77,545 bound volumes. 5,978 periodicals. 48,735 microforms. 2,005 audiovisuals. **Computers:** *Recommended operating system:* Windows 98/NT. School-owned computers available for student use.

EXTRACURRICULARS

Activities: Choral groups, concert band, literary magazine, music ensembles, pep band, student government, student newspaper, yearbook. **Organizations:** 33 registered organizations, 4 honor societies, 6 religious organizations. **Athletics (Intercollegiate):** *Men:* baseball, basketball, cross-country, golf, soccer, tennis. *Women:* basketball, cross-country, soccer, softball, tennis, volleyball.

ADMISSIONS

Selectivity Rating: 63 (of 100). **Freshman Academic Profile:** Average high school GPA 3.0. 8% in top 10% of high school class, 20% in top 25% of high school class, 63% in top 50% of high school class. Average SAT I Math 450, SAT I Math middle 50% range 400-520. Average SAT I Verbal 455, SAT I Verbal middle 50% range 390-520. Average ACT 18, ACT middle 50% range 15-20. TOEFL required of all international applicants, minimum TOEFL 500. **Basis for Candidate Selection:** *Very important factors considered include:* secondary school record, standardized test scores. *Important factors considered include:* class rank. *Other factors considered include:* alumni/ae relation, character/personal qualities, essays, interview, recommendations, talent/ability. **Freshman Admission Requirements:** High school diploma or GED is required. *Academic units required/recommended:* 4 total required; 16 total recommended; 4 English required, 4 English recommended, 3 math recommended, 3 science recommended, 2 foreign language recommended, 2 social studies recommended, 2 history recommended. **Freshman Admission Statistics:** 652 applied, 77% accepted, 50% of those accepted enrolled. **Transfer Admission Requirements:** *Items required:* high school transcript, college transcript. Minimum college GPA of 2.0 required. Lowest grade transferable C. **General Admission Information:** Application fee $20. Nonfall registration accepted. Admission may be deferred for a maximum of 1 year.

COSTS AND FINANCIAL AID

Tuition $9,900. Room & board $4,400. Required fees $110. Average book expense $800. **Required Forms and Deadlines:** FAFSA and state aid form. No deadline for regular filing. **Notification of Awards:** Applicants will be notified of awards on a rolling basis beginning on or about March 15. **Types of Aid:** *Need-based scholarships/grants:* Pell, SEOG, state scholarships/grants, private scholarships, the school's own gift aid. *Loans:* FFEL Subsidized Stafford, FFEL Unsubsidized Stafford, FFEL PLUS, Federal Perkins, Prospective Teacher Education Scholarship Loans, alternative loans. **Student Employment:** Federal Work-Study Program available. Off-campus job opportunities are excellent. **Financial Aid Statistics:** 69% freshmen, 62% undergrads receive some form of aid. Average freshman grant $2,945. Average freshman loan $2,433. Average income from on-campus job $0. **Financial Aid Phone:** 919-658-2502.

MOUNT SAINT MARY COLLEGE (NY)

330 Powell Avenue, Newburgh, NY 12550
Phone: 845-569-3248 **E-mail:** mtstmary@msmc.edu **CEEB Code:** 2423
Fax: 845-562-6762 **Web:** www.msmc.edu **ACT Code:** 2819

This private school was founded in 1960. It has a 70-acre campus.

STUDENTS AND FACULTY

Enrollment: 2,039. **Student Body:** Male 29%, female 71%, out-of-state 14%. **Ethnic Representation:** African American 11%, Asian 2%, Caucasian 79%, Hispanic 8%. **Retention and Graduation:** 80% freshmen return for sophomore year. 44% freshmen graduate within 4 years. 35% grads go on to further study within 1 year. 2% grads pursue business degrees. 3% grads pursue law degrees. 4% grads pursue medical degrees. **Faculty:** Student/faculty ratio 18:1. 62 full-time faculty, 80% hold PhDs. 100% faculty teach undergrads.

ACADEMICS

Degrees: Bachelor's, certificate, master's. **Academic Requirements:** General education including some course work in arts/fine arts, computer literacy, English (including composition), history, humanities, mathematics, philosophy, sciences (biological or physical), social science. **Classes:** 10-19 students in an average class. 10-19 students in an average lab/discussion section. **Majors with Highest Enrollment:** Nursing/registered nurse training (RN, ASN, BSN, MSN); business administration/management; education, general. **Disciplines with Highest Percentage of Degrees Awarded:** Business/marketing 26%, social sciences and history 15%, English 10%, psychology 8%, health professions and related sciences 8%. **Special Study Options:** Accelerated program, cooperative (work-study) program, cross registration, distance learning, double major, dual enrollment, student exchange program (domestic), honors program, independent study, internships, liberal arts/career combination, study abroad, teacher certification program.

FACILITIES

Housing: All-female, all-male, housing for disabled students. **Library Holdings:** 105,683 bound volumes. 860 periodicals. 708,609 microforms. 23,524 audiovisuals. **Special Academic Facilities/Equipment:** On-campus elementary school, television station and editing room, multimedia lab. **Computers:** *Recommended operating system:* Windows XP. School-owned computers available for student use.

EXTRACURRICULARS

Activities: Choral groups, concert band, dance, drama/theater, literary magazine, music ensembles, musical theater, radio station, student government, student newspaper, yearbook. **Organizations:** 28 registered organizations, 9 honor societies, 1 religious organization. **Athletics (Intercollegiate):** *Men:* baseball, basketball, soccer, swimming, tennis. *Women:* basketball, soccer, softball, swimming, tennis, volleyball.

ADMISSIONS

Selectivity Rating: 65 (of 100). **Freshman Academic Profile:** Average high school GPA 3.1. 11% in top 10% of high school class, 40% in top 25% of high school class, 75% in top 50% of high school class. 65% from public high schools. Average SAT I Math 508, SAT I Math middle 50% range 460-550. Average SAT I Verbal 510, SAT I Verbal middle 50% range 470-530. Average ACT 20, ACT middle 50% range 16-22. TOEFL required of all international applicants, minimum TOEFL 500. **Basis for Candidate Selection:** *Very important factors considered include:* class rank, secondary school record. *Important factors considered include:* interview, standardized test scores. *Other factors considered include:* alumni/ae relation, character/personal qualities, essays, extracurricular activities, recommendations, talent/ability, volunteer work, work experience. **Freshman Admission Requirements:** High school diploma or GED is required. *Academic units required/recommended:* 20 total recommended; 4 English recommended, 3 math recommended, 3 science recommended, 3 foreign language recommended, 4 social studies recommended, 3 elective recommended. **Freshman Admission Statistics:** 1,362 applied, 79% accepted, 33% of those accepted enrolled. **Transfer Admission Requirements:** *Items required:* college transcript. Minimum high school GPA of 2.0 required. Minimum college GPA of 2.0 required. Lowest grade transferable C. **General Admission Information:** Application fee $30. Priority application deadline April 1. Nonfall registration accepted. Admission may be deferred for a maximum of 1 year. Credit and/or placement offered for CEEB Advanced Placement tests.

COSTS AND FINANCIAL AID

Tuition $12,930. Room & board $6,520. Required fees $405. Average book expense $900. **Required Forms and Deadlines:** FAFSA and institution's own financial aid form. Priority filing deadline February 15. **Notification of Awards:** Applicants will be notified of awards on a rolling basis beginning on or about March 15. **Types of Aid:** *Need-based scholarships/grants:* Pell, SEOG, state scholarships/grants, private scholarships, the school's own gift aid, Federal Nursing. *Loans:* FFEL Subsidized Stafford, FFEL Unsubsidized Stafford, FFEL PLUS, Federal Perkins, Federal Nursing. **Student Employment:** Federal Work-Study Program available. Institutional employment available. Off-campus job opportunities are fair. **Financial Aid Statistics:** 73% freshmen, 70% undergrads receive some form of aid. Average freshman grant $3,600. Average freshman loan $2,500. Average income from on-campus job $1,300. **Financial Aid Phone:** 845-569-3195.

See page 1126.

MOUNT SAINT MARY'S COLLEGE (CA)

12001 Chalon Road, Los Angeles, CA 90049-1597
Phone: 310-954-4250 **E-mail:** admissions@msmc.la.edu **CEEB Code:** 4493
Fax: 310-954-4259 **Web:** www.msmc.la.edu **ACT Code:** 338

This private school, which is affiliated with the Roman Catholic Church, was founded in 1925. It has a 53-acre campus.

STUDENTS AND FACULTY

Enrollment: 1,694. **Student Body:** Male 5%, female 95%, international students represent 3 countries. **Ethnic Representation:** African American 11%, Asian 15%, Caucasian 18%, Hispanic 45%. **Retention and Graduation:** 76% freshmen return for sophomore year. 53% freshmen graduate within 4 years. **Faculty:** Student/faculty ratio 16:1. 82 full-time faculty, 41% hold PhDs. 95% faculty teach undergrads.

ACADEMICS

Degrees: Associate's, bachelor's, certificate, doctoral, master's, post-bachelor's certificate, terminal, transfer. **Academic Requirements:** General education including some course work in arts/fine arts, English (including composition), foreign languages, history, humanities, mathematics, philosophy, sciences (biological or physical), social science. **Classes:** 10-19 students in an average class. **Majors with Highest Enrollment:** Biology/biological sciences, general;

nursing/registered nurse training (RN, ASN, BSN, MSN); liberal arts and sciences/liberal studies. **Disciplines with Highest Percentage of Degrees Awarded:** Health professions and related sciences 27%, business/marketing 17%, biological life sciences 14%, social sciences and history 13%, liberal arts/general studies 12%. **Special Study Options:** Accelerated program, cross registration, double major, student exchange program (domestic), honors program, independent study, internships, student-designed major, study abroad, teacher certification program, weekend college.

FACILITIES

Housing: All-female, limited men's housing. **Library Holdings:** 140,000 bound volumes. 750 periodicals. 4,760 microforms. **Special Academic Facilities/Equipment:** Drudis-Biada Art Gallery. **Computers:** *Recommended operating system:* Windows 95. School-owned computers available for student use.

EXTRACURRICULARS

Activities: Choral groups, dance, drama/theater, literary magazine, music ensembles, student government, student newspaper, yearbook. **Organizations:** 29 registered organizations, 1 sorority.

ADMISSIONS

Selectivity Rating: 80 (of 100). **Freshman Academic Profile:** 68% from public high schools. SAT I Math middle 50% range 470-565. SAT I Verbal middle 50% range 460-570. TOEFL required of all international applicants, minimum TOEFL 550. **Basis for Candidate Selection:** *Very important factors considered include:* secondary school record, standardized test scores. *Important factors considered include:* essays, interview. *Other factors considered include:* alumni/ae relation, character/personal qualities, class rank, extracurricular activities, geographical residence, recommendations, talent/ability, volunteer work, work experience. **Freshman Admission Requirements:** High school diploma or GED is required. *Academic units required/recommended:* 25 total required; 30 total recommended; 4 English required, 3 math required, 4 math recommended, 2 science required, 3 science recommended, 2 science lab required, 3 science lab recommended, 2 foreign language required, 3 foreign language recommended, 2 social studies required, 3 social studies recommended, 2 history required, 3 history recommended. **Freshman Admission Statistics:** 819 applied, 89% accepted, 41% of those accepted enrolled. **Transfer Admission Requirements:** *Items required:* college transcript, essay, statement of good standing from prior school. Minimum college GPA of 2.4 required. Lowest grade transferable C. **General Admission Information:** Application fee $40. Priority application deadline March 1. Nonfall registration accepted. Admission may be deferred for a maximum of 1 year. Credit and/or placement offered for CEEB Advanced Placement tests.

COSTS AND FINANCIAL AID

Tuition $18,882. Room & board $7,832. Required fees $892. Average book expense $700. **Required Forms and Deadlines:** FAFSA, institution's own financial aid form and state aid form. Financial aid filing deadline May 1. Priority filing deadline March 1. **Notification of Awards:** Applicants will be notified of awards on or about February 1. **Types of Aid:** *Need-based scholarships/grants:* Pell, SEOG, state scholarships/grants, private scholarships, the school's own gift aid. *Loans:* FFEL Subsidized Stafford, FFEL Unsubsidized Stafford, FFEL PLUS, Federal Nursing, college/university loans from institutional funds. **Student Employment:** Federal Work-Study Program available. Institutional employment available. Off-campus job opportunities are good. **Financial Aid Phone:** 310-954-4190.

MOUNT SAINT MARY'S COLLEGE (MD)

16300 Old Emmitsburg Road, Emmitsburg, MD 21727
Phone: 301-447-5214 **E-mail:** admissions@msmary.edu **CEEB Code:** 5421
Fax: 301-447-5860 **Web:** www.msmary.edu **ACT Code:** 1726

This private school, which is affiliated with the Roman Catholic Church, was founded in 1808. It has a 1,400-acre campus.

STUDENTS AND FACULTY

Enrollment: 1,583. **Student Body:** Male 42%, female 58%, out-of-state 39%, international 1% (8 countries represented). **Ethnic Representation:** African American 5%, Asian 2%, Caucasian 89%, Hispanic 3%. **Retention and Graduation:** 80% freshmen return for sophomore year. 58% freshmen graduate within 4 years. 31% grads go on to further study within 1 year. 7% grads pursue business degrees. 1% grads pursue law degrees. 1% grads pursue medical degrees. **Faculty:** Student/faculty ratio 15:1. 90 full-time faculty, 88% hold PhDs. 92% faculty teach undergrads.

ACADEMICS

Degrees: Bachelor's, first professional, master's, post-bachelor's certificate. **Academic Requirements:** General education including some course work in arts/fine arts, computer literacy, English (including composition), foreign languages, history, humanities, mathematics, philosophy, sciences (biological or physical), social science, nonwestern culture and ethics, minority studies. **Classes:** 20-29 students in an average class. 10-19 students in an average lab/discussion section. **Majors with Highest Enrollment:** Business administration/management; elementary education and teaching; sociology. **Disciplines with Highest Percentage of Degrees Awarded:** Business/marketing 37%, social sciences and history 20%, education 12%, biological life sciences 6%, psychology 6%. **Special Study Options:** Accelerated program, cross registration, double major, dual enrollment, honors program, independent study, internships, liberal arts/career combination, student-designed major, study abroad, teacher certification program, weekend college, 3-2 with Johns Hopkins University in nursing.

FACILITIES

Housing: Coed, apartments for single students, housing for disabled students, theme houses. **Library Holdings:** 211,158 bound volumes. 905 periodicals. 17,885 microforms. 4,825 audiovisuals. **Special Academic Facilities/Equipment:** Historical art collection reflecting Catholic history in America and Marylandia. **Computers:** *Recommended operating system:* Windows NT/2000. School-owned computers available for student use.

EXTRACURRICULARS

Activities: Choral groups, concert band, dance, drama/theater, jazz band, literary magazine, music ensembles, musical theater, radio station, student government, student newspaper, television station, yearbook. **Organizations:** 55 registered organizations, 16 honor societies, 9 religious organizations. **Athletics (Intercollegiate):** *Men:* baseball, basketball, cross-country, golf, indoor track, lacrosse, soccer, tennis, track & field. *Women:* basketball, cross-country, golf, indoor track, lacrosse, soccer, softball, tennis, track & field.

ADMISSIONS

Selectivity Rating: 70 (of 100). **Freshman Academic Profile:** Average high school GPA 3.1. 15% in top 10% of high school class, 46% in top 25% of high school class, 76% in top 50% of high school class. 58% from public high schools. Average SAT I Math 540, SAT I Math middle 50% range 490-590. Average SAT I Verbal 540, SAT I Verbal middle 50% range 480-580. TOEFL required of all international applicants, minimum TOEFL 550. **Basis for Candidate Selection:** *Very important factors considered include:* secondary school record. *Important factors considered include:* standardized test scores. *Other factors considered include:* alumni/ae relation, character/personal qualities, class rank, extracurricular activities, recommendations, talent/ability, volunteer work, work experience. **Freshman Admission Requirements:** High school diploma or GED is required. *Academic units required/recommended:* 16 total required; 4 English required, 3 math required, 3 science required, 2 science lab required, 2 foreign language required, 3 social studies required, 1 elective required. **Freshman Admission Statistics:** 1,816 applied, 87% accepted, 25% of those accepted enrolled. **Transfer Admission Requirements:** *Items required:* college transcript, statement of good standing from prior school. Minimum college GPA of 2.0 required. Lowest grade transferable C. **General Admission Information:** Application fee $35. Priority application deadline March 1. Nonfall registration accepted. Admission may be deferred for a maximum of 1 year. Credit and/or placement offered for CEEB Advanced Placement tests.

COSTS AND FINANCIAL AID

Tuition $20,500. Room & board $7,400. Required fees $200. Average book expense $800. **Required Forms and Deadlines:** FAFSA and CSS/Financial Aid PROFILE. Financial aid filing deadline February 15. Priority filing deadline February 15. **Notification of Awards:** Applicants will be notified of awards on a rolling basis beginning on or about February 15. **Types of Aid:** *Need-based scholarships/grants:* Pell, SEOG, state scholarships/grants, private scholarships, the school's own gift aid. *Loans:* FFEL Subsidized Stafford, FFEL Unsubsidized Stafford, FFEL PLUS, Federal Perkins. **Student Employment:** Federal Work-Study Program available. Institutional employment available. Off-campus job opportunities are fair. **Financial Aid Statistics:** 69% freshmen, 63% undergrads receive some form of aid. Average freshman grant $9,320. Average freshman loan $3,133. Average income from on-campus job $1,200. **Financial Aid Phone:** 301-447-5207.

MOUNT SAINT VINCENT UNIVERSITY

Admissions Office, 215 Evaristus Hall, Halifax, NS B3M 2J6
Phone: 902-457-6128 **E-mail:** admissions@msvu.ca
Fax: 902-457-6498 **Web:** www.msvu.ca

This public school was founded in 1873. It has a 45-acre campus.

STUDENTS AND FACULTY

Enrollment: 2,953. **Student Body:** Male 16%, female 84%, international students represent 50 countries. **Faculty:** Student/faculty ratio 19:1. 140 full-time faculty, 74% hold PhDs. 100% faculty teach undergrads.

ACADEMICS

Degrees: Bachelor's, certificate, diploma, master's. **Academic Requirements:** General education including some course work in arts/fine arts, English (including composition), humanities, social science. **Majors with Highest Enrollment:** Business/commerce, general; education; liberal arts and sciences/liberal studies. **Disciplines with Highest Percentage of Degrees Awarded:** Education 29%, business/marketing 17%, home economics and vocational home economics 16%, communications/communication technologies 12%, liberal arts/general studies 8%. **Special Study Options:** Cooperative (work-study) program, distance learning, double major, honors program, independent study, internships, liberal arts/career combination, study abroad, teacher certification program.

FACILITIES

Housing: Coed, all-female, apartments for single students, housing for international students. **Library Holdings:** 204,005 bound volumes. 918 periodicals. 352,302 microforms. 649 audiovisuals. **Special Academic Facilities/Equipment:** Mount Saint Vincent Art Gallery. **Computers:** School-owned computers available for student use.

EXTRACURRICULARS

Activities: Choral groups, dance, drama/theater, student government, student newspaper. **Organizations:** 30 registered organizations. **Athletics (Intercollegiate):** *Men:* basketball. *Women:* basketball, soccer, volleyball.

ADMISSIONS

Selectivity Rating: 63 (of 100). **Freshman Academic Profile:** Average high school GPA 2.5. 25% in top 10% of high school class, 70% in top 25% of high school class, 100% in top 50% of high school class. 90% from public high schools. TOEFL required of all international applicants, minimum TOEFL 550. **Basis for Candidate Selection:** *Very important factors considered include:* secondary school record. *Important factors considered include:* class rank, standardized test scores. *Other factors considered include:* character/personal qualities, essays, extracurricular activities, recommendations, talent/ability, volunteer work, work experience. **Freshman Admission Requirements: Freshman Admission Statistics:** 1,172 applied, 72% accepted, 50% of those accepted enrolled. **Transfer Admission Requirements:** *Items required:* college transcript, statement of good standing from prior school. **General Admission Information:** Application fee $20. Regular application deadline June 15. Nonfall registration accepted. Admission may be deferred for a maximum of 1 year.

COSTS AND FINANCIAL AID

Room & board $4,775. Required fees $124. Average book expense $500. **Types of Aid:** *Need-based scholarships/grants:* Pell, SEOG, state scholarships/grants, private scholarships, the school's own gift aid. *Loans:* FFEL Subsidized Stafford, FFEL Unsubsidized Stafford, FFEL PLUS, Federal Perkins, college/university loans from institutional funds. **Student Employment:** Off-campus job opportunities are excellent. **Financial Aid Phone:** 902-457-6356.

MOUNT SENARIO COLLEGE

College Avenue West, Ladysmith, WI 54848
Phone: 715-532-5511 **E-mail:** admissions@mountsenario.edu
Fax: 715-532-7690 **Web:** www.mountsenario.edu

This private school was founded in 1930.

STUDENTS AND FACULTY

Enrollment: 672. **Student Body:** Male 59%, female 41%, out-of-state 13%, international 3% (4 countries represented). **Ethnic Representation:** African American 15%, Asian 2%, Caucasian 76%, Hispanic 3%, Native American 2%. **Retention and Graduation:** 21% freshmen return for sophomore year. 3% freshmen graduate within 4 years. 4% grads go on to further study within 1 year. 1% grads pursue business degrees. 1% grads pursue law degrees. **Faculty:** Student/faculty ratio 14:1. 22 full-time faculty, 36% hold PhDs. 100% faculty teach undergrads.

ACADEMICS

Degrees: Associate's, bachelor's. **Academic Requirements:** General education including some course work in arts/fine arts, English (including composition), history, humanities, mathematics, philosophy, sciences (biological or physical), social science. **Classes:** Under 10 students in an average class. Under 10 students in an average lab/discussion section. **Disciplines with Highest Percentage of Degrees Awarded:** Protective services/public administration 60%, business/marketing 17%, education 11%, parks and recreation 3%, biological life sciences 2%. **Special Study Options:** Cooperative (work-study) program, double major, English as a second language, independent study, internships, teacher certification program.

FACILITIES

Housing: Coed, modular housing units. **Library Holdings:** 37,068 bound volumes. 128 periodicals. 6,694 microforms. 221 audiovisuals.

EXTRACURRICULARS

Activities: Drama/theater, student government, student newspaper. **Organizations:** 7 honor societies, 2 religious organizations.

ADMISSIONS

Selectivity Rating: 63 (of 100). **Freshman Academic Profile:** Average high school GPA 2.6. 5% in top 10% of high school class, 15% in top 25% of high school class, 37% in top 50% of high school class. SAT I Math middle 50% range 250-470. SAT I Verbal middle 50% range 310-380. Average ACT 17, ACT middle 50% range 15-20. TOEFL required of all international applicants, minimum TOEFL 420. **Freshman Admission Requirements:** High school diploma or GED is required. *Academic units required/recommended:* 4 English recommended, 2 math recommended, 2 science recommended, 2 social studies recommended, 2 history recommended. **Freshman Admission Statistics:** 314 applied, 70% accepted, 50% of those accepted enrolled. **Transfer Admission Requirements:** *Items required:* high school transcript, college transcript. Lowest grade transferable C-. **General Admission Information:** Application fee $10. Nonfall registration accepted.

COSTS AND FINANCIAL AID

Tuition $12,800. Room & board $4,950. Required fees $0. Average book expense $650. **Required Forms and Deadlines:** FAFSA. Priority filing deadline April 15. **Notification of Awards:** Applicants will be notified of awards on a rolling basis. **Types of Aid:** *Need-based scholarships/grants:* Pell, SEOG, state scholarships/grants, private scholarships, the school's own gift aid. *Loans:* FFEL Subsidized Stafford, FFEL Unsubsidized Stafford, FFEL PLUS, Federal Perkins. **Student Employment:** Federal Work-Study Program available. Off-campus job opportunities are fair. **Financial Aid Statistics:** 95% freshmen, 93% undergrads receive some form of aid. Average freshman loan $4,315. Average income from on-campus job $800. **Financial Aid Phone:** 715-532-5511.

MOUNT UNION COLLEGE

1972 Clark Avenue, Alliance, OH 44601-3993
Phone: 800-334-6682 **E-mail:** admissn@muc.edu **CEEB Code:** 1492
Fax: 330-823-3457 **Web:** www.muc.edu

This private school was founded in 1846. It has a 224-acre campus.

STUDENTS AND FACULTY

Enrollment: 2,372. **Student Body:** Male 43%, female 57%, out-of-state 9%, international 1%. **Ethnic Representation:** African American 4%, Caucasian 93%. **Retention and Graduation:** 81% freshmen return for sophomore year. 53% freshmen graduate within 4 years. 19% grads go on to further study within 1 year. 4% grads pursue business degrees. 1% grads pursue law degrees. 2% grads pursue medical degrees. **Faculty:** Student/faculty ratio 14:1. 126 full-time faculty, 77% hold PhDs. 100% faculty teach undergrads.

ACADEMICS

Degrees: Bachelor's. **Academic Requirements:** General education including some course work in arts/fine arts, English (including composition), foreign languages, history, humanities, mathematics, philosophy, sciences (biological or physical), social science. **Classes:** 10-19 students in an average class. 10-19 students in an average lab/discussion section. **Majors with Highest Enroll-**

ment: Business administration/management; education, general; psychology, general. **Disciplines with Highest Percentage of Degrees Awarded:** Business/marketing 18%, education 17%, parks and recreation 12%, computer and information sciences 9%, biological life sciences 7%. **Special Study Options:** Accelerated program, cooperative (work-study) program, double major, English as a second language, honors program, independent study, internships, student-designed major, study abroad, teacher certification program.

FACILITIES

Housing: Coed, all-female, all-male, housing for disabled students, housing for international students, fraternities and/or sororities. **Library Holdings:** 228,850 bound volumes. 972 periodicals. 45,292 microforms. 500 audiovisuals. **Special Academic Facilities/Equipment:** Art gallery, ecological center, observatory, educational media center. **Computers:** School-owned computers available for student use.

EXTRACURRICULARS

Activities: Choral groups, concert band, dance, drama/theater, jazz band, literary magazine, marching band, music ensembles, musical theater, pep band, radio station, student government, student newspaper, yearbook. **Organizations:** 74 registered organizations, 18 honor societies, 17 religious organizations, 4 fraternities (16% men join), 5 sororities (17% women join). **Athletics (Intercollegiate):** *Men:* baseball, basketball, cross-country, diving, football, golf, indoor track, soccer, swimming, tennis, track & field, wrestling. *Women:* basketball, cheerleading, cross-country, diving, golf, indoor track, soccer, softball, swimming, tennis, track & field, volleyball.

ADMISSIONS

Selectivity Rating: 73 (of 100). **Freshman Academic Profile:** Average high school GPA 3.4. 19% in top 10% of high school class, 43% in top 25% of high school class, 75% in top 50% of high school class. 86% from public high schools. Average ACT 22, ACT middle 50% range 19-25. TOEFL required of all international applicants, minimum TOEFL 500. **Basis for Candidate Selection:** *Very important factors considered include:* class rank, secondary school record, standardized test scores. *Important factors considered include:* character/personal qualities, recommendations. *Other factors considered include:* alumni/ae relation, essays, extracurricular activities, minority status, talent/ability, volunteer work, work experience. **Freshman Admission Requirements:** High school diploma or GED is required. *Academic units required/recommended:* 16 total recommended; 4 English recommended, 3 math recommended, 3 science recommended, 2 science lab recommended, 2 foreign language recommended, 3 social studies recommended. **Freshman Admission Statistics:** 1,919 applied, 78% accepted, 39% of those accepted enrolled. **Transfer Admission Requirements:** *Items required:* high school transcript, college transcript, essay, statement of good standing from prior school. Minimum college GPA of 2.0 required. Lowest grade transferable C. **General Admission Information:** Application fee $2. Nonfall registration accepted. Credit and/or placement offered for CEEB Advanced Placement tests.

COSTS AND FINANCIAL AID

Tuition $16,240. Room & board $5,070. Required fees $910. Average book expense $600. **Required Forms and Deadlines:** FAFSA and institution's own financial aid form. Priority filing deadline April 1. **Notification of Awards:** Applicants will be notified of awards on or about March 15. **Types of Aid:** *Need-based scholarships/grants:* Pell, SEOG, state scholarships/grants, private scholarships, the school's own gift aid. *Loans:* FFEL Subsidized Stafford, FFEL Unsubsidized Stafford, FFEL PLUS, Federal Perkins, college/university loans from institutional funds. **Student Employment:** Federal Work-Study Program available. Institutional employment available. Off-campus job opportunities are good. **Financial Aid Statistics:** 80% freshmen, 78% undergrads receive some form of aid. Average freshman grant $8,110. Average freshman loan $4,187. Average income from on-campus job $1,129. **Financial Aid Phone:** 330-821-5320.

MOUNT VERNON COLLEGE

2100 Foxhall Road NW, Washington, DC 20007-1199
Phone: 800-682-4636 **E-mail:** mvcgw@gwu.edu **CEEB Code:** 5422
Fax: 202-625-4688 **Web:** www.mvc.gwu.edu **ACT Code:** 682

This private school was founded in 1875. It has a 26-acre campus.

STUDENTS AND FACULTY

Enrollment: 341. **Student Body:** Out-of-state 72%, international students represent 31 countries. **Ethnic Representation:** African American 18%, Asian 3%, Caucasian 74%, Hispanic 5%. **Retention and Graduation:** 7% grads go on to further study within 1 year. 2% grads pursue business degrees. 3% grads pursue law degrees.

ACADEMICS

Degrees: Bachelor's, doctoral, master's.

FACILITIES

Housing: Coed, all-female, all-male. **Library Holdings:** 50,000 bound volumes. **Computers:** *Recommended operating system:* Mac. School-owned computers available for student use.

EXTRACURRICULARS

Activities: Student government, student newspaper, yearbook. **Organizations:** 20 registered organizations, 1 honor society, 7 religious organizations.

ADMISSIONS

Selectivity Rating: 78 (of 100). **Freshman Academic Profile:** 70% from public high schools. Average SAT I Math 440. Average SAT I Verbal 402. Average ACT 20. TOEFL required of all international applicants, minimum TOEFL 500. **Freshman Admission Requirements:** High school diploma or GED is required. *Academic units required/recommended:* 15 total recommended; 4 English recommended, 3 math recommended, 3 science recommended, 2 foreign language recommended, 1 social studies recommended, 1 history recommended. **Transfer Admission Requirements:** Minimum college GPA of 2.0 required. Lowest grade transferable C-. **General Admission Information:** Early decision application deadline March 1. Regular application deadline rolling. Nonfall registration accepted. Credit and/or placement offered for CEEB Advanced Placement tests.

COSTS AND FINANCIAL AID

Room & board $7,730. Average book expense $500. **Required Forms and Deadlines:** FAFSA. **Types of Aid:** *Need-based scholarships/grants:* state scholarships/grants. *Loans:* FFEL Subsidized Stafford, FFEL PLUS. **Student Employment:** Federal Work-Study Program available. Institutional employment available. Off-campus job opportunities are excellent. **Financial Aid Statistics:** Average freshman loan $2,625. Average income from on-campus job $2,000. **Financial Aid Phone:** 202-625-4682.

MOUNT VERNON NAZARENE UNIVERSITY

800 Martinsburg Road, Mount Vernon, OH 43050
Phone: 740-392-6868 **E-mail:** admissions@mvnu.edu **CEEB Code:** 1531
Fax: 740-393-0511 **Web:** www.mvnu.edu **ACT Code:** 3372

This private school, which is affiliated with the Nazarene Church, was founded in 1964. It has a 401-acre campus.

STUDENTS AND FACULTY

Enrollment: 2,235. **Student Body:** Male 43%, female 57%, out-of-state 10%, international students represent 6 countries. **Ethnic Representation:** African American 3%, Asian 1%, Caucasian 91%, Hispanic 1%. **Retention and Graduation:** 74% freshmen return for sophomore year. 48% freshmen graduate within 4 years. 20% grads go on to further study within 1 year. 7% grads pursue business degrees. 2% grads pursue law degrees. 2% grads pursue medical degrees. **Faculty:** Student/faculty ratio 18:1. 72 full-time faculty, 63% hold PhDs. 100% faculty teach undergrads.

ACADEMICS

Degrees: Associate's, bachelor's, master's, terminal. **Academic Requirements:** General education including some course work in arts/fine arts, computer literacy, English (including composition), history, humanities, mathematics, philosophy, sciences (biological or physical), social science. **Classes:** 10-19 students in an average class. **Majors with Highest Enrollment:** Business administration/management; early childhood education and teaching; biology/biological sciences, general. **Disciplines with Highest Percentage of Degrees Awarded:** Business/marketing 54%, education 12%, biological life sciences 5%, philosophy/religion/theology 5%, visual and performing arts 4%. **Special Study Options:** Cooperative (work-study) program, cross registration, double major, dual enrollment, honors program, independent study, internships, study abroad, teacher certification program.

FACILITIES

Housing: All-female, all-male, apartments for single students, housing for disabled students. **Library Holdings:** 92,169 bound volumes. 586 periodicals. 11,146 microforms. 4,744 audiovisuals. **Special Academic Facilities/Equipment:** Art gallery, nature reserve. **Computers:** School-owned computers available for student use.

EXTRACURRICULARS

Activities: Choral groups, concert band, drama/theater, jazz band, literary magazine, music ensembles, musical theater, radio station, student government, student newspaper, yearbook. **Organizations:** 36 registered organizations, 2 honor societies, 11 religious organizations. **Athletics (Intercollegiate):** *Men:* baseball, basketball, golf, soccer. *Women:* basketball, soccer, softball, volleyball.

ADMISSIONS

Selectivity Rating: 67 (of 100). **Freshman Academic Profile:** Average high school GPA 3.3. 22% in top 10% of high school class, 49% in top 25% of high school class, 77% in top 50% of high school class. 84% from public high schools. Average SAT I Math 556, SAT I Math middle 50% range 500-610. Average SAT I Verbal 547, SAT I Verbal middle 50% range 480-600. Average ACT 23, ACT middle 50% range 20-25. TOEFL required of all international applicants, minimum TOEFL 500. **Basis for Candidate Selection:** *Very important factors considered include:* essays, recommendations, secondary school record, standardized test scores, state residency. *Important factors considered include:* class rank. *Other factors considered include:* character/personal qualities, extracurricular activities, geographical residence, interview, religious affiliation/commitment, talent/ability. **Freshman Admission Requirements:** High school diploma or GED is required. *Academic units required/recommended:* 21 total required; 21 total recommended; 4 English required, 4 English recommended, 3 math required, 3 math recommended, 2 science required, 3 science recommended, 1 science lab required, 3 science lab recommended, 3 foreign language recommended, 3 social studies required, 3 social studies recommended, 8 elective required, 8 elective recommended. **Freshman Admission Statistics:** 825 applied, 77% accepted, 56% of those accepted enrolled. **Transfer Admission Requirements:** *Items required:* high school transcript, college transcript, essay, standardized test score, statement of good standing from prior school. Minimum high school GPA of 2.5 required. Minimum college GPA of 2.0 required. Lowest grade transferable C. **General Admission Information:** Application fee $25. Regular application deadline May 31. Nonfall registration accepted. Admission may be deferred for a maximum of 1 year. Neither credit nor placement offered for CEEB Advanced Placement tests.

COSTS AND FINANCIAL AID

Tuition $13,794. Room & board $4,653. Required fees $486. Average book expense $900. **Required Forms and Deadlines:** FAFSA and institution's own financial aid form. No deadline for regular filing. Priority filing deadline March 15. **Notification of Awards:** Applicants will be notified of awards on a rolling basis beginning on or about February 15. **Types of Aid:** *Need-based scholarships/grants:* Pell, SEOG, state scholarships/grants, private scholarships, the school's own gift aid. *Loans:* FFEL Subsidized Stafford, FFEL Unsubsidized Stafford, FFEL PLUS, Federal Perkins, Bank One, City Bank, etc. private loans. **Student Employment:** Federal Work-Study Program available. Institutional employment available. Off-campus job opportunities are good. **Financial Aid Statistics:** 87% freshmen, 58% undergrads receive some form of aid. Average freshman grant $4,056. Average freshman loan $6,503. Average income from on-campus job $1,606. **Financial Aid Phone:** 800-287-3171.

MOUNTAIN STATE UNIVERSITY

609 South Kanawha Street, Beckley, WV 25801
Phone: 304-929-1433 **E-mail:** gomsu@mountainstate.edu
Fax: 304-253-3463 **Web:** www.mountainstate.edu

This private school was founded in 1933. It has a 7-acre campus.

STUDENTS AND FACULTY

Enrollment: 2,990. **Student Body:** Male 35%, female 65%, out-of-state 11%, international 5%. **Ethnic Representation:** African American 7%, Asian 1%, Caucasian 67%, Hispanic 1%, Native American 1%. **Faculty:** Student/faculty ratio 21:1. 65 full-time faculty, 32% hold PhDs.

ACADEMICS

Degrees: Associate's, bachelor's, certificate, master's, terminal, transfer. **Academic Requirements:** General education including some course work in arts/fine arts, computer literacy, English (including composition), humanities, mathematics, sciences (biological or physical), social science, freshman seminar. foreign languages and history are optional. **Classes:** Under 10 students in an average class. 10-19 students in an average lab/discussion section. **Majors with Highest Enrollment:** Nursing/registered nurse training (RN, ASN, BSN, MSN); health professions and related sciences; business administration/management. **Disciplines with Highest Percentage of Degrees Awarded:** Health professions and related sciences 38%, business/marketing 35%, interdisciplinary studies 13%, protective services/public administration 6%, other 5%. **Special Study Options:** Accelerated program, cooperative (work-study) program, cross registration, distance learning, double major, dual enrollment, external degree program, independent study, internships, liberal arts/career combination, student-designed major.

FACILITIES

Housing: Coed, athletic team houses (basketball and softball). **Library Holdings:** 90,929 bound volumes. 2,300 periodicals. 1,416 microforms. 5,269 audiovisuals. **Computers:** School-owned computers available for student use.

EXTRACURRICULARS

Activities: Literary magazine, student government. **Organizations:** 22 registered organizations, 5 honor societies, 1 religious organization, 25 fraternity. **Athletics (Intercollegiate):** *Men:* basketball, cheerleading. *Women:* cheerleading, softball, volleyball.

ADMISSIONS

Selectivity Rating: 63 (of 100). **Freshman Academic Profile:** 99% from public high schools. Average ACT 18. TOEFL required of all international applicants, minimum TOEFL 500. **Basis for Candidate Selection:** *Very important factors considered include:* standardized test scores. *Important factors considered include:* class rank, essays, recommendations, secondary school record. *Other factors considered include:* alumni/ae relation, character/personal qualities, extracurricular activities, talent/ability, volunteer work, work experience. **Freshman Admission Requirements:** High school diploma or GED is required. *Academic units required/recommended:* 4 English required, 4 English recommended, 2 math required, 2 math recommended, 2 science required, 2 science recommended, 2 science lab required, 2 science lab recommended, 3 social studies required, 3 social studies recommended, 2 history recommended. **Transfer Admission Requirements:** *Items required:* college transcript. Lowest grade transferable C. **General Admission Information:** Application fee $25. Nonfall registration accepted. Admission may be deferred for a maximum of 2 years. Credit offered for CEEB Advanced Placement tests.

COSTS AND FINANCIAL AID

Tuition $4,500. Room & board $2,500. Required fees $1,200. Average book expense $825. **Required Forms and Deadlines:** FAFSA and institution's own financial aid form. No deadline for regular filing. Priority filing deadline March 1. **Notification of Awards:** Applicants will be notified of awards on a rolling basis beginning on or about March 1. **Types of Aid:** *Need-based scholarships/grants:* Pell, SEOG, state scholarships/grants, private scholarships, the school's own gift aid. *Loans:* FFEL Subsidized Stafford, FFEL Unsubsidized Stafford, FFEL PLUS, alternative loans. **Student Employment:** Federal Work-Study Program available. Institutional employment available. Off-campus job opportunities are fair. **Financial Aid Statistics:** 87% freshmen, 88% undergrads receive some form of aid. Average freshman grant $3,528. Average freshman loan $2,311. **Financial Aid Phone:** 304-253-7351.

MUHLENBERG COLLEGE

2400 West Chew Street, Allentown, PA 18104-5596
Phone: 484-664-3200 **E-mail:** admission@muhlenberg.edu **CEEB Code:** 2424
Fax: 484-664-3234 **Web:** www.muhlenberg.edu **ACT Code:** 3640

This private school, which is affiliated with the Lutheran Church, was founded in 1848. It has an 81-acre campus.

STUDENTS AND FACULTY

Enrollment: 2,470. **Student Body:** Male 44%, female 56%, out-of-state 63%. **Ethnic Representation:** African American 2%, Asian 3%, Caucasian 90%, Hispanic 3%. **Retention and Graduation:** 93% freshmen return for sophomore year. 76% freshmen graduate within 4 years. 28% grads go on to further study within 1 year. 5% grads pursue law degrees. 6% grads pursue medical degrees. **Faculty:** Student/faculty ratio 13:1. 154 full-time faculty, 89% hold PhDs. 100% faculty teach undergrads.

ACADEMICS

Degrees: Associate's, bachelor's, certificate, transfer. **Academic Requirements:** General education including some course work in arts/fine arts, foreign languages, history, humanities, philosophy, sciences (biological or physical), social science, religious studies, nonwestern cultures, writing, reasoning, literature, and physical education. **Classes:** 10-19 students in an average class. 10-19 students in an average lab/discussion section. **Majors with Highest Enrollment:** Business administration/management; biology/biological sciences, general; psychology, general. **Disciplines with Highest Percentage of Degrees Awarded:** Business/marketing 25%, biological life sciences 14%, psychology 13%, social sciences and history 11%, visual and performing arts

10%. **Special Study Options:** Accelerated program, cross registration, double major, honors program, independent study, internships, student-designed major, study abroad, teacher certification program.

FACILITIES

Housing: Coed, all-female, apartments for single students, housing for disabled students, housing for international students, fraternities and/or sororities, college-owned houses in the neighborhood surrounding the campus. **Library Holdings:** 271,260 bound volumes. 1,088 periodicals. 133,121 microforms. 11,416 audiovisuals. **Special Academic Facilities/Equipment:** Martin Art Gallery, biology museum, Graver Arboretum, greenhouse, mainstage theatre, recital hall, 20-foot boat for marine studies, 40-acre Raker Environmental field Station, two electron microscopes, dance studios, experimental theatres, proscenium theatres. **Computers:** *Recommended operating system:* Windows NT/2000. School-owned computers available for student use.

EXTRACURRICULARS

Activities: Choral groups, concert band, dance, drama/theater, jazz band, literary magazine, music ensembles, musical theater, opera, pep band, radio station, student government, student newspaper, symphony orchestra, television station, yearbook. **Organizations:** 123 registered organizations, 15 honor societies, 6 religious organizations, 4 fraternities (27% men join), 4 sororities (22% women join). **Athletics (Intercollegiate):** *Men:* baseball, basketball, cheerleading, cross-country, football, golf, indoor track, lacrosse, soccer, tennis, track & field, wrestling. *Women:* basketball, cheerleading, cross-country, field hockey, golf, indoor track, lacrosse, soccer, softball, tennis, track & field, volleyball.

ADMISSIONS

Selectivity Rating: 82 (of 100). **Freshman Academic Profile:** Average high school GPA 3.7. 39% in top 10% of high school class, 75% in top 25% of high school class, 97% in top 50% of high school class. 70% from public high schools. Average SAT I Math 606, SAT I Math middle 50% range 560-650. Average SAT I Verbal 595, SAT I Verbal middle 50% range 550-640. TOEFL required of all international applicants, minimum TOEFL 550. **Basis for Candidate Selection:** *Very important factors considered include:* character/personal qualities, secondary school record, talent/ability. *Important factors considered include:* class rank, essays, extracurricular activities, interview, recommendations, standardized test scores, volunteer work. *Other factors considered include:* alumni/ae relation, geographical residence, minority status, work experience. **Freshman Admission Requirements:** High school diploma or GED is required. *Academic units required/recommended:* 16 total required; 4 English required, 3 math required, 2 science required, 3 science recommended, 2 science lab required, 2 foreign language required, 3 foreign language recommended, 2 history required, 1 elective required. **Freshman Admission Statistics:** 3,822 applied, 35% accepted, 41% of those accepted enrolled. **Transfer Admission Requirements:** *Items required:* high school transcript, college transcript, essay, interview, standardized test scores. Minimum college GPA of 2.5 required. Lowest grade transferable C-. **General Admission Information:** Application fee $40. Early decision application deadline January 15. Regular application deadline February 15. Nonfall registration accepted. Admission may be deferred for a maximum of 1 year. Credit and/or placement offered for CEEB Advanced Placement tests.

COSTS AND FINANCIAL AID

Tuition $23,250. Room & board $6,295. Required fees $205. Average book expense $750. **Required Forms and Deadlines:** FAFSA, institution's own financial aid form, CSS/Financial Aid PROFILE, noncustodial (divorced/separated) parent's statement and business/farm supplement. Financial aid filing deadline February 15. Priority filing deadline January 15. **Notification of Awards:** Applicants will be notified of awards on or about April 1. **Types of Aid:** *Need-based scholarships/grants:* Pell, SEOG, state scholarships/grants, private scholarships, the school's own gift aid. *Loans:* FFEL Subsidized Stafford, FFEL Unsubsidized Stafford, FFEL PLUS, Federal Perkins. **Student Employment:** Federal Work-Study Program available. Institutional employment available. Off-campus job opportunities are good. **Financial Aid Statistics:** 43% freshmen, 44% undergrads receive some form of aid. Average freshman grant $12,819. Average freshman loan $2,971. Average income from on-campus job $1,178. **Financial Aid Phone:** 484-664-3175.

MULTNOMAH BIBLE COLLEGE AND BIBLICAL SEMINARY

8435 Northeast Glisan Street, Portland, OR 97220-5898
Phone: 503-251-6485 **E-mail:** admiss@multnomah.edu
Fax: 503-254-1268 **Web:** www.multnomah.edu

This private school, which is affiliated with the Christian (Nondenominational) Church, was founded in 1936. It has a 25-acre campus.

STUDENTS AND FACULTY

Enrollment: 582. **Student Body:** Male 56%, female 44%, out-of-state 53%, international 1% (7 countries represented). **Ethnic Representation:** African American 1%, Asian 4%, Caucasian 93%, Hispanic 3%. **Retention and Graduation:** 73% freshmen return for sophomore year. **Faculty:** Student/faculty ratio 18:1. 22 full-time faculty, 54% hold PhDs.

ACADEMICS

Degrees: Bachelor's, first professional, master's, post-bachelor's certificate. **Academic Requirements:** General education including some course work in English (including composition), history, humanities, mathematics, philosophy, sciences (biological or physical), social science, minimum of 56 credit hours in Bible and theology required. **Classes:** 10-19 students in an average class. 10-19 students in an average lab/discussion section. **Majors with Highest Enrollment:** Bible/biblical studies; divinity/ministry (BD, MDiv); youth ministry. **Disciplines with Highest Percentage of Degrees Awarded:** Philosophy/religion/theology 100%. **Special Study Options:** Double major, internships, liberal arts/career combination.

FACILITIES

Housing: All-female, all-male, apartments for married students, apartments for single students. **Library Holdings:** 73,591 bound volumes. 369 periodicals. 7,780 microforms. 11,693 audiovisuals. **Special Academic Facilities/Equipment:** Prayer chapel, weight room, coffee shop. **Computers:** School-owned computers available for student use.

EXTRACURRICULARS

Activities: Choral groups, drama/theater, music ensembles, student government, student newspaper, yearbook. **Athletics (Intercollegiate):** *Men:* basketball. *Women:* volleyball.

ADMISSIONS

Selectivity Rating: 63 (of 100). **Freshman Academic Profile:** TOEFL required of all international applicants, minimum TOEFL 550. **Basis for Candidate Selection:** *Very important factors considered include:* recommendations, religious affiliation/commitment, secondary school record, standardized test scores. *Important factors considered include:* character/personal qualities, essays. *Other factors considered include:* alumni/ae relation, class rank, extracurricular activities, talent/ability, volunteer work, work experience. **Freshman Admission Requirements:** High school diploma or GED is required. *Academic units required/recommended:* 4 English recommended, 2 math recommended, 3 science recommended, 1 science lab recommended, 2 foreign language recommended, 3 social studies recommended, 2 history recommended. **Transfer Admission Requirements:** *Items required:* college transcript, essay, statement of good standing from prior school. Minimum college GPA of 2.0 required. Lowest grade transferable C. **General Admission Information:** Application fee $40. Priority application deadline March 1. Regular application deadline December 15. Nonfall registration accepted. Admission may be deferred. Credit offered for CEEB Advanced Placement tests.

COSTS AND FINANCIAL AID

Tuition $9,920. Room & board $4,450. Required fees $150. Average book expense $800. **Required Forms and Deadlines:** FAFSA and institution's own financial aid form. Financial aid filing deadline August 1. Priority filing deadline March 1. **Notification of Awards:** Applicants will be notified of awards on a rolling basis beginning on or about April 15. **Types of Aid:** *Need-based scholarships/grants:* Pell. *Loans:* Direct Subsidized Stafford, Direct Unsubsidized Stafford, Direct PLUS. **Student Employment:** Federal Work-Study Program available. Off-campus job opportunities are excellent. **Financial Aid Statistics:** 73% freshmen, 84% undergrads receive some form of aid. **Financial Aid Phone:** 503-251-5334.

MURRAY STATE UNIVERSITY

One Murray Street, Murray, KY 42071
Phone: 800-272-4678 **E-mail:** Admissions@murraystate.edu **CEEB Code:** 1494
Fax: 270-762-3050 **Web:** www.murraystate.edu **ACT Code:** 1532

This public school was founded in 1922. It has a 350-acre campus.

STUDENTS AND FACULTY

Enrollment: 8,083. **Student Body:** Male 41%, female 59%, out-of-state 26%, international 3% (64 countries represented). **Ethnic Representation:** African American 6%, Asian 1%, Caucasian 92%, Hispanic 1%. **Retention and Graduation:** 76% freshmen return for sophomore year. 32% freshmen graduate within 4 years. **Faculty:** Student/faculty ratio 16:1. 390 full-time faculty, 77% hold PhDs. 100% faculty teach undergrads.

ACADEMICS

Degrees: Associate's, bachelor's, master's. **Academic Requirements:** General education including some course work in arts/fine arts, computer literacy, English (including composition), history, humanities, mathematics, sciences (biological or physical), social science. **Classes:** Under 10 students in an average class. 10-19 students in an average lab/discussion section. **Disciplines with Highest Percentage of Degrees Awarded:** Business/marketing 17%, education 16%, communications/communication technologies 13%, health professions and related sciences 10%, engineering/engineering technology 7%. **Special Study Options:** Accelerated program, cooperative (work-study) program, cross registration, distance learning, double major, dual enrollment, English as a second language, student exchange program (domestic), external degree program, honors program, independent study, internships, study abroad, teacher certification program.

FACILITIES

Housing: Coed, all-female, all-male, apartments for married students, apartments for single students, housing for disabled students, fraternities and/or sororities. **Library Holdings:** 390,000 bound volumes. 109,600 periodicals. 194,800 microforms. 18,700 audiovisuals. **Computers:** School-owned computers available for student use.

EXTRACURRICULARS

Activities: Choral groups, concert band, dance, drama/theater, jazz band, literary magazine, marching band, music ensembles, musical theater, pep band, radio station, student government, student newspaper, symphony orchestra, television station, yearbook. **Organizations:** 160 registered organizations, 30 honor societies, 15 religious organizations, 13 fraternities (19% men join), 9 sororities (11% women join). **Athletics (Intercollegiate):** *Men:* baseball, basketball, cheerleading, crew, cross-country, equestrian, football, golf, rifle, rodeo, rugby, tennis, track & field. *Women:* basketball, cheerleading, crew, cross-country, equestrian, golf, rifle, rodeo, soccer, tennis, track & field, volleyball.

ADMISSIONS

Selectivity Rating: 79 (of 100). **Freshman Academic Profile:** Average high school GPA 3.5. 32% in top 10% of high school class, 65% in top 25% of high school class, 98% in top 50% of high school class. 80% from public high schools. Average ACT 23, ACT middle 50% range 20-25. TOEFL required of all international applicants, minimum TOEFL 500. **Basis for Candidate Selection:** *Very important factors considered include:* class rank, secondary school record, standardized test scores. *Important factors considered include:* alumni/ae relation, recommendations, talent/ability. *Other factors considered include:* character/personal qualities, essays, extracurricular activities, geographical residence, interview, minority status, state residency, volunteer work, work experience. **Freshman Admission Requirements:** High school diploma or GED is required. *Academic units required/recommended:* 21 total required; 4 English required, 3 math required, 4 math recommended, 3 science required, 4 science recommended, 2 foreign language recommended, 3 social studies required, 8 elective required. **Freshman Admission Statistics:** 2,740 applied, 88% accepted, 59% of those accepted enrolled. **Transfer Admission Requirements:** *Items required:* college transcript, statement of good standing from prior school. Minimum high school GPA of 2.0 required. Minimum college GPA of 4.0 required. Lowest grade transferable D. **General Admission Information:** Application fee $25. Regular application deadline August 3. Nonfall registration accepted. Admission may be deferred for a maximum of 1 year. Credit offered for CEEB Advanced Placement tests.

COSTS AND FINANCIAL AID

In-state tuition $2,540. Out-of-state tuition $7,620. Room & board $4,420. Required fees $490. Average book expense $700. **Required Forms and Deadlines:** FAFSA and institution's own financial aid form. Priority filing deadline April 1. **Notification of Awards:** Applicants will be notified of awards on a rolling basis beginning on or about April 15. **Types of Aid:** *Need-based scholarships/grants:* Pell, SEOG, state scholarships/grants, private scholarships, the school's own gift aid, Federal Nursing. *Loans:* Direct Subsidized Stafford, Direct Unsubsidized Stafford, Direct PLUS, FFEL Subsidized Stafford, FFEL Unsubsidized Stafford, FFEL PLUS, Federal Perkins, Federal Nursing, state loans, college/university loans from institutional funds. **Student Employment:** Federal Work-Study Program available. Institutional employment available. Off-campus job opportunities are good. **Financial Aid Statistics:** 45% freshmen, 44% undergrads receive some form of aid. Average freshman grant $4,575. Average freshman loan $1,845. Average income from on-campus job $1,845. **Financial Aid Phone:** 502-762-2546.

MUSKINGUM COLLEGE

163 Stormont Drive, New Concord, OH 43762
Phone: 614-826-8137 **E-mail:** adminfo@muskingum.edu **CEEB Code:** 1496
Fax: 614-826-8100 **Web:** www.muskingum.edu **ACT Code:** 3305

This private school, which is affiliated with the Presbyterian Church, was founded in 1837. It has a 215-acre campus.

STUDENTS AND FACULTY

Enrollment: 1,686. **Student Body:** Male 50%, female 50%, out-of-state 10%, international 2%. **Ethnic Representation:** African American 3%, Caucasian 95%, Hispanic 1%. **Retention and Graduation:** 77% freshmen return for sophomore year. 46% freshmen graduate within 4 years. 20% grads go on to further study within 1 year. 10% grads pursue business degrees. 15% grads pursue law degrees. 10% grads pursue medical degrees. **Faculty:** Student/faculty ratio 16:1. 93 full-time faculty, 83% hold PhDs. 100% faculty teach undergrads.

ACADEMICS

Degrees: Bachelor's, master's, post-bachelor's certificate, post-master's certificate. **Academic Requirements:** General education including some course work in arts/fine arts, computer literacy, English (including composition), humanities, mathematics, sciences (biological or physical), social science, speech, religion, physical education. **Classes:** 10-19 students in an average class. 20-29 students in an average lab/discussion section. **Majors with Highest Enrollment:** Business administration/management; history, general; elementary education and teaching. **Disciplines with Highest Percentage of Degrees Awarded:** Education 25%, business/marketing 23%, social sciences and history 13%, communications/communication technologies 9%, psychology 8%. **Special Study Options:** Accelerated program, double major, student exchange program (domestic), independent study, internships, student-designed major, study abroad, teacher certification program, English Support Program.

FACILITIES

Housing: Coed, all-female, all-male, apartments for single students, fraternities and/or sororities, cooperative housing. **Library Holdings:** 205,278 bound volumes. 835 periodicals. 152,800 microforms. 4,074 audiovisuals. **Special Academic Facilities/Equipment:** Art gallery, on-campus nursery school, electron microscope, 57-acre biology field station and mobile biology lab. **Computers:** School-owned computers available for student use.

EXTRACURRICULARS

Activities: Choral groups, concert band, dance, drama/theater, jazz band, literary magazine, marching band, music ensembles, musical theater, opera, pep band, radio station, student government, student newspaper, symphony orchestra, television station, yearbook. **Organizations:** 95 registered organizations, 14 honor societies, 4 religious organizations, 5 fraternities (35% men join), 5 sororities (40% women join). **Athletics (Intercollegiate):** *Men:* baseball, basketball, cheerleading, cross-country, football, golf, indoor track, soccer, tennis, track & field, wrestling. *Women:* basketball, cheerleading, cross-country, golf, indoor track, soccer, softball, tennis, track & field, volleyball.

ADMISSIONS

Selectivity Rating: 68 (of 100). **Freshman Academic Profile:** Average high school GPA 3.2. 23% in top 10% of high school class, 43% in top 25% of high school class, 74% in top 50% of high school class. 90% from public high schools. Average SAT I Math 520, SAT I Math middle 50% range 470-570. Average SAT I Verbal 530, SAT I Verbal middle 50% range 470-610. Average ACT 22, ACT middle 50% range 19-25. TOEFL required of all international applicants, minimum TOEFL 550. **Basis for Candidate Selection:** *Very important factors considered include:* secondary school record. *Important factors considered include:* class rank, recommendations, standardized test scores. *Other factors considered include:* alumni/ae relation, character/personal qualities, essays, extracurricular activities, geographical residence, interview, minority status, talent/ability. **Freshman Admission Requirements:** High school diploma or GED is required. *Academic units required/recommended:* 10 total required; 15 total recommended; 4 English required, 4 English recommended, 2 math required, 3 math recommended, 2 science required, 3 science recommended, 2 foreign language required, 2 foreign language recommended, 1 social studies required, 1 social studies recommended, 2 history required, 2 history recommended. **Freshman Admission Statistics:** 1,773 applied, 79% accepted, 32% of those accepted enrolled. **Transfer Admission Requirements:** *Items required:* high school transcript. Minimum college GPA of 2.0 required. Lowest grade transferable C. **General Admission Information:** Priority application deadline March 1. Regular application deadline August 1. Nonfall registration accepted. Admission may be deferred for a maximum of 1 year. Credit and/or placement offered for CEEB Advanced Placement tests.

COSTS AND FINANCIAL AID

Tuition $13,500. Room & board $5,600. Required fees $440. Average book expense $800. **Required Forms and Deadlines:** FAFSA. Priority filing deadline March 15. **Notification of Awards:** Applicants will be notified of awards on a rolling basis beginning on or about March 1. **Types of Aid:** *Need-based scholarships/grants:* Pell, SEOG, state scholarships/grants, private scholarships, the school's own gift aid. *Loans:* FFEL Subsidized Stafford, FFEL Unsubsidized Stafford, FFEL PLUS, Federal Perkins, college/university loans from institutional funds. **Student Employment:** Federal Work-Study Program available. Institutional employment available. Off-campus job opportunities are fair. **Financial Aid Statistics:** 80% freshmen, 76% undergrads receive some form of aid. Average freshman grant $9,000. Average freshman loan $3,600. Average income from on-campus job $800. **Financial Aid Phone:** 740-826-8139.

NAROPA COLLEGE AT NAROPA UNIVERSITY

2130 Araphahoe Avenue, Boulder, CO 80302
Phone: 303-546-3572 **E-mail:** admissions@naropa.edu **CEEB Code:** 908
Fax: 303-546-3583 **Web:** www.naropa.edu **ACT Code:** 4853

This private school was founded in 1974. It has a 5-acre campus.

STUDENTS AND FACULTY

Enrollment: 448. **Student Body:** Male 35%, female 65%, out-of-state 69%, international 4%. **Ethnic Representation:** African American 1%, Asian 2%, Caucasian 80%, Hispanic 3%, Native American 1%. **Retention and Graduation:** 78% freshmen return for sophomore year. **Faculty:** Student/faculty ratio 12:1. 31 full-time faculty, 48% hold PhDs.

ACADEMICS

Degrees: Bachelor's, certificate, first professional, master's, post-bachelor's certificate, post-master's certificate. **Academic Requirements:** General education including some course work in arts/fine arts, English (including composition), humanities, sciences (biological or physical), social science, contemplative practice (t'ai chi, meditation, Aikido), world wisdom (religious studies). **Classes:** 10-19 students in an average class. **Disciplines with Highest Percentage of Degrees Awarded:** Psychology 27%, visual and performing arts 22%, English 16%, interdisciplinary studies 11%, philosophy/religion/theology 8%. **Special Study Options:** Double major, dual enrollment, independent study, internships, student-designed major, study abroad, online courses.

FACILITIES

Housing: Coed. **Library Holdings:** 30,500 bound volumes. 155 periodicals. 0 microforms. 12,000 audiovisuals. **Special Academic Facilities/Equipment:** Maitri Rooms, meditation halls, 20-acre organic farm, Allen Ginsberg library and a preschool. **Computers:** School-owned computers available for student use.

EXTRACURRICULARS

Activities: Choral groups, dance, drama/theater, jazz band, literary magazine, student government, student newspaper. **Organizations:** 23 registered organizations.

ADMISSIONS

Selectivity Rating: 63 (of 100). **Freshman Academic Profile:** Average SAT I Math 535, SAT I Math middle 50% range 470-645. Average SAT I Verbal 546, SAT I Verbal middle 50% range 470-615. Average ACT 22, ACT middle 50% range 17-25. TOEFL required of all international applicants, minimum TOEFL 550. **Basis for Candidate Selection:** *Very important factors considered include:* essays, interview, recommendations, secondary school record. *Important factors considered include:* character/personal qualities, extracurricular activities, talent/ability, volunteer work. *Other factors considered include:* alumni/ae relation, minority status, standardized test scores, work experience. **Freshman Admission Requirements:** High school diploma or GED is required. *Academic units required/recommended:* 4 English recommended, 4 math recommended, 4 science recommended, 1 science lab recommended, 4 foreign language recommended, 3 social studies recommended, 3 history recommended, 3 elective recommended. **Freshman Admission Statistics:** 97 applied, 84% accepted, 49% of those accepted enrolled. **Transfer Admission Requirements:** *Items required:* college transcript, essay, interview. Lowest grade transferable C. **General Admission Information:** Application fee $35. Nonfall registration accepted. Admission may be deferred for a maximum of 1 year. Credit and/or placement offered for CEEB Advanced Placement tests.

COSTS AND FINANCIAL AID

Tuition $15,300. Required fees $560. Average book expense $600. **Required Forms and Deadlines:** FAFSA. No deadline for regular filing. **Notification of Awards:** Applicants will be notified of awards on a rolling basis beginning on or about April 1. **Types of Aid:** *Need-based scholarships/grants:* Pell, SEOG, private scholarships, the school's own gift aid. *Loans:* FFEL Subsidized Stafford, FFEL Unsubsidized Stafford, FFEL PLUS, Federal Perkins, private alternative loans. **Student Employment:** Federal Work-Study Program available. Off-campus job opportunities are good. **Financial Aid Statistics:** 76% freshmen, 66% undergrads receive some form of aid. Average freshman grant $7,088. Average freshman loan $4,992. **Financial Aid Phone:** 303-546-3534.

See page 1128.

NATIONAL UNIVERSITY

11255 North Torrey Pinos Road, La Jolla, CA 92037
Phone: 858-642-8180 **E-mail:** advisor@nu.edu **CEEB Code:** 4557
Fax: 858-642-8710 **Web:** www.nu.edu **ACT Code:** 20015

This private school was founded in 1971.

STUDENTS AND FACULTY

Enrollment: 4,776. **Student Body:** Male 43%, female 57%, out-of-state 0%, international 1% (70 countries represented). **Ethnic Representation:** African American 13%, Asian 9%, Caucasian 53%, Hispanic 19%, Native American 1%. **Retention and Graduation:** 40% freshmen return for sophomore year. **Faculty:** Student/faculty ratio 16:1. 151 full-time faculty, 86% hold PhDs. 100% faculty teach undergrads.

ACADEMICS

Degrees: Associate's, bachelor's, master's, post-bachelor's certificate, terminal, transfer. **Academic Requirements:** General education including some course work in arts/fine arts, computer literacy, English (including composition), humanities, mathematics, sciences (biological or physical), social science. **Classes:** 10-19 students in an average class. **Majors with Highest Enrollment:** Business/commerce, general; multi/interdisciplinary studies; criminal justice/law enforcement administration. **Disciplines with Highest Percentage of Degrees Awarded:** Business/marketing 24%, computer and information sciences 19%, interdisciplinary studies 18%, psychology 16%, liberal arts/general studies 9%. **Special Study Options:** Accelerated program, distance learning, double major, dual enrollment, English as a second language, teacher certification program.

FACILITIES

Library Holdings: 226,049 bound volumes. 2,794 periodicals. 2,530,352 microforms. 5,539 audiovisuals. **Computers:** School-owned computers available for student use.

EXTRACURRICULARS

Activities: Literary magazine.

ADMISSIONS

Selectivity Rating: 62 (of 100). **Freshman Academic Profile:** TOEFL required of all international applicants, minimum TOEFL 525. **Basis for Candidate Selection:** *Important factors considered include:* interview, work experience. *Other factors considered include:* essays, extracurricular activities. **Freshman Admission Requirements:** High school diploma or GED is required. **Freshman Admission Statistics:** 156 applied, 100% accepted, 36% of those accepted enrolled. **Transfer Admission Requirements:** *Items required:* high school transcript, college transcript, essay, interview, statement of good standing from prior school. Minimum college GPA of 2.0 required.

Lowest grade transferable C. **General Admission Information:** Application fee $60. Nonfall registration accepted. Admission may be deferred for a maximum of 1 year. Neither credit nor placement offered for CEEB Advanced Placement tests.

COSTS AND FINANCIAL AID

Tuition $7,965. Required fees $60. **Required Forms and Deadlines:** FAFSA, institution's own financial aid form and state aid form. No deadline for regular filing. **Notification of Awards:** Applicants will be notified of awards on a rolling basis. **Types of Aid:** *Need-based scholarships/grants:* Pell, SEOG, state scholarships/grants, private scholarships, the school's own gift aid. *Loans:* Direct Subsidized Stafford, Direct Unsubsidized Stafford, FFEL Subsidized Stafford, FFEL Unsubsidized Stafford, FFEL PLUS, Federal Perkins. **Student Employment:** Institutional employment available. Off-campus job opportunities are good. **Financial Aid Phone:** 619-573-7175.

NATIONAL-LOUIS UNIVERSITY

2840 Sheridan Road, Evanston, IL 60201
Phone: 847-465-0575 **E-mail:** nlnuinfo@wheeling1.nl.edu
Web: www.nl.edu **ACT Code:** 1094

This private school was founded in 1886.

STUDENTS AND FACULTY

Enrollment: 3,586. **Student Body:** Male 28%, female 72%, out-of-state 1%, international 1% (20 countries represented). **Ethnic Representation:** African American 26%, Asian 3%, Caucasian 57%, Hispanic 8%. **Retention and Graduation:** 60% freshmen return for sophomore year. 7% freshmen graduate within 4 years.

ACADEMICS

Degrees: Bachelor's, certificate, doctoral, master's, post-bachelor's certificate, post-master's certificate. **Academic Requirements:** General education including some course work in English (including composition), humanities, sciences (biological or physical), social science. **Special Study Options:** Accelerated program, distance learning, English as a second language, honors program, independent study, internships, general degree completion programs in liberal arts and business for upper level.

FACILITIES

Housing: Coed. **Library Holdings:** 131,934 bound volumes. 3,498 periodicals. 925,978 microforms. 5,043 audiovisuals. **Special Academic Facilities/ Equipment:** Pre K-8 elementary demonstration school. **Computers:** School-owned computers available for student use.

EXTRACURRICULARS

Activities: Drama/theater, musical theater, student government, student newspaper. **Organizations:** 15 registered organizations, 1 honor society, 2 religious organizations. **Athletics (Intercollegiate):** *Men:* soccer, softball, volleyball.

ADMISSIONS

Selectivity Rating: 63 (of 100). **Freshman Academic Profile:** 29% in top 25% of high school class, 89% in top 50% of high school class. Average ACT 18, ACT middle 50% range 15-20. **Basis for Candidate Selection:** *Very important factors considered include:* secondary school record. *Important factors considered include:* standardized test scores. *Other factors considered include:* class rank, essays, interview, recommendations. **Freshman Admission Requirements:** High school diploma or GED is required. *Academic units required/recommended:* 4 English recommended, 3 math recommended, 2 science recommended, 1 science lab recommended, 2 foreign language recommended, 3 social studies recommended. **Freshman Admission Statistics:** 320 applied, 100% accepted, 66% of those accepted enrolled. **Transfer Admission Requirements:** *Items required:* college transcript, statement of good standing from prior school. Minimum college GPA of 2.0 required. Lowest grade transferable C. **General Admission Information:** Application fee $25. Nonfall registration accepted. Admission may be deferred for a maximum of 2 years. Credit offered for CEEB Advanced Placement tests.

COSTS AND FINANCIAL AID

Tuition $13,095. Room & board $6,336. Average book expense $250. **Required Forms and Deadlines:** FAFSA and institution's own financial aid form. No deadline for regular filing. Priority filing deadline April 15. **Notification of Awards:** Applicants will be notified of awards on a rolling basis. **Types of Aid:** *Need-based scholarships/grants:* Pell, SEOG, state scholarships/grants, the school's own gift aid. *Loans:* Direct Subsidized Stafford, Direct Unsubsidized Stafford, Direct PLUS, Federal Perkins. **Student Employment:** Federal Work-Study Program available. Institutional employment available. Off-campus job opportunities are good. **Financial Aid Phone:** 800-443-5522.

NAZARETH COLLEGE OF ROCHESTER

4245 East Avenue, Rochester, NY 14618-3790
Phone: 585-389-2860 **E-mail:** admissions@naz.edu **CEEB Code:** 2511
Fax: 585-389-2826 **Web:** www.naz.edu **ACT Code:** 2826

This private school was founded in 1924. It has a 150-acre campus.

STUDENTS AND FACULTY

Enrollment: 1,969. **Student Body:** Male 25%, female 75%, out-of-state 6%, international students represent 8 countries. **Ethnic Representation:** African American 4%, Asian 2%, Caucasian 90%, Hispanic 2%. **Retention and Graduation:** 86% freshmen return for sophomore year. 62% freshmen graduate within 4 years. 42% grads go on to further study within 1 year. 1% grads pursue business degrees. 1% grads pursue law degrees. 1% grads pursue medical degrees. **Faculty:** Student/faculty ratio 13:1. 132 full-time faculty, 91% hold PhDs. 97% faculty teach undergrads.

ACADEMICS

Degrees: Bachelor's, master's, post-master's certificate. **Academic Requirements:** General education including some course work in arts/fine arts, computer literacy, English (including composition), foreign languages, history, humanities, mathematics, philosophy, sciences (biological or physical), social science. **Classes:** 10-19 students in an average class. 10-19 students in an average lab/discussion section. **Majors with Highest Enrollment:** Business administration/management; education, general; psychology, general. **Disciplines with Highest Percentage of Degrees Awarded:** Health professions and related sciences 21%, business/marketing 15%, social sciences and history 11%, psychology 11%, education 9%. **Special Study Options:** Cross registration, double major, student exchange program (domestic), honors program, independent study, internships, study abroad, teacher certification program.

FACILITIES

Housing: Coed, all-female, apartments for single students, housing for disabled students, substance free, quiet floor, language house floors, honors floor, first-year experience floor. **Library Holdings:** 162,593 bound volumes. 1,888 periodicals. 438,204 microforms. 12,236 audiovisuals. **Special Academic Facilities/Equipment:** Arts center, speech/hearing/language clinic, reading clinic, psychology center, center for service learning, Center for Teaching Excellence, and Center for International Education. **Computers:** School-owned computers available for student use.

EXTRACURRICULARS

Activities: Choral groups, concert band, dance, drama/theater, jazz band, music ensembles, radio station, student government, student newspaper, yearbook. **Organizations:** 33 registered organizations, 19 honor societies, 1 religious organization. **Athletics (Intercollegiate):** *Men:* basketball, cross-country, diving, equestrian, golf, lacrosse, soccer, swimming, tennis, track & field. *Women:* basketball, cheerleading, cross-country, diving, equestrian, field hockey, golf, lacrosse, soccer, swimming, tennis, track & field, volleyball.

ADMISSIONS

Selectivity Rating: 75 (of 100). **Freshman Academic Profile:** Average high school GPA 3.0. 31% in top 10% of high school class, 70% in top 25% of high school class, 90% in top 50% of high school class. 90% from public high schools. Average SAT I Math 562, SAT I Math middle 50% range 515-615. Average SAT I Verbal 569, SAT I Verbal middle 50% range 525-625. Average ACT 25, ACT middle 50% range 23-27. TOEFL required of all international applicants, minimum TOEFL 550. **Basis for Candidate Selection:** *Very important factors considered include:* class rank, secondary school record, standardized test scores. *Important factors considered include:* essays, interview, minority status, recommendations, volunteer work, work experience. *Other factors considered include:* alumni/ae relation, character/personal qualities, extracurricular activities, geographical residence, state residency, talent/ability. **Freshman Admission Requirements:** High school diploma or GED is required. *Academic units required/recommended:* 4 English required, 3 math required, 4 math recommended, 3 science required, 4 science recommended, 2 science lab required, 3 foreign language required, 4 foreign language recommended, 3 social studies required, 4 social studies recommended. **Freshman Admission Statistics:** 1,654 applied, 84% accepted, 28% of those accepted enrolled. **Transfer Admission Requirements:** *Items required:* college transcript, essay. Minimum college GPA of 2.5 required. Lowest grade transferable C. **General Admission Information:** Application fee $40. Early decision application deadline November 15. Regular application deadline February 15. Nonfall registration accepted. Admission may be deferred for a maximum of 1 year. Credit and/or placement offered for CEEB Advanced Placement tests.

COSTS AND FINANCIAL AID

Tuition $15,910. Room & board $6,930. Required fees $466. Average book expense $650. **Required Forms and Deadlines:** FAFSA. Financial aid filing deadline May 1. Priority filing deadline February 15. **Notification of Awards:** Applicants will be notified of awards on a rolling basis beginning on or about February 20. **Types of Aid:** *Need-based scholarships/grants:* Pell, SEOG, state scholarships/grants, private scholarships, the school's own gift aid. *Loans:* FFEL Subsidized Stafford, FFEL Unsubsidized Stafford, FFEL PLUS, Federal Perkins. **Student Employment:** Federal Work-Study Program available. Institutional employment available. Off-campus job opportunities are excellent. **Financial Aid Statistics:** 77% freshmen, 80% undergrads receive some form of aid. Average freshman grant $10,802. Average freshman loan $2,964. Average income from on-campus job $1,165. **Financial Aid Phone:** 585-389-2310.

See page 1130.

NEBRASKA METHODIST COLLEGE

8501 West Dodge Road, Omaha, NE 68114
Phone: 402-354-4879 **E-mail:** admissions@methodistcollege.edu **CEEB Code:** 6510
Fax: 402-354-8875 **Web:** www.methodistcollege.edu **ACT Code:** 2465

This private school, which is affiliated with the Methodist Church, was founded in 1891. It has a 6-acre campus.

STUDENTS AND FACULTY

Enrollment: 304. **Student Body:** Male 9%, female 91%, out-of-state 30%, international 1% (1 country represented). **Ethnic Representation:** African American 5%, Asian 1%, Caucasian 92%, Hispanic 2%. **Retention and Graduation:** 80% freshmen return for sophomore year. 10% grads go on to further study within 1 year. **Faculty:** Student/faculty ratio 10:1. 31 full-time faculty, 41% hold PhDs. 100% faculty teach undergrads.

ACADEMICS

Degrees: Associate's, bachelor's, certificate, master's, post-master's certificate. **Academic Requirements:** General education including some course work in computer literacy, English (including composition), humanities, mathematics, sciences (biological or physical), social science. **Classes:** 20-29 students in an average class. Under 10 students in an average lab/discussion section. **Majors with Highest Enrollment:** Nursing/registered nurse training (RN, ASN, BSN, MSN); diagnostic medical sonography/sonographer and ultrasound technician. **Disciplines with Highest Percentage of Degrees Awarded:** Health professions and related sciences 50%. **Special Study Options:** Accelerated program, independent study.

FACILITIES

Housing: Coed. **Library Holdings:** 15,176 bound volumes. 749 periodicals. 165 microforms. 609 audiovisuals. **Computers:** *Recommended operating system:* Windows NT/2000. School-owned computers available for student use.

EXTRACURRICULARS

Activities: Student government. **Organizations:** 11 registered organizations, 2 honor societies.

ADMISSIONS

Selectivity Rating: 63 (of 100). **Freshman Academic Profile:** Average high school GPA 3.6. 12% in top 10% of high school class, 12% in top 25% of high school class, 50% in top 50% of high school class. 90% from public high schools. Average ACT 20, ACT middle 50% range 18-22. TOEFL required of all international applicants, minimum TOEFL 550. **Basis for Candidate Selection:** *Very important factors considered include:* secondary school record, standardized test scores. *Important factors considered include:* character/personal qualities, class rank, essays, interview, recommendations. *Other factors considered include:* alumni/ae relation, geographical residence, minority status, state residency, volunteer work, work experience. **Freshman Admission Requirements:** High school diploma or GED is required. *Academic units required/recommended:* 4 English required, 3 math required, 2 science required, 2 science lab required, 2 social studies required. **Freshman Admission Statistics:** 54 applied, 83% accepted, 69% of those accepted enrolled. **Transfer Admission Requirements:** *Items required:* high school transcript, college transcript, essay, interview, statement of good standing from prior school. Minimum high school GPA of 2.0 required. Minimum college GPA of 2.0 required. Lowest grade transferable C. **General Admission Information:** Application fee $25. Priority application deadline January 1. Regular application deadline April 1. Nonfall registration accepted. Admission may be deferred for a maximum of 1 year. Credit offered for CEEB Advanced Placement tests.

COSTS AND FINANCIAL AID

Tuition $9,300. Room & board $1,500. Required fees $600. Average book expense $700. **Required Forms and Deadlines:** FAFSA and institution's own financial aid form. No deadline for regular filing. **Notification of Awards:** Applicants will be notified of awards on a rolling basis beginning on or about March 1. **Types of Aid:** *Need-based scholarships/grants:* Pell, SEOG, state scholarships/grants, private scholarships, the school's own gift aid. *Loans:* FFEL Subsidized Stafford, FFEL Unsubsidized Stafford, FFEL PLUS, Federal Perkins, Federal Nursing, college/university loans from institutional funds, alternative loans. **Student Employment:** Off-campus job opportunities are good. **Financial Aid Statistics:** 73% freshmen, 62% undergrads receive some form of aid. Average freshman grant $2,500. Average freshman loan $3,000. **Financial Aid Phone:** 402-354-4874.

NEBRASKA WESLEYAN UNIVERSITY

Admissions Office, 5000 Saint Paul Avenue, Lincoln, NE 68504
Phone: 402-465-2218 **E-mail:** admissions@nebrwesleyan.edu **CEEB Code:** 6470
Fax: 402-465-2179 **Web:** www.nebrwesleyan.edu **ACT Code:** 2474

This private school, which is affiliated with the Methodist Church, was founded in 1887. It has a 50-acre campus.

STUDENTS AND FACULTY

Enrollment: 1,559. **Student Body:** Male 45%, female 55%, out-of-state 6%, international students represent 9 countries. **Ethnic Representation:** African American 1%, Asian 2%, Caucasian 95%, Hispanic 1%. **Retention and Graduation:** 80% freshmen return for sophomore year. 52% freshmen graduate within 4 years. 30% grads go on to further study within 1 year. **Faculty:** Student/faculty ratio 14:1. 95 full-time faculty, 84% hold PhDs. 100% faculty teach undergrads.

ACADEMICS

Degrees: Bachelor's, certificate, master's. **Academic Requirements:** General education including some course work in arts/fine arts, English (including composition), foreign languages, humanities, mathematics, philosophy, sciences (biological or physical), social science, liberal arts seminar; health and human performance. **Classes:** 10-19 students in an average class. 10-19 students in an average lab/discussion section. **Majors with Highest Enrollment:** Business administration/management; biology/biological sciences, general; parks, recreation, leisure and fitness studies. **Disciplines with Highest Percentage of Degrees Awarded:** Business/marketing 25%, biological life sciences 11%, social sciences and history 10%, parks and recreation 10%, education 8%. **Special Study Options:** Double major, dual enrollment, student exchange program (domestic), independent study, internships, liberal arts/career combination, study abroad, teacher certification program, 3-2 engineering program with Washington University or Columbia University, Capitol Hill Internship Program in DC, Urban Life Center in Chicago.

FACILITIES

Housing: Coed, all-female, apartments for single students, fraternities and/or sororities. **Library Holdings:** 201,089 bound volumes. 665 periodicals. 4,547 microforms. 6,165 audiovisuals. **Special Academic Facilities/Equipment:** Art galleries, psychology/sleep lab, observatory and planetarium, greenhouse, laboratory theatre, herbarium, nuclear magnetic resonance laboratory. **Computers:** School-owned computers available for student use.

EXTRACURRICULARS

Activities: Choral groups, concert band, drama/theater, jazz band, literary magazine, music ensembles, musical theater, opera, pep band, student government, student newspaper, yearbook. **Organizations:** 87 registered organizations, 21 honor societies, 2 religious organizations, 4 fraternities (26% men join), 4 sororities (27% women join). **Athletics (Intercollegiate):** *Men:* baseball, basketball, cross-country, football, golf, indoor track, soccer, tennis, track & field. *Women:* basketball, cross-country, golf, indoor track, soccer, softball, tennis, track & field, volleyball.

ADMISSIONS

Selectivity Rating: 71 (of 100). **Freshman Academic Profile:** 22% in top 10% of high school class, 59% in top 25% of high school class, 89% in top 50% of high school class. Average ACT 24, ACT middle 50% range 21-27. TOEFL required of all international applicants, minimum TOEFL 525. **Basis for Candidate Selection:** *Very important factors considered include:* class rank, secondary school record, standardized test scores. *Important factors considered include:* character/personal qualities, interview, minority status, talent/ability. *Other factors considered include:* alumni/ae relation, essays, extracurricular activities, geographical residence, recommendations, volunteer work. **Freshman Admission Requirements:** High school diploma or GED is required. *Academic units required/recommended:* 4 English recommended, 4 math recommended, 4 science recommended, 4 foreign language recommended, 3 social studies recommended. **Freshman Admission Statistics:** 1,030 applied, 93% accepted, 35% of those accepted enrolled. **Transfer Admission Requirements:** *Items required:* college transcript, statement of good standing from prior school. Minimum college GPA of 2.0 required. Lowest grade transferable C-. **General Admission Information:** Application fee $20. Early decision application deadline November 15. Regular application deadline August 15. Nonfall registration accepted. Admission may be deferred for a maximum of 1 year. Credit offered for CEEB Advanced Placement tests.

COSTS AND FINANCIAL AID

Tuition $16,140. Room & board $4,530. Required fees $284. Average book expense $800. **Required Forms and Deadlines:** FAFSA. No deadline for regular filing. **Notification of Awards:** Applicants will be notified of awards on a rolling basis beginning on or about December 15. **Types of Aid:** *Need-based scholarships/grants:* Pell, SEOG, state scholarships/grants, private scholarships, the school's own gift aid. *Loans:* FFEL Subsidized Stafford, FFEL Unsubsidized Stafford, FFEL PLUS, Federal Perkins, United Methodist Loans. **Student Employment:** Federal Work-Study Program available. Institutional employment available. Off-campus job opportunities are excellent. **Financial Aid Statistics:** 77% freshmen, 71% undergrads receive some form of aid. Average freshman grant $6,958. Average freshman loan $2,621. Average income from on-campus job $1,110. **Financial Aid Phone:** 402-465-2212.

NEUMANN COLLEGE

One Neumann Drive, Aston, PA 19014
Phone: 610-558-5616 **E-mail:** neumann@neumann.edu **CEEB Code:** 2628
Fax: 610-558-5652 **Web:** www.neumann.edu **ACT Code:** 3649

This private school, which is affiliated with the Roman Catholic Church, was founded in 1965. It has a 37-acre campus.

STUDENTS AND FACULTY

Enrollment: 1,853. **Student Body:** Male 36%, female 64%, out-of-state 27%, international students represent 8 countries. **Ethnic Representation:** African American 13%, Asian 1%, Caucasian 78%, Hispanic 1%. **Retention and Graduation:** 71% freshmen return for sophomore year. 47% freshmen graduate within 4 years. 20% grads go on to further study within 1 year. 7% grads pursue business degrees. 2% grads pursue law degrees. 1% grads pursue medical degrees. **Faculty:** Student/faculty ratio 16:1. 67 full-time faculty, 62% hold PhDs. 98% faculty teach undergrads.

ACADEMICS

Degrees: Associate's, bachelor's, certificate, master's, post-master's certificate, terminal. **Academic Requirements:** General education including some course work in arts/fine arts, computer literacy, English (including composition), foreign languages, mathematics, philosophy, sciences (biological or physical), social science, religion, interdisciplinary studies, communication arts. **Classes:** 20-29 students in an average class. 20-29 students in an average lab/discussion section. **Majors with Highest Enrollment:** Nursing/registered nurse training (RN, ASN, BSN, MSN); education, general; business administration/management. **Disciplines with Highest Percentage of Degrees Awarded:** Liberal arts/general studies 28%, business/marketing 18%, education 17%, health professions and related sciences 12%, psychology 7%. **Special Study Options:** Accelerated program, cooperative (work-study) program, distance learning, double major, honors program, independent study, internships, liberal arts/career combination, student-designed major, study abroad, teacher certification program, weekend college.

FACILITIES

Housing: Coed, housing for disabled students, off-campus housing. **Library Holdings:** 90,000 bound volumes. 700 periodicals. 99,758 microforms. 36,562 audiovisuals. **Special Academic Facilities/Equipment:** Child development center. **Computers:** *Recommended operating system:* Windows NT/2000. School-owned computers available for student use.

EXTRACURRICULARS

Activities: Choral groups, dance, drama/theater, jazz band, literary magazine, music ensembles, musical theater, student government, student newspaper. **Organizations:** 14 registered organizations, 4 honor societies, 2 religious organizations. **Athletics (Intercollegiate):** *Men:* baseball, basketball, golf, ice hockey, lacrosse, soccer, tennis. *Women:* basketball, field hockey, ice hockey, lacrosse, soccer, softball, tennis, volleyball.

ADMISSIONS

Selectivity Rating: 66 (of 100). **Freshman Academic Profile:** Average high school GPA 3.0. 60% from public high schools. Average SAT I Math 440, SAT I Math middle 50% range 390-480. Average SAT I Verbal 450, SAT I Verbal middle 50% range 400-490. TOEFL required of all international applicants, minimum TOEFL 550. **Basis for Candidate Selection:** *Very important factors considered include:* extracurricular activities, recommendations, secondary school record, talent/ability. *Important factors considered include:* alumni/ae relation, character/personal qualities, class rank, interview, standardized test scores. *Other factors considered include:* minority status, religious affiliation/commitment, volunteer work. **Freshman Admission Requirements:** High school diploma or GED is required. *Academic units required/recommended:* 16 total required; 17 total recommended; 4 English required, 4 English recommended, 2 math required, 2 math recommended, 2 science required, 3 science recommended, 2 foreign language required, 2 foreign language recommended, 2 social studies required, 2 social studies recommended, 4 elective required, 4 elective recommended. **Freshman Admission Statistics:** 1,207 applied, 95% accepted, 33% of those accepted enrolled. **Transfer Admission Requirements:** *Items required:* college transcript. Minimum college GPA of 2.0 required. Lowest grade transferable C. **General Admission Information:** Application fee $35. Nonfall registration accepted. Admission may be deferred for a maximum of 1 year. Credit offered for CEEB Advanced Placement tests.

COSTS AND FINANCIAL AID

Tuition $15,060. Room & board $7,260. Required fees $590. Average book expense $1,300. **Required Forms and Deadlines:** FAFSA. No deadline for regular filing. **Notification of Awards:** Applicants will be notified of awards on a rolling basis beginning on or about March 1. **Types of Aid:** *Need-based scholarships/grants:* Pell, SEOG, state scholarships/grants, private scholarships, the school's own gift aid, Federal Nursing. *Loans:* Direct Subsidized Stafford, Direct Unsubsidized Stafford, Direct PLUS, FFEL Subsidized Stafford, FFEL Unsubsidized Stafford, FFEL PLUS, Federal Nursing. **Student Employment:** Federal Work-Study Program available. Institutional employment available. Off-campus job opportunities are excellent. **Financial Aid Statistics:** 95% freshmen, 90% undergrads receive some form of aid. Average freshman grant $15,000. Average freshman loan $2,800. Average income from on-campus job $5,000. **Financial Aid Phone:** 610-558-5521.

NEW COLLEGE OF CALIFORNIA

741 Valencia street, San Francisco, CA 94110
Phone: 415-437-3460 **CEEB Code:** 4555
Fax: 415-861-0461 **Web:** www.newcollege.edu

This private school was founded in 1971. It has a 1-acre campus.

STUDENTS AND FACULTY

Enrollment: 1,402. **Student Body:** Male 43%, female 57%, international students represent 6 countries. **Ethnic Representation:** African American 1%, Caucasian 96%, Hispanic 1%, Native American 1%. **Retention and Graduation:** 15% grads go on to further study within 1 year. 5% grads pursue law degrees.

ACADEMICS

Degrees: Associate's, bachelor's, certificate, diploma, first professional, master's, terminal. **Special Study Options:** Accelerated program, cooperative (work-study) program, distance learning, English as a second language, independent study, internships, liberal arts/career combination, student-designed major, study abroad, teacher certification program, weekend college.

FACILITIES

Library Holdings: 30,000 bound volumes. 100 periodicals. 100 microforms. **Special Academic Facilities/Equipment:** Arts studio, video editing lab, letter press lab. **Computers:** *Recommended operating system:* Mac. School-owned computers available for student use.

EXTRACURRICULARS

Activities: Choral groups, drama/theater, jazz band, literary magazine, student newspaper.

ADMISSIONS

Selectivity Rating: 60 (of 100). **Freshman Academic Profile:** TOEFL required of all international applicants, **Basis for Candidate Selection:** *Very* *important factors considered include:* secondary school record. *Important factors considered include:* geographical residence, interview, minority status, state residency, work experience. *Other factors considered include:* volunteer work. **Freshman Admission Requirements:** High school diploma or GED is required. **Transfer Admission Requirements:** *Items required:* high school transcript, college transcript, essay. Lowest grade transferable C. **General Admission Information:** Early decision application deadline March 1. Regular application deadline rolling. Nonfall registration accepted. Admission may be deferred.

COSTS AND FINANCIAL AID

Tuition $8,200. Average book expense $650. **Required Forms and Deadlines:** FAFSA, institution's own financial aid form and state aid form. No deadline for regular filing. Priority filing deadline March 2. **Notification of Awards:** Applicants will be notified of awards on a rolling basis beginning on or about May 15. **Types of Aid:** *Need-based scholarships/grants:* Pell, SEOG, state scholarships/grants, private scholarships, the school's own gift aid. *Loans:* Direct Subsidized Stafford, Direct Unsubsidized Stafford, FFEL PLUS, Federal Perkins. **Student Employment:** Federal Work-Study Program available. Off-campus job opportunities are good. **Financial Aid Statistics:** Average freshman grant $8,200. Average income from on-campus job $3,000. **Financial Aid Phone:** 415-241-1300.

NEW COLLEGE OF FLORIDA

5700 North Tamiami Trail, Sarasota, FL 34243-2197
Phone: 941-359-4269 **E-mail:** admissions@ncf.edu **CEEB Code:** 5506
Fax: 941-359-4435 **Web:** www.ncf.edu **ACT Code:** 750

This public school was founded in 1960. It has a 144-acre campus.

STUDENTS AND FACULTY

Enrollment: 650. **Student Body:** Out-of-state 24%, international 2% (8 countries represented). **Ethnic Representation:** African American 2%, Asian 3%, Caucasian 87%, Hispanic 6%. **Retention and Graduation:** 77% freshmen return for sophomore year. 47% freshmen graduate within 4 years. **Faculty:** Student/faculty ratio 11:1. 60 full-time faculty, 98% hold PhDs. 100% faculty teach undergrads.

ACADEMICS

Degrees: Bachelor's. **Academic Requirements:** Student must receive credit for the satisfactory completion of eight courses in the liberal arts curriculum of the college. These courses must include at least one course in each of the three divisions: humanities (including fine arts), social sciences (including behavioral sciences and history), and natural sciences (including mathematics). Other coursework requirements are defined by the student's individualized academic contract and, after declaration of an area of concentration (major), by academic contract within the framework of the concentration. **Classes:** 10-19 students in an average class. **Disciplines with Highest Percentage of Degrees Awarded:** Liberal arts/general studies 100%. **Special Study Options:** Accelerated program, cross registration, double major, student exchange program (domestic), honors program, independent study, internships, student-designed major, study abroad, Academic contract, January interterm (independent study), narrative evaluation/pass-fail.

FACILITIES

Housing: Coed, apartments for single students, housing for disabled students, wellness housing. **Library Holdings:** 256,581 bound volumes. 1,925 periodicals. 548,156 microforms. 4,195 audiovisuals. **Special Academic Facilities/Equipment:** Anthropology and psychology labs; electronic music lab; individual studio space for senior art students; marine biology research center with Living Ecosystem Teaching and Research Aquarium, wet lab, and seawater on tap; NMR; scanning electron microscope; inert atmosphere glovebox; transparent fume hoods; greenhouse. **Computers:** School-owned computers available for student use.

EXTRACURRICULARS

Activities: Choral groups, concert band, dance, drama/theater, literary magazine, music ensembles, musical theater, opera, radio station, student government, student newspaper, student-run film society. **Organizations:** 90 registered organizations.

ADMISSIONS

Selectivity Rating: 97 (of 100). **Freshman Academic Profile:** Average high school GPA 3.9. 51% in top 10% of high school class, 91% in top 25% of high school class, 97% in top 50% of high school class. 81% from public high schools. Average SAT I Math 637, SAT I Math middle 50% range 590-680. Average SAT I Verbal 693, SAT I Verbal middle 50% range 640-730. Average ACT 27, ACT middle 50% range 27-29. TOEFL required of all international applicants, minimum TOEFL 560. **Basis for Candidate Selection:** *Very important factors considered include:* essays, secondary school record. *Important factors considered include:* character/personal qualities, recommendations, standardized test scores. *Other factors considered include:* alumni/ae relation, class rank, extracurricular activities, geographical residence, interview, state residency, talent/ability, volunteer work, work experience. **Freshman Admission Requirements:** High school diploma or GED is required. *Academic units required/recommended:* 19 total required; 20 total recommended; 4 English required, 4 English recommended, 3 math required, 3 math recommended, 3 science required, 3 science recommended, 2 science lab required, 2 science lab recommended, 2 foreign language required, 2 foreign language recommended, 3 social studies required, 3 social studies recommended, 4 elective required, 5 elective recommended. **Freshman Admission Statistics:** 494 applied, 65% accepted, 50% of those accepted enrolled. **Transfer Admission Requirements:** *Items required:* high school transcript, college transcript, essay, standardized test score, statement of good standing from prior school. Minimum high school GPA of 2.0 required. Minimum college GPA of 2.0 required. Lowest grade transferable C. **General Admission Information:** Application fee $20. Priority application deadline February 1. Regular application deadline May 1. Nonfall registration accepted. Admission may be deferred for a maximum of 1 year. Neither credit nor placement offered for CEEB Advanced Placement tests.

COSTS AND FINANCIAL AID

In-state tuition $3,020. Out-of-state tuition $13,810. Room & board $5,394. Required fees $0. Average book expense $750. **Required Forms and Deadlines:** FAFSA. No deadline for regular filing. Priority filing deadline March 1. **Notification of Awards:** Applicants will be notified of awards on a rolling basis beginning on or about October 1. **Types of Aid:** *Need-based scholarships/grants:* Pell, state scholarships/grants, private scholarships, the school's own gift aid. *Loans:* FFEL Subsidized Stafford, FFEL Unsubsidized Stafford, FFEL PLUS. **Student Employment:** Institutional employment available. Off-campus job opportunities are good. **Financial Aid Statistics:** 45% freshmen, 42% undergrads receive some form of aid. Average freshman loan $2,181. **Financial Aid Phone:** 941-359-4255.

See page 1132.

NEW ENGLAND COLLEGE

26 Bridge Street, Henniker, NH 03242
Phone: 603-428-2223 **E-mail:** admission@nec.edu **CEEB Code:** 3657
Fax: 603-428-3155 **Web:** www.nec.edu **ACT Code:** 2513

This private school was founded in 1946. It has a 225-acre campus.

STUDENTS AND FACULTY

Enrollment: 836. **Student Body:** Male 48%, female 52%, out-of-state 74%, international 2%. **Ethnic Representation:** African American 1%, Asian 2%, Caucasian 83%, Hispanic 1%. **Retention and Graduation:** 66% freshmen return for sophomore year. 33% freshmen graduate within 4 years. 25% grads go on to further study within 1 year. 15% grads pursue business degrees. 2% grads pursue law degrees. **Faculty:** Student/faculty ratio 13:1. 53 full-time faculty, 54% hold PhDs. 100% faculty teach undergrads.

ACADEMICS

Degrees: Associate's, bachelor's, master's. **Academic Requirements:** General education including some course work in arts/fine arts, computer literacy, English (including composition), humanities, mathematics, sciences (biological or physical), social science. **Classes:** 10-19 students in an average class. 10-19 students in an average lab/discussion section. **Majors with Highest Enrollment:** Business administration/management; elementary education and teaching; psychology, general. **Disciplines with Highest Percentage of Degrees Awarded:** Business/marketing 20%, education 12%, communications/communication technologies 11%, visual and performing arts 9%, social sciences and history 9%. **Special Study Options:** Cross registration, distance learning, double major, English as a second language, student exchange program (domestic), honors program, independent study, internships, liberal arts/career combination, student-designed major, study abroad, teacher certification program.

FACILITIES

Housing: Coed, fraternities and/or sororities. **Library Holdings:** 106,000 bound volumes. 400 periodicals. 37,000 microforms. 2,200 audiovisuals. **Special Academic Facilities/Equipment:** New England Art Gallery, Graphic Design and Imaging Lab, Center for Educational Innovation (High Tech Building). **Computers:** School-owned computers available for student use.

EXTRACURRICULARS

Activities: Choral groups, dance, drama/theater, literary magazine, radio station, student government, student newspaper, yearbook. **Organizations:** 39 registered organizations, 1 honor society, 1 religious organization, 3 fraternities (15% men join), 2 sororities (10% women join). **Athletics (Intercollegiate):** *Men:* baseball, basketball, cross-country, ice hockey, lacrosse, soccer. *Women:* basketball, cheerleading, cross-country, field hockey, ice hockey, lacrosse, soccer, softball.

ADMISSIONS

Selectivity Rating: 64 (of 100). **Freshman Academic Profile:** Average high school GPA 2.6. 6% in top 10% of high school class, 15% in top 25% of high school class, 45% in top 50% of high school class. 74% from public high schools. Average SAT I Math 446, SAT I Math middle 50% range 380-500. Average SAT I Verbal 462, SAT I Verbal middle 50% range 400-510. TOEFL required of all international applicants, minimum TOEFL 550. **Basis for Candidate Selection:** *Very important factors considered include:* essays, extracurricular activities, interview, recommendations, secondary school record, talent/ability. *Important factors considered include:* character/personal qualities. *Other factors considered include:* alumni/ae relation, class rank, standardized test scores, volunteer work, work experience. **Freshman Admission Requirements:** High school diploma or GED is required. *Academic units required/recommended:* 12 total recommended; 4 English recommended, 3 math recommended, 3 science recommended, 1 science lab recommended, 2 foreign language recommended, 3 social studies recommended. **Freshman Admission Statistics:** 1,010 applied, 96% accepted, 25% of those accepted enrolled. **Transfer Admission Requirements:** *Items required:* high school transcript, college transcript, essay, statement of good standing from prior school. Lowest grade transferable C-. **General Admission Information:** Application fee $30. Nonfall registration accepted. Admission may be deferred for a maximum of 1 year. Credit and/or placement offered for CEEB Advanced Placement tests.

COSTS AND FINANCIAL AID

Tuition $18,382. Room & board $6,538. Required fees $504. Average book expense $450. **Required Forms and Deadlines:** FAFSA. No deadline for regular filing. Priority filing deadline April 1. **Notification of Awards:** Applicants will be notified of awards on a rolling basis beginning on or about April 15. **Types of Aid:** *Need-based scholarships/grants:* Pell, SEOG, state scholarships/grants, private scholarships, the school's own gift aid. *Loans:* Direct Subsidized Stafford, Direct Unsubsidized Stafford, Direct PLUS, FFEL Subsidized Stafford, FFEL Unsubsidized Stafford, FFEL PLUS, Federal Perkins, state loans. **Student Employment:** Federal Work-Study Program available. Institutional employment available. Off-campus job opportunities are good. **Financial Aid Statistics:** 65% freshmen, 65% undergrads receive some form of aid. Average freshman grant $9,849. Average freshman loan $8,465. Average income from on-campus job $1,500. **Financial Aid Phone:** 603-428-2488.

NEW ENGLAND CONSERVATORY OF MUSIC

290 Hunginton Avenue, Boston, MA 02115 **Phone:** 617-585-1101
E-mail: admissions@newenglandconservatory.edu **CEEB Code:** 3659
Fax: 617-369-5644 **Web:** www.newenglandconservatory.edu **ACT Code:** 1872

This private school was founded in 1867.

STUDENTS AND FACULTY

Enrollment: 362. **Student Body:** Male 53%, female 47%, international 18%. **Ethnic Representation:** African American 4%, Asian 9%, Caucasian 79%, Hispanic 4%, Native American 1%. **Retention and Graduation:** 92% freshmen return for sophomore year. 43% freshmen graduate within 4 years. **Faculty:** Student/faculty ratio 4:1. 88 full-time faculty. 53% faculty teach undergrads.

ACADEMICS

Degrees: Bachelor's, diploma, doctoral, master's. **Academic Requirements:** General education including some course work in arts/fine arts, English (including composition), history, humanities, career skills. **Majors with Highest Enrollment:** Violin, viola, guitar and other stringed instruments; jazz/jazz studies; voice and opera. **Disciplines with Highest Percentage of Degrees Awarded:** Visual and performing arts 69%. **Special Study Options:** Cross registration, dual enrollment, English as a second language, independent study, internships, study abroad.

FACILITIES

Housing: Coed. **Library Holdings:** 78,853 bound volumes. 275 periodicals. 298 microforms. 46,384 audiovisuals. **Special Academic Facilities/Equipment:** Rare instrument collection of over 200 pieces, recording and electronic music studios. Jordan Hall, the main concert hall, is a national historic landmark. **Computers:** School-owned computers available for student use.

EXTRACURRICULARS

Activities: Choral groups, concert band, jazz band, music ensembles, musical theater, opera, student government, symphony orchestra. **Organizations:** 7 registered organizations, 1 honor society, 1 religious organization, 16 fraternities.

ADMISSIONS

Selectivity Rating: 86 (of 100). **Freshman Academic Profile:** Average high school GPA 3.4. TOEFL required of all international applicants, minimum TOEFL 500. **Basis for Candidate Selection:** *Very important factors considered include:* talent/ability. *Other factors considered include:* class rank, essays, recommendations, secondary school record, standardized test scores. **Freshman Admission Requirements:** High school diploma or GED is required. **Freshman Admission Statistics:** 831 applied, 42% accepted, 31% of those accepted enrolled. **Transfer Admission Requirements:** *Items required:* college transcript, essay. Minimum high school GPA of 2.8 required. Minimum college GPA of 2.8 required. Lowest grade transferable C. **General Admission Information:** Application fee $100. Application deadline December 1. Nonfall registration accepted. Admission may be deferred for a maximum of 1 year. Credit offered for CEEB Advanced Placement tests.

COSTS AND FINANCIAL AID

Tuition $24,500. Room & board $10,250. Required fees $250. Average book expense $700. **Required Forms and Deadlines:** FAFSA and institution's own financial aid form. Priority filing deadline February 2. **Notification of Awards:** Applicants will be notified of awards on or about April 1. **Types of Aid:** *Need-based scholarships/grants:* Pell, SEOG, state scholarships/grants, private scholarships, the school's own gift aid. *Loans:* FFEL Subsidized Stafford, FFEL Unsubsidized Stafford, FFEL PLUS, Federal Perkins, state loans. **Student Employment:** Federal Work-Study Program available. Institutional employment available. Off-campus job opportunities are good. **Financial Aid Statistics:** Average freshman grant $9,756. Average freshman loan $2,727. Average income from on-campus job $1,200. **Financial Aid Phone:** 617-262-1120.

NEW JERSEY CITY UNIVERSITY

2039 Kennedy Boulevard, Jersey City, NJ 07305-1597
Phone: 201-200-3234 **E-mail:** admissions@jcsl.jcstate.edu **CEEB Code:** 2516
Fax: 201-200-2352 **Web:** www.njcu.edu

This public school was founded in 1927. It has a 17-acre campus.

STUDENTS AND FACULTY

Enrollment: 6,187. **Student Body:** Male 39%, female 61%, out-of-state 2%, international 2%. **Ethnic Representation:** African American 21%, Asian 10%, Caucasian 35%, Hispanic 33%. **Retention and Graduation:** 20% grads go on to further study within 1 year. 5% grads pursue business degrees. 1% grads pursue law degrees. 1% grads pursue medical degrees. **Faculty:** Student/faculty ratio 15:1. 238 full-time faculty, 79% hold PhDs. 100% faculty teach undergrads.

ACADEMICS

Degrees: Bachelor's, master's, post-master's certificate. **Academic Requirements:** General education including some course work in arts/fine arts, computer literacy, English (including composition), history, humanities, mathematics, sciences (biological or physical), social science. **Classes:** 10-19 students in an average class. **Disciplines with Highest Percentage of Degrees Awarded:** Business/marketing 21%, computer and information sciences 11%, other 10%, social sciences and history 10%, psychology 10%. **Special Study Options:** Accelerated program, cooperative (work-study) program, cross registration, distance learning, double major, English as a second language, honors program, independent study, internships, study abroad, teacher certification program, weekend college.

FACILITIES

Housing: Coed. **Library Holdings:** 212,786 bound volumes. 1,260 periodicals. 465,875 microforms. 2,234 audiovisuals. **Special Academic Facilities/Equipment:** Art galleries, lab school for special education, criminal justice institute, electron microscope, Raimondo Center for Urban Research and Public Policy. **Computers:** *Recommended operating system:* Windows NT/2000.

EXTRACURRICULARS

Activities: Concert band, drama/theater, jazz band, music ensembles, musical theater, opera, radio station, student government, student newspaper, student-run film society, yearbook. **Organizations:** 50 registered organizations, 2 religious organizations, 7 fraternities, 5 sororities. **Athletics (Intercollegiate):** *Men:* baseball, basketball, football, indoor track, soccer, track & field, volleyball. *Women:* basketball, cheerleading, cross-country, indoor track, soccer, softball, track & field, volleyball.

ADMISSIONS

Selectivity Rating: 73 (of 100). **Freshman Academic Profile:** Average high school GPA 2.7. 2% in top 10% of high school class, 9% in top 25% of high school class, 38% in top 50% of high school class. 75% from public high schools. SAT I Math middle 50% range 380-490. SAT I Verbal middle 50% range 390-490. TOEFL required of all international applicants, minimum TOEFL 500. **Basis for Candidate Selection:** *Very important factors considered include:* class rank, secondary school record, standardized test scores. *Important factors considered include:* essays, recommendations, talent/ability. *Other factors considered include:* alumni/ae relation, character/personal qualities, extracurricular activities, interview, volunteer work, work experience. **Freshman Admission Requirements:** High school diploma or GED is required. *Academic units required/recommended:* 4 English required, 4 English recommended, 4 math required, 4 math recommended, 4 science required, 4 science recommended, 2 science lab required, 3 science lab recommended, 2 foreign language recommended, 4 social studies required, 4 social studies recommended. **Freshman Admission Statistics:** 2,642 applied, 53% accepted, 49% of those accepted enrolled. **Transfer Admission Requirements:** *Items required:* college transcript. **General Admission Information:** Application fee $35. Regular application deadline April 1. Nonfall registration accepted. Admission may be deferred for a maximum of 1 year. Credit and/or placement offered for CEEB Advanced Placement tests.

COSTS AND FINANCIAL AID

In-state tuition $4,185. Out-of-state tuition $8,138. Room & board $6,198. Required fees $1,371. Average book expense $1,000. **Required Forms and Deadlines:** FAFSA and state aid form. Priority filing deadline April 15. **Notification of Awards:** Applicants will be notified of awards on or about May 15. **Types of Aid:** *Need-based scholarships/grants:* Pell, SEOG, state scholarships/grants, private scholarships, the school's own gift aid. *Loans:* Direct Subsidized Stafford, Direct Unsubsidized Stafford, Direct PLUS, Federal Perkins, state loans, college/university loans from institutional funds. **Student Employment:** Federal Work-Study Program available. Institutional employment available. Off-campus job opportunities are good. **Financial Aid Phone:** 201-200-3173.

NEW JERSEY INSTITUTE OF TECHNOLOGY

University Heights, Newark, NJ 07102
Phone: 973-596-3300 **E-mail:** admissions@njit.edu **CEEB Code:** 2513
Fax: 973-596-3461 **Web:** www.njit.edu **ACT Code:** 2580

This public school was founded in 1881. It has a 48-acre campus.

STUDENTS AND FACULTY

Enrollment: 5,730. **Student Body:** Male 79%, female 21%, out-of-state 4%, international 5%. **Ethnic Representation:** African American 11%, Asian 24%, Caucasian 37%, Hispanic 13%. **Retention and Graduation:** 80% freshmen return for sophomore year. 10% freshmen graduate within 4 years. 15% grads go on to further study within 1 year. 3% grads pursue business degrees. 2% grads pursue law degrees. 1% grads pursue medical degrees. **Faculty:** Student/faculty ratio 13:1. 409 full-time faculty, 100% hold PhDs. 70% faculty teach undergrads.

ACADEMICS

Degrees: Bachelor's, doctoral, master's, post-bachelor's certificate. **Academic Requirements:** General education including some course work in computer literacy, English (including composition), humanities, mathematics, sciences (biological or physical), general undergraduate requirements set a broad area of study for students including many humanities and social science courses at Rutgers Newark. **Majors with Highest Enrollment:** Computer science; computer engineering, general; electrical, electronics, and communications engineering. **Disciplines with Highest Percentage of Degrees Awarded:** Engineering/engineering technology 49%, computer and information sciences 28%, business/marketing 9%, architecture 8%, mathematics 2%. **Special Study Options:** Accelerated program, cooperative (work-study) program, distance learning, double major, English as a second language, honors program, independent study, internships, study abroad.

FACILITIES

Housing: Coed, fraternities and/or sororities. **Library Holdings:** 220,000 bound volumes. 2,500 periodicals. 7,325 microforms. 73,807 audiovisuals. **Special Academic Facilities/Equipment:** More than 50 research centers and sponsored research laboratories, including computer chip manufacturing center, manufacturing systems center. **Computers:** School-owned computers available for student use.

EXTRACURRICULARS

Activities: Dance, drama/theater, literary magazine, radio station, student government, student newspaper, student-run film society, yearbook. **Organizations:** 60 registered organizations, 8 honor societies, 5 religious organizations, 19 fraternities (7% men join), 8 sororities (5% women join). **Athletics (Intercollegiate):** *Men:* baseball, basketball, fencing, soccer, swimming, tennis, volleyball. *Women:* basketball, fencing, soccer, swimming, tennis, volleyball.

ADMISSIONS

Selectivity Rating: 80 (of 100). **Freshman Academic Profile:** 24% in top 10% of high school class, 59% in top 25% of high school class, 90% in top 50% of high school class. 80% from public high schools. Average SAT I Math 606, SAT I Math middle 50% range 550-650. Average SAT I Verbal 546, SAT I Verbal middle 50% range 490-590. TOEFL required of all international applicants, minimum TOEFL 550. **Basis for Candidate Selection:** *Very important factors considered include:* class rank, secondary school record, standardized test scores. *Other factors considered include:* character/personal qualities, essays, extracurricular activities, interview, recommendations, talent/ability, volunteer work, work experience. **Freshman Admission Requirements:** High school diploma or GED is required. *Academic units required/recommended:* 16 total required; 4 English required, 4 math required, 2 science required, 2 science lab required, 2 foreign language recommended, 1 social studies recommended, 1 history recommended, 2 elective recommended. **Freshman Admission Statistics:** 2,591 applied, 58% accepted, 44% of those accepted enrolled. **Transfer Admission Requirements:** *Items required:* high school transcript, college transcript, standardized test scores. Minimum college GPA of 2.0 required. Lowest grade transferable C. **General Admission Information:** Application fee $35. Priority application deadline April 1. Nonfall registration accepted. Admission may be deferred. Credit offered for CEEB Advanced Placement tests.

COSTS AND FINANCIAL AID

In-state tuition $6,758. Out-of-state tuition $11,710. Room & board $7,864. Required fees $1,148. Average book expense $1,000. **Required Forms and Deadlines:** FAFSA. **Types of Aid:** *Need-based scholarships/grants:* Pell, SEOG, state scholarships/grants, private scholarships, the school's own gift aid. *Loans:* Direct Subsidized Stafford, Direct Unsubsidized Stafford, Direct PLUS, FFEL Subsidized Stafford, FFEL Unsubsidized Stafford, FFEL PLUS, Federal Perkins, state loans, college/university loans from institutional funds. **Student Employment:** Federal Work-Study Program available. Institutional employment available. Off-campus job opportunities are good. **Financial Aid Statistics:** 65% freshmen, 57% undergrads receive some form of aid. Average freshman grant $4,400. Average freshman loan $2,500. Average income from on-campus job $1,600. **Financial Aid Phone:** 973-596-3480.

NEW MEXICO HIGHLANDS UNIVERSITY

NMHU Office of Student Recruitment, Box 9000, Las Vegas, NM 87701
Phone: 505-454-3593 **E-mail:** recruitment@nmhu.edu **CEEB Code:** 4532
Fax: 505-454-3511 **Web:** www.nmhu.edu **ACT Code:** 2640

This public school was founded in 1893. It has a 175-acre campus.

STUDENTS AND FACULTY

Enrollment: 2,054. **Student Body:** Out-of-state 12%, international 2% (8 countries represented). **Ethnic Representation:** African American 3%, Asian 1%, Caucasian 25%, Hispanic 67%, Native American 4%. **Retention and Graduation:** 53% freshmen return for sophomore year.

ACADEMICS

Degrees: Bachelor's, master's. **Special Study Options:** Cooperative (work-study) program.

FACILITIES

Housing: Coed, all-female, all-male, apartments for married students, apartments for single students. **Library Holdings:** 450,000 bound volumes. 2,394 periodicals. 107,000 microforms. **Computers:** *Recommended operating system:* Mac. School-owned computers available for student use.

EXTRACURRICULARS

Activities: Literary magazine, radio station, student government, student newspaper, television station, yearbook. **Organizations:** 13 honor societies, 5 religious organizations. **Athletics (Intercollegiate):** *Men:* baseball, basketball, cross-country, football. *Women:* basketball, cross-country, soccer, softball, volleyball.

ADMISSIONS

Selectivity Rating: 70 (of 100). **Freshman Academic Profile:** Average high school GPA 2.9. 5% in top 10% of high school class, 20% in top 25% of high school class, 65% in top 50% of high school class. 95% from public high schools. Average ACT 18. TOEFL required of all international applicants, minimum TOEFL 480. **Freshman Admission Requirements:** High school diploma is required and GED is not accepted. *Academic units required/recommended:* 4 English recommended, 2 math recommended, 3 science recommended, 1 foreign language recommended, 3 social studies recommended, 2 history recommended, 2 elective recommended. **Transfer Admission Requirements:** Minimum college GPA of 2.0 required. Lowest grade transferable C. **General Admission Information:** Early decision application deadline January 1. Regular application deadline August 1. Nonfall registration accepted. Credit and/or placement offered for CEEB Advanced Placement tests.

COSTS AND FINANCIAL AID

In-state tuition $1,782. Out-of-state tuition $7,122. Room & board $2,171. Required fees $80. Average book expense $600. **Required Forms and Deadlines:** FAFSA. **Types of Aid:** *Need-based scholarships/grants:* Pell, SEOG, state scholarships/grants, private scholarships, the school's own gift aid. *Loans:* FFEL Subsidized Stafford, FFEL Unsubsidized Stafford, FFEL PLUS, Federal Perkins, state loans, college/university loans from institutional funds. **Student Employment:** Federal Work-Study Program available. Institutional employment available. Off-campus job opportunities are fair. **Financial Aid Statistics:** Average freshman grant $1,250. **Financial Aid Phone:** 505-454-3317.

NEW MEXICO INSTITUTE OF MINING & TECHNOLOGY

Campus Station, 801 Leroy Place, Socorro, NM 87801
Phone: 505-835-5424 **E-mail:** admission@admin.nmt.edu **CEEB Code:** 4533
Fax: 505-835-5989 **Web:** www.nmt.edu **ACT Code:** 2642

This public school was founded in 1889. It has a 320-acre campus.

STUDENTS AND FACULTY

Enrollment: 1,336. **Student Body:** Male 65%, female 35%, out-of-state 16%, international 2% (30 countries represented). **Ethnic Representation:** African American 1%, Asian 4%, Caucasian 71%, Hispanic 21%, Native American 4%. **Retention and Graduation:** 82% freshmen return for sophomore year. 30% grads go on to further study within 1 year. **Faculty:** Student/faculty ratio 13:1. 126 full-time faculty, 94% hold PhDs. 85% faculty teach undergrads.

ACADEMICS

Degrees: Associate's, bachelor's, certificate, doctoral, master's, terminal. **Academic Requirements:** General education including some course work in computer literacy, English (including composition), humanities, mathematics, sciences (biological or physical), social science. **Classes:** Under 10 students in an average class. 10-19 students in an average lab/discussion section. **Majors with Highest Enrollment:** Computer science; electrical, electronics, and communications engineering; physics, general. **Disciplines with Highest Percentage of Degrees Awarded:** Engineering/engineering technology 47%, physical sciences 16%, computer and information sciences 15%, mathematics 8%, biological life sciences 6%. **Special Study Options:** Accelerated program, cooperative (work-study) program, distance learning, double major, dual enrollment, student exchange program (domestic), independent study, internships, student-designed major, teacher certification program.

FACILITIES

Housing: Coed, all-female, all-male, apartments for married students, apartments for single students. **Library Holdings:** 318,429 bound volumes. 883 periodicals. 214,665 microforms. 2,410 audiovisuals. **Special Academic Facilities/Equipment:** Mineral museum, observatory, radio telescope, seismic observatory and library, explosives labs. **Computers:** School-owned computers available for student use.

EXTRACURRICULARS

Activities: Choral groups, concert band, dance, drama/theater, jazz band, music ensembles, musical theater, radio station, student government, student newspaper. **Organizations:** 60 registered organizations, 7 honor societies, 3 religious organizations.

ADMISSIONS

Selectivity Rating: 83 (of 100). **Freshman Academic Profile:** Average high school GPA 3.6. 39% in top 10% of high school class, 66% in top 25% of high school class, 90% in top 50% of high school class. 80% from public high schools. Average SAT I Math 612, SAT I Math middle 50% range 540-680. Average SAT I Verbal 596, SAT I Verbal middle 50% range 540-660. Average ACT 26, ACT middle 50% range 24-29. TOEFL required of all international applicants, minimum TOEFL 540. **Basis for Candidate Selection:** *Very important factors considered include:* secondary school record, standardized test scores. *Other factors considered include:* class rank, extracurricular activities, talent/ability. **Freshman Admission Requirements:** High school diploma or GED is required. *Academic units required/recommended:* 15 total required; 18 total recommended; 4 English required, 4 English recommended, 3 math required, 4 math recommended, 2 science required, 4 science recommended, 2 science lab required, 3 science lab recommended, 2 foreign language recommended, 2 social studies required, 3 social studies recommended, 1 history required, 1 history recommended, 3 elective required. **Freshman Admission Statistics:** 482 applied, 63% accepted, 91% of those accepted enrolled. **Transfer Admission Requirements:** *Items required:* high school transcript, college transcript, statement of good standing from prior school. Minimum high school GPA of 2.5 required. Minimum college GPA of 2.0 required. Lowest grade transferable D. **General Admission Information:** Application fee $15. Priority application deadline March 1. Regular application deadline August 1. Nonfall registration accepted. Admission may be deferred for a maximum of 1 year. Credit and/or placement offered for CEEB Advanced Placement tests.

COSTS AND FINANCIAL AID

In-state tuition $2,053. Out-of-state tuition $8,264. Room & board $4,218. Required fees $858. Average book expense $800. **Required Forms and Deadlines:** FAFSA and institution's own financial aid form. Financial aid filing deadline June 1. Priority filing deadline March 1. **Notification of Awards:** Applicants will be notified of awards on a rolling basis beginning on or about April 1. **Types of Aid:** *Need-based scholarships/grants:* Pell, SEOG, state scholarships/grants, private scholarships, the school's own gift aid. *Loans:* FFEL Subsidized Stafford, FFEL Unsubsidized Stafford, FFEL PLUS, Federal Perkins, state loans. **Student Employment:** Federal Work-Study Program available. Institutional employment available. Off-campus job opportunities are fair. **Financial Aid Statistics:** 29% freshmen, 40% undergrads receive some form of aid. Average freshman grant $4,600. Average freshman loan $2,412. Average income from on-campus job $3,500. **Financial Aid Phone:** 505-835-5333.

NEW MEXICO STATE UNIVERSITY

Box 30001, MSC 3A, Las Cruces, NM 88003-8001
Phone: 505-646-3121 **E-mail:** admissions@nmsu.edu **CEEB Code:** 4531
Fax: 505-646-6330 **Web:** www.nmsu.edu **ACT Code:** 2638

This public school was founded in 1888. It has a 900-acre campus.

STUDENTS AND FACULTY

Enrollment: 12,531. **Student Body:** Male 46%, female 54%, out-of-state 18%, international 1%. **Ethnic Representation:** African American 3%, Asian 2%, Caucasian 25%, Hispanic 45%, Native American 3%. **Retention and Graduation:** 71% freshmen return for sophomore year. **Faculty:** Student/faculty ratio 19:1. 669 full-time faculty, 83% hold PhDs.

ACADEMICS

Degrees: Associate's, bachelor's, doctoral, master's. **Academic Requirements:** General education including some course work in English (including composition), mathematics. **Classes:** 10-19 students in an average class. 10-19 students in an average lab/discussion section. **Majors with Highest Enrollment:** Business administration/management; curriculum and instruction; electrical, electronics, and communications engineering. **Disciplines with Highest Percentage of Degrees Awarded:** Business/marketing 21%, education 14%, engineering/engineering technology 12%, protective services/public administration 7%, agriculture 6%. **Special Study Options:** Accelerated program, cooperative (work-study) program, cross registration, distance learning, double major, student exchange program (domestic), honors program, independent study, internships, student-designed major, study abroad, teacher certification program, weekend college.

FACILITIES

Housing: Coed, all-female, all-male, apartments for married students, apartments for single students, housing for disabled students, fraternities and/or sororities. **Library Holdings:** 1,642,678 bound volumes. 5,975 periodicals. 1,410,674 microforms. 34,845 audiovisuals. **Special Academic Facilities/ Equipment:** University and art department museums, theatre, horse farm, sports medicine training clinic, observatory, electron microscope, CRAY supercomputer. **Computers:** School-owned computers available for student use.

EXTRACURRICULARS

Activities: Choral groups, concert band, dance, drama/theater, jazz band, literary magazine, marching band, music ensembles, musical theater, opera, pep band, radio station, student government, student newspaper, symphony orchestra, television station. **Organizations:** 263 registered organizations, 24 honor societies, 23 religious organizations, 14 fraternities (4% men join), 5 sororities (3% women join). **Athletics (Intercollegiate):** *Men:* baseball, basketball, cross-country, football, golf, tennis. *Women:* basketball, cross-country, golf, softball, swimming, tennis, track & field, volleyball.

ADMISSIONS

Selectivity Rating: 72 (of 100). **Freshman Academic Profile:** Average high school GPA 3.4. 19% in top 10% of high school class, 48% in top 25% of high school class, 82% in top 50% of high school class. Average ACT 21, ACT middle 50% range 18-23. TOEFL required of all international applicants, minimum TOEFL 500. **Basis for Candidate Selection:** *Very important factors considered include:* secondary school record, standardized test scores. **Freshman Admission Requirements:** High school diploma or GED is required. *Academic units required/recommended:* 10 total required; 4 English required, 3 math required, 2 science required, 2 science lab required, 1 foreign language required. **Freshman Admission Statistics:** 5,706 applied, 81% accepted, 44% of those accepted enrolled. **Transfer Admission Requirements:** *Items required:* college transcript. Minimum college GPA of 2.0 required. Lowest grade transferable C. **General Admission Information:** Application fee $15. Nonfall registration accepted. Admission may be deferred for a maximum of 1 year. Credit offered for CEEB Advanced Placement tests.

COSTS AND FINANCIAL AID

In-state tuition $2,328. Out-of-state tuition $9,900. Room & board $4,422. Required fees $888. Average book expense $672. **Required Forms and Deadlines:** FAFSA and institution's own financial aid form. **Notification of Awards:** Applicants will be notified of awards on or about March 1. **Types of Aid:** *Need-based scholarships/grants:* the school's own gift aid. *Loans:* FFEL Subsidized Stafford, FFEL Unsubsidized Stafford, FFEL PLUS, Federal Perkins, college/university loans from institutional funds. **Student Employment:** Federal Work-Study Program available. Institutional employment available. Off-campus job opportunities are good. **Financial Aid Statistics:** 59% freshmen, 56% undergrads receive some form of aid. **Financial Aid Phone:** 505-646-4105.

NEW WORLD SCHOOL OF THE ARTS

300 NE 2nd Avenue, Miami, FL 33132
Phone: 305-237-7007 **E-mail:** nwsaadm@mdcc.edu
Fax: 305-237-3794 **Web:** www.mdcc.edu/nwsa

This public school was founded in 1984.

STUDENTS AND FACULTY

Enrollment: 350. **Student Body:** Out-of-state 35%. **Ethnic Representation:** African American 13%, Asian 5%, Caucasian 32%, Hispanic 47%. **Faculty:** Student/faculty ratio 10:1. 24 full-time faculty, 95% hold PhDs. 100% faculty teach undergrads.

ACADEMICS

Degrees: Associate's, bachelor's. **Academic Requirements:** General education including some course work in arts/fine arts, computer literacy, English (including composition), foreign languages, humanities, mathematics, sciences (biological or physical), social science. **Majors with Highest Enrollment:** Dance, general; graphic design; acting. **Disciplines with Highest Percentage of Degrees Awarded:** Visual and performing arts 100%. **Special Study Options:** Cooperative (work-study) program, distance learning, English as a second language, independent study, liberal arts/career combination.

FACILITIES

Special Academic Facilities/Equipment: Black box theater, art gallery, dance recital hall. **Computers:** *Recommended operating system:* Windows NT/2000. School-owned computers available for student use.

EXTRACURRICULARS

Activities: Choral groups, dance, drama/theater, jazz band, music ensembles, musical theater, opera, student government, student-run film society, symphony orchestra.

ADMISSIONS

Selectivity Rating: 63 (of 100). **Freshman Academic Profile:** 99% from public high schools. TOEFL required of all international applicants, minimum TOEFL 550. **Basis for Candidate Selection:** *Very important factors considered include:* talent/ability. *Other factors considered include:* character/ personal qualities, essays, extracurricular activities, interview, recommendations, secondary school record, standardized test scores. **Freshman Admission Requirements:** High school diploma or GED is required. **Transfer Admission Requirements:** *Items required:* high school transcript, college transcript, essay, interview. Lowest grade transferable C. **General Admission Information:** Credit and/or placement offered for CEEB Advanced Placement tests.

COSTS AND FINANCIAL AID

In-state tuition $7,000. Out-of-state tuition $12,000. Required fees $0. Average book expense $500. **Required Forms and Deadlines:** FAFSA. No deadline for regular filing. **Types of Aid:** *Need-based scholarships/grants:* Pell, SEOG, state scholarships/grants, private scholarships, the school's own gift aid. *Loans:* Direct Subsidized Stafford, Direct Unsubsidized Stafford, Direct PLUS, FFEL PLUS, Federal Perkins, state loans, college/university loans from institutional funds. **Student Employment:** Federal Work-Study Program available. Off-campus job opportunities are excellent. **Financial Aid Phone:** 305-237-7529.

NEW YORK INSTITUTE OF TECHNOLOGY

PO Box 8000, Northern Boulevard, Old Westbury, NY 11568
Phone: 516-686-7520 **E-mail:** admissions@nyit.edu **CEEB Code:** 2561
Fax: 516-686-7613 **Web:** www.nyit.edu **ACT Code:** 2832

This private school was founded in 1955. It has a 525-acre campus.

STUDENTS AND FACULTY

Enrollment: 5,472. **Student Body:** Male 62%, female 38%, out-of-state 7%, international 7%. **Ethnic Representation:** African American 14%, Asian 12%, Caucasian 37%, Hispanic 11%. **Retention and Graduation:** 73% freshmen return for sophomore year. 44% grads go on to further study within 1 year. 24% grads pursue business degrees. 6% grads pursue law degrees. 2% grads pursue medical degrees. **Faculty:** Student/faculty ratio 16:1. 283 full-time faculty, 87% hold PhDs. 90% faculty teach undergrads.

ACADEMICS

Degrees: Associate's, bachelor's, certificate, first professional, master's, post-bachelor's certificate, post-master's certificate, terminal, transfer. **Academic Requirements:** General education including some course work in computer literacy, English (including composition), history, mathematics, philosophy, sciences (biological or physical). All entering first-year freshmen, transfer students with less than 12 credits, and students on probation are required to complete the college success seminar. Additional required subjects are speech, behavioral sciences, and economics. Also, one course selected from either social science, fine arts, communication arts, or other liberal arts subject area. **Classes:** 10-19 students in an average class. 10-19 students in an average lab/ discussion section. **Majors with Highest Enrollment:** Radio and television; architecture (BArch, BA/BS, MArch, MA/MS, PhD); health professions and related sciences. **Disciplines with Highest Percentage of Degrees Awarded:** Business/marketing 21%, architecture 11%, health professions and related sciences 11%, communications/communication technologies 10%, engineering/engineering technology 9%. **Special Study Options:** Accelerated program, cooperative (work-study) program, cross registration, distance learning, double major, dual enrollment, English as a second language, honors program, independent study, internships, liberal arts/career combination, study abroad, teacher certification program, weekend college. Combined degree programs: life sciences (BS)/Osteopathic Medicine (DO); Architectural Technology (BS)/Energy Management (MS); Architectural Technology (BS)/ MBA; Mechanical Engineering (BS)/Energy Management (MS); Life Sciences (BS)/Physical Therapy (MS); Life Sciences (BS)/Occupational Therapy (MS); Behavioral Sciences (BS)/Law at Touro Law Center (JD).

FACILITIES

Housing: Coed, apartments for single students, housing for international students, fraternities and/or sororities. Special-interest housing for graduate, life sciences, first-year experience, student leaders, student government, international students, Greek Life organizations, and architecture students provided. For the Manhattan campus, housing is available off-campus. **Library Holdings:** 412,406 bound volumes. 3,212 periodicals. 749,346 microforms. 40,958 audiovisuals. **Special Academic Facilities/Equipment:** Center for Urban/Suburban Studies; Center for Neighborhood Revitalization; Parkinson's Disease Treatment Center; Center for Energy Policy & Research; academic computing labs; Center for Labor and Industrial Relations; Carleton Group (Advertising) LI News Tonight; Education Enterprise Zone; Center for Teaching and Learning with Technology; Production House; Motion Graphics Laboratory; Academic Health Care Center; Center for Business Information Technologies; de Seversky Culinary Arts Center. **Computers:** School-owned computers available for student use.

EXTRACURRICULARS

Activities: Choral groups, dance, drama/theater, literary magazine, musical theater, radio station, student government, student newspaper, student-run film society, television station, yearbook. **Organizations:** 100 registered organizations, 14 honor societies, 4 religious organizations, 5 fraternities (2% men join), 3 sororities (1% women join). **Athletics (Intercollegiate):** *Men:* baseball, basketball, cross-country, lacrosse, soccer, track & field. *Women:* basketball, cross-country, soccer, softball, track & field, volleyball.

ADMISSIONS

Selectivity Rating: 68 (of 100). **Freshman Academic Profile:** Average high school GPA 3.1. 60% from public high schools. Average SAT I Math 575, SAT I Math middle 50% range 510-620. Average SAT I Verbal 536, SAT I Verbal middle 50% range 480-570. TOEFL required of all international applicants, minimum TOEFL 500. **Basis for Candidate Selection:** *Very important factors considered include:* secondary school record. *Important factors considered include:* essays, interview, standardized test scores. *Other factors considered include:* character/personal qualities, class rank, extracurricular activities, recommendations, talent/ability, volunteer work, work experience. **Freshman Admission Requirements:** High school diploma or GED is required. *Academic units required/recommended:* 16 total required; 16 total recommended; 4 English required, 4 English recommended, 2 math required, 3 math recommended, 1 science required, 2 science recommended, 1 science lab required, 1 science lab recommended, 2 social studies required, 2 social studies recommended, 7 elective required, 7 elective recommended. **Freshman Admission Statistics:** 3,568 applied, 72% accepted, 35% of those accepted enrolled. **Transfer Admission Requirements:** *Items required:* college transcript, essay. Minimum college GPA of 2.0 required. Lowest grade transferable C-. **General Admission Information:** Application fee $50. Nonfall registration accepted. Admission may be deferred for a maximum of 1 year. Credit and/or placement offered for CEEB Advanced Placement tests.

COSTS AND FINANCIAL AID

Tuition $15,700. Room & board $7,680. Required fees $250. Average book expense $1,200. **Required Forms and Deadlines:** FAFSA. Priority filing deadline March 1. **Notification of Awards:** Applicants will be notified of awards on a rolling basis beginning on or about March 15. **Types of Aid:** *Need-based scholarships/grants:* Pell, SEOG, state scholarships/grants, private scholarships, the school's own gift aid. *Loans:* FFEL Subsidized Stafford, FFEL Unsubsidized Stafford, FFEL PLUS, Federal Perkins, Federal Nursing, alternative loans. **Student Employment:** Federal Work-Study Program available. Institutional employment available. Off-campus job opportunities are good. **Financial Aid Statistics:** 75% freshmen, 72% undergrads receive some form of aid. Average freshman grant $3,128. Average freshman loan $3,671. Average income from on-campus job $1,230. **Financial Aid Phone:** 516-686-7680.

NEW YORK SCHOOL OF INTERIOR DESIGN

107 East 70th Street, New York, NY 10021
Phone: 212-472-1500 **E-mail:** admissions@nysid.edu **CEEB Code:** 333
Fax: 212-472-1867 **Web:** www.nysid.edu **ACT Code:** 2829

This private school was founded in 1916.

STUDENTS AND FACULTY

Enrollment: 725. **Student Body:** Male 14%, female 86%, out-of-state 17%, international 3%. **Ethnic Representation:** African American 1%, Asian 11%, Caucasian 49%, Hispanic 6%. **Faculty:** Student/faculty ratio 9:1. 2 full-time faculty. 100% faculty teach undergrads.

ACADEMICS

Degrees: Associate's, bachelor's, certificate, master's, transfer. **Academic Requirements:** General education including some course work in arts/fine arts, computer literacy, English (including composition), history, humanities, mathematics, sciences (biological or physical), social science. **Classes:** 10-19 students in an average class. **Majors with Highest Enrollment:** Interior architecture; interior design. **Disciplines with Highest Percentage of Degrees Awarded:** Interior design 100%. **Special Study Options:** Independent study, internships, study abroad, weekend college.

FACILITIES

Library Holdings: 10,000 bound volumes. 98 periodicals. 100 audiovisuals. **Special Academic Facilities/Equipment:** Three galleries, lighting laboratory, student atelier. **Computers:** School-owned computers available for student use.

EXTRACURRICULARS

Organizations: 1 registered organization.

ADMISSIONS

Selectivity Rating: 60 (of 100). **Freshman Academic Profile:** Average high school GPA 3.0. Average SAT I Math 500. Average SAT I Verbal 500. TOEFL required of all international applicants, minimum TOEFL 550. **Basis for Candidate Selection:** *Very important factors considered include:* essays, secondary school record, talent/ability. *Important factors considered include:* recommendations, standardized test scores. *Other factors considered include:* character/personal qualities, class rank, extracurricular activities, interview, work experience. **Freshman Admission Requirements:** High school diploma or GED is required. *Academic units required/recommended:* 4 English recommended, 2 math recommended, 2 science recommended, 2 foreign language recommended. **Freshman Admission Statistics:** 97 applied, 46% accepted, 73% of those accepted enrolled. **Transfer Admission Requirements:** *Items required:* college transcript, essay. Minimum high school GPA of 2.5 required. Minimum college GPA of 2.5 required. Lowest grade transferable C. **General Admission Information:** Application fee $50. Nonfall registration accepted. Admission may be deferred for a maximum of 1 year. Credit and/or placement offered for CEEB Advanced Placement tests.

COSTS AND FINANCIAL AID

Tuition $17,920. Required fees $150. Average book expense $1,000. **Required Forms and Deadlines:** FAFSA and institution's own financial aid form. No deadline for regular filing. **Notification of Awards:** Applicants will be notified of awards on a rolling basis beginning on or about February 1. **Types of Aid:** *Need-based scholarships/grants:* Pell, SEOG, state scholarships/grants, private scholarships, the school's own gift aid. *Loans:* FFEL Subsidized Stafford, FFEL Unsubsidized Stafford, FFEL PLUS. **Student Employment:** Federal Work-Study Program available. Institutional employment available. Off-campus job opportunities are excellent. **Financial Aid Statistics:** 52% freshmen, 44% undergrads receive some form of aid. Average freshman grant $5,000. Average freshman loan $6,500. Average income from on-campus job $0. **Financial Aid Phone:** 212-472-1500.

See page 1134.

NEW YORK UNIVERSITY

22 Washington Square North, New York, NY 10011
Phone: 212-998-4500 **E-mail:** admissions@nyu.edu **CEEB Code:** 2562
Fax: 212-995-4902 **Web:** www.nyu.edu **ACT Code:** 2838

This private school was founded in 1831.

STUDENTS AND FACULTY

Enrollment: 19,490. **Student Body:** Male 40%, female 60%, out-of-state 51%, international 4% (137 countries represented). **Ethnic Representation:** African American 6%, Asian 15%, Caucasian 45%, Hispanic 7%. **Retention and Graduation:** 91% freshmen return for sophomore year. 23% grads go on to further study within 1 year. 6% grads pursue business degrees. 20% grads pursue law degrees. 13% grads pursue medical degrees. **Faculty:** Student/faculty ratio 12:1. 1,823 full-time faculty.

ACADEMICS

Degrees: Associate's, bachelor's, certificate, diploma, doctoral, first professional, first professional certificate, master's, post-bachelor's certificate, post-master's certificate, terminal, transfer. **Academic Requirements:** General education including some course work in arts/fine arts, computer literacy, English (including composition), foreign languages, history, humanities, mathematics, philosophy, sciences (biological or physical), social science, requirements vary according to specific degree programs at seven undergraduate colleges. **Classes:** 10-19 students in an average class. 20-29 students in an average lab/discussion section. **Disciplines with Highest Percentage of Degrees Awarded:** Visual and performing arts 23%, business/marketing 16%, social sciences and history 16%, communications/communication technologies 9%, liberal arts/general studies 8%. **Special Study Options:** Accelerated program, cross registration, distance learning, double major, English as a second language, student exchange program (domestic), honors program, independent study, internships, liberal arts/career combination, student-designed major, study abroad, teacher certification program, weekend college.

FACILITIES

Housing: Coed, housing for disabled students, fraternities and/or sororities, safe housing (substance-and-alcohol-free environment). **Library Holdings:** 4,172,898 bound volumes. 33,405 periodicals. 4,687,521 microforms. 92,989 audiovisuals. **Special Academic Facilities/Equipment:** Art galleries and exhibition spaces; institutes of fine arts, mathematics, and science; Center for Hellenic Studies; foreign language and cultural centers. **Computers:** School-owned computers available for student use.

EXTRACURRICULARS

Activities: Choral groups, concert band, dance, drama/theater, jazz band, literary magazine, music ensembles, musical theater, opera, pep band, radio station, student government, student newspaper, student-run film society, symphony orchestra, television station, yearbook. **Organizations:** 250 registered organizations, 13 fraternities (4% men join), 13 sororities (2% women join). **Athletics (Intercollegiate):** *Men:* basketball, cross-country, diving, fencing, golf, soccer, swimming, tennis, track & field, volleyball, wrestling. *Women:* basketball, cross-country, diving, fencing, soccer, swimming, tennis, track & field, volleyball.

ADMISSIONS

Selectivity Rating: 90 (of 100). **Freshman Academic Profile:** Average high school GPA 3.7. 70% in top 10% of high school class, 93% in top 25% of high school class, 100% in top 50% of high school class. 72% from public high schools. Average SAT I Math 666, SAT I Math middle 50% range 630-720. Average SAT I Verbal 672, SAT I Verbal middle 50% range 620-710. Average ACT 29, ACT middle 50% range 28-32. TOEFL required of all international applicants, minimum TOEFL 600. **Basis for Candidate Selection:** *Very important factors considered include:* essays, secondary school record, standardized test scores. *Important factors considered include:* character/personal qualities, class rank, extracurricular activities, recommendations, talent/ability. *Other factors considered include:* alumni/ae relation, minority status, volunteer work, work experience. **Freshman Admission Requirements:** High school diploma or GED is required. *Academic units required/recommended:* 18 total required; 4 English required, 3 math required, 4 math recommended, 3 science required, 2 science lab required, 2 foreign language required, 3 foreign language recommended, 4 history required. **Freshman Admission Statistics:** 29,581 applied, 28% accepted, 40% of those accepted enrolled. **Transfer Admission Requirements:** *Items required:* high school transcript, college transcript, essay, standardized test score, statement of good standing from prior school. Lowest grade transferable C. **General Admission Information:** Application fee $55. Priority application deadline November 15. Early decision application deadline November 15. Regular application deadline January 15. Nonfall registration accepted. Admission may be deferred for a maximum of 1 year. Credit offered for CEEB Advanced Placement tests.

COSTS AND FINANCIAL AID

Tuition $26,646. Room & board $10,430. Required fees $0. Average book expense $450. **Required Forms and Deadlines:** FAFSA, state aid form and Early decision applicants may submit an institutional form for an estimated award. Financial aid filing deadline February 15. **Notification of Awards:** Applicants will be notified of awards on a rolling basis beginning on or about April 1. **Types of Aid:** *Need-based scholarships/grants:* Pell, SEOG, state scholarships/grants, private scholarships, the school's own gift aid. *Loans:* FFEL Subsidized Stafford, FFEL Unsubsidized Stafford, FFEL PLUS, Federal Perkins, Federal Nursing. **Student Employment:** Federal Work-Study Program available. Institutional employment available. Off-campus job opportunities are excellent. **Financial Aid Statistics:** 61% freshmen, 55% undergrads receive some form of aid. Average freshman grant $18,444. Average freshman loan $4,384. **Financial Aid Phone:** 212-998-4444.

See page 1136.

NEWBERRY COLLEGE

2100 College Street, Newberry, SC 29108
Phone: 803-321-5127 **E-mail:** admissions@newberry.edu **CEEB Code:** 5493
Fax: 803-321-5138 **Web:** www.newberry.edu **ACT Code:** 3870

This private school, which is affiliated with the Lutheran Church, was founded in 1856. It has a 60-acre campus.

STUDENTS AND FACULTY

Enrollment: 748. **Student Body:** Male 56%, female 44%, out-of-state 12%, international 1% (9 countries represented). **Ethnic Representation:** African American 26%, Caucasian 72%, Hispanic 1%. **Retention and Graduation:** 66% freshmen return for sophomore year. 39% freshmen graduate within 4 years. 16% grads go on to further study within 1 year. **Faculty:** Student/faculty ratio 13:1. 44 full-time faculty, 65% hold PhDs. 100% faculty teach undergrads.

ACADEMICS

Degrees: Bachelor's. **Academic Requirements:** General education including some course work in arts/fine arts, computer literacy, English (including composition), foreign languages, history, humanities, mathematics, sciences (biological or physical), social science, religion speech. **Classes:** Under 10 students in an average class. 20-29 students in an average lab/discussion section. **Majors with Highest Enrollment:** Business administration/management; communications studies/speech communication and rhetoric; elementary education and teaching. **Disciplines with Highest Percentage of Degrees Awarded:** Business/marketing 19%, education 14%, social sciences and history 14%, parks and recreation 13%, biological life sciences 9%. **Special Study Options:** Cooperative (work-study) program, double major, dual enrollment, honors program, independent study, internships, liberal arts/career combination, student-designed major, study abroad, teacher certification program.

FACILITIES

Housing: Coed, all-female, all-male. **Library Holdings:** 77,460 bound volumes. 398 periodicals. 6,784 microforms. 1,369 audiovisuals. **Special Academic Facilities/Equipment:** TV studio. **Computers:** *Recommended operating system:* Windows NT/2000. School-owned computers available for student use.

EXTRACURRICULARS

Activities: Choral groups, concert band, drama/theater, jazz band, literary magazine, marching band, music ensembles, radio station, student government, student newspaper, television station, yearbook. **Organizations:** 50 registered organizations, 11 honor societies, 4 religious organizations, 5 fraternities (35% men join), 4 sororities (27% women join). **Athletics (Intercollegiate):** *Men:* baseball, basketball, cross-country, football, golf, soccer, tennis. *Women:* basketball, cheerleading, cross-country, golf, soccer, softball, tennis, volleyball.

ADMISSIONS

Selectivity Rating: 63 (of 100). **Freshman Academic Profile:** Average high school GPA 3.1. 12% in top 10% of high school class, 31% in top 25% of high school class, 63% in top 50% of high school class. Average SAT I Math 497, SAT I Math middle 50% range 440-560. Average SAT I Verbal 480, SAT I Verbal middle 50% range 430-540. Average ACT 20, ACT middle 50% range 18-22. TOEFL required of all international applicants, minimum TOEFL 525. **Basis for Candidate Selection:** *Very important factors considered include:* secondary school record, standardized test scores. *Important factors considered include:* class rank. *Other factors considered include:* alumni/ae relation, character/personal qualities, essays, extracurricular activities, geographical residence, interview, minority status, recommendations, religious affiliation/commitment, state residency, talent/ability, volunteer work, work experience. **Freshman Admission Requirements:** High school diploma or GED is required. *Academic units required/recommended:* 15 total required; 15 total recommended; 4 English required, 4 English recommended, 3 math required, 3 math recommended, 2 science required, 2 science recommended, 2 science lab required, 2 science lab recommended, 2 foreign language required, 2 foreign language recommended, 2 social studies required, 2 social studies recommended, 1 history required, 1 history recommended, 1 elective required, 1 elective recommended. **Freshman Admission Statistics:** 1,046 applied, 71% accepted, 34% of those accepted enrolled. **Transfer Admission Requirements:** *Items required:* college transcript. Minimum high school GPA of 2.0 required. Minimum college GPA of 2.0 required. Lowest grade transferable C. **General Admission Information:** Application fee $30. Priority application deadline January 30. Nonfall registration accepted. Admission may be deferred for a maximum of 2 years. Credit and/or placement offered for CEEB Advanced Placement tests.

COSTS AND FINANCIAL AID

Tuition $15,800. Room & board $4,910. Required fees $610. Average book expense $1,195. **Required Forms and Deadlines:** FAFSA and institution's own financial aid form. Priority filing deadline March 15. **Types of Aid:** *Need-based scholarships/grants:* Pell, SEOG, state scholarships/grants, private scholarships, the school's own gift aid. *Loans:* FFEL Subsidized Stafford, FFEL Unsubsidized Stafford, FFEL PLUS, Federal Perkins, state loans. **Student Employment:** Federal Work-Study Program available. Institutional employment available. Off-campus job opportunities are good. **Financial Aid Statistics:** 83% freshmen, 80% undergrads receive some form of aid. **Financial Aid Phone:** 803-321-5120.

NEWMAN UNIVERSITY

3100 McCormick Avenue, Wichita, KS 67213-2097
Phone: 316-942-4291 **E-mail:** admissions@newmanu.edu **CEEB Code:** 6615
Fax: 316-942-4483 **Web:** www.newmanu.edu **ACT Code:** 1452

This private school, which is affiliated with the Roman Catholic Church, was founded in 1933. It has a 53-acre campus.

STUDENTS AND FACULTY

Enrollment: 1,524. **Student Body:** Male 34%, female 66%, out-of-state 12%, international 2% (26 countries represented). **Ethnic Representation:** African American 6%, Asian 2%, Caucasian 84%, Hispanic 4%, Native American 1%. **Retention and Graduation:** 66% freshmen return for sophomore year. 21% freshmen graduate within 4 years. **Faculty:** Student/faculty ratio 11:1. 81 full-time faculty, 44% hold PhDs. 85% faculty teach undergrads.

ACADEMICS

Degrees: Associate's, bachelor's, master's, terminal, transfer. **Academic Requirements:** General education including some course work in arts/fine arts, English (including composition), history, humanities, mathematics, philosophy, sciences (biological or physical), social science, theology. **Classes:** 10-19 students in an average class. 10-19 students in an average lab/discussion section. **Disciplines with Highest Percentage of Degrees Awarded:** Education 30%, health professions and related sciences 24%, business/marketing 23%, biological life sciences 6%, psychology 4%. **Special Study Options:** Cooperative (work-study) program, cross registration, distance learning, double major, dual enrollment, independent study, internships, liberal arts/career combination, student-designed major, study abroad, teacher certification program.

FACILITIES

Housing: Coed, all-female, apartments for married students, apartments for single students, housing for disabled students. Freshmen required to live in college housing first 2 years if not living with parents. **Library Holdings:** 140,545 bound volumes. 506 periodicals. 86,053 microforms. 2,400 audiovisuals. **Special Academic Facilities/Equipment:** Cadaver lab, art gallery. **Computers:** *Recommended operating system:* Windows 98. School-owned computers available for student use.

EXTRACURRICULARS

Activities: Choral groups, drama/theater, literary magazine, student government, student newspaper. **Organizations:** 25 registered organizations, 3 honor societies, 2 religious organizations. **Athletics (Intercollegiate):** *Men:* baseball, basketball, golf, soccer. *Women:* basketball, golf, soccer, softball, volleyball.

ADMISSIONS

Selectivity Rating: 64 (of 100). **Freshman Academic Profile:** Average high school GPA 3.4. 18% in top 10% of high school class, 43% in top 25% of high school class, 78% in top 50% of high school class. 78% from public high schools. Average SAT I Math 511, SAT I Math middle 50% range 510-560. Average SAT I Verbal 553, SAT I Verbal middle 50% range 500-670. Average ACT 22, ACT middle 50% range 19-25. TOEFL required of all international applicants, minimum TOEFL 530. **Basis for Candidate Selection:** *Very important factors considered include:* secondary school record, standardized test scores. *Other factors considered include:* recommendations. **Freshman Admission Requirements:** High school diploma or GED is required. *Academic units required/recommended:* 4 English recommended, 3 math recommended, 3 science recommended, 3 social studies recommended. **Freshman Admission Statistics:** 340 applied, 84% accepted, 50% of those accepted enrolled. **Transfer Admission Requirements:** *Items required:* college transcript. Minimum college GPA of 2.0 required. Lowest grade transferable D. **General Admission Information:** Application fee $15. Nonfall registration accepted. Admission may be deferred for a maximum of 2 years. Credit offered for CEEB Advanced Placement tests.

COSTS AND FINANCIAL AID

Tuition $10,148. Room & board $3,950. Required fees $120. Average book expense $750. **Required Forms and Deadlines:** FAFSA and institution's own financial aid form. Priority filing deadline March 1. **Notification of Awards:** Applicants will be notified of awards on a rolling basis beginning on or about January 2. **Types of Aid:** *Need-based scholarships/grants:* Pell, SEOG, state scholarships/grants, private scholarships, the school's own gift aid. *Loans:* FFEL Subsidized Stafford, FFEL Unsubsidized Stafford, FFEL PLUS, Federal Perkins. **Student Employment:** Federal Work-Study Program available. Institutional employment available. Off-campus job opportunities are excellent. **Financial Aid Statistics:** 81% freshmen, 76% undergrads receive some form of aid. Average freshman grant $7,500. Average freshman loan $2,625. Average income from on-campus job $1,200. **Financial Aid Phone:** 316-942-4291.

NEWSCHOOL OF ARCHITECTURE AND DESIGN

1249 F Street, San Diego, CA 92101
Phone: (619) 235-4100 **E-mail:** pbinnis@newschoolarch.edu
Fax: (619) 235-4651 **Web:** www.newschoolarch.edu

This proprietary school was founded in 1980. It has a 10-acre campus.

STUDENTS AND FACULTY

Faculty: Student/faculty ratio 20:1. 5 full-time faculty, 40% hold PhDs. 100% faculty teach undergrads.

ACADEMICS

Degrees: Associate's, bachelor's, first professional, master's. **Academic Requirements:** General education including some course work in arts/fine arts, computer literacy, English (including composition), history, humanities, mathematics, philosophy, social science. **Disciplines with Highest Percentage of Degrees Awarded:** Architecture 5%. **Special Study Options:** Cooperative (work-study) program, independent study, internships, study abroad.

FACILITIES

Housing: None. **Computers:** *Recommended operating system:* Windows NT/2000. School-owned computers available for student use.

EXTRACURRICULARS

Activities: Student newspaper. **Organizations:** 2 registered organizations.

ADMISSIONS

Selectivity Rating: 63 (of 100). **Freshman Academic Profile:** 100% from public high schools. TOEFL required of all international applicants, minimum TOEFL 550. **Basis for Candidate Selection:** *Very important factors considered include:* interview. *Important factors considered include:* secondary school record, talent/ability. *Other factors considered include:* character/personal qualities, essays, extracurricular activities, recommendations, volunteer work. **Freshman Admission Requirements:** High school diploma or GED is required. **Freshman Admission Statistics:** 5 applied, 100% accepted, 100% of those accepted enrolled. **Transfer Admission Requirements:** *Items required:* high school transcript, college transcript, interview. Minimum high school GPA of 3.0 required. Minimum college GPA of 2.0 required. Lowest grade transferable C. **General Admission Information:** Application fee $75. Nonfall registration accepted. Admission may be deferred for a maximum of 1 year. Neither credit nor placement offered for CEEB Advanced Placement tests.

COSTS AND FINANCIAL AID

Types of Aid: *Need-based scholarships/grants:* Pell, SEOG, state scholarships/grants, private scholarships, the school's own gift aid. *Loans:* FFEL Subsidized Stafford, FFEL Unsubsidized Stafford, FFEL PLUS, Federal Perkins, college/university loans from institutional funds. **Student Employment:** Federal Work-Study Program available. Off-campus job opportunities are good. **Financial Aid Phone:** 619-235-4100.

NIAGARA COUNTY COMMUNITY COLLEGE

3111 Saunders Settlement Road, Sanborn, NY 14132-9460
Phone: 716-614-6200 **E-mail:** admiss@alpha.sunyniagara.cc.ny.us
Fax: 716-731-4053 **Web:** www.ntripc.org **ACT Code:** 2843

This public school was founded in 1962. It has a 287-acre campus.

STUDENTS AND FACULTY

Enrollment: 4,828. **Student Body:** Male 42%, female 58%, out-of-state 51%, international students represent 13 countries. **Ethnic Representation:** African American 5%, Asian 1%, Caucasian 87%, Hispanic 1%, Native American 2%. **Retention and Graduation:** 40% grads go on to further study within 1 year. **Faculty:** 100% faculty teach undergrads.

ACADEMICS

Degrees: Associate's, certificate, terminal, transfer. **Academic Requirements:** General education including some course work in English (including composition), social science, health and physical education. **Special Study Options:** Cooperative (work-study) program, cross registration, double major, dual enrollment, honors program, independent study, internships, student-designed major, study abroad.

FACILITIES

Library Holdings: 74,473 bound volumes. 564 periodicals. 91,976 microforms. 6,579 audiovisuals. **Special Academic Facilities/Equipment:** Art gallery. **Computers:** School-owned computers available for student use.

EXTRACURRICULARS

Activities: Choral groups, dance, drama/theater, jazz band, music ensembles, musical theater, radio station, student government, student newspaper, television station. **Organizations:** 1 honor society. **Athletics (Intercollegiate):** *Men:* baseball, basketball, golf, soccer, volleyball, wrestling. *Women:* basketball, golf, soccer, softball.

ADMISSIONS

Selectivity Rating: 63 (of 100). **Freshman Academic Profile:** Average high school GPA 2.5. 2% in top 10% of high school class, 11% in top 25% of high school class, 42% in top 50% of high school class. 90% from public high schools. TOEFL required of all international applicants, minimum TOEFL 450. **Freshman Admission Requirements:** High school diploma or GED is required. **Freshman Admission Statistics:** 2,001 applied, 100% accepted, 60% of those accepted enrolled. **Transfer Admission Requirements:** *Items required:* high school transcript, college transcript. Lowest grade transferable D. **General Admission Information:** Nonfall registration accepted.

COSTS AND FINANCIAL AID

In-state tuition $1,250. Out-of-state tuition $1,875. Required fees $60. **Types of Aid:** *Need-based scholarships/grants:* Pell, SEOG, state scholarships/grants, private scholarships, the school's own gift aid. *Loans:* FFEL Subsidized Stafford, FFEL Unsubsidized Stafford, FFEL PLUS, Federal Perkins, college/university loans from institutional funds. **Student Employment:** Federal Work-Study Program available. Institutional employment available. Off-campus job opportunities are good. **Financial Aid Statistics:** 92% undergrads receive some form of aid. Average income from on-campus job $1,100. **Financial Aid Phone:** 716-614-6200.

NIAGARA UNIVERSITY

Bailo Hall, PO Box 2011, Niagara Falls, NY 14109
Phone: 716-286-8700 **E-mail:** admissions@niagara.edu **CEEB Code:** 2558
Fax: 716-286-8710 **Web:** www.niagara.edu **ACT Code:** 2842

This private school, which is affiliated with the Roman Catholic Church, was founded in 1856. It has a 160-acre campus.

STUDENTS AND FACULTY

Enrollment: 2,635. **Student Body:** Male 40%, female 60%, out-of-state 8%, international 5% (12 countries represented). **Ethnic Representation:** African American 5%, Asian 1%, Caucasian 80%, Hispanic 2%, Native American 1%. **Retention and Graduation:** 77% freshmen return for sophomore year. 46% freshmen graduate within 4 years. 21% grads go on to further study within 1 year. 43% grads pursue business degrees. 2% grads pursue law degrees. 2% grads pursue medical degrees. **Faculty:** Student/faculty ratio 16:1. 135 full-time faculty, 91% hold PhDs. 97% faculty teach undergrads.

ACADEMICS

Degrees: Associate's, bachelor's, certificate, master's, post-bachelor's certificate, post-master's certificate. **Academic Requirements:** General education including some course work in English (including composition), history, humanities, mathematics, philosophy, sciences (biological or physical), social science. **Classes:** 20-29 students in an average class. 10-19 students in an average lab/discussion section. **Majors with Highest Enrollment:** Business/commerce, general; teacher education, multiple levels; criminal justice/law enforcement administration. **Disciplines with Highest Percentage of Degrees Awarded:** Business/marketing 28%, education 20%, protective services/public administration 10%, health professions and related sciences 9%, social sciences and history 7%. **Special Study Options:** Accelerated program, cooperative (work-study) program, cross registration, double major, dual enrollment, student exchange program (domestic), honors program, independent study, internships, study abroad, teacher certification program.

FACILITIES

Housing: Coed, all-female, apartments for single students. **Library Holdings:** 275,871 bound volumes. 4 periodicals. 78,833 microforms. 0 audiovisuals. **Special Academic Facilities/Equipment:** Castellani Art Museum.

EXTRACURRICULARS

Activities: Choral groups, dance, drama/theater, musical theater, radio station, student government, student newspaper, yearbook. **Organizations:** 70 registered organizations, 14 honor societies, 2 religious organizations. **Athletics (Intercollegiate):** *Men:* baseball, basketball, cross-country, diving, golf, ice hockey, lacrosse, soccer, swimming, tennis. *Women:* basketball, cross-country, diving, ice hockey, lacrosse, soccer, softball, swimming, tennis, volleyball.

ADMISSIONS

Selectivity Rating: 71 (of 100). **Freshman Academic Profile:** Average high school GPA 3.0. 14% in top 10% of high school class, 40% in top 25% of high school class, 73% in top 50% of high school class. Average SAT I Math 522, SAT I Math middle 50% range 460-570. Average SAT I Verbal 521, SAT I Verbal middle 50% range 470-570. ACT middle 50% range 19-26. TOEFL required of all international applicants, minimum TOEFL 500. **Basis for Candidate Selection:** *Very important factors considered include:* class rank, secondary school record. *Important factors considered include:* interview, recommendations, standardized test scores. *Other factors considered include:* alumni/ae relation, character/personal qualities, essays, extracurricular activities, talent/ability. **Freshman Admission Requirements:** High school diploma or GED is required. *Academic units required/recommended:* 16 total required; 4 English required, 2 math required, 2 science required, 2 foreign language required, 2 social studies required, 4 elective required. **Freshman Admission Statistics:** 2,703 applied, 83% accepted, 33% of those accepted enrolled. **Transfer Admission Requirements:** *Items required:* high school transcript, college transcript. Minimum college GPA of 2.0 required. Lowest grade transferable C. **General Admission Information:** Application fee $30. Regular application deadline August 1. Nonfall registration accepted. Admission may be deferred for a maximum of 1 year. Credit and/or placement offered for CEEB Advanced Placement tests.

COSTS AND FINANCIAL AID

Tuition $15,900. Room & board $7,300. Required fees $650. Average book expense $700. **Required Forms and Deadlines:** FAFSA and state aid form. No deadline for regular filing. Priority filing deadline February 15. **Notification of Awards:** Applicants will be notified of awards on a rolling basis beginning on or about March 1. **Types of Aid:** *Need-based scholarships/grants:* Pell, SEOG, state scholarships/grants, private scholarships, the school's own gift aid. *Loans:* Direct Subsidized Stafford, Direct Unsubsidized Stafford, Direct PLUS, Federal Perkins, Federal Nursing, state loans, college/university loans from institutional funds. **Student Employment:** Federal Work-Study Program available. Institutional employment available. Off-campus job opportunities are excellent. **Financial Aid Statistics:** 70% freshmen, 68% undergrads receive some form of aid. Average freshman grant $11,691. Average freshman loan $2,088. **Financial Aid Phone:** 716-286-8686.

See page 1138.

NICHOLLS STATE UNIVERSITY

PO Box 2004, Thibodaux, LA 70310
Phone: 985-448-4507 **E-mail:** nicholls@nicholls.edu **CEEB Code:** 6221
Fax: 985-448-4929 **Web:** www.nicholls.edu **ACT Code:** 1580

This public school was founded in 1948. It has a 210-acre campus.

STUDENTS AND FACULTY

Enrollment: 6,561. **Student Body:** Male 37%, female 63%, out-of-state 3%, international 1% (33 countries represented). **Ethnic Representation:** African American 16%, Asian 1%, Caucasian 77%, Hispanic 2%, Native American 2%. **Retention and Graduation:** 57% freshmen return for sophomore year. 7% freshmen graduate within 4 years. **Faculty:** Student/faculty ratio 23:1. 268 full-time faculty, 56% hold PhDs. 100% faculty teach undergrads.

ACADEMICS

Degrees: Associate's, bachelor's, certificate, master's, post-master's certificate. **Academic Requirements:** General education including some course work in arts/fine arts, computer literacy, English (including composition), humanities, mathematics, sciences (biological or physical), social science. **Classes:** 20-29 students in an average class. **Majors with Highest Enrollment:** Nursing/registered nurse training (RN, ASN, BSN, MSN); general studies; elementary education and teaching. **Disciplines with Highest Percentage of Degrees Awarded:** Business/marketing 24%, education 20%, liberal arts/general studies 11%, health professions and related sciences 10%, home economics and vocational home economics 9%. **Special Study Options:** Distance learning, dual enrollment, English as a second language, student exchange program (domestic), honors program, independent study, internships, study abroad, teacher certification program.

FACILITIES

Housing: Coed, all-female, all-male, apartments for married students, housing for disabled students, housing for international students. **Library Holdings:** 303,962 bound volumes. 1,341 periodicals. 396,049 microforms. 3,374 audiovisuals. **Computers:** School-owned computers available for student use.

EXTRACURRICULARS

Activities: Choral groups, concert band, dance, drama/theater, jazz band, literary magazine, marching band, music ensembles, musical theater, pep band, radio station, student government, student newspaper, student-run film society, television station, yearbook. **Organizations:** 41 registered organizations, 15 honor societies, 2 religious organizations, 8 fraternities (3% men join), 6 sororities (3% women join). **Athletics (Intercollegiate):** *Men:* baseball, basketball, cross-country, football, golf, indoor track, track & field. *Women:* basketball, cross-country, indoor track, soccer, softball, tennis, track & field, volleyball.

ADMISSIONS

Selectivity Rating: 63 (of 100). **Freshman Academic Profile:** Average high school GPA 2.9. 11% in top 10% of high school class, 30% in top 25% of high school class, 61% in top 50% of high school class. 72% from public high schools. SAT I Math middle 50% range 410-550. SAT I Verbal middle 50% range 410-530. Average ACT 19, ACT middle 50% range 17-21. TOEFL required of all international applicants, minimum TOEFL 500. **Basis for Candidate Selection:** *Important factors considered include:* class rank, geographical residence, secondary school record, standardized test scores, state residency. **Freshman Admission Requirements:** High school diploma or GED is required. *Academic units required/recommended:* 23 total required; 4 English required, 3 math required, 3 science required, 2 foreign language recommended, 1 social studies required, 2 history required, 7 elective required. **Freshman Admission Statistics:** 2,467 applied, 99% accepted, 61% of those accepted enrolled. **Transfer Admission Requirements:** *Items required:* college transcript, statement of good standing from prior school. Lowest grade transferable D. **General Admission Information:** Application fee $20. Nonfall registration accepted. Admission may be deferred. Credit and/or placement offered for CEEB Advanced Placement tests.

COSTS AND FINANCIAL AID

In-state tuition $2,037. Out-of-state tuition $7,485. Room & board $3,352. Required fees $417. Average book expense $1,000. **Required Forms and Deadlines:** FAFSA, institution's own financial aid form, state aid form and noncustodial (divorced/separated) parent's statement. Priority filing deadline April 14. **Notification of Awards:** Applicants will be notified of awards on a rolling basis. **Types of Aid:** *Need-based scholarships/grants:* Pell, SEOG, state scholarships/grants, private scholarships. *Loans:* FFEL Subsidized Stafford, FFEL Unsubsidized Stafford, FFEL PLUS, Federal Perkins. **Student Employment:** Federal Work-Study Program available. Institutional employment available. Off-campus job opportunities are fair. **Financial Aid Statistics:** 47% freshmen, 39% undergrads receive some form of aid. Average freshman grant $6,930. Average freshman loan $6,006. Average income from on-campus job $1,343. **Financial Aid Phone:** 504-448-4048.

NICHOLS COLLEGE

PO Box 5000, 124 Center Rd., Dudley, MA 01571-5000
Phone: 508-943-2055 **E-mail:** admissions@nichols.edu **CEEB Code:** 3666
Fax: 508-943-9885 **Web:** www.nichols.edu **ACT Code:** 1878

This private school was founded in 1815. It has a 210-acre campus.

STUDENTS AND FACULTY

Enrollment: 1,569. **Student Body:** Male 55%, female 45%, out-of-state 31%, international 1% (5 countries represented). **Ethnic Representation:** African American 5%, Asian 2%, Caucasian 90%, Hispanic 2%. **Retention and Graduation:** 64% freshmen return for sophomore year. 7% grads go on to further study within 1 year. 2% grads pursue business degrees. **Faculty:** Student/faculty ratio 18:1. 3,230 full-time faculty. 100% faculty teach undergrads.

ACADEMICS

Degrees: Associate's, bachelor's, master's. **Academic Requirements:** General education including some course work in arts/fine arts, computer literacy, English (including composition), history, humanities, mathematics, philosophy, sciences (biological or physical), social science. **Majors with Highest Enrollment:** Business administration/management; accounting; sports and fitness administration/management. **Disciplines with Highest Percentage of Degrees Awarded:** Business/marketing 90%, liberal arts/general studies 10%. **Special Study Options:** Cooperative (work-study) program, distance learning, double major, independent study, internships, liberal arts/career combination, study abroad, teacher certification program.

FACILITIES

Housing: Coed, 21-and-over housing. **Library Holdings:** 60,000 bound volumes. 450 periodicals. 3,800 microforms. 1,677 audiovisuals. **Computers:** *Recommended operating system:* Windows 95. School-owned computers available for student use.

EXTRACURRICULARS

Activities: Drama/theater, literary magazine, musical theater, radio station, student government, student newspaper, television station, yearbook. **Organizations:** 25 registered organizations, 7 honor societies, 1 religious organization. **Athletics (Intercollegiate):** *Men:* baseball, basketball, football, golf, ice hockey, lacrosse, soccer, tennis. *Women:* basketball, cheerleading, field hockey, lacrosse, soccer, softball, tennis.

ADMISSIONS

Selectivity Rating: 66 (of 100). **Freshman Academic Profile:** Average high school GPA 2.4. 1% in top 10% of high school class, 17% in top 25% of high school class, 34% in top 50% of high school class. 82% from public high schools. Average SAT I Math 477, SAT I Math middle 50% range 430-530. Average SAT I Verbal 461, SAT I Verbal middle 50% range 410-510. TOEFL required of all international applicants, minimum TOEFL 550. **Basis for Candidate Selection:** *Very important factors considered include:* essays, secondary school record. *Important factors considered include:* interview, recommendations, standardized test scores. *Other factors considered include:* alumni/ae relation, character/personal qualities, class rank, extracurricular activities, talent/ability, volunteer work, work experience. **Freshman Admission Requirements:** High school diploma or GED is required. *Academic units required/recommended:* 16 total required; 4 English required, 3 math required, 4 math recommended, 2 science required, 3 science recommended, 2 science lab required, 3 science lab recommended, 2 foreign language recommended, 2 social studies required, 5 elective required. **Freshman Admission Statistics:** 917 applied, 86% accepted, 35% of those accepted enrolled. **Transfer Admission Requirements:** *Items required:* high school transcript, college transcript, essay. Minimum college GPA of 2.0 required. Lowest grade transferable C. **General Admission Information:** Application fee $25. Nonfall registration accepted. Admission may be deferred for a maximum of 1 year. Neither credit nor placement offered for CEEB Advanced Placement tests.

COSTS AND FINANCIAL AID

Tuition $19,238. Room & board $7,912. Required fees $400. Average book expense $800. **Required Forms and Deadlines:** FAFSA. Financial aid filing deadline June 1. Priority filing deadline March 1. **Notification of Awards:** Applicants will be notified of awards on a rolling basis beginning on or about March 15. **Types of Aid:** *Need-based scholarships/grants:* Pell, SEOG, state scholarships/grants, private scholarships. *Loans:* FFEL Subsidized Stafford,

FFEL Unsubsidized Stafford, FFEL PLUS, state loans. **Student Employment:** Federal Work-Study Program available. Institutional employment available. Off-campus job opportunities are good. **Financial Aid Statistics:** 82% freshmen, 78% undergrads receive some form of aid. Average freshman grant $8,331. Average freshman loan $4,575. Average income from on-campus job $3,000. **Financial Aid Phone:** 508-213-2276.

NORFOLK STATE UNIVERSITY

700 Park Avenue, Norfolk, VA 23504
Phone: 757-823-8396 **E-mail:** admissions@nsu.edu **CEEB Code:** 5864
Fax: 757-823-2078 **Web:** www.nsu.edu **ACT Code:** 4425

This public school was founded in 1935. It has a 134-acre campus.

STUDENTS AND FACULTY

Enrollment: 5,968. **Student Body:** Male 38%, female 62%, out-of-state 31%, international 1% (38 countries represented). **Ethnic Representation:** African American 93%, Asian 1%, Caucasian 4%, Hispanic 1%. **Retention and Graduation:** 71% freshmen return for sophomore year. 10% freshmen graduate within 4 years. 7% grads go on to further study within 1 year. **Faculty:** Student/faculty ratio 16:1. 314 full-time faculty, 58% hold PhDs. 100% faculty teach undergrads.

ACADEMICS

Degrees: Associate's, bachelor's, certificate, doctoral, master's, transfer. **Academic Requirements:** General education including some course work in arts/fine arts, computer literacy, English (including composition), history, humanities, mathematics, sciences (biological or physical), social science, cultural electives, health and communication. **Classes:** 10-19 students in an average class. **Majors with Highest Enrollment:** Business administration/management; psychology, general; computer science. **Disciplines with Highest Percentage of Degrees Awarded:** Interdisciplinary studies 21%, business/marketing 18%, social sciences and history 13%, communications/communication technologies 8%, health professions and related sciences 7%. **Special Study Options:** Accelerated program, cooperative (work-study) program, cross registration, distance learning, double major, dual enrollment, honors program, independent study, internships, study abroad, teacher certification program.

FACILITIES

Housing: All-female, all-male. **Library Holdings:** 378,323 bound volumes. 124,460 periodicals. 18,919 microforms. 0 audiovisuals. **Special Academic Facilities/Equipment:** Museum; performing arts center research computer labs; L. Douglas Wilder Fine Arts Center; center for materials research. **Computers:** *Recommended operating system:* Windows NT/2000. School-owned computers available for student use.

EXTRACURRICULARS

Activities: Choral groups, concert band, dance, drama/theater, jazz band, marching band, music ensembles, radio station, student government, student newspaper, symphony orchestra, television station, yearbook. **Organizations:** 112 registered organizations, 16 honor societies, 4 religious organizations, 12 fraternities (10% men join), 8 sororities (10% women join). **Athletics (Intercollegiate):** *Men:* baseball, basketball, cross-country, football, indoor track, tennis, track & field. *Women:* basketball, cross-country, indoor track, softball, tennis, track & field, volleyball.

ADMISSIONS

Selectivity Rating: 64 (of 100). **Freshman Academic Profile:** Average high school GPA 2.6. 4% in top 10% of high school class, 20% in top 25% of high school class, 54% in top 50% of high school class. Average SAT I Math 430, SAT I Math middle 50% range 390-470. Average SAT I Verbal 430, SAT I Verbal middle 50% range 400-470. Average ACT 18, ACT middle 50% range 16-19. TOEFL required of all international applicants, minimum TOEFL 500. **Basis for Candidate Selection:** *Very important factors considered include:* recommendations, secondary school record, standardized test scores. *Important factors considered include:* class rank. *Other factors considered include:* alumni/ae relation, extracurricular activities, interview, state residency, talent/ability. **Freshman Admission Requirements:** High school diploma or GED is required. *Academic units required/recommended:* 22 total recommended; 4 English recommended, 3 math recommended, 3 science recommended, 3 history recommended, 9 elective recommended. **Freshman Admission Statistics:** 4,700 applied, 77% accepted, 32% of those accepted enrolled. **Transfer Admission Requirements:** *Items required:* college transcript, statement of good standing from prior school. Minimum high school GPA of 2.0 required. Minimum college GPA of 2.0 required. Lowest grade transferable C. **General Admission Information:** Application fee $25. Regular application deadline July 1. Nonfall registration accepted. Admission may be deferred for a maximum of 1 year. Credit and/or placement offered for CEEB Advanced Placement tests.

COSTS AND FINANCIAL AID

In-state tuition $1,658. Out-of-state tuition $10,065. Room & board $5,588. Required fees $1,638. Average book expense $1,000. **Required Forms and Deadlines:** FAFSA. Priority filing deadline April 15. **Notification of Awards:** Applicants will be notified of awards on a rolling basis beginning on or about February 1. **Types of Aid:** *Need-based scholarships/grants:* Pell, SEOG, state scholarships/grants, private scholarships, the school's own gift aid. *Loans:* Direct Subsidized Stafford, Direct Unsubsidized Stafford, FFEL PLUS, Federal Perkins, state loans, alternative loans. **Student Employment:** Federal Work-Study Program available. Institutional employment available. Off-campus job opportunities are good. **Financial Aid Statistics:** 75% freshmen, 64% undergrads receive some form of aid. Average freshman grant $5,246. Average freshman loan $2,625. **Financial Aid Phone:** 757-823-8381.

NORTH CAROLINA A&T STATE UNIVERSITY

1601 East Market Street, Greensboro, NC 27411
Phone: 336-334-7946 **E-mail:** uadmit@ncat.edu **CEEB Code:** 5003
Fax: 336-334-7478 **Web:** www.ncat.edu **ACT Code:** 3060

This public school was founded in 1891. It has a 181-acre campus.

STUDENTS AND FACULTY

Enrollment: 7,331. **Student Body:** Male 48%, female 52%, out-of-state 19%, international 1%. **Ethnic Representation:** African American 93%, Asian 1%, Caucasian 5%. **Retention and Graduation:** 77% freshmen return for sophomore year. 24% freshmen graduate within 4 years. 10% grads go on to further study within 1 year. 1% grads pursue business degrees. 1% grads pursue law degrees. 2% grads pursue medical degrees. **Faculty:** Student/faculty ratio 16:1. 404 full-time faculty, 90% hold PhDs.

ACADEMICS

Degrees: Bachelor's, doctoral, master's. **Academic Requirements:** General education including some course work in arts/fine arts, computer literacy, English (including composition), foreign languages, history, humanities, mathematics, sciences (biological or physical). **Classes:** 20-29 students in an average class. **Disciplines with Highest Percentage of Degrees Awarded:** Engineering/engineering technology 22%, business/marketing 18%, education 10%, physical sciences 7%, computer and information sciences 6%. **Special Study Options:** Cooperative (work-study) program, cross registration, distance learning, double major, external degree program, honors program, independent study, internships, study abroad, teacher certification program.

FACILITIES

Housing: Coed, all-female, all-male, honor student housing, graduate housing. **Library Holdings:** 507,036 bound volumes. 5,446 periodicals. 1,038,474 microforms. 34,025 audiovisuals. **Special Academic Facilities/Equipment:** Art gallery, African Heritage Center, child development laboratory, Microelectronics Center of North Carolina, planetarium, herbarium. **Computers:** School-owned computers available for student use.

EXTRACURRICULARS

Activities: Choral groups, concert band, dance, drama/theater, jazz band, literary magazine, marching band, music ensembles, musical theater, opera, pep band, radio station, student government, student newspaper, student-run film society, symphony orchestra, television station, yearbook. **Organizations:** 82 registered organizations, 6 honor societies, 1 religious organization, 4 fraternities (1% men join), 4 sororities (1% women join).

ADMISSIONS

Selectivity Rating: 70 (of 100). **Freshman Academic Profile:** Average high school GPA 2.9. 8% in top 10% of high school class, 17% in top 25% of high school class, 49% in top 50% of high school class. Average SAT I Math 451, SAT I Math middle 50% range 510-400. Average SAT I Verbal 446, SAT I Verbal middle 50% range 500-390. Average ACT 16, ACT middle 50% range 12-18. **Basis for Candidate Selection:** *Very important factors considered include:* secondary school record, state residency. *Important factors considered include:* standardized test scores. *Other factors considered include:* alumni/ae relation, character/personal qualities, class rank, extracurricular activities, geographical residence, recommendations, talent/ability, volunteer work, work experience. **Freshman Admission Requirements:** High school diploma or GED is required. *Academic units required/recommended:* 16 total required; 4 English required, 3 math required, 3 science required, 2 social studies required, 4 elective required. **Freshman Admission Statistics:** 4,810 applied, 83% accepted, 44% of those accepted enrolled. **Transfer Admission Requirements:** *Items required:* high school transcript. Minimum college GPA of 2.0 required. Lowest grade transferable C. **General Admission Information:** Application fee $35. Priority application deadline June 1. Nonfall registration accepted. Admission may be deferred.

COSTS AND FINANCIAL AID

In-state tuition $8,442. Out-of-state tuition $8,442. Room & board $4,470. Required fees $1,017. Average book expense $750. **Required Forms and Deadlines:** FAFSA. Priority filing deadline March 15. **Notification of Awards:** Applicants will be notified of awards on a rolling basis beginning on or about April 15. **Types of Aid:** *Need-based scholarships/grants:* Pell, SEOG, state scholarships/grants, private scholarships, the school's own gift aid, United Negro College Fund, Federal Nursing. *Loans:* Direct Subsidized Stafford, Direct Unsubsidized Stafford, Direct PLUS, Federal Perkins, alternative loans. **Student Employment:** Federal Work-Study Program available. Institutional employment available. Off-campus job opportunities are good. **Financial Aid Statistics:** 73% freshmen, 67% undergrads receive some form of aid. Average freshman grant $3,000. Average freshman loan $4,670. Average income from on-campus job $3,690. **Financial Aid Phone:** 910-334-7973.

NORTH CAROLINA CENTRAL UNIVERSITY

Fayetteville Street, Durham, NC 27707
Phone: 919-560-6298 **E-mail:** ebridges@wpo.nccu.edu **CEEB Code:** 5495
Fax: 919-530-7625 **Web:** www.nccu.edu **ACT Code:** 3132

This public school was founded in 1910. It has a 130-acre campus.

STUDENTS AND FACULTY

Enrollment: 4,762. **Student Body:** Male 35%, female 65%, out-of-state 10%, international 1% (17 countries represented). **Ethnic Representation:** African American 90%, Asian 1%, Caucasian 6%, Hispanic 1%. **Faculty:** Student/faculty ratio 13:1. 257 full-time faculty, 74% hold PhDs.

ACADEMICS

Degrees: Bachelor's, first professional, master's. **Academic Requirements:** General education including some course work in arts/fine arts, English (including composition), foreign languages, history, humanities, mathematics, sciences (biological or physical), social science. **Classes:** Under 10 students in an average class. Under 10 students in an average lab/discussion section. **Disciplines with Highest Percentage of Degrees Awarded:** Business/marketing 19%, social sciences and history 15%, health professions and related sciences 11%, protective services/public administration 9%, education 8%. **Special Study Options:** Cooperative (work-study) program, double major, honors program, independent study, internships, study abroad, teacher certification program, weekend college.

FACILITIES

Housing: Coed, all-female, all-male, Coed houses dormitory available. **Library Holdings:** 625,966 bound volumes. 6,435 periodicals. 1,344,956 microforms. 7,254 audiovisuals. **Special Academic Facilities/Equipment:** Treasury Room collection of primary resources on black life and culture, art museum with works of Afro-American culture. **Computers:** *Recommended operating system:* Windows 95. School-owned computers available for student use.

EXTRACURRICULARS

Activities: Choral groups, concert band, dance, drama/theater, jazz band, literary magazine, marching band, radio station, student government, student newspaper, yearbook. **Organizations:** 4 fraternities, 4 sororities. **Athletics (Intercollegiate):** *Men:* basketball, cross-country, football, golf, tennis, track & field. *Women:* basketball, cross-country, golf, softball, tennis, track & field, volleyball.

ADMISSIONS

Selectivity Rating: 63 (of 100). **Freshman Academic Profile:** Average high school GPA 2.6. 5% in top 10% of high school class, 18% in top 25% of high school class, 49% in top 50% of high school class. Average SAT I Math 427, SAT I Math middle 50% range 380-460. Average SAT I Verbal 425, SAT I Verbal middle 50% range 370-470. Average ACT 16, ACT middle 50% range 14-17. TOEFL required of all international applicants, minimum TOEFL 500. **Basis for Candidate Selection:** *Very important factors considered include:* secondary school record. *Important factors considered include:* class rank, standardized test scores. *Other factors considered include:* alumni/ae relation, essays, extracurricular activities, interview, minority status, recommendations, state residency, talent/ability. **Freshman Admission Requirements:** High school diploma or GED is required. *Academic units required/recommended:* 14 total required; 4 English required, 3 math required, 4 math recommended, 3 science required, 4 science recommended, 1 science lab required, 2 foreign language recommended, 2 social studies required, 2 history required, 2 history recommended. **Freshman Admission Statistics:** 2,184 applied, 88% accepted, 44% of those accepted enrolled. **Transfer Admission Requirements:** *Items required:* high school transcript, college transcript, statement of good standing from prior school. Minimum college GPA of 2.0 required. Lowest grade transferable C. **General Admission Information:** Application fee $30. Regular application deadline July 1. Nonfall registration accepted. Admission may be deferred for a maximum of 4 years. Credit offered for CEEB Advanced Placement tests.

COSTS AND FINANCIAL AID

In-state tuition $1,574. Out-of-state tuition $10,497. Room & board $4,206. Required fees $1,458. Average book expense $800. **Required Forms and Deadlines:** FAFSA. Priority filing deadline April 1. **Notification of Awards:** Applicants will be notified of awards on a rolling basis. **Types of Aid:** *Need-based scholarships/grants:* Pell, SEOG, state scholarships/grants, private scholarships, the school's own gift aid, United Negro College Fund, Federal Nursing. *Loans:* Direct Subsidized Stafford, Direct Unsubsidized Stafford, Direct PLUS, Federal Perkins. **Student Employment:** Federal Work-Study Program available. Off-campus job opportunities are fair. **Financial Aid Statistics:** 80% freshmen, 76% undergrads receive some form of aid. **Financial Aid Phone:** 919-530-6335.

NORTH CAROLINA SCHOOL OF THE ARTS

1533 South Main Street, PO Box 12189, Winston-Salem, NC 27127-2188
Phone: 336-770-3290 **E-mail:** admissions@ncarts.edu **CEEB Code:** 5512
Fax: 336-770-3370 **Web:** www.ncarts.edu **ACT Code:** 3133

This public school was founded in 1963. It has a 57-acre campus.

STUDENTS AND FACULTY

Enrollment: 738. **Student Body:** Male 59%, female 41%, out-of-state 52%, international 1%. **Ethnic Representation:** African American 10%, Asian 3%, Caucasian 85%, Hispanic 2%. **Retention and Graduation:** 75% freshmen return for sophomore year. 40% freshmen graduate within 4 years. **Faculty:** Student/faculty ratio 8:1. 135 full-time faculty. 100% faculty teach undergrads.

ACADEMICS

Degrees: Bachelor's, diploma, master's, post-master's certificate. **Academic Requirements:** General education including some course work in arts/fine arts. **Classes:** Under 10 students in an average class. **Majors with Highest Enrollment:** Technical theatre/theatre design and technology; cinematography and film/video production; music performance, general. **Disciplines with Highest Percentage of Degrees Awarded:** Visual and performing arts 100%. **Special Study Options:** Cooperative (work-study) program, English as a second language, independent study, internships, performing arts.

FACILITIES

Housing: Coed, all-female, all-male, apartments for single students, housing for disabled students. **Library Holdings:** 87,917 bound volumes. 490 periodicals. 25,053 microforms. 73,025 audiovisuals. **Computers:** *Recommended operating system:* Windows 95. School-owned computers available for student use.

EXTRACURRICULARS

Activities: Choral groups, dance, drama/theater, jazz band, literary magazine, music ensembles, musical theater, opera, student government, student-run film society, symphony orchestra, yearbook. **Organizations:** 8 registered organizations, 7 honor societies, 3 religious organizations.

ADMISSIONS

Selectivity Rating: 80 (of 100). **Freshman Academic Profile:** Average high school GPA 3.5. 16% in top 10% of high school class, 45% in top 25% of high school class, 78% in top 50% of high school class. Average SAT I Math 562, SAT I Math middle 50% range 500-620. Average SAT I Verbal 593, SAT I Verbal middle 50% range 540-640. Average ACT 23, ACT middle 50% range 20-25. TOEFL required of all international applicants, minimum TOEFL 550. **Basis for Candidate Selection:** *Very important factors considered include:* interview, recommendations, secondary school record, talent/ability. *Important factors considered include:* standardized test scores. *Other factors considered include:* character/personal qualities, extracurricular activities, minority status, work experience. **Freshman Admission Requirements:** High school diploma or GED is required. *Academic units required/recommended:* 20 total required;

4 English required, 3 math required, 3 science required, 1 science lab required, 2 foreign language recommended, 2 social studies required, 1 history required, 4 elective required. **Freshman Admission Statistics:** 744 applied, 46% accepted, 59% of those accepted enrolled. **Transfer Admission Requirements:** *Items required:* high school transcript, college transcript, interview, statement of good standing from prior school. Lowest grade transferable C. **General Admission Information:** Application fee $45. Regular application deadline March 1. Nonfall registration accepted. Admission may be deferred for a maximum of 1 year. Credit and/or placement offered for CEEB Advanced Placement tests.

COSTS AND FINANCIAL AID

In-state tuition $2,195. Out-of-state tuition $12,795. Room & board $5,115. Required fees $1,255. Average book expense $865. **Required Forms and Deadlines:** FAFSA. Priority filing deadline March 1. **Notification of Awards:** Applicants will be notified of awards on or about April 15. **Types of Aid:** *Need-based scholarships/grants:* Pell, SEOG, state scholarships/grants, private scholarships, the school's own gift aid. *Loans:* Direct Subsidized Stafford, Direct Unsubsidized Stafford, Direct PLUS, Federal Perkins. **Student Employment:** Federal Work-Study Program available. Institutional employment available. Off-campus job opportunities are good. **Financial Aid Statistics:** 64% freshmen, 47% undergrads receive some form of aid. **Financial Aid Phone:** 336-770-3297.

NORTH CAROLINA STATE UNIVERSITY

Box 7103, Raleigh, NC 27695
Phone: 919-515-2434 **E-mail:** undergrad_admissions@ncsu.edu **CEEB Code:** 5496
Fax: 919-515-5039 **Web:** www.ncsu.edu **ACT Code:** 3164

This public school was founded in 1887. It has a 2,110-acre campus.

STUDENTS AND FACULTY

Enrollment: 22,780. **Student Body:** Male 58%, female 42%, out-of-state 7%, international 1% (110 countries represented). **Ethnic Representation:** African American 10%, Asian 5%, Caucasian 82%, Hispanic 2%, Native American 1%. **Retention and Graduation:** 89% freshmen return for sophomore year. 28% freshmen graduate within 4 years. 29% grads go on to further study within 1 year. 14% grads pursue business degrees. 3% grads pursue law degrees. 7% grads pursue medical degrees. **Faculty:** Student/faculty ratio 16:1. 1,607 full-time faculty, 91% hold PhDs. 100% faculty teach undergrads.

ACADEMICS

Degrees: Associate's, bachelor's, doctoral, first professional, first professional certificate, master's, post-bachelor's certificate. **Academic Requirements:** General education including some course work in arts/fine arts, computer literacy, English (including composition), foreign languages, history, humanities, mathematics, sciences (biological or physical), social science. **Classes:** 20-29 students in an average class. 20-29 students in an average lab/discussion section. **Majors with Highest Enrollment:** Business administration/management; computer science; mechanical engineering. **Disciplines with Highest Percentage of Degrees Awarded:** Engineering/engineering technology 26%, business/marketing 14%, biological life sciences 9%, social sciences and history 7%, agriculture 7%. **Special Study Options:** Accelerated program, cooperative (work-study) program, cross registration, distance learning, double major, student exchange program (domestic), honors program, independent study, internships, liberal arts/career combination, student-designed major, study abroad, teacher certification program.

FACILITIES

Housing: Coed, all-female, all-male, apartments for married students, apartments for single students, housing for disabled students, housing for international students, fraternities and/or sororities. **Library Holdings:** 986,993 bound volumes. 17,050 periodicals. 4,923,689 microforms. 164,821 audiovisuals. **Special Academic Facilities/Equipment:** Art and arts/crafts galleries; research farms and forest; phytophotron with controlled atmosphere growth chambers; pulp/paper and wood products labs; processing equipment for fiber, fabric, and garment manufacture; electron microscopes; nuclear reactor; stable isotope lab. **Computers:** School-owned computers available for student use.

EXTRACURRICULARS

Activities: Choral groups, concert band, dance, drama/theater, jazz band, literary magazine, marching band, music ensembles, musical theater, pep band, radio station, student government, student newspaper, student-run film society, symphony orchestra, yearbook. **Organizations:** 353 registered organizations, 16 honor societies, 31 religious organizations, 29 fraternities (10% men join), 12 sororities (9% women join). **Athletics (Intercollegiate):** *Men:* baseball, basketball, cheerleading, cross-country, diving, football, golf, indoor track, rifle, soccer, swimming, tennis, track & field, wrestling. *Women:* basketball, cheerleading, cross-country, diving, golf, gymnastics, indoor track, rifle, soccer, swimming, tennis, track & field, volleyball.

ADMISSIONS

Selectivity Rating: 83 (of 100). **Freshman Academic Profile:** Average high school GPA 4. 37% in top 10% of high school class, 78% in top 25% of high school class, 98% in top 50% of high school class. 92% from public high schools. Average SAT I Math 615, SAT I Math middle 50% range 560-670. Average SAT I Verbal 578, SAT I Verbal middle 50% range 530-630. Average ACT 25, ACT middle 50% range 23-28. TOEFL required of all international applicants, minimum TOEFL 550. **Basis for Candidate Selection:** *Very important factors considered include:* class rank, secondary school record, standardized test scores. *Other factors considered include:* alumni/ae relation, character/personal qualities, essays, extracurricular activities, geographical residence, minority status, recommendations, state residency, talent/ability, volunteer work, work experience. **Freshman Admission Requirements:** High school diploma is required and GED is not accepted. *Academic units required/recommended:* 15 total required; 20 total recommended; 4 English required, 3 math required, 4 math recommended, 3 science required, 1 science lab required, 2 foreign language required, 1 social studies required, 1 history required, 4 elective recommended. **Freshman Admission Statistics:** 12,133 applied, 59% accepted, 51% of those accepted enrolled. **Transfer Admission Requirements:** *Items required:* college transcript. Minimum high school GPA of 2.0 required. Minimum college GPA of 2.0 required. Lowest grade transferable C-. **General Admission Information:** Application fee $55. Priority application deadline November 1. Regular application deadline February 1. Nonfall registration accepted. Admission may be deferred for a maximum of 1 year. Credit and/or placement offered for CEEB Advanced Placement tests.

COSTS AND FINANCIAL AID

In-state tuition $2,814. Out-of-state tuition $14,098. Room & board $5,917. Required fees $1,015. Average book expense $800. **Required Forms and Deadlines:** FAFSA and institution's own financial aid form. No deadline for regular filing. Priority filing deadline March 1. **Notification of Awards:** Applicants will be notified of awards on a rolling basis beginning on or about March 1. **Types of Aid:** *Need-based scholarships/grants:* Pell, SEOG, state scholarships/grants, private scholarships, the school's own gift aid. *Loans:* FFEL Subsidized Stafford, FFEL Unsubsidized Stafford, FFEL PLUS, Federal Perkins, state loans, college/university loans from institutional funds. **Student Employment:** Federal Work-Study Program available. Institutional employment available. Off-campus job opportunities are good. **Financial Aid Statistics:** 38% freshmen, 36% undergrads receive some form of aid. Average freshman grant $5,738. Average freshman loan $2,238. **Financial Aid Phone:** 919-515-2421.

NORTH CAROLINA WESLEYAN COLLEGE

3400 North Wesleyan Boulevard, Rocky Mount, NC 27804
Phone: 252-985-5200 **E-mail:** adm@ncwc.edu
Fax: 252-985-5309 **Web:** www.ncwc.edu

This private school, which is affiliated with the Methodist Church, was founded in 1956.

STUDENTS AND FACULTY

Enrollment: 753. **Student Body:** Male 41%, female 59%, out-of-state 14%. **Ethnic Representation:** African American 47%, Asian 1%, Caucasian 50%, Hispanic 1%, Native American 1%. **Retention and Graduation:** 61% freshmen return for sophomore year. 23% freshmen graduate within 4 years. **Faculty:** Student/faculty ratio 16:1. 46 full-time faculty, 71% hold PhDs. 100% faculty teach undergrads.

ACADEMICS

Degrees: Bachelor's. **Academic Requirements:** General education including some course work in computer literacy, English (including composition), history, humanities, mathematics, sciences (biological or physical), social science. **Classes:** 10-19 students in an average class. **Disciplines with Highest Percentage of Degrees Awarded:** Business/marketing 49%, computer and information sciences 24%, law/legal studies 10%, education 5%, psychology 5%. **Special Study Options:** Accelerated program, cooperative (work-study) program, cross registration, distance learning, double major, dual enrollment, honors program, independent study, internships, liberal arts/career combination, teacher certification program, weekend college.

FACILITIES

Housing: Coed, all-female, all-male, housing for disabled students. **Library Holdings:** 88,975 bound volumes. 11,245 periodicals. 30,720 microforms. 1,810 audiovisuals.

EXTRACURRICULARS

Activities: Choral groups, drama/theater, literary magazine, music ensembles, student government, student newspaper, yearbook. **Organizations:** 30 registered organizations, 2% men join fraternities, 2% women join sororities. **Athletics (Intercollegiate):** *Men:* baseball, basketball, golf, soccer, tennis. *Women:* basketball, soccer, softball, tennis, volleyball.

ADMISSIONS

Selectivity Rating: 67 (of 100). **Freshman Academic Profile:** Average high school GPA 2.8. 12% in top 10% of high school class, 23% in top 25% of high school class, 43% in top 50% of high school class. Average SAT I Math 450, SAT I Math middle 50% range 5-23. Average SAT I Verbal 459, SAT I Verbal middle 50% range 4-29. Average ACT 19. TOEFL required of all international applicants, minimum TOEFL 500. **Basis for Candidate Selection:** *Very important factors considered include:* secondary school record. *Important factors considered include:* character/personal qualities, class rank, extracurricular activities, interview, standardized test scores. *Other factors considered include:* alumni/ae relation, essays, recommendations, talent/ability, volunteer work. **Freshman Admission Requirements:** High school diploma or GED is required. *Academic units required/recommended:* 4 English recommended, 3 math recommended, 2 science lab recommended, 2 foreign language recommended, 2 social studies recommended. **Freshman Admission Statistics:** 852 applied, 62% accepted. **Transfer Admission Requirements:** *Items required:* high school transcript, college transcript, standardized test scores. Minimum college GPA of 2.0 required. Lowest grade transferable C. **General Admission Information:** Application fee $25. Regular application deadline July 30. Nonfall registration accepted. Credit and/or placement offered for CEEB Advanced Placement tests.

COSTS AND FINANCIAL AID

Tuition $10,725. Room & board $6,555. Required fees $1,000. Average book expense $675. **Required Forms and Deadlines:** FAFSA and state aid form. No deadline for regular filing. **Types of Aid:** *Need-based scholarships/grants:* Pell, SEOG, state scholarships/grants, private scholarships, the school's own gift aid. *Loans:* FFEL Subsidized Stafford, FFEL Unsubsidized Stafford, FFEL PLUS, Federal Perkins, alternative loans. **Student Employment:** Federal Work-Study Program available. **Financial Aid Statistics:** Average freshman loan $2,625. Average income from on-campus job $800. **Financial Aid Phone:** 919-985-5290.

NORTH CENTRAL COLLEGE

30 North Brainard Street., PO Box 3063, Naperville, IL 60566-7063
Phone: 630-637-5800 **E-mail:** ncadm@noctrl.edu **CEEB Code:** 1555
Fax: 630-637-5819 **Web:** www.northcentralcollege.edu **ACT Code:** 1096

This private school, which is affiliated with the Methodist Church, was founded in 1861. It has a 56-acre campus.

STUDENTS AND FACULTY

Enrollment: 2,116. **Student Body:** Male 42%, female 58%, out-of-state 9%, international 2% (26 countries represented). **Ethnic Representation:** African American 5%, Asian 2%, Caucasian 87%, Hispanic 4%. **Retention and Graduation:** 77% freshmen return for sophomore year. 57% freshmen graduate within 4 years. 11% grads go on to further study within 1 year. **Faculty:** Student/faculty ratio 14:1. 125 full-time faculty, 83% hold PhDs. 100% faculty teach undergrads.

ACADEMICS

Degrees: Bachelor's, master's. **Academic Requirements:** General education including some course work in English (including composition), humanities, mathematics, sciences (biological or physical), social science. **Classes:** 10-19 students in an average class. 10-19 students in an average lab/discussion section. **Majors with Highest Enrollment:** Business administration/management; organizational communication, general; elementary education and teaching. **Disciplines with Highest Percentage of Degrees Awarded:** Business/marketing 29%, social sciences and history 11%, education 8%, psychology 8%, computer and information sciences 7%. **Special Study Options:** Accelerated program, cooperative (work-study) program, cross registration, double major, student exchange program (domestic), honors program, independent study, internships, student-designed major, study abroad, teacher certification program, weekend college.

FACILITIES

Housing: Coed, all-female. **Library Holdings:** 145,707 bound volumes. 707 periodicals. 197,099 microforms. 3,367 audiovisuals. **Computers:** *Recommended operating system:* Windows NT/2000. School-owned computers available for student use.

EXTRACURRICULARS

Activities: Choral groups, concert band, drama/theater, jazz band, literary magazine, music ensembles, musical theater, radio station, student government, student newspaper, yearbook. **Organizations:** 45 registered organizations, 5 honor societies, 5 religious organizations. **Athletics (Intercollegiate):** *Men:* baseball, basketball, cross-country, football, golf, indoor track, soccer, swimming, tennis, track & field, wrestling. *Women:* basketball, cheerleading, cross-country, golf, indoor track, soccer, softball, swimming, tennis, track & field, volleyball.

ADMISSIONS

Selectivity Rating: 75 (of 100). **Freshman Academic Profile:** Average high school GPA 3.5. 20% in top 10% of high school class, 47% in top 25% of high school class, 78% in top 50% of high school class. 89% from public high schools. Average SAT I Math 564, SAT I Math middle 50% range 520-640. Average SAT I Verbal 555, SAT I Verbal middle 50% range 520-610. Average ACT 24, ACT middle 50% range 21-27. TOEFL required of all international applicants, minimum TOEFL 500. **Basis for Candidate Selection:** *Very important factors considered include:* character/personal qualities, class rank, secondary school record, standardized test scores. *Important factors considered include:* extracurricular activities, recommendations, talent/ability, volunteer work, work experience. *Other factors considered include:* alumni/ae relation, essays, interview. **Freshman Admission Requirements:** High school diploma or GED is required. *Academic units required/recommended:* 15 total required; 19 total recommended; 4 English required, 4 English recommended, 2 math required, 3 math recommended, 2 science required, 3 science recommended, 1 science lab required, 1 science lab recommended, 2 foreign language recommended, 2 social studies required, 2 social studies recommended, 2 history required, 2 history recommended, 3 elective required, 3 elective recommended. **Freshman Admission Statistics:** 1,504 applied, 74% accepted, 33% of those accepted enrolled. **Transfer Admission Requirements:** *Items required:* high school transcript, college transcript, standardized test scores. Minimum high school GPA of 2.3 required. Minimum college GPA of 2.3 required. Lowest grade transferable D. **General Admission Information:** Application fee $25. Nonfall registration accepted. Admission may be deferred for a maximum of 1 year. Credit and/or placement offered for CEEB Advanced Placement tests.

COSTS AND FINANCIAL AID

Tuition $17,997. Room & board $6,045. Required fees $180. Average book expense $925. **Required Forms and Deadlines:** FAFSA, institution's own financial aid form and Federal income tax returns for both the student and the parents. No deadline for regular filing. **Notification of Awards:** Applicants will be notified of awards on a rolling basis beginning on or about March 1. **Types of Aid:** *Need-based scholarships/grants:* Pell, SEOG, state scholarships/grants, private scholarships, the school's own gift aid. *Loans:* FFEL Subsidized Stafford, FFEL Unsubsidized Stafford, FFEL PLUS, Federal Perkins, state loans, college/university loans from institutional funds. **Student Employment:** Federal Work-Study Program available. Institutional employment available. Off-campus job opportunities are excellent. **Financial Aid Statistics:** 70% freshmen, 66% undergrads receive some form of aid. Average freshman grant $11,080. Average freshman loan $3,633. Average income from on-campus job $1,180. **Financial Aid Phone:** 630-637-5600.

NORTH CENTRAL UNIVERSITY

910 Elliot Avenue, Minneapolis, MN 55404
Phone: 612-343-4480 **E-mail:** admissions@northcentral.edu
Fax: 612-343-4146 **Web:** www.northcentral.edu

This private school, which is affiliated with the Pentecostal Church, was founded in 1930.

STUDENTS AND FACULTY

Enrollment: 1,172. **Student Body:** Male 43%, female 57%, out-of-state 58%, international 3%. **Ethnic Representation:** African American 5%, Asian 1%, Caucasian 91%, Hispanic 3%, Native American 1%. **Faculty:** Student/faculty ratio 18:1. 50 full-time faculty, 40% hold PhDs. 100% faculty teach undergrads.

ACADEMICS

Degrees: Associate's, bachelor's, certificate. **Academic Requirements:** General education including some course work in English (including composition), foreign languages, history, mathematics, sciences (biological or physical). **Disciplines with Highest Percentage of Degrees Awarded:** Philosophy/religion/theology 50%, education 15%, visual and performing arts 10%, psychology 8%, communications/communication technologies 5%. **Special Study Options:** Distance learning, double major, student exchange program (domestic).

FACILITIES

Housing: All-female, all-male, apartments for married students. **Computers:** School-owned computers available for student use.

EXTRACURRICULARS

Activities: Choral groups, concert band, drama/theater, music ensembles, radio station, student government, student newspaper, television station. **Athletics (Intercollegiate):** *Men:* basketball, soccer, track & field. *Women:* basketball, track & field, volleyball.

ADMISSIONS

Selectivity Rating: 67 (of 100). **Freshman Academic Profile:** Average ACT 21. TOEFL required of all international applicants, minimum TOEFL 500. **Basis for Candidate Selection:** *Very important factors considered include:* character/personal qualities, essays, recommendations, religious affiliation/commitment, secondary school record, standardized test scores. *Important factors considered include:* extracurricular activities, talent/ability, volunteer work. *Other factors considered include:* class rank, interview. **Freshman Admission Requirements:** High school diploma or GED is required. **Freshman Admission Statistics:** 737 applied, 62% accepted. **Transfer Admission Requirements:** *Items required:* high school transcript, college transcript, essay, statement of good standing from prior school. Minimum high school GPA of 2.2 required. Minimum college GPA of 2.0 required. Lowest grade transferable C. **General Admission Information:** Application fee $25. Regular application deadline June 1. Admission may be deferred for a maximum of 1 year.

COSTS AND FINANCIAL AID

Room & board $3,550. Required fees $600. Average book expense $450. **Required Forms and Deadlines:** FAFSA and state aid form. No deadline for regular filing. Priority filing deadline April 1. **Notification of Awards:** Applicants will be notified of awards on a rolling basis beginning on or about March 1. **Types of Aid:** *Need-based scholarships/grants:* Pell, SEOG, state scholarships/grants, private scholarships, the school's own gift aid. *Loans:* FFEL Subsidized Stafford, FFEL Unsubsidized Stafford, FFEL PLUS, Federal Perkins, state loans. **Student Employment:** Federal Work-Study Program available. Off-campus job opportunities are excellent. **Financial Aid Phone:** 800-289-6222.

NORTH DAKOTA STATE UNIVERSITY

Box 5454, Fargo, ND 58105-5454
Phone: 701-231-8643 **E-mail:** ndsu.admission@ndsu.nodak.edu **CEEB Code:** 6474
Fax: 701-231-8802 **Web:** www.ndsu.edu **ACT Code:** 3202

This public school was founded in 1890. It has a 258-acre campus.

STUDENTS AND FACULTY

Enrollment: 9,874. **Student Body:** Male 57%, female 43%, out-of-state 40%, international 1% (54 countries represented). **Ethnic Representation:** African American 1%, Asian 1%, Caucasian 96%, Native American 1%. **Retention and Graduation:** 69% freshmen return for sophomore year. 14% freshmen graduate within 4 years. 16% grads go on to further study within 1 year. 1% grads pursue business degrees. 1% grads pursue law degrees. 1% grads pursue medical degrees. **Faculty:** Student/faculty ratio 18:1. 495 full-time faculty, 82% hold PhDs. 99% faculty teach undergrads.

ACADEMICS

Degrees: Bachelor's, certificate, diploma, doctoral, first professional, master's. **Academic Requirements:** General education including some course work in arts/fine arts, computer literacy, English (including composition), humanities, mathematics, sciences (biological or physical), social science, wellness, diversity. **Classes:** 20-29 students in an average class. 20-29 students in an average lab/discussion section. **Majors with Highest Enrollment:** Civil engineering, general; mechanical engineering. **Disciplines with Highest Percentage of Degrees Awarded:** Engineering/engineering technology 16%, business/marketing 14%, agriculture 9%, architecture 8%, health professions and related sciences 8%. **Special Study Options:** Cooperative (work-study) program, cross registration, distance learning, double major, dual enrollment, English as a second language, honors program, independent study, internships, student-designed major, study abroad, teacher certification program.

FACILITIES

Housing: Coed, all-female, all-male, apartments for married students, learning communities, apartments for single students, and designated floors for nontraditional students, engineering, and architecture students. Freshmen under 19 years of age not living with a parent or guardian must live on campus. Housing is guaranteed. **Library Holdings:** 303,274 bound volumes. 4,497 periodicals. 168,008 microforms. 2,757 audiovisuals. **Special Academic Facilities/Equipment:** Art gallery, language lab, genetics institute, regional studies institute. **Computers:** School-owned computers available for student use.

EXTRACURRICULARS

Activities: Choral groups, concert band, drama/theater, jazz band, literary magazine, marching band, music ensembles, musical theater, pep band, radio station, student government, student newspaper. **Organizations:** 218 registered organizations, 22 honor societies, 12 religious organizations, 10 fraternities (4% men join), 5 sororities (2% women join). **Athletics (Intercollegiate):** *Men:* baseball, basketball, cross-country, football, golf, indoor track, track & field, wrestling. *Women:* basketball, cross-country, golf, indoor track, soccer, softball, track & field, volleyball.

ADMISSIONS

Selectivity Rating: 76 (of 100). **Freshman Academic Profile:** Average high school GPA 3.4. 93% from public high schools. SAT I Math middle 50% range 500-630. SAT I Verbal middle 50% range 470-610. Average ACT 23, ACT middle 50% range 20-26. TOEFL required of all international applicants, minimum TOEFL 525. **Basis for Candidate Selection:** *Very important factors considered include:* secondary school record, standardized test scores. *Other factors considered include:* class rank, recommendations. **Freshman Admission Requirements:** High school diploma or GED is required. *Academic units required/recommended:* 13 total required; 4 English required, 3 math required, 3 science required, 3 science lab required, 2 foreign language recommended, 3 social studies required. **Freshman Admission Statistics:** 3,547 applied, 60% accepted, 87% of those accepted enrolled. **Transfer Admission Requirements:** *Items required:* college transcript. Minimum college GPA of 2.0 required. Lowest grade transferable D. **General Admission Information:** Application fee $35. Nonfall registration accepted. Admission may be deferred for a maximum of 3 years. Credit and/or placement offered for CEEB Advanced Placement tests.

COSTS AND FINANCIAL AID

In-state tuition $2,904. Out-of-state tuition $7,754. Room & board $4,175. Required fees $602. Average book expense $700. **Required Forms and Deadlines:** FAFSA. No deadline for regular filing. Priority filing deadline April 15. **Notification of Awards:** Applicants will be notified of awards on a rolling basis beginning on or about March 15. **Types of Aid:** *Need-based scholarships/grants:* Pell, SEOG, state scholarships/grants, private scholarships, the school's own gift aid. *Loans:* FFEL Subsidized Stafford, FFEL Unsubsidized Stafford, FFEL PLUS, Federal Perkins, Federal Nursing, state loans, private loans from various lending institutions. **Student Employment:** Federal Work-Study Program available. Institutional employment available. Off-campus job opportunities are excellent. **Financial Aid Statistics:** Average freshman grant $2,512. Average freshman loan $2,801. Average income from on-campus job $1,848. **Financial Aid Phone:** 701-231-7533.

NORTH GEORGIA COLLEGE AND STATE UNIVERSITY

Office of Admissions, Dahlonega, GA 30597
Phone: 706-864-1800 **E-mail:** admissions@ngcsu.edu **CEEB Code:** 5497
Fax: 706-864-1478 **Web:** www.ngcsu.edu **ACT Code:** 848

This public school was founded in 1873. It has a 120-acre campus.

STUDENTS AND FACULTY

Enrollment: 3,681. **Student Body:** Male 37%, female 63%, out-of-state 4%, international 1% (34 countries represented). **Ethnic Representation:** African American 3%, Asian 1%, Caucasian 93%, Hispanic 2%, Native American 1%. **Retention and Graduation:** 74% freshmen return for sophomore year. 27% freshmen graduate within 4 years. 10% grads go on to further study within 1 year. 5% grads pursue business degrees. 1% grads pursue law degrees. 1% grads pursue medical degrees. **Faculty:** Student/faculty ratio 14:1. 208 full-time faculty, 63% hold PhDs.

ACADEMICS

Degrees: Associate's, bachelor's, certificate, master's, post-bachelor's certificate, post-master's certificate, transfer. **Academic Requirements:** General education including some course work in arts/fine arts, computer literacy, English (including composition), foreign languages, history, humanities, mathematics, philosophy, sciences (biological or physical), social science, leadership. **Classes:** 20-29 students in an average class. Under 10 students in an average lab/discussion section. **Special Study Options:** Cooperative (work-study) program, distance learning, double major, dual enrollment, English as a second language, student exchange program (domestic), honors program, independent study, internships, study abroad, teacher certification program.

FACILITIES

Housing: All-female, all-male, apartments for single students. Female cadets live in barracks with men. **Library Holdings:** 143,613 bound volumes. 2,544 periodicals. 755,688 microforms. 3,215 audiovisuals. **Special Academic Facilities/Equipment:** Planetarium, 2 art galleries, Hall of Fame, NGCSU Museum. **Computers:** School-owned computers available for student use.

EXTRACURRICULARS

Activities: Choral groups, concert band, drama/theater, jazz band, literary magazine, marching band, music ensembles, student government, student newspaper, symphony orchestra, yearbook. **Organizations:** 60 registered organizations, 12 honor societies, 8 religious organizations, 7 fraternities (4% men join), 4 sororities (6% women join). **Athletics (Intercollegiate):** *Men:* basketball, cross-country, rifle, soccer. *Women:* basketball, cross-country, rifle, soccer, softball, tennis.

ADMISSIONS

Selectivity Rating: 75 (of 100). **Freshman Academic Profile:** Average high school GPA 3.4. 21% in top 10% of high school class, 52% in top 25% of high school class, 84% in top 50% of high school class. 95% from public high schools. Average SAT I Math 526, SAT I Math middle 50% range 480-580. Average SAT I Verbal 541, SAT I Verbal middle 50% range 490-580. ACT middle 50% range 20-24. TOEFL required of all international applicants, minimum TOEFL 525. **Basis for Candidate Selection:** *Very important factors considered include:* secondary school record. *Important factors considered include:* standardized test scores. *Other factors considered include:* alumni/ae relation, class rank, extracurricular activities, recommendations, volunteer work, work experience. **Freshman Admission Requirements:** High school diploma or GED is required. *Academic units required/recommended:* 16 total required; 4 English required, 4 math required, 3 science required, 1 science lab required, 2 foreign language required, 3 social studies required, 3 history required. **Freshman Admission Statistics:** 2,100 applied, 57% accepted, 54% of those accepted enrolled. **Transfer Admission Requirements:** *Items required:* college transcript, standardized test score, statement of good standing from prior school. Minimum high school GPA of 2.0 required. Minimum college GPA of 2.0 required. Lowest grade transferable D. **General Admission Information:** Application fee $25. Regular application deadline July 1. Nonfall registration accepted. Credit offered for CEEB Advanced Placement tests.

COSTS AND FINANCIAL AID

In-state tuition $2,016. Out-of-state tuition $8,040. Room & board $4,000. Required fees $600. Average book expense $500. **Required Forms and Deadlines:** FAFSA and institution's own financial aid form. No deadline for regular filing. Priority filing deadline May 1. **Notification of Awards:** Applicants will be notified of awards on a rolling basis beginning on or about May 15. **Types of Aid:** *Need-based scholarships/grants:* Pell, SEOG, state scholarships/grants, private scholarships, the school's own gift aid. *Loans:* FFEL Subsidized Stafford, FFEL Unsubsidized Stafford, FFEL PLUS, Federal Perkins, state loans, college/university loans from institutional funds. **Student Employment:** Federal Work-Study Program available. Institutional employment available. Off-campus job opportunities are fair. **Financial Aid Phone:** 706-864-1412.

NORTH PARK UNIVERSITY

3225 West Foster Avenue, Chicago, IL 60625-4895
Phone: 773-244-5500 **E-mail:** admission@northpark.edu **CEEB Code:** 1556
Fax: 773-244-4953 **Web:** www.northpark.edu **ACT Code:** 1098

This private school was founded in 1891. It has a 30-acre campus.

STUDENTS AND FACULTY

Enrollment: 1,573. **Student Body:** Male 38%, female 62%, out-of-state 42%, international 6% (22 countries represented). **Ethnic Representation:** African American 12%, Asian 5%, Caucasian 65%, Hispanic 10%, Native American 1%. **Faculty:** Student/faculty ratio 16:1. 72 full-time faculty, 75% hold PhDs. 100% faculty teach undergrads.

ACADEMICS

Degrees: Bachelor's, certificate, doctoral, master's. **Academic Requirements:** General education including some course work in arts/fine arts, English (including composition), foreign languages, history, mathematics, philosophy, sciences (biological or physical), social science. **Special Study Options:** Accelerated program, double major, English as a second language, student exchange program (domestic), honors program, independent study, internships, liberal arts/career combination, student-designed major, study abroad, teacher certification program.

FACILITIES

Housing: All-female, all-male, apartments for married students, apartments for single students. **Library Holdings:** 250,000 bound volumes. **Special Academic Facilities/Equipment:** Art gallery, language lab, Swedish Historical Society Archives. **Computers:** School-owned computers available for student use.

EXTRACURRICULARS

Activities: Choral groups, concert band, drama/theater, jazz band, literary magazine, music ensembles, musical theater, opera, pep band, student government, student newspaper, symphony orchestra, yearbook. **Organizations:** 1 religious organization. **Athletics (Intercollegiate):** *Men:* baseball, basketball, cross-country, football, golf, soccer, tennis, track & field. *Women:* basketball, cross-country, golf, soccer, softball, tennis, track & field, volleyball.

ADMISSIONS

Selectivity Rating: 76 (of 100). **Freshman Academic Profile:** Average SAT I Math 570. Average SAT I Verbal 572. Average ACT 22.5. TOEFL required of all international applicants, minimum TOEFL 550. **Basis for Candidate Selection:** *Very important factors considered include:* secondary school record, standardized test scores. *Important factors considered include:* class rank, essays, recommendations. *Other factors considered include:* alumni/ae relation, extracurricular activities, interview, minority status, talent/ability. **Freshman Admission Requirements:** High school diploma or GED is required. *Academic units required/recommended:* 4 English recommended, 3 math recommended, 3 science recommended, 2 foreign language recommended, 1 social studies recommended, 1 history recommended. **Freshman Admission Statistics:** 1,020 applied, 74% accepted, 40% of those accepted enrolled. **Transfer Admission Requirements:** *Items required:* college transcript, essay, statement of good standing from prior school. Minimum college GPA of 2.0 required. Lowest grade transferable C. **General Admission Information:** Application fee $20. Priority application deadline August 15. Nonfall registration accepted. Credit offered for CEEB Advanced Placement tests.

COSTS AND FINANCIAL AID

Tuition $17,790. Room & board $5,830. Required fees $220. Average book expense $950. **Required Forms and Deadlines:** FAFSA. Financial aid filing deadline August 1. Priority filing deadline May 1. **Notification of Awards:** Applicants will be notified of awards on a rolling basis beginning on or about March 10. **Types of Aid:** *Need-based scholarships/grants:* Pell, SEOG, state scholarships/grants, private scholarships, the school's own gift aid, Federal Nursing. *Loans:* FFEL Subsidized Stafford, FFEL Unsubsidized Stafford, FFEL PLUS. **Student Employment:** Federal Work-Study Program available. Institutional employment available. Off-campus job opportunities are excellent. **Financial Aid Statistics:** 81% freshmen receive some form of aid. Average freshman grant $7,216. Average freshman loan $2,752. Average income from on-campus job $1,300. **Financial Aid Phone:** 773-244-5525.

NORTHEASTERN ILLINOIS UNIVERSITY

5500 North St. Louis Avenue, Chicago, IL 60625
Phone: 773-442-4000 **E-mail:** admrec@neiu.edu **CEEB Code:** 1090
Fax: 773-442-4020 **Web:** www.neiu.edu **ACT Code:** 993

This public school was founded in 1961. It has a 63-acre campus.

STUDENTS AND FACULTY

Enrollment: 8,674. **Student Body:** Male 38%, female 62%, out-of-state 1%, international 2%. **Ethnic Representation:** African American 14%, Asian 13%, Caucasian 44%, Hispanic 30%. **Retention and Graduation:** 69% freshmen return for sophomore year. 1% freshmen graduate within 4 years. 32% grads go on to further study within 1 year. 9% grads pursue business degrees. 3% grads pursue medical degrees. **Faculty:** Student/faculty ratio 17:1. 370 full-time faculty, 76% hold PhDs. 100% faculty teach undergrads.

ACADEMICS

Degrees: Bachelor's, master's. **Academic Requirements:** General education including some course work in arts/fine arts, computer literacy, English (including composition), humanities, mathematics, sciences (biological or physical), social science. **Classes:** 20-29 students in an average class. **Majors with Highest Enrollment:** Computer science; elementary education and teaching; liberal arts and sciences/liberal studies. **Disciplines with Highest Percentage of Degrees Awarded:** Education 25%, liberal arts/general studies 19%, computer and information sciences 13%, business/marketing 11%, social sciences and history 7%. **Special Study Options:** Cooperative (work-study) program, distance learning, double major, student exchange program (domestic), honors program, independent study, student-designed major, study abroad, teacher certification program.

FACILITIES

Library Holdings: 441,911 bound volumes. 3,421 periodicals. 899,200 microforms. 6,034 audiovisuals. **Special Academic Facilities/Equipment:** Learning center with audiovisual, TV, multimedia, film, photography, graphic arts, and electronic instructional equipment, listening room. **Computers:** School-owned computers available for student use.

EXTRACURRICULARS

Activities: Dance, drama/theater, jazz band, literary magazine, music ensembles, radio station, student government, student newspaper. **Organizations:** 42 registered organizations, 12 honor societies, 1 sorority.

ADMISSIONS

Selectivity Rating: 67 (of 100). **Freshman Academic Profile:** Average high school GPA 2.7. 5% in top 10% of high school class, 19% in top 25% of high school class, 48% in top 50% of high school class. 73% from public high schools. Average ACT 16, ACT middle 50% range 15-20. TOEFL required of all international applicants, minimum TOEFL 500. **Basis for Candidate Selection:** *Very important factors considered include:* class rank, secondary school record, standardized test scores. **Freshman Admission Requirements:** High school diploma or GED is required. *Academic units required/recommended:* 15 total required; 4 English required, 3 math required, 3 science required, 3 social studies required. **Freshman Admission Statistics:** 2,473 applied, 77% accepted, 55% of those accepted enrolled. **Transfer Admission Requirements:** *Items required:* college transcript, statement of good standing from prior school. Minimum college GPA of 2.0 required. Lowest grade transferable D. **General Admission Information:** Application fee $25. Regular application deadline July 2. Nonfall registration accepted. Admission may be deferred for a maximum of 1 year. Credit offered for CEEB Advanced Placement tests.

COSTS AND FINANCIAL AID

Average book expense $0. **Required Forms and Deadlines:** FAFSA and institution's own financial aid form. No deadline for regular filing. Priority filing deadline March 1. **Notification of Awards:** Applicants will be notified of awards on a rolling basis beginning on or about April 1. **Types of Aid:** *Need-based scholarships/grants:* Pell, SEOG, state scholarships/grants, private scholarships, the school's own gift aid. *Loans:* FFEL Subsidized Stafford, FFEL Unsubsidized Stafford, FFEL PLUS, Federal Perkins. **Student Employment:** Federal Work-Study Program available. Off-campus job opportunities are good. **Financial Aid Statistics:** 52% freshmen, 52% undergrads receive some form of aid. Average freshman loan $1,291. **Financial Aid Phone:** 773-442-5000.

NORTHEASTERN STATE UNIVERSITY

Office of Admissions and Records, 600 N. Grand, Tahlequah, OK 74464-2399
Phone: 918-456-5511 **E-mail:** nsuadmis@cherokee.nsuok.edu
Fax: 918-458-2342 **Web:** www.nsuok.edu **ACT Code:** 3408

This public school was founded in 1846. It has a 200-acre campus.

STUDENTS AND FACULTY

Enrollment: 7,777. **Student Body:** Male 41%, female 59%, out-of-state 6%, international 1% (40 countries represented). **Ethnic Representation:** African American 5%, Asian 1%, Caucasian 63%, Hispanic 1%, Native American 30%. **Faculty:** Student/faculty ratio 24:1. 306 full-time faculty.

ACADEMICS

Degrees: Bachelor's, first professional, master's, post-master's certificate. **Academic Requirements:** General education including some course work in computer literacy, English (including composition), history, humanities, mathematics, sciences (biological or physical), social science. **Disciplines with Highest Percentage of Degrees Awarded:** Education 25%, business/marketing 18%, health professions and related sciences 9%, protective services/public administration 8%, social sciences and history 6%. **Special Study Options:** Cooperative (work-study) program, distance learning, double major, dual enrollment, English as a second language, honors program, internships, teacher certification program, weekend college.

FACILITIES

Housing: Coed, all-female, all-male, apartments for married students, fraternities and/or sororities, apartments for single students with children. **Library Holdings:** 424,818 bound volumes. 3,983 periodicals. 742,695 microforms. 6,804 audiovisuals. **Special Academic Facilities/Equipment:** Indian Territory Genological Society. **Computers:** School-owned computers available for student use.

EXTRACURRICULARS

Activities: Choral groups, concert band, dance, drama/theater, jazz band, literary magazine, marching band, music ensembles, pep band, radio station, student government, student newspaper, symphony orchestra, television station, yearbook. **Organizations:** 80 registered organizations, 9 honor societies, 7 religious organizations, 4 fraternities (5% men join), 3 sororities (10% women join). **Athletics (Intercollegiate):** *Men:* baseball, basketball, cheerleading, football, golf, soccer. *Women:* basketball, cheerleading, golf, soccer, softball, tennis.

ADMISSIONS

Selectivity Rating: 65 (of 100). **Freshman Academic Profile:** Average high school GPA 3.2. 89% from public high schools. Average ACT 20. TOEFL required of all international applicants, minimum TOEFL 500. **Basis for Candidate Selection:** *Very important factors considered include:* class rank, secondary school record, standardized test scores. **Freshman Admission Requirements:** High school diploma or GED is required. *Academic units required/recommended:* 15 total required; 4 English required, 3 math required, 2 science required, 2 science lab required. **Transfer Admission Requirements:** *Items required:* college transcript. Minimum college GPA of 2.0 required. **General Admission Information:** Priority application deadline August 1. Nonfall registration accepted. Credit offered for CEEB Advanced Placement tests.

COSTS AND FINANCIAL AID

In-state tuition $2,275. Out-of-state tuition $5,268. Room & board $3,632. Required fees $150. Average book expense $560. **Required Forms and Deadlines:** FAFSA. No deadline for regular filing. **Notification of Awards:** Applicants will be notified of awards on a rolling basis beginning on or about March 30. **Types of Aid:** *Need-based scholarships/grants:* Pell, SEOG, state scholarships/grants, private scholarships. *Loans:* FFEL Subsidized Stafford, FFEL Unsubsidized Stafford, FFEL PLUS, Federal Perkins. **Student Employment:** Federal Work-Study Program available. Institutional employment available. Off-campus job opportunities are good. **Financial Aid Statistics:** 50% freshmen, 50% undergrads receive some form of aid. Average freshman grant $3,500. Average freshman loan $3,903. Average income from on-campus job $1,600. **Financial Aid Phone:** 918-458-2077.

NORTHEASTERN UNIVERSITY

360 Huntington Avenue, 150 Richards Hall, Boston, MA 02115
Phone: 617-373-2200 **E-mail:** admissions@neu.edu **CEEB Code:** 3667
Fax: 617-373-8780 **Web:** www.northeastern.edu **ACT Code:** 1880

This private school was founded in 1898. It has a 67-acre campus.

STUDENTS AND FACULTY

Enrollment: 14,144. **Student Body:** Out-of-state 63%, international students represent 110 countries. **Retention and Graduation:** 84% freshmen return for sophomore year. 17% grads go on to further study within 1 year. **Faculty:** Student/faculty ratio 16:1. 801 full-time faculty, 77% hold PhDs. 100% faculty teach undergrads.

ACADEMICS

Degrees: Associate's, bachelor's, certificate, doctoral, first professional, master's, post-bachelor's certificate, post-master's certificate. **Academic Requirements:** General education including some course work in English (including composition). **Classes:** 10-19 students in an average class. **Majors with Highest Enrollment:** Business/commerce, general; engineering, general; health services/allied health, general. **Disciplines with Highest Percentage of Degrees Awarded:** Business/marketing 26%, engineering/engineering technology 15%, health professions and related sciences 11%, protective services/public administration 9%, communications/communication technologies 8%. **Special Study Options:** Accelerated program, cooperative (work-study) program, cross registration, distance learning, double major, dual enrollment, English as a second language, student exchange program (domestic), honors program, independent study, internships, liberal arts/career combination, student-designed major, study abroad, teacher certification program, weekend college.

FACILITIES

Housing: Coed, all-female, apartments for single students, housing for disabled students, housing for international students, fraternities and/or sororities, honors halls, wellness hall, quiet hall, engineering hall, living and learning halls. **Library Holdings:** 710,843 bound volumes. 7,798 periodicals. 2,231,820 microforms. 17,981 audiovisuals. **Special Academic Facilities/Equipment:** Marine science center, African-American Institute, electron microscopy center, electromagnetic research center. **Computers:** School-owned computers available for student use.

EXTRACURRICULARS

Activities: Choral groups, concert band, dance, drama/theater, jazz band, literary magazine, music ensembles, musical theater, pep band, radio station, student government, student newspaper, symphony orchestra, yearbook. **Organizations:** 140 registered organizations, 13 honor societies, 10 religious organizations, 11 fraternities (4% men join), 8 sororities (3% women join). **Athletics (Intercollegiate):** *Men:* baseball, basketball, crew, cross-country, football, ice hockey, indoor track, soccer, tennis, track & field. *Women:* basketball, crew, cross-country, diving, field hockey, ice hockey, indoor track, soccer, swimming, tennis, track & field, volleyball.

ADMISSIONS

Selectivity Rating: 77 (of 100). **Freshman Academic Profile:** Average high school GPA 3.2. 21% in top 10% of high school class, 57% in top 25% of high school class, 88% in top 50% of high school class. Average SAT I Math 588, SAT I Math middle 50% range 540-640. Average SAT I Verbal 565, SAT I Verbal middle 50% range 520-620. Average ACT 24, ACT middle 50% range 22-27. TOEFL required of all international applicants, minimum TOEFL 550. **Basis for Candidate Selection:** *Very important factors considered include:* secondary school record. *Important factors considered include:* character/ personal qualities, class rank, essays, extracurricular activities, recommendations, standardized test scores, talent/ability. *Other factors considered include:* alumni/ae relation, geographical residence, minority status, volunteer work, work experience. **Freshman Admission Requirements:** High school diploma or GED is required. *Academic units required/recommended:* 17 total recommended; 4 English recommended, 3 math recommended, 3 science recommended, 2 science lab recommended, 2 foreign language recommended, 3 social studies recommended, 2 history recommended. **Freshman Admission Statistics:** 17,037 applied, 61% accepted, 28% of those accepted enrolled. **Transfer Admission Requirements:** *Items required:* college transcript, essay, statement of good standing from prior school. Minimum college GPA of 2.0 required. Lowest grade transferable C. **General Admission Information:** Application fee $50. Regular application deadline February 15. Nonfall registration accepted. Admission may be deferred for a maximum of 1 year. Credit and/or placement offered for CEEB Advanced Placement tests.

COSTS AND FINANCIAL AID

Tuition $24,266. Room & board $9,660. Required fees $201. Average book expense $900. **Required Forms and Deadlines:** FAFSA and CSS/Financial Aid PROFILE. No deadline for regular filing. Priority filing deadline February 15. **Notification of Awards:** Applicants will be notified of awards on a rolling basis beginning on or about February 15. **Types of Aid:** *Need-based scholarships/grants:* Pell, SEOG, state scholarships/grants, private scholarships, the school's own gift aid, Federal Nursing. *Loans:* FFEL Subsidized Stafford, FFEL Unsubsidized Stafford, FFEL PLUS, Federal Perkins, Federal Nursing, state loans, MEFA, TERI, Signature, Mass. No Interest Loan (NIL), CitiAssist. **Student Employment:** Federal Work-Study Program available. Institutional employment available. Off-campus job opportunities are excellent. **Financial Aid Statistics:** 67% freshmen, 63% undergrads receive some form of aid. Average freshman grant $12,321. Average freshman loan $3,028. **Financial Aid Phone:** 617-373-3190.

NORTHERN ARIZONA UNIVERSITY

PO Box 4084, Flagstaff, AZ 86011-4084
Phone: 928-523-5511 **E-mail:** undergraduate.admissions@nau.edu **CEEB Code:** 4006
Fax: 928-523-0226 **Web:** www.nau.edu **ACT Code:** 86

This public school was founded in 1899. It has a 740-acre campus.

STUDENTS AND FACULTY

Enrollment: 13,577. **Student Body:** Male 41%, female 59%, out-of-state 22%, international 2%. **Ethnic Representation:** African American 2%, Asian 2%, Caucasian 78%, Hispanic 10%, Native American 8%. **Retention and Graduation:** 67% freshmen return for sophomore year. 24% freshmen graduate within 4 years. **Faculty:** Student/faculty ratio 17:1. 708 full-time faculty, 83% hold PhDs. 90% faculty teach undergrads.

ACADEMICS

Degrees: Bachelor's, doctoral, first professional, master's. **Academic Requirements:** General education including some course work in arts/fine arts, computer literacy, English (including composition), foreign languages, history, humanities, mathematics, philosophy, sciences (biological or physical), social science, cultural diversity. **Classes:** 20-29 students in an average class. 20-29 students in an average lab/discussion section. **Majors with Highest Enrollment:** Elementary education and teaching; psychology, general; hotel/ motel administration/management. **Disciplines with Highest Percentage of Degrees Awarded:** Education 23%, business/marketing 18%, interdisciplinary studies 9%, social sciences and history 6%, protective services/public administration 6%. **Special Study Options:** Accelerated program, cooperative (work-study) program, distance learning, double major, English as a second language, student exchange program (domestic), honors program, independent study, internships, study abroad, teacher certification program.

FACILITIES

Housing: Coed, all-female, all-male, apartments for married students, housing for international students. **Library Holdings:** 633,417 bound volumes. 2,595 periodicals. 547,729 microforms. 31,746 audiovisuals. **Special Academic Facilities/Equipment:** Art gallery, art and music studios, observatory, multidisciplinary research center, 4,000-acre experimental forest. **Computers:** School-owned computers available for student use.

EXTRACURRICULARS

Activities: Choral groups, drama/theater, literary magazine, marching band, radio station, student government, student newspaper, symphony orchestra, yearbook. **Organizations:** 162 registered organizations, 23 honor societies, 7 religious organizations, 13 fraternities (9% men join), 7 sororities (7% women join). **Athletics (Intercollegiate):** *Men:* basketball, cross-country, football, tennis, track & field. *Women:* basketball, cross-country, diving, golf, soccer, swimming, tennis, track & field, volleyball.

ADMISSIONS

Selectivity Rating: 67 (of 100). **Freshman Academic Profile:** Average high school GPA 3.4, 26% in top 10% of high school class, 52% in top 25% of high school class, 82% in top 50% of high school class. Average SAT I Math 529, SAT I Math middle 50% range 470-590. Average SAT I Verbal 532, SAT I Verbal middle 50% range 480-590. Average ACT 22, ACT middle 50% range 20-25. TOEFL required of all international applicants, minimum TOEFL 500. **Basis for Candidate Selection:** *Very important factors considered include:* class rank, secondary school record, standardized test scores. **Freshman Admission Requirements:** High school diploma or equivalent is not required. *Academic units required/recommended:* 4 English required, 4 English recommended, 4 math required, 4 math recommended, 3 science required, 3 science recommended, 3 science lab required, 3 science lab recommended, 2 foreign language required, 1 social studies required, 1 history required. **Freshman Admission Statistics:** 7,912 applied, 81% accepted, 37% of those accepted enrolled. **Transfer Admission Requirements:** *Items required:* college transcript. Minimum college GPA of 2.0 required. Lowest grade transferable C. **General Admission Information:** Application fee $50. Priority application deadline March 1. Nonfall registration accepted. Credit and/or placement offered for CEEB Advanced Placement tests.

COSTS AND FINANCIAL AID

In-state tuition $2,412. Out-of-state tuition $7,790. Room & board $4,910. Required fees $76. Average book expense $750. **Required Forms and Deadlines:** FAFSA. Priority filing deadline February 14. **Notification of Awards:** Applicants will be notified of awards on a rolling basis beginning on or about February 14. **Types of Aid:** *Need-based scholarships/grants:* Pell, SEOG, state scholarships/grants, private scholarships, the school's own gift aid. *Loans:* Direct Subsidized Stafford, Direct Unsubsidized Stafford, Direct PLUS, Federal Perkins, Federal Nursing, college/university loans from institutional funds. **Student Employment:** Federal Work-Study Program available. Institutional employment available. Off-campus job opportunities are good. **Financial Aid Statistics:** 36% freshmen, 49% undergrads receive some form of aid. Average freshman grant $3,912. Average freshman loan $3,012. Average income from on-campus job $2,097. **Financial Aid Phone:** 928-523-4951.

NORTHERN ILLINOIS UNIVERSITY

Office of Admissions, Williston Hall 101, NIU, DeKalb, IL 60115-2857
Phone: 815-753-0446 **E-mail:** admissions-info@niu.edu **CEEB Code:** 1559
Fax: 815-753-1783 **Web:** www.reg.niu.edu **ACT Code:** 1102

This public school was founded in 1895. It has a 546-acre campus.

STUDENTS AND FACULTY

Enrollment: 17,468. **Student Body:** Male 47%, female 53%, out-of-state 4%, international 1%. **Ethnic Representation:** African American 13%, Asian 7%, Caucasian 71%, Hispanic 6%. **Retention and Graduation:** 24% freshmen graduate within 4 years. 10% grads go on to further study within 1 year. **Faculty:** Student/faculty ratio 17:1. 973 full-time faculty, 75% hold PhDs.

ACADEMICS

Degrees: Bachelor's, doctoral, first professional, master's. **Academic Requirements:** General education including some course work in English (including composition), foreign languages, humanities, mathematics, sciences (biological or physical), social science. **Classes:** 20-29 students in an average class. 20-29 students in an average lab/discussion section. **Disciplines with Highest Percentage of Degrees Awarded:** Business/marketing 24%, education 15%, social sciences and history 10%, English 9%, health professions and related sciences 8%. **Special Study Options:** Cooperative (work-study) program, distance learning, double major, dual enrollment, external degree program, honors program, independent study, internships, liberal arts/career combination, student-designed major, study abroad, teacher certification program.

FACILITIES

Housing: Coed, apartments for married students, housing for disabled students, fraternities and/or sororities. **Library Holdings:** 1,624,326 bound volumes. 18,394 periodicals. 2,971,571 microforms. 50,182 audiovisuals. **Special Academic Facilities/Equipment:** Art and anthropology museums, plant molecular biology center. **Computers:** School-owned computers available for student use.

EXTRACURRICULARS

Activities: Choral groups, concert band, dance, drama/theater, jazz band, opera, radio station, student government, student newspaper, student-run film society, symphony orchestra, television station. **Organizations:** 202 registered organizations, 18 religious organizations, 20 fraternities (11% men join), 12 sororities (7% women join). **Athletics (Intercollegiate):** *Men:* baseball, basketball, football, golf, soccer, swimming, wrestling. *Women:* basketball, golf, gymnastics, soccer, softball, swimming, tennis, volleyball.

ADMISSIONS

Selectivity Rating: 74 (of 100). **Freshman Academic Profile:** 10% in top 10% of high school class, 35% in top 25% of high school class, 74% in top 50% of high school class. Average ACT 22, ACT middle 50% range 20-25. TOEFL required of all international applicants, minimum TOEFL 525. **Basis for Candidate Selection:** *Very important factors considered include:* class rank, secondary school record, standardized test scores. *Other factors considered include:* essays, extracurricular activities, minority status, recommendations, talent/ability. **Freshman Admission Requirements:** High school diploma or GED is required. *Academic units required/recommended:* 15 total required; 4 English required, 2 math required, 4 math recommended, 2 science required, 4 science recommended, 1 science lab required, 2 science lab recommended, 1 foreign language required, 2 foreign language recommended, 2 social studies required, 3 social studies recommended, 1 history required. **Freshman Admission Statistics:** 13,421 applied, 64% accepted, 33% of those accepted enrolled. **Transfer Admission Requirements:** *Items required:* college transcript. Minimum college GPA of 2.0 required. Lowest grade transferable C. **General Admission Information:** Priority application deadline March 1. Regular application deadline August 1. Nonfall registration accepted. Credit and/or placement offered for CEEB Advanced Placement tests.

COSTS AND FINANCIAL AID

In-state tuition $4,347. Room & board $5,010. Average book expense $700. **Required Forms and Deadlines:** FAFSA, institution's own financial aid form, noncustodial (divorced/separated) parent's statement. Priority filing deadline March 1. **Notification of Awards:** Applicants will be notified of awards on a rolling basis beginning on or about April 15. **Types of Aid:** *Need-based scholarships/grants:* Pell, SEOG, state scholarships/grants, private scholarships, the school's own gift aid, Federal Nursing. *Loans:* FFEL Subsidized Stafford, FFEL Unsubsidized Stafford, FFEL PLUS, Federal Perkins. **Student Employment:** Federal Work-Study Program available. Institutional employment available. Off-campus job opportunities are good. **Financial Aid Statistics:** Average freshman grant $1,500. Average freshman loan $2,625. Average income from on-campus job $1,000. **Financial Aid Phone:** 815-753-1395.

NORTHERN KENTUCKY UNIVERSITY

Administrative Center 400, Nunn Drive, Highland Heights, KY 41099
Phone: 859-572-5220 **E-mail:** admitnku@nku.edu **CEEB Code:** 1574
Fax: 859-572-5566 **Web:** www.nku.edu **ACT Code:** 1566

This public school was founded in 1968. It has a 300-acre campus.

STUDENTS AND FACULTY

Enrollment: 12,136. **Student Body:** Male 41%, female 59%, out-of-state 23%, international 1% (43 countries represented). **Ethnic Representation:** African American 5%, Asian 1%, Caucasian 93%, Hispanic 1%. **Retention and Graduation:** 72% freshmen return for sophomore year. 11% freshmen graduate within 4 years. **Faculty:** Student/faculty ratio 17:1. 463 full-time faculty, 68% hold PhDs. 26% faculty teach undergrads.

ACADEMICS

Degrees: Associate's, bachelor's, certificate, first professional, master's. **Academic Requirements:** General education including some course work in English (including composition), history, humanities, mathematics, sciences (biological or physical), social science, diversity. **Classes:** 20-29 students in an average class. 20-29 students in an average lab/discussion section. **Disciplines with Highest Percentage of Degrees Awarded:** Business/marketing 24%, education 15%, social sciences and history 11%, English 10%, communications/communication technologies 6%. **Special Study Options:** Cooperative (work-study) program, cross registration, distance learning, double major, dual enrollment, student exchange program (domestic), honors program, independent study, internships, study abroad, teacher certification program.

FACILITIES

Housing: Coed, all-female, all-male, apartments for single students, housing for disabled students. **Library Holdings:** 325,721 bound volumes. 2,217 periodicals. 771,708 microforms. **Special Academic Facilities/Equipment:** Art gallery, biology, geology, and anthropology museums, research/technical center, two electron microscopes. **Computers:** School-owned computers available for student use.

EXTRACURRICULARS

Activities: Choral groups, drama/theater, jazz band, literary magazine, music ensembles, musical theater, pep band, radio station, student government, student newspaper, television station. **Organizations:** 100 registered organizations, 15 honor societies, 6 religious organizations, 6 fraternities (5% men join), 5 sororities (5% women join). **Athletics (Intercollegiate):** *Men:* baseball, basketball, cross-country, golf, soccer, tennis. *Women:* basketball, cross-country, soccer, softball, tennis, volleyball.

ADMISSIONS

Selectivity Rating: 65 (of 100). **Freshman Academic Profile:** SAT I Math middle 50% range 420-550. SAT I Verbal middle 50% range 410-540. Average ACT 20, ACT middle 50% range 17-22. TOEFL required of all international applicants, minimum TOEFL 500. **Freshman Admission Requirements:** High school diploma or GED is required. *Academic units required/recommended:* 4 total required; 3 English required, 3 math required, 1 science required, 2 science lab recommended, 3 foreign language required. **Freshman Admission Statistics:** 3,528 applied, 90% accepted, 62% of those accepted enrolled. **Transfer Admission Requirements:** *Items required:* college transcript. Minimum college GPA of 2.0 required. Lowest grade transferable C-. **General Admission Information:** Application fee $25. Priority application deadline February 1. Regular application deadline August 1. Nonfall registration accepted. Admission may be deferred for a maximum of 1 year. Credit offered for CEEB Advanced Placement tests.

COSTS AND FINANCIAL AID

In-state tuition $3,216. Out-of-state tuition $7,464. Room & board $4,862. Required fees $0. Average book expense $650. **Required Forms and Deadlines:** FAFSA. Priority filing deadline March 1. **Notification of Awards:** Applicants will be notified of awards on a rolling basis beginning on or about April 1. **Types of Aid:** *Need-based scholarships/grants:* Pell, SEOG, state scholarships/grants, private scholarships, the school's own gift aid. *Loans:* FFEL Subsidized Stafford, FFEL Unsubsidized Stafford, FFEL PLUS, Federal Perkins. **Student Employment:** Federal Work-Study Program available. Institutional employment available. Off-campus job opportunities are excellent. **Financial Aid Statistics:** 66% freshmen, 84% undergrads receive some form of aid. Average freshman grant $4,632. Average freshman loan $2,625. Average income from on-campus job $2,858. **Financial Aid Phone:** 606-572-5143.

NORTHERN MICHIGAN UNIVERSITY

1401 Presque Isle Avenue, 304 Cohodas, Marquette, MI 49855
Phone: 906-227-2650 **E-mail:** admiss@nmu.edu **CEEB Code:** 1560
Fax: 906-227-1747 **Web:** www.nmu.edu **ACT Code:** 2038

This public school was founded in 1899. It has a 300-acre campus.

STUDENTS AND FACULTY

Enrollment: 8,113. **Student Body:** Male 48%, female 52%, out-of-state 18%, international 1%. **Ethnic Representation:** African American 2%, Caucasian 93%, Hispanic 1%, Native American 2%, Asian 1%. **Retention and Graduation:** 71% freshmen return for sophomore year. **Faculty:** Student/faculty ratio 21:1. 311 full-time faculty, 85% hold PhDs.

ACADEMICS

Degrees: Associate's, bachelor's, certificate, diploma, master's, post-bachelor's certificate, post-master's certificate, terminal, transfer. **Academic Requirements:** General education including some course work in arts/fine arts, computer literacy, English (including composition), humanities, mathematics, sciences (biological or physical), social science. **Classes:** 20-29 students in an average class. **Disciplines with Highest Percentage of Degrees Awarded:** Education 19%, business/marketing 15%, social sciences and history 11%, protective services/public administration 8%, visual and performing arts 6%. **Special Study Options:** Distance learning, double major, dual enrollment, honors program, independent study, internships, liberal arts/career combination, student-designed major, study abroad, teacher certification program, weekend college, health promotion.

FACILITIES

Housing: Coed, apartments for married students, apartments for single students, housing for disabled students. **Library Holdings:** 1,111,373 bound volumes. 1,711 periodicals. 700,891 microforms. 19,167 audiovisuals. **Computers:** School-owned computers available for student use.

EXTRACURRICULARS

Activities: Choral groups, concert band, dance, drama/theater, jazz band, literary magazine, marching band, music ensembles, musical theater, opera, pep band, radio station, student government, student newspaper, student-run film society, symphony orchestra, television station. **Organizations:** 202 registered organizations, 4 fraternities (2% men join), 3 sororities (2% women join). **Athletics (Intercollegiate):** *Men:* basketball, cheerleading, football, golf, ice hockey, skiing (Nordic), wrestling. *Women:* basketball, cheerleading, cross-country, skiing (alpine), skiing (Nordic), soccer, swimming, tennis, volleyball.

ADMISSIONS

Selectivity Rating: 66 (of 100). **Freshman Academic Profile:** Average high school GPA 3.0. Average ACT 21. TOEFL required of all international applicants, minimum TOEFL 500. **Basis for Candidate Selection:** *Very important factors considered include:* secondary school record, standardized test scores. *Other factors considered include:* character/personal qualities, class rank, essays, extracurricular activities, interview, recommendations, talent/ability, volunteer work, work experience. **Freshman Admission Requirements:** High school diploma or GED is required. *Academic units required/recommended:* 12 total required; 16 total recommended; 4 English recommended, 3 math recommended, 2 science recommended, 3 foreign language recommended, 1 social studies recommended, 1 history recommended. **Freshman Admission Statistics:** 4,421 applied, 86% accepted, 50% of those accepted enrolled. **Transfer Admission Requirements:** *Items required:* high school transcript, college transcript, statement of good standing from prior school. Minimum college GPA of 2.0 required. Lowest grade transferable D-. **General Admission Information:** Application fee $25. Priority application deadline August 1. Nonfall registration accepted. Admission may be deferred. Credit and/or placement offered for CEEB Advanced Placement tests.

COSTS AND FINANCIAL AID

In-state tuition $4,128. Out-of-state tuition $7,080. Room & board $5,630. Required fees $652. Average book expense $600. **Required Forms and Deadlines:** FAFSA. No deadline for regular filing. Priority filing deadline February 20. **Notification of Awards:** Applicants will be notified of awards on a rolling basis beginning on or about April 1. **Types of Aid:** *Need-based scholarships/grants:* Pell, SEOG, state scholarships/grants, private scholarships, the school's own gift aid. *Loans:* Direct Subsidized Stafford, Direct Unsubsidized Stafford, Direct PLUS, Federal Perkins, state loans. **Student Employment:** Federal Work-Study Program available. Institutional employment available. Off-campus job opportunities are good. **Financial Aid Statistics:** 57% freshmen, 55% undergrads receive some form of aid. Average freshman grant $5,100. Average freshman loan $2,625. **Financial Aid Phone:** 906-227-2327.

NORTHERN STATE UNIVERSITY

1200 South Jay Street, Aberdeen, SD 57401-7198
Phone: 605-626-2544 **E-mail:** admissions1@northern.edu **CEEB Code:** 6487
Fax: 605-626-2431 **Web:** www.northern.edu **ACT Code:** 3916

This public school was founded in 1901. It has a 72-acre campus.

STUDENTS AND FACULTY

Enrollment: 2,740. **Student Body:** Male 41%, female 59%, out-of-state 15%, international 1% (10 countries represented). **Ethnic Representation:** African American 1%, Asian 1%, Caucasian 80%, Hispanic 1%, Native American 2%. **Retention and Graduation:** 69% freshmen return for sophomore year. 10% grads go on to further study within 1 year. 1% grads pursue business degrees. 1% grads pursue law degrees. 1% grads pursue medical degrees. **Faculty:** Student/faculty ratio 20:1. 110 full-time faculty, 77% hold PhDs.

ACADEMICS

Degrees: Associate's, bachelor's, certificate, master's. **Classes:** 10-19 students in an average class. **Majors with Highest Enrollment:** Business administration/management; elementary education and teaching; sociology. **Disciplines with Highest Percentage of Degrees Awarded:** Education 37%, business/marketing 34%, social sciences and history 11%, psychology 6%, biological life sciences 4%. **Special Study Options:** Accelerated program, cooperative (work-study) program, distance learning, double major, English as a second language, student exchange program (domestic), honors program, internships, student-designed major, study abroad, teacher certification program, international business.

FACILITIES

Housing: Coed, all-female, all-male, apartments for single students. **Library Holdings:** 187,734 bound volumes. 868 periodicals. 327,228 microforms. 3,385 audiovisuals. **Special Academic Facilities/Equipment:** Art galleries. **Computers:** *Recommended operating system:* Windows NT/2000. School-owned computers available for student use.

EXTRACURRICULARS

Activities: Choral groups, concert band, drama/theater, marching band, pep band, student government, student newspaper, yearbook. **Organizations:** 100 registered organizations, 5 honor societies, 3 religious organizations. **Athletics (Intercollegiate):** *Men:* baseball, basketball, cheerleading, cross-country, football, golf, ice hockey, indoor track, track & field, wrestling. *Women:* basketball, cheerleading, cross-country, golf, indoor track, soccer, softball, track & field, volleyball.

ADMISSIONS

Selectivity Rating: 63 (of 100). **Freshman Academic Profile:** 18% in top 10% of high school class, 45% in top 25% of high school class, 67% in top 50% of high school class. TOEFL required of all international applicants, minimum TOEFL 550. **Basis for Candidate Selection:** *Very important factors considered include:* class rank, secondary school record, standardized test scores. *Other factors considered include:* interview, talent/ability. **Freshman Admission Requirements:** High school diploma or GED is required. *Academic units required/recommended:* 13 total required; 4 English required, 3 math required, 3 science required, 3 science lab required, 3 social studies required. **Freshman Admission Statistics:** 902 applied, 92% accepted, 49% of those accepted enrolled. **Transfer Admission Requirements:** *Items required:* high school transcript, college transcript. Minimum college GPA of 2.0 required. Lowest grade transferable C. **General Admission Information:** Application fee $15. Regular application deadline August 15. Nonfall registration accepted. Credit offered for CEEB Advanced Placement tests.

COSTS AND FINANCIAL AID

In-state tuition $1,872. Out-of-state tuition $5,955. Room & board $2,740. Required fees $1,667. Average book expense $650. **Required Forms and Deadlines:** FAFSA. **Notification of Awards:** Applicants will be notified of awards on or about May 1. **Types of Aid:** *Need-based scholarships/grants:* Pell, SEOG, state scholarships/grants, private scholarships, the school's own gift aid. *Loans:* FFEL Subsidized Stafford, FFEL Unsubsidized Stafford, FFEL PLUS, Federal Perkins, college/university loans from institutional funds. **Student Employment:** Federal Work-Study Program available. Institutional employment available. Off-campus job opportunities are excellent. **Financial Aid**

Statistics: Average income from on-campus job $1,500. **Financial Aid Phone:** 605-626-2640.

NORTHLAND COLLEGE

1411 Ellis Avenue, Ashland, WI 54806-3999
Phone: 715-682-1224 **E-mail:** admit@northland.edu **CEEB Code:** 1561
Fax: 715-682-1258 **Web:** www.northland.edu **ACT Code:** 4624

This private school, which is affiliated with the United Church of Christ, was founded in 1892. It has a 130-acre campus.

STUDENTS AND FACULTY

Enrollment: 752. **Student Body:** Male 45%, female 55%, out-of-state 67%, international 3%. **Ethnic Representation:** African American 1%, Asian 1%, Caucasian 89%, Hispanic 1%, Native American 2%. **Retention and Graduation:** 66% freshmen return for sophomore year. 100% freshmen graduate within 4 years. **Faculty:** Student/faculty ratio 14:1. 48 full-time faculty, 81% hold PhDs. 100% faculty teach undergrads.

ACADEMICS

Degrees: Bachelor's. **Academic Requirements:** General education including some course work in arts/fine arts, English (including composition), history, humanities, mathematics, philosophy, sciences (biological or physical), social science. Student must take two multi-cultural-themed courses. **Classes:** 10-19 students in an average class. 20-29 students in an average lab/discussion section. **Majors with Highest Enrollment:** Natural resources/conservation, general; education, general; biology/biological sciences, general. **Disciplines with Highest Percentage of Degrees Awarded:** Education 32%, natural resources/environmental sciences 22%, biological life sciences 12%, physical sciences 10%, business/marketing 6%. **Special Study Options:** Cooperative (work-study) program, distance learning, double major, student exchange program (domestic), independent study, internships, liberal arts/career combination, student-designed major, study abroad, teacher certification program.

FACILITIES

Housing: Coed, all-female, all-male, apartments for single students, cooperative housing, theme houses focusing on a chosen theme and offering programming to the campus. **Library Holdings:** 75,000 bound volumes. 260 periodicals. 62,781 microforms. 1,146 audiovisuals. **Special Academic Facilities/Equipment:** Native American museum, language lab, field stations in nearby national forest, observatory. **Computers:** School-owned computers available for student use.

EXTRACURRICULARS

Activities: Choral groups, concert band, dance, drama/theater, jazz band, literary magazine, music ensembles, radio station, student government, student newspaper, student-run film society, symphony orchestra, yearbook. **Organizations:** 30 registered organizations, 1 honor society. **Athletics (Intercollegiate):** *Men:* baseball, basketball, cross-country, ice hockey, soccer. *Women:* basketball, cross-country, soccer, softball, volleyball.

ADMISSIONS

Selectivity Rating: 72 (of 100). **Freshman Academic Profile:** Average high school GPA 3.5. 20% in top 10% of high school class, 46% in top 25% of high school class, 74% in top 50% of high school class. Average SAT I Math 550, SAT I Math middle 50% range 490-570. Average SAT I Verbal 550, SAT I Verbal middle 50% range 510-590. Average ACT 24, ACT middle 50% range 21-26. TOEFL required of all international applicants, minimum TOEFL 550. **Basis for Candidate Selection:** *Very important factors considered include:* secondary school record. *Important factors considered include:* class rank, standardized test scores. *Other factors considered include:* alumni/ae relation, character/personal qualities, essays, extracurricular activities, geographical residence, interview, minority status, recommendations, talent/ability, volunteer work, work experience. **Freshman Admission Requirements:** High school diploma or GED is required. *Academic units required/recommended:* 3 total required; 17 total recommended; 3 English required, 4 English recommended, 3 math required, 3 math recommended, 3 science required, 3 science recommended, 2 science lab required, 2 science lab recommended, 2 foreign language recommended, 3 social studies required, 3 social studies recommended, 3 elective required, 4 elective recommended. **Freshman Admission Statistics:** 860 applied, 94% accepted, 23% of those accepted enrolled. **Transfer Admission Requirements:** *Items required:* high school transcript, college transcript, statement of good standing from prior school. Minimum college GPA of 2.0 required. Lowest grade transferable C. **General Admission Information:** Priority application deadline April 1. Nonfall registration accepted. Admission may be deferred for a maximum of 2 years. Credit and/or placement offered for CEEB Advanced Placement tests.

COSTS AND FINANCIAL AID

Tuition $17,070. Room & board $5,100. Required fees $580. Average book expense $600. **Required Forms and Deadlines:** FAFSA and institution's own financial aid form. Priority filing deadline April 15. **Notification of Awards:** Applicants will be notified of awards on a rolling basis beginning on or about March 1. **Types of Aid:** *Need-based scholarships/grants:* Pell, SEOG, state scholarships/grants, private scholarships, the school's own gift aid. *Loans:* Direct Subsidized Stafford, Direct Unsubsidized Stafford, Direct PLUS, Federal Perkins. **Student Employment:** Federal Work-Study Program available. Institutional employment available. Off-campus job opportunities are fair. **Financial Aid Statistics:** 76% freshmen, 78% undergrads receive some form of aid. Average freshman grant $9,250. Average freshman loan $3,437. Average income from on-campus job $1,000. **Financial Aid Phone:** 715-682-1255.

NORTHWEST CHRISTIAN COLLEGE

828 East 11th Avenue, Eugene, OR 97401
Phone: 541-684-7201 **E-mail:** admissions@nwcc.edu **CEEB Code:** 4543
Fax: 541-628-7317 **Web:** www.nwcc.edu **ACT Code:** 10101

This private school was founded in 1895.

STUDENTS AND FACULTY

Enrollment: 412. **Student Body:** Male 40%, female 60%, out-of-state 16%. **Ethnic Representation:** African American 5%, Asian 1%, Caucasian 87%, Hispanic 2%, Native American 1%. **Retention and Graduation:** 68% freshmen return for sophomore year. 13% freshmen graduate within 4 years. **Faculty:** Student/faculty ratio 15:1. 23 full-time faculty, 65% hold PhDs. 100% faculty teach undergrads.

ACADEMICS

Degrees: Associate's, bachelor's, certificate, master's, post-bachelor's certificate. **Academic Requirements:** General education including some course work in arts/fine arts, computer literacy, English (including composition), history, humanities, mathematics, philosophy, sciences (biological or physical), social science, biblical studies. **Majors with Highest Enrollment:** Business, management, marketing, and related support services; psychology, general; elementary education and teaching. **Disciplines with Highest Percentage of Degrees Awarded:** Business/marketing 61%, education 20%, psychology 5%, philosophy/religion/theology 5%, communications/communication technologies 3%. **Special Study Options:** Cooperative (work-study) program, distance learning, double major, English as a second language, internships, study abroad, teacher certification program.

FACILITIES

Housing: Coed, apartments for married students, apartments for single students. **Library Holdings:** 62,220 bound volumes. 261 periodicals. 128 microforms. 8,677 audiovisuals. **Computers:** School-owned computers available for student use.

EXTRACURRICULARS

Activities: Choral groups, drama/theater, literary magazine, music ensembles, student government, student newspaper, yearbook. **Athletics (Intercollegiate):** *Men:* basketball. *Women:* softball.

ADMISSIONS

Selectivity Rating: 63 (of 100). **Freshman Academic Profile:** Average high school GPA 3.3. 17% in top 10% of high school class, 36% in top 25% of high school class, 69% in top 50% of high school class. Average SAT I Math 509, SAT I Math middle 50% range 440-570. Average SAT I Verbal 515, SAT I Verbal middle 50% range 440-580. Average ACT 22, ACT middle 50% range 17-27. TOEFL required of all international applicants, minimum TOEFL 500. **Basis for Candidate Selection:** *Very important factors considered include:* secondary school record. *Important factors considered include:* class rank, essays, recommendations, standardized test scores. *Other factors considered include:* character/personal qualities, volunteer work. **Freshman Admission Requirements:** High school diploma or GED is required. *Academic units required/recommended:* 15 total recommended; 4 English recommended, 3 math recommended, 3 science recommended, 1 science lab recommended, 2 foreign language recommended, 2 social studies recommended, 1 history recommended. **Freshman Admission Statistics:** 178 applied, 75% accepted, 50% of those accepted enrolled. **Transfer Admission Requirements:** *Items required:* college transcript, essay, statement of good standing from prior school. Minimum high school GPA of 2.5 required. Minimum college GPA of 2.2

required. Lowest grade transferable C-. **General Admission Information:** Application fee $25. Nonfall registration accepted. Admission may be deferred for a maximum of 2 years. Credit and/or placement offered for CEEB Advanced Placement tests.

COSTS AND FINANCIAL AID

Tuition $15,435. Room & board $5,448. Required fees $0. Average book expense $750. **Required Forms and Deadlines:** FAFSA. Priority filing deadline March 1. **Notification of Awards:** Applicants will be notified of awards on a rolling basis beginning on or about April 1. **Types of Aid:** *Need-based scholarships/grants:* Pell, SEOG, private scholarships, the school's own gift aid. *Loans:* FFEL Subsidized Stafford, FFEL Unsubsidized Stafford, FFEL PLUS, Federal Perkins. **Student Employment:** Institutional employment available. Off-campus job opportunities are fair. **Financial Aid Phone:** 541-684-7210.

NORTHWEST COLLEGE

PO Box 579, Kirkland, WA 98083-0579
Phone: 425-889-5231 **E-mail:** admissions@ncag.edu **CEEB Code:** 4541
Fax: 425-889-5224 **Web:** www.nwcollege.edu **ACT Code:** 4466

This private school, which is affiliated with the Assemblies of God Church, was founded in 1934. It has a 56-acre campus.

STUDENTS AND FACULTY

Enrollment: 1,082. **Student Body:** Male 39%, female 61%, out-of-state 18%, international 3% (9 countries represented). **Ethnic Representation:** African American 2%, Asian 3%, Caucasian 80%, Hispanic 3%, Native American 1%. **Retention and Graduation:** 62% freshmen return for sophomore year. 35% freshmen graduate within 4 years. **Faculty:** Student/faculty ratio 18:1. 52 full-time faculty, 46% hold PhDs. 100% faculty teach undergrads.

ACADEMICS

Degrees: Associate's, bachelor's, certificate, diploma, master's, post-bachelor's certificate. **Academic Requirements:** General education including some course work in arts/fine arts, English (including composition), history, humanities, mathematics, philosophy, sciences (biological or physical), biblical studies. **Classes:** 20-29 students in an average class. 10-19 students in an average lab/discussion section. **Disciplines with Highest Percentage of Degrees Awarded:** Business/marketing 45%, philosophy/religion/theology 15%, education 14%, health professions and related sciences 6%, interdisciplinary studies 5%. **Special Study Options:** Accelerated program, double major, English as a second language, independent study, internships, liberal arts/career combination, study abroad, teacher certification program.

FACILITIES

Housing: All-female, all-male, apartments for married students, apartments for single students, apartments for students with dependent children. **Library Holdings:** 61,334 bound volumes. 1,007 periodicals. 33,484 microforms. 16,887 audiovisuals. **Computers:** *Recommended operating system:* Windows XP. School-owned computers available for student use.

EXTRACURRICULARS

Activities: Choral groups, concert band, drama/theater, music ensembles, musical theater, radio station, student government, student newspaper, symphony orchestra, yearbook. **Organizations:** 15 registered organizations, 9 religious organizations. **Athletics (Intercollegiate):** *Men:* basketball, cross-country, soccer, track & field. *Women:* basketball, cross-country, track & field, volleyball.

ADMISSIONS

Selectivity Rating: 79 (of 100). **Freshman Academic Profile:** Average high school GPA 3.3. 75% from public high schools. Average SAT I Math 500. Average SAT I Verbal 530. Average ACT 22. TOEFL required of all international applicants, minimum TOEFL 500. **Basis for Candidate Selection:** *Very important factors considered include:* character/personal qualities, essays, recommendations, secondary school record, standardized test scores. *Important factors considered include:* class rank, extracurricular activities, religious affiliation/commitment. *Other factors considered include:* alumni/ae relation, interview, talent/ability, volunteer work. **Freshman Admission Requirements:** High school diploma or GED is required. *Academic units required/recommended:* 16 total recommended; 4 English recommended, 3 math recommended, 2 science recommended, 2 foreign language recommended, 2 social studies recommended, 2 history recommended, 3 elective recommended. **Freshman Admission Statistics:** 312 applied, 89% accepted, 59% of those accepted enrolled. **Transfer Admission Requirements:** *Items required:* high school transcript, college transcript, essay, statement of good standing from prior school. Minimum high school GPA of 2.3 required. Minimum college GPA of 2.3 required. Lowest grade transferable C. **General Admission Information:** Application fee $30. Priority application deadline May 1. Regular application deadline August 1. Nonfall registration accepted. Admission may be deferred for a maximum of 1 year. Credit offered for CEEB Advanced Placement tests.

COSTS AND FINANCIAL AID

Tuition $12,550. Room & board $5,996. Required fees $308. Average book expense $850. **Required Forms and Deadlines:** FAFSA and institution's own financial aid form. No deadline for regular filing. Priority filing deadline March 1. **Notification of Awards:** Applicants will be notified of awards on a rolling basis beginning on or about April 15. **Types of Aid:** *Need-based scholarships/grants:* Pell, SEOG, state scholarships/grants, private scholarships, the school's own gift aid. *Loans:* FFEL Subsidized Stafford, FFEL Unsubsidized Stafford, FFEL PLUS, Federal Perkins, alternative (private) loans. **Student Employment:** Federal Work-Study Program available. Institutional employment available. Off-campus job opportunities are excellent. **Financial Aid Statistics:** 61% freshmen, 76% undergrads receive some form of aid. Average freshman grant $5,230. Average freshman loan $4,246. Average income from on-campus job $3,308. **Financial Aid Phone:** 425-889-5210.

NORTHWEST MISSOURI STATE UNIVERSITY

800 University Drive, Maryville, MO 64468
Phone: 800-633-1175 **E-mail:** admissions@mail.nwmissouri.edu **CEEB Code:** 6488
Fax: 660-562-1121 **Web:** www.nwmissouri.edu **ACT Code:** 2338

This public school was founded in 1905. It has a 240-acre campus.

STUDENTS AND FACULTY

Enrollment: 5,568. **Student Body:** Male 44%, female 56%, out-of-state 36%, international 2%. **Ethnic Representation:** African American 3%, Asian 1%, Caucasian 95%, Hispanic 1%. **Retention and Graduation:** 67% freshmen return for sophomore year. 26% freshmen graduate within 4 years. **Faculty:** 244 full-time faculty, 69% hold PhDs. 100% faculty teach undergrads.

ACADEMICS

Degrees: Bachelor's, master's, post-master's certificate. **Academic Requirements:** General education including some course work in arts/fine arts, computer literacy, English (including composition), history, humanities, mathematics, philosophy, sciences (biological or physical), social science. **Disciplines with Highest Percentage of Degrees Awarded:** Business/marketing 17%, education 13%, agriculture 10%, computer and information sciences 9%, health professions and related sciences 9%. **Special Study Options:** Accelerated program, distance learning, double major, dual enrollment, English as a second language, independent study, internships, study abroad, teacher certification program.

FACILITIES

Housing: Coed, all-female, all-male, housing for disabled students, housing for international students, fraternities and/or sororities. **Library Holdings:** 305,982 bound volumes. 1,469 periodicals. 503,862 microforms. 1,780 audiovisuals. **Special Academic Facilities/Equipment:** State history and art collections, earth/science museum, broadcasting museum, on-campus elementary lab school, biomass energy plant. **Computers:** School-owned computers available for student use.

EXTRACURRICULARS

Activities: Choral groups, concert band, dance, drama/theater, jazz band, literary magazine, marching band, music ensembles, musical theater, pep band, radio station, student government, student newspaper, student-run film society, television station, yearbook. **Organizations:** 174 registered organizations, 13 honor societies, 9 religious organizations, 10 fraternities (20% men join), 6 sororities (23% women join). **Athletics (Intercollegiate):** *Men:* baseball, basketball, cheerleading, cross-country, football, indoor track, rodeo, tennis, track & field. *Women:* basketball, cheerleading, cross-country, indoor track, rodeo, soccer, softball, tennis, track & field, volleyball.

ADMISSIONS

Selectivity Rating: 71 (of 100). **Freshman Academic Profile:** Average high school GPA 3.3. 10% in top 10% of high school class, 35% in top 25% of high school class, 74% in top 50% of high school class. 90% from public high schools. TOEFL required of all international applicants, minimum TOEFL 500. **Basis for Candidate Selection:** *Very important factors considered include:* class rank, secondary school record, standardized test scores. *Other factors considered include:* character/personal qualities, essays, extracurricular activities, interview, recommendations. **Freshman Admission Requirements:** High school diploma or GED is required. *Academic units required/recommended:* 16 total required; 4 English required, 3 math required, 2 science required, 3 science recommended, 1 science lab required, 3 social studies required, 4 elective required. **Freshman Admission Statistics:** 2,951 applied, 90% accepted. **Transfer Admission Requirements:** *Items required:* college transcript, statement of good standing from prior school. Minimum college GPA of 2.0 required. **General Admission Information:** Application fee $15. Nonfall registration accepted. Admission may be deferred.

COSTS AND FINANCIAL AID

In-state tuition $3,288. Out-of-state tuition $5,610. Room & board $4,556. Required fees $75. Average book expense $300. **Required Forms and Deadlines:** FAFSA. No deadline for regular filing. Priority filing deadline April 1. **Notification of Awards:** Applicants will be notified of awards on or about April 15. **Types of Aid:** *Need-based scholarships/grants:* Pell, SEOG, state scholarships/grants, private scholarships, the school's own gift aid. *Loans:* Direct Subsidized Stafford, Direct Unsubsidized Stafford, Direct PLUS, Federal Perkins, college/university loans from institutional funds. **Student Employment:** Federal Work-Study Program available. Institutional employment available. Off-campus job opportunities are fair. **Financial Aid Statistics:** 52% freshmen, 49% undergrads receive some form of aid. **Financial Aid Phone:** 660-562-1363.

NORTHWEST NAZARENE UNIVERSITY

623 Holly Street, Nampa, ID 83686
Phone: 208-467-8496 **E-mail:** admissions@nnu.edu **CEEB Code:** 4544
Fax: 208-467-8645 **Web:** www.nnu.edu **ACT Code:** 924

This private school, which is affiliated with the Nazarene Church, was founded in 1913. It has a 94-acre campus.

STUDENTS AND FACULTY

Enrollment: 1,110. **Student Body:** Male 45%, female 55%, out-of-state 68%. **Ethnic Representation:** African American 1%, Asian 1%, Caucasian 94%, Hispanic 2%, Native American 1%. **Retention and Graduation:** 68% freshmen return for sophomore year. 34% freshmen graduate within 4 years. 22% grads go on to further study within 1 year. 3% grads pursue business degrees. 5% grads pursue law degrees. 6% grads pursue medical degrees. **Faculty:** Student/faculty ratio 12:1. 90 full-time faculty, 67% hold PhDs. 98% faculty teach undergrads.

ACADEMICS

Degrees: Bachelor's, master's. **Academic Requirements:** General education including some course work in arts/fine arts, computer literacy, English (including composition), history, humanities, mathematics, philosophy, sciences (biological or physical), social science, religion (Bible and theology). **Classes:** 10-19 students in an average class. Under 10 students in an average lab/discussion section. **Disciplines with Highest Percentage of Degrees Awarded:** Education 21%, social sciences and history 14%, business/marketing 11%, philosophy/religion/theology 9%, biological life sciences 8%. **Special Study Options:** Cooperative (work-study) program, cross registration, distance learning, double major, honors program, independent study, internships, liberal arts/career combination, student-designed major, study abroad, teacher certification program.

FACILITIES

Housing: Coed, all-female, all-male, apartments for married students, apartments for single students, off-campus housing owned the University including rental homes and units. **Library Holdings:** 103,468 bound volumes. 794 periodicals. 146,909 microforms. 3,729 audiovisuals. **Computers:** *Recommended operating system:* Windows 95. School-owned computers available for student use.

EXTRACURRICULARS

Activities: Choral groups, concert band, drama/theater, jazz band, literary magazine, music ensembles, musical theater, pep band, student government, student newspaper, symphony orchestra, yearbook. **Organizations:** 21 registered organizations, 3 honor societies, 8 religious organizations. **Athletics (Intercollegiate):** *Men:* baseball, basketball, cheerleading, cross-country, golf, soccer, track & field. *Women:* basketball, cheerleading, cross-country, soccer, softball, track & field, volleyball.

ADMISSIONS

Selectivity Rating: 82 (of 100). **Freshman Academic Profile:** 23% in top 10% of high school class, 51% in top 25% of high school class, 79% in top 50% of high school class. 83% from public high schools. Average ACT 23, ACT middle 50% range 19-26. TOEFL required of all international applicants, minimum TOEFL 500. **Basis for Candidate Selection:** *Very important factors considered include:* recommendations, standardized test scores. *Important factors considered include:* character/personal qualities, class rank, secondary school record. *Other factors considered include:* alumni/ae relation, essays, extracurricular activities, religious affiliation/commitment, talent/ability, volunteer work, work experience. **Freshman Admission Requirements:** High school diploma or GED is required. *Academic units required/recommended:* 15 total recommended; 4 English recommended, 3 math recommended, 3 science recommended, 2 foreign language recommended, 3 social studies recommended, 1 history recommended. **Freshman Admission Statistics:** 681 applied, 77% accepted, 64% of those accepted enrolled. **Transfer Admission Requirements:** *Items required:* college transcript, essay. Minimum high school GPA of 2.0 required. Minimum college GPA of 1.7 required. Lowest grade transferable C-. **General Admission Information:** Application fee $25. Priority application deadline March 1. Nonfall registration accepted. Admission may be deferred for a maximum of 5 years. Credit and/or placement offered for CEEB Advanced Placement tests.

COSTS AND FINANCIAL AID

Tuition $14,520. Room & board $4,285. Required fees $540. Average book expense $750. **Required Forms and Deadlines:** FAFSA and institution's own financial aid form. Priority filing deadline March 1. **Notification of Awards:** Applicants will be notified of awards on a rolling basis beginning on or about April 1. **Types of Aid:** *Need-based scholarships/grants:* Pell, SEOG, state scholarships/grants, private scholarships, the school's own gift aid. *Loans:* FFEL Subsidized Stafford, FFEL Unsubsidized Stafford, FFEL PLUS, Federal Perkins, college/university loans from institutional funds, Bank Loans. **Student Employment:** Federal Work-Study Program available. Institutional employment available. Off-campus job opportunities are good. **Financial Aid Statistics:** 73% freshmen, 69% undergrads receive some form of aid. Average freshman grant $5,034. Average freshman loan $2,287. Average income from on-campus job $1,450. **Financial Aid Phone:** 208-467-8496.

NORTHWESTERN COLLEGE (IA)

101 7th St SW, Orange City, IA 51041
Phone: 712-707-7130 **E-mail:** admissions@nwciowa.edu **CEEB Code:** 6490
Fax: 712-707-7164 **Web:** www.nwciowa.edu **ACT Code:** 1346

This private school, which is affiliated with the Reformed Church, was founded in 1882. It has a 65-acre campus.

STUDENTS AND FACULTY

Enrollment: 1,313. **Student Body:** Male 39%, female 61%, out-of-state 44%, international 2% (14 countries represented). **Ethnic Representation:** Asian 1%, Caucasian 98%, Hispanic 1%. **Retention and Graduation:** 76% freshmen return for sophomore year. 47% freshmen graduate within 4 years. 10% grads go on to further study within 1 year. 1% grads pursue business degrees. 1% grads pursue law degrees. 3% grads pursue medical degrees. **Faculty:** Student/faculty ratio 16:1. 73 full-time faculty, 84% hold PhDs. 100% faculty teach undergrads.

ACADEMICS

Degrees: Associate's, bachelor's, certificate. **Academic Requirements:** General education including some course work in arts/fine arts, English (including composition), foreign languages, history, humanities, mathematics, philosophy, sciences (biological or physical), social science, eight hours of biblical studies. **Classes:** 10-19 students in an average class. **Majors with Highest Enrollment:** Business administration/management; education, general; biology/biological sciences, general. **Disciplines with Highest Percentage of Degrees Awarded:** Education 29%, business/marketing 19%, social sciences and history 10%, biological life sciences 9%, visual and performing arts 8%. **Special Study Options:** Double major, English as a second language, honors program, independent study, internships, liberal arts/career combination, student-designed major, study abroad, teacher certification program, American Studies Program (Washington, DC), Au Sable Institute of Environmental Studies Program (Michigan), Los Angeles Film Studies Semester, Chicago Metropolitan Studies Program (Chicago), China Studies Program (Xiaman, China), Middle East Studies Program (Cairo, Egypt), Oxford Summer Program (Oxford, England), Russian Studies Program, Contemporary Music Center (Martha's Vineyard, MA), Latin American Studies Program (Costa Rica).

FACILITIES

Housing: All-female, all-male, apartments for married students, apartments for single students, housing for disabled students. **Library Holdings:** 125,000 bound volumes. 615 periodicals. 110,000 microforms. 5,000 audiovisuals. **Special Academic Facilities/Equipment:** Language lab, Art Gallery. **Computers:** *Recommended operating system:* UNIX. School-owned computers available for student use.

EXTRACURRICULARS

Activities: Choral groups, concert band, dance, drama/theater, jazz band, literary magazine, music ensembles, musical theater, pep band, radio station, student government, student newspaper, symphony orchestra, television station, yearbook. **Organizations:** 30 registered organizations, 2 honor societies, 5 religious organizations. **Athletics (Intercollegiate):** *Men:* baseball, basketball, cheerleading, cross-country, football, golf, indoor track, soccer, tennis, track & field, wrestling. *Women:* basketball, cheerleading, cross-country, golf, indoor track, soccer, softball, tennis, track & field, volleyball.

ADMISSIONS

Selectivity Rating: 74 (of 100). **Freshman Academic Profile:** Average high school GPA 3.5. 24% in top 10% of high school class, 52% in top 25% of high school class, 85% in top 50% of high school class. 85% from public high schools. Average SAT I Math 576. Average SAT I Verbal 572. Average ACT 24, ACT middle 50% range 21-27. TOEFL required of all international applicants, minimum TOEFL 475. **Basis for Candidate Selection:** *Very important factors considered include:* secondary school record, standardized test scores. *Important factors considered include:* character/personal qualities, class rank, recommendations. *Other factors considered include:* essays, interview, religious affiliation/commitment, talent/ability. **Freshman Admission Requirements:** High school diploma or GED is required. *Academic units required/recommended:* 16 total recommended; 4 English recommended, 3 math recommended, 3 science recommended, 3 foreign language recommended, 3 social studies recommended. **Freshman Admission Statistics:** 1,150 applied, 83% accepted, 36% of those accepted enrolled. **Transfer Admission Requirements:** *Items required:* college transcript. Minimum college GPA of 2.0 required. Lowest grade transferable C-. **General Admission Information:** Application fee $25. Priority application deadline June 2. Nonfall registration accepted. Admission may be deferred for a maximum of 4 years. Credit and/or placement offered for CEEB Advanced Placement tests.

COSTS AND FINANCIAL AID

Tuition $15,290. Room & board $4,350. Required fees $0. Average book expense $600. **Required Forms and Deadlines:** FAFSA and institution's own financial aid form. No deadline for regular filing. Priority filing deadline April 1. **Notification of Awards:** Applicants will be notified of awards on a rolling basis beginning on or about March 15. **Types of Aid:** *Need-based scholarships/grants:* Pell, SEOG, state scholarships/grants, private scholarships, the school's own gift aid, United Negro College Fund. *Loans:* FFEL Subsidized Stafford, FFEL Unsubsidized Stafford, FFEL PLUS, Federal Perkins, college/university loans from institutional funds. **Student Employment:** Federal Work-Study Program available. Institutional employment available. Off-campus job opportunities are good. **Financial Aid Statistics:** 99% freshmen, 98% undergrads receive some form of aid. Average freshman grant $8,500. Average freshman loan $4,935. **Financial Aid Phone:** 712-737-7131.

NORTHWESTERN COLLEGE (MN)

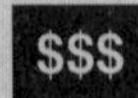

3003 Snelling Avenue North, Saint Paul, MN 55113-1598
Phone: 651-631-5111 **E-mail:** admissions@nwc.edu **CEEB Code:** 6489
Fax: 651-631-5680 **Web:** www.nwc.edu **ACT Code:** 2138

This private school, which is affiliated with the Protestant Church, was founded in 1902. It has a 103-acre campus.

STUDENTS AND FACULTY

Enrollment: 2,448. **Student Body:** Male 38%, female 62%, out-of-state 39%, international students represent 12 countries. **Ethnic Representation:** African American 4%, Asian 2%, Caucasian 91%, Hispanic 1%. **Retention and Graduation:** 80% freshmen return for sophomore year. 43% freshmen graduate within 4 years. 20% grads go on to further study within 1 year. 1% grads pursue business degrees. 1% grads pursue law degrees. 1% grads pursue medical degrees. **Faculty:** Student/faculty ratio 15:1. 78 full-time faculty, 66% hold PhDs. 100% faculty teach undergrads.

ACADEMICS

Degrees: Associate's, bachelor's, certificate, terminal, transfer. **Academic Requirements:** General education including some course work in arts/fine arts, computer literacy, English (including composition), history, mathematics, sciences (biological or physical), social science, Bible (30 credits for new freshmen; proportional amount for transfers), speech, literature or philosophy, physical health and wellness, global perspectives (satisfied by foreign language courses or specified courses with international/cross-cultural/multicultural emphasis), designated courses in major with written/oral communication emphasis. **Classes:** 10-19 students in an average class. 20-29 students in an average lab/discussion section. **Majors with Highest Enrollment:** Elementary education and teaching; business administration/management; psychology, general. **Disciplines with Highest Percentage of Degrees Awarded:** Education 23%, philosophy/religion/theology 16%, business/marketing 13%, visual and performing arts 9%, social sciences and history 9%. **Special Study Options:** Distance learning, double major, English as a second language (two English composition courses), student exchange program (domestic), honors program, independent study, internships, study abroad, teacher certification program.

FACILITIES

Housing: All-female, all-male, apartments for married students, apartments for single students, housing for disabled students. **Library Holdings:** 75,082 bound volumes. 560 periodicals. 281 microforms. 3,716 audiovisuals. **Special Academic Facilities/Equipment:** Art gallery, radio station, TV studio. **Computers:** *Recommended operating system:* Windows 95. School-owned computers available for student use.

EXTRACURRICULARS

Activities: Choral groups, concert band, drama/theater, jazz band, literary magazine, music ensembles, musical theater, opera, pep band, radio station, student government, student newspaper, symphony orchestra, yearbook. **Organizations:** 25 registered organizations, 4 honor societies, 5 religious organizations. **Athletics (Intercollegiate):** *Men:* baseball, basketball, cross-country, football, golf, soccer, tennis, track & field. *Women:* basketball, cheerleading, cross-country, golf, soccer, softball, tennis, track & field, volleyball.

ADMISSIONS

Selectivity Rating: 76 (of 100). **Freshman Academic Profile:** Average high school GPA 3.5. 23% in top 10% of high school class, 52% in top 25% of high school class, 80% in top 50% of high school class. 80% from public high schools. Average SAT I Math 563, SAT I Math middle 50% range 490-640. Average SAT I Verbal 566, SAT I Verbal middle 50% range 510-630. Average ACT 24, ACT middle 50% range 21-26. TOEFL required of all international applicants, minimum TOEFL 530. **Basis for Candidate Selection:** *Very important factors considered include:* character/personal qualities, essays, recommendations, religious affiliation/commitment. *Important factors considered include:* extracurricular activities, secondary school record, standardized test scores. *Other factors considered include:* class rank, interview, talent/ability. **Freshman Admission Requirements:** High school diploma or is required. *Academic units required/recommended:* 16 total recommended; 4 English recommended, 3 math recommended, 3 science recommended, 2 foreign language recommended, 3 social studies recommended, 1 elective recommended. **Freshman Admission Statistics:** 890 applied, 91% accepted, 53% of those accepted enrolled. **Transfer Admission Requirements:** *Items required:* high school transcript, college transcript, essay, statement of good standing from prior school. Minimum college GPA of 2.0 required. Lowest grade transferable C-. **General Admission Information:** Application fee $25. Priority application deadline June 15. Regular application deadline August 15. Nonfall registration accepted. Admission may be deferred for a maximum of 1 year. Credit offered for CEEB Advanced Placement tests.

COSTS AND FINANCIAL AID

Tuition $17,400. Room & board $5,620. Required fees $0. Average book expense $500. **Required Forms and Deadlines:** FAFSA and institution's own financial aid form. No deadline for regular filing. Priority filing deadline March 1. **Notification of Awards:** Applicants will be notified of awards on a rolling basis beginning on or about March 1. **Types of Aid:** *Need-based scholarships/grants:* Pell, SEOG, state scholarships/grants, private scholarships, the school's own gift aid. *Loans:* FFEL Subsidized Stafford, FFEL Unsubsidized Stafford, FFEL PLUS, Federal Perkins, state loans. **Student Employment:** Federal Work-Study Program available. Institutional employment available. Off-campus job opportunities are excellent. **Financial Aid Statistics:** 83% freshmen, 81% undergrads receive some form of aid. Average freshman grant $9,800. Average freshman loan $3,422. Average income from on-campus job $1,703. **Financial Aid Phone:** (651) 631-5212.

NORTHWESTERN OKLAHOMA STATE UNIVERSITY

709 Oklahoma Boulevard, Alva, OK 73717-2799
Phone: 580-327-8545 **E-mail:** krschroc@ranger1.nmalva.edu **CEEB Code:** 6493
Fax: 580-327-1881 **Web:** www.nwalva.edu **ACT Code:** 3412

This public school was founded in 1897. It has a 70-acre campus.

STUDENTS AND FACULTY

Enrollment: 1,648. **Student Body:** Male 45%, female 55%, out-of-state 14%, international 1%. **Ethnic Representation:** African American 5%, Caucasian 90%, Hispanic 1%, Native American 3%. **Retention and Graduation:** 54% freshmen return for sophomore year. 12% freshmen graduate within 4 years. **Faculty:** 100% faculty teach undergrads.

ACADEMICS

Degrees: Bachelor's, master's. **Special Study Options:** Accelerated program, cooperative (work-study) program, dual enrollment, English as a second language, honors program, independent study, internships, liberal arts/career combination, teacher certification program.

FACILITIES

Housing: Coed, fraternities and/or sororities. **Library Holdings:** 225,000 bound volumes. 1,411 periodicals. 650,000 microforms. 1,200 audiovisuals. **Special Academic Facilities/Equipment:** Natural history museum, instructional media center, TV production facility. **Computers:** *Recommended operating system:* Mac. School-owned computers available for student use.

EXTRACURRICULARS

Activities: Choral groups, drama/theater, literary magazine, marching band, radio station, student government, student newspaper, television station, yearbook. **Organizations:** 50 registered organizations, 1 honor society, 2 fraternities, 1 sorority. **Athletics (Intercollegiate):** *Men:* baseball, basketball, football, golf, softball, tennis, track & field. *Women:* basketball, softball.

ADMISSIONS

Selectivity Rating: 70 (of 100). **Freshman Academic Profile:** Average high school GPA 3.2. 8% in top 10% of high school class, 27% in top 25% of high school class, 64% in top 50% of high school class. ACT middle 50% range 18-23. TOEFL required of all international applicants, minimum TOEFL 500. **Freshman Admission Requirements:** High school diploma or GED is required. *Academic units required/recommended:* 15 total required; 4 English required, 3 math required, 2 science required, 2 science lab required, 1 social studies required, 2 history required, 3 elective required. **Freshman Admission Statistics:** 481 applied, 100% accepted, 67% of those accepted enrolled. **Transfer Admission Requirements:** Minimum college GPA of 2.0 required. Lowest grade transferable D. **General Admission Information:** Application fee $15. Regular application deadline rolling. Nonfall registration accepted. Credit and/or placement offered for CEEB Advanced Placement tests.

COSTS AND FINANCIAL AID

In-state tuition $1,830. Out-of-state tuition $4,340. Room & board $2,316. Required fees $125. Average book expense $500. **Required Forms and Deadlines:** FAFSA and institution's own financial aid form. **Types of Aid:** *Need-based scholarships/grants:* Pell, SEOG, state scholarships/grants, private scholarships, the school's own gift aid. *Loans:* FFEL Subsidized Stafford, FFEL Unsubsidized Stafford, FFEL PLUS, Federal Perkins, Federal Nursing, college/university loans from institutional funds. **Student Employment:** Federal Work-Study Program available. Institutional employment available. Off-campus job opportunities are good. **Financial Aid Statistics:** Average freshman grant $800. Average freshman loan $2,625. Average income from on-campus job $1,200. **Financial Aid Phone:** 405-327-8540.

NORTHWESTERN STATE UNIVERSITY

Roy Hall, Room 209, Natchitoches, LA 71497
Phone: 318-357-4503 **E-mail:** luckyj@nsula.edu **CEEB Code:** 6492
Fax: 318-357-4257 **Web:** www.nsula.edu

This public school was founded in 1884. It has a 940-acre campus.

STUDENTS AND FACULTY

Enrollment: 9,087. **Student Body:** Male 36%, female 64%, out-of-state 6%. **Ethnic Representation:** African American 30%, Asian 1%, Caucasian 61%, Hispanic 2%, Native American 2%. **Retention and Graduation:** 70% freshmen return for sophomore year. **Faculty:** Student/faculty ratio 30:1. 252 full-time faculty, 53% hold PhDs.

ACADEMICS

Degrees: Associate's, bachelor's, certificate, doctoral, master's, post-master's certificate. **Academic Requirements:** General education including some course work in arts/fine arts, computer literacy, English (including composition), history, mathematics, sciences (biological or physical), social science. **Classes:** Under 10 students in an average class. Under 10 students in an average lab/discussion section. **Majors with Highest Enrollment:** General studies; nursing/registered nurse training (RN, ASN, BSN, MSN); business administration/management. **Disciplines with Highest Percentage of Degrees Awarded:** Liberal arts/general studies 21%, health professions and related sciences 19%, business/marketing 14%, education 10%, protective services/public administration 9%. **Special Study Options:** Accelerated program, distance learning, double major, dual enrollment, student exchange program (domestic), honors program, internships, liberal arts/career combination, student-designed major, study abroad, teacher certification program, Louisiana Scholars' College.

FACILITIES

Housing: Coed, all-female, all-male, apartments for married students, apartments for single students, fraternities and/or sororities, University Colomns (privately owned on-campus housing). **Library Holdings:** 677,866 bound volumes. 1,749 periodicals. 126,460 microforms. 2,754 audiovisuals. **Special Academic Facilities/Equipment:** Natural history museum, Museum of Louisiana Education History, language lab, teacher education center, lab school.

EXTRACURRICULARS

Activities: Choral groups, concert band, dance, drama/theater, jazz band, literary magazine, marching band, music ensembles, musical theater, opera, pep band, radio station, student government, student newspaper, student-run film society, symphony orchestra, television station, yearbook. **Organizations:** 90 registered organizations, 5 religious organizations, 11 fraternities (11% men join), 8 sororities (10% women join). **Athletics (Intercollegiate):** *Men:* baseball, basketball, cheerleading, cross-country, football, golf, rifle, track & field. *Women:* basketball, cheerleading, cross-country, softball, tennis, track & field, volleyball.

ADMISSIONS

Selectivity Rating: 63 (of 100). **Freshman Academic Profile:** Average ACT 20, ACT middle 50% range 16-22. TOEFL required of all international applicants, minimum TOEFL 550. **Basis for Candidate Selection:** *Very important factors considered include:* class rank, secondary school record, standardized test scores. *Important factors considered include:* talent/ability. **Freshman Admission Requirements:** High school diploma or GED is required. *Academic units required/recommended:* 16 total recommended; 4 English recommended, 3 math recommended, 3 science recommended, 2 science lab recommended, 2 foreign language recommended, 1 social studies recommended, 2 history recommended, 1 fine arts recommended, .5 computer science/literacy recommended. **Freshman Admission Statistics:** 3,805 applied, 100% accepted, 54% of those accepted enrolled. **Transfer Admission Requirements:** Minimum college GPA of 2.0 required. Lowest grade transferable C. **General Admission Information:** Application fee $20. Priority application deadline August 1. Nonfall registration accepted.

COSTS AND FINANCIAL AID

Out-of-state tuition $7,850. Room & board $3,266. Required fees $669. Average book expense $1,125. **Required Forms and Deadlines:** FAFSA and institution's own financial aid form. No deadline for regular filing. **Notification of Awards:** Applicants will be notified of awards on a rolling basis. **Types of Aid:** *Need-based scholarships/grants:* Pell, SEOG, state scholarships/grants, private scholarships. *Loans:* FFEL Subsidized Stafford, FFEL Unsubsidized Stafford, FFEL PLUS, Federal Perkins, Federal Nursing. **Student Employment:** Federal Work-Study Program available. Institutional employment available. Off-campus job opportunities are fair. **Financial Aid Statistics:** 89%

freshmen, 87% undergrads receive some form of aid. Average freshman loan $3,186. Average income from on-campus job $1,102. **Financial Aid Phone:** 318-357-5961.

NORTHWESTERN UNIVERSITY

PO Box 3060, 1801 Hinman Avenue, Evanston, IL 60204-3060
Phone: 847-491-7271 **E-mail:** ug-admission@northwestern.edu **CEEB Code:** 1565
Web: www.northwestern.edu **ACT Code:** 1106

This private school was founded in 1851. It has a 240-acre campus.

STUDENTS AND FACULTY

Enrollment: 7,946. **Student Body:** Male 47%, female 53%, out-of-state 74%, international 5% (46 countries represented). **Ethnic Representation:** African American 7%, Asian 14%, Caucasian 66%, Hispanic 5%. **Retention and Graduation:** 96% freshmen return for sophomore year. 24% grads go on to further study within 1 year. **Faculty:** Student/faculty ratio 7:1. 922 full-time faculty, 100% hold PhDs. 100% faculty teach undergrads.

ACADEMICS

Degrees: Bachelor's, certificate, doctoral, first professional, master's, post-master's certificate. **Academic Requirements:** General education including some course work in arts/fine arts, English (including composition), foreign languages, humanities, mathematics, sciences (biological or physical), social science. **Majors with Highest Enrollment:** Journalism; speech and rhetorical studies; economics, general. **Disciplines with Highest Percentage of Degrees Awarded:** Social sciences and history 21%, engineering/engineering technology 15%, communications/communication technologies 12%, English 12%, visual and performing arts 10%. **Special Study Options:** Accelerated program, cooperative (work-study) program, double major, honors program, independent study, internships, student-designed major, study abroad, teacher certification program.

FACILITIES

Housing: Coed, all-female, all-male, fraternities and/or sororities. **Library Holdings:** 4,217,321 bound volumes. 39,423 periodicals. 4,110,673 microforms. 72,837 audiovisuals. **Special Academic Facilities/Equipment:** Art gallery, learning sciences institute, communicative disorders and materials and life sciences buildings, catalysis center, astronomical research center. **Computers:** School-owned computers available for student use.

EXTRACURRICULARS

Activities: Choral groups, concert band, dance, drama/theater, jazz band, literary magazine, marching band, music ensembles, musical theater, opera, pep band, radio station, student government, student newspaper, student-run film society, symphony orchestra, television station, yearbook. **Organizations:** 200 registered organizations, 18 honor societies, 32 religious organizations, 23 fraternities (30% men join), 17 sororities (40% women join). **Athletics (Intercollegiate):** *Men:* baseball, basketball, diving, football, golf, soccer, swimming, tennis, wrestling. *Women:* basketball, cross-country, diving, fencing, field hockey, golf, lacrosse, soccer, softball, swimming, tennis, volleyball.

ADMISSIONS

Selectivity Rating: 99 (of 100). **Freshman Academic Profile:** 82% in top 10% of high school class, 96% in top 25% of high school class, 99% in top 50% of high school class. 76% from public high schools. Average SAT I Math 703, SAT I Math middle 50% range 660-750. Average SAT I Verbal 675, SAT I Verbal middle 50% range 640-730. Average ACT 30, ACT middle 50% range 28-33. TOEFL required of all international applicants, minimum TOEFL 600. **Basis for Candidate Selection:** *Very important factors considered include:* class rank, essays, secondary school record, standardized test scores. *Important factors considered include:* character/personal qualities, extracurricular activities, recommendations, talent/ability. *Other factors considered include:* alumni/ae relation, interview, minority status, volunteer work, work experience. **Freshman Admission Requirements:** High school diploma or equivalent is not required. *Academic units required/recommended:* 16 total recommended; 4 English recommended, 4 math recommended, 2 science recommended, 2 science lab recommended, 2 foreign language recommended, 4 social studies recommended, 3 elective recommended. **Freshman Admission Statistics:** 14,283 applied, 33% accepted, 43% of those accepted enrolled. **Transfer Admission Requirements:** *Items required:* high school transcript, college transcript, essay, standardized test score, statement of good standing from prior school. Minimum college GPA of 3.0 required. Lowest grade transferable D. **General Admission Information:** Application fee $60. Early decision application deadline November 1. Regular application deadline January 1. Nonfall registration accepted. Admission may be deferred for a maximum of 1 year. Credit and/or placement offered for CEEB Advanced Placement tests.

COSTS AND FINANCIAL AID

Tuition $27,108. Room & board $8,446. Required fees $120. Average book expense $1,266. **Required Forms and Deadlines:** FAFSA, CSS/Financial Aid PROFILE, noncustodial (divorced/separated) parent's statement, business/farm supplement, and parent and student federal tax returns. Priority filing deadline February 1. **Notification of Awards:** Applicants will be notified of awards on or about April 15. **Types of Aid:** *Need-based scholarships/grants:* Pell, SEOG, state scholarships/grants, private scholarships, the school's own gift aid. *Loans:* FFEL Subsidized Stafford, FFEL Unsubsidized Stafford, FFEL PLUS, Federal Perkins, college/university loans from institutional funds. **Student Employment:** Federal Work-Study Program available. Institutional employment available. Off-campus job opportunities are excellent. **Financial Aid Statistics:** 45% freshmen, 44% undergrads receive some form of aid. Average freshman grant $22,515. Average freshman loan $2,660. **Financial Aid Phone:** 847-491-7400.

NORTHWOOD UNIVERSITY

4000 Whiting Drive, Midland, MI 48640
Phone: 989-837-4273 **E-mail:** admissions@northwood.edu **CEEB Code:** 1568
Fax: 989-837-4490 **Web:** www.northwood.edu **ACT Code:** 2041

This private school was founded in 1959. It has a 434-acre campus.

STUDENTS AND FACULTY

Enrollment: 3,361. **Student Body:** Male 53%, female 47%, out-of-state 13%, international 6%. **Ethnic Representation:** African American 18%, Asian 1%, Caucasian 77%, Hispanic 3%. **Retention and Graduation:** 73% freshmen return for sophomore year. 41% freshmen graduate within 4 years. 3% grads pursue business degrees. **Faculty:** Student/faculty ratio 34:1. 43 full-time faculty, 20% hold PhDs. 100% faculty teach undergrads.

ACADEMICS

Degrees: Associate's, bachelor's, master's, terminal, transfer. **Academic Requirements:** General education including some course work in computer literacy, English (including composition), humanities, mathematics, philosophy, sciences (biological or physical), social science. **Classes:** 20-29 students in an average class. **Majors with Highest Enrollment:** Marketing/marketing management, general; sports and fitness administration/management; business administration/management. **Disciplines with Highest Percentage of Degrees Awarded:** Business/marketing 97%, computer and information sciences 3%. **Special Study Options:** Accelerated program, cooperative (work-study) program, distance learning, double major, dual enrollment, English as a second language, external degree program, honors program, independent study, internships, study abroad, weekend college.

FACILITIES

Housing: All-female, all-male, apartments for single students. **Library Holdings:** 40,140 bound volumes. 402 periodicals. 46,540 microforms. 0 audiovisuals. **Computers:** School-owned computers available for student use.

EXTRACURRICULARS

Activities: Choral groups, dance, drama/theater, jazz band, pep band, student government, student newspaper, yearbook. **Organizations:** 46 registered organizations, 2 honor societies, 2 religious organizations, 6 fraternities (12% men join), 3 sororities (16% women join). **Athletics (Intercollegiate):** *Men:* baseball, basketball, cross-country, football, golf, soccer, tennis, track & field. *Women:* basketball, cross-country, golf, soccer, softball, tennis, track & field, volleyball.

ADMISSIONS

Selectivity Rating: 77 (of 100). **Freshman Academic Profile:** Average high school GPA 3.1. 9% in top 10% of high school class, 28% in top 25% of high school class, 55% in top 50% of high school class. 95% from public high schools. Average SAT I Math 488, SAT I Math middle 50% range 457-550. Average SAT I Verbal 473, SAT I Verbal middle 50% range 440-540. Average ACT 20, ACT middle 50% range 18-23. TOEFL required of all international applicants, minimum TOEFL 500. **Basis for Candidate Selection:** *Very important factors considered include:* secondary school record, standardized test scores. *Important factors considered include:* class rank, essays. *Other factors considered include:* alumni/ae relation, character/personal qualities, extracurricular activities, interview, recommendations. **Freshman Admission Requirements:** High school diploma or GED is required. *Academic units required/recommended:* 16 total recommended; 4 English recommended, 3 math recommended, 2 science recommended, 1 science lab recommended, 3 foreign language recommended, 3 social studies recommended. **Freshman Admission Statistics:** 1,452 applied, 86% accepted, 40% of those accepted enrolled. **Transfer Admission Requirements:** *Items required:* college transcript. Minimum college GPA of 2.0 required. Lowest grade transferable C. **General Admission Information:** Application fee $25. Nonfall registration accepted. Admission may be deferred for a maximum of 1 year. Credit and/or placement offered for CEEB Advanced Placement tests.

COSTS AND FINANCIAL AID

Required Forms and Deadlines: FAFSA. No deadline for regular filing. **Notification of Awards:** Applicants will be notified of awards on a rolling basis beginning on or about April 1. **Types of Aid:** *Need-based scholarships/grants:* Pell, SEOG, state scholarships/grants, private scholarships. *Loans:* FFEL Subsidized Stafford, FFEL Unsubsidized Stafford, FFEL PLUS, state loans. **Student Employment:** Federal Work-Study Program available. Institutional employment available. Off-campus job opportunities are good. **Financial Aid Statistics:** 64% freshmen, 61% undergrads receive some form of aid. Average freshman grant $8,968. Average freshman loan $2,120. **Financial Aid Phone:** 989-837-4230.

NORWICH UNIVERSITY

Admissions Office, 158 Harmon Drive, Northfield, VT 05663
Phone: 802-485-2001 **E-mail:** nuadm@norwich.edu
Fax: 802-485-2032 **Web:** www.norwich.edu

This private school was founded in 1819. It has a 1,125-acre campus.

STUDENTS AND FACULTY

Enrollment: 2,099. **Student Body:** Male 62%, female 38%, out-of-state 77%, international 3%. **Ethnic Representation:** African American 3%, Asian 2%, Caucasian 81%, Hispanic 4%. **Retention and Graduation:** 74% freshmen return for sophomore year. 10% grads go on to further study within 1 year. 2% grads pursue business degrees. 2% grads pursue law degrees. 1% grads pursue medical degrees. **Faculty:** Student/faculty ratio 13:1. 104 full-time faculty, 76% hold PhDs. 100% faculty teach undergrads.

ACADEMICS

Degrees: Bachelor's, master's, post-bachelor's certificate. **Academic Requirements:** General education including some course work in English (including composition), history, humanities, mathematics, sciences (biological or physical), social science. **Classes:** 10-19 students in an average class. **Majors with Highest Enrollment:** Liberal arts and sciences/liberal studies; criminal justice/law enforcement administration; architecture (BArch, BA/BS, MArch, MA/MS, PhD). **Disciplines with Highest Percentage of Degrees Awarded:** Liberal arts/general studies 39%, protective services/public administration 9%, social sciences and history 7%, business/marketing 6%, health professions and related sciences 6%. **Special Study Options:** Cooperative (work-study) program, distance learning, double major, English as a second language, honors program, independent study, internships, study abroad.

FACILITIES

Housing: Coed. **Library Holdings:** 256,530 bound volumes. 904 periodicals. 99,100 microforms. 1,501 audiovisuals. **Special Academic Facilities/Equipment:** museum, architecture and art building with gallery, new library. **Computers:** *Recommended operating system:* Windows NT/2000. School-owned computers available for student use.

EXTRACURRICULARS

Activities: Choral groups, concert band, drama/theater, jazz band, literary magazine, marching band, pep band, radio station, student government, student newspaper, yearbook. **Organizations:** 40 registered organizations, 8 honor societies, 4 religious organizations. **Athletics (Intercollegiate):** *Men:* baseball, basketball, cross-country, diving, football, ice hockey, lacrosse, rifle, rugby, soccer, swimming, track & field, volleyball, wrestling. *Women:* basketball, cross-country, diving, rifle, rugby, soccer, softball, swimming, track & field, volleyball.

ADMISSIONS

Selectivity Rating: 65 (of 100). **Freshman Academic Profile:** 8% in top 10% of high school class, 21% in top 25% of high school class, 43% in top 50% of high school class. 90% from public high schools. SAT I Math middle 50% range 440-570. SAT I Verbal middle 50% range 440-560. TOEFL required of all international applicants, minimum TOEFL 500. **Basis for Candidate Selection:** *Very important factors considered include:* secondary school record. *Important factors considered include:* extracurricular activities, talent/ability. *Other factors considered include:* alumni/ae relation, character/personal qualities, class rank, essays, interview, recommendations, standardized test scores, volunteer work, work experience. **Freshman Admission Requirements:** High school diploma or GED is required. *Academic units required/recommended:* 4 English required, 4 English recommended, 3 math required, 4 math recommended, 2 science required, 3 science recommended, 2 science lab required, 2 science lab recommended, 2 foreign language recommended. **Freshman Admission Statistics:** 1,473 applied, 91% accepted, 37% of those accepted enrolled. **Transfer Admission Requirements:** *Items required:* high school transcript, college transcript. Lowest grade transferable C-. **General Admission Information:** Application fee $35. Early decision application deadline November 15. Nonfall registration accepted. Admission may be deferred for a maximum of 1 year. Credit offered for CEEB Advanced Placement tests.

COSTS AND FINANCIAL AID

Tuition $16,710. Room & board $6,372. Required fees $350. Average book expense $500. **Types of Aid:** *Need-based scholarships/grants:* Pell, SEOG. *Loans:* Direct Subsidized Stafford, Direct Unsubsidized Stafford, FFEL Subsidized Stafford, FFEL Unsubsidized Stafford, FFEL PLUS, Federal Perkins. **Student Employment:** Federal Work-Study Program available. Institutional employment available. Off-campus job opportunities are fair. **Financial Aid Phone:** 802-485-2015.

NOTRE DAME COLLEGE (NH)

2321 Elm Street, Manchester, NH 03104-2299
Phone: 603-669-4298 **E-mail:** admissions@notredame.edu **CEEB Code:** 3670
Fax: 603-644-8316 **Web:** www.notredame.edu **ACT Code:** 2521

This private school, which is affiliated with the Roman Catholic Church, was founded in 1950. It has a 12-acre campus.

STUDENTS AND FACULTY

Enrollment: 685. **Student Body:** Male 24%, female 76%, out-of-state 31%, international students represent 3 countries. **Ethnic Representation:** African American 2%, Asian 1%, Caucasian 94%, Hispanic 1%. **Retention and Graduation:** 69% freshmen return for sophomore year. 41% freshmen graduate within 4 years. 40% grads go on to further study within 1 year. **Faculty:** 49 full-time faculty, 38% hold PhDs. 100% faculty teach undergrads.

ACADEMICS

Degrees: Associate's, bachelor's, certificate, master's. **Academic Requirements:** General education including some course work in arts/fine arts, English (including composition), history, humanities, mathematics, philosophy, sciences (biological or physical), social science, theology. **Classes:** 10-19 students in an average class. 20-29 students in an average lab/discussion section. **Disciplines with Highest Percentage of Degrees Awarded:** Agriculture 100%. **Special Study Options:** Accelerated program, cross registration, distance learning, double major, dual enrollment, English as a second language, independent study, internships, liberal arts/career combination, study abroad, teacher certification program, weekend college.

FACILITIES

Housing: Coed, all-female, all-male, apartments for single students. **Library Holdings:** 60,736 bound volumes. 750 periodicals. 26,400 microforms. 3,000 audiovisuals. **Special Academic Facilities/Equipment:** Center for the Health Sciences and the Arts with physical therapy clinic and counseling psychology center. **Computers:** *Recommended operating system:* Mac. School-owned computers available for student use.

EXTRACURRICULARS

Activities: Choral groups, drama/theater, literary magazine, musical theater, student government, student newspaper, yearbook. **Organizations:** 20 registered organizations, 2 honor societies, 3 religious organizations. **Athletics (Intercollegiate):** *Men:* basketball, soccer. *Women:* basketball, soccer, softball.

ADMISSIONS

Selectivity Rating: 71 (of 100). **Freshman Academic Profile:** Average high school GPA 2.8. Average SAT I Math 443, SAT I Math middle 50% range 390-510. Average SAT I Verbal 468, SAT I Verbal middle 50% range 410-520. TOEFL required of all international applicants, minimum TOEFL 500. **Basis for Candidate Selection:** *Very important factors considered include:* secondary school record, standardized test scores. *Other factors considered include:* character/personal qualities, class rank, essays, extracurricular activities, interview, recommendations, talent/ability, volunteer work, work experience. **Freshman Admission Requirements:** High school diploma or GED is required. *Academic units required/recommended:* 16 total required; 22 total recommended; 4 English required, 2 math required, 4 math recommended, 2 science required, 3 science recommended, 1 science lab required, 2 foreign language recommended, 3 social studies required, 2 history required, 3 elective required. **Freshman Admission Statistics:** 542 applied, 85% accepted, 27% of those accepted enrolled. **Transfer Admission Requirements:** *Items required:* high school transcript, college transcript. Minimum college GPA of 2.0 required. Lowest grade transferable C. **General Admission Information:** Application fee $25. Nonfall registration accepted. Admission may be deferred for a maximum of 1 year. Credit and/or placement offered for CEEB Advanced Placement tests.

COSTS AND FINANCIAL AID

Tuition $15,367. Room & board $6,213. Required fees $500. Average book expense $700. **Required Forms and Deadlines:** FAFSA and institution's own financial aid form. Priority filing deadline March 15. **Notification of Awards:** Applicants will be notified of awards on a rolling basis. **Types of Aid:** *Need-based scholarships/grants:* Pell, SEOG, state scholarships/grants, private scholarships. *Loans:* Direct Subsidized Stafford, Direct Unsubsidized Stafford, Direct PLUS, Federal Perkins, state loans. **Student Employment:** Federal Work-Study Program available. Institutional employment available. Off-campus job opportunities are excellent. **Financial Aid Statistics:** 95% freshmen, 61% undergrads receive some form of aid. Average freshman grant $5,500. Average freshman loan $2,625. Average income from on-campus job $1,000. **Financial Aid Phone:** 603-669-4298.

NOTRE DAME COLLEGE (OH)

4545 College Road, South Euclid, OH 44121
Phone: 216-381-1680 **E-mail:** admissions@ndc.edu **CEEB Code:** 3085
Fax: 216-381-3802 **Web:** www.ndc.edu **ACT Code:** 3302

This private school, which is affiliated with the Roman Catholic Church, was founded in 1922. It has a 53-acre campus.

STUDENTS AND FACULTY

Enrollment: 767. **Student Body:** Male 19%, female 81%, out-of-state 10%. **Ethnic Representation:** African American 26%, Asian 3%, Caucasian 65%, Hispanic 1%. **Retention and Graduation:** 100% freshmen return for sophomore year. 21% freshmen graduate within 4 years. 60% grads go on to further study within 1 year. 10% grads pursue business degrees. 5% grads pursue law degrees. 5% grads pursue medical degrees. **Faculty:** Student/faculty ratio 12:1. 26 full-time faculty, 69% hold PhDs. 100% faculty teach undergrads.

ACADEMICS

Degrees: Associate's, bachelor's, certificate, master's, post-bachelor's certificate. **Academic Requirements:** General education including some course work in arts/fine arts, computer literacy, English (including composition), foreign languages, history, mathematics, philosophy, sciences (biological or physical), social science, theology. **Classes:** 10-19 students in an average class. Under 10 students in an average lab/discussion section. **Special Study Options:** Cooperative (work-study) program, cross registration, distance learning, double major, independent study, internships, student-designed major, study abroad, teacher certification program, weekend college.

FACILITIES

Housing: All-female, all-male. **Library Holdings:** 59,159 bound volumes. 1,000 periodicals. 14,770 microforms. 9,983 audiovisuals. **Special Academic Facilities/Equipment:** Tolerance Resource Center. **Computers:** *Recommended operating system:* Windows NT/2000. School-owned computers available for student use.

EXTRACURRICULARS

Activities: Choral groups, drama/theater, literary magazine, student government, student newspaper, yearbook. **Organizations:** 22 registered organizations, 6 honor societies, 1 religious organization. **Athletics (Intercollegiate):** *Men:* basketball, cross-country, soccer, tennis, track & field. *Women:* basketball, cross-country, soccer, softball, tennis, track & field, volleyball.

ADMISSIONS

Selectivity Rating: 67 (of 100). **Freshman Academic Profile:** Average high school GPA 3.2. 12% in top 10% of high school class, 44% in top 25% of high school class, 78% in top 50% of high school class. 60% from public high schools. Average SAT I Math 520, SAT I Math middle 50% range 410-630. Average SAT I Verbal 600, SAT I Verbal middle 50% range 490-650. Average ACT 22, ACT middle 50% range 20-26. TOEFL required of all international applicants, minimum TOEFL 550. **Basis for Candidate Selection:** *Very important factors considered include:* recommendations, secondary school record, standardized test scores. *Important factors considered include:* class rank. *Other factors considered include:* extracurricular activities, interview. **Freshman Admission Requirements:** High school diploma or GED is required. *Academic units required/recommended:* 15 total recommended; 4 English recommended, 3 math recommended, 3 science recommended, 3 science lab recommended, 2 foreign language recommended, 2 social studies recommended, 1 history recommended, 1 elective recommended. **Freshman Admission Statistics:** 187 applied, 78% accepted, 56% of those accepted enrolled. **Transfer Admission Requirements:** *Items required:* high school transcript, college transcript, interview. Minimum college GPA of 2.5 required. Lowest grade transferable C. **General Admission Information:** Application fee $30. Nonfall registration accepted. Admission may be deferred for a maximum of 1 year. Credit offered for CEEB Advanced Placement tests.

COSTS AND FINANCIAL AID

Tuition $15,502. Room & board $5,906. Required fees $500. Average book expense $750. **Required Forms and Deadlines:** FAFSA. No deadline for regular filing. Priority filing deadline April 1. **Notification of Awards:** Applicants will be notified of awards on a rolling basis beginning on or about January 1. **Types of Aid:** *Need-based scholarships/grants:* Pell, SEOG, state scholarships/grants, private scholarships, the school's own gift aid. *Loans:* FFEL Subsidized Stafford, FFEL Unsubsidized Stafford, FFEL PLUS, Federal Perkins, state loans, college/university loans from institutional funds. **Student Employment:** Federal Work-Study Program available. Institutional employment available. Off-campus job opportunities are good. **Financial Aid Statistics:** 89% freshmen, 88% undergrads receive some form of aid. Average freshman grant $12,000. Average freshman loan $2,625. **Financial Aid Phone:** 216-381-1680.

NOTRE DAME DE NAMUR UNIVERSITY

1500 Ralston Avenue, Belmont, CA 94002
Phone: 650-593-1601 **E-mail:** admiss@ndnu.edu **CEEB Code:** 4063
Fax: 650-508-3426 **Web:** www.ndnu.edu **ACT Code:** 236

This private school, which is affiliated with the Roman Catholic Church, was founded in 1851. It has an 80-acre campus.

STUDENTS AND FACULTY

Enrollment: 813. **Student Body:** Male 35%, female 65%, out-of-state 20%, international 11%. **Ethnic Representation:** African American 8%, Asian 19%, Caucasian 40%, Hispanic 20%. **Retention and Graduation:** 89% freshmen return for sophomore year. 15% grads go on to further study within 1 year. 5% grads pursue business degrees. 1% grads pursue law degrees. 1% grads pursue medical degrees. **Faculty:** 100% faculty teach undergrads.

ACADEMICS

Degrees: Bachelor's, master's.

FACILITIES

Housing: Coed, all-female, all-male, apartments for single students. **Library Holdings:** 95,710 bound volumes. 718 periodicals. 35,369 microforms. 25 audiovisuals. **Special Academic Facilities/Equipment:** Student art museum, professional art gallery, archives of modern Christian art, theatre, early learning center for Montessori credential training, on-campus elementary school. **Computers:** School-owned computers available for student use.

EXTRACURRICULARS

Activities: Drama/theater, jazz band, literary magazine, student government, student newspaper. **Organizations:** 15 registered organizations, 3 honor societies, 1 religious organization. **Athletics (Intercollegiate):** *Men:* basketball, cheerleading, soccer, tennis, track & field. *Women:* basketball, cheerleading, cross-country, soccer, softball, tennis, track & field, volleyball.

ADMISSIONS

Selectivity Rating: 72 (of 100). **Freshman Academic Profile:** Average high school GPA 3.2. 14% in top 10% of high school class, 32% in top 25% of high school class, 69% in top 50% of high school class. 62% from public high schools. Average SAT I Math 470, SAT I Math middle 50% range 430-550. Average SAT I Verbal 465, SAT I Verbal middle 50% range 425-535. Average ACT 18, ACT middle 50% range 18-21. TOEFL required of all international applicants, minimum TOEFL 450. **Basis for Candidate Selection:** *Very important factors considered include:* secondary school record. *Important factors considered include:* essays, extracurricular activities, recommendations, standardized test scores. *Other factors considered include:* alumni/ae relation, character/personal qualities, class rank, interview, talent/ability, volunteer work, work experience. **Freshman Admission Requirements:** High school diploma or GED is required. *Academic units required/recommended:* 14 total required; 4 English required, 2 math required, 3 math recommended, 1 science required, 2 science recommended, 2 foreign language required, 3 foreign language recommended, 2 social studies required, 3 social studies recommended, 3 elective required. **Transfer Admission Requirements:** *Items required:* college transcript, essay. Minimum college GPA of 2.0 required. Lowest grade transferable C. **General Admission Information:** Application fee $35. Priority application deadline March 1. Regular application deadline June 1. Admission may be deferred for a maximum of 2 years. Credit offered for CEEB Advanced Placement tests.

COSTS AND FINANCIAL AID

Tuition $14,976. Room & board $6,400. Average book expense $672. **Required Forms and Deadlines:** FAFSA, CSS/Financial Aid PROFILE and state aid form. Priority filing deadline March 2. **Notification of Awards:** Applicants will be notified of awards on a rolling basis. **Types of Aid:** *Need-based scholarships/grants:* Pell, SEOG, state scholarships/grants, private scholarships, the school's own gift aid. *Loans:* Direct Subsidized Stafford, Direct Unsubsidized Stafford, FFEL Subsidized Stafford, FFEL Unsubsidized Stafford, FFEL PLUS, Federal Perkins. **Student Employment:** Federal Work-Study Program available. Institutional employment available. Off-campus job opportunities are excellent. **Financial Aid Statistics:** Average freshman grant $6,359. Average freshman loan $2,625. Average income from on-campus job $1,300. **Financial Aid Phone:** 650-508-3509.

NOVA SCOTIA COLLEGE OF ART AND DESIGN

5163 Duke Street, Halifax, NS B3J3J6
Phone: 902-494-8129 **E-mail:** admiss@nscad.ns.ca
Fax: 902-425-2987

This public school was founded in 1887. It has a 1-acre campus.

STUDENTS AND FACULTY

Enrollment: 842. **Student Body:** Male 32%, female 68%, out-of-state 54%. **Faculty:** Student/faculty ratio 11:1. 44 full-time faculty. 100% faculty teach undergrads.

ACADEMICS

Degrees: Bachelor's, master's. **Academic Requirements:** General education including some course work in arts/fine arts, English (including composition). **Disciplines with Highest Percentage of Degrees Awarded:** Visual and performing arts 100%. **Special Study Options:** Cooperative (work-study) program, distance learning, double major, student exchange program (domestic), honors program, independent study, internships, study abroad.

FACILITIES

Computers: School-owned computers available for student use.

EXTRACURRICULARS

Activities: Student government, student newspaper.

ADMISSIONS

Selectivity Rating: 63 (of 100). **Freshman Academic Profile:** TOEFL required of all international applicants, minimum TOEFL 575. **Basis for Candidate Selection:** *Very important factors considered include:* essays, secondary school record, talent/ability. *Other factors considered include:* character/personal qualities, interview, recommendations, standardized test scores, volunteer work, work experience. **Freshman Admission Requirements: Freshman Admission Statistics:** 247 applied, 43% accepted. **Transfer Admission Requirements:** *Items required:* college transcript, essay, statement of good standing from prior school. **General Admission Information:** Application fee $35. Regular application deadline May 15. Nonfall registration accepted. Admission may be deferred for a maximum of 1 year. Placement offered for CEEB Advanced Placement tests.

COSTS AND FINANCIAL AID

Required fees $250. **Types of Aid:** *Need-based scholarships/grants:* Pell, SEOG, state scholarships/grants, private scholarships, the school's own gift aid. *Loans:* FFEL Subsidized Stafford, FFEL Unsubsidized Stafford, FFEL PLUS, Federal Perkins, college/university loans from institutional funds. **Student Employment:** Institutional employment available. Off-campus job opportunities are fair. **Financial Aid Statistics:** Average freshman grant $1,600. Average freshman loan $7,500. **Financial Aid Phone:** 902-494-8130.

NOVA SOUTHEASTERN UNIVERSITY

3301 College Avenue, Ft. Lauderdale, FL 33314
Phone: 954-262-8000 **E-mail:** ncsinfo@nova.edu **CEEB Code:** 5514
Fax: 954-262-3811 **Web:** www.nova.edu **ACT Code:** 6706

This private school was founded in 1964. It has a 232-acre campus.

STUDENTS AND FACULTY

Enrollment: 4,700. **Student Body:** Male 26%, female 74%, international 10%. **Ethnic Representation:** African American 29%, Asian 3%, Caucasian 34%, Hispanic 26%. **Retention and Graduation:** 72% freshmen return for sophomore year. **Faculty:** Student/faculty ratio 14:1. 503 full-time faculty.

ACADEMICS

Degrees: Bachelor's, doctoral, first professional, first professional certificate, master's, post-master's certificate. **Academic Requirements:** General education including some course work in computer literacy, English (including composition), history, humanities, mathematics, sciences (biological or physical). **Classes:** 10-19 students in an average class. **Disciplines with Highest Percentage of Degrees Awarded:** Business/marketing 49%, education 20%, health professions and related sciences 9%, psychology 7%, biological life sciences 6%. **Special Study Options:** Accelerated program, cooperative (work-study) program, distance learning, dual enrollment, English as a second language, internships, study abroad, teacher certification program, dual admission programs with NSU graduate and professional school.

FACILITIES

Housing: Coed, apartments for married students, apartments for single students, housing for disabled students, housing for international students. **Library Holdings:** 395,927 bound volumes. 12,750 periodicals. 677,537 microforms. 12,421 audiovisuals. **Special Academic Facilities/Equipment:** Early childhood family center, university school for pre-kindergarten to grade 12, oceanographic center and lab, biofeedback and learning technology labs, audiology and speech language pathology clinics, psychology clinics. **Computers:** School-owned computers available for student use.

EXTRACURRICULARS

Activities: Choral groups, drama/theater, radio station, student government, student newspaper. **Organizations:** 43 registered organizations, 3 honor societies, 3 religious organizations, 4 fraternities, 4 sororities. **Athletics (Intercollegiate):** *Men:* baseball, basketball, cheerleading, cross-country, golf, soccer. *Women:* basketball, cheerleading, cross-country, golf, soccer, softball, volleyball.

ADMISSIONS

Selectivity Rating: 75 (of 100). **Freshman Academic Profile:** Average high school GPA 3.5. 24% in top 10% of high school class, 55% in top 25% of high school class, 85% in top 50% of high school class. 80% from public high schools. Average SAT I Math 524, SAT I Math middle 50% range 460-590. Average SAT I Verbal 515, SAT I Verbal middle 50% range 460-570. Average ACT 22. TOEFL required of all international applicants, minimum TOEFL 550. **Basis for Candidate Selection:** *Very important factors considered include:* character/personal qualities, secondary school record, standardized test scores. *Important factors considered include:* volunteer work, work experience. *Other factors considered include:* alumni/ae relation, class rank, extracurricular activities, interview, recommendations, talent/ability. **Freshman Admission Requirements:** High school diploma or GED is required. *Academic units required/recommended:* 4 English required, 3 math required, 3 science required, 2 foreign language recommended, 1 social studies required, 2 history required, 1 elective recommended. **Freshman Admission Statistics:** 817 applied, 73% accepted, 55% of those accepted enrolled. **Transfer Admission Requirements:** *Items required:* college transcript. Minimum college GPA of 2.5 required. Lowest grade transferable C. **General Admission Information:** Application fee $35. Nonfall registration accepted. Admission may be deferred for a maximum of 1 year. Credit offered for CEEB Advanced Placement tests.

COSTS AND FINANCIAL AID

Tuition $13,650. Room & board $6,484. Required fees $230. Average book expense $856. **Required Forms and Deadlines:** FAFSA and institution's own financial aid form. No deadline for regular filing. Priority filing deadline April 15. **Notification of Awards:** Applicants will be notified of awards on a rolling basis beginning on or about March 30. **Types of Aid:** *Need-based scholarships/grants:* Pell, SEOG, state scholarships/grants, private scholarships, the school's own gift aid. *Loans:* FFEL Subsidized Stafford, FFEL Unsubsidized Stafford, FFEL PLUS, Federal Perkins, college/university loans from institutional funds. **Student Employment:** Federal Work-Study Program available. Institutional employment available. Off-campus job opportunities are good. **Financial Aid**

Statistics: 73% freshmen, 72% undergrads receive some form of aid. **Financial Aid Phone:** 954-262-3380.

NYACK COLLEGE

1 South Boulevard, Nyack, NY 10960-3698
Phone: 845-358-1710 **E-mail:** enroll@nyack.edu **CEEB Code:** 2560
Fax: 845-358-3047 **Web:** www.nyackcollege.edu **ACT Code:** 2846

This private school was founded in 1882. It has a 102-acre campus.

STUDENTS AND FACULTY

Enrollment: 1,990. **Student Body:** Male 41%, female 59%, out-of-state 36%, international 4% (46 countries represented). **Ethnic Representation:** African American 31%, Asian 7%, Caucasian 37%, Hispanic 23%. **Retention and Graduation:** 64% freshmen return for sophomore year. **Faculty:** Student/faculty ratio 17:1. 83 full-time faculty, 62% hold PhDs. 86% faculty teach undergrads.

ACADEMICS

Degrees: Associate's, bachelor's, first professional, master's certificate, terminal, transfer. **Academic Requirements:** General education including some course work in arts/fine arts, English (including composition), foreign languages, history, humanities, mathematics, philosophy, sciences (biological or physical), social science, Bible/theology studies. **Classes:** 10-19 students in an average class. 10-19 students in an average lab/discussion section. **Disciplines with Highest Percentage of Degrees Awarded:** Business/marketing 55%, education 9%, liberal arts/general studies 9%, philosophy/religion/theology 8%, psychology 7%. **Special Study Options:** Accelerated program, distance learning, double major, English as a second language, honors program, independent study, internships, liberal arts/career combination, study abroad, teacher certification program.

FACILITIES

Housing: All-female, all-male, apartments for single students. **Library Holdings:** 127,271 bound volumes. 958 periodicals. 11,997 microforms. 4,739 audiovisuals. **Computers:** School-owned computers available for student use.

EXTRACURRICULARS

Activities: Choral groups, drama/theater, literary magazine, music ensembles, musical theater, radio station, student government, student newspaper, yearbook. **Organizations:** 1 honor society, 1 religious organization. **Athletics (Intercollegiate):** *Men:* baseball, basketball, cross-country, golf, soccer. *Women:* basketball, cross-country, soccer, softball, volleyball.

ADMISSIONS

Selectivity Rating: 73 (of 100). **Freshman Academic Profile:** Average high school GPA 2.8. 9% in top 10% of high school class, 23% in top 25% of high school class, 62% in top 50% of high school class. Average SAT I Math 466, SAT I Math middle 50% range 410-550. Average SAT I Verbal 487, SAT I Verbal middle 50% range 430-560. Average ACT 21, ACT middle 50% range 17-23. TOEFL required of all international applicants, minimum TOEFL 550. **Basis for Candidate Selection:** *Very important factors considered include:* class rank, interview, recommendations, religious affiliation/commitment, secondary school record, standardized test scores. *Important factors considered include:* character/personal qualities, essays, extracurricular activities. *Other factors considered include:* talent/ability, volunteer work, work experience. **Freshman Admission Requirements:** High school diploma or GED is required. *Academic units required/recommended:* 16 total required; 4 English recommended, 2 foreign language recommended, 4 elective recommended. **Freshman Admission Statistics:** 944 applied, 63% accepted, 53% of those accepted enrolled. **Transfer Admission Requirements:** *Items required:* college transcript, essay, statement of good standing from prior school. Lowest grade transferable C-. **General Admission Information:** Application fee $15. Nonfall registration accepted. Admission may be deferred. Credit offered for CEEB Advanced Placement tests.

COSTS AND FINANCIAL AID

Tuition $12,990. Required fees $800. **Required Forms and Deadlines:** FAFSA. Priority filing deadline March 1. **Notification of Awards:** Applicants will be notified of awards on a rolling basis beginning on or about March 1. **Types of Aid:** *Need-based scholarships/grants:* Pell, SEOG, state scholarships/grants, private scholarships, the school's own gift aid. *Loans:* FFEL Subsidized Stafford, FFEL Unsubsidized Stafford, FFEL PLUS, Federal Perkins. **Student Employment:** Federal Work-Study Program available. Institutional employment available. Off-campus job opportunities are excellent. **Financial Aid Statistics:** 87% freshmen, 77% undergrads receive some form of aid. **Financial Aid Phone:** 914-358-1710.

OAKLAND CITY UNIVERSITY

143 N. Lucretia Street, Oakland City, IN 47660
Phone: 812-749-4781 **E-mail:** ocuadmit@oak.edu
Fax: 812-749-1233 **Web:** www.oak.edu

This private school, which is affiliated with the Baptist Church, was founded in 1885.

STUDENTS AND FACULTY

Enrollment: 1,258. **Student Body:** Male 50%, female 50%, out-of-state 30%, international students represent 9 countries. **Ethnic Representation:** African American 12%, Caucasian 86%, Hispanic 2%. **Retention and Graduation:** 50% freshmen graduate within 4 years. 42% grads go on to further study within 1 year. 2% grads pursue business degrees. **Faculty:** Student/faculty ratio 16:1. 36 full-time faculty, 66% hold PhDs. 100% faculty teach undergrads.

ACADEMICS

Degrees: Associate's, bachelor's, certificate, doctoral, first professional, master's, terminal, transfer. **Academic Requirements:** General education including some course work in arts/fine arts, computer literacy, English (including composition), history, humanities, mathematics, philosophy, sciences (biological or physical), social science, New Testament. **Classes:** Under 10 students in an average class. **Disciplines with Highest Percentage of Degrees Awarded:** Business/marketing 65%, education 21%, philosophy/religion/theology 4%, computer and information sciences 2%, other 2%. **Special Study Options:** Accelerated program, cooperative (work-study) program, distance learning, double major, dual enrollment, external degree program, honors program, independent study, internships, teacher certification program.

FACILITIES

Housing: All-female, all-male, apartments for married students, apartments for single students, housing for disabled students. **Computers:** School-owned computers available for student use.

EXTRACURRICULARS

Activities: Choral groups, drama/theater, music ensembles, pep band, student government, student newspaper, yearbook. **Organizations:** 18 registered organizations, 5 honor societies, 3 religious organizations. **Athletics (Intercollegiate):** *Men:* baseball, basketball, cheerleading, cross-country, golf, soccer, volleyball. *Women:* basketball, cheerleading, cross-country, golf, soccer, softball, volleyball.

ADMISSIONS

Selectivity Rating: 63 (of 100). **Freshman Academic Profile:** 7% in top 10% of high school class, 18% in top 25% of high school class, 60% in top 50% of high school class. TOEFL required of all international applicants, minimum TOEFL 500. **Basis for Candidate Selection:** *Very important factors considered include:* secondary school record, standardized test scores. *Important factors considered include:* character/personal qualities, interview. *Other factors considered include:* class rank, essays, recommendations, talent/ability, volunteer work. **Freshman Admission Requirements:** High school diploma or GED is required. *Academic units required/recommended:* 12 total recommended; 4 English recommended, 3 math recommended, 3 science recommended, 2 social studies recommended. **Freshman Admission Statistics:** 382 applied, 100% accepted. **Transfer Admission Requirements:** *Items required:* high school transcript, college transcript, statement of good standing from prior school. Minimum high school GPA of 2.0 required. Minimum college GPA of 2.0 required. Lowest grade transferable C. **General Admission Information:** Application fee $35. Priority application deadline July 1. Regular application deadline August 27.

COSTS AND FINANCIAL AID

Tuition $12,000. Room & board $4,560. Required fees $320. Average book expense $1,000. **Required Forms and Deadlines:** FAFSA. Financial aid filing deadline March 2. **Notification of Awards:** Applicants will be notified of awards on a rolling basis beginning on or about June 2. **Student Employment:** Federal Work-Study Program available. Off-campus job opportunities are poor. **Financial Aid Statistics:** Average income from on-campus job $1,700. **Financial Aid Phone:** 812-749-1224.

OAKLAND UNIVERSITY

Office of Admissions, 101 North Foundation Hall, Rochester, MI 48309-4475
Phone: 248-370-3360 **E-mail:** ouinfo@oakland.edu **CEEB Code:** 1497
Fax: 248-370-4462 **Web:** www.oakland.edu **ACT Code:** 2033

This public school was founded in 1957. It has a 1,444-acre campus.

STUDENTS AND FACULTY

Enrollment: 12,634. **Student Body:** Male 37%, female 63%, out-of-state 2%, international 1%. **Ethnic Representation:** African American 7%, Asian 3%, Caucasian 77%, Hispanic 2%, Native American 1%. **Retention and Graduation:** 72% freshmen return for sophomore year. 11% freshmen graduate within 4 years. 20% grads go on to further study within 1 year. **Faculty:** Student/faculty ratio 21:1. 452 full-time faculty, 94% hold PhDs. 99% faculty teach undergrads.

ACADEMICS

Degrees: Bachelor's, doctoral, master's, post-bachelor's certificate, post-master's certificate. **Academic Requirements:** General education including some course work in arts/fine arts, computer literacy, English (including composition), foreign languages, history, humanities, mathematics, philosophy, sciences (biological or physical), social science, ethnic diversity. **Classes:** 20-29 students in an average class. 10-19 students in an average lab/discussion section. **Majors with Highest Enrollment:** Nursing/registered nurse training (RN, ASN, BSN, MSN); elementary education and teaching; psychology, general. **Disciplines with Highest Percentage of Degrees Awarded:** Education 22%, business/marketing 21%, health professions and related sciences 9%, engineering/engineering technology 8%, communications/communication technologies 8%. **Special Study Options:** Accelerated program, cooperative (work-study) program, distance learning, double major, English as a second language, honors program, independent study, internships, student-designed major, study abroad, teacher certification program.

FACILITIES

Housing: Coed, apartments for married students, apartments for single students, housing for disabled students, fraternities and/or sororities, living/learning communities, substance-free dorms. **Library Holdings:** 738,420 bound volumes. 1,660 periodicals. 1,161,993 microforms. 5,340 audiovisuals. **Special Academic Facilities/Equipment:** Art gallery, robotics lab, eye research institute, professional theater, Meadowbrook Hall. **Computers:** School-owned computers available for student use.

EXTRACURRICULARS

Activities: Choral groups, concert band, dance, drama/theater, jazz band, literary magazine, music ensembles, musical theater, pep band, radio station, student government, student newspaper, student-run film society, symphony orchestra. **Organizations:** 105 registered organizations, 5 honor societies, 11 religious organizations, 10 fraternities (1% men join), 9 sororities (2% women join). **Athletics (Intercollegiate):** *Men:* baseball, basketball, cross-country, diving, golf, soccer, swimming. *Women:* basketball, cross-country, diving, golf, soccer, softball, swimming, tennis, volleyball.

ADMISSIONS

Selectivity Rating: 75 (of 100). **Freshman Academic Profile:** Average high school GPA 3.2. 42% in top 25% of high school class, 88% in top 50% of high school class. 90% from public high schools. Average ACT 22, ACT middle 50% range 19-24. TOEFL required of all international applicants, minimum TOEFL 550. **Basis for Candidate Selection:** *Very important factors considered include:* secondary school record. *Important factors considered include:* character/personal qualities, extracurricular activities, recommendations, talent/ability, volunteer work. *Other factors considered include:* alumni/ae relation, essays, interview, work experience. **Freshman Admission Requirements:** High school diploma or GED is required. *Academic units required/recommended:* 4 English required, 3 math required, 3 science required, 2 foreign language recommended, 3 social studies required. **Freshman Admission Statistics:** 5,733 applied, 78% accepted, 42% of those accepted enrolled. **Transfer Admission Requirements:** *Items required:* college transcript, statement of good standing from prior school. Minimum high school GPA of 2.5 required. Minimum college GPA of 2.5 required. Lowest grade transferable C. **General Admission Information:** Application fee $25. Nonfall registration accepted. Admission may be deferred for a maximum of 1 year. Placement offered for CEEB Advanced Placement tests.

COSTS AND FINANCIAL AID

In-state tuition $4,545. Out-of-state tuition $11,340. Room & board $5,252. Required fees $486. Average book expense $580. **Required Forms and Deadlines:** FAFSA. No deadline for regular filing. Priority filing deadline February 21. **Notification of Awards:** Applicants will be notified of awards on a rolling basis beginning on or about March 15. **Types of Aid:** *Need-based scholarships/grants:* Pell, SEOG, state scholarships/grants, private scholarships, the school's own gift aid. *Loans:* Direct Subsidized Stafford, Direct Unsubsidized Stafford, Direct PLUS, Federal Perkins. **Student Employment:** Federal Work-Study Program available. Institutional employment available. Off-campus job opportunities are excellent. **Financial Aid Statistics:** 34% freshmen, 31% undergrads receive some form of aid. Average freshman grant $3,010. Average income from on-campus job $1,812. **Financial Aid Phone:** 248-370-2550.

OBERLIN COLLEGE

101 North Professor Street, Oberlin, OH 44074
Phone: 440-775-8411 **E-mail:** college.admissions@oberlin.edu **CEEB Code:** 1587
Fax: 440-775-6905 **Web:** www.oberlin.edu **ACT Code:** 3304

This private school was founded in 1833. It has a 450-acre campus.

STUDENTS AND FACULTY

Enrollment: 2,848. **Student Body:** Male 45%, female 55%, out-of-state 89%, international 6%. **Ethnic Representation:** African American 8%, Asian 6%, Caucasian 81%, Hispanic 4%, Native American 1%. **Retention and Graduation:** 88% freshmen return for sophomore year. 63% freshmen graduate within 4 years. 16% grads go on to further study within 1 year. 2% grads pursue business degrees. 3% grads pursue law degrees. 3% grads pursue medical degrees. **Faculty:** Student/faculty ratio 10:1. 272 full-time faculty, 94% hold PhDs. 100% faculty teach undergrads.

ACADEMICS

Degrees: Bachelor's, diploma, master's, post-master's certificate. **Academic Requirements:** General education including some course work in humanities, sciences (biological or physical), social science, cultural diversity, quantitative. **Classes:** 10-19 students in an average class. 10-19 students in an average lab/discussion section. **Majors with Highest Enrollment:** History, general; English language and literature, general; biology/biological sciences, general. **Disciplines with Highest Percentage of Degrees Awarded:** Visual and performing arts 29%, social sciences and history 16%, English 12%, biological life sciences 9%, area and ethnic studies 7%. **Special Study Options:** Double major, dual enrollment, English as a second language, student exchange program (domestic), honors program, independent study, internships, student-designed major, study abroad, teacher certification program, 5-year double-degree program with Conservatory of Music and College of Arts and Sciences, 3-2 engineering program.

FACILITIES

Housing: Coed, all-female, all-male, cooperative housing. **Library Holdings:** 1,541,260 bound volumes. 4,560 periodicals. 364,504 microforms. 59,186 audiovisuals. **Special Academic Facilities/Equipment:** Allen Memorial Art Museum, theaters, music performance halls. **Computers:** School-owned computers available for student use.

EXTRACURRICULARS

Activities: Choral groups, concert band, dance, drama/theater, jazz band, literary magazine, marching band, music ensembles, musical theater, opera, radio station, student government, student newspaper, student-run film society, symphony orchestra, yearbook. **Organizations:** 125 registered organizations, 3 honor societies, 10 religious organizations. **Athletics (Intercollegiate):** *Men:* baseball, basketball, cross-country, diving, football, golf, indoor track, lacrosse, soccer, swimming, tennis, track & field. *Women:* basketball, cross-country, diving, field hockey, golf, indoor track, lacrosse, soccer, softball, swimming, tennis, track & field, volleyball.

ADMISSIONS

Selectivity Rating: 91 (of 100). **Freshman Academic Profile:** Average high school GPA 3.5. 63% in top 10% of high school class, 93% in top 25% of high school class, 99% in top 50% of high school class. 66% from public high schools. Average SAT I Math 659, SAT I Math middle 50% range 610-710. Average SAT I Verbal 691, SAT I Verbal middle 50% range 630-740. Average ACT 30, ACT middle 50% range 26-31. TOEFL required of all international applicants, minimum TOEFL 600. **Basis for Candidate Selection:** *Very important factors considered include:* class rank, secondary school record, standardized test scores. *Important factors considered include:* character/personal qualities, essays, extracurricular activities, recommendations, talent/ability. *Other factors considered include:* alumni/ae relation, geographical residence, interview, minority status, state residency, volunteer work, work experience. **Freshman Admission Requirements:** High school diploma or GED is required.

Academic units required/recommended: 4 English recommended, 4 math recommended, 3 science recommended, 3 science lab recommended, 3 foreign language recommended, 3 social studies recommended. **Freshman Admission Statistics:** 5,934 applied, 33% accepted, 38% of those accepted enrolled. **Transfer Admission Requirements:** *Items required:* high school transcript, college transcript, essay, standardized test score, statement of good standing from prior school. Minimum college GPA of 3.0 required. Lowest grade transferable C-. **General Admission Information:** Application fee $35. Early decision application deadline November 15. Regular application deadline January 15. Admission may be deferred for a maximum of 1 year. Credit and/or placement offered for CEEB Advanced Placement tests.

COSTS AND FINANCIAL AID

Tuition $27,880. Room & board $6,830. Required fees $170. Average book expense $734. **Required Forms and Deadlines:** FAFSA, CSS/Financial Aid PROFILE, noncustodial (divorced/separated) parent's statement and business/farm supplement. Financial aid filing deadline February 15. Priority filing deadline February 1. **Notification of Awards:** Applicants will be notified of awards on or about April 15. **Types of Aid:** *Need-based scholarships/grants:* Pell, SEOG, state scholarships/grants, private scholarships, the school's own gift aid. *Loans:* Direct Subsidized Stafford, Direct Unsubsidized Stafford, Direct PLUS, Federal Perkins, college/university loans from institutional funds. **Student Employment:** Federal Work-Study Program available. Institutional employment available. Off-campus job opportunities are good. **Financial Aid Statistics:** 56% freshmen, 56% undergrads receive some form of aid. Average freshman grant $23,700. Average freshman loan $4,000. Average income from on-campus job $1,500. **Financial Aid Phone:** 440-775-8142.

See page 1140.

OCCIDENTAL COLLEGE

1600 Campus Road, Office of Admission, Los Angeles, CA 90041
Phone: 323-259-2700 **E-mail:** admission@oxy.edu **CEEB Code:** 4581
Fax: 323-341-4875 **Web:** www.oxy.edu **ACT Code:** 350

This private school was founded in 1887. It has a 120-acre campus.

STUDENTS AND FACULTY

Enrollment: 1,570. **Student Body:** Male 44%, female 56%, out-of-state 40%, international 3% (45 countries represented). **Ethnic Representation:** African American 6%, Asian 20%, Caucasian 57%, Hispanic 14%, Native American 1%. **Retention and Graduation:** 87% freshmen return for sophomore year. 67% freshmen graduate within 4 years. 30% grads go on to further study within 1 year. 5% grads pursue business degrees. 5% grads pursue law degrees. 5% grads pursue medical degrees. **Faculty:** Student/faculty ratio 11:1. 138 full-time faculty, 92% hold PhDs. 100% faculty teach undergrads.

ACADEMICS

Degrees: Bachelor's, master's. **Academic Requirements:** General education including some course work in arts/fine arts, English (including composition), foreign languages, history, humanities, mathematics, sciences (biological or physical). **Classes:** 10-19 students in an average class. 10-19 students in an average lab/discussion section. **Disciplines with Highest Percentage of Degrees Awarded:** Social sciences and history 27%, biological life sciences 17%, visual and performing arts 14%, psychology 7%, physical sciences 7%. **Special Study Options:** Accelerated program, cross registration, double major, student exchange program (domestic), honors program, independent study, internships, liberal arts/career combination, student-designed major, study abroad, teacher certification program.

FACILITIES

Housing: Coed, all-female, apartments for single students, fraternities and/or sororities. **Library Holdings:** 475,645 bound volumes. 1,270 periodicals. 399,104 microforms. 16,358 audiovisuals. **Special Academic Facilities/Equipment:** Ornithology museum, subcritical reactor, natural science, astronomical instrument, and geological collections, child psychology lab. **Computers:** *Recommended operating system:* Mac. School-owned computers available for student use.

EXTRACURRICULARS

Activities: Choral groups, dance, drama/theater, jazz band, literary magazine, music ensembles, musical theater, radio station, student government, student newspaper, student-run film society, symphony orchestra, yearbook. **Organizations:** 100 registered organizations, 5 honor societies, 15 religious organizations, 2 fraternities (15% men join), 3 sororities (15% women join). **Athletics (Intercollegiate):** *Men:* baseball, basketball, cross-country, diving, golf, soccer, swimming, tennis, track & field, water polo. *Women:* basketball, cross-country, diving, soccer, softball, swimming, tennis, track & field, volleyball, water polo.

ADMISSIONS

Selectivity Rating: 88 (of 100). **Freshman Academic Profile:** Average high school GPA 3.8. 51% in top 10% of high school class, 77% in top 25% of high school class, 95% in top 50% of high school class. 57% from public high schools. Average SAT I Math 610, SAT I Math middle 50% range 550-660. Average SAT I Verbal 610, SAT I Verbal middle 50% range 550-660. Average ACT 27. TOEFL required of all international applicants, minimum TOEFL 600. **Basis for Candidate Selection:** *Very important factors considered include:* class rank, essays, recommendations, secondary school record, standardized test scores. *Important factors considered include:* character/personal qualities, extracurricular activities, interview, talent/ability. *Other factors considered include:* alumni/ae relation, geographical residence, minority status, volunteer work, work experience. **Freshman Admission Requirements:** High school diploma or GED is required. *Academic units required/recommended:* 3 English required, 3 English recommended, 3 math required, 3 math recommended, 2 science required, 3 science recommended, 1 science lab required, 2 science lab recommended, 2 foreign language required, 3 foreign language recommended, 2 social studies required, 2 social studies recommended, 2 history recommended. **Freshman Admission Statistics:** 2,992 applied, 60% accepted, 23% of those accepted enrolled. **Transfer Admission Requirements:** *Items required:* high school transcript, college transcript, essay, standardized test scores. Minimum college GPA of 3.0 required. **General Admission Information:** Application fee $50. Early decision application deadline November 15. Regular application deadline January 15. Admission may be deferred for a maximum of 1 year. Credit offered for CEEB Advanced Placement tests.

COSTS AND FINANCIAL AID

Tuition $23,532. Room & board $6,880. Required fees $498. Average book expense $810. **Required Forms and Deadlines:** FAFSA, CSS/Financial Aid PROFILE, state aid form, noncustodial (divorced/separated) parent's statement, business/farm supplement and P. Financial aid filing deadline February 1. Priority filing deadline February 1. **Notification of Awards:** Applicants will be notified of awards on or about April 1. **Student Employment:** Federal Work-Study Program available. Institutional employment available. Off-campus job opportunities are excellent. **Financial Aid Statistics:** 54% freshmen, 60% undergrads receive some form of aid. Average freshman grant $19,000. Average freshman loan $3,000. Average income from on-campus job $2,000. **Financial Aid Phone:** 323-259-2548.

OGLETHORPE UNIVERSITY

$$$

4484 Peachtree Road, NE, Atlanta, GA 30319
Phone: 404-364-8307 **E-mail:** admission@oglethorpe.edu **CEEB Code:** 5521
Fax: 404-364-8500 **Web:** www.oglethorpe.edu **ACT Code:** 850

This private school was founded in 1835. It has a 118-acre campus.

STUDENTS AND FACULTY

Enrollment: 1,037. **Student Body:** Male 34%, female 66%, out-of-state 44%, international 6% (32 countries represented). **Ethnic Representation:** African American 21%, Asian 4%, Caucasian 70%, Hispanic 1%. **Retention and Graduation:** 81% freshmen return for sophomore year. 49% freshmen graduate within 4 years. 36% grads go on to further study within 1 year. 6% grads pursue business degrees. 9% grads pursue law degrees. 2% grads pursue medical degrees. **Faculty:** Student/faculty ratio 12:1. 55 full-time faculty, 92% hold PhDs. 100% faculty teach undergrads.

ACADEMICS

Degrees: Bachelor's, master's. **Academic Requirements:** General education including some course work in arts/fine arts, computer literacy, English (including composition), history, humanities, mathematics, philosophy, sciences (biological or physical), social science. **Classes:** 10-19 students in an average class. **Disciplines with Highest Percentage of Degrees Awarded:** Business/marketing 32%, communications/communication technologies 14%, social sciences and history 11%, psychology 10%, interdisciplinary studies 8%. **Special Study Options:** Accelerated program, cooperative (work-study) program, cross registration, double major, honors program, independent study, internships, liberal arts/career combination, student-designed major, study abroad, teacher certification program.

FACILITIES

Housing: Coed, all-female, all-male, fraternities and/or sororities. **Library Holdings:** 150,000 bound volumes. 710 periodicals. **Special Academic**

Facilities/Equipment: Art museum, Japanese elementary school, scanning electron microscope. **Computers:** *Recommended operating system:* Windows 95. School-owned computers available for student use.

EXTRACURRICULARS

Activities: Choral groups, dance, drama/theater, literary magazine, musical theater, radio station, student government, student newspaper, yearbook. **Organizations:** 57 registered organizations, 10 honor societies, 5 religious organizations, 4 fraternities (33% men join), 3 sororities (22% women join). **Athletics (Intercollegiate):** *Men:* baseball, basketball, cross-country, golf, soccer, tennis, track & field. *Women:* basketball, cheerleading, cross-country, golf, soccer, tennis, track & field, volleyball.

ADMISSIONS

Selectivity Rating: 85 (of 100). **Freshman Academic Profile:** Average high school GPA 3.7. 43% in top 10% of high school class, 73% in top 25% of high school class, 99% in top 50% of high school class. 77% from public high schools. Average SAT I Math 603, SAT I Math middle 50% range 540-650. Average SAT I Verbal 617, SAT I Verbal middle 50% range 560-680. Average ACT 26, ACT middle 50% range 23-29. Minimum TOEFL 550. **Basis for Candidate Selection:** *Very important factors considered include:* essays, interview, secondary school record. *Important factors considered include:* standardized test scores. *Other factors considered include:* alumni/ae relation, character/personal qualities, class rank, extracurricular activities, recommendations, talent/ability, volunteer work, work experience. **Freshman Admission Requirements:** High school diploma or GED is required. *Academic units required/recommended:* 4 English required, 4 English recommended, 3 math required, 4 math recommended, 2 science required, 3 science recommended, 2 foreign language recommended, 3 social studies required, 4 social studies recommended. **Freshman Admission Statistics:** 602 applied, 90% accepted, 35% of those accepted enrolled. **Transfer Admission Requirements:** *Items required:* college transcript, essay, statement of good standing from prior school. Minimum college GPA of 2.8 required. Lowest grade transferable C. **General Admission Information:** Application fee $30. Priority application deadline December 30. Nonfall registration accepted. Admission may be deferred for a maximum of 1 year. Neither credit nor placement offered for CEEB Advanced Placement tests.

COSTS AND FINANCIAL AID

Tuition $18,990. Room & board $6,360. Required fees $450. Average book expense $600. **Required Forms and Deadlines:** FAFSA, institution's own financial aid form and state aid form. No deadline for regular filing. Priority filing deadline March 1. **Notification of Awards:** Applicants will be notified of awards on a rolling basis beginning on or about January 1. **Types of Aid:** *Need-based scholarships/grants:* Pell, SEOG, state scholarships/grants, private scholarships, the school's own gift aid. *Loans:* Direct Subsidized Stafford, Direct Unsubsidized Stafford, Direct PLUS, FFEL Subsidized Stafford, FFEL Unsubsidized Stafford, FFEL PLUS, Federal Perkins. **Student Employment:** Federal Work-Study Program available. Institutional employment available. Off-campus job opportunities are excellent. **Financial Aid Statistics:** 66% freshmen, 61% undergrads receive some form of aid. Average freshman grant $11,018. Average freshman loan $2,934. Average income from on-campus job $1,200. **Financial Aid Phone:** 404-364-8356.

See page 1142.

OHIO DOMINICAN UNIVERSITY

1216 Sunbury Road, Coumbus, OH 42319-2099
Phone: 614-251-4500 **E-mail:** admissions@ohiodominican.edu **CEEB Code:** 1131
Fax: 614-251-0156 **Web:** www.ohiodominican.edu **ACT Code:** 3256

This private school, which is affiliated with the Roman Catholic Church, was founded in 1911. It has a 65-acre campus.

STUDENTS AND FACULTY

Enrollment: 2,250. **Student Body:** Male 29%, female 71%, out-of-state 1%, international 1% (1 country represented). **Ethnic Representation:** African American 27%, Asian 1%, Caucasian 69%, Hispanic 2%. **Retention and Graduation:** 62% freshmen return for sophomore year. 29% freshmen graduate within 4 years. **Faculty:** Student/faculty ratio 15:1. 62 full-time faculty, 87% hold PhDs. 100% faculty teach undergrads.

ACADEMICS

Degrees: Associate's, bachelor's, certificate, master's, terminal, transfer. **Academic Requirements:** General education including some course work in arts/fine arts, English (including composition), foreign languages, humanities, mathematics, philosophy, sciences (biological or physical), social science. **Classes:** 10-19 students in an average class. **Majors with Highest Enrollment:** Business administration/management; secondary education and teaching. **Disciplines with Highest Percentage of Degrees Awarded:** Business/marketing 38%, education 18%, computer and information sciences 7%, liberal arts/general studies 7%, communications/communication technologies 6%. **Special Study Options:** Cross registration, double major, dual enrollment, English as a second language, student exchange program (domestic), honors program, independent study, internships, study abroad, teacher certification program, weekend college.

FACILITIES

Housing: Coed. **Library Holdings:** 110,953 bound volumes. 553 periodicals. 6,849 microforms. 4,302 audiovisuals. **Special Academic Facilities/Equipment:** Wehrle Art Gallery. **Computers:** School-owned computers available for student use.

EXTRACURRICULARS

Activities: Choral groups, drama/theater, literary magazine, radio station, student government. **Organizations:** 23 registered organizations, 4 honor societies, 1 religious organization. **Athletics (Intercollegiate):** *Men:* baseball, basketball, golf, soccer, tennis. *Women:* basketball, golf, soccer, softball, tennis, volleyball.

ADMISSIONS

Selectivity Rating: 79 (of 100). **Freshman Academic Profile:** Average high school GPA 3.1. 9% in top 10% of high school class, 32% in top 25% of high school class, 65% in top 50% of high school class. 72% from public high schools. Average ACT 21, ACT middle 50% range 17-22. **Basis for Candidate Selection:** *Very important factors considered include:* secondary school record. *Important factors considered include:* standardized test scores. *Other factors considered include:* character/personal qualities, class rank, essays, extracurricular activities, interview, recommendations, talent/ability, volunteer work, work experience. **Freshman Admission Requirements:** High school diploma or GED is required. *Academic units required/recommended:* 16 total recommended; 4 English recommended, 3 math recommended, 3 science recommended, 3 foreign language recommended, 3 social studies recommended. **Freshman Admission Statistics:** 1,116 applied, 64% accepted, 37% of those accepted enrolled. **Transfer Admission Requirements:** *Items required:* college transcript, essay. Lowest grade transferable C. **General Admission Information:** Application fee $25. Priority application deadline April 1. Nonfall registration accepted. Admission may be deferred for a maximum of 1 year. Credit and/or placement offered for CEEB Advanced Placement tests.

COSTS AND FINANCIAL AID

Tuition $16,200. Room & board $5,370. Required fees $0. Average book expense $665. **Required Forms and Deadlines:** FAFSA. Priority filing deadline April 1. **Notification of Awards:** Applicants will be notified of awards on a rolling basis beginning on or about March 1. **Types of Aid:** *Need-based scholarships/grants:* Pell, SEOG, state scholarships/grants, private scholarships, the school's own gift aid. *Loans:* FFEL Subsidized Stafford, FFEL Unsubsidized Stafford, FFEL PLUS, Federal Perkins. **Student Employment:** Federal Work-Study Program available. Institutional employment available. Off-campus job opportunities are excellent. **Financial Aid Statistics:** Average income from on-campus job $1,200. **Financial Aid Phone:** 614-251-4640.

OHIO NORTHERN UNIVERSITY

525 South Main Street, Ada, OH 45810
Phone: 419-772-2260 **E-mail:** admissions-ug@onu.edu **CEEB Code:** 1591
Fax: 419-772-2313 **Web:** www.onu.edu **ACT Code:** 3310

This private school, which is affiliated with the Methodist Church, was founded in 1871. It has a 320-acre campus.

STUDENTS AND FACULTY

Enrollment: 2,281. **Student Body:** Male 53%, female 47%, out-of-state 12%, international 1% (15 countries represented). **Ethnic Representation:** African American 2%, Asian 1%, Caucasian 97%, Hispanic 1%. **Retention and Graduation:** 79% freshmen return for sophomore year. 30% freshmen graduate within 4 years. 19% grads go on to further study within 1 year. 1% grads pursue business degrees. 11% grads pursue law degrees. 8% grads pursue medical degrees. **Faculty:** Student/faculty ratio 13:1. 197 full-time faculty, 77% hold PhDs. 100% faculty teach undergrads.

ACADEMICS

Degrees: Bachelor's, first professional. **Academic Requirements:** General education including some course work in arts/fine arts, computer literacy,

English (including composition), history, humanities, mathematics, philosophy, sciences (biological or physical), social science. **Classes:** 10-19 students in an average class. **Majors with Highest Enrollment:** Biology/biological sciences, general; pharmacy (PharmD, BS/BPharm); industrial production technologies/technicians. **Disciplines with Highest Percentage of Degrees Awarded:** Engineering/engineering technology 24%, health professions and related sciences 18%, business/marketing 11%, education 9%, biological life sciences 9%. **Special Study Options:** Cooperative (work-study) program, distance learning, double major, dual enrollment, student exchange program (domestic), honors program, independent study, internships, liberal arts/career combination, study abroad, teacher certification program.

FACILITIES

Housing: Coed, all-female, all-male, apartments for single students, housing for disabled students, fraternities and/or sororities, honors residence halls. **Library Holdings:** 250,231 bound volumes. 9,220 periodicals. 280 microforms. 9,776 audiovisuals. **Special Academic Facilities/Equipment:** Art gallery, performing arts center, language lab, sports center, pharmacy museum. **Computers:** School-owned computers available for student use.

EXTRACURRICULARS

Activities: Choral groups, concert band, dance, drama/theater, jazz band, literary magazine, marching band, music ensembles, musical theater, opera, pep band, radio station, student government, student newspaper, symphony orchestra, television station, yearbook. **Organizations:** 150 registered organizations, 38 honor societies, 32 religious organizations, 8 fraternities (25% men join), 4 sororities (22% women join). **Athletics (Intercollegiate):** *Men:* baseball, basketball, cross-country, diving, football, golf, indoor track, soccer, swimming, tennis, track & field, wrestling. *Women:* basketball, cross-country, diving, golf, indoor track, soccer, softball, swimming, tennis, track & field, volleyball.

ADMISSIONS

Selectivity Rating: 78 (of 100). **Freshman Academic Profile:** Average high school GPA 3.6. 40% in top 10% of high school class, 69% in top 25% of high school class, 90% in top 50% of high school class. Average SAT I Math 590, SAT I Math middle 50% range 450-650. Average SAT I Verbal 560, SAT I Verbal middle 50% range 450-610. Average ACT 25, ACT middle 50% range 23-28. TOEFL required of all international applicants, minimum TOEFL 550. **Basis for Candidate Selection:** *Very important factors considered include:* secondary school record, standardized test scores. *Important factors considered include:* class rank, extracurricular activities, interview. *Other factors considered include:* alumni/ae relation, character/personal qualities, essays, minority status, recommendations, talent/ability, volunteer work, work experience. **Freshman Admission Requirements:** High school diploma or GED is required. *Academic units required/recommended:* 16 total required; 22 total recommended; 4 English required, 4 English recommended, 2 math required, 4 math recommended, 2 science required, 3 science recommended, 2 science lab required, 2 science lab recommended, 2 foreign language recommended, 2 social studies required, 3 social studies recommended, 2 history required, 2 history recommended, 4 elective required, 4 elective recommended. **Freshman Admission Statistics:** 2,469 applied, 89% accepted, 34% of those accepted enrolled. **Transfer Admission Requirements:** *Items required:* high school transcript, college transcript, statement of good standing from prior school. Minimum high school GPA of 2.0 required. Minimum college GPA of 2.0 required. Lowest grade transferable C. **General Admission Information:** Application fee $30. Priority application deadline December 15. Regular application deadline August 15. Nonfall registration accepted. Admission may be deferred for a maximum of 1 year. Credit and/or placement offered for CEEB Advanced Placement tests.

COSTS AND FINANCIAL AID

Tuition $24,240. Room & board $5,940. Required fees $210. Average book expense $900. **Required Forms and Deadlines:** FAFSA and institution's own financial aid form. Financial aid filing deadline June 1. Priority filing deadline April 15. **Notification of Awards:** Applicants will be notified of awards on a rolling basis beginning on or about February 15. **Types of Aid:** *Need-based scholarships/grants:* Pell, SEOG, state scholarships/grants, private scholarships, the school's own gift aid. *Loans:* FFEL Subsidized Stafford, FFEL Unsubsidized Stafford, FFEL PLUS, Federal Perkins, college/university loans from institutional funds, alternative loans, Federal Health Professions Loan. **Student Employment:** Federal Work-Study Program available. Institutional employment available. Off-campus job opportunities are good. **Financial Aid Statistics:** 86% freshmen, 83% undergrads receive some form of aid. Average income from on-campus job $1,639. **Financial Aid Phone:** 419-772-2272.

See page 1144.

OHIO STATE UNIVERSITY—COLUMBUS

Third Floor Lincoln Tower, 1800 Cannon Drive, Columbus, OH 43210
Phone: 614-292-3980 **E-mail:** telecounseling@fa.adm.ohio-state.edu
CEEB Code: 1592 **Fax:** 614-292-4818 **Web:** www.osu.edu **ACT Code:** 3312

This public school was founded in 1870. It has a 4,404-acre campus.

STUDENTS AND FACULTY

Enrollment: 36,855. **Student Body:** Male 52%, female 48%, out-of-state 11%, international 4% (89 countries represented). **Ethnic Representation:** African American 9%, Asian 6%, Caucasian 81%, Hispanic 2%. **Retention and Graduation:** 86% freshmen return for sophomore year. 25% freshmen graduate within 4 years. 25% grads go on to further study within 1 year. 2% grads pursue law degrees. 3% grads pursue medical degrees. **Faculty:** Student/faculty ratio 13:1. 2,713 full-time faculty, 99% hold PhDs.

ACADEMICS

Degrees: Bachelor's, doctoral, first professional, master's, post-master's certificate. **Academic Requirements:** General education including some course work in arts/fine arts, English (including composition), foreign languages, history, humanities, mathematics, sciences (biological or physical), social science. **Classes:** 10-19 students in an average class. 20-29 students in an average lab/discussion section. **Majors with Highest Enrollment:** English language and literature, general; biology/biological sciences, general; psychology, general. **Disciplines with Highest Percentage of Degrees Awarded:** Social sciences and history 15%, business/marketing 14%, home economics and vocational home economics 9%, engineering/engineering technology 8%, health professions and related sciences 7%. **Special Study Options:** Accelerated program, cooperative (work-study) program, cross registration, distance learning, double major, dual enrollment, English as a second language, student exchange program (domestic), honors program, independent study, internships, liberal arts/career combination, student-designed major, study abroad, teacher certification program.

FACILITIES

Housing: Coed, all-female, apartments for married students, housing for disabled students, housing for international students, fraternities and/or sororities, cooperative housing. **Library Holdings:** 5,491,498 bound volumes. 42,915 periodicals. 5,316,219 microforms. 35,969 audiovisuals. **Special Academic Facilities/Equipment:** Wexner Center for the Arts, zoology museum, geology museum, art and photography galleries, nuclear research reactor, electroscience lab, biomedical engineering center, cartoon art museum. **Computers:** School-owned computers available for student use.

EXTRACURRICULARS

Activities: Choral groups, concert band, dance, drama/theater, jazz band, literary magazine, marching band, music ensembles, musical theater, pep band, radio station, student government, student newspaper, student-run film society, television station, yearbook. **Organizations:** 550 registered organizations, 36 honor societies, 34 religious organizations, 33 fraternities (5% men join), 22 sororities (6% women join). **Athletics (Intercollegiate):** *Men:* baseball, basketball, cross-country, diving, fencing, football, golf, gymnastics, ice hockey, lacrosse, rifle, soccer, swimming, tennis, track & field, volleyball, wrestling. *Women:* basketball, crew, cross-country, diving, fencing, field hockey, golf, gymnastics, ice hockey, lacrosse, rifle, soccer, softball, swimming, tennis, track & field, volleyball.

ADMISSIONS

Selectivity Rating: 73 (of 100). **Freshman Academic Profile:** 33% in top 10% of high school class, 66% in top 25% of high school class, 91% in top 50% of high school class. 88% from public high schools. Average SAT I Math 594, SAT I Math middle 50% range 540-660. Average SAT I Verbal 575, SAT I Verbal middle 50% range 520-630. Average ACT 25, ACT middle 50% range 23-28. TOEFL required of all international applicants, minimum TOEFL 527. **Basis for Candidate Selection:** *Very important factors considered include:* class rank, secondary school record, standardized test scores. *Important factors considered include:* extracurricular activities, minority status, talent/ability, volunteer work, work experience. *Other factors considered include:* essays, geographical residence, recommendations, state residency. **Freshman Admission Requirements:** High school diploma or GED is required. *Academic units required/recommended:* 4 English required, 4 English recommended, 3 math required, 4 math recommended, 2 science required, 3 science recommended, 2 science lab required, 2 foreign language required, 3 foreign language recommended, 2 social studies required, 3 social studies recommended, 1 elective required, 1 elective recommended. **Transfer Admission Requirements:** *Items required:* college transcript. Minimum college GPA of 2.0 required. Lowest grade transferable C-. **General**

Admission Information: Application fee $30. Regular application deadline February 15. Nonfall registration accepted. Credit and/or placement offered for CEEB Advanced Placement tests.

COSTS AND FINANCIAL AID

In-state tuition $4,788. Out-of-state tuition $13,554. Room & board $6,031. Required fees $0. Average book expense $936. **Required Forms and Deadlines:** FAFSA. Priority filing deadline February 15. **Notification of Awards:** Applicants will be notified of awards on or about April 1. **Types of Aid:** *Need-based scholarships/grants:* Pell, SEOG, state scholarships/grants, private scholarships, the school's own gift aid. *Loans:* Direct Subsidized Stafford, Direct Unsubsidized Stafford, Direct PLUS, Federal Perkins, Federal Nursing, college/university loans from institutional funds. **Student Employment:** Federal Work-Study Program available. Institutional employment available. Off-campus job opportunities are good. **Financial Aid Statistics:** 48% freshmen, 45% undergrads receive some form of aid. Average freshman grant $3,410. Average freshman loan $2,702. **Financial Aid Phone:** 614-292-0300.

OHIO STATE UNIVERSITY—LIMA

4240 Campus Drive, Lima, OH 45804-3596
Phone: 419-995-8396 **E-mail:** admissions@lima.ohio-state.edu
Fax: 419-995-8483 **Web:** www.lima.ohio-state.edu **ACT Code:** 3237

This public school was founded in 1960. It has a 565-acre campus.

STUDENTS AND FACULTY

Enrollment: 1,293. **Student Body:** Male 43%, female 57%, out-of-state 1%. **Faculty:** Student/faculty ratio 15:1. 58 full-time faculty, 77% hold PhDs. 100% faculty teach undergrads.

ACADEMICS

Degrees: Associate's, bachelor's, master's. **Academic Requirements:** General education including some course work in English (including composition), foreign languages, humanities, mathematics, sciences (biological or physical), social science, electives. **Majors with Highest Enrollment:** Business/commerce, general; elementary education and teaching; psychology, general. **Special Study Options:** Cooperative (work-study) program, distance learning, honors program, independent study, internships, study abroad, teacher certification program.

FACILITIES

Housing: Commuter campus. **Special Academic Facilities/Equipment:** Geological fossils. **Computers:** School-owned computers available for student use.

EXTRACURRICULARS

Activities: Choral groups, dance, drama/theater, musical theater, student government. **Organizations:** 24 registered organizations, 2 honor societies, 1 religious organization. **Athletics (Intercollegiate):** *Men:* baseball, basketball. *Women:* basketball.

ADMISSIONS

Selectivity Rating: 80 (of 100). **Freshman Academic Profile:** 95% from public high schools. Average SAT I Math 570, SAT I Math middle 50% range 570-600. Average SAT I Verbal 510, SAT I Verbal middle 50% range 510-570. Average ACT 21, ACT middle 50% range 20-23. TOEFL required of all international applicants, minimum TOEFL 500. **Basis for Candidate Selection:** *Important factors considered include:* standardized test scores. **Freshman Admission Requirements:** High school diploma or GED is required. *Academic units required/recommended:* 4 English required, 4 English recommended, 4 math required, 4 math recommended, 2 science required, 3 science recommended, 2 foreign language required, 2 foreign language recommended, 3 social studies recommended, 3 history recommended, 1 elective required, 1 elective recommended. **Freshman Admission Statistics:** 548 applied, 96% accepted, 71% of those accepted enrolled. **Transfer Admission Requirements:** *Items required:* college transcript. Minimum college GPA of 2.0 required. Lowest grade transferable C-. **General Admission Information:** Application fee $30. Regular application deadline July 1. Nonfall registration accepted.

COSTS AND FINANCIAL AID

In-state tuition $3,927. Out-of-state tuition $13,350. Average book expense $750. **Required Forms and Deadlines:** FAFSA. Priority filing deadline April 1. **Types of Aid:** *Need-based scholarships/grants:* Pell, SEOG, state scholarships/grants, private scholarships. *Loans:* Direct Subsidized Stafford, Direct Unsubsidized Stafford, Direct PLUS, FFEL Subsidized Stafford, FFEL PLUS, Federal Perkins. **Student Employment:** Federal Work-Study Program available. Institutional employment available. Off-campus job opportunities are good. **Financial Aid Statistics:** 28% freshmen, 30% undergrads receive some form of aid. Average freshman grant $2,250. Average freshman loan $2,550. Average income from on-campus job $1,500. **Financial Aid Phone:** 419-995-8299.

OHIO STATE UNIVERSITY—MANSFIELD

1680 University Drive, Mansfield, OH 44906
Phone: 419-755-4011 **E-mail:** admissions@mansfield.ohio-state.edu
Fax: 419-755-4241 **Web:** www.mansfield.ohio-state.edu/

STUDENTS AND FACULTY

Enrollment: 1,225. **Student Body:** Out-of-state 1%.

ACADEMICS

Degrees: Associate's, bachelor's, master's.

EXTRACURRICULARS

Organizations: 1 honor society, 1 religious organization.

ADMISSIONS

Selectivity Rating: 63 (of 100). **General Admission Information:** Regular application deadline July 1.

COSTS AND FINANCIAL AID

In-state tuition $3,906. Out-of-state tuition $11,088. Room & board $5,800. Average book expense $600. **Types of Aid:** *Loans:* FFEL Subsidized Stafford, FFEL PLUS.

OHIO STATE UNIVERSITY—MARION

1465 Mount Vernon Avenue, Marion, OH 43302
Phone: 614-389-2361 **E-mail:** vanderlind.6@osu.edu
Fax: 614-292-5817

STUDENTS AND FACULTY

Enrollment: 1,060. **Student Body:** Out-of-state 1%.

EXTRACURRICULARS

Organizations: 1 honor society, 1 religious organization.

ADMISSIONS

Selectivity Rating: 63 (of 100). **Freshman Academic Profile:** TOEFL required of all international applicants, minimum TOEFL 500. **Freshman Admission Requirements: General Admission Information:** Regular application deadline July 1.

COSTS AND FINANCIAL AID

In-state tuition $3,906. Out-of-state tuition $11,088. Room & board $5,800. Average book expense $600. **Types of Aid:** *Loans:* FFEL Subsidized Stafford, FFEL PLUS. **Student Employment:** Federal Work-Study Program available.

OHIO STATE UNIVERSITY—NEWARK

1179 University Drive, Newark, OH 43055
Phone: 740-366-3321 **E-mail:** Vogelmeier.1@osu.edu
Fax: 740-364-9645 **Web:** www.newark.ohio-state.edu

This public school was founded in 1957.

STUDENTS AND FACULTY

Enrollment: 1,522. **Student Body:** Out-of-state 2%.

ACADEMICS

Degrees: Associate's, bachelor's, master's.

EXTRACURRICULARS

Organizations: 1 religious organization.

ADMISSIONS

Selectivity Rating: 74 (of 100). **Freshman Academic Profile:** Average SAT I Math 454, SAT I Math middle 50% range 390-550. Average SAT I Verbal 422, SAT I Verbal middle 50% range 370-510. Average ACT 21. **Freshman Admission Requirements: General Admission Information:** Regular application deadline July 1.

COSTS AND FINANCIAL AID

In-state tuition $3,906. Out-of-state tuition $11,088. Room & board $5,800. Required fees $85. Average book expense $750. **Types of Aid:** *Loans:* FFEL Subsidized Stafford, FFEL PLUS. **Student Employment:** Federal Work-Study Program available. Off-campus job opportunities are excellent. **Financial Aid Statistics:** Average income from on-campus job $1,500. **Financial Aid Phone:** 614-366-9364.

OHIO UNIVERSITY—ATHENS

120 Chubb Hall, Athens, OH 45701
Phone: 740-593-4100 **E-mail:** admissions.freshmen@ohiou.edu **CEEB Code:** 1593
Fax: 740-593-0560 **Web:** www.ohiou.edu **ACT Code:** 3314

This public school was founded in 1804. It has a 1,700-acre campus.

STUDENTS AND FACULTY

Enrollment: 17,343. **Student Body:** Male 45%, female 55%, out-of-state 9%, international 2% (100 countries represented). **Ethnic Representation:** African American 3%, Asian 1%, Caucasian 95%, Hispanic 1%. **Retention and Graduation:** 84% freshmen return for sophomore year. 45% freshmen graduate within 4 years. 25% grads go on to further study within 1 year. 3% grads pursue business degrees. 2% grads pursue law degrees. 1% grads pursue medical degrees. **Faculty:** Student/faculty ratio 20:1. 846 full-time faculty, 88% hold PhDs. 100% faculty teach undergrads.

ACADEMICS

Degrees: Associate's, bachelor's, doctoral, first professional, master's. **Academic Requirements:** General education including some course work in arts/fine arts, English (including composition), foreign languages, history, humanities, mathematics, philosophy, sciences (biological or physical), social science. **Classes:** 10-19 students in an average class. 10-19 students in an average lab/discussion section. **Disciplines with Highest Percentage of Degrees Awarded:** Education 12%, communications/communication technologies 12%, business/marketing 12%, English 10%, social sciences and history 9%. **Special Study Options:** Accelerated program, cooperative (work-study) program, cross registration, distance learning, double major, English as a second language, honors program, independent study, internships, liberal arts/career combination, student-designed major, study abroad, teacher certification program.

FACILITIES

Housing: Coed, all-female, all-male, apartments for married students, apartments for single students, housing for disabled students, housing for international students, fraternities and/or sororities, cooperative housing. **Library Holdings:** 2,405,884 bound volumes. 15,906 periodicals. 3,152,947 microforms. 111,579 audiovisuals. **Special Academic Facilities/Equipment:** Museum of American Art, Innovation Center, nuclear accelerator, electron microscope, biotech center. **Computers:** *Recommended operating system:* Windows 95. School-owned computers available for student use.

EXTRACURRICULARS

Activities: Choral groups, concert band, dance, drama/theater, jazz band, literary magazine, marching band, music ensembles, musical theater, opera, pep band, radio station, student government, student newspaper, student-run film society, symphony orchestra, television station, yearbook. **Organizations:** 315 registered organizations, 12 honor societies, 21 religious organizations, 21 fraternities (12% men join), 12 sororities (14% women join). **Athletics (Intercollegiate):** *Men:* baseball, basketball, cross-country, diving, football, golf, swimming, track & field, wrestling. *Women:* basketball, cross-country, diving, field hockey, golf, lacrosse, soccer, softball, swimming, track & field, volleyball.

ADMISSIONS

Selectivity Rating: 79 (of 100). **Freshman Academic Profile:** Average high school GPA 3.3. 18% in top 10% of high school class, 50% in top 25% of high school class, 90% in top 50% of high school class. 82% from public high schools. Average SAT I Math 550, SAT I Math middle 50% range 500-610. Average SAT I Verbal 540, SAT I Verbal middle 50% range 500-600. Average ACT 23, ACT middle 50% range 21-26. TOEFL required of all international applicants, minimum TOEFL 550. **Basis for Candidate Selection:** *Very important factors considered include:* class rank, secondary school record, standardized test scores. *Other factors considered include:* alumni/ae relation, essays, extracurricular activities, geographical residence, minority status, recommendations, state residency, talent/ability, work experience. **Freshman Admission Requirements:** High school diploma or GED is required. *Academic units required/recommended:* 19 total recommended; 4 English recommended, 3 math recommended, 3 science recommended, 2 foreign language recommended, 3 social studies recommended, 2 history recommended, 2 elective recommended. **Freshman Admission Statistics:** 13,195 applied, 75% accepted, 37% of those accepted enrolled. **Transfer Admission Requirements:** *Items required:* college transcript. Minimum college GPA of 2.5 required. Lowest grade transferable C-. **General Admission Information:** Application fee $40. Regular application deadline February 1. Nonfall registration accepted. Admission may be deferred for a maximum of 1 year. Credit and/or placement offered for CEEB Advanced Placement tests.

COSTS AND FINANCIAL AID

In-state tuition $6,336. Out-of-state tuition $13,818. Room & board $6,777. Required fees $0. Average book expense $810. **Required Forms and Deadlines:** FAFSA. Priority filing deadline March 15. **Notification of Awards:** Applicants will be notified of awards on or about April 1. **Types of Aid:** *Need-based scholarships/grants:* Pell, SEOG, state scholarships/grants, private scholarships, the school's own gift aid. *Loans:* Direct Subsidized Stafford, Direct Unsubsidized Stafford, Direct PLUS, Federal Perkins, college/university loans from institutional funds. **Student Employment:** Federal Work-Study Program available. Institutional employment available. Off-campus job opportunities are good. **Financial Aid Statistics:** 46% freshmen, 45% undergrads receive some form of aid. Average freshman grant $3,565. Average income from on-campus job $1,886. **Financial Aid Phone:** 740-593-4141.

OHIO UNIVERSITY—SOUTHERN

Office of Admissions, 1804 Liberty Avenue, Ironton, OH 45638-2214
Phone: 740-533-4600 **E-mail:** askousc@mail.southern.ohiou.edu
Fax: 740-533-4632 **Web:** www.southern.ohiou.edu

This public school was founded in 1956. It has a 9-acre campus.

STUDENTS AND FACULTY

Enrollment: 1,963. **Student Body:** Male 37%, female 63%, out-of-state 11%. **Ethnic Representation:** African American 2%, Caucasian 97%.

ACADEMICS

Degrees: Associate's, bachelor's, master's, terminal, transfer. **Academic Requirements:** General education including some course work in English (including composition), mathematics. **Special Study Options:** Distance learning, double major, independent study, student-designed major, teacher certification program, weekend college.

EXTRACURRICULARS

Activities: Choral groups, concert band, drama/theater, literary magazine, music ensembles, radio station, student government, television station.

ADMISSIONS

Selectivity Rating: 63 (of 100). **Transfer Admission Requirements:** *Items required:* college transcript. Lowest grade transferable C. **General Admission Information:** Application fee $20.

COSTS AND FINANCIAL AID

In-state tuition $3,087. Out-of-state tuition $3,219. Required fees $0. Average book expense $700. **Required Forms and Deadlines:** FAFSA. Priority filing deadline February 15. **Types of Aid:** *Need-based scholarships/grants:* Pell, SEOG, state scholarships/grants, private scholarships, the school's own gift aid. *Loans:* Direct Subsidized Stafford, Direct Unsubsidized Stafford, Direct PLUS, Federal Perkins.

OHIO UNIVERSITY—ZANESVILLE

Office of Admissions, 1425 Newark Road, Zanesville, OH 43701
Phone: 740-588-1439 **E-mail:** tumblin@ohiou.edu **CEEB Code:** 1593
Fax: 740-588-1444 **Web:** www.zanesville.ohiou.edu

This public school was founded in 1946. It has a 146-acre campus.

STUDENTS AND FACULTY

Enrollment: 1,779. **Student Body:** Male 41%, female 59%, out-of-state 5%. **Ethnic Representation:** African American 2%, Asian 1%, Caucasian 97%. **Retention and Graduation:** 55% freshmen return for sophomore year. **Faculty:** Student/faculty ratio 20:1. 100% faculty teach undergrads.

ACADEMICS

Degrees: Associate's, bachelor's, master's, terminal, transfer. **Academic Requirements:** General education including some course work in arts/fine arts, computer literacy, English (including composition), history, humanities, mathematics, sciences (biological or physical), social science. **Majors with Highest Enrollment:** Early childhood education and teaching; junior high/intermediate/middle school education and teaching; nursing/registered nurse training (RN, ASN, BSN, MSN). **Special Study Options:** Cooperative (work-study) program, cross registration, distance learning, double major, dual enrollment, external degree program, independent study, internships, liberal arts/career combination, student-designed major, study abroad, teacher certification program, weekend college.

FACILITIES

Housing: Apartments for married students, apartments for single students.

EXTRACURRICULARS

Activities: Music ensembles, radio station, student government. **Organizations:** 10 registered organizations, 3 honor societies. **Athletics (Intercollegiate):** *Men:* baseball, basketball, golf. *Women:* basketball, cheerleading, softball, volleyball.

ADMISSIONS

Selectivity Rating: 60 (of 100). **Freshman Academic Profile:** Average high school GPA 3.0. 20% in top 10% of high school class, 20% in top 25% of high school class, 50% in top 50% of high school class. **Freshman Admission Requirements:** High school diploma or GED is required. *Academic units required/recommended:* 4 English recommended, 3 math recommended, 3 science recommended, 2 science lab recommended, 2 foreign language recommended, 3 social studies recommended, 1 history recommended, 4 elective recommended. **Freshman Admission Statistics:** 503 applied, 100% accepted, 96% of those accepted enrolled. **Transfer Admission Requirements:** *Items required:* college transcript, statement of good standing from prior school. Minimum college GPA of 2.0 required. Lowest grade transferable C-. **General Admission Information:** Application fee $20. Nonfall registration accepted. Admission may be deferred for a maximum of 1 year.

COSTS AND FINANCIAL AID

In-state tuition $3,579. Out-of-state tuition $9,150. Required fees $15. Average book expense $400. **Student Employment:** Federal Work-Study Program available. Institutional employment available. Off-campus job opportunities are excellent.

OHIO VALLEY COLLEGE

#1 Campus View Drive, Vienna, WV 26105
Phone: 304-865-6200 **E-mail:** admissions@ovc.edu
Fax: 304-865-6001 **Web:** www.ovc.edu **ACT Code:** 4548

This private school was founded in 1960. It has a 267-acre campus.

STUDENTS AND FACULTY

Enrollment: 498. **Student Body:** Male 42%, female 58%, out-of-state 57%, international 7% (17 countries represented). **Ethnic Representation:** African American 4%, Asian 1%, Caucasian 93%, Hispanic 1%. **Retention and Graduation:** 65% freshmen return for sophomore year. 10% freshmen graduate within 4 years. **Faculty:** Student/faculty ratio 15:1. 19 full-time faculty, 42% hold PhDs. 100% faculty teach undergrads.

ACADEMICS

Degrees: Associate's, bachelor's. **Academic Requirements:** General education including some course work in arts/fine arts, computer literacy, English (including composition), history, humanities, mathematics, sciences (biological or physical), social science, Bible. **Classes:** 10-19 students in an average class. **Majors with Highest Enrollment:** Business administration/management; elementary education and teaching; psychology, general. **Disciplines with Highest Percentage of Degrees Awarded:** Business/marketing 34%, education 30%, psychology 18%, liberal arts/general studies 11%, philosophy/religion/theology 7%. **Special Study Options:** Double major, English as a second language, study abroad, teacher certification program, weekend college, adult education, degree completion program in business administration, Saturday college.

FACILITIES

Housing: All-female, all-male, apartments for married students, apartments for single students. **Library Holdings:** 32,020 bound volumes. 239 periodicals. 58,206 microforms. 6,615 audiovisuals. **Computers:** School-owned computers available for student use.

EXTRACURRICULARS

Activities: Choral groups, drama/theater, jazz band, music ensembles, student government, student newspaper, yearbook. **Organizations:** 10 registered organizations, 2 honor societies, 3 religious organizations, 4 fraternities (65% men join), 4 sororities (75% women join). **Athletics (Intercollegiate):** *Men:* baseball, basketball, cross-country, golf, soccer. *Women:* basketball, cheerleading, cross-country, soccer, softball, volleyball.

ADMISSIONS

Selectivity Rating: 63 (of 100). **Freshman Academic Profile:** Average high school GPA 3.0. 9% in top 10% of high school class, 22% in top 25% of high school class, 62% in top 50% of high school class. 95% from public high schools. Average SAT I Math 460. Average SAT I Verbal 500. Average ACT 21, ACT middle 50% range 18-24. TOEFL required of all international applicants, minimum TOEFL 420. **Basis for Candidate Selection:** *Very important factors considered include:* character/personal qualities, secondary school record, standardized test scores. *Important factors considered include:* alumni/ae relation, recommendations, talent/ability. *Other factors considered include:* class rank, essays, extracurricular activities, interview, religious affiliation/commitment. **Freshman Admission Requirements:** High school diploma or GED is required. *Academic units required/recommended:* 12 total recommended; 3 English recommended, 2 math recommended, 3 science recommended, 1 science lab recommended, 2 social studies recommended, 1 history recommended. **Freshman Admission Statistics:** 363 applied, 71% accepted, 43% of those accepted enrolled. **Transfer Admission Requirements:** *Items required:* high school transcript, college transcript, standardized test scores. Minimum high school GPA of 1.6 required. Minimum college GPA of 2.0 required. Lowest grade transferable D. **General Admission Information:** Application fee $20. Priority application deadline August 1. Regular application deadline August 20. Nonfall registration accepted. Admission may be deferred for a maximum of 1 year. Credit and/or placement offered for CEEB Advanced Placement tests.

COSTS AND FINANCIAL AID

Tuition $8,880. Room & board $4,840. Required fees $1,080. Average book expense $700. **Required Forms and Deadlines:** FAFSA. No deadline for regular filing. Priority filing deadline March 1. **Notification of Awards:** Applicants will be notified of awards on a rolling basis beginning on or about March 1. **Types of Aid:** *Need-based scholarships/grants:* Pell, SEOG, state scholarships/grants, private scholarships, the school's own gift aid. *Loans:* FFEL Subsidized Stafford, FFEL Unsubsidized Stafford, FFEL PLUS, Federal Perkins, Signature student loans. **Student Employment:** Federal Work-Study Program available. Institutional employment available. Off-campus job opportunities are good. **Financial Aid Statistics:** 82% freshmen, 60% undergrads receive some form of aid. Average freshman grant $4,531. Average freshman loan $2,970. Average income from on-campus job $800. **Financial Aid Phone:** 304-865-6075.

OHIO WESLEYAN UNIVERSITY

Admissions Office, 61 South Sandusky Street, Delaware, OH 43015
Phone: 740-368-3020 **E-mail:** owuadmit@owu.edu **CEEB Code:** 1594
Fax: 740-368-3314 **Web:** web.owu.edu **ACT Code:** 3316

This private school, which is affiliated with the Methodist Church, was founded in 1842. It has a 200-acre campus.

STUDENTS AND FACULTY

Enrollment: 1,935. **Student Body:** Male 46%, female 54%, out-of-state 40%, international 11% (52 countries represented). **Ethnic Representation:** African American 5%, Asian 2%, Caucasian 89%, Hispanic 2%. **Retention and Graduation:** 82% freshmen return for sophomore year. 59% freshmen graduate within 4 years. 34% grads go on to further study within 1 year. 3% grads pursue business degrees. 5% grads pursue law degrees. 7% grads pursue medical degrees. **Faculty:** Student/faculty ratio 13:1. 130 full-time faculty, 100% hold PhDs. 100% faculty teach undergrads.

ACADEMICS

Degrees: Bachelor's. **Academic Requirements:** General education including some course work in arts/fine arts, English (including composition), foreign languages, humanities, sciences (biological or physical), social science, one course that satisfied cultural diversity requirement. **Classes:** 10-19 students in an average class. 10-19 students in an average lab/discussion section. **Majors with Highest Enrollment:** Business/managerial economics; zoology/animal biology; psychology, general. **Disciplines with Highest Percentage of Degrees Awarded:** Social sciences and history 21%, business/marketing 16%, biological life sciences 14%, psychology 11%, education 9%. **Special Study Options:** Double major, honors program, independent study, internships, student-designed major, study abroad, teacher certification program.

FACILITIES

Housing: Coed, all-female, apartments for single students, housing for international students, fraternities and/or sororities. Special-interest houses: language, fine arts, honors, black culture, environmental, peace and justice, international, women's issues, and education. **Library Holdings:** 420,936 bound volumes. 1,084 periodicals. 107,768 microforms. 2,980 audiovisuals. **Special Academic Facilities/Equipment:** Perkins and Student Observatories; scanning electron microscope; Woltemade Center for Economics, Business and Entrepreneurship; 9-inch refractor telescope; Ross Museum. **Computers:** School-owned computers available for student use.

EXTRACURRICULARS

Activities: Choral groups, dance, drama/theater, jazz band, literary magazine, music ensembles, opera, pep band, radio station, student government, student newspaper, yearbook. **Organizations:** 85 registered organizations, 26 honor societies, 10 religious organizations, 13 fraternities (44% men join), 8 sororities (34% women join). **Athletics (Intercollegiate):** *Men:* baseball, basketball, cross-country, diving, football, golf, indoor track, lacrosse, sailing, soccer, swimming, tennis, track & field. *Women:* basketball, cross-country, diving, field hockey, indoor track, lacrosse, sailing, soccer, softball, swimming, tennis, track & field, volleyball.

ADMISSIONS

Selectivity Rating: 80 (of 100). **Freshman Academic Profile:** Average high school GPA 3.3. 26% in top 10% of high school class, 50% in top 25% of high school class, 76% in top 50% of high school class. 75% from public high schools. Average SAT I Math 608, SAT I Math middle 50% range 540-650. Average SAT I Verbal 602, SAT I Verbal middle 50% range 540-650. Average ACT 27, ACT middle 50% range 23-28. TOEFL required of all international applicants, minimum TOEFL 550. **Basis for Candidate Selection:** *Very important factors considered include:* character/personal qualities, interview, recommendations, secondary school record. *Important factors considered include:* alumni/ae relation, class rank, essays, extracurricular activities, geographical residence, minority status, standardized test scores, talent/ability, volunteer work. *Other factors considered include:* work experience. **Freshman Admission Requirements:** High school diploma or GED is required. *Academic units required/recommended:* 16 total recommended; 4 English recommended, 3 math recommended, 3 science recommended, 3 foreign language recommended, 3 social studies recommended. **Freshman Admission Statistics:** 2,212 applied, 80% accepted, 31% of those accepted enrolled. **Transfer Admission Requirements:** *Items required:* high school transcript, college transcript, essay, statement of good standing from prior school. Minimum college GPA of 2.5 required. Lowest grade transferable C-. **General Admission Information:** Application fee $35. Priority application deadline March 15. Early decision application deadline December 1. Nonfall registration accepted. Admission may be deferred for a maximum of 1 year. Credit and/or placement offered for CEEB Advanced Placement tests.

COSTS AND FINANCIAL AID

Tuition $24,000. Room & board $7,010. Required fees $200. Average book expense $800. **Required Forms and Deadlines:** FAFSA and institution's own financial aid form. Financial aid filing deadline May 15. Priority filing deadline March 15. **Notification of Awards:** Applicants will be notified of awards on a rolling basis beginning on or about January 15. **Types of Aid:** *Need-based scholarships/grants:* Pell, SEOG, state scholarships/grants, private scholarships, the school's own gift aid. *Loans:* FFEL Subsidized Stafford, FFEL Unsubsidized Stafford, FFEL PLUS, Federal Perkins, state loans, college/university loans from institutional funds. **Student Employment:** Federal Work-Study Program available. Institutional employment available. Off-campus job opportunities are excellent. **Financial Aid Statistics:** 60% freshmen, 55% undergrads receive some form of aid. Average freshman grant $12,861. Average freshman loan $3,586. Average income from on-campus job $1,175. **Financial Aid Phone:** 740-368-3050.

See page 1146.

OKLAHOMA BAPTIST UNIVERSITY

500 West University, Shawnee, OK 74804
Phone: 800-654-3285 **E-mail:** admissions@mail.okbu.edu **CEEB Code:** 6541
Fax: 405-878-2046 **Web:** www.okbu.edu **ACT Code:** 3414

This private school, which is affiliated with the Southern Baptist Church, was founded in 1910. It has a 200-acre campus.

STUDENTS AND FACULTY

Enrollment: 1,911. **Student Body:** Male 44%, female 56%, out-of-state 39%, international 1% (15 countries represented). **Ethnic Representation:** African American 3%, Asian 2%, Caucasian 88%, Hispanic 2%, Native American 6%. **Retention and Graduation:** 72% freshmen return for sophomore year. 48% freshmen graduate within 4 years. 35% grads go on to further study within 1 year. 10% grads pursue business degrees. 2% grads pursue law degrees. 3% grads pursue medical degrees. **Faculty:** Student/faculty ratio 14:1. 114 full-time faculty, 75% hold PhDs. 100% faculty teach undergrads.

ACADEMICS

Degrees: Bachelor's, master's. **Academic Requirements:** General education including some course work in arts/fine arts, computer literacy, English (including composition), foreign languages, history, humanities, mathematics, philosophy, sciences (biological or physical), social science, religion, speech, health concepts, health activity. **Classes:** 10-19 students in an average class. Under 10 students in an average lab/discussion section. **Majors with Highest Enrollment:** Elementary education and teaching; theological and ministerial studies; pre-medicine/pre-medical studies. **Disciplines with Highest Percentage of Degrees Awarded:** Education 23%, health professions and related sciences 13%, business/marketing 12%, philosophy/religion/theology 12%, psychology 8%. **Special Study Options:** Cooperative (work-study) program, double major, student exchange program (domestic), honors program, independent study, internships, student-designed major, study abroad, teacher certification program, semester-away programs available.

FACILITIES

Housing: All-female, all-male, apartments for married students, apartments for single students. **Library Holdings:** 230,000 bound volumes. 1,800 periodicals. 315,000 microforms. 7,600 audiovisuals. **Special Academic Facilities/Equipment:** Planetarium, Baptist Historical Society Archives. **Computers:** School-owned computers available for student use.

EXTRACURRICULARS

Activities: Choral groups, concert band, drama/theater, jazz band, literary magazine, music ensembles, musical theater, opera, pep band, student government, student newspaper, symphony orchestra, television station, yearbook. **Organizations:** 80 registered organizations, 15 honor societies, 5 religious organizations, 5 fraternities (12% men join), 5 sororities (5% women join). **Athletics (Intercollegiate):** *Men:* baseball, basketball, cheerleading, cross-country, golf, indoor track, tennis, track & field. *Women:* basketball, cheerleading, cross-country, golf, indoor track, softball, tennis, track & field.

ADMISSIONS

Selectivity Rating: 79 (of 100). **Freshman Academic Profile:** Average high school GPA 3.7. 45% in top 10% of high school class, 73% in top 25% of high school class, 92% in top 50% of high school class. 90% from public high schools. Average SAT I Math 560, SAT I Math middle 50% range 500-630. Average SAT I Verbal 580, SAT I Verbal middle 50% range 510-650. Average ACT 24, ACT middle 50% range 21-28. TOEFL required of all international applicants, minimum TOEFL 500. **Basis for Candidate Selection:** *Very important* *factors considered include:* secondary school record. *Important factors considered include:* class rank, extracurricular activities, standardized test scores. *Other factors considered include:* alumni/ae relation, character/personal qualities, essays, geographical residence, interview, recommendations, religious affiliation/commitment, state residency, talent/ability, volunteer work, work experience. **Freshman Admission Requirements:** High school diploma or GED is required. *Academic units required/recommended:* 17 total recommended; 4 English recommended, 3 math recommended, 3 science recommended, 2 science lab recommended, 2 foreign language recommended, 1 social studies recommended, 2 history recommended, 2 elective recommended. **Freshman Admission Statistics:** 958 applied, 86% accepted, 53% of those accepted enrolled. **Transfer Admission Requirements:** *Items required:* high school transcript, college transcript. Minimum college GPA of 2.5 required. Lowest grade transferable D. **General Admission Information:** Application fee $25. Priority application deadline March 15. Regular application deadline August 1. Nonfall registration accepted. Admission may be deferred for a maximum of 1 year. Credit and/or placement offered for CEEB Advanced Placement tests.

COSTS AND FINANCIAL AID

Tuition $10,300. Room & board $3,750. Required fees $740. Average book expense $650. **Required Forms and Deadlines:** FAFSA. No deadline for regular filing. Priority filing deadline March 1. **Notification of Awards:** Applicants will be notified of awards on or about April 1. **Types of Aid:** *Need-based scholarships/grants:* Pell, SEOG, state scholarships/grants, private scholarships, the school's own gift aid, Federal Nursing. *Loans:* FFEL Subsidized Stafford, FFEL Unsubsidized Stafford, FFEL PLUS, Federal Perkins, Federal Nursing, college/university loans from institutional funds. **Student Employment:** Federal Work-Study Program available. Institutional employment available. Off-campus job opportunities are excellent. **Financial Aid Statistics:** 62% freshmen, 60% undergrads receive some form of aid. Average freshman grant $3,480. Average freshman loan $2,903. Average income from on-campus job $1,350. **Financial Aid Phone:** 800-654-3285.

OKLAHOMA CHRISTIAN UNIVERSITY

PO Box 11000, Oklahoma City, OK 73136-1100
Phone: 405-425-5050 **E-mail:** Info@oc.edu
Fax: 405-425-5269 **Web:** www.oc.edu **ACT Code:** 3415

This private school, which is affiliated with the Church of Christ, was founded in 1950. It has a 200-acre campus.

STUDENTS AND FACULTY

Enrollment: 1,599. **Student Body:** Male 49%, female 51%, out-of-state 54%, international students represent 31 countries. **Ethnic Representation:** African American 7%, Asian 2%, Caucasian 84%, Hispanic 2%, Native American 3%. **Retention and Graduation:** 67% freshmen return for sophomore year. 20% freshmen graduate within 4 years. **Faculty:** Student/faculty ratio 13:1. 108 full-time faculty, 66% hold PhDs. 100% faculty teach undergrads.

ACADEMICS

Degrees: Bachelor's, master's. **Academic Requirements:** General education including some course work in arts/fine arts, English (including composition), history, humanities, mathematics, philosophy, sciences (biological or physical), social science, Bible. **Classes:** 10-19 students in an average class. **Majors with Highest Enrollment:** Business/commerce, general; liberal arts and sciences/liberal studies; biology/biological sciences, general. **Disciplines with Highest Percentage of Degrees Awarded:** Business/marketing 27%, education 13%, social sciences and history 11%, liberal arts/general studies 9%, communications/communication technologies 8%. **Special Study Options:** Cross registration, distance learning, double major, English as a second language, honors program, independent study, internships, student-designed major, study abroad, teacher certification program.

FACILITIES

Housing: All-female, all-male, apartments for married students, apartments for single students, housing for disabled students. **Library Holdings:** 99,916 bound volumes. 990 periodicals. 723,333 microforms. 10,232 audiovisuals. **Computers:** *Recommended operating system:* Windows XP. School-owned computers available for student use.

EXTRACURRICULARS

Activities: Choral groups, drama/theater, jazz band, music ensembles, radio station, student government, student newspaper, television station, yearbook. **Organizations:** 20 registered organizations, 5 honor societies, 2 religious organizations, 6 fraternities (15% men join), 6 sororities (18% women join). **Athletics (Intercollegiate):** *Men:* basketball, cross-country, golf, soccer, tennis, track & field. *Women:* basketball, cheerleading, cross-country, soccer, softball, tennis, track & field.

ADMISSIONS

Selectivity Rating: 75 (of 100). **Freshman Academic Profile:** Average SAT I Math 532, SAT I Math middle 50% range 490-620. Average SAT I Verbal 537, SAT I Verbal middle 50% range 490-610. Average ACT 23, ACT middle 50% range 18-26. TOEFL required of all international applicants, minimum TOEFL 500. **Basis for Candidate Selection:** *Other factors considered include:* class rank, secondary school record, standardized test scores. **Freshman Admission Requirements:** High school diploma or GED is required. **Freshman Admission Statistics:** 1,169 applied, 100% accepted, 37% of those accepted enrolled. **Transfer Admission Requirements:** *Items required:* high school transcript, college transcript, standardized test scores. Lowest grade transferable D. **General Admission Information:** Application fee $25. Nonfall registration accepted. Admission may be deferred for a maximum of 1 year. Credit offered for CEEB Advanced Placement tests.

COSTS AND FINANCIAL AID

Tuition $11,100. Room & board $4,500. Required fees $1,600. Average book expense $800. **Required Forms and Deadlines:** FAFSA and institution's own financial aid form. No deadline for regular filing. Priority filing deadline March 15. **Notification of Awards:** Applicants will be notified of awards on a rolling basis beginning on or about February 2. **Types of Aid:** *Need-based scholarships/grants:* Pell, SEOG, state scholarships/grants, private scholarships, the school's own gift aid. *Loans:* FFEL Subsidized Stafford, FFEL Unsubsidized Stafford, FFEL PLUS, Federal Perkins. **Student Employment:** Federal Work-Study Program available. Institutional employment available. Off-campus job opportunities are excellent. **Financial Aid Statistics:** 73% freshmen, 67% undergrads receive some form of aid. Average freshman grant $6,350. Average freshman loan $3,160. Average income from on-campus job $1,063. **Financial Aid Phone:** 405-425-5190.

OKLAHOMA CITY UNIVERSITY

2501 North Blackwelder, Oklahoma City, OK 73106
Phone: 405-521-5050 **E-mail:** uadmission@okcu.edu **CEEB Code:** 6543
Fax: 405-521-5264 **Web:** www.okcu.edu **ACT Code:** 3416

This private school, which is affiliated with the Methodist Church, was founded in 1904. It has a 68-acre campus.

STUDENTS AND FACULTY

Enrollment: 1,710. **Student Body:** Male 40%, female 60%, out-of-state 69%, international 22%. **Ethnic Representation:** African American 7%, Asian 3%, Caucasian 78%, Hispanic 4%, Native American 5%. **Retention and Graduation:** 86% freshmen return for sophomore year. 35% freshmen graduate within 4 years. **Faculty:** Student/faculty ratio 15:1. 168 full-time faculty, 72% hold PhDs. 83% faculty teach undergrads.

ACADEMICS

Degrees: Bachelor's, first professional, master's. **Academic Requirements:** General education including some course work in arts/fine arts, computer literacy, English (including composition), foreign languages, history, humanities, mathematics, philosophy, sciences (biological or physical), social science, religion. **Classes:** 10-19 students in an average class. Under 10 students in an average lab/discussion section. **Disciplines with Highest Percentage of Degrees Awarded:** Liberal arts/general studies 27%, visual and performing arts 18%, business/marketing 16%, health professions and related sciences 7%, communications/communication technologies 6%. **Special Study Options:** Accelerated program, cooperative (work-study) program, double major, English as a second language, student exchange program (domestic), external degree program, honors program, independent study, internships, student-designed major, study abroad, teacher certification program.

FACILITIES

Housing: All-female, all-male, apartments for married students, apartments for single students, housing for disabled students, fraternities and/or sororities. **Library Holdings:** 321,093 bound volumes. 5,498 periodicals. 923,958 microforms. 10,132 audiovisuals. **Special Academic Facilities/Equipment:** Art museum, audiovisual center, language lab. **Computers:** School-owned computers available for student use.

EXTRACURRICULARS

Activities: Choral groups, concert band, dance, drama/theater, jazz band, literary magazine, music ensembles, musical theater, opera, pep band, student government, student newspaper, television station, yearbook. **Organizations:** 35 registered organizations, 11 honor societies, 6 religious organizations, 3 fraternities (11% men join), 3 sororities (17% women join). **Athletics (Intercollegiate):** *Men:* baseball, basketball, cheerleading, golf, soccer, tennis. *Women:* basketball, cheerleading, golf, soccer, softball, tennis.

ADMISSIONS

Selectivity Rating: 74 (of 100). **Freshman Academic Profile:** Average high school GPA 3.5. 27% in top 10% of high school class, 52% in top 25% of high school class, 81% in top 50% of high school class. Average SAT I Math 520, SAT I Math middle 50% range 422-564. Average SAT I Verbal 550, SAT I Verbal middle 50% range 442-577. Average ACT 23, ACT middle 50% range 19-25. TOEFL required of all international applicants, minimum TOEFL 500. **Basis for Candidate Selection:** *Very important factors considered include:* class rank, essays, secondary school record, standardized test scores, talent/ability. *Important factors considered include:* character/personal qualities, extracurricular activities, minority status, volunteer work. *Other factors considered include:* alumni/ae relation, interview, recommendations, religious affiliation/commitment, work experience. **Freshman Admission Requirements:** High school diploma or GED is required. *Academic units required/recommended:* 15 total recommended; 4 English recommended, 3 math recommended, 3 science recommended, 1 science lab recommended, 2 foreign language recommended, 3 social studies recommended, 3 history recommended. **Freshman Admission Statistics:** 891 applied, 67% accepted, 37% of those accepted enrolled. **Transfer Admission Requirements:** *Items required:* college transcript, essay, statement of good standing from prior school. Minimum college GPA of 2.0 required. Lowest grade transferable C-. **General Admission Information:** Application fee $30. Priority application deadline March 30. Regular application deadline August 22. Nonfall registration accepted. Admission may be deferred for a maximum of 1 year. Credit and/or placement offered for CEEB Advanced Placement tests.

COSTS AND FINANCIAL AID

Tuition $10,480. Room & board $9,860. Required fees $400. Average book expense $900. **Required Forms and Deadlines:** FAFSA and tax returns if selected for verification. No deadline for regular filing. Priority filing deadline March 1. **Notification of Awards:** Applicants will be notified of awards on a rolling basis beginning on or about March 15. **Types of Aid:** *Need-based scholarships/grants:* Pell, SEOG, state scholarships/grants, private scholarships, the school's own gift aid, United Negro College Fund, Federal Nursing, Native American Grants. *Loans:* FFEL Subsidized Stafford, FFEL Unsubsidized Stafford, FFEL PLUS, Federal Perkins, Federal Nursing. **Student Employment:** Federal Work-Study Program available. Institutional employment available. Off-campus job opportunities are excellent. **Financial Aid Statistics:** 54% freshmen, 47% undergrads receive some form of aid. **Financial Aid Phone:** 405-521-5211.

OKLAHOMA PANHANDLE STATE UNIVERSITY

PO Box 430, Goodwell, OK 73939-0430
Phone: 580-349-1312 **E-mail:** opsu@opsu.edu
Fax: 508-349-2302 **Web:** www.opsu.edu **ACT Code:** 34026

This public school was founded in 1909. It has a 120-acre campus.

STUDENTS AND FACULTY

Enrollment: 1,226. **Student Body:** Male 46%, female 54%, out-of-state 49%, international 4%. **Ethnic Representation:** African American 4%, Caucasian 83%, Hispanic 11%, Native American 2%. **Retention and Graduation:** 70% freshmen return for sophomore year. **Faculty:** Student/faculty ratio 15:1. 44 full-time faculty, 43% hold PhDs. 100% faculty teach undergrads.

ACADEMICS

Degrees: Associate's, bachelor's, terminal. **Academic Requirements:** General education including some course work in arts/fine arts, computer literacy, English (including composition), history, humanities, mathematics, sciences (biological or physical), social science. **Classes:** 20-29 students in an average class. Under 10 students in an average lab/discussion section. **Majors with Highest Enrollment:** Agricultural business and management, general; computer and information sciences, general; education, general. **Disciplines with Highest Percentage of Degrees Awarded:** Agriculture 24%, education 22%, business/marketing 15%, computer and information sciences 8%, biological life sciences 8%. **Special Study Options:** Cooperative (work-study) program, distance learning, double major, dual enrollment, independent study, internships, liberal arts/career combination, teacher certification program.

FACILITIES

Housing: Coed, all-female, all-male, apartments for married students, apartments for single students. **Library Holdings:** 91,027 bound volumes. 462 periodicals. 12,840 microforms. 8,432 audiovisuals. **Computers:** School-owned computers available for student use.

EXTRACURRICULARS

Activities: Choral groups, concert band, drama/theater, jazz band, literary magazine, marching band, music ensembles, musical theater, radio station, student government, student newspaper, yearbook. **Organizations:** 8 registered organizations, 12 honor societies, 4 religious organizations. **Athletics (Intercollegiate):** *Men:* baseball, basketball, cheerleading, football, golf, rodeo. *Women:* basketball, cheerleading, cross-country, golf, rodeo, softball.

ADMISSIONS

Selectivity Rating: 64 (of 100). **Freshman Academic Profile:** 9% in top 10% of high school class, 18% in top 25% of high school class, 30% in top 50% of high school class. 99% from public high schools. Average ACT 18, ACT middle 50% range 27-19. TOEFL required of all international applicants, minimum TOEFL 500. **Freshman Admission Requirements:** High school diploma or GED is required. *Academic units required/recommended:* 15 total required; 4 English required, 3 math required, 2 science required, 2 science lab required, 1 social studies required, 2 history required, 3 elective required. **Freshman Admission Statistics:** 257 applied, 85% accepted, 100% of those accepted enrolled. **Transfer Admission Requirements:** *Items required:* high school transcript, college transcript, standardized test scores. **General Admission Information:** Nonfall registration accepted.

COSTS AND FINANCIAL AID

In-state tuition $2,055. Out-of-state tuition $3,840. Room & board $2,670. Required fees $441. Average book expense $180. **Required Forms and Deadlines:** FAFSA. **Notification of Awards:** Applicants will be notified of awards on a rolling basis. **Types of Aid:** *Need-based scholarships/grants:* Pell, SEOG, state scholarships/grants, private scholarships, the school's own gift aid. *Loans:* FFEL Subsidized Stafford, FFEL Unsubsidized Stafford, FFEL PLUS, Federal Perkins, college/university loans from institutional funds. **Student Employment:** Federal Work-Study Program available. Off-campus job opportunities are good. **Financial Aid Statistics:** Average freshman loan $2,625. Average income from on-campus job $1,900. **Financial Aid Phone:** 580-349-1580.

OKLAHOMA STATE UNIVERSITY

324 Student Union, Stillwater, OK 74078
Phone: 405-744-6858 **E-mail:** admit@okstate.edu **CEEB Code:** 6546
Fax: 405-744-5285 **Web:** www.okstate.edu **ACT Code:** 3424

This public school was founded in 1890. It has an 840-acre campus.

STUDENTS AND FACULTY

Enrollment: 18,043. **Student Body:** Male 51%, female 49%, out-of-state 12%, international 5% (111 countries represented). **Ethnic Representation:** African American 3%, Asian 2%, Caucasian 84%, Hispanic 2%, Native American 9%. **Retention and Graduation:** 80% freshmen return for sophomore year. 22% freshmen graduate within 4 years. **Faculty:** Student/faculty ratio 19:1. 964 full-time faculty, 90% hold PhDs. 58% faculty teach undergrads.

ACADEMICS

Degrees: Bachelor's, doctoral, first professional, master's. **Academic Requirements:** General education including some course work in English (including composition), history, humanities, mathematics, sciences (biological or physical), social science, American government and international dimension. **Classes:** 20-29 students in an average class. 10-19 students in an average lab/discussion section. **Majors with Highest Enrollment:** Business administration/management; accounting; education, general. **Disciplines with Highest Percentage of Degrees Awarded:** Business/marketing 29%, engineering/engineering technology 13%, agriculture 9%, education 8%, biological life sciences 6%. **Special Study Options:** Accelerated program, cooperative (work-study) program, cross registration, distance learning, double major, English as a second language, student exchange program (domestic), honors program, independent study, internships, student-designed major, study abroad, teacher certification program, weekend college.

FACILITIES

Housing: Coed, all-female, all-male, apartments for married students, apartments for single students, housing for disabled students, housing for international students, fraternities and/or sororities. **Library Holdings:**

2,409,875 bound volumes. 24,806 periodicals. 4,493,010 microforms. 510,548 audiovisuals. **Special Academic Facilities/Equipment:** Archaeology, art, history, and natural science museums, wellness center, laser research center. **Computers:** School-owned computers available for student use.

EXTRACURRICULARS

Activities: Choral groups, concert band, dance, drama/theater, jazz band, literary magazine, marching band, music ensembles, musical theater, opera, pep band, radio station, student government, student newspaper, symphony orchestra, television station. **Organizations:** 304 registered organizations, 32 honor societies, 30 religious organizations, 21 fraternities (14% men join), 15 sororities (18% women join). **Athletics (Intercollegiate):** *Men:* baseball, basketball, cross-country, football, golf, tennis, track & field, wrestling. *Women:* basketball, cross-country, equestrian, golf, soccer, softball, tennis, track & field.

ADMISSIONS

Selectivity Rating: 74 (of 100). **Freshman Academic Profile:** Average high school GPA 3.5. 27% in top 10% of high school class, 55% in top 25% of high school class, 85% in top 50% of high school class. 96% from public high schools. Average SAT I Math 559, SAT I Math middle 50% range 500-610. Average SAT I Verbal 552, SAT I Verbal middle 50% range 500-610. Average ACT 24, ACT middle 50% range 21-26. TOEFL required of all international applicants, minimum TOEFL 500. **Basis for Candidate Selection:** *Very important factors considered include:* class rank, secondary school record, standardized test scores. *Other factors considered include:* character/personal qualities, essays, extracurricular activities, interview, minority status, recommendations, talent/ability. **Freshman Admission Requirements:** High school diploma or GED is required. *Academic units required/recommended:* 15 total required; 3 total recommended; 4 English required, 3 math required, 2 science required, 2 science lab required, 2 foreign language recommended, 1 social studies required, 2 history required, 3 elective required. **Freshman Admission Statistics:** 5,639 applied, 92% accepted, 63% of those accepted enrolled. **Transfer Admission Requirements:** *Items required:* college transcript. Minimum high school GPA of 3.0 required. Minimum college GPA of 2.0 required. Lowest grade transferable D. **General Admission Information:** Application fee $25. Nonfall registration accepted. Credit offered for CEEB Advanced Placement tests.

COSTS AND FINANCIAL AID

In-state tuition $2,163. Out-of-state tuition $7,217. Room & board $5,150. Required fees $862. Average book expense $930. **Required Forms and Deadlines:** FAFSA. No deadline for regular filing. **Notification of Awards:** Applicants will be notified of awards on a rolling basis beginning on or about March 15. **Types of Aid:** *Need-based scholarships/grants:* Pell, SEOG, state scholarships/grants. *Loans:* Direct Subsidized Stafford, Direct Unsubsidized Stafford, Direct PLUS, Federal Perkins, college/university loans from institutional funds. **Student Employment:** Federal Work-Study Program available. Institutional employment available. Off-campus job opportunities are excellent. **Financial Aid Statistics:** 40% freshmen, 45% undergrads receive some form of aid. Average freshman grant $4,140. Average freshman loan $3,590. Average income from on-campus job $1,990. **Financial Aid Phone:** 405-744-7440.

OKLAHOMA WESLEYAN UNIVERSITY

2201 Silver Lake Road, Bartlesville, OK 74006
Phone: 800-468-6292 **E-mail:** admissions@bwc.edu **CEEB Code:** 6135
Fax: 918-335-6229 **ACT Code:** 3387

This private school was founded in 1972. It has a 127-acre campus.

STUDENTS AND FACULTY

Enrollment: 571. **Student Body:** Male 36%, female 64%, out-of-state 43%, international 6% (12 countries represented). **Ethnic Representation:** African American 3%, Asian 1%, Caucasian 85%, Hispanic 3%, Native American 8%. **Retention and Graduation:** 10% grads go on to further study within 1 year. 5% grads pursue business degrees. 2% grads pursue law degrees. 2% grads pursue medical degrees. **Faculty:** 100% faculty teach undergrads.

ACADEMICS

Degrees: Associate's, bachelor's, certificate. **Academic Requirements:** General education including some course work in computer literacy, English (including composition), history, humanities, mathematics, philosophy, sciences (biological or physical), social science, religion. **Special Study Options:** Double major, English as a second language, independent study, internships, student-designed major, study abroad.

FACILITIES

Housing: All-female, all-male. **Special Academic Facilities/Equipment:** LaQuinta Mansion. **Computers:** *Recommended operating system:* Mac. School-owned computers available for student use.

EXTRACURRICULARS

Activities: Choral groups, music ensembles, pep band, student government, student newspaper, yearbook. **Organizations:** 10 registered organizations, 2 honor societies, 3 religious organizations. **Athletics (Intercollegiate):** *Men:* baseball, basketball, cheerleading, golf, soccer. *Women:* basketball, cheerleading, soccer, softball, volleyball.

ADMISSIONS

Selectivity Rating: 79 (of 100). **Freshman Academic Profile:** Average high school GPA 3.6. 20% in top 10% of high school class, 40% in top 25% of high school class, 80% in top 50% of high school class. 90% from public high schools. Average SAT I Math 550. Average SAT I Verbal 500. Average ACT 22, ACT middle 50% range 19-25. TOEFL required of all international applicants, minimum TOEFL 500. **Basis for Candidate Selection:** *Very important factors considered include:* character/personal qualities, class rank, recommendations, religious affiliation/commitment, secondary school record, standardized test scores, state residency. *Important factors considered include:* alumni/ae relation, geographical residence, interview, minority status. *Other factors considered include:* extracurricular activities, talent/ability. **Freshman Admission Requirements:** High school diploma or GED is required. *Academic units required/recommended:* 15 total required; 4 English required, 2 math required, 1 science required, 1 science lab required, 1 social studies required, 1 history required, 6 elective required. **Freshman Admission Statistics:** 317 applied, 60% accepted, 62% of those accepted enrolled. **Transfer Admission Requirements:** *Items required:* high school transcript, college transcript, essay, statement of good standing from prior school. Minimum college GPA of 2.0 required. Lowest grade transferable D. **General Admission Information:** Application fee $25. Regular application deadline rolling. Nonfall registration accepted. Admission may be deferred for a maximum of 1 year. Credit and/or placement offered for CEEB Advanced Placement tests.

COSTS AND FINANCIAL AID

Tuition $8,200. Room & board $3,800. Required fees $500. **Types of Aid:** *Need-based scholarships/grants:* Pell, SEOG, state scholarships/grants, private scholarships, the school's own gift aid. *Loans:* Direct Subsidized Stafford, Direct Unsubsidized Stafford, Direct PLUS, Federal Perkins. **Student Employment:** Federal Work-Study Program available. Institutional employment available. Off-campus job opportunities are excellent. **Financial Aid Statistics:** Average freshman grant $3,000. Average freshman loan $4,000. Average income from on-campus job $1,913. **Financial Aid Phone:** 918-335-6282.

OLD DOMINION UNIVERSITY

108 Rollins Hall, 5215 Hampton Boulevard, Norfolk, VA 23529-0050
Phone: 757-683-3685 **E-mail:** admit@odu.edu **CEEB Code:** 5126
Fax: 757-683-3255 **Web:** www.odu.edu

This public school was founded in 1930. It has a 170-acre campus.

STUDENTS AND FACULTY

Enrollment: 13,578. **Student Body:** Male 43%, female 57%, out-of-state 8%, international 3%. **Ethnic Representation:** African American 24%, Asian 7%, Caucasian 61%, Hispanic 3%, Native American 1%. **Retention and Graduation:** 78% freshmen return for sophomore year. 17% freshmen graduate within 4 years. **Faculty:** Student/faculty ratio 16:1. 592 full-time faculty, 83% hold PhDs. 72% faculty teach undergrads.

ACADEMICS

Degrees: Bachelor's, doctoral, master's, post-master's certificate. **Academic Requirements:** General education including some course work in arts/fine arts, computer literacy, English (including composition), foreign languages, history, humanities, mathematics, philosophy, sciences (biological or physical), social science, oral communication and literature. **Classes:** Under 10 students in an average class. 20-29 students in an average lab/discussion section. **Majors with Highest Enrollment:** Community health services/liaison/counseling; nursing/registered nurse training (RN, ASN, BSN, MSN); multi/interdisciplinary studies. **Disciplines with Highest Percentage of Degrees Awarded:** Health professions and related sciences 22%, business/marketing 20%, engineering/engineering technology 10%, social sciences and history 10%, English 8%. **Special Study Options:** Accelerated program, cooperative (work-study) program, cross registration, distance learning, double major, dual enrollment, English as a second language, student exchange program (domestic), honors program, independent study, internships, liberal arts/career combination, student-designed major, study abroad, teacher certification program, weekend college, experiential learning.

FACILITIES

Housing: Coed, all-female, all-male, apartments for single students, housing for disabled students, housing for international students. **Library Holdings:** 985,801 bound volumes. 10,579 periodicals. 1,752,613 microforms. 40,628 audiovisuals. **Special Academic Facilities/Equipment:** Centers for urban research/service, economic education, and child study, planetarium, marine science research vessel, random wave pool. **Computers:** *Recommended operating system:* Windows NT/2000. School-owned computers available for student use.

EXTRACURRICULARS

Activities: Choral groups, concert band, dance, drama/theater, jazz band, literary magazine, music ensembles, musical theater, pep band, radio station, student government, student newspaper, yearbook. **Organizations:** 170 registered organizations, 19 honor societies, 17 religious organizations, 19 fraternities (8% men join), 9 sororities (5% women join). **Athletics (Intercollegiate):** *Men:* baseball, basketball, cheerleading, cross-country, diving, golf, sailing, soccer, swimming, tennis, volleyball, wrestling. *Women:* basketball, cheerleading, cross-country, diving, golf, lacrosse, sailing, soccer, swimming, tennis.

ADMISSIONS

Selectivity Rating: 66 (of 100). **Freshman Academic Profile:** Average high school GPA 3.2. 15% in top 10% of high school class, 47% in top 25% of high school class, 85% in top 50% of high school class. 90% from public high schools. Average SAT I Math 526, SAT I Math middle 50% range 470-580. Average SAT I Verbal 525, SAT I Verbal middle 50% range 470-560. Average ACT 19, ACT middle 50% range 17-20. TOEFL required of all international applicants, minimum TOEFL 550. **Basis for Candidate Selection:** *Very important factors considered include:* extracurricular activities, secondary school record, standardized test scores. *Important factors considered include:* class rank, essays, recommendations, volunteer work, work experience. *Other factors considered include:* alumni/ae relation, character/personal qualities, interview, talent/ability. **Freshman Admission Requirements:** High school diploma or GED is required. *Academic units required/recommended:* 16 total required; 4 English required, 3 math required, 3 science required, 2 science lab required, 3 foreign language required, 3 social studies recommended, 3 history required. **Freshman Admission Statistics:** 6,472 applied, 70% accepted, 39% of those accepted enrolled. **Transfer Admission Requirements:** *Items required:* college transcript, essay. Minimum high school GPA of 2.5 required. Minimum college GPA of 2.2 required. Lowest grade transferable C. **General Admission Information:** Application fee $30. Priority application deadline December 15. Regular application deadline March 15. Nonfall registration accepted. Admission may be deferred for a maximum of 1 year. Credit and/or placement offered for CEEB Advanced Placement tests.

COSTS AND FINANCIAL AID

In-state tuition $4,110. Out-of-state tuition $13,140. Room & board $5,498. Required fees $154. Average book expense $800. **Required Forms and Deadlines:** FAFSA. Financial aid filing deadline March 15. Priority filing deadline February 15. **Notification of Awards:** Applicants will be notified of awards on a rolling basis beginning on or about March 15. **Types of Aid:** *Need-based scholarships/grants:* Pell, SEOG, state scholarships/grants, private scholarships, the school's own gift aid. *Loans:* Direct Subsidized Stafford, Direct Unsubsidized Stafford, Direct PLUS, Federal Perkins. **Student Employment:** Federal Work-Study Program available. Institutional employment available. Off-campus job opportunities are excellent. **Financial Aid Statistics:** 53% freshmen, 54% undergrads receive some form of aid. Average freshman grant $4,381. Average freshman loan $2,425. Average income from on-campus job $2,884. **Financial Aid Phone:** 757-683-3683.

See page 1148.

OLIVET COLLEGE

320 S. Main St., Olivet, MI 49076
Phone: (269) 749-7635 **E-mail:** admissions@olivetcollege.edu **CEEB Code:** 1595
Fax: 269-749-3821 **Web:** www.olivetcollege.edu **ACT Code:** 2042

This private school, which is affiliated with the United Church of Christ, was founded in 1844. It has a 45-acre campus.

STUDENTS AND FACULTY

Enrollment: 912. **Student Body:** Male 54%, female 46%, out-of-state 5%, international 5%. **Ethnic Representation:** African American 17%, Asian 1%, Caucasian 76%, Hispanic 3%, Native American 2%. **Retention and Graduation:** 65% grads go on to further study within 1 year. 45% grads pursue business degrees. 20% grads pursue law degrees. 10% grads pursue medical degrees. **Faculty:** Student/faculty ratio 14:1. 46 full-time faculty, 45% hold PhDs. 99% faculty teach undergrads.

ACADEMICS

Degrees: Bachelor's, master's. **Academic Requirements:** General education including some course work in arts/fine arts, English (including composition), humanities, mathematics, sciences (biological or physical), social science. **Special Study Options:** Cooperative (work-study) program, dual enrollment, honors program, independent study, internships, liberal arts/career combination, student-designed major, study abroad, teacher certification program, Freshman Year Experience, portfolio assessment, Senior Experience, and service learning programs.

FACILITIES

Housing: Coed, all-female, all-male, apartments for single students, fraternities and/or sororities. **Library Holdings:** 96,791 bound volumes. 575 periodicals. 2,880 microforms. 1,689 audiovisuals. **Computers:** *Recommended operating system:* Windows NT/2000. School-owned computers available for student use.

EXTRACURRICULARS

Activities: Choral groups, drama/theater, music ensembles, musical theater, radio station, student government, student newspaper, yearbook. **Organizations:** 12 registered organizations, 1 honor society, 1 religious organization, 3 fraternities (8% men join), 3 sororities (8% women join). **Athletics (Intercollegiate):** *Men:* baseball, basketball, cross-country, diving, football, golf, soccer, swimming, track & field, wrestling. *Women:* basketball, cheerleading, cross-country, diving, golf, soccer, softball, swimming, tennis, track & field, volleyball.

ADMISSIONS

Selectivity Rating: 60 (of 100). **Freshman Academic Profile:** Average high school GPA 2.9. 93% from public high schools. Average SAT I Math 420. Average SAT I Verbal 450. Average ACT 18. TOEFL required of all international applicants, minimum TOEFL 500. **Basis for Candidate Selection:** *Very important factors considered include:* alumni/ae relation, character/personal qualities, extracurricular activities, secondary school record, standardized test scores, volunteer work, work experience. *Important factors considered include:* minority status, recommendations. *Other factors considered include:* class rank, essays, geographical residence, interview, religious affiliation/commitment, state residency, talent/ability. **Freshman Admission Requirements:** High school diploma or GED is required. *Academic units required/recommended:* 13 total recommended; 4 English recommended, 2 math recommended, 2 science recommended, 3 social studies recommended, 2 elective recommended. **Transfer Admission Requirements:** *Items required:* high school transcript, college transcript. Minimum college GPA of 2.0 required. Lowest grade transferable D. **General Admission Information:** Application fee $25. Priority application deadline August 1. Nonfall registration accepted. Admission may be deferred for a maximum of 1 year. Credit and/or placement offered for CEEB Advanced Placement tests.

COSTS AND FINANCIAL AID

Tuition $14,762. Room & board $4,802. Required fees $420. Average book expense $600. **Required Forms and Deadlines:** FAFSA. No deadline for regular filing. **Notification of Awards:** Applicants will be notified of awards on a rolling basis beginning on or about February 1. **Types of Aid:** *Need-based scholarships/grants:* Pell, SEOG, state scholarships/grants, private scholarships, the school's own gift aid. *Loans:* FFEL Subsidized Stafford, FFEL Unsubsidized Stafford, FFEL PLUS, Federal Perkins, state loans. **Student Employment:** Federal Work-Study Program available. Institutional employment available. Off-campus job opportunities are fair. **Financial Aid Statistics:** 71% freshmen, 84% undergrads receive some form of aid. Average freshman grant $7,500. Average freshman loan $3,741. Average income from on-campus job $850. **Financial Aid Phone:** 616-749-7645.

OLIVET NAZARENE UNIVERSITY

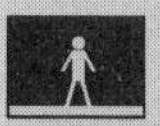

One University Avenue, Bourbonnais, IL 60914
Phone: 815-939-5203 **E-mail:** admissions@olivet.edu **CEEB Code:** 32
Fax: 815-935-4998 **Web:** www.olivet.edu **ACT Code:** 1112

This private school, which is affiliated with the Nazarene Church, was founded in 1907. It has a 200-acre campus.

STUDENTS AND FACULTY

Enrollment: 2,229. **Student Body:** Male 42%, female 58%, out-of-state 60%, international 1% (15 countries represented). **Ethnic Representation:** African American 7%, Asian 1%, Caucasian 90%, Hispanic 2%. **Retention and Graduation:** 75% freshmen return for sophomore year. 10% grads go on to further study within 1 year. 1% grads pursue business degrees. 1% grads pursue law degrees. 2% grads pursue medical degrees. **Faculty:** Student/faculty ratio 20:1. 86 full-time faculty, 67% hold PhDs. 100% faculty teach undergrads.

ACADEMICS

Degrees: Associate's, bachelor's, master's. **Academic Requirements:** General education including some course work in arts/fine arts, English (including composition), history, humanities, mathematics, sciences (biological or physical), social science, theology/Bible. **Disciplines with Highest Percentage of Degrees Awarded:** Business/marketing 16%, education 12%, health professions and related sciences 12%, social sciences and history 10%, protective services/public administration 8%. **Special Study Options:** Distance learning, double major, honors program, independent study, internships, student-designed major, study abroad, teacher certification program.

FACILITIES

Housing: All-female, all-male, apartments for married students, apartments for single students. **Library Holdings:** 160,039 bound volumes. 925 periodicals. 240,846 microforms. 6,818 audiovisuals. **Special Academic Facilities/Equipment:** Planetarium, telescope, Smartboard, ADAM (Biology) Counseling labs and Class rooms. **Computers:** *Recommended operating system:* Windows NT/2000. School-owned computers available for student use.

EXTRACURRICULARS

Activities: Choral groups, concert band, drama/theater, jazz band, literary magazine, music ensembles, musical theater, pep band, radio station, student government, student newspaper, symphony orchestra, yearbook. **Organizations:** 22 registered organizations, 5 honor societies, 1 religious organization. **Athletics (Intercollegiate):** *Men:* baseball, basketball, cheerleading, cross-country, football, golf, indoor track, soccer, tennis, track & field. *Women:* basketball, cheerleading, cross-country, indoor track, soccer, softball, tennis, track & field, volleyball.

ADMISSIONS

Selectivity Rating: 78 (of 100). **Freshman Academic Profile:** Average high school GPA 3.6. 34% in top 10% of high school class, 55% in top 25% of high school class, 90% in top 50% of high school class. 85% from public high schools. Average SAT I Math 600, SAT I Math middle 50% range 550-650. Average SAT I Verbal 580, SAT I Verbal middle 50% range 550-650. Average ACT 26, ACT middle 50% range 23-29. TOEFL required of all international applicants, minimum TOEFL 500. **Basis for Candidate Selection:** *Very important factors considered include:* character/personal qualities, class rank, essays, extracurricular activities, interview, recommendations, religious affiliation/commitment, secondary school record, standardized test scores. *Important factors considered include:* talent/ability. *Other factors considered include:* alumni/ae relation. **Freshman Admission Requirements:** High school diploma or GED is required. *Academic units required/recommended:* 15 total required; 20 total recommended; 4 English required, 4 English recommended, 3 math required, 3 math recommended, 3 science required, 3 science recommended, 3 science lab recommended, 2 foreign language recommended, 3 social studies required, 3 social studies recommended, 2 history required, 2 history recommended. **Freshman Admission Statistics:** 1,568 applied, 81% accepted, 45% of those accepted enrolled. **Transfer Admission Requirements:** *Items required:* college transcript, essay. Lowest grade transferable D-. **General Admission Information:** Priority application deadline December 1. Regular application deadline August 1. Nonfall registration accepted. Admission may be deferred for a maximum of 1 year. Credit and/or placement offered for CEEB Advanced Placement tests.

COSTS AND FINANCIAL AID

Tuition $14,160. Room & board $5,260. Required fees $820. Average book expense $800. **Required Forms and Deadlines:** No deadline for regular filing. **Notification of Awards:** Applicants will be notified of awards on or about January 15. **Types of Aid:** *Need-based scholarships/grants:* Pell, SEOG, state scholarships/grants, private scholarships, the school's own gift aid. *Loans:* FFEL Subsidized Stafford, FFEL Unsubsidized Stafford, FFEL PLUS, Federal Perkins. **Student Employment:** Federal Work-Study Program available. Off-campus job opportunities are excellent. **Financial Aid Statistics:** 76% freshmen, 71% undergrads receive some form of aid. Average freshman grant $4,228. Average income from on-campus job $1,000. **Financial Aid Phone:** 800-648-1463.

See page 1150.

ONONDAGA COMMUNITY COLLEGE

4941, Onondaga Road, Syracuse, NY 13215
Phone: 315-498-2201 **E-mail:** flynnm@sunyocc.edu
Fax: 315-469-2107 **Web:** sunyocc.edu

This public school was founded in 1961. It has a 181-acre campus.

STUDENTS AND FACULTY

Enrollment: 7,363. **Student Body:** Male 47%, female 53%. **Faculty:** Student/faculty ratio 17:1. 179 full-time faculty.

ACADEMICS

Degrees: Associate's, certificate. **Academic Requirements:** General education including some course work in humanities, mathematics, social science, health professions. **Classes:** 10-19 students in an average class. **Special Study Options:** Cooperative (work-study) program, double major, dual enrollment, English as a second language, honors program, independent study, internships, liberal arts/career combination, study abroad.

FACILITIES

Library Holdings: 87,534 bound volumes. 588 periodicals. 61,138 microforms. 3,205 audiovisuals. **Computers:** School-owned computers available for student use.

EXTRACURRICULARS

Activities: Choral groups, music ensembles, radio station, student government, student newspaper, television station. **Organizations:** 1 honor society. **Athletics (Intercollegiate):** *Men:* baseball, basketball, cross-country, lacrosse, tennis. *Women:* basketball, cross-country, softball, tennis, volleyball.

ADMISSIONS

Selectivity Rating: 63 (of 100). **Freshman Academic Profile:** 95% from public high schools. TOEFL required of all international applicants, minimum TOEFL 500. **Basis for Candidate Selection:** *Very important factors considered include:* secondary school record. *Other factors considered include:* character/personal qualities, interview, recommendations. **Freshman Admission Requirements:** High school diploma or equivalent is not required. *Academic units required/recommended:* 4 English recommended, 2 math recommended, 3 science recommended, 2 science lab recommended, 2 foreign language recommended, 4 social studies recommended, 4 history recommended. **Freshman Admission Statistics:** 2,899 applied, 79% accepted, 217% of those accepted enrolled. **Transfer Admission Requirements:** *Items required:* high school transcript, college transcript. Lowest grade transferable C. **General Admission Information:** Application fee $30. Nonfall registration accepted. Admission may be deferred for a maximum of 1 year.

COSTS AND FINANCIAL AID

Required Forms and Deadlines: FAFSA and state aid form. No deadline for regular filing. Priority filing deadline February 15. **Notification of Awards:** Applicants will be notified of awards on or about April 15. **Types of Aid:** *Need-based scholarships/grants:* Pell, SEOG, state scholarships/grants, Federal work study. *Loans:* FFEL Subsidized Stafford, FFEL Unsubsidized Stafford, FFEL PLUS. **Student Employment:** Federal Work-Study Program available. Off-campus job opportunities are excellent. **Financial Aid Statistics:** 55% freshmen, 62% undergrads receive some form of aid. Average freshman grant $1,400. **Financial Aid Phone:** 315-498-2291.

ORAL ROBERTS UNIVERSITY

7777 S. Lewis Avenue, Tulsa, OK 74171
Phone: 918-495-6518 **E-mail:** admissions@oru.edu **CEEB Code:** 6552
Fax: 918-495-6222 **Web:** www.oru.edu **ACT Code:** 3427

This private school has a 500-acre campus.

STUDENTS AND FACULTY

Enrollment: 3,041. **Student Body:** Male 41%, female 59%, out-of-state 64%, international 3%. **Ethnic Representation:** African American 17%, Asian 3%, Caucasian 69%, Hispanic 5%, Native American 2%. **Retention and Graduation:** 80% freshmen return for sophomore year. 38% freshmen graduate within 4 years. **Faculty:** Student/faculty ratio 16:1. 207 full-time faculty, 56% hold PhDs.

ACADEMICS

Degrees: Bachelor's, doctoral, first professional, master's. **Academic Requirements:** General education including some course work in English (including composition), foreign languages, history, humanities, mathematics, sciences (biological or physical), social science. **Classes:** 10-19 students in an average class. 20-29 students in an average lab/discussion section. **Disciplines with Highest Percentage of Degrees Awarded:** Business/marketing 22%, philosophy/religion/theology 19%, communications/communication technologies 14%, education 9%, visual and performing arts 7%. **Special Study Options:** Distance learning, double major, dual enrollment, English as a second language, external degree program, honors program, independent study, internships, liberal arts/career combination, student-designed major, study abroad, teacher certification program, weekend college.

FACILITIES

Housing: All-female, all-male. **Library Holdings:** 216,691 bound volumes. 600 periodicals. 49,936 microforms. 25,445 audiovisuals. **Special Academic Facilities/Equipment:** Dial Access Information Retrieval System, programmed learning facilities, early learning center, TV production studio. **Computers:** *Recommended operating system:* Mac. School-owned computers available for student use.

EXTRACURRICULARS

Activities: Choral groups, concert band, dance, drama/theater, jazz band, literary magazine, music ensembles, musical theater, opera, pep band, radio station, student government, student newspaper, student-run film society, symphony orchestra, television station, yearbook. **Athletics (Intercollegiate):** *Men:* basketball, cross-country, swimming, tennis, volleyball. *Women:* basketball, cross-country, swimming, tennis, volleyball.

ADMISSIONS

Selectivity Rating: 80 (of 100). **Freshman Academic Profile:** Average high school GPA 3.9. 27% in top 10% of high school class, 53% in top 25% of high school class, 78% in top 50% of high school class. Average SAT I Math 523, SAT I Math middle 50% range 470-590. Average SAT I Verbal 538, SAT I Verbal middle 50% range 480-600. Average ACT 23, ACT middle 50% range 20-26. TOEFL required of all international applicants, minimum TOEFL 500. **Basis for Candidate Selection:** *Very important factors considered include:* essays, secondary school record, standardized test scores. *Important factors considered include:* class rank, recommendations. **Freshman Admission Requirements:** High school diploma or GED is required. *Academic units required/recommended:* 16 total recommended; 4 English recommended, 2 math recommended, 1 science recommended, 1 science lab recommended, 2 foreign language recommended, 2 social studies recommended. **Transfer Admission Requirements:** *Items required:* high school transcript, college transcript, essay. Minimum college GPA of 2.0 required. Lowest grade transferable C. **General Admission Information:** Application fee $35. Nonfall registration accepted. Admission may be deferred for a maximum of 2 years. Credit and/or placement offered for CEEB Advanced Placement tests.

COSTS AND FINANCIAL AID

Tuition $12,600. Room & board $5,570. Required fees $380. Average book expense $1,000. **Required Forms and Deadlines:** FAFSA. No deadline for regular filing. Priority filing deadline March 15. **Notification of Awards:** Applicants will be notified of awards on a rolling basis beginning on or about February 15. **Types of Aid:** *Need-based scholarships/grants:* Pell, SEOG, state scholarships/grants, private scholarships, the school's own gift aid. *Loans:* FFEL Subsidized Stafford, FFEL Unsubsidized Stafford, FFEL PLUS, Federal Perkins, college/university loans from institutional funds. **Student Employment:** Federal Work-Study Program available. Institutional employment available. Off-campus job opportunities are good. **Financial Aid Statistics:** 72% freshmen, 67% undergrads receive some form of aid. Average freshman loan $8,467. Average income from on-campus job $1,800. **Financial Aid Phone:** 918-495-6510.

OREGON COLLEGE OF ART AND CRAFT

8245 Southwest Barnes Road, Portland, OR 97225
Phone: 503-297-5544 **E-mail:** dspencer@ocac.edu
Fax: 503-297-9651 **Web:** www.ocac.edu

This private school was founded in 1994. It has a 3-acre campus.

STUDENTS AND FACULTY

Enrollment: 92. **Student Body:** Male 27%, female 73%, international 1%. **Ethnic Representation:** Caucasian 80%, Hispanic 2%. **Faculty:** Student/faculty ratio 8:1.

ACADEMICS

Degrees: Bachelor's, certificate, post-bachelor's certificate. **Academic Requirements:** General education including some course work in arts/fine arts, English (including composition), history, humanities, sciences (biological or physical), social science. **Majors with Highest Enrollment:** Metal and jewelry arts; ceramic arts and ceramics; painting. **Disciplines with Highest Percentage of Degrees Awarded:** Visual and performing arts 87%. **Special Study Options:** Cooperative (work-study) program, double major, student exchange program (domestic), internships, study abroad.

FACILITIES

Library Holdings: 8,250 bound volumes. 90 periodicals. 28,000 audiovisuals. **Computers:** School-owned computers available for student use.

EXTRACURRICULARS

ADMISSIONS

Selectivity Rating: 62 (of 100). **Freshman Academic Profile:** TOEFL required of all international applicants, minimum TOEFL 550. **Freshman Admission Requirements:** High school diploma or GED is required. **Freshman Admission Statistics:** applied. **Transfer Admission Requirements:** *Items required:* high school transcript, college transcript, essay, interview. Minimum high school GPA of 2.5 required. Minimum college GPA of 2.0 required. Lowest grade transferable C. **General Admission Information:** Application fee $35. Priority application deadline February 15.

COSTS AND FINANCIAL AID

Tuition $13,200. Required fees $950. Average book expense $850. **Required Forms and Deadlines:** FAFSA. No deadline for regular filing. Priority filing deadline March 1. **Notification of Awards:** Applicants will be notified of awards on a rolling basis beginning on or about March 15. **Types of Aid:** *Need-based scholarships/grants:* Pell, SEOG, state scholarships/grants, private scholarships, the school's own gift aid. *Loans:* FFEL Subsidized Stafford, FFEL Unsubsidized Stafford; FFEL PLUS, state loans. **Student Employment:** Federal Work-Study Program available. Institutional employment available. **Financial Aid Statistics:** Average freshman grant $4,500. Average freshman loan $6,625. **Financial Aid Phone:** 503-297-5544.

OREGON HEALTH SCIENCES UNIVERSITY

3181 SW Sam Jackson Park Road, L-109, Portland, OR 97201-3098
Phone: 503-494-7800 **E-mail:** finaid@ohsu.edu
Fax: 503-494-4629 **Web:** www.ohsu.edu

STUDENTS AND FACULTY

Enrollment: 243. **Student Body:** International 4%. **Ethnic Representation:** African American 1%, Asian 6%, Caucasian 89%, Hispanic 2%, Native American 2%.

ACADEMICS

Degrees: Associate's, bachelor's, certificate, doctoral, first professional, first professional certificate, master's, post-master's certificate. **Special Study Options:** Distance learning.

FACILITIES

Housing: Single (coed) dorm (capacity 85), considerable housing for rent by students available in the local community. **Library Holdings:** 200,771 bound volumes.

EXTRACURRICULARS

Organizations: 2 religious organizations.

ADMISSIONS

Selectivity Rating: 60 (of 100). **General Admission Information:** Application fee $60. Regular application deadline rolling.

COSTS AND FINANCIAL AID

In-state tuition $4,939. Out-of-state tuition $12,272. Required fees $2,668. Average book expense $1,444. **Types of Aid:** *Need-based scholarships/grants:* Pell, SEOG, state scholarships/grants, private scholarships, the school's own gift aid. *Loans:* Direct Subsidized Stafford, Direct Unsubsidized Stafford, Direct PLUS, Federal Perkins, Federal Nursing, college/university loans from institutional funds. **Student Employment:** Federal Work-Study Program available. **Financial Aid Phone:** 503-494-7800.

OREGON INSTITUTE OF TECHNOLOGY

3201 Campus Drive, Klamath Falls, OR 97601
Phone: 541-885-1150 **E-mail:** oit@oit.edu **CEEB Code:** 4587
Fax: 541-885-1115 **Web:** www.oit.edu **ACT Code:** 3484

This public school was founded in 1947. It has a 173-acre campus.

STUDENTS AND FACULTY

Enrollment: 3,136. **Student Body:** Male 55%, female 45%, out-of-state 14%, international 1%. **Ethnic Representation:** African American 1%, Asian 6%, Caucasian 80%, Hispanic 4%, Native American 2%. **Retention and Graduation:** 69% freshmen return for sophomore year. 1% grads go on to further study within 1 year. **Faculty:** Student/faculty ratio 14:1. 123 full-time faculty, 36% hold PhDs. 100% faculty teach undergrads.

ACADEMICS

Degrees: Associate's, bachelor's, terminal, transfer. **Academic Requirements:** General education including some course work in computer literacy, English (including composition), humanities, mathematics, sciences (biological or physical), social science. **Classes:** 10-19 students in an average class. 10-19 students in an average lab/discussion section. **Majors with Highest Enrollment:** Mechanical engineering/mechanical technology/technician; computer engineering technology/technician; computer software technology/technician. **Disciplines with Highest Percentage of Degrees Awarded:** Engineering/engineering technology 50%, health professions and related sciences 24%, business/marketing 15%, psychology 10%, physical sciences 1%. **Special Study Options:** Cooperative (work-study) program, distance learning, double major, dual enrollment, student exchange program (domestic), external degree program, internships, study abroad.

FACILITIES

Housing: Coed. **Library Holdings:** 90,389 bound volumes. 1,764 periodicals. 150,550 microforms. 1,905 audiovisuals. **Special Academic Facilities/Equipment:** Historical library. **Computers:** School-owned computers available for student use.

EXTRACURRICULARS

Activities: Choral groups, jazz band, radio station, student government, student newspaper, television station. **Organizations:** 36 registered organizations, 1 honor society, 5 religious organizations, 4 fraternity, 1 sorority. **Athletics (Intercollegiate):** *Men:* baseball, basketball, cheerleading, cross-country, soccer, track & field. *Women:* basketball, cheerleading, cross-country, soccer, softball, track & field, volleyball.

ADMISSIONS

Selectivity Rating: 83 (of 100). **Freshman Academic Profile:** Average high school GPA 3.3. 16% in top 10% of high school class, 40% in top 25% of high school class, 76% in top 50% of high school class. SAT I Math middle 50% range 480-590. SAT I Verbal middle 50% range 450-580. ACT middle 50% range 18-24. TOEFL required of all international applicants, minimum TOEFL 520. **Basis for Candidate Selection:** *Very important factors considered include:* secondary school record. *Important factors considered include:* standardized test scores. *Other factors considered include:* character/personal qualities, class rank, geographical residence, minority status, state residency, work experience. **Freshman Admission Requirements:** High school diploma or GED is required. *Academic units required/recommended:* 14 total required; 16 total recommended; 4 English required, 4 English recommended, 3 math required, 4 math recommended, 2 science required, 3 science recommended, 1 science lab recommended, 2 foreign language required, 2 foreign language recommended, 3 social studies required, 3 social studies recommended. **Freshman Admission Statistics:** 792 applied, 61% accepted, 74% of those accepted enrolled. **Transfer Admission Requirements:** *Items required:* college transcript. Minimum college GPA of 2.0 required. Lowest grade transferable D. **General Admission Information:** Application fee $50. Priority application deadline March 1. Nonfall registration accepted. Admission may be deferred for a maximum of 1 year. Credit and/or placement offered for CEEB Advanced Placement tests.

COSTS AND FINANCIAL AID

In-state tuition $2,697. Out-of-state tuition $11,655. Room & board $5,154. Required fees $975. Average book expense $864. **Required Forms and Deadlines:** FAFSA. Priority filing deadline March 1. **Notification of Awards:** Applicants will be notified of awards on a rolling basis beginning on or about April 2. **Types of Aid:** *Need-based scholarships/grants:* Pell, SEOG, state scholarships/grants, private scholarships, the school's own gift aid. *Loans:* FFEL Subsidized Stafford, FFEL Unsubsidized Stafford, FFEL PLUS, Federal Perkins, college/university loans from institutional funds. **Student Employment:** Federal Work-Study Program available. Institutional employment available. Off-campus job opportunities are good. **Financial Aid Statistics:** 68% freshmen, 67% undergrads receive some form of aid. **Financial Aid Phone:** 541-885-1280.

OREGON STATE UNIVERSITY

104 Kerr Administration Building, Corvallis, OR 97331-2106
Phone: 541-737-4411 **E-mail:** osuadmit@orst.edu **CEEB Code:** 4586
Fax: 541-737-2482 **Web:** oregonstate.edu

This public school was founded in 1868. It has a 420-acre campus.

STUDENTS AND FACULTY

Enrollment: 15,413. **Student Body:** Male 53%, female 47%, out-of-state 12%, international 2%. **Ethnic Representation:** African American 1%, Asian 8%, Caucasian 82%, Hispanic 3%, Native American 1%. **Retention and Graduation:** 80% freshmen return for sophomore year. 27% freshmen graduate within 4 years. **Faculty:** Student/faculty ratio 21:1. 634 full-time faculty, 63% hold PhDs. 100% faculty teach undergrads.

ACADEMICS

Degrees: Bachelor's, doctoral, first professional, master's. **Academic Requirements:** General education including some course work in English (including composition), humanities, mathematics, sciences (biological or physical), social science, fitness, difference, power and discrimination. **Classes:** 20-29 students in an average class. 20-29 students in an average lab/discussion section. **Majors with Highest Enrollment:** Engineering, general; business administration/management; liberal arts and sciences/liberal studies. **Disciplines with Highest Percentage of Degrees Awarded:** Engineering/engineering technology 15%, business/marketing 14%, home economics and vocational home economics 8%, agriculture 8%, biological life sciences 7%. **Special Study Options:** Cooperative (work-study) program, distance learning, double major, dual enrollment, English as a second language, student exchange program (domestic), external degree program, honors program, internships, student-designed major, study abroad.

FACILITIES

Housing: Coed, all-female, all-male, apartments for married students, apartments for single students, housing for disabled students, housing for international students, fraternities and/or sororities, cooperative housing. **Library Holdings:** 1,403,451 bound volumes. 14,777 periodicals. 1,912,023 microforms. **Special Academic Facilities/Equipment:** Museums, galleries, collections, exhibits of cultural and scientific materials, language lab. **Computers:** School-owned computers available for student use.

EXTRACURRICULARS

Activities: Choral groups, concert band, dance, drama/theater, jazz band, literary magazine, marching band, music ensembles, musical theater, opera, pep band, radio station, student government, student newspaper, student-run film society, symphony orchestra, television station, yearbook. **Organizations:** 350 registered organizations, 29 honor societies, 23 religious organizations, 24 fraternities (13% men join), 13 sororities (12% women join). **Athletics (Intercollegiate):** *Men:* baseball, basketball, crew, football, golf, soccer, wrestling. *Women:* basketball, crew, golf, gymnastics, soccer, softball, swimming, volleyball.

ADMISSIONS

Selectivity Rating: 65 (of 100). **Freshman Academic Profile:** Average high school GPA 3.4. 17% in top 10% of high school class, 45% in top 25% of high school class, 80% in top 50% of high school class. Average SAT I Math 549, SAT I Math middle 50% range 480-610. Average SAT I Verbal 532, SAT I Verbal middle 50% range 470-590. Average ACT 23, ACT middle 50% range 20-26. TOEFL required of all international applicants, minimum TOEFL 550. **Basis**

for Candidate Selection: *Very important factors considered include:* secondary school record. *Other factors considered include:* character/personal qualities, essays, extracurricular activities, interview, recommendations, standardized test scores, talent/ability, volunteer work, work experience. **Freshman Admission Requirements:** High school diploma or GED is required. *Academic units required/recommended:* 4 English required, 3 math required, 2 science required, 1 science lab recommended, 2 foreign language required, 3 social studies required. **Freshman Admission Statistics:** 5,811 applied, 75% accepted, 70% of those accepted enrolled. **Transfer Admission Requirements:** *Items required:* college transcript, statement of good standing from prior school. Minimum college GPA of 2.3 required. Lowest grade transferable D. **General Admission Information:** Application fee $50. Priority application deadline February 1. Nonfall registration accepted. Admission may be deferred for a maximum of 1 year. Credit and/or placement offered for CEEB Advanced Placement tests.

COSTS AND FINANCIAL AID

In-state tuition $2,886. Out-of-state tuition $13,770. Room & board $5,976. Required fees $1,128. Average book expense $1,050. **Required Forms and Deadlines:** FAFSA. Financial aid filing deadline May 1. Priority filing deadline February 1. **Notification of Awards:** Applicants will be notified of awards on a rolling basis beginning on or about April 1. **Types of Aid:** *Need-based scholarships/grants:* Pell, SEOG, state scholarships/grants, private scholarships, the school's own gift aid. *Loans:* Direct Subsidized Stafford, Direct Unsubsidized Stafford, Direct PLUS, Federal Perkins, college/university loans from institutional funds. **Student Employment:** Federal Work-Study Program available. Institutional employment available. Off-campus job opportunities are good. **Financial Aid Phone:** 541-737-2241.

OTIS COLLEGE OF ART & DESIGN

9045 Lincoln Boulevard, Los Angeles, CA 90045
Phone: 310-665-6820 **E-mail:** otisinfo@otis.edu **CEEB Code:** 4394
Fax: 310-665-6821 **Web:** www.otis.edu **ACT Code:** 359

This private school was founded in 1918. It has a 5-acre campus.

STUDENTS AND FACULTY

Enrollment: 927. **Student Body:** Male 36%, female 64%, out-of-state 20%, international 12%. **Ethnic Representation:** African American 2%, Asian 34%, Caucasian 40%, Hispanic 12%. **Retention and Graduation:** 71% freshmen return for sophomore year. 26% freshmen graduate within 4 years. **Faculty:** Student/faculty ratio 12:1. 32 full-time faculty, 21% hold PhDs.

ACADEMICS

Degrees: Bachelor's, master's. **Academic Requirements:** General education including some course work in arts/fine arts, computer literacy, English (including composition), humanities, mathematics, sciences (biological or physical), social science. **Classes:** 10-19 students in an average class. **Majors with Highest Enrollment:** Animation, interactive technology, video graphics and special effects; fashion/apparel design; graphic design. **Disciplines with Highest Percentage of Degrees Awarded:** Visual and performing arts 100%. **Special Study Options:** English as a second language, student exchange program (domestic), honors program, independent study, internships, study abroad.

FACILITIES

Housing: Apartments for single students. **Library Holdings:** 42,000 bound volumes. 150 periodicals. 0 microforms. 2,500 audiovisuals. **Special Academic Facilities/Equipment:** Art gallery, student gallery, woodshop, metal shop, photo lab, digital media lab, printmaking lab, letterpress lab. **Computers:** School-owned computers available for student use.

EXTRACURRICULARS

Activities: Literary magazine, student government, student newspaper.

ADMISSIONS

Selectivity Rating: 73 (of 100). **Freshman Academic Profile:** Average high school GPA 3.1. SAT I Math middle 50% range 470-590. SAT I Verbal middle 50% range 430-580. ACT middle 50% range 20-25. TOEFL required of all international applicants, minimum TOEFL 550. **Basis for Candidate Selection:** *Very important factors considered include:* secondary school record, talent/ability. *Important factors considered include:* essays, standardized test scores. *Other factors considered include:* alumni/ae relation, character/personal qualities, extracurricular activities, interview, recommendations, volunteer work, work experience. **Freshman Admission Requirements:** High school diploma or GED is required. *Academic units required/recommended:* 4 English required, 4 English recommended, 3 math required, 4 math recommended, 2 science required, 4 science recommended, 1 science lab required, 4 science lab recommended, 2 foreign language recommended, 1 social studies required, 2 social studies recommended, 2 history required, 3 history recommended. **Freshman Admission Statistics:** 581 applied, 65% accepted, 39% of those accepted enrolled. **Transfer Admission Requirements:** *Items required:* high school transcript, college transcript, essay, statement of good standing from prior school. Minimum college GPA of 2.5 required. Lowest grade transferable C. **General Admission Information:** Application fee $50. Priority application deadline February 15. Nonfall registration accepted. Credit offered for CEEB Advanced Placement tests.

COSTS AND FINANCIAL AID

Tuition $22,292. Required fees $600. Average book expense $2,400. **Required Forms and Deadlines:** FAFSA and institution's own financial aid form. No deadline for regular filing. Priority filing deadline February 15. **Notification of Awards:** Applicants will be notified of awards on a rolling basis beginning on or about March 1. **Types of Aid:** *Need-based scholarships/grants:* Pell, SEOG, state scholarships/grants, private scholarships, the school's own gift aid. *Loans:* FFEL Subsidized Stafford, FFEL Unsubsidized Stafford, FFEL PLUS. **Student Employment:** Federal Work-Study Program available. Institutional employment available. Off-campus job opportunities are good. **Financial Aid Statistics:** 70% freshmen, 73% undergrads receive some form of aid. **Financial Aid Phone:** 310-665-6880.

See page 1152.

OTTAWA UNIVERSITY

1001 S. Cedar Street #17, Ottawa, KS 66067-3399
Phone: 785-242-5200 **E-mail:** admiss@ottawa.edu **CEEB Code:** 6547
Fax: 785-229-1008 **Web:** www.ottawa.edu **ACT Code:** 1446

This private school, which is affiliated with the American Baptist Church, was founded in 1865. It has a 64-acre campus.

STUDENTS AND FACULTY

Enrollment: 521. **Student Body:** Male 57%, female 43%, out-of-state 41%, international 6% (11 countries represented). **Ethnic Representation:** African American 11%, Asian 1%, Caucasian 84%, Hispanic 2%, Native American 2%. **Retention and Graduation:** 68% freshmen return for sophomore year. 17% freshmen graduate within 4 years. 15% grads go on to further study within 1 year. 26% grads pursue business degrees. 1% grads pursue law degrees. 2% grads pursue medical degrees. **Faculty:** 100% faculty teach undergrads.

ACADEMICS

Degrees: Bachelor's. **Academic Requirements:** General education including some course work in arts/fine arts, English (including composition), history, mathematics, sciences (biological or physical), social science. **Special Study Options:** Double major, English as a second language, internships, student-designed major, teacher certification program.

FACILITIES

Housing: All-female, all-male, apartments for married students. **Library Holdings:** 80,000 bound volumes. 320 periodicals. 21 microforms. 1,200 audiovisuals. **Special Academic Facilities/Equipment:** Art Collection, FM Radio Station. **Computers:** *Recommended operating system:* Windows 95. School-owned computers available for student use.

EXTRACURRICULARS

Activities: Choral groups, concert band, dance, drama/theater, jazz band, music ensembles, pep band, radio station, student government, student newspaper, yearbook. **Organizations:** 33 registered organizations, 3 honor societies, 4 religious organizations, 2 fraternities, 3 sororities. **Athletics (Intercollegiate):** *Men:* baseball, basketball, cheerleading, football, golf, indoor track, soccer, track & field. *Women:* basketball, cheerleading, indoor track, soccer, softball, track & field, volleyball.

ADMISSIONS

Selectivity Rating: 79 (of 100). **Freshman Academic Profile:** Average high school GPA 3.1. 7% in top 10% of high school class, 23% in top 25% of high school class, 73% in top 50% of high school class. 98% from public high schools. Average SAT I Math 540, SAT I Math middle 50% range 500-600. Average SAT I Verbal 570, SAT I Verbal middle 50% range 500-600. Average ACT 21, ACT middle 50% range 18-23. TOEFL required of all international applicants, minimum TOEFL 550. **Basis for Candidate Selection:** *Very important factors considered include:* class rank, secondary school record, standardized test scores. *Other factors considered include:* alumni/ae relation, character/personal qualities, essays, extracurricular activities, interview, recommendations, religious affiliation/commitment, talent/ability. **Freshman Admission Requirements:** High school diploma or GED is required. *Academic units required/recommended:* 16 total recommended; 4 English recommended, 3 math recommended, 2 science recommended, 2 foreign language recommended, 1 social studies recommended, 2 history recommended, 2 elective recommended. **Freshman Admission Statistics:** 630 applied, 68% accepted, 32% of those accepted enrolled. **Transfer Admission Requirements:** *Items required:* college transcript. Minimum college GPA of 2.5 required. Lowest grade transferable D. **General Admission Information:** Application fee $15. Priority application deadline April 1. Regular application deadline July 15. Nonfall registration accepted. Credit and/or placement offered for CEEB Advanced Placement tests.

COSTS AND FINANCIAL AID

Tuition $10,750. Room & board $4,640. Required fees $210. Average book expense $600. **Required Forms and Deadlines:** FAFSA, institution's own financial aid form and state aid form. **Types of Aid:** *Need-based scholarships/grants:* Pell, SEOG, state scholarships/grants, private scholarships, the school's own gift aid. *Loans:* FFEL Subsidized Stafford, FFEL Unsubsidized Stafford, FFEL PLUS, Federal Perkins, Federal Nursing, college/university loans from institutional funds. **Student Employment:** Federal Work-Study Program available. Institutional employment available. Off-campus job opportunities are excellent. **Financial Aid Statistics:** Average freshman grant $6,500. Average freshman loan $4,000. Average income from on-campus job $1,500. **Financial Aid Phone:** 785-242-5200.

OTTERBEIN COLLEGE

office of Admission, One Otterbein College, Westerville, OH 43081
Phone: 614-823-1500 **E-mail:** uotterb@otterbein.edu **CEEB Code:** 1597
Fax: 614-823-1200 **Web:** www.otterbein.edu **ACT Code:** 3318

This private school, which is affiliated with the Methodist Church, was founded in 1847. It has a 140-acre campus.

STUDENTS AND FACULTY

Enrollment: 2,624. **Student Body:** Male 34%, female 66%, out-of-state 11%, (26 countries represented). **Ethnic Representation:** African American 9%, Asian 1%, Caucasian 85%, Hispanic 1%. **Retention and Graduation:** 89% freshmen return for sophomore year. 2% grads pursue business degrees. 1% grads pursue law degrees. 4% grads pursue medical degrees. **Faculty:** Student/faculty ratio 13:1. 138 full-time faculty, 81% hold PhDs. 100% faculty teach undergrads.

ACADEMICS

Degrees: Bachelor's, master's. **Academic Requirements:** General education including some course work in arts/fine arts, English (including composition), foreign languages, history, humanities, mathematics, philosophy, sciences (biological or physical), social science. **Majors with Highest Enrollment:** Education, general; business administration/management; radio and television. **Disciplines with Highest Percentage of Degrees Awarded:** Business/marketing 19%, education 13%, communications/communication technologies 11%, visual and performing arts 11%, social sciences and history 9%. **Special Study Options:** Accelerated program, cooperative (work-study) program, cross registration, double major, student exchange program (domestic), honors program, internships, liberal arts/career combination, student-designed major, study abroad, teacher certification program, weekend college.

FACILITIES

Housing: All-female, all-male, apartments for single students, fraternities and/or sororities, theme housing. **Library Holdings:** 182,629 bound volumes. 1,012 periodicals. 312,944 microforms. 8,971 audiovisuals. **Special Academic Facilities/Equipment:** Language lab, horse stable, observatory and planetarium, Celestron 8-inch and 14-inch telescopes.

EXTRACURRICULARS

Activities: Choral groups, concert band, dance, drama/theater, jazz band, marching band, music ensembles, musical theater, opera, pep band, radio station, student government, student newspaper, symphony orchestra, television station, yearbook. **Organizations:** 90 registered organizations, 4 fraternities (27% men join), 6 sororities (27% women join). **Athletics (Intercollegiate):** *Men:* baseball, basketball, cheerleading, cross-country, equestrian, football, golf, indoor track, soccer, tennis, track & field. *Women:* basketball, cheerleading, cross-country, equestrian, golf, indoor track, soccer, softball, tennis, track & field, volleyball.

ADMISSIONS

Selectivity Rating: 72 (of 100). **Freshman Academic Profile:** Average high school GPA 3.3. Average SAT I Math 512. Average SAT I Verbal 524. Average ACT 23. TOEFL required of all international applicants, minimum TOEFL 500. **Basis for Candidate Selection:** *Important factors considered include:* class rank, secondary school record, standardized test scores. *Other factors considered include:* alumni/ae relation, character/personal qualities, essays, extracurricular activities, interview, minority status, recommendations, talent/ability, volunteer work, work experience. **Freshman Admission Requirements:** High school diploma or GED is required. *Academic units required/recommended:* 21 total recommended; 4 English recommended, 3 math recommended, 3 science recommended, 2 foreign language recommended, 3 social studies recommended. **Freshman Admission Statistics:** 2,185 applied, 81% accepted, 31% of those accepted enrolled. **Transfer Admission Requirements:** *Items required:* high school transcript, college transcript, standardized test scores. Minimum college GPA of 2.5 required. Lowest grade transferable C. **General Admission Information:** Application fee $25. Priority application deadline March 1. Nonfall registration accepted. Admission may be deferred for a maximum of 1 year. Credit and/or placement offered for CEEB Advanced Placement tests.

COSTS AND FINANCIAL AID

Tuition $16,911. Room & board $5,289. Average book expense $600. **Required Forms and Deadlines:** FAFSA. Priority filing deadline April 1. **Notification of Awards:** Applicants will be notified of awards on a rolling basis. **Types of Aid:** *Need-based scholarships/grants:* Pell, SEOG, state scholarships/grants, the school's own gift aid. *Loans:* Direct Subsidized Stafford, Direct Unsubsidized Stafford, Direct PLUS, Federal Perkins. **Student Employment:** Federal Work-Study Program available. Institutional employment available. Off-campus job opportunities are excellent. **Financial Aid Statistics:** Average income from on-campus job $1,500. **Financial Aid Phone:** 614-823-1502.

OUACHITA BAPTIST UNIVERSITY

410 Ouachita Street, Arkadelphia, AR 71998-0001
Phone: 870-245-5110 **E-mail:** admissions@alpha.obu.edu **CEEB Code:** 6549
Fax: 870-245-5500 **Web:** www.obu.edu **ACT Code:** 134

This private school, which is affiliated with the Southern Baptist Church, was founded in 1886. It has a 200-acre campus.

STUDENTS AND FACULTY

Enrollment: 1,536. **Student Body:** Male 46%, female 54%, out-of-state 42%, international 6%. **Ethnic Representation:** African American 3%, Caucasian 95%, Hispanic 1%. **Retention and Graduation:** 71% freshmen return for sophomore year. 41% freshmen graduate within 4 years. 33% grads go on to further study within 1 year. 4% grads pursue business degrees. 4% grads pursue law degrees. 9% grads pursue medical degrees. **Faculty:** 100% faculty teach undergrads.

ACADEMICS

Degrees: Bachelor's, terminal. **Academic Requirements:** General education including some course work in arts/fine arts, English (including composition), foreign languages, history, humanities, mathematics, sciences (biological or physical), social science, religion, physical education. **Special Study Options:** Cross registration, double major, dual enrollment, English as a second language, honors program, internships, study abroad, teacher certification program.

FACILITIES

Housing: All-female, all-male, apartments for married students, apartments for single students. **Library Holdings:** 119,437 bound volumes. 1,862 periodicals. 256,933 microforms. 8,043 audiovisuals. **Special Academic Facilities/Equipment:** Historical archives, Senator John McClellan collection, language lab, TV studio. **Computers:** School-owned computers available for student use.

EXTRACURRICULARS

Activities: Choral groups, concert band, drama/theater, marching band, music ensembles, musical theater, student government, student newspaper, television station, yearbook. **Organizations:** 60 registered organizations, 8 honor societies, 4 religious organizations, 5 fraternities (20% men join), 4 sororities (25% women join). **Athletics (Intercollegiate):** *Men:* baseball, basketball, cross-country, diving, football, golf, soccer, softball, swimming, tennis. *Women:* basketball, cross-country, diving, soccer, softball, swimming, tennis, volleyball.

ADMISSIONS

Selectivity Rating: 63 (of 100). **Freshman Academic Profile:** Average high school GPA 3.4. 32% in top 10% of high school class, 63% in top 25% of high

school class, 88% in top 50% of high school class. 95% from public high schools. Average SAT I Math 570, SAT I Math middle 50% range 438-624. Average SAT I Verbal 530, SAT I Verbal middle 50% range 423-662. Average ACT 23, ACT middle 50% range 20-27. TOEFL required of all international applicants, minimum TOEFL 550. **Basis for Candidate Selection:** *Very important factors considered include:* class rank, secondary school record, standardized test scores. *Important factors considered include:* interview. *Other factors considered include:* character/personal qualities, essays, extracurricular activities, recommendations, religious affiliation/commitment, talent/ability, volunteer work, work experience. **Freshman Admission Requirements:** High school diploma or GED is required. *Academic units required/recommended:* 4 English required, 2 math required, 3 math recommended, 2 science required, 3 science recommended, 2 foreign language recommended, 1 social studies required, 2 history required. **Freshman Admission Statistics:** 927 applied, 80% accepted, 49% of those accepted enrolled. **Transfer Admission Requirements:** *Items required:* college transcript, statement of good standing from prior school. Lowest grade transferable D. **General Admission Information:** Application fee $25. Nonfall registration accepted. Admission may be deferred for a maximum of 1 year. Credit offered for CEEB Advanced Placement tests.

COSTS AND FINANCIAL AID

Tuition $8,410. Room & board $3,100. Required fees $140. Average book expense $350. **Required Forms and Deadlines:** FAFSA and institution's own financial aid form. Financial aid filing deadline June 1. Priority filing deadline February 15. **Notification of Awards:** Applicants will be notified of awards on a rolling basis beginning on or about October 1. **Types of Aid:** *Need-based scholarships/grants:* Pell, SEOG, state scholarships/grants, private scholarships, the school's own gift aid. *Loans:* FFEL Subsidized Stafford, FFEL Unsubsidized Stafford, FFEL PLUS, Federal Perkins, college/university loans from institutional funds. **Student Employment:** Federal Work-Study Program available. Off-campus job opportunities are fair. **Financial Aid Statistics:** Average freshman grant $3,000. Average freshman loan $2,100. Average income from on-campus job $1,400. **Financial Aid Phone:** 870-245-5570.

OUR LADY OF THE HOLY CROSS COLLEGE

4123 Woodland Drive, New Orleans, LA 70131
Phone: 504-398-2175 **E-mail:** kkopecky@olhcc.edu **CEEB Code:** 6002
Fax: 504-391-2421 **Web:** www.olhcc.edu **ACT Code:** 1574

This private school, which is affiliated with the Roman Catholic Church, was founded in 1916. It has a 40-acre campus.

STUDENTS AND FACULTY

Enrollment: 1,199. **Student Body:** Male 22%, female 78%, out-of-state 0%, international 1% (0 countries represented). **Ethnic Representation:** African American 13%, Asian 3%, Caucasian 74%, Hispanic 5%, Native American 1%. **Retention and Graduation:** 63% freshmen return for sophomore year. **Faculty:** Student/faculty ratio 19:1. 38 full-time faculty, 60% hold PhDs.

ACADEMICS

Degrees: Associate's, bachelor's, master's, post-bachelor's certificate. **Academic Requirements:** General education including some course work in arts/fine arts, computer literacy, English (including composition), foreign languages, history, humanities, mathematics, philosophy, sciences (biological or physical), social science. **Classes:** 20-29 students in an average class. **Majors with Highest Enrollment:** Nursing/registered nurse training (RN, ASN, BSN, MSN); accounting and business/management; education, general. **Disciplines with Highest Percentage of Degrees Awarded:** Health professions and related sciences 30%, education 25%, business/marketing 18%, psychology 12%, liberal arts/general studies 6%. **Special Study Options:** Cross registration, distance learning, double major, dual enrollment, student exchange program (domestic), independent study, internships, liberal arts/career combination, study abroad, teacher certification program.

FACILITIES

Library Holdings: 83,631 bound volumes. 1,002 periodicals. 222,522 microforms. 11,949 audiovisuals. **Computers:** *Recommended operating system:* Windows NT/2000. School-owned computers available for student use.

EXTRACURRICULARS

Activities: Choral groups, drama/theater, literary magazine, student government, student newspaper, yearbook. **Organizations:** 18 registered organizations, 5 honor societies.

ADMISSIONS

Selectivity Rating: 63 (of 100). **Freshman Academic Profile:** 38% from public high schools. Average ACT 19. TOEFL required of all international applicants, minimum TOEFL 500. **Basis for Candidate Selection:** *Very important factors considered include:* secondary school record, standardized test scores. *Important factors considered include:* class rank, recommendations. *Other factors considered include:* minority status. **Freshman Admission Requirements:** High school diploma or GED is required. *Academic units required/recommended:* 16 total required; 4 English required, 2 math required, 2 science required, 2 foreign language required, 3 social studies required, 3 elective required. **Freshman Admission Statistics:** 320 applied, 97% accepted, 42% of those accepted enrolled. **Transfer Admission Requirements:** *Items required:* college transcript. Minimum high school GPA of 2.0 required. Minimum college GPA of 2.0 required. Lowest grade transferable C. **General Admission Information:** Application fee $15. Priority application deadline July 20. Nonfall registration accepted. Admission may be deferred for a maximum of 1 year. Placement offered for CEEB Advanced Placement tests.

COSTS AND FINANCIAL AID

Tuition $5,160. Required fees $400. Average book expense $0. **Required Forms and Deadlines:** FAFSA and institution's own financial aid form. Priority filing deadline April 15. **Notification of Awards:** Applicants will be notified of awards on or about July 2. **Types of Aid:** *Need-based scholarships/grants:* Pell, SEOG, state scholarships/grants, private scholarships, the school's own gift aid. *Loans:* FFEL Subsidized Stafford, FFEL Unsubsidized Stafford, FFEL PLUS. **Student Employment:** Federal Work-Study Program available. Off-campus job opportunities are good. **Financial Aid Statistics:** 33% freshmen, 54% undergrads receive some form of aid. Average freshman grant $674. Average freshman loan $2,625. Average income from on-campus job $1,238. **Financial Aid Phone:** 504-398-2164.

OUR LADY OF THE LAKE UNIVERSITY

Admissions Office, 411 South West 24th Street, San Antonio, TX 78207-4689
Phone: 210-434-6711 **E-mail:** admission@lake.ollusa.edu **CEEB Code:** 6550
Fax: 210-431-4036 **Web:** www.ollusa.edu **ACT Code:** 4140

This private school, which is affiliated with the Roman Catholic Church, was founded in 1895. It has a 75-acre campus.

STUDENTS AND FACULTY

Enrollment: 2,196. **Student Body:** Male 22%, female 78%, out-of-state 1%, international 1%. **Ethnic Representation:** African American 7%, Asian 1%, Caucasian 20%, Hispanic 68%. **Retention and Graduation:** 68% freshmen return for sophomore year. 14% freshmen graduate within 4 years. 30% grads go on to further study within 1 year. **Faculty:** Student/faculty ratio 15:1. 128 full-time faculty, 70% hold PhDs.

ACADEMICS

Degrees: Bachelor's, doctoral, master's. **Academic Requirements:** General education including some course work in arts/fine arts, computer literacy, English (including composition), history, humanities, mathematics, philosophy, sciences (biological or physical), social science, religion. **Classes:** 10-19 students in an average class. **Disciplines with Highest Percentage of Degrees Awarded:** Business/marketing 24%, psychology 13%, liberal arts/general studies 10%, education 7%, computer and information sciences 7%. **Special Study Options:** Cross registration, double major, dual enrollment, English as a second language, internships, teacher certification program, weekend college, summer terms.

FACILITIES

Housing: Coed, all-female, all-male, housing for disabled students. **Library Holdings:** 127,441 bound volumes. 32,047 periodicals. 7,177 microforms. 6,877 audiovisuals. **Special Academic Facilities/Equipment:** Lab school for children with language and learning disabilities, elementary demonstration school, intercultural institute for training and research, language lab. **Computers:** School-owned computers available for student use.

EXTRACURRICULARS

Activities: Choral groups, dance, drama/theater, music ensembles, student government, student newspaper, symphony orchestra, television station.

ADMISSIONS

Selectivity Rating: 72 (of 100). **Freshman Academic Profile:** Average high school GPA 3.2. 75% from public high schools. Average SAT I Math 472, SAT I Math middle 50% range 400-490. Average SAT I Verbal 490, SAT I Verbal middle 50% range 410-500. Average ACT 20, ACT middle 50% range 17-20.

TOEFL required of all international applicants, minimum TOEFL 525. **Basis for Candidate Selection:** *Very important factors considered include:* secondary school record, standardized test scores. *Important factors considered include:* class rank, recommendations. *Other factors considered include:* interview. **Freshman Admission Requirements:** High school diploma or GED is required. *Academic units required/recommended:* 16 total required; 4 English required, 2 math required, 2 science required, 2 foreign language required, 3 social studies required, 3 elective required. **Freshman Admission Statistics:** 2,285 applied, 61% accepted, 29% of those accepted enrolled. **Transfer Admission Requirements:** *Items required:* college transcript. Minimum high school GPA of 2.5 required. Minimum college GPA of 2.0 required. Lowest grade transferable D. **General Admission Information:** Application fee $25. Priority application deadline March 31. Nonfall registration accepted. Admission may be deferred for a maximum of 1 year. Credit and/or placement offered for CEEB Advanced Placement tests.

COSTS AND FINANCIAL AID

Tuition $12,528. Room & board $4,550. Required fees $258. Average book expense $720. **Required Forms and Deadlines:** FAFSA. No deadline for regular filing. **Notification of Awards:** Applicants will be notified of awards on a rolling basis beginning on or about February 15. **Types of Aid:** *Need-based scholarships/grants:* Pell, SEOG, state scholarships/grants, private scholarships, the school's own gift aid. *Loans:* FFEL Subsidized Stafford, FFEL Unsubsidized Stafford, FFEL PLUS, Federal Perkins, state loans, private loans. **Student Employment:** Federal Work-Study Program available. Institutional employment available. Off-campus job opportunities are good. **Financial Aid Statistics:** 98% freshmen, 89% undergrads receive some form of aid. Average freshman grant $2,100. Average freshman loan $2,952. Average income from on-campus job $1,206. **Financial Aid Phone:** 210-434-3960.

OXFORD COLLEGE OF EMORY UNIVERSITY

PO Box 1418, Oxford, GA 30054-1418
Phone: 770-784-8328 **E-mail:** oxadmission@learnlink.emory.edu **CEEB Code:** 5186
Fax: 770-784-8359 **Web:** www.emory.edu/OXFORD **ACT Code:** 851

This private school, which is affiliated with the Methodist Church, was founded in 1836. It has a 56-acre campus.

STUDENTS AND FACULTY

Enrollment: 554. **Student Body:** Out-of-state 43%, international 3%. **Ethnic Representation:** African American 13%, Asian 21%, Caucasian 54%, Hispanic 4%. **Retention and Graduation:** 89% freshmen return for sophomore year. **Faculty:** Student/faculty ratio 10:1. 43 full-time faculty, 93% hold PhDs. 100% faculty teach undergrads.

ACADEMICS

Degrees: Associate's, transfer. **Academic Requirements:** General education including some course work in English (including composition), foreign languages, history, humanities, mathematics, sciences (biological or physical), social science, physical education. **Classes:** 10-19 students in an average class. **Special Study Options:** Cross registration, double major, dual enrollment, independent study, internships, liberal arts/career combination, study abroad.

FACILITIES

Housing: Coed, all-female, housing for disabled students, themed housing (arts, diversity, and healthy living). **Library Holdings:** 80,099 bound volumes. 240 periodicals. 495 microforms. 556 audiovisuals. **Computers:** School-owned computers available for student use.

EXTRACURRICULARS

Activities: Choral groups, dance, drama/theater, literary magazine, music ensembles, student government, student newspaper, student-run film society, yearbook. **Organizations:** 53 registered organizations, 2 honor societies, 6 religious organizations. **Athletics (Intercollegiate):** *Men:* basketball, tennis. *Women:* soccer, tennis.

ADMISSIONS

Selectivity Rating: 63 (of 100). **Freshman Academic Profile:** Average ACT 26, ACT middle 50% range 24-28. SAT I Math middle 50% range 570-660. SAT I Verbal middle 50% range 550-650. TOEFL required of all international applicants, minimum TOEFL 600. **Basis for Candidate Selection:** *Very important factors considered include:* secondary school record. *Important factors considered include:* essays, extracurricular activities, recommendations, standardized test scores. *Other factors considered include:* alumni/ae relation, talent/ability. **Freshman Admission Requirements:** High school diploma or GED is required. *Academic units required/recommended:* 16 total required; 4 English required, 3 math required, 4 math recommended, 3 science required, 3 science lab required, 2 foreign language required, 2 social studies required, 5 elective required. **Freshman Admission Statistics:** 1,421 applied, 72% accepted, 27% of those accepted enrolled. **Transfer Admission Requirements:** *Items required:* college transcript, standardized test scores, statement of good standing from prior school. Minimum college GPA of 3.0 required. Lowest grade transferable C. **General Admission Information:** Application fee $40. Priority application deadline February 1. Admission may be deferred for a maximum of 1 year. Credit and placement offered for CEEB Advanced Placement tests.

COSTS AND FINANCIAL AID

Tuition $19,636. Room & board $5,978. Required fees $220. Average book expense $700. **Required Forms and Deadlines:** FAFSA and CSS/Financial Aid PROFILE. Financial aid filing deadline April 1. Priority filing deadline February 15. **Notification of Awards:** Applicants will be notified of awards on or about April 1. **Types of Aid:** *Need-based scholarships/grants:* Pell, SEOG, state scholarships/grants, private scholarships, the school's own gift aid. *Loans:* FFEL Subsidized Stafford, FFEL Unsubsidized Stafford, FFEL PLUS, Federal Perkins. **Student Employment:** Federal Work-Study Program available. Institutional employment available. Off-campus job opportunities are good. **Financial Aid Statistics:** 54% undergrads receive some form of aid. Average freshman grant $15,000. Average freshman loan $2,625. **Financial Aid Phone:** 770-784-8330.

PACE UNIVERSITY—NEW YORK CITY

1 Pace Plaza, New York, NY 10038
Phone: 212-346-1323 **E-mail:** infoctr@pace.edu **CEEB Code:** 2635
Fax: 212-346-1040 **Web:** www.pace.edu **ACT Code:** 2852

This private school was founded in 1906. It has a 1-acre campus.

STUDENTS AND FACULTY

Enrollment: 9,149. **Student Body:** Male 40%, female 60%, out-of-state 17%, international 4% (32 countries represented). **Ethnic Representation:** African American 12%, Asian 13%, Caucasian 46%, Hispanic 12%. **Retention and Graduation:** 77% freshmen return for sophomore year. 35% freshmen graduate within 4 years. **Faculty:** Student/faculty ratio 15:1. 438 full-time faculty, 87% hold PhDs.

ACADEMICS

Degrees: Associate's, bachelor's, certificate, diploma, doctoral, first professional, first professional certificate, master's, post-bachelor's certificate, post-master's certificate. **Academic Requirements:** General education including some course work in arts/fine arts, computer literacy, English (including composition), foreign languages, history, humanities, mathematics, philosophy, sciences (biological or physical), social science, speech. **Classes:** 20-29 students in an average class. Under 10 students in an average lab/discussion section. **Majors with Highest Enrollment:** Accounting; finance, general; information science/studies. **Disciplines with Highest Percentage of Degrees Awarded:** Business/marketing 46%, computer and information sciences 20%, health professions and related sciences 7%, communications/communication technologies 5%, psychology 5%. **Special Study Options:** Accelerated program, cooperative (work-study) program, cross registration, distance learning, double major, dual enrollment, English as a second language, honors program, independent study, internships, study abroad, teacher certification program, evening and freshman studies programs, pre-freshman summer program.

FACILITIES

Housing: Coed, apartments for single students, apartments housing for upperclassmen. **Library Holdings:** 811,957 bound volumes. 2,303 periodicals. 75,002 microforms. 976 audiovisuals. **Special Academic Facilities/Equipment:** Laboratory Theatre, Communication Center, language center, Center for the Arts, art gallery, English Language Institute. **Computers:** School-owned computers available for student use.

EXTRACURRICULARS

Activities: Choral groups, dance, drama/theater, literary magazine, musical theater, radio station, student government, student newspaper, student-run film society, television station, yearbook. **Organizations:** 60 registered organizations, 13 honor societies, 4 religious organizations, 6 fraternities (5% men join), 7 sororities (5% women join). **Athletics (Intercollegiate):** *Men:* baseball, basketball, cross-country, equestrian, football, golf, indoor track, lacrosse, tennis, track & field. *Women:* basketball, cross-country, equestrian, golf, indoor track, soccer, softball, tennis, track & field, volleyball.

ADMISSIONS

Selectivity Rating: 76 (of 100). **Freshman Academic Profile:** Average high school GPA 3.0. 13% in top 10% of high school class, 40% in top 25% of high school class, 83% in top 50% of high school class. 70% from public high schools. Average SAT I Math 537, SAT I Math middle 50% range 480-590. Average SAT I Verbal 518, SAT I Verbal middle 50% range 470-570. Average ACT 21, ACT middle 50% range 19-25. TOEFL required of all international applicants, minimum TOEFL 450. **Basis for Candidate Selection:** *Very important factors considered include:* secondary school record, standardized test scores. *Important factors considered include:* class rank. *Other factors considered include:* alumni/ae relation, character/personal qualities, essays, extracurricular activities, recommendations, talent/ability, volunteer work, work experience. **Freshman Admission Requirements:** High school diploma or GED is required. *Academic units required/recommended:* 16 total required; 20 total recommended; 4 English required, 4 English recommended, 3 math required, 4 math recommended, 2 science required, 2 science recommended, 2 science lab required, 2 science lab recommended, 2 foreign language required, 3 foreign language recommended, 1 social studies required, 2 social studies recommended, 2 history required, 2 history recommended, 2 elective required, 3 elective recommended. **Freshman Admission Statistics:** 7,644 applied, 79% accepted, 25% of those accepted enrolled. **Transfer Admission Requirements:** *Items required:* high school transcript, college transcript. Minimum college GPA of 2.5 required. Lowest grade transferable C. **General Admission Information:** Application fee $45. Priority application deadline February 1. Nonfall registration accepted. Admission may be deferred for a maximum of 1 year. Credit offered for CEEB Advanced Placement tests.

COSTS AND FINANCIAL AID

Tuition $17,800. Room & board $7,720. Required fees $380. Average book expense $720. **Required Forms and Deadlines:** FAFSA and state aid form. Priority filing deadline February 15. **Notification of Awards:** Applicants will be notified of awards on a rolling basis beginning on or about April 1. **Types of Aid:** *Need-based scholarships/grants:* Pell, SEOG, state scholarships/grants, private scholarships, the school's own gift aid, Federal Nursing. *Loans:* Direct Subsidized Stafford, Direct Unsubsidized Stafford, Direct PLUS, Federal Perkins, Federal Nursing. **Student Employment:** Federal Work-Study Program available. Institutional employment available. Off-campus job opportunities are excellent. **Financial Aid Statistics:** 81% freshmen, 84% undergrads receive some form of aid. Average freshman grant $7,438. Average freshman loan $4,849. Average income from on-campus job $3,600. **Financial Aid Phone:** 212-346-1300.

PACE UNIVERSITY—PLEASANTVILLE/BRIARCLIFF

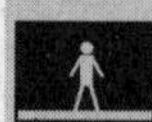

861 Bedford Road, Pleasantville, NY 10570
Phone: 914-773-3746 **E-mail:** infoctr@pace.edu **CEEB Code:** 2685
Fax: 914-773-3851 **Web:** www.pace.edu **ACT Code:** 2855

This private school was founded in 1906. It has a 198-acre campus.

STUDENTS AND FACULTY

Enrollment: 3,245. **Student Body:** Male 43%, female 57%, out-of-state 11%, international 3% (42 countries represented). **Ethnic Representation:** African American 10%, Asian 6%, Caucasian 58%, Hispanic 10%. **Retention and Graduation:** 75% freshmen return for sophomore year. 37% freshmen graduate within 4 years. **Faculty:** Student/faculty ratio 15:1. 151 full-time faculty, 79% hold PhDs.

ACADEMICS

Degrees: Associate's, bachelor's, certificate, diploma, doctoral, first professional, first professional certificate, master's, post-bachelor's certificate, post-master's certificate. **Academic Requirements:** General education including some course work in arts/fine arts, computer literacy, English (including composition), foreign languages, history, humanities, mathematics, philosophy, sciences (biological or physical), social science, speech. **Classes:** 20-29 students in an average class. Under 10 students in an average lab/discussion section. **Majors with Highest Enrollment:** Accounting; finance, general; computer science. **Disciplines with Highest Percentage of Degrees Awarded:** Business/marketing 42%, computer and information sciences 17%, health professions and related sciences 9%, psychology 5%, education 4%. **Special Study Options:** Accelerated program, cooperative (work-study) program, cross registration, distance learning, double major, dual enrollment, English as a second language, honors program, independent study, internships, study abroad, teacher certification program, evening and freshman studies program, pre-freshman summer program.

FACILITIES

Housing: Coed, apartments for single students, Apartment style for upperclassmen. **Library Holdings:** 706,132 bound volumes. 2,637 periodicals. 71,030 microforms. 976 audiovisuals. **Special Academic Facilities/Equipment:** Center for the arts, art gallery, laboratory theatre, communication center, language center, environmental center, English language institute. **Computers:** School-owned computers available for student use.

EXTRACURRICULARS

Activities: Choral groups, dance, drama/theater, literary magazine, musical theater, radio station, student government, student newspaper, student-run film society, television station, yearbook. **Organizations:** 40 registered organizations, 7 honor societies, 4 religious organizations, 7 fraternities (4% men join), 6 sororities (4% women join). **Athletics (Intercollegiate):** *Men:* baseball, basketball, cross-country, equestrian, football, golf, indoor track, lacrosse, tennis, track & field. *Women:* basketball, cross-country, equestrian, golf, indoor track, soccer, softball, tennis, track & field, volleyball.

ADMISSIONS

Selectivity Rating: 63 (of 100). **Freshman Academic Profile:** 20% in top 10% of high school class, 52% in top 25% of high school class, 86% in top 50% of high school class. 70% from public high schools. Average SAT I Math 540, SAT I Math middle 50% range 460-580. Average SAT I Verbal 514, SAT I Verbal middle 50% range 450-550. Average ACT 21, ACT middle 50% range 19-23. TOEFL required of all international applicants, minimum TOEFL 450. **Basis for Candidate Selection:** *Very important factors considered include:* secondary school record, standardized test scores. *Important factors considered include:* class rank. *Other factors considered include:* alumni/ae relation, character/personal qualities, essays, extracurricular activities, recommendations, talent/ability, volunteer work, work experience. **Freshman Admission Requirements:** High school diploma or GED is required. *Academic units required/recommended:* 16 total required; 20 total recommended; 4 English required, 4 English recommended, 3 math required, 4 math recommended, 2 science required, 2 science recommended, 2 science lab required, 2 science lab recommended, 2 foreign language required, 3 foreign language recommended, 1 social studies required, 2 social studies recommended, 2 history required, 2 history recommended, 2 elective required, 3 elective recommended. **Freshman Admission Statistics:** 2,051 applied, 92% accepted, 30% of those accepted enrolled. **Transfer Admission Requirements:** *Items required:* high school transcript, college transcript. Minimum college GPA of 2.5 required. Lowest grade transferable C. **General Admission Information:** Application fee $45. Priority application deadline February 1. Nonfall registration accepted. Admission may be deferred for a maximum of 1 year. Credit offered for CEEB Advanced Placement tests.

COSTS AND FINANCIAL AID

Tuition $16,650. Room & board $7,070. Required fees $380. Average book expense $720. **Required Forms and Deadlines:** FAFSA and state aid form. Priority filing deadline February 15. **Notification of Awards:** Applicants will be notified of awards on a rolling basis beginning on or about April 1. **Types of Aid:** *Need-based scholarships/grants:* Pell, SEOG, state scholarships/grants, private scholarships, the school's own gift aid, Federal Nursing. *Loans:* Direct Subsidized Stafford, Direct Unsubsidized Stafford, Direct PLUS, Federal Perkins, Federal Nursing. **Student Employment:** Off-campus job opportunities are excellent. **Financial Aid Statistics:** 74% freshmen, 84% undergrads receive some form of aid. Average freshman grant $5,011. Average freshman loan $3,392. Average income from on-campus job $3,600. **Financial Aid Phone:** 212-346-1300.

PACE UNIVERSITY—WHITE PLAINS

78 North Broadway, White Plains, NY 10603
Phone: 914-422-4000 **E-mail:** wpgrad@pace.edu **CEEB Code:** 2635
Fax: 914-773-3851 **Web:** www.pace.edu **ACT Code:** 2852

This private school was founded in 1906. It has a 13-acre campus.

STUDENTS AND FACULTY

Student Body: International students represent 42 countries. **Faculty:** Student/faculty ratio 12:1. 66 full-time faculty, 59% hold PhDs.

ACADEMICS

Degrees: Doctoral, first professional, master's, post-bachelor's certificate, post-master's certificate. **Special Study Options:** Cross registration, distance learning, double major, independent study, teacher certification program.

FACILITIES

Library Holdings: 161,207 bound volumes. 1,234 periodicals. 666,532 microforms. 482 audiovisuals. **Special Academic Facilities/Equipment:** Center for the arts, lab theatre, communication center, language center. **Computers:** School-owned computers available for student use.

EXTRACURRICULARS

Organizations: 106 registered organizations, 8 honor societies, 4 religious organizations, 5 fraternities, 4 sororities. **Athletics (Intercollegiate):** *Women:* basketball, cross-country, softball, tennis, volleyball.

ADMISSIONS

Selectivity Rating: 70 (of 100). **Freshman Academic Profile:** 25% in top 10% of high school class, 57% in top 25% of high school class, 87% in top 50% of high school class. **Freshman Admission Requirements: General Admission Information:** Application fee $35. Priority application deadline February 1. Nonfall registration accepted.

COSTS AND FINANCIAL AID

Student Employment: Federal Work-Study Program available. Off-campus job opportunities are excellent. **Financial Aid Phone:** 212-346-1300.

PACIFIC LUTHERAN UNIVERSITY

Office of Admissions, Tacoma, WA 98447-0003
Phone: 253-535-7151 **E-mail:** admissions@plu.edu **CEEB Code:** 4597
Fax: 253-536-5136 **Web:** www.plu.edu **ACT Code:** 4470

This private school, which is affiliated with the Lutheran Church, was founded in 1890. It has a 126-acre campus.

STUDENTS AND FACULTY

Enrollment: 3,133. **Student Body:** Male 37%, female 63%, out-of-state 29%, international 7%. **Ethnic Representation:** African American 2%, Asian 6%, Caucasian 82%, Hispanic 2%, Native American 1%. **Retention and Graduation:** 81% freshmen return for sophomore year. 47% freshmen graduate within 4 years. 19% grads go on to further study within 1 year. **Faculty:** Student/faculty ratio 13:1. 189 full-time faculty, 93% hold PhDs. 100% faculty teach undergrads.

ACADEMICS

Degrees: Bachelor's, master's, post-bachelor's certificate, post-master's certificate. **Academic Requirements:** General education including some course work in arts/fine arts, English (including composition), foreign languages, mathematics, philosophy, sciences (biological or physical), social science, religious studies, critical conversation, perspectives on diversity. **Classes:** 10-19 students in an average class. 10-19 students in an average lab/discussion section. **Majors with Highest Enrollment:** Business administration/management; education, general; biology/biological sciences, general. **Disciplines with Highest Percentage of Degrees Awarded:** Business/marketing 19%, education 16%, social sciences and history 9%, health professions and related sciences 9%, communications/communication technologies 6%. **Special Study Options:** Cooperative (work-study) program, double major, English as a second language, student exchange program (domestic), honors program, independent study, internships, liberal arts/career combination, student-designed major, study abroad, teacher certification program.

FACILITIES

Housing: Coed, all-female, apartments for married students, apartments for single students. **Library Holdings:** 367,628 bound volumes. 1,949 periodicals. 232,505 microforms. 13,965 audiovisuals. **Special Academic Facilities/Equipment:** Mary Baker Russell Music Center, Wekell Art Gallery, Keck Observatory, Rieke Science Center, Scandinavian Cultural Center. **Computers:** School-owned computers available for student use.

EXTRACURRICULARS

Activities: Choral groups, concert band, dance, drama/theater, jazz band, literary magazine, music ensembles, musical theater, opera, pep band, radio station, student government, student newspaper, student-run film society, symphony orchestra, television station, yearbook. **Organizations:** 58 registered organizations, 8 religious organizations. **Athletics (Intercollegiate):** *Men:* baseball, basketball, crew, cross-country, football, golf, soccer, swimming, tennis, track & field, volleyball, wrestling. *Women:* basketball, crew, cross-country, golf, soccer, softball, swimming, tennis, track & field, volleyball.

ADMISSIONS

Selectivity Rating: 74 (of 100). **Freshman Academic Profile:** Average high school GPA 3.6. 35% in top 10% of high school class, 66% in top 25% of high school class, 90% in top 50% of high school class. Average SAT I Math 558, SAT I Math middle 50% range 500-610. Average SAT I Verbal 559, SAT I Verbal middle 50% range 500-610. Average ACT 23, ACT middle 50% range 20-26. TOEFL required of all international applicants, minimum TOEFL 550. **Basis for Candidate Selection:** *Very important factors considered include:* essays, secondary school record. *Important factors considered include:* character/personal qualities, class rank, extracurricular activities, recommendations, standardized test scores, talent/ability, volunteer work. *Other factors considered include:* interview, work experience. **Freshman Admission Requirements:** High school diploma or GED is required. *Academic units required/recommended:* 17 total required; 6 total recommended; 4 English required, 2 math required, 3 math recommended, 2 science required, 2 science lab required, 2 foreign language required, 3 foreign language recommended, 2 social studies required, 3 elective required. **Freshman Admission Statistics:** 1,926 applied, 81% accepted, 40% of those accepted enrolled. **Transfer Admission Requirements:** *Items required:* high school transcript, college transcript, essay. Minimum college GPA of 2.5 required. Lowest grade transferable C-. **General Admission Information:** Application fee $35. Priority application deadline March 1. Nonfall registration accepted. Admission may be deferred for a maximum of 2 years. Credit and/or placement offered for CEEB Advanced Placement tests.

COSTS AND FINANCIAL AID

Tuition $18,500. Room & board $5,870. Required fees $0. Average book expense $720. **Required Forms and Deadlines:** FAFSA. Priority filing deadline January 31. **Notification of Awards:** Applicants will be notified of awards on a rolling basis beginning on or about April 1. **Types of Aid:** *Need-based scholarships/grants:* Pell, SEOG, state scholarships/grants, private scholarships, the school's own gift aid, Federal Nursing. *Loans:* FFEL Subsidized Stafford, FFEL Unsubsidized Stafford, FFEL PLUS, Federal Perkins, Federal Nursing, state loans, college/university loans from institutional funds. **Student Employment:** Federal Work-Study Program available. Institutional employment available. Off-campus job opportunities are excellent. **Financial Aid Statistics:** 68% freshmen, 70% undergrads receive some form of aid. Average freshman grant $10,782. Average freshman loan $4,048. Average income from on-campus job $1,972. **Financial Aid Phone:** 253-535-7161.

PACIFIC NORTHWEST COLLEGE OF ART

1241 NW Johnson Street, Portland, OR 97209
Phone: 503-821-8972 **E-mail:** admissions@pnca.edu **CEEB Code:** 4504
Fax: 503-821-8978 **Web:** www.pnca.edu **ACT Code:** 3477

This private school was founded in 1909. It has a 1-acre campus.

STUDENTS AND FACULTY

Enrollment: 298. **Student Body:** Male 43%, female 57%, out-of-state 20%, international 2%. **Ethnic Representation:** African American 2%, Asian 5%, Caucasian 88%, Hispanic 4%, Native American 2%. **Retention and Graduation:** 54% freshmen return for sophomore year. 21% freshmen graduate within 4 years. **Faculty:** Student/faculty ratio 12:1. 14 full-time faculty, 85% hold PhDs. 100% faculty teach undergrads.

ACADEMICS

Degrees: Bachelor's, certificate. **Academic Requirements:** General education including some course work in arts/fine arts, computer literacy, English (including composition), history, humanities, mathematics, sciences (biological or physical), social science, art history. **Classes:** 10-19 students in an average class. **Majors with Highest Enrollment:** Graphic design; photography; painting. **Disciplines with Highest Percentage of Degrees Awarded:** Visual and performing arts 100%. **Special Study Options:** Cooperative (work-study) program, cross registration, student exchange program (domestic), independent study, internships, student-designed major, study abroad.

FACILITIES

Library Holdings: 12,716 bound volumes. 65 periodicals. 0 microforms. 62,300 audiovisuals. **Special Academic Facilities/Equipment:** Student galleries, darkrooms, student painting studios, printmaking studio, computer labs. **Computers:** *Recommended operating system:* Mac. School-owned computers available for student use.

EXTRACURRICULARS

Activities: Student government, student-run film society. **Organizations:** 2 registered organizations.

ADMISSIONS

Selectivity Rating: 72 (of 100). **Freshman Academic Profile:** Average high school GPA 3.2. 0% in top 10% of high school class, 23% in top 25% of high school class, 46% in top 50% of high school class. 89% from public high schools. Average SAT I Math 509, SAT I Math middle 50% range 500-550. Average SAT I Verbal 531, SAT I Verbal middle 50% range 490-580. Average ACT 22, ACT middle 50% range 20-23. TOEFL required of all international applicants, minimum TOEFL 550. **Basis for Candidate Selection:** *Very important factors considered include:* talent/ability. *Important factors considered include:* essays, interview, recommendations, secondary school record. *Other factors considered include:* character/personal qualities, extracurricular activities. **Freshman Admission Requirements:** High school diploma or GED is required. **Freshman Admission Statistics:** 55 applied, 82% accepted, 40% of those accepted enrolled. **Transfer Admission Requirements:** *Items required:* college transcript, essay. Minimum college GPA of 2.0 required. Lowest grade transferable C. **General Admission Information:** Application fee $35. Priority application deadline March 1. Nonfall registration accepted. Admission may be deferred for a maximum of 2 years. Credit and/or placement offered for CEEB Advanced Placement tests.

COSTS AND FINANCIAL AID

Tuition $13,370. Required fees $787. Average book expense $794. **Required Forms and Deadlines:** FAFSA. Financial aid filing deadline August 30. Priority filing deadline March 1. **Notification of Awards:** Applicants will be notified of awards on a rolling basis beginning on or about April 1. **Types of Aid:** *Need-based scholarships/grants:* Pell, SEOG, state scholarships/grants, private scholarships, the school's own gift aid. *Loans:* FFEL Subsidized Stafford, FFEL Unsubsidized Stafford, FFEL PLUS. **Student Employment:** Federal Work-Study Program available. Off-campus job opportunities are good. **Financial Aid Statistics:** 82% freshmen, 57% undergrads receive some form of aid. Average freshman grant $3,851. Average freshman loan $5,741. Average income from on-campus job $1,000. **Financial Aid Phone:** 503-821-8972.

PACIFIC OAKS COLLEGE

5 Westmoreland Place, Pasadena, CA 91103
Phone: 626-397-1349 **E-mail:** admissions@pacificoaks.edu
Fax: 626-685-2531 **Web:** www.pacificoaks.edu

This private school was founded in 1945.

STUDENTS AND FACULTY

Enrollment: 258. **Student Body:** Out-of-state 19%, international students represent 7 countries. **Ethnic Representation:** African American 12%, Asian 4%, Caucasian 40%, Hispanic 29%, Native American 2%. **Faculty:** Student/faculty ratio 7:1. 29 full-time faculty, 58% hold PhDs. 100% faculty teach undergrads.

ACADEMICS

Degrees: Bachelor's, master's, post-bachelor's certificate, post-master's certificate. **Academic Requirements:** General education including some course work in social science. **Classes:** 10-19 students in an average class. **Disciplines with Highest Percentage of Degrees Awarded:** Social sciences and history 100%. **Special Study Options:** Accelerated program, distance learning, dual enrollment, independent study, student-designed major, teacher certification program, weekend college.

FACILITIES

Library Holdings: 19,500 bound volumes. 84 periodicals. 0 microforms. 197 audiovisuals. **Computers:** School-owned computers available for student use.

EXTRACURRICULARS

Activities: Student government. **Organizations:** 3 registered organizations.

ADMISSIONS

Selectivity Rating: 63 (of 100). **Freshman Academic Profile:** 0% from public high schools. TOEFL required of all international applicants, minimum TOEFL 550. **Freshman Admission Requirements:** High school diploma or GED is required. **Transfer Admission Requirements:** *Items required:* college transcript, essay. Minimum college GPA of 2.0 required. Lowest grade transferable C. **General Admission Information:** Application fee $55. Priority application deadline April 15. Regular application deadline June 1. Admission may be deferred for a maximum of 2 years.

COSTS AND FINANCIAL AID

Tuition $13,800. Required fees $60. Average book expense $0. **Required Forms and Deadlines:** FAFSA, institution's own financial aid form, state aid form, noncustodial (divorced/separated) parent's statement and H. Financial aid filing deadline April 15. Priority filing deadline April 15. **Notification of Awards:** Applicants will be notified of awards on a rolling basis beginning on or about May 1. **Types of Aid:** *Need-based scholarships/grants:* Pell, SEOG, state scholarships/grants, private scholarships, the school's own gift aid. *Loans:* FFEL Subsidized Stafford, FFEL Unsubsidized Stafford, FFEL PLUS, Federal Perkins. **Student Employment:** Federal Work-Study Program available. Institutional employment available. Off-campus job opportunities are good. **Financial Aid Statistics:** 40% undergrads receive some form of aid. **Financial Aid Phone:** 626-397-1350.

PACIFIC UNION COLLEGE

Enrollment Services, Angwin, CA 94508
Phone: 800-862-7080 **E-mail:** enroll@puc.edu **CEEB Code:** 4600
Fax: 707-965-6432 **Web:** www.puc.edu **ACT Code:** 362

This private school, which is affiliated with the Seventh-Day Adventist Church, was founded in 1882. It has a 200-acre campus.

STUDENTS AND FACULTY

Enrollment: 1,453. **Student Body:** Male 44%, female 56%, out-of-state 11%, international 10% (35 countries represented). **Ethnic Representation:** African American 6%, Asian 22%, Caucasian 52%, Hispanic 11%. **Faculty:** Student/faculty ratio 13:1. 106 full-time faculty, 47% hold PhDs. 100% faculty teach undergrads.

ACADEMICS

Degrees: Associate's, bachelor's, first professional, master's. **Academic Requirements:** General education including some course work in arts/fine arts, computer literacy, English (including composition), history, mathematics, philosophy, sciences (biological or physical), social science. **Classes:** 10-19 students in an average class. Under 10 students in an average lab/discussion section. **Disciplines with Highest Percentage of Degrees Awarded:** Business/marketing 25%, health professions and related sciences 16%, education 8%, biological life sciences 7%, visual and performing arts 7%. **Special Study Options:** Cooperative (work-study) program, double major, dual enrollment, English as a second language, external degree program, honors program, independent study, internships, liberal arts/career combination, student-designed major, study abroad, teacher certification program.

FACILITIES

Housing: All-female, all-male, apartments for married students. **Library Holdings:** 165,321 bound volumes. 839 periodicals. 119,612 microforms. 55,502 audiovisuals. **Special Academic Facilities/Equipment:** Art gallery, natural history collection, Pitcairn Island studies center, on-campus elementary and high schools, airport, flight training facility, observatory. **Computers:** School-owned computers available for student use.

EXTRACURRICULARS

Activities: Choral groups, concert band, drama/theater, literary magazine, music ensembles, musical theater, radio station, student government, student newspaper, student-run film society, symphony orchestra, yearbook. **Organizations:** 22 registered organizations, 8 honor societies. **Athletics (Intercollegiate):** *Men:* basketball, cross-country, volleyball. *Women:* basketball, cross-country, volleyball.

ADMISSIONS

Selectivity Rating: 76 (of 100). **Freshman Academic Profile:** SAT I Math middle 50% range 400-640. SAT I Verbal middle 50% range 430-680. ACT middle 50% range 18-27. TOEFL required of all international applicants, minimum TOEFL 525. **Basis for Candidate Selection:** *Very important factors considered include:* recommendations. *Important factors considered include:* character/personal qualities, secondary school record. *Other factors considered include:* interview, religious affiliation/commitment. **Freshman Admission Requirements:** High school diploma or GED is required. *Academic units required/recommended:* 8 total required; 4 English required, 2 math required, 3 math recommended, 1 science required, 3 science recommended, 2 foreign language recommended, 1 history required, 2 history recommended. **Freshman Admission Statistics:** 1,183 applied, 35% accepted, 93% of those accepted enrolled. **Transfer Admission Requirements:** *Items required:* high school transcript, college transcript. Minimum college GPA of 2.0 required. Lowest grade transferable C-. **General Admission Information:** Application fee $30. Nonfall registration accepted. Admission may be deferred for a maximum of 1 year. Credit offered for CEEB Advanced Placement tests.

COSTS AND FINANCIAL AID

Tuition $17,235. Room & board $4,902. Required fees $120. Average book expense $1,224. **Required Forms and Deadlines:** FAFSA, institution's own financial aid form, state aid form, business/farm supplement and Federal tax returns. No deadline for regular filing. **Notification of Awards:** Applicants will be notified of awards on a rolling basis. **Types of Aid:** *Need-based scholarships/ grants:* Pell, SEOG, state scholarships/grants, the school's own gift aid. *Loans:* Direct Subsidized Stafford, Direct Unsubsidized Stafford, Direct PLUS, FFEL Subsidized Stafford, FFEL Unsubsidized Stafford, FFEL PLUS, Federal Perkins, college/university loans from institutional funds. **Student Employment:** Federal Work-Study Program available. Institutional employment available. Off-campus job opportunities are good. **Financial Aid Statistics:** 75% freshmen, 90% undergrads receive some form of aid. Average freshman grant $8,438. Average freshman loan $4,025. Average income from on-campus job $1,200. **Financial Aid Phone:** 707-965-7200.

PACIFIC UNIVERSITY

2043 College Way, Forest Grove, OR 97116
Phone: 503-352-2218 **E-mail:** admissions@pacificu.edu **CEEB Code:** 4601
Fax: 503-352-2975 **Web:** www.pacificu.edu

This private school, which is affiliated with the United Church of Christ, was founded in 1849. It has a 60-acre campus.

STUDENTS AND FACULTY

Enrollment: 1,173. **Student Body:** Male 40%, female 60%, out-of-state 55%, international 1%. **Ethnic Representation:** Asian 21%, Caucasian 73%, Hispanic 3%, Native American 1%. **Retention and Graduation:** 75% freshmen return for sophomore year. 45% freshmen graduate within 4 years. 34% grads go on to further study within 1 year. 2% grads pursue business degrees. **Faculty:** Student/faculty ratio 11:1. 87 full-time faculty, 86% hold PhDs. 100% faculty teach undergrads.

ACADEMICS

Degrees: Bachelor's, doctoral, first professional, master's. **Academic Requirements:** General education including some course work in arts/fine arts, English (including composition), foreign languages, humanities, mathematics, sciences (biological or physical), social science, cross cultural studies. **Classes:** 10-19 students in an average class. 10-19 students in an average lab/discussion section. **Majors with Highest Enrollment:** Biology/ biological sciences, general; business administration/management; kinesiology and exercise science. **Disciplines with Highest Percentage of Degrees Awarded:** Business/marketing 12%, biological life sciences 11%, social sciences and history 11%, physical sciences 10%, parks and recreation 10%. **Special Study Options:** Cross registration, double major, English as a second language, student exchange program (domestic), honors program, independent study, internships, liberal arts/career combination, study abroad, teacher certification program.

FACILITIES

Housing: Coed, apartments for married students, apartments for single students, housing for disabled students, cooperative housing, Houses (limited number) available for married students. **Library Holdings:** 244,691 bound volumes. 1,180 periodicals. 60,065 microforms. 5,715 audiovisuals. **Special Academic Facilities/Equipment:** State History Museum, performing arts center, media center, humanitarian center, Holocaust Resource Center, politics/ law forum, Berglund Center for Internet Studies, electron microscopes. **Computers:** School-owned computers available for student use.

EXTRACURRICULARS

Activities: Choral groups, concert band, dance, drama/theater, jazz band, literary magazine, music ensembles, musical theater, radio station, student government, student newspaper, student-run film society, yearbook. **Organizations:** 40 registered organizations, 3 fraternities (4% men join), 3 sororities (8% women join). **Athletics (Intercollegiate):** *Men:* baseball, basketball, cross-country, golf, soccer, tennis, track & field, wrestling. *Women:* basketball, cross-country, golf, soccer, softball, tennis, track & field, volleyball.

ADMISSIONS

Selectivity Rating: 73 (of 100). **Freshman Academic Profile:** Average high school GPA 3.5. 31% in top 10% of high school class, 60% in top 25% of high school class, 90% in top 50% of high school class. 80% from public high schools. Average SAT I Math 560, SAT I Math middle 50% range 510-610. Average SAT I Verbal 550, SAT I Verbal middle 50% range 500-610. Average ACT 24, ACT middle 50% range 22-27. TOEFL required of all international applicants, minimum TOEFL 550, **Basis for Candidate Selection:** *Very important factors considered include:* recommendations, secondary school record, standardized test scores. *Important factors considered include:* class rank, essays, interview, volunteer work. *Other factors considered include:* alumni/ae relation, character/personal qualities, extracurricular activities, minority status, talent/ability, work experience. **Freshman Admission Requirements:** High school diploma or GED is required. *Academic units required/recommended:* 21 total recommended; 4 English recommended, 3 math recommended, 3 science recommended, 1 science lab recommended, 2 foreign language recommended, 3 social studies recommended, 1 history recommended, 4 elective recommended. **Freshman Admission Statistics:** 1,166 applied, 87% accepted, 27% of those accepted enrolled. **Transfer Admission Requirements:** *Items required:* college transcript, essay. Minimum college GPA of 2.7 required. Lowest grade transferable C-. **General Admission Information:** Application fee $30. Priority application deadline February 15. Regular application deadline August 15. Nonfall registration accepted. Admission may be deferred for a maximum of 1 year. Credit and/or placement offered for CEEB Advanced Placement tests.

COSTS AND FINANCIAL AID

Required Forms and Deadlines: FAFSA. Priority filing deadline February 15. **Notification of Awards:** Applicants will be notified of awards on a rolling basis beginning on or about March 1. **Types of Aid:** *Need-based scholarships/ grants:* Pell, SEOG, state scholarships/grants, private scholarships, the school's own gift aid. *Loans:* Direct Subsidized Stafford, Direct Unsubsidized Stafford, Direct PLUS, Federal Perkins, private alternative Loan. **Student Employment:** Federal Work-Study Program available. Institutional employment available. Off-campus job opportunities are good. **Financial Aid Statistics:** 77% freshmen, 78% undergrads receive some form of aid. Average freshman grant $10,594. Average freshman loan $4,564. Average income from on-campus job $1,179. **Financial Aid Phone:** 503-352-2222.

PAINE COLLEGE

1235 15th Street, Augusta, GA 30901-3182
Phone: 800-476-7703 **E-mail:** simpkins@mail.paine.edu
Fax: 706-821-8691 **Web:** www.paine.edu

This private school, which is affiliated with the Methodist Church, was founded in 1882.

STUDENTS AND FACULTY

Enrollment: 863. **Student Body:** Male 32%, female 68%, out-of-state 23%, international 1%. **Ethnic Representation:** African American 98%, Caucasian 2%. **Retention and Graduation:** 67% freshmen return for sophomore year. 6% grads go on to further study within 1 year.

ACADEMICS

Degrees: Bachelor's. **Special Study Options:** Accelerated program, cooperative (work-study) program, honors program, independent study, internships, study abroad.

FACILITIES

Housing: Coed. **Library Holdings:** 76,120 bound volumes. 350 periodicals. 6,833 microforms. 1,407 audiovisuals.

EXTRACURRICULARS

Activities: Literary magazine, student government, student newspaper, yearbook. **Organizations:** 1 honor society, 1 religious organization. **Athletics (Intercollegiate):** *Women:* basketball, cross-country, track & field, volleyball.

ADMISSIONS

Selectivity Rating: 60 (of 100). **Freshman Academic Profile:** Average high school GPA 2.6. Average SAT I Math 376. Average SAT I Verbal 335. Average ACT 16. TOEFL required of all international applicants, minimum TOEFL 500. **Freshman Admission Requirements:** High school diploma or GED is required. *Academic units required/recommended:* 16 total required; 4 English required, 2 math required, 3 math recommended, 2 science required, 2 science lab required, 2 foreign language recommended, 1 social studies required, 1 history required, 6 elective required. **General Admission Information:** Application fee $10. Regular application deadline August 1. Admission may be deferred.

COSTS AND FINANCIAL AID

Room & board $3,020. Required fees $420. Average book expense $500. **Types of Aid:** *Loans:* FFEL Subsidized Stafford, FFEL PLUS. **Student Employment:** Federal Work-Study Program available.

PALM BEACH ATLANTIC COLLEGE

PO Box 24708, 901 S. Flagler Dr., West Palm Beach, FL 33416-4708
Phone: 561-803-2100 **E-mail:** admit@pbac.edu **CEEB Code:** 5553
Fax: 561-803-2186 **Web:** www.pbac.edu **ACT Code:** 739

This private school was founded in 1968. It has a 25-acre campus.

STUDENTS AND FACULTY

Enrollment: 2,058. **Student Body:** Male 37%, female 63%, out-of-state 25%. **Ethnic Representation:** African American 15%, Asian 1%, Caucasian 73%, Hispanic 9%. **Retention and Graduation:** 72% freshmen return for sophomore year. **Faculty:** Student/faculty ratio 19:1. 75 full-time faculty, 72% hold PhDs.

ACADEMICS

Degrees: Associate's, bachelor's, master's. **Academic Requirements:** General education including some course work in arts/fine arts, English (including composition), humanities, mathematics, sciences (biological or physical), social science. **Classes:** 10-19 students in an average class. **Disciplines with Highest Percentage of Degrees Awarded:** Other 48%, business/marketing 11%, psychology 10%, communications/communication technologies 7%, education 5%. **Special Study Options:** Cooperative (work-study) program, distance learning, double major, dual enrollment, English as a second language, honors program, independent study, internships, study abroad, teacher certification program.

FACILITIES

Housing: All-female, all-male, apartments. **Library Holdings:** 81,016 bound volumes. 2,144 periodicals. 196,350 microforms. 3,178 audiovisuals.

EXTRACURRICULARS

Activities: Choral groups, concert band, dance, drama/theater, jazz band, literary magazine, marching band, music ensembles, musical theater, opera, pep band, radio station, student government, student newspaper, student-run film society, symphony orchestra, television station, yearbook. **Organizations:** 29 honor societies, 6 religious organizations. **Athletics (Intercollegiate):** *Men:* baseball, basketball, soccer.

ADMISSIONS

Selectivity Rating: 68 (of 100). **Freshman Academic Profile:** Average high school GPA 3.2. 17% in top 10% of high school class, 39% in top 25% of high school class, 70% in top 50% of high school class. SAT I Math middle 50% range 470-580. SAT I Verbal middle 50% range 470-570. ACT middle 50% range 20-25. TOEFL required of all international applicants, minimum TOEFL 550. **Basis for Candidate Selection:** *Important factors considered include:* character/personal qualities, class rank, essays, interview, recommendations, religious affiliation/commitment, secondary school record, standardized test scores, talent/ability. *Other factors considered include:* extracurricular activities, volunteer work, work experience. **Freshman Admission Requirements:** High school diploma or GED is required. *Academic units required/recommended:* 18 total required; 4 English required, 3 math required, 3 science required, 2 foreign language recommended, 3 social studies required, 5 elective required. **Freshman Admission Statistics:** 1,260 applied, 63% accepted, 55% of those accepted enrolled. **Transfer Admission Requirements:** *Items required:* high school transcript, college transcript, essay, statement of good standing from prior school. Minimum high school GPA of 2.5 required. Minimum college GPA of 2.0 required. Lowest grade transferable C. **General Admission Information:** Application fee $25. Nonfall registration accepted. Credit offered for CEEB Advanced Placement tests.

COSTS AND FINANCIAL AID

Tuition $11,540. Room & board $4,950. Required fees $130. Average book expense $740. **Required Forms and Deadlines:** FAFSA, institution's own financial aid form and state aid form. No deadline for regular filing. Priority filing deadline April 1. **Notification of Awards:** Applicants will be notified of awards on a rolling basis beginning on or about March 1. **Types of Aid:** *Need-based scholarships/grants:* Pell, SEOG, state scholarships/grants, private scholarships, the school's own gift aid. *Loans:* FFEL Subsidized Stafford, FFEL Unsubsidized Stafford, FFEL PLUS, Federal Perkins, college/university loans from institutional funds. **Student Employment:** Federal Work-Study Program available. Off-campus job opportunities are excellent. **Financial Aid Statistics:** 39% freshmen, 65% undergrads receive some form of aid. **Financial Aid Phone:** 561-803-2125.

PALMER COLLEGE OF CHIROPRACTIC

1000 Brady Street, Davenport, IA 52803
Phone: 563-884-5656 **E-mail:** pcadmit@palmer.edu
Fax: 563-884-5414 **Web:** www.palmer.edu

This private school was founded in 1897.

STUDENTS AND FACULTY

Enrollment: 1,650. **Faculty:** Student/faculty ratio 14:1.

ACADEMICS

Degrees: Associate's, bachelor's, first professional, master's.

FACILITIES

Special Academic Facilities/Equipment: Palmer Mansion, specific collections, David D. Palmer Library.

EXTRACURRICULARS

Organizations: 78 registered organizations, 1 honor society, 3 fraternities, 1 sorority. **Athletics (Intercollegiate):** *Men:* baseball, ice hockey, rugby, soccer. *Women:* soccer, softball.

ADMISSIONS

Selectivity Rating: 60 (of 100). **Transfer Admission Requirements:** Minimum college GPA of 2.5 required. **General Admission Information:** Application fee $50. Nonfall registration accepted. Admission may be deferred for a maximum of 3 times.

COSTS AND FINANCIAL AID

Tuition $4,665. Required fees $105. Average book expense $100. **Student Employment:** Federal Work-Study Program available. Institutional employment available. Off-campus job opportunities are excellent. **Financial Aid Phone:** 563-884-5889.

PARK UNIVERSITY

8700 River Park Drive, Campus Box 1, Parkville, MO 64152
Phone: 816-741-2000 **E-mail:** admissions@mail.park.edu **CEEB Code:** 6574
Fax: 816-741-4462 **Web:** www.park.edu **ACT Code:** 2340

This private school was founded in 1875. It has an 800-acre campus.

STUDENTS AND FACULTY

Enrollment: 9,870. **Student Body:** Male 50%, female 50%, out of state 77%, international 2% (93 countries represented). **Ethnic Representation:** African American 21%, Asian 2%, Caucasian 61%, Hispanic 15%, Native American 1%. **Retention and Graduation:** 71% freshmen return for sophomore year. 20% freshmen graduate within 4 years. 7% grads go on to further study within 1 year. 1% grads pursue business degrees. **Faculty:** Student/faculty ratio 14:1. 77 full-time faculty, 50% hold PhDs. 100% faculty teach undergrads.

ACADEMICS

Degrees: Associate's, bachelor's, master's. **Academic Requirements:** General education including some course work in computer literacy, English (including composition), foreign languages, humanities, mathematics, sciences (biological or physical), social science. **Majors with Highest Enrollment:** Business administration/management; human resources management/personnel administration, general; management information systems, general. **Disciplines with Highest Percentage of Degrees Awarded:** Business/marketing 70%, psychology 14%, protective services/public administration 8%, computer and information sciences 5%, education 2%. **Special Study Options:** Accelerated program, cross registration, distance learning, double major, dual enrollment, honors program, independent study, internships, student-designed major, study abroad, teacher certification program, weekend college.

FACILITIES

Housing: Coed, apartments for married students. **Library Holdings:** 144,870 bound volumes. 775 periodicals. 218,030 microforms. 850 audiovisuals. **Computers:** School-owned computers available for student use.

EXTRACURRICULARS

Activities: Choral groups, drama/theater, literary magazine, radio station, student government, student newspaper, symphony orchestra, yearbook. **Organizations:** 15 registered organizations, 4 honor societies, 13 religious organizations. **Athletics (Intercollegiate):** *Men:* baseball, basketball, cross-country, soccer, track & field, volleyball. *Women:* basketball, cross-country, golf, soccer, softball, track & field, volleyball.

ADMISSIONS

Selectivity Rating: 72 (of 100). **Freshman Academic Profile:** Average high school GPA 3.0. 14% in top 10% of high school class, 40% in top 25% of high school class, 78% in top 50% of high school class. 80% from public high schools. Average ACT 21, ACT middle 50% range 18-23. TOEFL required of all international applicants, minimum TOEFL 500. **Basis for Candidate Selection:** *Very important factors considered include:* class rank, secondary school record, standardized test scores. *Other factors considered include:* essays, recommendations. **Freshman Admission Requirements:** High school diploma or GED is required. *Academic units required/recommended:* 19 total recommended; 3 English recommended, 2 math recommended, 2 science recommended, 1 science lab recommended, 2 foreign language recommended, 3 social studies recommended, 1 history recommended, 6 elective recommended. **Freshman Admission Statistics:** 424 applied, 72% accepted, 52% of those accepted enrolled. **Transfer Admission Requirements:** *Items required:* high school transcript, college transcript. Minimum college GPA of 2.0 required. Lowest grade transferable C. **General Admission Information:** Application fee $25. Priority application deadline April 15. Regular application deadline July 1. Nonfall registration accepted. Admission may be deferred for a maximum of 1 year. Credit and/or placement offered for CEEB Advanced Placement tests.

COSTS AND FINANCIAL AID

Tuition $6,000. Room & board $5,180. Average book expense $800. **Required Forms and Deadlines:** FAFSA and institution's own financial aid form. Priority filing deadline April 1. **Notification of Awards:** Applicants will be notified of awards on a rolling basis. **Types of Aid:** *Need-based scholarships/grants:* Pell, SEOG, state scholarships/grants, private scholarships, the school's own gift aid. *Loans:* FFEL Subsidized Stafford, FFEL Unsubsidized Stafford, FFEL PLUS, Federal Perkins, college/university loans from institutional funds. **Student Employment:** Federal Work-Study Program available. Institutional employment available. Off-campus job opportunities are good. **Financial Aid Statistics:** 46% freshmen, 60% undergrads receive some form of aid. Average freshman grant $6,550. Average freshman loan $3,241. **Financial Aid Phone:** 816-741-2000.

PARSONS SCHOOL OF DESIGN

66 Fifth Avenue, New York, NY 10011
Phone: 877-528-3321 **E-mail:** customer@newschool.edu **CEEB Code:** 2638
Fax: 212-229-5166 **Web:** www.parsons.edu **ACT Code:** 2854

This private school was founded in 1896. It has a 2-acre campus.

STUDENTS AND FACULTY

Enrollment: 2,499. **Student Body:** Male 25%, female 75%, out-of-state 49%, international 29%. **Ethnic Representation:** African American 5%, Asian 27%, Caucasian 45%, Hispanic 9%. **Retention and Graduation:** 85% freshmen return for sophomore year. 42% freshmen graduate within 4 years. **Faculty:** Student/faculty ratio 5:1. 51 full-time faculty. 100% faculty teach undergrads.

ACADEMICS

Degrees: Associate's, bachelor's, certificate, master's. **Academic Requirements:** General education including some course work in arts/fine arts, computer literacy, English (including composition), humanities, social science. **Classes:** 10-19 students in an average class. **Majors with Highest Enrollment:** Design and visual communications, general; fashion/apparel design; illustration. **Disciplines with Highest Percentage of Degrees Awarded:** Visual and performing arts 57%, business/marketing 11%, architecture 2%. **Special Study Options:** Accelerated program, cooperative (work-study) program, cross registration, distance learning, dual enrollment, English as a second language, student exchange program (domestic), honors program, independent study, internships, liberal arts/career combination, student-designed major, study abroad, teacher certification program.

FACILITIES

Housing: Coed, apartments for single students, housing for disabled students. **Library Holdings:** 4,137,530 bound volumes. 22,150 periodicals. 4,656,806 microforms. 48,379 audiovisuals. **Special Academic Facilities/Equipment:** Fashion Education Center in New York's garment district with labs and studios for fashion design students. **Computers:** *Recommended operating system:* Windows NT/2000. School-owned computers available for student use.

EXTRACURRICULARS

Activities: Student government. **Organizations:** 3 registered organizations.

ADMISSIONS

Selectivity Rating: 80 (of 100). **Freshman Academic Profile:** Average high school GPA 3.0. Average SAT I Math 552, SAT I Math middle 50% range 490-620. Average SAT I Verbal 544, SAT I Verbal middle 50% range 450-600. Average ACT 24. TOEFL required of all international applicants, minimum TOEFL 550. **Basis for Candidate Selection:** *Very important factors considered include:* interview, secondary school record, standardized test scores, talent/ability. *Other factors considered include:* essays, extracurricular activities, recommendations. **Freshman Admission Requirements:** High school diploma or GED is required. *Academic units required/recommended:* 16 total required; 4 English recommended, 4 social studies recommended. **Freshman Admission Statistics:** 1,532 applied, 44% accepted, 48% of those accepted enrolled. **Transfer Admission Requirements:** *Items required:* college transcript. Minimum college GPA of 2.0 required. Lowest grade transferable C. **General Admission Information:** Application fee $40. Priority application deadline March 1. Nonfall registration accepted. Neither credit nor placement offered for CEEB Advanced Placement tests.

COSTS AND FINANCIAL AID

Tuition $23,900. Room & board $9,896. Required fees $575. Average book expense $2,062. **Required Forms and Deadlines:** FAFSA and state aid form. No deadline for regular filing. Priority filing deadline March 1. **Notification of Awards:** Applicants will be notified of awards on a rolling basis beginning on or about March 1. **Types of Aid:** *Need-based scholarships/grants:* Pell, SEOG, state scholarships/grants, private scholarships, the school's own gift aid. *Loans:* FFEL Subsidized Stafford, FFEL Unsubsidized Stafford, FFEL PLUS, Federal Perkins, college/university loans from institutional funds. **Student Employment:** Federal Work-Study Program available. Institutional employment available. Off-campus job opportunities are excellent. **Financial Aid Statistics:** 70% freshmen, 61% undergrads receive some form of aid. Average freshman grant $12,872. Average freshman loan $3,081. Average income from on-campus job $2,500. **Financial Aid Phone:** 212-229-8930.

PENNSYLVANIA COLLEGE OF ART & DESIGN

204 N. Prince Street, PO Box 59, Lancaster, PA 17608-0059
Phone: 717-396-7833 **E-mail:** admissions@pcad.edu **CEEB Code:** 2681
Fax: 717-396-1339 **Web:** www.pcad.edu **ACT Code:** 3569

This private school was founded in 1982.

STUDENTS AND FACULTY

Faculty: Student/faculty ratio 11:1. 10 full-time faculty, 70% hold PhDs. 100% faculty teach undergrads.

ACADEMICS

Degrees: Bachelor's, certificate. **Academic Requirements:** General education including some course work in arts/fine arts, English (including composition), humanities, mathematics, sciences (biological or physical), art history. **Special Study Options:** Internships.

FACILITIES

Library Holdings: 14,813 bound volumes. 54 periodicals. 24,090 audiovisuals. **Special Academic Facilities/Equipment:** Main Gallery, library. **Computers:** *Recommended operating system:* Mac. School-owned computers available for student use.

EXTRACURRICULARS

Activities: Student government, yearbook. **Organizations:** 2 registered organizations.

ADMISSIONS

Selectivity Rating: 60 (of 100). **Freshman Academic Profile:** TOEFL required of all international applicants, minimum TOEFL 500. **Basis for Candidate Selection:** *Very important factors considered include:* essays, interview, secondary school record, talent/ability. *Important factors considered include:* class rank, recommendations. *Other factors considered include:* character/personal qualities, extracurricular activities, volunteer work, work experience. **Freshman Admission Requirements:** High school diploma or GED is required. **Transfer Admission Requirements:** *Items required:* high school transcript, college transcript, essay, interview. Minimum college GPA of 2.0 required. Lowest grade transferable C. **General Admission Information:** Application fee $35. Admission may be deferred for a maximum of 1 year. Credit offered for CEEB Advanced Placement tests.

COSTS AND FINANCIAL AID

Tuition $11,100. Required fees $400. Average book expense $1,100. **Required Forms and Deadlines:** FAFSA. **Student Employment:** Federal Work-Study Program available. Institutional employment available. Off-campus job opportunities are good. **Financial Aid Phone:** 717-396-7833.

PENNSYLVANIA STATE UNIVERSITY—ABINGTON

106 Sutherland, Abington, PA 19001
Phone: 215-881-7600 **E-mail:** abingtonadmissions@psu.edu
Fax: 215-881-7317 **Web:** www.abington.psu.edu

This public school was founded in 1950. It has a 45-acre campus.

STUDENTS AND FACULTY

Enrollment: 3,316. **Student Body:** Male 49%, female 51%, out-of-state 4%. **Ethnic Representation:** African American 10%, Asian 12%, Caucasian 75%, Hispanic 4%. **Retention and Graduation:** 74% freshmen return for sophomore year. 13% freshmen graduate within 4 years. **Faculty:** Student/faculty ratio 20:1. 105 full-time faculty, 57% hold PhDs.

ACADEMICS

Degrees: Bachelor's, terminal. **Academic Requirements:** General education including some course work in arts/fine arts, English (including composition), foreign languages, humanities, mathematics, sciences (biological or physical), social science, intercultural/international competence. **Disciplines with Highest Percentage of Degrees Awarded:** Business/marketing 36%, protective services/public administration 22%, liberal arts/general studies 14%, English 7%, interdisciplinary studies 5%. **Special Study Options:** Accelerated program, cooperative (work-study) program, distance learning, double major, dual enrollment, English as a second language, student exchange program (domestic), external degree program, honors program, independent study, internships, liberal arts/career combination, student-designed major, study abroad.

FACILITIES

Library Holdings: 65,866 bound volumes. 318 periodicals. 12,417 microforms. 4,046 audiovisuals. **Computers:** School-owned computers available for student use.

EXTRACURRICULARS

Activities: Dance, drama/theater, literary magazine, music ensembles, student government, student newspaper. **Athletics (Intercollegiate):** *Men:* basketball, soccer, softball, tennis. *Women:* basketball, field hockey, softball, tennis, volleyball.

ADMISSIONS

Selectivity Rating: 63 (of 100). **Freshman Academic Profile:** Average high school GPA 3.1. 8% in top 10% of high school class, 26% in top 25% of high school class, 65% in top 50% of high school class. SAT I Math middle 50% range 410-550. SAT I Verbal middle 50% range 410-530. TOEFL required of all international applicants, minimum TOEFL 550. **Basis for Candidate Selection:** *Very important factors considered include:* secondary school record, standardized test scores. *Other factors considered include:* alumni/ae relation, character/personal qualities, class rank, essays, extracurricular activities, recommendations, talent/ability, volunteer work, work experience. **Freshman Admission Requirements:** High school diploma or GED is required. *Academic units required/recommended:* 4 English required, 3 math required, 3 science required, 2 foreign language required, 3 social studies required. **Freshman Admission Statistics:** 2,753 applied, 77% accepted, 36% of those accepted enrolled. **Transfer Admission Requirements:** *Items required:* high school transcript, college transcript. Lowest grade transferable C. **General Admission Information:** Application fee $50. Priority application deadline November 30. Nonfall registration accepted. Admission may be deferred for a maximum of 1 year.

COSTS AND FINANCIAL AID

In-state tuition $7,874. Out-of-state tuition $12,232. Room & board $5,660. Required fees $364. Average book expense $864. **Required Forms and Deadlines:** FAFSA. No deadline for regular filing. Priority filing deadline February 15. **Notification of Awards:** Applicants will be notified of awards on a rolling basis beginning on or about February 15. **Types of Aid:** *Need-based scholarships/grants:* Pell, SEOG, state scholarships/grants, private scholarships, the school's own gift aid. *Loans:* FFEL Subsidized Stafford, FFEL Unsubsidized Stafford, FFEL PLUS, Federal Perkins, college/university loans from institutional funds, private loans. **Financial Aid Statistics:** 59% freshmen, 56% undergrads receive some form of aid.

PENNSYLVANIA STATE UNIVERSITY—ALTOONA

E108 Raymond Smith Building, Altoona, PA 16601-3760
Phone: 814-949-5466 **E-mail:** aaadmit@psu.edu
Fax: 814-949-5564 **Web:** www.aa.psu.edu

This public school was founded in 1929.

STUDENTS AND FACULTY

Enrollment: 3,877. **Student Body:** Male 51%, female 49%, out-of-state 13%, international 1%. **Ethnic Representation:** African American 5%, Asian 2%, Caucasian 91%, Hispanic 2%. **Retention and Graduation:** 83% freshmen return for sophomore year. 23% freshmen graduate within 4 years. **Faculty:** Student/faculty ratio 21:1. 126 full-time faculty, 69% hold PhDs.

ACADEMICS

Degrees: Bachelor's, terminal, transfer. **Academic Requirements:** General education including some course work in arts/fine arts, English (including composition), foreign languages, humanities, mathematics, sciences (biological or physical), social science, intercultural/international competence. **Disciplines with Highest Percentage of Degrees Awarded:** Business/marketing 25%, protective services/public administration 24%, engineering/engineering technology 18%, home economics and vocational home economics 13%, liberal arts/general studies 10%. **Special Study Options:** Accelerated program, cooperative (work-study) program, cross registration, distance learning, double major, dual enrollment, English as a second language, honors program, independent study, internships, liberal arts/career combination, student-designed major, study abroad.

FACILITIES

Housing: Coed, suites. **Library Holdings:** 70,851 bound volumes. 308 periodicals. 58,596 microforms. 5,680 audiovisuals.

EXTRACURRICULARS

Activities: Choral groups, dance, drama/theater, jazz band, literary magazine, music ensembles, pep band, student government, student newspaper. **Organizations:** 6% men join fraternities, 5% women join sororities. **Athletics (Intercollegiate):** *Men:* basketball, diving, skiing (alpine), soccer, swimming, tennis, volleyball. *Women:* basketball, diving, skiing (alpine), swimming, tennis, volleyball.

ADMISSIONS

Selectivity Rating: 63 (of 100). **Freshman Academic Profile:** Average high school GPA 3.0. 7% in top 10% of high school class, 30% in top 25% of high school class, 73% in top 50% of high school class. SAT I Math middle 50% range 460-570. SAT I Verbal middle 50% range 450-540. TOEFL required of all international applicants, **Basis for Candidate Selection:** *Very important factors considered include:* secondary school record, standardized test scores. *Other factors considered include:* alumni/ae relation, character/personal qualities, class rank, essays, extracurricular activities, recommendations, talent/ability, volunteer work, work experience. **Freshman Admission Requirements:** High school diploma or GED is required. *Academic units required/recommended:* 4 English required, 3 math required, 3 science required, 2 foreign language required, 3 social studies required. **Freshman Admission Statistics:** 4,386 applied, 80% accepted, 39% of those accepted enrolled. **Transfer Admission Requirements:** *Items required:* high school transcript, college transcript. Lowest grade transferable C. **General Admission Information:** Application fee $50. Priority application deadline November 30. Nonfall registration accepted. Admission may be deferred for a maximum of 1 year.

COSTS AND FINANCIAL AID

In-state tuition $7,874. Out-of-state tuition $12,232. Room & board $5,660. Required fees $374. Average book expense $864. **Required Forms and Deadlines:** FAFSA. No deadline for regular filing. Priority filing deadline February 15. **Notification of Awards:** Applicants will be notified of awards on a rolling basis beginning on or about February 15. **Types of Aid:** *Need-based scholarships/grants:* Pell, SEOG, state scholarships/grants, private scholarships, the school's own gift aid. *Loans:* FFEL Subsidized Stafford, FFEL Unsubsidized Stafford, FFEL PLUS, Federal Perkins, college/university loans from institutional funds, private loans. **Financial Aid Statistics:** 63% freshmen, 66% undergrads receive some form of aid.

PENNSYLVANIA STATE UNIVERSITY—BEAVER

100 University Drive, Monaca, PA 15061-2799
Phone: 724-773-3800 **E-mail:** admissions@br.psu.edu
Fax: 724-773-3658 **Web:** www.br.psu.edu

This public school was founded in 1964. It has a 90-acre campus.

STUDENTS AND FACULTY

Enrollment: 784. **Student Body:** Male 64%, female 36%, out-of-state 5%. **Ethnic Representation:** African American 3%, Asian 2%, Caucasian 94%, Hispanic 1%. **Retention and Graduation:** 78% freshmen return for sophomore year. 16% freshmen graduate within 4 years. **Faculty:** Student/faculty ratio 16:1. 35 full-time faculty, 57% hold PhDs.

ACADEMICS

Degrees: Bachelor's, terminal, transfer. **Academic Requirements:** General education including some course work in arts/fine arts, English (including composition), foreign languages, humanities, mathematics, sciences (biological or physical), social science, intercultural/international competence. **Special Study Options:** Accelerated program, cross registration, distance learning, double major, dual enrollment, English as a second language, honors program, independent study, internships.

FACILITIES

Housing: Coed, townhouses. **Library Holdings:** 39,861 bound volumes. 222 periodicals. 9,506 microforms. 6,683 audiovisuals. **Computers:** School-owned computers available for student use.

EXTRACURRICULARS

Activities: Drama/theater, literary magazine, radio station, student government, student newspaper. **Athletics (Intercollegiate):** *Men:* baseball, basketball, fencing, ice hockey, tennis, track & field, volleyball. *Women:* basketball, fencing, ice hockey, softball, tennis, track & field, volleyball.

ADMISSIONS

Selectivity Rating: 63 (of 100). **Freshman Academic Profile:** Average high school GPA 2.9. 5% in top 10% of high school class, 27% in top 25% of high school class, 61% in top 50% of high school class. SAT I Math middle 50% range 450-550. SAT I Verbal middle 50% range 440-530. TOEFL required of all international applicants, minimum TOEFL 550. **Basis for Candidate Selection:** *Very important factors considered include:* secondary school record, standardized test scores. *Other factors considered include:* alumni/ae relation, character/personal qualities, class rank, essays, extracurricular activities, recommendations, talent/ability, volunteer work, work experience. **Freshman Admission Requirements:** High school diploma or GED is required. *Academic units required/recommended:* 4 English required, 3 math required, 3 science required, 2 foreign language required, 3 social studies required. **Freshman Admission Statistics:** 599 applied, 90% accepted, 49% of those accepted enrolled. **Transfer Admission Requirements:** *Items required:* high school transcript, college transcript. Lowest grade transferable C. **General Admission Information:** Application fee $50. Priority application deadline November 30. Nonfall registration accepted. Admission may be deferred for a maximum of 1 year.

COSTS AND FINANCIAL AID

In-state tuition $7,756. Out-of-state tuition $12,006. Room & board $5,660. Required fees $374. Average book expense $864. **Required Forms and Deadlines:** FAFSA. No deadline for regular filing. **Notification of Awards:** Applicants will be notified of awards on a rolling basis beginning on or about February 15. **Types of Aid:** *Need-based scholarships/grants:* Pell, SEOG, state scholarships/grants, private scholarships, the school's own gift aid. *Loans:* FFEL Subsidized Stafford, FFEL Unsubsidized Stafford, FFEL PLUS, Federal Perkins, college/university loans from institutional funds, private loans. **Financial Aid Statistics:** 63% freshmen, 63% undergrads receive some form of aid.

PENNSYLVANIA STATE UNIVERSITY—BERKS

14 Perkins Student Center, Reading, PA 19610-6009
Phone: 610-396-6060 **E-mail:** admissions@psu.edu
Fax: 610-396-6077 **Web:** www.bk.psu.edu

This public school was founded in 1924. It has a 241-acre campus.

STUDENTS AND FACULTY

Enrollment: 2,443. **Student Body:** Male 61%, female 39%, out-of-state 7%. **Ethnic Representation:** African American 6%, Asian 5%, Caucasian 86%, Hispanic 3%, international 1%. **Retention and Graduation:** 84% freshmen return for sophomore year. 19% freshmen graduate within 4 years. **Faculty:** Student/faculty ratio 19:1. 88 full-time faculty, 68% hold PhDs.

ACADEMICS

Degrees: Bachelor's, terminal, transfer. **Academic Requirements:** General education including some course work in arts/fine arts, English (including composition), foreign languages, humanities, mathematics, sciences (biological or physical), social science, intercultural/international competence. **Disciplines with Highest Percentage of Degrees Awarded:** Business/marketing 61%, engineering/engineering technology 15%, interdisciplinary studies 10%, computer and information sciences 9%, psychology 3%. **Special Study Options:** Accelerated program, cross registration, distance learning, dual enrollment, honors program, independent study, internships, study abroad.

FACILITIES

Housing: Coed, honor student housing, suites. **Library Holdings:** 49,520 bound volumes. 460 periodicals. 2,095 microforms. 2,336 audiovisuals. **Computers:** School-owned computers available for student use.

EXTRACURRICULARS

Activities: Choral groups, dance, drama/theater, pep band, radio station, student government, student newspaper, yearbook. **Athletics (Intercollegiate):** *Men:* baseball, basketball, fencing, soccer, tennis, volleyball. *Women:* fencing, softball, tennis, volleyball.

ADMISSIONS

Selectivity Rating: 63 (of 100). **Freshman Academic Profile:** Average high school GPA 2.8. 6% in top 10% of high school class, 22% in top 25% of high school class, 63% in top 50% of high school class. SAT I Math middle 50% range 450-560. SAT I Verbal middle 50% range 440-540. TOEFL required of all international applicants, minimum TOEFL 550. **Basis for Candidate Selection:** *Very important factors considered include:* secondary school record, standardized test scores. *Other factors considered include:* alumni/ae relation, character/personal qualities, class rank, essays, extracurricular activities, recommendations, talent/ability, volunteer work, work experience. **Freshman Admission Requirements:** High school diploma or GED is required. *Academic units required/recommended:* 4 English required, 3 math required, 3 science required, 2 foreign language required, 3 social studies required. **Freshman Admission Statistics:** 2,457 applied, 81% accepted, 42% of those accepted enrolled. **Transfer Admission Requirements:** *Items required:* high school transcript, college transcript. Lowest grade transferable C. **General Admission Information:** Application fee $50. Priority application deadline November 30. Nonfall registration accepted. Admission may be deferred for a maximum of 1 year.

COSTS AND FINANCIAL AID

In-state tuition $7,874. Out-of-state tuition $12,232. Room & board $5,660. Required fees $374. Average book expense $864. **Required Forms and Deadlines:** FAFSA. No deadline for regular filing. **Notification of Awards:** Applicants will be notified of awards on a rolling basis beginning on or about February 15. **Types of Aid:** *Need-based scholarships/grants:* Pell, SEOG, state scholarships/grants, private scholarships, the school's own gift aid. *Loans:* FFEL Subsidized Stafford, FFEL Unsubsidized Stafford, FFEL PLUS, Federal Perkins, college/university loans from institutional funds, private loans. **Financial Aid Statistics:** 51% freshmen, 51% undergrads receive some form of aid.

PENNSYLVANIA STATE UNIVERSITY—DELAWARE COUNTY

25 Yearsley Mill Road, Media, PA 19063-5596
Phone: 610-892-1200 **E-mail:** admissions-delco@psu.edu
Fax: 610-892-1357 **Web:** www.de.psu.edu

This public school was founded in 1966. It has an 87-acre campus.

STUDENTS AND FACULTY

Enrollment: 1,738. **Student Body:** Male 54%, female 46%, out-of-state 4%. **Ethnic Representation:** African American 12%, Asian 9%, Caucasian 77%, Hispanic 1%. **Retention and Graduation:** 72% freshmen return for sophomore year. 11% freshmen graduate within 4 years. **Faculty:** Student/faculty ratio 18:1. 65 full-time faculty, 61% hold PhDs.

ACADEMICS

Degrees: Bachelor's, terminal. **Academic Requirements:** General education including some course work in arts/fine arts, English (including composition), foreign languages, humanities, mathematics, sciences (biological or physical), social science, intercultural/international competence. **Disciplines with Highest Percentage of Degrees Awarded:** Business/marketing 42%, English 15%, education 14%, liberal arts/general studies 14%, home economics and vocational home economics 10%. **Special Study Options:** Accelerated program, cross registration, distance learning, double major, dual enrollment, English as a second language, honors program, independent study, internships, student-designed major, study abroad.

FACILITIES

Library Holdings: 59,930 bound volumes. 457 periodicals. 4,526 microforms. 3,987 audiovisuals. **Computers:** School-owned computers available for student use.

EXTRACURRICULARS

Activities: Drama/theater, literary magazine, student newspaper, student-run film society. **Athletics (Intercollegiate):** *Men:* baseball, basketball, ice hockey, rifle, soccer, tennis, volleyball. *Women:* basketball, ice hockey, rifle, soccer, tennis, volleyball.

ADMISSIONS

Selectivity Rating: 63 (of 100). **Freshman Academic Profile:** Average high school GPA 2.9. 8% in top 10% of high school class, 20% in top 25% of high school class, 53% in top 50% of high school class. SAT I Math middle 50% range 410-540. SAT I Verbal middle 50% range 400-510. TOEFL required of all international applicants, minimum TOEFL 550. **Basis for Candidate Selection:** *Very important factors considered include:* secondary school record, standardized test scores. *Other factors considered include:* alumni/ae relation, character/personal qualities, class rank, essays, extracurricular activities, recommendations, talent/ability, volunteer work, work experience. **Freshman Admission Requirements:** High school diploma or GED is required. *Academic units required/recommended:* 4 English required, 3 math required, 3 science required, 2 foreign language required, 3 social studies required. **Freshman Admission Statistics:** 1,399 applied, 80% accepted, 41% of those accepted enrolled. **Transfer Admission Requirements:** *Items required:* high school transcript, college transcript. Lowest grade transferable C. **General Admission Information:** Application fee $50. Priority application deadline November 30. Nonfall registration accepted. Admission may be deferred for a maximum of 1 year.

COSTS AND FINANCIAL AID

In-state tuition $7,756. Out-of-state tuition $12,006. Room & board $5,660. Required fees $364. Average book expense $864. **Required Forms and Deadlines:** FAFSA. No deadline for regular filing. **Notification of Awards:** Applicants will be notified of awards on a rolling basis beginning on or about February 15. **Types of Aid:** *Need-based scholarships/grants:* Pell, SEOG, state scholarships/grants, private scholarships, the school's own gift aid. *Loans:* FFEL Subsidized Stafford, FFEL Unsubsidized Stafford, FFEL PLUS, Federal Perkins, college/university loans from institutional funds, private loans. **Financial Aid Statistics:** 54% freshmen, 55% undergrads receive some form of aid.

PENNSYLVANIA STATE UNIVERSITY—DUBOIS

108 Hiller, Dubois, PA 15801-3199
Phone: 814-375-4720 **E-mail:** ds-admissions@psu.edu
Fax: 814-375-4784 **Web:** www.ds.psu.edu

This public school was founded in 1935. It has a 13-acre campus.

STUDENTS AND FACULTY

Enrollment: 953. **Student Body:** Male 48%, female 52%, out-of-state 1%. **Ethnic Representation:** African American 1%, Asian 1%, Caucasian 98%. **Retention and Graduation:** 73% freshmen return for sophomore year. 17% freshmen graduate within 4 years. **Faculty:** Student/faculty ratio 12:1. 48 full-time faculty, 60% hold PhDs.

ACADEMICS

Degrees: Bachelor's, terminal, transfer. **Academic Requirements:** General education including some course work in arts/fine arts, English (including composition), foreign languages, humanities, mathematics, sciences (biological or physical), social science, intercultural/international competence. **Classes:** 10-19 students in an average class. 10-19 students in an average lab/discussion section. **Disciplines with Highest Percentage of Degrees Awarded:** Business/marketing 47%, home economics and vocational home economics 44%, liberal arts/general studies 9%. **Special Study Options:** Accelerated program, cross registration, distance learning, double major, dual enrollment, honors program, independent study, internships, student-designed major.

FACILITIES

Housing: Independently owned housing nearby. **Library Holdings:** 43,710 bound volumes. 224 periodicals. 17,158 microforms. 1,091 audiovisuals. **Computers:** School-owned computers available for student use.

EXTRACURRICULARS

Activities: Choral groups, literary magazine, student government, student newspaper, student-run film society. **Athletics (Intercollegiate):** *Men:* basketball. *Women:* volleyball.

ADMISSIONS

Selectivity Rating: 63 (of 100). **Freshman Academic Profile:** Average high school GPA 2.8. 6% in top 10% of high school class, 29% in top 25% of high school class, 69% in top 50% of high school class. SAT I Math middle 50% range 435-540. SAT I Verbal middle 50% range 430-525. TOEFL required of all international applicants, minimum TOEFL 550. **Basis for Candidate Selection:** *Very important factors considered include:* secondary school record, standardized test scores. *Other factors considered include:* alumni/ae relation, character/personal qualities, class rank, essays, extracurricular activities, recommendations, talent/ability, volunteer work, work experience. **Freshman Admission Requirements:** High school diploma or GED is required. *Academic units required/recommended:* 4 English required, 3 math required, 3 science required, 2 foreign language required, 3 social studies required. **Freshman Admission Statistics:** 397 applied, 92% accepted, 58% of those accepted enrolled. **Transfer Admission Requirements:** *Items required:* high school transcript, college transcript. Lowest grade transferable C. **General Admission Information:** Application fee $50. Priority application deadline November 30. Nonfall registration accepted. Admission may be deferred for a maximum of 1 year.

COSTS AND FINANCIAL AID

In-state tuition $7,756. Out-of-state tuition $12,006. Room & board $5,660. Required fees $354. Average book expense $864. **Required Forms and Deadlines:** FAFSA. No deadline for regular filing. Priority filing deadline February 15. **Notification of Awards:** Applicants will be notified of awards on a rolling basis beginning on or about February 15. **Types of Aid:** *Need-based scholarships/grants:* Pell, SEOG, state scholarships/grants, private scholarships, the school's own gift aid. *Loans:* FFEL Subsidized Stafford, FFEL Unsubsidized Stafford, FFEL PLUS, Federal Perkins, college/university loans from institutional funds, private loans. **Financial Aid Statistics:** 76% freshmen, 79% undergrads receive some form of aid.

PENNSYLVANIA STATE UNIVERSITY—ERIE, THE BEHREND COLLEGE

Glenhill Farmhouse, Erie, PA 16563
Phone: 814-898-6100 **E-mail:** behrend.admissions@psu.edu
Fax: 814-898-6044 **Web:** www.pserie.psu.edu **ACT Code:** 3656

This public school was founded in 1948. It has a 732-acre campus.

STUDENTS AND FACULTY

Enrollment: 3,586. **Student Body:** Male 65%, female 35%, out-of-state 8%, international 1%. **Ethnic Representation:** African American 3%, Asian 2%, Caucasian 94%, Hispanic 1%. **Retention and Graduation:** 84% freshmen return for sophomore year. 27% freshmen graduate within 4 years. **Faculty:** Student/faculty ratio 16:1. 195 full-time faculty, 57% hold PhDs. 100% faculty teach undergrads.

ACADEMICS

Degrees: Bachelor's, master's, terminal, transfer. **Academic Requirements:** General education including some course work in arts/fine arts, English (including composition), foreign languages, humanities, mathematics, sciences (biological or physical), social science, intercultural/international competence. **Disciplines with Highest Percentage of Degrees Awarded:** Business/marketing 37%, engineering/engineering technology 28%, psychology 7%, communications/communication technologies 6%, biological life sciences 6%. **Special Study Options:** Accelerated program, cooperative (work-study) program, distance learning, double major, honors program, independent study, internships, liberal arts/career combination, study abroad, teacher certification program.

FACILITIES

Housing: Coed, all-female, all-male, apartments for single students, housing for disabled students, suites, special-interest housing. **Library Holdings:** 103,524 bound volumes. 810 periodicals. 58,349 microforms. 3,180 audiovisuals. **Special Academic Facilities/Equipment:** Observatory, plastics lab. **Computers:** *Recommended operating system:* Windows 3x. School-owned computers available for student use.

EXTRACURRICULARS

Activities: Choral groups, concert band, dance, drama/theater, jazz band, literary magazine, music ensembles, pep band, radio station, student government, student newspaper, student-run film society. **Organizations:** 75 registered organizations, 46 honor societies, 26 religious organizations, 6 fraternities (8% men join), 4 sororities (7% women join). **Athletics (Intercollegiate):** *Men:* baseball, basketball, cheerleading, cross-country, golf, soccer, swimming, tennis, track & field, water polo, wrestling. *Women:* basketball, cheerleading, cross-country, golf, soccer, softball, swimming, tennis, track & field, volleyball, water polo.

ADMISSIONS

Selectivity Rating: 81 (of 100). **Freshman Academic Profile:** Average high school GPA 3.2. 13% in top 10% of high school class, 41% in top 25% of high school class, 84% in top 50% of high school class. Average SAT I Math 538, SAT I Math middle 50% range 500-600. Average SAT I Verbal 520, SAT I Verbal middle 50% range 470-560. TOEFL required of all international applicants, minimum TOEFL 550. **Basis for Candidate Selection:** *Very important factors considered include:* secondary school record, standardized test scores. *Other factors considered include:* alumni/ae relation, character/personal qualities, class rank, essays, extracurricular activities, recommendations, talent/ability, volunteer work, work experience. **Freshman Admission Requirements:** High school diploma or GED is required. *Academic units required/recommended:* 4 English required, 3 math required, 3 science required, 2 foreign language required, 3 social studies required. **Freshman Admission Statistics:** 3,132 applied, 76% accepted, 37% of those accepted enrolled. **Transfer Admission Requirements:** *Items required:* high school transcript, college transcript. Lowest grade transferable C. **General Admission Information:** Application fee $50. Priority application deadline November 30. Nonfall registration accepted. Admission may be deferred for a maximum of 1 year. Credit offered for CEEB Advanced Placement tests.

COSTS AND FINANCIAL AID

In-state tuition $8,008. Out-of-state tuition $15,366. Room & board $5,660. Required fees $374. Average book expense $864. **Required Forms and Deadlines:** FAFSA. No deadline for regular filing. Priority filing deadline February 15. **Notification of Awards:** Applicants will be notified of awards on a rolling basis beginning on or about March 5. **Types of Aid:** *Need-based scholarships/grants:* Pell, SEOG, state scholarships/grants, private scholarships, the school's own gift aid. *Loans:* FFEL Subsidized Stafford, FFEL Unsubsidized Stafford, FFEL PLUS, Federal Perkins, college/university loans from institutional funds, private loans. **Student Employment:** Federal Work-Study Program available. Institutional employment available. Off-campus job opportunities are good. **Financial Aid Statistics:** 67% freshmen, 65% undergrads receive some form of aid. Average freshman loan $3,015. Average income from on-campus job $656. **Financial Aid Phone:** 814-898-6162.

PENNSYLVANIA STATE UNIVERSITY—FAYETTE

108 Williams Building, Route 119 North, Uniontown, PA 15401
Phone: 724-430-4130 **E-mail:** feadm@psu.edu
Fax: 724-430-4175 **Web:** www.fe.psu.edu

This public school was founded in 1934. It has a 193-acre campus.

STUDENTS AND FACULTY

Enrollment: 1,139. **Student Body:** Male 42%, female 58%, out-of-state 1%. **Ethnic Representation:** African American 4%, Caucasian 95%. **Retention and Graduation:** 75% freshmen return for sophomore year. 16% freshmen graduate within 4 years. **Faculty:** Student/faculty ratio 14:1. 52 full-time faculty, 53% hold PhDs.

ACADEMICS

Degrees: Bachelor's, terminal, transfer. **Academic Requirements:** General education including some course work in arts/fine arts, English (including composition), foreign languages, humanities, mathematics, sciences (biological or physical), social science, intercultural/international competence. **Disciplines with Highest Percentage of Degrees Awarded:** Business/marketing 42%, protective services/public administration 32%, home economics and vocational home economics 15%, liberal arts/general studies 11%. **Special Study Options:** Accelerated program, cross registration, distance learning, double major, dual enrollment, honors program, independent study, internships, student-designed major, weekend college.

FACILITIES

Library Holdings: 54,610 bound volumes. 187 periodicals. 6,556 microforms. 6,721 audiovisuals. **Computers:** School-owned computers available for student use.

EXTRACURRICULARS

Activities: Drama/theater, student government, student newspaper.

ADMISSIONS

Selectivity Rating: 63 (of 100). **Freshman Academic Profile:** Average high school GPA 2.9. 10% in top 10% of high school class, 38% in top 25% of high school class, 75% in top 50% of high school class. SAT I Math middle 50% range 410-540. SAT I Verbal middle 50% range 420-510. TOEFL required of all international applicants, minimum TOEFL 550. **Basis for Candidate Selection:** *Very important factors considered include:* secondary school record, standardized test scores. *Other factors considered include:* alumni/ae relation, character/personal qualities, class rank, essays, extracurricular activities, recommendations, talent/ability, volunteer work, work experience. **Freshman Admission Requirements:** High school diploma or GED is required. *Academic units required/recommended:* 4 English required, 3 math required, 3 science required, 2 foreign language required, 3 social studies required. **Freshman Admission Statistics:** 355 applied, 85% accepted, 59% of those accepted enrolled. **Transfer Admission Requirements:** *Items required:* high school transcript, college transcript. Lowest grade transferable C. **General Admission Information:** Application fee $50. Priority application deadline November 30. Nonfall registration accepted. Admission may be deferred for a maximum of 1 year.

COSTS AND FINANCIAL AID

In-state tuition $7,756. Out-of-state tuition $12,006. Room & board $5,660. Required fees $354. Average book expense $864. **Required Forms and Deadlines:** FAFSA. No deadline for regular filing. **Notification of Awards:**

Applicants will be notified of awards on a rolling basis beginning on or about February 15. **Types of Aid:** *Need-based scholarships/grants:* Pell, SEOG, state scholarships/grants, private scholarships, the school's own gift aid. *Loans:* FFEL Subsidized Stafford, FFEL Unsubsidized Stafford, FFEL PLUS, Federal Perkins, college/university loans from institutional funds, private loans. **Financial Aid Statistics:** 80% freshmen, 78% undergrads receive some form of aid.

PENNSYLVANIA STATE UNIVERSITY—HARRISBURG

Swatapa Bldg., 777 W. Harrisburg Pike, Middletown, PA 17057
Phone: 717-948-6250 **E-mail:** hbgadmit@psu.edu
Fax: 717-948-6325 **Web:** www.psu.edu

This public school was founded in 1966.

STUDENTS AND FACULTY

Enrollment: 1,710. **Student Body:** Male 50%, female 50%, out-of-state 4%, international 1%. **Ethnic Representation:** African American 5%, Asian 6%, Caucasian 87%, Hispanic 2%. **Faculty:** Student/faculty ratio 10:1. 156 full-time faculty, 84% hold PhDs.

ACADEMICS

Degrees: Bachelor's, certificate, doctoral, master's, post-bachelor's certificate, terminal. **Academic Requirements:** General education including some course work in arts/fine arts, English (including composition), foreign languages, humanities, mathematics, sciences (biological or physical), social science, intercultural/international competency. **Disciplines with Highest Percentage of Degrees Awarded:** Business/marketing 34%, engineering/engineering technology 16%, education 13%, protective services/public administration 11%, computer and information sciences 6%. **Special Study Options:** Accelerated program, cooperative (work-study) program, cross registration, distance learning, double major, dual enrollment, honors program, independent study, internships, study abroad, teacher certification program, weekend college.

FACILITIES

Housing: Apartments for married students, apartments for single students. **Library Holdings:** 285,171 bound volumes. 1,903 periodicals. 1,078,423 microforms. 5,144 audiovisuals.

EXTRACURRICULARS

Activities: Literary magazine, radio station, student government, student newspaper. **Organizations:** 2 honor societies, 1 religious organization. **Athletics (Intercollegiate):** *Men:* basketball, skiing (alpine), soccer, tennis, track & field, volleyball. *Women:* skiing (alpine), soccer, track & field, volleyball.

ADMISSIONS

Selectivity Rating: 60 (of 100). **Freshman Academic Profile:** Average high school GPA 2.9. 12% in top 10% of high school class, 18% in top 25% of high school class, 65% in top 50% of high school class. SAT I Math middle 50% range 480-590. SAT I Verbal middle 50% range 480-590. TOEFL required of all international applicants. **Basis for Candidate Selection:** *Very important factors considered include:* secondary school record, standardized test scores. *Other factors considered include:* alumni/ae relation, character/personal qualities, class rank, essays, extracurricular activities, recommendations, talent/ability, volunteer work, work experience. **Freshman Admission Requirements:** High school diploma or GED is required. *Academic units required/recommended:* 4 English required, 3 math required, 3 science required, 2 foreign language required, 3 social studies required. **Freshman Admission Statistics:** 237 applied, 13% accepted, 58% of those accepted enrolled. **Transfer Admission Requirements:** *Items required:* high school transcript, college transcript. Lowest grade transferable C. **General Admission Information:** Application fee $50. Priority application deadline November 30. Nonfall registration accepted. Admission may be deferred for a maximum of 1 year.

COSTS AND FINANCIAL AID

In-state tuition $8,008. Out-of-state tuition $15,366. Room & board $6,950. Required fees $354. Average book expense $864. **Required Forms and Deadlines:** FAFSA. No deadline for regular filing. Priority filing deadline February 15. **Notification of Awards:** Applicants will be notified of awards on a rolling basis beginning on or about February 15. **Types of Aid:** *Need-based scholarships/grants:* Pell, SEOG, state scholarships/grants, private scholarships, the school's own gift aid. *Loans:* FFEL Subsidized Stafford, FFEL Unsubsidized Stafford, FFEL PLUS, Federal Perkins, college/university loans from institutional funds, private loans. **Financial Aid Statistics:** 69% undergrads receive some form of aid.

PENNSYLVANIA STATE UNIVERSITY—HAZLETON

110 Admin. Building, 76 University Drive, Hazleton, PA 18202
Phone: 570-450-3142 **E-mail:** admissions-hn@psu.edu
Fax: 570-450-3182 **Web:** www.hn.psu.edu

This public school was founded in 1934. It has a 73-acre campus.

STUDENTS AND FACULTY

Enrollment: 1,236. **Student Body:** Male 59%, female 41%, out-of-state 15%. **Ethnic Representation:** African American 4%, Asian 4%, Caucasian 89%, Hispanic 3%. **Retention and Graduation:** 83% freshmen return for sophomore year. 23% freshmen graduate within 4 years. **Faculty:** Student/faculty ratio 17:1. 57 full-time faculty, 54% hold PhDs.

ACADEMICS

Degrees: Bachelor's, terminal, transfer. **Academic Requirements:** General education including some course work in arts/fine arts, English (including composition), foreign languages, humanities, mathematics, sciences (biological or physical), social science, intercultural/international competence. **Disciplines with Highest Percentage of Degrees Awarded:** Business/marketing 100%. **Special Study Options:** Accelerated program, cross registration, distance learning, double major, dual enrollment, honors program, independent study, internships.

FACILITIES

Housing: Coed, townhouses, suites. **Library Holdings:** 83,266 bound volumes. 996 periodicals. 8,991 microforms. 6,771 audiovisuals. **Computers:** School-owned computers available for student use.

EXTRACURRICULARS

Activities: Choral groups, drama/theater, radio station, student government, student newspaper. **Athletics (Intercollegiate):** *Men:* baseball, basketball, soccer, tennis. *Women:* softball, tennis, volleyball.

ADMISSIONS

Selectivity Rating: 63 (of 100). **Freshman Academic Profile:** Average high school GPA 2.9. 7% in top 10% of high school class, 27% in top 25% of high school class, 60% in top 50% of high school class. SAT I Math middle 50% range 440-550. SAT I Verbal middle 50% range 440-530. TOEFL required of all international applicants, minimum TOEFL 550. **Basis for Candidate Selection:** *Very important factors considered include:* secondary school record, standardized test scores. *Other factors considered include:* alumni/ae relation, character/personal qualities, class rank, essays, extracurricular activities, recommendations, talent/ability, volunteer work, work experience. **Freshman Admission Requirements:** High school diploma or GED is required. *Academic units required/recommended:* 4 English required, 3 math required, 3 science required, 2 foreign language required, 3 social studies required. **Freshman Admission Statistics:** 1,256 applied, 91% accepted, 47% of those accepted enrolled. **Transfer Admission Requirements:** *Items required:* high school transcript, college transcript. Lowest grade transferable C. **General Admission Information:** Application fee $50. Priority application deadline November 30. Nonfall registration accepted. Admission may be deferred for a maximum of 1 year.

COSTS AND FINANCIAL AID

In-state tuition $7,756. Out-of-state tuition $12,006. Room & board $5,660. Required fees $364. Average book expense $864. **Required Forms and Deadlines:** FAFSA. No deadline for regular filing. **Notification of Awards:** Applicants will be notified of awards on a rolling basis beginning on or about February 15. **Types of Aid:** *Need-based scholarships/grants:* Pell, SEOG, state scholarships/grants, private scholarships, the school's own gift aid. *Loans:* FFEL Subsidized Stafford, FFEL Unsubsidized Stafford, FFEL PLUS, Federal Perkins, college/university loans from institutional funds, private loans. **Financial Aid Statistics:** 64% freshmen, 63% undergrads receive some form of aid.

PENNSYLVANIA STATE UNIVERSITY—MCKEESPORT

101 Frable Bldg., 4000 University Drive, McKeesport, PA 15132
Phone: 412-675-9010 **E-mail:** psumk@psu.edu
Fax: 412-675-9056 **Web:** www.mk.psu.edu

STUDENTS AND FACULTY

Enrollment: 929. **Student Body:** Male 61%, female 39%, out-of-state 7%, international 1%. **Ethnic Representation:** African American 13%, Asian 3%, Caucasian 83%, Hispanic 2%. **Retention and Graduation:** 74% freshmen return for sophomore year. 16% freshmen graduate within 4 years. **Faculty:** Student/faculty ratio 17:1. 35 full-time faculty, 60% hold PhDs.

ACADEMICS

Degrees: Bachelor's, terminal, transfer. **Academic Requirements:** General education including some course work in arts/fine arts, English (including composition), foreign languages, humanities, mathematics, sciences (biological or physical), social science, intercultural/international competence. **Classes:** 20-29 students in an average class. 10-19 students in an average lab/discussion section. **Disciplines with Highest Percentage of Degrees Awarded:** Computers and information sciences 100%. **Special Study Options:** Accelerated program, cross registration, distance learning, double major, dual enrollment, honors program, independent study, internships.

FACILITIES

Housing: Coed. **Library Holdings:** 40,851 bound volumes. 300 periodicals. 10,538 microforms. 2,783 audiovisuals.

EXTRACURRICULARS

Activities: Dance, drama/theater, literary magazine, radio station, student government, student newspaper. **Athletics (Intercollegiate):** *Men:* basketball, diving, fencing, ice hockey, skiing (alpine), soccer, squash, swimming, tennis, track & field, volleyball. *Women:* diving, fencing, skiing (alpine), squash, swimming, tennis, track & field, volleyball.

ADMISSIONS

Selectivity Rating: 63 (of 100). **Freshman Academic Profile:** Average high school GPA 2.8. 5% in top 10% of high school class, 26% in top 25% of high school class, 61% in top 50% of high school class. SAT I Math middle 50% range 430-540. SAT I Verbal middle 50% range 420-530. **Basis for Candidate Selection:** *Very important factors considered include:* secondary school record, standardized test scores. *Other factors considered include:* alumni/ae relation, character/personal qualities, class rank, essays, extracurricular activities, recommendations, talent/ability, volunteer work, work experience. **Freshman Admission Requirements:** High school diploma or GED is required. *Academic units required/recommended:* 4 English required, 3 math required, 3 science required, 2 foreign language required, 3 social studies required. **Freshman Admission Statistics:** 553 applied, 89% accepted, 51% of those accepted enrolled. **Transfer Admission Requirements:** *Items required:* high school transcript, college transcript. Lowest grade transferable C. **General Admission Information:** Application fee $50. Priority application deadline November 30. Nonfall registration accepted. Admission may be deferred for a maximum of 1 year.

COSTS AND FINANCIAL AID

In-state tuition $7,756. Out-of-state tuition $12,006. Room & board $5,660. Required fees $354. Average book expense $864. **Required Forms and Deadlines:** FAFSA. No deadline for regular filing. Priority filing deadline February 15. **Notification of Awards:** Applicants will be notified of awards on a rolling basis beginning on or about February 15. **Types of Aid:** *Need-based scholarships/grants:* Pell, SEOG, state scholarships/grants, private scholarships, the school's own gift aid. *Loans:* FFEL Subsidized Stafford, FFEL Unsubsidized Stafford, FFEL PLUS, Federal Perkins, college/university loans from institutional funds, private loans. **Financial Aid Statistics:** 69% freshmen, 66% undergrads receive some form of aid.

PENNSYLVANIA STATE UNIVERSITY—MONT ALTO

1 Campus Drive, Mont Alto, PA 17237-9703
Phone: 717-749-6130 **E-mail:** psuma@psu.edu
Fax: 717-749-6132 **Web:** www.ma.psu.edu

This public school was founded in 1929. It has a 62-acre campus.

STUDENTS AND FACULTY

Enrollment: 1,087. **Student Body:** Male 42%, female 58%, out-of-state 15%. **Ethnic Representation:** African American 8%, Asian 4%, Caucasian 85%, Hispanic 3%. **Retention and Graduation:** 79% freshmen return for sophomore year. 18% freshmen graduate within 4 years. **Faculty:** Student/faculty ratio 13:1. 54 full-time faculty, 44% hold PhDs.

ACADEMICS

Degrees: Bachelor's, terminal. **Academic Requirements:** General education including some course work in arts/fine arts, English (including composition), foreign languages, humanities, mathematics, sciences (biological or physical), social science, intercultural/international competence. **Classes:** 10-19 students in an average class. 20-29 students in an average lab/discussion section. **Disciplines with Highest Percentage of Degrees Awarded:** Home economics and vocational home economics 64%, health professions and related sciences 28%, business/marketing 8%. **Special Study Options:** Accelerated program, cross registration, distance learning, double major, dual enrollment, honors program, independent study, internships.

FACILITIES

Housing: Coed, suites, special-interest housing. **Library Holdings:** 38,962 bound volumes. 273 periodicals. 19,744 microforms. 1,418 audiovisuals. **Computers:** School-owned computers available for student use.

EXTRACURRICULARS

Activities: Literary magazine, radio station, student government. **Athletics (Intercollegiate):** *Men:* basketball, soccer, tennis. *Women:* basketball, tennis.

ADMISSIONS

Selectivity Rating: 63 (of 100). **Freshman Academic Profile:** Average high school GPA 2.8. 8% in top 10% of high school class, 26% in top 25% of high school class, 66% in top 50% of high school class. SAT I Math middle 50% range 420-560. SAT I Verbal middle 50% range 430-540. TOEFL required of all international applicants, minimum TOEFL 550. **Basis for Candidate Selection:** *Very important factors considered include:* secondary school record, standardized test scores. *Other factors considered include:* alumni/ae relation, character/personal qualities, class rank, essays, extracurricular activities, recommendations, talent/ability, volunteer work, work experience. **Freshman Admission Requirements:** High school diploma or GED is required. *Academic units required/recommended:* 4 English required, 3 math required, 3 science required, 2 foreign language required, 3 social studies required. **Freshman Admission Statistics:** 658 applied, 88% accepted, 56% of those accepted enrolled. **Transfer Admission Requirements:** *Items required:* high school transcript, college transcript. Lowest grade transferable C. **General Admission Information:** Application fee $50. Priority application deadline November 30. Nonfall registration accepted. Admission may be deferred for a maximum of 1 year.

COSTS AND FINANCIAL AID

In-state tuition $7,756. Out-of-state tuition $12,006. Room & board $5,660. Required fees $364. Average book expense $864. **Required Forms and Deadlines:** FAFSA. No deadline for regular filing. **Notification of Awards:** Applicants will be notified of awards on a rolling basis beginning on or about February 15. **Types of Aid:** *Need-based scholarships/grants:* Pell, SEOG, state scholarships/grants, private scholarships, the school's own gift aid. *Loans:* FFEL Subsidized Stafford, FFEL Unsubsidized Stafford, FFEL PLUS, Federal Perkins, college/university loans from institutional funds, private loans. **Financial Aid Statistics:** 65% freshmen, 63% undergrads receive some form of aid.

PENNSYLVANIA STATE UNIVERSITY—NEW KENSINGTON

3550 7th Street Road, Route780, Upper Barrell, PA 15068-1798
Phone: 724-334-5466 **E-mail:** nkadmissions@psu.edu
Fax: 724-334-6111 **Web:** www.nk.psu.edu

This public school was founded in 1958. It has a 71-acre campus.

STUDENTS AND FACULTY

Enrollment: 1,079. **Student Body:** Male 60%, female 40%, out-of-state 2%. **Ethnic Representation:** African American 2%, Asian 2%, Caucasian 96%. **Retention and Graduation:** 73% freshmen return for sophomore year. 15% freshmen graduate within 4 years. **Faculty:** Student/faculty ratio 14:1. 40 full-time faculty, 55% hold PhDs.

ACADEMICS

Degrees: Bachelor's, terminal, transfer. **Academic Requirements:** General education including some course work in arts/fine arts, English (including composition), foreign languages, humanities, mathematics, sciences (biological or physical), social science, intercultural/international competence. **Classes:** Under 10 students in an average class. 10-19 students in an average lab/discussion section. **Disciplines with Highest Percentage of Degrees Awarded:** Computer and information sciences 53%, engineering/engineering technology 47%. **Special Study Options:** Accelerated program, cross registration, distance learning, double major, dual enrollment, honors program, independent study, internships.

FACILITIES

Housing: Independently owned housing nearby. **Library Holdings:** 28,897 bound volumes. 404 periodicals. 4,506 microforms. 4,294 audiovisuals. **Computers:** School-owned computers available for student use.

EXTRACURRICULARS

Activities: Choral groups, drama/theater, jazz band, literary magazine, student government, student newspaper. **Athletics (Intercollegiate):** *Men:* baseball, basketball, ice hockey, tennis, volleyball. *Women:* basketball, ice hockey, tennis, volleyball.

ADMISSIONS

Selectivity Rating: 63 (of 100). **Freshman Academic Profile:** Average high school GPA 2.9. 6% in top 10% of high school class, 25% in top 25% of high school class, 63% in top 50% of high school class. SAT I Math middle 50% range 430-550. SAT I Verbal middle 50% range 430-530. TOEFL required of all international applicants, minimum TOEFL 550. **Basis for Candidate Selection:** *Very important factors considered include:* secondary school record, standardized test scores. *Other factors considered include:* alumni/ae relation, character/personal qualities, class rank, essays, extracurricular activities, recommendations, talent/ability, volunteer work, work experience. **Freshman Admission Requirements:** High school diploma or GED is required. *Academic units required/recommended:* 4 English required, 3 math required, 3 science required, 2 foreign language required, 3 social studies required. **Freshman Admission Statistics:** 429 applied, 90% accepted, 57% of those accepted enrolled. **Transfer Admission Requirements:** *Items required:* high school transcript, college transcript. Lowest grade transferable C. **General Admission Information:** Application fee $50. Priority application deadline November 30. Nonfall registration accepted. Admission may be deferred for a maximum of 1 year.

COSTS AND FINANCIAL AID

In-state tuition $7,756. Out-of-state tuition $12,006. Room & board $5,660. Required fees $364. Average book expense $864. **Required Forms and Deadlines:** FAFSA. No deadline for regular filing. **Notification of Awards:** Applicants will be notified of awards on a rolling basis beginning on or about February 15. **Types of Aid:** *Need-based scholarships/grants:* Pell, SEOG, state scholarships/grants, private scholarships, the school's own gift aid. *Loans:* FFEL Subsidized Stafford, FFEL Unsubsidized Stafford, FFEL PLUS, Federal Perkins, college/university loans from institutional funds, private loans. **Financial Aid Statistics:** 64% freshmen, 63% undergrads receive some form of aid.

PENNSYLVANIA STATE UNIVERSITY—SCHUYLKILL

200 University Drive, A102 Admin. Bldg., Schuykill Haven, PA 17972-2208
Phone: 570-385-6242 **E-mail:** sl-admissions@psu.edu
Fax: 570-385-3672 **Web:** www.sl.psu.edu

This public school was founded in 1934. It has a 42-acre campus.

STUDENTS AND FACULTY

Enrollment: 1,062. **Student Body:** Male 41%, female 59%, out-of-state 11%. **Ethnic Representation:** African American 12%, Asian 4%, Caucasian 81%, Hispanic 3%. **Retention and Graduation:** 80% freshmen return for sophomore year. 20% freshmen graduate within 4 years. **Faculty:** Student/faculty ratio 15:1. 51 full-time faculty, 66% hold PhDs.

ACADEMICS

Degrees: Bachelor's, terminal, transfer. **Academic Requirements:** General education including some course work in arts/fine arts, English (including composition), foreign languages, humanities, mathematics, sciences (biological or physical), social science, intercultural/international competence. **Disciplines with Highest Percentage of Degrees Awarded:** Protective services/public administration 42%, business/marketing 28%, psychology 28%, liberal arts/general studies 2%. **Special Study Options:** Accelerated program, cooperative (work-study) program, distance learning, double major, dual enrollment, independent study, internships, study abroad.

FACILITIES

Housing: Apartments for single students. **Library Holdings:** 39,289 bound volumes. 518 periodicals. 27,466 microforms. 930 audiovisuals.

EXTRACURRICULARS

Activities: Choral groups, dance, drama/theater, musical theater, student government, student newspaper. **Athletics (Intercollegiate):** *Men:* basketball, cross-country, softball, tennis, volleyball. *Women:* basketball, cross-country, softball, tennis, volleyball.

ADMISSIONS

Selectivity Rating: 63 (of 100). **Freshman Academic Profile:** Average high school GPA 2.8. 8% in top 10% of high school class, 24% in top 25% of high school class, 62% in top 50% of high school class. SAT I Math middle 50% range 400-550. SAT I Verbal middle 50% range 410-530. TOEFL required of all international applicants, minimum TOEFL 550. **Basis for Candidate Selection:** *Very important factors considered include:* secondary school record, standardized test scores. *Other factors considered include:* alumni/ae relation, character/personal qualities, class rank, essays, extracurricular activities, recommendations, talent/ability, volunteer work, work experience. **Freshman Admission Requirements:** High school diploma or GED is required. *Academic units required/recommended:* 4 English required, 3 math required, 3 science required, 2 foreign language required, 3 social studies required. **Freshman Admission Statistics:** 70 applied, 87% accepted, 50% of those accepted enrolled. **Transfer Admission Requirements:** *Items required:* high school transcript, college transcript. Lowest grade transferable C. **General Admission Information:** Application fee $50. Priority application deadline November 30. Nonfall registration accepted. Admission may be deferred for a maximum of 1 year.

COSTS AND FINANCIAL AID

In-state tuition $7,756. Out-of-state tuition $12,006. Room & board $2,910. Required fees $354. Average book expense $864. **Required Forms and Deadlines:** FAFSA. No deadline for regular filing. **Notification of Awards:** Applicants will be notified of awards on a rolling basis beginning on or about February 15. **Types of Aid:** *Need-based scholarships/grants:* Pell, SEOG, state scholarships/grants, private scholarships, the school's own gift aid. *Loans:* FFEL Subsidized Stafford, FFEL Unsubsidized Stafford, FFEL PLUS, Federal Perkins, college/university loans from institutional funds, private loans. **Financial Aid Statistics:** 73% freshmen, 73% undergrads receive some form of aid.

PENNSYLVANIA STATE UNIVERSITY—SHENANGO

147 Shenango Avenue, Sharon, PA 16146
Phone: 412-983-2803 **E-mail:** psushenango@psu.edu
Fax: 724-983-2820 **Web:** www.shenango.psu.edu

This public school was founded in 1965. It has a 14-acre campus.

STUDENTS AND FACULTY

Enrollment: 938. **Student Body:** Male 36%, female 64%, out-of-state 11%. **Ethnic Representation:** African American 4%, Caucasian 93%, Hispanic 1%, Asian 1%. **Retention and Graduation:** 69% freshmen return for sophomore year. 11% freshmen graduate within 4 years. **Faculty:** Student/faculty ratio 15:1. 31 full-time faculty, 48% hold PhDs.

ACADEMICS

Degrees: Bachelor's, terminal, transfer. **Academic Requirements:** General education including some course work in arts/fine arts, English (including composition), foreign languages, humanities, mathematics, sciences (biological or physical), social science, intercultural/international competence. **Disciplines with Highest Percentage of Degrees Awarded:** Business/marketing 66%, home economics and vocational home economics 34%. **Special Study Options:** Accelerated program, cross registration, distance learning, double major, dual enrollment, honors program, independent study, internships, study abroad.

FACILITIES

Library Holdings: 25,273 bound volumes. 346 periodicals. 3,581 microforms. 2,064 audiovisuals. **Computers:** School-owned computers available for student use.

EXTRACURRICULARS

Activities: Literary magazine, student government.

ADMISSIONS

Selectivity Rating: 63 (of 100). **Freshman Academic Profile:** Average high school GPA 2.9. 4% in top 10% of high school class, 25% in top 25% of high school class, 55% in top 50% of high school class. SAT I Math middle 50% range 410-520. SAT I Verbal middle 50% range 410-530. TOEFL required of all international applicants, minimum TOEFL 550. **Basis for Candidate Selection:** *Very important factors considered include:* secondary school record, standardized test scores. *Other factors considered include:* alumni/ae relation, character/personal qualities, class rank, essays, extracurricular activities, recommendations, talent/ability, volunteer work, work experience. **Freshman Admission Requirements:** High school diploma or GED is required. *Academic units required/recommended:* 4 English required, 3 math required, 3 science required, 2 foreign language required, 3 social studies required. **Freshman Admission Statistics:** 264 applied, 93% accepted, 64% of those accepted enrolled. **Transfer Admission Requirements:** *Items required:* high school transcript, college transcript. Lowest grade transferable C. **General Admission Information:** Application fee $50. Priority application deadline November 30. Nonfall registration accepted. Admission may be deferred for a maximum of 1 year.

COSTS AND FINANCIAL AID

In-state tuition $7,756. Out-of-state tuition $12,006. Room & board $5,660. Required fees $364. Average book expense $864. **Required Forms and Deadlines:** FAFSA. No deadline for regular filing. **Notification of Awards:** Applicants will be notified of awards on a rolling basis beginning on or about February 15. **Types of Aid:** *Need-based scholarships/grants:* Pell, SEOG, state scholarships/grants, private scholarships, the school's own gift aid. *Loans:* FFEL Subsidized Stafford, FFEL Unsubsidized Stafford, FFEL PLUS, Federal Perkins, college/university loans from institutional funds, private loans. **Financial Aid Statistics:** 76% freshmen, 77% undergrads receive some form of aid.

PENNSYLVANIA STATE UNIVERSITY—UNIVERSITY PARK

201 Shields Building, University Park, University Park, PA 16802-3000
Phone: 814-865-5471 **E-mail:** admissions@psu.edu **CEEB Code:** 2660
Fax: 814-863-7590 **Web:** www.psu.edu **ACT Code:** 3656

This public school was founded in 1855. It has a 5,617-acre campus.

STUDENTS AND FACULTY

Enrollment: 34,829. **Student Body:** Male 54%, female 46%, out-of-state 24%, international 2%. **Ethnic Representation:** African American 4%, Asian 5%, Caucasian 87%, Hispanic 3%. **Retention and Graduation:** 93% freshmen return for sophomore year. 45% freshmen graduate within 4 years. **Faculty:** Student/faculty ratio 17:1. 2143 full-time faculty, 76% hold PhDs.

ACADEMICS

Degrees: Bachelor's, certificate, doctoral, master's, post-bachelor's certificate, terminal. **Academic Requirements:** General education including some course work in arts/fine arts, English (including composition), foreign languages, humanities, mathematics, sciences (biological or physical), social science, intercultural/international competence. **Disciplines with Highest Percentage of Degrees Awarded:** Business/marketing 23%, engineering/engineering technology 13%, education 8%, communications/communication technologies 8%, social sciences and history 5%. **Special Study Options:** Accelerated program, cooperative (work-study) program, cross registration, distance learning, double major, dual enrollment, English as a second language, student exchange program (domestic), external degree program, honors program, independent study, internships, liberal arts/career combination, student-designed major, study abroad, teacher certification program.

FACILITIES

Housing: Coed, all-female, all-male, apartments for married students, apartments for single students, housing for disabled students, housing for international students, fraternities and/or sororities, Suites, special-interest housing. **Library Holdings:** 3,117,880 bound volumes. 36,856 periodicals. 2,459,545 microforms. 146,254 audiovisuals. **Special Academic Facilities/Equipment:** Museums, theatres, language labs, weather station, nuclear reactor.

EXTRACURRICULARS

Activities: Choral groups, concert band, dance, drama/theater, jazz band, literary magazine, marching band, music ensembles, musical theater, opera, pep band, radio station, student government, student newspaper, student-run film society, symphony orchestra, television station, yearbook. **Organizations:** 400 registered organizations, 39 religious organizations, 55 fraternities (13% men join), 25 sororities (10% women join). **Athletics (Intercollegiate):** *Men:* baseball, basketball, cross-country, fencing, football, golf, gymnastics, lacrosse, soccer, swimming, tennis, track & field, volleyball, wrestling. *Women:* basketball, cross-country, fencing, field hockey, golf, gymnastics, lacrosse, soccer, softball, swimming, tennis, track & field, volleyball.

ADMISSIONS

Selectivity Rating: 86 (of 100). **Freshman Academic Profile:** Average high school GPA 3.5. 41% in top 10% of high school class, 78% in top 25% of high school class, 96% in top 50% of high school class. Average SAT I Math 617, SAT I Math middle 50% range 560-670. Average SAT I Verbal 593, SAT I Verbal middle 50% range 530-630. TOEFL required of all international applicants, minimum TOEFL 550. **Basis for Candidate Selection:** *Very important factors considered include:* secondary school record, standardized test scores. *Other factors considered include:* alumni/ae relation, character/personal qualities, class rank, essays, extracurricular activities, recommendations, talent/ability, volunteer work, work experience. **Freshman Admission Requirements:** High school diploma or GED is required. *Academic units required/recommended:* 4 English required, 3 math required, 3 science required, 2 foreign language required, 3 social studies required. **Freshman Admission Statistics:** 27,604 applied, 57% accepted, 38% of those accepted enrolled. **Transfer Admission Requirements:** *Items required:* high school transcript, college transcript. Lowest grade transferable C. **General Admission Information:** Application fee $50. Priority application deadline November 30. Nonfall registration accepted. Admission may be deferred for a maximum of 1 year. Credit offered for CEEB Advanced Placement tests.

COSTS AND FINANCIAL AID

In-state tuition $8,008. Out-of-state tuition $17,236. Room & board $5,660. Required fees $374. Average book expense $864. **Required Forms and Deadlines:** FAFSA. No deadline for regular filing. Priority filing deadline

February 15. **Notification of Awards:** Applicants will be notified of awards on a rolling basis beginning on or about February 15. **Types of Aid:** *Need-based scholarships/grants:* Pell, SEOG, state scholarships/grants, private scholarships, the school's own gift aid. *Loans:* FFEL Subsidized Stafford, FFEL Unsubsidized Stafford, FFEL PLUS, Federal Perkins, college/university loans from institutional funds, private loans. **Student Employment:** Federal Work-Study Program available. Off-campus job opportunities are good. **Financial Aid Statistics:** 44% freshmen, 49% undergrads receive some form of aid. Average freshman grant $2,800. Average freshman loan $3,193. Average income from on-campus job $1,065. **Financial Aid Phone:** 814-865-6301.

PENNSYLVANIA STATE UNIVERSITY—WILKES-BARRE

PO Box PSU, Lehman, PA 18627
Phone: 570-675-9238 **E-mail:** wbadmissions@psu.edu
Fax: 570-675-9113 **Web:** www.wb.psu.edu

This public school was founded in 1916. It has a 58-acre campus.

STUDENTS AND FACULTY

Enrollment: 805. **Student Body:** Male 64%, female 36%, out-of-state 3%. **Ethnic Representation:** African American 2%, Asian 2%, Caucasian 96%, Hispanic 1%. **Retention and Graduation:** 83% freshmen return for sophomore year. 19% freshmen graduate within 4 years. **Faculty:** Student/faculty ratio 13:1. 40 full-time faculty, 50% hold PhDs.

ACADEMICS

Degrees: Bachelor's, terminal, transfer. **Academic Requirements:** General education including some course work in arts/fine arts, English (including composition), foreign languages, humanities, mathematics, sciences (biological or physical), social science, intercultural/international competence. **Classes:** 10-19 students in an average class. **Disciplines with Highest Percentage of Degrees Awarded:** Business/marketing 56%, engineering/engineering technology 44%. **Special Study Options:** Accelerated program, cross registration, distance learning, double major, dual enrollment, honors program, independent study, internships.

FACILITIES

Housing: Independently owned housing nearby. **Library Holdings:** 35,697 bound volumes. 199 periodicals. 1,992 microforms. 394 audiovisuals. **Computers:** School-owned computers available for student use.

EXTRACURRICULARS

Activities: Radio station, student government, student newspaper. **Athletics (Intercollegiate):** *Men:* baseball, soccer, volleyball. *Women:* volleyball.

ADMISSIONS

Selectivity Rating: 63 (of 100). **Freshman Academic Profile:** Average high school GPA 2.9. 9% in top 10% of high school class, 30% in top 25% of high school class, 69% in top 50% of high school class. SAT I Math middle 50% range 430-560. SAT I Verbal middle 50% range 430-540. TOEFL required of all international applicants, minimum TOEFL 550. **Basis for Candidate Selection:** *Very important factors considered include:* secondary school record, standardized test scores. *Other factors considered include:* alumni/ae relation, character/personal qualities, class rank, essays, extracurricular activities, recommendations, talent/ability, volunteer work, work experience. **Freshman Admission Requirements:** High school diploma or GED is required. *Academic units required/recommended:* 4 English required, 3 math required, 3 science required, 2 foreign language required, 3 social studies required. **Freshman Admission Statistics:** 479 applied, 82% accepted, 45% of those accepted enrolled. **Transfer Admission Requirements:** *Items required:* high school transcript, college transcript. Lowest grade transferable C. **General Admission Information:** Application fee $50. Priority application deadline November 30. Nonfall registration accepted. Admission may be deferred for a maximum of 1 year.

COSTS AND FINANCIAL AID

In-state tuition $7,756. Out-of-state tuition $12,006. Room & board $5,660. Required fees $374. Average book expense $864. **Required Forms and Deadlines:** FAFSA. No deadline for regular filing. Priority filing deadline February 15. **Notification of Awards:** Applicants will be notified of awards on a rolling basis beginning on or about February 15. **Types of Aid:** *Need-based scholarships/grants:* Pell, SEOG, state scholarships/grants, private scholarships, the school's own gift aid. *Loans:* FFEL Subsidized Stafford, FFEL Unsubsidized Stafford, FFEL PLUS, Federal Perkins, college/university loans from institutional funds, private loans. **Financial Aid Statistics:** 62% freshmen, 63% undergrads receive some form of aid.

PENNSYLVANIA STATE UNIVERSITY—WORTHINGTON SCRANTON

120 Ridge View Drive, Dunmore, PA 18512-1699
Phone: 570-963-2500 **E-mail:** wsadmissions@psu.edu
Fax: 570-963-2524 **Web:** www.sn.psu.edu

This public school was founded in 1923. It has a 43-acre campus.

STUDENTS AND FACULTY

Enrollment: 1,357. **Student Body:** Male 51%, female 49%, out-of-state 2%. **Ethnic Representation:** African American 1%, Asian 1%, Caucasian 97%, Hispanic 1%. **Retention and Graduation:** 79% freshmen return for sophomore year. 12% freshmen graduate within 4 years. **Faculty:** Student/faculty ratio 14:1. 66 full-time faculty, 46% hold PhDs.

ACADEMICS

Degrees: Bachelor's, terminal. **Academic Requirements:** General education including some course work in arts/fine arts, English (including composition), foreign languages, humanities, mathematics, sciences (biological or physical), social science, intercultural/international competence. **Classes:** 10-19 students in an average class. 10-19 students in an average lab/discussion section. **Disciplines with Highest Percentage of Degrees Awarded:** Business/marketing 70%, home economics and vocational home economics 30%. **Special Study Options:** Accelerated program, cross registration, distance learning, double major, dual enrollment, honors program, independent study, internships.

FACILITIES

Library Holdings: 53,572 bound volumes. 102 periodicals. 23,130 microforms. 3,048 audiovisuals.

EXTRACURRICULARS

Activities: Drama/theater, literary magazine, music ensembles, student government, student newspaper. **Athletics (Intercollegiate):** *Men:* baseball, basketball, cross-country, soccer. *Women:* volleyball.

ADMISSIONS

Selectivity Rating: 63 (of 100). **Freshman Academic Profile:** Average high school GPA 2.8. 5% in top 10% of high school class, 19% in top 25% of high school class, 62% in top 50% of high school class. SAT I Math middle 50% range 420-520. SAT I Verbal middle 50% range 420-510. TOEFL required of all international applicants, minimum TOEFL 550. **Basis for Candidate Selection:** *Very important factors considered include:* secondary school record, standardized test scores. *Other factors considered include:* alumni/ae relation, character/personal qualities, class rank, essays, extracurricular activities, recommendations, talent/ability, volunteer work, work experience. **Freshman Admission Requirements:** High school diploma or GED is required. *Academic units required/recommended:* 4 English required, 3 math required, 3 science required, 2 foreign language required, 3 social studies required. **Freshman Admission Statistics:** 634 applied, 83% accepted, 50% of those accepted enrolled. **Transfer Admission Requirements:** *Items required:* high school transcript, college transcript. Lowest grade transferable C. **General Admission Information:** Application fee $50. Priority application deadline November 30. Nonfall registration accepted. Admission may be deferred for a maximum of 1 year.

COSTS AND FINANCIAL AID

In-state tuition $7,756. Out-of-state tuition $12,006. Room & board $5,660. Required fees $354. Average book expense $864. **Required Forms and Deadlines:** FAFSA. No deadline for regular filing. **Notification of Awards:** Applicants will be notified of awards on a rolling basis beginning on or about February 15. **Types of Aid:** *Need-based scholarships/grants:* Pell, SEOG, state scholarships/grants, private scholarships, the school's own gift aid. *Loans:* FFEL Subsidized Stafford, FFEL Unsubsidized Stafford, FFEL PLUS, Federal Perkins, college/university loans from institutional funds, private loans. **Financial Aid Statistics:** 68% freshmen, 69% undergrads receive some form of aid.

PENNSYLVANIA STATE UNIVERSITY—YORK

1031 Edgecomb Avenue, York, PA 17403-3398
Phone: 717-771-4040 **E-mail:** ykadmission@psu.edu
Fax: 717-771-4005 **Web:** www.yk.psu.edu

This public school was founded in 1926. It has a 52-acre campus.

STUDENTS AND FACULTY

Enrollment: 1,764. **Student Body:** Male 55%, female 45%, out-of-state 2%. **Ethnic Representation:** African American 4%, Asian 5%, Caucasian 88%, Hispanic 3%. **Retention and Graduation:** 75% freshmen return for sophomore year. 17% freshmen graduate within 4 years. **Faculty:** Student/faculty ratio 15:1. 66 full-time faculty, 60% hold PhDs.

ACADEMICS

Degrees: Bachelor's, terminal, transfer. **Academic Requirements:** General education including some course work in arts/fine arts, English (including composition), foreign languages, humanities, mathematics, sciences (biological or physical), social science, intercultural/international competence. **Classes:** 10-19 students in an average class. 10-19 students in an average lab/discussion section. **Disciplines with Highest Percentage of Degrees Awarded:** Business/marketing 92%, liberal arts/general studies 4%, interdisciplinary studies 4%. **Special Study Options:** Accelerated program, cross registration, distance learning, double major, dual enrollment, English as a second language, honors program, independent study, internships, student-designed major, study abroad, weekend college.

FACILITIES

Library Holdings: 49,996 bound volumes. 243 periodicals. 23,349 microforms. 3,567 audiovisuals.

EXTRACURRICULARS

Activities: Student government, student newspaper. **Athletics (Intercollegiate):** *Men:* basketball, soccer, tennis. *Women:* tennis, volleyball.

ADMISSIONS

Selectivity Rating: 63 (of 100). **Freshman Academic Profile:** Average high school GPA 2.7. 4% in top 10% of high school class, 18% in top 25% of high school class, 51% in top 50% of high school class. SAT I Math middle 50% range 430-560. SAT I Verbal middle 50% range 430-540. TOEFL required of all international applicants, minimum TOEFL 550. **Basis for Candidate Selection:** *Very important factors considered include:* secondary school record, standardized test scores. *Other factors considered include:* alumni/ae relation, character/personal qualities, class rank, essays, extracurricular activities, recommendations, talent/ability, volunteer work, work experience. **Freshman Admission Requirements:** High school diploma or GED is required. *Academic units required/recommended:* 4 English required, 3 math required, 3 science required, 2 foreign language required, 3 social studies required. **Freshman Admission Statistics:** 825 applied, 86% accepted, 49% of those accepted enrolled. **Transfer Admission Requirements:** *Items required:* high school transcript, college transcript. Lowest grade transferable C. **General Admission Information:** Application fee $50. Priority application deadline November 30. Nonfall registration accepted. Admission may be deferred for a maximum of 1 year.

COSTS AND FINANCIAL AID

In-state tuition $7,756. Out-of-state tuition $12,006. Room & board $5,660. Required fees $354. Average book expense $864. **Required Forms and Deadlines:** FAFSA. No deadline for regular filing. **Notification of Awards:** Applicants will be notified of awards on a rolling basis beginning on or about February 15. **Types of Aid:** *Need-based scholarships/grants:* Pell, SEOG, state scholarships/grants, private scholarships, the school's own gift aid. *Loans:* FFEL Subsidized Stafford, FFEL Unsubsidized Stafford, FFEL PLUS, Federal Perkins, college/university loans from institutional funds, private loans. **Financial Aid Statistics:** 60% freshmen, 60% undergrads receive some form of aid.

PEPPERDINE UNIVERSITY

24255 Pacific Coast Highway, Malibu, CA 90263-4392
Phone: 310-506-4392 **E-mail:** admission-seaver@pepperdine.edu **CEEB Code:** 4630
Fax: 310-506-4861 **Web:** www.pepperdine.edu **ACT Code:** 373

This private school, which is affiliated with the Church of Christ, was founded in 1937. It has an 830-acre campus.

STUDENTS AND FACULTY

Enrollment: 3,153. **Student Body:** Male 41%, female 59%, out-of-state 48%, international 6%. **Ethnic Representation:** African American 7%, Asian 10%, Caucasian 59%, Hispanic 12%, Native American 2%. **Retention and Graduation:** 89% freshmen return for sophomore year. 63% freshmen graduate within 4 years. 53% grads go on to further study within 1 year. 12% grads pursue business degrees. 9% grads pursue law degrees. 5% grads pursue medical degrees. **Faculty:** Student/faculty ratio 12:1. 366 full-time faculty, 96% hold PhDs. 100% faculty teach undergrads.

ACADEMICS

Degrees: Bachelor's, doctoral, first professional, master's. **Academic Requirements:** General education including some course work in arts/fine arts, English (including composition), foreign languages, history, humanities, mathematics, sciences (biological or physical), social science, speech and rhetoric, religion, physical education. **Classes:** 10-19 students in an average class. 10-19 students in an average lab/discussion section. **Majors with Highest Enrollment:** Business administration/management; organizational communication, general; psychology, general. **Disciplines with Highest Percentage of Degrees Awarded:** Business/marketing 42%, communications/communication technologies 20%, social sciences and history 8%, psychology 5%, liberal arts/general studies 4%. **Special Study Options:** Accelerated program, double major, honors program, independent study, internships, student-designed major, study abroad, teacher certification program, weekend college. 3-2 program engineering with University of Southern California, Washington University in St. Louis, Boston University.

FACILITIES

Housing: All-female, all-male, apartments for married students, apartments for single students, housing for disabled students. Freshmen and sophomores must live on campus or at home with parent or guardian if single and under age 21. **Library Holdings:** 315,078 bound volumes. 3,182 periodicals. 258,343 microforms. 5,044 audiovisuals. **Special Academic Facilities/Equipment:** Art museum, Japanese Tea House. **Computers:** School-owned computers available for student use.

EXTRACURRICULARS

Activities: Choral groups, concert band, dance, drama/theater, jazz band, literary magazine, music ensembles, musical theater, opera, pep band, radio station, student government, student newspaper, symphony orchestra, television station, yearbook. **Organizations:** 50 registered organizations, 5 honor societies, 8 religious organizations, 6 fraternities (24% men join), 8 sororities (29% women join). **Athletics (Intercollegiate):** *Men:* baseball, basketball, cross-country, golf, tennis, volleyball, water polo. *Women:* basketball, cheerleading, cross-country, diving, golf, soccer, swimming, tennis, volleyball.

ADMISSIONS

Selectivity Rating: 86 (of 100). **Freshman Academic Profile:** Average high school GPA 3.6. 72% in top 10% of high school class, 95% in top 25% of high school class, 99% in top 50% of high school class. Average SAT I Math 600, SAT I Math middle 50% range 550-660. Average SAT I Verbal 590, SAT I Verbal middle 50% range 540-640. Average ACT 26, ACT middle 50% range 23-28. TOEFL required of all international applicants, minimum TOEFL 550. **Basis for Candidate Selection:** *Very important factors considered include:* character/personal qualities, essays, extracurricular activities, recommendations, religious affiliation/commitment, secondary school record, standardized test scores. *Important factors considered include:* talent/ability, volunteer work. *Other factors considered include:* alumni/ae relation, interview, minority status, work experience. **Freshman Admission Requirements:** High school diploma or GED is required. *Academic units required/recommended:* 25 total recommended; 4 English recommended, 4 math recommended, 4 science recommended, 3 foreign language recommended, 3 social studies recommended, 3 history recommended, 2 elective recommended. **Freshman Admission Statistics:** 5,503 applied, 37% accepted, 39% of those accepted enrolled. **Transfer Admission Requirements:** *Items required:* high school transcript, college transcript, essay. Minimum college GPA of 3.0 required. Lowest grade transferable C. **General Admission Information:** Application fee $55. Priority application deadline January 15. Nonfall registration accepted. Credit and/or placement offered for CEEB Advanced Placement tests.

COSTS AND FINANCIAL AID

Tuition $26,280. Room & board $7,930. Required fees $90. Average book expense $800. **Required Forms and Deadlines:** FAFSA and institution's own financial aid form. Financial aid filing deadline February 15. Priority filing deadline April 1. **Notification of Awards:** Applicants will be notified of awards on or about April 15. **Types of Aid:** *Need-based scholarships/grants:* Pell, SEOG, state scholarships/grants, private scholarships, the school's own gift aid. *Loans:* FFEL Subsidized Stafford, FFEL Unsubsidized Stafford, FFEL PLUS, Federal Perkins, state loans, college/university loans from institutional funds. **Student Employment:** Federal Work-Study Program available. Institutional employment available. Off-campus job opportunities are excellent. **Financial Aid Statistics:** 58% freshmen, 56% undergrads receive some form of aid. Average freshman grant $24,235. Average freshman loan $5,363. Average income from on-campus job $2,000. **Financial Aid Phone:** 310-456-4301.

PERU STATE COLLEGE

Box 10, Peru, NE 68421-0010
Phone: 402-872-2221 **E-mail:** admissions@oakmail.peru.edu **CEEB Code:** 6468
Fax: 402-872-2296 **Web:** www.peru.edu **ACT Code:** 2470

This public school was founded in 1867. It has a 103-acre campus.

STUDENTS AND FACULTY

Enrollment: 1,454. **Student Body:** Male 45%, female 55%, out-of-state 15%, international 1% (5 countries represented). **Ethnic Representation:** African American 3%, Asian 1%, Caucasian 81%, Hispanic 2%, Native American 1%. **Retention and Graduation:** 55% freshmen return for sophomore year. 8% freshmen graduate within 4 years. 10% grads go on to further study within 1 year. 1% grads pursue business degrees. 1% grads pursue law degrees. 1% grads pursue medical degrees. **Faculty:** Student/faculty ratio 16:1. 41 full-time faculty, 73% hold PhDs. 100% faculty teach undergrads.

ACADEMICS

Degrees: Bachelor's, master's. **Academic Requirements:** General education including some course work in arts/fine arts, computer literacy, English (including composition), history, humanities, mathematics, sciences (biological or physical), social science. **Majors with Highest Enrollment:** Education, general; business administration/management; criminology. **Disciplines with Highest Percentage of Degrees Awarded:** Education 28%, biological life sciences 25%, interdisciplinary studies 24%, business/marketing 16%, social sciences and history 3%. **Special Study Options:** Accelerated program, cooperative (work-study) program, distance learning, double major, dual enrollment, honors program, independent study, internships, teacher certification program.

FACILITIES

Housing: Coed, all-female, all-male, apartments for married students, apartments for single students. **Library Holdings:** 105,698 bound volumes. 1,027 periodicals. 45,000 microforms. 0 audiovisuals. **Special Academic Facilities/Equipment:** TV studio, TV distance learning classroom. **Computers:** *Recommended operating system:* Windows 2000/XP. School-owned computers available for student use.

EXTRACURRICULARS

Activities: Choral groups, concert band, drama/theater, jazz band, literary magazine, marching band, music ensembles, musical theater, pep band, student government, student newspaper, yearbook. **Organizations:** 50 registered organizations, 8 honor societies. **Athletics (Intercollegiate):** *Men:* baseball, basketball, cheerleading, football. *Women:* basketball, cheerleading, softball, volleyball.

ADMISSIONS

Selectivity Rating: 69 (of 100). **Freshman Academic Profile:** Average high school GPA 3.0. 6% in top 10% of high school class, 23% in top 25% of high school class, 53% in top 50% of high school class. 95% from public high schools. Average ACT 19, ACT middle 50% range 25-. TOEFL required of all international applicants, minimum TOEFL 550. **Basis for Candidate Selection:** *Very important factors considered include:* secondary school record, standardized test scores. *Important factors considered include:* class rank, recommendations. **Freshman Admission Requirements:** High school diploma or GED is required. *Academic units required/recommended:* 12 total recommended; 4 English recommended, 3 math recommended, 2 science recommended, 2 science lab recommended, 2 foreign language recommended, 3 social studies recommended, 3 history recommended, 2 elective recommended. **Freshman Admission Statistics:** 504 applied, 62% accepted, 57% of those accepted enrolled. **Transfer Admission Requirements:** *Items required:* college transcript. Minimum college GPA of 2.0 required. Lowest grade transferable C. **General Admission Information:** Application fee $10. Nonfall registration accepted. Credit and/or placement offered for CEEB Advanced Placement tests.

COSTS AND FINANCIAL AID

In-state tuition $2,288. Out-of-state tuition $4,575. Room & board $4,010. Required fees $600. Average book expense $600. **Required Forms and Deadlines:** FAFSA and institution's own financial aid form. No deadline for regular filing. Priority filing deadline March 3. **Notification of Awards:** Applicants will be notified of awards on a rolling basis beginning on or about April 3. **Types of Aid:** *Need-based scholarships/grants:* Pell, SEOG, state scholarships/grants, the school's own gift aid. *Loans:* FFEL Subsidized Stafford, FFEL Unsubsidized Stafford, FFEL PLUS, Federal Perkins. **Student Employment:** Federal Work-Study Program available. Institutional employment available. Off-campus job opportunities are good. **Financial Aid Statistics:** Average freshman grant $1,088. Average freshman loan $2,600. Average income from on-campus job $1,000. **Financial Aid Phone:** 402-872-2228.

PFEIFFER UNIVERSITY

USPS 429-480, Misenheimer, NC 28109
Phone: 800-338-2060 **E-mail:** admis@jfh.pfeiffer.edu **CEEB Code:** 5536
Fax: 704-463-1363 **Web:** www.pfeifferuniv.edu

This private school, which is affiliated with the Methodist Church, was founded in 1885.

STUDENTS AND FACULTY

Enrollment: 847. **Student Body:** Out-of-state 34%, international 4%. **Ethnic Representation:** African American 11%, Caucasian 87%, Hispanic 1%, Native American 1%. **Retention and Graduation:** 68% freshmen return for sophomore year. 28% grads go on to further study within 1 year. 5% grads pursue business degrees. 2% grads pursue law degrees. 1% grads pursue medical degrees.

FACILITIES

Housing: Coed, all-female, all-male.

EXTRACURRICULARS

Activities: Literary magazine, radio station, student government, student newspaper, yearbook. **Organizations:** 60 registered organizations, 6 honor societies, 1 religious organization. **Athletics (Intercollegiate):** *Men:* baseball, basketball, cheerleading, cross-country, golf, soccer, softball, tennis. *Women:* basketball, cheerleading, field hockey, softball, swimming, tennis, volleyball.

ADMISSIONS

Selectivity Rating: 68 (of 100). **Freshman Academic Profile:** Average high school GPA 2.6. 19% in top 10% of high school class, 24% in top 25% of high school class, 57% in top 50% of high school class. Average SAT I Math 460, SAT I Math middle 50% range 420-510. Average SAT I Verbal 450, SAT I Verbal middle 50% range 410-520. Average ACT 19, ACT middle 50% range 16-20. TOEFL required of all international applicants, minimum TOEFL 500. **Freshman Admission Requirements: General Admission Information:** Regular application deadline rolling. Nonfall registration accepted. Credit offered for CEEB Advanced Placement tests.

COSTS AND FINANCIAL AID

Tuition $10,230. Room & board $1,860. Average book expense $500. **Required Forms and Deadlines:** FAFSA. **Types of Aid:** *Loans:* FFEL Subsidized Stafford, FFEL PLUS. **Student Employment:** Federal Work-Study Program available. Off-campus job opportunities are good. **Financial Aid Statistics:** Average freshman loan $3,207. Average income from on-campus job $1,250. **Financial Aid Phone:** 704-463-1360.

PHILADELPHIA BIBLICAL UNIVERSITY

200 Manor Avenue, Langhorne, PA 19047
Phone: 215-702-4235 **E-mail:** admissions@pbu.edu
Fax: 215-702-4248 **Web:** www.pbu.edu **ACT Code:** 3658

This private school, which is affiliated with the Protestant Church, was founded in 1913. It has a 105-acre campus.

STUDENTS AND FACULTY

Enrollment: 1,058. **Student Body:** Male 45%, female 55%, out-of-state 52%, international 3%. **Ethnic Representation:** African American 11%, Asian 2%, Caucasian 85%, Hispanic 1%. **Retention and Graduation:** 69% freshmen return for sophomore year. 43% freshmen graduate within 4 years. **Faculty:** Student/faculty ratio 15:1. 55 full-time faculty, 56% hold PhDs. 89% faculty teach undergrads.

ACADEMICS

Degrees: Associate's, bachelor's, certificate, first professional, master's, terminal, transfer. **Academic Requirements:** General education including some course work in English (including composition), foreign languages, history, humanities, philosophy, sciences (biological or physical), social science, Bible, cultural diversity, ministry, physical education. **Classes:** 10-19 students in an average class. **Majors with Highest Enrollment:** Bible/biblical studies; elementary education and teaching; social work. **Disciplines with Highest Percentage of Degrees Awarded:** Philosophy/religion/theology 70%, computer and information sciences 14%, protective services/public administration 9%, business/marketing 4%, trade and industry 3%. **Special Study Options:** Accelerated program, double major, dual enrollment, honors program, independent study, internships, study abroad, teacher certification program.

FACILITIES

Housing: All-female, all-male, housing for disabled students, housing for international students. **Library Holdings:** 96,988 bound volumes. 733 periodicals. 63,703 microforms. 13,740 audiovisuals. **Computers:** *Recommended operating system:* Windows 95. School-owned computers available for student use.

EXTRACURRICULARS

Activities: Choral groups, concert band, drama/theater, music ensembles, student government, student newspaper, symphony orchestra, yearbook. **Organizations:** 14 registered organizations, 4 honor societies, 3 religious organizations. **Athletics (Intercollegiate):** *Men:* baseball, basketball, cross-country, soccer, tennis, volleyball. *Women:* basketball, cross-country, field hockey, soccer, softball, tennis, volleyball.

ADMISSIONS

Selectivity Rating: 75 (of 100). **Freshman Academic Profile:** Average high school GPA 3.4. 19% in top 10% of high school class, 42% in top 25% of high school class, 77% in top 50% of high school class. 60% from public high schools. Average SAT I Math 525, SAT I Math middle 50% range 488-590. Average SAT I Verbal 550, SAT I Verbal middle 50% range 490-600. Average ACT 23, ACT middle 50% range 21-28. TOEFL required of all international applicants, minimum TOEFL 550. **Basis for Candidate Selection:** *Very important factors considered include:* character/personal qualities, essays, recommendations, religious affiliation/commitment, secondary school record, standardized test scores. *Important factors considered include:* class rank. *Other factors considered include:* extracurricular activities, interview, volunteer work. **Freshman Admission Requirements:** High school diploma or GED is required. *Academic units required/recommended:* 15 total recommended; 4 English recommended, 1 math recommended, 2 science recommended, 2 foreign language recommended, 3 social studies recommended. **Freshman Admission Statistics:** 508 applied, 66% accepted, 55% of those accepted enrolled. **Transfer Admission Requirements:** *Items required:* college transcript, essay. Minimum high school GPA of 2.0 required. Minimum college GPA of 2.0 required. Lowest grade transferable C. **General Admission Information:** Application fee $25. Regular application deadline August 1. Nonfall registration accepted. Admission may be deferred for a maximum of 1 year. Neither credit nor placement offered for CEEB Advanced Placement tests.

COSTS AND FINANCIAL AID

Tuition $11,700. Room & board $5,405. Required fees $290. Average book expense $750. **Required Forms and Deadlines:** FAFSA. No deadline for regular filing. Priority filing deadline May 1. **Notification of Awards:** Applicants will be notified of awards on a rolling basis beginning on or about March 15. **Types of Aid:** *Need-based scholarships/grants:* Pell, SEOG, state scholarships/grants, private scholarships, the school's own gift aid. *Loans:* FFEL Subsidized Stafford, FFEL Unsubsidized Stafford, FFEL PLUS. **Student Employment:** Federal Work-Study Program available. Institutional employment available. Off-campus job opportunities are excellent. **Financial Aid Statistics:** 65% freshmen, 78% undergrads receive some form of aid. Average freshman grant $3,411. Average freshman loan $2,451. Average income from on-campus job $800. **Financial Aid Phone:** 215-702-4247.

PHILADELPHIA UNIVERSITY

School House Lane & Henry Avenue, Philadelphia, PA 19144-5497
Phone: 215-951-2800 **E-mail:** admissions@philau.edu **CEEB Code:** 2666
Fax: 215-951-2907 **Web:** www.PhilaU.edu **ACT Code:** 3668

This private school was founded in 1884. It has a 100-acre campus.

STUDENTS AND FACULTY

Enrollment: 2,692. **Student Body:** Male 33%, female 67%, out-of-state 42%, international 3%. **Ethnic Representation:** African American 11%, Asian 4%, Caucasian 83%, Hispanic 3%. **Retention and Graduation:** 69% freshmen return for sophomore year. 34% freshmen graduate within 4 years. 24% grads go on to further study within 1 year. 11% grads pursue business degrees. 1% grads pursue law degrees. 5% grads pursue medical degrees. **Faculty:** Student/faculty ratio 13:1. 99 full-time faculty, 72% hold PhDs. 100% faculty teach undergrads.

ACADEMICS

Degrees: Associate's, bachelor's, certificate, master's, post-bachelor's certificate. **Academic Requirements:** General education including some course work in English (including composition), sciences (biological or physical), social science. **Classes:** 10-19 students in an average class. 10-19 students in an average lab/discussion section. **Majors with Highest Enrollment:** Business administration/management; architecture (BArch, BA/BS, MArch, MA/MS, PhD); fashion/apparel design. **Disciplines with Highest Percentage of Degrees Awarded:** Business/marketing 36%, visual and performing arts 20%, architecture 13%, health professions and related sciences 13%, computer and information sciences 7%. **Special Study Options:** Cooperative (work-study) program, distance learning, student exchange program (domestic), honors program, independent study, internships, study abroad.

FACILITIES

Housing: Coed, all-female, apartments. **Library Holdings:** 124,525 bound volumes. 2,150 periodicals. 1,361 microforms. 36,844 audiovisuals. **Special Academic Facilities/Equipment:** The Design Center; industrial design studios; graphic design studios; architecture design studios; CAD labs in fashion design, interior design, and architecture. **Computers:** *Recommended operating system:* Mac. School-owned computers available for student use.

EXTRACURRICULARS

Activities: Drama/theater, radio station, student government, student newspaper, yearbook. **Organizations:** 25 registered organizations, 3 religious organizations, 2 fraternities, 2 sororities. **Athletics (Intercollegiate):** *Men:* baseball, basketball, golf, soccer, tennis. *Women:* basketball, cheerleading, cross-country, field hockey, lacrosse, soccer, softball, tennis, track & field, volleyball.

ADMISSIONS

Selectivity Rating: 68 (of 100). **Freshman Academic Profile:** Average high school GPA 3.3. 15% in top 10% of high school class, 44% in top 25% of high school class, 80% in top 50% of high school class. Average SAT I Math 538, SAT I Math middle 50% range 490-580. Average SAT I Verbal 530, SAT I Verbal middle 50% range 490-570. TOEFL required of all international applicants, minimum TOEFL 500. **Basis for Candidate Selection:** *Very important factors considered include:* secondary school record, standardized test scores. *Important factors considered include:* class rank, extracurricular activities, interview, recommendations. *Other factors considered include:* alumni/ae relation, essays. **Freshman Admission Requirements:** High school diploma or GED is required. *Academic units required/recommended:* 4 English required, 4 English recommended, 3 math required, 4 math recommended, 3 science required, 4 science recommended, 2 science lab required, 2 foreign language recommended, 2 social studies required, 3 social studies recommended, 1 history required, 2 history recommended, 2 elective required. **Freshman Admission Statistics:** 3,541 applied, 70% accepted, 25% of those accepted enrolled. **Transfer Admission Requirements:** *Items required:* college transcript. Minimum college GPA of 2.4 required. Lowest grade transferable C. **General Admission Information:** Application fee $35. Nonfall registration accepted. Admission may be deferred for a maximum of 1 year. Credit and/or placement offered for CEEB Advanced Placement tests.

COSTS AND FINANCIAL AID

Tuition $18,744. Room & board $7,370. Required fees $60. Average book expense $1,000. **Required Forms and Deadlines:** FAFSA. Financial aid filing deadline April 15. **Notification of Awards:** Applicants will be notified of awards on a rolling basis beginning on or about February 2. **Types of Aid:** *Need-based scholarships/grants:* Pell, SEOG, state scholarships/grants, private scholarships, the school's own gift aid, gift scholarships from outside sources (not endowed money) for which University chooses recipients using a need component. *Loans:* FFEL Subsidized Stafford, FFEL Unsubsidized Stafford, FFEL PLUS, Federal Perkins, private alternative Loan Programs. **Student Employment:** Federal Work-Study Program available. Institutional employment available. Off-campus job opportunities are good. **Financial Aid Statistics:** 73% freshmen, 69% undergrads receive some form of aid. Average freshman grant $9,261. Average freshman loan $3,354. **Financial Aid Phone:** 215-951-2940.

PHILANDER SMITH COLLEGE

812 W. 13th Street, Little Rock, AR 72202
Phone: 501-370-5221 **E-mail:** admission@philander.edu **CEEB Code:** 6578
Fax: 501-370-5225 **Web:** www.philander.edu **ACT Code:** 136

This private school, which is affiliated with the Methodist Church, was founded in 1877. It has a 25-acre campus.

STUDENTS AND FACULTY

Enrollment: 918. **Student Body:** Male 36%, female 64%, out-of-state 7%, international 3%. **Ethnic Representation:** African American 99%. **Retention and Graduation:** 61% freshmen return for sophomore year. 6% freshmen graduate within 4 years. **Faculty:** Student/faculty ratio 26:1. 42 full-time faculty, 57% hold PhDs. 100% faculty teach undergrads.

ACADEMICS

Degrees: Bachelor's. **Academic Requirements:** General education including some course work in arts/fine arts, computer literacy, English (including composition), foreign languages, history, humanities, mathematics, philosophy, sciences (biological or physical), social science. **Classes:** Under 10 students in an average class. Under 10 students in an average lab/discussion section. **Disciplines with Highest Percentage of Degrees Awarded:** Business/marketing 35%, social sciences and history 23%, psychology 18%, education 12%, computer and information sciences 4%. **Special Study Options:** Cooperative (work-study) program, double major, independent study, internships, teacher certification program.

FACILITIES

Housing: All-female, all-male. **Library Holdings:** 60,000 bound volumes. 280 periodicals. 3,816 microforms. 196 audiovisuals.

EXTRACURRICULARS

Activities: Choral groups, drama/theater, student government, student newspaper, yearbook. **Organizations:** 25 registered organizations, 3 honor societies, 3 religious organizations, 4 fraternities (8% men join), 4 sororities (8% women join). **Athletics (Intercollegiate):** *Men:* basketball, cheerleading. *Women:* basketball, cheerleading, volleyball.

ADMISSIONS

Selectivity Rating: 65 (of 100). **Freshman Academic Profile:** Average high school GPA 3.0. 4% in top 10% of high school class, 23% in top 25% of high school class, 55% in top 50% of high school class. 80% from public high schools. Average SAT I Math 380, SAT I Math middle 50% range 380-45. Average SAT I Verbal 450, SAT I Verbal middle 50% range 450-330. Average ACT 16, ACT middle 50% range 22-16. TOEFL required of all international applicants, minimum TOEFL 500. **Basis for Candidate Selection:** *Very important factors considered include:* secondary school record, standardized test scores. **Freshman Admission Requirements:** High school diploma or GED is required. *Academic units required/recommended:* 16 total recommended; 3 English required, 2 math required, 2 science required, 2 foreign language required, 2 social studies required. **Freshman Admission Statistics:** 368 applied, 55% accepted, 84% of those accepted enrolled. **Transfer Admission Requirements:** *Items required:* high school transcript, college transcript, standardized test score, statement of good standing from prior school. Lowest grade transferable D. **General Admission Information:** Application fee $10. Nonfall registration accepted. Admission may be deferred for a maximum of 2 years.

COSTS AND FINANCIAL AID

Tuition $3,360. Room & board $2,746. Required fees $175. Average book expense $600. **Required Forms and Deadlines:** FAFSA and institution's own financial aid form. No deadline for regular filing. Priority filing deadline April 15. **Notification of Awards:** Applicants will be notified of awards on a rolling basis beginning on or about April 1. **Types of Aid:** *Need-based scholarships/grants:* Pell, SEOG, state scholarships/grants, private scholarships, the school's own gift aid, United Negro College Fund. *Loans:* Direct Subsidized Stafford, Direct Unsubsidized Stafford, Direct PLUS, FFEL Subsidized Stafford, FFEL PLUS, Federal Perkins. **Student Employment:** Federal Work-Study Program available. Institutional employment available. Off-campus job opportunities are good. **Financial Aid Statistics:** 96% freshmen, 88% undergrads receive some form of aid. Average freshman grant $2,700. Average freshman loan $2,700. Average income from on-campus job $2,318. **Financial Aid Phone:** 501-370-5350.

PIEDMONT COLLEGE

PO Box 10, Demorest, GA 30535
Phone: 706-776-0103 **E-mail:** admit@piedmont.edu **CEEB Code:** 5537
Fax: 706-776-6635 **Web:** www.piedmont.edu **ACT Code:** 853

This private school, which is affiliated with the Congregational Church, was founded in 1897. It has a 115-acre campus.

STUDENTS AND FACULTY

Enrollment: 910. **Student Body:** Male 38%, female 62%, out-of-state 4%, international students represent 12 countries. **Ethnic Representation:** African American 8%, Asian 1%, Caucasian 88%, Hispanic 2%. **Retention and Graduation:** 66% freshmen return for sophomore year. 39% grads go on to further study within 1 year. 10% grads pursue business degrees. **Faculty:** Student/faculty ratio 15:1. 92 full-time faculty, 78% hold PhDs.

ACADEMICS

Degrees: Bachelor's, master's, post-master's certificate. **Academic Requirements:** General education including some course work in arts/fine arts, computer literacy, English (including composition), foreign languages, history, humanities, mathematics, philosophy, sciences (biological or physical), social science. **Classes:** Under 10 students in an average class. **Disciplines with Highest Percentage of Degrees Awarded:** Business/marketing 26%, education 22%, social sciences and history 15%, visual and performing arts 10%, psychology 9%. **Special Study Options:** Accelerated program, distance learning, double major, dual enrollment, honors program, independent study, internships, teacher certification program.

FACILITIES

Housing: Coed, all-female, all-male, apartments for single students, housing for disabled students, some student houses. **Library Holdings:** 116,750 bound volumes. 366 periodicals. 48,462 microforms. 725 audiovisuals. **Special Academic Facilities/Equipment:** Art Gallery, observatory, child development center, distance learning center, Northeast Georgia Youth and Tech Center, botanical center, fitness center. **Computers:** *Recommended operating system:* Windows 95. School-owned computers available for student use.

EXTRACURRICULARS

Activities: Choral groups, concert band, drama/theater, music ensembles, opera, radio station, student government, student newspaper, yearbook. **Organizations:** 25 registered organizations, 5 honor societies, 3 religious organizations. **Athletics (Intercollegiate):** *Men:* baseball, basketball, cheerleading, golf, soccer, tennis. *Women:* basketball, cheerleading, golf, soccer, softball, tennis, volleyball.

ADMISSIONS

Selectivity Rating: 63 (of 100). **Freshman Academic Profile:** Average high school GPA 3.1. 14% in top 10% of high school class, 43% in top 25% of high school class, 73% in top 50% of high school class. Average SAT I Math 560, SAT I Math middle 50% range 460-560. Average SAT I Verbal 560, SAT I Verbal middle 50% range 440-560. Average ACT 22, ACT middle 50% range 18-22. TOEFL required of all international applicants, minimum TOEFL 550. **Basis for Candidate Selection:** *Very important factors considered include:* class rank, secondary school record, standardized test scores. *Important factors considered include:* essays. *Other factors considered include:* alumni/ae relation, extracurricular activities, interview, recommendations, talent/ability. **Freshman Admission Requirements:** High school diploma or GED is required. *Academic units required/recommended:* 21 total required; 21 total recommended; 4 English recommended, 3 math recommended, 3 science recommended, 2 science lab recommended, 2 foreign language recommended, 1 social studies recommended, 2 history recommended. **Freshman Admission Statistics:** 385 applied, 68% accepted, 55% of those accepted enrolled. **Transfer Admission Requirements:** *Items required:* college transcript, statement of good standing from prior school. Minimum high school GPA of 2.0 required. Minimum college GPA of 2.0 required. Lowest grade transferable D. **General Admission Information:** Regular application deadline June 2. Nonfall registration accepted. Admission may be deferred for a maximum of 1 year. Neither credit nor placement offered for CEEB Advanced Placement tests.

COSTS AND FINANCIAL AID

Tuition $12,500. Room & board $4,400. Average book expense $850. **Required Forms and Deadlines:** FAFSA, institution's own financial aid form and state aid form. No deadline for regular filing. Priority filing deadline May 2. **Notification of Awards:** Applicants will be notified of awards on a rolling basis. **Types of Aid:** *Need-based scholarships/grants:* Pell, SEOG, state scholarships/grants, private scholarships, the school's own gift aid. *Loans:* Direct Subsidized Stafford, Direct Unsubsidized Stafford, Direct PLUS. **Student Employment:** Federal Work-Study Program available. Institutional employment available. Off-campus job opportunities are good. **Financial Aid Statistics:** 87% freshmen, 87% undergrads receive some form of aid. Average freshman grant $7,540. Average freshman loan $2,625. Average income from on-campus job $1,000. **Financial Aid Phone:** 706-776-0114.

Admission Statistics: 517 applied, 100% accepted, 44% of those accepted enrolled. **Transfer Admission Requirements:** *Items required:* high school transcript, college transcript, standardized test score, statement of good standing from prior school. Minimum college GPA of 2.0 required. Lowest grade transferable C. **General Admission Information:** Priority application deadline March 15. Regular application deadline August 20. Nonfall registration accepted. Admission may be deferred. Credit and/or placement offered for CEEB Advanced Placement tests.

COSTS AND FINANCIAL AID

Tuition $9,000. Room & board $4,600. Required fees $0. Average book expense $1,500. **Required Forms and Deadlines:** FAFSA and institution's own financial aid form. Financial aid filing deadline August 20. Priority filing deadline March 15. **Notification of Awards:** Applicants will be notified of awards on a rolling basis beginning on or about January 15. **Types of Aid:** *Need-based scholarships/grants:* Pell, SEOG, state scholarships/grants, private scholarships, the school's own gift aid. *Loans:* FFEL Subsidized Stafford, FFEL Unsubsidized Stafford, FFEL PLUS, Federal Perkins, college/university loans from institutional funds. **Student Employment:** Federal Work-Study Program available. Institutional employment available. Off-campus job opportunities are fair. **Financial Aid Statistics:** 95% freshmen, 94% undergrads receive some form of aid. Average freshman grant $9,237. Average freshman loan $3,316. **Financial Aid Phone:** 606-218-5253.

PIKEVILLE COLLEGE

Admissions Office, 147 Sycamore Street., Pikeville, KY 41501
Phone: 606-218-5251 **E-mail:** wewantyou@pc.edu **CEEB Code:** 1980
Fax: 606-218-5255 **Web:** www.pc.edu **ACT Code:** 1540

This private school, which is affiliated with the Presbyterian Church, was founded in 1889. It has a 20-acre campus.

STUDENTS AND FACULTY

Enrollment: 957. **Student Body:** Male 40%, female 60%, out-of-state 19%, international students represent 10 countries. **Ethnic Representation:** African American 7%, Caucasian 90%, Hispanic 2%. **Retention and Graduation:** 58% freshmen return for sophomore year. 20% freshmen graduate within 4 years. 10% grads go on to further study within 1 year. 2% grads pursue business degrees. 1% grads pursue law degrees. 2% grads pursue medical degrees. **Faculty:** Student/faculty ratio 12:1. 67 full-time faculty, 38% hold PhDs. 100% faculty teach undergrads.

ACADEMICS

Degrees: Associate's, bachelor's, first professional, terminal, transfer. **Academic Requirements:** General education including some course work in computer literacy, English (including composition), history, humanities, mathematics, sciences (biological or physical), social science, religion and public speaking. **Classes:** 10-19 students in an average class. **Majors with Highest Enrollment:** Business administration/management; nursing/registered nurse training (RN, ASN, BSN, MSN); psychology, general. **Disciplines with Highest Percentage of Degrees Awarded:** Business/marketing 30%, psychology 30%, biological life sciences 11%, education 5%, communications/communication technologies 5%. **Special Study Options:** Double major, independent study, internships, liberal arts/career combination, study abroad, teacher certification program.

FACILITIES

Housing: Coed, all-female, all-male, apartments for married students. **Library Holdings:** 61,071 bound volumes. 8,302 periodicals. 31,451 microforms. 1,598 audiovisuals. **Computers:** School-owned computers available for student use.

EXTRACURRICULARS

Activities: Choral groups, concert band, dance, drama/theater, jazz band, literary magazine, pep band, student government, student newspaper, yearbook. **Organizations:** 24 registered organizations, 4 honor societies, 2 religious organizations. **Athletics (Intercollegiate):** *Men:* baseball, basketball, cheerleading, cross-country, football, golf, tennis. *Women:* basketball, cheerleading, cross-country, golf, softball, tennis, volleyball.

ADMISSIONS

Selectivity Rating: 63 (of 100). **Freshman Academic Profile:** Average high school GPA 3.2. 99% from public high schools. Average ACT 19, ACT middle 50% range 15-22. TOEFL required of all international applicants, minimum TOEFL 500. **Freshman Admission Requirements:** High school diploma or GED is required. *Academic units required/recommended:* 13 total recommended; 4 English recommended, 3 math recommended, 3 science recommended, 1 social studies recommended, 1 history recommended. **Freshman**

PINE MANOR COLLEGE

400 Heath Street, Chestnut Hill, MA 02467-2332
Phone: 617-731-7104 **E-mail:** admission@pmc.edu **CEEB Code:** 3689
Fax: 617-731-7102 **Web:** www.pmc.edu **ACT Code:** 1882

This private school was founded in 1911. It has a 60-acre campus.

STUDENTS AND FACULTY

Enrollment: 306. **Student Body:** Out-of-state 24%, international 15%. **Ethnic Representation:** African American 26%, Asian 4%, Caucasian 42%, Hispanic 19%, Native American 1%. **Retention and Graduation:** 72% freshmen return for sophomore year. 38% freshmen graduate within 4 years. 27% grads go on to further study within 1 year. 11% grads pursue business degrees. 1% grads pursue law degrees. 4% grads pursue medical degrees. **Faculty:** Student/faculty ratio 9:1. 30 full-time faculty, 80% hold PhDs. 100% faculty teach undergrads.

ACADEMICS

Degrees: Bachelor's, certificate, master's, transfer. **Academic Requirements:** General education including some course work in arts/fine arts, computer literacy, English (including composition), history, humanities, mathematics, sciences (biological or physical), social science, and portfolio. **Classes:** 10-19 students in an average class. 20-29 students in an average lab/discussion section. **Majors with Highest Enrollment:** Psychology, general; communications and media studies; business administration/management. **Disciplines with Highest Percentage of Degrees Awarded:** Biological life sciences 21%, psychology 18%, business/marketing 16%, communications/communication technologies 12%, visual and performing arts 11%. **Special Study Options:** Cross registration, double major, English as a second language, honors program, independent study, internships, liberal arts/career combination, student-designed major, study abroad, teacher certification program.

FACILITIES

Housing: All-female, housing for disabled students. **Library Holdings:** 64,647 bound volumes. 1,645 periodicals. 64,376 microforms. 4,085 audiovisuals. **Special Academic Facilities/Equipment:** Art gallery, communications center, child study center. **Computers:** *Recommended operating system:* Mac. School-owned computers available for student use.

EXTRACURRICULARS

Activities: Choral groups, dance, drama/theater, literary magazine, radio station, student government, student newspaper, yearbook. **Organizations:** 17 registered organizations, 1 honor society, 1 religious organization. **Athletics (Intercollegiate):** *Women:* basketball, cross-country, golf, soccer, softball, tennis, volleyball.

ADMISSIONS

Selectivity Rating: 71 (of 100). **Freshman Academic Profile:** Average high school GPA 2.4. 2% in top 10% of high school class, 20% in top 25% of high school class, 45% in top 50% of high school class. Average SAT I Math 420, SAT I Math middle 50% range 450-330. Average SAT I Verbal 440, SAT I Verbal middle 50% range 470-340. Average ACT 19, ACT middle 50% range 21-17. TOEFL required of all international applicants, minimum TOEFL 475. **Basis**

for Candidate Selection: *Very important factors considered include:* secondary school record, volunteer work. *Important factors considered include:* essays, extracurricular activities, recommendations. *Other factors considered include:* alumni/ae relation, character/personal qualities, class rank, minority status, standardized test scores, talent/ability, work experience. **Freshman Admission Requirements:** High school diploma or GED is required. *Academic units required/recommended:* 4 English recommended, 3 math recommended, 3 science recommended, 2 foreign language recommended, 2 social studies recommended. **Freshman Admission Statistics:** 471 applied, 75% accepted, 44% of those accepted enrolled. **Transfer Admission Requirements:** *Items required:* college transcript, essay, statement of good standing from prior school. Minimum college GPA of 2.0 required. Lowest grade transferable C-. **General Admission Information:** Application fee $25. Nonfall registration accepted. Admission may be deferred for a maximum of 1 year. Credit and/or placement offered for CEEB Advanced Placement tests.

COSTS AND FINANCIAL AID

Tuition $11,440. Room & board $7,245. Average book expense $500. **Required Forms and Deadlines:** FAFSA and institution's own financial aid form. Priority filing deadline March 15. **Notification of Awards:** Applicants will be notified of awards on a rolling basis beginning on or about March 1. **Types of Aid:** *Need-based scholarships/grants:* Pell, SEOG, state scholarships/grants, private scholarships, the school's own gift aid. *Loans:* FFEL Subsidized Stafford, FFEL Unsubsidized Stafford, FFEL PLUS, state loans. **Student Employment:** Federal Work-Study Program available. Institutional employment available. Off-campus job opportunities are excellent. **Financial Aid Statistics:** 84% freshmen, 76% undergrads receive some form of aid. Average freshman loan $2,436. **Financial Aid Phone:** 617-731-7129.

PITTSBURG STATE UNIVERSITY

1701 South Broadway, Pittsburg, KS 66762-5880
Phone: 620-235-4251 **E-mail:** psuadmit@pittstate.edu **CEEB Code:** 6336
Fax: 620-235-6003 **Web:** www.pittstate.edu **ACT Code:** 1449

This public school was founded in 1903. It has a 233-acre campus.

STUDENTS AND FACULTY

Enrollment: 5,470. **Student Body:** Male 52%, female 48%, international 5%. **Ethnic Representation:** African American 2%, Caucasian 79%, Hispanic 2%, Native American 2%. **Retention and Graduation:** 75% freshmen return for sophomore year. **Faculty:** Student/faculty ratio 23:1. 269 full-time faculty. 100% faculty teach undergrads.

ACADEMICS

Degrees: Associate's, bachelor's, certificate, master's, terminal. **Academic Requirements:** General education including some course work in arts/fine arts, computer literacy, foreign languages, history, humanities, mathematics, sciences (biological or physical), social science. **Disciplines with Highest Percentage of Degrees Awarded:** Education 13%, engineering/engineering technology 12%, business/marketing 9%, trade and industry 7%, psychology 7%. **Special Study Options:** Cooperative (work-study) program, distance learning, double major, dual enrollment, English as a second language, honors program, independent study, internships, student-designed major, study abroad, teacher certification program.

FACILITIES

Housing: Coed, apartments for married students. **Library Holdings:** 718,422 bound volumes. 4,512 periodicals. 797,204 microforms. 0 audiovisuals. **Special Academic Facilities/Equipment:** Planetarium, observatory. **Computers:** *Recommended operating system:* Windows 95.

EXTRACURRICULARS

Activities: Choral groups, concert band, dance, drama/theater, jazz band, literary magazine, marching band, music ensembles, musical theater, pep band, radio station, student government, student newspaper, symphony orchestra, television station, yearbook. **Organizations:** 131 registered organizations, 1 honor society, 13 religious organizations, 8 fraternities, 3 sororities. **Athletics (Intercollegiate):** *Men:* baseball, basketball, cheerleading, cross-country, football, golf, indoor track, track & field. *Women:* basketball, cheerleading, cross-country, indoor track, softball, track & field, volleyball.

ADMISSIONS

Selectivity Rating: 66 (of 100). **Freshman Academic Profile:** 32% in top 25% of high school class, 63% in top 50% of high school class. 86% from public high schools. Average ACT 21. TOEFL required of all international applicants, minimum TOEFL 520. **Basis for Candidate Selection:** *Very important factors considered include:* standardized test scores. *Other factors considered include:* class rank, secondary school record. **Freshman Admission Requirements:** High school diploma or GED is required. *Academic units required/recommended:* 4 English required, 3 math required, 3 science required, 1 science lab required, 3 social studies required. **Transfer Admission Requirements:** *Items required:* college transcript. Minimum college GPA of 2.0 required. **General Admission Information:** Application fee $25. Nonfall registration accepted. Credit and/or placement offered for CEEB Advanced Placement tests.

COSTS AND FINANCIAL AID

In-state tuition $2,338. Out-of-state tuition $7,192. Room & board $3,890. Required fees $0. Average book expense $300. **Required Forms and Deadlines:** FAFSA. Priority filing deadline March 1. **Notification of Awards:** Applicants will be notified of awards on a rolling basis beginning on or about April 1. **Types of Aid:** *Need-based scholarships/grants:* Pell, SEOG, state scholarships/grants, private scholarships, the school's own gift aid. *Loans:* FFEL Subsidized Stafford, FFEL Unsubsidized Stafford, FFEL PLUS, Federal Perkins, Federal Nursing, college/university loans from institutional funds. **Student Employment:** Federal Work-Study Program available. Institutional employment available. Off-campus job opportunities are good. **Financial Aid Statistics:** 52% freshmen, 55% undergrads receive some form of aid. Average freshman grant $750. Average income from on-campus job $3,500. **Financial Aid Phone:** 620-235-4240.

PITZER COLLEGE

1050 North Mills Avenue, Claremont, CA 91711-6101
Phone: 909-621-8129 **E-mail:** admission@pitzer.edu **CEEB Code:** 4619
Fax: 909-621-8770 **Web:** www.pitzer.edu **ACT Code:** 363

This private school was founded in 1963. It has a 35-acre campus.

STUDENTS AND FACULTY

Enrollment: 954. **Student Body:** Male 38%, female 62%, out-of-state 49%, international 3% (17 countries represented). **Ethnic Representation:** African American 6%, Asian 10%, Caucasian 48%, Hispanic 15%, Native American 1%. **Retention and Graduation:** 82% freshmen return for sophomore year. 52% freshmen graduate within 4 years. 8% grads pursue business degrees. 9% grads pursue law degrees. 5% grads pursue medical degrees. **Faculty:** Student/faculty ratio 12:1. 61 full-time faculty, 96% hold PhDs. 100% faculty teach undergrads.

ACADEMICS

Degrees: Bachelor's. **Academic Requirements:** General education including some course work in arts/fine arts, English (including composition), humanities, mathematics, sciences (biological or physical), social science, interdisciplinary and intercultural exploration; social responsibility. **Classes:** 10-19 students in an average class. **Majors with Highest Enrollment:** English language and literature, general; psychology, general; sociology. **Disciplines with Highest Percentage of Degrees Awarded:** Social sciences and history 28%, visual and performing arts 15%, psychology 11%, English 10%, business/marketing 8%. **Special Study Options:** Cross registration, double major, English as a second language, student exchange program (domestic), independent study, internships, liberal arts/career combination, student-designed major, study abroad.

FACILITIES

Housing: Coed, housing for disabled students, cooperative housing. **Library Holdings:** 2,000,000 bound volumes. 6,000 periodicals. 1,131,000 microforms. 606 audiovisuals. **Special Academic Facilities/Equipment:** Theatre arts center, black, Asian American and Chicano study centers, film, TV, and videotape studios, botanical garden, biological field station, medical center. **Computers:** *Recommended operating system:* Windows NT/2000. School-owned computers available for student use.

EXTRACURRICULARS

Activities: Choral groups, concert band, dance, drama/theater, literary magazine, music ensembles, musical theater, radio station, student government, student newspaper, student-run film society, symphony orchestra. **Organizations:** 64 registered organizations, 3 religious organizations. **Athletics (Intercollegiate):** *Men:* baseball, basketball, cross-country, diving, football, golf, soccer, swimming, tennis, track & field, water polo. *Women:* basketball, cross-country, diving, soccer, softball, swimming, tennis, track & field, volleyball, water polo.

ADMISSIONS

Selectivity Rating: 83 (of 100). **Freshman Academic Profile:** Average high school GPA 3.5. 22% in top 10% of high school class, 91% in top 50% of high school class. Average SAT I Math 610, SAT I Math middle 50% range 550-670.

Average SAT I Verbal 620, SAT I Verbal middle 50% range 570-670. Average ACT 25, ACT middle 50% range 23-27. TOEFL required of all international applicants, minimum TOEFL 590. **Basis for Candidate Selection:** *Very important factors considered include:* character/personal qualities, essays, extracurricular activities, minority status, recommendations, secondary school record, talent/ability, volunteer work. *Important factors considered include:* class rank, geographical residence, interview, standardized test scores, work experience. *Other factors considered include:* alumni/ae relation. **Freshman Admission Requirements:** High school diploma or GED is required. *Academic units required/recommended:* 4 English recommended, 3 math recommended, 3 science recommended, 3 science lab recommended, 3 foreign language recommended, 3 social studies recommended. **Freshman Admission Statistics:** 2,323 applied, 56% accepted, 18% of those accepted enrolled. **Transfer Admission Requirements:** *Items required:* college transcript, essay, statement of good standing from prior school. Minimum college GPA of 2.0 required. Lowest grade transferable C. **General Admission Information:** Application fee $50. Regular application deadline January 15. Admission may be deferred for a maximum of 1 year. Placement offered for CEEB Advanced Placement tests.

COSTS AND FINANCIAL AID

Average book expense $850. **Required Forms and Deadlines:** FAFSA, CSS/Financial Aid PROFILE, state aid form, noncustodial (divorced/separated) parent's statement and business/farm supplement. Financial aid filing deadline February 1. **Notification of Awards:** Applicants will be notified of awards on or about April 1. **Types of Aid:** *Need-based scholarships/grants:* Pell, SEOG, state scholarships/grants, private scholarships, the school's own gift aid. *Loans:* FFEL Subsidized Stafford, FFEL Unsubsidized Stafford, FFEL PLUS, Federal Perkins, college/university loans from institutional funds. **Student Employment:** Federal Work-Study Program available. Institutional employment available. Off-campus job opportunities are good. **Financial Aid Statistics:** 34% freshmen, 45% undergrads receive some form of aid. Average freshman grant $23,864. Average freshman loan $2,626. Average income from on-campus job $2,454. **Financial Aid Phone:** 909-621-8208.

See page 1154.

PLATTSBURGH STATE UNIVERSITY

1001 Kehoe Bldg., Plattsburgh, NY 12901
Phone: 518-564-2040 **E-mail:** admissions@plattsburgh.edu **CEEB Code:** 2544
Fax: 518-564-2045 **Web:** www.plattsburgh.edu **ACT Code:** 2944

This public school was founded in 1889. It has a 300-acre campus.

STUDENTS AND FACULTY

Enrollment: 5,459. **Student Body:** Male 42%, female 58%, out-of-state 3%, international 7% (19 countries represented). **Ethnic Representation:** African American 4%, Asian 2%, Caucasian 83%, Hispanic 3%. **Retention and Graduation:** 77% freshmen return for sophomore year. 33% freshmen graduate within 4 years. 34% grads go on to further study within 1 year. 2% grads pursue business degrees. 1% grads pursue law degrees. 1% grads pursue medical degrees. **Faculty:** Student/faculty ratio 18:1. 252 full-time faculty, 81% hold PhDs. 100% faculty teach undergrads.

ACADEMICS

Degrees: Bachelor's, certificate, master's, post-master's certificate. **Academic Requirements:** General education including some course work in arts/fine arts, computer literacy, English (including composition), foreign languages, humanities, mathematics, sciences (biological or physical), social science. **Classes:** 20-29 students in an average class. 20-29 students in an average lab/discussion section. **Majors with Highest Enrollment:** Special education, general; business administration/management; early childhood education and teaching. **Disciplines with Highest Percentage of Degrees Awarded:** Education 21%, business/marketing 18%, communications/communication technologies 9%, social sciences and history 9%, protective services/public administration 8%. **Special Study Options:** Cooperative (work-study) program, cross registration, distance learning, double major, dual enrollment, English as a second language, student exchange program (domestic), honors program, independent study, internships, liberal arts/career combination, student-designed major, study abroad, teacher certification program.

FACILITIES

Housing: Coed, housing for disabled students, housing for international students, wellness floor, substance-free building & floors, quiet floors, men's floor, women's floors, extended lodging. **Library Holdings:** 378,020 bound volumes. 1,407 periodicals. 925,213 microforms. 19,714 audiovisuals. **Special Academic Facilities/Equipment:** Art galleries, sculpture courtyard, theatre and concert halls, communications/lecture hall, interactive video for tele-courses, radio and TV broadcasting facilities, planetarium, on-site research center for biotechnology and environmental science, enzymology lab, electron microscope, remote sensing lab, NMR spectrophotometer, computer-operated infrared spectrophotometer, gas chromatograph, mass spectrometer, computerized liquid scintillation counter, facility for analysis of environmental pollutants in lake water, sediments and biota, lake research/sampling vessel with differential GPS navigation equipment, ubductively coupled plasma/mass spectrometer, ion chromatograph/high performance liquid chromatograph, mercury detector. **Computers:** School-owned computers available for student use.

EXTRACURRICULARS

Activities: Choral groups, concert band, drama/theater, jazz band, literary magazine, music ensembles, radio station, student government, student newspaper, student-run film society, symphony orchestra, television station, yearbook. **Organizations:** 90 registered organizations, 26 honor societies, 3 religious organizations, 7 fraternities (6% men join), 7 sororities (5% women join). **Athletics (Intercollegiate):** *Men:* basketball, cross-country, golf, ice hockey, indoor track, lacrosse, rugby, soccer, swimming, track & field. *Women:* basketball, cross-country, golf, ice hockey, indoor track, rugby, soccer, softball, swimming, tennis, track & field, volleyball.

ADMISSIONS

Selectivity Rating: 63 (of 100). **Freshman Academic Profile:** Average high school GPA 3.0. 10% in top 10% of high school class, 30% in top 25% of high school class, 75% in top 50% of high school class. 98% from public high schools. Average SAT I Math 525, SAT I Math middle 50% range 480-560. Average SAT I Verbal 530, SAT I Verbal middle 50% range 480-560. Average ACT 22, ACT middle 50% range 20-24. TOEFL required of all international applicants, minimum TOEFL 525. **Basis for Candidate Selection:** *Very important factors considered include:* interview, secondary school record, standardized test scores. *Important factors considered include:* alumni/ae relation, character/personal qualities, class rank, essays, extracurricular activities, minority status, recommendations, talent/ability. *Other factors considered include:* volunteer work, work experience. **Freshman Admission Requirements:** High school diploma or GED is required. *Academic units required/recommended:* 17 total required; 21 total recommended; 4 English required, 4 English recommended, 3 math required, 4 math recommended, 3 science required, 4 science recommended, 3 foreign language required, 3 foreign language recommended, 3 social studies required, 3 social studies recommended, 1 history required, 1 history recommended, 2 elective recommended. **Freshman Admission Statistics:** 5,138 applied, 60% accepted, 33% of those accepted enrolled. **Transfer Admission Requirements:** *Items required:* college transcript. Minimum college GPA of 2.3 required. Lowest grade transferable D. **General Admission Information:** Application fee $40. Early decision application deadline November 15. Priority application deadline March 1. Regular application deadline August 1. Nonfall registration accepted. Admission may be deferred for a maximum of 1 year. Credit and/or placement offered for CEEB Advanced Placement tests.

COSTS AND FINANCIAL AID

In-state tuition $3,400. Out-of-state tuition $8,300. Room & board $5,920. Required fees $829. Average book expense $750. **Required Forms and Deadlines:** FAFSA and state aid form. No deadline for regular filing. Priority filing deadline March 1. **Notification of Awards:** Applicants will be notified of awards on a rolling basis beginning on or about March 15. **Types of Aid:** *Need-based scholarships/grants:* Pell, SEOG, state scholarships/grants, private scholarships, the school's own gift aid, Scholarships for disadvantaged students, State Educational Opportunity Program. *Loans:* Direct Subsidized Stafford, Direct Unsubsidized Stafford, Direct PLUS, Federal Perkins, Federal Nursing, Grace Appleton Loan (privately endowed, administered by a trust company and awarded by the College). **Student Employment:** Federal Work-Study Program available. Institutional employment available. Off-campus job opportunities are good. **Financial Aid Statistics:** 54% freshmen, 56% undergrads receive some form of aid. Average freshman grant $4,703. Average freshman loan $2,553. Average income from on-campus job $1,100. **Financial Aid Phone:** 518-564-4076.

PLYMOUTH STATE COLLEGE

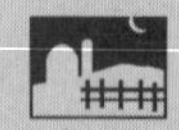

17 High Street, Plymouth, NH 03264
Phone: 603-535-2237 **E-mail:** pscadmit@mail.plymouth.edu **CEEB Code:** 3690
Fax: 603-535-2714 **Web:** www.plymouth.edu **ACT Code:** 2518

This public school was founded in 1871. It has a 170-acre campus.

STUDENTS AND FACULTY

Enrollment: 3,790. **Student Body:** Male 49%, female 51%, out-of-state 45%, international students represent 20 countries. **Ethnic Representation:** Asian 1%, Caucasian 90%, Hispanic 1%. **Retention and Graduation:** 74% freshmen return for sophomore year. 23% freshmen graduate within 4 years. 15% grads go on to further study within 1 year. 4% grads pursue business degrees. 1% grads pursue law degrees. **Faculty:** Student/faculty ratio 17:1. 170 full-time faculty, 87% hold PhDs. 100% faculty teach undergrads.

ACADEMICS

Degrees: Bachelor's, master's, post-bachelor's certificate, post-master's certificate. **Academic Requirements:** General education including some course work in arts/fine arts, computer literacy, English (including composition), history, humanities, mathematics, philosophy, sciences (biological or physical), social science, technological. **Classes:** 10-19 students in an average class. 10-19 students in an average lab/discussion section. **Majors with Highest Enrollment:** Elementary education and teaching; business administration/management; health and physical education, general. **Disciplines with Highest Percentage of Degrees Awarded:** Education 31%, business/marketing 18%, visual and performing arts 9%, social sciences and history 7%, psychology 6%. **Special Study Options:** Double major, student exchange program (domestic), honors program, independent study, internships, student-designed major, study abroad, teacher certification program.

FACILITIES

Housing: Coed, apartments for married students, apartments for single students, fraternities and/or sororities, nontraditional student apartments. **Library Holdings:** 296,479 bound volumes. 1,071 periodicals. 731,476 microforms. 20,993 audiovisuals. **Special Academic Facilities/Equipment:** Karl Drerup Art gallery, Silver Cultural Arts Center, Sylvestre Planetarium, Child Development & Family Center (NAEYC-accredited lab school for children 2-6 years old), meteorology lab, Geographic Information System Lab, psychology lab, graphic design computer lab. **Computers:** School-owned computers available for student use.

EXTRACURRICULARS

Activities: Choral groups, concert band, dance, drama/theater, jazz band, literary magazine, music ensembles, musical theater, radio station, student government, student newspaper, yearbook. **Organizations:** 80 registered organizations, 10 honor societies, 2 religious organizations, 2 fraternities (4% men join), 5 sororities (7% women join). **Athletics (Intercollegiate):** *Men:* baseball, basketball, football, ice hockey, lacrosse, skiing (alpine), soccer, wrestling. *Women:* basketball, diving, field hockey, lacrosse, skiing (alpine), soccer, softball, swimming, tennis, volleyball.

ADMISSIONS

Selectivity Rating: 63 (of 100). **Freshman Academic Profile:** Average high school GPA 2.8. 3% in top 10% of high school class, 15% in top 25% of high school class, 48% in top 50% of high school class. 98% from public high schools. Average SAT I Math 485, SAT I Math middle 50% range 430-540. Average SAT I Verbal 480, SAT I Verbal middle 50% range 430-530. Average ACT 18, ACT middle 50% range 17-21. TOEFL required of all international applicants, minimum TOEFL 520. **Basis for Candidate Selection:** *Very important factors considered include:* secondary school record. *Important factors considered include:* character/personal qualities, class rank, essays, recommendations, standardized test scores, talent/ability. *Other factors considered include:* alumni/ae relation, extracurricular activities, minority status, volunteer work, work experience. **Freshman Admission Requirements:** High school diploma or GED is required. *Academic units required/recommended:* 13 total required; 16 total recommended; 4 English required, 4 English recommended, 3 math required, 3 math recommended, 2 science required, 2 science recommended, 1 science lab required, 1 science lab recommended, 2 foreign language recommended, 2 social studies required, 2 social studies recommended, 1 history required, 2 history recommended. **Freshman Admission Statistics:** 3,573 applied, 77% accepted, 34% of those accepted enrolled. **Transfer Admission Requirements:** *Items required:* high school transcript, college transcript. Minimum college GPA of 2.0 required. Lowest grade transferable C. **General Admission Information:** Application fee $30. Regular application deadline April 1. Nonfall registration accepted. Admission may be deferred for a maximum of 1 year. Credit offered for CEEB Advanced Placement tests.

COSTS AND FINANCIAL AID

In-state tuition $4,450. Out-of-state tuition $10,110. Room & board $5,768. Required fees $1,406. Average book expense $700. **Required Forms and Deadlines:** FAFSA. Priority filing deadline March 2. **Notification of Awards:** Applicants will be notified of awards on a rolling basis beginning on or about March 2. **Types of Aid:** *Need-based scholarships/grants:* Pell, SEOG, state scholarships/grants, private scholarships, the school's own gift aid. *Loans:* FFEL Subsidized Stafford, FFEL Unsubsidized Stafford, FFEL PLUS, Federal Perkins. **Student Employment:** Federal Work-Study Program available. Institutional employment available. Off-campus job opportunities are good. **Financial Aid Statistics:** 59% freshmen, 58% undergrads receive some form of aid. Average freshman grant $4,016. Average freshman loan $2,806. Average income from on-campus job $840. **Financial Aid Phone:** 603-535-2338.

POINT LOMA NAZARENE UNIVERSITY

3900 Lomaland Drive, San Diego, CA 92106
Phone: 619-849-2273 **E-mail:** admissions@ptloma.edu **CEEB Code:** 4605
Fax: 619-849-2601 **Web:** www.ptloma.edu **ACT Code:** 370

This private school, which is affiliated with the Nazarene Church, was founded in 1902. It has a 90-acre campus.

STUDENTS AND FACULTY

Enrollment: 2,390. **Student Body:** Male 41%, female 59%, out-of-state 23%, international 1% (17 countries represented). **Ethnic Representation:** African American 2%, Asian 4%, Caucasian 85%, Hispanic 8%, Native American 1%. **Retention and Graduation:** 82% freshmen return for sophomore year. 43% freshmen graduate within 4 years. **Faculty:** Student/faculty ratio 16:1. 129 full-time faculty, 72% hold PhDs. 100% faculty teach undergrads.

ACADEMICS

Degrees: Bachelor's, master's, post-bachelor's certificate, post-master's certificate. **Academic Requirements:** General education including some course work in arts/fine arts, English (including composition), foreign languages, history, mathematics, philosophy, sciences (biological or physical), social science, 8 units of Bible and theology. **Majors with Highest Enrollment:** Business administration/management; liberal arts and sciences/liberal studies; psychology, general. **Disciplines with Highest Percentage of Degrees Awarded:** Health professions and related sciences 19%, business/marketing 16%, liberal arts/general studies 11%, education 9%, social sciences and history 9%. **Special Study Options:** Double major, independent study, internships, study abroad, teacher certification program.

FACILITIES

Housing: All-female, all-male, apartments for married students, apartments for single students. **Library Holdings:** 146,016 bound volumes. 836 periodicals. 74,171 microforms. 18,685 audiovisuals. **Special Academic Facilities/Equipment:** Language lab, on-campus preschool, electron microscope.

EXTRACURRICULARS

Activities: Choral groups, concert band, drama/theater, jazz band, literary magazine, music ensembles, opera, pep band, radio station, student government, student newspaper, yearbook. **Organizations:** 30 registered organizations, 2 honor societies, 7 religious organizations, 3 fraternities, 3 sororities. **Athletics (Intercollegiate):** *Men:* baseball, basketball, cross-country, golf, soccer, tennis, track & field. *Women:* basketball, cross-country, softball, tennis, track & field, volleyball.

ADMISSIONS

Selectivity Rating: 66 (of 100). **Freshman Academic Profile:** Average high school GPA 3.7. 32% in top 10% of high school class, 62% in top 25% of high school class, 90% in top 50% of high school class. 82% from public high schools. Average SAT I Math 572, SAT I Math middle 50% range 500-620. Average SAT I Verbal 563, SAT I Verbal middle 50% range 510-600. Average ACT 23, ACT middle 50% range 21-26. TOEFL required of all international applicants, minimum TOEFL 550. **Basis for Candidate Selection:** *Very important factors considered include:* character/personal qualities, secondary school record, standardized test scores. *Important factors considered include:* essays, recommendations. *Other factors considered include:* alumni/ae relation, class rank, extracurricular activities, religious affiliation/commitment, talent/ability. **Freshman Admission Requirements:** High school diploma or GED is required. *Academic units required/recommended:* 10 total recommended; 4 English recommended, 2 math recommended, 1 science recommended, 1 science lab recommended, 2 foreign language recommended, 1 history recommended. **Freshman Admission Statistics:** 1,404 applied, 73% accepted,

53% of those accepted enrolled. **Transfer Admission Requirements:** *Items required:* college transcript, standardized test score, statement of good standing from prior school. Minimum college GPA of 2.0 required. Lowest grade transferable D. **General Admission Information:** Application fee $45. Regular application deadline March 1. Nonfall registration accepted. Admission may be deferred. Credit offered for CEEB Advanced Placement tests.

COSTS AND FINANCIAL AID

Tuition $15,760. Room & board $6,380. Required fees $500. Average book expense $1,210. **Required Forms and Deadlines:** FAFSA and institution's own financial aid form. Priority filing deadline March 15. **Notification of Awards:** Applicants will be notified of awards on or about May 30. **Types of Aid:** *Need-based scholarships/grants:* Pell, SEOG, state scholarships/grants, private scholarships, the school's own gift aid. *Loans:* FFEL Subsidized Stafford, FFEL Unsubsidized Stafford, FFEL PLUS, Federal Perkins, Federal Nursing, state loans, college/university loans from institutional funds. **Student Employment:** Federal Work-Study Program available. Institutional employment available. Off-campus job opportunities are good. **Financial Aid Statistics:** 38% freshmen, 54% undergrads receive some form of aid. **Financial Aid Phone:** 619-849-2296.

POINT PARK COLLEGE

201 Wood Street, Pittsburgh, PA 15222
Phone: 412-392-3430 **E-mail:** enroll@ppc.edu **CEEB Code:** 2676
Fax: 412-391-1980 **Web:** www.ppc.edu **ACT Code:** 3530

This private school was founded in 1960.

STUDENTS AND FACULTY

Enrollment: 2,743. **Student Body:** Male 43%, female 57%, out-of-state 13%, international 2%. **Ethnic Representation:** African American 13%, Asian 1%, Caucasian 79%, Hispanic 1%. **Retention and Graduation:** 71% freshmen return for sophomore year. 37% freshmen graduate within 4 years. 12% grads go on to further study within 1 year. 9% grads pursue business degrees. 1% grads pursue law degrees. **Faculty:** Student/faculty ratio 14:1. 78 full-time faculty, 34% hold PhDs. 95% faculty teach undergrads.

ACADEMICS

Degrees: Associate's, bachelor's, certificate, master's. **Academic Requirements:** General education including some course work in arts/fine arts, computer literacy, English (including composition), foreign languages, history, humanities, mathematics, philosophy, sciences (biological or physical), social science. **Classes:** 10-19 students in an average class. **Majors with Highest Enrollment:** Business, management, marketing, and related support services; dance, general; drama and dramatics/theatre arts, general. **Disciplines with Highest Percentage of Degrees Awarded:** Business/marketing 27%, visual and performing arts 15%, communications/communication technologies 12%, engineering/engineering technology 10%, education 9%. **Special Study Options:** Accelerated program, cross registration, distance learning, double major, dual enrollment, English as a second language, honors program, independent study, internships, liberal arts/career combination, student-designed major, study abroad, teacher certification program, weekend college.

FACILITIES

Housing: Coed, quiet floors, single-gender floors. **Library Holdings:** 163,197 bound volumes. 765 periodicals. 29,911 microforms. 5,595 audiovisuals. **Special Academic Facilities/Equipment:** Theater, daycare center and elementary school, engineering technology labs, television and radio studios. **Computers:** School-owned computers available for student use.

EXTRACURRICULARS

Activities: Choral groups, dance, drama/theater, literary magazine, musical theater, radio station, student government, student newspaper, television station, yearbook. **Organizations:** 3 honor societies, 2 religious organizations. **Athletics (Intercollegiate):** *Men:* baseball, basketball, cross-country, soccer. *Women:* basketball, cross-country, softball, volleyball.

ADMISSIONS

Selectivity Rating: 67 (of 100). **Freshman Academic Profile:** Average high school GPA 3.2. 16% in top 10% of high school class, 25% in top 25% of high school class, 51% in top 50% of high school class. 10% from public high schools. Average SAT I Math 495, SAT I Math middle 50% range 419-606. Average SAT I Verbal 520, SAT I Verbal middle 50% range 433-638. Average ACT 22, ACT middle 50% range 17-27. TOEFL required of all international applicants, minimum TOEFL 500. **Basis for Candidate Selection:** *Very important factors considered include:* class rank, secondary school record, standardized test scores, talent/ability. *Important factors considered include:* character/personal qualities, essays, extracurricular activities, interview, recommendations, volunteer work, work experience. **Freshman Admission Requirements:** High school diploma or GED is required. *Academic units required/recommended:* 19 total recommended; 4 English recommended, 3 math recommended, 3 science recommended, 2 foreign language recommended, 3 social studies recommended, 3 history recommended, 1 elective recommended. **Freshman Admission Statistics:** 1,651 applied, 79% accepted, 25% of those accepted enrolled. **Transfer Admission Requirements:** *Items required:* high school transcript, college transcript. Minimum college GPA of 2.0 required. Lowest grade transferable C. **General Admission Information:** Application fee $20. Nonfall registration accepted. Admission may be deferred for a maximum of 2 years. Credit and/or placement offered for CEEB Advanced Placement tests.

COSTS AND FINANCIAL AID

Tuition $13,888. Room & board $6,098. Required fees $400. Average book expense $700. **Required Forms and Deadlines:** FAFSA. No deadline for regular filing. Priority filing deadline May 1. **Notification of Awards:** Applicants will be notified of awards on a rolling basis beginning on or about September 1. **Types of Aid:** *Need-based scholarships/grants:* Pell, SEOG, state scholarships/grants, private scholarships, the school's own gift aid. *Loans:* FFEL Subsidized Stafford, FFEL Unsubsidized Stafford, FFEL PLUS, Federal Perkins, college/university loans from institutional funds. **Student Employment:** Federal Work-Study Program available. Institutional employment available. Off-campus job opportunities are excellent. **Financial Aid Statistics:** 59% freshmen, 79% undergrads receive some form of aid. Average freshman grant $8,553. Average income from on-campus job $1,200. **Financial Aid Phone:** 412-392-3930.

See page 1156.

POLYTECHNIC UNIVERSITY

6 Metrotech Center, Brooklyn, NY 11201-2999
Phone: 718-260-3100 **E-mail:** admitme@poly.edu **CEEB Code:** 2668
Fax: 718-260-3446 **Web:** www.poly.edu **ACT Code:** 2860

This private school was founded in 1854. It has a 3-acre campus.

STUDENTS AND FACULTY

Enrollment: 1,685. **Student Body:** Male 81%, female 19%, out-of-state 3%, international 7%. **Ethnic Representation:** African American 11%, Asian 43%, Caucasian 29%, Hispanic 7%. **Retention and Graduation:** 80% freshmen return for sophomore year. 32% freshmen graduate within 4 years. 5% grads go on to further study within 1 year. **Faculty:** Student/faculty ratio 12:1. 160 full-time faculty, 89% hold PhDs. 100% faculty teach undergrads.

ACADEMICS

Degrees: Bachelor's, certificate, doctoral, master's. **Academic Requirements:** General education including some course work in computer literacy, English (including composition), history, humanities, mathematics, sciences (biological or physical), social science. **Classes:** 10-19 students in an average class. 20-29 students in an average lab/discussion section. **Majors with Highest Enrollment:** Computer science; computer engineering, general; electrical, electronics, and communications engineering. **Disciplines with Highest Percentage of Degrees Awarded:** Engineering/engineering technology 55%, computer and information sciences 37%, liberal arts/general studies 5%, mathematics 2%, physical sciences 1%. **Special Study Options:** Accelerated program, cooperative (work-study) program, distance learning, double major, dual enrollment, honors program, independent study, internships.

FACILITIES

Housing: Coed, fraternities and/or sororities. **Library Holdings:** 148,000 bound volumes. 613 periodicals. 56,620 microforms. 235 audiovisuals. **Special Academic Facilities/Equipment:** Electron microscope, supersonic wind tunnel, Art Displays in Student Center. **Computers:** School-owned computers available for student use.

EXTRACURRICULARS

Activities: Literary magazine, radio station, student government, student newspaper, student-run film society, yearbook. **Organizations:** 50 registered organizations, 10 honor societies, 3 religious organizations, 3 fraternities (3% men join), 1 sorority (4% women join). **Athletics (Intercollegiate):** *Men:* baseball, basketball, cross-country, soccer, tennis, track & field, volleyball. *Women:* basketball, cross-country, softball, tennis, track & field, volleyball.

ADMISSIONS

Selectivity Rating: 82 (of 100). **Freshman Academic Profile:** Average high school GPA 3.3. 82% from public high schools. Average SAT I Math 650, SAT I

Math middle 50% range 600-700. Average SAT I Verbal 550, SAT I Verbal middle 50% range 500-600. TOEFL required of all international applicants, minimum TOEFL 500. **Basis for Candidate Selection:** *Very important factors considered include:* secondary school record, standardized test scores. *Important factors considered include:* class rank. *Other factors considered include:* essays, interview, recommendations. **Freshman Admission Requirements:** High school diploma is required and GED is not accepted. *Academic units required/recommended:* 4 English required, 4 math required, 4 science required, 2 foreign language recommended, 3 social studies required, 2 elective required. **Freshman Admission Statistics:** 1,553 applied, 77% accepted, 34% of those accepted enrolled. **Transfer Admission Requirements:** *Items required:* college transcript. Minimum college GPA of 2.5 required. Lowest grade transferable C. **General Admission Information:** Application fee $45. Nonfall registration accepted. Admission may be deferred for a maximum of 1 year. Credit and/or placement offered for CEEB Advanced Placement tests.

COSTS AND FINANCIAL AID

Tuition $23,510. Room & board $8,000. Required fees $790. Average book expense $750. **Required Forms and Deadlines:** FAFSA. No deadline for regular filing. **Notification of Awards:** Applicants will be notified of awards on a rolling basis beginning on or about February 1. **Types of Aid:** *Need-based scholarships/grants:* Pell, SEOG, state scholarships/grants, private scholarships, the school's own gift aid. *Loans:* FFEL Subsidized Stafford, FFEL Unsubsidized Stafford, FFEL PLUS, Federal Perkins, college/university loans from institutional funds. **Student Employment:** Federal Work-Study Program available. Institutional employment available. Off-campus job opportunities are good. **Financial Aid Statistics:** 84% freshmen, 83% undergrads receive some form of aid. Average freshman grant $15,688. Average freshman loan $5,313. Average income from on-campus job $2,000. **Financial Aid Phone:** 718-260-3300.

POMONA COLLEGE

333 North College Way, Claremont, CA 91711-6312
Phone: 909-621-8134 **E-mail:** admissions@pomona.edu **CEEB Code:** 4607
Fax: 909-621-8952 **Web:** www.pomona.edu **ACT Code:** 372

This private school was founded in 1887. It has a 140-acre campus.

STUDENTS AND FACULTY

Enrollment: 1,551. **Student Body:** Male 50%, female 50%, out-of-state 66%, international 2%. **Ethnic Representation:** African American 6%, Asian 13%, Caucasian 60%, Hispanic 8%, Native American 1%. **Retention and Graduation:** 99% freshmen return for sophomore year. 83% freshmen graduate within 4 years. 40% grads go on to further study within 1 year. 6% grads pursue business degrees. 10% grads pursue law degrees. 10% grads pursue medical degrees. **Faculty:** Student/faculty ratio 9:1. 161 full-time faculty, 95% hold PhDs. 100% faculty teach undergrads.

ACADEMICS

Degrees: Bachelor's. **Academic Requirements:** General education including some course work in arts/fine arts, English (including composition), foreign languages, history, humanities, mathematics, sciences (biological or physical), social science, general education requirement. **Classes:** 10-19 students in an average class. 10-19 students in an average lab/discussion section. **Majors with Highest Enrollment:** English language and literature, general; biology/biological sciences, general; economics, general. **Disciplines with Highest Percentage of Degrees Awarded:** Social sciences and history 26%, interdisciplinary studies 16%, biological life sciences 13%, psychology 6%, physical sciences 6%. **Special Study Options:** Cross registration, double major, student exchange program (domestic), independent study, internships, student-designed major, study abroad, teacher certification program.

FACILITIES

Housing: Coed, language residence hall. **Library Holdings:** 2,232,086 bound volumes. 5,968 periodicals. 1,448,719 microforms. 16,524 audiovisuals. **Special Academic Facilities/Equipment:** Oldenborg Center for Foreign Languages, Museum of Art, Brackett Observatory. **Computers:** School-owned computers available for student use.

EXTRACURRICULARS

Activities: Choral groups, dance, drama/theater, jazz band, literary magazine, music ensembles, musical theater, radio station, student government, student newspaper, student-run film society, symphony orchestra, television station, yearbook. **Organizations:** 280 registered organizations, 3 honor societies, 5 religious organizations, 4 fraternities (5% men join). **Athletics (Intercollegiate):** *Men:* baseball, basketball, cross-country, diving, football, golf, soccer, squash, swimming, tennis, track & field, water polo. *Women:* basketball, cross-country, diving, golf, lacrosse, soccer, softball, squash, swimming, tennis, track & field, volleyball, water polo.

ADMISSIONS

Selectivity Rating: 97 (of 100). **Freshman Academic Profile:** Average high school GPA 3.9. 84% in top 10% of high school class, 89% in top 25% of high school class, 100% in top 50% of high school class. 61% from public high schools. Average SAT I Math 720, SAT I Math middle 50% range 680-750. Average SAT I Verbal 730, SAT I Verbal middle 50% range 690-760. Average ACT 32, ACT middle 50% range 30-33. TOEFL required of all international applicants, minimum TOEFL 600. **Basis for Candidate Selection:** *Very important factors considered include:* character/personal qualities, class rank, essays, extracurricular activities, interview, recommendations, secondary school record, standardized test scores, talent/ability. *Other factors considered include:* alumni/ae relation, geographical residence, minority status, volunteer work, work experience. **Freshman Admission Requirements:** High school diploma or equivalent is not required. *Academic units required/recommended:* 4 English required, 4 English recommended, 3 math required, 4 math recommended, 3 science required, 3 science recommended, 2 science lab required, 2 science lab recommended, 3 foreign language required, 4 foreign language recommended, 2 social studies required, 2 social studies recommended. **Freshman Admission Statistics:** 4,230 applied, 23% accepted, 39% of those accepted enrolled. **Transfer Admission Requirements:** *Items required:* high school transcript, college transcript, essay, standardized test score, statement of good standing from prior school. Lowest grade transferable C. **General Admission Information:** Application fee $55. Early decision application deadline November 15. Regular application deadline January 2. Admission may be deferred for a maximum of 1 year. Credit and/or placement offered for CEEB Advanced Placement tests.

COSTS AND FINANCIAL AID

Required Forms and Deadlines: FAFSA, CSS/Financial Aid PROFILE, state aid form, noncustodial (divorced/separated) parent's statement, business/farm supplement and Tax returns for both the student and parents. Financial aid filing deadline February 1. **Notification of Awards:** Applicants will be notified of awards on or about April 10. **Types of Aid:** *Need-based scholarships/grants:* Pell, SEOG, state scholarships/grants, private scholarships, the school's own gift aid. *Loans:* FFEL Subsidized Stafford, FFEL Unsubsidized Stafford, FFEL PLUS, Federal Perkins, college/university loans from institutional funds. **Student Employment:** Federal Work-Study Program available. Institutional employment available. Off-campus job opportunities are excellent. **Financial Aid Statistics:** 51% freshmen, 52% undergrads receive some form of aid. Average freshman grant $20,300. Average freshman loan $2,000. **Financial Aid Phone:** 909-621-8205.

PONTIFICAL COLLEGE JOSEPHINUM

7625 North High Street, Columbus, OH 43235-1498
Phone: 614-885-5585 **E-mail:** acrawford@pcj.edu
Fax: 614-885-2307 **Web:** www.pcj.edu

This private school, which is affiliated with the Roman Catholic Church, was founded in 1888.

STUDENTS AND FACULTY

Enrollment: 69. **Student Body:** Out-of-state 90%, international 1%. **Ethnic Representation:** Asian 4%, Caucasian 89%, Hispanic 7%. **Retention and Graduation:** 90% freshmen return for sophomore year. 95% grads go on to further study within 1 year.

ACADEMICS

Degrees: Bachelor's, first professional, master's. **Academic Requirements:** General education including some course work in arts/fine arts, English (including composition), foreign languages, history, humanities, mathematics, philosophy, sciences (biological or physical). **Disciplines with Highest Percentage of Degrees Awarded:** Philosophy/religion/theology 6%, English 3%, other 1%. **Special Study Options:** Cross registration, double major, honors program.

FACILITIES

Housing: All-male. **Computers:** School-owned computers available for student use.

EXTRACURRICULARS

Organizations: 1 religious organization.

ADMISSIONS

Selectivity Rating: 72 (of 100). **Freshman Academic Profile:** TOEFL required of all international applicants, minimum TOEFL 550. **Basis for Candidate Selection:** *Very important factors considered include:* recommendations, religious affiliation/commitment, secondary school record, standardized test scores. *Other factors considered include:* alumni/ae relation, essays, extracurricular activities, interview. **Freshman Admission Requirements:** High school diploma or GED is required. *Academic units required/recommended:* 10 total required; 18 total recommended; 4 English required, 2 math required, 4 math recommended, 1 science required, 4 science recommended, 1 foreign language required, 2 foreign language recommended, 2 social studies required, 4 social studies recommended. **Freshman Admission Statistics:** 9 applied, 100% accepted, 100% of those accepted enrolled. **Transfer Admission Requirements:** *Items required:* high school transcript, college transcript. Lowest grade transferable C. **General Admission Information:** Application fee $25.

COSTS AND FINANCIAL AID

Room & board $2,320. Required fees $70. Average book expense $350. **Types of Aid:** *Loans:* FFEL Subsidized Stafford, FFEL PLUS. **Student Employment:** Federal Work-Study Program available. **Financial Aid Statistics:** Average income from on-campus job $1,200. **Financial Aid Phone:** 614-885-5585.

PORTLAND STATE UNIVERSITY

PO Box 751, Portland, OR 97207
Phone: 503-725-3511 **E-mail:** admissions@pdx.edu **CEEB Code:** 4610
Fax: 503-725-5525 **Web:** www.pdx.edu **ACT Code:** 3492

This public school was founded in 1946. It has a 49-acre campus.

STUDENTS AND FACULTY

Enrollment: 15,808. **Student Body:** Male 46%, female 54%, out-of-state 10%, international 3%. **Ethnic Representation:** African American 3%, Asian 11%, Caucasian 69%, Hispanic 4%, Native American 1%. **Retention and Graduation:** 66% freshmen return for sophomore year. 10% freshmen graduate within 4 years. **Faculty:** Student/faculty ratio 19:1. 657 full-time faculty, 99% hold PhDs. 87% faculty teach undergrads.

ACADEMICS

Degrees: Bachelor's, certificate, doctoral, master's, post-bachelor's certificate. **Academic Requirements:** General education including some course work in university studies, a general education program, is required of all freshman inquiry (15 credits), sophomore inquiry (12 credit), upper division cluster (12 credits), upper division cluster (12 credits), and senior capstone (6 credits). students must also meet major requirements of the department. **Classes:** 10-19 students in an average class. Under 10 students in an average lab/discussion section. **Majors with Highest Enrollment:** Business administration/management; psychology, general; fine/studio arts, general. **Disciplines with Highest Percentage of Degrees Awarded:** Business/marketing 24%, social sciences and history 22%, psychology 7%, liberal arts/general studies 6%, communications/communication technologies 5%. **Special Study Options:** Accelerated program, cooperative (work-study) program, distance learning, double major, English as a second language, student exchange program (domestic), honors program, independent study, internships, study abroad, teacher certification program.

FACILITIES

Housing: Coed, apartments for married students, apartments for single students, housing for disabled students, fraternities and/or sororities, special housing for new students, apartments for students with dependent children. **Library Holdings:** 1,787,100 bound volumes. 8,698 periodicals. 2,330,129 microforms. 91,912 audiovisuals. **Special Academic Facilities/Equipment:** Art galleries, audiovisual resources, classroom multimedia computer systems, learning lab, child development center. **Computers:** School-owned computers available for student use.

EXTRACURRICULARS

Activities: Choral groups, concert band, dance, drama/theater, jazz band, literary magazine, music ensembles, musical theater, opera, radio station, student government, student newspaper, student-run film society, symphony orchestra. **Organizations:** 148 registered organizations, 8 religious organizations, 4 fraternities (2% men join), 4 sororities (2% women join). **Athletics (Intercollegiate):** *Men:* basketball, cross-country, football, indoor track, tennis, track & field, wrestling. *Women:* basketball, cross-country, golf, indoor track, soccer, softball, tennis, track & field, volleyball.

ADMISSIONS

Selectivity Rating: 63 (of 100). **Freshman Academic Profile:** Average high school GPA 3.2. Average SAT I Math 513, SAT I Math middle 50% range 460-570. Average SAT I Verbal 509, SAT I Verbal middle 50% range 450-580. Average ACT 22, ACT middle 50% range 19-24. TOEFL required of all international applicants, minimum TOEFL 525. **Basis for Candidate Selection:** *Very important factors considered include:* secondary school record, standardized test scores. **Freshman Admission Requirements:** High school diploma or GED is required. *Academic units required/recommended:* 14 total required; 1 total recommended; 4 English required, 3 math required, 2 science required, 1 science lab recommended, 2 foreign language required, 2 social studies required, 1 history required. **Freshman Admission Statistics:** 3,147 applied, 84% accepted, 57% of those accepted enrolled. **Transfer Admission Requirements:** *Items required:* college transcript. Minimum college GPA of 2.0 required. Lowest grade transferable C-. **General Admission Information:** Application fee $50. Priority application deadline June 1. Nonfall registration accepted. Admission may be deferred for a maximum of 1 year. Credit and/or placement offered for CEEB Advanced Placement tests.

COSTS AND FINANCIAL AID

In-state tuition $2,892. Out-of-state tuition $12,273. Room & board $7,500. Required fees $993. Average book expense $1,200. **Required Forms and Deadlines:** FAFSA. No deadline for regular filing. **Notification of Awards:** Applicants will be notified of awards on a rolling basis. **Types of Aid:** *Need-based scholarships/grants:* Pell, SEOG, state scholarships/grants, private scholarships, the school's own gift aid, United Negro College Fund. *Loans:* Direct Subsidized Stafford, Direct Unsubsidized Stafford, Direct PLUS, FFEL Subsidized Stafford, FFEL Unsubsidized Stafford, FFEL PLUS, Federal Perkins, state loans. **Student Employment:** Federal Work-Study Program available. Institutional employment available. Off-campus job opportunities are excellent. **Financial Aid Statistics:** 44% freshmen, 49% undergrads receive some form of aid. **Financial Aid Phone:** 503-725-3461.

PRAIRIE VIEW A&M UNIVERSITY

PO Box 3089, University Drive, Prarie View, TX 77446
Phone: 936-857-2626 **E-mail:** mary_gooch@pvamu.edu **CEEB Code:** 6580
Fax: 936-857-2699 **Web:** www.pvamu.edu **ACT Code:** 4202

This public school was founded in 1878. It has a 1,440-acre campus.

STUDENTS AND FACULTY

Enrollment: 5,754. **Student Body:** Male 44%, female 56%, out-of-state 5%, international 1%. **Ethnic Representation:** African American 94%, Asian 1%, Caucasian 3%, Hispanic 2%. **Retention and Graduation:** 14% grads go on to further study within 1 year. 13% grads pursue business degrees. 4% grads pursue law degrees. 21% grads pursue medical degrees. **Faculty:** Student/faculty ratio 20:1. 306 full-time faculty, 74% hold PhDs. 85% faculty teach undergrads.

ACADEMICS

Degrees: Bachelor's, doctoral, master's. **Academic Requirements:** General education including some course work in arts/fine arts, computer literacy, English (including composition), foreign languages, history, humanities, mathematics, philosophy, sciences (biological or physical), social science. **Classes:** 30-39 students in an average class. 20-29 students in an average lab/discussion section. **Majors with Highest Enrollment:** Biology/biological sciences, general; multi/interdisciplinary studies. **Disciplines with Highest Percentage of Degrees Awarded:** Business/marketing 18%, health professions and related sciences 17%, engineering/engineering technology 15%, protective services/public administration 12%, biological life sciences 6%. **Special Study Options:** Accelerated program, cooperative (work-study) program, distance learning, double major, dual enrollment, English as a second language, honors program, independent study, internships, liberal arts/career combination, teacher certification program, weekend college.

FACILITIES

Housing: Coed, all-female, all-male, apartments for single students. **Library Holdings:** 324,167 bound volumes. 18,201 periodicals. 618,663 microforms. 5,454 audiovisuals.

EXTRACURRICULARS

Activities: Choral groups, concert band, dance, drama/theater, jazz band, literary magazine, marching band, music ensembles, musical theater, radio station, student government, student newspaper, student-run film society, symphony orchestra, yearbook. **Organizations:** 21 registered organizations, 5 honor societies, 5 religious organizations, 4 fraternities, 4 sororities. **Athletics**

(Intercollegiate): *Men:* baseball, basketball, cross-country, equestrian, football, golf, tennis, track & field. *Women:* basketball, cross-country, equestrian, golf, softball, tennis, track & field, volleyball.

ADMISSIONS

Selectivity Rating: 63 (of 100). **Freshman Academic Profile:** Average high school GPA 2.8. 5% in top 10% of high school class, 6% in top 25% of high school class, 61% in top 50% of high school class. Average SAT I Math 417, SAT I Math middle 50% range 360-470. Average SAT I Verbal 413, SAT I Verbal middle 50% range 360-470. Average ACT 17, ACT middle 50% range 14-19. TOEFL required of all international applicants, minimum TOEFL 500. **Basis for Candidate Selection:** *Very important factors considered include:* secondary school record, standardized test scores. *Important factors considered include:* class rank. *Other factors considered include:* essays, extracurricular activities, interview, recommendations, talent/ability. **Freshman Admission Requirements:** High school diploma or GED is required. *Academic units required/recommended:* 16 total required; 18 total recommended; 4 English required, 4 English recommended, 3 math required, 4 math recommended, 3 science required, 3 science recommended, 2 foreign language recommended, 2 social studies required, 2 social studies recommended, 2 history recommended, 4 elective required. **Freshman Admission Statistics:** 2,643 applied, 97% accepted, 58% of those accepted enrolled. **Transfer Admission Requirements:** *Items required:* high school transcript, college transcript. Minimum high school GPA of 2.5 required. Minimum college GPA of 2.0 required. Lowest grade transferable C. **General Admission Information:** Application fee $25. Priority application deadline May 1. Regular application deadline July 1. Nonfall registration accepted. Admission may be deferred for a maximum of 2 years. Credit and/or placement offered for CEEB Advanced Placement tests.

COSTS AND FINANCIAL AID

Required Forms and Deadlines: FAFSA and institution's own financial aid form. Financial aid filing deadline April 1. **Notification of Awards:** Applicants will be notified of awards on or about June 1. **Student Employment:** Federal Work-Study Program available. Institutional employment available. Off-campus job opportunities are poor. **Financial Aid Statistics:** 89% freshmen, 91% undergrads receive some form of aid. Average freshman grant $4,500. Average income from on-campus job $3,050. **Financial Aid Phone:** 409-857-2424.

PRATT INSTITUTE

200 Willoughby Avenue, Brooklyn, NY 11205
Phone: 718-636-3669 **E-mail:** admissions@pratt.edu **CEEB Code:** 2669
Fax: 718-636-3670 **Web:** www.pratt.edu **ACT Code:** 2862

This private school was founded in 1887. It has a 25-acre campus.

STUDENTS AND FACULTY

Enrollment: 3,124. **Student Body:** Male 46%, female 54%, out-of-state 49%, international 11% (70 countries represented). **Ethnic Representation:** African American 8%, Asian 14%, Caucasian 70%, Hispanic 8%. **Retention and Graduation:** 87% freshmen return for sophomore year. 25% grads go on to further study within 1 year. 6% grads pursue business degrees. 1% grads pursue law degrees. **Faculty:** 73% hold PhDs. 100% faculty teach undergrads.

ACADEMICS

Degrees: Associate's, bachelor's, first professional, master's, terminal, transfer. **Academic Requirements:** General education including some course work in arts/fine arts, English (including composition), history, humanities, mathematics, philosophy, sciences (biological or physical), social science. **Classes:** 10-19 students in an average class. **Majors with Highest Enrollment:** Architecture (BArch, BA/BS, MArch, MA/MS, PhD); design and visual communications, general; fashion/apparel design. **Disciplines with Highest Percentage of Degrees Awarded:** Visual and performing arts 76%, architecture 24%. **Special Study Options:** Accelerated program, double major, English as a second language, student exchange program (domestic), independent study, internships, liberal arts/career combination, student-designed major, study abroad, teacher certification program, weekend college.

FACILITIES

Housing: Coed, apartments for single students, fraternities and/or sororities. **Library Holdings:** 172,000 bound volumes. 540 periodicals. 50,000 microforms. 2,921 audiovisuals. **Special Academic Facilities/Equipment:** Art gallery, fine arts center, printmaking center, computer graphics lab. **Computers:** School-owned computers available for student use.

EXTRACURRICULARS

Activities: Dance, drama/theater, jazz band, literary magazine, radio station, student government, student newspaper, student-run film society, yearbook. **Organizations:** 63 registered organizations, 4 honor societies, 3 religious organizations, 3 fraternities, 1 sorority. **Athletics (Intercollegiate):** *Men:* basketball, cross-country, indoor track, soccer, tennis, track & field. *Women:* basketball, cross-country, tennis, track & field, volleyball.

ADMISSIONS

Selectivity Rating: 83 (of 100). **Freshman Academic Profile:** Average high school GPA 3.4. 70% from public high schools. Average SAT I Math 562, SAT I Math middle 50% range 595-490. Average SAT I Verbal 553, SAT I Verbal middle 50% range 610-520. Average ACT 28, ACT middle 50% range 25-21. TOEFL required of all international applicants, minimum TOEFL 530. **Basis for Candidate Selection:** *Very important factors considered include:* secondary school record, standardized test scores, talent/ability. *Important factors considered include:* essays, interview, recommendations. *Other factors considered include:* alumni/ae relation, character/personal qualities, class rank, extracurricular activities, minority status, volunteer work, work experience. **Freshman Admission Requirements:** High school diploma or GED is required. *Academic units required/recommended:* 16 total recommended; 4 English recommended, 3 math recommended, 2 science recommended, 2 social studies recommended. **Freshman Admission Statistics:** 3,640 applied, 42% accepted, 39% of those accepted enrolled. **Transfer Admission Requirements:** *Items required:* college transcript, essay, statement of good standing from prior school. Lowest grade transferable C. **General Admission Information:** Application fee $40. Priority application deadline January 1. Early decision application deadline November 15. Regular application deadline February 1. Nonfall registration accepted. Admission may be deferred for a maximum of 1 year. Credit and/or placement offered for CEEB Advanced Placement tests.

COSTS AND FINANCIAL AID

Tuition $23,528. Room & board $8,186. Required fees $670. Average book expense $3,000. **Required Forms and Deadlines:** FAFSA and institution's own financial aid form. Priority filing deadline February 1. **Notification of Awards:** Applicants will be notified of awards on a rolling basis beginning on or about April 15. **Types of Aid:** *Need-based scholarships/grants:* Pell, SEOG, state scholarships/grants, the school's own gift aid. *Loans:* FFEL Subsidized Stafford, FFEL Unsubsidized Stafford, FFEL PLUS, Federal Perkins, college/university loans from institutional funds. **Student Employment:** Federal Work-Study Program available. Institutional employment available. Off-campus job opportunities are excellent. **Financial Aid Statistics:** 85% freshmen, 76% undergrads receive some form of aid. Average freshman grant $6,220. Average freshman loan $3,425. Average income from on-campus job $2,250. **Financial Aid Phone:** 718-636-3599.

PRESBYTERIAN COLLEGE

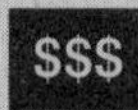

503 South Broad Street, Clinton, SC 29325
Phone: 864-833-8230 **E-mail:** admissions@presby.edu **CEEB Code:** 5540
Fax: 864-833-8481 **Web:** www.presby.edu **ACT Code:** 3874

This private school was founded in 1880. It has a 240-acre campus.

STUDENTS AND FACULTY

Enrollment: 1,212. **Student Body:** Male 46%, female 54%, out-of-state 38%, international students represent 9 countries. **Ethnic Representation:** African American 4%, Asian 1%, Caucasian 93%, Hispanic 1%. **Retention and Graduation:** 83% freshmen return for sophomore year. 61% freshmen graduate within 4 years. 16% grads go on to further study within 1 year. 7% grads pursue business degrees. 8% grads pursue law degrees. 9% grads pursue medical degrees. **Faculty:** Student/faculty ratio 13:1. 80 full-time faculty, 88% hold PhDs. 100% faculty teach undergrads.

ACADEMICS

Degrees: Bachelor's. **Academic Requirements:** General education including some course work in arts/fine arts, English (including composition), foreign languages, history, humanities, mathematics, sciences (biological or physical), social science. **Classes:** Under 10 students in an average class. **Disciplines with Highest Percentage of Degrees Awarded:** Business/marketing 23%, social sciences and history 22%, education 13%, biological life sciences 13%, psychology 10%. **Special Study Options:** Accelerated program, double major, dual enrollment, student exchange program (domestic), honors program, independent study, internships, liberal arts/career combination, study abroad, teacher certification program, 3-2 environmental science program, 3-2 engineering program, religious educational program.

FACILITIES

Housing: Coed, all-female, all-male, apartments for single students, housing for international students, fraternities and/or sororities. **Library Holdings:** 149,273 bound volumes. 797 periodicals. 13,690 microforms. 7,204 audiovisuals. **Special Academic Facilities/Equipment:** Art gallery, recital hall, media center, marine/ecological center, scanning and transmission electron microscopes, visible spectrophotometer. **Computers:** School-owned computers available for student use.

EXTRACURRICULARS

Activities: Choral groups, dance, drama/theater, literary magazine, music ensembles, pep band, radio station, student government, student newspaper, yearbook. **Organizations:** 60 registered organizations, 8 honor societies, 5 religious organizations, 7 fraternities (48% men join), 3 sororities (46% women join). **Athletics (Intercollegiate):** *Men:* baseball, basketball, cross-country, football, golf, rifle, soccer, tennis. *Women:* basketball, cross-country, golf, rifle, soccer, softball, tennis, volleyball.

ADMISSIONS

Selectivity Rating: 76 (of 100). **Freshman Academic Profile:** Average high school GPA 3.3. 25% in top 10% of high school class, 56% in top 25% of high school class, 86% in top 50% of high school class. 75% from public high schools. Average SAT I Math 555, SAT I Math middle 50% range 510-610. Average SAT I Verbal 563, SAT I Verbal middle 50% range 500-600. Average ACT 24, ACT middle 50% range 21-26. TOEFL required of all international applicants, minimum TOEFL 550. **Basis for Candidate Selection:** *Very important factors considered include:* secondary school record. *Important factors considered include:* class rank, essays, standardized test scores. *Other factors considered include:* alumni/ae relation, character/personal qualities, extracurricular activities, interview, recommendations, talent/ability. **Freshman Admission Requirements:** High school diploma or GED is required. *Academic units required/recommended:* 17 total required; 4 English required, 3 math required, 2 science required, 2 science lab required, 2 foreign language required, 3 foreign language recommended, 2 history required, 2 elective required. **Freshman Admission Statistics:** 1,034 applied, 79% accepted, 39% of those accepted enrolled. **Transfer Admission Requirements:** *Items required:* high school transcript, college transcript, essay, standardized test scores. Minimum high school GPA of 2.2 required. Minimum college GPA of 2.5 required. Lowest grade transferable C. **General Admission Information:** Application fee $30. Priority application deadline May 1. Nonfall registration accepted. Admission may be deferred for a maximum of 1 year. Neither credit nor placement offered for CEEB Advanced Placement tests.

COSTS AND FINANCIAL AID

Tuition $18,360. Room & board $5,810. Required fees $1,750. Average book expense $848. **Required Forms and Deadlines:** FAFSA and institution's own financial aid form. Priority filing deadline March 1. **Notification of Awards:** Applicants will be notified of awards on a rolling basis beginning on or about April 1. **Types of Aid:** *Need-based scholarships/grants:* Pell, SEOG, state scholarships/grants, private scholarships, the school's own gift aid. *Loans:* Direct Subsidized Stafford, Direct Unsubsidized Stafford, Direct PLUS, FFEL Subsidized Stafford, FFEL Unsubsidized Stafford, FFEL PLUS, Federal Perkins, college/university loans from institutional funds. **Student Employment:** Federal Work-Study Program available. Institutional employment available. Off-campus job opportunities are good. **Financial Aid Statistics:** 66% freshmen, 61% undergrads receive some form of aid. Average freshman grant $12,234. Average freshman loan $4,757. Average income from on-campus job $800. **Financial Aid Phone:** 864-833-8287.

PRESCOTT COLLEGE

220 Grove Avenue, Prescott, AZ 86301
Phone: 928-776-5180 **E-mail:** admissions@prescott.edu **CEEB Code:** 9295
Fax: 928-776-5242 **Web:** www.prescott.edu **ACT Code:** 5022

This private school was founded in 1966. It has a 4-acre campus.

STUDENTS AND FACULTY

Enrollment: 834. **Student Body:** Male 41%, female 59%, out-of-state 85%. **Ethnic Representation:** African American 1%, Asian 1%, Caucasian 85%, Hispanic 4%, Native American 5%. **Retention and Graduation:** 69% freshmen return for sophomore year. 37% freshmen graduate within 4 years. **Faculty:** Student/faculty ratio 12:1. 45 full-time faculty, 44% hold PhDs. 83% faculty teach undergrads.

ACADEMICS

Degrees: Bachelor's, certificate, master's. **Academic Requirements:** General education including some course work in English (including composition), mathematics. **Classes:** 10-19 students in an average class. **Majors with Highest Enrollment:** Elementary education and teaching; environmental science; parks, recreation, leisure and fitness studies. **Disciplines with Highest Percentage of Degrees Awarded:** Education 35%, natural resources/environmental sciences 17%, psychology 15%, visual and performing arts 6%, biological life sciences 4%. **Special Study Options:** Double major, external degree program, independent study, internships, liberal arts/career combination, student-designed major, teacher certification program.

FACILITIES

Library Holdings: 23,293 bound volumes. 262 periodicals. 1,364 audiovisuals.

EXTRACURRICULARS

Activities: Dance, drama/theater, literary magazine, student government, student newspaper. **Organizations:** 10 registered organizations.

ADMISSIONS

Selectivity Rating: 79 (of 100). **Freshman Academic Profile:** 73% from public high schools. SAT I Math middle 50% range 500-660. SAT I Verbal middle 50% range 450-610. Average ACT 25. **Basis for Candidate Selection:** *Very important factors considered include:* essays, recommendations, secondary school record. *Important factors considered include:* character/personal qualities, extracurricular activities, interview, volunteer work, work experience. *Other factors considered include:* standardized test scores, talent/ability. **Freshman Admission Requirements:** High school diploma or GED is required. **Freshman Admission Statistics:** 129 applied, 69% accepted, 49% of those accepted enrolled. **Transfer Admission Requirements:** *Items required:* college transcript, essay. Lowest grade transferable C. **General Admission Information:** Application fee $25. Priority application deadline February 1. Nonfall registration accepted. Admission may be deferred for a maximum of 1 year. Credit and/or placement offered for CEEB Advanced Placement tests.

COSTS AND FINANCIAL AID

Tuition $13,300. Required fees $130. Average book expense $600. **Required Forms and Deadlines:** FAFSA and institution's own financial aid form. No deadline for regular filing. **Notification of Awards:** Applicants will be notified of awards on a rolling basis beginning on or about April 1. **Types of Aid:** *Need-based scholarships/grants:* Pell, SEOG, state scholarships/grants, private scholarships, the school's own gift aid. *Loans:* FFEL Subsidized Stafford, FFEL Unsubsidized Stafford, FFEL PLUS, Federal Perkins, state loans, alternative loans. **Student Employment:** Federal Work-Study Program available. Institutional employment available. Off-campus job opportunities are fair. **Financial Aid Statistics:** 83% freshmen, 77% undergrads receive some form of aid. Average freshman grant $3,264. Average income from on-campus job $689. **Financial Aid Phone:** 928-776-5168.

PRESENTATION COLLEGE

1500 North Main Street, Aberdeen, SD 57401
Phone: 800-437-6060 **CEEB Code:** 6582
Fax: 605-229-8332 **Web:** www.presentation.edu **ACT Code:** 3918

This private school was founded in 1951. It has a 100-acre campus.

STUDENTS AND FACULTY

Enrollment: 461. **Student Body:** Male 22%, female 78%, out-of-state 19%. **Ethnic Representation:** African American 2%, Caucasian 86%, Native American 12%. **Faculty:** 100% faculty teach undergrads.

ACADEMICS

Degrees: Associate's, bachelor's, certificate. **Academic Requirements:** General education including some course work in arts/fine arts, English (including composition), humanities, mathematics, sciences (biological or physical), social science. **Special Study Options:** Accelerated program, distance learning, dual enrollment, external degree program.

FACILITIES

Housing: Coed. **Library Holdings:** 41,149 bound volumes. 274 periodicals. 61 microforms. 2,379 audiovisuals. **Computers:** *Recommended operating system:* Windows 95. School-owned computers available for student use.

EXTRACURRICULARS

Activities: Drama/theater, student government. **Organizations:** 2 honor societies, 1 religious organization. **Athletics (Intercollegiate):** *Men:* basketball. *Women:* basketball.

ADMISSIONS

Selectivity Rating: 60 (of 100). **Freshman Academic Profile:** Average high school GPA 2.9. 5% in top 10% of high school class, 19% in top 25% of high school class, 49% in top 50% of high school class. ACT middle 50% range 17-21. TOEFL required of all international applicants, minimum TOEFL 500. **Basis for Candidate Selection:** *Very important factors considered include:* class rank. *Important factors considered include:* secondary school record, standardized test scores. **Freshman Admission Requirements:** High school diploma or GED is required. *Academic units required/recommended:* 16 total recommended; 4 English recommended, 3 math recommended, 2 science recommended, 2 social studies recommended. **Transfer Admission Requirements:** *Items required:* high school transcript, college transcript, standardized test scores. Lowest grade transferable C. **General Admission Information:** Application fee $15. Regular application deadline rolling. Nonfall registration accepted.

COSTS AND FINANCIAL AID

Tuition $6,820. Room & board $3,100. Required fees $148. Average book expense $800. **Required Forms and Deadlines:** FAFSA. No deadline for regular filing. Priority filing deadline April 1. **Notification of Awards:** Applicants will be notified of awards on a rolling basis beginning on or about May 1. **Types of Aid:** *Loans:* Direct Subsidized Stafford, Direct Unsubsidized Stafford, Direct PLUS, Federal Perkins, college/university loans from institutional funds. **Student Employment:** Federal Work-Study Program available. Off-campus job opportunities are good. **Financial Aid Phone:** 605-229-8427.

PRINCETON UNIVERSITY

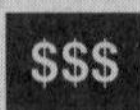

PO Box 430, Admission Office, Princeton, NJ 08544-0430
Phone: 609-258-3060 **CEEB Code:** 2672
Fax: 609-258-6743 **Web:** www.princeton.edu **ACT Code:** 2588

This private school was founded in 1746. It has a 600-acre campus.

STUDENTS AND FACULTY

Enrollment: 4,779. **Student Body:** Male 52%, female 48%, out-of-state 86%, international 7%. **Ethnic Representation:** African American 9%, Asian 13%, Caucasian 70%, Hispanic 7%, Native American 1%. **Retention and Graduation:** 99% freshmen return for sophomore year. 92% freshmen graduate within 4 years. **Faculty:** Student/faculty ratio 6:1. 736 full-time faculty, 92% hold PhDs.

ACADEMICS

Degrees: Bachelor's, certificate, doctoral, master's. **Majors with Highest Enrollment:** History, general; English language and literature, general; political science and government, general. **Disciplines with Highest Percentage of Degrees Awarded:** Social sciences and history 32%, engineering/engineering technology 20%, English 10%, biological life sciences 8%, protective services/public administration 7%. **Special Study Options:** Cross registration, independent study, student-designed major, study abroad, teacher certification program.

FACILITIES

Housing: Coed, apartments for married students, apartments for single students, housing for disabled students, cooperative housing. **Library Holdings:** 5,000,000 bound volumes. 30,000 periodicals. 3,000,000 microforms. **Special Academic Facilities/Equipment:** Art Museum, Natural History Museum, energy and environmental studies center, plasma physics lab, Center for Jewish Life, Center for Human Values, Woodrow Wilson School of Public and International Affairs. **Computers:** School-owned computers available for student use.

EXTRACURRICULARS

Activities: Choral groups, concert band, dance, drama/theater, jazz band, literary magazine, marching band, music ensembles, musical theater, opera, pep band, radio station, student government, student newspaper, symphony orchestra, yearbook. **Organizations:** 250 registered organizations, 30 honor societies, 24 religious organizations. **Athletics (Intercollegiate):** *Men:* baseball, basketball, cheerleading, crew, cross-country, diving, equestrian, fencing, football, golf, ice hockey, indoor track, lacrosse, rugby, sailing, skiing (Nordic), soccer, squash, swimming, tennis, track & field, volleyball, water polo, wrestling. *Women:* basketball, cheerleading, crew, cross-country, diving, equestrian, fencing, field hockey, golf, ice hockey, indoor track, lacrosse, rugby, sailing, skiing (Nordic), soccer, softball, squash, swimming, tennis, track & field, volleyball, water polo.

ADMISSIONS

Selectivity Rating: 99 (of 100). **Freshman Academic Profile:** 95% in top 10% of high school class, 99% in top 25% of high school class, 100% in top 50% of high school class. 55% from public high schools. TOEFL required of all international applicants, minimum TOEFL 630. **Basis for Candidate Selection:** *Very important factors considered include:* character/personal qualities, essays, extracurricular activities, recommendations, secondary school record, standardized test scores, talent/ability, volunteer work, work experience. *Important factors considered include:* alumni/ae relation, minority status. *Other factors considered include:* class rank, interview. **Freshman Admission Requirements:** High school diploma is required and GED is not accepted. *Academic units required/recommended:* 18 total recommended; 4 English recommended, 4 math recommended, 2 science recommended, 2 science lab recommended, 4 foreign language recommended, 2 history recommended. **Freshman Admission Statistics:** 14,521 applied, 11% accepted, 73% of those accepted enrolled. **General Admission Information:** Application fee $60. Early decision application deadline November 1. Regular application deadline January 1. Admission may be deferred for a maximum of 1 year. Credit and/or placement offered for CEEB Advanced Placement tests.

COSTS AND FINANCIAL AID

Tuition $28,540. Room & board $8,109. Required fees $0. Average book expense $790. **Required Forms and Deadlines:** FAFSA and institution's own financial aid form. Financial aid filing deadline February 1. **Notification of Awards:** Applicants will be notified of awards on or about April 1. **Types of Aid:** *Need-based scholarships/grants:* Pell, SEOG, state scholarships/grants, private scholarships, the school's own gift aid. *Loans:* FFEL Subsidized Stafford, FFEL Unsubsidized Stafford, FFEL PLUS, Federal Perkins, college/university loans from institutional funds. **Student Employment:** Federal Work-Study Program available. Institutional employment available. Off-campus job opportunities are good. **Financial Aid Statistics:** 46% freshmen, 43% undergrads receive some form of aid. Average freshman grant $23,000. Average freshman loan $0. Average income from on-campus job $2,000. **Financial Aid Phone:** 609-258-3330.

PRINCIPIA COLLEGE

1 Maybeck Place, Elsah, IL 62028
Phone: 618-374-5181 **E-mail:** collegeadmissions@prin.edu **CEEB Code:** 1630
Fax: 618-374-4000 **Web:** www.prin.edu/college **ACT Code:** 1118

This private school, which is affiliated with the Christian Science Church, was founded in 1898. It has a 2,600-acre campus.

STUDENTS AND FACULTY

Enrollment: 538. **Student Body:** Male 46%, female 54%, out-of-state 88%, international 12% (25 countries represented). **Ethnic Representation:** African American 1%, Asian 1%, Caucasian 93%, Hispanic 2%. **Retention and Graduation:** 84% freshmen return for sophomore year. 69% freshmen graduate within 4 years. 24% grads go on to further study within 1 year. 3% grads pursue business degrees. 3% grads pursue law degrees. **Faculty:** Student/faculty ratio 9:1. 51 full-time faculty, 62% hold PhDs. 100% faculty teach undergrads.

ACADEMICS

Degrees: Bachelor's. **Academic Requirements:** General education including some course work in arts/fine arts, English (including composition), foreign languages, history, humanities, mathematics, philosophy, sciences (biological or physical), social science, 1 Bible course, physical education. **Classes:** 10-19 students in an average class. **Majors with Highest Enrollment:** Business administration/management; sociology; fine/studio arts, general. **Disciplines with Highest Percentage of Degrees Awarded:** Visual and performing arts 22%, social sciences and history 18%, business/marketing 14%, biological life sciences 8%, English 8%. **Special Study Options:** Double major, independent study, internships, liberal arts/career combination, student-designed major, study abroad, teacher certification program.

FACILITIES

Housing: All-female, all-male, apartments for married students, apartments for single students. **Library Holdings:** 208,197 bound volumes. 10,547 periodicals. 204,211 microforms. 7,273 audiovisuals. **Special Academic Facilities/Equipment:** Science Center, School of Nations Museum & Classrooms, Voney Art Studio, School of Government, Merrick Wing for Performing Arts. **Computers:** School-owned computers available for student use.

EXTRACURRICULARS

Activities: Choral groups, dance, drama/theater, jazz band, music ensembles, musical theater, radio station, student government, student newspaper, television station, yearbook. **Organizations:** 32 registered organizations, 1 honor society, 1 religious organization. **Athletics (Intercollegiate):** *Men:* baseball, basketball, cross-country, diving, football, golf, soccer, swimming, tennis, track & field. *Women:* basketball, cross-country, diving, soccer, swimming, tennis, track & field, volleyball.

ADMISSIONS

Selectivity Rating: 81 (of 100). **Freshman Academic Profile:** Average high school GPA 3.3. 20% in top 10% of high school class, 18% in top 25% of high school class, 58% in top 50% of high school class. 63% from public high schools. Average SAT I Math 580, SAT I Math middle 50% range 520-660. Average SAT I Verbal 593, SAT I Verbal middle 50% range 530-660. Average ACT 25, ACT middle 50% range 20-29. TOEFL required of all international applicants, minimum TOEFL 550. **Basis for Candidate Selection:** *Very important factors considered include:* character/personal qualities, essays, religious affiliation/commitment, secondary school record. *Important factors considered include:* class rank, extracurricular activities, interview, recommendations, standardized test scores, talent/ability. *Other factors considered include:* alumni/ae relation, minority status, volunteer work, work experience. **Freshman Admission Requirements:** High school diploma or GED is required. *Academic units required/recommended:* 16 total required; 20 total recommended; 4 English required, 4 English recommended, 3 math required, 4 math recommended, 2 science required, 3 science recommended, 2 science lab required, 2 science lab recommended, 2 foreign language required, 3 foreign language recommended, 2 social studies required, 2 social studies recommended, 1 history required, 2 history recommended, 2 elective required, 2 elective recommended. **Freshman Admission Statistics:** 274 applied, 83% accepted, 63% of those accepted enrolled. **Transfer Admission Requirements:** *Items required:* high school transcript, college transcript, essay. Minimum high school GPA of 2.0 required. Minimum college GPA of 2.0 required. Lowest grade transferable C-. **General Admission Information:** Application fee $40. Priority application deadline January 15. Regular application deadline March 1. Nonfall registration accepted. Admission may be deferred for a maximum of 1 year. Credit and/or placement offered for CEEB Advanced Placement tests.

COSTS AND FINANCIAL AID

Tuition $18,270. Room & board $6,504. Required fees $270. Average book expense $1,500. **Required Forms and Deadlines:** institution's own financial aid form and CSS/Financial Aid PROFILE. Financial aid filing deadline April 1. Priority filing deadline February 1. **Notification of Awards:** Applicants will be notified of awards on or about April 1. **Types of Aid:** *Need-based scholarships/grants:* private scholarships, the school's own gift aid. *Loans:* college/university loans from institutional funds. **Student Employment:** Institutional employment available. Off-campus job opportunities are poor. **Financial Aid Statistics:** 68% freshmen, 61% undergrads receive some form of aid. Average freshman grant $13,282. Average freshman loan $3,000. Average income from on-campus job $2,830. **Financial Aid Phone:** 800-277-4648.

PROVIDENCE COLLEGE

River Avenue and Eaton Street, Providence, RI 02918
Phone: 401-865-2535 **E-mail:** pcadmiss@providence.edu **CEEB Code:** 3693
Fax: 401-865-2826 **Web:** www.providence.edu **ACT Code:** 3806

This private school, which is affiliated with the Roman Catholic Church, was founded in 1917. It has a 105-acre campus.

STUDENTS AND FACULTY

Enrollment: 4,371. **Student Body:** Male 42%, female 58%, out-of-state 75%, international 1%. **Ethnic Representation:** African American 2%, Asian 2%, Caucasian 86%, Hispanic 2%. **Retention and Graduation:** 92% freshmen return for sophomore year. 83% freshmen graduate within 4 years. **Faculty:** Student/faculty ratio 14:1. 249 full-time faculty, 87% hold PhDs. 100% faculty teach undergrads.

ACADEMICS

Degrees: Associate's, bachelor's, certificate, master's, terminal. **Academic Requirements:** General education including some course work in arts/fine arts, English (including composition), mathematics, philosophy, sciences (biological or physical), social science, development of western civilization, theology. **Classes:** 10-19 students in an average class. 10-19 students in an average lab/discussion section. **Majors with Highest Enrollment:** Marketing/marketing management, general; special education, general; biology/biological sciences, general. **Disciplines with Highest Percentage of Degrees Awarded:** Business/marketing 31%, social sciences and history 18%, education 13%, psychology 6%, English 6%. **Special Study Options:** Cooperative (work-study) program, cross registration, double major, honors program, independent study, internships, student-designed major, study abroad, teacher certification program.

FACILITIES

Housing: Coed, all-female, all-male, apartments for single students, housing for disabled students. **Library Holdings:** 397,630 bound volumes. 1,759 periodicals. 214,679 microforms. 278 audiovisuals. **Special Academic Facilities/Equipment:** Art gallery, theatre, science center complex, computer and language labs. **Computers:** School-owned computers available for student use.

EXTRACURRICULARS

Activities: Choral groups, concert band, dance, drama/theater, jazz band, literary magazine, music ensembles, pep band, radio station, student government, student newspaper, television station, yearbook. **Organizations:** 94 registered organizations, 17 honor societies, 2 religious organizations. **Athletics (Intercollegiate):** *Men:* basketball, cross-country, diving, ice hockey, indoor track, lacrosse, soccer, swimming, track & field. *Women:* basketball, cross-country, diving, field hockey, ice hockey, indoor track, soccer, softball, swimming, tennis, track & field, volleyball.

ADMISSIONS

Selectivity Rating: 83 (of 100). **Freshman Academic Profile:** Average high school GPA 3.4. 42% in top 10% of high school class, 80% in top 25% of high school class, 98% in top 50% of high school class. 63% from public high schools. Average SAT I Math 596, SAT I Math middle 50% range 550-640. Average SAT I Verbal 587, SAT I Verbal middle 50% range 540-630. Average ACT 25, ACT middle 50% range 23-27. TOEFL required of all international applicants, minimum TOEFL 550. **Basis for Candidate Selection:** *Very important factors considered include:* secondary school record. *Important factors considered include:* character/personal qualities, class rank, essays, extracurricular activities, recommendations, standardized test scores, talent/ability, volunteer work. *Other factors considered include:* alumni/ae relation, geographical residence, minority status, state residency, work experience. **Freshman Admission Requirements:** High school diploma is required and GED is not accepted. *Academic units required/recommended:* 16 total required; 18 total recommended; 4 English required, 4 English recommended, 3 math required, 4 math recommended, 3 science required, 4 science recommended, 2 science lab required, 3 science lab recommended, 3 foreign language required, 3 foreign language recommended, 1 social studies required, 1 social studies recommended, 2 history required, 2 history recommended. **Freshman Admission Statistics:** 7,354 applied, 49% accepted, 24% of those accepted enrolled. **Transfer Admission Requirements:** *Items required:* high school transcript, college transcript, essay, standardized test score, statement of good standing from prior school. Minimum college GPA of 3.0 required. Lowest grade transferable C. **General Admission Information:** Application fee $55. Regular application deadline January 15. Nonfall registration accepted. Admission may be deferred for a maximum of 1 year. Neither credit nor placement offered for CEEB Advanced Placement tests.

COSTS AND FINANCIAL AID

Tuition $19,375. Room & board $7,925. Required fees $320. Average book expense $650. **Required Forms and Deadlines:** FAFSA and CSS/Financial Aid PROFILE. Financial aid filing deadline February 1. Priority filing deadline February 1. **Notification of Awards:** Applicants will be notified of awards on or about April 1. **Types of Aid:** *Need-based scholarships/grants:* Pell, SEOG, state scholarships/grants, private scholarships, the school's own gift aid. *Loans:* Direct Subsidized Stafford, Direct Unsubsidized Stafford, Direct PLUS, FFEL Subsidized Stafford, FFEL Unsubsidized Stafford, FFEL PLUS, Federal Perkins. **Student Employment:** Federal Work-Study Program available. Institutional employment available. Off-campus job opportunities are excellent. **Financial Aid Statistics:** 55% freshmen, 52% undergrads receive some form of aid. Average freshman grant $9,200. Average freshman loan $4,125. Average income from on-campus job $1,800. **Financial Aid Phone:** 401-865-2286.

PURDUE UNIVERSITY—CALUMET

Office of Admissions, 2200 169th Street, Hammond, IN 46323-2094
Phone: 219-989-2213 **E-mail:** adms@calumet.purdue.edu **CEEB Code:** 1638
Fax: 219-989-2775 **Web:** www.calumet.purdue.edu **ACT Code:** 1233

This public school was founded in 1943. It has a 167-acre campus.

STUDENTS AND FACULTY

Enrollment: 8,350. **Student Body:** Male 45%, female 55%, out-of-state 7%. **Ethnic Representation:** African American 12%, Asian 1%, Caucasian 70%, Hispanic 14%. **Faculty:** 300 full-time faculty, 57% hold PhDs. 70% faculty teach undergrads.

ACADEMICS

Degrees: Associate's, bachelor's, certificate, master's, post-bachelor's certificate. **Academic Requirements:** General education including some course work in English (including composition), humanities, mathematics. **Classes:** 20-29 students in an average class. 10-19 students in an average lab/discussion section. **Special Study Options:** Accelerated program, cooperative (work-study) program, distance learning, double major, dual enrollment, independent study, internships, teacher certification program.

FACILITIES

Library Holdings: 215,830 bound volumes. 1,736 periodicals. 481,678 microforms. **Special Academic Facilities/Equipment:** Audiovisual services, urban development institute. **Computers:** School-owned computers available for student use.

EXTRACURRICULARS

Activities: Drama/theater, student government, student newspaper. **Organizations:** 25 honor societies, 2 religious organizations, 2 fraternities (1% men join), 5 sororities (2% women join). **Athletics (Intercollegiate):** *Men:* basketball. *Women:* basketball, cheerleading.

ADMISSIONS

Selectivity Rating: 63 (of 100). **Freshman Academic Profile:** 6% in top 10% of high school class, 20% in top 25% of high school class, 49% in top 50% of high school class. 88% from public high schools. SAT I Math middle 50% range 390-510. SAT I Verbal middle 50% range 400-520. TOEFL required of all international applicants, minimum TOEFL 550. **Basis for Candidate Selection:** *Very important factors considered include:* class rank, secondary school record, standardized test scores. **Freshman Admission Requirements:** High school diploma or GED is required. *Academic units required/recommended:* 14 total recommended; 4 English recommended, 2 math recommended, 2 science recommended, 2 foreign language recommended, 2 social studies recommended, 2 history recommended. **Freshman Admission Statistics:** 1,771 applied, 99% accepted, 68% of those accepted enrolled. **Transfer Admission Requirements:** *Items required:* high school transcript. Minimum college GPA of 2.0 required. Lowest grade transferable C. **General Admission Information:** Nonfall registration accepted. Admission may be deferred. Credit offered for CEEB Advanced Placement tests.

COSTS AND FINANCIAL AID

In-state tuition $2,262. Out-of-state tuition $5,688. Required fees $228. Average book expense $600. **Required Forms and Deadlines:** FAFSA. No deadline for regular filing. Priority filing deadline March 1. **Notification of Awards:** Applicants will be notified of awards on or about June 1. **Types of Aid:** *Need-based scholarships/grants:* Pell, SEOG, state scholarships/grants, private scholarships, the school's own gift aid. *Loans:* Direct Subsidized Stafford, Direct Unsubsidized Stafford, Direct PLUS, Federal Perkins. **Student Employment:** Federal Work-Study Program available. Institutional employment available. Off-campus job opportunities are excellent. **Financial Aid Statistics:** 58% freshmen, 64% undergrads receive some form of aid. **Financial Aid Phone:** 219-989-2301.

PURDUE UNIVERSITY—NORTH CENTRAL

1401 South U.S. Highway 421, Westville, IN 46391-9528
Phone: 219-785-5458 **E-mail:** admissions@purduenc.edu **CEEB Code:** 1640
Fax: 219-785-5538 **Web:** www.pnc.edu **ACT Code:** 1826

This public school was founded in 1948. It has a 296-acre campus.

STUDENTS AND FACULTY

Enrollment: 3,636. **Student Body:** Male 41%, female 59%, out-of-state 1%, international students represent 3 countries. **Ethnic Representation:** African American 3%, Asian 1%, Caucasian 88%, Hispanic 3%, Native American 1%. **Retention and Graduation:** 63% freshmen return for sophomore year. **Faculty:** Student/faculty ratio 18:1. 96 full-time faculty, 58% hold PhDs. 100% faculty teach undergrads.

ACADEMICS

Degrees: Associate's, bachelor's, certificate, master's. **Academic Requirements:** General education including some course work in computer literacy, English (including composition), humanities, mathematics, sciences (biological or physical), social science. **Classes:** 20-29 students in an average class. 10-19 students in an average lab/discussion section. **Majors with Highest Enrollment:** Business administration/management; elementary education and teaching; liberal arts and sciences/liberal studies. **Disciplines with Highest Percentage of Degrees Awarded:** Liberal arts/general studies 51%, business/marketing 24%, education 15%, English 5%, engineering/engineering technology 3%. **Special Study Options:** Distance learning, dual enrollment, independent study, internships, teacher certification program.

FACILITIES

Library Holdings: 87,675 bound volumes. 403 periodicals. 2,832 microforms. 602 audiovisuals. **Computers:** *Recommended operating system:* Windows 98/2000. School-owned computers available for student use.

EXTRACURRICULARS

Activities: Student government, student newspaper. **Organizations:** 13 registered organizations, 2 honor societies, 1 religious organization. **Athletics (Intercollegiate):** *Men:* baseball, basketball, cheerleading. *Women:* cheerleading.

ADMISSIONS

Selectivity Rating: 63 (of 100). **Freshman Academic Profile:** Average high school GPA 2.8. 5% in top 10% of high school class, 18% in top 25% of high school class, 49% in top 50% of high school class. 95% from public high schools. Average SAT I Math 473, SAT I Math middle 50% range 410-530. Average SAT I Verbal 471, SAT I Verbal middle 50% range 410-530. Average ACT 21, ACT middle 50% range 17-22. TOEFL required of all international applicants, minimum TOEFL 213. **Basis for Candidate Selection:** *Very important factors considered include:* secondary school record. *Important factors considered include:* class rank, standardized test scores. *Other factors considered include:* character/personal qualities, extracurricular activities, interview, recommendations, talent/ability, volunteer work, work experience. **Freshman Admission Requirements:** High school diploma or GED is required. *Academic units required/recommended:* 17 total required; 26 total recommended; 4 English required, 4 English recommended, 3 math required, 4 math recommended, 2 science required, 3 science recommended, 2 science lab required, 3 science lab recommended, 4 foreign language recommended, 1 social studies required, 2 social studies recommended, 1 history recommended, 5 elective required, 5 elective recommended. **Freshman Admission Statistics:** 1,089 applied, 91% accepted, 70% of those accepted enrolled. **Transfer Admission Requirements:** *Items required:* high school transcript, college transcript. Minimum high school GPA of 2.0 required. Minimum college GPA of 2.0 required. Lowest grade transferable C. **General Admission Information:** Priority application deadline August 1. Nonfall registration accepted. Admission may be deferred for a maximum of 1 year. Credit and/or placement offered for CEEB Advanced Placement tests.

COSTS AND FINANCIAL AID

In-state tuition $2,878. Out-of-state tuition $7,735. Required fees $280. Average book expense $800. **Required Forms and Deadlines:** FAFSA and state aid form. Priority filing deadline March 1. **Notification of Awards:** Applicants will be notified of awards on a rolling basis beginning on or about May 1. **Types of Aid:** *Need-based scholarships/grants:* Pell, SEOG, state scholarships/grants, private scholarships, the school's own gift aid. *Loans:* FFEL Subsidized Stafford, FFEL Unsubsidized Stafford, FFEL PLUS, Federal Perkins, college/university loans from institutional funds. **Student Employment:** Federal Work-Study Program available. Institutional employment available. Off-campus job opportunities are good. **Financial Aid Statistics:** 63% freshmen, 53%

undergrads receive some form of aid. Average freshman grant $3,000. Average freshman loan $2,800. **Financial Aid Phone:** 219-785-5493.

PURDUE UNIVERSITY—WEST LAFAYETTE

474 Stadium Mall Drive, Schleman Hall, Room 109, West Lafayette, IN 47907
Phone: 765-494-1776 **E-mail:** admissions@purdue.edu **CEEB Code:** 1631
Fax: 765-494-0544 **Web:** www.purdue.edu **ACT Code:** 1230

This public school was founded in 1,869. It has a 1,579-acre campus.

STUDENTS AND FACULTY

Enrollment: 30,908. **Student Body:** Male 58%, female 42%, out-of-state 24%, international 6% (120 countries represented). **Ethnic Representation:** African American 3%, Asian 5%, Caucasian 89%, Hispanic 2%. **Retention and Graduation:** 88% freshmen return for sophomore year. **Faculty:** Student/faculty ratio 16:1. 1,869 full-time faculty, 98% hold PhDs.

ACADEMICS

Degrees: Bachelor's, certificate, doctoral, first professional, master's, terminal. **Academic Requirements:** General education including some course work in computer literacy, English (including composition), history, humanities, mathematics, sciences (biological or physical), social science. **Classes:** 20-29 students in an average class. 20-29 students in an average lab/discussion section. **Disciplines with Highest Percentage of Degrees Awarded:** Engineering/engineering technology 25%, business/marketing 15%, education 8%, communications/communication technologies 6%, health professions and related sciences 6%. **Special Study Options:** Cooperative (work-study) program, cross registration, distance learning, double major, dual enrollment, student exchange program (domestic), honors program, independent study, internships, liberal arts/career combination, study abroad, teacher certification program.

FACILITIES

Housing: Coed, all-female, all-male, apartments for married students, apartments for single students, housing for disabled students, fraternities and/or sororities, cooperative housing. **Library Holdings:** 2,518,849 microforms. 12,733 audiovisuals. **Special Academic Facilities/Equipment:** Hall of music, child development lab, speech and hearing clinic, small animal veterinary clinic, horticulture park, linear accelerator, tornado simulator, nuclear accelerator. **Computers:** School-owned computers available for student use.

EXTRACURRICULARS

Activities: Choral groups, concert band, dance, drama/theater, jazz band, literary magazine, marching band, music ensembles, musical theater, pep band, radio station, student government, student newspaper, symphony orchestra, television station, yearbook. **Organizations:** 620 registered organizations, 59 honor societies, 39 religious organizations, 46 fraternities (18% men join), 25 sororities (17% women join). **Athletics (Intercollegiate):** *Men:* baseball, basketball, cross-country, diving, football, golf, indoor track, swimming, tennis, track & field, wrestling. *Women:* basketball, cross-country, diving, golf, indoor track, soccer, softball, swimming, tennis, track & field, volleyball.

ADMISSIONS

Selectivity Rating: 76 (of 100). **Freshman Academic Profile:** 28% in top 10% of high school class, 62% in top 25% of high school class, 93% in top 50% of high school class. Average SAT I Math 595, SAT I Math middle 50% range 530-660. Average SAT I Verbal 555, SAT I Verbal middle 50% range 500-610. Average ACT 26, ACT middle 50% range 23-28. TOEFL required of all international applicants, minimum TOEFL 550. **Basis for Candidate Selection:** *Very important factors considered include:* class rank, secondary school record, standardized test scores. *Other factors considered include:* alumni/ae relation, recommendations, state residency. **Freshman Admission Requirements:** High school diploma or GED is required. *Academic units required/recommended:* 4 English required, 3 math required, 2 science required, 3 science recommended, 2 science lab required, 3 science lab recommended, 2 foreign language recommended. **Freshman Admission Statistics:** 22,872 applied, 76% accepted, 36% of those accepted enrolled. **Transfer Admission Requirements:** *Items required:* college transcript. Minimum college GPA of 2.3 required. Lowest grade transferable C. **General Admission Information:** Application fee $30. Priority application deadline March 1. Nonfall registration accepted. Admission may be deferred for a maximum of 1 year. Credit and/or placement offered for CEEB Advanced Placement tests.

COSTS AND FINANCIAL AID

In-state tuition $3,872. Out-of-state tuition $12,904. Room & board $5,800. Required fees $0. Average book expense $780. **Required Forms and Deadlines:** FAFSA. Priority filing deadline March 1. **Notification of Awards:** Applicants will be notified of awards on or about April 15. **Types of Aid:** *Need-based scholarships/grants:* Pell, SEOG, state scholarships/grants, private scholarships, the school's own gift aid. *Loans:* FFEL Subsidized Stafford, FFEL Unsubsidized Stafford, FFEL PLUS, Federal Perkins, college/university loans from institutional funds. **Student Employment:** Federal Work-Study Program available. Institutional employment available. Off-campus job opportunities are good. **Financial Aid Statistics:** 38% freshmen, 37% undergrads receive some form of aid. **Financial Aid Phone:** 765-494-5050.

QUEENS UNIVERSITY OF CHARLOTTE

1900 Selwyn Avenue, Charlotte, NC 28274
Phone: 704-337-2212 **E-mail:** cas@queens.edu **CEEB Code:** 5560
Fax: 704-337-2403 **Web:** www.queens.edu **ACT Code:** 3148

This private school, which is affiliated with the Presbyterian Church, was founded in 1857. It has a 25-acre campus.

STUDENTS AND FACULTY

Enrollment: 1,205. **Student Body:** Male 24%, female 76%, international 4%. **Ethnic Representation:** African American 17%, Asian 1%, Caucasian 78%, Hispanic 3%. **Retention and Graduation:** 76% freshmen return for sophomore year. 51% freshmen graduate within 4 years. 25% grads go on to further study within 1 year. 13% grads pursue business degrees. 3% grads pursue law degrees. 1% grads pursue medical degrees. **Faculty:** Student/faculty ratio 13:1. 63 full-time faculty, 82% hold PhDs. 100% faculty teach undergrads.

ACADEMICS

Degrees: Bachelor's, master's, post-bachelor's certificate. **Academic Requirements:** General education including some course work in arts/fine arts, English (including composition), foreign languages, history, humanities, mathematics, sciences (biological or physical), social science. **Classes:** 10-19 students in an average class. 20-29 students in an average lab/discussion section. **Majors with Highest Enrollment:** Nursing/registered nurse training (RN, ASN, BSN, MSN); communications studies/speech communication and rhetoric; business administration/management. **Disciplines with Highest Percentage of Degrees Awarded:** Business/marketing 26%, communications/communication technologies 21%, health professions and related sciences 16%, English 8%, psychology 6%. **Special Study Options:** Cross registration, double major, dual enrollment, honors program, independent study, internships, liberal arts/career combination, study abroad, teacher certification program, weekend college.

FACILITIES

Housing: Coed, all-female, all-male. **Library Holdings:** 130,798 bound volumes. 592 periodicals. 80,571 microforms. 1,369 audiovisuals. **Special Academic Facilities/Equipment:** Three art galleries, rare books museum. **Computers:** School-owned computers available for student use.

EXTRACURRICULARS

Activities: Choral groups, dance, drama/theater, literary magazine, music ensembles, musical theater, student government, student newspaper, yearbook. **Organizations:** 40 registered organizations, 9 honor societies, 3 religious organizations, 18 fraternity, 4 sororities. **Athletics (Intercollegiate):** *Men:* basketball, cheerleading, cross-country, golf, lacrosse, soccer, tennis. *Women:* basketball, cheerleading, cross-country, golf, lacrosse, soccer, softball, tennis, volleyball.

ADMISSIONS

Selectivity Rating: 77 (of 100). **Freshman Academic Profile:** Average high school GPA 3.3. 25% in top 10% of high school class, 53% in top 25% of high school class, 84% in top 50% of high school class. 78% from public high schools. SAT I Math middle 50% range 480-580. SAT I Verbal middle 50% range 510-590. ACT middle 50% range 21-26. TOEFL required of all international applicants, minimum TOEFL 550. **Basis for Candidate Selection:** *Very important factors considered include:* character/personal qualities, recommendations, secondary school record, standardized test scores. *Important factors considered include:* class rank, essays, extracurricular activities, volunteer work. *Other factors considered include:* interview, talent/ability, work experience. **Freshman Admission Requirements:** High school diploma or GED is required. *Academic units required/recommended:* 4 English required, 3 math required, 2 science required, 1 science lab required, 2 foreign language required, 2 social studies required. **Freshman Admission Statistics:** 600 applied, 79% accepted, 41% of those accepted enrolled. **Transfer Admission Requirements:** *Items required:* high school transcript, college transcript, essay. Minimum college GPA of 2.0 required. Lowest grade transferable C. **General Admission Information:** Application fee $35. Nonfall registration accepted.

Admission may be deferred for a maximum of 1 year. Credit and/or placement offered for CEEB Advanced Placement tests.

COSTS AND FINANCIAL AID

Tuition $15,650. Room & board $6,190. Required fees $0. Average book expense $750. **Required Forms and Deadlines:** FAFSA. No deadline for regular filing. Priority filing deadline March 1. **Notification of Awards:** Applicants will be notified of awards on a rolling basis beginning on or about March 1. **Types of Aid:** *Need-based scholarships/grants:* Pell, SEOG, state scholarships/grants, private scholarships, the school's own gift aid, United Negro College Fund. *Loans:* FFEL Subsidized Stafford, FFEL Unsubsidized Stafford, FFEL PLUS, Federal Perkins. **Student Employment:** Federal Work-Study Program available. Institutional employment available. Off-campus job opportunities are good. **Financial Aid Statistics:** 68% freshmen, 59% undergrads receive some form of aid. Average income from on-campus job $1,500. **Financial Aid Phone:** 704-337-2225.

QUEENSBOROUGH COMMUNITY COLLEGE

222-05 56TH Avenue, Bayside, NY 11364
Phone: 718-631-6236 **E-mail:** wyarde@qcc.cuny.edu **CEEB Code:** 2751
Fax: 718-281-5208 **Web:** www.qcc.cuny.edu

This public school was founded in 1967. It has a 34-acre campus.

STUDENTS AND FACULTY

Enrollment: 11,704. **Student Body:** Male 42%, female 58%, out-of-state 1%, international 3%. **Ethnic Representation:** African American 28%, Asian 20%, Caucasian 29%, Hispanic 23%. **Faculty:** Student/faculty ratio 15:1. 248 full-time faculty, 61% hold PhDs. 100% faculty teach undergrads.

ACADEMICS

Degrees: Associate's, certificate, transfer. **Academic Requirements:** General education including some course work in arts/fine arts, computer literacy, English (including composition), foreign languages, history, humanities, mathematics, philosophy, sciences (biological or physical), social science. **Special Study Options:** Distance learning, double major, English as a second language, honors program, independent study, internships, liberal arts/career combination, study abroad, weekend college.

FACILITIES

Library Holdings: 150,000 bound volumes. 750 periodicals. **Special Academic Facilities/Equipment:** Oakland Art Gallery, performing arts center, The Holocaust Center. **Computers:** School-owned computers available for student use.

EXTRACURRICULARS

Activities: Dance, drama/theater, student government, student newspaper. **Organizations:** 37 registered organizations, 3 honor societies. **Athletics (Intercollegiate):** *Men:* baseball, basketball, cross-country, indoor track, soccer, swimming, tennis, volleyball. *Women:* basketball, cross-country, softball, swimming, tennis, volleyball.

ADMISSIONS

Selectivity Rating: 63 (of 100). **Freshman Academic Profile:** 65% from public high schools. Average SAT I Math 495. Average SAT I Verbal 512. TOEFL required of all international applicants, minimum TOEFL 475. **Basis for Candidate Selection:** *Other factors considered include:* class rank, secondary school record, standardized test scores. **Freshman Admission Requirements:** High school diploma or GED is required. **Freshman Admission Statistics:** 4,263 applied, 87% accepted, 61% of those accepted enrolled. **Transfer Admission Requirements:** *Items required:* high school transcript, college transcript. Minimum high school GPA of 2.1 required. Minimum college GPA of 2.0 required. Lowest grade transferable D. **General Admission Information:** Application fee $40. Nonfall registration accepted. Credit offered for CEEB Advanced Placement tests.

COSTS AND FINANCIAL AID

In-state tuition $2,500. Out-of-state tuition $3,076. Required fees $43. **Required Forms and Deadlines:** FAFSA and noncustodial (divorced/separated) parent's statement. **Types of Aid:** *Loans:* Direct Subsidized Stafford, Direct Unsubsidized Stafford, Direct PLUS. **Student Employment:** Federal Work-Study Program available. Institutional employment available. Off-campus job opportunities are good. **Financial Aid Phone:** 718-631-6367.

QUINCY UNIVERSITY

1800 College Avenue, Quincy, IL 62301
Phone: 217-228-5215 **E-mail:** admissions@quincy.edu **CEEB Code:** 1645
Fax: 217-228-5479 **Web:** www.quincy.edu **ACT Code:** 1120

This private school, which is affiliated with the Roman Catholic Church, was founded in 1860. It has a 75-acre campus.

STUDENTS AND FACULTY

Enrollment: 1,057. **Student Body:** Male 45%, female 55%, out-of-state 26%, international 1%. **Ethnic Representation:** African American 5%, Caucasian 84%, Hispanic 2%. **Retention and Graduation:** 74% freshmen return for sophomore year. 19% grads go on to further study within 1 year. 2% grads pursue business degrees. 3% grads pursue law degrees. 2% grads pursue medical degrees. **Faculty:** Student/faculty ratio 14:1. 58 full-time faculty, 86% hold PhDs. 100% faculty teach undergrads.

ACADEMICS

Degrees: Associate's, bachelor's, master's, transfer. **Academic Requirements:** General education including some course work in arts/fine arts, computer literacy, English (including composition), history, humanities, mathematics, philosophy, sciences (biological or physical), social science, theology. **Classes:** Under 10 students in an average class. Under 10 students in an average lab/discussion section. **Majors with Highest Enrollment:** Business administration/management; elementary education and teaching; psychology, general. **Disciplines with Highest Percentage of Degrees Awarded:** Business/marketing 27%, education 16%, social sciences and history 11%, computer and information sciences 7%, visual and performing arts 7%. **Special Study Options:** Accelerated program, distance learning, double major, dual enrollment, English as a second language, honors program, independent study, internships, student-designed major, study abroad, teacher certification program.

FACILITIES

Housing: Coed, all-female, all-male, apartments for married students, apartments for single students, housing for international students, fraternities and/or sororities. **Library Holdings:** 239,368 bound volumes. 725 periodicals. 182,025 microforms. 5,640 audiovisuals. **Special Academic Facilities/Equipment:** On-campus reading center for student teachers, television studio, computer art lab, computer writing lab, environmental field station, NPR radio station. **Computers:** School-owned computers available for student use.

EXTRACURRICULARS

Activities: Choral groups, concert band, dance, drama/theater, jazz band, literary magazine, music ensembles, musical theater, opera, pep band, radio station, student government, student newspaper, symphony orchestra, television station, yearbook. **Organizations:** 55 registered organizations, 6 honor societies, 4 religious organizations, 2 fraternities (5% men join), 2 sororities (6% women join). **Athletics (Intercollegiate):** *Men:* baseball, basketball, football, golf, soccer, tennis, volleyball. *Women:* basketball, golf, soccer, softball, tennis, track & field, volleyball.

ADMISSIONS

Selectivity Rating: 79 (of 100). **Freshman Academic Profile:** Average high school GPA 3.1. 10% in top 10% of high school class, 26% in top 25% of high school class, 61% in top 50% of high school class. 55% from public high schools. Average SAT I Math 521, SAT I Math middle 50% range 440-550. Average SAT I Verbal 524, SAT I Verbal middle 50% range 420-580. Average ACT 22, ACT middle 50% range 20-24. TOEFL required of all international applicants, minimum TOEFL 500. **Basis for Candidate Selection:** *Very important factors considered include:* secondary school record, standardized test scores. *Other factors considered include:* class rank, talent/ability. **Freshman Admission Requirements:** High school diploma or GED is required. *Academic units required/recommended:* 16 total recommended; 4 English required, 4 English recommended, 3 math recommended, 3 science recommended, 2 foreign language recommended, 2 social studies recommended, 2 history recommended. **Freshman Admission Statistics:** 1,034 applied, 97% accepted, 23% of those accepted enrolled. **Transfer Admission Requirements:** *Items required:* college transcript, statement of good standing from prior school. Minimum high school GPA of 2.0 required. Minimum college GPA of 2.0 required. Lowest grade transferable D. **General Admission Information:** Application fee $25. Nonfall registration accepted. Admission may be deferred for a maximum of 1 year. Credit offered for CEEB Advanced Placement tests.

COSTS AND FINANCIAL AID

Tuition $16,400. Room & board $5,480. Required fees $450. Average book expense $800. **Required Forms and Deadlines:** FAFSA. Priority filing

deadline April 15. **Notification of Awards:** Applicants will be notified of awards on a rolling basis beginning on or about February 15. **Types of Aid:** *Need-based scholarships/grants:* Pell, SEOG, state scholarships/grants, private scholarships, the school's own gift aid. *Loans:* FFEL Subsidized Stafford, FFEL Unsubsidized Stafford, FFEL PLUS, Federal Perkins. **Student Employment:** Federal Work-Study Program available. Institutional employment available. Off-campus job opportunities are good. **Financial Aid Statistics:** 74% freshmen, 76% undergrads receive some form of aid. Average freshman grant $10,556. Average freshman loan $2,625. Average income from on-campus job $1,500. **Financial Aid Phone:** 217-228-5260.

QUINNIPIAC UNIVERSITY

Mount Carmel Avenue, 275 Mount Carmel Avenue, Hamden, CT 06518
Phone: 203-582-8600 **E-mail:** admissions@quinnipiac.edu **CEEB Code:** 3712
Fax: 203-582-8906 **Web:** www.quinnipiac.edu **ACT Code:** 582

This private school was founded in 1929. It has a 400-acre campus.

STUDENTS AND FACULTY

Enrollment: 4,843. **Student Body:** Male 36%, female 64%, out-of-state 70%. **Ethnic Representation:** African American 2%, Asian 2%, Caucasian 87%, Hispanic 4%. **Retention and Graduation:** 85% freshmen return for sophomore year. 64% freshmen graduate within 4 years. 25% grads go on to further study within 1 year. 20% grads pursue business degrees. 10% grads pursue law degrees. 4% grads pursue medical degrees. **Faculty:** Student/faculty ratio 16:1. 265 full-time faculty, 80% hold PhDs. 83% faculty teach undergrads.

ACADEMICS

Degrees: Bachelor's, first professional, first professional certificate, master's, post-bachelor's certificate. **Academic Requirements:** General education including some course work in arts/fine arts, computer literacy, English (including composition), humanities, mathematics, philosophy, sciences (biological or physical), social science, management or economics. Foreign language is required in the college of liberal arts. **Classes:** 10-19 students in an average class. 10-19 students in an average lab/discussion section. **Majors with Highest Enrollment:** Physical therapy/therapist; mass communications/media studies; psychology, general. **Disciplines with Highest Percentage of Degrees Awarded:** Health professions and related sciences 30%, business/marketing 25%, communications/communication technologies 14%, computer and information sciences 7%, social sciences and history 7%. **Special Study Options:** Double major, dual enrollment, student exchange program (domestic), honors program, internships, liberal arts/career combination, student-designed major, study abroad, teacher certification program, online option for summer course offerings, one ESL course only.

FACILITIES

Housing: Coed, apartments for single students. **Library Holdings:** 285,000 bound volumes. 3,250 periodicals. 3,500 microforms. 3,300 audiovisuals. **Special Academic Facilities/Equipment:** Polling institute, Albert Schweitzer Institute, critical care nursing lab, electron microscope, computer center, radiology, television and radio broadcast/editing labs, news technology center. Lender family special collection room in library on the Irish famine. **Computers:** School-owned computers available for student use.

EXTRACURRICULARS

Activities: Choral groups, dance, drama/theater, pep band, radio station, student government, student newspaper, yearbook. **Organizations:** 70 registered organizations, 8 honor societies, 3 religious organizations, 4 fraternities (8% men join), 3 sororities (6% women join). **Athletics (Intercollegiate):** *Men:* baseball, basketball, cheerleading, cross-country, golf, ice hockey, indoor track, lacrosse, soccer, tennis. *Women:* basketball, cheerleading, cross-country, field hockey, ice hockey, indoor track, lacrosse, soccer, softball, tennis, volleyball.

ADMISSIONS

Selectivity Rating: 77 (of 100). **Freshman Academic Profile:** Average high school GPA 3.2. 21% in top 10% of high school class, 55% in top 25% of high school class, 89% in top 50% of high school class. 80% from public high schools. Average SAT I Math 545, SAT I Math middle 50% range 520-600. Average SAT I Verbal 540, SAT I Verbal middle 50% range 500-590. Average ACT 24, ACT middle 50% range 22-27. TOEFL required of all international applicants, minimum TOEFL 550. **Basis for Candidate Selection:** *Very important factors considered include:* secondary school record. *Important factors considered include:* class rank, essays, recommendations, standardized test scores. *Other factors considered include:* alumni/ae relation, extracurricular activities, interview, minority status, volunteer work, work experience. **Freshman Admission Requirements:** High school diploma or GED is required. *Academic units required/recommended:* 16 total required; 4 English required, 3 math required, 3 science required, 2 science lab required, 2 foreign language recommended, 2 social studies required, 3 elective required. **Freshman Admission Statistics:** 7,468 applied, 74% accepted, 25% of those accepted enrolled. **Transfer Admission Requirements:** *Items required:* college transcript, essay. Minimum college GPA of 2.5 required. Lowest grade transferable C. **General Admission Information:** Application fee $45. Priority application deadline February 15. Nonfall registration accepted. Admission may be deferred for a maximum of 1 year. Credit and/or placement offered for CEEB Advanced Placement tests.

COSTS AND FINANCIAL AID

Tuition $19,000. Room & board $8,980. Required fees $890. Average book expense $600. **Required Forms and Deadlines:** FAFSA. Priority filing deadline March 1. **Notification of Awards:** Applicants will be notified of awards on a rolling basis beginning on or about March 1. **Types of Aid:** *Need-based scholarships/grants:* Pell, SEOG, state scholarships/grants, private scholarships, the school's own gift aid, Federal Nursing. *Loans:* FFEL Subsidized Stafford, FFEL Unsubsidized Stafford, FFEL PLUS, Federal Perkins, Federal Nursing, state loans. **Student Employment:** Federal Work-Study Program available. Institutional employment available. Off-campus job opportunities are excellent. **Financial Aid Statistics:** 60% freshmen, 58% undergrads receive some form of aid. Average freshman grant $12,176. Average freshman loan $2,625. Average income from on-campus job $1,900. **Financial Aid Phone:** 203-582-8750.

See page 1158.

RADFORD UNIVERSITY

PO Box 6903, RU Station, Radford, VA 24142-6903
Phone: 540-831-5371 **E-mail:** ruadmiss@radford.edu **CEEB Code:** 5565
Fax: 540-831-5038 **Web:** www.radford.edu **ACT Code:** 4422

This public school was founded in 1910. It has a 177-acre campus.

STUDENTS AND FACULTY

Enrollment: 8,200. **Student Body:** Male 41%, female 59%, out-of-state 12%, international students represent 65 countries. **Ethnic Representation:** African American 6%, Asian 2%, Caucasian 89%, Hispanic 2%. **Retention and Graduation:** 79% freshmen return for sophomore year. 33% freshmen graduate within 4 years. 26% grads go on to further study within 1 year. **Faculty:** Student/faculty ratio 20:1. 358 full-time faculty, 84% hold PhDs. 90% faculty teach undergrads.

ACADEMICS

Degrees: Bachelor's, master's, post-master's certificate. **Academic Requirements:** General education including some course work in arts/fine arts, English (including composition), history, humanities, mathematics, philosophy, sciences (biological or physical), social science. **Classes:** 20-29 students in an average class. 20-29 students in an average lab/discussion section. **Majors with Highest Enrollment:** Business administration/management; multi/interdisciplinary studies; criminal justice/safety studies. **Disciplines with Highest Percentage of Degrees Awarded:** Business/marketing 22%, interdisciplinary studies 14%, protective services/public administration 9%, communications/communication technologies 8%, visual and performing arts 8%. **Special Study Options:** Accelerated program, distance learning, double major, dual enrollment, English as a second language, student exchange program (domestic), honors program, independent study, internships, student-designed major, study abroad, teacher certification program.

FACILITIES

Housing: Coed, all-female, apartments for married students, apartments for single students. **Library Holdings:** 552,687 bound volumes. 2,966 periodicals. 1,456,781 microforms. 12,614 audiovisuals. **Special Academic Facilities/Equipment:** On-campus preschool for elementary/early education student teachers, language lab, art gallery with sculpture garden, planetarium, Selu Conservancy, and on-campus speech/hearing clinic. **Computers:** School-owned computers available for student use.

EXTRACURRICULARS

Activities: Choral groups, concert band, dance, drama/theater, jazz band, music ensembles, musical theater, opera, radio station, student government, student newspaper, symphony orchestra, television station, yearbook. **Organizations:** 159 registered organizations, 23 honor societies, 18 religious organizations, 14 fraternities (13% men join), 11 sororities (14% women join). **Athletics (Intercollegiate):** *Men:* baseball, basketball, cross-country, golf, lacrosse, soccer, tennis, track & field. *Women:* basketball, cross-country, field hockey, golf, soccer, softball, tennis, track & field, volleyball.

ADMISSIONS

Selectivity Rating: 64 (of 100). **Freshman Academic Profile:** Average high school GPA 3.0. 6% in top 10% of high school class, 21% in top 25% of high school class, 77% in top 50% of high school class. 96% from public high schools. Average SAT I Math 492, SAT I Math middle 50% range 440-540. Average SAT I Verbal 499, SAT I Verbal middle 50% range 450-540. Average ACT 19, ACT middle 50% range 18-20. TOEFL required of all international applicants, minimum TOEFL 520. **Basis for Candidate Selection:** *Very important factors considered include:* secondary school record, standardized test scores. *Other factors considered include:* alumni/ae relation, character/personal qualities, class rank, essays, extracurricular activities, interview, recommendations, talent/ability, work experience. **Freshman Admission Requirements:** High school diploma or GED is required. *Academic units required/recommended:* 13 total required; 21 total recommended; 4 English required, 4 English recommended, 3 math required, 3 math recommended, 2 science required, 2 science recommended, 2 science lab required, 2 science lab recommended, 2 foreign language required, 2 foreign language recommended, 2 social studies required, 2 social studies recommended, 1 history recommended, 7 elective recommended. **Freshman Admission Statistics:** 6,278 applied, 75% accepted, 40% of those accepted enrolled. **Transfer Admission Requirements:** *Items required:* college transcript. Minimum college GPA of 2.0 required. Lowest grade transferable C. **General Admission Information:** Application fee $20. Priority application deadline April 1. Regular application deadline May 1. Nonfall registration accepted. Neither credit nor placement offered for CEEB Advanced Placement tests.

COSTS AND FINANCIAL AID

In-state tuition $3,594. Out-of-state tuition $10,292. Room & board $5,442. Required fees $1,570. Average book expense $700. **Required Forms and Deadlines:** FAFSA. Financial aid filing deadline March 1. **Notification of Awards:** Applicants will be notified of awards on a rolling basis. **Types of Aid:** *Need-based scholarships/grants:* Pell, SEOG, state scholarships/grants, private scholarships, the school's own gift aid. *Loans:* FFEL Subsidized Stafford, FFEL Unsubsidized Stafford, FFEL PLUS, Federal Perkins, Federal Nursing, state loans, college/university loans from institutional funds. **Student Employment:** Federal Work-Study Program available. Institutional employment available. Off-campus job opportunities are good. **Financial Aid Statistics:** 39% freshmen, 40% undergrads receive some form of aid. Average freshman grant $6,356. Average freshman loan $3,620. Average income from on-campus job $1,310. **Financial Aid Phone:** 540-831-5408.

See page 1160.

RAMAPO COLLEGE OF NEW JERSEY

505 Ramapo Valley Road, Mahwah, NJ 07430
Phone: 201-684-7300 **E-mail:** admissions@ramapo.edu **CEEB Code:** 2884
Fax: 201-684-7964 **Web:** www.ramapo.edu **ACT Code:** 2591

This public school was founded in 1971. It has a 300-acre campus.

STUDENTS AND FACULTY

Enrollment: 5,143. **Student Body:** Male 39%, female 61%, out-of-state 12%, international 3% (66 countries represented). **Ethnic Representation:** African American 7%, Asian 4%, Caucasian 80%, Hispanic 9%. **Retention and Graduation:** 84% freshmen return for sophomore year. 25% freshmen graduate within 4 years. **Faculty:** Student/faculty ratio 17:1. 168 full-time faculty, 95% hold PhDs. 100% faculty teach undergrads.

ACADEMICS

Degrees: Bachelor's, certificate, first professional, master's. **Academic Requirements:** General education including some course work in computer literacy, English (including composition), history, humanities, mathematics, sciences (biological or physical), social science. A course in values, ethics, and aesthetics as well as in global/multicultural disciplines is required. Senior seminar is to be taken in appropriate major required for graduation. **Classes:** 10-19 students in an average class. 10-19 students in an average lab/discussion section. **Majors with Highest Enrollment:** Business administration/management; communications studies/speech communication and rhetoric; psychology, general. **Disciplines with Highest Percentage of Degrees Awarded:** Business/marketing 23%, communications/communication technologies 14%, psychology 14%, computer and information sciences 9%, social sciences and history 7%. **Special Study Options:** Accelerated program, cooperative (work-study) program, double major, dual enrollment, English as a second language, student exchange program (domestic), external degree program, honors program, independent study, internships, liberal arts/career combination, student-designed major, study abroad, teacher certification program.

FACILITIES

Housing: Coed, apartments for single students, housing for disabled students, housing for international students, cooperative housing. Special arrangements are made from time to time. **Library Holdings:** 158,633 bound volumes. 670 periodicals. 19,079 microforms. 3,250 audiovisuals. **Special Academic Facilities/Equipment:** Art museum, media center, International Telecommunications Center, electron microscope. **Computers:** School-owned computers available for student use.

EXTRACURRICULARS

Activities: Choral groups, dance, drama/theater, literary magazine, music ensembles, musical theater, pep band, radio station, student government, student newspaper, student-run film society, television station, yearbook. **Organizations:** 85 registered organizations, 5 honor societies, 2 religious organizations, 6 fraternities (7% men join), 7 sororities (6% women join). **Athletics (Intercollegiate):** *Men:* baseball, basketball, skiing (cross-country), cross-country, soccer, softball, tennis, track & field, volleyball. *Women:* baseball, basketball, cheerleading, skiing (cross-country), cross-country, soccer, softball, tennis, track & field, volleyball.

ADMISSIONS

Selectivity Rating: 81 (of 100). **Freshman Academic Profile:** Average high school GPA 3.2. 19% in top 10% of high school class, 49% in top 25% of high school class, 92% in top 50% of high school class. Average SAT I Math 530, SAT I Math middle 50% range 490-580. Average SAT I Verbal 540, SAT I Verbal middle 50% range 480-580. TOEFL required of all international applicants, minimum TOEFL 550. **Basis for Candidate Selection:** *Very important factors considered include:* secondary school record. *Important factors considered include:* character/personal qualities, class rank, essays, extracurricular activities, interview, recommendations, standardized test scores, talent/ability. *Other factors considered include:* alumni/ae relation. **Freshman Admission Requirements:** High school diploma or GED is required. *Academic units required/recommended:* 16 total required; 4 English required, 3 math required, 3 science recommended, 2 science lab required, 2 foreign language recommended, 2 history required, 5 elective required. **Freshman Admission Statistics:** 3,549 applied, 42% accepted, 42% of those accepted enrolled. **Transfer Admission Requirements:** *Items required:* college transcript, essay, statement of good standing from prior school. Minimum college GPA of 2.5 required. Lowest grade transferable C. **General Admission Information:** Application fee $45. Regular application deadline March 15. Nonfall registration accepted. Admission may be deferred for a maximum of 1 year. Credit offered for CEEB Advanced Placement tests.

COSTS AND FINANCIAL AID

In-state tuition $4,836. Out-of-state tuition $8,738. Room & board $7,682. Required fees $1,939. Average book expense $850. **Required Forms and Deadlines:** FAFSA. No deadline for regular filing. Priority filing deadline March 1. **Notification of Awards:** Applicants will be notified of awards on a rolling basis beginning on or about April 1. **Types of Aid:** *Need-based scholarships/grants:* Pell, SEOG, state scholarships/grants, private scholarships, the school's own gift aid. *Loans:* Direct Subsidized Stafford, Direct Unsubsidized Stafford, Direct PLUS, Federal Perkins, Federal Nursing, state loans. **Student Employment:** Federal Work-Study Program available. Off-campus job opportunities are excellent. **Financial Aid Statistics:** 45% freshmen, 43% undergrads receive some form of aid. Average freshman grant $9,231. Average freshman loan $2,578. **Financial Aid Phone:** 201-529-7550.

RANDOLPH-MACON COLLEGE

P. O. Box 5005, Ashland, VA 23005
Phone: 804-752-7305 **E-mail:** admissions@rmc.edu **CEEB Code:** 5566
Fax: 804-752-4707 **Web:** www.rmc.edu **ACT Code:** 4386

This private school, which is affiliated with the Methodist Church, was founded in 1830. It has a 110-acre campus.

STUDENTS AND FACULTY

Enrollment: 1,154. **Student Body:** Male 50%, female 50%, out-of-state 35%, international 1% (12 countries represented). **Ethnic Representation:** African American 5%, Asian 1%, Caucasian 92%, Hispanic 2%. **Retention and Graduation:** 68% freshmen return for sophomore year. 70% freshmen graduate within 4 years. 25% grads go on to further study within 1 year. 3%

grads pursue business degrees. 4% grads pursue law degrees. 2% grads pursue medical degrees. **Faculty:** Student/faculty ratio 11:1. 88 full-time faculty, 93% hold PhDs. 100% faculty teach undergrads.

ACADEMICS

Degrees: Bachelor's. **Academic Requirements:** General education including some course work in arts/fine arts, computer literacy, English (including composition), foreign languages, history, humanities, mathematics, sciences (biological or physical), social science, philosophy or religion. **Classes:** 10-19 students in an average class. **Majors with Highest Enrollment:** Business/managerial economics; English language and literature, general; psychology, general. **Disciplines with Highest Percentage of Degrees Awarded:** Social sciences and history 25%, business/marketing 24%, psychology 11%, English 9%, visual and performing arts 6%. **Special Study Options:** Accelerated program, cross registration, double major, dual enrollment, student exchange program (domestic), honors program, independent study, internships, liberal arts/career combination, study abroad, teacher certification program.

FACILITIES

Housing: Coed, all-female, all-male, housing for disabled students, fraternities and/or sororities, Honors House; Community Service House; Special-interest Housing. **Library Holdings:** 152,257 bound volumes. 1,006 periodicals. 203,253 microforms. 5,184 audiovisuals. **Special Academic Facilities/Equipment:** Language lab, learning center, media center, greenhouse, observatory with telescope, electron microscopes, nuclear magnetic resonator, art gallery, new fine arts center. **Computers:** *Recommended operating system:* Windows NT/2000. School-owned computers available for student use.

EXTRACURRICULARS

Activities: Choral groups, dance, drama/theater, jazz band, literary magazine, musical theater, pep band, radio station, student government, student newspaper, student-run film society, television station, yearbook. **Organizations:** 104 registered organizations, 19 honor societies, 3 religious organizations, 6 fraternities (45% men join), 5 sororities (45% women join). **Athletics (Intercollegiate):** *Men:* baseball, basketball, football, golf, lacrosse, soccer, swimming, tennis. *Women:* basketball, field hockey, lacrosse, soccer, softball, swimming, tennis, volleyball.

ADMISSIONS

Selectivity Rating: 77 (of 100). **Freshman Academic Profile:** Average high school GPA 3.2. 20% in top 10% of high school class, 50% in top 25% of high school class, 81% in top 50% of high school class. 65% from public high schools. Average SAT I Math 552, SAT I Math middle 50% range 500-600. Average SAT I Verbal 560, SAT I Verbal middle 50% range 500-610. TOEFL required of all international applicants, minimum TOEFL 550. **Basis for Candidate Selection:** *Very important factors considered include:* secondary school record. *Important factors considered include:* class rank, recommendations, standardized test scores. *Other factors considered include:* alumni/ae relation, character/personal qualities, essays, extracurricular activities, interview, minority status, talent/ability, volunteer work. **Freshman Admission Requirements:** High school diploma or GED is required. *Academic units required/recommended:* 16 total required; 22 total recommended; 4 English required, 4 English recommended, 3 math required, 4 math recommended, 3 science required, 4 science recommended, 2 science lab required, 4 science lab recommended, 2 foreign language required, 4 foreign language recommended, 1 social studies required, 4 social studies recommended, 2 history required, 2 history recommended, 1 elective required. **Freshman Admission Statistics:** 1,689 applied, 78% accepted, 29% of those accepted enrolled. **Transfer Admission Requirements:** *Items required:* high school transcript, college transcript, essay, standardized test score, statement of good standing from prior school. Minimum college GPA of 2.0 required. Lowest grade transferable C. **General Admission Information:** Application fee $30. Priority application deadline February 1. Early decision application deadline December 1. Regular application deadline March 1. Nonfall registration accepted. Admission may be deferred for a maximum of 1 year. Credit and/or placement offered for CEEB Advanced Placement tests.

COSTS AND FINANCIAL AID

Tuition $19,480. Room & board $5,715. Required fees $565. Average book expense $600. **Required Forms and Deadlines:** FAFSA and state aid form. Priority filing deadline February 1. **Notification of Awards:** Applicants will be notified of awards on or about April 1. **Types of Aid:** *Need-based scholarships/grants:* Pell, SEOG, state scholarships/grants, private scholarships, the school's own gift aid. *Loans:* FFEL Subsidized Stafford, FFEL Unsubsidized Stafford, FFEL PLUS, Federal Perkins, college/university loans from institutional funds. **Student Employment:** Federal Work-Study Program available. Institutional employment available. Off-campus job opportunities are good. **Financial Aid Statistics:** 62% freshmen, 56% undergrads receive some form of aid. Average freshman grant $10,540. Average freshman loan $4,100. Average income from on-campus job $1,200. **Financial Aid Phone:** 804-752-7259.

RANDOLPH-MACON WOMAN'S COLLEGE

2500 Rivermont Avenue, Lynchburg, VA 24503-1526
Phone: 434-947-8100 **E-mail:** admissions@rmwc.edu **CEEB Code:** 5567
Fax: 434-947-8996 **Web:** www.rmwc.edu **ACT Code:** 4388

This private school, which is affiliated with the Methodist Church, was founded in 1891. It has a 100-acre campus.

STUDENTS AND FACULTY

Enrollment: 764. **Student Body:** Out-of-state 55%, international 11% (48 countries represented). **Ethnic Representation:** African American 8%, Asian 3%, Caucasian 85%, Hispanic 3%. **Retention and Graduation:** 77% freshmen return for sophomore year. 60% freshmen graduate within 4 years. 31% grads go on to further study within 1 year. 2% grads pursue business degrees. 6% grads pursue law degrees. 5% grads pursue medical degrees. **Faculty:** Student/faculty ratio 9:1. 77 full-time faculty, 89% hold PhDs. 100% faculty teach undergrads.

ACADEMICS

Degrees: Bachelor's. **Academic Requirements:** General education including some course work in arts/fine arts, English (including composition), foreign languages, history, humanities, mathematics, sciences (biological or physical), social science, cultural inquiry; global issues; women and gender; criticism, analysis and research; wellness/physical education; interdisciplinary. Note: an individual course may satisfy more than one general education requirement. **Classes:** 10-19 students in an average class. 10-19 students in an average lab/discussion section. **Majors with Highest Enrollment:** English language and literature, general; biology/biological sciences, general; psychology, general. **Disciplines with Highest Percentage of Degrees Awarded:** Social sciences and history 30%, psychology 14%, biological life sciences 13%, visual and performing arts 12%, English 12%. **Special Study Options:** Accelerated program, cross registration, double major, dual enrollment, student exchange program (domestic), honors program, independent study, internships, liberal arts/career combination, student-designed major, study abroad, teacher certification program, 7-college exchange with Washington and Lee University, Hollins University, Hampden-Sydney College, Mary Baldwin College, Sweet Briar College, and Randolph-Macon College. Junior year abroad program that includes Reading, England. American Culture Program, a 1-Semester program that includes study on-site at key locations in and near Virginia, open to R-MWC students and students from other colleges who are accepted through a special application process.

FACILITIES

Housing: All-female, Shared housing for nontraditional age students. **Library Holdings:** 197,332 bound volumes. 618 periodicals. 187,000 microforms. 3,600 audiovisuals. **Special Academic Facilities/Equipment:** Maier Museum of American Art recognized as one of the most outstanding college collections in the nation, computer-equipped classrooms (including wireless computer networks and smart boards), 100-acre equestrian center, language lab, science and math resource center, learning resources center, writing lab, nursery school, nature preserves, observatory, electron microscope. **Computers:** School-owned computers available for student use.

EXTRACURRICULARS

Activities: Choral groups, dance, drama/theater, literary magazine, music ensembles, radio station, student government, student newspaper, student-run film society, yearbook. **Organizations:** 35 registered organizations, 7 honor societies, 6 religious organizations. **Athletics (Intercollegiate):** *Women:* basketball, equestrian, field hockey, soccer, softball, swimming, tennis, volleyball.

ADMISSIONS

Selectivity Rating: 80 (of 100). **Freshman Academic Profile:** Average high school GPA 3.4. 39% in top 10% of high school class, 65% in top 25% of high school class, 93% in top 50% of high school class. 82% from public high schools. Average SAT I Math 564, SAT I Math middle 50% range 510-620. Average SAT I Verbal 592, SAT I Verbal middle 50% range 540-640. Average ACT 25, ACT middle 50% range 23-28. TOEFL required of all international applicants, minimum TOEFL 550. **Basis for Candidate Selection:** *Very important factors considered include:* character/personal qualities, essays, recommendations, secondary school record. *Important factors considered include:* class rank, extracurricular activities, standardized test scores, talent/ability. *Other factors considered include:* alumni/ae relation, interview, minority status, volunteer work, work experience. **Freshman Admission Requirements:** High school diploma or GED is required. *Academic units required/recommended:* 16 total required; 4 English required, 3 math required, 2 science required, 2 science lab required, 4 foreign language required, 2 history required, 2 elective required.

Freshman Admission Statistics: 723 applied, 85% accepted, 33% of those accepted enrolled. **Transfer Admission Requirements:** *Items required:* high school transcript, college transcript, essay, statement of good standing from prior school. Lowest grade transferable C-. **General Admission Information:** Application fee $35. Early decision application deadline November 15. Regular application deadline March 1. Nonfall registration accepted. Admission may be deferred for a maximum of 1 year. Credit and/or placement offered for CEEB Advanced Placement tests.

COSTS AND FINANCIAL AID

Required Forms and Deadlines: FAFSA and state aid form. No deadline for regular filing. Priority filing deadline March 1. **Notification of Awards:** Applicants will be notified of awards on a rolling basis beginning on or about March 1. **Types of Aid:** *Need-based scholarships/grants:* Pell, SEOG, state scholarships/grants, private scholarships, the school's own gift aid. *Loans:* FFEL Subsidized Stafford, FFEL Unsubsidized Stafford, FFEL PLUS, Federal Perkins. **Student Employment:** Federal Work-Study Program available. Institutional employment available. Off-campus job opportunities are good. **Financial Aid Statistics:** 65% freshmen, 62% undergrads receive some form of aid. Average freshman grant $14,400. Average freshman loan $2,461. **Financial Aid Phone:** 434-947-8128.

See page 1162.

REED COLLEGE

3203 SE Woodstock Boulevard, Portland, OR 97202-8199
Phone: 503-777-7511 **E-mail:** admission@reed.edu **CEEB Code:** 4654
Fax: 503-777-7553 **Web:** www.reed.edu **ACT Code:** 3494

This private school was founded in 1908. It has a 100-acre campus.

STUDENTS AND FACULTY

Enrollment: 1,363. **Student Body:** Male 46%, female 54%, out-of-state 79%, international 3% (38 countries represented). **Ethnic Representation:** African American 1%, Asian 5%, Caucasian 68%, Hispanic 4%, Native American 1%. **Retention and Graduation:** 85% freshmen return for sophomore year. 45% freshmen graduate within 4 years. 65% grads go on to further study within 1 year. 5% grads pursue business degrees. 7% grads pursue law degrees. 5% grads pursue medical degrees. **Faculty:** Student/faculty ratio 10:1. 118 full-time faculty, 87% hold PhDs. 100% faculty teach undergrads.

ACADEMICS

Degrees: Bachelor's, master's. **Academic Requirements:** General education including some course work in arts/fine arts, English (including composition), foreign languages, humanities, philosophy, sciences (biological or physical), social science. **Classes:** 10-19 students in an average class. 10-19 students in an average lab/discussion section. **Majors with Highest Enrollment:** Biology/biological sciences, general; psychology, general; English language and literature, general. **Disciplines with Highest Percentage of Degrees Awarded:** Social sciences and history 18%, biological life sciences 14%, physical sciences 11%, English 11%, psychology 10%. **Special Study Options:** Cross registration, double major, dual enrollment, student exchange program (domestic), independent study, internships, liberal arts/career combination, study abroad, Applied Physics and Electronic Science program with Oregon Graduate Institute (OGI)

FACILITIES

Housing: Coed, apartments for single students, housing for disabled students, Reed language houses accommodate upper-division students studying Chinese, French, German, Russian, and Spanish. First year students required to live on campus; exceptions granted for unusual situations. **Library Holdings:** 494,784 bound volumes. 1,872 periodicals. 235,794 microforms. 16,596 audiovisuals. **Special Academic Facilities/Equipment:** Art gallery, studio art building, language labs, computerized music listening lab, nuclear research reactor, 20 music practice rooms and MIDI lab, 800-seat auditorium, quantitative skills center, educational technology center. **Computers:** School-owned computers available for student use.

EXTRACURRICULARS

Activities: Choral groups, dance, drama/theater, literary magazine, music ensembles, radio station, student government, student newspaper, student-run film society, symphony orchestra. **Organizations:** 56 registered organizations, 1 honor society, 5 religious organizations.

ADMISSIONS

Selectivity Rating: 89 (of 100). **Freshman Academic Profile:** Average high school GPA 3.8. 51% in top 10% of high school class, 85% in top 25% of high school class, 100% in top 50% of high school class. 66% from public high schools. Average SAT I Math 704, SAT I Math middle 50% range 620-710. Average SAT I Verbal 667, SAT I Verbal middle 50% range 660-760. Average ACT 30, ACT middle 50% range 29-32. TOEFL required of all international applicants, minimum TOEFL 600. **Basis for Candidate Selection:** *Very important factors considered include:* essays, secondary school record. *Important factors considered include:* class rank, interview, recommendations, standardized test scores. *Other factors considered include:* alumni/ae relation, character/personal qualities, extracurricular activities, talent/ability, volunteer work, work experience. **Freshman Admission Requirements:** High school diploma or GED is required. *Academic units required/recommended:* 23 total recommended; 4 English recommended, 4 math recommended, 4 science recommended, 3 science lab recommended, 4 foreign language recommended, 1 social studies recommended, 3 history recommended. **Freshman Admission Statistics:** 1,847 applied, 55% accepted, 31% of those accepted enrolled. **Transfer Admission Requirements:** *Items required:* high school transcript, college transcript, essay, standardized test score, statement of good standing from prior school. Lowest grade transferable C-. **General Admission Information:** Application fee $40. Early decision application deadline November 15. Regular application deadline January 15. Admission may be deferred for a maximum of 1 year. Credit and/or placement offered for CEEB Advanced Placement tests.

COSTS AND FINANCIAL AID

Average book expense $950. **Required Forms and Deadlines:** FAFSA, institution's own financial aid form, CSS/Financial Aid PROFILE and noncustodial (divorced/separated) parent's statement. Financial aid filing deadline February 1. Priority filing deadline January 15. **Notification of Awards:** Applicants will be notified of awards on or about April 1. **Types of Aid:** *Need-based scholarships/grants:* Pell, SEOG, state scholarships/grants, private scholarships, the school's own gift aid. *Loans:* FFEL Subsidized Stafford, FFEL Unsubsidized Stafford, FFEL PLUS, Federal Perkins, state loans. **Student Employment:** Federal Work-Study Program available. Institutional employment available. Off-campus job opportunities are good. **Financial Aid Statistics:** 55% freshmen, 55% undergrads receive some form of aid. Average freshman grant $20,162. Average freshman loan $2,258. Average income from on-campus job $700. **Financial Aid Phone:** 800-547-4750.

See page 1164.

REEDLEY COLLEGE

995 North Reed Avenue, Reedley, CA 93654
Phone: 559-638-3641
Web: www.rc.cc.ca.us

STUDENTS AND FACULTY

Enrollment: 10,078. **Student Body:** Male 38%, female 62%, out-of-state 1%. **Ethnic Representation:** African American 3%, Asian 4%, Caucasian 40%, Hispanic 41%, Native American 2%. **Faculty:** Student/faculty ratio 25:1. 83 full-time faculty.

ACADEMICS

Degrees: Associate's, certificate, diploma, terminal, transfer. **Special Study Options:** Cooperative (work-study) program, distance learning, English as a second language, honors program, independent study, academic remediation, Advanced Placement credit, freshman honors college, learning disabilities services.

FACILITIES

Library Holdings: 36,000 bound volumes. 217 periodicals. 8,400 microforms. 50 audiovisuals.

ADMISSIONS

Selectivity Rating: 63 (of 100). High school diploma or GED is required.

COSTS AND FINANCIAL AID

In-state tuition $330. Out-of-state tuition $3,830. Room & board $3,820. Required fees $0. Average book expense $300. **Types of Aid:** *Need-based scholarships/grants:* Pell, SEOG, state scholarships/grants, private scholarships, the school's own gift aid. *Loans:* FFEL Subsidized Stafford, FFEL Unsubsidized Stafford, FFEL PLUS, Federal Perkins, college/university loans from institutional funds.

REGIS COLLEGE

 $$$  

235 Wellesley Street, Weston, MA 02493-1571
Phone: 781-768-7100 **E-mail:** admission@regiscollege.edu **CEEB Code:** 3723
Fax: 781-768-7071 **Web:** www.regiscollege.edu **ACT Code:** 1886

This private school, which is affiliated with the Roman Catholic Church, was founded in 1927. It has a 168-acre campus.

STUDENTS AND FACULTY

Enrollment: 782. **Student Body:** Out-of-state 14%, international 2%. **Ethnic Representation:** African American 6%, Asian 5%, Caucasian 49%, Hispanic 8%. **Retention and Graduation:** 74% freshmen return for sophomore year. 14% grads go on to further study within 1 year. 1% grads pursue business degrees. 2% grads pursue law degrees. 1% grads pursue medical degrees. **Faculty:** Student/faculty ratio 12:1. 50 full-time faculty, 84% hold PhDs. 81% faculty teach undergrads.

ACADEMICS

Degrees: Associate's, bachelor's, master's, post-master's certificate, terminal, transfer. **Academic Requirements:** General education including some course work in English (including composition), humanities, mathematics, sciences (biological or physical), social science, first year seminar and religious studies. **Classes:** 10-19 students in an average class. 10-19 students in an average lab/discussion section. **Majors with Highest Enrollment:** Communications studies/speech communication and rhetoric; nursing/registered nurse training (RN, ASN, BSN, MSN); business administration/management. **Disciplines with Highest Percentage of Degrees Awarded:** Social sciences and history 16%, communications/communication technologies 14%, health professions and related sciences 13%, business/marketing 11%, visual and performing arts 11%. **Special Study Options:** Cross registration, double major, English as a second language, student exchange program (domestic), honors program, independent study, internships, student-designed major, study abroad, teacher certification program.

FACILITIES

Housing: All-female, Quiet floors. **Library Holdings:** 133,565 bound volumes. 951 periodicals. 44,770 microforms. 5,684 audiovisuals. **Special Academic Facilities/Equipment:** Fine arts center, philatelic museum. **Computers:** School-owned computers available for student use.

EXTRACURRICULARS

Activities: Choral groups, dance, drama/theater, literary magazine, musical theater, radio station, student government, yearbook. **Organizations:** 29 registered organizations, 8 honor societies, 1 religious organization. **Athletics (Intercollegiate):** *Women:* basketball, crew, cross-country, diving, field hockey, soccer, softball, swimming, tennis, track & field, volleyball.

ADMISSIONS

Selectivity Rating: 66 (of 100). **Freshman Academic Profile:** Average high school GPA 3.2. 19% in top 10% of high school class, 48% in top 25% of high school class, 77% in top 50% of high school class. 79% from public high schools. Average SAT I Math 476, SAT I Math middle 50% range 410-520. Average SAT I Verbal 496, SAT I Verbal middle 50% range 420-570. TOEFL required of all international applicants, minimum TOEFL 500. **Basis for Candidate Selection:** *Very important factors considered include:* character/personal qualities, essays, recommendations, secondary school record. *Important factors considered include:* class rank, extracurricular activities, interview, standardized test scores, talent/ability, volunteer work. *Other factors considered include:* alumni/ae relation, work experience. **Freshman Admission Requirements:** High school diploma or GED is required. *Academic units required/recommended:* 16 total required; 20 total recommended; 4 English required, 4 English recommended, 3 math required, 3 math recommended, 2 science required, 3 science recommended, 1 science lab required, 1 science lab recommended, 2 foreign language required, 2 foreign language recommended, 2 social studies required, 2 social studies recommended, 2 history recommended, 3 elective required, 4 elective recommended. **Freshman Admission Statistics:** 574 applied, 84% accepted, 28% of those accepted enrolled. **Transfer Admission Requirements:** *Items required:* college transcript, essay, statement of good standing from prior school. Minimum college GPA of 2.0 required. Lowest grade transferable C-. **General Admission Information:** Application fee $30. Priority application deadline August 1. Nonfall registration accepted. Admission may be deferred for a maximum of 1 year. Credit and/or placement offered for CEEB Advanced Placement tests.

COSTS AND FINANCIAL AID

Tuition $18,400. Room & board $8,350. Required fees $0. Average book expense $900. **Required Forms and Deadlines:** FAFSA and institution's own financial aid form. No deadline for regular filing. Priority filing deadline March 1. **Notification of Awards:** Applicants will be notified of awards on a rolling basis beginning on or about March 1. **Types of Aid:** *Need-based scholarships/grants:* Pell, SEOG, state scholarships/grants, private scholarships, the school's own gift aid, Federal Nursing. *Loans:* FFEL Subsidized Stafford, FFEL Unsubsidized Stafford, FFEL PLUS, Federal Perkins, state loans, college/university loans from institutional funds. **Student Employment:** Federal Work-Study Program available. Institutional employment available. Off-campus job opportunities are fair. **Financial Aid Statistics:** 78% freshmen, 77% undergrads receive some form of aid. Average freshman grant $11,752. Average freshman loan $4,279. Average income from on-campus job $1,000. **Financial Aid Phone:** 781-768-7180.

REGIS UNIVERSITY

 $$$  

3333 Regis Boulevard, Denver, CO 80221-1099
Phone: 303-458-4900 **E-mail:** regisadm@regis.edu **CEEB Code:** 4656
Fax: 303-964-5534 **Web:** www.regis.edu **ACT Code:** 526

This private school, which is affiliated with the Roman Catholic Church, was founded in 1877. It has a 90-acre campus.

STUDENTS AND FACULTY

Enrollment: 1,200. **Student Body:** Out-of-state 58%, international 3% (23 countries represented). **Ethnic Representation:** African American 3%, Asian 3%, Caucasian 79%, Hispanic 8%, Native American 1%. **Retention and Graduation:** 79% freshmen return for sophomore year. **Faculty:** Student/faculty ratio 16:1. 68 full-time faculty, 97% hold PhDs. 100% faculty teach undergrads.

ACADEMICS

Degrees: Bachelor's, master's. **Academic Requirements:** General education including some course work in arts/fine arts, English (including composition), foreign languages, history, mathematics, philosophy, sciences (biological or physical), social science. **Special Study Options:** Cross registration, double major, honors program, independent study, internships, student-designed major, study abroad, teacher certification program.

FACILITIES

Housing: Coed. **Library Holdings:** 430,514 bound volumes. 7,850 periodicals. 155,296 microforms. 104,887 audiovisuals. **Special Academic Facilities/Equipment:** Language lab, wellness center. **Computers:** School-owned computers available for student use.

EXTRACURRICULARS

Activities: Choral groups, drama/theater, literary magazine, music ensembles, musical theater, radio station, student government, student newspaper, yearbook. **Organizations:** 40 registered organizations, 1 honor society, 1 religious organization. **Athletics (Intercollegiate):** *Men:* baseball, basketball, cross-country, golf, soccer. *Women:* basketball, cross-country, lacrosse, soccer, softball, volleyball.

ADMISSIONS

Selectivity Rating: 81 (of 100). **Freshman Academic Profile:** Average high school GPA 3.2. 21% in top 10% of high school class, 47% in top 25% of high school class, 70% in top 50% of high school class. 65% from public high schools. Average SAT I Math 543, SAT I Math middle 50% range 480-600. Average SAT I Verbal 546, SAT I Verbal middle 50% range 490-590. Average ACT 23, ACT middle 50% range 21-26. TOEFL required of all international applicants, minimum TOEFL 550. **Basis for Candidate Selection:** *Very important factors considered include:* secondary school record, standardized test scores. *Important factors considered include:* essays, recommendations. *Other factors considered include:* character/personal qualities, class rank, extracurricular activities, interview, talent/ability, volunteer work, work experience. **Freshman Admission Requirements:** High school diploma or GED is required. *Academic units required/recommended:* 16 total recommended; 4 English recommended, 2 math recommended, 2 science recommended, 2 foreign language recommended, 2 social studies recommended, 1 history recommended. **Freshman Admission Statistics:** 1,327 applied, 84% accepted, 27% of those accepted enrolled. **Transfer Admission Requirements:** *Items required:* college transcript, essay. Minimum college GPA of 2.0 required. Lowest grade transferable C. **General Admission Information:** Application fee $40. Nonfall registration accepted. Admission may be deferred for a maximum of 1 year. Credit and/or placement offered for CEEB Advanced Placement tests.

COSTS AND FINANCIAL AID

Tuition $18,400. Room & board $7,150. Required fees $170. Average book expense $550. **Required Forms and Deadlines:** FAFSA. Priority filing

deadline March 5. **Notification of Awards:** Applicants will be notified of awards on a rolling basis beginning on or about March 31. **Types of Aid:** *Need-based scholarships/grants:* Pell, SEOG, state scholarships/grants, the school's own gift aid. *Loans:* FFEL Subsidized Stafford, FFEL Unsubsidized Stafford, FFEL PLUS, Federal Perkins, Federal Nursing. **Student Employment:** Federal Work-Study Program available. Off-campus job opportunities are good. **Financial Aid Statistics:** Average freshman grant $9,896. Average income from on-campus job $1,800. **Financial Aid Phone:** 303-458-4066.

REINHARDT COLLEGE

7300 Reinhardt College Circle, Waleska, GA 30183
Phone: 770-720-5526 **E-mail:** admissions@reinhardt.edu
Fax: 770-720-5899 **Web:** www.reinhardt.edu **ACT Code:** 856

This private school, which is affiliated with the Methodist Church, was founded in 1883. It has a 600-acre campus.

STUDENTS AND FACULTY

Enrollment: 1,083. **Student Body:** Male 41%, female 59%, out-of-state 2%. **Retention and Graduation:** 4% freshmen graduate within 4 years. 50% grads go on to further study within 1 year. 40% grads pursue business degrees. 20% grads pursue law degrees. 15% grads pursue medical degrees. **Faculty:** Student/faculty ratio 15:1. 48 full-time faculty, 62% hold PhDs. 100% faculty teach undergrads.

ACADEMICS

Degrees: Associate's, bachelor's, transfer. **Academic Requirements:** General education including some course work in arts/fine arts, English (including composition), foreign languages, history, humanities, mathematics, philosophy, social science, religion. **Classes:** 10-19 students in an average class. **Disciplines with Highest Percentage of Degrees Awarded:** Business/marketing 31%, education 24%, communications/communication technologies 17%, liberal arts/general studies 9%, computer and information sciences 6%. **Special Study Options:** Accelerated program, double major, dual enrollment, external degree program, honors program, independent study, internships, study abroad, teacher certification program.

FACILITIES

Housing: Coed, all-female, all-male, honors house. **Library Holdings:** 44,350 bound volumes. 380 periodicals. 2,200 microforms. 9,500 audiovisuals. **Computers:** *Recommended operating system:* Windows 95. School-owned computers available for student use.

EXTRACURRICULARS

Activities: Choral groups, concert band, music ensembles, student government, student newspaper, student-run film society, television station, yearbook. **Organizations:** 1 registered organization, 1 honor society, 2 religious organizations. **Athletics (Intercollegiate):** *Men:* basketball, cheerleading, cross-country, golf, soccer. *Women:* basketball, cheerleading, cross-country, soccer, softball.

ADMISSIONS

Selectivity Rating: 63 (of 100). **Freshman Academic Profile:** Average high school GPA 3.0. Average SAT I Math 470, SAT I Math middle 50% range 410-520. Average SAT I Verbal 485, SAT I Verbal middle 50% range 420-540. Average ACT 20, ACT middle 50% range 17-21. TOEFL required of all international applicants, minimum TOEFL 500. **Basis for Candidate Selection:** *Very important factors considered include:* secondary school record, standardized test scores. *Important factors considered include:* interview. *Other factors considered include:* character/personal qualities, class rank, essays, extracurricular activities, recommendations, talent/ability. **Freshman Admission Requirements:** High school diploma or GED is required. *Academic units required/recommended:* 14 total required; 2 total recommended; 4 English required, 4 math required, 3 science required, 2 foreign language recommended, 3 social studies required. **Freshman Admission Statistics:** 546 applied, 85% accepted, 51% of those accepted enrolled. **Transfer Admission Requirements:** *Items required:* college transcript, statement of good standing from prior school. Minimum college GPA of 2.0 required. Lowest grade transferable C. **General Admission Information:** Application fee $25. Nonfall registration accepted. Admission may be deferred for a maximum of 2 years. Credit and/or placement offered for CEEB Advanced Placement tests.

COSTS AND FINANCIAL AID

Tuition $8,700. Room & board $4,885. Required fees $0. Average book expense $300. **Required Forms and Deadlines:** FAFSA and state aid form. No deadline for regular filing. Priority filing deadline May 1. **Notification of Awards:** Applicants will be notified of awards on or about April 1. **Types of Aid:** *Need-based scholarships/grants:* Pell, SEOG, state scholarships/grants, private scholarships, the school's own gift aid. *Loans:* FFEL Subsidized Stafford, FFEL Unsubsidized Stafford, FFEL PLUS. **Student Employment:** Federal Work-Study Program available. Institutional employment available. Off-campus job opportunities are excellent. **Financial Aid Statistics:** 51% freshmen receive some form of aid. **Financial Aid Phone:** 770-720-5667.

RENSSELAER POLYTECHNIC INSTITUTE

110 Eighth Street, Troy, NY 12180-3590
Phone: 518-276-6216 **E-mail:** admissions@rpi.edu **CEEB Code:** 2757
Fax: 518-276-4072 **Web:** www.rpi.edu **ACT Code:** 2866

This private school was founded in 1824. It has a 260-acre campus.

STUDENTS AND FACULTY

Enrollment: 5,139. **Student Body:** Male 75%, female 25%, out-of-state 47%, international 4%. **Ethnic Representation:** African American 4%, Asian 13%, Caucasian 71%, Hispanic 5%, Native American 1%. **Retention and Graduation:** 91% freshmen return for sophomore year. 54% freshmen graduate within 4 years. 24% grads go on to further study within 1 year. **Faculty:** Student/faculty ratio 16:1. 384 full-time faculty, 93% hold PhDs.

ACADEMICS

Degrees: Bachelor's, doctoral, master's. **Academic Requirements:** General education including some course work in English (including composition), humanities, mathematics, sciences (biological or physical), social science. **Classes:** 20-29 students in an average class. 10-19 students in an average lab/discussion section. **Disciplines with Highest Percentage of Degrees Awarded:** Engineering/engineering technology 53%, computer and information sciences 13%, business/marketing 13%, architecture 7%, biological life sciences 4%. **Special Study Options:** Accelerated program, cooperative (work-study) program, cross registration, distance learning, double major, dual enrollment, English as a second language, student exchange program (domestic), independent study, internships, liberal arts/career combination, student-designed major, study abroad.

FACILITIES

Housing: Coed, all-male, apartments for married students, apartments for single students, housing for disabled students, fraternities and/or sororities. **Library Holdings:** 312,500 bound volumes. 10,210 periodicals. 0 microforms. 91,435 audiovisuals. **Special Academic Facilities/Equipment:** Gallery, observatory, fresh water institute at Lake George, technology park, center for polymer synthesis, center for industrial innovation, wind tunnel, linear accelerator, incubator center. **Computers:** *Recommended operating system:* Windows NT/2000. School-owned computers available for student use.

EXTRACURRICULARS

Activities: Choral groups, concert band, dance, drama/theater, jazz band, literary magazine, music ensembles, musical theater, pep band, radio station, student government, student newspaper, student-run film society, yearbook. **Organizations:** 130 registered organizations, 29 fraternities (35% men join), 6 sororities (20% women join). **Athletics (Intercollegiate):** *Men:* baseball, basketball, cross-country, diving, football, golf, ice hockey, lacrosse, soccer, swimming, tennis, track & field. *Women:* basketball, cross-country, diving, field hockey, ice hockey, lacrosse, soccer, softball, swimming, tennis, track & field.

ADMISSIONS

Selectivity Rating: 83 (of 100). **Freshman Academic Profile:** 65% in top 10% of high school class, 91% in top 25% of high school class, 99% in top 50% of high school class. 79% from public high schools. Average SAT I Math 671, SAT I Math middle 50% range 640-720. Average SAT I Verbal 611, SAT I Verbal middle 50% range 580-680. Average ACT 27, ACT middle 50% range 24-28. TOEFL required of all international applicants, minimum TOEFL 550. **Basis for Candidate Selection:** *Very important factors considered include:* secondary school record. *Important factors considered include:* standardized test scores. *Other factors considered include:* alumni/ae relation, character/personal qualities, class rank, essays, extracurricular activities, geographical residence, minority status, recommendations, talent/ability, volunteer work, work experience. **Freshman Admission Requirements:** High school diploma or GED is required. *Academic units required/recommended:* 15 total required; 4 English required, 4 math required, 4 science required, 3 social studies required. **Freshman Admission Statistics:** 5,480 applied, 70% accepted, 27% of those accepted enrolled. **Transfer Admission Requirements:** *Items* *required:* college transcript, statement of good standing from prior school. Minimum college GPA of 3.0 required. Lowest grade transferable C. **General Admission Information:** Application fee $50. Early decision application deadline November 15. Regular application deadline January 1. Nonfall registration accepted. Admission may be deferred for a maximum of 1 year. Credit and/or placement offered for CEEB Advanced Placement tests.

COSTS AND FINANCIAL AID

Tuition $26,400. Room & board $8,902. Required fees $770. Average book expense $1,528. **Required Forms and Deadlines:** FAFSA. No deadline for regular filing. Priority filing deadline February 15. **Notification of Awards:** Applicants will be notified of awards on or about March 20. **Types of Aid:** *Need-based scholarships/grants:* Pell, SEOG, state scholarships/grants, private scholarships, the school's own gift aid. *Loans:* Direct Subsidized Stafford, Direct Unsubsidized Stafford, Direct PLUS, FFEL Subsidized Stafford, FFEL Unsubsidized Stafford, FFEL PLUS, Federal Perkins, college/university loans from institutional funds. **Student Employment:** Federal Work-Study Program available. Institutional employment available. Off-campus job opportunities are good. **Financial Aid Statistics:** 70% freshmen, 70% undergrads receive some form of aid. Average freshman grant $16,992. Average freshman loan $4,800. Average income from on-campus job $1,068. **Financial Aid Phone:** 518-276-6813.

See page 1166.

RHODE ISLAND COLLEGE

Office of Undergraduate Admissions, 600 Mt. Pleasant Avenue, Providence, RI 02908
Phone: 401-456-8234 **E-mail:** admissions@ric.edu **CEEB Code:** 3724
Fax: 401-456-8817 **Web:** www.ric.edu

This public school was founded in 1854. It has a 170-acre campus.

STUDENTS AND FACULTY

Enrollment: 7,098. **Student Body:** Male 33%, female 67%. **Ethnic Representation:** African American 4%, Asian 2%, Caucasian 77%, Hispanic 5%. **Retention and Graduation:** 74% freshmen return for sophomore year. 14% freshmen graduate within 4 years. **Faculty:** Student/faculty ratio 14:1. 306 full-time faculty, 84% hold PhDs. 90% faculty teach undergrads.

ACADEMICS

Degrees: Bachelor's, doctoral, master's, post-master's certificate. **Academic Requirements:** General education including some course work in arts/fine arts, English (including composition), history, mathematics, sciences (biological or physical), social science. **Classes:** 20-29 students in an average class. **Majors with Highest Enrollment:** History, general; communications studies/speech communication and rhetoric; psychology, general. **Disciplines with Highest Percentage of Degrees Awarded:** Education 33%, psychology 12%, business/marketing 10%, protective services/public administration 8%, health professions and related sciences 8%. **Special Study Options:** Double major, student exchange program (domestic), honors program, independent study, internships, student-designed major, study abroad, teacher certification program, weekend college.

FACILITIES

Housing: Coed, all-female, housing for disabled students. **Library Holdings:** 368,891 bound volumes. 1,766 periodicals. 920,820 microforms. 3,982 audiovisuals. **Special Academic Facilities/Equipment:** Art gallery, curriculum resource center, center for economic education, on-campus elementary school, closed-circuit TV studios. **Computers:** School-owned computers available for student use.

EXTRACURRICULARS

Activities: Choral groups, concert band, dance, drama/theater, jazz band, literary magazine, music ensembles, musical theater, radio station, student government, student newspaper, symphony orchestra, television station, yearbook. **Organizations:** 60 registered organizations, 4 honor societies, 3 religious organizations, 1 fraternity, 1 sorority. **Athletics (Intercollegiate):** *Men:* baseball, basketball, cross-country, soccer, tennis, track & field, wrestling. *Women:* basketball, cross-country, gymnastics, soccer, softball, tennis, track & field, volleyball.

ADMISSIONS

Selectivity Rating: 69 (of 100). **Freshman Academic Profile:** Average SAT I Math 484, SAT I Math middle 50% range 430-540. Average SAT I Verbal 490, SAT I Verbal middle 50% range 440-550. TOEFL required of all international applicants, minimum TOEFL 550. **Basis for Candidate Selection:** *Very important factors considered include:* class rank, secondary school record. *Important factors considered include:* essays, recommendations. *Other factors considered include:* alumni/ae relation, extracurricular activities, interview, standardized test scores, talent/ability, volunteer work, work experience. **Freshman Admission Requirements:** High school diploma or GED is required. *Academic units required/recommended:* 4 English required, 3 math required, 2 science required, 2 science lab required, 2 foreign language required, 2 social studies required, 4 elective required. **Transfer Admission Requirements:** *Items required:* college transcript. Lowest grade transferable C. **General Admission Information:** Application fee $25. Regular application deadline May 1. Nonfall registration accepted. Admission may be deferred. Credit and/or placement offered for CEEB Advanced Placement tests.

COSTS AND FINANCIAL AID

In-state tuition $3,086. Out-of-state tuition $8,850. Room & board $6,136. Required fees $675. Average book expense $650. **Required Forms and Deadlines:** FAFSA and institution's own financial aid form. Priority filing deadline March 1. **Notification of Awards:** Applicants will be notified of awards on a rolling basis beginning on or about March 15. **Types of Aid:** *Need-based scholarships/grants:* Pell, SEOG, state scholarships/grants, private scholarships, the school's own gift aid. *Loans:* FFEL Subsidized Stafford, FFEL Unsubsidized Stafford, FFEL PLUS, Federal Perkins, state loans. **Student Employment:** Federal Work-Study Program available. Institutional employment available. Off-campus job opportunities are good. **Financial Aid Statistics:** 63% freshmen receive some form of aid. Average income from on-campus job $1,000. **Financial Aid Phone:** 401-456-8033.

RHODE ISLAND SCHOOL OF DESIGN

2 College Street, Providence, RI 02903
Phone: 401-454-6300 **E-mail:** admissions@risd.edu **CEEB Code:** 3726
Fax: 401-454-6309 **Web:** www.risd.edu **ACT Code:** 3812

This private school was founded in 1877. It has a 13-acre campus.

STUDENTS AND FACULTY

Enrollment: 1,882. **Student Body:** International 10%. **Ethnic Representation:** African American 3%, Asian 13%, Caucasian 65%, Hispanic 5%. **Retention and Graduation:** 93% freshmen return for sophomore year. 3% grads go on to further study within 1 year. **Faculty:** Student/faculty ratio 11:1. 145 full-time faculty. 100% faculty teach undergrads.

ACADEMICS

Degrees: Bachelor's, master's. **Academic Requirements:** General education including some course work in arts/fine arts, English (including composition), history, philosophy, social science. **Classes:** 100+ students in an average class. 20-29 students in an average lab/discussion section. **Disciplines with Highest Percentage of Degrees Awarded:** Visual and performing arts 87%, architecture 13%. **Special Study Options:** Cross registration, student exchange program (domestic), independent study, internships, study abroad, continuing education program, 6-week pre-college summer program for secondary school students, summer workshops for undergraduate credit, 6-week winter session study abroad courses.

FACILITIES

Housing: Coed, apartments for single students. **Library Holdings:** 100,961 bound volumes. 419 periodicals. 1,855 microforms. 680,663 audiovisuals. **Special Academic Facilities/Equipment:** Art museum with over 45 galleries, extensive facilities for glassblowing, metalsmithing, lithography, sculpture, painting, and other art disciplines, nature lab. **Computers:** *Recommended operating system:* Mac. School-owned computers available for student use.

EXTRACURRICULARS

Activities: Student government, student newspaper, student-run film society, yearbook. **Organizations:** 35 registered organizations, 1 religious organization.

ADMISSIONS

Selectivity Rating: 91 (of 100). **Freshman Academic Profile:** Average high school GPA 3.3. 26% in top 10% of high school class, 58% in top 25% of high school class, 91% in top 50% of high school class. 60% from public high schools. Average SAT I Math 600. Average SAT I Verbal 603. Average ACT 25. TOEFL required of all international applicants, minimum TOEFL 580. **Basis for Candidate Selection:** *Very important factors considered include:* secondary school record, talent/ability. *Important factors considered include:* character/personal qualities, essays, recommendations, standardized test scores. *Other factors considered include:* alumni/ae relation, class rank, extracurricular activities, minority status, volunteer work, work experience. **Freshman Admission Requirements:** High school diploma or GED is required.

Freshman Admission Statistics: 2,524 applied, 32% accepted, 49% of those accepted enrolled. **Transfer Admission Requirements:** *Items required:* college transcript, essay. Lowest grade transferable C. **General Admission Information:** Application fee $45. Priority application deadline January 20. Regular application deadline February 15. Nonfall registration accepted. Admission may be deferred for a maximum of 1 year. Credit and/or placement offered for CEEB Advanced Placement tests.

COSTS AND FINANCIAL AID

Tuition $22,952. Room & board $6,830. Required fees $445. Average book expense $3,800. **Required Forms and Deadlines:** FAFSA and CSS/Financial Aid PROFILE. Financial aid filing deadline February 15. Priority filing deadline February 15. **Notification of Awards:** Applicants will be notified of awards on or about April 1. **Types of Aid:** *Need-based scholarships/grants:* Pell, SEOG, state scholarships/grants, private scholarships, the school's own gift aid. *Loans:* FFEL Subsidized Stafford, FFEL Unsubsidized Stafford, FFEL PLUS, Federal Perkins, college/university loans from institutional funds. **Student Employment:** Federal Work-Study Program available. Institutional employment available. Off-campus job opportunities are good. **Financial Aid Statistics:** 40% freshmen, 47% undergrads receive some form of aid. Average freshman grant $12,350. Average freshman loan $3,050. Average income from on-campus job $1,100. **Financial Aid Phone:** 401-454-6661.

RHODES COLLEGE

Office of Admissions, 2000 North Parkway, Memphis, TN 38112
Phone: 901-843-3700 **E-mail:** adminfo@rhodes.edu **CEEB Code:** 1730
Fax: 901-843-3631 **Web:** www.rhodes.edu **ACT Code:** 4008

This private school, which is affiliated with the Presbyterian Church, was founded in 1848. It has a 100-acre campus.

STUDENTS AND FACULTY

Enrollment: 1,541. **Student Body:** Male 44%, female 56%, out-of-state 71%, international 1% (13 countries represented). **Ethnic Representation:** African American 4%, Asian 3%, Caucasian 87%, Hispanic 1%. **Retention and Graduation:** 87% freshmen return for sophomore year. 71% freshmen graduate within 4 years. 34% grads go on to further study within 1 year. 6% grads pursue business degrees. 8% grads pursue law degrees. 7% grads pursue medical degrees. **Faculty:** Student/faculty ratio 11:1. 129 full-time faculty, 89% hold PhDs. 100% faculty teach undergrads.

ACADEMICS

Degrees: Bachelor's, master's. **Academic Requirements:** General education including some course work in arts/fine arts, English (including composition), foreign languages, humanities, sciences (biological or physical), social science. **Classes:** 10-19 students in an average class. 10-19 students in an average lab/ discussion section. **Majors with Highest Enrollment:** Business administration/management; English language and literature, general; biology/biological sciences, general. **Disciplines with Highest Percentage of Degrees Awarded:** Social sciences and history 39%, biological life sciences 14%, English 12%, business/marketing 11%, psychology 7%. **Special Study Options:** Cross registration, double major, dual enrollment, student exchange program (domestic), honors program, independent study, internships, student-designed major, study abroad, teacher certification program.

FACILITIES

Housing: Coed, all-female, all-male, substance-free, quiet study, restricted visitation, nonsmoking. American Studies Focus Program: first year students take 3 classes together (American history, literature and art), and live in close proximity to one another. **Library Holdings:** 270,761 bound volumes. 1,179 periodicals. 74,500 microforms. 990 audiovisuals. **Special Academic Facilities/Equipment:** Art gallery, anthropology museum, two reflecting telescopes, electron microscopes, cell culture lab, nuclear magnetic resonance instrument. **Computers:** School-owned computers available for student use.

EXTRACURRICULARS

Activities: Choral groups, concert band, drama/theater, literary magazine, music ensembles, musical theater, student government, student newspaper, student-run film society, symphony orchestra, yearbook. **Organizations:** 90 registered organizations, 14 honor societies, 8 religious organizations, 7 fraternities (55% men join), 5 sororities (58% women join). **Athletics (Intercollegiate):** *Men:* baseball, basketball, cross-country, football, golf, soccer, swimming, tennis, track & field. *Women:* basketball, cross-country, field hockey, golf, soccer, softball, swimming, tennis, track & field, volleyball.

ADMISSIONS

Selectivity Rating: 85 (of 100). **Freshman Academic Profile:** Average high school GPA 3.6. 50% in top 10% of high school class, 78% in top 25% of high school class, 95% in top 50% of high school class. Average SAT I Math 640, SAT I Math middle 50% range 600-690. Average SAT I Verbal 644, SAT I Verbal middle 50% range 590-700. Average ACT 28, ACT middle 50% range 26-30. TOEFL required of all international applicants, minimum TOEFL 550. **Basis for Candidate Selection:** *Very important factors considered include:* class rank, secondary school record, standardized test scores. *Important factors considered include:* alumni/ae relation, character/personal qualities, essays, extracurricular activities, interview, minority status, recommendations, talent/ ability. *Other factors considered include:* geographical residence, state residency, volunteer work, work experience. **Freshman Admission Requirements:** High school diploma or GED is required. *Academic units required/ recommended:* 16 total required; 4 English required, 3 math required, 4 math recommended, 2 science required, 2 science lab required, 2 foreign language required, 2 social studies required, 2 history required, 3 elective required. **Freshman Admission Statistics:** 2,345 applied, 70% accepted, 27% of those accepted enrolled. **Transfer Admission Requirements:** *Items required:* high school transcript, college transcript, essay, standardized test score statement of good standing from prior school. Minimum college GPA of 2.5 required. Lowest grade transferable C. **General Admission Information:** Application fee $40. Priority application deadline February 1. Early decision application deadline November 1. Regular application deadline February 1. Nonfall registration accepted. Admission may be deferred for a maximum of 1 year. Credit and/or placement offered for CEEB Advanced Placement tests.

COSTS AND FINANCIAL AID

Tuition $22,628. Room & board $6,382. Required fees $310. Average book expense $760. **Required Forms and Deadlines:** FAFSA, CSS/Financial Aid PROFILE and business/farm supplement. Priority filing deadline March 1. **Notification of Awards:** Applicants will be notified of awards on or about April 10. **Types of Aid:** *Need-based scholarships/grants:* Pell, SEOG, state scholarships/grants, private scholarships, the school's own gift aid. *Loans:* FFEL Subsidized Stafford, FFEL Unsubsidized Stafford, FFEL PLUS, Federal Perkins. **Student Employment:** Federal Work-Study Program available. Institutional employment available. Off-campus job opportunities are good. **Financial Aid Statistics:** 43% freshmen, 37% undergrads receive some form of aid. Average freshman grant $10,256. Average freshman loan $3,423. Average income from on-campus job $1,340. **Financial Aid Phone:** 901-843-3810.

RICE UNIVERSITY

PO Box 1892, MS-17, Houston, TX 77251-1892
Phone: 713-348-7423 **E-mail:** admission@rice.edu **CEEB Code:** 6609
Fax: 713-348-5952 **Web:** www.rice.edu **ACT Code:** 4152

This private school was founded in 1912. It has a 300-acre campus.

STUDENTS AND FACULTY

Enrollment: 2,787. **Student Body:** Male 53%, female 47%, out-of-state 46%, international 3%. **Ethnic Representation:** African American 7%, Asian 15%, Caucasian 56%, Hispanic 11%, Native American 1%. **Retention and Graduation:** 95% freshmen return for sophomore year. 74% freshmen graduate within 4 years. 35% grads go on to further study within 1 year. 6% grads pursue law degrees. 9% grads pursue medical degrees. **Faculty:** Student/ faculty ratio 5:1. 503 full-time faculty, 96% hold PhDs. 96% faculty teach undergrads.

ACADEMICS

Degrees: Bachelor's, doctoral, master's. **Academic Requirements:** General education including some course work in distribution requirements for graduation: 12 semester hours are required in each of three areas of study - humanities, social sciences, and natural sciences/engineering. **Classes:** Under 10 students in an average class. **Majors with Highest Enrollment:** Economics, general; biology/biological sciences, general; electrical, electronics, and communications engineering. **Disciplines with Highest Percentage of Degrees Awarded:** Social sciences and history 17%, engineering/engineering technology 14%, biological life sciences 9%, visual and performing arts 7%, foreign languages and literature 6%. **Special Study Options:** Accelerated program, cross registration, double major, dual enrollment, student exchange program (domestic), honors program, independent study, internships, liberal arts/career combination, student-designed major, study abroad, teacher certification program, 8-year guaranteed medical school program with the Baylor College of Medicine, 5-year joint degree BSE/MSE in engineering, 5-year joint degree BSE/MBA in engineering and business.

FACILITIES

Housing: Coed, housing for disabled students. **Library Holdings:** 2,100,000 bound volumes. 28,000 periodicals. 2,700,000 microforms. 51,000 audiovisuals. **Special Academic Facilities/Equipment:** Art gallery, museum, media center, language labs, computer labs, civil engineering lab, NASA equipment for students in space physics courses.

EXTRACURRICULARS

Activities: Choral groups, concert band, dance, drama/theater, jazz band, literary magazine, marching band, music ensembles, musical theater, opera, pep band, radio station, student government, student newspaper, student-run film society, symphony orchestra, television station, yearbook. **Organizations:** 290 registered organizations, 11 honor societies, 14 religious organizations. **Athletics (Intercollegiate):** *Men:* baseball, basketball, cross-country, football, golf, indoor track, tennis, track & field. *Women:* basketball, cross-country, indoor track, soccer, swimming, tennis, track & field, volleyball.

ADMISSIONS

Selectivity Rating: 98 (of 100). **Freshman Academic Profile:** 83% in top 10% of high school class, 92% in top 25% of high school class, 99% in top 50% of high school class. SAT I Math middle 50% range 670-770. SAT I Verbal middle 50% range 650-750. ACT middle 50% range 28-33. TOEFL required of all international applicants, minimum TOEFL 550. **Basis for Candidate Selection:** *Very important factors considered include:* character/personal qualities, class rank, essays, extracurricular activities, recommendations, secondary school record, standardized test scores, talent/ability. *Other factors considered include:* alumni/ae relation, geographical residence, interview, state residency, volunteer work, work experience. **Freshman Admission Requirements:** High school diploma or equivalent is not required. *Academic units required/recommended:* 16 total required; 4 English required, 3 math required, 2 science required, 2 science lab required, 2 foreign language required, 2 social studies required, 3 elective required. **Freshman Admission Statistics:** 7,079 applied, 24% accepted, 42% of those accepted enrolled. **Transfer Admission Requirements:** *Items required:* high school transcript, college transcript, essay, standardized test score statement of good standing from prior school. Minimum college GPA of 3.2 required. Lowest grade transferable C. **General Admission Information:** Application fee $35. Early decision application deadline November 1. Regular application deadline January 2. Admission may be deferred for a maximum of 2 years. Credit offered for CEEB Advanced Placement tests.

COSTS AND FINANCIAL AID

Required Forms and Deadlines: FAFSA, CSS/Financial Aid PROFILE, noncustodial (divorced/separated) parent's statement and business/farm supplement. Financial aid filing deadline March 1. Priority filing deadline March 1. **Notification of Awards:** Applicants will be notified of awards on a rolling basis. **Types of Aid:** *Need-based scholarships/grants:* Pell, SEOG, state scholarships/grants, private scholarships, the school's own gift aid. *Loans:* FFEL Subsidized Stafford, FFEL Unsubsidized Stafford, FFEL PLUS, Federal Perkins, college/university loans from institutional funds. **Student Employment:** Federal Work-Study Program available. Institutional employment available. Off-campus job opportunities are excellent. **Financial Aid Statistics:** 32% freshmen, 30% undergrads receive some form of aid. **Financial Aid Phone:** 713-348-4958.

RICHMOND, THE AMERICAN INTERNATIONAL UNIVERSITY IN LONDON

US Office of Admissions, 343 Congress Street - Suite 3100, Boston, MA 02210
Phone: 617-450-5617 **E-mail:** us_admissions@richmond.ac.uk **CEEB Code:** 823
Fax: 617-450-5601 **Web:** www.richmond.ac.uk **ACT Code:** 5244

This private school was founded in 1972.

STUDENTS AND FACULTY

Enrollment: 911. **Retention and Graduation:** 72% freshmen return for sophomore year. 35% grads go on to further study within 1 year. **Faculty:** Student/faculty ratio 16:1. 39 full-time faculty, 90% hold PhDs.

ACADEMICS

Degrees: Associate's, bachelor's, master's, post-bachelor's certificate, terminal. **Academic Requirements:** General education including some course work in arts/fine arts, computer literacy, English (including composition), foreign languages, history, humanities, mathematics, philosophy, sciences (biological or physical), social science. **Classes:** 10-19 students in an average class. 20-29 students in an average lab/discussion section. **Majors with Highest Enrollment:** Business administration/management; international relations and affairs; communications studies/speech communication and rhetoric. **Disciplines with Highest Percentage of Degrees Awarded:** Business/marketing 40%, social sciences and history 18%, computer and information sciences 13%, communications/communication technologies 13%, visual and performing arts 7%. **Special Study Options:** Cross registration, English as a second language, honors program, independent study, internships, liberal arts/career combination, study abroad.

FACILITIES

Housing: Coed, all-female, all-male. **Library Holdings:** 70,000 bound volumes. 300 periodicals. 87 microforms. 737 audiovisuals. **Computers:** *Recommended operating system:* Windows NT/2000. School-owned computers available for student use.

EXTRACURRICULARS

Activities: Choral groups, dance, drama/theater, literary magazine, music ensembles, student government, student newspaper, yearbook. **Athletics (Intercollegiate):** *Men:* basketball, rugby, soccer, softball, tennis, volleyball. *Women:* rugby, soccer, tennis, volleyball.

ADMISSIONS

Selectivity Rating: 63 (of 100). **Freshman Academic Profile:** Average high school GPA 3.2. 33% in top 10% of high school class, 36% in top 25% of high school class, 96% in top 50% of high school class. Average SAT I Math 540, SAT I Math middle 50% range 470-610. Average SAT I Verbal 570, SAT I Verbal middle 50% range 470-620. ACT middle 50% range 24-28. TOEFL required of all international applicants, minimum TOEFL 550. **Basis for Candidate Selection:** *Very important factors considered include:* essays, recommendations, secondary school record. *Important factors considered include:* extracurricular activities. *Other factors considered include:* alumni/ae relation, interview, standardized test scores, talent/ability. **Freshman Admission Requirements:** High school diploma or GED is required. *Academic units required/recommended:* 4 English required, 3 math required, 3 science required. **Freshman Admission Statistics:** 1,874 applied, 44% accepted, 21% of those accepted enrolled. **Transfer Admission Requirements:** *Items required:* college transcript, essay, statement of good standing from prior school. Minimum college GPA of 2.0 required. Lowest grade transferable C. **General Admission Information:** Application fee $50. Regular application deadline August 1. Nonfall registration accepted. Admission may be deferred for a maximum of 1 year. Credit and/or placement offered for CEEB Advanced Placement tests.

COSTS AND FINANCIAL AID

Tuition $16,650. Room & board $8,800. Required fees $0. Average book expense $1,000. **Required Forms and Deadlines:** FAFSA and institution's own financial aid form. Priority filing deadline April 1. **Notification of Awards:** Applicants will be notified of awards on a rolling basis. **Types of Aid:** *Need-based scholarships/grants:* private scholarships, the school's own gift aid. *Loans:* FFEL Subsidized Stafford, FFEL Unsubsidized Stafford, FFEL PLUS. **Student Employment:** Institutional employment available. Off-campus job opportunities are good. **Financial Aid Statistics:** Average freshman grant $4,000. Average freshman loan $2,500. Average income from on-campus job $1,500. **Financial Aid Phone:** 617-450-5617.

RIDER UNIVERSITY

2083 Lawrenceville Road, Lawrenceville, NJ 08648
Phone: 609-896-5042 **E-mail:** admissions@rider.edu **CEEB Code:** 2758
Fax: 609-895-6645 **Web:** www.rider.edu **ACT Code:** 2590

This private school was founded in 1865. It has a 353-acre campus.

STUDENTS AND FACULTY

Enrollment: 4,284. **Student Body:** Male 41%, female 59%, out-of-state 21%, international 2%. **Ethnic Representation:** African American 8%, Asian 4%, Caucasian 78%, Hispanic 5%. **Retention and Graduation:** 78% freshmen return for sophomore year. 43% freshmen graduate within 4 years. 15% grads go on to further study within 1 year. 3% grads pursue business degrees. 2% grads pursue law degrees. 1% grads pursue medical degrees. **Faculty:** Student/faculty ratio 12:1. 229 full-time faculty, 93% hold PhDs. 95% faculty teach undergrads.

ACADEMICS

Degrees: Associate's, bachelor's, master's, post-master's certificate. **Academic Requirements:** General education including some course work in English (including composition), history, humanities, mathematics, sciences (biological or physical), social science. **Classes:** 10-19 students in an average class. 10-19 students in an average lab/discussion section. **Majors with Highest Enrollment:** Communications studies/speech communication and rhetoric; elementary education and teaching; psychology, general. **Disciplines with Highest Percentage of Degrees Awarded:** Business/marketing 35%, education 16%, communications/communication technologies 13%, computer and information sciences 7%, psychology 7%. **Special Study Options:** Cooperative (work-study) program, cross registration, double major, English as a second language, honors program, independent study, internships, liberal arts/career combination, study abroad, teacher certification program, weekend college.

FACILITIES

Housing: Coed, all-female, apartments for single students, housing for disabled students, fraternities and/or sororities, suites, special-interest areas (wellness, first-year experience, learning community). **Library Holdings:** 460,574 bound volumes. 3,031 periodicals. 615,126 microforms. 17,857 audiovisuals. **Special Academic Facilities/Equipment:** Art gallery, Holocaust/Genocide Resource Center. **Computers:** School-owned computers available for student use.

EXTRACURRICULARS

Activities: Choral groups, concert band, dance, drama/theater, jazz band, literary magazine, music ensembles, musical theater, opera, pep band, radio station, student government, student newspaper, student-run film society, symphony orchestra, yearbook. **Organizations:** 81 registered organizations, 28 honor societies, 4 religious organizations, 8 fraternities (15% men join), 7 sororities (16% women join). **Athletics (Intercollegiate):** *Men:* baseball, basketball, cheerleading, cross-country, diving, golf, soccer, swimming, tennis, track & field, wrestling. *Women:* basketball, cheerleading, cross-country, diving, field hockey, soccer, softball, swimming, tennis, track & field, volleyball.

ADMISSIONS

Selectivity Rating: 73 (of 100). **Freshman Academic Profile:** Average high school GPA 3.1. 11% in top 10% of high school class, 37% in top 25% of high school class, 71% in top 50% of high school class. 80% from public high schools. Average SAT I Math 520, SAT I Math middle 50% range 470-580. Average SAT I Verbal 510, SAT I Verbal middle 50% range 470-560. TOEFL required of all international applicants, minimum TOEFL 550. **Basis for Candidate Selection:** *Very important factors considered include:* essays, secondary school record, standardized test scores. *Important factors considered include:* class rank, interview, recommendations. *Other factors considered include:* character/personal qualities, extracurricular activities, talent/ability. **Freshman Admission Requirements:** High school diploma or GED is required. *Academic units required/recommended:* 16 total required; 4 English required, 2 math required, 3 math recommended, 3 science recommended, 2 foreign language recommended, 2 social studies recommended, 2 history recommended. **Freshman Admission Statistics:** 4,091 applied, 82% accepted, 29% of those accepted enrolled. **Transfer Admission Requirements:** *Items required:* college transcript, essay. Minimum college GPA of 2.5 required. Lowest grade transferable C. **General Admission Information:** Application fee $40. Nonfall registration accepted. Admission may be deferred for a maximum of 1 year. Credit and/or placement offered for CEEB Advanced Placement tests.

COSTS AND FINANCIAL AID

Tuition $20,590. Room & board $8,060. Required fees $460. Average book expense $1,000. **Required Forms and Deadlines:** FAFSA. Financial aid filing deadline June 1. Priority filing deadline March 1. **Notification of Awards:** Applicants will be notified of awards on a rolling basis beginning on or about April 15. **Types of Aid:** *Need-based scholarships/grants:* Pell, SEOG, state scholarships/grants, private scholarships, the school's own gift aid. *Loans:* FFEL Subsidized Stafford, FFEL Unsubsidized Stafford, FFEL PLUS, Federal Perkins, state loans, college/university loans from institutional funds, alternative. **Student Employment:** Federal Work-Study Program available. Institutional employment available. Off-campus job opportunities are excellent. **Financial Aid Statistics:** 69% freshmen, 65% undergrads receive some form of aid. Average freshman grant $17,171. Average freshman loan $3,613. Average income from on-campus job $1,800. **Financial Aid Phone:** 609-896-5360.

See page 1168.

RINGLING SCHOOL OF ART & DESIGN

$$$

2700 N. Tamiami Trail, Sarasota, FL 34234
Phone: 941-351-5100 **E-mail:** admissions@rsad.edu **CEEB Code:** 5573
Fax: 941-359-7517 **Web:** www.rsad.edu **ACT Code:** 6724

This private school was founded in 1931. It has a 20-acre campus.

STUDENTS AND FACULTY

Enrollment: 1,015. **Student Body:** Male 53%, female 47%, out-of-state 45%, international 7% (34 countries represented). **Ethnic Representation:** African American 2%, Asian 4%, Caucasian 85%, Hispanic 8%, Native American 1%. **Retention and Graduation:** 79% freshmen return for sophomore year. 68% freshmen graduate within 4 years. 5% grads go on to further study within 1 year. **Faculty:** Student/faculty ratio 14:1. 54 full-time faculty, 72% hold PhDs. 100% faculty teach undergrads.

ACADEMICS

Degrees: Bachelor's. **Academic Requirements:** General education including some course work in arts/fine arts, English (including composition), history, humanities, mathematics, social science, environmental studies. **Classes:** 10-19 students in an average class. **Majors with Highest Enrollment:** Design and applied arts; graphic design; illustration. **Disciplines with Highest Percentage of Degrees Awarded:** Visual and performing arts 100%. **Special Study Options:** Student exchange program (domestic), independent study, internships, study abroad.

FACILITIES

Housing: Coed, apartments for married students, apartments for single students. **Library Holdings:** 42,436 bound volumes. 320 periodicals. 0 microforms. 113,143 audiovisuals. **Special Academic Facilities/Equipment:** Art gallery. **Computers:** School-owned computers available for student use.

EXTRACURRICULARS

Activities: Drama/theater, student government. **Organizations:** 24 registered organizations, 3 religious organizations, 2 fraternities (3% men join), 1 sorority (1% women join).

ADMISSIONS

Selectivity Rating: 85 (of 100). **Freshman Academic Profile:** Average SAT I Math 510, SAT I Math middle 50% range 430-560. Average SAT I Verbal 520, SAT I Verbal middle 50% range 460-600. ACT middle 50% range 17-20. TOEFL required of all international applicants, minimum TOEFL 500. **Basis for Candidate Selection:** *Very important factors considered include:* secondary school record, talent/ability. *Important factors considered include:* character/personal qualities, essays, extracurricular activities, recommendations. *Other factors considered include:* alumni/ae relation, geographical residence, interview, minority status, volunteer work, work experience. **Freshman Admission Requirements:** High school diploma or GED is required. **Freshman Admission Statistics:** 621 applied, 76% accepted, 41% of those accepted enrolled. **Transfer Admission Requirements:** *Items required:* high school transcript, college transcript, essay. Minimum high school GPA of 2.0 required. Minimum college GPA of 2.0 required. Lowest grade transferable C. **General Admission Information:** Application fee $35. Priority application deadline March 1. Admission may be deferred for a maximum of 2 years. Credit and/or placement offered for CEEB Advanced Placement tests.

COSTS AND FINANCIAL AID

Tuition $16,230. Room & board $7,844. Required fees $200. Average book expense $1,750. **Required Forms and Deadlines:** FAFSA. No deadline for regular filing. Priority filing deadline March 1. **Notification of Awards:** Applicants will be notified of awards on a rolling basis beginning on or about May 1. **Types of Aid:** *Need-based scholarships/grants:* Pell, SEOG, state scholarships/grants, private scholarships, the school's own gift aid. *Loans:* FFEL Subsidized Stafford, FFEL Unsubsidized Stafford, FFEL PLUS. **Student Employment:** Federal Work-Study Program available. Institutional employment available. Off-campus job opportunities are excellent. **Financial Aid Statistics:** 62% freshmen, 76% undergrads receive some form of aid. Average freshman grant $6,487. Average freshman loan $2,482. Average income from on-campus job $2,615. **Financial Aid Phone:** 941-351-5100.

RIPON COLLEGE

300 Seward Street, PO Box 248, Ripon, WI 54971
Phone: 920-748-8337 **E-mail:** adminfo@ripon.edu **CEEB Code:** 1664
Fax: 920-748-8335 **Web:** www.ripon.edu **ACT Code:** 4336

This private school, which is affiliated with the United Church of Christ, was founded in 1851. It has a 250-acre campus.

STUDENTS AND FACULTY

Enrollment: 987. **Student Body:** Male 47%, female 53%, out-of-state 32%, international 2%. **Ethnic Representation:** African American 2%, Asian 1%, Caucasian 89%, Hispanic 4%, Native American 1%. **Retention and Graduation:** 86% freshmen return for sophomore year. 48% freshmen graduate within 4 years. 10% grads go on to further study within 1 year. 3% grads pursue law degrees. 4% grads pursue medical degrees. **Faculty:** Student/faculty ratio 15:1. 47 full-time faculty, 95% hold PhDs. 100% faculty teach undergrads.

ACADEMICS

Degrees: Bachelor's. **Academic Requirements:** General education including some course work in arts/fine arts, English (including composition), foreign languages, humanities, mathematics, sciences (biological or physical), social science, PE and global studies. **Classes:** 10-19 students in an average class. 10-19 students in an average lab/discussion section. **Majors with Highest Enrollment:** Business administration/management; education, general; biology/biological sciences, general. **Disciplines with Highest Percentage of Degrees Awarded:** Social sciences and history 27%, business/marketing 13%, biological life sciences 9%, psychology 9%, visual and performing arts 7%. **Special Study Options:** Double major, student exchange program (domestic), internships, student-designed major, study abroad, teacher certification program.

FACILITIES

Housing: Coed, all-female, all-male, fraternities and/or sororities. **Library Holdings:** 169,523 bound volumes. 985 periodicals. 25,186 microforms. 662 audiovisuals. **Special Academic Facilities/Equipment:** Art gallery, language labs. **Computers:** *Recommended operating system:* Windows NT/2000. School-owned computers available for student use.

EXTRACURRICULARS

Activities: Choral groups, concert band, drama/theater, jazz band, literary magazine, music ensembles, musical theater, radio station, student government, student newspaper, symphony orchestra, yearbook. **Organizations:** 45 registered organizations, 13 honor societies, 1 religious organization, 5 fraternities (49% men join), 3 sororities (27% women join). **Athletics (Intercollegiate):** *Men:* baseball, basketball, cross-country, football, golf, indoor track, soccer, swimming, tennis, track & field. *Women:* basketball, cross-country, golf, indoor track, soccer, softball, swimming, tennis, track & field, volleyball.

ADMISSIONS

Selectivity Rating: 80 (of 100). **Freshman Academic Profile:** Average high school GPA 3.3. 26% in top 10% of high school class, 53% in top 25% of high school class, 85% in top 50% of high school class. 75% from public high schools. Average SAT I Math 602, SAT I Math middle 50% range 540-670. Average SAT I Verbal 599, SAT I Verbal middle 50% range 570-640. Average ACT 24, ACT middle 50% range 22-26. TOEFL required of all international applicants, minimum TOEFL 550. **Basis for Candidate Selection:** *Very important factors considered include:* interview, secondary school record. *Important factors considered include:* character/personal qualities, class rank, extracurricular activities, recommendations, standardized test scores. *Other factors considered include:* alumni/ae relation, essays, talent/ability, volunteer work. **Freshman Admission Requirements:** High school diploma or GED is required. *Academic units required/recommended:* 17 total required; 4 English required, 2 math required, 4 math recommended, 2 science required, 4 science recommended, 2 foreign language recommended, 2 social studies required, 4 social studies recommended. **Freshman Admission Statistics:** 934 applied, 84% accepted, 32% of those accepted enrolled. **Transfer Admission Requirements:** *Items required:* high school transcript, college transcript, essay, standardized test score statement of good standing from prior school. Minimum college GPA of 2.0 required. Lowest grade transferable C. **General Admission Information:** Application fee $30. Priority application deadline March 15. Nonfall registration accepted. Credit and/or placement offered for CEEB Advanced Placement tests.

COSTS AND FINANCIAL AID

Tuition $19,700. Room & board $5,055. Required fees $240. Average book expense $500. **Required Forms and Deadlines:** FAFSA. No deadline for regular filing. Priority filing deadline March 1. **Notification of Awards:** Applicants will be notified of awards on a rolling basis beginning on or about March 1. **Types of Aid:** *Need-based scholarships/grants:* Pell, SEOG, state scholarships/grants, private scholarships, the school's own gift aid. *Loans:* FFEL Subsidized Stafford, FFEL Unsubsidized Stafford, FFEL PLUS, Federal Perkins. **Student Employment:** Federal Work-Study Program available. Institutional employment available. Off-campus job opportunities are good. **Financial Aid Statistics:** 77% freshmen, 76% undergrads receive some form of aid. Average freshman grant $11,125. Average freshman loan $2,751. Average income from on-campus job $1,200. **Financial Aid Phone:** 920-748-8101.

See page 1170.

RIVIER COLLEGE

420 Main Street, Nashua, NH 03060
Phone: 603-897-8507 **E-mail:** rivadmit@rivier.edu **CEEB Code:** 3728
Fax: 603-891-1799 **Web:** www.rivier.edu **ACT Code:** 2520

This private school, which is affiliated with the Roman Catholic Church, was founded in 1933. It has a 68-acre campus.

STUDENTS AND FACULTY

Enrollment: 1,489. **Student Body:** Male 19%, female 81%, out-of-state 33%. **Ethnic Representation:** African American 3%, Asian 1%, Caucasian 85%, Hispanic 3%. **Retention and Graduation:** 70% freshmen return for sophomore year. 21% grads go on to further study within 1 year. 7% grads pursue business degrees. 1% grads pursue law degrees. 1% grads pursue medical degrees. **Faculty:** Student/faculty ratio 13:1. 80 full-time faculty, 60% hold PhDs. 88% faculty teach undergrads.

ACADEMICS

Degrees: Associate's, bachelor's, certificate, master's, post-bachelor's certificate, post-master's certificate. **Academic Requirements:** General education including some course work in arts/fine arts, English (including composition), foreign languages, history, humanities, mathematics, philosophy, sciences (biological or physical), social science, religious studies, service learning. **Classes:** 10-19 students in an average class. 10-19 students in an average lab/discussion section. **Disciplines with Highest Percentage of Degrees Awarded:** Education 24%, business/marketing 14%, health professions and related sciences 14%, psychology 11%, social sciences and history 8%. **Special Study Options:** Cross registration, double major, English as a second language, honors program, independent study, internships, study abroad, teacher certification program.

FACILITIES

Housing: Coed. **Library Holdings:** 107,200 bound volumes. 480 periodicals. 89,572 microforms. 29,094 audiovisuals. **Special Academic Facilities/Equipment:** Art gallery, Early Childhood Center/Laboratory School, language lab, TV microscope, video/laser disk system, photospectrometer, high-performance liquid chromatograph, digital imaging lab, several art studios including a photography darkroom. **Computers:** *Recommended operating system:* Windows 95. School-owned computers available for student use.

EXTRACURRICULARS

Activities: Choral groups, drama/theater, music ensembles, student government, student newspaper, yearbook. **Organizations:** 30 registered organizations, 2 honor societies, 2 religious organizations. **Athletics (Intercollegiate):** *Men:* baseball, basketball, cross-country, soccer, volleyball. *Women:* basketball, cross-country, soccer, softball, volleyball.

ADMISSIONS

Selectivity Rating: 64 (of 100). **Freshman Academic Profile:** Average high school GPA 2.9. 9% in top 10% of high school class, 24% in top 25% of high school class, 70% in top 50% of high school class. 80% from public high schools. Average SAT I Math 480, SAT I Math middle 50% range 410-530. Average SAT I Verbal 490, SAT I Verbal middle 50% range 430-540. TOEFL required of all international applicants, minimum TOEFL 500. **Basis for Candidate Selection:** *Very important factors considered include:* secondary school record. *Important factors considered include:* essays, extracurricular activities, recommendations, standardized test scores, talent/ability, volunteer work, work experience. *Other factors considered include:* character/personal qualities, class rank, interview. **Freshman Admission Requirements:** High school diploma or GED is required. *Academic units required/recommended:* 16 total recommended; 4 English recommended, 3 math recommended, 1 science recommended, 1 science lab recommended, 2 foreign language recommended, 2 social studies recommended, 1 history recommended, 3 elective recommended. **Freshman Admission Statistics:** 899 applied, 82% accepted, 43% of those accepted enrolled. **Transfer Admission Requirements:** *Items required:* college transcript. Minimum college GPA of 2.5 required. Lowest grade transferable C. **General Admission Information:** Application fee $25. Nonfall registration accepted. Admission may be deferred for a maximum of 1 year. Credit and/or placement offered for CEEB Advanced Placement tests.

COSTS AND FINANCIAL AID

Tuition $17,730. Room & board $6,916. Required fees $675. Average book expense $800. **Required Forms and Deadlines:** FAFSA. **Notification of Awards:** Applicants will be notified of awards on a rolling basis beginning on or about March 1. **Types of Aid:** *Need-based scholarships/grants:* Pell, SEOG, state scholarships/grants, private scholarships, the school's own gift aid. *Loans:* FFEL Subsidized Stafford, FFEL Unsubsidized Stafford, FFEL PLUS, Federal Perkins, Federal Nursing, state loans. **Student Employment:** Federal Work-Study Program available. Institutional employment available. Off-campus job opportunities are good. **Financial Aid Statistics:** 100% freshmen, 84% undergrads receive some form of aid. Average freshman grant $7,841. Average freshman loan $2,536. Average income from on-campus job $800. **Financial Aid Phone:** 603-897-8510.

See page 1172.

ROANOKE COLLEGE

221 College Lane, Salem, VA 24153-3794
Phone: 540-375-2270 **E-mail:** admissions@roanoke.edu **CEEB Code:** 5571
Fax: 540-375-2267 **Web:** www.roanoke.edu **ACT Code:** 4392

This private school, which is affiliated with the Lutheran Church, was founded in 1842. It has a 68-acre campus.

STUDENTS AND FACULTY

Enrollment: 1,822. **Student Body:** Male 39%, female 61%, out-of-state 41%, international 1% (17 countries represented). **Ethnic Representation:** African American 4%, Asian 2%, Caucasian 86%, Hispanic 2%. **Retention and Graduation:** 78% freshmen return for sophomore year. 60% freshmen graduate within 4 years. 20% grads go on to further study within 1 year. **Faculty:** Student/faculty ratio 14:1. 118 full-time faculty, 90% hold PhDs. 100% faculty teach undergrads.

ACADEMICS

Degrees: Bachelor's. **Academic Requirements:** General education including some course work in arts/fine arts, computer literacy, English (including composition), foreign languages, history, humanities, mathematics, philosophy, sciences (biological or physical), social science, co-curricular learning and service course; may intensive learning course. **Classes:** 10-19 students in an average class. 10-19 students in an average lab/discussion section. **Majors with Highest Enrollment:** Business administration/management; English language and literature, general; sociology. **Disciplines with Highest Percentage of Degrees Awarded:** Social sciences and history 26%, business/marketing 23%, psychology 11%, English 10%, biological life sciences 7%. **Special Study Options:** Accelerated program, cross registration, double major, dual enrollment, English as a second language, honors program, independent study, internships, liberal arts/career combination, study abroad, teacher certification program.

FACILITIES

Housing: Coed, all-female, all-male, apartments for single students, fraternities and/or sororities, theme housing. **Library Holdings:** 134,085 bound volumes. 719 periodicals. 307,716 microforms. 7,635 audiovisuals. **Special Academic Facilities/Equipment:** Fine arts center, community research center, language lab, church and society center. **Computers:** *Recommended operating system:* Windows XP. School-owned computers available for student use.

EXTRACURRICULARS

Activities: Choral groups, dance, drama/theater, jazz band, literary magazine, music ensembles, musical theater, pep band, radio station, student government, student newspaper, student-run film society, yearbook. **Organizations:** 50 registered organizations, 20 honor societies, 5 religious organizations, 3 fraternities (18% men join), 4 sororities (18% women join). **Athletics (Intercollegiate):** *Men:* baseball, basketball, cross-country, golf, indoor track, lacrosse, soccer, tennis, track & field. *Women:* basketball, cross-country, field hockey, indoor track, lacrosse, soccer, softball, tennis, track & field, volleyball.

ADMISSIONS

Selectivity Rating: 78 (of 100). **Freshman Academic Profile:** Average high school GPA 3.3. 28% in top 10% of high school class, 60% in top 25% of high school class, 94% in top 50% of high school class. 70% from public high schools. Average SAT I Math 554, SAT I Math middle 50% range 500-610. Average SAT I Verbal 560, SAT I Verbal middle 50% range 510-600. TOEFL required of all international applicants, minimum TOEFL 520. **Basis for Candidate Selection:** *Very important factors considered include:* character/personal qualities, class rank, secondary school record, standardized test scores. *Important factors considered include:* extracurricular activities, interview, recommendations. *Other factors considered include:* alumni/ae relation, essays, minority status, talent/ability, volunteer work, work experience. **Freshman Admission Requirements:** High school diploma or GED is required. *Academic units required/recommended:* 18 total required; 4 English required, 3 math required, 2 science required, 2 science lab required, 4 foreign language recommended, 2 social studies required, 5 elective required. **Freshman Admission Statistics:** 2,767 applied, 72% accepted, 23% of those accepted enrolled. **Transfer Admission Requirements:** *Items required:* high school transcript, college transcript, statement of good standing from prior school. Minimum college GPA of 2.2 required. Lowest grade transferable C-. **General Admission Information:** Application fee $30. Priority application deadline December 15. Early decision application deadline November 15. Regular application deadline March 1. Nonfall registration accepted. Admission may be deferred for a maximum of 2 years. Credit and/or placement offered for CEEB Advanced Placement tests.

COSTS AND FINANCIAL AID

Tuition $19,186. Room & board $6,338. Required fees $530. Average book expense $850. **Required Forms and Deadlines:** FAFSA and state aid form. No deadline for regular filing. Priority filing deadline March 1. **Notification of Awards:** Applicants will be notified of awards on a rolling basis beginning on or about December 25. **Types of Aid:** *Need-based scholarships/grants:* Pell, SEOG, state scholarships/grants, private scholarships, the school's own gift aid. *Loans:* FFEL Subsidized Stafford, FFEL Unsubsidized Stafford, FFEL PLUS, Federal Perkins, college/university loans from institutional funds. **Student Employment:** Federal Work-Study Program available. Institutional employment available. Off-campus job opportunities are excellent. **Financial Aid Statistics:** 75% freshmen, 70% undergrads receive some form of aid. Average freshman grant $9,815. Average freshman loan $4,584. Average income from on-campus job $1,200. **Financial Aid Phone:** 540-375-2235.

ROBERT MORRIS UNIVERSITY

881 Narrows Run Road, Moon Township, PA 15108-1189
Phone: 412-262-8206 **E-mail:** enrollmentoffice@rmu.edu **CEEB Code:** 2769
Fax: 412-299-2425 **Web:** www.rmu.edu **ACT Code:** 3674

This private school was founded in 1921. It has a 230-acre campus.

STUDENTS AND FACULTY

Enrollment: 3,747. **Student Body:** Male 51%, female 49%, out-of-state 8%, international 2% (26 countries represented). **Ethnic Representation:** African American 8%, Asian 1%, Caucasian 84%, Hispanic 1%. **Retention and Graduation:** 75% freshmen return for sophomore year. 26% freshmen graduate within 4 years. 5% grads go on to further study within 1 year. **Faculty:** Student/faculty ratio 19:1. 122 full-time faculty, 81% hold PhDs. 100% faculty teach undergrads.

ACADEMICS

Degrees: Bachelor's, doctoral, master's, post-bachelor's certificate. **Academic Requirements:** General education including some course work in computer literacy, English (including composition), history, humanities, mathematics, sciences (biological or physical), social science. **Classes:** 20-29 students in an average class. **Majors with Highest Enrollment:** Accounting; information science/studies; business administration/management. **Disciplines with Highest Percentage of Degrees Awarded:** Business/marketing 60%, computer and information sciences 24%, communications/communication technologies 9%, social sciences and history 2%, mathematics 2%. **Special Study Options:** Cooperative (work-study) program, cross registration, distance learning, double major, honors program, independent study, internships, study abroad, teacher certification program, weekend college. Evening, weekend, and 5-week/8-week programs.

FACILITIES

Housing: Coed, all-female, all-male, apartments for single students. **Library Holdings:** 187,897 bound volumes. 740 periodicals. 339,459 microforms. 2,994 audiovisuals. **Special Academic Facilities/Equipment:** "Learning Factory" - automated manufacturing facility for engineering students. **Computers:** School-owned computers available for student use.

EXTRACURRICULARS

Activities: Drama/theater, marching band, student government, television station. **Organizations:** 50 registered organizations, 2 honor societies, 2 religious organizations, 6 fraternities (4% men join), 2 sororities (3% women join). **Athletics (Intercollegiate):** *Men:* basketball, cheerleading, cross-country, football, golf, indoor track, soccer, tennis, track & field. *Women:* basketball, cheerleading, crew, cross-country, indoor track, soccer, softball, tennis, track & field, volleyball.

ADMISSIONS

Selectivity Rating: 63 (of 100). **Freshman Academic Profile:** Average high school GPA 3.1. 8% in top 10% of high school class, 24% in top 25% of high school class, 55% in top 50% of high school class. 81% from public high schools. Average SAT I Math 507, SAT I Math middle 50% range 450-560. Average SAT I Verbal 496, SAT I Verbal middle 50% range 440-540. ACT middle 50% range 19-23. TOEFL required of all international applicants, minimum TOEFL 500. **Basis for Candidate Selection:** *Very important factors considered include:* secondary school record, standardized test scores. *Important factors considered include:* character/personal qualities, class rank, extracurricular activities, interview, recommendations. *Other factors considered include:* essays, geographical residence, talent/ability, volunteer work. **Freshman Admission Requirements:** High school diploma or GED is required. *Academic units required/recommended:* 16 total required; 18 total recommended; 4 English required, 3 math required, 2 science required, 2 foreign language recommended, 4 social studies required, 3 elective required. **Freshman Admission Statistics:** 2,127 applied, 78% accepted, 29% of those accepted enrolled. **Transfer Admission Requirements:** *Items required:* high school transcript, college transcript, statement of good standing from prior school. Minimum college GPA of 2.0 required. Lowest grade transferable C. **General Admission Information:** Application fee $30. Priority application deadline December 1. Regular application deadline July 1. Nonfall registration accepted. Admission may be deferred for a maximum of 1 year. Credit and/or placement offered for CEEB Advanced Placement tests.

COSTS AND FINANCIAL AID

Tuition $12,720. Room & board $6,752. Required fees $0. Average book expense $800. **Required Forms and Deadlines:** FAFSA. No deadline for regular filing. Priority filing deadline May 1. **Notification of Awards:** Applicants will be notified of awards on a rolling basis beginning on or about March 1. **Types of Aid:** *Need-based scholarships/grants:* Pell, SEOG, state scholarships/grants, private scholarships, the school's own gift aid. *Loans:* FFEL Subsidized Stafford, FFEL Unsubsidized Stafford, FFEL PLUS, Federal Perkins. **Student Employment:** Federal Work-Study Program available. Institutional employment available. Off-campus job opportunities are excellent. **Financial Aid Statistics:** 84% freshmen, 82% undergrads receive some form of aid. Average freshman grant $13,095. Average freshman loan $1,163. **Financial Aid Phone:** 412-299-2450.

ROBERTS WESLEYAN COLLEGE

2301 Westside Drive, Rochester, NY 14624-1997
Phone: 585-594-6400 **E-mail:** admissions@roberts.edu **CEEB Code:** 2805
Fax: 585-594-6371 **Web:** www.roberts.edu **ACT Code:** 2759

This private school, which is affiliated with the Methodist Church, was founded in 1866. It has a 75-acre campus.

STUDENTS AND FACULTY

Enrollment: 1,266. **Student Body:** Male 33%, female 67%, out-of-state 14%, international 4%. **Ethnic Representation:** African American 5%, Asian 1%, Caucasian 80%, Hispanic 2%. **Retention and Graduation:** 81% freshmen return for sophomore year. 46% freshmen graduate within 4 years. 30% grads go on to further study within 1 year. 5% grads pursue business degrees. 5% grads pursue medical degrees. **Faculty:** Student/faculty ratio 14:1. 80 full-time faculty, 57% hold PhDs. 84% faculty teach undergrads.

ACADEMICS

Degrees: Associate's, bachelor's, master's. **Academic Requirements:** General education including some course work in arts/fine arts, English (including composition), foreign languages, history, humanities, mathematics, philosophy, sciences (biological or physical), social science, Old and New Testament, physical education. **Classes:** 10-19 students in an average class. 20-29 students in an average lab/discussion section. **Disciplines with Highest Percentage of Degrees Awarded:** Business/marketing 43%, education 14%, health professions and related sciences 10%, protective services/public administration 9%, philosophy/religion/theology 7%. **Special Study Options:** Cross registration, double major, honors program, internships, study abroad, teacher certification program.

FACILITIES

Housing: All-female, all-male, apartments for single students, housing for disabled students. **Library Holdings:** 115,921 bound volumes. 864 periodicals. 170,978 microforms. 3,662 audiovisuals. **Computers:** *Recommended operating system:* Windows NT/2000.

EXTRACURRICULARS

Activities: Choral groups, concert band, drama/theater, jazz band, music ensembles, musical theater, opera, radio station, student government, student newspaper, symphony orchestra, television station, yearbook. **Organizations:** 30 registered organizations, 10 religious organizations. **Athletics (Intercollegiate):** *Men:* basketball, cross-country, golf, indoor track, soccer, tennis, track & field. *Women:* basketball, cross-country, golf, indoor track, soccer, tennis, track & field, volleyball.

ADMISSIONS

Selectivity Rating: 71 (of 100). **Freshman Academic Profile:** Average high school GPA 3.2. 25% in top 10% of high school class, 55% in top 25% of high school class, 85% in top 50% of high school class. Average SAT I Math 552, SAT I Math middle 50% range 470-580. Average SAT I Verbal 555, SAT I Verbal middle 50% range 480-580. Average ACT 24, ACT middle 50% range 18-27. TOEFL required of all international applicants, minimum TOEFL 550. **Basis for Candidate Selection:** *Very important factors considered include:* character/personal qualities, essays, recommendations, secondary school record, standardized test scores. *Important factors considered include:* class rank, extracurricular activities, interview, religious affiliation/commitment. *Other factors considered include:* alumni/ae relation, geographical residence, minority status, state residency, talent/ability, volunteer work, work experience. **Freshman Admission Requirements:** High school diploma or GED is required. *Academic units required/recommended:* 12 total required; 4 English required, 2 math required, 3 math recommended, 1 science required, 3 science recommended, 1 science lab required, 3 science lab recommended, 3 foreign language recommended, 2 social studies required, 3 social studies recommended, 1 history required, 2 elective required. **Freshman Admission Statistics:** 708 applied, 82% accepted, 44% of those accepted enrolled. **Transfer Admission Requirements:** *Items required:* college transcript, essay. Minimum college GPA of 2.7 required. Lowest grade transferable C. **General Admission Information:** Application fee $35. Priority application deadline February 1. Regular application deadline rolling. Nonfall registration accepted. Admission may be deferred for a maximum of 1 year. Credit and/or placement offered for CEEB Advanced Placement tests.

COSTS AND FINANCIAL AID

Tuition $15,192. Room & board $5,746. Required fees $582. Average book expense $650. **Required Forms and Deadlines:** FAFSA, institution's own financial aid form and state aid form. No deadline for regular filing. Priority filing deadline March 15. **Notification of Awards:** Applicants will be notified of awards on a rolling basis beginning on or about March 15. **Types of Aid:** *Need-based scholarships/grants:* Pell, SEOG, state scholarships/grants, private scholarships, the school's own gift aid. *Loans:* FFEL Subsidized Stafford, FFEL Unsubsidized Stafford, FFEL PLUS, Federal Perkins. **Student Employment:** Federal Work-Study Program available. Institutional employment available. Off-campus job opportunities are good. **Financial Aid Statistics:** 86% freshmen, 86% undergrads receive some form of aid. Average freshman grant $4,961. Average freshman loan $4,679. Average income from on-campus job $1,500. **Financial Aid Phone:** 585-594-6150.

ROCHESTER COLLEGE

800 West Avon Road, Rochester Hills, MI 48307
Phone: 248-218-2031 **E-mail:** admissions@rc.edu **CEEB Code:** 1516
Fax: 248-218-2035 **Web:** www.rc.edu **ACT Code:** 2072

This private school, which is affiliated with the Church of Christ, was founded in 1959. It has an 83-acre campus.

STUDENTS AND FACULTY

Enrollment: 927. **Student Body:** Male 43%, female 57%, out-of-state 14%, international 3% (10 countries represented). **Ethnic Representation:** African American 11%, Asian 1%, Caucasian 86%, Hispanic 1%, Native American 1%. **Retention and Graduation:** 69% freshmen return for sophomore year. 8% freshmen graduate within 4 years. **Faculty:** Student/faculty ratio 15:1. 32 full-time faculty, 28% hold PhDs. 100% faculty teach undergrads.

ACADEMICS

Degrees: Associate's, bachelor's, transfer. **Academic Requirements:** General education including some course work in arts/fine arts, computer literacy, English (including composition), history, mathematics, sciences (biological or physical), social science, communication, literature, physical education. **Majors with Highest Enrollment:** Business administration/management; early childhood education and teaching; communications studies/speech communication and rhetoric. **Disciplines with Highest Percentage of Degrees Awarded:** Business/marketing 47%, education 11%, philosophy/religion/ theology 11%, psychology 10%, interdisciplinary studies 6%. **Special Study Options:** Accelerated program, cross registration, double major, dual enrollment, independent study, internships, liberal arts/career combination, study abroad, teacher certification program, weekend college.

FACILITIES

Housing: All-female, all-male, apartments for married students, housing for disabled students. **Library Holdings:** 68,922 bound volumes. 642 periodicals. 16,725 microforms. 956 audiovisuals. **Computers:** *Recommended operating system:* Windows 95. School-owned computers available for student use.

EXTRACURRICULARS

Activities: Choral groups, drama/theater, jazz band, music ensembles, student government, student newspaper, yearbook. **Organizations:** 19 registered organizations, 3 honor societies, 1 religious organization. **Athletics (Intercollegiate):** *Men:* baseball, basketball, cross-country, soccer, track & field. *Women:* basketball, cross-country, softball, track & field, volleyball.

ADMISSIONS

Selectivity Rating: 71 (of 100). **Freshman Academic Profile:** TOEFL required of all international applicants, minimum TOEFL 500. **Basis for Candidate Selection:** *Important factors considered include:* secondary school record, standardized test scores. *Other factors considered include:* interview. **Freshman Admission Requirements:** High school diploma or GED is required. **Freshman Admission Statistics:** 277 applied, 83% accepted. **Transfer Admission Requirements:** *Items required:* high school transcript, college transcript. Minimum college GPA of 2.0 required. Lowest grade transferable C. **General Admission Information:** Application fee $25. Nonfall registration accepted. Admission may be deferred for a maximum of 2 years. Credit and/or placement offered for CEEB Advanced Placement tests.

COSTS AND FINANCIAL AID

Tuition $9,462. Room & board $5,342. Required fees $600. Average book expense $600. **Required Forms and Deadlines:** FAFSA and institution's own financial aid form. No deadline for regular filing. Priority filing deadline August 1. **Notification of Awards:** Applicants will be notified of awards on a rolling basis beginning on or about June 1. **Types of Aid:** *Need-based scholarships/ grants:* Pell, SEOG, state scholarships/grants, private scholarships, the school's own gift aid. *Loans:* Direct Subsidized Stafford, Direct Unsubsidized Stafford, Direct PLUS, Federal Perkins. **Student Employment:** Federal Work-Study Program available. Institutional employment available. Off-campus job opportunities are excellent. **Financial Aid Statistics:** 67% freshmen receive some form of aid. **Financial Aid Phone:** 248-218-2028.

ROCHESTER INSTITUTE OF TECHNOLOGY

60 Lomb Memorial Drive, Rochester, NY 14623-5604
Phone: 585-475-6631 **E-mail:** admissions@rit.edu **CEEB Code:** 2760
Fax: 585-475-7424 **Web:** www.rit.edu **ACT Code:** 2870

This private school was founded in 1829. It has a 1,300-acre campus.

STUDENTS AND FACULTY

Enrollment: 12,279. **Student Body:** Male 69%, female 31%, out-of-state 40%, international 5% (90 countries represented). **Ethnic Representation:** African American 5%, Asian 7%, Caucasian 75%, Hispanic 3%. **Retention and Graduation:** 88% freshmen return for sophomore year. **Faculty:** Student/ faculty ratio 13:1. 684 full-time faculty, 80% hold PhDs. 95% faculty teach undergrads.

ACADEMICS

Degrees: Associate's, bachelor's, certificate, diploma, doctoral, master's, post-bachelor's certificate, terminal, transfer. **Academic Requirements:** General education including some course work in arts/fine arts, computer literacy, English (including composition), history, humanities, mathematics, philosophy, sciences (biological or physical), social science. **Classes:** 10-19 students in an average class. 10-19 students in an average lab/discussion section. **Majors with Highest Enrollment:** Information technology; mechanical engineering; photography. **Disciplines with Highest Percentage of Degrees Awarded:** Engineering/engineering technology 23%, visual and performing arts 21%, computer and information sciences 16%, business/marketing 10%. **Special Study Options:** Accelerated program, cooperative (work-study) program, cross registration, distance learning, English as a second language, student exchange program (domestic), honors program, independent study, internships, liberal arts/career combination, student-designed major, study abroad, teacher certification program, weekend college.

FACILITIES

Housing: Coed, apartments for married students, apartments for single students, housing for disabled students, housing for international students, fraternities and/or sororities, special-interest floors for selected majors/ groups, men's floors, women's floors. **Library Holdings:** 350,000 bound volumes. 15,000 periodicals. 438,000 microforms. 9,940 audiovisuals. **Special Academic Facilities/Equipment:** Art gallery; student-managed restaurant; media resource, TV, and graphic arts centers; center for imaging science; microelectronic engineering center; center for integrated manufacturing studies; packaging testing facility; observatory. **Computers:** School-owned computers available for student use.

EXTRACURRICULARS

Activities: Choral groups, concert band, dance, drama/theater, jazz band, literary magazine, music ensembles, musical theater, pep band, radio station, student government, student newspaper, student-run film society, yearbook. **Organizations:** 170 registered organizations, 9 honor societies, 5 religious organizations, 19 fraternities (7% men join), 10 sororities (5% women join). **Athletics (Intercollegiate):** *Men:* baseball, basketball, crew, cross-country, diving, ice hockey, indoor track, lacrosse, soccer, swimming, tennis, track & field, volleyball, wrestling. *Women:* basketball, crew, cross-country, diving, ice hockey, indoor track, lacrosse, soccer, softball, swimming, tennis, track & field, volleyball.

ADMISSIONS

Selectivity Rating: 85 (of 100). **Freshman Academic Profile:** Average high school GPA 3.7. 31% in top 10% of high school class, 65% in top 25% of high school class, 92% in top 50% of high school class. 85% from public high schools. SAT I Math middle 50% range 570-670. SAT I Verbal middle 50% range 540-640. ACT middle 50% range 25-28. TOEFL required of all international applicants, minimum TOEFL 525. **Basis for Candidate Selection:** *Very important factors considered include:* secondary school record. *Important factors considered include:* class rank, minority status, standardized test scores. *Other factors considered include:* alumni/ae relation, character/personal qualities, essays, extracurricular activities, geographical residence, interview, recommendations, talent/ability, volunteer work, work experience. **Freshman Admission Requirements:** High school diploma or GED is required. *Academic units required/recommended:* 22 total required; 22 total recommended; 4 English required, 4 English recommended, 2 math required, 3 math recommended, 2 science required, 3 science recommended, 1 science lab required, 2 science lab recommended, 3 foreign language recommended, 4 social studies required, 4 social studies recommended, 10 elective required, 5 elective recommended. **Freshman Admission Statistics:** 8,697 applied, 69% accepted, 39% of those accepted enrolled. **Transfer Admission Requirements:** *Items required:* college transcript. Minimum college GPA of 2.0 required. Lowest grade transferable C-. **General Admission Information:** Application fee $50. Priority application deadline February 15. Early decision application deadline December 15. Regular application deadline March 15. Nonfall registration accepted. Admission may be deferred for a maximum of 1 year. Credit and/or placement offered for CEEB Advanced Placement tests.

COSTS AND FINANCIAL AID

Tuition $19,470. Room & board $7,527. Required fees $510. Average book expense $600. **Required Forms and Deadlines:** FAFSA and state aid form. Priority filing deadline March 1. **Notification of Awards:** Applicants will be notified of awards on a rolling basis beginning on or about March 15. **Types of Aid:** *Need-based scholarships/grants:* Pell, SEOG, state scholarships/grants, private scholarships, the school's own gift aid. *Loans:* Direct Subsidized Stafford, Direct Unsubsidized Stafford, Direct PLUS, Federal Perkins, private bank loans. **Student Employment:** Federal Work-Study Program available. Institutional employment available. Off-campus job opportunities are excellent. **Financial Aid Statistics:** 70% freshmen, 67% undergrads receive some form of aid. Average freshman grant $9,800. Average freshman loan $3,900. Average income from on-campus job $2,000. **Financial Aid Phone:** 585-475-2186.

ROCKFORD COLLEGE

Office of Admission, 5050 East State Street, Rockford, IL 61108-2393
Phone: 815-226-4050 **E-mail:** admission@rockford.edu **CEEB Code:** 1665
Fax: 815-226-2822 **Web:** www.rockford.edu **ACT Code:** 1122

This private school was founded in 1847. It has a 130-acre campus.

STUDENTS AND FACULTY

Enrollment: 975. **Student Body:** Male 38%, female 62%, out-of-state 2%, international 2%. **Ethnic Representation:** African American 7%, Asian 2%, Caucasian 86%, Hispanic 4%. **Retention and Graduation:** 67% freshmen return for sophomore year. 26% grads go on to further study within 1 year. 14% grads pursue business degrees. **Faculty:** Student/faculty ratio 10:1. 75 full-time faculty, 68% hold PhDs. 100% faculty teach undergrads.

ACADEMICS

Degrees: Bachelor's, master's. **Academic Requirements:** General education including some course work in arts/fine arts, English (including composition), humanities, mathematics, sciences (biological or physical), social science. **Classes:** 10-19 students in an average class. Under 10 students in an average lab/discussion section. **Disciplines with Highest Percentage of Degrees Awarded:** Education 28%, business/marketing 22%, health professions and related sciences 11%, social sciences and history 9%, computer and information sciences 5%. **Special Study Options:** Double major, English as a second language, honors program, independent study, internships, student-designed major, study abroad, teacher certification program.

FACILITIES

Housing: Coed, all-female, all-male. **Library Holdings:** 140,000 bound volumes. 834 periodicals. 20 microforms. 9,723 audiovisuals. **Special Academic Facilities/Equipment:** Language lab, art gallery, sculpture garden. **Computers:** *Recommended operating system:* Windows 95. School-owned computers available for student use.

EXTRACURRICULARS

Activities: Choral groups, dance, drama/theater, literary magazine, music ensembles, musical theater, pep band, student government, student newspaper. **Organizations:** 25 registered organizations, 6 honor societies, 1 religious organization. **Athletics (Intercollegiate):** *Men:* baseball, basketball, cheerleading, football, golf, soccer, tennis. *Women:* basketball, cheerleading, soccer, softball, tennis, volleyball.

ADMISSIONS

Selectivity Rating: 77 (of 100). **Freshman Academic Profile:** Average high school GPA 3.1. 18% in top 10% of high school class, 41% in top 25% of high school class, 77% in top 50% of high school class. 87% from public high schools. Average SAT I Math 510, SAT I Math middle 50% range 490-550. Average SAT I Verbal 490, SAT I Verbal middle 50% range 460-570. Average ACT 21, ACT middle 50% range 18-27. TOEFL required of all international applicants, minimum TOEFL 560. **Basis for Candidate Selection:** *Very important factors considered include:* class rank, secondary school record, standardized test scores, talent/ability. *Other factors considered include:* alumni/ae relation, character/personal qualities, essays, extracurricular activities, interview, recommendations, volunteer work, work experience. **Freshman Admission Requirements:** High school diploma or GED is required. *Academic units required/recommended:* 16 total required; 4 English required, 2 math required, 2 science required, 2 foreign language required, 1 social studies required, 3 history required. **Freshman Admission Statistics:** 654 applied, 59% accepted, 34% of those accepted enrolled. **Transfer Admission Requirements:** *Items required:* college transcript. Minimum college GPA of 2.2 required. Lowest grade transferable C. **General Admission Information:** Application fee $35. Nonfall registration accepted. Admission may be deferred for a maximum of 2 years. Credit and/or placement offered for CEEB Advanced Placement tests.

COSTS AND FINANCIAL AID

Tuition $18,320. Room & board $5,930. Required fees $900. Average book expense $900. **Required Forms and Deadlines:** FAFSA and institution's own financial aid form. No deadline for regular filing. **Types of Aid:** *Need-based scholarships/grants:* Pell, SEOG, state scholarships/grants, private scholarships, the school's own gift aid. *Loans:* Direct Subsidized Stafford, Direct Unsubsidized Stafford, Direct PLUS, FFEL Subsidized Stafford, FFEL Unsubsidized Stafford, FFEL PLUS, Federal Perkins. **Student Employment:** Federal Work-Study Program available. Institutional employment available. Off-campus job opportunities are excellent. **Financial Aid Statistics:** 84% freshmen, 83% undergrads receive some form of aid. Average freshman grant $8,700. Average freshman loan $3,500. Average income from on-campus job $2,000. **Financial Aid Phone:** 815-226-3385.

See page 1174.

ROCKHURST UNIVERSITY

1100 Rockhurst Road, Kansas City, MO 64110
Phone: 816-501-4100 **E-mail:** admission@rockhurst.edu **CEEB Code:** 6611
Fax: 816-501-4241 **Web:** www.rockhurst.edu **ACT Code:** 2342

This private school, which is affiliated with the Roman Catholic Church, was founded in 1910. It has a 55-acre campus.

STUDENTS AND FACULTY

Enrollment: 2,020. **Student Body:** Male 44%, female 56%, out-of-state 28%, international 1%. **Ethnic Representation:** African American 9%, Asian 3%, Caucasian 81%, Hispanic 5%, Native American 1%. **Retention and Graduation:** 80% freshmen return for sophomore year. 51% freshmen graduate within 4 years. **Faculty:** Student/faculty ratio 10:1. 131 full-time faculty, 80% hold PhDs. 98% faculty teach undergrads.

ACADEMICS

Degrees: Bachelor's, certificate, master's, post-bachelor's certificate. **Academic Requirements:** General education including some course work in arts/fine arts, computer literacy, English (including composition), history, humanities, mathematics, philosophy, sciences (biological or physical), theology. **Classes:** 10-19 students in an average class. 10-19 students in an average lab/discussion section. **Majors with Highest Enrollment:** Nursing/registered nurse training (RN, ASN, BSN, MSN); biology/biological sciences, general; psychology, general. **Disciplines with Highest Percentage of Degrees Awarded:** Business/marketing 27%, health professions and related sciences 16%, psychology 14%, social sciences and history 9%, biological life sciences 6%. **Special Study Options:** Accelerated program, cooperative (work-study) program, cross registration, distance learning, double major, dual enrollment, student exchange program (domestic), honors program, independent study, internships, study abroad, teacher certification program.

FACILITIES

Housing: Coed, all-female, all-male, apartments for single students, townhouse village. **Library Holdings:** 597,800 bound volumes. 750 periodicals. 213,300 microforms. 3,339 audiovisuals. **Special Academic Facilities/Equipment:** Greenlease Art Gallery, Richardson Science Center. **Computers:** *Recommended operating system:* Windows NT/2000. School-owned computers available for student use.

EXTRACURRICULARS

Activities: Choral groups, drama/theater, literary magazine, music ensembles, musical theater, radio station, student government, student newspaper, yearbook. **Organizations:** 44 registered organizations, 4 honor societies, 6 religious organizations, 3 fraternities (21% men join), 3 sororities (33% women join). **Athletics (Intercollegiate):** *Men:* baseball, basketball, golf, soccer, tennis. *Women:* basketball, golf, soccer, tennis, volleyball.

ADMISSIONS

Selectivity Rating: 75 (of 100). **Freshman Academic Profile:** Average high school GPA 3.3. 25% in top 10% of high school class, 48% in top 25% of high school class, 71% in top 50% of high school class. 45% from public high schools. Average SAT I Math 557, SAT I Math middle 50% range 470-620. Average SAT I Verbal 543, SAT I Verbal middle 50% range 510-570. Average ACT 23, ACT middle 50% range 21-27. TOEFL required of all international applicants, minimum TOEFL 550. **Basis for Candidate Selection:** *Very important factors considered include:* class rank, recommendations, secondary school record, standardized test scores. *Important factors considered include:* character/personal qualities. *Other factors considered include:* alumni/ae relation, extracurricular activities, interview, talent/ability, volunteer work, work experience. **Freshman Admission Requirements:** High school diploma or GED is required. *Academic units required/recommended:* 16 total recommended; 4 English recommended, 3 math recommended, 3 science recommended, 1 science lab recommended, 4 elective recommended. **Freshman Admission Statistics:** 1,032 applied, 83% accepted, 25% of those accepted enrolled. **Transfer Admission Requirements:** *Items required:* college transcript, statement of good standing from prior school. Minimum college GPA of 2.3 required. Lowest grade transferable C. **General Admission Information:** Application fee $25. Priority application deadline January 15. Regular application deadline June 30. Nonfall registration accepted. Admission may be deferred for a maximum of 1 year. Credit and/or placement offered for CEEB Advanced Placement tests.

COSTS AND FINANCIAL AID

Average book expense $778. **Required Forms and Deadlines:** FAFSA and institution's own financial aid form. No deadline for regular filing. Priority filing deadline March 1. **Notification of Awards:** Applicants will be notified of awards on a rolling basis beginning on or about February 15. **Types of Aid:** *Need-based scholarships/grants:* Pell, SEOG, state scholarships/grants, private scholarships, the school's own gift aid. *Loans:* FFEL Subsidized Stafford, FFEL Unsubsidized Stafford, FFEL PLUS, Federal Perkins. **Student Employment:** Federal Work-Study Program available. Institutional employment available. Off-campus job opportunities are good. **Financial Aid Statistics:** 84% freshmen, 65% undergrads receive some form of aid. Average freshman grant $5,700. Average freshman loan $5,700. Average income from on-campus job $1,650. **Financial Aid Phone:** 816-501-4100.

ROCKY MOUNTAIN COLLEGE

1511 Poly Drive, Billings, MT 59102-1796
Phone: 406-657-1026 **E-mail:** admissions@rocky.edu **CEEB Code:** 4660
Fax: 406-259-9751 **Web:** www.rocky.edu **ACT Code:** 2426

This private school was founded in 1878. It has a 60-acre campus.

STUDENTS AND FACULTY

Enrollment: 813. **Student Body:** Male 48%, female 52%, out-of-state 28%, international 5% (20 countries represented). **Ethnic Representation:** African American 1%, Asian 2%, Caucasian 89%, Hispanic 2%, Native American 6%. **Retention and Graduation:** 75% freshmen return for sophomore year. 24% freshmen graduate within 4 years. 10% grads go on to further study within 1 year. 2% grads pursue medical degrees. **Faculty:** Student/faculty ratio 13:1. 44 full-time faculty, 70% hold PhDs. 100% faculty teach undergrads.

ACADEMICS

Degrees: Associate's, bachelor's, diploma, terminal, transfer. **Academic Requirements:** General education including some course work in arts/fine arts, computer literacy, English (including composition), history, humanities, mathematics, philosophy, sciences (biological or physical), social science, fitness focus, communication studies, religious thought. **Classes:** 10-19 students in an average class. 10-19 students in an average lab/discussion section. **Majors with Highest Enrollment:** Business administration/management; elementary education and teaching; airline/commercial/professional pilot and flight crew. **Disciplines with Highest Percentage of Degrees Awarded:** Business/marketing 29%, education 14%, health professions and related sciences 11%, biological life sciences 7%, parks and recreation 7%. **Special Study Options:** Accelerated program, cooperative (work-study) program, distance learning, double major, dual enrollment, English as a second language, honors program, independent study, internships, liberal arts/career combination, student-designed major, study abroad, teacher certification program, information technology program (degree completion).

FACILITIES

Housing: Coed, apartments for married students, apartments for single students, suites. **Library Holdings:** 67,877 bound volumes. 364 periodicals. 0 microforms. 782 audiovisuals. **Special Academic Facilities/Equipment:** Elementary school, city theater, museum, studio, flight simulator/flight school, equestrian facilities, geology collection. **Computers:** School-owned computers available for student use.

EXTRACURRICULARS

Activities: Choral groups, concert band, drama/theater, jazz band, literary magazine, marching band, music ensembles, musical theater, student government, student newspaper, yearbook. **Organizations:** 23 registered organizations, 1 honor society, 3 religious organizations. **Athletics (Intercollegiate):** *Men:* basketball, football, golf, skiing (alpine). *Women:* basketball, golf, skiing (alpine), soccer, volleyball.

ADMISSIONS

Selectivity Rating: 63 (of 100). **Freshman Academic Profile:** Average high school GPA 3.3. 12% in top 10% of high school class, 35% in top 25% of high school class, 68% in top 50% of high school class. 96% from public high schools. Average SAT I Math 508, SAT I Math middle 50% range 430-570. Average SAT I Verbal 512, SAT I Verbal middle 50% range 460-600. Average ACT 22, ACT middle 50% range 19-24. TOEFL required of all international applicants, minimum TOEFL 500. **Basis for Candidate Selection:** *Very important factors considered include:* secondary school record, standardized test scores. *Important factors considered include:* character/personal qualities, class rank. *Other factors considered include:* alumni/ae relation, essays, extracurricular activities, interview, recommendations, talent/ability, volunteer work, work experience. **Freshman Admission Requirements:** High school diploma or GED is required. *Academic units required/recommended:* 13 total required; 4 English required, 4 English recommended, 2 math required, 3 math recommended, 2 science required, 2 science recommended, 1 science lab required, 1 science lab recommended, 1 foreign language required, 2 foreign language recommended, 2 social studies required, 2 social studies recommended, 2 history required, 2 history recommended. **Freshman Admission Statistics:** 575 applied, 82% accepted, 34% of those accepted enrolled. **Transfer Admission Requirements:** *Items required:* college transcript. Minimum high school GPA of 2.5 required. Minimum college GPA of 2.0 required. Lowest grade transferable C-. **General Admission Information:** Application fee $25. Priority application deadline April 1. Nonfall registration accepted. Admission may be deferred for a maximum of 1 year. Credit and/or placement offered for CEEB Advanced Placement tests.

COSTS AND FINANCIAL AID

Tuition $13,300. Room & board $4,800. Required fees $165. Average book expense $800. **Required Forms and Deadlines:** FAFSA and institution's own financial aid form. No deadline for regular filing. Priority filing deadline April 1. **Notification of Awards:** Applicants will be notified of awards on a rolling basis beginning on or about February 1. **Types of Aid:** *Need-based scholarships/grants:* Pell, SEOG, state scholarships/grants, private scholarships, the school's own gift aid. *Loans:* FFEL Subsidized Stafford, FFEL Unsubsidized Stafford, FFEL PLUS, Federal Perkins. **Student Employment:** Federal Work-Study Program available. Institutional employment available. Off-campus job opportunities are good. **Financial Aid Statistics:** 92% freshmen, 73% undergrads receive some form of aid. Average freshman grant $6,216. Average freshman loan $2,600. Average income from on-campus job $715. **Financial Aid Phone:** 406-657-1031.

ROGER WILLIAMS UNIVERSITY

$$$

One Old Ferry Road, Bristol, RI 02809-0000
Phone: 401-254-3500 **E-mail:** admit@rwu.edu **CEEB Code:** 3729
Fax: 401-254-3557 **Web:** www.rwu.edu **ACT Code:** 3814

This private school was founded in 1956. It has a 140-acre campus.

STUDENTS AND FACULTY

Enrollment: 4,031. **Student Body:** Male 49%, female 51%, out-of-state 83%, international 2%. **Ethnic Representation:** African American 2%, Asian 1%, Caucasian 85%, Hispanic 2%. **Retention and Graduation:** 81% freshmen return for sophomore year. 25% grads go on to further study within 1 year. 2% grads pursue business degrees. 5% grads pursue law degrees. 1% grads pursue medical degrees. **Faculty:** Student/faculty ratio 17:1. 144 full-time faculty, 82% hold PhDs. 100% faculty teach undergrads.

ACADEMICS

Degrees: Associate's, bachelor's, first professional, master's. **Academic Requirements:** General education including some course work in arts/fine arts, English (including composition), history, humanities, mathematics, philosophy, sciences (biological or physical), social science. **Classes:** 20-29 students in an average class. 10-19 students in an average lab/discussion section. **Majors with Highest Enrollment:** Marketing/marketing management, general; legal studies, general; architecture (BArch, BA/BS, MArch, MA/MS, PhD). **Disciplines with Highest Percentage of Degrees Awarded:** Law/legal studies 24%, business/marketing 15%, engineering/engineering technology 9%, architecture 8%, computer and information sciences 6%. **Special Study Options:** Cooperative (work-study) program, distance learning, double major, dual enrollment, English as a second language, student exchange program (domestic), external degree program, honors program, independent study, internships, liberal arts/career combination, student-designed major, study abroad, teacher certification program.

FACILITIES

Housing: Coed, apartments for married students, apartments for single students, housing for disabled students, special-interest, academic theme housing, honors, wellness, nonsmoking. **Library Holdings:** 168,460 bound volumes. 1,118 periodicals. 69,748 microforms. 60,622 audiovisuals. **Special Academic Facilities/Equipment:** Center for Environmental and Economic Development, School of Law and law library, main library, architecture building and architecture library, performing arts center, Thomas J. Paolino Recreation Center. **Computers:** School-owned computers available for student use.

EXTRACURRICULARS

Activities: Choral groups, dance, drama/theater, literary magazine, radio station, student government, student newspaper, student-run film society, yearbook. **Organizations:** 54 registered organizations, 13 honor societies, 3 religious organizations. **Athletics (Intercollegiate):** *Men:* baseball, basketball, crew, cross-country, equestrian, golf, lacrosse, rugby, sailing, soccer, tennis, track

& field, volleyball, wrestling. *Women:* basketball, crew, cross-country, equestrian, golf, sailing, soccer, softball, tennis, track & field, volleyball.

ADMISSIONS

Selectivity Rating: 67 (of 100). **Freshman Academic Profile:** Average high school GPA 3.0. 12% in top 10% of high school class, 36% in top 25% of high school class, 69% in top 50% of high school class. 78% from public high schools. Average SAT I Math 536, SAT I Math middle 50% range 490-585. Average SAT I Verbal 531, SAT I Verbal middle 50% range 480-570. **Basis for Candidate Selection:** *Very important factors considered include:* essays, secondary school record, standardized test scores, talent/ability. *Important factors considered include:* character/personal qualities, class rank, extracurricular activities. *Other factors considered include:* alumni/ae relation, interview, recommendations, volunteer work, work experience. **Freshman Admission Requirements:** High school diploma or GED is required. *Academic units required/recommended:* 16 total required; 4 English required, 3 math required, 4 math recommended, 3 science required, 2 science lab required, 2 foreign language recommended, 3 social studies required, 2 history required. **Freshman Admission Statistics:** 4,793 applied, 84% accepted, 24% of those accepted enrolled. **Transfer Admission Requirements:** *Items required:* college transcript, essay. Minimum high school GPA of 2.0 required. Minimum college GPA of 2.5 required. Lowest grade transferable C. **General Admission Information:** Application fee $50. Priority application deadline March 1. Early decision application deadline December 1. Nonfall registration accepted. Admission may be deferred for a maximum of 1 year. Credit and/or placement offered for CEEB Advanced Placement tests.

COSTS AND FINANCIAL AID

Tuition $20,280. Room & board $9,375. Required fees $830. Average book expense $600. **Required Forms and Deadlines:** FAFSA and CSS/Financial Aid PROFILE. Financial aid filing deadline February 1. Priority filing deadline February 1. **Notification of Awards:** Applicants will be notified of awards on a rolling basis beginning on or about March 19. **Types of Aid:** *Need-based scholarships/grants:* Pell, SEOG, state scholarships/grants, private scholarships, the school's own gift aid. *Loans:* FFEL Subsidized Stafford, FFEL Unsubsidized Stafford, FFEL PLUS, Federal Perkins, state loans. **Student Employment:** Federal Work-Study Program available. Institutional employment available. Off-campus job opportunities are good. **Financial Aid Statistics:** 74% freshmen, 73% undergrads receive some form of aid. Average freshman grant $7,200. Average freshman loan $4,125. Average income from on-campus job $1,700. **Financial Aid Phone:** 800-458-7144.

ROLLINS COLLEGE

1000 Holt Avenue, Winter Park, FL 32789-4499
Phone: 407-646-2161 **E-mail:** admission@rollins.edu **CEEB Code:** 5572
Fax: 407-646-1502 **Web:** www.rollins.edu **ACT Code:** 748

This private school was founded in 1885. It has a 67-acre campus.

STUDENTS AND FACULTY

Enrollment: 1,723. **Student Body:** Out-of-state 48%, international 4% (31 countries represented). **Ethnic Representation:** African American 4%, Asian 3%, Caucasian 78%, Hispanic 8%, Native American 1%. **Retention and Graduation:** 86% freshmen return for sophomore year. 29% grads go on to further study within 1 year. 4% grads pursue business degrees. 4% grads pursue law degrees. 2% grads pursue medical degrees. **Faculty:** Student/faculty ratio 11:1. 177 full-time faculty, 81% hold PhDs. 100% faculty teach undergrads.

ACADEMICS

Degrees: Bachelor's, master's. **Academic Requirements:** General education including some course work in arts/fine arts, computer literacy, English (including composition), foreign languages, history, humanities, mathematics, philosophy, sciences (biological or physical), social science, oral communication, other cultures, literature, contemporary American society, decision making and valuation, writing, writing reinforcement, and personal fitness. **Classes:** 10-19 students in an average class. **Majors with Highest Enrollment:** International business; English language and literature, general; psychology, general. **Disciplines with Highest Percentage of Degrees Awarded:** Social sciences and history 27%, business/marketing 13%, visual and performing arts 13%, English 11%, psychology 9%. **Special Study Options:** Accelerated program, cross registration, double major, dual enrollment, honors program, independent study, internships, student-designed major, study abroad, teacher certification program.

FACILITIES

Housing: Coed, apartments for single students, housing for disabled students, fraternities and/or sororities. **Library Holdings:** 237,333 bound volumes. 2,259 periodicals. 96,410 microforms. 4,853 audiovisuals. **Special Academic Facilities/Equipment:** Art museum, theatres, fine arts center, language lab, skills development building, child development center, psychology center. **Computers:** School-owned computers available for student use.

EXTRACURRICULARS

Activities: Choral groups, dance, drama/theater, literary magazine, music ensembles, musical theater, pep band, radio station, student government, student newspaper, television station, yearbook. **Organizations:** 74 registered organizations, 5 honor societies, 4 religious organizations, 5 fraternities (38% men join), 6 sororities (40% women join). **Athletics (Intercollegiate):** *Men:* baseball, basketball, crew, cross-country, golf, sailing, soccer, swimming, tennis. *Women:* basketball, crew, cross-country, golf, sailing, soccer, softball, swimming, tennis, volleyball.

ADMISSIONS

Selectivity Rating: 84 (of 100). **Freshman Academic Profile:** Average high school GPA 3.4. 40% in top 10% of high school class, 71% in top 25% of high school class, 90% in top 50% of high school class. 55% from public high schools. Average SAT I Math 580, SAT I Math middle 50% range 530-630. Average SAT I Verbal 576, SAT I Verbal middle 50% range 530-620. Average ACT 24, ACT middle 50% range 22-26. TOEFL required of all international applicants, minimum TOEFL 550. **Basis for Candidate Selection:** *Very important factors considered include:* secondary school record. *Important factors considered include:* essays, extracurricular activities, recommendations, standardized test scores, talent/ability. *Other factors considered include:* alumni/ae relation, character/personal qualities, class rank, geographical residence, interview, minority status, religious affiliation/commitment, state residency, volunteer work, work experience. **Freshman Admission Requirements:** High school diploma or GED is required. *Academic units required/recommended:* 17 total required; 24 total recommended; 4 English required, 4 English recommended, 3 math required, 4 math recommended, 2 science required, 4 science recommended, 2 foreign language required, 3 foreign language recommended, 2 social studies required, 3 social studies recommended, 2 history required, 3 history recommended, 2 elective required, 3 elective recommended. **Freshman Admission Statistics:** 2,307 applied, 63% accepted, 32% of those accepted enrolled. **Transfer Admission Requirements:** *Items required:* high school transcript, college transcript, essay, standardized test scores. Minimum college GPA of 3.0 required. Lowest grade transferable C. **General Admission Information:** Application fee $40. Early decision application deadline November 15. Regular application deadline February 15. Nonfall registration accepted. Admission may be deferred. Credit and/or placement offered for CEEB Advanced Placement tests.

COSTS AND FINANCIAL AID

Tuition $23,205. Room & board $7,341. Required fees $677. Average book expense $520. **Required Forms and Deadlines:** FAFSA and institution's own financial aid form. Financial aid filing deadline March 1. Priority filing deadline February 15. **Notification of Awards:** Applicants will be notified of awards on a rolling basis beginning on or about March 1. **Types of Aid:** *Need-based scholarships/grants:* Pell, SEOG, state scholarships/grants, private scholarships, the school's own gift aid. *Loans:* Direct Subsidized Stafford, Direct Unsubsidized Stafford, Direct PLUS, Federal Perkins, college/university loans from institutional funds. **Student Employment:** Federal Work-Study Program available. Institutional employment available. Off-campus job opportunities are excellent. **Financial Aid Statistics:** 39% freshmen, 42% undergrads receive some form of aid. Average freshman grant $12,654. Average freshman loan $3,536. Average income from on-campus job $1,050. **Financial Aid Phone:** 407-646-2395.

ROOSEVELT UNIVERSITY

430 South Michigan Avenue, Chicago, IL 60605
Phone: 312-341-3500 **E-mail:** applyRU@roosevelt.edu **CEEB Code:** 1666
Fax: 312-341-3655 **Web:** www.roosevelt.edu **ACT Code:** 1124

This private school was founded in 1945. It has a 34-acre campus.

STUDENTS AND FACULTY

Enrollment: 4,307. **Student Body:** Male 33%, female 67%, out-of-state 4%, international 3%. **Ethnic Representation:** African American 27%, Asian 5%, Caucasian 47%, Hispanic 11%. **Retention and Graduation:** 51% freshmen return for sophomore year. 6% freshmen graduate within 4 years. **Faculty:** Student/faculty ratio 11:1. 202 full-time faculty. 95% faculty teach undergrads.

ACADEMICS

Degrees: Bachelor's, doctoral, master's. **Academic Requirements:** General education including some course work in English (including composition), history, humanities, mathematics, sciences (biological or physical), social science. **Classes:** 10-19 students in an average class. **Majors with Highest Enrollment:** Psychology, general; computer science; hospitality administration/management, general. **Disciplines with Highest Percentage of Degrees Awarded:** Business/marketing 34%, social sciences and history 10%, psychology 10%, computer and information sciences 9%, communications/communication technologies 7%. **Special Study Options:** Accelerated program, distance learning, double major, dual enrollment, English as a second language, honors program, independent study, internships, student-designed major, teacher certification program.

FACILITIES

Housing: Coed. **Library Holdings:** 233,016 bound volumes. 1,195 periodicals. 164,286 microforms. 9,897 audiovisuals. **Special Academic Facilities/Equipment:** The Chicago campus is approximately 1 mile from the Museum of Natural History, Aquarium, Planetarium and Contemporary Art museums and is 2 blocks from the Art Institute of Chicago. **Computers:** *Recommended operating system:* Windows NT/2000. School-owned computers available for student use.

EXTRACURRICULARS

Activities: Choral groups, concert band, drama/theater, jazz band, literary magazine, music ensembles, musical theater, opera, radio station, student government, student newspaper, symphony orchestra. **Organizations:** 34 registered organizations, 3 honor societies, 4 religious organizations, 7 fraternities, 2 sororities.

ADMISSIONS

Selectivity Rating: 65 (of 100). **Freshman Academic Profile:** Average high school GPA 3.0. 4% in top 10% of high school class, 14% in top 25% of high school class, 35% in top 50% of high school class. 80% from public high schools. SAT I Math middle 50% range 440-605. SAT I Verbal middle 50% range 475-655. Average ACT 21, ACT middle 50% range 17-24. TOEFL required of all international applicants, minimum TOEFL 525. **Basis for Candidate Selection:** *Very important factors considered include:* secondary school record. *Important factors considered include:* character/personal qualities, class rank, essays, interview, recommendations, standardized test scores. *Other factors considered include:* alumni/ae relation, extracurricular activities, minority status, talent/ability, volunteer work, work experience. **Freshman Admission Requirements:** High school diploma or GED is required. *Academic units required/recommended:* 15 total required; 19 total recommended; 4 English required, 4 English recommended, 3 math required, 4 math recommended, 3 science required, 3 science recommended, 2 science lab required, 2 science lab recommended, 2 foreign language recommended, 2 social studies required, 2 social studies recommended, 1 history required, 2 history recommended, 2 elective required, 2 elective recommended. **Freshman Admission Statistics:** 935 applied, 67% accepted, 45% of those accepted enrolled. **Transfer Admission Requirements:** *Items required:* college transcript, essay, statement of good standing from prior school. Minimum college GPA of 2.0 required. Lowest grade transferable D. **General Admission Information:** Application fee $25. Priority application deadline August 15. Regular application deadline September 1. Nonfall registration accepted. Admission may be deferred for a maximum of 1 year. Credit and/or placement offered for CEEB Advanced Placement tests.

COSTS AND FINANCIAL AID

Tuition $14,460. Room & board $6,750. Required fees $200. Average book expense $900. **Required Forms and Deadlines:** FAFSA and institution's own financial aid form. No deadline for regular filing. Priority filing deadline April 1. **Notification of Awards:** Applicants will be notified of awards on a rolling basis beginning on or about March 15. **Types of Aid:** *Need-based scholarships/grants:* Pell, SEOG, state scholarships/grants, private scholarships, the school's own gift aid. *Loans:* FFEL Subsidized Stafford, FFEL Unsubsidized Stafford, FFEL PLUS, Federal Perkins. **Student Employment:** Federal Work-Study Program available. Institutional employment available. Off-campus job opportunities are good. **Financial Aid Statistics:** 81% freshmen, 78% undergrads receive some form of aid. **Financial Aid Phone:** 312-341-2195.

ROSE-HULMAN INSTITUTE OF TECHNOLOGY

5500 Wabash Avenue-CM 1, Terre Haute, IN 47803-3999
Phone: 812-877-8213 **E-mail:** admis.ofc@rose-hulman.edu **CEEB Code:** 1668
Fax: 812-877-8941 **Web:** www.rose-hulman.edu **ACT Code:** 1232

This private school was founded in 1874. It has a 380-acre campus.

STUDENTS AND FACULTY

Enrollment: 1,642. **Student Body:** Male 82%, female 18%, out-of-state 51%, international 1% (12 countries represented). **Ethnic Representation:** African American 2%, Asian 3%, Caucasian 94%, Hispanic 1%. **Retention and Graduation:** 94% freshmen return for sophomore year. 65% freshmen graduate within 4 years. 20% grads go on to further study within 1 year. 2% grads pursue business degrees. 2% grads pursue law degrees. 1% grads pursue medical degrees. **Faculty:** Student/faculty ratio 13:1. 126 full-time faculty, 98% hold PhDs. 100% faculty teach undergrads.

ACADEMICS

Degrees: Bachelor's, master's. **Academic Requirements:** General education including some course work in computer literacy, English (including composition), humanities, mathematics, sciences (biological or physical), social science. **Classes:** 20-29 students in an average class. 20-29 students in an average lab/discussion section. **Majors with Highest Enrollment:** Electrical, electronics, and communications engineering; mechanical engineering; chemical engineering. **Disciplines with Highest Percentage of Degrees Awarded:** Engineering/engineering technology 81%, computer and information sciences 15%, physical sciences 3%, mathematics 1%. **Special Study Options:** Accelerated program, cooperative (work-study) program, cross registration, double major, independent study, study abroad.

FACILITIES

Housing: Coed, all-male, fraternities and/or sororities. **Library Holdings:** 77,348 bound volumes. 280 periodicals. 532 microforms. 493 audiovisuals. **Special Academic Facilities/Equipment:** Union Building contains collection of British watercolors; Moench Hall contains Western sculpture and eclectic art; Hadley Hall contains Hadley pottery and Salty Seamon paintings; Oakley Observatory. **Computers:** *Recommended operating system:* Windows XP. School-owned computers available for student use.

EXTRACURRICULARS

Activities: Choral groups, concert band, dance, drama/theater, jazz band, literary magazine, music ensembles, musical theater, pep band, radio station, student government, student newspaper, yearbook. **Organizations:** 60 registered organizations, 13 honor societies, 3 religious organizations, 8 fraternities (47% men join), 2 sororities (46% women join). **Athletics (Intercollegiate):** *Men:* baseball, basketball, cheerleading, cross-country, diving, football, golf, indoor track, rifle, soccer, swimming, tennis, track & field, wrestling. *Women:* basketball, cheerleading, cross-country, diving, golf, indoor track, rifle, soccer, softball, swimming, tennis, track & field, volleyball.

ADMISSIONS

Selectivity Rating: 92 (of 100). **Freshman Academic Profile:** 73% in top 10% of high school class, 96% in top 25% of high school class, 100% in top 50% of high school class. 87% from public high schools. Average SAT I Math 680, SAT I Math middle 50% range 640-720. Average SAT I Verbal 620, SAT I Verbal middle 50% range 570-670. Average ACT 29, ACT middle 50% range 27-31. TOEFL required of all international applicants, minimum TOEFL 550. **Basis for Candidate Selection:** *Very important factors considered include:* class rank, secondary school record, standardized test scores. *Important factors considered include:* character/personal qualities, minority status, recommendations. *Other factors considered include:* alumni/ae relation, extracurricular activities, interview, talent/ability, volunteer work, work experience. **Freshman Admission Requirements:** High school diploma is required and GED is not accepted. *Academic units required/recommended:* 16 total required; 4 English required, 4 math required, 5 math recommended, 2 science required, 3 science recommended, 2 science lab required, 2 social studies required, 4 elective required. **Freshman Admission Statistics:** 3,207 applied, 65% accepted, 22% of those accepted enrolled. **Transfer Admission Requirements:** *Items required:* college transcript, essay, statement of good standing from prior school. Minimum college GPA of 3.0 required. Lowest grade transferable C. **General Admission Information:** Application fee $40. Priority application deadline December 1. Regular application deadline March 1. Admission may be deferred for a maximum of 1 year. Credit and/or placement offered for CEEB Advanced Placement tests.

COSTS AND FINANCIAL AID

Tuition $22,562. Room & board $6,348. Required fees $435. Average book expense $900. **Required Forms and Deadlines:** FAFSA. No deadline for

regular filing. Priority filing deadline March 1. **Notification of Awards:** Applicants will be notified of awards on or about March 10. **Types of Aid:** *Need-based scholarships/grants:* Pell, SEOG, state scholarships/grants, the school's own gift aid. *Loans:* Direct Subsidized Stafford, Direct Unsubsidized Stafford, Direct PLUS, Federal Perkins. **Student Employment:** Federal Work-Study Program available. Institutional employment available. Off-campus job opportunities are good. **Financial Aid Statistics:** 77% freshmen, 73% undergrads receive some form of aid. Average freshman grant $5,649. Average freshman loan $5,000. Average income from on-campus job $1,500. **Financial Aid Phone:** 812-877-8259.

ROSEMONT COLLEGE

1400 Montgomery Avenue, Rosemont, PA 19010
Phone: 610-526-2966 **E-mail:** admissions@rosemont.edu **CEEB Code:** 2763
Fax: 610-520-4399 **Web:** www.rosemont.edu **ACT Code:** 3676

This private school, which is affiliated with the Roman Catholic Church, was founded in 1921. It has a 56-acre campus.

STUDENTS AND FACULTY

Enrollment: 732. **Student Body:** Out-of-state 35%, international 2%. **Ethnic Representation:** African American 19%, Asian 4%, Caucasian 58%, Hispanic 4%. **Retention and Graduation:** 73% freshmen return for sophomore year. 69% freshmen graduate within 4 years. 36% grads go on to further study within 1 year. 5% grads pursue business degrees. 2% grads pursue law degrees. 9% grads pursue medical degrees. **Faculty:** Student/faculty ratio 8:1. 35 full-time faculty, 91% hold PhDs. 100% faculty teach undergrads.

ACADEMICS

Degrees: Bachelor's, master's, post-bachelor's certificate. **Academic Requirements:** General education including some course work in arts/fine arts, computer literacy, English (including composition), foreign languages, history, humanities, mathematics, philosophy, sciences (biological or physical), social science, religious studies. **Classes:** Under 10 students in an average class. **Majors with Highest Enrollment:** English language and literature, general; psychology, general; social sciences, general. **Disciplines with Highest Percentage of Degrees Awarded:** Business/marketing 50%, psychology 9%, social sciences and history 8%, communications/communication technologies 6%, biological life sciences 5%. **Special Study Options:** Accelerated program, cross registration, double major, honors program, independent study, internships, liberal arts/career combination, student-designed major, study abroad, teacher certification program.

FACILITIES

Housing: All-female. **Library Holdings:** 158,000 bound volumes. 557 periodicals. 25,000 microforms. 2,700 audiovisuals. **Special Academic Facilities/Equipment:** McShain Performing Arts Center and Conwell Learning Center. **Computers:** School-owned computers available for student use.

EXTRACURRICULARS

Activities: Choral groups, concert band, dance, drama/theater, jazz band, literary magazine, marching band, music ensembles, musical theater, opera, pep band, radio station, student government, student newspaper, yearbook. **Organizations:** 23 registered organizations, 6 honor societies, 1 religious organization, 2% women join sororities. **Athletics (Intercollegiate):** *Women:* basketball, field hockey, lacrosse, softball, tennis, volleyball.

ADMISSIONS

Selectivity Rating: 82 (of 100). **Freshman Academic Profile:** Average high school GPA 3.5. 21% in top 10% of high school class, 48% in top 25% of high school class, 69% in top 50% of high school class. 61% from public high schools. Average SAT I Math 500, SAT I Math middle 50% range 460-600. Average SAT I Verbal 520, SAT I Verbal middle 50% range 480-620. TOEFL required of all international applicants, minimum TOEFL 500. **Basis for Candidate Selection:** *Very important factors considered include:* class rank, interview, secondary school record. *Important factors considered include:* essays, extracurricular activities, recommendations, standardized test scores, talent/ability, volunteer work. *Other factors considered include:* alumni/ae relation, character/personal qualities, work experience. **Freshman Admission Requirements:** High school diploma or GED is required. *Academic units required/recommended:* 18 total required; 4 English required, 2 math required, 2 science required, 2 science lab required, 2 foreign language required, 2 social studies required, 2 history required, 2 elective required. **Freshman Admission Statistics:** 234 applied, 77% accepted, 42% of those accepted enrolled. **Transfer Admission Requirements:** *Items required:* college transcript. Minimum college GPA of 2.5 required. Lowest grade transferable C. **General Admission Information:** Application fee $35. Nonfall registration accepted. Admission may be deferred for a maximum of 1 year. Credit and/or placement offered for CEEB Advanced Placement tests.

COSTS AND FINANCIAL AID

Tuition $16,800. Room & board $7,700. Required fees $800. Average book expense $1,000. **Required Forms and Deadlines:** FAFSA. No deadline for regular filing. Priority filing deadline March 1. **Notification of Awards:** Applicants will be notified of awards on a rolling basis beginning on or about February 15. **Types of Aid:** *Need-based scholarships/grants:* Pell, SEOG, state scholarships/grants, private scholarships, the school's own gift aid. *Loans:* FFEL Subsidized Stafford, FFEL Unsubsidized Stafford, FFEL PLUS, Federal Perkins, alternative loans offered, payment plans offered. **Student Employment:** Federal Work-Study Program available. Institutional employment available. Off-campus job opportunities are good. **Financial Aid Statistics:** 73% freshmen, 92% undergrads receive some form of aid. Average freshman grant $17,427. Average freshman loan $4,914. Average income from on-campus job $2,000. **Financial Aid Phone:** 610-527-0200.

ROWAN UNIVERSITY

201 Mullica Hill Road, Glassboro, NJ 08028
Phone: 856-256-4200 **E-mail:** admissions@rowan.edu **CEEB Code:** 2515
Fax: 856-256-4430 **Web:** www.rowan.edu **ACT Code:** 2560

This public school was founded in 1923. It has a 200-acre campus.

STUDENTS AND FACULTY

Enrollment: 8,324. **Student Body:** Male 42%, female 58%, out-of-state 2%, international students represent 31 countries. **Ethnic Representation:** African American 9%, Asian 3%, Caucasian 80%, Hispanic 6%. **Retention and Graduation:** 83% freshmen return for sophomore year. 37% freshmen graduate within 4 years. 48% grads go on to further study within 1 year. 9% grads pursue business degrees. 2% grads pursue law degrees. 2% grads pursue medical degrees. **Faculty:** Student/faculty ratio 14:1. 371 full-time faculty, 77% hold PhDs. 95% faculty teach undergrads.

ACADEMICS

Degrees: Bachelor's, doctoral, master's. **Academic Requirements:** General education including some course work in arts/fine arts, computer literacy, English (including composition), humanities, mathematics, sciences (biological or physical). Must select from bank 1 (history, humanities, language) or bank 2 (social and behavioral sciences). Must take writing intensive, multicultural/global, and public speaking courses. **Classes:** 20-29 students in an average class. **Majors with Highest Enrollment:** Communications, journalism, and related fields; early childhood education and teaching; business, management, marketing, and related support services. **Disciplines with Highest Percentage of Degrees Awarded:** Education 22%, business/marketing 17%, communications/communication technologies 15%, social sciences and history 9%, law/legal studies 6%. **Special Study Options:** Double major, English as a second language, student exchange program (domestic), honors program, independent study, internships, liberal arts/career combination, study abroad, teacher certification program.

FACILITIES

Housing: Coed, apartments for married students, apartments for single students, housing for disabled students, housing for international students. **Library Holdings:** 316,500 bound volumes. 1,858 periodicals. 478,692 microforms. 52,834 audiovisuals. **Special Academic Facilities/Equipment:** Concert hall, glass collection, student recreation center, on-campus early childhood demonstration center, greenhouse for biological studies, observatory. **Computers:** School-owned computers available for student use.

EXTRACURRICULARS

Activities: Choral groups, concert band, dance, drama/theater, jazz band, literary magazine, music ensembles, musical theater, opera, pep band, radio station, student government, student newspaper, student-run film society, symphony orchestra, television station, yearbook. **Organizations:** 90 registered organizations, 7 honor societies, 6 religious organizations, 13 fraternities, 12 sororities. **Athletics (Intercollegiate):** *Men:* baseball, basketball, cheerleading, cross-country, diving, football, golf, indoor track, soccer, swimming, track & field. *Women:* basketball, cheerleading, cross-country, diving, field hockey, indoor track, lacrosse, soccer, softball, swimming, tennis, track & field, volleyball.

ADMISSIONS

Selectivity Rating: 69 (of 100). **Freshman Academic Profile:** Average high school GPA 3.0. 20% in top 10% of high school class, 54% in top 25% of high

school class, 88% in top 50% of high school class. 90% from public high schools. Average SAT I Math 552, SAT I Math middle 50% range 510-610. Average SAT I Verbal 540, SAT I Verbal middle 50% range 500-590. TOEFL required of all international applicants, minimum TOEFL 550. **Basis for Candidate Selection:** *Very important factors considered include:* secondary school record. *Important factors considered include:* character/personal qualities, class rank, extracurricular activities, standardized test scores, talent/ability, volunteer work, work experience. *Other factors considered include:* interview, minority status, recommendations. **Freshman Admission Requirements:** High school diploma or GED is required. *Academic units required/recommended:* 16 total required; 18 total recommended; 4 English required, 3 math required, 4 math recommended. **Freshman Admission Statistics:** 6,881 applied, 44% accepted, 41% of those accepted enrolled. **Transfer Admission Requirements:** *Items required:* college transcript. Minimum college GPA of 2.0 required. Lowest grade transferable D-. **General Admission Information:** Application fee $50. Priority application deadline January 31. Regular application deadline March 15. Nonfall registration accepted. Admission may be deferred for a maximum of 1 year. Credit and/or placement offered for CEEB Advanced Placement tests.

COSTS AND FINANCIAL AID

In-state tuition $4,950. Out-of-state tuition $9,900. Room & board $6,846. Required fees $1,708. Average book expense $800. **Required Forms and Deadlines:** FAFSA. No deadline for regular filing. **Notification of Awards:** Applicants will be notified of awards on a rolling basis beginning on or about March 1. **Types of Aid:** *Need-based scholarships/grants:* Pell, SEOG, state scholarships/grants, private scholarships, the school's own gift aid. *Loans:* Direct Subsidized Stafford, Direct Unsubsidized Stafford, Direct PLUS, state loans. **Student Employment:** Federal Work-Study Program available. Institutional employment available. Off-campus job opportunities are excellent. **Financial Aid Statistics:** 80% freshmen, 66% undergrads receive some form of aid. Average freshman grant $4,429. Average freshman loan $2,292. Average income from on-campus job $2,200. **Financial Aid Phone:** 609-256-4250.

RUSSELL SAGE COLLEGE

Office of Admissions, 45 Ferry Street, Troy, NY 12180
Phone: 518-244-2217 **E-mail:** rscadm@sage.edu **CEEB Code:** 2764
Fax: 518-244-6880 **Web:** www.sage.edu/RSC **ACT Code:** 2876

This private school was founded in 1916. It has an 8-acre campus.

STUDENTS AND FACULTY

Enrollment: 819. **Student Body:** Out-of-state 9%, (1 country represented). **Ethnic Representation:** African American 6%, Asian 2%, Caucasian 78%, Hispanic 2%. **Retention and Graduation:** 80% freshmen return for sophomore year. 29% freshmen graduate within 4 years. 47% grads go on to further study within 1 year. 1% grads pursue business degrees. 3% grads pursue law degrees. **Faculty:** Student/faculty ratio 11:1. 56 full-time faculty, 67% hold PhDs. 100% faculty teach undergrads.

ACADEMICS

Degrees: Bachelor's, terminal. **Academic Requirements:** General education including some course work in arts/fine arts, computer literacy, English (including composition), humanities, sciences (biological or physical), social science, 1 technology intensive course, 3 cross-cultural courses (2 pre-determined). **Classes:** 10-19 students in an average class. 10-19 students in an average lab/discussion section. **Disciplines with Highest Percentage of Degrees Awarded:** Health professions and related sciences 38%, education 16%, biological life sciences 10%, psychology 7%, business/marketing 5%. **Special Study Options:** Accelerated program, cooperative (work-study) program, cross registration, double major, honors program, independent study, internships, liberal arts/career combination, student-designed major, study abroad, teacher certification program.

FACILITIES

Housing: All-female, honors housing, senior housing, Spanish & French housing, returning adult housing. **Library Holdings:** 371,686 bound volumes. 16,747 periodicals. 29,613 microforms. 34,485 audiovisuals. **Special Academic Facilities/Equipment:** Schact Fine Arts Center (home of NYS Theatre Institute), Robison Athletic and Recreational Center, state-of-the-art lab and research facilities in biology, historic 19th-century brownstones. **Computers:** *Recommended operating system:* Windows 95. School-owned computers available for student use.

EXTRACURRICULARS

Activities: Choral groups, dance, drama/theater, literary magazine, musical theater, student government, student newspaper, yearbook. **Organizations:** 40 registered organizations, 14 honor societies. **Athletics (Intercollegiate):** *Women:* basketball, soccer, softball, tennis, volleyball.

ADMISSIONS

Selectivity Rating: 71 (of 100). **Freshman Academic Profile:** Average high school GPA 3.3. 16% in top 10% of high school class, 59% in top 25% of high school class, 85% in top 50% of high school class. Average SAT I Math 524, SAT I Math middle 50% range 480-560. Average SAT I Verbal 518, SAT I Verbal middle 50% range 470-570. Average ACT 23, ACT middle 50% range 22-24. TOEFL required of all international applicants, minimum TOEFL 550. **Basis for Candidate Selection:** *Very important factors considered include:* secondary school record, standardized test scores. *Important factors considered include:* class rank, interview, recommendations. *Other factors considered include:* alumni/ae relation, character/personal qualities, essays, extracurricular activities, talent/ability, volunteer work, work experience. **Freshman Admission Requirements:** High school diploma or GED is required. *Academic units required/recommended:* 16 total required; 4 English required, 3 math required, 3 science required, 3 science lab required, 2 foreign language required, 4 social studies required. **Freshman Admission Statistics:** 367 applied, 57% accepted, 58% of those accepted enrolled. **Transfer Admission Requirements:** *Items required:* high school transcript, college transcript, statement of good standing from prior school. Minimum college GPA of 2.5 required. Lowest grade transferable C. **General Admission Information:** Application fee $30. Priority application deadline May 1. Early decision application deadline December 1. Nonfall registration accepted. Admission may be deferred for a maximum of 1 year. Credit and/or placement offered for CEEB Advanced Placement tests.

COSTS AND FINANCIAL AID

Tuition $17,200. Room & board $6,164. Required fees $480. Average book expense $800. **Required Forms and Deadlines:** FAFSA and state aid form. Priority filing deadline March 1. **Notification of Awards:** Applicants will be notified of awards on a rolling basis beginning on or about March 15. **Types of Aid:** *Need-based scholarships/grants:* Pell, SEOG, state scholarships/grants, the school's own gift aid. *Loans:* FFEL Subsidized Stafford, FFEL Unsubsidized Stafford, FFEL PLUS, Federal Perkins. **Student Employment:** Federal Work-Study Program available. Institutional employment available. Off-campus job opportunities are excellent. **Financial Aid Statistics:** 89% freshmen, 94% undergrads receive some form of aid. Average freshman grant $7,500. Average freshman loan $3,400. Average income from on-campus job $800. **Financial Aid Phone:** 518-244-2341.

RUST COLLEGE

150 Rust Avenue, Holly Springs, MS 38635
Phone: 662-252-8000 **E-mail:** jbmcdonald@rustcollege.edu
Fax: 662-252-8895 **Web:** www.rustcollege.edu **ACT Code:** 2240

This private school, which is affiliated with the Methodist Church, was founded in 1866. It has a 126-acre campus.

STUDENTS AND FACULTY

Enrollment: 943. **Student Body:** Male 33%, female 67%, out-of-state 31%, international 7% (7 countries represented). **Ethnic Representation:** African American 99%. **Retention and Graduation:** 60% freshmen return for sophomore year. 23% freshmen graduate within 4 years. 19% grads go on to further study within 1 year. 7% grads pursue medical degrees. **Faculty:** Student/faculty ratio 20:1. 43 full-time faculty, 46% hold PhDs. 100% faculty teach undergrads.

ACADEMICS

Degrees: Associate's, bachelor's. **Academic Requirements:** General education including some course work in arts/fine arts, computer literacy, English (including composition), history, humanities, mathematics, philosophy, sciences (biological or physical), social science, religion. **Classes:** 10-19 students in an average class. 10-19 students in an average lab/discussion section. **Majors with Highest Enrollment:** Business administration/management; computer science; biology/biological sciences, general. **Disciplines with Highest Percentage of Degrees Awarded:** Business/marketing 26%, biological life sciences 18%, computer and information sciences 12%, social sciences and history 9%, communications/communication technologies 7%. **Special Study Options:** Double major, honors program, independent study, internships, liberal arts/career combination, study abroad, teacher certification program, weekend college, Advanced Placement program, Adult Pathway program. Dual enrollment includes three dual degree programs with other institutions and one cooperative program with another institution.

FACILITIES

Housing: All-female, all-male, honors. **Library Holdings:** 126,353 bound volumes. 342 periodicals. 9,158 microforms. 1,510 audiovisuals. **Special Academic Facilities/Equipment:** Dr. Ron Trojcak Collection of African Tribal Art, which includes fabrics, masks, and statues used for religious ceremonies, weddings, ritual dance, and funerals. **Computers:** School-owned computers available for student use.

EXTRACURRICULARS

Activities: Choral groups, concert band, dance, drama/theater, marching band, music ensembles, pep band, radio station, student government, student newspaper, television station, yearbook. **Organizations:** 35 registered organizations, 7 honor societies, 5 religious organizations, 3 fraternities (6% men join), 4 sororities (2% women join). **Athletics (Intercollegiate):** *Men:* baseball, basketball, cheerleading, cross-country, tennis, track & field. *Women:* basketball, cheerleading, cross-country, softball, tennis, track & field, volleyball.

ADMISSIONS

Selectivity Rating: 84 (of 100). **Freshman Academic Profile:** Average high school GPA 2.7. 15% in top 10% of high school class, 30% in top 25% of high school class, 86% in top 50% of high school class. 98% from public high schools. Average ACT 16, ACT middle 50% range 14-17. TOEFL required of all international applicants, minimum TOEFL 540. **Basis for Candidate Selection:** *Very important factors considered include:* recommendations, talent/ability. *Important factors considered include:* standardized test scores. *Other factors considered include:* character/personal qualities, class rank, extracurricular activities, interview, secondary school record, state residency. **Freshman Admission Requirements:** High school diploma or GED is required. *Academic units required/recommended:* 19 total required; 4 English required, 3 math required, 3 science required, 3 social studies required, 6 elective required. **Freshman Admission Statistics:** 3,470 applied, 48% accepted, 18% of those accepted enrolled. **Transfer Admission Requirements:** *Items required:* high school transcript, college transcript, statement of good standing from prior school. Minimum high school GPA of 2.0 required. Minimum college GPA of 2.0 required. Lowest grade transferable C. **General Admission Information:** Application fee $10. Priority application deadline July 15. Nonfall registration accepted. Admission may be deferred for a maximum of 1 year. Credit offered for CEEB Advanced Placement tests.

COSTS AND FINANCIAL AID

Tuition $5,600. Room & board $2,600. Required fees $0. Average book expense $500. **Required Forms and Deadlines:** FAFSA, institution's own financial aid form and state aid form. No deadline for regular filing. Priority filing deadline May 1. **Notification of Awards:** Applicants will be notified of awards on a rolling basis beginning on or about June 1. **Types of Aid:** *Need-based scholarships/grants:* Pell, SEOG, state scholarships/grants, private scholarships, United Negro College Fund. *Loans:* FFEL Subsidized Stafford, FFEL Unsubsidized Stafford, FFEL PLUS, United Methodist. **Student Employment:** Federal Work-Study Program available. Off-campus job opportunities are good. **Financial Aid Statistics:** 88% freshmen, 100% undergrads receive some form of aid. Average freshman grant $3,625. Average freshman loan $1,350. Average income from on-campus job $1,600. **Financial Aid Phone:** 662-252-8000.

RUTGERS UNIVERSITY—CAMDEN COLLEGE OF ARTS & SCIENCES

406 Penn Street, Camden, NJ 08102
Phone: 856-225-6104 **E-mail:** admissions@asb-ugadm.rutgers.edu **CEEB Code:** 2765
Fax: 856-225-6498 **Web:** www.rutgers.edu **ACT Code:** 2592

This public school was founded in 1927. It has a 25-acre campus.

STUDENTS AND FACULTY

Enrollment: 3,716. **Student Body:** Male 41%, female 59%, out-of-state 3%, international 1% (13 countries represented). **Ethnic Representation:** African American 16%, Asian 7%, Caucasian 66%, Hispanic 6%. **Retention and Graduation:** 86% freshmen return for sophomore year. **Faculty:** Student/faculty ratio 12:1. 219 full-time faculty, 98% hold PhDs. 70% faculty teach undergrads.

ACADEMICS

Degrees: Bachelor's, first professional, master's. **Academic Requirements:** General education including some course work in arts/fine arts, English (including composition), foreign languages, history, humanities, mathematics, sciences (biological or physical), social science, 3 credits in an interdisciplinary course. **Classes:** 20-29 students in an average class. 10-19 students in an average lab/discussion section. **Disciplines with Highest Percentage of Degrees Awarded:** Business/marketing 26%, psychology 17%, social sciences and history 15%, biological life sciences 6%, protective services/public administration 6%. **Special Study Options:** Accelerated program, cooperative (work-study) program, cross registration, distance learning, double major, dual enrollment, English as a second language, honors program, independent study, liberal arts/career combination, student-designed major, study abroad, teacher certification program, 8 year BA/MD with University of Medicine and Dentistry of New Jersey; 5 year BA or BS/MA in Criminal Justice with School of Criminal Justice-Newark Campus; 2-3 dual bachelors degree with School of Engineering BA in Political Science/MPA.

FACILITIES

Housing: Coed, apartments for single students, housing for disabled students. **Library Holdings:** 3,777,538 bound volumes. 28,760 periodicals. **Special Academic Facilities/Equipment:** Art gallery, poetry center, music synthesizer, electron microscope, School of Law, theater. **Computers:** *Recommended operating system:* Mac. School-owned computers available for student use.

EXTRACURRICULARS

Activities: Drama/theater, literary magazine, radio station, student government, student newspaper, yearbook. **Organizations:** 50 registered organizations, 11 honor societies, 4 fraternities, 4 sororities. **Athletics (Intercollegiate):** *Men:* baseball, basketball, cross-country, golf, soccer, track & field. *Women:* basketball, cross-country, soccer, softball, track & field, volleyball.

ADMISSIONS

Selectivity Rating: 78 (of 100). **Freshman Academic Profile:** 15% in top 10% of high school class, 51% in top 25% of high school class, 89% in top 50% of high school class. SAT I Math middle 50% range 480-590. SAT I Verbal middle 50% range 470-580. TOEFL required of all international applicants, minimum TOEFL 550. **Basis for Candidate Selection:** *Very important factors considered include:* class rank, secondary school record, standardized test scores. *Other factors considered include:* essays, extracurricular activities, geographical residence, minority status, recommendations, state residency, volunteer work, work experience. **Freshman Admission Requirements:** High school diploma or GED is required. *Academic units required/recommended:* 16 total required; 4 English required, 3 math required, 4 math recommended, 2 science required, 2 foreign language required, 5 elective required. **Freshman Admission Statistics:** 5,414 applied, 59% accepted, 13% of those accepted enrolled. **Transfer Admission Requirements:** *Items required:* high school transcript, college transcript. Lowest grade transferable C. **General Admission Information:** Application fee $50. Priority application deadline December 1. Nonfall registration accepted. Admission may be deferred for a maximum of 1 year. Credit and/or placement offered for CEEB Advanced Placement tests.

COSTS AND FINANCIAL AID

In-state tuition $4,762. Out-of-state tuition $9,692. Room & board $5,322. Required fees $1,112. Average book expense $700. **Required Forms and Deadlines:** FAFSA. Priority filing deadline March 15. **Notification of Awards:** Applicants will be notified of awards on a rolling basis beginning on or about February 15. **Types of Aid:** *Need-based scholarships/grants:* Pell, SEOG, state scholarships/grants, private scholarships, the school's own gift aid. *Loans:* Direct Subsidized Stafford, Direct Unsubsidized Stafford, Direct PLUS, Federal Perkins, state loans, college/university loans from institutional funds. **Student Employment:** Federal Work-Study Program available. Institutional employment available. Off-campus job opportunities are good. **Financial Aid Statistics:** 52% freshmen, 61% undergrads receive some form of aid. **Financial Aid Phone:** 609-225-6039.

RUTGERS UNIVERSITY—COLLEGE OF NURSING

249 University Avenue, Newark, NJ 07102-1896
Phone: 973-353-5205 **E-mail:** admissions@asb-ugadm.rutgers.edu **CEEB Code:** 2765
Fax: 973-353-1440 **Web:** www.rutgers.edu **ACT Code:** 2592

This public school was founded in 1956. It has a 36-acre campus.

STUDENTS AND FACULTY

Enrollment: 466. **Student Body:** Male 8%, female 92%, out-of-state 4%, international 1% (2 countries represented). **Ethnic Representation:** African American 18%, Asian 17%, Caucasian 47%, Hispanic 12%. **Faculty:** Student/faculty ratio 11:1. 36 full-time faculty, 97% hold PhDs. 70% faculty teach undergrads.

ACADEMICS

Degrees: Bachelor's. **Academic Requirements:** General education including some course work in English (including composition), humanities, sciences (biological or physical), social science, nursing curriculum. **Disciplines with Highest Percentage of Degrees Awarded:** Health professions and related sciences 100%. **Special Study Options:** Distance learning, dual enrollment, English as a second language, honors program, internships.

FACILITIES

Housing: Coed, apartments for single students, housing for disabled students, fraternities and/or sororities. **Special Academic Facilities/Equipment:** Center for molecular and behavioral neuroscience, center for nursing research. **Computers:** *Recommended operating system:* Mac. School-owned computers available for student use.

EXTRACURRICULARS

Activities: Choral groups, concert band, drama/theater, literary magazine, radio station, student government, student newspaper, symphony orchestra, yearbook. **Organizations:** 80 registered organizations, 1 honor society, 7 fraternities, 7 sororities. **Athletics (Intercollegiate):** *Men:* baseball, basketball, soccer, tennis, volleyball. *Women:* basketball, softball, tennis, volleyball.

ADMISSIONS

Selectivity Rating: 85 (of 100). **Freshman Academic Profile:** 20% in top 10% of high school class, 67% in top 25% of high school class, 96% in top 50% of high school class. SAT I Math middle 50% range 500-580. SAT I Verbal middle 50% range 480-570. TOEFL required of all international applicants, minimum TOEFL 600. **Basis for Candidate Selection:** *Very important factors considered include:* class rank, secondary school record, standardized test scores. *Other factors considered include:* essays, extracurricular activities, geographical residence, minority status, recommendations, state residency, talent/ability, volunteer work, work experience. **Freshman Admission Requirements:** High school diploma or GED is required. *Academic units required/recommended:* 16 total required; 4 English required, 3 math required, 4 math recommended, 2 science required, 7 elective required. **Freshman Admission Statistics:** 711 applied, 26% accepted, 31% of those accepted enrolled. **Transfer Admission Requirements:** *Items required:* high school transcript, college transcript. Lowest grade transferable C. **General Admission Information:** Application fee $50. Priority application deadline December 15. Admission may be deferred for a maximum of 1 year. Credit and/or placement offered for CEEB Advanced Placement tests.

COSTS AND FINANCIAL AID

In-state tuition $4,762. Out-of-state tuition $9,692. Room & board $6,090. Required fees $1,030. Average book expense $800. **Required Forms and Deadlines:** FAFSA. No deadline for regular filing. Priority filing deadline March 15. **Notification of Awards:** Applicants will be notified of awards on a rolling basis beginning on or about February 15. **Types of Aid:** *Need-based scholarships/grants:* Pell, SEOG, state scholarships/grants, the school's own gift aid. *Loans:* Direct Subsidized Stafford, Direct Unsubsidized Stafford, Direct PLUS, Federal Perkins, state loans, college/university loans from institutional funds. **Student Employment:** Federal Work-Study Program available. Institutional employment available. Off-campus job opportunities are good. **Financial Aid Statistics:** 63% freshmen, 59% undergrads receive some form of aid. Average freshman grant $5,698. Average freshman loan $2,479. **Financial Aid Phone:** 973-353-5152.

RUTGERS UNIVERSITY—COLLEGE OF PHARMACY

Office of Admissions, 65 Davidson Road, New Brunswick, NJ 08903-2101
Phone: 732-932-4636 **E-mail:** admissions@asb-ugadm.rutgers.edu **CEEB Code:** 2765
Fax: 732-445-0237 **Web:** www.rutgers.edu **ACT Code:** 2592

This public school was founded in 1892. It has a 2,695-acre campus.

STUDENTS AND FACULTY

Enrollment: 825. **Student Body:** Male 36%, female 64%, out-of-state 15%, international 2% (9 countries represented). **Ethnic Representation:** African American 6%, Asian 46%, Caucasian 31%, Hispanic 7%. **Retention and Graduation:** 92% freshmen return for sophomore year. **Faculty:** Student/faculty ratio 11:1. 63 full-time faculty, 98% hold PhDs. 70% faculty teach undergrads.

ACADEMICS

Degrees: Doctoral, first professional. **Academic Requirements:** General education including some course work in English (including composition), humanities, mathematics, sciences (biological or physical), social science, pharmacy curriculum. **Disciplines with Highest Percentage of Degrees Awarded:** Health professions and related sciences 100%. **Special Study Options:** Distance learning, English as a second language, honors program, independent study, internships, study abroad.

FACILITIES

Housing: Coed, all-female, all-male, apartments for single students, housing for disabled students, fraternities and/or sororities, language and cultural houses, math/science house for women, substance-free/wellness house, first-year and transfer residence halls. **Library Holdings:** 6,362,037 bound volumes. 28,934 periodicals. 5,427,289 microforms. 119,880 audiovisuals. **Special Academic Facilities/Equipment:** Controlled drug-delivery research center, Institute for Environmental and Occupational Health Sciences. **Computers:** *Recommended operating system:* Mac. School-owned computers available for student use.

EXTRACURRICULARS

Activities: Choral groups, concert band, dance, drama/theater, jazz band, literary magazine, marching band, music ensembles, opera, pep band, radio station, student government, student newspaper, student-run film society, symphony orchestra, television station, yearbook. **Organizations:** 400 registered organizations, 3 honor societies, 29 fraternities, 15 sororities. **Athletics (Intercollegiate):** *Men:* baseball, basketball, cheerleading, crew, cross-country, diving, fencing, football, golf, indoor track, lacrosse, soccer, swimming, tennis, track & field, wrestling. *Women:* basketball, cheerleading, crew, cross-country, diving, fencing, field hockey, golf, gymnastics, indoor track, lacrosse, soccer, softball, swimming, tennis, track & field, volleyball.

ADMISSIONS

Selectivity Rating: 63 (of 100). **Freshman Academic Profile:** 67% in top 10% of high school class, 100% in top 25% of high school class, 100% in top 50% of high school class. SAT I Math middle 50% range 620-710. SAT I Verbal middle 50% range 580-650. TOEFL required of all international applicants, minimum TOEFL 550. **Basis for Candidate Selection:** *Very important factors considered include:* class rank, secondary school record, standardized test scores. *Other factors considered include:* essays, extracurricular activities, geographical residence, minority status, recommendations, state residency, talent/ability, volunteer work, work experience. **Freshman Admission Requirements:** High school diploma or GED is required. *Academic units required/recommended:* 16 total required; 4 English required, 3 math required, 4 math recommended, 2 science required, 2 foreign language required, 5 elective required. **Freshman Admission Statistics:** 1,401 applied, 45% accepted, 29% of those accepted enrolled. **Transfer Admission Requirements:** *Items required:* high school transcript, college transcript. Lowest grade transferable C. **General Admission Information:** Application fee $50. Priority application deadline December 15. Admission may be deferred for a maximum of 1 year. Credit and/or placement offered for CEEB Advanced Placement tests.

COSTS AND FINANCIAL AID

In-state tuition $5,286. Out-of-state tuition $10,754. Room & board $6,098. Required fees $1,290. Average book expense $800. **Required Forms and Deadlines:** FAFSA. No deadline for regular filing. Priority filing deadline March 15. **Notification of Awards:** Applicants will be notified of awards on a rolling basis beginning on or about February 15. **Types of Aid:** *Need-based scholarships/grants:* Pell, SEOG, state scholarships/grants, the school's own gift aid. *Loans:* Direct Subsidized Stafford, Direct Unsubsidized Stafford, Direct PLUS, Federal Perkins, state loans, college/university loans from institutional funds, Other Educational Loans. **Student Employment:** Federal Work-Study Program available. Institutional employment available. Off-campus job opportunities are good. **Financial Aid Statistics:** 43% freshmen, 47% undergrads receive some form of aid. Average freshman grant $5,122. Average freshman loan $3,005. Average income from on-campus job $1,374. **Financial Aid Phone:** 732-932-7057.

RUTGERS UNIVERSITY—COOK COLLEGE

65 Davidson Road, Piscataway, NJ 08854-8097
Phone: 732-932-4326 **E-mail:** admissions@asb-ugadm.rutgers.edu **CEEB Code:** 2765
Fax: 732-445-0237 **Web:** www.rutgers.edu **ACT Code:** 2592

This public school was founded in 1864. It has a 2,695-acre campus.

STUDENTS AND FACULTY

Enrollment: 3,231. **Student Body:** Male 50%, female 50%, out-of-state 9%, international 2% (23 countries represented). **Ethnic Representation:** African

American 6%, Asian 13%, Caucasian 68%, Hispanic 6%. **Retention and Graduation:** 91% freshmen return for sophomore year. 42% freshmen graduate within 4 years. **Faculty:** Student/faculty ratio 11:1. 256 full-time faculty, 97% hold PhDs. 70% faculty teach undergrads.

ACADEMICS

Degrees: Bachelor's. **Academic Requirements:** General education including some course work in computer literacy, English (including composition), humanities, sciences (biological or physical), 5 credits in interdisciplinary/ethical analysis, 6 credits in human diversity, 6-9 credits in economic and political systems. **Disciplines with Highest Percentage of Degrees Awarded:** Area and ethnic studies 25%, natural resources/environmental sciences 25%, agriculture 15%, education 9%, social sciences and history 9%. **Special Study Options:** Cooperative (work-study) program, distance learning, double major, dual enrollment, English as a second language, honors program, independent study, internships, student-designed major, study abroad, teacher certification program, 8-year BA/ or BS/MD, 5-year dual degree in bioresource engineering with the College of Engineering, BA/ or BS/MPP with School of Planning and Public Policy.

FACILITIES

Housing: Coed, all-male, apartments for single students, housing for disabled students, fraternities and/or sororities, cooperative housing, Substance-free/ wellness housing, transfer center, first-year residence. **Library Holdings:** 6,362,037 bound volumes. 28,934 periodicals. 5,427,289 microforms. 119,880 audiovisuals. **Special Academic Facilities/Equipment:** Center for Advanced Food Technology, Agricultural Experiment Station, Center for Agricultural Molecular Biology, Institute of Marine and Coastal Sciences, Center for Remote Sensing and Spatial Analysis, Ecopolicy Center, Center for Theoretical and Applied Genetics, Center for Advanced Biotechnology and Medicine. **Computers:** *Recommended operating system:* UNIX. School-owned computers available for student use.

EXTRACURRICULARS

Activities: Choral groups, concert band, dance, drama/theater, jazz band, literary magazine, marching band, music ensembles, opera, pep band, radio station, student government, student newspaper, student-run film society, symphony orchestra, television station, yearbook. **Organizations:** 400 registered organizations, 9 honor societies, 29 fraternities (8% men join), 15 sororities (5% women join). **Athletics (Intercollegiate):** *Men:* baseball, basketball, cheerleading, crew, cross-country, diving, fencing, football, golf, indoor track, lacrosse, soccer, swimming, tennis, track & field, wrestling. *Women:* basketball, cheerleading, crew, cross-country, diving, fencing, field hockey, golf, gymnastics, indoor track, lacrosse, soccer, softball, swimming, tennis, track & field, volleyball.

ADMISSIONS

Selectivity Rating: 63 (of 100). **Freshman Academic Profile:** 28% in top 10% of high school class, 71% in top 25% of high school class, 97% in top 50% of high school class. SAT I Math middle 50% range 540-630. SAT I Verbal middle 50% range 510-610. TOEFL required of all international applicants, minimum TOEFL 550. **Basis for Candidate Selection:** *Very important factors considered include:* class rank, secondary school record, standardized test scores. *Other factors considered include:* essays, extracurricular activities, geographical residence, minority status, recommendations, state residency, talent/ability, volunteer work, work experience. **Freshman Admission Requirements:** High school diploma or GED is required. *Academic units required/recommended:* 16 total required; 4 English required, 3 math required, 4 math recommended, 2 science required, 7 elective required. **Freshman Admission Statistics:** 6,673 applied, 64% accepted, 15% of those accepted enrolled. **Transfer Admission Requirements:** *Items required:* high school transcript, college transcript. Lowest grade transferable C. **General Admission Information:** Application fee $50. Priority application deadline December 15. Admission may be deferred for a maximum of 1 year. Credit and/or placement offered for CEEB Advanced Placement tests.

COSTS AND FINANCIAL AID

In-state tuition $5,286. Out-of-state tuition $10,754. Room & board $6,098. Required fees $1,258. Average book expense $800. **Required Forms and Deadlines:** FAFSA. Priority filing deadline March 15. **Notification of Awards:** Applicants will be notified of awards on a rolling basis beginning on or about February 15. **Types of Aid:** *Need-based scholarships/grants:* Pell, SEOG, state scholarships/grants, the school's own gift aid. *Loans:* Direct Subsidized Stafford, Direct Unsubsidized Stafford, Direct PLUS, Federal Perkins, state loans, college/university loans from institutional funds, Other Educational. **Student Employment:** Federal Work-Study Program available. Institutional employment available. Off-campus job opportunities are good. **Financial Aid Statistics:** 55% freshmen, 47% undergrads receive some form of aid. Average freshman grant $4,959. Average freshman loan $2,947. Average income from on-campus job $1,374. **Financial Aid Phone:** 732-932-7057.

RUTGERS UNIVERSITY—DOUGLASS COLLEGE

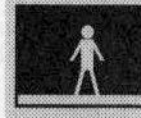

65 Davidson Road, Room 202, Piscataway, NJ 08854-8097
Phone: 732-932-4636 **E-mail:** admissions@asb-ugadm.rutgers.edu **CEEB Code:** 2765
Fax: 732-445-0237 **Web:** www.rutgers.edu **ACT Code:** 2592

This public school was founded in 1918. It has a 2,695-acre campus.

STUDENTS AND FACULTY

Enrollment: 3,099. **Student Body:** Out-of-state 7%, international 2% (25 countries represented). **Ethnic Representation:** African American 12%, Asian 14%, Caucasian 57%, Hispanic 8%. **Faculty:** Student/faculty ratio 15:1. 1,051 full-time faculty, 98% hold PhDs. 70% faculty teach undergrads.

ACADEMICS

Degrees: Bachelor's. **Academic Requirements:** General education including some course work in English (including composition), foreign languages, history, humanities, mathematics, sciences (biological or physical), social science, two courses related to the experience of women; one three-credit course in cross-cultural perspectives. **Disciplines with Highest Percentage of Degrees Awarded:** Social sciences and history 20%, psychology 20%, communications/communication technologies 10%, biological life sciences 10%, English 9%. **Special Study Options:** Cross registration, distance learning, double major, dual enrollment, English as a second language, honors program, independent study, internships, liberal arts/career combination, student-designed major, study abroad, teacher certification program, Washington semester, 8-year BA/ or BS/MD University of Medicine and Dentistry of New Jersey, 5-year dual degree with the School of Engineering, 5-year BA/MBA with Graduate School of Management, 5-year BA/ or BS/MPP with School of Planning and Public Policy, 5-year BA/ or BS/MEd in conjunction with the Graduate School of Education, BA/ or BS/MPH with School of Planning and Public Policy.

FACILITIES

Housing: All-female, apartments for single students, housing for disabled students, fraternities and/or sororities, language and cultural houses, special house for women in math/sciences/engineering, cooperative community house for single mothers with children. **Special Academic Facilities/Equipment:** Center for Women and Work; Institute for Research on Women; Center for Women's Global Leadership; Center for American Women and Politics; Center for Public Interest Polling; Douglass Project for Women in Math, Science, and Engineering; Walt Whitman Center for the Culture and Politics of Democracy. **Computers:** *Recommended operating system:* Mac. School-owned computers available for student use.

EXTRACURRICULARS

Activities: Choral groups, concert band, dance, drama/theater, jazz band, literary magazine, marching band, music ensembles, opera, pep band, radio station, student government, student newspaper, student-run film society, symphony orchestra, television station, yearbook. **Organizations:** 400 registered organizations, 15 sororities. **Athletics (Intercollegiate):** *Women:* basketball, cheerleading, crew, cross-country, diving, fencing, field hockey, golf, gymnastics, indoor track, lacrosse, soccer, softball, swimming, tennis, track & field, volleyball.

ADMISSIONS

Selectivity Rating: 77 (of 100). **Freshman Academic Profile:** 19% in top 10% of high school class, 53% in top 25% of high school class, 98% in top 50% of high school class. SAT I Math middle 50% range 490-590. SAT I Verbal middle 50% range 500-590. TOEFL required of all international applicants, minimum TOEFL 550. **Basis for Candidate Selection:** *Very important factors considered include:* class rank, secondary school record, standardized test scores. *Other factors considered include:* essays, extracurricular activities, geographical residence, minority status, recommendations, state residency, talent/ability, volunteer work, work experience. **Freshman Admission Requirements:** High school diploma or GED is required. *Academic units required/recommended:* 16 total required; 4 English required, 3 math required, 4 math recommended, 2 science required, 2 foreign language required, 5 elective required. **Freshman Admission Statistics:** 6,453 applied, 68% accepted, 15% of those accepted enrolled. **Transfer Admission Requirements:** *Items required:* high school transcript, college transcript. Lowest grade transferable C. **General Admission Information:** Application fee $50. Priority application deadline December 15. Admission may be deferred for a maximum of 1 year. Credit and/or placement offered for CEEB Advanced Placement tests.

COSTS AND FINANCIAL AID

In-state tuition $4,762. Out-of-state tuition $9,692. Room & board $6,098. Required fees $1,255. Average book expense $700. **Required Forms and**

Deadlines: FAFSA. No deadline for regular filing. Priority filing deadline March 15. **Notification of Awards:** Applicants will be notified of awards on a rolling basis beginning on or about February 15. **Types of Aid:** *Need-based scholarships/grants:* Pell, SEOG, state scholarships/grants, the school's own gift aid. *Loans:* Direct Subsidized Stafford, Direct Unsubsidized Stafford, Direct PLUS, Federal Perkins, state loans, college/university loans from institutional funds, other educational loans. **Student Employment:** Federal Work-Study Program available. Institutional employment available. Off-campus job opportunities are good. **Financial Aid Statistics:** 53% freshmen, 48% undergrads receive some form of aid. Average freshman grant $5,100. Average freshman loan $2,867. Average income from on-campus job $1,374. **Financial Aid Phone:** 732-932-7057.

RUTGERS UNIVERSITY—LIVINGSTON COLLEGE

65 Davidson Road, Piscataway, NJ 00854-8097
Phone: 732-932-4636 **E-mail:** admissions@asb-ugadm.rutgers.edu **CEEB Code:** 2765
Fax: 732-445-0237 **Web:** www.rutgers.edu **ACT Code:** 2592

This public school was founded in 1969. It has a 2,695-acre campus.

STUDENTS AND FACULTY

Enrollment: 3,536. **Student Body:** Male 48%, female 52%, out-of-state 8%, international 2% (30 countries represented). **Ethnic Representation:** African American 10%, Asian 18%, Caucasian 57%, Hispanic 8%. **Faculty:** Student/faculty ratio 15:1. 1,051 full-time faculty, 98% hold PhDs. 70% faculty teach undergrads.

ACADEMICS

Degrees: Bachelor's. **Academic Requirements:** General education including some course work in arts/fine arts, English (including composition), humanities, mathematics, sciences (biological or physical), social science, one course in areas of cultural perspectives and contemporary issues. **Disciplines with Highest Percentage of Degrees Awarded:** Social sciences and history 30%, protective services/public administration 16%, psychology 13%, communications/communication technologies 10%, business/marketing 6%. **Special Study Options:** Cross registration, distance learning, double major, dual enrollment, English as a second language, honors program, independent study, internships, liberal arts/career combination, student-designed major, study abroad.

FACILITIES

Housing: Coed, apartments for single students, housing for disabled students, fraternities and/or sororities, special-interest housing, leadership house, first-year residence, wellness/substance-free housing, transfer center. **Library Holdings:** 6,362,037 bound volumes. 28,934 periodicals. 5,427,289 microforms. 119,880 audiovisuals. **Special Academic Facilities/Equipment:** Art and geology museums, Center for Urban Policy Research, Center for International Business Education, Bureau of Government Research, Institute for Criminological Research, American Affordable Housing Institute, Institute for Ethnic Studies in Social Work, Center for Negotiation and Conflict Resolution. **Computers:** *Recommended operating system:* Mac. School-owned computers available for student use.

EXTRACURRICULARS

Activities: Choral groups, concert band, dance, drama/theater, jazz band, literary magazine, marching band, music ensembles, opera, pep band, radio station, student government, student newspaper, student-run film society, symphony orchestra, television station, yearbook. **Organizations:** 400 registered organizations, 1 honor society, 29 fraternities, 15 sororities. **Athletics (Intercollegiate):** *Men:* baseball, basketball, cheerleading, crew, cross-country, diving, fencing, football, golf, indoor track, lacrosse, soccer, swimming, tennis, track & field, wrestling. *Women:* basketball, cheerleading, crew, cross-country, diving, fencing, field hockey, golf, gymnastics, indoor track, lacrosse, soccer, softball, swimming, tennis, track & field, volleyball.

ADMISSIONS

Selectivity Rating: 77 (of 100). **Freshman Academic Profile:** 9% in top 10% of high school class, 42% in top 25% of high school class, 95% in top 50% of high school class. SAT I Math middle 50% range 520-610. SAT I Verbal middle 50% range 500-580. TOEFL required of all international applicants, minimum TOEFL 550. **Basis for Candidate Selection:** *Very important factors considered include:* class rank, secondary school record, standardized test scores. *Other factors considered include:* essays, extracurricular activities, geographical residence, minority status, recommendations, state residency, talent/ability, volunteer work, work experience. **Freshman Admission Requirements:** High school diploma or GED is required. *Academic units required/recommended:* 16 total required; 4 English required, 3 math required, 4 math recommended, 2 science required, 2 foreign language required, 5 elective required. **Freshman Admission Statistics:** 14,995 applied, 60% accepted, 9% of those accepted enrolled. **Transfer Admission Requirements:** *Items required:* high school transcript, college transcript. Lowest grade transferable C. **General Admission Information:** Application fee $50. Admission may be deferred for a maximum of 1 year. Credit and/or placement offered for CEEB Advanced Placement tests.

COSTS AND FINANCIAL AID

In-state tuition $4,762. Out-of-state tuition $9,692. Room & board $6,098. Required fees $1,276. Average book expense $700. **Required Forms and Deadlines:** FAFSA. No deadline for regular filing. Priority filing deadline March 15. **Notification of Awards:** Applicants will be notified of awards on a rolling basis beginning on or about February 15. **Types of Aid:** *Need-based scholarships/grants:* Pell, SEOG, state scholarships/grants, the school's own gift aid. *Loans:* Direct Subsidized Stafford, Direct Unsubsidized Stafford, Direct PLUS, Federal Perkins, state loans, college/university loans from institutional funds, Educational Loans. **Student Employment:** Federal Work-Study Program available. Institutional employment available. Off-campus job opportunities are good. **Financial Aid Statistics:** 51% freshmen, 49% undergrads receive some form of aid. Average freshman grant $5,423. Average freshman loan $2,923. Average income from on-campus job $1,374. **Financial Aid Phone:** 732-932-7057.

RUTGERS UNIVERSITY—MASON GROSS SCHOOL OF THE ARTS

65 Davidson Road, #202, Piscataway, NJ 08854-8097
Phone: 732-932-4636 **E-mail:** admissions@asb-ugadm.rutgers.edu **CEEB Code:** 2765
Fax: 732-445-0237 **Web:** www.rutgers.edu **ACT Code:** 2592

This public school was founded in 1976. It has a 2,695-acre campus.

STUDENTS AND FACULTY

Enrollment: 617. **Student Body:** Male 42%, female 58%, out-of-state 18%, international 1% (6 countries represented). **Ethnic Representation:** African American 5%, Asian 6%, Caucasian 77%, Hispanic 4%, Native American 1%. **Faculty:** Student/faculty ratio 6:1. 79 full-time faculty, 97% hold PhDs. 70% faculty teach undergrads.

ACADEMICS

Degrees: Bachelor's, doctoral, master's. **Academic Requirements:** General education including some course work in arts/fine arts, English (including composition), humanities, mathematics, sciences (biological or physical), social science. **Disciplines with Highest Percentage of Degrees Awarded:** Visual and performing arts 100%. **Special Study Options:** Cross registration, distance learning, English as a second language, honors program, internships, study abroad, teacher certification program.

FACILITIES

Housing: Coed, all-female, all-male, apartments for single students, housing for disabled students, fraternities and/or sororities, language and cultural houses, houses for women, substance-free/wellness house, freshman dorms. **Library Holdings:** 6,362,037 bound volumes. 28,934 periodicals. 5,427,289 microforms. 119,880 audiovisuals. **Special Academic Facilities/Equipment:** Agricultural, art, and geology museums, dance, music, and art studios, concert and recital halls, theatres, institute of jazz studies. **Computers:** *Recommended operating system:* Mac. School-owned computers available for student use.

EXTRACURRICULARS

Activities: Choral groups, concert band, dance, drama/theater, jazz band, literary magazine, marching band, music ensembles, opera, pep band, radio station, student government, student newspaper, student-run film society, symphony orchestra, television station, yearbook. **Organizations:** 400 registered organizations, 29 fraternities, 15 sororities. **Athletics (Intercollegiate):** *Men:* baseball, basketball, cheerleading, crew, cross-country, diving, fencing, football, golf, indoor track, lacrosse, soccer, swimming, tennis, track & field, wrestling. *Women:* basketball, cheerleading, crew, cross-country, diving, fencing, field hockey, golf, gymnastics, indoor track, lacrosse, soccer, softball, swimming, tennis, track & field, volleyball.

ADMISSIONS

Selectivity Rating: 88 (of 100). **Freshman Academic Profile:** 24% in top 10% of high school class, 48% in top 25% of high school class, 85% in top 50% of high school class. SAT I Math middle 50% range 490-620. SAT I Verbal middle 50% range 510-620. TOEFL required of all international applicants, minimum TOEFL 550. **Basis for Candidate Selection:** *Very important factors considered include:* class rank, interview, secondary school record, standardized test scores, talent/ability. *Other factors considered include:* essays, extracurricular activities, geographical residence, minority status, recommendations, state residency, volunteer work, work experience. **Freshman Admission Requirements:** High school diploma or GED is required. *Academic units required/recommended:* 16 total required; 4 English required, 3 math required, 2 foreign language recommended, 9 elective required. **Freshman Admission Statistics:** 1,603 applied, 22% accepted, 37% of those accepted enrolled. **Transfer Admission Requirements:** *Items required:* high school transcript, college transcript, interview. Lowest grade transferable C. **General Admission Information:** Application fee $50. Priority application deadline December 15. Admission may be deferred for a maximum of 1 year. Credit and/or placement offered for CEEB Advanced Placement tests.

COSTS AND FINANCIAL AID

In-state tuition $4,762. Out-of-state tuition $9,692. Room & board $6,098. Required fees $1,290. Average book expense $700. **Required Forms and Deadlines:** FAFSA. No deadline for regular filing. Priority filing deadline March 15. **Notification of Awards:** Applicants will be notified of awards on a rolling basis beginning on or about February 15. **Types of Aid:** *Need-based scholarships/grants:* Pell, SEOG, state scholarships/grants, the school's own gift aid. *Loans:* Direct Subsidized Stafford, Direct Unsubsidized Stafford, Direct PLUS, Federal Perkins, state loans, college/university loans from institutional funds, Other Education Loans. **Student Employment:** Federal Work-Study Program available. Institutional employment available. Off-campus job opportunities are good. **Financial Aid Statistics:** 36% freshmen, 41% undergrads receive some form of aid. Average freshman grant $3,780. Average freshman loan $3,218. Average income from on-campus job $1,374. **Financial Aid Phone:** 732-932-7057.

RUTGERS UNIVERSITY—NEWARK COLLEGE OF ARTS & SCIENCES

249 University Avenue, Newark, NJ 07102-1896
Phone: 973-353-1440 **E-mail:** admissions@asb-ugadm.rutgers.edu **CEEB Code:** 2765
Fax: 973-353-1440 **Web:** www.rutgers.edu **ACT Code:** 2592

This public school was founded in 1930. It has a 36-acre campus.

STUDENTS AND FACULTY

Enrollment: 5,873. **Student Body:** Male 42%, female 58%, out-of-state 6%, international 3%. **Ethnic Representation:** African American 21%, Asian 19%, Caucasian 31%, Hispanic 19%. **Faculty:** Student/faculty ratio 9:1. 388 full-time faculty, 97% hold PhDs. 70% faculty teach undergrads.

ACADEMICS

Degrees: Bachelor's, doctoral, first professional, master's. **Academic Requirements:** General education including some course work in arts/fine arts, English (including composition), humanities, mathematics, sciences (biological or physical), social science. **Disciplines with Highest Percentage of Degrees Awarded:** Business/marketing 27%, biological life sciences 14%, psychology 11%, protective services/public administration 11%, social sciences and history 10%. **Special Study Options:** Accelerated program, cross registration, distance learning, double major, dual enrollment, English as a second language, honors program, independent study, internships, liberal arts/career combination, student-designed major, study abroad, teacher certification program, 8-year BA/MD with University of Medicine and Dentistry of New Jersey, 5-year BA/ or BS/MA in criminal justice, 2+2 and 2+3 programs in engineering, 5-year BA/MBA, dual admission to School of Law.

FACILITIES

Housing: Coed, apartments for single students, housing for disabled students, fraternities and/or sororities. **Library Holdings:** 3,777,538 bound volumes. 28,760 periodicals. **Special Academic Facilities/Equipment:** Institute of jazz studies, TV/radio media center, animal behavior institute, molecular and behavioral neuroscience, center for crime prevention studies, center for negotiation and conflict resolution. **Computers:** *Recommended operating system:* Mac. School-owned computers available for student use.

EXTRACURRICULARS

Activities: Choral groups, drama/theater, literary magazine, radio station, student government, student newspaper, yearbook. **Organizations:** 13 honor societies, 7 fraternities, 7 sororities. **Athletics (Intercollegiate):** *Men:* baseball, basketball, soccer, tennis, volleyball. *Women:* basketball, softball, tennis, volleyball.

ADMISSIONS

Selectivity Rating: 77 (of 100). **Freshman Academic Profile:** 29% in top 10% of high school class, 63% in top 25% of high school class, 97% in top 50% of high school class. SAT I Math middle 50% range 490-600. SAT I Verbal middle 50% range 470-560. TOEFL required of all international applicants, minimum TOEFL 550. **Basis for Candidate Selection:** *Very important factors considered include:* class rank, secondary school record, standardized test scores. *Other factors considered include:* essays, extracurricular activities, geographical residence, minority status, recommendations, state residency, volunteer work, work experience. **Freshman Admission Requirements:** High school diploma or GED is required. *Academic units required/recommended:* 16 total required; 4 English required, 3 math required, 4 math recommended, 2 science required, 2 foreign language required, 5 elective required. **Freshman Admission Statistics:** 8,234 applied, 52% accepted, 18% of those accepted enrolled. **Transfer Admission Requirements:** *Items required:* high school transcript, college transcript. **General Admission Information:** Application fee $50. Priority application deadline December 1. Nonfall registration accepted. Credit and/or placement offered for CEEB Advanced Placement tests.

COSTS AND FINANCIAL AID

In-state tuition $4,762. Out-of-state tuition $9,692. Room & board $6,110. Required fees $1,052. Average book expense $700. **Required Forms and Deadlines:** FAFSA. Priority filing deadline March 15. **Notification of Awards:** Applicants will be notified of awards on a rolling basis beginning on or about February 15. **Types of Aid:** *Loans:* Direct Subsidized Stafford, Direct Unsubsidized Stafford, Direct PLUS, Federal Perkins, state loans, college/university loans from institutional funds. **Student Employment:** Federal Work-Study Program available. Institutional employment available. Off-campus job opportunities are good. **Financial Aid Statistics:** 49% freshmen, 60% undergrads receive some form of aid. Average freshman grant $5,291. Average freshman loan $2,730. **Financial Aid Phone:** 973-353-5357.

RUTGERS UNIVERSITY—RUTGERS COLLEGE

65 Davidson Road, Piscataway, NJ 08854-8097
Phone: 732-932-4636 **E-mail:** admissions@asb-ugadm.rutgers.edu **CEEB Code:** 2765
Fax: 732-445-0237 **Web:** www.rutgers.edu **ACT Code:** 2592

This public school was founded in 1766. It has a 2,695-acre campus.

STUDENTS AND FACULTY

Enrollment: 10,993. **Student Body:** Male 49%, female 51%, out-of-state 10%, international 3% (70 countries represented). **Ethnic Representation:** African American 7%, Asian 20%, Caucasian 56%, Hispanic 9%. **Faculty:** Student/faculty ratio 15:1. 1,051 full-time faculty, 98% hold PhDs. 70% faculty teach undergrads.

ACADEMICS

Degrees: Bachelor's. **Academic Requirements:** General education including some course work in English (including composition), humanities, mathematics, sciences (biological or physical), social science, one course of at least 3 credits about the nonwestern world. **Disciplines with Highest Percentage of Degrees Awarded:** Social sciences and history 24%, psychology 13%, biological life sciences 12%, business/marketing 10%, communications/communication technologies 7%. **Special Study Options:** Accelerated program, cross registration, distance learning, double major, dual enrollment, English as a second language, honors program, independent study, internships, liberal arts/career combination, student-designed major, study abroad, teacher certification program, Washington semester, 8-year BA/ or BS/MD, 5-year BA/ or BS/MBA, 5-year dual degree with School of Engineering, 5-year BA/ or BS/MEd with Graduate School of Education, BA/ or BS/MA in criminal justice, BA or BS/MPH, BA/ or BS/MPP with Edward J. Bloustein School of Planning and Public Policy.

FACILITIES

Housing: Coed, apartments for single students, housing for disabled students, fraternities and/or sororities, Special-interest housing, substance-free house, first-year residence, transfer center. **Library Holdings:** 6,362,037 bound volumes. 28,934 periodicals. 5,427,289 microforms. 119,880 audiovisuals. **Special Academic Facilities/Equipment:** Waksman Institute of Microbiology, Center for the Critical Analysis of Contemporary Culture, Eagleton Institute of Politics, Center for Historical Analysis, Center for the Study of Jewish Life, Center for Mathematical Sciences Research, Center for Molecular Biophysics and Biophysical Chemistry. **Computers:** *Recommended operating system:* Mac. School-owned computers available for student use.

EXTRACURRICULARS

Activities: Choral groups, concert band, dance, drama/theater, jazz band, literary magazine, marching band, music ensembles, opera, pep band, radio station, student government, student newspaper, student-run film society, symphony orchestra, television station, yearbook. **Organizations:** 400 registered organizations, 1 honor society, 22 religious organizations, 25 fraternities, 15 sororities. **Athletics (Intercollegiate):** *Men:* baseball, basketball, cheerleading, crew, cross-country, diving, fencing, football, golf, indoor track, lacrosse, soccer, swimming, tennis, track & field, wrestling. *Women:* basketball, cheerleading, crew, cross-country, diving, fencing, field hockey, golf, gymnastics, indoor track, lacrosse, soccer, softball, swimming, tennis, track & field, volleyball.

ADMISSIONS

Selectivity Rating: 88 (of 100). **Freshman Academic Profile:** 43% in top 10% of high school class, 82% in top 25% of high school class, 99% in top 50% of high school class. Average SAT I Math 612, SAT I Math middle 50% range 560-670. Average SAT I Verbal 591, SAT I Verbal middle 50% range 540-640. TOEFL required of all international applicants, minimum TOEFL 550. **Basis for Candidate Selection:** *Very important factors considered include:* class rank, secondary school record, standardized test scores. *Other factors considered include:* extracurricular activities, geographical residence, minority status, state residency, talent/ability, volunteer work, work experience. **Freshman Admission Requirements:** High school diploma or GED is required. *Academic units required/recommended:* 16 total required; 4 English required, 3 math required, 4 math recommended, 2 science required, 2 foreign language required, 5 elective required. **Freshman Admission Statistics:** 20,441 applied, 48% accepted, 25% of those accepted enrolled. **Transfer Admission Requirements:** *Items required:* high school transcript, college transcript. Lowest grade transferable C. **General Admission Information:** Application fee $50. Priority application deadline December 15. Admission may be deferred for a maximum of 1 year. Credit and/or placement offered for CEEB Advanced Placement tests.

COSTS AND FINANCIAL AID

In-state tuition $4,762. Out-of-state tuition $9,692. Room & board $6,098. Required fees $1,290. Average book expense $700. **Required Forms and Deadlines:** FAFSA. No deadline for regular filing. Priority filing deadline March 15. **Notification of Awards:** Applicants will be notified of awards on a rolling basis beginning on or about February 15. **Types of Aid:** *Need-based scholarships/grants:* Pell, SEOG, state scholarships/grants, the school's own gift aid. *Loans:* Direct Subsidized Stafford, Direct Unsubsidized Stafford, Direct PLUS, Federal Perkins, state loans, college/university loans from institutional funds, Other educational loans. **Student Employment:** Federal Work-Study Program available. Institutional employment available. Off-campus job opportunities are good. **Financial Aid Statistics:** 49% freshmen, 43% undergrads receive some form of aid. Average freshman grant $6,065. Average freshman loan $3,923. **Financial Aid Phone:** 732-932-7057.

RUTGERS UNIVERSITY—SCHOOL OF ENGINEERING

65 Davidson Road, Piscataway, NJ 08854-8097
Phone: 732-932-4636 **E-mail:** admissions@asb-ugadm.rutgers.edu **CEEB Code:** 2765
Fax: 732-445-0237 **Web:** www.rutgers.edu **ACT Code:** 2592

This public school was founded in 1914. It has a 2,695-acre campus.

STUDENTS AND FACULTY

Enrollment: 2,190. **Student Body:** Male 78%, female 22%, out-of-state 9%, international 6% (39 countries represented). **Ethnic Representation:** African American 7%, Asian 29%, Caucasian 51%, Hispanic 7%. **Faculty:** Student/faculty ratio 15:1. 139 full-time faculty, 97% hold PhDs. 70% faculty teach undergrads.

ACADEMICS

Degrees: Bachelor's. **Academic Requirements:** General education including some course work in English (including composition), humanities, mathematics, sciences (biological or physical), social science. **Disciplines with Highest Percentage of Degrees Awarded:** Engineering/engineering technology 100%. **Special Study Options:** Cooperative (work-study) program, distance learning, double major, dual enrollment, English as a second language, honors program, internships, liberal arts/career combination, student-designed major, study abroad, 5-year BS/MBA, 8-year BS/MD with University of Dentistry of New Jersey, 5-year dual degree in bioresource engineering with Cook College, 5-year BA/BS.

FACILITIES

Housing: Coed, all-female, all-male, apartments for single students, housing for disabled students, fraternities and/or sororities, cooperative housing. For students who are affiliated with Cook College: language and cultural houses, math/science/engineering house for women, substance-free/wellness house, first-year dorms, and transfer center. **Library Holdings:** 6,362,037 bound volumes. 28,934 periodicals. 5,427,289 microforms. 119,880 audiovisuals. **Special Academic Facilities/Equipment:** Agricultural, art, and geology museums, center for fiber optics materials research, center for ceramics research, center for advanced biotechnology and medicine, center for computer aids to industrial productivity, draw tower lab, massively parellel processor (MPP). **Computers:** *Recommended operating system:* Mac. School-owned computers available for student use.

EXTRACURRICULARS

Activities: Choral groups, concert band, dance, drama/theater, jazz band, literary magazine, marching band, music ensembles, opera, pep band, radio station, student government, student newspaper, student-run film society, symphony orchestra, television station, yearbook. **Organizations:** 400 registered organizations, 7 honor societies, 29 fraternities, 15 sororities. **Athletics (Intercollegiate):** *Men:* baseball, basketball, cheerleading, crew, cross-country, diving, fencing, football, golf, indoor track, lacrosse, soccer, swimming, tennis, track & field, wrestling. *Women:* basketball, cheerleading, crew, cross-country, diving, fencing, field hockey, golf, gymnastics, indoor track, lacrosse, soccer, softball, swimming, tennis, track & field, volleyball.

ADMISSIONS

Selectivity Rating: 84 (of 100). **Freshman Academic Profile:** 35% in top 10% of high school class, 73% in top 25% of high school class, 98% in top 50% of high school class. SAT I Math middle 50% range 610-710. SAT I Verbal middle 50% range 530-630. TOEFL required of all international applicants, minimum TOEFL 550. **Basis for Candidate Selection:** *Very important factors considered include:* class rank, secondary school record, standardized test scores. *Other factors considered include:* essays, extracurricular activities, minority status, recommendations, state residency, talent/ability, volunteer work, work experience. **Freshman Admission Requirements:** High school diploma or GED is required. *Academic units required/recommended:* 16 total required; 4 English required, 4 math required, 2 science required, 2 science lab required, 6 elective required. **Freshman Admission Statistics:** 3,806 applied, 68% accepted, 22% of those accepted enrolled. **Transfer Admission Requirements:** *Items required:* high school transcript, college transcript. Lowest grade transferable C. **General Admission Information:** Application fee $50. Priority application deadline December 15. Admission may be deferred for a maximum of 2 years. Credit and/or placement offered for CEEB Advanced Placement tests.

COSTS AND FINANCIAL AID

In-state tuition $5,286. Out-of-state tuition $10,754. Room & board $6,098. Required fees $1,290. Average book expense $800. **Required Forms and Deadlines:** FAFSA. No deadline for regular filing. Priority filing deadline March 15. **Notification of Awards:** Applicants will be notified of awards on a rolling basis beginning on or about February 15. **Types of Aid:** *Need-based scholarships/grants:* Pell, SEOG, state scholarships/grants, the school's own gift aid. *Loans:* Direct Subsidized Stafford, Direct Unsubsidized Stafford, Direct PLUS, Federal Perkins, state loans, college/university loans from institutional funds, Other Educational Loan. **Student Employment:** Federal Work-Study Program available. Institutional employment available. Off-campus job opportunities are good. **Financial Aid Statistics:** 50% freshmen, 45% undergrads receive some form of aid. Average freshman grant $5,814. **Financial Aid Phone:** 732-932-7057.

RUTGERS UNIVERSITY—UNIVERSITY COLLEGE AT CAMDEN

406 Penn Street, Camden, NJ 08102
Phone: 856-225-6104 **CEEB Code:** 2765
Fax: 856-225-6498 **Web:** www.rutgers.edu **ACT Code:** 2592

This public school was founded in 1927. It has a 25-acre campus.

STUDENTS AND FACULTY

Enrollment: 3,800. **Student Body:** Male 41%, female 59%, out-of-state 4%, international 1% (13 countries represented). **Ethnic Representation:** African American 15%, Asian 7%, Caucasian 68%, Hispanic 6%. **Retention and Graduation:** 82% freshmen return for sophomore year. **Faculty:** Student/faculty ratio 11:1. 222 full-time faculty, 99% hold PhDs. 70% faculty teach undergrads.

ACADEMICS

Degrees: Bachelor's, first professional, master's. **Academic Requirements:** General education including some course work in arts/fine arts, English (including composition), foreign languages, history, humanities, mathematics, sciences (biological or physical), social science. **Classes:** 20-29 students in an average class. 10-19 students in an average lab/discussion section. **Disciplines with Highest Percentage of Degrees Awarded:** Business/marketing 24%, psychology 17%, social sciences and history 16%, protective services/public administration 8%, health professions and related sciences 7%. **Special Study Options:** Accelerated program, cooperative (work-study) program, cross registration, distance learning, double major, dual enrollment, English as a second language, honors program, independent study, liberal arts/career combination, student-designed major, study abroad, teacher certification program, 8-year BA/MD with University of Medicine and Dentistry of New Jersey, 5-year BA/ or BS/MA in criminal justice with School of Criminal Justice-Newark, 2-3 dual bachelors degree with School of Engineering, BA in political science/MPA, BA/MS in biology, BA/MS in chemistry, BA/MA in English, BA/MA in history, BA/MA in liberal studies, BA/MS in mathematics, articulated bachelor's/dentistry program with University of Medicine and Dentistry of New Jersey.

FACILITIES

Housing: Coed, apartments for single students, housing for disabled students. **Library Holdings:** 714,447 bound volumes. 5,189 periodicals. 259,928 microforms. 326 audiovisuals. **Computers:** *Recommended operating system:* Mac. School-owned computers available for student use.

EXTRACURRICULARS

Activities: Drama/theater, literary magazine, radio station, student government, student newspaper, yearbook. **Organizations:** 50 registered organizations, 11 honor societies, 4 fraternities, 4 sororities. **Athletics (Intercollegiate):** *Men:* baseball, basketball, cross-country, golf, soccer, track & field. *Women:* basketball, cross-country, soccer, softball, track & field, volleyball.

ADMISSIONS

Selectivity Rating: 63 (of 100). **Freshman Academic Profile:** 20% in top 10% of high school class, 58% in top 25% of high school class, 97% in top 50% of high school class. SAT I Math middle 50% range 490-590. SAT I Verbal middle 50% range 480-580. TOEFL required of all international applicants, minimum TOEFL 550. **Basis for Candidate Selection:** *Very important factors considered include:* class rank, secondary school record, standardized test scores. *Other factors considered include:* essays, extracurricular activities, geographical residence, minority status, recommendations, volunteer work, work experience. **Freshman Admission Requirements:** High school diploma or GED is required. *Academic units required/recommended:* 16 total required; 4 English required, 3 math required, 4 math recommended, 2 science required, 2 foreign language required, 5 elective required. **Freshman Admission Statistics:** 6,430 applied, 54% accepted, 12% of those accepted enrolled. **Transfer Admission Requirements:** *Items required:* high school transcript, college transcript. **General Admission Information:** Application fee $50. Priority application deadline December 1. Nonfall registration accepted. Credit and/or placement offered for CEEB Advanced Placement tests.

COSTS AND FINANCIAL AID

In-state tuition $5,602. Out-of-state tuition $10,326. Room & board $5,322. Required fees $416. Average book expense $66. **Required Forms and Deadlines:** FAFSA. No deadline for regular filing. Priority filing deadline March 15. **Notification of Awards:** Applicants will be notified of awards on a rolling basis beginning on or about February 1. **Types of Aid:** *Need-based scholarships/grants:* Pell, SEOG, state scholarships/grants, private scholarships, the school's own gift aid, Outside Scholarships. *Loans:* Direct Subsidized Stafford, Direct Unsubsidized Stafford, Direct PLUS, Federal Perkins, state loans, college/university loans from institutional funds, Other Educational Loans. **Student Employment:** Federal Work-Study Program available. Institutional employment available. Off-campus job opportunities are good. **Financial Aid Statistics:** 65% freshmen, 62% undergrads receive some form of aid. **Financial Aid Phone:** 609-225-6039.

RUTGERS UNIVERSITY—UNIVERSITY COLLEGE AT NEW BRUNSWICK

65 Davidson Road, Piscataway, NJ 08854-8097
Phone: 732-932-4636 **CEEB Code:** 2765
Fax: 732-445-0237 **Web:** www.rutgers.edu **ACT Code:** 2592

This public school has a 2,695-acre campus.

STUDENTS AND FACULTY

Enrollment: 28,070. **Student Body:** Male 47%, female 53%, out-of-state 8%, international 3%. **Ethnic Representation:** African American 9%, Asian 20%, Caucasian 58%, Hispanic 8%. **Retention and Graduation:** 88% freshmen return for sophomore year. **Faculty:** Student/faculty ratio 14:1. 1,522 full-time faculty, 98% hold PhDs. 70% faculty teach undergrads.

ACADEMICS

Degrees: Bachelor's, doctoral, first professional, master's. **Academic Requirements:** General education including some course work in arts/fine arts, English (including composition), humanities, mathematics, sciences (biological or physical), social science. **Disciplines with Highest Percentage of Degrees Awarded:** Social sciences and history 24%, psychology 10%, communications/communication technologies 8%, biological life sciences 8%, engineering/engineering technology 7%. **Special Study Options:** Accelerated program, cooperative (work-study) program, cross registration, distance learning, double major, dual enrollment, English as a second language, honors program, independent study, liberal arts/career combination, student-designed major, study abroad, teacher certification program, Washington Semester, 8-year BA/ or BS/MD with University of Medicine and Dentistry of New Jersey, 5-year BA/MBA, 5-year dual degrees in liberal arts and engineering, 5-year BA/ or BS/MPP with Edward J. Bloustein School of Planning and Public Policy, 5-year BA/ or BS/MA in criminal justice with School of Criminal Justice in Newark, 6-year BA in biology/MS in physician assistant, 5-year BA or BS/MEd offered in conjunction with the Graduate School of Education, dual admission to Newark School of Law, BA/ or BS/MPH with Edward J. Bloustein School of Planning and Public Policy, articulated bachelor's/dentistry program with the University of Medicine and Dentistry of New Jersey.

FACILITIES

Housing: Coed, all-female, all-male, apartments for married students, apartments for single students, housing for disabled students, fraternities and/or sororities, cooperative housing, Special-interest housing, language and cultural houses, substance-free house, math/science/engineering house for women, first-year residence, transfer center, residence for single mothers and children. **Library Holdings:** 4,737,147 bound volumes. 17,182 periodicals. 3,280,875 microforms. 91,657 audiovisuals. **Computers:** *Recommended operating system:* Mac. School-owned computers available for student use.

EXTRACURRICULARS

Activities: Choral groups, concert band, dance, drama/theater, jazz band, literary magazine, marching band, music ensembles, opera, pep band, radio station, student government, student newspaper, student-run film society, symphony orchestra, television station, yearbook. **Organizations:** 400 registered organizations, 24 honor societies, 29 fraternities, 15 sororities. **Athletics (Intercollegiate):** *Men:* baseball, basketball, cheerleading, crew, cross-country, diving, fencing, football, golf, indoor track, lacrosse, soccer, swimming, tennis, track & field, wrestling. *Women:* basketball, cheerleading, crew, cross-country, diving, fencing, field hockey, golf, gymnastics, indoor track, lacrosse, soccer, softball, swimming, tennis, track & field, volleyball.

ADMISSIONS

Selectivity Rating: 63 (of 100). **Freshman Academic Profile:** 36% in top 10% of high school class, 75% in top 25% of high school class, 98% in top 50% of high school class. SAT I Math middle 50% range 550-670. SAT I Verbal middle 50% range 520-630. TOEFL required of all international applicants, minimum TOEFL 550. **Basis for Candidate Selection:** *Very important factors considered include:* class rank, interview, secondary school record, standardized test scores, talent/ability. *Other factors considered include:* essays, extracurricular activities, geographical residence, minority status, recommendations, state residency, volunteer work, work experience. **Freshman Admission Requirements:** High school diploma or GED is required. *Academic units required/recommended:* 16 total required; 4 English required, 3 math required, 4 math recommended, 2 science required, 2 foreign language required, 2 foreign language recommended, 5 elective required. **Freshman Admission Statistics:** 26,678 applied, 55% accepted, 34% of those accepted enrolled. **Transfer Admission Requirements:** *Items required:* high school transcript, college transcript. **General Admission Information:** Application fee $50.

Priority application deadline December 1. Nonfall registration accepted. Credit and/or placement offered for CEEB Advanced Placement tests.

COSTS AND FINANCIAL AID

In-state tuition $4,732. Out-of-state tuition $9,626. Room & board $5,314. Required fees $332. Average book expense $650. **Required Forms and Deadlines:** FAFSA. No deadline for regular filing. Priority filing deadline March 15. **Notification of Awards:** Applicants will be notified of awards on a rolling basis beginning on or about February 1. **Types of Aid:** *Need-based scholarships/grants:* Pell, SEOG, state scholarships/grants, private scholarships, the school's own gift aid, Outside Scholarships. *Loans:* Direct Subsidized Stafford, Direct Unsubsidized Stafford, Direct PLUS, Federal Perkins, state loans, college/university loans from institutional funds, Other Educational Loans. **Student Employment:** Federal Work-Study Program available. Institutional employment available. Off-campus job opportunities are good. **Financial Aid Statistics:** 49% freshmen, 47% undergrads receive some form of aid. Average freshman grant $5,828. Average freshman loan $2,928. Average income from on-campus job $1,374. **Financial Aid Phone:** 732-932-7057.

RUTGERS UNIVERSITY—UNIVERSITY COLLEGE AT NEWARK

249 University Avenue, Newark, NJ 07102-1896
Phone: 973-353-5205 **CEEB Code:** 2765
Fax: 973-353-1440 **Web:** www.rutgers.edu **ACT Code:** 2592

This public school was founded in 1930. It has a 36-acre campus.

STUDENTS AND FACULTY

Enrollment: 6,706. **Student Body:** Male 42%, female 58%, out-of-state 9%, international 4% (53 countries represented). **Ethnic Representation:** African American 20%, Asian 21%, Caucasian 31%, Hispanic 18%. **Retention and Graduation:** 84% freshmen return for sophomore year. **Faculty:** Student/faculty ratio 12:1. 382 full-time faculty, 98% hold PhDs. 70% faculty teach undergrads.

ACADEMICS

Degrees: Bachelor's, doctoral, first professional, master's. **Academic Requirements:** General education including some course work in computer literacy, humanities, mathematics, sciences (biological or physical), social science. **Classes:** 10-19 students in an average class. 10-19 students in an average lab/discussion section. **Disciplines with Highest Percentage of Degrees Awarded:** Business/marketing 26%, computer and information sciences 12%, social sciences and history 12%, psychology 11%, health professions and related sciences 10%. **Special Study Options:** Accelerated program, cross registration, distance learning, double major, dual enrollment, English as a second language, honors program, independent study, internships, liberal arts/career combination, student-designed major, study abroad, teacher certification program, 8-year BA/ or BS/MD with University of Medicine and Dentistry of New Jersey, 5-year BA/ or BS/MA in criminal justice, 2+2 and 2+3 in engineering, 5-year BA/MBA, dual admission to School of Law, BA in physics/BS in industrial engineering with New Jersey Institute of Technology, articulated bachelor's/dentistry program with University of Medicine and Dentistry of New Jersey. The Honors College of Rutgers University's Newark College of Arts and Sciences is a four-year program, a college within a college, providing by-invitation-only students with opportunities for enrichment both in and outside of the classroom. Students invited to join the Honors College benefit from small classes with first-rate faculty, co-curricular internships in major corporations and other institutions, and other special options. Reserved dormitory space, a substantial scholarship program, and research assistantships with faculty members combine to make the RU-Newark Honors College experience unique. For additional information, visit the Honors College web site: http://honors.newark.rutgers.edu or call 973-353-5860.

FACILITIES

Housing: Coed, apartments for single students, housing for disabled students, fraternities and/or sororities. **Library Holdings:** 941,103 bound volumes. 6,408 periodicals. 1,464,368 microforms. 34,994 audiovisuals. **Special Academic Facilities/Equipment:** Institute of Jazz Studies, TV/Radio media center, Institute of Animal Behavior, Center for Crime Prevention Studies, Center for Negotiation and Conflict Resolution, Center for Molecular and Behavioral Neuroscience, Center for Nursing Research. **Computers:** *Recommended operating system:* Mac. School-owned computers available for student use.

EXTRACURRICULARS

Activities: Choral groups, drama/theater, literary magazine, radio station, student government, student newspaper, yearbook. **Organizations:** 80 registered organizations, 16 honor societies, 7 fraternities, 7 sororities. **Athletics (Intercollegiate):** *Men:* baseball, basketball, soccer, tennis, volleyball. *Women:* basketball, softball, tennis, volleyball.

ADMISSIONS

Selectivity Rating: 63 (of 100). **Freshman Academic Profile:** 30% in top 10% of high school class, 67% in top 25% of high school class, 99% in top 50% of high school class. SAT I Math middle 50% range 490-600. SAT I Verbal middle 50% range 470-550. TOEFL required of all international applicants, minimum TOEFL 550. **Basis for Candidate Selection:** *Very important factors considered include:* class rank, secondary school record, standardized test scores. *Other factors considered include:* essays, extracurricular activities, geographical residence, minority status, recommendations, state residency, volunteer work, work experience. **Freshman Admission Requirements:** High school diploma or GED is required. *Academic units required/recommended:* 16 total required; 4 English required, 3 math required, 4 math recommended, 2 science required, 2 foreign language required, 5 elective required. **Freshman Admission Statistics:** 9,168 applied, 50% accepted, 19% of those accepted enrolled. **Transfer Admission Requirements:** *Items required:* high school transcript, college transcript. **General Admission Information:** Application fee $50. Priority application deadline December 1. Nonfall registration accepted. Credit and/or placement offered for CEEB Advanced Placement tests.

COSTS AND FINANCIAL AID

In-state tuition $4,262. Out-of-state tuition $8,676. Room & board $5,314. Required fees $416. Average book expense $650. **Required Forms and Deadlines:** FAFSA. No deadline for regular filing. Priority filing deadline March 15. **Notification of Awards:** Applicants will be notified of awards on a rolling basis beginning on or about February 1. **Types of Aid:** *Need-based scholarships/grants:* Pell, SEOG, state scholarships/grants, private scholarships, the school's own gift aid, Other Scholarships. *Loans:* Direct Subsidized Stafford, Direct Unsubsidized Stafford, Direct PLUS, Federal Perkins, state loans, college/university loans from institutional funds, Other Educational Loans. **Student Employment:** Federal Work-Study Program available. Institutional employment available. Off-campus job opportunities are good. **Financial Aid Statistics:** 58% freshmen, 60% undergrads receive some form of aid. Average freshman grant $5,331. Average freshman loan $2,693. **Financial Aid Phone:** 973-353-5357.

SACRED HEART UNIVERSITY

5151 Park Avenue, Fairfield, CT 06432-1000
Phone: 203-371-7880 **E-mail:** enroll@sacredheart.edu **CEEB Code:** 3780
Fax: 203-365-7607 **Web:** www.sacredheart.edu **ACT Code:** 589

This private school, which is affiliated with the Roman Catholic Church, was founded in 1963. It has a 56-acre campus.

STUDENTS AND FACULTY

Enrollment: 4,207. **Student Body:** Male 38%, female 62%, out-of-state 61%, international 1%. **Ethnic Representation:** African American 6%, Asian 1%, Caucasian 87%, Hispanic 5%. **Retention and Graduation:** 81% freshmen return for sophomore year. 47% freshmen graduate within 4 years. 37% grads go on to further study within 1 year. **Faculty:** Student/faculty ratio 13:1. 160 full-time faculty, 76% hold PhDs. 95% faculty teach undergrads.

ACADEMICS

Degrees: Associate's, bachelor's, certificate, first professional, master's, post-bachelor's certificate, post-master's certificate, terminal, transfer. **Academic Requirements:** General education including some course work in arts/fine arts, computer literacy, English (including composition), history, humanities, mathematics, philosophy, sciences (biological or physical), social science. **Classes:** 10-19 students in an average class. **Disciplines with Highest Percentage of Degrees Awarded:** Business/marketing 33%, psychology 17%, health professions and related sciences 11%, social sciences and history 7%, protective services/public administration 6%. **Special Study Options:** Accelerated program, cooperative (work-study) program, cross registration, distance learning, double major, English as a second language, student exchange program (domestic), honors program, independent study, internships, liberal arts/career combination, student-designed major, study abroad, teacher certification program, weekend college, off-campus study, semester in Luxembourg, combined degree program in physical therapy and occupational therapy, 3-2 bachelor's/MBA.

FACILITIES

Housing: Coed, apartments for single students, housing for disabled students, graduate student housing, thematic floors. **Library Holdings:** 98,000 bound volumes. 4,100 periodicals. 46,985 microforms. 1,063 audiovisuals. **Special Academic Facilities/Equipment:** WHRT student radio station, WSHU National Public Radio, Edgerton Center for the Performing Arts, Gallery of Contemporary Art. **Computers:** *Recommended operating system:* Windows NT/2000. School-owned computers available for student use.

EXTRACURRICULARS

Activities: Choral groups, concert band, dance, drama/theater, jazz band, literary magazine, marching band, music ensembles, musical theater, pep band, radio station, student government, student newspaper, student-run film society, yearbook. **Organizations:** 48 registered organizations, 11 honor societies, 3 religious organizations, 4 fraternities (7% men join), 6 sororities (6% women join). **Athletics (Intercollegiate):** *Men:* baseball, basketball, crew, cross-country, fencing, football, golf, ice hockey, indoor track, lacrosse, rugby, soccer, tennis, track & field, volleyball, wrestling. *Women:* basketball, cheerleading, crew, cross-country, diving, equestrian, fencing, field hockey, golf, ice hockey, indoor track, lacrosse, rugby, soccer, softball, swimming, tennis, track & field, volleyball.

ADMISSIONS

Selectivity Rating: 64 (of 100). **Freshman Academic Profile:** Average high school GPA 3.2. 18% in top 10% of high school class, 42% in top 25% of high school class, 80% in top 50% of high school class. Average SAT I Math 535, SAT I Math middle 50% range 500-580. Average SAT I Verbal 525, SAT I Verbal middle 50% range 490-570. TOEFL required of all international applicants, minimum TOEFL 500. **Basis for Candidate Selection:** *Very important factors considered include:* character/personal qualities, class rank, secondary school record, standardized test scores. *Important factors considered include:* essays, extracurricular activities, interview, recommendations, volunteer work. *Other factors considered include:* alumni/ae relation, geographical residence, minority status, religious affiliation/commitment, state residency, talent/ability, work experience. **Freshman Admission Requirements:** High school diploma or GED is required. *Academic units required/recommended:* 18 total required; 24 total recommended; 4 English required, 4 English recommended, 3 math required, 4 math recommended, 3 science required, 4 science recommended, 1 science lab required, 2 science lab recommended, 2 foreign language required, 4 foreign language recommended, 3 social studies required, 4 social studies recommended, 3 history required, 4 history recommended. **Freshman Admission Statistics:** 4,642 applied, 69% accepted, 31% of those accepted enrolled. **Transfer Admission Requirements:** *Items required:* high school transcript, college transcript, essay. Minimum high school GPA of 3.0 required. Minimum college GPA of 2.5 required. Lowest grade transferable C. **General Admission Information:** Application fee $50. Priority application deadline March 15. Early decision application deadline October 1. Nonfall registration accepted. Admission may be deferred for a maximum of 1 year. Credit and/or placement offered for CEEB Advanced Placement tests.

COSTS AND FINANCIAL AID

Tuition $19,260. Room & board $8,730. Average book expense $700. **Required Forms and Deadlines:** FAFSA and CSS/Financial Aid PROFILE. No deadline for regular filing. Priority filing deadline February 15. **Notification of Awards:** Applicants will be notified of awards on a rolling basis beginning on or about March 1. **Types of Aid:** *Need-based scholarships/grants:* Pell, SEOG, state scholarships/grants, private scholarships, the school's own gift aid, Federal Nursing. *Loans:* FFEL Subsidized Stafford, FFEL Unsubsidized Stafford, FFEL PLUS, Federal Perkins, state loans. **Student Employment:** Federal Work-Study Program available. Institutional employment available. Off-campus job opportunities are excellent. **Financial Aid Statistics:** 75% freshmen, 70% undergrads receive some form of aid. Average freshman grant $6,446. Average freshman loan $3,638. Average income from on-campus job $1,600. **Financial Aid Phone:** 203-371-7980.

SAGINAW VALLEY STATE UNIVERSITY

7400 Bay Road, University Center, MI 48710
Phone: 989-964-4200 **E-mail:** admissions@svsu.edu **CEEB Code:** 1766
Fax: 989-790-0180 **Web:** www.svsu.edu **ACT Code:** 2057

This public school was founded in 1963. It has a 782-acre campus.

STUDENTS AND FACULTY

Enrollment: 7,506. **Student Body:** Male 40%, female 60%, out-of-state 1%, international 3% (46 countries represented). **Ethnic Representation:** African American 6%, Asian 1%, Caucasian 86%, Hispanic 2%. **Retention and Graduation:** 63% freshmen return for sophomore year. 5% freshmen graduate within 4 years. **Faculty:** Student/faculty ratio 29:1. 233 full-time faculty, 77% hold PhDs. 100% faculty teach undergrads.

ACADEMICS

Degrees: Bachelor's, master's, post-master's certificate. **Academic Requirements:** General education including some course work in English (including composition), history, mathematics, philosophy, sciences (biological or physical), social science. **Classes:** 20-29 students in an average class. 10-19 students in an average lab/discussion section. **Majors with Highest Enrollment:** Elementary education and teaching; secondary education and teaching; criminal justice/safety studies. **Disciplines with Highest Percentage of Degrees Awarded:** Education 24%, business/marketing 16%, protective services/public administration 13%, health professions and related sciences 8%, social sciences and history 7%. **Special Study Options:** Accelerated program, cooperative (work-study) program, distance learning, double major, dual enrollment, English as a second language, honors program, independent study, internships, student-designed major, study abroad, teacher certification program.

FACILITIES

Housing: Coed, apartments for married students, apartments for single students, housing for disabled students. **Library Holdings:** 631,455 bound volumes. 1,113 periodicals. 360,554 microforms. 22,713 audiovisuals. **Special Academic Facilities/Equipment:** Sculpture gallery, fine arts center, center for health and physical education, independent testing lab, center for economic and business research, applied technology research center. **Computers:** School-owned computers available for student use.

EXTRACURRICULARS

Activities: Choral groups, concert band, drama/theater, jazz band, literary magazine, marching band, music ensembles, musical theater, pep band, student government, student newspaper. **Organizations:** 75 registered organizations, 3 honor societies, 4 religious organizations, 5 fraternities (2% men join), 3 sororities (2% women join). **Athletics (Intercollegiate):** *Men:* baseball, basketball, cross-country, football, golf, soccer, track & field. *Women:* basketball, cross-country, soccer, softball, tennis, track & field, volleyball.

ADMISSIONS

Selectivity Rating: 70 (of 100). **Freshman Academic Profile:** Average high school GPA 3.2. Average ACT 21, ACT middle 50% range 18-24. TOEFL required of all international applicants, minimum TOEFL 500. **Basis for Candidate Selection:** *Very important factors considered include:* secondary school record, standardized test scores. *Other factors considered include:* recommendations. **Freshman Admission Requirements:** High school diploma or GED is required. *Academic units required/recommended:* 4 English required, 4 English recommended, 3 math required, 4 math recommended, 2 science required, 4 science recommended, 2 foreign language recommended, 3 social studies required, 4 social studies recommended. **Freshman Admission Statistics:** 3,219 applied, 88% accepted, 41% of those accepted enrolled. **Transfer Admission Requirements:** *Items required:* college transcript. Minimum college GPA of 2.0 required. Lowest grade transferable C-. **General Admission Information:** Application fee $25. Nonfall registration accepted. Admission may be deferred for a maximum of 1 year. Credit and/or placement offered for CEEB Advanced Placement tests.

COSTS AND FINANCIAL AID

In-state tuition $4,382. Out-of-state tuition $9,288. Room & board $5,485. Required fees $558. Average book expense $800. **Required Forms and Deadlines:** FAFSA and state aid form. Priority filing deadline February 14. **Notification of Awards:** Applicants will be notified of awards on a rolling basis beginning on or about March 20. **Types of Aid:** *Need-based scholarships/grants:* Pell, SEOG, state scholarships/grants, private scholarships, the school's own gift aid. *Loans:* Direct Subsidized Stafford, Direct Unsubsidized Stafford. **Student Employment:** Federal Work-Study Program available. Institutional employment available. Off-campus job opportunities are good. **Financial Aid Statistics:** 39% freshmen, 35% undergrads receive some form of aid. Average freshman grant $5,071. Average freshman loan $2,686. Average income from on-campus job $1,532. **Financial Aid Phone:** 989-964-4103.

SAINT AMBROSE UNIVERSITY

518 West Locust Street, Davenport, IA 52803-2898
Phone: 563-333-6300 **E-mail:** admit@sau.edu/ **CEEB Code:** 6617
Fax: 563-333-6297 **Web:** www.sau.edu **ACT Code:** 1352

This private school, which is affiliated with the Roman Catholic Church, was founded in 1882. It has a 20-acre campus.

STUDENTS AND FACULTY

Enrollment: 2,454. **Student Body:** Male 41%, female 59%, out-of-state 37%, international 1% (25 countries represented). **Ethnic Representation:** African American 4%, Asian 1%, Caucasian 90%, Hispanic 5%. **Retention and Graduation:** 81% freshmen return for sophomore year. 55% freshmen graduate within 4 years. 25% grads go on to further study within 1 year. 8% grads pursue business degrees. 3% grads pursue law degrees. 2% grads pursue medical degrees. **Faculty:** Student/faculty ratio 17:1. 149 full-time faculty, 75% hold PhDs. 96% faculty teach undergrads.

ACADEMICS

Degrees: Bachelor's, certificate, doctoral, master's, post-bachelor's certificate, post-master's certificate. **Academic Requirements:** General education including some course work in arts/fine arts, English (including composition), foreign languages, history, humanities, mathematics, philosophy, sciences (biological or physical), social science, communication and theology and information literacy. **Classes:** 10-19 students in an average class. 10-19 students in an average lab/discussion section. **Majors with Highest Enrollment:** Business administration/management; elementary education and teaching; biology/biological sciences, general. **Disciplines with Highest Percentage of Degrees Awarded:** Business/marketing 24%, education 16%, psychology 13%, computer and information sciences 10%, communications/communication technologies 9%. **Special Study Options:** Accelerated program, cooperative (work-study) program, distance learning, double major, independent study, internships, liberal arts/career combination, student-designed major, study abroad, teacher certification program.

FACILITIES

Housing: Coed, all-female, all-male, apartments for single students, housing for disabled students. **Library Holdings:** 135,920 bound volumes. 735 periodicals. 6,465 microforms. 2,930 audiovisuals. **Special Academic Facilities/Equipment:** Art gallery, observatory, language lab, and distance learning classrooms (2). **Computers:** *Recommended operating system:* Windows 95. School-owned computers available for student use.

EXTRACURRICULARS

Activities: Choral groups, concert band, dance, drama/theater, jazz band, literary magazine, music ensembles, musical theater, pep band, radio station, student government, student newspaper, symphony orchestra, television station. **Organizations:** 42 registered organizations, 8 honor societies, 2 religious organizations. **Athletics (Intercollegiate):** *Men:* baseball, basketball, cheerleading, cross-country, football, golf, indoor track, soccer, tennis, track & field, volleyball. *Women:* basketball, cheerleading, cross-country, golf, indoor track, soccer, softball, tennis, track & field, volleyball.

ADMISSIONS

Selectivity Rating: 73 (of 100). **Freshman Academic Profile:** Average high school GPA 3.1. 13% in top 10% of high school class, 32% in top 25% of high school class, 65% in top 50% of high school class. 55% from public high schools. Average ACT 22, ACT middle 50% range 18-24. TOEFL required of all international applicants, minimum TOEFL 500. **Basis for Candidate Selection:** *Very important factors considered include:* class rank, secondary school record, standardized test scores. *Important factors considered include:* alumni/ae relation, character/personal qualities, recommendations. *Other factors considered include:* extracurricular activities, interview, talent/ability, volunteer work. **Freshman Admission Requirements:** High school diploma or GED is required. *Academic units required/recommended:* 18 total recommended; 4 English recommended, 3 math recommended, 2 science recommended, 2 science lab recommended, 1 foreign language recommended, 1 social studies recommended, 1 history recommended, 4 elective recommended. **Freshman Admission Statistics:** 1,150 applied, 85% accepted, 40% of those accepted enrolled. **Transfer Admission Requirements:** *Items required:* high school transcript, college transcript, standardized test score statement of good standing from prior school. Minimum high school GPA of 2.5 required. Minimum college GPA of 2.0 required. Lowest grade transferable D. **General Admission Information:** Application fee $25. Nonfall registration accepted. Admission may be deferred. Credit offered for CEEB Advanced Placement tests.

COSTS AND FINANCIAL AID

Tuition $16,540. Room & board $5,840. Required fees $0. Average book expense $756. **Required Forms and Deadlines:** FAFSA. No deadline for regular filing. Priority filing deadline March 15. **Notification of Awards:** Applicants will be notified of awards on a rolling basis beginning on or about February 1. **Types of Aid:** *Need-based scholarships/grants:* Pell, SEOG, state scholarships/grants, private scholarships, the school's own gift aid. *Loans:* FFEL Subsidized Stafford, FFEL Unsubsidized Stafford, FFEL PLUS, Federal Perkins, state loans. **Student Employment:** Federal Work-Study Program available. Institutional employment available. Off-campus job opportunities are excellent. **Financial Aid Statistics:** 74% freshmen, 73% undergrads receive some form of aid. Average freshman grant $7,550. Average freshman loan $4,065. Average income from on-campus job $1,866. **Financial Aid Phone:** 563-333-6314.

SAINT ANDREWS PRESBYTERIAN COLLEGE

1700 Dogwood Mile, Laurinburg, NC 28352
Phone: 910-277-5555 **E-mail:** admissions@sapc.edu **CEEB Code:** 5214
Fax: 910-277-5087 **Web:** www.sapc.edu **ACT Code:** 3146

This private school, which is affiliated with the Presbyterian Church, was founded in 1958. It has a 600-acre campus.

STUDENTS AND FACULTY

Enrollment: 613. **Student Body:** Male 38%, female 62%, out-of-state 43%, international 4% (20 countries represented). **Ethnic Representation:** African American 11%, Asian 2%, Caucasian 85%, Hispanic 1%, Native American 1%. **Retention and Graduation:** 63% freshmen return for sophomore year. 30% freshmen graduate within 4 years. 16% grads go on to further study within 1 year. 21% grads pursue law degrees. 1% grads pursue medical degrees. **Faculty:** Student/faculty ratio 9:1. 32 full-time faculty, 78% hold PhDs. 100% faculty teach undergrads.

ACADEMICS

Degrees: Bachelor's. **Academic Requirements:** General education including some course work in arts/fine arts, computer literacy, English (including composition), foreign languages, humanities, mathematics, sciences (biological or physical), social science. **Classes:** 10-19 students in an average class. 10-19 students in an average lab/discussion section. **Majors with Highest Enrollment:** Business administration/management; elementary education and teaching; English language and literature, general. **Disciplines with Highest Percentage of Degrees Awarded:** Business/marketing 31%, education 13%, English 10%, psychology 7%, communications/communication technologies 6%. **Special Study Options:** Double major, honors program, internships, student-designed major, study abroad, teacher certification program, weekend college.

FACILITIES

Housing: Coed, all-female, all-male, housing for disabled students, alcohol-free residence halls, adaptive living environment for disabled students. **Library Holdings:** 110,000 bound volumes. 434 periodicals. 13,848 microforms. 711 audiovisuals. **Special Academic Facilities/Equipment:** Art gallery, anthropology museum, science lab, electron microscopy center with three electron microscopes, psychology lab, artronics graphics computer, Scottish Heritage Foundation. **Computers:** *Recommended operating system:* Windows NT/2000. School-owned computers available for student use.

EXTRACURRICULARS

Activities: Choral groups, dance, drama/theater, literary magazine, musical theater, student government, student newspaper, yearbook. **Organizations:** 30 registered organizations, 3 honor societies, 1 religious organization. **Athletics (Intercollegiate):** *Men:* baseball, basketball, cross-country, equestrian, golf, lacrosse, soccer. *Women:* basketball, cross-country, equestrian, soccer, softball, tennis, volleyball.

ADMISSIONS

Selectivity Rating: 66 (of 100). **Freshman Academic Profile:** Average SAT I Math 488, SAT I Math middle 50% range 390-586. Average SAT I Verbal 509, SAT I Verbal middle 50% range 420-620. TOEFL required of all international applicants, minimum TOEFL 500. **Basis for Candidate Selection:** *Very important factors considered include:* standardized test scores. *Other factors considered include:* essays, interview, recommendations. **Freshman Admission Requirements:** High school diploma or GED is required. *Academic units required/recommended:* 11 total required; 4 English recommended, 3 math recommended, 2 science recommended, 2 foreign language recommended, 2 history recommended. **Freshman Admission Statistics:** 459 applied, 89%

accepted, 29% of those accepted enrolled. **Transfer Admission Requirements:** *Items required:* high school transcript, college transcript. Minimum college GPA of 2.0 required. Lowest grade transferable C-. **General Admission Information:** Application fee $30. Nonfall registration accepted. Admission may be deferred for a maximum of 1 year. Credit offered for CEEB Advanced Placement tests.

COSTS AND FINANCIAL AID

Tuition $14,540. Room & board $5,410. Required fees $220. Average book expense $800. **Required Forms and Deadlines:** FAFSA and state aid form. No deadline for regular filing. Priority filing deadline May 1. **Notification of Awards:** Applicants will be notified of awards on a rolling basis beginning on or about March 1. **Types of Aid:** *Need-based scholarships/grants:* Pell, SEOG, state scholarships/grants, private scholarships, the school's own gift aid. *Loans:* FFEL Subsidized Stafford, FFEL Unsubsidized Stafford, FFEL PLUS, Federal Perkins, state loans. **Student Employment:** Federal Work-Study Program available. Institutional employment available. Off-campus job opportunities are fair. **Financial Aid Statistics:** 74% freshmen, 81% undergrads receive some form of aid. Average freshman grant $6,600. Average freshman loan $2,590. **Financial Aid Phone:** 910-277-5560.

SAINT ANSELM COLLEGE

100 Saint Anselm Drive, Manchester, NH 03102-1310
Phone: 603-641-7500 **E-mail:** admissions@anselm.edu **CEEB Code:** 3748
Fax: 603-641-7550 **Web:** www.anselm.edu **ACT Code:** 2522

This private school, which is affiliated with the Roman Catholic Church, was founded in 1889. It has a 404-acre campus.

STUDENTS AND FACULTY

Enrollment: 1,956. **Student Body:** Male 43%, female 57%, out-of-state 77%, international 1% (15 countries represented). **Ethnic Representation:** Asian 1%, Caucasian 96%, Hispanic 1%. **Retention and Graduation:** 83% freshmen return for sophomore year. 14% grads go on to further study within 1 year. 1% grads pursue business degrees. 3% grads pursue law degrees. 1% grads pursue medical degrees. **Faculty:** Student/faculty ratio 14:1. 120 full-time faculty, 93% hold PhDs. 100% faculty teach undergrads.

ACADEMICS

Degrees: Bachelor's. **Academic Requirements:** General education including some course work in English (including composition), foreign languages, humanities, philosophy, sciences (biological or physical), theology. **Classes:** 10-19 students in an average class. 10-19 students in an average lab/discussion section. **Majors with Highest Enrollment:** Nursing; business administration/management; psychology, general. **Disciplines with Highest Percentage of Degrees Awarded:** Business/marketing 21%, social sciences and history 17%, psychology 12%, health professions and related sciences 11%, protective services/public administration 10%. **Special Study Options:** Cross registration, dual enrollment, student exchange program (domestic), honors program, independent study, internships, liberal arts/career combination, study abroad, teacher certification program.

FACILITIES

Housing: All-female, all-male, apartments for single students, housing for disabled students. **Library Holdings:** 222,000 bound volumes. 3,900 periodicals. 66,000 microforms. 8,000 audiovisuals. **Special Academic Facilities/Equipment:** Chapel Art Center, New Hampshire Institute of Politics, Izart Observatory, Koonz Theatre, Comisky Studio (Fine Arts), Poisson Hall. **Computers:** School-owned computers available for student use.

EXTRACURRICULARS

Activities: Choral groups, dance, drama/theater, jazz band, literary magazine, pep band, radio station, student government, student newspaper, television station, yearbook. **Organizations:** 74 registered organizations, 11 honor societies, 7 religious organizations. **Athletics (Intercollegiate):** *Men:* baseball, basketball, cross-country, football, golf, ice hockey, lacrosse, skiing (alpine), soccer, tennis. *Women:* basketball, cross-country, field hockey, lacrosse, skiing (alpine), soccer, softball, tennis, volleyball.

ADMISSIONS

Selectivity Rating: 86 (of 100). **Freshman Academic Profile:** Average high school GPA 3.1. 14% in top 10% of high school class, 47% in top 25% of high school class, 87% in top 50% of high school class. 65% from public high schools. Average SAT I Math 556, SAT I Math middle 50% range 510-600. Average SAT I Verbal 551, SAT I Verbal middle 50% range 510-600. Average ACT 23, ACT middle 50% range 21-25. TOEFL required of all international applicants, minimum TOEFL 550. **Basis for Candidate Selection:** *Very important factors considered include:* character/personal qualities, secondary school record. *Important factors considered include:* class rank, essays, recommendations, standardized test scores, talent/ability. *Other factors considered include:* alumni/ae relation, extracurricular activities, geographical residence, interview, minority status, volunteer work, work experience. **Freshman Admission Requirements:** High school diploma or GED is required. *Academic units required/recommended:* 18 total required; 20 total recommended; 4 English required, 3 math required, 4 math recommended, 3 science required, 4 science recommended, 3 science lab required, 2 foreign language required, 4 foreign language recommended, 2 social studies required, 1 history required, 2 history recommended, 3 elective required. **Freshman Admission Statistics:** 2,907 applied, 73% accepted, 27% of those accepted enrolled. **Transfer Admission Requirements:** *Items required:* high school transcript, college transcript, essay, standardized test score statement of good standing from prior school. Minimum high school GPA of 2.0 required. Minimum college GPA of 2.5 required. Lowest grade transferable C. **General Admission Information:** Application fee $50. Early decision application deadline December 1. Nonfall registration accepted. Admission may be deferred for a maximum of 1 year. Credit and/or placement offered for CEEB Advanced Placement tests.

COSTS AND FINANCIAL AID

Tuition $19,460. Room & board $7,350. Required fees $520. Average book expense $750. **Required Forms and Deadlines:** FAFSA, CSS/Financial Aid PROFILE and Federal tax returns for parent(s) and student. Priority filing deadline March 1. **Notification of Awards:** Applicants will be notified of awards on a rolling basis beginning on or about March 10. **Types of Aid:** *Need-based scholarships/grants:* Pell, SEOG, state scholarships/grants, private scholarships, the school's own gift aid. *Loans:* FFEL Subsidized Stafford, FFEL Unsubsidized Stafford, FFEL PLUS, Federal Perkins, GATE student loans. **Student Employment:** Federal Work-Study Program available. Institutional employment available. Off-campus job opportunities are excellent. **Financial Aid Statistics:** 91% freshmen, 82% undergrads receive some form of aid. Average freshman grant $7,904. Average freshman loan $2,401. Average income from on-campus job $630. **Financial Aid Phone:** 603-641-7110.

See page 1176.

SAINT AUGUSTINE'S COLLEGE

1315 Oakwood Avenue, Raleigh, NC 27610
Phone: 919-516-4016 **E-mail:** admissions@st-aug.edu
Fax: 919-516-5805 **Web:** www.st-aug.edu **ACT Code:** 3152

This private school, which is affiliated with the Episcopal Church, was founded in 1867. It has a 105-acre campus.

STUDENTS AND FACULTY

Enrollment: 1,502. **Student Body:** Male 48%, female 52%, out-of-state 44%, international 6% (22 countries represented). **Ethnic Representation:** African American 99%. **Retention and Graduation:** 62% freshmen return for sophomore year. 13% freshmen graduate within 4 years. 27% grads go on to further study within 1 year. 4% grads pursue business degrees. 2% grads pursue law degrees. **Faculty:** Student/faculty ratio 16:1. 76 full-time faculty, 65% hold PhDs. 100% faculty teach undergrads.

ACADEMICS

Degrees: Bachelor's. **Academic Requirements:** General education including some course work in arts/fine arts, computer literacy, English (including composition), foreign languages, history, humanities, mathematics, philosophy, sciences (biological or physical), social science. **Classes:** 10-19 students in an average class. 10-19 students in an average lab/discussion section. **Majors with Highest Enrollment:** Business administration/management; computer and information sciences, general; criminal justice/law enforcement administration. **Disciplines with Highest Percentage of Degrees Awarded:** Business/marketing 43%, social sciences and history 10%, parks and recreation 9%, computer and information sciences 8%, communications/communication technologies 8%. **Special Study Options:** Accelerated program, cooperative (work-study) program, cross registration, double major, honors program, independent study, internships, liberal arts/career combination, teacher certification program, weekend college.

FACILITIES

Housing: All-female, all-male. **Library Holdings:** 85,500 bound volumes. 300 periodicals. 500 microforms. 300 audiovisuals. **Special Academic Facilities/Equipment:** Radio & TV Station. **Computers:** *Recommended operating system:* Windows NT/2000. School-owned computers available for student use.

EXTRACURRICULARS

Activities: Choral groups, concert band, dance, drama/theater, jazz band, music ensembles, musical theater, pep band, radio station, student government, student newspaper, student-run film society, symphony orchestra, television station, yearbook. **Organizations:** 45 registered organizations, 8 honor societies, 1 religious organization, 4 fraternities (6% men join), 4 sororities (12% women join). **Athletics (Intercollegiate):** *Men:* baseball, basketball, cross-country, football, golf, indoor track, tennis, track & field. *Women:* basketball, cheerleading, cross-country, indoor track, softball, tennis, track & field, volleyball.

ADMISSIONS

Selectivity Rating: 71 (of 100). **Freshman Academic Profile:** Average high school GPA 2.5. 4% in top 10% of high school class, 16% in top 25% of high school class, 37% in top 50% of high school class. 95% from public high schools. Average SAT I Math 420, SAT I Math middle 50% range 210-690. Average SAT I Verbal 420, SAT I Verbal middle 50% range 260-670. Average ACT 17, ACT middle 50% range 15-23. TOEFL required of all international applicants, minimum TOEFL 500. **Basis for Candidate Selection:** *Very important factors considered include:* secondary school record. *Important factors considered include:* character/personal qualities, minority status, recommendations, state residency, talent/ability. *Other factors considered include:* alumni/ae relation, class rank, essays, extracurricular activities, geographical residence, interview, religious affiliation/commitment, standardized test scores, volunteer work, work experience. **Freshman Admission Requirements:** High school diploma or GED is required. *Academic units required/recommended:* 20 total required; 4 English required, 3 math required, 2 science required, 2 science lab recommended, 2 social studies required, 9 elective required. **Freshman Admission Statistics:** 1,287 applied, 66% accepted, 53% of those accepted enrolled. **Transfer Admission Requirements:** *Items required:* high school transcript, college transcript, standardized test score statement of good standing from prior school. Minimum high school GPA of 2.0 required. Minimum college GPA of 2.0 required. Lowest grade transferable C. **General Admission Information:** Application fee $25. Regular application deadline July 1. Nonfall registration accepted. Admission may be deferred for a maximum of 2 years. Credit offered for CEEB Advanced Placement tests.

COSTS AND FINANCIAL AID

Tuition $6,030. Room & board $4,960. Required fees $2,250. Average book expense $700. **Required Forms and Deadlines:** FAFSA and institution's own financial aid form. Financial aid filing deadline June 1. Priority filing deadline April 15. **Types of Aid:** *Need-based scholarships/grants:* Pell, SEOG, state scholarships/grants, private scholarships, the school's own gift aid, United Negro College Fund. *Loans:* FFEL Subsidized Stafford, FFEL Unsubsidized Stafford, FFEL PLUS, Federal Perkins. **Student Employment:** Federal Work-Study Program available. Institutional employment available. Off-campus job opportunities are excellent. **Financial Aid Statistics:** 87% freshmen, 89% undergrads receive some form of aid. Average freshman grant $5,025. Average freshman loan $4,942. Average income from on-campus job $1,000. **Financial Aid Phone:** 919-516-4133.

ST. BONAVENTURE UNIVERSITY

$$$

PO Box D, St. Bonaventure, NY 14778
Phone: 716-375-2400 **E-mail:** admissions@sbu.edu **CEEB Code:** 2793
Fax: 716-375-4005 **Web:** www.sbu.edu **ACT Code:** 2882

This private school, which is affiliated with the Roman Catholic Church, was founded in 1858. It has a 500-acre campus.

STUDENTS AND FACULTY

Enrollment: 2,229. **Student Body:** Male 46%, female 54%, out-of-state 21%. **Retention and Graduation:** 85% freshmen return for sophomore year. 57% freshmen graduate within 4 years. 30% grads go on to further study within 1 year. 7% grads pursue business degrees. 4% grads pursue law degrees. 2% grads pursue medical degrees. **Faculty:** Student/faculty ratio 15:1. 152 full-time faculty, 78% hold PhDs. 98% faculty teach undergrads.

ACADEMICS

Degrees: Bachelor's, master's, post-bachelor's certificate, post-master's certificate. **Academic Requirements:** General education including some course work in arts/fine arts, English (including composition), foreign languages, history, humanities, mathematics, philosophy, sciences (biological or physical), social science. **Classes:** 10-19 students in an average class. 10-19 students in an average lab/discussion section. **Majors with Highest Enrollment:** Journalism; elementary education and teaching; psychology, general. **Disciplines with Highest Percentage of Degrees Awarded:** Business/marketing 25%, education 22%, communications/communication technologies 14%, social sciences and history 13%, psychology 7%. **Special Study Options:** Accelerated program, cross registration, distance learning, double major, dual enrollment, English as a second language, student exchange program (domestic), honors program, independent study, internships, liberal arts/career combination, student-designed major, study abroad, teacher certification program, weekend college.

FACILITIES

Housing: Coed, all-female, all-male, apartments for single students, housing for disabled students. **Library Holdings:** 287,622 bound volumes. 1,584 periodicals. 630 microforms. 8,891 audiovisuals. **Special Academic Facilities/Equipment:** Quick Center for the Arts, digital conferencing and media center, Franciscan Center for Social Concern, Franciscan Institute. **Computers:** *Recommended operating system:* Windows NT/2000. School-owned computers available for student use.

EXTRACURRICULARS

Activities: Choral groups, concert band, dance, drama/theater, jazz band, literary magazine, music ensembles, pep band, radio station, student government, student newspaper, television station, yearbook. **Organizations:** 39 registered organizations, 3 honor societies, 6 religious organizations. **Athletics (Intercollegiate):** *Men:* baseball, basketball, cross-country, diving, golf, soccer, swimming, tennis. *Women:* basketball, cross-country, diving, lacrosse, soccer, softball, swimming, tennis.

ADMISSIONS

Selectivity Rating: 77 (of 100). **Freshman Academic Profile:** Average high school GPA 3.1. 12% in top 10% of high school class, 35% in top 25% of high school class, 70% in top 50% of high school class. 71% from public high schools. Average SAT I Math 531, SAT I Math middle 50% range 480-580. Average SAT I Verbal 523, SAT I Verbal middle 50% range 480-570. Average ACT 22, ACT middle 50% range 20-25. TOEFL required of all international applicants, minimum TOEFL 550. **Basis for Candidate Selection:** *Very important factors considered include:* character/personal qualities, interview, recommendations, secondary school record. *Important factors considered include:* essays, extracurricular activities, standardized test scores, talent/ability, volunteer work. *Other factors considered include:* alumni/ae relation, class rank, work experience. **Freshman Admission Requirements:** High school diploma or GED is required. *Academic units required/recommended:* 19 total recommended; 4 English required, 4 English recommended, 3 math required, 3 math recommended, 3 science required, 3 science recommended, 3 science lab recommended, 2 foreign language required, 2 foreign language recommended, 4 social studies required, 4 social studies recommended. **Freshman Admission Statistics:** 1,704 applied, 88% accepted, 39% of those accepted enrolled. **Transfer Admission Requirements:** *Items required:* high school transcript, college transcript, statement of good standing from prior school. Minimum college GPA of 2.0 required. Lowest grade transferable D. **General Admission Information:** Application fee $30. Priority application deadline February 1. Regular application deadline April 15. Nonfall registration accepted. Admission may be deferred for a maximum of 1 year. Credit and/or placement offered for CEEB Advanced Placement tests.

COSTS AND FINANCIAL AID

Tuition $16,210. Room & board $6,250. Required fees $635. Average book expense $600. **Required Forms and Deadlines:** FAFSA, institution's own financial aid form and state aid form. Priority filing deadline February 1. **Notification of Awards:** Applicants will be notified of awards on a rolling basis beginning on or about April 1. **Types of Aid:** *Need-based scholarships/grants:* Pell, SEOG, state scholarships/grants, private scholarships, the school's own gift aid. *Loans:* FFEL Subsidized Stafford, FFEL Unsubsidized Stafford, FFEL PLUS, Federal Perkins, college/university loans from institutional funds. **Student Employment:** Federal Work-Study Program available. Institutional employment available. Off-campus job opportunities are excellent. **Financial Aid Statistics:** 74% freshmen, 71% undergrads receive some form of aid. Average freshman grant $8,641. Average freshman loan $3,050. Average income from on-campus job $812. **Financial Aid Phone:** 716-375-2528.

ST. CHARLES BORROMENO SEMINARY

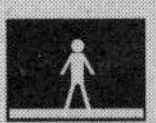

100 East Wynnewood Road, Wynnewood, PA 19096
Phone: 610-785-6271 **E-mail:** cao@adphila.org **CEEB Code:** 2794
Fax: 610-617-9267 **Web:** www.scs.edu **ACT Code:** 5923

This private school, which is affiliated with the Roman Catholic Church, was founded in 1832. It has a 77-acre campus.

STUDENTS AND FACULTY

Enrollment: 266. **Student Body:** Out-of-state 31%, international 1%. **Ethnic Representation:** African American 2%, Asian 10%, Caucasian 85%, Hispanic 3%. **Retention and Graduation:** 67% freshmen return for sophomore year. 43% freshmen graduate within 4 years. 95% grads go on to further study within 1 year. **Faculty:** Student/faculty ratio 7:1. 14 full-time faculty, 50% hold PhDs. 60% faculty teach undergrads.

ACADEMICS

Degrees: Bachelor's, first professional, master's. **Academic Requirements:** General education including some course work in English (including composition), foreign languages, history, humanities, mathematics, philosophy, sciences (biological or physical), social science, theology. **Classes:** 10-19 students in an average class. **Disciplines with Highest Percentage of Degrees Awarded:** Philosophy/religion/theology 100%. **Special Study Options:** Accelerated program, English as a second language, independent study.

FACILITIES

Housing: All-male. **Library Holdings:** 130,485 bound volumes. 564 periodicals. 443 microforms. 8,838 audiovisuals. **Computers:** School-owned computers available for student use.

EXTRACURRICULARS

Activities: Choral groups, drama/theater, student government, student newspaper. **Organizations:** 3 registered organizations, 1 honor society, 2 religious organizations.

ADMISSIONS

Selectivity Rating: 63 (of 100). **Freshman Academic Profile:** 38% in top 10% of high school class, 75% in top 25% of high school class, 88% in top 50% of high school class. 25% from public high schools. Average SAT I Math 570, SAT I Math middle 50% range 450-710. Average SAT I Verbal 575, SAT I Verbal middle 50% range 470-690. **Basis for Candidate Selection:** *Very important factors considered include:* character/personal qualities, essays, interview, recommendations, religious affiliation/commitment, secondary school record. *Important factors considered include:* class rank, standardized test scores. *Other factors considered include:* extracurricular activities, talent/ability, work experience. **Freshman Admission Requirements:** High school diploma or GED is required. *Academic units required/recommended:* 20 total recommended; 4 English recommended, 3 math recommended, 3 science recommended, 2 foreign language recommended, 3 social studies recommended. **Freshman Admission Statistics:** 8 applied, 100% accepted, 100% of those accepted enrolled. **Transfer Admission Requirements:** *Items required:* high school transcript, college transcript, essay. Minimum high school GPA of 2.0 required. Minimum college GPA of 2.0 required. Lowest grade transferable C. **General Admission Information:** Priority application deadline March 1. Regular application deadline July 15. Nonfall registration accepted. Credit and/or placement offered for CEEB Advanced Placement tests.

COSTS AND FINANCIAL AID

Tuition $9,150. Room & board $6,260. Average book expense $800.

SAINT CLOUD STATE UNIVERSITY

720 South 4th Avenue, Saint Cloud, MN 56301-4498
Phone: 320-255-2244 **E-mail:** scsu4u@stcloudstate.edu **CEEB Code:** 6679
Fax: 320-255-2243 **Web:** www.stcloudstate.edu **ACT Code:** 2144

This public school was founded in 1869. It has a 920-acre campus.

STUDENTS AND FACULTY

Enrollment: 14,513. **Student Body:** Male 46%, female 54%, out-of-state 15%, international 5% (84 countries represented). **Ethnic Representation:** African American 1%, Asian 2%, Caucasian 76%, Hispanic 1%, Native American 1%. **Retention and Graduation:** 69% freshmen return for sophomore year. **Faculty:** Student/faculty ratio 19:1. 659 full-time faculty. 98% faculty teach undergrads.

ACADEMICS

Degrees: Associate's, bachelor's, certificate, diploma, first professional certificate, master's, post-bachelor's certificate, post-master's certificate. **Academic Requirements:** General education including some course work in English (including composition), history, humanities, mathematics, philosophy, sciences (biological or physical), social science, wellness and fitness. Computer literacy is infused into the curriculum. **Classes:** 20-29 students in an average class. **Disciplines with Highest Percentage of Degrees Awarded:** Business/marketing 26%, education 21%, social sciences and history 8%, protective services/public administration 7%, communications/communication technologies 6%. **Special Study Options:** Accelerated program, cross registration, distance learning, double major, dual enrollment, English as a second language, honors program, independent study, internships, student-designed major, study abroad, teacher certification program.

FACILITIES

Housing: Coed. **Library Holdings:** 560,251 bound volumes. 1,487 periodicals. 1,647,066 microforms. 33,900 audiovisuals. **Special Academic Facilities/Equipment:** Art and anthropology museums, electron microscope, planetarium, G.I.S. and weather labs.

EXTRACURRICULARS

Activities: Choral groups, concert band, dance, drama/theater, music ensembles, musical theater, opera, radio station, student government, student newspaper, symphony orchestra, television station. **Organizations:** 230 registered organizations, 6 honor societies, 12 religious organizations, 5 fraternities, 4 sororities. **Athletics (Intercollegiate):** *Men:* baseball, basketball, cheerleading, cross-country, diving, football, golf, ice hockey, indoor track, rugby, swimming, tennis, track & field, wrestling. *Women:* basketball, cheerleading, skiing (cross-country), cross-country, diving, golf, ice hockey, indoor track, rugby, skiing (alpine), soccer, softball, swimming, tennis, track & field, volleyball.

ADMISSIONS

Selectivity Rating: 69 (of 100). **Freshman Academic Profile:** 7% in top 10% of high school class, 27% in top 25% of high school class, 70% in top 50% of high school class. 99% from public high schools. Average ACT 21. TOEFL required of all international applicants, minimum TOEFL 500. **Basis for Candidate Selection:** *Very important factors considered include:* class rank, secondary school record. *Important factors considered include:* standardized test scores. *Other factors considered include:* essays, extracurricular activities, minority status, recommendations, talent/ability. **Freshman Admission Requirements:** High school diploma or GED is required. *Academic units required/recommended:* 17 total required; 4 English required, 3 math required, 3 science required, 1 science lab required, 2 foreign language required, 3 social studies required, 1 history required. **Freshman Admission Statistics:** 5,733 applied, 76% accepted, 56% of those accepted enrolled. **Transfer Admission Requirements:** *Items required:* college transcript, statement of good standing from prior school. Minimum college GPA of 2.0 required. Lowest grade transferable C. **General Admission Information:** Application fee $20. Priority application deadline December 15. Regular application deadline June 1. Nonfall registration accepted. Admission may be deferred for a maximum of 2 years. Neither credit nor placement offered for CEEB Advanced Placement tests.

COSTS AND FINANCIAL AID

Average book expense $800. **Required Forms and Deadlines:** FAFSA, institution's own financial aid form, CSS/Financial Aid PROFILE, state aid form and noncustodial (divorced/separated) parent's statement. Financial aid filing deadline May 1. **Notification of Awards:** Applicants will be notified of awards on or about June 15. **Types of Aid:** *Need-based scholarships/grants:* Pell, SEOG, state scholarships/grants, the school's own gift aid. *Loans:* FFEL Subsidized Stafford, FFEL Unsubsidized Stafford, FFEL PLUS, Federal Perkins, state loans, college/university loans from institutional funds. **Student Employment:** Federal Work-Study Program available. Institutional employment available. Off-campus job opportunities are excellent. **Financial Aid Statistics:** 45% freshmen, 43% undergrads receive some form of aid. **Financial Aid Phone:** 320-255-2047.

ST. EDWARD'S UNIVERSITY

3001 South Congress Avenue, Austin, TX 78704-6489
Phone: 512-448-8500 **E-mail:** seu.admit@admin.stewards.edu **CEEB Code:** 6619
Fax: 512-464-8877 **Web:** www.stedwards.edu **ACT Code:** 4156

This private school, which is affiliated with the Roman Catholic Church, was founded in 1885. It has a 160-acre campus.

STUDENTS AND FACULTY

Enrollment: 3,402. **Student Body:** Male 44%, female 56%, out-of-state 5%, international 3% (44 countries represented). **Ethnic Representation:** African American 5%, Asian 3%, Caucasian 59%, Hispanic 30%, Native American 1%. **Retention and Graduation:** 75% freshmen return for sophomore year. 29% freshmen graduate within 4 years. **Faculty:** Student/faculty ratio 15:1. 125 full-time faculty, 78% hold PhDs. 78% faculty teach undergrads.

ACADEMICS

Degrees: Bachelor's, master's, post-bachelor's certificate. **Academic Requirements:** General education including some course work in arts/fine arts, computer literacy, English (including composition), foreign languages, history, humanities, mathematics, philosophy, sciences (biological or physical). **Classes:** 10-19 students in an average class. **Majors with Highest Enrollment:** Business administration/management; communications studies/speech communication and rhetoric; psychology, general. **Disciplines with Highest Percentage of Degrees Awarded:** Liberal arts/general studies 40%, business/marketing 21%, social sciences and history 7%, communications/communication technologies 6%, visual and performing arts 5%. **Special Study Options:** Double major, honors program, internships, liberal arts/career combination, study abroad, teacher certification program.

FACILITIES

Housing: Coed, all-female, all-male, apartments for single students. **Library Holdings:** 150,478 bound volumes. 977 periodicals. 101,435 microforms. 2,251 audiovisuals. **Special Academic Facilities/Equipment:** Fine arts building, photography labs. **Computers:** School-owned computers available for student use.

EXTRACURRICULARS

Activities: Choral groups, dance, drama/theater, literary magazine, musical theater, student government, student newspaper, yearbook. **Organizations:** 78 registered organizations, 6 honor societies, 6 religious organizations. **Athletics (Intercollegiate):** *Men:* baseball, basketball, golf, soccer, tennis. *Women:* basketball, soccer, softball, tennis, volleyball.

ADMISSIONS

Selectivity Rating: 66 (of 100). **Freshman Academic Profile:** 14% in top 10% of high school class, 41% in top 25% of high school class, 75% in top 50% of high school class. 75% from public high schools. Average SAT I Math 535, SAT I Math middle 50% range 490-580. Average SAT I Verbal 542, SAT I Verbal middle 50% range 490-580. Average ACT 22, ACT middle 50% range 20-25. TOEFL required of all international applicants, minimum TOEFL 500. **Basis for Candidate Selection:** *Very important factors considered include:* class rank, secondary school record, standardized test scores. *Important factors considered include:* essays. *Other factors considered include:* character/personal qualities, extracurricular activities, geographical residence, minority status, recommendations, religious affiliation/commitment, state residency, talent/ability, volunteer work, work experience. **Freshman Admission Requirements:** High school diploma or GED is required. *Academic units required/recommended:* 11 total required; 17 total recommended; 4 English required, 4 English recommended, 3 math required, 3 math recommended, 2 science required, 3 science recommended, 2 science lab required, 3 science lab recommended, 2 foreign language required, 3 foreign language recommended, 3 social studies recommended, 2 history recommended, 1 elective recommended. **Freshman Admission Statistics:** 1,511 applied, 70% accepted, 42% of those accepted enrolled. **Transfer Admission Requirements:** *Items required:* college transcript, essay. Minimum college GPA of 2.3 required. Lowest grade transferable C. **General Admission Information:** Application fee $30. Priority application deadline February 1. Regular application deadline July 1. Nonfall registration accepted. Admission may be deferred for a maximum of 1 year. Credit and/or placement offered for CEEB Advanced Placement tests.

COSTS AND FINANCIAL AID

Required Forms and Deadlines: FAFSA. No deadline for regular filing. Priority filing deadline April 15. **Notification of Awards:** Applicants will be notified of awards on a rolling basis beginning on or about February 1. **Types of Aid:** *Need-based scholarships/grants:* Pell, SEOG, state scholarships/grants, private scholarships, the school's own gift aid, United Negro College Fund, Endowed scholarships. *Loans:* FFEL Subsidized Stafford, FFEL Unsubsidized Stafford, FFEL PLUS, Federal Perkins, state loans, private alternative loans. **Student Employment:** Federal Work-Study Program available. Institutional employment available. Off-campus job opportunities are excellent. **Financial Aid Statistics:** 61% freshmen, 58% undergrads receive some form of aid. Average freshman grant $8,806. Average freshman loan $4,325. Average income from on-campus job $2,000. **Financial Aid Phone:** 512-448-8520.

See page 1178.

SAINT FRANCIS COLLEGE (NY)

180 Remsen Street, Brooklyn Heights, NY 11201
Phone: 718-522-2300 **E-mail:** glarkin@stfranciscollege.edu **CEEB Code:** 2796
Fax: 718-522-1274 **Web:** www.stfranciscollege.edu **ACT Code:** 2884

This private school, which is affiliated with the Roman Catholic Church, was founded in 1884. It has a 1-acre campus.

STUDENTS AND FACULTY

Enrollment: 2,336. **Student Body:** Male 40%, female 60%, out-of-state 1%, international 12%. **Ethnic Representation:** African American 22%, Asian 3%, Caucasian 60%, Hispanic 16%. **Retention and Graduation:** 84% freshmen return for sophomore year. 18% freshmen graduate within 4 years. 29% grads go on to further study within 1 year. 20% grads pursue business degrees. 2% grads pursue law degrees. 1% grads pursue medical degrees. **Faculty:** Student/faculty ratio 23:1. 66 full-time faculty. 100% faculty teach undergrads.

ACADEMICS

Degrees: Associate's, bachelor's, certificate. **Academic Requirements:** General education including some course work in arts/fine arts, English (including composition), history, humanities, philosophy, sciences (biological or physical), social science. **Disciplines with Highest Percentage of Degrees Awarded:** Business/marketing 37%, education 13%, liberal arts/general studies 13%, psychology 11%, social sciences and history 8%. **Special Study Options:** Accelerated program, double major, dual enrollment, honors program, independent study, internships, study abroad, teacher certification program. Accelerated biomedical science program with New York College of Podiatric Medicine. Medical technology program with 2 separate hospital clinical facilities. Joint affiliation with SUNY Health Science Center at Brooklyn offering pre-professional education in the fields of occupational therapy, medical sonography, and medical records administration. 7-year cooperative program with the New York University College of Dentistry.

FACILITIES

Library Holdings: 134,613 bound volumes. 570 periodicals. 236 microforms. 2,115 audiovisuals. **Computers:** School-owned computers available for student use.

EXTRACURRICULARS

Activities: Choral groups, drama/theater, literary magazine, student government, student newspaper, yearbook. **Organizations:** 25 registered organizations, 1 honor society, 1 religious organization, 1 fraternity (1% men join), 1 sorority (1% women join). **Athletics (Intercollegiate):** *Men:* baseball, basketball, cross-country, diving, soccer, swimming, tennis, track & field, water polo. *Women:* basketball, cross-country, softball, swimming, tennis, track & field, volleyball, water polo.

ADMISSIONS

Selectivity Rating: 70 (of 100). **Freshman Academic Profile:** Average high school GPA 3.0. 14% in top 10% of high school class, 30% in top 25% of high school class, 57% in top 50% of high school class. 41% from public high schools. Average SAT I Math 503, SAT I Math middle 50% range 440-560. Average SAT I Verbal 504, SAT I Verbal middle 50% range 450-560. TOEFL required of all international applicants, minimum TOEFL 500. **Basis for Candidate Selection:** *Very important factors considered include:* interview, secondary school record. *Important factors considered include:* class rank, essays, extracurricular activities, recommendations, standardized test scores. *Other factors considered include:* alumni/ae relation, talent/ability, volunteer work, work experience. **Freshman Admission Requirements:** High school diploma or GED is required. *Academic units required/recommended:* 16 total required; 4 English required, 2 math required, 2 science required, 2 foreign language recommended, 4 social studies required. **Freshman Admission Statistics:** 1,486 applied, 75% accepted, 41% of those accepted enrolled. **Transfer Admission Requirements:** *Items required:* high school transcript, college transcript, essay, statement of good standing from prior school. Minimum college GPA of 2.0 required. Lowest grade transferable C. **General Admission Information:** Application fee $20. Nonfall registration accepted. Admission may be deferred for a maximum of 1 year. Placement offered for CEEB Advanced Placement tests.

COSTS AND FINANCIAL AID

Tuition $8,830. Required fees $160. Average book expense $500. **Required Forms and Deadlines:** FAFSA, institution's own financial aid form and state aid form. Priority filing deadline February 15. **Notification of Awards:** Applicants will be notified of awards on a rolling basis beginning on or about March 15. **Student Employment:** Institutional employment available. Off-campus job opportunities are good. **Financial Aid Statistics:** 74% freshmen, 84% undergrads receive some form of aid. **Financial Aid Phone:** 718-489-5255.

SAINT FRANCIS UNIVERSITY (PA)

PO Box 600, Loretto, PA 15940
Phone: 814-472-3000 **E-mail:** admissions@francis.edu **CEEB Code:** 2797
Fax: 814-472-3335 **Web:** www.sfu.edu **ACT Code:** 3682

This private school, which is affiliated with the Roman Catholic Church, was founded in 1847. It has a 600-acre campus.

STUDENTS AND FACULTY

Enrollment: 1,470. **Student Body:** Male 38%, female 62%, out-of-state 22%, international 3% (11 countries represented). **Ethnic Representation:** African American 6%, Caucasian 86%, Hispanic 1%. **Retention and Graduation:** 79% freshmen return for sophomore year. 53% freshmen graduate within 4 years. 29% grads go on to further study within 1 year. 8% grads pursue business degrees. 3% grads pursue law degrees. 2% grads pursue medical degrees. **Faculty:** Student/faculty ratio 11:1. 87 full-time faculty, 72% hold PhDs. 99% faculty teach undergrads.

ACADEMICS

Degrees: Associate's, bachelor's, master's, post-bachelor's certificate. **Academic Requirements:** General education including some course work in arts/fine arts, computer literacy, English (including composition), foreign languages, history, humanities, mathematics, philosophy, sciences (biological or physical), social science, speech, religious studies. **Classes:** 10-19 students in an average class. 10-19 students in an average lab/discussion section. **Disciplines with Highest Percentage of Degrees Awarded:** Business/marketing 32%, health professions and related sciences 32%, education 14%, protective services/public administration 5%, psychology 4%. **Special Study Options:** Cooperative (work-study) program, distance learning, double major, honors program, independent study, internships, liberal arts/career combination, student-designed major, study abroad, teacher certification program.

FACILITIES

Housing: Coed, all-female, all-male, apartments for single students, fraternities and/or sororities. **Library Holdings:** 121,940 bound volumes. 5,386 periodicals. 6,805 microforms. 2,899 audiovisuals. **Special Academic Facilities/ Equipment:** Art museum, elementary-level library for education majors, physician assistant practice facilities, cadaver lab, physical therapy lab, Center for Excellence in Rural Medically Underserved Areas. **Computers:** *Recommended operating system:* Windows 95. School-owned computers available for student use.

EXTRACURRICULARS

Activities: Choral groups, dance, drama/theater, literary magazine, music ensembles, pep band, radio station, student government, student newspaper, student-run film society, television station, yearbook. **Organizations:** 50 registered organizations, 9 honor societies, 10 religious organizations, 1 fraternity (3% men join), 3 sororities (12% women join). **Athletics (Intercollegiate):** *Men:* basketball, cross-country, football, golf, indoor track, soccer, swimming, tennis, track & field, volleyball. *Women:* basketball, cross-country, field hockey, golf, indoor track, lacrosse, soccer, softball, swimming, tennis, track & field, volleyball.

ADMISSIONS

Selectivity Rating: 82 (of 100). **Freshman Academic Profile:** Average high school GPA 3.5. 23% in top 10% of high school class, 55% in top 25% of high school class, 80% in top 50% of high school class. 78% from public high schools. Average SAT I Math 530, SAT I Math middle 50% range 460-570. Average SAT I Verbal 550, SAT I Verbal middle 50% range 450-560. Average ACT 21, ACT middle 50% range 20-25. TOEFL required of all international applicants, minimum TOEFL 500. **Basis for Candidate Selection:** *Very important factors considered include:* secondary school record. *Important factors considered include:* character/personal qualities, class rank, extracurricular activities, standardized test scores, volunteer work. *Other factors considered include:* alumni/ae relation, essays, interview, recommendations, talent/ability, work experience. **Freshman Admission Requirements:** High school diploma or GED is required. *Academic units required/recommended:* 4 English required, 2 math required, 1 science required, 2 science recommended, 1 science lab required, 2 social studies required, 7 elective required. **Transfer Admission Requirements:** *Items required:* college transcript. Minimum college GPA of 2.0 required. Lowest grade transferable C. **General Admission Information:** Application fee $30. Priority application deadline April 1. Regular application deadline August 1. Nonfall registration accepted. Admission may be deferred for a maximum of 1 year. Credit offered for CEEB Advanced Placement tests.

COSTS AND FINANCIAL AID

Tuition $17,024. Room & board $7,346. Required fees $0. Average book expense $500. **Required Forms and Deadlines:** FAFSA and institution's own financial aid form. No deadline for regular filing. Priority filing deadline May 1. **Notification of Awards:** Applicants will be notified of awards on a rolling basis beginning on or about October 1. **Types of Aid:** *Need-based scholarships/grants:* Pell, SEOG, state scholarships/grants, private scholarships, the school's own gift aid. *Loans:* FFEL Subsidized Stafford, FFEL Unsubsidized Stafford, FFEL PLUS, Federal Perkins. **Student Employment:** Federal Work-Study Program available. Institutional employment available. Off-campus job opportunities are fair. **Financial Aid Statistics:** 83% freshmen, 85% undergrads receive some form of aid. Average freshman grant $13,222. Average freshman loan $2,500. Average income from on-campus job $800. **Financial Aid Phone:** 814-472-3010.

See page 1180.

SAINT JOHN FISHER COLLEGE

3690 East Avenue, Rochester, NY 14618-3597
Phone: 585-385-8064 **E-mail:** admissions@sjfc.edu **CEEB Code:** 2798
Fax: 585-385-8386 **Web:** www.sjfc.edu **ACT Code:** 2798

This private school, which is affiliated with the Roman Catholic Church, was founded in 1948. It has a 136-acre campus.

STUDENTS AND FACULTY

Enrollment: 2,350. **Student Body:** Male 40%, female 60%, out-of-state 2%, international students represent 11 countries. **Ethnic Representation:** African American 5%, Asian 1%, Caucasian 88%, Hispanic 2%, Native American 1%. **Retention and Graduation:** 82% freshmen return for sophomore year. 45% freshmen graduate within 4 years. 25% grads go on to further study within 1 year. 10% grads pursue business degrees. 8% grads pursue law degrees. 4% grads pursue medical degrees. **Faculty:** Student/faculty ratio 16:1. 121 full-time faculty, 87% hold PhDs. 100% faculty teach undergrads.

ACADEMICS

Degrees: Bachelor's, master's, post-bachelor's certificate. **Academic Requirements:** General education including some course work in English (including composition), humanities, mathematics, philosophy, sciences (biological or physical), social science. **Classes:** 10-19 students in an average class. Under 10 students in an average lab/discussion section. **Disciplines with Highest Percentage of Degrees Awarded:** Business/marketing 22%, social sciences and history 20%, psychology 12%, communications/communication technologies 10%, health professions and related sciences 8%. **Special Study Options:** Accelerated program, cross registration, double major, honors program, independent study, internships, liberal arts/career combination, student-designed major, study abroad, teacher certification program, weekend college.

FACILITIES

Housing: Coed. **Library Holdings:** 207,343 bound volumes. 1,214 periodicals. 193,805 microforms. 29,052 audiovisuals. **Special Academic Facilities/ Equipment:** Greenhouse, TV studio, language labs, human and animal psychology lab, marine aquarium, two electron microscopes, radiation lab, microbial fermenters, X-ray diffraction, spectrometer, microphotometer, reflecting telescopes. **Computers:** School-owned computers available for student use.

EXTRACURRICULARS

Activities: Choral groups, dance, drama/theater, literary magazine, musical theater, radio station, student government, student newspaper, television station, yearbook. **Organizations:** 40 registered organizations, 1 religious organization. **Athletics (Intercollegiate):** *Men:* baseball, basketball, cross-country, football, golf, lacrosse, soccer. *Women:* basketball, cheerleading, cross-country, lacrosse, soccer, softball, volleyball.

ADMISSIONS

Selectivity Rating: 73 (of 100). **Freshman Academic Profile:** Average high school GPA 3.3. 17% in top 10% of high school class, 49% in top 25% of high school class, 85% in top 50% of high school class. 65% from public high schools. Average SAT I Math 530, SAT I Math middle 50% range 490-580. Average SAT I Verbal 530, SAT I Verbal middle 50% range 480-570. Average ACT 23, ACT middle 50% range 20-24. TOEFL required of all international applicants, minimum TOEFL 550. **Basis for Candidate Selection:** *Important factors considered include:* character/personal qualities, class rank, recommendations, secondary school record, standardized test scores. *Other factors considered include:* alumni/ae relation, essays, extracurricular activities, interview, talent/ability, volunteer work, work experience. **Freshman Admission Requirements:** High school diploma or GED is required. *Academic units required/recommended:* 16 total required; 4 English recommended, 3 math recommended, 3 science recommended, 3 foreign language recommended, 4 social studies recommended. **Freshman Admission Statistics:** 1,939 applied, 72% accepted, 39% of those accepted enrolled. **Transfer Admission Requirements:** *Items required:* college transcript, statement of good standing from prior school. Minimum college GPA of 2.0 required. Lowest grade transferable C. **General Admission Information:** Application fee $25. Priority application deadline March 1. Early decision application deadline December 1. Nonfall registration accepted. Admission may be deferred for a maximum of 1 year. Credit and/or placement offered for CEEB Advanced Placement tests.

COSTS AND FINANCIAL AID

Tuition $16,100. Room & board $7,000. Required fees $350. Average book expense $500. **Required Forms and Deadlines:** FAFSA and state aid form. No deadline for regular filing. Priority filing deadline February 15. **Notification of Awards:** Applicants will be notified of awards on or about March 21. **Types of Aid:** *Need-based scholarships/grants:* Pell, SEOG, state scholarships/grants, private scholarships, the school's own gift aid. *Loans:* Direct Subsidized Stafford, Direct Unsubsidized Stafford, Direct PLUS, Federal Perkins. **Student Employment:** Federal Work-Study Program available. Institutional employment available. Off-campus job opportunities are excellent. **Financial Aid Statistics:** 85% freshmen, 81% undergrads receive some form of aid. Average freshman grant $12,500. Average freshman loan $2,625. **Financial Aid Phone:** 585-385-8042.

ST. JOHN'S COLLEGE (MD)

PO Box 2800, Annapolis, MD 21404
Phone: 410-626-2522 **E-mail:** admissions@sjca.edu **CEEB Code:** 5598
Fax: 410-269-7916 **Web:** www.sjca.edu **ACT Code:** 1732

This private school was founded in 1696. It has a 36-acre campus.

STUDENTS AND FACULTY

Enrollment: 465. **Student Body:** Male 55%, female 45%, out-of-state 85%, international 3% (15 countries represented). **Ethnic Representation:** Asian 2%, Caucasian 92%, Hispanic 3%. **Retention and Graduation:** 79% freshmen return for sophomore year. 52% freshmen graduate within 4 years. 15% grads go on to further study within 1 year. 7% grads pursue business degrees. 10% grads pursue law degrees. 6% grads pursue medical degrees. **Faculty:** Student/faculty ratio 8:1. 70 full-time faculty, 70% hold PhDs. 100% faculty teach undergrads.

ACADEMICS

Degrees: Bachelor's, master's. **Academic Requirements:** General education including some course work in English (including composition), foreign languages, history, humanities, mathematics, philosophy, sciences (biological or physical). **Classes:** 10-19 students in an average class. **Majors with Highest Enrollment:** Liberal arts and sciences, general studies and humanities. **Disciplines with Highest Percentage of Degrees Awarded:** Liberal arts/general studies 100%. **Special Study Options:** Students may spend one or more years at college's Santa Fe, New Mexico, campus.

FACILITIES

Housing: Coed, housing for disabled students. **Library Holdings:** 93,668 bound volumes. 114 periodicals. 412 microforms. 1,965 audiovisuals. **Special Academic Facilities/Equipment:** Art gallery, planetarium. **Computers:** School-owned computers available for student use.

EXTRACURRICULARS

Activities: Choral groups, dance, drama/theater, literary magazine, music ensembles, student government, student newspaper, student-run film society, yearbook. **Organizations:** 40 registered organizations, 3 religious organizations.

ADMISSIONS

Selectivity Rating: 85 (of 100). **Freshman Academic Profile:** 46% in top 10% of high school class, 74% in top 25% of high school class, 99% in top 50% of high school class. 67% from public high schools. SAT I Math middle 50% range 590-690. SAT I Verbal middle 50% range 660-750. TOEFL required of all international applicants, minimum TOEFL 600. **Basis for Candidate Selection:** *Very important factors considered include:* essays. *Important factors considered include:* alumni/ae relation, character/personal qualities, interview, recommendations, secondary school record. *Other factors considered include:* class rank, extracurricular activities, minority status, standardized test scores, talent/ability, volunteer work, work experience. **Freshman Admission Requirements:** High school diploma or GED is required. *Academic units required/recommended:* 4 English recommended, 3 math required, 4 math recommended, 3 science recommended, 3 science lab recommended, 2 foreign language required, 4 foreign language recommended, 2 social studies recommended, 2 history recommended. **Freshman Admission Statistics:** 450 applied, 71% accepted, 39% of those accepted enrolled. **Transfer Admission Requirements:** *Items required:* high school transcript, college transcript, essay. **General Admission Information:** Priority application deadline March 1. Nonfall registration accepted. Admission may be deferred for a maximum of 1 year. Neither credit nor placement offered for CEEB Advanced Placement tests.

COSTS AND FINANCIAL AID

Tuition $25,790. Room & board $6,770. Required fees $200. Average book expense $275. **Required Forms and Deadlines:** FAFSA, CSS/Financial Aid PROFILE, noncustodial (divorced/separated) parent's statement and business/farm supplement. No deadline for regular filing. Priority filing deadline February 15. **Notification of Awards:** Applicants will be notified of awards on a rolling basis beginning on or about November 1. **Types of Aid:** *Need-based scholarships/grants:* Pell, SEOG, state scholarships/grants, the school's own gift aid. *Loans:* FFEL Subsidized Stafford, FFEL Unsubsidized Stafford, FFEL PLUS, Federal Perkins, college/university loans from institutional funds. **Student Employment:** Federal Work-Study Program available. Institutional employment available. Off-campus job opportunities are excellent. **Financial Aid Statistics:** 53% freshmen, 56% undergrads receive some form of aid. Average freshman grant $14,207. Average freshman loan $3,125. Average income from on-campus job $2,494. **Financial Aid Phone:** 410-626-2502.

ST. JOHN'S COLLEGE (NM)

1160 Camino Cruz Blanca, Santa Fe, NM 87505
Phone: 505-984-6060 **E-mail:** admissions@mail.sjcsf.edu **CEEB Code:** 4737
Fax: 505-984-6162 **Web:** www.sjcsf.edu **ACT Code:** 2649

This private school was founded in 1696. It has a 250-acre campus.

STUDENTS AND FACULTY

Enrollment: 444. **Student Body:** Male 56%, female 44%, out-of-state 86%, international 2% (8 countries represented). **Ethnic Representation:** African American 1%, Asian 3%, Caucasian 89%, Hispanic 5%, Native American 2%. **Retention and Graduation:** 85% freshmen return for sophomore year. 41% freshmen graduate within 4 years. 75% grads go on to further study within 1 year. 7% grads pursue business degrees. 10% grads pursue law degrees. 6% grads pursue medical degrees. **Faculty:** Student/faculty ratio 8:1. 66 full-time faculty, 86% hold PhDs. 100% faculty teach undergrads.

ACADEMICS

Degrees: Bachelor's, master's. **Academic Requirements:** General education including some course work in arts/fine arts, English (including composition), foreign languages, history, humanities, mathematics, philosophy, sciences (biological or physical), social science. St. John's only offers an all-courses-required curriculum. **Classes:** 10-19 students in an average class. **Disciplines with Highest Percentage of Degrees Awarded:** Liberal arts/general studies 100%. **Special Study Options:** The Great Books Program. Also, students may spend a year or more on our Maryland Campus.

FACILITIES

Housing: Coed, all-female, all-male, apartments for married students, apartments for single students, housing for disabled students, single-sex suites, nonsmoking, nondrinking dorms. **Library Holdings:** 65,000 bound volumes.

135 periodicals. 0 microforms. 8,205 audiovisuals. **Special Academic Facilities/Equipment:** Art gallery. **Computers:** School-owned computers available for student use.

EXTRACURRICULARS

Activities: Choral groups, dance, drama/theater, jazz band, literary magazine, music ensembles, student government, student newspaper, student-run film society, yearbook. **Organizations:** 21 registered organizations. **Athletics (Intercollegiate):** *Men:* fencing. *Women:* fencing.

ADMISSIONS

Selectivity Rating: 82 (of 100). **Freshman Academic Profile:** 23% in top 10% of high school class, 46% in top 25% of high school class, 77% in top 50% of high school class. 85% from public high schools. Average SAT I Math 620, SAT I Math middle 50% range 560-650. Average SAT I Verbal 700, SAT I Verbal middle 50% range 630-720. Average ACT 27, ACT middle 50% range 26-30. TOEFL required of all international applicants, minimum TOEFL 550. **Basis for Candidate Selection:** *Very important factors considered include:* character/personal qualities, essays, interview, talent/ability. *Important factors considered include:* extracurricular activities, recommendations, secondary school record. *Other factors considered include:* class rank, standardized test scores, volunteer work, work experience. **Freshman Admission Requirements:** High school diploma or equivalent is not required. *Academic units required/recommended:* 18 total recommended; 3 math required, 4 math recommended, 3 science recommended, 3 science lab recommended, 2 foreign language required, 4 foreign language recommended, 2 social studies recommended, 2 history recommended. **Freshman Admission Statistics:** 358 applied, 80% accepted, 48% of those accepted enrolled. **Transfer Admission Requirements:** *Items required:* high school transcript, college transcript, essay, statement of good standing from prior school. Minimum college GPA of 3.0 required. **General Admission Information:** Priority application deadline March 1. Nonfall registration accepted. Admission may be deferred for a maximum of 1 year. Neither credit nor placement offered for CEEB Advanced Placement tests.

COSTS AND FINANCIAL AID

Tuition $27,210. Room & board $6,970. Required fees $200. Average book expense $275. **Required Forms and Deadlines:** FAFSA, CSS/Financial Aid PROFILE, noncustodial (divorced/separated) parent's statement and business/farm supplement. Priority filing deadline February 15. **Notification of Awards:** Applicants will be notified of awards on a rolling basis beginning on or about December 1. **Types of Aid:** *Need-based scholarships/grants:* Pell, SEOG, state scholarships/grants, private scholarships, the school's own gift aid. *Loans:* Direct Subsidized Stafford, Direct Unsubsidized Stafford, Direct PLUS, Federal Perkins, college/university loans from institutional funds. **Student Employment:** Federal Work-Study Program available. Institutional employment available. Off-campus job opportunities are good. **Financial Aid Statistics:** 71% freshmen, 71% undergrads receive some form of aid. Average freshman grant $19,021. Average freshman loan $3,245. Average income from on-campus job $2,015. **Financial Aid Phone:** 505-984-6058.

ST. JOHN'S UNIVERSITY (NY)

8000 Utopia Parkway, Jamaica, NY 11439
Phone: 718-990-2000 **E-mail:** admissions@stjohns.edu **CEEB Code:** 2799
Fax: 718-990-5728 **Web:** www.stjohns.edu **ACT Code:** 2888

This private school, which is affiliated with the Roman Catholic Church, was founded in 1870. It has a 96-acre campus.

STUDENTS AND FACULTY

Enrollment: 14,708. **Student Body:** Male 42%, female 58%, out-of-state 9%, international 3%. **Ethnic Representation:** African American 16%, Asian 14%, Caucasian 44%, Hispanic 16%. **Retention and Graduation:** 82% freshmen return for sophomore year. 43% freshmen graduate within 4 years. 18% grads go on to further study within 1 year. 3% grads pursue business degrees. 3% grads pursue law degrees. 1% grads pursue medical degrees. **Faculty:** Student/faculty ratio 19:1. 551 full-time faculty, 89% hold PhDs. 91% faculty teach undergrads.

ACADEMICS

Degrees: Associate's, bachelor's, certificate, diploma, doctoral, first professional, master's, post-bachelor's certificate, post-master's certificate, terminal, transfer. **Academic Requirements:** General education including some course work in arts/fine arts, English (including composition), foreign languages, history, mathematics, philosophy, sciences (biological or physical), social science, theology. **Classes:** 20-29 students in an average class. 20-29 students in an average lab/discussion section. **Majors with Highest Enrollment:** Pharmacy (PharmD, BS/BPharm); finance, general; criminal justice/law enforcement administration. **Disciplines with Highest Percentage of Degrees Awarded:** Business/marketing 31%, health professions and related sciences 16%, computer and information sciences 11%, education 8%, communications/communication technologies 8%. **Special Study Options:** Accelerated program, cross registration, distance learning, double major, dual enrollment, English as a second language, honors program, independent study, internships, liberal arts/career combination, study abroad, teacher certification program, weekend college.

FACILITIES

Housing: Coed. Some off-campus apartments are available on a limited basis on the Staten Island campus. **Library Holdings:** 1,162,637 bound volumes. 16,014 periodicals. 2,766,265 microforms. 22,376 audiovisuals. **Special Academic Facilities/Equipment:** University Gallery; Chung-Cheng Art Gallery; instructional media center; Institute of Asian Studies; health education resource center; Center for Psychological Services and Clinical Studies; TV center; speech and hearing clinic. **Computers:** School-owned computers available for student use.

EXTRACURRICULARS

Activities: Choral groups, dance, drama/theater, jazz band, literary magazine, pep band, radio station, student government, student newspaper, student-run film society, television station, yearbook. **Organizations:** 175 registered organizations, 32 honor societies, 6 religious organizations, 23 fraternities (8% men join), 22 sororities (7% women join). **Athletics (Intercollegiate):** *Men:* baseball, basketball, fencing, golf, soccer, swimming, tennis, track & field. *Women:* basketball, fencing, soccer, softball, swimming, tennis, track & field, volleyball.

ADMISSIONS

Selectivity Rating: 69 (of 100). **Freshman Academic Profile:** Average high school GPA 3.0. 19% in top 10% of high school class, 24% in top 25% of high school class, 74% in top 50% of high school class. 59% from public high schools. Average SAT I Math 535, SAT I Math middle 50% range 480-580. Average SAT I Verbal 516, SAT I Verbal middle 50% range 460-560. TOEFL required of all international applicants, minimum TOEFL 500. **Basis for Candidate Selection:** *Very important factors considered include:* secondary school record. *Important factors considered include:* class rank, essays, recommendations, standardized test scores. *Other factors considered include:* character/personal qualities, extracurricular activities, interview, talent/ability, volunteer work, work experience. **Freshman Admission Requirements:** High school diploma or GED is required. *Academic units required/recommended:* 16 total required; 4 English required. **Freshman Admission Statistics:** 12,274 applied, 75% accepted, 32% of those accepted enrolled. **Transfer Admission Requirements:** *Items required:* high school transcript, college transcript. Minimum college GPA of 3.0 required. Lowest grade transferable C. **General Admission Information:** Application fee $40. Nonfall registration accepted. Admission may be deferred for a maximum of 1 year. Credit and/or placement offered for CEEB Advanced Placement tests.

COSTS AND FINANCIAL AID

Tuition $17,850. Room & board $9,700. Required fees $480. Average book expense $1,000. **Required Forms and Deadlines:** FAFSA and state aid form. Priority filing deadline February 1. **Notification of Awards:** Applicants will be notified of awards on a rolling basis beginning on or about April 1. **Types of Aid:** *Need-based scholarships/grants:* Pell, SEOG, state scholarships/grants, private scholarships, the school's own gift aid. *Loans:* FFEL Subsidized Stafford, FFEL Unsubsidized Stafford, FFEL PLUS, Federal Perkins. **Student Employment:** Federal Work-Study Program available. Institutional employment available. Off-campus job opportunities are fair. **Financial Aid Statistics:** 80% freshmen, 76% undergrads receive some form of aid. Average freshman grant $4,527. Average freshman loan $3,749. Average income from on-campus job $4,000. **Financial Aid Phone:** 718-990-2000.

See page 1182.

SAINT JOHN'S UNIVERSITY/ COLLEGE OF SAINT BENEDICT

PO Box 7155, Collegeville, MN 56321-7155
Phone: 320-363-2196 **E-mail:** admissions@csbsju.edu **CEEB Code:** 6624
Fax: 320-363-3206 **Web:** www.csbsju.edu **ACT Code:** 2140

This private school, which is affiliated with the Roman Catholic Church, was founded in 1857. It has a 2,400-acre campus.

STUDENTS AND FACULTY

Enrollment: 3,969. **Student Body:** Male 48%, female 52%, out-of-state 14%, international 3% (35 countries represented). **Ethnic Representation:** Asian 2%, Caucasian 96%, Hispanic 1%. **Retention and Graduation:** 90% freshmen return for sophomore year. 70% freshmen graduate within 4 years. 15% grads go on to further study within 1 year. 2% grads pursue law degrees. 3% grads pursue medical degrees. **Faculty:** Student/faculty ratio 13:1. 287 full-time faculty, 89% hold PhDs. 100% faculty teach undergrads.

ACADEMICS

Degrees: Bachelor's, first professional, master's. **Academic Requirements:** General education including some course work in arts/fine arts, English (including composition), foreign languages, history, humanities, mathematics, philosophy, sciences (biological or physical), social science, gender perspectives, global perspectives. Students are required to take first-year symposium and senior seminar. **Classes:** 20-29 students in an average class. 10-19 students in an average lab/discussion section. **Majors with Highest Enrollment:** Nursing/registered nurse training (RN, ASN, BSN, MSN); business administration/management; biology/biological sciences, general. **Disciplines with Highest Percentage of Degrees Awarded:** Business/marketing 22%, English 15%, social sciences and history 13%, education 7%, psychology 7%. **Special Study Options:** Accelerated program, cross registration, double major, dual enrollment, English as a second language, honors program, independent study, internships, liberal arts/career combination, student-designed major, study abroad, teacher certification program.

FACILITIES

Housing: All-female, all-male, apartments for single students, housing for disabled students, global initiative group, service learning/social justice floor, Christian living floor, health and wellness floor. **Library Holdings:** 805,376 bound volumes. 5,735 periodicals. 196,563 microforms. 22,452 audiovisuals. **Special Academic Facilities/Equipment:** Monastic manuscript library (world's largest medieval library), art gallery, natural science museum, nature preserve, arboretum. **Computers:** *Recommended operating system:* Windows 2000. School-owned computers available for student use.

EXTRACURRICULARS

Activities: Choral groups, concert band, dance, drama/theater, jazz band, literary magazine, music ensembles, musical theater, opera, radio station, student government, student newspaper, symphony orchestra, yearbook. **Organizations:** 80 registered organizations, 2 honor societies, 5 religious organizations. **Athletics (Intercollegiate):** *Men:* baseball, basketball, cross-country, diving, football, golf, ice hockey, skiing (Nordic), soccer, swimming, tennis, track & field, wrestling. *Women:* basketball, cross-country, diving, golf, ice hockey, skiing (Nordic), soccer, softball, swimming, tennis, track & field, volleyball.

ADMISSIONS

Selectivity Rating: 81 (of 100). **Freshman Academic Profile:** Average high school GPA 3.7. 30% in top 10% of high school class, 66% in top 25% of high school class, 93% in top 50% of high school class. 77% from public high schools. Average SAT I Math 605, SAT I Math middle 50% range 560-660. Average SAT I Verbal 585, SAT I Verbal middle 50% range 530-650. Average ACT 25, ACT middle 50% range 22-28. TOEFL required of all international applicants, minimum TOEFL 500. **Basis for Candidate Selection:** *Very important factors considered include:* class rank, essays, secondary school record, standardized test scores. *Important factors considered include:* alumni/ae relation, character/personal qualities, extracurricular activities, geographical residence, minority status, recommendations, religious affiliation/commitment, state residency, talent/ability, volunteer work, work experience. *Other factors considered include:* interview. **Freshman Admission Requirements:** High school diploma or GED is required. *Academic units required/recommended:* 17 total recommended; 4 English recommended, 3 math recommended, 2 science recommended, 2 science lab recommended, 2 foreign language recommended, 2 social studies recommended, 4 elective recommended. **Freshman Admission Statistics:** 2,375 applied, 86% accepted, 48% of those accepted enrolled. **Transfer Admission Requirements:** *Items required:* high school transcript, college transcript, essay, statement of good standing from prior school. Minimum college GPA of 2.7 required. Lowest grade transferable C. **General Admission Information:** Application fee $30. Priority application deadline February 1. Nonfall registration accepted. Admission may be deferred for a maximum of 1 year. Credit and/or placement offered for CEEB Advanced Placement tests.

COSTS AND FINANCIAL AID

Tuition $18,916. Room & board $5,789. Required fees $310. Average book expense $600. **Required Forms and Deadlines:** FAFSA, institution's own financial aid form and Federal tax forms and W-2. Priority filing deadline March 15. **Notification of Awards:** Applicants will be notified of awards on a rolling basis beginning on or about March 15. **Types of Aid:** *Need-based scholarships/grants:* Pell, SEOG, state scholarships/grants, private scholarships, the school's own gift aid. *Loans:* FFEL Subsidized Stafford, FFEL Unsubsidized Stafford, FFEL PLUS, Federal Perkins, state loans, various private loans. **Student Employment:** Federal Work-Study Program available. Institutional employment available. Off-campus job opportunities are good. **Financial Aid Statistics:** 67% freshmen, 63% undergrads receive some form of aid. Average freshman grant $11,656. Average freshman loan $4,365. Average income from on-campus job $2,100. **Financial Aid Phone:** 320-363-3664.

SAINT JOSEPH COLLEGE (CT)

1678 Asylum Avenue, West Hartford, CT 06117
Phone: 860-231-5216 **E-mail:** admissions@mercy.sjc.edu **CEEB Code:** 3754
Fax: 860-233-5695 **Web:** www.sjc.edu **ACT Code:** 588

This private school, which is affiliated with the Roman Catholic Church, was founded in 1932. It has an 84-acre campus.

STUDENTS AND FACULTY

Enrollment: 1,169. **Student Body:** Male 1%, female 99%, out-of-state 23%. **Ethnic Representation:** African American 15%, Asian 2%, Caucasian 70%, Hispanic 6%. **Retention and Graduation:** 76% freshmen return for sophomore year. 63% freshmen graduate within 4 years. 25% grads go on to further study within 1 year. 3% grads pursue business degrees. 1% grads pursue law degrees. 2% grads pursue medical degrees. **Faculty:** Student/faculty ratio 11:1. 75 full-time faculty, 81% hold PhDs. 75% faculty teach undergrads.

ACADEMICS

Degrees: Bachelor's, certificate, master's. **Academic Requirements:** General education including some course work in English (including composition), mathematics, sciences (biological or physical), social science. **Classes:** 10-19 students in an average class. 10-19 students in an average lab/discussion section. **Disciplines with Highest Percentage of Degrees Awarded:** Health professions and related sciences 17%, education 16%, social sciences and history 15%, psychology 9%, natural resources/environmental sciences 9%. **Special Study Options:** Accelerated program, cross registration, distance learning, double major, honors program, independent study, internships, liberal arts/career combination, student-designed major, study abroad, teacher certification program, weekend college, undergrads may take grad-level classes. Exchange programs abroad in Australia (Brisbane/Queensland University), Denmark (Aabenrau School of Business), and Japan (Seissen Junior College).

FACILITIES

Housing: All-female. **Library Holdings:** 135,500 bound volumes. 595 periodicals. 58,772 microforms. 3,530 audiovisuals. **Special Academic Facilities/Equipment:** Art gallery, computer labs, Freshwater Institute, language lab, nursing lab, pre-K school, school for exceptional children. **Computers:** School-owned computers available for student use.

EXTRACURRICULARS

Activities: Choral groups, dance, drama/theater, literary magazine, student government, yearbook. **Organizations:** 24 registered organizations, 3 honor societies. **Athletics (Intercollegiate):** *Women:* basketball, cross-country, soccer, softball, swimming, tennis, volleyball.

ADMISSIONS

Selectivity Rating: 67 (of 100). **Freshman Academic Profile:** 9% in top 10% of high school class, 21% in top 25% of high school class, 56% in top 50% of high school class. 79% from public high schools. Average SAT I Math 486, SAT I Math middle 50% range 420-530. Average SAT I Verbal 500, SAT I Verbal middle 50% range 440-550. TOEFL required of all international applicants, minimum TOEFL 530. **Basis for Candidate Selection:** *Very important factors considered include:* secondary school record, standardized test scores.

Other factors considered include: alumni/ae relation, character/personal qualities, essays, extracurricular activities, interview, recommendations, talent/ability, volunteer work. **Freshman Admission Requirements:** High school diploma or GED is required. *Academic units required/recommended:* 16 total required; 4 English recommended, 3 math recommended, 3 science recommended, 2 foreign language recommended, 2 social studies recommended, 2 history recommended. **Freshman Admission Statistics:** 669 applied, 76% accepted, 41% of those accepted enrolled. **Transfer Admission Requirements:** *Items required:* high school transcript, college transcript, essay, statement of good standing from prior school. Minimum college GPA of 2.5 required. Lowest grade transferable C. **General Admission Information:** Application fee $35. Priority application deadline May 1. Nonfall registration accepted. Admission may be deferred for a maximum of 1 year. Credit and/or placement offered for CEEB Advanced Placement tests.

COSTS AND FINANCIAL AID

Tuition $19,110. Room & board $8,210. Required fees $500. Average book expense $850. **Required Forms and Deadlines:** FAFSA. Financial aid filing deadline February 15. Priority filing deadline June 30. **Notification of Awards:** Applicants will be notified of awards on a rolling basis beginning on or about March 1. **Types of Aid:** *Need-based scholarships/grants:* Pell, SEOG, state scholarships/grants, private scholarships, the school's own gift aid. *Loans:* FFEL Subsidized Stafford, FFEL Unsubsidized Stafford, FFEL PLUS, Federal Perkins, state loans, Connecticut Family Education Loan Program. **Student Employment:** Federal Work-Study Program available. Institutional employment available. Off-campus job opportunities are good. **Financial Aid Statistics:** 93% freshmen, 94% undergrads receive some form of aid. Average freshman grant $12,398. Average freshman loan $2,804. Average income from on-campus job $858. **Financial Aid Phone:** 860-231-5223.

See page 1184.

SAINT JOSEPH SEMINARY COLLEGE

75376 River Road, St. Benedict, LA 70457
Phone: 985-867-2248 **E-mail:** registrar@sjasc.edu **CEEB Code:** 6689
Fax: 985-867-2270 **Web:** www.sjasc.edu **ACT Code:** 1604

This private school, which is affiliated with the Roman Catholic Church, was founded in 1891. It has a 1,200-acre campus.

STUDENTS AND FACULTY

Enrollment: 248. **Student Body:** Male 48%, female 52%, out-of-state 39%. **Ethnic Representation:** African American 3%, Asian 5%, Caucasian 68%, Hispanic 23%. **Retention and Graduation:** 100% freshmen return for sophomore year. 100% freshmen graduate within 4 years. **Faculty:** Student/faculty ratio 7:1. 6 full-time faculty, 66% hold PhDs. 100% faculty teach undergrads.

ACADEMICS

Degrees: Bachelor's. **Academic Requirements:** General education including some course work in arts/fine arts, English (including composition), foreign languages, history, mathematics, philosophy, sciences (biological or physical), social science, religious studies. **Classes:** Under 10 students in an average class. 10-19 students in an average lab/discussion section. **Disciplines with Highest Percentage of Degrees Awarded:** Liberal arts/general studies 100%. **Special Study Options:** Cooperative (work-study) program, English as a second language, independent study, study abroad.

FACILITIES

Housing: All-male. **Library Holdings:** 63,000 bound volumes. 155 periodicals. 4,084 microforms. 1,298 audiovisuals. **Computers:** School-owned computers available for student use.

EXTRACURRICULARS

Activities: Choral groups, literary magazine, student government, yearbook. **Organizations:** 1 registered organization, 1 religious organization.

ADMISSIONS

Selectivity Rating: 63 (of 100). **Freshman Academic Profile:** TOEFL required of all international applicants, minimum TOEFL 550. **Basis for Candidate Selection:** *Very important factors considered include:* character/personal qualities, religious affiliation/commitment, secondary school record. *Important factors considered include:* recommendations, standardized test scores. *Other factors considered include:* class rank, extracurricular activities, interview, volunteer work. **Freshman Admission Requirements:** High school diploma or GED is required. *Academic units required/recommended:* 17 total required; 17 total recommended; 3 English required, 3 English recommended, 2 math required, 2 math recommended, 2 science required, 2 science recommended, 2 foreign language required, 2 foreign language recommended, 1 history required, 1 history recommended. **Freshman Admission Statistics:** 9 applied, 100% accepted, 100% of those accepted enrolled. **Transfer Admission Requirements:** *Items required:* high school transcript, college transcript, standardized test scores. Minimum high school GPA of 2.0 required. Minimum college GPA of 1.7 required. Lowest grade transferable C. **General Admission Information:** Regular application deadline rolling. Nonfall registration accepted. Neither credit nor placement offered for CEEB Advanced Placement tests.

COSTS AND FINANCIAL AID

Tuition $6,450. Room & board $4,750. Average book expense $600. **Required Forms and Deadlines:** institution's own financial aid form and state aid form. No deadline for regular filing. **Notification of Awards:** Applicants will be notified of awards on a rolling basis beginning on or about March 1. **Types of Aid:** *Need-based scholarships/grants:* Pell, SEOG, state scholarships/grants, private scholarships, the school's own gift aid. *Loans:* FFEL Subsidized Stafford, FFEL Unsubsidized Stafford, FFEL PLUS, Federal Perkins. **Student Employment:** Federal Work-Study Program available. Institutional employment available. Off-campus job opportunities are poor. **Financial Aid Statistics:** 44% freshmen, 43% undergrads receive some form of aid. **Financial Aid Phone:** 985-867-2229.

SAINT JOSEPH'S COLLEGE (IN)

PO Box 890, Rensselaer, IN 47978
Phone: 219-866-6170 **E-mail:** admissions@saintjoe.edu **CEEB Code:** 1697
Fax: 219-866-6122 **Web:** www.saintjoe.edu **ACT Code:** 1240

This private school, which is affiliated with the Roman Catholic Church, was founded in 1889. It has a 180-acre campus.

STUDENTS AND FACULTY

Enrollment: 972. **Student Body:** Male 42%, female 58%, out-of-state 28%, international students represent 3 countries. **Ethnic Representation:** African American 3%, Asian 1%, Caucasian 91%, Hispanic 4%. **Retention and Graduation:** 67% freshmen return for sophomore year. 48% freshmen graduate within 4 years. 25% grads go on to further study within 1 year. 4% grads pursue business degrees. 20% grads pursue law degrees. 20% grads pursue medical degrees. **Faculty:** Student/faculty ratio 15:1. 54 full-time faculty, 83% hold PhDs. 100% faculty teach undergrads.

ACADEMICS

Degrees: Associate's, bachelor's, certificate, diploma, master's, terminal. **Academic Requirements:** General education including some course work in arts/fine arts, computer literacy, English (including composition), history, humanities, philosophy, sciences (biological or physical), social science. **Classes:** 10-19 students in an average class. 10-19 students in an average lab/discussion section. **Majors with Highest Enrollment:** Business administration/management; elementary education and teaching; biology/biological sciences, general. **Disciplines with Highest Percentage of Degrees Awarded:** Business/marketing 21%, education 19%, protective services/public administration 9%, communications/communication technologies 8%, social sciences and history 8%. **Special Study Options:** Accelerated program, cross registration, double major, dual enrollment, honors program, independent study, internships, liberal arts/career combination, student-designed major, study abroad, teacher certification program.

FACILITIES

Housing: Coed, all-female, all-male, apartments for single students, housing for disabled students. **Library Holdings:** 157,481 bound volumes. 498 periodicals. 63,979 microforms. 22,416 audiovisuals. **Computers:** *Recommended operating system:* Windows 95. School-owned computers available for student use.

EXTRACURRICULARS

Activities: Choral groups, concert band, dance, drama/theater, jazz band, literary magazine, marching band, music ensembles, musical theater, pep band, radio station, student government, student newspaper, student-run film society, television station, yearbook. **Organizations:** 47 registered organizations, 4 honor societies, 12 religious organizations. **Athletics (Intercollegiate):** *Men:* baseball, basketball, cross-country, football, golf, soccer, tennis, track & field. *Women:* basketball, cross-country, golf, soccer, softball, tennis, track & field, volleyball.

ADMISSIONS

Selectivity Rating: 68 (of 100). **Freshman Academic Profile:** Average high school GPA 3.1. 20% in top 10% of high school class, 44% in top 25% of high school class, 67% in top 50% of high school class. Average SAT I Math 504, SAT I Math middle 50% range 440-560. Average SAT I Verbal 502, SAT I Verbal middle 50% range 450-560. Average ACT 22, ACT middle 50% range 19-25. TOEFL required of all international applicants, minimum TOEFL 550. **Basis for Candidate Selection:** *Very important factors considered include:* class rank, recommendations, secondary school record, standardized test scores. *Important factors considered include:* character/personal qualities, interview. *Other factors considered include:* alumni/ae relation, essays, extracurricular activities, talent/ability, volunteer work, work experience. **Freshman Admission Requirements:** High school diploma or GED is required. *Academic units required/recommended:* 15 total recommended; 4 English recommended, 3 math recommended, 3 science recommended, 2 science lab recommended, 2 foreign language recommended, 3 social studies recommended. **Freshman Admission Statistics:** 971 applied, 77% accepted, 33% of those accepted enrolled. **Transfer Admission Requirements:** *Items required:* college transcript. Minimum college GPA of 2.0 required. Lowest grade transferable C-. **General Admission Information:** Application fee $25. Priority application deadline December 1. Early decision application deadline October 1. Nonfall registration accepted. Admission may be deferred for a maximum of 2 years. Credit offered for CEEB Advanced Placement tests.

COSTS AND FINANCIAL AID

Tuition $16,900. Room & board $5,800. Required fees $160. Average book expense $700. **Required Forms and Deadlines:** FAFSA. No deadline for regular filing. Priority filing deadline March 1. **Notification of Awards:** Applicants will be notified of awards on a rolling basis beginning on or about March 1. **Types of Aid:** *Need-based scholarships/grants:* Pell, SEOG, state scholarships/grants, private scholarships, the school's own gift aid. *Loans:* FFEL Subsidized Stafford, FFEL Unsubsidized Stafford, FFEL PLUS, Federal Perkins. **Student Employment:** Federal Work-Study Program available. Institutional employment available. Off-campus job opportunities are fair. **Financial Aid Statistics:** 82% freshmen, 81% undergrads receive some form of aid. Average freshman grant $8,000. Average freshman loan $2,900. Average income from on-campus job $800. **Financial Aid Phone:** 219-866-6163.

SAINT JOSEPH'S COLLEGE (ME)

278 Whites Bridge Road, Standish, ME 04084-5263
Phone: 207-893-7746 **E-mail:** admissions@sjcme.edu **CEEB Code:** 3755
Fax: 207-893-7862 **Web:** www.sjcme.edu **ACT Code:** 1659

This private school, which is affiliated with the Roman Catholic Church, was founded in 1912. It has a 331-acre campus.

STUDENTS AND FACULTY

Enrollment: 975. **Student Body:** Male 33%, female 67%, out-of-state 34%. **Ethnic Representation:** African American 1%, Asian 1%, Caucasian 87%, Hispanic 1%. **Retention and Graduation:** 72% freshmen return for sophomore year. 49% freshmen graduate within 4 years. 11% grads go on to further study within 1 year. 13% grads pursue business degrees. 13% grads pursue law degrees. 26% grads pursue medical degrees. **Faculty:** Student/faculty ratio 13:1. 59 full-time faculty, 96% hold PhDs. 99% faculty teach undergrads.

ACADEMICS

Degrees: Associate's, bachelor's, master's. **Academic Requirements:** General education including some course work in English (including composition), history, mathematics, philosophy, sciences (biological or physical). **Classes:** 10-19 students in an average class. 10-19 students in an average lab/discussion section. **Majors with Highest Enrollment:** Nursing/registered nurse training (RN, ASN, BSN, MSN); business administration/management; elementary education and teaching. **Disciplines with Highest Percentage of Degrees Awarded:** Liberal arts/general studies 29%, health professions and related sciences 25%, education 15%, business/marketing 12%, communications/communication technologies 4%. **Special Study Options:** Cross registration, distance learning, double major, external degree program, honors program, independent study, internships, liberal arts/career combination, study abroad, teacher certification program.

FACILITIES

Housing: Coed, all-female, all-male, substance-free housing. **Library Holdings:** 95,650 bound volumes. 392 periodicals. 6,863 microforms. 1,200 audiovisuals. **Special Academic Facilities/Equipment:** radio studio. **Computers:** School-owned computers available for student use.

EXTRACURRICULARS

Activities: Drama/theater, literary magazine, musical theater, radio station, student government, student newspaper, yearbook. **Organizations:** 30 registered organizations, 2 honor societies, 1 religious organization. **Athletics (Intercollegiate):** *Men:* baseball, basketball, golf, soccer. *Women:* basketball, field hockey, soccer, softball, volleyball.

ADMISSIONS

Selectivity Rating: 75 (of 100). **Freshman Academic Profile:** Average high school GPA 3.1. 18% in top 10% of high school class, 25% in top 25% of high school class, 70% in top 50% of high school class. 84% from public high schools. Average SAT I Math 494, SAT I Math middle 50% range 430-560. Average SAT I Verbal 484, SAT I Verbal middle 50% range 420-540. Average ACT 20. TOEFL required of all international applicants, minimum TOEFL 500. **Basis for Candidate Selection:** *Very important factors considered include:* secondary school record, standardized test scores. *Important factors considered include:* character/personal qualities, class rank, essays, extracurricular activities, interview, recommendations, talent/ability, volunteer work. *Other factors considered include:* work experience. **Freshman Admission Requirements:** High school diploma or GED is required. *Academic units required/recommended:* 18 total required; 4 English required, 3 math required, 2 science required, 2 science lab required, 2 foreign language required, 1 social studies required, 2 history required. **Freshman Admission Statistics:** 1,129 applied, 82% accepted, 32% of those accepted enrolled. **Transfer Admission Requirements:** *Items required:* high school transcript, college transcript, essay, statement of good standing from prior school. Minimum college GPA of 2.0 required. Lowest grade transferable C. **General Admission Information:** Nonfall registration accepted. Admission may be deferred. Credit and/or placement offered for CEEB Advanced Placement tests.

COSTS AND FINANCIAL AID

Tuition $16,150. Room & board $6,980. Required fees $590. Average book expense $600. **Required Forms and Deadlines:** FAFSA and institution's own financial aid form. Priority filing deadline March 1. **Notification of Awards:** Applicants will be notified of awards on a rolling basis beginning on or about March 1. **Types of Aid:** *Need-based scholarships/grants:* Pell, SEOG, state scholarships/grants, private scholarships, the school's own gift aid, Federal Nursing. *Loans:* FFEL Subsidized Stafford, FFEL Unsubsidized Stafford, FFEL PLUS, Federal Perkins, Federal Nursing, state loans. **Student Employment:** Federal Work-Study Program available. Institutional employment available. Off-campus job opportunities are good. **Financial Aid Statistics:** 89% freshmen, 89% undergrads receive some form of aid. Average freshman grant $9,533. Average freshman loan $3,515. Average income from on-campus job $905. **Financial Aid Phone:** 800-752-1266.

See page 1186.

ST. JOSEPH'S COLLEGE—BROOKLYN

245 Clinton Avenue, Brooklyn, NY 11205
Phone: 718-636-6868 **E-mail:** brooklynas@sjcny.edu **CEEB Code:** 2802
Fax: 718-636-8303 **Web:** www.sjcny.edu **ACT Code:** 2890

This private school was founded in 1916. It has a 2-acre campus.

STUDENTS AND FACULTY

Enrollment: 1,256. **Student Body:** Male 22%, female 78%, out-of-state 1%, international students represent 2 countries. **Ethnic Representation:** African American 39%, Asian 4%, Caucasian 49%, Hispanic 8%. **Retention and Graduation:** 86% freshmen return for sophomore year. 54% freshmen graduate within 4 years. 40% grads go on to further study within 1 year. 1% grads pursue business degrees. 3% grads pursue law degrees. 3% grads pursue medical degrees. **Faculty:** Student/faculty ratio 13:1. 46 full-time faculty, 69% hold PhDs. 100% faculty teach undergrads.

ACADEMICS

Degrees: Bachelor's, certificate, master's. **Academic Requirements:** General education including some course work in arts/fine arts, computer literacy, English (including composition), foreign languages, history, humanities, mathematics, philosophy, sciences (biological or physical), social science. **Classes:** 10-19 students in an average class. 10-19 students in an average lab/discussion section. **Disciplines with Highest Percentage of Degrees Awarded:** Health professions and related sciences 50%, education 18%, business/marketing 17%, biological life sciences 3%, psychology 3%. **Special Study Options:** Accelerated program, double major, honors program, independent study, internships, liberal arts/career combination, teacher certification program. Five-year affiliated program: BA/BS + MS in Computer

Science from Polytechnic University. Six-year affiliated program: BS/DPM with New York College of Podiatric Medicine.

FACILITIES

Library Holdings: 100,000 bound volumes. 436 periodicals. 4,198 microforms. 4,482 audiovisuals. **Special Academic Facilities/Equipment:** Child study center, on-campus laboratory preschool, videoconferencing center, Internet access. **Computers:** *Recommended operating system:* Windows 95. School-owned computers available for student use.

EXTRACURRICULARS

Activities: Choral groups, drama/theater, musical theater, student government, student newspaper, yearbook. **Organizations:** 24 registered organizations, 5 honor societies, 1 religious organization, 1 fraternity (1% men join), 1 sorority (6% women join). **Athletics (Intercollegiate):** *Men:* basketball, cross-country, track. *Women:* basketball, cheerleading, cross-country, softball, volleyball.

ADMISSIONS

Selectivity Rating: 66 (of 100). **Freshman Academic Profile:** 16% in top 10% of high school class, 49% in top 25% of high school class, 67% in top 50% of high school class. 18% from public high schools. Average SAT I Math 494. Average SAT I Verbal 515. TOEFL required of all international applicants, minimum TOEFL 550. **Basis for Candidate Selection:** *Very important factors considered include:* secondary school record, standardized test scores. *Important factors considered include:* class rank. *Other factors considered include:* alumni/ae relation, character/personal qualities, essays, extracurricular activities, interview, recommendations, volunteer work, work experience. **Freshman Admission Requirements:** High school diploma or GED is required. *Academic units required/recommended:* 4 English required, 3 math required, 2 science required, 2 foreign language required, 4 social studies required, 3 elective required. **Freshman Admission Statistics:** 460 applied, 49% accepted, 40% of those accepted enrolled. **Transfer Admission Requirements:** *Items required:* college transcript, interview. Minimum college GPA of 2.0 required. **General Admission Information:** Application fee $25. Nonfall registration accepted. Admission may be deferred for a maximum of 1 year. Credit and/or placement offered for CEEB Advanced Placement tests.

COSTS AND FINANCIAL AID

Tuition $10,050. Required fees $322. Average book expense $600. **Required Forms and Deadlines:** FAFSA, institution's own financial aid form and state aid form. Priority filing deadline February 25. **Notification of Awards:** Applicants will be notified of awards on a rolling basis beginning on or about April 15. **Types of Aid:** *Need-based scholarships/grants:* Pell, SEOG, state scholarships/grants, private scholarships, the school's own gift aid. *Loans:* FFEL Subsidized Stafford, FFEL Unsubsidized Stafford, FFEL PLUS, Federal Perkins. **Student Employment:** Federal Work-Study Program available. Institutional employment available. Off-campus job opportunities are excellent. **Financial Aid Statistics:** 68% freshmen, 64% undergrads receive some form of aid. Average freshman grant $5,000. Average freshman loan $2,625. Average income from on-campus job $1,200. **Financial Aid Phone:** 718-636-6808.

ST. JOSEPH'S COLLEGE—PATCHOGUE

155 West Roe Boulevard, Patchogue, NY 11772
Phone: 631-447-3219 **E-mail:** admissionspatchogue@sjcny.edu **CEEB Code:** 2802
Fax: 631-447-1734 **Web:** www.sjcny.edu **ACT Code:** 2923

This private school was founded in 1916. It has a 27-acre campus.

STUDENTS AND FACULTY

Enrollment: 3,115. **Student Body:** Male 22%, female 78%, out-of-state 0%. **Ethnic Representation:** African American 3%, Asian 1%, Caucasian 84%, Hispanic 5%. **Retention and Graduation:** 96% freshmen return for sophomore year. 39% freshmen graduate within 4 years. 32% grads go on to further study within 1 year. 1% grads pursue business degrees. 1% grads pursue law degrees. 1% grads pursue medical degrees. **Faculty:** Student/faculty ratio 15:1. 110 full-time faculty, 39% hold PhDs. 100% faculty teach undergrads.

ACADEMICS

Degrees: Bachelor's, certificate, master's. **Academic Requirements:** General education including some course work in arts/fine arts, English (including composition), humanities, sciences (biological or physical), social science. **Classes:** 20-29 students in an average class. 20-29 students in an average lab/discussion section. **Disciplines with Highest Percentage of Degrees Awarded:** Education 41%, business/marketing 18%, health professions and related sciences 17%, social sciences and history 8%, psychology 5%. **Special Study Options:** Accelerated program, cross registration, double major, internships, liberal arts/career combination, teacher certification program, weekend college.

FACILITIES

Library Holdings: 68,131 bound volumes. 518 periodicals. 3,697 microforms. 11,653 audiovisuals. **Computers:** School-owned computers available for student use.

EXTRACURRICULARS

Activities: Choral groups, dance, drama/theater, jazz band, literary magazine, music ensembles, musical theater, student government, student newspaper, yearbook. **Organizations:** 27 registered organizations, 8 honor societies, 2 religious organizations, 1 fraternity (1% men join), 1 sorority (1% women join). **Athletics (Intercollegiate):** *Men:* baseball, basketball, cross-country, soccer, tennis. *Women:* basketball, cheerleading, cross-country, equestrian, soccer, softball, swimming, tennis, volleyball.

ADMISSIONS

Selectivity Rating: 63 (of 100). **Freshman Academic Profile:** Average high school GPA 3.5. 18% in top 10% of high school class, 50% in top 25% of high school class, 95% in top 50% of high school class. 84% from public high schools. Average SAT I Math 527, SAT I Math middle 50% range 470-560. Average SAT I Verbal 521, SAT I Verbal middle 50% range 470-560. Average ACT 20, ACT middle 50% range 18-21. TOEFL required of all international applicants, minimum TOEFL 500. **Basis for Candidate Selection:** *Very important factors considered include:* standardized test scores. *Important factors considered include:* recommendations. *Other factors considered include:* class rank, essays, interview, secondary school record. **Freshman Admission Requirements:** High school diploma or GED is required. *Academic units required/recommended:* 4 English required, 3 math required, 2 science required, 2 foreign language required, 4 social studies required, 3 elective required. **Freshman Admission Statistics:** 634 applied, 78% accepted, 48% of those accepted enrolled. **Transfer Admission Requirements:** *Items required:* college transcript. Minimum college GPA of 2.0 required. **General Admission Information:** Application fee $25. Nonfall registration accepted. Admission may be deferred for a maximum of 2 years. Credit offered for CEEB Advanced Placement tests.

COSTS AND FINANCIAL AID

Tuition $9,750. Required fees $332. **Required Forms and Deadlines:** FAFSA and institution's own financial aid form. No deadline for regular filing. Priority filing deadline February 25. **Notification of Awards:** Applicants will be notified of awards on a rolling basis. **Types of Aid:** *Need-based scholarships/grants:* Pell, SEOG, state scholarships/grants, private scholarships, the school's own gift aid. *Loans:* FFEL Subsidized Stafford, FFEL Unsubsidized Stafford, FFEL PLUS, Federal Perkins. **Student Employment:** Federal Work-Study Program available. Institutional employment available. Off-campus job opportunities are good. **Financial Aid Statistics:** 72% freshmen, 50% undergrads receive some form of aid. Average freshman grant $800. Average freshman loan $2,200. Average income from on-campus job $1,500. **Financial Aid Phone:** 631-447-3214.

SAINT JOSEPH'S UNIVERSITY (PA)

5600 City Avenue, Philadelphia, PA 19131
Phone: 610-660-1300 **E-mail:** admi@sju.edu **CEEB Code:** 2801
Fax: 610-660-1314 **Web:** www.sju.edu **ACT Code:** 3684

This private school, which is affiliated with the Roman Catholic Church, was founded in 1851. It has a 60-acre campus.

STUDENTS AND FACULTY

Enrollment: 4,584. **Student Body:** Male 47%, female 53%, out-of-state 50%, international 1% (24 countries represented). **Ethnic Representation:** African American 7%, Asian 3%, Caucasian 83%, Hispanic 2%. **Retention and Graduation:** 85% freshmen return for sophomore year. 68% freshmen graduate within 4 years. 25% grads go on to further study within 1 year. 4% grads pursue business degrees. 1% grads pursue law degrees. 4% grads pursue medical degrees. **Faculty:** Student/faculty ratio 14:1. 240 full-time faculty, 90% hold PhDs. 100% faculty teach undergrads.

ACADEMICS

Degrees: Associate's, bachelor's, certificate, doctoral, master's, terminal. **Academic Requirements:** General education including some course work in arts/fine arts, English (including composition), foreign languages, history, humanities, mathematics, philosophy, sciences (biological or physical), social science. **Classes:** 10-19 students in an average class. 10-19 students in an average lab/discussion section. **Majors with Highest Enrollment:** Marketing/

marketing management, general; marketing; business administration/management. **Disciplines with Highest Percentage of Degrees Awarded:** Business/marketing 42%, social sciences and history 14%, education 11%, psychology 8%, English 6%. **Special Study Options:** Distance learning, double major, English as a second language, honors program, independent study, internships, student-designed major, study abroad, teacher certification program, weekend college, off-campus study in Jesuit student exchange.

FACILITIES

Housing: Coed, all-female, all-male, apartments for single students. **Library Holdings:** 347,877 bound volumes. 1,423 periodicals. 808,309 microforms. 3,949 audiovisuals. **Special Academic Facilities/Equipment:** Moot Board Room, Financial Trading Room. **Computers:** School-owned computers available for student use.

EXTRACURRICULARS

Activities: Choral groups, drama/theater, jazz band, literary magazine, musical theater, pep band, radio station, student government, student newspaper, yearbook. **Organizations:** 70 registered organizations, 7 honor societies, 3 fraternities (7% men join), 3 sororities (8% women join). **Athletics (Intercollegiate):** *Men:* baseball, basketball, cheerleading, crew, cross-country, golf, indoor track, lacrosse, soccer, tennis, track & field. *Women:* basketball, cheerleading, crew, cross-country, field hockey, indoor track, soccer, softball, tennis, track & field.

ADMISSIONS

Selectivity Rating: 81 (of 100). **Freshman Academic Profile:** Average high school GPA 3.3. 49% in top 10% of high school class, 89% in top 25% of high school class, 98% in top 50% of high school class. 52% from public high schools. Average SAT I Math 607, SAT I Math middle 50% range 520-620. Average SAT I Verbal 603, SAT I Verbal middle 50% range 510-620. Average ACT 27. TOEFL required of all international applicants, minimum TOEFL 550. **Basis for Candidate Selection:** *Very important factors considered include:* secondary school record. *Important factors considered include:* essays, recommendations, standardized test scores. *Other factors considered include:* character/personal qualities, class rank, extracurricular activities, volunteer work, work experience. **Freshman Admission Requirements:** High school diploma is required and GED is not accepted. *Academic units required/recommended:* 15 total required; 17 total recommended; 4 English required, 3 math required, 2 science required, 3 science recommended, 1 science lab required, 2 foreign language required, 1 social studies recommended, 1 history required, 2 elective required. **Freshman Admission Statistics:** 7,051 applied, 55% accepted, 31% of those accepted enrolled. **Transfer Admission Requirements:** *Items required:* high school transcript, college transcript, statement of good standing from prior school. Minimum college GPA of 2.5 required. Lowest grade transferable C. **General Admission Information:** Application fee $45. Nonfall registration accepted. Admission may be deferred for a maximum of 1 year. Credit offered for CEEB Advanced Placement tests.

COSTS AND FINANCIAL AID

Tuition $22,410. Room & board $9,040. Required fees $0. Average book expense $800. **Required Forms and Deadlines:** FAFSA. Financial aid filing deadline May 1. Priority filing deadline February 15. **Notification of Awards:** Applicants will be notified of awards on a rolling basis beginning on or about March 15. **Types of Aid:** *Need-based scholarships/grants:* Pell, SEOG, state scholarships/grants, private scholarships, the school's own gift aid. *Loans:* FFEL Subsidized Stafford, FFEL Unsubsidized Stafford, FFEL PLUS, Federal Perkins. **Student Employment:** Federal Work-Study Program available. Institutional employment available. Off-campus job opportunities are good. **Financial Aid Statistics:** 71% freshmen, 55% undergrads receive some form of aid. Average freshman grant $8,434. Average freshman loan $10,940. **Financial Aid Phone:** 610-660-1556.

ST. LAWRENCE UNIVERSITY

Payson Hall, Canton, NY 13617
Phone: 315-229-5261 **E-mail:** admissions@stlawu.edu **CEEB Code:** 2805
Fax: 315-229-5818 **Web:** www.stlawu.edu **ACT Code:** 2896

This private school was founded in 1856. It has a 1,000-acre campus.

STUDENTS AND FACULTY

Enrollment: 2,150. **Student Body:** Male 47%, female 53%, out-of-state 46%, international 4%. **Ethnic Representation:** African American 2%, Asian 1%, Caucasian 74%, Hispanic 2%. **Retention and Graduation:** 87% freshmen return for sophomore year. 65% freshmen graduate within 4 years. 23% grads go on to further study within 1 year. 1% grads pursue business degrees. 4% grads pursue law degrees. 6% grads pursue medical degrees. **Faculty:** Student/faculty ratio 12:1. 165 full-time faculty, 99% hold PhDs. 99% faculty teach undergrads.

ACADEMICS

Degrees: Bachelor's, master's, post-master's certificate. **Academic Requirements:** General education including some course work in arts/fine arts, humanities, sciences (biological or physical), social science, one course in mathematics and foreign language, two courses from two different departments on diversity issues. **Classes:** 10-19 students in an average class. 10-19 students in an average lab/discussion section. **Majors with Highest Enrollment:** English language and literature, general; psychology, general; economics, general. **Disciplines with Highest Percentage of Degrees Awarded:** Social sciences and history 36%, biological life sciences 13%, psychology 12%, English 11%, visual and performing arts 8%. **Special Study Options:** Cross registration, double major, student exchange program (domestic), independent study, internships, student-designed major, study abroad, teacher certification program.

FACILITIES

Housing: Coed, housing for international students, fraternities and/or sororities, theme cottages and theme areas. **Library Holdings:** 533,463 bound volumes. 2,065 periodicals. 590,375 microforms. 4,242 audiovisuals. **Special Academic Facilities/Equipment:** Art gallery, language lab, center for international education, mobile environmental research facility, 76-acre forest preserve, two electron microscopes, microscopy and sleep labs, neuroscience lab. **Computers:** *Recommended operating system:* Windows 95. School-owned computers available for student use.

EXTRACURRICULARS

Activities: Choral groups, dance, drama/theater, literary magazine, music ensembles, pep band, radio station, student government, student newspaper, student-run film society, television station, yearbook. **Organizations:** 100 registered organizations, 19 honor societies, 3 religious organizations, 4 fraternities (15% men join), 4 sororities (23% women join). **Athletics (Intercollegiate):** *Men:* baseball, basketball, crew, skiing (cross-country), cross-country, diving, equestrian, football, golf, ice hockey, indoor track, lacrosse, skiing (alpine), skiing (Nordic), soccer, squash, swimming, tennis, track & field. *Women:* basketball, crew, skiing (cross-country), cross-country, diving, equestrian, field hockey, golf, ice hockey, indoor track, lacrosse, skiing (alpine), skiing (Nordic), soccer, softball, squash, swimming, tennis, track & field, volleyball.

ADMISSIONS

Selectivity Rating: 86 (of 100). **Freshman Academic Profile:** Average high school GPA 3.3. 31% in top 10% of high school class, 62% in top 25% of high school class, 92% in top 50% of high school class. 72% from public high schools. Average SAT I Math 570, SAT I Math middle 50% range 520-620. Average SAT I Verbal 570, SAT I Verbal middle 50% range 520-620. Average ACT 24, ACT middle 50% range 21-27. TOEFL required of all international applicants, minimum TOEFL 600. **Basis for Candidate Selection:** *Very important factors considered include:* character/personal qualities, recommendations, secondary school record. *Important factors considered include:* class rank, essays, extracurricular activities, interview, minority status, standardized test scores. *Other factors considered include:* alumni/ae relation, geographical residence, talent/ability, volunteer work, work experience. **Freshman Admission Requirements:** High school diploma or GED is required. *Academic units required/recommended:* 20 total recommended; 4 English recommended, 4 math recommended, 4 science recommended, 4 foreign language recommended, 2 social studies recommended, 2 history recommended. **Freshman Admission Statistics:** 2,867 applied, 65% accepted, 33% of those accepted enrolled. **Transfer Admission Requirements:** *Items required:* high school transcript, college transcript, essay, standardized test scores. Lowest grade transferable C. **General Admission Information:** Application fee $50. Early decision application deadline November 15. Regular application deadline February 15. Nonfall registration accepted. Admission may be deferred for a maximum of 1 year. Credit offered for CEEB Advanced Placement tests.

COSTS AND FINANCIAL AID

Average book expense $650. **Required Forms and Deadlines:** FAFSA, institution's own financial aid form, noncustodial (divorced/separated) parent's statement and Income Tax Returns/W-2s. Financial aid filing deadline February 15. Priority filing deadline February 15. **Notification of Awards:** Applicants will be notified of awards on or about March 30. **Types of Aid:** *Need-based scholarships/grants:* Pell, SEOG, state scholarships/grants, the school's own gift aid. *Loans:* Direct Subsidized Stafford, Direct Unsubsidized Stafford, FFEL Subsidized Stafford, FFEL Unsubsidized Stafford, FFEL PLUS, Federal Perkins, college/university loans from institutional funds, Gate Student Loan Program. **Student Employment:** Federal Work-Study Program available. Institutional employment available. Off-campus job opportunities are poor. **Financial Aid Statistics:** 69% freshmen, 69% undergrads receive some form of aid. Average freshman grant $16,662. Average freshman loan $3,910. Average income from on-campus job $1,140. **Financial Aid Phone:** 315-229-5265.

See page 1188.

SAINT LEO UNIVERSITY

Office of Admission, MC 2008 PO Box 6665, Saint Leo, FL 33574-6665
Phone: 352-588-8283 **E-mail:** admission@saintleo.edu **CEEB Code:** 5638
Fax: 352-588-8257 **Web:** www.saintleo.edu **ACT Code:** 755

This private school, which is affiliated with the Roman Catholic Church, was founded in 1889. It has a 153-acre campus.

STUDENTS AND FACULTY

Enrollment: 1,004. **Student Body:** Male 43%, female 57%, out-of-state 22%, international 5% (27 countries represented). **Ethnic Representation:** African American 8%, Asian 2%, Caucasian 68%, Hispanic 9%, Native American 1%. **Retention and Graduation:** 68% freshmen return for sophomore year. 30% freshmen graduate within 4 years. **Faculty:** Student/faculty ratio 15:1. 55 full-time faculty, 85% hold PhDs. 100% faculty teach undergrads.

ACADEMICS

Degrees: Associate's, bachelor's, master's. **Academic Requirements:** General education including some course work in arts/fine arts, computer literacy, English (including composition), history, humanities, mathematics, philosophy, sciences (biological or physical), social science, physical education. **Classes:** 10-19 students in an average class. **Majors with Highest Enrollment:** Business administration/management; elementary education and teaching; sports and fitness administration/management. **Disciplines with Highest Percentage of Degrees Awarded:** Business/marketing 21%, social sciences and history 20%, education 15%, English 14%, computer and information sciences 7%. **Special Study Options:** Distance learning, double major, dual enrollment, English as a second language, honors program, independent study, internships, liberal arts/career combination, study abroad, teacher certification program, weekend college, Internet-based instruction.

FACILITIES

Housing: Coed, all-female, all-male, housing for disabled students, freshmen-only housing, special housing for international graduate students. **Library Holdings:** 141,521 bound volumes. 700 periodicals. 28,290 microforms. 6,437 audiovisuals. **Computers:** School-owned computers available for student use.

EXTRACURRICULARS

Activities: Choral groups, concert band, drama/theater, literary magazine, music ensembles, student government, student newspaper, television station, yearbook. **Organizations:** 26 registered organizations, 6 honor societies, 2 religious organizations, 7 fraternities (12% men join), 6 sororities (10% women join). **Athletics (Intercollegiate):** *Men:* baseball, basketball, cross-country, golf, soccer, tennis. *Women:* basketball, cross-country, golf, soccer, softball, tennis, volleyball.

ADMISSIONS

Selectivity Rating: 64 (of 100). **Freshman Academic Profile:** Average high school GPA 3.1. 6% in top 10% of high school class, 23% in top 25% of high school class, 63% in top 50% of high school class. 70% from public high schools. Average SAT I Math 480, SAT I Math middle 50% range 420-530. Average SAT I Verbal 470, SAT I Verbal middle 50% range 420-520. Average ACT 20, ACT middle 50% range 19-22. TOEFL required of all international applicants, minimum TOEFL 550. **Basis for Candidate Selection:** *Very important factors considered include:* character/personal qualities, recommendations, secondary school record. *Important factors considered include:* alumni/ae relation, essays, extracurricular activities, interview, standardized test scores. *Other factors considered include:* class rank, minority status, talent/ability, volunteer work, work experience. **Freshman Admission Requirements:** High school diploma or GED is required. *Academic units required/recommended:* 16 total recommended; 4 English recommended, 3 math recommended, 2 science recommended, 2 foreign language recommended, 3 social studies recommended, 2 elective recommended. **Freshman Admission Statistics:** 1,334 applied, 68% accepted, 31% of those accepted enrolled. **Transfer Admission Requirements:** *Items required:* college transcript, essay. Minimum college GPA of 2.0 required. Lowest grade transferable D. **General Admission Information:** Application fee $35. Priority application deadline March 1. Regular application deadline August 15. Nonfall registration accepted. Admission may be deferred for a maximum of 1 year. Credit offered for CEEB Advanced Placement tests.

COSTS AND FINANCIAL AID

Tuition $12,750. Room & board $6,834. Required fees $220. Average book expense $1,200. **Required Forms and Deadlines:** FAFSA. Priority filing deadline March 1. **Notification of Awards:** Applicants will be notified of awards on a rolling basis beginning on or about March 1. **Types of Aid:** *Need-based scholarships/grants:* Pell, SEOG, state scholarships/grants, private scholarships, the school's own gift aid. *Loans:* FFEL Subsidized Stafford, FFEL Unsubsidized Stafford, FFEL PLUS, Federal Perkins. **Student Employment:** Federal Work-Study Program available. Institutional employment available. Off-campus job opportunities are good. **Financial Aid Statistics:** 70% freshmen, 70% undergrads receive some form of aid. Average freshman grant $9,110. Average freshman loan $2,625. Average income from on-campus job $1,500. **Financial Aid Phone:** 800-240-7658.

ST. LOUIS COLLEGE OF PHARMACY

4588 Parkview Place, St. Louis, MO 63110
Phone: 314-367-8700 **E-mail:** pkulage@stlcop.edu **CEEB Code:** 6626
Fax: 314-367-2784 **Web:** www.stlcop.edu **ACT Code:** 2346

This private school was founded in 1864. It has a 7-acre campus.

STUDENTS AND FACULTY

Enrollment: 814. **Student Body:** Male 34%, female 66%, out-of-state 28%. **Ethnic Representation:** African American 4%, Asian 16%, Caucasian 77%, Hispanic 1%. **Retention and Graduation:** 83% freshmen return for sophomore year. **Faculty:** Student/faculty ratio 13:1. 64 full-time faculty, 92% hold PhDs.

ACADEMICS

Degrees: First professional, master's. **Academic Requirements:** General education including some course work in English (including composition), history, humanities, mathematics, sciences (biological or physical), social science. **Classes:** 20-29 students in an average class. 20-29 students in an average lab/discussion section. **Disciplines with Highest Percentage of Degrees Awarded:** Health professions and related sciences 100%.

FACILITIES

Housing: Coed, apartments for married students, apartments for single students, fraternities and/or sororities. **Library Holdings:** 56,636 bound volumes. 282 periodicals. 5,259 microforms. 1,003 audiovisuals. **Computers:** School-owned computers available for student use.

EXTRACURRICULARS

Activities: Choral groups, concert band, drama/theater, literary magazine, musical theater, student government, student newspaper, yearbook. **Organizations:** 2 honor societies, 6 religious organizations, 5 fraternities. **Athletics (Intercollegiate):** *Men:* basketball, cheerleading, cross-country. *Women:* cheerleading, cross-country, volleyball.

ADMISSIONS

Selectivity Rating: 82 (of 100). **Freshman Academic Profile:** Average high school GPA 3.4. 20% in top 10% of high school class, 35% in top 25% of high school class, 98% in top 50% of high school class. SAT I Math middle 50% range 628-687. SAT I Verbal middle 50% range 536-562. Average ACT 24, ACT middle 50% range 25-26. TOEFL required of all international applicants, minimum TOEFL 550. **Basis for Candidate Selection:** *Very important factors considered include:* secondary school record, standardized test scores. *Important factors considered include:* class rank. *Other factors considered include:* alumni/ae relation, character/personal qualities, essays, extracurricular activities, recommendations, volunteer work, work experience. **Freshman Admission Requirements:** High school diploma or GED is required. *Academic units required/recommended:* 4 English required, 3 math required, 2 science required, 3 science recommended, 2 science lab required. **Freshman Admission Statistics:** 356 applied, 80% accepted, 59% of those accepted enrolled. **Transfer Admission Requirements:** *Items required:* high school transcript, college transcript, essay. Minimum college GPA of 3.0 required. Lowest grade transferable C. **General Admission Information:** Application fee $35. Priority application deadline April 2. Regular application deadline April 2. Nonfall registration accepted. Credit offered for CEEB Advanced Placement tests.

COSTS AND FINANCIAL AID

Tuition $13,625. Room & board $5,364. Required fees $120. Average book expense $1,000. **Required Forms and Deadlines:** FAFSA and institution's own financial aid form. No deadline for regular filing. Priority filing deadline March 2. **Notification of Awards:** Applicants will be notified of awards on a rolling basis beginning on or about February 19. **Types of Aid:** *Need-based scholarships/grants:* Pell, SEOG, state scholarships/grants, private scholarships, the school's own gift aid. *Loans:* FFEL Subsidized Stafford, FFEL Unsubsidized Stafford, FFEL PLUS, Federal Perkins, Health Professions Loan. **Student Employment:** Federal Work-Study Program available. Institutional employment available. Off-campus job opportunities are excellent.

Financial Aid Statistics: 88% freshmen, 77% undergrads receive some form of aid. Average freshman grant $5,080. Average freshman loan $8,000. Average income from on-campus job $800. **Financial Aid Phone:** 314-367-8700.

SAINT LOUIS UNIVERSITY

221 North Grand Boulevard, Saint Louis, MO 63103
Phone: 314-977-2500 **E-mail:** admitme@slu.edu **CEEB Code:** 6629
Fax: 314-977-7136 **Web:** www.slu.edu **ACT Code:** 2352

This private school, which is affiliated with the Roman Catholic Church, was founded in 1818. It has a 300-acre campus.

STUDENTS AND FACULTY

Enrollment: 7,178. **Student Body:** Male 46%, female 54%, out-of-state 47%, international 3% (73 countries represented). **Ethnic Representation:** African American 7%, Asian 4%, Caucasian 73%, Hispanic 3%. **Retention and Graduation:** 87% freshmen return for sophomore year. 54% freshmen graduate within 4 years. **Faculty:** Student/faculty ratio 12:1. 591 full-time faculty, 91% hold PhDs.

ACADEMICS

Degrees: Associate's, bachelor's, certificate, doctoral, first professional, master's, post-bachelor's certificate, post-master's certificate, terminal. **Academic Requirements:** General education including some course work in arts/fine arts, English (including composition), foreign languages, history, mathematics, philosophy, sciences (biological or physical), social science, theological studies. **Classes:** 10-19 students in an average class. 20-29 students in an average lab/discussion section. **Majors with Highest Enrollment:** Communications studies/speech communication and rhetoric; biology/biological sciences, general; psychology, general. **Disciplines with Highest Percentage of Degrees Awarded:** Business/marketing 30%, psychology 10%, communications/communication technologies 9%, health professions and related sciences 9%, social sciences and history 7%. **Special Study Options:** Accelerated program, cross registration, distance learning, double major, dual enrollment, English as a second language, student exchange program (domestic), honors program, independent study, internships, student-designed major, study abroad, teacher certification program.

FACILITIES

Housing: Coed, all-female, apartments for single students, housing for disabled students, fraternities and/or sororities, theme housing in cooperation with other departments. Theme housing includes MICAH House (social justice floor in residence halls), classic living (wellness floor in residence halls), and German, French, and Spanish houses. **Library Holdings:** 1,340,251 bound volumes. 12,881 periodicals. 2,466,911 microforms. 195,651 audiovisuals. **Special Academic Facilities/Equipment:** Art gallery, museum. **Computers:** School-owned computers available for student use.

EXTRACURRICULARS

Activities: Choral groups, concert band, drama/theater, jazz band, musical theater, pep band, radio station, student government, student newspaper. **Organizations:** 101 registered organizations, 12 honor societies, 12 religious organizations, 11 fraternities (16% men join), 4 sororities (17% women join). **Athletics (Intercollegiate):** *Men:* baseball, basketball, cheerleading, cross-country, diving, golf, ice hockey, rifle, soccer, swimming, tennis. *Women:* basketball, cheerleading, cross-country, diving, field hockey, rifle, soccer, softball, swimming, tennis, volleyball.

ADMISSIONS

Selectivity Rating: 77 (of 100). **Freshman Academic Profile:** Average high school GPA 3.5. 32% in top 10% of high school class, 61% in top 25% of high school class, 88% in top 50% of high school class. Average SAT I Math 595, SAT I Math middle 50% range 530-655. Average SAT I Verbal 585, SAT I Verbal middle 50% range 530-640. Average ACT 26, ACT middle 50% range 23-28. TOEFL required of all international applicants, minimum TOEFL 525. **Basis for Candidate Selection:** *Important factors considered include:* secondary school record, standardized test scores. *Other factors considered include:* character/personal qualities, essays, extracurricular activities, recommendations, volunteer work. **Freshman Admission Requirements:** High school diploma or GED is required. *Academic units required/recommended:* 16 total recommended; 4 English recommended, 3 math recommended, 2 science recommended, 2 foreign language recommended, 2 social studies recommended, 3 elective recommended. **Freshman Admission Statistics:** 5,992 applied, 72% accepted, 33% of those accepted enrolled. **Transfer Admission Requirements:** *Items required:* college transcript. Minimum high school GPA of 2.5 required. Minimum college GPA of 2.0 required. Lowest grade transferable C. **General Admission Information:** Application fee $25. Priority application deadline December 1. Regular application deadline August 1. Nonfall registration accepted. Admission may be deferred for a maximum of 1 year. Credit and/or placement offered for CEEB Advanced Placement tests.

COSTS AND FINANCIAL AID

Tuition $20,840. Room & board $7,310. Required fees $168. Average book expense $1,040. **Required Forms and Deadlines:** FAFSA. Financial aid filing deadline May 1. Priority filing deadline April 1. **Notification of Awards:** Applicants will be notified of awards on a rolling basis beginning on or about January 15. **Types of Aid:** *Need-based scholarships/grants:* Pell, SEOG, state scholarships/grants, private scholarships, the school's own gift aid. *Loans:* FFEL Subsidized Stafford, FFEL Unsubsidized Stafford, FFEL PLUS, Federal Perkins, Federal Nursing, short-term loans. **Student Employment:** Federal Work-Study Program available. Off-campus job opportunities are excellent. **Financial Aid Statistics:** 73% freshmen, 67% undergrads receive some form of aid. Average freshman grant $13,575. Average freshman loan $6,797. **Financial Aid Phone:** 314-977-2350.

SAINT MARTIN'S COLLEGE

5300 Pacific Avenue SE, Lacey, WA 98503
Phone: 360-438-4311 **E-mail:** admissions@stmartin.edu **CEEB Code:** 4674
Fax: 360-412-6189 **Web:** www.stmartin.edu **ACT Code:** 4474

This private school, which is affiliated with the Roman Catholic Church, was founded in 1895. It has a 304-acre campus.

STUDENTS AND FACULTY

Enrollment: 1,121. **Student Body:** Male 44%, female 56%, out-of-state 7%, international 5%. **Ethnic Representation:** African American 10%, Asian 2%, Caucasian 67%, Hispanic 6%, Native American 9%. **Retention and Graduation:** 70% freshmen return for sophomore year. 43% freshmen graduate within 4 years. 14% grads go on to further study within 1 year. 8% grads pursue business degrees. 2% grads pursue law degrees. 2% grads pursue medical degrees. **Faculty:** Student/faculty ratio 14:1. 55 full-time faculty, 85% hold PhDs. 100% faculty teach undergrads.

ACADEMICS

Degrees: Associate's, bachelor's, master's, post-bachelor's certificate. **Academic Requirements:** General education including some course work in arts/fine arts, computer literacy, English (including composition), foreign languages, history, humanities, mathematics, philosophy, sciences (biological or physical), social science, religious studies. **Classes:** Under 10 students in an average class. Under 10 students in an average lab/discussion section. **Majors with Highest Enrollment:** Business administration/management; elementary education and teaching; biology/biological sciences, general. **Disciplines with Highest Percentage of Degrees Awarded:** Business/marketing 27%, social sciences and history 19%, psychology 15%, education 11%, protective services/public administration 9%. **Special Study Options:** Double major, English as a second language, student exchange program (domestic), independent study, internships, liberal arts/career combination, study abroad, teacher certification program.

FACILITIES

Housing: Coed. **Library Holdings:** 84,220 bound volumes. 852 periodicals. 110,800 microforms. 1,239 audiovisuals. **Special Academic Facilities/Equipment:** Arts Education Building. **Computers:** *Recommended operating system:* Windows 95. School-owned computers available for student use.

EXTRACURRICULARS

Activities: Choral groups, concert band, drama/theater, pep band, student government, student newspaper, yearbook. **Organizations:** 30 registered organizations, 2 honor societies, 1 religious organization, 4% men join fraternities, 4% women join sororities. **Athletics (Intercollegiate):** *Men:* baseball, basketball, cross-country, golf, track & field. *Women:* basketball, cross-country, golf, softball, track & field, volleyball.

ADMISSIONS

Selectivity Rating: 71 (of 100). **Freshman Academic Profile:** Average high school GPA 3.3. 22% in top 10% of high school class, 45% in top 25% of high school class, 76% in top 50% of high school class. Average SAT I Math 566, SAT I Math middle 50% range 420-550. Average SAT I Verbal 553, SAT I Verbal middle 50% range 450-560. Average ACT 23, ACT middle 50% range 17-22. TOEFL required of all international applicants, minimum TOEFL 525. **Basis for Candidate Selection:** *Very important factors considered include:* essays, secondary school record, standardized test scores. *Important factors considered include:* character/personal qualities, extracurricular activities, recommendations, volunteer work. *Other factors considered include:* interview, talent/ability. **Freshman Admission Requirements:** High school diploma or GED is required. *Academic units required/recommended:* 4 English recommended, 2 math recommended, 2 science recommended, 1 science lab recommended, 1 foreign language recommended, 2 social studies recommended, 3 elective recommended. **Freshman Admission Statistics:** 380 applied, 92% accepted. **Transfer Admission Requirements:** *Items required:* college transcript, essay. Minimum high school GPA of 2.5 required. Minimum college GPA of 2.3 required. Lowest grade transferable C. **General Admission Information:** Application fee $35. Priority application deadline March 1. Regular application deadline August 1. Nonfall registration accepted. Credit offered for CEEB Advanced Placement tests.

COSTS AND FINANCIAL AID

Tuition $17,600. Room & board $5,300. Required fees $230. Average book expense $720. **Required Forms and Deadlines:** FAFSA. No deadline for regular filing. Priority filing deadline March 1. **Notification of Awards:** Applicants will be notified of awards on a rolling basis beginning on or about March 15. **Types of Aid:** *Need-based scholarships/grants:* Pell, SEOG, state scholarships/grants, private scholarships, the school's own gift aid. *Loans:* Direct Subsidized Stafford, Direct Unsubsidized Stafford, FFEL PLUS, Federal Perkins, college/university loans from institutional funds. **Student Employment:** Federal Work-Study Program available. Institutional employment available. Off-campus job opportunities are good. **Financial Aid Statistics:** 90% freshmen, 87% undergrads receive some form of aid. Average freshman grant $9,498. Average freshman loan $4,682. **Financial Aid Phone:** 360-438-4397.

500. **Basis for Candidate Selection:** *Very important factors considered include:* secondary school record, standardized test scores. *Important factors considered include:* character/personal qualities, extracurricular activities, interview, recommendations, talent/ability, volunteer work, work experience. *Other factors considered include:* alumni/ae relation. **Freshman Admission Requirements:** High school diploma or GED is required. *Academic units required/recommended:* 12 total required; 26 total recommended; 4 English required, 4 English recommended, 2 math required, 4 math recommended, 2 science required, 4 science recommended, 2 science lab recommended, 2 foreign language required, 2 foreign language recommended, 2 social studies recommended, 2 history required, 4 history recommended, 2 elective recommended. **Freshman Admission Statistics:** 292 applied, 83% accepted, 32% of those accepted enrolled. **Transfer Admission Requirements:** *Items required:* college transcript. Minimum college GPA of 2.0 required. Lowest grade transferable C. **General Admission Information:** Application fee $20. Nonfall registration accepted. Credit and/or placement offered for CEEB Advanced Placement tests.

COSTS AND FINANCIAL AID

Tuition $12,070. Room & board $4,880. Average book expense $600. **Required Forms and Deadlines:** FAFSA. **Types of Aid:** *Need-based scholarships/grants:* Pell, SEOG, state scholarships/grants, private scholarships, the school's own gift aid. *Loans:* FFEL Subsidized Stafford, FFEL Unsubsidized Stafford, FFEL PLUS, Federal Perkins. **Student Employment:** Federal Work-Study Program available. Institutional employment available. Off-campus job opportunities are good. **Financial Aid Statistics:** 87% freshmen receive some form of aid. Average freshman grant $9,406. Average freshman loan $2,420. Average income from on-campus job $800. **Financial Aid Phone:** 800-752-7043.

SAINT MARY COLLEGE (KS)

4100 South Fourth Street Trafficway, Leavenworth, KS 66048
Phone: 913-758-6118 **E-mail:** admis@hub.smcks.edu **CEEB Code:** 6630
Fax: 913-758-6140 **Web:** www.smcks.edu **ACT Code:** 1455

This private school, which is affiliated with the Roman Catholic Church, was founded in 1923. It has a 240-acre campus.

STUDENTS AND FACULTY

Enrollment: 506. **Student Body:** Male 35%, female 65%, out-of-state 24%. **Ethnic Representation:** African American 11%, Asian 2%, Caucasian 79%, Hispanic 4%, Native American 1%. **Retention and Graduation:** 52% freshmen return for sophomore year. 28% freshmen graduate within 4 years. **Faculty:** Student/faculty ratio 10:1. 47 full-time faculty, 63% hold PhDs. 100% faculty teach undergrads.

ACADEMICS

Degrees: Associate's, bachelor's, master's, transfer. **Academic Requirements:** General education including some course work in arts/fine arts, English (including composition), foreign languages, history, humanities, mathematics, philosophy, sciences (biological or physical), social science. **Classes:** Under 10 students in an average class. **Disciplines with Highest Percentage of Degrees Awarded:** Education 24%, psychology 19%, business/marketing 17%, English 9%, biological life sciences 7%. **Special Study Options:** Accelerated program, cooperative (work-study) program, distance learning, double major, dual enrollment, honors program, independent study, internships, liberal arts/career combination, student-designed major, study abroad, teacher certification program.

FACILITIES

Housing: Coed. **Library Holdings:** 100,000 bound volumes. 1,675 periodicals. 5,012 microforms. **Special Academic Facilities/Equipment:** Lincoln Library Collection and an Art Gallery. **Computers:** School-owned computers available for student use.

EXTRACURRICULARS

Activities: Choral groups, concert band, drama/theater, literary magazine, musical theater, student government, student newspaper. **Organizations:** 22 registered organizations, 3 honor societies, 2 religious organizations. **Athletics (Intercollegiate):** *Men:* baseball, basketball, football, soccer, tennis. *Women:* basketball, golf, soccer, softball, tennis, volleyball.

ADMISSIONS

Selectivity Rating: 74 (of 100). **Freshman Academic Profile:** 2% in top 10% of high school class, 5% in top 25% of high school class, 27% in top 50% of high school class. 80% from public high schools. Average ACT 21, ACT middle 50% range 12-25. TOEFL required of all international applicants, minimum TOEFL

SAINT MARY-OF-THE-WOODS COLLEGE

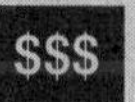

Office of Admissions, Guerin Hall, Saint Mary-of-the-Woods, IN 47876-0068
Phone: 812-535-5106 **E-mail:** smwcadms@smwc.edu **CEEB Code:** 1704
Fax: 812-535-4900 **Web:** www.smwc.edu **ACT Code:** 1242

This private school, which is affiliated with the Roman Catholic Church, was founded in 1840. It has a 200-acre campus.

STUDENTS AND FACULTY

Enrollment: 1,775. **Student Body:** Male 22%, female 78%, put-of-state 28%, international students represent 5 countries. **Ethnic Representation:** African American 3%, Caucasian 95%, Hispanic 1%, Native American 1%. **Retention and Graduation:** 68% freshmen return for sophomore year. 54% freshmen graduate within 4 years. 15% grads go on to further study within 1 year. 1% grads pursue business degrees. 3% grads pursue law degrees. 3% grads pursue medical degrees. **Faculty:** Student/faculty ratio 12:1. 60 full-time faculty, 71% hold PhDs. 100% faculty teach undergrads.

ACADEMICS

Degrees: Associate's, bachelor's, certificate, master's, post-bachelor's certificate, terminal, transfer. **Academic Requirements:** General education including some course work in arts/fine arts, computer literacy, English (including composition), foreign languages, history, humanities, mathematics, philosophy, sciences (biological or physical), social science, integrative studies. **Classes:** Under 10 students in an average class. **Majors with Highest Enrollment:** Equestrian/equine studies; elementary education and teaching; pre-medicine/pre-medical studies. **Disciplines with Highest Percentage of Degrees Awarded:** Education 27%, business/marketing 20%, psychology 8%, liberal arts/general studies 8%, visual and performing arts 6%. **Special Study Options:** Accelerated program, cross registration, distance learning, double major, student exchange program (domestic), external degree program, independent study, internships, student-designed major, study abroad, teacher certification program.

FACILITIES

Housing: All-female, housing for disabled students, Housing for single mothers with one child. **Library Holdings:** 151,389 bound volumes. 284 periodicals. 641 microforms. 479 audiovisuals. **Computers:** *Recommended operating system:* Windows 95. School-owned computers available for student use.

EXTRACURRICULARS

Activities: Choral groups, drama/theater, jazz band, literary magazine, music ensembles, musical theater, student government, student newspaper. **Organizations:** 30 registered organizations, 1 honor society, 1 religious organization. **Athletics (Intercollegiate):** *Women:* basketball, equestrian, soccer, softball.

ADMISSIONS

Selectivity Rating: 69 (of 100). **Freshman Academic Profile:** Average high school GPA 3.2. 15% in top 10% of high school class, 41% in top 25% of high school class, 80% in top 50% of high school class. 85% from public high schools. Average SAT I Math 490, SAT I Math middle 50% range 440-530. Average SAT I Verbal 513, SAT I Verbal middle 50% range 450-550. Average ACT 22, ACT middle 50% range 18-25. TOEFL required of all international applicants, minimum TOEFL 500. **Basis for Candidate Selection:** *Very important factors considered include:* secondary school record. *Important factors considered include:* character/personal qualities, class rank, essays, extracurricular activities, recommendations, standardized test scores, volunteer work. *Other factors considered include:* interview, talent/ability. **Freshman Admission Requirements:** High school diploma or GED is required. *Academic units required/recommended:* 15 total required; 4 English required, 3 math required, 3 science required, 3 science lab required, 2 foreign language required, 3 social studies required. **Freshman Admission Statistics:** 258 applied, 83% accepted, 45% of those accepted enrolled. **Transfer Admission Requirements:** *Items required:* college transcript, essay. Minimum college GPA of 2.0 required. Lowest grade transferable C. **General Admission Information:** Application fee $30. Nonfall registration accepted. Admission may be deferred for a maximum of 1 year. Credit and/or placement offered for CEEB Advanced Placement tests.

COSTS AND FINANCIAL AID

Tuition $15,890. Room & board $6,010. Required fees $480. Average book expense $900. **Required Forms and Deadlines:** FAFSA and institution's own financial aid form. Financial aid filing deadline March 1. **Notification of Awards:** Applicants will be notified of awards on a rolling basis beginning on or about December 1. **Types of Aid:** *Need-based scholarships/grants:* Pell, SEOG, state scholarships/grants, the school's own gift aid. *Loans:* Direct Subsidized Stafford, Direct Unsubsidized Stafford, Direct PLUS, FFEL Subsidized Stafford, FFEL Unsubsidized Stafford, FFEL PLUS, Federal Perkins. **Student Employment:** Federal Work-Study Program available. Institutional employment available. Off-campus job opportunities are excellent. **Financial Aid Statistics:** 56% freshmen, 66% undergrads receive some form of aid. Average freshman grant $5,000. Average freshman loan $2,625. Average income from on-campus job $600. **Financial Aid Phone:** 812-535-5109.

SAINT MARY'S COLLEGE (CA)

PO Box 4800, Moraga, CA 94575-4800
Phone: 925-631-4224 **E-mail:** smcadmit@stmarys-ca.edu **CEEB Code:** 4675
Fax: 925-376-7193 **Web:** www.stmarys-ca.edu **ACT Code:** 386

This private school, which is affiliated with the Roman Catholic Church, was founded in 1863. It has a 420-acre campus.

STUDENTS AND FACULTY

Enrollment: 3,401. **Student Body:** Male 40%, female 60%, out-of-state 11%, international 2% (21 countries represented). **Ethnic Representation:** African American 6%, Asian 10%, Caucasian 60%, Hispanic 18%, Native American 1%. **Retention and Graduation:** 88% freshmen return for sophomore year. 63% freshmen graduate within 4 years. 18% grads go on to further study within 1 year. **Faculty:** Student/faculty ratio 13:1. 193 full-time faculty, 94% hold PhDs. 100% faculty teach undergrads.

ACADEMICS

Degrees: Bachelor's, certificate, doctoral, master's. **Academic Requirements:** General education including some course work in English (including composition), foreign languages, humanities, mathematics, sciences (biological or physical), social science, collegiate seminar. **Classes:** 20-29 students in an average class. **Majors with Highest Enrollment:** Business administration/management; communications studies/speech communication and rhetoric; political science and government. **Disciplines with Highest Percentage of Degrees Awarded:** Business/marketing 25%, communications/communication technologies 14%, social sciences and history 14%, psychology 12%, liberal arts/general studies 11%. **Special Study Options:** Cross registration, double major, student exchange program (domestic), external degree program, honors program, independent study, internships, liberal arts/career combination, student-designed major, study abroad, teacher certification program, weekend college.

FACILITIES

Housing: Coed, all-male, apartments for single students, housing for disabled students. **Library Holdings:** 207,076 bound volumes. 1,070 periodicals. 479,591 microforms. 6,296 audiovisuals. **Special Academic Facilities/Equipment:** Hearst Art Gallery. **Computers:** School-owned computers available for student use.

EXTRACURRICULARS

Activities: Choral groups, dance, drama/theater, jazz band, literary magazine, music ensembles, pep band, radio station, student government, student newspaper, television station, yearbook. **Organizations:** 51 registered organizations, 1 religious organization. **Athletics (Intercollegiate):** *Men:* baseball, basketball, cross-country, football, golf, soccer, tennis. *Women:* basketball, crew, cross-country, golf, lacrosse, soccer, softball, tennis, volleyball.

ADMISSIONS

Selectivity Rating: 79 (of 100). **Freshman Academic Profile:** Average high school GPA 3.4. 57% from public high schools. Average SAT I Math 552, SAT I Math middle 50% range 500-600. Average SAT I Verbal 551, SAT I Verbal middle 50% range 500-600. TOEFL required of all international applicants, minimum TOEFL 525. **Basis for Candidate Selection:** *Very important factors considered include:* secondary school record, standardized test scores. *Important factors considered include:* essays, recommendations. *Other factors considered include:* alumni/ae relation, character/personal qualities, class rank, extracurricular activities, geographical residence, interview, minority status, religious affiliation/commitment, talent/ability, volunteer work, work experience. **Freshman Admission Requirements:** High school diploma or GED is required. *Academic units required/recommended:* 16 total required; 17 total recommended; 4 English required, 4 English recommended, 3 math required, 4 math recommended, 2 science required, 3 science recommended, 1 science lab required, 1 science lab recommended, 2 foreign language required, 3 foreign language recommended, 1 social studies required, 1 social studies recommended, 1 history required, 1 history recommended, 3 elective required, 3 elective recommended. **Freshman Admission Statistics:** 3,021 applied, 85% accepted, 25% of those accepted enrolled. **Transfer Admission Requirements:** *Items required:* high school transcript, college transcript, essay. Minimum high school GPA of 2.0 required. Minimum college GPA of 2.5 required. Lowest grade transferable C-. **General Admission Information:** Application fee $45. Priority application deadline November 30. Regular application deadline February 1. Nonfall registration accepted. Admission may be deferred for a maximum of 1 year. Credit and/or placement offered for CEEB Advanced Placement tests.

COSTS AND FINANCIAL AID

Tuition $20,750. Room & board $8,550. Required fees $135. Average book expense $846. **Required Forms and Deadlines:** FAFSA and state aid form. Financial aid filing deadline March 2. Priority filing deadline March 2. **Notification of Awards:** Applicants will be notified of awards on a rolling basis beginning on or about April 15. **Types of Aid:** *Need-based scholarships/grants:* Pell, SEOG, state scholarships/grants, private scholarships, the school's own gift aid. *Loans:* FFEL Subsidized Stafford, FFEL Unsubsidized Stafford, FFEL PLUS, Federal Perkins. **Student Employment:** Federal Work-Study Program available. Institutional employment available. Off-campus job opportunities are excellent. **Financial Aid Statistics:** 66% freshmen, 60% undergrads receive some form of aid. Average freshman loan $3,818. Average income from on-campus job $1,867. **Financial Aid Phone:** 925-631-4370.

SAINT MARY'S COLLEGE (IN)

Admission office, Notre Dame, IN 46556
Phone: 219-284-4587 **E-mail:** admission@saintmarys.edu **CEEB Code:** 1702
Fax: 219-284-4841 **Web:** www.saintmarys.edu **ACT Code:** 1244

This private school, which is affiliated with the Roman Catholic Church, was founded in 1844. It has a 275-acre campus.

STUDENTS AND FACULTY

Enrollment: 1,492. **Student Body:** Out-of-state 72%, international 1% (12 countries represented). **Ethnic Representation:** African American 1%, Asian 2%, Caucasian 91%, Hispanic 5%. **Retention and Graduation:** 82% freshmen return for sophomore year. 71% freshmen graduate within 4 years. 22% grads go on to further study within 1 year. 8% grads pursue business degrees. 3% grads pursue law degrees. 1% grads pursue medical degrees. **Faculty:** Student/faculty ratio 12:1. 114 full-time faculty. 100% faculty teach undergrads.

ACADEMICS

Degrees: Bachelor's. **Academic Requirements:** General education including some course work in arts/fine arts, computer literacy, English (including composition), foreign languages, history, mathematics, philosophy, sciences (biological or physical), social science, religious studies. **Classes:** 20-29 students in an average class. 10-19 students in an average lab/discussion section. **Majors with Highest Enrollment:** Business administration/management; elementary education and teaching; communications studies/speech communication and rhetoric. **Disciplines with Highest Percentage of Degrees Awarded:**

Business/marketing 15%, education 14%, communications/communication technologies 13%, social sciences and history 10%, biological life sciences 9%. **Special Study Options:** Accelerated program, cooperative (work-study) program, cross registration, double major, student exchange program (domestic), independent study, internships, liberal arts/career combination, student-designed major, study abroad, teacher certification program.

FACILITIES

Housing: All-female. **Library Holdings:** 210,812 bound volumes. 776 periodicals. 14,276 microforms. 2,471 audiovisuals. **Special Academic Facilities/Equipment:** Art gallery, early childhood development center, language lab, electron microscope. **Computers:** School-owned computers available for student use.

EXTRACURRICULARS

Activities: Choral groups, dance, drama/theater, literary magazine, marching band, music ensembles, musical theater, opera, radio station, student government, student newspaper, yearbook. **Organizations:** 80 registered organizations, 10 honor societies. **Athletics (Intercollegiate):** *Women:* basketball, cross-country, diving, golf, soccer, softball, swimming, tennis, volleyball.

ADMISSIONS

Selectivity Rating: 79 (of 100). **Freshman Academic Profile:** Average high school GPA 3.7. 34% in top 10% of high school class, 70% in top 25% of high school class, 95% in top 50% of high school class. 52% from public high schools. Average SAT I Math 563, SAT I Math middle 50% range 520-610. Average SAT I Verbal 578, SAT I Verbal middle 50% range 530-630. Average ACT 25, ACT middle 50% range 22-27. TOEFL required of all international applicants, minimum TOEFL 550. **Basis for Candidate Selection:** *Very important factors considered include:* essays, secondary school record, standardized test scores. *Important factors considered include:* class rank, extracurricular activities, recommendations, talent/ability. *Other factors considered include:* alumni/ae relation, interview, minority status, volunteer work, work experience. **Freshman Admission Requirements:** High school diploma or GED is required. *Academic units required/recommended:* 16 total required; 4 English required, 4 English recommended, 3 math required, 4 math recommended, 2 science required, 4 science recommended, 2 science lab required, 2 foreign language required, 4 foreign language recommended, 2 social studies required, 4 elective required. **Freshman Admission Statistics:** 997 applied, 82% accepted, 46% of those accepted enrolled. **Transfer Admission Requirements:** *Items required:* high school transcript, college transcript, essay. Minimum college GPA of 3.0 required. Lowest grade transferable C. **General Admission Information:** Application fee $30. Priority application deadline March 1. Early decision application deadline November 15. Nonfall registration accepted. Admission may be deferred for a maximum of 1 year. Credit and/or placement offered for CEEB Advanced Placement tests.

COSTS AND FINANCIAL AID

Required Forms and Deadlines: FAFSA and CSS/Financial Aid PROFILE. Priority filing deadline March 1. **Notification of Awards:** Applicants will be notified of awards on a rolling basis beginning on or about December 15. **Types of Aid:** *Need-based scholarships/grants:* Pell, SEOG, state scholarships/grants, private scholarships, the school's own gift aid. *Loans:* FFEL Subsidized Stafford, FFEL Unsubsidized Stafford, FFEL PLUS, Federal Perkins, college/university loans from institutional funds. **Student Employment:** Federal Work-Study Program available. Institutional employment available. Off-campus job opportunities are excellent. **Financial Aid Statistics:** 62% freshmen, 61% undergrads receive some form of aid. Average freshman grant $16,306. Average freshman loan $12,719. Average income from on-campus job $3,307. **Financial Aid Phone:** 219-284-4557.

SAINT MARY'S COLLEGE OF AVE MARIA UNIVERSITY (MI)

3535 Indian Trail, Orchard Lake, MI 48324
Phone: 248-683-1757 **E-mail:** info@stmarys.avemaria.edu **CEEB Code:** 1753
Fax: 248-683-1756 **Web:** www.stmarys.avemaria.edu **ACT Code:** 2053

This private school, which is affiliated with the Roman Catholic Church, was founded in 1885. It has a 100-acre campus.

STUDENTS AND FACULTY

Enrollment: 381. **Student Body:** Male 60%, female 40%, out-of-state 1%, international 29% (17 countries represented). **Ethnic Representation:** African American 12%, Asian 2%, Caucasian 80%, Hispanic 1%. **Retention and Graduation:** 29% freshmen graduate within 4 years. **Faculty:** Student/faculty ratio 14:1. 11 full-time faculty. 100% faculty teach undergrads.

ACADEMICS

Degrees: Bachelor's, certificate. **Academic Requirements:** General education including some course work in arts/fine arts, computer literacy, English (including composition), foreign languages, history, humanities, mathematics, philosophy, sciences (biological or physical), social science, theology. **Classes:** 100+ students in an average class. Under 10 students in an average lab/discussion section. **Disciplines with Highest Percentage of Degrees Awarded:** Communications/communication technologies 32%, social sciences and history 21%, psychology 14%, biological life sciences 7%, health professions and related sciences 7%. **Special Study Options:** Double major, English as a second language, independent study, internships.

FACILITIES

Housing: All-female, all-male. **Library Holdings:** 74,342 bound volumes. 327 periodicals. 0 microforms. 1,384 audiovisuals. **Computers:** School-owned computers available for student use.

EXTRACURRICULARS

Activities: Choral groups, drama/theater, student government. **Organizations:** 3 registered organizations, 1 religious organization. **Athletics (Intercollegiate):** *Men:* baseball, basketball, soccer. *Women:* cheerleading, soccer.

ADMISSIONS

Selectivity Rating: 63 (of 100). **Freshman Academic Profile:** Average high school GPA 2.7. 15% in top 10% of high school class, 30% in top 25% of high school class, 51% in top 50% of high school class. 80% from public high schools. Average SAT I Math 458. Average SAT I Verbal 455. Average ACT 20. TOEFL required of all international applicants, minimum TOEFL 500. **Basis for Candidate Selection:** *Important factors considered include:* secondary school record, standardized test scores. *Other factors considered include:* character/personal qualities, extracurricular activities, interview, talent/ability. **Freshman Admission Requirements:** High school diploma or GED is required. *Academic units required/recommended:* 2 math recommended, 2 science recommended, 2 science lab recommended, 3 social studies recommended. **Freshman Admission Statistics:** 120 applied, 80% accepted, 47% of those accepted enrolled. **Transfer Admission Requirements:** *Items required:* high school transcript, college transcript. Minimum college GPA of 2.0 required. Lowest grade transferable C. **General Admission Information:** Application fee $25. Regular application deadline August 15. Nonfall registration accepted. Admission may be deferred for a maximum of 1 year.

COSTS AND FINANCIAL AID

Tuition $7,380. Room & board $4,900. Required fees $72. **Required Forms and Deadlines:** FAFSA and institution's own financial aid form. Financial aid filing deadline April 30. Priority filing deadline February 21. **Notification of Awards:** Applicants will be notified of awards on or about May 30. **Types of Aid:** *Need-based scholarships/grants:* Pell, SEOG, state scholarships/grants, private scholarships, the school's own gift aid. *Loans:* FFEL Subsidized Stafford, FFEL Unsubsidized Stafford, FFEL PLUS, state loans. **Student Employment:** Federal Work-Study Program available. Institutional employment available. Off-campus job opportunities are good. **Financial Aid Statistics:** 61% freshmen, 68% undergrads receive some form of aid. Average freshman grant $4,637. Average freshman loan $2,616. Average income from on-campus job $2,663. **Financial Aid Phone:** 248-683-0508.

ST. MARY'S COLLEGE OF MARYLAND

Admissions Office, 18952 E. Fisher Rd., St Mary's City, MD 20686-3001
Phone: 240-895-5000 **E-mail:** admissions@smcm.edu **CEEB Code:** 5601
Fax: 240-895-5001 **Web:** www.smcm.edu **ACT Code:** 1736

This public school was founded in 1840. It has a 319-acre campus.

STUDENTS AND FACULTY

Enrollment: 1,823. **Student Body:** Male 40%, female 60%, out-of-state 15%, (25 countries represented). **Ethnic Representation:** African American 7%, Asian 4%, Caucasian 82%, Hispanic 3%, Native American 1%. **Retention and Graduation:** 91% freshmen return for sophomore year. 71% freshmen graduate within 4 years. 30% grads go on to further study within 1 year. 2% grads pursue business degrees. 3% grads pursue law degrees. 1% grads pursue medical degrees. **Faculty:** Student/faculty ratio 12:1. 118 full-time faculty, 97% hold PhDs. 100% faculty teach undergrads.

ACADEMICS

Degrees: Bachelor's. **Academic Requirements:** General education including some course work in arts/fine arts, English (including composition), foreign languages, history, humanities, mathematics, philosophy, sciences (biological or physical), social science. **Classes:** 10-19 students in an average class. 10-19 students in an average lab/discussion section. **Majors with Highest Enrollment:** Biology/biological sciences, general; economics, general; psychology, general. **Disciplines with Highest Percentage of Degrees Awarded:** Social sciences and history 37%, psychology 18%, biological life sciences 15%, visual and performing arts 7%, English 5%. **Special Study Options:** Cooperative (work-study) program, double major, dual enrollment, student exchange program (domestic), honors program, independent study, internships, student-designed major, study abroad, teacher certification program.

FACILITIES

Housing: Coed, all-female, all-male, apartments for single students, housing for disabled students, townhouse-style residences for single students. **Library Holdings:** 153,827 bound volumes. 1,797 periodicals. 44,990 microforms. 16,109 audiovisuals. **Special Academic Facilities/Equipment:** Art gallery, archaeological sites, historic St. Mary's City, historic state house of early Maryland settlers, electron microscope, freshwater and saltwater research facilities, research boat. **Computers:** *Recommended operating system:* Windows XP - 98. School-owned computers available for student use.

EXTRACURRICULARS

Activities: Choral groups, concert band, dance, drama/theater, jazz band, literary magazine, music ensembles, musical theater, radio station, student government, student newspaper, student-run film society, symphony orchestra, television station, yearbook. **Organizations:** 64 registered organizations, 8 honor societies, 2 religious organizations. **Athletics (Intercollegiate):** *Men:* baseball, basketball, lacrosse, sailing, soccer, swimming, tennis. *Women:* basketball, field hockey, lacrosse, sailing, soccer, swimming, tennis, volleyball.

ADMISSIONS

Selectivity Rating: 90 (of 100). **Freshman Academic Profile:** Average high school GPA 3.5. 44% in top 10% of high school class, 79% in top 25% of high school class, 97% in top 50% of high school class. 80% from public high schools. Average SAT I Math 608, SAT I Math middle 50% range 560-650. Average SAT I Verbal 624, SAT I Verbal middle 50% range 570-670. TOEFL required of all international applicants, minimum TOEFL 550. **Basis for Candidate Selection:** *Very important factors considered include:* essays, secondary school record, standardized test scores. *Important factors considered include:* extracurricular activities, recommendations, talent/ability. *Other factors considered include:* alumni/ae relation, character/personal qualities, geographical residence, interview, minority status, state residency, volunteer work, work experience. **Freshman Admission Requirements:** High school diploma or GED is required. *Academic units required/recommended:* 20 total required; 22 total recommended; 4 English required, 3 math required, 3 science required, 2 science lab recommended, 2 foreign language recommended, 3 social studies required, 7 elective required. **Freshman Admission Statistics:** 1,884 applied, 59% accepted, 38% of those accepted enrolled. **Transfer Admission Requirements:** *Items required:* college transcript, essay. Minimum high school GPA of 2.0 required. Minimum college GPA of 2.5 required. Lowest grade transferable C-. **General Admission Information:** Application fee $25. Priority application deadline December 1. Early decision application deadline December 1. Regular application deadline January 15. Nonfall registration accepted. Credit and/or placement offered for CEEB Advanced Placement tests.

COSTS AND FINANCIAL AID

In-state tuition $6,925. Out-of-state tuition $12,260. Room & board $6,613. Required fees $1,157. Average book expense $870. **Required Forms and Deadlines:** FAFSA. Financial aid filing deadline March 1. Priority filing deadline March 1. **Notification of Awards:** Applicants will be notified of awards on or about April 1. **Types of Aid:** *Need-based scholarships/grants:* Pell, SEOG, state scholarships/grants, private scholarships, the school's own gift aid. *Loans:* FFEL Subsidized Stafford, FFEL Unsubsidized Stafford, FFEL PLUS, Federal Perkins. **Student Employment:** Federal Work-Study Program available. Institutional employment available. Off-campus job opportunities are good. **Financial Aid Statistics:** 42% freshmen, 45% undergrads receive some form of aid. Average freshman grant $4,000. Average freshman loan $2,625. Average income from on-campus job $969. **Financial Aid Phone:** 240-895-3000.

ST. MARY'S UNIVERSITY (TX)

One Camino Santa Maria, San Antonio, TX 78228
Phone: 210-436-3126 **E-mail:** uadm@stmarytx.edu **CEEB Code:** 6637
Fax: 210-431-6742 **Web:** www.stmarytx.edu **ACT Code:** 4158

This private school, which is affiliated with the Roman Catholic Church, was founded in 1852. It has a 135-acre campus.

STUDENTS AND FACULTY

Enrollment: 2,725. **Student Body:** Male 41%, female 59%, out-of-state 4%, international 4%. **Ethnic Representation:** African American 3%, Asian 2%, Caucasian 22%, Hispanic 71%. **Retention and Graduation:** 80% freshmen return for sophomore year. 36% freshmen graduate within 4 years. **Faculty:** Student/faculty ratio 15:1. 185 full-time faculty, 87% hold PhDs.

ACADEMICS

Degrees: Bachelor's, doctoral, first professional, master's. **Academic Requirements:** General education including some course work in arts/fine arts, computer literacy, English (including composition), foreign languages, history, humanities, mathematics, philosophy, sciences (biological or physical), social science. **Classes:** 20-29 students in an average class. 10-19 students in an average lab/discussion section. **Disciplines with Highest Percentage of Degrees Awarded:** Business/marketing 31%, social sciences and history 12%, biological life sciences 11%, psychology 7%, communications/communication technologies 6%. **Special Study Options:** Cooperative (work-study) program, cross registration, distance learning, double major, English as a second language, honors program, independent study, internships, liberal arts/career combination, study abroad, teacher certification program.

FACILITIES

Housing: Coed, all-female, all-male, 22 years old or above/nontraditional dorms. **Library Holdings:** 481,137 bound volumes. 1,126 periodicals. 131,324 microforms. 3,104 audiovisuals. **Special Academic Facilities/Equipment:** Art gallery, earth sciences museum. **Computers:** School-owned computers available for student use.

EXTRACURRICULARS

Activities: Choral groups, concert band, dance, drama/theater, jazz band, literary magazine, music ensembles, musical theater, pep band, student government, student newspaper. **Organizations:** 55 registered organizations, 10 honor societies, 12 religious organizations, 5 fraternities (14% men join), 4 sororities (11% women join). **Athletics (Intercollegiate):** *Men:* baseball, basketball, golf, soccer, tennis. *Women:* basketball, soccer, softball, tennis, volleyball.

ADMISSIONS

Selectivity Rating: 78 (of 100). **Freshman Academic Profile:** Average high school GPA 3.5. 29% in top 10% of high school class, 59% in top 25% of high school class, 84% in top 50% of high school class. 74% from public high schools. Average SAT I Math 536, SAT I Math middle 50% range 480-590. Average SAT I Verbal 538, SAT I Verbal middle 50% range 470-580. Average ACT 22, ACT middle 50% range 20-24. TOEFL required of all international applicants, minimum TOEFL 550. **Basis for Candidate Selection:** *Very important factors considered include:* character/personal qualities, recommendations, talent/ability. *Important factors considered include:* class rank, essays, secondary school record, standardized test scores, volunteer work. *Other factors considered include:* alumni/ae relation, extracurricular activities, interview, religious affiliation/commitment, work experience. **Freshman Admission Requirements:** High school diploma or GED is required. *Academic units required/recommended:* 4 English required, 4 English recommended, 3 math required, 4 math recommended, 3 science required, 4 science recommended, 1 science lab required, 2 foreign language required, 3 foreign language recommended, 3 social studies required, 4 social studies recommended, 1 elective required. **Freshman Admission Statistics:** 1,664 applied, 85% accepted, 47% of those accepted enrolled. **Transfer Admission Requirements:** *Items required:* college transcript, essay, statement of good standing from prior school. Minimum college GPA of 2.5 required. Lowest grade transferable C. **General Admission Information:** Application fee $30. Priority application deadline March 1. Nonfall registration accepted. Admission may be deferred for a maximum of 2 years. Credit and/or placement offered for CEEB Advanced Placement tests.

COSTS AND FINANCIAL AID

Tuition $14,727. Room & board $6,246. Required fees $500. Average book expense $1,500. **Required Forms and Deadlines:** FAFSA. No deadline for regular filing. Priority filing deadline February 15. **Notification of Awards:** Applicants will be notified of awards on a rolling basis beginning on or about

March 15. **Types of Aid:** *Need-based scholarships/grants:* Pell, SEOG, state scholarships/grants, private scholarships, the school's own gift aid. *Loans:* FFEL Subsidized Stafford, FFEL Unsubsidized Stafford, FFEL PLUS, Federal Perkins, state loans. **Student Employment:** Federal Work-Study Program available. Institutional employment available. Off-campus job opportunities are good. **Financial Aid Statistics:** 72% freshmen, 71% undergrads receive some form of aid. Average freshman grant $10,523. Average freshman loan $3,503. **Financial Aid Phone:** 210-436-3141.

SAINT MARY'S UNIVERSITY OF MINNESOTA

700 Terrace Heights #2, Winona, MN 55987-1399
Phone: 507-457-1600 **E-mail:** admissions@smumn.edu **CEEB Code:** 6632
Fax: 507-457-1722 **Web:** www.smumn.edu **ACT Code:** 2148

This private school, which is affiliated with the Roman Catholic Church, was founded in 1912. It has a 400-acre campus.

STUDENTS AND FACULTY

Enrollment: 1,654. **Student Body:** Male 47%, female 53%, out-of-state 31%, international 2% (21 countries represented). **Ethnic Representation:** African American 2%, Asian 1%, Caucasian 81%, Hispanic 2%. **Retention and Graduation:** 71% freshmen return for sophomore year. 55% freshmen graduate within 4 years. 20% grads go on to further study within 1 year. 2% grads pursue business degrees. 3% grads pursue law degrees. 1% grads pursue medical degrees. **Faculty:** Student/faculty ratio 12:1. 107 full-time faculty, 74% hold PhDs. 100% faculty teach undergrads.

ACADEMICS

Degrees: Bachelor's, certificate, doctoral, master's, post-bachelor's certificate, post-master's certificate. **Academic Requirements:** General education including some course work in arts/fine arts, English (including composition), history, humanities, mathematics, philosophy, sciences (biological or physical), social science. **Classes:** 10-19 students in an average class. 10-19 students in an average lab/discussion section. **Majors with Highest Enrollment:** Marketing/marketing management, general; early childhood education and teaching; biology/biological sciences, general. **Disciplines with Highest Percentage of Degrees Awarded:** Business/marketing 32%, biological life sciences 7%, visual and performing arts 7%, protective services/public administration 7%, engineering/engineering technology 6%. **Special Study Options:** Accelerated program, cooperative (work-study) program, cross registration, double major, English as a second language, honors program, independent study, internships, student-designed major, study abroad, teacher certification program.

FACILITIES

Housing: Coed, all-female, all-male, apartments for single students, housing for disabled students, housing for international students. **Library Holdings:** 130,944 bound volumes. 708 periodicals. 141,141 microforms. 8,281 audiovisuals. **Special Academic Facilities/Equipment:** Art gallery, performance center, technology center, laboratories, observatory. **Computers:** School-owned computers available for student use.

EXTRACURRICULARS

Activities: Choral groups, concert band, dance, drama/theater, jazz band, literary magazine, music ensembles, musical theater, radio station, student government, student newspaper, student-run film society, symphony orchestra, yearbook. **Organizations:** 80 registered organizations, 13 honor societies, 5 religious organizations. **Athletics (Intercollegiate):** *Men:* baseball, basketball, cross-country, diving, golf, ice hockey, indoor track, skiing (Nordic), soccer, swimming, tennis, track & field. *Women:* basketball, cross-country, diving, golf, ice hockey, indoor track, skiing (Nordic), soccer, softball, swimming, tennis, track & field, volleyball.

ADMISSIONS

Selectivity Rating: 73 (of 100). **Freshman Academic Profile:** Average high school GPA 3.1. 17% in top 10% of high school class, 42% in top 25% of high school class, 74% in top 50% of high school class. 67% from public high schools. SAT I Math middle 50% range 480-550. SAT I Verbal middle 50% range 490-560. Average ACT 22, ACT middle 50% range 19-25. TOEFL required of all international applicants, minimum TOEFL 520. **Basis for Candidate Selection:** *Very important factors considered include:* secondary school record, standardized test scores. *Important factors considered include:* character/personal qualities, class rank, interview, talent/ability. *Other factors considered include:* alumni/ae relation, essays, extracurricular activities, minority status, recommendations, volunteer work. **Freshman Admission Requirements:** High school diploma or GED is required. *Academic units required/recommended:* 18 total required; 4 English required, 3 math required, 3 science required, 1 science lab required, 2 social studies required, 6 elective required. **Freshman Admission Statistics:** 1,122 applied, 79% accepted, 45% of those accepted enrolled. **Transfer Admission Requirements:** *Items required:* high school transcript, college transcript, statement of good standing from prior school. Minimum college GPA of 2.0 required. Lowest grade transferable C. **General Admission Information:** Application fee $25. Priority application deadline April 1. Regular application deadline May 1. Nonfall registration accepted. Admission may be deferred for a maximum of 1 year. Credit and/or placement offered for CEEB Advanced Placement tests.

COSTS AND FINANCIAL AID

Tuition $15,280. Room & board $4,920. Required fees $415. Average book expense $800. **Required Forms and Deadlines:** FAFSA. No deadline for regular filing. Priority filing deadline March 15. **Notification of Awards:** Applicants will be notified of awards on a rolling basis beginning on or about March 1. **Types of Aid:** *Need-based scholarships/grants:* Pell, SEOG, state scholarships/grants, private scholarships, the school's own gift aid, Federal Nursing. *Loans:* FFEL Subsidized Stafford, FFEL Unsubsidized Stafford, FFEL PLUS, Federal Perkins, state loans. **Student Employment:** Federal Work-Study Program available. Institutional employment available. Off-campus job opportunities are good. **Financial Aid Statistics:** 62% freshmen, 58% undergrads receive some form of aid. Average freshman grant $8,700. Average freshman loan $3,734. **Financial Aid Phone:** 507-457-1437.

SAINT MICHAEL'S COLLEGE

One Winooski Park, Colchester, VT 05439
Phone: 802-654-3000 **E-mail:** admission@smcvt.edu **CEEB Code:** 3757
Fax: 802-654-2591 **Web:** www.smcvt.edu **ACT Code:** 4312

This private school, which is affiliated with the Roman Catholic Church, was founded in 1904. It has a 440-acre campus.

STUDENTS AND FACULTY

Enrollment: 2,040. **Student Body:** Male 44%, female 56%, out-of-state 75%, international 2% (17 countries represented). **Ethnic Representation:** African American 1%, Asian 1%, Caucasian 96%, Hispanic 1%. **Retention and Graduation:** 91% freshmen return for sophomore year. 69% freshmen graduate within 4 years. 13% grads go on to further study within 1 year. 13% grads pursue business degrees. 4% grads pursue law degrees. 4% grads pursue medical degrees. **Faculty:** Student/faculty ratio 13:1. 144 full-time faculty, 83% hold PhDs. 100% faculty teach undergrads.

ACADEMICS

Degrees: Bachelor's, master's, post-bachelor's certificate, post-master's certificate. **Academic Requirements:** General education including some course work in arts/fine arts, English (including composition), foreign languages, history, humanities, philosophy, sciences (biological or physical), social science, religious studies. **Classes:** 10-19 students in an average class. 10-19 students in an average lab/discussion section. **Majors with Highest Enrollment:** Business administration/management; English language and literature, general; psychology, general. **Disciplines with Highest Percentage of Degrees Awarded:** Business/marketing 27%, social sciences and history 15%, psychology 14%, English 9%, education 8%. **Special Study Options:** Double major, English as a second language, honors program, independent study, internships, liberal arts/career combination, student-designed major, study abroad, teacher certification program.

FACILITIES

Housing: Coed, all-female, all-male, apartments for single students, housing for disabled students, housing for international students, cooperative housing, theme housing, substance-free housing. **Library Holdings:** 141,000 bound volumes. 1,003 periodicals. 124,000 microforms. 7,525 audiovisuals. **Special Academic Facilities/Equipment:** Holcomb Observatory, McCarthy Arts Center Gallery. **Computers:** *Recommended operating system:* Windows. School-owned computers available for student use.

EXTRACURRICULARS

Activities: Choral groups, concert band, dance, drama/theater, jazz band, literary magazine, music ensembles, musical theater, radio station, student government, student newspaper, yearbook. **Organizations:** 40 registered organizations, 8 honor societies, 1 religious organization. **Athletics (Intercollegiate):** *Men:* baseball, basketball, skiing (cross-country), cross-country, diving, golf, ice hockey, lacrosse, skiing (alpine), skiing (Nordic), soccer, swimming, tennis. *Women:* basketball, skiing (cross-country), cross-country, diving, field hockey, ice hockey, lacrosse, skiing (alpine), skiing (Nordic), soccer, softball, swimming, tennis, volleyball.

ADMISSIONS

Selectivity Rating: 88 (of 100). **Freshman Academic Profile:** 17% in top 10% of high school class, 50% in top 25% of high school class, 86% in top 50% of high school class. 68% from public high schools. Average SAT I Math 556, SAT I Math middle 50% range 500-610. Average SAT I Verbal 557, SAT I Verbal middle 50% range 510-600. TOEFL required of all international applicants, minimum TOEFL 550. **Basis for Candidate Selection:** *Very important factors considered include:* class rank, secondary school record, standardized test scores. *Important factors considered include:* character/personal qualities, essays, recommendations. *Other factors considered include:* alumni/ae relation, extracurricular activities, geographical residence, interview, minority status, talent/ability, volunteer work, work experience. **Freshman Admission Requirements:** High school diploma or GED is required. *Academic units required/recommended:* 16 total required; 20 total recommended; 4 English required, 4 English recommended, 3 math required, 4 math recommended, 3 science required, 4 science recommended, 2 science lab required, 3 science lab recommended, 3 foreign language required, 4 foreign language recommended, 3 history required, 4 history recommended. **Freshman Admission Statistics:** 2,552 applied, 68% accepted, 31% of those accepted enrolled. **Transfer Admission Requirements:** *Items required:* high school transcript, college transcript, essay, standardized test scores. Minimum college GPA of 3.0 required. Lowest grade transferable C-. **General Admission Information:** Application fee $45. Priority application deadline November 15. Regular application deadline February 1. Admission may be deferred for a maximum of 1 year. Credit and/or placement offered for CEEB Advanced Placement tests.

COSTS AND FINANCIAL AID

Tuition $22,220. Room & board $7,680. Required fees $200. Average book expense $800. **Required Forms and Deadlines:** FAFSA, institution's own financial aid form and Parent and Student Federal Tax forms and W-2s. Financial aid filing deadline March 15. Priority filing deadline March 15. **Notification of Awards:** Applicants will be notified of awards on or about April 10. **Types of Aid:** *Need-based scholarships/grants:* Pell, SEOG, state scholarships/grants, private scholarships, the school's own gift aid. *Loans:* FFEL Subsidized Stafford, FFEL Unsubsidized Stafford, FFEL PLUS, Federal Perkins. **Student Employment:** Federal Work-Study Program available. Institutional employment available. Off-campus job opportunities are good. **Financial Aid Statistics:** 66% freshmen, 63% undergrads receive some form of aid. Average freshman grant $11,258. Average freshman loan $4,297. Average income from on-campus job $1,275. **Financial Aid Phone:** 802-654-3243.

See page 1190.

ST. NORBERT COLLEGE

100 Grant Street, De Pere, WI 54115
Phone: 920-403-3005 **E-mail:** admit@snc.edu **CEEB Code:** 1706
Fax: 920-403-4072 **Web:** www.snc.edu **ACT Code:** 4644

This private school, which is affiliated with the Roman Catholic Church, was founded in 1898. It has an 89-acre campus.

STUDENTS AND FACULTY

Enrollment: 2,072. **Student Body:** Male 43%, female 57%, out-of-state 28%, international 2% (27 countries represented). **Ethnic Representation:** African American 1%, Asian 1%, Caucasian 93%, Hispanic 2%, Native American 1%. **Retention and Graduation:** 82% freshmen return for sophomore year. 70% freshmen graduate within 4 years. 22% grads go on to further study within 1 year. **Faculty:** Student/faculty ratio 14:1. 122 full-time faculty, 91% hold PhDs. 100% faculty teach undergrads.

ACADEMICS

Degrees: Bachelor's, master's. **Academic Requirements:** General education including some course work in arts/fine arts, computer literacy, English (including composition), history, humanities, mathematics, philosophy, sciences (biological or physical), social science, religion or theology. **Classes:** 10-19 students in an average class. 10-19 students in an average lab/discussion section. **Majors with Highest Enrollment:** Business administration/management; communications studies/speech communication and rhetoric; elementary education and teaching. **Disciplines with Highest Percentage of Degrees Awarded:** Business/marketing 28%, education 14%, communications/ communication technologies 13%, social sciences and history 10%, biological life sciences 7%. **Special Study Options:** Cooperative (work-study) program, distance learning, double major, English as a second language, honors program, independent study, internships, liberal arts/career combination, student-designed major, study abroad, teacher certification program, Richmond College International Internships; Washington Semester.

FACILITIES

Housing: Coed, all-female, apartments for single students, housing for disabled students, townhouses, off-campus college owned housing. **Library Holdings:** 115,553 bound volumes. 690 periodicals. 28,322 microforms. 7,625 audiovisuals. **Special Academic Facilities/Equipment:** Art gallery, language lab, nursery school, electron microscope, Center for Leadership and Service, Bemis International Center, videoconferencing capabilities, Center for Adaptive Education and Assistive Technology. **Computers:** School-owned computers available for student use.

EXTRACURRICULARS

Activities: Choral groups, concert band, drama/theater, jazz band, literary magazine, music ensembles, musical theater, radio station, student government, student newspaper, television station. **Organizations:** 64 registered organizations, 14 honor societies, 3 religious organizations, 5 fraternities (15% men join), 5 sororities (15% women join). **Athletics (Intercollegiate):** *Men:* baseball, basketball, cheerleading, cross-country, football, golf, ice hockey, indoor track, soccer, tennis, track & field. *Women:* basketball, cheerleading, cross-country, diving, golf, indoor track, soccer, softball, swimming, tennis, track & field, volleyball.

ADMISSIONS

Selectivity Rating: 84 (of 100). **Freshman Academic Profile:** Average high school GPA 3.4. 32% in top 10% of high school class, 60% in top 25% of high school class, 92% in top 50% of high school class. 80% from public high schools. Average ACT 24, ACT middle 50% range 21-27. TOEFL required of all international applicants, minimum TOEFL 550. **Basis for Candidate Selection:** *Very important factors considered include:* secondary school record. *Important factors considered include:* recommendations, standardized test scores. *Other factors considered include:* alumni/ae relation, character/personal qualities, class rank, essays, extracurricular activities, interview, talent/ability, volunteer work, work experience. **Freshman Admission Requirements:** High school diploma or GED is required. *Academic units required/recommended:* 18 total recommended; 4 English recommended, 3 math recommended, 3 science recommended, 2 science lab recommended, 2 foreign language recommended, 2 social studies recommended, 2 history recommended. **Freshman Admission Statistics:** 1,714 applied, 83% accepted, 35% of those accepted enrolled. **Transfer Admission Requirements:** *Items required:* high school transcript, college transcript, essay, standardized test scores, statement of good standing from prior school. Minimum college GPA of 2.5 required. Lowest grade transferable C. **General Admission Information:** Application fee $25. Priority application deadline April 1. Early decision application deadline December 1. Nonfall registration accepted. Admission may be deferred for a maximum of 1 year. Credit and/or placement offered for CEEB Advanced Placement tests.

COSTS AND FINANCIAL AID

Tuition $18,834. Room & board $5,440. Required fees $250. Average book expense $450. **Required Forms and Deadlines:** FAFSA, institution's own financial aid form, parent's tax return and student's tax return. Priority filing deadline March 1. **Notification of Awards:** Applicants will be notified of awards on a rolling basis beginning on or about March 15. **Types of Aid:** *Need-based scholarships/grants:* Pell, SEOG, state scholarships/grants, private scholarships, the school's own gift aid. *Loans:* Direct Subsidized Stafford, Direct Unsubsidized Stafford, Direct PLUS, Federal Perkins, college/university loans from institutional funds. **Student Employment:** Federal Work-Study Program available. Institutional employment available. Off-campus job opportunities are good. **Financial Aid Statistics:** 66% freshmen, 64% undergrads receive some form of aid. Average freshman grant $9,715. Average freshman loan $3,495. Average income from on-campus job $1,019. **Financial Aid Phone:** 920-403-3071.

ST. OLAF COLLEGE

1520 St. Olaf Avenue, Northfield, MN 55057-1098
Phone: 507-646-3025 **E-mail:** admissions@stolaf.edu **CEEB Code:** 6638
Fax: 507-646-3832 **Web:** www.stolaf.edu **ACT Code:** 2150

This private school, which is affiliated with the Lutheran Church, was founded in 1874. It has a 300-acre campus.

STUDENTS AND FACULTY

Enrollment: 3,041. **Student Body:** Male 41%, female 59%, out-of-state 47%, international 1% (28 countries represented). **Ethnic Representation:** African American 1%, Asian 4%, Caucasian 89%, Hispanic 1%. **Retention and Graduation:** 93% freshmen return for sophomore year. 73% freshmen graduate within 4 years. 25% grads go on to further study within 1 year. 2% grads pursue law degrees. 3% grads pursue medical degrees. **Faculty:** Student/faculty ratio 13:1. 192 full-time faculty, 88% hold PhDs. 100% faculty teach undergrads.

ACADEMICS

Degrees: Bachelor's. **Academic Requirements:** General education including some course work in arts/fine arts, English (including composition), foreign languages, history, humanities, mathematics, philosophy, sciences (biological or physical), social science, religion, physical activity. **Classes:** 20-29 students in an average class. 10-19 students in an average lab/discussion section. **Majors with Highest Enrollment:** Economics, general; biology/biological sciences, general; English language and literature, general. **Disciplines with Highest Percentage of Degrees Awarded:** Social sciences and history 21%, biological life sciences 14%, visual and performing arts 14%, English 10%, psychology 9%. **Special Study Options:** Cross registration, double major, independent study, internships, student-designed major, study abroad, teacher certification program.

FACILITIES

Housing: Coed, honors houses, language houses, quiet halls, first-year-only dorms. Disabled students accommodated in dorm of their choice. **Library Holdings:** 654,950 bound volumes. 1,616 periodicals. 6,567 microforms. 16,194 audiovisuals. **Special Academic Facilities/Equipment:** Norwegian-American history museum, Finstad Office for Entrepreneurial Studies, Kierkegaard Library. **Computers:** School-owned computers available for student use.

EXTRACURRICULARS

Activities: Choral groups, concert band, dance, drama/theater, jazz band, literary magazine, music ensembles, musical theater, opera, pep band, radio station, student government, student newspaper, student-run film society, symphony orchestra, yearbook. **Organizations:** 98 registered organizations, 15 honor societies, 9 religious organizations. **Athletics (Intercollegiate):** *Men:* baseball, basketball, cross-country, diving, football, golf, ice hockey, indoor track, skiing (alpine), skiing (Nordic), soccer, swimming, tennis, track & field, wrestling. *Women:* basketball, cross-country, diving, golf, ice hockey, indoor track, skiing (alpine), skiing (Nordic), soccer, softball, swimming, tennis, track & field, volleyball.

ADMISSIONS

Selectivity Rating: 86 (of 100). **Freshman Academic Profile:** Average high school GPA 3.6. 50% in top 10% of high school class, 79% in top 25% of high school class, 97% in top 50% of high school class. 85% from public high schools. Average SAT I Math 635, SAT I Math middle 50% range 580-690. Average SAT I Verbal 639, SAT I Verbal middle 50% range 590-690. Average ACT 27, ACT middle 50% range 25-30. TOEFL required of all international applicants, minimum TOEFL 550. **Basis for Candidate Selection:** *Very important factors considered include:* secondary school record. *Important factors considered include:* essays, recommendations, standardized test scores. *Other factors considered include:* alumni/ae relation, character/personal qualities, class rank, extracurricular activities, geographical residence, interview, minority status, religious affiliation/commitment, state residency, talent/ability, volunteer work, work experience. **Freshman Admission Requirements:** High school diploma or GED is required. *Academic units required/recommended:* 15 total recommended; 4 English recommended, 4 math recommended, 3 science recommended, 1 science lab recommended, 2 foreign language recommended. **Freshman Admission Statistics:** 2,624 applied, 73% accepted, 41% of those accepted enrolled. **Transfer Admission Requirements:** *Items required:* high school transcript, college transcript, essay, standardized test scores, statement of good standing from prior school. Minimum college GPA of 3.0 required. Lowest grade transferable C. **General Admission Information:** Application fee $35. Priority application deadline February 1. Early decision application deadline November 15. Nonfall registration accepted. Admission may be deferred for a maximum of 1 year. Credit and/or placement offered for CEEB Advanced Placement tests.

COSTS AND FINANCIAL AID

Required Forms and Deadlines: FAFSA, CSS/Financial Aid PROFILE and noncustodial (divorced/separated) parent's statement. No deadline for regular filing. Priority filing deadline February 15. **Notification of Awards:** Applicants will be notified of awards on a rolling basis beginning on or about March 1. **Types of Aid:** *Need-based scholarships/grants:* Pell, SEOG, state scholarships/grants, private scholarships, the school's own gift aid. *Loans:* FFEL Subsidized Stafford, FFEL Unsubsidized Stafford, FFEL PLUS, Federal Perkins, Federal Nursing, state loans, college/university loans from institutional funds. **Student Employment:** Federal Work-Study Program available. Institutional employment available. Off-campus job opportunities are fair. **Financial Aid Statistics:** 60% freshmen, 58% undergrads receive some form of aid. Average freshman grant $12,210. Average freshman loan $3,680. Average income from on-campus job $1,100. **Financial Aid Phone:** 507-646-3019.

SAINT PAUL'S COLLEGE

115 College Drive, Lawrenceville, VA 23868
Phone: 434-848-1856 **E-mail:** admissions@saintpauls.edu
Fax: 804-848-6407 **Web:** www.saintpauls.edu **ACT Code:** 4394

This private school, which is affiliated with the Episcopal Church, was founded in 1888. It has a 185-acre campus.

STUDENTS AND FACULTY

Enrollment: 700. **Student Body:** Male 50%, female 50%, out-of-state 31%, international 1% (5 countries represented). **Ethnic Representation:** African American 97%, Caucasian 2%. **Retention and Graduation:** 16% freshmen graduate within 4 years. 10% grads go on to further study within 1 year. **Faculty:** Student/faculty ratio 17:1. 33 full-time faculty, 57% hold PhDs. 100% faculty teach undergrads.

ACADEMICS

Degrees: Bachelor's. **Academic Requirements:** General education including some course work in arts/fine arts, computer literacy, English (including composition), foreign languages, history, humanities, mathematics, philosophy, sciences (biological or physical), social science. **Classes:** Under 10 students in an average class. Under 10 students in an average lab/discussion section. **Majors with Highest Enrollment:** Business administration/management; criminal justice/police science; sociology. **Disciplines with Highest Percentage of Degrees Awarded:** Business/marketing 67%, protective services/public administration 11%, social sciences and history 9%, English 5%, computer and information sciences 3%. **Special Study Options:** Accelerated program, cooperative (work-study) program, honors program, independent study, internships, liberal arts/career combination, study abroad, teacher certification program, U.S. Army ROTC.

FACILITIES

Housing: All-female, all-male, apartments for single students. **Library Holdings:** 42,828 bound volumes. 174 periodicals. 29,000 microforms. 1,041 audiovisuals. **Special Academic Facilities/Equipment:** The Saul Building (1888) the first classroom built on SPC campus. **Computers:** *Recommended operating system:* Windows 95. School-owned computers available for student use.

EXTRACURRICULARS

Activities: Choral groups, dance, drama/theater, jazz band, pep band, student government. **Organizations:** 2 honor societies, 2 religious organizations, 2 fraternities (7% men join), 3 sororities (7% women join). **Athletics (Intercollegiate):** *Men:* baseball, basketball, cross-country, golf, indoor track, tennis, track & field. *Women:* basketball, cross-country, indoor track, softball, tennis, track & field, volleyball.

ADMISSIONS

Selectivity Rating: 66 (of 100). **Freshman Academic Profile:** Average high school GPA 2.5. 3% in top 10% of high school class, 8% in top 25% of high school class, 23% in top 50% of high school class. 95% from public high schools. Average SAT I Math 365, SAT I Math middle 50% range 300-430. Average SAT I Verbal 335, SAT I Verbal middle 50% range 300-370. Average ACT 15, ACT middle 50% range 13-17. **Basis for Candidate Selection:** *Important factors considered include:* character/personal qualities, class rank, essays, extracurricular activities, interview, recommendations, secondary school record, standardized test scores, talent/ability. *Other factors considered include:* volunteer work, work experience. **Freshman Admission Requirements:** High school diploma or GED is required. *Academic units required/recommended:* 8 total required; 10 total recommended; 4 English required, 4 English recommended, 2 math required, 2 math recommended, 2 science required, 2 science recommended, 2 social studies recommended. **Freshman Admission Statistics:** 870 applied, 92% accepted, 34% of those accepted enrolled. **Transfer Admission Requirements:** *Items required:* high school transcript, college transcript, essay, statement of good standing from prior school. Minimum high school GPA of 2.0 required. Minimum college GPA of 2.0 required. **General Admission Information:** Application fee $20. Nonfall registration accepted.

COSTS AND FINANCIAL AID

Tuition $8,070. Room & board $4,940. Required fees $650. Average book expense $600. **Required Forms and Deadlines:** FAFSA. Financial aid filing deadline June 30. Priority filing deadline March 30. **Notification of Awards:** Applicants will be notified of awards on a rolling basis beginning on or about January 7. **Types of Aid:** *Need-based scholarships/grants:* Pell, SEOG, state scholarships/grants, private scholarships, the school's own gift aid, United Negro College Fund. *Loans:* Direct Subsidized Stafford, Direct Unsubsidized Stafford, Direct PLUS. **Student Employment:** Federal Work-Study Program available. Off-campus job opportunities are fair. **Financial Aid Statistics:** 99% freshmen, 93% undergrads receive some form of aid. Average freshman loan $2,336. Average income from on-campus job $1,300. **Financial Aid Phone:** (434)848-6495.

SAINT PETER'S COLLEGE

2641 Kennedy Boulevard, Jersey City, NJ 07306
Phone: 201-915-9213 **E-mail:** admissions@spc.edu **CEEB Code:** 2806
Fax: 201-432-5860 **Web:** www.spc.edu **ACT Code:** 2604

This private school, which is affiliated with the Roman Catholic Church, was founded in 1872. It has a 10-acre campus.

STUDENTS AND FACULTY

Enrollment: 2,389. **Student Body:** Male 44%, female 56%, out-of-state 12%, international 2% (9 countries represented). **Ethnic Representation:** African American 15%, Asian 7%, Caucasian 50%, Hispanic 25%. **Retention and Graduation:** 73% freshmen return for sophomore year. 27% freshmen graduate within 4 years. 27% grads go on to further study within 1 year. 6% grads pursue business degrees. 5% grads pursue law degrees. 7% grads pursue medical degrees. **Faculty:** 100% faculty teach undergrads.

ACADEMICS

Degrees: Associate's, bachelor's, certificate, diploma, master's, post-bachelor's certificate, terminal, transfer. **Academic Requirements:** General education including some course work in arts/fine arts, computer literacy, English (including composition), foreign languages, history, humanities, mathematics, philosophy, sciences (biological or physical), social science, theology. **Special Study Options:** Cooperative (work-study) program, double major, honors program, independent study, internships, liberal arts/career combination, student-designed major, study abroad, teacher certification program, weekend college.

FACILITIES

Housing: Coed, all-female, all-male, apartments for single students. **Library Holdings:** 282,031 bound volumes. 1,702 periodicals. 62,279 microforms. 3,749 audiovisuals. **Special Academic Facilities/Equipment:** TV production facilities, center for government affairs. **Computers:** *Recommended operating system:* Mac. School-owned computers available for student use.

EXTRACURRICULARS

Activities: Choral groups, drama/theater, literary magazine, radio station, student government, student newspaper, yearbook. **Organizations:** 50 registered organizations, 13 honor societies. **Athletics (Intercollegiate):** *Men:* baseball, basketball, cheerleading, cross-country, diving, football, golf, soccer, swimming, tennis, track & field. *Women:* basketball, cheerleading, cross-country, diving, soccer, softball, swimming, tennis, track & field, volleyball.

ADMISSIONS

Selectivity Rating: 78 (of 100). **Freshman Academic Profile:** Average high school GPA 2.8. 14% in top 10% of high school class, 36% in top 25% of high school class, 69% in top 50% of high school class. Average SAT I Math 460, SAT I Math middle 50% range 410-530. Average SAT I Verbal 460, SAT I Verbal middle 50% range 410-520. TOEFL required of all international applicants, minimum TOEFL 500. **Basis for Candidate Selection:** *Very important factors considered include:* secondary school record. *Important factors considered include:* class rank, essays, recommendations, standardized test scores. *Other factors considered include:* character/personal qualities, extracurricular activities, interview, talent/ability, volunteer work, work experience. **Freshman Admission Requirements:** High school diploma or GED is required. *Academic units required/recommended:* 16 total required; 4 English required, 3 math required, 2 science required, 1 science lab required, 2 foreign language required, 2 history required, 3 elective required. **Transfer Admission Requirements:** *Items required:* college transcript, essay. Minimum college GPA of 2.0 required. Lowest grade transferable C. **General Admission Information:** Application fee $30. Regular application deadline rolling. Nonfall registration accepted. Admission may be deferred for a maximum of 2 years. Credit offered for CEEB Advanced Placement tests.

COSTS AND FINANCIAL AID

Required Forms and Deadlines: FAFSA. No deadline for regular filing. Priority filing deadline March 15. **Notification of Awards:** Applicants will be notified of awards on a rolling basis beginning on or about February 15. **Types of Aid:** *Need-based scholarships/grants:* Pell, SEOG, state scholarships/grants, the school's own gift aid. *Loans:* FFEL Subsidized Stafford, FFEL Unsubsidized Stafford, FFEL PLUS, Federal Perkins, state loans. **Student Employment:** Federal Work-Study Program available. Institutional employment available. Off-campus job opportunities are excellent. **Financial Aid Statistics:** Average freshman grant $7,800. Average freshman loan $2,500. Average income from on-campus job $1,500. **Financial Aid Phone:** 201-915-9308.

ST. THOMAS AQUINAS COLLEGE

125 Route 340, Sparkill, NY 10976
Phone: 914-398-4100 **E-mail:** admissions@stac.edu **CEEB Code:** 2807
Fax: 914-398-4224 **Web:** www.stac.edu **ACT Code:** 2897

This private school was founded in 1952. It has a 43-acre campus.

STUDENTS AND FACULTY

Enrollment: 2,038. **Student Body:** Male 42%, female 58%, out-of-state 35%, international 1%. **Ethnic Representation:** African American 5%, Asian 4%, Caucasian 81%, Hispanic 10%. **Retention and Graduation:** 77% freshmen return for sophomore year. 47% freshmen graduate within 4 years. 36% grads go on to further study within 1 year. 5% grads pursue business degrees. 4% grads pursue law degrees. 2% grads pursue medical degrees. **Faculty:** 100% faculty teach undergrads.

ACADEMICS

Degrees: Associate's, bachelor's, master's, post-master's certificate. **Academic Requirements:** General education including some course work in arts/fine arts, computer literacy, English (including composition), foreign languages, humanities, mathematics, philosophy, sciences (biological or physical), social science. **Special Study Options:** Student exchange program (domestic), honors program, independent study, internships, liberal arts/career combination, study abroad, teacher certification program, undergrads may take grad-level classes, cooperative education program in engineering, 3-2 engineering programs with George Washington University and Manhattan College, foreign exchange program in England.

FACILITIES

Housing: All-female, all-male. **Library Holdings:** 102,000 bound volumes. 825 periodicals. 98,671 microforms. 870 audiovisuals. **Special Academic Facilities/Equipment:** On-campus preschool, language lab. **Computers:** *Recommended operating system:* Mac. School-owned computers available for student use.

EXTRACURRICULARS

Activities: Choral groups, drama/theater, literary magazine, radio station, student government, student newspaper, yearbook. **Organizations:** 1 religious organization. **Athletics (Intercollegiate):** *Men:* baseball, basketball, cross-country, golf, soccer, volleyball. *Women:* basketball, soccer, softball, volleyball.

ADMISSIONS

Selectivity Rating: 76 (of 100). **Freshman Academic Profile:** Average high school GPA 2.8. 15% in top 10% of high school class, 48% in top 25% of high school class, 88% in top 50% of high school class. 80% from public high schools. Average SAT I Math 490. Average SAT I Verbal 510. TOEFL required of all international applicants, minimum TOEFL 500. **Basis for Candidate Selection:** *Very important factors considered include:* interview, recommendations, secondary school record. *Important factors considered include:* essays, extracurricular activities, standardized test scores. *Other factors considered include:* alumni/ae relation, character/personal qualities, class rank, talent/ability, volunteer work, work experience. **Freshman Admission Requirements:** High school diploma or GED is required. *Academic units required/recommended:* 17 total required; 4 English required, 2 math required, 2 science required, 1 foreign language required, 1 history required, 7 elective required. **Transfer Admission Requirements:** *Items required:* college transcript. Minimum college GPA of 2.0 required. Lowest grade transferable C. **General Admission Information:** Application fee $25. Early decision application deadline December 15. Regular application deadline rolling. Nonfall registration accepted. Admission may be deferred. Credit and/or placement offered for CEEB Advanced Placement tests.

COSTS AND FINANCIAL AID

Tuition $11,100. Room & board $6,910. Required fees $200. Average book expense $500. **Required Forms and Deadlines:** FAFSA and institution's own financial aid form. **Types of Aid:** *Need-based scholarships/grants:* Pell, SEOG, private scholarships, the school's own gift aid. *Loans:* FFEL Subsidized Stafford, FFEL Unsubsidized Stafford, FFEL PLUS, Federal Perkins, college/university loans from institutional funds. **Student Employment:** Federal

Work-Study Program available. Institutional employment available. Off-campus job opportunities are good. **Financial Aid Statistics:** Average freshman grant $3,800. Average freshman loan $6,500. Average income from on-campus job $1,200. **Financial Aid Phone:** 914-398-4097.

ST. THOMAS UNIVERSITY

1540 Northwest 32nd Avenue, Miami, FL 33054
Phone: 305-628-6546 **E-mail:** signup@stu.edu **CEEB Code:** 5076
Fax: 305-628-6591 **Web:** www.stu.edu **ACT Code:** 719

This private school, which is affiliated with the Roman Catholic Church, was founded in 1961. It has a 140-acre campus.

STUDENTS AND FACULTY

Enrollment: 1,205. **Student Body:** Male 39%, female 61%, out-of-state 3%, international 15% (52 countries represented). **Ethnic Representation:** African American 30%, Caucasian 10%, Hispanic 57%. **Retention and Graduation:** 60% freshmen return for sophomore year. 25% freshmen graduate within 4 years. **Faculty:** Student/faculty ratio 14:1. 91 full-time faculty, 62% hold PhDs. 100% faculty teach undergrads.

ACADEMICS

Degrees: Bachelor's, first professional, master's, post-bachelor's certificate, post-master's certificate. **Academic Requirements:** General education including some course work in computer literacy, English (including composition), history, mathematics, philosophy, sciences (biological or physical), social science, religious studies. **Classes:** 10-19 students in an average class. 20-29 students in an average lab/discussion section. **Disciplines with Highest Percentage of Degrees Awarded:** Business/marketing 50%, protective services/public administration 14%, communications/communication technologies 8%, education 6%, social sciences and history 5%. **Special Study Options:** Distance learning, double major, dual enrollment, honors program, independent study, liberal arts/career combination, teacher certification program.

FACILITIES

Housing: All-female, all-male. **Library Holdings:** 154,017 bound volumes. 898 periodicals. 319,889 microforms. 7,894 audiovisuals. **Special Academic Facilities/Equipment:** Multimedia computer equipment, TV studio, Art Atrium Gallery. **Computers:** School-owned computers available for student use.

EXTRACURRICULARS

Activities: Choral groups, literary magazine, music ensembles, student government, student newspaper, television station, yearbook. **Organizations:** 26 registered organizations, 4 honor societies, 2 religious organizations, 3 fraternities, 2 sororities. **Athletics (Intercollegiate):** *Men:* baseball, cross-country, golf, soccer, tennis. *Women:* cross-country, soccer, softball, tennis, volleyball.

ADMISSIONS

Selectivity Rating: 63 (of 100). **Freshman Academic Profile:** Average high school GPA 2.9. 68% from public high schools. Average SAT I Math 477, SAT I Math middle 50% range 368-483. Average SAT I Verbal 482, SAT I Verbal middle 50% range 368-490. Average ACT 19, ACT middle 50% range 16-19. TOEFL required of all international applicants, minimum TOEFL 525. **Basis for Candidate Selection:** *Very important factors considered include:* class rank, secondary school record, standardized test scores. *Other factors considered include:* alumni/ae relation, character/personal qualities, essays, extracurricular activities, interview, recommendations, talent/ability, volunteer work. **Freshman Admission Requirements:** High school diploma or GED is required. *Academic units required/recommended:* 4 English required, 3 math required, 2 science required, 3 social studies required, 6 elective required. **Freshman Admission Statistics:** 767 applied, 55% accepted, 39% of those accepted enrolled. **Transfer Admission Requirements:** *Items required:* college transcript, statement of good standing from prior school. Minimum high school GPA of 2.0 required. Minimum college GPA of 2.0 required. Lowest grade transferable C-. **General Admission Information:** Application fee $40. Nonfall registration accepted. Admission may be deferred for a maximum of 1 year. Credit and/or placement offered for CEEB Advanced Placement tests.

COSTS AND FINANCIAL AID

Tuition $13,350. Room & board $4,400. Required fees $630. Average book expense $700. **Required Forms and Deadlines:** FAFSA and state aid form. No deadline for regular filing. Priority filing deadline April 1. **Notification of Awards:** Applicants will be notified of awards on a rolling basis beginning on or about March 15. **Types of Aid:** *Need-based scholarships/grants:* Pell, SEOG, state scholarships/grants, private scholarships, the school's own gift aid. *Loans:* FFEL Subsidized Stafford, FFEL Unsubsidized Stafford, FFEL PLUS, Federal Perkins. **Student Employment:** Federal Work-Study Program available. Institutional employment available. Off-campus job opportunities are good. **Financial Aid Statistics:** 69% freshmen, 65% undergrads receive some form of aid. Average freshman grant $4,800. Average freshman loan $2,625. Average income from on-campus job $1,600. **Financial Aid Phone:** 305-628-6547.

SAINT VINCENT COLLEGE

Office of Admission & Financial Aid, 300 Fraser Purchase Rd., Latrobe, PA 15650-2690
Phone: 724-537-4540 **E-mail:** admission@stvincent.edu **CEEB Code:** 2808
Fax: 724-532-5069 **Web:** www.stvincent.edu **ACT Code:** 3686

This private school, which is affiliated with the Roman Catholic Church, was founded in 1846. It has a 200-acre campus.

STUDENTS AND FACULTY

Enrollment: 1,371. **Student Body:** Male 49%, female 51%, out-of-state 16%, international 2% (20 countries represented). **Ethnic Representation:** African American 3%, Asian 1%, Caucasian 94%, Hispanic 1%. **Retention and Graduation:** 83% freshmen return for sophomore year. 59% freshmen graduate within 4 years. 28% grads go on to further study within 1 year. 1% grads pursue business degrees. 5% grads pursue law degrees. 4% grads pursue medical degrees. **Faculty:** Student/faculty ratio 14:1. 75 full-time faculty, 84% hold PhDs. 100% faculty teach undergrads.

ACADEMICS

Degrees: Bachelor's, certificate, master's. **Academic Requirements:** General education including some course work in arts/fine arts, English (including composition), foreign languages, history, mathematics, philosophy, sciences (biological or physical), social science, religious studies. **Classes:** 20-29 students in an average class. 20-29 students in an average lab/discussion section. **Majors with Highest Enrollment:** Communications studies/speech communication and rhetoric; biology/biological sciences, general; psychology, general. **Disciplines with Highest Percentage of Degrees Awarded:** Business/marketing 20%, social sciences and history 17%, psychology 10%, communications/communication technologies 8%, biological life sciences 8%. **Special Study Options:** Accelerated program, cooperative (work-study) program, cross registration, double major, dual enrollment, honors program, independent study, internships, liberal arts/career combination, study abroad, teacher certification program.

FACILITIES

Housing: Coed. **Library Holdings:** 268,324 bound volumes. 791 periodicals. 98,880 microforms. 3,966 audiovisuals. **Special Academic Facilities/Equipment:** Art gallery, life sciences research center, spectrophotometer, spectrometer, physiograph work stations, data acquisition work station, planetarium, observatory, radio telescope, instructional technology resource center. **Computers:** School-owned computers available for student use.

EXTRACURRICULARS

Activities: Choral groups, dance, drama/theater, literary magazine, music ensembles, pep band, radio station, student government, student newspaper, television station, yearbook. **Organizations:** 55 registered organizations, 9 honor societies, 2 religious organizations. **Athletics (Intercollegiate):** *Men:* baseball, basketball, cross-country, golf, lacrosse, soccer, tennis. *Women:* basketball, cross-country, golf, lacrosse, soccer, softball, volleyball.

ADMISSIONS

Selectivity Rating: 73 (of 100). **Freshman Academic Profile:** Average high school GPA 3.5. 30% in top 10% of high school class, 57% in top 25% of high school class, 81% in top 50% of high school class. 77% from public high schools. SAT I Math middle 50% range 480-610. SAT I Verbal middle 50% range 488-600. ACT middle 50% range 21-27. TOEFL required of all international applicants, minimum TOEFL 525. **Basis for Candidate Selection:** *Very important factors considered include:* class rank, secondary school record. *Important factors considered include:* character/personal qualities, essays, standardized test scores. *Other factors considered include:* alumni/ae relation, extracurricular activities, interview, recommendations, talent/ability, volunteer work. **Freshman Admission Requirements:** High school diploma or GED is required. *Academic units required/recommended:* 16 total required; 20 total recommended; 4 English required, 4 English recommended, 3 math required, 3 math recommended, 1 science required, 3 science recommended, 1 science lab required, 1 science lab recommended, 2 foreign language recommended, 3 social studies required, 3 social studies recommended, 5 elective required, 5 elective recommended. **Freshman Admission Statistics:** 1,005 applied, 84% accepted, 39% of those accepted enrolled. **Transfer Admission Requirements:** *Items required:* high school transcript, college transcript, essay. Minimum college GPA of 2.5 required. Lowest grade transferable C. **General Admission Information:** Application fee $25. Priority application deadline February 1. Regular application deadline May 1. Nonfall registration accepted. Admission may be deferred for a maximum of 1 year. Credit and/or placement offered for CEEB Advanced Placement tests.

COSTS AND FINANCIAL AID

Tuition $18,080. Room & board $5,784. Required fees $350. Average book expense $1,500. **Required Forms and Deadlines:** FAFSA and state aid form. Financial aid filing deadline May 1. Priority filing deadline March 1. **Notification of Awards:** Applicants will be notified of awards on a rolling basis beginning on or about March 1. **Types of Aid:** *Need-based scholarships/grants:* Pell, SEOG, state scholarships/grants, private scholarships, the school's own gift aid, United Negro College Fund. *Loans:* FFEL Subsidized Stafford, FFEL Unsubsidized Stafford, FFEL PLUS, Federal Perkins. **Student Employment:** Federal Work-Study Program available. Institutional employment available. Off-campus job opportunities are good. **Financial Aid Statistics:** 84% freshmen, 77% undergrads receive some form of aid. Average freshman grant $11,124. Average freshman loan $2,896. Average income from on-campus job $734. **Financial Aid Phone:** 724-537-4540.

SAINT XAVIER UNIVERSITY

3700 West 103rd Street., Chicago, IL 60655
Phone: 773-298-3050 **E-mail:** admissions@sxu.edu **CEEB Code:** 1708
Fax: 773-298-3076 **Web:** www.sxu.edu **ACT Code:** 1134

This private school, which is affiliated with the Roman Catholic Church, was founded in 1847. It has a 55-acre campus.

STUDENTS AND FACULTY

Enrollment: 2,958. **Student Body:** Male 28%, female 72%, out-of-state 3%, (19 countries represented). **Ethnic Representation:** African American 17%, Asian 2%, Caucasian 63%, Hispanic 12%. **Retention and Graduation:** 77% freshmen return for sophomore year. 29% freshmen graduate within 4 years. 10% grads go on to further study within 1 year. **Faculty:** Student/faculty ratio 15:1. 151 full-time faculty, 83% hold PhDs.

ACADEMICS

Degrees: Bachelor's, certificate, master's, post-bachelor's certificate, post-master's certificate. **Academic Requirements:** General education including some course work in English (including composition), history, humanities, mathematics, philosophy, sciences (biological or physical), social science. **Classes:** 20-29 students in an average class. 10-19 students in an average lab/discussion section. **Majors with Highest Enrollment:** Nursing/registered nurse training (RN, ASN, BSN, MSN); business administration/management; elementary education and teaching. **Disciplines with Highest Percentage of Degrees Awarded:** Education 23%, health professions and related sciences 22%, business/marketing 18%, psychology 7%, liberal arts/general studies 6%. **Special Study Options:** Accelerated program, cooperative (work-study) program, double major, English as a second language, student exchange program (domestic), honors program, independent study, internships, liberal arts/career combination, student-designed major, study abroad, teacher certification program, weekend college.

FACILITIES

Housing: Coed. **Library Holdings:** 170,753 bound volumes. 717 periodicals. 10,519 microforms. 2,350 audiovisuals. **Computers:** School-owned computers available for student use.

EXTRACURRICULARS

Activities: Choral groups, concert band, jazz band, literary magazine, marching band, music ensembles, pep band, radio station, student government, student newspaper, student-run film society, symphony orchestra, yearbook. **Organizations:** 41 registered organizations, 2 honor societies, 2 religious organizations. **Athletics (Intercollegiate):** *Men:* baseball, basketball, football, soccer. *Women:* basketball, cross-country, soccer, softball, volleyball.

ADMISSIONS

Selectivity Rating: 79 (of 100). **Freshman Academic Profile:** Average high school GPA 3.2. 16% in top 10% of high school class, 42% in top 25% of high school class, 75% in top 50% of high school class. 55% from public high schools. ACT middle 50% range 19-24. TOEFL required of all international applicants, minimum TOEFL 550. **Basis for Candidate Selection:** *Very important factors considered include:* secondary school record. *Important factors considered include:* standardized test scores. *Other factors considered include:* alumni/ae relation, character/personal qualities, class rank, essays, extracurricular activities, geographical residence, interview, minority status, recommendations, religious affiliation/commitment, state residency, talent/ability, volunteer work, work experience. **Freshman Admission Requirements:** High school diploma or GED is required. *Academic units required/recommended:* 16 total recommended; 4 English recommended, 3 math recommended, 2 foreign language recommended, 3 elective recommended. **Freshman Admission Statistics:** 6,702 applied, 18% accepted, 32% of those accepted enrolled. **Transfer Admission Requirements:** *Items required:* college transcript. Minimum high school GPA of 2.5 required. Minimum college GPA of 2.5 required. Lowest grade transferable C. **General Admission Information:** Application fee $25. Nonfall registration accepted. Admission may be deferred. Credit offered for CEEB Advanced Placement tests.

COSTS AND FINANCIAL AID

Tuition $15,750. Room & board $6,233. Required fees $130. Average book expense $900. **Required Forms and Deadlines:** FAFSA. Priority filing deadline March 1. **Notification of Awards:** Applicants will be notified of awards on a rolling basis beginning on or about February 15. **Types of Aid:** *Need-based scholarships/grants:* Pell, SEOG, state scholarships/grants, private scholarships, the school's own gift aid. *Loans:* FFEL Subsidized Stafford, FFEL Unsubsidized Stafford, FFEL PLUS, Federal Perkins. **Student Employment:** Federal Work-Study Program available. Institutional employment available. Off-campus job opportunities are excellent. **Financial Aid Statistics:** 86% freshmen, 81% undergrads receive some form of aid. Average freshman grant $9,086. Average freshman loan $2,711. Average income from on-campus job $936. **Financial Aid Phone:** 773-298-3070.

SALEM COLLEGE

PO Box 10548, Winston-Salem, NC 27108
Phone: 336-721-2621 **E-mail:** admissions@salem.edu **CEEB Code:** 5607
Fax: 336-917-5572 **Web:** www.salem.edu **ACT Code:** 3156

This private school, which is affiliated with the Moravian Church, was founded in 1772. It has a 57-acre campus.

STUDENTS AND FACULTY

Enrollment: 870. **Student Body:** Male 3%, female 97%, out-of-state 47%, international 4%. **Ethnic Representation:** African American 22%, Asian 1%, Caucasian 72%, Hispanic 2%, Native American 1%. **Retention and Graduation:** 78% freshmen return for sophomore year. 63% freshmen graduate within 4 years. 20% grads go on to further study within 1 year. 2% grads pursue business degrees. 2% grads pursue law degrees. **Faculty:** Student/faculty ratio 13:1. 45 full-time faculty, 91% hold PhDs. 96% faculty teach undergrads.

ACADEMICS

Degrees: Bachelor's, master's. **Academic Requirements:** General education including some course work in arts/fine arts, English (including composition), foreign languages, history, humanities, mathematics, sciences (biological or physical), social science. **Classes:** 10-19 students in an average class. Under 10 students in an average lab/discussion section. **Majors with Highest Enrollment:** Business administration/management; communications, journalism, and related fields; sociology. **Disciplines with Highest Percentage of Degrees Awarded:** Social sciences and history 24%, business/marketing 13%, communications/communication technologies 11%, visual and performing arts 11%, psychology 10%. **Special Study Options:** Cross registration, double major, dual enrollment, honors program, independent study, internships, liberal arts/career combination, student-designed major, study abroad, teacher certification program.

FACILITIES

Housing: All-female, apartments for single students. **Library Holdings:** 128,072 bound volumes. 427 periodicals. 291,566 microforms. 13,735 audiovisuals. **Special Academic Facilities/Equipment:** Art gallery, fine arts center, Center for Women Writers, videoconferencing center. **Computers:** School-owned computers available for student use.

EXTRACURRICULARS

Activities: Choral groups, dance, drama/theater, literary magazine, marching band, music ensembles, musical theater, student government, student newspaper, yearbook. **Organizations:** 26 registered organizations, 14 honor societies, 7 religious organizations. **Athletics (Intercollegiate):** *Women:* basketball, cross-country, equestrian, field hockey, soccer, softball, swimming, tennis, volleyball.

ADMISSIONS

Selectivity Rating: 81 (of 100). **Freshman Academic Profile:** Average high school GPA 3.5. 30% in top 10% of high school class, 59% in top 25% of high school class, 87% in top 50% of high school class. 84% from public high schools. Average SAT I Math 530, SAT I Math middle 50% range 480-610. Average SAT I Verbal 570, SAT I Verbal middle 50% range 500-640. Average ACT 23, ACT middle 50% range 20-26. TOEFL required of all international applicants, minimum TOEFL 550. **Basis for Candidate Selection:** *Very important factors considered include:* secondary school record. *Important factors considered include:* essays, extracurricular activities, interview, recommendations, standardized test scores. *Other factors considered include:* alumni/ae relation, character/personal qualities, class rank, minority status, talent/ability, volunteer work, work experience. **Freshman Admission Requirements:** High school diploma or GED is required. *Academic units required/recommended:* 16 total recommended; 4 English recommended, 3 math recommended, 3 science recommended, 2 foreign language recommended, 2 social studies recommended. **Freshman Admission Statistics:** 411 applied, 76% accepted, 48% of those accepted enrolled. **Transfer Admission Requirements:** *Items required:* high school transcript, college transcript, essay, standardized test scores, statement of good standing from prior school. Minimum college GPA of 2.0 required. Lowest grade transferable C-. **General Admission Information:** Application fee $25. Priority application deadline March 1. Nonfall registration accepted. Admission may be deferred for a maximum of 1 year. Credit and/or placement offered for CEEB Advanced Placement tests.

COSTS AND FINANCIAL AID

Tuition $14,780. Room & board $8,870. Required fees $215. Average book expense $600. **Required Forms and Deadlines:** FAFSA, institution's own financial aid form and state aid form. No deadline for regular filing. Priority filing deadline March 1. **Notification of Awards:** Applicants will be notified of awards on a rolling basis beginning on or about February 12. **Types of Aid:** *Need-based scholarships/grants:* Pell, SEOG, state scholarships/grants, private scholarships, the school's own gift aid. *Loans:* FFEL Subsidized Stafford, FFEL Unsubsidized Stafford, FFEL PLUS, Federal Perkins. **Student Employment:** Federal Work-Study Program available. Institutional employment available. Off-campus job opportunities are good. **Financial Aid Statistics:** 53% freshmen, 60% undergrads receive some form of aid. **Financial Aid Phone:** 336-721-2808.

See page 1192.

SALEM INTERNATIONAL UNIVERSITY

223 West Main Street, Salem, WV 26426-0500
Phone: 304-782-5336 **E-mail:** admissions@salemiu.edu **CEEB Code:** 5608
Fax: 304-782-5592 **Web:** www.salemiu.edu **ACT Code:** 4530

This private school was founded in 1888. It has a 300-acre campus.

STUDENTS AND FACULTY

Enrollment: 443. **Student Body:** Male 53%, female 47%, out-of-state 56%, international 39% (20 countries represented). **Ethnic Representation:** African American 14%, Asian 1%, Caucasian 75%, Hispanic 3%, Native American 2%. **Retention and Graduation:** 69% freshmen return for sophomore year. 3% grads go on to further study within 1 year. 2% grads pursue business degrees. 1% grads pursue law degrees. 1% grads pursue medical degrees. **Faculty:** Student/faculty ratio 14:1. 33 full-time faculty, 69% hold PhDs. 100% faculty teach undergrads.

ACADEMICS

Degrees: Associate's, bachelor's, master's, post-master's certificate. **Academic Requirements:** General education including some course work in arts/fine arts, computer literacy, English (including composition), foreign languages, history, humanities, mathematics, sciences (biological or physical), social science, a variety of international courses (global business and international perspectives, global issues, etc.). **Classes:** Under 10 students in an average class. **Majors with Highest Enrollment:** Business administration/management; computer science; biology/biological sciences, general. **Disciplines with Highest Percentage of Degrees Awarded:** Communications/communication technologies 16%, protective services/public administration 13%, business/marketing 11%, English 10%, agriculture 9%. **Special Study Options:** Distance learning, double major, English as a second language, independent study, internships, liberal arts/career combination, study abroad. Undergrads may take grad-level classes. Foreign exchange programs: exchange programs abroad in Japan (Teikyo University, Hachioji) and Germany (Teikyo University Berlin). Combined Bachelor's/Graduate degree in molecular biology.

FACILITIES

Housing: Coed, all-female, all-male. **Library Holdings:** 179,918 bound volumes. 398 periodicals. 278,224 microforms. 827 audiovisuals. **Special Academic Facilities/Equipment:** Living museum of culture and crafts of West Virginia settlers, Fort New Salem, biotechnology labs, equestrian center. **Computers:** School-owned computers available for student use.

EXTRACURRICULARS

Activities: Choral groups, dance, student government, student newspaper, television station, yearbook. **Organizations:** 20 registered organizations, 1 honor society, 2 religious organizations, 4 fraternities (5% men join), 4 sororities (7% women join). **Athletics (Intercollegiate):** *Men:* baseball, basketball, cheerleading, equestrian, golf, soccer, swimming, tennis, water polo. *Women:* basketball, cheerleading, equestrian, soccer, softball, swimming, tennis, volleyball, water polo.

ADMISSIONS

Selectivity Rating: 66 (of 100). **Freshman Academic Profile:** Average high school GPA 3.0. 7% in top 10% of high school class, 27% in top 25% of high school class, 47% in top 50% of high school class. Average SAT I Math 498, SAT I Math middle 50% range 420-570. Average SAT I Verbal 454, SAT I Verbal middle 50% range 380-550. Average ACT 20, ACT middle 50% range 16-22. TOEFL required of all international applicants, minimum TOEFL 500. **Basis for Candidate Selection:** *Very important factors considered include:* secondary school record, standardized test scores. *Important factors considered include:* extracurricular activities, recommendations. *Other factors considered include:* alumni/ae relation, character/personal qualities, essays, interview, talent/ability. **Freshman Admission Requirements:** High school diploma or GED is required. *Academic units required/recommended:* 16 total recommended; 4 English recommended, 2 math recommended, 2 science recommended, 2 foreign language recommended, 3 social studies recommended. **Freshman Admission Statistics:** 251 applied, 99% accepted, 24% of those accepted enrolled. **Transfer Admission Requirements:** *Items required:* high school transcript, college transcript, statement of good standing from prior school. Minimum college GPA of 2.5 required. Lowest grade transferable C. **General Admission Information:** Application fee $25. Nonfall registration accepted. Admission may be deferred for a maximum of 1 year. Credit and/or placement offered for CEEB Advanced Placement tests.

COSTS AND FINANCIAL AID

Tuition $13,770. Room & board $4,632. Required fees $280. Average book expense $550. **Required Forms and Deadlines:** FAFSA and institution's own financial aid form. No deadline for regular filing. Priority filing deadline April 15. **Notification of Awards:** Applicants will be notified of awards on a rolling basis beginning on or about February 15. **Types of Aid:** *Need-based scholarships/grants:* Pell, SEOG, state scholarships/grants, private scholarships, the school's own gift aid. *Loans:* Direct Subsidized Stafford, Direct Unsubsidized Stafford, Direct PLUS, FFEL Subsidized Stafford, FFEL Unsubsidized Stafford, FFEL PLUS, Federal Perkins, college/university loans from institutional funds. **Student Employment:** Federal Work-Study Program available. Institutional employment available. Off-campus job opportunities are fair. **Financial Aid Statistics:** 65% freshmen, 61% undergrads receive some form of aid. Average freshman grant $4,231. Average freshman loan $4,600. Average income from on-campus job $2,000. **Financial Aid Phone:** 304-782-5205.

SALEM STATE COLLEGE

352 Lafayette Street, Salem, MA 01970
Phone: 978-542-6200 **E-mail:** admissions@salemstate.edu **CEEB Code:** 3522
Fax: 978-542-6893 **Web:** www.salemstate.edu

This public school was founded in 1854. It has a 108-acre campus.

STUDENTS AND FACULTY

Enrollment: 6,404. **Student Body:** Male 37%, female 63%, out-of-state 2%, international 4%. **Ethnic Representation:** African American 4%, Asian 2%, Caucasian 84%, Hispanic 4%, Native American 1%. **Retention and Graduation:** 72% freshmen return for sophomore year. **Faculty:** 277 full-time faculty, 68% hold PhDs.

ACADEMICS

Degrees: Bachelor's, master's, post-master's certificate. **Academic Requirements:** General education including some course work in arts/fine arts, computer literacy, English (including composition), history, humanities, mathematics, philosophy, sciences (biological or physical), social science, speech, health, physical education. **Classes:** 10-19 students in an average class. 10-19 students in an average lab/discussion section. **Disciplines with Highest Percentage of Degrees Awarded:** Business/marketing 23%, education 16%, protective services/public administration 12%, social sciences and history 11%, health professions and related sciences 11%. **Special Study Options:** Double major, English as a second language, honors program, independent study, internships, student-designed major, study abroad, teacher certification program.

FACILITIES

Housing: Coed, apartments for single students, housing for disabled students, substance-free housing, scholar-in-residence, academic achievement. **Library Holdings:** 217,842 bound volumes. 1,914 periodicals. 230,788 microforms. 79,000 audiovisuals. **Special Academic Facilities/Equipment:** Aquaculture center, on-campus elementary school, color TV studio, instructional media center. **Computers:** School-owned computers available for student use.

EXTRACURRICULARS

Activities: Choral groups, dance, drama/theater, literary magazine, radio station, student government, student newspaper, yearbook. **Organizations:** 1 religious organization. **Athletics (Intercollegiate):** *Men:* baseball, basketball, cross-country, diving, golf, ice hockey, lacrosse, soccer, swimming, tennis, track & field. *Women:* basketball, cross-country, diving, field hockey, lacrosse, soccer, softball, swimming, tennis, track & field, volleyball.

ADMISSIONS

Selectivity Rating: 74 (of 100). **Freshman Academic Profile:** Average high school GPA 2.8. Average SAT I Math 428, SAT I Math middle 50% range 430-530. Average SAT I Verbal 393, SAT I Verbal middle 50% range 450-570. ACT middle 50% range 19-21. TOEFL required of all international applicants, minimum TOEFL 500. **Basis for Candidate Selection:** *Very important factors considered include:* secondary school record, standardized test scores. *Other factors considered include:* alumni/ae relation, character/personal qualities, extracurricular activities, interview, recommendations, talent/ability, volunteer work, work experience. **Freshman Admission Requirements:** High school diploma or GED is required. *Academic units required/recommended:* 16 total required; 18 total recommended; 4 English required, 4 English recommended, 3 math required, 3 math recommended, 3 science required, 3 science recommended, 2 science lab required, 2 science lab recommended, 2 foreign language required, 2 foreign language recommended, 2 social studies required, 2 social studies recommended, 2 history required, 3 history recommended, 2 elective recommended. **Freshman Admission Statistics:** 4,099 applied, 72% accepted, 31% of those accepted enrolled. **Transfer Admission Requirements:** *Items required:* college transcript. Minimum high school GPA of 3.0 required. Minimum college GPA of 2.0 required. Lowest grade transferable C-. **General Admission Information:** Application fee $25. Priority application deadline April 1. Nonfall registration accepted. Admission may be deferred. Credit and/or placement offered for CEEB Advanced Placement tests.

COSTS AND FINANCIAL AID

In-state tuition $910. Out-of-state tuition $7,050. Room & board $5,428. Required fees $3,028. Average book expense $800. **Required Forms and Deadlines:** FAFSA. Financial aid filing deadline February 28. Priority filing deadline April 1. **Notification of Awards:** Applicants will be notified of awards on a rolling basis beginning on or about April 1. **Types of Aid:** *Need-based scholarships/grants:* Pell, SEOG, state scholarships/grants, private scholarships, the school's own gift aid. *Loans:* Direct Subsidized Stafford, Direct Unsubsidized Stafford, FFEL PLUS, Federal Perkins, Federal Nursing, state loans, TERI, other alternative loan programs. **Student Employment:** Federal Work-Study Program available. Institutional employment available. Off-campus job opportunities are good. **Financial Aid Statistics:** 49% freshmen, 51% undergrads receive some form of aid. **Financial Aid Phone:** 978-542-6112.

SALISBURY UNIVERSITY

Admissions Office, 1101 Camden Avenue, Salisbury, MD 21801
Phone: 410-543-6161 **E-mail:** admissions@salisbury.edu **CEEB Code:** 5403
Fax: 410-546-6016 **Web:** www.salisbury.edu **ACT Code:** 1716

This public school was founded in 1925. It has a 144-acre campus.

STUDENTS AND FACULTY

Enrollment: 6,206. **Student Body:** Male 43%, female 57%, out-of-state 18%, international 1%. **Ethnic Representation:** African American 6%, Asian 2%, Caucasian 85%, Hispanic 2%. **Retention and Graduation:** 81% freshmen return for sophomore year. 50% freshmen graduate within 4 years. 29% grads go on to further study within 1 year. 4% grads pursue business degrees. 2% grads pursue law degrees. 1% grads pursue medical degrees. **Faculty:** Student/faculty ratio 17:1. 298 full-time faculty, 80% hold PhDs. 100% faculty teach undergrads.

ACADEMICS

Degrees: Bachelor's, master's. **Academic Requirements:** General education including some course work in arts/fine arts, computer literacy, English (including composition), history, humanities, mathematics, sciences (biological or physical), social science. **Classes:** 20-29 students in an average class. 20-29 students in an average lab/discussion section. **Majors with Highest Enrollment:** Business administration/management; communications studies/speech communication and rhetoric; elementary education and teaching. **Disciplines with Highest Percentage of Degrees Awarded:** Business/marketing 21%, education 18%, communications/communication technologies 10%, biological life sciences 8%, social sciences and history 8%. **Special Study Options:** Accelerated program, double major, dual enrollment, English as a second language, external degree program, honors program, independent study, internships, liberal arts/career combination, student-designed major, study abroad, teacher certification program.

FACILITIES

Housing: Coed, all-female, all-male, apartments for single students, housing for international students, wellness, quiet study, world living/learning option (community of international and American students). **Library Holdings:** 253,958 bound volumes. 1,711 periodicals. 738,503 microforms. 10,690 audiovisuals. **Special Academic Facilities/Equipment:** Arboretum, University Galleries, Scarborough Student Leadership Center, Research Center for Delmarva History and Culture, Small Business Development Center, Ward Museum of Wildfowl Art. **Computers:** *Recommended operating system:* Windows 95/98/2000/NT. School-owned computers available for student use.

EXTRACURRICULARS

Activities: Choral groups, concert band, dance, drama/theater, jazz band, literary magazine, music ensembles, musical theater, pep band, radio station, student government, student newspaper, student-run film society, symphony orchestra, television station, yearbook. **Organizations:** 100 registered organizations, 20 honor societies, 8 religious organizations, 4 fraternities (5% men join), 4 sororities (7% women join). **Athletics (Intercollegiate):** *Men:* baseball, basketball, cross-country, football, lacrosse, soccer, swimming, tennis, track & field. *Women:* basketball, cross-country, field hockey, lacrosse, soccer, softball, swimming, tennis, track & field, volleyball.

ADMISSIONS

Selectivity Rating: 84 (of 100). **Freshman Academic Profile:** Average high school GPA 3.4. 22% in top 10% of high school class, 55% in top 25% of high school class, 87% in top 50% of high school class. 80% from public high schools. Average SAT I Math 571, SAT I Math middle 50% range 530-610. Average SAT I Verbal 555, SAT I Verbal middle 50% range 520-600. TOEFL required of all international applicants, minimum TOEFL 595. **Basis for Candidate Selection:** *Very important factors considered include:* secondary school record. *Important factors considered include:* class rank, standardized test scores. *Other factors considered include:* alumni/ae relation, character/personal qualities, essays, extracurricular activities, geographical residence, minority status, recommendations, state residency, talent/ability, volunteer work, work experience. **Freshman Admission Requirements:** High school diploma or GED is required. *Academic units required/recommended:* 14 total required; 18 total recommended; 4 English required, 4 English recommended, 3 math required, 4 math recommended, 3 science required, 4 science recommended, 2 science lab required, 3 science lab recommended, 2 foreign language required, 3 foreign language recommended, 3 social studies required, 3 social studies recommended. **Freshman Admission Statistics:** 5,298 applied, 50% accepted. **Transfer Admission Requirements:** *Items required:* college transcript. Minimum college GPA of 2.0 required. Lowest grade transferable C. **General Admission Information:** Application fee $30. Early decision application deadline December 15. Regular application deadline January 15. Nonfall registration accepted. Credit offered for CEEB Advanced Placement tests.

COSTS AND FINANCIAL AID

In-state tuition $4,804. Out-of-state tuition $10,568. Room & board $6,530. Required fees $1,430. Average book expense $675. **Required Forms and Deadlines:** FAFSA. Financial aid filing deadline December 31. Priority filing deadline February 1. **Notification of Awards:** Applicants will be notified of awards on a rolling basis beginning on or about April 1. **Types of Aid:** *Need-based scholarships/grants:* Pell, SEOG, state scholarships/grants, the school's own gift aid. *Loans:* Direct Subsidized Stafford, Direct Unsubsidized Stafford, Direct PLUS, Federal Perkins. **Student Employment:** Federal Work-Study Program available. Institutional employment available. Off-campus job opportunities are good. **Financial Aid Statistics:** 43% freshmen, 39% undergrads receive some form of aid. **Financial Aid Phone:** 410-543-6165.

SALISH-KOOTENAI COLLEGE

Attn: Jackie Moran, PO Box 117, Pablo, MT 59855
Phone: 406-675-4800 **E-mail:** jackie_moran@skc.edu
Fax: 406-275-4810 **Web:** www.skc.edu

This private school was founded in 1977.

STUDENTS AND FACULTY

Enrollment: 1,088. **Student Body:** Male 39%, female 61%, out-of state 27%. **Ethnic Representation:** Caucasian 20%, Native American 79%. **Faculty:** Student/faculty ratio 35:1.

ACADEMICS

Degrees: Associate's, bachelor's, certificate. **Special Study Options:** Cooperative (work-study) program, distance learning.

FACILITIES

Housing: Apartments for married students, apartments for single students. **Computers:** School-owned computers available for student use.

EXTRACURRICULARS

Activities: Student government. **Athletics (Intercollegiate):** *Men:* baseball, basketball. *Women:* basketball.

ADMISSIONS

Selectivity Rating: 63 (of 100). High school diploma or GED is required. **Freshman Admission Statistics:** 133 applied, 81% accepted, 100% of those accepted enrolled. **Transfer Admission Requirements:** *Items required:* high school transcript, college transcript. Lowest grade transferable C. **General Admission Information:** Priority application deadline July 1. Nonfall registration accepted.

COSTS AND FINANCIAL AID

Tuition $1,620. Required fees $687. Average book expense $750. **Financial Aid Statistics:** 24% freshmen, 49% undergrads receive some form of aid. **Financial Aid Phone:** 406-675-4800.

SALVE REGINA UNIVERSITY

100 Ochre Point Avenue, Newport, RI 02840-4192
Phone: 401-341-2908 **E-mail:** sruadmis@salve.edu **CEEB Code:** 3759
Fax: 401-848-2823 **Web:** www.salve.edu **ACT Code:** 3816

This private school, which is affiliated with the Roman Catholic Church, was founded in 1947. It has a 70-acre campus.

STUDENTS AND FACULTY

Enrollment: 1,916. **Student Body:** Male 31%, female 69%, out-of-state 83%, international 2% (16 countries represented). **Ethnic Representation:** African American 1%, Asian 1%, Caucasian 90%, Hispanic 2%. **Retention and Graduation:** 78% freshmen return for sophomore year. 55% freshmen graduate within 4 years. 26% grads go on to further study within 1 year. 12% grads pursue business degrees. 5% grads pursue law degrees. 1% grads pursue medical degrees. **Faculty:** Student/faculty ratio 13:1. 105 full-time faculty, 68% hold PhDs. 95% faculty teach undergrads.

ACADEMICS

Degrees: Associate's, bachelor's, doctoral, master's, post-master's certificate. **Academic Requirements:** General education including some course work in arts/fine arts, English (including composition), foreign languages, history, humanities, mathematics, philosophy, sciences (biological or physical), social science, two courses in religious studies. **Classes:** 10-19 students in an average class. 20-29 students in an average lab/discussion section. **Majors with Highest Enrollment:** Business administration/management; special education, general; criminal justice/law enforcement administration. **Disciplines with Highest Percentage of Degrees Awarded:** Education 21%, business/marketing 19%, protective services/public administration 13%, social sciences and history 7%, psychology 6%. **Special Study Options:** Accelerated program, distance learning, double major, English as a second language, student exchange program (domestic), honors program, independent study, internships, liberal arts/career combination, study abroad, teacher certification program.

FACILITIES

Housing: Coed, all-female, all-male, apartments for single students, housing for disabled students, unique housing options in Newport's historic buildings as well as in the more traditional-style dormitories. One dormitory option includes a "Living & Learning" setting. Off-campus housing in downtown area. **Library Holdings:** 139,161 bound volumes. 1,041 periodicals. 43,146 microforms. 19,420 audiovisuals. **Special Academic Facilities/Equipment:** Art gallery, theater, technology center. **Computers:** *Recommended operating system:* Windows 95. School-owned computers available for student use.

EXTRACURRICULARS

Activities: Choral groups, concert band, dance, drama/theater, jazz band, literary magazine, music ensembles, radio station, student government, student newspaper, yearbook. **Organizations:** 30 registered organizations, 12 honor societies, 2 religious organizations. **Athletics (Intercollegiate):** *Men:* baseball, basketball, football, ice hockey, lacrosse, sailing, soccer, tennis. *Women:* basketball, cross-country, field hockey, ice hockey, lacrosse, sailing, soccer, softball, tennis, track & field, volleyball.

ADMISSIONS

Selectivity Rating: 66 (of 100). **Freshman Academic Profile:** Average high school GPA 3.2. 10% in top 10% of high school class, 38% in top 25% of high school class, 77% in top 50% of high school class. 65% from public high schools. Average SAT I Math 518, SAT I Math middle 50% range 480-560. Average SAT I Verbal 525, SAT I Verbal middle 50% range 490-560. ACT middle 50% range 19-21. TOEFL required of all international applicants, minimum TOEFL 500. **Basis for Candidate Selection:** *Very important factors considered include:* class rank, secondary school record, standardized test scores. *Important factors considered include:* character/personal qualities, essays, extracurricular activities, recommendations, talent/ability, volunteer work, work experience. *Other factors considered include:* alumni/ae relation, minority status. **Freshman Admission Requirements:** High school diploma or GED is required. *Academic units required/recommended:* 16 total required; 4 English required, 3 math required, 2 science required, 2 science lab required, 2 foreign language required, 1 social studies required, 4 elective required. **Freshman Admission Statistics:** 3,528 applied, 59% accepted, 25% of those accepted enrolled. **Transfer Admission Requirements:** *Items required:* high school transcript, college transcript, essay. Minimum high school GPA of 2.3 required. Minimum college GPA of 2.3 required. Lowest grade transferable C. **General Admission Information:** Application fee $40. Priority application deadline March 1. Nonfall registration accepted. Admission may be deferred for a maximum of 1 year. Credit and/or placement offered for CEEB Advanced Placement tests.

COSTS AND FINANCIAL AID

Average book expense $700. **Required Forms and Deadlines:** FAFSA, institution's own financial aid form, CSS/Financial Aid PROFILE, noncustodial (divorced/separated) parent's statement, and business/farm supplement. No deadline for regular filing. Priority filing deadline March 1. **Notification of Awards:** Applicants will be notified of awards on a rolling basis beginning on or about April 1. **Types of Aid:** *Need-based scholarships/grants:* Pell, SEOG, state scholarships/grants, private scholarships, the school's own gift aid. *Loans:* FFEL Subsidized Stafford, FFEL Unsubsidized Stafford, FFEL PLUS, Federal Perkins, Federal Nursing, state loans, college/university loans from institutional funds, private loans. **Student Employment:** Federal Work-Study Program available. Institutional employment available. Off-campus job opportunities are excellent. **Financial Aid Statistics:** 69% freshmen, 65% undergrads receive some form of aid. Average freshman grant $10,100. Average freshman loan $3,609. Average income from on-campus job $1,000. **Financial Aid Phone:** 401-341-2901.

SAM HOUSTON STATE UNIVERSITY

Box 2418, SHSU, Huntsville, TX 77341-2418
Phone: 936-294-1828 **E-mail:** admissions@shsu.edu **CEEB Code:** 6643
Fax: 936-294-3758 **Web:** www.shsu.edu **ACT Code:** 4162

This public school was founded in 1879. It has a 2,143-acre campus.

STUDENTS AND FACULTY

Enrollment: 11,222. **Student Body:** Male 43%, female 57%, out-of-state 1%, international 1%. **Ethnic Representation:** African American 15%, Asian 1%, Caucasian 74%, Hispanic 9%. **Retention and Graduation:** 63% freshmen return for sophomore year. 13% freshmen graduate within 4 years. 18% grads go on to further study within 1 year. 2% grads pursue business degrees. **Faculty:** Student/faculty ratio 21:1. 390 full-time faculty, 78% hold PhDs. 90% faculty teach undergrads.

ACADEMICS

Degrees: Bachelor's, doctoral, master's. **Academic Requirements:** General education including some course work in arts/fine arts, computer literacy, English (including composition), history, humanities, mathematics, sciences (biological or physical), social science. **Classes:** 20-29 students in an average class. 20-29 students in an average lab/discussion section. **Majors with Highest Enrollment:** Business administration/management; multi/interdisciplinary studies; criminal justice/safety studies. **Disciplines with Highest Percentage of Degrees Awarded:** Business/marketing 25%, interdisciplinary studies 17%, protective services/public administration 13%, education 7%, social sciences and history 6%. **Special Study Options:** Cooperative (work-study) program, distance learning, double major, student exchange program (domestic), honors program, independent study, internships, teacher certification program, weekend college, undergrads may take grad-level classes, 3-2 engineering program with Texas A&M University.

FACILITIES

Housing: Coed, all-female, all-male, apartments for married students, apartments for single students, fraternities and/or sororities. **Library Holdings:** 1,849,801 bound volumes. 3,263 periodicals. 1,111,264 microforms. 19,716 audiovisuals. **Special Academic Facilities/Equipment:** Sam Houston Memorial Museum, on-campus elementary school, communications center for photography, radio, TV, and film, agricultural complex and university farm. **Computers:** School-owned computers available for student use.

EXTRACURRICULARS

Activities: Choral groups, concert band, dance, drama/theater, jazz band, marching band, music ensembles, musical theater, pep band, radio station, student government, student newspaper, symphony orchestra, television station, yearbook. **Organizations:** 164 registered organizations, 14 fraternities, 13 sororities. **Athletics (Intercollegiate):** *Men:* baseball, basketball, cross-country, football, golf, indoor track, rodeo, tennis, track & field. *Women:* basketball, cheerleading, cross-country, golf, indoor track, rodeo, softball, tennis, track & field, volleyball.

ADMISSIONS

Selectivity Rating: 63 (of 100). **Freshman Academic Profile:** 11% in top 10% of high school class, 42% in top 25% of high school class, 83% in top 50% of high school class. Average SAT I Math 501, SAT I Math middle 50% range 450-550. Average SAT I Verbal 496, SAT I Verbal middle 50% range 450-550. Average ACT 21, ACT middle 50% range 18-23. TOEFL required of all international applicants, minimum TOEFL 550. **Basis for Candidate Selection:** *Very important factors considered include:* class rank, standardized test scores. *Important factors considered include:* secondary school record. *Other factors considered include:* interview. **Freshman Admission Requirements:** High school diploma or GED is required. *Academic units required/recommended:* 4 English recommended, 2 math recommended, 2 science recommended, 1 social studies recommended, 1 history recommended. **Freshman Admission Statistics:** 5,777 applied, 70% accepted, 42% of those accepted enrolled. **Transfer Admission Requirements:** *Items required:* college transcript. Minimum college GPA of 2.0 required. Lowest grade transferable D. **General Admission Information:** Application fee $20. Priority application deadline August 1. Regular application deadline August 1. Nonfall registration accepted. Credit and/or placement offered for CEEB Advanced Placement tests.

COSTS AND FINANCIAL AID

In-state tuition $2,070. Out-of-state tuition $8,400. Room & board $3,672. Required fees $748. Average book expense $650. **Required Forms and Deadlines:** FAFSA and institution's own financial aid form. Financial aid filing deadline May 31. Priority filing deadline March 31. **Notification of Awards:** Applicants will be notified of awards on a rolling basis beginning on or about June 1. **Types of Aid:** *Need-based scholarships/grants:* Pell, SEOG, state scholarships/grants, the school's own gift aid. *Loans:* FFEL Subsidized Stafford, FFEL Unsubsidized Stafford, FFEL PLUS, Federal Perkins, state loans, college/university loans from institutional funds. **Student Employment:** Federal Work-Study Program available. Institutional employment available. Off-campus job opportunities are good. **Financial Aid Statistics:** 44% freshmen, 40% undergrads receive some form of aid. Average freshman grant $2,499. Average freshman loan $2,413. Average income from on-campus job $2,500. **Financial Aid Phone:** 936-294-1724.

SAMFORD UNIVERSITY

Best 351

800 Lakeshore Drive, Birmingham, AL 35229
Phone: 205-726-3673 **E-mail:** admiss@samford.edu **CEEB Code:** 1302
Fax: 205-726-2171 **Web:** www.samford.edu **ACT Code:** 16

This private school, which is affiliated with the Baptist Church, was founded in 1841. It has a 180-acre campus.

STUDENTS AND FACULTY

Enrollment: 2,853. **Student Body:** Male 37%, female 63%, out-of-state 52%. **Ethnic Representation:** African American 6%, Asian 1%, Caucasian 90%, Hispanic 1%. **Retention and Graduation:** 80% freshmen return for sophomore year. **Faculty:** Student/faculty ratio 13:1. 256 full-time faculty, 80% hold PhDs. 72% faculty teach undergrads.

ACADEMICS

Degrees: Associate's, bachelor's, certificate, doctoral, first professional, master's, post-master's certificate, terminal. **Academic Requirements:** General education including some course work in arts/fine arts, English (including composition), foreign languages, history, humanities, mathematics, sciences (biological or physical), social science, fitness, health, religion. **Classes:** 10-19 students in an average class. Under 10 students in an average lab/discussion section. **Majors with Highest Enrollment:** Nursing/registered nurse training (RN, ASN, BSN, MSN); business administration/management; human development and family studies, general. **Disciplines with Highest Percentage of Degrees Awarded:** Business/marketing 17%, education 14%, social sciences and history 11%, health professions and related sciences 9%, philosophy/religion/theology 7%. **Special Study Options:** Accelerated program, cross registration, double major, dual enrollment, student exchange program (domestic), honors program, independent study, internships, study abroad, teacher certification program.

FACILITIES

Housing: All-female, all-male, housing for disabled students, fraternities and/or sororities. **Library Holdings:** 439,760 bound volumes. 3,724 periodicals. 1,281,780 microforms. 14,362 audiovisuals. **Special Academic Facilities/Equipment:** Language lab, observatory, reflective telescope, geographic information systems lab, global center. **Computers:** School-owned computers available for student use.

EXTRACURRICULARS

Activities: Choral groups, concert band, dance, drama/theater, jazz band, literary magazine, marching band, music ensembles, musical theater, pep band, radio station, student government, student newspaper, symphony orchestra, yearbook. **Organizations:** 133 registered organizations, 20 honor societies, 20 religious organizations, 7 fraternities (30% men join), 8 sororities (31% women join). **Athletics (Intercollegiate):** *Men:* baseball, basketball, cross-country, football, golf, tennis, track & field. *Women:* basketball, cross-country, golf, soccer, softball, tennis, track & field, volleyball.

ADMISSIONS

Selectivity Rating: 78 (of 100). **Freshman Academic Profile:** Average high school GPA 3.7. 42% in top 10% of high school class, 66% in top 25% of high school class, 90% in top 50% of high school class. 64% from public high schools. Average SAT I Math 581, SAT I Math middle 50% range 530-640. Average SAT I Verbal 572, SAT I Verbal middle 50% range 520-620. Average ACT 25, ACT middle 50% range 22-28. TOEFL required of all international applicants, minimum TOEFL 550. **Basis for Candidate Selection:** *Very important factors considered include:* character/personal qualities, recommendations, secondary school record, standardized test scores. *Important factors considered include:* class rank, essays, extracurricular activities, religious affiliation/commitment, talent/ability. *Other factors considered include:* alumni/ae relation, geographical residence, interview, minority status, state residency, volunteer work, work experience. **Freshman Admission Requirements:** High school diploma or GED is required. *Academic units required/recommended:* 4 English required, 3 math required, 2 science recommended, 2 science lab recommended, 2 foreign language recommended, 3 social studies recommended, 3 history recommended, 3 elective recommended. **Freshman Admission Statistics:** 1,954 applied, 89% accepted, 38% of those accepted enrolled. **Transfer Admission Requirements:** *Items required:* college transcript, essay, statement of good standing from prior school. Minimum college GPA of 2.5 required. Lowest grade transferable C-. **General Admission Information:** Application fee $25. Priority application deadline June 1. Regular application deadline August 15. Nonfall registration accepted. Admission may be deferred for a maximum of 1 year. Credit and/or placement offered for CEEB Advanced Placement tests.

COSTS AND FINANCIAL AID

Required Forms and Deadlines: FAFSA. No deadline for regular filing. Priority filing deadline March 15. **Notification of Awards:** Applicants will be notified of awards on a rolling basis beginning on or about March 1. **Types of Aid:** *Need-based scholarships/grants:* Pell, SEOG, state scholarships/grants, private scholarships, the school's own gift aid, United Negro College Fund. *Loans:* FFEL Subsidized Stafford, FFEL Unsubsidized Stafford, FFEL PLUS, Federal Perkins, college/university loans from institutional funds. **Student Employment:** Federal Work-Study Program available. Institutional employment available. Off-campus job opportunities are excellent. **Financial Aid Statistics:** 40% freshmen, 41% undergrads receive some form of aid. Average freshman grant $2,446. Average freshman loan $8,693. Average income from on-campus job $642. **Financial Aid Phone:** 800-888-7245.

SAMUEL MERRITT COLLEGE

370 Hawthorne Avenue, Oakland, CA 94609
Phone: 510-869-6576 **E-mail:** admission@samuelmerritt.edu **CEEB Code:** 412
Fax: 510-869-6525 **Web:** www.samuelmerritt.edu **ACT Code:** 4750

This private school was founded in 1909. It has a 1-acre campus.

STUDENTS AND FACULTY

Enrollment: 286. **Student Body:** Male 12%, female 88%, out-of-state 1%, international 1% (2 countries represented). **Ethnic Representation:** African American 10%, Asian 19%, Caucasian 58%, Hispanic 7%, Native American 2%. **Retention and Graduation:** 67% freshmen return for sophomore year. 81% freshmen graduate within 4 years. 1% grads go on to further study within 1 year. **Faculty:** 48% faculty teach undergrads.

ACADEMICS

Degrees: Bachelor's, master's, post-master's certificate. **Academic Requirements:** General education including some course work in English (including composition), humanities, mathematics, philosophy, sciences (biological or physical), social science. **Special Study Options:** Accelerated program, double major, dual enrollment, independent study, internships, study abroad.

FACILITIES

Housing: Coed. **Library Holdings:** 10,500 bound volumes. 528 periodicals. 75 microforms. 800 audiovisuals. **Computers:** School-owned computers available for student use.

EXTRACURRICULARS

Activities: Student government, student newspaper. **Organizations:** 11 registered organizations, 1 honor society. **Athletics (Intercollegiate):** *Men:* baseball, basketball, crew, cross-country, football, golf, rugby, soccer, tennis, volleyball. *Women:* basketball, crew, cross-country, soccer, tennis, volleyball.

ADMISSIONS

Selectivity Rating: 63 (of 100). **Freshman Academic Profile:** Average high school GPA 3.2. Average SAT I Math 510, SAT I Math middle 50% range 435-570. Average SAT I Verbal 505, SAT I Verbal middle 50% range 415-525. Average ACT 21, ACT middle 50% range 17-23. TOEFL required of all international applicants, minimum TOEFL 550. **Basis for Candidate Selection:** *Very important factors considered include:* secondary school record, standardized test scores. *Important factors considered include:* character/personal qualities, recommendations, volunteer work. *Other factors considered include:* essays, extracurricular activities, interview, talent/ability, work experience. **Freshman Admission Requirements:** High school diploma or GED is required. *Academic units required/recommended:* 3 English required, 2 math required, 2 science required, 2 science lab required, 2 social studies required. **Freshman Admission Statistics:** 43 applied, 63% accepted, 33% of those accepted enrolled. **Transfer Admission Requirements:** *Items required:* college transcript, essay. Minimum college GPA of 2.5 required. Lowest grade transferable C-. **General Admission Information:** Application fee $35. Regular application deadline May 1. Nonfall registration accepted. Admission may be deferred for a maximum of 1 year. Credit offered for CEEB Advanced Placement tests.

COSTS AND FINANCIAL AID

Tuition $14,560. Required fees $65. Average book expense $864. **Required Forms and Deadlines:** FAFSA. No deadline for regular filing. Priority filing deadline March 2. **Notification of Awards:** Applicants will be notified of awards on a rolling basis beginning on or about April 15. **Types of Aid:** *Need-based scholarships/grants:* Pell, SEOG, state scholarships/grants, private scholarships, the school's own gift aid. *Loans:* FFEL Subsidized Stafford, FFEL Unsubsidized Stafford, FFEL PLUS, Federal Nursing, college/university loans from institutional funds. **Student Employment:** Federal Work-Study Program available. Institutional employment available. Off-campus job opportunities are excellent. **Financial Aid Statistics:** Average freshman grant $4,782. Average freshman loan $2,625. Average income from on-campus job $1,000. **Financial Aid Phone:** 510-869-6131.

SAN DIEGO STATE UNIVERSITY

5500 Campanile Drive, San Diego, CA 92182-7455
Phone: 619-594-7800 **CEEB Code:** 4682
Fax: 619-594-1250 **Web:** www.sdsu.edu **ACT Code:** 398

This public school was founded in 1897. It has a 300-acre campus.

STUDENTS AND FACULTY

Enrollment: 27,846. **Student Body:** Male 42%, female 58%, out-of-state 3%, international 3%. **Ethnic Representation:** African American 4%, Asian 15%, Caucasian 46%, Hispanic 21%, Native American 1%. **Retention and Graduation:** 79% freshmen return for sophomore year. 7% freshmen graduate within 4 years. 3% grads go on to further study within 1 year. **Faculty:** Student/faculty ratio 19:1. 1,050 full-time faculty, 90% hold PhDs. 100% faculty teach undergrads.

ACADEMICS

Degrees: Bachelor's, certificate, doctoral, master's, post-bachelor's certificate, post-master's certificate. **Academic Requirements:** General education including some course work in arts/fine arts, English (including composition), foreign languages, history, humanities, mathematics, philosophy, sciences (biological or physical), social science. **Classes:** 20-29 students in an average class. 20-29 students in an average lab/discussion section. **Majors with Highest Enrollment:** Business administration/management; international business; liberal arts and sciences/liberal studies. **Disciplines with Highest Percentage of Degrees Awarded:** Business/marketing 15%, social sciences and history 12%, protective services/public administration 10%, liberal arts/general studies 9%, psychology 8%. **Special Study Options:** Cross registration, distance learning, double major, dual enrollment, English as a second language, student exchange program (domestic), honors program, independent study, internships, student-designed major, study abroad, teacher certification program.

FACILITIES

Housing: Coed, apartments for single students, housing for international students, fraternities and/or sororities. **Library Holdings:** 1,342,735 bound volumes. 8,245 periodicals. 4,262,120 microforms. 12,616 audiovisuals. **Special Academic Facilities/Equipment:** Art gallery, theatre, recital hall, research bureaus for labor economics, marine studies and social science, audiovisual center, electronic boardroom, multimedia interactive fine arts technology lab, Palomar Observatory (off-campus), field studies stations (off-campus). **Computers:** School-owned computers available for student use.

EXTRACURRICULARS

Activities: Choral groups, concert band, dance, drama/theater, jazz band, literary magazine, marching band, music ensembles, musical theater, opera, pep band, radio station, student government, student newspaper, student-run film society, symphony orchestra, television station. **Organizations:** 178 registered organizations, 27 honor societies, 15 religious organizations, 21 fraternities (7% men join), 22 sororities (6% women join). **Athletics (Intercollegiate):** *Men:* baseball, basketball, football, golf, soccer, tennis, volleyball. *Women:* basketball, crew, cross-country, diving, golf, soccer, softball, swimming, tennis, track & field, volleyball, water polo.

ADMISSIONS

Selectivity Rating: 78 (of 100). **Freshman Academic Profile:** Average high school GPA 3.4. 83% from public high schools. Average SAT I Math 538, SAT I Math middle 50% range 460-590. Average SAT I Verbal 514, SAT I Verbal middle 50% range 450-560. Average ACT 22, ACT middle 50% range 19-24. TOEFL required of all international applicants, minimum TOEFL 550. **Basis for Candidate Selection:** *Very important factors considered include:* secondary school record, standardized test scores. *Important factors considered include:* geographical residence, state residency. **Freshman Admission Requirements:** High school diploma or GED is required. *Academic units required/recommended:* 15 total required; 4 English required, 3 math required, 1 science required, 2 science recommended, 1 science lab required, 2 foreign language required, 1 social studies recommended, 1 history required, 3 elective required. **Freshman Admission Statistics:** 29,217 applied, 54% accepted, 26% of those accepted enrolled. **Transfer Admission Requirements:** *Items required:* college transcript. Minimum high school GPA of 2.0 required. Minimum college GPA of 2.0 required. Lowest grade transferable D-. **General**

Admission Information: Application fee $55. Regular application deadline November 30. Credit offered for CEEB Advanced Placement tests.

COSTS AND FINANCIAL AID

In-state tuition $1,428. Out-of-state tuition $8,460. Room & board $8,307. Required fees $442. Average book expense $1,206. **Required Forms and Deadlines:** FAFSA and state aid form. No deadline for regular filing. **Notification of Awards:** Applicants will be notified of awards on a rolling basis beginning on or about February 15. **Types of Aid:** *Need-based scholarships/grants:* Pell, SEOG, state scholarships/grants, private scholarships, the school's own gift aid, Federal Nursing. *Loans:* Direct Subsidized Stafford, Direct Unsubsidized Stafford, Direct PLUS, Federal Perkins, college/university loans from institutional funds. **Student Employment:** Federal Work-Study Program available. Institutional employment available. Off-campus job opportunities are excellent. **Financial Aid Statistics:** 45% freshmen, 41% undergrads receive some form of aid. Average income from on-campus job $3,000. **Financial Aid Phone:** 619-594-6323.

SAN FRANCISCO ART INSTITUTE

800 Chestnut Street, San Francisco, CA 94133
Phone: 415-749-4600 **E-mail:** admissions@sfai.edu **CEEB Code:** 4036
Fax: 415-749-4592 **Web:** www.sfai.edu

This private school was founded in 1871. It has a 4-acre campus.

STUDENTS AND FACULTY

Enrollment: 500. **Student Body:** Male 49%, female 51%, international 8%. **Ethnic Representation:** African American 3%, Asian 8%, Caucasian 77%, Hispanic 11%, Native American 1%. **Faculty:** Student/faculty ratio 8:1. 34 full-time faculty.

ACADEMICS

Degrees: Bachelor's, certificate, master's, post-bachelor's certificate. **Academic Requirements:** General education including some course work in arts/fine arts, English (including composition), history, humanities, mathematics, sciences (biological or physical), social science. **Classes:** 10-19 students in an average class. **Disciplines with Highest Percentage of Degrees Awarded:** Visual and performing arts 100%. **Special Study Options:** Accelerated program, double major, English as a second language, student exchange program (domestic), independent study, internships, study abroad.

FACILITIES

Housing: We have a partnership with Mills College in Oakland, California, whereby students can arrange to stay in a coed dorm on their campus, which is shared with students from Berkeley and the San Francisco Conservatory of Music. **Library Holdings:** 35,500 bound volumes. 210 periodicals. 0 microforms. 121,100 audiovisuals. **Special Academic Facilities/Equipment:** Art gallery. **Computers:** School-owned computers available for student use.

EXTRACURRICULARS

Activities: Student government, student newspaper, student-run film society.

ADMISSIONS

Selectivity Rating: 81 (of 100). **Freshman Academic Profile:** TOEFL required of all international applicants, minimum TOEFL 500. **Basis for Candidate Selection:** *Very important factors considered include:* essays, talent/ability. *Important factors considered include:* recommendations. *Other factors considered include:* interview, secondary school record, standardized test scores. **Freshman Admission Requirements:** High school diploma or GED is required. **Freshman Admission Statistics:** 197 applied, 61% accepted, 30% of those accepted enrolled. **Transfer Admission Requirements:** *Items required:* college transcript, essay. Lowest grade transferable C. **General Admission Information:** Application fee $50. Regular application deadline September 1. Nonfall registration accepted. Admission may be deferred for a maximum of 1 year. Credit offered for CEEB Advanced Placement tests.

COSTS AND FINANCIAL AID

Tuition $20,200. Required fees $498. Average book expense $1,400. **Required Forms and Deadlines:** FAFSA. California residents must submit California Grant GPA Verification Form to California Student Aid Commission (CSAC). Priority filing deadline March 1. **Notification of Awards:** Applicants will be notified of awards on a rolling basis beginning on or about March 31. **Types of Aid:** *Need-based scholarships/grants:* Pell, SEOG, state scholarships/grants, the school's own gift aid. *Loans:* Direct Subsidized Stafford, Direct Unsubsidized Stafford, Direct PLUS, alternative Educational Loans. **Student Employment:** Federal Work-Study Program available. Off-campus job opportunities are good. **Financial Aid Statistics:** 54% freshmen, 69% undergrads receive some form of aid. **Financial Aid Phone:** 415-749-4520.

SAN FRANCISCO CONSERVATORY OF MUSIC

1201 Ortega Street, San Francisco, CA 94122
Phone: 415-759-3431 **E-mail:** sed@sfcm.edu **CEEB Code:** 4744
Fax: 417-759-3499 **Web:** www.sfcm.edu

This private school was founded in 1917. It has a 5-acre campus.

STUDENTS AND FACULTY

Enrollment: 136. **Student Body:** Male 45%, female 55%, out-of-state 41%, international 16%. **Ethnic Representation:** African American 6%, Asian 16%, Caucasian 68%, Hispanic 9%, Native American 1%. **Retention and Graduation:** 85% freshmen return for sophomore year. 60% freshmen graduate within 4 years. 50% grads go on to further study within 1 year. 5% grads pursue law degrees. **Faculty:** Student/faculty ratio 7:1. 26 full-time faculty, 23% hold PhDs. 100% faculty teach undergrads.

ACADEMICS

Degrees: Bachelor's, diploma, master's, post-master's certificate. **Academic Requirements:** General education including some course work in arts/fine arts, English (including composition), history. **Classes:** Under 10 students in an average class. **Disciplines with Highest Percentage of Degrees Awarded:** Visual and performing arts 100%. **Special Study Options:** Independent study.

FACILITIES

Library Holdings: 36,821 bound volumes. 80 periodicals. 0 microforms. 14,614 audiovisuals. **Special Academic Facilities/Equipment:** Performance hall, electronic composition studio. **Computers:** School-owned computers available for student use.

EXTRACURRICULARS

Activities: Choral groups, music ensembles, musical theater, opera, student government, symphony orchestra.

ADMISSIONS

Selectivity Rating: 79 (of 100). **Freshman Academic Profile:** 71% from public high schools. Average SAT I Math 576, SAT I Math middle 50% range 530-630. Average SAT I Verbal 585, SAT I Verbal middle 50% range 490-700. TOEFL required of all international applicants, minimum TOEFL 500. **Basis for Candidate Selection:** *Very important factors considered include:* talent/ability. *Important factors considered include:* secondary school record. *Other factors considered include:* character/personal qualities, class rank, essays, extracurricular activities, recommendations, standardized test scores. **Freshman Admission Requirements:** High school diploma or GED is required. *Academic units required/recommended:* 3 English recommended, 3 foreign language recommended. **Freshman Admission Statistics:** 110 applied, 64% accepted, 30% of those accepted enrolled. **Transfer Admission Requirements:** *Items required:* high school transcript, college transcript. Minimum high school GPA of 2.0 required. Minimum college GPA of 2.0 required. Lowest grade transferable C. **General Admission Information:** Application fee $70. Priority application deadline February 15. Nonfall registration accepted. Credit offered for CEEB Advanced Placement tests.

COSTS AND FINANCIAL AID

Tuition $20,500. Required fees $280. Average book expense $850. **Required Forms and Deadlines:** FAFSA and institution's own financial aid form. Priority filing deadline March 1. **Notification of Awards:** Applicants will be notified of awards on a rolling basis beginning on or about March 15. **Types of Aid:** *Need-based scholarships/grants:* Pell, SEOG, state scholarships/grants, the school's own gift aid. *Loans:* FFEL Subsidized Stafford, FFEL Unsubsidized Stafford, FFEL PLUS, Federal Perkins. **Student Employment:** Federal Work-Study Program available. Institutional employment available. Off-campus job opportunities are excellent. **Financial Aid Statistics:** 75% freshmen, 71% undergrads receive some form of aid. Average freshman grant $8,660. Average freshman loan $4,000. Average income from on-campus job $1,000. **Financial Aid Phone:** 415-759-3422.

SAN FRANCISCO STATE UNIVERSITY

1600 Holloway Avenue, San Francisco, CA 94132
Phone: 415-338-6486 **E-mail:** ugadmit@sfsu.edu **CEEB Code:** 4684
Fax: 415-338-7196 **Web:** www.sfsu.edu

This public school was founded in 1899. It has a 130-acre campus.

STUDENTS AND FACULTY

Enrollment: 20,828. **Student Body:** Male 41%, female 59%, out-of-state 1%, international 7%. **Ethnic Representation:** African American 7%, Asian 34%, Caucasian 27%, Hispanic 13%, Native American 1%. **Retention and Graduation:** 74% freshmen return for sophomore year. 6% freshmen graduate within 4 years. **Faculty:** Student/faculty ratio 20:1. 887 full-time faculty, 70% hold PhDs.

ACADEMICS

Degrees: Bachelor's, certificate, doctoral, master's, post-bachelor's certificate. **Academic Requirements:** General education including some course work in arts/fine arts, English (including composition), foreign languages, history, humanities, mathematics, sciences (biological or physical), social science. **Classes:** 20-29 students in an average class. 20-29 students in an average lab/discussion section. **Disciplines with Highest Percentage of Degrees Awarded:** Business/marketing 24%, social sciences and history 10%, visual and performing arts 9%, psychology 8%, liberal arts/general studies 8%. **Special Study Options:** Accelerated program, cooperative (work-study) program, cross registration, distance learning, double major, dual enrollment, English as a second language, student exchange program (domestic), honors program, independent study, internships, liberal arts/career combination, student-designed major, study abroad, teacher certification program.

FACILITIES

Housing: Coed, apartments for married students, apartments for single students, housing for disabled students, housing for international students. **Library Holdings:** 780,230 bound volumes. 5,679 periodicals. 2,209,455 microforms. 72,245 audiovisuals. **Special Academic Facilities/Equipment:** Museum of anthropology and ancient Egyptian artifacts, on-campus elementary school, telescopes. **Computers:** School-owned computers available for student use.

EXTRACURRICULARS

Activities: Choral groups, concert band, dance, drama/theater, jazz band, literary magazine, marching band, music ensembles, musical theater, opera, pep band, radio station, student government, student newspaper, student-run film society, symphony orchestra, television station. **Organizations:** 12 fraternities (3% men join), 9 sororities (2% women join). **Athletics (Intercollegiate):** *Men:* baseball, basketball, cross-country, soccer, tennis, track & field, wrestling. *Women:* basketball, cross-country, field hockey, soccer, softball, swimming, tennis, track & field, volleyball.

ADMISSIONS

Selectivity Rating: 77 (of 100). **Freshman Academic Profile:** Average high school GPA 3.0. 79% from public high schools. Average SAT I Math 500, SAT I Math middle 50% range 430-560. Average SAT I Verbal 488, SAT I Verbal middle 50% range 420-560. Average ACT 19, ACT middle 50% range 17-24. TOEFL required of all international applicants, minimum TOEFL 550. **Basis for Candidate Selection:** *Very important factors considered include:* secondary school record, standardized test scores. *Other factors considered include:* recommendations, state residency. **Freshman Admission Requirements:** High school diploma or GED is required. *Academic units required/recommended:* 4 English required, 3 math required, 1 science required, 1 science lab required, 2 foreign language required, 1 history required, 3 elective required. **Freshman Admission Statistics:** 11,900 applied, 61% accepted, 27% of those accepted enrolled. **Transfer Admission Requirements:** *Items required:* college transcript, statement of good standing from prior school. Minimum high school GPA of 2.0 required. Minimum college GPA of 2.0 required. Lowest grade transferable D. **General Admission Information:** Application fee $55. Regular application deadline rolling. Nonfall registration accepted. Credit offered for CEEB Advanced Placement tests.

COSTS AND FINANCIAL AID

Average book expense $810. **Required Forms and Deadlines:** FAFSA. No deadline for regular filing. Priority filing deadline March 2. **Notification of Awards:** Applicants will be notified of awards on a rolling basis beginning on or about January 31. **Types of Aid:** *Need-based scholarships/grants:* Pell, SEOG, state scholarships/grants, private scholarships, the school's own gift aid. *Loans:* Direct Subsidized Stafford, Direct Unsubsidized Stafford, FFEL PLUS, Federal Perkins. **Student Employment:** Federal Work-Study Program available. Institutional employment available. Off-campus job opportunities are good. **Financial Aid Statistics:** 43% freshmen, 46% undergrads receive some form of aid. Average freshman grant $2,126. Average freshman loan $1,551. Average income from on-campus job $3,081. **Financial Aid Phone:** 415-338-7000.

SAN JOSE STATE UNIVERSITY

1 Washington Square, San Jose, CA 95112-0001
Phone: 408-283-7500 **E-mail:** contact@sjsu.edu **CEEB Code:** 4687
Fax: 408-924-2050 **Web:** www.sjsu.edu

This public school was founded in 1857. It has a 104-acre campus.

STUDENTS AND FACULTY

Enrollment: 22,784. **Student Body:** Male 49%, female 51%, out-of-state 0%, international 4%. **Ethnic Representation:** African American 5%, Asian 41%, Caucasian 23%, Hispanic 16%, Native American 1%. **Retention and Graduation:** 80% freshmen return for sophomore year. 5% freshmen graduate within 4 years. 6% grads pursue business degrees. **Faculty:** Student/faculty ratio 17:1.

ACADEMICS

Degrees: Bachelor's, master's. **Academic Requirements:** General education including some course work in arts/fine arts, English (including composition), foreign languages, history, humanities, mathematics, philosophy, sciences (biological or physical), social science. **Classes:** 20-29 students in an average class. 10-19 students in an average lab/discussion section. **Disciplines with Highest Percentage of Degrees Awarded:** Business/marketing 22%, computer and information sciences 15%, engineering/engineering technology 13%, visual and performing arts 7%, education 5%. **Special Study Options:** Accelerated program, cooperative (work-study) program, cross registration, distance learning, double major, dual enrollment, English as a second language, external degree program, honors program, independent study, internships, student-designed major, study abroad, teacher certification program.

FACILITIES

Housing: Coed, housing for international students, fraternities and/or sororities. **Library Holdings:** 1,101,995 bound volumes. 2,504 periodicals. 1,621,426 microforms. 37,146 audiovisuals. **Special Academic Facilities/Equipment:** Child development lab, Chicano resource center, Beethoven Studies Center, John Steinbeck Research Center, art metal foundry, natural history living museum (science education), science resource center, deep-sea research ship, electro-acoustical/recording studios, nuclear science and engineering labs.

EXTRACURRICULARS

Activities: Choral groups, concert band, dance, drama/theater, jazz band, literary magazine, marching band, music ensembles, musical theater, opera, pep band, radio station, student government, student newspaper, symphony orchestra. **Organizations:** 15 fraternities, 9 sororities. **Athletics (Intercollegiate):** *Men:* baseball, basketball, cheerleading, football, golf, gymnastics, softball, swimming, volleyball, water polo. *Women:* basketball, cheerleading, cross-country, golf, softball, swimming, volleyball, water polo.

ADMISSIONS

Selectivity Rating: 65 (of 100). **Freshman Academic Profile:** Average high school GPA 3.1. Average SAT I Math 507. Average SAT I Verbal 465. Average ACT 19. TOEFL required of all international applicants, minimum TOEFL 550. **Basis for Candidate Selection:** *Very important factors considered include:* secondary school record, standardized test scores. *Other factors considered include:* state residency. **Freshman Admission Requirements:** High school diploma or GED is required. *Academic units required/recommended:* 15 total required; 4 English required, 3 math required, 1 science required, 1 science lab required, 2 foreign language required, 1 history required, 3 elective required. **Freshman Admission Statistics:** 13,453 applied, 72% accepted, 28% of those accepted enrolled. **Transfer Admission Requirements:** *Items required:* statement of good standing from prior school. Minimum college GPA of 2.0 required. Lowest grade transferable C. **General Admission Information:** Application fee $55. Priority application deadline November 30. Nonfall registration accepted. Credit and/or placement offered for CEEB Advanced Placement tests.

COSTS AND FINANCIAL AID

Required fees $2,059. Average book expense $1,224. **Required Forms and Deadlines:** FAFSA. Priority filing deadline March 2. **Notification of Awards:** Applicants will be notified of awards on a rolling basis beginning on or about

April 15. **Types of Aid:** *Need-based scholarships/grants:* Pell, SEOG, state scholarships/grants, private scholarships, the school's own gift aid. *Loans:* FFEL Subsidized Stafford, FFEL Unsubsidized Stafford, FFEL PLUS, Federal Perkins, college/university loans from institutional funds. **Student Employment:** Federal Work-Study Program available. Institutional employment available. Off-campus job opportunities are good. **Financial Aid Statistics:** 45% freshmen, 40% undergrads receive some form of aid. Average freshman grant $3,337. Average freshman loan $2,782. Average income from on-campus job $2,925. **Financial Aid Phone:** 408-924-6100.

SANTA CLARA UNIVERSITY

500 El Camino Real, Santa Clara, CA 95053
Phone: 406-554-4700 **CEEB Code:** 4851
Fax: 408-554-5255 **Web:** www.scu.edu

This private school, which is affiliated with the Roman Catholic Church, was founded in 1851. It has a 104-acre campus.

STUDENTS AND FACULTY

Enrollment: 4,394. **Student Body:** Male 45%, female 55%, out-of-state 34%, international 2%. **Ethnic Representation:** African American 2%, Asian 20%, Caucasian 59%, Hispanic 14%, Native American 1%. **Retention and Graduation:** 28% grads go on to further study within 1 year. 1% grads pursue business degrees. 3% grads pursue law degrees. 4% grads pursue medical degrees. **Faculty:** Student/faculty ratio 12:1. 74% faculty teach undergrads.

ACADEMICS

Degrees: Bachelor's, doctoral, first professional, first professional certificate, master's, post-bachelor's certificate, post-master's certificate. **Academic Requirements:** General education including some course work in arts/fine arts, computer literacy, English (including composition), foreign languages, history, humanities, mathematics, philosophy, sciences (biological or physical), social science, ethics. **Classes:** 20-29 students in an average class. 10-19 students in an average lab/discussion section. **Disciplines with Highest Percentage of Degrees Awarded:** Business/marketing 33%, social sciences and history 15%, engineering/engineering technology 10%, communications/communication technologies 9%, psychology 8%. **Special Study Options:** Accelerated program, cooperative (work-study) program, double major, student exchange program (domestic), honors program, independent study, internships, student-designed major, study abroad, teacher certification program.

FACILITIES

Housing: Coed. **Library Holdings:** 639,691 bound volumes. 11,952 periodicals. 2,007,913 microforms. 12,622 audiovisuals. **Special Academic Facilities/Equipment:** Art and history museum, mission church, theatre, media lab, retail management institute, computer design center, engineering labs, Markkula Center for Applied Ethics, and Center for Science, Technology, and Society. **Computers:** School-owned computers available for student use.

EXTRACURRICULARS

Activities: Choral groups, concert band, dance, drama/theater, jazz band, literary magazine, music ensembles, musical theater, opera, pep band, radio station, student government, student newspaper, symphony orchestra, television station, yearbook. **Organizations:** 55 registered organizations, 13 honor societies, 2 religious organizations, 5 fraternities, 3 sororities. **Athletics (Intercollegiate):** *Men:* baseball, basketball, crew, cross-country, golf, soccer, tennis, water polo. *Women:* basketball, crew, cross-country, golf, soccer, softball, tennis, volleyball, water polo.

ADMISSIONS

Selectivity Rating: 80 (of 100). **Freshman Academic Profile:** Average high school GPA 3.6. 41% in top 10% of high school class, 75% in top 25% of high school class, 96% in top 50% of high school class. 54% from public high schools. Average SAT I Math 618, SAT I Math middle 50% range 560-660. Average SAT I Verbal 601, SAT I Verbal middle 50% range 550-650. Average ACT 27, ACT middle 50% range 23-28. TOEFL required of all international applicants, minimum TOEFL 550. **Basis for Candidate Selection:** *Very important factors considered include:* essays, recommendations, secondary school record, standardized test scores. *Important factors considered include:* character/personal qualities, extracurricular activities, talent/ability, volunteer work. *Other factors considered include:* alumni/ae relation, class rank, geographical residence, minority status, work experience. **Freshman Admission Requirements:** High school diploma is required and GED is not accepted. *Academic units required/recommended:* 18 total required; 19 total recommended; 4 English required, 4 English recommended, 4 math required, 4 math recommended, 3 science required, 4 science recommended, 1 science lab required, 2 science lab recommended, 3 foreign language required, 4 foreign language recommended, 1 social studies required, 2 social studies recommended, 1 history required, 2 history recommended, 2 elective required, 2 elective recommended. **Freshman Admission Statistics:** 5,842 applied, 70% accepted, 28% of those accepted enrolled. **Transfer Admission Requirements:** *Items required:* college transcript, essay. Minimum college GPA of 3.3 required. Lowest grade transferable C. **General Admission Information:** Application fee $50. Regular application deadline January 15. Nonfall registration accepted. Admission may be deferred for a maximum of 1 year. Credit and/or placement offered for CEEB Advanced Placement tests.

COSTS AND FINANCIAL AID

Required Forms and Deadlines: FAFSA and CSS/Financial Aid PROFILE. No deadline for regular filing. Priority filing deadline February 1. **Notification of Awards:** Applicants will be notified of awards on a rolling basis beginning on or about April 1. **Types of Aid:** *Need-based scholarships/grants:* Pell, SEOG, state scholarships/grants, private scholarships, the school's own gift aid. *Loans:* Direct Subsidized Stafford, Direct Unsubsidized Stafford, Direct PLUS, Federal Perkins, private alternative loans. **Student Employment:** Federal Work-Study Program available. Institutional employment available. Off-campus job opportunities are excellent. **Financial Aid Statistics:** 48% freshmen, 48% undergrads receive some form of aid. Average freshman grant $7,728. Average freshman loan $2,512. **Financial Aid Phone:** 408-554-4505.

SARAH LAWRENCE COLLEGE

One Mead Way, Bronxville, NY 10708-5999
Phone: 914-395-2510 **E-mail:** slcadmit@slc.edu **CEEB Code:** 2810
Fax: 914-395-2515 **Web:** www.slc.edu **ACT Code:** 2904

This private school was founded in 1926. It has a 41-acre campus.

STUDENTS AND FACULTY

Enrollment: 1,226. **Student Body:** Male 26%, female 74%, out-of-state 79%, international 2%. **Ethnic Representation:** African American 6%, Asian 5%, Caucasian 77%, Hispanic 4%, Native American 1%. **Retention and Graduation:** 91% freshmen return for sophomore year. 65% freshmen graduate within 4 years. 30% grads go on to further study within 1 year. 5% grads pursue business degrees. 15% grads pursue law degrees. 4% grads pursue medical degrees. **Faculty:** Student/faculty ratio 6:1. 180 full-time faculty. 100% faculty teach undergrads.

ACADEMICS

Degrees: Bachelor's, master's. **Academic Requirements:** Students must complete 120 credit hours and meet distribution requirements in 3 of 4 areas: history and social sciences; natural sciences and math; humanities; and creative and performing arts. **Classes:** 10-19 students in an average class. **Disciplines with Highest Percentage of Degrees Awarded:** Liberal arts/general studies 100%. **Special Study Options:** Double major, student exchange program (domestic), independent study, internships, student-designed major, study abroad, teacher certification program, Sarah Lawrence College has no formal majors, however students may concentrate in subject areas. All students design their own educational programs (with faculty advisement), so the equivalent of a "double major" is available.

FACILITIES

Housing: Coed, all-female, all-male. **Library Holdings:** 193,581 bound volumes. 1,260 periodicals. 21,172 microforms. 8,674 audiovisuals. **Special Academic Facilities/Equipment:** Performing arts center including a concert hall, dance studio, and theatres; science center;, child development institute; early childhood center; greenhouse. **Computers:** School-owned computers available for student use.

EXTRACURRICULARS

Activities: Choral groups, dance, drama/theater, jazz band, literary magazine, music ensembles, musical theater, radio station, student government, student newspaper, student-run film society, symphony orchestra, yearbook. **Organizations:** 20 registered organizations, 1 religious organization. **Athletics (Intercollegiate):** *Men:* basketball, crew, cross-country, equestrian, tennis. *Women:* crew, cross-country, equestrian, swimming, tennis, volleyball.

ADMISSIONS

Selectivity Rating: 90 (of 100). **Freshman Academic Profile:** Average high school GPA 3.6. 34% in top 10% of high school class, 77% in top 25% of high school class, 97% in top 50% of high school class. 65% from public high schools. Average SAT I Math 590, SAT I Math middle 50% range 530-650. Average SAT

I Verbal 660, SAT I Verbal middle 50% range 610-710. Average ACT 27, ACT middle 50% range 24-29. TOEFL required of all international applicants, minimum TOEFL 600. **Basis for Candidate Selection:** *Very important factors considered include:* character/personal qualities, essays, recommendations, secondary school record. *Important factors considered include:* extracurricular activities, talent/ability, volunteer work, work experience. *Other factors considered include:* alumni/ae relation, class rank, geographical, residence, interview, minority status, standardized test scores. **Freshman Admission Requirements:** High school diploma or equivalent is not required. *Academic units required/recommended:* 4 English required, 4 English recommended, 2 math required, 4 math recommended, 2 science required, 4 science recommended, 2 foreign language required, 4 foreign language recommended, 4 social studies recommended, 2 history required, 4 history recommended. **Freshman Admission Statistics:** 2,667 applied, 40% accepted, 30% of those accepted enrolled. **Transfer Admission Requirements:** *Items required:* high school transcript, college transcript, essay. Minimum college GPA of 3.0 required. Lowest grade transferable C. **General Admission Information:** Application fee $50. Early decision application deadline November 15. Regular application deadline February 1. Admission may be deferred for a maximum of 1 year. Credit offered for CEEB Advanced Placement tests.

COSTS AND FINANCIAL AID

Tuition $28,680. Room & board $10,494. Required fees $680. Average book expense $600. **Required Forms and Deadlines:** FAFSA, CSS/Financial Aid PROFILE, and noncustodial (divorced/separated) parent's statement. Financial aid filing deadline February 1. Priority filing deadline February 1. **Notification of Awards:** Applicants will be notified of awards on or about April 1. **Types of Aid:** *Need-based scholarships/grants:* Pell, SEOG, state scholarships/grants, private scholarships, the school's own gift aid. *Loans:* FFEL Subsidized Stafford, FFEL Unsubsidized Stafford, FFEL PLUS, Federal Perkins. **Student Employment:** Federal Work-Study Program available. Institutional employment available. Off-campus job opportunities are good. **Financial Aid Statistics:** 46% freshmen, 51% undergrads receive some form of aid. Average freshman grant $18,268. Average freshman loan $2,370. Average income from on-campus job $1,800. **Financial Aid Phone:** 914-395-2570.

SAVANNAH COLLEGE OF ART AND DESIGN

PO Box 3146, Savannah, GA 31402-3146
Phone: 912-525-5100 **E-mail:** admission@scad.edu **CEEB Code:** 5631
Fax: 912-525-5986 **Web:** www.scad.edu **ACT Code:** 855

This private school was founded in 1978.

STUDENTS AND FACULTY

Enrollment: 5,055. **Student Body:** Male 52%, female 48%, out-of-state 81%, international 7% (75 countries represented). **Ethnic Representation:** African American 5%, Asian 2%, Caucasian 50%, Hispanic 3%. **Retention and Graduation:** 81% freshmen return for sophomore year. 44% freshmen graduate within 4 years. 10% grads go on to further study within 1 year. **Faculty:** Student/faculty ratio 19:1. 282 full-time faculty, 73% hold PhDs. 100% faculty teach undergrads.

ACADEMICS

Degrees: Bachelor's, master's. **Academic Requirements:** General education including some course work in arts/fine arts, computer literacy, English (including composition), humanities, mathematics, social science. **Classes:** 10-19 students in an average class. **Majors with Highest Enrollment:** Computer graphics; graphic design; photography. **Disciplines with Highest Percentage of Degrees Awarded:** Visual and performing arts 95%, architecture 5%. **Special Study Options:** Double major, English as a second language, independent study, internships, study abroad.

FACILITIES

Housing: Coed, all-female, all-male, apartments for single students, housing for disabled students. **Library Holdings:** 85,000 bound volumes. 917 periodicals. 6,112 microforms. 3,976 audiovisuals. **Special Academic Facilities/Equipment:** Art galleries; computer, video, photography, and design labs; Earle W. Newton Center for British-American Studies.

EXTRACURRICULARS

Activities: Choral groups, dance, drama/theater, literary magazine, music ensembles, musical theater, radio station, student government, student newspaper, student-run film society. **Organizations:** 45 registered organizations, 3 honor societies, 3 religious organizations. **Athletics (Intercollegiate):** *Men:* baseball, basketball, cheerleading, crew, cross-country, equestrian, golf, soccer, tennis. *Women:* basketball, cheerleading, crew, cross-country, equestrian, golf, soccer, softball, tennis, volleyball.

ADMISSIONS

Selectivity Rating: 78 (of 100). **Freshman Academic Profile:** Average SAT I Math 536, SAT I Math middle 50% range 480-600. Average SAT I Verbal 556, SAT I Verbal middle 50% range 490-620. Average ACT 23, ACT middle 50% range 20-26. TOEFL required of all international applicants, minimum TOEFL 500. **Basis for Candidate Selection:** *Very important factors considered include:* interview, recommendations, talent/ability. *Important factors considered include:* character/personal qualities, class rank, secondary school record, standardized test scores. *Other factors considered include:* alumni/ae relation, extracurricular activities. **Freshman Admission Requirements:** High school diploma or GED is required. **Freshman Admission Statistics:** 3,471 applied, 83% accepted, 37% of those accepted enrolled. **Transfer Admission Requirements:** *Items required:* college transcript. Minimum college GPA of 2.0 required. Lowest grade transferable C. **General Admission Information:** Application fee $50. Priority application deadline April 1. Nonfall registration accepted. Admission may be deferred for a maximum of 2 years. Credit offered for CEEB Advanced Placement tests.

COSTS AND FINANCIAL AID

Tuition $17,955. Room & board $7,620. Required fees $500. Average book expense $1,500. **Required Forms and Deadlines:** FAFSA, institution's own financial aid form and state aid form. No deadline for regular filing. Priority filing deadline April 1. **Notification of Awards:** Applicants will be notified of awards on a rolling basis beginning on or about April 1. **Types of Aid:** *Need-based scholarships/grants:* Pell, SEOG, state scholarships/grants, private scholarships, the school's own gift aid. *Loans:* Direct Subsidized Stafford, Direct Unsubsidized Stafford, Direct PLUS, Federal Perkins. **Student Employment:** Federal Work-Study Program available. Institutional employment available. Off-campus job opportunities are excellent. **Financial Aid Statistics:** 48% freshmen, 46% undergrads receive some form of aid. Average freshman grant $3,700. Average freshman loan $2,500. Average income from on-campus job $2,500. **Financial Aid Phone:** 912-525-6109.

See page 1194.

SAVANNAH STATE UNIVERSITY

College Station, PO Box 20209, Savannah, GA 31404
Phone: 912-356-2181 **E-mail:** SSUAdmissions@savstate.edu **CEEB Code:** 5609
Fax: 912-356-2256 **ACT Code:** 858

This public school was founded in 1890. It has a 165-acre campus.

STUDENTS AND FACULTY

Enrollment: 2,822. **Student Body:** Out-of-state 15%, international 2% (18 countries represented). **Ethnic Representation:** African American 81%, Caucasian 18%, Hispanic 1%. **Retention and Graduation:** 7% grads go on to further study within 1 year.

ACADEMICS

Degrees: Bachelor's, master's. **Special Study Options:** Internships, study abroad. Undergrads may take grad-level classes. Off-campus study: summer quarter programs in New York City and Europe; apprenticeships with artists or designers and internships with museums, agencies, media production companies, architectural firms, and other companies in the U.S. or abroad. Foreign Exchange Programs: study abroad in England, France, Germany, Italy, and Spain.

FACILITIES

Housing: Coed, all-female, all-male, fraternities and/or sororities. **Library Holdings:** 173,702 bound volumes. 757 periodicals. 500,211 microforms. **Computers:** *Recommended operating system:* Mac.

EXTRACURRICULARS

Organizations: 8 honor societies, 3 religious organizations, 5 fraternities (38% men join), 4 sororities (39% women join).

ADMISSIONS

Selectivity Rating: 63 (of 100). **Freshman Academic Profile:** 12% in top 10% of high school class, 39% in top 25% of high school class, 77% in top 50% of high school class. 94% from public high schools. **Freshman Admission Requirements:** High school diploma is required and GED is not accepted. *Academic units required/recommended:* 18 total recommended; 4 English recommended, 3 math recommended, 3 science recommended, 2 foreign language recommended, 3 social studies recommended, 3 elective recommended. **Transfer Admission Requirements:** Minimum college GPA of 2.0 required. Lowest grade transferable D. **General Admission Information:** Early decision application deadline March 1. Regular application deadline September 1. Nonfall registration accepted. Credit and/or placement offered for CEEB Advanced Placement tests.

COSTS AND FINANCIAL AID

Room & board $3,495. Average book expense $750. **Required Forms and Deadlines:** FAFSA and institution's own financial aid form. **Types of Aid:** *Need-based scholarships/grants:* state scholarships/grants. *Loans:* FFEL Subsidized Stafford, FFEL PLUS. **Student Employment:** Off-campus job opportunities are good. **Financial Aid Phone:** 912-356-2253.

SCHENECTADY COUNTY COMMUNITY COLLEGE

Office of Admissions, 78 Washington Avenue, Schenectady, NY 12305
Phone: 518-381-1366 **E-mail:** dinellre@gw.sunysccc.edu
Fax: 518-381-1477 **Web:** www.sunysccc.edu

This public school was founded in 1967. It has a 50-acre campus.

STUDENTS AND FACULTY

Enrollment: 3,334. **Student Body:** Male 45%, female 55%, international students represent 2 countries. **Ethnic Representation:** African American 7%, Asian 2%, Caucasian 87%, Hispanic 3%, Native American 1%. **Faculty:** Student/faculty ratio 20:1. 64 full-time faculty, 20% hold PhDs. 100% faculty teach undergrads.

ACADEMICS

Degrees: Associate's, certificate, diploma, terminal, transfer. **Academic Requirements:** General education including some course work in English (including composition), humanities, mathematics, sciences (biological or physical), social science. **Special Study Options:** Cooperative (work-study) program, cross registration, distance learning, dual enrollment, English as a second language, internships, liberal arts/career combination.

FACILITIES

Library Holdings: 72,578 bound volumes. 678 periodicals. 69,916 microforms. 5,038 audiovisuals. **Computers:** School-owned computers available for student use.

EXTRACURRICULARS

Athletics (Intercollegiate): *Men:* baseball, basketball, soccer. *Women:* basketball, softball.

ADMISSIONS

Selectivity Rating: 60 (of 100). **Freshman Academic Profile:** TOEFL required of all international applicants, minimum TOEFL 213. **Freshman Admission Requirements:** High school diploma or GED is required. **Transfer Admission Requirements:** *Items required:* high school transcript. Lowest grade transferable C. **General Admission Information:** Nonfall registration accepted. Credit and/or placement offered for CEEB Advanced Placement tests.

COSTS AND FINANCIAL AID

In-state tuition $2,340. Out-of-state tuition $4,680. Required fees $115. Average book expense $700. **Required Forms and Deadlines:** FAFSA and state aid form. No deadline for regular filing. **Notification of Awards:** Applicants will be notified of awards on a rolling basis. **Types of Aid:** *Need-based scholarships/grants:* Pell, SEOG, state scholarships/grants, the school's own gift aid. *Loans:* Direct Subsidized Stafford, Direct Unsubsidized Stafford, Direct PLUS. **Student Employment:** Federal Work-Study Program available. Off-campus job opportunities are excellent. **Financial Aid Phone:** 518-381-1352.

SCHOOL OF RISK MANAGEMENT, INSURANCE, AND ACTUARIAL SCIENCE

101 Murray Street, New York, NY 10007
Phone: 212-815-9232 **E-mail:** admissions@tci.edu
Fax: 212-964-3381 **Web:** www.tci.edu

This private school was founded in 1901.

STUDENTS AND FACULTY

Enrollment: 338. **Student Body:** Male 48%, female 52%, international 11% (17 countries represented). **Ethnic Representation:** African American 17%, Asian 9%, Caucasian 61%, Hispanic 12%. **Retention and Graduation:** 94% freshmen return for sophomore year. 20% freshmen graduate within 4 years. **Faculty:** 100% faculty teach undergrads.

ACADEMICS

Academic Requirements: General education including some course work in English (including composition), foreign languages, history. **Special Study Options:** Distance learning, double major, English as a second language, internships, weekend college.

FACILITIES

Housing: Coed. **Library Holdings:** 114,997 bound volumes. 1,172 periodicals. 142 microforms. 127 audiovisuals.

EXTRACURRICULARS

Activities: Drama/theater, student government, student newspaper. **Organizations:** 10 honor societies, 1 religious organization, 21 fraternity.

ADMISSIONS

Selectivity Rating: 85 (of 100). **Freshman Academic Profile:** Average SAT I Math 601, SAT I Math middle 50% range 70-30. Average SAT I Verbal 533, SAT I Verbal middle 50% range 30-70. TOEFL required of all international applicants, minimum TOEFL 550. **Basis for Candidate Selection:** *Very important factors considered include:* secondary school record, standardized test scores. *Important factors considered include:* essays, extracurricular activities, interview, recommendations. *Other factors considered include:* alumni/ae relation, character/personal qualities, talent/ability, volunteer work, work experience. **Freshman Admission Requirements:** High school diploma or GED is required. *Academic units required/recommended:* 18 total required; 4 English required, 3 math required, 3 math recommended, 3 science required, 1 science lab required, 1 foreign language required, 1 social studies required, 1 history required, 4 elective required. **Freshman Admission Statistics:** 62 applied, 60% accepted, 27% of those accepted enrolled. **Transfer Admission Requirements:** *Items required:* high school transcript, college transcript, essay, interview. Minimum high school GPA of 2.5 required. Minimum college GPA of 2.5 required. Lowest grade transferable C. **General Admission Information:** Application fee $30. Priority application deadline December 1. Early decision application deadline December 1. Regular application deadline August 1. Nonfall registration accepted. Admission may be deferred. Credit offered for CEEB Advanced Placement tests.

COSTS AND FINANCIAL AID

Tuition $14,252. Room & board $9,140. Required fees $360. Average book expense $900. **Required Forms and Deadlines:** FAFSA, institution's own financial aid form, and state aid form. No deadline for regular filing. **Notification of Awards:** Applicants will be notified of awards on a rolling basis. **Types of Aid:** *Need-based scholarships/grants:* Pell, SEOG, state scholarships/grants, private scholarships, the school's own gift aid, Co-op Education Sponsorship tuition payments. *Loans:* FFEL Subsidized Stafford, FFEL Unsubsidized Stafford, FFEL PLUS, Federal Perkins, college/university loans from institutional funds, private loans. **Student Employment:** Institutional employment available. Off-campus job opportunities are excellent. **Financial Aid Statistics:** 60% freshmen, 52% undergrads receive some form of aid. Average freshman grant $11,350. Average freshman loan $2,494. Average income from on-campus job $4,500. **Financial Aid Phone:** 212-815-9222.

SCHOOL OF THE ART INSTITUTE OF CHICAGO

37 South Wabash Avenue, Chicago, IL 60603
Phone: 312-899-5219 **E-mail:** admiss@artic.edu **CEEB Code:** 1713
Fax: 312-899-1840 **Web:** www.artic.edu **ACT Code:** 1136

This private school was founded in 1866.

STUDENTS AND FACULTY

Enrollment: 1,819. **Student Body:** Male 39%, female 61%, out-of-state 72%, international 14% (40 countries represented). **Ethnic Representation:** African American 3%, Asian 11%, Caucasian 75%, Hispanic 7%, Native American 1%. **Retention and Graduation:** 78% freshmen return for sophomore year. **Faculty:** Student/faculty ratio 13:1. 107 full-time faculty.

ACADEMICS

Degrees: Bachelor's, certificate, master's, post-bachelor's certificate. **Academic Requirements:** General education including some course work in arts/fine arts, English (including composition), history, humanities, mathematics, philosophy, sciences (biological or physical), social science, art history. Foundation program includes drawing, sculpture, and time arts. **Classes:** 10-19 students in an average class. 10-19 students in an average lab/discussion section. **Disciplines with Highest Percentage of Degrees Awarded:** Visual and performing arts 99%, interior architecture 1%. **Special Study Options:** Cooperative (work-study) program, cross registration, double major, dual enrollment, English as a second language, student exchange program (domestic), independent study, internships, student-designed major, study abroad, teacher certification program.

FACILITIES

Housing: Coed. **Library Holdings:** 60,000 bound volumes. 360 periodicals. 155 microforms, 2,700 audiovisuals. **Special Academic Facilities/Equipment:** Affiliated with the Art Institute of Chicago. **Computers:** School-owned computers available for student use.

EXTRACURRICULARS

Activities: Student government, student newspaper, television station. **Organizations:** 32 registered organizations, 1 religious organization.

ADMISSIONS

Selectivity Rating: 77 (of 100). **Freshman Academic Profile:** Average SAT I Verbal 500. Average ACT 20. TOEFL required of all international applicants, minimum TOEFL 527. **Basis for Candidate Selection:** *Very important factors considered include:* secondary school record, standardized test scores. *Important factors considered include:* character/personal qualities, essays, interview, recommendations, talent/ability. **Freshman Admission Requirements:** High school diploma or GED is required. **Transfer Admission Requirements:** *Items required:* college transcript, essay. Minimum college GPA of 2.0 required. Lowest grade transferable C. **General Admission Information:** Application fee $65. Priority application deadline March 1. Regular application deadline August 15. Nonfall registration accepted. Admission may be deferred for a maximum of 1 year. Credit and/or placement offered for CEEB Advanced Placement tests.

COSTS AND FINANCIAL AID

Tuition $22,500. Required fees $0. Average book expense $2,160. **Required Forms and Deadlines:** FAFSA and institution's own financial aid form. No deadline for regular filing. Priority filing deadline March 15. **Notification of Awards:** Applicants will be notified of awards on a rolling basis beginning on or about April 1. **Types of Aid:** *Need-based scholarships/grants:* Pell, SEOG, state scholarships/grants, private scholarships, the school's own gift aid. *Loans:* FFEL Subsidized Stafford, FFEL Unsubsidized Stafford, FFEL PLUS, Federal Perkins, alternative/private. **Student Employment:** Federal Work-Study Program available. Institutional employment available. Off-campus job opportunities are good. **Financial Aid Phone:** 312-899-5106.

See page 1196.

SCHOOL OF THE MUSEUM OF FINE ARTS

230 The Fenway, Boston, MA 02115
Phone: 617-369-3626 **E-mail:** admissions@smfa.edu **CEEB Code:** 3794
Fax: 617-369-4264 **Web:** www.smfa.edu **ACT Code:** 1895

This private school was founded in 1876. It has a 14-acre campus.

STUDENTS AND FACULTY

Enrollment: 1,247. **Student Body:** Male 34%, female 66%, international 4%. **Ethnic Representation:** African American 2%, Asian 5%, Caucasian 87%, Hispanic 5%, Native American 1%.

ACADEMICS

Degrees: Bachelor's, certificate, diploma, master's, post-bachelor's certificate. **Academic Requirements:** General education including some course work in arts/fine arts, English (including composition), history, humanities. **Disciplines with Highest Percentage of Degrees Awarded:** Visual and performing arts 100%. **Special Study Options:** Cross registration, double major, dual enrollment, English as a second language, student exchange program (domestic), independent study, internships, liberal arts/career combination, student-designed major, study abroad, teacher certification program, weekend college, combined degree opportunity (BFA or BFE + BS or BA).

FACILITIES

Housing: Coed, all-female, Professional off-campus housing assistance. **Library Holdings:** 17,000 bound volumes. 100 periodicals. **Special Academic Facilities/Equipment:** Museum of Fine Arts, Boston; art galleries.

ADMISSIONS

Selectivity Rating: 71 (of 100). **Freshman Academic Profile:** TOEFL required of all international applicants, minimum TOEFL 550. **Basis for Candidate Selection:** *Very important factors considered include:* essays, secondary school record, talent/ability. *Important factors considered include:* recommendations, standardized test scores. *Other factors considered include:* alumni/ae relation, character/personal qualities, class rank, extracurricular activities, geographical residence, interview, state residency, volunteer work, work experience. **Freshman Admission Requirements:** High school diploma or GED is required. **Transfer Admission Requirements:** *Items required:* college transcript, essay, statement of good standing from prior school. **General Admission Information:** Application fee $50. Regular application deadline February 1. Nonfall registration accepted. Admission may be deferred for a maximum of 1 year.

COSTS AND FINANCIAL AID

Required Forms and Deadlines: FAFSA, institution's own financial aid form, and CSS/Financial Aid PROFILE. **Types of Aid:** *Need-based scholarships/grants:* Pell, SEOG, state scholarships/grants, the school's own gift aid. *Loans:* FFEL Subsidized Stafford, FFEL Unsubsidized Stafford, FFEL PLUS, state loans. **Student Employment:** Federal Work-Study Program available. Institutional employment available. Off-campus job opportunities are excellent. **Financial Aid Phone:** 617-369-3645.

SCHOOL OF VISUAL ARTS

209 East 23rd Street, New York, NY 10010
Phone: 212-592-2100 **E-mail:** admissions@sva.edu **CEEB Code:** 2835
Fax: 212-592-2116 **Web:** www.schoolofvisualarts.edu **ACT Code:** 2895

This proprietary school was founded in 1947.

STUDENTS AND FACULTY

Enrollment: 4,867. **Student Body:** Male 45%, female 55%, out-of-state 38%, international 7% (51 countries represented). **Ethnic Representation:** African American 5%, Asian 13%, Caucasian 64%, Hispanic 11%, Native American 1%. **Retention and Graduation:** 84% freshmen return for sophomore year. 47% freshmen graduate within 4 years. 6% grads go on to further study within 1 year. **Faculty:** Student/faculty ratio 8:1. 148 full-time faculty, 31% hold PhDs. 87% faculty teach undergrads.

ACADEMICS

Degrees: Bachelor's, master's. **Academic Requirements:** General education including some course work in arts/fine arts, computer literacy, English (including composition), foreign languages, history, humanities, philosophy, sciences (biological or physical), social science. **Classes:** 10-19 students in an average class. **Majors with Highest Enrollment:** Graphic design; cinematography and film/video production; photography. **Disciplines with Highest Percentage of Degrees Awarded:** Visual and performing arts 100%. **Special Study Options:** Cross registration, double major, English as a second language, student exchange program (domestic), independent study, internships, study abroad, teacher certification program.

FACILITIES

Housing: Coed, all-female, all-male, apartments for single students, placement assistance for housing in the New York City area. **Library Holdings:** 70,000 bound volumes. 278 periodicals. 1,070 microforms. 404,000 audiovisuals. **Special Academic Facilities/Equipment:** Art museum, student galleries, animation studio, amphitheater. **Computers:** *Recommended operating system:* Mac. School-owned computers available for student use.

EXTRACURRICULARS

Activities: Drama/theater, literary magazine, radio station, student government, student newspaper, student-run film society, yearbook. **Organizations:** 12 registered organizations.

ADMISSIONS

Selectivity Rating: 76 (of 100). **Freshman Academic Profile:** Average high school GPA 3.1. 60% from public high schools. Average SAT I Math 540, SAT I Math middle 50% range 460-570. Average SAT I Verbal 530, SAT I Verbal middle 50% range 470-590. Average ACT 22, ACT middle 50% range 20-24. TOEFL required of all international applicants, minimum TOEFL 550. **Basis for Candidate Selection:** *Very important factors considered include:* essays, secondary school record. *Important factors considered include:* character/personal qualities, interview, recommendations, standardized test scores, talent/ability. *Other factors considered include:* alumni/ae relation, class rank, extracurricular activities, volunteer work. **Freshman Admission Requirements:** High school diploma or GED is required. **Freshman Admission Statistics:** 1,876 applied, 69% accepted, 40% of those accepted enrolled. **Transfer Admission Requirements:** *Items required:* college transcript, essay. Minimum high school GPA of 2.5 required. Minimum college GPA of 2.5 required. Lowest grade transferable C. **General Admission Information:** Application fee $45. Priority application deadline March 1. Early decision application deadline December 1. Nonfall registration accepted. Admission may be deferred for a maximum of 1 year. Credit offered for CEEB Advanced Placement tests.

COSTS AND FINANCIAL AID

Room & board $10,000. Required fees $500. Average book expense $2,500. **Required Forms and Deadlines:** FAFSA and state aid form. No deadline for regular filing. Priority filing deadline February 1. **Notification of Awards:** Applicants will be notified of awards on a rolling basis beginning on or about February 1. **Types of Aid:** *Need-based scholarships/grants:* Pell, SEOG, state scholarships/grants, private scholarships, the school's own gift aid, alternate loans. *Loans:* FFEL Subsidized Stafford, FFEL Unsubsidized Stafford, FFEL PLUS, Federal Perkins. **Student Employment:** Federal Work-Study Program available. Institutional employment available. Off-campus job opportunities are excellent. **Financial Aid Statistics:** 61% freshmen, 57% undergrads receive some form of aid. Average freshman grant $4,500. Average freshman loan $5,000. Average income from on-campus job $5,000. **Financial Aid Phone:** 212-592-2030.

See page 1198.

SCHREINER UNIVERSITY

2100 Memorial Boulevard, Kerrville, TX 78028-5697
Phone: 830-792-7217 **E-mail:** admissions@schreiner.edu **CEEB Code:** 6647
Fax: 830-792-7226 **Web:** www.schreiner.edu **ACT Code:** 4168

This private school, which is affiliated with the Presbyterian Church, was founded in 1923. It has a 175-acre campus.

STUDENTS AND FACULTY

Enrollment: 739. **Student Body:** Male 42%, female 58%, out-of-state 2%, international 1%. **Ethnic Representation:** African American 2%, Asian 1%, Caucasian 79%, Hispanic 17%, Native American 1%. **Retention and Graduation:** 59% freshmen return for sophomore year. 30% freshmen graduate within 4 years. 5% grads go on to further study within 1 year. 1% grads pursue law degrees. **Faculty:** Student/faculty ratio 13:1. 50 full-time faculty, 64% hold PhDs. 99% faculty teach undergrads.

ACADEMICS

Degrees: Associate's, bachelor's, certificate, master's, post-bachelor's certificate. **Academic Requirements:** General education including some course work in arts/fine arts, computer literacy, English (including composition), foreign languages, history, humanities, mathematics, philosophy, sciences (biological or physical), social science. **Classes:** 10-19 students in an average class. 10-19 students in an average lab/discussion section. **Majors with Highest Enrollment:** Business administration/management; kinesiology and exercise science; psychology, general. **Disciplines with Highest Percentage of Degrees Awarded:** Business/marketing 25%, parks and recreation 14%, liberal arts/general studies 13%, English 13%, biological life sciences 12%. **Special Study Options:** Accelerated program, cooperative (work-study) program, distance learning, double major, English as a second language, honors program, independent study, internships, liberal arts/career combination, student-designed major, study abroad, teacher certification program, weekend college.

FACILITIES

Housing: Coed, all-male, apartments for married students, apartments for single students, housing for disabled students. **Library Holdings:** 69,873 bound volumes. 225 periodicals. 593 microforms. 477 audiovisuals. **Computers:** School-owned computers available for student use.

EXTRACURRICULARS

Activities: Choral groups, drama/theater, literary magazine, music ensembles, musical theater, student government, student newspaper, symphony orchestra, yearbook. **Organizations:** 31 registered organizations, 5 honor societies, 6 religious organizations, 2 fraternities (7% men join), 1 sorority (5% women join). **Athletics (Intercollegiate):** *Men:* baseball, basketball, cross-country, golf, soccer, tennis. *Women:* basketball, cross-country, golf, soccer, softball, tennis, volleyball.

ADMISSIONS

Selectivity Rating: 63 (of 100). **Freshman Academic Profile:** Average high school GPA 3.4. 15% in top 10% of high school class, 36% in top 25% of high school class, 69% in top 50% of high school class. 87% from public high schools. Average SAT I Math 488, SAT I Math middle 50% range 430-550. Average SAT I Verbal 492, SAT I Verbal middle 50% range 420-540. Average ACT 20, ACT middle 50% range 19-23. TOEFL required of all international applicants, minimum TOEFL 550. **Basis for Candidate Selection:** *Very important factors considered include:* secondary school record. *Important factors considered include:* class rank, interview, standardized test scores. *Other factors considered include:* character/personal qualities, essays, extracurricular activities, recommendations, talent/ability, volunteer work, work experience. **Freshman Admission Requirements:** High school diploma or GED is required. *Academic units required/recommended:* 4 English recommended, 3 math recommended, 2 science recommended, 2 science lab recommended, 2 social studies recommended. **Freshman Admission Statistics:** 583 applied, 67% accepted, 48% of those accepted enrolled. **Transfer Admission Requirements:** *Items required:* college transcript, statement of good standing from prior school. Minimum college GPA of 2.0 required. Lowest grade transferable D. **General Admission Information:** Application fee $25. Priority application deadline May 1. Regular application deadline August 1. Nonfall registration accepted. Admission may be deferred for a maximum of 1 year. Credit and/or placement offered for CEEB Advanced Placement tests.

COSTS AND FINANCIAL AID

Tuition $12,602. Room & board $6,654. Required fees $400. Average book expense $800. **Required Forms and Deadlines:** FAFSA and institution's own financial aid form. Priority filing deadline April 1. **Notification of Awards:** Applicants will be notified of awards on a rolling basis beginning on or about December 15. **Types of Aid:** *Need-based scholarships/grants:* Pell, SEOG, state scholarships/grants, private scholarships, the school's own gift aid. *Loans:* FFEL Subsidized Stafford, FFEL Unsubsidized Stafford, FFEL PLUS, state loans. **Student Employment:** Federal Work-Study Program available. Institutional employment available. Off-campus job opportunities are good. **Financial Aid Statistics:** 57% freshmen, 72% undergrads receive some form of aid. Average freshman grant $9,053. Average freshman loan $5,439. Average income from on-campus job $335. **Financial Aid Phone:** 830-792-7230.

SCRIPPS COLLEGE

Best 351

1030 Columbia Avenue, Mailbox #1265, Claremont, CA 91711
Phone: 909-621-8149 **E-mail:** admission@scrippscollege.edu **CEEB Code:** 4693
Fax: 909-607-7508 **Web:** www.scrippscollege.edu **ACT Code:** 426

This private school was founded in 1926. It has a 30-acre campus.

STUDENTS AND FACULTY

Enrollment: 798. **Student Body:** Out-of-state 52%, international 2% (16 countries represented). **Ethnic Representation:** African American 4%, Asian 14%, Caucasian 60%, Hispanic 6%, Native American 1%. **Retention and Graduation:** 88% freshmen return for sophomore year. 63% freshmen graduate within 4 years. 40% grads go on to further study within 1 year. 7% grads pursue business degrees. 10% grads pursue law degrees. 2% grads pursue medical degrees. **Faculty:** Student/faculty ratio 11:1. 59 full-time faculty, 96% hold PhDs. 100% faculty teach undergrads.

ACADEMICS

Degrees: Bachelor's, post-bachelor's certificate. **Academic Requirements:** General education including some course work in arts/fine arts, English (including composition), foreign languages, humanities, mathematics, sciences (biological or physical), social science, women's studies. **Classes:** 10-19 students in an average lab/discussion section. **Majors with Highest Enrollment:** English language and literature, general; biology/biological sciences, general; psychology, general. **Disciplines with Highest Percentage of Degrees Awarded:** Social sciences and history 23%, visual and performing arts 17%, area and ethnic studies 13%, English 10%, biological life sciences 9%. **Special Study Options:** Accelerated program, cross registration, double major, dual enrollment, student exchange program (domestic), honors program, independent study, internships, student-designed major, study abroad.

FACILITIES

Housing: All-female, apartments for single students, housing for disabled students, off-campus houses for single students. **Library Holdings:** 2,088,476 bound volumes. 5,733 periodicals. 1,444,465 microforms. 4,361 audiovisuals. **Special Academic Facilities/Equipment:** Art center, music complex, dance studio, humanities museum and institute, science center, biological field station. **Computers:** *Recommended operating system:* Mac. School-owned computers available for student use.

EXTRACURRICULARS

Activities: Choral groups, dance, drama/theater, literary magazine, music ensembles, radio station, student government, student newspaper, symphony orchestra, yearbook. **Organizations:** 200 registered organizations, 5 honor societies, 7 religious organizations. **Athletics (Intercollegiate):** *Women:* basketball, cross-country, diving, golf, soccer, softball, swimming, tennis, track & field, volleyball, water polo.

ADMISSIONS

Selectivity Rating: 84 (of 100). **Freshman Academic Profile:** Average high school GPA 3.8. 62% in top 10% of high school class, 86% in top 25% of high school class, 100% in top 50% of high school class. 63% from public high schools. Average SAT I Math 641, SAT I Math middle 50% range 600-690. Average SAT I Verbal 666, SAT I Verbal middle 50% range 620-720. Average ACT 28, ACT middle 50% range 26-30. TOEFL required of all international applicants, minimum TOEFL 600. **Basis for Candidate Selection:** *Very important factors considered include:* alumni/ae relation, character/personal qualities, extracurricular activities, interview, recommendations, secondary school record. *Important factors considered include:* class rank, essays, geographical residence, minority status, standardized test scores, state residency, talent/ability, volunteer work, work experience. **Freshman Admission Requirements:** High school diploma or GED is required. *Academic units required/recommended:* 4 English recommended, 4 math recommended, 4 science recommended, 4 foreign language recommended. **Freshman Admission Statistics:** 1,371 applied, 58% accepted, 28% of those accepted enrolled. **Transfer Admission Requirements:** *Items required:* high school transcript, college transcript, essay, standardized test scores, statement of good standing from prior school. Minimum college GPA of 3.0 required. Lowest grade transferable C. **General Admission Information:** Application fee $50. Early decision application deadline November 1. Regular application deadline February 1. Nonfall registration accepted. Admission may be deferred for a maximum of 1 year. Credit offered for CEEB Advanced Placement tests.

COSTS AND FINANCIAL AID

Tuition $25,568. Room & board $8,300. Required fees $132. Average book expense $800. **Required Forms and Deadlines:** FAFSA, CSS/Financial Aid PROFILE, noncustodial (divorced/separated) parent's statement, business/farm supplement, verification worksheet, and parent and student federal tax returns. No deadline for regular filing. Priority filing deadline February 1. **Notification of Awards:** Applicants will be notified of awards on or about April 1. **Types of Aid:** *Need-based scholarships/grants:* Pell, SEOG, state scholarships/grants, private scholarships, the school's own gift aid, Federal work-study. *Loans:* FFEL Subsidized Stafford, FFEL Unsubsidized Stafford, FFEL PLUS, Federal Perkins, college/university loans from institutional funds. **Student Employment:** Federal Work-Study Program available. Institutional employment available. Off-campus job opportunities are fair. **Financial Aid Statistics:** 49% freshmen, 46% undergrads receive some form of aid. Average freshman grant $20,140. Average freshman loan $2,998. **Financial Aid Phone:** 909-621-8275.

See page 1200.

SEATTLE PACIFIC UNIVERSITY

3307 3rd Avenue West, Seattle, WA 98119-1997
Phone: 206-281-2021 **E-mail:** admissions@spu.edu **CEEB Code:** 4694
Fax: 206-281-2669 **Web:** www.spu.edu **ACT Code:** 4476

This private school, which is affiliated with the Methodist Church, was founded in 1891. It has a 35-acre campus.

STUDENTS AND FACULTY

Enrollment: 2,818. **Student Body:** Male 34%, female 66%, out-of-state 35%, international 2%. **Ethnic Representation:** African American 2%, Asian 5%, Caucasian 86%, Hispanic 2%, Native American 1%. **Retention and Graduation:** 80% freshmen return for sophomore year. 37% freshmen graduate within 4 years. 12% grads go on to further study within 1 year. 1% grads pursue business degrees. 1% grads pursue law degrees. 3% grads pursue medical degrees. **Faculty:** Student/faculty ratio 16:1. 174 full-time faculty, 88% hold PhDs. 99% faculty teach undergrads.

ACADEMICS

Degrees: Bachelor's, certificate, doctoral, master's, post-master's certificate. **Academic Requirements:** General education including some course work in arts/fine arts, English (including composition), foreign languages, history, humanities, mathematics, sciences (biological or physical), social science, biblical literature and Christian perspectives. **Classes:** 10-19 students in an average class. Under 10 students in an average lab/discussion section. **Disciplines with Highest Percentage of Degrees Awarded:** Health professions and related sciences 14%, business/marketing 13%, social sciences and history 10%, psychology 8%, biological life sciences 7%. **Special Study Options:** Cooperative (work-study) program, distance learning, double major, English as a second language, student exchange program (domestic), external degree program, honors program, independent study, internships, liberal arts/career combination, student-designed major, study abroad, teacher certification program, weekend college.

FACILITIES

Housing: Coed, all-female, apartments for married students, apartments for single students, theme housing. **Library Holdings:** 169,527 bound volumes. 1,336 periodicals. 498,997 microforms. 3,002 audiovisuals. **Special Academic Facilities/Equipment:** Art gallery, language lab, instructional media center, performing arts theatre, science learning center. Island campus used for seminars, summer workshops, and field work in botany and marine biology. **Computers:** School-owned computers available for student use.

EXTRACURRICULARS

Activities: Choral groups, drama/theater, jazz band, literary magazine, music ensembles, pep band, radio station, student government, student newspaper, symphony orchestra, yearbook. **Organizations:** 37 registered organizations, 1 honor society, 1 religious organization. **Athletics (Intercollegiate):** *Men:* basketball, cheerleading, crew, cross-country, soccer, track & field. *Women:* basketball, cheerleading, crew, cross-country, gymnastics, soccer, track & field, volleyball.

ADMISSIONS

Selectivity Rating: 68 (of 100). **Freshman Academic Profile:** Average high school GPA 3.6. 24% in top 10% of high school class, 53% in top 25% of high school class, 83% in top 50% of high school class. 60% from public high schools. Average SAT I Math 569, SAT I Math middle 50% range 510-620. Average SAT I Verbal 577, SAT I Verbal middle 50% range 530-630. Average ACT 24, ACT middle 50% range 21-27. TOEFL required of all international applicants, minimum TOEFL 550. **Basis for Candidate Selection:** *Very important factors considered include:* character/personal qualities, essays, recommendations, secondary school record, standardized test scores. *Important factors* *considered include:* interview, religious affiliation/commitment. *Other factors considered include:* alumni/ae relation, extracurricular activities, talent/ability, volunteer work, work experience. **Freshman Admission Requirements:** High school diploma or GED is required. *Academic units required/recommended:* 4 English recommended, 3 math recommended, 3 science recommended, 3 foreign language recommended, 1 social studies recommended, 2 history recommended. **Freshman Admission Statistics:** 1,564 applied, 96% accepted. **Transfer Admission Requirements:** *Items required:* high school transcript, college transcript, essay, statement of good standing from prior school. Minimum college GPA of 2.5 required. Lowest grade transferable C. **General Admission Information:** Application fee $45. Priority application deadline March 1. Regular application deadline June 1. Nonfall registration accepted. Admission may be deferred for a maximum of 2 years. Credit offered for CEEB Advanced Placement tests.

COSTS AND FINANCIAL AID

Tuition $17,592. Room & board $6,660. Required fees $90. Average book expense $711. **Required Forms and Deadlines:** FAFSA. Financial aid filing deadline January 1. Priority filing deadline January 31. **Notification of Awards:** Applicants will be notified of awards on a rolling basis beginning on or about April 15. **Types of Aid:** *Need-based scholarships/grants:* Pell, SEOG, state scholarships/grants, private scholarships, the school's own gift aid. *Loans:* FFEL Subsidized Stafford, FFEL Unsubsidized Stafford, FFEL PLUS, Federal Perkins, Federal Nursing, college/university loans from institutional funds. **Student Employment:** Federal Work-Study Program available. Institutional employment available. Off-campus job opportunities are excellent. **Financial Aid Statistics:** 62% freshmen, 61% undergrads receive some form of aid. Average freshman grant $9,944. Average freshman loan $4,833. Average income from on-campus job $1,326. **Financial Aid Phone:** 206-281-2061.

SEATTLE UNIVERSITY

Admissions Office, 900 Broadway, Seattle, WA 98122-4340
Phone: 206-296-2000 **E-mail:** admissions@seattleu.edu **CEEB Code:** 4695
Fax: 206-296-5656 **Web:** www.seattleu.edu **ACT Code:** 4478

This private school, which is affiliated with the Roman Catholic-Jesuit Church, was founded in 1891. It has a 46-acre campus.

STUDENTS AND FACULTY

Enrollment: 3,561. **Student Body:** Male 39%, female 61%, out-of-state 32%, international 9% (69 countries represented). **Ethnic Representation:** African American 5%, Asian 24%, Caucasian 54%, Hispanic 7%, Native American 1%. **Retention and Graduation:** 81% freshmen return for sophomore year. 43% freshmen graduate within 4 years. **Faculty:** Student/faculty ratio 14:1. 335 full-time faculty, 87% hold PhDs. 73% faculty teach undergrads.

ACADEMICS

Degrees: Bachelor's, certificate, doctoral, first professional, master's, post-bachelor's certificate, post-master's certificate. **Academic Requirements:** General education including some course work in arts/fine arts, English (including composition), history, humanities, mathematics, philosophy, sciences (biological or physical), social science, theology & religious studies. **Classes:** 20-29 students in an average class. 20-29 students in an average lab/discussion section. **Majors with Highest Enrollment:** Nursing/registered nurse training (RN, ASN, BSN, MSN); finance, general; marketing/marketing management, general. **Disciplines with Highest Percentage of Degrees Awarded:** Business/marketing 28%, health professions and related sciences 8%, social sciences and history 7%, liberal arts/general studies 7%, engineering/engineering technology 6%. **Special Study Options:** Accelerated program, cross registration, double major, honors program, independent study, internships, student-designed major, study abroad.

FACILITIES

Housing: Coed, apartments for single students, housing for disabled students, single-sex floors. **Library Holdings:** 141,478 bound volumes. 2,701 periodicals. 555,909 microforms. 5,649 audiovisuals. **Special Academic Facilities/Equipment:** Observatory, electron microscope. **Computers:** School-owned computers available for student use.

EXTRACURRICULARS

Activities: Choral groups, drama/theater, literary magazine, music ensembles, musical theater, radio station, student government, student newspaper. **Organizations:** 65 registered organizations. **Athletics (Intercollegiate):** *Men:* basketball, cross-country, soccer, swimming, track & field. *Women:* basketball, cross-country, soccer, softball, swimming, track & field, volleyball.

ADMISSIONS

Selectivity Rating: 81 (of 100). **Freshman Academic Profile:** Average high school GPA 3.5. 28% in top 10% of high school class, 58% in top 25% of high school class, 86% in top 50% of high school class. Average SAT I Math 561, SAT I Math middle 50% range 500-620. Average SAT I Verbal 562, SAT I Verbal middle 50% range 500-610. Average ACT 26, ACT middle 50% range 23-29. TOEFL required of all international applicants, minimum TOEFL 520. **Basis for Candidate Selection:** *Very important factors considered include:* recommendations, secondary school record, standardized test scores, volunteer work. *Important factors considered include:* class rank, essays, extracurricular activities, geographical residence, talent/ability. *Other factors considered include:* alumni/ae relation, character/personal qualities, interview, minority status, state residency, work experience. **Freshman Admission Requirements:** High school diploma or GED is required. *Academic units required/recommended:* 18 total required; 4 English required, 3 math required, 2 science required, 3 science recommended, 2 science lab required, 3 science lab recommended, 2 foreign language required, 2 foreign language recommended, 3 social studies required, 2 elective required. **Freshman Admission Statistics:** 2,951 applied, 82% accepted, 28% of those accepted enrolled. **Transfer Admission Requirements:** *Items required:* college transcript, essay. Minimum high school GPA of 2.5 required. Minimum college GPA of 2.5 required. Lowest grade transferable C. **General Admission Information:** Application fee $45. Priority application deadline February 2. Regular application deadline July 2. Nonfall registration accepted. Admission may be deferred for a maximum of 1 year. Credit and/or placement offered for CEEB Advanced Placement tests.

COSTS AND FINANCIAL AID

Tuition $17,865. Room & board $6,318. Required fees $0. Average book expense $900. **Required Forms and Deadlines:** FAFSA. Priority filing deadline February 2. **Notification of Awards:** Applicants will be notified of awards on a rolling basis beginning on or about April 2. **Types of Aid:** *Need-based scholarships/grants:* Pell, SEOG, state scholarships/grants, private scholarships, the school's own gift aid. *Loans:* Direct Subsidized Stafford, Direct Unsubsidized Stafford, Direct PLUS, Federal Perkins, Federal Nursing. **Student Employment:** Federal Work-Study Program available. Institutional employment available. Off-campus job opportunities are excellent. **Financial Aid Statistics:** 69% freshmen, 65% undergrads receive some form of aid. **Financial Aid Phone:** 206-296-2000.

See page 1202.

SETON HALL UNIVERSITY

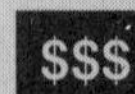

Enrollment Services, 400 South Orange Avenue, South Orange, NJ 07079
Phone: 973-761-9332 **E-mail:** thehall@shu.edu **CEEB Code:** 2811
Fax: 973-275-2040 **Web:** www.shu.edu **ACT Code:** 2606

This private school, which is affiliated with the Roman Catholic Church, was founded in 1856. It has a 58-acre campus.

STUDENTS AND FACULTY

Enrollment: 5,080. **Student Body:** Male 48%, female 52%, out-of-state 21%, international 2%. **Ethnic Representation:** African American 11%, Asian 9%, Caucasian 54%, Hispanic 9%. **Retention and Graduation:** 78% freshmen return for sophomore year. 36% freshmen graduate within 4 years. 36% grads go on to further study within 1 year. 5% grads pursue business degrees. 7% grads pursue law degrees. 9% grads pursue medical degrees. **Faculty:** Student/faculty ratio 14:1. 393 full-time faculty, 90% hold PhDs. 65% faculty teach undergrads.

ACADEMICS

Degrees: Bachelor's, doctoral, first professional, master's, post-master's certificate. **Academic Requirements:** General education including some course work in English (including composition), mathematics, philosophy, sciences (biological or physical), social science, oral communication. **Classes:** 10-19 students in an average class. 10-19 students in an average lab/discussion section. **Majors with Highest Enrollment:** Finance, general; communications studies/speech communication and rhetoric; nursing/registered nurse training (RN, ASN, BSN, MSN). **Disciplines with Highest Percentage of Degrees Awarded:** Business/marketing 23%, education 11%, social sciences and history 9%, communications/communication technologies 8%, protective services/public administration 8%. **Special Study Options:** Accelerated program, cooperative (work-study) program, cross registration, distance learning, double major, dual enrollment, English as a second language, honors program, independent study, internships, liberal arts/career combination, study abroad, teacher certification program.

FACILITIES

Housing: Coed, apartments for single students, housing for disabled students, first-year student dorms, all-female floors, academic teaming floors, alcohol-free floors, professional lifestyles floor. **Library Holdings:** 506,042 bound volumes. 1,475 periodicals. 530,000 microforms. 2,225 audiovisuals. **Special Academic Facilities/Equipment:** Art, natural history, and Native American museums, theatre-in-the-round, archaeological research center, TV studio. **Computers:** *Recommended operating system:* Windows XP. School-owned computers available for student use.

EXTRACURRICULARS

Activities: Choral groups, drama/theater, pep band, radio station, student government, student newspaper, television station, yearbook. **Organizations:** 100 registered organizations, 13 honor societies, 3 religious organizations, 11 fraternities (6% men join), 12 sororities (5% women join). **Athletics (Intercollegiate):** *Men:* baseball, basketball, cross-country, diving, golf, soccer, swimming, track & field. *Women:* basketball, cross-country, diving, soccer, softball, swimming, tennis, track & field, volleyball.

ADMISSIONS

Selectivity Rating: 77 (of 100). **Freshman Academic Profile:** Average high school GPA 3.2. 24% in top 10% of high school class, 50% in top 25% of high school class, 80% in top 50% of high school class. 70% from public high schools. Average SAT I Math 548, SAT I Math middle 50% range 490-600. Average SAT I Verbal 539, SAT I Verbal middle 50% range 480-590. Average ACT 25, ACT middle 50% range 22-27. TOEFL required of all international applicants, minimum TOEFL 550. **Basis for Candidate Selection:** *Very important factors considered include:* essays, recommendations, secondary school record, standardized test scores. *Important factors considered include:* extracurricular activities, volunteer work, work experience. *Other factors considered include:* character/personal qualities, class rank, interview, talent/ability. **Freshman Admission Requirements:** High school diploma or GED is required. *Academic units required/recommended:* 16 total required; 4 English required, 3 math required, 1 science required, 1 science lab required, 2 foreign language required, 2 social studies required, 4 elective required. **Freshman Admission Statistics:** 5,575 applied, 85% accepted, 25% of those accepted enrolled. **Transfer Admission Requirements:** *Items required:* high school transcript, college transcript, essay. Minimum college GPA of 2.5 required. Lowest grade transferable C. **General Admission Information:** Application fee $45. Priority application deadline March 1. Nonfall registration accepted. Admission may be deferred for a maximum of 1 year. Credit and/or placement offered for CEEB Advanced Placement tests.

COSTS AND FINANCIAL AID

Tuition $18,780. Room & board $8,302. Required fees $2,050. Average book expense $1,100. **Required Forms and Deadlines:** FAFSA. No deadline for regular filing. **Notification of Awards:** Applicants will be notified of awards on a rolling basis beginning on or about March 15. **Types of Aid:** *Need-based scholarships/grants:* Pell, SEOG, state scholarships/grants, private scholarships, the school's own gift aid. *Loans:* Direct Subsidized Stafford, Direct Unsubsidized Stafford, Direct PLUS, Federal Perkins, state loans, college/university loans from institutional funds. **Student Employment:** Federal Work-Study Program available. Institutional employment available. Off-campus job opportunities are excellent. **Financial Aid Phone:** 973-761-9332.

See page 1204.

SETON HILL UNIVERSITY

Seton Hill Drive, Greensburg, PA 15601
Phone: 724-838-4255 **E-mail:** admit@setonhill.edu **CEEB Code:** 2812
Fax: 724-830-1294 **Web:** www.setonhill.edu **ACT Code:** 3688

This private school, which is affiliated with the Roman Catholic Church, was founded in 1883. It has a 200-acre campus.

STUDENTS AND FACULTY

Enrollment: 1,188. **Student Body:** Male 21%, female 79%, out-of-state 15%, international 2% (12 countries represented). **Ethnic Representation:** African American 7%, Asian 1%, Caucasian 89%, Hispanic 1%. **Retention and Graduation:** 72% freshmen return for sophomore year. 54% freshmen graduate within 4 years. 32% grads go on to further study within 1 year. 37% grads pursue business degrees. 6% grads pursue law degrees. 1% grads pursue medical degrees. **Faculty:** Student/faculty ratio 13:1. 61 full-time faculty, 81% hold PhDs. 100% faculty teach undergrads.

ACADEMICS

Degrees: Bachelor's, certificate, master's, post-bachelor's certificate. **Academic Requirements:** General education including some course work in arts/fine arts, computer literacy, English (including composition), foreign languages, history, humanities, mathematics, philosophy, sciences (biological or physical), religious studies. **Classes:** 10-19 students in an average class. **Majors with Highest Enrollment:** Marketing/marketing management, general; psychology, general; fine/studio arts, general. **Disciplines with Highest Percentage of Degrees Awarded:** Business/marketing 38%, health professions and related sciences 12%, visual and performing arts 8%, home economics and vocational home economics 6%, education 4%. **Special Study Options:** Accelerated program, cross registration, distance learning, double major, English as a second language, student exchange program (domestic), honors program, independent study, internships, liberal arts/career combination, student-designed major, study abroad, teacher certification program, weekend college.

FACILITIES

Housing: Coed, all-female, all-male. **Library Holdings:** 80,730 bound volumes. 361 periodicals. 5,103 microforms. 6,185 audiovisuals. **Special Academic Facilities/Equipment:** Art gallery, concert hall, theatre, nursery school, kindergarten, smart classrooms. **Computers:** School-owned computers available for student use.

EXTRACURRICULARS

Activities: Choral groups, drama/theater, jazz band, literary magazine, music ensembles, musical theater, student government, student newspaper, symphony orchestra, television station, yearbook. **Organizations:** 25 registered organizations, 8 honor societies, 3 religious organizations. **Athletics (Intercollegiate):** *Men:* baseball, basketball, cross-country, equestrian, golf, soccer. *Women:* basketball, cross-country, equestrian, field hockey, golf, soccer, softball, tennis, volleyball.

ADMISSIONS

Selectivity Rating: 69 (of 100). **Freshman Academic Profile:** Average high school GPA 3.2. 19% in top 10% of high school class, 46% in top 25% of high school class, 78% in top 50% of high school class. SAT I Math middle 50% range 440-560. SAT I Verbal middle 50% range 450-550. TOEFL required of all international applicants, minimum TOEFL 500. **Basis for Candidate Selection:** *Very important factors considered include:* interview, secondary school record. *Important factors considered include:* character/personal qualities, class rank, extracurricular activities, standardized test scores, talent/ability. *Other factors considered include:* alumni/ae relation, essays, recommendations, volunteer work, work experience. **Freshman Admission Requirements:** High school diploma or GED is required. *Academic units required/recommended:* 15 total required; 15 total recommended; 4 English required, 4 English recommended, 2 math required, 2 math recommended, 1 science required, 1 science recommended, 1 science lab required, 1 science lab recommended, 2 foreign language recommended, 2 social studies required, 2 social studies recommended, 4 elective required, 4 elective recommended. **Freshman Admission Statistics:** 912 applied, 83% accepted, 27% of those accepted enrolled. **Transfer Admission Requirements:** *Items required:* high school transcript, college transcript, statement of good standing from prior school. Minimum college GPA of 2.0 required. Lowest grade transferable C. **General Admission Information:** Application fee $30. Priority application deadline May 1. Regular application deadline August 15. Nonfall registration accepted. Admission may be deferred for a maximum of 1 year. Credit and/or placement offered for CEEB Advanced Placement tests.

COSTS AND FINANCIAL AID

Tuition $17,370. Room & board $5,900. Required fees $0. Average book expense $1,000. **Required Forms and Deadlines:** FAFSA, institution's own financial aid form and state aid form. No deadline for regular filing. **Notification of Awards:** Applicants will be notified of awards on a rolling basis beginning on or about December 1. **Types of Aid:** *Need-based scholarships/grants:* Pell, SEOG, state scholarships/grants, private scholarships, the school's own gift aid, United Negro College Fund. *Loans:* FFEL Subsidized Stafford, FFEL Unsubsidized Stafford, FFEL PLUS, Federal Perkins, college/university loans from institutional funds. **Student Employment:** Federal Work-Study Program available. Institutional employment available. Off-campus job opportunities are good. **Financial Aid Statistics:** 93% freshmen, 88% undergrads receive some form of aid. Average freshman grant $15,000. Average freshman loan $3,200. Average income from on-campus job $1,200. **Financial Aid Phone:** 724-838-4293.

See page 1206.

SHAW UNIVERSITY

118 East South Street, Raleigh, NC 27601
Phone: 919-546-8275 **E-mail:** admission@shawu.edu **CEEB Code:** 5612
Fax: 919-546-8271 **Web:** www.shawuniversity.edu **ACT Code:** 3158

This private school, which is affiliated with the Baptist Church, was founded in 1865. It has a 30-acre campus.

STUDENTS AND FACULTY

Enrollment: 2,535. **Student Body:** Male 38%, female 62%, out-of-state 25%, international 3% (10 countries represented). **Ethnic Representation:** African American 88%, Caucasian 2%. **Retention and Graduation:** 69% freshmen return for sophomore year. 17% freshmen graduate within 4 years. **Faculty:** Student/faculty ratio 15:1. 85 full-time faculty, 68% hold PhDs. 94% faculty teach undergrads.

ACADEMICS

Degrees: Associate's, bachelor's, first professional, master's. **Academic Requirements:** General education including some course work in computer literacy, English (including composition), humanities, mathematics, sciences (biological or physical), social science. **Classes:** Under 10 students in an average class. **Majors with Highest Enrollment:** Business administration/management; criminal justice/safety studies; sociology. **Disciplines with Highest Percentage of Degrees Awarded:** Business/marketing 29%, protective services/public administration 21%, social sciences and history 10%, psychology 7%, philosophy/religion/theology 7%. **Special Study Options:** Accelerated program, cross registration, double major, dual enrollment, honors program, independent study, internships, student-designed major, study abroad, teacher certification program, weekend college.

FACILITIES

Housing: All-female, all-male. **Library Holdings:** 152,132 bound volumes. 113 periodicals. 99,700 microforms. 840 audiovisuals. **Special Academic Facilities/Equipment:** TV and film production facilities, curriculum and materials center. **Computers:** School-owned computers available for student use.

EXTRACURRICULARS

Activities: Choral groups, concert band, dance, drama/theater, jazz band, marching band, music ensembles, musical theater, pep band, radio station, student government, student newspaper, yearbook. **Organizations:** 4 honor societies, 4 fraternities (4% men join), 4 sororities (5% women join). **Athletics (Intercollegiate):** *Men:* baseball, basketball, cheerleading, cross-country, indoor track, tennis, track & field. *Women:* basketball, cheerleading, cross-country, indoor track, softball, tennis, track & field, volleyball.

ADMISSIONS

Selectivity Rating: 63 (of 100). **Freshman Academic Profile:** Average high school GPA 2.3. 3% in top 10% of high school class, 5% in top 25% of high school class, 25% in top 50% of high school class. 90% from public high schools. Average SAT I Math 370, SAT I Math middle 50% range 310-420. Average SAT I Verbal 372, SAT I Verbal middle 50% range 320-420. **Basis for Candidate Selection:** *Very important factors considered include:* talent/ability. *Important factors considered include:* character/personal qualities, class rank, essays, extracurricular activities, secondary school record, standardized test scores, state residency, volunteer work. *Other factors considered include:* alumni/ae relation, geographical residence, interview, recommendations, work experience. **Freshman Admission Requirements:** High school diploma or GED is required. *Academic units required/recommended:* 18 total required; 3 English required, 2 math required, 2 science required, 2 social studies required, 9 elective required. **Freshman Admission Statistics:** 3,471 applied, 57% accepted, 28% of those accepted enrolled. **Transfer Admission Requirements:** *Items required:* college transcript. Lowest grade transferable C. **General Admission Information:** Application fee $25. Priority application deadline July 30. Regular application deadline July 30. Nonfall registration accepted. Admission may be deferred. Credit and/or placement offered for CEEB Advanced Placement tests.

COSTS AND FINANCIAL AID

Average book expense $700. **Required Forms and Deadlines:** FAFSA. **Notification of Awards:** Applicants will be notified of awards on a rolling basis beginning on or about April 30. **Types of Aid:** *Need-based scholarships/grants:* Pell, SEOG, state scholarships/grants, private scholarships, the school's own gift aid, United Negro College Fund. *Loans:* Direct Subsidized Stafford, Direct Unsubsidized Stafford, Direct PLUS, Federal Perkins, state loans for education majors. **Student Employment:** Federal Work-Study Program available. Institutional employment available. Off-campus job opportunities are excellent. **Financial Aid Statistics:** 94% freshmen, 76% undergrads receive some form of aid. Average freshman grant $5,058. Average freshman loan $5,365. **Financial Aid Phone:** 919-546-8240.

SHAWNEE STATE UNIVERSITY

940 Second Street, Portsmouth, OH 45662
Phone: 740-351-4778 **E-mail:** to_ssu@shawnee.edu **CEEB Code:** 1790
Fax: 740-351-3111 **Web:** www.shawnee.edu **ACT Code:** 3336

This public school was founded in 1986. It has a 50-acre campus.

STUDENTS AND FACULTY

Enrollment: 3,606. **Student Body:** Male 38%, female 62%, out-of-state 9%. **Ethnic Representation:** African American 3%, Caucasian 87%, Hispanic 1%, Native American 1%. **Retention and Graduation:** 58% freshmen return for sophomore year. 19% freshmen graduate within 4 years. **Faculty:** Student/faculty ratio 18:1. 121 full-time faculty, 48% hold PhDs. 100% faculty teach undergrads.

ACADEMICS

Degrees: Associate's, bachelor's, certificate. **Academic Requirements:** General education including some course work in arts/fine arts, English (including composition), history, humanities, mathematics, philosophy, sciences (biological or physical), social science, ethics, cultural perspectives, capstone. **Classes:** 10-19 students in an average class. Under 10 students in an average lab/discussion section. **Majors with Highest Enrollment:** Business administration/management; nursing/registered nurse training (RN, ASN, BSN, MSN); dental hygiene/hygienist. **Disciplines with Highest Percentage of Degrees Awarded:** Business/marketing 18%, social sciences and history 14%, health professions and related sciences 12%, biological life sciences 11%, education 10%. **Special Study Options:** Distance learning, double major, honors program, independent study, internships, student-designed major, study abroad, teacher certification program.

FACILITIES

Housing: Coed, off-campus housing list available. **Library Holdings:** 152,961 bound volumes. 6,906 periodicals. 39,946 microforms. 19,316 audiovisuals. **Special Academic Facilities/Equipment:** Vern Riffe Center for the Arts. **Computers:** School-owned computers available for student use.

EXTRACURRICULARS

Activities: Choral groups, drama/theater, literary magazine, music ensembles, musical theater, student government, student newspaper. **Organizations:** 30 registered organizations, 2 honor societies, 2 religious organizations, 3 fraternities (5% men join), 2 sororities (3% women join). **Athletics (Intercollegiate):** *Men:* baseball, basketball, cross-country, golf, soccer. *Women:* basketball, cross-country, soccer, softball, tennis, volleyball.

ADMISSIONS

Selectivity Rating: 63 (of 100). **Freshman Academic Profile:** 11% in top 10% of high school class, 26% in top 25% of high school class, 56% in top 50% of high school class. Average ACT 19, ACT middle 50% range 16-21. TOEFL required of all international applicants, minimum TOEFL 500. **Freshman Admission Requirements:** High school diploma or GED is required. *Academic units required/recommended:* 16 total recommended; 4 English recommended, 3 math recommended, 3 science recommended, 2 foreign language recommended, 3 social studies recommended, 1 elective recommended. **Freshman Admission Statistics:** 2,478 applied, 100% accepted, 29% of those accepted enrolled. **Transfer Admission Requirements:** *Items required:* high school transcript, college transcript. Minimum college GPA of 2.0 required. Lowest grade transferable C. **General Admission Information:** Nonfall registration accepted. Credit and/or placement offered for CEEB Advanced Placement tests.

COSTS AND FINANCIAL AID

In-state tuition $3,528. Out-of-state tuition $6,624. Room & board $5,421. Required fees $522. Average book expense $900. **Required Forms and Deadlines:** FAFSA and institution's own financial aid form. Priority filing deadline June 15. **Notification of Awards:** Applicants will be notified of awards on a rolling basis beginning on or about May 1. **Types of Aid:** *Need-based scholarships/grants:* Pell, SEOG, state scholarships/grants, private scholarships, the school's own gift aid. *Loans:* FFEL Subsidized Stafford, FFEL Unsubsidized Stafford, FFEL PLUS, state loans. **Student Employment:** Federal Work-Study Program available. Institutional employment available. Off-campus job opportunities are fair. **Financial Aid Statistics:** 64% freshmen, 67% undergrads receive some form of aid. Average income from on-campus job $3,100. **Financial Aid Phone:** 740-351-4243.

SHELDON JACKSON COLLEGE

801 Lincoln Street, Sitka, AK 99835
Phone: 800-478-4556 **E-mail:** elower@sj-alaska.edu **CEEB Code:** 4742
Fax: 907-747-6366 **Web:** www.sj-alaska.edu **ACT Code:** 74

This private school, which is affiliated with the Presbyterian Church, was founded in 1878. It has a 300-acre campus.

STUDENTS AND FACULTY

Enrollment: 158. **Student Body:** Male 42%, female 58%, out-of-state 70%. **Ethnic Representation:** Asian 3%, Caucasian 72%, Hispanic 2%, Native American 23%. **Retention and Graduation:** 42% freshmen return for sophomore year. 20% grads go on to further study within 1 year. 10% grads pursue law degrees. **Faculty:** Student/faculty ratio 10:1. 30 full-time faculty, 53% hold PhDs. 100% faculty teach undergrads.

ACADEMICS

Degrees: Associate's, bachelor's, certificate. **Academic Requirements:** General education including some course work in arts/fine arts, computer literacy, English (including composition), history, humanities, mathematics, philosophy, sciences (biological or physical), social science. **Classes:** Under 10 students in an average class. **Disciplines with Highest Percentage of Degrees Awarded:** Education 58%, natural resources/environmental sciences 33%, interdisciplinary studies 8%. **Special Study Options:** Cooperative (work-study) program, cross registration, double major, student exchange program (domestic), independent study, internships, liberal arts/career combination, student-designed major, teacher certification program.

FACILITIES

Housing: Coed, apartments for married students, off-campus housing for students over 21. **Library Holdings:** 80,000 bound volumes. 325 periodicals. **Special Academic Facilities/Equipment:** Sheldon Jackson Museum. **Computers:** School-owned computers available for student use.

EXTRACURRICULARS

Activities: Choral groups, concert band, music ensembles, student government. **Organizations:** 10 registered organizations, 2 honor societies, 1 religious organization.

ADMISSIONS

Selectivity Rating: 63 (of 100). **Freshman Academic Profile:** 90% from public high schools. TOEFL required of all international applicants, minimum TOEFL 550. **Basis for Candidate Selection:** *Other factors considered include:* alumni/ae relation, character/personal qualities, extracurricular activities, geographical residence, minority status, religious affiliation/commitment, secondary school record, state residency, volunteer work, work experience. **Freshman Admission Requirements:** High school diploma or GED is required. *Academic units required/recommended:* 4 English recommended, 4 math recommended, 4 science recommended, 2 science lab recommended, 4 social studies recommended. **Transfer Admission Requirements:** *Items required:* college transcript. Minimum high school GPA of 2.0 required. Minimum college GPA of 2.0 required. Lowest grade transferable C. **General Admission Information:** Application fee $25. Priority application deadline January 31. Nonfall registration accepted. Admission may be deferred for a maximum of 1 year. Credit offered for CEEB Advanced Placement tests.

COSTS AND FINANCIAL AID

Tuition $9,400. Room & board $6,920. Required fees $370. Average book expense $750. **Required Forms and Deadlines:** FAFSA. No deadline for regular filing. Priority filing deadline May 2. **Notification of Awards:** Applicants will be notified of awards on a rolling basis beginning on or about April 2. **Types of Aid:** *Need-based scholarships/grants:* Pell, SEOG, state scholarships/grants, private scholarships, the school's own gift aid, endowments. *Loans:* FFEL Subsidized Stafford, FFEL Unsubsidized Stafford, Federal Perkins, state loans, endowments. **Student Employment:** Federal Work-Study Program available. Institutional employment available. Off-campus job opportunities are excellent. **Financial Aid Statistics:** 85% freshmen, 82% undergrads receive some form of aid. Average freshman grant $1,500. Average freshman loan $6,000. Average income from on-campus job $2,000. **Financial Aid Phone:** 800-478-4556.

SHENANDOAH UNIVERSITY

1460 University Drive, Winchester, VA 22601-5195
Phone: 540-665-4581 **E-mail:** admit@su.edu **CEEB Code:** 5613
Fax: 540-665-4627 **Web:** www.su.edu **ACT Code:** 5613

This private school, which is affiliated with the Methodist Church, was founded in 1875. It has a 100-acre campus.

STUDENTS AND FACULTY

Enrollment: 1,391. **Student Body:** Male 44%, female 56%, out-of-state 38%, international 4% (41 countries represented). **Ethnic Representation:** African American 9%, Asian 1%, Caucasian 87%, Hispanic 2%. **Retention and Graduation:** 66% freshmen return for sophomore year. 24% freshmen graduate within 4 years. 40% grads go on to further study within 1 year. 16% grads pursue business degrees. 1% grads pursue law degrees. 1% grads pursue medical degrees. **Faculty:** Student/faculty ratio 8:1. 167 full-time faculty, 77% hold PhDs. 71% faculty teach undergrads.

ACADEMICS

Degrees: Associate's, bachelor's, certificate, doctoral, first professional, master's, post-bachelor's certificate, post-master's certificate, terminal. **Academic Requirements:** General education including some course work in computer literacy, English (including composition), foreign languages, history, humanities, mathematics, philosophy, sciences (biological or physical), social science. **Classes:** Under 10 students in an average class. 10-19 students in an average lab/discussion section. **Majors with Highest Enrollment:** Nursing/registered nurse training (RN, ASN, BSN, MSN); business administration/management; drama and dramatics/theatre arts, general. **Disciplines with Highest Percentage of Degrees Awarded:** Visual and performing arts 29%, business/marketing 20%, education 15%, health professions and related sciences 12%, psychology 11%. **Special Study Options:** Accelerated program, distance learning, double major, English as a second language, independent study, internships, liberal arts/career combination, study abroad, teacher certification program.

FACILITIES

Housing: Coed, all-female, apartments for married students, apartments for single students, apartments for students with dependent children. **Library Holdings:** 123,628 bound volumes. 1,150 periodicals. 134,169 microforms. 17,823 audiovisuals. **Computers:** *Recommended operating system:* Windows NT/2000. School-owned computers available for student use.

EXTRACURRICULARS

Activities: Choral groups, concert band, dance, drama/theater, jazz band, music ensembles, musical theater, opera, radio station, student government, student newspaper, symphony orchestra, television station. **Organizations:** 55 registered organizations, 9 honor societies, 2 religious organizations. **Athletics (Intercollegiate):** *Men:* baseball, basketball, cheerleading, cross-country, football, golf, lacrosse, soccer, tennis. *Women:* basketball, cheerleading, cross-country, lacrosse, soccer, softball, tennis, volleyball.

ADMISSIONS

Selectivity Rating: 73 (of 100). **Freshman Academic Profile:** Average high school GPA 3.0. 16% in top 10% of high school class, 35% in top 25% of high school class, 64% in top 50% of high school class. Average SAT I Math 504, SAT I Math middle 50% range 430-570. Average SAT I Verbal 513, SAT I Verbal middle 50% range 450-580. Average ACT 20, ACT middle 50% range 17-23. TOEFL required of all international applicants, minimum TOEFL 450. **Basis for Candidate Selection:** *Very important factors considered include:* interview, secondary school record, talent/ability. *Important factors considered include:* extracurricular activities, standardized test scores, volunteer work. *Other factors considered include:* alumni/ae relation, character/personal qualities, essays, recommendations, work experience. **Freshman Admission Requirements:** High school diploma or GED is required. *Academic units required/recommended:* 15 total required; 4 English required, 3 math required, 4 math recommended, 2 science required, 4 science recommended, 1 science lab required, 2 foreign language required, 3 foreign language recommended, 2 elective required, 4 elective recommended. **Freshman Admission Statistics:** 1,312 applied, 80% accepted, 31% of those accepted enrolled. **Transfer Admission Requirements:** *Items required:* high school transcript, college transcript, statement of good standing from prior school. Minimum college GPA of 2.0 required. Lowest grade transferable C. **General Admission Information:** Application fee $30. Priority application deadline March 1. Nonfall registration accepted. Admission may be deferred for a maximum of 1 year. Credit and/or placement offered for CEEB Advanced Placement tests.

COSTS AND FINANCIAL AID

Tuition $17,510. Average book expense $1,000. **Required Forms and Deadlines:** FAFSA and state aid form. Priority filing deadline March 1. **Notification of Awards:** Applicants will be notified of awards on a rolling basis beginning on or about March 15. **Types of Aid:** *Need-based scholarships/grants:* Pell, SEOG, state scholarships/grants, private scholarships, the school's own gift aid. *Loans:* Direct Subsidized Stafford, Direct Unsubsidized Stafford, Direct PLUS, Federal Perkins, Federal Nursing, college/university loans from institutional funds. **Student Employment:** Federal Work-Study Program available. Institutional employment available. Off-campus job opportunities are good. **Financial Aid Statistics:** 67% freshmen, 91% undergrads receive some form of aid. Average freshman grant $12,780. Average freshman loan $3,095. Average income from on-campus job $1,500. **Financial Aid Phone:** 540-665-4538.

SHEPHERD COLLEGE

Office of Admissions, PO Box 3210, Shepherdstown, WV 25443-3210
Phone: 304-876-5212 **E-mail:** admoff@shepherd.edu **CEEB Code:** 5615
Fax: 304-876-5165 **Web:** www.shepherd.edu **ACT Code:** 4532

This public school was founded in 1871. It has a 320-acre campus.

STUDENTS AND FACULTY

Enrollment: 4,676. **Student Body:** Male 42%, female 58%, out-of-state 33%, international 1% (24 countries represented). **Ethnic Representation:** African American 6%, Asian 1%, Caucasian 91%, Hispanic 2%, Native American 1%. **Retention and Graduation:** 62% freshmen return for sophomore year. 19% freshmen graduate within 4 years. 8% grads go on to further study within 1 year. 7% grads pursue business degrees. 16% grads pursue law degrees. 5% grads pursue medical degrees. **Faculty:** Student/faculty ratio 19:1. 115 full-time faculty, 73% hold PhDs. 100% faculty teach undergrads.

ACADEMICS

Degrees: Associate's, bachelor's. **Academic Requirements:** General education including some course work in arts/fine arts, computer literacy, English (including composition), history, humanities, mathematics, sciences (biological or physical), social science, physical education. **Classes:** 20-29 students in an average class. **Majors with Highest Enrollment:** Teacher education, multiple levels; business administration/management; parks, recreation, and leisure studies. **Disciplines with Highest Percentage of Degrees Awarded:** Education 15%, liberal arts/general studies 13%, business/marketing 12%, parks and recreation 10%, computer and information sciences 9%. **Special Study Options:** Cooperative (work-study) program, double major, honors program, internships, study abroad, teacher certification program.

FACILITIES

Housing: Coed, housing for disabled students, fraternities and/or sororities. **Library Holdings:** 183,197 bound volumes. 918 periodicals. 245,794 microforms. 11,393 audiovisuals. **Special Academic Facilities/Equipment:** Nursery school, elementary education lab, art galleries, theatres. **Computers:** School-owned computers available for student use.

EXTRACURRICULARS

Activities: Choral groups, concert band, drama/theater, jazz band, literary magazine, marching band, music ensembles, musical theater, pep band, radio station, student government, student newspaper, symphony orchestra. **Organizations:** 54 registered organizations, 5 honor societies, 1 religious organization, 4 fraternities (1% men join), 3 sororities (1% women join). **Athletics (Intercollegiate):** *Men:* baseball, basketball, cross-country, football, golf, soccer, tennis. *Women:* basketball, cross-country, soccer, softball, tennis, volleyball.

ADMISSIONS

Selectivity Rating: 82 (of 100). **Freshman Academic Profile:** Average high school GPA 3.0. 20% in top 10% of high school class, 85% in top 25% of high school class, 95% in top 50% of high school class. 70% from public high schools. Average SAT I Math 498, SAT I Math middle 50% range 450-540. Average SAT I Verbal 512, SAT I Verbal middle 50% range 460-560. Average ACT 20, ACT middle 50% range 18-23. TOEFL required of all international applicants, minimum TOEFL 550. **Basis for Candidate Selection:** *Very important factors considered include:* secondary school record, standardized test scores. *Other factors considered include:* alumni/ae relation, character/personal qualities, class rank, extracurricular activities, geographical residence, recommendations, state residency, talent/ability, volunteer work. **Freshman Admission Requirements:** High school diploma or GED is required. *Academic units required/recommended:* 21 total required; 4 English required, 3 math required, 3 math recommended, 2 science required, 3 science recommended, 2 science lab required, 3 science lab recommended, 2 foreign language recommended, 3 social studies required, 3 social studies recommended, 1 history required, 1 history recommended, 10 elective required. **Transfer Admission Requirements:** *Items required:* college transcript, statement of good standing from prior school. Minimum college GPA of 2.0 required. Lowest grade transferable D. **General Admission Information:** Application fee $35. Priority application deadline February 1. Regular application deadline June 15. Nonfall registration accepted. Admission may be deferred for a maximum of 1 year. Credit offered for CEEB Advanced Placement tests.

COSTS AND FINANCIAL AID

In-state tuition $2,866. Out-of-state tuition $6,982. Room & board $4,739. Average book expense $800. **Required Forms and Deadlines:** FAFSA and state aid form. No deadline for regular filing. Priority filing deadline March 1. **Notification of Awards:** Applicants will be notified of awards on a rolling basis beginning on or about March 25. **Types of Aid:** *Need-based scholarships/grants:* Pell, SEOG, state scholarships/grants, private scholarships, the school's own gift aid. *Loans:* Direct Subsidized Stafford, Direct Unsubsidized Stafford, Direct PLUS, Federal Perkins, Federal Nursing. **Student Employment:** Institutional employment available. Off-campus job opportunities are good. **Financial Aid Statistics:** 48% freshmen, 47% undergrads receive some form of aid. Average freshman grant $3,038. Average income from on-campus job $2,300. **Financial Aid Phone:** 304-876-5470.

SHERIDAN COLLEGE

1430 Trafalgar Road, Oakville, ON L6H 2L1
Phone: 905-815-4007 **E-mail:** international@sheridanc.on.ca
Fax: 905-815-4004 **Web:** www.sheridanc.on.ca

STUDENTS AND FACULTY

Enrollment: 9,806. **Student Body:** Out-of-state 1%.

ACADEMICS

Degrees: Diploma, post-bachelor's certificate. **Academic Requirements:** General education including some course work in computer literacy. **Special Study Options:** Cooperative (work-study) program, English as a second language, internships.

FACILITIES

Housing: Coed, housing for disabled students, off-campus housing.

EXTRACURRICULARS

Activities: Literary magazine, student government.

ADMISSIONS

Selectivity Rating: 63 (of 100). High school diploma is required and GED is not accepted. **Transfer Admission Requirements:** *Items required:* high school transcript. Lowest grade transferable C. **General Admission Information:** Application fee $65. Priority application deadline March 1. Regular application deadline June 1. Nonfall registration accepted. Admission may be deferred for a maximum of 1 year.

COSTS AND FINANCIAL AID

Types of Aid: *Loans:* Direct Subsidized Stafford, Direct Unsubsidized Stafford, FFEL Subsidized Stafford, FFEL Unsubsidized Stafford.

SHIMER COLLEGE

PO Box 500, Waukegan, IL 60079-0500
Phone: 847-249-7175 **E-mail:** admiss@shimer.edu **CEEB Code:** 1717
Fax: 847-249-8798 **Web:** www.shimer.edu **ACT Code:** 1142

This private school was founded in 1853. It has a 3-acre campus.

STUDENTS AND FACULTY

Enrollment: 115. **Student Body:** Male 57%, female 43%, out-of-state 60%, international 3%. **Ethnic Representation:** African American 6%, Asian 1%, Caucasian 88%, Hispanic 5%. **Retention and Graduation:** 50% grads go on to further study within 1 year. 10% grads pursue law degrees. **Faculty:** Student/faculty ratio 8:1. 13 full-time faculty, 84% hold PhDs. 100% faculty teach undergrads.

ACADEMICS

Degrees: Bachelor's, post-bachelor's certificate. **Academic Requirements:** General education including some course work in arts/fine arts, English (including composition), history, humanities, mathematics, philosophy, sciences (biological or physical), social science. **Classes:** 10-19 students in an average class. **Disciplines with Highest Percentage of Degrees Awarded:** Liberal arts/general studies 100%. **Special Study Options:** Internships, study abroad, weekend college.

FACILITIES

Housing: Coed, apartments for married students, apartments for single students. **Computers:** School-owned computers available for student use.

EXTRACURRICULARS

Activities: Drama/theater, student government, student newspaper.

ADMISSIONS

Selectivity Rating: 63 (of 100). **Freshman Academic Profile: Basis for Candidate Selection:** *Very important factors considered include:* essays, interview, recommendations. *Important factors considered include:* secondary school record, talent/ability. *Other factors considered include:* character/personal qualities, class rank, extracurricular activities, standardized test scores. **Freshman Admission Requirements:** High school diploma or equivalent is not required. **Freshman Admission Statistics:** 32 applied, 75% accepted, 96% of those accepted enrolled. **Transfer Admission Requirements:** *Items required:* high school transcript, college transcript, essay, interview. Lowest grade transferable C. **General Admission Information:** Application fee $25. Nonfall registration accepted. Admission may be deferred for a maximum of 2 years.

COSTS AND FINANCIAL AID

Tuition $15,550. Room & board $2,530. Required fees $80. Average book expense $940. **Required Forms and Deadlines:** FAFSA and CSS/Financial Aid PROFILE. **Types of Aid:** *Need-based scholarships/grants:* Pell, SEOG, state scholarships/grants, private scholarships, the school's own gift aid. *Loans:* Direct Subsidized Stafford, Direct Unsubsidized Stafford, Direct PLUS, FFEL Subsidized Stafford, FFEL Unsubsidized Stafford, FFEL PLUS, Federal Perkins. **Student Employment:** Federal Work-Study Program available. Institutional employment available. Off-campus job opportunities are good. **Financial Aid Statistics:** Average freshman grant $4,250. Average freshman loan $2,625. Average income from on-campus job $1,500. **Financial Aid Phone:** 847-249-7180.

SHIPPENSBURG UNIVERSITY OF PENNSYLVANIA

Old Main 105, 1871 Old Main Drive Shippensburg University, Shippensburg, PA 17257-2299
Phone: 717-477-1231 **E-mail:** admiss@ship.edu **CEEB Code:** 2657
Fax: 717-477-4016 **Web:** www.ship.edu **ACT Code:** 3714

This public school was founded in 1871. It has a 200-acre campus.

STUDENTS AND FACULTY

Enrollment: 6,413. **Student Body:** Male 46%, female 54%, out-of-state 6%, international 1% (40 countries represented). **Ethnic Representation:** African American 4%, Asian 1%, Caucasian 93%, Hispanic 1%. **Retention and Graduation:** 79% freshmen return for sophomore year. 36% freshmen graduate within 4 years. **Faculty:** Student/faculty ratio 19:1. 302 full-time faculty, 88% hold PhDs. 90% faculty teach undergrads.

ACADEMICS

Degrees: Bachelor's, master's, post-master's certificate. **Academic Requirements:** General education including some course work in English (including composition); history; humanities; mathematics; sciences (biological or physical); social science; political, economic, and geographic sciences; diversity. **Classes:** 20-29 students in an average class. 10-19 students in an average lab/discussion section. **Majors with Highest Enrollment:** Journalism; elementary education and teaching; criminal justice/safety studies. **Disciplines with Highest Percentage of Degrees Awarded:** Business/marketing 24%, education 17%, protective services/public administration 13%, social sciences and history 9%, communications/communication technologies 8%. **Special Study Options:** Accelerated program, cooperative (work-study) program, double major, dual enrollment, honors program, independent study, internships, study abroad, teacher certification program, distance learning, Raider Plan.

FACILITIES

Housing: Coed, all-female, apartments for single students, off-campus apartment complex. **Library Holdings:** 449,590 bound volumes. 1,757 periodicals. 1,294,417 microforms. 76,583 audiovisuals. **Special Academic Facilities/Equipment:** art gallery, vertebrate museum, on-campus elementary school, planetarium, electron microscope, NMR spectrometer, greenhouse, herbarium. **Computers:** School-owned computers available for student use.

EXTRACURRICULARS

Activities: Choral groups, concert band, dance, drama/theater, jazz band, literary magazine, marching band, music ensembles, musical theater, radio station, student government, student newspaper, television station, yearbook. **Organizations:** 239 registered organizations, 17 honor societies, 7 religious organizations, 10 fraternities (6% men join), 9 sororities (8% women join). **Athletics (Intercollegiate):** *Men:* baseball, basketball, cross-country, football, soccer, swimming, track & field, wrestling. *Women:* basketball, cross-country, field hockey, lacrosse, soccer, softball, swimming, tennis, track & field, volleyball.

ADMISSIONS

Selectivity Rating: 75 (of 100). **Freshman Academic Profile:** Average high school GPA 3.2. 9% in top 10% of high school class, 34% in top 25% of high school class, 75% in top 50% of high school class. 90% from public high schools. Average SAT I Math 533, SAT I Math middle 50% range 480-580. Average SAT I Verbal 526, SAT I Verbal middle 50% range 480-560. TOEFL required of all international applicants, minimum TOEFL 550. **Basis for Candidate Selection:** *Very important factors considered include:* class rank, secondary school record, standardized test scores. *Other factors considered include:* character/personal qualities, essays, extracurricular activities, interview, recommendations, volunteer work. **Freshman Admission Requirements:** High school diploma or GED is required. *Academic units required/recommended:* 15 total recommended; 4 English recommended, 3 math recommended, 3 science recommended, 3 science lab recommended, 2 foreign language recommended. **Freshman Admission Statistics:** 5,769 applied, 69% accepted, 38% of those accepted enrolled. **Transfer Admission Requirements:** *Items required:* college transcript, statement of good standing from prior school. Minimum college GPA of 2.2 required. Lowest grade transferable C. **General Admission Information:** Application fee $30. Nonfall registration accepted. Admission may be deferred for a maximum of 1 year. Credit and/or placement offered for CEEB Advanced Placement tests.

COSTS AND FINANCIAL AID

In-state tuition $4,378. Out-of-state tuition $10,946. Room & board $4,864. Required fees $1,124. Average book expense $800. **Required Forms and Deadlines:** FAFSA. No deadline for regular filing. Priority filing deadline March 15. **Notification of Awards:** Applicants will be notified of awards on a rolling basis beginning on or about February 15. **Types of Aid:** *Need-based scholarships/grants:* Pell, SEOG, state scholarships/grants, private scholarships, the school's own gift aid. *Loans:* FFEL Subsidized Stafford, FFEL Unsubsidized Stafford, FFEL PLUS, Federal Perkins, college/university loans from institutional funds, FFEL Consolidation Loans, alternative loans. **Student Employment:** Federal Work-Study Program available. Institutional employment available. Off-campus job opportunities are fair. **Financial Aid Statistics:** 52% freshmen, 47% undergrads receive some form of aid. Average income from on-campus job $1,500. **Financial Aid Phone:** 717-477-1131.

SHORTER COLLEGE

315 Shorter Avenue, Box 1, Rome, GA 30165
Phone: 706-233-7319 **E-mail:** admissions@shorter.edu **CEEB Code:** 5616
Fax: 706-233-7224 **Web:** www.shorter.edu **ACT Code:** 860

This private school, which is affiliated with the Southern Baptist Church, was founded in 1873. It has a 150-acre campus.

STUDENTS AND FACULTY

Enrollment: 925. **Student Body:** Male 34%, female 66%, out-of-state 89%, international 3%. **Ethnic Representation:** African American 4%, Asian 1%, Caucasian 92%, Hispanic 1%. **Retention and Graduation:** 71% freshmen return for sophomore year. 37% freshmen graduate within 4 years. 30% grads go on to further study within 1 year. **Faculty:** Student/faculty ratio 11:1. 65 full-time faculty, 72% hold PhDs. 100% faculty teach undergrads.

ACADEMICS

Degrees: Associate's, bachelor's, master's, transfer. **Academic Requirements:** General education including some course work in arts/fine arts, computer literacy, English (including composition), foreign languages, history, mathematics, sciences (biological or physical), social science, interdisciplinary courses, religion. **Classes:** 10-19 students in an average class. 20-29 students in an average lab/discussion section. **Disciplines with Highest Percentage of**

Degrees Awarded: Education 28%, business/marketing 14%, philosophy/religion/theology 10%, biological life sciences 9%, visual and performing arts 9%. **Special Study Options:** Cross registration, double major, dual enrollment, student exchange program (domestic), honors program, independent study, internships, student-designed major, study abroad, teacher certification program.

FACILITIES

Housing: All-female, all-male, apartments for married students, apartments for single students, housing for disabled students. **Library Holdings:** 100,366 bound volumes. 596 periodicals. 7,165 microforms. 11,226 audiovisuals. **Computers:** School-owned computers available for student use.

EXTRACURRICULARS

Activities: Choral groups, concert band, dance, drama/theater, literary magazine, music ensembles, musical theater, opera, radio station, student government, student newspaper, student-run film society, television station, yearbook. **Organizations:** 32 registered organizations, 10 honor societies, 3 religious organizations, 2 fraternities (16% men join), 3 sororities (29% women join). **Athletics (Intercollegiate):** *Men:* baseball, basketball, cross-country, golf, tennis. *Women:* basketball, cross-country, golf, soccer, tennis.

ADMISSIONS

Selectivity Rating: 73 (of 100). **Freshman Academic Profile:** Average high school GPA 3.4. 26% in top 10% of high school class, 62% in top 25% of high school class, 81% in top 50% of high school class. 95% from public high schools. Average SAT I Math 522, SAT I Math middle 50% range 470-590. Average SAT I Verbal 531, SAT I Verbal middle 50% range 480-600. Average ACT 22, ACT middle 50% range 20-25. TOEFL required of all international applicants, minimum TOEFL 500. **Basis for Candidate Selection:** *Very important factors considered include:* secondary school record, standardized test scores. *Important factors considered include:* essays, talent/ability. *Other factors considered include:* alumni/ae relation, character/personal qualities, class rank, extracurricular activities, interview, recommendations, volunteer work, work experience. **Freshman Admission Requirements:** High school diploma or GED is required. *Academic units required/recommended:* 16 total required; 4 English required, 4 math required, 3 science required, 2 foreign language required, 3 history required. **Freshman Admission Statistics:** 580 applied, 83% accepted, 45% of those accepted enrolled. **Transfer Admission Requirements:** *Items required:* college transcript, statement of good standing from prior school. Minimum high school GPA of 2.0 required. Minimum college GPA of 2.0 required. Lowest grade transferable C. **General Admission Information:** Application fee $25. Priority application deadline March 15. Regular application deadline August 25. Nonfall registration accepted. Admission may be deferred for a maximum of 2 years. Credit and/or placement offered for CEEB Advanced Placement tests.

COSTS AND FINANCIAL AID

Tuition $10,400. Room & board $5,565. Required fees $240. Average book expense $700. **Required Forms and Deadlines:** FAFSA, institution's own financial aid form and state aid form. No deadline for regular filing. Priority filing deadline April 1. **Notification of Awards:** Applicants will be notified of awards on a rolling basis beginning on or about March 1. **Types of Aid:** *Need-based scholarships/grants:* Pell, SEOG, state scholarships/grants, private scholarships, the school's own gift aid. *Loans:* FFEL Subsidized Stafford, FFEL Unsubsidized Stafford, FFEL PLUS, Federal Perkins, college/university loans from institutional funds. **Student Employment:** Federal Work-Study Program available. Institutional employment available. Off-campus job opportunities are good. **Financial Aid Statistics:** 64% freshmen, 67% undergrads receive some form of aid. Average freshman grant $7,076. Average freshman loan $1,200. Average income from on-campus job $1,296. **Financial Aid Phone:** 706-233-7227.

SIENA COLLEGE

515 Loudon Road, Loudonville, NY 12211
Phone: 518-783-2423 **E-mail:** admit@siena.edu **CEEB Code:** 2814
Fax: 518-783-2436 **Web:** www.siena.edu **ACT Code:** 2878

This private school, which is affiliated with the Roman Catholic Church, was founded in 1938. It has a 155-acre campus.

STUDENTS AND FACULTY

Enrollment: 3,405. **Student Body:** Male 43%, female 57%, out-of-state 20%, international students represent 6 countries. **Ethnic Representation:** African American 2%, Asian 2%, Caucasian 90%, Hispanic 3%. **Retention and Graduation:** 88% freshmen return for sophomore year. 63% freshmen graduate within 4 years. 20% grads go on to further study within 1 year. 3% grads pursue law degrees. 3% grads pursue medical degrees. **Faculty:** Student/faculty ratio 14:1. 166 full-time faculty, 85% hold PhDs. 100% faculty teach undergrads.

ACADEMICS

Degrees: Bachelor's, certificate. **Academic Requirements:** General education including some course work in arts/fine arts, English (including composition), history, humanities, mathematics, philosophy, sciences (biological or physical), social science, religious studies. **Classes:** 20-29 students in an average class. 10-19 students in an average lab/discussion section. **Majors with Highest Enrollment:** Accounting; marketing/marketing management, general; English/language arts teacher education. **Disciplines with Highest Percentage of Degrees Awarded:** Business/marketing 47%, social sciences and history 16%, English 10%, biological life sciences 9%, psychology 8%. **Special Study Options:** Accelerated program, cross registration, double major, honors program, independent study, internships, study abroad, teacher certification program, semester in Washington, DC.

FACILITIES

Housing: Coed, on-campus townhouses. **Library Holdings:** 314,942 bound volumes. 1,063 periodicals. 27,404 microforms. 5,179 audiovisuals. **Computers:** School-owned computers available for student use.

EXTRACURRICULARS

Activities: Choral groups, concert band, dance, drama/theater, literary magazine, music ensembles, musical theater, pep band, radio station, student government, student newspaper, student-run film society, symphony orchestra, yearbook. **Organizations:** 75 registered organizations, 17 honor societies, 1 religious organization. **Athletics (Intercollegiate):** *Men:* baseball, basketball, cross-country, football, golf, lacrosse, soccer, tennis. *Women:* basketball, cross-country, diving, field hockey, golf, lacrosse, soccer, softball, swimming, tennis, volleyball, water polo.

ADMISSIONS

Selectivity Rating: 74 (of 100). **Freshman Academic Profile:** 24% in top 10% of high school class, 63% in top 25% of high school class, 94% in top 50% of high school class. Average SAT I Math 567, SAT I Math middle 50% range 520-610. Average SAT I Verbal 550, SAT I Verbal middle 50% range 510-590. Average ACT 26, ACT middle 50% range 24-27. TOEFL required of all international applicants, minimum TOEFL 550. **Basis for Candidate Selection:** *Very important factors considered include:* secondary school record. *Important factors considered include:* essays, recommendations, standardized test scores. *Other factors considered include:* alumni/ae relation, character/personal qualities, class rank, extracurricular activities, talent/ability, volunteer work, work experience. **Freshman Admission Requirements:** High school diploma or GED is required. *Academic units required/recommended:* 14 total required; 19 total recommended; 4 English required, 4 English recommended, 3 math required, 4 math recommended, 3 science required, 4 science recommended, 3 science lab required, 4 science lab recommended, 3 foreign language recommended, 1 social studies required, 1 social studies recommended, 3 history required, 3 history recommended. **Freshman Admission Statistics:** 3,945 applied, 58% accepted, 30% of those accepted enrolled. **Transfer Admission Requirements:** *Items required:* college transcript, statement of good standing from prior school. Minimum college GPA of 2.5 required. Lowest grade transferable C-. **General Admission Information:** Application fee $40. Priority application deadline March 1. Early decision application deadline December 1. Regular application deadline March 1. Nonfall registration accepted. Admission may be deferred for a maximum of 1 year. Credit and/or placement offered for CEEB Advanced Placement tests.

COSTS AND FINANCIAL AID

Tuition $16,405. Room & board $7,010. Required fees $540. Average book expense $745. **Required Forms and Deadlines:** FAFSA and state aid form. Priority filing deadline February 1. **Notification of Awards:** Applicants will be notified of awards on or about April 1. **Types of Aid:** *Need-based scholarships/grants:* Pell, SEOG, state scholarships/grants, private scholarships, the school's own gift aid, Siena Grants, Franciscan Community Grants. *Loans:* FFEL Subsidized Stafford, FFEL Unsubsidized Stafford, FFEL PLUS, Federal Perkins. **Student Employment:** Federal Work-Study Program available. Institutional employment available. Off-campus job opportunities are good. **Financial Aid Statistics:** 70% freshmen, 69% undergrads receive some form of aid. Average income from on-campus job $1,000. **Financial Aid Phone:** 518-783-2427.

See page 1208.

SIENA HEIGHTS UNIVERSITY

1247 East Siena Heights Drive, Adrian, MI 49221
Phone: 517-263-0731 **E-mail:** admissions@alpha.sienahts.edu **CEEB Code:** 1719
Fax: 517-264-7704 **ACT Code:** 2052

This private school, which is affiliated with the Roman Catholic Church, was founded in 1919. It has a 140-acre campus.

STUDENTS AND FACULTY

Enrollment: 993. **Student Body:** Out-of-state 16%, international 2% (6 countries represented). **Ethnic Representation:** African American 4%, Asian 1%, Caucasian 88%, Hispanic 7%. **Retention and Graduation:** 68% freshmen return for sophomore year. 14% grads go on to further study within 1 year. 2% grads pursue law degrees. 1% grads pursue medical degrees.

ACADEMICS

Degrees: Associate's, bachelor's, master's. **Special Study Options:** Cooperative (work-study) program, study abroad. Undergrads may take grad-level classes. Cooperative education programs: arts, business, computer science, education, health professions, humanities, natural science, social/behavioral science. Combined degree programs: 2-2 pre-engineering programs with University of Detroit and University of Michigan. Foreign exchange program: study abroad in Italy. Continuing education classes.

FACILITIES

Housing: Coed, fraternities and/or sororities. **Library Holdings:** 120,407 bound volumes. 451 periodicals. 24,997 microforms. 5,284 audiovisuals. **Special Academic Facilities/Equipment:** Art gallery, Montessori school, language lab. **Computers:** *Recommended operating system:* Mac. School-owned computers available for student use.

EXTRACURRICULARS

Organizations: 2 fraternities (5% men join), 2 sororities (5% women join). **Athletics (Intercollegiate):** *Men:* baseball, basketball, cross-country, soccer, tennis, track & field, wrestling. *Women:* basketball, cross-country, softball, tennis, track & field, volleyball.

ADMISSIONS

Selectivity Rating: 74 (of 100). **Freshman Academic Profile:** 78% from public high schools. Average ACT 21. TOEFL required of all international applicants, minimum TOEFL 500. **Freshman Admission Requirements:** High school diploma is required and GED is not accepted. *Academic units required/recommended:* 4 English recommended, 2 math recommended, 1 science recommended, 2 foreign language recommended, 2 social studies recommended, 2 history recommended. **Transfer Admission Requirements:** Minimum college GPA of 2.0 required. Lowest grade transferable C. **General Admission Information:** Regular application deadline August 15. Nonfall registration accepted. Credit and/or placement offered for CEEB Advanced Placement tests.

COSTS AND FINANCIAL AID

Room & board $4,630. Average book expense $575. **Required Forms and Deadlines:** FAFSA. **Notification of Awards:** Applicants will be notified of awards on or about March 1. **Types of Aid:** *Need-based scholarships/grants:* Pell, SEOG, state scholarships/grants, private scholarships, the school's own gift aid. *Loans:* FFEL Subsidized Stafford, FFEL Unsubsidized Stafford, FFEL PLUS, Federal Perkins, state loans, college/university loans from institutional funds. **Student Employment:** Federal Work-Study Program available. Institutional employment available. Off-campus job opportunities are good. **Financial Aid Statistics:** Average freshman grant $2,200. Average income from on-campus job $1,275. **Financial Aid Phone:** 517-264-7130.

SIERRA NEVADA COLLEGE

999 Tahoe Blvd., Incline Village, NV 89451
Phone: 775-831-1314 **E-mail:** admissions@sierraneveda.edu
Fax: 702-831-1347 **Web:** www.sierraneveda.edu

This private school was founded in 1969. It has a 25-acre campus.

STUDENTS AND FACULTY

Enrollment: 297. **Student Body:** Male 53%, female 47%, out-of-state 70%, international 3%. **Ethnic Representation:** African American 1%, Asian 3%, Caucasian 80%, Hispanic 1%, Native American 1%. **Retention and Graduation:** 60% freshmen return for sophomore year. 20% freshmen graduate within 4 years. 33% grads go on to further study within 1 year. **Faculty:** Student/faculty ratio 8:1. 19 full-time faculty. 100% faculty teach undergrads.

ACADEMICS

Degrees: Bachelor's, post-bachelor's certificate. **Academic Requirements:** General education including some course work in arts/fine arts, computer literacy, English (including composition), foreign languages, history, humanities, mathematics, sciences (biological or physical), entrepreneurship. **Majors with Highest Enrollment:** Environmental science; business, management, marketing, and related support services; humanities/humanistic studies. **Disciplines with Highest Percentage of Degrees Awarded:** Business/marketing 50%, biological life sciences 15%, psychology 10%, natural resources/environmental sciences 10%, computer and information sciences 5%. **Special Study Options:** Honors program, internships, study abroad, teacher certification program.

FACILITIES

Housing: Coed. **Special Academic Facilities/Equipment:** McLean Observatory. **Computers:** School-owned computers available for student use.

EXTRACURRICULARS

Activities: Literary magazine, student government, student newspaper. **Organizations:** 10 registered organizations, 1 honor society, 2 religious organizations. **Athletics (Intercollegiate):** *Men:* equestrian, skiing (alpine). *Women:* equestrian, skiing (alpine).

ADMISSIONS

Selectivity Rating: 64 (of 100). **Freshman Academic Profile:** Average high school GPA 3.2. 13% in top 10% of high school class, 30% in top 25% of high school class, 70% in top 50% of high school class. 60% from public high schools. Average SAT I Math 512, SAT I Math middle 50% range 440-570. Average SAT I Verbal 540, SAT I Verbal middle 50% range 470-590. ACT middle 50% range 21-26. TOEFL required of all international applicants, minimum TOEFL 500. **Basis for Candidate Selection:** *Important factors considered include:* essays, recommendations, secondary school record. *Other factors considered include:* alumni/ae relation, character/personal qualities, class rank, extracurricular activities, geographical residence, interview, minority status, standardized test scores, talent/ability, volunteer work, work experience. **Freshman Admission Requirements:** High school diploma or GED is required. *Academic units required/recommended:* 4 English recommended, 3 math recommended, 2 science recommended, 2 foreign language recommended, 2 social studies recommended, 2 history recommended. **Transfer Admission Requirements:** *Items required:* college transcript, essay. Lowest grade transferable C. **General Admission Information:** Priority application deadline February 15. Nonfall registration accepted. Admission may be deferred for a maximum of 1 year. Credit and/or placement offered for CEEB Advanced Placement tests.

COSTS AND FINANCIAL AID

Tuition $18,750. Room & board $6,586. Required fees $120. Average book expense $650. **Required Forms and Deadlines:** FAFSA. No deadline for regular filing. Priority filing deadline April 1. **Notification of Awards:** Applicants will be notified of awards on a rolling basis beginning on or about March 1. **Types of Aid:** *Need-based scholarships/grants:* Pell, SEOG, state scholarships/grants, private scholarships, the school's own gift aid. *Loans:* Direct Subsidized Stafford, Direct PLUS. **Student Employment:** Federal Work-Study Program available. Institutional employment available. Off-campus job opportunities are excellent. **Financial Aid Statistics:** 88% freshmen, 90% undergrads receive some form of aid. Average freshman grant $15,750. Average freshman loan $3,000. **Financial Aid Phone:** 775-831-7799.

SILVER LAKE COLLEGE

2406 South Alverno Road, Manitowoc, WI 54220
Phone: 920-686-6175 **E-mail:** admslc@silver.sl.edu **CEEB Code:** 1300
Fax: 920-684-7082 **Web:** www.sl.edu **ACT Code:** 4586

This private school, which is affiliated with the Roman Catholic Church, was founded in 1935. It has a 30-acre campus.

STUDENTS AND FACULTY

Enrollment: 733. **Student Body:** Male 31%, female 69%, out-of-state 2%. **Ethnic Representation:** African American 1%, Asian 2%, Caucasian 88%, Hispanic 2%, Native American 5%. **Retention and Graduation:** 64% freshmen return for sophomore year. 10% freshmen graduate within 4 years. 15% grads go on to further study within 1 year. **Faculty:** Student/faculty ratio 9:1. 44 full-time faculty, 50% hold PhDs. 98% faculty teach undergrads.

ACADEMICS

Degrees: Associate's, bachelor's, certificate, master's, post-bachelor's certificate. **Academic Requirements:** General education including some course work in arts/fine arts, computer literacy, English (including composition), history, humanities, mathematics, philosophy, sciences (biological or physical), social science. **Classes:** Under 10 students in an average class. **Disciplines with Highest Percentage of Degrees Awarded:** Business/marketing 50%, education 26%, psychology 10%, engineering/engineering technology 4%, computer and information sciences 2%. **Special Study Options:** Accelerated program, double major, independent study, internships, student-designed major, teacher certification program.

FACILITIES

Housing: Apartments for single students. **Library Holdings:** 60,466 bound volumes. 296 periodicals. 2,154 microforms. 11,458 audiovisuals. **Computers:** School-owned computers available for student use.

EXTRACURRICULARS

Activities: Choral groups, concert band, dance, jazz band, literary magazine, music ensembles, student government, student newspaper. **Organizations:** 14 registered organizations, 6 honor societies, 1 religious organization. **Athletics (Intercollegiate):** *Women:* basketball.

ADMISSIONS

Selectivity Rating: 69 (of 100). **Freshman Academic Profile:** Average high school GPA 3.1. 4% in top 10% of high school class, 4% in top 25% of high school class, 64% in top 50% of high school class. 75% from public high schools. Average ACT 19, ACT middle 50% range 17-20. TOEFL required of all international applicants, minimum TOEFL 550. **Basis for Candidate Selection:** *Very important factors considered include:* secondary school record, standardized test scores. *Important factors considered include:* character/personal qualities. *Other factors considered include:* alumni/ae relation, class rank, interview, recommendations. **Freshman Admission Requirements:** High school diploma or GED is required. *Academic units required/recommended:* 16 total required; 3 English required, 2 math required, 1 science required, 1 science lab required, 1 social studies required, 1 history required, 7 elective required. **Transfer Admission Requirements:** *Items required:* college transcript. Minimum college GPA of 2.0 required. Lowest grade transferable C. **General Admission Information:** Application fee $35. Nonfall registration accepted. Admission may be deferred.

COSTS AND FINANCIAL AID

Tuition $14,350. Required fees $0. Average book expense $600. **Required Forms and Deadlines:** FAFSA and institution's own financial aid form. No deadline for regular filing. Priority filing deadline April 15. **Notification of Awards:** Applicants will be notified of awards on a rolling basis beginning on or about May 1. **Types of Aid:** *Need-based scholarships/grants:* Pell, SEOG, state scholarships/grants, private scholarships, the school's own gift aid. *Loans:* FFEL Subsidized Stafford, FFEL Unsubsidized Stafford, FFEL PLUS, state loans. **Student Employment:** Federal Work-Study Program available. Off-campus job opportunities are good. **Financial Aid Statistics:** 97% freshmen, 63% undergrads receive some form of aid. Average freshman grant $13,016. Average freshman loan $2,313. **Financial Aid Phone:** 920-686-6122.

SIMMONS COLLEGE

300 The Fenway, Boston, MA 02115
Phone: 617-521-2051 **E-mail:** ugadm@simmons.edu **CEEB Code:** 3761
Fax: 617-521-3190 **Web:** www.simmons.edu **ACT Code:** 1892

This private school was founded in 1899. It has a 12-acre campus.

STUDENTS AND FACULTY

Enrollment: 1,224. **Student Body:** Out-of-state 43%, international 4% (26 countries represented). **Ethnic Representation:** African American 7%, Asian 7%, Caucasian 75%, Hispanic 4%. **Retention and Graduation:** 82% freshmen return for sophomore year. 70% freshmen graduate within 4 years. 20% grads go on to further study within 1 year. 5% grads pursue business degrees. 2% grads pursue law degrees. 1% grads pursue medical degrees. **Faculty:** Student/faculty ratio 9:1. 175 full-time faculty, 64% hold PhDs. 100% faculty teach undergrads.

ACADEMICS

Degrees: Bachelor's, diploma, doctoral, master's, post-bachelor's certificate, post-master's certificate. **Academic Requirements:** General education including some course work in foreign languages, humanities, mathematics, sciences (biological or physical), multidisciplinary core course. **Classes:** 10-19 students in an average class. **Majors with Highest Enrollment:** Nursing/registered nurse training (RN, ASN, BSN, MSN); physical therapy/therapist; psychology, general. **Disciplines with Highest Percentage of Degrees Awarded:** Health professions and related sciences 27%, social sciences and history 15%, biological life sciences 12%, communications/communication technologies 9%, business/marketing 8%. **Special Study Options:** Accelerated program, cooperative (work-study) program, cross registration, double major, English as a second language, student exchange program (domestic), honors program, independent study, internships, liberal arts/career combination, student-designed major, study abroad, teacher certification program.

FACILITIES

Housing: Coed, all-female, housing for disabled students. Special-interest housing options: limited visitation floor, quiet floor, community service floor, wellness residence. **Library Holdings:** 235,431 bound volumes. 1,675 periodicals. 9,599 microforms. 5,725 audiovisuals. **Special Academic Facilities/Equipment:** Art gallery, media center, science center with dream/sleep analysis lab, physical therapy clinic areas, sports center with pool and spa. **Computers:** School-owned computers available for student use.

EXTRACURRICULARS

Activities: Choral groups, dance, drama/theater, literary magazine, music ensembles, student government, student newspaper, symphony orchestra, yearbook. **Organizations:** 70 registered organizations, 1 honor society, 4 religious organizations. **Athletics (Intercollegiate):** *Women:* basketball, crew, cross-country, diving, field hockey, soccer, softball, swimming, tennis, track & field, volleyball.

ADMISSIONS

Selectivity Rating: 77 (of 100). **Freshman Academic Profile:** Average high school GPA 3.1. 24% in top 10% of high school class, 56% in top 25% of high school class, 88% in top 50% of high school class. 81% from public high schools. Average SAT I Math 542, SAT I Math middle 50% range 490-590. Average SAT I Verbal 554, SAT I Verbal middle 50% range 500-600. Average ACT 23, ACT middle 50% range 19-25. TOEFL required of all international applicants, minimum TOEFL 560. **Basis for Candidate Selection:** *Very important factors considered include:* secondary school record. *Important factors considered include:* character/personal qualities, class rank, essays, recommendations, standardized test scores. *Other factors considered include:* alumni/ae relation, extracurricular activities, interview, talent/ability, volunteer work, work experience. **Freshman Admission Requirements:** High school diploma or GED is required. *Academic units required/recommended:* 15 total required; 4 English required, 3 math required, 4 math recommended, 3 science required, 3 science recommended, 3 foreign language required, 4 foreign language recommended, 3 social studies required, 4 social studies recommended. **Freshman Admission Statistics:** 1,704 applied, 68% accepted, 26% of those accepted enrolled. **Transfer Admission Requirements:** *Items required:* high school transcript, college transcript, essay, standardized test scores, statement of good standing from prior school. Minimum college GPA of 2.8 required. Lowest grade transferable C-. **General Admission Information:** Application fee $35. Regular application deadline February 2. Nonfall registration accepted. Admission may be deferred for a maximum of 1 year. Credit and/or placement offered for CEEB Advanced Placement tests.

COSTS AND FINANCIAL AID

Tuition $22,000. Room & board $9,100. Required fees $668. Average book expense $600. **Required Forms and Deadlines:** FAFSA, CSS/Financial Aid PROFILE, noncustodial (divorced/separated) parent's statement, business/farm supplement, and parents' income tax return. Priority filing deadline February 1. **Notification of Awards:** Applicants will be notified of awards on a rolling basis. **Types of Aid:** *Need-based scholarships/grants:* Pell, SEOG, state scholarships/grants, private scholarships, the school's own gift aid. *Loans:* FFEL Subsidized Stafford, FFEL Unsubsidized Stafford, FFEL PLUS, Federal Perkins, state loans, college/university loans from institutional funds. **Student Employment:** Federal Work-Study Program available. Institutional employment available. Off-campus job opportunities are good. **Financial Aid Statistics:** 77% freshmen, 73% undergrads receive some form of aid. Average income from on-campus job $2,000. **Financial Aid Phone:** 617-521-2036.

SIMON FRASER UNIVERSITY

Office of the Registrar, 8888 University Drive, Burnaby, BC V5A 1S6
Phone: 604-291-3224 **E-mail:** undergraduate-admissions@sfu.ca
Fax: 604-291-4969 **Web:** www.sfu.ca

This public school has a 400-acre campus.

STUDENTS AND FACULTY

Enrollment: 17,185. **Student Body:** Male 43%, female 57%, out-of-state 7%. **Faculty:** Student/faculty ratio 22:1.

ACADEMICS

Degrees: Bachelor's, certificate, diploma, doctoral, master's, post-master's certificate. **Classes:** 10-19 students in an average class. 10-19 students in an average lab/discussion section. **Majors with Highest Enrollment:** Business administration/management; communications and media studies; psychology, general. **Disciplines with Highest Percentage of Degrees Awarded:** Social sciences and history 28%, business/marketing 14%, psychology 8%, biological life sciences 7%, liberal arts/general studies 7%. **Special Study Options:** Cooperative (work-study) program, distance learning, double major, student exchange program (domestic), honors program, independent study, study abroad, teacher certification program.

FACILITIES

Housing: Coed, all-female, apartments for married students, housing for disabled students. **Library Holdings:** 1,306,397 bound volumes. 16,331 periodicals. 1,160,877 microforms. 148,910 audiovisuals.

EXTRACURRICULARS

Activities: Dance, drama/theater, radio station, student government, student newspaper, student-run film society.

ADMISSIONS

Selectivity Rating: 60 (of 100). **Freshman Academic Profile:** Average high school GPA 3.2. **Basis for Candidate Selection:** *Very important factors considered include:* class rank, secondary school record, standardized test scores. **Freshman Admission Requirements: Transfer Admission Requirements:** *Items required:* high school transcript, college transcript. **General Admission Information:** Application fee $25. Early decision application deadline May 1. Regular application deadline April 30. Nonfall registration accepted.

COSTS AND FINANCIAL AID

Required fees $209. Average book expense $540. **Types of Aid:** *Need-based scholarships/grants:* Pell, SEOG, state scholarships/grants, private scholarships, the school's own gift aid. *Loans:* FFEL Subsidized Stafford, FFEL Unsubsidized Stafford, FFEL PLUS, Federal Perkins, college/university loans from institutional funds.

SIMON'S ROCK COLLEGE OF BARD

84 Alford Road, Great Barrington, MA 01230
Phone: 413-528-7312 **E-mail:** admit@simons-rock.edu **CEEB Code:** 3795
Fax: 413-528-7334 **Web:** www.simons-rock.edu **ACT Code:** 1893

This private school was founded in 1964. It has a 275-acre campus.

STUDENTS AND FACULTY

Enrollment: 409. **Student Body:** Male 41%, female 59%, out-of-state 80%, international 1%. **Ethnic Representation:** African American 3%, Asian 5%, Caucasian 74%, Hispanic 3%. **Retention and Graduation:** 78% freshmen return for sophomore year. 73% freshmen graduate within 4 years. 4% grads go on to further study within 1 year. **Faculty:** Student/faculty ratio 8:1. 35 full-time faculty, 91% hold PhDs. 100% faculty teach undergrads.

ACADEMICS

Degrees: Associate's, bachelor's. **Academic Requirements:** General education including some course work in arts/fine arts, English (including composition), foreign languages, history, humanities, mathematics, sciences (biological or physical), social science, year-long first-year seminar, sophomore-year seminar, BA seminar within area of concentration. **Classes:** 10-19 students in an average class. 10-19 students in an average lab/discussion section. **Majors with Highest Enrollment:** Dramatic/theatre arts and stagecraft; mathematics, general; ethnic, cultural minority, and gender studies. **Disciplines with Highest Percentage of Degrees Awarded:** Visual and performing arts 32%, English 13%, natural resources/environmental sciences 11%, psychology 10%, mathematics 10%. **Special Study Options:** Accelerated program, cooperative (work-study) program, cross registration, dual enrollment, student exchange program (domestic), independent study, internships, student-designed major, study abroad.

FACILITIES

Housing: Coed, all-female, all-male, apartments for single students. **Library Holdings:** 65,370 bound volumes. 437 periodicals. 7,500 microforms. 4,032 audiovisuals. **Special Academic Facilities/Equipment:** Arts center, Fisher Science & Academic Center. **Computers:** School-owned computers available for student use.

EXTRACURRICULARS

Activities: Choral groups, dance, drama/theater, jazz band, literary magazine, music ensembles, radio station, student government, student newspaper, student-run film society, yearbook. **Organizations:** 21 registered organizations, 3 religious organizations. **Athletics (Intercollegiate):** *Men:* basketball, soccer, swimming. *Women:* basketball, soccer, swimming.

ADMISSIONS

Selectivity Rating: 91 (of 100). **Freshman Academic Profile:** 70% from public high schools. Average SAT I Math 600, SAT I Math middle 50% range 490-640. Average SAT I Verbal 640, SAT I Verbal middle 50% range 580-660. Average ACT 26, ACT middle 50% range 22-28. TOEFL required of all international applicants, minimum TOEFL 550. **Basis for Candidate Selection:** *Very important factors considered include:* character/personal qualities, essays, interview, recommendations, talent/ability. *Important factors considered include:* extracurricular activities, secondary school record, standardized test scores, volunteer work. *Other factors considered include:* alumni/ae relation, minority status, work experience. **Freshman Admission Requirements:** High school diploma or equivalent is not required. *Academic units required/recommended:* 15 total recommended; 2 English recommended, 2 math recommended, 2 science recommended, 1 science lab recommended, 2 foreign language recommended, 2 social studies recommended, 2 history recommended, 2 elective recommended. **Freshman Admission Statistics:** 480 applied, 50% accepted, 64% of those accepted enrolled. **Transfer Admission Requirements:** *Items required:* college transcript, essay, statement of good standing from prior school. Minimum high school GPA of 3.0 required. Minimum college GPA of 2.0 required. Lowest grade transferable C. **General Admission Information:** Application fee $40. Regular application deadline July 1. Admission may be deferred for a maximum of 1 year.

COSTS AND FINANCIAL AID

Tuition $27,180. Room & board $7,160. Required fees $235. Average book expense $1,000. **Required Forms and Deadlines:** FAFSA, CSS/Financial Aid PROFILE and noncustodial (divorced/separated) parent's statement. Financial aid filing deadline June 15. Priority filing deadline April 30. **Notification of Awards:** Applicants will be notified of awards on a rolling basis beginning on or about April 15. **Types of Aid:** *Need-based scholarships/grants:* Pell, SEOG, state scholarships/grants, private scholarships, the school's own gift aid. *Loans:* Direct Subsidized Stafford, Direct Unsubsidized Stafford, Direct PLUS, FFEL Subsidized Stafford, FFEL Unsubsidized Stafford, FFEL PLUS, Federal Perkins, state loans. **Student Employment:** Federal Work-Study Program available. Institutional employment available. Off-campus job opportunities are good. **Financial Aid Statistics:** 68% freshmen, 63% undergrads receive some form of aid. **Financial Aid Phone:** 413-528-7297.

SIMPSON COLLEGE (IA)

701 North C Street, Indianola, IA 50125
Phone: 515-961-1624 **E-mail:** admiss@simpson.edu **CEEB Code:** 6650
Fax: 515-961-1870 **Web:** www.simpson.edu **ACT Code:** 1354

This private school, which is affiliated with the Methodist Church, was founded in 1860. It has a 63-acre campus.

STUDENTS AND FACULTY

Enrollment: 1,845. **Student Body:** Male 41%, female 59%, out-of-state 10%, international 2% (13 countries represented). **Ethnic Representation:** African American 1%, Asian 1%, Caucasian 95%, Hispanic 1%. **Retention and Graduation:** 78% freshmen return for sophomore year. 56% freshmen graduate within 4 years. 11% grads go on to further study within 1 year. 1% grads pursue business degrees. 2% grads pursue law degrees. 2% grads pursue medical degrees. **Faculty:** Student/faculty ratio 14:1. 84 full-time faculty, 86% hold PhDs. 100% faculty teach undergrads.

ACADEMICS

Degrees: Bachelor's, post-bachelor's certificate. **Academic Requirements:** General education including some course work in arts/fine arts, English (including composition), history, humanities, mathematics, sciences (biological or physical), social science, senior. **Classes:** 10-19 students in an average class. 10-19 students in an average lab/discussion section. **Disciplines with Highest Percentage of Degrees Awarded:** Business/marketing 20%, education 13%, social sciences and history 10%, protective services/public administration 8%, computer and information sciences 7%. **Special Study Options:** Accelerated program, cooperative (work-study) program, double major, English as a second language, honors program, independent study, internships, liberal arts/career combination, student-designed major, study abroad, teacher certification program, weekend college, international program.

FACILITIES

Housing: Coed, all-female, all-male, apartments for single students, fraternities and/or sororities, theme housing. Groups of students petition for theme houses on a yearly basis. **Library Holdings:** 151,359 bound volumes. 599 periodicals. 12,374 microforms. 5,357 audiovisuals. **Special Academic Facilities/ Equipment:** Human cadaver lab, Dunn Library, antebellum collection. **Computers:** School-owned computers available for student use.

EXTRACURRICULARS

Activities: Choral groups, concert band, dance, drama/theater, jazz band, literary magazine, music ensembles, opera, pep band, radio station, student government, student newspaper, yearbook. **Organizations:** 89 registered organizations, 15 honor societies, 17 religious organizations, 4 fraternities (27% men join), 4 sororities (24% women join). **Athletics (Intercollegiate):** *Men:* baseball, basketball, cheerleading, cross-country, football, golf, indoor track, soccer, tennis, track & field, wrestling. *Women:* basketball, cheerleading, cross-country, golf, indoor track, soccer, softball, swimming, tennis, track & field, volleyball.

ADMISSIONS

Selectivity Rating: 76 (of 100). **Freshman Academic Profile:** 21% in top 10% of high school class, 57% in top 25% of high school class, 90% in top 50% of high school class. 96% from public high schools. Average ACT 24, ACT middle 50% range 22-27. TOEFL required of all international applicants, minimum TOEFL 550. **Basis for Candidate Selection:** *Very important factors considered include:* class rank, secondary school record, standardized test scores. *Important factors considered include:* character/personal qualities, recommendations. *Other factors considered include:* alumni/ae relation, extracurricular activities, interview, volunteer work. **Freshman Admission Requirements:** High school diploma or GED is required. *Academic units required/recommended:* 16 total recommended; 4 English recommended, 3 math recommended, 3 science recommended, 3 science lab recommended, 3 foreign language recommended, 3 social studies recommended. **Freshman Admission Statistics:** 1,177 applied, 85% accepted, 38% of those accepted enrolled. **Transfer Admission Requirements:** *Items required:* high school transcript, college transcript, standardized test scores. Minimum college GPA of 2.5 required. Lowest grade transferable C-. **General Admission Information:** Priority application deadline May 1. Nonfall registration accepted. Admission may be deferred for a maximum of 2 years. Credit and/or placement offered for CEEB Advanced Placement tests.

COSTS AND FINANCIAL AID

Tuition $16,475. Room & board $5,561. Required fees $174. Average book expense $800. **Required Forms and Deadlines:** FAFSA. No deadline for regular filing. Priority filing deadline April 1. **Notification of Awards:** Applicants will be notified of awards on a rolling basis beginning on or about March 15. **Types of Aid:** *Need-based scholarships/grants:* Pell, SEOG, state scholarships/grants, private scholarships, the school's own gift aid. *Loans:* FFEL Subsidized Stafford, FFEL Unsubsidized Stafford, FFEL PLUS, Federal Perkins, state loans, college/university loans from institutional funds, private educational loans. **Student Employment:** Federal Work-Study Program available. Institutional employment available. Off-campus job opportunities are fair. **Financial Aid Statistics:** 87% freshmen, 86% undergrads receive some form of aid. Average freshman grant $17,224. Average freshman loan $2,845. Average income from on-campus job $735. **Financial Aid Phone:** 515-961-1630.

SIMPSON COLLEGE AND GRADUATE SCHOOL

2211 College View Drive, Redding, CA 96003
Phone: 530-226-4606 **E-mail:** admissions@simpsonca.edu
Fax: 530-226-4861 **Web:** www.simpsonca.edu **ACT Code:** 430

This private school was founded in 1921. It has a 60-acre campus.

STUDENTS AND FACULTY

Enrollment: 1,031. **Student Body:** Male 36%, female 64%, international 1% (5 countries represented). **Ethnic Representation:** Asian 5%, Caucasian 88%, Hispanic 4%, Native American 1%. **Faculty:** Student/faculty ratio 23:1. 40 full-time faculty, 60% hold PhDs. 89% faculty teach undergrads.

ACADEMICS

Degrees: Associate's, bachelor's, certificate, master's. **Academic Requirements:** General education including some course work in arts/fine arts, English (including composition), history, humanities, mathematics, philosophy, sciences (biological or physical), social science, Bible, theology. **Classes:** Under 10 students in an average class. 10-19 students in an average lab/discussion section. **Disciplines with Highest Percentage of Degrees Awarded:** Business/ marketing 26%, liberal arts/general studies 26%, psychology 21%, philosophy/ religion/theology 12%, education 8%. **Special Study Options:** Accelerated program, distance learning, double major, student exchange program (domestic), honors program, independent study, internships, student-designed major, study abroad, teacher certification program, weekend college.

FACILITIES

Housing: All-female, all-male, apartments for married students, housing for disabled students. **Library Holdings:** 79,812 bound volumes. 327 periodicals. 209,181 microforms. 2,296 audiovisuals. **Computers:** School-owned computers available for student use.

EXTRACURRICULARS

Activities: Choral groups, music ensembles, pep band, student government, student newspaper, yearbook. **Organizations:** 10 registered organizations, 2 religious organizations. **Athletics (Intercollegiate):** *Men:* baseball, basketball, soccer. *Women:* basketball, cheerleading, soccer, volleyball.

ADMISSIONS

Selectivity Rating: 63 (of 100). **Freshman Academic Profile:** Average high school GPA 3.4. Average SAT I Math 495, SAT I Math middle 50% range 440-550. Average SAT I Verbal 510, SAT I Verbal middle 50% range 450-570. TOEFL required of all international applicants, minimum TOEFL 500. **Basis for Candidate Selection:** *Very important factors considered include:* character/personal qualities, religious affiliation/commitment, secondary school record, standardized test scores. *Important factors considered include:* recommendations. *Other factors considered include:* class rank, extracurricular activities, interview, talent/ability, volunteer work, work experience. **Freshman Admission Requirements:** High school diploma or GED is required. *Academic units required/recommended:* 4 English recommended, 3 math recommended, 2 science recommended, 2 foreign language recommended, 3 social studies recommended. **Freshman Admission Statistics:** 766 applied, 66% accepted, 41% of those accepted enrolled. **Transfer Admission Requirements:** *Items required:* college transcript, statement of good standing from prior school. Minimum college GPA of 2.0 required. Lowest grade transferable C. **General Admission Information:** Application fee $20. Priority application deadline March 1. Nonfall registration accepted. Admission may be deferred for a maximum of 2 years. Credit and/or placement offered for CEEB Advanced Placement tests.

COSTS AND FINANCIAL AID

Tuition $14,760. Room & board $5,470. Required fees $0. Average book expense $750. **Required Forms and Deadlines:** FAFSA and institution's own financial aid form. No deadline for regular filing. Priority filing deadline March 2. **Notification of Awards:** Applicants will be notified of awards on a rolling basis beginning on or about March 30. **Types of Aid:** *Need-based scholarships/ grants:* Pell, SEOG, state scholarships/grants, private scholarships, the school's own gift aid, restricted institutional aid. *Loans:* FFEL Subsidized Stafford, FFEL Unsubsidized Stafford, FFEL PLUS, Federal Perkins, state loans, college/university loans from institutional funds, private lender loans. **Student Employment:** Federal Work-Study Program available. Institutional employment available. Off-campus job opportunities are good. **Financial Aid Statistics:** 92% freshmen, 91% undergrads receive some form of aid. Average income from on-campus job $2,100. **Financial Aid Phone:** 530-224-5600.

SKIDMORE COLLEGE

815 North Broadway, Saratoga Springs, NY 12866-1632
Phone: 518-580-5570 **E-mail:** admissions@skidmore.edu **CEEB Code:** 2815
Fax: 518-580-5584 **Web:** www.skidmore.edu **ACT Code:** 2906

This private school was founded in 1903. It has an 850-acre campus.

STUDENTS AND FACULTY

Enrollment: 2,506. **Student Body:** Male 40%, female 60%, out-of-state 71%, international 1%. **Ethnic Representation:** African American 3%, Asian 5%, Caucasian 75%, Hispanic 4%. **Retention and Graduation:** 91% freshmen return for sophomore year. 71% freshmen graduate within 4 years. 15% grads go on to further study within 1 year. 1% grads pursue business degrees. 3% grads pursue law degrees. 1% grads pursue medical degrees. **Faculty:** Student/faculty ratio 11:1. 192 full-time faculty, 83% hold PhDs. 100% faculty teach undergrads.

ACADEMICS

Degrees: Bachelor's, master's. **Academic Requirements:** General education including some course work in arts/fine arts, English (including composition), foreign languages, humanities, mathematics, sciences (biological or physical), social science, interdisciplinary study, nonwestern, cultural diversity. **Classes:** 10-19 students in an average class. 10-19 students in an average lab/discussion section. **Disciplines with Highest Percentage of Degrees Awarded:** Visual and performing arts 17%, social sciences and history 15%, business/marketing 14%, English 9%, psychology 8%. **Special Study Options:** Accelerated program, cross registration, distance learning, double major, dual enrollment, external degree program, honors program, independent study, internships, liberal arts/career combination, student-designed major, study abroad, teacher certification program.

FACILITIES

Housing: Coed, all-female, all-male, apartments for single students, housing for disabled students. **Library Holdings:** 372,769 bound volumes. 1,983 periodicals. 233,986 microforms. 137,110 audiovisuals. **Special Academic Facilities/Equipment:** Tang Teaching Museum and Art Gallery; center for child study; art, music, dance, and theatre facilities; electron microscope; spectrometer; Center for Information Technology Services. **Computers:** School-owned computers available for student use.

EXTRACURRICULARS

Activities: Choral groups, concert band, dance, drama/theater, jazz band, literary magazine, music ensembles, musical theater, opera, radio station, student government, student newspaper, student-run film society, symphony orchestra, television station, yearbook. **Organizations:** 80 registered organizations, 10 honor societies, 3 religious organizations. **Athletics (Intercollegiate):** *Men:* baseball, basketball, crew, diving, equestrian, golf, ice hockey, lacrosse, soccer, swimming, tennis. *Women:* basketball, crew, diving, equestrian, field hockey, lacrosse, soccer, softball, swimming, tennis, volleyball.

ADMISSIONS

Selectivity Rating: 83 (of 100). **Freshman Academic Profile:** Average high school GPA 3.4. 41% in top 10% of high school class, 74% in top 25% of high school class, 97% in top 50% of high school class. 60% from public high schools. Average SAT I Math 620, SAT I Math middle 50% range 580-660. Average SAT I Verbal 630, SAT I Verbal middle 50% range 580-670. Average ACT 27, ACT middle 50% range 25-28. TOEFL required of all international applicants, minimum TOEFL 580. **Basis for Candidate Selection:** *Very important factors considered include:* recommendations, secondary school record. *Important factors considered include:* character/personal qualities, class rank, essays, extracurricular activities, standardized test scores, talent/ability, volunteer work, work experience. *Other factors considered include:* alumni/ae relation, geographical residence, interview, minority status. **Freshman Admission Requirements:** High school diploma or GED is required. *Academic units required/recommended:* 4 English recommended, 4 math recommended, 4 science recommended, 3 science lab recommended, 4 foreign language recommended, 4 social studies recommended. **Freshman Admission Statistics:** 5,606 applied, 46% accepted, 25% of those accepted enrolled. **Transfer Admission Requirements:** *Items required:* high school transcript, college transcript, essay, standardized test scores, statement of good standing from prior school. Minimum college GPA of 2.7 required. Lowest grade transferable C. **General Admission Information:** Application fee $50. Early decision application deadline December 1. Regular application deadline January 15. Nonfall registration accepted. Admission may be deferred for a maximum of 2 years. Credit and/or placement offered for CEEB Advanced Placement tests.

COSTS AND FINANCIAL AID

Tuition $27,700. Room & board $7,835. Required fees $280. Average book expense $650. **Required Forms and Deadlines:** FAFSA, CSS/Financial Aid PROFILE and state aid form. Financial aid filing deadline January 15. **Notification of Awards:** Applicants will be notified of awards on or about April 1. **Types of Aid:** *Need-based scholarships/grants:* Pell, SEOG, state scholarships/grants, the school's own gift aid. *Loans:* FFEL Subsidized Stafford, FFEL Unsubsidized Stafford, FFEL PLUS, Federal Perkins. **Student Employment:** Federal Work-Study Program available. Institutional employment available. Off-campus job opportunities are good. **Financial Aid Statistics:** 40% freshmen, 42% undergrads receive some form of aid. Average freshman grant $17,342. Average freshman loan $2,336. Average income from on-campus job $644. **Financial Aid Phone:** 518-580-5750.

See page 1210.

SLIPPERY ROCK UNIVERSITY OF PENNSYLVANIA

Office of Admissions, Maltby Center, Slippery Rock, PA 16057
Phone: 724-738-2015 **E-mail:** apply@sru.edu **CEEB Code:** 2658
Fax: 724-738-2913 **Web:** www.sru.edu **ACT Code:** 3716

This public school was founded in 1889. It has a 600-acre campus.

STUDENTS AND FACULTY

Enrollment: 6,814. **Student Body:** Male 43%, female 57%, out-of-state 4%, international 3% (56 countries represented). **Ethnic Representation:** African American 4%, Asian 1%, Caucasian 92%, Hispanic 1%. **Retention and Graduation:** 74% freshmen return for sophomore year. 21% freshmen graduate within 4 years. 12% grads go on to further study within 1 year. 1% grads pursue business degrees. 1% grads pursue law degrees. 1% grads pursue medical degrees. **Faculty:** Student/faculty ratio 18:1. 361 full-time faculty, 77% hold PhDs. 100% faculty teach undergrads.

ACADEMICS

Degrees: Bachelor's, doctoral, master's, post-bachelor's certificate, post-master's certificate. **Academic Requirements:** General education including some course work in arts/fine arts, English (including composition), history, humanities, mathematics, sciences (biological or physical), social science. **Classes:** 20-29 students in an average class. 10-19 students in an average lab/discussion section. **Majors with Highest Enrollment:** Business/managerial operations; elementary education and teaching; health and physical education, general. **Disciplines with Highest Percentage of Degrees Awarded:** Education 23%, business/marketing 13%, parks and recreation 13%, health professions and related sciences 8%, communications/communication technologies 7%. **Special Study Options:** Accelerated program, cross registration, distance learning, double major, student exchange program (domestic), honors program, independent study, internships, study abroad, teacher certification program.

FACILITIES

Housing: Coed, all-female, apartments for single students, housing for disabled students. Special-interest residence hall floors in education, humanities & fine arts, honors, wellness, technology, math/science, intensive study, ROTC, nontraditional/grad. **Library Holdings:** 533,718 bound volumes. 667 periodicals. 1,497,469 microforms. 22,707 audiovisuals. **Special Academic Facilities/Equipment:** Special education school for student teachers, physical therapy clinic, microvideo system, planetarium, electron microscope. **Computers:** School-owned computers available for student use.

EXTRACURRICULARS

Activities: Choral groups, concert band, dance, drama/theater, jazz band, literary magazine, marching band, music ensembles, musical theater, radio station, student government, student newspaper, student-run film society, symphony orchestra, television station, yearbook. **Organizations:** 170 registered organizations, 35 honor societies, 7 religious organizations, 12 fraternities (8% men join), 9 sororities (7% women join). **Athletics (Intercollegiate):** *Men:* baseball, basketball, cross-country, diving, football, golf, soccer, swimming, tennis, track & field, water polo, wrestling. *Women:* basketball, cross-country, diving, field hockey, golf, soccer, softball, swimming, tennis, track & field, volleyball, water polo.

ADMISSIONS

Selectivity Rating: 67 (of 100). **Freshman Academic Profile:** Average high school GPA 3.1. 7% in top 10% of high school class, 26% in top 25% of high

school class, 63% in top 50% of high school class. 80% from public high schools. Average SAT I Math 478, SAT I Math middle 50% range 430-520. Average SAT I Verbal 480, SAT I Verbal middle 50% range 430-520. Average ACT 20, ACT middle 50% range 17-22. TOEFL required of all international applicants, minimum TOEFL 500. **Basis for Candidate Selection:** *Very important factors considered include:* secondary school record, standardized test scores. *Other factors considered include:* alumni/ae relation, character/personal qualities, class rank, essays, extracurricular activities, interview, recommendations, state residency, talent/ability. **Freshman Admission Requirements:** High school diploma or GED is required. *Academic units required/recommended:* 16 total recommended; 4 English recommended, 3 math recommended, 3 science recommended, 2 foreign language recommended, 4 social studies recommended. **Freshman Admission Statistics:** 3,859 applied, 49% accepted, 75% of those accepted enrolled. **Transfer Admission Requirements:** *Items required:* college transcript, statement of good standing from prior school. Minimum college GPA of 2.0 required. Lowest grade transferable C. **General Admission Information:** Application fee $25. Priority application deadline May 1. Nonfall registration accepted. Admission may be deferred for a maximum of 1 year. Credit offered for CEEB Advanced Placement tests.

COSTS AND FINANCIAL AID

In-state tuition $4,378. Out-of-state tuition $10,946. Room & board $4,400. Required fees $1,170. Average book expense $650. **Required Forms and Deadlines:** FAFSA. Priority filing deadline May 1. **Notification of Awards:** Applicants will be notified of awards on a rolling basis beginning on or about March 15. **Types of Aid:** *Need-based scholarships/grants:* Pell, SEOG, state scholarships/grants, private scholarships, the school's own gift aid. *Loans:* FFEL Subsidized Stafford, FFEL Unsubsidized Stafford, FFEL PLUS, Federal Perkins. **Student Employment:** Federal Work-Study Program available. Institutional employment available. Off-campus job opportunities are excellent. **Financial Aid Statistics:** 64% freshmen, 60% undergrads receive some form of aid. Average freshman grant $2,835. Average freshman loan $2,183. Average income from on-campus job $1,710. **Financial Aid Phone:** 724-738-2044.

SMITH COLLEGE

7 College Lane, Northampton, MA 01063
Phone: 413-585-2500 **E-mail:** admission@smith.edu **CEEB Code:** 3762
Fax: 413-585-2527 **Web:** www.smith.edu **ACT Code:** 1894

This private school was founded in 1871. It has a 125-acre campus.

STUDENTS AND FACULTY

Enrollment: 2,647. **Student Body:** Out-of-state 76%, international 6% (55 countries represented). **Ethnic Representation:** African American 5%, Asian 10%, Caucasian 62%, Hispanic 6%, Native American 1%. **Retention and Graduation:** 90% freshmen return for sophomore year. 76% freshmen graduate within 4 years. 17% grads go on to further study within 1 year. 3% grads pursue law degrees. 1% grads pursue medical degrees. **Faculty:** Student/faculty ratio 9:1. 287 full-time faculty, 94% hold PhDs. 100% faculty teach undergrads.

ACADEMICS

Degrees: Bachelor's, doctoral, master's, post-bachelor's certificate, post-master's certificate. **Classes:** 10-19 students in an average class. 10-19 students in an average lab/discussion section. **Majors with Highest Enrollment:** Psychology, general; economics, general; political science and government, general. **Disciplines with Highest Percentage of Degrees Awarded:** Social sciences and history 27%, biological life sciences 12%, visual and performing arts 12%, area and ethnic studies 10%, English 10%. **Special Study Options:** Accelerated program, cross registration, double major, student exchange program (domestic), honors program, independent study, internships, student-designed major, study abroad, teacher certification program.

FACILITIES

Housing: All-female, cooperative housing, apartment complex for limited number of juniors and seniors, senior house, French-speaking house, and Ada Comstock (nontraditional age) House. **Library Holdings:** 1,296,828 bound volumes. 6,530 periodicals. 141,932 microforms. 65,135 audiovisuals. **Special Academic Facilities/Equipment:** Art museum; printing, darkroom, and sculpture facilities; dance, electronic music, television, and theatre studios; recital hall; rehearsal rooms; multimedia language lab; early childhood/elementary education campus school; two electronic classrooms; physiology and horticultural labs; animal care facilities; two electron microscopes; greenhouses; observatories. **Computers:** School-owned computers available for student use.

EXTRACURRICULARS

Activities: Choral groups, concert band, dance, drama/theater, jazz band, literary magazine, music ensembles, radio station, student government, student newspaper, student-run film society, symphony orchestra, television station, yearbook. **Organizations:** 121 registered organizations, 3 honor societies, 15 religious organizations. **Athletics (Intercollegiate):** *Women:* basketball, crew, cross-country, diving, equestrian, field hockey, indoor track, lacrosse, skiing (alpine), soccer, softball, squash, swimming, tennis, track & field, volleyball.

ADMISSIONS

Selectivity Rating: 97 (of 100). **Freshman Academic Profile:** Average high school GPA 3.8. 58% in top 10% of high school class, 90% in top 25% of high school class, 99% in top 50% of high school class. 74% from public high schools. Average SAT I Math 630, SAT I Math middle 50% range 580-670. Average SAT I Verbal 650, SAT I Verbal middle 50% range 590-700. Average ACT 27, ACT middle 50% range 24-30. TOEFL required of all international applicants, minimum TOEFL 600. **Basis for Candidate Selection:** *Very important factors considered include:* character/personal qualities, recommendations, secondary school record. *Important factors considered include:* class rank, essays, extracurricular activities, interview, standardized test scores, talent/ability. *Other factors considered include:* alumni/ae relation, minority status, volunteer work, work experience. **Freshman Admission Requirements:** High school diploma or equivalent is not required. *Academic units required/recommended:* 15 total recommended; 4 English recommended, 3 math recommended, 3 science recommended, 3 science lab recommended, 3 foreign language recommended, 2 history recommended. **Freshman Admission Statistics:** 3,074 applied, 53% accepted, 42% of those accepted enrolled. **Transfer Admission Requirements:** *Items required:* high school transcript, college transcript, essay, statement of good standing from prior school. Lowest grade transferable C. **General Admission Information:** Application fee $50. Early decision application deadline November 15. Regular application deadline January 15. Admission may be deferred for a maximum of 1 year. Credit and/or placement offered for CEEB Advanced Placement tests.

COSTS AND FINANCIAL AID

Tuition $23,400. Room & board $8,160. Required fees $184. Average book expense $1,500. **Required Forms and Deadlines:** FAFSA, institution's own financial aid form, CSS/Financial Aid PROFILE, noncustodial (divorced/separated) parent's statement and business/farm supplement. Financial aid filing deadline February 1. **Notification of Awards:** Applicants will be notified of awards on or about April 1. **Types of Aid:** *Need-based scholarships/grants:* Pell, SEOG, state scholarships/grants, the school's own gift aid. *Loans:* Direct Subsidized Stafford, Direct Unsubsidized Stafford, FFEL PLUS, Federal Perkins, state loans, college/university loans from institutional funds. **Student Employment:** Federal Work-Study Program available. Institutional employment available. Off-campus job opportunities are excellent. **Financial Aid Statistics:** 61% freshmen, 64% undergrads receive some form of aid. Average freshman grant $21,874. Average freshman loan $2,674. **Financial Aid Phone:** 413-585-2530.

SOJOURNER DOUGLASS COLLEGE

500 North Caroline Street, Baltimore, MD 21205
Phone: 410-276-0306 **E-mail:** dsamuels@host.sdc.edu
Fax: 410-276-1593 **Web:** www.sdc.edu

STUDENTS AND FACULTY

Enrollment: 1,046. **Student Body:** Male 15%, female 85%. **Ethnic Representation:** African American 98%, Caucasian 2%.

ACADEMICS

Degrees: Bachelor's, master's.

EXTRACURRICULARS

Organizations: 6 religious organizations.

ADMISSIONS

Selectivity Rating: 60 (of 100). **General Admission Information:** Regular application deadline July 31.

COSTS AND FINANCIAL AID

Average book expense $400. **Types of Aid:** *Loans:* FFEL Subsidized Stafford, FFEL PLUS.

SOKA UNIVERSITY OF AMERICA

1 University Drive, Admission Office, Aliso Viejo, CA 92656-4105
Phone: 949-480-4150 **E-mail:** admission@soka.edu
Fax: 949-480-4151 **Web:** www.soka.edu/homeav.html **ACT Code:** 467

This private school was founded in 2001. It has a 103-acre campus.

STUDENTS AND FACULTY

Enrollment: 202. **Student Body:** Out-of-state 50%, international 50% (23 countries represented). **Ethnic Representation:** African American 9%, Asian 32%, Caucasian 55%, Hispanic 4%. **Retention and Graduation:** 96% freshmen return for sophomore year. **Faculty:** Student/faculty ratio 6:1. 30 full-time faculty, 100% hold PhDs. 100% faculty teach undergrads.

ACADEMICS

Degrees: Bachelor's. **Academic Requirements:** General education including some course work in arts/fine arts, computer literacy, English (including composition), foreign languages, history, humanities, mathematics, philosophy, sciences (biological or physical), social science. Courses stress multicultural, ethnic, and/or gender-related content. **Classes:** 10-19 students in an average class. **Special Study Options:** Independent study, internships, liberal arts/career combination, study abroad.

FACILITIES

Housing: Coed, housing for disabled students. **Library Holdings:** 35,000 bound volumes. 174 periodicals. 1 microforms. 332 audiovisuals. **Special Academic Facilities/Equipment:** Art gallery, athenaeum. **Computers:** *Recommended operating system:* Windows XP. School-owned computers available for student use.

EXTRACURRICULARS

Activities: Choral groups, concert band, dance, music ensembles, student government, student newspaper, student-run film society, symphony orchestra, yearbook. **Organizations:** 35 registered organizations, 1 religious organization.

ADMISSIONS

Selectivity Rating: 63 (of 100). **Freshman Academic Profile:** Average high school GPA 3.5. Average SAT I Verbal 503, SAT I Verbal middle 50% range 450-570. Average SAT I Math 626, SAT I Math range 580-690. Average ACT 26, ACT middle 50% range 23-29. TOEFL required of all international applicants, minimum TOEFL 550. **Basis for Candidate Selection:** *Very important factors considered include:* character/personal qualities, class rank, essays, recommendations, secondary school record. *Important factors considered include:* extracurricular activities, geographical residence, standardized test scores, state residency, talent/ability. *Other factors considered include:* alumni/ae relation, interview, volunteer work, work experience. **Freshman Admission Requirements:** High school diploma or GED is required. *Academic units required/recommended:* 17 total recommended; 4 English recommended, 3 math recommended, 2 science recommended, 2 science lab recommended, 2 foreign language recommended, 2 social studies recommended, 2 history recommended. **Freshman Admission Statistics:** 221 applied, 54% accepted, 73% of those accepted enrolled. **General Admission Information:** Application fee $45. Priority application deadline October 1. Regular application deadline January 15. Admission may be deferred for a maximum of 1 year. Neither credit nor placement offered for CEEB Advanced Placement tests.

COSTS AND FINANCIAL AID

Tuition $17,510. Room & board $8,000. Required fees $0. Average book expense $1,000. **Required Forms and Deadlines:** FAFSA and institution's own financial aid form. Financial aid filing deadline March 1. Priority filing deadline March 1. **Notification of Awards:** Applicants will be notified of awards on or about March 15. **Types of Aid:** *Need-based scholarships/grants:* private scholarships, the school's own gift aid. *Loans:* college/university loans from institutional funds. **Student Employment:** Institutional employment available. Off-campus job opportunities are good. **Financial Aid Statistics:** 80% freshmen, 86% undergrads receive some form of aid. Average freshman grant $14,371. Average freshman loan $5,458. Average income from on-campus job $3,024. **Financial Aid Phone:** 949-480-4138.

SONOMA STATE UNIVERSITY

1801 East Cotati Avenue, Rohnert Park, CA 94928
Phone: 707-664-2778 **E-mail:** admitme.@sonoma.edu **CEEB Code:** 4723
Fax: 707-664-2060 **Web:** www.sonoma.edu **ACT Code:** 431

This public school was founded in 1960. It has a 275-acre campus.

STUDENTS AND FACULTY

Enrollment: 6,278. **Student Body:** Male 36%, female 64%, out-of-state 1%, international 2%. **Ethnic Representation:** African American 2%, Asian 5%, Caucasian 65%, Hispanic 10%, Native American 1%. **Retention and Graduation:** 75% freshmen return for sophomore year. 19% freshmen graduate within 4 years. 25% grads go on to further study within 1 year. 10% grads pursue business degrees. 2% grads pursue law degrees. 2% grads pursue medical degrees. **Faculty:** Student/faculty ratio 21:1. 241 full-time faculty, 93% hold PhDs. 98% faculty teach undergrads.

ACADEMICS

Degrees: Bachelor's, master's. **Academic Requirements:** General education including some course work in arts/fine arts, English (including composition), history, humanities, mathematics, sciences (biological or physical), social science, U.S. and California goverment, ethnic studies. **Classes:** 10-19 students in an average class. 10-19 students in an average lab/discussion section. **Majors with Highest Enrollment:** Business administration/management; liberal arts and sciences/liberal studies; psychology, general. **Disciplines with Highest Percentage of Degrees Awarded:** Business/marketing 18%, social sciences and history 15%, psychology 11%, liberal arts/general studies 11%, communications/communication technologies 6%. **Special Study Options:** Accelerated program, cooperative (work-study) program, cross registration, distance learning, double major, dual enrollment, English as a second language, student exchange program (domestic), external degree program, honors program, independent study, internships, liberal arts/career combination, student-designed major, study abroad, teacher certification program.

FACILITIES

Housing: Coed, apartments for single students, housing for international students, housing for focused learning communities, freshman seminar dorms, healthy living dorms, women in math/science dorms. **Library Holdings:** 666,393 bound volumes. 1,071 periodicals. 1,655,701 microforms. 25,805 audiovisuals. **Special Academic Facilities/Equipment:** Performing arts center, observatory, electron microscope, seismograph, information technology center, environmental technology center, high technology high school. **Computers:** *Recommended operating system:* Mac /Windows NT/2000. School-owned computers available for student use.

EXTRACURRICULARS

Activities: Choral groups, dance, drama/theater, jazz band, literary magazine, music ensembles, musical theater, opera, pep band, radio station, student government, student newspaper, symphony orchestra. **Organizations:** 101 registered organizations, 6 honor societies, 4 religious organizations, 4 fraternities (6% men join), 4 sororities (5% women join). **Athletics (Intercollegiate):** *Men:* baseball, basketball, soccer, tennis. *Women:* basketball, cross-country, soccer, softball, tennis, track & field, volleyball.

ADMISSIONS

Selectivity Rating: 71 (of 100). **Freshman Academic Profile:** Average high school GPA 3.1. 11% in top 10% of high school class, 38% in top 25% of high school class, 77% in top 50% of high school class. 87% from public high schools. Average SAT I Math 516, SAT I Math middle 50% range 470-570. Average SAT I Verbal 514, SAT I Verbal middle 50% range 460-570. TOEFL required of all international applicants, minimum TOEFL 500. **Basis for Candidate Selection:** *Very important factors considered include:* secondary school record, standardized test scores. *Important factors considered include:* geographical residence, minority status, state residency. **Freshman Admission Requirements:** High school diploma or GED is required. *Academic units required/recommended:* 16 total required; 4 English required, 3 math required, 2 science required, 1 science lab required, 2 foreign language required, 1 history required, 3 elective required. **Freshman Admission Statistics:** 5,006 applied, 92% accepted, 23% of those accepted enrolled. **Transfer Admission Requirements:** *Items required:* college transcript. Minimum high school GPA of 2.0 required. Minimum college GPA of 2.0 required. Lowest grade transferable D. **General Admission Information:** Application fee $55. Priority application deadline November 30. Regular application deadline January 31. Nonfall registration accepted. Credit and/or placement offered for CEEB Advanced Placement tests.

COSTS AND FINANCIAL AID

In-state tuition $0. Out-of-state tuition $7,380. Room & board $6,921. Required fees $2,032. Average book expense $846. **Required Forms and Deadlines:** FAFSA. Priority filing deadline January 31. **Notification of Awards:** Applicants will be notified of awards on a rolling basis beginning on or about March 15. **Types of Aid:** *Need-based scholarships/grants:* Pell, SEOG, state scholarships/grants, private scholarships, the school's own gift aid. *Loans:* Direct Subsidized Stafford, Direct Unsubsidized Stafford, Direct PLUS, Federal Perkins. **Student Employment:** Federal Work-Study Program available. Institutional employment available. Off-campus job opportunities are good. **Financial Aid Statistics:** 34% freshmen, 37% undergrads receive some form of aid. Average freshman grant $1,200. Average freshman loan $2,454. Average income from on-campus job $1,833. **Financial Aid Phone:** 707-664-2389.

SOUTH CAROLINA STATE UNIVERSITY

300 College Street Northeast, Orangeburg, SC 29117-0001
Phone: 800-260-5956 **CEEB Code:** 5618
Fax: 803-536-8990 **ACT Code:** 3876

This public school was founded in 1896. It has a 147-acre campus.

STUDENTS AND FACULTY

Enrollment: 4,911. **Student Body:** Out-of-state 8%, international 1% (21 countries represented). **Ethnic Representation:** African American 93%, Caucasian 7%.

ACADEMICS

Degrees: Associate's, bachelor's, master's. **Special Study Options:** Cooperative (work-study) program, study abroad.

FACILITIES

Housing: Coed, apartments for married students. **Library Holdings:** 1,337 periodicals. 654,907 microforms. **Special Academic Facilities/Equipment:** Museum, planetarium, language lab. **Computers:** *Recommended operating system:* Mac. School-owned computers available for student use.

EXTRACURRICULARS

Organizations: 1 religious organization, 4 fraternities, 4 sororities.

ADMISSIONS

Selectivity Rating: 63 (of 100). **Freshman Academic Profile:** 7% in top 10% of high school class, 16% in top 25% of high school class, 60% in top 50% of high school class. 98% from public high schools. TOEFL required of all international applicants, minimum TOEFL 550. **Freshman Admission Requirements:** High school diploma is required and GED is not accepted. *Academic units required/recommended:* 16 total required; 4 English required, 3 math required, 2 science required, 2 foreign language required, 2 social studies required, 1 history required, 2 elective required. **Transfer Admission Requirements:** Minimum college GPA of 2.0 required. Lowest grade transferable C. **General Admission Information:** Regular application deadline July 31. Nonfall registration accepted. Credit and/or placement offered for CEEB Advanced Placement tests.

COSTS AND FINANCIAL AID

Room & board $4,100. Required fees $75. Average book expense $1,000. **Required Forms and Deadlines:** FAFSA. **Notification of Awards:** Applicants will be notified of awards on or about June 15. **Types of Aid:** *Loans:* FFEL Subsidized Stafford, FFEL PLUS. **Student Employment:** Institutional employment available. **Financial Aid Phone:** 803-536-7067.

SOUTH DAKOTA SCHOOL OF MINES & TECHNOLOGY

501 East St. Joseph Street, Rapid City, SD 57701-3995
Phone: 800-544-8162 **E-mail:** admissions@sdsmt.edu **CEEB Code:** 6652
Fax: 605-394-6131 **Web:** www.sdsmt.edu **ACT Code:** 3922

This public school was founded in 1885. It has a 120-acre campus.

STUDENTS AND FACULTY

Enrollment: 2,094. **Student Body:** Male 68%, female 32%, out-of-state 26%, international 1% (18 countries represented). **Ethnic Representation:** Asian 1%, Caucasian 88%, Hispanic 1%, Native American 2%. **Retention and Graduation:** 71% freshmen return for sophomore year. 11% freshmen graduate within 4 years. **Faculty:** Student/faculty ratio 16:1. 101 full-time faculty, 80% hold PhDs. 100% faculty teach undergrads.

ACADEMICS

Degrees: Associate's, bachelor's, doctoral, master's, terminal. **Academic Requirements:** General education including some course work in computer literacy, English (including composition), humanities, mathematics, sciences (biological or physical), social science. **Classes:** 20-29 students in an average class. **Majors with Highest Enrollment:** Civil engineering, general; mechanical engineering; multi/interdisciplinary studies. **Disciplines with Highest Percentage of Degrees Awarded:** Engineering/engineering technology 71%, interdisciplinary studies 10%, computer and information sciences 8%, physical sciences 8%, mathematics 3%. **Special Study Options:** Cooperative (work-study) program, cross registration, distance learning, double major, dual enrollment, English as a second language, independent study, internships, student-designed major, study abroad, MS degree in technology management via the Internet, BS in interdisciplinary sciences is essentially a student-designed major. Cooperative program with National American University, a private college in Rapid City.

FACILITIES

Housing: Coed, fraternities and/or sororities. **Library Holdings:** 219,961 bound volumes. 496 periodicals. 122,867 microforms. 1,610 audiovisuals. **Special Academic Facilities/Equipment:** Museum of geology and paleontology, electron microscope, engineering/mining experiment station, institute of atmospheric science and other research institutes. **Computers:** School-owned computers available for student use.

EXTRACURRICULARS

Activities: Choral groups, concert band, drama/theater, jazz band, music ensembles, pep band, radio station, student government, student newspaper. **Organizations:** 65 registered organizations, 6 honor societies, 9 religious organizations, 4 fraternities, 2 sororities. **Athletics (Intercollegiate):** *Men:* basketball, cross-country, football, golf, indoor track, track & field. *Women:* basketball, cross-country, indoor track, track & field, volleyball.

ADMISSIONS

Selectivity Rating: 78 (of 100). **Freshman Academic Profile:** Average high school GPA 3.3. 17% in top 10% of high school class, 44% in top 25% of high school class, 77% in top 50% of high school class. 93% from public high schools. SAT I Math middle 50% range 520-650. SAT I Verbal middle 50% range 490-620. Average ACT 24, ACT middle 50% range 21-27. TOEFL required of all international applicants, minimum TOEFL 530. **Basis for Candidate Selection:** *Very important factors considered include:* secondary school record, standardized test scores. *Important factors considered include:* class rank. *Other factors considered include:* character/personal qualities, extracurricular activities, talent/ability, volunteer work, work experience. **Freshman Admission Requirements:** High school diploma or GED is required. *Academic units required/recommended:* 20 total required; 4 English required, 3 math required, 3 science required, 3 science lab required, 2 foreign language recommended, 3 social studies required. **Freshman Admission Statistics:** 883 applied, 98% accepted, 51% of those accepted enrolled. **Transfer Admission Requirements:** *Items required:* college transcript, statement of good standing from prior school. Minimum high school GPA of 2.0 required. Minimum college GPA of 2.0 required. Lowest grade transferable C. **General Admission Information:** Application fee $20. Nonfall registration accepted. Admission may be deferred for a maximum of 1 year. Credit and/or placement offered for CEEB Advanced Placement tests.

COSTS AND FINANCIAL AID

In-state tuition $1,950. Out-of-state tuition $6,200. Room & board $3,484. Required fees $2,009. Average book expense $850. **Required Forms and Deadlines:** FAFSA and Freshman Scholarship Application Form. No deadline for regular filing. Priority filing deadline March 15. **Notification of Awards:** Applicants will be notified of awards on a rolling basis beginning on or about May 1. **Types of Aid:** *Need-based scholarships/grants:* Pell, SEOG, the school's own gift aid, LEAP. *Loans:* FFEL Subsidized Stafford, FFEL Unsubsidized Stafford, FFEL PLUS, Federal Perkins. **Student Employment:** Federal Work-Study Program available. Institutional employment available. Off-campus job opportunities are excellent. **Financial Aid Statistics:** 50% freshmen, 52% undergrads receive some form of aid. Average freshman grant $3,290. Average freshman loan $4,110. Average income from on-campus job $1,407. **Financial Aid Phone:** 605-394-2400.

SOUTH DAKOTA STATE UNIVERSITY

Box 2201, Brookings, SD 57007-0649
Phone: 605-688-4121 **E-mail:** sdsu_admissions@sdstate.edu **CEEB Code:** 6653
Fax: 605-688-6891 **Web:** www.sdstate.edu **ACT Code:** 3924

This public school was founded in 1881. It has a 272-acre campus.

STUDENTS AND FACULTY

Enrollment: 8,445. **Student Body:** Male 47%, female 53%, out-of-state 25%, international 1% (19 countries represented). **Ethnic Representation:** Caucasian 93%, Native American 1%. **Retention and Graduation:** 75% freshmen return for sophomore year. **Faculty:** Student/faculty ratio 18:1. 486 full-time faculty, 75% hold PhDs.

ACADEMICS

Degrees: Associate's, bachelor's, doctoral, first professional, master's. **Academic Requirements:** General education including some course work in arts/fine arts, computer literacy, English (including composition), history, humanities, mathematics, sciences (biological or physical), social science, wellness. **Disciplines with Highest Percentage of Degrees Awarded:** Health professions and related sciences 17%, agriculture 14%, social sciences and history 13%, engineering/engineering technology 11%, home economics and vocational home economics 6%. **Special Study Options:** Accelerated program, cooperative (work-study) program, distance learning, double major, dual enrollment, student exchange program (domestic), honors program, independent study, internships, study abroad, teacher certification program.

FACILITIES

Housing: Coed, apartments for married students, apartments for single students, housing for disabled students, fraternities and/or sororities. **Library Holdings:** 538,358 bound volumes. 3,284 periodicals. 835,017 microforms. 2,060 audiovisuals. **Special Academic Facilities/Equipment:** Art museum, agricultural heritage museum, bio-stress lab, electron microscope, animal disease research and diagnostic lab, McCrory Gardens. **Computers:** *Recommended operating system:* Windows 95.

EXTRACURRICULARS

Activities: Choral groups, concert band, dance, drama/theater, jazz band, marching band, music ensembles, musical theater, opera, pep band, radio station, student government, student newspaper, symphony orchestra, television station, yearbook. **Organizations:** 190 registered organizations, 33 honor societies, 7 religious organizations, 4 fraternities, 3 sororities. **Athletics (Intercollegiate):** *Men:* baseball, basketball, cheerleading, cross-country, diving, football, golf, indoor track, swimming, tennis, track & field, wrestling. *Women:* basketball, cheerleading, cross-country, diving, golf, indoor track, soccer, softball, swimming, tennis, track & field, volleyball.

ADMISSIONS

Selectivity Rating: 67 (of 100). **Freshman Academic Profile:** Average high school GPA 3.3. 13% in top 10% of high school class, 36% in top 25% of high school class, 70% in top 50% of high school class. Average ACT 22, ACT middle 50% range 19-25. TOEFL required of all international applicants, minimum TOEFL 500. **Basis for Candidate Selection:** *Very important factors considered include:* class rank, secondary school record, standardized test scores. **Freshman Admission Requirements:** High school diploma or GED is required. *Academic units required/recommended:* 4 English required, 3 math required, 3 science required, 3 science lab required, 3 social studies required. **Freshman Admission Statistics:** 3,343 applied, 94% accepted. **Transfer Admission Requirements:** *Items required:* high school transcript, college transcript, statement of good standing from prior school. Minimum college GPA of 2.0 required. Lowest grade transferable C. **General Admission Information:** Application fee $20. Nonfall registration accepted. Admission may be deferred for a maximum of 1 year. Credit and/or placement offered for CEEB Advanced Placement tests.

COSTS AND FINANCIAL AID

In-state tuition $2,185. Out-of-state tuition $6,945. Room & board $3,500. Required fees $2,108. Average book expense $700. **Required Forms and Deadlines:** FAFSA. No deadline for regular filing. Priority filing deadline March 7. **Notification of Awards:** Applicants will be notified of awards on a rolling basis beginning on or about April 5. **Types of Aid:** *Need-based scholarships/grants:* Pell, SEOG, private scholarships, the school's own gift aid, United Negro College Fund, Federal Nursing, Agency awards. *Loans:* FFEL Subsidized Stafford, FFEL Unsubsidized Stafford, FFEL PLUS, Federal Perkins, Federal Nursing, college/university loans from institutional funds, alternative loans from private sources. **Student Employment:** Federal Work-Study Program available. Institutional employment available. Off-campus job opportunities are excellent. **Financial Aid Statistics:** 68% freshmen, 72% undergrads receive some form of aid. Average freshman grant $5,475. Average freshman loan $1,940. **Financial Aid Phone:** 605-688-4695.

SOUTHAMPTON COLLEGE OF LONG ISLAND UNIVERSITY

239 Montauk Highway, Southampton, NY 11968
Phone: 631-287-8200 **E-mail:** admissions@southampton.liunet.edu **CEEB Code:** 2853
Fax: 516-287-8130 **Web:** www.southampton.liu.edu **ACT Code:** 2853

This private school was founded in 1963. It has a 110-acre campus.

STUDENTS AND FACULTY

Enrollment: 3,021. **Student Body:** Male 43%, female 57%, out-of-state 27%, international 1% (20 countries represented). **Ethnic Representation:** African American 6%, Asian 2%, Caucasian 69%, Hispanic 5%, Native American 1%. **Retention and Graduation:** 89% freshmen return for sophomore year. 40% grads go on to further study within 1 year. 8% grads pursue business degrees. 1% grads pursue law degrees. 1% grads pursue medical degrees. **Faculty:** Student/faculty ratio 17:1. 64 full-time faculty, 70% hold PhDs. 100% faculty teach undergrads.

ACADEMICS

Degrees: Bachelor's, master's, post-bachelor's certificate. **Academic Requirements:** General education including some course work in arts/fine arts, English (including composition), humanities, sciences (biological or physical), social science. **Majors with Highest Enrollment:** Marine biology and biological oceanography; biopsychology; business administration/management. **Disciplines with Highest Percentage of Degrees Awarded:** Interdisciplinary studies 32%, biological life sciences 21%, liberal arts/general studies 7%, education 6%, business/marketing 5%. **Special Study Options:** Accelerated program, cooperative (work-study) program, distance learning, double major, dual enrollment, English as a second language, student exchange program (domestic), honors program, independent study, internships, liberal arts/career combination, student-designed major, study abroad, teacher certification program. Undergrads may take grad-level classes. Co-Op programs: arts, business, education, health professions, humanities, natural science, social/behavioral science, all majors. Off-campus study: United Nations, Semester at Sea. Other special programs: travel abroad through Friends World Program.

FACILITIES

Housing: Coed, all-female, apartments for single students, housing for disabled students. **Library Holdings:** 115,380 bound volumes. 665 periodicals. 140,400 microforms. 886 audiovisuals. **Special Academic Facilities/Equipment:** Art galleries, on-campus nursery school, psychobiology lab, marine station and fleet of research vessels, Silicon Graphics Computer Lab. **Computers:** School-owned computers available for student use.

EXTRACURRICULARS

Activities: Choral groups, dance, drama/theater, literary magazine, music ensembles, musical theater, radio station, student government, student newspaper, student-run film society, television station, yearbook. **Organizations:** 40 registered organizations, 5 honor societies, 2 religious organizations. **Athletics (Intercollegiate):** *Men:* basketball, lacrosse, soccer, tennis, volleyball. *Women:* basketball, soccer, softball, tennis, volleyball.

ADMISSIONS

Selectivity Rating: 67 (of 100). **Freshman Academic Profile:** Average high school GPA 3.2. 19% in top 10% of high school class, 49% in top 25% of high school class, 84% in top 50% of high school class. 87% from public high schools. Average SAT I Math 531, SAT I Math middle 50% range 480-580. Average SAT

I Verbal 551, SAT I Verbal middle 50% range 490-600. Average ACT 24, ACT middle 50% range 21-27. TOEFL required of all international applicants, minimum TOEFL 525. **Basis for Candidate Selection:** *Very important factors considered include:* secondary school record, standardized test scores, talent/ability. *Important factors considered include:* character/personal qualities, essays, extracurricular activities, interview, recommendations. *Other factors considered include:* alumni/ae relation, class rank, volunteer work, work experience. **Freshman Admission Requirements:** High school diploma or GED is required. *Academic units required/recommended:* 4 English required, 4 English recommended, 3 math required, 4 math recommended, 3 science required, 4 science recommended, 1 science lab recommended, 2 foreign language recommended, 2 social studies required, 2 social studies recommended, 2 history required, 2 history recommended, 1 elective required, 1 elective recommended. **Freshman Admission Statistics:** 1,470 applied, 62% accepted, 29% of those accepted enrolled. **Transfer Admission Requirements:** *Items required:* high school transcript, college transcript, statement of good standing from prior school. Minimum college GPA of 2.0 required. Lowest grade transferable C. **General Admission Information:** Application fee $30. Priority application deadline February 1. Early decision application deadline December 1. Nonfall registration accepted. Admission may be deferred for a maximum of 1 year. Credit and/or placement offered for CEEB Advanced Placement tests.

COSTS AND FINANCIAL AID

Average book expense $800. **Required Forms and Deadlines:** FAFSA, institution's own financial aid form and state aid form. No deadline for regular filing. **Notification of Awards:** Applicants will be notified of awards on a rolling basis beginning on or about February 10. **Types of Aid:** *Need-based scholarships/grants:* Pell, SEOG, state scholarships/grants, private scholarships, the school's own gift aid, Center for Creative Retirement Awards for nontraditional students. *Loans:* Direct Subsidized Stafford, Direct Unsubsidized Stafford, Direct PLUS, Federal Perkins. **Student Employment:** Federal Work-Study Program available. Institutional employment available. Off-campus job opportunities are good. **Financial Aid Statistics:** 75% freshmen, 74% undergrads receive some form of aid. Average income from on-campus job $700. **Financial Aid Phone:** 516-287-8321.

SOUTHEAST MISSOURI STATE UNIVERSITY

One University Plaza, Mail Stop 3550, Cape Girardeau, MO 63701
Phone: 573-651-2590 **E-mail:** admissions@semo.edu **CEEB Code:** 6655
Fax: 573-651-5936 **Web:** www.semo.edu **ACT Code:** 2366

This public school was founded in 1873. It has a 200-acre campus.

STUDENTS AND FACULTY

Enrollment: 8,351. **Student Body:** Male 41%, female 59%, out-of-state 13%, international 2%. **Ethnic Representation:** African American 7%, Asian 1%, Caucasian 91%, Hispanic 1%. **Retention and Graduation:** 73% freshmen return for sophomore year. 24% freshmen graduate within 4 years. **Faculty:** Student/faculty ratio 18:1. 388 full-time faculty, 85% hold PhDs. 94% faculty teach undergrads.

ACADEMICS

Degrees: Associate's, bachelor's, certificate, master's, post-master's certificate. **Academic Requirements:** General education including some course work in arts/fine arts, English (including composition), history, humanities, mathematics, sciences (biological or physical). **Classes:** 20-29 students in an average class. **Majors with Highest Enrollment:** Communications studies/speech communication and rhetoric; elementary education and teaching; business administration/management. **Disciplines with Highest Percentage of Degrees Awarded:** Education 21%, business/marketing 17%, protective services/public administration 7%, liberal arts/general studies 7%, communications/communication technologies 6%. **Special Study Options:** Accelerated program, distance learning, double major, dual enrollment, English as a second language, student exchange program (domestic), honors program, independent study, internships, liberal arts/career combination, student-designed major, study abroad, teacher certification program.

FACILITIES

Housing: Coed, fraternities and/or sororities, apartments for students with dependents. **Library Holdings:** 411,992 bound volumes. 2,781 periodicals. 1,253,490 microforms. 9,400 audiovisuals. **Special Academic Facilities/Equipment:** University Museum, Center for Faulkner Studies, Center for Earthquake Studies, Center for Teaching & Learning, Clinical Education Lab, Writing Center, university demonstration farm, bird sanctuary, 4 corporate video studios, 2 radio stations. **Computers:** *Recommended operating system:* Windows 95. School-owned computers available for student use.

EXTRACURRICULARS

Activities: Choral groups, concert band, dance, drama/theater, jazz band, literary magazine, marching band, music ensembles, musical theater, opera, pep band, radio station, student government, student newspaper, symphony orchestra. **Organizations:** 122 registered organizations, 8 honor societies, 12 religious organizations, 11 fraternities (14% men join), 9 sororities (12% women join). **Athletics (Intercollegiate):** *Men:* baseball, basketball, cross-country, football, golf, indoor track, track & field. *Women:* basketball, cross-country, gymnastics, indoor track, soccer, softball, tennis, track & field, volleyball.

ADMISSIONS

Selectivity Rating: 71 (of 100). **Freshman Academic Profile:** Average high school GPA 3.3. 13% in top 10% of high school class, 35% in top 25% of high school class, 67% in top 50% of high school class. Average ACT 22, ACT middle 50% range 19-25. TOEFL required of all international applicants, minimum TOEFL 500. **Basis for Candidate Selection:** *Very important factors considered include:* secondary school record, standardized test scores. *Other factors considered include:* class rank. **Freshman Admission Requirements:** High school diploma or GED is required. *Academic units required/recommended:* 17 total required; 22 total recommended; 4 English required, 4 English recommended, 3 math required, 4 math recommended, 3 science required, 4 science recommended, 1 science lab required, 1 science lab recommended, 2 foreign language recommended, 2 social studies required, 2 social studies recommended, 1 history required, 1 history recommended, 3 elective required, 3 elective recommended. **Freshman Admission Statistics:** 3,197 applied, 57% accepted, 86% of those accepted enrolled. **Transfer Admission Requirements:** *Items required:* college transcript, standardized test scores. Minimum college GPA of 2.0 required. Lowest grade transferable D. **General Admission Information:** Application fee $20. Priority application deadline December 15. Regular application deadline August 1. Nonfall registration accepted. Admission may be deferred for a maximum of 1 year. Credit offered for CEEB Advanced Placement tests.

COSTS AND FINANCIAL AID

In-state tuition $3,744. Out-of-state tuition $6,819. Room & board $4,938. Required fees $291. Average book expense $350. **Required Forms and Deadlines:** FAFSA. No deadline for regular filing. **Notification of Awards:** Applicants will be notified of awards on a rolling basis beginning on or about April 1. **Types of Aid:** *Need-based scholarships/grants:* Pell, SEOG, state scholarships/grants, private scholarships, the school's own gift aid. *Loans:* FFEL Subsidized Stafford, FFEL Unsubsidized Stafford, FFEL PLUS, Federal Perkins, state loans. **Student Employment:** Federal Work-Study Program available. Institutional employment available. Off-campus job opportunities are excellent. **Financial Aid Statistics:** 47% freshmen, 42% undergrads receive some form of aid. Average freshman grant $3,496. Average freshman loan $4,580. Average income from on-campus job $1,141. **Financial Aid Phone:** 573-651-2253.

SOUTHEASTERN COLLEGE OF THE ASSEMBLIES OF GOD

1000 Longfellow Boulevard, Lakeland, FL 33801-6099
Phone: 863-667-5081 **E-mail:** admission@secollege.edu **CEEB Code:** 5621
Fax: 863-667-5200 **Web:** www.secollege.edu **ACT Code:** 754

This private school, which is affiliated with the Assemblies of God Church, was founded in 1935. It has a 60-acre campus.

STUDENTS AND FACULTY

Enrollment: 1,078. **Student Body:** Male 51%, female 49%, out-of-state 44%, international 1% (18 countries represented). **Ethnic Representation:** African American 4%, Asian 1%, Caucasian 86%, Hispanic 8%, Native American 1%. **Retention and Graduation:** 65% freshmen return for sophomore year. 17% freshmen graduate within 4 years. **Faculty:** Student/faculty ratio 28:1. 44 full-time faculty, 59% hold PhDs. 100% faculty teach undergrads.

ACADEMICS

Degrees: Bachelor's. **Academic Requirements:** General education including some course work in English (including composition), foreign languages, humanities, mathematics, sciences (biological or physical), social science, religion. **Classes:** 10-19 students in an average class. **Majors with Highest Enrollment:** Theological studies and religious vocations; youth ministry;

psychology, general. **Disciplines with Highest Percentage of Degrees Awarded:** Philosophy/religion/theology 29%, education 27%, psychology 15%, business/marketing 8%, communications/communication technologies 7%. **Special Study Options:** Accelerated program, double major, dual enrollment, independent study, internships, study abroad, teacher certification program, learning disabilities services.

FACILITIES

Housing: Coed, all-female, all-male. **Library Holdings:** 94,167 bound volumes. 600 periodicals. 974 microforms. 2,390 audiovisuals. **Special Academic Facilities/Equipment:** Art museum, environmental studies institute, center for teaching and learning, writing center, clinical education lab, farm. **Computers:** *Recommended operating system:* Windows 95. School-owned computers available for student use.

EXTRACURRICULARS

Activities: Choral groups, concert band, drama/theater, jazz band, literary magazine, marching band, music ensembles, opera, radio station, student government, student newspaper, television station, yearbook. **Organizations:** 18 registered organizations, 3 honor societies. **Athletics (Intercollegiate):** *Men:* baseball, basketball, golf, soccer. *Women:* basketball, volleyball.

ADMISSIONS

Selectivity Rating: 63 (of 100). **Freshman Academic Profile:** TOEFL required of all international applicants, minimum TOEFL 500. **Freshman Admission Requirements:** High school diploma or GED is required. **Freshman Admission Statistics:** 361 applied, 83% accepted, 78% of those accepted enrolled. **Transfer Admission Requirements:** *Items required:* high school transcript, college transcript, essay, standardized test scores, statement of good standing from prior school. Lowest grade transferable C. **General Admission Information:** Application fee $40. Regular application deadline August 1. Nonfall registration accepted. Admission may be deferred. Credit offered for CEEB Advanced Placement tests.

COSTS AND FINANCIAL AID

Required Forms and Deadlines: FAFSA, institution's own financial aid form and state aid form. No deadline for regular filing. Priority filing deadline May 1. **Notification of Awards:** Applicants will be notified of awards on a rolling basis beginning on or about May 10. **Types of Aid:** *Need-based scholarships/grants:* Pell, SEOG, state scholarships/grants, private scholarships, the school's own gift aid. *Loans:* FFEL Subsidized Stafford, FFEL Unsubsidized Stafford, FFEL PLUS, Federal Perkins. **Student Employment:** Federal Work-Study Program available. Institutional employment available. Off-campus job opportunities are excellent. **Financial Aid Phone:** 863-667-5026.

SOUTHEASTERN LOUISIANA UNIVERSITY

SLU 10752, Hammond, LA 70402
Phone: 985-549-2066 **E-mail:** jmercante@selu.edu
Fax: 985-549-5632 **Web:** www.selu.edu **ACT Code:** 1608

This public school was founded in 1925. It has a 375-acre campus.

STUDENTS AND FACULTY

Enrollment: 13,388. **Student Body:** Male 38%, female 62%, out-of-state 2%, international 1% (41 countries represented). **Ethnic Representation:** African American 15%, Asian 1%, Caucasian 81%, Hispanic 2%, Native American 1%. **Retention and Graduation:** 68% freshmen return for sophomore year. 5% freshmen graduate within 4 years. **Faculty:** Student/faculty ratio 26:1. 477 full-time faculty, 57% hold PhDs. 95% faculty teach undergrads.

ACADEMICS

Degrees: Associate's, bachelor's, master's. **Academic Requirements:** General education including some course work in arts/fine arts, computer literacy, English (including composition), foreign languages, history, humanities, mathematics, philosophy, sciences (biological or physical), social science. **Classes:** 20-29 students in an average class. **Majors with Highest Enrollment:** Nursing/registered nurse training (RN, ASN, BSN, MSN); elementary education and teaching; biology/biological sciences, general. **Disciplines with Highest Percentage of Degrees Awarded:** Business/marketing 30%, education 18%, protective services/public administration 8%, liberal arts/general studies 8%, health professions and related sciences 7%. **Special Study Options:** Cross registration, distance learning, double major, student exchange program (domestic), honors program, independent study, internships, liberal arts/career combination, study abroad, teacher certification program.

FACILITIES

Housing: Coed, apartments for married students, apartments for single students, fraternities and/or sororities. **Library Holdings:** 572,563 bound volumes. 2,381 periodicals. 769,303 microforms. 48,752 audiovisuals. **Computers:** School-owned computers available for student use.

EXTRACURRICULARS

Activities: Choral groups, dance, drama/theater, pep band, radio station, student government, student newspaper, television station, yearbook. **Organizations:** 74 registered organizations, 9 honor societies, 6 religious organizations, 9 fraternities (5% men join), 8 sororities (3% women join). **Athletics (Intercollegiate):** *Men:* baseball, basketball, cheerleading, cross-country, golf, indoor track, tennis, track & field. *Women:* basketball, cheerleading, cross-country, indoor track, soccer, softball, tennis, track & field, volleyball.

ADMISSIONS

Selectivity Rating: 65 (of 100). **Freshman Academic Profile:** Average ACT 20, ACT middle 50% range 17-22. TOEFL required of all international applicants, minimum TOEFL 500. **Basis for Candidate Selection:** *Other factors considered include:* class rank, secondary school record, standardized test scores. **Freshman Admission Requirements:** High school diploma or GED is required. *Academic units required/recommended:* 18 total recommended; 4 English recommended, 3 math recommended, 3 science recommended, 3 social studies recommended, 5 elective recommended. **Freshman Admission Statistics:** 3,480 applied, 91% accepted, 80% of those accepted enrolled. **Transfer Admission Requirements:** *Items required:* college transcript, statement of good standing from prior school. Minimum college GPA of 2.0 required. Lowest grade transferable D. **General Admission Information:** Application fee $20. Regular application deadline July 15. Nonfall registration accepted. Admission may be deferred for a maximum of 1 year. Credit and/or placement offered for CEEB Advanced Placement tests.

COSTS AND FINANCIAL AID

In-state tuition $2,618. Out-of-state tuition $7,946. Room & board $3,720. Required fees $0. Average book expense $1,000. **Required Forms and Deadlines:** FAFSA and institution's own financial aid form. No deadline for regular filing. Priority filing deadline May 1. **Notification of Awards:** Applicants will be notified of awards on a rolling basis beginning on or about March 1. **Types of Aid:** *Need-based scholarships/grants:* Pell, SEOG, state scholarships/grants, private scholarships, the school's own gift aid, Federal Nursing. *Non need based (college administered):* state, academic, creative arts/performance, special achievments/activities, special characteristics, athletic. *Loans:* FFEL Subsidized Stafford, FFEL Unsubsidized Stafford, FFEL PLUS, Federal Perkins, college/university loans from institutional funds. **Student Employment:** Federal Work-Study Program available. Institutional employment available. Off-campus job opportunities are good. **Financial Aid Statistics:** 34% freshmen, 62% undergrads receive some form of aid. Average freshman grant $1,278. Average freshman loan $1,838. Average income from on-campus job $685. **Financial Aid Phone:** 985-549-2244.

SOUTHEASTERN OKLAHOMA STATE UNIVERSITY

1405 North 4th Avenue, PMB 4225, Durant, OK 74701-0609
Phone: 580-745-2060 **E-mail:** admissions@sosu.edu **CEEB Code:** 6657
Fax: 580-745-7502 **Web:** www.sosu.edu **ACT Code:** 3438

This public school was founded in 1909. It has a 165-acre campus.

STUDENTS AND FACULTY

Enrollment: 3,637. **Student Body:** Male 47%, female 53%, out-of-state 22%, international 2% (25 countries represented). **Ethnic Representation:** African American 5%, Caucasian 65%, Hispanic 1%, Native American 28%. **Retention and Graduation:** 51% freshmen return for sophomore year. 15% freshmen graduate within 4 years. **Faculty:** Student/faculty ratio 19:1. 155 full-time faculty, 66% hold PhDs. 100% faculty teach undergrads.

ACADEMICS

Degrees: Bachelor's, master's, post-master's certificate. **Academic Requirements:** General education including some course work in computer literacy, English (including composition), history, mathematics, sciences (biological or physical), social science. **Classes:** 20-29 students in an average class. 20-29 students in an average lab/discussion section. **Disciplines with Highest Percentage of Degrees Awarded:** Education 22%, business/marketing 16%, engineering/engineering technology 9%, psychology 8%, communications/communication technologies 7%. **Special Study Options:** Distance learning, double major, honors program, independent study, internships, teacher certification program.

FACILITIES

Housing: Coed, all-female, all-male, apartments for married students, housing for disabled students. **Library Holdings:** 187,971 bound volumes. 671 periodicals. 457,438 microforms. 5,291 audiovisuals. **Computers:** School-owned computers available for student use.

EXTRACURRICULARS

Activities: Choral groups, concert band, dance, drama/theater, jazz band, literary magazine, marching band, music ensembles, musical theater, opera, pep band, radio station, student government, student newspaper, yearbook. **Organizations:** 70 registered organizations, 11 honor societies, 11 religious organizations, 4 fraternities (4% men join), 3 sororities (6% women join). **Athletics (Intercollegiate):** *Men:* baseball, basketball, football, softball, tennis, volleyball. *Women:* basketball, cross-country, softball, tennis, volleyball.

ADMISSIONS

Selectivity Rating: 66 (of 100). **Freshman Academic Profile:** Average high school GPA 3.2. 14% in top 10% of high school class, 41% in top 25% of high school class, 78% in top 50% of high school class. 99% from public high schools. Average ACT 20, ACT middle 50% range 18-23. TOEFL required of all international applicants, minimum TOEFL 550. **Basis for Candidate Selection:** *Very important factors considered include:* class rank, secondary school record, standardized test scores. *Other factors considered include:* interview, recommendations, state residency, talent/ability. **Freshman Admission Requirements:** High school diploma or GED is required. *Academic units required/recommended:* 4 English required, 3 math required, 2 science required, 2 science lab required, 2 history required, 3 elective required. **Freshman Admission Statistics:** 1,021 applied, 68% accepted, 86% of those accepted enrolled. **Transfer Admission Requirements:** *Items required:* college transcript, statement of good standing from prior school. Minimum college GPA of 2.0 required. Lowest grade transferable D. **General Admission Information:** Application fee $20. Nonfall registration accepted. Credit offered for CEEB Advanced Placement tests.

COSTS AND FINANCIAL AID

In-state tuition $1,682. Out-of-state tuition $4,674. Room & board $2,670. Required fees $722. Average book expense $600. **Required Forms and Deadlines:** FAFSA and institution's own financial aid form. No deadline for regular filing. Priority filing deadline March 1. **Notification of Awards:** Applicants will be notified of awards on a rolling basis beginning on or about May 1. **Types of Aid:** *Need-based scholarships/grants:* Pell, SEOG, state scholarships/grants. *Loans:* FFEL Subsidized Stafford, FFEL Unsubsidized Stafford, FFEL PLUS, Federal Perkins. **Student Employment:** Federal Work-Study Program available. Institutional employment available. Off-campus job opportunities are good. **Financial Aid Statistics:** 77% freshmen, 76% undergrads receive some form of aid. Average freshman grant $1,000. Average freshman loan $2,000. Average income from on-campus job $1,000. **Financial Aid Phone:** 405-745-2186.

SOUTHEASTERN UNIVERSITY

501 Eye Street, SW, Washington, DC 20024
Phone: 202-265-5343 **E-mail:** admissions@admin.seu.edu
Fax: 202-488-8093 **Web:** www.seu.edu

This private school was founded in 1879. It has a 1-acre campus.

STUDENTS AND FACULTY

Enrollment: 513. **Student Body:** Male 31%, female 69%, out-of-state 44%, international 13% (51 countries represented). **Ethnic Representation:** African American 84%, Asian 4%, Caucasian 2%, Hispanic 9%. **Retention and Graduation:** 50% freshmen return for sophomore year. 8% freshmen graduate within 4 years. **Faculty:** Student/faculty ratio 11:1. 16 full-time faculty, 56% hold PhDs. 100% faculty teach undergrads.

ACADEMICS

Degrees: Associate's, bachelor's, certificate, master's. **Academic Requirements:** General education including some course work in arts/fine arts, computer literacy, English (including composition), humanities, mathematics, social science. **Classes:** Under 10 students in an average class. **Disciplines with Highest Percentage of Degrees Awarded:** Business/marketing 38%, computer and information sciences 30%, liberal arts/general studies 28%, protective services/public administration 4%. **Special Study Options:** Accelerated program, cooperative (work-study) program, double major, English as a second language, honors program, independent study, internships, weekend college.

FACILITIES

Housing: No housing available. **Library Holdings:** 57,000 bound volumes. 300 periodicals. 2,000 microforms. 273 audiovisuals. **Computers:** School-owned computers available for student use.

EXTRACURRICULARS

Activities: Student government, student newspaper. **Organizations:** 6 registered organizations, 2 fraternities (2% men join), 2 sororities (2% women join).

ADMISSIONS

Selectivity Rating: 63 (of 100). **Freshman Academic Profile:** 99% from public high schools. TOEFL required of all international applicants, minimum TOEFL 500. **Basis for Candidate Selection:** *Other factors considered include:* alumni/ae relation, character/personal qualities, class rank, essays, interview, recommendations, secondary school record, standardized test scores, talent/ability. **Freshman Admission Requirements:** High school diploma or GED is required. *Academic units required/recommended:* 4 English recommended, 3 math recommended, 2 science recommended, 2 foreign language recommended, 2 social studies recommended, 2 history recommended. **Transfer Admission Requirements:** *Items required:* high school transcript, college transcript. Minimum high school GPA of 2.0 required. Minimum college GPA of 2.0 required. Lowest grade transferable C. **General Admission Information:** Application fee $45. Nonfall registration accepted. Admission may be deferred for a maximum of 1 year. Credit and/or placement offered for CEEB Advanced Placement tests.

COSTS AND FINANCIAL AID

Tuition $8,100. Required fees $525. **Required Forms and Deadlines:** FAFSA and institution's own financial aid form. No deadline for regular filing. Priority filing deadline August 15. **Notification of Awards:** Applicants will be notified of awards on a rolling basis beginning on or about August 15. **Types of Aid:** *Need-based scholarships/grants:* Pell, SEOG, state scholarships/grants, private scholarships, the school's own gift aid. *Loans:* FFEL Subsidized Stafford, FFEL Unsubsidized Stafford, FFEL PLUS, Federal Perkins. **Student Employment:** Federal Work-Study Program available. Institutional employment available. Off-campus job opportunities are excellent. **Financial Aid Statistics:** 65% freshmen, 43% undergrads receive some form of aid. Average freshman grant $2,100. Average freshman loan $2,625. **Financial Aid Phone:** 202-488-8162.

SOUTHERN ADVENTIST UNIVERSITY

PO Box 370, Collegedale, TN 37315
Phone: 423-238-2844 **E-mail:** admissions@southern.edu **CEEB Code:** 3518
Fax: 423-238-3005 **Web:** www.southern.edu **ACT Code:** 4006

This private school, which is affiliated with the Seventh-Day Adventist Church, was founded in 1892. It has a 1,000-acre campus.

STUDENTS AND FACULTY

Enrollment: 2,199. **Student Body:** Male 46%, female 54%, out-of-state 68%, international 4%. **Ethnic Representation:** African American 8%, Asian 4%, Caucasian 77%, Hispanic 11%, Native American 1%. **Retention and Graduation:** 71% freshmen return for sophomore year. 31% freshmen graduate within 4 years. 15% grads go on to further study within 1 year. 1% grads pursue business degrees. 4% grads pursue medical degrees. **Faculty:** Student/faculty ratio 16:1. 118 full-time faculty, 62% hold PhDs. 100% faculty teach undergrads.

ACADEMICS

Degrees: Associate's, bachelor's, certificate, master's. **Academic Requirements:** General education including some course work in arts/fine arts, English (including composition), history, mathematics, philosophy, sciences (biological or physical), social science. **Classes:** 20-29 students in an average class. 10-19 students in an average lab/discussion section. **Majors with Highest Enrollment:** Nursing/registered nurse training (RN, ASN, BSN, MSN); education, general; theology/theological studies. **Disciplines with Highest Percentage of Degrees Awarded:** Business/marketing 16%, health professions and related sciences 12%, visual and performing arts 10%, philosophy/religion/theology 10%, education 8%. **Special Study Options:** Double major, dual enrollment, English as a second language, honors program, independent study, internships, study abroad, teacher certification program.

FACILITIES

Housing: All-female, all-male, apartments for married students. **Library Holdings:** 144,846 bound volumes. 1,096 periodicals. 451,365 microforms.

5,045 audiovisuals. **Special Academic Facilities/Equipment:** Near-Eastern archaeology teaching collection. **Computers:** School-owned computers available for student use.

EXTRACURRICULARS

Activities: Choral groups, concert band, drama/theater, music ensembles, radio station, student government, student newspaper, student-run film society, symphony orchestra, television station, yearbook. **Organizations:** 30 registered organizations, 7 honor societies, 3 religious organizations.

ADMISSIONS

Selectivity Rating: 73 (of 100). **Freshman Academic Profile:** Average high school GPA 3.3. 16% from public high schools. SAT I Math middle 50% range 20-28. SAT I Verbal middle 50% range 24-32. Average ACT 22, ACT middle 50% range 19-26. TOEFL required of all international applicants, minimum TOEFL 550. **Basis for Candidate Selection:** *Very important factors considered include:* character/personal qualities, secondary school record, standardized test scores. *Important factors considered include:* interview, religious affiliation/commitment. *Other factors considered include:* alumni/ae relation, class rank, extracurricular activities, minority status, recommendations, talent/ability. **Freshman Admission Requirements:** High school diploma or GED is required. *Academic units required/recommended:* 18 total required; 24 total recommended; 3 English required, 4 English recommended, 2 math required, 3 math recommended, 2 science required, 3 science recommended, 1 science lab required, 2 science lab recommended, 2 foreign language recommended, 1 social studies required, 1 social studies recommended, 2 history required, 2 history recommended, 7 elective required, 7 elective recommended. **Freshman Admission Statistics:** 1,293 applied, 76% accepted, 49% of those accepted enrolled. **Transfer Admission Requirements:** *Items required:* high school transcript, college transcript, standardized test scores. Minimum high school GPA of 2.0 required. Minimum college GPA of 2.0 required. Lowest grade transferable D-. **General Admission Information:** Application fee $25. Regular application deadline September 8. Nonfall registration accepted. Admission may be deferred for a maximum of 1 year. Credit and/or placement offered for CEEB Advanced Placement tests.

COSTS AND FINANCIAL AID

Tuition $12,400. Room & board $4,280. Required fees $400. Average book expense $900. **Required Forms and Deadlines:** FAFSA and state aid form. No deadline for regular filing. Priority filing deadline March 31. **Notification of Awards:** Applicants will be notified of awards on a rolling basis beginning on or about April 15. **Types of Aid:** *Need-based scholarships/grants:* Pell, SEOG, state scholarships/grants, private scholarships, the school's own gift aid. *Loans:* FFEL Subsidized Stafford, FFEL Unsubsidized Stafford, FFEL PLUS, Federal Perkins, Federal Nursing, college/university loans from institutional funds. **Student Employment:** Federal Work-Study Program available. Institutional employment available. Off-campus job opportunities are excellent. **Financial Aid Statistics:** 65% freshmen, 50% undergrads receive some form of aid. Average freshman grant $3,541. Average freshman loan $2,182. Average income from on-campus job $2,000. **Financial Aid Phone:** 423-238-2835.

SOUTHERN ARKANSAS UNIVERSITY

100 E. University, Magnolia, AR 71753
Phone: 870-235-4040 **E-mail:** muleriders@saumag.edu **CEEB Code:** 142
Web: www.saumag.edu **ACT Code:** 142

This public school was founded in 1909. It has a 731-acre campus.

STUDENTS AND FACULTY

Enrollment: 2,855. **Student Body:** Male 44%, female 56%, out-of-state 21%, international 4%. **Ethnic Representation:** African American 27%, Caucasian 71%, Hispanic 1%. **Retention and Graduation:** 64% freshmen return for sophomore year. 12% freshmen graduate within 4 years. 1% grads pursue business degrees. 1% grads pursue law degrees. 1% grads pursue medical degrees. **Faculty:** Student/faculty ratio 19:1. 126 full-time faculty, 61% hold PhDs. 100% faculty teach undergrads.

ACADEMICS

Degrees: Associate's, bachelor's, master's. **Academic Requirements:** General education including some course work in arts/fine arts, English (including composition), history, humanities, mathematics, sciences (biological or physical), social science. **Classes:** 20-29 students in an average class. 10-19 students in an average lab/discussion section. **Disciplines with Highest Percentage of Degrees Awarded:** Business/marketing 30%; education 20%; communications/communication technologies 6%; protective services/public administration 6%; agriculture 6%. **Special Study Options:** Distance learning, double major, dual enrollment, internships, teacher certification program.

FACILITIES

Housing: Coed, all-female, all-male. **Library Holdings:** 197,635 bound volumes. 1,235 periodicals. 989,591 microforms. 12,223 audiovisuals. **Computers:** School-owned computers available for student use.

EXTRACURRICULARS

Activities: Choral groups, concert band, drama/theater, jazz band, marching band, music ensembles, pep band, radio station, student government, student newspaper, yearbook. **Organizations:** 80 registered organizations, 9 honor societies, 6 religious organizations, 8 fraternities (11% men join), 7 sororities (10% women join). **Athletics (Intercollegiate):** *Men:* baseball, basketball, cheerleading, cross-country, football, golf, rodeo, swimming, track & field. *Women:* basketball, cheerleading, cross-country, rodeo, softball, swimming, track & field, volleyball.

ADMISSIONS

Selectivity Rating: 63 (of 100). **Freshman Academic Profile:** 39% in top 25% of high school class, 72% in top 50% of high school class. 99% from public high schools. Average ACT 21, ACT middle 50% range 18-23. TOEFL required of all international applicants, minimum TOEFL 500. **Basis for Candidate Selection:** *Very important factors considered include:* class rank, secondary school record, standardized test scores. *Other factors considered include:* recommendations. **Freshman Admission Requirements:** High school diploma or GED is required. *Academic units required/recommended:* 4 English recommended, 3 math recommended, 3 science recommended, 3 science lab recommended, 3 social studies recommended. **Freshman Admission Statistics:** 1,166 applied, 99% accepted, 49% of those accepted enrolled. **Transfer Admission Requirements:** *Items required:* college transcript, statement of good standing from prior school. Lowest grade transferable C. **General Admission Information:** Regular application deadline August 28. Nonfall registration accepted. Admission may be deferred. Credit offered for CEEB Advanced Placement tests.

COSTS AND FINANCIAL AID

In-state tuition $2,784. Out-of-state tuition $4,272. Room & board $3,220. Required fees $280. Average book expense $800. **Required Forms and Deadlines:** FAFSA. Priority filing deadline July 2. **Notification of Awards:** Applicants will be notified of awards on a rolling basis beginning on or about April 15. **Types of Aid:** *Need-based scholarships/grants:* Pell, SEOG, state scholarships/grants, private scholarships, the school's own gift aid. *Loans:* FFEL Subsidized Stafford, FFEL Unsubsidized Stafford, FFEL PLUS, Federal Perkins. **Student Employment:** Federal Work-Study Program available. Institutional employment available. Off-campus job opportunities are fair. **Financial Aid Statistics:** 52% freshmen, 56% undergrads receive some form of aid. Average freshman grant $2,423. Average freshman loan $1,818. Average income from on-campus job $2,200. **Financial Aid Phone:** 870-235-4023.

SOUTHERN CONNECTICUT STATE UNIVERSITY

SCSU-Admissions House, 131 Farnham Avenue, New Haven, CT 06515-1202
Phone: 203-392-5656 **E-mail:** adminfo@scsu.ctstateu.edu **CEEB Code:** 3662
Fax: 203-392-5727 **Web:** www.southernct.edu

This public school was founded in 1893. It has a 168-acre campus.

STUDENTS AND FACULTY

Enrollment: 7,624. **Student Body:** Male 41%, female 59%, out-of-state 5%, international 2% (39 countries represented). **Ethnic Representation:** African American 11%, Asian 2%, Caucasian 72%, Hispanic 5%. **Retention and Graduation:** 71% freshmen return for sophomore year. 18% freshmen graduate within 4 years. 27% grads go on to further study within 1 year. **Faculty:** 85% faculty teach undergrads.

ACADEMICS

Degrees: Bachelor's, master's, post-master's certificate. **Academic Requirements:** General education including some course work in arts/fine arts, English (including composition), foreign languages, history, humanities, mathematics, philosophy, sciences (biological or physical), social science. **Special Study Options:** Accelerated program, cooperative (work-study) program, cross registration, double major, student exchange program (domestic), external degree program, honors program, independent study, internships, liberal arts/career combination, student-designed major, study abroad, teacher certification program. Undergrads may take grad-level classes. Cooperative education programs in arts, business, computer science, education, health professions, humanities, natural science, social/behavioral science, and technologies. Exchange programs with other members of state university system. Study abroad in England, France, and Spain. Evening division.

FACILITIES

Housing: Coed, apartments for single students, housing for disabled students. Freshmen have their own residence halls. Students must be 19 or older to live in upper-classman residence halls. **Library Holdings:** 1,100,000 bound volumes. 2,567 periodicals. 789,998 microforms. 4,418 audiovisuals. **Special Academic Facilities/Equipment:** Art gallery, language lab, child development center, communication disorders center, planetarium and observatory, closed-circuit TV center. **Computers:** *Recommended operating system:* Mac. School-owned computers available for student use.

EXTRACURRICULARS

Activities: Choral groups, concert band, drama/theater, literary magazine, marching band, music ensembles, pep band, radio station, student government, student newspaper, yearbook. **Organizations:** 63 registered organizations, 3 religious organizations, 2 fraternities, 4 sororities (1% women join). **Athletics (Intercollegiate):** *Men:* baseball, basketball, cross-country, football, golf, gymnastics, ice hockey, indoor track, rugby, soccer, softball, swimming, track & field, volleyball, wrestling. *Women:* basketball, cheerleading, cross-country, field hockey, golf, gymnastics, indoor track, rugby, soccer, softball, swimming, track & field, volleyball.

ADMISSIONS

Selectivity Rating: 75 (of 100). **Freshman Academic Profile:** 5% in top 10% of high school class, 22% in top 25% of high school class, 57% in top 50% of high school class. 88% from public high schools. Average SAT I Math 451, SAT I Math middle 50% range 440-530. Average SAT I Verbal 466, SAT I Verbal middle 50% range 460-540. TOEFL required of all international applicants, minimum TOEFL 525. **Basis for Candidate Selection:** *Very important factors considered include:* class rank, secondary school record. *Important factors considered include:* essays, extracurricular activities, recommendations, standardized test scores. *Other factors considered include:* minority status, talent/ability. **Freshman Admission Requirements:** High school diploma or GED is required. *Academic units required/recommended:* 15 total required; 4 English required, 3 math required, 2 science required, 2 foreign language required, 2 social studies required, 2 history required. **Freshman Admission Statistics:** 3,607 applied, 70% accepted, 44% of those accepted enrolled. **Transfer Admission Requirements:** *Items required:* college transcript, essay, statement of good standing from prior school. Minimum college GPA of 2.0 required. Lowest grade transferable C-. **General Admission Information:** Application fee $40. Regular application deadline May 1. Nonfall registration accepted. Admission may be deferred. Credit offered for CEEB Advanced Placement tests.

COSTS AND FINANCIAL AID

Out-of-state tuition $6,874. Room & board $5,934. Required fees $1,905. Average book expense $750. **Required Forms and Deadlines:** FAFSA, institution's own financial aid form, and business/farm supplement. Financial aid filing deadline April 15. Priority filing deadline April 15. **Notification of Awards:** Applicants will be notified of awards on a rolling basis beginning on or about April 21. **Types of Aid:** *Need-based scholarships/grants:* Pell, SEOG, state scholarships/grants, the school's own gift aid. *Loans:* FFEL Subsidized Stafford, FFEL Unsubsidized Stafford, FFEL PLUS, Federal Perkins. **Student Employment:** Federal Work-Study Program available. Institutional employment available. Off-campus job opportunities are good. **Financial Aid Statistics:** 58% freshmen, 67% undergrads receive some form of aid. Average freshman grant $2,600. Average freshman loan $2,625. Average income from on-campus job $1,400. **Financial Aid Phone:** 203-392-5222.

SOUTHERN ILLINOIS UNIVERSITY—CARBONDALE

Admissions & Records, Carbondale, IL 62901-4701
Phone: 618-453-4381 **E-mail:** admrec@siuc.edu **CEEB Code:** 1726
Fax: 618-453-3250 **Web:** www.siuc.edu **ACT Code:** 1144

This public school was founded in 1869. It has a 1,128-acre campus.

STUDENTS AND FACULTY

Enrollment: 16,863. **Student Body:** Male 56%, female 44%, out-of-state 15%, international 3% (120 countries represented). **Ethnic Representation:** African American 13%, Asian 1%, Caucasian 69%, Hispanic 3%. **Retention and Graduation:** 32% grads go on to further study within 1 year. **Faculty:** Student/faculty ratio 17:1. 894 full-time faculty, 75% hold PhDs. 87% faculty teach undergrads.

ACADEMICS

Degrees: Associate's, bachelor's, doctoral, first professional, first professional certificate, master's, post-bachelor's certificate, post-master's certificate. **Academic Requirements:** General education including some course work in arts/fine arts, English (including composition), humanities, mathematics, sciences (biological or physical), social science, human health, integrative studies, interdisciplinary & multicultural studies. **Classes:** 20-29 students in an average class. 10-19 students in an average lab/discussion section. **Majors with Highest Enrollment:** Trade and industrial teacher education; electrical and electronic engineering technologies/technicians; hospital and health care facilities administration/management. **Disciplines with Highest Percentage of Degrees Awarded:** Education 22%, engineering/engineering technology 13%, business/marketing 10%, health professions and related sciences 8%, protective services/public administration 6%. **Special Study Options:** Accelerated program, cooperative (work-study) program, distance learning, double major, dual enrollment, English as a second language, honors program, independent study, internships, study abroad, teacher certification program.

FACILITIES

Housing: Coed, all-female, all-male, apartments for married students, housing for disabled students, fraternities and/or sororities. Many privately owned facilities are within walking distance of the campus. **Library Holdings:** 4,165,239 bound volumes. 18,271 periodicals. 4,242,929 microforms. 371,180 audiovisuals. **Special Academic Facilities/Equipment:** Art, natural history, and science museums, outdoor education center, Center for Crime Studies, advertising and public relations agencies, child development lab, community human services center, airport training facility, archaeological research center, fisheries and wildlife research labs, coal research center, electron microscopy center. **Computers:** School-owned computers available for student use.

EXTRACURRICULARS

Activities: Choral groups, concert band, dance, drama/theater, jazz band, literary magazine, marching band, music ensembles, musical theater, opera, pep band, radio station, student government, student newspaper, television station. **Organizations:** 375 registered organizations, 30 honor societies, 25 religious organizations, 12 fraternities (6% men join), 9 sororities (5% women join). **Athletics (Intercollegiate):** *Men:* baseball, basketball, cheerleading, cross-country, diving, football, golf, indoor track, rodeo, swimming, tennis, track & field. *Women:* basketball, cheerleading, cross-country, diving, golf, indoor track, softball, swimming, tennis, track & field, volleyball.

ADMISSIONS

Selectivity Rating: 70 (of 100). **Freshman Academic Profile:** 9% in top 10% of high school class, 26% in top 25% of high school class, 58% in top 50% of high school class. SAT I Math middle 50% range 450-595. SAT I Verbal middle 50% range 440-560. Average ACT 22, ACT middle 50% range 19-24. TOEFL required of all international applicants, minimum TOEFL 520. **Basis for Candidate Selection:** *Very important factors considered include:* class rank, standardized test scores. **Freshman Admission Requirements:** High school diploma or GED is required. *Academic units required/recommended:* 15 total required; 4 English required, 3 math required, 3 science required, 3 social studies required, 2 elective required. **Freshman Admission Statistics:** 8,073 applied, 78% accepted, 40% of those accepted enrolled. **Transfer Admission Requirements:** *Items required:* high school transcript, college transcript, standardized test scores. Minimum college GPA of 2.0 required. Lowest grade transferable D. **General Admission Information:** Application fee $30. Nonfall registration accepted. Admission may be deferred. Credit and/or placement offered for CEEB Advanced Placement tests.

COSTS AND FINANCIAL AID

In-state tuition $3,011. Out-of-state tuition $6,021. Room & board $4,903. Required fees $1,103. Average book expense $660. **Required Forms and Deadlines:** FAFSA. Priority filing deadline April 1. **Notification of Awards:** Applicants will be notified of awards on a rolling basis beginning on or about February 15. **Types of Aid:** *Need-based scholarships/grants:* Pell, SEOG, state scholarships/grants, private scholarships, the school's own gift aid. *Loans:* Direct Subsidized Stafford, Direct Unsubsidized Stafford, Direct PLUS, Federal Perkins, college/university loans from institutional funds. **Student Employment:** Federal Work-Study Program available. Institutional employment available. Off-campus job opportunities are good. **Financial Aid Statistics:** 50% freshmen, 51% undergrads receive some form of aid. Average freshman grant $6,990. Average freshman loan $2,129. Average income from on-campus job $1,375. **Financial Aid Phone:** 618-453-4334.

SOUTHERN ILLINOIS UNIVERSITY—EDWARDSVILLE

PO Box 1600, Edwardsville, IL 62026-1080
Phone: 618-650-3705 **E-mail:** admis@siue.edu **CEEB Code:** 1759
Fax: 618-650-5013 **Web:** www.siue.edu **ACT Code:** 1147

This public school was founded in 1957. It has a 2,660-acre campus.

STUDENTS AND FACULTY

Enrollment: 10,014. **Student Body:** Male 44%, female 56%, international 1% (63 countries represented). **Ethnic Representation:** African American 11%, Asian 1%, Caucasian 86%, Hispanic 2%. **Retention and Graduation:** 69% freshmen return for sophomore year. 31% grads go on to further study within 1 year. 1% grads pursue law degrees. 1% grads pursue medical degrees. **Faculty:** Student/faculty ratio 17:1. 494 full-time faculty, 83% hold PhDs. 100% faculty teach undergrads.

ACADEMICS

Degrees: Bachelor's, first professional, first professional certificate, master's, post-bachelor's certificate, post-master's certificate. **Academic Requirements:** General education including some course work in arts/fine arts, computer literacy, English (including composition), history, humanities, mathematics, philosophy, sciences (biological or physical), social science, interdisciplinary studies. **Classes:** 20-29 students in an average class. 20-29 students in an average lab/discussion section. **Majors with Highest Enrollment:** Business/managerial economics. **Disciplines with Highest Percentage of Degrees Awarded:** Business/marketing 25%, education 15%, social sciences and history 10%, health professions and related sciences 8%, biological life sciences 6%. **Special Study Options:** Accelerated program, cooperative (work-study) program, cross registration, distance learning, double major, English as a second language, honors program, independent study, internships, student-designed major, study abroad, teacher certification program, weekend college, independent study. Elementary and secondary teacher certificate programs in art, music, social studies, English, kinesiology, biology, chemistry, foreign languages, history, math, physics, speech communication.

FACILITIES

Housing: Coed, apartments for married students, apartments for single students, housing for disabled students, fraternities and/or sororities, focused interest communities. **Library Holdings:** 783,050 bound volumes. 14,807 periodicals. 1,658,847 microforms. 29,183 audiovisuals. **Special Academic Facilities/Equipment:** Art gallery, anthropology museum, language lab, center for advanced manufacturing and production, technology commercialization center, electron microscope, psychomotor skills lab, new engineering building and lab. **Computers:** *Recommended operating system:* Windows 95. School-owned computers available for student use.

EXTRACURRICULARS

Activities: Choral groups, concert band, dance, drama/theater, jazz band, literary magazine, music ensembles, musical theater, pep band, radio station, student government, student newspaper, student-run film society, symphony orchestra. **Organizations:** 140 registered organizations, 15 honor societies, 9 religious organizations, 10 fraternities, 7 sororities. **Athletics (Intercollegiate):** *Men:* baseball, basketball, cross-country, soccer, tennis, track & field, wrestling. *Women:* basketball, cross-country, golf, soccer, softball, tennis, track & field, volleyball.

ADMISSIONS

Selectivity Rating: 67 (of 100). **Freshman Academic Profile:** 14% in top 10% of high school class, 41% in top 25% of high school class, 78% in top 50% of high school class. Average ACT 22, ACT middle 50% range 19-25. TOEFL required of all international applicants, minimum TOEFL 550. **Basis for Candidate Selection:** *Very important factors considered include:* class rank, standardized test scores. *Important factors considered include:* secondary school record. **Freshman Admission Requirements:** High school diploma or GED is required. *Academic units required/recommended:* 15 total required; 4 English required, 3 math required, 3 science required, 3 science lab required, 2 foreign language recommended, 3 social studies required, 2 elective required. **Freshman Admission Statistics:** 4,263 applied, 79% accepted, 49% of those accepted enrolled. **Transfer Admission Requirements:** *Items required:* college transcript. Minimum college GPA of 2.0 required. Lowest grade transferable D. **General Admission Information:** Application fee $30. Regular application deadline May 31. Nonfall registration accepted. Admission may be deferred for a maximum of 1 year. Credit and/or placement offered for CEEB Advanced Placement tests.

COSTS AND FINANCIAL AID

In-state tuition $3,198. Out-of-state tuition $6,396. Room & board $6,214. Required fees $823. Average book expense $620. **Required Forms and Deadlines:** FAFSA. Financial aid filing deadline June 1. Priority filing deadline March 1. **Notification of Awards:** Applicants will be notified of awards on a rolling basis beginning on or about March 15. **Types of Aid:** *Need-based scholarships/grants:* Pell, SEOG, state scholarships/grants, private scholarships, the school's own gift aid, Federal Nursing, Presidential Scholars Program, Chancellor's Scholars Program, Johnetta Haley Scholarship Program, Provost Scholarship. *Loans:* Direct Subsidized Stafford, Direct Unsubsidized Stafford, Direct PLUS, Federal Perkins, college/university loans from institutional funds. **Student Employment:** Federal Work-Study Program available. Institutional employment available. Off-campus job opportunities are good. **Financial Aid Statistics:** 47% freshmen, 46% undergrads receive some form of aid. Average freshman grant $2,046. Average freshman loan $2,208. Average income from on-campus job $1,348. **Financial Aid Phone:** 618-650-3880.

SOUTHERN METHODIST UNIVERSITY

PO Box 750181, Dallas, TX 75275-0181
Phone: 214-768-2058 **E-mail:** enrol_serv@mail.smu.edu **CEEB Code:** 6660
Fax: 214-768-0103 **Web:** www.smu.edu **ACT Code:** 4171

This private school, which is affiliated with the Methodist Church, was founded in 1911. It has a 165-acre campus.

STUDENTS AND FACULTY

Enrollment: 6,210. **Student Body:** Male 46%, female 54%, out-of-state 36%, international 5% (92 countries represented). **Ethnic Representation:** African American 6%, Asian 7%, Caucasian 78%, Hispanic 9%, Native American 1%. **Retention and Graduation:** 86% freshmen return for sophomore year. 56% freshmen graduate within 4 years. **Faculty:** Student/faculty ratio 12:1. 535 full-time faculty, 83% hold PhDs.

ACADEMICS

Degrees: Bachelor's, doctoral, first professional, master's, post-bachelor's certificate. **Academic Requirements:** General education including some course work in arts/fine arts, computer literacy, English (including composition), history, humanities, mathematics, philosophy, sciences (biological or physical), social science. **Classes:** 10-19 students in an average class. 10-19 students in an average lab/discussion section. **Majors with Highest Enrollment:** Finance, general; marketing/marketing management, general; psychology, general. **Disciplines with Highest Percentage of Degrees Awarded:** Business/marketing 28%, social sciences and history 18%, communications/communication technologies 14%, visual and performing arts 9%, psychology 9%. **Special Study Options:** Accelerated program, cooperative (work-study) program, distance learning, double major, English as a second language, student exchange program (domestic), honors program, independent study, internships, student-designed major, study abroad, teacher certification program.

FACILITIES

Housing: Coed, apartments for married students, apartments for single students, fraternities and/or sororities, theme residence halls. **Library Holdings:** 2,577,345 bound volumes. 11,727 periodicals. 803,898 microforms. 39,444 audiovisuals. **Special Academic Facilities/Equipment:** Art, natural history, and paleontology museums; southwest film/video archives; sculpture garden; performing arts theatres; pollen analysis and geothermal labs; electron microbe lab; microscopy lab; seismological observatory; institute of technology services; TV studio. **Computers:** *Recommended operating system:* Windows 95. School-owned computers available for student use.

EXTRACURRICULARS

Activities: Choral groups, concert band, dance, drama/theater, jazz band, literary magazine, marching band, music ensembles, musical theater, opera, pep band, radio station, student government, student newspaper, student-run film society, symphony orchestra, yearbook. **Organizations:** 130 registered organizations, 15 honor societies, 26 religious organizations, 15 fraternities (37% men join), 12 sororities (38% women join). **Athletics (Intercollegiate):** *Men:* basketball, cross-country, diving, football, golf, soccer, swimming, tennis, track & field. *Women:* basketball, crew, cross-country, diving, golf, soccer, swimming, tennis, track & field, volleyball.

ADMISSIONS

Selectivity Rating: 82 (of 100). **Freshman Academic Profile:** Average high school GPA 3.5. 35% in top 10% of high school class, 65% in top 25% of high

school class, 91% in top 50% of high school class. 61% from public high schools. SAT I Math middle 50% range 550-650. SAT I Verbal middle 50% range 540-630. ACT middle 50% range 23-28. TOEFL required of all international applicants, minimum TOEFL 550. **Basis for Candidate Selection:** *Very important factors considered include:* essays, recommendations, secondary school record, standardized test scores. *Important factors considered include:* character/personal qualities, class rank, extracurricular activities, talent/ability, volunteer work, work experience. *Other factors considered include:* alumni/ae relation, interview. **Freshman Admission Requirements:** High school diploma is required and GED is not accepted. *Academic units required/recommended:* 15 total required; 4 English required, 4 English recommended, 3 math required, 4 math recommended, 3 science required, 4 science recommended, 2 science lab required, 3 science lab recommended, 2 foreign language required, 3 foreign language recommended, 1 social studies required, 2 social studies recommended, 2 history required, 3 history recommended. **Freshman Admission Statistics:** 6,152 applied, 66% accepted, 34% of those accepted enrolled. **Transfer Admission Requirements:** *Items required:* high school transcript, college transcript, essay. Minimum college GPA of 2.5 required. Lowest grade transferable C-. **General Admission Information:** Application fee $50. Priority application deadline January 15. Nonfall registration accepted. Admission may be deferred for a maximum of 1 year. Credit and/or placement offered for CEEB Advanced Placement tests.

COSTS AND FINANCIAL AID

Tuition $19,466. Room & board $7,954. Required fees $2,476. Average book expense $600. **Required Forms and Deadlines:** FAFSA. Priority filing deadline February 1. **Notification of Awards:** Applicants will be notified of awards on a rolling basis beginning on or about March 15. **Types of Aid:** *Need-based scholarships/grants:* Pell, SEOG, state scholarships/grants, private scholarships, the school's own gift aid. *Loans:* FFEL Subsidized Stafford, FFEL Unsubsidized Stafford, FFEL PLUS, Federal Perkins, state loans, college/university loans from institutional funds. **Student Employment:** Federal Work-Study Program available. Institutional employment available. Off-campus job opportunities are excellent. **Financial Aid Statistics:** 37% freshmen, 37% undergrads receive some form of aid. **Financial Aid Phone:** 214-768-3417.

SOUTHERN NAZARENE UNIVERSITY

6729 Northwest 39th Expressway, Bethany, OK 73008-2694
Phone: 800-648-9899 **E-mail:** rmeek@snu.edu **CEEB Code:** 6036
Fax: 405-491-6320 **Web:** www.snu.edu **ACT Code:** 3384

This private school, which is affiliated with the Nazarene Church, was founded in 1899. It has a 40-acre campus.

STUDENTS AND FACULTY

Enrollment: 1,536. **Student Body:** Out-of-state 55%, international 5% (18 countries represented). **Ethnic Representation:** African American 5%, Asian 1%, Caucasian 92%, Hispanic 1%, Native American 1%. **Retention and Graduation:** 37% grads go on to further study within 1 year. 14% grads pursue business degrees. 5% grads pursue law degrees. 3% grads pursue medical degrees.

ACADEMICS

Degrees: Bachelor's, master's. **Special Study Options:** Study abroad, American Studies Program (Washington, DC). Los Angeles Film Studies Program (California). Undergrads may take grad-level classes. Study abroad in Costa Rica and England may be arranged elsewhere.

FACILITIES

Housing: Coed, all-female, all-male, apartments for married students. **Library Holdings:** 112,673 bound volumes. 667 periodicals. 180,152 microforms. **Special Academic Facilities/Equipment:** On-campus lab school, recital hall, concert grand piano, tracker pipe organ, seven-foot double French harpsichord, media center, anatomy lab, laser labs. **Computers:** *Recommended operating system:* Mac. School-owned computers available for student use.

EXTRACURRICULARS

Activities: Student government, student newspaper, yearbook. **Organizations:** 50 registered organizations, 3 religious organizations. **Athletics (Intercollegiate):** *Men:* basketball, cheerleading, cross-country, golf, soccer, softball, tennis, track & field, volleyball. *Women:* basketball, cheerleading, cross-country, golf, soccer, softball, tennis, track & field, volleyball.

ADMISSIONS

Selectivity Rating: 65 (of 100). **Freshman Academic Profile:** 14% in top 10% of high school class, 43% in top 25% of high school class, 91% in top 50% of high school class. 90% from public high schools. TOEFL required of all international applicants, minimum TOEFL 500. **Freshman Admission Requirements:** High school diploma is required and GED is not accepted. *Academic units required/recommended:* 23 total required; 4 English required, 3 math required, 2 science required, 2 foreign language required, 1 social studies required, 2 history required, 7 elective required. **Transfer Admission Requirements:** Minimum college GPA of 2.0 required. Lowest grade transferable D. **General Admission Information:** Regular application deadline August 15. Nonfall registration accepted. Credit and/or placement offered for CEEB Advanced Placement tests.

COSTS AND FINANCIAL AID

Room & board $4,028. Required fees $348. Average book expense $350. **Required Forms and Deadlines:** FAFSA and institution's own financial aid form. **Types of Aid:** *Need-based scholarships/grants:* Pell, SEOG, state scholarships/grants, private scholarships, the school's own gift aid. *Loans:* FFEL Subsidized Stafford, FFEL Unsubsidized Stafford, FFEL PLUS, Federal Perkins, college/university loans from institutional funds. **Student Employment:** Federal Work-Study Program available. Institutional employment available. Off-campus job opportunities are good. **Financial Aid Statistics:** Average freshman loan $2,077. Average income from on-campus job $2,000. **Financial Aid Phone:** 405-491-6310.

SOUTHERN NEW HAMPSHIRE UNIVERSITY

2500 North River Road, Manchester, NH 03108
Phone: 603-645-9611 **E-mail:** admission@snhu.edu **CEEB Code:** 3649
Fax: 603-645-9693 **Web:** www.snhu.edu **ACT Code:** 2514

This private school was founded in 1932. It has a 280-acre campus.

STUDENTS AND FACULTY

Enrollment: 3,907. **Student Body:** Male 45%, female 55%, out-of-state 70%, international 4%. **Ethnic Representation:** African American 2%, Asian 1%, Caucasian 51%, Hispanic 2%. **Retention and Graduation:** 75% freshmen return for sophomore year. 1% grads go on to further study within 1 year. **Faculty:** Student/faculty ratio 17:1. 110 full-time faculty, 57% hold PhDs. 70% faculty teach undergrads.

ACADEMICS

Degrees: Associate's, bachelor's, certificate, doctoral, master's, post-bachelor's certificate, transfer. **Academic Requirements:** General education including some course work in computer literacy, English (including composition), history, humanities, mathematics, philosophy, social science. **Majors with Highest Enrollment:** Business/managerial operations; culinary arts/chef training; psychology, general. **Disciplines with Highest Percentage of Degrees Awarded:** Business/marketing 67%, other 28%, education 1%, computer and information sciences 1%, social sciences and history 1%. **Special Study Options:** Accelerated program, cooperative (work-study) program, cross registration, distance learning, double major, English as a second language, student exchange program (domestic), honors program, independent study, internships, liberal arts/career combination, study abroad, teacher certification program, weekend college.

FACILITIES

Housing: Coed, apartments for single students, townhouses, wellness housing, single-sex areas in residence halls. **Library Holdings:** 112,998 bound volumes. 1,800 periodicals. 320,236 microforms. 2,105 audiovisuals. **Special Academic Facilities/Equipment:** Museum. **Computers:** School-owned computers available for student use.

EXTRACURRICULARS

Activities: Drama/theater, radio station, student government, student newspaper, yearbook. **Organizations:** 40 registered organizations, 3 honor societies, 4 religious organizations, 4 fraternities (10% men join), 4 sororities (10% women join). **Athletics (Intercollegiate):** *Men:* baseball, basketball, cheerleading, crew, cross-country, golf, ice hockey, lacrosse, soccer, tennis. *Women:* basketball, cheerleading, crew, cross-country, soccer, softball, tennis, volleyball.

ADMISSIONS

Selectivity Rating: 69 (of 100). **Freshman Academic Profile:** Average high school GPA 2.7. 3% in top 10% of high school class, 20% in top 25% of high school class, 44% in top 50% of high school class. 85% from public high schools. Average SAT I Math 476, SAT I Math middle 50% range 420-530. Average SAT I Verbal 475, SAT I Verbal middle 50% range 430-520. Average ACT 20. TOEFL required of all international applicants, minimum TOEFL 500. **Basis**

for Candidate Selection: *Very important factors considered include:* essays, extracurricular activities, interview, recommendations, secondary school record. *Important factors considered include:* class rank, standardized test scores. *Other factors considered include:* alumni/ae relation, character/personal qualities, minority status, talent/ability, volunteer work, work experience. **Freshman Admission Requirements:** High school diploma or GED is required. *Academic units required/recommended:* 16 total required; 20 total recommended; 4 English required, 4 English recommended, 2 math required, 4 math recommended, 2 science required, 3 science recommended, 1 science lab required, 3 science lab recommended, 2 foreign language recommended, 2 social studies recommended, 2 history required, 2 history recommended. **Transfer Admission Requirements:** *Items required:* high school transcript, college transcript, essay. Minimum college GPA of 2.0 required. Lowest grade transferable C-. **General Admission Information:** Application fee $25. Nonfall registration accepted. Admission may be deferred for a maximum of 1 year. Credit and/or placement offered for CEEB Advanced Placement tests.

COSTS AND FINANCIAL AID

Tuition $16,536. Room & board $7,066. Required fees $250. Average book expense $600. **Required Forms and Deadlines:** FAFSA. Priority filing deadline March 15. **Notification of Awards:** Applicants will be notified of awards on a rolling basis. **Types of Aid:** *Need-based scholarships/grants:* Pell, SEOG, state scholarships/grants, private scholarships, the school's own gift aid. *Loans:* FFEL Subsidized Stafford, FFEL Unsubsidized Stafford, FFEL PLUS, Federal Perkins. **Student Employment:** Federal Work-Study Program available. Institutional employment available. Off-campus job opportunities are good. **Financial Aid Statistics:** Average freshman grant $5,500. Average freshman loan $3,600. Average income from on-campus job $1,544. **Financial Aid Phone:** 603-645-9645.

See page 1212.

SOUTHERN OREGON UNIVERSITY

Office of Admissions, 1250 Siskiyou Blvd., Ashland, OR 97520-5032
Phone: 541-552-6411 **E-mail:** admissions@sou.edu **CEEB Code:** 4702
Fax: 541-552-6614 **Web:** www.sou.edu **ACT Code:** 3496

This public school was founded in 1926. It has a 175-acre campus.

STUDENTS AND FACULTY

Enrollment: 4,917. **Student Body:** Male 43%, female 57%, out-of-state 20%, international 2% (32 countries represented). **Ethnic Representation:** African American 1%, Asian 4%, Caucasian 82%, Hispanic 4%, Native American 2%. **Retention and Graduation:** 67% freshmen return for sophomore year. **Faculty:** Student/faculty ratio 19:1. 189 full-time faculty, 82% hold PhDs.

ACADEMICS

Degrees: Bachelor's, master's, post-bachelor's certificate. **Academic Requirements:** General education including some course work in arts/fine arts, English (including composition), foreign languages, mathematics, sciences (biological or physical), social science. **Classes:** 20-29 students in an average class. 20-29 students in an average lab/discussion section. **Disciplines with Highest Percentage of Degrees Awarded:** Social sciences and history 20%, business/marketing 16%, communications/communication technologies 10%, visual and performing arts 9%, psychology 8%. **Special Study Options:** Accelerated program, cooperative (work-study) program, cross registration, distance learning, double major, dual enrollment, English as a second language, student exchange program (domestic), honors program, independent study, internships, liberal arts/career combination, student-designed major, study abroad, teacher certification program.

FACILITIES

Housing: Coed, apartments for married students, apartments for single students, housing for disabled students, housing for international students. Special quiet, substance-free, nonsmoking, older students, or freshman-only residence halls. **Library Holdings:** 272,319 bound volumes. 2,040 periodicals. 793,114 microforms. 20,241 audiovisuals. **Special Academic Facilities/ Equipment:** Art and history museums, art galleries, on-campus preschool and kindergarten, National Guard armory, United States Wildlife Forensics Lab.

EXTRACURRICULARS

Activities: Choral groups, concert band, dance, drama/theater, jazz band, literary magazine, music ensembles, musical theater, opera, pep band, radio station, student government, student newspaper, symphony orchestra, television station. **Organizations:** 52 registered organizations, 13 honor societies, 5 religious organizations. **Athletics (Intercollegiate):** *Men:* basketball, cross-country, football, track & field, wrestling. *Women:* basketball, cross-country, soccer, tennis, track & field, volleyball.

ADMISSIONS

Selectivity Rating: 81 (of 100). **Freshman Academic Profile:** Average high school GPA 3.2. 90% from public high schools. TOEFL required of all international applicants, minimum TOEFL 540. **Basis for Candidate Selection:** *Very important factors considered include:* secondary school record, standardized test scores. *Other factors considered include:* class rank, essays, extracurricular activities, interview, minority status, recommendations, talent/ ability, volunteer work, work experience. **Freshman Admission Requirements:** High school diploma or GED is required. *Academic units required/ recommended:* 14 total required; 4 English required, 3 math required, 2 science required, 2 foreign language required, 3 social studies required. **Freshman Admission Statistics:** 2,169 applied, 85% accepted, 48% of those accepted enrolled. **Transfer Admission Requirements:** *Items required:* college transcript, statement of good standing from prior school. Minimum college GPA of 2.2 required. Lowest grade transferable C. **General Admission Information:** Application fee $50. Priority application deadline July 1. Nonfall registration accepted. Admission may be deferred. Credit and/or placement offered for CEEB Advanced Placement tests.

COSTS AND FINANCIAL AID

Required Forms and Deadlines: FAFSA. No deadline for regular filing. **Notification of Awards:** Applicants will be notified of awards on a rolling basis beginning on or about April 1. **Types of Aid:** *Need-based scholarships/grants:* Pell, SEOG, state scholarships/grants, private scholarships, the school's own gift aid. *Loans:* Direct Subsidized Stafford, Direct Unsubsidized Stafford, Direct PLUS, Federal Perkins, college/university loans from institutional funds. **Student Employment:** Federal Work-Study Program available. Institutional employment available. Off-campus job opportunities are good. **Financial Aid Statistics:** 61% freshmen, 56% undergrads receive some form of aid. **Financial Aid Phone:** 541-552-6161.

SOUTHERN POLYTECHNIC STATE UNIVERSITY

1100 South Marietta Parkway, Marietta, GA 30060-2896
Phone: 770-528-7281 **E-mail:** admissions@spsu.edu **CEEB Code:** 5626
Fax: 770-528-7292 **Web:** www.spsu.edu **ACT Code:** 865

This public school was founded in 1948. It has a 200-acre campus.

STUDENTS AND FACULTY

Enrollment: 3,084. **Student Body:** Male 83%, female 17%, out-of-state 4%, international 5%. **Ethnic Representation:** African American 23%, Asian 7%, Caucasian 66%, Hispanic 3%. **Retention and Graduation:** 66% freshmen return for sophomore year. **Faculty:** Student/faculty ratio 20:1. 136 full-time faculty, 57% hold PhDs. 98% faculty teach undergrads.

ACADEMICS

Degrees: Associate's, bachelor's, certificate, master's, post-bachelor's certificate. **Academic Requirements:** General education including some course work in arts/fine arts, English (including composition), humanities, mathematics, sciences (biological or physical), social science, speech and science, technology and society, science/math/technology. **Classes:** 20-29 students in an average class. Under 10 students in an average lab/discussion section. **Majors with Highest Enrollment:** Computer science; electrical, electronic, and communications engineering technology/technician; mechanical engineering/mechanical technology/technician. **Disciplines with Highest Percentage of Degrees Awarded:** Engineering/engineering technology 64%, computer and information sciences 18%, business/marketing 9%, architecture 4%, English 3%. **Special Study Options:** Cooperative (work-study) program, cross registration, distance learning, double major, dual enrollment, independent study, internships, study abroad.

FACILITIES

Housing: Coed, Privately-owned student apartments on campus property. **Library Holdings:** 117,963 bound volumes. 1,320 periodicals. 56,619 microforms. 60 audiovisuals. **Computers:** School-owned computers available for student use.

EXTRACURRICULARS

Activities: Radio station, student government, student newspaper. **Organizations:** 24 registered organizations, 1 honor society, 3 religious organizations, 6 fraternities (5% men join), 3 sororities (2% women join). **Athletics (Intercollegiate):** *Men:* baseball, basketball, tennis. *Women:* basketball.

ADMISSIONS

Selectivity Rating: 64 (of 100). **Freshman Academic Profile:** Average high school GPA 3.2. 95% from public high schools. Average SAT I Math 562, SAT I Math middle 50% range 510-610. Average SAT I Verbal 535, SAT I Verbal middle 50% range 490-580. Average ACT 22, ACT middle 50% range 20-24. TOEFL required of all international applicants, minimum TOEFL 550. **Basis for Candidate Selection:** *Very important factors considered include:* secondary school record, standardized test scores. **Freshman Admission Requirements:** High school diploma is required and GED is not accepted. *Academic units required/recommended:* 18 total required; 4 English required, 4 math required, 3 science required, 2 science lab required, 2 foreign language required, 3 social studies required, 2 history required, 2 elective required. **Freshman Admission Statistics:** 918 applied, 65% accepted, 62% of those accepted enrolled. **Transfer Admission Requirements:** *Items required:* college transcript. Minimum college GPA of 2.0 required. Lowest grade transferable C. **General Admission Information:** Application fee $20. Regular application deadline August 1. Nonfall registration accepted. Credit and/or placement offered for CEEB Advanced Placement tests.

COSTS AND FINANCIAL AID

In-state tuition $2,010. Out-of-state tuition $8,040. Room & board $4,806. Required fees $442. Average book expense $1,000. **Required Forms and Deadlines:** FAFSA. Priority filing deadline March 15. **Notification of Awards:** Applicants will be notified of awards on a rolling basis beginning on or about May 15. **Types of Aid:** *Need-based scholarships/grants:* Pell, SEOG, state scholarships/grants, private scholarships, the school's own gift aid. *Loans:* Direct Subsidized Stafford, Direct Unsubsidized Stafford, Direct PLUS, Federal Perkins, college/university loans from institutional funds. **Student Employment:** Federal Work-Study Program available. Institutional employment available. Off-campus job opportunities are excellent. **Financial Aid Statistics:** 37% freshmen, 35% undergrads receive some form of aid. **Financial Aid Phone:** 770-528-7290.

SOUTHERN UNIVERSITY AND A&M COLLEGE

PO Box 9901, Baton Rouge, LA 70813
Phone: 225-771-2430 **E-mail:** admit@subr.edu **CEEB Code:** 6663
Fax: 225-771-2500 **Web:** subr.edu **ACT Code:** 1610

This public school was founded in 1880. It has an 884-acre campus.

STUDENTS AND FACULTY

Enrollment: 7,352. **Student Body:** Male 41%, female 59%, out-of-state 14%, international 1% (35 countries represented). **Ethnic Representation:** African American 98%, Asian 1%, Caucasian 1%. **Retention and Graduation:** 68% freshmen return for sophomore year. 7% freshmen graduate within 4 years. 19% grads go on to further study within 1 year. **Faculty:** Student/faculty ratio 16:1. 422 full-time faculty, 67% hold PhDs.

ACADEMICS

Degrees: Associate's, bachelor's, certificate, doctoral, master's. **Academic Requirements:** General education including some course work in arts/fine arts, computer literacy, English (including composition), history, humanities, mathematics, sciences (biological or physical), social science. **Classes:** 20-29 students in an average class. 20-29 students in an average lab/discussion section. **Majors with Highest Enrollment:** Computer science; nursing/registered nurse training (RN, ASN, BSN, MSN); business administration/management. **Disciplines with Highest Percentage of Degrees Awarded:** Business/ marketing 14%, health professions and related sciences 14%, engineering/ engineering technology 9%, social sciences and history 9%, parks and recreation 8%. **Special Study Options:** Cooperative (work-study) program, cross registration, distance learning, double major, dual enrollment, student exchange program (domestic), honors program, independent study, internships, study abroad, teacher certification program, weekend college.

FACILITIES

Housing: All-female, all-male, housing for disabled students. **Library Holdings:** 807,825 bound volumes. 1,753 periodicals. 674,787 microforms. 42,217 audiovisuals. **Special Academic Facilities/Equipment:** Jazz institute, Southern Museum of Art. **Computers:** *Recommended operating system:* Windows NT/2000. School-owned computers available for student use.

EXTRACURRICULARS

Activities: Choral groups, concert band, dance, drama/theater, jazz band, literary magazine, marching band, music ensembles, musical theater, pep band, student government, student newspaper, yearbook. **Organizations:** 74 registered organizations, 5 honor societies, 6 religious organizations, 5 fraternities (1% men join), 4 sororities (2% women join). **Athletics (Intercollegiate):** *Men:* baseball, basketball, cross-country, football, golf, tennis, track & field. *Women:* basketball, cross-country, golf, softball, tennis, track & field, volleyball.

ADMISSIONS

Selectivity Rating: 67 (of 100). **Freshman Academic Profile:** 4% in top 10% of high school class, 10% in top 25% of high school class, 37% in top 50% of high school class. 75% from public high schools. Average ACT 17, ACT middle 50% range 15-19. TOEFL required of all international applicants, minimum TOEFL 500. **Basis for Candidate Selection:** *Very important factors considered include:* secondary school record, standardized test scores. *Other factors considered include:* talent/ability. **Freshman Admission Requirements:** High school diploma or GED is required. *Academic units required/ recommended:* 13 total required; 4 English required, 3 math required, 3 science required, 2 social studies required, 1 history required. **Freshman Admission Statistics:** 3,626 applied, 54% accepted, 60% of those accepted enrolled. **Transfer Admission Requirements:** *Items required:* high school transcript, college transcript, standardized test scores, statement of good standing from prior school. Minimum high school GPA of 2.3 required. Minimum college GPA of 2.0 required. Lowest grade transferable C. **General Admission Information:** Application fee $5. Regular application deadline July 1. Nonfall registration accepted. Admission may be deferred for a maximum of 1 year. Credit offered for CEEB Advanced Placement tests.

COSTS AND FINANCIAL AID

In-state tuition $2,702. Out-of-state tuition $8,494. Room & board $4,306. Required fees $0. Average book expense $1,200. **Required Forms and Deadlines:** FAFSA and institution's own financial aid form. Priority filing deadline May 15. **Notification of Awards:** Applicants will be notified of awards on a rolling basis beginning on or about June 30. **Types of Aid:** *Need-based scholarships/grants:* Pell, SEOG, state scholarships/grants, private scholarships, the school's own gift aid. *Loans:* Direct Subsidized Stafford, Direct Unsubsidized Stafford, Direct PLUS, FFEL Subsidized Stafford, FFEL Unsubsidized Stafford, FFEL PLUS, college/university loans from institutional funds. **Student Employment:** Federal Work-Study Program available. Institutional employment available. Off-campus job opportunities are good. **Financial Aid Statistics:** 77% freshmen, 77% undergrads receive some form of aid. Average freshman grant $2,625. Average freshman loan $2,625. Average income from on-campus job $1,000. **Financial Aid Phone:** 504-771-2790.

SOUTHERN UNIVERSITY AND AGRICULTURAL AND MECHANICAL COLLEGE

3050 Maritn Luther King Jr. Drive, Shreveport, LA 71107
Phone: 318-674-3342
Fax: 318-674-3338 **ACT Code:** 1613

This public school was founded in 1967. It has a 101-acre campus.

STUDENTS AND FACULTY

Enrollment: 1,345. **Student Body:** Male 31%, female 69%, out-of-state 2%, international students represent 3 countries. **Ethnic Representation:** African American 90%, Caucasian 9%. **Faculty:** 100% faculty teach undergrads.

ACADEMICS

Degrees: Associate's, certificate, diploma. **Academic Requirements:** General education including some course work in arts/fine arts, computer literacy, English (including composition), humanities, mathematics, sciences (biological or physical), social science. **Special Study Options:** Cooperative (work-study) program, cross registration, double major, dual enrollment, honors program, independent study, internships, teacher certification program, weekend college.

FACILITIES

Library Holdings: 47,686 bound volumes. 2,170 periodicals. 25,241 microforms. 1,361 audiovisuals. **Special Academic Facilities/Equipment:** Academic Career Enhancement Lab (ACE), Aerospace Technology Center, Rad Tech Lab/CAD Lab. **Computers:** *Recommended operating system:* Windows 95. School-owned computers available for student use.

EXTRACURRICULARS

Activities: Choral groups, student government, student newspaper. **Organizations:** 17 registered organizations, 1 honor society, 2 religious organizations. **Athletics (Intercollegiate):** *Men:* basketball. *Women:* basketball.

ADMISSIONS

Selectivity Rating: 60 (of 100). **Freshman Academic Profile:** Average high school GPA 2.0. 90% from public high schools. ACT middle 50% range 13-16. TOEFL required of all international applicants, minimum TOEFL 500. **Basis for Candidate Selection:** *Very important factors considered include:* secondary school record. *Other factors considered include:* standardized test scores, state residency. **Freshman Admission Requirements:** High school diploma or GED is required. *Academic units required/recommended:* 24 total required; 24 total recommended; 4 English required, 4 English recommended, 3 math required, 3 math recommended, 3 science required, 3 science recommended, 1 foreign language required, 1 foreign language recommended, 1 social studies required, 1 social studies recommended, 3 history required, 3 history recommended, 9 elective required, 9 elective recommended. **Freshman Admission Statistics:** 458 applied, 100% accepted, 100% of those accepted enrolled. **Transfer Admission Requirements:** *Items required:* college transcript. Minimum college GPA of 2.0 required. Lowest grade transferable C. **General Admission Information:** Regular application deadline rolling. Nonfall registration accepted. Admission may be deferred.

COSTS AND FINANCIAL AID

In-state tuition $1,104. Out-of-state tuition $2,394. Average book expense $300. **Required Forms and Deadlines:** FAFSA and institution's own financial aid form. Priority filing deadline April 1. **Notification of Awards:** Applicants will be notified of awards on a rolling basis. **Types of Aid:** *Need-based scholarships/grants:* Pell, SEOG, state scholarships/grants, private scholarships, the school's own gift aid. *Loans:* Direct Subsidized Stafford, Direct Unsubsidized Stafford, Direct PLUS. **Student Employment:** Federal Work-Study Program available. Off-campus job opportunities are fair. **Financial Aid Statistics:** Average freshman grant $4,200. Average freshman loan $2,625. **Financial Aid Phone:** 318-674-3494.

SOUTHERN UNIVERSITY OF NEW ORLEANS

6400 Press Drive, New Orleans, LA 70126
Phone: 504-286-5314
Fax: 504-286-5320

This private school was founded in 1959.

STUDENTS AND FACULTY

Enrollment: 4,500. **Student Body:** Out-of-state 5%. **Retention and Graduation:** 39% grads go on to further study within 1 year. 30% grads pursue business degrees. 6% grads pursue law degrees.

EXTRACURRICULARS

Athletics (Intercollegiate): *Men:* basketball, cross-country, tennis, track & field. *Women:* basketball, cross-country, tennis, track & field.

ADMISSIONS

Selectivity Rating: 66 (of 100). **Freshman Academic Profile:** 10% in top 10% of high school class, 30% in top 25% of high school class, 70% in top 50% of high school class. TOEFL required of all international applicants, **Freshman Admission Requirements: General Admission Information:** Regular application deadline rolling.

COSTS AND FINANCIAL AID

Average book expense $800. **Types of Aid:** *Loans:* FFEL Subsidized Stafford, FFEL PLUS.

SOUTHERN UTAH UNIVERSITY

Admissions Office, 351 West Center, Cedar City, UT 84720
Phone: 435-586-7740 **E-mail:** adminfo@suu.edu **CEEB Code:** 4092
Fax: 435-865-8223 **Web:** www.suu.edu **ACT Code:** 4271

This public school was founded in 1897. It has a 113-acre campus.

STUDENTS AND FACULTY

Enrollment: 5,680. **Student Body:** Male 44%, female 56%, out-of-state 16%, international 1% (7 countries represented). **Ethnic Representation:** African American 1%, Asian 1%, Caucasian 93%, Hispanic 2%, Native American 1%. **Retention and Graduation:** 58% freshmen return for sophomore year. 9% freshmen graduate within 4 years. **Faculty:** Student/faculty ratio 21:1. 221 full-time faculty, 64% hold PhDs.

ACADEMICS

Degrees: Associate's, bachelor's, certificate, diploma, master's, terminal, transfer. **Academic Requirements:** General education including some course work in arts/fine arts, computer literacy, English (including composition), history, humanities, mathematics, philosophy, sciences (biological or physical), social science. **Classes:** Under 10 students in an average class. Under 10 students in an average lab/discussion section. **Disciplines with Highest Percentage of Degrees Awarded:** Education 29%, business/marketing 15%, communications/communication technologies 8%, social sciences and history 7%, psychology 6%. **Special Study Options:** Cooperative (work-study) program, distance learning, double major, English as a second language, honors program, independent study, internships, liberal arts/career combination, teacher certification program, weekend college.

FACILITIES

Housing: Coed, all-female, all-male, apartments for single students, housing for disabled students, fraternities and/or sororities. **Library Holdings:** 182,553 bound volumes. 1,100 periodicals. 673,985 microforms. 17,969 audiovisuals. **Special Academic Facilities/Equipment:** Art gallery, natural history museum, farm and ranch, TV studio. **Computers:** *Recommended operating system:* Mac. School-owned computers available for student use.

EXTRACURRICULARS

Activities: Choral groups, concert band, dance, drama/theater, jazz band, literary magazine, marching band, music ensembles, musical theater, opera, pep band, radio station, student government, student newspaper, symphony orchestra, television station, yearbook. **Organizations:** 3 religious organizations, 2 fraternities (3% men join), 3 sororities (3% women join). **Athletics (Intercollegiate):** *Men:* baseball, basketball, cross-country, football, golf, track & field. *Women:* basketball, cross-country, gymnastics, softball, tennis, track & field.

ADMISSIONS

Selectivity Rating: 65 (of 100). **Freshman Academic Profile:** Average high school GPA 3.4. 18% in top 10% of high school class, 42% in top 25% of high school class, 76% in top 50% of high school class. 95% from public high schools. Average SAT I Math 487, SAT I Math middle 50% range 440-540. Average SAT I Verbal 498, SAT I Verbal middle 50% range 450-550. Average ACT 22, ACT middle 50% range 18-24. TOEFL required of all international applicants, minimum TOEFL 500. **Basis for Candidate Selection:** *Very important factors considered include:* secondary school record, standardized test scores. **Freshman Admission Requirements:** High school diploma or GED is required. *Academic units required/recommended:* 4 English recommended, 3 math recommended, 2 science recommended, 1 science lab recommended, 2 social studies recommended. **Freshman Admission Statistics:** 1,398 applied, 81% accepted, 59% of those accepted enrolled. **Transfer Admission Requirements:** *Items required:* college transcript. Minimum high school GPA of 2.0 required. Minimum college GPA of 2.3 required. Lowest grade transferable D. **General Admission Information:** Application fee $25. Nonfall registration accepted. Admission may be deferred for a maximum of 1 year. Credit and/or placement offered for CEEB Advanced Placement tests.

COSTS AND FINANCIAL AID

In-state tuition $1,888. Out-of-state tuition $6,882. Room & board $5,224. Required fees $462. Average book expense $1,036. **Required Forms and Deadlines:** FAFSA, institution's own financial aid form and Institutional verification form. No deadline for regular filing. **Notification of Awards:** Applicants will be notified of awards on a rolling basis beginning on or about February 1. **Types of Aid:** *Need-based scholarships/grants:* Pell, SEOG, state scholarships/grants, private scholarships, the school's own gift aid. *Loans:* FFEL Subsidized Stafford, FFEL Unsubsidized Stafford, FFEL PLUS, Federal Perkins, college/university loans from institutional funds. **Student Employment:** Federal Work-Study Program available. Institutional employment available. Off-campus job opportunities are good. **Financial Aid Statistics:** Average income from on-campus job $2,000. **Financial Aid Phone:** 801-586-7735.

SOUTHERN VERMONT COLLEGE

982 Mansion Drive, Bennington, VT 05201
Phone: 802-447-6304 **E-mail:** admis@svc.edu **CEEB Code:** 3796
Fax: 802-447-4695 **Web:** www.svc.edu **ACT Code:** 4310

This private school was founded in 1974. It has a 371-acre campus.

STUDENTS AND FACULTY

Enrollment: 448. **Student Body:** Male 36%, female 64%, out-of-state 66%, international 1%. **Ethnic Representation:** African American 6%, Caucasian 79%, Hispanic 2%. **Retention and Graduation:** 61% freshmen return for sophomore year. **Faculty:** Student/faculty ratio 11:1. 16 full-time faculty, 25% hold PhDs. 100% faculty teach undergrads.

ACADEMICS

Degrees: Associate's, bachelor's, terminal, transfer. **Academic Requirements:** General education including some course work in arts/fine arts, computer literacy, English (including composition), history, humanities, mathematics, philosophy, sciences (biological or physical), social science, environmental studies elective. **Disciplines with Highest Percentage of Degrees Awarded:** Business/marketing 28%, protective services/public administration 21%, health professions and related sciences 11%, communications/communication technologies 10%, natural resources/environmental sciences 10%. **Special Study Options:** Accelerated program, cooperative (work-study) program, distance learning, double major, dual enrollment, honors program, independent study, internships, liberal arts/career combination, student-designed major, study abroad.

FACILITIES

Housing: Coed, apartment-style residence halls and courtyard. **Library Holdings:** 26,000 bound volumes. 1,504 periodicals. 0 microforms. 380 audiovisuals. **Special Academic Facilities/Equipment:** Mountaineers Field House and Fitness Center, dining hall, student center, Everett Mansion. **Computers:** School-owned computers available for student use.

EXTRACURRICULARS

Activities: Drama/theater, literary magazine, music ensembles, radio station, student government, student newspaper, yearbook. **Organizations:** 14 registered organizations, 1 honor society. **Athletics (Intercollegiate):** *Men:* baseball, basketball, cross-country, soccer. *Women:* basketball, cross-country, soccer, softball, volleyball.

ADMISSIONS

Selectivity Rating: 69 (of 100). **Freshman Academic Profile:** Average high school GPA 2.6. 0% in top 10% of high school class, 5% in top 25% of high school class, 35% in top 50% of high school class. 85% from public high schools. SAT I Math middle 50% range 340-550. SAT I Verbal middle 50% range 380-580. ACT middle 50% range 15-25. TOEFL required of all international applicants, minimum TOEFL 500. **Basis for Candidate Selection:** *Very important factors considered include:* class rank, secondary school record, standardized test scores. *Important factors considered include:* character/personal qualities, essays, extracurricular activities, interview, recommendations, talent/ability, volunteer work, work experience. **Freshman Admission Requirements:** High school diploma or GED is required. *Academic units required/recommended:* 16 total recommended; 4 English required, 2 math required, 2 science recommended, 2 foreign language recommended, 3 social studies recommended, 2 history recommended. **Freshman Admission Statistics:** 351 applied, 63% accepted, 42% of those accepted enrolled. **Transfer Admission Requirements:** *Items required:* high school transcript, college transcript, essay. Minimum college GPA of 2.0 required. Lowest grade transferable C. **General Admission Information:** Application fee $30. Nonfall registration accepted. Admission may be deferred for a maximum of 1 year. Credit offered for CEEB Advanced Placement tests.

COSTS AND FINANCIAL AID

Tuition $11,695. Room & board $5,990. Required fees $0. Average book expense $500. **Required Forms and Deadlines:** FAFSA and institution's own financial aid form. Financial aid filing deadline May 1. Priority filing deadline March 1. **Notification of Awards:** Applicants will be notified of awards on or about March 1. **Types of Aid:** *Need-based scholarships/grants:* Pell, SEOG, state scholarships/grants, private scholarships, the school's own gift aid, Southern Vermont College Opportunity Grant, Everett Scholarship, Leadership Scholarship, Vermont Resident Scholarship, TRIO Scholarship. *Loans:* Direct Subsidized Stafford, Direct Unsubsidized Stafford, Direct PLUS. **Student Employment:** Federal Work-Study Program available. Institutional employment available. Off-campus job opportunities are good. **Financial Aid Statistics:** 72% freshmen, 80% undergrads receive some form of aid. Average freshman grant $5,040. **Financial Aid Phone:** 877-563-6076.

See page 1214.

SOUTHERN WESLEYAN UNIVERSITY

Wesleyan Drive, PO Box 1020, Central, SC 29630-1020
Phone: 864-644-5903 **E-mail:** admissions@swu.edu
Fax: 864-644-5093 **Web:** www.swu.edu **ACT Code:** 3837

This private school, which is affiliated with the Methodist Church, was founded in 1906. It has a 210-acre campus.

STUDENTS AND FACULTY

Enrollment: 2,024. **Student Body:** Male 37%, female 63%, out-of-state 13%, international 1% (8 countries represented). **Ethnic Representation:** African American 29%, Caucasian 66%, Hispanic 1%, Native American 1%. **Retention and Graduation:** 71% freshmen return for sophomore year. 26% freshmen graduate within 4 years. **Faculty:** Student/faculty ratio 12:1. 49 full-time faculty, 73% hold PhDs. 100% faculty teach undergrads.

ACADEMICS

Degrees: Associate's, bachelor's, master's. **Academic Requirements:** General education including some course work in arts/fine arts, computer literacy, English (including composition), history, humanities, mathematics, philosophy, sciences (biological or physical), social science, religion, aesthetics, computer science, physical education, interdisciplinary seminars. **Classes:** 10-19 students in an average class. Under 10 students in an average lab/discussion section. **Majors with Highest Enrollment:** Elementary education and teaching; religion/religious studies; business administration/management. **Disciplines with Highest Percentage of Degrees Awarded:** Business/marketing 75%, education 9%, biological life sciences 3%, psychology 3%, philosophy/religion/theology 3%. **Special Study Options:** Cooperative (work-study) program, cross registration, double major, honors program, independent study, internships, study abroad, teacher certification program.

FACILITIES

Housing: Coed, all-female, apartments for single students, housing for disabled students. **Library Holdings:** 84,340 bound volumes. 520 periodicals. 160 microforms. 3,291 audiovisuals. **Computers:** *Recommended operating system:* Windows 2000. School-owned computers available for student use.

EXTRACURRICULARS

Activities: Choral groups, concert band, drama/theater, jazz band, literary magazine, music ensembles, musical theater, student government, yearbook. **Organizations:** 8 registered organizations, 1 honor society, 6 religious organizations. **Athletics (Intercollegiate):** *Men:* baseball, basketball, cheerleading, cross-country, golf, soccer. *Women:* basketball, cheerleading, cross-country, soccer, softball, volleyball.

ADMISSIONS

Selectivity Rating: 63 (of 100). **Freshman Academic Profile:** Average high school GPA 3.4. 23% in top 10% of high school class, 45% in top 25% of high school class, 72% in top 50% of high school class. Average SAT I Math 516, SAT I Math middle 50% range 450-570. Average SAT I Verbal 516, SAT I Verbal middle 50% range 460-560. Average ACT 19, ACT middle 50% range 17-21. TOEFL required of all international applicants, minimum TOEFL 500. **Basis for Candidate Selection:** *Very important factors considered include:* class rank, recommendations, secondary school record, standardized test scores. *Important factors considered include:* character/personal qualities, extracurricular activities, interview, talent/ability. **Freshman Admission Requirements:** High school diploma or GED is required. *Academic units required/recommended:* 12 total required; 18 total recommended; 4 English required, 4 English recommended, 2 math required, 3 math recommended, 2 science required, 3 science recommended, 2 foreign language recommended, 2 social studies required, 2 social studies recommended, 2 history recommended, 2 elective required, 3 elective recommended. **Freshman Admission Statistics:** 284 applied, 69% accepted, 57% of those accepted enrolled. **Transfer Admission Requirements:** *Items required:* college transcript, statement of good standing from prior school. Minimum high school GPA of 2.0 required. Minimum college GPA of 2.0 required. Lowest grade transferable C. **General Admission Information:** Application fee $25. Admission may be deferred. Credit and/or placement offered for CEEB Advanced Placement tests.

COSTS AND FINANCIAL AID

Tuition $13,000. Room & board $4,700. Required fees $450. Average book expense $900. **Required Forms and Deadlines:** FAFSA and institution's own financial aid form. Financial aid filing deadline June 30. Priority filing deadline June 30. **Notification of Awards:** Applicants will be notified of awards on a rolling basis beginning on or about March 1. **Types of Aid:** *Need-based scholarships/grants:* Pell, SEOG, state scholarships/grants, private scholarships, the school's own gift aid. *Loans:* FFEL Subsidized Stafford, FFEL Unsubsidized Stafford, FFEL PLUS, Federal Perkins, state. **Student**

Employment: Federal Work-Study Program available. Institutional employment available. Off-campus job opportunities are good. **Financial Aid Statistics:** 84% freshmen, 80% undergrads receive some form of aid. Average freshman grant $7,569. Average freshman loan $3,470. Average income from on-campus job $1,150. **Financial Aid Phone:** 864-644-5501.

SOUTHWEST BAPTIST UNIVERSITY

1600 University Avenue, Bolivar, MO 65613-2597
Phone: 417-328-1810 **E-mail:** admitme@sbuniv.edu
Fax: 417-328-1808 **Web:** www.sbuniv.edu **ACT Code:** 2368

This private school, which is affiliated with the Southern Baptist Church, was founded in 1878. It has a 100-acre campus.

STUDENTS AND FACULTY

Enrollment: 2,714. **Student Body:** Male 34%, female 66%, out-of-state 24%international students represent 7 countries. **Retention and Graduation:** 77% freshmen return for sophomore year. 32% freshmen graduate within 4 years. **Faculty:** Student/faculty ratio 17:1. 99 full-time faculty, 63% hold PhDs. 100% faculty teach undergrads.

ACADEMICS

Degrees: Associate's, bachelor's, certificate, diploma, master's. **Academic Requirements:** General education including some course work in arts/fine arts, computer literacy, English (including composition), history, humanities, mathematics, sciences (biological or physical), social science. **Classes:** 10-19 students in an average class. 10-19 students in an average lab/discussion section. **Majors with Highest Enrollment:** Elementary education and teaching; business administration/management; theological studies and religious vocations. **Disciplines with Highest Percentage of Degrees Awarded:** Education 26%, psychology 19%, philosophy/religion/theology 13%, health professions and related sciences 12%, business/marketing 11%. **Special Study Options:** Double major, independent study, internships, study abroad, teacher certification program.

FACILITIES

Housing: All-female, all-male. **Library Holdings:** 169,084 bound volumes. 730 periodicals. 446,803 microforms. 10,497 audiovisuals. **Computers:** School-owned computers available for student use.

EXTRACURRICULARS

Activities: Choral groups, concert band, drama/theater, jazz band, music ensembles, musical theater, opera, pep band, student government, student newspaper, symphony orchestra, television station, yearbook. **Organizations:** 50 registered organizations, 9 honor societies, 12 religious organizations. **Athletics (Intercollegiate):** *Men:* baseball, basketball, cross-country, football, golf, indoor track, tennis. *Women:* basketball, cheerleading, cross-country, indoor track, soccer, softball, tennis, volleyball.

ADMISSIONS

Selectivity Rating: 74 (of 100). **Freshman Academic Profile:** Average high school GPA 3.4. 27% in top 10% of high school class, 50% in top 25% of high school class, 77% in top 50% of high school class. SAT I Math middle 50% range 450-600. SAT I Verbal middle 50% range 450-590. Average ACT 23, ACT middle 50% range 20-25. TOEFL required of all international applicants, minimum TOEFL 550. **Basis for Candidate Selection:** *Very important factors considered include:* standardized test scores. *Important factors considered include:* secondary school record. *Other factors considered include:* alumni/ae relation, character/personal qualities, essays, extracurricular activities, recommendations, religious affiliation/commitment. **Freshman Admission Requirements:** High school diploma or GED is required. *Academic units required/recommended:* 4 English recommended, 3 math recommended, 3 science recommended, 2 foreign language recommended, 2 social studies recommended, 2 history recommended. **Freshman Admission Statistics:** 884 applied, 85% accepted, 64% of those accepted enrolled. **Transfer Admission Requirements:** *Items required:* college transcript, standardized test scores. Minimum high school GPA of 2.0 required. Minimum college GPA of 2.0 required. Lowest grade transferable D. **General Admission Information:** Application fee $25. Nonfall registration accepted. Admission may be deferred for a maximum of 1 year. Credit offered for CEEB Advanced Placement tests.

COSTS AND FINANCIAL AID

Tuition $10,300. Room & board $3,260. Required fees $62. Average book expense $500. **Required Forms and Deadlines:** FAFSA. No deadline for regular filing. Priority filing deadline March 15. **Notification of Awards:** Applicants will be notified of awards on a rolling basis beginning on or about March 1. **Types of Aid:** *Need-based scholarships/grants:* Pell, SEOG, state scholarships/grants, private scholarships, the school's own gift aid. *Loans:* FFEL Subsidized Stafford, FFEL Unsubsidized Stafford, FFEL PLUS, Federal Perkins, college/university loans from institutional funds. **Student Employment:** Federal Work-Study Program available. Institutional employment available. Off-campus job opportunities are good. **Financial Aid Statistics:** 78% freshmen, 84% undergrads receive some form of aid. Average freshman grant $3,500. Average freshman loan $3,500. Average income from on-campus job $1,000. **Financial Aid Phone:** 417-328-1822.

SOUTHWEST MISSOURI STATE UNIVERSITY

901 South National, Springfield, MO 65804
Phone: 417-836-5517 **E-mail:** smsuinfo@smsu.edu **CEEB Code:** 6665
Fax: 417-836-6334 **Web:** www.smsu.edu **ACT Code:** 2370

This public school was founded in 1906. It has a 450-acre campus.

STUDENTS AND FACULTY

Enrollment: 15,448. **Student Body:** Male 45%, female 55%, out-of-state 8%, international 2%. **Ethnic Representation:** African American 3%, Asian 1%, Caucasian 90%, Hispanic 1%, Native American 1%. **Retention and Graduation:** 73% freshmen return for sophomore year. 14% freshmen graduate within 4 years. 18% grads go on to further study within 1 year. 10% grads pursue business degrees. 2% grads pursue law degrees. 2% grads pursue medical degrees. **Faculty:** Student/faculty ratio 18:1. 731 full-time faculty, 79% hold PhDs. 94% faculty teach undergrads.

ACADEMICS

Degrees: Bachelor's, master's. **Academic Requirements:** General education including some course work in computer literacy, English (including composition), history, humanities, mathematics, sciences (biological or physical), social science. **Classes:** 20-29 students in an average class. 20-29 students in an average lab/discussion section. **Disciplines with Highest Percentage of Degrees Awarded:** Business/marketing 35%, education 15%, communications/communication technologies 7%, visual and performing arts 5%, social sciences and history 5%. **Special Study Options:** Accelerated program, cooperative (work-study) program, distance learning, double major, dual enrollment, English as a second language, student exchange program (domestic), honors program, independent study, internships, student-designed major, study abroad, teacher certification program.

FACILITIES

Housing: Coed, apartments for married students, apartments for single students, housing for disabled students, housing for international students, fraternities and/or sororities, graduate student housing, nontraditional student housing, upper-class student housing, honor student housing, transfer student housing. **Library Holdings:** 1,699,866 bound volumes. 4,238 periodicals. 1,010,550 microforms. 33,547 audiovisuals. **Special Academic Facilities/Equipment:** On-campus laboratory school (K-12), 125-acre Darr Agricultural Center, Baker Observatory, Bull Shoals Field Station, electron microscope, molecular beam epitaxy laboratory, ion implantation laboratory, art & design gallery, student exhibition center, Coger Theatre, Ellis Recital Hall, instructional TV studio, computer animation studio, foundry, Wehr Band Hall, multimedia lab, language lab, Juanita K. Hammons Hall for the Performing Arts. **Computers:** School-owned computers available for student use.

EXTRACURRICULARS

Activities: Choral groups, concert band, dance, drama/theater, jazz band, literary magazine, marching band, music ensembles, musical theater, pep band, radio station, student government, student newspaper, student-run film society, symphony orchestra, television station. **Organizations:** 240 registered organizations, 40 honor societies, 26 religious organizations, 13 fraternities (13% men join), 10 sororities (12% women join). **Athletics (Intercollegiate):** *Men:* baseball, basketball, cross-country, diving, football, golf, indoor track, soccer, swimming, tennis, track & field, volleyball. *Women:* basketball, cross-country, diving, field hockey, golf, indoor track, soccer, softball, swimming, tennis, track & field, volleyball.

ADMISSIONS

Selectivity Rating: 70 (of 100). **Freshman Academic Profile:** Average high school GPA 3.5. 19% in top 10% of high school class, 46% in top 25% of high school class, 79% in top 50% of high school class. 93% from public high schools. Average ACT 24, ACT middle 50% range 21-26. TOEFL required of all international applicants, minimum TOEFL 500. **Basis for Candidate Selection:** *Very important factors considered include:* class rank, secondary school record, standardized test scores. *Other factors considered include:* alumni/ae relation, character/personal qualities, essays, extracurricular activities, interview, minority status, recommendations, talent/ability, volunteer work, work experience. **Freshman Admission Requirements:** High school diploma or GED is required. *Academic units required/recommended:* 16 total required; 4 English required, 3 math required, 2 science required, 1 science lab required, 3 social studies required, 3 elective required. **Freshman Admission Statistics:** 6,892 applied, 80% accepted, 50% of those accepted enrolled. **Transfer Admission Requirements:** *Items required:* college transcript. Minimum college GPA of 2.0 required. Lowest grade transferable D. **General Admission Information:** Application fee $25. Priority application deadline February 2. Regular application deadline August 2. Nonfall registration accepted. Credit and/or placement offered for CEEB Advanced Placement tests.

COSTS AND FINANCIAL AID

In-state tuition $4,274. Out-of-state tuition $8,114. Room & board $4,850. Required fees $434. Average book expense $400. **Required Forms and Deadlines:** FAFSA. Priority filing deadline March 30. **Notification of Awards:** Applicants will be notified of awards on a rolling basis beginning on or about April 30. **Types of Aid:** *Need-based scholarships/grants:* Pell, SEOG, state scholarships/grants, private scholarships, the school's own gift aid. *Loans:* FFEL Subsidized Stafford, FFEL Unsubsidized Stafford, FFEL PLUS, Federal Perkins, state loans, college/university loans from institutional funds. **Student Employment:** Federal Work-Study Program available. Institutional employment available. Off-campus job opportunities are excellent. **Financial Aid Statistics:** 45% freshmen, 47% undergrads receive some form of aid. Average freshman grant $3,340. Average freshman loan $2,274. Average income from on-campus job $2,237. **Financial Aid Phone:** 417-836-5262.

SOUTHWEST STATE UNIVERSITY

Admission Office, 1501 State Street, Marshall, MN 56258
Phone: 800-642-0684 **E-mail:** shearerr@southwest.msus.edu **CEEB Code:** 6703
Fax: 507-537-7154 **Web:** www.southwest.msus.edu **ACT Code:** 2151

This public school was founded in 1963. It has a 216-acre campus.

STUDENTS AND FACULTY

Enrollment: 2,900. **Student Body:** Out-of-state 17%, international 1%. **Ethnic Representation:** African American 3%, Asian 2%, Caucasian 91%, Hispanic 2%, Native American 2%. **Retention and Graduation:** 66% freshmen return for sophomore year. 8% freshmen graduate within 4 years.

ACADEMICS

Degrees: Associate's, bachelor's, master's. **Special Study Options:** Study abroad.

FACILITIES

Housing: Apartments for single students. **Library Holdings:** 165,000 bound volumes. 800 periodicals. 37,000 microforms. 12,000 audiovisuals. **Special Academic Facilities/Equipment:** Art gallery, natural history museum, science museum, planetarium, greenhouse, wildlife area. **Computers:** *Recommended operating system:* Mac. School-owned computers available for student use.

EXTRACURRICULARS

Activities: Literary magazine, radio station, student government, student newspaper, television station, yearbook. **Organizations:** 65 registered organizations, 1 honor society, 5 religious organizations. **Athletics (Intercollegiate):** *Men:* cross-country track. *Women:* basketball, cross-country, softball, tennis, volleyball.

ADMISSIONS

Selectivity Rating: 71 (of 100). **Freshman Academic Profile:** 17% in top 10% of high school class, 41% in top 25% of high school class, 81% in top 50% of high school class. Average ACT 20, ACT middle 50% range 19-24. TOEFL required of all international applicants, minimum TOEFL 500. **Freshman Admission Requirements:** High school diploma is required and GED is not accepted. *Academic units required/recommended:* 16 total recommended; 4 English recommended, 3 math recommended, 3 science recommended, 2 foreign language recommended, 3 social studies recommended, 1 history recommended. **Transfer Admission Requirements:** Minimum college GPA of 2.0 required. Lowest grade transferable C. **General Admission Information:** Application fee $20. Regular application deadline rolling. Nonfall registration accepted. Credit offered for CEEB Advanced Placement tests.

COSTS AND FINANCIAL AID

In-state tuition $2,648. Out-of-state tuition $5,965. Room & board $3,000. Required fees $484. Average book expense $800. **Required Forms and Deadlines:** FAFSA and institution's own financial aid form. **Types of Aid:** *Need-based scholarships/grants:* Pell, SEOG, state scholarships/grants, private scholarships, the school's own gift aid. *Loans:* FFEL Subsidized Stafford, FFEL Unsubsidized Stafford, FFEL PLUS, Federal Perkins, college/university loans from institutional funds. **Student Employment:** Federal Work-Study Program available. Institutional employment available. Off-campus job opportunities are excellent. **Financial Aid Statistics:** Average freshman grant $1,331. Average freshman loan $2,521. Average income from on-campus job $2,602. **Financial Aid Phone:** 507-537-6281.

SOUTHWEST TEXAS STATE UNIVERSITY

429 North Guadalupe St., San Marcos, TX 78666
Phone: 512-245-2364 **E-mail:** admissions@swt.edu **CEEB Code:** 6667
Fax: 512-245-9020 **Web:** www.swt.edu **ACT Code:** 4178

This public school was founded in 1899. It has a 427-acre campus.

STUDENTS AND FACULTY

Enrollment: 21,089. **Student Body:** Male 45%, female 55%, out-of-state 1%, international 1% (74 countries represented). **Ethnic Representation:** African American 5%, Asian 2%, Caucasian 73%, Hispanic 19%, Native American 1%. **Retention and Graduation:** 76% freshmen return for sophomore year. 17% freshmen graduate within 4 years. **Faculty:** Student/faculty ratio 26:1. 684 full-time faculty, 78% hold PhDs. 89% faculty teach undergrads.

ACADEMICS

Degrees: Bachelor's, doctoral, master's, post-bachelor's certificate. **Academic Requirements:** General education including some course work in arts/fine arts, computer literacy, English (including composition), foreign languages, history, humanities, mathematics, philosophy, sciences (biological or physical), social science. **Classes:** 20-29 students in an average class. 10-19 students in an average lab/discussion section. **Majors with Highest Enrollment:** Multi/interdisciplinary studies; business administration/management; marketing/marketing management, general. **Disciplines with Highest Percentage of Degrees Awarded:** Business/marketing 23%, interdisciplinary studies 14%, social sciences and history 7%, parks and recreation 7%, visual and performing arts 6%. **Special Study Options:** Cross registration, distance learning, double major, dual enrollment, English as a second language, honors program, independent study, internships, liberal arts/career combination, study abroad, teacher certification program, weekend college.

FACILITIES

Housing: Coed, all-female, all-male, apartments for married students, apartments for single students, fraternities and/or sororities, nonsmoking, honors. Access for the disabled, but not separate housing. **Library Holdings:** 732,524 bound volumes. 7,117 periodicals. 1,809,139 microforms. 30,644 audiovisuals. **Special Academic Facilities/Equipment:** Child development center, aquifer research center, two demonstration farms, physical anthropology and archaeology laboratories. Southwestern Writers Collection. **Computers:** School-owned computers available for student use.

EXTRACURRICULARS

Activities: Choral groups, concert band, dance, drama/theater, jazz band, literary magazine, marching band, music ensembles, musical theater, opera, pep band, radio station, student government, student newspaper, student-run film society, symphony orchestra, yearbook. **Organizations:** 242 registered organizations, 31 honor societies, 31 religious organizations, 21 fraternities (5% men join), 8 sororities (5% women join). **Athletics (Intercollegiate):** *Men:* baseball, basketball, cheerleading, cross-country, football, golf, track & field. *Women:* basketball, cheerleading, cross-country, golf, soccer, softball, tennis, track & field, volleyball.

ADMISSIONS

Selectivity Rating: 64 (of 100). **Freshman Academic Profile:** 12% in top 10% of high school class, 49% in top 25% of high school class, 93% in top 50% of high school class. Average SAT I Math 520, SAT I Math middle 50% range 480-560. Average SAT I Verbal 510, SAT I Verbal middle 50% range 470-560. Average ACT 21, ACT middle 50% range 19-23. TOEFL required of all international applicants, minimum TOEFL 550. **Basis for Candidate Selection:** *Very important factors considered include:* class rank, standardized test scores. *Important factors considered include:* essays. *Other factors considered include:* secondary school record, talent/ability. **Freshman Admission Requirements:** High school diploma or GED is required. *Academic units required/recommended:* 16 total required; 21 total recommended; 4 English required, 4 English recommended, 3 math required, 3 math recommended, 3 science required, 3 science recommended, 2 science lab required, 2 science lab recommended, 2 foreign language required, 3 foreign language recommended, 3 social studies required, 4 social studies recommended, 2 elective recommended. **Freshman Admission Statistics:** 10,269 applied, 56% accepted, 47% of those accepted enrolled. **Transfer Admission Requirements:** *Items required:* college transcript, statement of good standing from prior school. Minimum college GPA of 2.2 required. Lowest grade transferable D. **General Admission Information:** Application fee $40. Regular application deadline July 1. Nonfall registration accepted. Admission may be deferred. Credit offered for CEEB Advanced Placement tests.

COSTS AND FINANCIAL AID

In-state tuition $2,640. Out-of-state tuition $9,180. Room & board $5,296. Required fees $1,110. Average book expense $950. **Required Forms and Deadlines:** FAFSA. No deadline for regular filing. Priority filing deadline April 1. **Notification of Awards:** Applicants will be notified of awards on a rolling basis beginning on or about May 1. **Types of Aid:** *Need-based scholarships/grants:* Pell, SEOG, state scholarships/grants, private scholarships. *Loans:* Direct Subsidized Stafford, Direct Unsubsidized Stafford, Direct PLUS, FFEL Subsidized Stafford, FFEL Unsubsidized Stafford, FFEL PLUS, Federal Perkins, college/university loans from institutional funds, alternative loans. **Student Employment:** Federal Work-Study Program available. Institutional employment available. Off-campus job opportunities are good. **Financial Aid Statistics:** 38% freshmen, 42% undergrads receive some form of aid. Average freshman grant $2,624. Average freshman loan $2,444. Average income from on-campus job $2,970. **Financial Aid Phone:** 512-245-2315.

SOUTHWESTERN ADVENTIST UNIVERSITY

PO Box 567, Keene, TX 76059
Phone: 800-433-2240 **E-mail:** illingworth@swac.edu
Fax: 817-645-3921 **Web:** www.swac.edu

This private school, which is affiliated with the Seventh-Day Adventist Church, was founded in 1893.

STUDENTS AND FACULTY

Enrollment: 1,065. **Student Body:** Out-of-state 46%, international students represent 35 countries. **Retention and Graduation:** 63% freshmen return for sophomore year. 28% grads go on to further study within 1 year. 5% grads pursue business degrees. 3% grads pursue law degrees. 10% grads pursue medical degrees. **Faculty:** 100% faculty teach undergrads.

FACILITIES

Housing: Coed, all-female, all-male.

EXTRACURRICULARS

Organizations: 2 honor societies, 2 religious organizations.

ADMISSIONS

Selectivity Rating: 60 (of 100). **Freshman Academic Profile:** Average high school GPA 3.3. 15% in top 10% of high school class, 37% in top 25% of high school class, 65% in top 50% of high school class. 30% from public high schools. Average SAT I Math 464, SAT I Math middle 50% range 400-540. Average SAT I Verbal 503, SAT I Verbal middle 50% range 450-570. Average ACT 21, ACT middle 50% range 18-23. TOEFL required of all international applicants, minimum TOEFL 520. **Freshman Admission Requirements: General Admission Information:** Regular application deadline September 10. Credit and/or placement offered for CEEB Advanced Placement tests.

COSTS AND FINANCIAL AID

Room & board $4,084. Required fees $100. Average book expense $536. **Types of Aid:** *Loans:* FFEL Subsidized Stafford, FFEL PLUS. **Student Employment:** Federal Work-Study Program available. Off-campus job opportunities are fair. **Financial Aid Statistics:** Average income from on-campus job $2,140. **Financial Aid Phone:** 817-645-3921.

SOUTHWESTERN CHRISTIAN UNIVERSITY

PO Box 340, Bethany, OK 73008
Phone: 405-789-7661 **E-mail:** admissions@swcu.edu
Fax: 405-495-0078 **Web:** www.swcu.edu **ACT Code:** 3439

This private school, which is affiliated with the Pentecostal Church, was founded in 1946. It has a 11-acre campus.

STUDENTS AND FACULTY

Enrollment: 122. **Student Body:** Male 58%, female 42%, out-of-state 30%, international 4%. **Ethnic Representation:** African American 4%, Asian 1%, Caucasian 87%, Hispanic 3%, Native American 5%. **Retention and Graduation:** 42% freshmen return for sophomore year. 15% freshmen graduate within 4 years. **Faculty:** Student/faculty ratio 8:1. 5 full-time faculty, 20% hold PhDs.

ACADEMICS

Degrees: Associate's, bachelor's, certificate, diploma, master's. **Academic Requirements:** General education including some course work in computer literacy, English (including composition), history, humanities, mathematics, sciences (biological or physical), social science, Bible. **Classes:** 10-19 students in an average class. **Disciplines with Highest Percentage of Degrees Awarded:** Theology 100%. **Special Study Options:** Cooperative (work-study) program, double major, internships.

FACILITIES

Housing: All-female, all-male.

EXTRACURRICULARS

Activities: Choral groups, music ensembles, musical theater, student government. **Organizations:** 10 honor societies, 4 religious organizations. **Athletics (Intercollegiate):** *Men:* basketball, golf. *Women:* basketball, volleyball.

ADMISSIONS

Selectivity Rating: 60 (of 100). **Freshman Academic Profile:** Average high school GPA 3.4. 11% in top 10% of high school class, 30% in top 25% of high school class, 55% in top 50% of high school class. ACT middle 50% range 19-21. TOEFL required of all international applicants, minimum TOEFL 550. **Basis for Candidate Selection:** *Very important factors considered include:* recommendations, secondary school record. *Important factors considered include:* character/personal qualities, class rank, standardized test scores. *Other factors considered include:* essays, extracurricular activities, interview, religious affiliation/commitment, talent/ability. **Freshman Admission Requirements:** High school diploma or GED is required. **Transfer Admission Requirements:** *Items required:* college transcript, statement of good standing from prior school. Minimum college GPA of 2.5 required. Lowest grade transferable C. **General Admission Information:** Application fee $30. Priority application deadline May 15. Early decision application deadline March 15. Regular application deadline July 15. Nonfall registration accepted. Admission may be deferred for a maximum of 1 year.

COSTS AND FINANCIAL AID

Tuition $6,000. Room & board $3,400. Required fees $300. Average book expense $300. **Types of Aid:** *Loans:* FFEL Subsidized Stafford, FFEL PLUS. **Student Employment:** Federal Work-Study Program available. Off-campus job opportunities are excellent. **Financial Aid Statistics:** Average income from on-campus job $800. **Financial Aid Phone:** 405-789-7661.

SOUTHWESTERN COLLEGE

100 College Street, Winfield, KS 67156
Phone: 620-229-6236 **E-mail:** scadmit@sckans.edu **CEEB Code:** 6670
Fax: 620-229-6344 **Web:** www.sckans.edu **ACT Code:** 1464

This private school, which is affiliated with the Methodist Church, was founded in 1885. It has an 85-acre campus.

STUDENTS AND FACULTY

Enrollment: 1,137. **Student Body:** Male 51%, female 49%, out-of-state 15%, international 3% (9 countries represented). **Ethnic Representation:** African American 6%, Asian 2%, Caucasian 83%, Hispanic 4%, Native American 2%. **Retention and Graduation:** 68% freshmen return for sophomore year. 41% freshmen graduate within 4 years. 16% grads go on to further study within 1 year. **Faculty:** Student/faculty ratio 13:1. 54 full-time faculty, 55% hold PhDs. 100% faculty teach undergrads.

ACADEMICS

Degrees: Bachelor's, master's. **Academic Requirements:** General education including some course work in English (including composition). **Classes:** 10-19 students in an average class. 10-19 students in an average lab/discussion section. **Majors with Highest Enrollment:** Business administration/management; management science, general; biology/biological sciences, general. **Disciplines with Highest Percentage of Degrees Awarded:** Business/marketing 48%, computer and information sciences 14%, biological life sciences 7%, education 6%, health professions and related sciences 6%. **Special Study Options:** Accelerated program, cooperative (work-study) program, double major, student exchange program (domestic), honors program, independent study, internships, liberal arts/career combination, student-designed major, study abroad, teacher certification program, weekend college.

FACILITIES

Housing: Coed, all-female, all-male, apartments for married students, apartments for single students. **Library Holdings:** 77,000 bound volumes. 1,800 periodicals. 3,740 microforms. 350 audiovisuals. **Special Academic Facilities/Equipment:** Ruth Warren Abbott Horticulture Lab, Floyd and Ethel Moore Biological Field Station. **Computers:** *Recommended operating system:* Windows XP. School-owned computers available for student use.

EXTRACURRICULARS

Activities: Choral groups, concert band, dance, drama/theater, jazz band, literary magazine, music ensembles, musical theater, pep band, radio station, student government, student newspaper, student-run film society, symphony orchestra, television station, yearbook. **Organizations:** 17 registered organizations, 3 honor societies, 10 religious organizations, 2 fraternities (8% men join), 1 sorority (7% women join). **Athletics (Intercollegiate):** *Men:* basketball, cheerleading, cross-country, football, golf, indoor track, soccer, tennis, track & field. *Women:* basketball, cheerleading, cross-country, golf, indoor track, soccer, tennis, track & field, volleyball.

ADMISSIONS

Selectivity Rating: 66 (of 100). **Freshman Academic Profile:** Average high school GPA 3.3. 24% in top 10% of high school class, 46% in top 25% of high school class, 74% in top 50% of high school class. 94% from public high schools. TOEFL required of all international applicants, minimum TOEFL 550. **Basis for Candidate Selection:** *Very important factors considered include:* essays, secondary school record, standardized test scores. *Important factors considered include:* character/personal qualities, extracurricular activities, interview, volunteer work. *Other factors considered include:* alumni/ae relation, class rank, recommendations, talent/ability, work experience. **Freshman Admission Requirements:** High school diploma or GED is required. *Academic units required/recommended:* 12 total required; 1 total recommended; 4 English required, 3 math required, 2 science required, 1 science lab required, 1 foreign language recommended, 1 social studies required, 1 history required. **Freshman Admission Statistics:** 353 applied, 74% accepted, 41% of those accepted enrolled. **Transfer Admission Requirements:** *Items required:* college transcript, essay. Minimum college GPA of 2.0 required. Lowest grade transferable C. **General Admission Information:** Application fee $20. Priority application deadline February 1. Regular application deadline August 1. Nonfall registration accepted. Admission may be deferred for a maximum of 3 years. Credit and/or placement offered for CEEB Advanced Placement tests.

COSTS AND FINANCIAL AID

Tuition $13,922. Room & board $4,736. Required fees $0. Average book expense $600. **Required Forms and Deadlines:** FAFSA and institution's own financial aid form. Financial aid filing deadline August 1. Priority filing deadline July 1. **Notification of Awards:** Applicants will be notified of awards on a rolling basis. **Types of Aid:** *Need-based scholarships/grants:* Pell, SEOG, state scholarships/grants, the school's own gift aid. *Loans:* Direct Subsidized Stafford, Direct Unsubsidized Stafford, Direct PLUS, FFEL Subsidized Stafford, FFEL Unsubsidized Stafford, FFEL PLUS, Federal Perkins. **Student Employment:** Federal Work-Study Program available. Institutional employment available. Off-campus job opportunities are good. **Financial Aid Statistics:** 86% freshmen, 81% undergrads receive some form of aid. Average freshman grant $7,522. Average freshman loan $4,647. Average income from on-campus job $730. **Financial Aid Phone:** 620-229-6215.

SOUTHWESTERN OKLAHOMA STATE UNIVERSITY

100 Campus Drive, Weatherford, OK 73096
Phone: 580-774-3795 **E-mail:** phillic@swosu.edu **CEEB Code:** 6673
Fax: 580-774-3795 **Web:** www.swosu.edu **ACT Code:** 3340

This public school was founded in 1901. It has a 73-acre campus.

STUDENTS AND FACULTY

Enrollment: 4,015. **Student Body:** Male 44%, female 56%, out-of-state 10%, international 3%. **Ethnic Representation:** African American 4%, Asian 1%, Caucasian 85%, Hispanic 4%, Native American 6%. **Retention and Graduation:** 65% freshmen return for sophomore year. **Faculty:** Student/faculty ratio 20:1. 195 full-time faculty, 63% hold PhDs.

ACADEMICS

Degrees: Bachelor's, first professional, master's. **Academic Requirements:** General education including some course work in arts/fine arts, computer literacy, English (including composition), history, humanities, mathematics, sciences (biological or physical), social science, wellness, international & cultural studies. **Classes:** 20-29 students in an average class. 10-19 students in an average lab/discussion section. **Disciplines with Highest Percentage of Degrees Awarded:** Business/marketing 24%, education 22%, health professions and related sciences 12%, visual and performing arts 8%, engineering/engineering technology 5%. **Special Study Options:** Accelerated program, distance learning, double major, dual enrollment, independent study, internships, student-designed major, teacher certification program, weekend college.

FACILITIES

Housing: All-female, all-male, apartments for married students. **Library Holdings:** 217,051 bound volumes. 1,230 periodicals. 1,223,309 microforms. 6,718 audiovisuals. **Special Academic Facilities/Equipment:** Writing lab, museum. **Computers:** *Recommended operating system:* Mac. School-owned computers available for student use.

EXTRACURRICULARS

Activities: Choral groups, concert band, drama/theater, jazz band, marching band, music ensembles, musical theater, pep band, student government, student newspaper, symphony orchestra, yearbook. **Organizations:** 3 religious organizations, 3 fraternities, 3 sororities. **Athletics (Intercollegiate):** *Men:* baseball, basketball, football, golf, tennis, track & field. *Women:* basketball, tennis.

ADMISSIONS

Selectivity Rating: 63 (of 100). **Freshman Academic Profile:** Average high school GPA 3.4. 18% in top 10% of high school class, 41% in top 25% of high school class, 71% in top 50% of high school class. 98% from public high schools. Average ACT 21, ACT middle 50% range 18-24. TOEFL required of all international applicants, minimum TOEFL 500. **Basis for Candidate Selection:** *Very important factors considered include:* class rank, secondary school record, standardized test scores. **Freshman Admission Requirements:** High school diploma or GED is required. *Academic units required/recommended:* 15 total required; 17 total recommended; 4 English required, 4 English recommended, 3 math required, 3 math recommended, 2 science required, 2 science recommended, 2 science lab required, 2 science lab recommended, 1 social studies required, 1 social studies recommended, 2 history required, 2 history recommended, 2 elective recommended. **Freshman Admission Statistics:** 1,395 applied, 94% accepted, 71% of those accepted enrolled. **Transfer Admission Requirements:** *Items required:* college transcript. Minimum college GPA of 2.0 required. Lowest grade transferable D. **General Admission Information:** Application fee $15. Nonfall registration accepted. Admission may be deferred for a maximum of 1 year. Credit and/or placement offered for CEEB Advanced Placement tests.

COSTS AND FINANCIAL AID

In-state tuition $1,700. Out-of-state tuition $4,853. Room & board $2,680. Required fees $748. Average book expense $772. **Required Forms and Deadlines:** FAFSA and institution's own financial aid form. Financial aid filing deadline March 1. Priority filing deadline March 1. **Types of Aid:** *Need-based scholarships/grants:* Pell, SEOG, state scholarships/grants, private scholarships, the school's own gift aid. *Loans:* FFEL Subsidized Stafford, FFEL Unsubsidized Stafford, FFEL PLUS, alternative loans through various institutions. **Student Employment:** Federal Work-Study Program available. Institutional employment available. Off-campus job opportunities are fair. **Financial Aid Statistics:** 58% freshmen, 58% undergrads receive some form of aid. **Financial Aid Phone:** 405-774-3786.

SOUTHWESTERN UNIVERSITY

Admissions Office, PO Box 770, Georgetown, TX 78627-0770
Phone: 512-863-1200 **E-mail:** admission@southwestern.edu **CEEB Code:** 6674
Fax: 512-863-9601 **Web:** www.southwestern.edu **ACT Code:** 4186

This private school, which is affiliated with the Methodist Church, was founded in 1840. It has a 703-acre campus.

STUDENTS AND FACULTY

Enrollment: 1,266. **Student Body:** Male 41%, female 59%, out-of-state 6%, international students represent 10 countries. **Ethnic Representation:** African American 3%, Asian 3%, Caucasian 78%, Hispanic 13%. **Retention and Graduation:** 83% freshmen return for sophomore year. 57% freshmen graduate within 4 years. 24% grads go on to further study within 1 year. 1% grads pursue business degrees. 6% grads pursue law degrees. 3% grads pursue medical degrees. **Faculty:** Student/faculty ratio 10:1. 107 full-time faculty, 93% hold PhDs. 100% faculty teach undergrads.

ACADEMICS

Degrees: Bachelor's. **Academic Requirements:** General education including some course work in arts/fine arts, computer literacy, English (including composition), foreign languages, history, humanities, mathematics, philosophy, sciences (biological or physical), social science. **Classes:** 10-19 students in an average class. Under 10 students in an average lab/discussion section. **Majors with Highest Enrollment:** Business/commerce, general; communications studies/speech communication and rhetoric; biology/biological sciences, general. **Disciplines with Highest Percentage of Degrees Awarded:** Business/marketing 16%, social sciences and history 15%, communications/ communication technologies 12%, psychology 10%, education 8%. **Special Study Options:** Double major, independent study, internships, student-designed major, study abroad, teacher certification program.

FACILITIES

Housing: Coed, all-female, all-male, apartments for single students, housing for disabled students, fraternities and/or sororities. **Library Holdings:** 210,848 bound volumes. 1,473 periodicals. 51,380 microforms. 10,533 audiovisuals. **Special Academic Facilities/Equipment:** Alma Thomas Fine Arts Center, Red and Charline McCombs Campus Center, Corbin J. Robertson Center for Fitness and Wellness, Fountainwood Astronomical Observatory. **Computers:** School-owned computers available for student use.

EXTRACURRICULARS

Activities: Choral groups, concert band, dance, drama/theater, jazz band, literary magazine, music ensembles, musical theater, student government, student newspaper, student-run film society, symphony orchestra, television station, yearbook. **Organizations:** 92 registered organizations, 7 honor societies, 6 religious organizations, 3 fraternities (34% men join), 4 sororities (33% women join). **Athletics (Intercollegiate):** *Men:* baseball, basketball, cross-country, diving, golf, lacrosse, soccer, swimming, tennis. *Women:* basketball, cross-country, diving, golf, soccer, swimming, tennis, volleyball.

ADMISSIONS

Selectivity Rating: 84 (of 100). **Freshman Academic Profile:** Average high school GPA 3.5. 60% in top 10% of high school class, 91% in top 25% of high school class, 99% in top 50% of high school class. 84% from public high schools. Average SAT I Math 615, SAT I Math middle 50% range 570-670. Average SAT I Verbal 621, SAT I Verbal middle 50% range 570-660. Average ACT 26, ACT middle 50% range 24-29. TOEFL required of all international applicants, minimum TOEFL 570. **Basis for Candidate Selection:** *Very important factors considered include:* secondary school record. *Important factors considered include:* class rank, essays, extracurricular activities, interview, recommendations, standardized test scores. *Other factors considered include:* alumni/ae relation, character/personal qualities, geographical residence, religious affiliation/commitment, talent/ability. **Freshman Admission Requirements:** High school diploma or GED is required. *Academic units required/recommended:* 17 total recommended; 4 English recommended, 4 math recommended, 3 science recommended, 2 science lab recommended, 2 foreign language recommended, 3 social studies recommended, 3 history recommended, 1 elective recommended. **Freshman Admission Statistics:** 1,572 applied, 61% accepted, 36% of those accepted enrolled. **Transfer Admission Requirements:** *Items required:* high school transcript, college transcript, essay, standardized test scores. Minimum high school GPA of 3.0 required. Minimum college GPA of 3.0 required. Lowest grade transferable C. **General Admission Information:** Application fee $40. Priority application deadline January 15. Early decision application deadline November 1. Regular application deadline February 15. Admission may be deferred for a maximum of 1 year. Credit offered for CEEB Advanced Placement tests.

COSTS AND FINANCIAL AID

Required Forms and Deadlines: FAFSA and institution's own financial aid form. Priority filing deadline March 1. **Notification of Awards:** Applicants will be notified of awards on a rolling basis beginning on or about February 15. **Types of Aid:** *Need-based scholarships/grants:* Pell, SEOG, state scholarships/ grants, private scholarships, the school's own gift aid. *Loans:* FFEL Subsidized Stafford, FFEL Unsubsidized Stafford, FFEL PLUS, Federal Perkins, state loans, college/university loans from institutional funds; Gold, Silver Star private Educational Loan Program. **Student Employment:** Federal Work-Study Program available. Institutional employment available. Off-campus job opportunities are good. **Financial Aid Statistics:** 56% freshmen, 51% undergrads receive some form of aid. Average freshman grant $12,116. Average freshman loan $3,008. Average income from on-campus job $1,103. **Financial Aid Phone:** 512-863-1259.

SPALDING UNIVERSITY

851 South Fourth Street, Louisville, KY 40203
Phone: 502-585-7111 **E-mail:** admission@spalding.edu **CEEB Code:** 1552
Fax: 502-992-2418 **Web:** www.spalding.edu **ACT Code:** 1534

This private school, which is affiliated with the Roman Catholic Church, was founded in 1814. It has a 6-acre campus.

STUDENTS AND FACULTY

Enrollment: 964. **Student Body:** Male 24%, female 76%, out-of-state 18%, international 6% (25 countries represented). **Ethnic Representation:** African American 13%, Asian 1%, Caucasian 85%, Hispanic 1%. **Retention and Graduation:** 90% freshmen return for sophomore year. 35% freshmen graduate within 4 years. 69% grads go on to further study within 1 year. **Faculty:** Student/faculty ratio 12:1. 82 full-time faculty, 75% hold PhDs. 80% faculty teach undergrads.

ACADEMICS

Degrees: Associate's, bachelor's, certificate, doctoral, master's. **Academic Requirements:** General education including some course work in arts/fine arts, computer literacy, English (including composition), history, humanities, mathematics, philosophy, sciences (biological or physical), social science. **Classes:** 10-19 students in an average class. **Disciplines with Highest Percentage of Degrees Awarded:** Health professions and related sciences 24%, business/marketing 21%, psychology 10%, education 8%, liberal arts/ general studies 5%. **Special Study Options:** Accelerated program, cooperative (work-study) program, cross registration, double major, independent study, internships, liberal arts/career combination, study abroad, teacher certification program, weekend college.

FACILITIES

Housing: All-female, all-male. **Library Holdings:** 185,498 bound volumes. 592 periodicals. 54 microforms. 4,713 audiovisuals. **Special Academic Facilities/Equipment:** Huff Gallery.

EXTRACURRICULARS

Activities: Choral groups, drama/theater, student government, student newspaper. **Organizations:** 30 registered organizations, 7 honor societies, 2 religious organizations. **Athletics (Intercollegiate):** *Men:* basketball, cross-country, golf, soccer. *Women:* basketball, soccer, softball, volleyball.

ADMISSIONS

Selectivity Rating: 69 (of 100). **Freshman Academic Profile:** Average high school GPA 3.1. 15% in top 10% of high school class, 25% in top 25% of high school class, 19% in top 50% of high school class. SAT I Math middle 50% range 390-595. SAT I Verbal middle 50% range 350-590. Average ACT 20, ACT middle 50% range 19-23. TOEFL required of all international applicants, minimum TOEFL 535. **Basis for Candidate Selection:** *Very important factors considered include:* secondary school record, standardized test scores. *Important factors considered include:* class rank, essays, extracurricular activities, interview, recommendations. *Other factors considered include:* character/personal qualities, talent/ability. **Freshman Admission Requirements:** High school diploma or GED is required. *Academic units required/ recommended:* 4 English recommended, 3 math recommended, 4 science recommended, 2 foreign language recommended. **Freshman Admission Statistics:** 373 applied, 74% accepted, 33% of those accepted enrolled. **Transfer Admission Requirements:** *Items required:* college transcript, statement of good standing from prior school. Minimum high school GPA of 2.0 required. Minimum college GPA of 2.5 required. Lowest grade transferable C. **General Admission Information:** Application fee $20. Priority application deadline February 15. Regular application deadline August 1. Admission may be deferred for a maximum of 1 year. Credit and/or placement offered for CEEB Advanced Placement tests.

COSTS AND FINANCIAL AID

Required Forms and Deadlines: FAFSA and institution's own financial aid form. No deadline for regular filing. Priority filing deadline March 1. **Notification of Awards:** Applicants will be notified of awards on a rolling basis beginning on or about March 1. **Types of Aid:** *Need-based scholarships/grants:* Pell, SEOG, state scholarships/grants, private scholarships, the school's own gift aid. *Loans:* FFEL Subsidized Stafford, FFEL Unsubsidized Stafford, FFEL PLUS, Federal Perkins, Federal Nursing. **Student Employment:** Federal Work-Study Program available. Institutional employment available. Off-campus job opportunities are fair. **Financial Aid Statistics:** 38% freshmen, 65% undergrads receive some form of aid. Average freshman grant $3,384. Average freshman loan $3,152. Average income from on-campus job $1,400. **Financial Aid Phone:** 502-588-7185.

SPELMAN COLLEGE

350 Spelman Lane, South West, Atlanta, GA 30314
Phone: 800-982-2411 **E-mail:** admiss@spelman.edu **CEEB Code:** 5628
Fax: 404-215-7788 **Web:** www.spelman.edu **ACT Code:** 794

This private school was founded in 1881. It has a 32-acre campus.

STUDENTS AND FACULTY

Enrollment: 1,899. **Student Body:** Out-of-state 75%, international 3%. **Ethnic Representation:** African American 100%. **Faculty:** 100% faculty teach undergrads.

ACADEMICS

Degrees: Bachelor's. **Special Study Options:** Student exchange program (domestic), study abroad. Combined degree programs: 3-2 engineering programs with Auburn University, Boston University, Georgia Tech, and Rochester University. Off-campus study: Washington, DC, and New York Semester. Exchange programs with Mills College, Mount Holyoke College, Pomona College, Simmons College, Smith College, Vassar College, and Wellesley College. Pre-medicine program with Boston University. Study abroad in numerous countries.

FACILITIES

Housing: Coed, all-female. **Library Holdings:** 404,991 bound volumes. 1,739 periodicals. 385,538 microforms. **Special Academic Facilities/Equipment:** Nursery-elementary school for child development majors, language lab, electron microscope.

EXTRACURRICULARS

Activities: Student government, student newspaper, yearbook. **Organizations:** 17 registered organizations, 1 honor society, 2 religious organizations, 4 sororities (1% women join).

ADMISSIONS

Selectivity Rating: 89 (of 100). **Freshman Academic Profile:** Average high school GPA 3.1. 84% from public high schools. Average SAT I Math 524, SAT I Math middle 50% range 500-599. Average SAT I Verbal 549, SAT I Verbal middle 50% range 500-600. Average ACT 22, ACT middle 50% range 21-24. **Freshman Admission Requirements:** High school diploma or GED is required. *Academic units required/recommended:* 15 total required; 4 English required, 2 math required, 3 math recommended, 2 science required, 3 science recommended, 2 foreign language required, 3 foreign language recommended, 2 social studies required, 2 elective required. **Transfer Admission Requirements:** Minimum college GPA of 2.0 required. Lowest grade transferable C. **General Admission Information:** Early decision application deadline November 15. Regular application deadline February 1. Nonfall registration accepted. Credit offered for CEEB Advanced Placement tests.

COSTS AND FINANCIAL AID

Tuition $9,250. Room & board $6,560. Required fees $1,600. Average book expense $750. **Required Forms and Deadlines:** FAFSA and institution's own financial aid form. **Notification of Awards:** Applicants will be notified of awards on or about April 2. **Types of Aid:** *Loans:* FFEL Subsidized Stafford, FFEL PLUS. **Student Employment:** Federal Work-Study Program available. Institutional employment available. Off-campus job opportunities are fair. **Financial Aid Phone:** 404-681-3643.

See page 1216.

SPRING ARBOR UNIVERSITY

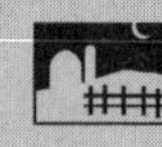

106 East Main Street, Spring Arbor, MI 49283-9799
Phone: 517-750-6458 **E-mail:** admissions@admin.arbor.edu **CEEB Code:** 1732
Fax: 517-750-6620 **Web:** www.arbor.edu **ACT Code:** 2056

This private school was founded in 1873. It has a 120-acre campus.

STUDENTS AND FACULTY

Enrollment: 2,441. **Student Body:** Male 30%, female 70%, out-of-state 13%, international 1% (12 countries represented). **Ethnic Representation:** African American 11%, Caucasian 85%, Hispanic 2%, Native American 1%. **Retention and Graduation:** 78% freshmen return for sophomore year. 36% freshmen graduate within 4 years. 15% grads go on to further study within 1 year. **Faculty:** Student/faculty ratio 15:1. 68 full-time faculty, 61% hold PhDs. 100% faculty teach undergrads.

ACADEMICS

Degrees: Associate's, bachelor's, master's. **Academic Requirements:** General education including some course work in arts/fine arts, English (including composition), history, humanities, philosophy, sciences (biological or physical), social science, cross-culture and Christian perspectives core. **Classes:** 10-19 students in an average class. **Majors with Highest Enrollment:** Business/managerial operations; family systems; English language and literature, general. **Disciplines with Highest Percentage of Degrees Awarded:** Business/marketing 47%, home economics and vocational home economics 20%, education 6%, health professions and related sciences 6%, English 4%. **Special Study Options:** Accelerated program, cross registration, distance learning, double major, dual enrollment, English as a second language, honors program, internships, student-designed major, study abroad, teacher certification program, weekend college. Undergrads may take grad-level classes. Off-campus study: Washington, DC, and Au Sable Institute of Environmental Studies Program (Michigan). Study programs available in Latin America, Middle East, Oxford Honors, Jerusalem University, Russia at St. Petersburg, People's Republic of China at Sichuan College.

FACILITIES

Housing: All-female, all-male, apartments for married students, housing for disabled students. **Library Holdings:** 90,042 bound volumes. 667 periodicals. 375,439 microforms. 2,025 audiovisuals. **Special Academic Facilities/Equipment:** Radio and TV studios, commercial writing/computer graphics lab, science center. **Computers:** School-owned computers available for student use.

EXTRACURRICULARS

Activities: Choral groups, concert band, jazz band, music ensembles, radio station, student government, student newspaper, yearbook. **Athletics (Intercollegiate):** *Men:* baseball, basketball, cross-country, golf, indoor track, soccer, tennis, track & field. *Women:* basketball, cross-country, indoor track, soccer, softball, tennis, track & field, volleyball.

ADMISSIONS

Selectivity Rating: 69 (of 100). **Freshman Academic Profile:** Average high school GPA 3.4. 24% in top 10% of high school class, 49% in top 25% of high school class, 81% in top 50% of high school class. Average ACT 23, ACT middle 50% range 19-25. TOEFL required of all international applicants, minimum TOEFL 525. **Basis for Candidate Selection:** *Very important factors considered include:* character/personal qualities, religious affiliation/commitment, secondary school record, standardized test scores. *Other factors considered include:* alumni/ae relation, class rank, essays, extracurricular activities, interview, minority status, recommendations, talent/ability. **Freshman Admission Requirements:** High school diploma or GED is required. *Academic units required/recommended:* 4 English recommended, 2 math recommended, 2 science recommended, 2 foreign language recommended, 2 social studies recommended. **Freshman Admission Statistics:** 793 applied, 87% accepted, 44% of those accepted enrolled. **Transfer Admission Requirements:** *Items required:* college transcript, essay. Minimum college GPA of 2.0 required. Lowest grade transferable C. **General Admission Information:** Application fee $30. Priority application deadline February 15. Regular application deadline August 1. Nonfall registration accepted. Admission may be deferred. Credit offered for CEEB Advanced Placement tests.

COSTS AND FINANCIAL AID

Tuition $13,800. Room & board $5,080. Required fees $216. Average book expense $600. **Required Forms and Deadlines:** FAFSA. Priority filing deadline February 15. **Notification of Awards:** Applicants will be notified of awards on a rolling basis beginning on or about April 2. **Types of Aid:** *Need-based scholarships/grants:* Pell, SEOG, state scholarships/grants, private scholarships, the school's own gift aid. *Loans:* FFEL Subsidized Stafford, FFEL Unsubsidized Stafford, FFEL PLUS, Federal Perkins, state loans. **Student Employment:** Federal Work-Study Program available. Institutional employment available. Off-campus job opportunities are good. **Financial Aid Statistics:** 51% freshmen, 47% undergrads receive some form of aid. **Financial Aid Phone:** 517-750-6468.

SPRING HILL COLLEGE

4000 Dauphin Street, Mobile, AL 36608
Phone: 251-380-3030 **E-mail:** admit@shc.edu **CEEB Code:** 1733
Fax: 251-460-2186 **Web:** www.shc.edu **ACT Code:** 0042

This private school, which is affiliated with the Roman Catholic Church, was founded in 1830. It has a 450-acre campus.

STUDENTS AND FACULTY

Enrollment: 1,221. **Student Body:** Male 36%, female 64%, out-of-state 48%, international 1% (8 countries represented). **Ethnic Representation:** African American 13%, Asian 1%, Caucasian 78%, Hispanic 5%, Native American 1%. **Retention and Graduation:** 77% freshmen return for sophomore year. 48% freshmen graduate within 4 years. 28% grads go on to further study within 1 year. 5% grads pursue business degrees. 3% grads pursue law degrees. 2% grads pursue medical degrees. **Faculty:** Student/faculty ratio 14:1. 69 full-time faculty, 91% hold PhDs. 100% faculty teach undergrads.

ACADEMICS

Degrees: Associate's, bachelor's, certificate, master's, post-bachelor's certificate, terminal. **Academic Requirements:** General education including some course work in arts/fine arts, English (including composition), foreign languages, history, mathematics, philosophy, sciences (biological or physical), social science, theology. **Classes:** 10-19 students in an average class. 20-29 students in an average lab/discussion section. **Majors with Highest Enrollment:** Business administration/management; communications studies/speech communication and rhetoric; biology/biological sciences, general. **Disciplines with Highest Percentage of Degrees Awarded:** Business/marketing 22%, communications/communication technologies 18%, biological life sciences 10%, health professions and related sciences 10%, education 7%. **Special Study Options:** Accelerated program, distance learning, double major, dual enrollment, honors program, independent study, internships, student-designed major, study abroad, teacher certification program.

FACILITIES

Housing: Coed, all-female, all-male, apartments for single students. **Library Holdings:** 180,098 bound volumes. 573 periodicals. 295,471 microforms. 757 audiovisuals. **Special Academic Facilities/Equipment:** Public radio broadcasting station, theater. **Computers:** School-owned computers available for student use.

EXTRACURRICULARS

Activities: Choral groups, dance, drama/theater, literary magazine, student government, student newspaper, yearbook. **Organizations:** 33 registered organizations, 3 honor societies, 4 religious organizations, 2 fraternities (16% men join), 3 sororities (25% women join). **Athletics (Intercollegiate):** *Men:* baseball, basketball, cross-country, golf, soccer, swimming, tennis. *Women:* basketball, cross-country, golf, soccer, softball, swimming, tennis, volleyball.

ADMISSIONS

Selectivity Rating: 71 (of 100). **Freshman Academic Profile:** Average high school GPA 3.4. 23% in top 10% of high school class, 48% in top 25% of high school class, 77% in top 50% of high school class. 37% from public high schools. Average SAT I Math 550, SAT I Math middle 50% range 500-610. Average SAT I Verbal 561, SAT I Verbal middle 50% range 500-620. Average ACT 24, ACT middle 50% range 21-27. TOEFL required of all international applicants, minimum TOEFL 550. **Basis for Candidate Selection:** *Very important factors considered include:* class rank, essays, secondary school record, standardized test scores. *Important factors considered include:* recommendations, volunteer work. *Other factors considered include:* alumni/ae relation, character/personal qualities, extracurricular activities, interview, talent/ability, work experience. **Freshman Admission Requirements:** High school diploma or GED is required. *Academic units required/recommended:* 16 total required; 20 total recommended; 4 English required, 4 English recommended, 3 math required, 3 math recommended, 3 science required, 3 science recommended, 2 science lab required, 2 science lab recommended, 2 foreign language recommended, 2 social studies required, 2 social studies recommended, 1 history required, 2 history recommended, 3 elective required, 4 elective recommended. **Freshman Admission Statistics:** 988 applied, 81% accepted, 37% of those accepted enrolled. **Transfer Admission Requirements:** *Items required:* college transcript, essay, statement of good standing from prior school. Minimum college GPA of 2.5 required. Lowest grade transferable C-. **General Admission Information:** Application fee $25. Priority application deadline January 15. Regular application deadline July 1. Nonfall registration accepted. Admission may be deferred. Credit and/or placement offered for CEEB Advanced Placement tests.

COSTS AND FINANCIAL AID

Required Forms and Deadlines: FAFSA and institution's own financial aid form. No deadline for regular filing. Priority filing deadline March 1. **Notification of Awards:** Applicants will be notified of awards on a rolling basis beginning on or about March 1. **Types of Aid:** *Need-based scholarships/grants:* Pell, SEOG, state scholarships/grants, private scholarships, the school's own gift aid, Bedsole scholarships, funded/endowed scholarships. *Loans:* FFEL Subsidized Stafford, FFEL Unsubsidized Stafford, FFEL PLUS, Federal Perkins, alternative loans (CitiAssist, Signature). **Student Employment:** Federal Work-Study Program available. Institutional employment available. Off-campus job opportunities are good. **Financial Aid Statistics:** 68% freshmen, 67% undergrads receive some form of aid. Average freshman grant $12,528. Average freshman loan $3,530. Average income from on-campus job $920. **Financial Aid Phone:** 251-380-3460.

SPRINGFIELD COLLEGE

263 Alden Street, Springfield, MA 01109
Phone: 413-748-3136 **E-mail:** admissions@spfldcol.edu **CEEB Code:** 3763
Fax: 413-748-3694 **Web:** www.spfldcol.edu

This private school was founded in 1885. It has an 80-acre campus.

STUDENTS AND FACULTY

Enrollment: 2,046. **Student Body:** Out-of-state 66%, international 3% (18 countries represented). **Ethnic Representation:** African American 4%, Asian 1%, Caucasian 92%, Hispanic 2%, Native American 1%. **Retention and Graduation:** 82% freshmen return for sophomore year. 58% freshmen graduate within 4 years. 20% grads go on to further study within 1 year. **Faculty:** 85% faculty teach undergrads.

ACADEMICS

Degrees: Bachelor's, doctoral, master's. **Academic Requirements:** General education including some course work in arts/fine arts, computer literacy, English (including composition), foreign languages, history, humanities, mathematics, philosophy, sciences (biological or physical), social science, physical education. **Special Study Options:** Cooperative (work-study) program, cross registration, distance learning, double major, English as a second language, independent study, internships, liberal arts/career combination, study abroad, teacher certification program, weekend college.

FACILITIES

Housing: Coed, all-female, all-male, apartments for single students. **Library Holdings:** 242,945 bound volumes. 641 periodicals. 628,721 microforms. 2,398 audiovisuals. **Special Academic Facilities/Equipment:** International center, college-operated summer day camp, hypermedia lab, centers for allied health sciences (emergency medical services management, occupational therapy, and physician assistant).

EXTRACURRICULARS

Activities: Dance, drama/theater, literary magazine, musical theater, radio station, student government, student newspaper, yearbook. **Athletics (Intercollegiate):** *Men:* baseball, basketball, cross-country, diving, football, golf, gymnastics, lacrosse, soccer, swimming, tennis, track & field, volleyball, wrestling. *Women:* basketball, cross-country, diving, field hockey, golf, gymnastics, lacrosse, soccer, softball, swimming, tennis, track & field, volleyball.

ADMISSIONS

Selectivity Rating: 75 (of 100). **Freshman Academic Profile:** 14% in top 10% of high school class, 35% in top 25% of high school class, 76% in top 50% of high school class. 84% from public high schools. Average SAT I Math 510, SAT I Math middle 50% range 450-550. Average SAT I Verbal 500, SAT I Verbal middle 50% range 440-550. TOEFL required of all international applicants, minimum TOEFL 525. **Basis for Candidate Selection:** *Other factors considered include:* alumni/ae relation, character/personal qualities, class rank, essays, extracurricular activities, geographical residence, interview, minority status, recommendations, religious affiliation/commitment, secondary school record, talent/ability, volunteer work, work experience. **Freshman Admission Requirements:** High school diploma or GED is required. *Academic units required/recommended:* 16 total required; 4 English recommended, 2 math recommended, 2 science recommended, 2 foreign language recommended, 2 social studies recommended, 4 elective recommended.

Freshman Admission Statistics: 2,249 applied, 59% accepted. **Transfer Admission Requirements:** *Items required:* college transcript, essay, interview, statement of good standing from prior school. Minimum college GPA of 2.5 required. Lowest grade transferable C. **General Admission Information:** Application fee $40. Priority application deadline March 15. Early decision application deadline December 1. Regular application deadline April 11. Nonfall registration accepted. Admission may be deferred for a maximum of 1 year. Credit and/or placement offered for CEEB Advanced Placement tests.

COSTS AND FINANCIAL AID

Room & board $5,856. Average book expense $950. **Required Forms and Deadlines:** FAFSA and CSS/Financial Aid PROFILE. **Types of Aid:** *Need-based scholarships/grants:* Pell, SEOG, state scholarships/grants, private scholarships, the school's own gift aid. *Loans:* FFEL Subsidized Stafford, FFEL Unsubsidized Stafford, FFEL PLUS, Federal Perkins, college/university loans from institutional funds. **Student Employment:** Federal Work-Study Program available. Institutional employment available. Off-campus job opportunities are good. **Financial Aid Statistics:** Average freshman grant $7,393. Average freshman loan $1,500. Average income from on-campus job $1,100. **Financial Aid Phone:** 413-748-3108.

STANFORD UNIVERSITY

Undergraduate Admission, Old Student Union, Stanford, CA 94305-3005
Phone: 650-723-2091 **E-mail:** undergrad.admissions@forsythe.stanford.edu **CEEB Code:** 4704 **Fax:** 650-723-6050 **Web:** www.stanford.edu **ACT Code:** 434

This private school was founded in 1885. It has an 8,180-acre campus.

STUDENTS AND FACULTY

Enrollment: 7,360. **Student Body:** Male 49%, female 51%, out-of-state 50%, international 5%. **Ethnic Representation:** African American 10%, Asian 26%, Caucasian 48%, Hispanic 12%, Native American 2%. **Retention and Graduation:** 98% freshmen return for sophomore year. 77% freshmen graduate within 4 years. 35% grads go on to further study within 1 year. **Faculty:** Student/faculty ratio 7:1. 1,688 full-time faculty, 98% hold PhDs.

ACADEMICS

Degrees: Bachelor's, doctoral, first professional, master's. **Academic Requirements:** General education including some course work in English (including composition), foreign languages, humanities, mathematics, sciences (biological or physical), social science. Undergrads complete at least 180 units, including requirements for the major, a writing requirement, 1 year of a foreign language, and courses in the following areas: (1) introduction to the humanities, (2) natural sciences, applied science & technology, mathematics, (3) humanities & social sciences, (4) world cultures, American cultures, and gender studies. **Classes:** 10-19 students in an average class. 10-19 students in an average lab/discussion section. **Majors with Highest Enrollment:** Biology/biological sciences, general; economics, general; computer science. **Disciplines with Highest Percentage of Degrees Awarded:** Social sciences and history 28%, engineering/engineering technology 12%, computer and information sciences 12%, interdisciplinary studies 11%, biological life sciences 7%. **Special Study Options:** Double major; student exchange program (domestic); honors program; independent study; internships; student-designed major; study abroad; marine research center; Stanford in Washington, DC.

FACILITIES

Housing: Coed, all-female, apartments for married students, apartments for single students, housing for disabled students, fraternities and/or sororities, cooperative housing. Also, academic, crosscultural, language theme, and ethnic theme houses. **Library Holdings:** 7,000,000 bound volumes. 44,504 periodicals. 4,975,102 microforms. 1,244,441 audiovisuals. **Special Academic Facilities/Equipment:** Art museum, marine station, observatory, biological preserve, linear accelerator. **Computers:** School-owned computers available for student use.

EXTRACURRICULARS

Activities: Choral groups, concert band, dance, drama/theater, jazz band, literary magazine, marching band, music ensembles, musical theater, radio station, student government, student newspaper, student-run film society, symphony orchestra, television station, yearbook. **Organizations:** 600 registered organizations, 50 religious organizations, 15 fraternities, 8 sororities. **Athletics (Intercollegiate):** *Men:* baseball, basketball, crew, cross-country, diving, fencing, football, golf, gymnastics, sailing, soccer, swimming, tennis, track & field, volleyball, water polo, wrestling. *Women:* basketball, crew, cross-country, diving, fencing, field hockey, golf, gymnastics, lacrosse, sailing, soccer, softball, swimming, tennis, track & field, volleyball, water polo.

ADMISSIONS

Selectivity Rating: 99 (of 100). **Freshman Academic Profile:** Average high school GPA 3.9. 88% in top 10% of high school class, 97% in top 25% of high school class, 99% in top 50% of high school class. 65% from public high schools. SAT I Math middle 50% range 690-780. SAT I Verbal middle 50% range 660-760. ACT middle 50% range 28-33. **Basis for Candidate Selection:** *Very important factors considered include:* character/personal qualities, class rank, essays, recommendations, secondary school record, standardized test scores. *Important factors considered include:* extracurricular activities, talent/ability. *Other factors considered include:* alumni/ae relation, geographical residence, minority status, volunteer work, work experience. **Freshman Admission Requirements:** High school diploma or GED is required. *Academic units required/recommended:* 20 total recommended; 4 English recommended, 4 math recommended, 3 science recommended, 3 science lab recommended, 3 foreign language recommended, 2 social studies recommended, 1 history recommended. **Freshman Admission Statistics:** 18,599 applied, 13% accepted, 69% of those accepted enrolled. **Transfer Admission Requirements:** *Items required:* high school transcript, college transcript, essay, standardized test scores, statement of good standing from prior school. Lowest grade transferable C-. **General Admission Information:** Application fee $65. Early decision application deadline November 1. Regular application deadline December 15. Admission may be deferred for a maximum of 2 years. Credit and/or placement offered for CEEB Advanced Placement tests.

COSTS AND FINANCIAL AID

Tuition $27,204. Room & board $8,680. Average book expense $1,155. **Required Forms and Deadlines:** FAFSA and CSS/Financial Aid PROFILE. Priority filing deadline February 1. **Notification of Awards:** Applicants will be notified of awards on a rolling basis beginning on or about April 2. **Types of Aid:** *Need-based scholarships/grants:* Pell, SEOG, state scholarships/grants, private scholarships, the school's own gift aid. *Loans:* FFEL Subsidized Stafford, FFEL Unsubsidized Stafford, FFEL PLUS, Federal Perkins, GATES. **Student Employment:** Federal Work-Study Program available. Institutional employment available. Off-campus job opportunities are excellent. **Financial Aid Statistics:** 47% freshmen, 44% undergrads receive some form of aid. Average freshman grant $25,334. **Financial Aid Phone:** 650-723-3058.

STATE UNIVERSITY OF NEW YORK AT ALBANY

Office of Undergraduate Admissions, 1400 Washington Ave., Albany, NY 12222
Phone: 518-442-5435 **E-mail:** ugadmissions@albany.edu **CEEB Code:** 2532
Fax: 518-442-5383 **Web:** www.albany.edu **ACT Code:** 2926

This public school was founded in 1844. It has a 560-acre campus.

STUDENTS AND FACULTY

Enrollment: 11,953. **Student Body:** Male 50%, female 50%, out-of-state 5%, international 2% (87 countries represented). **Ethnic Representation:** African American 9%, Asian 6%, Caucasian 65%, Hispanic 7%. **Retention and Graduation:** 84% freshmen return for sophomore year. 53% freshmen graduate within 4 years. 33% grads go on to further study within 1 year. 2% grads pursue business degrees. 6% grads pursue law degrees. 4% grads pursue medical degrees. **Faculty:** Student/faculty ratio 21:1. 610 full-time faculty, 90% hold PhDs. 91% faculty teach undergrads.

ACADEMICS

Degrees: Bachelor's, doctoral, master's, post-master's certificate. **Academic Requirements:** General education including some course work in arts/fine arts, foreign languages, history, humanities, mathematics, sciences (biological or physical), social science. 30 credits of course work in the areas noted above as well as in national and international perspectives, pluralism and diversity, communication and reasoning competencies. For details see www.albany.edu/gened/index.html. **Classes:** 20-29 students in an average class. 10-19 students in an average lab/discussion section. **Majors with Highest Enrollment:** Business administration/management; English language and literature, general; psychology, general. **Disciplines with Highest Percentage of Degrees Awarded:** Social sciences and history 25%, business/marketing 16%, psychology 14%, English 10%, communications/communication technologies 7%. **Special Study Options:** Accelerated program, cross registration, distance learning, double major, dual enrollment, English as a second language, student exchange program (domestic), honors program, independent study, internships, student-designed major, study abroad, teacher certification program, accelerated 5-year bachelor's/master's programs in 40 fields, internships with New York State legislature, combined Bachelors/Law degree with Albany Law school, 3+2 engineering programs with RPI, SUNY Binghamton, SUNY New Paltz, and Clarkson.

FACILITIES

Housing: Coed, all-female, all-male, apartments for married students, apartments for single students, housing for international students. Disabled Student Services provides individualized services including accessible housing information. **Library Holdings:** 1,192,938 bound volumes. 28,055 periodicals. 2,782,393 microforms. 10,115 audiovisuals. **Special Academic Facilities/ Equipment:** Performing arts center, art museum, art and dance studios, sculpture foundry, nuclear accelerator and advanced materials facilities, peptide synthesis facility, recombinant DNA sequencing laboratories, and atmospheric science's Whiteface Mountain Observational Facility. **Computers:** School-owned computers available for student use.

EXTRACURRICULARS

Activities: Choral groups, concert band, dance, drama/theater, jazz band, literary magazine, music ensembles, musical theater, pep band, radio station, student government, student newspaper, symphony orchestra, yearbook. **Organizations:** 160 registered organizations, 20 honor societies, 9 religious organizations, 19 fraternities (4% men join), 15 sororities (5% women join). **Athletics (Intercollegiate):** *Men:* baseball, basketball, crew, cross-country, football, indoor track, lacrosse, rugby, skiing (alpine), soccer, track & field. *Women:* basketball, crew, cross-country, field hockey, golf, indoor track, lacrosse, rugby, skiing (alpine), soccer, softball, tennis, track & field, volleyball.

ADMISSIONS

Selectivity Rating: 79 (of 100). **Freshman Academic Profile:** Average high school GPA 3.6. 16% in top 10% of high school class, 54% in top 25% of high school class, 92% in top 50% of high school class. Average SAT I Math 583, SAT I Math middle 50% range 520-610. Average SAT I Verbal 567, SAT I Verbal middle 50% range 500-600. TOEFL required of all international applicants, minimum TOEFL 550. **Basis for Candidate Selection:** *Very important factors considered include:* character/personal qualities, class rank, secondary school record, standardized test scores. *Important factors considered include:* essays, recommendations. *Other factors considered include:* extracurricular activities, geographical residence, minority status, talent/ability, volunteer work. **Freshman Admission Requirements:** High school diploma or GED is required. *Academic units required/recommended:* 18 total required; 4 English required, 2 math required, 4 math recommended, 2 science required, 3 science recommended, 2 science lab required, 3 science lab recommended, 3 foreign language recommended, 3 social studies required, 2 history required, 5 elective required. **Freshman Admission Statistics:** 17,667 applied, 56% accepted, 23% of those accepted enrolled. **Transfer Admission Requirements:** *Items required:* college transcript, essay, statement of good standing from prior school. Lowest grade transferable C. **General Admission Information:** Application fee $40. Priority application deadline December 1. Regular application deadline March 1. Nonfall registration accepted. Admission may be deferred for a maximum of 1 year. Credit and/or placement offered for CEEB Advanced Placement tests.

COSTS AND FINANCIAL AID

In-state tuition $3,400. Out-of-state tuition $8,300. Room & board $7,052. Required fees $1,420. Average book expense $800. **Required Forms and Deadlines:** FAFSA. NY State residents will receive an Express TAP Application one month after filing FAFSA. Priority filing deadline March 15. **Notification of Awards:** Applicants will be notified of awards on a rolling basis beginning on or about April 1. **Types of Aid:** *Need-based scholarships/grants:* Pell, SEOG, state scholarships/grants, private scholarships, the school's own gift aid. *Loans:* FFEL Subsidized Stafford, FFEL Unsubsidized Stafford, FFEL PLUS, Federal Perkins, college/university loans from institutional funds. **Student Employment:** Federal Work-Study Program available. Institutional employment available. Off-campus job opportunities are good. **Financial Aid Statistics:** 54% freshmen, 53% undergrads receive some form of aid. Average freshman grant $4,310. Average freshman loan $4,113. **Financial Aid Phone:** 518-442-5757.

STATE UNIVERSITY OF NEW YORK AT FARMINGDALE

Admissions, Route 110, Farmingdale, NY 11735
Phone: 631-420-2200 **E-mail:** admissions@farmingdale.edu
Fax: 631-420-2633 **Web:** www.farmingdale.edu

This public school was founded in 1912. It has a 380-acre campus.

STUDENTS AND FACULTY

Student Body: Out-of-state 0%. **Ethnic Representation:** African American 15%, Asian 4%, Caucasian 62%, Hispanic 9%. **Faculty:** Student/faculty ratio 21:1. 187 full-time faculty, 49% hold PhDs. 100% faculty teach undergrads.

ACADEMICS

Degrees: Associate's, bachelor's, certificate, terminal, transfer. **Academic Requirements:** General education including some course work in English (including composition), humanities, mathematics, sciences (biological or physical), social science. **Classes:** 20-29 students in an average class. **Disciplines with Highest Percentage of Degrees Awarded:** Engineering/ engineering technology 47%, business/marketing 37%, trade and industry 16%. **Special Study Options:** Distance learning, double major, dual enrollment, internships, study abroad.

FACILITIES

Housing: Coed. **Library Holdings:** 239,885 bound volumes. 1,079 periodicals. 76,970 microforms. 3,456 audiovisuals. **Computers:** School-owned computers available for student use.

EXTRACURRICULARS

Activities: Drama/theater, radio station, student government, student newspaper, yearbook. **Athletics (Intercollegiate):** *Men:* baseball, basketball, cross-country, golf, indoor track, lacrosse, soccer, track & field. *Women:* basketball, cross-country, indoor track, soccer, softball, track & field, volleyball.

ADMISSIONS

Selectivity Rating: 63 (of 100). **Freshman Academic Profile:** Average SAT I Math 460, SAT I Math middle 50% range 400-520. Average SAT I Verbal 445, SAT I Verbal middle 50% range 390-500. TOEFL required of all international applicants, minimum TOEFL 500. **Basis for Candidate Selection:** *Very important factors considered include:* class rank, secondary school record. *Important factors considered include:* talent/ability. *Other factors considered include:* alumni/ae relation, character/personal qualities, extracurricular activities, interview, recommendations, standardized test scores, volunteer work, work experience. **Freshman Admission Requirements:** High school diploma or GED is required. *Academic units required/recommended:* 4 English required, 4 English recommended, 2 math required, 4 math recommended, 1 science required, 3 science recommended, 1 science lab required, 3 science lab recommended, 4 social studies required, 4 social studies recommended. **Freshman Admission Statistics:** 2,382 applied, 68% accepted, 56% of those accepted enrolled. **Transfer Admission Requirements:** *Items required:* high school transcript, college transcript, statement of good standing from prior school. Minimum college GPA of 2.0 required. Lowest grade transferable C. **General Admission Information:** Application fee $30. Nonfall registration accepted. Admission may be deferred for a maximum of 1 year. Credit and/or placement offered for CEEB Advanced Placement tests.

COSTS AND FINANCIAL AID

Average book expense $800. **Required Forms and Deadlines:** FAFSA and institution's own financial aid form. **Notification of Awards:** Applicants will be notified of awards on a rolling basis. **Types of Aid:** *Need-based scholarships/ grants:* Pell, SEOG, state scholarships/grants. *Loans:* Direct Subsidized Stafford, Direct Unsubsidized Stafford, Direct PLUS, FFEL Subsidized Stafford, FFEL Unsubsidized Stafford, FFEL PLUS, Federal Perkins, Federal Nursing, state loans. **Student Employment:** Federal Work-Study Program available. Institutional employment available. Off-campus job opportunities are good.

STATE UNIVERSITY OF NEW YORK AT NEW PALTZ

75 S. Manheim Boulevard, Suite 1, New Paltz, NY 12561-2499
Phone: 845-257-3200 **E-mail:** admissions@newpaltz.edu **CEEB Code:** 2541
Fax: 914-257-3209 **Web:** www.newpaltz.edu **ACT Code:** 2938

This public school was founded in 1828. It has a 216-acre campus.

STUDENTS AND FACULTY

Enrollment: 6,187. **Student Body:** Male 36%, female 64%, out-of-state 5%, international 2% (30 countries represented). **Ethnic Representation:** African American 7%, Asian 4%, Caucasian 67%, Hispanic 9%. **Retention and Graduation:** 84% freshmen return for sophomore year. 33% freshmen graduate within 4 years. 38% grads go on to further study within 1 year. **Faculty:** Student/faculty ratio 17:1. 296 full-time faculty, 87% hold PhDs. 98% faculty teach undergrads.

ACADEMICS

Degrees: Bachelor's, doctoral, master's, post-master's certificate. **Academic Requirements:** General education including some course work in arts/fine arts, computer literacy, English (including composition), foreign languages, history, humanities, mathematics, philosophy, sciences (biological or physical), social science. **Classes:** 10-19 students in an average class. **Majors with Highest Enrollment:** Business administration/management; special education, general; sociology. **Disciplines with Highest Percentage of Degrees Awarded:** Education 43%, business/marketing 11%, English 8%, visual and performing arts 7%, social sciences and history 6%. **Special Study Options:** Cooperative (work-study) program, cross registration, distance learning, double major, English as a second language, honors program, independent study, internships, liberal arts/career combination, student-designed major, study abroad, teacher certification program.

FACILITIES

Housing: Coed, all-female, all-male, housing for disabled students. **Library Holdings:** 515,000 bound volumes. 1,500 periodicals. 1,000,000 microforms. 106 audiovisuals. **Special Academic Facilities/Equipment:** Samuel Dorsky Museum of Art, Resnick Engineering Hall, Coykendall Media Center, Communication Disorders Training Center & Clinic, Music Therapy Training Center & Clinic, Shepherd Recital Hall, Honors Center, Martin Luther King Jr. Study Center, Fournier Mass Spectrometer, Raymond Kurdt Theatre Collection. **Computers:** School-owned computers available for student use.

EXTRACURRICULARS

Activities: Choral groups, concert band, dance, drama/theater, jazz band, music ensembles, musical theater, radio station, student government, student newspaper, symphony orchestra, television station, yearbook. **Organizations:** 135 registered organizations, 8 honor societies, 10 religious organizations, 10 fraternities (3% men join), 14 sororities (2% women join). **Athletics (Intercollegiate):** *Men:* baseball, basketball, cheerleading, cross-country, diving, soccer, swimming, tennis, track & field, volleyball. *Women:* basketball, cheerleading, cross-country, diving, field hockey, lacrosse, soccer, softball, swimming, tennis, track & field, volleyball.

ADMISSIONS

Selectivity Rating: 84 (of 100). **Freshman Academic Profile:** Average high school GPA 3.2. 15% in top 10% of high school class, 36% in top 25% of high school class, 93% in top 50% of high school class. 92% from public high schools. Average SAT I Math 566, SAT I Math middle 50% range 510-600. Average SAT I Verbal 564, SAT I Verbal middle 50% range 510-600. TOEFL required of all international applicants, minimum TOEFL 550. **Basis for Candidate Selection:** *Very important factors considered include:* class rank, secondary school record, standardized test scores. *Other factors considered include:* character/personal qualities, essays, extracurricular activities, recommendations, talent/ability. **Freshman Admission Requirements:** High school diploma or GED is required. *Academic units required/recommended:* 17 total required; 21 total recommended; 4 English required, 4 English recommended, 3 math required, 4 math recommended, 3 science required, 4 science recommended, 3 science lab required, 3 science lab recommended, 3 foreign language required, 4 foreign language recommended, 3 social studies required, 3 social studies recommended, 1 history required, 1 history recommended. **Freshman Admission Statistics:** 10,372 applied, 40% accepted, 23% of those accepted enrolled. **Transfer Admission Requirements:** *Items required:* college transcript, statement of good standing from prior school. Minimum high school GPA of 3.0 required. Minimum college GPA of 2.5 required. Lowest grade transferable C. **General Admission Information:** Application fee $40. Priority application deadline January 15. Regular application deadline May 1. Nonfall registration accepted. Admission may be deferred for a maximum of 1 year. Credit and/or placement offered for CEEB Advanced Placement tests.

COSTS AND FINANCIAL AID

In-state tuition $3,400. Out-of-state tuition $8,300. Room & board $6,110. Required fees $766. Average book expense $1,000. **Required Forms and Deadlines:** FAFSA and state aid form. Financial aid filing deadline March 15. Priority filing deadline March 15. **Notification of Awards:** Applicants will be notified of awards on a rolling basis beginning on or about April 1. **Types of Aid:** *Need-based scholarships/grants:* Pell, SEOG, state scholarships/grants, private scholarships, the school's own gift aid, Federal Nursing. *Loans:* Direct Subsidized Stafford, Direct Unsubsidized Stafford, Direct PLUS. **Student Employment:** Federal Work-Study Program available. Institutional employment available. Off-campus job opportunities are good. **Financial Aid Statistics:** 53% freshmen, 53% undergrads receive some form of aid. Average freshman grant $2,625. Average freshman loan $2,200. Average income from on-campus job $800. **Financial Aid Phone:** 914-257-3250.

STATE UNIVERSITY OF NEW YORK COLLEGE AT BROCKPORT

350 New Campus Drive, Brockport, NY 14420
Phone: 585-395-2751 **E-mail:** admit@brockport.edu **CEEB Code:** 2537
Fax: 585-395-5452 **Web:** www.brockport.edu **ACT Code:** 2928

This public school was founded in 1867. It has a 435-acre campus.

STUDENTS AND FACULTY

Enrollment: 6,959. **Student Body:** Male 43%, female 57%, out-of-state 2%, international 1% (27 countries represented). **Ethnic Representation:** African American 6%, Asian 1%, Caucasian 82%, Hispanic 2%. **Retention and Graduation:** 77% freshmen return for sophomore year. 29% freshmen graduate within 4 years. 23% grads go on to further study within 1 year. 3% grads pursue business degrees. 4% grads pursue law degrees. 4% grads pursue medical degrees. **Faculty:** Student/faculty ratio 18:1. 313 full-time faculty, 68% hold PhDs. 95% faculty teach undergrads.

ACADEMICS

Degrees: Bachelor's, master's, post-master's certificate. **Academic Requirements:** General education including some course work in arts/fine arts, computer literacy, English (including composition), foreign languages, history, humanities, mathematics, sciences (biological or physical), social science, oral communication, western civilization, world civilization, science & technology, women's studies, diversity, contemporary issues. **Classes:** 20-29 students in an average class. 20-29 students in an average lab/discussion section. **Majors with Highest Enrollment:** Business administration/management; physical education teaching and coaching; psychology, general. **Disciplines with Highest Percentage of Degrees Awarded:** Business/marketing 15%, health professions and related sciences 13%, education 12%, protective services/public administration 12%, social sciences and history 10%. **Special Study Options:** Accelerated program, cross registration, distance learning, double major, dual enrollment, honors program, independent study, internships, student-designed major, study abroad, teacher certification program.

FACILITIES

Housing: Coed, housing for disabled students, housing for international students, first-year experience, transfer hall, substance-free floors, 24-hour quiet floor, adult/international floor. **Library Holdings:** 584,687 bound volumes. 1,800 periodicals. 2,044,866 microforms. 8,228 audiovisuals. **Special Academic Facilities/Equipment:** Theatre, leadership development institute, greenhouse, planetarium, electron microscope, art galleries, aquaculture ponds, newly renovated science building, environmental science deciduous woodlot, new meteorology lab with on-campus Doppler radar station. **Computers:** School-owned computers available for student use.

EXTRACURRICULARS

Activities: Choral groups, dance, drama/theater, literary magazine, radio station, student government, student newspaper, television station. **Organizations:** 46 registered organizations, 20 honor societies, 5 religious organizations, 5 fraternities (1% men join), 4 sororities (1% women join). **Athletics (Intercollegiate):** *Men:* baseball, basketball, cross-country, diving, football, ice hockey, indoor track, lacrosse, soccer, swimming, track & field, wrestling. *Women:* basketball, cross-country, diving, field hockey, gymnastics, indoor track, lacrosse, soccer, softball, swimming, tennis, track & field, volleyball.

ADMISSIONS

Selectivity Rating: 70 (of 100). **Freshman Academic Profile:** Average high school GPA 3.4. 10% in top 10% of high school class, 38% in top 25% of high school class, 82% in top 50% of high school class. Average SAT I Math 534, SAT I Math middle 50% range 490-580. Average SAT I Verbal 518, SAT I Verbal middle 50% range 470-560. Average ACT 22, ACT middle 50% range 20-24. TOEFL required of all international applicants, minimum TOEFL 530. **Basis for Candidate Selection:** *Very important factors considered include:* class rank, secondary school record, standardized test scores. *Important factors considered include:* essays, extracurricular activities, recommendations, talent/ability. *Other factors considered include:* character/personal qualities, interview, volunteer work, work experience. **Freshman Admission Requirements:** High school diploma or GED is required. *Academic units required/recommended:* 18 total required; 4 English required, 3 math required, 3 science required, 1 science lab required, 3 foreign language recommended, 4 social studies required, 4 elective required. **Freshman Admission Statistics:** 7,350 applied, 51% accepted, 26% of those accepted enrolled. **Transfer Admission Requirements:** *Items required:* college transcript. Minimum college GPA of 2.3 required. Lowest grade transferable D-. **General Admission Information:** Application fee $40. Priority application deadline February 1. Nonfall registration accepted. Admission may be deferred for a maximum of 1 year. Credit and/or placement offered for CEEB Advanced Placement tests.

COSTS AND FINANCIAL AID

Required Forms and Deadlines: FAFSA and state aid form. No deadline for regular filing. Priority filing deadline February 15. **Notification of Awards:** Applicants will be notified of awards on a rolling basis. **Types of Aid:** *Need-based scholarships/grants:* Pell, SEOG, state scholarships/grants, private scholarships, the school's own gift aid. *Loans:* Direct Subsidized Stafford, Direct Unsubsidized Stafford, Direct PLUS, Federal Perkins, Federal Nursing, alternative bank loans. **Student Employment:** Federal Work-Study Program available. Institutional employment available. Off-campus job opportunities are good. **Financial Aid Statistics:** 60% freshmen, 64% undergrads receive some form of aid. Average freshman grant $2,695. Average freshman loan $2,715. Average income from on-campus job $835. **Financial Aid Phone:** 585-395-2501.

STATE UNIVERSITY OF NEW YORK COLLEGE AT BUFFALO

1300 Elmwood Avenue, Buffalo, NY 14222
Phone: 716-878-4017 **E-mail:** admissio@buffalostate.edu
Fax: 716-878-6100 **Web:** www.buffalostate.edu

This public school was founded in 1867. It has a 115-acre campus.

STUDENTS AND FACULTY

Enrollment: 9,495. **Student Body:** Male 40%, female 60%, out-of-state 1%, international 1%. **Ethnic Representation:** African American 11%, Asian 1%, Caucasian 74%, Hispanic 3%, Native American 1%. **Retention and Graduation:** 75% freshmen return for sophomore year. 12% freshmen graduate within 4 years. 27% grads go on to further study within 1 year. 2% grads pursue business degrees. 4% grads pursue law degrees. **Faculty:** Student/faculty ratio 16:1. 411 full-time faculty, 78% hold PhDs. 100% faculty teach undergrads.

ACADEMICS

Degrees: Bachelor's, master's, post-master's certificate. **Classes:** 10-19 students in an average class. 10-19 students in an average lab/discussion section. **Disciplines with Highest Percentage of Degrees Awarded:** Education 37%, business/marketing 13%, social sciences and history 9%, protective services/public administration 9%, computer and information sciences 5%. **Special Study Options:** Cooperative (work-study) program, cross registration, distance learning, double major, dual enrollment, English as a second language, student exchange program (domestic), honors program, independent study, internships, liberal arts/career combination, study abroad, teacher certification program.

FACILITIES

Housing: Coed, apartments for married students, housing for international students, apartments for students with dependent children. **Library Holdings:** 489,069 bound volumes. 2,874 periodicals. 943,930 microforms. 22,189 audiovisuals. **Special Academic Facilities/Equipment:** Art center, anthropology museum, concert hall with pipe organ, nature preserve. **Computers:** School-owned computers available for student use.

EXTRACURRICULARS

Activities: Choral groups, concert band, dance, drama/theater, jazz band, literary magazine, music ensembles, radio station, student government, student newspaper, student-run film society, yearbook. **Organizations:** 85 registered organizations, 2 religious organizations, 8 fraternities (1% men join), 11 sororities (1% women join). **Athletics (Intercollegiate):** *Men:* basketball, cross-country, diving, football, ice hockey, indoor track, soccer, swimming, track & field. *Women:* basketball, cross-country, diving, ice hockey, indoor track, lacrosse, soccer, softball, swimming, tennis, track & field, volleyball.

ADMISSIONS

Selectivity Rating: 71 (of 100). **Freshman Academic Profile:** Average high school GPA 3.3. 7% in top 10% of high school class, 25% in top 25% of high school class, 70% in top 50% of high school class. Average SAT I Math 491, SAT I Math middle 50% range 450-540. Average SAT I Verbal 490, SAT I Verbal middle 50% range 450-540. TOEFL required of all international applicants, minimum TOEFL 500. **Basis for Candidate Selection:** *Very important factors considered include:* secondary school record, standardized test scores. *Important factors considered include:* class rank. *Other factors considered include:* character (personal qualities), essays, extracurricular activities, interview, recommendations, talent/ability, volunteer work, work experience. **Freshman Admission Requirements:** High school diploma or GED is required. *Academic units required/recommended:* 17 total recommended; 4 English recommended, 2 math required, 3 math recommended, 2 science required, 3 science recommended, 3 foreign language recommended, 4 history recommended. **Freshman Admission Statistics:** 7,852 applied, 54% accepted, 32% of those accepted enrolled. **Transfer Admission Requirements:** *Items required:* college transcript, statement of good standing from prior school. Minimum college GPA of 2.0 required. **General Admission Information:** Application fee $30. Early decision application deadline November 15. Nonfall registration accepted. Admission may be deferred for a maximum of 1 year. Credit offered for CEEB Advanced Placement tests.

COSTS AND FINANCIAL AID

In-state tuition $3,400. Out-of-state tuition $8,300. Room & board $5,640. Required fees $709. Average book expense $800. **Required Forms and Deadlines:** FAFSA. No deadline for regular filing. **Notification of Awards:** Applicants will be notified of awards on a rolling basis beginning on or about April 15. **Types of Aid:** *Need-based scholarships/grants:* Pell, SEOG, state scholarships/grants, private scholarships, the school's own gift aid. *Loans:* Direct Subsidized Stafford, Direct Unsubsidized Stafford, Direct PLUS, FFEL Subsidized Stafford, FFEL Unsubsidized Stafford, FFEL PLUS, Federal Perkins. **Student Employment:** Federal Work-Study Program available. Institutional employment available. Off-campus job opportunities are good. **Financial Aid Statistics:** 65% freshmen, 60% undergrads receive some form of aid. Average freshman grant $870. Average freshman loan $1,145. Average income from on-campus job $1,044. **Financial Aid Phone:** 716-829-3724.

STATE UNIVERSITY OF NEW YORK COLLEGE AT CORTLAND

PO Box 2000, Cortland, NY 13045
Phone: 607-753-4712 **E-mail:** admissions@cortland.edu
Fax: 607-753-5998 **Web:** www.cortland.edu

This public school was founded in 1868. It has a 191-acre campus.

STUDENTS AND FACULTY

Enrollment: 5,781. **Student Body:** Male 40%, female 60%, out-of-state 2%, international students represent 14 countries. **Ethnic Representation:** African American 2%, Asian 1%, Caucasian 88%, Hispanic 3%. **Retention and Graduation:** 76% freshmen return for sophomore year. 48% freshmen graduate within 4 years. **Faculty:** Student/faculty ratio 15:1. 272 full-time faculty, 79% hold PhDs. 97% faculty teach undergrads.

ACADEMICS

Degrees: Bachelor's, master's, post-bachelor's certificate, post-master's certificate. **Academic Requirements:** General education including some course work in computer literacy, English (including composition), foreign languages, history, humanities, mathematics, sciences (biological or physical), social science. **Classes:** 20-29 students in an average class. 20-29 students in an average lab/discussion section. **Disciplines with Highest Percentage of Degrees Awarded:** Education 61%, social sciences and history 13%, psychology 6%, communications/communication technologies 5%, 4%. **Special Study Options:** Cooperative (work-study) program, cross registration, distance learning, double major, dual enrollment, student exchange program (domestic), honors program, independent study, internships, liberal arts/career combination, student-designed major, study abroad, teacher certification program.

FACILITIES

Housing: Coed, apartments for single students, housing for international students, fraternities and/or sororities. **Library Holdings:** 82,257 bound volumes. 2,943 periodicals. 351,020 microforms. 4,557 audiovisuals. **Special Academic Facilities/Equipment:** Natural science museum, greenhouse, center for speech and hearing disorders, classrooms with integrated technologies, specialized labs. **Computers:** School-owned computers available for student use.

EXTRACURRICULARS

Activities: Choral groups, concert band, dance, drama/theater, jazz band, literary magazine, music ensembles, musical theater, radio station, student government, student newspaper, student-run film society, symphony orchestra, television station, yearbook. **Organizations:** 100 registered organizations, 15 honor societies, 4 fraternities, 1 sorority. **Athletics (Intercollegiate):** *Men:* baseball, basketball, skiing (cross-country), cross-country, diving, football, gymnastics, ice hockey, indoor track, lacrosse, soccer, swimming, track & field, wrestling. *Women:* basketball, skiing (cross-country), cross-country, diving, field hockey, golf, gymnastics, ice hockey, indoor track, lacrosse, soccer, softball, swimming, tennis, track & field, volleyball.

ADMISSIONS

Selectivity Rating: 75 (of 100). **Freshman Academic Profile:** Average high school GPA 3.2. 6% in top 10% of high school class, 38% in top 25% of high school class, 87% in top 50% of high school class. 91% from public high schools. Average SAT I Math 520, SAT I Math middle 50% range 480-550. Average SAT I Verbal 520, SAT I Verbal middle 50% range 500-570. Average ACT 23. TOEFL required of all international applicants, minimum TOEFL 550. **Basis for Candidate Selection:** *Very important factors considered include:* secondary school record, standardized test scores. *Important factors considered include:* essays, extracurricular activities, recommendations, talent/ability. *Other factors considered include:* alumni/ae relation, class rank, geographical residence, interview, minority status, state residency, volunteer work, work experience. **Freshman Admission Requirements:** High school diploma or GED is required. *Academic units required/recommended:* 20 total required; 23 total recommended; 4 English required, 3 math required, 4 math recommended, 3 science required, 4 science recommended, 3 science lab required, 3 foreign language required, 4 foreign language recommended, 4 social studies required. **Freshman Admission Statistics:** 9,278 applied, 46% accepted, 25% of those accepted enrolled. **Transfer Admission Requirements:** *Items required:* high school transcript, college transcript. Minimum college GPA of 2.5 required. Lowest grade transferable C. **General Admission Information:** Application fee $40. Priority application deadline March 1. Early decision application deadline November 15. Nonfall registration accepted. Admission may be deferred for a maximum of 1 year. Credit offered for CEEB Advanced Placement tests.

COSTS AND FINANCIAL AID

In-state tuition $3,400. Out-of-state tuition $8,300. Room & board $6,700. Required fees $865. Average book expense $700. **Required Forms and Deadlines:** FAFSA. Financial aid filing deadline April 1. **Notification of Awards:** Applicants will be notified of awards on a rolling basis beginning on or about March 1. **Types of Aid:** *Need-based scholarships/grants:* Pell, SEOG, state scholarships/grants, private scholarships, the school's own gift aid. *Loans:* Direct Subsidized Stafford, Direct Unsubsidized Stafford, Direct PLUS. **Student Employment:** Federal Work-Study Program available. Institutional employment available. Off-campus job opportunities are good. **Financial Aid Statistics:** 61% freshmen, 60% undergrads receive some form of aid. **Financial Aid Phone:** 607-753-4717.

STATE UNIVERSITY OF NEW YORK COLLEGE AT FREDONIA

178 Central Avenue, Fredonia, NY 14063
Phone: 716-673-3251 **E-mail:** admissions.office@fredonia.edu **CEEB Code:** 2539
Fax: 716-673-3249 **Web:** www.fredonia.edu **ACT Code:** 2934

This public school was founded in 1826. It has a 266-acre campus.

STUDENTS AND FACULTY

Enrollment: 4,990. **Student Body:** Male 41%, female 59%, out-of-state 2%, international 1% (8 countries represented). **Ethnic Representation:** African American 1%, Asian 1%, Caucasian 95%, Hispanic 2%, Native American 1%. **Retention and Graduation:** 81% freshmen return for sophomore year. 45% freshmen graduate within 4 years. 29% grads go on to further study within 1 year. **Faculty:** Student/faculty ratio 18:1. 254 full-time faculty, 83% hold PhDs. 100% faculty teach undergrads.

ACADEMICS

Degrees: Bachelor's, master's, post-master's certificate. **Academic Requirements:** General education including some course work in arts/fine arts, English (including composition), foreign languages, history, humanities, mathematics, sciences (biological or physical), social science. **Classes:** Under 10 students in an average class. 20-29 students in an average lab/discussion section. **Majors with Highest Enrollment:** Business administration/management; elementary education and teaching; music teacher education. **Disciplines with Highest Percentage of Degrees Awarded:** Education 35%, business/marketing 11%, communications/communication technologies 9%, visual and performing arts 9%, psychology 8%. **Special Study Options:** Cross registration, distance learning, double major, student exchange program (domestic), honors program, independent study, internships, liberal arts/career combination, student-designed major, study abroad, teacher certification program.

FACILITIES

Housing: Coed, all-female, all-male, apartments for single students, housing for disabled students, smoke-free residence hall option. **Library Holdings:** 396,000 bound volumes. 2,270 periodicals. 1,052,956 microforms. 17,607 audiovisuals. **Special Academic Facilities/Equipment:** Art center, education and local history museums, teacher education research center, developmental reading center, Sheldon Communications Lab, smart classrooms, greenhouse. **Computers:** School-owned computers available for student use.

EXTRACURRICULARS

Activities: Choral groups, concert band, dance, drama/theater, jazz band, literary magazine, music ensembles, musical theater, opera, radio station, student government, student newspaper, symphony orchestra, television station. **Organizations:** 118 registered organizations, 22 honor societies, 5 religious organizations, 4 fraternities (5% men join), 3 sororities (3% women join). **Athletics (Intercollegiate):** *Men:* baseball, basketball, cheerleading, cross-country, diving, ice hockey, indoor track, soccer, swimming, tennis, track & field. *Women:* basketball, cheerleading, cross-country, diving, indoor track, lacrosse, soccer, softball, swimming, tennis, track & field, volleyball.

ADMISSIONS

Selectivity Rating: 77 (of 100). **Freshman Academic Profile:** Average high school GPA 3.3. 15% in top 10% of high school class, 45% in top 25% of high school class, 90% in top 50% of high school class. 75% from public high schools. Average SAT I Math 561, SAT I Math middle 50% range 510-590. Average SAT I Verbal 557, SAT I Verbal middle 50% range 510-590. Average ACT 24, ACT middle 50% range 21-26. TOEFL required of all international applicants, minimum TOEFL 500. **Basis for Candidate Selection:** *Very important factors considered include:* secondary school record. *Important factors considered include:* class rank, extracurricular activities, recommendations, standardized test scores. *Other factors considered include:* alumni/ae relation, character/personal qualities, essays, minority status, talent/ability, volunteer work, work experience. **Freshman Admission Requirements:** High school diploma or GED is required. *Academic units required/recommended:* 17 total required; 19 total recommended; 4 English required, 4 English recommended, 3 math required, 4 math recommended, 3 science required, 4 science recommended, 3 foreign language required, 3 foreign language recommended, 4 social studies required, 4 social studies recommended. **Freshman Admission Statistics:** 6,178 applied, 53% accepted, 33% of those accepted enrolled. **Transfer Admission Requirements:** *Items required:* college transcript. Minimum college GPA of 2.0 required. Lowest grade transferable D. **General Admission Information:** Application fee $40. Early decision application deadline November 1. Nonfall registration accepted. Admission may be deferred for a maximum of 1 year. Credit and/or placement offered for CEEB Advanced Placement tests.

COSTS AND FINANCIAL AID

In-state tuition $3,400. Out-of-state tuition $8,300. Room & board $5,960. Required fees $973. Average book expense $620. **Required Forms and Deadlines:** FAFSA and state aid form. Priority filing deadline February 7. **Notification of Awards:** Applicants will be notified of awards on a rolling basis beginning on or about March 15. **Types of Aid:** *Need-based scholarships/grants:* Pell, SEOG, state scholarships/grants, private scholarships, the school's own gift aid. *Loans:* FFEL Subsidized Stafford, FFEL Unsubsidized Stafford, FFEL PLUS, Federal Perkins. **Student Employment:** Federal Work-Study Program available. Institutional employment available. Off-campus job opportunities are good. **Financial Aid Statistics:** 62% freshmen, 58% undergrads receive some form of aid. Average freshman grant $2,581. Average freshman loan $2,944. Average income from on-campus job $1,000. **Financial Aid Phone:** 716-673-3253.

STATE UNIVERSITY OF NEW YORK COLLEGE AT GENESEO

1 College Circle, Geneseo, NY 14454-1401
Phone: 585-245-5571 **E-mail:** admissions@geneseo.edu **CEEB Code:** 2540
Fax: 585-245-5550 **Web:** www.geneseo.edu **ACT Code:** 2936

This public school was founded in 1871. It has a 220-acre campus.

STUDENTS AND FACULTY

Enrollment: 5,387. **Student Body:** Male 36%, female 64%, out-of-state 1%, international 1%. **Ethnic Representation:** African American 2%, Asian 5%, Caucasian 90%, Hispanic 3%. **Retention and Graduation:** 91% freshmen return for sophomore year. 67% freshmen graduate within 4 years. 36% grads go on to further study within 1 year. 1% grads pursue business degrees. 2% grads pursue law degrees. 2% grads pursue medical degrees. **Faculty:** Student/faculty ratio 19:1. 252 full-time faculty, 84% hold PhDs. 100% faculty teach undergrads.

ACADEMICS

Degrees: Bachelor's, master's. **Academic Requirements:** General education including some course work in arts/fine arts, English (including composition), foreign languages, history, humanities, mathematics, sciences (biological or physical), social science, critical writing & reading, nonwestern traditions, numeric & symbolic reasoning. **Classes:** 20-29 students in an average class. **Majors with Highest Enrollment:** Special education, general; psychology, general; business administration/management. **Disciplines with Highest Percentage of Degrees Awarded:** Education 23%, social sciences and history 16%, business/marketing 13%, psychology 9%, communications/communication technologies 6%. **Special Study Options:** Cross registration, double major, honors program, independent study, internships, study abroad, teacher certification program, Albany semester, Washington semester, 3/2 engineering, 3/2 MBA, 3/2 master's in forestry, 4/1 MBA, 2/3 physical therapy, 3/4 dentistry, 3/4 optometry, 3/4 osteopathic medicine.

FACILITIES

Housing: Coed, town houses, and special-interest housing. Some fraternities and sororities have housing independent of college. **Library Holdings:** 524,692 bound volumes. 2,048 periodicals. 822,758 microforms. 21,463 audiovisuals. **Special Academic Facilities/Equipment:** Three theatres, electron microscopes, new technology building. **Computers:** School-owned computers available for student use.

EXTRACURRICULARS

Activities: Choral groups, dance, drama/theater, jazz band, literary magazine, music ensembles, musical theater, radio station, student government, student newspaper, symphony orchestra, television station, yearbook. **Organizations:** 163 registered organizations, 13 honor societies, 5 religious organizations, 10 fraternities (10% men join), 10 sororities (12% women join). **Athletics (Intercollegiate):** *Men:* basketball, cross-country, diving, ice hockey, indoor track, lacrosse, soccer, swimming, track & field. *Women:* basketball, cross-country, diving, field hockey, indoor track, lacrosse, soccer, softball, swimming, tennis, track & field, volleyball.

ADMISSIONS

Selectivity Rating: 92 (of 100). **Freshman Academic Profile:** Average high school GPA 3.7. 49% in top 10% of high school class, 81% in top 25% of high school class, 99% in top 50% of high school class. 94% from public high schools. Average SAT I Math 626, SAT I Math middle 50% range 590-660. Average SAT I Verbal 619, SAT I Verbal middle 50% range 580-650. Average ACT 27, ACT middle 50% range 25-28. TOEFL required of all international applicants, minimum TOEFL 525. **Basis for Candidate Selection:** *Very important factors considered include:* class rank, secondary school record, standardized test scores. *Important factors considered include:* essays, extracurricular activities, minority status, recommendations, talent/ability. *Other factors considered include:* character/personal qualities, volunteer work. **Freshman Admission Requirements:** High school diploma or GED is required. *Academic units required/recommended:* 20 total recommended; 4 English recommended, 4 math recommended, 4 science recommended, 4 foreign language recommended, 4 social studies recommended. **Transfer Admission Requirements:** *Items required:* college transcript. Minimum college GPA of 2.0 required. Lowest grade transferable D. **General Admission Information:** Application fee $30. Early decision application deadline November 15. Regular application deadline January 15. Nonfall registration accepted. Admission may be deferred for a maximum of 1 year. Credit offered for CEEB Advanced Placement tests.

COSTS AND FINANCIAL AID

In-state tuition $3,400. Out-of-state tuition $8,300. Room & board $5,660. Required fees $910. Average book expense $700. **Required Forms and Deadlines:** FAFSA and state aid form. Priority filing deadline February 15. **Notification of Awards:** Applicants will be notified of awards on a rolling basis beginning on or about March 15. **Types of Aid:** *Need-based scholarships/grants:* Pell, SEOG, state scholarships/grants, private scholarships, the school's own gift aid. *Loans:* FFEL Subsidized Stafford, FFEL Unsubsidized Stafford, FFEL PLUS, Federal Perkins, state loans, alternative loans. **Student Employment:** Federal Work-Study Program available. Institutional employment available. Off-campus job opportunities are fair. **Financial Aid Statistics:** 45% freshmen, 47% undergrads receive some form of aid. Average freshman grant $1,585. Average freshman loan $2,975. Average income from on-campus job $1,500. **Financial Aid Phone:** 585-245-5731.

STATE UNIVERSITY OF NEW YORK COLLEGE AT OLD WESTBURY

PO Box 307, Old Westbury, NY 11568-0307
Phone: 516-876-3073 **E-mail:** enroll@oldwestbury.edu **CEEB Code:** 2866
Fax: 516-876-3307 **Web:** www.oldwestbury.edu

This public school was founded in 1948. It has a 605-acre campus.

STUDENTS AND FACULTY

Enrollment: 3,147. **Student Body:** Male 40%, female 60%, out-of-state 1%, international 1%. **Ethnic Representation:** African American 28%, Asian 8%, Caucasian 32%, Hispanic 15%. **Retention and Graduation:** 73% freshmen return for sophomore year. 22% freshmen graduate within 4 years. **Faculty:** Student/faculty ratio 21:1. 124 full-time faculty, 78% hold PhDs. 100% faculty teach undergrads.

ACADEMICS

Degrees: Bachelor's, certificate. **Academic Requirements:** General education including some course work in mathematics. **Majors with Highest Enrollment:** Accounting; elementary education and teaching; psychology, general. **Disciplines with Highest Percentage of Degrees Awarded:** Business/marketing 29%, education 16%, social sciences and history 13%, computer and information sciences 11%, communications/communication technologies 9%. **Special Study Options:** Cooperative (work-study) program, cross registration, distance learning, double major, English as a second language, honors program, independent study, internships, study abroad, teacher certification program, disabled student services.

FACILITIES

Housing: Coed. **Library Holdings:** 216,289 bound volumes. 862 periodicals. 187,833 microforms. 4,119 audiovisuals. **Special Academic Facilities/Equipment:** Art gallery, language lab, TV studio, Maguire Theatre. **Computers:** School-owned computers available for student use.

EXTRACURRICULARS

Activities: Choral groups, radio station, student government, student newspaper, yearbook. **Organizations:** 55 registered organizations, 1 honor society, 2 religious organizations, 7 fraternities, 6 sororities. **Athletics (Intercollegiate):** *Men:* baseball, basketball, cross-country, soccer, tennis. *Women:* basketball, cross-country, softball, tennis, volleyball.

ADMISSIONS

Selectivity Rating: 68 (of 100). **Freshman Academic Profile:** Average high school GPA 3.0. Average SAT I Math 459, SAT I Math middle 50% range 410-500. Average SAT I Verbal 443, SAT I Verbal middle 50% range 395-490. Average ACT 18, ACT middle 50% range 15-20. TOEFL required of all international applicants, minimum TOEFL 500. **Basis for Candidate Selection:** *Very important factors considered include:* essays, standardized test scores. *Important factors considered include:* character/personal qualities, extracurricular activities, volunteer work, work experience. *Other factors considered include:* class rank, interview, recommendations, talent/ability. **Freshman Admission Requirements:** High school diploma or GED is required. *Academic units required/recommended:* 18 total recommended; 4 English recommended, 3 math recommended, 3 science recommended, 3 science lab recommended, 2 foreign language recommended, 2 social studies recommended, 2 history recommended, 2 elective recommended. **Freshman Admission Statistics:** 2,970 applied, 52% accepted, 19% of those accepted enrolled. **Transfer Admission Requirements:** *Items required:* college transcript, statement of good standing from prior school. Minimum high school GPA of 3.0 required. Minimum college GPA of 2.0 required. Lowest grade transferable C. **General Admission Information:** Application fee $30. Nonfall registration accepted. Admission may be deferred for a maximum of 1 year. Credit and/or placement offered for CEEB Advanced Placement tests.

COSTS AND FINANCIAL AID

In-state tuition $3,400. Out-of-state tuition $8,300. Room & board $6,190. Required fees $691. Average book expense $500. **Required Forms and Deadlines:** FAFSA, institution's own financial aid form and state aid form. Financial aid filing deadline April 21. Priority filing deadline April 21. **Notification of Awards:** Applicants will be notified of awards on a rolling basis. **Types of Aid:** *Loans:* FFEL Subsidized Stafford, FFEL Unsubsidized Stafford, FFEL PLUS, Federal Perkins, Federal Pell Grants, Federal Supplemental Education Opportunity Grants, State Educational Opportunity Program Grants, Supplemental State Tuition Grants, Aid for Part-Time Study Grants, Tuition Assistance Program, Federal Parent Loans, alternative loans. **Student Employment:** Federal Work-Study Program available. Institutional employment available. Off-campus job opportunities are good. **Financial Aid Statistics:** 66% freshmen, 55% undergrads receive some form of aid. Average income from on-campus job $952. **Financial Aid Phone:** 516-876-3222.

STATE UNIVERSITY OF NEW YORK COLLEGE AT ONEONTA

Alumni Hall 116, State University College, Oneonta, NY 13820
Phone: 607-436-2524 **E-mail:** admissions@oneonta.edu **CEEB Code:** 2542
Fax: 607-436-3074 **Web:** www.oneonta.edu **ACT Code:** 2940

This public school was founded in 1889. It has a 250-acre campus.

STUDENTS AND FACULTY

Enrollment: 5,477. **Student Body:** Male 40%, female 60%, out-of-state 2%, international 1% (19 countries represented). **Ethnic Representation:** African American 3%, Asian 1%, Caucasian 83%, Hispanic 4%. **Retention and Graduation:** 74% freshmen return for sophomore year. 28% freshmen graduate within 4 years. 36% grads go on to further study within 1 year. **Faculty:** Student/faculty ratio 18:1. 245 full-time faculty, 75% hold PhDs. 99% faculty teach undergrads.

ACADEMICS

Degrees: Bachelor's, master's, post-master's certificate. **Academic Requirements:** General education including some course work in arts/fine arts, computer literacy, English (including composition), foreign languages, history, humanities, mathematics, philosophy, sciences (biological or physical), social science. **Classes:** 10-19 students in an average class. **Majors with Highest Enrollment:** Business/managerial economics; elementary education and teaching; psychology, general. **Disciplines with Highest Percentage of Degrees Awarded:** Education 30%, home economics and vocational home economics 12%, business/marketing 11%, visual and performing arts 10%, social sciences and history 9%. **Special Study Options:** Cross registration, distance learning, double major, English as a second language, honors program, independent study, internships, liberal arts/career combination, study abroad. Variety of 3-1, 3-2, and 2-2 programs with other colleges and universities.

FACILITIES

Housing: Coed, housing for international students, special-interest wings in residence halls. **Library Holdings:** 549,243 bound volumes. 14,452 periodicals. 1,131,652 microforms. 30,772 audiovisuals. **Special Academic Facilities/Equipment:** Science discovery center, biological field station, weather station, planetarium, observatory, college camp. **Computers:** School-owned computers available for student use.

EXTRACURRICULARS

Activities: Choral groups, concert band, dance, drama/theater, jazz band, literary magazine, music ensembles, musical theater, opera, pep band, radio station, student government, student newspaper, student-run film society, symphony orchestra, television station, yearbook. **Organizations:** 70 registered organizations, 14 honor societies, 4 religious organizations, 3 sororities (7% women join). **Athletics (Intercollegiate):** *Men:* baseball, basketball, cross-country, indoor track, lacrosse, soccer, swimming, tennis, track & field, wrestling. *Women:* basketball, cross-country, diving, field hockey, indoor track, lacrosse, soccer, softball, swimming, tennis, track & field, volleyball.

ADMISSIONS

Selectivity Rating: 67 (of 100). **Freshman Academic Profile:** Average high school GPA 3.1. 9% in top 10% of high school class, 34% in top 25% of high school class, 88% in top 50% of high school class. 92% from public high schools. Average SAT I Math 541, SAT I Math middle 50% range 500-580. Average SAT I Verbal 536, SAT I Verbal middle 50% range 490-570. Average ACT 22, ACT middle 50% range 21-24. TOEFL required of all international applicants, minimum TOEFL 500. **Basis for Candidate Selection:** *Very important factors considered include:* secondary school record. *Important factors considered include:* character/personal qualities, extracurricular activities, interview, recommendations, standardized test scores, talent/ability, volunteer work. *Other factors considered include:* alumni/ae relation, class rank, essays, minority status, work experience. **Freshman Admission Requirements:** High school diploma or GED is required. *Academic units required/recommended:* 16 total required; 4 English required, 2 math required, 3 math recommended, 2 science required, 3 science recommended, 2 science lab required, 2 foreign language required, 3 foreign language recommended, 3 social studies required. **Freshman Admission Statistics:** 10,304 applied, 47% accepted, 22% of those accepted enrolled. **Transfer Admission Requirements:** *Items required:* college transcript. Minimum college GPA of 2.0 required. Lowest grade transferable C-. **General Admission Information:** Application fee $30. Priority application deadline February 1. Early decision application deadline November 1. Nonfall registration accepted. Admission may be deferred for a maximum of 1 year. Credit offered for CEEB Advanced Placement tests.

COSTS AND FINANCIAL AID

In-state tuition $3,400. Out-of-state tuition $8,300. Room & board $6,158. Required fees $906. Average book expense $800. **Required Forms and Deadlines:** FAFSA. No deadline for regular filing. Priority filing deadline March 15. **Notification of Awards:** Applicants will be notified of awards on a rolling basis beginning on or about March 1. **Types of Aid:** *Need-based scholarships/grants:* Pell, SEOG, state scholarships/grants, private scholarships, the school's own gift aid. *Loans:* Direct Subsidized Stafford, Direct Unsubsidized Stafford, Direct PLUS, FFEL Subsidized Stafford, FFEL Unsubsidized Stafford, FFEL PLUS, Federal Perkins, state loans, college/university loans from institutional funds. **Student Employment:** Federal Work-Study Program available. Institutional employment available. Off-campus job opportunities are good. **Financial Aid Statistics:** 57% freshmen, 61% undergrads receive some form of aid. Average freshman grant $6,395. Average freshman loan $2,934. Average income from on-campus job $1,675. **Financial Aid Phone:** 607-436-2532.

STATE UNIVERSITY OF NEW YORK COLLEGE AT OSWEGO

211 Culkin Hall, Oswego, NY 13126
Phone: 315-312-2250 **E-mail:** admiss@oswego.edu **CEEB Code:** 2543
Fax: 315-312-3260 **Web:** www.oswego.edu **ACT Code:** 2942

This public school was founded in 1861. It has a 696-acre campus.

STUDENTS AND FACULTY

Enrollment: 7,337. **Student Body:** Male 46%, female 54%, out-of-state 2%, international 1% (21 countries represented). **Ethnic Representation:** African American 4%, Asian 2%, Caucasian 91%, Hispanic 3%, Native American 1%. **Retention and Graduation:** 78% freshmen return for sophomore year. 45% freshmen graduate within 4 years. 14% grads go on to further study within 1 year. 7% grads pursue business degrees. 4% grads pursue law degrees. 9% grads pursue medical degrees. **Faculty:** Student/faculty ratio 20:1. 310 full-time faculty, 76% hold PhDs. 93% faculty teach undergrads.

ACADEMICS

Degrees: Bachelor's, master's, post-bachelor's certificate, post-master's certificate. **Academic Requirements:** General education including some course work in arts/fine arts, computer literacy, English (including composition), foreign languages, history, humanities, mathematics, philosophy, sciences (biological or physical), social science. **Classes:** 20-29 students in an average class. 20-29 students in an average lab/discussion section. **Disciplines with Highest Percentage of Degrees Awarded:** Education 28%, business/marketing 20%, communications/communication technologies 8%, social sciences and history 8%, psychology 8%. **Special Study Options:** Cooperative (work-study) program, distance learning, double major, dual enrollment, English as a second language, student exchange program (domestic), honors program, independent study, internships, study abroad, teacher certification program.

FACILITIES

Housing: Coed, fraternities and/or sororities, single rooms for nontraditional students. Johnson Hall first year experience residence hall for incoming freshmen only. Hart Hall global living and learning center. **Library Holdings:** 467,346 bound volumes. 1,477 periodicals. 2,106,494 microforms. 36,172 audiovisuals. **Special Academic Facilities/Equipment:** Art galleries, biological field station, curriculum materials center, electron microscopy lab, planetarium. **Computers:** School-owned computers available for student use.

EXTRACURRICULARS

Activities: Choral groups, concert band, dance, drama/theater, jazz band, literary magazine, music ensembles, musical theater, opera, radio station, student government, student newspaper, student-run film society, symphony orchestra, television station, yearbook. **Organizations:** 118 registered organizations, 12 honor societies, 5 religious organizations, 16 fraternities (12% men join), 12 sororities (12% women join). **Athletics (Intercollegiate):** *Men:* baseball, basketball, cross-country, diving, golf, ice hockey, indoor track, lacrosse, soccer, swimming, tennis, track & field, wrestling. *Women:* basketball, cross-country, diving, field hockey, golf, indoor track, lacrosse, soccer, softball, swimming, tennis, track & field, volleyball.

ADMISSIONS

Selectivity Rating: 68 (of 100). **Freshman Academic Profile:** Average high school GPA 3.1. 9% in top 10% of high school class, 42% in top 25% of high school class, 87% in top 50% of high school class. 94% from public high schools. Average SAT I Math 545, SAT I Math middle 50% range 520-590. Average SAT I Verbal 539, SAT I Verbal middle 50% range 500-590. Average ACT 24, ACT middle 50% range 21-25. TOEFL required of all international applicants, minimum TOEFL 550. **Basis for Candidate Selection:** *Very important factors considered include:* secondary school record. *Important factors considered include:* class rank, recommendations, standardized test scores. *Other factors considered include:* alumni/ae relation, character/personal qualities, essays, extracurricular activities, interview, minority status, talent/ability, volunteer work, work experience. **Freshman Admission Requirements:** High school diploma or GED is required. *Academic units required/recommended:* 18 total required; 4 English required, 4 English recommended, 3 math required, 4 math recommended, 3 science required, 4 science recommended, 2 science lab required, 3 science lab recommended, 2 foreign language required, 4 foreign language recommended, 4 social studies required, 2 history recommended. **Freshman Admission Statistics:** 7,697 applied, 58% accepted, 31% of those accepted enrolled. **Transfer Admission Requirements:** *Items required:* college transcript. Minimum college GPA of 2.5 required. Lowest grade transferable C. **General Admission Information:** Application fee $40. Early decision application deadline November 15. Nonfall registration accepted. Admission may be deferred for a maximum of 1 year. Credit offered for CEEB Advanced Placement tests.

COSTS AND FINANCIAL AID

In-state tuition $3,400. Out-of-state tuition $8,300. Room & board $7,194. Required fees $894. Average book expense $825. **Required Forms and Deadlines:** FAFSA. No deadline for regular filing. Priority filing deadline April 1. **Notification of Awards:** Applicants will be notified of awards on a rolling basis beginning on or about April 1. **Types of Aid:** *Need-based scholarships/grants:* Pell, SEOG, state scholarships/grants. *Loans:* FFEL Subsidized Stafford, FFEL Unsubsidized Stafford, FFEL PLUS, Federal Perkins. **Student Employment:** Federal Work-Study Program available. Institutional employment available. Off-campus job opportunities are fair. **Financial Aid Statistics:** 61% freshmen, 65% undergrads receive some form of aid. Average freshman grant $2,300. Average freshman loan $2,625. Average income from on-campus job $950. **Financial Aid Phone:** 315-312-2248.

STATE UNIVERSITY OF NEW YORK COLLEGE AT POTSDAM

44 Pierrepont Avenue, Potsdam, NY 13676
Phone: 315-267-2180 **E-mail:** admissions@potsdam.edu **CEEB Code:** 2545
Fax: 315-267-2163 **Web:** www.potsdam.edu **ACT Code:** 2946

This public school was founded in 1816. It has a 240-acre campus.

STUDENTS AND FACULTY

Enrollment: 3,475. **Student Body:** Male 41%, female 59%, out-of-state 3%, international 2% (10 countries represented). **Ethnic Representation:** African American 2%, Asian 1%, Caucasian 84%, Hispanic 2%, Native American 2%. **Retention and Graduation:** 75% freshmen return for sophomore year. 33% grads go on to further study within 1 year. 9% grads pursue business degrees. 3% grads pursue law degrees. 5% grads pursue medical degrees. **Faculty:** Student/faculty ratio 18:1. 238 full-time faculty, 72% hold PhDs. 95% faculty teach undergrads.

ACADEMICS

Degrees: Bachelor's, master's. **Academic Requirements:** General education including some course work in arts/fine arts, English (including composition), foreign languages, history, humanities, mathematics, philosophy, sciences (biological or physical), social science. **Classes:** 10-19 students in an average class. 10-19 students in an average lab/discussion section. **Majors with Highest Enrollment:** Elementary education and teaching; psychology, general; music teacher education. **Disciplines with Highest Percentage of Degrees Awarded:** Social sciences and history 25%, psychology 15%, education 13%, English 12%, visual and performing arts 9%. **Special Study Options:** Cross registration, distance learning, double major, dual enrollment, student exchange program (domestic), honors program, independent study, internships, liberal arts/career combination, student-designed major, study abroad, teacher certification program. Combined degree options: engineering with Clarkson University and SUNY Binghamton; accounting, engineering, or management with SUNY Utica/Rome.

FACILITIES

Housing: Coed, all-female, apartments for single students, housing for disabled students, housing for international students, First-Year Experience, substance-free. **Library Holdings:** 319,870 bound volumes. 1,253 periodicals. 743,042 microforms. 17,120 audiovisuals. **Special Academic Facilities/Equipment:** Art gallery, anthropology museum, ecology museum, three performance halls, theatre, synthesizer music studios, planetarium, electron microscope, nuclear magnetic resonator, seismograph. **Computers:** School-owned computers available for student use.

EXTRACURRICULARS

Activities: Choral groups, concert band, dance, drama/theater, jazz band, literary magazine, music ensembles, musical theater, opera, pep band, radio station, student government, student newspaper, symphony orchestra, yearbook. **Organizations:** 100 registered organizations. **Athletics (Intercollegiate):** *Men:* basketball, cross-country, diving, golf, ice hockey, lacrosse, soccer, swimming. *Women:* basketball, cheerleading, cross-country, diving, equestrian, lacrosse, soccer, softball, swimming, tennis, volleyball.

ADMISSIONS

Selectivity Rating: 69 (of 100). **Freshman Academic Profile:** 11% in top 10% of high school class, 37% in top 25% of high school class, 78% in top 50% of high school class. Average SAT I Math 533, SAT I Math middle 50% range 480-580. Average SAT I Verbal 534, SAT I Verbal middle 50% range 470-590. Average ACT 23, ACT middle 50% range 20-26. TOEFL required of all international applicants, minimum TOEFL 520. **Basis for Candidate Selection:** *Very important factors considered include:* secondary school record, standardized test scores. *Important factors considered include:* class rank, talent/ability. *Other factors considered include:* alumni/ae relation, character/personal qualities, essays, extracurricular activities, interview, recommendations, volunteer work, work experience. **Freshman Admission Requirements:** High school diploma or GED is required. *Academic units required/recommended:* 17 total required; 20 total recommended; 4 English required, 4 English recommended, 3 math required, 4 math recommended, 2 science required, 3 science recommended, 1 science lab required, 2 science lab recommended, 3 foreign language required, 4 foreign language recommended, 4 social studies required, 4 social studies recommended. **Freshman Admission Statistics:** 3,397 applied, 67% accepted, 28% of those accepted enrolled. **Transfer Admission Requirements:** *Items required:* college transcript, statement of good standing from prior school. Minimum college GPA of 2.0 required. Lowest grade transferable D. **General Admission Information:** Application fee $30. Nonfall registration accepted. Admission may be deferred for a maximum of 1 year. Credit and/or placement offered for CEEB Advanced Placement tests.

COSTS AND FINANCIAL AID

In-state tuition $3,400. Out-of-state tuition $8,300. Room & board $6,390. Required fees $729. Average book expense $800. **Required Forms and Deadlines:** FAFSA and state aid form. No deadline for regular filing. Priority filing deadline March 1. **Notification of Awards:** Applicants will be notified of awards on a rolling basis beginning on or about February 15. **Types of Aid:** *Need-based scholarships/grants:* Pell, SEOG, state scholarships/grants, private scholarships, the school's own gift aid. *Loans:* Direct Subsidized Stafford, Direct Unsubsidized Stafford, Direct PLUS, Federal Perkins, alternative loans. **Student Employment:** Federal Work-Study Program available. Institutional employment available. Off-campus job opportunities are good. **Financial Aid Statistics:** 67% freshmen, 67% undergrads receive some form of aid. Average freshman grant $4,042. Average freshman loan $6,290. **Financial Aid Phone:** 315-267-2162.

STATE UNIVERSITY OF NEW YORK COLLEGE AT PURCHASE

Admissions Office, 735 Anderson Hill Road, Purchase, NY 10577-1400
Phone: 914-251-6300 **E-mail:** admissn@purchase.edu **CEEB Code:** 2878
Fax: 914-251-6314 **Web:** www.purchase.edu **ACT Code:** 2931

This public school was founded in 1967. It has a 550-acre campus.

STUDENTS AND FACULTY

Enrollment: 3,920. **Student Body:** Male 44%, female 56%, out-of-state 15%, international 2% (30 countries represented). **Ethnic Representation:** African American 8%, Asian 4%, Caucasian 71%, Hispanic 10%. **Retention and Graduation:** 72% freshmen return for sophomore year. 25% freshmen graduate within 4 years. **Faculty:** Student/faculty ratio 17:1. 136 full-time faculty. 100% faculty teach undergrads.

ACADEMICS

Degrees: Bachelor's, certificate, master's, post-master's certificate. **Academic Requirements:** General education including some course work in English (including composition), foreign languages, history, humanities, mathematics, sciences (biological or physical), social science, critical thinking, information management; some arts majors are exempt. **Classes:** 10-19 students in an average class. 10-19 students in an average lab/discussion section. **Majors with Highest Enrollment:** Music performance, general; liberal arts and sciences/ liberal studies; psychology, general. **Disciplines with Highest Percentage of Degrees Awarded:** Visual and performing arts 48%, liberal arts/general studies 21%, social sciences and history 15%, English 7%, mathematics 4%. **Special Study Options:** Cross registration, distance learning, double major, English as a second language, independent study, internships, liberal arts/career combination, student-designed major, study abroad.

FACILITIES

Housing: Coed, apartments for single students, housing for disabled students, housing for international students. **Library Holdings:** 281,686 bound volumes. 1,990 periodicals. 247,057 microforms. 15,578 audiovisuals. **Special Academic Facilities/Equipment:** Museum, four-theatre performing arts center, visual arts facility, children's center, recording studio, electron microscopes. **Computers:** School-owned computers available for student use.

EXTRACURRICULARS

Activities: Choral groups, dance, drama/theater, jazz band, radio station, student government, student newspaper, student-run film society, television station. **Organizations:** 23 registered organizations. **Athletics (Intercollegiate):** *Men:* basketball, cross-country, soccer, tennis, volleyball. *Women:* basketball, cross-country, soccer, softball, tennis, volleyball.

ADMISSIONS

Selectivity Rating: 63 (of 100). **Freshman Academic Profile:** Average SAT I Math 528, SAT I Math middle 50% range 470-580. Average SAT I Verbal 559, SAT I Verbal middle 50% range 500-600. TOEFL required of all international applicants, minimum TOEFL 550. **Basis for Candidate Selection:** *Very important factors considered include:* essays, secondary school record, standardized test scores. *Important factors considered include:* recommendations. *Other factors considered include:* extracurricular activities, interview, talent/ability. **Freshman Admission Requirements:** High school diploma or GED is required. **Freshman Admission Statistics:** 7,102 applied, 37% accepted, 26% of those accepted enrolled. **Transfer Admission Requirements:** *Items required:* college transcript. Minimum college GPA of 2.5 required. Lowest grade transferable D. **General Admission Information:** Application fee $40. Priority application deadline March 1. Early decision application deadline November 1. Nonfall registration accepted. Admission may be deferred for a maximum of 1 year. Credit and/or placement offered for CEEB Advanced Placement tests.

COSTS AND FINANCIAL AID

In-state tuition $3,400. Out-of-state tuition $8,300. Room & board $6,860. Required fees $827. Average book expense $750. **Required Forms and Deadlines:** FAFSA and state aid form. NYS Tuition Assistance Program applicable for NYS residents. Priority filing deadline March 15. **Notification of Awards:** Applicants will be notified of awards on a rolling basis beginning on or about March 1. **Types of Aid:** *Need-based scholarships/grants:* Pell, SEOG, state scholarships/grants, private scholarships, the school's own gift aid. *Loans:* FFEL Subsidized Stafford, FFEL Unsubsidized Stafford, FFEL PLUS, Federal Perkins. **Student Employment:** Federal Work-Study Program available. Institutional employment available. Off-campus job opportunities are excellent. **Financial Aid Statistics:** 52% freshmen, 49% undergrads receive some form of aid. Average freshman grant $1,500. Average freshman loan $3,076. Average income from on-campus job $1,073. **Financial Aid Phone:** 914-251-6350.

STATE UNIVERSITY OF NEW YORK COLLEGE OF A&T AT COBLESKILL

Office of Admissions, Cobleskill, NY 12043
Phone: 518-255-5525 **E-mail:** admwpc@cobleskill.edu **CEEB Code:** 2524
Fax: 518-255-6769 **Web:** www.cobleskill.edu **ACT Code:** 2914

This public school was founded in 1916. It has a 750-acre campus.

STUDENTS AND FACULTY

Enrollment: 2,443. **Student Body:** Male 53%, female 47%, out-of-state 8%, international 2% (7 countries represented). **Ethnic Representation:** African American 6%, Asian 1%, Caucasian 84%, Hispanic 4%, Native American 1%. **Retention and Graduation:** 63% grads go on to further study within 1 year. **Faculty:** Student/faculty ratio 19:1. 107 full-time faculty, 29% hold PhDs. 100% faculty teach undergrads.

ACADEMICS

Degrees: Associate's, bachelor's, certificate, terminal, transfer. **Academic Requirements:** General education including some course work in arts/fine arts, English (including composition), foreign languages, history, humanities, mathematics, sciences (biological or physical), social science. The SUNY trustees general education requirements include the above areas, plus western civilization and world cultures. For associate degrees, a student must take 3 credits in 7 of the 10 areas; for the bachelor's, a student must take 3 credits in each of the 10 areas. **Classes:** 20-29 students in an average class. 10-19 students in an average lab/discussion section. **Disciplines with Highest Percentage of Degrees Awarded:** Agriculture 20%, computer and information sciences 1%. **Special Study Options:** Distance learning, English as a second language, honors program, independent study, internships, study abroad, weekend college.

FACILITIES

Housing: Coed, all-female, all-male, separate housing for older students. **Library Holdings:** 76,919 bound volumes. 327 periodicals. 32,405 microforms. 12,601 audiovisuals. **Special Academic Facilities/Equipment:** Art museum, 650-acre agricultural campus, distance learning classrooms, ski area, adult study center. **Computers:** *Recommended operating system:* Windows 98, NT, or 2000. School-owned computers available for student use.

EXTRACURRICULARS

Activities: Choral groups, drama/theater, jazz band, music ensembles, musical theater, student government, yearbook. **Organizations:** 40 registered organizations, 1 honor society, 1 religious organization. **Athletics (Intercollegiate):** *Men:* baseball, basketball, cross-country, diving, golf, lacrosse, soccer, swimming, tennis, track & field, wrestling. *Women:* basketball, cross-country, diving, golf, soccer, softball, swimming, tennis, track & field, volleyball.

ADMISSIONS

Selectivity Rating: 63 (of 100). **Freshman Academic Profile:** Average high school GPA 2.4. 3% in top 10% of high school class, 11% in top 25% of high school class, 35% in top 50% of high school class. 98% from public high schools. Average SAT I Math 461, SAT I Math middle 50% range 400-510. Average SAT I Verbal 457, SAT I Verbal middle 50% range 400-510. Average ACT 20, ACT middle 50% range 16-22. TOEFL required of all international applicants, minimum TOEFL 500. **Basis for Candidate Selection:** *Very important factors considered include:* secondary school record. *Important factors considered include:* class rank. *Other factors considered include:* alumni/ae relation, essays, extracurricular activities, geographical residence, interview, recommendations, standardized test scores, talent/ability, volunteer work, work experience. **Freshman Admission Requirements:** High school diploma or GED is required. *Academic units required/recommended:* 4 English required, 4 English recommended, 1 math required, 3 math recommended, 1 science required, 3 science recommended, 2 science lab recommended, 3 social studies recommended. **Freshman Admission Statistics:** 2,966 applied, 92% accepted, 36% of those accepted enrolled. **Transfer Admission Requirements:** *Items required:* college transcript, statement of good standing from prior school. Lowest grade transferable C. **General Admission Information:** Application fee $30. Priority application deadline May 1. Regular application deadline rolling. Nonfall registration accepted. Admission may be deferred for a maximum of 1 year. Credit offered for CEEB Advanced Placement tests.

COSTS AND FINANCIAL AID

In-state tuition $3,400. Out-of-state tuition $8,300. Room & board $6,600. Required fees $861. Average book expense $1,000. **Required Forms and Deadlines:** FAFSA and state aid form. Financial aid filing deadline March 15. **Notification of Awards:** Applicants will be notified of awards on or about April 15. **Types of Aid:** *Need-based scholarships/grants:* Pell, SEOG, state scholarships/grants, private scholarships, the school's own gift aid. *Loans:* FFEL Subsidized Stafford, FFEL Unsubsidized Stafford, FFEL PLUS, Federal Perkins. **Student Employment:** Federal Work-Study Program available. Institutional employment available. Off-campus job opportunities are good. **Financial Aid Statistics:** 83% freshmen, 70% undergrads receive some form of aid. Average freshman grant $4,700. Average freshman loan $2,480. Average income from on-campus job $720. **Financial Aid Phone:** 518-255-5623.

STATE UNIVERSITY OF NEW YORK COLLEGE OF A&T AT MORRISVILLE

PO Box 901, Morrisville, NY 13408
Phone: 315-684-6046 **E-mail:** admissions@morrisville.edu **CEEB Code:** 2527
Fax: 315-684-6427 **Web:** www.morrisville.edu

This public school was founded in 1908. It has a 150-acre campus.

STUDENTS AND FACULTY

Enrollment: 2,899. **Student Body:** Male 52%, female 48%, out-of-state 3%, international 2%. **Ethnic Representation:** African American 14%, Asian 1%, Caucasian 73%, Hispanic 4%, Native American 2%. **Faculty:** Student/faculty ratio 15:1. 123 full-time faculty, 14% hold PhDs.

ACADEMICS

Degrees: Associate's, bachelor's, certificate, terminal, transfer. **Academic Requirements:** General education including some course work in computer literacy, English (including composition), humanities, mathematics, sciences (biological or physical), social science. **Classes:** 10-19 students in an average class. 10-19 students in an average lab/discussion section. **Special Study Options:** Cooperative (work-study) program, cross registration, distance learning, double major, dual enrollment, honors program, internships, student-designed major.

FACILITIES

Housing: Coed, housing for disabled students, housing for international students. **Library Holdings:** 90,000 bound volumes. 500 periodicals. 1,500 audiovisuals. **Special Academic Facilities/Equipment:** Wildlife museum, equine institute, aquaculture center, dairy complex, automotive performance center, IcePlex, recreation building, wood products technology building, greenhouse/horticulture complex. **Computers:** School-owned computers available for student use.

EXTRACURRICULARS

Activities: Choral groups, dance, drama/theater, jazz band, music ensembles, musical theater, pep band, radio station, student government, student newspaper, yearbook. **Organizations:** 43 registered organizations, 1 honor society. **Athletics (Intercollegiate):** *Men:* baseball, basketball, cheerleading, cross-country, diving, equestrian, football, ice hockey, lacrosse, skiing (alpine), soccer, swimming, track & field, wrestling. *Women:* basketball, cheerleading, cross-country, diving, equestrian, field hockey, lacrosse, skiing (alpine), soccer, softball, swimming, tennis, track & field, volleyball.

ADMISSIONS

Selectivity Rating: 63 (of 100). **Freshman Academic Profile:** Average SAT I Math 440, SAT I Math middle 50% range 390-520. Average SAT I Verbal 440, SAT I Verbal middle 50% range 390-510. Average ACT 18, ACT middle 50% range 18-21. TOEFL required of all international applicants, minimum TOEFL 500. **Basis for Candidate Selection:** *Very important factors considered include:* secondary school record. *Important factors considered include:* interview, work experience. *Other factors considered include:* alumni/ae relation, character/personal qualities, class rank, extracurricular activities, recommendations, standardized test scores, state residency. **Freshman Admission Requirements:** High school diploma or GED is required. *Academic units required/recommended:* 4 total required; 10 total recommended; 4 English required, 4 English recommended, 3 math recommended, 3 science recommended, 2 science lab recommended. **Freshman Admission Statistics:** 3,474 applied, 77% accepted, 49% of those accepted enrolled. **Transfer Admission Requirements:** *Items required:* high school transcript, college transcript. Minimum high school GPA of 2.5 required. Minimum college GPA of 2.0 required. Lowest grade transferable C. **General Admission Information:** Application fee $30. Nonfall registration accepted. Admission may be deferred for a maximum of 1 year.

COSTS AND FINANCIAL AID

In-state tuition $3,200. Out-of-state tuition $5,200. Room & board $6,100. Required fees $1,045. Average book expense $800. **Required Forms and Deadlines:** FAFSA. No deadline for regular filing. Priority filing deadline February 1. **Notification of Awards:** Applicants will be notified of awards on a rolling basis beginning on or about February 25. **Types of Aid:** *Need-based scholarships/grants:* Pell, SEOG, state scholarships/grants, the school's own gift aid. *Loans:* FFEL Subsidized Stafford, FFEL Unsubsidized Stafford, FFEL PLUS, Federal Perkins, Federal Nursing. **Student Employment:** Federal Work-Study Program available. Institutional employment available. Off-campus job opportunities are good. **Financial Aid Statistics:** 72% freshmen, 81% undergrads receive some form of aid. **Financial Aid Phone:** 315-684-6289.

STATE UNIVERSITY OF NEW YORK COLLEGE OF ENVIRONMENTAL SCIENCE AND FORESTRY

106 Bray Hall, SUNY-ESF, Syracuse, NY 13210
Phone: 315-470-6600 **E-mail:** esfinfo@esf.edu **CEEB Code:** 2530
Fax: 315-470-6933 **Web:** www.esf.edu **ACT Code:** 2948

This public school was founded in 1911. It has a 12-acre campus.

STUDENTS AND FACULTY

Enrollment: 1,171. **Student Body:** Male 63%, female 37%, out-of-state 20%, international 1% (18 countries represented). **Ethnic Representation:** African American 3%, Asian 1%, Caucasian 92%, Hispanic 2%. **Faculty:** 100% faculty teach undergrads.

ACADEMICS

Degrees: Associate's, bachelor's, doctoral, master's, terminal, transfer. **Academic Requirements:** General education including some course work in English (including composition), mathematics, sciences (biological or physical), social science. **Special Study Options:** Cooperative (work-study) program, cross registration, distance learning, honors program, internships, study abroad, teacher certification program.

FACILITIES

Housing: Coed, all-female, all-male, apartments for married students, apartments for single students, housing for international students, fraternities and/or sororities. **Library Holdings:** 122,377 bound volumes. 3,000 periodicals. 189,433 microforms. 732 audiovisuals. **Special Academic Facilities/Equipment:** Museums, art galleries, plant growth & animal environmental simulation chambers, wildlife collection, electron microscope, paper machine, photogrammetric & geodetic facilities. **Computers:** *Recommended operating system:* Windows 3x. School-owned computers available for student use.

EXTRACURRICULARS

Activities: Choral groups, concert band, dance, drama/theater, jazz band, literary magazine, marching band, music ensembles, musical theater, pep band, radio station, student government, student newspaper, symphony orchestra, yearbook. **Organizations:** 300 registered organizations, 1 honor society, 6 religious organizations, 10% men join fraternities, 10% women join sororities. **Athletics (Intercollegiate):** *Men:* baseball, basketball, cheerleading, crew, skiing (cross-country), cross-country, equestrian, fencing, football, golf, gymnastics, ice hockey, indoor track, lacrosse, rifle, rugby, sailing, skiing (alpine), skiing (Nordic), soccer, softball, squash, swimming, tennis, track & field, volleyball. *Women:* basketball, cheerleading, crew, skiing (cross-country), cross-country, equestrian, fencing, field hockey, golf, gymnastics, ice hockey, indoor track, lacrosse, rugby, sailing, skiing (alpine), skiing (Nordic), soccer, softball, squash, swimming, tennis, track & field, volleyball.

ADMISSIONS

Selectivity Rating: 63 (of 100). **Freshman Academic Profile:** Average high school GPA 3.6. 31% in top 10% of high school class, 67% in top 25% of high school class, 98% in top 50% of high school class. 90% from public high schools. Average SAT I Math 585, SAT I Math middle 50% range 530-640. Average SAT I Verbal 575, SAT I Verbal middle 50% range 530-600. Average ACT 26, ACT middle 50% range 23-28. TOEFL required of all international applicants, minimum TOEFL 550. **Basis for Candidate Selection:** *Very important factors considered include:* essays, secondary school record, standardized test scores. *Important factors considered include:* character/personal qualities, class rank, extracurricular activities, recommendations, volunteer work. *Other factors considered include:* alumni/ae relation, interview, work experience. **Freshman Admission Requirements:** High school diploma is required and GED is not accepted. *Academic units required/recommended:* 4 English required, 3 math required, 4 math recommended, 3 science required, 4 science recommended, 3 science lab required, 4 science lab recommended, 3 foreign language recommended, 4 social studies required. **Freshman Admission Statistics:** 587 applied, 50% accepted, 49% of those accepted enrolled. **Transfer Admission Requirements:** *Items required:* college transcript. Minimum college GPA of 2.0 required. Lowest grade transferable C. **General Admission Information:** Application fee $30. Priority application deadline March 1. Early decision application deadline November 15. Regular application deadline rolling. Nonfall registration accepted. Admission may be deferred for a maximum of 1 year. Credit offered for CEEB Advanced Placement tests.

COSTS AND FINANCIAL AID

In-state tuition $3,400. Out-of-state tuition $8,300. Room & board $8,310. Required fees $362. Average book expense $700. **Required Forms and Deadlines:** FAFSA and state aid form. No deadline for regular filing. Priority filing deadline March 1. **Notification of Awards:** Applicants will be notified of awards on a rolling basis beginning on or about March 15. **Types of Aid:** *Need-based scholarships/grants:* Pell, SEOG, state scholarships/grants, private scholarships, the school's own gift aid. *Loans:* FFEL Subsidized Stafford, FFEL Unsubsidized Stafford, FFEL PLUS, Federal Perkins. **Student Employment:** Federal Work-Study Program available. Institutional employment available. Off-campus job opportunities are excellent. **Financial Aid Statistics:** 71% freshmen, 83% undergrads receive some form of aid. Average freshman grant $8,625. Average freshman loan $2,625. Average income from on-campus job $800. **Financial Aid Phone:** 315-470-6670.

STATE UNIVERSITY OF NEW YORK COLLEGE OF TECHNOLOGY AT CANTON

French Hall, SUNY Canton, Canton, NY 13617
Phone: 315-386-7123 **E-mail:** admissions@canton.edu **CEEB Code:** 2523
Fax: 315-386-7929 **Web:** www.canton.edu **ACT Code:** 2912

This public school was founded in 1906. It has a 555-acre campus.

STUDENTS AND FACULTY

Enrollment: 2,422. **Student Body:** Male 51%, female 49%, international students represent 5 countries. **Ethnic Representation:** African American 8%, Caucasian 86%, Hispanic 3%, Native American 2%. **Retention and Graduation:** 81% freshmen return for sophomore year. 45% grads go on to further study within 1 year. **Faculty:** Student/faculty ratio 23:1. 83 full-time faculty, 20% hold PhDs. 100% faculty teach undergrads.

ACADEMICS

Degrees: Associate's, bachelor's, certificate, terminal, transfer. **Academic Requirements:** General education including some course work in computer literacy, English (including composition), mathematics, sciences (biological or physical), social science. **Classes:** 20-29 students in an average class. 10-19 students in an average lab/discussion section. **Majors with Highest Enrollment:** Computer/information technology services administration and management; criminal justice/law enforcement administration. **Special Study Options:** Cooperative (work-study) program, cross registration, distance learning, dual enrollment, internships, liberal arts/career combination, student-designed major.

FACILITIES

Housing: Coed. **Library Holdings:** 69,388 bound volumes. 382 periodicals. 5,245 microforms. 1,782 audiovisuals. **Special Academic Facilities/ Equipment:** Criminal investigation labs, radio station, distance learning classrooms. **Computers:** *Recommended operating system:* Windows 95. School-owned computers available for student use.

EXTRACURRICULARS

Activities: Choral groups, literary magazine, radio station, student government, student newspaper, yearbook. **Organizations:** 50 registered organizations, 2 honor societies, 1 religious organization, 3 fraternities, 3 sororities. **Athletics (Intercollegiate):** *Men:* basketball, football, ice hockey, lacrosse, soccer. *Women:* basketball, soccer, softball, volleyball.

ADMISSIONS

Selectivity Rating: 62 (of 100). **Freshman Academic Profile:** TOEFL required of all international applicants, minimum TOEFL 550. **Basis for Candidate Selection:** *Very important factors considered include:* secondary school record. *Other factors considered include:* character/personal qualities, class rank, extracurricular activities, interview, recommendations, standardized test scores, talent/ability, work experience. **Freshman Admission Requirements:** High school diploma or GED is required. *Academic units required/recommended:* 12 total recommended; 4 English recommended, 2 math recommended, 2 science recommended, 4 social studies recommended. **Freshman Admission Statistics:** 1,830 applied, 98% accepted, 45% of those accepted enrolled. **Transfer Admission Requirements:** *Items required:* high school transcript, college transcript. Lowest grade transferable C. **General Admission Information:** Application fee $40. Priority application deadline March 15. Nonfall registration accepted. Admission may be deferred for a maximum of 1 year.

COSTS AND FINANCIAL AID

In-state tuition $3,200. Out-of-state tuition $5,000. Room & board $6,490. Required fees $980. Average book expense $800. **Required Forms and Deadlines:** FAFSA and state aid form. No deadline for regular filing. Priority filing deadline March 15. **Notification of Awards:** Applicants will be notified of awards on a rolling basis beginning on or about February 3. **Types of Aid:** *Need-based scholarships/grants:* Pell, SEOG, private scholarships. *Loans:* Direct Subsidized Stafford, Direct Unsubsidized Stafford, Direct PLUS, Federal Perkins. **Student Employment:** Federal Work-Study Program available. Institutional employment available. Off-campus job opportunities are fair. **Financial Aid Phone:** 315-386-7616.

STATE UNIVERSITY OF NEW YORK COLLEGE OF TECHNOLOGY AT DELHI

Bush Hall, 2 Main St., Delhi, NY 13753
Phone: 607-746-4550 **E-mail:** enroll@Delhi.edu
Fax: 607-746-4104 **Web:** www.delhi.edu

STUDENTS AND FACULTY

Enrollment: 1,893. **Student Body:** Male 55%, female 45%, out-of-state 4%, international 1%. **Ethnic Representation:** African American 11%, Asian 1%, Caucasian 81%, Hispanic 7%. **Faculty:** Student/faculty ratio 15:1.

ACADEMICS

Degrees: Associate's, bachelor's, certificate, terminal, transfer. **Special Study Options:** Distance learning, English as a second language, honors program, internships, student-designed major, weekend college.

FACILITIES

Housing: Coed. **Library Holdings:** 47,909 bound volumes. 318 periodicals. 160 microforms. 713 audiovisuals.

EXTRACURRICULARS

Activities: Choral groups, dance, drama/theater, music ensembles, musical theater, radio station, student government, student newspaper, yearbook. **Organizations:** 12% men join fraternities, 6% women join sororities. **Athletics (Intercollegiate):** *Men:* basketball, cross-country, diving, golf, indoor track, lacrosse, soccer, swimming, tennis, track & field, wrestling. *Women:* basketball, cross-country, diving, golf, indoor track, soccer, softball, swimming, tennis, track & field, volleyball.

ADMISSIONS

Selectivity Rating: 63 (of 100). **Freshman Academic Profile: Basis for Candidate Selection:** *Very important factors considered include:* secondary school record. *Important factors considered include:* character/personal qualities, recommendations, talent/ability. *Other factors considered include:* alumni/ae relation, class rank, essays, extracurricular activities, geographical residence, interview, standardized test scores, state residency, volunteer work, work experience. **Freshman Admission Requirements:** High school diploma or GED is required. *Academic units required/recommended:* 4 English required, 1 math required, 2 math recommended, 1 science required, 2 science recommended, 1 science lab recommended, 3 social studies required, 1 history required. **Transfer Admission Requirements:** *Items required:* high school transcript, college transcript. Lowest grade transferable C. **General Admission Information:** Application fee $30. Nonfall registration accepted. Admission may be deferred for a maximum of 1 year.

COSTS AND FINANCIAL AID

In-state tuition $3,200. Average book expense $650. **Financial Aid Statistics:** 81% undergrads receive some form of aid.

STATE UNIVERSITY OF NEW YORK COLLEGE OF TECHNOLOGY AT FARMINGDALE

2350 Broadhollow Rd., Farmingdale, NY 11735
Phone: 631-420-2000 **E-mail:** admissions@farmingdale.edu
Web: www.farmingdale.edu

STUDENTS AND FACULTY

Enrollment: 5,700. **Student Body:** Out-of-state 2%.

ACADEMICS

Academic Requirements: General education including some course work in computer literacy, English (including composition), mathematics, sciences (biological or physical), social science. **Special Study Options:** Cooperative (work-study) program, cross registration, distance learning, dual enrollment, internships, liberal arts/career combination, student-designed major.

FACILITIES

Housing: Coed, housing for disabled students, fraternities and/or sororities. **Library Holdings:** 69,388 bound volumes. 382 periodicals. 5,245 microforms. 1,782 audiovisuals.

EXTRACURRICULARS

Activities: Literary magazine, pep band, radio station, student government, student newspaper, yearbook. **Organizations:** 1% men join fraternities, 1% women join sororities. **Athletics (Intercollegiate):** *Men:* basketball, football, ice hockey, lacrosse, soccer. *Women:* basketball, soccer, softball, volleyball.

ADMISSIONS

Selectivity Rating: 63 (of 100). **Transfer Admission Requirements:** *Items required:* high school transcript, college transcript, statement of good standing from prior school. Minimum high school GPA of 2.0 required. Minimum college GPA of 2.0 required. Lowest grade transferable 2.0.

COSTS AND FINANCIAL AID

In-state tuition $3,200. Out-of-state tuition $5,000. Room & board $5,230. Required fees $510. Average book expense $700. **Types of Aid:** *Need-based scholarships/grants:* Pell, SEOG, state scholarships/grants, private scholarships.

STATE UNIVERSITY OF NEW YORK EMPIRE STATE COLLEGE

2 Union Avenue, Saratoga, NY 12866
Phone: 518-587-2100 **E-mail:** admissions@esc.edu **CEEB Code:** 2214
Fax: 518-580-0105 **Web:** www.esc.edu **ACT Code:** 2737

This public school was founded in 1971.

STUDENTS AND FACULTY

Enrollment: 9,110. **Student Body:** Male 45%, female 55%, out-of-state 2%, international 3%. **Ethnic Representation:** African American 13%, Asian 2%, Caucasian 69%, Hispanic 7%, Native American 1%. **Retention and Graduation:** 40% grads go on to further study within 1 year. **Faculty:** Student/faculty ratio 22:1. 133 full-time faculty, 81% hold PhDs. 99% faculty teach undergrads.

ACADEMICS

Degrees: Associate's, bachelor's, master's. **Special Study Options:** Cross registration, distance learning, double major, dual enrollment, external degree program, independent study, internships, student-designed major, study abroad.

FACILITIES

Computers: School-owned computers available for student use.

EXTRACURRICULARS

Activities: Literary magazine.

ADMISSIONS

Selectivity Rating: 63 (of 100). **Freshman Academic Profile: Basis for Candidate Selection:** *Very important factors considered include:* character/personal qualities, essays. *Important factors considered include:* interview. *Other factors considered include:* recommendations, secondary school record, talent/ability. **Freshman Admission Requirements:** High school diploma or GED is required. **Transfer Admission Requirements:** *Items required:* high school transcript, essay. Lowest grade transferable C. **General Admission Information:** Nonfall registration accepted. Admission may be deferred for a maximum of 3 years.

COSTS AND FINANCIAL AID

In-state tuition $3,400. Out-of-state tuition $8,300. Required fees $455. **Required Forms and Deadlines:** FAFSA and state aid form. **Types of Aid:** *Need-based scholarships/grants:* Pell, SEOG, state scholarships/grants, private scholarships, the school's own gift aid. *Loans:* FFEL Subsidized Stafford, FFEL Unsubsidized Stafford, FFEL PLUS, Federal Perkins. **Student Employment:** Federal Work-Study Program available. **Financial Aid Phone:** 518-587-2100.

STATE UNIVERSITY OF NEW YORK INSTITUTE OF TECHNOLOGY

PO Box 3050, Utica, NY 13504
Phone: 315-792-7500 **E-mail:** admissions@sunyit.edu **CEEB Code:** 2896
Fax: 315-792-7837 **Web:** www.sunyit.edu **ACT Code:** 2953

This public school was founded in 1966. It has an 850-acre campus.

STUDENTS AND FACULTY

Enrollment: 1,974. **Student Body:** Male 50%, female 50%, out-of-state 1%, international 2%. **Ethnic Representation:** African American 6%, Asian 3%, Caucasian 84%, Hispanic 3%. **Faculty:** Student/faculty ratio 19:1. 85 full-time faculty.

ACADEMICS

Degrees: Bachelor's, master's, post-master's certificate. **Academic Requirements:** General education including some course work in arts/fine arts, computer literacy, English (including composition), foreign languages, history, humanities, mathematics, sciences (biological or physical), social science. **Majors with Highest Enrollment:** Nursing/registered nurse training (RN, ASN, BSN, MSN); business administration/management; computer science. **Disciplines with Highest Percentage of Degrees Awarded:** Business/marketing 26%, engineering/engineering technology 21%, computer and information sciences 17%, health professions and related sciences 13%, communications/communication technologies 8%. **Special Study Options:** Accelerated program, cross registration, distance learning, double major, English as a second language, independent study, internships.

FACILITIES

Housing: Coed, housing for disabled students. **Library Holdings:** 169,722 bound volumes. 819 periodicals. **Special Academic Facilities/Equipment:** Gannett Gallery, New York State Telecommunications Museum. **Computers:** School-owned computers available for student use.

EXTRACURRICULARS

Activities: Jazz band, radio station, student government, student newspaper, television station, yearbook. **Organizations:** 30 registered organizations, 4 honor societies, 1 religious organization. **Athletics (Intercollegiate):** *Men:* baseball, basketball, golf, lacrosse, soccer. *Women:* basketball, cross-country, golf, soccer, softball, volleyball.

ADMISSIONS

Selectivity Rating: 63 (of 100). **Freshman Academic Profile:** TOEFL required of all international applicants, minimum TOEFL 550. **Freshman Admission Requirements: Transfer Admission Requirements:** *Items required:* college transcript. Minimum college GPA of 2.0 required. Lowest grade transferable D. **General Admission Information:** Application fee $30. Admission may be deferred for a maximum of 1 year. Neither credit nor placement offered for CEEB Advanced Placement tests.

COSTS AND FINANCIAL AID

In-state tuition $3,400. Out-of-state tuition $8,300. Room & board $6,560. Required fees $764. Average book expense $750. **Required Forms and Deadlines:** FAFSA and institution's own financial aid form. **Notification of Awards:** Applicants will be notified of awards on a rolling basis. **Types of Aid:** *Need-based scholarships/grants:* Pell, SEOG, state scholarships/grants, private scholarships. *Loans:* Direct Subsidized Stafford, Direct Unsubsidized Stafford, Direct PLUS, Federal Perkins, Federal Nursing. **Student Employment:** Federal Work-Study Program available. Institutional employment available. Off-campus job opportunities are good. **Financial Aid Statistics:** 81% undergrads receive some form of aid. **Financial Aid Phone:** 315-792-7210.

STATE UNIVERSITY OF NEW YORK MARITIME COLLEGE

Fort Schuyler, Throg's Neck, NY 10465-4198
Phone: 800-642-1874 **E-mail:** edmaritime@aol.com
Fax: 718-409-7392

STUDENTS AND FACULTY

Enrollment: 646.

FACILITIES

Housing: Coed, apartments for single students.

EXTRACURRICULARS

Organizations: 14 registered organizations, 2 religious organizations. **Athletics (Intercollegiate):** *Men:* baseball, basketball, crew, cross-country, lacrosse, rifle, rugby, sailing, soccer, softball, swimming, tennis, wrestling. *Women:* basketball, crew, cross-country, rifle, sailing, softball, swimming, tennis.

ADMISSIONS

Selectivity Rating: 60 (of 100). **Freshman Academic Profile:** TOEFL required of all international applicants, minimum TOEFL 500. **Freshman Admission Requirements: General Admission Information:** Early decision application deadline December 1. Regular application deadline rolling.

COSTS AND FINANCIAL AID

In-state tuition $3,400. Out-of-state tuition $8,300. Room & board $5,420. Required fees $175. Average book expense $500. **Types of Aid:** *Loans:* FFEL Subsidized Stafford, FFEL PLUS. **Student Employment:** Federal Work-Study Program available. **Financial Aid Statistics:** Average income from on-campus job $800.

STATE UNIVERSITY OF NEW YORK UPSTATE MEDICAL UNIVERSITY

155 Elizabeth Blackwell Street, Syracuse, NY 13210
Phone: 315-464-4570 **E-mail:** vavonesd@upstate.edu **CEEB Code:** 2547
Fax: 315-464-8867 **Web:** www.upstate.edu **ACT Code:** 2981

This public school was founded in 1850. It has a 25-acre campus.

STUDENTS AND FACULTY

Enrollment: 308. **Student Body:** Male 23%, female 77%, out-of-state 2%. **Ethnic Representation:** African American 4%, Asian 2%, Caucasian 93%, Native American 1%. **Retention and Graduation:** 3% grads go on to further study within 1 year.

ACADEMICS

Degrees: Bachelor's, certificate, doctoral, first professional, master's, post-master's certificate. **Special Study Options:** Accelerated program, independent study.

FACILITIES

Housing: Coed, apartments for married students, apartments for single students. **Library Holdings:** 189,999 bound volumes. 1,438 periodicals. 29,515 audiovisuals. **Special Academic Facilities/Equipment:** 350-bed tertiary care hospital.

EXTRACURRICULARS

Activities: Student government, yearbook.

ADMISSIONS

Selectivity Rating: 63 (of 100). **Freshman Academic Profile: Basis for Candidate Selection:** *Very important factors considered include:* class rank, interview. *Important factors considered include:* essays, extracurricular activities, geographical residence, minority status, recommendations, state residency. *Other factors considered include:* character/personal qualities, standardized test scores, volunteer work, work experience. **Freshman Admission Requirements:** High school diploma or GED is required. *Academic units required/recommended:* 13 total recommended; 4 English recommended, 3 math recommended, 3 science recommended, 3 social studies recommended. **Transfer Admission Requirements:** *Items required:* high school transcript, college transcript, essay, interview, statement of good standing from prior school. Minimum college GPA of 2.0 required. Lowest grade transferable C-. **General Admission Information:** Application fee $30. Admission may be deferred for a maximum of 1 year.

COSTS AND FINANCIAL AID

Out-of-state tuition $8,300. Room & board $5,680. Required fees $410. Average book expense $730. **Required Forms and Deadlines:** FAFSA. Priority filing deadline April 1. **Notification of Awards:** Applicants will be notified of awards on a rolling basis beginning on or about June 1. **Types of Aid:** *Need-based scholarships/grants:* Pell, SEOG, state scholarships/grants, the school's own gift aid. *Loans:* FFEL Subsidized Stafford, FFEL Unsubsidized Stafford, FFEL PLUS, Federal Perkins. **Student Employment:** Federal Work-Study Program available. Institutional employment available. Off-campus job opportunities are excellent. **Financial Aid Statistics:** 64% undergrads receive some form of aid. Average income from on-campus job $950. **Financial Aid Phone:** 315-464-4329.

STATE UNIVERSITY OF WEST GEORGIA

1600 Maple Street, Carrollton, GA 30118
Phone: 770-836-6416 **E-mail:** admiss@westga.edu **CEEB Code:** 5900
Fax: 770-836-4659 **Web:** www.westga.edu **ACT Code:** 878

This public school was founded in 1906. It has a 394-acre campus.

STUDENTS AND FACULTY

Enrollment: 7,661. **Student Body:** Male 40%, female 60%, out-of-state 4%, international 1% (37 countries represented). **Ethnic Representation:** African American 23%, Asian 1%, Caucasian 75%, Hispanic 1%. **Retention and Graduation:** 72% freshmen return for sophomore year. 10% freshmen graduate within 4 years. **Faculty:** Student/faculty ratio 23:1. 344 full-time faculty, 81% hold PhDs. 91% faculty teach undergrads.

ACADEMICS

Degrees: Bachelor's, doctoral, master's, post-master's certificate. **Academic Requirements:** General education including some course work in arts/fine arts, computer literacy, English (including composition), foreign languages, history, humanities, mathematics, sciences (biological or physical), social science. **Classes:** 20-29 students in an average class. 20-29 students in an average lab/discussion section. **Majors with Highest Enrollment:** Business administration/management; elementary education and teaching; biology/biological sciences, general. **Disciplines with Highest Percentage of Degrees Awarded:** Business/marketing 28%, education 20%, social sciences and history 10%, psychology 8%, health professions and related sciences 8%. **Special Study Options:** Accelerated program, cooperative (work-study) program, distance learning, double major, dual enrollment, external degree program, honors program, independent study, internships, study abroad, teacher certification program, weekend college.

FACILITIES

Housing: Coed, all-female, all-male, housing for disabled students, housing for international students, fraternities and/or sororities. **Library Holdings:** 378,656 bound volumes. 1,342 periodicals. 1,104,126 microforms. 9,494 audiovisuals. **Special Academic Facilities/Equipment:** Archaeological laboratory, art gallery, electron microscope, observatory, preschool, performing arts center, TV studio. **Computers:** School-owned computers available for student use.

EXTRACURRICULARS

Activities: Choral groups, concert band, dance, drama/theater, jazz band, literary magazine, marching band, music ensembles, musical theater, opera, pep band, radio station, student government, student newspaper, television station. **Organizations:** 86 registered organizations, 31 honor societies, 12 religious organizations, 11 fraternities (7% men join), 10 sororities (11% women join). **Athletics (Intercollegiate):** *Men:* baseball, basketball, cheerleading, cross-country, football, tennis. *Women:* basketball, cheerleading, cross-country, softball, tennis, volleyball.

ADMISSIONS

Selectivity Rating: 72 (of 100). **Freshman Academic Profile:** Average high school GPA 3.0. 96% from public high schools. Average SAT I Math 505, SAT I Math middle 50% range 450-550. Average SAT I Verbal 509, SAT I Verbal middle 50% range 460-550. Average ACT 21, ACT middle 50% range 18-22. TOEFL required of all international applicants, minimum TOEFL 523. **Basis for Candidate Selection:** *Very important factors considered include:* secondary school record, standardized test scores. **Freshman Admission**

Requirements: High school diploma is required and GED is not accepted. *Academic units required/recommended:* 16 total required; 4 English required, 4 math required, 3 science required, 2 science lab required, 2 foreign language required, 3 social studies required. **Freshman Admission Statistics:** 4,451 applied, 64% accepted, 63% of those accepted enrolled. **Transfer Admission Requirements:** *Items required:* college transcript. Minimum college GPA of 2.0 required. Lowest grade transferable D. **General Admission Information:** Application fee $20. Priority application deadline June 1. Regular application deadline July 31. Nonfall registration accepted. Admission may be deferred for a maximum of 1 year. Credit and/or placement offered for CEEB Advanced Placement tests.

COSTS AND FINANCIAL AID

In-state tuition $2,010. Out-of-state tuition $8,040. Room & board $4,244. Required fees $548. Average book expense $600. **Required Forms and Deadlines:** FAFSA. No deadline for regular filing. Priority filing deadline April 1. **Notification of Awards:** Applicants will be notified of awards on a rolling basis beginning on or about May 15. **Types of Aid:** *Need-based scholarships/grants:* Pell, SEOG, state scholarships/grants, private scholarships, the school's own gift aid. *Loans:* Direct Subsidized Stafford, Direct Unsubsidized Stafford, Direct PLUS, Federal Perkins, college/university loans from institutional funds. **Student Employment:** Federal Work-Study Program available. Institutional employment available. Off-campus job opportunities are good. **Financial Aid Statistics:** 51% freshmen, 34% undergrads receive some form of aid. Average freshman grant $4,268. Average freshman loan $1,911. Average income from on-campus job $4,560. **Financial Aid Phone:** 770-836-6421.

STEPHEN F. AUSTIN STATE UNIVERSITY

PO Box 13051, SFA Station, Nacogdoches, TX 75962
Phone: 936-468-2504 **E-mail:** admissions@sfasu.edu **CEEB Code:** 6682
Fax: 936-468-3849 **Web:** www.sfasu.edu **ACT Code:** 4188

This public school was founded in 1923. It has a 401-acre campus.

STUDENTS AND FACULTY

Enrollment: 9,783. **Student Body:** Male 42%, female 58%, out-of-state 2%, international 1% (49 countries represented). **Ethnic Representation:** African American 16%, Asian 1%, Caucasian 76%, Hispanic 6%, Native American 1%. **Retention and Graduation:** 58% freshmen return for sophomore year. 17% freshmen graduate within 4 years. 22% grads go on to further study within 1 year. **Faculty:** Student/faculty ratio 21:1. 416 full-time faculty, 75% hold PhDs. 98% faculty teach undergrads.

ACADEMICS

Degrees: Bachelor's, doctoral, master's. **Academic Requirements:** General education including some course work in arts/fine arts, computer literacy, English (including composition), history, humanities, mathematics, sciences (biological or physical), social science, communication. **Classes:** 20-29 students in an average class. 10-19 students in an average lab/discussion section. **Majors with Highest Enrollment:** Marketing/marketing management, general; multi/interdisciplinary studies; health and physical education, general. **Disciplines with Highest Percentage of Degrees Awarded:** Business/marketing 24%, interdisciplinary studies 19%, health professions and related sciences 8%, parks and recreation 6%, communications/communication technologies 5%. **Special Study Options:** Accelerated program, distance learning, double major, dual enrollment, honors program, independent study, internships, liberal arts/career combination, student-designed major, study abroad, teacher certification program.

FACILITIES

Housing: Coed, all-female, all-male, apartments for married students, apartments for single students, housing for disabled students, fraternities and/or sororities, apartments for students with dependent children. **Library Holdings:** 981,951 bound volumes. 3,194 periodicals. 1,345,793 microforms. 10,436 audiovisuals. **Special Academic Facilities/Equipment:** Stone Fort Museum, planetarium, arboretum, observatory, GIS lab, Forest Resources Institute, soils analysis lab, East Texas Historical Association, East Texas Research Center, science research center, research feed mill. **Computers:** School-owned computers available for student use.

EXTRACURRICULARS

Activities: Choral groups, concert band, dance, drama/theater, jazz band, literary magazine, marching band, music ensembles, musical theater, opera, pep band, radio station, student government, student newspaper, student-run film society, symphony orchestra, television station, yearbook. **Organizations:** 220 registered organizations, 19 honor societies, 21 religious organizations, 23 fraternities (14% men join), 16 sororities (12% women join). **Athletics (Intercollegiate):** *Men:* basketball, cross-country, football, golf, indoor track, track & field. *Women:* basketball, cross-country, indoor track, soccer, softball, tennis, track & field, volleyball.

ADMISSIONS

Selectivity Rating: 76 (of 100). **Freshman Academic Profile:** 11% in top 10% of high school class, 37% in top 25% of high school class, 80% in top 50% of high school class. 90% from public high schools. Average SAT I Math 487, SAT I Math middle 50% range 440-560. Average SAT I Verbal 484, SAT I Verbal middle 50% range 440-550. Average ACT 20, ACT middle 50% range 19-23. TOEFL required of all international applicants, minimum TOEFL 550. **Basis for Candidate Selection:** *Very important factors considered include:* class rank, standardized test scores. **Freshman Admission Requirements:** High school diploma or GED is required. *Academic units required/recommended:* 17 total recommended; 4 English recommended, 3 math recommended, 2 science recommended, 2 science lab recommended, 2 foreign language recommended, 4 social studies recommended. **Freshman Admission Statistics:** 5,836 applied, 76% accepted, 46% of those accepted enrolled. **Transfer Admission Requirements:** *Items required:* college transcript. Minimum college GPA of 2.0 required. Lowest grade transferable D. **General Admission Information:** Application fee $25. Nonfall registration accepted. Credit and/or placement offered for CEEB Advanced Placement tests.

COSTS AND FINANCIAL AID

In-state tuition $2,310. Out-of-state tuition $8,850. Room & board $4,546. Required fees $791. Average book expense $874. **Required Forms and Deadlines:** FAFSA and institution's own financial aid form. Financial aid filing deadline April 15. Priority filing deadline April 1. **Notification of Awards:** Applicants will be notified of awards on a rolling basis beginning on or about May 1. **Types of Aid:** *Need-based scholarships/grants:* Pell, SEOG, state scholarships/grants, private scholarships, the school's own gift aid. *Loans:* FFEL Subsidized Stafford, FFEL Unsubsidized Stafford, FFEL PLUS, Federal Perkins, state loans, college/university loans from institutional funds, alternative loans. **Student Employment:** Federal Work-Study Program available. Institutional employment available. Off-campus job opportunities are fair. **Financial Aid Statistics:** 52% freshmen, 51% undergrads receive some form of aid. Average freshman grant $5,000. Average freshman loan $2,625. Average income from on-campus job $4,100. **Financial Aid Phone:** 936-468-2403.

STEPHENS COLLEGE

1200 East Broadway, Box 2121, Columbia, MO 65215
Phone: 573-876-7207 **E-mail:** apply@wc.stephens.edu **CEEB Code:** 6683
Fax: 573-876-7237 **Web:** www.stephens.edu **ACT Code:** 2374

This private school was founded in 1833. It has an 86-acre campus.

STUDENTS AND FACULTY

Enrollment: 596. **Student Body:** Male 5%, female 95%, out-of-state 57%, international students represent 5 countries. **Ethnic Representation:** African American 9%, Asian 1%, Caucasian 84%, Hispanic 4%, Native American 1%. **Retention and Graduation:** 83% freshmen return for sophomore year. 38% freshmen graduate within 4 years. **Faculty:** Student/faculty ratio 10:1. 47 full-time faculty, 70% hold PhDs. 100% faculty teach undergrads.

ACADEMICS

Degrees: Associate's, bachelor's, master's. **Academic Requirements:** General education including some course work in arts/fine arts, computer literacy, English (including composition), history, humanities, mathematics, philosophy, sciences (biological or physical), social science. **Classes:** Under 10 students in an average class. Under 10 students in an average lab/discussion section. **Majors with Highest Enrollment:** Fashion/apparel design; drama and dramatics/theatre arts, general; education, general. **Disciplines with Highest Percentage of Degrees Awarded:** Visual and performing arts 20%, other 16%, education 11%, interdisciplinary studies 7%, English 6%. **Special Study Options:** Cross registration, distance learning, double major, dual enrollment, external degree program, independent study, internships, liberal arts/career combination, student-designed major, study abroad, teacher certification program.

FACILITIES

Housing: All-female, apartments for single students. **Library Holdings:** 120,626 bound volumes. 534 periodicals. 11,067 microforms. 4,764 audiovisuals. **Special Academic Facilities/Equipment:** Art gallery and historical costume collections; on-campus preschool, kindergarten, and elementary school; language lab. **Computers:** School-owned computers available for student use.

EXTRACURRICULARS

Activities: Choral groups, dance, drama/theater, literary magazine, music ensembles, musical theater, radio station, student government, student newspaper, television station, yearbook. **Organizations:** 45 registered organizations, 10 honor societies, 5 religious organizations, 2 sororities (8% women join). **Athletics (Intercollegiate):** *Women:* basketball, soccer, swimming, tennis, volleyball.

ADMISSIONS

Selectivity Rating: 73 (of 100). **Freshman Academic Profile:** Average high school GPA 3.5. 43% in top 10% of high school class, 67% in top 25% of high school class, 88% in top 50% of high school class. 75% from public high schools. Average SAT I Math 513, SAT I Math middle 50% range 480-580. Average SAT I Verbal 566, SAT I Verbal middle 50% range 510-630. Average ACT 24, ACT middle 50% range 21-26. TOEFL required of all international applicants, minimum TOEFL 550. **Basis for Candidate Selection:** *Very important factors considered include:* character/personal qualities, essays, recommendations, secondary school record, standardized test scores. *Important factors considered include:* extracurricular activities, interview, talent/ability, volunteer work. *Other factors considered include:* work experience. **Freshman Admission Requirements:** High school diploma or GED is required. *Academic units required/recommended:* 12 total recommended; 4 English recommended, 2 math recommended, 2 science recommended, 2 foreign language recommended, 2 social studies recommended. **Freshman Admission Statistics:** 335 applied, 83% accepted, 44% of those accepted enrolled. **Transfer Admission Requirements:** *Items required:* high school transcript, college transcript, statement of good standing from prior school. Minimum college GPA of 2.0 required. Lowest grade transferable C. **General Admission Information:** Application fee $25. Nonfall registration accepted. Admission may be deferred for a maximum of 1 year. Credit offered for CEEB Advanced Placement tests.

COSTS AND FINANCIAL AID

Tuition $16,715. Room & board $5,690. Required fees $0. Average book expense $600. **Required Forms and Deadlines:** FAFSA. No deadline for regular filing. Priority filing deadline March 1. **Notification of Awards:** Applicants will be notified of awards on a rolling basis beginning on or about February 1. **Types of Aid:** *Need-based scholarships/grants:* Pell, SEOG, state scholarships/grants, private scholarships, the school's own gift aid. *Loans:* Direct Subsidized Stafford, Direct Unsubsidized Stafford, Direct PLUS, Federal Perkins. **Student Employment:** Federal Work-Study Program available. Institutional employment available. Off-campus job opportunities are excellent. **Financial Aid Statistics:** 73% freshmen, 65% undergrads receive some form of aid. Average freshman grant $10,600. Average freshman loan $2,000. Average income from on-campus job $1,000. **Financial Aid Phone:** 573-876-7106.

STERLING COLLEGE

PO Box 98, Sterling, KS 67579
Phone: 620-278-4275 **E-mail:** admissions@sterling.edu **CEEB Code:** 6684
Fax: 620-278-4416 **Web:** www.sterling.edu **ACT Code:** 1466

This private school, which is affiliated with the Presbyterian Church, was founded in 1887. It has a 42-acre campus.

STUDENTS AND FACULTY

Enrollment: 466. **Student Body:** Male 47%, female 53%, out-of-state 39%, international 3%. **Ethnic Representation:** African American 6%, Asian 1%, Caucasian 87%, Hispanic 4%, Native American 2%. **Retention and Graduation:** 71% freshmen return for sophomore year. 36% freshmen graduate within 4 years. 10% grads go on to further study within 1 year. 2% grads pursue business degrees. 1% grads pursue law degrees. 2% grads pursue medical degrees. **Faculty:** Student/faculty ratio 11:1. 33 full-time faculty, 51% hold PhDs. 100% faculty teach undergrads.

ACADEMICS

Degrees: Bachelor's. **Academic Requirements:** General education including some course work in arts/fine arts, computer literacy, English (including composition), history, humanities, mathematics, philosophy, sciences (biological or physical), social science, religion. **Classes:** Under 10 students in an average class. Under 10 students in an average lab/discussion section. **Disciplines with Highest Percentage of Degrees Awarded:** Business/marketing 15%, education 14%, philosophy/religion/theology 11%, parks and recreation 11%, biological life sciences 10%. **Special Study Options:** Double major, dual enrollment, independent study, internships, student-designed major, study abroad, teacher certification program.

FACILITIES

Housing: All-female, all-male. **Library Holdings:** 76,637 bound volumes. 350 periodicals. 2,120 microforms. 2,159 audiovisuals. **Special Academic Facilities/Equipment:** History/cultural museum. **Computers:** School-owned computers available for student use.

EXTRACURRICULARS

Activities: Choral groups, concert band, drama/theater, jazz band, literary magazine, music ensembles, musical theater, pep band, student government, student newspaper, yearbook. **Organizations:** 2 registered organizations, 1 honor society, 2 religious organizations. **Athletics (Intercollegiate):** *Men:* baseball, basketball, cross-country, football, soccer, tennis, track & field. *Women:* basketball, cheerleading, cross-country, soccer, softball, tennis, track & field, volleyball.

ADMISSIONS

Selectivity Rating: 69 (of 100). **Freshman Academic Profile:** Average high school GPA 3.4. 28% in top 10% of high school class, 41% in top 25% of high school class, 71% in top 50% of high school class. 80% from public high schools. Average SAT I Math 530. Average SAT I Verbal 560. Average ACT 23, ACT middle 50% range 20-27. TOEFL required of all international applicants, minimum TOEFL 520. **Basis for Candidate Selection:** *Very important factors considered include:* character/personal qualities, secondary school record, standardized test scores. *Important factors considered include:* essays, extracurricular activities, interview, religious affiliation/commitment, volunteer work. *Other factors considered include:* alumni/ae relation, class rank, recommendations, talent/ability, work experience. **Freshman Admission Requirements:** High school diploma or GED is required. *Academic units required/recommended:* 4 English recommended, 3 math recommended, 2 science recommended, 1 science lab recommended, 2 foreign language recommended, 2 social studies recommended, 2 history recommended, 1 elective recommended. **Freshman Admission Statistics:** 359 applied, 57% accepted, 48% of those accepted enrolled. **Transfer Admission Requirements:** *Items required:* college transcript, essay. Minimum college GPA of 2.2 required. Lowest grade transferable C-. **General Admission Information:** Application fee $25. Priority application deadline February 15. Nonfall registration accepted. Admission may be deferred for a maximum of 1 year. Credit offered for CEEB Advanced Placement tests.

COSTS AND FINANCIAL AID

Tuition $12,750. Room & board $5,240. Required fees $100. Average book expense $600. **Required Forms and Deadlines:** FAFSA. No deadline for regular filing. Priority filing deadline March 15. **Notification of Awards:** Applicants will be notified of awards on a rolling basis beginning on or about March 1. **Types of Aid:** *Need-based scholarships/grants:* Pell, SEOG, state scholarships/grants, private scholarships, the school's own gift aid. *Loans:* FFEL Subsidized Stafford, FFEL Unsubsidized Stafford, FFEL PLUS, Federal Perkins, college/university loans from institutional funds. **Student Employment:** Federal Work-Study Program available. Institutional employment available. Off-campus job opportunities are fair. **Financial Aid Statistics:** 82% freshmen, 86% undergrads receive some form of aid. Average freshman grant $6,000. Average freshman loan $2,625. Average income from on-campus job $1,100. **Financial Aid Phone:** 316-278-4226.

STETSON UNIVERSITY

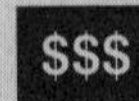

421 N. Woodland Boulevard, Unit 8378, DeLand, FL 32723
Phone: 386-822-7100 **E-mail:** admissions@stetson.edu **CEEB Code:** 5630
Fax: 386-822-7112 **Web:** www.stetson.edu **ACT Code:** 756

This private school was founded in 1883. It has a 170-acre campus.

STUDENTS AND FACULTY

Enrollment: 2,142. **Student Body:** Male 42%, female 58%, out-of-state 23%, international 3% (43 countries represented). **Ethnic Representation:** African American 4%, Asian 2%, Caucasian 85%, Hispanic 5%. **Retention and Graduation:** 77% freshmen return for sophomore year. 50% freshmen graduate within 4 years. 35% grads go on to further study within 1 year. 11% grads pursue business degrees. 7% grads pursue law degrees. 1% grads pursue medical degrees. **Faculty:** Student/faculty ratio 11:1. 196 full-time faculty, 89% hold PhDs. 98% faculty teach undergrads.

ACADEMICS

Degrees: Bachelor's, first professional, master's, post-master's certificate. **Academic Requirements:** General education including some course work in arts/fine arts, English (including composition), foreign languages, history, humanities, mathematics, philosophy, sciences (biological or physical), social science, religious studies. **Classes:** 10-19 students in an average class. 10-19 students in an average lab/discussion section. **Disciplines with Highest Percentage of Degrees Awarded:** Business/marketing 36%, social sciences and history 9%, visual and performing arts 8%, parks and recreation 7%, education 6%. **Special Study Options:** Accelerated program, double major, dual enrollment, honors program, independent study, internships, liberal arts/career combination, student-designed major, study abroad, teacher certification program.

FACILITIES

Housing: Coed, all-female, all-male, fraternities and/or sororities. **Library Holdings:** 377,319 bound volumes. 10,079 periodicals. 1,035,968 microforms. 18,769 audiovisuals. **Special Academic Facilities/Equipment:** Language lab, art gallery, greenhouse with growth chambers, mineral museum, electron microscopes. **Computers:** School-owned computers available for student use.

EXTRACURRICULARS

Activities: Choral groups, concert band, dance, drama/theater, jazz band, literary magazine, music ensembles, musical theater, opera, pep band, radio station, student government, student newspaper, symphony orchestra, yearbook. **Organizations:** 95 registered organizations, 19 honor societies, 10 religious organizations, 7 fraternities (33% men join), 6 sororities (29% women join). **Athletics (Intercollegiate):** *Men:* baseball, basketball, crew, cross-country, golf, soccer, tennis. *Women:* basketball, crew, cross-country, golf, soccer, softball, tennis, volleyball.

ADMISSIONS

Selectivity Rating: 81 (of 100). **Freshman Academic Profile:** Average high school GPA 3.6. 32% in top 10% of high school class, 61% in top 25% of high school class, 90% in top 50% of high school class. 75% from public high schools. Average SAT I Math 557, SAT I Math middle 50% range 500-610. Average SAT I Verbal 566, SAT I Verbal middle 50% range 510-620. Average ACT 24, ACT middle 50% range 21-27. TOEFL required of all international applicants, minimum TOEFL 550. **Basis for Candidate Selection:** *Very important factors considered include:* secondary school record. *Important factors considered include:* character/personal qualities, class rank, essays, extracurricular activities, interview, recommendations, standardized test scores, talent/ability, volunteer work, work experience. *Other factors considered include:* alumni/ae relation, geographical residence, minority status, state residency. **Freshman Admission Requirements:** High school diploma or GED is required. *Academic units required/recommended:* 16 total required; 4 English required, 3 math required, 3 science required, 2 foreign language required, 2 social studies required, 2 elective required. **Transfer Admission Requirements:** *Items required:* high school transcript, college transcript, essay, standardized test scores. Minimum college GPA of 2.0 required. Lowest grade transferable C-. **General Admission Information:** Application fee $40. Priority application deadline January 1. Early decision application deadline November 1. Regular application deadline March 1. Nonfall registration accepted. Admission may be deferred for a maximum of 1 year. Credit and/or placement offered for CEEB Advanced Placement tests.

COSTS AND FINANCIAL AID

Tuition $20,425. Room & board $6,855. Required fees $1,080. Average book expense $800. **Required Forms and Deadlines:** FAFSA and institution's own financial aid form. Financial aid filing deadline February 15. **Notification of Awards:** Applicants will be notified of awards on a rolling basis. **Types of Aid:** *Need-based scholarships/grants:* Pell, SEOG, state scholarships/grants, private scholarships, the school's own gift aid. *Loans:* FFEL Subsidized Stafford, FFEL Unsubsidized Stafford, FFEL PLUS, Federal Perkins, state loans, college/university loans from institutional funds. **Student Employment:** Federal Work-Study Program available. Institutional employment available. Off-campus job opportunities are good. **Financial Aid Statistics:** 59% freshmen, 58% undergrads receive some form of aid. **Financial Aid Phone:** 386-822-7120.

STEVENS INSTITUTE OF TECHNOLOGY

1 Castle Point on Hudson, Hoboken, NJ 07030
Phone: 201-216-5194 **E-mail:** admissions@stevens-tech.edu **CEEB Code:** 2819
Fax: 201-216-8348 **Web:** www.stevens.edu **ACT Code:** 2610

This private school was founded in 1870. It has a 55-acre campus.

STUDENTS AND FACULTY

Enrollment: 1,729. **Student Body:** Male 75%, female 25%, out-of-state 35%, international 7% (68 countries represented). **Ethnic Representation:** African American 5%, Asian 25%, Caucasian 51%, Hispanic 10%. **Retention and Graduation:** 16% grads go on to further study within 1 year. 39% grads pursue medical degrees. **Faculty:** Student/faculty ratio 9:1. 171 full-time faculty, 93% hold PhDs. 100% faculty teach undergrads.

ACADEMICS

Degrees: Bachelor's, doctoral, first professional, master's, post-bachelor's certificate. **Academic Requirements:** General education including some course work in computer literacy, English (including composition), humanities, mathematics, sciences (biological or physical). Core varies by major. **Classes:** 20-29 students in an average class. 10-19 students in an average lab/discussion section. **Majors with Highest Enrollment:** Computer science; computer engineering, general; mechanical engineering. **Disciplines with Highest Percentage of Degrees Awarded:** Engineering/engineering technology 78%, computer and information sciences 13%, biological life sciences 7%, physical sciences 1%. **Special Study Options:** Accelerated program, cooperative (work-study) program, cross registration, distance learning, double major, dual enrollment, honors program, independent study, internships, study abroad.

FACILITIES

Housing: Coed, all-female, all-male, fraternities and/or sororities, Lore-El Center for Women in Engineering and Science. **Special Academic Facilities/Equipment:** Art museum, electron microscope, ocean engineering lab, HDTV research facility, advanced telecommunications institute, environmental lab, design/manufacturing institute, wind tunnel, robotics lab, product management center, polymer processing institute, DeBaun Theater, a multimedia facility, wireless campus network. **Computers:** *Recommended operating system:* Windows NT/2000. School-owned computers available for student use.

EXTRACURRICULARS

Activities: Choral groups, dance, drama/theater, jazz band, literary magazine, music ensembles, musical theater, radio station, student government, student newspaper, television station, yearbook. **Organizations:** 70 registered organizations, 7 honor societies, 9 religious organizations, 9 fraternities (30% men join), 3 sororities (33% women join). **Athletics (Intercollegiate):** *Men:* baseball, basketball, cross-country, fencing, indoor track, lacrosse, soccer, tennis, track & field, volleyball. *Women:* basketball, cross-country, fencing, indoor track, lacrosse, soccer, swimming, tennis, track & field, volleyball.

ADMISSIONS

Selectivity Rating: 85 (of 100). **Freshman Academic Profile:** Average high school GPA 3.8. SAT I Math middle 50% range 610-730. SAT I Verbal middle 50% range 540-660. TOEFL required of all international applicants, minimum TOEFL 550. **Basis for Candidate Selection:** *Very important factors considered include:* interview, secondary school record, standardized test scores. *Important factors considered include:* character/personal qualities, class rank, extracurricular activities, talent/ability. *Other factors considered include:* alumni/ae relation, essays, recommendations, volunteer work, work experience. **Freshman Admission Requirements:** High school diploma is required and GED is not accepted. *Academic units required/recommended:* 4 English required, 4 English recommended, 4 math required, 4 math recommended, 3 science required, 4 science recommended, 3 science lab required, 4 science lab recommended, 2 foreign language recommended, 2 social studies recommended, 2 history recommended, 4 elective recommended. **Freshman Admission Statistics:** 2,049 applied, 50% accepted, 38% of those accepted enrolled. **Transfer Admission Requirements:** *Items required:* college transcript, interview. Minimum high school GPA of 3.0 required. Minimum college GPA of 2.0 required. Lowest grade transferable C. **General Admission Information:** Application fee $45. Priority application deadline November 15. Early decision application deadline November 1. Regular application deadline February 15. Admission may be deferred for a maximum of 1 year. Credit and/or placement offered for CEEB Advanced Placement tests.

COSTS AND FINANCIAL AID

Tuition $24,500. Room & board $8,100. Required fees $250. Average book expense $900. **Required Forms and Deadlines:** FAFSA. No deadline for regular filing. Priority filing deadline February 15. **Notification of Awards:** Applicants will be notified of awards on a rolling basis beginning on or about March 30. **Types of Aid:** *Need-based scholarships/grants:* Pell, SEOG, state scholarships/grants, private scholarships, the school's own gift aid. *Loans:* Direct Subsidized Stafford, Direct Unsubsidized Stafford, Direct PLUS, Federal Perkins, state loans, Signature Loans, TERI Loans. **Student Employment:** Federal Work-Study Program available. Institutional employment available. Off-campus job opportunities are excellent. **Financial Aid Statistics:** 74% freshmen, 70% undergrads receive some form of aid. Average freshman grant $19,140. Average freshman loan $2,500. Average income from on-campus job $1,300. **Financial Aid Phone:** 201-216-5194.

See page 1218.

STILLMAN COLLEGE

3600 Stillman Boulevard, Tuscalusa, AL 35403
Phone: 800-841-5722 **CEEB Code:** 1739
Fax: 205-366-8996 **Web:** www.stillman.edu

This private school, which is affiliated with the Presbyterian Church, was founded in 1876.

STUDENTS AND FACULTY

Enrollment: 913. **Student Body:** Out-of-state 30%.

FACILITIES

Housing: Coed.

EXTRACURRICULARS

Activities: Student government, student newspaper, yearbook. **Organizations:** 17 registered organizations, 5 honor societies, 2 religious organizations. **Athletics (Intercollegiate):** *Women:* basketball, cross-country, tennis.

ADMISSIONS

Selectivity Rating: 63 (of 100). **Freshman Academic Profile:** TOEFL required of all international applicants, minimum TOEFL 500. **Freshman Admission Requirements: General Admission Information:** Regular application deadline August 1.

COSTS AND FINANCIAL AID

Room & board $3,100. Required fees $60. Average book expense $250. **Types of Aid:** *Need-based scholarships/grants:* Pell, SEOG, state scholarships/grants, private scholarships, the school's own gift aid. *Loans:* FFEL Subsidized Stafford, FFEL Unsubsidized Stafford, FFEL PLUS, Federal Perkins, college/university loans from institutional funds. **Student Employment:** Federal Work-Study Program available. **Financial Aid Statistics:** Average freshman grant $3,000. Average income from on-campus job $608.

STOCKTON COLLEGE OF NEW JERSEY

Jim Leeds Road, PO Box 195, Pomona, NJ 08240
Phone: 609-652-4261 **E-mail:** admissions@stockton.edu **CEEB Code:** 2889
Fax: 609-748-5541 **Web:** www.stockton.edu

This public school was founded in 1969. It has a 1,600-acre campus.

STUDENTS AND FACULTY

Enrollment: 6,138. **Student Body:** Male 42%, female 58%, out-of-state 2%, international 1% (21 countries represented). **Ethnic Representation:** African American 8%, Asian 5%, Caucasian 82%, Hispanic 5%. **Retention and Graduation:** 83% freshmen return for sophomore year. 33% freshmen graduate within 4 years. 39% grads go on to further study within 1 year. 10% grads pursue business degrees. 4% grads pursue law degrees. 2% grads pursue medical degrees. **Faculty:** Student/faculty ratio 19:1. 218 full-time faculty, 94% hold PhDs. 97% faculty teach undergrads.

ACADEMICS

Degrees: Bachelor's, master's. **Academic Requirements:** General education including some course work in English (including composition), history, humanities, mathematics, sciences (biological or physical), social science, writing. **Classes:** 20-29 students in an average class. Under 10 students in an average lab/discussion section. **Majors with Highest Enrollment:** Business administration/management; biology/biological sciences, general; psychology, general. **Disciplines with Highest Percentage of Degrees Awarded:** Business/marketing 17%, social sciences and history 16%, biological life sciences 13%, psychology 11%, computer and information sciences 7%. **Special Study Options:** Accelerated program, cross registration, distance learning, double major, dual enrollment, honors program, independent study, internships, liberal arts/career combination, student-designed major, study abroad, teacher certification program, Service learning.

FACILITIES

Housing: All-female, all-male, apartments for single students, wellness (substance free) housing, academic housing. **Library Holdings:** 246,834 bound volumes. 1,360 periodicals. 354,795 microforms. 14,227 audiovisuals. **Special Academic Facilities/Equipment:** Observatory, Nacote Creek Field Station, Holocaust resource center. **Computers:** School-owned computers available for student use.

EXTRACURRICULARS

Activities: Choral groups, concert band, dance, drama/theater, literary magazine, music ensembles, musical theater, pep band, radio station, student government, student newspaper, television station, yearbook. **Organizations:** 80 registered organizations, 5 honor societies, 4 religious organizations, 9 fraternities (5% men join), 9 sororities (5% women join). **Athletics (Intercollegiate):** *Men:* baseball, basketball, cheerleading, cross-country, indoor track, lacrosse, soccer, track & field. *Women:* basketball, cheerleading, crew, cross-country, field hockey, indoor track, soccer, softball, tennis, track & field, volleyball.

ADMISSIONS

Selectivity Rating: 86 (of 100). **Freshman Academic Profile:** Average high school GPA 3.2. 15% in top 10% of high school class, 56% in top 25% of high school class, 95% in top 50% of high school class. 74% from public high schools. Average SAT I Math 553, SAT I Math middle 50% range 480-590. Average SAT I Verbal 543, SAT I Verbal middle 50% range 490-560. Average ACT 25, ACT middle 50% range 19-23. TOEFL required of all international applicants, minimum TOEFL 550. **Basis for Candidate Selection:** *Very important factors considered include:* class rank, secondary school record, standardized test scores. *Important factors considered include:* essays, extracurricular activities. *Other factors considered include:* alumni/ae relation, character/personal qualities, recommendations, talent/ability, volunteer work, work experience. **Freshman Admission Requirements:** High school diploma or GED is required. *Academic units required/recommended:* 16 total required; 4 English required, 3 math required, 2 science required, 2 science lab required, 2 social studies required, 5 elective required. **Freshman Admission Statistics:** 3,642 applied, 40% accepted, 55% of those accepted enrolled. **Transfer Admission Requirements:** *Items required:* college transcript. Minimum college GPA of 2.5 required. Lowest grade transferable C. **General Admission Information:** Application fee $35. Priority application deadline February 1. Regular application deadline May 1. Nonfall registration accepted. Credit and/or placement offered for CEEB Advanced Placement tests.

COSTS AND FINANCIAL AID

In-state tuition $4,352. Out-of-state tuition $7,040. Room & board $6,290. Required fees $1,248. Average book expense $825. **Required Forms and Deadlines:** FAFSA. Priority filing deadline March 1. **Notification of Awards:** Applicants will be notified of awards on a rolling basis beginning on or about April 1. **Types of Aid:** *Need-based scholarships/grants:* Pell, SEOG, state scholarships/grants. *Loans:* FFEL Subsidized Stafford, FFEL Unsubsidized Stafford, FFEL PLUS, Federal Perkins, state loans. **Student Employment:** Federal Work-Study Program available. Institutional employment available. Off-campus job opportunities are excellent. **Financial Aid Statistics:** 54% freshmen, 52% undergrads receive some form of aid. Average freshman grant $4,847. Average freshman loan $5,645. Average income from on-campus job $1,682. **Financial Aid Phone:** 609-652-4201.

See page 1220.

STONEHILL COLLEGE

320 Washington Street, Easton, MA 02357-5610
Phone: 508-565-1373 **E-mail:** admissions@stonehill.edu **CEEB Code:** 3770
Fax: 508-565-1545 **Web:** www.stonehill.edu **ACT Code:** 1918

This private school, which is affiliated with the Roman Catholic Church, was founded in 1948. It has a 375-acre campus.

STUDENTS AND FACULTY

Enrollment: 2,602. **Student Body:** Male 40%, female 60%, out-of-state 39%, international 1% (15 countries represented). **Ethnic Representation:** African American 2%, Asian 2%, Caucasian 92%, Hispanic 3%. **Retention and Graduation:** 91% freshmen return for sophomore year. 76% freshmen graduate within 4 years. 13% grads go on to further study within 1 year. 4% grads pursue business degrees. 2% grads pursue law degrees. 1% grads pursue medical degrees. **Faculty:** Student/faculty ratio 15:1. 126 full-time faculty, 82% hold PhDs. 100% faculty teach undergrads.

ACADEMICS

Degrees: Bachelor's, certificate, master's. **Academic Requirements:** General education including some course work in English (including composition), foreign languages, history, mathematics, philosophy, sciences (biological or physical), social science, religious studies, learning communities (2 courses with an integrative seminar), senior year capstone course (connects major to general education). **Classes:** 20-29 students in an average class. 20-29 students in an average lab/discussion section. **Majors with Highest Enrollment:** Elementary education and teaching; psychology, general; communications studies/speech communication and rhetoric. **Disciplines with Highest Percentage of Degrees Awarded:** Business/marketing 24%, social sciences and history 14%, education 12%, psychology 11%, communications/communication technologies 8%. **Special Study Options:** Cross registration, double major, dual enrollment, honors program, independent study, internships, liberal arts/career combination, student-designed major, study abroad, teacher certification program, Stonehill Undergraduate Research Experience (SURE) Program.

FACILITIES

Housing: Coed, all-female, housing for disabled students, substance-free/ wellness housing. Special-interest housing proposals considered for groups. **Library Holdings:** 194,587 bound volumes. 1,612 periodicals. 346,043 microforms. 4,588 audiovisuals. **Special Academic Facilities/Equipment:** Institute for Law and Society, observatory, Stonehill Industrial History Center. **Computers:** *Recommended operating system:* WindowsME,Windows2000 Home. School-owned computers available for student use.

EXTRACURRICULARS

Activities: Choral groups, dance, drama/theater, literary magazine, music ensembles, musical theater, pep band, radio station, student government, student newspaper, yearbook. **Organizations:** 54 registered organizations, 13 honor societies, 9 religious organizations. **Athletics (Intercollegiate):** *Men:* baseball, basketball, cross-country, football, ice hockey, indoor track, soccer, tennis, track & field. *Women:* basketball, cross-country, equestrian, field hockey, indoor track, lacrosse, soccer, softball, tennis, track & field, volleyball.

ADMISSIONS

Selectivity Rating: 79 (of 100). **Freshman Academic Profile:** Average high school GPA 3.5. 51% in top 10% of high school class, 92% in top 25% of high school class, 100% in top 50% of high school class. 74% from public high schools. Average SAT I Math 600, SAT I Math middle 50% range 560-640. Average SAT I Verbal 590, SAT I Verbal middle 50% range 540-630. Average ACT 25, ACT middle 50% range 22-27. TOEFL required of all international applicants, minimum TOEFL 550. **Basis for Candidate Selection:** *Very important factors considered include:* class rank, secondary school record, standardized test scores. *Important factors considered include:* character/personal qualities, essays, extracurricular activities, recommendations, talent/ability. *Other factors considered include:* alumni/ae relation, geographical residence, minority status, volunteer work, work experience. **Freshman Admission Requirements:** High school diploma or GED is required. *Academic units required/recommended:* 16 total required; 21 total recommended; 4 English required, 4 English recommended, 3 math required, 4 math recommended, 1 science required, 3 science recommended, 1 science lab required, 2 science lab recommended, 2 foreign language required, 3 foreign language recommended, 3 history required, 4 history recommended, 3 elective required, 3 elective recommended. **Freshman Admission Statistics:** 5,331 applied, 42% accepted, 25% of those accepted enrolled. **Transfer Admission Requirements:** *Items required:* high school transcript, college transcript, essay. Minimum college GPA of 2.0 required. Lowest grade transferable C. **General Admission Information:** Application fee $50. Early decision application deadline November 1. Regular application deadline January 15. Nonfall registration accepted. Admission may be deferred for a maximum of 1 year. Credit and/or placement offered for CEEB Advanced Placement tests.

COSTS AND FINANCIAL AID

Tuition $19,094. Room & board $9,172. Required fees $814. Average book expense $740. **Required Forms and Deadlines:** FAFSA, CSS/Financial Aid PROFILE, noncustodial (divorced/separated) parent's statement, business/farm supplement and Verification Form (provided by Institution). Financial aid filing deadline February 1. Priority filing deadline February 1. **Notification of Awards:** Applicants will be notified of awards on or about April 1. **Types of Aid:** *Need-based scholarships/grants:* Pell, SEOG, state scholarships/grants, private scholarships, the school's own gift aid. *Loans:* Direct Subsidized Stafford, Direct Unsubsidized Stafford, Direct PLUS, Federal Perkins, state loans. **Student Employment:** Federal Work-Study Program available. Institutional employment available. Off-campus job opportunities are good. **Financial Aid Statistics:** 70% freshmen, 66% undergrads receive some form of aid. Average freshman grant $11,620. Average freshman loan $4,259. Average income from on-campus job $750. **Financial Aid Phone:** 508-565-1088.

STONY BROOK UNIVERSITY (STATE UNIVERSITY OF NEW YORK)

Office of Admissions, Stony Brook, NY 11794-1901
Phone: 631-632-6868 **E-mail:** ugadmissions@notes.cc.sunysb.edu **CEEB Code:** 2548
Fax: 631-632-9898 **Web:** www.stonybrook.edu **ACT Code:** 2952

This public school was founded in 1957. It has a 1,100-acre campus.

STUDENTS AND FACULTY

Enrollment: 14,224. **Student Body:** Male 52%, female 48%, out-of-state 3%, international 4%. **Ethnic Representation:** African American 10%, Asian 25%, Caucasian 37%, Hispanic 8%. **Retention and Graduation:** 85% freshmen return for sophomore year. 35% freshmen graduate within 4 years. **Faculty:** Student/faculty ratio 18:1. 871 full-time faculty, 94% hold PhDs.

ACADEMICS

Degrees: Bachelor's, doctoral, first professional, first professional certificate, master's, post-bachelor's certificate, post-master's certificate. **Academic Requirements:** General education including some course work in arts/fine arts, English (including composition), foreign languages, history, humanities, mathematics, philosophy, sciences (biological or physical), social science. **Classes:** 10-19 students in an average class. 20-29 students in an average lab/ discussion section. **Majors with Highest Enrollment:** Psychology, general; computer science; business administration/management. **Disciplines with Highest Percentage of Degrees Awarded:** Social sciences and history 22%, health professions and related sciences 16%, psychology 11%, biological life sciences 10%, computer and information sciences 9%. **Special Study Options:** Cross registration, distance learning, double major, English as a second language, student exchange program (domestic), honors program, independent study, internships, student-designed major, study abroad, teacher certification program, Albany Semester, undergrads may take grad-level courses, BS/MS programs, BE/MS, BS/MA, Living Learning Centers in residence halls, Honors College, undergraduate research and creative activities program where undergraduates work with faculty on research projects, university learning communities, (WISE) Women in Science & Engineering.

FACILITIES

Housing: Coed, apartments for married students, apartments for single students, housing for disabled students, single-sex floors, living learning centers. **Library Holdings:** 2,136,801 bound volumes. 10,319 periodicals. 3,810,919 microforms. 54,826 audiovisuals. **Special Academic Facilities/Equipment:** Fine arts center, natural sciences museum, federated learning center, curriculum development center, economic research bureau, instructional resource center, marine sciences research center, Van de Graaff accelerator. **Computers:** School-owned computers available for student use.

EXTRACURRICULARS

Activities: Choral groups, concert band, dance, drama/theater, jazz band, literary magazine, music ensembles, musical theater, opera, pep band, radio station, student government, student newspaper, student-run film society, symphony orchestra, yearbook. **Organizations:** 214 registered organizations, 11 honor societies, 17 religious organizations, 16 fraternities, 15 sororities. **Athletics (Intercollegiate):** *Men:* baseball, basketball, cross-country, diving, football, indoor track, lacrosse, soccer, swimming, tennis, track & field. *Women:* basketball, cross-country, diving, indoor track, lacrosse, soccer, softball, swimming, tennis, track & field, volleyball.

ADMISSIONS

Selectivity Rating: 80 (of 100). **Freshman Academic Profile:** Average high school GPA 3.5. 26% in top 10% of high school class, 63% in top 25% of high school class, 93% in top 50% of high school class. 90% from public high schools. Average SAT I Math 599, SAT I Math middle 50% range 550-650. Average SAT I Verbal 545, SAT I Verbal middle 50% range 500-590. TOEFL required of all international applicants, minimum TOEFL 550. **Basis for Candidate Selection:** *Very important factors considered include:* secondary school record, standardized test scores. *Important factors considered include:* character/ personal qualities, interview, recommendations, talent/ability. *Other factors considered include:* alumni/ae relation, class rank, essays, extracurricular activities, volunteer work, work experience. **Freshman Admission Requirements:** High school diploma or GED is required. *Academic units required/ recommended:* 14 total required; 19 total recommended; 4 English required, 4 English recommended, 3 math required, 4 math recommended, 3 science required, 4 science recommended, 2 foreign language required, 3 foreign language recommended, 4 social studies required, 4 social studies recommended. **Freshman Admission Statistics:** 16,849 applied, 54% accepted, 27% of those accepted enrolled. **Transfer Admission Requirements:** *Items required:* college transcript, statement of good standing from prior school.

Minimum college GPA of 2.5 required. Lowest grade transferable C. **General Admission Information:** Application fee $40. Priority application deadline November 15. Nonfall registration accepted. Admission may be deferred for a maximum of 1 year. Credit and/or placement offered for CEEB Advanced Placement tests.

COSTS AND FINANCIAL AID

In-state tuition $3,400. Out-of-state tuition $8,300. Room & board $6,974. Required fees $958. Average book expense $900. **Required Forms and Deadlines:** FAFSA. No deadline for regular filing. **Notification of Awards:** Applicants will be notified of awards on a rolling basis beginning on or about March 1. **Types of Aid:** *Need-based scholarships/grants:* Pell, SEOG, state scholarships/grants. *Loans:* FFEL Subsidized Stafford, FFEL Unsubsidized Stafford, FFEL PLUS, Federal Perkins. **Student Employment:** Federal Work-Study Program available. Institutional employment available. Off-campus job opportunities are excellent. **Financial Aid Statistics:** 50% freshmen, 60% undergrads receive some form of aid. Average freshman grant $4,043. Average freshman loan $2,153. Average income from on-campus job $1,518. **Financial Aid Phone:** 631-632-6840.

See page 1222.

STRAYER UNIVERSITY

1025 15th Street, NW, Washington, DC 20005
Phone: 202-408-2400 **E-mail:** washington@strayer.edu
Fax: 202-289-1831 **Web:** www.strayer.edu **ACT Code:** 694

This proprietary school was founded in 1892.

STUDENTS AND FACULTY

Enrollment: 13,397. **Student Body:** Male 42%, female 58%, out-of-state 5%, international 4% (110 countries represented). **Ethnic Representation:** African American 45%, Asian 5%, Caucasian 35%, Hispanic 4%. **Faculty:** Student/faculty ratio 20:1. 137 full-time faculty, 33% hold PhDs. 100% faculty teach undergrads.

ACADEMICS

Degrees: Associate's, bachelor's, diploma, master's, post-bachelor's certificate, transfer. **Academic Requirements:** General education including some course work in arts/fine arts, computer literacy, English (including composition), humanities, mathematics, social science. **Disciplines with Highest Percentage of Degrees Awarded:** Computer and information sciences 61%, business/marketing 39%. **Special Study Options:** Accelerated program, cooperative (work-study) program, distance learning, double major, internships, weekend college.

FACILITIES

Library Holdings: 34,000 bound volumes. 1,600 periodicals. 400 audiovisuals. **Computers:** *Recommended operating system:* Windows 95. School-owned computers available for student use.

EXTRACURRICULARS

Activities: Student newspaper. **Organizations:** 9 registered organizations, 2 honor societies.

ADMISSIONS

Selectivity Rating: 63 (of 100). **Freshman Academic Profile:** TOEFL required of all international applicants, minimum TOEFL 400. **Basis for Candidate Selection:** *Very important factors considered include:* secondary school record, work experience. *Important factors considered include:* alumni/ae relation, interview, recommendations, talent/ability. *Other factors considered include:* character/personal qualities, extracurricular activities, standardized test scores. **Freshman Admission Requirements:** High school diploma or GED is required. *Academic units required/recommended:* 14 total recommended; 3 English recommended, 3 math recommended, 2 foreign language recommended, 1 social studies recommended, 1 history recommended, 4 elective recommended. **Freshman Admission Statistics:** 71% of those accepted enrolled. **Transfer Admission Requirements:** *Items required:* college transcript. Lowest grade transferable C. **General Admission Information:** Application fee $25. Regular application deadline rolling. Nonfall registration accepted. Admission may be deferred for a maximum of 2 years. Credit and/or placement offered for CEEB Advanced Placement tests.

COSTS AND FINANCIAL AID

Required Forms and Deadlines: FAFSA. No deadline for regular filing. **Notification of Awards:** Applicants will be notified of awards on a rolling basis. **Types of Aid:** *Need-based scholarships/grants:* Pell, SEOG, the school's own gift aid. *Loans:* Direct Subsidized Stafford, Direct Unsubsidized Stafford, Direct PLUS, FFEL Subsidized Stafford, FFEL Unsubsidized Stafford, FFEL PLUS, Federal Perkins. **Student Employment:** Federal Work-Study Program available. Institutional employment available. Off-campus job opportunities are excellent. **Financial Aid Phone:** 202-408-2400.

SUFFOLK UNIVERSITY

8 Ashburton Place, Boston, MA 02108
Phone: 617-573-8460 **E-mail:** admission@suffolk.edu **CEEB Code:** 3771
Fax: 617-742-4291 **Web:** www.suffolk.edu **ACT Code:** 1920

This private school was founded in 1906.

STUDENTS AND FACULTY

Enrollment: 3,962. **Student Body:** Male 41%, female 59%, out-of-state 14%, international 12%. **Ethnic Representation:** African American 4%, Asian 7%, Caucasian 68%, Hispanic 5%. **Retention and Graduation:** 74% freshmen return for sophomore year. 33% freshmen graduate within 4 years. 27% grads go on to further study within 1 year. 7% grads pursue business degrees. 5% grads pursue law degrees. 1% grads pursue medical degrees. **Faculty:** Student/faculty ratio 12:1. 320 full-time faculty, 93% hold PhDs. 90% faculty teach undergrads.

ACADEMICS

Degrees: Associate's, bachelor's, certificate, diploma, doctoral, first professional, master's, post-bachelor's certificate. **Academic Requirements:** General education including some course work in computer literacy, English (including composition), foreign languages, humanities, mathematics, philosophy, sciences (biological or physical), social science. **Classes:** 20-29 students in an average class. 10-19 students in an average lab/discussion section. **Majors with Highest Enrollment:** Communications studies/speech communication and rhetoric; sociology; business administration/management. **Disciplines with Highest Percentage of Degrees Awarded:** Business/marketing 38%, law/legal studies 12%, communications/communication technologies 11%, computer and information sciences 8%, psychology 8%. **Special Study Options:** Accelerated program, cooperative (work-study) program, cross registration, distance learning, double major, dual enrollment, English as a second language, student exchange program (domestic), external degree program, honors program, independent study, internships, study abroad.

FACILITIES

Housing: Coed. **Library Holdings:** 300,900 bound volumes. 5,330 periodicals. 262,000 microforms. 319 audiovisuals. **Special Academic Facilities/Equipment:** Marine biology field station in Maine, art gallery, Walsh Theatre. **Computers:** School-owned computers available for student use.

EXTRACURRICULARS

Activities: Choral groups, dance, drama/theater, literary magazine, musical theater, radio station, student government, student newspaper, television station, yearbook. **Organizations:** 45 registered organizations, 24 honor societies, 3 religious organizations, 2 fraternities (1% men join). **Athletics (Intercollegiate):** *Men:* baseball, basketball, cross-country, golf, ice hockey, soccer, tennis. *Women:* basketball, cross-country, tennis, volleyball.

ADMISSIONS

Selectivity Rating: 72 (of 100). **Freshman Academic Profile:** Average high school GPA 2.9. 11% in top 10% of high school class, 32% in top 25% of high school class, 66% in top 50% of high school class. 67% from public high schools. Average SAT I Math 499, SAT I Math middle 50% range 450-550. Average SAT I Verbal 500, SAT I Verbal middle 50% range 440-550. TOEFL required of all international applicants, minimum TOEFL 525. **Basis for Candidate Selection:** *Very important factors considered include:* secondary school record. *Important factors considered include:* class rank, essays, recommendations, standardized test scores. *Other factors considered include:* alumni/ae relation, character/personal qualities, extracurricular activities, interview. **Freshman Admission Requirements:** High school diploma or GED is required. *Academic units required/recommended:* 4 English required, 3 math required, 2 science required, 1 science lab required, 2 foreign language required, 1 history required, 4 elective required. **Freshman Admission Statistics:** 3,466 applied, 84% accepted, 27% of those accepted enrolled. **Transfer Admission Requirements:** *Items required:* high school transcript, college transcript, essay. Minimum college GPA of 2.5 required. Lowest grade transferable C. **General Admission Information:** Application fee $40. Nonfall registration accepted. Admission may be deferred for a maximum of 1 year. Credit and/or placement offered for CEEB Advanced Placement tests.

COSTS AND FINANCIAL AID

Tuition $17,610. Room & board $10,290. Required fees $80. Average book expense $1,000. **Required Forms and Deadlines:** FAFSA and institution's own financial aid form. No deadline for regular filing. Priority filing deadline March 1. **Notification of Awards:** Applicants will be notified of awards on a rolling basis beginning on or about March 1. **Types of Aid:** *Need-based scholarships/grants:* Pell, SEOG, state scholarships/grants, private scholarships, the school's own gift aid. *Loans:* Direct Subsidized Stafford, Direct Unsubsidized Stafford, Direct PLUS, Federal Perkins. **Student Employment:** Federal Work-Study Program available. Institutional employment available. Off-campus job opportunities are excellent. **Financial Aid Statistics:** 64% freshmen, 57% undergrads receive some form of aid. Average freshman grant $7,100. Average freshman loan $5,400. Average income from on-campus job $1,860. **Financial Aid Phone:** 617-573-8470.

SUL ROSS STATE UNIVERSITY

Box C-2, Alpine, TX 79832
Phone: 915-837-8050 **E-mail:** admissions@sulross.edu **CEEB Code:** 6685
Fax: 915-837-8431 **Web:** www.sulross.edu **ACT Code:** 4190

This public school was founded in 1917. It has a 650-acre campus.

STUDENTS AND FACULTY

Enrollment: 1,402. **Student Body:** Male 52%, female 48%, out-of-state 2%, (5 countries represented). **Ethnic Representation:** African American 4%, Asian 1%, Caucasian 44%, Hispanic 48%, Native American 1%. **Retention and Graduation:** 48% freshmen return for sophomore year. 7% freshmen graduate within 4 years. 10% grads go on to further study within 1 year. 1% grads pursue business degrees. 1% grads pursue law degrees. 1% grads pursue medical degrees. **Faculty:** Student/faculty ratio 13:1. 88 full-time faculty, 71% hold PhDs. 99% faculty teach undergrads.

ACADEMICS

Degrees: Associate's, bachelor's, certificate, master's. **Academic Requirements:** General education including some course work in arts/fine arts, English (including composition), history, humanities, mathematics, sciences (biological or physical), social science, political science. **Classes:** 10-19 students in an average class. Under 10 students in an average lab/discussion section. **Majors with Highest Enrollment:** Multi/interdisciplinary studies; health and physical education, general; criminal justice/safety studies. **Disciplines with Highest Percentage of Degrees Awarded:** Education 16%, interdisciplinary studies 15%, business/marketing 10%, agriculture 9%, communications/communication technologies 6%. **Special Study Options:** Distance learning, honors program, internships, teacher certification program.

FACILITIES

Housing: Coed, apartments for married students, apartments for single students. **Library Holdings:** 245,567 bound volumes. 1,350 periodicals. 549,490 microforms. 7,011 audiovisuals. **Special Academic Facilities/Equipment:** Museum, range animal science ranch, planetarium, observatory, scanning electron microscope, automated electron probe microanalyzer, computer-controlled X-ray fluorescence analyzer. **Computers:** *Recommended operating system:* Windows NT/2000. School-owned computers available for student use.

EXTRACURRICULARS

Activities: Choral groups, drama/theater, literary magazine, music ensembles, pep band, radio station, student government, student newspaper, yearbook. **Organizations:** 30 registered organizations, 10 honor societies, 3 religious organizations. **Athletics (Intercollegiate):** *Men:* baseball, basketball, cheerleading, football, rodeo, tennis, track & field. *Women:* basketball, cheerleading, rodeo, softball, tennis, track & field, volleyball.

ADMISSIONS

Selectivity Rating: 66 (of 100). **Freshman Academic Profile:** 5% in top 10% of high school class, 18% in top 25% of high school class, 55% in top 50% of high school class. 95% from public high schools. Average SAT I Math 440. Average SAT I Verbal 440. Average ACT 17, ACT middle 50% range 15-19. TOEFL required of all international applicants, minimum TOEFL 520. **Basis for Candidate Selection:** *Very important factors considered include:* class rank. *Important factors considered include:* minority status, standardized test scores, state residency. *Other factors considered include:* geographical residence, secondary school record. **Freshman Admission Requirements:** High school diploma or GED is required. *Academic units required/recommended:* 25 total recommended; 4 English recommended, 4 math recommended, 4 science recommended, 3 foreign language recommended, 2 social studies recommended, 2 history recommended, 2 elective recommended. **Freshman Admission Statistics:** 1,021 applied, 73% accepted, 43% of those accepted enrolled. **Transfer Admission Requirements:** Minimum college GPA of 1.8 required. Lowest grade transferable D. **General Admission Information:** Nonfall registration accepted. Admission may be deferred for a maximum of 1 year. Neither credit nor placement offered for CEEB Advanced Placement tests.

COSTS AND FINANCIAL AID

In-state tuition $2,040. Out-of-state tuition $8,580. Room & board $3,850. Required fees $992. Average book expense $692. **Required Forms and Deadlines:** FAFSA and institution's own financial aid form. No deadline for regular filing. **Notification of Awards:** Applicants will be notified of awards on a rolling basis beginning on or about April 1. **Types of Aid:** *Need-based scholarships/grants:* Pell, SEOG, state scholarships/grants, the school's own gift aid, Federal Nursing. *Loans:* FFEL Subsidized Stafford, FFEL Unsubsidized Stafford, FFEL PLUS, college/university loans from institutional funds. **Student Employment:** Federal Work-Study Program available. Institutional employment available. Off-campus job opportunities are poor. **Financial Aid Statistics:** 67% freshmen, 70% undergrads receive some form of aid. Average freshman grant $1,800. Average freshman loan $2,625. Average income from on-campus job $2,000. **Financial Aid Phone:** 915-837-8055.

SULLIVAN COUNTY COMMUNITY COLLEGE

112 College Road, Loch Sheldrake, NY 12759
Phone: 845-434-5750 **E-mail:** admissions@sullivan.suny.edu
Fax: 845-434-4806

This public school was founded in 1962. It has a 405-acre campus.

STUDENTS AND FACULTY

Enrollment: 1,552. **Student Body:** Male 39%, female 61%, out-of-state 29%. **Ethnic Representation:** African American 21%, Asian 2%, Caucasian 66%, Hispanic 12%. **Faculty:** Student/faculty ratio 15:1. 40 full-time faculty. 100% faculty teach undergrads.

ACADEMICS

Degrees: Associate's, certificate, terminal, transfer. **Academic Requirements:** General education including some course work in English (including composition), history, humanities, mathematics, sciences (biological or physical), social science. **Special Study Options:** Distance learning, double major, honors program, internships.

FACILITIES

Housing: Approved dorm and apartment-style off-campus housing. **Library Holdings:** 65,699 bound volumes. 400 periodicals. 300 microforms. 4,928 audiovisuals. **Computers:** School-owned computers available for student use.

EXTRACURRICULARS

Activities: Student government, student newspaper. **Organizations:** 1 honor society. **Athletics (Intercollegiate):** *Men:* basketball, golf. *Women:* basketball, softball, volleyball.

ADMISSIONS

Selectivity Rating: 63 (of 100). **Freshman Admission Statistics:** 1,183 applied, 95% accepted, 54% of those accepted enrolled. **Transfer Admission Requirements:** *Items required:* high school transcript, college transcript. Lowest grade transferable C. **General Admission Information:** Nonfall registration accepted. Admission may be deferred for a maximum of 2 years.

COSTS AND FINANCIAL AID

In-state tuition $2,500. Out-of-state tuition $5,000. Required fees $156. Average book expense $700. **Required Forms and Deadlines:** FAFSA, institution's own financial aid form and state aid form. No deadline for regular filing. Priority filing deadline April 15. **Notification of Awards:** Applicants will be notified of awards on a rolling basis beginning on or about May 15. **Types of Aid:** *Need-based scholarships/grants:* Pell, SEOG, state scholarships/grants, the school's own gift aid. *Loans:* FFEL Subsidized Stafford, FFEL Unsubsidized Stafford, FFEL PLUS, Federal Perkins. **Student Employment:** Federal Work-Study Program available. Off-campus job opportunities are fair. **Financial Aid Statistics:** 47% freshmen, 52% undergrads receive some form of aid. Average freshman grant $1,324. Average freshman loan $1,886. **Financial Aid Phone:** 845-434-5750.

SUSQUEHANNA UNIVERSITY

 $$$  

514 University Avenue, Selinsgrove, PA 17870
Phone: 570-372-4260 **E-mail:** suadmiss@susqu.edu **CEEB Code:** 2820
Fax: 570-372-2722 **Web:** www.susqu.edu **ACT Code:** 3720

This private school, which is affiliated with the Lutheran Church, was founded in 1858. It has a 220-acre campus.

STUDENTS AND FACULTY

Enrollment: 1,995. **Student Body:** Male 42%, female 58%, out-of-state 38%, international 1%. **Ethnic Representation:** African American 2%, Asian 2%, Caucasian 93%, Hispanic 2%. **Retention and Graduation:** 88% freshmen return for sophomore year. 72% freshmen graduate within 4 years. 24% grads go on to further study within 1 year. 1% grads pursue business degrees. 2% grads pursue law degrees. 2% grads pursue medical degrees. **Faculty:** Student/faculty ratio 14:1. 112 full-time faculty, 88% hold PhDs. 100% faculty teach undergrads.

ACADEMICS

Degrees: Associate's, bachelor's. **Academic Requirements:** General education including some course work in arts/fine arts, computer literacy, English (including composition), foreign languages, history, humanities, mathematics, sciences (biological or physical), social science, philosophy or religion. **Classes:** 10-19 students in an average class. 10-19 students in an average lab/discussion section. **Majors with Highest Enrollment:** Business administration/management; communications studies/speech communication and rhetoric; biology/biological sciences, general. **Disciplines with Highest Percentage of Degrees Awarded:** Business/marketing 27%, communications/communication technologies 12%, education 9%, computer and information sciences 9%, social sciences and history 9%. **Special Study Options:** Accelerated program, cross registration, double major, dual enrollment, student exchange program (domestic), honors program, independent study, internships, student-designed major, study abroad, teacher certification program.

FACILITIES

Housing: Coed, all-female, all-male, apartments for single students, housing for international students, fraternities and/or sororities, scholars' house. Student volunteers in Susquehanna's nationally recognized Project House System have the privilege of living together in University-owned houses, in Shobrt Hall apartment-suites, or in the upper level of Seibert Hall, one of the landmark historic buildings on campus. Seibert Hall is also home to international students and student volunteers in the Student Association for Cultural Awareness, and includes dedicated space for multicultural and international programming. **Library Holdings:** 279,149 bound volumes. 11,078 periodicals. 119,392 microforms. 21,052 audiovisuals. **Special Academic Facilities/Equipment:** Art gallery, electronic music lab, child development center, foreign language broadcast system, teaching theatre, greenhouse, rare book room, ecological field station, electron microscope, reflecting telescope, fluorescent microscopes, video conference center, and the new Business and Communications Building featuring three multimedia classrooms, three computer laboratories/classrooms, conference and seminar rooms, student team study rooms and alcoves, two video studios, seminar/observation rooms and a room for faculty instructional development. The building facilitates use of laptop computers by offering informational technology dataports for every seat in the classrooms, team study areas, and student lounges and faculty offices. **Computers:** *Recommended operating system:* Windows 2000Pro or Windows XPro. School-owned computers available for student use.

EXTRACURRICULARS

Activities: Choral groups, concert band, dance, drama/theater, jazz band, literary magazine, music ensembles, musical theater, opera, pep band, radio station, student government, student newspaper, student-run film society, symphony orchestra, yearbook. **Organizations:** 100 registered organizations, 22 honor societies, 11 religious organizations, 4 fraternities (25% men join), 4 sororities (28% women join). **Athletics (Intercollegiate):** *Men:* baseball, basketball, crew, cross-country, football, golf, indoor track, lacrosse, soccer, swimming, tennis, track & field. *Women:* basketball, crew, cross-country, field hockey, golf, indoor track, lacrosse, soccer, softball, swimming, tennis, track & field, volleyball.

ADMISSIONS

Selectivity Rating: 79 (of 100). **Freshman Academic Profile:** 38% in top 10% of high school class, 72% in top 25% of high school class, 97% in top 50% of high school class. 86% from public high schools. SAT I Math middle 50% range 540-630. SAT I Verbal middle 50% range 530-620. TOEFL required of all international applicants, minimum TOEFL 550. **Basis for Candidate Selection:** *Very important factors considered include:* class rank, secondary school record, standardized test scores. *Important factors considered include:* character/personal qualities, essays, interview, minority status, recommendations, talent/ability. *Other factors considered include:* alumni/ae relation, extracurricular activities, geographical residence, religious affiliation/commitment, state residency, volunteer work, work experience. **Freshman Admission Requirements:** High school diploma or GED is required. *Academic units required/recommended:* 18 total required; 22 total recommended; 4 English required, 4 English recommended, 3 math required, 4 math recommended, 3 science required, 4 science recommended, 2 science lab required, 3 science lab recommended, 2 foreign language required, 3 foreign language recommended, 1 social studies required, 2 social studies recommended, 1 history required, 1 history recommended. **Freshman Admission Statistics:** 2,411 applied, 63% accepted, 33% of those accepted enrolled. **Transfer Admission Requirements:** *Items required:* high school transcript, college transcript, essay, standardized test scores, statement of good standing from prior school. Minimum college GPA of 2.5 required. Lowest grade transferable C-. **General Admission Information:** Application fee $35. Early decision application deadline January 1. Regular application deadline March 1. Nonfall registration accepted. Admission may be deferred for a maximum of 1 year. Credit and/or placement offered for CEEB Advanced Placement tests.

COSTS AND FINANCIAL AID

Tuition $21,930. Room & board $6,260. Required fees $320. Average book expense $600. **Required Forms and Deadlines:** FAFSA, CSS/Financial Aid PROFILE, state aid form and business/farm supplement. Financial aid filing deadline May 1. Priority filing deadline March 1. **Notification of Awards:** Applicants will be notified of awards on a rolling basis beginning on or about January 15. **Types of Aid:** *Need-based scholarships/grants:* Pell, SEOG, state scholarships/grants, private scholarships, the school's own gift aid. *Loans:* FFEL Subsidized Stafford, FFEL Unsubsidized Stafford, FFEL PLUS, Federal Perkins, college/university loans from institutional funds. **Student Employment:** Federal Work-Study Program available. Institutional employment available. Off-campus job opportunities are good. **Financial Aid Statistics:** 65% freshmen, 68% undergrads receive some form of aid. Average freshman grant $10,515. Average freshman loan $3,300. Average income from on-campus job $835. **Financial Aid Phone:** 570-372-4450.

SWARTHMORE COLLEGE

 $$$  

500 College Avenue, Swarthmore, PA 19081
Phone: 610-328-8300 **E-mail:** admissions@swarthmore.edu **CEEB Code:** 2821
Fax: 610-328-8580 **Web:** www.swarthmore.edu **ACT Code:** 3722

This private school was founded in 1864. It has a 357-acre campus.

STUDENTS AND FACULTY

Enrollment: 1,479. **Student Body:** Out-of-state 83%, international 6%. **Ethnic Representation:** African American 7%, Asian 17%, Caucasian 58%, Hispanic 9%, Native American 1%. **Retention and Graduation:** 96% freshmen return for sophomore year. 86% freshmen graduate within 4 years. 23% grads go on to further study within 1 year. 2% grads pursue law degrees. 3% grads pursue medical degrees. **Faculty:** Student/faculty ratio 8:1. 167 full-time faculty, 98% hold PhDs. 100% faculty teach undergrads.

ACADEMICS

Degrees: Bachelor's. **Academic Requirements:** General education including some course work in foreign languages, humanities, sciences (biological or physical), social science. **Classes:** 10-19 students in an average class. 10-19 students in an average lab/discussion section. **Majors with Highest Enrollment:** Biology/biological sciences, general; economics, general; political science and government, general. **Disciplines with Highest Percentage of Degrees Awarded:** Social sciences and history 33%, biological life sciences 13%, foreign languages and literature 8%, English 8%, philosophy/religion/theology 7%. **Special Study Options:** Cross registration, double major, dual enrollment, student exchange program (domestic), honors program, independent study, internships, student-designed major, study abroad, teacher certification program.

FACILITIES

Housing: Coed, all-female, all-male, overflow housing available in a nearby condominium. **Library Holdings:** 567,875 bound volumes. 4,949 periodicals. 72,308 microforms. 19,751 audiovisuals. **Special Academic Facilities/Equipment:** 330-acre arboretum; observatory; performing arts center with art gallery; solar energy laboratory; Friends Historical Library; Peace Collection in library; a stadium complex including lights, a 400-meter dual durometer track, and a synthetic grass field for soccer, lacrosse, and field hockey; a state-of-the-art fitness center and three indoor tennis courts on a Rebound Ace surface; new $77 million environmentally friendly science center, specially designed for interdisciplinary and student-faculty collaboration. **Computers:** School-owned computers available for student use.

EXTRACURRICULARS

Activities: Choral groups, dance, drama/theater, jazz band, literary magazine, music ensembles, musical theater, radio station, student government, student newspaper, student-run film society, symphony orchestra, yearbook. **Organizations:** 100 registered organizations, 3 honor societies, 7 religious organizations, 2 fraternities (6% men join). **Athletics (Intercollegiate):** *Men:* baseball, basketball, cross-country, golf, indoor track, lacrosse, soccer, swimming, tennis, track & field. *Women:* basketball, cross-country, field hockey, indoor track, lacrosse, soccer, softball, swimming, tennis, track & field, volleyball.

ADMISSIONS

Selectivity Rating: 98 (of 100). **Freshman Academic Profile:** 90% in top 10% of high school class, 99% in top 25% of high school class, 100% in top 50% of high school class. 55% from public high schools. Average SAT I Math 715, SAT I Math middle 50% range 680-760. Average SAT I Verbal 718, SAT I Verbal middle 50% range 670-770. **Basis for Candidate Selection:** *Very important factors considered include:* character/personal qualities, class rank, essays, recommendations, secondary school record, standardized test scores. *Important factors considered include:* extracurricular activities. *Other factors considered include:* alumni/ae relation, geographical residence, interview, minority status, talent/ability, volunteer work, work experience. **Freshman Admission Requirements:** High school diploma or equivalent is not required. **Freshman Admission Statistics:** 3,886 applied, 24% accepted, 40% of those accepted enrolled. **Transfer Admission Requirements:** *Items required:* high school transcript, college transcript, essay, standardized test scores, statement of good standing from prior school. Lowest grade transferable C. **General Admission Information:** Application fee $60. Early decision application deadline November 15. Regular application deadline January 1. Admission may be deferred for a maximum of 1 year. Credit and/or placement offered for CEEB Advanced Placement tests.

COSTS AND FINANCIAL AID

Tuition $27,272. Room & board $8,530. Required fees $290. Average book expense $944. **Required Forms and Deadlines:** FAFSA, institution's own financial aid form, CSS/Financial Aid PROFILE, state aid form, noncustodial (divorced/separated) parent's statement, business/farm supplement, Federal Tax Return, W-2 Statements and Year-end paycheck stub. Financial aid filing deadline February 15. Priority filing deadline February 15. **Notification of Awards:** Applicants will be notified of awards on or about April 1. **Types of Aid:** *Need-based scholarships/grants:* Pell, SEOG, state scholarships/grants, private scholarships, the school's own gift aid. *Loans:* FFEL Subsidized Stafford, FFEL Unsubsidized Stafford, FFEL PLUS, Federal Perkins, state loans, college/university loans from institutional funds. **Student Employment:** Federal Work-Study Program available. Institutional employment available. Off-campus job opportunities are fair. **Financial Aid Statistics:** 48% freshmen, 49% undergrads receive some form of aid. Average freshman grant $21,656. Average freshman loan $1,989. Average income from on-campus job $1,450. **Financial Aid Phone:** 610-328-8358.

SWEET BRIAR COLLEGE

PO Box B, Sweet Briar, VA 24595
Phone: 434-381-6142 **E-mail:** admissions@sbc.edu **CEEB Code:** 5634
Fax: 434-381-6152 **Web:** www.sbc.edu **ACT Code:** 4406

This private school was founded in 1901. It has a 3,300-acre campus.

STUDENTS AND FACULTY

Enrollment: 688. **Student Body:** Male 3%, female 97%, out-of-state 57%, international 2% (15 countries represented). **Ethnic Representation:** African American 4%, Asian 2%, Caucasian 90%, Hispanic 3%, Native American 1%. **Retention and Graduation:** 82% freshmen return for sophomore year. 61% freshmen graduate within 4 years. 25% grads go on to further study within 1 year. 5% grads pursue law degrees. 3% grads pursue medical degrees. **Faculty:** Student/faculty ratio 7:1. 70 full-time faculty, 94% hold PhDs. 100% faculty teach undergrads.

ACADEMICS

Degrees: Bachelor's. **Academic Requirements:** General education including some course work in arts/fine arts, English (including composition), foreign languages, humanities, sciences (biological or physical), social science, physical education and nonwestern studies. **Classes:** Under 10 students in an average class. **Majors with Highest Enrollment:** English language and literature, general; liberal arts and sciences/liberal studies; biology/biological sciences, general. **Disciplines with Highest Percentage of Degrees Awarded:** Social sciences and history 30%, visual and performing arts 17%, biological life sciences 13%, English 13%, foreign languages and literature 7%. **Special Study Options:** Accelerated program, cross registration, double major, dual enrollment, student exchange program (domestic), honors program, independent study, internships, liberal arts/career combination, student-designed major, study abroad, teacher certification program.

FACILITIES

Housing: All-female, substance-free dorm area. **Library Holdings:** 177,710 bound volumes. 996 periodicals. 430,311 microforms. 6,816 audiovisuals. **Special Academic Facilities/Equipment:** Art museum and galleries, college and local history museums, kindergarten/nursery school, riding center, electron microscope, DNA sequencing equipment, nuclear resonance spectrometer. **Computers:** School-owned computers available for student use.

EXTRACURRICULARS

Activities: Choral groups, dance, drama/theater, literary magazine, music ensembles, musical theater, radio station, student government, student newspaper, student-run film society, symphony orchestra, television station, yearbook. **Organizations:** 62 registered organizations, 9 honor societies, 3 religious organizations. **Athletics (Intercollegiate):** *Women:* field hockey, lacrosse, soccer, swimming, tennis, volleyball.

ADMISSIONS

Selectivity Rating: 81 (of 100). **Freshman Academic Profile:** Average high school GPA 3.5. 30% in top 10% of high school class, 59% in top 25% of high school class, 90% in top 50% of high school class. 77% from public high schools. Average SAT I Math 550, SAT I Math middle 50% range 490-610. Average SAT I Verbal 590, SAT I Verbal middle 50% range 530-660. Average ACT 26, ACT middle 50% range 22-27. TOEFL required of all international applicants, minimum TOEFL 580. **Basis for Candidate Selection:** *Very important factors considered include:* secondary school record. *Important factors considered include:* class rank, essays, extracurricular activities, recommendations, standardized test scores. *Other factors considered include:* alumni/ae relation, character/personal qualities, interview, minority status, talent/ability, volunteer work, work experience. **Freshman Admission Requirements:** High school diploma or GED is required. *Academic units required/recommended:* 16 total required; 20 total recommended; 4 English required, 4 English recommended, 3 math required, 4 math recommended, 3 science required, 4 science recommended, 2 science lab required, 2 science lab recommended, 3 foreign language required, 4 foreign language recommended, 1 social studies required, 2 social studies recommended, 2 history required, 2 history recommended. **Freshman Admission Statistics:** 420 applied, 86% accepted, 42% of those accepted enrolled. **Transfer Admission Requirements:** *Items required:* high school transcript, college transcript, essay, standardized test scores, statement of good standing from prior school. Minimum college GPA of 2.5 required. Lowest grade transferable C-. **General Admission Information:** Application fee $25. Early decision application deadline December 1. Regular application deadline February 1. Nonfall registration accepted. Admission may be deferred for a maximum of 1 year. Credit and/or placement offered for CEEB Advanced Placement tests.

COSTS AND FINANCIAL AID

Tuition $18,760. Room & board $7,660. Required fees $150. Average book expense $600. **Required Forms and Deadlines:** FAFSA, noncustodial (divorced/separated) parent's statement and business/farm supplement. Priority filing deadline March 1. **Notification of Awards:** Applicants will be notified of awards on a rolling basis beginning on or about March 1. **Types of Aid:** *Need-based scholarships/grants:* Pell, SEOG, state scholarships/grants, private scholarships, the school's own gift aid. *Loans:* Direct Subsidized Stafford, Direct Unsubsidized Stafford, Direct PLUS, Federal Perkins, college/university loans from institutional funds. **Student Employment:** Federal Work-Study Program available. Institutional employment available. Off-campus job opportunities are good. **Financial Aid Statistics:** Average freshman grant $9,494. Average freshman loan $2,876. **Financial Aid Phone:** 434-381-6156.

See page 1224.

SYRACUSE UNIVERSITY

201 Tolley, Administration Building, Syracuse, NY 13244
Phone: 315-443-3611 **E-mail:** orange@syr.edu **CEEB Code:** 2823
Fax: 315-443-4226 **Web:** www.syracuse.edu **ACT Code:** 2968

This private school was founded in 1870. It has a 200-acre campus.

STUDENTS AND FACULTY

Enrollment: 10,936. **Student Body:** Male 44%, female 56%, out-of-state 56%, international 3% (61 countries represented). **Ethnic Representation:** African American 6%, Asian 5%, Caucasian 73%, Hispanic 4%. **Retention and Graduation:** 92% freshmen return for sophomore year. 61% freshmen graduate within 4 years. 14% grads go on to further study within 1 year. 1% grads pursue business degrees. 3% grads pursue law degrees. 2% grads pursue medical degrees. **Faculty:** Student/faculty ratio 12:1. 859 full-time faculty, 86% hold PhDs. 98% faculty teach undergrads.

ACADEMICS

Degrees: Bachelor's, doctoral, first professional, master's, post-master's certificate. **Academic Requirements:** General education including some course work in English (including composition), humanities, mathematics, sciences (biological or physical), social science. Arts and sciences liberal arts core required for most students. **Classes:** 10-19 students in an average class. 20-29 students in an average lab/discussion section. **Majors with Highest Enrollment:** Information science/studies; psychology, general; political science and government, general. **Disciplines with Highest Percentage of Degrees Awarded:** Business/marketing 15%, communications/communication technologies 14%, social sciences and history 13%, visual and performing arts 11%, computer and information sciences 8%. **Special Study Options:** Accelerated program, cooperative (work-study) program, distance learning, double major, dual enrollment, English as a second language, external degree program, honors program, independent study, internships, liberal arts/career combination, student-designed major, study abroad, teacher certification program, undergraduate research, pre-professional programs and minors.

FACILITIES

Housing: Coed, apartments for married students, apartments for single students, fraternities and/or sororities, international living center and language groups (limited), single-sex floors and wings, learning communities and interest/theme housing. **Library Holdings:** 3,115,566 bound volumes. 14,462 periodicals. 4,697,965 microforms. 858,500 audiovisuals. **Special Academic Facilities/Equipment:** Institute for Sensory Research, Center for Public and Community Service, Child Care & Child Development Laboratory School, English Language Institute, Center for Undergraduate Research and Innovative Learning, Audio Archives, Global Collaboratory Multimedia Classroom, Center for Science & Technology, and Community Darkrooms, Lowe Art Gallery, Theatre Complex, Computer Applications Center, CAD Studio, Laser Spectroscopy Labs, Gerontology Center and a Speech/Hearing Clinic. **Computers:** School-owned computers available for student use.

EXTRACURRICULARS

Activities: Choral groups, concert band, dance, drama/theater, jazz band, literary magazine, marching band, music ensembles, musical theater, opera, pep band, radio station, student government, student newspaper, student-run film society, symphony orchestra, television station, yearbook. **Organizations:** 300 registered organizations, 15 honor societies, 26 religious organizations, 22 fraternities (8% men join), 20 sororities (13% women join). **Athletics (Intercollegiate):** *Men:* basketball, crew, cross-country, diving, football, indoor track, lacrosse, soccer, swimming, track & field. *Women:* basketball, crew, cross-country, diving, field hockey, indoor track, lacrosse, soccer, softball, swimming, tennis, track & field, volleyball.

ADMISSIONS

Selectivity Rating: 88 (of 100). **Freshman Academic Profile:** Average high school GPA 3.5. 41% in top 10% of high school class, 79% in top 25% of high school class, 98% in top 50% of high school class. 78% from public high schools. SAT I Math middle 50% range 570-660. SAT I Verbal middle 50% range 550-640. TOEFL required of all international applicants, minimum TOEFL 550. **Basis for Candidate Selection:** *Very important factors considered include:* character/personal qualities, class rank, essays, interview, recommendations, secondary school record, standardized test scores. *Important factors considered include:* talent/ability. *Other factors considered include:* alumni/ae relation, extracurricular activities, minority status, volunteer work, work experience. **Freshman Admission Requirements:** High school diploma or GED is required. *Academic units required/recommended:* 20 total required; 21 total recommended; 4 English required, 4 English recommended, 3 math required, 3 math recommended, 3 science required, 3 science recommended, 3 science lab required, 3 science lab recommended, 2 foreign language required, 3 foreign language recommended, 3 social studies required, 3 social studies recommended, 5 elective required, 5 elective recommended. **Freshman Admission Statistics:** 13,644 applied, 69% accepted, 31% of those accepted enrolled. **Transfer Admission Requirements:** *Items required:* college transcript, essay. Minimum college GPA of 2.5 required. Lowest grade transferable C. **General Admission Information:** Application fee $50. Early decision application deadline November 15. Regular application deadline January 1. Nonfall registration accepted. Admission may be deferred for a maximum of 1 year. Credit and/or placement offered for CEEB Advanced Placement tests.

COSTS AND FINANCIAL AID

Tuition $22,800. Room & board $9,510. Required fees $624. Average book expense $1,104. **Required Forms and Deadlines:** FAFSA and CSS/Financial Aid PROFILE. Financial aid filing deadline February 1. Priority filing deadline February 1. **Notification of Awards:** Applicants will be notified of awards on or about April 1. **Types of Aid:** *Need-based scholarships/grants:* Pell, SEOG, state scholarships/grants, the school's own gift aid. *Loans:* FFEL Subsidized Stafford, FFEL Unsubsidized Stafford, FFEL PLUS, Federal Perkins, Federal Nursing. **Student Employment:** Federal Work-Study Program available. Institutional employment available. Off-campus job opportunities are good. **Financial Aid Statistics:** 55% freshmen, 56% undergrads receive some form of aid. Average freshman grant $13,400. Average freshman loan $3,300. Average income from on-campus job $1,000. **Financial Aid Phone:** 315-443-1513.

TABOR COLLEGE

400 South Jefferson, Hillsboro, KS 67063
Phone: 620-947-3121 **E-mail:** admissions@tabor.edu
Fax: 620-947-6276 **Web:** www.tabor.edu **ACT Code:** 1468

This private school, which is affiliated with the Mennonite Church, was founded in 1908. It has a 30-acre campus.

STUDENTS AND FACULTY

Enrollment: 572. **Student Body:** Male 53%, female 47%, out-of-state 40%, international 1%. **Ethnic Representation:** African American 4%, Asian 8%, Caucasian 85%, Hispanic 2%, Native American 1%. **Retention and Graduation:** 72% freshmen return for sophomore year. 36% freshmen graduate within 4 years. 15% grads go on to further study within 1 year. **Faculty:** 100% faculty teach undergrads.

ACADEMICS

Degrees: Associate's, bachelor's, diploma, master's. **Academic Requirements:** General education including some course work in arts/fine arts, computer literacy, English (including composition), history, humanities, mathematics, philosophy, sciences (biological or physical), social science, Bible, crosscultural experience. **Disciplines with Highest Percentage of Degrees Awarded:** Business/marketing 32%, education 20%, philosophy/religion/theology 17%, communications/communication technologies 6%, biological life sciences 5%. **Special Study Options:** Accelerated program, cross registration, distance learning, double major, student exchange program (domestic), honors program, independent study, internships, student-designed major, study abroad, teacher certification program.

FACILITIES

Housing: All-female, all-male, off-campus housing. **Library Holdings:** 85,000 bound volumes. 450 periodicals. 1,000 microforms. 945 audiovisuals. **Special Academic Facilities/Equipment:** Center for Mennonite Brethren Studies, historic church. **Computers:** School-owned computers available for student use.

EXTRACURRICULARS

Activities: Choral groups, concert band, dance, drama/theater, jazz band, music ensembles, pep band, student government, student newspaper, yearbook. **Organizations:** 27 registered organizations, 9 religious organizations. **Athletics (Intercollegiate):** *Men:* baseball, basketball, cheerleading, cross-country, football, golf, indoor track, soccer, tennis, track & field. *Women:* basketball, cheerleading, cross-country, golf, indoor track, soccer, softball, tennis, track & field, volleyball.

ADMISSIONS

Selectivity Rating: 60 (of 100). **Freshman Academic Profile:** Average high school GPA 3.4. 18% in top 10% of high school class, 40% in top 25% of high school class, 71% in top 50% of high school class. 83% from public high schools.

Average ACT 23. TOEFL required of all international applicants, minimum TOEFL 525. **Basis for Candidate Selection:** *Very important factors considered include:* character/personal qualities, essays, recommendations, secondary school record, standardized test scores. *Important factors considered include:* interview, religious affiliation/commitment. *Other factors considered include:* class rank, volunteer work. **Freshman Admission Requirements:** High school diploma or GED is required. *Academic units required/recommended:* 4 English recommended, 2 math recommended, 2 science recommended, 1 science lab recommended, 2 foreign language recommended, 1 social studies recommended, 2 history recommended. **Transfer Admission Requirements:** *Items required:* college transcript, essay, standardized test scores, statement of good standing from prior school. Minimum college GPA of 2.0 required. Lowest grade transferable C-. **General Admission Information:** Application fee $20. Priority application deadline May 1. Regular application deadline August 1. Nonfall registration accepted. Admission may be deferred for a maximum of 4 years.

COSTS AND FINANCIAL AID

Tuition $13,314. Room & board $4,900. Required fees $320. Average book expense $600. **Required Forms and Deadlines:** FAFSA and institution's own financial aid form. Financial aid filing deadline March 1. Priority filing deadline March 1. **Notification of Awards:** Applicants will be notified of awards on a rolling basis beginning on or about March 1. **Types of Aid:** *Need-based scholarships/grants:* Pell, SEOG, state scholarships/grants, private scholarships, the school's own gift aid. *Loans:* FFEL Subsidized Stafford, FFEL Unsubsidized Stafford, FFEL PLUS, Federal Perkins. **Student Employment:** Federal Work-Study Program available. Institutional employment available. Off-campus job opportunities are good. **Financial Aid Statistics:** 82% freshmen, 76% undergrads receive some form of aid. Average freshman grant $2,990. Average freshman loan $1,500. Average income from on-campus job $1,500. **Financial Aid Phone:** 800-822-6799.

TALLADEGA COLLEGE

627 West Battle Street, Talladega, AL 35160
Phone: 256-761-6219 **E-mail:** be2long@talladega.edu
Fax: 205-362-2268 **Web:** www.talladega.edu

This private school, which is affiliated with the United Church of Christ, was founded in 1867. It has a 350-acre campus.

STUDENTS AND FACULTY

Enrollment: 455. **Student Body:** Male 39%, female 61%, out-of-state 44%, international students represent 9 countries. **Ethnic Representation:** African American 98%, Caucasian 2%. **Retention and Graduation:** 61% freshmen return for sophomore year. 24% freshmen graduate within 4 years. **Faculty:** Student/faculty ratio 9:1. 40 full-time faculty, 100% hold PhDs. 100% faculty teach undergrads.

ACADEMICS

Degrees: Bachelor's. **Academic Requirements:** General education including some course work in computer literacy, English (including composition), humanities, mathematics, sciences (biological or physical), social science. **Disciplines with Highest Percentage of Degrees Awarded:** Biological life sciences 22%, business/marketing 21%, computer and information sciences 10%, English 8%, education 5%. **Special Study Options:** Double major, dual enrollment, internships, study abroad.

FACILITIES

Housing: All-female, all-male, apartments for single students, honors houses. **Library Holdings:** 87,008 bound volumes. 88 periodicals. 100 microforms. 300 audiovisuals. **Special Academic Facilities/Equipment:** Goodnow Art Building, TC Coffee House, The Pub, Savery Library, Swayne Hall, DeForest Chapel. **Computers:** School-owned computers available for student use.

EXTRACURRICULARS

Activities: Choral groups, dance, drama/theater, jazz band, student government, student newspaper, yearbook. **Organizations:** 31 registered organizations, 2 honor societies, 2 religious organizations, 4 fraternities (1% men join), 4 sororities (3% women join). **Athletics (Intercollegiate):** *Men:* baseball, basketball, cross-country, golf. *Women:* basketball, cross-country, golf, volleyball.

ADMISSIONS

Selectivity Rating: 72 (of 100). **Freshman Academic Profile:** Average SAT I Math 354, SAT I Math middle 50% range 300-400. Average SAT I Verbal 380, SAT I Verbal middle 50% range 340-440. Average ACT 17, ACT middle 50% range 15-18. TOEFL required of all international applicants, minimum TOEFL 500. **Basis for Candidate Selection:** *Very important factors considered include:* character/personal qualities, secondary school record, standardized test scores. *Important factors considered include:* class rank, extracurricular activities. *Other factors considered include:* alumni/ae relation, essays, recommendations, talent/ability, volunteer work, work experience. **Freshman Admission Requirements:** High school diploma is required and GED is not accepted. *Academic units required/recommended:* 22 total required; 4 English required, 2 math required, 2 science required, 3 social studies required, 9 elective required. **Freshman Admission Statistics:** 1,098 applied, 22% accepted, 33% of those accepted enrolled. **Transfer Admission Requirements:** *Items required:* high school transcript, college transcript, statement of good standing from prior school. Minimum college GPA of 2.0 required. Lowest grade transferable C. **General Admission Information:** Application fee $25. Admission may be deferred for a maximum of 1 year. Credit and/or placement offered for CEEB Advanced Placement tests.

COSTS AND FINANCIAL AID

Tuition $5,666. Room & board $2,964. Required fees $418. Average book expense $1,000. **Required Forms and Deadlines:** FAFSA. No deadline for regular filing. Priority filing deadline March 15. **Notification of Awards:** Applicants will be notified of awards on a rolling basis beginning on or about April 17. **Types of Aid:** *Need-based scholarships/grants:* Pell, SEOG, state scholarships/grants, United Negro College Fund. *Loans:* Direct Subsidized Stafford, Direct Unsubsidized Stafford, Direct PLUS, FFEL Subsidized Stafford, FFEL Unsubsidized Stafford, FFEL PLUS, Federal Perkins. **Student Employment:** Federal Work-Study Program available. Off-campus job opportunities are fair. **Financial Aid Statistics:** 95% freshmen, 82% undergrads receive some form of aid. Average freshman grant $4,097. Average freshman loan $2,498. Average income from on-campus job $1,000. **Financial Aid Phone:** 256-761-6237.

TARLETON STATE UNIVERSITY

PO Box T-0030, Tarleton Station, Stephenville, TX 76402
Phone: 254-968-9125 **E-mail:** uadm@tarleton.edu **CEEB Code:** 6817
Fax: 254-968-9951 **Web:** www.tarleton.edu **ACT Code:** 4204

This public school was founded in 1899. It has a 120-acre campus.

STUDENTS AND FACULTY

Enrollment: 6,970. **Student Body:** Male 45%, female 55%, out-of-state 4%, international 1%. **Ethnic Representation:** African American 7%, Asian 1%, Caucasian 84%, Hispanic 7%, Native American 1%. **Retention and Graduation:** 62% freshmen return for sophomore year. 14% freshmen graduate within 4 years. **Faculty:** Student/faculty ratio 18:1. 308 full-time faculty, 60% hold PhDs. 92% faculty teach undergrads.

ACADEMICS

Degrees: Bachelor's, master's. **Academic Requirements:** General education including some course work in arts/fine arts, English (including composition), history, humanities, mathematics, sciences (biological or physical), social science, wellness course. **Classes:** 20-29 students in an average class. 10-19 students in an average lab/discussion section. **Majors with Highest Enrollment:** Multi/interdisciplinary studies; health and physical education, general; management science, general. **Disciplines with Highest Percentage of Degrees Awarded:** Business/marketing 27%, agriculture 14%, interdisciplinary studies 10%, protective services/public administration 8%, parks and recreation 8%. **Special Study Options:** Distance learning, double major, dual enrollment, honors program, internships, study abroad, teacher certification program. Undergrads may take grad-level classes.

FACILITIES

Housing: Coed, all-female, all-male, apartments for married students, apartments for single students, fraternities and/or sororities. **Library Holdings:** 293,149 bound volumes. 3,000 periodicals. 898,265 microforms. 7,954 audiovisuals. **Computers:** School-owned computers available for student use.

EXTRACURRICULARS

Activities: Choral groups, concert band, dance, drama/theater, jazz band, literary magazine, marching band, music ensembles, musical theater, pep band, student government, student newspaper, symphony orchestra, yearbook. **Organizations:** 104 registered organizations, 10 honor societies, 3 religious organizations, 5 fraternities (3% men join), 3 sororities (2% women join). **Athletics (Intercollegiate):** *Men:* baseball, basketball, cheerleading, cross-country, football, rodeo, track & field. *Women:* basketball, cheerleading, cross-country, golf, rodeo, softball, tennis, track & field, volleyball.

ADMISSIONS

Selectivity Rating: 66 (of 100). **Freshman Academic Profile:** 8% in top 10% of high school class, 30% in top 25% of high school class, 68% in top 50% of high school class. 99% from public high schools. Average SAT I Math 488, SAT I Math middle 50% range 430-530. Average SAT I Verbal 488, SAT I Verbal middle 50% range 430-520. Average ACT 20, ACT middle 50% range 18-22. TOEFL required of all international applicants, minimum TOEFL 520. **Basis for Candidate Selection:** *Very important factors considered include:* class rank, secondary school record, standardized test scores. **Freshman Admission Requirements:** High school diploma or GED is required. *Academic units required/recommended:* 19 total required; 4 English required, 3 math required, 2 science required, 3 science recommended, 2 science lab required, 2 foreign language recommended, 2 social studies recommended, 1 history required, 2 elective required, 4 elective recommended. **Freshman Admission Statistics:** 1,933 applied, 95% accepted, 63% of those accepted enrolled. **Transfer Admission Requirements:** *Items required:* college transcript. Minimum college GPA of 2.0 required. Lowest grade transferable D. **General Admission Information:** Application fee $25. Regular application deadline August 1. Nonfall registration accepted. Credit offered for CEEB Advanced Placement tests.

COSTS AND FINANCIAL AID

In-state tuition $1,608. Out-of-state tuition $6,768. Room & board $3,636. Required fees $458. Average book expense $731. **Required Forms and Deadlines:** FAFSA. Financial aid filing deadline October 15. Priority filing deadline April 1. **Types of Aid:** *Need-based scholarships/grants:* Pell, state scholarships/grants, private scholarships, the school's own gift aid. *Loans:* Direct Subsidized Stafford, Direct Unsubsidized Stafford, Direct PLUS, Federal Perkins, college/university loans from institutional funds. **Student Employment:** Federal Work-Study Program available. Institutional employment available. Off-campus job opportunities are good. **Financial Aid Statistics:** 48% freshmen, 59% undergrads receive some form of aid. Average income from on-campus job $1,715. **Financial Aid Phone:** 254-968-9070.

TAYLOR UNIVERSITY—FORT WAYNE

1025 West Rudisill Boulevard, Fort Wayne, IN 46807
Phone: 219-744-8689 **E-mail:** admissions_f@tayloru.edu **CEEB Code:** 1227
Fax: 219-744-8660 **Web:** www.tayloru.edu/fw **ACT Code:** 1192

This private school, which is affiliated with the Protestant Church, was founded in 1846. It has a 32-acre campus.

STUDENTS AND FACULTY

Enrollment: 633. **Student Body:** Male 37%, female 63%, out-of-state 25%, international students represent 3 countries. **Ethnic Representation:** African American 8%, Asian 1%, Caucasian 85%, Hispanic 1%. **Retention and Graduation:** 71% freshmen return for sophomore year. 21% freshmen graduate within 4 years. **Faculty:** Student/faculty ratio 14:1. 26 full-time faculty, 61% hold PhDs. 100% faculty teach undergrads.

ACADEMICS

Degrees: Associate's, bachelor's, terminal, transfer. **Academic Requirements:** General education including some course work in arts/fine arts, computer literacy, English (including composition), history, humanities, mathematics, philosophy, sciences (biological or physical), social science, biblical studies, communications, physical fitness, crosscultural studies. **Classes:** Under 10 students in an average class. 10-19 students in an average lab/discussion section. **Majors with Highest Enrollment:** Elementary education and teaching; pastoral studies/counseling; psychology, general. **Disciplines with Highest Percentage of Degrees Awarded:** Philosophy/religion/theology 44%, protective services/public administration 20%, education 13%, business/marketing 8%, communications/communication technologies 6%. **Special Study Options:** Accelerated program, cooperative (work-study) program, distance learning, double major, student exchange program (domestic), independent study, internships, student-designed major, study abroad, teacher certification program, weekend college.

FACILITIES

Housing: All-female, all-male, apartments for single students. **Library Holdings:** 78,662 bound volumes. 487 periodicals. 29,815 microforms. 4,699 audiovisuals. **Computers:** *Recommended operating system:* Windows NT/2000. School-owned computers available for student use.

EXTRACURRICULARS

Activities: Choral groups, drama/theater, jazz band, music ensembles, student government, student newspaper, yearbook. **Organizations:** 11 registered organizations, 1 religious organization. **Athletics (Intercollegiate):** *Men:* basketball, cheerleading, soccer. *Women:* basketball, cheerleading, volleyball.

ADMISSIONS

Selectivity Rating: 63 (of 100). **Freshman Academic Profile:** Average high school GPA 3.1. 13% in top 10% of high school class, 36% in top 25% of high school class, 60% in top 50% of high school class. 65% from public high schools. Average SAT I Math 488, SAT I Math middle 50% range 425-540. Average SAT I Verbal 499, SAT I Verbal middle 50% range 425-555. Average ACT 22, ACT middle 50% range 18-25. TOEFL required of all international applicants, minimum TOEFL 550. **Basis for Candidate Selection:** *Very important factors considered include:* religious affiliation/commitment, secondary school record. *Important factors considered include:* character/personal qualities, essays, interview, recommendations, standardized test scores. *Other factors considered include:* class rank, extracurricular activities, volunteer work, work experience. **Freshman Admission Requirements:** High school diploma or GED is required. *Academic units required/recommended:* 17 total required; 2 total recommended; 4 English required, 3 math required, 3 science required, 3 science lab required, 2 foreign language recommended, 2 social studies required, 2 history required. **Freshman Admission Statistics:** 457 applied, 84% accepted, 37% of those accepted enrolled. **Transfer Admission Requirements:** *Items required:* high school transcript, college transcript, essay, statement of good standing from prior school. Minimum college GPA of 2.5 required. Lowest grade transferable C-. **General Admission Information:** Application fee $20. Priority application deadline December 15. Regular application deadline August 15. Nonfall registration accepted. Admission may be deferred for a maximum of 2 years. Neither credit nor placement offered for CEEB Advanced Placement tests.

COSTS AND FINANCIAL AID

Required Forms and Deadlines: FAFSA and institution's own financial aid form. Priority filing deadline March 1. **Notification of Awards:** Applicants will be notified of awards on a rolling basis beginning on or about March 1. **Types of Aid:** *Need-based scholarships/grants:* Pell, SEOG, state scholarships/grants, private scholarships, the school's own gift aid, endowed-donor scholarships. *Loans:* FFEL Subsidized Stafford, FFEL Unsubsidized Stafford, FFEL PLUS, Federal Perkins. **Student Employment:** Federal Work-Study Program available. Institutional employment available. Off-campus job opportunities are excellent. **Financial Aid Statistics:** 81% freshmen, 81% undergrads receive some form of aid. Average freshman grant $10,523. Average freshman loan $3,877. **Financial Aid Phone:** 219-744-8644.

TAYLOR UNIVERSITY—UPLAND

236 West Reade Avenue, Upland, IN 46989-1001
Phone: 765-998-5134 **E-mail:** admissions_u@tayloru.edu **CEEB Code:** 1802
Fax: 765-998-4925 **Web:** www.tayloru.edu **ACT Code:** 1248

This private school was founded in 1846. It has a 250-acre campus.

STUDENTS AND FACULTY

Enrollment: 1,869. **Student Body:** Male 48%, female 52%, out-of-state 69%, international 2% (25 countries represented). **Ethnic Representation:** African American 1%, Asian 1%, Caucasian 95%, Hispanic 2%. **Retention and Graduation:** 88% freshmen return for sophomore year. 72% freshmen graduate within 4 years. 17% grads go on to further study within 1 year. 2% grads pursue business degrees. 1% grads pursue law degrees. 2% grads pursue medical degrees. **Faculty:** Student/faculty ratio 15:1. 118 full-time faculty, 78% hold PhDs. 100% faculty teach undergrads.

ACADEMICS

Degrees: Associate's, bachelor's. **Academic Requirements:** General education including some course work in arts/fine arts, computer literacy, English (including composition), history, humanities, philosophy, sciences (biological or physical), social science. BA degree candidates must complete a foreign language requirement. **Classes:** 10-19 students in an average class. Under 10 students in an average lab/discussion section. **Majors with Highest Enrollment:** Business/managerial operations; elementary education and teaching; Bible/biblical studies. **Disciplines with Highest Percentage of Degrees Awarded:** Business/marketing 20%, education 17%, philosophy/religion/theology 11%, communications/communication technologies 8%, social sciences and history 8%. **Special Study Options:** Cooperative (work-study) program, distance learning, double major, student exchange program (domestic), honors program, independent study, internships, student-designed major, study abroad, teacher certification program.

FACILITIES

Housing: All-female, all-male, apartments for married students, apartments for single students. **Library Holdings:** 193,343 bound volumes. 902 periodicals.

10,534 microforms. 6,653 audiovisuals. **Special Academic Facilities/ Equipment:** Compton Art Gallery, Edwin W. Brown Collection/C.S. Lewis and Friends. **Computers:** School-owned computers available for student use.

EXTRACURRICULARS

Activities: Choral groups, concert band, drama/theater, jazz band, literary magazine, music ensembles, musical theater, pep band, radio station, student government, student newspaper, symphony orchestra, television station, yearbook. **Organizations:** 30 registered organizations, 6 honor societies. **Athletics (Intercollegiate):** *Men:* baseball, basketball, cross-country, football, golf, soccer, tennis, track & field. *Women:* basketball, cross-country, soccer, softball, tennis, track & field, volleyball.

ADMISSIONS

Selectivity Rating: 86 (of 100). **Freshman Academic Profile:** 36% in top 10% of high school class, 68% in top 25% of high school class, 91% in top 50% of high school class. 79% from public high schools. Average SAT I Math 593, SAT I Math middle 50% range 550-650. Average SAT I Verbal 593, SAT I Verbal middle 50% range 550-650. Average ACT 26, ACT middle 50% range 23-29. TOEFL required of all international applicants, minimum TOEFL 550. **Basis for Candidate Selection:** *Very important factors considered include:* character/personal qualities, class rank, essays, interview, recommendations, religious affiliation/commitment, secondary school record, standardized test scores. *Important factors considered include:* extracurricular activities, talent/ability. *Other factors considered include:* alumni/ae relation, geographical residence, minority status, state residency, volunteer work, work experience. **Freshman Admission Requirements:** High school diploma or GED is required. *Academic units required/recommended:* 15 total required; 21 total recommended; 4 English required, 4 English recommended, 3 math required, 4 math recommended, 3 science required, 4 science recommended, 3 science lab required, 4 science lab recommended, 2 foreign language recommended, 2 history required, 3 history recommended. **Freshman Admission Statistics:** 1,325 applied, 78% accepted, 44% of those accepted enrolled. **Transfer Admission Requirements:** *Items required:* high school transcript, college transcript, essay, standardized test scores, statement of good standing from prior school. **General Admission Information:** Application fee $25. Priority application deadline February 15. Nonfall registration accepted. Admission may be deferred for a maximum of 1 year. Credit and/or placement offered for CEEB Advanced Placement tests.

COSTS AND FINANCIAL AID

Tuition $17,270. Room & board $5,130. Required fees $220. Average book expense $600. **Required Forms and Deadlines:** FAFSA, institution's own financial aid form, and business/farm supplement. Financial aid filing deadline March 1. **Notification of Awards:** Applicants will be notified of awards on a rolling basis beginning on or about March 1. **Types of Aid:** *Need-based scholarships/grants:* Pell, SEOG, state scholarships/grants, private scholarships, the school's own gift aid. *Loans:* FFEL Subsidized Stafford, FFEL Unsubsidized Stafford, FFEL PLUS, Federal Perkins, college/university loans from institutional funds. **Student Employment:** Federal Work-Study Program available. Institutional employment available. Off-campus job opportunities are poor. **Financial Aid Statistics:** 56% freshmen, 56% undergrads receive some form of aid. Average freshman grant $7,200. Average freshman loan $3,300. Average income from on-campus job $850. **Financial Aid Phone:** 765-998-5358.

TCU

Office of Admissions, TCU Box 297013, Fort Worth, TX 76129
Phone: 817-257-7490 **E-mail:** frogmail@tcu.edu **CEEB Code:** 6820
Fax: 817-257-7268 **Web:** www.tcu.edu **ACT Code:** 4206

This private school, which is affiliated with the Disciples of Christ Church, was founded in 1873. It has a 300-acre campus.

STUDENTS AND FACULTY

Enrollment: 6,851. **Student Body:** Male 42%, female 58%, out-of-state 23%, international 4% (75 countries represented). **Ethnic Representation:** African American 5%, Asian 2%, Caucasian 83%, Hispanic 6%, Native American 1%. **Retention and Graduation:** 81% freshmen return for sophomore year. **Faculty:** Student/faculty ratio 15:1. 415 full-time faculty, 90% hold PhDs. 97% faculty teach undergrads.

ACADEMICS

Degrees: Bachelor's, certificate, doctoral, first professional, first professional certificate, master's, post-bachelor's certificate. **Academic Requirements:** General education including some course work in arts/fine arts, English (including composition), foreign languages, history, humanities, mathematics, sciences (biological or physical), social science. **Classes:** 10-19 students in an average class. 10-19 students in an average lab/discussion section. **Disciplines with Highest Percentage of Degrees Awarded:** Business/marketing 29%, communications/communication technologies 16%, education 7%, home economics and vocational home economics 7%, visual and performing arts 6%. **Special Study Options:** Cross registration, distance learning, double major, English as a second language, honors program, independent study, internships, liberal arts/career combination, study abroad, teacher certification program.

FACILITIES

Housing: Coed, all-female, all-male, apartments for married students, apartments for single students, fraternities and/or sororities, designated rooms available for ADA needs. **Library Holdings:** 1,299,875 bound volumes. 4,629 periodicals. 610,764 microforms. 57,562 audiovisuals. **Special Academic Facilities/Equipment:** Art exhibition hall, Tandy Film Library, speech/hearing clinic, TV studios, computer labs, observatory, Moncrief Meteorite, special collections, alumni and visitors' center, cable TV, radio station, performance hall, variety of athletic facilities.

EXTRACURRICULARS

Activities: Choral groups, concert band, dance, drama/theater, jazz band, literary magazine, marching band, music ensembles, musical theater, opera, pep band, radio station, student government, student newspaper, television station, yearbook. **Organizations:** 193 registered organizations, 29 honor societies, 19 religious organizations, 13 fraternities (34% men join), 16 sororities (38% women join). **Athletics (Intercollegiate):** *Men:* baseball, basketball, cross-country, diving, football, golf, indoor track, soccer, swimming, tennis, track & field. *Women:* basketball, cross-country, diving, golf, indoor track, rifle, soccer, swimming, tennis, track & field, volleyball.

ADMISSIONS

Selectivity Rating: 80 (of 100). **Freshman Academic Profile:** 28% in top 10% of high school class, 64% in top 25% of high school class, 94% in top 50% of high school class. 94% from public high schools. SAT I Math middle 50% range 520-630. SAT I Verbal middle 50% range 510-620. ACT middle 50% range 21-27. TOEFL required of all international applicants, minimum TOEFL 550. **Basis for Candidate Selection:** *Very important factors considered include:* character/personal qualities, class rank, essays, recommendations, secondary school record, standardized test scores. *Important factors considered include:* extracurricular activities, geographical residence, minority status, religious affiliation/commitment, talent/ability, volunteer work, work experience. *Other factors considered include:* alumni/ae relation, interview. **Freshman Admission Requirements:** High school diploma is required and GED is not accepted. *Academic units required/recommended:* 17 total required; 24 total recommended; 4 English required, 4 English recommended, 3 math required, 4 math recommended, 3 science required, 4 science recommended, 2 foreign language required, 4 foreign language recommended, 3 social studies required, 4 social studies recommended, 2 elective required, 4 elective recommended. **Freshman Admission Statistics:** 6,137 applied, 71% accepted, 33% of those accepted enrolled. **Transfer Admission Requirements:** *Items required:* college transcript, essay. Minimum college GPA of 2.0 required. Lowest grade transferable C. **General Admission Information:** Application fee $35. Regular application deadline February 15. Nonfall registration accepted. Admission may be deferred for a maximum of 1 year. Credit and/or placement offered for CEEB Advanced Placement tests.

COSTS AND FINANCIAL AID

Tuition $13,500. Room & board $4,870. Required fees $1,540. Average book expense $720. **Required Forms and Deadlines:** FAFSA and institution's own financial aid form. Financial aid filing deadline May 1. Priority filing deadline May 1. **Notification of Awards:** Applicants will be notified of awards on a rolling basis beginning on or about March 1. **Types of Aid:** *Need-based scholarships/grants:* Pell, SEOG, state scholarships/grants, private scholarships, the school's own gift aid, United Negro College Fund. *Loans:* FFEL Subsidized Stafford, FFEL Unsubsidized Stafford, FFEL PLUS, Federal Perkins, Federal Nursing, state loans, college/university loans from institutional funds. **Student Employment:** Federal Work-Study Program available. Institutional employment available. Off-campus job opportunities are excellent. **Financial Aid Statistics:** 42% freshmen, 40% undergrads receive some form of aid. **Financial Aid Phone:** 817-257-7858.

TEIKYO LORETTO HEIGHTS UNIVERSITY

3001 South Federal Boulevard, Denver, CO 80236
Phone: 303-937-4219
Fax: 303-937-4224 **Web:** www.tlhu.edu

STUDENTS AND FACULTY

Enrollment: 200.

ACADEMICS

Degrees: Associate's, bachelor's. **Special Study Options:** English as a second language, study abroad.

FACILITIES

Housing: All-female, all-male.

ADMISSIONS

Selectivity Rating: 60 (of 100). High school diploma or GED is required. **Transfer Admission Requirements:** *Items required:* college transcript, essay. Lowest grade transferable C. **General Admission Information:** Regular application deadline June 30. Nonfall registration accepted.

COSTS AND FINANCIAL AID

Tuition $13,600. Room & board $5,400.

TEIKYO POST UNIVERSITY

PO Box 2540, Waterbury, CT 06723
Phone: 203-596-4520 **E-mail:** tpuadmis@teikyopost.edu **CEEB Code:** 3698
Fax: 203-756-5810 **Web:** www.teikyopost.edu **ACT Code:** 580

This private school was founded in 1890. It has a 60-acre campus.

STUDENTS AND FACULTY

Enrollment: 1,378. **Student Body:** Male 37%, female 63%, out-of-state 17%, international 3%. **Ethnic Representation:** African American 19%, Asian 2%, Caucasian 67%, Hispanic 8%, Native American 1%. **Retention and Graduation:** 78% freshmen return for sophomore year. 10% grads go on to further study within 1 year. 32% grads pursue business degrees. 1% grads pursue law degrees. **Faculty:** Student/faculty ratio 11:1. 29 full-time faculty, 75% hold PhDs. 100% faculty teach undergrads.

ACADEMICS

Degrees: Associate's, bachelor's, certificate, post-bachelor's certificate, terminal, transfer. **Academic Requirements:** General education including some course work in computer literacy, English (including composition), history, humanities, mathematics, sciences (biological or physical), social science. **Classes:** 10-19 students in an average class. 10-19 students in an average lab/discussion section. **Majors with Highest Enrollment:** Business administration/management; general studies; psychology, general. **Disciplines with Highest Percentage of Degrees Awarded:** Business/marketing 60%, liberal arts/general studies 14%, psychology 11%, agriculture 4%, protective services/public administration 3%. **Special Study Options:** Accelerated program, cooperative (work-study) program, cross registration, distance learning, double major, English as a second language, independent study, internships, liberal arts/career combination, study abroad, weekend college.

FACILITIES

Housing: Coed, apartments for married students, apartments for single students. **Library Holdings:** 106,127 bound volumes. 500 periodicals. 5,000 microforms. 885 audiovisuals. **Computers:** *Recommended operating system:* Windows NT/2000. School-owned computers available for student use.

EXTRACURRICULARS

Activities: Choral groups, drama/theater, literary magazine, student government, student newspaper. **Organizations:** 20 registered organizations, 2 honor societies, 3 religious organizations. **Athletics (Intercollegiate):** *Men:* baseball, basketball, cross-country, equestrian, golf, soccer. *Women:* basketball, cross-country, equestrian, soccer, softball, volleyball.

ADMISSIONS

Selectivity Rating: 63 (of 100). **Freshman Academic Profile:** Average high school GPA 2.3. 8% in top 10% of high school class, 27% in top 25% of high school class, 39% in top 50% of high school class. 90% from public high schools. Average SAT I Math 430. Average SAT I Verbal 460. Average ACT 18. TOEFL required of all international applicants, minimum TOEFL 500. **Basis for Candidate Selection:** *Important factors considered include:* character/personal qualities, essays, interview, recommendations, secondary school record, standardized test scores. *Other factors considered include:* alumni/ae relation, class rank, extracurricular activities, talent/ability, volunteer work, work experience. **Freshman Admission Requirements:** High school diploma or GED is required. *Academic units required/recommended:* 16 total required; 16 total recommended; 4 English required, 4 English recommended, 2 math required, 2 math recommended, 2 science required, 2 science recommended, 1 science lab required, 1 science lab recommended, 2 foreign language required, 2 foreign language recommended, 1 social studies required, 1 social studies recommended, 2 history required, 2 history recommended, 2 elective required, 2 elective recommended. **Freshman Admission Statistics:** 1,109 applied, 36% accepted, 62% of those accepted enrolled. **Transfer Admission Requirements:** *Items required:* college transcript. Minimum college GPA of 2.0 required. Lowest grade transferable C-. **General Admission Information:** Application fee $40. Early decision application deadline November 1. Nonfall registration accepted. Admission may be deferred for a maximum of 1 year. Credit and/or placement offered for CEEB Advanced Placement tests.

COSTS AND FINANCIAL AID

Tuition $16,050. Room & board $6,800. Required fees $450. Average book expense $800. **Required Forms and Deadlines:** FAFSA. No deadline for regular filing. Priority filing deadline March 1. **Notification of Awards:** Applicants will be notified of awards on a rolling basis beginning on or about April 1. **Types of Aid:** *Need-based scholarships/grants:* Pell, SEOG, state scholarships/grants, private scholarships, the school's own gift aid. *Loans:* Direct Subsidized Stafford, Direct Unsubsidized Stafford, Direct PLUS, FFEL Subsidized Stafford, FFEL Unsubsidized Stafford, FFEL PLUS, Federal Perkins, state loans. **Student Employment:** Federal Work-Study Program available. Institutional employment available. Off-campus job opportunities are good. **Financial Aid Statistics:** 100% freshmen, 100% undergrads receive some form of aid. Average freshman grant $13,500. Average freshman loan $2,625. Average income from on-campus job $2,056. **Financial Aid Phone:** 203-596-4526.

TEMPLE UNIVERSITY

1801 North Broad Street, Philadelphia, PA 19122-6096
Phone: 215-204-7200 **E-mail:** tuadm@mail.temple.edu **CEEB Code:** 2906
Fax: 215-204-5694 **Web:** www.temple.edu **ACT Code:** 3724

This public school was founded in 1888. It has a 362-acre campus.

STUDENTS AND FACULTY

Enrollment: 21,429. **Student Body:** Male 42%, female 58%, out-of-state 25%, international 4% (130 countries represented). **Ethnic Representation:** African American 23%, Asian 8%, Caucasian 57%, Hispanic 4%. **Retention and Graduation:** 81% freshmen return for sophomore year. **Faculty:** Student/faculty ratio 14:1. 1,232 full-time faculty, 81% hold PhDs.

ACADEMICS

Degrees: Associate's, bachelor's, certificate, diploma, doctoral, first professional, first professional certificate, master's, post-master's certificate, terminal, transfer. **Academic Requirements:** General education including some course work in arts/fine arts, computer literacy, English (including composition), foreign languages, history, humanities, mathematics, philosophy, sciences (biological or physical), social science, intellectual heritage. **Classes:** 20-29 students in an average class. 20-29 students in an average lab/discussion section. **Majors with Highest Enrollment:** Elementary education and teaching; journalism; psychology, general. **Disciplines with Highest Percentage of Degrees Awarded:** Business/marketing 20%, education 14%, visual and performing arts 11%, communications/communication technologies 10%, social sciences and history 7%. **Special Study Options:** Cooperative (work-study) program, cross registration, distance learning, double major, dual enrollment, English as a second language, student exchange program (domestic), honors program, independent study, internships, liberal arts/career combination, student-designed major, study abroad, teacher certification program.

FACILITIES

Housing: Coed, apartments for married students, apartments for single students, housing for disabled students, fraternities and/or sororities, learning communities. **Library Holdings:** 5,086,211 bound volumes. 16,755 periodicals. 2,694,297 microforms. 10,138,110 audiovisuals. **Special Academic Facilities/Equipment:** Blockson Collection, Urban Archives, observatory. **Computers:** School-owned computers available for student use.

EXTRACURRICULARS

Activities: Choral groups, concert band, dance, drama/theater, jazz band, literary magazine, marching band, music ensembles, opera, pep band, radio station, student government, student newspaper, student-run film society, symphony orchestra, yearbook. **Organizations:** 158 registered organizations, 23 honor societies, 6 religious organizations, 13 fraternities (1% men join), 12 sororities (1% women join). **Athletics (Intercollegiate):** *Men:* baseball, basketball, cheerleading, crew, football, golf, gymnastics, indoor track, soccer, tennis, track & field. *Women:* basketball, cheerleading, crew, fencing, field hockey, gymnastics, indoor track, lacrosse, soccer, softball, tennis, track & field, volleyball.

ADMISSIONS

Selectivity Rating: 79 (of 100). **Freshman Academic Profile:** Average high school GPA 3.2. 17% in top 10% of high school class, 47% in top 25% of high school class, 86% in top 50% of high school class. 78% from public high schools. Average SAT I Math 521, SAT I Math middle 50% range 480-580. Average SAT I Verbal 521, SAT I Verbal middle 50% range 480-580. ACT middle 50% range 19-24. TOEFL required of all international applicants, minimum TOEFL 525. **Basis for Candidate Selection:** *Very important factors considered include:* class rank, secondary school record. *Important factors considered include:* standardized test scores. *Other factors considered include:* alumni/ae relation, character/personal qualities, essays, extracurricular activities, recommendations, talent/ability, volunteer work, work experience. **Freshman Admission Requirements:** High school diploma or GED is required. *Academic units required/recommended:* 16 total required; 22 total recommended; 4 English required, 4 English recommended, 3 math required, 4 math recommended, 2 science required, 3 science recommended, 1 science lab required, 2 science lab recommended, 2 foreign language required, 2 foreign language recommended, 2 social studies required, 2 social studies recommended, 1 history required, 2 history recommended, 1 elective required, 3 elective recommended. **Freshman Admission Statistics:** 15,316 applied, 78% accepted, 29% of those accepted enrolled. **Transfer Admission Requirements:** *Items required:* high school transcript, college transcript, essay, statement of good standing from prior school. Minimum college GPA of 2.3 required. Lowest grade transferable C-. **General Admission Information:** Application fee $35. Regular application deadline April 1. Nonfall registration accepted. Admission may be deferred for a maximum of 1 year. Credit and/or placement offered for CEEB Advanced Placement tests.

COSTS AND FINANCIAL AID

In-state tuition $7,602. Out-of-state tuition $13,856. Room & board $7,112. Required fees $460. Average book expense $800. **Required Forms and Deadlines:** FAFSA. Priority filing deadline March 1. **Notification of Awards:** Applicants will be notified of awards on a rolling basis beginning on or about February 15. **Types of Aid:** *Need-based scholarships/grants:* Pell, SEOG, state scholarships/grants, private scholarships, the school's own gift aid, Federal Nursing. *Loans:* FFEL Subsidized Stafford, FFEL Unsubsidized Stafford, FFEL PLUS, Federal Perkins, Federal Nursing, college/university loans from institutional funds. **Student Employment:** Federal Work-Study Program available. Institutional employment available. Off-campus job opportunities are excellent. **Financial Aid Statistics:** 70% freshmen, 67% undergrads receive some form of aid. **Financial Aid Phone:** 215-204-8760.

See page 1226.

TENNESSEE STATE UNIVERSITY

3500 John Merritt Boulevard, Nashville, TN 37209-1561
Phone: 615-963-3101 **E-mail:** jcade@tnstate.edu **CEEB Code:** 1803
Fax: 615-963-5108 **Web:** www.tnstate.edu **ACT Code:** 4010

This public school was founded in 1912. It has a 465-acre campus.

STUDENTS AND FACULTY

Enrollment: 7,239. **Student Body:** Male 38%, female 62%, out-of-state 49%, international 1% (54 countries represented). **Ethnic Representation:** African American 84%, Asian 1%, Caucasian 15%, Hispanic 1%. **Retention and Graduation:** 77% freshmen return for sophomore year. 14% freshmen graduate within 4 years. 20% grads go on to further study within 1 year. **Faculty:** Student/faculty ratio 22:1. 383 full-time faculty, 73% hold PhDs. 83% faculty teach undergrads.

ACADEMICS

Degrees: Associate's, bachelor's, doctoral, master's. **Academic Requirements:** General education including some course work in arts/fine arts, English (including composition), foreign languages, history, humanities, mathematics, philosophy, sciences (biological or physical), social science. **Classes:** Under 10 students in an average class. 10-19 students in an average lab/discussion section. **Majors with Highest Enrollment:** Business/managerial economics; nursing/registered nurse training (RN, ASN, BSN, MSN); liberal arts and sciences, general studies and humanities. **Disciplines with Highest Percentage of Degrees Awarded:** Interdisciplinary studies 20%, health professions and related sciences 10%, business/marketing 9%, psychology 9%, engineering/engineering technology 8%. **Special Study Options:** Cooperative (work-study) program, cross registration, double major, student exchange program (domestic), honors program, independent study, internships, liberal arts/career combination, teacher certification program, on-line degree (courses offered via Internet approved by Tennessee Board of Regents).

FACILITIES

Housing: Coed, all-female, all-male, apartments for single students. **Library Holdings:** 743,741 bound volumes. 439,138 periodicals. 997,321 microforms. 44,832 audiovisuals. **Special Academic Facilities/Equipment:** Eight structural buildings on the national register of historic places, Hiran V. Gordon Art Gallery. **Computers:** *Recommended operating system:* Windows NT/2000. School-owned computers available for student use.

EXTRACURRICULARS

Activities: Choral groups, drama/theater, jazz band, marching band, music ensembles, radio station, student government, student newspaper, yearbook. **Organizations:** 82 registered organizations, 8 honor societies, 4 religious organizations, 4 fraternities (29% men join), 5 sororities (12% women join). **Athletics (Intercollegiate):** *Men:* basketball, cheerleading, cross-country, football, golf, indoor track, tennis, track & field. *Women:* basketball, cheerleading, cross-country, indoor track, softball, tennis, track & field, volleyball.

ADMISSIONS

Selectivity Rating: 77 (of 100). **Freshman Academic Profile:** Average high school GPA 3.0. 96% from public high schools. SAT I Math middle 50% range 430-510. SAT I Verbal middle 50% range 430-510. Average ACT 19, ACT middle 50% range 18-21. TOEFL required of all international applicants, minimum TOEFL 500. **Basis for Candidate Selection:** *Very important factors considered include:* standardized test scores, state residency. *Important factors considered include:* class rank, geographical residence, recommendations, secondary school record. *Other factors considered include:* alumni/ae relation, character/personal qualities, extracurricular activities, talent/ability. **Freshman Admission Requirements:** High school diploma or GED is required. *Academic units required/recommended:* 15 total required; 4 English required, 3 math required, 2 science required, 1 science lab required, 2 foreign language required, 1 social studies required, 1 history required, 1 elective required. **Freshman Admission Statistics:** 6,344 applied, 35% accepted, 59% of those accepted enrolled. **Transfer Admission Requirements:** *Items required:* college transcript. Minimum college GPA of 2.9 required. Lowest grade transferable C. **General Admission Information:** Application fee $15. Regular application deadline August 1. Nonfall registration accepted. Credit offered for CEEB Advanced Placement tests.

COSTS AND FINANCIAL AID

In-state tuition $3,272. Out-of-state tuition $10,230. Room & board $3,060. Required fees $150. Average book expense $850. **Required Forms and Deadlines:** FAFSA, CSS/Financial Aid PROFILE and noncustodial (divorced/separated) parent's statement. **Types of Aid:** *Need-based scholarships/grants:* Pell, SEOG. *Loans:* Direct Subsidized Stafford, Direct Unsubsidized Stafford, Direct PLUS, FFEL Subsidized Stafford, FFEL Unsubsidized Stafford, FFEL PLUS, Federal Perkins. **Student Employment:** Federal Work-Study Program available. Off-campus job opportunities are good. **Financial Aid Statistics:** 43% freshmen receive some form of aid. Average freshman grant $2,844. Average freshman loan $2,966. **Financial Aid Phone:** 615-963-5701.

TENNESSEE TECHNOLOGICAL UNIVERSITY

PO Box 5006, Cookeville, TN 38505-0001
Phone: 931-372-3888 **E-mail:** admissions@tntech.edu **CEEB Code:** 1804
Fax: 931-372-6250 **Web:** www.tntech.edu **ACT Code:** 4012

This public school was founded in 1915. It has a 235-acre campus.

STUDENTS AND FACULTY

Enrollment: 7,251. **Student Body:** Male 54%, female 46%, out-of-state 5%, international 1%. **Ethnic Representation:** African American 4%, Asian 1%, Caucasian 93%, Hispanic 1%. **Retention and Graduation:** 70% freshmen return for sophomore year. 12% freshmen graduate within 4 years. **Faculty:**

Student/faculty ratio 18:1. 371 full-time faculty, 78% hold PhDs. 99% faculty teach undergrads.

ACADEMICS

Degrees: Bachelor's, doctoral, master's. **Academic Requirements:** General education including some course work in computer literacy, English (including composition), history, humanities, mathematics, sciences (biological or physical), social science. **Classes:** 20-29 students in an average class. 10-19 students in an average lab/discussion section. **Disciplines with Highest Percentage of Degrees Awarded:** Business/marketing 27%, engineering/engineering technology 22%, education 20%, social sciences and history 5%, agriculture 4%. **Special Study Options:** Cooperative (work-study) program, dual enrollment, honors program, internships, study abroad, teacher certification program.

FACILITIES

Housing: Coed, all-female, all-male, apartments for married students, housing for disabled students. **Library Holdings:** 624,952 bound volumes. 3,843 periodicals. 1,402,436 microforms. 18,138 audiovisuals. **Special Academic Facilities/Equipment:** 300-acre farm lab, electric power center, water resources center, manufacturing center. **Computers:** School-owned computers available for student use.

EXTRACURRICULARS

Activities: Choral groups, concert band, dance, drama/theater, jazz band, literary magazine, marching band, music ensembles, musical theater, opera, pep band, radio station, student government, student newspaper, symphony orchestra, yearbook. **Organizations:** 186 registered organizations, 14 honor societies, 16 religious organizations, 16 fraternities (12% men join), 6 sororities (8% women join). **Athletics (Intercollegiate):** *Men:* baseball, basketball, cheerleading, cross-country, football, golf, rifle, tennis. *Women:* basketball, cheerleading, cross-country, golf, indoor track, rifle, soccer, softball, tennis, track & field, volleyball.

ADMISSIONS

Selectivity Rating: 71 (of 100). **Freshman Academic Profile:** Average high school GPA 3.1. 21% in top 10% of high school class, 49% in top 25% of high school class, 80% in top 50% of high school class. 90% from public high schools. SAT I Math middle 50% range 470-610. SAT I Verbal middle 50% range 460-610. Average ACT 22, ACT middle 50% range 19-25. TOEFL required of all international applicants, minimum TOEFL 500. **Basis for Candidate Selection:** *Very important factors considered include:* secondary school record, standardized test scores. *Other factors considered include:* alumni/ae relation, character/personal qualities, class rank, extracurricular activities, interview, recommendations, talent/ability. **Freshman Admission Requirements:** High school diploma or GED is required. *Academic units required/recommended:* 14 total required; 4 English required, 3 math required, 2 science required, 1 science lab required, 2 foreign language required, 1 social studies required, 1 history required. **Freshman Admission Statistics:** 3,294 applied, 79% accepted, 53% of those accepted enrolled. **Transfer Admission Requirements:** *Items required:* college transcript. Minimum college GPA of 2.0 required. Lowest grade transferable D. **General Admission Information:** Application fee $15. Priority application deadline December 15. Regular application deadline August 1. Nonfall registration accepted. Admission may be deferred for a maximum of 1 year. Credit and/or placement offered for CEEB Advanced Placement tests.

COSTS AND FINANCIAL AID

In-state tuition $2,748. Out-of-state tuition $10,246. Room & board $5,198. Required fees $540. Average book expense $720. **Required Forms and Deadlines:** FAFSA and p. No deadline for regular filing. Priority filing deadline March 15. **Notification of Awards:** Applicants will be notified of awards on a rolling basis beginning on or about April 15. **Types of Aid:** *Need-based scholarships/grants:* Pell, SEOG, state scholarships/grants, private scholarships, the school's own gift aid. *Loans:* Direct Subsidized Stafford, Direct Unsubsidized Stafford, FFEL PLUS, Federal Perkins, state loans, college/university loans from institutional funds. **Student Employment:** Federal Work-Study Program available. Institutional employment available. Off-campus job opportunities are excellent. **Financial Aid Statistics:** 42% freshmen, 43% undergrads receive some form of aid. Average freshman grant $3,419. Average freshman loan $1,862. **Financial Aid Phone:** 931-372-3073.

TENNESSEE TEMPLE UNIVERSITY

Office of Admissions, 1815 Union Avenue, Chattanooga, TN 37404
Phone: 423-493-4371 **E-mail:** ttuinfo@tntemple.edu
Fax: 423-493-4497 **Web:** www.tntemple.edu

STUDENTS AND FACULTY

Faculty: Student/faculty ratio 14:1.

ACADEMICS

Degrees: Associate's, bachelor's, diploma, master's. **Academic Requirements:** General education including some course work in computer literacy, English (including composition), history, humanities, mathematics, philosophy, social science, Bible and theology. **Special Study Options:** Dual enrollment, external degree program, internships.

FACILITIES

Housing: All-female, all-male.

EXTRACURRICULARS

Activities: Choral groups, drama/theater, music ensembles, pep band, radio station, student government, symphony orchestra, television station, yearbook. **Athletics (Intercollegiate):** *Men:* baseball, basketball, cheerleading, soccer, wrestling. *Women:* basketball, cheerleading, volleyball.

ADMISSIONS

Selectivity Rating: 60 (of 100).

COSTS AND FINANCIAL AID

Tuition $5,000. Room & board $4,000. Required fees $950. Average book expense $800.

TENNESSEE WESLEYAN COLLEGE

PO Box 40, Athens, TN 37371-0040
Phone: 423-746-5286 **E-mail:** cawoodr@twcnet.edu
Fax: 423-745-9335 **Web:** www.twcnet.edu **ACT Code:** 4014

This private school, which is affiliated with the Methodist Church, was founded in 1857. It has a 40-acre campus.

STUDENTS AND FACULTY

Enrollment: 803. **Student Body:** Male 34%, female 66%, out-of-state 8%, international 4% (24 countries represented). **Ethnic Representation:** African American 3%, Caucasian 96%, Hispanic 1%. **Retention and Graduation:** 61% freshmen return for sophomore year. **Faculty:** Student/faculty ratio 17:1. 43 full-time faculty, 72% hold PhDs.

ACADEMICS

Degrees: Bachelor's. **Academic Requirements:** General education including some course work in arts/fine arts, computer literacy, English (including composition), foreign languages, history, humanities, mathematics, philosophy, sciences (biological or physical), social science. **Classes:** 10-19 students in an average class. Under 10 students in an average lab/discussion section. **Disciplines with Highest Percentage of Degrees Awarded:** Business/marketing 40%, psychology 15%, protective services/public administration 10%, parks and recreation 10%, computer and information sciences 7%. **Special Study Options:** Cooperative (work-study) program, double major, dual enrollment, English as a second language, student exchange program (domestic), honors program, internships, liberal arts/career combination, student-designed major, study abroad, teacher certification program.

FACILITIES

Housing: Coed, all-female, all-male, apartments for single students, housing for disabled students.

EXTRACURRICULARS

Activities: Choral groups, drama/theater, literary magazine, music ensembles, musical theater, student government, student newspaper, yearbook. **Organizations:** 19 registered organizations, 1 honor society, 3 religious organizations, 2 sororities (10% women join). **Athletics (Intercollegiate):** *Men:* baseball, basketball, cross-country, golf, soccer, tennis. *Women:* basketball, cheerleading, cross-country, soccer, softball, tennis, volleyball.

ADMISSIONS

Selectivity Rating: 73 (of 100). **Freshman Academic Profile:** Average high school GPA 3.3. Average ACT 22. TOEFL required of all international applicants, minimum TOEFL 500. **Basis for Candidate Selection:** *Very important factors considered include:* recommendations, secondary school record, standardized test scores. *Important factors considered include:* class rank, essays, extracurricular activities. *Other factors considered include:* alumni/ae relation, character/personal qualities, interview, talent/ability, volunteer work. **Freshman Admission Requirements:** High school diploma or GED is required. *Academic units required/recommended:* 17 total recommended; 4 English recommended, 2 math recommended, 2 science recommended, 1 social studies recommended, 1 history recommended. **Freshman Admission Statistics:** 560 applied, 81% accepted, 30% of those accepted enrolled. **Transfer Admission Requirements:** *Items required:* college transcript. Minimum college GPA of 2.0 required. Lowest grade transferable D. **General Admission Information:** Application fee $25. Nonfall registration accepted. Admission may be deferred. Credit and/or placement offered for CEEB Advanced Placement tests.

COSTS AND FINANCIAL AID

Tuition $10,000. Room & board $4,380. Required fees $240. Average book expense $800. **Required Forms and Deadlines:** FAFSA and institution's own financial aid form. Financial aid filing deadline March 1. Priority filing deadline March 1. **Notification of Awards:** Applicants will be notified of awards on a rolling basis beginning on or about March 1. **Types of Aid:** *Need-based scholarships/grants:* Pell, SEOG, state scholarships/grants, private scholarships, the school's own gift aid. *Loans:* Direct Subsidized Stafford, Direct Unsubsidized Stafford, Direct PLUS, Federal Perkins. **Student Employment:** Federal Work-Study Program available. Institutional employment available. Off-campus job opportunities are good. **Financial Aid Statistics:** 69% freshmen, 62% undergrads receive some form of aid. Average freshman grant $3,000. Average freshman loan $2,625. Average income from on-campus job $750. **Financial Aid Phone:** 423-746-5215.

TEXAS A&M UNIVERSITY—COLLEGE STATION

Admissions Counseling, College Station, TX 77843-1265
Phone: 979-845-3741 **E-mail:** admissions@tamu.edu **CEEB Code:** 6003
Fax: 979-847-8737 **Web:** www.tamu.edu **ACT Code:** 4198

This public school was founded in 1876. It has a 5,200-acre campus.

STUDENTS AND FACULTY

Enrollment: 36,603. **Student Body:** Male 51%, female 49%, out-of-state 3%, international 1% (115 countries represented). **Ethnic Representation:** African American 2%, Asian 3%, Caucasian 84%, Hispanic 9%, Native American 1%. **Retention and Graduation:** 89% freshmen return for sophomore year. 30% freshmen graduate within 4 years. **Faculty:** Student/faculty ratio 21:1. 1,917 full-time faculty, 91% hold PhDs. 75% faculty teach undergrads.

ACADEMICS

Degrees: Bachelor's, doctoral, first professional, master's, post-bachelor's certificate. **Academic Requirements:** General education including some course work in arts/fine arts, computer literacy, English (including composition), foreign languages, history, humanities, mathematics, philosophy, sciences (biological or physical), social science. **Classes:** 20-29 students in an average class. 10-19 students in an average lab/discussion section. **Majors with Highest Enrollment:** Operations management and supervision; biological and physical sciences; psychology, general. **Disciplines with Highest Percentage of Degrees Awarded:** Business/marketing 17%, engineering/engineering technology 15%, agriculture 12%, social sciences and history 10%, interdisciplinary studies 10%. **Special Study Options:** Accelerated program, cooperative (work-study) program, cross registration, distance learning, double major, dual enrollment, English as a second language, student exchange program (domestic), honors program, independent study, internships, study abroad, teacher certification program.

FACILITIES

Housing: Coed, all-female, all-male, apartments for married students, apartments for single students, housing for disabled students, fraternities and/or sororities. **Library Holdings:** 4,425,478 bound volumes. 39,459 periodicals. 5,304,146 microforms. 318,876 audiovisuals. **Special Academic Facilities/Equipment:** Bush Library/Museum; Jordan International Collection; Corps of Cadets Center/Museum; Forsyth Center Gallery; MSC Visual Arts Gallery; J. Wayne Stark University Center Galleries. **Computers:** School-owned computers available for student use.

EXTRACURRICULARS

Activities: Choral groups, concert band, dance, drama/theater, jazz band, literary magazine, marching band, music ensembles, musical theater, radio station, student government, student newspaper, student-run film society, symphony orchestra, television station, yearbook. **Organizations:** 658 registered organizations, 27 honor societies, 52 religious organizations, 26 fraternities (4% men join), 20 sororities (6% women join). **Athletics (Intercollegiate):** *Men:* baseball, basketball, cross-country, diving, football, golf, indoor track, rifle, swimming, tennis, track & field. *Women:* basketball, cross-country, diving, equestrian, golf, indoor track, rifle, soccer, softball, swimming, tennis, track & field, volleyball.

ADMISSIONS

Selectivity Rating: 83 (of 100). **Freshman Academic Profile:** 55% in top 10% of high school class, 89% in top 25% of high school class, 99% in top 50% of high school class. Average SAT I Math 602, SAT I Math middle 50% range 550-660. Average SAT I Verbal 576, SAT I Verbal middle 50% range 520-630. Average ACT 25, ACT middle 50% range 22-27. TOEFL required of all international applicants, minimum TOEFL 550. **Basis for Candidate Selection:** *Very important factors considered include:* class rank, extracurricular activities, secondary school record, standardized test scores, state residency, talent/ability. *Important factors considered include:* essays, volunteer work, work experience. *Other factors considered include:* alumni/ae relation, character/personal qualities, geographical residence, recommendations. **Freshman Admission Requirements:** High school diploma or GED is required. *Academic units required/recommended:* 16 total required; 19 total recommended; 4 English required, 4 English recommended, 3 math required, 3 math recommended, 2 science required, 3 science recommended, 2 science lab required, 2 science lab recommended, 2 foreign language required, 3 foreign language recommended, 2 social studies required, 2 social studies recommended, 1 history required, 1 history recommended. **Freshman Admission Statistics:** 17,284 applied, 68% accepted, 59% of those accepted enrolled. **Transfer Admission Requirements:** *Items required:* high school transcript, college transcript. Minimum college GPA of 2.2 required. Lowest grade transferable D. **General Admission Information:** Application fee $50. Regular application deadline February 15. Nonfall registration accepted. Credit offered for CEEB Advanced Placement tests.

COSTS AND FINANCIAL AID

In-state tuition $2,640. Out-of-state tuition $9,180. Room & board $6,030. Required fees $2,108. Average book expense $818. **Required Forms and Deadlines:** FAFSA, institution's own financial aid form and Financial Aid Transcripts (for transfer students). Priority filing deadline March 1. **Notification of Awards:** Applicants will be notified of awards on a rolling basis beginning on or about April 15. **Types of Aid:** *Need-based scholarships/grants:* Pell, SEOG, state scholarships/grants, private scholarships, the school's own gift aid. *Loans:* FFEL Subsidized Stafford, FFEL Unsubsidized Stafford, FFEL PLUS, Federal Perkins, state loans, college/university loans from institutional funds. **Student Employment:** Federal Work-Study Program available. Institutional employment available. Off-campus job opportunities are good. **Financial Aid Statistics:** 29% freshmen, 28% undergrads receive some form of aid. Average freshman grant $3,280. Average freshman loan $4,350. Average income from on-campus job $1,934. **Financial Aid Phone:** 979-845-3236.

TEXAS A&M UNIVERSITY—COMMERCE

PO Box 3011, Commerce, TX 75429
Phone: 903-886-5106 **E-mail:** admissions@tamu-commerce.edu
Fax: 903-886-5888 **Web:** www.tamu-commerce.edu **ACT Code:** 6188

This public school was founded in 1889. It has a 140-acre campus.

STUDENTS AND FACULTY

Enrollment: 4,815. **Student Body:** Male 41%, female 59%, out-of-state 4%, international 1%. **Ethnic Representation:** African American 18%, Asian 1%, Caucasian 75%, Hispanic 5%, Native American 1%. **Faculty:** Student/faculty ratio 17:1. 283 full-time faculty. 17% faculty teach undergrads.

ACADEMICS

Degrees: Bachelor's, doctoral, master's. **Academic Requirements:** General education including some course work in arts/fine arts, English (including composition), foreign languages, history, humanities, mathematics, sciences (biological or physical), social science, government. **Classes:** 10-19 students in an average class. **Majors with Highest Enrollment:** Business administration/management; criminal justice/safety studies; computer and information sciences, general. **Disciplines with Highest Percentage of Degrees**

Awarded: Visual and performing arts 5%, social sciences and history 4%, physical sciences 2%, agriculture 2%, computer and information sciences 1%. **Special Study Options:** Cooperative (work-study) program, distance learning, double major, dual enrollment, honors program, independent study, internships, study abroad, teacher certification program, weekend college (for graduate students only). Selected courses available online.

FACILITIES

Housing: Coed, all-female, all-male, apartments for married students, apartments for single students, housing for disabled students, housing for international students, fraternities and/or sororities. **Library Holdings:** 1,060,435 bound volumes. 1,711 periodicals. 1,096,031 microforms. 49,849 audiovisuals. **Computers:** School-owned computers available for student use.

EXTRACURRICULARS

Activities: Choral groups, concert band, dance, drama/theater, jazz band, literary magazine, marching band, music ensembles, musical theater, pep band, radio station, student government, student newspaper, student-run film society, television station, yearbook. **Organizations:** 110 registered organizations, 12 honor societies, 10 religious organizations, 9 fraternities (11% men join), 9 sororities (8% women join). **Athletics (Intercollegiate):** *Men:* basketball, cheerleading, cross-country, football, golf, track & field. *Women:* basketball, cheerleading, cross-country, golf, soccer, track & field, volleyball.

ADMISSIONS

Selectivity Rating: 63 (of 100). **Freshman Academic Profile:** Average high school GPA 3.4. 13% in top 10% of high school class, 26% in top 25% of high school class, 33% in top 50% of high school class. 98% from public high schools. Average SAT I Math 550, SAT I Math middle 50% range 410-560. Average SAT I Verbal 535, SAT I Verbal middle 50% range 410-540. Average ACT 21, ACT middle 50% range 19-22. TOEFL required of all international applicants, minimum TOEFL 500. **Basis for Candidate Selection:** *Very important factors considered include:* class rank, secondary school record, standardized test scores. *Other factors considered include:* work experience. **Freshman Admission Requirements:** High school diploma or GED is required. *Academic units required/recommended:* 12 total required; 4 English required, 3 math required, 2 science required, 2 foreign language recommended. **Freshman Admission Statistics:** 2,565 applied, 54% accepted, 48% of those accepted enrolled. **Transfer Admission Requirements:** *Items required:* college transcript, standardized test scores, statement of good standing from prior school. Minimum college GPA of 2.0 required. Lowest grade transferable D. **General Admission Information:** Application fee $25. Priority application deadline June 1. Regular application deadline August 1. Nonfall registration accepted. Admission may be deferred for a maximum of 1 year. Credit and/or placement offered for CEEB Advanced Placement tests.

COSTS AND FINANCIAL AID

In-state tuition $3,224. Out-of-state tuition $9,764. Room & board $4,786. Required fees $0. Average book expense $900. **Required Forms and Deadlines:** FAFSA and institution's own financial aid form. No deadline for regular filing. Priority filing deadline May 1. **Notification of Awards:** Applicants will be notified of awards on a rolling basis beginning on or about June 1. **Types of Aid:** *Need-based scholarships/grants:* Pell, SEOG, state scholarships/grants, private scholarships, the school's own gift aid. *Loans:* Direct Subsidized Stafford, Direct Unsubsidized Stafford, FFEL Subsidized Stafford, FFEL Unsubsidized Stafford, FFEL PLUS, Federal Perkins. **Student Employment:** Federal Work-Study Program available. Institutional employment available. Off-campus job opportunities are good. **Financial Aid Statistics:** 56% freshmen, 56% undergrads receive some form of aid. Average income from on-campus job $2,500. **Financial Aid Phone:** 903-886-5096.

TEXAS A&M UNIVERSITY—CORPUS CHRISTI

6300 Ocean Drive, Corpus Christi, TX 78412
Phone: 361-825-2624 **E-mail:** Judith.Perales@mail.tamucc.edu **CEEB Code:** 366
Fax: 361-825-5887 **Web:** www.tamucc.edu **ACT Code:** 4045

This public school was founded in 1947. It has a 240-acre campus.

STUDENTS AND FACULTY

Enrollment: 6,098. **Student Body:** Male 40%, female 60%, out-of-state 3%, international 1%. **Ethnic Representation:** African American 2%, Asian 2%, Caucasian 59%, Hispanic 37%. **Retention and Graduation:** 65% freshmen return for sophomore year. 13% freshmen graduate within 4 years. **Faculty:** Student/faculty ratio 16:1. 141 full-time faculty. 87% faculty teach undergrads.

ACADEMICS

Degrees: Bachelor's, doctoral, master's. **Academic Requirements:** General education including some course work in arts/fine arts, computer literacy, English (including composition), foreign languages, history, mathematics, philosophy, sciences (biological or physical), social science. **Classes:** 20-29 students in an average class. 20-29 students in an average lab/discussion section. **Majors with Highest Enrollment:** Biology/biological sciences, general. **Disciplines with Highest Percentage of Degrees Awarded:** Business/marketing 20%, interdisciplinary studies 18%, psychology 9%, protective services/public administration 7%, social sciences and history 6%. **Special Study Options:** Cooperative (work-study) program, distance learning, double major, independent study, internships, teacher certification program.

FACILITIES

Housing: Coed, apartments for single students. **Library Holdings:** 731,586 bound volumes. 1,901 periodicals. 536,059 microforms. 6,012 audiovisuals. **Special Academic Facilities/Equipment:** Weil Gallery, S. Texas Institute for the Arts. **Computers:** School-owned computers available for student use.

EXTRACURRICULARS

Activities: Choral groups, concert band, dance, drama/theater, jazz band, literary magazine, marching band, music ensembles, musical theater, opera, pep band, student government, student newspaper, student-run film society, symphony orchestra, yearbook. **Organizations:** 50 registered organizations, 15 honor societies, 4 religious organizations, 5 fraternities, 5 sororities. **Athletics (Intercollegiate):** *Men:* baseball, basketball, cross-country, tennis, track & field. *Women:* basketball, cross-country, golf, softball, tennis, track & field, volleyball.

ADMISSIONS

Selectivity Rating: 63 (of 100). **Freshman Academic Profile:** 15% in top 10% of high school class, 45% in top 25% of high school class, 83% in top 50% of high school class. Average SAT I Math 480, SAT I Math middle 50% range 410-527. Average SAT I Verbal 481, SAT I Verbal middle 50% range 530-518. Average ACT 20, ACT middle 50% range 17-23. TOEFL required of all international applicants, minimum TOEFL 550. **Basis for Candidate Selection:** *Very important factors considered include:* class rank, secondary school record. *Important factors considered include:* standardized test scores. *Other factors considered include:* character/personal qualities, extracurricular activities, recommendations, talent/ability, volunteer work, work experience. **Freshman Admission Requirements:** High school diploma or GED is required. *Academic units required/recommended:* 15 total required; 4 English required, 3 math required, 3 science required, 2 foreign language required, 3 social studies required. **Freshman Admission Statistics:** 3,114 applied, 85% accepted, 38% of those accepted enrolled. **Transfer Admission Requirements:** *Items required:* college transcript, statement of good standing from prior school. Minimum college GPA of 2.0 required. Lowest grade transferable D. **General Admission Information:** Application fee $20. Regular application deadline July 1. Nonfall registration accepted. Credit offered for CEEB Advanced Placement tests.

COSTS AND FINANCIAL AID

Required Forms and Deadlines: FAFSA and institution's own financial aid form. Priority filing deadline April 1. **Notification of Awards:** Applicants will be notified of awards on a rolling basis beginning on or about May 1. **Types of Aid:** *Need-based scholarships/grants:* Pell, SEOG, state scholarships/grants, the school's own gift aid. *Loans:* FFEL Subsidized Stafford, FFEL Unsubsidized Stafford, FFEL PLUS, Federal Perkins, college/university loans from institutional funds. **Student Employment:** Federal Work-Study Program available. Institutional employment available. Off-campus job opportunities are good. **Financial Aid Statistics:** 48% freshmen, 50% undergrads receive some form of aid. Average freshman grant $2,000. **Financial Aid Phone:** 361-825-2338.

TEXAS A&M UNIVERSITY—GALVESTON

Admissions Office, PO Box 1675, Galveston, TX 77553
Phone: 409-740-4414 **E-mail:** seaaggie@tamug.tamu.edu **CEEB Code:** 6835
Fax: 409-740-4731 **Web:** www.tamug.edu **ACT Code:** 6592

This public school was founded in 1963. It has a 150-acre campus.

STUDENTS AND FACULTY

Enrollment: 1,517. **Student Body:** Male 53%, female 47%, out-of-state 19%, international 1% (6 countries represented). **Ethnic Representation:** African American 2%, Asian 2%, Caucasian 84%, Hispanic 11%, Native American 1%. **Retention and Graduation:** 69% grads go on to further study within 1 year.

6% grads pursue business degrees. 2% grads pursue law degrees. 3% grads pursue medical degrees. **Faculty:** Student/faculty ratio 16:1. 83 full-time faculty, 73% hold PhDs. 99% faculty teach undergrads.

ACADEMICS

Degrees: Bachelor's, master's. **Academic Requirements:** General education including some course work in computer literacy, English (including composition), foreign languages, history, humanities, mathematics, sciences (biological or physical), social science. **Classes:** 10-19 students in an average class. **Majors with Highest Enrollment:** Marine biology and biological oceanography; business administration/management; marine science/merchant marine officer. **Disciplines with Highest Percentage of Degrees Awarded:** Biological life sciences 45%, business/marketing 21%, trade and industry 12%, physical sciences 10%, engineering/engineering technology 7%. **Special Study Options:** Accelerated program, cooperative (work-study) program, double major, dual enrollment, independent study, internships, study abroad, teacher certification program, Merchant Marine Certification, NROTC, naval sciences.

FACILITIES

Housing: Coed, all-female, housing for disabled students, privatized apartment housing available next to campus. **Library Holdings:** 83,883 bound volumes. 431 periodicals. 54,187 microforms. 2,757 audiovisuals. **Special Academic Facilities/Equipment:** USTS Texas Clipper II, Radar School/Ship Bridge Simulator, Engineering Laboratory Building, Sea Camp, Center for Bioacoustics, Center for Marine Training and Safety/TEEX, Laboratory for Oceanographic and Environmental Research, Galveston Bay Information Center, Center for Ports and Waterways, Coastal Zone Laboratory, GulfCet, Marine Mammal Research Program, Naval Science, Texas State Maritime Academy, Texas Institute of Oceanography, Texas Marine Mammal Stranding Network, Sea Turtle/Fisheries Ecology Lab. **Computers:** *Recommended operating system:* Windows XP Professional. School-owned computers available for student use.

EXTRACURRICULARS

Activities: Choral groups, dance, drama/theater, literary magazine, student government, student newspaper, television station, yearbook. **Organizations:** 51 registered organizations, 16 honor societies, 4 religious organizations. **Athletics (Intercollegiate):** *Men:* crew, sailing. *Women:* crew, sailing.

ADMISSIONS

Selectivity Rating: 80 (of 100). **Freshman Academic Profile:** 14% in top 10% of high school class, 50% in top 25% of high school class, 87% in top 50% of high school class. 83% from public high schools. Average SAT I Math 553, SAT I Math middle 50% range 502-643. Average SAT I Verbal 545, SAT I Verbal middle 50% range 476-618. Average ACT 25, ACT middle 50% range 21-28. TOEFL required of all international applicants, minimum TOEFL 550. **Basis for Candidate Selection:** *Very important factors considered include:* class rank, secondary school record, standardized test scores. *Important factors considered include:* character/personal qualities, essays, extracurricular activities, recommendations, talent/ability, volunteer work, work experience. *Other factors considered include:* alumni/ae relation, interview. **Freshman Admission Requirements:** High school diploma or GED is required. *Academic units required/recommended:* 4 English required, 4 English recommended, 3 math required, 4 math recommended, 3 science required, 4 science recommended, 2 science lab required, 3 foreign language recommended, 3 social studies recommended. **Freshman Admission Statistics:** 1,148 applied, 84% accepted, 50% of those accepted enrolled. **Transfer Admission Requirements:** *Items required:* high school transcript, college transcript, essay. Minimum college GPA of 2.5 required. Lowest grade transferable C. **General Admission Information:** Application fee $35. Priority application deadline March 1. Nonfall registration accepted. Admission may be deferred. Credit offered for CEEB Advanced Placement tests.

COSTS AND FINANCIAL AID

In-state tuition $2,760. Out-of-state tuition $10,006. Room & board $4,692. Required fees $826. Average book expense $800. **Required Forms and Deadlines:** FAFSA. No deadline for regular filing. **Notification of Awards:** Applicants will be notified of awards on or about March 15. **Types of Aid:** *Need-based scholarships/grants:* Pell, SEOG, state scholarships/grants, private scholarships, the school's own gift aid. *Loans:* Direct Subsidized Stafford, Direct Unsubsidized Stafford, Direct PLUS, FFEL Subsidized Stafford, FFEL Unsubsidized Stafford, FFEL PLUS, Federal Perkins, college/university loans from institutional funds. **Student Employment:** Federal Work-Study Program available. Institutional employment available. Off-campus job opportunities are excellent. **Financial Aid Statistics:** 43% freshmen, 44% undergrads receive some form of aid. Average freshman grant $4,459. Average freshman loan $3,686. Average income from on-campus job $2,100. **Financial Aid Phone:** 409-740-4500.

TEXAS A&M UNIVERSITY—KINGSVILLE

$

700 University Blvd., MSC 114, Kingsville TX 78363
Phone: 361-593-2115 **Fax:** 361-593-2195
E-mail: ksossrx@tamuk.edu **Web:** www.tamuk.edu

STUDENTS AND FACULTY

Enrollment: 5,287, male 51%, female 49%, out-of-state 2%, international 1%. **Ethnic Representation:** African American 5%, Asian 1%, Caucasian 27%, Hispanic 67%. **Retention and Graduation:** 59% freshmen return for sophomore year. 6% freshmen graduate within 4 years. **Faculty:** Student/faculty ratio 15:1. 276 full-time faculty, 69% hold PhDs.

ACADEMICS

Degrees: Bachelor's, doctoral, master's, post-bachelor's certificate, post-master's certificate. **Academic Requirements:** General education including some course work in arts/fine arts, computer literacy, English (including composition), history, humanities, mathematics, sciences (biological or physical), social science. **Disciplines with Highest Percentage of Degrees Awarded:** Engineering/engineering technology 17%, business/marketing 15%, interdisciplinary studies 14%, social sciences and history 10%, parks and recreation 10%. **Special Study Options:** Accelerated program, cooperative (work-study) program, distance learning, double major, English as a second language, honors program, internships, study abroad, teacher certification program.

FACILITIES

Housing: Coed, all-female, all-male, apartments for married students. **Library Holdings:** 358,466 bound volumes. 2,304 periodicals. 183,416 microforms. 3,224 audiovisuals.

EXTRACURRICULARS

Activities: Choral groups, concert band, dance, drama/theater, jazz band, marching band, music ensembles, musical theater, pep band, radio station, student government, student newspaper, television station. **Organizations:** 2% of men join fraternities, 2% of women join sororities.

ADMISSIONS

Selectivity Rating: 62 (of 100). **Freshman Academic Profile:** ACT middle 50% range 21-28. **Basis for Candidate Selection:** *Important factors considered include:* class rank, secondary school record, standardized test scores. **Freshman Admission Requirements:** High school diploma or GED is required. *Academic units required/recommended:* 24 total recommended; 4 English recommended, 3 math recommended, 3 science recommended, 3 foreign language recommended, 4 social studies recommended, 3 history recommended, 3 elective recommended. **Freshman Admission Statistics:** 2,105 applied, 99% accepted, 43% of those accepted enrolled. **Transfer Admission Requirements:** Minimum college GPA of 2.0 required. Lowest grade transferable F. **General Admission Information:** Application fee $15. Admission may be deferred.

COSTS AND FINANCIAL AID

In-state tuition $1,380. Out-of-state tuition $7,590. Room & board $3,966. Required fees $1,602. Average book expense $614.

TEXAS COLLEGE

2404 North Grand Avenue, Tyler, TX 75702
Phone: 903-593-8311 **E-mail:** afrancis@texacollege.edu
Fax: 903-593-0588 **Web:** www.texascollege.edu

This private school, which is affiliated with the Methodist Church, was founded in 1894.

STUDENTS AND FACULTY

Enrollment: 511. **Student Body:** Male 37%, female 63%, out-of-state 33%. **Ethnic Representation:** African American 96%, Asian 1%, Caucasian 1%, Hispanic 2%. **Retention and Graduation:** 25% freshmen graduate within 4 years. 7% grads go on to further study within 1 year.

ACADEMICS

Degrees: Associate's, bachelor's. **Majors with Highest Enrollment:** Business administration/management; computer science; sociology. **Disciplines with Highest Percentage of Degrees Awarded:** Biological life sciences 10%, education 7%, social sciences and history 6%, visual and performing arts 4%, business/marketing 3%.

FACILITIES

Housing: All-female, all-male, apartments for single students, off-campus housing for students. **Computers:** School-owned computers available for student use.

EXTRACURRICULARS

Activities: Choral groups, jazz band, student government, student newspaper, yearbook. **Organizations:** 27 registered organizations, 1 religious organization. **Athletics (Intercollegiate):** *Men:* baseball, basketball, cheerleading, softball, track & field. *Women:* basketball, cheerleading, softball, track & field, volleyball.

ADMISSIONS

Selectivity Rating: 63 (of 100). **Freshman Academic Profile:** 15% in top 10% of high school class, 26% in top 25% of high school class, 50% in top 50% of high school class. **Basis for Candidate Selection:** *Very important factors considered include:* secondary school record. **Freshman Admission Requirements:** High school diploma or GED is required. *Academic units required/recommended:* 16 total required; 4 English required, 2 math required, 2 science required, 2 social studies required, 2 history required, 4 elective required. **Freshman Admission Statistics:** 981 applied, 26% accepted, 44% of those accepted enrolled. **Transfer Admission Requirements:** *Items required:* college transcript, statement of good standing from prior school. Lowest grade transferable C. **General Admission Information:** Application fee $10. Priority application deadline August 1. Early decision application deadline August 15. Regular application deadline August 1. Nonfall registration accepted.

COSTS AND FINANCIAL AID

Tuition $6,305. Room & board $2,930. Required fees $445. Average book expense $556. **Required Forms and Deadlines:** FAFSA and institution's own financial aid form. No deadline for regular filing. Priority filing deadline April 15. **Notification of Awards:** Applicants will be notified of awards on a rolling basis beginning on or about April 15. **Types of Aid:** *Need-based scholarships/grants:* Pell, SEOG, state scholarships/grants, private scholarships, the school's own gift aid. *Loans:* Federal Perkins, state loans, college/university loans from institutional funds. **Student Employment:** Federal Work-Study Program available. Off-campus job opportunities are good. **Financial Aid Statistics:** Average freshman grant $6,000. **Financial Aid Phone:** 903-593-8311.

TEXAS LUTHERAN UNIVERSITY

1000 West Court Street, Seguin, TX 78155
Phone: 800-771-8521 **E-mail:** admissions@tlu.edu **CEEB Code:** 6823
Fax: 830-372-8096 **Web:** www.tlu.edu **ACT Code:** 4214

This private school, which is affiliated with the Lutheran Church, was founded in 1891. It has a 161-acre campus.

STUDENTS AND FACULTY

Enrollment: 1,460. **Student Body:** Male 46%, female 54%, out-of-state 5%, international 3%. **Ethnic Representation:** African American 7%, Asian 2%, Caucasian 73%, Hispanic 17%, Native American 1%. **Retention and Graduation:** 63% freshmen return for sophomore year. 27% freshmen graduate within 4 years. 17% grads go on to further study within 1 year. 5% grads pursue business degrees. 3% grads pursue law degrees. 5% grads pursue medical degrees. **Faculty:** Student/faculty ratio 15:1. 70 full-time faculty, 74% hold PhDs. 100% faculty teach undergrads.

ACADEMICS

Degrees: Bachelor's. **Academic Requirements:** General education including some course work in arts/fine arts, English (including composition), history, humanities, mathematics, sciences (biological or physical), social science, theology. **Classes:** 10-19 students in an average class. **Disciplines with Highest Percentage of Degrees Awarded:** Business/marketing 31%, education 16%, biological life sciences 10%, psychology 10%, social sciences and history 6%. **Special Study Options:** Double major, dual enrollment, honors program, independent study, internships, student-designed major, study abroad, teacher certification program, senior seminars.

FACILITIES

Housing: Coed, all-female, all-male, apartments for married students, apartments for single students, housing for disabled students. **Library Holdings:** 156,321 bound volumes. 633 periodicals. 115,445 microforms. 10,298 audiovisuals. **Special Academic Facilities/Equipment:** Mexican-American Studies Center, geological museum. **Computers:** School-owned computers available for student use.

EXTRACURRICULARS

Activities: Choral groups, concert band, drama/theater, jazz band, literary magazine, music ensembles, musical theater, pep band, student government, student newspaper, symphony orchestra, yearbook. **Organizations:** 55 registered organizations, 10 honor societies, 3 religious organizations, 5 fraternities (17% men join), 4 sororities (16% women join). **Athletics (Intercollegiate):** *Men:* baseball, basketball, football, golf, soccer, tennis. *Women:* basketball, cross-country, golf, soccer, softball, tennis, track & field, volleyball.

ADMISSIONS

Selectivity Rating: 66 (of 100). **Freshman Academic Profile:** Average high school GPA 3.4. 24% in top 10% of high school class, 57% in top 25% of high school class, 84% in top 50% of high school class. 88% from public high schools. Average SAT I Math 526, SAT I Math middle 50% range 480-580. Average SAT I Verbal 520, SAT I Verbal middle 50% range 470-550. Average ACT 21, ACT middle 50% range 19-25. TOEFL required of all international applicants, minimum TOEFL 550. **Basis for Candidate Selection:** *Very important factors considered include:* class rank, secondary school record. *Important factors considered include:* essays, recommendations, standardized test scores, volunteer work. *Other factors considered include:* character/personal qualities, extracurricular activities, interview, work experience. **Freshman Admission Requirements:** High school diploma or GED is required. *Academic units required/recommended:* 21 total recommended; 4 English recommended, 3 math recommended, 3 science recommended, 2 science lab recommended, 2 foreign language recommended, 3 social studies recommended, 2 history recommended, 4 elective recommended. **Freshman Admission Statistics:** 857 applied, 81% accepted, 48% of those accepted enrolled. **Transfer Admission Requirements:** *Items required:* high school transcript, college transcript, essay. Minimum college GPA of 2.3 required. Lowest grade transferable C. **General Admission Information:** Application fee $25. Priority application deadline May 1. Regular application deadline August 1. Nonfall registration accepted. Credit and/or placement offered for CEEB Advanced Placement tests.

COSTS AND FINANCIAL AID

Tuition $13,440. Room & board $4,120. Required fees $100. Average book expense $1,200. **Required Forms and Deadlines:** FAFSA. Priority filing deadline April 15. **Notification of Awards:** Applicants will be notified of awards on a rolling basis beginning on or about March 1. **Types of Aid:** *Need-based scholarships/grants:* Pell, SEOG, state scholarships/grants, private scholarships, the school's own gift aid. *Loans:* FFEL Subsidized Stafford, FFEL Unsubsidized Stafford, FFEL PLUS, Federal Perkins, state loans, Key, Signature. **Student Employment:** Federal Work-Study Program available. Institutional employment available. Off-campus job opportunities are fair. **Financial Aid Statistics:** 67% freshmen, 62% undergrads receive some form of aid. Average freshman grant $6,053. Average freshman loan $2,995. Average income from on-campus job $800. **Financial Aid Phone:** 830-372-8075.

TEXAS SOUTHERN UNIVERSITY

3100 Cleburne Street, Houston, TX 77004
Phone: 713-313-7420 **CEEB Code:** 6824
Fax: 713-313-4317 **Web:** www.tsu.edu **ACT Code:** 4216

This public school was founded in 1949. It has a 125-acre campus.

STUDENTS AND FACULTY

Enrollment: 8,832. **Student Body:** Out-of-state 9%, international 7% (40 countries represented). **Ethnic Representation:** African American 84%, Asian 2%, Caucasian 4%, Hispanic 8%, Native American 1%. **Retention and Graduation:** 46% grads go on to further study within 1 year. 11% grads pursue business degrees. 15% grads pursue law degrees. 3% grads pursue medical degrees.

ACADEMICS

Degrees: Bachelor's, master's. **Special Study Options:** Cooperative (work-study) program.

FACILITIES

Housing: Coed, all-female, all-male, apartments for single students. **Library Holdings:** 747,785 bound volumes. 2,398 periodicals. 349,969 microforms. **Special Academic Facilities/Equipment:** Excellence in education center, hunger and world peace center, minority institute reserve center. **Computers:** *Recommended operating system:* Mac.

EXTRACURRICULARS

Activities: Radio station, student government, television station, yearbook. **Organizations:** 64 registered organizations, 10 honor societies, 15 religious organizations, 4 fraternities (15% men join), 4 sororities (15% women join).

ADMISSIONS

Selectivity Rating: 72 (of 100). **Freshman Academic Profile:** 15% in top 10% of high school class, 85% in top 25% of high school class, 95% in top 50% of high school class. 90% from public high schools. TOEFL required of all international applicants, **Freshman Admission Requirements:** High school diploma or GED is required. *Academic units required/recommended:* 15 total recommended; 4 English recommended, 2 math recommended, 2 science recommended, 2 social studies recommended. **Transfer Admission Requirements:** Minimum college GPA of 2.0 required. Lowest grade transferable D. **General Admission Information:** Early decision application deadline June 15. Regular application deadline August 15. Nonfall registration accepted.

COSTS AND FINANCIAL AID

In-state tuition $2,058. Out-of-state tuition $7,180. Room & board $4,000. Required fees $152. Average book expense $600. **Required Forms and Deadlines:** FAFSA and institution's own financial aid form. **Types of Aid:** *Need-based scholarships/grants:* state scholarships/grants. *Loans:* FFEL Subsidized Stafford, FFEL PLUS. **Student Employment:** Federal Work-Study Program available. Institutional employment available. Off-campus job opportunities are good. **Financial Aid Statistics:** Average income from on-campus job $900. **Financial Aid Phone:** 713-527-7530.

TEXAS TECH UNIVERSITY

PO Box 45005, Lubbock, TX 79409-5005
Phone: 806-742-1480 **E-mail:** nsr@ttu.edu **CEEB Code:** 6827
Fax: 806-742-0980 **Web:** www.ttu.edu **ACT Code:** 4220

This public school was founded in 1923. It has a 1,839-acre campus.

STUDENTS AND FACULTY

Enrollment: 22,768. **Student Body:** Male 55%, female 45%, out-of-state 5%, international 1%. **Ethnic Representation:** African American 3%, Asian 2%, Caucasian 83%, Hispanic 11%, Native American 1%. **Retention and Graduation:** 82% freshmen return for sophomore year. 22% freshmen graduate within 4 years. **Faculty:** Student/faculty ratio 20:1. 977 full-time faculty, 93% hold PhDs. 100% faculty teach undergrads.

ACADEMICS

Degrees: Bachelor's, doctoral, first professional, master's. **Academic Requirements:** General education including some course work in arts/fine arts, English (including composition), foreign languages, history, humanities, mathematics, philosophy, sciences (biological or physical), social science, speech. **Classes:** 20-29 students in an average class. 20-29 students in an average lab/discussion section. **Majors with Highest Enrollment:** Finance, general; marketing/marketing management, general; multi/interdisciplinary studies. **Disciplines with Highest Percentage of Degrees Awarded:** Business/marketing 31%, interdisciplinary studies 9%, home economics and vocational home economics 8%, engineering/engineering technology 7%, communications/communication technologies 6%. **Special Study Options:** Accelerated program, cooperative (work-study) program, cross registration, distance learning, double major, dual enrollment, English as a second language, student exchange program (domestic), external degree program, honors program, independent study, internships, liberal arts/career combination, student-designed major, study abroad, teacher certification program. Undergrads may take grad-level classes.

FACILITIES

Housing: Coed, all-female, all-male, apartments for single students, housing for disabled students, housing for international students. **Library Holdings:** 2,234,274 bound volumes. 18,082 periodicals. 2,121,127 microforms. 82,191 audiovisuals. **Special Academic Facilities/Equipment:** Museum, child development center, textile research center, agricultural research center, planetarium, ranching heritage center, semi-arid land studies center, ranching heritage center, seismological observatory. **Computers:** School-owned computers available for student use.

EXTRACURRICULARS

Activities: Choral groups, concert band, dance, drama/theater, jazz band, literary magazine, marching band, music ensembles, musical theater, opera, pep band, radio station, student government, student newspaper, student-run film society, symphony orchestra, television station, yearbook. **Organizations:** 370 registered organizations, 28 honor societies, 33 religious organizations, 29 fraternities (13% men join), 20 sororities (18% women join). **Athletics (Intercollegiate):** *Men:* baseball, basketball, cross-country, football, golf, tennis, track & field. *Women:* basketball, cross-country, golf, soccer, softball, tennis, track & field, volleyball.

ADMISSIONS

Selectivity Rating: 74 (of 100). **Freshman Academic Profile:** 22% in top 10% of high school class, 53% in top 25% of high school class, 89% in top 50% of high school class. Average SAT I Math 566, SAT I Math middle 50% range 500-610. Average SAT I Verbal 546, SAT I Verbal middle 50% range 480-590. Average ACT 24, ACT middle 50% range 21-26. TOEFL required of all international applicants, minimum TOEFL 550. **Basis for Candidate Selection:** *Very important factors considered include:* class rank, secondary school record, standardized test scores. *Important factors considered include:* alumni/ae relation, character/personal qualities, extracurricular activities, talent/ability, volunteer work, work experience. *Other factors considered include:* essays, recommendations. **Freshman Admission Requirements:** High school diploma is required and GED is not accepted. *Academic units required/recommended:* 17 total required; 4 English required, 3 math required, 2 science required, 2 science lab required, 2 foreign language required, 2 social studies required, 3 elective required. **Freshman Admission Statistics:** 13,101 applied, 69% accepted, 50% of those accepted enrolled. **Transfer Admission Requirements:** *Items required:* college transcript, statement of good standing from prior school. Minimum college GPA of 2.2 required. Lowest grade transferable C. **General Admission Information:** Application fee $50. Nonfall registration accepted. Credit and/or placement offered for CEEB Advanced Placement tests.

COSTS AND FINANCIAL AID

Required Forms and Deadlines: FAFSA and institution's own financial aid form. No deadline for regular filing. Priority filing deadline May 1. **Notification of Awards:** Applicants will be notified of awards on a rolling basis beginning on or about May 1. **Types of Aid:** *Need-based scholarships/grants:* Pell, SEOG, state scholarships/grants, private scholarships, the school's own gift aid. *Loans:* FFEL Subsidized Stafford, FFEL Unsubsidized Stafford, FFEL PLUS, Federal Perkins, state loans, college/university loans from institutional funds. **Student Employment:** Federal Work-Study Program available. Institutional employment available. Off-campus job opportunities are excellent. **Financial Aid Statistics:** 32% freshmen, 37% undergrads receive some form of aid. **Financial Aid Phone:** 806-742-3681.

See page 1228.

TEXAS WESLEYAN UNIVERSITY

1201 Wesleyan, Fort Worth, TX 76105-1536
Phone: 817-531-4422 **E-mail:** info@txwesleyan.edu **CEEB Code:** 6828
Fax: 817-531-7515 **Web:** www.txwesleyan.edu **ACT Code:** 4222

This private school, which is affiliated with the Methodist Church, was founded in 1890. It has a 75-acre campus.

STUDENTS AND FACULTY

Enrollment: 1,630. **Student Body:** Male 36%, female 64%, out-of-state 1%, international 2% (32 countries represented). **Ethnic Representation:** African American 19%, Asian 2%, Caucasian 58%, Hispanic 18%, Native American 1%. **Retention and Graduation:** 58% freshmen return for sophomore year. **Faculty:** Student/faculty ratio 15:1. 110 full-time faculty, 82% hold PhDs.

ACADEMICS

Degrees: Bachelor's, first professional, master's. **Academic Requirements:** General education including some course work in arts/fine arts, English (including composition), history, humanities, mathematics, sciences (biological or physical), social science, religion. **Classes:** 10-19 students in an average class. **Majors with Highest Enrollment:** Business administration/management; radio and television; psychology, general. **Disciplines with Highest Percentage of Degrees Awarded:** Business/marketing 31%, education 26%, interdisciplinary studies 8%, psychology 6%, visual and performing arts 4%. **Special Study Options:** English as a second language, independent study, internships, study abroad, teacher certification program, weekend college.

FACILITIES

Housing: Coed, all-female, all-male. **Library Holdings:** 192,885 bound volumes. 610 periodicals. 457,424 microforms. 5,302 audiovisuals. **Special Academic Facilities/Equipment:** Art gallery. **Computers:** School-owned computers available for student use.

EXTRACURRICULARS

Activities: Choral groups, concert band, drama/theater, jazz band, literary magazine, music ensembles, musical theater, opera, pep band, student government, student newspaper. **Organizations:** 55 registered organizations, 7 honor societies, 5 religious organizations, 3 fraternities, 2 sororities. **Athletics (Intercollegiate):** *Men:* baseball, basketball, cheerleading, golf, soccer, tennis. *Women:* basketball, cheerleading, soccer, softball, tennis, volleyball.

ADMISSIONS

Selectivity Rating: 71 (of 100). **Freshman Academic Profile:** Average high school GPA 3.3. 14% in top 10% of high school class, 37% in top 25% of high school class, 68% in top 50% of high school class. 94% from public high schools. Average SAT I Math 472, SAT I Math middle 50% range 430-550. Average SAT I Verbal 486, SAT I Verbal middle 50% range 450-550. Average ACT 20, ACT middle 50% range 17-23. TOEFL required of all international applicants, minimum TOEFL 550. **Basis for Candidate Selection:** *Very important factors considered include:* character/personal qualities, secondary school record. *Important factors considered include:* class rank, essays, interview, recommendations, standardized test scores. *Other factors considered include:* alumni/ae relation, extracurricular activities, talent/ability, volunteer work, work experience. **Freshman Admission Requirements:** High school diploma or GED is required. *Academic units required/recommended:* 20 total recommended; 4 English recommended, 4 math recommended, 2 science recommended, 2 social studies recommended, 1 history recommended, 7 elective recommended. **Freshman Admission Statistics:** 335 applied, 55% accepted, 76% of those accepted enrolled. **Transfer Admission Requirements:** *Items required:* college transcript. Minimum college GPA of 2.0 required. Lowest grade transferable D. **General Admission Information:** Application fee $25. Nonfall registration accepted. Admission may be deferred for a maximum of 1 year. Credit offered for CEEB Advanced Placement tests.

COSTS AND FINANCIAL AID

Tuition $10,306. Room & board $3,990. Required fees $970. Average book expense $675. **Required Forms and Deadlines:** FAFSA and institution's own financial aid form. Priority filing deadline April 15. **Notification of Awards:** Applicants will be notified of awards on a rolling basis beginning on or about April 15. **Types of Aid:** *Need-based scholarships/grants:* Pell, SEOG, state scholarships/grants, private scholarships, the school's own gift aid. *Loans:* FFEL Subsidized Stafford, FFEL Unsubsidized Stafford, FFEL PLUS, state loans, college/university loans from institutional funds. **Student Employment:** Federal Work-Study Program available. Institutional employment available. Off-campus job opportunities are excellent. **Financial Aid Statistics:** Average freshman grant $2,000. Average freshman loan $2,364. Average income from on-campus job $2,334. **Financial Aid Phone:** 817-531-4420.

TEXAS WOMAN'S UNIVERSITY

PO Box 425589, Denton, TX 76204-5589
Phone: 940-898-3188 **E-mail:** admissions@twu.edu **CEEB Code:** 6826
Fax: 940-898-3081 **Web:** www.twu.edu **ACT Code:** 4224

This public school was founded in 1901. It has a 270-acre campus.

STUDENTS AND FACULTY

Enrollment: 5,752. **Student Body:** Out-of-state 3%, international 4%. **Ethnic Representation:** African American 14%, Asian 2%, Caucasian 74%, Hispanic 8%, Native American 1%.

ACADEMICS

Degrees: Bachelor's, doctoral, master's. **Special Study Options:** Cross registration, distance learning, double major, dual enrollment, honors program, independent study, internships, study abroad, teacher certification program.

FACILITIES

Housing: Coed, all-female, apartments for married students, apartments for single students, housing for international students. **Library Holdings:** 788,271 bound volumes. 2,899 periodicals. 652,861 microforms. **Special Academic Facilities/Equipment:** Museum, radiation lab, language lab, lab nursery school, radio and TV studio. **Computers:** *Recommended operating system:* Mac. School-owned computers available for student use.

EXTRACURRICULARS

Activities: Choral groups, dance, drama/theater, jazz band, music ensembles, musical theater, student government, student newspaper, television station. **Organizations:** 5 sororities (2% women join). **Athletics (Intercollegiate):** *Women:* basketball, gymnastics, tennis, volleyball.

ADMISSIONS

Selectivity Rating: 66 (of 100). **Freshman Academic Profile:** TOEFL required of all international applicants, minimum TOEFL 550. **Freshman Admission Requirements:** High school diploma is required and GED is not accepted. *Academic units required/recommended:* 16 total required; 4 English required, 3 math required, 2 science required, 3 social studies required, 3 elective required. **Transfer Admission Requirements:** *Items required:* college transcript, statement of good standing from prior school. Minimum college GPA of 2.0 required. Lowest grade transferable D. **General Admission Information:** Early decision application deadline March 1. Regular application deadline July 15. Nonfall registration accepted. Credit and/or placement offered for CEEB Advanced Placement tests.

COSTS AND FINANCIAL AID

In-state tuition $2,084. Out-of-state tuition $7,196. Room & board $3,578. Required fees $60. Average book expense $730. **Required Forms and Deadlines:** FAFSA and institution's own financial aid form. **Types of Aid:** *Need-based scholarships/grants:* Pell, SEOG, state scholarships/grants, private scholarships, the school's own gift aid, Federal Nursing. *Loans:* FFEL Subsidized Stafford, FFEL Unsubsidized Stafford, FFEL PLUS, Federal Perkins, Federal Nursing, state loans, college/university loans from institutional funds. **Student Employment:** Federal Work-Study Program available. Institutional employment available. Off-campus job opportunities are good. **Financial Aid Statistics:** Average freshman grant $1,700. Average income from on-campus job $1,700. **Financial Aid Phone:** 817-898-3050.

THIEL COLLEGE

75 College Avenue, Greenville, PA 16125
Phone: 724-589-2345 **E-mail:** admission@thiel.edu **CEEB Code:** 2910
Fax: 724-589-2013 **Web:** www.thiel.edu **ACT Code:** 3730

This private school, which is affiliated with the Lutheran Church, was founded in 1866. It has a 135-acre campus.

STUDENTS AND FACULTY

Enrollment: 1,279. **Student Body:** Male 51%, female 49%, out-of-state 26%, international 4% (12 countries represented). **Ethnic Representation:** African American 8%, Caucasian 80%, Hispanic 1%. **Retention and Graduation:** 64% freshmen return for sophomore year. 32% freshmen graduate within 4 years. 13% grads go on to further study within 1 year. 12% grads pursue business degrees. **Faculty:** Student/faculty ratio 15:1. 61 full-time faculty, 70% hold PhDs. 100% faculty teach undergrads.

ACADEMICS

Degrees: Associate's, bachelor's. **Academic Requirements:** General education including some course work in arts/fine arts, English (including composition), foreign languages, history, humanities, mathematics, sciences (biological or physical). **Classes:** Under 10 students in an average class. 10-19 students in an average lab/discussion section. **Majors with Highest Enrollment:** Business administration/management; biology/biological sciences, general; psychology, general. **Disciplines with Highest Percentage of Degrees Awarded:** Business/marketing 32%, social sciences and history 16%, psychology 15%, health professions and related sciences 8%, communications/communication technologies 5%. **Special Study Options:** Cooperative (work-study) program, double major, English as a second language, honors program, internships, liberal arts/career combination, study abroad, teacher certification program.

FACILITIES

Housing: Coed, all-female, apartments for single students, fraternities and/or sororities, living & learning housing. **Library Holdings:** 131,176 bound volumes. 532 periodicals. 39,970 microforms. 6,463 audiovisuals. **Special Academic Facilities/Equipment:** Art gallery, language lab, center for productive retirement, enterprise institute. **Computers:** *Recommended operating system:* Windows ME. School-owned computers available for student use.

EXTRACURRICULARS

Activities: Choral groups, concert band, drama/theater, literary magazine, musical theater, radio station, student government, student newspaper, symphony orchestra, yearbook, pep band. **Organizations:** 40 registered organizations, 8 honor societies, 4 religious organizations, 4 fraternities (10% men join), 4 sororities (19% women join). **Athletics (Intercollegiate):** *Men:* baseball, basketball, cheerleading, cross-country, football, golf, indoor track, soccer, tennis, track & field, wrestling. *Women:* basketball, cheerleading, cross-country, golf, indoor track, lacrosse, soccer, softball, tennis, track & field, volleyball.

ADMISSIONS

Selectivity Rating: 67 (of 100). **Freshman Academic Profile:** Average high school GPA 3.0. 9% in top 10% of high school class, 27% in top 25% of high school class, 64% in top 50% of high school class. 88% from public high schools. Average SAT I Math 488, SAT I Math middle 50% range 420-550. Average SAT I Verbal 485, SAT I Verbal middle 50% range 420-540. Average ACT 20, ACT middle 50% range 17-22. TOEFL required of all international applicants, minimum TOEFL 450. **Basis for Candidate Selection:** *Very important factors considered include:* secondary school record. *Important factors considered include:* character/personal qualities, class rank, extracurricular activities, interview, recommendations, standardized test scores, talent/ability.

Other factors considered include: alumni/ae relation, essays, volunteer work, work experience. **Freshman Admission Requirements:** High school diploma or GED is required. *Academic units required/recommended:* 13 total recommended; 4 English recommended, 2 math recommended, 2 science recommended, 2 science lab recommended, 2 foreign language recommended, 3 social studies recommended. **Freshman Admission Statistics:** 1,537 applied, 81% accepted, 32% of those accepted enrolled. **Transfer Admission Requirements:** *Items required:* college transcript. Minimum high school GPA of 2.0 required. Minimum college GPA of 2.0 required. Lowest grade transferable C. **General Admission Information:** Application fee $25. Priority application deadline April 1. Regular application deadline August 15. Nonfall registration accepted. Admission may be deferred for a maximum of 1 year. Credit and/or placement offered for CEEB Advanced Placement tests.

COSTS AND FINANCIAL AID

Tuition $11,688. Room & board $5,974. Required fees $757. Average book expense $600. **Required Forms and Deadlines:** FAFSA and state aid form. No deadline for regular filing. Priority filing deadline March 1. **Notification of Awards:** Applicants will be notified of awards on a rolling basis beginning on or about February 1. **Types of Aid:** *Need-based scholarships/grants:* Pell, SEOG, state scholarships/grants, private scholarships, the school's own gift aid. *Loans:* FFEL Subsidized Stafford, FFEL Unsubsidized Stafford, FFEL PLUS, Federal Perkins, college/university loans from institutional funds. **Student Employment:** Federal Work-Study Program available. Institutional employment available. Off-campus job opportunities are fair. **Financial Aid Statistics:** 86% freshmen, 82% undergrads receive some form of aid. Average freshman grant $7,662. Average freshman loan $4,600. **Financial Aid Phone:** 724-589-2250.

THOMAS AQUINAS COLLEGE

10000 North Ojai Road, Santa Paula, CA 93060
Phone: 805-525-4417 **E-mail:** admissions@thomasaquinas.edu **CEEB Code:** 4828
Fax: 805-525-9342 **Web:** www.thomasaquinas.edu **ACT Code:** 425

This private school, which is affiliated with the Roman Catholic Church, was founded in 1971. It has a 170-acre campus.

STUDENTS AND FACULTY

Enrollment: 330. **Student Body:** Out-of-state 48%, international 8% (5 countries represented). **Ethnic Representation:** Asian 4%, Caucasian 87%, Hispanic 8%. **Retention and Graduation:** 89% freshmen return for sophomore year. 99% freshmen graduate within 4 years. 36% grads go on to further study within 1 year. 2% grads pursue business degrees. 11% grads pursue law degrees. 4% grads pursue medical degrees. **Faculty:** Student/faculty ratio 10:1. 30 full-time faculty, 73% hold PhDs. 100% faculty teach undergrads.

ACADEMICS

Degrees: Bachelor's. **Academic Requirements:** General education including some course work in English (including composition), foreign languages, history, humanities, mathematics, philosophy, sciences (biological or physical), social science, theology, music, logic, rhetoric. **Classes:** 10-19 students in an average class. **Disciplines with Highest Percentage of Degrees Awarded:** Liberal arts/general studies 100%. **Special Study Options:** The sole academic program offered is a "cross-disciplinary" curriculum of liberal education through reading and analyzing the "Great Books," with special emphasis on theology, philosophy, mathematics, laboratory science, and literature.

FACILITIES

Housing: All-female, all-male. Students living with their families may live off campus. **Library Holdings:** 51,000 bound volumes. 80 periodicals. 7,900 microforms. 2,200 audiovisuals. **Computers:** School-owned computers available for student use.

EXTRACURRICULARS

Activities: Choral groups, drama/theater, literary magazine, music ensembles. **Organizations:** 2 registered organizations, 3 religious organizations.

ADMISSIONS

Selectivity Rating: 83 (of 100). **Freshman Academic Profile:** Average high school GPA 3.6. 44% in top 10% of high school class, 84% in top 25% of high school class, 100% in top 50% of high school class. 23% from public high schools. Average SAT I Math 626, SAT I Math middle 50% range 570-670. Average SAT I Verbal 669, SAT I Verbal middle 50% range 620-710. Average ACT 28, ACT middle 50% range 27-30. TOEFL required of all international applicants, minimum TOEFL 550. **Basis for Candidate Selection:** *Very important factors considered include:* character/personal qualities, essays, recommendations, secondary school record. *Important factors considered include:* religious affiliation/commitment, standardized test scores. *Other factors considered include:* extracurricular activities, interview, talent/ability, volunteer work, work experience. **Freshman Admission Requirements:** High school diploma or GED is required. *Academic units required/recommended:* 19 total recommended; 4 English recommended, 3 math recommended, 3 science recommended, 2 foreign language recommended, 2 history recommended, 5 elective recommended. **Freshman Admission Statistics:** 189 applied, 80% accepted, 68% of those accepted enrolled. **General Admission Information:** Admission may be deferred for a maximum of 1 year. Neither credit nor placement offered for CEEB Advanced Placement tests.

COSTS AND FINANCIAL AID

Tuition $17,000. Room & board $5,000. Required fees $0. Average book expense $450. **Required Forms and Deadlines:** FAFSA, institution's own financial aid form, state aid form, noncustodial (divorced/separated) parent's statement and Tax return. No deadline for regular filing. **Notification of Awards:** Applicants will be notified of awards on a rolling basis beginning on or about November 1. **Types of Aid:** *Need-based scholarships/grants:* state scholarships/grants, private scholarships, the school's own gift aid. *Loans:* FFEL Subsidized Stafford, FFEL Unsubsidized Stafford, FFEL PLUS, college/university loans from institutional funds, Canadian student Loans. **Student Employment:** Off-campus job opportunities are good. **Financial Aid Statistics:** 73% freshmen, 71% undergrads receive some form of aid. Average freshman grant $7,714. Average freshman loan $2,625. **Financial Aid Phone:** 800-634-9797.

THOMAS COLLEGE

180 West River Road, Waterville, ME 04901
Phone: 207-859-1101 **E-mail:** admiss@thomas.edu **CEEB Code:** 2052
Fax: 207-859-1114 **Web:** www.thomas.edu **ACT Code:** 1663

This private school was founded in 1894. It has a 70-acre campus.

STUDENTS AND FACULTY

Enrollment: 671. **Student Body:** Male 47%, female 53%, out-of-state 16%. **Ethnic Representation:** African American 1%, Caucasian 93%. **Retention and Graduation:** 64% freshmen return for sophomore year. 41% freshmen graduate within 4 years. 7% grads go on to further study within 1 year. 7% grads pursue business degrees. **Faculty:** Student/faculty ratio 12:1. 22 full-time faculty, 54% hold PhDs. 100% faculty teach undergrads.

ACADEMICS

Degrees: Associate's, bachelor's, master's. **Academic Requirements:** General education including some course work in computer literacy, English (including composition), history, humanities, mathematics, philosophy, sciences (biological or physical), social science. **Classes:** 10-19 students in an average class. **Majors with Highest Enrollment:** Accounting; accounting and finance; computer and information sciences, general. **Disciplines with Highest Percentage of Degrees Awarded:** Business/marketing 74%, computer and information sciences 24%, education 2%. **Special Study Options:** Cooperative (work-study) program, cross registration, independent study, internships, study abroad, teacher certification program, double major.

FACILITIES

Housing: Coed, apartments for single students. **Library Holdings:** 23,000 bound volumes. 3,050 periodicals. 500 microforms. 440 audiovisuals. **Computers:** *Recommended operating system:* Windows XP. School-owned computers available for student use.

EXTRACURRICULARS

Activities: Drama/theater, student government, student newspaper, yearbook. **Organizations:** 20 registered organizations, 3 honor societies, 1 fraternity (3% men join), 2 sororities (5% women join). **Athletics (Intercollegiate):** *Men:* baseball, basketball, golf, soccer, tennis. *Women:* basketball, field hockey, soccer, softball, volleyball.

ADMISSIONS

Selectivity Rating: 63 (of 100). **Freshman Academic Profile:** Average high school GPA 2.8. 6% in top 10% of high school class, 22% in top 25% of high school class, 58% in top 50% of high school class. Average SAT I Math 469, SAT I Math middle 50% range 410-530. Average SAT I Verbal 449, SAT I Verbal middle 50% range 420-510. TOEFL required of all international applicants, minimum TOEFL 530. **Basis for Candidate Selection:** *Very important factors considered include:* secondary school record. *Important factors considered include:* class rank, essays, recommendations, standardized test scores. *Other factors considered include:* alumni/ae relation, character/personal qualities, extracurricular activities, interview, talent/ability, volunteer work, work experience. **Freshman Admission Requirements:** High school diploma or GED is required. *Academic units required/recommended:* 16 total required; 4 English required, 3 math required, 3 science required, 2 foreign language required, 2 social studies required, 2 elective required. **Freshman Admission Statistics:** 428 applied, 93% accepted, 46% of those accepted enrolled. **Transfer Admission Requirements:** *Items required:* high school transcript, college transcript, essay. Minimum high school GPA of 2.0 required. Minimum college GPA of 2.0 required. Lowest grade transferable C. **General Admission Information:** Application fee $25. Nonfall registration accepted. Admission may be deferred for a maximum of 2 years. Credit and/or placement offered for CEEB Advanced Placement tests.

COSTS AND FINANCIAL AID

Tuition $13,570. Room & board $6,070. Required fees $320. Average book expense $700. **Required Forms and Deadlines:** FAFSA. No deadline for regular filing. Priority filing deadline February 15. **Notification of Awards:** Applicants will be notified of awards on a rolling basis beginning on or about March 15. **Types of Aid:** *Need-based scholarships/grants:* Pell, SEOG, state scholarships/grants, private scholarships, the school's own gift aid. *Loans:* Direct Subsidized Stafford, Direct Unsubsidized Stafford, Direct PLUS, Federal Perkins. **Student Employment:** Federal Work-Study Program available. Institutional employment available. Off-campus job opportunities are excellent. **Financial Aid Statistics:** 93% freshmen, 89% undergrads receive some form of aid. Average freshman grant $8,261. Average freshman loan $5,760. **Financial Aid Phone:** 207-859-1105.

THOMAS EDISON STATE COLLEGE

101 West State Street, Trenton, NJ 08608-1176
Phone: 609-984-1150 **E-mail:** info@tesc.edu **CEEB Code:** 2612
Fax: 609-984-8447 **Web:** www.tesc.edu **ACT Code:** 274872

This public school was founded in 1972. It has a 2-acre campus.

STUDENTS AND FACULTY

Enrollment: 9,012. **Student Body:** Out-of-state 44%, international 3%. **Ethnic Representation:** African American 10%, Asian 2%, Caucasian 67%, Hispanic 4%, Native American 1%.

ACADEMICS

Degrees: Associate's, bachelor's, certificate, master's. **Academic Requirements:** General education including some course work in English (including composition), humanities, mathematics, sciences (biological or physical), social science. **Majors with Highest Enrollment:** Business administration/management; liberal arts and sciences/liberal studies; multi/interdisciplinary studies. **Disciplines with Highest Percentage of Degrees Awarded:** Liberal arts/general studies 38%, physical sciences 16%, business/marketing 12%, psychology 6%, social sciences and history 5%. **Special Study Options:** Distance learning, double major, dual enrollment, external degree program, independent study, joint degree with University of Medicine and Dentistry of New Jersey, BS in health sciences.

FACILITIES

Computers: School-owned computers available for student use.

ADMISSIONS

Selectivity Rating: 67 (of 100). **Freshman Academic Profile:** TOEFL required of all international applicants, minimum TOEFL 500. **Freshman Admission Requirements:** High school diploma or GED is required. **Transfer Admission Requirements:** *Items required:* high school transcript, college transcript. Minimum college GPA of 2.0 required. Lowest grade transferable D. **General Admission Information:** Application fee $75. Regular application deadline rolling. Nonfall registration accepted. Credit offered for CEEB Advanced Placement tests.

COSTS AND FINANCIAL AID

Required Forms and Deadlines: FAFSA and institution's own financial aid form. No deadline for regular filing. **Notification of Awards:** Applicants will be notified of awards on a rolling basis. **Types of Aid:** *Need-based scholarships/grants:* Pell, state scholarships/grants, private scholarships. *Loans:* FFEL Subsidized Stafford, FFEL Unsubsidized Stafford, FFEL PLUS. **Student Employment:** Off-campus job opportunities are good. **Financial Aid Phone:** 609-633-9658.

THOMAS JEFFERSON UNIVERSITY

$$$

130 South 9th Street, Suite 1610, Philadelphia, PA 19107
Phone: 215-503-8890 **E-mail:** admissions.chp@mail.tju.edu **CEEB Code:** 2903
Fax: 215-503-7241 **Web:** www.tju.edu/chp

STUDENTS AND FACULTY

Enrollment: 838. **Student Body:** Male 17%, female 83%, out-of-state 27%, international 5%. **Ethnic Representation:** African American 11%, Asian 7%, Caucasian 79%, Hispanic 2%.

ACADEMICS

Degrees: Associate's, bachelor's, master's, post-bachelor's certificate, transfer. **Special Study Options:** Independent study, internships, study abroad.

FACILITIES

Housing: Coed, apartments for married students, apartments for single students, housing for disabled students.

EXTRACURRICULARS

Activities: Choral groups, student government, student newspaper, student-run film society, yearbook.

ADMISSIONS

Selectivity Rating: 63 (of 100). **Freshman Admission Statistics:** 1,170 applied, 57% accepted. **Transfer Admission Requirements:** *Items required:* college transcript, essay, statement of good standing from prior school. Minimum college GPA of 2.5 required. Lowest grade transferable C. **General Admission Information:** Priority application deadline February 1.

COSTS AND FINANCIAL AID

Tuition $17,500. Average book expense $1,150.

THOMAS MORE COLLEGE

333 Thomas More Parkway, Crestview Hill, KY 41017
Phone: 859-344-3332 **E-mail:** robert.mcdermott@thomasmore.edu **CEEB Code:** 3892
Fax: 859-344-3444 **Web:** www.thomasmore.edu **ACT Code:** 1560

This private school, which is affiliated with the Roman Catholic Church, was founded in 1921. It has a 100-acre campus.

STUDENTS AND FACULTY

Enrollment: 1,272. **Student Body:** Male 45%, female 55%, out-of-state 34%. **Ethnic Representation:** African American 4%, Caucasian 79%, Hispanic 1%, Native American 1%. **Retention and Graduation:** 71% freshmen return for sophomore year. 31% freshmen graduate within 4 years. 22% grads go on to further study within 1 year. 5% grads pursue business degrees. 11% grads pursue law degrees. 21% grads pursue medical degrees. **Faculty:** Student/faculty ratio 12:1. 77 full-time faculty, 67% hold PhDs. 100% faculty teach undergrads.

ACADEMICS

Degrees: Associate's, bachelor's, certificate, master's, terminal, transfer. **Academic Requirements:** General education including some course work in arts/fine arts, computer literacy, English (including composition), foreign languages, history, humanities, mathematics, philosophy, sciences (biological or physical), social science. **Classes:** 10-19 students in an average class. 10-19 students in an average lab/discussion section. **Disciplines with Highest Percentage of Degrees Awarded:** Business/marketing 49%, biological life sciences 8%, health professions and related sciences 7%, social sciences and history 6%, education 4%. **Special Study Options:** Accelerated program, cooperative (work-study) program, cross registration, double major, dual enrollment, honors program, independent study, internships, liberal arts/career combination, student-designed major, study abroad, teacher certification program, weekend college.

FACILITIES

Housing: Coed, all-female, all-male. **Library Holdings:** 126,923 bound volumes. 606 periodicals. 49,145 microforms. 2,136 audiovisuals. **Computers:** School-owned computers available for student use.

EXTRACURRICULARS

Activities: Drama/theater, literary magazine, student government, student newspaper. **Organizations:** 29 registered organizations, 5 honor societies, 1 religious organization. **Athletics (Intercollegiate):** *Men:* baseball, basketball, football, soccer, tennis. *Women:* basketball, golf, soccer, softball, tennis, volleyball.

ADMISSIONS

Selectivity Rating: 73 (of 100). **Freshman Academic Profile:** Average high school GPA 2.9. 7% in top 10% of high school class, 31% in top 25% of high school class, 55% in top 50% of high school class. 71% from public high schools. Average SAT I Math 490, SAT I Math middle 50% range 430-520. Average SAT I Verbal 480, SAT I Verbal middle 50% range 410-540. Average ACT 20, ACT middle 50% range 17-23. TOEFL required of all international applicants, minimum TOEFL 515. **Basis for Candidate Selection:** *Very important factors considered include:* secondary school record. *Important factors considered include:* class rank, recommendations, standardized test scores. *Other factors considered include:* character/personal qualities, essays, extracurricular activities, interview, talent/ability, volunteer work. **Freshman Admission Requirements:** High school diploma or GED is required. *Academic units required/recommended:* 15 total required; 2 total recommended; 4 English required, 3 math required, 3 science required, 1 science lab required, 2 foreign language required, 3 social studies required. **Freshman Admission Statistics:** 1,197 applied, 79% accepted, 26% of those accepted enrolled. **Transfer Admission Requirements:** *Items required:* college transcript, statement of good standing from prior school. Minimum college GPA of 2.0 required. Lowest grade transferable C. **General Admission Information:** Application fee $25. Priority application deadline March 15. Nonfall registration accepted. Admission may be deferred for a maximum of 1 year. Credit and/or placement offered for CEEB Advanced Placement tests.

COSTS AND FINANCIAL AID

Tuition $13,200. Room & board $3,800. Required fees $350. Average book expense $700. **Required Forms and Deadlines:** FAFSA. Priority filing deadline March 15. **Notification of Awards:** Applicants will be notified of awards on or about March 15. **Types of Aid:** *Need-based scholarships/grants:* Pell, SEOG, state scholarships/grants, private scholarships, the school's own gift aid. *Loans:* FFEL Subsidized Stafford, FFEL Unsubsidized Stafford, FFEL PLUS, Federal Perkins, Federal Nursing, college/university loans from institutional funds. **Student Employment:** Federal Work-Study Program available. Institutional employment available. Off-campus job opportunities are excellent. **Financial Aid Statistics:** 64% freshmen, 66% undergrads receive some form of aid. Average freshman grant $4,052. Average freshman loan $4,377. Average income from on-campus job $1,318. **Financial Aid Phone:** 859-344-3319.

THOMAS MORE COLLEGE OF LIBERAL ARTS

6 Manchester Street, Merrimack, NH 03054-4818
Phone: 603-880-8308 **E-mail:** admissions@thomasmorecollege.edu
Fax: 603-880-9280 **Web:** www.thomasmorecollege.edu **ACT Code:** 3892

This private school, which is affiliated with the Roman Catholic Church, was founded in 1978. It has a 13-acre campus.

STUDENTS AND FACULTY

Enrollment: 71. **Student Body:** Male 44%, female 56%, out-of-state 88%, international 6%. **Ethnic Representation:** Hispanic 5%, Native American 2%. **Retention and Graduation:** 59% freshmen return for sophomore year. 28% freshmen graduate within 4 years. 52% grads go on to further study within 1 year. 2% grads pursue business degrees. 8% grads pursue law degrees. 2% grads pursue medical degrees. **Faculty:** Student/faculty ratio 7:1. 7 full-time faculty, 71% hold PhDs. 100% faculty teach undergrads.

ACADEMICS

Degrees: Bachelor's. **Academic Requirements:** General education including some course work in arts/fine arts, English (including composition), foreign languages, history, humanities, mathematics, philosophy, sciences (biological or physical), social science, theology. **Classes:** 10-19 students in an average class. **Disciplines with Highest Percentage of Degrees Awarded:** Philosophy/religion/theology 55%, literature 45%. **Special Study Options:** Study abroad.

FACILITIES

Housing: All-female, all-male. **Library Holdings:** 50,000 bound volumes. 15 periodicals. 0 microforms. 1,000 audiovisuals. **Computers:** School-owned computers available for student use.

EXTRACURRICULARS

Activities: Choral groups.

ADMISSIONS

Selectivity Rating: 63 (of 100). **Freshman Academic Profile:** 12% from public high schools. **Basis for Candidate Selection:** *Very important factors considered include:* character/personal qualities, essays, interview, recommendations. *Important factors considered include:* talent/ability. *Other factors considered include:* class rank, extracurricular activities, religious affiliation/commitment, secondary school record, standardized test scores. **Freshman Admission Requirements:** High school diploma or GED is required. *Academic units required/recommended:* 17 total required; 4 English required, 3 math required, 2 science required, 2 science lab required, 2 foreign language required, 2 social studies required, 2 history required. **Freshman Admission Statistics:** 27 applied, 100% accepted, 48% of those accepted enrolled. **Transfer Admission Requirements:** *Items required:* college transcript, essay. Lowest grade transferable C. **General Admission Information:** Application fee $25. Nonfall registration accepted. Admission may be deferred. Neither credit nor placement offered for CEEB Advanced Placement tests.

COSTS AND FINANCIAL AID

Tuition $10,000. Room & board $7,700. Average book expense $525. **Required Forms and Deadlines:** FAFSA. Priority filing deadline May 1. **Notification of Awards:** Applicants will be notified of awards on a rolling basis beginning on or about May 15. **Types of Aid:** *Need-based scholarships/grants:* Pell, SEOG, state scholarships/grants, the school's own gift aid. *Loans:* FFEL Subsidized Stafford, FFEL Unsubsidized Stafford, FFEL PLUS. **Student Employment:** Off-campus job opportunities are good. **Financial Aid Statistics:** 80% freshmen, 90% undergrads receive some form of aid. **Financial Aid Phone:** 603-880-8308.

TIFFIN UNIVERSITY

155 Miami Street, Tiffin, OH 44883
Phone: 419-447-6443 **E-mail:** admiss@tiffin.edu
Fax: 419-443-5006 **Web:** www.tiffin.edu **ACT Code:** 3334

This private school was founded in 1888. It has a 91-acre campus.

STUDENTS AND FACULTY

Enrollment: 1,007. **Student Body:** Male 56%, female 44%, out-of-state 12%, international 4% (20 countries represented). **Ethnic Representation:** African American 13%, Asian 2%, Caucasian 83%, Hispanic 2%. **Retention and Graduation:** 53% freshmen return for sophomore year. 15% grads go on to further study within 1 year. 13% grads pursue business degrees. 4% grads pursue law degrees. **Faculty:** Student/faculty ratio 25:1. 52 full-time faculty, 63% hold PhDs. 100% faculty teach undergrads.

ACADEMICS

Degrees: Associate's, bachelor's, master's. **Academic Requirements:** General education including some course work in arts/fine arts, computer literacy, English (including composition), history, humanities, mathematics, philosophy, social science. **Majors with Highest Enrollment:** Business administration/management; accounting and finance; criminal justice/law enforcement administration. **Disciplines with Highest Percentage of Degrees Awarded:** Business/marketing 73%, protective services/public administration 20%, computer and information sciences 3%, liberal arts/general studies 2%, communications/communication technologies 1%. **Special Study Options:** Accelerated program, cooperative (work-study) program, distance learning, double major, dual enrollment, student exchange program (domestic), external degree program, independent study, internships, student-designed major, study abroad, weekend college.

FACILITIES

Housing: Coed, apartments for single students, housing for disabled students, fraternities and/or sororities, small residences. **Library Holdings:** 29,779 bound volumes. 250 periodicals. 33,250 microforms. 544 audiovisuals. **Special Academic Facilities/Equipment:** University Art Gallery, multimedia lab. **Computers:** School-owned computers available for student use.

EXTRACURRICULARS

Activities: Choral groups, concert band, drama/theater, jazz band, marching band, music ensembles, pep band, student government, student newspaper. **Organizations:** 25 registered organizations, 1 honor society, 1 religious organization, 2 fraternities (1% men join), 2 sororities (1% women join). **Athletics (Intercollegiate):** *Men:* baseball, basketball, cheerleading, cross-country, football, golf, indoor track, soccer, tennis, track & field. *Women:* basketball, cheerleading, cross-country, golf, indoor track, soccer, softball, tennis, track & field, volleyball.

ADMISSIONS

Selectivity Rating: 63 (of 100). **Freshman Academic Profile:** Average high school GPA 2.9. 10% in top 10% of high school class, 31% in top 25% of high school class, 68% in top 50% of high school class. Average SAT I Math 415. Average SAT I Verbal 410. Average ACT 19, ACT middle 50% range 19-29. TOEFL required of all international applicants, minimum TOEFL 500. **Basis for Candidate Selection:** *Very important factors considered include:* secondary school record, standardized test scores. *Important factors considered include:* character/personal qualities, class rank. *Other factors considered include:* alumni/ae relation, essays, extracurricular activities, interview, recommendations, volunteer work, work experience. **Freshman Admission Requirements:** High school diploma or GED is required. *Academic units required/recommended:* 13 total recommended; 4 English required, 4 English recommended, 3 math required, 3 math recommended, 1 science required, 1 science recommended, 1 science lab recommended, 2 foreign language recommended, 2 social studies required, 2 social studies recommended, 1 history required, 1 history recommended. **Freshman Admission Statistics:** 1,424 applied, 73% accepted, 25% of those accepted enrolled. **Transfer Admission Requirements:** *Items required:* high school transcript, college transcript. Minimum college GPA of 2.0 required. Lowest grade transferable C. **General Admission Information:** Application fee $20. Nonfall registration accepted. Admission may be deferred for a maximum of 1 year. Credit and/or placement offered for CEEB Advanced Placement tests.

COSTS AND FINANCIAL AID

Tuition $12,850. Room & board $5,700. Required fees $35. Average book expense $850. **Required Forms and Deadlines:** FAFSA. No deadline for regular filing. Priority filing deadline March 3. **Notification of Awards:** Applicants will be notified of awards on a rolling basis beginning on or about March 1. **Types of Aid:** *Need-based scholarships/grants:* Pell, SEOG, state scholarships/grants, private scholarships, the school's own gift aid. *Loans:* Direct Subsidized Stafford, Direct Unsubsidized Stafford, Direct PLUS, Federal Perkins, college/university loans from institutional funds. **Student Employment:** Federal Work-Study Program available. Institutional employment available. Off-campus job opportunities are fair. **Financial Aid Statistics:** 86% freshmen, 86% undergrads receive some form of aid. Average freshman grant $4,300. Average freshman loan $2,625. Average income from on-campus job $1,000. **Financial Aid Phone:** 419-448-3415.

TOCCOA FALLS COLLEGE

Toccoa Falls College, Office of Admissions, Toccoa Falls, GA 30598
Phone: 800-868-3257 **E-mail:** admissions@toccoafalls.edu
Fax: 706-282-6012 **Web:** www.toccoafalls.edu

This private school was founded in 1907. It has a 1,100-acre campus.

STUDENTS AND FACULTY

Enrollment: 916. **Student Body:** Male 43%, female 57%, out-of-state 61%. **Ethnic Representation:** African American 2%, Asian 4%, Caucasian 89%, Hispanic 2%. **Retention and Graduation:** 68% freshmen return for sophomore year. 24% freshmen graduate within 4 years. **Faculty:** Student/faculty ratio 14:1. 54 full-time faculty, 50% hold PhDs. 100% faculty teach undergrads.

ACADEMICS

Degrees: Associate's, bachelor's, certificate, diploma. **Academic Requirements:** General education including some course work in computer literacy, English (including composition), humanities, social science, public speaking, 30 hours of Bible and doctrine. **Classes:** Under 10 students in an average class. **Disciplines with Highest Percentage of Degrees Awarded:** Philosophy/religion/theology 43%, psychology 21%, education 19%, communications/communication technologies 7%, English 3%. **Special Study Options:** Accelerated program, double major, independent study, internships.

FACILITIES

Housing: All-female, all-male, apartments for married students, apartments for single students. **Library Holdings:** 106,106 bound volumes. 294 periodicals. 22,864 microforms. 5,161 audiovisuals. **Computers:** School-owned computers available for student use.

EXTRACURRICULARS

Activities: Choral groups, concert band, drama/theater, music ensembles, radio station, student government, student newspaper, yearbook. **Athletics (Intercollegiate):** *Men:* baseball, basketball, football, golf, soccer, softball, tennis, volleyball. *Women:* basketball, cheerleading, golf, soccer, softball, tennis, volleyball.

ADMISSIONS

Selectivity Rating: 70 (of 100). **Freshman Academic Profile:** Average high school GPA 3.2. 15% in top 10% of high school class, 40% in top 25% of high school class, 69% in top 50% of high school class. 92% from public high schools. Average SAT I Math 488, SAT I Math middle 50% range 400-580. Average SAT I Verbal 510, SAT I Verbal middle 50% range 410-610. Average ACT 22, ACT middle 50% range 20-25. TOEFL required of all international applicants, minimum TOEFL 500. **Basis for Candidate Selection:** *Very important factors considered include:* character/personal qualities, essays, recommendations, religious affiliation/commitment, secondary school record, standardized test scores. *Important factors considered include:* extracurricular activities, talent/ability. *Other factors considered include:* interview, volunteer work, work experience. **Freshman Admission Requirements:** High school diploma or GED is required. *Academic units required/recommended:* 15 total recommended; 4 English recommended, 3 math recommended, 3 science recommended, 2 foreign language recommended, 3 history recommended. **Freshman Admission Statistics:** 769 applied, 82% accepted, 33% of those accepted enrolled. **Transfer Admission Requirements:** *Items required:* college transcript, essay. Minimum college GPA of 2.0 required. Lowest grade transferable C-. **General Admission Information:** Application fee $20. Nonfall registration accepted. Admission may be deferred for a maximum of 2 years. Credit and/or placement offered for CEEB Advanced Placement tests.

COSTS AND FINANCIAL AID

Tuition $9,600. Room & board $4,170. Required fees $450. Average book expense $500. **Required Forms and Deadlines:** FAFSA and institution's own financial aid form. Priority filing deadline March 1. **Notification of Awards:** Applicants will be notified of awards on a rolling basis beginning on or about March 1. **Types of Aid:** *Need-based scholarships/grants:* Pell, SEOG, state scholarships/grants, private scholarships, the school's own gift aid. *Loans:* FFEL Subsidized Stafford, FFEL Unsubsidized Stafford, FFEL PLUS, Federal Perkins, state loans, college/university loans from institutional funds. **Student Employment:** Federal Work-Study Program available. Off-campus job opportunities are good. **Financial Aid Statistics:** Average freshman grant $3,238. Average freshman loan $4,264. Average income from on-campus job $1,784. **Financial Aid Phone:** 800-868-3257.

TOUGALOO COLLEGE

500 West Country Line Road, Tougaloo, MS 39174
Phone: 888-424-2566 **E-mail:** slaterJa@mail.tougaloo.edu
Fax: 601-977-6185 **Web:** tougaloo.edu

This private school was founded in 1869.

STUDENTS AND FACULTY

Enrollment: 967. **Student Body:** Male 28%, female 72%, out-of-state 14%. **Ethnic Representation:** African American 100%. **Retention and Graduation:** 78% freshmen return for sophomore year. 25% freshmen graduate within 4 years. 55% grads go on to further study within 1 year. 5% grads pursue business degrees. 10% grads pursue law degrees. 10% grads pursue medical degrees. **Faculty:** Student/faculty ratio 14:1. 60 full-time faculty, 63% hold PhDs. 100% faculty teach undergrads.

ACADEMICS

Degrees: Associate's, bachelor's, certificate, transfer. **Academic Requirements:** General education including some course work in computer literacy, English (including composition), foreign languages, history, humanities, mathematics, sciences (biological or physical), social science. **Classes:** 20-29 students in an average class. 10-19 students in an average lab/discussion section. **Disciplines with Highest Percentage of Degrees Awarded:** Psychology 23%, other 20%, social sciences and history 20%, biological life sciences 12%, English 10%. **Special Study Options:** Cooperative (work-study) program, double major, dual enrollment, student exchange program (domestic), independent study, internships, liberal arts/career combination, study abroad, teacher certification program.

FACILITIES

Housing: All-female, all-male. **Library Holdings:** 109,350 bound volumes. 303 periodicals. 7,332 microforms. 1,423 audiovisuals. **Special Academic Facilities/Equipment:** Bailey-Ward Black Collection. **Computers:** School-owned computers available for student use.

EXTRACURRICULARS

Activities: Choral groups, drama/theater, literary magazine, student government, student newspaper, yearbook. **Organizations:** 20 registered organizations, 2 honor societies, 7 religious organizations, 4 fraternities (10% men join),

4 sororities (10% women join). **Athletics (Intercollegiate):** *Men:* basketball, cross-country, golf. *Women:* basketball, cross-country, golf, softball.

ADMISSIONS

Selectivity Rating: 75 (of 100). **Freshman Academic Profile:** Average high school GPA 3.2. 95% from public high schools. Average SAT I Math 483. Average SAT I Verbal 477. Average ACT 18, ACT middle 50% range 16-21. TOEFL required of all international applicants, minimum TOEFL 500. **Basis for Candidate Selection:** *Important factors considered include:* character/personal qualities, recommendations, secondary school record, standardized test scores, talent/ability. *Other factors considered include:* alumni/ae relation, class rank, essays, extracurricular activities, interview. **Freshman Admission Requirements:** High school diploma or GED is required. *Academic units required/recommended:* 16 total required; 16 total recommended; 3 English required, 4 English recommended, 2 math required, 3 math recommended, 2 science required, 3 science recommended, 2 foreign language recommended, 1 social studies required, 2 social studies recommended, 1 history required, 2 history recommended, 7 elective required, 7 elective recommended. **Freshman Admission Statistics:** 646 applied, 99% accepted, 39% of those accepted enrolled. **Transfer Admission Requirements:** *Items required:* high school transcript, college transcript, standardized test score statement of good standing from prior school. Lowest grade transferable C. **General Admission Information:** Application fee $5. Nonfall registration accepted.

COSTS AND FINANCIAL AID

Tuition $6,400. Room & board $3,060. Required fees $340. Average book expense $600. **Required Forms and Deadlines:** FAFSA, institution's own financial aid form and CSS/Financial Aid PROFILE. **Types of Aid:** *Need-based scholarships/grants:* Pell, SEOG, state scholarships/grants, private scholarships, the school's own gift aid, United Negro College Fund. *Loans:* Direct Subsidized Stafford, Federal Perkins. **Student Employment:** Federal Work-Study Program available. Off-campus job opportunities are good. **Financial Aid Statistics:** Average freshman grant $4,292. Average freshman loan $2,783. **Financial Aid Phone:** 601-977-6134.

TOURO COLLEGE

1602 Avenue J, Brooklyn, NY 11230
Phone: 718-252-7800 **E-mail:** lasadmit@touro.edu **CEEB Code:** 2902
Fax: 718-253-6479 **Web:** www.touro.edu **ACT Code:** 2961

This private school was founded in 1971.

STUDENTS AND FACULTY

Enrollment: 8,741. **Student Body:** Male 31%, female 69%. **Ethnic Representation:** African American 16%, Asian 5%, Caucasian 66%, Hispanic 13%. **Faculty:** Student/faculty ratio 12:1. 282 full-time faculty.

ACADEMICS

Degrees: Associate's, bachelor's, certificate, doctoral, first professional, master's, post-bachelor's certificate. **Academic Requirements:** General education including some course work in computer literacy, English (including composition), humanities, mathematics, sciences (biological or physical). **Special Study Options:** Accelerated program, distance learning, double major, dual enrollment, English as a second language, honors program, independent study, internships, student-designed major, study abroad, teacher certification program. Undergrads may take grad-level classes.

FACILITIES

Housing: All-female, all-male. **Library Holdings:** 213,100 bound volumes. 400 periodicals. 14,500 microforms. 1,491 audiovisuals.

EXTRACURRICULARS

Activities: Literary magazine, student government, student newspaper, yearbook. **Organizations:** 33 honor societies, 18 religious organizations.

ADMISSIONS

Selectivity Rating: 72 (of 100). **Freshman Academic Profile:** TOEFL required of all international applicants, minimum TOEFL 500. **Basis for Candidate Selection:** *Very important factors considered include:* secondary school record. *Important factors considered include:* essays, interview, recommendations, standardized test scores. *Other factors considered include:* alumni/ae relation, extracurricular activities, minority status. **Freshman Admission Requirements:** High school diploma or GED is required. *Academic units required/recommended:* 12 total required; 4 English required, 2 math required, 2 science required, 2 foreign language required, 2 history required. **Freshman Admission Statistics:** 5,891 applied, 45% accepted, 83% of those accepted enrolled. **Transfer Admission Requirements:** *Items required:* college transcript. Minimum college GPA of 2.5 required. Lowest grade transferable C. **General Admission Information:** Application fee $35. Nonfall registration accepted. Credit and/or placement offered for CEEB Advanced Placement tests.

COSTS AND FINANCIAL AID

Tuition $9,900. Required fees $300. Average book expense $778. **Required Forms and Deadlines:** FAFSA and state aid form. Financial aid filing deadline June 1. Priority filing deadline May 15. **Notification of Awards:** Applicants will be notified of awards on or about August 15. **Types of Aid:** *Need-based scholarships/grants:* Pell, SEOG, state scholarships/grants, the school's own gift aid. *Loans:* FFEL Subsidized Stafford, FFEL Unsubsidized Stafford, FFEL PLUS, Federal Perkins. **Student Employment:** Federal Work-Study Program available. Institutional employment available. Off-campus job opportunities are excellent. **Financial Aid Statistics:** Average freshman grant $3,000. **Financial Aid Phone:** 212-463-0400.

TOWSON UNIVERSITY

8000 York Road, Towson, MD 21252-0001
Phone: 410-704-2113 **E-mail:** admissions@towson.edu **CEEB Code:** 5404
Fax: 410-704-3030 **Web:** www.towson.edu **ACT Code:** 1718

This public school was founded in 1866. It has a 321-acre campus.

STUDENTS AND FACULTY

Enrollment: 14,296. **Student Body:** Male 40%, female 60%, out-of-state 19%, international 2%. **Ethnic Representation:** African American 10%, Asian 3%, Caucasian 80%, Hispanic 2%. **Retention and Graduation:** 86% freshmen return for sophomore year. 30% freshmen graduate within 4 years. **Faculty:** Student/faculty ratio 17:1. 585 full-time faculty, 76% hold PhDs.

ACADEMICS

Degrees: Bachelor's, doctoral, master's, post-bachelor's certificate, post-master's certificate. **Academic Requirements:** General education including some course work in English (including composition), humanities, mathematics, sciences (biological or physical), social science. **Classes:** 20-29 students in an average class. Under 10 students in an average lab/discussion section. **Majors with Highest Enrollment:** Business administration/management; elementary education and teaching; mass communications/media studies. **Disciplines with Highest Percentage of Degrees Awarded:** Business/marketing 19%, communications/communication technologies 15%, education 12%, social sciences and history 10%, psychology 9%. **Special Study Options:** Accelerated program, cross registration, distance learning, double major, dual enrollment, English as a second language, student exchange program (domestic), honors program, independent study, internships, student-designed major, study abroad, teacher certification program.

FACILITIES

Housing: Coed, apartments for married students, apartments for single students, housing for disabled students, housing for international students, honors hall, alcohol-free floors, academic emphasis floors, smoke-free floors, nontraditional aged areas. **Library Holdings:** 364,468 bound volumes. 2,164 periodicals. 830,286 microforms. 14,174 audiovisuals. **Special Academic Facilities/Equipment:** Art galleries, animal museum, Asian art collection, elementary school, media center, speech/language clinic, planetarium/observatory, herbarium, electron microscope, argon laser. **Computers:** School-owned computers available for student use.

EXTRACURRICULARS

Activities: Choral groups, concert band, dance, drama/theater, jazz band, literary magazine, marching band, music ensembles, musical theater, opera, pep band, radio station, student government, student newspaper, student-run film society, symphony orchestra, television station, yearbook. **Organizations:** 112 registered organizations, 15 honor societies, 14 religious organizations, 14 fraternities (8% men join), 10 sororities (7% women join). **Athletics (Intercollegiate):** *Men:* baseball, basketball, cheerleading, cross-country, diving, football, golf, lacrosse, soccer, swimming, tennis, track & field. *Women:* basketball, cheerleading, cross-country, diving, field hockey, gymnastics, lacrosse, soccer, softball, swimming, tennis, track & field, volleyball.

ADMISSIONS

Selectivity Rating: 66 (of 100). **Freshman Academic Profile:** Average high school GPA 3.5. 15% in top 10% of high school class, 41% in top 25% of high school class, 78% in top 50% of high school class. Average SAT I Math 555, SAT I Math middle 50% range 510-600. Average SAT I Verbal 540, SAT I Verbal middle 50% range 500-580. Average ACT 23. **Basis for Candidate Selection:**

Very important factors considered include: class rank, secondary school record. *Important factors considered include:* recommendations, standardized test scores, talent/ability. *Other factors considered include:* alumni/ae relation, character/personal qualities, essays, extracurricular activities, geographical residence, interview, minority status, state residency, volunteer work, work experience. **Freshman Admission Requirements:** High school diploma or GED is required. *Academic units required/recommended:* 24 total required; 4 English required, 4 English recommended, 3 math required, 4 math recommended, 3 science required, 3 science recommended, 3 science lab required, 3 science lab recommended, 2 foreign language required, 4 foreign language recommended, 3 social studies required, 4 social studies recommended, 6 elective required. **Freshman Admission Statistics:** 10,824 applied, 58% accepted, 35% of those accepted enrolled. **Transfer Admission Requirements:** *Items required:* college transcript. Minimum high school GPA of 3.0 required. Minimum college GPA of 2.5 required. Lowest grade transferable D. **General Admission Information:** Application fee $35. Priority application deadline October 2. Regular application deadline March 1. Admission may be deferred.

COSTS AND FINANCIAL AID

In-state tuition $3,956. Out-of-state tuition $11,602. Room & board $6,322. Required fees $1,698. Average book expense $800. **Required Forms and Deadlines:** FAFSA. No deadline for regular filing. Priority filing deadline March 1. **Notification of Awards:** Applicants will be notified of awards on a rolling basis beginning on or about March 15. **Types of Aid:** *Need-based scholarships/grants:* Pell, SEOG, state scholarships/grants, private scholarships, the school's own gift aid. *Loans:* Direct Subsidized Stafford, Direct Unsubsidized Stafford, Direct PLUS, Federal Perkins. **Student Employment:** Federal Work-Study Program available. Institutional employment available. Off-campus job opportunities are excellent. **Financial Aid Statistics:** 45% freshmen, 38% undergrads receive some form of aid. Average freshman grant $5,334. Average freshman loan $3,147. Average income from on-campus job $1,056. **Financial Aid Phone:** 410-704-4236.

See page 1230.

TRANSYLVANIA UNIVERSITY

300 North Broadway, Lexington, KY 40508-1797
Phone: 859-233-8242 **E-mail:** admissions@mail.transy.edu **CEEB Code:** 1808
Fax: 859-233-8797 **Web:** www.transy.edu **ACT Code:** 1550

This private school, which is affiliated with the Disciples of Christ Church, was founded in 1780. It has a 35-acre campus.

STUDENTS AND FACULTY

Enrollment: 1,108. **Student Body:** Male 42%, female 58%, out-of-state 18%. **Ethnic Representation:** African American 2%, Asian 2%, Caucasian 88%, Hispanic 1%. **Retention and Graduation:** 80% freshmen return for sophomore year. 59% freshmen graduate within 4 years. 44% grads go on to further study within 1 year. 3% grads pursue business degrees. 11% grads pursue law degrees. 10% grads pursue medical degrees. **Faculty:** Student/faculty ratio 13:1. 78 full-time faculty, 91% hold PhDs. 100% faculty teach undergrads.

ACADEMICS

Degrees: Bachelor's. **Academic Requirements:** General education including some course work in arts/fine arts, English (including composition), foreign languages, humanities, mathematics, sciences (biological or physical), social science, western civilization, and nonwestern civilization. **Classes:** 10-19 students in an average class. **Majors with Highest Enrollment:** Business/commerce, general; biology/biological sciences, general; psychology, general. **Disciplines with Highest Percentage of Degrees Awarded:** Business/marketing 32%, biological life sciences 17%, social sciences and history 16%, psychology 6%, education 5%. **Special Study Options:** Double major, independent study, internships, liberal arts/career combination, student-designed major, study abroad, teacher certification program.

FACILITIES

Housing: Coed, all-female, all-male, apartments for single students, housing for disabled students. **Library Holdings:** 93,019 bound volumes. 500 periodicals. 13,128 microforms. 1,860 audiovisuals. **Special Academic Facilities/Equipment:** Art gallery, Museum of Early Scientific Apparatus, medical museum, language lab, transmission electron microscope. **Computers:** *Recommended operating system:* Windows 95. School-owned computers available for student use.

EXTRACURRICULARS

Activities: Choral groups, concert band, dance, drama/theater, jazz band, literary magazine, music ensembles, musical theater, opera, pep band, radio station, student government, student newspaper, yearbook. **Organizations:** 55 registered organizations, 10 honor societies, 3 religious organizations, 4 fraternities (60% men join), 4 sororities (60% women join). **Athletics (Intercollegiate):** *Men:* baseball, basketball, cheerleading, cross-country, diving, golf, soccer, swimming, tennis. *Women:* basketball, cheerleading, cross-country, diving, field hockey, golf, soccer, softball, swimming, tennis, volleyball.

ADMISSIONS

Selectivity Rating: 77 (of 100). **Freshman Academic Profile:** Average high school GPA 3.5. 42% in top 10% of high school class, 75% in top 25% of high school class, 97% in top 50% of high school class. 89% from public high schools. Average SAT I Math 588, SAT I Math middle 50% range 530-650. Average SAT I Verbal 592, SAT I Verbal middle 50% range 530-650. Average ACT 26, ACT middle 50% range 23-29. TOEFL required of all international applicants, minimum TOEFL 550. **Basis for Candidate Selection:** *Very important factors considered include:* secondary school record, standardized test scores. *Important factors considered include:* class rank, essays, extracurricular activities, recommendations. *Other factors considered include:* alumni/ae relation, character/personal qualities, geographical residence, interview, talent/ability. **Freshman Admission Requirements:** High school diploma or GED is required. *Academic units required/recommended:* 12 total required; 16 total recommended; 4 English required, 4 English recommended, 3 math required, 3 math recommended, 3 science required, 3 science recommended, 2 foreign language recommended, 2 social studies required, 2 social studies recommended, 1 history recommended, 1 elective recommended. **Freshman Admission Statistics:** 1,179 applied, 87% accepted, 32% of those accepted enrolled. **Transfer Admission Requirements:** *Items required:* high school transcript, college transcript, essay, standardized test scores. Minimum high school GPA of 2.7 required. Minimum college GPA of 2.7 required. Lowest grade transferable C. **General Admission Information:** Application fee $30. Priority application deadline December 2. Regular application deadline February 2. Nonfall registration accepted. Admission may be deferred for a maximum of 1 year. Credit and/or placement offered for CEEB Advanced Placement tests.

COSTS AND FINANCIAL AID

Tuition $16,170. Room & board $5,940. Required fees $620. Average book expense $600. **Required Forms and Deadlines:** FAFSA. Priority filing deadline March 1. **Notification of Awards:** Applicants will be notified of awards on a rolling basis beginning on or about March 15. **Types of Aid:** *Need-based scholarships/grants:* Pell, SEOG, state scholarships/grants, private scholarships, the school's own gift aid. *Loans:* FFEL Subsidized Stafford, FFEL Unsubsidized Stafford, FFEL PLUS, Federal Perkins, college/university loans from institutional funds. **Student Employment:** Federal Work-Study Program available. Off-campus job opportunities are good. **Financial Aid Statistics:** 57% freshmen, 60% undergrads receive some form of aid. Average freshman grant $9,493. Average freshman loan $1,866. **Financial Aid Phone:** 859-233-8239.

See page 1232.

TREVECCA NAZARENE UNIVERSITY

333 Murfreesboro Road, Nashville, TN 37210
Phone: 615-248-1320 **E-mail:** admissions_und@trevecca.edu
Fax: 615-248-7406 **Web:** www.trevecca.edu **ACT Code:** 4016

This private school, which is affiliated with the Nazarene Church, was founded in 1901. It has a 65-acre campus.

STUDENTS AND FACULTY

Enrollment: 1,185. **Student Body:** Male 41%, female 59%, out-of-state 36%, international 2% (16 countries represented). **Ethnic Representation:** African American 7%, Caucasian 82%, Hispanic 2%. **Retention and Graduation:** 66% freshmen return for sophomore year. 20% freshmen graduate within 4 years. **Faculty:** Student/faculty ratio 16:1. 74 full-time faculty, 67% hold PhDs. 89% faculty teach undergrads.

ACADEMICS

Degrees: Associate's, bachelor's, doctoral, master's, post-master's certificate. **Academic Requirements:** General education including some course work in arts/fine arts, computer literacy, English (including composition), foreign languages, history, humanities, mathematics, philosophy, sciences (biological or physical), social science, religion. **Classes:** 10-19 students in an average class. **Majors with Highest Enrollment:** Business administration/management; early childhood education and teaching; religion/religious studies. **Disciplines with Highest Percentage of Degrees Awarded:** Business/marketing 61%, communications/communication technologies 8%, biological life sciences 6%, philosophy/religion/theology 6%, education 5%. **Special Study Options:** Double major, internships, teacher certification program, Adult degree completion program.

FACILITIES

Housing: All-female, all-male, apartments for married students, apartments for single students. **Library Holdings:** 100,231 bound volumes. 507 periodicals. 285,736 microforms. 3,060 audiovisuals. **Computers:** School-owned computers available for student use.

EXTRACURRICULARS

Activities: Choral groups, concert band, drama/theater, literary magazine, music ensembles, musical theater, pep band, radio station, student government, student newspaper, symphony orchestra, yearbook. **Organizations:** 26 registered organizations, 1 honor society, 1 religious organization. **Athletics (Intercollegiate):** *Men:* baseball, basketball, golf, soccer. *Women:* basketball, golf, soccer, softball, volleyball.

ADMISSIONS

Selectivity Rating: 71 (of 100). **Freshman Academic Profile:** Average high school GPA 3.2. 24% in top 10% of high school class, 44% in top 25% of high school class, 74% in top 50% of high school class. Average SAT I Math 528. Average SAT I Verbal 553. Average ACT 22, ACT middle 50% range 18-25. TOEFL required of all international applicants, minimum TOEFL 500. **Basis for Candidate Selection:** *Very important factors considered include:* character/personal qualities, secondary school record, standardized test scores. *Other factors considered include:* class rank, extracurricular activities, interview, recommendations, talent/ability. **Freshman Admission Requirements:** High school diploma or GED is required. *Academic units required/recommended:* 15 total recommended; 4 English recommended, 2 math recommended, 1 science recommended, 2 foreign language recommended, 1 social studies recommended, 1 history recommended, 4 elective recommended. **Freshman Admission Statistics:** 535 applied, 82% accepted, 49% of those accepted enrolled. **Transfer Admission Requirements:** *Items required:* college transcript. Lowest grade transferable D. **General Admission Information:** Application fee $25. Priority application deadline July 1. Nonfall registration accepted. Admission may be deferred. Neither credit nor placement offered for CEEB Advanced Placement tests.

COSTS AND FINANCIAL AID

Tuition $11,960. Room & board $5,408. Required fees $0. Average book expense $772. **Required Forms and Deadlines:** FAFSA. Priority filing deadline March 1. **Notification of Awards:** Applicants will be notified of awards on a rolling basis beginning on or about March 20. **Types of Aid:** *Need-based scholarships/grants:* Pell, SEOG, state scholarships/grants, private scholarships, the school's own gift aid. *Loans:* FFEL Subsidized Stafford, FFEL Unsubsidized Stafford, FFEL PLUS, Federal Perkins. **Student Employment:** Federal Work-Study Program available. Institutional employment available. Off-campus job opportunities are excellent. **Financial Aid Statistics:** 57% freshmen, 49% undergrads receive some form of aid. Average freshman grant $3,708. Average freshman loan $3,540. **Financial Aid Phone:** 615-248-1242.

TRINITY CHRISTIAN COLLEGE

6601 West College Drive, Palos Heights, IL 60463
Phone: 708-239-4708 **E-mail:** admissions@trnty.edu **CEEB Code:** 1820
Fax: 708-239-4826 **Web:** www.trnty.edu **ACT Code:** 1165

This private school was founded in 1959. It has a 47-acre campus.

STUDENTS AND FACULTY

Enrollment: 1,135. **Student Body:** Male 38%, female 62%, out-of-state 42%, international 2% (4 countries represented). **Ethnic Representation:** African American 6%, Asian 2%, Caucasian 84%, Hispanic 4%. **Retention and Graduation:** 75% freshmen return for sophomore year. 45% freshmen graduate within 4 years. 12% grads go on to further study within 1 year. 3% grads pursue business degrees. 1% grads pursue law degrees. 1% grads pursue medical degrees. **Faculty:** Student/faculty ratio 12:1. 56 full-time faculty, 60% hold PhDs. 100% faculty teach undergrads.

ACADEMICS

Degrees: Bachelor's. **Academic Requirements:** General education including some course work in arts/fine arts, English (including composition), history, humanities, mathematics, philosophy, sciences (biological or physical), social science. **Classes:** 10-19 students in an average class. **Majors with Highest Enrollment:** Nursing/registered nurse training (RN, ASN, BSN, MSN); business administration/management; elementary education and teaching. **Disciplines with Highest Percentage of Degrees Awarded:** Education 26%, business/marketing 23%, communications/communication technologies 9%, psychology 8%, health professions and related sciences 8%. **Special Study Options:** Cooperative (work-study) program, double major, honors program, independent study, internships, liberal arts/career combination, study abroad, teacher certification program.

FACILITIES

Housing: Coed, apartments for single students. **Library Holdings:** 77,833 bound volumes. 441 periodicals. 40,450 microforms. 762 audiovisuals. **Special Academic Facilities/Equipment:** Dutch Heritage Center. **Computers:** *Recommended operating system:* Windows XP. School-owned computers available for student use.

EXTRACURRICULARS

Activities: Choral groups, concert band, drama/theater, jazz band, literary magazine, music ensembles, student government, student newspaper, yearbook. **Organizations:** 15 registered organizations, 2 honor societies, 1 religious organization. **Athletics (Intercollegiate):** *Men:* baseball, basketball, cross-country, soccer, track & field, volleyball. *Women:* basketball, cross-country, soccer, softball, track & field, volleyball.

ADMISSIONS

Selectivity Rating: 70 (of 100). **Freshman Academic Profile:** Average high school GPA 3.3. 15% in top 10% of high school class, 33% in top 25% of high school class, 65% in top 50% of high school class. 44% from public high schools. Average SAT I Math 510, SAT I Math middle 50% range 420-600. Average SAT I Verbal 572, SAT I Verbal middle 50% range 530-620. Average ACT 23, ACT middle 50% range 19-26. TOEFL required of all international applicants, minimum TOEFL 500. **Basis for Candidate Selection:** *Very important factors considered include:* recommendations, secondary school record, standardized test scores. *Important factors considered include:* character/personal qualities, extracurricular activities, interview. *Other factors considered include:* alumni/ae relation, class rank, essays, geographical residence, minority status, religious affiliation/commitment, state residency, talent/ability, volunteer work, work experience. **Freshman Admission Requirements:** High school diploma or GED is required. *Academic units required/recommended:* 16 total required; 18 total recommended; 2 English required, 4 English recommended, 2 math required, 4 math recommended, 2 science required, 3 science recommended, 2 foreign language recommended, 2 social studies required, 3 social studies recommended, 2 history recommended. **Freshman Admission Statistics:** 538 applied, 91% accepted, 38% of those accepted enrolled. **Transfer Admission Requirements:** *Items required:* college transcript, essay, interview. Minimum college GPA of 2.0 required. Lowest grade transferable C. **General Admission Information:** Application fee $20. Nonfall registration accepted. Admission may be deferred for a maximum of 1 year. Credit and/or placement offered for CEEB Advanced Placement tests.

COSTS AND FINANCIAL AID

Tuition $14,460. Room & board $5,700. Required fees $0. Average book expense $675. **Required Forms and Deadlines:** FAFSA and institution's own financial aid form. No deadline for regular filing. **Notification of Awards:** Applicants will be notified of awards on a rolling basis beginning on or about April 1. **Types of Aid:** *Need-based scholarships/grants:* Pell, SEOG, state scholarships/grants, private scholarships, the school's own gift aid. *Loans:* FFEL Subsidized Stafford, FFEL Unsubsidized Stafford, FFEL PLUS, Federal Perkins, Federal Nursing. **Student Employment:** Federal Work-Study Program available. Institutional employment available. Off-campus job opportunities are excellent. **Financial Aid Statistics:** 72% freshmen, 75% undergrads receive some form of aid. Average freshman grant $6,211. Average freshman loan $3,939. Average income from on-campus job $1,298. **Financial Aid Phone:** 708-239-4706.

TRINITY COLLEGE (CT)

Best 351

300 Summit Street, Hartford, CT 06016
Phone: 860-297-2180 **E-mail:** admissions.office@trincoll.edu **CEEB Code:** 3899
Fax: 860-297-2287 **Web:** www.trincoll.edu **ACT Code:** 598

This private school was founded in 1823. It has a 100-acre campus.

STUDENTS AND FACULTY

Enrollment: 2,098. **Student Body:** Male 48%, female 52%, out-of-state 78%, international 2% (35 countries represented). **Ethnic Representation:** African American 6%, Asian 6%, Caucasian 69%, Hispanic 5%. **Retention and Graduation:** 93% freshmen return for sophomore year. 77% freshmen graduate within 4 years. 19% grads go on to further study within 1 year. 1% grads pursue business degrees. 4% grads pursue law degrees. 1% grads pursue medical degrees. **Faculty:** Student/faculty ratio 9:1. 197 full-time faculty, 89% hold PhDs. 100% faculty teach undergrads.

ACADEMICS

Degrees: Bachelor's, master's. **Academic Requirements:** General education including some course work in arts/fine arts, humanities, sciences (biological or physical), social science, numerical and symbolic reasoning. **Classes:** 10-19 students in an average class. 20-29 students in an average lab/discussion section. **Majors with Highest Enrollment:** History, general; economics, general; political science and government, general. **Disciplines with Highest Percentage of Degrees Awarded:** Social sciences and history 44%, English 8%, biological life sciences 6%, visual and performing arts 6%, area and ethnic studies 6%. **Special Study Options:** Cross registration, double major, honors program, independent study, internships, student-designed major, study abroad, teacher certification program, 5-year BS/MS in electrical engineering or mechanical engineering with Rensselaer Polytechnic Institute.

FACILITIES

Housing: Coed, housing for disabled students, fraternities and/or sororities, community service dorm, quiet dorm, wellness and substance-free, 21+ only, cooking. All dorms are nonsmoking. **Library Holdings:** 988,536 bound volumes. 2,434 periodicals. 432,790 microforms. 226,532 audiovisuals. **Special Academic Facilities/Equipment:** Watkinson Library. **Computers:** School-owned computers available for student use.

EXTRACURRICULARS

Activities: Choral groups, dance, drama/theater, jazz band, literary magazine, music ensembles, musical theater, radio station, student government, student newspaper, student-run film society, television station, yearbook. **Organizations:** 112 registered organizations, 5 honor societies, 5 religious organizations, 7 fraternities (27% men join), 7 sororities (22% women join). **Athletics (Intercollegiate):** *Men:* baseball, basketball, crew, cross-country, diving, equestrian, fencing, football, golf, ice hockey, indoor track, lacrosse, rifle, rugby, sailing, soccer, softball, squash, swimming, tennis, track & field, wrestling. *Women:* basketball, crew, cross-country, diving, equestrian, fencing, field hockey, ice hockey, indoor track, lacrosse, rifle, rugby, sailing, soccer, softball, squash, swimming, tennis, track & field, volleyball.

ADMISSIONS

Selectivity Rating: 94 (of 100). **Freshman Academic Profile:** 56% in top 10% of high school class, 83% in top 25% of high school class, 98% in top 50% of high school class. 54% from public high schools. Average SAT I Math 642, SAT I Math middle 50% range 600-690. Average SAT I Verbal 630, SAT I Verbal middle 50% range 590-690. Average ACT 27, ACT middle 50% range 24-29. TOEFL required of all international applicants, minimum TOEFL 550. **Basis for Candidate Selection:** *Very important factors considered include:* secondary school record. *Important factors considered include:* character/personal qualities, class rank, essays, extracurricular activities, interview, minority status, recommendations, standardized test scores, talent/ability. *Other factors considered include:* alumni/ae relation, geographical residence, volunteer work, work experience. **Freshman Admission Requirements:** High school diploma or GED is required. *Academic units required/recommended:* 16 total required; 4 English required, 3 math required, 2 science required, 2 science lab required, 2 foreign language required, 2 history required. **Freshman Admission Statistics:** 5,417 applied, 36% accepted, 28% of those accepted enrolled. **Transfer Admission Requirements:** *Items required:* high school transcript, college transcript, essay, standardized test scores, statement of good standing from prior school. Minimum college GPA of 3.0 required. Lowest grade transferable C-. **General Admission Information:** Application fee $50. Early decision application deadline November 15. Regular application deadline January 15. Admission may be deferred for a maximum of 1 year. Credit and/or placement offered for CEEB Advanced Placement tests.

COSTS AND FINANCIAL AID

Tuition $27,170. Room & board $7,380. Required fees $1,432. Average book expense $850. **Required Forms and Deadlines:** FAFSA, CSS/Financial Aid PROFILE, noncustodial (divorced/separated) parent's statement and Federal Income tax returns. Financial aid filing deadline February 1. **Notification of Awards:** Applicants will be notified of awards on or about April 1. **Types of Aid:** *Need-based scholarships/grants:* Pell, SEOG, state scholarships/grants, private scholarships, the school's own gift aid. *Loans:* Direct Subsidized Stafford, Direct Unsubsidized Stafford, Direct PLUS, FFEL Subsidized Stafford, FFEL Unsubsidized Stafford, FFEL PLUS, Federal Perkins, college/university loans from institutional funds. **Student Employment:** Federal Work-Study Program available. Institutional employment available. Off-campus job opportunities are good. **Financial Aid Statistics:** 44% freshmen, 47% undergrads receive some form of aid. Average freshman grant $25,000. Average freshman loan $3,521. Average income from on-campus job $1,500. **Financial Aid Phone:** 860-297-2046.

See page 1234.

TRINITY COLLEGE (DC)

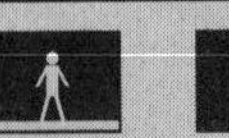

125 Michigan Avenue, NE, Washington, DC 20017
Phone: 202-884-9400 **E-mail:** admissions@trinitydc.edu **CEEB Code:** 5796
Fax: 202-884-9403 **Web:** www.trinitydc.edu **ACT Code:** 696

This private school was founded in 1897. It has a 26-acre campus.

STUDENTS AND FACULTY

Enrollment: 1,035. **Student Body:** Out-of-state 14%, international students represent 42 countries. **Ethnic Representation:** African American 60%, Asian 3%, Caucasian 13%, Hispanic 10%. **Retention and Graduation:** 75% freshmen return for sophomore year. 44% freshmen graduate within 4 years. **Faculty:** Student/faculty ratio 10:1. 48 full-time faculty, 89% hold PhDs. 90% faculty teach undergrads.

ACADEMICS

Degrees: Bachelor's, master's, post-bachelor's certificate. **Academic Requirements:** General education including some course work in arts/fine arts, computer literacy, English (including composition), foreign languages, history, humanities, mathematics, philosophy, sciences (biological or physical), social science. **Classes:** 10-19 students in an average class. **Disciplines with Highest Percentage of Degrees Awarded:** Interdisciplinary studies 21%, business/marketing 20%, education 13%, communications/communication technologies 12%, social sciences and history 10%. **Special Study Options:** Accelerated program, cross registration, double major, English as a second language, student exchange program (domestic), honors program, independent study, internships, liberal arts/career combination, student-designed major, study abroad, teacher certification program, weekend college.

FACILITIES

Housing: All-female, housing for disabled students. **Library Holdings:** 210,899 bound volumes. 498 periodicals. 6,541 microforms. 13,500 audiovisuals. **Special Academic Facilities/Equipment:** Art gallery, media technology center, writing center, Marilley Computer Lab. **Computers:** *Recommended operating system:* Windows 98 and Windows NT. School-owned computers available for student use.

EXTRACURRICULARS

Activities: Student government, student newspaper, student-run film society, yearbook. **Organizations:** 35 registered organizations, 3 honor societies. **Athletics (Intercollegiate):** *Women:* crew, field hockey, indoor track, lacrosse, soccer, tennis.

ADMISSIONS

Selectivity Rating: 76 (of 100). **Freshman Academic Profile:** Average SAT I Math 450, SAT I Math middle 50% range 410-490. Average SAT I Verbal 500, SAT I Verbal middle 50% range 450-560. TOEFL required of all international applicants, minimum TOEFL 450. **Basis for Candidate Selection:** *Very important factors considered include:* essays, secondary school record. *Important factors considered include:* extracurricular activities, recommendations, standardized test scores. *Other factors considered include:* alumni/ae relation, class rank, geographical residence, interview, volunteer work, work experience. **Freshman Admission Requirements:** High school diploma or GED is required. *Academic units required/recommended:* 17 total required; 4 English required, 3 math required, 3 science required, 1 science lab required, 2 foreign language required, 1 social studies required, 2 history required, 1 elective required. **Freshman Admission Statistics:** 277 applied, 95% accepted, 69% of those accepted enrolled. **Transfer Admission Requirements:** *Items required:* college transcript, essay. Minimum college GPA of 2.0 required. Lowest grade transferable C. **General Admission Information:** Application fee $35. Nonfall registration accepted. Admission may be deferred for a maximum of 1 year. Credit and/or placement offered for CEEB Advanced Placement tests.

COSTS AND FINANCIAL AID

Tuition $13,875. Room & board $6,500. Required fees $150. Average book expense $600. **Required Forms and Deadlines:** FAFSA. Priority filing deadline April 1. **Notification of Awards:** Applicants will be notified of awards on a rolling basis beginning on or about January 15. **Types of Aid:** *Need-based scholarships/grants:* Pell, SEOG, state scholarships/grants, private scholarships, the school's own gift aid. *Loans:* FFEL Subsidized Stafford, FFEL Unsubsidized Stafford, FFEL PLUS, Federal Perkins. **Student Employment:** Federal Work-Study Program available. Institutional employment available. Off-campus job opportunities are excellent. **Financial Aid Statistics:** 79% freshmen, 67% undergrads receive some form of aid. Average freshman grant $9,000. Average freshman loan $2,625. Average income from on-campus job $1,000. **Financial Aid Phone:** 202-884-9530.

TRINITY INTERNATIONAL UNIVERSITY

 $$$  

2065 Half Day Road, Deerfield, IL 60015
Phone: 847-317-7000 **E-mail:** tcdadm@tiu.edu **CEEB Code:** 1810
Fax: 847-317-8097 **Web:** www.tiu.edu **ACT Code:** 1150

This private school was founded in 1897. It has a 111-acre campus.

STUDENTS AND FACULTY

Enrollment: 1,162. **Student Body:** Male 42%, female 58%, out-of-state 38%, international 1% (37 countries represented). **Ethnic Representation:** African American 11%, Asian 3%, Caucasian 79%, Hispanic 3%. **Retention and Graduation:** 89% freshmen return for sophomore year. 22% freshmen graduate within 4 years. **Faculty:** Student/faculty ratio 16:1. 40 full-time faculty, 60% hold PhDs. 50% faculty teach undergrads.

ACADEMICS

Degrees: Bachelor's, certificate, doctoral, first professional, master's. **Academic Requirements:** General education including some course work in arts/fine arts, English (including composition), foreign languages, history, humanities, mathematics, philosophy, sciences (biological or physical), social science, Bible. **Classes:** 10-19 students in an average class. 10-19 students in an average lab/discussion section. **Majors with Highest Enrollment:** Business administration/management; elementary education and teaching; pastoral studies/counseling. **Disciplines with Highest Percentage of Degrees Awarded:** Education 24%, business/marketing 18%, philosophy/religion/theology 18%, liberal arts/general studies 14%, psychology 9%. **Special Study Options:** Accelerated program, cooperative (work-study) program, cross registration, distance learning, double major, dual enrollment, student exchange program (domestic), honors program, independent study, internships, liberal arts/career combination, student-designed major, study abroad, teacher certification program, TIPS (Training Institute for Pastoral Study), REACH (for nontraditional students with previous college credit), graduate courses.

FACILITIES

Housing: All-female, all-male, apartments for married students, apartments for single students, housing for disabled students, housing for international students. **Library Holdings:** 155,811 bound volumes. 1,332 periodicals. 141,840 microforms. 4,332 audiovisuals. **Computers:** School-owned computers available for student use.

EXTRACURRICULARS

Activities: Choral groups, concert band, dance, drama/theater, jazz band, literary magazine, music ensembles, musical theater, opera, pep band, student government, student newspaper, symphony orchestra, yearbook. **Organizations:** 20 registered organizations, 2 honor societies, 2 religious organizations. **Athletics (Intercollegiate):** *Men:* baseball, basketball, cross-country, football, soccer, volleyball. *Women:* basketball, cross-country, soccer, softball, volleyball.

ADMISSIONS

Selectivity Rating: 73 (of 100). **Freshman Academic Profile:** Average high school GPA 3.2. 13% in top 10% of high school class, 35% in top 25% of high school class, 66% in top 50% of high school class. Average SAT I Math 522, SAT I Math middle 50% range 450-560. Average SAT I Verbal 542, SAT I Verbal middle 50% range 480-580. Average ACT 23, ACT middle 50% range 19-25. TOEFL required of all international applicants, minimum TOEFL 530. **Basis for Candidate Selection:** *Very important factors considered include:* secondary school record, standardized test scores. *Important factors considered include:* character/personal qualities, essays, recommendations, religious affiliation/commitment. *Other factors considered include:* class rank, extracurricular activities, talent/ability, volunteer work. **Freshman Admission Requirements:** High school diploma or GED is required. *Academic units required/recommended:* 15 total required; 3 English required, 2 math required, 2 science required, 1 science lab required, 2 foreign language required, 2 social studies required, 3 elective required. **Freshman Admission Statistics:** 455 applied, 84% accepted, 40% of those accepted enrolled. **Transfer Admission Requirements:** *Items required:* high school transcript, college transcript, essay. Minimum college GPA of 2.0 required. Lowest grade transferable C-. **General Admission Information:** Application fee $25. Nonfall registration accepted. Admission may be deferred for a maximum of 2 years. Credit and/or placement offered for CEEB Advanced Placement tests.

COSTS AND FINANCIAL AID

Tuition $16,100. Room & board $5,510. Required fees $250. Average book expense $840. **Required Forms and Deadlines:** FAFSA. No deadline for regular filing. Priority filing deadline April 1. **Notification of Awards:** Applicants will be notified of awards on a rolling basis beginning on or about February 15. **Types of Aid:** *Need-based scholarships/grants:* Pell, SEOG, state scholarships/grants, private scholarships, the school's own gift aid. *Loans:* FFEL Subsidized Stafford, FFEL Unsubsidized Stafford, FFEL PLUS, Federal Perkins. **Student Employment:** Federal Work-Study Program available. Institutional employment available. Off-campus job opportunities are excellent. **Financial Aid Statistics:** 60% freshmen, 76% undergrads receive some form of aid. Average freshman grant $12,921. Average freshman loan $3,964. **Financial Aid Phone:** 847-317-8060.

TRINITY LUTHERAN COLLEGE

4221 228th Avenue SE, Issaquah, WA 98029
Phone: 425-961-5510 **E-mail:** admission@lbi.edu
Fax: 425-392-0404 **Web:** www.lbi.edu

This private school, which is affiliated with the Lutheran Church, was founded in 1944.

STUDENTS AND FACULTY

Enrollment: 132. **Student Body:** Male 38%, female 62%, out-of-state 41%. **Ethnic Representation:** African American 5%, Asian 6%, Caucasian 88%, Hispanic 1%. **Retention and Graduation:** 75% freshmen return for sophomore year. **Faculty:** 100% faculty teach undergrads.

ACADEMICS

Degrees: Associate's, bachelor's, diploma, post-bachelor's certificate, terminal, transfer. **Special Study Options:** Double major, English as a second language, internships, study abroad.

FACILITIES

Housing: Coed. **Library Holdings:** 31,000 bound volumes. 217 periodicals.

EXTRACURRICULARS

Activities: Choral groups, drama/theater. **Organizations:** 4 honor societies. **Athletics (Intercollegiate):** *Men:* basketball, softball, tennis, volleyball. *Women:* basketball, softball, tennis, volleyball.

ADMISSIONS

Selectivity Rating: 60 (of 100). **Freshman Academic Profile:** 0% in top 10% of high school class, 33% in top 25% of high school class, 60% in top 50% of high school class. TOEFL required of all international applicants, minimum TOEFL 500. **Freshman Admission Requirements: Transfer Admission Requirements:** Lowest grade transferable C-. **General Admission Information:** Application fee $30. Regular application deadline August 15.

COSTS AND FINANCIAL AID

Tuition $5,750. Room & board $4,525. Average book expense $500. **Types of Aid:** *Loans:* FFEL Subsidized Stafford, FFEL PLUS. **Financial Aid Statistics:** Average income from on-campus job $1,750. **Financial Aid Phone:** 800-843-5659.

TRINITY UNIVERSITY

  $$$   

715 Stadium Drive, San Antonio, TX 78212
Phone: 210-999-7207 **E-mail:** Admissions@Trinity.edu **CEEB Code:** 6831
Fax: 210-999-8164 **Web:** www.Trinity.edu **ACT Code:** 4226

This private school, which is affiliated with the Presbyterian Church, was founded in 1869. It has a 117-acre campus.

STUDENTS AND FACULTY

Enrollment: 2,406. **Student Body:** Male 48%, female 52%, out-of-state 30%, international 1%. **Ethnic Representation:** African American 2%, Asian 6%, Caucasian 71%, Hispanic 11%. **Retention and Graduation:** 88% freshmen return for sophomore year. 64% freshmen graduate within 4 years. 29% grads go on to further study within 1 year. 11% grads pursue business degrees. 12% grads pursue law degrees. 5% grads pursue medical degrees. **Faculty:** Student/faculty ratio 11:1. 211 full-time faculty, 98% hold PhDs. 100% faculty teach undergrads.

ACADEMICS

Degrees: Bachelor's, master's. **Academic Requirements:** General education including some course work in arts/fine arts, computer literacy, English (including composition), foreign languages, humanities, sciences (biological or physical), social science. **Classes:** 10-19 students in an average class. 20-29 students in an average lab/discussion section. **Majors with Highest Enroll-**

ment: Business administration/management; mass communications/media studies; foreign languages/modern languages, general. **Disciplines with Highest Percentage of Degrees Awarded:** Business/marketing 23%, social sciences and history 20%, computer and information sciences 7%, communications/communication technologies 7%, biological life sciences 7%. **Special Study Options:** Accelerated program, double major, honors program, independent study, internships, liberal arts/career combination, study abroad, teacher certification program.

FACILITIES

Housing: Coed. **Library Holdings:** 898,527 bound volumes. 2,311 periodicals. 290,702 microforms. 24,742 audiovisuals. **Special Academic Facilities/ Equipment:** Steiren Theatre, Richardson Communication Center, Ruth Taylor Arts Complex, Laurie Auditorium. **Computers:** *Recommended operating system:* Windows 2000/XP. School-owned computers available for student use.

EXTRACURRICULARS

Activities: Choral groups, concert band, dance, drama/theater, jazz band, literary magazine, music ensembles, musical theater, opera, pep band, radio station, student government, student newspaper, student-run film society, symphony orchestra, television station, yearbook. **Organizations:** 106 registered organizations, 24 honor societies, 11 religious organizations, 8 fraternities, 6 sororities. **Athletics (Intercollegiate):** *Men:* baseball, basketball, cross-country, diving, football, golf, soccer, swimming, tennis, track & field. *Women:* basketball, cross-country, diving, golf, soccer, softball, swimming, tennis, track & field, volleyball.

ADMISSIONS

Selectivity Rating: 84 (of 100). **Freshman Academic Profile:** Average high school GPA 3.5. 49% in top 10% of high school class, 83% in top 25% of high school class, 97% in top 50% of high school class. 67% from public high schools. Average SAT I Math 640, SAT I Math middle 50% range 610-690. Average SAT I Verbal 631, SAT I Verbal middle 50% range 580-690. Average ACT 28, ACT middle 50% range 27-31. TOEFL required of all international applicants, minimum TOEFL 570. **Basis for Candidate Selection:** *Very important factors considered include:* character/personal qualities, class rank, secondary school record, standardized test scores. *Important factors considered include:* essays, extracurricular activities, recommendations, talent/ability. *Other factors considered include:* alumni/ae relation, geographical residence, interview, state residency, volunteer work, work experience. **Freshman Admission Requirements:** High school diploma or GED is required. *Academic units required/ recommended:* 19 total required; 20 total recommended; 4 English required, 4 English recommended, 3 math required, 4 math recommended, 3 science required, 3 science recommended, 2 science lab required, 3 science lab recommended, 2 foreign language required, 3 foreign language recommended, 3 social studies required, 3 social studies recommended, 1 elective required. **Freshman Admission Statistics:** 3,108 applied, 69% accepted, 31% of those accepted enrolled. **Transfer Admission Requirements:** *Items required:* high school transcript, college transcript, essay, standardized test scores, statement of good standing from prior school. Minimum college GPA of 3.0 required. Lowest grade transferable C-. **General Admission Information:** Application fee $20. Priority application deadline February 1. Early decision application deadline November 1. Nonfall registration accepted. Admission may be deferred for a maximum of 1 year. Credit and/or placement offered for CEEB Advanced Placement tests.

COSTS AND FINANCIAL AID

Tuition $17,214. Room & board $7,040. Required fees $640. Average book expense $612. **Required Forms and Deadlines:** FAFSA. Financial aid filing deadline April 1. Priority filing deadline February 1. **Notification of Awards:** Applicants will be notified of awards on or about April 1. **Types of Aid:** *Need-based scholarships/grants:* Pell, SEOG, state scholarships/grants, private scholarships, the school's own gift aid. *Loans:* FFEL Subsidized Stafford, FFEL Unsubsidized Stafford, FFEL PLUS, Federal Perkins, state loans, college/ university loans from institutional funds. **Student Employment:** Federal Work-Study Program available. Institutional employment available. Off-campus job opportunities are good. **Financial Aid Statistics:** 43% freshmen, 41% undergrads receive some form of aid. Average freshman grant $8,719. Average freshman loan $4,729. Average income from on-campus job $1,253. **Financial Aid Phone:** 210-999-8315.

TRINITY WESTERN UNIVERSITY

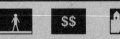

PO Box 1409, Blaine, WA 98231
Phone: 604-513-2019 **E-mail:** admissions@twu.ca **CEEB Code:** 876
Fax: 604-513-2064 **Web:** www.twu.ca **ACT Code:** 5242

This private school was founded in 1962. It has a 100-acre campus.

STUDENTS AND FACULTY

Enrollment: 2,379. **Student Body:** Male 44%, female 56%. **Retention and Graduation:** 80% freshmen return for sophomore year. 15% grads go on to further study within 1 year. 3% grads pursue law degrees. 3% grads pursue medical degrees. **Faculty:** Student/faculty ratio 18:1. 77 full-time faculty, 89% hold PhDs. 100% faculty teach undergrads.

ACADEMICS

Degrees: Bachelor's, certificate, diploma, first professional, master's. **Academic Requirements:** General education including some course work in arts/fine arts, English (including composition), history, philosophy, sciences (biological or physical), social science. **Disciplines with Highest Percentage of Degrees Awarded:** Liberal arts/general studies 18%, psychology 10%, education 8%, business/marketing 8%, biological life sciences 8%. **Special Study Options:** Cooperative (work-study) program, double major, English as a second language, honors program, internships, study abroad.

FACILITIES

Housing: All-female, all-male, apartments for single students, housing for disabled students, housing for international students. **Library Holdings:** 115,626 bound volumes. 2,316 periodicals. 256,089 microforms. 3,002 audiovisuals. **Special Academic Facilities/Equipment:** Museum of Biblical History. **Computers:** *Recommended operating system:* Windows 95. School-owned computers available for student use.

EXTRACURRICULARS

Activities: Choral groups, concert band, dance, drama/theater, jazz band, music ensembles, pep band, student government, student newspaper, yearbook. **Organizations:** 33 registered organizations. **Athletics (Intercollegiate):** *Men:* basketball, cross-country, ice hockey, rugby, soccer, track & field, volleyball. *Women:* basketball, cross-country, rugby, soccer, track & field, volleyball.

ADMISSIONS

Selectivity Rating: 63 (of 100). **Freshman Academic Profile:** Average high school GPA 3.4. 80% from public high schools. Average SAT I Math 550. Average SAT I Verbal 570. Average ACT 26. TOEFL required of all international applicants, minimum TOEFL 570. **Basis for Candidate Selection:** *Very important factors considered include:* recommendations, secondary school record, standardized test scores. *Important factors considered include:* essays. *Other factors considered include:* character/personal qualities, class rank, extracurricular activities, religious affiliation/commitment, talent/ability. **Freshman Admission Requirements:** High school diploma or GED is required. *Academic units required/recommended:* 4 English required, 3 math required, 2 science required, 1 science lab required, 2 social studies required, 2 elective required. **Freshman Admission Statistics:** 1,371 applied, 78% accepted, 39% of those accepted enrolled. **Transfer Admission Requirements:** *Items required:* high school transcript, college transcript, essay. Minimum college GPA of 2.0 required. Lowest grade transferable D. **General Admission Information:** Application fee $35. Priority application deadline February 28. Regular application deadline June 15. Nonfall registration accepted. Admission may be deferred. Credit and/or placement offered for CEEB Advanced Placement tests.

COSTS AND FINANCIAL AID

Tuition $10,350. Room & board $5,990. Required fees $120. Average book expense $800. **Required Forms and Deadlines:** institution's own financial aid form. Financial aid filing deadline March 15. **Notification of Awards:** Applicants will be notified of awards on a rolling basis beginning on or about April 1. **Types of Aid:** *Need-based scholarships/grants:* state scholarships/grants, private scholarships, the school's own gift aid. *Loans:* Direct Subsidized Stafford, Direct Unsubsidized Stafford, Direct PLUS. **Student Employment:** Institutional employment available. Off-campus job opportunities are good. **Financial Aid Statistics:** 56% freshmen, 57% undergrads receive some form of aid. Average freshman grant $1,800. Average income from on-campus job $1,000. **Financial Aid Phone:** 604-513-2061.

TRI-STATE UNIVERSITY

1 University Avenue, Angola, IN 46703
Phone: 260-665-4132 **E-mail:** admit@tristate.edu **CEEB Code:** 1811
Fax: 260-665-4578 **Web:** www.tristate.edu **ACT Code:** 1250

This private school was founded in 1884. It has a 400-acre campus.

STUDENTS AND FACULTY

Enrollment: 1,267. **Student Body:** Male 64%, female 36%, out-of-state 38%, international 3% (20 countries represented). **Ethnic Representation:** African American 2%, Asian 1%, Caucasian 89%, Hispanic 1%. **Retention and Graduation:** 68% freshmen return for sophomore year. 5% grads go on to further study within 1 year. 5% grads pursue business degrees. 2% grads pursue law degrees. **Faculty:** Student/faculty ratio 16:1. 64 full-time faculty, 62% hold PhDs. 100% faculty teach undergrads.

ACADEMICS

Degrees: Associate's, bachelor's. **Academic Requirements:** General education including some course work in computer literacy, English (including composition), humanities, mathematics, sciences (biological or physical), social science. **Classes:** 10-19 students in an average class. 10-19 students in an average lab/discussion section. **Majors with Highest Enrollment:** Mechanical engineering; civil engineering, general; business administration/management. **Disciplines with Highest Percentage of Degrees Awarded:** Engineering/engineering technology 50%, business/marketing 24%, education 9%, protective services/public administration 4%, trade and industry 3%. **Special Study Options:** Cooperative (work-study) program, distance learning, double major, internships, teacher certification program.

FACILITIES

Housing: Coed. **Library Holdings:** 141,543 bound volumes. 336 periodicals. 1,792 microforms. 625 audiovisuals. **Special Academic Facilities/Equipment:** Lewis Hershey Museum; Wells Gallery of Engravings; Zollner Golf Course. **Computers:** *Recommended operating system:* Windows NT/2000. School-owned computers available for student use.

EXTRACURRICULARS

Activities: Choral groups, drama/theater, pep band, radio station, student government, student newspaper, yearbook. **Organizations:** 35 registered organizations, 13 honor societies, 3 religious organizations, 8 fraternities (25% men join), 6 sororities (15% women join). **Athletics (Intercollegiate):** *Men:* baseball, basketball, cross-country, football, golf, indoor track, soccer, tennis, track & field. *Women:* basketball, cross-country, golf, indoor track, soccer, softball, tennis, track & field, volleyball.

ADMISSIONS

Selectivity Rating: 63 (of 100). **Freshman Academic Profile:** Average high school GPA 3.2. 19% in top 10% of high school class, 46% in top 25% of high school class, 77% in top 50% of high school class. 80% from public high schools. Average SAT I Math 533, SAT I Math middle 50% range 470-590. Average SAT I Verbal 500, SAT I Verbal middle 50% range 440-550. Average ACT 22, ACT middle 50% range 19-25. TOEFL required of all international applicants, minimum TOEFL 550. **Basis for Candidate Selection:** *Very important factors considered include:* secondary school record, standardized test scores. *Important factors considered include:* class rank, extracurricular activities, interview, recommendations. *Other factors considered include:* alumni/ae relation, character/personal qualities, talent/ability, volunteer work, work experience. **Freshman Admission Requirements:** High school diploma or GED is required. *Academic units required/recommended:* 17 total required; 4 English required, 2 math required, 2 science required, 2 science lab required, 2 social studies required, 2 history required, 5 elective required. **Freshman Admission Statistics:** 1,352 applied, 74% accepted, 29% of those accepted enrolled. **Transfer Admission Requirements:** *Items required:* high school transcript, college transcript, statement of good standing from prior school. Minimum college GPA of 2.0 required. Lowest grade transferable C. **General Admission Information:** Application fee $20. Priority application deadline March 1. Regular application deadline June 1. Nonfall registration accepted. Admission may be deferred for a maximum of 1 year. Credit and/or placement offered for CEEB Advanced Placement tests.

COSTS AND FINANCIAL AID

Average book expense $700. **Required Forms and Deadlines:** FAFSA. Financial aid filing deadline June 1. Priority filing deadline March 1. **Notification of Awards:** Applicants will be notified of awards on a rolling basis beginning on or about February 1. **Types of Aid:** *Need-based scholarships/grants:* Pell, SEOG, state scholarships/grants, private scholarships, the school's own gift aid. *Loans:* FFEL Subsidized Stafford, FFEL Unsubsidized Stafford, FFEL PLUS. **Student Employment:** Federal Work-Study Program available. Institutional employment available. Off-campus job opportunities are excellent. **Financial Aid Statistics:** 99% freshmen, 90% undergrads receive some form of aid. Average freshman grant $6,800. Average freshman loan $2,452. Average income from on-campus job $1,200. **Financial Aid Phone:** 260-665-4175.

TROY STATE UNIVERSITY—DOTHAN

PO Box 8368, Dothan, AL 36304-0368
Phone: 334-983-6556 **E-mail:** arivers@tsud.edu
Fax: 334-983-6322 **Web:** www.tsud.edu **ACT Code:** 15

This public school was founded in 1864. It has a 265-acre campus.

STUDENTS AND FACULTY

Enrollment: 1,538. **Student Body:** Male 35%, female 65%, out-of-state 9%. **Ethnic Representation:** African American 19%, Asian 2%, Caucasian 73%, Hispanic 3%, Native American 1%. **Retention and Graduation:** 42% freshmen return for sophomore year. **Faculty:** Student/faculty ratio 14:1. 59 full-time faculty, 79% hold PhDs. 78% faculty teach undergrads.

ACADEMICS

Degrees: Associate's, bachelor's, master's, post-master's certificate. **Academic Requirements:** General education including some course work in English (including composition), history, humanities, mathematics, sciences (biological or physical), social science. **Classes:** 10-19 students in an average class. 10-19 students in an average lab/discussion section. **Majors with Highest Enrollment:** Computer science; accounting; elementary education and teaching. **Disciplines with Highest Percentage of Degrees Awarded:** Business/marketing 39%, education 23%, computer and information sciences 13%, psychology 9%, social sciences and history 6%. **Special Study Options:** Cooperative (work-study) program, distance learning, double major, independent study, internships, teacher certification program, weekend college.

FACILITIES

Library Holdings: 101,136 bound volumes. 455 periodicals. 283,829 microforms. 14,282 audiovisuals. **Computers:** School-owned computers available for student use.

EXTRACURRICULARS

Activities: Student government. **Organizations:** 18 registered organizations, 6 honor societies, 1 religious organization.

ADMISSIONS

Selectivity Rating: 63 (of 100). **Freshman Academic Profile:** 98% from public high schools. Average ACT 22, ACT middle 50% range 20-25. TOEFL required of all international applicants, minimum TOEFL 550. **Basis for Candidate Selection:** *Very important factors considered include:* secondary school record, standardized test scores. **Freshman Admission Requirements:** High school diploma or GED is required. **Freshman Admission Statistics:** 112 applied, 69% accepted, 83% of those accepted enrolled. **Transfer Admission Requirements:** *Items required:* college transcript, statement of good standing from prior school. Lowest grade transferable D. **General Admission Information:** Application fee $20. Nonfall registration accepted. Admission may be deferred for a maximum of 1 year.

COSTS AND FINANCIAL AID

In-state tuition $3,220. Out-of-state tuition $6,440. Required fees $312. Average book expense $600. **Required Forms and Deadlines:** FAFSA and institution's own financial aid form. No deadline for regular filing. Priority filing deadline May 1. **Notification of Awards:** Applicants will be notified of awards on a rolling basis beginning on or about February 1. **Types of Aid:** *Need-based scholarships/grants:* Pell, SEOG, private scholarships, the school's own gift aid. *Loans:* Direct Subsidized Stafford, Direct Unsubsidized Stafford, Federal Perkins, college/university loans from institutional funds. **Student Employment:** Federal Work-Study Program available. Off-campus job opportunities are fair.

TROY STATE UNIVERSITY—MONTGOMERY

PO Drawer 4419, Montgomery, AL 36103-4419
Phone: 334-241-9506 **E-mail:** admit@tsum.edu
Fax: 334-241-5448 **Web:** www.tsum.edu

This public school was founded in 1965. It has a 6-acre campus.

STUDENTS AND FACULTY

Enrollment: 2,831. **Student Body:** Male 34%, female 66%. **Ethnic Representation:** African American 43%, Asian 1%, Caucasian 47%, Hispanic 1%. **Faculty:** Student/faculty ratio 20:1. 36 full-time faculty, 97% hold PhDs. 100% faculty teach undergrads.

ACADEMICS

Degrees: Associate's, bachelor's, master's, post-master's certificate, terminal. **Academic Requirements:** General education including some course work in arts/fine arts, computer literacy, English (including composition), history, humanities, mathematics, philosophy, sciences (biological or physical), social science. **Classes:** 10-19 students in an average class. **Majors with Highest Enrollment:** Liberal arts and sciences/liberal studies; business administration/management; human resources management/personnel administration, general. **Disciplines with Highest Percentage of Degrees Awarded:** Business/marketing 57%, psychology 16%, social sciences and history 12%, computer and information sciences 6%, liberal arts/general studies 5%. **Special Study Options:** Accelerated program, cross registration, distance learning, double major, dual enrollment, external degree program, honors program, independent study, teacher certification program, weekend college.

FACILITIES

Housing: No on-campus housing available. **Library Holdings:** 26,041 bound volumes. 476 periodicals. 72,991 microforms. 9,194 audiovisuals. **Special Academic Facilities/Equipment:** W. A. Gayle Planetarium, Davis Theater, Rosa L. Parks Library & Museum. **Computers:** School-owned computers available for student use.

EXTRACURRICULARS

Organizations: 7 registered organizations, 2 honor societies.

ADMISSIONS

Selectivity Rating: 63 (of 100). **Basis for Candidate Selection:** *Very important factors considered include:* secondary school record. *Other factors considered include:* standardized test scores. **Freshman Admission Requirements:** High school diploma or GED is required. *Academic units required/recommended:* 11 total required; 15 total recommended; 3 English required, 4 English recommended. **Freshman Admission Statistics:** 451 applied, 100% accepted, 55% of those accepted enrolled. **Transfer Admission Requirements:** *Items required:* college transcript, statement of good standing from prior school. Minimum college GPA of 2.0 required. Lowest grade transferable C. **General Admission Information:** Application fee $20. Nonfall registration accepted. Admission may be deferred for a maximum of 1 year.

COSTS AND FINANCIAL AID

Required Forms and Deadlines: FAFSA and institution's own financial aid form. Financial aid filing deadline May 1. **Notification of Awards:** Applicants will be notified of awards on a rolling basis. **Types of Aid:** *Need-based scholarships/grants:* Pell, SEOG, state scholarships/grants, private scholarships. *Loans:* FFEL Subsidized Stafford, FFEL Unsubsidized Stafford, FFEL PLUS. **Student Employment:** Federal Work-Study Program available. Off-campus job opportunities are good. **Financial Aid Statistics:** 55% freshmen, 43% undergrads receive some form of aid. **Financial Aid Phone:** 334-241-9520.

TROY STATE UNIVERSITY—TROY

111 Adams Administration, Troy, AL 36082
Phone: 334-670-3179 **E-mail:** bstar@trojan.troyst.edu **CEEB Code:** 1738
Fax: 334-670-3733 **Web:** www.troyst.edu **ACT Code:** 48

This public school was founded in 1887. It has a 577-acre campus.

STUDENTS AND FACULTY

Enrollment: 4,607. **Student Body:** Male 40%, female 60%, out-of-state 14%, international 6%. **Ethnic Representation:** African American 24%, Asian 1%, Caucasian 71%, Hispanic 1%, Native American 1%. **Retention and Graduation:** 74% freshmen return for sophomore year. 40% freshmen graduate within 4 years. **Faculty:** Student/faculty ratio 19:1. 209 full-time faculty, 61% hold PhDs. 100% faculty teach undergrads.

ACADEMICS

Degrees: Associate's, bachelor's, master's, post-master's certificate. **Academic Requirements:** General education including some course work in arts/fine arts, computer literacy, English (including composition), history, humanities, mathematics, sciences (biological or physical). **Classes:** 10-19 students in an average class. 20-29 students in an average lab/discussion section. **Majors with Highest Enrollment:** Business administration/management; elementary education and teaching; nursing/registered nurse training (RN, ASN, BSN, MSN). **Disciplines with Highest Percentage of Degrees Awarded:** Business/marketing 25%, education 24%, protective services/public administration 11%, health professions and related sciences 9%, communications/communication technologies 6%. **Special Study Options:** Distance learning, double major, dual enrollment, English as a second language, honors program, independent study, internships, study abroad, teacher certification program.

FACILITIES

Housing: Coed, all-female, all-male, apartments for married students, apartments for single students, housing for international students, fraternities and/or sororities, substance-free housing, honor student housing. **Library Holdings:** 646,982 bound volumes. 4,190 periodicals. 1,362,063 microforms. 10,065 audiovisuals. **Computers:** School-owned computers available for student use.

EXTRACURRICULARS

Activities: Choral groups, concert band, dance, drama/theater, jazz band, marching band, music ensembles, musical theater, pep band, student government, student newspaper, television station, yearbook. **Organizations:** 110 registered organizations, 20 honor societies, 10 religious organizations, 11 fraternities (18% men join), 8 sororities (19% women join). **Athletics (Intercollegiate):** *Men:* baseball, basketball, cheerleading, cross-country, football, golf, tennis, track & field. *Women:* basketball, cheerleading, cross-country, golf, soccer, softball, tennis, track & field, volleyball.

ADMISSIONS

Selectivity Rating: 79 (of 100). **Freshman Academic Profile:** Average high school GPA 3.2. 48% in top 25% of high school class, 82% in top 50% of high school class. ACT middle 50% range 17-24. TOEFL required of all international applicants, minimum TOEFL 500. **Basis for Candidate Selection:** *Very important factors considered include:* character/personal qualities, secondary school record. *Important factors considered include:* extracurricular activities, standardized test scores. *Other factors considered include:* recommendations. **Freshman Admission Requirements:** High school diploma or GED is required. *Academic units required/recommended:* 15 total required; 3 English required. **Freshman Admission Statistics:** 2,438 applied, 72% accepted, 49% of those accepted enrolled. **Transfer Admission Requirements:** *Items required:* college transcript. Minimum college GPA of 2.0 required. Lowest grade transferable D. **General Admission Information:** Application fee $20. Nonfall registration accepted. Admission may be deferred for a maximum of 1 year. Credit and/or placement offered for CEEB Advanced Placement tests.

COSTS AND FINANCIAL AID

Required Forms and Deadlines: FAFSA and institution's own financial aid form. No deadline for regular filing. Priority filing deadline May 1. **Notification of Awards:** Applicants will be notified of awards on a rolling basis beginning on or about May 1. **Types of Aid:** *Need-based scholarships/grants:* Pell, SEOG, state scholarships/grants, private scholarships, the school's own gift aid. *Loans:* FFEL Subsidized Stafford, FFEL Unsubsidized Stafford, FFEL PLUS, Federal Perkins. **Student Employment:** Federal Work-Study Program available. Institutional employment available. Off-campus job opportunities are good. **Financial Aid Statistics:** 54% freshmen, 68% undergrads receive some form of aid. Average income from on-campus job $2,295. **Financial Aid Phone:** 334-670-3186.

TRUMAN STATE UNIVERSITY

McClain Hall 205, 100 East Normal, Kirksville, MO 63501
Phone: 660-785-4114 **E-mail:** admissions@truman.edu **CEEB Code:** 6483
Fax: 660-785-7456 **Web:** www.truman.edu **ACT Code:** 2336

This public school was founded in 1867. It has a 140-acre campus.

STUDENTS AND FACULTY

Enrollment: 5,636. **Student Body:** Male 41%, female 59%, out-of-state 24%, international 4% (49 countries represented). **Ethnic Representation:** African American 4%, Asian 2%, Caucasian 90%, Hispanic 2%. **Retention and Graduation:** 85% freshmen return for sophomore year. 40% freshmen graduate within 4 years. 41% grads go on to further study within 1 year. **Faculty:** Student/faculty ratio 15:1. 366 full-time faculty, 84% hold PhDs. 97% faculty teach undergrads.

ACADEMICS

Degrees: Bachelor's, master's. **Academic Requirements:** General education including some course work in arts/fine arts, computer literacy, English (including composition), foreign languages, history, humanities, mathematics, sciences (biological or physical), social science. **Classes:** 20-29 students in an average class. 20-29 students in an average lab/discussion section. **Majors with Highest Enrollment:** Business administration/management; English language and literature, general; biology/biological sciences, general. **Disciplines with Highest Percentage of Degrees Awarded:** Business/marketing 22%, English 11%, biological life sciences 10%, psychology 10%, social sciences and history 9%. **Special Study Options:** Double major, dual enrollment, honors program, internships, study abroad, teacher certification program.

FACILITIES

Housing: Coed, all-female, apartments for married students, apartments for single students, housing for international students, sorority housing. **Library Holdings:** 481,424 bound volumes. 3,197 periodicals. 1,514,497 microforms. 36,724 audiovisuals. **Special Academic Facilities/Equipment:** Art gallery, local history and artifacts museum, human performance lab, greenhouse, observatory, IR and NMR instrumentation. **Computers:** School-owned computers available for student use.

EXTRACURRICULARS

Activities: Choral groups, concert band, dance, drama/theater, jazz band, literary magazine, marching band, music ensembles, musical theater, pep band, radio station, student government, student newspaper, symphony orchestra, television station, yearbook. **Organizations:** 221 registered organizations, 37 honor societies, 17 religious organizations, 19 fraternities (30% men join), 11 sororities (21% women join). **Athletics (Intercollegiate):** *Men:* baseball, basketball, cross-country, football, golf, indoor track, soccer, swimming, tennis, track & field, wrestling. *Women:* basketball, cross-country, golf, indoor track, soccer, softball, swimming, tennis, track & field, volleyball.

ADMISSIONS

Selectivity Rating: 82 (of 100). **Freshman Academic Profile:** Average high school GPA 3.8. 47% in top 10% of high school class, 82% in top 25% of high school class, 98% in top 50% of high school class. 78% from public high schools. Average SAT I Math 606, SAT I Math middle 50% range 550-660. Average SAT I Verbal 614, SAT I Verbal middle 50% range 560-680. Average ACT 27, ACT middle 50% range 25-30. TOEFL required of all international applicants, minimum TOEFL 550. **Basis for Candidate Selection:** *Very important factors considered include:* class rank, secondary school record, standardized test scores. *Important factors considered include:* essays, extracurricular activities. *Other factors considered include:* alumni/ae relation, character/personal qualities, geographical residence, interview, minority status, recommendations, state residency, talent/ability, volunteer work, work experience. **Freshman Admission Requirements:** High school diploma or GED is required. *Academic units required/recommended:* 16 total required; 17 total recommended; 4 English required, 3 math required, 4 math recommended, 3 science required, 2 foreign language required, 3 social studies required. **Freshman Admission Statistics:** 5,132 applied, 79% accepted, 36% of those accepted enrolled. **Transfer Admission Requirements:** *Items required:* high school transcript, college transcript, essay, standardized test scores. Minimum high school GPA of 2.7 required. Minimum college GPA of 2.7 required. Lowest grade transferable D. **General Admission Information:** Priority application deadline November 15. Regular application deadline March 1. Nonfall registration accepted. Admission may be deferred for a maximum of 1 year. Credit and/or placement offered for CEEB Advanced Placement tests.

COSTS AND FINANCIAL AID

In-state tuition $4,144. Out-of-state tuition $7,544. Room & board $4,928. Required fees $56. Average book expense $600. **Required Forms and Deadlines:** FAFSA and institution's own financial aid form. Priority filing deadline April 1. **Notification of Awards:** Applicants will be notified of awards on a rolling basis beginning on or about April 15. **Types of Aid:** *Need-based scholarships/grants:* Pell, SEOG, state scholarships/grants, private scholarships, the school's own gift aid. *Loans:* FFEL Subsidized Stafford, FFEL Unsubsidized Stafford, FFEL PLUS, Federal Perkins, Federal Nursing, state loans, college/university loans from institutional funds. **Student Employment:** Federal Work-Study Program available. Institutional employment available. Off-campus job opportunities are good. **Financial Aid Statistics:** 26% freshmen, 36% undergrads receive some form of aid. Average freshman grant $4,103. Average freshman loan $3,462. Average income from on-campus job $917. **Financial Aid Phone:** 660-785-4130.

TUFTS UNIVERSITY

Bendetson Hall, Medford, MA 02155
Phone: 617-627-3170 **E-mail:** admissions.inquiry@ase.tufts.edu **CEEB Code:** 3901
Fax: 617-627-3860 **Web:** www.tufts.edu **ACT Code:** 1922

This private school was founded in 1852. It has a 150-acre campus.

STUDENTS AND FACULTY

Enrollment: 4,910. **Student Body:** Male 45%, female 55%, out-of-state 76%, international 7%. **Ethnic Representation:** African American 8%, Asian 14%, Caucasian 58%, Hispanic 9%. **Retention and Graduation:** 96% freshmen return for sophomore year. 81% freshmen graduate within 4 years. 35% grads go on to further study within 1 year. **Faculty:** Student/faculty ratio 9:1. 716 full-time faculty. 100% faculty teach undergrads.

ACADEMICS

Degrees: Bachelor's, doctoral, first professional, master's, post-master's certificate. **Academic Requirements:** General education including some course work in arts/fine arts, English (including composition), foreign languages, humanities, mathematics, sciences (biological or physical), social science. **Classes:** 10-19 students in an average class. 10-19 students in an average lab/discussion section. **Disciplines with Highest Percentage of Degrees Awarded:** Social sciences and history 35%, engineering/engineering technology 15%, visual and performing arts 8%, English 8%, biological life sciences 7%. **Special Study Options:** Cross registration, double major, student exchange program (domestic), honors program, independent study, internships, liberal arts/career combination, student-designed major, study abroad, teacher certification program.

FACILITIES

Housing: Coed, all-female, housing for disabled students, fraternities and/or sororities, cooperative housing, special-interest housing. **Library Holdings:** 1,475,800 bound volumes. 5,204 periodicals. 1,180,500 microforms. 33,800 audiovisuals. **Special Academic Facilities/Equipment:** Language lab, nutrition institute, research lab for physical electronics, bioelectrical and biochemical labs, computer-aided design (CAD) facility, electro-optics technology, and environmental management centers. **Computers:** School-owned computers available for student use.

EXTRACURRICULARS

Activities: Choral groups, concert band, dance, drama/theater, jazz band, literary magazine, marching band, music ensembles, musical theater, pep band, radio station, student government, student newspaper, student-run film society, symphony orchestra, television station, yearbook. **Organizations:** 160 registered organizations, 4 honor societies, 5 religious organizations, 10 fraternities (15% men join), 3 sororities (4% women join). **Athletics (Intercollegiate):** *Men:* baseball, basketball, cheerleading, crew, cross-country, diving, equestrian, fencing, football, golf, ice hockey, indoor track, lacrosse, rugby, sailing, skiing (alpine), skiing (Nordic), soccer, squash, swimming, tennis, track & field. *Women:* basketball, cheerleading, crew, cross-country, diving, equestrian, fencing, field hockey, indoor track, lacrosse, rugby, sailing, skiing (alpine), skiing (Nordic), soccer, softball, squash, swimming, tennis, track & field, volleyball.

ADMISSIONS

Selectivity Rating: 97 (of 100). **Freshman Academic Profile:** 72% in top 10% of high school class, 94% in top 25% of high school class, 100% in top 50% of high school class. 61% from public high schools. SAT I Math middle 50% range 640-720. SAT I Verbal middle 50% range 610-710. ACT middle 50% range 26-31. TOEFL required of all international applicants, minimum TOEFL 100. **Basis for Candidate Selection:** *Very important factors considered include:* secondary school record. *Important factors considered include:* character/personal qualities, class rank, essays, extracurricular activities, minority status, recommendations, standardized test scores, talent/ability, volunteer work, work experience. *Other factors considered include:* alumni/ae relation, geographical residence, interview. **Freshman Admission Requirements:** High school diploma or GED is required. *Academic units required/ recommended:* 4 English recommended, 3 math recommended, 2 science recommended, 3 foreign language recommended, 2 history recommended. **Freshman Admission Statistics:** 14,308 applied, 27% accepted, 34% of those accepted enrolled. **Transfer Admission Requirements:** *Items required:* high school transcript, college transcript, essay, standardized test scores, statement of good standing from prior school. Lowest grade transferable C. **General Admission Information:** Application fee $60. Early decision application deadline November 15. Regular application deadline January 1. Admission may be deferred for a maximum of 1 year. Credit and/or placement offered for CEEB Advanced Placement tests.

COSTS AND FINANCIAL AID

Tuition $26,213. Room & board $7,987. Required fees $679. Average book expense $700. **Required Forms and Deadlines:** FAFSA, CSS/Financial Aid PROFILE, noncustodial (divorced/separated) parent's statement, business/farm supplement, and parent and student federal income tax returns. Financial aid filing deadline February 15. Priority filing deadline February 15. **Notification of Awards:** Applicants will be notified of awards on or about April 5. **Types of Aid:** *Need-based scholarships/grants:* Pell, SEOG, state scholarships/grants, private scholarships, the school's own gift aid. *Loans:* FFEL Subsidized Stafford, FFEL Unsubsidized Stafford, FFEL PLUS, Federal Perkins, state loans, college/university loans from institutional funds. **Student Employment:** Federal Work-Study Program available. Institutional employment available. Off-campus job opportunities are good. **Financial Aid Statistics:** 36% freshmen, 41% undergrads receive some form of aid. Average freshman grant $19,183. Average freshman loan $3,356. **Financial Aid Phone:** 617-627-2000.

TULANE UNIVERSITY

6823 St. Charles Avenue, New Orleans, LA 70118
Phone: 504-865-5260 **E-mail:** undergrad.admission@tulane.edu **CEEB Code:** 6832
Fax: 504-862-8715 **Web:** www.tulane.edu **ACT Code:** 1614

This private school was founded in 1834. It has a 110-acre campus.

STUDENTS AND FACULTY

Enrollment: 7,701. **Student Body:** Male 47%, female 53%, out-of-state 66%, international 3% (100 countries represented). **Ethnic Representation:** African American 9%, Asian 5%, Caucasian 73%, Hispanic 4%. **Retention and Graduation:** 87% freshmen return for sophomore year. 63% freshmen graduate within 4 years. 32% grads go on to further study within 1 year. 10% grads pursue business degrees. 8% grads pursue law degrees. 7% grads pursue medical degrees. **Faculty:** Student/faculty ratio 10:1. 518 full-time faculty, 88% hold PhDs. 89% faculty teach undergrads.

ACADEMICS

Degrees: Associate's, bachelor's, doctoral, first professional, master's, post-bachelor's certificate. **Academic Requirements:** General education including some course work in arts/fine arts, computer literacy, English (including composition), foreign languages, humanities, mathematics, philosophy, sciences (biological or physical), social science. **Classes:** 10-19 students in an average class. 10-19 students in an average lab/discussion section. **Majors with Highest Enrollment:** Engineering, general; social sciences, general; business/ commerce, general. **Disciplines with Highest Percentage of Degrees Awarded:** Business/marketing 21%, social sciences and history 18%, engineering/engineering technology 10%, biological life sciences 8%, psychology 8%. **Special Study Options:** Accelerated program, cooperative (work-study) program, cross registration, double major, English as a second language, student exchange program (domestic), external degree program, honors program, independent study, internships, student-designed major, study abroad, teacher certification program.

FACILITIES

Housing: Coed, all-female, apartments for married students, apartments for single students, housing for disabled students, housing for international students, fraternities and/or sororities, special-interest floors. **Library Holdings:** 2,285,029 bound volumes. 15,308 periodicals. 2,534,540 microforms. 92,904 audiovisuals. **Special Academic Facilities/Equipment:** Art gallery, jazz and architecture archives, Louisiana collection of historical materials, language labs, research facilities and research centers covering many areas, coordinated (interdisciplinary scientific) research instrumentation facility, Middle American Research Institute. **Computers:** School-owned computers available for student use.

EXTRACURRICULARS

Activities: Choral groups, concert band, dance, drama/theater, jazz band, literary magazine, music ensembles, musical theater, pep band, radio station, student government, student newspaper, student-run film society, television station. **Organizations:** 200 registered organizations, 35 honor societies, 12 religious organizations, 15 fraternities (12% men join), 9 sororities (15% women join). **Athletics (Intercollegiate):** *Men:* baseball, basketball, crew, cross-country, football, golf, tennis, track & field, wrestling. *Women:* basketball, crew, cross-country, golf, soccer, tennis, track & field, volleyball.

ADMISSIONS

Selectivity Rating: 84 (of 100). **Freshman Academic Profile:** 58% in top 10% of high school class, 92% in top 25% of high school class, 99% in top 50% of high school class. 55% from public high schools. Average SAT I Math 634, SAT I Math middle 50% range 610-700. Average SAT I Verbal 648, SAT I Verbal middle 50% range 630-710. ACT middle 50% range 28-32. TOEFL required of all international applicants, minimum TOEFL 550. **Basis for Candidate Selection:** *Very important factors considered include:* class rank, secondary school record, standardized test scores. *Important factors considered include:* essays, recommendations. *Other factors considered include:* alumni/ae relation, character/personal qualities, extracurricular activities, geographical residence, talent/ability, volunteer work, work experience. **Freshman Admission Requirements:** High school diploma or GED is required. *Academic units required/recommended:* 4 English required, 4 English recommended, 3 math required, 4 math recommended, 3 science required, 4 science recommended, 3 science lab required, 3 science lab recommended, 2 foreign language required, 3 foreign language recommended, 3 social studies required, 3 social studies recommended, 3 history required, 3 history recommended. **Freshman Admission Statistics:** 12,985 applied, 56% accepted. **Transfer Admission Requirements:** *Items required:* college transcript, statement of good standing from prior school. Minimum college GPA of 3.0 required. Lowest grade transferable C-. **General Admission Information:** Application fee $55. Priority application deadline November 1. Early decision application deadline November 1. Regular application deadline January 15. Admission may be deferred for a maximum of 1 year. Credit and/or placement offered for CEEB Advanced Placement tests.

COSTS AND FINANCIAL AID

Tuition $26,100. Room & board $7,392. Required fees $2,210. Average book expense $1,000. **Required Forms and Deadlines:** FAFSA, CSS/Financial Aid PROFILE, noncustodial (divorced/separated) parent's statement and business/ farm supplement. Financial aid filing deadline February 1. Priority filing deadline February 1. **Notification of Awards:** Applicants will be notified of awards on a rolling basis beginning on or about February 1. **Types of Aid:** *Need-based scholarships/grants:* Pell, SEOG, state scholarships/grants, private scholarships. *Loans:* FFEL Subsidized Stafford, FFEL Unsubsidized Stafford, FFEL PLUS, Federal Perkins. **Student Employment:** Federal Work-Study Program available. Institutional employment available. Off-campus job opportunities are good. **Financial Aid Statistics:** 46% freshmen, 43% undergrads receive some form of aid. Average freshman grant $15,700. Average freshman loan $3,460. **Financial Aid Phone:** 504-865-5723.

TUSCULUM COLLEGE

PO Box 5047, Greenville, TN 37743
Phone: 423-636-7312 **E-mail:** admissions@tusculum.edu **CEEB Code:** 1812
Fax: 423-638-7166 **Web:** www.tusculum.edu **ACT Code:** 4018

This private school, which is affiliated with the Presbyterian Church, was founded in 1794. It has a 142-acre campus.

STUDENTS AND FACULTY

Enrollment: 1,137. **Student Body:** Male 46%, female 54%, out-of-state 57%, international 1% (8 countries represented). **Ethnic Representation:** African American 7%, Caucasian 91%, Hispanic 1%. **Retention and Graduation:** 60% freshmen return for sophomore year. 27% freshmen graduate within 4 years. 10% grads go on to further study within 1 year. 5% grads pursue business degrees. 1% grads pursue law degrees. 2% grads pursue medical degrees. **Faculty:** 100% faculty teach undergrads.

ACADEMICS

Degrees: Bachelor's, master's. **Academic Requirements:** General education including some course work in computer literacy, English (including composition), history, humanities, mathematics, philosophy. **Special Study Options:** Double major, independent study, internships, student-designed major, study abroad, teacher certification program, 16-month accelerated evening program for nontraditional students.

FACILITIES

Housing: All-female, all-male. **Library Holdings:** 67,202 bound volumes. 1,000 periodicals. 210,798 microforms. 966 audiovisuals. **Special Academic Facilities/Equipment:** The Andrew Johnson Presidential Museum and Library. The College Archives. The Charles Coffin Collection. **Computers:** *Recommended operating system:* Mac. School-owned computers available for student use.

EXTRACURRICULARS

Activities: Choral groups, drama/theater, pep band, radio station, student government, student newspaper, yearbook. **Organizations:** 12 registered organizations, 2 religious organizations. **Athletics (Intercollegiate):** *Men:* baseball, basketball, cheerleading, cross-country, football, golf, soccer, tennis. *Women:* basketball, cheerleading, cross-country, golf, soccer, softball, tennis, volleyball.

ADMISSIONS

Selectivity Rating: 72 (of 100). **Freshman Academic Profile:** Average high school GPA 2.9. 16% in top 10% of high school class, 42% in top 25% of high school class, 78% in top 50% of high school class. Average SAT I Math 490, SAT I Math middle 50% range 430-550. Average SAT I Verbal 500, SAT I Verbal middle 50% range 450-540. Average ACT 21, ACT middle 50% range 19-23. TOEFL required of all international applicants, minimum TOEFL 550. **Basis for Candidate Selection:** *Very important factors considered include:* essays, secondary school record, standardized test scores. *Important factors considered include:* class rank, recommendations. *Other factors considered include:* character/personal qualities, extracurricular activities, interview, talent/ability. **Freshman Admission Requirements:** High school diploma or GED is required. *Academic units required/recommended:* 14 total required; 4 English required, 3 math required, 2 science required, 2 foreign language required, 3 social studies required. **Transfer Admission Requirements:** *Items required:* college transcript, essay. Minimum college GPA of 2.0 required. Lowest grade transferable D. **General Admission Information:** Regular application deadline rolling. Nonfall registration accepted. Admission may be deferred for a maximum of 1 year. Credit offered for CEEB Advanced Placement tests.

COSTS AND FINANCIAL AID

Tuition $11,800. Room & board $3,900. **Student Employment:** Federal Work-Study Program available. Institutional employment available. Off-campus job opportunities are good. **Financial Aid Phone:** 423-636-7376.

TUSKEGEE UNIVERSITY

Old Administration Building, Suite 101, Tuskegee, AL 36088
Phone: 334-727-8500 **E-mail:** admissions@tusk.edu **CEEB Code:** 1813
Fax: 334-724-4402 **Web:** www.tusk.edu **ACT Code:** 50

This private school was founded in 1881. It has a 5,200-acre campus.

STUDENTS AND FACULTY

Enrollment: 2,608. **Student Body:** Male 43%, female 57%, out-of-state 58%, international 1%. **Ethnic Representation:** African American 81%. **Retention and Graduation:** 77% freshmen return for sophomore year. 22% freshmen graduate within 4 years. 20% grads go on to further study within 1 year. 4% grads pursue business degrees. 2% grads pursue law degrees. 3% grads pursue medical degrees. **Faculty:** Student/faculty ratio 13:1. 218 full-time faculty, 70% hold PhDs.

ACADEMICS

Degrees: Bachelor's, doctoral, first professional, master's. **Academic Requirements:** General education including some course work in arts/fine arts, English (including composition), history, mathematics, sciences (biological or physical), social science. **Classes:** 10-19 students in an average class. **Majors with Highest Enrollment:** Veterinary medicine (DVM); electrical, electronics, and communications engineering; marine biology and biological oceanography. **Disciplines with Highest Percentage of Degrees Awarded:** Engineering/engineering technology 20%, business/marketing 17%, biological life sciences 12%, agriculture 8%, health professions and related sciences 7%. **Special Study Options:** Cooperative (work-study) program, double major, honors program, independent study, internships, teacher certification program.

FACILITIES

Housing: Coed, all-female, all-male, apartments for married students, apartments for single students. **Library Holdings:** 317,003 bound volumes. 81,182 periodicals. 287,500 microforms. 4,115 audiovisuals. **Special Academic Facilities/Equipment:** Agricultural and natural history museum, electron microscopes, two nursery schools. **Computers:** School-owned computers available for student use.

EXTRACURRICULARS

Activities: Choral groups, drama/theater, marching band, student government, student newspaper, yearbook. **Organizations:** 36 registered organizations, 22 honor societies, 6 religious organizations, 5 fraternities (6% men join), 6 sororities (5% women join). **Athletics (Intercollegiate):** *Men:* baseball, basketball, cheerleading, cross-country, diving, fencing, football, golf, gymnastics, indoor track, rifle, soccer, swimming, tennis, track & field, volleyball. *Women:* basketball, cheerleading, cross-country, diving, fencing, golf, gymnastics, indoor track, rifle, soccer, swimming, tennis, track & field, volleyball.

ADMISSIONS

Selectivity Rating: 73 (of 100). **Freshman Academic Profile:** Average high school GPA 3.2. 20% in top 10% of high school class, 59% in top 25% of high school class, 100% in top 50% of high school class. Average SAT I Math 438, SAT I Math middle 50% range 370-550. Average SAT I Verbal 441, SAT I Verbal middle 50% range 340-540. Average ACT 19, ACT middle 50% range 17-20. TOEFL required of all international applicants, minimum TOEFL 500. **Basis for Candidate Selection:** *Very important factors considered include:* recommendations, secondary school record, standardized test scores, talent/ability. *Important factors considered include:* alumni/ae relation, class rank. *Other factors considered include:* character/personal qualities, essays, geographical residence, interview, state residency, volunteer work, work experience. **Freshman Admission Requirements:** High school diploma or GED is required. *Academic units required/recommended:* 16 total required; 4 English required, 3 math required, 2 science required, 3 social studies required, 4 elective required. **Freshman Admission Statistics:** 1,902 applied, 81% accepted, 49% of those accepted enrolled. **Transfer Admission Requirements:** *Items required:* college transcript. Minimum college GPA of 2.0 required. Lowest grade transferable C. **General Admission Information:** Application fee $25. Nonfall registration accepted. Credit and/or placement offered for CEEB Advanced Placement tests.

COSTS AND FINANCIAL AID

Tuition $11,060. Room & board $5,940. Required fees $250. Average book expense $848. **Required Forms and Deadlines:** FAFSA, institution's own financial aid form and CSS/Financial Aid PROFILE. Priority filing deadline March 31. **Types of Aid:** *Need-based scholarships/grants:* Pell, SEOG, state scholarships/grants, private scholarships, the school's own gift aid, United Negro College Fund, Federal Nursing. *Loans:* Direct Subsidized Stafford, Direct Unsubsidized Stafford, Direct PLUS, FFEL Subsidized Stafford, FFEL Unsubsidized Stafford, FFEL PLUS, Federal Perkins, Federal Nursing, state loans, college/university loans from institutional funds. **Student Employment:** Federal Work-Study Program available. Institutional employment available. Off-campus job opportunities are good. **Financial Aid Statistics:** 66% freshmen, 66% undergrads receive some form of aid. Average freshman grant $2,500. Average freshman loan $2,625. Average income from on-campus job $1,540. **Financial Aid Phone:** 334-727-8210.

ULSTER COMMUNITY COLLEGE

Admissions Office, SUNY at Ulster, Stone Ridge, NY 12484
Phone: 914-687-5018 **E-mail:** admissions@sunyulster.edu
Fax: 914-687-5090 **Web:** www.sunyulster.edu

This public school was founded in 1962. It has a 160-acre campus.

STUDENTS AND FACULTY

Enrollment: 2,884. **Student Body:** Male 41%, female 59%, international students represent 3 countries. **Ethnic Representation:** African American 5%, Asian 2%, Caucasian 88%, Hispanic 5%. **Faculty:** Student/faculty ratio 11:1. 60 full-time faculty, 11% hold PhDs. 100% faculty teach undergrads.

ACADEMICS

Degrees: Associate's, certificate, diploma, terminal, transfer. **Academic Requirements:** General education including some course work in computer literacy, English (including composition), history, humanities, mathematics, sciences (biological or physical), social science. **Classes:** 10-19 students in an average class. Under 10 students in an average lab/discussion section. **Special Study Options:** Cooperative (work-study) program, cross registration, distance learning, English as a second language, honors program, independent study, internships, liberal arts/career combination, student-designed major.

FACILITIES

Library Holdings: 71,063 bound volumes. 480 periodicals. 22,656 microforms. 4,141 audiovisuals. **Computers:** School-owned computers available for student use.

EXTRACURRICULARS

Activities: Choral groups, drama/theater, radio station, student government, student newspaper. **Organizations:** 16 registered organizations, 1 honor society, 1 religious organization. **Athletics (Intercollegiate):** *Men:* baseball, basketball, golf, soccer, tennis. *Women:* basketball, softball, tennis, volleyball.

ADMISSIONS

Selectivity Rating: 60 (of 100). **Freshman Academic Profile:** 99% from public high schools.

COSTS AND FINANCIAL AID

Types of Aid: *Need-based scholarships/grants:* Pell, SEOG, state scholarships/grants, private scholarships, the school's own gift aid. *Loans:* FFEL Subsidized Stafford, FFEL Unsubsidized Stafford, FFEL PLUS, Federal Perkins, college/university loans from institutional funds. **Student Employment:** Federal Work-Study Program available. Institutional employment available. Off-campus job opportunities are good. **Financial Aid Statistics:** Average freshman grant $2,323. Average freshman loan $788. **Financial Aid Phone:** 914-687-5058.

UNION COLLEGE (KY)

310 College Street, Box 5, Barbourville, KY 40906-1499
Phone: 606-546-1657 **E-mail:** enroll@unionky.edu
Fax: 606-546-1667 **Web:** www.unionky.edu **ACT Code:** 1552

This private school, which is affiliated with the Methodist Church, was founded in 1879. It has a 110-acre campus.

STUDENTS AND FACULTY

Enrollment: 618. **Student Body:** Male 49%, female 51%, international 4% (12 countries represented). **Ethnic Representation:** African American 9%, Asian 1%, Caucasian 86%, Hispanic 2%, Native American 1%. **Retention and Graduation:** 57% freshmen return for sophomore year. 22% freshmen graduate within 4 years. **Faculty:** Student/faculty ratio 10:1. 49 full-time faculty, 69% hold PhDs. 100% faculty teach undergrads.

ACADEMICS

Degrees: Bachelor's, master's. **Academic Requirements:** General education including some course work in arts/fine arts, English (including composition), history, humanities, mathematics, philosophy, sciences (biological or physical), social science. **Classes:** 10-19 students in an average class. 10-19 students in an average lab/discussion section. **Disciplines with Highest Percentage of Degrees Awarded:** Psychology 15%, social sciences and history 8%, protective services/public administration 5%, physical sciences 1%. **Special Study Options:** Accelerated program, cooperative (work-study) program, double major, dual enrollment, external degree program, independent study, internships, study abroad, teacher certification program.

FACILITIES

Housing: Coed, all-female, all-male, apartments for married students, apartments for single students. **Library Holdings:** 176,710 bound volumes. 642 periodicals. 437,024 microforms. 5,169 audiovisuals. **Special Academic Facilities/Equipment:** Lincoln Collection. **Computers:** School-owned computers available for student use.

EXTRACURRICULARS

Activities: Choral groups, drama/theater, literary magazine, music ensembles, musical theater, student government, student newspaper. **Organizations:** 33 registered organizations, 6 religious organizations. **Athletics (Intercollegiate):** *Men:* baseball, basketball, cheerleading, football, golf, soccer, tennis. *Women:* basketball, cheerleading, golf, soccer, softball, tennis, volleyball.

ADMISSIONS

Selectivity Rating: 63 (of 100). **Freshman Academic Profile:** Average high school GPA 3.0. 5% in top 10% of high school class, 23% in top 25% of high school class, 46% in top 50% of high school class. Average ACT 19. TOEFL required of all international applicants, minimum TOEFL 550. **Basis for Candidate Selection:** *Very important factors considered include:* secondary school record, standardized test scores. *Important factors considered include:* class rank, extracurricular activities, interview, volunteer work. *Other factors considered include:* alumni/ae relation, character/personal qualities, essays, recommendations, talent/ability. **Freshman Admission Requirements:** High school diploma or GED is required. *Academic units required/recommended:* 21 total required; 4 English required, 3 math required, 2 science required, 2 science lab required, 2 foreign language recommended, 1 social studies required, 1 history required, 8 elective required. **Freshman Admission Statistics:** 594 applied, 51% accepted, 46% of those accepted enrolled.

Transfer Admission Requirements: *Items required:* college transcript. Minimum college GPA of 2.0 required. Lowest grade transferable C. **General Admission Information:** Application fee $20. Priority application deadline May 1. Regular application deadline September 5. Nonfall registration accepted. Admission may be deferred for a maximum of 1 year.

COSTS AND FINANCIAL AID

Tuition $12,480. Room & board $4,250. Required fees $50. Average book expense $550. **Required Forms and Deadlines:** FAFSA. No deadline for regular filing. Priority filing deadline March 15. **Notification of Awards:** Applicants will be notified of awards on a rolling basis beginning on or about April 1. **Types of Aid:** *Need-based scholarships/grants:* Pell, SEOG, state scholarships/grants, private scholarships, the school's own gift aid. *Loans:* FFEL Subsidized Stafford, FFEL Unsubsidized Stafford, FFEL PLUS, Federal Perkins, college/university loans from institutional funds. **Student Employment:** Federal Work-Study Program available. Institutional employment available. Off-campus job opportunities are good. **Financial Aid Statistics:** 99% freshmen, 100% undergrads receive some form of aid. **Financial Aid Phone:** 800-489-8646.

UNION COLLEGE (NE)

3800 South 48th Street, Lincoln, NE 68506-4300
Phone: 402-486-2504 **E-mail:** ucenrol@ucollege.edu
Fax: 402-486-2895 **Web:** www.ucollege.edu **ACT Code:** 2480

This private school, which is affiliated with the Seventh-Day Adventist Church, was founded in 1891.

STUDENTS AND FACULTY

Enrollment: 951. **Student Body:** Male 43%, female 57%, out-of-state 77%, international 13% (34 countries represented). **Ethnic Representation:** African American 3%, Asian 2%, Caucasian 80%, Hispanic 5%, Native American 1%. **Retention and Graduation:** 71% freshmen return for sophomore year. 28% freshmen graduate within 4 years. 21% grads go on to further study within 1 year. 5% grads pursue business degrees. 2% grads pursue law degrees. 6% grads pursue medical degrees. **Faculty:** Student/faculty ratio 14:1. 49 full-time faculty, 44% hold PhDs. 100% faculty teach undergrads.

ACADEMICS

Degrees: Associate's, bachelor's. **Academic Requirements:** General education including some course work in arts/fine arts, computer literacy, English (including composition), history, humanities, mathematics, sciences (biological or physical), social science. **Classes:** Under 10 students in an average class. **Disciplines with Highest Percentage of Degrees Awarded:** Health professions and related sciences 34%, business/marketing 19%, education 9%, philosophy/religion/theology 6%, computer and information sciences 5%. **Special Study Options:** Cross registration, distance learning, double major, dual enrollment, English as a second language, honors program, independent study, internships, student-designed major, study abroad, teacher certification program.

FACILITIES

Housing: All-female, all-male, apartments for married students, apartments for single students. **Library Holdings:** 147,813 bound volumes. 1,357 periodicals. 1,026 microforms. 3,278 audiovisuals. **Computers:** *Recommended operating system:* Windows NT/2000. School-owned computers available for student use.

EXTRACURRICULARS

Activities: Choral groups, concert band, drama/theater, literary magazine, music ensembles, student government, student newspaper, yearbook. **Organizations:** 1 honor society, 3 religious organizations. **Athletics (Intercollegiate):** *Men:* basketball, volleyball. *Women:* basketball, volleyball.

ADMISSIONS

Selectivity Rating: 63 (of 100). **Freshman Academic Profile:** 21% in top 10% of high school class, 25% in top 25% of high school class, 35% in top 50% of high school class. 10% from public high schools. SAT I Math middle 50% range 18-25. SAT I Verbal middle 50% range 20-28. ACT middle 50% range 20-26. TOEFL required of all international applicants, minimum TOEFL 550. **Basis for Candidate Selection:** *Very important factors considered include:* character/personal qualities, recommendations, secondary school record, standardized test scores. *Important factors considered include:* extracurricular activities, interview, religious affiliation/commitment. *Other factors considered include:* class rank, essays, talent/ability. **Freshman Admission Requirements:** High school diploma or GED is required. *Academic units required/recommended:* 20 total required; 3 English required, 4 English recommended,

2 math required, 3 math recommended, 2 science required, 3 science recommended, 1 science lab required, 1 foreign language recommended, 1 social studies required, 1 history required, 3 elective required. **Freshman Admission Statistics:** 458 applied, 55% accepted, 69% of those accepted enrolled. **Transfer Admission Requirements:** *Items required:* high school transcript, college transcript. Minimum college GPA of 2.0 required. Lowest grade transferable C-. **General Admission Information:** Nonfall registration accepted.

COSTS AND FINANCIAL AID

Room & board $3,484. Required fees $0. Average book expense $800. **Required Forms and Deadlines:** FAFSA. No deadline for regular filing. Priority filing deadline May 2. **Notification of Awards:** Applicants will be notified of awards on a rolling basis. **Types of Aid:** *Need-based scholarships/grants:* Pell, SEOG, state scholarships/grants, private scholarships, the school's own gift aid. *Loans:* FFEL Subsidized Stafford, FFEL Unsubsidized Stafford, FFEL PLUS, Federal Perkins, Federal Nursing, college/university loans from institutional funds. **Student Employment:** Federal Work-Study Program available. Off-campus job opportunities are good. **Financial Aid Statistics:** 73% freshmen, 61% undergrads receive some form of aid. Average income from on-campus job $1,200. **Financial Aid Phone:** 402-488-2505.

UNION COLLEGE (NY)

Grant Hall, Schenectady, NY 12308
Phone: 518-388-6112 **E-mail:** admissions@union.edu **CEEB Code:** 2920
Fax: 518-388-6986 **Web:** www.union.edu **ACT Code:** 2970

This private school was founded in 1795. It has a 100-acre campus.

STUDENTS AND FACULTY

Enrollment: 2,147. **Student Body:** Male 53%, female 47%, out-of-state 54%, international 2% (21 countries represented). **Ethnic Representation:** African American 4%, Asian 5%, Caucasian 86%, Hispanic 4%. **Retention and Graduation:** 93% freshmen return for sophomore year. 80% freshmen graduate within 4 years. 33% grads go on to further study within 1 year. 4% grads pursue business degrees. 5% grads pursue law degrees. 7% grads pursue medical degrees. **Faculty:** Student/faculty ratio 11:1. 208 full-time faculty, 93% hold PhDs. 100% faculty teach undergrads.

ACADEMICS

Degrees: Bachelor's, master's. **Academic Requirements:** General education including some course work in English (including composition), history, mathematics, sciences (biological or physical), social science, and foreign language or cultural diversity track or foreign study. **Classes:** 10-19 students in an average class. 10-19 students in an average lab/discussion section. **Majors with Highest Enrollment:** Psychology, general; political science and government, general; economics, general. **Disciplines with Highest Percentage of Degrees Awarded:** Social sciences and history 34%, engineering/engineering technology 11%, psychology 11%, liberal arts/general studies 11%, biological life sciences 8%. **Special Study Options:** Accelerated program, cooperative (work-study) program, cross registration, double major, dual enrollment, English as a second language, honors program, independent study, internships, liberal arts/career combination, student-designed major, study abroad, teacher certification program.

FACILITIES

Housing: Coed, all-female, all-male, apartments for single students, fraternities and/or sororities, cooperative housing, theme housing. **Library Holdings:** 301,101 bound volumes. 1,988 periodicals. 816,829 microforms. 8,450 audiovisuals. **Special Academic Facilities/Equipment:** Horticultural garden; theater; Nott Memorial; high technology classroom and laboratory building, which contains a multimedia auditorium, collaborative computer classrooms, and a 20-inch remote-controlled telescope; superconducting nuclear magnetic resonance spectrometer; two electron microscopes; tandem pelletron positive ion accelerator. **Computers:** School-owned computers available for student use.

EXTRACURRICULARS

Activities: Choral groups, concert band, dance, drama/theater, jazz band, literary magazine, music ensembles, radio station, student government, student newspaper, student-run film society, symphony orchestra, yearbook. **Organizations:** 100 registered organizations, 12 honor societies, 5 religious organizations, 14 fraternities (21% men join), 4 sororities (25% women join). **Athletics (Intercollegiate):** *Men:* baseball, basketball, crew, cross-country, football, ice hockey, indoor track, lacrosse, soccer, swimming, tennis, track & field. *Women:* basketball, crew, cross-country, field hockey, ice hockey, indoor track, lacrosse, soccer, softball, swimming, tennis, track & field, volleyball.

ADMISSIONS

Selectivity Rating: 91 (of 100). **Freshman Academic Profile:** Average high school GPA 3.5. 58% in top 10% of high school class, 81% in top 25% of high school class, 96% in top 50% of high school class. 70% from public high schools. Average SAT I Math 640, SAT I Math middle 50% range 590-680. Average SAT I Verbal 600, SAT I Verbal middle 50% range 550-650. TOEFL required of all international applicants, minimum TOEFL 600. **Basis for Candidate Selection:** *Very important factors considered include:* class rank, secondary school record. *Important factors considered include:* alumni/ae relation, character/personal qualities, essays, extracurricular activities, interview, minority status, recommendations, talent/ability, volunteer work. *Other factors considered include:* geographical residence, standardized test scores, state residency, work experience. **Freshman Admission Requirements:** High school diploma or GED is required. *Academic units required/recommended:* 16 total required; 24 total recommended; 4 English required, 4 English recommended, 3 math required, 4 math recommended, 2 science required, 4 science recommended, 2 science lab required, 4 science lab recommended, 2 foreign language required, 4 foreign language recommended, 1 social studies required, 2 social studies recommended, 1 history required, 2 history recommended. **Freshman Admission Statistics:** 3,828 applied, 45% accepted, 33% of those accepted enrolled. **Transfer Admission Requirements:** *Items required:* high school transcript, college transcript, essay, statement of good standing from prior school. Minimum college GPA of 3.0 required. Lowest grade transferable C. **General Admission Information:** Application fee $50. Early decision application deadline November 15. Regular application deadline January 15. Admission may be deferred for a maximum of 1 year. Credit and/or placement offered for CEEB Advanced Placement tests.

COSTS AND FINANCIAL AID

Tuition $27,246. Room & board $6,738. Required fees $268. Average book expense $450. **Required Forms and Deadlines:** FAFSA, CSS/Financial Aid PROFILE, state aid form, noncustodial (divorced/separated) parent's statement and business/farm supplement. Financial aid filing deadline February 1. Priority filing deadline February 1. **Notification of Awards:** Applicants will be notified of awards on or about April 1. **Types of Aid:** *Need-based scholarships/grants:* Pell, SEOG, state scholarships/grants, private scholarships, the school's own gift aid. *Loans:* FFEL Subsidized Stafford, FFEL Unsubsidized Stafford, FFEL PLUS, Federal Perkins, college/university loans from institutional funds. **Student Employment:** Federal Work-Study Program available. Institutional employment available. Off-campus job opportunities are good. **Financial Aid Statistics:** 48% freshmen, 51% undergrads receive some form of aid. Average freshman grant $19,846. Average freshman loan $2,745. Average income from on-campus job $800. **Financial Aid Phone:** 518-388-6123.

See page 1236.

UNION INSTITUTE & UNIVERSITY

440 East McMillan Street, Cincinnati, OH 45206
Phone: 513-861-6400 **E-mail:** admissions@tui.edu
Fax: 513-861-3238 **Web:** www.tui.edu

This private school was founded in 1964.

STUDENTS AND FACULTY

Enrollment: 652. **Student Body:** Male 34%, female 66%, out-of-state 7%, international students represent 16 countries. **Ethnic Representation:** African American 36%, Asian 1%, Caucasian 42%, Hispanic 9%. **Retention and Graduation:** 62% freshmen return for sophomore year. 20% freshmen graduate within 4 years. 25% grads go on to further study within 1 year. **Faculty:** 32% faculty teach undergrads.

ACADEMICS

Degrees: Bachelor's, doctoral, master's, post-master's certificate. **Academic Requirements:** General education including some course work in humanities and arts, language and communications, natural sciences and mathematics, social sciences. **Special Study Options:** Distance learning, double major, external degree program, independent study, student-designed major.

FACILITIES

Library Holdings: 4,469 bound volumes. 0 periodicals. 0 microforms. 18 audiovisuals. **Computers:** School-owned computers available for student use.

ADMISSIONS

Selectivity Rating: 63 (of 100). **Freshman Academic Profile: Basis for Candidate Selection:** *Very important factors considered include:* character/personal qualities, essays, interview, recommendations. *Important factors* *considered include:* talent/ability, volunteer work, work experience. *Other factors considered include:* extracurricular activities. **Freshman Admission Requirements:** High school diploma or equivalent is not required. **Freshman Admission Statistics:** 26 applied, 62% accepted, 88% of those accepted enrolled. **Transfer Admission Requirements:** *Items required:* college transcript, essay, interview. Lowest grade transferable C. **General Admission Information:** Application fee $50. Regular application deadline October 8. Nonfall registration accepted. Admission may be deferred for a maximum of 1 year. Credit offered for CEEB Advanced Placement tests.

COSTS AND FINANCIAL AID

Required Forms and Deadlines: FAFSA, institution's own financial aid form and F. Financial aid filing deadline August 1. **Notification of Awards:** Applicants will be notified of awards on a rolling basis beginning on or about May 1. **Types of Aid:** *Need-based scholarships/grants:* Pell, SEOG, state scholarships/grants, private scholarships, the school's own gift aid. *Loans:* FFEL Subsidized Stafford, FFEL Unsubsidized Stafford, FFEL PLUS, Federal Perkins. **Student Employment:** Federal Work-Study Program available. Off-campus job opportunities are good. **Financial Aid Statistics:** 73% freshmen, 77% undergrads receive some form of aid. Average freshman grant $4,000. Average freshman loan $6,625. Average income from on-campus job $4,500. **Financial Aid Phone:** 513-861-6400.

UNION UNIVERSITY

1050 Union University Drive, Jackson, TN 38305-3697
Phone: 731-661-5000 **E-mail:** cgriffin@uu.edu **CEEB Code:** 1826
Fax: 731-661-5017 **Web:** www.uu.edu **ACT Code:** 4020

This private school, which is affiliated with the Southern Baptist Church, was founded in 1823. It has a 290-acre campus.

STUDENTS AND FACULTY

Enrollment: 1,935. **Student Body:** Male 42%, female 58%, out-of-state 30%, international 2% (23 countries represented). **Ethnic Representation:** African American 7%, Asian 1%, Caucasian 91%, Hispanic 1%. **Retention and Graduation:** 75% freshmen return for sophomore year. 40% grads go on to further study within 1 year. **Faculty:** Student/faculty ratio 12:1. 146 full-time faculty, 79% hold PhDs. 100% faculty teach undergrads.

ACADEMICS

Degrees: Associate's, bachelor's, diploma, doctoral, master's, post-master's certificate, terminal. **Academic Requirements:** General education including some course work in arts/fine arts, Christian studies, computer literacy, English (including composition), history, humanities, mathematics, oral communication, sciences (biological or physical), social science. **Classes:** 10-19 students in an average class. Under 10 students in an average lab/discussion section. **Majors with Highest Enrollment:** Elementary education and teaching; Christian studies; Nursing/registered nurse training (RN, ASN, BSN, MSN). **Disciplines with Highest Percentage of Degrees Awarded:** Business/marketing 30%, education 12%, health professions and related sciences 12%, philosophy/religion/theology 10%, visual and performing arts 5%. **Special Study Options:** Accelerated program, cooperative (work-study) program, cross registration, distance learning, double major, dual enrollment, student exchange program (domestic), honors program, independent study, internships, study abroad, teacher certification program.

FACILITIES

Housing: All-female, all-male, apartments for married students, apartments for single students, apartment-style housing, family housing. **Library Holdings:** 135,877 bound volumes. 655 periodicals. 466,987 microforms. 11,526 audiovisuals. **Special Academic Facilities/Equipment:** Elementary education lab, 21st-century classroom, TV communications truck, nursing/health assessment labs, health and wellness center, art gallery. **Computers:** School-owned computers available for student use.

EXTRACURRICULARS

Activities: Choral groups, concert band, drama/theater, jazz band, literary magazine, music ensembles, musical theater, opera, student government, student newspaper, symphony orchestra, yearbook. **Organizations:** 73 registered organizations, 13 honor societies, 7 religious organizations, 3 fraternities (25% men join), 3 sororities (22% women join). **Athletics (Intercollegiate):** *Men:* baseball, basketball, cheerleading, golf, soccer, tennis. *Women:* basketball, cheerleading, cross-country, softball, tennis, volleyball.

ADMISSIONS

Selectivity Rating: 82 (of 100). **Freshman Academic Profile:** Average high school GPA 3.5. 37% in top 10% of high school class, 65% in top 25% of high school class, 89% in top 50% of high school class. 73% from public high schools. SAT I Math middle 50% range 500-640. SAT I Verbal middle 50% range 510-650. Average ACT 24, ACT middle 50% range 21-28. TOEFL required of all international applicants, minimum TOEFL 500. **Basis for Candidate Selection:** *Very important factors considered include:* character/personal qualities, class rank, interview, secondary school record, standardized test scores. *Important factors considered include:* alumni/ae relation, essays, extracurricular activities, recommendations, religious affiliation/commitment, talent/ability, volunteer work. *Other factors considered include:* work experience. **Freshman Admission Requirements:** High school diploma or GED is required. *Academic units required/recommended:* 20 total required; 21 total recommended; 4 English required, 4 English recommended, 3 math required, 4 math recommended, 3 science required, 4 science recommended, 2 science lab required, 3 science lab recommended, 2 foreign language required, 2 foreign language recommended, 2 social studies required, 2 social studies recommended, 1 history required, 2 history recommended, 3 elective required, 2 elective recommended. **Freshman Admission Statistics:** 1,011 applied, 88% accepted, 48% of those accepted enrolled. **Transfer Admission Requirements:** *Items required:* college transcript, statement of good standing from prior school. Minimum college GPA of 2.5 required. Lowest grade transferable C. **General Admission Information:** Application fee $25. Priority application deadline March 2. Nonfall registration accepted. Admission may be deferred for a maximum of 1 year. Credit offered for CEEB Advanced Placement tests.

COSTS AND FINANCIAL AID

Tuition $13,200. Room & board $4,300. Required fees $500. Average book expense $600. **Required Forms and Deadlines:** FAFSA and institution's own financial aid form. Priority filing deadline January 15. **Notification of Awards:** Applicants will be notified of awards on a rolling basis beginning on or about February 15. **Types of Aid:** *Need-based scholarships/grants:* Pell, SEOG, state scholarships/grants, private scholarships, the school's own gift aid. *Loans:* FFEL Subsidized Stafford, FFEL Unsubsidized Stafford, FFEL PLUS, Federal Perkins, college/university loans from institutional funds, alternative. **Student Employment:** Federal Work-Study Program available. Institutional employment available. Off-campus job opportunities are excellent. **Financial Aid Statistics:** 61% freshmen, 56% undergrads receive some form of aid. Average freshman grant $4,500. Average freshman loan $1,900. Average income from on-campus job $800. **Financial Aid Phone:** 731-661-5015.

UNITED STATES AIR FORCE ACADEMY

HQ USAFA/ RRS, 2304 Cadet Drive, Suite 200, USAF Academy, CO 80840-5025
Phone: 719-333-2520 **E-mail:** rr_webmail@usafa.af.mil
Fax: 719-333-3012 **Web:** www.usafa.edu **ACT Code:** 530

This public school was founded in 1954. It has a 18,000-acre campus.

STUDENTS AND FACULTY

Enrollment: 4,219. **Student Body:** Out-of-state 95%, international 1% (22 countries represented). **Ethnic Representation:** African American 6%, Asian 5%, Caucasian 82%, Hispanic 6%, Native American 1%. **Retention and Graduation:** 89% freshmen return for sophomore year. 76% freshmen graduate within 4 years. 6% grads go on to further study within 1 year. 1% grads pursue medical degrees. **Faculty:** Student/faculty ratio 8:1. 531 full-time faculty, 57% hold PhDs. 100% faculty teach undergrads.

ACADEMICS

Degrees: Bachelor's. **Academic Requirements:** General education including some course work in computer literacy, English (including composition), foreign languages, history, humanities, mathematics, philosophy, sciences (biological or physical), social science, physical education courses, flight course, military arts and sciences. **Classes:** 10-19 students in an average class. 10-19 students in an average lab/discussion section. **Majors with Highest Enrollment:** Business administration/management; engineering, general; social sciences, general. **Disciplines with Highest Percentage of Degrees Awarded:** Engineering/engineering technology 27%, business/marketing 20%, social sciences and history 14%, biological life sciences 8%, psychology 7%. **Special Study Options:** Double major, English as a second language, student exchange program (domestic), independent study, student-designed major, study abroad, academically at-risk program, hospital instruction program, extra instruction program, summer programs.

FACILITIES

Housing: Coed. **Library Holdings:** 492,000 bound volumes. 1,600 periodicals. 663,000 microforms. 4,385 audiovisuals. **Special Academic Facilities/Equipment:** Language learning center, laser and optics research center,

USAFA observatory, department of engineering mechanics lab, visitor's center, consolidated educational training facility, planetarium, Air Force Academy cadet chapel, American Legion Memorial Tower, Clune Arena for athletic and speaking events, air garden, Falcon Stadium, aeronautics laboratory, meteorology lab, Arnold Hall Broadway Theatre, ballroom and conference rooms, historical displays. **Computers:** *Recommended operating system:* Windows NT/2000. School-owned computers available for student use.

EXTRACURRICULARS

Activities: Choral groups, dance, drama/theater, marching band, musical theater, pep band, radio station, student government, student newspaper, television station, yearbook. **Organizations:** 110 registered organizations, 2 honor societies. **Athletics (Intercollegiate):** *Men:* baseball, basketball, cheerleading, cross-country, diving, fencing, football, golf, gymnastics, ice hockey, indoor track, lacrosse, rifle, soccer, swimming, tennis, track & field, water polo, wrestling. *Women:* basketball, cheerleading, cross-country, diving, fencing, gymnastics, indoor track, rifle, soccer, swimming, tennis, track & field, volleyball.

ADMISSIONS

Selectivity Rating: 99 (of 100). **Freshman Academic Profile:** Average high school GPA 3.8. 57% in top 10% of high school class, 85% in top 25% of high school class, 98% in top 50% of high school class. Average SAT I Math 659, SAT I Math middle 50% range 617-700. Average SAT I Verbal 635, SAT I Verbal middle 50% range 590-680. **Basis for Candidate Selection:** *Very important factors considered include:* character/personal qualities, interview, secondary school record, standardized test scores. *Important factors considered include:* class rank, extracurricular activities, volunteer work, work experience. *Other factors considered include:* essays, minority status, recommendations, talent/ability. **Freshman Admission Requirements:** High school diploma is required and GED is not accepted. *Academic units required/recommended:* 4 English recommended, 4 math recommended, 4 science recommended, 4 science lab recommended, 2 foreign language recommended, 3 social studies recommended, 1 elective recommended. **Freshman Admission Statistics:** 9,041 applied, 17% accepted, 79% of those accepted enrolled. **Transfer Admission Requirements:** *Items required:* high school transcript, college transcript, essay, interview, standardized test scores. Minimum high school GPA of 2.0 required. Minimum college GPA of 2.0 required. Lowest grade transferable C. **General Admission Information:** Regular application deadline January 31. Credit and/or placement offered for CEEB Advanced Placement tests.

COSTS AND FINANCIAL AID

In-state tuition $0. Out-of-state tuition $0. Room & board $0. Required fees $0. Average book expense $0. **Student Employment:** Off-campus job opportunities are poor.

See page 1238.

UNITED STATES COAST GUARD ACADEMY

31 Mohegan Avenue, New London, CT 06320-8103
Phone: 800-883-8724 **E-mail:** admissions@cga.uscg.mil **CEEB Code:** 5708
Fax: 860-701-6700 **Web:** www.cga.edu **ACT Code:** 600

This public school was founded in 1876.

STUDENTS AND FACULTY

Enrollment: 985. **Student Body:** Out-of-state 93%, international 2%. **Ethnic Representation:** African American 5%, Asian 5%, Caucasian 82%, Hispanic 6%, Native American 1%. **Retention and Graduation:** 83% freshmen return for sophomore year. 70% freshmen graduate within 4 years. **Faculty:** Student/faculty ratio 10:1. 100% faculty teach undergrads.

ACADEMICS

Degrees: Bachelor's. **Academic Requirements:** General education including some course work in computer literacy, English (including composition), foreign languages, history, humanities, mathematics, philosophy, sciences (biological or physical), social science, nautical sciences, engineering. **Classes:** 20-29 students in an average class. 10-19 students in an average lab/discussion section. **Majors with Highest Enrollment:** Civil engineering, general; electrical, electronics, and communications engineering; environmental/environmental health engineering. **Disciplines with Highest Percentage of Degrees Awarded:** Engineering/engineering technology 29%, other 24%, social sciences and history 21%, physical sciences 15%, mathematics 11%. **Special Study Options:** Double major, student exchange program (domestic), honors program, independent study, internships.

FACILITIES

Housing: Coed. **Library Holdings:** 1,900 bound volumes. 761 periodicals. 6,912 microforms. 76 audiovisuals. **Special Academic Facilities/Equipment:** Coast Guard Museum, library, visitors center. **Computers:** *Recommended operating system:* Windows NT/2000.

EXTRACURRICULARS

Activities: Choral groups, concert band, drama/theater, jazz band, marching band, music ensembles, musical theater, pep band, student government, yearbook. **Organizations:** 3 religious organizations. **Athletics (Intercollegiate):** *Men:* baseball, basketball, crew, cross-country, diving, football, ice hockey, indoor track, rifle, sailing, soccer, swimming, tennis, track & field, wrestling. *Women:* basketball, cheerleading, crew, cross-country, diving, indoor track, rifle, sailing, soccer, softball, swimming, track & field, volleyball.

ADMISSIONS

Selectivity Rating: 98 (of 100). **Freshman Academic Profile:** 48% in top 10% of high school class, 88% in top 25% of high school class, 100% in top 50% of high school class. Average SAT I Math 640, SAT I Math middle 50% range 610-680. Average SAT I Verbal 620, SAT I Verbal middle 50% range 580-670. Average ACT 27, ACT middle 50% range 25-30. TOEFL required of all international applicants, minimum TOEFL 500. **Basis for Candidate Selection:** *Very important factors considered include:* character/personal qualities, class rank, extracurricular activities, secondary school record, standardized test scores. *Important factors considered include:* essays, recommendations, talent/ability. *Other factors considered include:* alumni/ae relation, interview, minority status, volunteer work, work experience. **Freshman Admission Requirements:** High school diploma or GED is required. *Academic units required/recommended:* 4 English required, 4 math required. **General Admission Information:** Regular application deadline December 15.

COSTS AND FINANCIAL AID

In-state tuition $0. Out-of-state tuition $0. Required fees $3,000. Average book expense $0.

UNITED STATES INTERNATIONAL UNIVERSITY

10455 Pomerado Road, San Diego, CA 92131
Phone: 619-635-4772 **E-mail:** admissions@usiu.edu **CEEB Code:** 4039
Fax: 619-635-4739 **Web:** www.usiu.edu **ACT Code:** 443

This private school was founded in 1952. It has a 160-acre campus.

STUDENTS AND FACULTY

Enrollment: 401. **Student Body:** Male 46%, female 54%, out-of-state 60%, international 47%. **Ethnic Representation:** African American 7%, Asian 9%, Caucasian 43%, Hispanic 29%, Native American 2%. **Retention and Graduation:** 37% freshmen return for sophomore year.

ACADEMICS

Degrees: Associate's, bachelor's, doctoral, master's, post-bachelor's certificate, post-master's certificate. **Academic Requirements:** General education including some course work in computer literacy, English (including composition), foreign languages, humanities, mathematics, sciences (biological or physical), social science. **Special Study Options:** English as a second language, student exchange program (domestic), honors program, internships, study abroad, teacher certification program.

FACILITIES

Housing: Coed, all-female, all-male, housing for disabled students. **Library Holdings:** 161,000 bound volumes. 1,000 periodicals. 301,587 microforms. **Computers:** School-owned computers available for student use.

EXTRACURRICULARS

Activities: Drama/theater, radio station, student government, student newspaper, television station, yearbook. **Organizations:** 17 registered organizations, 3 honor societies. **Athletics (Intercollegiate):** *Men:* cross-country, soccer, tennis. *Women:* cross-country, soccer, tennis, volleyball.

ADMISSIONS

Selectivity Rating: 70 (of 100). **Freshman Academic Profile:** Average high school GPA 2.9. Average SAT I Math 452, SAT I Math middle 50% range 430-580. Average SAT I Verbal 463, SAT I Verbal middle 50% range 400-560. Average ACT 19, ACT middle 50% range 19-23. TOEFL required of all international applicants, minimum TOEFL 550. **Basis for Candidate Selection:** *Very important factors considered include:* secondary school record, standardized test scores. *Important factors considered include:* essays, recommendations. *Other factors considered include:* character/personal qualities, extracurricular activities, interview, talent/ability, volunteer work. **Freshman Admission Requirements:** *Academic units required/recommended:* 16 total required; 4 English required, 3 math required, 2 science required, 2 foreign language required, 3 social studies required. **Freshman Admission Statistics:** 399 applied, 59% accepted, 13% of those accepted enrolled. **Transfer Admission Requirements:** *Items required:* high school transcript, college transcript, essay. Minimum college GPA of 2.5 required. Lowest grade transferable C. **General Admission Information:** Application fee $40. Priority application deadline March 2. Regular application deadline rolling. Nonfall registration accepted. Admission may be deferred for a maximum of 1 year. Credit offered for CEEB Advanced Placement tests.

COSTS AND FINANCIAL AID

Tuition $12,015. Room & board $5,040. Required fees $300. Average book expense $660. **Required Forms and Deadlines:** FAFSA, institution's own financial aid form, state aid form and noncustodial (divorced/separated) parent's statement. No deadline for regular filing. Priority filing deadline March 2. **Notification of Awards:** Applicants will be notified of awards on a rolling basis beginning on or about March 15. **Types of Aid:** *Need-based scholarships/grants:* Pell, SEOG, state scholarships/grants, private scholarships, the school's own gift aid. *Loans:* FFEL Subsidized Stafford, FFEL Unsubsidized Stafford, FFEL PLUS, Federal Perkins. **Student Employment:** Federal Work-Study Program available. Institutional employment available. Off-campus job opportunities are excellent. **Financial Aid Statistics:** Average freshman grant $4,276. Average freshman loan $2,116. Average income from on-campus job $3,450. **Financial Aid Phone:** 858-635-4559.

UNITED STATES MERCHANT MARINE ACADEMY

Office of Admissions, Kings Point, NY 11024-1699
Phone: 516-773-5391 **E-mail:** admissions@usmma.edu **CEEB Code:** 2923
Fax: 516-773-5390 **Web:** www.usmma.edu **ACT Code:** 2974

This public school was founded in 1943. It has an 82-acre campus.

STUDENTS AND FACULTY

Enrollment: 943. **Student Body:** Out-of-state 87%, international 2% (4 countries represented). **Retention and Graduation:** 92% freshmen return for sophomore year. 70% freshmen graduate within 4 years. 3% grads go on to further study within 1 year. 2% grads pursue law degrees. **Faculty:** Student/faculty ratio 12:1. 80 full-time faculty.

ACADEMICS

Degrees: Bachelor's. **Academic Requirements:** General education including some course work in computer literacy, humanities, mathematics, sciences (biological or physical), sea year. All students must complete at least 300 days aboard ship during their sophomore and junior years. **Majors with Highest Enrollment:** Naval architecture and marine engineering; transportation and materials moving services. **Disciplines with Highest Percentage of Degrees Awarded:** Trade and industry 56%, engineering/engineering technology 44%. **Special Study Options:** Honors program, internships.

FACILITIES

Housing: Coed. **Library Holdings:** 185,000 bound volumes. 950 periodicals. 15,269 microforms. 3,389 audiovisuals. **Special Academic Facilities/Equipment:** American Merchant Marine Museum. **Computers:** School-owned computers available for student use.

EXTRACURRICULARS

Activities: Choral groups, concert band, drama/theater, marching band, student government, student newspaper, yearbook. **Organizations:** 3 religious organizations. **Athletics (Intercollegiate):** *Men:* baseball, basketball, crew, cross-country, diving, football, golf, lacrosse, rifle, sailing, soccer, swimming, tennis, track & field, volleyball, water polo, wrestling. *Women:* basketball, crew, cross-country, diving, golf, rifle, sailing, softball, swimming, tennis, track & field, volleyball.

ADMISSIONS

Selectivity Rating: 99 (of 100). **Freshman Academic Profile:** Average high school GPA 3.6. 16% in top 10% of high school class, 54% in top 25% of high school class, 94% in top 50% of high school class. 50% from public high schools. Average SAT I Math 612, SAT I Math middle 50% range 560-670. Average SAT I Verbal 607, SAT I Verbal middle 50% range 550-660. Average ACT 27. TOEFL required of all international applicants, minimum TOEFL 520. **Basis for Candidate Selection:** *Very important factors considered include:* character/personal qualities, secondary school record, standardized test scores. *Important factors considered include:* class rank, essays, extracurricular activities, recommendations, talent/ability. *Other factors considered include:* interview, minority status, state residency, volunteer work, work experience. **Freshman Admission Requirements:** High school diploma is required and GED is not accepted. *Academic units required/recommended:* 18 total required; 4 English required, 4 English recommended, 3 math required, 4 math recommended, 3 science required, 4 science recommended, 1 science lab required, 2 science lab recommended, 2 foreign language recommended, 4 social studies recommended, 8 elective required. **Freshman Admission Statistics:** 1,558 applied, 25% accepted, 74% of those accepted enrolled. **Transfer Admission Requirements:** *Items required:* high school transcript, college transcript, essay, standardized test scores, statement of good standing from prior school. **General Admission Information:** Early decision application deadline November 1. Regular application deadline March 1.

COSTS AND FINANCIAL AID

Required fees $1,871. **Required Forms and Deadlines:** FAFSA and institution's own financial aid form. Financial aid filing deadline May 1. **Notification of Awards:** Applicants will be notified of awards on a rolling basis beginning on or about January 31. **Types of Aid:** *Need-based scholarships/grants:* Pell. *Loans:* FFEL Subsidized Stafford, FFEL Unsubsidized Stafford, FFEL PLUS. **Student Employment:** Off-campus job opportunities are poor. **Financial Aid Statistics:** 27% freshmen, 14% undergrads receive some form of aid. Average freshman loan $2,625. **Financial Aid Phone:** 516-773-5295.

UNITED STATES MILITARY ACADEMY

600 Thayer Road, West Point, NY 10996-1797
Phone: 845-938-4041 **E-mail:** 8dad@exmail.usma.army.mil **CEEB Code:** 2924
Fax: 845-938-3021 **Web:** www.usma.edu **ACT Code:** 2976

This public school was founded in 1802. It has a 16,080-acre campus.

STUDENTS AND FACULTY

Enrollment: 4,154. **Student Body:** Out-of-state 92%, international 1%. **Ethnic Representation:** African American 8%, Asian 5%, Caucasian 79%, Hispanic 6%, Native American 1%. **Retention and Graduation:** 92% freshmen return for sophomore year. 83% freshmen graduate within 4 years. 100% grads go on to further study within 1 year. 2% grads pursue medical degrees. **Faculty:** Student/faculty ratio 7:1. 575 full-time faculty, 38% hold PhDs. 100% faculty teach undergrads.

ACADEMICS

Degrees: Bachelor's. **Academic Requirements:** General education including some course work in computer literacy, English (including composition), foreign languages, history, humanities, mathematics, philosophy, sciences (biological or physical), social science, military science. **Disciplines with Highest Percentage of Degrees Awarded:** Engineering/engineering technology 31%, social sciences and history 24%, physical sciences 16%, foreign languages and literature 8%, computer and information sciences 3%. **Special Study Options:** Double major, student exchange program (domestic), honors program, individual advanced study, individual advanced developments.

FACILITIES

Housing: Coed. Coed dorms are called barracks. **Library Holdings:** 442,169 bound volumes. 1,963 periodicals. 1,232 microforms. 1,266 audiovisuals. **Special Academic Facilities/Equipment:** West Point Museum (oldest of U.S. army museums). **Computers:** *Recommended operating system:* Windows NT. School-owned computers available for student use.

EXTRACURRICULARS

Activities: Choral groups, drama/theater, literary magazine, marching band, music ensembles, pep band, radio station, student government, student newspaper, television station, yearbook. **Organizations:** 105 registered organizations, 7 honor societies, 2 religious organizations. **Athletics (Intercollegiate):** *Men:* baseball, basketball, cross-country, diving, football, golf, gymnastics, ice hockey, indoor track, lacrosse, rifle, soccer, swimming, tennis, track & field, wrestling. *Women:* basketball, cross-country, diving, indoor track, rifle, soccer, softball, swimming, tennis, track & field.

ADMISSIONS

Selectivity Rating: 99 (of 100). **Freshman Academic Profile:** Average high school GPA 3.7. 50% in top 10% of high school class, 81% in top 25% of high school class, 97% in top 50% of high school class. 86% from public high schools. Average SAT I Math 641, SAT I Math middle 50% range 590-680. Average SAT

I Verbal 627, SAT I Verbal middle 50% range 570-670. Average ACT 28, ACT middle 50% range 26-30. **Basis for Candidate Selection:** *Very important factors considered include:* essays, extracurricular activities, recommendations, secondary school record, standardized test scores. *Important factors considered include:* character/personal qualities, interview, minority status, talent/ability. *Other factors considered include:* geographical residence, volunteer work, work experience. **Freshman Admission Requirements:** High school diploma or GED is required. *Academic units required/recommended:* 19 total recommended; 4 English recommended, 4 math recommended, 2 science recommended, 2 science lab recommended, 2 foreign language recommended, 3 social studies recommended, 1 history recommended, 3 elective recommended. **Freshman Admission Statistics:** 11,473 applied, 13% accepted, 74% of those accepted enrolled. **General Admission Information:** Priority application deadline December 1. Regular application deadline March 21. Placement offered for CEEB Advanced Placement tests.

COSTS AND FINANCIAL AID

Average book expense $664. **Financial Aid Phone:** 845-938-3516.

See page 1240.

UNITED STATES NAVAL ACADEMY

117 Decatur Road, Annapolis, MD 21402
Phone: 410-293-4361 **E-mail:** webmail@gwmail.usna.com **CEEB Code:** 5809
Fax: 410-295-1815 **Web:** www.usna.edu **ACT Code:** 1742

This public school was founded in 1845. It has a 338-acre campus.

STUDENTS AND FACULTY

Enrollment: 4,309. **Student Body:** Out-of-state 94%, international 1% (24 countries represented). **Ethnic Representation:** African American 6%, Asian 4%, Caucasian 80%, Hispanic 8%, Native American 1%. **Retention and Graduation:** 90% freshmen return for sophomore year. 85% freshmen graduate within 4 years. 5% grads go on to further study within 1 year. 1% grads pursue medical degrees. **Faculty:** Student/faculty ratio 7:1. 560 full-time faculty, 58% hold PhDs. 100% faculty teach undergrads.

ACADEMICS

Degrees: Bachelor's. **Academic Requirements:** General education including some course work in English (including composition), history, humanities, mathematics, sciences (biological or physical), social science, engineering, naval science, military law, ethics, leadership. **Classes:** 10-19 students in an average class. **Majors with Highest Enrollment:** Systems engineering; economics, general; political science and government, general. **Disciplines with Highest Percentage of Degrees Awarded:** Social sciences and history 38%, engineering/engineering technology 34%, physical sciences 14%, computer and information sciences 6%, English 5%. **Special Study Options:** Double major, student exchange program (domestic), honors program, independent study, voluntary graduate education program.

FACILITIES

Housing: Coed. **Library Holdings:** 316,777 bound volumes. 1,892 periodicals. 0 microforms. 0 audiovisuals. **Special Academic Facilities/Equipment:** Naval history museum, Naval Institute, propulsion lab, subsonic and supersonic wind tunnels, flight simulator, subcritical nuclear reactor, 120/380-foot tow tanks, satellite dish, coastal chamber facilities, extensive fleet of small craft (power and sail), oceanographic research vessel. **Computers:** *Recommended operating system:* Windows NT/2000. School-owned computers available for student use.

EXTRACURRICULARS

Activities: Choral groups, concert band, drama/theater, jazz band, literary magazine, marching band, musical theater, pep band, radio station, student government, yearbook. **Organizations:** 70 registered organizations, 10 honor societies, 8 religious organizations. **Athletics (Intercollegiate):** *Men:* baseball, basketball, crew, cross-country, diving, football, golf, gymnastics, indoor track, lacrosse, rifle, sailing, soccer, squash, swimming, tennis, track & field, water polo, wrestling. *Women:* basketball, crew, cross-country, diving, indoor track, lacrosse, rifle, sailing, soccer, swimming, track & field, volleyball.

ADMISSIONS

Selectivity Rating: 99 (of 100). **Freshman Academic Profile:** 57% in top 10% of high school class, 84% in top 25% of high school class, 96% in top 50% of high school class. 60% from public high schools. Average SAT I Math 663, SAT I Math middle 50% range 560-670. Average SAT I Verbal 637, SAT I Verbal middle 50% range 530-640. TOEFL required of all international applicants, minimum TOEFL 500. **Basis for Candidate Selection:** *Very important factors considered include:* character/personal qualities, class rank, essays, extracurricular activities, interview, recommendations, secondary school record, standardized test scores. *Important factors considered include:* talent/ability. *Other factors considered include:* alumni/ae relation, geographical residence, minority status, state residency, volunteer work, work experience. **Freshman Admission Requirements:** High school diploma or equivalent is not required. *Academic units required/recommended:* 4 English recommended, 4 math recommended, 2 science recommended, 1 science lab recommended, 2 foreign language recommended, 2 history recommended. **Freshman Admission Statistics:** 12,331 applied, 12% accepted, 83% of those accepted enrolled. **General Admission Information:** Regular application deadline February 15. Credit and/or placement offered for CEEB Advanced Placement tests.

COSTS AND FINANCIAL AID

In-state tuition $0. Out-of-state tuition $0. Room & board $0. Required fees $0. Average book expense $0. **Financial Aid Statistics:** Average freshman grant $0. Average freshman loan $0. Average income from on-campus job $0.

UNITY COLLEGE

PO Box 532, Unity, ME 04988-0532
Phone: 207-948-3131 **E-mail:** admissions@unity.edu **CEEB Code:** 3925
Fax: 207-948-6277 **Web:** www.unity.edu

This private school was founded in 1965. It has a 205-acre campus.

STUDENTS AND FACULTY

Enrollment: 512. **Student Body:** Male 69%, female 31%, out-of-state 64%, international 1%. **Ethnic Representation:** African American 1%, Caucasian 99%. **Retention and Graduation:** 67% freshmen return for sophomore year. 13% freshmen graduate within 4 years. 3% grads go on to further study within 1 year. **Faculty:** Student/faculty ratio 14:1. 34 full-time faculty, 61% hold PhDs. 100% faculty teach undergrads.

ACADEMICS

Degrees: Associate's, bachelor's. **Academic Requirements:** General education including some course work in arts/fine arts, computer literacy, English (including composition), history, humanities, mathematics, philosophy, sciences (biological or physical), social science. **Special Study Options:** Accelerated program, cooperative (work-study) program, double major, dual enrollment, independent study, internships, student-designed major.

FACILITIES

Housing: Coed, residential cottages. **Library Holdings:** 45,000 bound volumes. 500 periodicals. 0 microforms. 750 audiovisuals. **Special Academic Facilities/Equipment:** The Indian Museum, a collection of Indian artifacts. **Computers:** School-owned computers available for student use.

EXTRACURRICULARS

Activities: Drama/theater, radio station, student government, student newspaper, yearbook. **Organizations:** 27 registered organizations, 1 honor society, 2 religious organizations. **Athletics (Intercollegiate):** *Men:* basketball, cross-country track. *Women:* cross-country, volleyball.

ADMISSIONS

Selectivity Rating: 63 (of 100). **Freshman Academic Profile:** Average high school GPA 2.7. 3% in top 10% of high school class, 13% in top 25% of high school class, 48% in top 50% of high school class. 98% from public high schools. Average SAT I Math 480, SAT I Math middle 50% range 500-510. Average SAT I Verbal 510, SAT I Verbal middle 50% range 480-500. TOEFL required of all international applicants, minimum TOEFL 500. **Basis for Candidate Selection:** *Very important factors considered include:* essays, interview, recommendations, secondary school record. *Important factors considered include:* character/personal qualities, extracurricular activities, talent/ability. *Other factors considered include:* alumni/ae relation, standardized test scores, volunteer work, work experience. **Freshman Admission Requirements:** High school diploma or GED is required. *Academic units required/recommended:* 18 total recommended; 4 English required, 4 math recommended, 2 science required, 2 foreign language recommended, 4 social studies recommended. **Freshman Admission Statistics:** 500 applied, 92% accepted, 34% of those accepted enrolled. **Transfer Admission Requirements:** *Items required:* high school transcript, college transcript, essay. Minimum high school GPA of 2.0 required. Minimum college GPA of 2.0 required. Lowest grade transferable C. **General Admission Information:** Application fee $25. Nonfall registration accepted. Admission may be deferred for a maximum of 2 years. Credit and/or placement offered for CEEB Advanced Placement tests.

COSTS AND FINANCIAL AID

Tuition $12,330. Room & board $5,300. Required fees $560. Average book expense $450. **Required Forms and Deadlines:** FAFSA and institution's own financial aid form. Financial aid filing deadline April 15. Priority filing deadline March 1. **Notification of Awards:** Applicants will be notified of awards on a rolling basis beginning on or about March 15. **Types of Aid:** *Need-based scholarships/grants:* Pell, SEOG, state scholarships/grants, private scholarships, the school's own gift aid. *Loans:* FFEL Subsidized Stafford, FFEL Unsubsidized Stafford, FFEL PLUS. **Student Employment:** Federal Work-Study Program available. Off-campus job opportunities are fair. **Financial Aid Statistics:** 78% freshmen, 75% undergrads receive some form of aid. Average freshman grant $5,973. Average freshman loan $6,499. **Financial Aid Phone:** 207-948-3131.

UNIVERSITY AT BUFFALO (STATE UNIVERSITY OF NEW YORK)

Buffalo, NY 14214
Phone: 716-645-6900 **E-mail:** ub-admissions@buffalo.edu
Fax: 716-645-6411 **Web:** www.buffalo.edu

This public school was founded in 1846. It has a 1,346-acre campus.

STUDENTS AND FACULTY

Enrollment: 16,600. **Student Body:** Male 55%, female 45%, out-of-state 2%, international 5% (106 countries represented). **Ethnic Representation:** African American 8%, Asian 10%, Caucasian 71%, Hispanic 4%. **Retention and Graduation:** 86% freshmen return for sophomore year. 34% freshmen graduate within 4 years. 26% grads go on to further study within 1 year. **Faculty:** Student/faculty ratio 14:1. 1,248 full-time faculty, 96% hold PhDs. 64% faculty teach undergrads.

ACADEMICS

Degrees: Associate's, bachelor's, doctoral, first professional, first professional certificate, master's, post-master's certificate. **Academic Requirements:** General education including some course work in arts/fine arts, computer literacy, English (including composition), foreign languages, history, humanities, mathematics, sciences (biological or physical), social science. **Classes:** 20-29 students in an average class. 20-29 students in an average lab/discussion section. **Majors with Highest Enrollment:** Business administration/management; psychology, general; engineering, general. **Disciplines with Highest Percentage of Degrees Awarded:** Business/marketing 16%, social sciences and history 12%, engineering/engineering technology 10%, psychology 9%, communications/communication technologies 8%. **Special Study Options:** Accelerated program, cooperative (work-study) program, cross registration, distance learning, double major, dual enrollment, English as a second language, student exchange program (domestic), honors program, independent study, internships, student-designed major, study abroad, teacher certification program.

FACILITIES

Housing: Coed, apartments for married students, apartments for single students, housing for disabled students, housing for international students. **Library Holdings:** 2,000,000 bound volumes. 32,179 periodicals. 5,322,129 microforms. 160,000 audiovisuals. **Special Academic Facilities/Equipment:** Arts center, anthropology museum, concert hall with pipe organ, nature preserve, health and sciences center, national earthquake center, nuclear reactor, pharmacy museum, document analysis & recognition center, numerous research centers. **Computers:** School-owned computers available for student use.

EXTRACURRICULARS

Activities: Choral groups, concert band, dance, drama/theater, jazz band, literary magazine, marching band, music ensembles, musical theater, pep band, radio station, student government, student newspaper, student-run film society, symphony orchestra, yearbook. **Organizations:** 180 registered organizations, 29 honor societies, 10 religious organizations, 10 fraternities (1% men join), 13 sororities (1% women join). **Athletics (Intercollegiate):** *Men:* baseball, basketball, skiing (cross-country), cross-country, diving, football, soccer, swimming, tennis, track & field, wrestling. *Women:* basketball, crew, skiing (cross-country), cross-country, diving, soccer, softball, swimming, tennis, track & field, volleyball.

ADMISSIONS

Selectivity Rating: 82 (of 100). **Freshman Academic Profile:** Average high school GPA 3.1. 21% in top 10% of high school class, 57% in top 25% of high school class, 92% in top 50% of high school class. Average SAT I Math 578, SAT I Math middle 50% range 520-630. Average SAT I Verbal 551, SAT I Verbal middle 50% range 500-600. Average ACT 24, ACT middle 50% range 21-27. TOEFL required of all international applicants, minimum TOEFL 550. **Basis for Candidate Selection:** *Very important factors considered include:* class rank, secondary school record, standardized test scores. *Other factors considered include:* essays, extracurricular activities, minority status, recommendations, talent/ability, volunteer work. **Freshman Admission Requirements:** High school diploma or GED is required. *Academic units required/recommended:* 17 total recommended; 4 English recommended, 3 math recommended, 3 science recommended, 3 foreign language recommended, 4 social studies recommended. **Freshman Admission Statistics:** 16,057 applied, 61% accepted, 31% of those accepted enrolled. **Transfer Admission Requirements:** *Items required:* college transcript. Minimum college GPA of 2.0 required. Lowest grade transferable D. **General Admission Information:** Application fee $40. Priority application deadline November 1. Early decision application deadline November 1. Nonfall registration accepted. Credit offered for CEEB Advanced Placement tests.

COSTS AND FINANCIAL AID

In-state tuition $3,400. Out-of-state tuition $8,300. Room & board $6,512. Required fees $1,450. Average book expense $750. **Required Forms and Deadlines:** FAFSA. Priority filing deadline March 1. **Notification of Awards:** Applicants will be notified of awards on a rolling basis beginning on or about February 1. **Types of Aid:** *Need-based scholarships/grants:* Pell, SEOG, state scholarships/grants, private scholarships, the school's own gift aid, Federal Nursing. *Loans:* Direct Subsidized Stafford, Direct Unsubsidized Stafford, Direct PLUS, Federal Perkins, Federal Nursing, college/university loans from institutional funds. **Student Employment:** Federal Work-Study Program available. Institutional employment available. Off-campus job opportunities are good. **Financial Aid Statistics:** 65% freshmen, 52% undergrads receive some form of aid. Average freshman grant $890. Average freshman loan $1,155. Average income from on-campus job $1,050. **Financial Aid Phone:** 716-829-3724.

UNIVERSITY COLLEGE OF THE CARIBOO

UCC Admissions, PO Box 3010, Kamloops, BC V2C 5N3
Phone: 250-828-5071 **E-mail:** admissions@cariboo.bc.ca
Fax: 250-371-5513 **Web:** www.cariboo.bc.ca

This public school was founded in 1970. It has a 200-acre campus.

STUDENTS AND FACULTY

Enrollment: 7,958. **Student Body:** Male 43%, female 57%, out-of-state 7%, international students represent 43 countries. **Faculty:** Student/faculty ratio 20:1. 375 full-time faculty, 28% hold PhDs. 100% faculty teach undergrads.

ACADEMICS

Degrees: Associate's, bachelor's, certificate, diploma, post-bachelor's certificate, terminal, transfer. **Academic Requirements:** General education including some course work in arts/fine arts, computer literacy, English (including composition), humanities, mathematics, sciences (biological or physical), social science. **Classes:** 20-29 students in an average class. 10-19 students in an average lab/discussion section. **Majors with Highest Enrollment:** Business administration/management; education, general; English language and literature, general. **Disciplines with Highest Percentage of Degrees Awarded:** Liberal arts/general studies 15%, business/marketing 13%, education 10%, protective services/public administration 10%, natural resources/environmental sciences 9%. **Special Study Options:** Cooperative (work-study) program, distance learning, double major, English as a second language, honors program, internships, liberal arts/career combination, study abroad.

FACILITIES

Housing: Coed. **Library Holdings:** 158,500 bound volumes. 900 periodicals. 42,500 microforms. 8,200 audiovisuals. **Computers:** *Recommended operating system:* Windows 95. School-owned computers available for student use.

EXTRACURRICULARS

Activities: Choral groups, drama/theater, literary magazine, radio station, student government, student newspaper. **Organizations:** 5 religious organizations. **Athletics (Intercollegiate):** *Men:* baseball, basketball, soccer, volleyball. *Women:* basketball, soccer, volleyball.

ADMISSIONS

Selectivity Rating: 63 (of 100). **Freshman Academic Profile:** 95% from public high schools. **Basis for Candidate Selection:** *Very important factors considered* *include:* secondary school record. *Important factors considered include:* standardized test scores. *Other factors considered include:* character/personal qualities, interview, minority status, recommendations, talent/ability, volunteer work, work experience. **Freshman Admission Requirements: Transfer Admission Requirements:** *Items required:* high school transcript, college transcript. **General Admission Information:** Application fee $60. Regular application deadline March 1. Nonfall registration accepted. Admission may be deferred for a maximum of 1 year. Neither credit nor placement offered for CEEB Advanced Placement tests.

COSTS AND FINANCIAL AID

Room & board $2,100. Required fees $200. Average book expense $1,000. **Types of Aid:** *Need-based scholarships/grants:* Pell, SEOG, state scholarships/grants, private scholarships, the school's own gift aid. *Loans:* FFEL Subsidized Stafford, FFEL Unsubsidized Stafford, FFEL PLUS, Federal Perkins, college/university loans from institutional funds. **Student Employment:** Off-campus job opportunities are good. **Financial Aid Phone:** 250-828-5000.

UNIVERSITY COLLEGE OF THE FRASER VALLEY

33844 King Road, Abbotsford, BC V25 7M8
Phone: 604-854-4501 **E-mail:** reginfo@ucfv.bc.ca
Fax: 604-854-4501

This public school was founded in 1974.

STUDENTS AND FACULTY

Enrollment: 5,987. **Student Body:** Male 40%, female 60%. **Faculty:** 100% faculty teach undergrads.

ACADEMICS

Degrees: Associate's, bachelor's, certificate, diploma, terminal, transfer. **Academic Requirements:** General education including some course work in English (including composition), humanities. **Majors with Highest Enrollment:** Visual and performing arts, general; business administration/management; criminal justice/law enforcement administration. **Disciplines with Highest Percentage of Degrees Awarded:** Protective services/public administration 21%, social sciences and history 15%, home economics and vocational home economics 13%, business/marketing 11%, physical sciences 9%. **Special Study Options:** Cooperative (work-study) program, distance learning, double major, English as a second language, student-designed major, study abroad.

EXTRACURRICULARS

Activities: Drama/theater, student government, student newspaper. **Athletics (Intercollegiate):** *Men:* basketball, soccer. *Women:* basketball, soccer.

ADMISSIONS

Selectivity Rating: 60 (of 100). **Freshman Academic Profile: Basis for Candidate Selection:** *Important factors considered include:* secondary school record. *Other factors considered include:* interview, talent/ability, volunteer work, work experience. **Freshman Admission Requirements: General Admission Information:** Application fee $15. Regular application deadline March 31. Nonfall registration accepted.

COSTS AND FINANCIAL AID

Types of Aid: *Need-based scholarships/grants:* Pell, SEOG, state scholarships/grants, private scholarships, the school's own gift aid. *Loans:* FFEL Subsidized Stafford, FFEL Unsubsidized Stafford, FFEL PLUS, Federal Perkins, college/university loans from institutional funds. **Financial Aid Phone:** 604-864-4601.

UNIVERSITY OF NORTHERN BRITISH COLUMBIA

Prince George, BC V2N 4Z9
Phone: 250-960-6300 **E-mail:** registrar-info@unbc.ca
Fax: 250-960-6330

This public school was founded in 1990.

STUDENTS AND FACULTY

Enrollment: 3,582. **Student Body:** Male 50%, female 50%, out-of-state 8%, international students represent 25 countries. **Faculty:** Student/faculty ratio 16:1. 144 full-time faculty.

ACADEMICS

Degrees: Bachelor's, certificate, doctoral, master's. **Academic Requirements:** General education including some course work in humanities, sciences (biological or physical). **Majors with Highest Enrollment:** Forest sciences; computer science; accounting. **Special Study Options:** Accelerated program, cooperative (work-study) program, distance learning, double major, student exchange program (domestic), honors program, independent study, study abroad, teacher certification program.

FACILITIES

Housing: Coed. **Library Holdings:** 773,459 bound volumes.

EXTRACURRICULARS

Activities: Radio station, student government, student newspaper. **Organizations:** 1 honor society, 1 religious organization, 1 sorority. **Athletics (Intercollegiate):** *Men:* basketball. *Women:* basketball.

ADMISSIONS

Selectivity Rating: 60 (of 100). **Freshman Academic Profile:** Average high school GPA 2.5. **Basis for Candidate Selection:** *Very important factors considered include:* secondary school record. **Freshman Admission Requirements: Transfer Admission Requirements:** *Items required:* college transcript. **General Admission Information:** Application fee $5. Regular application deadline July 15. Nonfall registration accepted.

COSTS AND FINANCIAL AID

Room & board $2,450. Required fees $70. Average book expense $500. **Types of Aid:** *Need-based scholarships/grants:* Pell, SEOG, state scholarships/grants, private scholarships, the school's own gift aid. *Loans:* FFEL Subsidized Stafford, FFEL Unsubsidized Stafford, FFEL PLUS, Federal Perkins, college/university loans from institutional funds. **Student Employment:** Off-campus job opportunities are excellent. **Financial Aid Phone:** 250-960-6364.

UNIVERSITY OF ADVANCING TECHNOLOGY

2625 W. Baseline Rd., Tempe, AZ 85283
Phone: 602-383-8228 **E-mail:** admissions@uat.edu
Fax: 602-383-8222 **Web:** www.uat.edu

This proprietary school was founded in 1983.

STUDENTS AND FACULTY

Enrollment: 924. **Student Body:** International 2%. **Ethnic Representation:** African American 4%, Asian 3%, Caucasian 74%, Hispanic 15%, Native American 2%.

ACADEMICS

Degrees: Associate's, bachelor's, certificate, diploma, master's. **Academic Requirements:** General education including some course work in computer literacy, English (including composition), history, humanities, mathematics, sciences (biological or physical). **Special Study Options:** Accelerated program, distance learning, double major, internships.

ADMISSIONS

Selectivity Rating: 60 (of 100). **Freshman Academic Profile:** TOEFL required of all international applicants, minimum TOEFL 500. **Basis for Candidate Selection:** *Very important factors considered include:* interview. *Other factors considered include:* standardized test scores. **Freshman Admission Requirements:** High school diploma or GED is required. **Transfer Admission Requirements:** *Items required:* high school transcript, college transcript, statement of good standing from prior school. Minimum high school GPA of 2.0 required. Minimum college GPA of 2.0 required. Lowest grade transferable C. **General Admission Information:** Application fee $100. Nonfall registration accepted. Admission may be deferred.

COSTS AND FINANCIAL AID

Types of Aid: *Need-based scholarships/grants:* state scholarships/grants, private scholarships. *Loans:* Direct Subsidized Stafford, Direct Unsubsidized Stafford, Direct PLUS. **Financial Aid Phone:** 602-383-8228.

UNIVERSITY OF AKRON

381 Butchel Common, Akron, OH 44325-2001
Phone: 330-972-7100 **E-mail:** admissions@uakron.edu **CEEB Code:** 1829
Fax: 330-972-7022 **Web:** www.uakron.edu **ACT Code:** 3338

This public school was founded in 1870. It has a 170-acre campus.

STUDENTS AND FACULTY

Enrollment: 20,182. **Student Body:** Male 45%, female 55%, out-of-state 2%, international 1%. **Ethnic Representation:** African American 15%, Asian 2%, Caucasian 80%, Hispanic 1%, Native American 1%. **Retention and Graduation:** 67% freshmen return for sophomore year. **Faculty:** Student/faculty ratio 17:1. 779 full-time faculty, 82% hold PhDs. 97% faculty teach undergrads.

ACADEMICS

Degrees: Associate's, bachelor's, certificate, doctoral, first professional, master's. **Academic Requirements:** General education including some course work in arts/fine arts, computer literacy, English (including composition), foreign languages, history, humanities, mathematics, sciences (biological or physical), social science, cultural diversity, communication. **Classes:** 10-19 students in an average class. 20-29 students in an average lab/discussion section. **Majors with Highest Enrollment:** Nursing/registered nurse training (RN, ASN, BSN, MSN); business administration/management; elementary education and teaching. **Disciplines with Highest Percentage of Degrees Awarded:** Business/marketing 21%, education 15%, engineering/engineering technology 12%, health professions and related sciences 10%, communications/communication technologies 6%. **Special Study Options:** Accelerated program, cooperative (work-study) program, distance learning, double major, dual enrollment, English as a second language, honors program, independent study, internships, student-designed major, study abroad, teacher certification program, Undergrads may take grad-level classes. Co-op programs: arts, business, computer science, engineering, home economics, humanities, natural science, technologies.

FACILITIES

Housing: Coed, all-female, all-male, apartments for single students, housing for disabled students, housing for international students, fraternities and/or sororities. **Library Holdings:** 1,163,501 bound volumes. 12,849 periodicals. 1,940,630 microforms. 43,448 audiovisuals. **Special Academic Facilities/ Equipment:** Performing arts hall, nursery center, language lab, speech and hearing center, nursing learning resource labs, institute of polymer science and engineering, chemical lab, institute for health and social policy, Bliss Institute of Applied Politics. **Computers:** *Recommended operating system:* Windows NT/ 2000. School-owned computers available for student use.

EXTRACURRICULARS

Activities: Choral groups, concert band, dance, drama/theater, jazz band, marching band, music ensembles, musical theater, opera, pep band, radio station, student government, student newspaper, symphony orchestra, television station, yearbook. **Organizations:** 230 registered organizations, 3 honor societies, 2 religious organizations, 18 fraternities, 9 sororities. **Athletics (Intercollegiate):** *Men:* baseball, basketball, cheerleading, cross-country, football, golf, indoor track, rifle, soccer, track & field, volleyball. *Women:* basketball, cheerleading, cross-country, diving, indoor track, rifle, soccer, softball, swimming, tennis, track & field, volleyball.

ADMISSIONS

Selectivity Rating: 63 (of 100). **Freshman Academic Profile:** Average high school GPA 2.8. 10% in top 10% of high school class, 26% in top 25% of high school class, 53% in top 50% of high school class. Average SAT I Math 471, SAT I Math middle 50% range 420-580. Average SAT I Verbal 477, SAT I Verbal middle 50% range 420-570. Average ACT 20, ACT middle 50% range 17-23. TOEFL required of all international applicants, minimum TOEFL 500. **Basis for Candidate Selection:** *Very important factors considered include:* secondary school record, standardized test scores. *Important factors considered include:* class rank. **Freshman Admission Requirements:** High school diploma or GED is required. *Academic units required/recommended:* 15 total recommended; 4 English recommended, 3 math recommended, 3 science recommended, 2 foreign language recommended, 3 social studies recommended. **Freshman Admission Statistics:** 7,945 applied, 85% accepted, 50% of those accepted enrolled. **Transfer Admission Requirements:** *Items required:* college transcript, statement of good standing from prior school. **General Admission Information:** Application fee $30. Priority application deadline February 1. Regular application deadline rolling. Nonfall registration accepted. Admission may be deferred. Credit offered for CEEB Advanced Placement tests.

COSTS AND FINANCIAL AID

In-state tuition $4,350. Out-of-state tuition $10,552. Room & board $5,600. Required fees $580. Average book expense $750. **Required Forms and Deadlines:** FAFSA and institution's own financial aid form. No deadline for regular filing. **Notification of Awards:** Applicants will be notified of awards on a rolling basis beginning on or about April 15. **Types of Aid:** *Need-based scholarships/grants:* Pell, state scholarships/grants. *Loans:* FFEL Subsidized Stafford, FFEL Unsubsidized Stafford, FFEL PLUS, Federal Perkins, Federal Nursing, college/university loans from institutional funds. **Student Employment:** Federal Work-Study Program available. Institutional employment available. Off-campus job opportunities are excellent. **Financial Aid Statistics:** 69% freshmen, 62% undergrads receive some form of aid. Average freshman grant $2,500. Average income from on-campus job $3,600. **Financial Aid Phone:** 330-972-7032.

UNIVERSITY OF ALABAMA—BIRMINGHAM

Office of Undergraduate Admissions, HUC 260, 1530 3rd Avenue South, Birmingham, AL 35294-1150 **Phone:** 205-934-8221 **E-mail:** undergradadmit@uab.edu
CEEB Code: 1856 **Fax:** 205-975-7114 **Web:** www.uab.edu **ACT Code:** 56

This public school was founded in 1969. It has a 265-acre campus.

STUDENTS AND FACULTY

Enrollment: 10,501. **Student Body:** Male 41%, female 59%, out-of-state 5%, international 3% (77 countries represented). **Ethnic Representation:** African American 32%, Asian 3%, Caucasian 61%, Hispanic 1%. **Retention and Graduation:** 72% freshmen return for sophomore year. 12% freshmen graduate within 4 years. 15% grads go on to further study within 1 year. **Faculty:** Student/faculty ratio 18:1. 756 full-time faculty, 87% hold PhDs.

ACADEMICS

Degrees: Bachelor's, certificate, doctoral, first professional, master's, post-bachelor's certificate, post-master's certificate. **Academic Requirements:** General education including some course work in arts/fine arts, computer literacy, English (including composition), foreign languages, history, mathematics, philosophy, sciences (biological or physical), social science, literature. **Classes:** 20-29 students in an average class. 10-19 students in an average lab/ discussion section. **Majors with Highest Enrollment:** Communications studies/speech communication and rhetoric; biology/biological sciences, general; psychology, general. **Disciplines with Highest Percentage of Degrees Awarded:** Business/marketing 18%, health professions and related sciences 14%, education 12%, psychology 10%, social sciences and history 8%. **Special Study Options:** Cooperative (work-study) program, cross registration, distance learning, double major, dual enrollment, honors program, independent study, internships, student-designed major, study abroad, teacher certification program, weekend college.

FACILITIES

Housing: Coed, all-female, apartments for married students, apartments for single students. **Library Holdings:** 853,445 bound volumes. 3,934 periodicals. 1,271,750 microforms. 78,017 audiovisuals. **Special Academic Facilities/ Equipment:** Museum of health sciences. **Computers:** School-owned computers available for student use.

EXTRACURRICULARS

Activities: Choral groups, concert band, dance, drama/theater, jazz band, literary magazine, marching band, music ensembles, musical theater, pep band, radio station, student government, student newspaper. **Organizations:** 150 registered organizations, 45 honor societies, 9 religious organizations, 9 fraternities (6% men join), 8 sororities (6% women join). **Athletics (Intercollegiate):** *Men:* baseball, basketball, football, golf, rifle, soccer, tennis. *Women:* basketball, cross-country, golf, indoor track, rifle, soccer, softball, swimming, tennis, track & field, volleyball.

ADMISSIONS

Selectivity Rating: 71 (of 100). **Freshman Academic Profile:** Average high school GPA 3.1. 17% in top 10% of high school class, 41% in top 25% of high school class, 74% in top 50% of high school class. Average ACT 22, ACT middle 50% range 19-25. TOEFL required of all international applicants, minimum TOEFL 500. **Basis for Candidate Selection:** *Very important factors considered include:* secondary school record, standardized test scores. **Freshman Admission Requirements:** High school diploma or GED is required. *Academic units required/recommended:* 12 total required; 4 English required, 2 math required, 2 science required, 2 social studies required. **Freshman Admission Statistics:** 3,532 applied, 91% accepted, 46% of those accepted enrolled. **Transfer Admission Requirements:** *Items required:* college transcript, statement of good standing from prior school. Minimum college GPA of 2.0 required. **General Admission Information:** Application fee $25. Regular application deadline August 1. Nonfall registration accepted. Admission may be deferred for a maximum of 1 year. Credit offered for CEEB Advanced Placement tests.

COSTS AND FINANCIAL AID

In-state tuition $3,150. Out-of-state tuition $7,080. Required fees $730. Average book expense $900. **Required Forms and Deadlines:** FAFSA and institution's own financial aid form. No deadline for regular filing. Priority filing deadline April 1. **Notification of Awards:** Applicants will be notified of awards on or about April 15. **Types of Aid:** *Need-based scholarships/grants:* Pell, SEOG, state scholarships/grants, the school's own gift aid. *Loans:* Direct Subsidized Stafford, Direct Unsubsidized Stafford, Direct PLUS, Federal Perkins, state loans, college/university loans from institutional funds. **Student Employment:** Federal Work-Study Program available. Institutional employment available. Off-campus job opportunities are excellent. **Financial Aid Statistics:** 49% freshmen, 54% undergrads receive some form of aid. **Financial Aid Phone:** 205-934-8223.

UNIVERSITY OF ALABAMA—HUNTSVILLE

301 Sparkman Drive, Huntsville, AL 35899
Phone: 256-824-6070 **E-mail:** admitme@email.uah.edu **CEEB Code:** 1854
Fax: 256-824-6073 **Web:** www.uah.edu **ACT Code:** 53

This public school was founded in 1950. It has a 376-acre campus.

STUDENTS AND FACULTY

Enrollment: 5,598. **Student Body:** Male 50%, female 50%, out-of-state 13%, international 3% (98 countries represented). **Ethnic Representation:** African American 15%, Asian 4%, Caucasian 77%, Hispanic 2%, Native American 2%. **Retention and Graduation:** 72% freshmen return for sophomore year. 10% freshmen graduate within 4 years. 15% grads go on to further study within 1 year. 2% grads pursue business degrees. 1% grads pursue law degrees. 1% grads pursue medical degrees. **Faculty:** Student/faculty ratio 15:1. 275 full-time faculty, 90% hold PhDs.

ACADEMICS

Degrees: Bachelor's, doctoral, master's, post-bachelor's certificate, post-master's certificate. **Academic Requirements:** General education including some course work in arts/fine arts, computer literacy, English (including composition), history, humanities, mathematics, sciences (biological or physical), social science. **Classes:** 20-29 students in an average class. 20-29 students in an average lab/discussion section. **Majors with Highest Enrollment:** Nursing/registered nurse training (RN, ASN, BSN, MSN); management information systems, general; electrical, electronics, and communications engineering. **Disciplines with Highest Percentage of Degrees Awarded:** Business/marketing 27%, engineering/engineering technology 24%, health professions and related sciences 20%, computer and information sciences 6%, biological life sciences 5%. **Special Study Options:** Accelerated program, cooperative (work-study) program, cross registration, distance learning, double major, dual enrollment, English as a second language, honors program, independent study, internships, liberal arts/career combination, teacher certification program, 3-2 program in engineering.

FACILITIES

Housing: Coed, apartments for married students, apartments for single students, fraternities and/or sororities. **Library Holdings:** 277,878 bound volumes. 1,120 periodicals. 735,299 microforms. 2,677 audiovisuals. **Special Academic Facilities/Equipment:** Art museum and galleries, optics building, centers for applied optics, micro-gravity research, robotics, solar research, space plasma, and aeronomic research. **Computers:** School-owned computers available for student use.

EXTRACURRICULARS

Activities: Choral groups, concert band, dance, drama/theater, jazz band, literary magazine, music ensembles, musical theater, opera, pep band, student government, student newspaper, symphony orchestra. **Organizations:** 126 registered organizations, 22 honor societies, 7 religious organizations, 6 fraternities (5% men join), 5 sororities (5% women join). **Athletics (Intercollegiate):** *Men:* baseball, basketball, cross-country, ice hockey, soccer, tennis. *Women:* basketball, cross-country, soccer, softball, tennis, track & field, volleyball.

ADMISSIONS

Selectivity Rating: 73 (of 100). **Freshman Academic Profile:** Average high school GPA 3.4. 31% in top 10% of high school class, 60% in top 25% of high school class, 89% in top 50% of high school class. 87% from public high schools. Average SAT I Math 577, SAT I Math middle 50% range 510-640. Average SAT I Verbal 562, SAT I Verbal middle 50% range 500-630. Average ACT 25, ACT middle 50% range 22-27. TOEFL required of all international applicants, minimum TOEFL 500. **Basis for Candidate Selection:** *Very important factors considered include:* secondary school record, standardized test scores. **Freshman Admission Requirements:** High school diploma or GED is required. *Academic units required/recommended:* 20 total required; 4 English required, 3 math required, 2 science required, 3 social studies required, 8 elective required. **Freshman Admission Statistics:** 1,537 applied, 91% accepted, 45% of those accepted enrolled. **Transfer Admission Requirements:** *Items required:* college transcript. Minimum college GPA of 2.0 required. Lowest grade transferable D. **General Admission Information:** Application fee $20. Priority application deadline August 15. Regular application deadline August 15. Nonfall registration accepted. Admission may be deferred for a maximum of 1 year. Credit and/or placement offered for CEEB Advanced Placement tests.

COSTS AND FINANCIAL AID

In-state tuition $3,764. Out-of-state tuition $7,940. Room & board $4,700. Required fees $0. Average book expense $720. **Required Forms and Deadlines:** FAFSA and institution's own financial aid form. Financial aid filing deadline July 31. Priority filing deadline April 1. **Notification of Awards:** Applicants will be notified of awards on a rolling basis. **Types of Aid:** *Need-based scholarships/grants:* Pell, SEOG, state scholarships/grants, private scholarships, the school's own gift aid. *Loans:* Direct Subsidized Stafford, Direct Unsubsidized Stafford, Direct PLUS, college/university loans from institutional funds. **Student Employment:** Federal Work-Study Program available. Institutional employment available. Off-campus job opportunities are excellent. **Financial Aid Statistics:** 43% freshmen, 41% undergrads receive some form of aid. Average freshman grant $2,726. Average freshman loan $3,618. Average income from on-campus job $3,500. **Financial Aid Phone:** 256-824-6241.

UNIVERSITY OF ALABAMA—TUSCALOOSA

Box 870132, Tuscaloosa, AL 35487-0132
Phone: 205-348-5666 **E-mail:** admissions@ua.edu **CEEB Code:** 1830
Fax: 205-348-9046 **Web:** www.ua.edu **ACT Code:** 52

This public school was founded in 1831. It has a 1,000-acre campus.

STUDENTS AND FACULTY

Enrollment: 15,441. **Student Body:** Male 47%, female 53%, out-of-state 20%, international 1%. **Ethnic Representation:** African American 15%, Asian 1%, Caucasian 83%, Hispanic 1%, Native American 1%. **Retention and Graduation:** 83% freshmen return for sophomore year. 36% freshmen graduate within 4 years. **Faculty:** Student/faculty ratio 18:1. 882 full-time faculty, 92% hold PhDs. 76% faculty teach undergrads.

ACADEMICS

Degrees: Bachelor's, doctoral, first professional, master's, post-master's certificate. **Academic Requirements:** General education including some course work in arts/fine arts, computer literacy, English (including composition), foreign languages, history, humanities, mathematics, sciences (biological or physical), social science. **Classes:** 10-19 students in an average class. 10-19 students in an average lab/discussion section. **Majors with Highest Enrollment:** Finance, general; marketing/marketing management, general; public administration. **Disciplines with Highest Percentage of Degrees Awarded:** Business/marketing 31%, communications/communication technologies 12%, education 8%, home economics and vocational home economics 7%, engineering/engineering technology 6%. **Special Study Options:** Accelerated program, cooperative (work-study) program, cross registration, distance learning, double major, dual enrollment, English as a second language, student exchange program (domestic), external degree program, honors program, independent study, internships, liberal arts/career combination, student-designed major, study abroad, teacher certification program, weekend college.

FACILITIES

Housing: Coed, all-female, all-male, apartments for married students, apartments for single students, housing for disabled students, fraternities and/or sororities, academically based residential college, special-interest housing, alcohol-/tobacco-free housing, apartments for visiting scholars. **Library**

Holdings: 2,261,449 bound volumes. 16,590 periodicals. 3,715,144 microforms. 495,484 audiovisuals. **Special Academic Facilities/Equipment:** Art gallery, natural history museum, concert hall, archaeological site and museum, arboretum, observatory, simulated coal mine, robotics lab, wind tunnel, artificial intelligence lab, jet propulsion engine mini-lab, special collections building. **Computers:** School-owned computers available for student use.

EXTRACURRICULARS

Activities: Choral groups, concert band, dance, drama/theater, jazz band, literary magazine, marching band, music ensembles, musical theater, opera, pep band, radio station, student government, student newspaper, student-run film society, symphony orchestra, television station, yearbook. **Organizations:** 222 registered organizations, 66 honor societies, 22 religious organizations, 27 fraternities (16% men join), 19 sororities (24% women join). **Athletics (Intercollegiate):** *Men:* baseball, basketball, cross-country, diving, football, golf, swimming, tennis, track & field. *Women:* basketball, cross-country, diving, golf, gymnastics, soccer, softball, swimming, tennis, track & field, volleyball.

ADMISSIONS

Selectivity Rating: 80 (of 100). **Freshman Academic Profile:** Average high school GPA 3.4. 27% in top 10% of high school class, 54% in top 25% of high school class, 82% in top 50% of high school class. 89% from public high schools. Average SAT I Math 546, SAT I Math middle 50% range 490-620. Average SAT I Verbal 547, SAT I Verbal middle 50% range 490-620. Average ACT 23, ACT middle 50% range 21-26. TOEFL required of all international applicants, minimum TOEFL 500. **Basis for Candidate Selection:** *Very important factors considered include:* secondary school record. *Important factors considered include:* class rank, standardized test scores. *Other factors considered include:* alumni/ae relation, character/personal qualities, essays, extracurricular activities, interview, recommendations, talent/ability, volunteer work, work experience. **Freshman Admission Requirements:** High school diploma or GED is required. *Academic units required/recommended:* 15 total required; 19 total recommended; 4 English required, 4 English recommended, 3 math required, 4 math recommended, 3 science required, 4 science recommended, 2 science lab required, 1 foreign language required, 2 foreign language recommended, 3 social studies required, 4 social studies recommended, 1 history required, 1 history recommended, 5 elective required, 5 elective recommended. **Freshman Admission Statistics:** 7,322 applied, 85% accepted, 43% of those accepted enrolled. **Transfer Admission Requirements:** *Items required:* college transcript. Minimum college GPA of 2.0 required. Lowest grade transferable D. **General Admission Information:** Application fee $25. Priority application deadline March 1. Regular application deadline July 1. Nonfall registration accepted. Admission may be deferred for a maximum of 1 year. Credit and/or placement offered for CEEB Advanced Placement tests.

COSTS AND FINANCIAL AID

In-state tuition $3,556. Out-of-state tuition $9,624. Room & board $4,232. Required fees $0. Average book expense $700. **Required Forms and Deadlines:** FAFSA. No deadline for regular filing. Priority filing deadline March 1. **Notification of Awards:** Applicants will be notified of awards on or about April 1. **Types of Aid:** *Need-based scholarships/grants:* Pell, SEOG, state scholarships/grants, private scholarships, the school's own gift aid, Federal Nursing. *Loans:* Direct Subsidized Stafford, Direct Unsubsidized Stafford, Direct PLUS, Federal Perkins, college/university loans from institutional funds. **Student Employment:** Federal Work-Study Program available. Institutional employment available. Off-campus job opportunities are good. **Financial Aid Statistics:** 30% freshmen, 46% undergrads receive some form of aid. Average freshman grant $5,174. Average freshman loan $4,667. **Financial Aid Phone:** 205-348-6756.

UNIVERSITY OF ALASKA—ANCHORAGE

3211 Providence Drive, Anchorage, AK 99508-8046
Phone: 907-786-1480 **CEEB Code:** 4896
Fax: 907-786-4888 **Web:** www.uaa.alaska.edu **ACT Code:** 137

This public school was founded in 1954. It has a 428-acre campus.

STUDENTS AND FACULTY

Enrollment: 15,091. **Student Body:** Male 39%, female 61%, out-of-state 5%, international 1%. **Ethnic Representation:** African American 5%, Asian 5%, Caucasian 73%, Hispanic 5%, Native American 9%. **Retention and Graduation:** 64% freshmen return for sophomore year. 16% freshmen graduate within 4 years. **Faculty:** Student/faculty ratio 18:1. 487 full-time faculty, 64% hold PhDs. 94% faculty teach undergrads.

ACADEMICS

Degrees: Associate's, bachelor's, certificate, diploma, master's. **Academic Requirements:** General education including some course work in arts/fine arts, English (including composition), history, humanities, mathematics, sciences (biological or physical), social science, these are for baccalaureate degree seeking only. **Classes:** Under 10 students in an average lab/discussion section. **Disciplines with Highest Percentage of Degrees Awarded:** Education 17%, business/marketing 17%, health professions and related sciences 11%, social sciences and history 9%, psychology 7%. **Special Study Options:** Cooperative (work-study) program, cross registration, distance learning, double major, dual enrollment, English as a second language, student exchange program (domestic), honors program, independent study, internships, liberal arts/career combination, student-designed major, study abroad, teacher certification program.

FACILITIES

Housing: Coed, apartments for single students, housing for disabled students, housing for international students, floors for Alaska natives studying engineering, nursing housing, honor housing, language & cultures, first-year students under age 20 housing, healthy lifestyle housing, quiet lifestyle housing, WWAME program housing, Far East exchange program housing. **Library Holdings:** 894,080 bound volumes. 3,833 periodicals. 579,920 microforms. 9,006 audiovisuals. **Special Academic Facilities/Equipment:** Kimura and student Center Galleries. **Computers:** School-owned computers available for student use.

EXTRACURRICULARS

Activities: Choral groups, dance, drama/theater, jazz band, literary magazine, music ensembles, radio station, student government, student newspaper. **Organizations:** 70 registered organizations, 5 honor societies, 5 religious organizations, 2 fraternities, (1% men join), 2 sororities, (1% women join). **Athletics (Intercollegiate):** *Men:* basketball, cross-country, ice hockey, skiing (alpine), skiing (Nordic). *Women:* basketball, cross-country, gymnastics, skiing (alpine), skiing (Nordic), volleyball.

ADMISSIONS

Selectivity Rating: 63 (of 100). **Freshman Academic Profile:** 7% in top 10% of high school class, 22% in top 25% of high school class, 39% in top 50% of high school class. SAT I Math middle 50% range 440-550. SAT I Verbal middle 50% range 430-560. ACT middle 50% range 18-24. TOEFL required of all international applicants, minimum TOEFL 450. **Basis for Candidate Selection:** *Very important factors considered include:* secondary school record. *Other factors considered include:* class rank, standardized test scores, talent/ability. **Freshman Admission Requirements:** High school diploma or GED is required. *Academic units required/recommended:* 4 English recommended, 2 math recommended, 3 science recommended, 1 foreign language recommended, 3 social studies recommended, 1 history recommended. **Freshman Admission Statistics:** 2,001 applied, 87% accepted, 78% of those accepted enrolled. **Transfer Admission Requirements:** *Items required:* college transcript, statement of good standing from prior school. Minimum high school GPA of 2.5 required. Minimum college GPA of 2.0 required. Lowest grade transferable C. **General Admission Information:** Application fee $45. Priority application deadline April 1. Regular application deadline September 10. Nonfall registration accepted. Admission may be deferred for a maximum of 2 years. Credit offered for CEEB Advanced Placement tests.

COSTS AND FINANCIAL AID

Out-of-state tuition $8,197. Room & board $6,030. Required fees $352. Average book expense $897. **Required Forms and Deadlines:** FAFSA and institution's own financial aid form. Financial aid filing deadline August 30. Priority filing deadline April 1. **Notification of Awards:** Applicants will be notified of awards on a rolling basis beginning on or about June 1. **Types of Aid:** *Need-based scholarships/grants:* Pell, SEOG, state scholarships/grants, private scholarships, the school's own gift aid. *Loans:* Direct Subsidized Stafford, Direct Unsubsidized Stafford, Direct PLUS, Federal Perkins, state loans. **Student Employment:** Federal Work-Study Program available. Institutional employment available. Off-campus job opportunities are good. **Financial Aid Statistics:** 26% freshmen, 34% undergrads receive some form of aid. **Financial Aid Phone:** 907-786-1586.

UNIVERSITY OF ALASKA—FAIRBANKS

PO Box 757480, Fairbanks, AK 99775-7480
Phone: 907-474-7500 **E-mail:** fyapply@uaf.edu **CEEB Code:** 4866
Fax: 907-474-5379 **Web:** www.uaf.edu **ACT Code:** 64

This public school was founded in 1917. It has a 2,250-acre campus.

STUDENTS AND FACULTY

Enrollment: 6,727. **Student Body:** Male 42%, female 58%, out-of-state 15%, international 1%. **Ethnic Representation:** African American 4%, Asian 3%, Caucasian 68%, Hispanic 3%, Native American 17%. **Retention and Graduation:** 70% freshmen return for sophomore year. 7% freshmen graduate within 4 years. 42% grads go on to further study within 1 year. 20% grads pursue business degrees. 5% grads pursue law degrees. 10% grads pursue medical degrees. **Faculty:** Student/faculty ratio 10:1. 426 full-time faculty. 79% faculty teach undergrads.

ACADEMICS

Degrees: Associate's, bachelor's, certificate, doctoral, master's, terminal. **Academic Requirements:** General education including some course work in arts/fine arts, English (including composition), history, humanities, mathematics, philosophy, sciences (biological or physical), social science. **Classes:** Under 10 students in an average class. Under 10 students in an average lab/discussion section. **Majors with Highest Enrollment:** Education, general; business administration/management; biology/biological sciences, general. **Disciplines with Highest Percentage of Degrees Awarded:** Engineering/engineering technology 12%, protective services/public administration 12%, business/marketing 10%, social sciences and history 9%, education 8%. **Special Study Options:** Accelerated program, cooperative (work-study) program, distance learning, double major, dual enrollment, student exchange program (domestic), honors program, independent study, internships, student-designed major, study abroad, teacher certification program.

FACILITIES

Housing: Coed, apartments for married students, apartments for single students, housing for disabled students, fraternities and/or sororities, Alaska Native Cultural Housing. **Library Holdings:** 608,575 bound volumes. 2,754 periodicals. 1,131,516 microforms. 664,448 audiovisuals. **Special Academic Facilities/Equipment:** Museum of Natural/Cultural History of Alaska and the North, Cray supercomputer, extensive telecommunication network, geophysical institute, NASA earth station, Poker Flat Research Range, electron microscope, microprobe. **Computers:** School-owned computers available for student use.

EXTRACURRICULARS

Activities: Choral groups, concert band, dance, drama/theater, jazz band, literary magazine, music ensembles, musical theater, opera, pep band, radio station, student government, student newspaper, student-run film society, symphony orchestra, television station. **Organizations:** 114 registered organizations, 4 honor societies, 8 religious organizations, 3 fraternity, 1 sorority. **Athletics (Intercollegiate):** *Men:* basketball, skiing (cross-country), ice hockey, rifle. *Women:* basketball, skiing (cross-country), diving, rifle, swimming, volleyball.

ADMISSIONS

Selectivity Rating: 69 (of 100). **Freshman Academic Profile:** Average high school GPA 3.1. 12% in top 10% of high school class, 31% in top 25% of high school class, 60% in top 50% of high school class. Average SAT I Math 513, SAT I Math middle 50% range 450-580. Average SAT I Verbal 517, SAT I Verbal middle 50% range 460-590. Average ACT 21, ACT middle 50% range 18-24. TOEFL required of all international applicants, minimum TOEFL 550. **Basis for Candidate Selection:** *Very important factors considered include:* secondary school record, standardized test scores. **Freshman Admission Requirements:** High school diploma or GED is required. *Academic units required/recommended:* 16 total required; 4 English required, 3 math required, 3 science required, 1 science lab required, 2 foreign language recommended, 3 social studies required, 3 elective required. **Freshman Admission Statistics:** 1,721 applied, 85% accepted, 64% of those accepted enrolled. **Transfer Admission Requirements:** *Items required:* college transcript. Minimum college GPA of 2.0 required. Lowest grade transferable C. **General Admission Information:** Application fee $35. Regular application deadline August 1. Nonfall registration accepted. Admission may be deferred for a maximum of 1 year. Credit and/or placement offered for CEEB Advanced Placement tests.

COSTS AND FINANCIAL AID

In-state tuition $2,880. Out-of-state tuition $8,610. Room & board $4,950. Required fees $970. Average book expense $650. **Required Forms and Deadlines:** FAFSA. Priority filing deadline July 1. **Notification of Awards:** Applicants will be notified of awards on a rolling basis beginning on or about March 1. **Types of Aid:** *Need-based scholarships/grants:* Pell, SEOG, private scholarships, the school's own gift aid. *Loans:* Direct Subsidized Stafford, Direct Unsubsidized Stafford, FFEL Subsidized Stafford, FFEL Unsubsidized Stafford, FFEL PLUS, state loans. **Student Employment:** Federal Work-Study Program available. Institutional employment available. Off-campus job opportunities are good. **Financial Aid Phone:** 907-474-7256.

UNIVERSITY OF ALASKA—SOUTHEAST

11120 Glacier Highway, Juneau, AK 99801-8681
Phone: 907-465-6462 **E-mail:** jngaw@acad1.alaska.edu **CEEB Code:** 4897
Fax: 907-465-6365 **Web:** www.jun.alaska.edu **ACT Code:** 153

This public school was founded in 1972. It has a 198-acre campus.

STUDENTS AND FACULTY

Enrollment: 2,782. **Student Body:** Out-of-state 20%, international 1% (8 countries represented). **Ethnic Representation:** African American 1%, Asian 2%, Caucasian 88%, Hispanic 1%, Native American 8%.

ACADEMICS

Degrees: Associate's, bachelor's, master's. **Special Study Options:** Cooperative (work-study) program, study abroad. Undergrads may take grad-level classes. Co-op programs: business, computer science, humanities.

FACILITIES

Housing: Coed, apartments for married students, apartments for single students. **Library Holdings:** 100,000 bound volumes. 1,500 periodicals. **Computers:** *Recommended operating system:* Mac. School-owned computers available for student use.

EXTRACURRICULARS

ADMISSIONS

Selectivity Rating: 63 (of 100). **Freshman Academic Profile:** 13% in top 10% of high school class, 31% in top 25% of high school class, 64% in top 50% of high school class. 94% from public high schools. TOEFL required of all international applicants, minimum TOEFL 500. **Freshman Admission Requirements:** High school diploma is required and GED is not accepted. *Academic units required/recommended:* 11 total recommended; 4 English recommended, 2 math recommended, 2 science recommended, 3 social studies recommended. **Transfer Admission Requirements:** Minimum college GPA of 2.0 required. Lowest grade transferable C. **General Admission Information:** Regular application deadline September 5. Nonfall registration accepted. Credit offered for CEEB Advanced Placement tests.

COSTS AND FINANCIAL AID

In-state tuition $2,168. Out-of-state tuition $6,428. Room & board $7,650. Required fees $134. Average book expense $529. **Required Forms and Deadlines:** FAFSA, institution's own financial aid form and state aid form. **Notification of Awards:** Applicants will be notified of awards on or about May 1. **Types of Aid:** *Need-based scholarships/grants:* state scholarships/grants. *Loans:* FFEL Subsidized Stafford, FFEL PLUS. **Student Employment:** Federal Work-Study Program available. Institutional employment available. Off-campus job opportunities are good. **Financial Aid Statistics:** Average income from on-campus job $1,800. **Financial Aid Phone:** 907-465-6255.

UNIVERSITY OF ALBERTA

120 Administration Building, Edmonton, Alberta, AB T6G 2M7
Phone: 780-492-3113 **E-mail:** registrar@ualberta.ca
Fax: 780-492-7172 **Web:** www.ualberta.ca

This public school was founded in 1908.

STUDENTS AND FACULTY

Enrollment: 27,241. **Student Body:** Male 44%, female 56%, out-of-state 12%. **Faculty:** Student/faculty ratio 14:1. 1,456 full-time faculty.

ACADEMICS

Degrees: Bachelor's, certificate, diploma, doctoral, first professional, master's. **Academic Requirements:** General education including some course work in

English (including composition), sciences (biological or physical). **Majors with Highest Enrollment:** Education, general; biology/biological sciences, general; psychology, general. **Disciplines with Highest Percentage of Degrees Awarded:** Other 49%, education 21%, engineering/engineering technology 10%, business/marketing 8%, health professions and related sciences 5%. **Special Study Options:** Cooperative (work-study) program, distance learning, English as a second language, student exchange program (domestic), honors program, independent study, internships, student-designed major, study abroad, teacher certification program.

FACILITIES

Housing: Coed, apartments for married students, apartments for single students, housing for disabled students, Family accommodations. **Library Holdings:** 4,550,496 bound volumes. 25,673 periodicals. 3,102,505 microforms. 0 audiovisuals. **Computers:** School-owned computers available for student use.

EXTRACURRICULARS

Activities: Choral groups, concert band, dance, drama/theater, jazz band, music ensembles, radio station, student government, student newspaper, student-run film society. **Organizations:** 250 registered organizations, 9 fraternities, 4 sororities. **Athletics (Intercollegiate):** *Men:* basketball, cross-country, football, ice hockey, indoor track. *Women:* basketball, cross-country, field hockey, ice hockey, indoor track.

ADMISSIONS

Selectivity Rating: 60 (of 100). **Freshman Academic Profile:** Average high school GPA 3.2. TOEFL required of all international applicants, minimum TOEFL 580. **Basis for Candidate Selection:** *Very important factors considered include:* secondary school record. *Important factors considered include:* standardized test scores, talent/ability. *Other factors considered include:* interview, minority status. **Freshman Admission Requirements:** High school diploma is required and GED is not accepted. **Transfer Admission Requirements:** *Items required:* college transcript. **General Admission Information:** Application fee $41. Regular application deadline May 2. Nonfall registration accepted.

COSTS AND FINANCIAL AID

In-state tuition $3,770. Out-of-state tuition $3,770. Room & board $4,500. Required fees $440. Average book expense $1,000. **Notification of Awards:** Applicants will be notified of awards on a rolling basis. **Types of Aid:** *Loans:* college/university loans from institutional funds, Alberta Student Finance Board, Canada Student Loans Program, Cooperative Education Plan, Federal Canadian, Provincial Grants. **Student Employment:** Institutional employment available. Off-campus job opportunities are good. **Financial Aid Phone:** (780) 492-3483.

UNIVERSITY OF ARIZONA

PO Box 210011, Tucson, AZ 85721-0011
CEEB Code: 4832
Fax: 520-621-9799 **Web:** www.arizona.edu **ACT Code:** 96

This public school was founded in 1885. It has a 355-acre campus.

STUDENTS AND FACULTY

Enrollment: 28,278. **Student Body:** Male 47%, female 53%, out-of-state 30%, international 4%. **Ethnic Representation:** African American 3%, Asian 6%, Caucasian 70%, Hispanic 15%, Native American 2%. **Retention and Graduation:** 29% freshmen graduate within 4 years. 42% grads go on to further study within 1 year. **Faculty:** Student/faculty ratio 19:1. 1375 full-time faculty, 98% hold PhDs. 77% faculty teach undergrads.

ACADEMICS

Degrees: Bachelor's, doctoral, first professional, master's, post-bachelor's certificate. **Academic Requirements:** General education including some course work in arts/fine arts, English (including composition), foreign languages, humanities, mathematics, sciences (biological or physical), social science. **Classes:** 20-29 students in an average class. 20-29 students in an average lab/discussion section. **Majors with Highest Enrollment:** Psychology, general; political science and government, general; communications studies/speech communication and rhetoric. **Disciplines with Highest Percentage of Degrees Awarded:** Business/marketing 19%, social sciences and history 11%, communications/communication technologies 9%, education 9%, biological life sciences 8%. **Special Study Options:** Distance learning, double major, dual enrollment, English as a second language, student exchange program (domestic), honors program, independent study, internships, study abroad, teacher certification program, weekend college.

FACILITIES

Housing: Coed, all-female, all-male, apartments for single students, fraternities and/or sororities. **Library Holdings:** 4,359,195 bound volumes. 23,790 periodicals. 5,287,401 microforms. 51,136 audiovisuals. **Special Academic Facilities/Equipment:** Art, photography, and natural history museums; tree-ring lab; planetarium; optical sciences center; nuclear reactor. **Computers:** School-owned computers available for student use.

EXTRACURRICULARS

Activities: Choral groups, concert band, dance, drama/theater, jazz band, marching band, music ensembles, pep band, radio station, student government, student newspaper, television station, yearbook. **Organizations:** 13 honor societies, 13 religious organizations, 25 fraternities (11% men join), 20 sororities (13% women join). **Athletics (Intercollegiate):** *Men:* baseball, basketball, cross-country, diving, football, golf, swimming, tennis, track & field. *Women:* basketball, cross-country, diving, golf, gymnastics, indoor track, soccer, softball, swimming, tennis, track & field, volleyball.

ADMISSIONS

Selectivity Rating: 75 (of 100). **Freshman Academic Profile:** 32% in top 10% of high school class, 59% in top 25% of high school class, 87% in top 50% of high school class. 90% from public high schools. Average SAT I Math 556, SAT I Math middle 50% range 500-620. Average SAT I Verbal 543, SAT I Verbal middle 50% range 490-600. Average ACT 23, ACT middle 50% range 21-26. **Basis for Candidate Selection:** *Very important factors considered include:* secondary school record. *Important factors considered include:* class rank, standardized test scores. *Other factors considered include:* character/personal qualities, essays, extracurricular activities, geographical residence, interview, minority status, recommendations, state residency, talent/ability, volunteer work, work experience. **Freshman Admission Requirements:** High school diploma or GED is required. *Academic units required/recommended:* 16 total required; 16 total recommended; 4 English required, 4 English recommended, 4 math required, 4 math recommended, 3 science required, 3 science recommended, 3 science lab required, 3 science lab recommended, 2 foreign language required, 2 foreign language recommended, 1 social studies required, 1 social studies recommended, 1 history required, 1 history recommended. **Freshman Admission Statistics:** 19,832 applied, 86% accepted, 34% of those accepted enrolled. **Transfer Admission Requirements:** *Items required:* college transcript. Minimum college GPA of 2.5 required. Lowest grade transferable C. **General Admission Information:** Application fee $50. Priority application deadline October 1. Regular application deadline April 1. Nonfall registration accepted. Credit offered for CEEB Advanced Placement tests.

COSTS AND FINANCIAL AID

In-state tuition $2,508. Out-of-state tuition $11,028. Room & board $6,568. Required fees $85. Average book expense $735. **Required Forms and Deadlines:** FAFSA. Priority filing deadline March 1. **Notification of Awards:** Applicants will be notified of awards on a rolling basis beginning on or about April 1. **Types of Aid:** *Need-based scholarships/grants:* Pell, SEOG, state scholarships/grants, private scholarships, the school's own gift aid, Federal Nursing. *Loans:* FFEL Subsidized Stafford, FFEL Unsubsidized Stafford, FFEL PLUS, Federal Perkins, Federal Nursing, college/university loans from institutional funds. **Student Employment:** Federal Work-Study Program available. Institutional employment available. Off-campus job opportunities are good. **Financial Aid Statistics:** 36% freshmen, 47% undergrads receive some form of aid. **Financial Aid Phone:** 520-621-1858.

UNIVERSITY OF ARKANSAS—FAYETTEVILLE

200 Silas Hunt Hall, Fayetteville, AR 72701
Phone: 479-575-5346 **E-mail:** uofa@uark.edu **CEEB Code:** 6866
Fax: 479-575-7515 **Web:** www.uark.edu **ACT Code:** 144

This public school was founded in 1871. It has a 345-acre campus.

STUDENTS AND FACULTY

Enrollment: 12,889. **Student Body:** Male 51%, female 49%, out-of-state 11%, international 3%. **Ethnic Representation:** African American 6%, Asian 3%, Caucasian 86%, Hispanic 2%, Native American 2%. **Retention and Graduation:** 82% freshmen return for sophomore year. 22% freshmen graduate within 4 years. **Faculty:** Student/faculty ratio 16:1. 791 full-time faculty. 100% faculty teach undergrads.

ACADEMICS

Degrees: Bachelor's, doctoral, first professional, master's, post-master's certificate. **Academic Requirements:** General education including some course work in arts/fine arts, English (including composition), foreign languages, history, humanities, mathematics, sciences (biological or physical), social science. **Classes:** 20-29 students in an average class. 20-29 students in an average lab/discussion section. **Majors with Highest Enrollment:** Marketing/ marketing management, general; computer science; curriculum and instruction. **Disciplines with Highest Percentage of Degrees Awarded:** Business/ marketing 21%, engineering/engineering technology 12%, education 7%, communications/communication technologies 7%, computer and information sciences 6%. **Special Study Options:** Accelerated program, cooperative (work-study) program, distance learning, double major, English as a second language, honors program, independent study, internships, study abroad, teacher certification program.

FACILITIES

Housing: Coed, all-female, all-male, apartments for married students, apartments for single students, housing for international students, fraternities and/or sororities, substance-free halls, apartments for students with children, special-interest floors, student outreach and academic resource, first-year experience program area, honors housing. Several residences remain open over holidays and winter break. **Library Holdings:** 851,714 bound volumes. 14,168 periodicals. 3,840,006 microforms. 22,606 audiovisuals. **Special Academic Facilities/Equipment:** Public Radio-KUAF, High Density Electronics Center, University of Arkansas Museum, Reynolds Center for Enterprise Development, Center for Excellence in Poultry Science, Genesis Small Business Incubation Center, Chemical Hazards Research Center, Honors College. **Computers:** School-owned computers available for student use.

EXTRACURRICULARS

Activities: Choral groups, concert band, dance, drama/theater, jazz band, literary magazine, marching band, music ensembles, musical theater, opera, pep band, radio station, student government, student newspaper, student-run film society, symphony orchestra, television station, yearbook. **Organizations:** 230 registered organizations, 60 honor societies, 23 religious organizations, 15 fraternities (14% men join), 12 sororities (18% women join). **Athletics (Intercollegiate):** *Men:* baseball, basketball, cross-country, football, golf, tennis, track & field. *Women:* basketball, cross-country, diving, football, golf, soccer, softball, swimming, tennis, track & field, volleyball.

ADMISSIONS

Selectivity Rating: 81 (of 100). **Freshman Academic Profile:** Average high school GPA 3.6. 36% in top 10% of high school class, 65% in top 25% of high school class, 91% in top 50% of high school class. 95% from public high schools. Average SAT I Math 587, SAT I Math middle 50% range 520-650. Average SAT I Verbal 576, SAT I Verbal middle 50% range 510-640. Average ACT 25, ACT middle 50% range 22-28. TOEFL required of all international applicants, minimum TOEFL 550. **Basis for Candidate Selection:** *Very important factors considered include:* secondary school record, standardized test scores. *Important factors considered include:* class rank. *Other factors considered include:* alumni/ae relation, character/personal qualities, essays, extracurricular activities, geographical residence, state residency, talent/ability, volunteer work, work experience. **Freshman Admission Requirements:** High school diploma or GED is required. *Academic units required/recommended:* 16 total required; 4 English required, 3 math required, 3 science required, 2 science lab required, 2 foreign language recommended, 3 social studies required, 3 elective required. **Freshman Admission Statistics:** 5,025 applied, 86% accepted, 52% of those accepted enrolled. **Transfer Admission Requirements:** *Items required:* college transcript, statement of good standing from prior school. Minimum high school GPA of 3.0 required. Minimum college GPA of 2.0 required. Lowest grade transferable C. **General Admission Information:** Application fee $30. Priority application deadline November 15. Regular application deadline August 15. Nonfall registration accepted. Admission may be deferred for a maximum of 1 year. Credit and/or placement offered for CEEB Advanced Placement tests.

COSTS AND FINANCIAL AID

In-state tuition $3,573. Out-of-state tuition $9,945. Room & board $4,744. Required fees $883. Average book expense $800. **Required Forms and Deadlines:** FAFSA. No deadline for regular filing. Priority filing deadline March 15. **Notification of Awards:** Applicants will be notified of awards on a rolling basis beginning on or about April 1. **Types of Aid:** *Need-based scholarships/grants:* Pell, SEOG, state scholarships/grants, private scholarships, the school's own gift aid. *Loans:* FFEL Subsidized Stafford, FFEL Unsubsidized Stafford, FFEL PLUS, Federal Perkins, state loans, college/ university loans from institutional funds. **Student Employment:** Federal Work-Study Program available. Institutional employment available. Off-campus job opportunities are excellent. **Financial Aid Statistics:** 42% freshmen, 44% undergrads receive some form of aid. Average freshman grant $5,854. Average freshman loan $4,169. **Financial Aid Phone:** 479-575-3806.

See page 1242.

UNIVERSITY OF ARKANSAS—LITTLE ROCK

2801 South University Avenue, Little Rock, AR 72204
Phone: 501-569-3127 **E-mail:** admissions@ualr.edu **CEEB Code:** 6368
Fax: 501-569-8915 **Web:** www.ualr.edu **ACT Code:** 132

This public school was founded in 1927. It has a 150-acre campus.

STUDENTS AND FACULTY

Enrollment: 8,559. **Student Body:** Out-of-state 2%, international 3%. **Ethnic Representation:** African American 21%, Asian 4%, Caucasian 73%, Hispanic 1%, Native American 1%. **Retention and Graduation:** 59% freshmen return for sophomore year. 25% grads go on to further study within 1 year. 1% grads pursue business degrees. 4% grads pursue law degrees.

ACADEMICS

Degrees: Associate's, bachelor's, certificate, doctoral, master's, post-bachelor's certificate. **Academic Requirements:** General education including some course work in English (including composition), mathematics.

FACILITIES

Housing: Coed, all-female, all-male, fraternities and/or sororities. **Library Holdings:** 394,780 bound volumes. 862 periodicals. 9,794 microforms. **Special Academic Facilities/Equipment:** Language lab, observatory, planetarium, electron microscope, particle accelerator, nuclear magnetic resonator. **Computers:** *Recommended operating system:* Mac. School-owned computers available for student use.

EXTRACURRICULARS

Activities: Radio station, student government, student newspaper, television station, yearbook. **Organizations:** 98 registered organizations, 37 honor societies, 16 religious organizations, 5 fraternities (2% men join), 5 sororities (2% women join). **Athletics (Intercollegiate):** *Men:* basketball, cross-country, diving, soccer, swimming, tennis. *Women:* basketball, golf, soccer, swimming, tennis, track & field, volleyball.

ADMISSIONS

Selectivity Rating: 71 (of 100). **Freshman Academic Profile:** Average high school GPA 2.5. Average ACT 19. TOEFL required of all international applicants, minimum TOEFL 525. **Freshman Admission Requirements:** High school diploma or GED is required. *Academic units required/recommended:* 16 total recommended; 4 English recommended, 3 math recommended, 2 science recommended, 2 science lab recommended, 2 foreign language recommended, 1 social studies recommended, 2 history recommended. **Transfer Admission Requirements:** *Items required:* college transcript. Minimum college GPA of 2.0 required. Lowest grade transferable C. **General Admission Information:** Early decision application deadline August 1. Regular application deadline August 1. Nonfall registration accepted. Credit offered for CEEB Advanced Placement tests.

COSTS AND FINANCIAL AID

In-state tuition $1,131. Out-of-state tuition $2,916. Room & board $2,435. Required fees $138. Average book expense $1,000. **Required Forms and Deadlines:** FAFSA and state aid form. **Types of Aid:** *Need-based scholarships/ grants:* state scholarships/grants. *Loans:* FFEL Subsidized Stafford, FFEL PLUS. **Student Employment:** Federal Work-Study Program available. Institutional employment available. Off-campus job opportunities are good. **Financial Aid Phone:** 501-569-3130.

UNIVERSITY OF ARKANSAS—MONTICELLO

UAM PO Box 3600, Monticello, AR 71656
Phone: 870 460-1034 **E-mail:** johnsonj@uamont.edu **CEEB Code:** 6007
Fax: 870 460-1035 **Web:** www.uamont.edu **ACT Code:** 110

This public school was founded in 1910. It has a 1,600-acre campus.

STUDENTS AND FACULTY

Enrollment: 2,200. **Student Body:** Out-of-state 8%, international 1%. **Ethnic Representation:** African American 15%, Asian 1%, Caucasian 82%, Hispanic 1%, Native American 1%.

ACADEMICS

Degrees: Associate's, bachelor's, master's. **Special Study Options:** Cooperative (work-study) program.

FACILITIES

Housing: Coed, apartments for married students. **Library Holdings:** 126,229 bound volumes. 862 periodicals. 9,794 microforms. **Special Academic Facilities/Equipment:** Natural history museum, language lab, university farm and forest, instructional resource center, planetarium. **Computers:** *Recommended operating system:* Mac. School-owned computers available for student use.

EXTRACURRICULARS

Activities: Student government, yearbook. **Organizations:** 57 registered organizations, 1 honor society, 1 religious organization. **Athletics (Intercollegiate):** *Men:* baseball, basketball, football, golf. *Women:* basketball, cheerleading, cross-country, softball, tennis, track & field.

ADMISSIONS

Selectivity Rating: 68 (of 100). **Freshman Academic Profile:** 98% from public high schools. Average ACT 19. TOEFL required of all international applicants, minimum TOEFL 500. **Freshman Admission Requirements:** High school diploma is required and GED is not accepted. *Academic units required/recommended:* 20 total recommended; 3 English required, 4 English recommended, 2 math required, 4 math recommended, 3 science recommended, 2 foreign language recommended, 4 social studies recommended. **Transfer Admission Requirements:** Minimum college GPA of 2.0 required. Lowest grade transferable C. **General Admission Information:** Regular application deadline August 16. Nonfall registration accepted. Credit offered for CEEB Advanced Placement tests.

COSTS AND FINANCIAL AID

In-state tuition $2,040. Out-of-state tuition $4,248. Room & board $2,930. Average book expense $600. **Required Forms and Deadlines:** FAFSA. **Types of Aid:** *Need-based scholarships/grants:* state scholarships/grants. *Loans:* FFEL Subsidized Stafford, FFEL PLUS. **Student Employment:** Federal Work-Study Program available. Institutional employment available. Off-campus job opportunities are good. **Financial Aid Statistics:** Average freshman grant $946. Average freshman loan $1,907. Average income from on-campus job $971. **Financial Aid Phone:** 870-460-1050.

UNIVERSITY OF ARKANSAS—PINE BLUFF

1200 North University Drive, Mail Slot 4983, Pine Bluff, AR 71601
Phone: 870-575-8486 **E-mail:** fulton_e@uapb.edu; johnson_f@uapb.edu
CEEB Code: 6004 **Fax:** 870-543-8014 **Web:** www.uapb.edu **ACT Code:** 108

This public school was founded in 1873. It has a 295-acre campus.

STUDENTS AND FACULTY

Enrollment: 3,425. **Student Body:** Out-of-state 15%. **Ethnic Representation:** African American 82%, Caucasian 18%.

ACADEMICS

Degrees: Associate's, bachelor's, master's.

FACILITIES

Housing: Coed. **Library Holdings:** 113,658 bound volumes. 810 periodicals. 96,255 microforms. **Special Academic Facilities/Equipment:** Fine arts gallery, child care center, 240-acre farm. **Computers:** School-owned computers available for student use.

EXTRACURRICULARS

Organizations: 4 honor societies, 5 religious organizations, 4 fraternities (5% men join), 4 sororities (2% women join). **Athletics (Intercollegiate):** *Men:* basketball, cross-country, football, track & field, volleyball. *Women:* basketball, track & field, volleyball.

ADMISSIONS

Selectivity Rating: 63 (of 100). **Freshman Academic Profile:** TOEFL required of all international applicants, minimum TOEFL 500. **Freshman Admission Requirements:** High school diploma is required and GED is not accepted. *Academic units required/recommended:* 4 English required, 3 math required, 2 science required, 2 foreign language required, 1 social studies required, 2 history required, 2 elective required. **Transfer Admission Requirements:** Minimum college GPA of 2.0 required. **General Admission Information:** Regular application deadline rolling. Nonfall registration accepted.

COSTS AND FINANCIAL AID

In-state tuition $1,680. Out-of-state tuition $3,888. Room & board $3,470. Required fees $265. Average book expense $600. **Required Forms and Deadlines:** FAFSA, institution's own financial aid form and state aid form. **Notification of Awards:** Applicants will be notified of awards on or about February 1. **Types of Aid:** *Need-based scholarships/grants:* state scholarships/grants. *Loans:* FFEL Subsidized Stafford, FFEL PLUS. **Student Employment:** Federal Work-Study Program available. Institutional employment available. Off-campus job opportunities are good. **Financial Aid Statistics:** Average income from on-campus job $1,000. **Financial Aid Phone:** 501-543-8302.

UNIVERSITY OF BALTIMORE

$

1420 North Charles Street, Baltimore, MD 21201
Phone: 410-837-4777 **E-mail:** admissions@ubmall.ubalt.edu **CEEB Code:** 5810
Fax: 410-837-4793 **Web:** www.ubalt.edu

This public school was founded in 1925. It has a 47-acre campus.

STUDENTS AND FACULTY

Enrollment: 2,008. **Student Body:** Male 38%, female 62%, out-of-state 1%, international 4%. **Ethnic Representation:** African American 34%, Asian 3%, Caucasian 51%, Hispanic 2%, Native American 1%. **Retention and Graduation:** 10% grads go on to further study within 1 year. 7% grads pursue business degrees. 1% grads pursue law degrees. **Faculty:** Student/faculty ratio 16:1. 169 full-time faculty, 88% hold PhDs. 100% faculty teach undergrads.

ACADEMICS

Degrees: Bachelor's, certificate, doctoral, first professional, first professional certificate, master's, post-bachelor's certificate, post-master's certificate. **Academic Requirements:** General education including some course work in arts/fine arts, computer literacy, English (including composition), history, mathematics, philosophy, sciences (biological or physical), social science. **Classes:** 20-29 students in an average class. **Majors with Highest Enrollment:** Business/commerce, general; criminal justice/police science; health/health care administration/management. **Disciplines with Highest Percentage of Degrees Awarded:** Business/marketing 43%, protective services/public administration 11%, health professions and related sciences 9%, interdisciplinary studies 7%, computer and information sciences 5%. **Special Study Options:** Accelerated program, cooperative (work-study) program, distance learning, honors program, internships, student-designed major, study abroad, weekend college.

FACILITIES

Computers: *Recommended operating system:* Windows NT/2000. School-owned computers available for student use.

EXTRACURRICULARS

Activities: Literary magazine, student government, student newspaper. **Organizations:** 26 registered organizations, 10 honor societies.

ADMISSIONS

Selectivity Rating: 63 (of 100). **Freshman Academic Profile:** TOEFL required of all international applicants, minimum TOEFL 550. **Freshman Admission Requirements: Transfer Admission Requirements:** *Items required:* college transcript. Minimum college GPA of 2.0 required. Lowest grade transferable C. **General Admission Information:** Application fee $20.

COSTS AND FINANCIAL AID

In-state tuition $3,888. Out-of-state tuition $12,658. Room & board $1,108. Required fees $1,108. Average book expense $746. **Student Employment:** Federal Work-Study Program available. Off-campus job opportunities are good. **Financial Aid Statistics:** Average income from on-campus job $4,286. **Financial Aid Phone:** 410-837-4763.

UNIVERSITY OF BRIDGEPORT

 $$  

380 University Avenue, Bridgeport, CT 06601
Phone: 203-576-4552 **E-mail:** admit@.bridgeport.edu **CEEB Code:** 3914
Fax: 203-576-4941 **Web:** www.bridgeport.edu **ACT Code:** 602

This private school was founded in 1927. It has an 86-acre campus.

STUDENTS AND FACULTY

Enrollment: 1,212. **Student Body:** Male 47%, female 53%, out-of-state 37%, international 42% (73 countries represented). **Ethnic Representation:** African American 30%, Asian 8%, Caucasian 44%, Hispanic 14%. **Retention and Graduation:** 78% freshmen return for sophomore year. 42% freshmen graduate within 4 years. 15% grads go on to further study within 1 year. 10% grads pursue business degrees. 10% grads pursue law degrees. 5% grads pursue medical degrees. **Faculty:** Student/faculty ratio 12:1. 94 full-time faculty, 92% hold PhDs. 100% faculty teach undergrads.

ACADEMICS

Degrees: Associate's, bachelor's, doctoral, first professional, master's, post-master's certificate. **Academic Requirements:** General education including some course work in arts/fine arts, English (including composition), history, humanities, mathematics, philosophy, sciences (biological or physical), social science. **Classes:** 10-19 students in an average class. **Disciplines with Highest Percentage of Degrees Awarded:** Business/marketing 31%, liberal arts/general studies 21%, protective services/public administration 10%, health professions and related sciences 8%, biological life sciences 7%. **Special Study Options:** Accelerated program, cooperative (work-study) program, cross registration, distance learning, double major, English as a second language, honors program, independent study, internships, liberal arts/career combination, student-designed major, study abroad, teacher certification program, weekend college.

FACILITIES

Housing: Coed, men's and women's floors. **Library Holdings:** 272,430 bound volumes. 2,117 periodicals. 1,051,159 microforms. 5,485 audiovisuals. **Computers:** School-owned computers available for student use.

EXTRACURRICULARS

Activities: Choral groups, literary magazine, music ensembles, student government, student newspaper, yearbook. **Organizations:** 51 registered organizations, 11 honor societies, 6 religious organizations, 2 fraternities (2% men join), 4 sororities (2% women join). **Athletics (Intercollegiate):** *Men:* baseball, basketball, cross-country, soccer. *Women:* basketball, cross-country, gymnastics, soccer, softball, volleyball.

ADMISSIONS

Selectivity Rating: 66 (of 100). **Freshman Academic Profile:** Average high school GPA 2.9. 10% in top 10% of high school class, 30% in top 25% of high school class, 61% in top 50% of high school class. 89% from public high schools. Average SAT I Math 494, SAT I Math middle 50% range 410-570. Average SAT I Verbal 471, SAT I Verbal middle 50% range 400-530. Average ACT 16, ACT middle 50% range 16-17. TOEFL required of all international applicants, minimum TOEFL 500. **Basis for Candidate Selection:** *Very important factors considered include:* secondary school record, standardized test scores. *Important factors considered include:* character/personal qualities, class rank, essays, recommendations, talent/ability. *Other factors considered include:* alumni/ae relation, extracurricular activities, interview, volunteer work, work experience. **Freshman Admission Requirements:** High school diploma or GED is required. *Academic units required/recommended:* 16 total required; 16 total recommended; 4 English required, 4 English recommended, 3 math required, 3 math recommended, 2 science required, 2 science recommended, 2 science lab required, 2 science lab recommended, 2 social studies required, 2 social studies recommended, 5 elective required, 5 elective recommended. **Freshman Admission Statistics:** 1,732 applied, 78% accepted, 14% of those accepted enrolled. **Transfer Admission Requirements:** *Items required:* college transcript, essay. Lowest grade transferable C-. **General Admission Information:** Application fee $25. Priority application deadline April 1. Nonfall registration accepted. Admission may be deferred for a maximum of 1 year. Credit and/or placement offered for CEEB Advanced Placement tests.

COSTS AND FINANCIAL AID

Tuition $14,150. Room & board $7,070. Required fees $841. Average book expense $750. **Required Forms and Deadlines:** FAFSA, institution's own financial aid form and state aid form. No deadline for regular filing. Priority filing deadline April 1. **Notification of Awards:** Applicants will be notified of awards on a rolling basis beginning on or about April 1. **Types of Aid:** *Need-based scholarships/grants:* Pell, SEOG, state scholarships/grants, private scholarships, the school's own gift aid. *Loans:* Direct PLUS, FFEL Subsidized Stafford, FFEL Unsubsidized Stafford, FFEL PLUS, Federal Perkins. **Student Employment:** Federal Work-Study Program available. Off-campus job opportunities are good. **Financial Aid Statistics:** 34% freshmen, 44% undergrads receive some form of aid. Average freshman grant $7,118. Average freshman loan $4,625. Average income from on-campus job $1,000. **Financial Aid Phone:** 203-576-4568.

UNIVERSITY OF BRITISH COLUMBIA

Room 1206, 1874 East Mall, Vancouver, BC V6T1Z1
Phone: 604-822-8999 **E-mail:** international.reception@ubc.ca
Fax: 604-822-3599 **Web:** www.welcome.ubc.ca

This public school was founded in 1908. It has a 1,000-acre campus.

STUDENTS AND FACULTY

Enrollment: 28,030. **Student Body:** Male 44%, female 56%, out-of-state 6%, international students represent 127 countries. **Retention and Graduation:** 50% grads go on to further study within 1 year. **Faculty:** Student/faculty ratio 15:1. 1883 full-time faculty, 98% hold PhDs.

ACADEMICS

Degrees: Associate's, bachelor's, certificate, diploma, doctoral, master's, post-bachelor's certificate, post-master's certificate. **Academic Requirements:** General education including some course work in English (including composition), foreign languages, humanities, sciences (biological or physical), social science. **Classes:** 30-39 students in an average class. 10-19 students in an average lab/discussion section. **Majors with Highest Enrollment:** Elementary education and teaching; secondary education and teaching; psychology, general. **Disciplines with Highest Percentage of Degrees Awarded:** Other 15%, education 13%, business/marketing 9%, biological life sciences 8%, health professions and related sciences 8%. **Special Study Options:** Accelerated program, cooperative (work-study) program, distance learning, double major, dual enrollment, English as a second language, student exchange program (domestic), honors program, independent study, internships, liberal arts/career combination, student-designed major, study abroad, teacher certification program.

FACILITIES

Housing: Coed, all-female, all-male, apartments for married students, housing for disabled students, fraternities and/or sororities, theme housing. **Library Holdings:** 4,000,000 bound volumes. 26,016 periodicals. 4,900,000 microforms. 1,500,000 audiovisuals. **Special Academic Facilities/Equipment:** Museum of Anthropology, geological museum, TRIUMF, subatomic particle research, botanical gardens, Belkin Gallery, Chan Centre for Performing Arts, Liu International Studies Centre, St. John's College (Graduate College), Pulp and Paper Centre, Centre for Integrated Systems Research, Wall Centre for Interdisciplinary Studies. **Computers:** School-owned computers available for student use.

EXTRACURRICULARS

Activities: Choral groups, concert band, dance, drama/theater, jazz band, literary magazine, music ensembles, opera, radio station, student government, student newspaper, student-run film society, symphony orchestra, television station. **Organizations:** 200 registered organizations, 1 honor society, 6% men join fraternities, 2% women join sororities. **Athletics (Intercollegiate):** *Men:* baseball, basketball, cheerleading, crew, cross-country, field hockey, football, golf, ice hockey, rugby, skiing (alpine), skiing (Nordic), soccer, swimming, track & field, volleyball. *Women:* basketball, cheerleading, crew, cross-country, field hockey, golf, ice hockey, rugby, skiing (alpine), skiing (Nordic), soccer, swimming, track & field, volleyball.

ADMISSIONS

Selectivity Rating: 63 (of 100). **Freshman Academic Profile:** 98% from public high schools. Average SAT I Math 650. Average SAT I Verbal 650. Average ACT 27. TOEFL required of all international applicants, minimum TOEFL 550. **Basis for Candidate Selection:** *Very important factors considered include:* secondary school record. *Other factors considered include:* essays, extracurricular activities, recommendations, standardized test scores, talent/ability. **Freshman Admission Requirements:** High school diploma is required and GED is not accepted. *Academic units required/recommended:* 8 total required; 4 English required, 3 math required, 1 elective required. **Transfer Admission Requirements:** *Items required:* college transcript. **General Admission Information:** Application fee $63. Priority application deadline February 15. Regular application deadline March 31. Nonfall registration accepted. Credit and/or placement offered for CEEB Advanced Placement tests.

COSTS AND FINANCIAL AID

In-state tuition $2,295. Out-of-state tuition $2,295. Room & board $3,515. Required fees $180. Average book expense $543. **Required Forms and Deadlines:** Institution's own financial aid form. Financial aid filing deadline October 1. Priority filing deadline June 30. **Notification of Awards:** Applicants will be notified of awards on or about December 31. **Types of Aid:** *Loans:* FFEL Subsidized Stafford, FFEL Unsubsidized Stafford, FFEL PLUS. **Student Employment:** Institutional employment available. Off-campus job opportunities are fair. **Financial Aid Statistics:** Average freshman grant $1,720. Average freshman loan $4,237. **Financial Aid Phone:** 604-822-5111.

UNIVERSITY OF CALIFORNIA—BERKELEY

Office of Undergraduate Admission and Relations, 110 Sproul Hall #5800, Berkeley, CA 94720-5800 **Phone:** 510-642-3175 **E-mail:** ouars@uclink.berkeley.edu
CEEB Code: 4833 **Fax:** 510-642-7333 **Web:** www.berkeley.edu **ACT Code:** 444

This public school was founded in 1868. It has a 1,232-acre campus.

STUDENTS AND FACULTY

Enrollment: 23,835. **Student Body:** Male 46%, female 54%, out-of-state 11%, international 3%. **Ethnic Representation:** African American 4%, Asian 43%, Caucasian 31%, Hispanic 10%, Native American 1%. **Retention and Graduation:** 51% freshmen graduate within 4 years. **Faculty:** Student/faculty ratio 16:1. 1,442 full-time faculty, 97% hold PhDs. 100% faculty teach undergrads.

ACADEMICS

Degrees: Bachelor's, doctoral, first professional, master's. **Academic Requirements:** General education including some course work in English (including composition), history. **Classes:** 10-19 students in an average class. **Majors with Highest Enrollment:** Computer engineering, general; English language and literature, general; political science and government, general. **Disciplines with Highest Percentage of Degrees Awarded:** Social sciences and history 21%, biological life sciences 13%, engineering/engineering technology 12%, interdisciplinary studies 11%, English 7%. **Special Study Options:** Accelerated program, cross registration, distance learning, double major, dual enrollment, English as a second language, student exchange program (domestic), honors program, independent study, internships, student-designed major, study abroad, teacher certification program.

FACILITIES

Housing: Coed, all-female, all-male, apartments for married students, apartments for single students, housing for disabled students, housing for international students, fraternities and/or sororities, cooperative housing, theme program housing. **Library Holdings:** 13,915,488 bound volumes. 181,071 periodicals. 6,442,253 microforms. 100,560 audiovisuals. **Special Academic Facilities/Equipment:** Lawrence Berkeley National Lab; Pacific Film Archive; earthquake data center; museums of art, anthropology, natural history, and paleontology; botanical garden. **Computers:** School-owned computers available for student use.

EXTRACURRICULARS

Activities: Choral groups, concert band, dance, drama/theater, jazz band, literary magazine, marching band, music ensembles, pep band, radio station, student government, student newspaper, student-run film society, symphony orchestra, television station, yearbook. **Organizations:** 300 registered organizations, 6 honor societies, 28 religious organizations, 38 fraternities (11% men join), 19 sororities (10% women join). **Athletics (Intercollegiate):** *Men:* baseball, basketball, crew, cross-country, diving, football, golf, gymnastics, rugby, sailing, soccer, swimming, tennis, track & field, water polo. *Women:* basketball, crew, cross-country, diving, field hockey, golf, gymnastics, lacrosse, sailing, soccer, softball, swimming, tennis, track & field, volleyball, water polo.

ADMISSIONS

Selectivity Rating: 96 (of 100). **Freshman Academic Profile:** 98% in top 10% of high school class, 100% in top 25% of high school class, 100% in top 50% of high school class. 85% from public high schools. Average SAT I Math 671, SAT I Math middle 50% range 610-740. Average SAT I Verbal 629, SAT I Verbal middle 50% range 570-700. TOEFL required of all international applicants, minimum TOEFL 550. **Basis for Candidate Selection:** *Very important factors considered include:* essays, secondary school record, state residency. *Important factors considered include:* character/personal qualities, extracurricular activities, standardized test scores, talent/ability, volunteer work, work experience. *Other factors considered include:* geographical residence. **Freshman Admission Requirements:** High school diploma or GED is required. *Academic units required/recommended:* 15 total required; 4 English required, 3 math required, 4 math recommended, 2 science required, 3 science recommended, 2 science lab required, 3 science lab recommended, 2 foreign language required, 3 foreign language recommended, 2 social studies required, 2 history required, 2 elective required. **Transfer Admission Requirements:** *Items required:* essay. Minimum college GPA of 2.0 required. Lowest grade transferable D. **General Admission Information:** Application fee $40. Regular application deadline October 30. Nonfall registration accepted. Neither credit nor placement offered for CEEB Advanced Placement tests.

COSTS AND FINANCIAL AID

In-state tuition $0. Out-of-state tuition $11,502. Room & board $10,047. Required fees $4,200. Average book expense $1,072. **Required Forms and Deadlines:** FAFSA and state aid form. No deadline for regular filing. Priority filing deadline March 2. **Notification of Awards:** Applicants will be notified of awards on a rolling basis. **Types of Aid:** *Need-based scholarships/grants:* Pell, SEOG, state scholarships/grants, private scholarships, the school's own gift aid. *Loans:* Direct Subsidized Stafford, Direct Unsubsidized Stafford, Direct PLUS, Federal Perkins. **Student Employment:** Federal Work-Study Program available. Institutional employment available. Off-campus job opportunities are excellent. **Financial Aid Statistics:** 48% freshmen, 45% undergrads receive some form of aid. **Financial Aid Phone:** 510-642-6442.

UNIVERSITY OF CALIFORNIA—DAVIS

Undergraduate Admissions and Outreach Services, 175 Mrak Hall, Davis, CA 95616
Phone: 530-752-2971 **E-mail:** thinkucd@ucdavis.edu **CEEB Code:** 4834
Fax: 530-752-1280 **Web:** www.ucdavis.edu **ACT Code:** 454

This public school was founded in 1905. It has a 5,200-acre campus.

STUDENTS AND FACULTY

Enrollment: 20,388. **Student Body:** Male 44%, female 56%, out-of-state 4%, international 1%. **Ethnic Representation:** African American 3%, Asian 35%, Caucasian 44%, Hispanic 10%, Native American 1%. **Retention and Graduation:** 99% freshmen return for sophomore year. 27% freshmen graduate within 4 years. 40% grads go on to further study within 1 year. 2% grads pursue business degrees. 4% grads pursue law degrees. 4% grads pursue medical degrees. **Faculty:** Student/faculty ratio 19:1. 1,694 full-time faculty, 97% hold PhDs.

ACADEMICS

Degrees: Bachelor's, doctoral, first professional, master's, post-bachelor's certificate. **Academic Requirements:** General education including some course work in English (including composition), 3 courses in arts & humanities, 3 courses in science & engineering, 3 courses in social sciences, 1 course in social-cultural diversity. **Classes:** 20-29 students in an average class. 20-29 students in an average lab/discussion section. **Disciplines with Highest Percentage of Degrees Awarded:** Biological life sciences 17%, social sciences and history 17%, engineering/engineering technology 11%, business/marketing 7%, psychology 7%. **Special Study Options:** Accelerated program, cross registration, double major, dual enrollment, English as a second language, honors program, independent study, internships, student-designed major, study abroad, teacher certification program, off-campus study in Washington, DC.

FACILITIES

Housing: Coed, all-female, all-male, apartments for married students, apartments for single students, housing for international students, fraternities and/or sororities, cooperative housing, multi-ethnic program, integrated studies (honors) program, outdoor experiences program, quiet hall, health sciences program, science floor. **Library Holdings:** 3,180,865 bound volumes. 44,614 periodicals. 3,948,731 microforms. 14,047 audiovisuals. **Special Academic Facilities/Equipment:** Art galleries, 150-acre university arboretum, equestrian center, craft center, student experimental farm, nuclear lab, human performance lab, natural reserves, early childhood lab, raptor center, primate research center. **Computers:** School-owned computers available for student use.

EXTRACURRICULARS

Activities: Choral groups, concert band, dance, drama/theater, jazz band, literary magazine, marching band, music ensembles, pep band, radio station, student government, student newspaper, symphony orchestra, yearbook. **Organizations:** 364 registered organizations, 1 honor society, 28 fraternities (9% men join), 21 sororities (9% women join). **Athletics (Intercollegiate):** *Men:* baseball, basketball, cross-country, diving, football, golf, indoor track, soccer, swimming, tennis, track & field, water polo, wrestling. *Women:* basketball, crew, cross-country, diving, golf, gymnastics, indoor track, lacrosse, soccer, softball, swimming, tennis, track & field, volleyball, water polo.

ADMISSIONS

Selectivity Rating: 84 (of 100). **Freshman Academic Profile:** Average high school GPA 3.7. 95% in top 10% of high school class, 100% in top 25% of high school class, 100% in top 50% of high school class. 85% from public high schools. Average SAT I Math 600, SAT I Math middle 50% range 560-660. Average SAT I Verbal 565, SAT I Verbal middle 50% range 500-620. Average ACT 24, ACT middle 50% range 21-27. TOEFL required of all international applicants, minimum TOEFL 500. **Basis for Candidate Selection:** *Very important factors considered include:* essays, secondary school record, standardized test scores. *Important factors considered include:* extracurricular activities, state residency, talent/ability, volunteer work, work experience. *Other factors considered include:* geographical residence. **Freshman Admission Requirements:** High school diploma or GED is required. *Academic units required/recommended:* 15 total required; 4 English required, 4 English recommended, 3 math required, 4 math recommended, 2 science required, 3 science recommended, 2 science lab required, 3 science lab recommended, 2 foreign language required, 3 foreign language recommended, 2 history required, 2 elective required, 2 elective recommended. **Transfer Admission Requirements:** *Items required:* high school transcript, college transcript, essay, statement of good standing from prior school. Minimum college GPA of 2.0 required. Lowest grade transferable D-. **General Admission Information:** Application fee $40. Regular application deadline November 30. Nonfall registration accepted. Credit and/or placement offered for CEEB Advanced Placement tests.

COSTS AND FINANCIAL AID

In-state tuition $0. Out-of-state tuition $10,704. Room & board $5,762. Required fees $4,594. Average book expense $1,146. **Required Forms and Deadlines:** FAFSA. **Student Employment:** Federal Work-Study Program available. Institutional employment available. Off-campus job opportunities are good. **Financial Aid Statistics:** 49% freshmen, 50% undergrads receive some form of aid. Average freshman grant $5,427. Average freshman loan $4,985. Average income from on-campus job $1,500. **Financial Aid Phone:** 530-752-2390.

UNIVERSITY OF CALIFORNIA—IRVINE

Office of Admissions, 204 Administration Bldg., Irvine, CA 92697-1075
Phone: 949-824-6703 **E-mail:** oars@uci.edu **CEEB Code:** 4859
Fax: 949-824-2711 **Web:** www.uci.edu

This public school was founded in 1965. It has a 1,489-acre campus.

STUDENTS AND FACULTY

Enrollment: 17,723. **Student Body:** Male 48%, female 52%, out-of-state 4%, international 2%. **Ethnic Representation:** African American 2%, Asian 53%, Caucasian 24%, Hispanic 12%. **Retention and Graduation:** 92% freshmen return for sophomore year. 33% freshmen graduate within 4 years. 5% grads pursue business degrees. 4% grads pursue law degrees. 7% grads pursue medical degrees. **Faculty:** Student/faculty ratio 17:1. 845 full-time faculty.

ACADEMICS

Degrees: Bachelor's, doctoral, first professional, master's, post-bachelor's certificate. **Academic Requirements:** General education including some course work in arts/fine arts, computer literacy, English (including composition), foreign languages, history, humanities, mathematics, sciences (biological or physical), social science, writing, and multicultural & international/global issues. **Classes:** 20-29 students in an average class. 20-29 students in an average lab/discussion section. **Majors with Highest Enrollment:** Biology/biological sciences, general; social sciences, general; economics, general. **Special Study Options:** Cooperative (work-study) program, distance learning, double major, English as a second language, honors program, independent study, internships, study abroad, teacher certification program.

FACILITIES

Housing: Coed, all-female, apartments for married students, apartments for single students, housing for disabled students, housing for international students, fraternities and/or sororities, cooperative housing, trailer park. **Library Holdings:** 2,510,108 bound volumes. 25,774 periodicals. 2,536,465 microforms. 100,301 audiovisuals. **Special Academic Facilities/Equipment:** Museum of systemic biology, freshwater marsh reserve, electron microscope, nuclear reactor, laser institute, research facilities. **Computers:** School-owned computers available for student use.

EXTRACURRICULARS

Activities: Choral groups, concert band, dance, drama/theater, jazz band, literary magazine, music ensembles, musical theater, opera, pep band, radio station, student government, student newspaper, student-run film society, symphony orchestra, yearbook. **Organizations:** 289 registered organizations, 65 honor societies, 8% men join fraternities, 8% women join sororities. **Athletics (Intercollegiate):** *Men:* baseball, basketball, cheerleading, crew, cross-country, diving, golf, sailing, soccer, swimming, tennis, track & field, volleyball, water polo. *Women:* basketball, cheerleading, crew, cross-country, diving, golf, sailing, soccer, swimming, tennis, track & field, volleyball, water polo.

ADMISSIONS

Selectivity Rating: 79 (of 100). **Freshman Academic Profile:** Average high school GPA 3.7. 95% in top 10% of high school class, 100% in top 25% of high school class, 100% in top 50% of high school class. 61% from public high schools. SAT I Math middle 50% range 550-660. SAT I Verbal middle 50% range 520-610. TOEFL required of all international applicants, minimum TOEFL 550. **Basis for Candidate Selection:** *Very important factors considered include:* essays, secondary school record, standardized test scores. *Important factors considered include:* character/personal qualities, extracurricular activities, talent/ability, volunteer work. *Other factors considered include:* work experience. **Freshman Admission Requirements:** High school diploma or GED is required. *Academic units required/recommended:* 17 total required; 21 total recommended; 4 English required, 4 English recommended, 3 math required, 4 math recommended, 2 science required, 3 science recommended, 2 science lab required, 3 science lab recommended, 2 foreign language required, 3 foreign language recommended, 1 social studies required, 1 social studies recommended, 1 history required, 1 history recommended, 2 elective required, 2 elective recommended. **Freshman Admission Statistics:** 29,178 applied, 59% accepted, 28% of those accepted enrolled. **Transfer Admission Requirements:** *Items required:* college transcript, statement of good standing from prior school. Minimum college GPA of 2.0 required. Lowest grade transferable C. **General Admission Information:** Application fee $40. Priority application deadline November 30. Credit offered for CEEB Advanced Placement tests.

COSTS AND FINANCIAL AID

In-state tuition $4,556. Out-of-state tuition $15,630. Room & board $7,098. Required fees $4,556. Average book expense $1,350. **Required Forms and Deadlines:** FAFSA. Priority filing deadline March 2. **Notification of Awards:** Applicants will be notified of awards on or about May 1. **Types of Aid:** *Need-based scholarships/grants:* Pell, SEOG, the school's own gift aid. *Loans:* Direct Subsidized Stafford, Direct Unsubsidized Stafford, Direct PLUS, FFEL Subsidized Stafford, Federal Perkins. **Student Employment:** Federal Work-Study Program available. Institutional employment available. Off-campus job opportunities are excellent. **Financial Aid Statistics:** 38% freshmen, 47% undergrads receive some form of aid. Average freshman grant $1,466. Average income from on-campus job $1,200. **Financial Aid Phone:** 949-824-6261.

UNIVERSITY OF CALIFORNIA—LOS ANGELES

405 Hilgard Avenue, Box 951436, Los Angeles, CA 90095-1436
Phone: 310-825-3101 **E-mail:** ugadm@saonet.ucla.edu **CEEB Code:** 4837
Fax: 310-206-1206 **Web:** www.ucla.edu **ACT Code:** 448

This public school was founded in 1919. It has a 419-acre campus.

STUDENTS AND FACULTY

Enrollment: 24,899. **Student Body:** Male 44%, female 56%, out-of-state 3%, international 3% (100 countries represented). **Ethnic Representation:** African American 4%, Asian 39%, Caucasian 34%, Hispanic 15%. **Retention and Graduation:** 96% freshmen return for sophomore year. 47% freshmen graduate within 4 years. **Faculty:** Student/faculty ratio 17:1. 1,855 full-time faculty, 98% hold PhDs.

ACADEMICS

Degrees: Bachelor's, doctoral, first professional, master's. **Academic Requirements:** General education including some course work in arts/fine arts, English (including composition), foreign languages, history, humanities, mathematics, sciences (biological or physical), social science. **Classes:** 10-19 students in an average class. 20-29 students in an average lab/discussion section. **Disciplines with Highest Percentage of Degrees Awarded:** Social sciences and history 43%, psychology 14%, biological life sciences 11%, English 7%, engineering/engineering technology 6%. **Special Study Options:** Cross registration, distance learning, double major, English as a second language, student exchange program (domestic), honors program, independent study, internships, liberal arts/career combination, student-designed major, study abroad, teacher certification program.

FACILITIES

Housing: Coed, apartments for married students, apartments for single students, fraternities and/or sororities, cooperative housing. **Library Holdings:** 7,517,303 bound volumes. 93,854 periodicals. 6,055,632 microforms. 4,614,721 audiovisuals. **Special Academic Facilities/Equipment:** Art gallery, cultural history museum, sculpture garden, graphic arts center, numerous study centers, research institutes.

EXTRACURRICULARS

Activities: Choral groups, concert band, dance, drama/theater, jazz band, literary magazine, marching band, music ensembles, opera, pep band, radio station, student government, student newspaper, student-run film society, symphony orchestra, yearbook. **Organizations:** 700 registered organizations, 18 honor societies, 30 religious organizations, 27 fraternities (11% men join), 18 sororities (9% women join). **Athletics (Intercollegiate):** *Men:* baseball, basketball, cross-country, football, golf, soccer, tennis, track & field, volleyball, water polo. *Women:* basketball, cross-country, golf, gymnastics, soccer, softball, swimming, tennis, track & field, volleyball, water polo.

ADMISSIONS

Selectivity Rating: 94 (of 100). **Freshman Academic Profile:** 97% in top 10% of high school class, 80% from public high schools. Average SAT I Math 660, SAT I Math middle 50% range 590-720. Average SAT I Verbal 617, SAT I Verbal middle 50% range 550-670. Average ACT 26, ACT middle 50% range 22-29. TOEFL required of all international applicants, minimum TOEFL 550. **Basis for Candidate Selection:** *Very important factors considered include:* character/personal qualities, essays, secondary school record, standardized test scores, state residency, talent/ability, volunteer work. *Important factors considered include:* extracurricular activities. *Other factors considered include:* work experience. **Freshman Admission Requirements:** High school diploma or GED is required. *Academic units required/recommended:* 4 English required, 3 math required, 4 math recommended, 2 science required, 3 science recommended, 2 science lab required, 3 science lab recommended, 2 foreign language required, 3 foreign language recommended, 2 history required, 2 elective required. **Freshman Admission Statistics:** 43,443 applied, 24% accepted, 41% of those accepted enrolled. **Transfer Admission Requirements:** *Items required:* college transcript, essay, statement of good standing from prior school. Minimum college GPA of 2.4 required. Lowest grade transferable D. **General Admission Information:** Application fee $40. Regular application deadline November 30. Credit and/or placement offered for CEEB Advanced Placement tests.

COSTS AND FINANCIAL AID

In-state tuition $0. Out-of-state tuition $10,244. Room & board $8,565. Required fees $3,698. Average book expense $1,116. **Required Forms and Deadlines:** FAFSA. No deadline for regular filing. Priority filing deadline March 2. **Notification of Awards:** Applicants will be notified of awards on a rolling basis beginning on or about March 15. **Types of Aid:** *Need-based scholarships/grants:* Pell, SEOG, state scholarships/grants, private scholarships, the school's own gift aid, United Negro College Fund, Federal Nursing, National Merit Scholarship. *Loans:* FFEL Subsidized Stafford, FFEL Unsubsidized Stafford, FFEL PLUS, Federal Perkins, Federal Nursing, state loans, college/university loans from institutional funds. **Student Employment:** Federal Work-Study Program available. Institutional employment available. Off-campus job opportunities are good. **Financial Aid Statistics:** 49% freshmen, 50% undergrads receive some form of aid. Average freshman grant $6,492. Average freshman loan $2,660. Average income from on-campus job $1,138. **Financial Aid Phone:** 310-206-0400.

UNIVERSITY OF CALIFORNIA—RIVERSIDE

Best 351

1120 Hinderaker Hall, Riverside, CA 92521

Phone: 909-787-4531 **E-mail:** discover@pop.ucr.edu **CEEB Code:** 4839

Fax: 909-787-6344 **Web:** www.ucr.edu

This public school was founded in 1954. It has a 1,200-acre campus.

STUDENTS AND FACULTY

Enrollment: 14,124. **Student Body:** Male 46%, female 54%, out-of-state 1%, international 2% (22 countries represented). **Ethnic Representation:** African American 6%, Asian 41%, Caucasian 23%, Hispanic 23%. **Retention and Graduation:** 85% freshmen return for sophomore year. 39% freshmen graduate within 4 years. 37% grads go on to further study within 1 year. 4% grads pursue business degrees. 3% grads pursue law degrees. 5% grads pursue medical degrees. **Faculty:** Student/faculty ratio 19:1. 647 full-time faculty, 97% hold PhDs. 100% faculty teach undergrads.

ACADEMICS

Degrees: Bachelor's, doctoral, master's. **Academic Requirements:** General education including some course work in arts/fine arts, English (including composition), foreign languages, history, humanities, mathematics, philosophy, sciences (biological or physical), social science, ethnic studies. **Classes:** 20-29 students in an average class. 20-29 students in an average lab/discussion section. **Majors with Highest Enrollment:** Business administration/management; biology/biological sciences, general; social sciences, general. **Disciplines with Highest Percentage of Degrees Awarded:** Business/marketing 28%, social sciences and history 20%, biological life sciences 11%, psychology 9%, liberal arts/general studies 8%. **Special Study Options:** Accelerated program, cooperative (work-study) program, cross registration, distance learning, double major, dual enrollment, English as a second language, student exchange program (domestic), honors program, independent study, internships, student-designed major, study abroad, teacher certification program, accelerated 7-year MD program in cooperation with UCLA School of Medicine.

FACILITIES

Housing: Coed, apartments for married students, apartments for single students, housing for international students, fraternities and/or sororities, family housing and duplexes. 9 special interest halls available including academic, honors, multicultural. **Library Holdings:** 2,081,146 bound volumes. 21,323 periodicals. 1,701,311 microforms. 141,663 audiovisuals. **Special Academic Facilities/Equipment:** Art gallery, photography museum, botanical gardens, audiovisual resource center/studios, media resource center, statistical consulting center, citrus research center and agricultural experiment station, air pollution research center, center for environmental research and technology, center for social and behavioral science research, dry lands research institute, water resources center, geophysics and planetary physics institutes, center for bibliographical studies. **Computers:** School-owned computers available for student use.

EXTRACURRICULARS

Activities: Choral groups, concert band, dance, drama/theater, jazz band, literary magazine, music ensembles, musical theater, pep band, radio station, student government, student newspaper, student-run film society, symphony orchestra, yearbook. **Organizations:** 200 registered organizations, 10 honor societies, 11 religious organizations, 16 fraternities (3% men join), 14 sororities (3% women join). **Athletics (Intercollegiate):** *Men:* baseball, basketball, cross-country, golf, soccer, tennis, track & field. *Women:* basketball, cross-country, golf, soccer, softball, tennis, track & field, volleyball.

ADMISSIONS

Selectivity Rating: 80 (of 100). **Freshman Academic Profile:** Average high school GPA 3.5. 94% in top 10% of high school class, 100% in top 25% of high school class, 100% in top 50% of high school class. 90% from public high schools. Average SAT I Math 553, SAT I Math middle 50% range 490-620. Average SAT I Verbal 504, SAT I Verbal middle 50% range 440-560. Average ACT 21, ACT middle 50% range 18-23. TOEFL required of all international applicants, minimum TOEFL 550. **Basis for Candidate Selection:** *Very important factors considered include:* secondary school record, standardized test scores. *Important factors considered include:* essays. *Other factors considered include:* extracurricular activities, recommendations, talent/ability, volunteer work, work experience. **Freshman Admission Requirements:** High school diploma or GED is required. *Academic units required/recommended:* 15 total required; 4 English required, 3 math required, 2 science required, 2 science lab required, 2 foreign language required, 2 history required, 1 elective required. **Freshman Admission Statistics:** 22,975 applied, 86% accepted, 18% of those accepted enrolled. **Transfer Admission Requirements:** *Items required:* high school transcript, college transcript, essay, statement of good standing from prior school. Minimum high school GPA of 2.0 required. Minimum college GPA of 2.0 required. **General Admission Information:** Application fee $40. Priority application deadline November 1. Regular application deadline November 30. Nonfall registration accepted. Credit and/or placement offered for CEEB Advanced Placement tests.

COSTS AND FINANCIAL AID

In-state tuition $0. Out-of-state tuition $11,775. Room & board $8,200. Required fees $4,421. Average book expense $1,300. **Required Forms and Deadlines:** FAFSA and state aid form. Priority filing deadline March 2. **Notification of Awards:** Applicants will be notified of awards on a rolling basis beginning on or about March 1. **Types of Aid:** *Need-based scholarships/grants:* Pell, SEOG, state scholarships/grants, private scholarships, the school's own gift aid. *Loans:* Direct Subsidized Stafford, Direct Unsubsidized Stafford, Direct PLUS, Federal Perkins, college/university loans from institutional funds. **Student Employment:** Federal Work-Study Program available. Institutional employment available. Off-campus job opportunities are excellent. **Financial Aid Statistics:** 60% freshmen, 61% undergrads receive some form of aid. Average freshman grant $7,648. Average freshman loan $9,672. Average income from on-campus job $2,000. **Financial Aid Phone:** 909-787-3878.

UNIVERSITY OF CALIFORNIA—SAN DIEGO

9500 Gilman Drive, 0021, La Jolla, CA 92093-0021
Phone: 858-534-4831 **E-mail:** admissionsinfo@ucsd.edu **CEEB Code:** 4836
Fax: 858-534-5723 **Web:** www.ucsd.edu

This public school was founded in 1959. It has a 1,976-acre campus.

STUDENTS AND FACULTY

Enrollment: 15,840. **Student Body:** Male 49%, female 51%, out-of-state 2%, international 1% (70 countries represented). **Ethnic Representation:** African American 2%, Asian 38%, Caucasian 43%, Hispanic 2%, Native American 1%. **Retention and Graduation:** 93% freshmen return for sophomore year. 49% grads pursue business degrees. 8% grads pursue law degrees. 8% grads pursue medical degrees. **Faculty:** Student/faculty ratio 19:1.

ACADEMICS

Degrees: Bachelor's, doctoral, master's. **Academic Requirements:** General education including some course work in arts/fine arts, English (including composition), foreign languages, history, humanities, mathematics, sciences (biological or physical), social science. **Classes:** 10-19 students in an average class. 20-29 students in an average lab/discussion section. **Disciplines with Highest Percentage of Degrees Awarded:** Social sciences and history 42%, other 41%, engineering/engineering technology 12%, visual and performing arts 5%. **Special Study Options:** Accelerated program, cooperative (work-study) program, double major, English as a second language, student exchange program (domestic), honors program, independent study, internships, student-designed major, study abroad, teacher certification program, summer sessions for credit, special services for students with learning disabilities, research programs, freshman honors program, in-depth academic assignments working in small groups or one-to-one with faculty.

FACILITIES

Housing: Coed, apartments for married students, apartments for single students, housing for disabled students, housing for international students, International House for international students and others interested in international living. **Library Holdings:** 2,616,776 bound volumes. 24,986 periodicals. 2,880,645 microforms. 87,625 audiovisuals. **Special Academic Facilities/Equipment:** Art galleries, center for U.S.-Mexican studies, music recording studio, audiovisual center, center for music experimentation, aquarium, oceanographic institute, structural lab, supercomputer, electron microscopes. **Computers:** School-owned computers available for student use.

EXTRACURRICULARS

Activities: Choral groups, dance, drama/theater, jazz band, literary magazine, music ensembles, musical theater, pep band, radio station, student government, student newspaper, television station. **Organizations:** 275 registered organizations, 5 honor societies, 19 fraternities (10% men join), 14 sororities (10% women join). **Athletics (Intercollegiate):** *Men:* baseball, basketball, crew, cross-country, diving, fencing, golf, soccer, swimming, tennis, track & field, volleyball, water polo. *Women:* basketball, crew, cross-country, fencing, soccer, softball, swimming, tennis, track & field, volleyball, water polo.

ADMISSIONS

Selectivity Rating: 84 (of 100). **Freshman Academic Profile:** 95% in top 10% of high school class, 100% in top 25% of high school class, 100% in top 50% of high school class. Average SAT I Math 647. Average SAT I Verbal 609. Average ACT 25. TOEFL required of all international applicants, minimum TOEFL 550. **Basis for Candidate Selection:** *Very important factors considered include:* essays, secondary school record, standardized test scores, talent/ability, volunteer work, work experience. **Freshman Admission Requirements:** High school diploma or GED is required. *Academic units required/recommended:* 15 total required; 4 English required, 3 math required, 4 math recommended, 2 science required, 3 science recommended, 2 science lab required, 3 science lab recommended, 2 foreign language required, 3 foreign language recommended, 2 history required, 2 elective required. **Freshman Admission Statistics:** 32,318 applied, 41% accepted, 26% of those accepted enrolled. **Transfer Admission Requirements:** *Items required:* high school transcript, college transcript, essay. Minimum college GPA of 2.8 required. Lowest grade transferable D. **General Admission Information:** Application fee $40. Regular application deadline November 30. Credit and/or placement offered for CEEB Advanced Placement tests.

COSTS AND FINANCIAL AID

In-state tuition $3,848. Out-of-state tuition $13,652. Room & board $7,134. Required fees $3,848. Average book expense $886. **Required Forms and Deadlines:** FAFSA and state aid form. Financial aid filing deadline June 1. Priority filing deadline March 2. **Notification of Awards:** Applicants will be notified of awards on a rolling basis beginning on or about March 15. **Types of Aid:** *Need-based scholarships/grants:* Pell, SEOG, state scholarships/grants, private scholarships, the school's own gift aid. *Loans:* FFEL Subsidized Stafford, FFEL Unsubsidized Stafford, FFEL PLUS, Federal Perkins, college/university loans from institutional funds, alternative loans. **Student Employment:** Federal Work-Study Program available. Institutional employment available. Off-campus job opportunities are excellent. **Financial Aid Statistics:** 58% freshmen, 61% undergrads receive some form of aid. Average freshman grant $5,014. Average freshman loan $4,668. **Financial Aid Phone:** 858-534-4480.

UNIVERSITY OF CALIFORNIA—SANTA BARBARA

Undergraduate Admissions, 1234 Cheadle Hall-University of California, Santa Barbara, CA 93106-2014 **Phone:** 805-893-2881 **E-mail:** appinfo@sa.ucsb.edu **CEEB Code:** 4835 **Fax:** 805-893-2676 **Web:** www.ucsb.edu

This public school was founded in 1909. It has a 989-acre campus.

STUDENTS AND FACULTY

Enrollment: 17,724. **Student Body:** Male 46%, female 54%, out-of-state 5%, international 1%. **Ethnic Representation:** African American 3%, Asian 14%, Caucasian 57%, Hispanic 15%, Native American 1%. **Retention and Graduation:** 91% freshmen return for sophomore year. 39% freshmen graduate within 4 years. 39% grads go on to further study within 1 year. 5% grads pursue business degrees. 15% grads pursue law degrees. 2% grads pursue medical degrees. **Faculty:** Student/faculty ratio 17:1. 835 full-time faculty.

ACADEMICS

Degrees: Bachelor's, doctoral, master's, post-bachelor's certificate, post-master's certificate. **Academic Requirements:** General education including some course work in arts/fine arts, English (including composition), foreign languages, history, humanities, mathematics, philosophy, sciences (biological or physical), social science. **Classes:** 10-19 students in an average class. 20-29 students in an average lab/discussion section. **Disciplines with Highest Percentage of Degrees Awarded:** Social sciences and history 24%, business/marketing 12%, biological life sciences 8%, visual and performing arts 8%, communications/communication technologies 6%. **Special Study Options:** Accelerated program, cooperative (work-study) program, cross registration, distance learning, double major, English as a second language, student exchange program (domestic), honors program, independent study, internships, student-designed major, study abroad, teacher certification program. Undergrads may take grad-level classes. Off-campus study: Washington, DC.

FACILITIES

Housing: Coed, apartments for married students, apartments for single students, fraternities and/or sororities, cooperative housing. **Library Holdings:** 2,674,331 bound volumes. 18,898 periodicals. 3,669,358 microforms. 103,495 audiovisuals. **Special Academic Facilities/Equipment:** Art museum; centers for black studies, Chicano studies, and study of developing nations; institutes for applied behavioral sciences, community/organizational research, marine science, and theoretical physics; Channel Islands Field Station. **Computers:** School-owned computers available for student use.

EXTRACURRICULARS

Activities: Choral groups, concert band, dance, drama/theater, jazz band, literary magazine, music ensembles, musical theater, opera, pep band, radio station, student government, student newspaper, student-run film society, symphony orchestra, television station, yearbook. **Organizations:** 255 registered organizations, 4 honor societies, 6 religious organizations, 19 fraternities (8% men join), 18 sororities (10% women join). **Athletics (Intercollegiate):** *Men:* baseball, basketball, crew, cross-country, diving, football, golf, gymnastics, soccer, softball, squash, swimming, tennis, track & field, volleyball, water polo. *Women:* basketball, crew, cross-country, diving, football, golf, gymnastics, soccer, softball, squash, swimming, tennis, track & field, volleyball, water polo.

ADMISSIONS

Selectivity Rating: 82 (of 100). **Freshman Academic Profile:** Average high school GPA 3.7. 82% from public high schools. Average SAT I Math 612, SAT I Math middle 50% range 560-670. Average SAT I Verbal 580, SAT I Verbal middle 50% range 530-630. Average ACT 25, ACT middle 50% range 22-27. TOEFL required of all international applicants, minimum TOEFL 500. **Basis for Candidate Selection:** *Very important factors considered include:* essays, extracurricular activities, standardized test scores, talent/ability, volunteer work,

work experience. **Freshman Admission Requirements:** High school diploma or GED is required. *Academic units required/recommended:* 15 total required; 4 English required, 3 math required, 4 math recommended, 2 science required, 2 science lab required, 3 science lab recommended, 2 foreign language required, 3 foreign language recommended, 1 social studies required, 2 history required, 2 elective required. **Freshman Admission Statistics:** 34,022 applied, 50% accepted, 21% of those accepted enrolled. **Transfer Admission Requirements:** *Items required:* high school transcript, college transcript, essay. Minimum college GPA of 2.4 required. Lowest grade transferable D. **General Admission Information:** Application fee $40. Regular application deadline November 30. Nonfall registration accepted. Credit and/or placement offered for CEEB Advanced Placement tests.

COSTS AND FINANCIAL AID

Required Forms and Deadlines: FAFSA. Financial aid filing deadline May 31. Priority filing deadline March 2. **Notification of Awards:** Applicants will be notified of awards on a rolling basis beginning on or about March 15. **Types of Aid:** *Need-based scholarships/grants:* Pell, SEOG, state scholarships/grants, the school's own gift aid. *Loans:* Direct PLUS, Federal Perkins. **Student Employment:** Federal Work-Study Program available. Institutional employment available. Off-campus job opportunities are fair. **Financial Aid Statistics:** 43% freshmen, 42% undergrads receive some form of aid. Average freshman grant $4,673. Average freshman loan $3,742. **Financial Aid Phone:** 805-893-2432.

UNIVERSITY OF CALIFORNIA—SANTA CRUZ

Office of Admissions, Cook House, 1156 High Street, Santa Cruz, CA 95064
Phone: 831-459-4008 **E-mail:** admissions@ucsc.edu **CEEB Code:** 4860
Fax: 831-459-4452 **Web:** www.ucsc.edu

This public school was founded in 1965. It has a 2,000-acre campus.

STUDENTS AND FACULTY

Enrollment: 12,881. **Student Body:** Male 44%, female 56%, out-of-state 5%, international 1%. **Ethnic Representation:** African American 2%, Asian 17%, Caucasian 54%, Hispanic 14%, Native American 1%. **Retention and Graduation:** 87% freshmen return for sophomore year. 40% freshmen graduate within 4 years. **Faculty:** Student/faculty ratio 19:1. 508 full-time faculty, 98% hold PhDs.

ACADEMICS

Degrees: Bachelor's, certificate, doctoral, master's. **Academic Requirements:** General education including some course work in arts/fine arts, English (including composition), history, humanities, mathematics, sciences (biological or physical), social science. A writing-intensive course is required, and an ethnic/third world course is required. Also, a senior examination or equivalent body of work is required of all seniors prior to graduation. **Classes:** 20-29 students in an average class. 10-19 students in an average lab/discussion section. **Majors with Highest Enrollment:** Psychology, general; biology/biological sciences, general; English language and literature, general. **Disciplines with Highest Percentage of Degrees Awarded:** Social sciences and history 22%, biological life sciences 13%, visual and performing arts 12%, psychology 11%, English 9%. **Special Study Options:** Accelerated program, cooperative (work-study) program, double major, dual enrollment, English as a second language, student exchange program (domestic), honors program, independent study, internships, student-designed major, study abroad, teacher certification program.

FACILITIES

Housing: Coed, all-female, apartments for married students, apartments for single students, housing for international students. **Library Holdings:** 1,302,295 bound volumes. 9,023 periodicals. 831,193 microforms. 41,187 audiovisuals. **Special Academic Facilities/Equipment:** Eloise Pickard Smith Gallery, Mary Porter Sesnon Gallery, Center for Agroecology, Interdisciplinary Sciences Building, Wellness Center, Seymour Discovery Center at Long Marine Laboratory.

EXTRACURRICULARS

Activities: Choral groups, dance, drama/theater, literary magazine, music ensembles, radio station, student government, student newspaper, student-run film society, symphony orchestra. **Organizations:** 100 registered organizations, 1 honor society, 11 religious organizations, 9 fraternities (1% men join), 7 sororities (1% women join). **Athletics (Intercollegiate):** *Men:* basketball, diving, soccer, swimming, tennis, volleyball, water polo. *Women:* basketball, diving, soccer, swimming, tennis, volleyball, water polo.

ADMISSIONS

Selectivity Rating: 80 (of 100). **Freshman Academic Profile:** Average high school GPA 3.5. 96% from public high schools. Average SAT I Math 573, SAT I Math middle 50% range 520-630. Average SAT I Verbal 564, SAT I Verbal middle 50% range 500-620. Average ACT 23, ACT middle 50% range 21-26. TOEFL required of all international applicants, minimum TOEFL 550. **Basis for Candidate Selection:** *Very important factors considered include:* class rank, secondary school record, standardized test scores, state residency. *Important factors considered include:* essays. *Other factors considered include:* character/personal qualities, extracurricular activities, geographical residence, recommendations, talent/ability, volunteer work, work experience. **Freshman Admission Requirements:** High school diploma or GED is required. *Academic units required/recommended:* 15 total required; 18 total recommended; 4 English required, 4 English recommended, 3 math required, 4 math recommended, 2 science required, 3 science recommended, 2 foreign language required, 3 foreign language recommended, 1 social studies required, 1 social studies recommended, 1 history required, 1 history recommended, 2 elective required, 2 elective recommended. **Freshman Admission Statistics:** 20,616 applied, 80% accepted, 19% of those accepted enrolled. **Transfer Admission Requirements:** *Items required:* college transcript, essay. Minimum college GPA of 2.4 required. Lowest grade transferable D. **General Admission Information:** Application fee $40. Regular application deadline November 30. Nonfall registration accepted. Neither credit nor placement offered for CEEB Advanced Placement tests.

COSTS AND FINANCIAL AID

In-state tuition $0. Out-of-state tuition $12,379. Room & board $9,355. Required fees $4,300. Average book expense $1,170. **Required Forms and Deadlines:** FAFSA and state aid form. Financial aid filing deadline May 1. Priority filing deadline March 2. **Notification of Awards:** Applicants will be notified of awards on a rolling basis beginning on or about April 1. **Types of Aid:** *Need-based scholarships/grants:* Pell, SEOG, state scholarships/grants, private scholarships, the school's own gift aid. *Loans:* Direct Subsidized Stafford, Direct Unsubsidized Stafford, Direct PLUS, Federal Perkins, college/university loans from institutional funds. **Student Employment:** Federal Work-Study Program available. Institutional employment available. Off-campus job opportunities are good. **Financial Aid Statistics:** 41% freshmen, 47% undergrads receive some form of aid. **Financial Aid Phone:** 831-459-2963.

UNIVERSITY OF CENTRAL ARKANSAS

201 Donaghey Avenue, Conway, AR 72035
Phone: 501-450-3128 **E-mail:** admissions@mail.uca.edu **CEEB Code:** 6012
Fax: 501-450-5228 **Web:** www.uca.edu

This public school was founded in 1907. It has a 256-acre campus.

STUDENTS AND FACULTY

Enrollment: 7,663. **Student Body:** Male 41%, female 59%, out-of-state 5%, international 2% (52 countries represented). **Ethnic Representation:** African American 16%, Asian 1%, Caucasian 78%, Hispanic 1%, Native American 1%. **Retention and Graduation:** 70% freshmen return for sophomore year. 13% freshmen graduate within 4 years. 8% grads pursue business degrees. 1% grads pursue law degrees. 1% grads pursue medical degrees. **Faculty:** Student/faculty ratio 18:1. 407 full-time faculty, 69% hold PhDs. 100% faculty teach undergrads.

ACADEMICS

Degrees: Associate's, bachelor's, doctoral, master's. **Academic Requirements:** General education including some course work in arts/fine arts, English (including composition), history, humanities, mathematics, sciences (biological or physical), social science. **Classes:** 20-29 students in an average class. **Majors with Highest Enrollment:** Business/commerce, general; education, general; health services/allied health, general. **Disciplines with Highest Percentage of Degrees Awarded:** Business/marketing 24%, education 15%, health professions and related sciences 15%, social sciences and history 7%, home economics and vocational home economics 6%. **Special Study Options:** Accelerated program, cooperative (work-study) program, distance learning, double major, dual enrollment, English as a second language, honors program, independent study, internships, liberal arts/career combination, study abroad, teacher certification program, 5 year professional program in Physical and Occupational Therapy.

FACILITIES

Housing: Coed, all-female, all-male, apartments for married students, apartments for single students, housing for disabled students, housing for international students, fraternities and/or sororities, residential college. **Library Holdings:** 587,714 bound volumes. 1,824 periodicals. 104,740 microforms. 11,147 audiovisuals. **Special Academic Facilities/Equipment:** Greenhouse, observatory, Baum Gallery, Hughes Residential College, HPER Center. **Computers:** School-owned computers available for student use.

EXTRACURRICULARS

Activities: Choral groups, concert band, dance, drama/theater, jazz band, literary magazine, marching band, music ensembles, musical theater, opera, pep band, radio station, student government, student newspaper, student-run film society, symphony orchestra, television station, yearbook. **Organizations:** 95 registered organizations, 16 honor societies, 8 religious organizations, 9 fraternities (10% men join), 9 sororities (10% women join). **Athletics (Intercollegiate):** *Men:* baseball, basketball, cheerleading, cross-country, football, golf, soccer, tennis, track & field. *Women:* basketball, cheerleading, cross-country, golf, soccer, softball, tennis, volleyball.

ADMISSIONS

Selectivity Rating: 73 (of 100). **Freshman Academic Profile:** Average high school GPA 3.3. 26% in top 10% of high school class, 57% in top 25% of high school class, 85% in top 50% of high school class. 96% from public high schools. Average ACT 23, ACT middle 50% range 20-27. TOEFL required of all international applicants, minimum TOEFL 500. **Basis for Candidate Selection:** *Very important factors considered include:* class rank, secondary school record, standardized test scores. *Other factors considered include:* character/personal qualities, extracurricular activities, talent/ability. **Freshman Admission Requirements:** High school diploma or GED is required. *Academic units required/recommended:* 4 English recommended, 3 math recommended, 3 science recommended, 1 social studies recommended, 2 history recommended. **Freshman Admission Statistics:** 3,622 applied, 83% accepted, 59% of those accepted enrolled. **Transfer Admission Requirements:** *Items required:* college transcript, statement of good standing from prior school. Minimum college GPA of 2.0 required. Lowest grade transferable C. **General Admission Information:** Nonfall registration accepted. Admission may be deferred for a maximum of 1 year. Credit and/or placement offered for CEEB Advanced Placement tests.

COSTS AND FINANCIAL AID

In-state tuition $3,312. Out-of-state tuition $6,624. Room & board $3,600. Required fees $678. Average book expense $600. **Required Forms and Deadlines:** FAFSA. No deadline for regular filing. Priority filing deadline February 15. **Notification of Awards:** Applicants will be notified of awards on a rolling basis. **Types of Aid:** *Need-based scholarships/grants:* Pell, SEOG, state scholarships/grants, the school's own gift aid, Federal Work Study. *Loans:* Direct Subsidized Stafford, Direct Unsubsidized Stafford, Direct PLUS, Federal Perkins, state loans. **Student Employment:** Federal Work-Study Program available. Institutional employment available. Off-campus job opportunities are good. **Financial Aid Statistics:** Average freshman grant $2,017. Average freshman loan $2,519. Average income from on-campus job $1,500. **Financial Aid Phone:** 501-450-3140.

UNIVERSITY OF CENTRAL FLORIDA

PO Box 160111, Orlando, FL 32816-0111
Phone: 407-823-3000 **E-mail:** admission@mail.ucf.edu **CEEB Code:** 5233
Fax: 407-823-5625 **Web:** www.ucf.edu **ACT Code:** 735

This public school was founded in 1963. It has a 1,415-acre campus.

STUDENTS AND FACULTY

Enrollment: 32,044. **Student Body:** Male 45%, female 55%, out-of-state 6%, international 1%. **Ethnic Representation:** African American 8%, Asian 5%, Caucasian 71%, Hispanic 11%, Native American 1%. **Retention and Graduation:** 81% freshmen return for sophomore year. 26% freshmen graduate within 4 years. **Faculty:** Student/faculty ratio 24:1. 1,093 full-time faculty, 77% hold PhDs. 100% faculty teach undergrads.

ACADEMICS

Degrees: Associate's, bachelor's, certificate, doctoral, master's, post-bachelor's certificate. **Academic Requirements:** General education including some course work in English (including composition), history, humanities, mathematics, sciences (biological or physical), social science. **Classes:** 20-29 students in an average class. 30-39 students in an average lab/discussion section. **Disciplines with Highest Percentage of Degrees Awarded:** Business/marketing 27%, education 10%, psychology 9%, health professions and related sciences 9%, communications/communication technologies 7%. **Special Study Options:** Cooperative (work-study) program, distance learning, double major, dual enrollment, English as a second language, honors program, internships, study abroad, teacher certification program.

FACILITIES

Housing: Coed, all-female, all-male, apartments for single students, fraternities and/or sororities, affiliated student residences available across street from campus with university resident assistants. On-campus: honors center, living learning communities, lead scholars center. **Library Holdings:** 1,152,653 bound volumes. 9,866 periodicals. 2,372,416 microforms. 35,233 audiovisuals. **Special Academic Facilities/Equipment:** Center for research and education in optics and lasers, new student union, communications building, health and public affairs building. **Computers:** School-owned computers available for student use.

EXTRACURRICULARS

Activities: Choral groups, concert band, drama/theater, jazz band, literary magazine, marching band, music ensembles, musical theater, pep band, radio station, student government, student newspaper, student-run film society, symphony orchestra. **Organizations:** 240 registered organizations, 16 fraternities (12% men join), 9 sororities (13% women join). **Athletics (Intercollegiate):** *Men:* baseball, basketball, cheerleading, cross-country, football, golf, soccer, tennis. *Women:* basketball, cheerleading, crew, cross-country, golf, soccer, softball, tennis, track & field, volleyball.

ADMISSIONS

Selectivity Rating: 76 (of 100). **Freshman Academic Profile:** Average high school GPA 3.7. 33% in top 10% of high school class, 85% in top 25% of high school class, 90% in top 50% of high school class. Average SAT I Math 590, SAT I Math middle 50% range 520-620. Average SAT I Verbal 577, SAT I Verbal middle 50% range 510-610. Average ACT 26, ACT middle 50% range 22-26. TOEFL required of all international applicants, minimum TOEFL 550. **Basis for Candidate Selection:** *Very important factors considered include:* secondary school record, standardized test scores. *Important factors considered include:* essays. *Other factors considered include:* alumni/ae relation, character/personal qualities, class rank, extracurricular activities, geographical residence, interview, recommendations, state residency, talent/ability, volunteer work, work experience. **Freshman Admission Requirements:** High school diploma or GED is required. *Academic units required/recommended:* 19 total required; 4 English required, 3 math required, 3 science required, 2 science lab required, 2 foreign language required, 3 social studies required, 4 elective required. **Freshman Admission Statistics:** 19,307 applied, 62% accepted, 47% of those accepted enrolled. **Transfer Admission Requirements:** *Items required:* high school transcript, college transcript. Minimum college GPA of 2.0 required. Lowest grade transferable D. **General Admission Information:** Application fee $20. Priority application deadline March 1. Regular application deadline May 1. Nonfall registration accepted. Credit offered for CEEB Advanced Placement tests.

COSTS AND FINANCIAL AID

In-state tuition $2,640. Out-of-state tuition $12,049. Room & board $6,215. Required fees $180. Average book expense $800. **Required Forms and Deadlines:** FAFSA. Financial aid filing deadline June 1. Priority filing deadline March 1. **Notification of Awards:** Applicants will be notified of awards on a rolling basis beginning on or about March 15. **Types of Aid:** *Need-based scholarships/grants:* Pell, SEOG, state scholarships/grants, private scholarships, the school's own gift aid. *Loans:* FFEL Subsidized Stafford, FFEL Unsubsidized Stafford, FFEL PLUS, Federal Perkins. **Student Employment:** Federal Work-Study Program available. Institutional employment available. Off-campus job opportunities are excellent. **Financial Aid Statistics:** 39% freshmen, 32% undergrads receive some form of aid. **Financial Aid Phone:** 407-823-2827.

UNIVERSITY OF CENTRAL OKLAHOMA

100 North University Drive, Edmond, OK 73034
Phone: 405-974-2338 **E-mail:** admituco@ucok.edu **CEEB Code:** 6091
Fax: 405-341-4964 **Web:** www.ucok.edu **ACT Code:** 3390

This public school was founded in 1890. It has a 200-acre campus.

STUDENTS AND FACULTY

Enrollment: 11,790. **Student Body:** Male 43%, female 57%, out-of-state 2%, international 9% (109 countries represented). **Ethnic Representation:** African American 7%, Asian 3%, Caucasian 81%, Hispanic 3%, Native American 6%. **Retention and Graduation:** 67% freshmen return for sophomore year. 8% freshmen graduate within 4 years. **Faculty:** Student/faculty ratio 22:1. 386 full-time faculty, 72% hold PhDs. 95% faculty teach undergrads.

ACADEMICS

Degrees: Bachelor's, certificate, master's. **Academic Requirements:** General education including some course work in English (including composition), history, humanities, mathematics, sciences (biological or physical). **Classes:** 20-29 students in an average class. Under 10 students in an average lab/discussion section. **Majors with Highest Enrollment:** Management information systems, general; finance, general; accounting. **Disciplines with Highest Percentage of Degrees Awarded:** Business/marketing 28%, education 18%, liberal arts/general studies 14%, other 6%, social sciences and history 5%. **Special Study Options:** Accelerated program, distance learning, double major, dual enrollment, English as a second language, honors program, independent study, internships, teacher certification program.

FACILITIES

Housing: Coed, all-female, all-male, apartments for married students, apartments for single students, fraternities and/or sororities. **Library Holdings:** 438,975 bound volumes. 5,244 periodicals. 989,936 microforms. 30,202 audiovisuals. **Special Academic Facilities/Equipment:** Art and history museums, archives. **Computers:** *Recommended operating system:* Windows NT/2000. School-owned computers available for student use.

EXTRACURRICULARS

Activities: Choral groups, concert band, dance, drama/theater, jazz band, marching band, music ensembles, musical theater, pep band, radio station, student government, student newspaper, symphony orchestra, television station, yearbook. **Organizations:** 150 registered organizations, 19 honor societies, 12 religious organizations, 7 fraternities (5% men join), 5 sororities (7% women join). **Athletics (Intercollegiate):** *Men:* baseball, basketball, cross-country, football, golf, tennis, track & field, wrestling. *Women:* basketball, cheerleading, cross-country, soccer, softball, tennis, track & field, volleyball.

ADMISSIONS

Selectivity Rating: 65 (of 100). **Freshman Academic Profile:** Average high school GPA 3.2. 13% in top 10% of high school class, 24% in top 25% of high school class, 42% in top 50% of high school class. 96% from public high schools. Average ACT 21, ACT middle 50% range 18-23. TOEFL required of all international applicants, minimum TOEFL 500. **Basis for Candidate Selection:** *Very important factors considered include:* class rank, secondary school record, standardized test scores. *Other factors considered include:* extracurricular activities, talent/ability. **Freshman Admission Requirements:** High school diploma or GED is required. *Academic units required/recommended:* 15 total required; 16 total recommended; 4 English required, 4 English recommended, 3 math required, 4 math recommended, 2 science required, 3 science recommended, 2 science lab required, 2 science lab recommended, 2 foreign language recommended, 1 social studies required, 1 social studies recommended, 2 history required, 2 history recommended, 3 elective required. **Freshman Admission Statistics:** 6,701 applied, 96% accepted, 32% of those accepted enrolled. **Transfer Admission Requirements:** *Items required:* college transcript, statement of good standing from prior school. Minimum college GPA of 2.0 required. Lowest grade transferable D. **General Admission Information:** Application fee $15. Nonfall registration accepted. Admission may be deferred. Credit and/or placement offered for CEEB Advanced Placement tests.

COSTS AND FINANCIAL AID

In-state tuition $1,572. Out-of-state tuition $4,318. Room & board $3,138. Required fees $495. Average book expense $900. **Required Forms and Deadlines:** FAFSA and institution's own financial aid form. No deadline for regular filing. Priority filing deadline May 15. **Notification of Awards:** Applicants will be notified of awards on a rolling basis beginning on or about April 15. **Types of Aid:** *Need-based scholarships/grants:* Pell, SEOG, state scholarships/grants, private scholarships, the school's own gift aid. *Loans:* FFEL Subsidized Stafford, FFEL Unsubsidized Stafford, FFEL PLUS. **Student Employment:** Federal Work-Study Program available. Institutional employment available. Off-campus job opportunities are excellent. **Financial Aid Statistics:** 38% freshmen, 46% undergrads receive some form of aid. Average freshman grant $1,200. Average freshman loan $2,000. Average income from on-campus job $2,400. **Financial Aid Phone:** 405-974-2303.

UNIVERSITY OF CENTRAL TEXAS

1901 South Clear Creek Drive, PO Box 1416, Killeen, TX 76540-1416
Phone: 245-526-8262 **E-mail:** uct10@vvm.com **CEEB Code:** 6756
Fax: 254-526-8403 **Web:** www.vvm.com/uct **ACT Code:** 4055

This private school was founded in 1973. It has a 10-acre campus.

STUDENTS AND FACULTY

Enrollment: 1,117. **Student Body:** Male 43%, female 57%, out-of-state 10%, international 1% (10 countries represented). **Ethnic Representation:** African American 19%, Asian 3%, Caucasian 66%, Hispanic 9%, Native American 1%.

ACADEMICS

Degrees: Bachelor's, master's. **Academic Requirements:** General education including some course work in computer literacy, English (including composition), humanities, mathematics, social science. **Special Study Options:** Cooperative (work-study) program, teacher certification program.

FACILITIES

Library Holdings: 22,687 bound volumes. 327 periodicals. 20,241 microforms. 4,299 audiovisuals. **Computers:** *Recommended operating system:* Windows 95. School-owned computers available for student use.

EXTRACURRICULARS

Organizations: 1 honor society.

ADMISSIONS

Selectivity Rating: 63 (of 100). **Freshman Academic Profile:** TOEFL required of all international applicants, minimum TOEFL 515. **Freshman Admission Requirements:** High school diploma or GED is required. **Transfer Admission Requirements:** *Items required:* college transcript. Minimum college GPA of 2.0 required. Lowest grade transferable D. **General Admission Information:** Regular application deadline rolling. Nonfall registration accepted.

COSTS AND FINANCIAL AID

Tuition $3,144. Room & board $3,449. Required fees $40. Average book expense $800. **Required Forms and Deadlines:** FAFSA, institution's own financial aid form and state aid form. **Types of Aid:** *Need-based scholarships/grants:* Pell, SEOG, state scholarships/grants. *Loans:* FFEL Subsidized Stafford, FFEL Unsubsidized Stafford, FFEL PLUS. **Student Employment:** Federal Work-Study Program available. Off-campus job opportunities are excellent. **Financial Aid Phone:** 254-526-8262.

UNIVERSITY OF CHARLESTON

2300 MacCorkle Avenue Southeast, Charleston, WV 25304-1099
Phone: 304-357-4750 **E-mail:** admissions@uchaswv.edu **CEEB Code:** 5419
Fax: 304-357-4781 **Web:** www.uchaswv.edu **ACT Code:** 4528

This private school was founded in 1888. It has a 40-acre campus.

STUDENTS AND FACULTY

Enrollment: 1,037. **Student Body:** Male 33%, female 67%, out-of-state 19%, international 3%. **Ethnic Representation:** African American 4%, Asian 1%, Caucasian 83%, Hispanic 1%, Native American 1%. **Retention and Graduation:** 65% freshmen return for sophomore year. 39% freshmen graduate within 4 years. 14% grads go on to further study within 1 year. 2% grads pursue business degrees. 1% grads pursue law degrees. 3% grads pursue medical degrees. **Faculty:** Student/faculty ratio 12:1. 67 full-time faculty, 35% hold PhDs. 100% faculty teach undergrads.

ACADEMICS

Degrees: Associate's, bachelor's, master's. **Academic Requirements:** General education including some course work in computer literacy, English (including composition), history, humanities, mathematics, sciences (biological or physical), social science. All incoming freshmen must participate in learning communities. **Classes:** 10-19 students in an average class. **Majors with Highest Enrollment:** Nursing/registered nurse training (RN, ASN, BSN, MSN); business administration/management; education, general. **Disciplines with Highest Percentage of Degrees Awarded:** Health professions and related sciences 34%, business/marketing 16%, biological life sciences 9%, education 7%, visual and performing arts 7%. **Special Study Options:**

Accelerated program, cooperative (work-study) program, double major, dual enrollment, independent study, internships, student-designed major, study abroad, teacher certification program. Co-op programs in arts, business, health professions, political science. Off-campus study in Washington, DC.

FACILITIES

Housing: Coed. **Library Holdings:** 114,954 bound volumes. 7,068 periodicals. 172,753 microforms. 3,408 audiovisuals. **Special Academic Facilities/Equipment:** Frankenberger Art Gallery. **Computers:** School-owned computers available for student use.

EXTRACURRICULARS

Activities: Choral groups, drama/theater, music ensembles, musical theater, student government, student newspaper. **Organizations:** 40 registered organizations, 8 honor societies, 2 religious organizations, 2 fraternities (4% men join), 3 sororities (4% women join). **Athletics (Intercollegiate):** *Men:* baseball, basketball, crew, cross-country, football, golf, indoor track, soccer, swimming, tennis, track & field. *Women:* basketball, cheerleading, crew, cross-country, indoor track, soccer, softball, swimming, tennis, track & field, volleyball.

ADMISSIONS

Selectivity Rating: 64 (of 100). **Freshman Academic Profile:** Average high school GPA 3.1. 21% in top 10% of high school class, 80% in top 50% of high school class. Average SAT I Math 500, SAT I Math middle 50% range 400-560. Average SAT I Verbal 502, SAT I Verbal middle 50% range 450-570. Average ACT 21, ACT middle 50% range 19-24. TOEFL required of all international applicants, minimum TOEFL 500. **Basis for Candidate Selection:** *Very important factors considered include:* secondary school record, standardized test scores. *Important factors considered include:* class rank, essays, interview. *Other factors considered include:* alumni/ae relation, character/personal qualities, extracurricular activities, recommendations, talent/ability, volunteer work. **Freshman Admission Requirements:** High school diploma or GED is required. *Academic units required/recommended:* 16 total recommended; 4 English recommended, 3 math recommended, 3 science recommended, 1 foreign language recommended, 3 social studies recommended, 2 history recommended. **Freshman Admission Statistics:** 939 applied, 75% accepted, 25% of those accepted enrolled. **Transfer Admission Requirements:** *Items required:* college transcript. Minimum college GPA of 2.0 required. Lowest grade transferable C. **General Admission Information:** Application fee $25. Early decision application deadline December 15. Nonfall registration accepted. Admission may be deferred for a maximum of 2 years. Credit and/or placement offered for CEEB Advanced Placement tests.

COSTS AND FINANCIAL AID

Tuition $16,500. Room & board $6,000. Average book expense $500. **Required Forms and Deadlines:** FAFSA. No deadline for regular filing. Priority filing deadline March 1. **Notification of Awards:** Applicants will be notified of awards on a rolling basis beginning on or about March 1. **Types of Aid:** *Need-based scholarships/grants:* Pell, SEOG, state scholarships/grants, private scholarships, the school's own gift aid. *Loans:* FFEL Subsidized Stafford, FFEL Unsubsidized Stafford, FFEL PLUS, Federal Perkins, Federal Nursing. **Student Employment:** Federal Work-Study Program available. Institutional employment available. Off-campus job opportunities are excellent. **Financial Aid Statistics:** 77% freshmen, 88% undergrads receive some form of aid. Average freshman grant $6,500. Average freshman loan $2,875. Average income from on-campus job $1,000. **Financial Aid Phone:** 304-357-4760.

UNIVERSITY OF CHICAGO

1116 East 59th Street, Chicago, IL 60637
Phone: 773-702-8650 **CEEB Code:** 1832
Fax: 773-702-4199 **Web:** www.uchicago.edu **ACT Code:** 1152

This private school was founded in 1892. It has a 190-acre campus.

STUDENTS AND FACULTY

Enrollment: 4,236. **Student Body:** Male 50%, female 50%, out-of-state 78%, international 8% (34 countries represented). **Ethnic Representation:** African American 4%, Asian 16%, Caucasian 71%, Hispanic 8%. **Retention and Graduation:** 95% freshmen return for sophomore year. 78% freshmen graduate within 4 years. 35% grads go on to further study within 1 year. 8% grads pursue law degrees. 8% grads pursue medical degrees. **Faculty:** Student/faculty ratio 4:1. 1,600 full-time faculty, 6% hold PhDs. 90% faculty teach undergrads.

ACADEMICS

Degrees: Bachelor's, doctoral, first professional, master's. **Academic Requirements:** General education including some course work in arts/fine arts, humanities, mathematics, sciences (biological or physical), social science, civilizations. **Disciplines with Highest Percentage of Degrees Awarded:** Social sciences and history 40%, biological life sciences 15%, mathematics 6%, English 6%, psychology 5%. **Special Study Options:** Accelerated program, double major, student exchange program (domestic), independent study, internships, student-designed major, study abroad.

FACILITIES

Housing: Coed, apartments for married students, fraternities and/or sororities. **Library Holdings:** 5,854,014 bound volumes. 40,711 periodicals. 0 microforms. 0 audiovisuals. **Special Academic Facilities/Equipment:** Two art galleries, archaeology museum, Court Theatre, on-campus lab school (pre-K-12), Argonne National Lab, Enrico Fermi Institute, observatory, two telescopes, accelerator lab.

EXTRACURRICULARS

Activities: Choral groups, concert band, dance, drama/theater, jazz band, literary magazine, music ensembles, musical theater, pep band, radio station, student government, student newspaper, student-run film society, symphony orchestra. **Organizations:** 200 registered organizations, 9 fraternities (12% men join), 2 sororities (5% women join). **Athletics (Intercollegiate):** *Men:* baseball, basketball, cross-country, diving, football, indoor track, soccer, swimming, tennis, track & field, wrestling. *Women:* basketball, cross-country, diving, indoor track, soccer, softball, swimming, tennis, track & field, volleyball.

ADMISSIONS

Selectivity Rating: 96 (of 100). **Freshman Academic Profile:** 79% in top 10% of high school class, 94% in top 25% of high school class, 100% in top 50% of high school class. 70% from public high schools. SAT I Math middle 50% range 650-750. SAT I Verbal middle 50% range 660-750. ACT middle 50% range 28-32. TOEFL required of all international applicants, minimum TOEFL 600. **Basis for Candidate Selection:** *Very important factors considered include:* essays, recommendations, secondary school record. *Important factors considered include:* character/personal qualities, class rank, standardized test scores, talent/ability. *Other factors considered include:* alumni/ae relation, extracurricular activities, interview, minority status, volunteer work, work experience. **Freshman Admission Requirements:** High school diploma or equivalent is not required. *Academic units required/recommended:* 4 English recommended, 4 math recommended, 4 science recommended, 3 foreign language recommended, 2 social studies recommended, 2 history recommended. **Freshman Admission Statistics:** 8,139 applied, 42% accepted, 33% of those accepted enrolled. **Transfer Admission Requirements:** *Items required:* high school transcript, college transcript, essay, standardized test scores, statement of good standing from prior school. **General Admission Information:** Application fee $60. Regular application deadline January 1. Admission may be deferred for a maximum of 2 years. Credit and/or placement offered for CEEB Advanced Placement tests.

COSTS AND FINANCIAL AID

Tuition $27,324. Room & board $8,728. Required fees $501. Average book expense $1,061. **Student Employment:** Federal Work-Study Program available. Institutional employment available. Off-campus job opportunities are excellent. **Financial Aid Statistics:** 58% freshmen, 56% undergrads receive some form of aid. Average freshman grant $20,616. Average freshman loan $4,000. **Financial Aid Phone:** 773-702-8666.

UNIVERSITY OF CINCINNATI

PO Box 210091, Cincinnati, OH 45221-0091
Phone: 513-556-1100 **E-mail:** admissions@uc.edu **CEEB Code:** 1833
Fax: 513-556-1105 **Web:** www.uc.edu **ACT Code:** 3340

This public school was founded in 1819. It has a 392-acre campus.

STUDENTS AND FACULTY

Enrollment: 19,204. **Student Body:** Male 51%, female 49%, out-of-state 7%, international 1% (113 countries represented). **Ethnic Representation:** African American 14%, Asian 3%, Caucasian 78%, Hispanic 1%. **Retention and Graduation:** 74% freshmen return for sophomore year. 14% freshmen graduate within 4 years. **Faculty:** Student/faculty ratio 18:1. 1,333 full-time faculty, 57% hold PhDs.

ACADEMICS

Degrees: Associate's, bachelor's, certificate, doctoral, first professional, master's, post-bachelor's certificate, terminal, transfer. **Classes:** 10-19 students in an average class. **Disciplines with Highest Percentage of Degrees Awarded:** Business/marketing 20%, engineering/engineering technology 11%, visual and performing arts 9%, social sciences and history 8%, health professions and related sciences 8%. **Special Study Options:** Accelerated program, cooperative (work-study) program, distance learning, double major, English as a second language, honors program, independent study, internships, liberal arts/career combination, study abroad, teacher certification program, weekend college.

FACILITIES

Housing: Coed, all-female, all-male, fraternities and/or sororities. **Library Holdings:** 16,560 periodicals. 2,405,442 microforms. 51,224 audiovisuals. **Special Academic Facilities/Equipment:** Art museum, language lab, observatory.

EXTRACURRICULARS

Activities: Choral groups, concert band, dance, drama/theater, jazz band, marching band, music ensembles, musical theater, opera, pep band, radio station, student government, student newspaper, student-run film society, symphony orchestra, yearbook. **Organizations:** 250 registered organizations, 16 honor societies, 23 religious organizations, 23 fraternities, 10 sororities. **Athletics (Intercollegiate):** *Men:* baseball, basketball, cheerleading, cross-country, diving, football, golf, soccer, swimming, track & field. *Women:* basketball, cheerleading, cross-country, diving, golf, indoor track, soccer, swimming, tennis, track & field, volleyball.

ADMISSIONS

Selectivity Rating: 76 (of 100). **Freshman Academic Profile:** Average high school GPA 3.0. 12% in top 10% of high school class, 30% in top 25% of high school class, 61% in top 50% of high school class. Average SAT I Math 556, SAT I Math middle 50% range 460-610. Average SAT I Verbal 548, SAT I Verbal middle 50% range 460-590. Average ACT 23, ACT middle 50% range 19-26. TOEFL required of all international applicants, minimum TOEFL 515. **Basis for Candidate Selection:** *Very important factors considered include:* secondary school record, standardized test scores. *Important factors considered include:* class rank. **Freshman Admission Requirements:** High school diploma is required and GED is not accepted. *Academic units required/recommended:* 16 total required; 4 English required, 3 math required, 2 science required, 2 foreign language required, 2 social studies required, 1 history required, 2 elective required. **Freshman Admission Statistics:** 9,899 applied, 88% accepted, 45% of those accepted enrolled. **Transfer Admission Requirements:** *Items required:* college transcript. Lowest grade transferable C. **General Admission Information:** Application fee $35. Regular application deadline July 31. Nonfall registration accepted.

COSTS AND FINANCIAL AID

In-state tuition $5,715. Out-of-state tuition $16,089. Room & board $6,774. Required fees $1,221. Average book expense $790. **Required Forms and Deadlines:** FAFSA. No deadline for regular filing. **Notification of Awards:** Applicants will be notified of awards on a rolling basis beginning on or about March 15. **Types of Aid:** *Need-based scholarships/grants:* Pell, SEOG, state scholarships/grants, private scholarships, the school's own gift aid, Federal Nursing. *Loans:* FFEL Subsidized Stafford, FFEL Unsubsidized Stafford, FFEL PLUS, Federal Perkins, Federal Nursing, state loans, college/university loans from institutional funds. **Student Employment:** Federal Work-Study Program available. Institutional employment available. Off-campus job opportunities are good. **Financial Aid Statistics:** 55% freshmen, 47% undergrads receive some form of aid. Average freshman loan $2,319. **Financial Aid Phone:** 513-556-6982.

UNIVERSITY OF COLORADO—BOULDER

552 UCB, Boulder, CO 80309-0030
Phone: 303-492-6301 **E-mail:** apply@colorado.edu **CEEB Code:** 4841
Fax: 303-492-7115 **Web:** www.colorado.edu **ACT Code:** 532

This public school was founded in 1876. It has a 600-acre campus.

STUDENTS AND FACULTY

Enrollment: 25,158. **Student Body:** Male 53%, female 47%, out-of-state 33%, international 1% (100 countries represented). **Ethnic Representation:** African American 2%, Asian 6%, Caucasian 81%, Hispanic 6%, Native American 1%. **Retention and Graduation:** 83% freshmen return for sophomore year. 39% freshmen graduate within 4 years. 44% grads go on to further study within 1 year. 6% grads pursue business degrees. 7% grads pursue law degrees. 11% grads pursue medical degrees. **Faculty:** Student/faculty ratio 16:1. 1,225 full-time faculty, 84% hold PhDs. 75% faculty teach undergrads.

ACADEMICS

Degrees: Bachelor's, doctoral, first professional, master's. **Academic Requirements:** General education including some course work in English (including composition), foreign languages, history, humanities, mathematics, sciences (biological or physical), social science, critical thinking, cultural and gender diversity, United States context. **Classes:** 10-19 students in an average class. 20-29 students in an average lab/discussion section. **Majors with Highest Enrollment:** Psychology, general; communications; cell/cellular and molecular biology. **Disciplines with Highest Percentage of Degrees Awarded:** Social sciences and history 21%, business/marketing 14%, communications/communication technologies 11%, engineering/engineering technology 8%, biological life sciences 8%. **Special Study Options:** Accelerated program, cooperative (work-study) program, cross registration, distance learning, double major, dual enrollment, English as a second language, student exchange program (domestic), honors program, independent study, internships, liberal arts/career combination, student-designed major, study abroad, teacher certification program, undergraduate research opportunities, concurrent bachelor's/master's programs. Small-group academic programs include residence hall academic programs, FallFEST, and president's leadership class.

FACILITIES

Housing: Coed, apartments for married students, housing for disabled students. **Library Holdings:** 2,179,492 bound volumes. 24,337 periodicals. 6,199,844 microforms. 70,198 audiovisuals. **Special Academic Facilities/Equipment:** Art galleries, natural history museum, outdoor theatre, auditorium/concert hall, planetarium, electron microscope. **Computers:** School-owned computers available for student use.

EXTRACURRICULARS

Activities: Choral groups, concert band, dance, drama/theater, jazz band, literary magazine, marching band, music ensembles, musical theater, opera, pep band, radio station, student government, student newspaper, student-run film society, symphony orchestra, television station. **Organizations:** 286 registered organizations, 17 honor societies, 27 religious organizations, 17 fraternities (8% men join), 15 sororities (12% women join). **Athletics (Intercollegiate):** *Men:* basketball, cross-country, football, golf, skiing (alpine), skiing (Nordic), tennis, track & field. *Women:* basketball, cross-country, golf, skiing (alpine), skiing (Nordic), soccer, tennis, track & field, volleyball.

ADMISSIONS

Selectivity Rating: 84 (of 100). **Freshman Academic Profile:** Average high school GPA 3.5. 23% in top 10% of high school class, 56% in top 25% of high school class, 91% in top 50% of high school class. Average SAT I Math 590, SAT I Math middle 50% range 540-640. Average SAT I Verbal 569, SAT I Verbal middle 50% range 520-620. Average ACT 25, ACT middle 50% range 22-27. TOEFL required of all international applicants, minimum TOEFL 500. **Basis for Candidate Selection:** *Very important factors considered include:* class rank, secondary school record, standardized test scores. *Important factors considered include:* essays, geographical residence, minority status, recommendations, state residency. *Other factors considered include:* alumni/ae relation, character/personal qualities, extracurricular activities, talent/ability, volunteer work, work experience. **Freshman Admission Requirements:** High school diploma or GED is required. *Academic units required/recommended:* 16 total required; 4 English required, 3 math required, 3 science required, 2 science lab required, 3 foreign language required, 3 social studies required, 1 history required. **Freshman Admission Statistics:** 19,152 applied, 80% accepted, 36% of those accepted enrolled. **Transfer Admission Requirements:** *Items required:* high school transcript, college transcript, essay. Lowest grade transferable C-. **General Admission Information:** Application fee $40. Regular application deadline January 15. Nonfall registration accepted. Admission may be deferred for a maximum of 1 year. Credit and/or placement offered for CEEB Advanced Placement tests.

COSTS AND FINANCIAL AID

In-state tuition $2,776. Out-of-state tuition $18,120. Room & board $6,272. Required fees $799. Average book expense $1,142. **Required Forms and Deadlines:** FAFSA and Tax return required. No deadline for regular filing. Priority filing deadline April 1. **Notification of Awards:** Applicants will be notified of awards on a rolling basis beginning on or about February 1. **Types of Aid:** *Need-based scholarships/grants:* Pell, SEOG, state scholarships/grants, private scholarships, the school's own gift aid. *Loans:* Direct Subsidized Stafford, Direct Unsubsidized Stafford, Direct PLUS, Federal Perkins, college/university loans from institutional funds, private lenders. **Student Employment:** Federal Work-Study Program available. Institutional employment available. Off-campus job opportunities are excellent. **Financial Aid Statistics:** 24% freshmen, 25% undergrads receive some form of aid. Average freshman grant $2,875. Average freshman loan $2,842. Average income from on-campus job $1,789. **Financial Aid Phone:** 303-492-5091.

UNIVERSITY OF COLORADO—COLORADO SPRINGS

Admissions Office, PO Box 7150, Colorado Springs, CO 80933-7150
Phone: 719-262-3383 **E-mail:** admrec@mail.uccs.edu **CEEB Code:** 4874
Fax: 719-262-3116 **Web:** www.uccs.edu **ACT Code:** 535

This public school was founded in 1965. It has a 504-acre campus.

STUDENTS AND FACULTY

Enrollment: 5,649. **Student Body:** Male 39%, female 61%, out-of-state 11%, (35 countries represented). **Retention and Graduation:** 17% freshmen graduate within 4 years. **Faculty:** Student/faculty ratio 16:1. 265 full-time faculty, 43% hold PhDs. 93% faculty teach undergrads.

ACADEMICS

Degrees: Bachelor's, diploma, doctoral, master's. **Academic Requirements:** General education including some course work in English (including composition), mathematics, sciences (biological or physical), social science. **Classes:** 20-29 students in an average class. **Disciplines with Highest Percentage of Degrees Awarded:** Business/marketing 20%, social sciences and history 19%, psychology 14%, communications/communication technologies 13%, health professions and related sciences 8%. **Special Study Options:** Distance learning, double major, dual enrollment, independent study, study abroad, teacher certification program.

FACILITIES

Housing: Coed, all-female, all-male, housing for disabled students. **Library Holdings:** 391,638 bound volumes. 2,201 periodicals. 642,082 microforms. 5,229 audiovisuals. **Special Academic Facilities/Equipment:** Gallery of contemporary art. **Computers:** School-owned computers available for student use.

EXTRACURRICULARS

Activities: Choral groups, dance, drama/theater, literary magazine, student government, student newspaper. **Organizations:** 55 registered organizations, 7 religious organizations, 1 sorority (1% women join). **Athletics (Intercollegiate):** *Men:* basketball, cross-country, golf, soccer, tennis, track & field. *Women:* basketball, cross-country, softball, tennis, track & field, volleyball.

ADMISSIONS

Selectivity Rating: 77 (of 100). **Freshman Academic Profile:** Average high school GPA 3.4. 13% in top 10% of high school class, 48% in top 25% of high school class, 74% in top 50% of high school class. Average SAT I Math 532, SAT I Math middle 50% range 470-600. Average SAT I Verbal 526, SAT I Verbal middle 50% range 470-590. Average ACT 23; ACT middle 50% range 20-26. TOEFL required of all international applicants, minimum TOEFL 550. **Basis for Candidate Selection:** *Very important factors considered include:* class rank, secondary school record. *Important factors considered include:* standardized test scores. *Other factors considered include:* alumni/ae relation, character/personal qualities, extracurricular activities, geographical residence, minority status, recommendations, state residency, talent/ability. **Freshman Admission Requirements:** High school diploma or GED is required. *Academic units required/recommended:* 15 total required; 4 English required, 3 math required, 4 math recommended, 3 science required, 2 science lab required, 2 foreign language required, 2 social studies required, 1 elective required. **Transfer Admission Requirements:** *Items required:* high school transcript, college transcript. Minimum college GPA of 2.0 required. Lowest grade transferable C. **General Admission Information:** Application fee $45. Priority application deadline April 1. Regular application deadline July 1. Nonfall registration accepted. Admission may be deferred. Neither credit nor placement offered for CEEB Advanced Placement tests.

COSTS AND FINANCIAL AID

In-state tuition $3,312. Out-of-state tuition $16,536. Room & board $5,893. Required fees $770. Average book expense $648. **Required Forms and Deadlines:** FAFSA. No deadline for regular filing. Priority filing deadline April 1. **Notification of Awards:** Applicants will be notified of awards on a rolling basis beginning on or about April 15. **Types of Aid:** *Need-based scholarships/grants:* Pell, SEOG, state scholarships/grants, private scholarships, the school's own gift aid. *Loans:* FFEL Subsidized Stafford, FFEL Unsubsidized Stafford, FFEL PLUS, Federal Perkins, college/university loans from institutional funds. **Student Employment:** Federal Work-Study Program available. Institutional employment available. Off-campus job opportunities are good. **Financial Aid Statistics:** 35% freshmen, 46% undergrads receive some form of aid. **Financial Aid Phone:** 719-262-3460.

UNIVERSITY OF COLORADO—DENVER

PO Box 173364, Campus Box 167, Denver, CO 80217
Phone: 303-556-3287 **E-mail:** admissions@carbon.cudenver.edu **CEEB Code:** 4875
Fax: 303-556-4838 **Web:** www.cudenver.edu **ACT Code:** 533

This public school was founded in 1912. It has a 127-acre campus.

STUDENTS AND FACULTY

Student Body: Out-of-state 2%, international students represent 84 countries. **Retention and Graduation:** 67% freshmen return for sophomore year. 14% freshmen graduate within 4 years. **Faculty:** Student/faculty ratio 14:1. 482 full-time faculty, 82% hold PhDs. 100% faculty teach undergrads.

ACADEMICS

Degrees: Bachelor's, doctoral, master's, post-master's certificate. **Academic Requirements:** General education including some course work in arts/fine arts, English (including composition), humanities, mathematics, sciences (biological or physical), social science, behavioral science, and multicultural diversity. **Disciplines with Highest Percentage of Degrees Awarded:** Business/marketing 26%, social sciences and history 20%, engineering/engineering technology 9%, communications/communication technologies 8%, psychology 8%. **Special Study Options:** Accelerated program, cooperative (work-study) program, cross registration, distance learning, double major, English as a second language, honors program, independent study, internships, student-designed major, study abroad, teacher certification program, weekend college.

FACILITIES

Library Holdings: 588,582 bound volumes. 4,364 periodicals. 1,008,065 microforms. 15,720 audiovisuals. **Computers:** *Recommended operating system:* Windows 98 and Windows NT. School-owned computers available for student use.

EXTRACURRICULARS

Activities: Choral groups, dance, drama/theater, jazz band, music ensembles, musical theater, student government, student newspaper. **Organizations:** 60 registered organizations, 8 honor societies, 1 religious organization.

ADMISSIONS

Selectivity Rating: 72 (of 100). **Freshman Academic Profile:** 80% from public high schools. Average SAT I Math 526. Average SAT I Verbal 518. Average ACT 22. TOEFL required of all international applicants, minimum TOEFL 525. **Basis for Candidate Selection:** *Very important factors considered include:* class rank, secondary school record, standardized test scores. *Important factors considered include:* essays, recommendations. *Other factors considered include:* alumni/ae relation, character/personal qualities, extracurricular activities, interview, talent/ability, volunteer work. **Freshman Admission Requirements:** High school diploma or GED is required. *Academic units required/recommended:* 16 total required; 16 total recommended; 4 English required, 4 English recommended, 3 math required, 3 math recommended, 3 science required, 3 science recommended, 2 science lab required, 2 science lab recommended, 3 foreign language required, 3 foreign language recommended, 2 social studies required, 2 social studies recommended, 1 elective required, 1 elective recommended. **Freshman Admission Statistics:** 1,778 applied, 70% accepted, 51% of those accepted enrolled. **Transfer Admission Requirements:** *Items required:* college transcript. Minimum high school GPA of 2.5 required. Minimum college GPA of 2.5 required. Lowest grade transferable C. **General Admission Information:** Application fee $40. Priority application deadline July 22. Nonfall registration accepted. Admission may be deferred for a maximum of 1 year. Credit and/or placement offered for CEEB Advanced Placement tests.

COSTS AND FINANCIAL AID

Required Forms and Deadlines: FAFSA and institution's own financial aid form. No deadline for regular filing. Priority filing deadline April 1. **Notification of Awards:** Applicants will be notified of awards on a rolling basis beginning on or about May 1. **Types of Aid:** *Need-based scholarships/grants:* Pell, SEOG, state scholarships/grants, private scholarships, the school's own gift aid, alternative loans. *Loans:* FFEL Subsidized Stafford, FFEL Unsubsidized Stafford, FFEL PLUS, Federal Perkins. **Student Employment:** Federal Work-Study Program available. Institutional employment available. Off-campus job opportunities are good. **Financial Aid Statistics:** 66% freshmen, 39% undergrads receive some form of aid. Average freshman grant $1,500. **Financial Aid Phone:** 303-556-2886.

UNIVERSITY OF CONNECTICUT

2131 Hillside Road, Unit 3088, Storrs, CT 06269-3088
Phone: 860-486-3137 **E-mail:** beahusky@uconn.edu **CEEB Code:** 3915
Fax: 860-486-1476 **Web:** www.uconn.edu **ACT Code:** 604

This public school was founded in 1881. It has a 4,104-acre campus.

STUDENTS AND FACULTY

Enrollment: 14,716. **Student Body:** Male 48%, female 52%, out-of-state 23%, international 1% (107 countries represented). **Ethnic Representation:** African American 5%, Asian 6%, Caucasian 75%, Hispanic 5%. **Retention and Graduation:** 88% freshmen return for sophomore year. 43% freshmen graduate within 4 years. 33% grads go on to further study within 1 year. 11% grads pursue business degrees. 6% grads pursue law degrees. 4% grads pursue medical degrees. **Faculty:** Student/faculty ratio 17:1. 886 full-time faculty, 95% hold PhDs.

ACADEMICS

Degrees: Associate's, bachelor's, doctoral, first professional, master's, post-bachelor's certificate, post-master's certificate, terminal, transfer. **Academic Requirements:** General education including some course work in arts/fine arts, computer literacy, English (including composition), foreign languages, history, humanities, mathematics, philosophy, sciences (biological or physical), social science. **Classes:** 10-19 students in an average class. 10-19 students in an average lab/discussion section. **Majors with Highest Enrollment:** Human development and family studies, general; general studies; psychology, general. **Disciplines with Highest Percentage of Degrees Awarded:** Business/marketing 17%, social sciences and history 13%, liberal arts/general studies 9%, home economics and vocational home economics 8%, communications/communication technologies 7%. **Special Study Options:** Accelerated program, cooperative (work-study) program, distance learning, double major, dual enrollment, English as a second language, student exchange program (domestic), honors program, independent study, internships, liberal arts/career combination, student-designed major, study abroad, teacher certification program, winter inter-session, summer session, and urban semester.

FACILITIES

Housing: Coed, all-female, all-male, apartments for married students, apartments for single students, housing for disabled students, housing for international students, fraternities and/or sororities, special-interest, honors, engineering, foreign languages, substance-free, older student housing, freshman-year-experience housing. **Library Holdings:** 2,987,772 bound volumes. 17,378 periodicals. 4,323,086 microforms. 61,417 audiovisuals. **Special Academic Facilities/Equipment:** Art and natural history museums, child development labs, national undersea research center, arboretum, institute for social inquiry, institute of materials science, electron microscope labs. **Computers:** School-owned computers available for student use.

EXTRACURRICULARS

Activities: Choral groups, concert band, dance, drama/theater, jazz band, literary magazine, marching band, music ensembles, musical theater, opera, pep band, radio station, student government, student newspaper, student-run film society, symphony orchestra, television station, yearbook. **Organizations:** 226 registered organizations, 29 honor societies, 9 religious organizations, 18 fraternities (7% men join), 9 sororities (7% women join). **Athletics (Intercollegiate):** *Men:* baseball, basketball, cross-country, diving, football, golf, ice hockey, indoor track, soccer, swimming, tennis, track & field. *Women:* basketball, crew, cross-country, diving, field hockey, ice hockey, indoor track, lacrosse, soccer, softball, swimming, tennis, track & field, volleyball.

ADMISSIONS

Selectivity Rating: 79 (of 100). **Freshman Academic Profile:** 26% in top 10% of high school class, 65% in top 25% of high school class, 96% in top 50% of high school class. Average SAT I Math 584, SAT I Math middle 50% range 530-630. Average SAT I Verbal 565, SAT I Verbal middle 50% range 520-610. TOEFL required of all international applicants, minimum TOEFL 550. **Basis for Candidate Selection:** *Very important factors considered include:* class rank, secondary school record, standardized test scores, talent/ability. *Important factors considered include:* character/personal qualities, essays, extracurricular activities, minority status, recommendations, volunteer work. *Other factors considered include:* alumni/ae relation, geographical residence, state residency, work experience. **Freshman Admission Requirements:** High school diploma or GED is required. *Academic units required/recommended:* 16 total required; 4 English required, 3 math required, 2 science required, 2 science lab required, 2 foreign language required, 3 foreign language recommended, 2 social studies required, 3 elective required. **Freshman Admission Statistics:** 13,760 applied, 62% accepted, 37% of those accepted enrolled. **Transfer Admission Requirements:** *Items required:* high school transcript, college transcript, essay. Minimum college GPA of 2.5 required. Lowest grade transferable C-. **General Admission Information:** Application fee $50. Regular application deadline March 1. Nonfall registration accepted. Admission may be deferred for a maximum of 1 year. Credit and/or placement offered for CEEB Advanced Placement tests.

COSTS AND FINANCIAL AID

In-state tuition $5,260. Out-of-state tuition $16,044. Room & board $6,888. Required fees $1,540. Average book expense $725. **Required Forms and Deadlines:** FAFSA. No deadline for regular filing. Priority filing deadline March 1. **Notification of Awards:** Applicants will be notified of awards on a rolling basis beginning on or about March 1. **Types of Aid:** *Need-based scholarships/grants:* Pell, SEOG, state scholarships/grants, private scholarships, the school's own gift aid. *Loans:* FFEL Subsidized Stafford, FFEL Unsubsidized Stafford, FFEL PLUS, Federal Perkins. **Student Employment:** Federal Work-Study Program available. Institutional employment available. Off-campus job opportunities are good. **Financial Aid Statistics:** 48% freshmen, 47% undergrads receive some form of aid. Average freshman grant $5,124. Average freshman loan $3,108. Average income from on-campus job $1,741. **Financial Aid Phone:** 860-486-2819.

UNIVERSITY OF DALLAS

1845 East Northgate Drive, Irving, TX 75062
Phone: 972-721-5266 **E-mail:** ugadmis@acad.udallas.edu **CEEB Code:** 6868
Fax: 972-721-5017 **Web:** www.udallas.edu **ACT Code:** 4234

This private school, which is affiliated with the Roman Catholic Church, was founded in 1956. It has a 750-acre campus.

STUDENTS AND FACULTY

Enrollment: 1,218. **Student Body:** Male 44%, female 56%, out-of-state 41%, international 2%. **Ethnic Representation:** African American 2%, Asian 7%, Caucasian 67%, Hispanic 15%. **Retention and Graduation:** 80% freshmen return for sophomore year. 56% freshmen graduate within 4 years. 64% grads go on to further study within 1 year. 13% grads pursue business degrees. 5% grads pursue law degrees. 16% grads pursue medical degrees. **Faculty:** Student/faculty ratio 12:1. 130 full-time faculty, 93% hold PhDs. 100% faculty teach undergrads.

ACADEMICS

Degrees: Bachelor's, doctoral, master's. **Academic Requirements:** General education including some course work in arts/fine arts, English (including composition), foreign languages, history, mathematics, philosophy, sciences (biological or physical), social science, theology, economics. **Classes:** 10-19 students in an average class. 10-19 students in an average lab/discussion section. **Majors with Highest Enrollment:** English language and literature, general; biology/biological sciences, general; political science and government, general. **Disciplines with Highest Percentage of Degrees Awarded:** Social sciences and history 25%, English 16%, biological life sciences 15%, visual and performing arts 10%, philosophy/religion/theology 10%. **Special Study Options:** Accelerated program, cooperative (work-study) program, distance learning, double major, dual enrollment, independent study, internships, liberal arts/career combination, student-designed major, study abroad, teacher certification program, and university campus in Rome, Italy.

FACILITIES

Housing: Coed, all-female, all-male, apartments for single students, and dorms at University's campus in Rome, Italy. **Library Holdings:** 232,472 bound volumes. 767 periodicals. 75,488 microforms. 1,922 audiovisuals. **Special Academic Facilities/Equipment:** Art gallery, theater, language science, and computer labs, observatory. **Computers:** School-owned computers available for student use.

EXTRACURRICULARS

Activities: Choral groups, dance, drama/theater, literary magazine, music ensembles, musical theater, student government, student newspaper, student-run film society, yearbook. **Organizations:** 30 registered organizations, 4 honor societies, 7 religious organizations. **Athletics (Intercollegiate):** *Men:* baseball, basketball, cross-country, golf, soccer, tennis. *Women:* basketball, cross-country, golf, soccer, softball, tennis, volleyball.

ADMISSIONS

Selectivity Rating: 80 (of 100). **Freshman Academic Profile:** 38% in top 10% of high school class, 66% in top 25% of high school class, 89% in top 50% of high school class. 49% from public high schools. Average SAT I Math 582,

SAT I Math middle 50% range 520-640. Average SAT I Verbal 593, SAT I Verbal middle 50% range 520-670. Average ACT 25, ACT middle 50% range 22-29. TOEFL required of all international applicants, minimum TOEFL 550. **Basis for Candidate Selection:** *Very important factors considered include:* class rank, essays, secondary school record, standardized test scores. *Important factors considered include:* recommendations. *Other factors considered include:* alumni/ae relation, character/personal qualities, extracurricular activities, talent/ ability, volunteer work, work experience. **Freshman Admission Requirements:** High school diploma or GED is required. *Academic units required/ recommended:* 23 total required; 27 total recommended; 4 English required, 4 English recommended, 3 math required, 3 math recommended, 3 science required, 4 science recommended, 2 foreign language required, 4 foreign language recommended, 2 social studies required, 3 social studies recommended, 1 history required, 4 elective required. **Freshman Admission Statistics:** 1,183 applied, 90% accepted, 29% of those accepted enrolled. **Transfer Admission Requirements:** *Items required:* college transcript, essay, statement of good standing from prior school. Minimum college GPA of 3.0 required. Lowest grade transferable C. **General Admission Information:** Application fee $50. Priority application deadline December 1. Regular application deadline January 15. Nonfall registration accepted. Admission may be deferred for a maximum of 1 year. Credit and/or placement offered for CEEB Advanced Placement tests.

COSTS AND FINANCIAL AID

Tuition $17,612. Room & board $6,494. Required fees $450. Average book expense $850. **Required Forms and Deadlines:** FAFSA and institution's own financial aid form. Financial aid filing deadline March 1. Priority filing deadline March 1. **Notification of Awards:** Applicants will be notified of awards on a rolling basis beginning on or about March 15. **Types of Aid:** *Need-based scholarships/grants:* Pell, SEOG, state scholarships/grants, private scholarships, the school's own gift aid. *Loans:* FFEL Subsidized Stafford, FFEL Unsubsidized Stafford, FFEL PLUS, Federal Perkins, state loans. **Student Employment:** Federal Work-Study Program available. Institutional employment available. Off-campus job opportunities are good. **Financial Aid Statistics:** 61% freshmen, 61% undergrads receive some form of aid. Average freshman grant $7,991. Average freshman loan $4,750. Average income from on-campus job $1,335. **Financial Aid Phone:** 972-721-5266.

See page 1244.

UNIVERSITY OF DAYTON

300 College Park, Dayton, OH 45469-1300
Phone: 937-229-4411 **E-mail:** admission@udayton.edu **CEEB Code:** 1834
Fax: 937-229-4729 **Web:** www.udayton.edu **ACT Code:** 3342

This private school, which is affiliated with the Roman Catholic Church, was founded in 1850. It has a 123-acre campus.

STUDENTS AND FACULTY

Enrollment: 7,085. **Student Body:** Male 50%, female 50%, out-of-state 33%, international 1% (46 countries represented). **Ethnic Representation:** African American 4%, Asian 1%, Caucasian 89%, Hispanic 2%. **Retention and Graduation:** 90% freshmen return for sophomore year. 57% freshmen graduate within 4 years. **Faculty:** Student/faculty ratio 15:1. 407 full-time faculty, 95% hold PhDs. 88% faculty teach undergrads.

ACADEMICS

Degrees: Bachelor's, doctoral, first professional, master's. **Academic Requirements:** General education including some course work in arts/fine arts, English (including composition), history, humanities, mathematics, philosophy, sciences (biological or physical), social science, oral communication competencies. **Classes:** 20-29 students in an average class. 10-19 students in an average lab/discussion section. **Majors with Highest Enrollment:** Communications studies/speech communication and rhetoric; marketing/marketing management, general; education, general. **Disciplines with Highest Percentage of Degrees Awarded:** Business/marketing 22%, engineering/ engineering technology 15%, education 11%, communications/communication technologies 10%, social sciences and history 6%. **Special Study Options:** Accelerated program, cooperative (work-study) program, cross registration, double major, dual enrollment, English as a second language, student exchange program (domestic), honors program, independent study, internships, liberal arts/career combination, study abroad, teacher certification program, domestic exchange program only among other Marianist institutions.

FACILITIES

Housing: Coed, all-female, all-male, apartments for single students, housing for disabled students, housing for international students, fraternities and/or sororities, university-owned houses. **Library Holdings:** 605,500 bound volumes. 2,953 periodicals. 806,101 microforms. 1,763 audiovisuals. **Special Academic Facilities/Equipment:** Student art gallery, information sciences center, children's learning center, Marian Library, research institute. **Computers:** *Recommended operating system:* Windows XP. School-owned computers available for student use.

EXTRACURRICULARS

Activities: Choral groups, concert band, dance, drama/theater, jazz band, literary magazine, marching band, music ensembles, musical theater, opera, pep band, radio station, student government, student newspaper, symphony orchestra, television station, yearbook. **Organizations:** 200 registered organizations, 19 honor societies, 14 fraternities (15% men join), 10 sororities (18% women join). **Athletics (Intercollegiate):** *Men:* baseball, basketball, cross-country, football, golf, soccer, tennis. *Women:* basketball, crew, cross-country, golf, soccer, softball, tennis, track & field, volleyball.

ADMISSIONS

Selectivity Rating: 78 (of 100). **Freshman Academic Profile:** 18% in top 10% of high school class, 41% in top 25% of high school class, 75% in top 50% of high school class. 51% from public high schools. Average SAT I Math 575, SAT I Math middle 50% range 510-630. Average SAT I Verbal 557, SAT I Verbal middle 50% range 500-610. Average ACT 24, ACT middle 50% range 22-27. TOEFL required of all international applicants, minimum TOEFL 550. **Basis for Candidate Selection:** *Very important factors considered include:* secondary school record. *Important factors considered include:* class rank, standardized test scores, talent/ability. *Other factors considered include:* alumni/ ae relation, character/personal qualities, essays, extracurricular activities, interview, minority status, recommendations, volunteer work, work experience. **Freshman Admission Requirements:** High school diploma or GED is required. *Academic units required/recommended:* 16 total recommended; 4 English recommended, 3 math recommended, 2 science recommended, 3 social studies recommended, 4 elective recommended. **Freshman Admission Statistics:** 7,496 applied, 84% accepted, 26% of those accepted enrolled. **Transfer Admission Requirements:** *Items required:* high school transcript, college transcript. Minimum college GPA of 2.0 required. Lowest grade transferable C. **General Admission Information:** Priority application deadline January 1. Nonfall registration accepted. Admission may be deferred. Credit and/or placement offered for CEEB Advanced Placement tests.

COSTS AND FINANCIAL AID

Required Forms and Deadlines: FAFSA. Priority filing deadline March 31. **Notification of Awards:** Applicants will be notified of awards on a rolling basis beginning on or about February 20. **Types of Aid:** *Need-based scholarships/ grants:* Pell, SEOG, state scholarships/grants, private scholarships. *Loans:* FFEL Subsidized Stafford, FFEL Unsubsidized Stafford, FFEL PLUS, Federal Perkins, state loans, college/university loans from institutional funds, GATE. **Student Employment:** Federal Work-Study Program available. Institutional employment available. Off-campus job opportunities are good. **Financial Aid Statistics:** 63% freshmen, 56% undergrads receive some form of aid. Average freshman grant $6,406. Average freshman loan $4,263. Average income from on-campus job $1,522. **Financial Aid Phone:** 937-229-4311.

UNIVERSITY OF DELAWARE

Admissions Office, 116 Hullihen Hall, Newark, DE 19716-6210
Phone: 302-831-8123 **E-mail:** admissions@udel.edu **CEEB Code:** 5811
Fax: 302-831-6905 **Web:** www.udel.edu **ACT Code:** 634

This public school was founded in 1743. It has a 1,000-acre campus.

STUDENTS AND FACULTY

Enrollment: 17,486. **Student Body:** Male 42%, female 58%, out-of-state 59%, international 1% (100 countries represented). **Ethnic Representation:** African American 5%, Asian 3%, Caucasian 88%, Hispanic 3%. **Retention and Graduation:** 89% freshmen return for sophomore year. 55% freshmen graduate within 4 years. 20% grads go on to further study within 1 year. **Faculty:** Student/faculty ratio 12:1. 1119 full-time faculty, 84% hold PhDs. 95% faculty teach undergrads.

ACADEMICS

Degrees: Associate's, bachelor's, doctoral, master's. **Academic Requirements:** General education including some course work in computer literacy, English (including composition), foreign languages, humanities, mathematics, sciences (biological or physical), social science; one course emphasizing multicultural, ethnic, and/or gender-related content. **Classes:** 20-29 students in an average class. 20-29 students in an average lab/discussion section. **Disciplines with Highest Percentage of Degrees Awarded:** Social sciences and history 17%, business/marketing 16%, education 10%, home economics and vocational home economics 6%, engineering/engineering technology 5%. **Special Study Options:** Accelerated program, cooperative (work-study) program, distance learning, double major, dual enrollment, English as a second language, honors program, independent study, internships, liberal arts/career combination, student-designed major, study abroad, teacher certification program.

FACILITIES

Housing: Coed, all-female, apartments for married students, apartments for single students, housing for disabled students, fraternities and/or sororities, special-interest communities. **Library Holdings:** 2,540,162 bound volumes. 13,541 periodicals. 3,307,290 microforms. 16,315 audiovisuals. **Special Academic Facilities/Equipment:** Lammont du Pont Laboratory, biotechnology center, Fischer Greenhouse Laboratory, 23,000-seat Delaware Football Stadium, 350-acre agricultural teaching and research complex, 35-acre woodlot harboring numerous wild species of animals and birds, 28 micro-computing sites, 6-acre Morris Library containing 2.3 million books and 120 networked databases, 2 student/University centers, art conservation laboratories at Winterthur Museum & Gardens, Bob Carpenter Sports/Convocation Center, livestock arena and working farm, composites manufacturing science laboratory, Delaware Field House, Fred P. Rullo Stadium, Gerald Culley foreign language media center, historic costume & textile collection, laboratory for the analysis of cultural materials, medical technology laboratories, the mineralogical museum, nursing practice laboratories, orthopedic and biomechanical engineering center, Rust & Gold ice skating arenas, textiles, botanical gardens, the University gallery, University honors center, University laboratory preschool, Vita Nova, 40+ research centers & institutes. **Computers:** School-owned computers available for student use.

EXTRACURRICULARS

Activities: Choral groups, concert band, dance, drama/theater, jazz band, literary magazine, marching band, music ensembles, musical theater, opera, pep band, radio station, student government, student newspaper, student-run film society, symphony orchestra, television station. **Organizations:** 200 registered organizations, 36 honor societies, 18 religious organizations, 15 fraternities (15% men join), 15 sororities (15% women join). **Athletics (Intercollegiate):** *Men:* baseball, basketball, cross-country, diving, football, golf, indoor track, lacrosse, soccer, swimming, tennis, track & field. *Women:* basketball, crew, cross-country, diving, field hockey, indoor track, lacrosse, soccer, softball, swimming, tennis, track & field, volleyball.

ADMISSIONS

Selectivity Rating: 83 (of 100). **Freshman Academic Profile:** Average high school GPA 3.5. 34% in top 10% of high school class, 75% in top 25% of high school class, 97% in top 50% of high school class. 80% from public high schools. SAT I Math middle 50% range 550-650. SAT I Verbal middle 50% range 530-620. ACT middle 50% range 22-27. TOEFL required of all international applicants, minimum TOEFL 550. **Basis for Candidate Selection:** *Very important factors considered include:* essays, secondary school record. *Important factors considered include:* character/personal qualities, class rank, extracurricular activities, geographical residence, recommendations, standardized test scores, state residency, talent/ability. *Other factors considered include:* alumni/ae relation, minority status, volunteer work, work experience. **Freshman Admission Requirements:** High school diploma or GED is required. *Academic units required/recommended:* 16 total required; 19 total recommended; 4 English required, 4 English recommended, 2 math required, 4 math recommended, 2 science required, 3 science recommended, 1 science lab required, 2 foreign language required, 4 foreign language recommended, 1 social studies required, 2 social studies recommended, 2 history required, 2 history recommended, 3 elective required. **Freshman Admission Statistics:** 20,365 applied, 48% accepted, 35% of those accepted enrolled. **Transfer Admission Requirements:** *Items required:* high school transcript, college transcript, essay. Minimum college GPA of 2.5 required. Lowest grade transferable C. **General Admission Information:** Application fee $55. Priority application deadline January 15. Early decision application deadline November 15. Regular application deadline February 15. Nonfall registration accepted. Admission may be deferred for a maximum of 1 year. Credit and/or placement offered for CEEB Advanced Placement tests.

COSTS AND FINANCIAL AID

In-state tuition $5,190. Out-of-state tuition $14,720. Room & board $5,822. Required fees $570. Average book expense $800. **Required Forms and Deadlines:** FAFSA. Financial aid filing deadline March 15. Priority filing deadline February 1. **Notification of Awards:** Applicants will be notified of awards on a rolling basis beginning on or about March 15. **Types of Aid:** *Need-based scholarships/grants:* Pell, SEOG, state scholarships/grants, private scholarships, the school's own gift aid. *Loans:* Direct Subsidized Stafford, Direct Unsubsidized Stafford, Direct PLUS, Federal Perkins, Federal Nursing. **Student Employment:** Federal Work-Study Program available. Institutional employment available. Off-campus job opportunities are good. **Financial Aid Statistics:** 43% freshmen, 37% undergrads receive some form of aid. Average freshman grant $4,200. Average freshman loan $3,500. **Financial Aid Phone:** 302-831-8761.

UNIVERSITY OF DENVER

$$$

University Hall, Room 155, 2199 S. University Blvd., Denver, CO 80208
Phone: 303-871-2036 **E-mail:** admission@du.edu **CEEB Code:** 4842
Fax: 303-871-3301 **Web:** www.du.edu **ACT Code:** 534

This private school, which is affiliated with the Methodist Church, was founded in 1864. It has a 125-acre campus.

STUDENTS AND FACULTY

Enrollment: 3,809. **Student Body:** Male 42%, female 58%, out-of-state 56%, international 6%. **Ethnic Representation:** African American 4%, Asian 5%, Caucasian 81%, Hispanic 6%, Native American 1%. **Retention and Graduation:** 84% freshmen return for sophomore year. 57% freshmen graduate within 4 years. **Faculty:** Student/faculty ratio 13:1. 402 full-time faculty, 89% hold PhDs.

ACADEMICS

Degrees: Bachelor's, doctoral, first professional, master's. **Academic Requirements:** General education including some course work in English (including composition), foreign languages, humanities, mathematics, sciences (biological or physical), social science. **Classes:** 10-19 students in an average class. 10-19 students in an average lab/discussion section. **Disciplines with Highest Percentage of Degrees Awarded:** Business/marketing 41%, communications/communication technologies 11%, social sciences and history 10%, biological life sciences 7%, visual and performing arts 6%. **Special Study Options:** Accelerated program, cooperative (work-study) program, double major, English as a second language, honors program, independent study, internships, student-designed major, study abroad, weekend college, Learning Disabilities Services.

FACILITIES

Housing: Coed, fraternities and/or sororities. **Library Holdings:** 1,268,928 bound volumes. 5,788 periodicals. 970,022 microforms. 1,736 audiovisuals. **Special Academic Facilities/Equipment:** Art gallery, fine arts center, centers for Judaic and Latin American studies, anthropology museum, center for child study, center for gifted and talented children, regional conservation center, high altitude research lab, law enforcement technology center, observatory. **Computers:** *Recommended operating system:* Mac. School-owned computers available for student use.

EXTRACURRICULARS

Activities: Choral groups, concert band, dance, drama/theater, jazz band, music ensembles, musical theater, pep band, student government, student newspaper, yearbook. **Organizations:** 120 registered organizations, 8 honor societies, 9 fraternities (15% men join), 4 sororities (10% women join). **Athletics (Intercollegiate):** *Men:* basketball, skiing (cross-country), cross-country, golf, ice hockey, lacrosse, skiing (alpine), soccer, swimming, tennis. *Women:* basketball, skiing (cross-country), cross-country, golf, gymnastics, lacrosse, skiing (alpine), soccer, swimming, tennis, volleyball.

ADMISSIONS

Selectivity Rating: 78 (of 100). **Freshman Academic Profile:** Average high school GPA 3.4. 32% in top 10% of high school class, 57% in top 25% of high school class, 85% in top 50% of high school class. Average SAT I Math 569, SAT I Math middle 50% range 500-610. Average SAT I Verbal 555, SAT I Verbal middle 50% range 510-610. Average ACT 24, ACT middle 50% range 21-27. TOEFL required of all international applicants, minimum TOEFL 500. **Basis for Candidate Selection:** *Very important factors considered include:* secondary school record. *Important factors considered include:* character/personal qualities, class rank, extracurricular activities, standardized test scores, talent/ability, volunteer work, work experience. *Other factors considered include:* alumni/ae relation, essays, geographical residence, interview, recommendations. **Freshman Admission Requirements:** High school diploma or GED is required. *Academic units required/recommended:* 4 English required, 4 math required, 3 science required, 2 science lab required, 2 foreign language required. **Freshman Admission Statistics:** 3,303 applied, 84% accepted, 30% of those accepted enrolled. **Transfer Admission Requirements:** *Items required:* college transcript, essay. Lowest grade transferable C.

General Admission Information: Application fee $45. Nonfall registration accepted. Admission may be deferred. Credit and/or placement offered for CEEB Advanced Placement tests.

COSTS AND FINANCIAL AID

Tuition $18,936. Room & board $6,165. Required fees $504. **Required Forms and Deadlines:** FAFSA. Priority filing deadline February 15. **Notification of Awards:** Applicants will be notified of awards on or about April 1. **Types of Aid:** *Need-based scholarships/grants:* Pell, SEOG, state scholarships/grants, private scholarships, the school's own gift aid. *Loans:* Direct Subsidized Stafford, Direct Unsubsidized Stafford, Direct PLUS, FFEL Subsidized Stafford, FFEL Unsubsidized Stafford, FFEL PLUS, Federal Perkins, college/university loans from institutional funds. **Student Employment:** Federal Work-Study Program available. Institutional employment available. Off-campus job opportunities are excellent. **Financial Aid Statistics:** 52% freshmen, 53% undergrads receive some form of aid. Average freshman grant $9,800. Average freshman loan $6,500. Average income from on-campus job $1,350. **Financial Aid Phone:** 303-871-2681.

UNIVERSITY OF DETROIT MERCY

PO Box 19900, Detroit, MI 48219
Phone: 313-993-1245 **E-mail:** admissions@udmercy.edu **CEEB Code:** 1835
Fax: 313-993-3326 **Web:** www.udmercy.edu **ACT Code:** 2060

This private school, which is affiliated with the Roman Catholic-Jesuit Church, was founded in 1877. It has a 70-acre campus.

STUDENTS AND FACULTY

Enrollment: 3,543. **Student Body:** Male 34%, female 66%, out-of-state 8%, international 2%. **Ethnic Representation:** African American 34%, Asian 2%, Caucasian 51%, Hispanic 2%, Native American 1%. **Retention and Graduation:** 77% freshmen return for sophomore year. 25% freshmen graduate within 4 years. 20% grads go on to further study within 1 year. 8% grads pursue business degrees. 4% grads pursue law degrees. 3% grads pursue medical degrees.

ACADEMICS

Degrees: Associate's, bachelor's, certificate, doctoral, first professional, first professional certificate, master's, post-bachelor's certificate, post-master's certificate, terminal, transfer. **Academic Requirements:** General education including some course work in arts/fine arts, computer literacy, English (including composition), history, humanities, mathematics, philosophy, sciences (biological or physical), social science. **Disciplines with Highest Percentage of Degrees Awarded:** Health professions and related sciences 22%, business/marketing 15%, engineering/engineering technology 13%, biological life sciences 7%, protective services/public administration 7%. **Special Study Options:** Accelerated program, cooperative (work-study) program, double major, dual enrollment, English as a second language, honors program, independent study, internships, study abroad, teacher certification program, weekend college.

FACILITIES

Housing: Coed, apartments for married students, fraternities and/or sororities. **Library Holdings:** 784,696 bound volumes. 311 periodicals. 19,459 microforms. 10,217 audiovisuals. **Computers:** *Recommended operating system:* Windows 3x. School-owned computers available for student use.

EXTRACURRICULARS

Activities: Dance, drama/theater, literary magazine, pep band, radio station, student government, student newspaper. **Organizations:** 55 registered organizations, 1 honor society, 7 fraternities, 3 sororities. **Athletics (Intercollegiate):** *Men:* baseball, basketball, cheerleading, cross-country, fencing, golf, indoor track, soccer, track & field. *Women:* basketball, cheerleading, cross-country, fencing, indoor track, soccer, softball, tennis, track & field.

ADMISSIONS

Selectivity Rating: 75 (of 100). **Freshman Academic Profile:** Average high school GPA 3.2. 23% in top 10% of high school class, 53% in top 25% of high school class, 82% in top 50% of high school class. Average ACT 21, ACT middle 50% range 19-26. **Basis for Candidate Selection:** *Very important factors considered include:* class rank, secondary school record. *Important factors considered include:* standardized test scores. *Other factors considered include:* character/personal qualities, extracurricular activities, recommendations, volunteer work. **Freshman Admission Requirements:** High school diploma or GED is required. *Academic units required/recommended:* 16 total required; 4 English required, 3 math required, 4 math recommended, 2 science required, 3 science recommended, 1 science lab required, 1 social studies required, 1 history required, 4 elective required. **Transfer Admission Requirements:** *Items required:* college transcript, statement of good standing from prior school. Minimum college GPA of 2.0 required. Lowest grade transferable C. **General Admission Information:** Application fee $25. Priority application deadline April 1. Regular application deadline July 1. Nonfall registration accepted. Admission may be deferred for a maximum of 1 year. Credit and/or placement offered for CEEB Advanced Placement tests.

COSTS AND FINANCIAL AID

Tuition $13,350. Room & board $5,380. Required fees $222. Average book expense $674. **Required Forms and Deadlines:** FAFSA. Priority filing deadline April 1. **Notification of Awards:** Applicants will be notified of awards on a rolling basis. **Types of Aid:** *Need-based scholarships/grants:* Pell, SEOG, state scholarships/grants, private scholarships, the school's own gift aid, Federal Nursing. *Loans:* FFEL Subsidized Stafford, FFEL Unsubsidized Stafford, FFEL PLUS, Federal Perkins, Federal Nursing, college/university loans from institutional funds. **Student Employment:** Federal Work-Study Program available. Institutional employment available. Off-campus job opportunities are good. **Financial Aid Statistics:** Average freshman grant $8,800. Average freshman loan $4,425. **Financial Aid Phone:** 313-993-1350.

UNIVERSITY OF DUBUQUE

2000 University Avenue, Dubuque, IA 52001-5050
Phone: 319-589-3200 **E-mail:** admssns@dbq.edu **CEEB Code:** 6869
Fax: 319-589-3690 **Web:** www.dbq.edu **ACT Code:** 1358

This private school, which is affiliated with the Presbyterian Church, was founded in 1852. It has a 56-acre campus.

STUDENTS AND FACULTY

Enrollment: 843. **Student Body:** Male 65%, female 35%, out-of-state 48%. **Ethnic Representation:** African American 12%, Asian 1%, Caucasian 81%, Hispanic 3%, Native American 1%. **Retention and Graduation:** 68% freshmen return for sophomore year. 25% freshmen graduate within 4 years. 16% grads go on to further study within 1 year. 5% grads pursue business degrees. 1% grads pursue medical degrees. **Faculty:** Student/faculty ratio 14:1. 45 full-time faculty, 62% hold PhDs. 100% faculty teach undergrads.

ACADEMICS

Degrees: Associate's, bachelor's, doctoral, master's. **Academic Requirements:** General education including some course work in computer literacy, English (including composition), history, humanities, mathematics, sciences (biological or physical), social science. **Classes:** 10-19 students in an average class. Under 10 students in an average lab/discussion section. **Majors with Highest Enrollment:** Business administration/management; animation, interactive technology, video graphics and special effects; airline/commercial/professional pilot and flight crew. **Disciplines with Highest Percentage of Degrees Awarded:** Education 17%, computer and information sciences 12%, business/marketing 11%, other 9%, parks and recreation 9%. **Special Study Options:** Cooperative (work-study) program, cross registration, double major, dual enrollment, independent study, internships, liberal arts/career combination, study abroad, teacher certification program. Undergrads may take grad-level classes. Off-campus study: semester-away programs.

FACILITIES

Housing: Coed, apartments for married students, apartments for single students, housing for disabled students, houses and townhouses. **Library Holdings:** 166,331 bound volumes. 565 periodicals. 20,000 microforms. 525 audiovisuals. **Special Academic Facilities/Equipment:** Art gallery, language labs, electron microscope, gas chromatograph/mass spectrometer, floating science lab on the Mississippi River, computer graphics/interactive media studios, multimedia project production studio in the new Charles C. Myers Library. **Computers:** *Recommended operating system:* Windows NT/2000. School-owned computers available for student use.

EXTRACURRICULARS

Activities: Choral groups, dance, drama/theater, music ensembles, pep band, student government, student newspaper, student-run film society, yearbook. **Organizations:** 35 registered organizations, 2 honor societies, 3 religious organizations, 5 fraternities (6% men join), 3 sororities (5% women join). **Athletics (Intercollegiate):** *Men:* baseball, basketball, cross-country, football, golf, indoor track, soccer, tennis, track & field, wrestling. *Women:* basketball, cross-country, golf, indoor track, soccer, softball, tennis, track & field, volleyball.

ADMISSIONS

Selectivity Rating: 72 (of 100). **Freshman Academic Profile:** Average high school GPA 3.0. 7% in top 10% of high school class, 21% in top 25% of high school class, 51% in top 50% of high school class. 85% from public high schools. SAT I Math middle 50% range 410-520. SAT I Verbal middle 50% range 370-520. Average ACT 22, ACT middle 50% range 18-23. TOEFL required of all international applicants, minimum TOEFL 500. **Basis for Candidate Selection:** *Very important factors considered include:* character/personal qualities, class rank, essays, recommendations, secondary school record, standardized test scores. *Important factors considered include:* interview. *Other factors considered include:* alumni/ae relation, extracurricular activities, volunteer work, work experience. **Freshman Admission Requirements:** High school diploma or GED is required. *Academic units required/recommended:* 16 total required; 4 English required, 3 math required, 3 science required, 3 social studies required, 3 elective required. **Freshman Admission Statistics:** 625 applied, 78% accepted, 49% of those accepted enrolled. **Transfer Admission Requirements:** *Items required:* high school transcript, college transcript, essay. Minimum college GPA of 2.0 required. Lowest grade transferable C. **General Admission Information:** Application fee $25. Nonfall registration accepted. Admission may be deferred for a maximum of 1 year. Credit offered for CEEB Advanced Placement tests.

COSTS AND FINANCIAL AID

Tuition $14,990. Room & board $5,020. Required fees $160. Average book expense $750. **Required Forms and Deadlines:** FAFSA. No deadline for regular filing. **Notification of Awards:** Applicants will be notified of awards on a rolling basis beginning on or about March 1. **Types of Aid:** *Need-based scholarships/grants:* Pell, SEOG, state scholarships/grants, private scholarships, the school's own gift aid. *Loans:* FFEL Subsidized Stafford, FFEL Unsubsidized Stafford, FFEL PLUS, Federal Perkins, state loans, college/university loans from institutional funds. **Student Employment:** Federal Work-Study Program available. Institutional employment available. Off-campus job opportunities are excellent. **Financial Aid Statistics:** 89% freshmen, 94% undergrads receive some form of aid. Average freshman grant $12,500. Average freshman loan $3,400. Average income from on-campus job $1,500. **Financial Aid Phone:** 319-589-3170.

UNIVERSITY OF EVANSVILLE

1800 Lincoln Avenue, Evansville, IN 47722
Phone: 812-479-2468 **E-mail:** admission@evansville.edu **CEEB Code:** 1208
Fax: 812-474-4076 **Web:** www.evansville.edu **ACT Code:** 1188

This private school, which is affiliated with the Methodist Church, was founded in 1854. It has a 75-acre campus.

STUDENTS AND FACULTY

Enrollment: 2,590. **Student Body:** Male 40%, female 60%, out-of-state 33%, international 5% (48 countries represented). **Ethnic Representation:** African American 2%, Asian 1%, Caucasian 77%, Hispanic 1%, Native American 3%. **Retention and Graduation:** 79% freshmen return for sophomore year. 71% freshmen graduate within 4 years. 17% grads go on to further study within 1 year. **Faculty:** Student/faculty ratio 13:1. 168 full-time faculty, 86% hold PhDs. 100% faculty teach undergrads.

ACADEMICS

Degrees: Associate's, bachelor's, master's. **Academic Requirements:** General education including some course work in arts/fine arts, computer literacy, English (including composition), foreign languages, history, humanities, mathematics, philosophy, sciences (biological or physical), social science, world cultures and health & wellness. **Classes:** 10-19 students in an average class. 10-19 students in an average lab/discussion section. **Majors with Highest Enrollment:** Physical therapy/therapist; elementary education and teaching; drama and dramatics/theatre arts, general. **Disciplines with Highest Percentage of Degrees Awarded:** Health professions and related sciences 19%, business/marketing 13%, visual and performing arts 11%, engineering/engineering technology 9%, education 9%. **Special Study Options:** Cooperative (work-study) program, double major, English as a second language, student exchange program (domestic), honors program, independent study, internships, student-designed major, study abroad. Co-op programs in computer science, engineering, chemistry, and business.

FACILITIES

Housing: Coed, all-female, all-male, apartments for single students, fraternities and/or sororities. **Library Holdings:** 275,980 bound volumes. 1,320 periodicals. 458,241 microforms. 10,775 audiovisuals. **Computers:** *Recommended operating system:* Windows NT 4.1.

EXTRACURRICULARS

Activities: Choral groups, concert band, dance, drama/theater, jazz band, literary magazine, music ensembles, musical theater, opera, pep band, radio station, student government, student newspaper, symphony orchestra, yearbook. **Organizations:** 130 registered organizations, 13 honor societies, 15 religious organizations, 6 fraternities (25% men join), 4 sororities (25% women join). **Athletics (Intercollegiate):** *Men:* baseball, basketball, cheerleading, cross-country, diving, golf, soccer, swimming, tennis. *Women:* basketball, cheerleading, cross-country, diving, golf, soccer, softball, swimming, tennis, volleyball.

ADMISSIONS

Selectivity Rating: 73 (of 100). **Freshman Academic Profile:** Average high school GPA 3.5. 31% in top 10% of high school class, 63% in top 25% of high school class, 90% in top 50% of high school class. Average SAT I Math 559. Average SAT I Verbal 559. Average ACT 26. TOEFL required of all international applicants, minimum TOEFL 500. **Basis for Candidate Selection:** *Very important factors considered include:* secondary school record, standardized test scores. *Important factors considered include:* extracurricular activities. *Other factors considered include:* character/personal qualities, class rank, essays, recommendations, talent/ability, volunteer work, work experience. **Freshman Admission Requirements:** High school diploma or GED is required. *Academic units required/recommended:* 4 English required, 3 math required, 2 science required, 2 science lab required, 2 foreign language recommended, 1 social studies recommended, 2 history recommended, 2 elective recommended. **Transfer Admission Requirements:** *Items required:* high school transcript, college transcript, statement of good standing from prior school. Minimum college GPA of 2.0 required. Lowest grade transferable C. **General Admission Information:** Application fee $35. Regular application deadline February 1. Nonfall registration accepted. Admission may be deferred for a maximum of 1 year. Credit offered for CEEB Advanced Placement tests.

COSTS AND FINANCIAL AID

Tuition $17,900. Room & board $5,610. Required fees $330. Average book expense $700. **Required Forms and Deadlines:** FAFSA. Priority filing deadline March 1. **Notification of Awards:** Applicants will be notified of awards on a rolling basis beginning on or about March 15. **Types of Aid:** *Need-based scholarships/grants:* Pell, SEOG, state scholarships/grants, private scholarships, the school's own gift aid. *Loans:* FFEL Subsidized Stafford, FFEL Unsubsidized Stafford, FFEL PLUS, Federal Perkins, Federal Nursing. **Student Employment:** Federal Work-Study Program available. Institutional employment available. Off-campus job opportunities are good. **Financial Aid Statistics:** 73% freshmen, 68% undergrads receive some form of aid. Average freshman grant $10,106. Average freshman loan $3,066. Average income from on-campus job $1,057. **Financial Aid Phone:** 812-479-2364.

UNIVERSITY OF FINDLAY

1000 North Main Street, Findlay, OH 45840
Phone: 419-424-4732 **E-mail:** admissions@findlay.edu **CEEB Code:** 1223
Fax: 419-434-4898 **Web:** www.findlay.edu **ACT Code:** 3272

This private school was founded in 1882. It has a 175-acre campus.

STUDENTS AND FACULTY

Enrollment: 3,381. **Student Body:** Male 43%, female 57%, out-of-state 20%, international 1%. **Ethnic Representation:** African American 4%, Asian 4%, Caucasian 73%, Hispanic 2%. **Retention and Graduation:** 72% freshmen return for sophomore year. 32% freshmen graduate within 4 years. 18% grads go on to further study within 1 year. 3% grads pursue business degrees. 4% grads pursue law degrees. 1% grads pursue medical degrees. **Faculty:** Student/faculty ratio 16:1. 160 full-time faculty, 50% hold PhDs. 90% faculty teach undergrads.

ACADEMICS

Degrees: Associate's, bachelor's, master's. **Academic Requirements:** General education including some course work in arts/fine arts, computer literacy, English (including composition), foreign languages, humanities, mathematics, philosophy, sciences (biological or physical), social science. **Classes:** 10-19 students in an average class. **Disciplines with Highest Percentage of Degrees Awarded:** Health professions and related sciences 28%, business/marketing 16%, education 13%, engineering/engineering technology 6%, computer and information sciences 6%. **Special Study Options:** Accelerated program, cooperative (work-study) program, distance learning, double major, dual enrollment, English as a second language, external degree program, honors program, independent study, internships, liberal arts/career combination, student-designed major, study abroad, teacher certification program, weekend college, 3-2 in engineering with Ohio Northern University; Toledo and Washington University in St. Louis, BS in nursing with Mount Carmel College of Nursing, 3-1 arrangement with Art Institute Consortium.

FACILITIES

Housing: All-female, all-male, apartments for single students, housing for disabled students, housing for international students, fraternities and/or sororities, honors house, special-interest houses. **Library Holdings:** 135,000 bound volumes. 1,050 periodicals. 133,104 microforms. 2,000 audiovisuals. **Special Academic Facilities/Equipment:** Fine arts pavilion, planetarium, Mazza Gallery (Children's Book Illustrations.). **Computers:** School-owned computers available for student use.

EXTRACURRICULARS

Activities: Choral groups, concert band, drama/theater, jazz band, literary magazine, marching band, music ensembles, musical theater, pep band, radio station, student government, student newspaper, student-run film society, television station, yearbook. **Organizations:** 40 registered organizations, 1 honor society, 1 religious organization, 3 fraternities (2% men join), 2 sororities (2% women join). **Athletics (Intercollegiate):** *Men:* baseball, basketball, cross-country, diving, equestrian, football, golf, ice hockey, indoor track, soccer, swimming, tennis, track & field, volleyball, wrestling. *Women:* basketball, cross-country, diving, equestrian, golf, ice hockey, indoor track, soccer, softball, swimming, tennis, track & field, volleyball.

ADMISSIONS

Selectivity Rating: 72 (of 100). **Freshman Academic Profile:** Average high school GPA 3.2. 10% in top 10% of high school class, 33% in top 25% of high school class, 70% in top 50% of high school class. 92% from public high schools. Average SAT I Math 510, SAT I Math middle 50% range 440-580. Average SAT I Verbal 520, SAT I Verbal middle 50% range 450-580. Average ACT 23. TOEFL required of all international applicants, minimum TOEFL 500. **Basis for Candidate Selection:** *Very important factors considered include:* secondary school record, standardized test scores. *Important factors considered include:* interview. *Other factors considered include:* alumni/ae relation, character/personal qualities, class rank, essays, extracurricular activities, recommendations, religious affiliation/commitment, talent/ability, volunteer work. **Freshman Admission Requirements:** High school diploma or GED is required. *Academic units required/recommended:* 16 total recommended; 4 English recommended, 2 math recommended, 4 science recommended, 2 foreign language recommended, 2 social studies recommended, 1 history recommended, 1 elective recommended. **Freshman Admission Statistics:** 2,404 applied, 84% accepted, 35% of those accepted enrolled. **Transfer Admission Requirements:** *Items required:* college transcript. Minimum college GPA of 2.0 required. Lowest grade transferable C. **General Admission Information:** Regular application deadline July 1. Nonfall registration accepted. Admission may be deferred for a maximum of 1 year. Credit and/or placement offered for CEEB Advanced Placement tests.

COSTS AND FINANCIAL AID

Tuition $17,088. Room & board $6,434. Required fees $440. Average book expense $600. **Required Forms and Deadlines:** FAFSA. Financial aid filing deadline August 1. Priority filing deadline March 1. **Notification of Awards:** Applicants will be notified of awards on a rolling basis beginning on or about March 1. **Types of Aid:** *Need-based scholarships/grants:* Pell, SEOG, state scholarships/grants, private scholarships, the school's own gift aid. *Loans:* Direct Subsidized Stafford, Direct Unsubsidized Stafford, Direct PLUS, Federal Perkins, college/university loans from institutional funds. **Student Employment:** Federal Work-Study Program available. Institutional employment available. Off-campus job opportunities are excellent. **Financial Aid Statistics:** 81% freshmen, 74% undergrads receive some form of aid. Average freshman grant $5,750. Average freshman loan $2,200. Average income from on-campus job $600. **Financial Aid Phone:** 419-424-4791.

UNIVERSITY OF FLORIDA

201 Criser Hall, Box 114000, Gainesville, FL 32611-4000
Phone: 352-392-1365 **CEEB Code:** 5812
Fax: 904-392-3987 **Web:** www.ufl.edu

This public school was founded in 1853. It has a 2,000-acre campus.

STUDENTS AND FACULTY

Enrollment: 34,031. **Student Body:** Male 47%, female 53%, out-of-state 5%, international 1%. **Ethnic Representation:** African American 8%, Asian 7%, Caucasian 72%, Hispanic 11%, Native American 1%. **Retention and Graduation:** 93% freshmen return for sophomore year. 43% freshmen graduate within 4 years. **Faculty:** Student/faculty ratio 22:1. 1,601 full-time faculty, 95% hold PhDs.

ACADEMICS

Degrees: Bachelor's, doctoral, first professional, master's. **Classes:** 20-29 students in an average class. 10-19 students in an average lab/discussion section. **Disciplines with Highest Percentage of Degrees Awarded:** Business/marketing 21%, engineering/engineering technology 11%, social sciences and history 11%, communications/communication technologies 10%, health professions and related sciences 6%. **Special Study Options:** Accelerated program, cooperative (work-study) program, cross registration, distance learning, double major, dual enrollment, English as a second language, student exchange program (domestic), external degree program, honors program, independent study, internships, liberal arts/career combination, student-designed major, study abroad, teacher certification program, weekend college, Adult/Continuing Education, TV-delivered credit-bearing courses.

FACILITIES

Housing: Coed, all-female, apartments for married students, apartments for single students, housing for disabled students, housing for international students, fraternities and/or sororities, cooperative housing, Honors Residential College at Hume Hall, International House at Weaver Hall, "quiet/study" floors, faculty-in-residence program, first-year experience program, wellness floor, no-visitation-by-opposite sex floor. **Library Holdings:** 5,024,637 bound volumes. 28,103 periodicals. 6,701,512 microforms. 36,078 audiovisuals. **Special Academic Facilities/Equipment:** Natural history museum, art museum, art gallery, center for the performing arts, Aeolian Skinner organ, cast-bell carillon, citrus research center, coastal engineering wave tank, 100-kilowatt training and research reactor, academic computing center, microkelvin lab, self-contained intensive care hyperbaric chamber. **Computers:** School-owned computers available for student use.

EXTRACURRICULARS

Activities: Choral groups, concert band, dance, drama/theater, jazz band, literary magazine, marching band, music ensembles, musical theater, pep band, radio station, student government, student newspaper, student-run film society, symphony orchestra, television station, yearbook. **Organizations:** 500 registered organizations, 29 fraternities (15% men join), 18 sororities (15% women join). **Athletics (Intercollegiate):** *Men:* baseball, basketball, cross-country, diving, football, golf, swimming, tennis, track & field. *Women:* basketball, cross-country, diving, golf, gymnastics, soccer, softball, swimming, tennis, track & field, volleyball.

ADMISSIONS

Selectivity Rating: 88 (of 100). **Freshman Academic Profile:** Average high school GPA 3.8. 71% in top 10% of high school class, 89% in top 25% of high school class, 97% in top 50% of high school class. SAT I Math middle 50% range 580-680. SAT I Verbal middle 50% range 550-660. ACT middle 50% range 24-29. **Freshman Admission Requirements:** High school diploma or GED is required. *Academic units required/recommended:* 15 total required; 4 English required, 3 math required, 3 science required, 2 science lab required, 2 foreign language required, 3 social studies required. **Freshman Admission Statistics:** 20,119 applied, 58% accepted, 56% of those accepted enrolled. **Transfer Admission Requirements:** *Items required:* high school transcript, college transcript, standardized test scores. Minimum college GPA of 2.0 required. **General Admission Information:** Application fee $20. Early decision application deadline October 1. Regular application deadline January 13. Nonfall registration accepted. Credit and/or placement offered for CEEB Advanced Placement tests.

COSTS AND FINANCIAL AID

In-state tuition $2,581. Out-of-state tuition $12,046. Room & board $5,640. Required fees $0. Average book expense $780. **Required Forms and Deadlines:** FAFSA. Priority filing deadline March 15. **Notification of Awards:** Applicants will be notified of awards on a rolling basis beginning on or about April 1. **Types of Aid:** *Need-based scholarships/grants:* Pell, SEOG, state scholarships/grants, private scholarships, the school's own gift aid. *Loans:* Direct Subsidized Stafford, Direct Unsubsidized Stafford, Direct PLUS, Federal Perkins, college/university loans from institutional funds. **Student Employment:** Federal Work-Study Program available. Institutional employment available. Off-campus job opportunities are fair. **Financial Aid Statistics:** 34% freshmen, 34% undergrads receive some form of aid. Average freshman grant $3,994. Average freshman loan $2,341. Average income from on-campus job $1,574. **Financial Aid Phone:** 352-392-1275.

UNIVERSITY OF GEORGIA

Terrell Hall, Athens, GA 30602
Phone: 706-542-8776 **E-mail:** undergrad@admissions.uga.edu **CEEB Code:** 5813
Fax: 706-542-1466 **Web:** www.uga.edu

This public school was founded in 1785. It has a 614-acre campus.

STUDENTS AND FACULTY

Enrollment: 24,983. **Student Body:** Male 44%, female 56%, out-of-state 9%, international 1%. **Ethnic Representation:** African American 5%, Asian 4%, Caucasian 89%, Hispanic 2%. **Retention and Graduation:** 93% freshmen return for sophomore year. 43% freshmen graduate within 4 years. 34% grads go on to further study within 1 year. 10% grads pursue business degrees. 4% grads pursue law degrees. 4% grads pursue medical degrees. **Faculty:** Student/faculty ratio 13:1. 1,709 full-time faculty, 94% hold PhDs. 80% faculty teach undergrads.

ACADEMICS

Degrees: Associate's, bachelor's, doctoral, first professional, master's, post-master's certificate. **Academic Requirements:** General education including some course work in arts/fine arts, English (including composition), foreign languages, history, humanities, mathematics, sciences (biological or physical), social science, physical education, environmental literacy. **Classes:** 20-29 students in an average class. **Disciplines with Highest Percentage of Degrees Awarded:** Business/marketing 30%, education 11%, social sciences and history 10%, communications/communication technologies 7%, biological life sciences 7%. **Special Study Options:** Accelerated program, cooperative (work-study) program, cross registration, distance learning, double major, dual enrollment, English as a second language, student exchange program (domestic), honors program, independent study, internships, liberal arts/career combination, student-designed major, study abroad, teacher certification program. Undergrads may take grad-level classes. Off-campus study in Washington, DC. Governor's intern programs. Co-op programs in agriculture, arts, business, computer science, education, home economics, humanities, natural science, social/behavioral science, technologies, and vocational arts.

FACILITIES

Housing: Coed, all-female, all-male, apartments for married students, apartments for single students, housing for disabled students, housing for international students, fraternities and/or sororities, graduate apartments. Transfer, honors, and language halls are available. **Library Holdings:** 3,789,228 bound volumes. 46,431 periodicals. 6,202,440 microforms. 108,672 audiovisuals. **Special Academic Facilities/Equipment:** Art and natural history museums, state botanical garden, language lab. **Computers:** School-owned computers available for student use.

EXTRACURRICULARS

Activities: Choral groups, concert band, dance, drama/theater, jazz band, literary magazine, marching band, music ensembles, musical theater, opera, pep band, radio station, student government, student newspaper, student-run film society, symphony orchestra, television station, yearbook. **Organizations:** 433 registered organizations, 48 honor societies, 20 religious organizations, 25 fraternities (16% men join), 22 sororities (17% women join). **Athletics (Intercollegiate):** *Men:* baseball, basketball, cheerleading, cross-country, diving, equestrian, football, golf, swimming, tennis, track & field. *Women:* basketball, cheerleading, cross-country, diving, equestrian, golf, gymnastics, soccer, softball, swimming, tennis, track & field, volleyball.

ADMISSIONS

Selectivity Rating: 85 (of 100). **Freshman Academic Profile:** Average high school GPA 3.7. 87% from public high schools. Average SAT I Math 611, SAT I Math middle 50% range 560-650. Average SAT I Verbal 604, SAT I Verbal middle 50% range 550-640. ACT middle 50% range 24-29. TOEFL required of all international applicants, minimum TOEFL 550. **Basis for Candidate Selection:** *Very important factors considered include:* secondary school record, standardized test scores. *Other factors considered include:* essays, extracurricular activities, recommendations, state residency, talent/ability, volunteer work, work experience. **Freshman Admission Requirements:** High school diploma or GED is required. *Academic units required/recommended:* 20 total required; 4 English required, 4 math required, 3 science required, 2 science lab required, 2 foreign language required, 3 social studies required, 4 elective required. **Freshman Admission Statistics:** 12,786 applied, 65% accepted, 51% of those accepted enrolled. **Transfer Admission Requirements:** *Items required:* college transcript. Minimum college GPA of 2.5 required. Lowest grade transferable D. **General Admission Information:** Application fee $50. Regular application deadline February 1. Nonfall registration accepted. Credit and/or placement offered for CEEB Advanced Placement tests.

COSTS AND FINANCIAL AID

Average book expense $610. **Required Forms and Deadlines:** FAFSA. Financial aid filing deadline August 1. Priority filing deadline March 3. **Notification of Awards:** Applicants will be notified of awards on a rolling basis. **Types of Aid:** *Need-based scholarships/grants:* Pell, SEOG, state scholarships/grants, private scholarships, the school's own gift aid. *Loans:* Direct Subsidized Stafford, Direct Unsubsidized Stafford, Direct PLUS, Federal Perkins, college/university loans from institutional funds. **Student Employment:** Federal Work-Study Program available. Institutional employment available. Off-campus job opportunities are good. **Financial Aid Statistics:** 27% freshmen, 26% undergrads receive some form of aid. **Financial Aid Phone:** 706-542-6147.

UNIVERSITY OF GREAT FALLS

1301 20th Street South, Great Falls, MT 59405
Phone: 406-791-5200 **E-mail:** enroll@ugf.edu **CEEB Code:** 4058
Fax: 406-791-5209 **Web:** www.ugf.edu **ACT Code:** 2410

This private school, which is affiliated with the Roman Catholic Church, was founded in 1932. It has a 44-acre campus.

STUDENTS AND FACULTY

Enrollment: 717. **Student Body:** Male 27%, female 73%, out-of-state 5%, international 2%. **Ethnic Representation:** African American 2%, Asian 1%, Caucasian 83%, Hispanic 2%, Native American 7%. **Retention and Graduation:** 41% freshmen return for sophomore year. 22% freshmen graduate within 4 years. 5% grads go on to further study within 1 year. 12% grads pursue business degrees. 33% grads pursue law degrees. **Faculty:** Student/faculty ratio 9:1. 40 full-time faculty, 55% hold PhDs. 100% faculty teach undergrads.

ACADEMICS

Degrees: Associate's, bachelor's, master's. **Academic Requirements:** General education including some course work in arts/fine arts, computer literacy, English (including composition), foreign languages, history, humanities, mathematics, philosophy, sciences (biological or physical), social science, speech, literature, religion. **Classes:** Under 10 students in an average class. **Majors with Highest Enrollment:** Elementary education and teaching; legal assistant/paralegal; criminal justice/safety studies. **Disciplines with Highest Percentage of Degrees Awarded:** Education 27%, protective services/public administration 26%, computer and information sciences 13%, business/marketing 8%, psychology 6%. **Special Study Options:** Accelerated program, cooperative (work-study) program, distance learning, double major, dual enrollment, independent study, internships, liberal arts/career combination, teacher certification program, weekend college.

FACILITIES

Housing: Coed, apartments for married students, apartments for single students, housing for disabled students. **Library Holdings:** 101,110 bound volumes. 549 periodicals. 21,299 microforms. 4,069 audiovisuals. **Special Academic Facilities/Equipment:** Art museum. **Computers:** School-owned computers available for student use.

EXTRACURRICULARS

Activities: Choral groups, concert band, drama/theater, literary magazine, music ensembles, musical theater, student government, student newspaper. **Organizations:** 10 registered organizations, 1 honor society, 1 religious organization. **Athletics (Intercollegiate):** *Men:* basketball. *Women:* basketball, volleyball.

ADMISSIONS

Selectivity Rating: 66 (of 100). **Freshman Academic Profile:** Average high school GPA 2.9. 7% in top 10% of high school class, 21% in top 25% of high school class, 47% in top 50% of high school class. 99% from public high schools. Average SAT I Math 470, SAT I Math middle 50% range 440-520. Average SAT I Verbal 465, SAT I Verbal middle 50% range 420-540. Average ACT 21, ACT middle 50% range 17-24. TOEFL required of all international applicants, minimum TOEFL 500. **Basis for Candidate Selection:** *Very important factors considered include:* interview. *Important factors considered include:* extracurricular activities, religious affiliation/commitment, secondary school record, standardized test scores, volunteer work. *Other factors considered include:* character/personal qualities, class rank, essays, minority status, recommendations, talent/ability, work experience. **Freshman Admission Requirements:** High school diploma or GED is required. *Academic units required/recommended:* 20 total required; 22 total recommended; 4 English required, 4 English recommended, 3 math required, 3 math recommended, 3 science required, 3 science recommended, 1 science lab required, 1 science lab recommended, 2 foreign language recommended, 1 social studies required, 2 social studies recommended, 3 history required, 3 history recommended, 5 elective required, 3 elective recommended. **Freshman Admission Statistics:** 196 applied, 96% accepted, 58% of those accepted enrolled. **Transfer Admission Requirements:** *Items required:* college transcript. Minimum college GPA of 2.0 required. Lowest grade transferable C. **General Admission Information:** Application fee $25. Priority application deadline June 1. Regular application deadline August 31. Nonfall registration accepted. Admission may be deferred for a maximum of 1 year. Credit offered for CEEB Advanced Placement tests.

COSTS AND FINANCIAL AID

Tuition $11,500. Room & board $5,100. Required fees $260. Average book expense $750. **Required Forms and Deadlines:** FAFSA. No deadline for regular filing. Priority filing deadline March 1. **Notification of Awards:** Applicants will be notified of awards on a rolling basis beginning on or about March 1. **Types of Aid:** *Need-based scholarships/grants:* Pell, SEOG, state scholarships/grants, private scholarships, the school's own gift aid. *Loans:* FFEL Subsidized Stafford, FFEL Unsubsidized Stafford, FFEL PLUS, Federal Perkins. **Student Employment:** Federal Work-Study Program available. Institutional employment available. Off-campus job opportunities are good. **Financial Aid Statistics:** 80% freshmen, 83% undergrads receive some form of aid. Average freshman grant $1,750. Average freshman loan $2,625. Average income from on-campus job $3,000. **Financial Aid Phone:** 406-791-5235.

UNIVERSITY OF GUELPH

Admission Services, Level 3, University Centre, Guelph, ON N1G 2W1
Phone: 519-821-2130 **E-mail:** info@registrar.uoguelph.ca
Fax: 519-766-9481 **Web:** www.uoguelph.ca

This public school was founded in 1964. It has a 1,200-acre campus.

STUDENTS AND FACULTY

Enrollment: 14,126. **Student Body:** Male 37%, female 63%. **Ethnic Representation:** African American 17%, Asian 17%, Caucasian 17%, Hispanic 17%, Native American 17%. **Retention and Graduation:** 91% freshmen return for sophomore year. 43% freshmen graduate within 4 years. **Faculty:** Student/faculty ratio 22:1. 692 full-time faculty.

ACADEMICS

Degrees: Bachelor's, diploma, doctoral, first professional, master's. **Academic Requirements:** General education including some course work in humanities, sciences (biological or physical), social science. **Majors with Highest Enrollment:** Biology/biological sciences, general; physical sciences. **Disciplines with Highest Percentage of Degrees Awarded:** Biological life sciences 23%, social sciences and history 20%, liberal arts/general studies 13%, business/marketing 12%, home economics and vocational home economics 5%. **Special Study Options:** Cooperative (work-study) program, distance learning, double major, English as a second language, external degree program, honors program, independent study, student-designed major, study abroad.

FACILITIES

Housing: Coed, all-female, all-male, apartments for married students, housing for disabled students, housing for international students. **Library Holdings:** 2,500,000 bound volumes. 7,600 periodicals. 1,520,555 microforms. 17,000 audiovisuals. **Special Academic Facilities/Equipment:** Art Gallery, Arboretum.

EXTRACURRICULARS

Activities: Choral groups, dance, drama/theater, jazz band, music ensembles, musical theater, radio station, student government, student newspaper. **Organizations:** 100 registered organizations. **Athletics (Intercollegiate):** *Men:* baseball, basketball, skiing (cross-country), cross-country, football, golf, ice hockey, indoor track, lacrosse, rugby, skiing (Nordic), soccer, swimming, volleyball, wrestling. *Women:* basketball, skiing (cross-country), cross-country, field hockey, ice hockey, indoor track, lacrosse, rugby, skiing (Nordic), soccer, swimming, volleyball, wrestling.

ADMISSIONS

Selectivity Rating: 60 (of 100). **Freshman Academic Profile:** Average high school GPA 3.5. TOEFL required of all international applicants, minimum TOEFL 600. **Basis for Candidate Selection:** *Very important factors considered include:* secondary school record. *Important factors considered include:* class rank, standardized test scores. *Other factors considered include:* character/personal qualities, extracurricular activities, recommendations, talent/ability, volunteer work, work experience. **Freshman Admission Requirements:** High school diploma is required and GED is not accepted. *Academic units required/recommended:* 4 English recommended, 4 math recommended, 4 science recommended, 2 social studies recommended, 2 history recommended. **Freshman Admission Statistics:** 18,222 applied, 78% accepted, 26% of those accepted enrolled. **Transfer Admission Requirements:** *Items required:* high school transcript, college transcript. **General Admission Information:** Application fee $85. Priority application deadline April 1. Regular application deadline June 1. Nonfall registration accepted. Credit and/or placement offered for CEEB Advanced Placement tests.

COSTS AND FINANCIAL AID

In-state tuition $3,794. Out-of-state tuition $3,794. Room & board $5,766. Required fees $681. Average book expense $1,000. **Required Forms and Deadlines:** Institution's own financial aid form. No deadline for regular filing. **Notification of Awards:** Applicants will be notified of awards on a rolling basis. **Types of Aid:** *Need-based scholarships/grants:* Pell, the school's own gift aid, University of Guelph Work-Study Program. **Student Employment:** Off-campus job opportunities are good.

UNIVERSITY OF HARTFORD

200 Bloomfield Avenue, West Hartford, CT 06117
Phone: 860-768-4296 **E-mail:** admissions@mail.hartford.edu **CEEB Code:** 3436
Fax: 860-768-4961 **Web:** www.hartford.edu **ACT Code:** 606

This private school was founded in 1877. It has a 320-acre campus.

STUDENTS AND FACULTY

Enrollment: 5,542. **Student Body:** Male 48%, female 52%, out-of-state 61%, international 3%. **Ethnic Representation:** African American 9%, Asian 2%, Caucasian 75%, Hispanic 4%. **Retention and Graduation:** 74% freshmen return for sophomore year. 42% freshmen graduate within 4 years. 23% grads go on to further study within 1 year. 12% grads pursue business degrees. 2% grads pursue law degrees. 2% grads pursue medical degrees. **Faculty:** Student/faculty ratio 12:1. 328 full-time faculty, 78% hold PhDs. 100% faculty teach undergrads.

ACADEMICS

Degrees: Associate's, bachelor's, certificate, diploma, doctoral, master's, post-bachelor's certificate, post-master's certificate. **Academic Requirements:** General education including some course work in arts/fine arts, computer literacy, English (including composition), foreign languages, history, humanities, mathematics, philosophy, sciences (biological or physical), social science. **Classes:** 10-19 students in an average class. Under 10 students in an average lab/discussion section. **Majors with Highest Enrollment:** Communications studies/speech communication and rhetoric; psychology, general; physical therapy/therapist. **Disciplines with Highest Percentage of Degrees Awarded:** Health professions and related sciences 18%, visual and performing arts 17%, business/marketing 13%, engineering/engineering technology 10%, communications/communication technologies 10%. **Special Study Options:** Cooperative (work-study) program, cross registration, distance learning, double major, dual enrollment, English as a second language, student exchange program (domestic), honors program, independent study, internships, liberal arts/career combination, student-designed major, study abroad, teacher certification program.

FACILITIES

Housing: Coed, all-female, apartments for single students, housing for disabled students, honors housing. **Library Holdings:** 452,060 bound volumes. 2,121 periodicals. 325,018 microforms. 30,811 audiovisuals. **Special Academic Facilities/Equipment:** Museum of presidential memorabilia, art gallery, off-campus child care center for student teaching, learning skills and language lab, audiovisual aids center, 8,000-acre environmental center. **Computers:** School-owned computers available for student use.

EXTRACURRICULARS

Activities: Choral groups, concert band, dance, drama/theater, jazz band, literary magazine, music ensembles, musical theater, opera, radio station, student government, student newspaper, symphony orchestra, television station, yearbook. **Organizations:** 54 registered organizations, 19 honor societies, 3 religious organizations, 7 fraternities, 7 sororities. **Athletics (Intercollegiate):** *Men:* baseball, basketball, cross-country, golf, lacrosse, soccer, tennis, track & field. *Women:* basketball, cross-country, golf, soccer, softball, tennis, track & field, volleyball.

ADMISSIONS

Selectivity Rating: 73 (of 100). **Freshman Academic Profile:** 74% from public high schools. Average SAT I Math 531, SAT I Math middle 50% range 480-580. Average SAT I Verbal 528, SAT I Verbal middle 50% range 480-570. Average ACT 23, ACT middle 50% range 20-24. TOEFL required of all international applicants, minimum TOEFL 550. **Basis for Candidate Selection:** *Very important factors considered include:* secondary school record. *Important factors considered include:* class rank, standardized test scores. *Other factors considered include:* character/personal qualities, essays, extracurricular activities, interview, recommendations, talent/ability. **Freshman Admission Requirements:** High school diploma or GED is required. *Academic units required/recommended:* 16 total required; 4 English required, 2 math required, 3 math recommended, 2 science required, 3 science recommended, 2 foreign language recommended, 2 social studies required, 3 social studies recommended, 2 history required, 4 elective required. **Freshman Admission Statistics:** 10,145 applied, 69% accepted, 19% of those accepted enrolled. **Transfer Admission Requirements:** *Items required:* college transcript. Minimum college GPA of 2.3 required. Lowest grade transferable C-. **General Admission Information:** Application fee $35. Nonfall registration accepted. Admission may be deferred for a maximum of 1 year. Credit offered for CEEB Advanced Placement tests.

COSTS AND FINANCIAL AID

Required Forms and Deadlines: FAFSA and institution's own financial aid form. Priority filing deadline February 1. **Notification of Awards:** Applicants will be notified of awards on a rolling basis beginning on or about March 1. **Types of Aid:** *Need-based scholarships/grants:* Pell, SEOG, state scholarships/grants, private scholarships, the school's own gift aid. *Loans:* Direct Subsidized Stafford, Direct Unsubsidized Stafford, Direct PLUS, Federal Perkins. **Student Employment:** Federal Work-Study Program available. Institutional employment available. Off-campus job opportunities are good. **Financial Aid Statistics:** 63% freshmen, 61% undergrads receive some form of aid. Average freshman grant $16,216. Average freshman loan $5,081. **Financial Aid Phone:** 860-768-4296.

See page 1246.

UNIVERSITY OF HAWAII—HILO

200 West Kawili Street, Hilo, HI 96720-4091
Phone: 808-974-7414 **E-mail:** uhhadm@hawaii.edu
Fax: 808-933-0861 **Web:** www.uhh.hawaii.edu **ACT Code:** 904

This public school was founded in 1970. It has a 225-acre campus.

STUDENTS AND FACULTY

Enrollment: 2,904. **Student Body:** Male 40%, female 60%, out-of-state 35%, international 11%. **Ethnic Representation:** African American 1%, Asian 47%, Caucasian 35%, Hispanic 2%, Native American 1%. **Retention and Graduation:** 66% freshmen return for sophomore year. 11% freshmen graduate within 4 years. **Faculty:** Student/faculty ratio 13:1. 169 full-time faculty, 73% hold PhDs. 100% faculty teach undergrads.

ACADEMICS

Degrees: Bachelor's, master's. **Academic Requirements:** General education including some course work in English (including composition), humanities, mathematics, sciences (biological or physical), social science, world cultures, Hawaiian/Asian/Pacific, writing intensive. **Classes:** 10-19 students in an average class. 10-19 students in an average lab/discussion section. **Majors with Highest Enrollment:** Business, management, marketing, and related support services; psychology, general; marine biology and biological oceanography. **Disciplines with Highest Percentage of Degrees Awarded:** Social sciences and history 21%, psychology 18%, business/marketing 13%, biological life sciences 8%, interdisciplinary studies 8%. **Special Study Options:** Cross registration, distance learning, double major, dual enrollment, English as a second language, student exchange program (domestic), honors program, independent study, internships, student-designed major, study abroad, teacher certification program.

FACILITIES

Housing: Coed, apartments for married students, apartments for single students, housing for disabled students. **Library Holdings:** 266,113 bound volumes. 1,552 periodicals. 482,559 microforms. 11,909 audiovisuals. **Computers:** *Recommended operating system:* Windows 2000/NT. School-owned computers available for student use.

EXTRACURRICULARS

Activities: Choral groups, dance, drama/theater, jazz band, literary magazine, music ensembles, student government, student newspaper. **Organizations:** 43 registered organizations, 4 religious organizations. **Athletics (Intercollegiate):** *Men:* baseball, basketball, cross-country, golf, tennis. *Women:* cross-country, softball, tennis, volleyball.

ADMISSIONS

Selectivity Rating: 76 (of 100). **Freshman Academic Profile:** Average high school GPA 3.2. 21% in top 10% of high school class, 52% in top 25% of high school class, 82% in top 50% of high school class. Average SAT I Math 510, SAT I Math middle 50% range 440-580. Average SAT I Verbal 490, SAT I Verbal middle 50% range 430-550. TOEFL required of all international applicants, minimum TOEFL 500. **Basis for Candidate Selection:** *Very important factors considered include:* secondary school record, standardized test scores. *Important factors considered include:* class rank. *Other factors considered include:* essays, extracurricular activities, recommendations, talent/ability. **Freshman Admission Requirements:** High school diploma or GED is required. *Academic units required/recommended:* 17 total required; 18 total recommended; 4 English required, 4 English recommended, 3 math required, 4 math recommended, 3 science required, 4 science recommended, 3 science lab required, 3 science lab recommended, 2 foreign language recommended, 2 social studies recommended, 2 history recommended, 7 elective required. **Freshman Admission Statistics:** 1,572 applied, 59% accepted, 48% of those accepted enrolled. **Transfer Admission Requirements:** *Items required:* college transcript. Minimum high school GPA of 3.0 required. Minimum college GPA of 2.0 required. Lowest grade transferable C. **General Admission Information:** Application fee $25. Priority application deadline March 1. Regular application deadline July 1. Nonfall registration accepted. Admission may be deferred. Credit offered for CEEB Advanced Placement tests.

COSTS AND FINANCIAL AID

Required Forms and Deadlines: FAFSA, institution's own financial aid form and Institution's own financial aid form is submitted only when applicant is selected. No deadline for regular filing. Priority filing deadline March 1. **Notification of Awards:** Applicants will be notified of awards on a rolling basis beginning on or about April 12. **Types of Aid:** *Need-based scholarships/grants:* Pell, SEOG, state scholarships/grants, private scholarships, the school's own gift aid. *Loans:* FFEL Subsidized Stafford, FFEL Unsubsidized Stafford, FFEL PLUS, Federal Perkins, state loans. **Student Employment:** Federal Work-Study Program available. Institutional employment available. Off-campus job opportunities are fair. **Financial Aid Statistics:** 37% freshmen, 41% undergrads receive some form of aid. Average freshman grant $3,216. Average freshman loan $1,287. Average income from on-campus job $1,832. **Financial Aid Phone:** 808-974-7323.

UNIVERSITY OF HAWAII—MANOA

2600 Campus Road, SSC Room 001, Honolulu, HI 96822
Phone: 808-956-8975 **E-mail:** ar-info@hawaii.edu **CEEB Code:** 4867
Web: www.uhm.hawaii.edu **ACT Code:** 902

This public school was founded in 1907. It has a 320-acre campus.

STUDENTS AND FACULTY

Enrollment: 12,054. **Student Body:** Male 44%, female 56%, out-of-state 17%, international 6% (77 countries represented). **Ethnic Representation:** African American 1%, Asian 77%, Caucasian 20%, Hispanic 2%. **Retention and Graduation:** 79% freshmen return for sophomore year. 10% freshmen graduate within 4 years. **Faculty:** Student/faculty ratio 12:1. 1,043 full-time faculty, 84% hold PhDs.

ACADEMICS

Degrees: Bachelor's, doctoral, first professional, master's, post-bachelor's certificate. **Academic Requirements:** General education including some course work in arts/fine arts, English (including composition), foreign languages, history, humanities, sciences (biological or physical), social science. **Classes:** 10-19 students in an average class. 10-19 students in an average lab/discussion section. **Majors with Highest Enrollment:** Biology/biological sciences, general; psychology, general; art/art studies, general. **Disciplines with Highest Percentage of Degrees Awarded:** Business/marketing 25%, social sciences and history 10%, education 8%, biological life sciences 6%, communications/communication technologies 5%. **Special Study Options:** Accelerated program, cooperative (work-study) program, distance learning, double major, English as a second language, student exchange program (domestic), honors program, independent study, internships, student-designed major, study abroad, teacher certification program.

FACILITIES

Housing: Coed, all-female, all-male, apartments for married students, apartments for single students, housing for disabled students, housing for international students. **Library Holdings:** 1,964,814 bound volumes. 26,767 periodicals. 5,947,837 microforms. 50,365 audiovisuals. **Special Academic Facilities/Equipment:** Language lab, urban and regional planning program, environmental center, water resources research center, institute of marine biology, center on aging, biomedical research center, population genetics lab, institute of astronomy/geophysics, John Young Museum of Art. **Computers:** School-owned computers available for student use.

EXTRACURRICULARS

Activities: Choral groups, concert band, dance, drama/theater, jazz band, literary magazine, marching band, music ensembles, radio station, student government, student newspaper, student-run film society. **Organizations:** 163 registered organizations, 15 honor societies, 16 religious organizations, 3 fraternities, 5 sororities. **Athletics (Intercollegiate):** *Men:* baseball, basketball, diving, football, golf, sailing, swimming, tennis, volleyball. *Women:* basketball, cross-country, diving, golf, sailing, soccer, softball, swimming, tennis, track & field, volleyball, water polo.

ADMISSIONS

Selectivity Rating: 81 (of 100). **Freshman Academic Profile:** Average high school GPA 3.3. 23% in top 10% of high school class, 58% in top 25% of high school class, 90% in top 50% of high school class. 67% from public high schools. Average SAT I Math 563, SAT I Math middle 50% range 510-610. Average SAT I Verbal 525, SAT I Verbal middle 50% range 470-570. TOEFL required of all international applicants, minimum TOEFL 500. **Basis for Candidate Selection:** *Very important factors considered include:* secondary school record, standardized test scores. *Important factors considered include:* class rank, state residency. *Other factors considered include:* character/personal qualities, essays, extracurricular activities, geographical residence, interview, recommendations, talent/ability. **Freshman Admission Requirements:** High school diploma or GED is required. *Academic units required/recommended:* 4 English required, 3 math required, 3 science required, 2 foreign language recommended, 3 social studies required, 4 elective required. **Freshman Admission Statistics:** 4,565 applied, 71% accepted, 51% of those accepted enrolled. **Transfer Admission Requirements:** *Items required:* college transcript. Minimum high school GPA of 2.8 required. Minimum college GPA of 2.5 required. Lowest grade transferable D. **General Admission Information:** Application fee $25. Priority application deadline November 1. Regular application deadline June 1. Nonfall registration accepted. Credit and/or placement offered for CEEB Advanced Placement tests.

COSTS AND FINANCIAL AID

In-state tuition $3,216. Out-of-state tuition $9,696. Room & board $5,089. Required fees $133. Average book expense $1,017. **Required Forms and Deadlines:** FAFSA and institution's own financial aid form. Priority filing deadline March 15. **Notification of Awards:** Applicants will be notified of awards on a rolling basis beginning on or about March 26. **Types of Aid:** *Need-based scholarships/grants:* Pell, SEOG, state scholarships/grants, private scholarships, the school's own gift aid, Federal Nursing. *Loans:* FFEL Subsidized Stafford, FFEL Unsubsidized Stafford, FFEL PLUS, Federal Perkins, Federal Nursing, state loans, college/university loans from institutional funds. **Student Employment:** Federal Work-Study Program available. Institutional employment available. Off-campus job opportunities are fair. **Financial Aid Statistics:** 28% freshmen, 30% undergrads receive some form of aid. Average freshman grant $3,015. Average freshman loan $1,420. Average income from on-campus job $3,775. **Financial Aid Phone:** 808-956-7251.

UNIVERSITY OF HAWAII—WEST OAHU

96-129 Ala Ike, Pearl City, HI 96782
Phone: 808-454-4700 **E-mail:** studsr@uhwo.hawaii.edu
Fax: 808-453-6075 **Web:** www.uhwo.hawaii.edu

This public school was founded in 1976.

STUDENTS AND FACULTY

Enrollment: 834. **Student Body:** Male 30%, female 70%, out-of-state 8%. **Faculty:** Student/faculty ratio 15:1. 23 full-time faculty. 100% faculty teach undergrads.

ACADEMICS

Degrees: Bachelor's, certificate. **Academic Requirements:** General education including some course work in English (including composition), humanities, mathematics, sciences (biological or physical), social science. **Majors with Highest Enrollment:** Psychology, general; business administration/management; public administration. **Special Study Options:** Accelerated program, distance learning, double major, independent study, internships, student-designed major, weekend college.

EXTRACURRICULARS

Activities: Student government.

ADMISSIONS

Selectivity Rating: 63 (of 100). **Freshman Academic Profile:** TOEFL required of all international applicants, minimum TOEFL 550. **Freshman Admission Requirements:** High school diploma or equivalent is not required. **Transfer Admission Requirements:** *Items required:* college transcript. Minimum college GPA of 2.0 required. Lowest grade transferable D. **General Admission Information:** Application fee $10.

COSTS AND FINANCIAL AID

In-state tuition $2,112. Out-of-state tuition $7,248. Required fees $20. Average book expense $1,017. **Types of Aid:** *Need-based scholarships/grants:* Pell, SEOG, state scholarships/grants, private scholarships. *Loans:* FFEL Subsidized Stafford, FFEL Unsubsidized Stafford. **Student Employment:** Federal Work-Study Program available. Institutional employment available. **Financial Aid Phone:** 808-454-4700.

UNIVERSITY OF HOUSTON—CLEAR LAKE

2700 Bay Area Boulevard, Houston, TX 77058-1080
Phone: 281-283-7600 **E-mail:** admissions@cl.uh.edu **CEEB Code:** 6916
Fax: 281-283-2530 **Web:** www.uhcl.edu

This public school was founded in 1974.

STUDENTS AND FACULTY

Enrollment: 4,017. **Student Body:** Male 36%, female 64%, international 3%. **Ethnic Representation:** African American 8%, Asian 7%, Caucasian 70%, Hispanic 16%. **Faculty:** Student/faculty ratio 16:1. 227 full-time faculty. 72% faculty teach undergrads.

ACADEMICS

Degrees: Bachelor's, master's, post-bachelor's certificate, post-master's certificate. **Classes:** 20-29 students in an average class. **Disciplines with Highest Percentage of Degrees Awarded:** Business/marketing 29%, interdisciplinary studies 21%, liberal arts/general studies 8%, social sciences and history 7%, psychology 7%. **Special Study Options:** Cooperative (work-study) program, distance learning, double major, dual enrollment, independent study, internships, student-designed major, study abroad, teacher certification program, weekend college.

FACILITIES

Housing: Limited apartments on campus; one has 136 units. **Library Holdings:** 2,222,020 bound volumes. 984 periodicals. 1,889,865 microforms. 795 audiovisuals. **Computers:** *Recommended operating system:* Windows NT/2000. School-owned computers available for student use.

EXTRACURRICULARS

Activities: Literary magazine, student government, student newspaper. **Organizations:** 70 registered organizations, 16 honor societies, 2 religious organizations.

ADMISSIONS

Selectivity Rating: 60 (of 100). **Freshman Academic Profile:** TOEFL required of all international applicants, minimum TOEFL 550. **Freshman Admission Requirements: Transfer Admission Requirements:** *Items required:* college transcript, statement of good standing from prior school. Minimum college GPA of 2.0 required. Lowest grade transferable C. **General Admission Information:** Application fee $35. Regular application deadline March 11. Nonfall registration accepted. Admission may be deferred.

COSTS AND FINANCIAL AID

In-state tuition $2,980. Out-of-state tuition $9,250. Required fees $525. Average book expense $765. **Required Forms and Deadlines:** FAFSA and institution's own financial aid form. No deadline for regular filing. Priority filing deadline April 1. **Notification of Awards:** Applicants will be notified of awards on a rolling basis beginning on or about June 1. **Types of Aid:** *Need-based scholarships/grants:* Pell, SEOG, state scholarships/grants, the school's own gift aid. *Loans:* FFEL Subsidized Stafford, FFEL Unsubsidized Stafford, FFEL PLUS, Federal Perkins, state loans. **Student Employment:** Off-campus job opportunities are excellent. **Financial Aid Statistics:** 37% undergrads receive some form of aid. **Financial Aid Phone:** 281-283-2480.

UNIVERSITY OF HOUSTON—DOWNTOWN

Admissions Office, One Main Street, Houston, TX 77002-1001
Phone: 713-221-8522 **E-mail:** uhdadmit@dt.uh.edu
Fax: 713-221-8157 **Web:** www.uhd.edu

This public school was founded in 1974.

STUDENTS AND FACULTY

Enrollment: 10,423. **Student Body:** Male 40%, female 60%, out-of-state 4%, international 3%. **Ethnic Representation:** African American 28%, Asian 10%, Caucasian 25%, Hispanic 36%. **Retention and Graduation:** 63% freshmen return for sophomore year. **Faculty:** Student/faculty ratio 20:1. 244 full-time faculty, 78% hold PhDs.

ACADEMICS

Degrees: Bachelor's, master's. **Academic Requirements:** General education including some course work in arts/fine arts, computer literacy, English (including composition), history, humanities, mathematics, sciences (biological or physical), social science, literature, political science, speech. **Classes:** 20-29 students in an average class. 20-29 students in an average lab/discussion section. **Disciplines with Highest Percentage of Degrees Awarded:** Business/marketing 44%, liberal arts/general studies 20%, protective services/public administration 9%, interdisciplinary studies 8%, psychology 5%. **Special Study Options:** Cooperative (work-study) program, cross registration, distance learning, double major, dual enrollment, English as a second language, honors program, independent study, internships, student-designed major, study abroad, teacher certification program, weekend college.

EXTRACURRICULARS

Activities: Drama/theater, jazz band, literary magazine, student government, student newspaper. **Organizations:** 66 registered organizations, 6 honor societies, 4 religious organizations.

ADMISSIONS

Selectivity Rating: 63 (of 100). **Freshman Academic Profile:** TOEFL required of all international applicants, minimum TOEFL 550. **Freshman Admission Requirements:** High school diploma or GED is required. *Academic units required/recommended:* 24 total recommended; 4 English recommended, 3 math recommended, 3 science recommended, 2 foreign language recommended, 4 social studies recommended. **Freshman Admission Statistics:** 1,761 applied, 100% accepted, 55% of those accepted enrolled. **Transfer Admission Requirements:** *Items required:* college transcript. Lowest grade transferable C. **General Admission Information:** Application fee $10. Regular application deadline August 1. Nonfall registration accepted. Admission may be deferred.

COSTS AND FINANCIAL AID

In-state tuition $2,684. Out-of-state tuition $9,224. **Required Forms and Deadlines:** FAFSA and institution's own financial aid form. No deadline for regular filing. Priority filing deadline April 1. **Notification of Awards:** Applicants will be notified of awards on a rolling basis beginning on or about June 1. **Types of Aid:** *Need-based scholarships/grants:* Pell, SEOG, state scholarships/grants, private scholarships, the school's own gift aid. *Loans:* FFEL Subsidized Stafford, FFEL Unsubsidized Stafford, FFEL PLUS. **Student Employment:** Federal Work-Study Program available.

UNIVERSITY OF HOUSTON—HOUSTON

Office of Admissions, 122 E. Cullen Building, Houston, TX 77204-2023
Phone: 713-743-1010 **E-mail:** admissions@uh.edu **CEEB Code:** 6870
Fax: 713-743-9633 **Web:** www.uh.edu **ACT Code:** 4236

This public school was founded in 1927. It has a 557-acre campus.

STUDENTS AND FACULTY

Enrollment: 26,283. **Student Body:** Male 48%, female 52%, out-of-state 2%, international 4% (126 countries represented). **Ethnic Representation:** African American 16%, Asian 22%, Caucasian 39%, Hispanic 22%. **Retention and Graduation:** 79% freshmen return for sophomore year. 11% freshmen graduate within 4 years. **Faculty:** Student/faculty ratio 21:1. 1,052 full-time faculty, 84% hold PhDs. 45% faculty teach undergrads.

ACADEMICS

Degrees: Bachelor's, doctoral, first professional, master's. **Academic Requirements:** General education including some course work in arts/fine arts, English (including composition), history, humanities, mathematics, sciences (biological or physical), social science. **Classes:** Under 10 students in an average class. Under 10 students in an average lab/discussion section. **Majors with Highest Enrollment:** Business/commerce, general; psychology, general; engineering, general. **Disciplines with Highest Percentage of Degrees Awarded:** Business/marketing 35%, engineering/engineering technology 9%, psychology 9%, social sciences and history 7%, communications/communication technologies 6%. **Special Study Options:** Accelerated program, cooperative (work-study) program, cross registration, distance learning, double major, dual enrollment, English as a second language, student exchange program (domestic), honors program, independent study, internships, study abroad, teacher certification program, weekend college, academic enrichment programs, certification programs, affiliated studies, and continuing education.

FACILITIES

Housing: Coed, apartments for married students, apartments for single students, housing for disabled students, fraternities and/or sororities. Special housing for honors, upper-level, and graduate students.**Library Holdings:** 2,123,257 bound volumes. 20,276 periodicals. 4,023,252 microforms. 8,834 audiovisuals. **Special Academic Facilities/Equipment:** Art gallery, language lab, human development lab school, University Hilton (staffed in part by students in College of Hotel and Restaurant Management), opera studio. **Computers:** School-owned computers available for student use.

EXTRACURRICULARS

Activities: Choral groups, concert band, dance, drama/theater, jazz band, literary magazine, marching band, music ensembles, musical theater, opera, pep band, radio station, student government, student newspaper, student-run film society, symphony orchestra, television station, yearbook. **Organizations:** 300 registered organizations, 25 honor societies, 28 religious organizations, 26 fraternities (3% men join), 16 sororities (3% women join). **Athletics (Intercollegiate):** *Men:* baseball, basketball, cross-country, diving, football, golf, indoor track, swimming, tennis, track & field, volleyball, water polo. *Women:* basketball, cross-country, diving, golf, indoor track, soccer, softball, swimming, tennis, track & field, volleyball, water polo.

ADMISSIONS

Selectivity Rating: 72 (of 100). **Freshman Academic Profile:** Average high school GPA 3.1. 21% in top 10% of high school class, 46% in top 25% of high school class, 79% in top 50% of high school class. Average SAT I Math 534, SAT I Math middle 50% range 470-590. Average SAT I Verbal 508, SAT I Verbal middle 50% range 450-560. Average ACT 21, ACT middle 50% range 18-23. TOEFL required of all international applicants, minimum TOEFL 550. **Basis for Candidate Selection:** *Very important factors considered include:* class rank, secondary school record, standardized test scores. *Important factors considered include:* talent/ability. *Other factors considered include:* alumni/ae relation, essays, geographical residence, recommendations. **Freshman Admission Requirements:** High school diploma or GED is required. *Academic units required/recommended:* 4 English required, 3 math required, 2 science required, 2 science lab required, 2 foreign language recommended, 2 social studies required, 2 history required. **Freshman Admission Statistics:** 8,175 applied, 78% accepted, 54% of those accepted enrolled. **Transfer Admission Requirements:** *Items required:* college transcript. Minimum college GPA of 2.0 required. Lowest grade transferable C-. **General Admission Information:** Application fee $40. Priority application deadline January 15. Regular application deadline May 1. Nonfall registration accepted. Admission may be deferred for a maximum of 1 year. Credit and/or placement offered for CEEB Advanced Placement tests.

COSTS AND FINANCIAL AID

In-state tuition $1,320. Out-of-state tuition $7,860. Room & board $5,694. Required fees $2,028. Average book expense $900. **Required Forms and Deadlines:** FAFSA. No deadline for regular filing. Priority filing deadline April 1. **Notification of Awards:** Applicants will be notified of awards on a rolling basis beginning on or about April 1. **Types of Aid:** *Need-based scholarships/grants:* Pell, SEOG, state scholarships/grants, private scholarships, the school's own gift aid, United Negro College Fund. *Loans:* FFEL Subsidized Stafford, FFEL Unsubsidized Stafford, FFEL PLUS, Federal Perkins. **Student Employment:** Federal Work-Study Program available. Institutional employment available. Off-campus job opportunities are excellent. **Financial Aid Statistics:** 45% freshmen, 56% undergrads receive some form of aid. Average freshman grant $2,166. Average freshman loan $3,006. Average income from on-campus job $2,198. **Financial Aid Phone:** 713-743-1010.

UNIVERSITY OF HOUSTON—VICTORIA

Enrollment Management Office, UHV, Victoria, TX 77901-4450
Phone: 361-788-6222 **E-mail:** urbanom@jade.vic.uh.edu
Fax: 361-572-9377 **Web:** www.vic.uh.edu

STUDENTS AND FACULTY

Enrollment: 832. **Student Body:** Male 27%, female 73%, international students represent 3 countries. **Ethnic Representation:** African American 7%, Asian 3%, Caucasian 74%, Hispanic 17%. **Retention and Graduation:** 81% freshmen return for sophomore year. 70% freshmen graduate within 4 years. **Faculty:** Student/faculty ratio 16:1. 38 full-time faculty, 94% hold PhDs.

ACADEMICS

Degrees: Bachelor's, master's. **Academic Requirements:** General education including some course work in computer literacy, English (including composition), history, mathematics, sciences (biological or physical), social science. **Disciplines with Highest Percentage of Degrees Awarded:** Education 28%, business/marketing 21%, computer and information sciences 10%, psychology 10%, English 8%. **Special Study Options:** Distance learning, double major, independent study, internships, teacher certification program.

FACILITIES

Library Holdings: 217,692 bound volumes. 603 periodicals. 526,043 microforms. 7,608 audiovisuals. **Computers:** School-owned computers available for student use.

EXTRACURRICULARS

Activities: Student government. **Organizations:** 12 honor societies, 2 religious organizations.

ADMISSIONS

Selectivity Rating: 60 (of 100). **Freshman Academic Profile:** TOEFL required of all international applicants, minimum TOEFL 500. **Freshman Admission Requirements: Transfer Admission Requirements:** *Items required:* college transcript, standardized test scores, statement of good standing from prior school. Minimum college GPA of 2.0 required. Lowest grade transferable C.

COSTS AND FINANCIAL AID

In-state tuition $912. Out-of-state tuition $6,096. Required fees $1,104. **Student Employment:** Federal Work-Study Program available.

UNIVERSITY OF IDAHO

UI Admissions Office, PO Box 444264, Moscow, ID 83844-4264
Phone: 208-885-6326 **E-mail:** admappl@uidaho.edu **CEEB Code:** 4843
Fax: 208-885-9119 **Web:** www.its.uidaho.edu/uihome/ **ACT Code:** 928

This public school was founded in 1889. It has a 1,450-acre campus.

STUDENTS AND FACULTY

Enrollment: 9,368. **Student Body:** Male 54%, female 46%, out-of-state 19%, international 2%. **Ethnic Representation:** African American 1%, Asian 2%, Caucasian 88%, Hispanic 3%, Native American 1%. **Retention and Graduation:** 78% freshmen return for sophomore year. 16% freshmen graduate within 4 years. **Faculty:** Student/faculty ratio 19:1. 570 full-time faculty, 82% hold PhDs. 70% faculty teach undergrads.

ACADEMICS

Degrees: Bachelor's, certificate, doctoral, first professional, master's, post-master's certificate. **Academic Requirements:** General education including some course work in foreign languages, history, mathematics, philosophy, social science, communications. **Classes:** 10-19 students in an average class. 10-19 students in an average lab/discussion section. **Disciplines with Highest Percentage of Degrees Awarded:** Education 14%, business/marketing 13%, natural resources/environmental sciences 9%, engineering/engineering technology 8%, social sciences and history 7%. **Special Study Options:** Accelerated program, cooperative (work-study) program, cross registration, distance learning, double major, dual enrollment, English as a second language, student exchange program (domestic), honors program, independent study, internships, student-designed major, study abroad, teacher certification program.

FACILITIES

Housing: Coed, all-female, all-male, apartments for married students, apartments for single students, housing for disabled students, housing for international students, fraternities and/or sororities, cooperative housing. **Library Holdings:** 1,355,911 bound volumes. 14,230 periodicals. 1,465,210 microforms. 8,717 audiovisuals. **Special Academic Facilities/Equipment:** On-campus preschool, experimental forest, electron microscope. **Computers:** School-owned computers available for student use.

EXTRACURRICULARS

Activities: Choral groups, concert band, dance, drama/theater, jazz band, literary magazine, marching band, music ensembles, musical theater, opera, pep band, radio station, student government, student newspaper, student-run film society, symphony orchestra, television station, yearbook. **Organizations:** 130 registered organizations, 1 religious organization, 18 fraternities, 8 sororities.

ADMISSIONS

Selectivity Rating: 74 (of 100). **Freshman Academic Profile:** Average high school GPA 3.4. 18% in top 10% of high school class, 45% in top 25% of high school class, 76% in top 50% of high school class. Average SAT I Math 559. Average SAT I Verbal 549. Average ACT 23. **Basis for Candidate Selection:** *Very important factors considered include:* secondary school record, standardized test scores. **Freshman Admission Requirements:** High school diploma or GED is required. *Academic units required/recommended:* 15 total required; 4 English required, 3 math required, 3 science required, 1 science lab required, 1 foreign language required, 3 social studies required, 2 elective required. **Freshman Admission Statistics:** 3,936 applied, 82% accepted, 53% of those accepted enrolled. **Transfer Admission Requirements:** *Items required:* high school transcript, college transcript. Lowest grade transferable D. **General Admission Information:** Application fee $40. Priority application deadline August 1. Nonfall registration accepted. Admission may be deferred for a maximum of 2 years.

COSTS AND FINANCIAL AID

In-state tuition $0. Out-of-state tuition $6,720. Room & board $6,550. Required fees $3,044. Average book expense $1,188. **Required Forms and Deadline:** FAFSA. No deadline for regular filing. Priority filing deadline February 15. **Notification of Awards:** Applicants will be notified of awards on or about March 28. **Types of Aid:** *Need-based scholarships/grants:* Pell, SEOG, state scholarships/grants, private scholarships, school's own gift aid. *Loans:* Direct Subsidized Stafford, Direct Unsubsidized Stafford, Direct PLUS, Federal Perkins, college loans from institutional funds. **Student Employment:** Federal Work-Study Program available. Institutional employment available. Off-campus job opportunities are good. **Financial Aid Statistics:** 59% freshmen, 54% undergrads receive some form of aid. **Financial Aid Phone:** 208-885-6312.

UNIVERSITY OF ILLINOIS—CHICAGO

Box 5220, Chicago, IL 60680
Phone: 312-996-4350 **E-mail:** uicadmit@uic.edu **CEEB Code:** 1851
Fax: 312-413-7628 **Web:** www.uic.edu **ACT Code:** 1155

This public school was founded in 1982. It has a 218-acre campus.

STUDENTS AND FACULTY

Enrollment: 15,887. **Student Body:** Male 45%, female 55%, out-of-state 2%, international 2% (87 countries represented). **Ethnic Representation:** African American 10%, Asian 24%, Caucasian 45%, Hispanic 17%. **Retention and Graduation:** 79% freshmen return for sophomore year. 9% freshmen graduate within 4 years. **Faculty:** Student/faculty ratio 14:1. 1,249 full-time faculty, 87% hold PhDs. 82% faculty teach undergrads.

ACADEMICS

Degrees: Bachelor's, doctoral, first professional, first professional certificate, master's. **Academic Requirements:** General education including some course work in English (including composition), humanities, sciences (biological or physical), social science. **Classes:** 20-29 students in an average class. 20-29 students in an average lab/discussion section. **Majors with Highest Enrollment:** Information science/studies; biology/biological sciences, general; psychology, general. **Disciplines with Highest Percentage of Degrees Awarded:** Business/marketing 21%, engineering/engineering technology 11%, psychology 11%, health professions and related sciences 9%, biological life sciences 8%. **Special Study Options:** Accelerated program, cooperative (work-study) program, distance learning, double major, English as a second language, student exchange program (domestic), honors program, independent study, internships, student-designed major, study abroad, teacher certification program, concurrent registration at another campus of the university of Illinois.

FACILITIES

Housing: Coed, apartments for single students, honors floor, special-interest floors, Presidential Award House. **Library Holdings:** 2,022,611 bound volumes. 16,234 periodicals. 3,423,008 microforms. 28,066 audiovisuals. **Special Academic Facilities/Equipment:** Art galleries, multimedia lecture centers, Jane Addams's Hull House Museum, James Woodworth Prairie Preserve, convention/sports/entertainment center, laboratory facilities. **Computers:** School-owned computers available for student use.

EXTRACURRICULARS

Activities: Choral groups, concert band, dance, drama/theater, jazz band, literary magazine, music ensembles, musical theater, pep band, radio station, student government, student newspaper. **Organizations:** 200 registered organizations, 11 fraternities (3% men join), 13 sororities (3% women join). **Athletics (Intercollegiate):** *Men:* baseball, basketball, cross-country, diving, gymnastics, soccer, swimming, tennis, track & field. *Women:* basketball, cross-country, diving, gymnastics, softball, swimming, tennis, track & field, volleyball.

ADMISSIONS

Selectivity Rating: 78 (of 100). **Freshman Academic Profile:** 24% in top 10% of high school class, 60% in top 25% of high school class, 93% in top 50% of high school class. 79% from public high schools. Average ACT 23, ACT middle 50% range 21-26. TOEFL required of all international applicants, minimum TOEFL 520. **Basis for Candidate Selection:** *Very important factors considered include:* class rank, secondary school record, standardized test scores. *Other factors considered include:* character/personal qualities, essays, minority status, recommendations, talent/ability, volunteer work, work experience. **Freshman Admission Requirements:** High school diploma or GED is required. *Academic units required/recommended:* 16 total required; 4 English required, 3 math required, 3 math recommended, 3 science required, 3 science lab required, 4 foreign language recommended, 2 social studies required, 1 history required, 3 elective required. **Freshman Admission Statistics:** 9,512 applied, 64% accepted, 45% of those accepted enrolled. **Transfer Admission Requirements:** *Items required:* college transcript, statement of good standing from prior school. Minimum college GPA of 2.2 required. Lowest grade transferable D. **General Admission Information:** Application fee $40. Priority application deadline February 28. Regular application deadline May 1. Nonfall registration accepted. Credit and/or placement offered for CEEB Advanced Placement tests.

COSTS AND FINANCIAL AID

In-state tuition $3,330. Out-of-state tuition $9,990. Room & board $6,206. Required fees $1,614. Average book expense $850. **Required Forms and Deadlines:** FAFSA. No deadline for regular filing. Priority filing deadline March 1. **Notification of Awards:** Applicants will be notified of awards on a rolling basis beginning on or about April 15. **Types of Aid:** *Need-based scholarships/grants:* Pell, SEOG, state scholarships/grants, private scholarships, the school's own gift aid, Federal Nursing. *Loans:* Direct Subsidized Stafford, Direct Unsubsidized Stafford, Direct PLUS, Federal Perkins, Federal Nursing, college/university loans from institutional funds. **Student Employment:** Federal Work-Study Program available. Institutional employment available. Off-campus job opportunities are excellent. **Financial Aid Statistics:** 47% freshmen, 51% undergrads receive some form of aid. Average freshman grant $9,000. Average freshman loan $2,600. Average income from on-campus job $2,200. **Financial Aid Phone:** 312-996-5563.

UNIVERSITY OF ILLINOIS—SPRINGFIELD

PO Box 19243, Springfield, IL 62794-9243
Phone: 217-206-6626 **E-mail:** admissions@uis.edu
Fax: 217-786-6620 **Web:** www.uis.edu

This public school was founded in 1969. It has a 746-acre campus.

STUDENTS AND FACULTY

Enrollment: 2,445. **Student Body:** Male 38%, female 62%, out-of-state 1%, international 1%. **Ethnic Representation:** African American 8%, Asian 2%, Caucasian 88%, Hispanic 2%. **Faculty:** Student/faculty ratio 15:1. 170 full-time faculty, 100% hold PhDs. 100% faculty teach undergrads.

ACADEMICS

Degrees: Bachelor's, certificate, doctoral, master's, post-bachelor's certificate. **Academic Requirements:** General education including some course work in English (including composition), history, humanities, mathematics, sciences (biological or physical), social science. **Majors with Highest Enrollment:** Business administration/management; psychology, general; liberal arts and sciences/liberal studies. **Disciplines with Highest Percentage of Degrees Awarded:** Business/marketing 34%, other 15%, psychology 12%, communications/communication technologies 8%, protective services/public administration 6%. **Special Study Options:** Distance learning, double major, student exchange program (domestic), external degree program, independent study, liberal arts/career combination, teacher certification program, weekend college.

FACILITIES

Housing: Coed, apartments for married students, apartments for single students, housing for international students. **Library Holdings:** 521,389 bound volumes. 2,014 periodicals. 1,840,667 microforms. 40,171 audiovisuals. **Special Academic Facilities/Equipment:** Norris L. Brookens Library, Sangamon Auditorium, Observatory. **Computers:** *Recommended operating system:* Windows NT/2000. School-owned computers available for student use.

EXTRACURRICULARS

Activities: Choral groups, radio station, student government, student newspaper, television station. **Organizations:** 4 religious organizations. **Athletics (Intercollegiate):** *Men:* basketball, soccer, tennis. *Women:* basketball, tennis, volleyball.

ADMISSIONS

Selectivity Rating: 63 (of 100). **Freshman Academic Profile:** TOEFL required of all international applicants, minimum TOEFL 500. **Basis for Candidate Selection:** *Other factors considered include:* class rank, essays, interview, recommendations, secondary school record, standardized test scores. **Freshman Admission Requirements:** High school diploma or GED is required. *Academic units required/recommended:* 15 total required; 4 English required, 3 math required, 3 science required, 2 foreign language required, 3 social studies required. **Freshman Admission Statistics:** 316 applied, 65% accepted, 57% of those accepted enrolled. **Transfer Admission Requirements:** Minimum college GPA of 2.5 required. Lowest grade transferable C.

COSTS AND FINANCIAL AID

Room & board $6,075. Average book expense $900. **Required Forms and Deadlines:** FAFSA and institution's own financial aid form. Financial aid filing deadline November 15. Priority filing deadline April 1. **Notification of Awards:** Applicants will be notified of awards on a rolling basis beginning on or about January 1. **Types of Aid:** *Need-based scholarships/grants:* Pell, SEOG, state scholarships/grants, private scholarships, the school's own gift aid. *Loans:* FFEL Subsidized Stafford, FFEL Unsubsidized Stafford, FFEL PLUS, Federal Perkins, college/university loans from institutional funds. **Student Employment:** Federal Work-Study Program available. Off-campus job opportunities are excellent. **Financial Aid Statistics:** 40% freshmen, 46% undergrads receive some form of aid. Average freshman grant $100. Average freshman loan $100. **Financial Aid Phone:** 217-206-6724.

UNIVERSITY OF ILLINOIS— URBANA-CHAMPAIGN

901 West Illinois Street, Urbana, IL 61801
Phone: 217-333-0302 **E-mail:** admissions@oar.uiuc.edu **CEEB Code:** 4607
Fax: 217-333-9758 **Web:** www.uiuc.edu **ACT Code:** 1154

This public school was founded in 1867. It has a 1,472-acre campus.

STUDENTS AND FACULTY

Enrollment: 28,750. **Student Body:** Male 52%, female 48%, out-of-state 7%, international 2% (51 countries represented). **Ethnic Representation:** African American 7%, Asian 14%, Caucasian 72%, Hispanic 6%. **Retention and Graduation:** 93% freshmen return for sophomore year. 52% freshmen graduate within 4 years. 34% grads go on to further study within 1 year. 12% grads pursue law degrees. 6% grads pursue medical degrees. **Faculty:** Student/faculty ratio 15:1. 2,240 full-time faculty, 89% hold PhDs. 89% faculty teach undergrads.

ACADEMICS

Degrees: Bachelor's, doctoral, first professional, master's. **Academic Requirements:** General education including some course work in English (including composition), humanities, mathematics, philosophy, sciences (biological or physical), cultural studies. **Classes:** 20-29 students in an average class. 20-29 students in an average lab/discussion section. **Majors with Highest Enrollment:** Biology/biological sciences, general; psychology, general. **Disciplines with Highest Percentage of Degrees Awarded:** Engineering/engineering technology 17%, business/marketing 17%, social sciences and history 11%, biological life sciences 7%, English 7%. **Special Study Options:** Accelerated program, cooperative (work-study) program, cross registration, distance learning, double major, dual enrollment, English as a second language, honors program, independent study, internships, liberal arts/career combination, student-designed major, study abroad, teacher certification program.

FACILITIES

Housing: Coed, all-female, all-male, apartments for married students, housing for disabled students, fraternities and/or sororities, cooperative housing. **Library Holdings:** 9,647,652 bound volumes. 91,054 periodicals. 8,976,026 microforms. 159,365 audiovisuals. **Special Academic Facilities/Equipment:** Art and natural history museums, performing arts center, National Center for Supercomputing Applications. **Computers:** School-owned computers available for student use.

EXTRACURRICULARS

Activities: Choral groups, concert band, dance, drama/theater, jazz band, literary magazine, marching band, music ensembles, musical theater, opera, pep band, radio station, student government, student newspaper, student-run film society, symphony orchestra, television station, yearbook. **Organizations:** 850 registered organizations, 50 honor societies, 55 fraternities (17% men join), 30 sororities (22% women join). **Athletics (Intercollegiate):** *Men:* baseball, basketball, cheerleading, cross-country, football, golf, gymnastics, tennis, track & field, wrestling. *Women:* basketball, cheerleading, cross-country, diving, golf, gymnastics, soccer, softball, swimming, tennis, track & field, volleyball.

ADMISSIONS

Selectivity Rating: 85 (of 100). **Freshman Academic Profile:** 55% in top 10% of high school class, 86% in top 25% of high school class, 99% in top 50% of high school class. Average SAT I Math 660, SAT I Math middle 50% range 600-720. Average SAT I Verbal 613, SAT I Verbal middle 50% range 550-670. Average ACT 27, ACT middle 50% range 25-30. TOEFL required of all international applicants, minimum TOEFL 550. **Basis for Candidate Selection:** *Very important factors considered include:* class rank, secondary school record, standardized test scores. *Important factors considered include:* essays, minority status, talent/ability. *Other factors considered include:* character/personal qualities, extracurricular activities, geographical residence, recommendations, state residency, volunteer work, work experience. **Freshman Admission Requirements:** High school diploma or GED is required. *Academic units required/recommended:* 4 English required, 3 math required, 2 science required, 2 science lab required, 2 foreign language required, 2 social studies required, 2 elective required. **Freshman Admission Statistics:** 19,930 applied, 62% accepted, 51% of those accepted enrolled. **Transfer Admission Requirements:** *Items required:* high school transcript, college transcript. Minimum college GPA of 2.3 required. Lowest grade transferable D. **General Admission Information:** Application fee $40. Regular application deadline January 1. Nonfall registration accepted. Admission may be deferred for a maximum of 1 year. Credit and/or placement offered for CEEB Advanced Placement tests.

COSTS AND FINANCIAL AID

In-state tuition $5,226. Out-of-state tuition $13,046. Room & board $6,090. Required fees $1,304. Average book expense $740. **Required Forms and Deadlines:** FAFSA. Financial aid filing deadline March 15. Priority filing deadline March 15. **Notification of Awards:** Applicants will be notified of awards on or about April 1. **Types of Aid:** *Need-based scholarships/grants:* Pell, SEOG, state scholarships/grants, private scholarships, the school's own gift aid. *Loans:* Direct Subsidized Stafford, Direct Unsubsidized Stafford, Direct PLUS, Federal Perkins, college/university loans from institutional funds. **Student Employment:** Federal Work-Study Program available. Institutional employment available. Off-campus job opportunities are excellent. **Financial Aid Statistics:** 40% freshmen, 38% undergrads receive some form of aid. **Financial Aid Phone:** 217-333-0100.

UNIVERSITY OF INDIANAPOLIS

1400 East Hanna Avenue, Indianapolis, IN 46227-3697
Phone: 317-788-3216 **E-mail:** admissions@uindy.edu **CEEB Code:** 1321
Fax: 317-788-3300 **Web:** admissions.uindy.edu **ACT Code:** 1204

This private school, which is affiliated with the Methodist Church, was founded in 1902. It has a 65-acre campus.

STUDENTS AND FACULTY

Enrollment: 2,868. **Student Body:** Male 33%, female 67%, out-of-state 8%, international 4% (60 countries represented). **Ethnic Representation:** African American 10%, Asian 1%, Caucasian 81%, Hispanic 1%. **Retention and Graduation:** 72% freshmen return for sophomore year. 47% freshmen graduate within 4 years. 25% grads go on to further study within 1 year. **Faculty:** Student/faculty ratio 14:1. 160 full-time faculty, 75% hold PhDs. 100% faculty teach undergrads.

ACADEMICS

Degrees: Associate's, bachelor's, doctoral, master's. **Academic Requirements:** General education including some course work in arts/fine arts, computer literacy, English (including composition), foreign languages, history, humanities, mathematics, philosophy, sciences (biological or physical), social science, wellness. **Classes:** Under 10 students in an average class. Under 10 students in an average lab/discussion section. **Majors with Highest Enrollment:** Nursing/registered nurse training (RN, ASN, BSN, MSN); business administration/management; education, general. **Disciplines with Highest Percentage of Degrees Awarded:** Business/marketing 25%, education 17%, biological life sciences 9%, health professions and related sciences 8%, psychology 7%. **Special Study Options:** Accelerated program, cross registration, distance learning, double major, dual enrollment, English as a second language, honors program, independent study, internships, student-designed major, study abroad, teacher certification program.

FACILITIES

Housing: Coed, all-female, apartments for married students, apartments for single students. **Library Holdings:** 173,363 bound volumes. 1,015 periodicals. 15,551 microforms. 5,324 audiovisuals. **Special Academic Facilities/Equipment:** Developmental preschool, art gallery, observatory. **Computers:** School-owned computers available for student use.

EXTRACURRICULARS

Activities: Choral groups, concert band, dance, drama/theater, jazz band, literary magazine, music ensembles, musical theater, pep band, radio station, student government, student newspaper, yearbook. **Organizations:** 60 registered organizations, 8 honor societies, 3 religious organizations. **Athletics (Intercollegiate):** *Men:* baseball, basketball, cross-country, football, golf, soccer, swimming, tennis, track & field, wrestling. *Women:* basketball, cross-country, golf, soccer, softball, swimming, tennis, track & field, volleyball.

ADMISSIONS

Selectivity Rating: 70 (of 100). **Freshman Academic Profile:** Average high school GPA 3.1. 21% in top 10% of high school class, 51% in top 25% of high school class, 84% in top 50% of high school class. Average SAT I Math 512, SAT I Math middle 50% range 450-560. Average SAT I Verbal 503, SAT I Verbal middle 50% range 450-550. ACT middle 50% range 19-24. TOEFL required of all international applicants, minimum TOEFL 500. **Basis for Candidate Selection:** *Very important factors considered include:* secondary school record. *Important factors considered include:* class rank, standardized test scores. *Other factors considered include:* extracurricular activities, interview, recommendations. **Freshman Admission Requirements:** High school diploma or GED is required. *Academic units required/recommended:* 15 total recommended; 4 English recommended, 3 math recommended, 3 science recommended, 2 science lab recommended, 2 foreign language recommended, 3 social studies recommended. **Freshman Admission Statistics:** 2,194 applied, 80% accepted, 32% of those accepted enrolled. **Transfer Admission Requirements:** *Items required:* high school transcript, college transcript, standardized test scores, statement of good standing from prior school. Minimum college GPA of 2.0 required. Lowest grade transferable C-. **General Admission Information:** Application fee $20. Nonfall registration accepted. Admission may be deferred for a maximum of 1 year. Credit offered for CEEB Advanced Placement tests.

COSTS AND FINANCIAL AID

Average book expense $600. **Required Forms and Deadlines:** FAFSA and institution's own financial aid form. No deadline for regular filing. Priority filing deadline March 1. **Notification of Awards:** Applicants will be notified of awards on a rolling basis beginning on or about March 1. **Types of Aid:** *Need-based scholarships/grants:* Pell, SEOG, state scholarships/grants, private scholarships, the school's own gift aid. *Loans:* FFEL Subsidized Stafford, FFEL Unsubsidized Stafford, FFEL PLUS, Federal Perkins. **Student Employment:** Federal Work-Study Program available. Institutional employment available. Off-campus job opportunities are excellent. **Financial Aid Statistics:** 80% freshmen, 72% undergrads receive some form of aid. Average freshman grant $7,353. Average freshman loan $2,233. Average income from on-campus job $746. **Financial Aid Phone:** 317-788-3217.

UNIVERSITY OF IOWA

107 Calvin Hall, Iowa City, IA 52242
Phone: 319-335-3847 **E-mail:** admissions@uiowa.edu **CEEB Code:** 6681
Fax: 319-333-1535 **Web:** www.uiowa.edu **ACT Code:** 1356

This public school was founded in 1847. It has a 1,900-acre campus.

STUDENTS AND FACULTY

Enrollment: 20,487. **Student Body:** Male 45%, female 55%, out-of-state 33%, international 1% (122 countries represented). **Ethnic Representation:** African American 2%, Asian 3%, Caucasian 88%, Hispanic 2%. **Retention and Graduation:** 83% freshmen return for sophomore year. 38% freshmen graduate within 4 years. **Faculty:** Student/faculty ratio 15:1. 1,595 full-time faculty, 96% hold PhDs. 100% faculty teach undergrads.

ACADEMICS

Degrees: Bachelor's, certificate, doctoral, first professional, first professional certificate, master's, post-master's certificate. **Academic Requirements:** General education including some course work in English (including composition), foreign languages, history, humanities, mathematics, sciences (biological or physical), social science. **Classes:** 10-19 students in an average class. 20-29 students in an average lab/discussion section. **Majors with Highest Enrollment:** Business administration/management; communications studies/speech communication and rhetoric; psychology, general. **Disciplines with Highest Percentage of Degrees Awarded:** Business/marketing 21%, social sciences and history 13%, communications/communication technologies 10%, English 8%, visual and performing arts 7%. **Special Study Options:** Accelerated program, cooperative (work-study) program, distance learning, double major, dual enrollment, English as a second language, student exchange program (domestic), external degree program, honors program, independent study, internships, liberal arts/career combination, student-designed major, study abroad, teacher certification program.

FACILITIES

Housing: Coed, apartments for married students, apartments for single students, housing for disabled students, fraternities and/or sororities, quiet houses. Learning Communities for the following students: honors; health sciences; performing arts; business and entrepreneurship; women in science and engineering; men in engineering; students with international interests. **Library Holdings:** 4,027,546 bound volumes. 44,644 periodicals. 6,640,879 microforms. 267,192 audiovisuals. **Special Academic Facilities/Equipment:** Art and natural history museums, information arcade, newspaper production lab, TV lab, survey research facilities, electron microscope, laser facility, Oakdale Research Park, National Advanced Driving Simulator. **Computers:** School-owned computers available for student use.

EXTRACURRICULARS

Activities: Choral groups, concert band, dance, drama/theater, jazz band, literary magazine, marching band, music ensembles, musical theater, opera, pep band, radio station, student government, student newspaper, student-run film society, symphony orchestra. **Organizations:** 362 registered organizations, 21 honor societies, 23 fraternities (12% men join), 17 sororities (13% women join). **Athletics (Intercollegiate):** *Men:* baseball, basketball, cheerleading, cross-country, diving, football, golf, gymnastics, indoor track, swimming, tennis, track & field, wrestling. *Women:* basketball, cheerleading, crew, cross-country, diving, field hockey, golf, gymnastics, indoor track, soccer, softball, swimming, tennis, track & field, volleyball.

ADMISSIONS

Selectivity Rating: 80 (of 100). **Freshman Academic Profile:** Average high school GPA 3.5. 21% in top 10% of high school class, 50% in top 25% of high school class, 89% in top 50% of high school class. 89% from public high schools. SAT I Math middle 50% range 540-670. SAT I Verbal middle 50% range 520-650. ACT middle 50% range 22-27. TOEFL required of all international applicants, minimum TOEFL 530. **Basis for Candidate Selection:** *Very important factors considered include:* class rank, secondary school record, standardized test scores. *Other factors considered include:* alumni/ae relation, minority status, state residency, talent/ability. **Freshman Admission Requirements:** High school diploma or GED is required. *Academic units required/recommended:* 15 total required; 4 English required, 3 math required, 3 science required, 2 foreign language required, 4 foreign language recommended, 3 social studies required. **Freshman Admission Statistics:** 13,079 applied, 84% accepted, 38% of those accepted enrolled. **Transfer Admission Requirements:** *Items required:* high school transcript, college transcript. Minimum college GPA of 2.3 required. Lowest grade transferable D. **General Admission Information:** Application fee $30. Regular application deadline April 1. Priority deadline February 1. Nonfall registration accepted. Admission may be deferred for a maximum of 1 year. Credit and/or placement offered for CEEB Advanced Placement tests.

COSTS AND FINANCIAL AID

In-state tuition $4,342. Out-of-state tuition $14,634. Room & board $5,930. Required fees $651. Average book expense $840. **Required Forms and Deadlines:** FAFSA and institution's own financial aid form. No deadline for regular filing. Priority filing deadline January 1. **Notification of Awards:** Applicants will be notified of awards on a rolling basis beginning on or about March 1. **Types of Aid:** *Need-based scholarships/grants:* Pell, SEOG, state scholarships/grants, private scholarships, the school's own gift aid, Federal Nursing. *Loans:* Direct Subsidized Stafford, Direct Unsubsidized Stafford, Direct PLUS, Federal Perkins, Federal Nursing, college/university loans from institutional funds. **Student Employment:** Federal Work-Study Program available. Institutional employment available. Off-campus job opportunities are excellent. **Financial Aid Statistics:** 38% freshmen, 42% undergrads receive some form of aid. Average freshman grant $1,650. Average freshman loan $2,250. Average income from on-campus job $2,000. **Financial Aid Phone:** 319-335-1450.

UNIVERSITY OF JUDAISM

 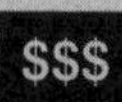 

15600 Mulholland Drive, Bel Air, CA 90077
Phone: 310-476-9777 **E-mail:** admissions@uj.edu **CEEB Code:** 2741
Fax: 310-471-3657 **Web:** www.uj.edu **ACT Code:** 462

This private school, which is affiliated with the Jewish faith, was founded in 1947. It has a 28-acre campus.

STUDENTS AND FACULTY

Enrollment: 155. **Student Body:** Male 41%, female 59%, out-of-state 45%, international 5% (5 countries represented). **Ethnic Representation:** African American 5%, Asian 1%, Caucasian 80%, Hispanic 13%. **Retention and Graduation:** 70% freshmen return for sophomore year. 55% freshmen graduate within 4 years. **Faculty:** Student/faculty ratio 7:1. 19 full-time faculty, 84% hold PhDs. 25% faculty teach undergrads.

ACADEMICS

Degrees: Bachelor's, master's. **Academic Requirements:** General education including some course work in arts/fine arts, computer literacy, English (including composition), foreign languages, history, humanities, mathematics, sciences (biological or physical), social science, Jewish and western civilization, world cultures. **Classes:** 10-19 students in an average class. **Majors with Highest Enrollment:** Area studies; biological and biomedical sciences; psychology, general. **Disciplines with Highest Percentage of Degrees Awarded:** Business/marketing 4%, area and ethnic studies 4%, liberal arts/general studies 3%, social sciences and history 2%, psychology 2%. **Special Study Options:** Accelerated program, cross registration, double major, honors program, independent study, internships, student-designed major, study abroad.

FACILITIES

Housing: Coed, apartments for married students, apartments for single students. **Library Holdings:** 105,000 bound volumes. 400 periodicals. **Computers:** *Recommended operating system:* Windows NT/2000. School-owned computers available for student use.

EXTRACURRICULARS

Activities: Choral groups, drama/theater, literary magazine, radio station, student government, student newspaper, yearbook.

ADMISSIONS

Selectivity Rating: 78 (of 100). **Freshman Academic Profile:** Average high school GPA 3.1. 21% in top 10% of high school class, 14% in top 25% of high school class, 58% in top 50% of high school class. 70% from public high schools. Average SAT I Math 600, SAT I Math middle 50% range 510-650. Average SAT I Verbal 600, SAT I Verbal middle 50% range 550-600. Average ACT 26. TOEFL required of all international applicants, minimum TOEFL 550. **Basis for Candidate Selection:** *Very important factors considered include:* essays, extracurricular activities, recommendations, secondary school record. *Important factors considered include:* character/personal qualities, class rank, interview, standardized test scores, volunteer work. *Other factors considered include:* talent/ability. **Freshman Admission Requirements:** High school diploma or GED is required. *Academic units required/recommended:* 18 total recommended; 4 English recommended, 3 math recommended, 3 science recommended, 2 science lab recommended, 2 foreign language recommended, 2 social studies recommended, 2 history recommended. **Freshman Admission Statistics:** 109 applied, 73% accepted, 46% of those accepted enrolled. **Transfer Admission Requirements:** *Items required:* high school transcript, college transcript, essay. Minimum high school GPA of 3.0 required. Minimum college GPA of 3.0 required. Lowest grade transferable C. **General Admission Information:** Application fee $35. Priority application deadline January 31. Early decision application deadline November 15. Nonfall registration accepted. Admission may be deferred for a maximum of 1 year. Credit offered for CEEB Advanced Placement tests.

COSTS AND FINANCIAL AID

Tuition $16,000. Room & board $9,100. Required fees $590. Average book expense $650. **Required Forms and Deadlines:** FAFSA, institution's own financial aid form and state aid form. No deadline for regular filing. Priority filing deadline March 2. **Notification of Awards:** Applicants will be notified of awards on a rolling basis. **Types of Aid:** *Need-based scholarships/grants:* Pell, state scholarships/grants, private scholarships, the school's own gift aid. *Loans:* FFEL Subsidized Stafford, FFEL Unsubsidized Stafford, FFEL PLUS. **Student Employment:** Federal Work-Study Program available. Institutional employment available. Off-campus job opportunities are good. **Financial Aid Statistics:** 74% freshmen, 73% undergrads receive some form of aid. Average freshman grant $12,448. Average freshman loan $5,433. Average income from on-campus job $1,700. **Financial Aid Phone:** 310-476-9777.

UNIVERSITY OF KANSAS

Office of Admissions and Scholarships, 1502 Iowa Street, Lawrence, KS 66045
Phone: 785-864-3911 **E-mail:** adm@ku.edu **CEEB Code:** 6871
Fax: 785-864-5017 **Web:** www.ku.edu **ACT Code:** 1470

This public school was founded in 1866. It has a 1,000-acre campus.

STUDENTS AND FACULTY

Enrollment: 20,605. **Student Body:** Male 48%, female 52%, out-of-state 24%, international 3% (118 countries represented). **Ethnic Representation:** African American 3%, Asian 4%, Caucasian 88%, Hispanic 3%, Native American 1%. **Retention and Graduation:** 81% freshmen return for sophomore year. 26% freshmen graduate within 4 years. 19% grads go on to further study within 1 year. **Faculty:** Student/faculty ratio 19:1. 1,194 full-time faculty, 91% hold PhDs. 100% faculty teach undergrads.

ACADEMICS

Degrees: Bachelor's, doctoral, first professional, first professional certificate, master's, post-master's certificate. **Academic Requirements:** General education including some course work in English (including composition), foreign languages, humanities, mathematics, sciences (biological or physical), social science, oral communication/logic, western civilization, nonwestern civilization. **Classes:** 20-29 students in an average class. 10-19 students in an average lab/discussion section. **Majors with Highest Enrollment:** Biology/biological sciences, general; psychology, general; business administration/management. **Disciplines with Highest Percentage of Degrees Awarded:** Business/marketing 11%, health professions and related sciences 11%, English 10%, communications/communication technologies 9%, social sciences and history 9%. **Special Study Options:** Accelerated program, cooperative (work-study) program, distance learning, double major, dual enrollment, English as a second language, honors program, independent study, internships, study abroad, teacher certification program, off-campus study in Washington DC.

FACILITIES

Housing: Coed, all-female, apartments for married students, apartments for single students, fraternities and/or sororities, cooperative housing. **Library Holdings:** 4,623,079 bound volumes. 33,874 periodicals. 3,489,807 microforms. 51,153 audiovisuals. **Special Academic Facilities/Equipment:** Performing arts center, museums of art, anthropology, classical, entomology, invertebrate paleontology, and natural history, film studio, 464-bed hospital for clinical learning, herbarium, space technology center, observatory, laser lab, organ recital hall, Robert J. Dole Institute for Politics, Center for International Business, 12 libraries, Institute for Life Span Studies, information and telecommunication technology center, student operated radio and television stations, flight research lab. **Computers:** School-owned computers available for student use.

EXTRACURRICULARS

Activities: Choral groups, concert band, dance, drama/theater, jazz band, literary magazine, marching band, music ensembles, musical theater, opera, pep band, radio station, student government, student newspaper, symphony orchestra, television station, yearbook. **Organizations:** 367 registered organizations, 16 honor societies, 37 religious organizations, 26 fraternities (15% men join), 20 sororities (18% women join). **Athletics (Intercollegiate):** *Men:* baseball, basketball, cross-country, football, golf, indoor track, track & field. *Women:* basketball, crew, cross-country, diving, golf, indoor track, soccer, softball, swimming, tennis, track & field, volleyball.

ADMISSIONS

Selectivity Rating: 81 (of 100). **Freshman Academic Profile:** Average high school GPA 3.4. 28% in top 10% of high school class, 56% in top 25% of high school class, 87% in top 50% of high school class. Average ACT 24, ACT middle 50% range 21-27. **Basis for Candidate Selection:** *Very important factors considered include:* class rank, secondary school record, standardized test scores. *Important factors considered include:* geographical residence, state residency. *Other factors considered include:* alumni/ae relation, character/personal qualities, essays, extracurricular activities, minority status, recommendations, talent/ability, volunteer work, work experience. **Freshman Admission Requirements:** High school diploma or GED is required. *Academic units required/recommended:* 14 total required; 17 total recommended; 4 English required, 4 English recommended, 3 math required, 4 math recommended, 3 science required, 3 science recommended, 1 science lab required, 1 science lab recommended, 2 foreign language recommended, 3 social studies required, 3 social studies recommended. **Freshman Admission Statistics:** 9,573 applied, 67% accepted, 63% of those accepted enrolled. **Transfer Admission Requirements:** *Items required:* college transcript. Minimum high school GPA of 2.5 required. Minimum college GPA of 2.5 required. Lowest grade transferable C. **General Admission Information:** Application fee $25. Priority application deadline January 15. Regular application deadline April 1. Nonfall registration accepted. Admission may be deferred. Credit and/or placement offered for CEEB Advanced Placement tests.

COSTS AND FINANCIAL AID

In-state tuition $2,921. Out-of-state tuition $10,124. Room & board $4,642. Required fees $563. Average book expense $750. **Required Forms and Deadlines:** FAFSA. Financial aid filing deadline March 1. **Notification of Awards:** Applicants will be notified of awards on a rolling basis beginning on or about April 1. **Types of Aid:** *Need-based scholarships/grants:* Pell, SEOG, state scholarships/grants, private scholarships, the school's own gift aid. *Loans:* Direct Subsidized Stafford, Direct Unsubsidized Stafford, Direct PLUS, Federal Perkins, college/university loans from institutional funds. **Student Employment:** Federal Work-Study Program available. Institutional employment available. Off-campus job opportunities are excellent. **Financial Aid Statistics:** 32% freshmen, 34% undergrads receive some form of aid. Average freshman grant $3,777. Average freshman loan $2,502. Average income from on-campus job $3,300. **Financial Aid Phone:** 785-864-4700.

UNIVERSITY OF KENTUCKY

100 Funkhouser Building, Lexington, KY 40506
Phone: 859-257-2000 **E-mail:** admission@uky.edu **CEEB Code:** 1837
Fax: 859-257-3823 **Web:** www.uky.edu **ACT Code:** 1554

This public school was founded in 1865. It has a 687-acre campus.

STUDENTS AND FACULTY

Enrollment: 17,830. **Student Body:** Male 48%, female 52%, out-of-state 14%, international 1% (113 countries represented). **Ethnic Representation:** African American 5%, Asian 2%, Caucasian 91%, Hispanic 1%. **Retention and Graduation:** 79% freshmen return for sophomore year. 27% freshmen graduate within 4 years. **Faculty:** Student/faculty ratio 16:1. 1,202 full-time faculty, 86% hold PhDs. 76% faculty teach undergrads.

ACADEMICS

Degrees: Bachelor's, doctoral, first professional, master's, post-bachelor's certificate, post-master's certificate. **Academic Requirements:** General education including some course work in English (including composition), foreign languages, history, humanities, mathematics, sciences (biological or physical), social science. **Classes:** 20-29 students in an average class. **Disciplines with Highest Percentage of Degrees Awarded:** Business/marketing 23%, communications/communication technologies 9%, engineering/engineering technology 7%, education 7%, social sciences and history 7%. **Special Study Options:** Accelerated program, cooperative (work-study) program, distance learning, double major, dual enrollment, English as a second language, student exchange program (domestic), honors program, independent study, internships, student-designed major, study abroad, teacher certification program, weekend college.

FACILITIES

Housing: Coed, all-female, all-male, apartments for married students, apartments for single students, housing for disabled students, housing for international students, fraternities and/or sororities. **Library Holdings:** 2,989,443 bound volumes. 25,917 periodicals. 6,202,256 microforms. 82,722 audiovisuals. **Special Academic Facilities/Equipment:** Anthropology and art museums; Center for the Humanities; centers for equine research, cancer research, and robotics; pharmacy manufacturing lab. **Computers:** School-owned computers available for student use.

EXTRACURRICULARS

Activities: Choral groups, concert band, dance, drama/theater, jazz band, literary magazine, marching band, music ensembles, musical theater, opera, pep band, radio station, student government, student newspaper, symphony orchestra, yearbook. **Organizations:** 277 registered organizations, 28 honor societies, 20 religious organizations, 19 fraternities (16% men join), 16 sororities (20% women join). **Athletics (Intercollegiate):** *Men:* baseball, basketball, cross-country, diving, football, golf, indoor track, rifle, soccer, swimming, tennis, track & field. *Women:* basketball, cross-country, diving, golf, gymnastics, indoor track, rifle, soccer, softball, swimming, tennis, track & field, volleyball.

ADMISSIONS

Selectivity Rating: 79 (of 100). **Freshman Academic Profile:** 26% in top 10% of high school class, 54% in top 25% of high school class, 84% in top 50% of high school class. Average ACT 25, ACT middle 50% range 21-26. SAT I Math middle 50% range 510-630. SAT I Verbal middle 50% range 500-620. TOEFL required of all international applicants, minimum TOEFL 527. **Basis for Candidate Selection:** *Very important factors considered include:* secondary school record, standardized test scores. *Important factors considered include:* class rank, extracurricular activities, minority status, state residency, talent/ability, volunteer work, work experience. *Other factors considered include:* character/personal qualities, essays, geographical residence, recommendations. **Freshman Admission Requirements:** High school diploma or GED is required. *Academic units required/recommended:* 22 total required; 22 total recommended; 4 English required, 4 English recommended, 3 math required, 4 math recommended, 3 science required, 3 science recommended, 2 foreign language recommended, 3 social studies required, 3 social studies recommended. **Freshman Admission Statistics:** 8,879 applied, 82% accepted, 51% of those accepted enrolled. **Transfer Admission Requirements:** *Items required:* college transcript, statement of good standing from prior school. Minimum college GPA of 2.0 required. Lowest grade transferable D. **General Admission Information:** Application fee $30. Priority application deadline February 15. Regular application deadline February 15. Nonfall registration accepted. Credit and/or placement offered for CEEB Advanced Placement tests.

COSTS AND FINANCIAL AID

In-state tuition $3,480. Out-of-state tuition $10,032. Room & board $4,050. Required fees $495. Average book expense $600. **Required Forms and Deadlines:** FAFSA. Priority filing deadline February 15. **Notification of Awards:** Applicants will be notified of awards on a rolling basis beginning on or about May 1. **Types of Aid:** *Need-based scholarships/grants:* Pell, SEOG, state scholarships/grants, private scholarships, the school's own gift aid. *Loans:* Federal Perkins, Federal Nursing. **Student Employment:** Federal Work-Study Program available. Institutional employment available. Off-campus job opportunities are excellent. **Financial Aid Statistics:** 32% freshmen, 34% undergrads receive some form of aid. Average freshman grant $3,525. Average freshman loan $3,769. **Financial Aid Phone:** 859-257-3172.

UNIVERSITY OF KING'S COLLEGE

Registrar's Office, Halifax, NS B3H 2A1
Phone: 902-422-1271 **E-mail:** admissions@ukings.ns.ca
Fax: 902-423-3357 **Web:** www.ukings.ns.ca

This public school was founded in 1789. It has a 3-acre campus.

STUDENTS AND FACULTY

Enrollment: 910. **Student Body:** Out-of-state 54%, international students represent 6 countries. **Faculty:** Student/faculty ratio 30:1. 27 full-time faculty, 92% hold PhDs. 100% faculty teach undergrads.

ACADEMICS

Degrees: Bachelor's. **Academic Requirements:** General education including some course work in foreign languages, humanities, sciences (biological or physical), writing credit (specified classes in arts and science qualify). **Majors with Highest Enrollment:** Journalism; history, general; English language and literature, general. **Special Study Options:** Cooperative (work-study) program, double major, honors program, internships, study abroad.

FACILITIES

Housing: Coed, all-female, all-male.

EXTRACURRICULARS

Activities: Choral groups, dance, drama/theater, literary magazine, radio station, student government, student newspaper, student-run film society, yearbook. **Athletics (Intercollegiate):** *Men:* basketball, soccer, volleyball. *Women:* basketball, soccer, volleyball.

ADMISSIONS

Selectivity Rating: 63 (of 100). **Freshman Academic Profile:** TOEFL required of all international applicants, minimum TOEFL 580. **Basis for Candidate Selection:** *Very important factors considered include:* secondary school record, standardized test scores. **Freshman Admission Requirements: Transfer Admission Requirements:** *Items required:* college transcript. **General Admission Information:** Application fee $30. Priority application deadline March 1. Regular application deadline June 1.

COSTS AND FINANCIAL AID

Room & board $5,865. Required fees $0. Average book expense $900. **Types of Aid:** *Need-based scholarships/grants:* Pell, SEOG, state scholarships/grants, private scholarships, the school's own gift aid. *Loans:* FFEL Subsidized Stafford, FFEL Unsubsidized Stafford, FFEL PLUS, Federal Perkins, college/university loans from institutional funds. **Student Employment:** Off-campus job opportunities are good.

UNIVERSITY OF LA VERNE

1950 Third Street, La Verne, CA 91750
Phone: 909-593-3511 **E-mail:** admissions@ulv.edu **CEEB Code:** 4381
Fax: 909-392-2714 **Web:** www.ulv.edu **ACT Code:** 295

This private school was founded in 1891. It has a 34-acre campus.

STUDENTS AND FACULTY

Enrollment: 1,439. **Student Body:** Male 38%, female 62%, out-of-state 5%, international 2%. **Ethnic Representation:** African American 10%, Asian 6%, Caucasian 36%, Hispanic 37%, Native American 1%. **Retention and Graduation:** 83% freshmen return for sophomore year. 28% freshmen graduate within 4 years. **Faculty:** Student/faculty ratio 11:1. 109 full-time faculty, 80% hold PhDs. 72% faculty teach undergrads.

ACADEMICS

Degrees: Bachelor's, certificate, doctoral, first professional, master's, post-bachelor's certificate, post-master's certificate. **Academic Requirements:** General education including some course work in arts/fine arts, English (including composition), foreign languages, history, humanities, mathematics, philosophy, sciences (biological or physical), social science, community service, interdisciplinary coursework. **Classes:** 10-19 students in an average class. 10-19 students in an average lab/discussion section. **Majors with Highest Enrollment:** Business administration/management; liberal arts and sciences/liberal studies; psychology, general. **Disciplines with Highest Percentage of Degrees Awarded:** Business/marketing 23%, social sciences and history 17%, liberal arts/general studies 15%, psychology 10%, communications/communication technologies 9%. **Special Study Options:** Accelerated program, distance learning, double major, English as a second language, student exchange program (domestic), honors program, independent study, internships, liberal arts/career combination, student-designed major, study abroad, teacher certification program, weekend college.

FACILITIES

Housing: Coed, all-female, housing for international students. **Library Holdings:** 215,000 bound volumes. 4,500 periodicals. **Special Academic Facilities/Equipment:** Photography and art galleries, archaeology laboratory and two archaeology collections, live fauna collection. **Computers:** *Recommended operating system:* Windows 95. School-owned computers available for student use.

EXTRACURRICULARS

Activities: Choral groups, dance, drama/theater, jazz band, literary magazine, music ensembles, musical theater, radio station, student government, student newspaper, television station, yearbook. **Organizations:** 40 registered organizations, 2 honor societies, 3 fraternities (7% men join), 3 sororities (10% women join). **Athletics (Intercollegiate):** *Men:* baseball, basketball, cross-country, diving, football, golf, soccer, swimming, tennis, track & field, volleyball, water polo. *Women:* basketball, cross-country, diving, soccer, softball, swimming, tennis, track & field, volleyball, water polo.

ADMISSIONS

Selectivity Rating: 63 (of 100). **Freshman Academic Profile:** Average high school GPA 3.5. 33% in top 10% of high school class, 66% in top 25% of high school class, 92% in top 50% of high school class. Average SAT I Math 512, SAT I Math middle 50% range 460-568. Average SAT I Verbal 500, SAT I Verbal middle 50% range 440-540. Average ACT 20, ACT middle 50% range 17-21. TOEFL required of all international applicants, minimum TOEFL 550. **Basis**

for Candidate Selection: *Very important factors considered include:* character/personal qualities, essays, recommendations, secondary school record, standardized test scores. *Important factors considered include:* extracurricular activities. *Other factors considered include:* alumni/ae relation, class rank, interview, talent/ability, volunteer work, work experience. **Freshman Admission Requirements:** High school diploma or GED is required. *Academic units required/recommended:* 14 total required; 19 total recommended; 4 English required, 4 English recommended, 3 math required, 4 math recommended, 2 science required, 2 science recommended, 1 science lab required, 2 science lab recommended, 2 foreign language recommended, 2 social studies required, 2 social studies recommended, 3 history required, 3 history recommended, 2 elective recommended. **Freshman Admission Statistics:** 1,261 applied, 61% accepted, 39% of those accepted enrolled. **Transfer Admission Requirements:** *Items required:* college transcript, essay. Minimum college GPA of 2.5 required. Lowest grade transferable C-. **General Admission Information:** Application fee $50. Priority application deadline February 1. Regular application deadline February 1. Nonfall registration accepted. Admission may be deferred for a maximum of 1 year. Credit and/or placement offered for CEEB Advanced Placement tests.

COSTS AND FINANCIAL AID

Tuition $20,500. Room & board $7,750. Required fees $0. Average book expense $1,206. **Required Forms and Deadlines:** FAFSA and state aid form. No deadline for regular filing. Priority filing deadline March 2. **Notification of Awards:** Applicants will be notified of awards on a rolling basis beginning on or about March 15. **Types of Aid:** *Need-based scholarships/grants:* Pell, SEOG, state scholarships/grants, private scholarships, the school's own gift aid. *Loans:* FFEL Subsidized Stafford, FFEL Unsubsidized Stafford, FFEL PLUS, Federal Perkins, college/university loans from institutional funds. **Student Employment:** Federal Work-Study Program available. Institutional employment available. Off-campus job opportunities are good. **Financial Aid Statistics:** 91% freshmen, 86% undergrads receive some form of aid. Average freshman grant $16,726. Average freshman loan $6,031. **Financial Aid Phone:** 909-593-3511.

UNIVERSITY OF LETHBRIDGE

4401 University Drive, Lethbridge, AB T1K 3M4
Phone: 403-320-5700 **E-mail:** inquiries@uleth.ca
Fax: 403-329-5159 **Web:** www.uleth.ca **ACT Code:** 5202

This public school was founded in 1967. It has a 568-acre campus.

STUDENTS AND FACULTY

Enrollment: 6,675. **Student Body:** Male 43%, female 57%, out-of-state 17%. **Faculty:** Student/faculty ratio 15:1.

ACADEMICS

Degrees: Bachelor's, certificate, diploma, doctoral, master's, post-bachelor's certificate. **Academic Requirements:** General education including some course work in 4 semester courses in each of fine arts and humanities, social sciences, and sciences. **Classes:** 10-19 students in an average class. 10-19 students in an average lab/discussion section. **Majors with Highest Enrollment:** Business administration/management; kinesiology and exercise science; psychology, general. **Disciplines with Highest Percentage of Degrees Awarded:** Business/marketing 31%, education 12%, social sciences and history 9%, visual and performing arts 8%, psychology 5%. **Special Study Options:** Accelerated program, cooperative (work-study) program, double major, English as a second language, student exchange program (domestic), honors program, independent study, internships, student-designed major, study abroad, teacher certification program, applied studies.

FACILITIES

Housing: Coed, apartments for married students, apartments for single students, housing for disabled students, townhouses for single and married students and students with families. **Library Holdings:** 1,300,000 bound volumes. 1,740 periodicals. 800,000 microforms. 3,500 audiovisuals. **Special Academic Facilities/Equipment:** Art gallery. **Computers:** School-owned computers available for student use.

EXTRACURRICULARS

Activities: Choral groups, dance, drama/theater, jazz band, literary magazine, music ensembles, musical theater, radio station, student government, student newspaper, student-run film society, symphony orchestra. **Athletics (Intercollegiate):** *Men:* basketball, ice hockey, soccer, swimming, track & field. *Women:* basketball, ice hockey, rugby, soccer, swimming, track & field.

ADMISSIONS

Selectivity Rating: 63 (of 100). **Freshman Academic Profile: Basis for Candidate Selection:** *Very important factors considered include:* secondary school record. *Other factors considered include:* class rank, standardized test scores. **Freshman Admission Requirements: Transfer Admission Requirements:** *Items required:* college transcript. **General Admission Information:** Application fee $38. Priority application deadline April 1. Regular application deadline June 1. Nonfall registration accepted. Admission may be deferred.

COSTS AND FINANCIAL AID

Room & board $2,426. Required fees $369. Average book expense $630. **Types of Aid:** *Need-based scholarships/grants:* Pell, SEOG, state scholarships/grants, private scholarships, the school's own gift aid. *Loans:* FFEL Subsidized Stafford, FFEL Unsubsidized Stafford, FFEL PLUS, Federal Perkins, college/university loans from institutional funds. **Student Employment:** Institutional employment available. Off-campus job opportunities are good. **Financial Aid Statistics:** Average freshman grant $1,260. **Financial Aid Phone:** 403-329-2585.

UNIVERSITY OF LOUISIANA—LAFAYETTE

PO Drawer 41210, Lafayette, LA 70504
Phone: 337-482-6457 **E-mail:** admissions@louisiana.edu **CEEB Code:** 6672
Fax: 337-482-6195 **Web:** www.louisiana.edu **ACT Code:** 1612

This public school was founded in 1898. It has a 1,375-acre campus.

STUDENTS AND FACULTY

Enrollment: 14,341. **Student Body:** Male 42%, female 58%, out-of-state 3%, international 2%. **Ethnic Representation:** African American 19%, Asian 2%, Caucasian 76%, Hispanic 2%, Native American 1%. **Retention and Graduation:** 72% freshmen return for sophomore year. 6% freshmen graduate within 4 years. **Faculty:** Student/faculty ratio 24:1. 532 full-time faculty, 75% hold PhDs.

ACADEMICS

Degrees: Bachelor's, doctoral, master's, post-master's certificate. **Academic Requirements:** General education including some course work in arts/fine arts, computer literacy, English (including composition), humanities, mathematics, sciences (biological or physical), social science, communication. **Classes:** 20-29 students in an average class. **Disciplines with Highest Percentage of Degrees Awarded:** Business/marketing 19%, liberal arts/general studies 15%, education 14%, engineering/engineering technology 10%, health professions and related sciences 9%. **Special Study Options:** Cooperative (work-study) program, cross registration, distance learning, double major, dual enrollment, student exchange program (domestic), honors program, independent study, internships, student-designed major, study abroad, teacher certification program.

FACILITIES

Housing: All-female, all-male, apartments for married students, fraternities and/or sororities. **Library Holdings:** 425,034 bound volumes. 4,290 periodicals. 810,609 microforms. 5,727 audiovisuals. **Special Academic Facilities/Equipment:** Art, experimental farm, museum, natural history museum adjacent to campus, primate center, high technology center, two Van de Graaff nuclear center electron microscopy centers, CAD/CAM factory of the future. **Computers:** School-owned computers available for student use.

EXTRACURRICULARS

Activities: Choral groups, concert band, dance, drama/theater, jazz band, literary magazine, marching band, music ensembles, musical theater, opera, radio station, student government, student newspaper, student-run film society, yearbook. **Organizations:** 192 registered organizations, 10 honor societies, 11 religious organizations, 13 fraternities (5% men join), 8 sororities (5% women join). **Athletics (Intercollegiate):** *Men:* baseball, basketball, cheerleading, cross-country, football, golf, indoor track, tennis, track & field. *Women:* basketball, cheerleading, cross-country, indoor track, soccer, softball, tennis, track & field, volleyball.

ADMISSIONS

Selectivity Rating: 63 (of 100). **Freshman Academic Profile:** Average high school GPA 3.1. 0% in top 10% of high school class, 38% in top 25% of high school class, 82% in top 50% of high school class. 70% from public high schools. Average ACT 21, ACT middle 50% range 18-23. TOEFL required of all international applicants, minimum TOEFL 450. **Basis for Candidate Selection:** *Very important factors considered include:* class rank, secondary school record, standardized test scores. **Freshman Admission Requirements:**

High school diploma or GED is required. *Academic units required/recommended:* 4 English required, 3 math required, 3 science required, 2 social studies required, 1 history required, 4 elective required. **Freshman Admission Statistics:** 4,308 applied, 85% accepted, 65% of those accepted enrolled. **Transfer Admission Requirements:** *Items required:* college transcript. **General Admission Information:** Application fee $20. Nonfall registration accepted. Admission may be deferred. Credit and/or placement offered for CEEB Advanced Placement tests.

COSTS AND FINANCIAL AID

In-state tuition $2,440. Out-of-state tuition $8,620. Room & board $2,896. Required fees $0. Average book expense $1,000. **Required Forms and Deadlines:** FAFSA and institution's own financial aid form. No deadline for regular filing. Priority filing deadline March 1. **Notification of Awards:** Applicants will be notified of awards on a rolling basis beginning on or about April 1. **Types of Aid:** *Need-based scholarships/grants:* Pell, SEOG, state scholarships/grants, private scholarships, the school's own gift aid, Federal Nursing. *Loans:* Direct Subsidized Stafford, FFEL Subsidized Stafford, FFEL Unsubsidized Stafford, FFEL PLUS, Federal Perkins, Federal Nursing. **Student Employment:** Federal Work-Study Program available. Institutional employment available. Off-campus job opportunities are excellent. **Financial Aid Statistics:** 58% freshmen, 50% undergrads receive some form of aid. Average freshman grant $2,453. Average freshman loan $4,338. **Financial Aid Phone:** 337-482-6506.

UNIVERSITY OF LOUISIANA—MONROE

700 University Avenue, Monroe, LA 71209
Phone: 318-342-5252 **E-mail:** rehood@ulm.edu **CEEB Code:** 6482
Fax: 318-342-5274 **Web:** www.ulm.edu **ACT Code:** 1598

This public school was founded in 1931. It has a 238-acre campus.

STUDENTS AND FACULTY

Enrollment: 8,669. **Student Body:** Male 39%, female 61%, out-of-state 7%, international 1% (47 countries represented). **Ethnic Representation:** African American 22%, Asian 2%, Caucasian 75%, Hispanic 1%. **Retention and Graduation:** 8% freshmen graduate within 4 years. **Faculty:** Student/faculty ratio 17:1. 100% faculty teach undergrads.

ACADEMICS

Degrees: Associate's, bachelor's, certificate, doctoral, master's, post-master's certificate. **Academic Requirements:** General education including some course work in arts/fine arts, computer literacy, English (including composition), foreign languages, history, humanities, mathematics, sciences (biological or physical). **Special Study Options:** Accelerated program, cooperative (work-study) program, distance learning, English as a second language, honors program, internships, teacher certification program.

FACILITIES

Housing: Coed, all-female, all-male, fraternities and/or sororities. **Library Holdings:** 595,351 bound volumes. 2,902 periodicals. 433,624 microforms. 77 audiovisuals. **Special Academic Facilities/Equipment:** Agricultural farm lab, soil/plant analysis lab, climatic research center, herbarium, preschool child lab, educational media center, cancer research center. **Computers:** School-owned computers available for student use.

EXTRACURRICULARS

Activities: Choral groups, concert band, dance, drama/theater, jazz band, literary magazine, marching band, music ensembles, musical theater, pep band, radio station, student government, student newspaper, television station, yearbook. **Organizations:** 128 registered organizations, 22 honor societies, 11 religious organizations, 8 fraternities (3% men join), 8 sororities (2% women join). **Athletics (Intercollegiate):** *Men:* baseball, basketball, cheerleading, cross-country, football, golf, indoor track, swimming, tennis, track & field. *Women:* basketball, cheerleading, cross-country, indoor track, softball, swimming, tennis, track & field, volleyball.

ADMISSIONS

Selectivity Rating: 64 (of 100). **Freshman Academic Profile:** 41% in top 25% of high school class, 74% in top 50% of high school class. 79% from public high schools. Average ACT 19, ACT middle 50% range 16-22. TOEFL required of all international applicants, minimum TOEFL 600. **Freshman Admission Requirements:** High school diploma or GED is required. *Academic units required/recommended:* 16 total recommended; 4 English recommended, 3 math recommended, 3 science recommended, 2 foreign language recommended, 2 social studies recommended, 1 history recommended, 1 elective recommended. **Freshman Admission Statistics:** 2,657 applied, 92% accepted, 74% of those accepted enrolled. **Transfer Admission Requirements:** *Items required:* high school transcript, college transcript. **General Admission Information:** Application fee $15. Nonfall registration accepted. Credit and/or placement offered for CEEB Advanced Placement tests.

COSTS AND FINANCIAL AID

Out-of-state tuition $2,400. Room & board $3,380. Required fees $282. Average book expense $668. **Required Forms and Deadlines:** FAFSA. **Types of Aid:** *Need-based scholarships/grants:* Pell, private scholarships, the school's own gift aid. **Student Employment:** Federal Work-Study Program available. Off-campus job opportunities are good. **Financial Aid Statistics:** Average freshman grant $1,200. Average income from on-campus job $1,000. **Financial Aid Phone:** 318-342-5320.

UNIVERSITY OF LOUISVILLE

Admissions Office, Louisville, KY 40292
Phone: 502-852-6531 **E-mail:** admitme@gwise.louisville.edu **CEEB Code:** 1838
Fax: 502-852-4776 **Web:** www.louisville.edu **ACT Code:** 1556

This public school was founded in 1798. It has a 170-acre campus.

STUDENTS AND FACULTY

Enrollment: 14,458. **Student Body:** Male 47%, female 53%, out-of-state 11%, international 1%. **Ethnic Representation:** African American 14%, Asian 3%, Caucasian 82%, Hispanic 1%. **Retention and Graduation:** 74% freshmen return for sophomore year. 10% freshmen graduate within 4 years. **Faculty:** Student/faculty ratio 13:1. 726 full-time faculty, 92% hold PhDs.

ACADEMICS

Degrees: Associate's, bachelor's, certificate, diploma, doctoral, first professional, master's, post-bachelor's certificate, post-master's certificate, terminal, transfer. **Academic Requirements:** General education including some course work in arts/fine arts, computer literacy, English (including composition), foreign languages, history, humanities, mathematics, sciences (biological or physical), social science. **Classes:** 20-29 students in an average class. **Disciplines with Highest Percentage of Degrees Awarded:** Communications/communication technologies 22%, social sciences and history 11%, engineering/engineering technology 10%, psychology 8%, computer and information sciences 7%. **Special Study Options:** Accelerated program, cooperative (work-study) program, cross registration, distance learning, double major, dual enrollment, English as a second language, student exchange program (domestic), external degree program, honors program, independent study, internships, student-designed major, study abroad, teacher certification program, weekend college.

FACILITIES

Housing: Coed, apartments for married students, apartments for single students, housing for disabled students, fraternities and/or sororities, suite-style rooms. **Library Holdings:** 1,833,386 bound volumes. 16,078 periodicals. 2,122,902 microforms. 33,109 audiovisuals. **Special Academic Facilities/Equipment:** Natural history and art museums, planetarium, numerous institutes and centers. **Computers:** School-owned computers available for student use.

EXTRACURRICULARS

Activities: Choral groups, concert band, dance, drama/theater, jazz band, marching band, music ensembles, pep band, radio station, student government, student newspaper. **Organizations:** 14 fraternities (10% men join), 9 sororities (6% women join). **Athletics (Intercollegiate):** *Men:* baseball, basketball, cheerleading, cross-country, diving, fencing, football, golf, ice hockey, soccer, softball, swimming, tennis, track & field. *Women:* basketball, cheerleading, crew, cross-country, diving, fencing, field hockey, golf, soccer, softball, swimming, tennis, track & field, volleyball.

ADMISSIONS

Selectivity Rating: 72 (of 100). **Freshman Academic Profile:** Average high school GPA 3.4. 12% in top 10% of high school class, 27% in top 25% of high school class, 44% in top 50% of high school class. Average ACT 23. TOEFL required of all international applicants, minimum TOEFL 550. **Basis for Candidate Selection:** *Very important factors considered include:* secondary school record, standardized test scores. *Important factors considered include:* class rank. *Other factors considered include:* character/personal qualities, essays, extracurricular activities, geographical residence, interview, recommendations, talent/ability, volunteer work, work experience. **Freshman Admission Requirements:** High school diploma or GED is required. *Academic units* *required/recommended:* 20 total required; 4 English required, 3 math required, 4 math recommended, 3 science required, 4 science recommended, 1 science lab required, 2 foreign language recommended, 3 social studies required, 7 elective required. **Freshman Admission Statistics:** 5,306 applied, 77% accepted, 57% of those accepted enrolled. **Transfer Admission Requirements:** *Items required:* college transcript. Minimum high school GPA of 2.5 required. Minimum college GPA of 2.0 required. Lowest grade transferable D. **General Admission Information:** Application fee $25. Regular application deadline August 25. Priority application deadline April 1. Nonfall registration accepted. Credit and/or placement offered for CEEB Advanced Placement tests.

COSTS AND FINANCIAL AID

In-state tuition $4,344. Out-of-state tuition $11,856. Room & board $3,672. Required fees $0. Average book expense $700. **Required Forms and Deadlines:** FAFSA. No deadline for regular filing. Priority filing deadline March 1. **Notification of Awards:** Applicants will be notified of awards on a rolling basis beginning on or about April 1. **Types of Aid:** *Need-based scholarships/grants:* Pell, SEOG, state scholarships/grants, private scholarships, the school's own gift aid. *Loans:* FFEL Subsidized Stafford, FFEL Unsubsidized Stafford, FFEL PLUS, Federal Perkins, Federal Nursing. **Student Employment:** Federal Work-Study Program available. Institutional employment available. Off-campus job opportunities are excellent. **Financial Aid Statistics:** 52% freshmen, 46% undergrads receive some form of aid. **Financial Aid Phone:** 502-852-5511.

THE UNIVERSITY OF MAINE

5713 Chadbourne Hall, Orono, ME 04469-5713
Phone: 207-581-1561 **E-mail:** um-admit@maine.edu **CEEB Code:** 3916
Fax: 207-581-1213 **Web:** www.umaine.edu **ACT Code:** 1664

This public school was founded in 1865. It has a 3,300-acre campus.

STUDENTS AND FACULTY

Enrollment: 8,817. **Student Body:** Male 48%, female 52%, out-of-state 14%, international 2% (73 countries represented). **Ethnic Representation:** African American 1%, Asian 1%, Caucasian 95%, Hispanic 1%, Native American 2%. **Retention and Graduation:** 79% freshmen return for sophomore year. 27% freshmen graduate within 4 years. 19% grads go on to further study within 1 year. **Faculty:** Student/faculty ratio 15:1. 509 full-time faculty, 86% hold PhDs. 76% faculty teach undergrads.

ACADEMICS

Degrees: Bachelor's, doctoral, master's, post-bachelor's certificate, post-master's certificate. **Academic Requirements:** General education including some course work in arts/fine arts, English (including composition), foreign languages, humanities, mathematics, sciences (biological or physical), social science, population & environment, cultural diversity/international perspectives. **Classes:** 20-29 students in an average class. 10-19 students in an average lab/discussion section. **Majors with Highest Enrollment:** Business administration/management; education, general; engineering, general. **Disciplines with Highest Percentage of Degrees Awarded:** Education 15%, engineering/engineering technology 14%, business/marketing 11%, social sciences and history 8%, health professions and related sciences 7%. **Special Study Options:** Cooperative (work-study) program, distance learning, double major, English as a second language, student exchange program (domestic), honors program, independent study, internships, liberal arts/career combination, student-designed major, study abroad, teacher certification program.

FACILITIES

Housing: Coed, all-female, apartments for married students, apartments for single students, housing for disabled students, housing for international students, honors college housing, graduate student housing, smoke-free, chem-free, clusters for engineering and science majors. **Library Holdings:** 851,736 bound volumes. 16,667 periodicals. 2,312,184 microforms. 25,137 audiovisuals. **Special Academic Facilities/Equipment:** Anthropology museum, digital media lab, folklore and oral history museum, art museum, Canadian-American center, social sciences research institute, exceptional child research lab, preschool, experimental farms, land/water resources center, center for marine studies, planetarium/observatory, electron microscopes, farm museum, paper-making machine, aquaculture production facility, woodland preserve, botanical garden, arts center, Franco-American Center. **Computers:** School-owned computers available for student use.

EXTRACURRICULARS

Activities: Choral groups, concert band, dance, drama/theater, jazz band, marching band, music ensembles, musical theater, opera, pep band, radio station, student government, student newspaper, student-run film society, symphony orchestra. **Organizations:** 248 registered organizations, 43 honor societies, 9 religious organizations, 13 fraternities, 6 sororities. **Athletics (Intercollegiate):** *Men:* baseball, basketball, cross-country, diving, football, ice hockey, indoor track, soccer, swimming, track & field. *Women:* basketball, cross-country, diving, field hockey, ice hockey, indoor track, soccer, softball, swimming, track & field, volleyball.

ADMISSIONS

Selectivity Rating: 76 (of 100). **Freshman Academic Profile:** Average high school GPA 3.2. 23% in top 10% of high school class, 50% in top 25% of high school class, 89% in top 50% of high school class. Average SAT I Math 547, SAT I Math middle 50% range 490-610. Average SAT I Verbal 539, SAT I Verbal middle 50% range 480-590. Average ACT 23, ACT middle 50% range 20-26. TOEFL required of all international applicants, minimum TOEFL 530. **Basis for Candidate Selection:** *Very important factors considered include:* secondary school record, standardized test scores. *Important factors considered include:* class rank, essays. *Other factors considered include:* alumni/ae relation, recommendations, state residency. **Freshman Admission Requirements:** High school diploma or GED is required. *Academic units required/recommended:* 17 total required; 24 total recommended; 4 English required, 4 English recommended, 3 math required, 4 math recommended, 2 science required, 3 science recommended, 2 science lab required, 3 science lab recommended, 2 foreign language required, 2 foreign language recommended, 2 social studies required, 3 social studies recommended, 1 history recommended, 2 elective required, 4 elective recommended. **Freshman Admission Statistics:** 5,249 applied, 79% accepted, 43% of those accepted enrolled. **Transfer Admission Requirements:** *Items required:* high school transcript, college transcript. Minimum college GPA of 2.0 required. Lowest grade transferable C-. **General Admission Information:** Application fee $40. Nonfall registration accepted. Admission may be deferred for a maximum of 1 year. Credit offered for CEEB Advanced Placement tests.

COSTS AND FINANCIAL AID

In-state tuition $4,380. Out-of-state tuition $12,450. Room & board $5,922. Required fees $1,170. Average book expense $700. **Required Forms and Deadlines:** FAFSA. Priority filing deadline March 1. **Notification of Awards:** Applicants will be notified of awards on a rolling basis beginning on or about March 15. **Types of Aid:** *Need-based scholarships/grants:* Pell, SEOG, state scholarships/grants, private scholarships, the school's own gift aid. *Loans:* FFEL Subsidized Stafford, FFEL Unsubsidized Stafford, FFEL PLUS, Federal Perkins, state loans. **Student Employment:** Federal Work-Study Program available. Institutional employment available. Off-campus job opportunities are good. **Financial Aid Statistics:** 73% freshmen, 57% undergrads receive some form of aid. Average freshman grant $5,329. Average freshman loan $2,974. Average income from on-campus job $1,538. **Financial Aid Phone:** 207-581-1324.

UNIVERSITY OF MAINE—AUGUSTA

46 University Drive, Augusta, ME 04330
Phone: 207-621-3185 **E-mail:** umaar@maine.edu **CEEB Code:** 3929
Fax: 207-621-3116 **Web:** www.uma.maine.edu

This public school was founded in 1965. It has a 180-acre campus.

STUDENTS AND FACULTY

Enrollment: 5,722. **Student Body:** Male 25%, female 75%. **Faculty:** Student/faculty ratio 22:1. 95 full-time faculty, 38% hold PhDs. 100% faculty teach undergrads.

ACADEMICS

Degrees: Associate's, bachelor's, certificate, terminal, transfer. **Academic Requirements:** General education including some course work in arts/fine arts, computer literacy, English (including composition), humanities, mathematics, social science. **Disciplines with Highest Percentage of Degrees Awarded:** Health professions and related sciences 41%, business/marketing 22%, protective services/public administration 9%, social sciences and history 8%, library sciences 6%. **Special Study Options:** Cooperative (work-study) program, cross registration, distance learning, double major, dual enrollment, external degree program, honors program, independent study, internships, student-designed major, study abroad.

FACILITIES

Library Holdings: 44,000 bound volumes. 560 periodicals. 12,300 microforms. 1,350 audiovisuals. **Special Academic Facilities/Equipment:** Jewett Gallery.

EXTRACURRICULARS

Activities: Choral groups, concert band, jazz band, music ensembles, pep band, student government, student newspaper. **Organizations:** 2 registered organizations, 1 honor society. **Athletics (Intercollegiate):** *Men:* basketball, soccer, softball, tennis, volleyball. *Women:* basketball, soccer, softball, tennis, volleyball.

ADMISSIONS

Selectivity Rating: 63 (of 100). **Freshman Academic Profile:** 10% in top 10% of high school class, 35% in top 25% of high school class, 59% in top 50% of high school class. 88% from public high schools. Average SAT I Math 456, SAT I Math middle 50% range 400-630. Average SAT I Verbal 472, SAT I Verbal middle 50% range 410-660. TOEFL required of all international applicants, minimum TOEFL 500. **Basis for Candidate Selection:** *Important factors considered include:* class rank. *Other factors considered include:* character/personal qualities, essays, interview, recommendations, secondary school record, standardized test scores, talent/ability. **Freshman Admission Requirements:** High school diploma or GED is required. **Transfer Admission Requirements:** *Items required:* high school transcript, college transcript, statement of good standing from prior school. Minimum college GPA of 2.0 required. Lowest grade transferable C. **General Admission Information:** Application fee $25. Early decision application deadline November 1. Nonfall registration accepted. Admission may be deferred for a maximum of 1 year. Credit offered for CEEB Advanced Placement tests.

COSTS AND FINANCIAL AID

In-state tuition $3,420. Out-of-state tuition $8,310. Required fees $870. Average book expense $702. **Required Forms and Deadlines:** FAFSA. Priority filing deadline March 1. **Notification of Awards:** Applicants will be notified of awards on a rolling basis beginning on or about March 15. **Types of Aid:** *Need-based scholarships/grants:* Pell, SEOG, state scholarships/grants, private scholarships, the school's own gift aid. *Loans:* Direct Subsidized Stafford, Direct Unsubsidized Stafford, FFEL Subsidized Stafford, FFEL Unsubsidized Stafford, FFEL PLUS, Federal Perkins, Federal Nursing, state loans. **Student Employment:** Federal Work-Study Program available. Institutional employment available. Off-campus job opportunities are good. **Financial Aid Statistics:** 49% freshmen, 85% undergrads receive some form of aid. Average freshman grant $5,290. Average freshman loan $2,581. **Financial Aid Phone:** 207-621-3160.

UNIVERSITY OF MAINE—FARMINGTON

246 Main Street, Farmington, ME 04938
Phone: 207-778-7050 **E-mail:** umfadmit@maine.edu **CEEB Code:** 3506
Fax: 207-778-8182 **Web:** www.umf.maine.edu **ACT Code:** 1640

This public school was founded in 1863. It has a 50-acre campus.

STUDENTS AND FACULTY

Enrollment: 2,395. **Student Body:** Male 33%, female 67%, out-of-state 17%, international 1% (19 countries represented). **Ethnic Representation:** Caucasian 98%, Native American 1%. **Retention and Graduation:** 74% freshmen return for sophomore year. 40% freshmen graduate within 4 years. 12% grads go on to further study within 1 year. 4% grads pursue business degrees. 2% grads pursue law degrees. 2% grads pursue medical degrees. **Faculty:** Student/faculty ratio 15:1. 120 full-time faculty, 82% hold PhDs. 100% faculty teach undergrads.

ACADEMICS

Degrees: Bachelor's, certificate. **Academic Requirements:** General education including some course work in arts/fine arts, English (including composition), humanities, mathematics, sciences (biological or physical), social science, health and physical fitness. **Classes:** 10-19 students in an average class. 10-19 students in an average lab/discussion section. **Majors with Highest Enrollment:** Elementary education and teaching; psychology, general; business/managerial economics. **Disciplines with Highest Percentage of Degrees Awarded:** Education 47%, psychology 11%, interdisciplinary studies 10%, health professions and related sciences 10%, English 6%. **Special Study Options:** Accelerated program, cooperative (work-study) program, cross registration, distance learning, double major, dual enrollment, student exchange program (domestic), honors program, independent study, internships, liberal arts/career combination, student-designed major, study abroad, teacher certification program, SALT, documentary field study in Portland.

FACILITIES

Housing: Coed, all-female, apartments for single students, housing for international students, chemical-free community, quiet floors, international experiences program. **Library Holdings:** 104,313 bound volumes. 2,399 periodicals. 78,903 microforms. 8,572 audiovisuals. **Special Academic Facilities/Equipment:** Art gallery, health and fitness center, computer center, Mantor Library, Alumni theater, Nordica Auditorium. **Computers:** School-owned computers available for student use.

EXTRACURRICULARS

Activities: Choral groups, dance, drama/theater, jazz band, literary magazine, music ensembles, musical theater, radio station, student government, student newspaper, student-run film society, yearbook. **Organizations:** 52 registered organizations, 3 honor societies, 3 religious organizations. **Athletics (Intercollegiate):** *Men:* baseball, basketball, cross-country, golf, soccer. *Women:* basketball, cross-country, field hockey, soccer, softball, volleyball.

ADMISSIONS

Selectivity Rating: 68 (of 100). **Freshman Academic Profile:** Average high school GPA 3.2. 13% in top 10% of high school class, 49% in top 25% of high school class, 83% in top 50% of high school class. 88% from public high schools. Average SAT I Math 522, SAT I Math middle 50% range 470-580. Average SAT I Verbal 530, SAT I Verbal middle 50% range 480-580. TOEFL required of all international applicants, minimum TOEFL 550. **Basis for Candidate Selection:** *Very important factors considered include:* class rank, secondary school record. *Important factors considered include:* character/personal qualities, essays, extracurricular activities, geographical residence, interview, recommendations, state residency, talent/ability, volunteer work, work experience. *Other factors considered include:* alumni/ae relation, minority status, standardized test scores. **Freshman Admission Requirements:** High school diploma or GED is required. *Academic units required/recommended:* 19 total recommended; 4 English required, 4 English recommended, 3 math required, 5 math recommended, 2 science required, 2 science recommended, 2 science lab required, 2 science lab recommended, 2 foreign language required, 2 foreign language recommended, 2 social studies required, 2 social studies recommended, 2 history recommended, 3 elective recommended. **Freshman Admission Statistics:** 1,410 applied, 71% accepted, 47% of those accepted enrolled. **Transfer Admission Requirements:** *Items required:* high school transcript, college transcript, essay. Minimum college GPA of 2.0 required. Lowest grade transferable C-. **General Admission Information:** Application fee $40. Priority application deadline March 1. Regular application deadline April 15. Nonfall registration accepted. Admission may be deferred for a maximum of 1 year. Credit and/or placement offered for CEEB Advanced Placement tests.

COSTS AND FINANCIAL AID

In-state tuition $3,990. Out-of-state tuition $9,750. Room & board $5,064. Required fees $492. Average book expense $600. **Required Forms and Deadlines:** FAFSA. Financial aid filing deadline March 1. **Notification of Awards:** Applicants will be notified of awards on a rolling basis beginning on or about March 15. **Types of Aid:** *Need-based scholarships/grants:* Pell, SEOG, state scholarships/grants, private scholarships, the school's own gift aid, Native American scholarships, waivers. *Loans:* FFEL Subsidized Stafford, FFEL Unsubsidized Stafford, FFEL PLUS, Federal Perkins, state loans, Teachers for Maine Loans. **Student Employment:** Federal Work-Study Program available. Institutional employment available. Off-campus job opportunities are good. **Financial Aid Statistics:** 66% freshmen, 61% undergrads receive some form of aid. Average freshman grant $4,000. Average freshman loan $2,751. **Financial Aid Phone:** 207-778-7100.

See page 1248.

UNIVERSITY OF MAINE—FORT KENT

23 University Drive, Fort Kent, ME 04743
Phone: 207-834-7500 **E-mail:** umfkadm@maine.maine.edu **CEEB Code:** 3393
Fax: 207-834-7609 **Web:** www.umfk.maine.edu **ACT Code:** 1642

This public school was founded in 1878. It has a 52-acre campus.

STUDENTS AND FACULTY

Enrollment: 926. **Student Body:** Male 36%, female 64%, out-of-state 31%, international 3%. **Ethnic Representation:** African American 1%, Asian 1%, Caucasian 96%, Native American 1%. **Retention and Graduation:** 78% freshmen return for sophomore year. **Faculty:** Student/faculty ratio 18:1. 33 full-time faculty, 69% hold PhDs. 100% faculty teach undergrads.

ACADEMICS

Degrees: Associate's, bachelor's. **Academic Requirements:** General education including some course work in arts/fine arts, computer literacy, English (including composition), foreign languages, history, humanities, mathematics, sciences (biological or physical), social science. **Classes:** 10-19 students in an average class. **Majors with Highest Enrollment:** Elementary education and teaching; Nursing/registered nurse training (RN, ASN, BSN, MSN); business administration/management. **Disciplines with Highest Percentage of Degrees Awarded:** Education 48%, business/marketing 12%, psychology 11%, health professions and related sciences 10%, social sciences and history 6%. **Special Study Options:** Cooperative (work-study) program, distance learning, double major, student exchange program (domestic), external degree program, honors program, independent study, internships, student-designed major, study abroad, teacher certification program.

FACILITIES

Housing: Coed. **Library Holdings:** 63,408 bound volumes. 381 periodicals. 83 microforms. 1,200 audiovisuals. **Computers:** *Recommended operating system:* Windows 95. School-owned computers available for student use.

EXTRACURRICULARS

Activities: Choral groups, dance, drama/theater, jazz band, literary magazine, musical theater, radio station, student government, student newspaper. **Organizations:** 25 registered organizations, 3 honor societies, 1 religious organization, 5% men join fraternities, 1 sorority (2% women join). **Athletics (Intercollegiate):** *Men:* basketball, cross-country, golf, skiing (alpine), soccer. *Women:* basketball, cheerleading, cross-country, golf, skiing (alpine), soccer.

ADMISSIONS

Selectivity Rating: 63 (of 100). **Freshman Academic Profile:** Average high school GPA 2.7. 11% in top 10% of high school class, 25% in top 25% of high school class, 59% in top 50% of high school class. 96% from public high schools. Average SAT I Math 420. Average SAT I Verbal 450. TOEFL required of all international applicants, minimum TOEFL 500. **Basis for Candidate Selection:** *Very important factors considered include:* secondary school record. *Important factors considered include:* essays, talent/ability. *Other factors considered include:* character/personal qualities, class rank, extracurricular activities, interview, recommendations, standardized test scores, volunteer work, work experience. **Freshman Admission Requirements:** High school diploma or GED is required. *Academic units required/recommended:* 4 English required, 2 math required, 2 science required, 2 science lab required, 2 social studies required. **Freshman Admission Statistics:** 260 applied, 93% accepted, 54% of those accepted enrolled. **Transfer Admission Requirements:** *Items required:* college transcript. Lowest grade transferable D. **General Admission Information:** Application fee $25. Nonfall registration accepted. Admission may be deferred for a maximum of 1 year.

COSTS AND FINANCIAL AID

In-state tuition $3,120. Out-of-state tuition $7,590. Room & board $4,000. Required fees $254. Average book expense $650. **Required Forms and Deadlines:** FAFSA. No deadline for regular filing. Priority filing deadline March 15. **Types of Aid:** *Need-based scholarships/grants:* Pell, SEOG, state scholarships/grants, private scholarships, the school's own gift aid. *Loans:* FFEL Subsidized Stafford, FFEL Unsubsidized Stafford, FFEL PLUS, Federal Perkins, state loans. **Student Employment:** Federal Work-Study Program available. Institutional employment available. Off-campus job opportunities are good. **Financial Aid Statistics:** Average freshman grant $3,440. Average freshman loan $2,923. Average income from on-campus job $1,000. **Financial Aid Phone:** 207-834-7605.

UNIVERSITY OF MAINE—MACHIAS

Office of Admissions, 9 O'Brien Avenue, Machias, ME 04654
Phone: 207-255-1318 **E-mail:** ummadmissions@maine.edu **CEEB Code:** 3956
Fax: 207-255-1363 **Web:** www.umm.maine.edu

This public school was founded in 1909. It has a 42-acre campus.

STUDENTS AND FACULTY

Enrollment: 1,068. **Student Body:** Male 29%, female 71%, out-of-state 23%, international 4%. **Ethnic Representation:** African American 1%, Asian 1%, Caucasian 95%, Native American 3%. **Retention and Graduation:** 80% freshmen return for sophomore year. 10% freshmen graduate within 4 years. **Faculty:** Student/faculty ratio 15:1. 35 full-time faculty, 74% hold PhDs. 100% faculty teach undergrads.

ACADEMICS

Degrees: Associate's, bachelor's, transfer. **Academic Requirements:** General education including some course work in arts/fine arts, English (including composition), history, humanities, mathematics, sciences (biological or physical), social science, personal wellness. **Classes:** 10-19 students in an average class. 10-19 students in an average lab/discussion section. **Majors with Highest Enrollment:** Business administration/management; biology/biological sciences, general; parks, recreation and leisure facilities management. **Disciplines with Highest Percentage of Degrees Awarded:** Business/marketing 17%, biological life sciences 14%, parks and recreation 14%, health professions and related sciences 12%, social sciences and history 11%. **Special Study Options:** Cooperative (work-study) program, distance learning, double major, dual enrollment, English as a second language, external degree program, honors program, independent study, internships, student-designed major, study abroad, teacher certification program.

FACILITIES

Housing: Coed, all-female. **Library Holdings:** 82,664 bound volumes. 316 periodicals. 4,750 microforms. 3,647 audiovisuals. **Special Academic Facilities/Equipment:** Art Gallery. **Computers:** School-owned computers available for student use.

EXTRACURRICULARS

Activities: Choral groups, dance, drama/theater, literary magazine, music ensembles, musical theater, pep band, radio station, student government. **Organizations:** 38 registered organizations, 4 fraternities (15% men join), 4 sororities (3% women join). **Athletics (Intercollegiate):** *Men:* basketball, cross-country, soccer. *Women:* basketball, cross-country, soccer, volleyball.

ADMISSIONS

Selectivity Rating: 75 (of 100). **Freshman Academic Profile:** Average high school GPA 3.0. Average SAT I Math 453, SAT I Math middle 50% range 390-520. Average SAT I Verbal 472, SAT I Verbal middle 50% range 420-530. Average ACT 21, ACT middle 50% range 17-26. TOEFL required of all international applicants, minimum TOEFL 500. **Basis for Candidate Selection:** *Very important factors considered include:* interview, secondary school record. *Important factors considered include:* character/personal qualities, class rank, essays, extracurricular activities, recommendations. *Other factors considered include:* standardized test scores, talent/ability, volunteer work, work experience. **Freshman Admission Requirements:** High school diploma or GED is required. *Academic units required/recommended:* 11 total required; 5 total recommended; 4 English required, 3 math required, 2 science required, 2 science lab required, 2 foreign language recommended, 2 social studies required, 3 elective recommended. **Freshman Admission Statistics:** 478 applied, 83% accepted, 39% of those accepted enrolled. **Transfer Admission Requirements:** *Items required:* high school transcript, college transcript. Minimum college GPA of 2.0 required. Lowest grade transferable C-. **General Admission Information:** Application fee $25. Nonfall registration accepted. Admission may be deferred for a maximum of 1 year. Credit offered for CEEB Advanced Placement tests.

COSTS AND FINANCIAL AID

In-state tuition $3,905. Out-of-state tuition $9,215. Room & board $4,880. Required fees $485. Average book expense $650. **Required Forms and Deadlines:** FAFSA. Priority filing deadline March 1. **Notification of Awards:** Applicants will be notified of awards on a rolling basis beginning on or about February 15. **Types of Aid:** *Need-based scholarships/grants:* Pell, SEOG, state scholarships/grants, private scholarships, the school's own gift aid. *Loans:* FFEL Subsidized Stafford, FFEL Unsubsidized Stafford, FFEL PLUS, Federal Perkins. **Student Employment:** Federal Work-Study Program available. Institutional employment available. Off-campus job opportunities are good. **Financial Aid Statistics:** 71% freshmen, 77% undergrads receive some form of aid. Average freshman grant $5,099. Average freshman loan $2,700. Average income from on-campus job $1,200. **Financial Aid Phone:** 207-255-1203.

UNIVERSITY OF MAINE—PRESQUE ISLE

Office of Admissions, 181 Main Street, Presque Isle, ME 04769
Phone: 207-768-9532 **E-mail:** adventure@umpi.maine.edu **CEEB Code:** 3008
Fax: 207-768-9777 **Web:** www.umpi.maine.edu

This public school was founded in 1903. It has a 150-acre campus.

STUDENTS AND FACULTY

Enrollment: 1,560. **Student Body:** Male 35%, female 65%, out-of-state 3%, international 11% (6 countries represented). **Ethnic Representation:** African American 1%, Asian 1%, Caucasian 94%, Hispanic 1%, Native American 3%.

Retention and Graduation: 61% freshmen return for sophomore year. 20% grads go on to further study within 1 year. 1% grads pursue medical degrees. **Faculty:** Student/faculty ratio 14:1. 60 full-time faculty, 76% hold PhDs. 100% faculty teach undergrads.

ACADEMICS

Degrees: Associate's, bachelor's, certificate. **Academic Requirements:** General education including some course work in arts/fine arts, English (including composition), foreign languages, history, humanities, mathematics, philosophy, sciences (biological or physical), social science. **Classes:** 10-19 students in an average class. 10-19 students in an average lab/discussion section. **Majors with Highest Enrollment:** Education, general; social work; liberal arts and sciences/liberal studies. **Disciplines with Highest Percentage of Degrees Awarded:** Liberal arts/general studies 46%, education 19%, protective services/public administration 9%, parks and recreation 8%, business/marketing 6%. **Special Study Options:** Accelerated program, distance learning, double major, dual enrollment, student exchange program (domestic), honors program, independent study, internships, liberal arts/career combination, student-designed major, study abroad, teacher certification program.

FACILITIES

Housing: Coed, apartments for married students, apartments for single students, apartments for students with dependent children. **Library Holdings:** 455,372 bound volumes. 2,500 periodicals. 440,453 microforms. 1,281 audiovisuals. **Special Academic Facilities/Equipment:** Museum and art gallery. **Computers:** School-owned computers available for student use.

EXTRACURRICULARS

Activities: Concert band, drama/theater, music ensembles, musical theater, radio station, student government, student newspaper. **Organizations:** 27 registered organizations, 1 honor society, 1 religious organization, 1 fraternity (1% men join), 1 sorority (1% women join). **Athletics (Intercollegiate):** *Men:* baseball, basketball, cross-country, golf, soccer. *Women:* basketball, cross-country, soccer, softball, volleyball.

ADMISSIONS

Selectivity Rating: 64 (of 100). **Freshman Academic Profile:** Average high school GPA 3.0. 5% in top 10% of high school class, 19% in top 25% of high school class, 58% in top 50% of high school class. Average SAT I Math 462, SAT I Math middle 50% range 410-510. Average SAT I Verbal 464, SAT I Verbal middle 50% range 400-530. TOEFL required of all international applicants, minimum TOEFL 550. **Basis for Candidate Selection:** *Very important factors considered include:* class rank, essays, recommendations, secondary school record. *Important factors considered include:* interview. *Other factors considered include:* alumni/ae relation, character/personal qualities, extracurricular activities, minority status, standardized test scores, state residency, talent/ability, volunteer work, work experience. **Freshman Admission Requirements:** High school diploma or GED is required. *Academic units required/recommended:* 16 total recommended; 4 English recommended, 3 math recommended, 2 science recommended, 2 science lab recommended, 2 foreign language recommended, 3 social studies recommended, 2 elective recommended. **Freshman Admission Statistics:** 532 applied, 86% accepted, 60% of those accepted enrolled. **Transfer Admission Requirements:** *Items required:* high school transcript, college transcript, essay. Minimum high school GPA of 2.0 required. Minimum college GPA of 2.0 required. Lowest grade transferable C-. **General Admission Information:** Application fee $25. Nonfall registration accepted. Admission may be deferred for a maximum of 1 year. Credit offered for CEEB Advanced Placement tests.

COSTS AND FINANCIAL AID

In-state tuition $3,420. Out-of-state tuition $8,580. Room & board $4,494. Required fees $430. Average book expense $650. **Required Forms and Deadlines:** FAFSA. Priority filing deadline April 1. **Notification of Awards:** Applicants will be notified of awards on a rolling basis beginning on or about March 1. **Types of Aid:** *Need-based scholarships/grants:* Pell, SEOG, state scholarships/grants, private scholarships, the school's own gift aid. *Loans:* Direct Subsidized Stafford, Direct Unsubsidized Stafford, Direct PLUS, FFEL Subsidized Stafford, FFEL Unsubsidized Stafford, FFEL PLUS, Federal Perkins, state loans, college/university loans from institutional funds. **Student Employment:** Federal Work-Study Program available. Institutional employment available. Off-campus job opportunities are fair. **Financial Aid Statistics:** 73% freshmen, 67% undergrads receive some form of aid. **Financial Aid Phone:** 207-768-9510.

UNIVERSITY OF MANITOBA

424 University Centre, Winnipeg, MB R3T 2N2
Phone: 204-474-8808 **E-mail:** admissions@umanitoba.ca
Fax: 204-474-7554 **Web:** www.umanitoba.ca

This public school was founded in 1877. It has a 274-acre campus.

STUDENTS AND FACULTY

Enrollment: 20,534. **Student Body:** Male 43%, female 57%, out-of-state 12%. **Faculty:** 1,423 full-time faculty, 93% hold PhDs. 100% faculty teach undergrads.

ACADEMICS

Degrees: Bachelor's, certificate, diploma, doctoral, first professional, master's. **Academic Requirements:** General education including some course work in English (including composition), mathematics. **Classes:** 20-29 students in an average class. **Special Study Options:** Cooperative (work-study) program, distance learning, double major, honors program, independent study, internships, teacher certification program, weekend college.

FACILITIES

Housing: Coed. **Library Holdings:** 2,000,000 bound volumes. 9,000 periodicals. 2,000,000 microforms. **Special Academic Facilities/Equipment:** Planetarium, zoological museum, archives, art galleries. **Computers:** School-owned computers available for student use.

EXTRACURRICULARS

Activities: Choral groups, concert band, drama/theater, jazz band, music ensembles, radio station, student government, student newspaper. **Organizations:** 40 registered organizations, 5 religious organizations. **Athletics (Intercollegiate):** *Men:* basketball, skiing (cross-country), cross-country, diving, football, golf, gymnastics, ice hockey, swimming, track & field, volleyball, wrestling. *Women:* basketball, skiing (cross-country), cross-country, diving, field hockey, golf, gymnastics, ice hockey, swimming, track & field, volleyball, wrestling.

ADMISSIONS

Selectivity Rating: 63 (of 100). **Freshman Academic Profile:** TOEFL required of all international applicants, minimum TOEFL 550. **Basis for Candidate Selection:** *Very important factors considered include:* secondary school record. **Freshman Admission Requirements:** High school diploma or GED is required. *Academic units required/recommended:* 4 English required, 4 English recommended, 4 math required, 4 math recommended, 4 science recommended, 3 science lab recommended. **Transfer Admission Requirements:** *Items required:* college transcript. **General Admission Information:** Application fee $35. Early decision application deadline December 1. Regular application deadline July 1. Nonfall registration accepted. Credit offered for CEEB Advanced Placement tests.

COSTS AND FINANCIAL AID

Room & board $5,343. Required fees $450. Average book expense $1,200. **Types of Aid:** *Need-based scholarships/grants:* private scholarships, the school's own gift aid. **Student Employment:** Institutional employment available. Off-campus job opportunities are good. **Financial Aid Phone:** 204-474-8197.

UNIVERSITY OF MARY

7500 University Drive, Bismarck, ND 58504
Phone: 701-255-7500 **E-mail:** dfehr@umary.edu **CEEB Code:** 6428
Fax: 701-255-7687 **Web:** www.umary.edu **ACT Code:** 3201

This private school, which is affiliated with the Roman Catholic Church, was founded in 1959. It has a 107-acre campus.

STUDENTS AND FACULTY

Enrollment: 1,934. **Student Body:** Male 37%, female 63%. **Ethnic Representation:** Caucasian 94%, Native American 1%. **Retention and Graduation:** 70% freshmen return for sophomore year. 4% grads pursue business degrees. 2% grads pursue law degrees. **Faculty:** Student/faculty ratio 17:1. 100% faculty teach undergrads.

ACADEMICS

Degrees: Associate's, bachelor's, doctoral, master's. **Academic Requirements:** General education including some course work in arts/fine arts, English (including composition), history, humanities, mathematics, philosophy, sciences (biological or physical), social science. **Majors with Highest Enrollment:** Business administration/management; Nursing/registered nurse training (RN, ASN, BSN, MSN); health services/allied health, general. **Special Study Options:** Accelerated program, cooperative (work-study) program, distance learning, double major, dual enrollment, external degree program, honors program, independent study, internships, study abroad, teacher certification program.

FACILITIES

Housing: All-female, all-male, apartments for single students. **Library Holdings:** 55,000 bound volumes. 550 periodicals. 2,500 audiovisuals. **Special Academic Facilities/Equipment:** Art gallery. **Computers:** *Recommended operating system:* Windows 95. School-owned computers available for student use.

EXTRACURRICULARS

Activities: Choral groups, concert band, drama/theater, jazz band, literary magazine, music ensembles, musical theater, pep band, radio station, student government, student newspaper, television station, yearbook. **Organizations:** 50 registered organizations, 5 honor societies, 6 religious organizations. **Athletics (Intercollegiate):** *Men:* baseball, basketball, cross-country, football, golf, indoor track, soccer, tennis, track & field, wrestling. *Women:* basketball, cheerleading, cross-country, golf, indoor track, soccer, softball, tennis, track & field, volleyball.

ADMISSIONS

Selectivity Rating: 72 (of 100). **Freshman Academic Profile:** Average high school GPA 3.4. 9% in top 10% of high school class, 38% in top 25% of high school class, 71% in top 50% of high school class. Average ACT 23, ACT middle 50% range 19-24. TOEFL required of all international applicants, minimum TOEFL 500. **Basis for Candidate Selection:** *Very important factors considered include:* standardized test scores. *Important factors considered include:* class rank, recommendations, secondary school record. *Other factors considered include:* character/personal qualities, essays, interview. **Freshman Admission Requirements:** High school diploma or GED is required. *Academic units required/recommended:* 4 English recommended, 2 math recommended, 2 science recommended, 3 social studies recommended. **Freshman Admission Statistics:** 943 applied, 95% accepted, 48% of those accepted enrolled. **Transfer Admission Requirements:** *Items required:* college transcript. Minimum college GPA of 2.0 required. Lowest grade transferable D. **General Admission Information:** Application fee $15. Regular application deadline August 23. Nonfall registration accepted. Admission may be deferred for a maximum of 1 year. Credit and/or placement offered for CEEB Advanced Placement tests.

COSTS AND FINANCIAL AID

Tuition $9,200. Room & board $3,540. Required fees $300. Average book expense $610. **Required Forms and Deadlines:** FAFSA. Priority filing deadline May 1. **Notification of Awards:** Applicants will be notified of awards on a rolling basis. **Types of Aid:** *Need-based scholarships/grants:* Pell, SEOG, state scholarships/grants, private scholarships, the school's own gift aid. *Loans:* FFEL Subsidized Stafford, FFEL Unsubsidized Stafford, FFEL PLUS, Federal Perkins, Federal Nursing. **Student Employment:** Federal Work-Study Program available. Institutional employment available. Off-campus job opportunities are good. **Financial Aid Statistics:** Average freshman grant $3,000. Average freshman loan $3,500. Average income from on-campus job $1,000. **Financial Aid Phone:** 701-255-7500.

UNIVERSITY OF MARY HARDIN-BAYLOR

UMHB Box 8004, 900 College Street, Belton, TX 76513
Phone: 254-295-4520 **E-mail:** admission@umhb.edu **CEEB Code:** 6396
Fax: 254-295-5049 **Web:** www.umhb.edu **ACT Code:** 4128

This private school, which is affiliated with the Baptist Church, was founded in 1845. It has a 100-acre campus.

STUDENTS AND FACULTY

Enrollment: 2,474. **Student Body:** Male 35%, female 65%, out-of-state 2%, international 1% (10 countries represented). **Ethnic Representation:** African American 11%, Asian 2%, Caucasian 76%, Hispanic 10%. **Retention and Graduation:** 63% freshmen return for sophomore year. 23% freshmen graduate within 4 years. 10% grads go on to further study within 1 year. **Faculty:** Student/faculty ratio 16:1. 120 full-time faculty, 67% hold PhDs. 100% faculty teach undergrads.

ACADEMICS

Degrees: Bachelor's, master's. **Academic Requirements:** General education including some course work in computer literacy, English (including composition), history, sciences (biological or physical), social science. **Classes:** 10-19 students in an average class. 20-29 students in an average lab/discussion section. **Majors with Highest Enrollment:** Nursing/registered nurse training (RN, ASN, BSN, MSN); computer science; education, general. **Disciplines with Highest Percentage of Degrees Awarded:** Education 20%, business/marketing 12%, liberal arts/general studies 12%, health professions and related sciences 10%, computer and information sciences 9%. **Special Study Options:** Accelerated program, double major, dual enrollment, English as a second language, honors program, independent study, internships, study abroad, teacher certification program, tuition exchange program with other participating universities. Undergrads may take grad-level classes.

FACILITIES

Housing: All-female, all-male, apartments for single students, housing for disabled students. **Library Holdings:** 192,526 bound volumes. 1,631 periodicals. 387,817 microforms. 5,484 audiovisuals. **Special Academic Facilities/Equipment:** Language lab, language institute. **Computers:** School-owned computers available for student use.

EXTRACURRICULARS

Activities: Choral groups, concert band, drama/theater, jazz band, literary magazine, marching band, music ensembles, musical theater, opera, pep band, student government, student newspaper, yearbook. **Organizations:** 28 registered organizations, 4 honor societies. **Athletics (Intercollegiate):** *Men:* baseball, basketball, cross-country, football, golf, soccer, tennis. *Women:* basketball, cross-country, golf, soccer, softball, tennis, volleyball.

ADMISSIONS

Selectivity Rating: 66 (of 100). **Freshman Academic Profile:** 14% in top 10% of high school class, 39% in top 25% of high school class, 68% in top 50% of high school class. 92% from public high schools. SAT I Math middle 50% range 470-560. SAT I Verbal middle 50% range 470-550. ACT middle 50% range 19-24. **Basis for Candidate Selection:** *Very important factors considered include:* secondary school record, standardized test scores. *Important factors considered include:* class rank. *Other factors considered include:* essays, interview. **Freshman Admission Requirements:** High school diploma or GED is required. *Academic units required/recommended:* 22 total required; 4 English required, 3 math required, 2 social studies required. **Freshman Admission Statistics:** 747 applied, 92% accepted, 70% of those accepted enrolled. **Transfer Admission Requirements:** *Items required:* college transcript. Minimum college GPA of 2.0 required. Lowest grade transferable C. **General Admission Information:** Application fee $35. Nonfall registration accepted. Admission may be deferred. Credit offered for CEEB Advanced Placement tests.

COSTS AND FINANCIAL AID

Average book expense $750. **Required Forms and Deadlines:** FAFSA, institution's own financial aid form and state aid form. No deadline for regular filing. Priority filing deadline March 2. **Notification of Awards:** Applicants will be notified of awards on a rolling basis beginning on or about March 2. **Types of Aid:** *Need-based scholarships/grants:* Pell, SEOG, state scholarships/grants, the school's own gift aid. *Loans:* FFEL Subsidized Stafford, FFEL Unsubsidized Stafford, FFEL PLUS, college/university loans from institutional funds. **Student Employment:** Federal Work-Study Program available. Institutional employment available. Off-campus job opportunities are good. **Financial Aid Statistics:** 69% freshmen, 73% undergrads receive some form of aid. Average income from on-campus job $2,300. **Financial Aid Phone:** 817-939-4515.

UNIVERSITY OF MARYLAND, BALTIMORE COUNTY

1000 Hilltop Circle, Baltimore, MD 21250
Phone: 410-455-2291 **E-mail:** admissions@umbc.edu **CEEB Code:** 5835
Fax: 410-455-1094 **Web:** www.umbc.edu **ACT Code:** 1751

This public school was founded in 1966. It has a 500-acre campus.

STUDENTS AND FACULTY

Enrollment: 9,549. **Student Body:** Male 52%, female 48%, out-of-state 8%, international 5%. **Ethnic Representation:** African American 16%, Asian 20%,

Caucasian 59%, Hispanic 3%, Native American 1%. **Retention and Graduation:** 83% freshmen return for sophomore year. 44% grads go on to further study within 1 year. 1% grads pursue business degrees. 1% grads pursue law degrees. 5% grads pursue medical degrees. **Faculty:** Student/faculty ratio 17:1. 471 full-time faculty, 85% hold PhDs. 100% faculty teach undergrads.

ACADEMICS

Degrees: Bachelor's, doctoral, master's, post-bachelor's certificate. **Academic Requirements:** General education including some course work in arts/fine arts, English (including composition), foreign languages, humanities, mathematics, sciences (biological or physical), social science. **Classes:** 10-19 students in an average class. 10-19 students in an average lab/discussion section. **Majors with Highest Enrollment:** Information technology; psychology, general; visual and performing arts, general. **Disciplines with Highest Percentage of Degrees Awarded:** Computer and information sciences 28%, social sciences and history 15%, visual and performing arts 11%, psychology 11%, biological life sciences 10%. **Special Study Options:** Cooperative (work-study) program, cross registration, distance learning, double major, English as a second language, honors program, independent study, internships, liberal arts/career combination, student-designed major, study abroad, teacher certification program.

FACILITIES

Housing: Coed, apartments for single students, same-sex floors, honors floors. **Library Holdings:** 749,618 bound volumes. 4,282 periodicals. 1,036,790 microforms. 39,007 audiovisuals. **Special Academic Facilities/Equipment:** Albin O. Kuhn Library and Gallery, Center for Art and Visual Culture, women's center, Center for Environmental Science, Center for Photonics Technology, Center for Women and Information Technology, Center on Research and Teaching in Social Work, Howard Hughes Medical Institute at UMBC, imaging research center, Institute for Global Electronic Commerce, Joint Center for Earth Systems Technology, Laboratory for Healthcare Informatics, Maryland Center for Telecommunications Research, Maryland Institute for Policy Analysis and Research, bwtech@umbc Research and Technology Park, Shriver Center, UMBC Technology Center, Goddard Earth Science and Technology Center. **Computers:** School-owned computers available for student use.

EXTRACURRICULARS

Activities: Choral groups, concert band, dance, drama/theater, jazz band, literary magazine, music ensembles, musical theater, opera, pep band, radio station, student government, student newspaper, student-run film society, symphony orchestra, television station. **Organizations:** 170 registered organizations, 24 honor societies, 14 religious organizations, 11 fraternities (3% men join), 10 sororities (3% women join). **Athletics (Intercollegiate):** *Men:* baseball, basketball, cross-country, diving, lacrosse, soccer, swimming, tennis, track & field. *Women:* basketball, cross-country, diving, field hockey, lacrosse, soccer, softball, swimming, tennis, track & field, volleyball.

ADMISSIONS

Selectivity Rating: 80 (of 100). **Freshman Academic Profile:** Average high school GPA 3.5. 30% in top 10% of high school class, 60% in top 25% of high school class, 90% in top 50% of high school class. 84% from public high schools. Average SAT I Math 621, SAT I Math middle 50% range 570-670. Average SAT I Verbal 592, SAT I Verbal middle 50% range 540-640. Average ACT 25, ACT middle 50% range 23-28. TOEFL required of all international applicants, minimum TOEFL 220. **Basis for Candidate Selection:** *Very important factors considered include:* secondary school record, standardized test scores. *Important factors considered include:* class rank, essays, recommendations. *Other factors considered include:* character/personal qualities, extracurricular activities, interview, talent/ability, volunteer work, work experience. **Freshman Admission Requirements:** High school diploma or GED is required. *Academic units required/recommended:* 22 total required; 23 total recommended; 4 English required, 4 English recommended, 3 math required, 4 math recommended, 3 science required, 3 science recommended, 2 science lab required, 2 science lab recommended, 2 foreign language required, 2 foreign language recommended, 2 social studies required, 2 social studies recommended, 2 history required, 2 history recommended, 4 elective required, 4 elective recommended. **Freshman Admission Statistics:** 5,211 applied, 63% accepted, 41% of those accepted enrolled. **Transfer Admission Requirements:** *Items required:* college transcript. Minimum college GPA of 2.0 required. Lowest grade transferable C-. **General Admission Information:** Application fee $50. Priority application deadline November 1. Regular application deadline February 1. Nonfall registration accepted. Admission may be deferred. Credit and/or placement offered for CEEB Advanced Placement tests.

COSTS AND FINANCIAL AID

In-state tuition $4,614. Out-of-state tuition $10,798. Room & board $6,780. Required fees $1,748. Average book expense $800. **Required Forms and Deadlines:** FAFSA. No deadline for regular filing. Priority filing deadline March 1. **Notification of Awards:** Applicants will be notified of awards on a rolling basis beginning on or about March 15. **Types of Aid:** *Need-based scholarships/grants:* Pell, SEOG, state scholarships/grants, private scholarships, the school's own gift aid. *Loans:* FFEL Subsidized Stafford, FFEL Unsubsidized Stafford, FFEL PLUS, Federal Perkins. **Student Employment:** Federal Work-Study Program available. Institutional employment available. Off-campus job opportunities are excellent. **Financial Aid Statistics:** 53% freshmen, 54% undergrads receive some form of aid. Average freshman grant $6,212. Average freshman loan $2,566. Average income from on-campus job $1,132. **Financial Aid Phone:** 410-455-2387.

UNIVERSITY OF MARYLAND, COLLEGE PARK

Mitchell Building, College Park, MD 20742-5235
Phone: 301-314-8385 **E-mail:** um-admit@uga.umd.edu **CEEB Code:** 5814
Fax: 301-314-9693 **Web:** www.maryland.edu **ACT Code:** 1746

This public school was founded in 1856. It has a 1,580-acre campus.

STUDENTS AND FACULTY

Enrollment: 25,179. **Student Body:** Male 51%, female 49%, out-of-state 25%, international 3%. **Ethnic Representation:** African American 13%, Asian 14%, Caucasian 61%, Hispanic 5%. **Retention and Graduation:** 92% freshmen return for sophomore year. 41% freshmen graduate within 4 years. 33% grads go on to further study within 1 year. 2% grads pursue business degrees. 9% grads pursue law degrees. 4% grads pursue medical degrees. **Faculty:** Student/faculty ratio 13:1. 1,621 full-time faculty, 90% hold PhDs.

ACADEMICS

Degrees: Bachelor's, certificate, doctoral, first professional, master's, post-bachelor's certificate, post-master's certificate. **Academic Requirements:** General education including some course work in arts/fine arts, English (including composition), history, humanities, mathematics, sciences (biological or physical), social science, one diversity course, two advanced studies courses (upper-level classes) outside of one's major. **Classes:** 20-29 students in an average class. 20-29 students in an average lab/discussion section. **Majors with Highest Enrollment:** Political science and government; criminology; computer science. **Disciplines with Highest Percentage of Degrees Awarded:** Social sciences and history 20%, business/marketing 17%, engineering/engineering technology 9%, biological life sciences 9%, English 8%. **Special Study Options:** Accelerated program, cooperative (work-study) program, cross registration, distance learning, double major, dual enrollment, English as a second language, student exchange program (domestic), external degree program, honors program, independent study, internships, student-designed major, study abroad, teacher certification program, living learning programs, Gemstone program, honors humanities, first-year focus, CIVICUS program, College Park Scholars, Beyond the Classroom, Global Communities, Jimenez-Porter Writers' House.

FACILITIES

Housing: Coed, all-female, apartments for single students, housing for disabled students, housing for international students, fraternities and/or sororities, cooperative housing, Gemstone program, College Park Scholars, language house, honors house, international house, smoke-free/alcohol-free. **Library Holdings:** 2,956,648 bound volumes. 33,858 periodicals. 5,473,621 microforms. 283,669 audiovisuals. **Special Academic Facilities/Equipment:** Aerospace buoyancy lab, art gallery, international piano archives, center for architectural design and research, model nuclear reactor, wind tunnel. **Computers:** School-owned computers available for student use.

EXTRACURRICULARS

Activities: Choral groups, concert band, dance, drama/theater, jazz band, literary magazine, marching band, music ensembles, musical theater, opera, pep band, radio station, student government, student newspaper, student-run film society, symphony orchestra, television station, yearbook. **Organizations:** 300 registered organizations, 48 honor societies, 27 fraternities (9% men join), 20 sororities (10% women join). **Athletics (Intercollegiate):** *Men:* baseball, basketball, cross-country, football, golf, indoor track, lacrosse, soccer, swimming, tennis, track & field, wrestling. *Women:* basketball, cross-country, field hockey, golf, gymnastics, indoor track, lacrosse, soccer, softball, swimming, tennis, track & field, volleyball.

ADMISSIONS

Selectivity Rating: 81 (of 100). **Freshman Academic Profile:** Average high school GPA 3.9. 58% in top 10% of high school class, 90% in top 25% of high school class, 100% in top 50% of high school class. SAT I Math middle 50% range 600-700. SAT I Verbal middle 50% range 570-670. TOEFL required of all international applicants, minimum TOEFL 575. **Basis for Candidate Selection:** *Very important factors considered include:* secondary school record, standardized test scores. *Important factors considered include:* class rank, essays, recommendations, state residency, talent/ability. *Other factors considered include:* alumni/ae relation, character/personal qualities, extracurricular activities, geographical residence, minority status, volunteer work, work experience. **Freshman Admission Requirements:** High school diploma or GED is required. *Academic units required/recommended:* 16 total required; 17 total recommended; 4 English required, 3 math required, 4 math recommended, 2 science required, 2 science lab required, 2 foreign language required, 3 social studies required. **Freshman Admission Statistics:** 23,117 applied, 43% accepted, 39% of those accepted enrolled. **Transfer Admission Requirements:** *Items required:* college transcript. Lowest grade transferable C. **General Admission Information:** Application fee $45. Priority application deadline December 1. Regular application deadline January 20. Nonfall registration accepted. Admission may be deferred for a maximum of 1 year. Credit and/or placement offered for CEEB Advanced Placement tests.

COSTS AND FINANCIAL AID

In-state tuition $4,572. Out-of-state tuition $13,336. Room & board $7,241. Required fees $1,098. Average book expense $808. **Required Forms and Deadlines:** FAFSA. Financial aid filing deadline June 30. Priority filing deadline February 15. **Notification of Awards:** Applicants will be notified of awards on or about April 1. **Types of Aid:** *Need-based scholarships/grants:* Pell, SEOG, state scholarships/grants, private scholarships, the school's own gift aid. *Loans:* FFEL Subsidized Stafford, FFEL Unsubsidized Stafford, FFEL PLUS, Federal Perkins. **Student Employment:** Federal Work-Study Program available. Institutional employment available. Off-campus job opportunities are excellent. **Financial Aid Statistics:** 40% freshmen, 40% undergrads receive some form of aid. Average freshman grant $4,858. Average freshman loan $3,301. **Financial Aid Phone:** 301-314-9000.

UNIVERSITY OF MARYLAND, EASTERN SHORE

Office of Admissions, Backbone Road, Princess Anne, MD 21853
Phone: 410-651-6410 **E-mail:** ccmills@mail.umes.edu **CEEB Code:** 5400
Fax: 410-651-7922 **Web:** www.umes.edu **ACT Code:** 1752

This public school was founded in 1886. It has a 620-acre campus.

STUDENTS AND FACULTY

Enrollment: 2,704. **Student Body:** Male 43%, female 57%, out-of-state 26%, international students represent 44 countries. **Ethnic Representation:** African American 80%, Asian 1%, Caucasian 14%, Hispanic 1%. **Retention and Graduation:** 76% freshmen return for sophomore year. 19% freshmen graduate within 4 years. 15% grads go on to further study within 1 year. 4% grads pursue business degrees. 2% grads pursue law degrees. 2% grads pursue medical degrees. **Faculty:** Student/faculty ratio 18:1. 133 full-time faculty, 65% hold PhDs.

ACADEMICS

Degrees: Bachelor's, doctoral, master's, terminal. **Academic Requirements:** General education including some course work in arts/fine arts, English (including composition), foreign languages, history, humanities, mathematics, sciences (biological or physical), social science. **Classes:** Under 10 students in an average class. **Disciplines with Highest Percentage of Degrees Awarded:** Business/marketing 20%, protective services/public administration 13%, education 9%, biological life sciences 9%, health professions and related sciences 9%. **Special Study Options:** Accelerated program, cooperative (work-study) program, cross registration, distance learning, double major, honors program, independent study, internships, teacher certification program, hotel/restaurant management semester, NASA program, study possible at Wallops Island (Virginia), other off-campus study opportunities in marine research.

FACILITIES

Housing: Coed, all-female, all-male. **Library Holdings:** 175,090 bound volumes. 173,624 periodicals. 6,001 microforms. 19,026 audiovisuals. **Special Academic Facilities/Equipment:** Art museum, performing arts center, college farm, academic center. **Computers:** School-owned computers available for student use.

EXTRACURRICULARS

Activities: Choral groups, concert band, dance, drama/theater, jazz band, literary magazine, music ensembles, radio station, student government, student newspaper, student-run film society, symphony orchestra, television station, yearbook. **Organizations:** 60 registered organizations, 4 honor societies, 4 religious organizations, 3 fraternities (5% men join), 2 sororities (5% women join). **Athletics (Intercollegiate):** *Men:* baseball, basketball, cross-country, tennis, track & field. *Women:* basketball, cheerleading, cross-country, softball, tennis, track & field, volleyball.

ADMISSIONS

Selectivity Rating: 79 (of 100). **Freshman Academic Profile:** Average high school GPA 2.7. 90% from public high schools. Average SAT I Math 410. Average SAT I Verbal 430. TOEFL required of all international applicants, minimum TOEFL 500. **Basis for Candidate Selection:** *Very important factors considered include:* character/personal qualities, secondary school record, standardized test scores, talent/ability. *Important factors considered include:* alumni/ae relation, class rank, essays, extracurricular activities, interview. *Other factors considered include:* recommendations, volunteer work, work experience. **Freshman Admission Requirements:** High school diploma or GED is required. *Academic units required/recommended:* 20 total required; 24 total recommended; 4 English required, 3 math required, 2 science required, 2 science lab required, 2 foreign language required, 3 social studies required, 6 elective required. **Freshman Admission Statistics:** 3,073 applied, 51% accepted, 52% of those accepted enrolled. **Transfer Admission Requirements:** *Items required:* high school transcript, college transcript, essay. Minimum college GPA of 2.0 required. Lowest grade transferable C. **General Admission Information:** Application fee $25. Priority application deadline March 1. Regular application deadline July 15. Nonfall registration accepted. Credit offered for CEEB Advanced Placement tests.

COSTS AND FINANCIAL AID

In-state tuition $3,994. Out-of-state tuition $8,497. Room & board $4,930. Required fees $604. Average book expense $700. **Required Forms and Deadlines:** FAFSA. No deadline for regular filing. Priority filing deadline March 1. **Notification of Awards:** Applicants will be notified of awards on or about April 1. **Types of Aid:** *Need-based scholarships/grants:* Pell, SEOG, state scholarships/grants, private scholarships, the school's own gift aid. *Loans:* Direct Subsidized Stafford, Direct Unsubsidized Stafford, Direct PLUS, Federal Perkins, college/university loans from institutional funds. **Student Employment:** Federal Work-Study Program available. Institutional employment available. Off-campus job opportunities are fair. **Financial Aid Statistics:** Average income from on-campus job $1,381. **Financial Aid Phone:** 410-651-6172.

UNIVERSITY OF MARYLAND, UNIVERSITY COLLEGE

3501 University Blvd. East, Adelphi, MD 20783
Phone: 301-985-7000 **E-mail:** umucinfo@nova.umuc.edu
Fax: 301-985-7364 **Web:** www.umuc.edu **ACT Code:** 20097

This public school was founded in 1947.

STUDENTS AND FACULTY

Enrollment: 16,990. **Student Body:** Male 58%, female 42%, out-of-state 25%, international 2%. **Ethnic Representation:** African American 34%, Asian 6%, Caucasian 47%, Hispanic 5%, Native American 1%. **Faculty:** Student/faculty ratio 19:1. 76 full-time faculty, 84% hold PhDs.

ACADEMICS

Degrees: Associate's, bachelor's, certificate, doctoral, master's, post-bachelor's certificate. **Academic Requirements:** General education including some course work in computer literacy, English (including composition), humanities, mathematics, sciences (biological or physical), social science. **Classes:** 20-29 students in an average class. **Majors with Highest Enrollment:** Business administration/management; information science/studies; multi/interdisciplinary studies. **Disciplines with Highest Percentage of Degrees Awarded:** Interdisciplinary studies 95%, computer and information sciences 3%, business/marketing 1%. **Special Study Options:** Accelerated program, cooperative (work-study) program, cross registration, distance learning, double major, dual enrollment, external degree program, weekend college.

FACILITIES

Library Holdings: 5,807 bound volumes. 31 periodicals. 0 microforms. 0 audiovisuals. **Computers:** School-owned computers available for student use.

ADMISSIONS

Selectivity Rating: 63 (of 100). **Freshman Academic Profile:** TOEFL required of all international applicants, minimum TOEFL 550. **Freshman Admission Requirements:** High school diploma or GED is required. **Freshman Admission Statistics:** 970 applied, 100% accepted, 41% of those accepted enrolled. **Transfer Admission Requirements:** *Items required:* high school transcript, college transcript. Minimum college GPA of 2.0 required. Lowest grade transferable D. **General Admission Information:** Application fee $30. Nonfall registration accepted. Admission may be deferred for a maximum of 2 years. Credit and/or placement offered for CEEB Advanced Placement tests.

COSTS AND FINANCIAL AID

In-state tuition $4,944. Out-of-state tuition $9,216. Required fees $120. Average book expense $1,362. **Required Forms and Deadlines:** FAFSA and institution's own financial aid form. No deadline for regular filing. Priority filing deadline June 1. **Notification of Awards:** Applicants will be notified of awards on a rolling basis beginning on or about May 1. **Types of Aid:** *Need-based scholarships/grants:* Pell, SEOG, state scholarships/grants, private scholarships, the school's own gift aid. *Loans:* Direct Subsidized Stafford, Direct Unsubsidized Stafford, Direct PLUS, Federal Perkins. **Student Employment:** Off-campus job opportunities are good. **Financial Aid Statistics:** 46% freshmen, 49% undergrads receive some form of aid. **Financial Aid Phone:** 301-985-7000.

UNIVERSITY OF MASSACHUSETTS—AMHERST

Office of Undergraduate Admissions, 37 Mather Drive, Amherst, MA 01003-9291
Phone: 413-545-0222 **E-mail:** mail@admissions.umass.edu **CEEB Code:** 3917
Fax: 413-545-4312 **Web:** www.umass.edu **ACT Code:** 1924

This public school was founded in 1863. It has a 1,463-acre campus.

STUDENTS AND FACULTY

Enrollment: 18,606. **Student Body:** Male 49%, female 51%, out-of-state 18%, international 2% (114 countries represented). **Ethnic Representation:** African American 5%, Asian 7%, Caucasian 76%, Hispanic 4%. **Retention and Graduation:** 83% freshmen return for sophomore year. 41% freshmen graduate within 4 years. 16% grads go on to further study within 1 year. 13% grads pursue business degrees. 12% grads pursue law degrees. 6% grads pursue medical degrees. **Faculty:** Student/faculty ratio 19:1. 1,063 full-time faculty, 93% hold PhDs. 88% faculty teach undergrads.

ACADEMICS

Degrees: Associate's, bachelor's, doctoral, master's, post-master's certificate, terminal. **Academic Requirements:** General education including some course work in arts/fine arts, English (including composition), foreign languages, history, humanities, mathematics, sciences (biological or physical), social science, social & cultural diversity. **Classes:** 20-29 students in an average class. 20-29 students in an average lab/discussion section. **Majors with Highest Enrollment:** Communications studies/speech communication and rhetoric; English language and literature, general; biology/biological sciences, general. **Disciplines with Highest Percentage of Degrees Awarded:** Social sciences and history 17%, business/marketing 16%, communications/communication technologies 9%, psychology 7%, engineering/engineering technology 5%. **Special Study Options:** Cooperative (work-study) program, cross registration, distance learning, double major, dual enrollment, English as a second language, student exchange program (domestic), honors program, independent study, internships, student-designed major, study abroad, teacher certification program. Residential academic programs. University Without Walls offers individualized degrees to working adults for whom the conventional route for obtaining a bachelor's degree is difficult or impossible.

FACILITIES

Housing: Coed, all-female, all-male, apartments for married students, apartments for single students, housing for disabled students, housing for international students, fraternities and/or sororities, special-interest housing, residential academic programs. **Library Holdings:** 3,089,191 bound volumes. 14,022 periodicals. 2,493,063 microforms. 18,468 audiovisuals. **Special Academic Facilities/Equipment:** Computer science complex, population research institute, polymer research institute. **Computers:** School-owned computers available for student use.

EXTRACURRICULARS

Activities: Choral groups, concert band, dance, drama/theater, jazz band, literary magazine, marching band, music ensembles, musical theater, opera, pep band, radio station, student government, student newspaper, student-run film society, symphony orchestra, television station, yearbook. **Organizations:** 200 registered organizations, 40 honor societies, 12 religious organizations, 21 fraternities (3% men join), 12 sororities (7% women join). **Athletics (Intercollegiate):** *Men:* baseball, basketball, cheerleading, cross-country, diving, football, ice hockey, indoor track, lacrosse, skiing (alpine), soccer, swimming, track & field. *Women:* basketball, cheerleading, crew, cross-country, diving, field hockey, indoor track, lacrosse, skiing (alpine), soccer, softball, swimming, tennis, track & field.

ADMISSIONS

Selectivity Rating: 75 (of 100). **Freshman Academic Profile:** Average high school GPA 3.4. 21% in top 10% of high school class, 56% in top 25% of high school class, 92% in top 50% of high school class. 90% from public high schools. Average SAT I Math 571, SAT I Math middle 50% range 510-630. Average SAT I Verbal 554, SAT I Verbal middle 50% range 500-620. TOEFL required of all international applicants, minimum TOEFL 550. **Basis for Candidate Selection:** *Very important factors considered include:* essays, secondary school record. *Important factors considered include:* character/personal qualities, extracurricular activities, standardized test scores, state residency, talent/ability. *Other factors considered include:* alumni/ae relation, class rank, minority status, recommendations, volunteer work, work experience. **Freshman Admission Requirements:** High school diploma or GED is required. *Academic units required/recommended:* 16 total required; 4 English required, 3 math required, 3 science required, 2 science lab required, 2 foreign language required, 2 social studies required, 2 elective required. **Freshman Admission Statistics:** 20,449 applied, 58% accepted, 28% of those accepted enrolled. **Transfer Admission Requirements:** *Items required:* college transcript, essay. Minimum college GPA of 2.5 required. Lowest grade transferable C-. **General Admission Information:** Application fee $40. Regular application deadline January 15. Nonfall registration accepted. Credit and/or placement offered for CEEB Advanced Placement tests.

COSTS AND FINANCIAL AID

Average book expense $500. **Required Forms and Deadlines:** FAFSA. Priority filing deadline March 1. **Notification of Awards:** Applicants will be notified of awards on a rolling basis beginning on or about April 1. **Types of Aid:** *Need-based scholarships/grants:* Pell, SEOG, state scholarships/grants, private scholarships, the school's own gift aid. *Loans:* Direct Subsidized Stafford, Direct Unsubsidized Stafford, Direct PLUS, Federal Perkins, state loans, William D. Ford Federal Direct (Subsidized & Unsubsidized) Loans. **Student Employment:** Federal Work-Study Program available. Institutional employment available. Off-campus job opportunities are good. **Financial Aid Statistics:** 46% freshmen, 44% undergrads receive some form of aid. Average income from on-campus job $1,800. **Financial Aid Phone:** 413-545-0801.

UNIVERSITY OF MASSACHUSETTS—BOSTON

100 Morrissey Boulevard, Boston, MA 02125-3393
Phone: 617-287-6100 **E-mail:** undergrad@umb.edu **CEEB Code:** 3924
Fax: 617-287-5999 **Web:** www.umb.edu

This public school was founded in 1964. It has a 177-acre campus.

STUDENTS AND FACULTY

Enrollment: 10,071. **Student Body:** Male 43%, female 57%, out-of-state 4%, international 5% (74 countries represented). **Ethnic Representation:** African American 15%, Asian 12%, Caucasian 51%, Hispanic 7%. **Retention and Graduation:** 70% freshmen return for sophomore year. 10% freshmen graduate within 4 years. **Faculty:** Student/faculty ratio 15:1. 427 full-time faculty. 100% faculty teach undergrads.

ACADEMICS

Degrees: Bachelor's, certificate, doctoral, master's, post-bachelor's certificate, post-master's certificate. **Academic Requirements:** General education including some course work in arts/fine arts, computer literacy, English (including composition), foreign languages, history, humanities, mathematics, philosophy, sciences (biological or physical), social science. **Classes:** 20-29 students in an average class. 10-19 students in an average lab/discussion section. **Majors with Highest Enrollment:** Business/commerce, general; education, general; social sciences, general. **Disciplines with Highest Percentage of Degrees Awarded:** Business/marketing 20%, social sciences and history 18%, psychology 12%, protective services/public administration 11%, health professions and related sciences 10%. **Special Study Options:** Accelerated program, cooperative (work-study) program, cross registration, distance learning, double major, dual enrollment, English as a second language, student exchange program (domestic), honors program, independent study, internships, liberal arts/career combination, student-designed major, study abroad, teacher certification program.

FACILITIES

Housing: University housing referral service. **Library Holdings:** 443,194 bound volumes. 2,784 periodicals. 827,117 microforms. 1,885 audiovisuals. **Special Academic Facilities/Equipment:** Art gallery, tropical greenhouse, observatory, adaptive computer lab. **Computers:** School-owned computers available for student use.

EXTRACURRICULARS

Activities: Choral groups, concert band, dance, drama/theater, jazz band, literary magazine, music ensembles, musical theater, radio station, student government, student newspaper, student-run film society, yearbook. **Organizations:** 76 registered organizations, 1 honor society. **Athletics (Intercollegiate):** *Men:* baseball, basketball, cross-country, golf, ice hockey, lacrosse, sailing, soccer, softball, squash, tennis, track & field, volleyball. *Women:* basketball, cross-country, sailing, soccer, softball, squash, tennis, track & field, volleyball.

ADMISSIONS

Selectivity Rating: 69 (of 100). **Freshman Academic Profile:** Average high school GPA 2.8. 7% in top 10% of high school class, 30% in top 25% of high school class, 76% in top 50% of high school class. Average SAT I Math 531, SAT I Math middle 50% range 480-590. Average SAT I Verbal 515, SAT I Verbal middle 50% range 460-570. TOEFL required of all international applicants, minimum TOEFL 500. **Basis for Candidate Selection:** *Very important factors considered include:* character/personal qualities, secondary school record, standardized test scores. *Important factors considered include:* essays, recommendations. *Other factors considered include:* extracurricular activities, interview, talent/ability, volunteer work, work experience. **Freshman Admission Requirements:** High school diploma or GED is required. *Academic units required/recommended:* 16 total required; 4 English required, 3 math required, 3 science required, 2 science lab required, 2 foreign language required, 1 social studies required, 1 history required, 2 elective required. **Freshman Admission Statistics:** 2,704 applied, 55% accepted, 39% of those accepted enrolled. **Transfer Admission Requirements:** *Items required:* college transcript, essay, statement of good standing from prior school. Minimum high school GPA of 2.0 required. Minimum college GPA of 2.0 required. Lowest grade transferable C-. **General Admission Information:** Application fee $40. Priority application deadline March 1. Nonfall registration accepted. Admission may be deferred for a maximum of 1 year. Credit offered for CEEB Advanced Placement tests.

COSTS AND FINANCIAL AID

In-state tuition $1,714. Out-of-state tuition $9,758. Required fees $3,508. Average book expense $0. **Required Forms and Deadlines:** FAFSA. No deadline for regular filing. Priority filing deadline March 1. **Notification of Awards:** Applicants will be notified of awards on a rolling basis beginning on or about April 1. **Types of Aid:** *Need-based scholarships/grants:* Pell, SEOG, state scholarships/grants, private scholarships, the school's own gift aid. *Loans:* FFEL Subsidized Stafford, FFEL Unsubsidized Stafford, FFEL PLUS, Federal Perkins, state loans, TERI, CitiAssist, Educaid. **Student Employment:** Federal Work-Study Program available. Institutional employment available. Off-campus job opportunities are excellent. **Financial Aid Statistics:** 64% freshmen, 46% undergrads receive some form of aid. Average freshman grant $4,421. Average freshman loan $2,896. **Financial Aid Phone:** 617-287-6300.

UNIVERSITY OF MASSACHUSETTS—DARTMOUTH

285 Old Westport Road, Dartmouth, MA 02747-2300
Phone: 508-999-8605 **E-mail:** admissions@umassd.edu **CEEB Code:** 3786
Fax: 508-999-8755 **Web:** www.umassd.edu **ACT Code:** 1906

This public school was founded in 1895. It has a 710-acre campus.

STUDENTS AND FACULTY

Enrollment: 7,309. **Student Body:** Male 48%, female 52%, out-of-state 7%, international students represent 49 countries. **Ethnic Representation:** African American 6%, Asian 2%, Caucasian 79%, Hispanic 2%, Native American 1%. **Retention and Graduation:** 79% freshmen return for sophomore year. 29% freshmen graduate within 4 years. **Faculty:** Student/faculty ratio 16:1. 321 full-time faculty, 86% hold PhDs. 100% faculty teach undergrads.

ACADEMICS

Degrees: Bachelor's, certificate, doctoral, master's, post-bachelor's certificate, post-master's certificate. **Academic Requirements:** General education including some course work in arts/fine arts, computer literacy, English (including composition), humanities, mathematics, sciences (biological or physical), social science. **Classes:** 10-19 students in an average class. 20-29 students in an average lab/discussion section. **Majors with Highest Enrollment:** Psychology, general; nursing; sociology. **Disciplines with Highest Percentage of Degrees Awarded:** Business/marketing 24%, social sciences and history 19%, visual and performing arts 11%, engineering/engineering technology 9%, psychology 9%. **Special Study Options:** Cooperative (work-study) program, cross registration, distance learning, double major, dual enrollment, honors program, independent study, internships, student-designed major, study abroad, teacher certification program.

FACILITIES

Housing: Coed, apartments for single students, housing for disabled students, apartments for upperclassmen and graduate students, program-dedicated suites. **Library Holdings:** 288,189 bound volumes. 2,925 periodicals. 810,127 microforms. 12,980 audiovisuals. **Special Academic Facilities/Equipment:** Art gallery, language center, center for Jewish culture, Robert F. Kennedy assassination archives, electron microscope, observatory, marine research vessels, Advanced Manufacturing and Technology Center, School of Marine Science and Technology. **Computers:** School-owned computers available for student use.

EXTRACURRICULARS

Activities: Choral groups, concert band, dance, drama/theater, jazz band, literary magazine, music ensembles, musical theater, pep band, radio station, student government, student newspaper, symphony orchestra, yearbook. **Organizations:** 92 registered organizations, 7 honor societies, 6 religious organizations, 3 fraternities, 1 sorority. **Athletics (Intercollegiate):** *Men:* baseball, basketball, cheerleading, cross-country, diving, equestrian, football, golf, ice hockey, indoor track, lacrosse, soccer, swimming, tennis, track & field. *Women:* basketball, cheerleading, cross-country, diving, equestrian, field hockey, golf, indoor track, lacrosse, soccer, softball, swimming, tennis, track & field, volleyball.

ADMISSIONS

Selectivity Rating: 80 (of 100). **Freshman Academic Profile:** Average high school GPA 3.0. 10% in top 10% of high school class, 34% in top 25% of high school class, 74% in top 50% of high school class. 85% from public high schools. Average SAT I Math 539, SAT I Math middle 50% range 490-590. Average SAT I Verbal 527, SAT I Verbal middle 50% range 480-570. TOEFL required of all international applicants, minimum TOEFL 500. **Basis for Candidate Selection:** *Very important factors considered include:* secondary school record, standardized test scores. *Other factors considered include:* alumni/ae relation, character/personal qualities, class rank, essays, extracurricular activities, recommendations, talent/ability, volunteer work, work experience. **Freshman Admission Requirements:** High school diploma or GED is required. *Academic units required/recommended:* 16 total required; 4 English required, 3 math required, 3 science required, 2 science lab required, 2 foreign language required, 1 social studies required, 1 history required, 2 elective required. **Freshman Admission Statistics:** 6,039 applied, 70% accepted, 36% of those accepted enrolled. **Transfer Admission Requirements:** *Items required:* college transcript, essay, statement of good standing from prior school. Minimum high school GPA of 3.0 required. Minimum college GPA of 2.5 required. Lowest grade transferable C-. **General Admission Information:** Application fee $35. Early decision application deadline November 15. Nonfall registration accepted. Admission may be deferred for a maximum of 1 year. Credit and/or placement offered for CEEB Advanced Placement tests.

COSTS AND FINANCIAL AID

In-state tuition $1,417. Out-of-state tuition $8,099. Room & board $6,526. Required fees $3,712. Average book expense $600. **Required Forms and Deadlines:** FAFSA. Priority filing deadline March 1. **Types of Aid:** *Need-based scholarships/grants:* Pell, SEOG, state scholarships/grants, private scholarships, the school's own gift aid. *Loans:* Direct Subsidized Stafford, Direct Unsubsidized Stafford, Direct PLUS, Federal Perkins, Federal Nursing, state loans. **Student Employment:** Federal Work-Study Program available. Institutional employment available. Off-campus job opportunities are good. **Financial Aid Statistics:** 48% freshmen, 52% undergrads receive some form of aid. **Financial Aid Phone:** 508-999-8632.

See page 1250.

UNIVERSITY OF MASSACHUSETTS—LOWELL

Office of Undergrad Admissions, 883 Broadway Street Room 110, Lowell, MA 01854-5104
Phone: 978-934-3931 **E-mail:** admissions@uml.edu **CEEB Code:** 3911
Fax: 978-934-3086 **Web:** www.uml.edu **ACT Code:** 1854

This public school was founded in 1894. It has a 150-acre campus.

STUDENTS AND FACULTY

Enrollment: 9,334. **Student Body:** Male 60%, female 40%, out-of-state 11%, international 2% (73 countries represented). **Ethnic Representation:** African American 2%, Asian 8%, Caucasian 54%, Hispanic 3%. **Retention and Graduation:** 74% freshmen return for sophomore year. 22% freshmen graduate within 4 years. **Faculty:** Student/faculty ratio 15:1. 359 full-time faculty, 93% hold PhDs.

ACADEMICS

Degrees: Associate's, bachelor's, doctoral, master's, post-master's certificate. **Academic Requirements:** General education including some course work in English (including composition), foreign languages, history, humanities, mathematics, sciences (biological or physical), social science. **Classes:** 10-19 students in an average class. **Disciplines with Highest Percentage of Degrees Awarded:** Business/marketing 24%, engineering/engineering technology 13%, protective services/public administration 11%, health professions and related sciences 11%, computer and information sciences 9%. **Special Study Options:** Accelerated program, cooperative (work-study) program, cross registration, distance learning, double major, dual enrollment, honors program, internships, liberal arts/career combination, study abroad, teacher certification program.

FACILITIES

Housing: Coed, all-female, all-male, apartments for married students, apartments for single students, housing for disabled students, cooperative housing. **Library Holdings:** 810,849 bound volumes. 1,865 periodicals. 1,701,316 microforms. 7,205 audiovisuals. **Special Academic Facilities/Equipment:** Language lab, media center, audiovisual department, on-campus elementary school, centers for learning, center for productivity enhancement, center for field studies, center for performing and visual art, center for health promotion, research nuclear reactor. New recreation center includes multicourt gymnasium, 1/8-mile indoor elevated track, aerobics room, game rooms, locker rooms, sauna, meeting rooms, and indoor/outdoor food court. **Computers:** School-owned computers available for student use.

EXTRACURRICULARS

Activities: Choral groups, concert band, dance, drama/theater, jazz band, literary magazine, marching band, music ensembles, pep band, radio station, student government, student newspaper, student-run film society, yearbook. **Organizations:** 100 registered organizations, 16 honor societies, 4 religious organizations. **Athletics (Intercollegiate):** *Men:* baseball, basketball, crew, cross-country, football, ice hockey, indoor track, lacrosse, soccer, track & field. *Women:* basketball, crew, cross-country, field hockey, indoor track, soccer, softball, track & field, volleyball.

ADMISSIONS

Selectivity Rating: 66 (of 100). **Freshman Academic Profile:** Average high school GPA 3.1. 13% in top 10% of high school class, 25% in top 25% of high school class, 39% in top 50% of high school class. 98% from public high schools. Average SAT I Math 552, SAT I Math middle 50% range 500-610. Average SAT I Verbal 529, SAT I Verbal middle 50% range 480-580. TOEFL required of all international applicants, minimum TOEFL 500. **Basis for Candidate Selection:** *Very important factors considered include:* secondary school record, standardized test scores. *Important factors considered include:* class rank, essays, recommendations. *Other factors considered include:* character/personal qualities, extracurricular activities, interview, talent/ability, volunteer work, work experience. **Freshman Admission Requirements:** High school diploma or GED is required. *Academic units required/recommended:* 16 total required; 4 English required, 3 math required, 3 science required, 2 science lab required, 2 foreign language required, 2 social studies required, 2 elective required. **Freshman Admission Statistics:** 3,583 applied, 63% accepted, 45% of those accepted enrolled. **Transfer Admission Requirements:** *Items required:* college transcript. Minimum college GPA of 2.0 required. Lowest grade transferable C-. **General Admission Information:** Application fee $20. Priority application deadline July 1. Nonfall registration accepted. Admission may be deferred for a maximum of 1 year. Credit offered for CEEB Advanced Placement tests.

COSTS AND FINANCIAL AID

In-state tuition $1,454. Out-of-state tuition $8,567. Room & board $5,464. Required fees $3,759. Average book expense $500. **Required Forms and Deadlines:** FAFSA. Priority filing deadline March 1. **Notification of Awards:** Applicants will be notified of awards on a rolling basis beginning on or about March 24. **Types of Aid:** *Need-based scholarships/grants:* Pell, SEOG, state scholarships/grants, private scholarships, the school's own gift aid. *Loans:* Direct Subsidized Stafford, Direct Unsubsidized Stafford, Direct PLUS, Federal Perkins, state loans. **Student Employment:** Federal Work-Study Program available. Institutional employment available. Off-campus job opportunities are good. **Financial Aid Statistics:** 41% freshmen, 42% undergrads receive some form of aid. Average freshman grant $3,745. Average freshman loan $1,936. Average income from on-campus job $2,710. **Financial Aid Phone:** 978-934-4220.

THE UNIVERSITY OF MEMPHIS

229 Administration Building, Memphis, TN 38152
Phone: 901-678-2111 **E-mail:** recruitment@memphis.edu **CEEB Code:** 1459
Fax: 901-678-3053 **Web:** www.memphis.edu **ACT Code:** 3992

This public school was founded in 1912. It has a 1,178-acre campus.

STUDENTS AND FACULTY

Enrollment: 15,485. **Student Body:** Out-of-state 12%, international 4% (84 countries represented). **Ethnic Representation:** African American 23%, Asian 2%, Caucasian 74%, Hispanic 1%.

ACADEMICS

Degrees: Bachelor's, certificate, doctoral, master's, terminal, transfer. **Academic Requirements:** General education including some course work in arts/fine arts, computer literacy, English (including composition), foreign languages, history, humanities, mathematics, philosophy, sciences (biological or physical), social science. **Special Study Options:** Distance learning, double major, dual enrollment, English as a second language, student exchange program (domestic), honors program, independent study, internships, student-designed major, study abroad, teacher certification program.

FACILITIES

Housing: Coed, all-female, all-male, apartments for married students, apartments for single students, fraternities and/or sororities, townhouses for single students. **Library Holdings:** 1,138,952 bound volumes. 12,239 periodicals. 3,062,580 microforms. **Special Academic Facilities/Equipment:** Indian museum and village, music archive, center for study of higher education, center for river studies, center for research on women, center for earthquake research and information, biological field station. **Computers:** *Recommended operating system:* Mac. School-owned computers available for student use.

EXTRACURRICULARS

Activities: Choral groups, concert band, dance, drama/theater, jazz band, marching band, music ensembles, musical theater, opera, pep band, radio station, student government, student newspaper, student-run film society, symphony orchestra, television station. **Organizations:** 27 honor societies, 12 religious organizations, 11 fraternities (8% men join), 7 sororities (8% women join). **Athletics (Intercollegiate):** *Men:* baseball, basketball, cheerleading, cross-country, football, golf, rifle, soccer, tennis, track & field, volleyball. *Women:* basketball, cheerleading, golf, soccer, tennis, track & field, volleyball.

ADMISSIONS

Selectivity Rating: 73 (of 100). **Freshman Academic Profile:** 80% from public high schools. Average ACT 22. TOEFL required of all international applicants, minimum TOEFL 500. **Freshman Admission Requirements:** High school diploma is required and GED is not accepted. *Academic units required/recommended:* 14 total required; 16 total recommended; 3 math required, 4 math recommended, 2 science required, 3 science recommended, 2 foreign language required, 2 social studies recommended. **Transfer Admission Requirements:** Minimum college GPA of 2.0 required. Lowest grade transferable C. **General Admission Information:** Regular application deadline August 1. Nonfall registration accepted. Credit and/or placement offered for CEEB Advanced Placement tests.

COSTS AND FINANCIAL AID

Room & board $3,995. Average book expense $500. **Required Forms and Deadlines:** FAFSA, institution's own financial aid form and CSS/Financial Aid PROFILE. **Notification of Awards:** Applicants will be notified of awards on or about June 1. **Types of Aid:** *Need-based scholarships/grants:* Pell, SEOG, state scholarships/grants, private scholarships, the school's own gift aid, Federal Nursing. *Loans:* FFEL Subsidized Stafford, FFEL Unsubsidized Stafford, FFEL PLUS, Federal Perkins, college/university loans from institutional funds. **Student Employment:** Federal Work-Study Program available. Institutional employment available. Off-campus job opportunities are excellent. **Financial**

Aid Statistics: Average freshman grant $2,000. Average freshman loan $2,350. **Financial Aid Phone:** 901-678-2303.

UNIVERSITY OF MIAMI

Office of Admission, PO Box 248025, Coral Gables, FL 33124-4616
Phone: 305-284-4323 **E-mail:** admission@miami.edu **CEEB Code:** 5815
Fax: 305-284-2507 **Web:** www.miami.edu **ACT Code:** 760

This private school was founded in 1925. It has a 260-acre campus.

STUDENTS AND FACULTY

Enrollment: 9,794. **Student Body:** Male 43%, female 57%, out-of-state 44%, international 7%. **Ethnic Representation:** African American 10%, Asian 6%, Caucasian 54%, Hispanic 27%. **Retention and Graduation:** 86% freshmen return for sophomore year. 53% freshmen graduate within 4 years. 35% grads go on to further study within 1 year. 10% grads pursue medical degrees. **Faculty:** Student/faculty ratio 13:1. 837 full-time faculty, 86% hold PhDs.

ACADEMICS

Degrees: Bachelor's, certificate, doctoral, first professional, master's, post-bachelor's certificate, post-master's certificate. **Academic Requirements:** General education including some course work in arts/fine arts, English (including composition), history, humanities, mathematics, sciences (biological or physical), social science. **Classes:** 10-19 students in an average class. 10-19 students in an average lab/discussion section. **Disciplines with Highest Percentage of Degrees Awarded:** Business/marketing 24%, visual and performing arts 12%, biological life sciences 10%, communications/communication technologies 8%, engineering/engineering technology 7%. **Special Study Options:** Accelerated program, distance learning, double major, dual enrollment, English as a second language, student exchange program (domestic), honors program, independent study, internships, student-designed major, study abroad, teacher certification program, weekend college, learning communities.

FACILITIES

Housing: Coed, apartments for single students, housing for disabled students, fraternities and/or sororities. **Library Holdings:** 1,415,781 bound volumes. 16,305 periodicals. 3,541,773 microforms. 109,900 audiovisuals. **Special Academic Facilities/Equipment:** Art museum, concert hall, cinema, wellness center. **Computers:** School-owned computers available for student use.

EXTRACURRICULARS

Activities: Choral groups, concert band, dance, drama/theater, jazz band, literary magazine, marching band, music ensembles, musical theater, opera, pep band, radio station, student government, student newspaper, student-run film society, symphony orchestra, television station, yearbook. **Organizations:** 165 registered organizations, 55 honor societies, 12 religious organizations, 14 fraternities (13% men join), 9 sororities (13% women join). **Athletics (Intercollegiate):** *Men:* baseball, basketball, cheerleading, cross-country, football, indoor track, tennis, track & field. *Women:* basketball, cheerleading, crew, cross-country, diving, golf, indoor track, soccer, swimming, tennis, track & field, volleyball.

ADMISSIONS

Selectivity Rating: 86 (of 100). **Freshman Academic Profile:** Average high school GPA 4. 55% in top 10% of high school class, 87% in top 25% of high school class, 98% in top 50% of high school class. SAT I Math middle 50% range 570-670. SAT I Verbal middle 50% range 550-650. ACT middle 50% range 25-30. TOEFL required of all international applicants, minimum TOEFL 550. **Basis for Candidate Selection:** *Very important factors considered include:* class rank, essays, recommendations, secondary school record, standardized test scores. *Other factors considered include:* alumni/ae relation, character/personal qualities, extracurricular activities, geographical residence, minority status, state residency, talent/ability, volunteer work, work experience. **Freshman Admission Requirements:** High school diploma or GED is required. *Academic units required/recommended:* 16 total recommended; 4 English recommended, 4 math recommended, 3 science recommended, 2 science lab recommended, 2 foreign language recommended, 3 social studies recommended. **Freshman Admission Statistics:** 15,909 applied, 44% accepted, 30% of those accepted enrolled. **Transfer Admission Requirements:** *Items required:* college transcript, statement of good standing from prior school. Minimum college GPA of 2.8 required. Lowest grade transferable C. **General Admission Information:** Application fee $50. Early decision application deadline November 15. Regular application deadline February 15. Nonfall registration accepted. Admission may be deferred for a maximum of 1 year. Credit and/or placement offered for CEEB Advanced Placement tests.

COSTS AND FINANCIAL AID

Tuition $24,378. Room & board $8,062. Required fees $432. Average book expense $775. **Required Forms and Deadlines:** FAFSA. Priority filing deadline February 15. **Notification of Awards:** Applicants will be notified of awards on a rolling basis beginning on or about March 1. **Types of Aid:** *Need-based scholarships/grants:* Pell, SEOG, state scholarships/grants, private scholarships, the school's own gift aid, Federal Nursing. *Loans:* FFEL Subsidized Stafford, FFEL Unsubsidized Stafford, FFEL PLUS, Federal Perkins, Federal Nursing, Signature Student Loan (alternative Loan Program). **Student Employment:** Federal Work-Study Program available. Institutional employment available. Off-campus job opportunities are excellent. **Financial Aid Statistics:** 57% freshmen, 54% undergrads receive some form of aid. **Financial Aid Phone:** 305-284-5212.

UNIVERSITY OF MICHIGAN—ANN ARBOR

1220 Student Activities Building, 515 E. Jefferson, Ann Arbor, MI 48109-1316
Phone: 734-764-7433 **E-mail:** ugadmiss@umich.edu **CEEB Code:** 3129
Fax: 734-936-0740 **Web:** www.umich.edu **ACT Code:** 2062

This public school was founded in 1817. It has a 3,129-acre campus.

STUDENTS AND FACULTY

Enrollment: 24,472. **Student Body:** Male 49%, female 51%, out-of-state 31%, international 4% (90 countries represented). **Ethnic Representation:** African American 8%, Asian 13%, Caucasian 67%, Hispanic 5%, Native American 1%. **Retention and Graduation:** 95% freshmen return for sophomore year. 61% freshmen graduate within 4 years. 34% grads go on to further study within 1 year. 1% grads pursue business degrees. 5% grads pursue law degrees. 5% grads pursue medical degrees. **Faculty:** Student/faculty ratio 15:1. 2,176 full-time faculty, 91% hold PhDs.

ACADEMICS

Degrees: Bachelor's, certificate, doctoral, first professional, first professional certificate, master's, post-bachelor's certificate, post-master's certificate. **Academic Requirements:** Academic requirements vary by program. For the college of literature, science, and the arts most students must fulfill requirements in English (including composition), race and ethnicity (one course), and foreign language and must complete 9 semester hours each of humanities, social science, and natural science/mathematics. All students admitted to the college must also meet the quantitative reasoning requirement. To graduate, students must complete 120 to 128 semester hours, including 24 to 30 in a major field, with a minimum GPA. **Classes:** 10-19 students in an average class. 20-29 students in an average lab/discussion section. **Majors with Highest Enrollment:** Engineering, general; English language and literature, general; psychology, general. **Disciplines with Highest Percentage of Degrees Awarded:** Social sciences and history 18%, engineering/engineering technology 16%, psychology 9%, biological life sciences 7%, visual and performing arts 7%. **Special Study Options:** Accelerated program, cooperative (work-study) program, cross registration, distance learning, double major, dual enrollment, English as a second language, student exchange program (domestic), honors program, independent study, internships, liberal arts/career combination, student-designed major, study abroad, teacher certification program, weekend college.

FACILITIES

Housing: Coed, all-female, apartments for married students, apartments for single students, housing for disabled students, housing for international students, fraternities and/or sororities, cooperative housing, living/ learning communities, substance-free dorms. **Library Holdings:** 7,484,343 bound volumes. 69,849 periodicals. 7,766,136 microforms. 73,568 audiovisuals. **Special Academic Facilities/Equipment:** Anthropology, archaeology, art, natural science, paleontology, and zoology museums; audiovisual center, planetarium; electron microscope; biology station; geology camp; athletic campus; medical center; nuclear lab; botanical garden; herbarium; arboretum. **Computers:** School-owned computers available for student use.

EXTRACURRICULARS

Activities: Choral groups, concert band, dance, drama/theater, jazz band, literary magazine, marching band, music ensembles, musical theater, opera, pep band, radio station, student government, student newspaper, student-run film society, symphony orchestra, television station, yearbook. **Organizations:** 900 registered organizations, 21 honor societies, 57 religious organizations, 37 fraternities (16% men join), 21 sororities (15% women join). **Athletics (Intercollegiate):** *Men:* baseball, basketball, cross-country, diving, football, golf, gymnastics, ice hockey, indoor track, soccer, swimming, tennis, track &

field, wrestling. *Women:* basketball, crew, cross-country, diving, field hockey, golf, gymnastics, indoor track, soccer, softball, swimming, tennis, track & field, volleyball, water polo.

ADMISSIONS

Selectivity Rating: 91 (of 100). **Freshman Academic Profile:** Average high school GPA 3.8. 80% from public high schools. Average SAT I Math 652, SAT I Math middle 50% range 610-720. Average SAT I Verbal 617, SAT I Verbal middle 50% range 570-670. Average ACT 27, ACT middle 50% range 26-30. TOEFL required of all international applicants, minimum TOEFL 560. **Basis for Candidate Selection:** *Very important factors considered include:* secondary school record. *Important factors considered include:* class rank, minority status, standardized test scores, state residency, talent/ability. *Other factors considered include:* alumni/ae relation, character/personal qualities, essays, extracurricular activities, geographical residence, recommendations, volunteer work. **Freshman Admission Requirements:** High school diploma or GED is required. *Academic units required/recommended:* 15 total required; 18 total recommended; 4 English required, 4 English recommended, 3 math required, 4 math recommended, 2 science required, 3 science recommended, 1 science lab recommended, 2 foreign language required, 4 foreign language recommended, 3 social studies required, 3 social studies recommended, 2 history recommended. **Freshman Admission Statistics:** 25,108 applied, 49% accepted, 42% of those accepted enrolled. **Transfer Admission Requirements:** *Items required:* high school transcript, college transcript, essay, statement of good standing from prior school. Minimum college GPA of 3.0 required. Lowest grade transferable C. **General Admission Information:** Application fee $40. Regular application deadline February 1. Nonfall registration accepted. Admission may be deferred for a maximum of 1 year. Credit and/or placement offered for CEEB Advanced Placement tests.

COSTS AND FINANCIAL AID

In-state tuition $6,620. Out-of-state tuition $22,500. Room & board $6,366. Required fees $187. Average book expense $756. **Required Forms and Deadlines:** FAFSA and parent and student income tax return. Financial aid filing deadline September 30. Priority filing deadline February 15. **Notification of Awards:** Applicants will be notified of awards on a rolling basis beginning on or about March 15. **Types of Aid:** *Need-based scholarships/grants:* Pell, SEOG, state scholarships/grants, private scholarships, the school's own gift aid. *Loans:* Direct Subsidized Stafford, Direct Unsubsidized Stafford, Direct PLUS, Federal Perkins, Federal Nursing, state loans, college/university loans from institutional funds, Michigan Loan Program, Health Professional student loans. **Student Employment:** Federal Work-Study Program available. Institutional employment available. Off-campus job opportunities are excellent. **Financial Aid Statistics:** 34% freshmen, 38% undergrads receive some form of aid. Average freshman grant $5,937. Average freshman loan $1,920. Average income from on-campus job $3,000. **Financial Aid Phone:** 734-763-6600.

UNIVERSITY OF MICHIGAN—DEARBORN

4901 Evergreen Road, Dearborn, MI 48128-1491
Phone: 313-593-5100 **E-mail:** admissions@umd.umich.edu **CEEB Code:** 1861
Fax: 313-436-9167 **Web:** www.umd.umich.edu **ACT Code:** 2074

This public school was founded in 1959. It has a 210-acre campus.

STUDENTS AND FACULTY

Enrollment: 6,326. **Student Body:** Male 46%, female 54%, out-of-state 2%, international 1%. **Ethnic Representation:** African American 7%, Asian 6%, Caucasian 76%, Hispanic 2%, Native American 1%. **Retention and Graduation:** 79% freshmen return for sophomore year. 8% freshmen graduate within 4 years. 10% grads go on to further study within 1 year. **Faculty:** Student/faculty ratio 15:1. 259 full-time faculty, 88% hold PhDs.

ACADEMICS

Degrees: Bachelor's, master's, post-bachelor's certificate. **Classes:** 20-29 students in an average class. 10-19 students in an average lab/discussion section. **Disciplines with Highest Percentage of Degrees Awarded:** Education 20%, business/marketing 20%, engineering/engineering technology 16%, social sciences and history 9%, psychology 7%. **Special Study Options:** Accelerated program, cooperative (work-study) program, cross registration, distance learning, double major, dual enrollment, honors program, independent study, internships, liberal arts/career combination, student-designed major, study abroad, teacher certification program.

FACILITIES

Housing: Fraternities and/or sororities. **Library Holdings:** 1,064,690 bound volumes. 1,231 periodicals. 518,716 microforms. 3,918 audiovisuals. **Special Academic Facilities/Equipment:** Museum at Henry Ford estate, child development center, CAD/CAM robotics lab, environmental study area, Armenian center. **Computers:** *Recommended operating system:* Mac. School-owned computers available for student use.

EXTRACURRICULARS

Activities: Drama/theater, literary magazine, radio station, student government, student newspaper, student-run film society, television station. **Organizations:** 2 honor societies, 24 religious organizations, 5 fraternities (4% men join), 4 sororities (4% women join). **Athletics (Intercollegiate):** *Men:* basketball, volleyball. *Women:* basketball, volleyball.

ADMISSIONS

Selectivity Rating: 77 (of 100). **Freshman Academic Profile:** Average high school GPA 3.4. 25% in top 10% of high school class, 60% in top 25% of high school class, 94% in top 50% of high school class. 83% from public high schools. Average ACT 23, ACT middle 50% range 21-26. TOEFL required of all international applicants, minimum TOEFL 550. **Basis for Candidate Selection:** *Very important factors considered include:* secondary school record, standardized test scores. *Other factors considered include:* class rank, essays, interview, recommendations. **Freshman Admission Requirements:** High school diploma or GED is required. *Academic units required/recommended:* 4 English recommended, 4 math recommended, 3 science recommended, 1 science lab recommended, 3 foreign language recommended, 3 social studies recommended. **Freshman Admission Statistics:** 2,334 applied, 65% accepted, 47% of those accepted enrolled. **Transfer Admission Requirements:** *Items required:* high school transcript, college transcript. Minimum college GPA of 2.5 required. Lowest grade transferable C. **General Admission Information:** Application fee $30. Regular application deadline rolling. Nonfall registration accepted. Admission may be deferred. Credit and/or placement offered for CEEB Advanced Placement tests.

COSTS AND FINANCIAL AID

In-state tuition $4,915. Out-of-state tuition $11,883. Required fees $90. Average book expense $800. **Required Forms and Deadlines:** FAFSA. Priority filing deadline April 1. **Notification of Awards:** Applicants will be notified of awards on a rolling basis beginning on or about May 1. **Types of Aid:** *Need-based scholarships/grants:* Pell, SEOG, state scholarships/grants, private scholarships, the school's own gift aid. *Loans:* Direct Subsidized Stafford, Direct Unsubsidized Stafford, Direct PLUS, Federal Perkins, state loans, college/university loans from institutional funds. **Student Employment:** Federal Work-Study Program available. Institutional employment available. Off-campus job opportunities are good. **Financial Aid Statistics:** 29% freshmen, 33% undergrads receive some form of aid. Average freshman grant $1,789. Average freshman loan $2,100. Average income from on-campus job $1,400. **Financial Aid Phone:** 313-593-5300.

UNIVERSITY OF MICHIGAN—FLINT

University Pavilion Suite 245, Flint, MI 48502
Phone: 810-762-3300 **E-mail:** admissions@umflint.edu **CEEB Code:** 1853
Fax: 810-762-3272 **Web:** www.flint.umich.edu **ACT Code:** 2063

This public school was founded in 1956. It has a 70-acre campus.

STUDENTS AND FACULTY

Enrollment: 5,877. **Student Body:** Male 36%, female 64%, out-of-state 1%. **Ethnic Representation:** African American 10%, Asian 1%, Caucasian 78%, Hispanic 2%, Native American 1%. **Retention and Graduation:** 72% freshmen return for sophomore year. 10% freshmen graduate within 4 years. **Faculty:** Student/faculty ratio 16:1. 209 full-time faculty, 72% hold PhDs.

ACADEMICS

Degrees: Bachelor's, master's, post-bachelor's certificate. **Academic Requirements:** General education including some course work in arts/fine arts, English (including composition), foreign languages, history, humanities, mathematics, philosophy, sciences (biological or physical), social science. **Classes:** 20-29 students in an average class. 20-29 students in an average lab/discussion section. **Disciplines with Highest Percentage of Degrees Awarded:** Education 19%, business/marketing 15%, health professions and related sciences 13%, protective services/public administration 9%, social sciences and history 7%. **Special Study Options:** Cooperative (work-study) program, distance learning, double major, dual enrollment, honors program, independent study, internships, student-designed major, study abroad, teacher certification program.

FACILITIES

Library Holdings: 267,062 bound volumes. 1,111 periodicals. 18,758 microforms. 18,063 audiovisuals. **Computers:** School-owned computers available for student use.

EXTRACURRICULARS

Activities: Choral groups, concert band, dance, drama/theater, jazz band, literary magazine, music ensembles, musical theater, student government, student newspaper, symphony orchestra, television station. **Organizations:** 60 registered organizations, 1 honor society, 1 religious organization, 5 fraternities (1% men join), 5 sororities (1% women join).

ADMISSIONS

Selectivity Rating: 70 (of 100). **Freshman Academic Profile:** Average high school GPA 3.3. 16% in top 10% of high school class, 45% in top 25% of high school class, 80% in top 50% of high school class. 80% from public high schools. SAT I Math middle 50% range 482-650. SAT I Verbal middle 50% range 537-597. Average ACT 22, ACT middle 50% range 19-24. TOEFL required of all international applicants, minimum TOEFL 550. **Basis for Candidate Selection:** *Very important factors considered include:* secondary school record, standardized test scores. *Important factors considered include:* extracurricular activities. *Other factors considered include:* alumni/ae relation, class rank, essays, geographical residence, interview, recommendations, talent/ability. **Freshman Admission Requirements:** High school diploma or GED is required. *Academic units required/recommended:* 12 total required; 21 total recommended; 4 English required, 4 English recommended, 3 math required, 4 math recommended, 2 science required, 4 science recommended, 2 science lab recommended, 2 foreign language recommended, 3 social studies required, 3 social studies recommended, 2 history recommended. **Freshman Admission Statistics:** 1,357 applied, 79% accepted, 49% of those accepted enrolled. **Transfer Admission Requirements:** *Items required:* high school transcript, college transcript. Minimum college GPA of 2.0 required. Lowest grade transferable C. **General Admission Information:** Application fee $30. Priority application deadline May 1. Early decision application deadline January 15. Regular application deadline September 2. Nonfall registration accepted. Admission may be deferred for a maximum of 1 year. Credit and/or placement offered for CEEB Advanced Placement tests.

COSTS AND FINANCIAL AID

In-state tuition $4,494. Out-of-state tuition $8,988. Required fees $258. **Required Forms and Deadlines:** FAFSA. Priority filing deadline February 23. **Notification of Awards:** Applicants will be notified of awards on a rolling basis beginning on or about March 15. **Types of Aid:** *Need-based scholarships/grants:* Pell, SEOG, state scholarships/grants, private scholarships, the school's own gift aid. *Loans:* Direct Subsidized Stafford, Direct Unsubsidized Stafford, Direct PLUS, Federal Perkins. **Student Employment:** Federal Work-Study Program available. Off-campus job opportunities are excellent. **Financial Aid Statistics:** 47% freshmen, 53% undergrads receive some form of aid. Average freshman grant $2,820. Average freshman loan $2,820. Average income from on-campus job $1,300. **Financial Aid Phone:** 810-762-3444.

UNIVERSITY OF MINNESOTA—CROOKSTON

170 Owen Hall, 2900 University Avenue, Crookston, MN 56716-5001
Phone: 218-281-8569 **E-mail:** info@mail.crk.umn.edu
Fax: 218-281-8575 **Web:** www.crk.umn.edu **ACT Code:** 2129

This public school was founded in 1966. It has a 237-acre campus.

STUDENTS AND FACULTY

Enrollment: 2,387. **Student Body:** Male 45%, female 55%, out-of-state 28%, international 1%. **Ethnic Representation:** African American 3%, Asian 2%, Caucasian 89%, Hispanic 1%, Native American 1%. **Faculty:** Student/faculty ratio 15:1. 55 full-time faculty, 45% hold PhDs. 100% faculty teach undergrads.

ACADEMICS

Degrees: Associate's, bachelor's. **Academic Requirements:** General education including some course work in computer literacy, English (including composition), humanities, mathematics, sciences (biological or physical), technology applications. **Classes:** 10-19 students in an average class. 10-19 students in an average lab/discussion section. **Majors with Highest Enrollment:** Business administration/management; information technology; natural resources/conservation, general. **Disciplines with Highest Percentage of Degrees Awarded:** Agriculture 31%, business/marketing 18%, other 12%, computer and information sciences 10%, natural resources/environmental sciences 7%. **Special Study Options:** Distance learning, double major, internships, liberal arts/career combination, study abroad, pilot license preparation.

FACILITIES

Housing: Coed, apartments for single students. **Library Holdings:** 32,481 bound volumes. 667 periodicals. 25,779 microforms. 1,670 audiovisuals. **Special Academic Facilities/Equipment:** Red River Valley Natural History Area, Northwerst Research and Outreach Center, UMC Horse Riding Arena, Valley Technology Park. **Computers:** *Recommended operating system:* Windows XP. School-owned computers available for student use.

EXTRACURRICULARS

Activities: Choral groups, drama/theater, music ensembles, pep band, student government. **Organizations:** 32 registered organizations, 1 honor society, 1 religious organization, 2 fraternities, 1 sorority. **Athletics (Intercollegiate):** *Men:* baseball, basketball, football, golf, ice hockey. *Women:* basketball, equestrian, golf, soccer, softball, volleyball.

ADMISSIONS

Selectivity Rating: 63 (of 100). **Freshman Academic Profile:** ACT middle 50% range 19-25. TOEFL required of all international applicants, minimum TOEFL 500. **Basis for Candidate Selection:** *Very important factors considered include:* class rank, secondary school record, standardized test scores. **Freshman Admission Requirements:** High school diploma or GED is required. *Academic units required/recommended:* 4 English recommended, 3 math recommended, 3 science recommended, 2 foreign language recommended, 2 social studies recommended. **Freshman Admission Statistics:** 521 applied, 86% accepted, 64% of those accepted enrolled. **Transfer Admission Requirements:** *Items required:* college transcript. Minimum college GPA of 2.0 required. Lowest grade transferable D. **General Admission Information:** Application fee $25. Priority application deadline March 15. Regular application deadline July 15. Nonfall registration accepted. Admission may be deferred for a maximum of 1 year.

COSTS AND FINANCIAL AID

In-state tuition $4,800. Out-of-state tuition $4,800. Room & board $4,510. Required fees $1,304. Average book expense $700. **Required Forms and Deadlines:** FAFSA. No deadline for regular filing. Priority filing deadline March 31. **Notification of Awards:** Applicants will be notified of awards on a rolling basis beginning on or about March 1. **Types of Aid:** *Need-based scholarships/grants:* Pell, SEOG, state scholarships/grants, private scholarships, the school's own gift aid. *Loans:* Direct Subsidized Stafford, Direct Unsubsidized Stafford, Direct PLUS, Federal Perkins. **Student Employment:** Federal Work-Study Program available. Institutional employment available. Off-campus job opportunities are fair. **Financial Aid Statistics:** 65% freshmen, 68% undergrads receive some form of aid. Average freshman grant $5,154. Average freshman loan $5,064. **Financial Aid Phone:** 218-281-8563.

UNIVERSITY OF MINNESOTA—DULUTH

23 Solon Campus Center, 1117 University Drive, Duluth, MN 55812-3000
Phone: 218-726-7171 **E-mail:** umdadmis@d.umn.edu **CEEB Code:** 6873
Fax: 218-726-7040 **Web:** www.d.umn.edu **ACT Code:** 2157

This public school was founded in 1947. It has a 247-acre campus.

STUDENTS AND FACULTY

Enrollment: 9,144. **Student Body:** Male 49%, female 51%, out-of-state 13%, international 2% (25 countries represented). **Ethnic Representation:** African American 1%, Asian 2%, Caucasian 91%, Hispanic 1%, Native American 1%. **Retention and Graduation:** 74% freshmen return for sophomore year. 20% grads go on to further study within 1 year. **Faculty:** Student/faculty ratio 20:1. 363 full-time faculty, 76% hold PhDs. 100% faculty teach undergrads.

ACADEMICS

Degrees: Bachelor's, first professional, master's, post-bachelor's certificate. **Academic Requirements:** General education including some course work in arts/fine arts, computer literacy, English (including composition), sciences (biological or physical), social science, cultural diversity and international perspectives. **Classes:** 20-29 students in an average class. **Majors with Highest Enrollment:** Business administration/management; elementary education and teaching; biology/biological sciences, general. **Disciplines with Highest Percentage of Degrees Awarded:** Biological life sciences 18%, computer and information sciences 16%, business/marketing 10%, social sciences and history 10%, area and ethnic studies 9%. **Special Study Options:** Accelerated program, cross registration, double major, dual enrollment, independent study, internships, student-designed major, study abroad, teacher certification program.

FACILITIES

Housing: Coed, all-female, all-male, apartments for single students. **Library Holdings:** 704,145 bound volumes. 4,500 periodicals. 750,000 microforms. 15,245 audiovisuals. **Special Academic Facilities/Equipment:** Art museum, planetarium, theatre. **Computers:** School-owned computers available for student use.

EXTRACURRICULARS

Activities: Choral groups, concert band, dance, drama/theater, jazz band, music ensembles, musical theater, pep band, radio station, student government, student newspaper. **Organizations:** 120 registered organizations, 10 honor societies, 7 religious organizations, 2 fraternities (1% men join), 2 sororities (1% women join). **Athletics (Intercollegiate):** *Men:* baseball, basketball, cross-country, football, ice hockey, soccer, track & field. *Women:* basketball, cross-country, ice hockey, soccer, softball, tennis, track & field, volleyball.

ADMISSIONS

Selectivity Rating: 70 (of 100). **Freshman Academic Profile:** Average high school GPA 3.2. 15% in top 10% of high school class, 41% in top 25% of high school class, 83% in top 50% of high school class. 95% from public high schools. Average ACT 23, ACT middle 50% range 20-24. TOEFL required of all international applicants, minimum TOEFL 550. **Basis for Candidate Selection:** *Very important factors considered include:* class rank, standardized test scores. *Important factors considered include:* secondary school record. *Other factors considered include:* essays, minority status, recommendations, talent/ability. **Freshman Admission Requirements:** High school diploma or GED is required. *Academic units required/recommended:* 14 total required; 4 English required, 3 math required, 3 science required, 2 foreign language required, 2 social studies required. **Freshman Admission Statistics:** 6,202 applied, 77% accepted, 43% of those accepted enrolled. **Transfer Admission Requirements:** *Items required:* high school transcript, college transcript. Minimum college GPA of 2.0 required. Lowest grade transferable D. **General Admission Information:** Application fee $35. Priority application deadline February 1. Regular application deadline August 1. Nonfall registration accepted. Admission may be deferred for a maximum of 1 year. Credit offered for CEEB Advanced Placement tests.

COSTS AND FINANCIAL AID

In-state tuition $5,580. Out-of-state tuition $15,840. Room & board $4,960. Required fees $887. Average book expense $1,020. **Required Forms and Deadlines:** FAFSA. No deadline for regular filing. Priority filing deadline March 31. **Notification of Awards:** Applicants will be notified of awards on a rolling basis. **Types of Aid:** *Need-based scholarships/grants:* Pell, SEOG, state scholarships/grants, private scholarships, the school's own gift aid. *Loans:* Direct Subsidized Stafford, Direct Unsubsidized Stafford, Direct PLUS, Federal Perkins, state loans. **Student Employment:** Federal Work-Study Program available. Institutional employment available. Off-campus job opportunities are good. **Financial Aid Statistics:** 50% freshmen, 51% undergrads receive some form of aid. **Financial Aid Phone:** 218-726-8000.

UNIVERSITY OF MINNESOTA—MORRIS

600 E 4th Street, Morris, MN 56267
Phone: 320-589-6035 **E-mail:** admisfa@mrs.umn.edu **CEEB Code:** 6890
Fax: 320-589-1673 **Web:** www.mrs.umn.edu **ACT Code:** 2155

This public school was founded in 1959. It has a 130-acre campus.

STUDENTS AND FACULTY

Enrollment: 1,910. **Student Body:** Male 40%, female 60%, out-of-state 18%, international 1%. **Ethnic Representation:** African American 3%, Asian 3%, Caucasian 82%, Hispanic 2%, Native American 7%. **Retention and Graduation:** 84% freshmen return for sophomore year. 49% freshmen graduate within 4 years. 32% grads go on to further study within 1 year. 4% grads pursue business degrees. 4% grads pursue law degrees. 4% grads pursue medical degrees. **Faculty:** Student/faculty ratio 14:1. 126 full-time faculty, 90% hold PhDs. 100% faculty teach undergrads.

ACADEMICS

Degrees: Bachelor's, certificate. **Academic Requirements:** General education including some course work in arts/fine arts, computer literacy, English (including composition), foreign languages, humanities, mathematics, sciences (biological or physical), social science, first year experience. **Classes:** 10-19 students in an average class. 10-19 students in an average lab/discussion section. **Majors with Highest Enrollment:** Elementary education and teaching; biology/biological sciences, general; economics, general. **Disciplines with Highest Percentage of Degrees Awarded:** Social sciences and history 19%, English 14%, education 10%, biological life sciences 10%, computer and information sciences 7%. **Special Study Options:** Accelerated program, cooperative (work-study) program, distance learning, double major, English as a second language, student exchange program (domestic), honors program, independent study, internships, student-designed major, study abroad, teacher certification program.

FACILITIES

Housing: Coed, all-female, all-male, apartments for single students, housing for disabled students. **Library Holdings:** 329,561 bound volumes. 6,911 periodicals. 218,549 microforms. 1,923 audiovisuals. **Special Academic Facilities/Equipment:** Art gallery. **Computers:** School-owned computers available for student use.

EXTRACURRICULARS

Activities: Choral groups, concert band, dance, drama/theater, jazz band, literary magazine, music ensembles, radio station, student government, student newspaper, symphony orchestra, television station. **Organizations:** 80 registered organizations, 5 honor societies, 10 religious organizations, 11 fraternity. **Athletics (Intercollegiate):** *Men:* baseball, basketball, football, golf, indoor track, tennis, track & field, wrestling. *Women:* basketball, cross-country, golf, indoor track, soccer, softball, tennis, track & field, volleyball, wrestling.

ADMISSIONS

Selectivity Rating: 84 (of 100). **Freshman Academic Profile:** 45% in top 10% of high school class, 75% in top 25% of high school class, 98% in top 50% of high school class. 80% from public high schools. Average SAT I Math 620, SAT I Math middle 50% range 560-670. Average SAT I Verbal 600, SAT I Verbal middle 50% range 550-650. Average ACT 25, ACT middle 50% range 24-28. TOEFL required of all international applicants, minimum TOEFL 600. **Basis for Candidate Selection:** *Very important factors considered include:* class rank, secondary school record, standardized test scores. *Important factors considered include:* essays, extracurricular activities, minority status, recommendations, talent/ability, volunteer work, work experience. *Other factors considered include:* alumni/ae relation, interview. **Freshman Admission Requirements:** High school diploma or GED is required. *Academic units required/recommended:* 14 total required; 4 English required, 3 math required, 3 science required, 2 foreign language required, 2 social studies required. **Freshman Admission Statistics:** 1,297 applied, 82% accepted. **Transfer Admission Requirements:** *Items required:* high school transcript, college transcript, essay. Minimum college GPA of 2.5 required. Lowest grade transferable D. **General Admission Information:** Application fee $35. Priority application deadline November 15. Regular application deadline March 15. Nonfall registration accepted. Admission may be deferred for a maximum of 1 year. Credit and/or placement offered for CEEB Advanced Placement tests.

COSTS AND FINANCIAL AID

In-state tuition $6,381. Out-of-state tuition $6,381. Room & board $4,680. Required fees $878. Average book expense $600. **Required Forms and Deadlines:** FAFSA and institution's own financial aid form. No deadline for regular filing. Priority filing deadline March 1. **Notification of Awards:** Applicants will be notified of awards on a rolling basis beginning on or about March 15. **Types of Aid:** *Need-based scholarships/grants:* Pell, SEOG, state scholarships/grants, private scholarships, the school's own gift aid. *Loans:* Direct Subsidized Stafford, Direct Unsubsidized Stafford, Direct PLUS, Federal Perkins, state loans, college/university loans from institutional funds, SELF Loan. **Student Employment:** Federal Work-Study Program available. Institutional employment available. Off-campus job opportunities are good. **Financial Aid Statistics:** 64% freshmen, 66% undergrads receive some form of aid. Average freshman grant $4,629. Average freshman loan $3,412. **Financial Aid Phone:** 320-589-6035.

UNIVERSITY OF MINNESOTA—TWIN CITIES

240 Williamson Hall, 231 Pillsbury Drive SE, Minneapolis, MN 55455-0115
Phone: 612-625-2008 **E-mail:** admissions@tc.umn.edu **CEEB Code:** 6874
Fax: 612-626-1693 **Web:** www.umn.edu/tc/ **ACT Code:** 2156

This public school was founded in 1851. It has a 2,000-acre campus.

STUDENTS AND FACULTY

Enrollment: 32,457. **Student Body:** Male 47%, female 53%, out-of-state 26%, international 2%. **Ethnic Representation:** African American 4%, Asian 8%, Caucasian 82%, Hispanic 2%, Native American 1%. **Retention and Graduation:** 84% freshmen return for sophomore year. 26% freshmen graduate within 4 years. **Faculty:** Student/faculty ratio 15:1. 2,711 full-time faculty, 96% hold PhDs.

ACADEMICS

Degrees: Bachelor's, certificate, diploma, doctoral, first professional, master's, post-bachelor's certificate, post-master's certificate. **Academic Requirements:** General education including some course work in arts/fine arts, computer literacy, English (including composition), foreign languages, history, humanities, mathematics, philosophy, sciences (biological or physical), social science. **Classes:** 10-19 students in an average class. 10-19 students in an average lab/discussion section. **Disciplines with Highest Percentage of Degrees Awarded:** Social sciences and history 14%, engineering/engineering technology 10%, business/marketing 10%, psychology 7%, English 7%. **Special Study Options:** Accelerated program, cooperative (work-study) program, cross registration, distance learning, double major, dual enrollment, English as a second language, student exchange program (domestic), external degree program, honors program, independent study, liberal arts/career combination, programs in foreign service and pre-social work, Phi Beta Kappa, pass/fail grading option, internships, student-designed major, study abroad, teacher certification program, minors offered in most areas. Students may register in the College of Continuing Education and take courses in any division for BA or BS degrees. Qualified undergraduates may take graduate-level classes. Pre-professional programs in law, medicine, veterinary science, pharmacy, dentistry, architecture, biology, education, journalism, landscape architecture, management, medical technology, mortuary science, nursing, and occupational/physical therapy.

FACILITIES

Housing: Coed, apartments for married students, apartments for single students, housing for disabled students, housing for international students, fraternities and/or sororities, cooperative housing, honors housing, residential college (academic programs in residence). Eight conventional residence halls, plus three new apartment-style residence halls. Housing application, $25 nonrefundable residence hall application fee, and $100 residence hall advance payment (refundable), required by May 1 for guaranteed freshman housing. Off-campus housing office provides off-campus housing listings. **Library Holdings:** 5,700,000 bound volumes. 45,000 periodicals. 5,700,000 microforms. 1,185,373 audiovisuals. **Special Academic Facilities/Equipment:** Frederick R. Weisman Art Museum, Bell Museum of Natural History, Ted Mann Concert Hall, Recreational Sports Center, Civil Engineering Building, Basic Sciences/Biomedical Engineering Building. **Computers:** School-owned computers available for student use.

EXTRACURRICULARS

Activities: Choral groups, dance, drama/theater, jazz band, literary magazine, marching band, music ensembles, musical theater, opera, pep band, radio station, student government, student newspaper, student-run film society, symphony orchestra, television station, yearbook. **Organizations:** 350 registered organizations, 21 honor societies, 10 religious organizations, 22 fraternities, 12 sororities. **Athletics (Intercollegiate):** *Men:* baseball, basketball, cross-country, diving, football, golf, gymnastics, ice hockey, indoor track, swimming, tennis, track & field, wrestling. *Women:* baseball, basketball, cross-country, diving, golf, gymnastics, ice hockey, indoor track, soccer, softball, swimming, tennis, track & field, volleyball.

ADMISSIONS

Selectivity Rating: 80 (of 100). **Freshman Academic Profile:** 30% in top 10% of high school class, 65% in top 25% of high school class, 92% in top 50% of high school class. Average SAT I Math 611, SAT I Math middle 50% range 550-670. Average SAT I Verbal 588, SAT I Verbal middle 50% range 540-660. Average ACT 25, ACT middle 50% range 22-28. TOEFL required of all international applicants, minimum TOEFL 550. **Basis for Candidate Selection:** *Very important factors considered include:* class rank, secondary school record, standardized test scores. *Other factors considered include:* character/personal qualities, essays, extracurricular activities, geographical residence, interview, minority status, state residency, talent/ability, volunteer work, work experience. **Freshman Admission Requirements:** High school diploma or GED is required. *Academic units required/recommended:* 16 total required; 4 English required, 3 math required, 3 science required, 2 foreign language required, 3 social studies required, 1 history required. **Freshman Admission Statistics:** 14,724 applied, 74% accepted, 47% of those accepted enrolled. **Transfer Admission Requirements:** *Items required:* college transcript. Minimum college GPA of 2.0 required. Lowest grade transferable D. **General Admission Information:** Application fee $35. Priority application deadline December 15. Nonfall registration accepted. Admission may be deferred for a maximum of 1 year. Credit and/or placement offered for CEEB Advanced Placement tests.

COSTS AND FINANCIAL AID

In-state tuition $5,420. Out-of-state tuition $15,994. Room & board $5,696. Required fees $860. Average book expense $730. **Required Forms and Deadlines:** FAFSA. No deadline for regular filing. Priority filing deadline January 15. **Notification of Awards:** Applicants will be notified of awards on a rolling basis. **Types of Aid:** *Need-based scholarships/grants:* Pell, SEOG, state scholarships/grants, private scholarships, the school's own gift aid, NSS, ROTC scholarships, academic merit scholarships, athletic scholarships, aid for undergraduate international students. *Loans:* Direct Subsidized Stafford, Direct Unsubsidized Stafford, Direct PLUS, Federal Perkins, Federal Nursing, state loans, college/university loans from institutional funds, NSL, private loans. **Student Employment:** Federal Work-Study Program available. Institutional employment available. Off-campus job opportunities are excellent. **Financial Aid Statistics:** 48% freshmen, 46% undergrads receive some form of aid. Average freshman grant $4,292. Average freshman loan $3,587. **Financial Aid Phone:** 612-624-1665.

UNIVERSITY OF MISSISSIPPI

145 Martindale, University, MS 38677
Phone: 662-915-7226 **E-mail:** admissions@olemiss.edu **CEEB Code:** 1840
Fax: 662-915-5869 **Web:** www.olemiss.edu **ACT Code:** 2250

This public school was founded in 1844. It has a 2,500-acre campus.

STUDENTS AND FACULTY

Enrollment: 10,661. **Student Body:** Male 47%, female 53%, out-of-state 32%, international 1% (68 countries represented). **Ethnic Representation:** African American 13%, Asian 1%, Caucasian 85%. **Retention and Graduation:** 75% freshmen return for sophomore year. 33% freshmen graduate within 4 years. **Faculty:** Student/faculty ratio 21:1. 527 full-time faculty, 83% hold PhDs.

ACADEMICS

Degrees: Bachelor's, certificate, doctoral, first professional, master's. **Academic Requirements:** General education including some course work in arts/fine arts, English (including composition), humanities, mathematics, sciences (biological or physical), social science, university studies (the mission, values, and constituencies of a comprehensive public university and ethical and social concerns affecting its functioning). **Classes:** 10-19 students in an average class. 20-29 students in an average lab/discussion section. **Majors with Highest Enrollment:** Business administration/management; marketing/marketing management, general; elementary education and teaching. **Disciplines with Highest Percentage of Degrees Awarded:** Business/marketing 33%, education 11%, social sciences and history 7%, protective services/public administration 6%, health professions and related sciences 6%. **Special Study Options:** Accelerated program, cooperative (work-study) program, distance learning, double major, English as a second language, honors program, independent study, internships, study abroad, teacher certification program.

FACILITIES

Housing: All-female, all-male, apartments for married students, housing for disabled students, housing for international students, fraternities and/or sororities, Graduate/Older Students. **Library Holdings:** 1,251,189 bound volumes. 6,867 periodicals. 2,558,796 microforms. 30,584 audiovisuals. **Special Academic Facilities/Equipment:** McDonnell Barksdale Honors College, Croft Institute for International Studies, National Food Service Management Institute, Mississippi Center for Supercomputing Research, art and archaeology museums, women's studies center, Center for Study of Southern Culture, William Faulkner Home, Marine Minerals Research Institute, Center for Computational Hydroscience & Engineering, National Center for Physical Acoustics Natural Products Development Center, small business development center, center for population studies, biological field station, center for wireless communication, center for archaeological research. **Computers:** School-owned computers available for student use.

EXTRACURRICULARS

Activities: Choral groups, concert band, dance, drama/theater, jazz band, literary magazine, marching band, music ensembles, musical theater, pep band, radio station, student government, student newspaper, symphony orchestra, television station, yearbook. **Organizations:** 200 registered organizations, 27 honor societies, 21 religious organizations, 19 fraternities (32% men join), 13 sororities (34% women join). **Athletics (Intercollegiate):** *Men:* baseball, basketball, cross-country, football, golf, indoor track, tennis, track & field. *Women:* basketball, cross-country, golf, indoor track, rifle, soccer, softball, tennis, track & field, volleyball.

ADMISSIONS

Selectivity Rating: 77 (of 100). **Freshman Academic Profile:** Average high school GPA 3.4. 35% in top 10% of high school class, 52% in top 25% of high school class, 85% in top 50% of high school class. 70% from public high schools. Average ACT 23, ACT middle 50% range 20-26. TOEFL required of all international applicants, minimum TOEFL 550. **Basis for Candidate Selection:** *Very important factors considered include:* secondary school record. *Important factors considered include:* class rank, standardized test scores. *Other factors considered include:* alumni/ae relation, state residency, talent/ability.

Freshman Admission Requirements: High school diploma or GED is required. *Academic units required/recommended:* 15 total required; 4 English required, 3 math required, 4 math recommended, 3 science required, 4 science recommended, 3 science lab required, 1 foreign language required, 2 foreign language recommended, 1 social studies required, 2 social studies recommended, 2 history required, 1 elective required. **Freshman Admission Statistics:** 7,603 applied, 67% accepted, 44% of those accepted enrolled. **Transfer Admission Requirements:** *Items required:* college transcript. Minimum college GPA of 2.0 required. Lowest grade transferable D. **General Admission Information:** Application fee $25. Priority application deadline June 15. Regular application deadline July 20. Nonfall registration accepted. Credit offered for CEEB Advanced Placement tests.

COSTS AND FINANCIAL AID

In-state tuition $3,916. Out-of-state tuition $8,826. Room & board $5,200. Required fees $0. Average book expense $800. **Required Forms and Deadlines:** FAFSA. No deadline for regular filing. Priority filing deadline March 15. **Notification of Awards:** Applicants will be notified of awards on a rolling basis beginning on or about April 1. **Types of Aid:** *Need-based scholarships/grants:* Pell, SEOG, state scholarships/grants, private scholarships, the school's own gift aid. *Loans:* FFEL Subsidized Stafford, FFEL Unsubsidized Stafford, FFEL PLUS, Federal Perkins, college/university loans from institutional funds. **Student Employment:** Federal Work-Study Program available. Institutional employment available. Off-campus job opportunities are good. **Financial Aid Statistics:** 34% freshmen, 38% undergrads receive some form of aid. **Financial Aid Phone:** 662-915-7175.

UNIVERSITY OF MISSOURI—COLUMBIA

230 Jesse Hall, Columbia, MO 65211
Phone: 573-882-7786 **E-mail:** admissions@missouri.edu **CEEB Code:** 6875
Fax: 573-882-7887 **Web:** www.missouri.edu **ACT Code:** 2382

This public school was founded in 1839. It has a 1,348-acre campus.

STUDENTS AND FACULTY

Enrollment: 17,346. **Student Body:** Male 47%, female 53%, out-of-state 11%, international 3% (87 countries represented). **Ethnic Representation:** African American 7%, Asian 3%, Caucasian 86%, Hispanic 1%. **Retention and Graduation:** 83% freshmen return for sophomore year. 29% freshmen graduate within 4 years.

ACADEMICS

Degrees: Bachelor's, doctoral, first professional, master's, post-master's certificate. **Academic Requirements:** General education including some course work in computer literacy, English (including composition), history, mathematics. Two 9-credit clusters outside major area of study in social/behavioral sciences, physical/biological sciences, or humanistic studies/fine arts. **Special Study Options:** Accelerated program, cooperative (work-study) program, distance learning, double major, dual enrollment, honors program, independent study, internships, student-designed major, study abroad, teacher certification program.

FACILITIES

Housing: Coed, all-female, all-male, apartments for married students, housing for disabled students, housing for international students, fraternities and/or sororities, freshmen-interest housing. **Library Holdings:** 2,816,515 bound volumes. 1,758,729 periodicals. 6,450,139 microforms. 15,908 audiovisuals. **Special Academic Facilities/Equipment:** Art/archaeology, anthropology, entomology, geology, and natural history museums, NBC-TV affiliate, freedom of information center, herbarium, agricultural research farm, equine center, nuclear reactor, observatory, child development lab, engineering experiment station. **Computers:** *Recommended operating system:* Mac. School-owned computers available for student use.

EXTRACURRICULARS

Activities: Choral groups, concert band, drama/theater, jazz band, literary magazine, marching band, music ensembles, opera, radio station, student government, student newspaper, symphony orchestra, television station, yearbook. **Organizations:** 406 registered organizations, 32 honor societies, 25 religious organizations, 31 fraternities (25% men join), 17 sororities (24% women join). **Athletics (Intercollegiate):** *Men:* baseball, basketball, cross-country, diving, football, golf, swimming, track & field, wrestling. *Women:* basketball, diving, golf, gymnastics, softball, swimming, tennis, track & field, volleyball.

ADMISSIONS

Selectivity Rating: 78 (of 100). **Freshman Academic Profile:** 34% in top 10% of high school class, 73% in top 25% of high school class, 91% in top 50% of high school class. Average ACT 25, ACT middle 50% range 24-29. TOEFL required of all international applicants, minimum TOEFL 500. **Basis for Candidate Selection:** *Very important factors considered include:* class rank, standardized test scores. **Freshman Admission Requirements:** High school diploma or GED is required. *Academic units required/recommended:* 17 total required; 4 English required, 4 math required, 3 science required, 1 science lab required, 2 foreign language required, 3 social studies required, 1 elective required. **Freshman Admission Statistics:** 8,092 applied, 80% accepted, 55% of those accepted enrolled. **Transfer Admission Requirements:** *Items required:* college transcript. Minimum college GPA of 2.0 required. Lowest grade transferable C. **General Admission Information:** Application fee $25. Priority application deadline May 1. Regular application deadline rolling. Nonfall registration accepted. Admission may be deferred for a maximum of 1 year. Credit and/or placement offered for CEEB Advanced Placement tests.

COSTS AND FINANCIAL AID

Required Forms and Deadlines: FAFSA. Priority filing deadline March 1. **Notification of Awards:** Applicants will be notified of awards on a rolling basis beginning on or about April 1. **Types of Aid:** *Need-based scholarships/grants:* Pell, SEOG, state scholarships/grants, private scholarships, the school's own gift aid, Federal Nursing. *Loans:* Direct Subsidized Stafford, Direct Unsubsidized Stafford, Direct PLUS, Federal Perkins, Federal Nursing, state loans, college/university loans from institutional funds, Auxiliary loans. **Student Employment:** Federal Work-Study Program available. Institutional employment available. Off-campus job opportunities are excellent. **Financial Aid Statistics:** Average freshman grant $4,217. Average freshman loan $3,377. Average income from on-campus job $1,299. **Financial Aid Phone:** 573-882-7506.

UNIVERSITY OF MISSOURI—KANSAS CITY

5100 Rockhill Road, 101 AC, Kansas City, MO 64114
Phone: 816-235-1111 **E-mail:** admit@umkc.edu **CEEB Code:** 6872
Fax: 816-235-5544 **Web:** www.umkc.edu **ACT Code:** 2380

This public school was founded in 1929. It has a 191-acre campus.

STUDENTS AND FACULTY

Enrollment: 8,870. **Student Body:** Male 40%, female 60%, out-of-state 19%, international 3%. **Ethnic Representation:** African American 14%, Asian 6%, Caucasian 69%, Hispanic 4%, Native American 1%. **Retention and Graduation:** 73% freshmen return for sophomore year. 16% freshmen graduate within 4 years. **Faculty:** Student/faculty ratio 9:1. 524 full-time faculty, 85% hold PhDs.

ACADEMICS

Degrees: Bachelor's, doctoral, first professional, first professional certificate, master's, post-master's certificate. **Academic Requirements:** General education including some course work in English (including composition), foreign languages, history, humanities, mathematics, sciences (biological or physical). **Classes:** 10-19 students in an average class. Under 10 students in an average lab/discussion section. **Majors with Highest Enrollment:** Computer and information sciences, general; liberal arts and sciences/liberal studies; psychology, general. **Disciplines with Highest Percentage of Degrees Awarded:** Liberal arts/general studies 20%, business/marketing 13%, education 8%, psychology 8%, computer and information sciences 7%. **Special Study Options:** Accelerated program, cooperative (work-study) program, double major, dual enrollment, honors program, independent study, internships, study abroad, teacher certification program.

FACILITIES

Housing: Coed, apartments for married students, apartments for single students. **Library Holdings:** 796,206 bound volumes. 6,951 periodicals. 2,350,917 microforms. 449,074 audiovisuals. **Special Academic Facilities/Equipment:** Art gallery, professional theater, geosciences museums, language lab. **Computers:** School-owned computers available for student use.

EXTRACURRICULARS

Activities: Choral groups, concert band, dance, drama/theater, jazz band, music ensembles, student government, student newspaper. **Organizations:** 150 registered organizations, 33 honor societies, 13 religious organizations, 5 fraternities, 8 sororities. **Athletics (Intercollegiate):** *Men:* basketball, cross-country, golf, rifle, soccer, tennis, track & field. *Women:* basketball, cheerleading, cross-country, golf, rifle, softball, tennis, track & field, volleyball.

ADMISSIONS

Selectivity Rating: 79 (of 100). **Freshman Academic Profile:** 34% in top 10% of high school class, 59% in top 25% of high school class, 84% in top 50% of high school class. Average ACT 25, ACT middle 50% range 21-28. TOEFL required of all international applicants, minimum TOEFL 500. **Basis for Candidate Selection:** *Very important factors considered include:* class rank, secondary school record, standardized test scores. *Other factors considered include:* character/personal qualities, essays, extracurricular activities, interview, recommendations, talent/ability, volunteer work, work experience. **Freshman Admission Requirements:** High school diploma or GED is required. *Academic units required/recommended:* 17 total required; 4 English required, 4 math required, 3 science required, 1 science lab required, 2 foreign language required, 3 social studies required. **Freshman Admission Statistics:** 2,480 applied, 78% accepted, 39% of those accepted enrolled. **Transfer Admission Requirements:** *Items required:* college transcript. Minimum college GPA of 2.0 required. Lowest grade transferable D. **General Admission Information:** Application fee $25. Priority application deadline April 1. Nonfall registration accepted. Admission may be deferred for a maximum of 1 year. Credit offered for CEEB Advanced Placement tests.

COSTS AND FINANCIAL AID

In-state tuition $4,585. Out-of-state tuition $13,997. Room & board $5,100. Required fees $791. Average book expense $825. **Required Forms and Deadlines:** FAFSA. No deadline for regular filing. Priority filing deadline March 1. **Notification of Awards:** Applicants will be notified of awards on a rolling basis beginning on or about April 15. **Types of Aid:** *Need-based scholarships/grants:* Pell, SEOG, state scholarships/grants, private scholarships, the school's own gift aid, United Negro College Fund, Federal Nursing. *Loans:* FFEL Subsidized Stafford, FFEL Unsubsidized Stafford, FFEL PLUS, Federal Perkins, Federal Nursing, state loans, college/university loans from institutional funds, alternative loans. **Student Employment:** Federal Work-Study Program available. Institutional employment available. Off-campus job opportunities are excellent. **Financial Aid Phone:** 816-235-1154.

UNIVERSITY OF MISSOURI—ROLLA

106 Parker Hall, Rolla, MO 65409
Phone: 573-341-4165 **E-mail:** admissions@umr.edu **CEEB Code:** 6876
Fax: 573-341-4082 **Web:** www.umr.edu **ACT Code:** 2398

This public school was founded in 1870. It has a 284-acre campus.

STUDENTS AND FACULTY

Enrollment: 3,849. **Student Body:** Male 77%, female 23%, out-of-state 22%, international 3% (38 countries represented). **Ethnic Representation:** African American 5%, Asian 3%, Caucasian 86%, Hispanic 2%, Native American 1%. **Retention and Graduation:** 84% freshmen return for sophomore year. 16% freshmen graduate within 4 years. 17% grads go on to further study within 1 year. **Faculty:** Student/faculty ratio 14:1. 311 full-time faculty, 89% hold PhDs. 88% faculty teach undergrads.

ACADEMICS

Degrees: Bachelor's, doctoral, master's, post-bachelor's certificate. **Academic Requirements:** General education including some course work in computer literacy, English (including composition), history, humanities, mathematics, sciences (biological or physical), social science. **Classes:** 20-29 students in an average class. 10-19 students in an average lab/discussion section. **Majors with Highest Enrollment:** Computer science; electrical, electronics, and communications engineering; mechanical engineering. **Disciplines with Highest Percentage of Degrees Awarded:** Engineering/engineering technology 75%, computer and information sciences 12%, psychology 3%, physical sciences 3%, biological life sciences 2%. **Special Study Options:** Accelerated program, cooperative (work-study) program, distance learning, double major, dual enrollment, English as a second language, honors program, independent study, internships, study abroad, teacher certification program.

FACILITIES

Housing: Coed, apartments for married students, apartments for single students, housing for disabled students, fraternities and/or sororities, religious-based housing. **Library Holdings:** 435,008 bound volumes. 1,580 periodicals. 51,443 microforms. 6,268 audiovisuals. **Special Academic Facilities/ Equipment:** Writing center; student design center; nuclear reactor; observatory; explosives testing lab; underground mine; museum of rocks, minerals, and gemstones; centers for environmental research, water resources, industrial research, and rock mechanics research; geophysical observatory; computerized manufacturing system. **Computers:** *Recommended operating system:* Windows NT/2000. School-owned computers available for student use.

EXTRACURRICULARS

Activities: Choral groups, concert band, drama/theater, jazz band, literary magazine, marching band, music ensembles, musical theater, pep band, radio station, student government, student newspaper, yearbook. **Organizations:** 197 registered organizations, 32 honor societies, 16 religious organizations, 20 fraternities (27% men join), 6 sororities (24% women join). **Athletics (Intercollegiate):** *Men:* baseball, basketball, cross-country, football, golf, indoor track, soccer, swimming, tennis, track & field. *Women:* basketball, cross-country, indoor track, soccer, softball, track & field.

ADMISSIONS

Selectivity Rating: 83 (of 100). **Freshman Academic Profile:** Average high school GPA 3.5. 40% in top 10% of high school class, 70% in top 25% of high school class, 94% in top 50% of high school class. 85% from public high schools. Average ACT 27, ACT middle 50% range 25-30. TOEFL required of all international applicants, minimum TOEFL 550. **Basis for Candidate Selection:** *Very important factors considered include:* class rank, secondary school record, standardized test scores. *Important factors considered include:* recommendations. *Other factors considered include:* character/personal qualities, essays, extracurricular activities, interview, talent/ability, volunteer work, work experience. **Freshman Admission Requirements:** High school diploma or GED is required. *Academic units required/recommended:* 17 total required; 4 English required, 4 math required, 3 science required, 1 science lab required, 2 foreign language required, 3 social studies required. **Freshman Admission Statistics:** 1,976 applied, 92% accepted. **Transfer Admission Requirements:** *Items required:* college transcript. Minimum college GPA of 2.0 required. Lowest grade transferable D. **General Admission Information:** Application fee $35. Priority application deadline December 1. Regular application deadline July 1. Nonfall registration accepted. Admission may be deferred for a maximum of 2 years. Credit offered for CEEB Advanced Placement tests.

COSTS AND FINANCIAL AID

In-state tuition $4,602. Out-of-state tuition $13,755. Room & board $5,230. Required fees $778. Average book expense $850. **Required Forms and Deadlines:** FAFSA. No deadline for regular filing. Priority filing deadline March 1. **Notification of Awards:** Applicants will be notified of awards on a rolling basis beginning on or about April 1. **Types of Aid:** *Need-based scholarships/grants:* Pell, SEOG, state scholarships/grants, private scholarships, the school's own gift aid, United Negro College Fund. *Loans:* Direct Subsidized Stafford, Direct Unsubsidized Stafford, Federal Perkins, state loans, college/university loans from institutional funds. **Student Employment:** Federal Work-Study Program available. Institutional employment available. Off-campus job opportunities are excellent. **Financial Aid Statistics:** 49% freshmen, 50% undergrads receive some form of aid. Average freshman grant $5,900. Average freshman loan $3,400. Average income from on-campus job $1,000. **Financial Aid Phone:** 800-522-0938.

UNIVERSITY OF MISSOURI—SAINT LOUIS

351 Millenium Student Center, 8001 Natural Bridge Road, Saint Louis, MO 63121-4499
Phone: 314-516-8675 **E-mail:** admissionsu@umsl.edu **CEEB Code:** 6889
Fax: 314-516-5310 **Web:** www.umsl.edu **ACT Code:** 2383

This public school was founded in 1963. It has a 320-acre campus.

STUDENTS AND FACULTY

Enrollment: 12,715. **Student Body:** Male 40%, female 60%, out-of-state 4%, international 2%. **Ethnic Representation:** African American 14%, Asian 3%, Caucasian 75%, Hispanic 1%. **Retention and Graduation:** 67% freshmen return for sophomore year. **Faculty:** Student/faculty ratio 19:1. 299 full-time faculty, 95% hold PhDs.

ACADEMICS

Degrees: Bachelor's, doctoral, first professional, master's, post-bachelor's certificate. **Academic Requirements:** General education including some course work in English (including composition), foreign languages, history, humanities, mathematics, sciences (biological or physical), social science. **Classes:** 20-29 students in an average class. 10-19 students in an average lab/discussion section. **Majors with Highest Enrollment:** Business administration/management; education, general; criminology. **Disciplines with Highest Percentage of Degrees Awarded:** Business/marketing 29%, education 16%, social sciences and history 11%, communications/communication technologies 7%, psychology 7%. **Special Study Options:** Accelerated program, cooperative (work-study) program, cross registration, distance learning, double major, dual enrollment, English as a second language, student exchange program (domestic), honors program, independent study, internships, student-designed major, study abroad, teacher certification program.

FACILITIES

Housing: Coed, apartments for married students, apartments for single students, housing for and older in residence halls and condominiums. **Library Holdings:** 782,431 bound volumes. 3,570 periodicals. 1,283,526 microforms. 3,878 audiovisuals. **Special Academic Facilities/Equipment:** Art galleries, language, writing labs, math labs, mercantile library, observatory, radio station. **Computers:** School-owned computers available for student use.

EXTRACURRICULARS

Activities: Choral groups, jazz band, literary magazine, music ensembles, musical theater, pep band, student government, student newspaper. **Organizations:** 140 registered organizations, 16 honor societies, 9 religious organizations, 2 fraternities (1% men join), 3 sororities (1% women join). **Athletics (Intercollegiate):** *Men:* baseball, basketball, golf, soccer, tennis. *Women:* basketball, golf, soccer, softball, tennis, volleyball.

ADMISSIONS

Selectivity Rating: 69 (of 100). **Freshman Academic Profile:** 19% in top 10% of high school class, 46% in top 25% of high school class, 77% in top 50% of high school class. 82% from public high schools. SAT I Math middle 50% range 520-630. SAT I Verbal middle 50% range 490-690. Average ACT 23, ACT middle 50% range 21-26. TOEFL required of all international applicants, minimum TOEFL 500. **Basis for Candidate Selection:** *Very important factors considered include:* class rank, secondary school record, standardized test scores. *Other factors considered include:* essays, recommendations. **Freshman Admission Requirements:** High school diploma or GED is required. *Academic units required/recommended:* 17 total required; 4 English required, 4 math required, 3 science required, 1 science lab required, 2 foreign language required, 3 social studies required. **Transfer Admission Requirements:** *Items required:* college transcript. Minimum college GPA of 2.0 required. Lowest grade transferable D. **General Admission Information:** Application fee $25. Priority application deadline July 1. Nonfall registration accepted. Admission may be deferred for a maximum of 1 year. Credit and/or placement offered for CEEB Advanced Placement tests.

COSTS AND FINANCIAL AID

In-state tuition $5,116. Out-of-state tuition $13,561. Room & board $6,700. Required fees $569. Average book expense $824. **Required Forms and Deadlines:** FAFSA. No deadline for regular filing. Priority filing deadline April 1. **Notification of Awards:** Applicants will be notified of awards on a rolling basis beginning on or about April 1. **Types of Aid:** *Need-based scholarships/grants:* Pell, SEOG, state scholarships/grants, private scholarships, the school's own gift aid. *Loans:* Direct Subsidized Stafford, Direct Unsubsidized Stafford, FFEL PLUS, Federal Perkins, Federal Nursing, state loans. **Student Employment:** Federal Work-Study Program available. Institutional employment available. Off-campus job opportunities are good. **Financial Aid Statistics:** 43% freshmen, 47% undergrads receive some form of aid. Average freshman grant $1,874. Average freshman loan $2,639. Average income from on-campus job $2,472. **Financial Aid Phone:** 314-516-5526.

UNIVERSITY OF MOBILE

5437 Parkway Drive, PO Box 13220, Mobile, AL 36663-0220
Phone: 251-442-2287 **E-mail:** adminfo@mail.umobile.edu **CEEB Code:** 1515
Fax: 251-442-2498 **Web:** www.umobile.edu **ACT Code:** 29

This private school, which is affiliated with the Baptist Church, was founded in 1961. It has an 830-acre campus.

STUDENTS AND FACULTY

Enrollment: 1,802. **Student Body:** Male 32%, female 68%, out-of-state 11%, international 1%. **Ethnic Representation:** African American 22%, Caucasian 60%, Hispanic 1%, Native American 2%. **Faculty:** Student/faculty ratio 17:1. 87 full-time faculty, 60% hold PhDs. 100% faculty teach undergrads.

ACADEMICS

Degrees: Associate's, bachelor's, master's. **Academic Requirements:** General education including some course work in arts/fine arts, computer literacy, English (including composition), history, humanities, mathematics, philosophy, sciences (biological or physical), social science, religion. **Classes:** 10-19 students in an average class. Under 10 students in an average lab/discussion section. **Majors with Highest Enrollment:** Nursing/registered nurse training (RN, ASN, BSN, MSN); business administration/management; elementary education and teaching. **Disciplines with Highest Percentage of Degrees Awarded:** Education 24%, business/marketing 18%, health professions and related sciences 13%, interdisciplinary studies 12%, social sciences and history 7%. **Special Study Options:** Accelerated program, cooperative (work-study) program, double major, honors program, independent study, internships, liberal arts/career combination, teacher certification program.

FACILITIES

Housing: All-female, all-male, housing for disabled students. **Library Holdings:** 66,399 bound volumes. 874 periodicals. 252 microforms. 1,150 audiovisuals. **Special Academic Facilities/Equipment:** Art gallery, forest learning center, mineral museum. **Computers:** School-owned computers available for student use.

EXTRACURRICULARS

Activities: Choral groups, concert band, dance, drama/theater, jazz band, music ensembles, musical theater, pep band, student government, student newspaper, symphony orchestra, yearbook. **Organizations:** 52 registered organizations, 12 honor societies, 3 religious organizations. **Athletics (Intercollegiate):** *Men:* baseball, basketball, cheerleading, cross-country, golf, indoor track, soccer, track & field. *Women:* basketball, cheerleading, cross-country, golf, indoor track, soccer, softball, tennis, track & field.

ADMISSIONS

Selectivity Rating: 73 (of 100). **Freshman Academic Profile:** 76% from public high schools. Average ACT 22, ACT middle 50% range 19-28. TOEFL required of all international applicants, minimum TOEFL 500. **Basis for Candidate Selection:** *Very important factors considered include:* secondary school record, standardized test scores. *Other factors considered include:* class rank, interview, recommendations. **Freshman Admission Requirements:** High school diploma or GED is required. *Academic units required/recommended:* 22 total recommended; 4 English recommended, 3 math recommended, 2 social studies recommended, 3 history recommended. **Freshman Admission Statistics:** 477 applied, 100% accepted, 49% of those accepted enrolled. **Transfer Admission Requirements:** *Items required:* college transcript. Minimum college GPA of 2.0 required. Lowest grade transferable C. **General Admission Information:** Application fee $30. Nonfall registration accepted. Admission may be deferred for a maximum of 1 year. Credit offered for CEEB Advanced Placement tests.

COSTS AND FINANCIAL AID

Tuition $8,940. Room & board $5,000. Required fees $100. Average book expense $500. **Required Forms and Deadlines:** FAFSA, institution's own financial aid form and state aid form. Priority filing deadline March 13. **Notification of Awards:** Applicants will be notified of awards on or about April 1. **Types of Aid:** *Need-based scholarships/grants:* Pell, SEOG, state scholarships/grants, private scholarships, the school's own gift aid. *Loans:* FFEL Subsidized Stafford, FFEL Unsubsidized Stafford, FFEL PLUS, Federal Perkins. **Student Employment:** Federal Work-Study Program available. Institutional employment available. Off-campus job opportunities are fair. **Financial Aid Statistics:** 84% freshmen, 61% undergrads receive some form of aid. Average income from on-campus job $1,545. **Financial Aid Phone:** 251-442-2252.

UNIVERSITY OF MONTANA COLLEGE OF TECHNOLOGY

909 South Avenue West, Missoula, MT 59801
Phone: 406-243-7882 **E-mail:** kathrynb@selway.umt.edu **CEEB Code:** 4489
Fax: 406-243-7899 **Web:** www.cte.umt.edu **ACT Code:** 2422

This public school was founded in 1893. It has a 220-acre campus.

STUDENTS AND FACULTY

Enrollment: 10,501. **Student Body:** Male 47%, female 53%, out-of-state 31%, international 3%. **Ethnic Representation:** African American 1%, Asian 1%, Caucasian 88%, Hispanic 1%, Native American 3%. **Retention and Graduation:** 68% freshmen return for sophomore year. 15% freshmen graduate within 4 years. 42% grads go on to further study within 1 year. 9% grads pursue business degrees. 7% grads pursue law degrees. 9% grads pursue medical degrees. **Faculty:** 100% faculty teach undergrads.

ACADEMICS

Degrees: Associate's, bachelor's, certificate, doctoral, first professional, master's, terminal, transfer. **Academic Requirements:** General education including some course work in computer literacy, English (including composition), mathematics, social science. **Special Study Options:** Cooperative (work-study) program, cross registration, distance learning, double major, dual enrollment, English as a second language, student exchange program (domestic), honors program, independent study, internships, study abroad, teacher certification program, combined programs with other institutions.

FACILITIES

Housing: Coed, all-female, all-male, apartments for married students, apartments for single students, housing for disabled students, housing for international students, fraternities and/or sororities. **Library Holdings:** 570,287 bound volumes. 6,248 periodicals. 238,184 microforms. 118,190 audiovisuals. **Special Academic Facilities/Equipment:** Bureau of business and economic research, clinical psychology center, environmental studies lab, geology field camp biological research center. **Computers:** *Recommended operating system:* Mac.

EXTRACURRICULARS

Activities: Choral groups, concert band, dance, drama/theater, jazz band, marching band, music ensembles, musical theater, pep band, radio station, student government, student newspaper, symphony orchestra, television station. **Organizations:** 117 registered organizations, 8 honor societies, 15 religious organizations, 7 fraternities (5% men join), 4 sororities (5% women join).

ADMISSIONS

Selectivity Rating: 63 (of 100). **Freshman Academic Profile:** Average SAT I Math 530. Average SAT I Verbal 540. Average ACT 23. TOEFL required of all international applicants, minimum TOEFL 500. **Freshman Admission Requirements:** High school diploma or GED is required. *Academic units required/recommended:* 4 English recommended, 3 math recommended, 2 science recommended, 1 science lab recommended, 2 foreign language recommended, 3 social studies recommended. **Freshman Admission Statistics:** 852 applied, 85% accepted, 70% of those accepted enrolled. **Transfer Admission Requirements:** *Items required:* college transcript. Minimum college GPA of 2.0 required. Lowest grade transferable D. **General Admission Information:** Application fee $30. Priority application deadline March 1. Nonfall registration accepted. Admission may be deferred for a maximum of 1 year. Credit and/or placement offered for CEEB Advanced Placement tests.

COSTS AND FINANCIAL AID

In-state tuition $2,365. Out-of-state tuition $5,085. Room & board $4,000. **Required Forms and Deadlines:** FAFSA and institution's own financial aid form. Priority filing deadline March 1. **Notification of Awards:** Applicants will be notified of awards on a rolling basis beginning on or about May 1. **Types of Aid:** *Need-based scholarships/grants:* Pell, SEOG, state scholarships/grants. *Loans:* FFEL Subsidized Stafford, FFEL Unsubsidized Stafford, FFEL PLUS, Federal Perkins. **Student Employment:** Federal Work-Study Program available. Institutional employment available. Off-campus job opportunities are excellent. **Financial Aid Statistics:** 47% freshmen, 48% undergrads receive some form of aid. Average freshman grant $2,500. Average freshman loan $2,849. Average income from on-campus job $1,200. **Financial Aid Phone:** 406-243-5373.

UNIVERSITY OF MONTANA—MISSOULA

103 Lommasson Center, Missoula, MT 59812
Phone: 406-243-6266 **E-mail:** admiss@selway.umt.edu **CEEB Code:** 4489
Fax: 406-243-5711 **Web:** www.umt.edu **ACT Code:** 2422

This public school was founded in 1893. It has a 220-acre campus.

STUDENTS AND FACULTY

Enrollment: 10,828. **Student Body:** Male 47%, female 53%, out-of-state 26%, international 2%. **Ethnic Representation:** Asian 1%, Caucasian 90%, Hispanic 1%, Native American 3%. **Retention and Graduation:** 69% freshmen return for sophomore year. 18% freshmen graduate within 4 years. 42% grads go on to further study within 1 year. 9% grads pursue business degrees. 7% grads pursue law degrees. 9% grads pursue medical degrees. **Faculty:** Student/faculty ratio 22:1. 486 full-time faculty, 80% hold PhDs. 100% faculty teach undergrads.

ACADEMICS

Degrees: Associate's, bachelor's, certificate, diploma, doctoral, first professional, master's, post-master's certificate. **Academic Requirements:** General education including some course work in arts/fine arts, English (including composition), foreign languages, history, mathematics, sciences (biological or physical), social science, ethical and human values. **Classes:** 10-19 students in an average class. 20-29 students in an average lab/discussion section. **Majors with Highest Enrollment:** Business, management, marketing, and related support services; education, general; English language and literature, general. **Disciplines with Highest Percentage of Degrees Awarded:** Business/marketing 22%, social sciences and history 14%, natural resources/environmental sciences 9%, English 9%, education 8%. **Special Study Options:** Cooperative (work-study) program, cross registration, distance learning, double major, dual enrollment, English as a second language, student exchange program (domestic), external degree program, honors program, independent study, internships, study abroad, teacher certification program. Combined bachelor's/graduate programs with other institutions: Bachelor of Nursing in Missoula and MPA Program at Helena in cooperation with Montana State University—Bozeman.

FACILITIES

Housing: Coed, all-female, all-male, apartments for married students, apartments for single students, housing for disabled students, housing for international students, fraternities and/or sororities, honors floors, international floors, quiet floors, activity dorms. **Library Holdings:** 889,280 bound volumes. 6,654 periodicals. 298,909 microforms. 65,645 audiovisuals. **Special Academic Facilities/Equipment:** Bureau of business and economic research, clinical psychology center, environmental studies lab, geology field camp, biological research center, biomedical research center. **Computers:** School-owned computers available for student use.

EXTRACURRICULARS

Activities: Choral groups, concert band, dance, drama/theater, jazz band, marching band, music ensembles, musical theater, pep band, radio station, student government, student newspaper. **Organizations:** 126 registered organizations, 11 honor societies, 15 religious organizations, 8 fraternities (6% men join), 4 sororities (5% women join). **Athletics (Intercollegiate):** *Men:* basketball, cheerleading, cross-country, football, indoor track, tennis, track & field. *Women:* basketball, cheerleading, cross-country, golf, indoor track, soccer, tennis, track & field, volleyball.

ADMISSIONS

Selectivity Rating: 76 (of 100). **Freshman Academic Profile:** Average high school GPA 3.2. 14% in top 10% of high school class, 33% in top 25% of high school class, 66% in top 50% of high school class. 56% from public high schools. Average SAT I Math 540, SAT I Math middle 50% range 470-590. Average SAT I Verbal 550, SAT I Verbal middle 50% range 450-600. Average ACT 22, ACT middle 50% range 20-25. TOEFL required of all international applicants, minimum TOEFL 500. **Basis for Candidate Selection:** *Very important factors considered include:* class rank, standardized test scores. *Important factors considered include:* extracurricular activities, secondary school record, talent/ability. *Other factors considered include:* interview, minority status, recommendations, volunteer work, work experience. **Freshman Admission Requirements:** High school diploma or GED is required. *Academic units required/recommended:* 4 English required, 3 math required, 2 science required, 2 science lab required, 3 social studies required. **Freshman Admission Statistics:** 3,560 applied, 88% accepted, 61% of those accepted enrolled. **Transfer Admission Requirements:** *Items required:* college transcript, statement of good standing from prior school. Minimum college GPA of 2.0 required. Lowest grade transferable D. **General Admission Information:** Application fee $30. Nonfall registration accepted. Admission may be deferred for a maximum of 1 year. Credit and/or placement offered for CEEB Advanced Placement tests.

COSTS AND FINANCIAL AID

In-state tuition $2,873. Out-of-state tuition $9,868. Room & board $5,090. Required fees $1,115. Average book expense $700. **Required Forms and Deadlines:** FAFSA and institution's own financial aid form. No deadline for regular filing. Priority filing deadline March 1. **Notification of Awards:** Applicants will be notified of awards on a rolling basis beginning on or about April 1. **Types of Aid:** *Need-based scholarships/grants:* Pell, SEOG, state scholarships/grants, private scholarships, the school's own gift aid. *Loans:* FFEL Subsidized Stafford, FFEL Unsubsidized Stafford, FFEL PLUS, Federal Perkins. **Student Employment:** Federal Work-Study Program available. Institutional employment available. Off-campus job opportunities are excellent. **Financial Aid Statistics:** 48% freshmen, 50% undergrads receive some form of aid. Average freshman grant $2,500. Average freshman loan $2,849. Average income from on-campus job $1,200. **Financial Aid Phone:** 406-243-5373.

UNIVERSITY OF MONTANA—WESTERN

710 South Atlantic, Dillon, MT 59725
Phone: 406-683-7331 **E-mail:** admissions@umwestern.edu **CEEB Code:** 4945
Fax: 406-683-7493 **Web:** www.umwestern.edu **ACT Code:** 2428

This public school was founded in 1893. It has a 34-acre campus.

STUDENTS AND FACULTY

Enrollment: 1,142. **Student Body:** Male 40%, female 60%, out-of-state 13%, international 1% (3 countries represented). **Ethnic Representation:** Asian 2%,

Caucasian 82%, Hispanic 2%, Native American 3%. **Retention and Graduation:** 29% freshmen return for sophomore year. 50% grads go on to further study within 1 year. **Faculty:** Student/faculty ratio 19:1. 4,748 full-time faculty. 100% faculty teach undergrads.

ACADEMICS

Degrees: Associate's, bachelor's. **Academic Requirements:** General education including some course work in arts/fine arts, computer literacy, English (including composition), history, humanities, mathematics, sciences (biological or physical), social science. **Classes:** 10-19 students in an average class. **Majors with Highest Enrollment:** Business administration/management; environmental studies; elementary education and teaching. **Disciplines with Highest Percentage of Degrees Awarded:** Education 69%, liberal arts/general studies 30%, interdisciplinary studies 1%. **Special Study Options:** Cooperative (work-study) program, distance learning, double major, dual enrollment, honors program, independent study, internships, teacher certification program.

FACILITIES

Housing: Coed, all-female, all-male, apartments for married students, apartments for single students, housing for disabled students. Students with fewer than 30 credits not living with family required to live in dorm. Transfer students under 21 with less than 30 credits not living with parents must live in dorm. **Library Holdings:** 90,431 bound volumes. 359 periodicals. 5,792 microforms. 3,863 audiovisuals. **Special Academic Facilities/Equipment:** Art gallery, outdoor education center, learning center. **Computers:** School-owned computers available for student use.

EXTRACURRICULARS

Activities: Choral groups, drama/theater, literary magazine, music ensembles, pep band, radio station, student government, student newspaper, yearbook. **Organizations:** 25 registered organizations, 2 honor societies, 2 religious organizations. **Athletics (Intercollegiate):** *Men:* basketball, cheerleading, football, golf, rodeo. *Women:* basketball, cheerleading, golf, rodeo, volleyball.

ADMISSIONS

Selectivity Rating: 64 (of 100). **Freshman Academic Profile:** Average high school GPA 2.9. 5% in top 10% of high school class, 17% in top 25% of high school class, 44% in top 50% of high school class. 96% from public high schools. Average SAT I Math 466, SAT I Math middle 50% range 330-570. Average SAT I Verbal 457, SAT I Verbal middle 50% range 350-560. Average ACT 18, ACT middle 50% range 15-25. TOEFL required of all international applicants, minimum TOEFL 500. **Basis for Candidate Selection:** *Very important factors considered include:* class rank, secondary school record, standardized test scores. *Other factors considered include:* alumni/ae relation, extracurricular activities, minority status, state residency, talent/ability. **Freshman Admission Requirements:** High school diploma or GED is required. *Academic units required/recommended:* 16 total required; 4 English required, 3 math required, 2 science required, 2 science lab required, 3 social studies required, 4 elective required. **Freshman Admission Statistics:** 321 applied, 100% accepted, 79% of those accepted enrolled. **Transfer Admission Requirements:** *Items required:* college transcript. Minimum college GPA of 2.0 required. Lowest grade transferable C. **General Admission Information:** Application fee $30. Priority application deadline July 1. Regular application deadline July 1. Nonfall registration accepted. Admission may be deferred. Credit and/or placement offered for CEEB Advanced Placement tests.

COSTS AND FINANCIAL AID

In-state tuition $2,875. Out-of-state tuition $10,380. Room & board $4,500. Required fees $720. Average book expense $675. **Required Forms and Deadlines:** FAFSA. Priority filing deadline March 1. **Notification of Awards:** Applicants will be notified of awards on a rolling basis beginning on or about March 1. **Types of Aid:** *Need-based scholarships/grants:* Pell, SEOG, state scholarships/grants, the school's own gift aid. *Loans:* FFEL Subsidized Stafford, FFEL Unsubsidized Stafford, FFEL PLUS, Federal Perkins. **Student Employment:** Federal Work-Study Program available. Institutional employment available. Off-campus job opportunities are good. **Financial Aid Statistics:** 83% freshmen, 91% undergrads receive some form of aid. Average freshman grant $1,000. Average freshman loan $2,625. Average income from on-campus job $1,350. **Financial Aid Phone:** 406-683-7511.

UNIVERSITY OF MONTEVALLO

Station 6030, Montevallo, AL 35115
Phone: 205-665-6000 **E-mail:** admissions@montevallo.edu **CEEB Code:** 1004
Fax: 205-655-6042 **Web:** www.montevallo.edu **ACT Code:** 4

This public school was founded in 1896. It has a 160-acre campus.

STUDENTS AND FACULTY

Enrollment: 2,515. **Student Body:** Male 32%, female 68%, out-of-state 5%, international 2%. **Ethnic Representation:** African American 13%, Caucasian 82%, Asian 1%, Hispanic 1%, Native American 1%. **Retention and Graduation:** 74% freshmen return for sophomore year. 22% freshmen graduate within 4 years. 40% grads go on to further study within 1 year. 1% grads pursue business degrees. 18% grads pursue law degrees. 1% grads pursue medical degrees. **Faculty:** Student/faculty ratio 16:1. 132 full-time faculty, 76% hold PhDs.

ACADEMICS

Degrees: Bachelor's, master's. **Academic Requirements:** General education including some course work in arts/fine arts, computer literacy, English (including composition), foreign languages, history, mathematics, philosophy, sciences (biological or physical), social science, communication studies (speech), kinesiology activities (PE), health, and psychology or philosophy, human behavior and inquiry, writing reinforcement. **Majors with Highest Enrollment:** Elementary education and teaching; English language and literature, general; art/art studies, general. **Special Study Options:** Accelerated program, cross registration, double major, dual enrollment, student exchange program (domestic), honors program, independent study, internships, study abroad, teacher certification program, academic remediation, and learning disabilities services.

FACILITIES

Housing: Coed, all-female, all-male, fraternities and/or sororities. **Library Holdings:** 159,026 bound volumes. 794 periodicals. 782,366 microforms. 3,185 audiovisuals. **Special Academic Facilities/Equipment:** Art gallery, child development, speech and hearing, traffic safety, and undergraduate liberal studies centers, mass communications center with cable TV broadcasting capabilities. **Computers:** School-owned computers available for student use.

EXTRACURRICULARS

Activities: Choral groups, concert band, dance, drama/theater, jazz band, literary magazine, music ensembles, musical theater, student government, student newspaper, television station, yearbook. **Organizations:** 8 honor societies, 3 religious organizations, 7 fraternities (23% men join), 7 sororities (23% women join). **Athletics (Intercollegiate):** *Men:* baseball, basketball, cheerleading, golf, tennis. *Women:* basketball, cheerleading, golf, tennis, volleyball.

ADMISSIONS

Selectivity Rating: 77 (of 100). **Freshman Academic Profile:** 90% from public high schools. Average ACT 22, ACT middle 50% range 19-25. **Basis for Candidate Selection:** *Very important factors considered include:* secondary school record, standardized test scores. *Other factors considered include:* alumni/ae relation, character/personal qualities, class rank, extracurricular activities, interview, recommendations, talent/ability, work experience. **Freshman Admission Requirements:** *Academic units required/recommended:* 16 total required; 4 English required, 2 math required, 3 math recommended, 2 science required, 3 science recommended, 2 foreign language recommended, 2 social studies required, 2 history required, 4 elective required. **Freshman Admission Statistics:** 1,329 applied, 74% accepted, 52% of those accepted enrolled. **Transfer Admission Requirements:** *Items required:* college transcript. Minimum college GPA of 2.0 required. Lowest grade transferable D. **General Admission Information:** Application fee $25. Regular application deadline August 1. Nonfall registration accepted. Admission may be deferred for a maximum of 2 years.

COSTS AND FINANCIAL AID

In-state tuition $4,050. Out-of-state tuition $8,100. Room & board $3,638. Required fees $284. Average book expense $600. **Required Forms and Deadlines:** FAFSA and institution's own financial aid form. **Types of Aid:** *Need-based scholarships/grants:* state scholarships/grants. *Loans:* FFEL Subsidized Stafford, FFEL PLUS. **Student Employment:** Federal Work-Study Program available. Institutional employment available. Off-campus job opportunities are good. **Financial Aid Statistics:** Average freshman grant $1,828. Average freshman loan $2,428. Average income from on-campus job $3,100. **Financial Aid Phone:** 205-665-6050.

UNIVERSITY OF NEBRASKA—KEARNEY

905 West 25th, Kearney, NE 68849
Phone: 800-532-7639 **E-mail:** admissionsug@unk.edu **CEEB Code:** 6467
Fax: 308-865-8987 **Web:** www.unk.edu **ACT Code:** 2468

This public school was founded in 1903. It has a 235-acre campus.

STUDENTS AND FACULTY

Enrollment: 5,886. **Student Body:** Male 44%, female 56%, out-of-state 6%, international 3%. **Ethnic Representation:** African American 1%, Asian 1%, Caucasian 91%, Hispanic 2%.

ACADEMICS

Degrees: Bachelor's, master's. **Academic Requirements:** General education including some course work in arts/fine arts, English (including composition), history, humanities, mathematics, sciences (biological or physical), social science, personal development such as healthful living, personal money management, and computers in society. **Special Study Options:** Distance learning, double major, English as a second language, student exchange program (domestic), external degree program, honors program, internships, study abroad, teacher certification program.

FACILITIES

Housing: Coed, all-female, all-male, apartments for married students, apartments for single students, fraternities and/or sororities. **Library Holdings:** 505,616 bound volumes. 1,677 periodicals. 997,940 microforms. 75,981 audiovisuals. **Special Academic Facilities/Equipment:** Art gallery, language lab, museum of Nebraska art. **Computers:** *Recommended operating system:* Mac. School-owned computers available for student use.

EXTRACURRICULARS

Activities: Choral groups, concert band, dance, drama/theater, jazz band, literary magazine, marching band, music ensembles, musical theater, opera, pep band, radio station, student government, student newspaper, symphony orchestra, television station. **Organizations:** 1 religious organization, 10 fraternities (9% men join), 6 sororities (9% women join). **Athletics (Intercollegiate):** *Men:* baseball, basketball, cross-country, diving, football, golf, soccer, softball, swimming, tennis, volleyball. *Women:* basketball, cross-country, diving, football, golf, soccer, softball, swimming, tennis, volleyball.

ADMISSIONS

Selectivity Rating: 67 (of 100). **Freshman Academic Profile:** 90% from public high schools. TOEFL required of all international applicants, minimum TOEFL 520. **Basis for Candidate Selection:** *Very important factors considered include:* class rank, secondary school record, standardized test scores. *Other factors considered include:* religious affiliation/commitment, talent/ability. **Freshman Admission Requirements:** High school diploma or GED is required. *Academic units required/recommended:* 4 English required, 3 math required, 3 science required, 1 science lab required, 2 foreign language required, 1 social studies required, 2 history required, 1 elective required. **Freshman Admission Statistics:** 2,672 applied. **Transfer Admission Requirements:** *Items required:* high school transcript, college transcript. Minimum college GPA of 2.0 required. Lowest grade transferable C. **General Admission Information:** Application fee $25. Regular application deadline August 1. Nonfall registration accepted. Credit and/or placement offered for CEEB Advanced Placement tests.

COSTS AND FINANCIAL AID

In-state tuition $2,715. Out-of-state tuition $5,550. Room & board $4,156. Required fees $498. Average book expense $700. **Required Forms and Deadlines:** FAFSA, institution's own financial aid form and C. No deadline for regular filing. Priority filing deadline March 1. **Notification of Awards:** Applicants will be notified of awards on or about May 1. **Types of Aid:** *Need-based scholarships/grants:* Pell, SEOG, state scholarships/grants, private scholarships, the school's own gift aid. *Loans:* FFEL Subsidized Stafford, FFEL Unsubsidized Stafford, FFEL PLUS, Federal Perkins. **Student Employment:** Federal Work-Study Program available. Institutional employment available. Off-campus job opportunities are excellent. **Financial Aid Phone:** 308-865-8520.

UNIVERSITY OF NEBRASKA—LINCOLN

1410 Q Street, Lincoln, NE 68588-0417
Phone: 402-472-2023 **E-mail:** nuhusker@unl.edu **CEEB Code:** 6877
Fax: 402-472-0670 **Web:** www.unl.edu **ACT Code:** 2482

This public school was founded in 1869. It has a 628-acre campus.

STUDENTS AND FACULTY

Enrollment: 18,118. **Student Body:** Male 52%, female 48%, out-of-state 14%, international 3% (124 countries represented). **Ethnic Representation:** African American 2%, Asian 2%, Caucasian 89%, Hispanic 2%. **Retention and Graduation:** 82% freshmen return for sophomore year. 18% freshmen graduate within 4 years. **Faculty:** Student/faculty ratio 19:1. 1,057 full-time faculty, 93% hold PhDs.

ACADEMICS

Degrees: Associate's, bachelor's, certificate, doctoral, first professional, master's, post-master's certificate, terminal. **Academic Requirements:** General education including some course work in arts/fine arts, English (including composition), foreign languages, history, humanities, mathematics, sciences (biological or physical), social science; and race, ethnicity & gender studies. **Classes:** 20-29 students in an average class. 20-29 students in an average lab/discussion section. **Disciplines with Highest Percentage of Degrees Awarded:** Business/marketing 21%, engineering/engineering technology 12%, education 10%, communications/communication technologies 8%, agriculture 8%. **Special Study Options:** Accelerated program, cooperative (work-study) program, cross registration, distance learning, double major, dual enrollment, English as a second language, student exchange program (domestic), honors program, independent study, internships, liberal arts/career combination, student-designed major, study abroad, teacher certification program.

FACILITIES

Housing: Coed, all-female, all-male, apartments for married students, apartments for single students, housing for disabled students, housing for international students, fraternities and/or sororities, cooperative housing. **Library Holdings:** 1,184,824 bound volumes. 21,309 periodicals. 3,480,580 microforms. 73,405 audiovisuals. **Special Academic Facilities/Equipment:** Art gallery, performing arts center, food industries complex, planetarium, center for mass spectrometry, natural science museum, animal science complex, veterinary animal research/diagnosis center. **Computers:** School-owned computers available for student use.

EXTRACURRICULARS

Activities: Choral groups, concert band, dance, drama/theater, jazz band, literary magazine, marching band, music ensembles, musical theater, opera, pep band, radio station, student government, student newspaper, student-run film society, symphony orchestra, television station, yearbook. **Organizations:** 335 registered organizations, 57 honor societies, 25 religious organizations, 26 fraternities (15% men join), 16 sororities (17% women join). **Athletics (Intercollegiate):** *Men:* baseball, basketball, cheerleading, cross-country, football, golf, gymnastics, indoor track, tennis, track & field, wrestling. *Women:* basketball, cheerleading, cross-country, diving, golf, gymnastics, indoor track, rifle, soccer, softball, swimming, tennis, track & field, volleyball.

ADMISSIONS

Selectivity Rating: 91 (of 100). **Freshman Academic Profile:** 26% in top 10% of high school class, 53% in top 25% of high school class, 85% in top 50% of high school class. Average SAT I Math 589, SAT I Math middle 50% range 520-660. Average SAT I Verbal 570, SAT I Verbal middle 50% range 500-640. Average ACT 24, ACT middle 50% range 21-27. TOEFL required of all international applicants, minimum TOEFL 525. **Basis for Candidate Selection:** *Very important factors considered include:* class rank, secondary school record, standardized test scores. *Important factors considered include:* talent/ability. *Other factors considered include:* alumni/ae relation, geographical residence, minority status, recommendations. **Freshman Admission Requirements:** High school diploma or GED is required. *Academic units required/recommended:* 16 total required; 4 English required, 4 math required, 3 science required, 1 science lab required, 2 foreign language required, 3 social studies required, 1 history recommended. **Freshman Admission Statistics:** 7,631 applied, 90% accepted, 53% of those accepted enrolled. **Transfer Admission Requirements:** *Items required:* high school transcript, college transcript. Minimum college GPA of 2.0 required. Lowest grade transferable D. **General Admission Information:** Application fee $25. Priority application deadline January 15. Regular application deadline June 30. Nonfall registration accepted. Neither credit nor placement offered for CEEB Advanced Placement tests.

COSTS AND FINANCIAL AID

In-state tuition $3,345. Out-of-state tuition $9,938. Room & board $4,875. Required fees $780. Average book expense $756. **Required Forms and Deadlines:** FAFSA. No deadline for regular filing. **Notification of Awards:** Applicants will be notified of awards on a rolling basis beginning on or about April 15. **Types of Aid:** *Need-based scholarships/grants:* Pell, SEOG, state scholarships/grants, private scholarships, the school's own gift aid. *Loans:* Direct Subsidized Stafford, Direct Unsubsidized Stafford, Direct PLUS, Federal Perkins, college/university loans from institutional funds. **Student Employment:** Federal Work-Study Program available. Institutional employment available. Off-campus job opportunities are excellent. **Financial Aid Statistics:** 41% freshmen, 40% undergrads receive some form of aid. Average freshman grant $3,934. Average freshman loan $2,588. **Financial Aid Phone:** 402-472-2030.

UNIVERSITY OF NEBRASKA—OMAHA

Office of Admissions, 6001 Dodge Street, EAB Room 103, Omaha, NE 68182
Phone: 402-554-2393 **E-mail:** unoadm@unomaha.edu **CEEB Code:** 6420
Fax: 402-554-3472 **Web:** www.unomaha.edu **ACT Code:** 2464

This public school was founded in 1908. It has a 158-acre campus.

STUDENTS AND FACULTY

Enrollment: 11,333. **Student Body:** Male 47%, female 53%, out-of-state 8%, international 3% (83 countries represented). **Ethnic Representation:** African American 6%, Asian 3%, Caucasian 85%, Hispanic 3%. **Retention and Graduation:** 73% freshmen return for sophomore year. 8% freshmen graduate within 4 years. **Faculty:** Student/faculty ratio 18:1. 462 full-time faculty, 81% hold PhDs.

ACADEMICS

Degrees: Bachelor's, doctoral, master's, post-bachelor's certificate, post-master's certificate. **Academic Requirements:** General education including some course work in English (including composition), humanities, mathematics, sciences (biological or physical), social science, cultural diversity. **Classes:** 20-29 students in an average class. Under 10 students in an average lab/discussion section. **Majors with Highest Enrollment:** Elementary education and teaching; criminal justice/safety studies; management information systems, general. **Disciplines with Highest Percentage of Degrees Awarded:** Business/marketing 26%, education 18%, protective services/public administration 13%, social sciences and history 6%, psychology 6%. **Special Study Options:** Cooperative (work-study) program, distance learning, double major, English as a second language, student exchange program (domestic), honors program, independent study, internships, student-designed major, study abroad, teacher certification program.

FACILITIES

Housing: Coed. **Library Holdings:** 750,000 bound volumes. 3,000 periodicals. 2,000,000 microforms. 7,000 audiovisuals. **Special Academic Facilities/Equipment:** Center for Afghanistan studies, language lab, physical education facility. **Computers:** School-owned computers available for student use.

EXTRACURRICULARS

Activities: Choral groups, concert band, dance, drama/theater, jazz band, literary magazine, marching band, music ensembles, musical theater, opera, pep band, radio station, student government, student newspaper, student-run film society, symphony orchestra, television station. **Organizations:** 96 registered organizations, 16 honor societies, 7 religious organizations, 9 fraternities (7% men join), 7 sororities (4% women join). **Athletics (Intercollegiate):** *Men:* baseball, basketball, football, ice hockey, wrestling. *Women:* basketball, cross-country, diving, golf, soccer, softball, swimming, tennis, volleyball.

ADMISSIONS

Selectivity Rating: 66 (of 100). **Freshman Academic Profile:** 13% in top 10% of high school class, 36% in top 25% of high school class, 70% in top 50% of high school class. 82% from public high schools. Average ACT 22, ACT middle 50% range 20-25. TOEFL required of all international applicants, minimum TOEFL 500. **Basis for Candidate Selection:** *Very important factors considered include:* class rank, secondary school record, standardized test scores. *Other factors considered include:* character/personal qualities. **Freshman Admission Requirements:** High school diploma or GED is required. *Academic units required/recommended:* 16 total required; 4 English required, 3 math required, 3 science required, 1 science lab required, 2 foreign language required, 1 social studies required, 2 history required, 1 elective required. **Freshman Admission Statistics:** 4,094 applied, 86% accepted, 49% of those accepted enrolled. **Transfer Admission Requirements:** *Items required:* college transcript, statement of good standing from prior school. Minimum college GPA of 2.0 required. Lowest grade transferable C. **General Admission Information:** Application fee $40. Regular application deadline August 1. Nonfall registration accepted. Credit offered for CEEB Advanced Placement tests.

COSTS AND FINANCIAL AID

In-state tuition $3,060. Out-of-state tuition $9,008. Room & board $4,517. Required fees $492. Average book expense $700. **Required Forms and Deadlines:** FAFSA. Priority filing deadline March 1. **Notification of Awards:** Applicants will be notified of awards on a rolling basis beginning on or about April 15. **Types of Aid:** *Need-based scholarships/grants:* Pell, SEOG, state scholarships/grants, private scholarships, the school's own gift aid. *Loans:* FFEL Subsidized Stafford, FFEL Unsubsidized Stafford, FFEL PLUS, Federal Perkins, college/university loans from institutional funds. **Student Employment:** Federal Work-Study Program available. Institutional employment available. Off-campus job opportunities are good. **Financial Aid Statistics:** 47% freshmen, 41% undergrads receive some form of aid. Average freshman grant $2,550. Average freshman loan $2,000. Average income from on-campus job $2,700. **Financial Aid Phone:** 402-554-2327.

UNIVERSITY OF NEVADA—LAS VEGAS

4505 Maryland Parkway, Box 451021, Las Vegas, NV 89154
Phone: 702-895-2030 **E-mail:** Undergraduate.Recruitment@ccmail.nevada.edu
CEEB Code: 4861 **Fax:** 702-895-1200 **Web:** www.unlv.edu **ACT Code:** 2496

This public school was founded in 1957. It has a 337-acre campus.

STUDENTS AND FACULTY

Enrollment: 19,761. **Student Body:** Male 44%, female 56%, out-of-state 21%, international 4% (84 countries represented). **Ethnic Representation:** African American 8%, Asian 14%, Caucasian 60%, Hispanic 10%, Native American 1%. **Retention and Graduation:** 72% freshmen return for sophomore year. 12% freshmen graduate within 4 years. **Faculty:** Student/faculty ratio 19:1. 755 full-time faculty, 89% hold PhDs. 88% faculty teach undergrads.

ACADEMICS

Degrees: Bachelor's, certificate, doctoral, first professional, master's, post-bachelor's certificate, post-master's certificate. **Academic Requirements:** General education including some course work in arts/fine arts, computer literacy, English (including composition), history, humanities, mathematics, philosophy, sciences (biological or physical), social science. **Classes:** 20-29 students in an average class. 20-29 students in an average lab/discussion section. **Majors with Highest Enrollment:** Hotel/motel administration/management; communications studies/speech communication and rhetoric; elementary education and teaching. **Disciplines with Highest Percentage of Degrees Awarded:** Business/marketing 33%, education 17%, communications/communication technologies 7%, protective services/public administration 7%, social sciences and history 6%. **Special Study Options:** Cooperative (work-study) program, distance learning, double major, English as a second language, student exchange program (domestic), honors program, independent study, internships, student-designed major, study abroad, teacher certification program.

FACILITIES

Housing: Coed, one all-female floor, handicapped-accessible suites in all complexes. **Library Holdings:** 1,034,288 bound volumes. 9,536 periodicals. 2,458,497 microforms. 120,128 audiovisuals. **Special Academic Facilities/Equipment:** Art galleries, National Supercomputing Center for Energy and Environment, natural history museum, arboretum, 3 theaters, concert hall, law school, dental school, International Gaming Institute, professional practice school for teachers. **Computers:** School-owned computers available for student use.

EXTRACURRICULARS

Activities: Choral groups, dance, drama/theater, jazz band, marching band, music ensembles, musical theater, pep band, radio station, student government, student newspaper, student-run film society, television station. **Organizations:** 24 honor societies, 14 religious organizations, 8 fraternities (7% men join), 6 sororities (5% women join). **Athletics (Intercollegiate):** *Men:* baseball, basketball, football, golf, soccer, swimming, tennis. *Women:* basketball, cross-country, equestrian, golf, soccer, softball, swimming, tennis, track & field, volleyball.

ADMISSIONS

Selectivity Rating: 73 (of 100). **Freshman Academic Profile:** Average high school GPA 3.2. 19% in top 10% of high school class, 49% in top 25% of high

school class, 85% in top 50% of high school class. Average SAT I Math 510, SAT I Math middle 50% range 450-570. Average SAT I Verbal 499, SAT I Verbal middle 50% range 430-560. Average ACT 21, ACT middle 50% range 19-24. TOEFL required of all international applicants, minimum TOEFL 500. **Basis for Candidate Selection:** *Very important factors considered include:* secondary school record. *Other factors considered include:* standardized test scores. **Freshman Admission Requirements:** High school diploma or GED is required. *Academic units required/recommended:* 13 total required; 13 total recommended; 4 English required, 4 English recommended, 3 math required, 3 math recommended, 3 science required, 3 science recommended, 2 science lab required, 2 science lab recommended, 3 social studies required, 3 social studies recommended. **Freshman Admission Statistics:** 5,538 applied, 82% accepted, 55% of those accepted enrolled. **Transfer Admission Requirements:** *Items required:* college transcript, statement of good standing from prior school. Minimum college GPA of 2.0 required. Lowest grade transferable D. **General Admission Information:** Application fee $40. Priority application deadline May 1. Nonfall registration accepted. Admission may be deferred for a maximum of 1 year. Credit and/or placement offered for CEEB Advanced Placement tests.

COSTS AND FINANCIAL AID

In-state tuition $2,670. Out-of-state tuition $11,157. Room & board $6,140. Required fees $126. Average book expense $850. **Required Forms and Deadlines:** FAFSA and institution's own financial aid form. No deadline for regular filing. Priority filing deadline February 1. **Notification of Awards:** Applicants will be notified of awards on a rolling basis beginning on or about April 1. **Types of Aid:** *Need-based scholarships/grants:* Pell, SEOG, state scholarships/grants, private scholarships, the school's own gift aid. *Loans:* Direct Subsidized Stafford, Direct Unsubsidized Stafford, Direct PLUS, Federal Perkins, state loans, college/university loans from institutional funds. **Student Employment:** Federal Work-Study Program available. Institutional employment available. Off-campus job opportunities are excellent. **Financial Aid Statistics:** 44% freshmen, 42% undergrads receive some form of aid. Average freshman grant $5,660. Average freshman loan $2,505. Average income from on-campus job $3,680. **Financial Aid Phone:** 702-895-3424.

UNIVERSITY OF NEVADA—RENO

Mailstop 120, Reno, NV 89557
Phone: 775-784-4700 **E-mail:** Undergraduate: asknevada@unr.edu **CEEB Code:** 4844
Fax: 775-784-4283 **Web:** www.unr.edu **ACT Code:** 2497

This public school was founded in 1864. It has a 200-acre campus.

STUDENTS AND FACULTY

Enrollment: 11,752. **Student Body:** Male 45%, female 55%, out-of-state 18%, international 3% (56 countries represented). **Ethnic Representation:** African American 3%, Asian 7%, Caucasian 77%, Hispanic 7%, Native American 1%. **Retention and Graduation:** 74% freshmen return for sophomore year. **Faculty:** Student/faculty ratio 17:1. 652 full-time faculty, 86% hold PhDs.

ACADEMICS

Degrees: Bachelor's, doctoral, first professional, master's, post-bachelor's certificate, post-master's certificate. **Academic Requirements:** General education including some course work in arts/fine arts, English (including composition), humanities, mathematics, sciences (biological or physical), social science, capstone courses which tie the core curriculum to the student's major. **Classes:** 20-29 students in an average class. 20-29 students in an average lab/discussion section. **Disciplines with Highest Percentage of Degrees Awarded:** Education 16%, business/marketing 12%, health professions and related sciences 9%, engineering/engineering technology 8%, social sciences and history 8%. **Special Study Options:** Distance learning, double major, dual enrollment, English as a second language, student exchange program (domestic), honors program, independent study, internships, study abroad, teacher certification program.

FACILITIES

Housing: Coed, all-female, all-male, apartments for married students, apartments for single students, housing for disabled students. **Library Holdings:** 1,082,941 bound volumes. 18,656 periodicals. 3,638,929 microforms. 460,751 audiovisuals. **Special Academic Facilities/Equipment:** Audiovisual center, theatres, state historical society, atmospherium/planetarium, seismological lab, research institutes, agricultural experimentation station. **Computers:** *Recommended operating system:* Mac. School-owned computers available for student use.

EXTRACURRICULARS

Activities: Choral groups, concert band, dance, drama/theater, jazz band, literary magazine, marching band, music ensembles, musical theater, opera, pep band, radio station, student government, student newspaper, yearbook. **Organizations:** 100 registered organizations, 12 honor societies, 6 religious organizations, 11 fraternities (8% men join), 4 sororities (7% women join). **Athletics (Intercollegiate):** *Men:* basketball, skiing (cross-country), cross-country, diving, softball, swimming, tennis, track & field, volleyball. *Women:* basketball, skiing (cross-country), cross-country, diving, soccer, softball, swimming, tennis, track & field, volleyball.

ADMISSIONS

Selectivity Rating: 66 (of 100). **Freshman Academic Profile:** Average high school GPA 3.4. Average SAT I Math 489, SAT I Math middle 50% range 480-590. Average SAT I Verbal 435, SAT I Verbal middle 50% range 470-580. Average ACT 22, ACT middle 50% range 20-25. TOEFL required of all international applicants, minimum TOEFL 500. **Basis for Candidate Selection:** *Very important factors considered include:* secondary school record. *Other factors considered include:* standardized test scores. **Freshman Admission Requirements:** High school diploma is required and GED is not accepted. *Academic units required/recommended:* 13 total required; 4 English required, 3 math required, 3 science required, 2 science lab required, 3 social studies required. **Freshman Admission Statistics:** 3,509 applied, 95% accepted, 60% of those accepted enrolled. **Transfer Admission Requirements:** *Items required:* college transcript. Minimum college GPA of 2.0 required. Lowest grade transferable D-. **General Admission Information:** Application fee $40. Priority application deadline March 1. Nonfall registration accepted. Admission may be deferred. Credit and/or placement offered for CEEB Advanced Placement tests.

COSTS AND FINANCIAL AID

In-state tuition $2,670. Out-of-state tuition $11,157. Room & board $6,580. Required fees $132. Average book expense $1,000. **Required Forms and Deadlines:** FAFSA. No deadline for regular filing. Priority filing deadline February 1. **Notification of Awards:** Applicants will be notified of awards on a rolling basis beginning on or about April 1. **Types of Aid:** *Need-based scholarships/grants:* Pell, SEOG, private scholarships, the school's own gift aid. *Loans:* FFEL Subsidized Stafford, FFEL Unsubsidized Stafford, FFEL PLUS, Federal Perkins, Federal Nursing, college/university loans from institutional funds. **Student Employment:** Federal Work-Study Program available. Institutional employment available. Off-campus job opportunities are excellent. **Financial Aid Statistics:** 32% freshmen, 31% undergrads receive some form of aid. Average income from on-campus job $3,000. **Financial Aid Phone:** 702-784-4666.

UNIVERSITY OF NEW ENGLAND

Hills Beach Road, Biddeford, ME 04005
Phone: 207-283-0171 **E-mail:** jshea@mailbox.une.edu
Fax: 207-294-5900 **Web:** www.une.edu

This private school was founded in 1831. It has a 550-acre campus.

STUDENTS AND FACULTY

Enrollment: 1,869. **Student Body:** Male 19%, female 81%, out-of-state 50%, international 28%. **Ethnic Representation:** African American 1%, Caucasian 93%. **Retention and Graduation:** 71% freshmen return for sophomore year. 51% freshmen graduate within 4 years. **Faculty:** Student/faculty ratio 11:1. 130 full-time faculty, 96% hold PhDs. 100% faculty teach undergrads.

ACADEMICS

Degrees: Associate's, bachelor's, certificate, diploma, first professional, master's, post-bachelor's certificate, post-master's certificate, terminal. **Academic Requirements:** General education including some course work in arts/fine arts, English (including composition), humanities, mathematics, sciences (biological or physical), social science, environmental issues, citizenship, critical thinking. **Classes:** 20-29 students in an average class. 10-19 students in an average lab/discussion section. **Disciplines with Highest Percentage of Degrees Awarded:** Health professions and related sciences 69%, biological life sciences 7%, business/marketing 6%, education 4%, parks and recreation 4%. **Special Study Options:** Cross registration, distance learning, double major, English as a second language, honors program, independent study, internships, student-designed major, study abroad, teacher certification program.

FACILITIES

Housing: Coed, all-female, wellness house. **Library Holdings:** 46,030 bound volumes. 1,210 periodicals. 7,304 microforms. 9,536 audiovisuals. **Special Academic Facilities/Equipment:** Payson Museum, Alfond Center for Health Sciences. **Computers:** School-owned computers available for student use.

EXTRACURRICULARS

Activities: Choral groups, dance, student government, student newspaper, yearbook. **Organizations:** 36 registered organizations, 1 honor society. **Athletics (Intercollegiate):** *Men:* basketball, cross-country, lacrosse, soccer. *Women:* basketball, cross-country, lacrosse, soccer, softball, volleyball.

ADMISSIONS

Selectivity Rating: 73 (of 100). **Freshman Academic Profile:** Average high school GPA 3.2. 17% in top 10% of high school class, 46% in top 25% of high school class, 80% in top 50% of high school class. Average SAT I Math 509, SAT I Math middle 50% range 460-540. Average SAT I Verbal 511, SAT I Verbal middle 50% range 460-530. TOEFL required of all international applicants, minimum TOEFL 550. **Basis for Candidate Selection:** *Very important factors considered include:* interview, secondary school record. *Other factors considered include:* alumni/ae relation, character/personal qualities, class rank, extracurricular activities, geographical residence, standardized test scores, talent/ability, volunteer work, work experience. **Freshman Admission Requirements:** High school diploma or GED is required. *Academic units required/recommended:* 4 English required, 3 math required, 4 math recommended, 3 science required, 4 science recommended, 2 science lab required, 3 science lab recommended, 2 foreign language recommended, 2 social studies required, 4 social studies recommended, 2 history required, 4 history recommended, 4 elective recommended. **Freshman Admission Statistics:** 959 applied, 72% accepted, 43% of those accepted enrolled. **Transfer Admission Requirements:** Minimum college GPA of 2.5 required. Lowest grade transferable C-. **General Admission Information:** Application fee $40. Early decision application deadline November 15. Nonfall registration accepted. Admission may be deferred for a maximum of 1 year. Credit and/or placement offered for CEEB Advanced Placement tests.

COSTS AND FINANCIAL AID

Tuition $15,740. Room & board $6,420. Required fees $585. Average book expense $800. **Required Forms and Deadlines:** FAFSA, tax returns, and verification worksheet. Financial aid filing deadline May 1. Priority filing deadline March 1. **Notification of Awards:** Applicants will be notified of awards on a rolling basis beginning on or about March 15. **Types of Aid:** *Need-based scholarships/grants:* Pell, SEOG, state scholarships/grants, private scholarships, the school's own gift aid. *Loans:* FFEL Subsidized Stafford, FFEL Unsubsidized Stafford, FFEL PLUS, Federal Perkins, Federal Nursing. **Student Employment:** Federal Work-Study Program available. Institutional employment available. Off-campus job opportunities are good. **Financial Aid Statistics:** 86% freshmen, 69% undergrads receive some form of aid. Average freshman grant $7,933. Average freshman loan $9,090. Average income from on-campus job $1,000. **Financial Aid Phone:** 207-283-0171.

UNIVERSITY OF NEW HAMPSHIRE—DURHAM

4 Garrison Avenue, Durham, NH 03824
Phone: 603-862-1360 **E-mail:** admissions@unh.edu **CEEB Code:** 3918
Fax: 603-862-0077 **Web:** www.unh.edu **ACT Code:** 2524

This public school was founded in 1866. It has a 2,600-acre campus.

STUDENTS AND FACULTY

Enrollment: 11,496. **Student Body:** Male 43%, female 57%, out-of-state 43%, international 1% (28 countries represented). **Ethnic Representation:** African American 1%, Asian 2%, Caucasian 90%, Hispanic 1%. **Retention and Graduation:** 85% freshmen return for sophomore year. 50% freshmen graduate within 4 years. **Faculty:** Student/faculty ratio 14:1. 596 full-time faculty, 90% hold PhDs. 77% faculty teach undergrads.

ACADEMICS

Degrees: Associate's, bachelor's, doctoral, master's, post-bachelor's certificate, post-master's certificate, terminal. **Academic Requirements:** General education including some course work in arts/fine arts, English (including composition), history, humanities, mathematics, philosophy, sciences (biological or physical), social science, 8-component general education requirement, intensive writing requirement. **Classes:** 10-19 students in an average class. 10-19 students in an average lab/discussion section. **Majors with Highest Enrollment:** Business administration/management; English language and literature, general; psychology, general. **Disciplines with Highest Percentage of Degrees Awarded:** Business/marketing 14%, social sciences and history 14%, health professions and related sciences 9%, English 8%, communications/communication technologies 7%. **Special Study Options:** Cross registration, double major, English as a second language, student exchange program (domestic), honors program, independent study, internships, student-designed major, study abroad, teacher certification program.

FACILITIES

Housing: Coed, all-female, apartments for married students, apartments for single students, housing for international students, fraternities and/or sororities, special-interest minidorms, substance-free housing. **Library Holdings:** 1,101,496 bound volumes. 13,217 periodicals. 2,505,640 microforms. 24,247 audiovisuals. **Special Academic Facilities/Equipment:** Art galleries, language lab, marine science labs, observatory, electron microscope. **Computers:** School-owned computers available for student use.

EXTRACURRICULARS

Activities: Choral groups, concert band, dance, drama/theater, jazz band, literary magazine, marching band, music ensembles, musical theater, pep band, radio station, student government, student newspaper, student-run film society, symphony orchestra, television station, yearbook. **Organizations:** 150 registered organizations, 22 honor societies, 9 religious organizations, 10 fraternities (5% men join), 5 sororities (5% women join). **Athletics (Intercollegiate):** *Men:* basketball, skiing (cross-country), cross-country, diving, football, ice hockey, indoor track, skiing (alpine), skiing (Nordic), soccer, swimming, tennis, track & field. *Women:* basketball, crew, skiing (cross-country), cross-country, diving, field hockey, gymnastics, ice hockey, indoor track, lacrosse, skiing (alpine), skiing (Nordic), soccer, swimming, tennis, track & field, volleyball.

ADMISSIONS

Selectivity Rating: 78 (of 100). **Freshman Academic Profile:** 18% in top 10% of high school class, 53% in top 25% of high school class, 94% in top 50% of high school class. 78% from public high schools. Average SAT I Math 558, SAT I Math middle 50% range 510-610. Average SAT I Verbal 546, SAT I Verbal middle 50% range 500-590. TOEFL required of all international applicants, minimum TOEFL 550. **Basis for Candidate Selection:** *Very important factors considered include:* secondary school record. *Important factors considered include:* class rank, essays, recommendations, standardized test scores, state residency. *Other factors considered include:* alumni/ae relation, character/personal qualities, extracurricular activities, geographical residence, minority status, talent/ability, volunteer work, work experience. **Freshman Admission Requirements:** High school diploma or GED is required. *Academic units required/recommended:* 18 total recommended; 4 English recommended, 4 math recommended, 4 science recommended, 4 science lab recommended, 3 foreign language recommended, 3 social studies recommended. **Freshman Admission Statistics:** 10,376 applied, 77% accepted, 34% of those accepted enrolled. **Transfer Admission Requirements:** *Items required:* high school transcript, college transcript, essay. Minimum college GPA of 2.5 required. Lowest grade transferable C. **General Admission Information:** Application fee $35. Regular application deadline February 1. Nonfall registration accepted. Admission may be deferred for a maximum of 1 year. Credit and/or placement offered for CEEB Advanced Placement tests.

COSTS AND FINANCIAL AID

Average book expense $1,300. **Required Forms and Deadlines:** FAFSA. Priority filing deadline March 1. **Notification of Awards:** Applicants will be notified of awards on a rolling basis beginning on or about March 1. **Types of Aid:** *Need-based scholarships/grants:* Pell, SEOG, state scholarships/grants, private scholarships, the school's own gift aid. *Loans:* FFEL Subsidized Stafford, FFEL Unsubsidized Stafford, FFEL PLUS, Federal Perkins, state loans, college/university loans from institutional funds. **Student Employment:** Federal Work-Study Program available. Institutional employment available. Off-campus job opportunities are excellent. **Financial Aid Statistics:** 54% freshmen, 53% undergrads receive some form of aid. Average freshman grant $6,630. Average freshman loan $3,538. Average income from on-campus job $1,695. **Financial Aid Phone:** 603-862-3600.

UNIVERSITY OF NEW HAMPSHIRE—MANCHESTER

400 Commercial Street, Manchester, NH 03101
Phone: 603-629-4150 **E-mail:** unhm.admissions@unh.edu **CEEB Code:** 2094
Fax: 603-623-2745 **Web:** www.unh.edu/unhm

This public school was founded in 1985.

STUDENTS AND FACULTY

Enrollment: 1,123. **Student Body:** Male 39%, female 61%, out-of-state 1%, international students represent 5 countries. **Ethnic Representation:** African American 2%, Asian 1%, Caucasian 95%, Hispanic 1%. **Faculty:** Student/faculty ratio 18:1. 23 full-time faculty, 78% hold PhDs. 100% faculty teach undergrads.

ACADEMICS

Degrees: Associate's, bachelor's. **Academic Requirements:** General education including some course work in arts/fine arts, English (including composition), foreign languages, history, mathematics, philosophy, sciences (biological or physical), social science, foreign culture. **Classes:** 10-19 students in an average class. **Disciplines with Highest Percentage of Degrees Awarded:** Health professions and related sciences 27%, psychology 21%, social sciences and history 18%, communications/communication technologies 16%, English 13%. **Special Study Options:** Cross registration, double major, English as a second language, student exchange program (domestic), independent study, internships, study abroad, teacher certification program.

FACILITIES

Library Holdings: 21,054 bound volumes. 535 periodicals. 56,000 microforms. 1,256 audiovisuals. **Computers:** School-owned computers available for student use.

EXTRACURRICULARS

Activities: Student government.

ADMISSIONS

Selectivity Rating: 63 (of 100). **Freshman Academic Profile:** 3% in top 10% of high school class, 15% in top 25% of high school class, 52% in top 50% of high school class. Average SAT I Math 500, SAT I Math middle 50% range 440-550. Average SAT I Verbal 509, SAT I Verbal middle 50% range 460-550. TOEFL required of all international applicants. **Basis for Candidate Selection:** *Very important factors considered include:* secondary school record. *Important factors considered include:* class rank, essays, recommendations, standardized test scores. *Other factors considered include:* alumni/ae relation, character/personal qualities, extracurricular activities, interview, minority status, state residency, talent/ability, volunteer work, work experience. **Freshman Admission Requirements:** High school diploma or GED is required. *Academic units required/recommended:* 4 English required, 3 math required, 4 math recommended, 3 science lab required, 4 science lab recommended, 2 foreign language required, 3 foreign language recommended, 2 social studies required. **Freshman Admission Statistics:** 218 applied, 74% accepted, 66% of those accepted enrolled. **Transfer Admission Requirements:** *Items required:* high school transcript, college transcript, essay, statement of good standing from prior school. Minimum college GPA of 2.5 required. Lowest grade transferable C. **General Admission Information:** Application fee $50. Priority application deadline April 1. Regular application deadline June 15. Nonfall registration accepted. Admission may be deferred for a maximum of 1 year. Credit offered for CEEB Advanced Placement tests.

COSTS AND FINANCIAL AID

In-state tuition $4,630. Out-of-state tuition $12,190. Required fees $54. Average book expense $700. **Required Forms and Deadlines:** FAFSA, noncustodial (divorced/separated) parent's statement and business/farm supplement. Priority filing deadline May 1. **Notification of Awards:** Applicants will be notified of awards on a rolling basis beginning on or about April 1. **Types of Aid:** *Need-based scholarships/grants:* Pell, SEOG, state scholarships/grants, private scholarships, the school's own gift aid. *Loans:* FFEL Subsidized Stafford, FFEL Unsubsidized Stafford, FFEL PLUS, Federal Perkins, outside loans. **Student Employment:** Federal Work-Study Program available. Institutional employment available. Off-campus job opportunities are excellent. **Financial Aid Phone:** 603-629-4114.

UNIVERSITY OF NEW HAVEN

300 Orange Avenue, West Haven, CT 06516
Phone: 203-932-7319 **E-mail:** adminfo@newhaven.edu **CEEB Code:** 3663
Fax: 203-931-6093 **Web:** www.newhaven.edu **ACT Code:** 576

This private school was founded in 1920. It has a 78-acre campus.

STUDENTS AND FACULTY

Enrollment: 2,546. **Student Body:** Male 56%, female 44%, out-of-state 34%, international 5%. **Ethnic Representation:** African American 12%, Asian 1%, Caucasian 63%, Hispanic 7%, Native American 1%. **Retention and Graduation:** 74% freshmen return for sophomore year. **Faculty:** Student/faculty ratio 11:1. 175 full-time faculty, 90% hold PhDs. 82% faculty teach undergrads.

ACADEMICS

Degrees: Associate's, bachelor's, master's, post-bachelor's certificate. **Academic Requirements:** General education including some course work in arts/fine arts, computer literacy, English (including composition), history, humanities, mathematics, philosophy, sciences (biological or physical), social science. **Classes:** 10-19 students in an average class. 10-19 students in an average lab/discussion section. **Majors with Highest Enrollment:** Business administration/management; engineering, general; criminal justice/law enforcement administration. **Disciplines with Highest Percentage of Degrees Awarded:** Protective services/public administration 39%, business/marketing 23%, engineering/engineering technology 14%, biological life sciences 3%, visual and performing arts 3%. **Special Study Options:** Accelerated program, cooperative (work-study) program, cross registration, double major, dual enrollment, English as a second language, honors program, independent study, internships, student-designed major, study abroad.

FACILITIES

Housing: Coed, apartments for single students. **Library Holdings:** 165,044 bound volumes. 1,294 periodicals. 516,054 microforms. 605 audiovisuals. **Special Academic Facilities/Equipment:** Art gallery, forensic science lab, radio station, TV station, Theater Orchestra New England, music & sound recording studio. **Computers:** School-owned computers available for student use.

EXTRACURRICULARS

Activities: Choral groups, dance, drama/theater, music ensembles, musical theater, pep band, radio station, student government, student newspaper, television station, yearbook. **Organizations:** 40 registered organizations, 5 honor societies, 1 religious organization, 2 fraternities (2% men join), 3 sororities (2% women join). **Athletics (Intercollegiate):** *Men:* baseball, basketball, cross-country, football, golf, indoor track, lacrosse, soccer, track & field, volleyball. *Women:* basketball, cheerleading, cross-country, golf, indoor track, lacrosse, soccer, softball, tennis, track & field, volleyball.

ADMISSIONS

Selectivity Rating: 72 (of 100). **Freshman Academic Profile:** Average high school GPA 2.8. 10% in top 10% of high school class, 35% in top 25% of high school class, 62% in top 50% of high school class. 85% from public high schools. Average SAT I Math 500, SAT I Math middle 50% range 430-560. Average SAT I Verbal 495, SAT I Verbal middle 50% range 440-550. TOEFL required of all international applicants, minimum TOEFL 520. **Basis for Candidate Selection:** *Very important factors considered include:* secondary school record, standardized test scores. *Important factors considered include:* class rank, essays, recommendations. *Other factors considered include:* alumni/ae relation, character/personal qualities, extracurricular activities, interview, talent/ability, volunteer work, work experience. **Freshman Admission Requirements:** High school diploma or GED is required. *Academic units required/recommended:* 16 total required; 4 English required, 3 math required, 2 science required, 2 foreign language recommended, 2 social studies recommended, 2 history required, 3 elective required. **Freshman Admission Statistics:** 2,917 applied, 71% accepted, 29% of those accepted enrolled. **Transfer Admission Requirements:** *Items required:* high school transcript, college transcript. Minimum high school GPA of 2.5 required. Minimum college GPA of 2.0 required. Lowest grade transferable C. **General Admission Information:** Application fee $50. Nonfall registration accepted. Admission may be deferred for a maximum of 1 year. Credit and/or placement offered for CEEB Advanced Placement tests.

COSTS AND FINANCIAL AID

Tuition $17,480. Room & board $8,040. Required fees $482. Average book expense $750. **Required Forms and Deadlines:** FAFSA, institution's own financial aid form and tax returns. Priority filing deadline March 2. **Notification of Awards:** Applicants will be notified of awards on a rolling basis beginning on or about March 15. **Types of Aid:** *Need-based scholarships/grants:* Pell, SEOG, state scholarships/grants, private scholarships, the school's own gift aid. *Loans:* FFEL Subsidized Stafford, FFEL Unsubsidized Stafford, FFEL PLUS, Federal Perkins. **Student Employment:** Federal Work-Study Program available. Institutional employment available. Off-campus job opportunities are excellent. **Financial Aid Statistics:** 76% freshmen, 73% undergrads receive some form of aid. Average freshman grant $7,768. Average freshman loan $4,884. Average income from on-campus job $900. **Financial Aid Phone:** 203-932-7315.

See page 1252.

UNIVERSITY OF NEW MEXICO

Student Services Center 150, MSC06 3720 1 University of New Mexico, Albuquerque, NM 87131-0001 **Phone:** 505-277-2446 **E-mail:** apply@unm.edu **CEEB Code:** 4845 **Fax:** 505-277-6686 **Web:** www.unm.edu **ACT Code:** 2650

This public school was founded in 1889. It has a 769-acre campus.

STUDENTS AND FACULTY

Enrollment: 17,166. **Student Body:** Male 43%, female 57%, out-of-state 19%, international 1%. **Ethnic Representation:** African American 3%, Asian 4%, Caucasian 51%, Hispanic 34%, Native American 7%. **Retention and Graduation:** 76% freshmen return for sophomore year. **Faculty:** Student/faculty ratio 16:1. 872 full-time faculty, 88% hold PhDs.

ACADEMICS

Degrees: Associate's, bachelor's, certificate, diploma, doctoral, first professional, master's, post-master's certificate. **Academic Requirements:** General education including some course work in arts/fine arts, English (including composition), foreign languages, humanities, mathematics, sciences (biological or physical), social science. **Classes:** 20-29 students in an average class. 20-29 students in an average lab/discussion section. **Majors with Highest Enrollment:** Elementary education and teaching; general studies; psychology, general. **Disciplines with Highest Percentage of Degrees Awarded:** Business/marketing 16%, education 13%, health professions and related sciences 10%, social sciences and history 8%, liberal arts/general studies 8%. **Special Study Options:** Accelerated program, cooperative (work-study) program, distance learning, double major, dual enrollment, English as a second language, student exchange program (domestic), honors program, independent study, internships, student-designed major, study abroad, teacher certification program, weekend college.

FACILITIES

Housing: Coed, apartments for married students, apartments for single students, housing for disabled students, fraternities and/or sororities. Special living options include graduate and senior housing, academic floors, scholars wing, and outdoor/wellness units. Computer Science and Engineering unit also available. **Library Holdings:** 2,473,170 bound volumes. 339,266 periodicals. 4,628,643 microforms. 1,850,221 audiovisuals. **Special Academic Facilities/Equipment:** Museums of art, anthropology, geology, and Southwestern biology; lithography institute; meteoritics institute; electron and electron scanning microscopes; nuclear reactor. **Computers:** School-owned computers available for student use.

EXTRACURRICULARS

Activities: Choral groups, concert band, dance, drama/theater, jazz band, literary magazine, marching band, music ensembles, musical theater, opera, pep band, radio station, student government, student newspaper, symphony orchestra, television station, yearbook. **Organizations:** 250 registered organizations, 15 honor societies, 23 religious organizations, 9 fraternities, 4 sororities. **Athletics (Intercollegiate):** *Men:* baseball, basketball, skiing (cross-country), cross-country, football, golf, indoor track, skiing (alpine), skiing (Nordic), soccer, tennis, track & field. *Women:* basketball, skiing (cross-country), cross-country, diving, golf, indoor track, skiing (alpine), skiing (Nordic), soccer, softball, swimming, tennis, track & field, volleyball.

ADMISSIONS

Selectivity Rating: 75 (of 100). **Freshman Academic Profile:** Average high school GPA 3.3. 18% in top 10% of high school class, 46% in top 25% of high school class, 79% in top 50% of high school class. Average SAT I Math 540, SAT I Math middle 50% range 480-600. Average SAT I Verbal 580, SAT I Verbal middle 50% range 510-630. Average ACT 22, ACT middle 50% range 19-24. TOEFL required of all international applicants, minimum TOEFL 520. **Basis for Candidate Selection:** *Very important factors considered include:* secondary school record. *Important factors considered include:* class rank, standardized test scores. *Other factors considered include:* essays, recommendations. **Freshman Admission Requirements:** High school diploma or GED is required. *Academic units required/recommended:* 13 total required; 4 English required, 3 math required, 2 science required, 1 science lab required, 2 foreign language required, 2 social studies required, 1 history required. **Freshman Admission Statistics:** 6,232 applied, 77% accepted, 59% of those accepted enrolled. **Transfer Admission Requirements:** *Items required:* college transcript. Minimum high school GPA of 2.3 required. Minimum college GPA of 2.0 required. Lowest grade transferable C. **General Admission Information:** Application fee $20. Regular application deadline June 15. Nonfall registration accepted. Admission may be deferred for a maximum of 1 year. Credit and/or placement offered for CEEB Advanced Placement tests.

COSTS AND FINANCIAL AID

In-state tuition $3,026. Out-of-state tuition $11,424. Room & board $5,217. Required fees $0. Average book expense $720. **Required Forms and Deadlines:** FAFSA. No deadline for regular filing. Priority filing deadline March 1. **Notification of Awards:** Applicants will be notified of awards on a rolling basis beginning on or about April 15. **Types of Aid:** *Need-based scholarships/grants:* Pell, SEOG, state scholarships/grants, private scholarships, the school's own gift aid, Federal Nursing. *Loans:* Direct Subsidized Stafford, Direct Unsubsidized Stafford, Federal Perkins, Federal Nursing, state loans, college/university loans from institutional funds. **Student Employment:** Federal Work-Study Program available. Institutional employment available. Off-campus job opportunities are excellent. **Financial Aid Statistics:** 40% freshmen, 45% undergrads receive some form of aid. **Financial Aid Phone:** 505-277-2041.

UNIVERSITY OF NEW ORLEANS

Admissions Office, Lakefront, New Orleans, LA 70148 **Phone:** 504-280-6595 **E-mail:** admissions@uno.edu **CEEB Code:** 6379 **Fax:** 504-280-5522 **Web:** www.uno.edu **ACT Code:** 1591

This public school was founded in 1956. It has a 195-acre campus.

STUDENTS AND FACULTY

Enrollment: 13,189. **Student Body:** Male 43%, female 57%, out-of-state 6%, international 3%. **Ethnic Representation:** African American 24%, Asian 6%, Caucasian 57%, Hispanic 6%. **Retention and Graduation:** 68% freshmen return for sophomore year. 4% freshmen graduate within 4 years. **Faculty:** Student/faculty ratio 25:1. 480 full-time faculty, 71% hold PhDs.

ACADEMICS

Degrees: Bachelor's, certificate, doctoral, master's, post-bachelor's certificate. **Academic Requirements:** General education including some course work in arts/fine arts, English (including composition), foreign languages, history, humanities, mathematics, sciences (biological or physical), social science. **Classes:** 20-29 students in an average class. **Majors with Highest Enrollment:** Business administration/management; liberal arts and sciences/liberal studies; engineering science. **Disciplines with Highest Percentage of Degrees Awarded:** Business/marketing 35%, liberal arts/general studies 13%, education 10%, engineering/engineering technology 7%, social sciences and history 7%. **Special Study Options:** Cooperative (work-study) program, cross registration, distance learning, double major, dual enrollment, English as a second language, student exchange program (domestic), honors program, independent study, internships, student-designed major, study abroad, teacher certification program, weekend college.

FACILITIES

Housing: Coed, apartments for married students, apartments for single students, housing for disabled students, on-campus housing. **Library Holdings:** 896,000 bound volumes. 13,030 periodicals. 2,385,500 microforms. 125,600 audiovisuals. **Special Academic Facilities/Equipment:** Performing arts center, audiovisual center, TV studio, Eisenhower leadership studies center, child care center, Louisiana collection.

EXTRACURRICULARS

Activities: Choral groups, concert band, dance, drama/theater, jazz band, literary magazine, music ensembles, musical theater, opera, pep band, radio station, student government, student newspaper, student-run film society, yearbook. **Organizations:** 100 registered organizations, 27 honor societies, 2 religious organizations, 8 fraternities (2% men join), 6 sororities (2% women join). **Athletics (Intercollegiate):** *Men:* baseball, basketball, cross-country, golf, indoor track, swimming, tennis, track & field. *Women:* basketball, cross-country, golf, indoor track, swimming, tennis, track & field, volleyball.

ADMISSIONS

Selectivity Rating: 74 (of 100). **Freshman Academic Profile:** 62% from public high schools. Average SAT I Math 535, SAT I Math middle 50% range 450-590. Average SAT I Verbal 553, SAT I Verbal middle 50% range 480-610. Average ACT 21, ACT middle 50% range 18-23. TOEFL required of all international applicants, minimum TOEFL 550. **Basis for Candidate Selection:** *Very important factors considered include:* secondary school record, standardized test scores. *Other factors considered include:* alumni/ae relation, character/personal qualities, class rank, essays, extracurricular activities, interview, recommendations, state residency, talent/ability, volunteer work, work experience. **Freshman Admission Requirements:** High school diploma or GED is required. *Academic units required/recommended:* 4 English required, 3 math required, 3 science required, 2 foreign language required, 3 social studies required, 2 elective required. **Freshman Admission Statistics:** 5,011 applied, 66% accepted, 59% of those accepted enrolled. **Transfer Admission Requirements:** *Items required:* college transcript. Minimum high school GPA of 2.0 required. Minimum college GPA of 2.0 required. Lowest grade transferable D. **General Admission Information:** Application fee $20. Priority application deadline July 1. Regular application deadline August 31. Nonfall registration accepted. Admission may be deferred for a maximum of 1 year. Credit offered for CEEB Advanced Placement tests.

COSTS AND FINANCIAL AID

In-state tuition $2,876. Out-of-state tuition $9,920. Room & board $3,888. Required fees $150. Average book expense $1,150. **Required Forms and Deadlines:** FAFSA and institution's own financial aid form. Priority filing deadline May 15. **Notification of Awards:** Applicants will be notified of awards on a rolling basis beginning on or about April 20. **Types of Aid:** *Need-based scholarships/grants:* Pell, SEOG, state scholarships/grants, private scholarships, the school's own gift aid. *Loans:* FFEL Subsidized Stafford, FFEL Unsubsidized Stafford, FFEL PLUS, Federal Perkins, college/university loans from institutional funds. **Student Employment:** Federal Work-Study Program available. Institutional employment available. Off-campus job opportunities are excellent. **Financial Aid Statistics:** 27% freshmen, 30% undergrads receive some form of aid. Average freshman grant $3,500. Average freshman loan $2,600. Average income from on-campus job $2,950. **Financial Aid Phone:** 504-280-6603.

UNIVERSITY OF NORTH ALABAMA

UNA Box 5011, Florence, AL 35632-0001
Phone: 256-765-4318 **E-mail:** admis1@unanov.una.edu
Fax: 256-765-4329 **Web:** www.una.edu **ACT Code:** 14

This public school was founded in 1830. It has a 125-acre campus.

STUDENTS AND FACULTY

Enrollment: 4,826. **Student Body:** Male 41%, female 59%, out-of-state 21%, international 3% (36 countries represented). **Ethnic Representation:** African American 12%, Asian 1%, Caucasian 79%, Hispanic 1%, Native American 2%. **Retention and Graduation:** 11% freshmen graduate within 4 years. **Faculty:** Student/faculty ratio 22:1. 200 full-time faculty, 70% hold PhDs. 100% faculty teach undergrads.

ACADEMICS

Degrees: Bachelor's, master's, post-master's certificate. **Academic Requirements:** General education including some course work in arts/fine arts, computer literacy, English (including composition), foreign languages, history, humanities, mathematics, sciences (biological or physical), social science. **Classes:** 10-19 students in an average class. 20-29 students in an average lab/discussion section. **Majors with Highest Enrollment:** Nursing/registered nurse training (RN, ASN, BSN, MSN); business administration/management; secondary education and teaching. **Disciplines with Highest Percentage of Degrees Awarded:** Business/marketing 23%, education 14%, health professions and related sciences 7%, English 7%, social sciences and history 6%. **Special Study Options:** Accelerated program, cooperative (work-study) program, distance learning, double major, dual enrollment, English as a second language, independent study, internships, student-designed major, teacher certification program, weekend college.

FACILITIES

Housing: Coed, all-female, all-male, apartments for married students, apartments for single students, housing for international students, fraternities and/or sororities. **Library Holdings:** 358,393 bound volumes. 3,126 periodicals. 1,006,142 microforms. 9,898 audiovisuals. **Special Academic Facilities/Equipment:** On-campus lab school (N-6), planetarium, observatory, art gallery. **Computers:** School-owned computers available for student use.

EXTRACURRICULARS

Activities: Choral groups, concert band, drama/theater, jazz band, literary magazine, marching band, music ensembles, musical theater, pep band, radio station, student government, student newspaper, yearbook. **Organizations:** 98 registered organizations, 19 honor societies, 8 religious organizations, 8 fraternities (4% men join), 6 sororities (5% women join). **Athletics (Intercollegiate):** *Men:* baseball, basketball, cross-country, football, golf, tennis. *Women:* basketball, cross-country, soccer, softball, tennis, volleyball.

ADMISSIONS

Selectivity Rating: 71 (of 100). **Freshman Academic Profile:** Average high school GPA 2.9. 44% in top 25% of high school class, 76% in top 50% of high school class. 99% from public high schools. Average SAT I Math 486, SAT I Math middle 50% range 450-510. Average SAT I Verbal 455, SAT I Verbal middle 50% range 410-500. Average ACT 21, ACT middle 50% range 18-23. TOEFL required of all international applicants, minimum TOEFL 500. **Basis for Candidate Selection:** *Very important factors considered include:* class rank, standardized test scores. *Important factors considered include:* character/personal qualities, secondary school record. **Freshman Admission Requirements:** High school diploma or GED is required. *Academic units required/recommended:* 13 total required; 4 English required, 2 math required, 2 science required, 2 foreign language required, 3 social studies required. **Freshman Admission Statistics:** 1,590 applied, 80% accepted, 62% of those accepted enrolled. **Transfer Admission Requirements:** *Items required:* college transcript. Minimum college GPA of 2.0 required. Lowest grade transferable C. **General Admission Information:** Application fee $25. Regular application deadline August 1. Nonfall registration accepted. Admission may be deferred. Credit offered for CEEB Advanced Placement tests.

COSTS AND FINANCIAL AID

In-state tuition $3,480. Out-of-state tuition $6,960. Room & board $4,034. Required fees $340. **Required Forms and Deadlines:** FAFSA. No deadline for regular filing. Priority filing deadline April 1. **Notification of Awards:** Applicants will be notified of awards on a rolling basis beginning on or about May 31. **Types of Aid:** *Need-based scholarships/grants:* Pell, SEOG, state scholarships/grants, private scholarships, the school's own gift aid. *Loans:* FFEL Subsidized Stafford, FFEL Unsubsidized Stafford, FFEL PLUS, Federal Perkins. **Student Employment:** Federal Work-Study Program available. Off-campus job opportunities are excellent. **Financial Aid Statistics:** 53% freshmen, 46% undergrads receive some form of aid. **Financial Aid Phone:** 256-765-4278.

UNIVERSITY OF NORTH CAROLINA—ASHEVILLE

CPO #2210, 117 Lipinsky Hall, Asheville, NC 28804-8510
Phone: 828-251-6481 **E-mail:** admissions@unca.edu **CEEB Code:** 5013
Fax: 828-251-6482 **Web:** www.unca.edu **ACT Code:** 3064

This public school was founded in 1927. It has a 265-acre campus.

STUDENTS AND FACULTY

Enrollment: 3,351. **Student Body:** Male 43%, female 57%, out-of-state 11%, international 1%. **Ethnic Representation:** African American 2%, Asian 2%, Caucasian 92%, Hispanic 1%, Native American 1%. **Retention and Graduation:** 78% freshmen return for sophomore year. 31% freshmen graduate within 4 years. 21% grads go on to further study within 1 year. 1% grads pursue business degrees. 1% grads pursue law degrees. 1% grads pursue medical degrees. **Faculty:** Student/faculty ratio 14:1. 179 full-time faculty, 85% hold PhDs. 100% faculty teach undergrads.

ACADEMICS

Degrees: Bachelor's, certificate, master's, post-bachelor's certificate. **Academic Requirements:** General education including some course work in arts/fine arts, English (including composition), foreign languages, humanities, mathematics, sciences (biological or physical), social science, library research, health and wellness. **Classes:** 10-19 students in an average class. 10-19 students in an average lab/discussion section. **Majors with Highest Enrollment:** Business administration/management; environmental science; psychology, general. **Disciplines with Highest Percentage of Degrees Awarded:** Social sciences and history 20%, business/marketing 16%, psychology 14%, visual and performing arts 10%, natural resources/environmental sciences 7%. **Special Study Options:** Cross registration, distance learning, double major, dual enrollment, honors program, independent study, internships, liberal arts/career combination, student-designed major, study abroad, teacher certification program.

FACILITIES

Housing: Coed, all-female, all-male, housing for disabled students, substance-free dorms, 24-hour quiet dorms. **Library Holdings:** 254,179 bound volumes. 2,014 periodicals. 822,833 microforms. 9,816 audiovisuals. **Special Academic Facilities/Equipment:** Undergraduate research center, Steelcase Teleconference Center, music recording center, botanical gardens, arboretum, environmental quality institute, creative retirement center. **Computers:** School-owned computers available for student use.

EXTRACURRICULARS

Activities: Choral groups, concert band, dance, drama/theater, jazz band, literary magazine, music ensembles, musical theater, pep band, student government, student newspaper. **Organizations:** 50 registered organizations, 14 honor societies, 10 religious organizations, 4 fraternities (5% men join), 2 sororities (4% women join). **Athletics (Intercollegiate):** *Men:* baseball, basketball, cheerleading, cross-country, soccer, tennis, track & field. *Women:* basketball, cheerleading, cross-country, soccer, tennis, track & field, volleyball.

ADMISSIONS

Selectivity Rating: 82 (of 100). **Freshman Academic Profile:** Average high school GPA 3.7. 24% in top 10% of high school class, 61% in top 25% of high school class, 97% in top 50% of high school class. Average SAT I Math 574, SAT I Math middle 50% range 520-630. Average SAT I Verbal 586, SAT I Verbal middle 50% range 530-640. Average ACT 24, ACT middle 50% range 21-27. TOEFL required of all international applicants, minimum TOEFL 550. **Basis for Candidate Selection:** *Very important factors considered include:* class rank, secondary school record. *Important factors considered include:* standardized test scores. *Other factors considered include:* alumni/ae relation, character/personal qualities, essays, extracurricular activities, geographical residence, interview, recommendations, state residency, talent/ability, volunteer work, work experience. **Freshman Admission Requirements:** High school diploma is required and GED is not accepted. *Academic units required/recommended:* 12 total required; 18 total recommended; 4 English required, 3 math required, 4 math recommended, 3 science required, 4 science recommended, 2 science lab required, 3 science lab recommended, 2 foreign language recommended, 1 social studies required, 1 history required, 4 elective recommended. **Freshman Admission Statistics:** 1,937 applied, 67% accepted, 33% of those accepted enrolled. **Transfer Admission Requirements:** *Items required:* college transcript, statement of good standing from prior school. Minimum college GPA of 2.5 required. Lowest grade transferable C. **General Admission Information:** Application fee $50. Priority application deadline October 15. Regular application deadline March 15. Nonfall registration accepted. Admission may be deferred for a maximum of 1 year. Credit and/or placement offered for CEEB Advanced Placement tests.

COSTS AND FINANCIAL AID

In-state tuition $1,592. Out-of-state tuition $9,997. Room & board $4,650. Required fees $1,365. Average book expense $800. **Required Forms and Deadlines:** FAFSA. No deadline for regular filing. Priority filing deadline March 1. **Notification of Awards:** Applicants will be notified of awards on a rolling basis beginning on or about March 15. **Types of Aid:** *Need-based scholarships/grants:* Pell, SEOG, state scholarships/grants, private scholarships, the school's own gift aid. *Loans:* Direct Subsidized Stafford, Direct Unsubsidized Stafford, Direct PLUS, Federal Perkins, state loans, college/university loans from institutional funds. **Student Employment:** Federal Work-Study Program available. Institutional employment available. Off-campus job opportunities are good. **Financial Aid Statistics:** 38% freshmen, 39% undergrads receive some form of aid. Average freshman grant $3,660. Average freshman loan $4,102. Average income from on-campus job $1,382. **Financial Aid Phone:** 828-251-6535.

UNIVERSITY OF NORTH CAROLINA— CHAPEL HILL

Office of Undergraduate Admissions, Jackson Hall 153A - Campus Box #2200, Chapel Hill, NC 27599 **Phone:** 919-966-3621 **E-mail:** uadm@email.unc.edu
CEEB Code: 5816 **Fax:** 919-962-3045 **Web:** www.unc.edu **ACT Code:** 3162

This public school was founded in 1789. It has a 729-acre campus.

STUDENTS AND FACULTY

Enrollment: 15,961. **Student Body:** Male 40%, female 60%, out-of-state 18%, international 1% (100 countries represented). **Ethnic Representation:** African American 11%, Asian 6%, Caucasian 79%, Hispanic 2%, Native American 1%. **Retention and Graduation:** 95% freshmen return for sophomore year. 67% freshmen graduate within 4 years. 27% grads go on to further study within 1 year. 5% grads pursue law degrees. 3% grads pursue medical degrees. **Faculty:** Student/faculty ratio 14:1. 1,356 full-time faculty, 83% hold PhDs. 68% faculty teach undergrads.

ACADEMICS

Degrees: Bachelor's, certificate, diploma, doctoral, first professional, master's, post-master's certificate. **Academic Requirements:** General education including some course work in arts/fine arts, English (including composition), foreign languages, history, humanities, mathematics, philosophy, sciences (biological or physical), social science, cultural diversity. **Classes:** 20-29 students in an average class. 10-19 students in an average lab/discussion section. **Majors with Highest Enrollment:** Business administration/management; communications studies/speech communication and rhetoric; psychology, general. **Disciplines with Highest Percentage of Degrees Awarded:** Social sciences and history 16%, communications/communication technologies 18%, business/marketing 11%, psychology 10%, biological life sciences 9%. **Special Study Options:** Cross registration, distance learning, double major, dual enrollment, honors program, independent study, internships, student-designed major, study abroad, teacher certification program.

FACILITIES

Housing: Coed, all-female, all-male, apartments for married students, housing for disabled students, housing for international students, fraternities and/or sororities, substance-free housing. Students with interests in arts, international relations, or foreign languages may live in the co-ed Carmichael Residence Hall. **Library Holdings:** 2,573,328 bound volumes. 42,635 periodicals. 4,648,209 microforms. 225,151 audiovisuals. **Special Academic Facilities/Equipment:** Art museum, folklore council, institute of folk music, communications center, Institute of Latin American studies, institute of fisheries research, institute of natural science, research laboratory of anthropology, planetarium, theatre. **Computers:** *Recommended operating system:* Windows 95/98/NT/00/XP. School-owned computers available for student use.

EXTRACURRICULARS

Activities: Choral groups, concert band, dance, drama/theater, jazz band, literary magazine, marching band, music ensembles, musical theater, pep band, radio station, student government, student newspaper, student-run film society, symphony orchestra, television station, yearbook. **Organizations:** 476 registered organizations, 29 honor societies, 40 religious organizations, 29 fraternities, 20 sororities. **Athletics (Intercollegiate):** *Men:* baseball, basketball, cross-country, diving, fencing, football, golf, indoor track, lacrosse, soccer, swimming, tennis, track & field, wrestling. *Women:* basketball, crew, cross-country, diving, fencing, field hockey, golf, gymnastics, indoor track, lacrosse, soccer, softball, swimming, tennis, track & field, volleyball.

ADMISSIONS

Selectivity Rating: 91 (of 100). **Freshman Academic Profile:** 71% in top 10% of high school class, 94% in top 25% of high school class, 99% in top 50% of high school class. 83% from public high schools. Average SAT I Math 642, SAT I Math middle 50% range 600-690. Average SAT I Verbal 625, SAT I Verbal middle 50% range 580-680. Average ACT 27, ACT middle 50% range 24-30. TOEFL required of all international applicants, minimum TOEFL 600. **Basis for Candidate Selection:** *Very important factors considered include:* character/personal qualities, class rank, essays, extracurricular activities, recommendations, secondary school record, standardized test scores, state residency, talent/ability. *Important factors considered include:* alumni/ae relation, minority status, volunteer work, work experience. **Freshman Admission Requirements:** High school diploma is required and GED is not accepted. *Academic units required/recommended:* 4 English required, 4 English recommended, 3 math required, 4 math recommended, 3 science required, 4 science recommended, 1 science lab required, 1 science lab recommended, 2 foreign language required, 4 foreign language recommended, 1 social studies required, 3 social studies recommended, 1 history required, 2 elective required. **Freshman Admission Statistics:** 17,141 applied, 35% accepted, 57% of those accepted enrolled. **Transfer Admission Requirements:** *Items required:* high school transcript, college transcript, essay, statement of good standing from prior school. Minimum college GPA of 2.0 required. Lowest grade transferable C. **General Admission Information:** Application fee $55. Regular application deadline January 15. Admission may be deferred for a maximum of 1 year. Credit and/or placement offered for CEEB Advanced Placement tests.

COSTS AND FINANCIAL AID

In-state tuition $2,814. Out-of-state tuition $14,098. Room & board $5,805. Required fees $1,042. Average book expense $800. **Required Forms and Deadlines:** FAFSA and CSS/Financial Aid PROFILE. Priority filing deadline March 1. **Notification of Awards:** Applicants will be notified of awards on a rolling basis beginning on or about March 15. **Types of Aid:** *Need-based scholarships/grants:* Pell, SEOG, state scholarships/grants, private scholarships, the school's own gift aid, State grants. *Loans:* FFEL Subsidized Stafford, FFEL Unsubsidized Stafford, FFEL PLUS, Federal Perkins, state loans, college/university loans from institutional funds, alternative loans. **Student Employ-**

ment: Federal Work-Study Program available. Institutional employment available. Off-campus job opportunities are good. **Financial Aid Statistics:** 29% freshmen, 29% undergrads receive some form of aid. Average freshman grant $5,845. Average freshman loan $2,684. **Financial Aid Phone:** 919-962-8396.

UNIVERSITY OF NORTH CAROLINA—CHARLOTTE

9201 University City Boulevard, Charlotte, NC 28223-0001
Phone: 704-687-2213 **E-mail:** unccadm@email.uncc.edu **CEEB Code:** 5105
Fax: 704-687-6483 **Web:** www.uncc.edu **ACT Code:** 3163

This public school was founded in 1946. It has a 1,000-acre campus.

STUDENTS AND FACULTY

Enrollment: 15,364. **Student Body:** Male 46%, female 54%, out-of-state 10%, international 2% (79 countries represented). **Ethnic Representation:** African American 17%, Asian 5%, Caucasian 75%, Hispanic 2%. **Retention and Graduation:** 76% freshmen return for sophomore year. 24% freshmen graduate within 4 years. 13% grads go on to further study within 1 year. **Faculty:** Student/faculty ratio 16:1. 727 full-time faculty, 87% hold PhDs. 93% faculty teach undergrads.

ACADEMICS

Degrees: Bachelor's, doctoral, master's, post-master's certificate. **Academic Requirements:** General education including some course work in arts/fine arts, computer literacy, English (including composition), foreign languages, history, humanities, mathematics, philosophy, sciences (biological or physical), social science. **Classes:** 20-29 students in an average class. 10-19 students in an average lab/discussion section. **Disciplines with Highest Percentage of Degrees Awarded:** Business/marketing 26%, engineering/engineering technology 10%, social sciences and history 10%, psychology 8%, education 6%. **Special Study Options:** Cooperative (work-study) program, cross registration, distance learning, double major, English as a second language, student exchange program (domestic), honors program, independent study, internships, study abroad, teacher certification program, weekend college.

FACILITIES

Housing: Coed, all-female, all-male, apartments for single students, housing for disabled students, housing for international students, fraternities and/or sororities, separate floors in high-rise dorms and apartments. **Library Holdings:** 1,718,107 bound volumes. 11,084 periodicals. 120,934 microforms. 10,481 audiovisuals. **Special Academic Facilities/Equipment:** Urban studies and community service institute, mock court room, applied research center, language lab, 63-acre ecological reserve, botanical and horticultural complex, tropical rainforest conservatory. **Computers:** School-owned computers available for student use.

EXTRACURRICULARS

Activities: Choral groups, concert band, dance, drama/theater, jazz band, literary magazine, music ensembles, opera, pep band, student government, student newspaper, student-run film society, yearbook. **Organizations:** 193 registered organizations, 38 honor societies, 15 religious organizations, 14 fraternities (6% men join), 8 sororities (5% women join). **Athletics (Intercollegiate):** *Men:* baseball, basketball, cross-country, golf, soccer, tennis, track & field. *Women:* basketball, cross-country, soccer, softball, tennis, track & field, volleyball.

ADMISSIONS

Selectivity Rating: 68 (of 100). **Freshman Academic Profile:** Average high school GPA 3.5. 14% in top 10% of high school class, 45% in top 25% of high school class, 89% in top 50% of high school class. Average SAT I Math 542, SAT I Math middle 50% range 500-590. Average SAT I Verbal 523, SAT I Verbal middle 50% range 470-570. Average ACT 21, ACT middle 50% range 19-24. TOEFL required of all international applicants, minimum TOEFL 500. **Basis for Candidate Selection:** *Very important factors considered include:* secondary school record, standardized test scores. *Other factors considered include:* alumni/ae relation, character/personal qualities, extracurricular activities, geographical residence, recommendations, state residency, talent/ability, volunteer work, work experience. **Freshman Admission Requirements:** High school diploma or GED is required. *Academic units required/recommended:* 16 total required; 4 English required, 3 math required, 3 science required, 1 science lab required, 2 foreign language required, 2 social studies required, 1 history recommended, 2 elective required. **Freshman Admission Statistics:** 8,112 applied, 70% accepted, 43% of those accepted enrolled. **Transfer Admission Requirements:** *Items required:* high school transcript, college transcript. Minimum high school GPA of 2.0 required. Minimum college GPA of 2.0 required. Lowest grade transferable C. **General Admission Information:** Application fee $35. Regular application deadline July 1. Nonfall registration accepted. Admission may be deferred. Credit and/or placement offered for CEEB Advanced Placement tests.

COSTS AND FINANCIAL AID

In-state tuition $1,813. Out-of-state tuition $11,132. Room & board $4,856. Required fees $1,135. Average book expense $900. **Required Forms and Deadlines:** FAFSA. No deadline for regular filing. Priority filing deadline April 1. **Notification of Awards:** Applicants will be notified of awards on a rolling basis beginning on or about April 1. **Types of Aid:** *Need-based scholarships/grants:* Pell, SEOG, state scholarships/grants, private scholarships, the school's own gift aid. *Loans:* FFEL Subsidized Stafford, FFEL Unsubsidized Stafford, FFEL PLUS, Federal Perkins, state loans, college/university loans from institutional funds. **Student Employment:** Federal Work-Study Program available. Institutional employment available. Off-campus job opportunities are excellent. **Financial Aid Statistics:** 44% freshmen, 42% undergrads receive some form of aid. Average freshman grant $2,285. Average freshman loan $2,700. Average income from on-campus job $1,600. **Financial Aid Phone:** 704-687-2461.

UNIVERSITY OF NORTH CAROLINA—GREENSBORO

123 Mossman Building, Greensboro, NC 27402-6170
Phone: 336-334-5243 **E-mail:** undergrad_admissions@uncg.edu **CEEB Code:** 5913
Fax: 336-334-4180 **Web:** www.uncg.edu **ACT Code:** 3166

This public school was founded in 1891. It has a 200-acre campus.

STUDENTS AND FACULTY

Enrollment: 10,751. **Student Body:** Male 33%, female 67%, out-of-state 9%, international 1%. **Ethnic Representation:** African American 20%, Asian 3%, Caucasian 73%, Hispanic 2%. **Retention and Graduation:** 74% freshmen return for sophomore year. 25% freshmen graduate within 4 years. **Faculty:** Student/faculty ratio 15:1. 666 full-time faculty, 83% hold PhDs.

ACADEMICS

Degrees: Bachelor's, doctoral, master's, post-bachelor's certificate, post-master's certificate. **Academic Requirements:** General education including some course work in arts/fine arts, English (including composition), foreign languages, history, humanities, mathematics, philosophy, sciences (biological or physical), social science. **Classes:** 20-29 students in an average class. 20-29 students in an average lab/discussion section. **Majors with Highest Enrollment:** Nursing/registered nurse training (RN, ASN, BSN, MSN); business administration/management; elementary education and teaching. **Disciplines with Highest Percentage of Degrees Awarded:** Business/marketing 24%, education 10%, health professions and related sciences 10%, social sciences and history 9%, visual and performing arts 8%. **Special Study Options:** Cross registration, distance learning, double major, dual enrollment, honors program, independent study, internships, study abroad, teacher certification program.

FACILITIES

Housing: Coed, all-female, apartments for single students, housing for international students. **Library Holdings:** 844,448 bound volumes. 8,714 periodicals. 1,400,761 microforms. 59,027 audiovisuals. **Special Academic Facilities/Equipment:** 42-acre recreational site, art gallery, 45,000-square-foot student center, new music building, new science building. **Computers:** School-owned computers available for student use.

EXTRACURRICULARS

Activities: Choral groups, concert band, dance, drama/theater, jazz band, literary magazine, music ensembles, musical theater, opera, pep band, radio station, student government, student newspaper, student-run film society, symphony orchestra. **Organizations:** 150 registered organizations, 11 religious organizations, 10 fraternities (8% men join), 9 sororities (6% women join). **Athletics (Intercollegiate):** *Men:* baseball, basketball, cross-country, golf, soccer, tennis, track & field, wrestling. *Women:* basketball, cross-country, golf, soccer, softball, tennis, track & field, volleyball.

ADMISSIONS

Selectivity Rating: 69 (of 100). **Freshman Academic Profile:** Average high school GPA 3.4. 12% in top 10% of high school class, 42% in top 25% of high

school class, 85% in top 50% of high school class. 95% from public high schools. Average SAT I Math 514, SAT I Math middle 50% range 470-570. Average SAT I Verbal 519, SAT I Verbal middle 50% range 460-570. TOEFL required of all international applicants, minimum TOEFL 550. **Basis for Candidate Selection:** *Important factors considered include:* secondary school record, standardized test scores. *Other factors considered include:* class rank. **Freshman Admission Requirements:** High school diploma or GED is required. *Academic units required/recommended:* 15 total required; 4 English required, 3 math required, 3 science required, 1 science lab required, 2 foreign language required, 1 social studies required, 1 history required, 1 elective required. **Freshman Admission Statistics:** 7,065 applied, 76% accepted, 39% of those accepted enrolled. **Transfer Admission Requirements:** *Items required:* college transcript. Minimum college GPA of 2.0 required. Lowest grade transferable C-. **General Admission Information:** Application fee $35. Priority application deadline March 1. Regular application deadline August 1. Nonfall registration accepted. Credit and/or placement offered for CEEB Advanced Placement tests.

COSTS AND FINANCIAL AID

In-state tuition $1,717. Out-of-state tuition $12,091. Room & board $4,460. Required fees $1,288. Average book expense $1,156. **Required Forms and Deadlines:** FAFSA. No deadline for regular filing. Priority filing deadline March 1. **Notification of Awards:** Applicants will be notified of awards on a rolling basis beginning on or about April 1. **Types of Aid:** *Need-based scholarships/grants:* Pell, SEOG, state scholarships/grants, private scholarships, the school's own gift aid. *Loans:* FFEL Subsidized Stafford, FFEL Unsubsidized Stafford, FFEL PLUS, Federal Perkins, state loans. **Student Employment:** Federal Work-Study Program available. Institutional employment available. Off-campus job opportunities are good. **Financial Aid Statistics:** 48% freshmen, 60% undergrads receive some form of aid. **Financial Aid Phone:** 910-334-5702.

UNIVERSITY OF NORTH CAROLINA—PEMBROKE

One University Drive, PO Box 1510, Pembroke, NC 28372
Phone: 910-521-6262 **E-mail:** admissions@papa.uncp.edu **CEEB Code:** 5534
Fax: 910-521-6497 **Web:** www.uncp.edu **ACT Code:** 3138

This public school was founded in 1887. It has a 126-acre campus.

STUDENTS AND FACULTY

Enrollment: 3,951. **Student Body:** Male 37%, female 63%, out-of-state 4%, international 1%. **Ethnic Representation:** African American 22%, Asian 2%, Caucasian 52%, Hispanic 2%, Native American 23%. **Retention and Graduation:** 72% freshmen return for sophomore year. 18% freshmen graduate within 4 years. 15% grads go on to further study within 1 year. **Faculty:** Student/faculty ratio 17:1. 180 full-time faculty, 71% hold PhDs. 99% faculty teach undergrads.

ACADEMICS

Degrees: Bachelor's, master's. **Academic Requirements:** General education including some course work in arts/fine arts, computer literacy, English (including composition), history, humanities, mathematics, philosophy, sciences (biological or physical), social science, physical education. **Classes:** 10-19 students in an average class. 10-19 students in an average lab/discussion section. **Disciplines with Highest Percentage of Degrees Awarded:** Protective services/public administration 15%, education 14%, business/marketing 14%, social sciences and history 14%, biological life sciences 10%. **Special Study Options:** Accelerated program, cross registration, distance learning, double major, dual enrollment, English as a second language, student exchange program (domestic), external degree program, honors program, independent study, internships, student-designed major, study abroad, teacher certification program.

FACILITIES

Housing: Coed, all-female, all-male, fraternities and/or sororities, Apartments for students to lease. **Library Holdings:** 308,667 bound volumes. 1,561 periodicals. 666,648 microforms. 1,856 audiovisuals. **Special Academic Facilities/Equipment:** Native American Resources Center and Museum. **Computers:** *Recommended operating system:* Windows 3x. School-owned computers available for student use.

EXTRACURRICULARS

Activities: Choral groups, concert band, drama/theater, jazz band, music ensembles, musical theater, student government, student newspaper, television station, yearbook. **Organizations:** 70 registered organizations, 11 honor societies, 3 religious organizations, 10 fraternities (5% men join), 8 sororities (8% women join). **Athletics (Intercollegiate):** *Men:* baseball, basketball, cheerleading, cross-country, golf, soccer, track & field, wrestling. *Women:* basketball, cheerleading, cross-country, soccer, softball, tennis, track & field, volleyball.

ADMISSIONS

Selectivity Rating: 63 (of 100). **Freshman Academic Profile:** Average high school GPA 3.0. 9% in top 10% of high school class, 40% in top 25% of high school class, 60% in top 50% of high school class. 98% from public high schools. Average SAT I Math 471, SAT I Math middle 50% range 520-420. Average SAT I Verbal 463, SAT I Verbal middle 50% range 500-420. Average ACT 19. TOEFL required of all international applicants, minimum TOEFL 500. **Basis for Candidate Selection:** *Very important factors considered include:* class rank, secondary school record, standardized test scores. *Other factors considered include:* alumni/ae relation, character/personal qualities, essays, interview, recommendations, talent/ability. **Freshman Admission Requirements:** High school diploma or GED is required. *Academic units required/recommended:* 13 total required; 17 total recommended; 4 English required, 4 English recommended, 3 math required, 4 math recommended, 3 science required, 3 science recommended, 1 science lab required, 1 science lab recommended, 2 foreign language recommended, 1 social studies required, 1 social studies recommended, 1 history required, 2 history recommended. **Freshman Admission Statistics:** 1,422 applied, 85% accepted, 60% of those accepted enrolled. **Transfer Admission Requirements:** *Items required:* high school transcript, college transcript, statement of good standing from prior school. Minimum high school GPA of 2.0 required. Minimum college GPA of 2.0 required. Lowest grade transferable C. **General Admission Information:** Application fee $40. Priority application deadline July 15. Nonfall registration accepted. Admission may be deferred. Credit and/or placement offered for CEEB Advanced Placement tests.

COSTS AND FINANCIAL AID

In-state tuition $1,394. Out-of-state tuition $10,313. Room & board $4,240. Required fees $971. Average book expense $800. **Required Forms and Deadlines:** FAFSA. No deadline for regular filing. Priority filing deadline March 15. **Notification of Awards:** Applicants will be notified of awards on a rolling basis beginning on or about April 15. **Types of Aid:** *Need-based scholarships/grants:* Pell, SEOG, state scholarships/grants, private scholarships, the school's own gift aid. *Loans:* FFEL Subsidized Stafford, FFEL Unsubsidized Stafford, FFEL PLUS, Federal Perkins, college/university loans from institutional funds. **Student Employment:** Federal Work-Study Program available. Off-campus job opportunities are good. **Financial Aid Statistics:** 64% freshmen, 64% undergrads receive some form of aid. Average freshman grant $2,623. Average freshman loan $2,625. **Financial Aid Phone:** 910-521-6255.

UNIVERSITY OF NORTH CAROLINA—WILMINGTON

601 South College Rd., Wilmington, NC 28403
Phone: 910-962-3243 **E-mail:** admissions@uncwil.edu **CEEB Code:** 5907
Fax: 910-962-3038 **Web:** www.uncwil.edu **ACT Code:** 3174

This public school was founded in 1947. It has a 650-acre campus.

STUDENTS AND FACULTY

Enrollment: 9,803. **Student Body:** Male 40%, female 60%, out-of-state 14%, international 1%. **Ethnic Representation:** African American 4%, Asian 1%, Caucasian 92%, Hispanic 2%, Native American 1%. **Retention and Graduation:** 80% freshmen return for sophomore year. 34% freshmen graduate within 4 years. 9% grads go on to further study within 1 year. 1% grads pursue business degrees. 1% grads pursue law degrees. 1% grads pursue medical degrees. **Faculty:** Student/faculty ratio 16:1. 434 full-time faculty, 86% hold PhDs. 100% faculty teach undergrads.

ACADEMICS

Degrees: Bachelor's, doctoral, master's. **Academic Requirements:** General education including some course work in arts/fine arts, computer literacy, English (including composition), foreign languages, history, humanities, mathematics, sciences (biological or physical), social science. **Classes:** 30-39 students in an average class. 10-19 students in an average lab/discussion section. **Majors with Highest Enrollment:** Communications studies/speech communication and rhetoric; marine biology and biological oceanography; psychology, general. **Disciplines with Highest Percentage of Degrees Awarded:** Business/marketing 27%, English 13%, education 11%, biological life sciences 8%, psychology 7%. **Special Study Options:** Accelerated program, cooperative (work-study) program, distance learning, double major, English as a second language, student exchange program (domestic), honors program, independent study, internships, study abroad, teacher certification program, 2+2 engineering program.

FACILITIES

Housing: Coed, all-female, apartments for single students, housing for international students, honors dorm. **Library Holdings:** 503,093 bound volumes. 3,626 periodicals. 773,426 microforms. 10,901 audiovisuals. **Special Academic Facilities/Equipment:** Museum of World Culture, wildflower preserve, center for marine science research. **Computers:** School-owned computers available for student use.

EXTRACURRICULARS

Activities: Choral groups, concert band, dance, drama/theater, jazz band, literary magazine, music ensembles, musical theater, opera, pep band, radio station, student government, student newspaper, student-run film society, symphony orchestra, television station. **Organizations:** 129 registered organizations; 9 honor societies, 12 fraternities, 12 sororities. **Athletics (Intercollegiate):** *Men:* baseball, basketball, cross-country, golf, soccer, swimming, tennis, track & field. *Women:* basketball, cross-country, golf, soccer, softball, swimming, tennis, track & field, volleyball.

ADMISSIONS

Selectivity Rating: 65 (of 100). **Freshman Academic Profile:** Average high school GPA 3.6. 20% in top 10% of high school class, 52% in top 25% of high school class, 94% in top 50% of high school class. Average SAT I Math 560, SAT I Math middle 50% range 520-610. Average SAT I Verbal 545, SAT I Verbal middle 50% range 500-590. ACT middle 50% range 18-24. TOEFL required of all international applicants, minimum TOEFL 580. **Basis for Candidate Selection:** *Very important factors considered include:* secondary school record, standardized test scores, state residency. *Important factors considered include:* class rank. *Other factors considered include:* alumni/ae relation, character/personal qualities, essays, extracurricular activities, geographical residence, minority status, recommendations, talent/ability, volunteer work, work experience. **Freshman Admission Requirements:** High school diploma or GED is required. *Academic units required/recommended:* 4 English required, 3 math required, 3 science required, 1 science lab required, 2 foreign language required, 2 social studies required, 1 history required, 5 elective required. **Freshman Admission Statistics:** 7,188 applied, 55% accepted, 41% of those accepted enrolled. **Transfer Admission Requirements:** *Items required:* high school transcript, college transcript. Minimum college GPA of 2.2 required. Lowest grade transferable C. **General Admission Information:** Application fee $45. Priority application deadline November 1. Regular application deadline February 1. Nonfall registration accepted. Credit and/or placement offered for CEEB Advanced Placement tests.

COSTS AND FINANCIAL AID

In-state tuition $1,622. Out-of-state tuition $10,741. Room & board $5,378. Required fees $1,452. Average book expense $775. **Required Forms and Deadlines:** FAFSA and institution's own financial aid form. No deadline for regular filing. **Notification of Awards:** Applicants will be notified of awards on a rolling basis beginning on or about January 15. **Types of Aid:** *Need-based scholarships/grants:* Pell, SEOG, state scholarships/grants, private scholarships, the school's own gift aid. *Loans:* Direct Subsidized Stafford, Direct Unsubsidized Stafford, Direct PLUS, Federal Perkins, state loans, college/university loans from institutional funds. **Student Employment:** Federal Work-Study Program available. Institutional employment available. Off-campus job opportunities are good. **Financial Aid Statistics:** 30% freshmen, 35% undergrads receive some form of aid. **Financial Aid Phone:** 910-962-3177.

UNIVERSITY OF NORTH DAKOTA

PO Box 8135, Grand Forks, ND 58202
Phone: 800-225-5863 **E-mail:** enrollment_services@mail.und.nodak.edu
CEEB Code: 6878 **Fax:** 701-777-4857 **Web:** www.und.edu **ACT Code:** 3218

This public school was founded in 1883. It has a 540-acre campus.

STUDENTS AND FACULTY

Enrollment: 10,277. **Student Body:** Male 53%, female 47%, out-of-state 42%, international 2% (61 countries represented). **Ethnic Representation:** African American 1%, Asian 1%, Caucasian 95%, Hispanic 1%, Native American 3%. **Retention and Graduation:** 79% freshmen return for sophomore year. 21% grads go on to further study within 1 year. 1% grads pursue business degrees. 1% grads pursue law degrees. **Faculty:** Student/faculty ratio 18:1. 466 full-time faculty. 85% faculty teach undergrads.

ACADEMICS

Degrees: Bachelor's, doctoral, first professional, master's, post-master's certificate. **Academic Requirements:** General education including some course work in arts/fine arts, English (including composition), humanities, sciences (biological or physical), social science. **Classes:** 20-29 students in an average class. 20-29 students in an average lab/discussion section. **Majors with Highest Enrollment:** Nursing/registered nurse training (RN, ASN, BSN, MSN); elementary education and teaching; aeronautics/aviation/aerospace science and technology, general. **Disciplines with Highest Percentage of Degrees Awarded:** Business/marketing 15%, trade and industry 14%, health professions and related sciences 11%, education 9%, social sciences and history 8%. **Special Study Options:** Accelerated program, cooperative (work-study) program, cross registration, distance learning, double major, dual enrollment, English as a second language, student exchange program (domestic), external degree program, honors program, independent study, internships, liberal arts/career combination, student-designed major, study abroad, teacher certification program, weekend college.

FACILITIES

Housing: Coed, all-female, all-male, apartments for married students, apartments for single students, housing for disabled students, fraternities and/or sororities. **Library Holdings:** 915,739 bound volumes. 7,192 periodicals. 1,305,871 microforms. 18,310 audiovisuals. **Special Academic Facilities/Equipment:** Hughes Fine Arts Center, Burtness Theatre, North Dakota Museum of Art, Chester Fritz Auditorium, mining/mineral resources research institute/energy research center, remote sensing institute, aviation facilities, meteorology data center. **Computers:** School-owned computers available for student use.

EXTRACURRICULARS

Activities: Choral groups, concert band, dance, drama/theater, jazz band, literary magazine, marching band, music ensembles, musical theater, pep band, student government, student newspaper, student-run film society, symphony orchestra, television station. **Organizations:** 250 registered organizations, 30 honor societies, 16 religious organizations, 13 fraternities (9% men join), 7 sororities (9% women join). **Athletics (Intercollegiate):** *Men:* baseball, basketball, cross-country, diving, football, golf, ice hockey, indoor track, swimming, track & field. *Women:* basketball, cross-country, diving, golf, ice hockey, indoor track, soccer, softball, swimming, tennis, track & field, volleyball.

ADMISSIONS

Selectivity Rating: 77 (of 100). **Freshman Academic Profile:** Average high school GPA 3.4. 16% in top 10% of high school class, 40% in top 25% of high school class, 74% in top 50% of high school class. 85% from public high schools. Average ACT 23, ACT middle 50% range 20-26. TOEFL required of all international applicants, minimum TOEFL 525. **Basis for Candidate Selection:** *Very important factors considered include:* secondary school record, standardized test scores. *Other factors considered include:* class rank, essays, recommendations. **Freshman Admission Requirements:** High school diploma or GED is required. *Academic units required/recommended:* 4 English required, 3 math required, 3 science required, 3 science lab required, 1 foreign language recommended, 3 social studies required. **Freshman Admission Statistics:** 3,628 applied, 72% accepted, 77% of those accepted enrolled. **Transfer Admission Requirements:** *Items required:* college transcript. Minimum high school GPA of 2.3 required. Minimum college GPA of 2.0 required. Lowest grade transferable F. **General Admission Information:** Application fee $35. Regular application deadline July 1. Nonfall registration accepted. Admission may be deferred. Credit and/or placement offered for CEEB Advanced Placement tests.

COSTS AND FINANCIAL AID

Out-of-state tuition $8,594. Room & board $3,987. Required fees $708. Average book expense $700. **Required Forms and Deadlines:** FAFSA. Priority filing deadline April 15. **Notification of Awards:** Applicants will be notified of awards on or about May 15. **Types of Aid:** *Need-based scholarships/grants:* Pell, SEOG, state scholarships/grants, private scholarships, the school's own gift aid. *Loans:* FFEL Subsidized Stafford, FFEL Unsubsidized Stafford, FFEL PLUS, Federal Perkins, Federal Nursing, college/university loans from institutional funds. **Student Employment:** Federal Work-Study Program available. Institutional employment available. Off-campus job opportunities are excellent. **Financial Aid Statistics:** 47% freshmen, 53% undergrads receive some form of aid. Average freshman grant $2,512. Average freshman loan $5,102. Average income from on-campus job $1,810. **Financial Aid Phone:** 701-777-3121.

UNIVERSITY OF NORTH FLORIDA

4567 St. Johns Bluff Road, South, Jacksonville, FL 32224-2645
Phone: 904-620-2624 **E-mail:** osprey@unf.edu **CEEB Code:** 9841
Fax: 904-620-2414 **Web:** www.unf.edu **ACT Code:** 5490

This public school was founded in 1965. It has a 1,300-acre campus.

STUDENTS AND FACULTY

Enrollment: 11,618. **Student Body:** Male 42%, female 58%, out-of-state 5%, international 1%. **Ethnic Representation:** African American 10%, Asian 6%, Caucasian 78%, Hispanic 5%. **Retention and Graduation:** 76% freshmen return for sophomore year. **Faculty:** Student/faculty ratio 22:1. 383 full-time faculty, 95% hold PhDs. 84% faculty teach undergrads.

ACADEMICS

Degrees: Associate's, bachelor's, certificate, doctoral, master's, post-bachelor's certificate, post-master's certificate, terminal, transfer. **Academic Requirements:** General education including some course work in arts/fine arts, computer literacy, English (including composition), foreign languages, history, humanities, mathematics, philosophy, sciences (biological or physical), social science, cultural diversity. **Classes:** 20-29 students in an average class. 10-19 students in an average lab/discussion section. **Majors with Highest Enrollment:** Health professions and related sciences; psychology, general; communications studies/speech communication and rhetoric. **Disciplines with Highest Percentage of Degrees Awarded:** Business/marketing 21%, education 15%, health professions and related sciences 13%, communications/communication technologies 8%, computer and information sciences 7%. **Special Study Options:** Accelerated program, cooperative (work-study) program, distance learning, double major, dual enrollment, English as a second language, honors program, independent study, internships, student-designed major, study abroad, teacher certification program, weekend college.

FACILITIES

Housing: Coed, apartments for married students, apartments for single students, housing for disabled students, fraternities and/or sororities, suite-style housing. **Library Holdings:** 746,604 bound volumes. 3,466 periodicals. 1,281,531 microforms. 67,208 audiovisuals. **Special Academic Facilities/Equipment:** Art gallery, bird sanctuary and wildlife preserve. **Computers:** School-owned computers available for student use.

EXTRACURRICULARS

Activities: Choral groups, concert band, dance, drama/theater, jazz band, literary magazine, music ensembles, pep band, radio station, student government, student newspaper, television station. **Organizations:** 141 registered organizations, 8 honor societies, 14 religious organizations, 8 fraternities (6% men join), 7 sororities (5% women join). **Athletics (Intercollegiate):** *Men:* baseball, basketball, cheerleading, cross-country, golf, soccer, tennis, track & field. *Women:* basketball, cheerleading, cross-country, soccer, softball, swimming, tennis, track & field, volleyball.

ADMISSIONS

Selectivity Rating: 71 (of 100). **Freshman Academic Profile:** Average high school GPA 3.4. 22% in top 10% of high school class, 55% in top 25% of high school class, 86% in top 50% of high school class. Average SAT I Math 567, SAT I Math middle 50% range 500-600. Average SAT I Verbal 570, SAT I Verbal middle 50% range 500-600. Average ACT 22, ACT middle 50% range 20-23. TOEFL required of all international applicants, minimum TOEFL 500. **Basis for Candidate Selection:** *Very important factors considered include:* secondary school record, standardized test scores. *Other factors considered include:* class rank, essays, extracurricular activities, recommendations, talent/ability, volunteer work, work experience. **Freshman Admission Requirements:** High school diploma or GED is required. *Academic units required/recommended:* 19 total required; 4 English required, 3 math required, 3 science required, 1 science lab required, 2 foreign language required, 3 social studies required, 4 elective required. **Freshman Admission Statistics:** 7,188 applied, 70% accepted, 39% of those accepted enrolled. **Transfer Admission Requirements:** *Items required:* college transcript. Minimum high school GPA of 2.0 required. Minimum college GPA of 2.0 required. Lowest grade transferable D. **General Admission Information:** Application fee $20. Priority application deadline December 31. Regular application deadline July 2. Nonfall registration accepted. Admission may be deferred for a maximum of 1 year. Credit offered for CEEB Advanced Placement tests.

COSTS AND FINANCIAL AID

In-state tuition $1,670. Out-of-state tuition $9,182. Room & board $5,420. Average book expense $600. **Required Forms and Deadlines:** FAFSA and Financial aid transcript for transfer students. Priority filing deadline April 1. **Notification of Awards:** Applicants will be notified of awards on a rolling basis beginning on or about March 15. **Types of Aid:** *Need-based scholarships/grants:* Pell, SEOG, state scholarships/grants, the school's own gift aid, 2-2 Scholarships jointly sponsored with Florida Community College at Jacksonville. *Loans:* FFEL Subsidized Stafford, FFEL Unsubsidized Stafford, FFEL PLUS, Federal Perkins. **Student Employment:** Federal Work-Study Program available. Institutional employment available. Off-campus job opportunities are excellent. **Financial Aid Statistics:** 62% freshmen, 61% undergrads receive some form of aid. Average freshman grant $1,734. Average freshman loan $3,219. Average income from on-campus job $5,414. **Financial Aid Phone:** 904-620-2604.

UNIVERSITY OF NORTH TEXAS

PO Box 311277, Denton, TX 76203-1277
Phone: 940-565-2681 **E-mail:** undergrad@unt.edu **CEEB Code:** 6481
Fax: 940-565-2408 **Web:** www.unt.edu **ACT Code:** 4136

This public school was founded in 1890. It has a 794-acre campus.

STUDENTS AND FACULTY

Enrollment: 22,618. **Student Body:** Male 45%, female 55%, out-of-state 4%, international 3%. **Ethnic Representation:** African American 11%, Asian 5%, Caucasian 72%, Hispanic 10%, Native American 1%. **Retention and Graduation:** 74% freshmen return for sophomore year. 11% freshmen graduate within 4 years. **Faculty:** Student/faculty ratio 17:1. 799 full-time faculty, 80% hold PhDs. 61% faculty teach undergrads.

ACADEMICS

Degrees: Bachelor's, doctoral, master's, post-bachelor's certificate. **Academic Requirements:** General education including some course work in arts/fine arts, computer literacy, English (including composition), foreign languages, history, humanities, mathematics, philosophy, sciences (biological or physical), social science. **Classes:** 20-29 students in an average class. 20-29 students in an average lab/discussion section. **Majors with Highest Enrollment:** Computer science; elementary education and teaching; psychology, general. **Disciplines with Highest Percentage of Degrees Awarded:** Business/marketing 28%, interdisciplinary studies 12%, visual and performing arts 9%, social sciences and history 8%, communications/communication technologies 7%. **Special Study Options:** Accelerated program, cooperative (work-study) program, cross registration, distance learning, dual enrollment, English as a second language, student exchange program (domestic), honors program, independent study, internships, study abroad, teacher certification program, weekend college.

FACILITIES

Housing: Coed, all-female, apartments for single students, housing for disabled students, fraternities and/or sororities, cooperative housing. **Library Holdings:** 1,989,141 bound volumes. 14,994 periodicals. 3,206,516 microforms. 16,007 audiovisuals. **Special Academic Facilities/Equipment:** Laser facilities, sky theater, Murchison Performing Arts Center. **Computers:** School-owned computers available for student use.

EXTRACURRICULARS

Activities: Choral groups, concert band, dance, drama/theater, jazz band, literary magazine, marching band, music ensembles, musical theater, opera, pep band, radio station, student government, student newspaper, student-run film society, symphony orchestra, television station, yearbook. **Organizations:** 254 registered organizations, 25 honor societies, 33 religious organizations, 17 fraternities (5% men join), 10 sororities (4% women join). **Athletics (Intercollegiate):** *Men:* basketball, cross-country, football, golf, track & field. *Women:* basketball, cross-country, diving, golf, soccer, softball, swimming, tennis, track & field, volleyball.

ADMISSIONS

Selectivity Rating: 72 (of 100). **Freshman Academic Profile:** 15% in top 10% of high school class, 44% in top 25% of high school class, 83% in top 50% of high school class. Average SAT I Math 544, SAT I Math middle 50% range 480-600. Average SAT I Verbal 541, SAT I Verbal middle 50% range 480-600. Average ACT 22, ACT middle 50% range 20-25. TOEFL required of all international applicants, minimum TOEFL 550. **Basis for Candidate Selection:** *Very important factors considered include:* class rank, secondary school record, standardized test scores. *Important factors considered include:* recommendations. *Other factors considered include:* character/personal qualities, essays, extracurricular activities, volunteer work, work experience. **Freshman Admission Requirements:** High school diploma or GED is required. *Academic units required/recommended:* 23 total required; 4 English required, 4 math required, 3 science required, 3 foreign language required, 4 social studies required, 3 elective required. **Freshman Admission Statistics:**

8,003 applied, 70% accepted, 54% of those accepted enrolled. **Transfer Admission Requirements:** *Items required:* college transcript. Minimum college GPA of 2.0 required. Lowest grade transferable D. **General Admission Information:** Application fee $40. Nonfall registration accepted. Admission may be deferred for a maximum of 1 year. Credit offered for CEEB Advanced Placement tests.

COSTS AND FINANCIAL AID

Required Forms and Deadlines: FAFSA. No deadline for regular filing. Priority filing deadline June 1. **Notification of Awards:** Applicants will be notified of awards on a rolling basis beginning on or about April 1. **Types of Aid:** *Need-based scholarships/grants:* Pell, SEOG, state scholarships/grants, the school's own gift aid. *Loans:* FFEL Subsidized Stafford, FFEL Unsubsidized Stafford, FFEL PLUS, state loans, college/university loans from institutional funds. **Student Employment:** Federal Work-Study Program available. Institutional employment available. Off-campus job opportunities are excellent. **Financial Aid Statistics:** 36% freshmen, 38% undergrads receive some form of aid. Average freshman grant $2,281. Average freshman loan $2,625. Average income from on-campus job $6,500. **Financial Aid Phone:** 940-565-2302.

UNIVERSITY OF NORTHERN COLORADO

UNC Admissions Office, Greeley, CO 80639
Phone: 970-351-2881 **E-mail:** unc@mail.unco.edu **CEEB Code:** 4074
Fax: 970-351-2984 **Web:** www.unco.edu **ACT Code:** 502

This public school was founded in 1890. It has a 236-acre campus.

STUDENTS AND FACULTY

Enrollment: 10,161. **Student Body:** Male 39%, female 61%, out-of-state 10%. **Ethnic Representation:** African American 2%, Asian 4%, Caucasian 82%, Hispanic 8%, Native American 1%. **Retention and Graduation:** 68% freshmen return for sophomore year. 8% grads go on to further study within 1 year. **Faculty:** Student/faculty ratio 20:1. 439 full-time faculty, 77% hold PhDs. 100% faculty teach undergrads.

ACADEMICS

Degrees: Bachelor's, doctoral, master's. **Academic Requirements:** General education including some course work in arts/fine arts, English (including composition), history, mathematics, sciences (biological or physical), social science. **Classes:** 20-29 students in an average class. 20-29 students in an average lab/discussion section. **Majors with Highest Enrollment:** Business/managerial operations; multi/interdisciplinary studies; psychology, general. **Disciplines with Highest Percentage of Degrees Awarded:** Social sciences and history 18%, business/marketing 16%, communications/communication technologies 10%, visual and performing arts 9%, psychology 9%. **Special Study Options:** Cooperative (work-study) program, cross registration, distance learning, double major, dual enrollment, English as a second language, student exchange program (domestic), external degree program, honors program, independent study, internships, student-designed major, study abroad, teacher certification program.

FACILITIES

Housing: Coed, all-female, apartments for married students, apartments for single students, housing for disabled students, fraternities and/or sororities. **Library Holdings:** 1,002,163 bound volumes. 3,621 periodicals. 1,213,058 microforms. 44,843 audiovisuals. **Special Academic Facilities/Equipment:** Art museum, music library, James A. Michener Collection. **Computers:** School-owned computers available for student use.

EXTRACURRICULARS

Activities: Choral groups, concert band, dance, drama/theater, jazz band, literary magazine, marching band, music ensembles, musical theater, opera, pep band, radio station, student government, student newspaper, student-run film society, symphony orchestra. **Organizations:** 111 registered organizations, 7 honor societies, 12 fraternities (7% men join), 8 sororities (4% women join). **Athletics (Intercollegiate):** *Men:* baseball, basketball, football, golf, tennis, track & field, wrestling. *Women:* basketball, cross-country, golf, soccer, softball, swimming, tennis, track & field, volleyball.

ADMISSIONS

Selectivity Rating: 70 (of 100). **Freshman Academic Profile:** Average high school GPA 3.3. 13% in top 10% of high school class, 33% in top 25% of high school class, 71% in top 50% of high school class. 94% from public high schools. Average SAT I Math 522, SAT I Math middle 50% range 470-570. Average SAT I Verbal 525, SAT I Verbal middle 50% range 470-580. Average ACT 22, ACT middle 50% range 20-25. TOEFL required of all international applicants, minimum TOEFL 520. **Basis for Candidate Selection:** *Very important factors considered include:* class rank, secondary school record, standardized test scores. *Important factors considered include:* recommendations. *Other factors considered include:* character/personal qualities, extracurricular activities, interview, minority status, state residency, talent/ability, work experience. **Freshman Admission Requirements:** High school diploma or GED is required. *Academic units required/recommended:* 15 total required; 4 English recommended, 3 math required, 2 science recommended, 1 science lab recommended, 2 social studies recommended. **Freshman Admission Statistics:** 6,961 applied, 72% accepted, 39% of those accepted enrolled. **Transfer Admission Requirements:** *Items required:* college transcript, statement of good standing from prior school. Minimum high school GPA of 2.9 required. Minimum college GPA of 2.5 required. Lowest grade transferable C. **General Admission Information:** Application fee $30. Regular application deadline August 1. Nonfall registration accepted. Admission may be deferred for a maximum of 1 year. Credit offered for CEEB Advanced Placement tests.

COSTS AND FINANCIAL AID

In-state tuition $2,290. Out-of-state tuition $10,584. Room & board $5,560. Required fees $694. Average book expense $875. **Required Forms and Deadlines:** FAFSA. Priority filing deadline March 1. **Notification of Awards:** Applicants will be notified of awards on or about April 15. **Types of Aid:** *Need-based scholarships/grants:* Pell, SEOG, state scholarships/grants, private scholarships, the school's own gift aid. *Loans:* FFEL Subsidized Stafford, FFEL Unsubsidized Stafford, FFEL PLUS, Federal Perkins, college/university loans from institutional funds. **Student Employment:** Federal Work-Study Program available. Institutional employment available. Off-campus job opportunities are good. **Financial Aid Statistics:** 34% freshmen, 35% undergrads receive some form of aid. Average freshman grant $3,195. Average freshman loan $6,080. Average income from on-campus job $1,175. **Financial Aid Phone:** 970-351-2502.

UNIVERSITY OF NORTHERN IOWA

1227 West 27th Street, Cedar Falls, IA 50614-0018
Phone: 319-273-2281 **E-mail:** admissions@uni.edu **CEEB Code:** 6307
Fax: 319-273-2885 **Web:** www.uni.edu **ACT Code:** 1322

This public school was founded in 1876. It has an 865-acre campus.

STUDENTS AND FACULTY

Enrollment: 12,397. **Student Body:** Male 42%, female 58%, out-of-state 5%, international 2%. **Ethnic Representation:** African American 3%, Asian 1%, Caucasian 95%, Hispanic 2%. **Retention and Graduation:** 81% freshmen return for sophomore year. 33% freshmen graduate within 4 years. 12% grads go on to further study within 1 year. 1% grads pursue business degrees. 1% grads pursue law degrees. 1% grads pursue medical degrees. **Faculty:** Student/faculty ratio 16:1. 678 full-time faculty, 78% hold PhDs.

ACADEMICS

Degrees: Bachelor's, doctoral, master's. **Academic Requirements:** General education including some course work in arts/fine arts, English (including composition), foreign languages, history, humanities, mathematics, philosophy, sciences (biological or physical), social science. **Classes:** 20-29 students in an average class. 20-29 students in an average lab/discussion section. **Majors with Highest Enrollment:** Accounting; communications, journalism, and related fields; elementary education and teaching. **Disciplines with Highest Percentage of Degrees Awarded:** Education 22%, business/marketing 22%, social sciences and history 8%, communications/communication technologies 7%, liberal arts/general studies 6%. **Special Study Options:** Accelerated program, cooperative (work-study) program, distance learning, double major, dual enrollment, English as a second language, student exchange program (domestic), honors program, independent study, internships, student-designed major, study abroad, teacher certification program.

FACILITIES

Housing: Coed, all-female, all-male, apartments for married students, apartments for single students, fraternities and/or sororities. Facilities accessible by persons with disabilities. **Library Holdings:** 760,595 bound volumes. 7,226 periodicals. 1,081,088 microforms. 22,883 audiovisuals. **Special Academic Facilities/Equipment:** Natural history museum, art gallery, greenhouse and biological preserves, lakeside biology lab and field lab for conservation problems, educational media center, curriculum lab, on-campus school for student teachers, NASA Regional Teacher Resource Center, speech and hearing clinic, small business development center, Iowa Waste Reduction Center, center for applied research in metal casting, satellite video production truck with three cameras, performing arts center. Iowa Communications Network provides two-way audio/video link between classrooms across the state. **Computers:** School-owned computers available for student use.

EXTRACURRICULARS

Activities: Choral groups, concert band, dance, drama/theater, jazz band, literary magazine, marching band, music ensembles, musical theater, opera, pep band, radio station, student government, student newspaper, symphony orchestra, yearbook. **Organizations:** 184 registered organizations, 8 fraternities (4% men join), 4 sororities (4% women join). **Athletics (Intercollegiate):** *Men:* baseball, basketball, cross-country, diving, football, golf, indoor track, track & field, wrestling. *Women:* basketball, cross-country, diving, golf, indoor track, soccer, softball, swimming, tennis, track & field, volleyball.

ADMISSIONS

Selectivity Rating: 75 (of 100). **Freshman Academic Profile:** 18% in top 10% of high school class, 48% in top 25% of high school class, 90% in top 50% of high school class. SAT I Math middle 50% range 438-582. SAT I Verbal middle 50% range 448-572. Average ACT 23, ACT middle 50% range 20-25. TOEFL required of all international applicants, minimum TOEFL 550. **Basis for Candidate Selection:** *Very important factors considered include:* class rank, secondary school record, standardized test scores. *Other factors considered include:* interview, minority status, recommendations, state residency, talent/ability. **Freshman Admission Requirements:** High school diploma or GED is required. *Academic units required/recommended:* 15 total required; 4 English required, 3 math required, 3 science required, 1 science lab recommended, 2 foreign language recommended, 3 social studies required, 2 elective required. **Freshman Admission Statistics:** 4,446 applied, 80% accepted, 52% of those accepted enrolled. **Transfer Admission Requirements:** *Items required:* college transcript. Lowest grade transferable D. **General Admission Information:** Application fee $30. Regular application deadline August 15. Nonfall registration accepted. Admission may be deferred for a maximum of 6 years. Credit and/or placement offered for CEEB Advanced Placement tests.

COSTS AND FINANCIAL AID

In-state tuition $4,342. Out-of-state tuition $11,300. Room & board $4,640. Required fees $574. Average book expense $776. **Required Forms and Deadlines:** FAFSA. No deadline for regular filing. **Notification of Awards:** Applicants will be notified of awards on a rolling basis beginning on or about March 1. **Types of Aid:** *Need-based scholarships/grants:* Pell, SEOG, state scholarships/grants, private scholarships, the school's own gift aid. *Loans:* Direct Subsidized Stafford, Direct Unsubsidized Stafford, Direct PLUS, Federal Perkins, state loans, private, alternative loans. **Student Employment:** Federal Work-Study Program available. Institutional employment available. Off-campus job opportunities are good. **Financial Aid Statistics:** 56% freshmen, 57% undergrads receive some form of aid. Average freshman grant $3,076. Average freshman loan $5,196. Average income from on-campus job $1,649. **Financial Aid Phone:** 319-273-2700.

UNIVERSITY OF NOTRE DAME

220 Main Building, Notre Dame, IN 46556
Phone: 574-631-7505 **E-mail:** admissio.1@nd.edu **CEEB Code:** 1841
Fax: 574-631-8865 **Web:** www.nd.edu **ACT Code:** 1252

This private school, which is affiliated with the Roman Catholic Church, was founded in 1842. It has a 1,250-acre campus.

STUDENTS AND FACULTY

Enrollment: 8,261. **Student Body:** Male 53%, female 47%, out-of-state 88%, international 3% (80 countries represented). **Ethnic Representation:** African American 3%, Asian 4%, Caucasian 84%, Hispanic 8%, Native American 1%. **Retention and Graduation:** 34% grads go on to further study within 1 year. 4% grads pursue business degrees. 8% grads pursue law degrees. 9% grads pursue medical degrees. **Faculty:** Student/faculty ratio 12:1. 760 full-time faculty, 98% hold PhDs. 94% faculty teach undergrads.

ACADEMICS

Degrees: Bachelor's, doctoral, first professional, master's. **Academic Requirements:** General education including some course work in arts/fine arts, English (including composition), foreign languages, history, humanities, mathematics, philosophy, sciences (biological or physical), social science, physical education, theology. **Classes:** 10-19 students in an average class. 10-19 students in an average lab/discussion section. **Majors with Highest Enrollment:** Pre-medicine/pre-medical studies; business administration/management; engineering, general. **Disciplines with Highest Percentage of Degrees Awarded:** Business/marketing 32%, social sciences and history 19%, engineering/engineering technology 9%, health professions and related sciences 6%, biological life sciences 5%. **Special Study Options:** Accelerated program, cooperative (work-study) program, cross registration, distance learning, double major, dual enrollment, student exchange program (domestic), honors program, independent study, internships, liberal arts/career combination, student-designed major, study abroad, teacher certification program (only available through cross registration with St. Mary's College).

FACILITIES

Housing: All-female, all-male. **Library Holdings:** 2,673,446 bound volumes. 19,232 periodicals. 2,074,436 microforms. 23,497 audiovisuals. **Special Academic Facilities/Equipment:** Art Museum, theater, germ-free research facility, radiation laboratory. **Computers:** School-owned computers available for student use.

EXTRACURRICULARS

Activities: Choral groups, concert band, dance, drama/theater, jazz band, literary magazine, marching band, music ensembles, musical theater, opera, pep band, radio station, student government, student newspaper, student-run film society, symphony orchestra, yearbook. **Organizations:** 270 registered organizations, 10 honor societies, 7 religious organizations. **Athletics (Intercollegiate):** *Men:* baseball, basketball, cross-country, diving, fencing, football, golf, ice hockey, lacrosse, soccer, swimming, tennis, track & field. *Women:* basketball, crew, cross-country, diving, fencing, golf, lacrosse, soccer, softball, swimming, tennis, track & field, volleyball.

ADMISSIONS

Selectivity Rating: 99 (of 100). **Freshman Academic Profile:** 82% in top 10% of high school class, 95% in top 25% of high school class, 100% in top 50% of high school class. 50% from public high schools. Average SAT I Math 685, SAT I Math middle 50% range 650-730. Average SAT I Verbal 665, SAT I Verbal middle 50% range 620-720. Average ACT 31, ACT middle 50% range 30-33. TOEFL required of all international applicants, minimum TOEFL 550. **Basis for Candidate Selection:** *Very important factors considered include:* character/personal qualities, class rank, essays, extracurricular activities, recommendations, secondary school record, standardized test scores, talent/ability. *Other factors considered include:* alumni/ae relation, minority status, religious affiliation/commitment, volunteer work, work experience. **Freshman Admission Requirements:** High school diploma is required and GED is not accepted. *Academic units required/recommended:* 16 total required; 23 total recommended; 4 English required, 4 English recommended, 3 math required, 4 math recommended, 2 science required, 4 science recommended, 2 foreign language required, 4 foreign language recommended, 2 history required, 4 history recommended, 3 elective required, 3 elective recommended. **Freshman Admission Statistics:** 9,744 applied, 34% accepted, 58% of those accepted enrolled. **Transfer Admission Requirements:** *Items required:* high school transcript, college transcript, essay, standardized test score, statement of good standing from prior school. Minimum college GPA of 3.0 required. Lowest grade transferable C. **General Admission Information:** Application fee $50. Regular application deadline January 9. Admission may be deferred for a maximum of 1 year. Credit and/or placement offered for CEEB Advanced Placement tests.

COSTS AND FINANCIAL AID

Tuition $25,510. Room & board $6,510. Required fees $342. Average book expense $850. **Required Forms and Deadlines:** FAFSA, CSS/Financial Aid PROFILE, noncustodial (divorced/separated) parent's statement, business/farm supplement, signed federal income tax return and W-2 forms. Financial aid filing deadline February 15. Priority filing deadline February 15. **Notification of Awards:** Applicants will be notified of awards on or about April 1. **Types of Aid:** *Need-based scholarships/grants:* Pell, SEOG, state scholarships/grants, private scholarships, the school's own gift aid, Alumni Club Scholarships. *Loans:* FFEL Subsidized Stafford, FFEL Unsubsidized Stafford, FFEL PLUS, Federal Perkins, privately funded student loan. **Student Employment:** Federal Work-Study Program available. Institutional employment available. Off-campus job opportunities are good. **Financial Aid Statistics:** 46% freshmen, 40% undergrads receive some form of aid. Average income from on-campus job $1,800. **Financial Aid Phone:** 574-631-6436.

See page 1254.

UNIVERSITY OF OKLAHOMA

1000 Asp Avenue, Norman, OK 73019-4076
Phone: 405-325-2252 **E-mail:** admrec@ou.edu **CEEB Code:** 6879
Fax: 405-325-7124 **Web:** www.ou.edu **ACT Code:** 6879

This public school was founded in 1890. It has a 3,500-acre campus.

STUDENTS AND FACULTY

Enrollment: 20,193. **Student Body:** Male 50%, female 50%, out-of-state 21%, international 3% (100 countries represented). **Ethnic Representation:** African American 6%, Asian 5%, Caucasian 76%, Hispanic 4%, Native American 8%. **Retention and Graduation:** 84% freshmen return for sophomore year. 20% freshmen graduate within 4 years. **Faculty:** Student/faculty ratio 21:1. 1,201 full-time faculty, 86% hold PhDs.

ACADEMICS

Degrees: Bachelor's, certificate, doctoral, first professional, master's, post-master's certificate. **Academic Requirements:** General education including some course work in arts/fine arts, computer literacy, English (including composition), foreign languages, history, humanities, mathematics, philosophy, sciences (biological or physical), social science, communication. **Classes:** 20-29 students in an average class. 20-29 students in an average lab/discussion section. **Majors with Highest Enrollment:** Management information systems, general; psychology, general; sociology. **Disciplines with Highest Percentage of Degrees Awarded:** Business/marketing 24%, engineering/engineering technology 9%, social sciences and history 9%, health professions and related sciences 9%, communications/communication technologies 8%. **Special Study Options:** Accelerated program, cooperative (work-study) program, distance learning, double major, dual enrollment, English as a second language, external degree program, honors program, independent study, internships, liberal arts/career combination, student-designed major, study abroad, teacher certification program, weekend college.

FACILITIES

Housing: Coed, all-female, all-male, apartments for married students, apartments for single students, housing for disabled students, housing for international students, fraternities and/or sororities, honors house, cultural housing. **Library Holdings:** 4,067,801 bound volumes. 28,614 periodicals. 4,046,619 microforms. 13,507 audiovisuals. **Special Academic Facilities/Equipment:** Art and natural history museums, linguistics institute, Institute of Asian Affairs, biological field station, energy center. **Computers:** School-owned computers available for student use.

EXTRACURRICULARS

Activities: Choral groups, concert band, dance, drama/theater, jazz band, literary magazine, marching band, music ensembles, musical theater, opera, pep band, radio station, student government, student newspaper, student-run film society, symphony orchestra, television station, yearbook. **Organizations:** 275 registered organizations, 11 honor societies, 33 religious organizations, 19 fraternities (17% men join), 12 sororities (25% women join). **Athletics (Intercollegiate):** *Men:* baseball, basketball, cheerleading, cross-country, football, golf, gymnastics, indoor track, tennis, track & field, wrestling. *Women:* basketball, cheerleading, cross-country, golf, gymnastics, indoor track, soccer, softball, tennis, track & field, volleyball.

ADMISSIONS

Selectivity Rating: 77 (of 100). **Freshman Academic Profile:** Average high school GPA 3.6. 32% in top 10% of high school class, 67% in top 25% of high school class, 91% in top 50% of high school class. Average SAT I Math 591. Average SAT I Verbal 582. Average ACT 25, ACT middle 50% range 23-28. TOEFL required of all international applicants, minimum TOEFL 550. **Basis for Candidate Selection:** *Important factors considered include:* class rank, secondary school record, standardized test scores. *Other factors considered include:* essays, recommendations, state residency. **Freshman Admission Requirements:** High school diploma or GED is required. *Academic units required/recommended:* 15 total required; 4 English required, 3 math required, 2 science required, 2 science lab required, 3 foreign language recommended, 1 social studies required, 2 history required, 3 elective required. **Freshman Admission Statistics:** 7,248 applied, 89% accepted, 60% of those accepted enrolled. **Transfer Admission Requirements:** *Items required:* college transcript. Minimum college GPA of 2.0 required. Lowest grade transferable D. **General Admission Information:** Application fee $25. Regular application deadline June 1. Nonfall registration accepted. Credit and/or placement offered for CEEB Advanced Placement tests.

COSTS AND FINANCIAL AID

In-state tuition $2,163. Out-of-state tuition $7,311. Room & board $5,030. Required fees $766. Average book expense $913. **Required Forms and Deadlines:** FAFSA and institution's own financial aid form. No deadline for regular filing. Priority filing deadline March 1. **Notification of Awards:** Applicants will be notified of awards on a rolling basis beginning on or about March 15. **Types of Aid:** *Need-based scholarships/grants:* Pell, SEOG, state scholarships/grants, private scholarships, the school's own gift aid, United Negro College Fund. *Loans:* FFEL Subsidized Stafford, FFEL Unsubsidized Stafford, FFEL PLUS, Federal Perkins, Federal Nursing, college/university loans from institutional funds. **Student Employment:** Federal Work-Study Program available. Institutional employment available. Off-campus job opportunities are excellent. **Financial Aid Statistics:** 48% freshmen, 49% undergrads receive some form of aid. Average freshman grant $3,711. Average freshman loan $4,996. Average income from on-campus job $4,187. **Financial Aid Phone:** 405-325-4521.

UNIVERSITY OF OREGON

1217 University of Oregon, Eugene, OR 97403-1217
Phone: 541-346-3201 **E-mail:** uoadmit@oregon.uoregon.edu **CEEB Code:** 4846
Fax: 541-346-5815 **Web:** www.uoregon.edu

This public school was founded in 1876. It has a 295-acre campus.

STUDENTS AND FACULTY

Enrollment: 16,041. **Student Body:** Male 46%, female 54%, out-of-state 26%, international 5%. **Ethnic Representation:** African American 2%, Asian 6%, Caucasian 79%, Hispanic 3%, Native American 1%. **Retention and Graduation:** 84% freshmen return for sophomore year. 38% freshmen graduate within 4 years. 20% grads go on to further study within 1 year. 2% grads pursue business degrees. 1% grads pursue law degrees. 2% grads pursue medical degrees. **Faculty:** Student/faculty ratio 18:1. 795 full-time faculty, 97% hold PhDs. 100% faculty teach undergrads.

ACADEMICS

Degrees: Bachelor's, doctoral, first professional, master's, post-bachelor's certificate. **Academic Requirements:** General education including some course work in English (including composition), foreign languages, humanities, mathematics, sciences (biological or physical), social science. Bachelor of Arts requires proficiency in a foreign language. Bachelor of Science requires proficiency in mathematics or computer & information science. **Classes:** 20-29 students in an average class. **Majors with Highest Enrollment:** Journalism; business administration/management; psychology, general. **Disciplines with Highest Percentage of Degrees Awarded:** Social sciences and history 25%, business/marketing 12%, communications/communication technologies 9%, psychology 8%, visual and performing arts 7%. **Special Study Options:** Cooperative (work-study) program, cross registration, distance learning, double major, dual enrollment, English as a second language, student exchange program (domestic), honors program, independent study, internships, student-designed major, study abroad, teacher certification program, Semester at Sea program.

FACILITIES

Housing: Coed, single-sex floors, apartments for married students, apartments for single students, housing for disabled students, fraternities and/or sororities. **Library Holdings:** 2,490,169 bound volumes. 17,840 periodicals. 2,887,172 microforms. 1,221,894 audiovisuals. **Special Academic Facilities/Equipment:** Art, natural history, geology, anthropology, and law museums, research institutes, marine biology center, observatory. **Computers:** School-owned computers available for student use.

EXTRACURRICULARS

Activities: Choral groups, concert band, dance, drama/theater, jazz band, literary magazine, marching band, music ensembles, musical theater, opera, pep band, radio station, student government, student newspaper, student-run film society, symphony orchestra. **Organizations:** 250 registered organizations, 26 honor societies, 24 religious organizations, 14 fraternities (10% men join), 9 sororities (10% women join). **Athletics (Intercollegiate):** *Men:* basketball, cross-country, football, golf, tennis, track & field, wrestling. *Women:* basketball, cross-country, golf, soccer, softball, tennis, track & field, volleyball.

ADMISSIONS

Selectivity Rating: 80 (of 100). **Freshman Academic Profile:** Average high school GPA 3.5. 21% in top 10% of high school class, 52% in top 25% of high school class, 85% in top 50% of high school class. 90% from public high schools. Average SAT I Math 551, SAT I Math middle 50% range 494-608. Average SAT I Verbal 551, SAT I Verbal middle 50% range 492-610. TOEFL required of all international applicants, minimum TOEFL 500. **Basis for Candidate Selection:** *Very important factors considered include:* secondary school record, standardized test scores. **Freshman Admission Requirements:** High school diploma or GED is required. *Academic units required/recommended:* 14 total required; 4 English required, 3 math required, 2 science required, 1 science lab recommended, 2 foreign language required, 3 social studies required. **Freshman Admission Statistics:** 9,889 applied, 86% accepted, 39% of those accepted enrolled. **Transfer Admission Requirements:** *Items required:* college transcript. Minimum college GPA of 2.3 required. Lowest grade transferable D. **General Admission Information:** Application fee $50. Regular application deadline January 15. Nonfall registration accepted. Credit offered for CEEB Advanced Placement tests.

COSTS AND FINANCIAL AID

In-state tuition $2,907. Out-of-state tuition $13,896. Room & board $6,252. Required fees $1,323. Average book expense $876. **Required Forms and Deadlines:** FAFSA. Priority filing deadline March 1. **Notification of Awards:** Applicants will be notified of awards on a rolling basis beginning on or about April 1. **Types of Aid:** *Need-based scholarships/grants:* Pell, SEOG, state scholarships/grants, private scholarships, the school's own gift aid. *Loans:* Direct Subsidized Stafford, Direct Unsubsidized Stafford, Direct PLUS, Federal Perkins, college/university loans from institutional funds. **Student Employment:** Federal Work-Study Program available. Institutional employment available. Off-campus job opportunities are good. **Financial Aid Statistics:** 39% freshmen, 45% undergrads receive some form of aid. **Financial Aid Phone:** 541-346-3221.

See page 1256.

UNIVERSITY OF PENNSYLVANIA

1 College Hall, Philadelphia, PA 19104
Phone: 215-898-7507 **E-mail:** info@admissions.ugao.upenn.edu **CEEB Code:** 2926
Fax: 215-898-9670 **Web:** www.upenn.edu **ACT Code:** 3668

This private school was founded in 1740. It has a 260-acre campus.

STUDENTS AND FACULTY

Enrollment: 9,742. **Student Body:** Male 51%, female 49%, out-of-state 81%, international 9%. **Ethnic Representation:** African American 6%, Asian 20%, Caucasian 55%, Hispanic 6%. **Retention and Graduation:** 97% freshmen return for sophomore year. 84% freshmen graduate within 4 years. 20% grads go on to further study within 1 year. 1% grads pursue business degrees. 7% grads pursue law degrees. 5% grads pursue medical degrees. **Faculty:** Student/faculty ratio 6:1. 1,344 full-time faculty, 100% hold PhDs.

ACADEMICS

Degrees: Associate's, bachelor's, doctoral, first professional, first professional certificate, master's, post-master's certificate. **Academic Requirements:** General education including some course work in English (including composition), foreign languages, history, humanities, mathematics, philosophy, sciences (biological or physical), social science. **Classes:** 10-19 students in an average class. **Majors with Highest Enrollment:** Finance, general; psychology, general; economics, general. **Disciplines with Highest Percentage of Degrees Awarded:** Social sciences and history 26%, business/marketing 19%, engineering/engineering technology 10%, psychology 9%, biological life sciences 4%. **Special Study Options:** Accelerated program, cross registration, distance learning, double major, dual enrollment, English as a second language, student exchange program (domestic), honors program, independent study, internships, liberal arts/career combination, student-designed major, study abroad, teacher certification program.

FACILITIES

Housing: Coed, apartments for single students, housing for disabled students, fraternities and/or sororities, private off-campus. **Library Holdings:** 5,152,960 bound volumes. 40,840 periodicals. 3,875,003 microforms. 53,578 audiovisuals. **Special Academic Facilities/Equipment:** Art gallery, anthropology museum, institute for contemporary art, language lab, large animal research center, primate research center, arboretum, observatory, wind tunnel, electron microscope. **Computers:** School-owned computers available for student use.

EXTRACURRICULARS

Activities: Choral groups, concert band, dance, drama/theater, jazz band, literary magazine, marching band, music ensembles, musical theater, opera, pep band, radio station, student government, student newspaper, student-run film society, symphony orchestra, television station, yearbook. **Organizations:** 300 registered organizations, 34 fraternities (11% men join), 10 sororities (8% women join). **Athletics (Intercollegiate):** *Men:* baseball, basketball, crew, cross-country, diving, fencing, football, golf, lacrosse, soccer, squash, swimming, tennis, track & field, wrestling. *Women:* basketball, crew, cross-country, diving, fencing, field hockey, golf, gymnastics, lacrosse, soccer, softball, squash, swimming, tennis, track & field, volleyball.

ADMISSIONS

Selectivity Rating: 99 (of 100). **Freshman Academic Profile:** Average high school GPA 3.8. 91% in top 10% of high school class, 98% in top 25% of high school class, 100% in top 50% of high school class. 56% from public high schools. Average SAT I Math 715, SAT I Math middle 50% range 680-760. Average SAT I Verbal 687, SAT I Verbal middle 50% range 650-740. Average ACT 30, ACT middle 50% range 28-32. TOEFL required of all international applicants, minimum TOEFL 600. **Basis for Candidate Selection:** *Very important factors considered include:* character/personal qualities, essays, recommendations, secondary school record. *Important factors considered include:* alumni/ae relation, extracurricular activities, standardized test scores. *Other factors considered include:* class rank, geographical residence, interview, minority status, talent/ability, volunteer work, work experience. **Freshman Admission Requirements:** High school diploma or GED is required. *Academic units required/recommended:* 17 total required; 4 English required, 4 math required, 3 science required, 3 foreign language required, 3 social studies required, 2 history required. **Freshman Admission Statistics:** 18,784 applied, 21% accepted, 62% of those accepted enrolled. **Transfer Admission Requirements:** *Items required:* high school transcript, college transcript, essay, standardized test scores, statement of good standing from prior school. Lowest grade transferable C. **General Admission Information:** Application fee $60. Early decision application deadline November 1. Regular application deadline January 1. Admission may be deferred for a maximum of 1 year. Credit and/or placement offered for CEEB Advanced Placement tests.

COSTS AND FINANCIAL AID

Tuition $25,078. Room & board $8,224. Required fees $2,910. Average book expense $760. **Required Forms and Deadlines:** FAFSA, institution's own financial aid form, CSS/Financial Aid PROFILE and Parent & student federal income tax returns(for verification). Priority filing deadline February 15. **Notification of Awards:** Applicants will be notified of awards on or about April 1. **Types of Aid:** *Need-based scholarships/grants:* Pell, SEOG, state scholarships/grants, private scholarships, the school's own gift aid. *Loans:* FFEL Subsidized Stafford, FFEL Unsubsidized Stafford, FFEL PLUS, Federal Perkins, Federal Nursing, college/university loans from institutional funds, Penn guaranteed loan. **Student Employment:** Federal Work-Study Program available. Institutional employment available. Off-campus job opportunities are excellent. **Financial Aid Statistics:** 41% freshmen, 42% undergrads receive some form of aid. Average freshman grant $26,447. **Financial Aid Phone:** 215-898-1988.

UNIVERSITY OF PHOENIX

Mail Stop 10-0030, 4615 E. Elwood St., Phoenix, AZ 85040-1958
Phone: 480-317-6000
Fax: 480-594-1758 **Web:** www.phoenix.edu

This private school was founded in 1976.

STUDENTS AND FACULTY

Student Body: International 4%. **Ethnic Representation:** African American 4%, Asian 1%, Caucasian 16%, Hispanic 4%. **Faculty:** Student/faculty ratio 13:1. 222 full-time faculty, 23% hold PhDs.

ACADEMICS

Degrees: Associate's, bachelor's, certificate, doctoral, master's, post-bachelor's certificate, post-master's certificate. **Academic Requirements:** General education including some course work in computer literacy, English (including composition), humanities, mathematics, sciences (biological or physical), social science. **Majors with Highest Enrollment:** Management information systems, general; computer and information sciences, general; business administration/management. **Disciplines with Highest Percentage of Degrees Awarded:** Business/marketing 86%, health professions and related sciences 7%, computer and information sciences 6%, protective services/public administration 1%. **Special Study Options:** Accelerated program, distance learning, double major, dual enrollment, English as a second language, independent study, teacher certification program, weekend college.

FACILITIES

Library Holdings: 15,456 bound volumes. 7,055 periodicals. 434,197 microforms. 373 audiovisuals.

EXTRACURRICULARS

Organizations: 2 honor societies.

ADMISSIONS

Selectivity Rating: 60 (of 100). **Freshman Academic Profile:** TOEFL required of all international applicants, minimum TOEFL 550. **Basis for Candidate Selection:** *Very important factors considered include:* work experience. *Other factors considered include:* recommendations. **Freshman Admission Requirements:** High school diploma or GED is required. **Transfer Admission Requirements:** *Items required:* college transcript. Lowest grade transferable C-. **General Admission Information:** Application fee $85. Nonfall registration accepted.

COSTS AND FINANCIAL AID

Required Forms and Deadlines: FAFSA and institution's own financial aid form. No deadline for regular filing. **Types of Aid:** *Need-based scholarships/grants:* Pell, SEOG. *Loans:* FFEL Subsidized Stafford, FFEL Unsubsidized Stafford, FFEL PLUS, Federal Perkins. **Financial Aid Phone:** 480-735-3000.

UNIVERSITY OF PITTSBURGH—BRADFORD

Office of Admissions - Hanley Library, 300 Campus Drive, Bradford, PA 16701
Phone: 814-362-7555 **E-mail:** Admissions@www.upb.pitt.edu **CEEB Code:** 2935
Fax: 814-362-7578 **Web:** www.upb.pitt.edu **ACT Code:** 3731

This public school was founded in 1963. It has a 125-acre campus.

STUDENTS AND FACULTY

Enrollment: 1,352. **Student Body:** Male 38%, female 62%, out-of-state 13%, (2 countries represented). **Ethnic Representation:** African American 2%, Asian 1%, Caucasian 93%, Hispanic 1%. **Retention and Graduation:** 67% freshmen return for sophomore year. 20% freshmen graduate within 4 years. 20% grads go on to further study within 1 year. 10% grads pursue business degrees. 8% grads pursue law degrees. 7% grads pursue medical degrees. **Faculty:** Student/faculty ratio 13:1. 70 full-time faculty, 70% hold PhDs. 100% faculty teach undergrads.

ACADEMICS

Degrees: Associate's, bachelor's, post-bachelor's certificate, terminal, transfer. **Academic Requirements:** General education including some course work in arts/fine arts, computer literacy, English (including composition), history, humanities, mathematics, philosophy, sciences (biological or physical), social science. **Classes:** 10-19 students in an average class. 10-19 students in an average lab/discussion section. **Majors with Highest Enrollment:** Business administration/management; criminal justice/law enforcement administration; social sciences, general. **Disciplines with Highest Percentage of Degrees Awarded:** Business/marketing 25%, social sciences and history 13%, protective services/public administration 11%, psychology 9%, parks and recreation 8%. **Special Study Options:** Cross registration, distance learning, double major, dual enrollment, external degree program, independent study, internships, study abroad, teacher certification program.

FACILITIES

Housing: Coed, apartments for single students, housing for disabled students. **Library Holdings:** 83,104 bound volumes. 440 periodicals. 14,433 microforms. 3,277 audiovisuals. **Computers:** School-owned computers available for student use.

EXTRACURRICULARS

Activities: Choral groups, dance, drama/theater, literary magazine, radio station, student government, student newspaper. **Organizations:** 57 registered organizations, 7 honor societies, 1 religious organization, 3 fraternities (3% men join), 3 sororities (3% women join). **Athletics (Intercollegiate):** *Men:* baseball, basketball, cross-country, golf, soccer. *Women:* basketball, cross-country, golf, soccer, softball, volleyball.

ADMISSIONS

Selectivity Rating: 63 (of 100). **Freshman Academic Profile:** Average high school GPA 3.0. 4% in top 10% of high school class, 25% in top 25% of high school class, 62% in top 50% of high school class. Average SAT I Math 492, SAT I Math middle 50% range 440-540. Average SAT I Verbal 492, SAT I Verbal middle 50% range 440-540. Average ACT 20, ACT middle 50% range 16-22. TOEFL required of all international applicants, minimum TOEFL 550. **Basis for Candidate Selection:** *Very important factors considered include:* secondary school record. *Important factors considered include:* interview, standardized test scores. *Other factors considered include:* alumni/ae relation, character/personal qualities, class rank, essays, extracurricular activities, recommendations, talent/ability, volunteer work, work experience. **Freshman Admission Requirements:** High school diploma or GED is required. *Academic units required/recommended:* 15 total required; 20 total recommended; 4 English required, 4 English recommended, 2 math required, 2 math recommended, 1 science required, 3 science recommended, 1 science lab required, 1 science lab recommended, 2 foreign language required, 2 foreign language recommended, 1 social studies recommended, 1 history required, 1 history recommended, 5 elective required, 6 elective recommended. **Freshman Admission Statistics:** 644 applied, 92% accepted, 51% of those accepted enrolled. **Transfer Admission Requirements:** *Items required:* college transcript. Minimum college GPA of 2.0 required. Lowest grade transferable C-. **General Admission Information:** Application fee $35. Priority application deadline May 1. Nonfall registration accepted. Admission may be deferred for a maximum of 1 year. Credit and/or placement offered for CEEB Advanced Placement tests.

COSTS AND FINANCIAL AID

Out-of-state tuition $16,676. Room & board $5,470. Required fees $584. Average book expense $800. **Required Forms and Deadlines:** FAFSA and Donor Scholarship Application. No deadline for regular filing. Priority filing deadline March 1. **Notification of Awards:** Applicants will be notified of awards on a rolling basis beginning on or about April 1. **Types of Aid:** *Need-based scholarships/grants:* Pell, SEOG, state scholarships/grants, private scholarships, the school's own gift aid. *Loans:* FFEL Subsidized Stafford, FFEL Unsubsidized Stafford, FFEL PLUS, Federal Perkins. **Student Employment:** Federal Work-Study Program available. Institutional employment available. Off-campus job opportunities are good. **Financial Aid Statistics:** 80% freshmen, 82% undergrads receive some form of aid. **Financial Aid Phone:** 814-362-7550.

See page 1258.

UNIVERSITY OF PITTSBURGH—GREENSBURG

1150 Mount Pleasant Road, Greensburg, PA 15601
Phone: 724-836-9880 **E-mail:** upgadmit@pitt.edu **CEEB Code:** 2936
Fax: 724-836-7160 **Web:** www.pitt.edu/~upg **ACT Code:** 3733

This public school was founded in 1963. It has a 217-acre campus.

STUDENTS AND FACULTY

Enrollment: 1,888. **Student Body:** Male 44%, female 56%, out-of-state 2%. **Ethnic Representation:** African American 2%, Asian 1%, Caucasian 92%, Hispanic 1%. **Retention and Graduation:** 74% freshmen return for sophomore year. 21% grads go on to further study within 1 year. 4% grads pursue business degrees. 1% grads pursue law degrees. 1% grads pursue medical degrees. **Faculty:** Student/faculty ratio 19:1. 72 full-time faculty, 87% hold PhDs. 100% faculty teach undergrads.

ACADEMICS

Degrees: Bachelor's. **Academic Requirements:** General education including some course work in arts/fine arts, computer literacy, English (including composition), foreign languages, history, humanities, mathematics, philosophy, sciences (biological or physical), social science. **Classes:** 20-29 students in an average class. 20-29 students in an average lab/discussion section. **Disciplines with Highest Percentage of Degrees Awarded:** Business/marketing 26%, psychology 23%, social sciences and history 20%, English 7%, communications/communication technologies 5%. **Special Study Options:** Cooperative (work-study) program, cross registration, distance learning, double major, dual enrollment, student exchange program (domestic), independent study, internships, student-designed major, study abroad, teacher certification program.

FACILITIES

Housing: Coed, apartments for single students, housing for disabled students. **Library Holdings:** 75,942 bound volumes. 418 periodicals. 8,297 microforms. 1,604 audiovisuals. **Computers:** *Recommended operating system:* Windows 95. School-owned computers available for student use.

EXTRACURRICULARS

Activities: Choral groups, concert band, dance, drama/theater, literary magazine, music ensembles, pep band, student government, student newspaper, student-run film society. **Organizations:** 25 registered organizations. **Athletics (Intercollegiate):** *Men:* baseball, basketball, cross-country, golf, soccer, tennis. *Women:* basketball, cross-country, golf, soccer, softball, tennis, volleyball.

ADMISSIONS

Selectivity Rating: 67 (of 100). **Freshman Academic Profile:** Average high school GPA 3.2. 9% in top 10% of high school class, 35% in top 25% of high school class, 82% in top 50% of high school class. 95% from public high schools. Average SAT I Math 521, SAT I Math middle 50% range 480-560. Average SAT I Verbal 518, SAT I Verbal middle 50% range 480-560. TOEFL required of all international applicants, minimum TOEFL 550. **Basis for Candidate Selection:** *Very important factors considered include:* class rank, secondary school record, standardized test scores. *Important factors considered include:* interview. *Other factors considered include:* alumni/ae relation, character/personal qualities, essays, extracurricular activities, recommendations, talent/ability, volunteer work. **Freshman Admission Requirements:** High school diploma or GED is required. *Academic units required/recommended:* 15 total required; 20 total recommended; 4 English required, 4 English recommended, 2 math required, 4 math recommended, 1 science required, 2 science recommended, 1 science lab required, 2 science lab recommended, 3 foreign language recommended, 2 social studies required, 2 social studies recommended, 2 history required, 2 history recommended, 1 elective required, 1 elective recommended. **Freshman Admission Statistics:** 1,291 applied, 67% accepted, 59% of those accepted enrolled. **Transfer Admission Requirements:** *Items required:* high school transcript, college transcript. Minimum college GPA of 2.5 required. Lowest grade transferable C. **General Admission Information:** Application fee $35. Regular application deadline August 15. Nonfall registration accepted. Admission may be deferred for a maximum of 1 year. Credit and/or placement offered for CEEB Advanced Placement tests.

COSTS AND FINANCIAL AID

In-state tuition $7,868. Out-of-state tuition $16,676. Room & board $6,250. Required fees $600. Average book expense $600. **Required Forms and Deadlines:** FAFSA and institution's own financial aid form. Financial aid filing deadline May 1. Priority filing deadline March 1. **Notification of Awards:** Applicants will be notified of awards on a rolling basis beginning on or about April 1. **Types of Aid:** *Need-based scholarships/grants:* Pell, SEOG, state scholarships/grants, private scholarships, the school's own gift aid, United Negro College Fund. *Loans:* FFEL Subsidized Stafford, FFEL Unsubsidized Stafford, FFEL PLUS, Federal Perkins. **Student Employment:** Federal Work-Study Program available. Institutional employment available. Off-campus job opportunities are excellent. **Financial Aid Statistics:** Average freshman grant $6,500. Average freshman loan $2,500. Average income from on-campus job $2,100. **Financial Aid Phone:** 724-836-9881.

UNIVERSITY OF PITTSBURGH—JOHNSTOWN

450 Schoolhouse Road, 157 Blackington Hall, Johnstown, PA 15904
Phone: 814-269-7050 **E-mail:** upjadmit@pitt.edu **CEEB Code:** 2934
Fax: 814-269-7044 **Web:** www.upj.pitt.edu

This public school was founded in 1927. It has a 650-acre campus.

STUDENTS AND FACULTY

Enrollment: 3,122. **Student Body:** Male 47%, female 53%, out-of-state 1%. **Ethnic Representation:** African American 1%, Asian 1%, Caucasian 96%. **Retention and Graduation:** 1% grads pursue business degrees. 1% grads pursue law degrees. 2% grads pursue medical degrees. **Faculty:** Student/faculty ratio 19:1. 136 full-time faculty, 63% hold PhDs. 100% faculty teach undergrads.

ACADEMICS

Degrees: Associate's, bachelor's, certificate. **Academic Requirements:** General education including some course work in English (including composition), history, humanities, mathematics, sciences (biological or physical), social science. **Classes:** 20-29 students in an average class. 10-19 students in an average lab/discussion section. **Disciplines with Highest Percentage of Degrees Awarded:** Business/marketing 21%, education 18%, social sciences and history 11%, English 11%, engineering/engineering technology 10%. **Special Study Options:** Accelerated program, cooperative (work-study) program, cross registration, distance learning, double major, independent study, internships, liberal arts/career combination, student-designed major, study abroad, teacher certification program.

FACILITIES

Housing: Coed, apartments for single students, townhouses, lodges, single-sex residence upon request. **Library Holdings:** 145,507 bound volumes. 405 periodicals. 20,718 microforms. 711 audiovisuals. **Special Academic Facilities/Equipment:** Art museum, performing arts center, language lab. **Computers:** School-owned computers available for student use.

EXTRACURRICULARS

Activities: Choral groups, concert band, dance, drama/theater, literary magazine, music ensembles, musical theater, radio station, student government, student newspaper, television station, yearbook. **Organizations:** 59 registered organizations, 11 honor societies, 3 religious organizations, 4 fraternities (6% men join), 4 sororities (6% women join). **Athletics (Intercollegiate):** *Men:* baseball, basketball, soccer, wrestling. *Women:* basketball, cheerleading, cross-country, track & field, volleyball.

ADMISSIONS

Selectivity Rating: 73 (of 100). **Freshman Academic Profile:** Average high school GPA 3.2. 13% in top 10% of high school class, 34% in top 25% of high school class, 73% in top 50% of high school class. Average SAT I Math 506, SAT I Math middle 50% range 470-570. Average SAT I Verbal 510, SAT I Verbal middle 50% range 460-550. Average ACT 21, ACT middle 50% range 19-23. TOEFL required of all international applicants, minimum TOEFL 550. **Basis for Candidate Selection:** *Very important factors considered include:* class rank, secondary school record. *Important factors considered include:* interview, standardized test scores. *Other factors considered include:* character/personal qualities, essays, extracurricular activities, minority status, recommendations, talent/ability, volunteer work, work experience. **Freshman Admission Requirements:** High school diploma or GED is required. *Academic units required/recommended:* 15 total required; 4 English required, 2 math required, 3 math recommended, 2 science required, 1 science lab required, 2 science lab recommended, 2 foreign language required, 4 social studies required. **Freshman Admission Statistics:** 2,721 applied, 84% accepted, 35% of those accepted enrolled. **Transfer Admission Requirements:** *Items required:* high school transcript, college transcript, standardized test scores. Minimum college GPA of 2.0 required. Lowest grade transferable C. **General Admission Information:** Application fee $35. Nonfall registration accepted. Admission may be deferred for a maximum of 1 year. Credit and/or placement offered for CEEB Advanced Placement tests.

COSTS AND FINANCIAL AID

Required Forms and Deadlines: FAFSA. Financial aid filing deadline April 1. Priority filing deadline April 1. **Notification of Awards:** Applicants will be notified of awards on a rolling basis beginning on or about March 15. **Types of Aid:** *Need-based scholarships/grants:* Pell, SEOG, state scholarships/grants, private scholarships, the school's own gift aid. *Loans:* FFEL Subsidized Stafford, FFEL Unsubsidized Stafford, FFEL PLUS, Federal Perkins. **Student Employment:** Federal Work-Study Program available. Institutional employment available. Off-campus job opportunities are excellent. **Financial Aid Statistics:** 77% freshmen, 82% undergrads receive some form of aid. Average freshman grant $3,906. Average freshman loan $3,892. Average income from on-campus job $1,550. **Financial Aid Phone:** 814-269-7045.

UNIVERSITY OF PITTSBURGH—PITTSBURGH

4227 Fifth Avenue, First Floor Alumni Hall, Pittsburgh, PA 15260
Phone: 412-624-7488 **E-mail:** oafa@pitt.edu **CEEB Code:** 2927
Fax: 412-648-8815 **Web:** www.pitt.edu **ACT Code:** 3734

This public school was founded in 1787. It has a 132-acre campus.

STUDENTS AND FACULTY

Enrollment: 17,910. **Student Body:** Male 48%, female 52%, out-of-state 15%, international 1%. **Ethnic Representation:** African American 9%, Asian 4%, Caucasian 83%, Hispanic 1%. **Retention and Graduation:** 88% freshmen return for sophomore year. 43% grads go on to further study within 1 year. 5% grads pursue business degrees. 4% grads pursue law degrees. 4% grads pursue medical degrees. **Faculty:** Student/faculty ratio 17:1. 1,285 full-time faculty, 92% hold PhDs.

ACADEMICS

Degrees: Bachelor's, certificate, doctoral, first professional, master's, post-bachelor's certificate, post-master's certificate. **Academic Requirements:** General education including some course work in arts/fine arts, English (including composition), foreign languages, history, humanities, mathematics, philosophy, sciences (biological or physical), social science. **Classes:** 10-19 students in an average class. 20-29 students in an average lab/discussion section. **Disciplines with Highest Percentage of Degrees Awarded:** Business/marketing 13%, social sciences and history 13%, English 11%, psychology 10%, engineering/engineering technology 9%. **Special Study Options:** Accelerated program, cooperative (work-study) program, cross registration, distance learning, double major, dual enrollment, English as a second language, external degree program, honors program, independent study, internships, liberal arts/

career combination, student-designed major, study abroad, teacher certification program, weekend college.

FACILITIES

Housing: Coed, all-female, apartments for single students, fraternities and/or sororities. **Library Holdings:** 3,807,550 bound volumes. 35,458 periodicals. 3,989,779 microforms. 840,253 audiovisuals. **Special Academic Facilities/ Equipment:** Stephen Foster Memorial, observatory. **Computers:** School-owned computers available for student use.

EXTRACURRICULARS

Activities: Choral groups, concert band, dance, drama/theater, jazz band, literary magazine, marching band, music ensembles, pep band, radio station, student government, student newspaper, student-run film society, symphony orchestra, television station, yearbook. **Organizations:** 250 registered organizations, 23 honor societies, 17 fraternities (10% men join), 11 sororities (7% women join). **Athletics (Intercollegiate):** *Men:* baseball, basketball, cross-country, diving, football, soccer, swimming, track & field, wrestling. *Women:* basketball, cross-country, diving, gymnastics, soccer, softball, swimming, tennis, track & field, volleyball.

ADMISSIONS

Selectivity Rating: 84 (of 100). **Freshman Academic Profile:** 34% in top 10% of high school class, 68% in top 25% of high school class, 97% in top 50% of high school class. Average SAT I Math 607, SAT I Math middle 50% range 540-640. Average SAT I Verbal 595, SAT I Verbal middle 50% range 530-630. Average ACT 26, ACT middle 50% range 23-28. TOEFL required of all international applicants, minimum TOEFL 500. **Basis for Candidate Selection:** *Very important factors considered include:* secondary school record, standardized test scores. *Important factors considered include:* class rank. *Other factors considered include:* essays, extracurricular activities, interview, recommendations, talent/ability, volunteer work, work experience. **Freshman Admission Requirements:** High school diploma or GED is required. *Academic units required/recommended:* 15 total required; 4 English required, 3 math required, 3 science required, 3 science lab required, 3 foreign language recommended, 1 social studies required, 4 elective required. **Freshman Admission Statistics:** 15,438 applied, 60% accepted, 35% of those accepted enrolled. **Transfer Admission Requirements:** *Items required:* high school transcript, college transcript. Lowest grade transferable C. **General Admission Information:** Application fee $35. Priority application deadline March 1. Nonfall registration accepted. Admission may be deferred for a maximum of 1 year. Credit offered for CEEB Advanced Placement tests.

COSTS AND FINANCIAL AID

In-state tuition $7,868. Out-of-state tuition $16,676. Room & board $6,470. Required fees $660. Average book expense $700. **Required Forms and Deadlines:** FAFSA and institution's own financial aid form. No deadline for regular filing. Priority filing deadline March 1. **Notification of Awards:** Applicants will be notified of awards on a rolling basis beginning on or about March 15. **Types of Aid:** *Need-based scholarships/grants:* Pell, SEOG, the school's own gift aid, College Work-Study Program (CWS). *Loans:* FFEL Subsidized Stafford, FFEL Unsubsidized Stafford, FFEL PLUS, Federal Perkins, Federal Nursing, VA, HEAL. **Student Employment:** Federal Work-Study Program available. Institutional employment available. Off-campus job opportunities are excellent. **Financial Aid Statistics:** 56% freshmen, 55% undergrads receive some form of aid. **Financial Aid Phone:** 412-624-7488.

UNIVERSITY OF PORTLAND

5000 North Willamette Blvd., Portland, OR 97203-7147
Phone: 503-943-7147 **E-mail:** admissio@up.edu **CEEB Code:** 4847
Fax: 503-283-7315 **Web:** www.up.edu **ACT Code:** 3500

This private school, which is affiliated with the Roman Catholic Church, was founded in 1901. It has a 130-acre campus.

STUDENTS AND FACULTY

Enrollment: 2,691. **Student Body:** Male 41%, female 59%, out-of-state 55%, international 2% (44 countries represented). **Ethnic Representation:** African American 1%, Asian 10%, Caucasian 82%, Hispanic 3%, Native American 1%. **Retention and Graduation:** 83% freshmen return for sophomore year. 57% freshmen graduate within 4 years. **Faculty:** Student/faculty ratio 13:1. 170 full-time faculty, 93% hold PhDs. 100% faculty teach undergrads.

ACADEMICS

Degrees: Bachelor's, master's, post-master's certificate. **Academic Requirements:** General education including some course work in arts/fine arts, English (including composition), history, mathematics, philosophy, sciences (biological or physical), social science. **Classes:** 20-29 students in an average class. 10-19 students in an average lab/discussion section. **Disciplines with Highest Percentage of Degrees Awarded:** Business/marketing 17%, engineering/ engineering technology 12%, biological life sciences 12%, health professions and related sciences 12%, education 9%. **Special Study Options:** Cross registration, double major, honors program, independent study, internships, liberal arts/career combination, study abroad, teacher certification program.

FACILITIES

Housing: Coed, all-female, all-male, rental houses. **Library Holdings:** 350,000 bound volumes. 1,400 periodicals. 540,073 microforms. 11,044 audiovisuals. **Special Academic Facilities/Equipment:** Art gallery, observatory. **Computers:** School-owned computers available for student use.

EXTRACURRICULARS

Activities: Choral groups, concert band, drama/theater, music ensembles, musical theater, pep band, radio station, student government, student newspaper, student-run film society, yearbook. **Organizations:** 40 registered organizations, 15 honor societies, 9 religious organizations. **Athletics (Intercollegiate):** *Men:* baseball, basketball, cross-country, soccer, tennis, track & field. *Women:* basketball, cross-country, soccer, tennis, track & field, volleyball.

ADMISSIONS

Selectivity Rating: 77 (of 100). **Freshman Academic Profile:** Average high school GPA 3.6. 35% in top 10% of high school class, 67% in top 25% of high school class, 92% in top 50% of high school class. 60% from public high schools. Average SAT I Math 575, SAT I Math middle 50% range 540-640. Average SAT I Verbal 565, SAT I Verbal middle 50% range 520-630. TOEFL required of all international applicants, minimum TOEFL 525. **Basis for Candidate Selection:** *Very important factors considered include:* secondary school record, standardized test scores. *Important factors considered include:* class rank, essays, extracurricular activities, recommendations, talent/ability, volunteer work. *Other factors considered include:* alumni/ae relation, character/personal qualities, geographical residence, interview, minority status, religious affiliation/ commitment, work experience. **Freshman Admission Requirements:** High school diploma or GED is required. *Academic units required/recommended:* 3 English required, 4 English recommended, 2 math required, 3 math recommended, 2 science required, 2 science recommended, 2 social studies required, 2 social studies recommended, 2 history required, 2 history recommended, 7 elective required, 2 elective recommended. **Freshman Admission Statistics:** 2,571 applied, 80% accepted, 36% of those accepted enrolled. **Transfer Admission Requirements:** *Items required:* college transcript, essay. Minimum high school GPA of 3.0 required. Minimum college GPA of 2.5 required. Lowest grade transferable C. **General Admission Information:** Application fee $45. Priority application deadline February 1. Regular application deadline June 1. Nonfall registration accepted. Admission may be deferred for a maximum of 1 year. Credit and/or placement offered for CEEB Advanced Placement tests.

COSTS AND FINANCIAL AID

Tuition $18,930. Room & board $5,872. Required fees $720. Average book expense $300. **Required Forms and Deadlines:** FAFSA and institution's own financial aid form. Priority filing deadline March 1. **Notification of Awards:** Applicants will be notified of awards on or about April 1. **Types of Aid:** *Need-based scholarships/grants:* Pell, SEOG, state scholarships/grants, private scholarships, the school's own gift aid. *Loans:* FFEL Subsidized Stafford, FFEL Unsubsidized Stafford, FFEL PLUS, Federal Perkins, Federal Nursing, college/university loans from institutional funds. **Student Employment:** Federal Work-Study Program available. Institutional employment available. Off-campus job opportunities are good. **Financial Aid Statistics:** 62% freshmen, 58% undergrads receive some form of aid. Average freshman grant $10,397. Average freshman loan $3,070. Average income from on-campus job $1,300. **Financial Aid Phone:** 503-943-7311.

UNIVERSITY OF PRINCE EDWARD ISLAND

Office of the Registrar, Charlottetown, PE C1A 4P3
Phone: 902-566-0439 **E-mail:** registrar@upei.ca
Fax: 902-566-0795 **Web:** www.upei.ca

This public school was founded in 1969. It has a 130-acre campus.

STUDENTS AND FACULTY

Enrollment: 2,870. **Student Body:** Male 36%, female 64%, out-of-state 20%. **Faculty:** Student/faculty ratio 13:1.

ACADEMICS

Degrees: Bachelor's, certificate, diploma, doctoral, first professional, master's. **Academic Requirements:** General education including some course work in English (including composition). **Majors with Highest Enrollment:** Biology/biological sciences, general; business administration/management; psychology, general. **Special Study Options:** Cooperative (work-study) program, double major, English as a second language, student exchange program (domestic), honors program, teacher certification program.

FACILITIES

Housing: Coed, all-female, all-male, apartments for single students. **Computers:** *Recommended operating system:* Windows 95.

EXTRACURRICULARS

Activities: Choral groups, concert band, drama/theater, music ensembles, radio station, student government, student newspaper, yearbook. **Organizations:** 25 registered organizations, 3 religious organizations. **Athletics (Intercollegiate):** *Men:* basketball, ice hockey, soccer. *Women:* basketball, field hockey, rugby, soccer, volleyball.

ADMISSIONS

Selectivity Rating: 60 (of 100). **Freshman Academic Profile:** Average high school GPA 3.3. 90% from public high schools. TOEFL required of all international applicants, minimum TOEFL 550. **Basis for Candidate Selection:** *Very important factors considered include:* secondary school record. *Important factors considered include:* class rank, recommendations. **Freshman Admission Requirements: Transfer Admission Requirements:** *Items required:* college transcript. **General Admission Information:** Application fee $23. Regular application deadline July 1. Nonfall registration accepted. Neither credit nor placement offered for CEEB Advanced Placement tests.

COSTS AND FINANCIAL AID

Room & board $3,900. Required fees $160. Average book expense $500. **Types of Aid:** *Need-based scholarships/grants:* Pell, SEOG, state scholarships/grants, private scholarships, the school's own gift aid. *Loans:* FFEL Subsidized Stafford, FFEL Unsubsidized Stafford, FFEL PLUS, Federal Perkins, college/university loans from institutional funds.

UNIVERSITY OF PUGET SOUND

Best 351

1500 North Warner, Tacoma, WA 98416
Phone: 253-879-3211 **E-mail:** admission@ups.edu **CEEB Code:** 4067
Fax: 253-879-3993 **Web:** www.ups.edu **ACT Code:** 4450

This private school was founded in 1888. It has a 97-acre campus.

STUDENTS AND FACULTY

Enrollment: 2,604. **Student Body:** Male 40%, female 60%, out-of-state 69%, international 1% (20 countries represented). **Ethnic Representation:** African American 2%, Asian 10%, Caucasian 78%, Hispanic 3%, Native American 1%. **Retention and Graduation:** 88% freshmen return for sophomore year. 62% freshmen graduate within 4 years. 31% grads go on to further study within 1 year. 2% grads pursue business degrees. 2% grads pursue law degrees. 2% grads pursue medical degrees. **Faculty:** Student/faculty ratio 11:1. 218 full-time faculty, 84% hold PhDs. 97% faculty teach undergrads.

ACADEMICS

Degrees: Bachelor's, first professional, master's, post-master's certificate. **Academic Requirements:** General education including some course work in arts/fine arts, English (including composition), history, humanities, mathematics, sciences (biological or physical), social science, science in context. **Classes:** 10-19 students in an average class. 10-19 students in an average lab/discussion section. **Majors with Highest Enrollment:** Business administration/management; English language and literature, general; psychology, general. **Disciplines with Highest Percentage of Degrees Awarded:** Social sciences and history 20%, business/marketing 18%, English 11%, psychology 10%, visual and performing arts 7%. **Special Study Options:** Cooperative (work-study) program, double major, honors program, independent study, internships, student-designed major, study abroad, teacher certification program.

FACILITIES

Housing: Coed, all-female, housing for disabled students, fraternities and/or sororities, small residential houses, theme floors in halls. **Library Holdings:** 343,787 bound volumes. 5,609 periodicals. 350,276 microforms. 17,328 audiovisuals. **Special Academic Facilities/Equipment:** Art gallery, natural history museum, transmission and scanning electron microscope, spectrophotometer, exercise science lab, observatory, paleomagnetic & X-ray lab, physiology labs, Spectrometer Gas Chromatography Mass Spectral Detector (GCMS), DNA sequencer. **Computers:** School-owned computers available for student use.

EXTRACURRICULARS

Activities: Choral groups, concert band, dance, drama/theater, jazz band, literary magazine, music ensembles, musical theater, opera, radio station, student government, student newspaper, student-run film society, symphony orchestra, yearbook. **Organizations:** 40 registered organizations, 14 honor societies, 10 religious organizations, 4 fraternities (20% men join), 5 sororities (29% women join). **Athletics (Intercollegiate):** *Men:* baseball, basketball, crew, cross-country, football, golf, skiing (alpine), soccer, swimming, tennis, track & field. *Women:* basketball, crew, cross-country, golf, lacrosse, skiing (alpine), soccer, softball, swimming, tennis, track & field, volleyball.

ADMISSIONS

Selectivity Rating: 86 (of 100). **Freshman Academic Profile:** Average high school GPA 3.6. 43% in top 10% of high school class, 75% in top 25% of high school class, 94% in top 50% of high school class. 77% from public high schools. Average SAT I Math 622, SAT I Math middle 50% range 580-670. Average SAT I Verbal 631, SAT I Verbal middle 50% range 580-685. Average ACT 27, ACT middle 50% range 25-29. TOEFL required of all international applicants, minimum TOEFL 550. **Basis for Candidate Selection:** *Very important factors considered include:* secondary school record, standardized test scores. *Important factors considered include:* alumni/ae relation, character/personal qualities, essays, extracurricular activities, minority status, recommendations, talent/ability. *Other factors considered include:* class rank, interview, volunteer work, work experience. **Freshman Admission Requirements:** High school diploma or GED is required. *Academic units required/recommended:* 19 total recommended; 4 English recommended, 4 math recommended, 4 science recommended, 4 science lab recommended, 3 foreign language recommended, 3 social studies recommended, 3 history recommended. **Freshman Admission Statistics:** 4,154 applied, 72% accepted, 22% of those accepted enrolled. **Transfer Admission Requirements:** *Items required:* college transcript, essay, statement of good standing from prior school. Minimum college GPA of 2.0 required. Lowest grade transferable D. **General Admission Information:** Application fee $40. Priority application deadline February 1. Early decision application deadline November 15. Regular application deadline May 1. Nonfall registration accepted. Admission may be deferred for a maximum of 1 year. Credit and/or placement offered for CEEB Advanced Placement tests.

COSTS AND FINANCIAL AID

Tuition $25,190. Room & board $6,400. Required fees $170. Average book expense $1,000. **Required Forms and Deadlines:** FAFSA. Financial aid filing deadline February 1. Priority filing deadline February 1. **Notification of Awards:** Applicants will be notified of awards on a rolling basis beginning on or about March 15. **Types of Aid:** *Need-based scholarships/grants:* Pell, SEOG, state scholarships/grants, private scholarships, the school's own gift aid. *Loans:* FFEL Subsidized Stafford, FFEL Unsubsidized Stafford, FFEL PLUS, Federal Perkins, state loans, private education loans. **Student Employment:** Federal Work-Study Program available. Institutional employment available. Off-campus job opportunities are excellent. **Financial Aid Statistics:** 59% freshmen, 57% undergrads receive some form of aid. Average freshman grant $10,448. Average freshman loan $5,981. Average income from on-campus job $2,500. **Financial Aid Phone:** 253-879-3214.

UNIVERSITY OF REDLANDS

PO Box 3080, Redlands, CA 92373-0999
Phone: 909-335-4074 **E-mail:** admissions@redlands.edu **CEEB Code:** 4848
Fax: 909-335-4089 **Web:** www.redlands.edu **ACT Code:** 464

This private school was founded in 1907. It has a 140-acre campus.

STUDENTS AND FACULTY

Enrollment: 2,088. **Student Body:** Male 40%, female 60%, out-of-state 26%, international 2% (10 countries represented). **Ethnic Representation:** African American 3%, Asian 5%, Caucasian 62%, Hispanic 12%, Native American 1%. **Retention and Graduation:** 80% freshmen return for sophomore year. **Faculty:** Student/faculty ratio 13:1. 144 full-time faculty, 84% hold PhDs. 100% faculty teach undergrads.

ACADEMICS

Degrees: Bachelor's, master's, post-bachelor's certificate, post-master's certificate. **Academic Requirements:** General education including some course work in arts/fine arts, computer literacy, English (including composition), foreign languages, history, humanities, mathematics, philosophy, sciences (biological or physical), social science. **Classes:** 10-19 students in an average class. **Majors with Highest Enrollment:** Business administration/management; liberal arts and sciences, general studies and humanities; sociology. **Disciplines with Highest Percentage of Degrees Awarded:** Liberal arts/general studies 29%, social sciences and history 17%, business/marketing 15%, English 9%, psychology 7%. **Special Study Options:** Cross registration, double major, student exchange program (domestic), honors program, independent study, internships, liberal arts/career combination, student-designed major, study abroad, teacher certification program.

FACILITIES

Housing: Coed, all-female, all-male, apartments for married students, apartments for single students, housing for disabled students, fraternities and/or sororities, abroad programming, apartments for students with dependent children. **Library Holdings:** 251,053 bound volumes. 7,786 periodicals. 307,788 microforms. 9,151 audiovisuals. **Special Academic Facilities/Equipment:** Art gallery, Far East art collection, Southwest collection, center for communicative disorders, language lab, Helen and Vernon Farquar Anthropology Lab, physics laser photonics lab, Irvine Map Library, geographic information system lab. **Computers:** School-owned computers available for student use.

EXTRACURRICULARS

Activities: Choral groups, concert band, dance, drama/theater, jazz band, literary magazine, music ensembles, musical theater, opera, student government, student newspaper, symphony orchestra, yearbook. **Organizations:** 100 registered organizations, 11 honor societies, 7 religious organizations, 7 fraternities (22% men join), 5 sororities (51% women join). **Athletics (Intercollegiate):** *Men:* baseball, basketball, cross-country, diving, football, golf, soccer, swimming, tennis, track & field, water polo. *Women:* basketball, cross-country, diving, lacrosse, soccer, softball, swimming, tennis, track & field, volleyball, water polo.

ADMISSIONS

Selectivity Rating: 74 (of 100). **Freshman Academic Profile:** Average high school GPA 3.5. 33% in top 10% of high school class, 69% in top 25% of high school class, 93% in top 50% of high school class. Average SAT I Math 574, SAT I Math middle 50% range 520-630. Average SAT I Verbal 565, SAT I Verbal middle 50% range 520-610. Average ACT 24, ACT middle 50% range 21-26. TOEFL required of all international applicants, minimum TOEFL 550. **Basis for Candidate Selection:** *Very important factors considered include:* essays, recommendations, secondary school record. *Important factors considered include:* character/personal qualities, standardized test scores. *Other factors considered include:* alumni/ae relation, extracurricular activities, geographical residence, interview, minority status, talent/ability, volunteer work, work experience. **Freshman Admission Requirements:** High school diploma or GED is required. *Academic units required/recommended:* 13 total required; 16 total recommended; 4 English required, 3 math required, 2 science required, 3 science recommended, 2 science lab required, 3 science lab recommended, 2 foreign language required, 3 foreign language recommended, 2 social studies required, 3 social studies recommended, 2 history recommended. **Freshman Admission Statistics:** 2,499 applied, 76% accepted, 32% of those accepted enrolled. **Transfer Admission Requirements:** *Items required:* high school transcript, college transcript, essay, statement of good standing from prior school. Minimum college GPA of 2.5 required. Lowest grade transferable C. **General Admission Information:** Application fee $40. Priority application deadline February 1. Regular application deadline December 15. Nonfall registration accepted. Admission may be deferred for a maximum of 1 year. Credit and/or placement offered for CEEB Advanced Placement tests.

COSTS AND FINANCIAL AID

Tuition $22,450. Room & board $8,114. Required fees $300. Average book expense $850. **Required Forms and Deadlines:** FAFSA and GPA Verification form for California Residents. Priority filing deadline March 2. **Notification of Awards:** Applicants will be notified of awards on a rolling basis beginning on or about February 28. **Types of Aid:** *Need-based scholarships/grants:* Pell, SEOG, state scholarships/grants, private scholarships, the school's own gift aid. *Loans:* FFEL Subsidized Stafford, FFEL Unsubsidized Stafford, FFEL PLUS, Federal Perkins, college/university loans from institutional funds, alternative loans. **Student Employment:** Federal Work-Study Program available. Institutional employment available. Off-campus job opportunities are good. **Financial Aid Statistics:** 68% freshmen, 71% undergrads receive some form of aid. Average freshman grant $11,887. Average freshman loan $3,860. Average income from on-campus job $1,250. **Financial Aid Phone:** 909-335-4047.

UNIVERSITY OF REGINA

3737 Wascana Parkway, Regina, SK S4S 0A2
Phone: 306-585-4591 **E-mail:** admissions.office@uregina.ca
Fax: 306-585-5203 **Web:** www.uregina.ca

This public school was founded in 1974.

STUDENTS AND FACULTY

Enrollment: 10,918. **Student Body:** Male 41%, female 59%, international 3% (44 countries represented). **Faculty:** Student/faculty ratio 26:1.

ACADEMICS

Degrees: Bachelor's, certificate, diploma, doctoral, master's. **Academic Requirements:** General education including some course work in English (including composition), humanities, social science. **Majors with Highest Enrollment:** Elementary education and teaching; computer science; business administration/management. **Special Study Options:** Cooperative (work-study) program, double major, English as a second language, student exchange program (domestic), honors program, independent study, internships, liberal arts/career combination, study abroad, teacher certification program, weekend college.

FACILITIES

Housing: Coed. **Library Holdings:** 2,400,000 bound volumes. **Special Academic Facilities/Equipment:** Student-run art gallery.

EXTRACURRICULARS

Activities: Choral groups, concert band, dance, drama/theater, jazz band, literary magazine, music ensembles, student government, student newspaper, student-run film society. **Organizations:** 70 registered organizations. **Athletics (Intercollegiate):** *Men:* basketball, cross-country, football, ice hockey, swimming, track & field, volleyball, wrestling. *Women:* basketball, cross-country, ice hockey, soccer, swimming, track & field, volleyball, wrestling.

ADMISSIONS

Selectivity Rating: 60 (of 100). **Freshman Academic Profile:** TOEFL required of all international applicants, minimum TOEFL 550. **Basis for Candidate Selection:** *Very important factors considered include:* secondary school record. *Other factors considered include:* essays, standardized test scores. **Freshman Admission Requirements:** High school diploma or GED is required. *Academic units required/recommended:* 2 English required, 2 English recommended, 2 math recommended, 2 science recommended, 1 social studies recommended. **Transfer Admission Requirements:** *Items required:* high school transcript, college transcript, statement of good standing from prior school. **General Admission Information:** Application fee $60. Regular application deadline July 1. Nonfall registration accepted.

COSTS AND FINANCIAL AID

In-state tuition $3,030. Out-of-state tuition $3,030. Room & board $5,000. Required fees $300. Average book expense $1,500. **Financial Aid Phone:** 306-585-4325.

UNIVERSITY OF RHODE ISLAND

Undergraduate Admissions Office, 14 Upper College Road, Kingston, RI 02881-2020
Phone: 401-874-7000 **E-mail:** uriadmit@etal.uri.edu **CEEB Code:** 3919
Fax: 401-874-5523 **Web:** www.uri.edu **ACT Code:** 3818

This public school was founded in 1892. It has a 1,250-acre campus.

STUDENTS AND FACULTY

Enrollment: 10,784. **Student Body:** Male 44%, female 56%, out-of-state 38%. **Ethnic Representation:** African American 4%, Asian 3%, Caucasian 77%, Hispanic 4%. **Retention and Graduation:** 80% freshmen return for sophomore year. 33% freshmen graduate within 4 years. **Faculty:** Student/faculty ratio 18:1. 671 full-time faculty, 91% hold PhDs. 83% faculty teach undergrads.

ACADEMICS

Degrees: Bachelor's, doctoral, first professional, master's, post-bachelor's certificate. **Academic Requirements:** General education including some course work in arts/fine arts, English (including composition), foreign languages, humanities, mathematics, sciences (biological or physical), social science, history or philosophy. **Classes:** 20-29 students in an average class. 10-19 students in an average lab/discussion section. **Majors with Highest Enrollment:** Pharmacy (PharmD, BS/BPharm); communications studies/speech communication and rhetoric; psychology, general. **Disciplines with Highest Percentage of Degrees Awarded:** Business/marketing 17%, personal and miscellaneous services 11%, health professions and related sciences 11%, communications/communication technologies 10%, education 8%. **Special Study Options:** Accelerated program, cooperative (work-study) program, cross registration, distance learning, double major, dual enrollment, student exchange program (domestic), honors program, independent study, internships, liberal arts/career combination, student-designed major, study abroad, teacher certification program.

FACILITIES

Housing: Coed, apartments for married students, apartments for single students, fraternities and/or sororities, three women's floors. **Library Holdings:** 836,056 bound volumes. 9,361 periodicals. 1,622,726 microforms. 10,457 audiovisuals. **Special Academic Facilities/Equipment:** Center for robotic research, animal science farm, planetarium, Watson House Museum, Narragansett Bay Campus for Marine Sciences, American Historic Textiles Museum, aquaculture center, fisheries and marine technology laboratory, biotechnology center, human performance laboratory. **Computers:** School-owned computers available for student use.

EXTRACURRICULARS

Activities: Choral groups, concert band, dance, drama/theater, jazz band, literary magazine, marching band, music ensembles, musical theater, opera, pep band, radio station, student government, student newspaper, yearbook. **Organizations:** 100 registered organizations, 40 honor societies, 9 fraternities (7% men join), 11 sororities (11% women join). **Athletics (Intercollegiate):** *Men:* baseball, basketball, cross-country, diving, football, golf, indoor track, soccer, swimming, tennis, track & field. *Women:* basketball, crew, cross-country, diving, equestrian, field hockey, gymnastics, indoor track, soccer, softball, swimming, tennis, track & field, volleyball.

ADMISSIONS

Selectivity Rating: 72 (of 100). **Freshman Academic Profile:** Average high school GPA 3.4. 16% in top 10% of high school class, 59% in top 25% of high school class, 89% in top 50% of high school class. 92% from public high schools. Average SAT I Math 562, SAT I Math middle 50% range 500-610. Average SAT I Verbal 549, SAT I Verbal middle 50% range 490-590. TOEFL required of all international applicants, minimum TOEFL 550. **Basis for Candidate Selection:** *Very important factors considered include:* secondary school record. *Important factors considered include:* character/personal qualities, class rank, geographical residence, minority status, standardized test scores, state residency, talent/ability. *Other factors considered include:* alumni/ae relation, essays, extracurricular activities, interview, recommendations, volunteer work, work experience. **Freshman Admission Requirements:** High school diploma or GED is required. *Academic units required/recommended:* 18 total required; 18 total recommended; 4 English required, 4 English recommended, 3 math required, 4 math recommended, 2 science required, 3 science recommended, 2 science lab required, 2 science lab recommended, 2 foreign language required, 3 foreign language recommended, 2 social studies required, 3 social studies recommended, 5 elective required, 5 elective recommended. **Freshman Admission Statistics:** 11,072 applied, 69% accepted, 31% of those accepted enrolled. **Transfer Admission Requirements:** *Items required:* high school transcript, college transcript, statement of good standing from prior school. Minimum college GPA of 2.4 required. Lowest grade transferable C. **General Admission Information:** Application fee $45. Priority application deadline December 15. Regular application deadline March 1. Nonfall registration accepted. Credit and/or placement offered for CEEB Advanced Placement tests.

COSTS AND FINANCIAL AID

In-state tuition $3,864. Out-of-state tuition $13,334. Room & board $7,402. Required fees $1,990. Average book expense $800. **Required Forms and Deadlines:** FAFSA. No deadline for regular filing. Priority filing deadline March 1. **Notification of Awards:** Applicants will be notified of awards on a rolling basis beginning on or about March 15. **Types of Aid:** *Need-based scholarships/grants:* Pell, SEOG, state scholarships/grants, private scholarships, the school's own gift aid. *Loans:* Direct Subsidized Stafford, Direct Unsubsidized Stafford, Direct PLUS, Federal Perkins, Federal Nursing, college/university loans from institutional funds, Health professions loan. **Student Employment:** Federal Work-Study Program available. Institutional employment available. Off-campus job opportunities are excellent. **Financial Aid Statistics:** 74% freshmen, 72% undergrads receive some form of aid. Average income from on-campus job $1,500. **Financial Aid Phone:** 401-874-2314.

UNIVERSITY OF RICHMOND

 $$$   

28 Westhampton Way, Richmond, VA 23173
Phone: 804-289-8640 **E-mail:** admissions@richmond.edu **CEEB Code:** 5569
Fax: 804-287-6003 **Web:** www.richmond.edu **ACT Code:** 4410

This private school was founded in 1830. It has a 350-acre campus.

STUDENTS AND FACULTY

Enrollment: 2,998. **Student Body:** Male 47%, female 53%, out-of-state 84%, international 4% (70 countries represented). **Ethnic Representation:** African American 5%, Asian 4%, Caucasian 89%, Hispanic 2%. **Retention and Graduation:** 93% freshmen return for sophomore year. 79% freshmen graduate within 4 years. 25% grads go on to further study within 1 year. 1% grads pursue business degrees. 5% grads pursue law degrees. 4% grads pursue medical degrees. **Faculty:** Student/faculty ratio 10:1. 274 full-time faculty, 87% hold PhDs. 100% faculty teach undergrads.

ACADEMICS

Degrees: Associate's, bachelor's, certificate, diploma, first professional, master's, post-bachelor's certificate. **Academic Requirements:** General education including some course work in arts/fine arts, English (including composition), foreign languages, history, humanities, mathematics, philosophy, sciences (biological or physical), social science, core class. **Classes:** 20-29 students in an average class. **Majors with Highest Enrollment:** Business administration/management; biology/biological sciences, general; political science and government, general. **Disciplines with Highest Percentage of Degrees Awarded:** Business/marketing 31%, social sciences and history 20%, English 8%, biological life sciences 6%, psychology 6%. **Special Study Options:** Accelerated program, cross registration, double major, English as a second language, student exchange program (domestic), honors program, independent study, internships, student-designed major, study abroad, teacher certification program.

FACILITIES

Housing: All-female, all-male, apartments for single students, housing for international students. **Library Holdings:** 1,049,365 bound volumes. 703,111 periodicals. 82,324 microforms. 15,892 audiovisuals. **Special Academic Facilities/Equipment:** Art gallery, mineral museum, Virginia Baptist Archives, language lab, neuroscience lab, speech center, music technology lab, Jepson School of Leadership. **Computers:** School-owned computers available for student use.

EXTRACURRICULARS

Activities: Choral groups, concert band, dance, drama/theater, jazz band, literary magazine, music ensembles, musical theater, pep band, radio station, student government, student newspaper, symphony orchestra, television station, yearbook. **Organizations:** 225 registered organizations, 22 honor societies, 16 religious organizations, 8 fraternities (32% men join), 8 sororities (49% women join). **Athletics (Intercollegiate):** *Men:* baseball, basketball, cheerleading, cross-country, football, golf, indoor track, soccer, tennis, track & field. *Women:* basketball, cheerleading, cross-country, diving, field hockey, golf, indoor track, lacrosse, soccer, swimming, tennis, track & field.

ADMISSIONS

Selectivity Rating: 91 (of 100). **Freshman Academic Profile:** 55% in top 10% of high school class, 95% in top 25% of high school class, 99% in top 50% of high school class. 70% from public high schools. SAT I Math middle 50% range 620-700. SAT I Verbal middle 50% range 600-690. ACT middle 50% range 27-30. TOEFL required of all international applicants, minimum TOEFL 550. **Basis for Candidate Selection:** *Very important factors considered include:* secondary school record. *Important factors considered include:* character/personal qualities, class rank, essays, standardized test scores, talent/ability. *Other factors considered include:* alumni/ae relation, extracurricular activities, geographical residence, minority status, recommendations, state residency, volunteer work, work experience. **Freshman Admission Requirements:** High school diploma or GED is required. *Academic units required/recommended:* 16 total required; 20 total recommended; 4 English required, 4 English recommended, 3 math required, 4 math recommended, 2 science required, 4 science recommended, 2 science lab required, 4 science lab recommended, 2 foreign language required, 4 foreign language recommended, 2 history required, 4 history recommended. **Freshman Admission Statistics:** 5,895 applied, 41% accepted, 33% of those accepted enrolled. **Transfer Admission Requirements:** *Items required:* high school transcript, college transcript, essay, statement of good standing from prior school. Minimum college GPA of 2.0 required. Lowest grade transferable C. **General Admission Information:** Application fee $40. Early decision application deadline November 15. Regular application deadline January 15. Admission may be deferred for a maximum of 1 year. Credit and/or placement offered for CEEB Advanced Placement tests.

COSTS AND FINANCIAL AID

Tuition $23,730. Room & board $5,160. Required fees $0. Average book expense $1,000. **Required Forms and Deadlines:** FAFSA and institution's own financial aid form. Financial aid filing deadline February 25. **Notification of Awards:** Applicants will be notified of awards on or about April 1. **Types of Aid:** *Need-based scholarships/grants:* Pell, SEOG, state scholarships/grants, private scholarships, the school's own gift aid. *Loans:* Direct Subsidized Stafford, Direct Unsubsidized Stafford, Direct PLUS, Federal Perkins. **Student Employment:** Federal Work-Study Program available. Institutional employment available. Off-campus job opportunities are good. **Financial Aid Statistics:** 34% freshmen, 30% undergrads receive some form of aid. Average income from on-campus job $1,300. **Financial Aid Phone:** 804-289-8438.

UNIVERSITY OF RIO GRANDE

218 North College Avenue, Admissions, Rio Grande, OH 45774
Phone: 740-245-7206 **E-mail:** mabell@urgrgcc.edu **CEEB Code:** 1663
Fax: 740-245-7260 **Web:** www.urgrgcc.edu or www.rio.edu **ACT Code:** 3324

This private school was founded in 1876. It has a 68-acre campus.

STUDENTS AND FACULTY

Enrollment: 1,897. **Student Body:** Male 41%, female 59%, out-of-state 5%, international 2%. **Ethnic Representation:** African American 1%, Caucasian 75%. **Retention and Graduation:** 65% freshmen return for sophomore year. **Faculty:** Student/faculty ratio 16:1. 81 full-time faculty, 44% hold PhDs. 100% faculty teach undergrads.

ACADEMICS

Degrees: Associate's, bachelor's, certificate, master's. **Academic Requirements:** General education including some course work in arts/fine arts, English (including composition), history, humanities, mathematics, philosophy, sciences (biological or physical), social science, communications. Computer literacy pending, along with other changes in the general education requirements, effective fall 2000. **Classes:** Under 10 students in an average class. Under 10 students in an average lab/discussion section. **Special Study Options:** Accelerated program, cooperative (work-study) program, distance learning, double major, dual enrollment, English as a second language, honors program, independent study, internships, liberal arts/career combination, student-designed major, study abroad, teacher certification program.

FACILITIES

Housing: Coed, all-female, all-male. **Library Holdings:** 59,368 bound volumes. 1,043 periodicals. 334,870 microforms. 1,938 audiovisuals. **Special Academic Facilities/Equipment:** Archives of local and college history, art museum, fine woodworking, theater, art annex. **Computers:** *Recommended operating system:* Windows, any version. School-owned computers available for student use.

EXTRACURRICULARS

Activities: Choral groups, concert band, drama/theater, jazz band, literary magazine, music ensembles, musical theater, pep band, radio station, student government, student newspaper, television station, yearbook. **Organizations:** 34 registered organizations, 4 honor societies, 3 religious organizations, 4 fraternities (25% men join), 5 sororities (25% women join). **Athletics (Intercollegiate):** *Men:* baseball, basketball, cross-country, indoor track, soccer, track & field. *Women:* basketball, cheerleading, cross-country, indoor track, softball, track & field, volleyball.

ADMISSIONS

Selectivity Rating: 69 (of 100). **Freshman Academic Profile:** Average high school GPA 2.8. 15% in top 10% of high school class, 35% in top 25% of high school class, 90% in top 50% of high school class. 95% from public high schools. Average ACT 19, ACT middle 50% range 16-30. TOEFL required of all international applicants, minimum TOEFL 500. **Freshman Admission Requirements:** High school diploma is required and GED is not accepted. *Academic units required/recommended:* 4 English required, 2 math required, 2 science required. **Transfer Admission Requirements:** *Items required:* high school transcript, college transcript, statement of good standing from prior school. Lowest grade transferable C. **General Admission Information:** Nonfall registration accepted. Credit and/or placement offered for CEEB Advanced Placement tests.

COSTS AND FINANCIAL AID

Tuition $8,976. Room & board $5,442. Required fees $367. Average book expense $900. **Required Forms and Deadlines:** FAFSA, institution's own financial aid form and state aid form. No deadline for regular filing. **Notification of Awards:** Applicants will be notified of awards on a rolling basis beginning on or about February 15. **Types of Aid:** *Need-based scholarships/grants:* Pell, state scholarships/grants, private scholarships, the school's own gift aid. *Loans:* Direct Subsidized Stafford, Direct Unsubsidized Stafford, Direct PLUS, FFEL Subsidized Stafford, FFEL PLUS, Federal Perkins, Federal Nursing, college/university loans from institutional funds. **Student Employment:** Federal Work-Study Program available. Institutional employment available. Off-campus job opportunities are fair. **Financial Aid Statistics:** 85% freshmen, 85% undergrads receive some form of aid. **Financial Aid Phone:** 614-245-7218.

UNIVERSITY OF ROCHESTER

Box 270251, Rochester, NY 14627-0251
Phone: 585-275-3221 **E-mail:** admit@admissions.rochester.edu **CEEB Code:** 2928
Fax: 585-461-4595 **Web:** www.rochester.edu **ACT Code:** 2980

This private school was founded in 1850. It has a 90-acre campus.

STUDENTS AND FACULTY

Enrollment: 4,665. **Student Body:** Male 54%, female 46%, out-of-state 50%, international 4%. **Ethnic Representation:** African American 5%, Asian 13%, Caucasian 66%, Hispanic 4%. **Retention and Graduation:** 95% freshmen return for sophomore year. 62% freshmen graduate within 4 years. 60% grads go on to further study within 1 year. 2% grads pursue business degrees. 10% grads pursue law degrees. 9% grads pursue medical degrees. **Faculty:** Student/faculty ratio 8:1. 499 full-time faculty, 89% hold PhDs.

ACADEMICS

Degrees: Bachelor's, certificate, doctoral, first professional, master's, post-bachelor's certificate, post-master's certificate. **Academic Requirements:** General education including some course work in humanities, sciences (biological or physical), social science. **Classes:** 10-19 students in an average class. **Disciplines with Highest Percentage of Degrees Awarded:** Other 13%, psychology 12%, biological life sciences 11%, visual and performing arts 10%, law/legal studies 10%. **Special Study Options:** Cross registration, double major, dual enrollment, English as a second language, honors program, independent study, internships, liberal arts/career combination, student-designed major, study abroad, teacher certification program, "Take 5" 5th year tuition free to supplement regular requirements, Washington semester program and Rochester Curriculum (clusters), Quest (1st year courses emphasizing how to learn).

FACILITIES

Housing: Coed, all-female, all-male, apartments for married students, apartments for single students, housing for disabled students, housing for international students, fraternities and/or sororities, freshman housing, special-interest themes, community learning center. **Library Holdings:** 1,479,605 bound volumes. 11,432 periodicals. 4,145,264 microforms. 71,100 audiovisuals. **Special Academic Facilities/Equipment:** Art center and gallery, African and African-American studies institute, center for women's studies, visual science and space science centers, institute of optics, observatory, laser energetics and nuclear structure research labs, electron microscopes, Judaic studies center, political economy institute, sign language research center, biomedical ultrasound center, Polish and Central European studies center, electronic imaging systems center, center for future health. **Computers:** School-owned computers available for student use.

EXTRACURRICULARS

Activities: Choral groups, concert band, dance, drama/theater, jazz band, literary magazine, music ensembles, musical theater, opera, pep band, radio station, student government, student newspaper, student-run film society, symphony orchestra, yearbook. **Organizations:** 170 registered organizations, 6 honor societies, 14 religious organizations, 17 fraternities (26% men join), 11 sororities (19% women join). **Athletics (Intercollegiate):** *Men:* baseball, basketball, cross-country, diving, football, golf, indoor track, soccer, swimming, tennis, track & field. *Women:* basketball, cross-country, diving, field hockey, golf, indoor track, lacrosse, soccer, softball, swimming, tennis, track & field, volleyball.

ADMISSIONS

Selectivity Rating: 88 (of 100). **Freshman Academic Profile:** 60% in top 10% of high school class, 88% in top 25% of high school class, 99% in top 50% of high school class. Average SAT I Math 687, SAT I Math middle 50% range 620-710. Average SAT I Verbal 665, SAT I Verbal middle 50% range 600-700. Average ACT 30, ACT middle 50% range 27-32. TOEFL required of all international applicants, minimum TOEFL 550. **Basis for Candidate Selection:** *Very important factors considered include:* secondary school record, standardized test scores. *Important factors considered include:* character/personal qualities, class rank, essays, recommendations, talent/ability. *Other factors considered include:* alumni/ae relation, extracurricular activities, minority status, volunteer work, work experience. **Freshman Admission Requirements:** High school diploma or GED is required. *Academic units required/recommended:* 4 total recommended; 4 English recommended, 4 math recommended, 3 science recommended, 4 science lab recommended, 2 foreign language recommended, 2 social studies recommended. **Freshman Admission Statistics:** 10,930 applied, 49% accepted, 21% of those accepted enrolled. **Transfer Admission Requirements:** *Items required:* high school transcript, college transcript, essay, standardized test scores. Minimum college GPA of 3.0 required. Lowest grade transferable C. **General Admission Information:** Application fee $50. Early decision application deadline November 15. Regular application deadline January 20. Nonfall registration accepted. Admission may be deferred for a maximum of 1 year. Credit and/or placement offered for CEEB Advanced Placement tests.

COSTS AND FINANCIAL AID

Tuition $24,150. Room & board $8,185. Required fees $644. Average book expense $575. **Required Forms and Deadlines:** FAFSA, CSS/Financial Aid PROFILE, state aid form and noncustodial (divorced/separated) parent's statement. Financial aid filing deadline February 1. Priority filing deadline February 1. **Notification of Awards:** Applicants will be notified of awards on or about April 1. **Types of Aid:** *Need-based scholarships/grants:* Pell, SEOG, state scholarships/grants, private scholarships, the school's own gift aid. **Student Employment:** Federal Work-Study Program available. Institutional employment available. Off-campus job opportunities are excellent. **Financial Aid Statistics:** 55% freshmen, 59% undergrads receive some form of aid. **Financial Aid Phone:** 716-275-3226.

See page 1260.

UNIVERSITY OF ST. FRANCIS (IL)

500 Wilcox Street, Joliet, IL 60435
Phone: 800-735-7500 **E-mail:** admissions@stfrancis.edu **CEEB Code:** 1130
Fax: 815-740-5032 **Web:** www.stfrancis.edu **ACT Code:** 1000

This private school, which is affiliated with the Roman Catholic Church, was founded in 1920. It has a 17-acre campus.

STUDENTS AND FACULTY

Enrollment: 1,362. **Student Body:** Male 32%, female 68%, out-of-state 3%. **Ethnic Representation:** African American 9%, Asian 2%, Caucasian 76%, Hispanic 7%. **Retention and Graduation:** 80% freshmen return for sophomore year. 6% grads go on to further study within 1 year. 2% grads pursue law degrees. 1% grads pursue medical degrees. **Faculty:** Student/faculty ratio 10:1. 74 full-time faculty, 55% hold PhDs. 100% faculty teach undergrads.

ACADEMICS

Degrees: Bachelor's, master's, post-bachelor's certificate. **Academic Requirements:** General education including some course work in arts/fine arts, computer literacy, English (including composition), history, mathematics, philosophy, sciences (biological or physical), social science. **Classes:** 10-19 students in an average class. **Majors with Highest Enrollment:** Mass communications/media studies; education, general; nursing/registered nurse training (RN, ASN, BSN, MSN). **Disciplines with Highest Percentage of Degrees Awarded:** Health professions and related sciences 25%, education 23%, business/marketing 22%, parks and recreation 7%, communications/communication technologies 5%. **Special Study Options:** Accelerated program, distance learning, double major, dual enrollment, independent study, internships, liberal arts/career combination, student-designed major, study abroad, teacher certification program.

FACILITIES

Housing: Coed, apartments for married students, apartments for single students. **Library Holdings:** 105,121 bound volumes. 953 periodicals. 2,549 microforms. 8,601 audiovisuals. **Special Academic Facilities/Equipment:** Nuclear magnetic resonance spectrometer. **Computers:** School-owned computers available for student use.

EXTRACURRICULARS

Activities: Choral groups, drama/theater, literary magazine, radio station, student government, student newspaper, television station. **Organizations:** 24 registered organizations, 12 honor societies, 2 religious organizations. **Athletics (Intercollegiate):** *Men:* baseball, basketball, football, golf, soccer, tennis. *Women:* cheerleading, cross-country, golf, softball, volleyball.

ADMISSIONS

Selectivity Rating: 63 (of 100). **Freshman Academic Profile:** Average high school GPA 3.2. 12% in top 10% of high school class, 30% in top 25% of high school class, 80% in top 50% of high school class. 55% from public high schools. Average ACT 21, ACT middle 50% range 18-23. TOEFL required of all international applicants, minimum TOEFL 550. **Basis for Candidate Selection:** *Very important factors considered include:* class rank, secondary school record, standardized test scores. *Other factors considered include:* essays, extracurricular activities, interview, recommendations, talent/ability, volunteer work. **Freshman Admission Requirements:** High school diploma or GED is required. *Academic units required/recommended:* 16 total required; 4 English required, 2 math required, 2 science required, 1 science lab required, 1 foreign language recommended, 2 social studies required. **Freshman Admission Statistics:** 664 applied, 69% accepted, 32% of those accepted enrolled. **Transfer Admission Requirements:** *Items required:* college transcript. Minimum college GPA of 2.0 required. Lowest grade transferable C. **General Admission Information:** Application fee $20. Priority application deadline September 1. Nonfall registration accepted. Admission may be deferred for a maximum of 1 year. Credit and/or placement offered for CEEB Advanced Placement tests.

COSTS AND FINANCIAL AID

Required Forms and Deadlines: FAFSA and institution's own financial aid form. No deadline for regular filing. Priority filing deadline May 1. **Notification of Awards:** Applicants will be notified of awards on a rolling basis beginning on or about February 15. **Types of Aid:** *Need-based scholarships/grants:* Pell, SEOG, state scholarships/grants, private scholarships, the school's own gift aid. *Loans:* Direct Subsidized Stafford, Direct Unsubsidized Stafford, Direct PLUS, Federal Perkins, college/university loans from institutional funds. **Student Employment:** Federal Work-Study Program available. Institutional employment available. Off-campus job opportunities are good. **Financial Aid Statistics:** 79% freshmen, 65% undergrads receive some form of aid. Average freshman grant $6,883. Average freshman loan $2,986. Average income from on-campus job $995. **Financial Aid Phone:** 815-740-3403.

THE UNIVERSITY OF SAINT FRANCIS (IN)

2701 Spring Street, Fort Wayne, IN 46808
Phone: 219-434-3279 **CEEB Code:** 1693
Fax: 219-434-3183 **ACT Code:** 1238

This private school, which is affiliated with the Roman Catholic Church, was founded in 1890. It has a 70-acre campus.

STUDENTS AND FACULTY

Enrollment: 794. **Student Body:** Male 35%, female 65%, out-of-state 16%, international 1%. **Ethnic Representation:** African American 6%, Asian 1%, Caucasian 81%, Hispanic 2%, Native American 1%. **Retention and Graduation:** 74% freshmen return for sophomore year. 1% grads pursue business degrees. 1% grads pursue law degrees. 1% grads pursue medical degrees. **Faculty:** 95% faculty teach undergrads.

ACADEMICS

Degrees: Associate's, bachelor's, certificate, master's, terminal, transfer. **Academic Requirements:** General education including some course work in computer literacy, humanities, mathematics, philosophy, sciences (biological or physical), social science.

FACILITIES

Housing: Coed. **Library Holdings:** 85,742 bound volumes. 13,834 periodicals. 1,276,539 microforms. 1,098 audiovisuals. **Computers:** School-owned computers available for student use.

EXTRACURRICULARS

Activities: Radio station, student government, student newspaper, television station, yearbook. **Organizations:** 25 registered organizations, 1 honor society. **Athletics (Intercollegiate):** *Men:* baseball, basketball, cheerleading, cross-country, football, golf, soccer, track & field. *Women:* basketball, cheerleading, cross-country, soccer, softball, tennis, track & field, volleyball.

ADMISSIONS

Selectivity Rating: 77 (of 100). **Freshman Academic Profile:** Average high school GPA 2.9. 12% in top 10% of high school class, 32% in top 25% of high school class, 73% in top 50% of high school class. Average SAT I Math 473, SAT I Math middle 50% range 420-540. Average SAT I Verbal 480, SAT I Verbal middle 50% range 440-530. Average ACT 21, ACT middle 50% range 18-24. TOEFL required of all international applicants, minimum TOEFL 500. **Basis for Candidate Selection:** *Very important factors considered include:* class rank, secondary school record, standardized test scores. *Other factors considered include:* alumni/ae relation, character/personal qualities, essays, interview, minority status, recommendations, religious affiliation/commitment, talent/ability, volunteer work. **Freshman Admission Requirements:** High school diploma or GED is required. *Academic units required/recommended:* 16 total recommended; 4 English recommended, 3 math recommended, 2 science recommended, 2 science lab recommended, 2 foreign language recommended, 2 social studies recommended, 2 history recommended, 1 elective recommended. **Freshman Admission Statistics:** 522 applied, 82% accepted. **Transfer Admission Requirements:** *Items required:* college transcript. Minimum college GPA of 2.0 required. Lowest grade transferable C. **General Admission Information:** Application fee $20. Priority application deadline August 1. Regular application deadline rolling. Nonfall registration accepted. Admission may be deferred for a maximum of 1 year. Credit and/or placement offered for CEEB Advanced Placement tests.

COSTS AND FINANCIAL AID

Tuition $10,310. Room & board $4,270. Required fees $400. Average book expense $600. **Required Forms and Deadlines:** FAFSA and institution's own financial aid form. Priority filing deadline March 1. **Notification of Awards:** Applicants will be notified of awards on a rolling basis beginning on or about March 15. **Types of Aid:** *Need-based scholarships/grants:* Pell, SEOG, state scholarships/grants, private scholarships, the school's own gift aid. *Loans:* Direct Subsidized Stafford, Direct Unsubsidized Stafford, Direct PLUS, Federal Perkins, college/university loans from institutional funds. **Student Employment:** Federal Work-Study Program available. Institutional employment available. Off-campus job opportunities are excellent. **Financial Aid Statistics:** Average freshman grant $10,872. Average freshman loan $2,560. Average income from on-campus job $1,300. **Financial Aid Phone:** 219-434-3283.

UNIVERSITY OF SAINT THOMAS (MN)

2115 Summit Avenue, #32-F1, St. Paul, MN 55105-1096
Phone: 651-962-6150 **E-mail:** admissions@stthomas.edu **CEEB Code:** 6110
Fax: 651-962-6160 **Web:** www.stthomas.edu **ACT Code:** 2102

This private school, which is affiliated with the Roman Catholic Church, was founded in 1885. It has a 78-acre campus.

STUDENTS AND FACULTY

Enrollment: 5,429. **Student Body:** Male 48%, female 52%, out-of-state 17%, international 1%. **Ethnic Representation:** African American 2%, Asian 6%, Caucasian 89%, Hispanic 2%, Native American 1%. **Retention and Graduation:** 87% freshmen return for sophomore year. 52% freshmen graduate within 4 years. 32% grads go on to further study within 1 year. 2% grads pursue business degrees. 2% grads pursue law degrees. 3% grads pursue medical degrees. **Faculty:** Student/faculty ratio 14:1. 399 full-time faculty, 86% hold PhDs.

ACADEMICS

Degrees: Bachelor's, certificate, doctoral, first professional, master's, post-bachelor's certificate, post-master's certificate. **Academic Requirements:** General education including some course work in arts/fine arts, computer literacy, English (including composition), foreign languages, history, mathematics, philosophy, sciences (biological or physical), social science, faith and Catholic tradition, human diversity, health and fitness. **Classes:** 20-29 students in an average class. 10-19 students in an average lab/discussion section. **Majors with Highest Enrollment:** Business administration/management; teacher education, multiple levels. **Disciplines with Highest Percentage of Degrees Awarded:** Business/marketing 43%, social sciences and history 11%, communications/communication technologies 10%, computer and information sciences 5%, biological life sciences 5%. **Special Study Options:** Cross registration, double major, English as a second language, student exchange program (domestic), honors program, independent study, internships, student-designed major, study abroad, teacher certification program.

FACILITIES

Housing: All-female, all-male, apartments for single students, housing for disabled students. **Library Holdings:** 440,073 bound volumes. 4,168 periodicals. 964,335 microforms. 3,516 audiovisuals. **Special Academic Facilities/Equipment:** Seminary. **Computers:** *Recommended operating system:* Windows NT/2000. School-owned computers available for student use.

EXTRACURRICULARS

Activities: Choral groups, concert band, dance, drama/theater, jazz band, literary magazine, music ensembles, pep band, student government, student newspaper, yearbook. **Organizations:** 79 registered organizations, 4 religious organizations. **Athletics (Intercollegiate):** *Men:* baseball, basketball, cross-country, diving, football, golf, ice hockey, indoor track, soccer, swimming, tennis, track & field. *Women:* basketball, cross-country, diving, golf, ice hockey, indoor track, soccer, softball, swimming, tennis, track & field, volleyball.

ADMISSIONS

Selectivity Rating: 74 (of 100). **Freshman Academic Profile:** Average high school GPA 3.6. 26% in top 10% of high school class, 58% in top 25% of high school class, 90% in top 50% of high school class. 75% from public high schools. Average SAT I Math 587, SAT I Math middle 50% range 530-640. Average SAT I Verbal 571, SAT I Verbal middle 50% range 520-620. Average ACT 25, ACT middle 50% range 22-27. TOEFL required of all international applicants, minimum TOEFL 550. **Basis for Candidate Selection:** *Very important factors considered include:* secondary school record. *Important factors considered include:* class rank, essays, standardized test scores. *Other factors considered include:* alumni/ae relation, character/personal qualities, extracurricular activities, geographical residence, minority status, recommendations, talent/ability, volunteer work. **Freshman Admission Requirements:** High school diploma or GED is required. *Academic units required/recommended:* 4 English recommended, 3 math required, 4 math recommended, 2 science recommended, 4 foreign language recommended. **Freshman Admission Statistics:** 3,094 applied, 87% accepted, 41% of those accepted enrolled. **Transfer Admission Requirements:** *Items required:* high school transcript, college transcript, essay, statement of good standing from prior school. Minimum college GPA of 2.3 required. Lowest grade transferable C-. **General Admission Information:** Application fee $30. Nonfall registration accepted. Admission may be deferred for a maximum of 1 year. Credit and/or placement offered for CEEB Advanced Placement tests.

COSTS AND FINANCIAL AID

Tuition $19,120. Room & board $5,858. Required fees $348. Average book expense $600. **Required Forms and Deadlines:** FAFSA. No deadline for regular filing. Priority filing deadline April 1. **Notification of Awards:** Applicants will be notified of awards on a rolling basis beginning on or about March 1. **Types of Aid:** *Need-based scholarships/grants:* Pell, SEOG, state scholarships/grants, private scholarships, the school's own gift aid. *Loans:* FFEL Subsidized Stafford, FFEL Unsubsidized Stafford, FFEL PLUS, Federal Perkins, state loans, private loans. **Student Employment:** Federal Work-Study Program available. Institutional employment available. Off-campus job opportunities are excellent. **Financial Aid Statistics:** 54% freshmen, 55% undergrads receive some form of aid. Average freshman grant $8,143. Average freshman loan $3,723. Average income from on-campus job $1,159. **Financial Aid Phone:** 612-962-6550.

UNIVERSITY OF ST. THOMAS

3800 Montrose Boulevard, Houston, TX 77006-4696
Phone: 713-525-3500 **E-mail:** admissions@stthom.edu **CEEB Code:** 6880
Fax: 713-525-3558 **Web:** www.stthom.edu **ACT Code:** 4238

This private school, which is affiliated with the Roman Catholic Church, was founded in 1947. It has a 21-acre campus.

STUDENTS AND FACULTY

Enrollment: 1,933. **Student Body:** Male 38%, female 62%, out-of-state 3%, international 3% (54 countries represented). **Ethnic Representation:** African American 6%, Asian 13%, Caucasian 43%, Hispanic 30%, Native American 1%. **Retention and Graduation:** 77% freshmen return for sophomore year. 25% freshmen graduate within 4 years. **Faculty:** Student/faculty ratio 14:1. 117 full-time faculty, 87% hold PhDs. 100% faculty teach undergrads.

ACADEMICS

Degrees: Bachelor's, diploma, doctoral, first professional, master's. **Academic Requirements:** General education including some course work in arts/fine arts, English (including composition), foreign languages, history, mathematics, philosophy, sciences (biological or physical), social science, theology, oral communication. **Classes:** 10-19 students in an average class. 10-19 students in an average lab/discussion section. **Majors with Highest Enrollment:** Business administration/management; biology/biological sciences, general; international relations and affairs. **Disciplines with Highest Percentage of Degrees Awarded:** Liberal arts/general studies 22%, business/marketing 21%, education 13%, social sciences and history 13%, communications/communication technologies 6%. **Special Study Options:** Cross registration, distance learning, double major, English as a second language, honors program, independent study, internships, study abroad, teacher certification program, first-year experiences, learning communities, service learning, senior capstone or culminating academic experiences, undergraduate research/creative projects.

FACILITIES

Housing: Apartments for single students, houses, Living-Learning Center housing. **Library Holdings:** 206,410 bound volumes. 10,000 periodicals. 539,919 microforms. 1,125 audiovisuals. **Special Academic Facilities/ Equipment:** Learning & Writing Center, Chapel of St. Basil. **Computers:** *Recommended operating system:* Windows 95. School-owned computers available for student use.

EXTRACURRICULARS

Activities: Choral groups, concert band, drama/theater, jazz band, literary magazine, music ensembles, musical theater, student government, student newspaper. **Organizations:** 78 registered organizations, 24 honor societies, 2 religious organizations.

ADMISSIONS

Selectivity Rating: 90 (of 100). **Freshman Academic Profile:** Average high school GPA 3.6. 26% in top 10% of high school class, 57% in top 25% of high school class, 85% in top 50% of high school class. Average SAT I Math 576, SAT I Math middle 50% range 530-630. Average SAT I Verbal 568, SAT I Verbal middle 50% range 520-620. Average ACT 25, ACT middle 50% range 23-27. TOEFL required of all international applicants, minimum TOEFL 550. **Basis for Candidate Selection:** *Very important factors considered include:* class rank, secondary school record, standardized test scores. *Important factors considered include:* extracurricular activities. *Other factors considered include:* character/personal qualities, essays, interview, recommendations, talent/ability, volunteer work, work experience. **Freshman Admission Requirements:** High school diploma or GED is required. *Academic units required/recommended:* 18 total required; 19 total recommended; 4 English required, 4 English recommended, 3 math required, 3 math recommended, 2 science required, 3 science recommended, 1 science lab required, 2 science lab recommended, 2 foreign language required, 2 foreign language recommended, 2 social studies required, 2 social studies recommended, 1 history required, 1 history recommended, 4 elective required, 4 elective recommended. **Freshman Admission Statistics:** 823 applied, 81% accepted, 43% of those accepted enrolled. **Transfer Admission Requirements:** *Items required:* college transcript, statement of good standing from prior school. Minimum college GPA of 2.2 required. Lowest grade transferable C. **General Admission Information:** Application fee $35. Priority application deadline February 1. Nonfall registration accepted. Admission may be deferred for a maximum of 1 year. Credit and/or placement offered for CEEB Advanced Placement tests.

COSTS AND FINANCIAL AID

Tuition $13,800. Room & board $6,070. Required fees $112. Average book expense $700. **Required Forms and Deadlines:** FAFSA. No deadline for regular filing. Priority filing deadline March 1. **Notification of Awards:** Applicants will be notified of awards on a rolling basis beginning on or about March 1. **Types of Aid:** *Need-based scholarships/grants:* Pell, SEOG, state scholarships/grants, the school's own gift aid. *Loans:* FFEL Subsidized Stafford, FFEL Unsubsidized Stafford, FFEL PLUS, Federal Perkins, state loans. **Student Employment:** Federal Work-Study Program available. Institutional employment available. Off-campus job opportunities are excellent. **Financial Aid Statistics:** 63% freshmen, 54% undergrads receive some form of aid. **Financial Aid Phone:** 713-525-2170.

UNIVERSITY OF SAN DIEGO

 $$$   

5998 Alcala Park, San Diego, CA 92110-2492
Phone: 619-260-4506 **E-mail:** admissions@sandiego.edu **CEEB Code:** 4849
Fax: 619-260-6836 **Web:** www.sandiego.edu **ACT Code:** 394

This private school, which is affiliated with the Roman Catholic Church, was founded in 1949. It has a 180-acre campus.

STUDENTS AND FACULTY

Enrollment: 4,837. **Student Body:** Male 39%, female 61%, out-of-state 39%, international 3% (63 countries represented). **Ethnic Representation:** African American 2%, Asian 7%, Caucasian 70%, Hispanic 16%, Native American 1%. **Retention and Graduation:** 85% freshmen return for sophomore year. 52% freshmen graduate within 4 years. 20% grads go on to further study within 1 year. **Faculty:** Student/faculty ratio 15:1. 328 full-time faculty, 96% hold PhDs. 100% faculty teach undergrads.

ACADEMICS

Degrees: Bachelor's, doctoral, first professional, first professional certificate, master's, post-bachelor's certificate, post-master's certificate. **Academic Requirements:** General education including some course work in arts/fine arts, English (including composition), foreign languages, history, humanities, mathematics, philosophy, sciences (biological or physical), social science, religion. **Classes:** 10-19 students in an average class. 10-19 students in an average lab/discussion section. **Majors with Highest Enrollment:** Business administration/management; communications studies/speech communication and rhetoric; psychology, general. **Disciplines with Highest Percentage of Degrees Awarded:** Business/marketing 34%, social sciences and history 16%, communications/communication technologies 11%, psychology 7%, liberal arts/ general studies 6%. **Special Study Options:** Double major, honors program, independent study, internships, study abroad, teacher certification program.

FACILITIES

Housing: Coed, all-female, apartments for single students, housing for disabled students. **Library Holdings:** 714,082 bound volumes. 10,451 periodicals. 839,992 microforms. 8,624 audiovisuals. **Special Academic Facilities/ Equipment:** Art gallery, peace & justice institute, child development center, language labs. **Computers:** School-owned computers available for student use.

EXTRACURRICULARS

Activities: Choral groups, dance, drama/theater, jazz band, literary magazine, music ensembles, musical theater, student government, student newspaper, symphony orchestra, television station, yearbook. **Organizations:** 65 registered organizations, 5 honor societies, 3 religious organizations, 5 fraternities (15% men join), 5 sororities (25% women join). **Athletics (Intercollegiate):** *Men:* baseball, basketball, crew, cross-country, football, golf, soccer, tennis. *Women:* basketball, crew, cross-country, diving, soccer, softball, swimming, tennis, volleyball.

ADMISSIONS

Selectivity Rating: 75 (of 100). **Freshman Academic Profile:** Average high school GPA 3.7. 46% in top 10% of high school class, 82% in top 25% of high school class, 97% in top 50% of high school class. 65% from public high schools. Average SAT I Math 590, SAT I Math middle 50% range 540-640. Average SAT I Verbal 570, SAT I Verbal middle 50% range 520-620. Average ACT 26, ACT middle 50% range 23-27. TOEFL required of all international applicants, minimum TOEFL 550. **Basis for Candidate Selection:** *Very important factors considered include:* secondary school record, standardized test scores. *Important factors considered include:* character/personal qualities, essays, extracurricular activities, recommendations, talent/ability. *Other factors considered include:* alumni/ae relation, class rank, minority status, religious affiliation/commitment, volunteer work, work experience. **Freshman Admission Requirements:** High school diploma or GED is required. *Academic units required/recommended:* 20 total recommended; 4 English recommended, 4 math recommended, 4 science recommended, 4 science lab recommended, 4 foreign language recommended, 4 social studies recommended. **Freshman Admission Statistics:** 6,815 applied, 53% accepted, 29% of those accepted enrolled. **Transfer Admission Requirements:** *Items required:* high school transcript, college transcript, essay. Minimum college GPA of 3.0 required. Lowest grade transferable C-. **General Admission Information:** Application fee $55. Priority application deadline January 5. Regular application deadline January 5. Nonfall registration accepted. Admission may be deferred for a maximum of 1 year. Credit and/or placement offered for CEEB Advanced Placement tests.

COSTS AND FINANCIAL AID

Tuition $21,880. Room & board $9,130. Required fees $108. Average book expense $1,206. **Required Forms and Deadlines:** FAFSA and institution's own financial aid form. Financial aid filing deadline February 20. **Notification of Awards:** Applicants will be notified of awards on a rolling basis beginning on or about March 1. **Types of Aid:** *Need-based scholarships/grants:* Pell, SEOG, state scholarships/grants, private scholarships, the school's own gift aid. *Loans:* FFEL Subsidized Stafford, FFEL Unsubsidized Stafford, FFEL PLUS, Federal Perkins, state loans, college/university loans from institutional funds, Non-Federal loan programs. **Student Employment:** Federal Work-Study Program available. Institutional employment available. Off-campus job opportunities are excellent. **Financial Aid Statistics:** 51% freshmen, 47% undergrads receive some form of aid. Average freshman grant $19,729. Average freshman loan $4,605. Average income from on-campus job $2,100. **Financial Aid Phone:** 619-260-4514.

UNIVERSITY OF SAN FRANCISCO

2130 Fulton Street, San Francisco, CA 94117
Phone: 415-422-6563 **E-mail:** admission@usfca.edu **CEEB Code:** 4850
Fax: 415-422-2217 **Web:** www.usfca.edu

This private school, which is affiliated with the Roman Catholic Church, was founded in 1855. It has a 55-acre campus.

STUDENTS AND FACULTY

Enrollment: 4,695. **Student Body:** Male 37%, female 63%, out-of-state 22%, international 7% (78 countries represented). **Ethnic Representation:** African American 6%, Asian 27%, Caucasian 42%, Hispanic 14%, Native American 1%. **Retention and Graduation:** 83% freshmen return for sophomore year. 40% freshmen graduate within 4 years. 1% grads pursue medical degrees. **Faculty:** Student/faculty ratio 15:1. 290 full-time faculty, 92% hold PhDs. 75% faculty teach undergrads.

ACADEMICS

Degrees: Bachelor's, certificate, doctoral, first professional, master's, post-master's certificate. **Academic Requirements:** General education including some course work in arts/fine arts, English (including composition), history, humanities, philosophy, sciences (biological or physical), social science, ethics. **Classes:** 10-19 students in an average class. 10-19 students in an average lab/discussion section. **Majors with Highest Enrollment:** Business administration/management; psychology, general; Nursing/registered nurse training (RN, ASN, BSN, MSN). **Disciplines with Highest Percentage of Degrees Awarded:** Business/marketing 22%, computer and information sciences 16%, interdisciplinary studies 12%, social sciences and history 11%, psychology 7%. **Special Study Options:** Accelerated program, cross registration, distance learning, double major, English as a second language, student exchange program (domestic), external degree program, honors program, independent study, internships, liberal arts/career combination, student-designed major, study abroad, teacher certification program.

FACILITIES

Housing: Coed, all-female, apartments for single students. Several off-campus buildings with flats have been purchased and converted into multiple student housing units. **Library Holdings:** 1,148,737 bound volumes. 5,560 periodicals. 788,402 microforms. 4,591 audiovisuals. **Special Academic Facilities/Equipment:** Rare book room, Ricci Institute for Chinese-Western Cultural History. **Computers:** School-owned computers available for student use.

EXTRACURRICULARS

Activities: Choral groups, dance, drama/theater, literary magazine, music ensembles, musical theater, pep band, radio station, student government, student newspaper, yearbook. **Organizations:** 60 registered organizations, 14 honor societies, 4 fraternities (2% men join), 4 sororities (2% women join). **Athletics (Intercollegiate):** *Men:* baseball, basketball, cross-country, golf, rifle, soccer, tennis. *Women:* basketball, cross-country, golf, rifle, soccer, tennis, volleyball.

ADMISSIONS

Selectivity Rating: 80 (of 100). **Freshman Academic Profile:** Average high school GPA 3.3. 20% in top 10% of high school class, 54% in top 25% of high school class, 90% in top 50% of high school class. 53% from public high schools. SAT I Math middle 50% range 500-610. SAT I Verbal middle 50% range 490-600. ACT middle 50% range 20-26. TOEFL required of all international applicants, minimum TOEFL 550. **Basis for Candidate Selection:** *Very important factors considered include:* recommendations, secondary school record, standardized test scores. *Important factors considered include:* class rank, essays. *Other factors considered include:* alumni/ae relation, character/personal qualities, extracurricular activities, interview, minority status, talent/ability, volunteer work. **Freshman Admission Requirements:** High school diploma or GED is required. *Academic units required/recommended:* 20 total recommended; 4 English recommended, 3 math recommended, 2 science recommended, 2 science lab recommended, 2 foreign language recommended, 3 social studies recommended, 6 elective recommended. **Freshman Admission Statistics:** 3,590 applied, 82% accepted, 28% of those accepted enrolled. **Transfer Admission Requirements:** *Items required:* college transcript, essay. Minimum college GPA of 2.5 required. Lowest grade transferable C. **General Admission Information:** Application fee $55. Priority application deadline February 1. Nonfall registration accepted. Admission may be deferred. Credit offered for CEEB Advanced Placement tests.

COSTS AND FINANCIAL AID

Tuition $23,220. Room & board $9,350. Required fees $120. Average book expense $800. **Required Forms and Deadlines:** FAFSA. Priority filing deadline February 15. **Types of Aid:** *Need-based scholarships/grants:* Pell, SEOG, state scholarships/grants, private scholarships, the school's own gift aid, Federal Nursing. *Loans:* Direct PLUS, FFEL PLUS, Federal Perkins, Federal Nursing. **Student Employment:** Federal Work-Study Program available. Institutional employment available. Off-campus job opportunities are excellent. **Financial Aid Statistics:** 59% freshmen, 56% undergrads receive some form of aid. Average freshman grant $6,654. Average freshman loan $4,684. Average income from on-campus job $2,000. **Financial Aid Phone:** 415-422-6303.

See page 1262.

UNIVERSITY OF SCIENCE AND ARTS OF OKLAHOMA

1727 West Alabama, Chickasha, OK 73018
Phone: 405-574-1204 **E-mail:** jwevans@usao.edu **CEEB Code:** 6544
Fax: 405-574-1220 **Web:** www.usao.edu **ACT Code:** 3418

This public school was founded in 1908. It has a 75-acre campus.

STUDENTS AND FACULTY

Enrollment: 1,490. **Student Body:** Male 36%, female 64%, out-of-state 4%, international 2% (21 countries represented). **Ethnic Representation:** African American 6%, Asian 1%, Caucasian 78%, Hispanic 2%, Native American 13%. **Retention and Graduation:** 56% freshmen return for sophomore year. 11% freshmen graduate within 4 years. 24% grads go on to further study within 1 year. 1% grads pursue business degrees. 1% grads pursue law degrees. **Faculty:** Student/faculty ratio 19:1. 53 full-time faculty, 86% hold PhDs. 100% faculty teach undergrads.

ACADEMICS

Degrees: Bachelor's. **Academic Requirements:** General education including some course work in arts/fine arts, computer literacy, English (including composition), history, humanities, mathematics, philosophy, sciences (biological or physical), social science. **Classes:** 10-19 students in an average class. 20-29 students in an average lab/discussion section. **Majors with Highest Enrollment:** Business administration/management; elementary education and teaching; art/art studies, general. **Disciplines with Highest Percentage of Degrees Awarded:** Business/marketing 18%, education 17%, parks and recreation 12%, social sciences and history 9%, psychology 9%. **Special Study Options:** Accelerated program, distance learning, double major, independent study, internships, liberal arts/career combination, student-designed major, study abroad, teacher certification program.

FACILITIES

Housing: Coed, apartments for single students, housing for disabled students. **Library Holdings:** 72,395 bound volumes. 137 periodicals. 152,567 microforms. 4,187 audiovisuals. **Special Academic Facilities/Equipment:** Language labs, speech and hearing clinic, multiple computer labs, interactive television. **Computers:** School-owned computers available for student use.

EXTRACURRICULARS

Activities: Choral groups, concert band, drama/theater, jazz band, pep band, student government, student newspaper, television station. **Organizations:** 27 registered organizations, 3 honor societies, 4 religious organizations, 1 fraternity (2% men join), 2 sororities. **Athletics (Intercollegiate):** *Men:* baseball, basketball, soccer, tennis. *Women:* basketball, soccer, softball, tennis.

ADMISSIONS

Selectivity Rating: 64 (of 100). **Freshman Academic Profile:** 12% in top 10% of high school class, 37% in top 25% of high school class, 72% in top 50% of high school class. 99% from public high schools. Average ACT 20, ACT middle 50% range 18-23. TOEFL required of all international applicants, minimum TOEFL 500. **Basis for Candidate Selection:** *Very important factors considered include:* class rank, secondary school record, standardized test scores. *Important factors considered include:* talent/ability. *Other factors considered include:* character/personal qualities. **Freshman Admission Requirements:** High school diploma or GED is required. *Academic units required/recommended:* 15 total required; 22 total recommended; 4 English required, 3 math required, 4 math recommended, 2 science required, 3 science recommended, 2 science lab required, 3 science lab recommended, 2 foreign language recommended, 1 social studies required, 2 history required, 3 elective required. **Freshman Admission Statistics:** 471 applied, 82% accepted, 75% of those accepted enrolled. **Transfer Admission Requirements:** *Items required:* college transcript, statement of good standing from prior school. Minimum college GPA of 2.0 required. Lowest grade transferable D. **General Admission Information:** Application fee $15. Regular application deadline September 3. Nonfall registration accepted. Admission may be deferred for a maximum of 1 year. Credit offered for CEEB Advanced Placement tests.

COSTS AND FINANCIAL AID

In-state tuition $1,699. Out-of-state tuition $4,794. Room & board $3,000. Required fees $546. Average book expense $800. **Required Forms and Deadlines:** FAFSA and institution's own financial aid form. No deadline for regular filing. Priority filing deadline March 15. **Notification of Awards:** Applicants will be notified of awards on a rolling basis beginning on or about March 15. **Types of Aid:** *Need-based scholarships/grants:* Pell, SEOG, state scholarships/grants, private scholarships, the school's own gift aid. *Loans:* FFEL Subsidized Stafford, FFEL Unsubsidized Stafford, FFEL PLUS, Federal Perkins. **Student Employment:** Federal Work-Study Program available. Institutional employment available. Off-campus job opportunities are good. **Financial Aid Statistics:** 75% freshmen, 72% undergrads receive some form of aid. Average freshman grant $3,974. Average freshman loan $1,889. Average income from on-campus job $1,016. **Financial Aid Phone:** 405-574-1240.

THE UNIVERSITY OF SCRANTON

800 Linden Street, Scranton, PA 18510-4699
Phone: 570-941-7540 **E-mail:** admissions@scranton.edu **CEEB Code:** 2929
Fax: 570-941-5928 **Web:** www.scranton.edu **ACT Code:** 3736

This private school, which is affiliated with the Roman Catholic Church, was founded in 1888. It has a 50-acre campus.

STUDENTS AND FACULTY

Enrollment: 4,060. **Student Body:** Male 42%, female 58%, out-of-state 48%, international 1%. **Ethnic Representation:** African American 1%, Asian 2%, Caucasian 87%, Hispanic 3%. **Retention and Graduation:** 87% freshmen return for sophomore year. 66% freshmen graduate within 4 years. 30% grads go on to further study within 1 year. 17% grads pursue business degrees. 4% grads pursue law degrees. 3% grads pursue medical degrees. **Faculty:** Student/faculty ratio 13:1. 243 full-time faculty, 85% hold PhDs. 98% faculty teach undergrads.

ACADEMICS

Degrees: Associate's, bachelor's, certificate, master's, post-bachelor's certificate, post-master's certificate. **Academic Requirements:** General education including some course work in computer literacy, English (including composition), history, humanities, mathematics, philosophy, sciences (biological or physical), social science. **Classes:** 10-19 students in an average class. 10-19 students in an average lab/discussion section. **Disciplines with Highest Percentage of Degrees Awarded:** Business/marketing 19%, health professions and related sciences 14%, education 13%, communications/communication technologies 9%, biological life sciences 9%. **Special Study Options:** Accelerated program, cross registration, distance learning, double major, dual enrollment, student exchange program (domestic), honors program, independent study, internships, liberal arts/career combination, study abroad, teacher certification program, combined baccalaureate/master's degree program.

FACILITIES

Housing: Coed, all-female, all-male, apartments for single students, single-family dwellings converted to theme houses. **Library Holdings:** 443,144 bound volumes. 1,750 periodicals. 507,750 microforms. 13,085 audiovisuals. **Special Academic Facilities/Equipment:** Art gallery, fine arts facility, theatre, center for music groups, language lab, microbiology institute, electron microscope, greenhouse. **Computers:** School-owned computers available for student use.

EXTRACURRICULARS

Activities: Choral groups, concert band, dance, drama/theater, jazz band, literary magazine, music ensembles, radio station, student government, student newspaper, symphony orchestra, television station, yearbook. **Organizations:** 90 registered organizations, 26 honor societies, 14 religious organizations. **Athletics (Intercollegiate):** *Men:* baseball, basketball, cross-country, golf, ice hockey, lacrosse, soccer, swimming, tennis, wrestling. *Women:* basketball, cross-country, field hockey, lacrosse, soccer, softball, swimming, tennis, volleyball.

ADMISSIONS

Selectivity Rating: 85 (of 100). **Freshman Academic Profile:** Average high school GPA 3.4. 30% in top 10% of high school class, 64% in top 25% of high school class, 91% in top 50% of high school class. 52% from public high schools. Average SAT I Math 562, SAT I Math middle 50% range 520-620. Average SAT I Verbal 565, SAT I Verbal middle 50% range 510-610. TOEFL required of all international applicants, minimum TOEFL 500. **Basis for Candidate Selection:** *Very important factors considered include:* secondary school record. *Important factors considered include:* class rank, standardized test scores. *Other factors considered include:* alumni/ae relation, character/personal qualities, essays, extracurricular activities, interview, minority status, recommendations, talent/ability, volunteer work, work experience. **Freshman Admission Requirements:** High school diploma or GED is required. *Academic units required/recommended:* 16 total required; 16 total recommended; 4 English required, 4 English recommended, 3 math required, 4 math recommended, 1 science required, 2 science recommended, 2 foreign language required, 2 foreign language recommended, 2 social studies required, 3 social studies recommended. **Freshman Admission Statistics:** 5,121 applied, 70% accepted, 27% of those accepted enrolled. **Transfer Admission Requirements:** *Items required:* high school transcript, college transcript. Minimum college GPA of 2.7 required. Lowest grade transferable C. **General Admission Information:** Application fee $40. Regular application deadline March 1. Nonfall registration accepted. Admission may be deferred for a maximum of 1 year. Credit and/or placement offered for CEEB Advanced Placement tests.

COSTS AND FINANCIAL AID

Tuition $20,248. Room & board $8,770. Required fees $200. Average book expense $900. **Required Forms and Deadlines:** FAFSA. No deadline for regular filing. Priority filing deadline February 15. **Notification of Awards:** Applicants will be notified of awards on a rolling basis beginning on or about March 1. **Types of Aid:** *Need-based scholarships/grants:* Pell, SEOG, state scholarships/grants, private scholarships, the school's own gift aid. *Loans:* FFEL Subsidized Stafford, FFEL Unsubsidized Stafford, FFEL PLUS, Federal Perkins. **Student Employment:** Federal Work-Study Program available. Institutional employment available. Off-campus job opportunities are good. **Financial Aid Statistics:** 68% freshmen, 63% undergrads receive some form of aid. Average freshman grant $10,217. Average freshman loan $3,300. Average income from on-campus job $894. **Financial Aid Phone:** 570-941-7700.

See page 1264.

UNIVERSITY OF SIOUX FALLS

1101 West 22nd Street, Sioux Falls, SD 57105
Phone: 605-331-6600 **E-mail:** admissions@usiouxfalls.edu **CEEB Code:** 6651
Fax: 605-331-6615 **Web:** www.usiouxfalls.edu **ACT Code:** 3920

This private school, which is affiliated with the American Baptist Church, was founded in 1883. It has a 26-acre campus.

STUDENTS AND FACULTY

Enrollment: 1,186. **Student Body:** Male 44%, female 56%, out-of-state 36%. **Ethnic Representation:** African American 2%, Caucasian 96%, Hispanic 1%, Native American 1%, international 1%. **Retention and Graduation:** 61% freshmen return for sophomore year. 43% freshmen graduate within 4 years. 14% grads go on to further study within 1 year. **Faculty:** Student/faculty ratio 18:1. 47 full-time faculty, 72% hold PhDs. 100% faculty teach undergrads.

ACADEMICS

Degrees: Associate's, bachelor's, master's, post-master's certificate, transfer. **Academic Requirements:** General education including some course work in arts/fine arts, computer literacy, English (including composition), history, humanities, mathematics, sciences (biological or physical), social science, communication, religion, wellness. **Classes:** 10-19 students in an average class. 20-29 students in an average lab/discussion section. **Majors with Highest Enrollment:** Business administration/management; teacher education, multiple levels. **Special Study Options:** Accelerated program, cross registration, distance learning, double major, dual enrollment, honors program, independent study, internships, liberal arts/career combination, student-designed major, study abroad, teacher certification program.

FACILITIES

Housing: Coed, all-female, all-male, apartments for married students, apartments for single students. **Library Holdings:** 97,797 bound volumes. 388 periodicals. 3,261 microforms. 5,276 audiovisuals. **Special Academic Facilities/Equipment:** Education curriculum lab, physiology lab, autoclave for research in diagnostic medicine. **Computers:** School-owned computers available for student use.

EXTRACURRICULARS

Activities: Choral groups, concert band, drama/theater, jazz band, literary magazine, music ensembles, musical theater, radio station, student government, student newspaper, television station. **Organizations:** 8 registered organizations, 2 honor societies, 3 religious organizations. **Athletics (Intercollegiate):** *Men:* baseball, basketball, cross-country, football, golf, indoor track, soccer, tennis, track & field. *Women:* basketball, cross-country, golf, indoor track, soccer, softball, tennis, track & field, volleyball.

ADMISSIONS

Selectivity Rating: 68 (of 100). **Freshman Academic Profile:** Average high school GPA 3.3. 16% in top 10% of high school class, 41% in top 25% of high school class, 72% in top 50% of high school class. ACT middle 50% range 19-24. TOEFL required of all international applicants, minimum TOEFL 500. **Basis for Candidate Selection:** *Very important factors considered include:* class rank, secondary school record, standardized test scores. *Other factors considered include:* interview, recommendations. **Freshman Admission Requirements:** High school diploma or GED is required. *Academic units required/recommended:* 4 English recommended, 3 math recommended, 2 science recommended, 3 social studies recommended, 3 history recommended. **Freshman Admission Statistics:** 488 applied, 98% accepted, 44% of those accepted enrolled. **Transfer Admission Requirements:** *Items required:* high school transcript, college transcript, statement of good standing from prior school. Minimum college GPA of 2.0 required. Lowest grade transferable C. **General Admission Information:** Application fee $25. Nonfall registration accepted. Admission may be deferred for a maximum of 3 years. Credit and/or placement offered for CEEB Advanced Placement tests.

COSTS AND FINANCIAL AID

Tuition $13,900. Room & board $4,000. Required fees $50. Average book expense $700. **Required Forms and Deadlines:** FAFSA. Priority filing deadline March 1. **Notification of Awards:** Applicants will be notified of awards on a rolling basis beginning on or about March 1. **Types of Aid:** *Need-based scholarships/grants:* Pell, SEOG, private scholarships, the school's own gift aid. *Loans:* Direct Subsidized Stafford, Direct Unsubsidized Stafford, Direct PLUS, FFEL Subsidized Stafford, FFEL Unsubsidized Stafford, FFEL PLUS, Federal Perkins, state loans. **Student Employment:** Federal Work-Study Program available. Off-campus job opportunities are excellent. **Financial Aid Statistics:** 77% freshmen, 79% undergrads receive some form of aid. **Financial Aid Phone:** 605-331-6623.

UNIVERSITY OF SOUTH ALABAMA

182 Administration Building, Mobile, AL 36688-0002
Phone: 334-460-6141 **E-mail:** admiss@jaguar1.usouthal.edu **CEEB Code:** 1880
Fax: 334-460-7023 **Web:** www.usouthal.edu **ACT Code:** 59

This public school was founded in 1963. It has a 1,215-acre campus.

STUDENTS AND FACULTY

Enrollment: 9,360. **Student Body:** Male 43%, female 57%, out-of-state 25%, international 5% (93 countries represented). **Ethnic Representation:** African American 14%, Asian 3%, Caucasian 81%, Hispanic 1%, Native American 1%. **Retention and Graduation:** 63% freshmen return for sophomore year. 11% freshmen graduate within 4 years.

ACADEMICS

Degrees: Bachelor's, certificate, doctoral, first professional, master's, post-bachelor's certificate, post-master's certificate. **Special Study Options:** Cooperative (work-study) program, double major, English as a second language, student-designed major, study abroad, teacher certification program.

FACILITIES

Housing: All-female, all-male, apartments for married students, apartments for single students, fraternities and/or sororities. **Library Holdings:** 253,412 bound volumes. 3,981 periodicals. 1,434,711 microforms. 13,349 audiovisuals. **Special Academic Facilities/Equipment:** Museum/gallery complex, three hospitals, center for clinical education in health programs, engineering labs. **Computers:** *Recommended operating system:* Mac. School-owned computers available for student use.

EXTRACURRICULARS

Activities: Student government, student newspaper. **Organizations:** 2 honor societies, 1 religious organization, 10 fraternities (8% men join), 8 sororities (6% women join). **Athletics (Intercollegiate):** *Men:* baseball, basketball, cross-country, golf, tennis, track & field. *Women:* basketball, cross-country, golf, soccer, tennis, track & field, volleyball.

ADMISSIONS

Selectivity Rating: 80 (of 100). **Freshman Academic Profile:** Average high school GPA 3.1. 92% from public high schools. Average ACT 23. TOEFL required of all international applicants, minimum TOEFL 500. **Freshman Admission Requirements:** High school diploma or GED is required. *Academic units required/recommended:* 16 total recommended; 4 English recommended, 3 math recommended, 2 science recommended, 2 social studies recommended, 2 history recommended, 3 elective recommended. **Freshman Admission Statistics:** 2,661 applied, 94% accepted, 48% of those accepted enrolled. **Transfer Admission Requirements:** Minimum college GPA of 2.0 required. Lowest grade transferable C. **General Admission Information:** Application fee $25. Regular application deadline September 10. Nonfall registration accepted. Credit and/or placement offered for CEEB Advanced Placement tests.

COSTS AND FINANCIAL AID

In-state tuition $2,475. Out-of-state tuition $4,950. Room & board $2,883. Required fees $201. Average book expense $600. **Required Forms and Deadlines:** FAFSA, institution's own financial aid form and state aid form. **Types of Aid:** *Need-based scholarships/grants:* Pell, SEOG, state scholarships/grants, private scholarships, the school's own gift aid. *Loans:* FFEL Subsidized Stafford, FFEL Unsubsidized Stafford, FFEL PLUS, Federal Perkins, college/university loans from institutional funds. **Student Employment:** Federal Work-Study Program available. Institutional employment available. Off-campus job opportunities are excellent. **Financial Aid Statistics:** Average freshman grant $1,600. Average freshman loan $2,700. Average income from on-campus job $1,500. **Financial Aid Phone:** 334-460-6231.

UNIVERSITY OF SOUTH CAROLINA—AIKEN

471 University Parkway, Aiken, SC 29801
Phone: 803-641-3366 **E-mail:** admit@sc.edu
Fax: 803-641-3727 **Web:** www.usca.sc.edu

This public school was founded in 1961. It has a 453-acre campus.

STUDENTS AND FACULTY

Enrollment: 3,148. **Student Body:** Male 34%, female 66%, out-of-state 14%, international 1% (16 countries represented). **Ethnic Representation:** African American 20%, Asian 1%, Caucasian 76%, Hispanic 2%. **Retention and Graduation:** 71% freshmen return for sophomore year. 10% freshmen graduate within 4 years.

ACADEMICS

Degrees: Associate's, bachelor's, master's. **Academic Requirements:** General education including some course work in English (including composition), foreign languages, history, humanities, mathematics, sciences (biological or physical), social science. **Special Study Options:** Accelerated program, cooperative (work-study) program, cross registration, double major, dual enrollment, English as a second language, honors program, independent study, internships, student-designed major, study abroad, teacher certification program.

FACILITIES

Housing: Apartments for single students. **Library Holdings:** 142,230 bound volumes. 827 periodicals. **Special Academic Facilities/Equipment:** Ruth Patrick Science Education Center, Etherredge Center (Fine Arts Center), Wellness Center. **Computers:** School-owned computers available for student use.

EXTRACURRICULARS

Activities: Choral groups, dance, drama/theater, literary magazine, music ensembles, musical theater, student government, student newspaper. **Organizations:** 6 honor societies, 6 religious organizations, 3 fraternities, 3 sororities.

ADMISSIONS

Selectivity Rating: 74 (of 100). **Freshman Academic Profile:** Average high school GPA 2.9. 16% in top 10% of high school class, 37% in top 25% of high school class, 75% in top 50% of high school class. Average SAT I Math 482. Average SAT I Verbal 490. Average ACT 21. **Basis for Candidate Selection:** *Very important factors considered include:* secondary school record. *Important factors considered include:* standardized test scores. *Other factors considered include:* class rank, essays, extracurricular activities, interview, recommendations. **Freshman Admission Requirements:** *Academic units required/ recommended:* 16 total recommended; 4 English recommended, 3 math recommended, 3 science recommended, 2 foreign language recommended, 4 social studies recommended. **Transfer Admission Requirements:** *Items required:* college transcript, statement of good standing from prior school. Minimum college GPA of 2.0 required. Lowest grade transferable C. **General Admission Information:** Application fee $25. Priority application deadline August 1. Regular application deadline August 20. Nonfall registration accepted. Admission may be deferred for a maximum of 1 year.

COSTS AND FINANCIAL AID

Out-of-state tuition $7,544. Room & board $3,890. Required fees $140. Average book expense $800. **Required Forms and Deadlines:** FAFSA and institution's own financial aid form. Priority filing deadline March 15. **Notification of Awards:** Applicants will be notified of awards on a rolling basis beginning on or about May 20. **Types of Aid:** *Loans:* FFEL Subsidized Stafford, FFEL PLUS. **Student Employment:** Federal Work-Study Program available. Institutional employment available. Off-campus job opportunities are good. **Financial Aid Statistics:** Average freshman grant $1,380. Average freshman loan $1,850. Average income from on-campus job $1,600. **Financial Aid Phone:** 803-648-6851.

UNIVERSITY OF SOUTH CAROLINA—COLUMBIA

Office of Undergraduate Admissions, University of South Carolina, Columbia, SC 29208
Phone: 803-777-7700 **E-mail:** admissions-ugrad@sc.edu **CEEB Code:** 5818
Fax: 803-777-0101 **Web:** www.sc.edu **ACT Code:** 3880

This public school was founded in 1801. It has a 351-acre campus.

STUDENTS AND FACULTY

Enrollment: 16,567. **Student Body:** Male 46%, female 54%, out-of-state 13%, international 2%. **Ethnic Representation:** African American 17%, Asian 3%, Caucasian 74%, Hispanic 1%. **Retention and Graduation:** 82% freshmen return for sophomore year. 33% freshmen graduate within 4 years. **Faculty:** Student/faculty ratio 17:1. 1,015 full-time faculty, 89% hold PhDs. 61% faculty teach undergrads.

ACADEMICS

Degrees: Associate's, bachelor's, doctoral, first professional, master's, post-bachelor's certificate, post-master's certificate. **Academic Requirements:** General education including some course work in arts/fine arts, computer literacy, English (including composition), foreign languages, history, humanities, mathematics, philosophy, sciences (biological or physical), social science. **Classes:** 20-29 students in an average class. 20-29 students in an average lab/ discussion section. **Disciplines with Highest Percentage of Degrees Awarded:** Business/marketing 29%, social sciences and history 11%, communications/communication technologies 8%, biological life sciences 7%, visual and performing arts 7%. **Special Study Options:** Accelerated program, cooperative (work-study) program, cross registration, distance learning, double major, dual enrollment, English as a second language, student exchange program (domestic), external degree program, honors program, independent study, internships, liberal arts/career combination, student-designed major, study abroad, teacher certification program, weekend college, alternative spring break, Dobson Internship Program, Students Educating and Empowering for Diversity.

FACILITIES

Housing: Coed, all-female, all-male, apartments for married students, apartments for single students, housing for disabled students, housing for international students, fraternities and/or sororities, honors housing (undergraduate), wellness, residential college, pre-medical, engineering community, athletic, Greek, teaching fellows. **Library Holdings:** 3,333,764 bound volumes. 21,836 periodicals. 5,008,383 microforms. 45,930 audiovisuals. **Special Academic Facilities/Equipment:** Art gallery, movie theater, McKissick Museum, South Caroliniana Library, Gibbes Planetarium, Melton Observatory, Filtration Research Engineering Demonstration Unit, Belser Arboretum, A.C. Moore Gardens. **Computers:** School-owned computers available for student use.

EXTRACURRICULARS

Activities: Choral groups, concert band, dance, drama/theater, jazz band, literary magazine, marching band, music ensembles, musical theater, opera, pep band, radio station, student government, student newspaper, symphony orchestra. **Organizations:** 275 registered organizations, 34 honor societies, 9 religious organizations, 18 fraternities (17% men join), 12 sororities (17% women join). **Athletics (Intercollegiate):** *Men:* baseball, basketball, diving, football, golf, soccer, swimming, tennis, track & field. *Women:* basketball, cross-country, diving, equestrian, golf, soccer, softball, swimming, tennis, track & field, volleyball.

ADMISSIONS

Selectivity Rating: 74 (of 100). **Freshman Academic Profile:** Average high school GPA 3.7. 24% in top 10% of high school class, 56% in top 25% of high school class, 88% in top 50% of high school class. Average SAT I Math 569, SAT I Math middle 50% range 510-620. Average SAT I Verbal 555, SAT I Verbal middle 50% range 500-610. Average ACT 24, ACT middle 50% range 21-26. TOEFL required of all international applicants, minimum TOEFL 550. **Basis for Candidate Selection:** *Very important factors considered include:* secondary school record, standardized test scores. *Other factors considered include:* recommendations, talent/ability. **Freshman Admission Requirements:** High school diploma or GED is required. *Academic units required/ recommended:* 19 total required; 4 English required, 3 math required, 3 science required, 3 science lab required, 2 foreign language required, 2 social studies required, 1 history required, 4 elective required. **Freshman Admission Statistics:** 12,016 applied, 70% accepted, 42% of those accepted enrolled. **Transfer Admission Requirements:** *Items required:* college transcript. Minimum college GPA of 2.3 required. Lowest grade transferable C-. **General Admission Information:** Application fee $40. Priority application deadline January 1. Regular application deadline February 15. Nonfall registration accepted. Credit offered for CEEB Advanced Placement tests.

COSTS AND FINANCIAL AID

In-state tuition $4,784. Out-of-state tuition $12,904. Room & board $5,064. Required fees $200. Average book expense $607. **Required Forms and Deadlines:** FAFSA. Priority filing deadline April 1. **Notification of Awards:** Applicants will be notified of awards on a rolling basis beginning on or about May 1. **Types of Aid:** *Need-based scholarships/grants:* Pell, SEOG, state scholarships/grants, private scholarships, the school's own gift aid, United Negro College Fund, Federal Nursing. *Loans:* FFEL Subsidized Stafford, FFEL Unsubsidized Stafford, FFEL PLUS, Federal Perkins, Federal Nursing. **Student Employment:** Federal Work-Study Program available. Institutional employment available. Off-campus job opportunities are excellent. **Financial Aid Statistics:** 43% freshmen, 44% undergrads receive some form of aid. Average freshman grant $3,261. Average freshman loan $2,806. Average income from on-campus job $1,517. **Financial Aid Phone:** 803-777-8134.

UNIVERSITY OF SOUTH CAROLINA—SPARTANBURG

800 University Way, Spartanburg, SC 29303
Phone: 864-503-5246 **E-mail:** dstewart@uscs.edu **CEEB Code:** 5850
Fax: 864-503-5727 **Web:** www.uscs.edu **ACT Code:** 3889

This public school was founded in 1967. It has a 298-acre campus.

STUDENTS AND FACULTY

Enrollment: 4,249. **Student Body:** Male 35%, female 65%, out-of-state 5%, international 2%. **Ethnic Representation:** African American 27%, Asian 2%, Caucasian 67%, Hispanic 2%. **Retention and Graduation:** 67% freshmen return for sophomore year. 17% freshmen graduate within 4 years. 20% grads go on to further study within 1 year. **Faculty:** Student/faculty ratio 18:1. 174 full-time faculty, 79% hold PhDs. 100% faculty teach undergrads.

ACADEMICS

Degrees: Associate's, bachelor's, master's, terminal. **Academic Requirements:** General education including some course work in arts/fine arts, computer literacy, English (including composition), foreign languages, history, humanities, mathematics, sciences (biological or physical), social science. **Classes:** 20-29 students in an average class. 20-29 students in an average lab/ discussion section. **Majors with Highest Enrollment:** Nursing/registered nurse training (RN, ASN, BSN, MSN); business administration/management; education, general. **Disciplines with Highest Percentage of Degrees Awarded:** Business/marketing 21%, education 19%, liberal arts/general studies 15%, health professions and related sciences 14%, psychology 7%. **Special**

Study Options: Accelerated program, cross registration, distance learning, double major, student exchange program (domestic), honors program, independent study, internships, student-designed major, study abroad, teacher certification program.

FACILITIES

Housing: Apartments for single students. **Library Holdings:** 156,558 bound volumes. 3,151 periodicals. 58,426 microforms. 11,119 audiovisuals. **Special Academic Facilities/Equipment:** Campus Life Center; performing arts building, including 450-seat theater; arts studies film theater; recital hall; language laboratory; Quality Institute. **Computers:** School-owned computers available for student use.

EXTRACURRICULARS

Activities: Choral groups, dance, drama/theater, jazz band, literary magazine, music ensembles, musical theater, student government, student newspaper. **Organizations:** 61 registered organizations, 5 religious organizations, 2 fraternities (4% men join), 3 sororities (4% women join). **Athletics (Intercollegiate):** *Men:* baseball, basketball, cross-country, soccer, tennis. *Women:* basketball, cross-country, soccer, softball, tennis, volleyball.

ADMISSIONS

Selectivity Rating: 60 (of 100). **Freshman Academic Profile:** Average high school GPA 3.4. 10% in top 10% of high school class, 36% in top 25% of high school class, 59% in top 50% of high school class. Average SAT I Math 485, SAT I Math middle 50% range 405-500. Average SAT I Verbal 472, SAT I Verbal middle 50% range 431-536. TOEFL required of all international applicants, minimum TOEFL 500. **Basis for Candidate Selection:** *Very important factors considered include:* secondary school record, standardized test scores. *Other factors considered include:* class rank, recommendations. **Freshman Admission Requirements:** High school diploma or GED is required. *Academic units required/recommended:* 20 total required; 4 English required, 3 math required, 3 science required, 2 science lab required, 2 foreign language required, 2 social studies required, 1 history required, 4 elective required. **Transfer Admission Requirements:** *Items required:* college transcript, statement of good standing from prior school. Minimum college GPA of 2.0 required. Lowest grade transferable C. **General Admission Information:** Application fee $35. Priority application deadline August 15. Nonfall registration accepted. Admission may be deferred for a maximum of 1 year. Credit offered for CEEB Advanced Placement tests.

COSTS AND FINANCIAL AID

In-state tuition $4,098. Out-of-state tuition $8,990. Room & board $4,164. Required fees $220. Average book expense $700. **Required Forms and Deadlines:** FAFSA and scholarship application. Financial aid filing deadline July 15. Priority filing deadline March 1. **Notification of Awards:** Applicants will be notified of awards on a rolling basis. **Types of Aid:** *Need-based scholarships/grants:* Pell, SEOG, state scholarships/grants, private scholarships, the school's own gift aid. *Loans:* FFEL Subsidized Stafford, FFEL Unsubsidized Stafford, FFEL PLUS, Federal Perkins, Federal Nursing, state loans. **Student Employment:** Federal Work-Study Program available. Institutional employment available. Off-campus job opportunities are excellent. **Financial Aid Statistics:** 61% freshmen, 55% undergrads receive some form of aid. Average freshman grant $1,475. Average freshman loan $1,311. Average income from on-campus job $1,200. **Financial Aid Phone:** 864-503-5340.

THE UNIVERSITY OF SOUTH DAKOTA

414 East Clark, Vermillion, SD 57069
Phone: 605-677-5434 **E-mail:** admiss@usd.edu **CEEB Code:** 6881
Fax: 605-677-6753 **Web:** www.usd.edu **ACT Code:** 3928

This public school was founded in 1862. It has a 216-acre campus.

STUDENTS AND FACULTY

Enrollment: 5,769. **Student Body:** Male 39%, female 61%, out-of-state 23%, international 1% (38 countries represented). **Ethnic Representation:** African American 1%, Asian 1%, Caucasian 90%, Hispanic 1%, Native American 2%. **Retention and Graduation:** 76% freshmen return for sophomore year. 42% freshmen graduate within 4 years. 24% grads go on to further study within 1 year. 4% grads pursue business degrees. 3% grads pursue law degrees. 6% grads pursue medical degrees. **Faculty:** Student/faculty ratio 14:1. 283 full-time faculty, 79% hold PhDs. 94% faculty teach undergrads.

ACADEMICS

Degrees: Associate's, bachelor's, certificate, doctoral, first professional, master's, post-bachelor's certificate, post-master's certificate, terminal. **Academic Requirements:** General education including some course work in arts/fine arts, computer literacy, English (including composition), history, humanities, mathematics, sciences (biological or physical), social science. **Classes:** Under 10 students in an average class. **Majors with Highest Enrollment:** Business administration/management; psychology, general; biology/biological sciences, general. **Disciplines with Highest Percentage of Degrees Awarded:** Business/marketing 21%, education 13%, health professions and related sciences 12%, psychology 10%, biological life sciences 8%. **Special Study Options:** Cooperative (work-study) program, distance learning, double major, dual enrollment, English as a second language, student exchange program (domestic), honors program, internships, liberal arts/career combination, student-designed major, study abroad, teacher certification program.

FACILITIES

Housing: Coed, all-female, apartments for married students, apartments for single students, housing for disabled students, fraternities and/or sororities, apartments for students with dependent children. **Library Holdings:** 335,757 bound volumes. 2,852 periodicals. 673,116 microforms. 30,885 audiovisuals. **Special Academic Facilities/Equipment:** W.H. Over State Museum, America's Shrine to Music Museum, Warren M. Lee Center for Fine Arts with numerous galleries, the Oscar Howe Art Gallery in the Old Main Building, Business Research Bureau, Center for Instructional Design and Delivery, Center for Disabilities, Governmental Research Bureau, State Data Center, Federal Technical Procurement Center, Family Business Initiative, Institute of American Indian Studies, Native American Cultural Center, Honors Program, South Dakota geological survey, archaeology lab, child welfare training institute, human factors lab, speech and hearing center, social science research institute, telecommunication center, disaster mental health institute. **Computers:** *Recommended operating system:* Windows 2000/XP. School-owned computers available for student use.

EXTRACURRICULARS

Activities: Choral groups, concert band, dance, drama/theater, jazz band, marching band, music ensembles, musical theater, opera, pep band, radio station, student government, student newspaper, symphony orchestra, television station. **Organizations:** 114 registered organizations, 11 honor societies, 7 religious organizations, 8 fraternities (20% men join), 4 sororities (12% women join). **Athletics (Intercollegiate):** *Men:* baseball, basketball, cross-country, diving, football, golf, indoor track, swimming, tennis, track & field. *Women:* basketball, cross-country, diving, golf, indoor track, soccer, softball, swimming, tennis, track & field, volleyball.

ADMISSIONS

Selectivity Rating: 73 (of 100). **Freshman Academic Profile:** Average high school GPA 3.1. 10% in top 10% of high school class, 31% in top 25% of high school class, 63% in top 50% of high school class. 93% from public high schools. Average ACT 22, ACT middle 50% range 19-25. TOEFL required of all international applicants, minimum TOEFL 560. **Basis for Candidate Selection:** *Very important factors considered include:* class rank, secondary school record, standardized test scores. *Other factors considered include:* essays, extracurricular activities, minority status, recommendations, talent/ability. **Freshman Admission Requirements:** High school diploma or GED is required. *Academic units required/recommended:* 16 total required; 17 total recommended; 4 English required, 3 math required, 3 science required, 3 science lab required, 3 social studies required. **Freshman Admission Statistics:** 2,539 applied, 86% accepted, 51% of those accepted enrolled. **Transfer Admission Requirements:** *Items required:* high school transcript, college transcript, standardized test score, statement of good standing from prior school. Minimum college GPA of 2.0 required. Lowest grade transferable D. **General Admission Information:** Application fee $20. Nonfall registration accepted. Credit and/or placement offered for CEEB Advanced Placement tests.

COSTS AND FINANCIAL AID

In-state tuition $1,950. Out-of-state tuition $6,200. Room & board $3,278. Required fees $1,922. Average book expense $700. **Required Forms and Deadlines:** FAFSA. No deadline for regular filing. Priority filing deadline March 15. **Notification of Awards:** Applicants will be notified of awards on a rolling basis beginning on or about May 3. **Types of Aid:** *Need-based scholarships/grants:* Pell, SEOG, private scholarships, the school's own gift aid, Federal Nursing. *Loans:* FFEL Subsidized Stafford, FFEL Unsubsidized Stafford, FFEL PLUS, Federal Perkins, Federal Nursing, college/university loans from institutional funds. **Student Employment:** Federal Work-Study Program available. Institutional employment available. Off-campus job opportunities are good. **Financial Aid Statistics:** 58% freshmen, 59% undergrads receive some form of aid. Average freshman grant $2,127. Average freshman loan $2,065. Average income from on-campus job $1,200. **Financial Aid Phone:** 605-677-5446.

UNIVERSITY OF SOUTH FLORIDA

4202 East Fowler Avenue, SVC-1036, Tampa, FL 33620-9951
Phone: 813-974-3350 **E-mail:** jglassma@admin.usf.edu **CEEB Code:** 5828
Fax: 813-974-9689 **Web:** www.usf.edu **ACT Code:** 761

This public school was founded in 1956. It has a 1,931-acre campus.

STUDENTS AND FACULTY

Enrollment: 29,986. **Student Body:** Male 41%, female 59%, out-of-state 5%, international 1%. **Ethnic Representation:** African American 13%, Asian 6%, Caucasian 68%, Hispanic 11%. **Retention and Graduation:** 22% grads go on to further study within 1 year. **Faculty:** Student/faculty ratio 17:1. 1,535 full-time faculty, 87% hold PhDs. 50% faculty teach undergrads.

ACADEMICS

Degrees: Associate's, bachelor's, doctoral, first professional, master's, post-bachelor's certificate. **Academic Requirements:** General education including some course work in arts/fine arts, English (including composition), foreign languages, history, humanities, mathematics, sciences (biological or physical), social science. **Classes:** 20-29 students in an average class. 10-19 students in an average lab/discussion section. **Majors with Highest Enrollment:** Marketing/marketing management, general; curriculum and instruction; social sciences, general. **Disciplines with Highest Percentage of Degrees Awarded:** Business/marketing 25%, education 15%, social sciences and history 10%, psychology 7%, English 7%. **Special Study Options:** Accelerated program, cooperative (work-study) program, cross registration, distance learning, double major, dual enrollment, student exchange program (domestic), honors program, internships, study abroad, teacher certification program, weekend college.

FACILITIES

Housing: Coed, all-female, apartments for married students, apartments for single students, housing for disabled students, housing for international students, fraternities and/or sororities, cooperative housing, grad students only, medical students only. **Library Holdings:** 1,700,000 bound volumes. 15,263 periodicals. 4,200,000 microforms. 154,199 audiovisuals. **Special Academic Facilities/Equipment:** Art museum and galleries, planetarium, contemporary art museum, graphic studio, galleries, anthropology museum. **Computers:** School-owned computers available for student use.

EXTRACURRICULARS

Activities: Choral groups, concert band, dance, drama/theater, jazz band, literary magazine, marching band, music ensembles, musical theater, opera, pep band, radio station, student government, student newspaper, student-run film society, symphony orchestra, television station. **Organizations:** 200 registered organizations, 20 honor societies, 21 religious organizations, 13 fraternities (6% men join), 11 sororities (4% women join). **Athletics (Intercollegiate):** *Men:* baseball, basketball, cheerleading, cross-country, football, golf, indoor track, soccer, tennis, track & field. *Women:* basketball, cheerleading, cross-country, golf, indoor track, sailing, soccer, softball, tennis, track & field, volleyball.

ADMISSIONS

Selectivity Rating: 79 (of 100). **Freshman Academic Profile:** Average high school GPA 3.6. 20% in top 10% of high school class, 44% in top 25% of high school class, 88% in top 50% of high school class. 91% from public high schools. Average SAT I Math 532, SAT I Math middle 50% range 480-580. Average SAT I Verbal 524, SAT I Verbal middle 50% range 470-570. Average ACT 26. TOEFL required of all international applicants, minimum TOEFL 550. **Basis for Candidate Selection:** *Very important factors considered include:* secondary school record. *Important factors considered include:* standardized test scores. *Other factors considered include:* character/personal qualities, essays, extracurricular activities, minority status, recommendations, talent/ability. **Freshman Admission Requirements:** High school diploma or GED is required. *Academic units required/recommended:* 19 total required; 4 English required, 3 math required, 3 science required, 2 science lab required, 2 foreign language required, 3 social studies required, 4 elective required. **Freshman Admission Statistics:** 13,535 applied, 62% accepted, 49% of those accepted enrolled. **Transfer Admission Requirements:** *Items required:* college transcript, statement of good standing from prior school. Minimum college GPA of 2.0 required. Lowest grade transferable D. **General Admission Information:** Application fee $20. Regular application deadline June 1. Nonfall registration accepted. Credit and/or placement offered for CEEB Advanced Placement tests.

COSTS AND FINANCIAL AID

In-state tuition $2,700. Out-of-state tuition $12,244. Room & board $6,110. Required fees $34. Average book expense $700. **Required Forms and Deadlines:** FAFSA. No deadline for regular filing. Priority filing deadline March 1. **Notification of Awards:** Applicants will be notified of awards on a rolling basis beginning on or about March 15. **Types of Aid:** *Need-based scholarships/grants:* Pell, SEOG, state scholarships/grants, private scholarships, the school's own gift aid. *Loans:* FFEL Subsidized Stafford, FFEL Unsubsidized Stafford, FFEL PLUS, Federal Perkins, college/university loans from institutional funds. **Student Employment:** Federal Work-Study Program available. Institutional employment available. Off-campus job opportunities are excellent. **Financial Aid Statistics:** 42% freshmen, 57% undergrads receive some form of aid. **Financial Aid Phone:** 813-974-4700.

UNIVERSITY OF SOUTHERN CALIFORNIA

$$$

University Park, Los Angeles, CA 90089-0911
Phone: 213-740-1111 **E-mail:** admitusc@usc.edu **CEEB Code:** 4852
Fax: 213-740-1556 **Web:** www.usc.edu **ACT Code:** 470

This private school was founded in 1880. It has a 155-acre campus.

STUDENTS AND FACULTY

Enrollment: 16,145. **Student Body:** Male 50%, female 50%, out-of-state 33%, international 7%. **Ethnic Representation:** African American 7%, Asian 23%, Caucasian 52%, Hispanic 14%, Native American 1%. **Retention and Graduation:** 94% freshmen return for sophomore year. 57% freshmen graduate within 4 years. **Faculty:** Student/faculty ratio 10:1. 1,406 full-time faculty, 86% hold PhDs.

ACADEMICS

Degrees: Bachelor's, doctoral, first professional, first professional certificate, master's, post-bachelor's certificate, post-master's certificate. **Academic Requirements:** General education including some course work in English (including composition), foreign languages, humanities, mathematics, sciences (biological or physical), social science. USC core curriculum is designed to help students acquire the analytical tools to question things often taken for granted and to understand the values at issue in contemporary society. The core sharpens students' skills in critical thinking, learning to weigh competing theories, evaluating new evidence, and articulating an informed, individual point of view. **Classes:** 10-19 students in an average class. 20-29 students in an average lab/discussion section. **Majors with Highest Enrollment:** Communications studies/speech communication and rhetoric; psychology, general; business administration/management. **Disciplines with Highest Percentage of Degrees Awarded:** Business/marketing 25%, visual and performing arts 14%, social sciences and history 14%, communications/communication technologies 9%, engineering/engineering technology 7%. **Special Study Options:** Accelerated program, cooperative (work-study) program, cross registration, double major, English as a second language, student exchange program (domestic), honors program, independent study, internships, liberal arts/career combination, student-designed major, study abroad, teacher certification program, learning communities, freshman seminar program, research opportunities, interdisciplinary study. In addition, students can select from 79 majors and over 100 minors.

FACILITIES

Housing: Coed, apartments for married students, apartments for single students, housing for disabled students, housing for international students, fraternities and/or sororities, faculty-in-residence programs, honors housing, different types of academic and ethnic-themed floors, new internationally themed residence hall. **Library Holdings:** 3,526,134 bound volumes. 28,561 periodicals. 5,795,818 microforms. 3,231,602 audiovisuals. **Special Academic Facilities/Equipment:** Art museums, wind tunnels, cinema scoring sound stage, media labs, recording studios, exercise physiology lab, many specialized engineering and health laboratories. **Computers:** School-owned computers available for student use.

EXTRACURRICULARS

Activities: Choral groups, concert band, dance, drama/theater, jazz band, literary magazine, marching band, music ensembles, musical theater, opera, pep band, radio station, student government, student newspaper, student-run film society, symphony orchestra, television station, yearbook. **Organizations:** 303 registered organizations, 41 honor societies, 54 religious organizations, 25 fraternities (16% men join), 18 sororities (17% women join). **Athletics (Intercollegiate):** *Men:* baseball, basketball, cross-country, diving, football, golf, swimming, tennis, track & field, volleyball, water polo. *Women:* basketball, crew, cross-country, diving, golf, soccer, swimming, tennis, track & field, volleyball, water polo.

ADMISSIONS

Selectivity Rating: 83 (of 100). **Freshman Academic Profile:** Average high school GPA 4. 80% in top 10% of high school class, 90% in top 25% of high school class, 99% in top 50% of high school class. 62% from public high schools. Average SAT I Math 683, SAT I Math middle 50% range 640-720. Average SAT I Verbal 652, SAT I Verbal middle 50% range 600-700. Average ACT 30, ACT middle 50% range 27-31. **Basis for Candidate Selection:** *Very important factors considered include:* secondary school record, standardized test scores, talent/ability. *Important factors considered include:* character/personal qualities, essays, extracurricular activities, interview, recommendations. *Other factors considered include:* alumni/ae relation, minority status, volunteer work, work experience. **Freshman Admission Requirements:** High school diploma is required and GED is not accepted. *Academic units required/recommended:* 16 total required; 4 English required, 3 math required, 4 math recommended, 2 science required, 4 science recommended, 2 science lab required, 3 science lab recommended, 2 foreign language required, 3 foreign language recommended, 2 social studies required, 3 social studies recommended, 3 elective required. **Freshman Admission Statistics:** 28,362 applied, 30% accepted, 32% of those accepted enrolled. **Transfer Admission Requirements:** *Items required:* high school transcript, college transcript, essay. Lowest grade transferable C-. **General Admission Information:** Application fee $65. Priority application deadline December 10. Regular application deadline January 10. Nonfall registration accepted. Credit offered for CEEB Advanced Placement tests.

COSTS AND FINANCIAL AID

Tuition $26,464. Room & board $8,512. Required fees $490. Average book expense $644. **Required Forms and Deadlines:** FAFSA, CSS/Financial Aid PROFILE, business/farm supplement, parent and student federal income tax form with all schedules and W-2s. Income documentation for non-filers. Financial aid filing deadline February 28. Priority filing deadline January 21. **Notification of Awards:** Applicants will be notified of awards on a rolling basis beginning on or about March 15. **Types of Aid:** *Need-based scholarships/grants:* Pell, SEOG, state scholarships/grants, private scholarships, the school's own gift aid. *Loans:* FFEL Subsidized Stafford, FFEL Unsubsidized Stafford, FFEL PLUS, Federal Perkins, credit ready, credit-based loans from private sources. **Student Employment:** Federal Work-Study Program available. Institutional employment available. Off-campus job opportunities are excellent. **Financial Aid Statistics:** 43% freshmen, 50% undergrads receive some form of aid. Average freshman grant $24,917. Average freshman loan $3,016. **Financial Aid Phone:** 213-740-1111.

UNIVERSITY OF SOUTHERN COLORADO

Admissions, 2200 Bonforte Boulevard, Pueblo, CO 81001
Phone: 719-549-2461 **E-mail:** info@uscolo.edu **CEEB Code:** 4611
Fax: 719-549-2419 **Web:** www.uscolo.edu **ACT Code:** 524

This public school was founded in 1933. It has a 275-acre campus.

STUDENTS AND FACULTY

Enrollment: 6,078. **Student Body:** Male 40%, female 60%, out-of-state 7%, international 2% (57 countries represented). **Ethnic Representation:** African American 4%, Asian 3%, Caucasian 59%, Hispanic 31%, Native American 2%. **Retention and Graduation:** 64% freshmen return for sophomore year. 12% freshmen graduate within 4 years. **Faculty:** Student/faculty ratio 17:1. 150 full-time faculty, 74% hold PhDs. 100% faculty teach undergrads.

ACADEMICS

Degrees: Bachelor's, master's. **Academic Requirements:** General education including some course work in arts/fine arts, computer literacy, English (including composition), history, humanities, mathematics, sciences (biological or physical), social science. **Classes:** 20-29 students in an average class. 10-19 students in an average lab/discussion section. **Majors with Highest Enrollment:** Business, management, marketing, and related support services; computer science; sociology. **Disciplines with Highest Percentage of Degrees Awarded:** Social sciences and history 29%, business/marketing 17%, psychology 8%, engineering/engineering technology 6%, communications/communication technologies 6%. **Special Study Options:** Accelerated program, cooperative (work-study) program, cross registration, distance learning, double major, dual enrollment, English as a second language, student exchange program (domestic), external degree program, honors program, independent study, internships, study abroad, teacher certification program, weekend college.

FACILITIES

Housing: Coed, apartments for single students, housing for disabled students. **Library Holdings:** 174,376 bound volumes. 1,574 periodicals. 7,519 microforms. 19,436 audiovisuals. **Special Academic Facilities/Equipment:** Recital hall, public television and nature center, raptor on the Arkansas River, rehabilitation center. **Computers:** School-owned computers available for student use.

EXTRACURRICULARS

Activities: Choral groups, concert band, dance, jazz band, literary magazine, music ensembles, pep band, radio station, student government, student newspaper, symphony orchestra, television station. **Organizations:** 55 registered organizations, 6 honor societies, 4 religious organizations, 3 fraternities, 1 sorority. **Athletics (Intercollegiate):** *Men:* baseball, basketball, golf, soccer, tennis. *Women:* basketball, soccer, softball, tennis, volleyball.

ADMISSIONS

Selectivity Rating: 65 (of 100). **Freshman Academic Profile:** Average high school GPA 3.1. 2% in top 10% of high school class, 9% in top 25% of high school class, 39% in top 50% of high school class. 85% from public high schools. Average SAT I Math 482, SAT I Math middle 50% range 430-540. Average SAT I Verbal 492, SAT I Verbal middle 50% range 430-550. Average ACT 20, ACT middle 50% range 18-23. TOEFL required of all international applicants, minimum TOEFL 500. **Basis for Candidate Selection:** *Very important factors considered include:* secondary school record, standardized test scores. *Important factors considered include:* class rank. *Other factors considered include:* character/personal qualities, essays, interview, minority status, recommendations, talent/ability, volunteer work, work experience. **Freshman Admission Requirements:** High school diploma or GED is required. *Academic units required/recommended:* 13 total recommended; 4 English recommended, 3 math recommended, 2 science recommended, 1 science lab recommended, 2 foreign language recommended, 2 social studies recommended. **Freshman Admission Statistics:** 1,665 applied, 95% accepted, 42% of those accepted enrolled. **Transfer Admission Requirements:** *Items required:* college transcript. Minimum high school GPA of 2.0 required. Minimum college GPA of 2.0 required. Lowest grade transferable C. **General Admission Information:** Application fee $25. Priority application deadline March 1. Regular application deadline August 1. Nonfall registration accepted. Admission may be deferred. Credit and/or placement offered for CEEB Advanced Placement tests.

COSTS AND FINANCIAL AID

In-state tuition $2,060. Out-of-state tuition $9,976. Room & board $5,624. Required fees $560. Average book expense $858. **Required Forms and Deadlines:** FAFSA. No deadline for regular filing. Priority filing deadline March 1. **Notification of Awards:** Applicants will be notified of awards on a rolling basis beginning on or about March 1. **Types of Aid:** *Need-based scholarships/grants:* Pell, SEOG, state scholarships/grants, private scholarships, the school's own gift aid. *Loans:* FFEL Subsidized Stafford, FFEL Unsubsidized Stafford, FFEL PLUS, Federal Perkins. **Student Employment:** Federal Work-Study Program available. Institutional employment available. Off-campus job opportunities are excellent. **Financial Aid Statistics:** 81% freshmen, 65% undergrads receive some form of aid. Average freshman grant $1,800. Average freshman loan $2,625. Average income from on-campus job $1,740. **Financial Aid Phone:** 719-549-2753.

UNIVERSITY OF SOUTHERN INDIANA

8600 University Boulevard, Evansville, IN 47712
Phone: 812-464-1765 **E-mail:** enroll@usi.edu **CEEB Code:** 1335
Fax: 812-465-7154 **Web:** www.usi.edu **ACT Code:** 1207

This public school was founded in 1965. It has a 300-acre campus.

STUDENTS AND FACULTY

Enrollment: 8,998. **Student Body:** Male 40%, female 60%, out-of-state 11%, international students represent 33 countries. **Ethnic Representation:** African American 4%, Asian 1%, Caucasian 95%, Hispanic 1%. **Retention and Graduation:** 61% freshmen return for sophomore year. 11% freshmen graduate within 4 years. **Faculty:** Student/faculty ratio 18:1. 283 full-time faculty, 63% hold PhDs. 100% faculty teach undergrads.

ACADEMICS

Degrees: Associate's, bachelor's, certificate, diploma, master's, post-bachelor's certificate, terminal, transfer. **Academic Requirements:** General education including some course work in arts/fine arts, computer literacy, English (including composition), history, humanities, mathematics, philosophy, sciences (biological or physical), social science. **Classes:** 20-29 students in an average class. 20-29 students in an average lab/discussion section. **Majors with Highest Enrollment:** Business administration/management; advertising; elementary education and teaching. **Disciplines with Highest Percentage of Degrees Awarded:** Business/marketing 20%, education 18%, communications/

communication technologies 12%, health professions and related sciences 12%, social sciences and history 7%. **Special Study Options:** Cooperative (work-study) program, distance learning, double major, English as a second language, honors program, independent study, internships, study abroad, teacher certification program.

FACILITIES

Housing: Coed, apartments for married students, apartments for single students, fraternities and/or sororities. **Library Holdings:** 234,406 bound volumes. 3,035 periodicals. 576,908 microforms. 7,924 audiovisuals. **Computers:** School-owned computers available for student use.

EXTRACURRICULARS

Activities: Choral groups, dance, drama/theater, jazz band, literary magazine, pep band, radio station, student government, student newspaper. **Organizations:** 103 registered organizations, 12 honor societies, 7 religious organizations, 5 fraternities (4% men join), 5 sororities (3% women join). **Athletics (Intercollegiate):** *Men:* baseball, basketball, cross-country, golf, soccer, tennis. *Women:* basketball, cross-country, golf, soccer, softball, tennis, volleyball.

ADMISSIONS

Selectivity Rating: 63 (of 100). **Freshman Academic Profile:** Average high school GPA 2.9. 8% in top 10% of high school class, 25% in top 25% of high school class, 56% in top 50% of high school class. Average SAT I Math 471, SAT I Math middle 50% range 410-520. Average SAT I Verbal 468, SAT I Verbal middle 50% range 410-520. Average ACT 20, ACT middle 50% range 17-22. TOEFL required of all international applicants, minimum TOEFL 525. **Basis for Candidate Selection:** *Very important factors considered include:* secondary school record. *Important factors considered include:* class rank. *Other factors considered include:* alumni/ae relation, character/personal qualities, essays, extracurricular activities, interview, recommendations, standardized test scores, talent/ability, work experience. **Freshman Admission Requirements:** High school diploma or GED is required. *Academic units required/recommended:* 18 total recommended; 4 English recommended, 4 math recommended, 3 science recommended, 2 foreign language recommended, 2 social studies recommended, 2 history recommended, 2 elective recommended. **Freshman Admission Statistics:** 4,258 applied, 94% accepted, 51% of those accepted enrolled. **Transfer Admission Requirements:** *Items required:* high school transcript, college transcript. Minimum college GPA of 2.0 required. Lowest grade transferable C-. **General Admission Information:** Application fee $25. Regular application deadline August 15. Nonfall registration accepted. Credit and/or placement offered for CEEB Advanced Placement tests.

COSTS AND FINANCIAL AID

In-state tuition $3,390. Out-of-state tuition $8,288. Room & board $4,940. Required fees $135. Average book expense $800. **Required Forms and Deadlines:** FAFSA and institution's own financial aid form. Financial aid filing deadline March 1. **Notification of Awards:** Applicants will be notified of awards on a rolling basis beginning on or about April 15. **Types of Aid:** *Need-based scholarships/grants:* Pell, SEOG, state scholarships/grants, private scholarships, the school's own gift aid. *Loans:* FFEL Subsidized Stafford, FFEL Unsubsidized Stafford, FFEL PLUS, Federal Perkins. **Student Employment:** Federal Work-Study Program available. Institutional employment available. Off-campus job opportunities are excellent. **Financial Aid Statistics:** 57% freshmen, 54% undergrads receive some form of aid. Average freshman grant $3,359. Average freshman loan $3,018. Average income from on-campus job $1,267. **Financial Aid Phone:** 812-464-1767.

UNIVERSITY OF SOUTHERN MAINE

37 College Avenue, Gorham, ME 04038
Phone: 207-780-5670 **E-mail:** usmadm@usm.maine.edu **CEEB Code:** 3691
Fax: 207-780-5640 **Web:** www.usm.maine.edu **ACT Code:** 1644

This public school was founded in 1878. It has a 144-acre campus.

STUDENTS AND FACULTY

Enrollment: 9,017. **Student Body:** Male 39%, female 61%, out-of-state 13%, international students represent 40 countries. **Ethnic Representation:** African American 1%, Asian 1%, Caucasian 96%, Hispanic 1%, Native American 1%. **Faculty:** Student/faculty ratio 13:1. 404 full-time faculty, 74% hold PhDs. 90% faculty teach undergrads.

ACADEMICS

Degrees: Associate's, bachelor's, certificate, doctoral, first professional, master's, post-master's certificate, terminal, transfer. **Academic Requirements:** General education including some course work in arts/fine arts, English (including composition), history, humanities, mathematics, philosophy, sciences (biological or physical), social science, interdisciplinary, other times/other cultures. **Majors with Highest Enrollment:** Surgical nurse/nursing; business/commerce, general; psychology, general. **Disciplines with Highest Percentage of Degrees Awarded:** Social sciences and history 21%, business/marketing 14%, health professions and related sciences 12%, communications/communication technologies 9%, visual and performing arts 6%. **Special Study Options:** Accelerated program, cooperative (work-study) program, cross registration, distance learning, double major, English as a second language, student exchange program (domestic), honors program, independent study, internships, liberal arts/career combination, student-designed major, study abroad, teacher certification program, weekend college, pre-engineering program with University of Maine at Orono, living/learning scholars program. Greater Portland Alliance includes cross registration with University of New England, St. Joseph's (Maine), Southern Maine Technical College, and Maine College of Art.

FACILITIES

Housing: Coed, apartments for married students, apartments for single students, housing for disabled students, fraternities and/or sororities, Fine Arts House, Russell Scholars (living/learning), chemical-free floor, 24-hour quiet floor, community living program. **Library Holdings:** 431,978 bound volumes. 3,339 periodicals. 1,124,225 microforms. 2,556 audiovisuals. **Special Academic Facilities/Equipment:** Southworth Planetarium, Osher Map Collection and Smith Center for Cartographic Education, WMPG (radio station), GTV (cable TV station), *Free Press* (campus newspaper), various art galleries on all three campuses. **Computers:** *Recommended operating system:* Windows NT/2000. School-owned computers available for student use.

EXTRACURRICULARS

Activities: Choral groups, concert band, dance, drama/theater, jazz band, literary magazine, music ensembles, musical theater, opera, radio station, student government, student newspaper, symphony orchestra, television station, yearbook. **Organizations:** 100 registered organizations, 2 honor societies, 3 religious organizations, 4 fraternities (4% men join), 4 sororities (4% women join). **Athletics (Intercollegiate):** *Men:* baseball, basketball, cheerleading, cross-country, golf, ice hockey, indoor track, lacrosse, soccer, tennis, track & field, wrestling. *Women:* basketball, cheerleading, cross-country, field hockey, golf, ice hockey, indoor track, lacrosse, soccer, softball, tennis, track & field, volleyball.

ADMISSIONS

Selectivity Rating: 68 (of 100). **Freshman Academic Profile:** Average high school GPA 3.0. 8% in top 10% of high school class, 30% in top 25% of high school class, 70% in top 50% of high school class. Average SAT I Math 512, SAT I Math middle 50% range 460-560. Average SAT I Verbal 516, SAT I Verbal middle 50% range 470-560. ACT middle 50% range 18-23. TOEFL required of all international applicants, minimum TOEFL 550. **Basis for Candidate Selection:** *Very important factors considered include:* class rank, secondary school record, standardized test scores. *Important factors considered include:* essays, recommendations. *Other factors considered include:* alumni/ae relation, character/personal qualities, extracurricular activities, geographical residence, interview, minority status, state residency, talent/ability, volunteer work, work experience. **Freshman Admission Requirements:** High school diploma or GED is required. *Academic units required/recommended:* 16 total required; 4 English required, 3 math required, 4 math recommended, 2 science required, 3 science recommended, 2 science lab required, 3 science lab recommended, 2 foreign language required, 3 foreign language recommended, 2 social studies required, 3 social studies recommended, 2 history required, 3 history recommended. **Freshman Admission Statistics:** 3,664 applied, 75% accepted, 35% of those accepted enrolled. **Transfer Admission Requirements:** *Items required:* high school transcript, college transcript, essay. Minimum college GPA of 2.0 required. Lowest grade transferable C-. **General Admission Information:** Application fee $40. Priority application deadline February 15. Regular application deadline rolling. Nonfall registration accepted. Admission may be deferred for a maximum of 1 year. Credit and/or placement offered for CEEB Advanced Placement tests.

COSTS AND FINANCIAL AID

In-state tuition $4,020. Out-of-state tuition $11,190. Room & board $5,738. Required fees $776. Average book expense $800. **Required Forms and Deadlines:** FAFSA. No deadline for regular filing. Priority filing deadline February 15. **Notification of Awards:** Applicants will be notified of awards on a rolling basis beginning on or about March 15. **Types of Aid:** *Need-based scholarships/grants:* Pell, SEOG, state scholarships/grants, private scholarships, the school's own gift aid. *Loans:* FFEL Subsidized Stafford, FFEL Unsubsidized Stafford, FFEL PLUS, Federal Perkins, Federal Nursing, state loans. **Student Employment:** Federal Work-Study Program available. Institutional employment available. Off-campus job opportunities are excellent. **Financial Aid Statistics:** 67% freshmen, 75% undergrads receive some form of aid. Average freshman grant $4,022. Average freshman loan $7,144. **Financial Aid Phone:** 207-780-5250.

UNIVERSITY OF SOUTHERN MISSISSIPPI

Box 5011, Hattiesburg, MS 39406
Phone: 601-266-5000 **E-mail:** admissions@usm.edu **CEEB Code:** 1479
Fax: 601-266-5148 **Web:** www.usm.edu **ACT Code:** 2218

This public school was founded in 1910. It has a 1,090-acre campus.

STUDENTS AND FACULTY

Enrollment: 12,612. **Student Body:** Male 39%, female 61%, out-of-state 14%, international 2%. **Ethnic Representation:** African American 21%, Asian 1%, Caucasian 77%, Hispanic 1%. **Retention and Graduation:** 74% freshmen return for sophomore year. 2% freshmen graduate within 4 years. 6% grads pursue business degrees. 1% grads pursue law degrees. 1% grads pursue medical degrees. **Faculty:** Student/faculty ratio 19:1. 641 full-time faculty, 83% hold PhDs. 95% faculty teach undergrads.

ACADEMICS

Degrees: Bachelor's, doctoral, master's. **Academic Requirements:** General education including some course work in arts/fine arts, English (including composition), history, humanities, mathematics, sciences (biological or physical), social science, human wellness. **Classes:** 10-19 students in an average class. Under 10 students in an average lab/discussion section. **Disciplines with Highest Percentage of Degrees Awarded:** Business/marketing 22%, education 15%, health professions and related sciences 10%, psychology 7%, communications/communication technologies 6%. **Special Study Options:** Accelerated program, cooperative (work-study) program, distance learning, double major, dual enrollment, English as a second language, honors program, study abroad, teacher certification program.

FACILITIES

Housing: All-female, all-male, apartments for married students, housing for disabled students, fraternities and/or sororities. **Library Holdings:** 972,812 bound volumes. 21,653 periodicals. 3,908,549 microforms. 21,001 audiovisuals. **Special Academic Facilities/Equipment:** English language institute, human performance and recreation facility, language lab, research institute, speech/hearing clinic, institute of microbiology, polymer science facility. **Computers:** School-owned computers available for student use.

EXTRACURRICULARS

Activities: Choral groups, concert band, dance, drama/theater, jazz band, literary magazine, marching band, music ensembles, musical theater, opera, pep band, radio station, student government, student newspaper, student-run film society, symphony orchestra, yearbook. **Organizations:** 202 registered organizations, 9 honor societies, 13 fraternities (18% men join), 12 sororities (19% women join). **Athletics (Intercollegiate):** *Men:* baseball, basketball, cross-country, football, golf, tennis, track & field. *Women:* basketball, cross-country, golf, softball, tennis, track & field, volleyball.

ADMISSIONS

Selectivity Rating: 72 (of 100). **Freshman Academic Profile:** Average high school GPA 3.3. 37% in top 10% of high school class, 49% in top 25% of high school class, 81% in top 50% of high school class. Average ACT 22, ACT middle 50% range 19-24. TOEFL required of all international applicants, minimum TOEFL 525. **Basis for Candidate Selection:** *Very important factors considered include:* secondary school record, standardized test scores. *Important factors considered include:* class rank, interview. *Other factors considered include:* alumni/ae relation, talent/ability. **Freshman Admission Requirements:** High school diploma or GED is required. *Academic units required/recommended:* 16 total required; 4 English required, 3 math required, 3 science required, 2 science lab required, 2 foreign language required, 1 social studies required, 2 history required. **Freshman Admission Statistics:** 4,553 applied, 63% accepted, 44% of those accepted enrolled. **Transfer Admission Requirements:** *Items required:* college transcript. Minimum college GPA of 2.0 required. Lowest grade transferable C. **General Admission Information:** Nonfall registration accepted. Credit and/or placement offered for CEEB Advanced Placement tests.

COSTS AND FINANCIAL AID

In-state tuition $3,782. Out-of-state tuition $8,660. Room & board $4,460. Required fees $0. Average book expense $700. **Required Forms and Deadlines:** FAFSA and institution's own financial aid form. No deadline for regular filing. Priority filing deadline March 15. **Types of Aid:** *Need-based scholarships/grants:* Pell, SEOG, state scholarships/grants, private scholarships, Federal Nursing. *Loans:* FFEL Subsidized Stafford, FFEL Unsubsidized Stafford, FFEL PLUS, Federal Perkins, Federal Nursing. **Student Employment:** Federal Work-Study Program available. Institutional employment available. Off-campus job opportunities are good. **Financial Aid Statistics:** 45% freshmen, 59% undergrads receive some form of aid. Average freshman grant $2,298. Average income from on-campus job $2,800. **Financial Aid Phone:** 601-266-4774.

UNIVERSITY OF TAMPA

401 West Kennedy Boulevard, Tampa, FL 33606-1490
Phone: 813-253-6211 **E-mail:** admissions@ut.edu **CEEB Code:** 5819
Fax: 813-258-7398 **Web:** www.ut.edu **ACT Code:** 762

This private school was founded in 1931. It has a 90-acre campus.

STUDENTS AND FACULTY

Enrollment: 3,730. **Student Body:** Male 37%, female 63%, out-of-state 50%, international 5% (70 countries represented). **Ethnic Representation:** African American 8%, Asian 2%, Caucasian 68%, Hispanic 10%. **Retention and Graduation:** 71% freshmen return for sophomore year. 36% freshmen graduate within 4 years. 16% grads go on to further study within 1 year. 5% grads pursue business degrees. 4% grads pursue law degrees. 6% grads pursue medical degrees. **Faculty:** Student/faculty ratio 17:1. 164 full-time faculty, 87% hold PhDs. 100% faculty teach undergrads.

ACADEMICS

Degrees: Associate's, bachelor's, certificate, master's. **Academic Requirements:** General education including some course work in computer literacy, English (including composition), humanities, mathematics, sciences (biological or physical), social science. **Classes:** 10-19 students in an average class. 10-19 students in an average lab/discussion section. **Majors with Highest Enrollment:** Business administration/management; mass communications/media studies; biology/biological sciences, general. **Disciplines with Highest Percentage of Degrees Awarded:** Business/marketing 25%, social sciences and history 16%, communications/communication technologies 10%, education 9%, computer and information sciences 8%. **Special Study Options:** Double major, dual enrollment, English as a second language, student exchange program (domestic), honors program, independent study, internships, study abroad, teacher certification program.

FACILITIES

Housing: Coed, all-female, apartments for single students. **Library Holdings:** 252,147 bound volumes. 10,854 periodicals. 16,661 microforms. 4,181 audiovisuals. **Special Academic Facilities/Equipment:** Victorian art and furniture museum, theatres, studios, music center, language lab, fully equipped research vessel for marine science, H. B. Plant Museum, marine science research center on Tampa Bay. **Computers:** School-owned computers available for student use.

EXTRACURRICULARS

Activities: Choral groups, concert band, dance, drama/theater, jazz band, literary magazine, music ensembles, musical theater, opera, pep band, radio station, student government, student newspaper, student-run film society, symphony orchestra, television station, yearbook. **Organizations:** 102 registered organizations, 21 honor societies, 5 religious organizations, 7 fraternities (16% men join), 8 sororities (12% women join). **Athletics (Intercollegiate):** *Men:* baseball, basketball, cross-country, golf, soccer, swimming. *Women:* basketball, crew, cross-country, soccer, softball, swimming, tennis, volleyball.

ADMISSIONS

Selectivity Rating: 68 (of 100). **Freshman Academic Profile:** Average high school GPA 3.2. 18% in top 10% of high school class, 49% in top 25% of high school class, 85% in top 50% of high school class. 75% from public high schools. Average SAT I Math 539, SAT I Math middle 50% range 500-580. Average SAT I Verbal 546, SAT I Verbal middle 50% range 490-580. Average ACT 22, ACT middle 50% range 20-25. TOEFL required of all international applicants, minimum TOEFL 550. **Basis for Candidate Selection:** *Very important factors considered include:* secondary school record, standardized test scores. *Important factors considered include:* character/personal qualities, essays, recommendations, talent/ability. *Other factors considered include:* alumni/ae relation, class rank, extracurricular activities, geographical residence, interview, state residency, volunteer work, work experience. **Freshman Admission Requirements:** High school diploma or GED is required. *Academic units required/recommended:* 15 total required; 4 English required, 2 math required,

2 science required, 2 science lab required, 2 foreign language recommended, 2 social studies required, 5 elective required. **Freshman Admission Statistics:** 4,169 applied, 68% accepted, 35% of those accepted enrolled. **Transfer Admission Requirements:** *Items required:* college transcript. Minimum high school GPA of 2.5 required. Minimum college GPA of 2.0 required. Lowest grade transferable C. **General Admission Information:** Application fee $35. Priority application deadline May 1. Nonfall registration accepted. Admission may be deferred for a maximum of 1 year. Credit and/or placement offered for CEEB Advanced Placement tests.

COSTS AND FINANCIAL AID

Tuition $16,150. Room & board $6,130. Required fees $882. Average book expense $765. **Required Forms and Deadlines:** FAFSA. No deadline for regular filing. **Notification of Awards:** Applicants will be notified of awards on a rolling basis beginning on or about February 1. **Types of Aid:** *Need-based scholarships/grants:* Pell, SEOG, state scholarships/grants, private scholarships, the school's own gift aid. *Loans:* FFEL Subsidized Stafford, FFEL Unsubsidized Stafford, FFEL PLUS, Federal Perkins, college/university loans from institutional funds. **Student Employment:** Federal Work-Study Program available. Institutional employment available. Off-campus job opportunities are excellent. **Financial Aid Statistics:** 57% freshmen, 45% undergrads receive some form of aid. Average freshman grant $15,393. Average freshman loan $2,717. Average income from on-campus job $2,000. **Financial Aid Phone:** 813-253-6219.

See page 1266.

UNIVERSITY OF TENNESSEE—CHATTANOOGA

615 McCallie Avenue, 131 Hooper Hall, Chattanooga, TN 37403
Phone: 423-425-4662 **E-mail:** Yancy-Freeman@utc.edu **CEEB Code:** 1831
Fax: 423-425-4157 **Web:** www.utc.edu **ACT Code:** 4022

This public school was founded in 1886. It has a 116-acre campus.

STUDENTS AND FACULTY

Enrollment: 7,133. **Student Body:** Male 43%, female 57%, out-of-state 8%, international students represent 49 countries. **Ethnic Representation:** African American 20%, Asian 3%, Caucasian 76%, Hispanic 1%, international 1%. **Retention and Graduation:** 73% freshmen return for sophomore year. 19% freshmen graduate within 4 years. **Faculty:** Student/faculty ratio 16:1. 348 full-time faculty, 83% hold PhDs. 95% faculty teach undergrads.

ACADEMICS

Degrees: Bachelor's, master's, post-bachelor's certificate, post-master's certificate. **Academic Requirements:** General education including some course work in arts/fine arts, computer literacy, English (including composition), humanities, mathematics, sciences (biological or physical), social science. **Disciplines with Highest Percentage of Degrees Awarded:** Business/marketing 26%, education 9%, home economics and vocational home economics 8%, psychology 7%, protective services/public administration 7%. **Special Study Options:** Cooperative (work-study) program, cross registration, distance learning, double major, dual enrollment, English as a second language, honors program, independent study, internships, study abroad, teacher certification program.

FACILITIES

Housing: Coed, apartments for married students, apartments for single students, fraternities and/or sororities. **Library Holdings:** 491,179 bound volumes. 2,488 periodicals. 1,403,102 microforms. 17,567 audiovisuals. **Special Academic Facilities/Equipment:** Walker Teaching Resource Center; Jones Observatory; Institute of Archaeology; Odor Research Center. **Computers:** School-owned computers available for student use.

EXTRACURRICULARS

Activities: Choral groups, concert band, dance, drama/theater, jazz band, marching band, music ensembles, pep band, radio station, student government, student newspaper, student-run film society, symphony orchestra. **Organizations:** 130 registered organizations, 19 honor societies, 9 religious organizations, 12 fraternities, 7 sororities. **Athletics (Intercollegiate):** *Men:* basketball, crew, cross-country, football, golf, tennis, track & field, wrestling. *Women:* basketball, crew, cross-country, soccer, softball, tennis, track & field, volleyball.

ADMISSIONS

Selectivity Rating: 84 (of 100). **Freshman Academic Profile:** Average high school GPA 3.1. Average ACT 21, ACT middle 50% range 18-24. TOEFL required of all international applicants, minimum TOEFL 500. **Basis for Candidate Selection:** *Very important factors considered include:* secondary school record, standardized test scores. *Important factors considered include:* essays. *Other factors considered include:* minority status. **Freshman Admission Requirements:** High school diploma or GED is required. *Academic units required/recommended:* 4 English required, 3 math required, 2 science required, 2 science lab required, 2 foreign language required, 2 social studies required, 1 history required. **Freshman Admission Statistics:** 2,686 applied, 55% accepted, 82% of those accepted enrolled. **Transfer Admission Requirements:** *Items required:* college transcript. Minimum college GPA of 1.0 required. Lowest grade transferable D. **General Admission Information:** Application fee $25. Priority application deadline August 1. Nonfall registration accepted. Admission may be deferred. Credit and/or placement offered for CEEB Advanced Placement tests.

COSTS AND FINANCIAL AID

Average book expense $800. **Notification of Awards:** Applicants will be notified of awards on a rolling basis. **Student Employment:** Federal Work-Study Program available. Institutional employment available. Off-campus job opportunities are good. **Financial Aid Phone:** 423-425-4677.

UNIVERSITY OF TENNESSEE—KNOXVILLE

320 Student Service Building, Circle Park Drive, Knoxville, TN 37996-0230
Phone: 865-974-2184 **E-mail:** admissions@tennessee.edu **CEEB Code:** 1843
Fax: 865-974-6341 **Web:** www.tennessee.edu **ACT Code:** 4026

This public school was founded in 1794. It has a 561-acre campus.

STUDENTS AND FACULTY

Enrollment: 19,956. **Student Body:** Male 49%, female 51%, out-of-state 14%, international 1% (90 countries represented). **Ethnic Representation:** African American 7%, Asian 3%, Caucasian 88%, Hispanic 1%. **Retention and Graduation:** 76% freshmen return for sophomore year. 28% freshmen graduate within 4 years. **Faculty:** Student/faculty ratio 19:1. 1,215 full-time faculty, 85% hold PhDs. 88% faculty teach undergrads.

ACADEMICS

Degrees: Bachelor's, doctoral, first professional, first professional certificate, master's, post-bachelor's certificate, post-master's certificate. **Academic Requirements:** General education including some course work in arts/fine arts, English (including composition), foreign languages, history, humanities, mathematics, philosophy, sciences (biological or physical), social science. **Classes:** 20-29 students in an average class. 10-19 students in an average lab/discussion section. **Disciplines with Highest Percentage of Degrees Awarded:** Business/marketing 18%, social sciences and history 13%, psychology 9%, communications/communication technologies 8%, engineering/engineering technology 7%. **Special Study Options:** Accelerated program, cooperative (work-study) program, distance learning, double major, English as a second language, honors program, independent study, internships, liberal arts/career combination, student-designed major, study abroad, teacher certification program.

FACILITIES

Housing: Coed, all-female, all-male, apartments for married students, apartments for single students, fraternities and/or sororities. **Library Holdings:** 24,437,024 bound volumes. 17,628 periodicals. 3,781,232 microforms. 175,541 audiovisuals. **Special Academic Facilities/Equipment:** Comprehensive museum of anthropology, archaeology, art, geology, natural history, and medicine, theatre-in-the-round, child development lab, livestock farms, robotics research center, electron microscope, McClung Museum. **Computers:** School-owned computers available for student use.

EXTRACURRICULARS

Activities: Choral groups, concert band, dance, drama/theater, jazz band, literary magazine, marching band, music ensembles, musical theater, opera, pep band, radio station, student government, student newspaper, student-run film society, symphony orchestra, yearbook. **Organizations:** 331 registered organizations, 51 honor societies, 32 religious organizations, 26 fraternities (15% men join), 17 sororities (20% women join). **Athletics (Intercollegiate):** *Men:* baseball, basketball, cheerleading, cross-country, diving, football, golf, indoor track, swimming, tennis, track & field, volleyball. *Women:* basketball, cheerleading, crew, cross-country, diving, golf, indoor track, soccer, softball, swimming, tennis, track & field, volleyball.

ADMISSIONS

Selectivity Rating: 77 (of 100). **Freshman Academic Profile:** Average high school GPA 3.4. 27% in top 10% of high school class, 54% in top 25% of high school class, 83% in top 50% of high school class. Average SAT I Math 549, SAT I Math middle 50% range 500-610. Average SAT I Verbal 551, SAT I Verbal middle 50% range 500-600. Average ACT 24, ACT middle 50% range 21-26.

TOEFL required of all international applicants, minimum TOEFL 523. **Basis for Candidate Selection:** *Very important factors considered include:* secondary school record, standardized test scores. *Important factors considered include:* essays, state residency, talent/ability. *Other factors considered include:* alumni/ae relation, character/personal qualities, class rank, extracurricular activities, interview, minority status, recommendations, volunteer work, work experience. **Freshman Admission Requirements:** High school diploma or GED is required. *Academic units required/recommended:* 14 total required; 4 English required, 3 math required, 2 science required, 1 science lab required, 2 foreign language required, 1 social studies required, 1 history required. **Freshman Admission Statistics:** 9,350 applied, 88% accepted, 45% of those accepted enrolled. **Transfer Admission Requirements;** *Items required:* high school transcript, college transcript, standardized test scores. Minimum college GPA of 2.0 required. Lowest grade transferable C. **General Admission Information:** Application fee $25. Priority application deadline November 1. Regular application deadline February 1. Nonfall registration accepted. Admission may be deferred. Credit offered for CEEB Advanced Placement tests.

COSTS AND FINANCIAL AID

In-state tuition $3,476. Out-of-state tuition $11,578. Room & board $4,912. Required fees $550. Average book expense $1,090. **Required Forms and Deadlines:** FAFSA, institution's own financial aid form and Academic College Scholarship Application. No deadline for regular filing. Priority filing deadline March 1. **Notification of Awards:** Applicants will be notified of awards on a rolling basis beginning on or about April 1. **Types of Aid:** *Need-based scholarships/grants:* Pell, SEOG, state scholarships/grants, private scholarships, the school's own gift aid. *Loans:* FFEL Subsidized Stafford, FFEL Unsubsidized Stafford, FFEL PLUS, Federal Perkins, college/university loans from institutional funds. **Student Employment:** Federal Work-Study Program available. Off-campus job opportunities are good. **Financial Aid Statistics:** 31% freshmen, 33% undergrads receive some form of aid. **Financial Aid Phone:** 865-974-3131.

UNIVERSITY OF TENNESSEE—MARTIN

200 Hall-Moody, Administrative Building, Martin, TN 38238
Phone: 731-587-7020 **E-mail:** jrayburn@utm.edu
Fax: 731-587-7029 **Web:** www.utm.edu **ACT Code:** 4032

This public school was founded in 1900. It has a 250-acre campus.

STUDENTS AND FACULTY

Enrollment: 5,300. **Student Body:** Male 43%, female 57%, out-of-state 6%, international 3%. **Ethnic Representation:** African American 16%, Asian 1%, Caucasian 82%, Hispanic 1%. **Retention and Graduation:** 67% freshmen return for sophomore year. 13% freshmen graduate within 4 years. 16% grads go on to further study within 1 year. 5% grads pursue business degrees. 3% grads pursue law degrees. 2% grads pursue medical degrees. **Faculty:** Student/faculty ratio 18:1. 243 full-time faculty, 68% hold PhDs. 100% faculty teach undergrads.

ACADEMICS

Degrees: Bachelor's, master's. **Academic Requirements:** General education including some course work in computer literacy, English (including composition), history, humanities, mathematics, philosophy, sciences (biological or physical), social science. **Classes:** 10-19 students in an average class. 20-29 students in an average lab/discussion section. **Majors with Highest Enrollment:** Nursing/registered nurse training (RN, ASN, BSN, MSN); business/commerce, general; agriculture, general. **Disciplines with Highest Percentage of Degrees Awarded:** Business/marketing 26%, education 16%, agriculture 8%, biological life sciences 6%, communications/communication technologies 5%. **Special Study Options:** Accelerated program, cooperative (work-study) program, distance learning, double major, dual enrollment, English as a second language, honors program, independent study, internships, liberal arts/career combination, student-designed major, study abroad, teacher certification program.

FACILITIES

Housing: Coed, all-female, all-male, apartments for married students, apartments for single students, housing for disabled students, fraternities and/or sororities, honors floor, Spanish language suite, Japanese language suite, freshman only, year-round living for people who do not go home at breaks. **Library Holdings:** 372,008 bound volumes. 1,607 periodicals. 666,729 microforms. 11,669 audiovisuals. **Computers:** School-owned computers available for student use.

EXTRACURRICULARS

Activities: Choral groups, concert band, dance, drama/theater, jazz band, literary magazine, marching band, music ensembles, musical theater, opera, pep band, radio station, student government, student newspaper, student-run film society, television station, yearbook. **Organizations:** 121 registered organizations, 17 honor societies, 7 religious organizations, 9 fraternities (21% men join), 8 sororities (18% women join). **Athletics (Intercollegiate):** *Men:* baseball, basketball, cheerleading, football, golf, rifle, rodeo, tennis, track & field. *Women:* basketball, cheerleading, cross-country, rifle, rodeo, soccer, softball, tennis, track & field, volleyball.

ADMISSIONS

Selectivity Rating: 82 (of 100). **Freshman Academic Profile:** Average high school GPA 3.2. 17% in top 10% of high school class, 38% in top 25% of high school class, 65% in top 50% of high school class. Average ACT 21, ACT middle 50% range 18-24. TOEFL required of all international applicants, minimum TOEFL 500. **Basis for Candidate Selection:** *Very important factors considered include:* secondary school record, standardized test scores. **Freshman Admission Requirements:** High school diploma or GED is required. *Academic units required/recommended:* 14 total required; 4 English required, 3 math required, 2 science required, 1 science lab required, 2 foreign language required, 2 history required. **Freshman Admission Statistics:** 2,324 applied, 55% accepted, 84% of those accepted enrolled. **Transfer Admission Requirements:** *Items required:* high school transcript, college transcript. Minimum college GPA of 2.0 required. Lowest grade transferable D. **General Admission Information:** Application fee $25. Priority application deadline August 1. Regular application deadline August 1. Nonfall registration accepted. Admission may be deferred. Credit and/or placement offered for CEEB Advanced Placement tests.

COSTS AND FINANCIAL AID

In-state tuition $2,172. Out-of-state tuition $7,432. Room & board $3,606. Required fees $484. Average book expense $850. **Required Forms and Deadlines:** FAFSA. No deadline for regular filing. **Notification of Awards:** Applicants will be notified of awards on a rolling basis beginning on or about May 1. **Types of Aid:** *Need-based scholarships/grants:* Pell, SEOG, state scholarships/grants, private scholarships, TN Minority Teaching Fellowships, TN Teachers Scholars Program. *Loans:* FFEL Subsidized Stafford, FFEL Unsubsidized Stafford, FFEL PLUS, Federal Perkins. **Student Employment:** Federal Work-Study Program available. Institutional employment available. Off-campus job opportunities are good. **Financial Aid Statistics:** 55% freshmen, 52% undergrads receive some form of aid. Average freshman grant $5,615. Average freshman loan $3,131. Average income from on-campus job $1,514. **Financial Aid Phone:** 731-587-7040.

UNIVERSITY OF TEXAS MEDICAL BRANCH

301 University Boulevard, Galveston, TX 77555-1305
Phone: 409-772-1215 **E-mail:** student.admissions@utmb.edu **CEEB Code:** 6887
Fax: 409-772-4466 **Web:** www.utmb.edu

This public school was founded in 1891. It has an 85-acre campus.

STUDENTS AND FACULTY

Enrollment: 557. **Student Body:** Male 15%, female 85%, international 1% (5 countries represented). **Ethnic Representation:** African American 14%, Asian 7%, Caucasian 59%, Hispanic 17%, Native American 1%. **Faculty:** Student/faculty ratio 4:1. 81 full-time faculty.

ACADEMICS

Degrees: Bachelor's, doctoral, first professional, master's. **Academic Requirements:** General education including some course work in arts/fine arts, computer literacy, English (including composition), history, humanities, mathematics, sciences (biological or physical), social science. **Majors with Highest Enrollment:** Clinical laboratory science/medical technology/technologist; nursing/registered nurse training (RN, ASN, BSN, MSN); occupational therapy/therapist. **Disciplines with Highest Percentage of Degrees Awarded:** Health professions and related sciences 100%. **Special Study Options:** Distance learning, independent study, internships.

FACILITIES

Housing: Coed, apartments for married students, apartments for single students, fraternities and/or sororities. **Library Holdings:** 248,370 bound volumes. 1,980 periodicals. 0 microforms. 960 audiovisuals. **Computers:** School-owned computers available for student use.

EXTRACURRICULARS

Activities: Student government, student newspaper, yearbook.

ADMISSIONS

Selectivity Rating: 60 (of 100). **Freshman Academic Profile:** TOEFL required of all international applicants, minimum TOEFL 550. **Transfer Admission Requirements:** *Items required:* college transcript. Minimum college GPA of 2.0 required. Lowest grade transferable C. **General Admission Information:** Application fee $30. Regular application deadline varies. Nonfall registration accepted.

COSTS AND FINANCIAL AID

Required Forms and Deadlines: FAFSA and institution's own financial aid form. No deadline for regular filing. **Notification of Awards:** Applicants will be notified of awards on a rolling basis. **Types of Aid:** *Need-based scholarships/grants:* Pell, SEOG, state scholarships/grants, private scholarships, the school's own gift aid. *Loans:* Direct Subsidized Stafford, Direct Unsubsidized Stafford, Direct PLUS, Federal Perkins, Federal Nursing, state loans, college/university loans from institutional funds. **Student Employment:** Federal Work-Study Program available. Institutional employment available. Off-campus job opportunities are good. **Financial Aid Phone:** 409-772-4955.

UNIVERSITY OF TEXAS—ARLINGTON

Office of Admissions, PO Box 19111, Arlington, TX 76019-0088
Phone: 817-272-6287 **E-mail:** admissions@uta.edu **CEEB Code:** 6013
Fax: 817-272-3435 **Web:** www.uta.edu **ACT Code:** 4200

This public school was founded in 1895. It has a 390-acre campus.

STUDENTS AND FACULTY

Enrollment: 17,650. **Student Body:** Male 47%, female 53%, out-of-state 2%, international 5%. **Ethnic Representation:** African American 14%, Asian 12%, Caucasian 60%, Hispanic 13%, Native American 1%. **Retention and Graduation:** 70% freshmen return for sophomore year. 12% freshmen graduate within 4 years. **Faculty:** Student/faculty ratio 23:1. 678 full-time faculty. 100% faculty teach undergrads.

ACADEMICS

Degrees: Bachelor's, doctoral, master's, post-bachelor's certificate, post-master's certificate. **Academic Requirements:** General education including some course work in arts/fine arts, computer literacy, English (including composition), foreign languages, history, mathematics, sciences (biological or physical), social science, liberal arts elective (philosophy, fine arts, etc.). **Classes:** 10-19 students in an average class. **Majors with Highest Enrollment:** Nursing; management information systems, general; real estate. **Disciplines with Highest Percentage of Degrees Awarded:** Business/marketing 32%, health professions and related sciences 10%, engineering/engineering technology 9%, social sciences and history 7%, interdisciplinary studies 6%. **Special Study Options:** Cooperative (work-study) program, cross registration, distance learning, double major, English as a second language, honors program, independent study, internships, student-designed major, study abroad, teacher certification program.

FACILITIES

Housing: Coed, all-female, all-male, apartments for married students, apartments for single students, fraternities and/or sororities, family housing (priority given to students with dependent children). **Library Holdings:** 1,119,526 bound volumes. 3,977 periodicals. 1,470,177 microforms. 5,240 audiovisuals. **Special Academic Facilities/Equipment:** Cartographic history library, maps collection, minority cultures collection, library of Texana and Mexican war material, planetarium, Automation and Robotics Research Institute, Wave Scattering Research Center. **Computers:** School-owned computers available for student use.

EXTRACURRICULARS

Activities: Choral groups, concert band, dance, drama/theater, jazz band, marching band, music ensembles, opera, radio station, student government, student newspaper, symphony orchestra. **Organizations:** 224 registered organizations, 23 honor societies, 16 religious organizations, 12 fraternities (5% men join), 10 sororities (4% women join). **Athletics (Intercollegiate):** *Men:* baseball, basketball, cross-country, golf, tennis, track & field. *Women:* basketball, cross-country, softball, tennis, track & field, volleyball.

ADMISSIONS

Selectivity Rating: 64 (of 100). **Freshman Academic Profile:** 18% in top 10% of high school class, 48% in top 25% of high school class, 79% in top 50% of high school class. Average SAT I Math 531, SAT I Math middle 50% range 470-590. Average SAT I Verbal 513, SAT I Verbal middle 50% range 460-560. Average ACT 21, ACT middle 50% range 18-23. TOEFL required of all international applicants, minimum TOEFL 550. **Basis for Candidate Selection:** *Very important factors considered include:* class rank, secondary school record, standardized test scores. *Other factors considered include:* alumni/ae relation, character/personal qualities, essays, extracurricular activities, geographical residence, interview, recommendations, state residency, talent/ability, volunteer work, work experience. **Freshman Admission Requirements:** High school diploma or GED is required. *Academic units required/recommended:* 20 total required; 4 English required, 4 English recommended, 3 math required, 4 math recommended, 3 science required, 3 science recommended, 2 foreign language required, 3 foreign language recommended, 3 social studies required, 4 social studies recommended, 5 elective required, 2 elective recommended. **Freshman Admission Statistics:** 4,791 applied, 90% accepted, 51% of those accepted enrolled. **Transfer Admission Requirements:** *Items required:* high school transcript, college transcript, standardized test scores. Minimum college GPA of 2.0 required. Lowest grade transferable C. **General Admission Information:** Application fee $25. Priority application deadline June 1. Nonfall registration accepted. Admission may be deferred for a maximum of 1 year. Credit offered for CEEB Advanced Placement tests.

COSTS AND FINANCIAL AID

Out-of-state tuition $9,180. Room & board $4,607. Required fees $1,484. Average book expense $600. **Required Forms and Deadlines:** FAFSA. No deadline for regular filing. Priority filing deadline June 1. **Notification of Awards:** Applicants will be notified of awards on a rolling basis beginning on or about May 1. **Types of Aid:** *Need-based scholarships/grants:* Pell, SEOG, state scholarships/grants, private scholarships, the school's own gift aid. *Loans:* FFEL Subsidized Stafford, FFEL Unsubsidized Stafford, FFEL PLUS, Federal Perkins, state loans, college/university loans from institutional funds. **Student Employment:** Federal Work-Study Program available. Institutional employment available. Off-campus job opportunities are excellent. **Financial Aid Statistics:** 40% freshmen, 42% undergrads receive some form of aid. Average freshman grant $1,839. Average freshman loan $2,552. **Financial Aid Phone:** 817-272-3561.

UNIVERSITY OF TEXAS—AUSTIN

Office of Admissions/Freshmen Admission Center, PO Box 8058, Austin, TX 78713-8058
Phone: 512-475-7440 **E-mail:** frmn@uts.cc.utexas.edu **CEEB Code:** 6882
Fax: 512-475-7475 **Web:** www.utexas.edu **ACT Code:** 4240

This public school was founded in 1883. It has a 350-acre campus.

STUDENTS AND FACULTY

Enrollment: 39,661. **Student Body:** Male 49%, female 51%, out-of-state 5%, international 3% (126 countries represented). **Ethnic Representation:** African American 4%, Asian 17%, Caucasian 64%, Hispanic 14%. **Retention and Graduation:** 91% freshmen return for sophomore year. 39% freshmen graduate within 4 years. **Faculty:** Student/faculty ratio 19:1. 2,476 full-time faculty, 97% hold PhDs.

ACADEMICS

Degrees: Bachelor's, doctoral, first professional, master's. **Academic Requirements:** General education including some course work in arts/fine arts, English (including composition), foreign languages, history, humanities, mathematics, sciences (biological or physical), social science. **Classes:** 10-19 students in an average class. 10-19 students in an average lab/discussion section. **Majors with Highest Enrollment:** Psychology, general; economics, general; multi/interdisciplinary studies. **Disciplines with Highest Percentage of Degrees Awarded:** Social sciences and history 15%, business/marketing 14%, communications/communication technologies 13%, engineering/engineering technology 10%, biological life sciences 6%. **Special Study Options:** Accelerated program, cooperative (work-study) program, distance learning, double major, dual enrollment, English as a second language, honors program, independent study, internships, liberal arts/career combination, student-designed major, study abroad, teacher certification program.

FACILITIES

Housing: Coed, all-female, all-male, apartments for married students, apartments for single students, cooperative housing, Honors Residence, Living Learning Centers (first-time freshmen). **Library Holdings:** 4,346,398 bound volumes. 49,771 periodicals. 5,954,373 microforms. 622,610 audiovisuals. **Special Academic Facilities/Equipment:** Art gallery, Lyndon Baines Johnson Library/Museum, Performing Arts Center, Texas Memorial Museum, Humanities Research Center.

EXTRACURRICULARS

Activities: Choral groups, concert band, dance, drama/theater, jazz band, literary magazine, marching band, music ensembles, musical theater, opera, pep band, radio station, student government, student newspaper, student-run film society, symphony orchestra, television station, yearbook. **Organizations:** 750 registered organizations, 95 religious organizations, 29 fraternities (10% men join), 22 sororities (14% women join). **Athletics (Intercollegiate):** *Men:* baseball, basketball, cross-country, diving, football, golf, swimming, tennis, track & field. *Women:* basketball, crew, cross-country, diving, golf, soccer, softball, swimming, tennis, track & field, volleyball.

ADMISSIONS

Selectivity Rating: 88 (of 100). **Freshman Academic Profile:** 53% in top 10% of high school class, 87% in top 25% of high school class, 99% in top 50% of high school class. Average SAT I Math 626, SAT I Math middle 50% range 570-680. Average SAT I Verbal 596, SAT I Verbal middle 50% range 540-650. Average ACT 26, ACT middle 50% range 22-28. TOEFL required of all international applicants, minimum TOEFL 550. **Basis for Candidate Selection:** *Very important factors considered include:* class rank, secondary school record. *Important factors considered include:* essays, extracurricular activities, standardized test scores, talent/ability, volunteer work, work experience. *Other factors considered include:* character/personal qualities, geographical residence, recommendations, state residency. **Freshman Admission Requirements:** High school diploma or GED is required. *Academic units required/recommended:* 16 total required; 4 English required, 3 math required, 4 math recommended, 2 science required, 3 science recommended, 2 foreign language required, 3 foreign language recommended, 3 social studies required, 2 elective required. **Freshman Admission Statistics:** 22,179 applied, 61% accepted, 59% of those accepted enrolled. **Transfer Admission Requirements:** *Items required:* college transcript. Minimum college GPA of 3.0 required. Lowest grade transferable C. **General Admission Information:** Application fee $50. Regular application deadline February 1. Nonfall registration accepted. Admission may be deferred for a maximum of 1 year. Credit and/or placement offered for CEEB Advanced Placement tests.

COSTS AND FINANCIAL AID

In-state tuition $2,640. Out-of-state tuition $9,180. Room & board $5,975. Required fees $1,310. Average book expense $736. **Required Forms and Deadlines:** FAFSA. No deadline for regular filing. Priority filing deadline April 1. **Notification of Awards:** Applicants will be notified of awards on a rolling basis beginning on or about March 15. **Types of Aid:** *Need-based scholarships/grants:* Pell, SEOG, state scholarships/grants, private scholarships, the school's own gift aid, Federal Nursing. *Loans:* FFEL Subsidized Stafford, FFEL Unsubsidized Stafford, FFEL PLUS, Federal Perkins, state loans, college/university loans from institutional funds. **Student Employment:** Federal Work-Study Program available. Institutional employment available. Off-campus job opportunities are good. **Financial Aid Statistics:** 46% freshmen, 48% undergrads receive some form of aid. Average freshman grant $4,280. Average freshman loan $3,100. **Financial Aid Phone:** 512-475-6282.

UNIVERSITY OF TEXAS—BROWNSVILLE

80 Fort Brown, Brownsville, TX 78520
Phone: 956-544-8295 **E-mail:** admissions@utb.edu **CEEB Code:** 6825
Fax: 956-983-7810 **Web:** www.utb.edu

STUDENTS AND FACULTY

Enrollment: 9,198. **Student Body:** Male 39%, female 61%, out-of-state 0%. **Ethnic Representation:** Caucasian 4%, Hispanic 95%. **Faculty:** Student/faculty ratio 17:1. 289 full-time faculty, 49% hold PhDs.

ACADEMICS

Degrees: Associate's, bachelor's, certificate, master's, terminal, transfer. **Academic Requirements:** General education including some course work in arts/fine arts, English (including composition), foreign languages, history, humanities, mathematics, sciences (biological or physical), social science. **Classes:** Under 10 students in an average class. 10-19 students in an average lab/discussion section. **Majors with Highest Enrollment:** Spanish language and literature; business administration/management; liberal arts and sciences/liberal studies. **Disciplines with Highest Percentage of Degrees Awarded:** Business/marketing 21%, social sciences and history 13%, foreign languages and literature 12%, protective services/public administration 8%, liberal arts/general studies 8%. **Special Study Options:** Cooperative (work-study) program, distance learning, double major, dual enrollment, English as a second language, independent study, internships, teacher certification program.

FACILITIES

Library Holdings: 159,006 bound volumes. 56,965 periodicals. 755,861 microforms. 4,569 audiovisuals.

EXTRACURRICULARS

Activities: Choral groups, dance, jazz band, music ensembles, student government, student newspaper, yearbook. **Athletics (Intercollegiate):** *Men:* baseball, golf. *Women:* golf, volleyball.

ADMISSIONS

Selectivity Rating: 63 (of 100). **Freshman Academic Profile:** 95% from public high schools. **Freshman Admission Requirements:** High school diploma or equivalent is not required. **Freshman Admission Statistics:** 1,901 applied, 100% accepted, 74% of those accepted enrolled. **Transfer Admission Requirements:** *Items required:* college transcript. Minimum college GPA of 2.0 required. Lowest grade transferable D. **General Admission Information:** Nonfall registration accepted. Admission may be deferred for a maximum of 1 year. Credit offered for CEEB Advanced Placement tests.

COSTS AND FINANCIAL AID

Required Forms and Deadlines: FAFSA. Financial aid filing deadline June 1. Priority filing deadline April 1. **Notification of Awards:** Applicants will be notified of awards on or about May 1. **Types of Aid:** *Need-based scholarships/grants:* Pell, SEOG, state scholarships/grants, private scholarships, the school's own gift aid. *Loans:* FFEL Subsidized Stafford, FFEL Unsubsidized Stafford, FFEL PLUS, college/university loans from institutional funds. **Student Employment:** Federal Work-Study Program available. Institutional employment available. Off-campus job opportunities are good. **Financial Aid Phone:** 956-544-8277.

UNIVERSITY OF TEXAS—DALLAS

PO Box 830688, MC 11, Richardson, TX 75083-0688
Phone: 972-883-2342 **E-mail:** admissions-status@utdallas.edu **CEEB Code:** 6897
Fax: 972-883-6803 **Web:** www.utdallas.edu **ACT Code:** 4243

This public school was founded in 1969. It has a 455-acre campus.

STUDENTS AND FACULTY

Enrollment: 7,959. **Student Body:** Male 51%, female 49%, out-of-state 3%, international 5% (137 countries represented). **Ethnic Representation:** African American 8%, Asian 22%, Caucasian 59%, Hispanic 9%, Native American 1%. **Retention and Graduation:** 80% freshmen return for sophomore year. 30% freshmen graduate within 4 years. **Faculty:** Student/faculty ratio 20:1. 390 full-time faculty, 97% hold PhDs. 94% faculty teach undergrads.

ACADEMICS

Degrees: Bachelor's, doctoral, master's, post-bachelor's certificate, post-master's certificate. **Academic Requirements:** General education including some course work in arts/fine arts, computer literacy, English (including composition), history, humanities, mathematics, sciences (biological or physical), social science. **Classes:** 10-19 students in an average class. 10-19 students in an average lab/discussion section. **Majors with Highest Enrollment:** Business administration/management; computer science; electrical, electronics, and communications engineering. **Disciplines with Highest Percentage of Degrees Awarded:** Business/marketing 31%, computer and information sciences 17%, interdisciplinary studies 12%, social sciences and history 8%, psychology 8%. **Special Study Options:** Accelerated program, cooperative (work-study) program, cross registration, distance learning, double major, dual enrollment, honors program, independent study, internships, student-designed major, study abroad, teacher certification program.

FACILITIES

Housing: Apartments for married students, apartments for single students. In addition there are privately owned and operated apartments on campus that are restricted to UTD students. UTD provides security, activities, and resident advisors for the apartments. **Library Holdings:** 754,491 bound volumes. 3,078 periodicals. 1,878,345 microforms. 5,080 audiovisuals. **Special Academic Facilities/Equipment:** Callier Center, History of Aviation Collection, Wineburgh Philatelic Research Library. **Computers:** School-owned computers available for student use.

EXTRACURRICULARS

Activities: Dance, drama/theater, student government, student newspaper. **Organizations:** 115 registered organizations, 6 honor societies, 22 religious organizations, 4 fraternities (5% men join), 4 sororities (3% women join). **Athletics (Intercollegiate):** *Men:* baseball, basketball, cross-country, golf, soccer, tennis. *Women:* basketball, cross-country, golf, soccer, softball, tennis.

ADMISSIONS

Selectivity Rating: 85 (of 100). **Freshman Academic Profile:** Average high school GPA 3.4. 38% in top 10% of high school class, 70% in top 25% of high school class, 96% in top 50% of high school class. 93% from public high schools. Average SAT I Math 616, SAT I Math middle 50% range 560-680. Average SAT I Verbal 586, SAT I Verbal middle 50% range 530-650. ACT middle 50% range 22-28. TOEFL required of all international applicants, minimum TOEFL 550. **Basis for Candidate Selection:** *Very important factors considered include:* class rank, secondary school record, standardized test scores. *Important factors considered include:* essays, extracurricular activities. *Other factors considered include:* character/personal qualities, geographical residence, state residency, talent/ability, volunteer work, work experience. **Freshman Admission Requirements:** High school diploma or GED is required. *Academic units required/recommended:* 18 total required; 24 total recommended; 4 English required, 4 English recommended, 4 math required, 4 math recommended, 3 science required, 3 science recommended, 3 science lab required, 3 science lab recommended, 2 foreign language required, 3 foreign language recommended, 3 social studies required, 4 social studies recommended, 2 elective required, 2 elective recommended. **Freshman Admission Statistics:** 4,086 applied, 53% accepted, 42% of those accepted enrolled. **Transfer Admission Requirements:** *Items required:* college transcript. Minimum college GPA of 2.5 required. Lowest grade transferable C. **General Admission Information:** Application fee $50. Regular application deadline August 1. Nonfall registration accepted. Admission may be deferred for a maximum of 1 year. Credit and/or placement offered for CEEB Advanced Placement tests.

COSTS AND FINANCIAL AID

In-state tuition $1,320. Out-of-state tuition $7,860. Room & board $6,032. Required fees $3,455. Average book expense $1,000. **Required Forms and Deadlines:** FAFSA. Financial aid filing deadline April 30. Priority filing deadline March 12. **Notification of Awards:** Applicants will be notified of awards on a rolling basis beginning on or about April 15. **Types of Aid:** *Need-based scholarships/grants:* Pell, SEOG, state scholarships/grants, private scholarships, the school's own gift aid. *Loans:* Direct Subsidized Stafford, Direct Unsubsidized Stafford, FFEL Subsidized Stafford, FFEL Unsubsidized Stafford, FFEL PLUS, Federal Perkins, state loans, college/university loans from institutional funds. **Student Employment:** Federal Work-Study Program available. Institutional employment available. Off-campus job opportunities are excellent. **Financial Aid Statistics:** 40% freshmen, 38% undergrads receive some form of aid. Average freshman grant $4,668. Average freshman loan $2,024. Average income from on-campus job $5,167. **Financial Aid Phone:** 972-883-2941.

UNIVERSITY OF TEXAS—EL PASO

500 W. University Ave., El Paso, TX 79968
Phone: 915-747-5576 **E-mail:** admission@utep.edu **CEEB Code:** 6829
Fax: 915-747-8893 **Web:** www.utep.edu **ACT Code:** 4223

This public school was founded in 1913. It has a 330-acre campus.

STUDENTS AND FACULTY

Enrollment: 14,384. **Student Body:** Male 45%, female 55%, out-of-state 3%, international 11%. **Ethnic Representation:** African American 3%, Asian 1%, Caucasian 12%, Hispanic 83%. **Retention and Graduation:** 69% freshmen return for sophomore year. 3% freshmen graduate within 4 years. **Faculty:** Student/faculty ratio 19:1. 593 full-time faculty. 88% faculty teach undergrads.

ACADEMICS

Degrees: Bachelor's, doctoral, master's. **Academic Requirements:** General education including some course work in arts/fine arts, English (including composition), foreign languages, mathematics, sciences (biological or physical). **Classes:** 20-29 students in an average class. 10-19 students in an average lab/discussion section. **Majors with Highest Enrollment:** Business administration/management; engineering, general; general studies. **Disciplines with Highest Percentage of Degrees Awarded:** Business/marketing 24%, interdisciplinary studies 19%, engineering/engineering technology 8%, health professions and related sciences 8%, social sciences and history 5%. **Special Study Options:** Cooperative (work-study) program, distance learning, dual enrollment, honors program, independent study, internships, study abroad, teacher certification program, weekend college.

FACILITIES

Housing: Coed, apartments for married students, apartments for single students, fraternities and/or sororities. **Library Holdings:** 1,080,588 bound volumes. 2,833 periodicals. 1,760,984 microforms. 9,995 audiovisuals. **Special Academic Facilities/Equipment:** Cross-cultural ethnic study center, natural history and cultural museum, solar pond and solar house, electron microscope, atmospheric and acoustic research lab, seismic observatory. **Computers:** School-owned computers available for student use.

EXTRACURRICULARS

Activities: Choral groups, concert band, dance, drama/theater, jazz band, marching band, music ensembles, musical theater, opera, pep band, radio station, student government, student newspaper, symphony orchestra. **Organizations:** 1 honor society, 1 religious organization, 6 fraternities, 4 sororities. **Athletics (Intercollegiate):** *Men:* basketball, cross-country, football, golf, indoor track, tennis, track & field, volleyball. *Women:* basketball, cross-country, golf, indoor track, rifle, soccer, tennis, track & field, volleyball.

ADMISSIONS

Selectivity Rating: 70 (of 100). **Freshman Academic Profile:** Average high school GPA 3.5. 15% in top 10% of high school class, 40% in top 25% of high school class, 70% in top 50% of high school class. 94% from public high schools. Average SAT I Math 454, SAT I Math middle 50% range 400-510. Average SAT I Verbal 448, SAT I Verbal middle 50% range 390-510. Average ACT 18, ACT middle 50% range 16-21. **Basis for Candidate Selection:** *Very important factors considered include:* class rank, state residency. *Important factors considered include:* geographical residence, secondary school record, standardized test scores. *Other factors considered include:* alumni/ae relation, character/personal qualities, extracurricular activities, interview, talent/ability, volunteer work, work experience. **Freshman Admission Requirements:** High school diploma or GED is required. *Academic units required/recommended:* 22 total recommended; 4 English recommended, 4 math recommended, 3 science recommended, 3 foreign language recommended, 4 social studies recommended. **Freshman Admission Statistics:** 3,724 applied, 94% accepted, 67% of those accepted enrolled. **Transfer Admission Requirements:** *Items required:* college transcript. Minimum college GPA of 2.0 required. Lowest grade transferable D. **General Admission Information:** Priority application deadline May 1. Regular application deadline July 31. Nonfall registration accepted. Admission may be deferred.

COSTS AND FINANCIAL AID

In-state tuition $2,064. Out-of-state tuition $7,296. Room & board $4,255. Required fees $732. Average book expense $842. **Required Forms and Deadlines:** FAFSA and institution's own financial aid form. Priority filing deadline March 15. **Notification of Awards:** Applicants will be notified of awards on or about June 30. **Types of Aid:** *Need-based scholarships/grants:* Pell, SEOG, state scholarships/grants, the school's own gift aid, Federal Nursing. *Loans:* FFEL Subsidized Stafford, FFEL Unsubsidized Stafford, FFEL PLUS, Federal Perkins, college/university loans from institutional funds. **Student Employment:** Federal Work-Study Program available. Institutional employment available. Off-campus job opportunities are good. **Financial Aid Statistics:** 58% freshmen, 52% undergrads receive some form of aid. Average freshman grant $5,193. Average freshman loan $2,658. Average income from on-campus job $1,840. **Financial Aid Phone:** 915-747-5204.

UNIVERSITY OF TEXAS—HOUSTON HEALTH SCIENCE CENTER

PO Box 20036, Houston, TX 77225
Phone: 713-500-3333 **E-mail:** uthschro@admin4.hsc.uth.tmc.edu
Fax: 713-500-3356 **Web:** www.uth.tmc.edu

This public school was founded in 1972.

STUDENTS AND FACULTY

Enrollment: 359. **Student Body:** Male 10%, female 90%, out-of-state 13%, international 1%. **Ethnic Representation:** African American 14%, Asian 11%, Caucasian 60%, Hispanic 14%. **Faculty:** 924 full-time faculty.

ACADEMICS

Degrees: Bachelor's, certificate, doctoral, first professional, master's, post-master's certificate. **Disciplines with Highest Percentage of Degrees Awarded:** Health professions and related sciences 100%.

FACILITIES

Housing: University owns an apartment complex located approximately 1.5 miles from campus. It is competitively priced with other apartment complexes in the area and does not cater exclusively to students. **Special Academic Facilities/Equipment:** The student's learning experience takes place in the heart of the Texas Medical Center, among state-of-the-art hospitals and research facilities.

EXTRACURRICULARS

Activities: Student government.

ADMISSIONS

Selectivity Rating: 63 (of 100). **Freshman Academic Profile:** TOEFL required of all international applicants, minimum TOEFL 565. **Transfer Admission Requirements:** *Items required:* college transcript, interview, standardized test score, statement of good standing from prior school. Minimum college GPA of 2.8 required. Lowest grade transferable C. **General Admission Information:** Application fee $10. Regular application deadline January 1.

COSTS AND FINANCIAL AID

In-state tuition $3,690. Out-of-state tuition $15,705. Required fees $656. Average book expense $2,400. **Required Forms and Deadlines:** FAFSA and institution's own financial aid form. No deadline for regular filing. Priority filing deadline March 1. **Types of Aid:** *Need-based scholarships/grants:* Pell, SEOG, state scholarships/grants, the school's own gift aid, Federal Nursing, outside scholarships. *Loans:* FFEL Subsidized Stafford, FFEL Unsubsidized Stafford, FFEL PLUS, Federal Perkins, Federal Nursing, college/university loans from institutional funds, outside loans. **Student Employment:** Off-campus job opportunities are excellent. **Financial Aid Statistics:** 92% undergrads receive some form of aid. **Financial Aid Phone:** 713-500-3860.

UNIVERSITY OF TEXAS—PAN AMERICAN

Office of Admissions & Records, 1201 West University Drive, Edinburg, TX 78541
Phone: 956-381-2201 **E-mail:** admissions@panam.edu
Fax: 956-381-2212 **Web:** www.panam.edu **ACT Code:** 4142

This public school was founded in 1927.

STUDENTS AND FACULTY

Enrollment: 12,529. **Student Body:** Male 42%, female 58%, out-of-state 1%, international 1%. **Ethnic Representation:** African American 1%, Asian 1%, Caucasian 6%, Hispanic 88%. **Retention and Graduation:** 64% freshmen return for sophomore year. 6% freshmen graduate within 4 years. 5% grads go on to further study within 1 year. 5% grads pursue business degrees. **Faculty:** Student/faculty ratio 22:1. 460 full-time faculty.

ACADEMICS

Degrees: Bachelor's, doctoral, master's, post-bachelor's certificate, post-master's certificate. **Academic Requirements:** General education including some course work in arts/fine arts, computer literacy, English (including composition), foreign languages, history, humanities, mathematics, philosophy, sciences (biological or physical), social science. **Classes:** 30-39 students in an average class. 20-29 students in an average lab/discussion section. **Majors with Highest Enrollment:** Nursing/registered nurse training (RN, ASN, BSN, MSN); business administration/management; multi/interdisciplinary studies. **Disciplines with Highest Percentage of Degrees Awarded:** Interdisciplinary studies 21%, business/marketing 17%, health professions and related sciences 10%, protective services/public administration 8%, social sciences and history 7%. **Special Study Options:** Cooperative (work-study) program, distance learning, double major, dual enrollment, student exchange program (domestic), honors program, independent study, internships, study abroad, teacher certification program, weekend college.

FACILITIES

Housing: All-female, all-male, apartments for married students, apartments for single students. **Library Holdings:** 505,641 bound volumes. 8,135 periodicals. 1,073,330 microforms. 25,862 audiovisuals.

EXTRACURRICULARS

Activities: Choral groups, concert band, dance, drama/theater, jazz band, music ensembles, student government, student newspaper, symphony orchestra. **Organizations:** 90 registered organizations, 5 honor societies, 7 religious organizations, 7 fraternities (1% men join), 1 sorority (1% women join). **Athletics (Intercollegiate):** *Men:* baseball, basketball, cross-country, golf, tennis, track & field, volleyball.

ADMISSIONS

Selectivity Rating: 63 (of 100). **Freshman Academic Profile:** 18% in top 10% of high school class, 44% in top 25% of high school class, 75% in top 50% of high school class. 99% from public high schools. Average SAT I Math 455, SAT I Math middle 50% range 390-510. Average SAT I Verbal 445, SAT I Verbal middle 50% range 380-500. Average ACT 18, ACT middle 50% range 15-20. TOEFL required of all international applicants, minimum TOEFL 550. **Basis for Candidate Selection:** *Important factors considered include:* secondary school record, standardized test scores. **Freshman Admission Requirements:** High school diploma or GED is required. *Academic units required/recommended:* 24 total required; 4 English required, 3 math required, 3 science required, 2 foreign language required, 4 social studies required, 3 social studies recommended, 4 elective required, 3 elective recommended. **Freshman Admission Statistics:** 5,728 applied, 72% accepted, 50% of those accepted enrolled. **Transfer Admission Requirements:** *Items required:* college transcript. Minimum college GPA of 2.0 required. Lowest grade transferable D. **General Admission Information:** Priority application deadline February 1. Regular application deadline July 10. Nonfall registration accepted.

COSTS AND FINANCIAL AID

In-state tuition $2,100. Out-of-state tuition $8,370. Room & board $4,333. Required fees $619. Average book expense $600. **Required Forms and Deadlines:** FAFSA. No deadline for regular filing. Priority filing deadline February 28. **Notification of Awards:** Applicants will be notified of awards on a rolling basis beginning on or about March 1. **Types of Aid:** *Need-based scholarships/grants:* Pell, SEOG, state scholarships/grants, private scholarships. *Loans:* FFEL Subsidized Stafford, FFEL Unsubsidized Stafford, FFEL PLUS, Federal Perkins, state loans, college/university loans from institutional funds. **Student Employment:** Federal Work-Study Program available. Off-campus job opportunities are fair. **Financial Aid Statistics:** 88% freshmen, 82% undergrads receive some form of aid. Average freshman grant $1,700. Average income from on-campus job $1,800.

UNIVERSITY OF TEXAS—PERMIAN BASIN

4901 East University Blvd., Odessa, TX 79762-0001
Phone: 915-552-2605 **E-mail:** admissions@utpb.edu **CEEB Code:** 448
Fax: 915-552-3605 **Web:** www.utpb.edu **ACT Code:** 4225

This public school was founded in 1969. It has a 588-acre campus.

STUDENTS AND FACULTY

Enrollment: 2,012. **Student Body:** Male 35%, female 65%, out-of-state 2%. **Ethnic Representation:** African American 6%, Asian 1%, Caucasian 90%, Hispanic 1%, Native American 1%. **Retention and Graduation:** 61% freshmen return for sophomore year. **Faculty:** Student/faculty ratio 18:1. 103 full-time faculty, 84% hold PhDs. 100% faculty teach undergrads.

ACADEMICS

Degrees: Bachelor's, master's. **Academic Requirements:** General education including some course work in computer literacy, English (including composition), history, humanities, mathematics, sciences (biological or physical), Texas higher education coordinating board core curriculum courses. **Classes:** 10-19 students in an average class. 10-19 students in an average lab/discussion section. **Majors with Highest Enrollment:** History, general; Spanish language and literature; humanities/humanistic studies. **Disciplines with Highest Percentage of Degrees Awarded:** Social sciences and history 22%, business/marketing 16%, liberal arts/general studies 12%, psychology 8%, foreign languages and literature 8%. **Special Study Options:** Accelerated program, cross registration, distance learning, double major, independent study, internships, teacher certification program.

FACILITIES

Housing: Apartments for married students, apartments for single students, housing for disabled students. **Library Holdings:** 257,531 bound volumes. 723 periodicals. 1,074,900 microforms. 6,322 audiovisuals. **Special Academic Facilities/Equipment:** Ellen Noel Art Center, applied psychology lab, visual arts studio. **Computers:** School-owned computers available for student use.

EXTRACURRICULARS

Activities: Choral groups, dance, drama/theater, literary magazine, pep band, radio station, student government, student newspaper. **Organizations:** 30 registered organizations, 3 honor societies, 3 religious organizations. **Athletics (Intercollegiate):** *Men:* baseball, basketball, soccer, swimming. *Women:* basketball, cheerleading, soccer, softball, swimming, volleyball.

ADMISSIONS

Selectivity Rating: 73 (of 100). **Freshman Academic Profile:** 21% in top 10% of high school class, 46% in top 25% of high school class, 83% in top 50% of high school class. 99% from public high schools. Average SAT I Math 477, SAT I Math middle 50% range 420-530. Average SAT I Verbal 486, SAT I

Verbal middle 50% range 440-530. Average ACT 20, ACT middle 50% range 18-22. TOEFL required of all international applicants, minimum TOEFL 550. **Basis for Candidate Selection:** *Very important factors considered include:* class rank, secondary school record, standardized test scores. *Important factors considered include:* recommendations. **Freshman Admission Requirements:** High school diploma or GED is required. *Academic units required/recommended:* 20 total required; 4 English required, 3 math required, 2 science required, 2 foreign language recommended, 2 social studies required, 1 history required, 6 elective required. **Freshman Admission Statistics:** 453 applied, 88% accepted, 57% of those accepted enrolled. **Transfer Admission Requirements:** *Items required:* college transcript. Minimum college GPA of 2.0 required. Lowest grade transferable C. **General Admission Information:** Priority application deadline July 15. Regular application deadline August 15. Nonfall registration accepted. Admission may be deferred for a maximum of 1 year. Credit offered for CEEB Advanced Placement tests.

COSTS AND FINANCIAL AID

Required Forms and Deadlines: FAFSA and institution's own financial aid form. No deadline for regular filing. Priority filing deadline May 1. **Notification of Awards:** Applicants will be notified of awards on a rolling basis beginning on or about June 1. **Types of Aid:** *Need-based scholarships/grants:* Pell, SEOG, state scholarships/grants, private scholarships, the school's own gift aid. *Loans:* FFEL Subsidized Stafford, FFEL Unsubsidized Stafford, FFEL PLUS, state loans. **Student Employment:** Federal Work-Study Program available. Institutional employment available. Off-campus job opportunities are good. **Financial Aid Statistics:** 67% freshmen, 68% undergrads receive some form of aid. Average freshman grant $1,200. Average freshman loan $2,625. Average income from on-campus job $1,375. **Financial Aid Phone:** 915-552-2620.

UNIVERSITY OF TEXAS—SAN ANTONIO

6900 North Loop 1604 West, San Antonio, TX 78249-0617
Phone: 210-458-4530 **E-mail:** prospects@utsa.edu **CEEB Code:** 6919
Fax: 210-458-7716 **Web:** www.utsa.edu **ACT Code:** 4239

This public school was founded in 1969. It has a 600-acre campus.

STUDENTS AND FACULTY

Enrollment: 16,026. **Student Body:** Male 45%, female 55%, out-of-state 4%, international 2% (66 countries represented). **Ethnic Representation:** African American 6%, Asian 4%, Caucasian 39%, Hispanic 51%. **Retention and Graduation:** 64% freshmen return for sophomore year. 5% freshmen graduate within 4 years. 4% grads go on to further study within 1 year. **Faculty:** Student/faculty ratio 24:1. 460 full-time faculty, 87% hold PhDs. 44% faculty teach undergrads.

ACADEMICS

Degrees: Bachelor's, doctoral, master's. **Academic Requirements:** General education including some course work in arts/fine arts, computer literacy, English (including composition), foreign languages, history, humanities, mathematics, philosophy, sciences (biological or physical), social science. **Classes:** 10-19 students in an average class. **Majors with Highest Enrollment:** Biotechnology; biology/biological sciences, general; computer science. **Disciplines with Highest Percentage of Degrees Awarded:** Business/marketing 29%, interdisciplinary studies 15%, biological life sciences 8%, social sciences and history 8%, psychology 7%. **Special Study Options:** Accelerated program, cooperative (work-study) program, distance learning, double major, dual enrollment, English as a second language, honors program, independent study, internships, study abroad, teacher certification program. 2+2 Programs with Alamo Community College District, Southwest Texas Junior College, Laredo Junior College, The Victoria College, Del Mar College, Coastal Bend College, and Austin Community College.

FACILITIES

Housing: Coed, apartments for married students, apartments for single students. **Library Holdings:** 386,546 bound volumes. 2,930 periodicals. 2,477,888 microforms. 24,752 audiovisuals. **Special Academic Facilities/Equipment:** Art gallery, audiovisual center, Institute of Texan Cultures Museum. **Computers:** School-owned computers available for student use.

EXTRACURRICULARS

Activities: Choral groups, concert band, drama/theater, jazz band, literary magazine, music ensembles, musical theater, pep band, student government, student newspaper, symphony orchestra, yearbook. **Organizations:** 140 registered organizations, 9 religious organizations, 10 fraternities (2% men join), 9 sororities (2% women join). **Athletics (Intercollegiate):** *Men:* baseball, basketball, cross-country, golf, tennis, track & field. *Women:* basketball, cross-country, softball, tennis, track & field, volleyball.

ADMISSIONS

Selectivity Rating: 70 (of 100). **Freshman Academic Profile:** 14% in top 10% of high school class, 41% in top 25% of high school class, 77% in top 50% of high school class. 94% from public high schools. Average SAT I Math 494, SAT I Math middle 50% range 450-550. Average SAT I Verbal 497, SAT I Verbal middle 50% range 440-550. Average ACT 20, ACT middle 50% range 18-23. TOEFL required of all international applicants, minimum TOEFL 500. **Basis for Candidate Selection:** *Very important factors considered include:* class rank, secondary school record, standardized test scores. *Other factors considered include:* extracurricular activities, recommendations, talent/ability, volunteer work, work experience. **Freshman Admission Requirements:** High school diploma or GED is required. *Academic units required/recommended:* 14 total recommended; 4 English recommended, 3 math recommended, 2 science recommended, 2 foreign language recommended, 2 social studies recommended. **Freshman Admission Statistics:** 5,519 applied, 99% accepted, 47% of those accepted enrolled. **Transfer Admission Requirements:** *Items required:* college transcript. Minimum college GPA of 2.0 required. Lowest grade transferable C. **General Admission Information:** Application fee $25. Priority application deadline April 1. Regular application deadline July 1. Nonfall registration accepted. Credit and/or placement offered for CEEB Advanced Placement tests.

COSTS AND FINANCIAL AID

In-state tuition $3,096. Out-of-state tuition $10,656. Room & board $8,151. Required fees $1,368. Average book expense $771. **Required Forms and Deadlines:** FAFSA. Priority filing deadline March 31. **Notification of Awards:** Applicants will be notified of awards on a rolling basis beginning on or about March 1. **Types of Aid:** *Need-based scholarships/grants:* Pell, SEOG, state scholarships/grants, private scholarships, the school's own gift aid. *Loans:* FFEL Subsidized Stafford, FFEL Unsubsidized Stafford, FFEL PLUS, Federal Perkins, state loans, college/university loans from institutional funds. **Student Employment:** Federal Work-Study Program available. Institutional employment available. Off-campus job opportunities are good. **Financial Aid Phone:** 210-458-4154.

UNIVERSITY OF TEXAS—TYLER

3900 University Boulevard, Tyler, TX 75799
Phone: 903-566-7202 **E-mail:** admissions@mail.uttyl.edu
Fax: 903-566-7068 **Web:** www.uttyler.edu

This public school was founded in 1971. It has a 204-acre campus.

STUDENTS AND FACULTY

Enrollment: 3,026. **Student Body:** Male 38%, female 62%, out-of-state 1%, international 2% (39 countries represented). **Ethnic Representation:** African American 9%, Asian 1%, Caucasian 84%, Hispanic 4%, Native American 1%. **Retention and Graduation:** 59% freshmen return for sophomore year. **Faculty:** Student/faculty ratio 141:1. 165 full-time faculty, 77% hold PhDs.

ACADEMICS

Degrees: Bachelor's, master's. **Classes:** 10-19 students in an average class. **Disciplines with Highest Percentage of Degrees Awarded:** Interdisciplinary studies 25%, health professions and related sciences 22%, business/marketing 16%, engineering/engineering technology 6%, social sciences and history 6%. **Special Study Options:** Cooperative (work-study) program, cross registration, distance learning, double major, English as a second language, student exchange program (domestic), independent study, internships, liberal arts/career combination, student-designed major, study abroad, teacher certification program.

FACILITIES

Housing: University Pines Apartment complex. **Library Holdings:** 136,402 bound volumes. 1,546 periodicals. 615,328 microforms. 10,864 audiovisuals. **Computers:** School-owned computers available for student use.

EXTRACURRICULARS

Activities: Choral groups, concert band, drama/theater, jazz band, literary magazine, music ensembles, musical theater, opera, student government, student newspaper. **Organizations:** 34 registered organizations, 11 honor societies, 2 religious organizations. **Athletics (Intercollegiate):** *Men:* basketball, cheerleading, cross-country, golf, soccer, tennis. *Women:* basketball, cheerleading, cross-country, golf, soccer, tennis, volleyball.

ADMISSIONS

Selectivity Rating: 63 (of 100). **Freshman Academic Profile:** 20% in top 10% of high school class, 29% in top 25% of high school class. Average SAT I Math 534, SAT I Math middle 50% range 490-580. Average SAT I Verbal 533, SAT I Verbal middle 50% range 480-580. Average ACT 23, ACT middle 50% range 20-24. TOEFL required of all international applicants, minimum TOEFL 550. **Basis for Candidate Selection:** *Very important factors considered include:* class rank, standardized test scores. *Other factors considered include:* extracurricular activities, volunteer work, work experience. **Freshman Admission Requirements:** High school diploma or GED is required. *Academic units required/recommended:* 4 English required, 3 math required, 3 science required, 4 science recommended, 3 science lab recommended, 2 foreign language required, 3 social studies required. **Freshman Admission Statistics:** 1,168 applied, 54% accepted, 49% of those accepted enrolled. **Transfer Admission Requirements:** *Items required:* college transcript. Minimum college GPA of 2.0 required. Lowest grade transferable C. **General Admission Information:** Nonfall registration accepted. Admission may be deferred for a maximum of 1 year.

COSTS AND FINANCIAL AID

Out-of-state tuition $9,180. Required fees $772. **Required Forms and Deadlines:** FAFSA. No deadline for regular filing. Priority filing deadline April 1. **Notification of Awards:** Applicants will be notified of awards on a rolling basis beginning on or about April 15. **Types of Aid:** *Need-based scholarships/grants:* Pell, SEOG, state scholarships/grants, private scholarships, the school's own gift aid, Texas Grant Program, Teach for Texas Conditional Program. *Loans:* FFEL Subsidized Stafford, FFEL Unsubsidized Stafford, FFEL PLUS, Federal Perkins. **Student Employment:** Federal Work-Study Program available. Off-campus job opportunities are good. **Financial Aid Statistics:** 44% freshmen, 54% undergrads receive some form of aid. **Financial Aid Phone:** 903-566-7180.

UNIVERSITY OF THE ARTS

320 South Broad Street, Philadelphia, PA 19102
Phone: 215-717-6049 **E-mail:** admissions@uarts.edu **CEEB Code:** 2664
Fax: 215-717-6045 **Web:** www.uarts.edu **ACT Code:** 3664

This private school was founded in 1876. It has a 18-acre campus.

STUDENTS AND FACULTY

Enrollment: 1,923. **Student Body:** Male 44%, female 56%, out-of-state 61%, international 2%. **Ethnic Representation:** African American 8%, Asian 4%, Caucasian 73%, Hispanic 4%. **Retention and Graduation:** 78% freshmen return for sophomore year. 53% freshmen graduate within 4 years. 68% grads go on to further study within 1 year. **Faculty:** Student/faculty ratio 10:1. 111 full-time faculty, 54% hold PhDs. 90% faculty teach undergrads.

ACADEMICS

Degrees: Bachelor's, certificate, diploma, master's, post-bachelor's certificate. **Academic Requirements:** General education including some course work in arts/fine arts, computer literacy, English (including composition), history, humanities, mathematics, sciences (biological or physical), social science. **Classes:** 10-19 students in an average class. **Majors with Highest Enrollment:** Graphic design; drama and dramatics/theatre arts, general; photography. **Disciplines with Highest Percentage of Degrees Awarded:** Visual and performing arts 91%, education 3%, communications/communication technologies 3%, interdisciplinary studies 3%. **Special Study Options:** Accelerated program, cross registration, double major, dual enrollment, English as a second language, student exchange program (domestic), independent study, internships, study abroad, teacher certification program.

FACILITIES

Housing: Coed, apartments for single students. **Library Holdings:** 123,175 bound volumes. 538 periodicals. 461 microforms. 321,710 audiovisuals. **Special Academic Facilities/Equipment:** Rosenwald-Wolf Gallery, Merriam Theater, Arts Bank, Borowsky Center for Publication Arts. **Computers:** School-owned computers available for student use.

EXTRACURRICULARS

Activities: Choral groups, concert band, dance, drama/theater, jazz band, music ensembles, musical theater, student government. **Organizations:** 5 registered organizations, 1 religious organization.

ADMISSIONS

Selectivity Rating: 63 (of 100). **Freshman Academic Profile:** Average high school GPA 3.1. 9% in top 10% of high school class, 23% in top 25% of high school class, 52% in top 50% of high school class. 85% from public high schools. Average SAT I Math 520, SAT I Math middle 50% range 470-580. Average SAT I Verbal 540, SAT I Verbal middle 50% range 490-600. TOEFL required of all international applicants, minimum TOEFL 500. **Basis for Candidate Selection:** *Very important factors considered include:* interview, secondary school record, talent/ability. *Important factors considered include:* character/personal qualities, class rank, essays, extracurricular activities, standardized test scores. *Other factors considered include:* alumni/ae relation, minority status, recommendations, volunteer work, work experience. **Freshman Admission Requirements:** High school diploma or GED is required. *Academic units required/recommended:* 4 total required; 13 total recommended; 4 English required, 3 math recommended, 2 science recommended, 2 foreign language recommended, 2 social studies recommended, 2 history recommended. **Freshman Admission Statistics:** 2,007 applied, 47% accepted, 47% of those accepted enrolled. **Transfer Admission Requirements:** *Items required:* high school transcript, college transcript, essay, standardized test scores. Minimum college GPA of 2.0 required. Lowest grade transferable C. **General Admission Information:** Application fee $50. Priority application deadline March 1. Nonfall registration accepted. Admission may be deferred for a maximum of 1 year. Credit and/or placement offered for CEEB Advanced Placement tests.

COSTS AND FINANCIAL AID

Tuition $19,630. Room & board $7,100. Required fees $850. Average book expense $2,000. **Required Forms and Deadlines:** FAFSA. No deadline for regular filing. Priority filing deadline February 15. **Notification of Awards:** Applicants will be notified of awards on a rolling basis beginning on or about March 15. **Types of Aid:** *Need-based scholarships/grants:* Pell, SEOG, state scholarships/grants, the school's own gift aid, merit scholarships. *Loans:* FFEL Subsidized Stafford, FFEL Unsubsidized Stafford, FFEL PLUS, Federal Perkins, state loans, alternative loans. **Student Employment:** Federal Work-Study Program available. Institutional employment available. Off-campus job opportunities are excellent. **Financial Aid Statistics:** 75% freshmen, 75% undergrads receive some form of aid. Average freshman grant $6,000. Average freshman loan $2,625. Average income from on-campus job $1,200. **Financial Aid Phone:** 800-616-2787.

UNIVERSITY OF THE DISTRICT OF COLUMBIA

4200 Connecticut Avenue Northwest, Washington, DC 20008
Phone: 202-274-5010 **E-mail:** lflannagan@udc.edu **CEEB Code:** 5929
Fax: 202-274-5552 **Web:** www.udc.edu **ACT Code:** 695

This public school was founded in 1976. It has a 21-acre campus.

STUDENTS AND FACULTY

Enrollment: 10,004. **Student Body:** Out-of-state 13%. **Ethnic Representation:** African American 89%, Asian 4%, Caucasian 4%, Hispanic 4%. **Retention and Graduation:** 61% freshmen return for sophomore year. 6% grads go on to further study within 1 year. 3% grads pursue business degrees. 1% grads pursue law degrees. 1% grads pursue medical degrees.

ACADEMICS

Degrees: Associate's, bachelor's, master's. **Special Study Options:** Cooperative (work-study) program, Business, Computer Science, Home Economics, Technologies.

FACILITIES

Library Holdings: 522,123 bound volumes. 1,983 periodicals. 605,281 microforms. **Special Academic Facilities/Equipment:** Theatre, greenhouse. **Computers:** School-owned computers available for student use.

EXTRACURRICULARS

Activities: Literary magazine, radio station, student government, television station. **Organizations:** 28 registered organizations, 3 fraternities (5% men join), 3 sororities (5% women join). **Athletics (Intercollegiate):** *Men:* basketball, cross-country, soccer, tennis. *Women:* basketball, tennis, track & field, volleyball.

ADMISSIONS

Selectivity Rating: 63 (of 100). **Freshman Academic Profile:** 90% from public high schools. TOEFL required of all international applicants, minimum TOEFL 550. **Freshman Admission Requirements:** High school diploma is required and GED is not accepted. **Transfer Admission Requirements:** Minimum college GPA of 2.0 required. Lowest grade transferable C. **General Admission Information:** Early decision application deadline June 1. Regular application deadline June 14. Nonfall registration accepted. Placement offered for CEEB Advanced Placement tests.

COSTS AND FINANCIAL AID

In-state tuition $2,360. Out-of-state tuition $5,660. Required fees $115. Average book expense $800. **Required Forms and Deadlines:** FAFSA and institution's own financial aid form. **Types of Aid:** *Loans:* FFEL Subsidized Stafford, FFEL PLUS. **Student Employment:** Federal Work-Study Program available. Institutional employment available. Off-campus job opportunities are good. **Financial Aid Statistics:** Average freshman loan $1,300. Average income from on-campus job $1,950. **Financial Aid Phone:** 202-274-5060.

UNIVERSITY OF THE INCARNATE WORD

4301 Broadway, Box 285, San Antonio, TX 78209-6397
Phone: 210-829-6005 **E-mail:** admis@universe.uiwtx.edu
Fax: 210-829-3921 **Web:** www.uiw.edu **ACT Code:** 4106

This private school, which is affiliated with the Roman Catholic Church, was founded in 1881. It has a 57-acre campus.

STUDENTS AND FACULTY

Enrollment: 3,522. **Student Body:** Male 34%, female 66%, out-of-state 2%, international 8%. **Ethnic Representation:** African American 7%, Asian 2%, Caucasian 28%, Hispanic 56%. **Retention and Graduation:** 63% freshmen return for sophomore year. 12% freshmen graduate within 4 years. 67% grads go on to further study within 1 year. **Faculty:** Student/faculty ratio 14:1. 131 full-time faculty, 79% hold PhDs. 100% faculty teach undergrads.

ACADEMICS

Degrees: Bachelor's, doctoral, master's, post-bachelor's certificate, post-master's certificate. **Academic Requirements:** General education including some course work in arts/fine arts, computer literacy, English (including composition), foreign languages, history, humanities, mathematics, philosophy, sciences (biological or physical), social science. **Classes:** 10-19 students in an average class. 10-19 students in an average lab/discussion section. **Majors with Highest Enrollment:** Nursing/registered nurse training (RN, ASN, BSN, MSN); business administration/management; education, general. **Disciplines with Highest Percentage of Degrees Awarded:** Business/marketing 30%, health professions and related sciences 11%, other 8%, liberal arts/general studies 8%, education 7%. **Special Study Options:** Accelerated program, cooperative (work-study) program, cross registration, distance learning, double major, dual enrollment, English as a second language, student exchange program (domestic), honors program, independent study, internships, study abroad, teacher certification program.

FACILITIES

Housing: Coed, all-female, all-male, apartments for single students. **Library Holdings:** 225,852 bound volumes. 577 periodicals. 235,498 microforms. 36,845 audiovisuals. **Computers:** *Recommended operating system:* Windows NT/2000. School-owned computers available for student use.

EXTRACURRICULARS

Activities: Choral groups, dance, drama/theater, jazz band, literary magazine, music ensembles, musical theater, student government, student newspaper, yearbook. **Organizations:** 17 registered organizations, 2 honor societies, 2 religious organizations, 1 fraternity (3% men join), 2 sororities. **Athletics (Intercollegiate):** *Men:* baseball, basketball, cheerleading, cross-country, golf, soccer, tennis. *Women:* baseball, basketball, cheerleading, cross-country, golf, soccer, softball, swimming, tennis, volleyball.

ADMISSIONS

Selectivity Rating: 66 (of 100). **Freshman Academic Profile:** Average high school GPA 3.3. 19% in top 10% of high school class, 46% in top 25% of high school class, 70% in top 50% of high school class. 85% from public high schools. Average SAT I Math 499, SAT I Math middle 50% range 430-540. Average SAT I Verbal 500, SAT I Verbal middle 50% range 430-540. Average ACT 20, ACT middle 50% range 17-23. TOEFL required of all international applicants, minimum TOEFL 550. **Basis for Candidate Selection:** *Very important factors considered include:* secondary school record. *Important factors considered include:* standardized test scores. *Other factors considered include:* alumni/ae relation, character/personal qualities, class rank, extracurricular activities, geographical residence, interview, minority status, recommendations, talent/ability, volunteer work, work experience. **Freshman Admission Requirements:** High school diploma or GED is required. *Academic units required/recommended:* 16 total required; 16 total recommended; 4 English required, 4 English recommended, 2 math required, 2 math recommended, 2 science required, 2 science recommended, 2 foreign language required, 2 foreign language recommended, 3 social studies required, 3 social studies recommended, 2 elective required, 2 elective recommended. **Freshman Admission Statistics:** 1,350 applied, 33% accepted, 94% of those accepted enrolled. **Transfer Admission Requirements:** *Items required:* college transcript. Minimum high school GPA of 2.0 required. Minimum college GPA of 2.5 required. Lowest grade transferable C. **General Admission Information:** Application fee $20. Nonfall registration accepted. Admission may be deferred for a maximum of 5 years. Credit and/or placement offered for CEEB Advanced Placement tests.

COSTS AND FINANCIAL AID

Tuition $14,000. Room & board $5,510. Required fees $328. Average book expense $800. **Required Forms and Deadlines:** FAFSA and institution's own financial aid form. No deadline for regular filing. Priority filing deadline April 1. **Notification of Awards:** Applicants will be notified of awards on a rolling basis beginning on or about February 1. **Types of Aid:** *Need-based scholarships/grants:* Pell, SEOG, state scholarships/grants, private scholarships, the school's own gift aid, Federal Nursing. *Loans:* FFEL Subsidized Stafford, FFEL Unsubsidized Stafford, FFEL PLUS, Federal Perkins, Federal Nursing, state loans, private loans. **Student Employment:** Federal Work-Study Program available. Institutional employment available. Off-campus job opportunities are good. **Financial Aid Statistics:** 76% freshmen, 75% undergrads receive some form of aid. Average freshman grant $5,380. Average freshman loan $4,028. Average income from on-campus job $3,407. **Financial Aid Phone:** 210-829-6008.

UNIVERSITY OF THE OZARKS

415 College Avenue, Clarksville, AR 72830
Phone: 479-979-1227 **E-mail:** jdecker@ozarks.edu **CEEB Code:** 6111
Fax: 479-979-1355 **Web:** www.ozarks.edu **ACT Code:** 120

This private school, which is affiliated with the Presbyterian Church, was founded in 1834. It has a 56-acre campus.

STUDENTS AND FACULTY

Enrollment: 703. **Student Body:** Male 45%, female 55%, out-of-state 41%, international 17% (18 countries represented). **Ethnic Representation:** African American 4%, Asian 2%, Caucasian 90%, Hispanic 2%, Native American 2%. **Retention and Graduation:** 63% freshmen return for sophomore year. **Faculty:** Student/faculty ratio 14:1. 43 full-time faculty, 86% hold PhDs. 100% faculty teach undergrads.

ACADEMICS

Degrees: Bachelor's. **Academic Requirements:** General education including some course work in computer literacy, English (including composition), humanities, sciences (biological or physical). **Disciplines with Highest Percentage of Degrees Awarded:** Business/marketing 38%, education 12%, biological life sciences 8%, communications/communication technologies 5%, psychology 5%. **Special Study Options:** Double major, liberal arts/career combination, study abroad, teacher certification program.

FACILITIES

Housing: Coed, apartments for single students. **Library Holdings:** 125,000 bound volumes. 536 periodicals. 9,516 microforms. 4,000 audiovisuals. **Special Academic Facilities/Equipment:** Walton Fine Arts Center, Stephens Gallery, Smith-Broyles Science Center, Walker Hall Teacher Education and Communications Center. **Computers:** *Recommended operating system:* Win NT. School-owned computers available for student use.

EXTRACURRICULARS

Activities: Choral groups, drama/theater, literary magazine, music ensembles, student government, television station, yearbook. **Organizations:** 40 registered organizations, 5 honor societies, 6 religious organizations. **Athletics (Intercollegiate):** *Men:* baseball, basketball, cheerleading, cross-country, golf, soccer, tennis. *Women:* basketball, cheerleading, cross-country, soccer, softball, tennis.

ADMISSIONS

Selectivity Rating: 74 (of 100). **Freshman Academic Profile:** Average high school GPA 3.4. 23% in top 10% of high school class, 44% in top 25% of high school class, 77% in top 50% of high school class. 87% from public high schools. Average SAT I Math 505, SAT I Math middle 50% range 440-550. Average SAT I Verbal 509, SAT I Verbal middle 50% range 490-560. Average ACT 22, ACT middle 50% range 19-25. TOEFL required of all international applicants, minimum TOEFL 500. **Basis for Candidate Selection:** *Very important factors considered include:* secondary school record, standardized test scores. *Important factors considered include:* character/personal qualities. *Other factors considered include:* alumni/ae relation, class rank, essays, extracurricular activities, geographical residence, interview, recommendations, talent/ability, volunteer work. **Freshman Admission Requirements:** High school diploma or GED is required. *Academic units required/recommended:* 18 total required; 4 English required, 4 math required, 3 science required, 2 science lab required, 2 foreign language required, 1 social studies required, 2 history required. **Freshman Admission Statistics:** 548 applied, 85% accepted, 51% of those accepted enrolled. **Transfer Admission Requirements:** *Items required:* college transcript. Minimum high school GPA of 2.0 required. Minimum college GPA of 2.0 required. Lowest grade transferable C. **General Admission Information:** Application fee $10. Priority application deadline April 1. Early decision application deadline March 15. Nonfall registration accepted. Credit and/or placement offered for CEEB Advanced Placement tests.

COSTS AND FINANCIAL AID

Required Forms and Deadlines: FAFSA and institution's own financial aid form. Priority filing deadline February 15. **Notification of Awards:** Applicants will be notified of awards on a rolling basis beginning on or about March 15. **Types of Aid:** *Need-based scholarships/grants:* Pell, SEOG, state scholarships/grants, private scholarships, the school's own gift aid. *Loans:* FFEL Subsidized Stafford, FFEL Unsubsidized Stafford, FFEL PLUS, Federal Perkins, college/university loans from institutional funds. **Student Employment:** Federal Work-Study Program available. Institutional employment available. Off-campus job opportunities are fair. **Financial Aid Statistics:** 59% freshmen, 51% undergrads receive some form of aid. Average freshman grant $12,555. Average freshman loan $2,378. Average income from on-campus job $1,878. **Financial Aid Phone:** 479-979-1221.

UNIVERSITY OF THE PACIFIC

3601 Pacific Avenue, Stockton, CA 95211
Phone: 209-946-2211 **E-mail:** admissions@uop.edu **CEEB Code:** 4065
Fax: 209-946-2413 **Web:** www.uop.edu **ACT Code:** 240

This private school was founded in 1851. It has a 175-acre campus.

STUDENTS AND FACULTY

Enrollment: 3,233. **Student Body:** Male 42%, female 58%, out-of-state 11%, international 3% (50 countries represented). **Ethnic Representation:** African American 3%, Asian 27%, Caucasian 51%, Hispanic 10%, Native American 1%. **Retention and Graduation:** 85% freshmen return for sophomore year. 44% freshmen graduate within 4 years. **Faculty:** Student/faculty ratio 13:1. 378 full-time faculty, 91% hold PhDs.

ACADEMICS

Degrees: Bachelor's, doctoral, first professional, master's. **Academic Requirements:** General education including some course work in arts/fine arts, computer literacy, English (including composition), foreign languages, history, humanities, mathematics, philosophy, sciences (biological or physical), social science, mentoring. **Classes:** Under 10 students in an average class. 10-19 students in an average lab/discussion section. **Majors with Highest Enrollment:** Business administration/management; physical education teaching and coaching; biology/biological sciences, general. **Disciplines with Highest Percentage of Degrees Awarded:** Business/marketing 20%, biological life sciences 12%, social sciences and history 10%, engineering/engineering technology 9%, education 8%. **Special Study Options:** Accelerated program, cooperative (work-study) program, double major, dual enrollment, English as a second language, student exchange program (domestic), honors program, independent study, internships, liberal arts/career combination, student-designed major, study abroad, teacher certification program.

FACILITIES

Housing: Coed, apartments for married students, apartments for single students, fraternities and/or sororities. **Library Holdings:** 268,365 bound volumes. 1,361 periodicals. 675,806 microforms. 10,110 audiovisuals. **Special Academic Facilities/Equipment:** John Muir Collection, Dave & Iola Brubeck Collection, Brubeck Institute for Jazz Studies, Reynolds Art Gallery. **Computers:** School-owned computers available for student use.

EXTRACURRICULARS

Activities: Choral groups, concert band, dance, drama/theater, jazz band, music ensembles, musical theater, pep band, student government, student newspaper, yearbook. **Organizations:** 90 registered organizations, 13 honor societies, 6 religious organizations, 6 fraternities (20% men join), 4 sororities (21% women join). **Athletics (Intercollegiate):** *Men:* baseball, basketball, cheerleading, golf, swimming, tennis, volleyball, water polo. *Women:* basketball, cheerleading, cross-country, field hockey, soccer, softball, swimming, tennis, volleyball, water polo.

ADMISSIONS

Selectivity Rating: 75 (of 100). **Freshman Academic Profile:** Average high school GPA 3.5. 46% in top 10% of high school class, 74% in top 25% of high school class, 95% in top 50% of high school class. 82% from public high schools. Average SAT I Math 595, SAT I Math middle 50% range 540-650. Average SAT I Verbal 559, SAT I Verbal middle 50% range 510-610. Average ACT 24, ACT middle 50% range 22-26. TOEFL required of all international applicants, minimum TOEFL 475. **Basis for Candidate Selection:** *Very important factors considered include:* secondary school record. *Important factors considered include:* essays, extracurricular activities, recommendations, standardized test scores. *Other factors considered include:* alumni/ae relation, character/personal qualities, class rank, geographical residence, minority status, talent/ability, volunteer work, work experience. **Freshman Admission Requirements:** High school diploma or GED is required. *Academic units required/recommended:* 16 total required; 4 English recommended, 3 math recommended, 2 science recommended, 2 science lab recommended, 2 foreign language recommended, 1 history recommended, 3 elective recommended. **Freshman Admission Statistics:** 3,736 applied, 71% accepted, 26% of those accepted enrolled. **Transfer Admission Requirements:** *Items required:* college transcript, essay. Minimum college GPA of 2.5 required. Lowest grade transferable D. **General Admission Information:** Application fee $50. Priority application deadline January 15. Nonfall registration accepted. Credit and/or placement offered for CEEB Advanced Placement tests.

COSTS AND FINANCIAL AID

Tuition $22,180. Room & board $7,198. Required fees $375. Average book expense $1,206. **Required Forms and Deadlines:** FAFSA. No deadline for regular filing. Priority filing deadline February 15. **Notification of Awards:** Applicants will be notified of awards on a rolling basis beginning on or about March 15. **Types of Aid:** *Need-based scholarships/grants:* Pell, SEOG, state scholarships/grants, private scholarships, the school's own gift aid. *Loans:* Direct Subsidized Stafford, Direct Unsubsidized Stafford, Direct PLUS, FFEL Subsidized Stafford, FFEL Unsubsidized Stafford, FFEL PLUS, Federal Perkins, state loans. **Student Employment:** Federal Work-Study Program available. Institutional employment available. Off-campus job opportunities are good. **Financial Aid Statistics:** 65% freshmen, 68% undergrads receive some form of aid. **Financial Aid Phone:** 209-946-2421.

UNIVERSITY OF THE SCIENCES IN PHILADELPHIA

600 South 43rd Street, Admission Office, Philadelphia, PA 19104-4495
Phone: 215-596-8810 **E-mail:** admit@usip.edu **CEEB Code:** 2663
Fax: 215 596 8821 **Web:** www.usip.edu **ACT Code:** 3671

This private school was founded in 1821. It has a 30-acre campus.

STUDENTS AND FACULTY

Enrollment: 1,240. **Student Body:** Male 31%, female 69%, out-of-state 45%, international 2%. **Ethnic Representation:** African American 6%, Asian 29%, Caucasian 53%, Hispanic 2%. **Retention and Graduation:** 83% freshmen return for sophomore year. 8% freshmen graduate within 4 years. **Faculty:** Student/faculty ratio 12:1. 146 full-time faculty, 78% hold PhDs. 95% faculty teach undergrads.

ACADEMICS

Degrees: Bachelor's, doctoral, first professional, master's, post-bachelor's certificate. **Academic Requirements:** General education including some course work in computer literacy, English (including composition), history, humanities, mathematics, sciences (biological or physical), social science. **Classes:** 10-19 students in an average class. 10-19 students in an average lab/discussion section. **Majors with Highest Enrollment:** Pharmacy (PharmD, BS/BPharm); physical therapy/therapist; biology/biological sciences, general. **Disciplines with Highest Percentage of Degrees Awarded:** Health professions and related sciences 59%, biological life sciences 25%, business/marketing 12%, psychology 2%, physical sciences 1%. **Special Study Options:** Cooperative (work-study) program, distance learning, double major, English as a second language, honors program, internships, teacher certification program, academic remediation, advanced placement credit, learning disabilities services, off-campus study.

FACILITIES

Housing: Coed, fraternities and/or sororities. **Library Holdings:** 84,848 bound volumes. 6,500 periodicals. 33,685 microforms. 5,965 audiovisuals. **Special Academic Facilities/Equipment:** Pharmacy museum, electron microscope. **Computers:** *Recommended operating system:* Windows XP Pro. School-owned computers available for student use.

EXTRACURRICULARS

Activities: Choral groups, concert band, drama/theater, literary magazine, musical theater, student government, student newspaper, yearbook. **Organizations:** 50 registered organizations, 5 honor societies, 4 religious organizations, 8 fraternities, 6 sororities. **Athletics (Intercollegiate):** *Men:* baseball, basketball, cross-country, golf, rifle, tennis. *Women:* basketball, cross-country, golf, rifle, softball, tennis, volleyball.

ADMISSIONS

Selectivity Rating: 82 (of 100). **Freshman Academic Profile:** Average high school GPA 3.5. 27% in top 10% of high school class, 63% in top 25% of high school class, 92% in top 50% of high school class. Average SAT I Math 570, SAT I Math middle 50% range 520-610. Average SAT I Verbal 540, SAT I Verbal middle 50% range 500-590. ACT middle 50% range 18-21. TOEFL required of all international applicants, minimum TOEFL 550. **Basis for Candidate Selection:** *Very important factors considered include:* class rank, secondary school record, standardized test scores. *Important factors considered include:* character/personal qualities, talent/ability, volunteer work. *Other factors considered include:* alumni/ae relation, essays, extracurricular activities, interview, recommendations, work experience. **Freshman Admission Requirements:** High school diploma or GED is required. *Academic units required/recommended:* 16 total required; 4 English required, 3 math required, 3 science required, 3 science lab required, 3 social studies required. **Freshman Admission Statistics:** 2,080 applied, 79% accepted, 22% of those accepted enrolled. **Transfer Admission Requirements:** *Items required:* college transcript, essay. Minimum high school GPA of 3.0 required. Lowest grade transferable C. **General Admission Information:** Application fee $45. Admission may be deferred for a maximum of 1 year. Credit offered for CEEB Advanced Placement tests.

COSTS AND FINANCIAL AID

Tuition $19,338. Average book expense $1,000. **Required Forms and Deadlines:** FAFSA. Financial aid filing deadline March 15. Priority filing deadline March 15. **Notification of Awards:** Applicants will be notified of awards on a rolling basis beginning on or about January 15. **Types of Aid:** *Need-based scholarships/grants:* Pell, SEOG, state scholarships/grants, private scholarships, the school's own gift aid. *Loans:* FFEL Subsidized Stafford, FFEL Unsubsidized Stafford, FFEL PLUS, Federal Perkins, college/university loans from institutional funds. **Student Employment:** Federal Work-Study Program available. Institutional employment available. Off-campus job opportunities are good. **Financial Aid Statistics:** 100% freshmen, 73% undergrads receive some form of aid. **Financial Aid Phone:** 215-596-8894.

THE UNIVERSITY OF THE SOUTH

735 University Avenue, Sewanee, TN 37383-1000
Phone: 931-598-1238 **E-mail:** collegeadmission@sewanee.edu **CEEB Code:** 1842
Fax: 931-538-3248 **Web:** www.sewanee.edu **ACT Code:** 4924

This private school, which is affiliated with the Episcopal Church, was founded in 1857. It has a 10,000-acre campus.

STUDENTS AND FACULTY

Enrollment: 1,340. **Student Body:** Male 47%, female 53%, out-of-state 76%, international 2% (25 countries represented). **Ethnic Representation:** African American 5%, Asian 1%, Caucasian 93%, Hispanic 1%. **Retention and Graduation:** 82% freshmen return for sophomore year. 72% freshmen graduate within 4 years. 38% grads go on to further study within 1 year. 4% grads pursue business degrees. 6% grads pursue law degrees. 4% grads pursue medical degrees. **Faculty:** Student/faculty ratio 10:1. 124 full-time faculty, 96% hold PhDs. 100% faculty teach undergrads.

ACADEMICS

Degrees: Bachelor's, doctoral, first professional, first professional certificate, master's. **Academic Requirements:** General education including some course work in arts/fine arts, English (including composition), foreign languages, history, humanities, mathematics, philosophy, sciences (biological or physical), social science, physical education. **Classes:** 10-19 students in an average class. 10-19 students in an average lab/discussion section. **Disciplines with Highest Percentage of Degrees Awarded:** Social sciences and history 29%, English 13%, visual and performing arts 12%, foreign languages and literature 10%, philosophy/religion/theology 8%. **Special Study Options:** Double major, independent study, internships, student-designed major, study abroad, teacher certification program.

FACILITIES

Housing: Coed, all-female, all-male, apartments for married students, housing for disabled students, fraternities and/or sororities, substance-free housing, language houses. **Library Holdings:** 648,459 bound volumes. 3,444 periodicals. 328,090 microforms. 72,964 audiovisuals. **Special Academic Facilities/Equipment:** Art gallery, observatory, keyboard collection, materials analysis lab with electron microscope. **Computers:** School-owned computers available for student use.

EXTRACURRICULARS

Activities: Choral groups, dance, drama/theater, literary magazine, music ensembles, musical theater, radio station, student government, student newspaper, student-run film society, symphony orchestra, yearbook. **Organizations:** 110 registered organizations, 9 honor societies, 11 religious organizations, 11 fraternities (45% men join), 6 sororities (43% women join). **Athletics (Intercollegiate):** *Men:* baseball, basketball, crew, cross-country, diving, equestrian, fencing, football, golf, soccer, swimming, tennis, track & field. *Women:* basketball, cheerleading, crew, cross-country, diving, equestrian, fencing, field hockey, golf, soccer, swimming, tennis, track & field, volleyball.

ADMISSIONS

Selectivity Rating: 87 (of 100). **Freshman Academic Profile:** Average high school GPA 3.4. 35% in top 10% of high school class, 69% in top 25% of high school class, 94% in top 50% of high school class. 52% from public high schools. SAT I Math middle 50% range 550-650. SAT I Verbal middle 50% range 560-660. ACT middle 50% range 24-28. TOEFL required of all international applicants, minimum TOEFL 550. **Basis for Candidate Selection:** *Very important factors considered include:* recommendations, secondary school record. *Important factors considered include:* character/personal qualities, essays, extracurricular activities, standardized test scores, volunteer work, work experience. *Other factors considered include:* alumni/ae relation, class rank, geographical residence, interview, minority status, talent/ability. **Freshman Admission Requirements:** High school diploma is required and GED is not accepted. *Academic units required/recommended:* 13 total required; 20 total recommended; 4 English required, 4 English recommended, 3 math required, 4 math recommended, 2 science required, 4 science recommended, 2 science lab required, 3 science lab recommended, 2 foreign language required, 4 foreign language recommended, 1 social studies required, 2 social studies recommended, 1 history required, 2 history recommended. **Freshman Admission Statistics:** 1,669 applied, 71% accepted, 31% of those accepted enrolled. **Transfer Admission Requirements:** *Items required:* high school transcript, college transcript, essay, standardized test score, statement of good standing from prior school. Lowest grade transferable C. **General Admission Information:** Application fee $45. Early decision application deadline November 15. Regular application deadline February 1. Admission may be deferred for a maximum of 1 year. Credit and/or placement offered for CEEB Advanced Placement tests.

COSTS AND FINANCIAL AID

Tuition $21,140. Room & board $5,950. Required fees $200. Average book expense $600. **Required Forms and Deadlines:** FAFSA and institution's own financial aid form. Priority filing deadline March 1. **Notification of Awards:** Applicants will be notified of awards on or about April 1. **Types of Aid:** *Need-based scholarships/grants:* Pell, SEOG, state scholarships/grants, private scholarships, the school's own gift aid. *Loans:* FFEL Subsidized Stafford, FFEL Unsubsidized Stafford, FFEL PLUS, Federal Perkins, state loans, college/university loans from institutional funds, private alternative loans. **Student Employment:** Federal Work-Study Program available. Institutional employment available. Off-campus job opportunities are fair. **Financial Aid Statistics:** 38% freshmen, 40% undergrads receive some form of aid. Average income from on-campus job $1,000. **Financial Aid Phone:** 931-598-1312.

UNIVERSITY OF THE VIRGIN ISLANDS

2 John Brewers Bay, St. Thomas, VI 00802
Phone: 340-693-1150 **E-mail:** admissions@uvi.edu **CEEB Code:** 879
Fax: 340-693-1155 **Web:** www.uvi.edu

This public school was founded in 1962.

STUDENTS AND FACULTY

Enrollment: 2,538. **Student Body:** Male 21%, female 79%, out-of-state 36%, international 5%. **Ethnic Representation:** African American 76%, Asian 1%, Caucasian 2%, Hispanic 3%. **Faculty:** Student/faculty ratio 14:1. 99 full-time faculty, 67% hold PhDs.

ACADEMICS

Degrees: Associate's, master's. **Academic Requirements:** General education including some course work in computer literacy, English (including composition), foreign languages, history, humanities, mathematics, social science. **Disciplines with Highest Percentage of Degrees Awarded:** Business/marketing 37%, education 17%, biological life sciences 13%, foreign languages and literature 10%, social sciences and history 6%. **Special Study Options:** Distance learning, dual enrollment, student exchange program (domestic), independent study, internships.

FACILITIES

Housing: All-female, all-male. **Library Holdings:** 96,422 bound volumes. 782 periodicals. 684 audiovisuals. **Computers:** *Recommended operating system:* Windows 95. School-owned computers available for student use.

EXTRACURRICULARS

Activities: Choral groups, concert band, dance, drama/theater, jazz band, music ensembles, student government, student newspaper, yearbook. **Organizations:** 27 registered organizations, 2 honor societies, 2 religious organizations, 23 fraternities, 3 sororities. **Athletics (Intercollegiate):** *Men:* basketball, soccer, swimming, tennis, volleyball. *Women:* basketball, swimming, tennis, volleyball.

ADMISSIONS

Selectivity Rating: 63 (of 100). **Freshman Academic Profile:** SAT I Math middle 50% range 330-450. SAT I Verbal middle 50% range 360-470. **Basis for Candidate Selection:** *Very important factors considered include:* secondary school record. *Other factors considered include:* standardized test scores, state residency. **Freshman Admission Requirements:** High school diploma or GED is required. *Academic units required/recommended:* 11 total recommended; 4 English recommended, 2 math recommended, 2 science recommended, 1 foreign language recommended, 2 social studies recommended. **Freshman Admission Statistics:** 854 applied, 73% accepted, 45% of those accepted enrolled. **Transfer Admission Requirements:** *Items required:* high school transcript, college transcript, statement of good standing from prior school. Minimum college GPA of 2.0 required. Lowest grade transferable C. **General Admission Information:** Application fee $20. Priority application deadline February 1. Regular application deadline April 30. Nonfall registration accepted. Admission may be deferred.

COSTS AND FINANCIAL AID

Types of Aid: *Need-based scholarships/grants:* Pell. **Financial Aid Statistics:** Average freshman grant $1,342. **Financial Aid Phone:** 340-693-1090.

UNIVERSITY OF TOLEDO

2801 West Bancroft, Toledo, OH 43606
Phone: 419-530-8700 **E-mail:** enroll@utnet.utoledo.edu **CEEB Code:** 1845
Fax: 419-530-5713 **Web:** www.utoledo.edu **ACT Code:** 3344

This public school was founded in 1872. It has a 400-acre campus.

STUDENTS AND FACULTY

Enrollment: 17,563. **Student Body:** Male 49%, female 51%, out-of-state 3%, international 2%. **Ethnic Representation:** African American 12%, Asian 2%, Caucasian 77%, Hispanic 2%. **Retention and Graduation:** 72% freshmen return for sophomore year. 11% freshmen graduate within 4 years. **Faculty:** Student/faculty ratio 18:1. 687 full-time faculty, 79% hold PhDs.

ACADEMICS

Degrees: Associate's, bachelor's, certificate, doctoral, first professional, master's, post-bachelor's certificate, post-master's certificate. **Academic Requirements:** General education including some course work in arts/fine arts, English (including composition), humanities, mathematics, sciences (biological or physical), social science. **Majors with Highest Enrollment:** Marketing/marketing management, general; education, general; engineering, general. **Disciplines with Highest Percentage of Degrees Awarded:** Business/marketing 18%, engineering/engineering technology 15%, education 15%, health professions and related sciences 9%, interdisciplinary studies 7%. **Special Study Options:** Accelerated program, cooperative (work-study) program, cross registration, distance learning, double major, dual enrollment, student exchange program (domestic), honors program, independent study, internships, liberal arts/career combination, student-designed major, study abroad, teacher certification program, weekend college.

FACILITIES

Housing: Coed, all-female, all-male, housing for disabled students, housing for international students, fraternities and/or sororities. **Library Holdings:** 1,326,010 bound volumes. 4,754 periodicals. 1,627,384 microforms. 4,695 audiovisuals. **Special Academic Facilities/Equipment:** Language lab, arboretum, planetariums, two observatories, electron microscope. **Computers:** School-owned computers available for student use.

EXTRACURRICULARS

Activities: Choral groups, concert band, dance, drama/theater, jazz band, literary magazine, marching band, music ensembles, musical theater, opera, pep band, radio station, student government, student newspaper, student-run film society, symphony orchestra, television station. **Organizations:** 200 registered organizations, 14 fraternities (5% men join), 13 sororities (5% women join). **Athletics (Intercollegiate):** *Men:* baseball, basketball, cheerleading, cross-country, diving, football, golf, indoor track, lacrosse, softball, swimming, tennis, track & field, volleyball. *Women:* basketball, cheerleading, cross-country, diving, golf, indoor track, lacrosse, softball, swimming, tennis, track & field, volleyball.

ADMISSIONS

Selectivity Rating: 65 (of 100). **Freshman Academic Profile:** 15% in top 10% of high school class, 35% in top 25% of high school class, 63% in top 50% of high school class. Average SAT I Math 517, SAT I Math middle 50% range 450-590. Average SAT I Verbal 503, SAT I Verbal middle 50% range 440-560. Average ACT 21, ACT middle 50% range 19-24. TOEFL required of all international applicants, minimum TOEFL 500. **Basis for Candidate Selection:** *Very important factors considered include:* state residency. *Important factors considered include:* standardized test scores. *Other factors considered include:* recommendations, talent/ability. **Freshman Admission Requirements:** High school diploma or GED is required. *Academic units required/recommended:* 3 English required, 4 English recommended, 3 math required, 3 math recommended, 3 science recommended, 1 science lab recommended, 2 foreign language recommended, 2 social studies required, 2 social studies recommended, 1 history recommended. **Freshman Admission Statistics:** 9,248 applied, 97% accepted, 42% of those accepted enrolled. **Transfer Admission Requirements:** *Items required:* college transcript. Minimum college GPA of 2.0 required. Lowest grade transferable C. **General Admission Information:** Application fee $40. Nonfall registration accepted. Admission may be deferred for a maximum of 1 year. Credit and/or placement offered for CEEB Advanced Placement tests.

COSTS AND FINANCIAL AID

In-state tuition $4,805. Out-of-state tuition $13,258. Room & board $6,630. Required fees $1,044. Average book expense $690. **Required Forms and Deadlines:** FAFSA. Priority filing deadline April 1. **Notification of Awards:** Applicants will be notified of awards on a rolling basis beginning on or about April 1. **Types of Aid:** *Need-based scholarships/grants:* Pell, SEOG, state scholarships/grants, private scholarships, the school's own gift aid. *Loans:* Direct Subsidized Stafford, Direct Unsubsidized Stafford, Direct PLUS, Federal Perkins, state. **Student Employment:** Federal Work-Study Program available. Institutional employment available. Off-campus job opportunities are good. **Financial Aid Phone:** 419-530-2056.

UNIVERSITY OF TORONTO

315 Bloor Street West, Toronto, ON M5S1A3
Phone: 416-978-2190 **E-mail:** ask@adm.utoronto.ca **CEEB Code:** 982
Fax: 416-978-7022 **Web:** www.myfuture.utoronto.ca or www.utoronto.ca

This public school was founded in 1827.

STUDENTS AND FACULTY

Enrollment: 40,341. **Student Body:** Male 44%, female 56%, out-of-state 4%, international 4%. **Retention and Graduation:** 95% freshmen return for sophomore year. **Faculty:** Student/faculty ratio 15:1. 2,710 full-time faculty.

ACADEMICS

Degrees: Bachelor's, certificate, diploma, doctoral, first professional, master's. **Classes:** 10-19 students in an average class. **Majors with Highest Enrollment:** Environmental studies; computer science; English language and literature, general. **Special Study Options:** Cooperative (work-study) program, double major, English as a second language, student exchange program (domestic), honors program, internships, study abroad, teacher certification program.

FACILITIES

Housing: Coed, all-female, all-male, apartments for married students, cooperative housing. **Library Holdings:** 10,306,621 bound volumes. 53,547 periodicals. 5,033,479 microforms. 1,202,358 audiovisuals. **Computers:** School-owned computers available for student use.

EXTRACURRICULARS

Activities: Choral groups, concert band, dance, drama/theater, jazz band, literary magazine, music ensembles, opera, radio station, student government, student newspaper, student-run film society, symphony orchestra. **Organizations:** 200 registered organizations. **Athletics (Intercollegiate):** *Men:* baseball, basketball, crew, skiing (cross-country), cross-country, fencing, football, golf, ice hockey, indoor track, lacrosse, rugby, skiing (Nordic), soccer, squash, swimming, tennis, track & field, volleyball, water polo, wrestling. *Women:* basketball, crew, skiing (cross-country), cross-country, fencing, field hockey, ice hockey, indoor track, lacrosse, rugby, skiing (Nordic), soccer, squash, swimming, tennis, track & field, volleyball, water polo, wrestling.

ADMISSIONS

Selectivity Rating: 82 (of 100). **Freshman Academic Profile:** Average high school GPA 3.0. **Basis for Candidate Selection:** *Very important factors considered include:* class rank, secondary school record, standardized test scores. **Freshman Admission Requirements:** High school diploma or GED is required. **Freshman Admission Statistics:** 54,474 applied, 60% accepted, 38% of those accepted enrolled. **Transfer Admission Requirements:** *Items required:* high school transcript, college transcript, standardized test scores. **General Admission Information:** Application fee $47. Regular application deadline March 1.

COSTS AND FINANCIAL AID

In-state tuition $3,951. Out-of-state tuition $8,755. Room & board $4,930. Required fees $527. Average book expense $1,050. **Student Employment:** Federal Work-Study Program available. Off-campus job opportunities are excellent. **Financial Aid Phone:** 416-978-2190.

UNIVERSITY OF TULSA

600 South College Ave., Tulsa, OK 74104
Phone: 918-631-2307 **E-mail:** admission@utulsa.edu **CEEB Code:** 6883
Fax: 918-631-5003 **Web:** www.utulsa.edu **ACT Code:** 3444

This private school, which is affiliated with the Presbyterian Church, was founded in 1894. It has a 200-acre campus.

STUDENTS AND FACULTY

Enrollment: 2,691. **Student Body:** Male 48%, female 52%, out-of-state 24%, international 11% (71 countries represented). **Ethnic Representation:** African American 9%, Asian 3%, Caucasian 72%, Hispanic 3%, Native American 6%. **Retention and Graduation:** 80% freshmen return for sophomore year. 43% freshmen graduate within 4 years. 29% grads go on to further study within 1 year. 5% grads pursue business degrees. 5% grads pursue law degrees. 6% grads pursue medical degrees. **Faculty:** Student/faculty ratio 11:1. 297 full-time faculty, 95% hold PhDs. 100% faculty teach undergrads.

ACADEMICS

Degrees: Bachelor's, doctoral, first professional, first professional certificate, master's, post-bachelor's certificate. **Academic Requirements:** General education including some course work in arts/fine arts, computer literacy, English (including composition), foreign languages, history, humanities, mathematics, philosophy, sciences (biological or physical), social science. **Classes:** 10-19 students in an average class. 10-19 students in an average lab/discussion section. **Majors with Highest Enrollment:** Business administration/management; computer science; biology/biological sciences, general. **Disciplines with Highest Percentage of Degrees Awarded:** Business/marketing 23%, engineering/engineering technology 18%, visual and performing arts 9%, social sciences and history 8%, health professions and related sciences 6%. **Special Study Options:** Accelerated program, double major, English as a second language, honors program, independent study, internships, liberal arts/career combination, student-designed major, study abroad, teacher certification program.

FACILITIES

Housing: Coed, all-female, all-male, apartments for married students, apartments for single students, housing for disabled students, fraternities and/or sororities, Honors House. **Library Holdings:** 940,105 bound volumes. 6,317 periodicals. 3,001,114 microforms. 13,320 audiovisuals. **Special Academic Facilities/Equipment:** Alexandre Hogue Art Gallery, biotechnology institute, Center for Communicative Disorders, charge-coupled camera microscope, Donald W. Reynolds Center (site of a state-of-the-art athletic training program), education technology lab, electron microscopes, Kendall Theatre, McFarlin Library Special Collections (focus on American, British, and Irish literature of the late 19th and early 20th centuries and on Native American history and law), 3 multimedia "boardroom-style" classrooms, ONEOK Multimedia Auditorium, Sadie Adwan Communication Lab, Sidney Born Technical Library (contains an outstanding collection concerning energy, most notably petroleum), Sun Computer work stations, world's largest research flow-loop in petroleum. **Computers:** School-owned computers available for student use.

EXTRACURRICULARS

Activities: Choral groups, concert band, drama/theater, jazz band, literary magazine, marching band, music ensembles, musical theater, opera, pep band, radio station, student government, student newspaper, symphony orchestra, television station, yearbook. **Organizations:** 286 registered organizations, 36 honor societies, 21 religious organizations, 7 fraternities (21% men join), 9 sororities (23% women join). **Athletics (Intercollegiate):** *Men:* basketball, cheerleading, cross-country, football, golf, indoor track, soccer, tennis, track & field. *Women:* basketball, cheerleading, crew, cross-country, golf, indoor track, soccer, softball, tennis, track & field, volleyball.

ADMISSIONS

Selectivity Rating: 79 (of 100). **Freshman Academic Profile:** Average high school GPA 3.7. 57% in top 10% of high school class, 75% in top 25% of high school class, 100% in top 50% of high school class. 78% from public high schools. Average SAT I Math 620, SAT I Math middle 50% range 540-700. Average SAT I Verbal 610, SAT I Verbal middle 50% range 540-700. Average ACT 26, ACT middle 50% range 22-30. TOEFL required of all international applicants, minimum TOEFL 500. **Basis for Candidate Selection:** *Very important factors considered include:* class rank, interview, secondary school record. *Important factors considered include:* extracurricular activities, recommendations, standardized test scores, talent/ability. *Other factors considered include:* alumni/ae relation, character/personal qualities, essays, minority status, volunteer work, work experience. **Freshman Admission Requirements:** High school diploma or GED is required. *Academic units required/recommended:* 16 total recommended; 4 English recommended, 3 math recommended, 3 science recommended, 2 science lab recommended, 2 foreign language recommended, 1 social studies recommended, 2 history recommended, 1 elective recommended. **Freshman Admission Statistics:** 2,077 applied, 73% accepted, 36% of those accepted enrolled. **Transfer Admission Requirements:** *Items required:* college transcript, essay, statement of good standing from prior school. Minimum college GPA of 2.5 required. Lowest grade transferable C. **General Admission Information:** Application fee $35. Priority application deadline February 1. Nonfall registration accepted. Admission may be deferred for a maximum of 1 year. Credit and/or placement offered for CEEB Advanced Placement tests.

COSTS AND FINANCIAL AID

Tuition $15,656. Room & board $5,610. Required fees $80. Average book expense $1,200. **Required Forms and Deadlines:** FAFSA and institution's own financial aid form. Priority filing deadline April 1. **Notification of Awards:** Applicants will be notified of awards on a rolling basis beginning on or about March 1. **Types of Aid:** *Need-based scholarships/grants:* Pell, SEOG, state scholarships/grants, private scholarships, the school's own gift aid. *Loans:* FFEL Subsidized Stafford, FFEL Unsubsidized Stafford, FFEL PLUS, Federal Perkins. **Student Employment:** Federal Work-Study Program available. Institutional employment available. Off-campus job opportunities are excellent. **Financial Aid Statistics:** 48% freshmen, 50% undergrads receive some form of aid. Average freshman grant $10,574. Average freshman loan $4,686. Average income from on-campus job $2,000. **Financial Aid Phone:** 918-631-2526.

UNIVERSITY OF UTAH

201 South 1460 East, Room 250S, Salt Lake City, UT 84112-9057
Phone: 801-581-7281 **E-mail:** admiss@saff.utah.edu **CEEB Code:** 4853
Fax: 801-585-7864 **Web:** www.utah.edu **ACT Code:** 4274

This public school was founded in 1850. It has a 1,500-acre campus.

STUDENTS AND FACULTY

Enrollment: 22,648. **Student Body:** Male 56%, female 44%, out-of-state 7%, international 3%. **Ethnic Representation:** African American 1%, Asian 4%, Caucasian 83%, Hispanic 4%, Native American 1%. **Retention and Graduation:** 78% freshmen return for sophomore year. 20% freshmen graduate within 4 years. **Faculty:** Student/faculty ratio 16:1. 1,042 full-time faculty, 93% hold PhDs. 87% faculty teach undergrads.

ACADEMICS

Degrees: Bachelor's, certificate, doctoral, first professional, master's, post-bachelor's certificate. **Academic Requirements:** General education including some course work in arts/fine arts, English (including composition), history, humanities, mathematics, sciences (biological or physical), social science. **Classes:** 10-19 students in an average class. 20-29 students in an average lab/discussion section. **Majors with Highest Enrollment:** Business administration/management; pre-medicine/pre-medical studies; special education, general. **Disciplines with Highest Percentage of Degrees Awarded:** Social sciences and history 20%, business/marketing 17%, architecture 11%, communications/communication technologies 9%, engineering/engineering technology 5%. **Special Study Options:** Accelerated program, cooperative (work-study) program, distance learning, double major, English as a second language, student exchange program (domestic), honors program, independent study, internships, student-designed major, study abroad, teacher certification program.

FACILITIES

Housing: All-female, all-male, apartments for married students, apartments for single students, fraternities and/or sororities. **Library Holdings:** 2,991,692 bound volumes. 33,517 periodicals. 3,543,837 microforms. 62,356 audiovisuals. **Special Academic Facilities/Equipment:** Museums of natural history and fine arts, government institute, environmental biological research facilities, human genetics lab. **Computers:** School-owned computers available for student use.

EXTRACURRICULARS

Activities: Choral groups, concert band, dance, drama/theater, jazz band, literary magazine, marching band, music ensembles, musical theater, opera, pep band, radio station, student government, student newspaper, student-run film society, symphony orchestra, television station. **Organizations:** 170 registered organizations, 20 honor societies, 2 religious organizations, 7 fraternities (5% men join), 6 sororities (5% women join). **Athletics (Intercollegiate):** *Men:* baseball, basketball, skiing (cross-country), cross-country, diving, football, golf, indoor track, skiing (alpine), swimming, tennis, track & field. *Women:* basketball, skiing (cross-country), cross-country, diving, gymnastics, indoor track, skiing (alpine), soccer, softball, swimming, tennis, track & field, volleyball.

ADMISSIONS

Selectivity Rating: 71 (of 100). **Freshman Academic Profile:** 26% in top 10% of high school class, 49% in top 25% of high school class, 79% in top 50% of high school class. Average high school GPA 3.5. 95% from public high schools. Average ACT 24, ACT middle 50% range 20-26. TOEFL required of all international applicants, minimum TOEFL 500. **Basis for Candidate Selection:** *Very important factors considered include:* secondary school record, standardized test scores. *Important factors considered include:* talent/ability. *Other factors considered include:* class rank, extracurricular activities, interview, minority status, recommendations. **Freshman Admission Requirements:** High school diploma or GED is required. *Academic units required/recommended:* 15 total required; 4 English required, 2 math required, 2 science required, 1 science lab required, 2 foreign language required, 1 history required, 4 elective required. **Freshman Admission Statistics:** 5,802 applied, 90% accepted, 54% of those accepted enrolled. **Transfer Admission Requirements:** *Items required:* college transcript. Minimum college GPA of 2.5 required. Lowest grade transferable D-. **General Admission Information:** Application fee $35. Priority application deadline February 15. Regular application deadline May 15. Nonfall registration accepted. Admission may be deferred for a maximum of 1 year. Credit and/or placement offered for CEEB Advanced Placement tests.

COSTS AND FINANCIAL AID

Room & board $5,036. Average book expense $1,086. **Required Forms and Deadlines:** FAFSA. No deadline for regular filing. Priority filing deadline March 15. **Notification of Awards:** Applicants will be notified of awards on a rolling basis beginning on or about April 24. **Types of Aid:** *Need-based scholarships/grants:* Pell, SEOG, state scholarships/grants, private scholarships, the school's own gift aid. *Loans:* FFEL Subsidized Stafford, FFEL Unsubsidized Stafford, FFEL PLUS, Federal Perkins, Federal Nursing, college/university loans from institutional funds. **Student Employment:** Federal Work-Study Program available. Institutional employment available. Off-campus job opportunities are good. **Financial Aid Statistics:** 28% freshmen, 36% undergrads receive some form of aid. **Financial Aid Phone:** 801-581-6211.

UNIVERSITY OF VERMONT

Office of Admissions, 194 South Prospect Street, Burlington, VT 05401-3596
Phone: 802-656-3370 **E-mail:** admissions@uvm.edu **CEEB Code:** 3920
Fax: 802-656-8611 **Web:** www.uvm.edu **ACT Code:** 4322

This public school was founded in 1791. It has a 425-acre campus.

STUDENTS AND FACULTY

Enrollment: 8,792. **Student Body:** Male 44%, female 56%, out-of-state 61%, international 1% (40 countries represented). **Ethnic Representation:** African American 1%, Asian 2%, Caucasian 94%, Hispanic 2%. **Retention and Graduation:** 84% freshmen return for sophomore year. 52% freshmen graduate within 4 years. 22% grads go on to further study within 1 year. 2% grads pursue business degrees. 2% grads pursue law degrees. 2% grads pursue medical degrees. **Faculty:** Student/faculty ratio 13:1. 548 full-time faculty, 84% hold PhDs. 85% faculty teach undergrads.

ACADEMICS

Degrees: Associate's, bachelor's, certificate, doctoral, first professional, master's, post-bachelor's certificate, post-master's certificate, terminal. **Academic Requirements:** General education including some course work in arts/fine arts, English (including composition), humanities, mathematics, sciences (biological or physical), social science, race & cultural awareness. **Classes:** 10-19 students in an average class. 10-19 students in an average lab/discussion section. **Majors with Highest Enrollment:** Business administration/management; English language and literature, general; psychology, general. **Disciplines with Highest Percentage of Degrees Awarded:** Social sciences and history 17%, business/marketing 10%, natural resources/environmental sciences 9%, agriculture 9%, psychology 8%. **Special Study Options:** Cooperative (work-study) program, distance learning, double major, honors program, independent study, internships, liberal arts/career combination, student-designed major, study abroad, teacher certification program, limited English as a Second Language offerings available, Evening University option in six programs.

FACILITIES

Housing: Coed, apartments for married students, apartments for single students, fraternities and/or sororities, cooperative housing. **Library Holdings:** 2,410,250 bound volumes. 20,216 periodicals. 1,856,634 microforms. 36,531 audiovisuals. **Special Academic Facilities/Equipment:** Art/ethnography museum, chemistry/physics library, medical library, on-campus preschool, government research and world affairs centers, agricultural experiment station, horse farm, multinuclear magnetic resonance spectrometers, mass spectrometer. **Computers:** School-owned computers available for student use.

EXTRACURRICULARS

Activities: Choral groups, concert band, dance, drama/theater, jazz band, literary magazine, music ensembles, musical theater, pep band, radio station, student government, student newspaper, student-run film society, television station. **Organizations:** 110 registered organizations, 23 honor societies, 5 religious organizations, 10 fraternities (9% men join), 5 sororities (6% women join). **Athletics (Intercollegiate):** *Men:* baseball, basketball, skiing (cross-country), cross-country, diving, golf, ice hockey, lacrosse, skiing (alpine), skiing (Nordic), soccer, swimming, tennis. *Women:* basketball, skiing (cross-country), cross-country, diving, field hockey, ice hockey, indoor track, lacrosse, skiing (alpine), skiing (Nordic), soccer, softball, swimming, tennis, track & field.

ADMISSIONS

Selectivity Rating: 77 (of 100). **Freshman Academic Profile:** 19% in top 10% of high school class, 55% in top 25% of high school class, 91% in top 50% of high school class. 70% from public high schools. Average SAT I Math 574, SAT I Math middle 50% range 520-620. Average SAT I Verbal 568, SAT I Verbal middle 50% range 520-620. Average ACT 24, ACT middle 50% range 22-27. TOEFL required of all international applicants, minimum TOEFL 550. **Basis for Candidate Selection:** *Very important factors considered include:* secondary school record. *Important factors considered include:* alumni/ae relation, character/personal qualities, class rank, essays, minority status, standardized test scores, state residency. *Other factors considered include:* extracurricular activities, geographical residence, interview, recommendations, talent/ability, volunteer work, work experience. **Freshman Admission Requirements:** High school diploma or GED is required. *Academic units required/recommended:* 16 total required; 4 English required, 3 math required, 2 science required, 1 science lab required, 2 foreign language required, 3 social studies required. **Freshman Admission Statistics:** 9,776 applied, 71% accepted, 26% of those accepted enrolled. **Transfer Admission Requirements:** *Items required:* high school transcript, college transcript, essay.

Minimum college GPA of 2.5 required. Lowest grade transferable C. **General Admission Information:** Application fee $45. Early decision application deadline November 1. Regular application deadline January 15. Nonfall registration accepted. Admission may be deferred for a maximum of 1 year. Credit and/or placement offered for CEEB Advanced Placement tests.

COSTS AND FINANCIAL AID

In-state tuition $8,320. Out-of-state tuition $20,810. Room & board $6,378. Required fees $674. Average book expense $696. **Required Forms and Deadlines:** FAFSA. Financial aid filing deadline March 15. Priority filing deadline February 10. **Notification of Awards:** Applicants will be notified of awards on a rolling basis beginning on or about March 15. **Types of Aid:** *Need-based scholarships/grants:* Pell, SEOG, state scholarships/grants, private scholarships, the school's own gift aid, Federal Nursing. *Loans:* FFEL Subsidized Stafford, FFEL Unsubsidized Stafford, FFEL PLUS, Federal Perkins, Federal Nursing, college/university loans from institutional funds. **Student Employment:** Federal Work-Study Program available. Institutional employment available. Off-campus job opportunities are excellent. **Financial Aid Statistics:** 54% freshmen, 50% undergrads receive some form of aid. Average freshman grant $8,208. Average freshman loan $4,239. **Financial Aid Phone:** 802-656-3156.

See page 1268.

UNIVERSITY OF VIRGINIA

Office of Admission, PO Box 400160, Charlottesville, VA 22904-4160
Phone: 434-982-3200 **E-mail:** undergradadmission@virginia.edu **CEEB Code:** 5820
Fax: 434-924-3587 **Web:** www.virginia.edu **ACT Code:** 4412

This public school was founded in 1819. It has a 1,160-acre campus.

STUDENTS AND FACULTY

Enrollment: 13,805. **Student Body:** Male 46%, female 54%, out-of-state 28%, international 4% (97 countries represented). **Ethnic Representation:** African American 10%, Asian 11%, Caucasian 73%, Hispanic 3%. **Retention and Graduation:** 97% freshmen return for sophomore year. 83% freshmen graduate within 4 years. 39% grads go on to further study within 1 year. **Faculty:** Student/faculty ratio 16:1. 1099 full-time faculty, 92% hold PhDs.

ACADEMICS

Degrees: Bachelor's, doctoral, first professional, master's, post-master's certificate. **Academic Requirements:** General education including some course work in English (including composition), foreign languages, history, humanities, mathematics, sciences (biological or physical), social science, nonwestern perspectives. **Classes:** 10-19 students in an average class. 10-19 students in an average lab/discussion section. **Majors with Highest Enrollment:** Business/commerce, general; psychology, general; economics, general. **Disciplines with Highest Percentage of Degrees Awarded:** Social sciences and history 28%, engineering/engineering technology 10%, business/marketing 10%, English 8%, psychology 7%. **Special Study Options:** Accelerated program, cooperative (work-study) program, double major, English as a second language, honors program, independent study, internships, student-designed major, study abroad, teacher certification program.

FACILITIES

Housing: Coed, apartments for married students, apartments for single students, fraternities and/or sororities, four foreign language houses, three residential colleges. **Library Holdings:** 3,398,441 bound volumes. 55,843 periodicals. 5,395,261 microforms. 84,035 audiovisuals. **Special Academic Facilities/Equipment:** Art museum, center for studies in political economy, bureau of public administration, experimental farm, biological station, labs, observatory/planetarium, nuclear information center. **Computers:** School-owned computers available for student use.

EXTRACURRICULARS

Activities: Choral groups, dance, drama/theater, jazz band, literary magazine, music ensembles, musical theater, opera, pep band, radio station, student government, student newspaper, student-run film society, symphony orchestra, television station, yearbook. **Organizations:** 300 registered organizations, 24 honor societies, 10 religious organizations, 32 fraternities (30% men join), 22 sororities (30% women join). **Athletics (Intercollegiate):** *Men:* baseball, basketball, cross-country, diving, football, golf, indoor track, lacrosse, soccer, swimming, tennis, track & field, wrestling. *Women:* basketball, crew, cross-country, diving, field hockey, golf, indoor track, lacrosse, soccer, softball, swimming, tennis, track & field, volleyball.

ADMISSIONS

Selectivity Rating: 94 (of 100). **Freshman Academic Profile:** Average high school GPA 4. 84% in top 10% of high school class, 97% in top 25% of high school class, 99% in top 50% of high school class. 75% from public high schools. Average SAT I Math 668, SAT I Math middle 50% range 620-720. Average SAT I Verbal 647, SAT I Verbal middle 50% range 600-700. Average ACT 28, ACT middle 50% range 25-31. TOEFL required of all international applicants, minimum TOEFL 600. **Basis for Candidate Selection:** *Very important factors considered include:* alumni/ae relation, minority status, secondary school record, state residency. *Important factors considered include:* character/personal qualities, class rank, essays, extracurricular activities, recommendations, standardized test scores, talent/ability. *Other factors considered include:* geographical residence, volunteer work, work experience. **Freshman Admission Requirements:** High school diploma or GED is required. *Academic units required/recommended:* 16 total required; 4 English required, 4 math required, 5 math recommended, 2 science required, 4 science recommended, 2 foreign language required, 5 foreign language recommended, 1 social studies required, 3 social studies recommended. **Freshman Admission Statistics:** 14,320 applied, 39% accepted, 54% of those accepted enrolled. **Transfer Admission Requirements:** *Items required:* high school transcript, college transcript, essay, statement of good standing from prior school. Minimum college GPA of 2.0 required. Lowest grade transferable C. **General Admission Information:** Application fee $40. Early decision application deadline November 1. Regular application deadline January 2. Admission may be deferred for a maximum of 1 year. Credit and/or placement offered for CEEB Advanced Placement tests.

COSTS AND FINANCIAL AID

Required Forms and Deadlines: FAFSA and institution's own financial aid form. Priority filing deadline March 1. **Notification of Awards:** Applicants will be notified of awards on or about April 5. **Types of Aid:** *Need-based scholarships/grants:* Pell, SEOG, state scholarships/grants, private scholarships, the school's own gift aid. *Loans:* Direct Subsidized Stafford, Direct Unsubsidized Stafford, Direct PLUS, Federal Perkins, Federal Nursing, college/university loans from institutional funds. **Student Employment:** Federal Work-Study Program available. Institutional employment available. Off-campus job opportunities are fair. **Financial Aid Statistics:** 22% freshmen, 21% undergrads receive some form of aid. **Financial Aid Phone:** 434-982-6000.

UNIVERSITY OF VIRGINIA'S COLLEGE AT WISE

1 College Avenue, Wise, VA 24293
Phone: 540-328-0102 **E-mail:** admissions@uvawise.edu **CEEB Code:** 5124
Fax: 540-328-0251 **Web:** www.uvawise.edu **ACT Code:** 4343

This public school was founded in 1954. It has a 367-acre campus.

STUDENTS AND FACULTY

Enrollment: 1,447. **Student Body:** Male 44%, female 56%, out-of-state 6%. **Ethnic Representation:** African American 5%, Asian 1%, Caucasian 93%, Hispanic 1%. **Retention and Graduation:** 67% freshmen return for sophomore year. 25% freshmen graduate within 4 years. 14% grads go on to further study within 1 year. 4% grads pursue business degrees. 6% grads pursue law degrees. 1% grads pursue medical degrees. **Faculty:** Student/faculty ratio 15:1. 65 full-time faculty, 80% hold PhDs. 100% faculty teach undergrads.

ACADEMICS

Degrees: Bachelor's. **Academic Requirements:** General education including some course work in arts/fine arts, computer literacy, English (including composition), foreign languages, history, humanities, mathematics, sciences (biological or physical), social science, literature, physical education. **Classes:** 20-29 students in an average class. 20-29 students in an average lab/discussion section. **Disciplines with Highest Percentage of Degrees Awarded:** Business/marketing 29%, social sciences and history 25%, psychology 14%, English 8%, biological life sciences 7%. **Special Study Options:** Accelerated program, cooperative (work-study) program, distance learning, double major, dual enrollment, honors program, independent study, internships, student-designed major, study abroad, teacher certification program.

FACILITIES

Housing: Coed, all-female, all-male, apartments for single students, housing for disabled students. **Library Holdings:** 95,861 bound volumes. 1,029 periodicals. 62,155 microforms. 11,582 audiovisuals. **Computers:** School-owned computers available for student use.

EXTRACURRICULARS

Activities: Choral groups, concert band, dance, drama/theater, literary magazine, music ensembles, musical theater, pep band, radio station, student government, student newspaper, television station, yearbook. **Organizations:** 40 registered organizations, 3 honor societies, 3 religious organizations, 3 fraternities (13% men join), 2 sororities (8% women join). **Athletics (Intercollegiate):** *Men:* baseball, basketball, cross-country, football, golf, tennis, track & field. *Women:* basketball, cross-country, softball, tennis, track & field, volleyball.

ADMISSIONS

Selectivity Rating: 71 (of 100). **Freshman Academic Profile:** Average high school GPA 3.3. 23% in top 10% of high school class, 52% in top 25% of high school class, 83% in top 50% of high school class. 99% from public high schools. Average SAT I Math 496, SAT I Math middle 50% range 420-520. Average SAT I Verbal 511, SAT I Verbal middle 50% range 430-550. Average ACT 20, ACT middle 50% range 16-23. TOEFL required of all international applicants, minimum TOEFL 550. **Basis for Candidate Selection:** *Very important factors considered include:* secondary school record. *Important factors considered include:* class rank, standardized test scores, talent/ability. *Other factors considered include:* character/personal qualities, essays, extracurricular activities, interview, minority status, recommendations, volunteer work, work experience. **Freshman Admission Requirements:** High school diploma or GED is required. *Academic units required/recommended:* 13 total required; 4 English required, 3 math required, 2 science required, 2 science lab required, 2 foreign language required, 2 history required. **Freshman Admission Statistics:** 814 applied, 73% accepted, 47% of those accepted enrolled. **Transfer Admission Requirements:** *Items required:* college transcript. Minimum high school GPA of 2.3 required. Minimum college GPA of 2.3 required. Lowest grade transferable C-. **General Admission Information:** Application fee $15. Priority application deadline April 1. Regular application deadline August 1. Nonfall registration accepted. Admission may be deferred for a maximum of 1 year. Credit and/or placement offered for CEEB Advanced Placement tests.

COSTS AND FINANCIAL AID

In-state tuition $1,885. Out-of-state tuition $8,379. Room & board $4,696. Required fees $1,445. Average book expense $638. **Required Forms and Deadlines:** FAFSA. Priority filing deadline April 1. **Notification of Awards:** Applicants will be notified of awards on a rolling basis beginning on or about April 1. **Types of Aid:** *Need-based scholarships/grants:* Pell, SEOG, state scholarships/grants, private scholarships, the school's own gift aid. *Loans:* FFEL Subsidized Stafford, FFEL Unsubsidized Stafford, FFEL PLUS, Federal Perkins, state loans, college/university loans from institutional funds. **Student Employment:** Federal Work-Study Program available. Institutional employment available. Off-campus job opportunities are fair. **Financial Aid Statistics:** 70% freshmen, 70% undergrads receive some form of aid. Average freshman grant $2,510. Average freshman loan $1,362. Average income from on-campus job $900. **Financial Aid Phone:** 540-328-0193.

UNIVERSITY OF WASHINGTON

1410 NE Campus Parkway, 320 Schmitz, Box 355840, Seattle, WA 98195-5840
Phone: 206-543-9686 **E-mail:** askuwadm@u.washington.edu **CEEB Code:** 4854
Fax: 206-685-3655 **Web:** www.washington.edu **ACT Code:** 4484

This public school was founded in 1861. It has a 680-acre campus.

STUDENTS AND FACULTY

Enrollment: 28,362. **Student Body:** Male 48%, female 52%, out-of-state 15%, international 3%. **Ethnic Representation:** African American 3%, Asian 25%, Caucasian 56%, Hispanic 4%, Native American 1%. **Retention and Graduation:** 90% freshmen return for sophomore year. 40% freshmen graduate within 4 years. 38% grads go on to further study within 1 year. **Faculty:** Student/faculty ratio 11:1. 2,764 full-time faculty, 93% hold PhDs.

ACADEMICS

Degrees: Bachelor's, doctoral, first professional, master's. **Academic Requirements:** General education including some course work in English (including composition), humanities, mathematics, sciences (biological or physical), social science. **Classes:** 20-29 students in an average class. 20-29 students in an average lab/discussion section. **Disciplines with Highest Percentage of Degrees Awarded:** Social sciences and history 18%, business/marketing 14%, engineering/engineering technology 9%, English 7%, biological life sciences 6%. **Special Study Options:** Accelerated program, cooperative (work-study) program, cross registration, distance learning, double major, dual enrollment, English as a second language, student exchange program (domestic), external degree program, honors program, independent study, internships, liberal arts/career combination, student-designed major, study abroad, teacher certification program, weekend college, Friday Harbor Labs.

FACILITIES

Housing: Coed, apartments for married students, apartments for single students, housing for disabled students, housing for international students, fraternities and/or sororities, special-interest houses. **Library Holdings:** 6,274,225 bound volumes. 45,587 periodicals. 7,387,734 microforms. 1,546,283 audiovisuals. **Special Academic Facilities/Equipment:** Art gallery, anthropology and natural history museum, arboretum, closed-circuit TV studio. **Computers:** School-owned computers available for student use.

EXTRACURRICULARS

Activities: Choral groups, concert band, dance, drama/theater, jazz band, literary magazine, marching band, music ensembles, musical theater, opera, student government, student newspaper, television station. **Organizations:** 250 registered organizations, 4 honor societies, 7 religious organizations, 30 fraternities (12% men join), 18 sororities (11% women join). **Athletics (Intercollegiate):** *Men:* baseball, basketball, crew, cross-country, football, golf, soccer, swimming, tennis, track & field. *Women:* basketball, crew, cross-country, golf, gymnastics, soccer, softball, swimming, tennis, track & field, volleyball.

ADMISSIONS

Selectivity Rating: 82 (of 100). **Freshman Academic Profile:** Average high school GPA 3.7. 44% in top 10% of high school class, 80% in top 25% of high school class, 97% in top 50% of high school class. SAT I Math middle 50% range 550-660. SAT I Verbal middle 50% range 510-630. ACT middle 50% range 22-28. **Basis for Candidate Selection:** *Very important factors considered include:* secondary school record. *Important factors considered include:* standardized test scores, state residency. *Other factors considered include:* alumni/ae relation, class rank, essays, extracurricular activities, talent/ability, volunteer work, work experience. **Freshman Admission Requirements:** High school diploma or equivalent is not required. *Academic units required/recommended:* 4 English required, 4 English recommended, 3 math required, 4 math recommended, 2 science required, 3 science recommended, 1 science lab required, 2 science lab recommended, 2 foreign language required, 3 foreign language recommended, 3 social studies required, 4 social studies recommended. **Freshman Admission Statistics:** 15,950 applied, 68% accepted, 44% of those accepted enrolled. **Transfer Admission Requirements:** *Items required:* high school transcript, college transcript. Minimum high school GPA of 2.0 required. Minimum college GPA of 2.7 required. Lowest grade transferable D. **General Admission Information:** Application fee $36. Regular application deadline January 15. Nonfall registration accepted. Credit and/or placement offered for CEEB Advanced Placement tests.

COSTS AND FINANCIAL AID

In-state tuition $4,167. Out-of-state tuition $14,868. Room & board $8,430. Required fees $469. Average book expense $822. **Required Forms and Deadlines:** FAFSA. Priority filing deadline February 28. **Notification of Awards:** Applicants will be notified of awards on a rolling basis beginning on or about April 1. **Types of Aid:** *Need-based scholarships/grants:* Pell, SEOG, state scholarships/grants, private scholarships, the school's own gift aid. *Loans:* Direct Subsidized Stafford, Direct Unsubsidized Stafford, Direct PLUS, Federal Perkins, Federal Nursing, college/university loans from institutional funds. **Student Employment:** Federal Work-Study Program available. Institutional employment available. Off-campus job opportunities are good. **Financial Aid Statistics:** 33% freshmen, 40% undergrads receive some form of aid. Average freshman loan $3,376. **Financial Aid Phone:** 206-543-6101.

UNIVERSITY OF WATERLOO

200 University Avenue West, Waterloo, ON N2L 3G1
Phone: 519-888-4567, extension 3777 **E-mail:** watquest@uwaterloo.ca
Fax: 519-746-2882 **Web:** www.findoutmore.uwaterloo.ca

This public school was founded in 1957. It has a 900-acre campus.

STUDENTS AND FACULTY

Enrollment: 21,108. **Student Body:** Male 49%, female 51%, out-of-state 2%. **Retention and Graduation:** 98% freshmen return for sophomore year. **Faculty:** Student/faculty ratio 15:1. 769 full-time faculty. 100% faculty teach undergrads.

ACADEMICS

Degrees: Bachelor's, certificate, diploma, doctoral, first professional, master's. **Majors with Highest Enrollment:** Mathematics, general; computer science; kinesiology and exercise science. **Disciplines with Highest Percentage of**

Degrees Awarded: Engineering/engineering technology 24%, computer and information sciences 9%, social sciences and history 9%, mathematics 8%. **Special Study Options:** Accelerated program, cooperative (work-study) program, cross registration, distance learning, double major, student exchange program (domestic), external degree program, honors program, independent study, internships, liberal arts/career combination, student-designed major, study abroad.

FACILITIES

Housing: Coed, all-female, all-male, apartments for single students. **Library Holdings:** 3,793,234 bound volumes. 13,228 periodicals. 1,485,000 microforms. 0 audiovisuals. **Special Academic Facilities/Equipment:** State-of-the-art high-tech computer, engineering and science labs; optometry and applied health studies clinics and labs; art galleries; theatres; games, earth sciences/biology, historic, and optometry museums; art and architecture studios; multimedia-link rooms; observatory; greenhouse. **Computers:** School-owned computers available for student use.

EXTRACURRICULARS

Activities: Choral groups, dance, drama/theater, literary magazine, music ensembles, radio station, student government, student newspaper, student-run film society, yearbook. **Organizations:** 80 registered organizations, 1 fraternity (1% men join), 1 sorority (1% women join). **Athletics (Intercollegiate):** *Men:* baseball, basketball, cross-country, football, golf, ice hockey, indoor track, rugby, skiing (Nordic), soccer, squash, swimming, tennis, track & field, volleyball. *Women:* basketball, cross-country, field hockey, ice hockey, indoor track, rugby, skiing (Nordic), soccer, swimming, tennis, track & field, volleyball.

ADMISSIONS

Selectivity Rating: 60 (of 100). **Freshman Academic Profile:** 80% in top 10% of high school class. TOEFL required of all international applicants, minimum TOEFL 600. **Basis for Candidate Selection:** *Very important factors considered include:* secondary school record. *Other factors considered include:* class rank, essays, extracurricular activities, interview, recommendations, standardized test scores, talent/ability, volunteer work, work experience. **Freshman Admission Requirements:** High school diploma is required and GED is not accepted. **Transfer Admission Requirements:** *Items required:* high school transcript. **General Admission Information:** Application fee $95. Regular application deadline May 1. Nonfall registration accepted.

COSTS AND FINANCIAL AID

In-state tuition $3,952. Out-of-state tuition $3,952. Room & board $5,950. Required fees $0. Average book expense $800. **Required Forms and Deadlines:** Institution's own financial aid form. Financial aid filing deadline July 1. Priority filing deadline July 1. **Notification of Awards:** Applicants will be notified of awards on or about September 1. **Student Employment:** Institutional employment available. Off-campus job opportunities are good. **Financial Aid Statistics:** 47% undergrads receive some form of aid. **Financial Aid Phone:** 519-888-4567.

UNIVERSITY OF WEST ALABAMA

Station 4, Livingston, AL 35470
Phone: 888-636-8800 **E-mail:** admissions@umamail.westal.edu **CEEB Code:** 1737
Fax: 205-652-3522 **Web:** www.uwa.edu **ACT Code:** 24

This public school was founded in 1835. It has a 600-acre campus.

STUDENTS AND FACULTY

Enrollment: 1,595. **Student Body:** Male 45%, female 55%, out-of-state 26%, international 1%. **Ethnic Representation:** African American 40%, Caucasian 59%. **Retention and Graduation:** 25% freshmen return for sophomore year. 14% freshmen graduate within 4 years. 15% grads go on to further study within 1 year. 1% grads pursue business degrees. 1% grads pursue law degrees. 1% grads pursue medical degrees. **Faculty:** Student/faculty ratio 19:1. 80 full-time faculty, 61% hold PhDs. 100% faculty teach undergrads.

ACADEMICS

Degrees: Associate's, bachelor's, master's, terminal. **Academic Requirements:** General education including some course work in arts/fine arts, computer literacy, English (including composition), foreign languages, history, humanities, mathematics, philosophy, sciences (biological or physical). **Disciplines with Highest Percentage of Degrees Awarded:** Education 24%, business/marketing 16%, parks and recreation 10%, computer and information sciences 9%, social sciences and history 8%. **Special Study Options:** Cooperative (work-study) program, distance learning, double major, student exchange program (domestic), honors program, internships, teacher certification program.

FACILITIES

Housing: Coed, all-female, all-male, apartments for married students, apartments for single students, housing for disabled students, fraternities and/or sororities. **Library Holdings:** 118,000 bound volumes. 882 periodicals. 485,657 microforms. **Computers:** School-owned computers available for student use.

EXTRACURRICULARS

Activities: Choral groups, concert band, dance, drama/theater, literary magazine, marching band, music ensembles, musical theater, pep band, radio station, student government, student newspaper, television station, yearbook. **Organizations:** 30 registered organizations, 8 honor societies, 5 religious organizations, 7 fraternities (20% men join), 6 sororities (15% women join). **Athletics (Intercollegiate):** *Men:* baseball, basketball, cheerleading, cross-country, football, rodeo. *Women:* basketball, cheerleading, cross-country, rodeo, softball, volleyball.

ADMISSIONS

Selectivity Rating: 68 (of 100). **Freshman Academic Profile:** 88% from public high schools. Average ACT 19, ACT middle 50% range 17-22. TOEFL required of all international applicants, minimum TOEFL 500. **Basis for Candidate Selection:** *Very important factors considered include:* secondary school record, standardized test scores. **Freshman Admission Requirements:** High school diploma or GED is required. *Academic units required/recommended:* 15 total required; 3 English required, 3 math required, 3 science required, 3 social studies required, 3 elective required. **Freshman Admission Statistics:** 1,038 applied, 66% accepted, 49% of those accepted enrolled. **Transfer Admission Requirements:** *Items required:* college transcript, statement of good standing from prior school. Minimum college GPA of 2.0 required. Lowest grade transferable C. **General Admission Information:** Application fee $20. Nonfall registration accepted. Credit and/or placement offered for CEEB Advanced Placement tests.

COSTS AND FINANCIAL AID

In-state tuition $2,504. Out-of-state tuition $5,008. Room & board $2,822. Required fees $390. Average book expense $600. **Required Forms and Deadlines:** FAFSA. Priority filing deadline April 1. **Notification of Awards:** Applicants will be notified of awards on a rolling basis beginning on or about June 1. **Types of Aid:** *Need-based scholarships/grants:* Pell, SEOG, state scholarships/grants, private scholarships, the school's own gift aid. *Loans:* FFEL Subsidized Stafford, FFEL Unsubsidized Stafford, FFEL PLUS, Federal Perkins, college/university loans from institutional funds. **Student Employment:** Federal Work-Study Program available. Off-campus job opportunities are good. **Financial Aid Statistics:** 69% undergrads receive some form of aid. Average freshman grant $3,111. Average freshman loan $2,724. Average income from on-campus job $1,317. **Financial Aid Phone:** 205-652-3576.

UNIVERSITY OF WEST FLORIDA

11000 University Parkway, Pensacola, FL 32514-5750
Phone: 850-474-2230 **E-mail:** admissions@uwf.edu **CEEB Code:** 5833
Fax: 850-474-3360 **Web:** uwf.edu (do not use www) **ACT Code:** 771

This public school was founded in 1963. It has a 1,600-acre campus.

STUDENTS AND FACULTY

Enrollment: 7,595. **Student Body:** Male 42%, female 58%, out-of-state 13%, international 1% (82 countries represented). **Ethnic Representation:** African American 10%, Asian 5%, Caucasian 77%, Hispanic 4%, Native American 1%. **Retention and Graduation:** 73% freshmen return for sophomore year. **Faculty:** Student/faculty ratio 20:1. 245 full-time faculty, 79% hold PhDs.

ACADEMICS

Degrees: Associate's, bachelor's, diploma, doctoral, master's. **Academic Requirements:** General education including some course work in English (including composition), mathematics. **Classes:** 20-29 students in an average class. 20-29 students in an average lab/discussion section. **Majors with Highest Enrollment:** Communications studies/speech communication and rhetoric; computer science; psychology, general. **Disciplines with Highest Percentage of Degrees Awarded:** Business/marketing 19%, education 11%, protective services/public administration 11%, communications/communication technologies 9%, psychology 9%. **Special Study Options:** Cooperative (work-study) program, distance learning, dual enrollment, student exchange program (domestic), honors program, independent study, internships, study abroad, teacher certification program, learning disability services.

FACILITIES

Housing: Coed, apartments for married students, apartments for single students, fraternities and/or sororities. Special facilities for the disabled are provided. **Library Holdings:** 414,418 bound volumes. 3,236 periodicals. 1,635,474 microforms. 4,303 audiovisuals. **Special Academic Facilities/ Equipment:** Archeology museum; instructional media center; biology, chemistry, physics, and psychology labs; property on the Gulf of Mexico for marine and ecology research. **Computers:** *Recommended operating system:* Windows XP/2000. School-owned computers available for student use.

EXTRACURRICULARS

Activities: Choral groups, concert band, drama/theater, jazz band, music ensembles, radio station, student government, student newspaper, television station. **Organizations:** 97 registered organizations, 14 honor societies, 8 religious organizations, 9 fraternities (5% men join), 8 sororities (5% women join). **Athletics (Intercollegiate):** *Men:* baseball, basketball, cross-country, golf, soccer, tennis. *Women:* basketball, cross-country, golf, soccer, softball, tennis, volleyball.

ADMISSIONS

Selectivity Rating: 76 (of 100). **Freshman Academic Profile:** Average high school GPA 3.4. 90% from public high schools. Average SAT I Math 542, SAT I Math middle 50% range 500-590. Average SAT I Verbal 543, SAT I Verbal middle 50% range 490-600. Average ACT 23, ACT middle 50% range 21-26. TOEFL required of all international applicants, minimum TOEFL 525. **Basis for Candidate Selection:** *Very important factors considered include:* secondary school record, standardized test scores, talent/ability. *Important factors considered include:* alumni/ae relation. *Other factors considered include:* character/personal qualities, class rank, essays, extracurricular activities, geographical residence, interview, minority status, recommendations, state residency, volunteer work, work experience. **Freshman Admission Requirements:** High school diploma or GED is required. *Academic units required/ recommended:* 19 total required; 4 English required, 3 math required, 3 science required, 2 science lab required, 2 foreign language required, 3 social studies required, 4 elective required. **Freshman Admission Statistics:** 2,569 applied, 78% accepted, 47% of those accepted enrolled. **Transfer Admission Requirements:** *Items required:* high school transcript, standardized test scores. Minimum high school GPA of 2.0 required. Minimum college GPA of 2.0 required. Lowest grade transferable C. **General Admission Information:** Application fee $20. Regular application deadline June 30. Nonfall registration accepted. Admission may be deferred for a maximum of 1 year. Credit offered for CEEB Advanced Placement tests.

COSTS AND FINANCIAL AID

In-state tuition $1,754. Out-of-state tuition $10,392. Room & board $6,000. Required fees $885. Average book expense $800. **Required Forms and Deadlines:** FAFSA and institution's own financial aid form. **Types of Aid:** *Need-based scholarships/grants:* Pell, SEOG, state scholarships/grants, private scholarships, the school's own gift aid. *Loans:* Direct Subsidized Stafford, Direct Unsubsidized Stafford, Direct PLUS, Federal Perkins, college/university loans from institutional funds. **Student Employment:** Federal Work-Study Program available. Institutional employment available. Off-campus job opportunities are good. **Financial Aid Phone:** 850-474-2400.

UNIVERSITY OF WEST LOS ANGELES

1155 West Arbor Vitae Street, Inglewood, CA 90301
Phone: 310-342-5254 **E-mail:** lfreeman@uwla.edu
Fax: 310-342-5295 **Web:** www.uwla.edu

This private school was founded in 1966. It has a 4-acre campus.

STUDENTS AND FACULTY

Enrollment: 64. **Ethnic Representation:** African American 63%, Asian 6%, Caucasian 20%, Hispanic 11%. **Faculty:** Student/faculty ratio 30:1. 10 full-time faculty, 100% hold PhDs.

ACADEMICS

Degrees: Bachelor's, certificate, first professional certificate. **Academic Requirements:** General education including some course work in English (including composition). **Classes:** 10-19 students in an average class. **Special Study Options:** Independent study, internships, extension, evening, and weekend courses.

FACILITIES

Housing: No on-campus housing. **Computers:** School-owned computers available for student use.

EXTRACURRICULARS

Activities: Student newspaper.

ADMISSIONS

Selectivity Rating: 60 (of 100). High school diploma or equivalent is not required. **Transfer Admission Requirements:** *Items required:* college transcript, essay. Minimum high school GPA of 3.5 required. Minimum college GPA of 2.0 required. Lowest grade transferable C. **General Admission Information:** Application fee $55. Admission may be deferred.

COSTS AND FINANCIAL AID

Tuition $235. Required fees $120. Average book expense $175. **Types of Aid:** *Need-based scholarships/grants:* Pell, SEOG, private scholarships. *Loans:* Direct Subsidized Stafford, Direct Unsubsidized Stafford, Direct PLUS, FFEL Subsidized Stafford, FFEL Unsubsidized Stafford, FFEL PLUS. **Student Employment:** Off-campus job opportunities are fair. **Financial Aid Phone:** 310-342-5257.

THE UNIVERSITY OF WESTERN ONTARIO

Stevenson-Lawson Bldg. Rm. 165, London, ON N6A5B8
Phone: 519-661-2150 **E-mail:** reg-admissions@uwo.ca
Fax: 519-661-3710 **Web:** www.uwo.ca

This public school was founded in 1878. It has a 383-acre campus.

STUDENTS AND FACULTY

Enrollment: 20,548. **Student Body:** Male 46%, female 54%. **Retention and Graduation:** 95% freshmen return for sophomore year. **Faculty:** Student/ faculty ratio 18:1. 1,204 full-time faculty.

ACADEMICS

Degrees: Bachelor's, certificate, diploma, doctoral, master's. **Academic Requirements:** General education including some course work in arts/fine arts, sciences (biological or physical), social science. **Majors with Highest Enrollment:** Education, general; biology/biological sciences, general. **Special Study Options:** Distance learning, double major, student exchange program (domestic), honors program, internships, liberal arts/career combination, student-designed major, study abroad, teacher certification program.

FACILITIES

Housing: Coed, all-female, all-male, apartments for married students, apartments for single students, housing for disabled students. **Library Holdings:** 2,511,107 bound volumes. 12,577 periodicals. 3,697,538 microforms. 1,293,239 audiovisuals.

EXTRACURRICULARS

Activities: Choral groups, jazz band, marching band, music ensembles, opera, radio station, student government, student newspaper, symphony orchestra, television station. **Organizations:** 122 registered organizations, 20 religious organizations, 21 fraternities, 6 sororities. **Athletics (Intercollegiate):** *Men:* basketball, cheerleading, crew, cross-country, fencing, football, golf, ice hockey, rugby, soccer, squash, swimming, tennis, track & field, volleyball, water polo, wrestling. *Women:* cheerleading, crew, cross-country, fencing, field hockey, rugby, soccer, squash, swimming, tennis, track & field, volleyball, wrestling.

ADMISSIONS

Selectivity Rating: 63 (of 100). **Freshman Academic Profile:** TOEFL required of all international applicants, minimum TOEFL 200. **Basis for Candidate Selection:** *Very important factors considered include:* secondary school record, standardized test scores. *Other factors considered include:* class rank, recommendations. **Freshman Admission Requirements:** High school diploma is required and GED is not accepted. *Academic units required/ recommended:* 4 English required. **Freshman Admission Statistics:** 25,776 applied, 64% accepted, 27% of those accepted enrolled. **Transfer Admission Requirements:** *Items required:* college transcript. **General Admission Information:** Application fee $85. Priority application deadline March 30. Regular application deadline June 1. Admission may be deferred for a maximum of 1 year. Credit offered for CEEB Advanced Placement tests.

COSTS AND FINANCIAL AID

In-state tuition $3,920. Out-of-state tuition $3,920. Room & board $5,600. Required fees $831. Average book expense $2,000. **Required Forms and Deadlines:** FAFSA, institution's own financial aid form and state aid form. No deadline for regular filing. **Notification of Awards:** Applicants will be notified of awards on a rolling basis beginning on or about March 1. **Types of Aid:** *Need-based scholarships/grants:* state scholarships/grants, private scholarships, the school's own gift aid, Federal Bursaries, grants. *Loans:* Federal, provincial loans administered by governments. **Student Employment:** Institutional employment available. Off-campus job opportunities are good. **Financial Aid Phone:** 519-661-3775.

UNIVERSITY OF WISCONSIN—EAU CLAIRE

105 Garfield Avenue, Eau Claire, WI 54701
Phone: 715-836-5415 **E-mail:** admissions@uwec.edu **CEEB Code:** 1913
Fax: 715-836-2409 **Web:** www.uwec.edu **ACT Code:** 4670

This public school was founded in 1916. It has a 333-acre campus.

STUDENTS AND FACULTY

Enrollment: 10,364. **Student Body:** Male 40%, female 60%, out-of-state 22%, international 1% (47 countries represented). **Ethnic Representation:** African American 1%, Asian 2%, Caucasian 95%, Hispanic 1%, Native American 1%. **Retention and Graduation:** 80% freshmen return for sophomore year. 15% freshmen graduate within 4 years. 9% grads go on to further study within 1 year. **Faculty:** Student/faculty ratio 21:1. 418 full-time faculty, 85% hold PhDs. 100% faculty teach undergrads.

ACADEMICS

Degrees: Associate's, bachelor's, certificate, first professional certificate, master's, post-bachelor's certificate, post-master's certificate, terminal, transfer. **Academic Requirements:** General education including some course work in arts/fine arts, computer literacy, English (including composition), foreign languages, history, humanities, mathematics, philosophy, sciences (biological or physical), social science. **Classes:** 20-29 students in an average class. 10-19 students in an average lab/discussion section. **Majors with Highest Enrollment:** Nursing/registered nurse training (RN, ASN, BSN, MSN); elementary education and teaching; biology/biological sciences, general. **Disciplines with Highest Percentage of Degrees Awarded:** Business/marketing 29%, health professions and related sciences 11%, education 8%, communications/communication technologies 8%, social sciences and history 7%. **Special Study Options:** Cooperative (work-study) program, distance learning, double major, dual enrollment, English as a second language, student exchange program (domestic), honors program, independent study, internships, study abroad, teacher certification program, program with University of Wisconsin Stout in early childhood education.

FACILITIES

Housing: Coed, all-female, all-male, apartments for single students. **Library Holdings:** 605,639 bound volumes. 2,570 periodicals. 1,351,524 microforms. 14,545 audiovisuals. **Special Academic Facilities/Equipment:** Art gallery, human development center, bird museum, field station, planetarium. **Computers:** *Recommended operating system:* Windows NT/2000. School-owned computers available for student use.

EXTRACURRICULARS

Activities: Choral groups, concert band, dance, drama/theater, jazz band, literary magazine, marching band, music ensembles, musical theater, opera, pep band, radio station, student government, student newspaper, student-run film society, symphony orchestra, television station. **Organizations:** 150 registered organizations, 27 honor societies, 14 religious organizations, 5 fraternities (1% men join), 3 sororities (1% women join). **Athletics (Intercollegiate):** *Men:* basketball, skiing (cross-country), diving, football, golf, ice hockey, swimming, tennis, track & field, wrestling. *Women:* basketball, skiing (cross-country), diving, golf, gymnastics, ice hockey, soccer, softball, swimming, tennis, track & field, volleyball.

ADMISSIONS

Selectivity Rating: 74 (of 100). **Freshman Academic Profile:** 21% in top 10% of high school class, 56% in top 25% of high school class, 93% in top 50% of high school class. 94% from public high schools. Average SAT I Math 588, SAT I Math middle 50% range 528-643. Average SAT I Verbal 558, SAT I Verbal middle 50% range 483-625. Average ACT 23, ACT middle 50% range 21-25. TOEFL required of all international applicants, minimum TOEFL 525. **Basis for Candidate Selection:** *Very important factors considered include:* secondary school record. *Important factors considered include:* class rank, standardized test scores. *Other factors considered include:* essays, extracurricular activities, interview, minority status, recommendations, talent/ability, volunteer work, work experience. **Freshman Admission Requirements:** High school diploma or GED is required. *Academic units required/recommended:* 17 total required; 4 English required, 3 math required, 3 science required, 2 foreign language required, 3 social studies required, 2 elective required. **Freshman Admission Statistics:** 6,777 applied, 68% accepted, 44% of those accepted enrolled. **Transfer Admission Requirements:** *Items required:* high school transcript, college transcript, standardized test score, statement of good standing from prior school. Minimum college GPA of 2.0 required. Lowest grade transferable D-. **General Admission Information:** Application fee $35. Priority application deadline February 1. Nonfall registration accepted. Credit and/or placement offered for CEEB Advanced Placement tests.

COSTS AND FINANCIAL AID

In-state tuition $3,722. Out-of-state tuition $13,768. Room & board $3,910. Required fees $0. Average book expense $370. **Required Forms and Deadlines:** FAFSA. No deadline for regular filing. Priority filing deadline April 15. **Notification of Awards:** Applicants will be notified of awards on a rolling basis beginning on or about April 15. **Types of Aid:** *Need-based scholarships/grants:* Pell, SEOG, state scholarships/grants, private scholarships, the school's own gift aid, Federal Nursing. *Loans:* Direct Subsidized Stafford, Direct Unsubsidized Stafford, Direct PLUS, Federal Perkins, college/university loans from institutional funds, private. **Student Employment:** Federal Work-Study Program available. Institutional employment available. Off-campus job opportunities are good. **Financial Aid Statistics:** 37% freshmen, 39% undergrads receive some form of aid. Average freshman grant $2,749. Average freshman loan $3,505. Average income from on-campus job $1,871. **Financial Aid Phone:** 715-836-3373.

UNIVERSITY OF WISCONSIN—GREEN BAY

2420 Nicolet Drive, Green Bay, WI 53411-7001
Phone: 920-465-2111 **E-mail:** admissions@uwgb.edu **CEEB Code:** 1859
Fax: 920-465-5754 **Web:** www.uwgb.edu **ACT Code:** 4688

This public school was founded in 1965. It has a 700-acre campus.

STUDENTS AND FACULTY

Enrollment: 5,101. **Student Body:** Male 34%, female 66%, out-of-state 4%, international 1% (30 countries represented). **Ethnic Representation:** African American 1%, Asian 2%, Caucasian 91%, Hispanic 1%, Native American 2%. **Retention and Graduation:** 73% freshmen return for sophomore year. 15% freshmen graduate within 4 years. 20% grads go on to further study within 1 year. 5% grads pursue business degrees. 2% grads pursue law degrees. 3% grads pursue medical degrees. **Faculty:** Student/faculty ratio 23:1. 173 full-time faculty, 84% hold PhDs. 99% faculty teach undergrads.

ACADEMICS

Degrees: Associate's, bachelor's, master's, post-bachelor's certificate. **Academic Requirements:** General education including some course work in arts/fine arts, English (including composition), humanities, mathematics, sciences (biological or physical), social science, ethnic studies, other culture studies. **Classes:** 20-29 students in an average class. 20-29 students in an average lab/discussion section. **Majors with Highest Enrollment:** Business administration/management; human development and family studies, general; biological and biomedical sciences. **Disciplines with Highest Percentage of Degrees Awarded:** Business/marketing 23%, psychology 18%, interdisciplinary studies 11%, biological life sciences 8%, education 6%. **Special Study Options:** Cooperative (work-study) program, cross registration, distance learning, double major, dual enrollment, English as a second language, student exchange program (domestic), external degree program, independent study, internships, liberal arts/career combination, student-designed major, study abroad, teacher certification program.

FACILITIES

Housing: Coed, apartments for single students, suites with private bedrooms. **Library Holdings:** 333,482 bound volumes. 5,512 periodicals. 714,166 microforms. 45,396 audiovisuals. **Special Academic Facilities/Equipment:** 290-acre arboretum, herbarium, regional performing arts center. **Computers:** *Recommended operating system:* Windows NT/2000. School-owned computers available for student use.

EXTRACURRICULARS

Activities: Choral groups, concert band, dance, drama/theater, jazz band, literary magazine, music ensembles, musical theater, pep band, student government, student newspaper. **Organizations:** 64 registered organizations, 3 honor societies, 3 religious organizations, 2 fraternities (1% men join), 2 sororities (1% women join). **Athletics (Intercollegiate):** *Men:* basketball, cheerleading, skiing (cross-country), cross-country, diving, golf, soccer, swimming, tennis. *Women:* basketball, cheerleading, skiing (cross-country), cross-country, diving, soccer, softball, swimming, tennis, volleyball.

ADMISSIONS

Selectivity Rating: 73 (of 100). **Freshman Academic Profile:** Average high school GPA 3.4. 20% in top 10% of high school class, 50% in top 25% of high

school class, 94% in top 50% of high school class. 90% from public high schools. Average ACT 23, ACT middle 50% range 20-25. TOEFL required of all international applicants, minimum TOEFL 550. **Basis for Candidate Selection:** *Very important factors considered include:* secondary school record, standardized test scores. *Important factors considered include:* extracurricular activities, talent/ability, volunteer work, work experience. *Other factors considered include:* essays, geographical residence, interview, minority status, recommendations, state residency. **Freshman Admission Requirements:** High school diploma or GED is required. *Academic units required/recommended:* 17 total required; 19 total recommended; 4 English required, 4 English recommended, 3 math required, 3 math recommended, 3 science required, 3 science recommended, 1 science lab required, 1 science lab recommended, 2 foreign language recommended, 3 social studies required, 3 social studies recommended, 4 elective required, 4 elective recommended. **Freshman Admission Statistics:** 2,598 applied, 76% accepted, 45% of those accepted enrolled. **Transfer Admission Requirements:** *Items required:* college transcript, statement of good standing from prior school. Minimum college GPA of 2.5 required. Lowest grade transferable D. **General Admission Information:** Application fee $35. Priority application deadline January 1. Nonfall registration accepted. Admission may be deferred for a maximum of 1 year. Credit and/or placement offered for CEEB Advanced Placement tests.

COSTS AND FINANCIAL AID

In-state tuition $3,000. Out-of-state tuition $13,046. Room & board $4,000. Required fees $1,023. Average book expense $700. **Required Forms and Deadlines:** FAFSA. Priority filing deadline April 15. **Notification of Awards:** Applicants will be notified of awards on a rolling basis beginning on or about November 1. **Types of Aid:** *Need-based scholarships/grants:* Pell, SEOG, state scholarships/grants, private scholarships, the school's own gift aid. *Loans:* FFEL Subsidized Stafford, FFEL Unsubsidized Stafford, FFEL PLUS, Federal Perkins. **Student Employment:** Federal Work-Study Program available. Institutional employment available. Off-campus job opportunities are excellent. **Financial Aid Statistics:** 51% freshmen, 50% undergrads receive some form of aid. Average freshman grant $3,445. Average freshman loan $2,856. **Financial Aid Phone:** 920-465-2075.

UNIVERSITY OF WISCONSIN—LACROSSE

1725 State Street, LaCrosse, WI 54601-3742
Phone: 608-785-8939 **E-mail:** admissions@uwlax.edu **CEEB Code:** 1914
Fax: 608-785-8940 **Web:** www.uwlax.edu **ACT Code:** 4672

This public school was founded in 1909. It has a 120-acre campus.

STUDENTS AND FACULTY

Enrollment: 8,148. **Student Body:** Male 41%, female 59%, out-of-state 16%, international 1% (42 countries represented). **Ethnic Representation:** African American 1%, Asian 2%, Caucasian 94%, Hispanic 1%, Native American 1%. **Retention and Graduation:** 85% freshmen return for sophomore year. 23% freshmen graduate within 4 years. 21% grads go on to further study within 1 year. **Faculty:** Student/faculty ratio 21:1. 375 full-time faculty, 76% hold PhDs. 100% faculty teach undergrads.

ACADEMICS

Degrees: Associate's, bachelor's, master's, terminal. **Academic Requirements:** General education including some course work in arts/fine arts, computer literacy, English (including composition), history, humanities, mathematics, sciences (biological or physical), social science. **Classes:** 20-29 students in an average class. 20-29 students in an average lab/discussion section. **Majors with Highest Enrollment:** Parks, recreation and leisure studies; social sciences, general; marketing/marketing management, general. **Disciplines with Highest Percentage of Degrees Awarded:** Business/marketing 26%, parks and recreation 13%, social sciences and history 12%, biological life sciences 9%, health professions and related sciences 9%. **Special Study Options:** Cooperative (work-study) program, cross registration, distance learning, double major, dual enrollment, English as a second language, honors program, independent study, internships, study abroad, teacher certification program.

FACILITIES

Housing: Coed, all-female, housing for disabled students, housing for international students, fraternities and/or sororities. There is a small amount of special housing for international students. **Library Holdings:** 660,159 bound volumes. 1,603 periodicals. 1,186,736 microforms. 1,648 audiovisuals. **Special Academic Facilities/Equipment:** Greenhouse, planetarium, Health Science Center, Mississippi Valley Archaeology Center, River Studies Center, Business Development Center, La Crosse Exercise & Health Program. **Computers:** School-owned computers available for student use.

EXTRACURRICULARS

Activities: Choral groups, concert band, dance, drama/theater, jazz band, marching band, music ensembles, musical theater, pep band, radio station, student government, student newspaper, symphony orchestra, television station. **Organizations:** 120 registered organizations, 12 honor societies, 10 religious organizations, 3 fraternities (1% men join), 2 sororities (1% women join). **Athletics (Intercollegiate):** *Men:* baseball, basketball, cross-country, diving, football, golf, indoor track, swimming, tennis, track & field, wrestling. *Women:* basketball, cross-country, diving, gymnastics, indoor track, soccer, softball, swimming, tennis, track & field, volleyball.

ADMISSIONS

Selectivity Rating: 74 (of 100). **Freshman Academic Profile:** Average high school GPA 3.5. 27% in top 10% of high school class, 70% in top 25% of high school class, 98% in top 50% of high school class. Average ACT 24, ACT middle 50% range 22-26. TOEFL required of all international applicants, minimum TOEFL 550. **Basis for Candidate Selection:** *Very important factors considered include:* class rank, secondary school record, standardized test scores. *Important factors considered include:* interview, minority status. *Other factors considered include:* character/personal qualities, essays, extracurricular activities, geographical residence, recommendations, state residency, talent/ability, volunteer work, work experience. **Freshman Admission Requirements:** High school diploma or GED is required. *Academic units required/recommended:* 17 total required; 21 total recommended; 4 English required, 4 English recommended, 3 math required, 4 math recommended, 3 science required, 4 science recommended, 2 science lab required, 2 science lab recommended, 3 foreign language recommended, 3 social studies required, 4 social studies recommended, 4 elective required, 2 elective recommended. **Freshman Admission Statistics:** 5,027 applied, 66% accepted, 47% of those accepted enrolled. **Transfer Admission Requirements:** *Items required:* college transcript, statement of good standing from prior school. Minimum college GPA of 3.0 required. Lowest grade transferable D. **General Admission Information:** Application fee $35. Priority application deadline January 3. Nonfall registration accepted. Credit offered for CEEB Advanced Placement tests.

COSTS AND FINANCIAL AID

In-state tuition $4,229. Out-of-state tuition $13,850. Room & board $3,800. Required fees $0. Average book expense $350. **Required Forms and Deadlines:** FAFSA and institution's own financial aid form. Priority filing deadline March 15. **Notification of Awards:** Applicants will be notified of awards on a rolling basis beginning on or about April 15. **Types of Aid:** *Need-based scholarships/grants:* Pell, SEOG, state scholarships/grants, private scholarships, the school's own gift aid. *Loans:* FFEL Subsidized Stafford, FFEL Unsubsidized Stafford, FFEL PLUS, Federal Perkins, state loans, college/university loans from institutional funds. **Student Employment:** Federal Work-Study Program available. Institutional employment available. Off-campus job opportunities are excellent. **Financial Aid Statistics:** 57% freshmen, 57% undergrads receive some form of aid. Average freshman grant $400. Average freshman loan $1,885. Average income from on-campus job $1,500. **Financial Aid Phone:** 608-785-8604.

UNIVERSITY OF WISCONSIN—MADISON

Armory and Gymnasium, 716 Langdon Street, Madison, WI 53706-1481
Phone: 608-262-3961 **E-mail:** onwisconsin@admissions.wisc.edu **CEEB Code:** 1846
Fax: 608-262-7706 **Web:** www.wisc.edu **ACT Code:** 4656

This public school was founded in 1848. It has a 932-acre campus.

STUDENTS AND FACULTY

Enrollment: 29,708. **Student Body:** Male 47%, female 53%, out-of-state 30%, international 3% (100 countries represented). **Ethnic Representation:** African American 2%, Asian 5%, Caucasian 90%, Hispanic 2%, Native American 1%. **Retention and Graduation:** 92% freshmen return for sophomore year. 41% freshmen graduate within 4 years. **Faculty:** Student/faculty ratio 13:1. 2,367 full-time faculty, 92% hold PhDs. 90% faculty teach undergrads.

ACADEMICS

Degrees: Bachelor's, doctoral, first professional, first professional certificate, master's, post-master's certificate. **Academic Requirements:** General education including some course work in English (including composition), foreign languages, humanities, mathematics, sciences (biological or physical), social science, ethnic studies. **Classes:** 10-19 students in an average class. 20-29 students in an average lab/discussion section. **Majors with Highest Enrollment:** Psychology, general; communications studies/speech communication and rhetoric; political science and government, general. **Disciplines with Highest Percentage of Degrees Awarded:** Social sciences and history 20%, business/marketing 16%, biological life sciences 9%, engineering/engineering technology 8%, communications/communication technologies 8%. **Special Study Options:** Accelerated program, cooperative (work-study) program, distance learning, double major, dual enrollment, English as a second language, honors program, independent study, internships, liberal arts/career combination, student-designed major, study abroad, teacher certification program.

FACILITIES

Housing: Coed, all-female, all-male, apartments for married students, apartments for single students, housing for international students, fraternities and/or sororities, cooperative housing, Residential Learning Communities. **Library Holdings:** 6,434,749 bound volumes. 43,770 periodicals. 4,630,939 microforms. **Special Academic Facilities/Equipment:** Art, physics, and geology museums, nuclear reactor, biotron, electron microscopes. **Computers:** School-owned computers available for student use.

EXTRACURRICULARS

Activities: Choral groups, concert band, dance, drama/theater, jazz band, literary magazine, marching band, music ensembles, musical theater, opera, pep band, radio station, student government, student newspaper, student-run film society, symphony orchestra, television station, yearbook. **Organizations:** 600 registered organizations, 25 honor societies, 21 religious organizations, 25 fraternities (9% men join), 9 sororities (8% women join). **Athletics (Intercollegiate):** *Men:* basketball, cheerleading, crew, cross-country, football, golf, ice hockey, indoor track, soccer, swimming, tennis, track & field, wrestling. *Women:* basketball, cheerleading, crew, cross-country, golf, ice hockey, indoor track, soccer, softball, swimming, tennis, track & field, volleyball.

ADMISSIONS

Selectivity Rating: 91 (of 100). **Freshman Academic Profile:** Average high school GPA 3.6. 55% in top 10% of high school class, 93% in top 25% of high school class, 94% in top 50% of high school class. 70% from public high schools. Average SAT I Math 652, SAT I Math middle 50% range 610-710. Average SAT I Verbal 613, SAT I Verbal middle 50% range 570-680. Average ACT 27, ACT middle 50% range 25-29. TOEFL required of all international applicants, minimum TOEFL 550. **Basis for Candidate Selection:** *Very important factors considered include:* class rank, secondary school record. *Important factors considered include:* recommendations, standardized test scores, state residency, talent/ability. *Other factors considered include:* alumni/ae relation, character/personal qualities, essays, extracurricular activities, interview, minority status, volunteer work, work experience. **Freshman Admission Requirements:** High school diploma or GED is required. *Academic units required/recommended:* 17 total required; 20 total recommended; 4 English required, 4 English recommended, 3 math required, 4 math recommended, 3 science required, 4 science recommended, 2 foreign language required, 2 foreign language recommended, 3 social studies required, 4 social studies recommended. **Freshman Admission Statistics:** 21,211 applied, 60% accepted, 43% of those accepted enrolled. **Transfer Admission Requirements:** *Items required:* high school transcript, college transcript, essay, standardized test scores. Lowest grade transferable D. **General Admission Information:** Application fee $35. Priority application deadline February 1. Regular application deadline February 1. Nonfall registration accepted. Admission may be deferred for a maximum of 1 year. Credit and/or placement offered for CEEB Advanced Placement tests.

COSTS AND FINANCIAL AID

In-state tuition $4,840. Out-of-state tuition $20,240. Room & board $6,130. Required fees $0. Average book expense $820. **Required Forms and Deadlines:** FAFSA and institution's own financial aid form. No deadline for regular filing. **Notification of Awards:** Applicants will be notified of awards on a rolling basis beginning on or about April 1. **Types of Aid:** *Need-based scholarships/grants:* Pell, SEOG, state scholarships/grants, private scholarships, the school's own gift aid. *Loans:* FFEL Subsidized Stafford, FFEL Unsubsidized Stafford, FFEL PLUS, Federal Perkins, Federal Nursing, state loans, college/university loans from institutional funds. **Student Employment:** Federal Work-Study Program available. Institutional employment available. Off-campus job opportunities are excellent. **Financial Aid Statistics:** 30% freshmen, 31% undergrads receive some form of aid. **Financial Aid Phone:** 608-262-3060.

UNIVERSITY OF WISCONSIN—MILWAUKEE

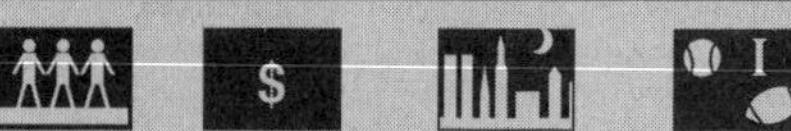

PO Box 749, Milwaukee, WI 53201
Phone: 414-229-3800 **E-mail:** uwmlook@des.uwm.edu **CEEB Code:** 1473
Fax: 414-229-6940 **Web:** www.uwm.edu **ACT Code:** 4658

This public school was founded in 1956. It has a 93-acre campus.

STUDENTS AND FACULTY

Enrollment: 20,259. **Student Body:** Male 45%, female 55%, out-of-state 2%, international 1%. **Ethnic Representation:** African American 8%, Asian 4%, Caucasian 82%, Hispanic 4%, Native American 1%. **Retention and Graduation:** 73% freshmen return for sophomore year.

ACADEMICS

Degrees: Bachelor's, certificate, doctoral, master's, post-bachelor's certificate, post-master's certificate. **Academic Requirements:** General education including some course work in arts/fine arts, English (including composition), foreign languages, humanities, mathematics, sciences (biological or physical), social science. **Classes:** 20-29 students in an average class. 10-19 students in an average lab/discussion section. **Disciplines with Highest Percentage of Degrees Awarded:** Business/marketing 22%, education 9%, social sciences and history 9%, visual and performing arts 8%, health professions and related sciences 8%. **Special Study Options:** Accelerated program, cooperative (work-study) program, cross registration, distance learning, double major, English as a second language, honors program, independent study, internships, student-designed major, study abroad, teacher certification program.

FACILITIES

Housing: Coed, apartments for married students. **Library Holdings:** 1,449,333 bound volumes. 8,240 periodicals. 1,696,803 microforms. 37,376 audiovisuals. **Special Academic Facilities/Equipment:** Art and geology museums, childhood education center, foreign language resource center, Great Lakes research facility and environmental studies field station, planetarium. **Computers:** *Recommended operating system:* Mac. School-owned computers available for student use.

EXTRACURRICULARS

Activities: Choral groups, concert band, dance, drama/theater, jazz band, literary magazine, music ensembles, radio station, student government, student newspaper, student-run film society, symphony orchestra. **Organizations:** 250 registered organizations, 1 honor society, 4 religious organizations, 8 fraternities, 4 sororities. **Athletics (Intercollegiate):** *Men:* baseball, basketball, cross-country, diving, soccer, swimming, track & field. *Women:* basketball, cross-country, soccer, swimming, tennis, track & field, volleyball.

ADMISSIONS

Selectivity Rating: 71 (of 100). **Freshman Academic Profile:** 8% in top 10% of high school class, 29% in top 25% of high school class, 69% in top 50% of high school class. SAT I Math middle 50% range 490-610. SAT I Verbal middle 50% range 470-600. Average ACT 22, ACT middle 50% range 20-25. TOEFL required of all international applicants, minimum TOEFL 500. **Basis for Candidate Selection:** *Very important factors considered include:* class rank, secondary school record. *Important factors considered include:* standardized test scores. *Other factors considered include:* essays, recommendations, state residency, talent/ability. **Freshman Admission Requirements:** High school diploma or GED is required. *Academic units required/recommended:* 17 total required; 19 total recommended; 4 English required, 4 English recommended, 3 math required, 3 math recommended, 3 science required, 3 science recommended, 1 science lab required, 1 science lab recommended, 2 foreign language recommended, 3 social studies required, 3 social studies recommended, 4 elective required, 4 elective recommended. **Freshman Admission Statistics:** 8,412 applied, 78% accepted, 50% of those accepted enrolled. **Transfer Admission Requirements:** *Items required:* college transcript. Minimum college GPA of 2.0 required. Lowest grade transferable D-. **General Admission Information:** Application fee $35. Regular admission deadline August 1. Priority admission deadline June 30. Nonfall registration accepted. Admission may be deferred. Credit offered for CEEB Advanced Placement tests.

COSTS AND FINANCIAL AID

In-state tuition $3,738. Out-of-state tuition $16,490. Room & board $4,400. Required fees $618. Average book expense $712. **Required Forms and Deadlines:** FAFSA. No deadline for regular filing. Priority filing deadline March 1. **Notification of Awards:** Applicants will be notified of awards on a rolling basis beginning on or about April 15. **Types of Aid:** *Need-based scholarships/grants:* Pell, SEOG, state scholarships/grants, private scholarships. *Loans:* Direct Subsidized Stafford, Direct Unsubsidized Stafford, Direct PLUS, Federal Perkins, Federal Nursing. **Student Employment:** Federal Work-Study Program available. Institutional employment available. Off-campus job opportunities are good. **Financial Aid Statistics:** Average freshman grant $3,069. **Financial Aid Phone:** 414-229-4541.

UNIVERSITY OF WISCONSIN—OSHKOSH

Dempsey Hall 135, 800 Algoma Boulevard, Oshkosh, WI 54901
Phone: 920-424-0202 **E-mail:** oshadmuw@uwosh.edu **CEEB Code:** 1916
Fax: 920-424-1098 **Web:** www.uwosh.edu **ACT Code:** 4674

This public school was founded in 1871. It has a 192-acre campus.

STUDENTS AND FACULTY

Enrollment: 9,749. **Student Body:** Male 41%, female 59%, out-of-state 24%, international 1% (32 countries represented). **Ethnic Representation:** African American 1%, Asian 2%, Caucasian 95%, Hispanic 1%, Native American 1%. **Retention and Graduation:** 72% freshmen return for sophomore year. 15% freshmen graduate within 4 years. **Faculty:** Student/faculty ratio 20:1. 420 full-time faculty, 98% hold PhDs. 99% faculty teach undergrads.

ACADEMICS

Degrees: Associate's, bachelor's, master's. **Academic Requirements:** General education including some course work in English (including composition), humanities, mathematics, sciences (biological or physical), social science, physical education, nonwestern culture, speech. **Classes:** 20-29 students in an average class. 20-29 students in an average lab/discussion section. **Majors with Highest Enrollment:** Elementary education and teaching; business administration/management; nursing/registered nurse training (RN, ASN, BSN, MSN). **Disciplines with Highest Percentage of Degrees Awarded:** Business/marketing 25%, education 18%, communications/communication technologies 10%, protective services/public administration 9%, health professions and related sciences 9%. **Special Study Options:** Accelerated program, distance learning, double major, English as a second language, external degree program, honors program, independent study, internships, student-designed major, study abroad, teacher certification program, weekend college.

FACILITIES

Housing: Coed. **Library Holdings:** 487,000 bound volumes. 743,604 periodicals. 1,275,000 microforms. 7,000 audiovisuals. **Special Academic Facilities/Equipment:** Art gallery, ceramics lab, electron microscope. **Computers:** School-owned computers available for student use.

EXTRACURRICULARS

Activities: Choral groups, concert band, drama/theater, jazz band, literary magazine, music ensembles, musical theater, pep band, radio station, student government, student newspaper, student-run film society, symphony orchestra, television station. **Organizations:** 175 registered organizations, 15 honor societies, 6 religious organizations, 8 fraternities (5% men join), 5 sororities (5% women join). **Athletics (Intercollegiate):** *Men:* baseball, basketball, cross-country, diving, football, indoor track, rifle, soccer, swimming, tennis, track & field, wrestling. *Women:* basketball, cross-country, diving, golf, gymnastics, indoor track, rifle, soccer, softball, swimming, tennis, track & field, volleyball.

ADMISSIONS

Selectivity Rating: 81 (of 100). **Freshman Academic Profile:** Average high school GPA 3.1. 8% in top 10% of high school class, 32% in top 25% of high school class, 81% in top 50% of high school class. Average ACT 22, ACT middle 50% range 19-24. TOEFL required of all international applicants, minimum TOEFL 525. **Basis for Candidate Selection:** *Very important factors considered include:* class rank, secondary school record, standardized test scores. *Other factors considered include:* essays, minority status, recommendations. **Freshman Admission Requirements:** High school diploma or GED is required. *Academic units required/recommended:* 17 total required; 4 English required, 3 math required, 3 science required, 3 science lab required, 3 social studies required, 4 elective required. **Freshman Admission Statistics:** 4,270 applied, 57% accepted, 74% of those accepted enrolled. **Transfer Admission Requirements:** *Items required:* college transcript. Minimum college GPA of 2.0 required. Lowest grade transferable D. **General Admission Information:** Application fee $35. Priority application deadline December 1. Regular application deadline August 1. Nonfall registration accepted. Admission may be deferred for a maximum of 1 year. Credit offered for CEEB Advanced Placement tests.

COSTS AND FINANCIAL AID

In-state tuition $3,670. Out-of-state tuition $14,320. Room & board $3,970. Average book expense $700. **Required Forms and Deadlines:** FAFSA. Priority filing deadline March 15. **Notification of Awards:** Applicants will be notified of awards on or about April 1. **Types of Aid:** *Need-based scholarships/grants:* Pell, SEOG, state scholarships/grants, private scholarships, the school's own gift aid, Federal Nursing. *Loans:* FFEL Subsidized Stafford, FFEL Unsubsidized Stafford, FFEL PLUS, Federal Perkins, Federal Nursing, college/university loans from institutional funds. **Student Employment:** Federal Work-Study Program available. Institutional employment available. Off-campus job opportunities are good. **Financial Aid Statistics:** Average freshman grant $2,000. Average freshman loan $2,500. Average income from on-campus job $2,000. **Financial Aid Phone:** 920-424-3377.

UNIVERSITY OF WISCONSIN—PARKSIDE

Box 2000, Kenosha, WI 53141
Phone: 262-595-2355 **E-mail:** matthew.jensen@uwp.edu **CEEB Code:** 1860
Fax: 262-595-2008 **Web:** www.uwp.edu **ACT Code:** 4690

This public school was founded in 1968. It has a 700-acre campus.

STUDENTS AND FACULTY

Enrollment: 4,815. **Student Body:** Male 42%, female 58%, out-of-state 9%, international 1% (28 countries represented). **Ethnic Representation:** African American 9%, Asian 3%, Caucasian 81%, Hispanic 7%. **Retention and Graduation:** 63% freshmen return for sophomore year. 13% grads go on to further study within 1 year. **Faculty:** Student/faculty ratio 21:1. 185 full-time faculty, 77% hold PhDs. 100% faculty teach undergrads.

ACADEMICS

Degrees: Bachelor's, certificate, master's. **Academic Requirements:** General education including some course work in arts/fine arts, English (including composition), foreign languages, mathematics, sciences (biological or physical), social science. **Classes:** Under 10 students in an average class. 10-19 students in an average lab/discussion section. **Majors with Highest Enrollment:** Business administration/management; communications and media studies; criminal justice/law enforcement administration. **Disciplines with Highest Percentage of Degrees Awarded:** Business/marketing 29%, social sciences and history 15%, communications/communication technologies 8%, visual and performing arts 8%, protective services/public administration 8%. **Special Study Options:** Accelerated program, distance learning, double major, dual enrollment, English as a second language, student exchange program (domestic), honors program, independent study, internships, liberal arts/career combination, study abroad, teacher certification program, weekend college, cooperative nursing program with University of Wisconsin-Milwaukee.

FACILITIES

Housing: Coed. **Library Holdings:** 400,000 bound volumes. 1,590 periodicals. 981,400 microforms. 21,220 audiovisuals. **Special Academic Facilities/Equipment:** Language lab, electron microscope. **Computers:** School-owned computers available for student use.

EXTRACURRICULARS

Activities: Choral groups, concert band, drama/theater, jazz band, music ensembles, musical theater, radio station, student government, student newspaper. **Organizations:** 48 registered organizations, 5 honor societies, 1 religious organization, 3 fraternities, 3 sororities. **Athletics (Intercollegiate):** *Men:* baseball, basketball, cross-country, golf, soccer, track & field, wrestling. *Women:* basketball, cross-country, soccer, softball, track & field, volleyball.

ADMISSIONS

Selectivity Rating: 63 (of 100). **Freshman Academic Profile:** 8% in top 10% of high school class, 26% in top 25% of high school class, 59% in top 50% of high school class. 92% from public high schools. Average ACT 20. TOEFL required of all international applicants, minimum TOEFL 525. **Basis for Candidate Selection:** *Very important factors considered include:* class rank, secondary school record, standardized test scores. *Other factors considered include:* alumni/ae relation, character/personal qualities, essays, extracurricular activities, interview, minority status, recommendations, talent/ability, volunteer work, work experience. **Freshman Admission Requirements:** High school diploma or GED is required. *Academic units required/recommended:* 17 total required; 22 total recommended; 4 English required, 4 English recommended, 3 math required, 4 math recommended, 3 science required, 4 science recommended, 1 science lab required, 2 science lab recommended, 2 foreign language recommended, 3 social studies required, 3 social studies recommended, 1 history recommended, 4 elective required, 4 elective recommended. **Freshman Admission Statistics:** 1,966 applied, 76% accepted, 62% of those accepted enrolled. **Transfer Admission Requirements:** *Items required:* high school transcript, college transcript, statement of good standing from prior school. Minimum college GPA of 2.0 required. Lowest grade transferable D-.

General Admission Information: Application fee $35. Priority application deadline March 1. Regular application deadline August 1. Nonfall registration accepted. Admission may be deferred for a maximum of 1 year. Credit and/or placement offered for CEEB Advanced Placement tests.

COSTS AND FINANCIAL AID

In-state tuition $3,532. Out-of-state tuition $13,578. Room & board $5,056. **Required Forms and Deadlines:** FAFSA. No deadline for regular filing. Priority filing deadline April 1. **Notification of Awards:** Applicants will be notified of awards on a rolling basis beginning on or about March 1. **Types of Aid:** *Need-based scholarships/grants:* Pell, SEOG, state scholarships/grants, the school's own gift aid. *Loans:* FFEL Subsidized Stafford, FFEL Unsubsidized Stafford, FFEL PLUS, Federal Perkins. **Student Employment:** Federal Work-Study Program available. Institutional employment available. Off-campus job opportunities are excellent. **Financial Aid Statistics:** 43% freshmen, 46% undergrads receive some form of aid. Average freshman grant $1,800. Average income from on-campus job $2,500. **Financial Aid Phone:** 262-595-2574.

UNIVERSITY OF WISCONSIN—PLATTEVILLE

1 University Plaza, Platteville, WI 53818
Phone: 608-342-1125 **E-mail:** schumacr@uwplatt.edu **CEEB Code:** 1917
Fax: 608-342-1122 **Web:** uwplatt.edu **ACT Code:** 4676

This public school was founded in 1881. It has a 400-acre campus.

STUDENTS AND FACULTY

Enrollment: 5,506. **Student Body:** Male 61%, female 39%, out-of-state 11%, international 1%. **Ethnic Representation:** African American 1%, Asian 1%, Caucasian 96%, Hispanic 1%. **Retention and Graduation:** 77% freshmen return for sophomore year. **Faculty:** Student/faculty ratio 21:1. 244 full-time faculty, 74% hold PhDs. 100% faculty teach undergrads.

ACADEMICS

Degrees: Associate's, bachelor's, certificate, diploma, master's. **Academic Requirements:** General education including some course work in arts/fine arts, computer literacy, English (including composition), foreign languages, history, humanities, mathematics, philosophy, sciences (biological or physical), social science. **Classes:** Under 10 students in an average class. 10-19 students in an average lab/discussion section. **Disciplines with Highest Percentage of Degrees Awarded:** Engineering/engineering technology 35%, business/marketing 13%, education 11%, agriculture 9%, law/legal studies 6%. **Special Study Options:** Cooperative (work-study) program, distance learning, double major, dual enrollment, student exchange program (domestic), external degree program, honors program, independent study, internships, liberal arts/career combination, student-designed major, study abroad, teacher certification program.

FACILITIES

Housing: Coed, all-female, all-male, fraternities and/or sororities. **Library Holdings:** 321,456 bound volumes. 1,280 periodicals. 996,402 microforms. 13,879 audiovisuals. **Special Academic Facilities/Equipment:** Electron microscope. **Computers:** School-owned computers available for student use.

EXTRACURRICULARS

Activities: Choral groups, concert band, dance, drama/theater, jazz band, literary magazine, marching band, music ensembles, musical theater, opera, pep band, radio station, student government, student newspaper, student-run film society, symphony orchestra, television station, yearbook. **Organizations:** 3 religious organizations, 9 fraternities (8% men join), 5 sororities (4% women join). **Athletics (Intercollegiate):** *Men:* baseball, basketball, cross-country, football, soccer, track & field, wrestling. *Women:* basketball, cross-country, soccer, softball, tennis, track & field, volleyball.

ADMISSIONS

Selectivity Rating: 74 (of 100). **Freshman Academic Profile:** 10% in top 10% of high school class, 35% in top 25% of high school class, 72% in top 50% of high school class. 94% from public high schools. Average ACT 23, ACT middle 50% range 18-26. TOEFL required of all international applicants, minimum TOEFL 550. **Basis for Candidate Selection:** *Very important factors considered include:* class rank, secondary school record, standardized test scores. *Other factors considered include:* extracurricular activities, interview, recommendations, talent/ability. **Freshman Admission Requirements:** High school diploma or GED is required. *Academic units required/recommended:* 17 total required; 4 English required, 3 math required, 3 math recommended, 3 science required, 2 science lab required, 3 social studies required, 4 elective required. **Freshman Admission Statistics:** 2,530 applied, 87% accepted, 51% of those accepted enrolled. **Transfer Admission Requirements:** *Items required:* college transcript, statement of good standing from prior school. Minimum college GPA of 2.0 required. Lowest grade transferable D. **General Admission Information:** Application fee $35. Nonfall registration accepted. Credit offered for CEEB Advanced Placement tests.

COSTS AND FINANCIAL AID

In-state tuition $3,000. Out-of-state tuition $13,046. Room & board $3,978. Required fees $723. Average book expense $500. **Required Forms and Deadlines:** FAFSA. No deadline for regular filing. Priority filing deadline January 3. **Notification of Awards:** Applicants will be notified of awards on a rolling basis beginning on or about April 15. **Types of Aid:** *Need-based scholarships/grants:* state scholarships/grants. *Loans:* FFEL Subsidized Stafford, FFEL Unsubsidized Stafford, FFEL PLUS, Federal Perkins. **Student Employment:** Federal Work-Study Program available. Institutional employment available. Off-campus job opportunities are good. **Financial Aid Statistics:** Average income from on-campus job $1,500. **Financial Aid Phone:** 608-342-1836.

UNIVERSITY OF WISCONSIN—RIVER FALLS

410 South Third Street, 112 South Hall, River Falls, WI 54022
Phone: 715 425-3500 **E-mail:** admit@uwrf.edu **CEEB Code:** 1918
Fax: 715-425-0676 **Web:** www.uwrf.edu **ACT Code:** 4678

This public school was founded in 1874. It has a 225-acre campus.

STUDENTS AND FACULTY

Enrollment: 5,285. **Student Body:** Male 39%, female 61%, out-of-state 48%, international 1%. **Ethnic Representation:** African American 1%, Asian 3%, Caucasian 94%, Hispanic 1%, international students represent 18 countries. **Retention and Graduation:** 73% freshmen return for sophomore year. 3% grads pursue business degrees. 2% grads pursue law degrees. 2% grads pursue medical degrees. **Faculty:** Student/faculty ratio 19:1. 82% faculty teach undergrads.

ACADEMICS

Degrees: Bachelor's, certificate, master's, post-bachelor's certificate, post-master's certificate. **Academic Requirements:** General education including some course work in arts/fine arts, English (including composition), humanities, mathematics, sciences (biological or physical), social science. **Special Study Options:** Accelerated program, cooperative (work-study) program, distance learning, double major, dual enrollment, English as a second language, student exchange program (domestic), honors program, independent study, internships, study abroad, teacher certification program.

FACILITIES

Housing: Coed, all-female, fraternities and/or sororities. **Library Holdings:** 448,088 bound volumes. 1,660 periodicals. 471,621 microforms. 7,500 audiovisuals. **Special Academic Facilities/Equipment:** Local history museum, 20-inch reflecting telescope, observatory, electron microscope, greenhouse, lab farms, educational technology center. **Computers:** School-owned computers available for student use.

EXTRACURRICULARS

Activities: Choral groups, concert band, dance, drama/theater, jazz band, literary magazine, music ensembles, musical theater, pep band, radio station, student government, student newspaper, symphony orchestra, television station. **Organizations:** 120 registered organizations, 9 honor societies, 12 religious organizations, 5 fraternities (5% men join), 4 sororities (5% women join). **Athletics (Intercollegiate):** *Men:* basketball, cross-country, football, ice hockey, indoor track, swimming. *Women:* basketball, cross-country, golf, ice hockey, indoor track, soccer, softball, swimming, tennis, track & field, volleyball.

ADMISSIONS

Selectivity Rating: 75 (of 100). **Freshman Academic Profile:** 17% in top 10% of high school class, 48% in top 25% of high school class, 88% in top 50% of high school class. 95% from public high schools. Average ACT 23, ACT middle 50% range 21-24. TOEFL required of all international applicants, minimum TOEFL 500. **Basis for Candidate Selection:** *Very important factors considered include:* class rank, secondary school record, standardized test scores. *Other factors considered include:* recommendations. **Freshman Admission Requirements:** High school diploma or GED is required. *Academic units required/recommended:* 17 total required; 4 English required, 3 math required, 3 science required, 2 foreign language recommended, 3 social studies required, 4 elective required. **Freshman Admission Statistics:** 2,690 applied, 74% accepted, 56% of those accepted enrolled. **Transfer Admission Requirements:** *Items required:* college transcript, statement of good standing from prior school. Minimum college GPA of 2.6 required. Lowest grade transferable D. **General Admission Information:** Application fee $35. Priority application deadline January 1. Regular application deadline January 1. Nonfall registration accepted. Admission may be deferred for a maximum of 1 year. Credit and/or placement offered for CEEB Advanced Placement tests.

COSTS AND FINANCIAL AID

In-state tuition $3,876. Out-of-state tuition $13,922. Room & board $3,690. Required fees $0. Average book expense $200. **Required Forms and Deadlines:** FAFSA and institution's own financial aid form. Priority filing deadline March 15. **Notification of Awards:** Applicants will be notified of awards on a rolling basis beginning on or about April 1. **Types of Aid:** *Need-based scholarships/grants:* Pell, SEOG, state scholarships/grants, private scholarships. *Loans:* Direct Subsidized Stafford, Direct Unsubsidized Stafford, Direct PLUS, Federal Perkins. **Student Employment:** Federal Work-Study Program available. Institutional employment available. Off-campus job opportunities are good. **Financial Aid Statistics:** Average freshman grant $4,080. Average freshman loan $2,616. Average income from on-campus job $1,200. **Financial Aid Phone:** 715-425-3141.

UNIVERSITY OF WISCONSIN—STEVENS POINT

Student Services Center, Stevens Point, WI 54481
Phone: 715-346-2441 **E-mail:** admiss@uwsp.edu **CEEB Code:** 1919
Fax: 715-346-3957 **Web:** www.uwsp.edu **ACT Code:** 4680

This public school was founded in 1894. It has a 335-acre campus.

STUDENTS AND FACULTY

Enrollment: 8,466. **Student Body:** Male 44%, female 56%, out-of-state 8%, international 2% (30 countries represented). **Ethnic Representation:** African American 1%, Asian 2%, Caucasian 96%, Hispanic 1%, Native American 1%. **Retention and Graduation:** 79% freshmen return for sophomore year. 20% freshmen graduate within 4 years. 16% grads go on to further study within 1 year. **Faculty:** Student/faculty ratio 20:1. 367 full-time faculty, 82% hold PhDs. 100% faculty teach undergrads.

ACADEMICS

Degrees: Associate's, bachelor's, certificate, master's. **Academic Requirements:** General education including some course work in English (including composition), history, humanities, mathematics, sciences (biological or physical), social science. **Classes:** 20-29 students in an average class. 20-29 students in an average lab/discussion section. **Disciplines with Highest Percentage of Degrees Awarded:** Social sciences and history 12%, natural resources/environmental sciences 12%, communications/communication technologies 10%, business/marketing 10%, education 9%. **Special Study Options:** Accelerated program, cooperative (work-study) program, distance learning, double major, dual enrollment, English as a second language, independent study, internships, student-designed major, study abroad, teacher certification program.

FACILITIES

Housing: Coed, all-female, all-male, alcohol-free house, eco hall, international program hall, language house, nonsmoking floors, quiet floors, tobacco-free hall, nontraditional hall, wellness emphasis program. **Library Holdings:** 978,112 bound volumes. 8,470 periodicals. 899,878 microforms. 32,916 audiovisuals. **Special Academic Facilities/Equipment:** Art galleries, costume and goblet collections, museum of natural history, early childhood study institute, communicative disorders center, map center, observatory, planetarium, Foucault pendulum, nature preserve, environmental station, groundwater center, herbarium, aviary, wellness institute. **Computers:** School-owned computers available for student use.

EXTRACURRICULARS

Activities: Choral groups, concert band, dance, drama/theater, jazz band, literary magazine, music ensembles, musical theater, opera, pep band, radio station, student government, student newspaper, student-run film society, symphony orchestra, television station. **Organizations:** 150 registered organizations, 6 honor societies, 6 religious organizations, 4 fraternities (2% men join), 3 sororities (1% women join). **Athletics (Intercollegiate):** *Men:* baseball, basketball, cross-country, diving, football, ice hockey, swimming, track & field, wrestling. *Women:* basketball, cross-country, diving, golf, ice hockey, soccer, softball, swimming, tennis, track & field, volleyball.

ADMISSIONS

Selectivity Rating: 73 (of 100). **Freshman Academic Profile:** Average high school GPA 3.4. 16% in top 10% of high school class, 48% in top 25% of high school class, 96% in top 50% of high school class. Average SAT I Math 557, SAT I Math middle 50% range 480-650. Average SAT I Verbal 582, SAT I Verbal middle 50% range 500-650. Average ACT 23, ACT middle 50% range 21-25. TOEFL required of all international applicants, minimum TOEFL 550. **Basis for Candidate Selection:** *Very important factors considered include:* class rank, secondary school record, standardized test scores. *Important factors considered include:* talent/ability. *Other factors considered include:* character/personal qualities, extracurricular activities, minority status, recommendations, work experience. **Freshman Admission Requirements:** High school diploma or GED is required. *Academic units required/recommended:* 17 total required; 4 English required, 3 math required, 3 science required, 2 foreign language recommended, 3 social studies required, 4 elective required. **Freshman Admission Statistics:** 4,450 applied, 72% accepted, 46% of those accepted enrolled. **Transfer Admission Requirements:** *Items required:* high school transcript, college transcript, statement of good standing from prior school. Lowest grade transferable D. **General Admission Information:** Application fee $35. Regular application deadline rolling. Nonfall registration accepted. Admission may be deferred. Credit and/or placement offered for CEEB Advanced Placement tests.

COSTS AND FINANCIAL AID

In-state tuition $3,000. Out-of-state tuition $13,046. Room & board $3,816. Required fees $631. Average book expense $450. **Required Forms and Deadlines:** FAFSA. Financial aid filing deadline July 15. Priority filing deadline March 15. **Notification of Awards:** Applicants will be notified of awards on a rolling basis beginning on or about May 1. **Types of Aid:** *Need-based scholarships/grants:* Pell, SEOG, state scholarships/grants, private scholarships, the school's own gift aid. *Loans:* FFEL Subsidized Stafford, FFEL Unsubsidized Stafford, FFEL PLUS, Federal Perkins. **Student Employment:** Federal Work-Study Program available. Institutional employment available. Off-campus job opportunities are excellent. **Financial Aid Statistics:** 39% freshmen, 42% undergrads receive some form of aid. **Financial Aid Phone:** 715-346-4771.

UNIVERSITY OF WISCONSIN—STOUT

Admissions UW-Stout, Menomonie, WI 54751
Phone: 715-232-1411 **E-mail:** admissions@uwstout.edu **CEEB Code:** 1740
Fax: 715-232-1667 **Web:** www.uwstout.edu **ACT Code:** 4652

This public school was founded in 1891. It has a 110-acre campus.

STUDENTS AND FACULTY

Enrollment: 7,316. **Student Body:** Male 52%, female 48%, out-of-state 29%, international students represent 30 countries. **Ethnic Representation:** African American 1%, Asian 2%, Caucasian 95%, Hispanic 1%. **Retention and Graduation:** 73% freshmen return for sophomore year. 15% freshmen graduate within 4 years. 9% grads go on to further study within 1 year. **Faculty:** Student/faculty ratio 19:1. 294 full-time faculty, 71% hold PhDs. 100% faculty teach undergrads.

ACADEMICS

Degrees: Bachelor's, master's, post-master's certificate. **Academic Requirements:** General education including some course work in arts/fine arts, English (including composition), history, humanities, mathematics, philosophy, sciences (biological or physical), social science. **Classes:** 20-29 students in an average class. 20-29 students in an average lab/discussion section. **Majors with Highest Enrollment:** Business administration/management; early childhood education and teaching; design and applied arts. **Disciplines with Highest Percentage of Degrees Awarded:** Business/marketing 31%, education 22%, engineering/engineering technology 17%, visual and performing arts 10%, home economics and vocational home economics 9%. **Special Study Options:** Accelerated program, cooperative (work-study) program, cross registration, distance learning, double major, dual enrollment, student exchange program (domestic), external degree program, honors program, independent study, internships, study abroad, teacher certification program.

FACILITIES

Housing: Coed, housing for disabled students, freshmen housing, smoke-free housing, upperclass/graduate housing, alcohol-free housing. **Library Holdings:** 229,986 bound volumes. 1,784 periodicals. 1,153,387 microforms. 16,142 audiovisuals. **Special Academic Facilities/Equipment:** Specialized labs support degree programs throughout the campus. Furlong Art Gallery in Michael's Hall. **Computers:** School-owned computers available for student use.

EXTRACURRICULARS

Activities: Choral groups, concert band, drama/theater, jazz band, literary magazine, marching band, music ensembles, pep band, radio station, student government, student newspaper, student-run film society. **Organizations:** 120 registered organizations, 1 honor society, 10 religious organizations, 5 fraternities (2% men join), 3 sororities (4% women join). **Athletics (Intercollegiate):** *Men:* baseball, basketball, cross-country, football, ice hockey, track & field. *Women:* basketball, cross-country, gymnastics, soccer, softball, tennis, track & field, volleyball.

ADMISSIONS

Selectivity Rating: 63 (of 100). **Freshman Academic Profile:** Average high school GPA 3.2. 8% in top 10% of high school class, 33% in top 25% of high school class, 82% in top 50% of high school class. Average ACT 21, ACT middle 50% range 19-23. TOEFL required of all international applicants, minimum TOEFL 500. **Basis for Candidate Selection:** *Very important factors considered include:* class rank, secondary school record, standardized test scores. *Other factors considered include:* alumni/ae relation, character/personal qualities, extracurricular activities, interview, minority status, recommendations, talent/ability, volunteer work, work experience. **Freshman Admission Requirements:** High school diploma or GED is required. *Academic units required/recommended:* 4 English required, 3 math required, 3 science required, 2 foreign language recommended, 3 social studies required, 4 elective required. **Freshman Admission Statistics:** 3,383 applied, 70% accepted, 55% of those accepted enrolled. **Transfer Admission Requirements:** *Items required:* college transcript, statement of good standing from prior school. Minimum college GPA of 2.0 required. Lowest grade transferable D. **General Admission Information:** Application fee $35. Priority application deadline January 1. Nonfall registration accepted. Credit offered for CEEB Advanced Placement tests.

COSTS AND FINANCIAL AID

In-state tuition $3,150. Out-of-state tuition $13,196. Room & board $3,830. Required fees $607. Average book expense $300. **Required Forms and Deadlines:** FAFSA. No deadline for regular filing. Priority filing deadline April 1. **Notification of Awards:** Applicants will be notified of awards on a rolling basis beginning on or about April 1. **Types of Aid:** *Need-based scholarships/grants:* Pell, SEOG, state scholarships/grants, private scholarships, the school's own gift aid, BIA, GearUp. *Loans:* FFEL Subsidized Stafford, FFEL Unsubsidized Stafford, FFEL PLUS, Federal Perkins, alternative educational loans. **Student Employment:** Federal Work-Study Program available. Institutional employment available. Off-campus job opportunities are good. **Financial Aid Statistics:** 51% freshmen, 50% undergrads receive some form of aid. Average freshman grant $2,612. Average freshman loan $4,189. Average income from on-campus job $1,330. **Financial Aid Phone:** 715-232-1363.

UNIVERSITY OF WISCONSIN—SUPERIOR

Belknap & Catlin, PO Box 2000, Superior, WI 54880
Phone: 715-394-8230 **E-mail:** admissions@uwsuper.edu **CEEB Code:** 1920
Fax: 715-394-8107 **Web:** www.uwsuper.edu **ACT Code:** 4682

This public school was founded in 1893. It has a 230-acre campus.

STUDENTS AND FACULTY

Enrollment: 2,513. **Student Body:** Male 41%, female 59%, out-of-state 46%, international 6%. **Ethnic Representation:** African American 1%, Asian 1%, Caucasian 95%, Hispanic 1%, Native American 2%. **Retention and Graduation:** 71% freshmen return for sophomore year. 5% freshmen graduate within 4 years. **Faculty:** Student/faculty ratio 17:1. 102 full-time faculty, 83% hold PhDs. 100% faculty teach undergrads.

ACADEMICS

Degrees: Associate's, bachelor's, certificate, diploma, first professional, master's, post-master's certificate, terminal, transfer. **Academic Requirements:** General education including some course work in arts/fine arts, computer literacy, English (including composition), history, humanities, mathematics, philosophy, sciences (biological or physical), social science, communicating arts, health promotion & human performance. **Classes:** 10-19 students in an average class. 10-19 students in an average lab/discussion section. **Majors with Highest Enrollment:** Business/managerial economics; biology/biological sciences, general; education, general. **Disciplines with Highest Percentage of Degrees Awarded:** Education 21%, business/marketing 21%, social sciences and history 10%, interdisciplinary studies 10%, biological life sciences 8%. **Special Study Options:** Cooperative (work-study) program, cross registration, distance learning, double major, dual enrollment, English as a second language, student exchange program (domestic), external degree program, honors program, independent study, internships, liberal arts/career combination, student-designed major, study abroad, teacher certification program, undergraduate research opportunities.

FACILITIES

Housing: Coed, all-female, residence hall rooms for married couples. **Library Holdings:** 455,313 bound volumes. 753 periodicals. 105,398 microforms. 5,467 audiovisuals. **Special Academic Facilities/Equipment:** TV, radio, and film facilities, observatory, greenhouse, two art galleries, recital hall, four theaters, aquaculture demonstration site under construction, health & wellness center under construction. **Computers:** School-owned computers available for student use.

EXTRACURRICULARS

Activities: Choral groups, concert band, dance, drama/theater, jazz band, music ensembles, radio station, student government, student newspaper, symphony orchestra, television station. **Organizations:** 45 registered organizations, 1 honor society, 1 religious organization. **Athletics (Intercollegiate):** *Men:* baseball, basketball, cross-country, ice hockey, soccer, track & field. *Women:* basketball, cross-country, golf, ice hockey, soccer, softball, track & field, volleyball.

ADMISSIONS

Selectivity Rating: 73 (of 100). **Freshman Academic Profile:** 10% in top 10% of high school class, 35% in top 25% of high school class, 76% in top 50% of high school class. 95% from public high schools. SAT I Math middle 50% range 440-560. SAT I Verbal middle 50% range 450-580. Average ACT 22, ACT middle 50% range 20-24. TOEFL required of all international applicants, minimum TOEFL 525. **Basis for Candidate Selection:** *Very important factors considered include:* class rank, secondary school record, standardized test scores. *Important factors considered include:* minority status. *Other factors considered include:* essays, extracurricular activities, interview, recommendations. **Freshman Admission Requirements:** High school diploma or GED is required. *Academic units required/recommended:* 17 total required; 4 English required, 3 math required, 3 science required, 2 foreign language recommended, 3 social studies required, 4 elective required. **Freshman Admission Statistics:** 747 applied, 76% accepted, 55% of those accepted enrolled. **Transfer Admission Requirements:** *Items required:* college transcript, statement of good standing from prior school. Minimum college GPA of 2.0 required. Lowest grade transferable D-. **General Admission Information:** Application fee $35. Priority application deadline April 1. Nonfall registration accepted. Admission may be deferred for a maximum of 1 year. Credit offered for CEEB Advanced Placement tests.

COSTS AND FINANCIAL AID

In-state tuition $3,464. Out-of-state tuition $13,510. Room & board $3,962. Average book expense $690. **Required Forms and Deadlines:** FAFSA. Financial aid filing deadline May 15. Priority filing deadline April 15. **Notification of Awards:** Applicants will be notified of awards on a rolling basis beginning on or about April 15. **Types of Aid:** *Need-based scholarships/grants:* Pell, SEOG, state scholarships/grants, private scholarships, the school's own gift aid. *Loans:* Direct Subsidized Stafford, Direct Unsubsidized Stafford, Federal Perkins, state loans, college/university loans from institutional funds. **Student Employment:** Federal Work-Study Program available. Institutional employment available. Off-campus job opportunities are excellent. **Financial Aid Statistics:** 47% freshmen, 45% undergrads receive some form of aid. Average freshman loan $2,037. **Financial Aid Phone:** 715-394-8274.

UNIVERSITY OF WISCONSIN—WHITEWATER

800 West Main Street, Baker Hall, Whitewater, WI 53190-1791
Phone: 262-472-1440 **E-mail:** uwwadmit@uww.edu **CEEB Code:** 1921
Fax: 262-472-1515 **Web:** www.uww.edu **ACT Code:** 4684

This public school was founded in 1868. It has a 385-acre campus.

STUDENTS AND FACULTY

Enrollment: 9,351. **Student Body:** Male 47%, female 53%, out-of-state 7%, international 1% (57 countries represented). **Ethnic Representation:** African American 4%, Asian 2%, Caucasian 92%, Hispanic 2%. **Retention and Graduation:** 74% freshmen return for sophomore year. 16% freshmen graduate within 4 years. **Faculty:** Student/faculty ratio 20:1. 384 full-time faculty, 76% hold PhDs. 100% faculty teach undergrads.

ACADEMICS

Degrees: Associate's, bachelor's, master's, transfer. **Academic Requirements:** General education including some course work in arts/fine arts, English (including composition), history, humanities, mathematics, sciences (biological or physical), social science. **Classes:** Under 10 students in an average class. **Majors with Highest Enrollment:** Education, general; communications studies/speech communication and rhetoric; social work. **Disciplines with Highest Percentage of Degrees Awarded:** Business/marketing 36%, education 14%, communications/communication technologies 14%, social sciences and history 9%, protective services/public administration 7%. **Special Study Options:** Accelerated program, cooperative (work-study) program, distance learning, double major, external degree program, honors program, independent study, internships, student-designed major, study abroad, teacher certification program.

FACILITIES

Housing: Coed, all-female, housing for disabled students, housing for international students, fraternities and/or sororities. **Library Holdings:** 533,330 bound volumes. 346,187 periodicals. 1,144,129 microforms. 18,617 audiovisuals. **Special Academic Facilities/Equipment:** Two electron microscopes, state-of-the-art theater/auditorium. **Computers:** School-owned computers available for student use.

EXTRACURRICULARS

Activities: Choral groups, concert band, dance, drama/theater, jazz band, literary magazine, marching band, music ensembles, musical theater, opera, pep band, radio station, student government, student newspaper, symphony orchestra, television station, yearbook. **Organizations:** 130 registered organizations, 4 honor societies, 8 religious organizations, 9 fraternities, 8 sororities. **Athletics (Intercollegiate):** *Men:* baseball, basketball, cross-country, diving, football, indoor track, soccer, swimming, tennis, track & field, wrestling. *Women:* basketball, cross-country, diving, golf, gymnastics, indoor track, soccer, softball, swimming, tennis, track & field, volleyball.

ADMISSIONS

Selectivity Rating: 71 (of 100). **Freshman Academic Profile:** 11% in top 10% of high school class, 35% in top 25% of high school class, 80% in top 50% of high school class. Average ACT 22, ACT middle 50% range 19-24. TOEFL required of all international applicants, minimum TOEFL 500. **Basis for Candidate Selection:** *Very important factors considered include:* class rank, secondary school record, standardized test scores. *Other factors considered include:* alumni/ae relation, character/personal qualities, essays, extracurricular activities, interview, minority status, recommendations, talent/ability, volunteer work, work experience. **Freshman Admission Requirements:** High school diploma or GED is required. *Academic units required/recommended:* 17 total required; 20 total recommended; 4 English required, 4 English recommended, 3 math required, 4 math recommended, 3 science required, 4 science recommended, 2 foreign language required, 2 foreign language recommended, 3 social studies required, 4 social studies recommended, 4 elective required, 4 elective recommended. **Transfer Admission Requirements:** *Items required:* high school transcript, college transcript, statement of good standing from prior school. Minimum college GPA of 2.0 required. Lowest grade transferable D-. **General Admission Information:** Application fee $35. Priority application deadline January 1. Nonfall registration accepted. Admission may be deferred for a maximum of 1 year. Credit offered for CEEB Advanced Placement tests.

COSTS AND FINANCIAL AID

In-state tuition $3,367. Out-of-state tuition $11,878. Room & board $3,570. Required fees $591. Average book expense $650. **Required Forms and Deadlines:** FAFSA. Priority filing deadline March 15. **Notification of Awards:** Applicants will be notified of awards on a rolling basis beginning on or about April 15. **Types of Aid:** *Need-based scholarships/grants:* Pell, SEOG, state scholarships/grants, private scholarships, the school's own gift aid. *Loans:* Direct Subsidized Stafford, Direct Unsubsidized Stafford, Direct PLUS, Federal Perkins. **Student Employment:** Federal Work-Study Program available. Institutional employment available. Off-campus job opportunities are good. **Financial Aid Statistics:** 40% undergrads receive some form of aid. Average income from on-campus job $500. **Financial Aid Phone:** 414-472-1130.

UNIVERSITY OF WYOMING

Admissions Office, PO Box 3435, Laramie, WY 82071
Phone: 307-766-5160 **E-mail:** Why-Wyo@uwyo.edu **CEEB Code:** 4855
Fax: 307-766-4042 **Web:** www.uwyo.edu **ACT Code:** 5006

This public school was founded in 1886. It has a 785-acre campus.

STUDENTS AND FACULTY

Enrollment: 9,250. **Student Body:** Male 47%, female 53%, out-of-state 26%, international 1%. **Ethnic Representation:** African American 1%, Asian 1%, Caucasian 87%, Hispanic 4%, Native American 1%. **Retention and Graduation:** 78% freshmen return for sophomore year. 21% freshmen graduate within 4 years. 22% grads go on to further study within 1 year. 9% grads pursue business degrees. 10% grads pursue law degrees. 5% grads pursue medical degrees. **Faculty:** Student/faculty ratio 15:1. 612 full-time faculty, 86% hold PhDs. 97% faculty teach undergrads.

ACADEMICS

Degrees: Bachelor's, certificate, doctoral, first professional, master's, post-master's certificate. **Academic Requirements:** General education including some course work in arts/fine arts, English (including composition), humanities, mathematics, sciences (biological or physical), social science, physical education, U.S. & Wyoming Constitutions, global diversity, first-year seminar. **Classes:** 20-29 students in an average class. 10-19 students in an average lab/discussion section. **Disciplines with Highest Percentage of Degrees Awarded:** Education 17%, business/marketing 15%, engineering/engineering technology 9%, social sciences and history 7%, health professions and related sciences 6%. **Special Study Options:** Accelerated program, distance learning, double major, dual enrollment, student exchange program (domestic), external degree program, honors program, independent study, internships, student-designed major, study abroad, teacher certification program.

FACILITIES

Housing: Coed, apartments for married students, apartments for single students, housing for disabled students, fraternities and/or sororities, floor-specific living plans in the dorms. **Library Holdings:** 1,297,778 bound volumes. 13,256 periodicals. 2,929,792 microforms. 4,161 audiovisuals. **Special Academic Facilities/Equipment:** Art gallery, geology museum, American Heritage Center, 2 herbariums, national park research center, art museum, planetarium, environmental biology lab, anthropology museum, vertebrate museum, on-site elementary school, history research center, state veterinary lab, water resources research institute, infrared telescope observatory, lysimeter lab, electron microscopes. **Computers:** School-owned computers available for student use.

EXTRACURRICULARS

Activities: Choral groups, concert band, dance, drama/theater, jazz band, literary magazine, marching band, music ensembles, musical theater, opera, pep band, radio station, student government, student newspaper, student-run film society, symphony orchestra, television station, yearbook. **Organizations:** 183 registered organizations, 18 honor societies, 14 religious organizations, 9 fraternities (8% men join), 4 sororities (5% women join). **Athletics (Intercollegiate):** *Men:* basketball, cheerleading, cross-country, diving, football, golf, rodeo, swimming, track & field, wrestling. *Women:* basketball, cross-country, diving, football, golf, rodeo, soccer, swimming, tennis, track & field, volleyball.

ADMISSIONS

Selectivity Rating: 75 (of 100). **Freshman Academic Profile:** Average high school GPA 3.4. 20% in top 10% of high school class, 45% in top 25% of high school class, 76% in top 50% of high school class. SAT I Math middle 50% range 480-600. SAT I Verbal middle 50% range 460-580. Average ACT 23, ACT middle 50% range 20-26. TOEFL required of all international applicants, minimum TOEFL 525. **Basis for Candidate Selection:** *Very important factors considered include:* secondary school record, standardized test scores. *Important factors considered include:* essays, recommendations. *Other factors considered include:* character/personal qualities, extracurricular activities, geographical residence, interview, state residency, talent/ability. **Freshman Admission Requirements:** High school diploma or GED is required. *Academic units required/recommended:* 13 total required; 19 total recommended; 4 English required, 4 English recommended, 3 math required, 3 math recommended, 3 science required, 3 science recommended, 3 science lab required, 3 science lab recommended. **Freshman Admission Statistics:** 2,954 applied, 95% accepted, 52% of those accepted enrolled. **Transfer Admission Requirements:** *Items required:* college transcript. Minimum college GPA of 2.0 required. Lowest grade transferable D. **General Admission Information:** Application fee $30. Priority application deadline March 1. Regular application deadline August 10. Nonfall registration accepted. Admission may be deferred for a maximum of 1 year. Credit offered for CEEB Advanced Placement tests.

COSTS AND FINANCIAL AID

In-state tuition $2,400. Out-of-state tuition $8,064. Room & board $5,120. Required fees $597. Average book expense $800. **Required Forms and Deadlines:** FAFSA and institution's own financial aid form. No deadline for regular filing. Priority filing deadline February 1. **Notification of Awards:** Applicants will be notified of awards on a rolling basis beginning on or about April 10. **Types of Aid:** *Need-based scholarships/grants:* Pell, SEOG, state scholarships/grants, private scholarships, the school's own gift aid. *Loans:* FFEL Subsidized Stafford, FFEL Unsubsidized Stafford, FFEL PLUS, Federal Perkins, private. **Student Employment:** Federal Work-Study Program available. Institutional employment available. Off-campus job opportunities are good. **Financial Aid Statistics:** 44% freshmen, 48% undergrads receive some form of aid. Average freshman grant $3,562. Average freshman loan $1,848. **Financial Aid Phone:** 307-766-2116.

See page 1270.

UPPER IOWA UNIVERSITY

Parker Fox Hall Box 1859, Fayette, IA 52142-1859
Phone: 800-553-4150 **E-mail:** admission@uiu.edu
Fax: 319-425-5277 **Web:** www.uiu.edu

This private school was founded in 1857. It has an 80-acre campus.

STUDENTS AND FACULTY

Enrollment: 697. **Student Body:** Male 59%, female 41%, out-of-state 40%, international 1%. **Ethnic Representation:** African American 12%, Asian 4%, Caucasian 75%, Hispanic 5%. **Retention and Graduation:** 62% freshmen return for sophomore year. 8% grads go on to further study within 1 year. 2% grads pursue business degrees. 1% grads pursue law degrees. 1% grads pursue medical degrees. **Faculty:** Student/faculty ratio 16:1. 37 full-time faculty, 27% hold PhDs.

ACADEMICS

Degrees: Associate's, bachelor's, master's, transfer. **Academic Requirements:** General education including some course work in arts/fine arts, computer literacy, English (including composition), history, humanities, mathematics, sciences (biological or physical). **Classes:** 10-19 students in an average class. 10-19 students in an average lab/discussion section. **Disciplines with Highest Percentage of Degrees Awarded:** Business/marketing 62%, social sciences and history 15%, protective services/public administration 9%, education 7%, biological life sciences 3%. **Special Study Options:** Accelerated program, distance learning, double major, dual enrollment, external degree program, independent study, internships, student-designed major, teacher certification program.

FACILITIES

Housing: Coed, all-female, all-male. **Library Holdings:** 132,175 bound volumes. 287 periodicals. 8,895 microforms. 4,040 audiovisuals. **Computers:** School-owned computers available for student use.

EXTRACURRICULARS

Activities: Choral groups, concert band, drama/theater, jazz band, music ensembles, pep band, student government, student newspaper, yearbook. **Organizations:** 40 registered organizations, 1 honor society, 1 religious organization, 6 fraternities (30% men join), 6 sororities (30% women join). **Athletics (Intercollegiate):** *Men:* baseball, basketball, cheerleading, skiing (cross-country), cross-country, football, golf, soccer, softball, tennis, track & field, wrestling. *Women:* basketball, cheerleading, skiing (cross-country), cross-country, golf, soccer, softball, tennis, track & field, volleyball.

ADMISSIONS

Selectivity Rating: 65 (of 100). **Freshman Academic Profile:** Average high school GPA 2.7. 5% in top 10% of high school class, 18% in top 25% of high school class, 74% in top 50% of high school class. Average SAT I Math 420. Average SAT I Verbal 370. Average ACT 22. TOEFL required of all international applicants, minimum TOEFL 550. **Basis for Candidate Selection:** *Very important factors considered include:* secondary school record, standardized test scores. *Important factors considered include:* character/personal qualities, class rank. *Other factors considered include:* alumni/ae relation, essays, extracurricular activities, interview, recommendations, talent/ability, volunteer work, work experience. **Freshman Admission Requirements:** High school diploma or GED is required. *Academic units required/recommended:* 4 English recommended, 3 math recommended, 3 science recommended, 1 science lab recommended, 2 social studies recommended, 1 history recommended. **Freshman Admission Statistics:** 510 applied, 75% accepted, 29% of those accepted enrolled. **Transfer Admission Requirements:** *Items required:* high school transcript, college transcript. Minimum high school GPA of 2.0 required. Minimum college GPA of 2.0 required. **General Admission Information:** Application fee $15. Nonfall registration accepted. Admission may be deferred for a maximum of 2 years. Credit and/or placement offered for CEEB Advanced Placement tests.

COSTS AND FINANCIAL AID

Tuition $11,290. Room & board $4,364. Average book expense $1,160. **Required Forms and Deadlines:** FAFSA. No deadline for regular filing. Priority filing deadline June 1. **Notification of Awards:** Applicants will be notified of awards on a rolling basis. **Types of Aid:** *Need-based scholarships/grants:* Pell, SEOG, state scholarships/grants, private scholarships, the school's own gift aid. *Loans:* FFEL Subsidized Stafford, FFEL Unsubsidized Stafford, FFEL PLUS, Federal Perkins. **Student Employment:** Federal Work-Study Program available. Off-campus job opportunities are fair. **Financial Aid Statistics:** 44% undergrads receive some form of aid. Average freshman grant $5,775. Average freshman loan $2,500. Average income from on-campus job $675. **Financial Aid Phone:** 319-425-5274.

URBANA UNIVERSITY

579 College Way, Urbana, OH 43078-2091
Phone: 937-484-1356 **E-mail:** admiss@urbana.edu
Fax: 937-484-1389 **Web:** www.urbana.edu **ACT Code:** 3346

This private school was founded in 1850. It has a 128-acre campus.

STUDENTS AND FACULTY

Enrollment: 1,338. **Student Body:** Male 44%, female 56%, out-of-state 4%, international students represent 5 countries. **Ethnic Representation:** African American 12%, Caucasian 86%, Hispanic 1%, Native American 1%. **Faculty:** 100% faculty teach undergrads.

ACADEMICS

Degrees: Associate's, bachelor's, master's, post-bachelor's certificate. **Academic Requirements:** General education including some course work in arts/fine arts, computer literacy, English (including composition), history, humanities, mathematics, philosophy, sciences (biological or physical), social science. **Special Study Options:** Accelerated program, cooperative (work-study) program, cross registration, honors program, independent study, internships, teacher certification program.

FACILITIES

Housing: All-female, all-male, apartments for single students. **Library Holdings:** 80,000 bound volumes. 1,000 periodicals. 10,142 microforms. 2,292 audiovisuals. **Special Academic Facilities/Equipment:** Johnny Appleseed Museum, Barclay Hall, Bailey Hall, Lewis and Jean Moore Math/Science Center. **Computers:** *Recommended operating system:* Windows 95. School-owned computers available for student use.

EXTRACURRICULARS

Activities: Choral groups, drama/theater, pep band, student government, student newspaper. **Organizations:** 37 honor societies, 11 religious organizations. **Athletics (Intercollegiate):** *Men:* baseball, basketball, football, golf, soccer. *Women:* basketball, cheerleading, soccer, softball, volleyball.

ADMISSIONS

Selectivity Rating: 67 (of 100). **Freshman Academic Profile:** 8% in top 10% of high school class, 23% in top 25% of high school class, 35% in top 50% of high school class. ACT middle 50% range 17-21. TOEFL required of all international applicants, minimum TOEFL 500. **Basis for Candidate Selection:** *Very important factors considered include:* secondary school record, standardized test scores. *Important factors considered include:* essays, extracurricular activities. *Other factors considered include:* alumni/ae relation, character/personal qualities, class rank, interview, minority status, recommendations, talent/ability, volunteer work, work experience. **Freshman Admission Requirements:** High school diploma or GED is required. *Academic units required/recommended:* 4 English required, 2 math required, 2 science required, 2 social studies required, 2 elective recommended. **Freshman Admission Statistics:** 520 applied, 57% accepted, 62% of those accepted enrolled. **Transfer Admission Requirements:** *Items required:* high school transcript, college transcript, essay. Minimum college GPA of 2.0 required. Lowest grade transferable C. **General Admission Information:** Application fee $25. Nonfall registration accepted. Admission may be deferred.

COSTS AND FINANCIAL AID

Tuition $11,862. Room & board $5,000. Required fees $200. Average book expense $500. **Required Forms and Deadlines:** FAFSA and institution's own financial aid form. No deadline for regular filing. **Notification of Awards:** Applicants will be notified of awards on a rolling basis. **Types of Aid:** *Need-based scholarships/grants:* Pell, SEOG, state scholarships/grants, private scholarships, the school's own gift aid, Phi Theta Kappa Scholarship. *Loans:* Direct Subsidized Stafford, Direct Unsubsidized Stafford, Direct PLUS, Federal Perkins. **Student Employment:** Federal Work-Study Program available. Institutional employment available. Off-campus job opportunities are good. **Financial Aid Statistics:** Average freshman loan $5,000. Average income from on-campus job $1,000. **Financial Aid Phone:** 937-484-1355.

URSINUS COLLEGE

Ursinus College, Admissions Office, Collegeville, PA 19426
Phone: 610-409-3200 **E-mail:** admissions@ursinus.edu **CEEB Code:** 2931
Fax: 610-409-3662 **Web:** www.ursinus.edu **ACT Code:** 3738

This private school was founded in 1869. It has a 165-acre campus.

STUDENTS AND FACULTY

Enrollment: 1,324. **Student Body:** Male 43%, female 57%, out-of-state 36%, international 3%. **Ethnic Representation:** African American 8%, Asian 4%, Caucasian 86%, Hispanic 2%. **Retention and Graduation:** 90% freshmen return for sophomore year. 74% freshmen graduate within 4 years. 33% grads go on to further study within 1 year. 5% grads pursue business degrees. 5% grads pursue law degrees. 12% grads pursue medical degrees. **Faculty:** Student/faculty ratio 11:1. 96 full-time faculty, 91% hold PhDs. 100% faculty teach undergrads.

ACADEMICS

Degrees: Bachelor's. **Academic Requirements:** General education including some course work in arts/fine arts, English (including composition), foreign languages, humanities, mathematics, sciences (biological or physical), social science. **Classes:** Under 10 students in an average class. 10-19 students in an average lab/discussion section. **Majors with Highest Enrollment:** Biology/biological sciences, general; psychology, general; economics, general. **Disciplines with Highest Percentage of Degrees Awarded:** Business/marketing 19%, social sciences and history 19%, biological life sciences 17%, communications/communication technologies 8%, psychology 8%. **Special Study Options:** Accelerated program, double major, student exchange program (domestic), honors program, independent study, internships, liberal arts/career combination, student-designed major, study abroad, teacher certification program.

FACILITIES

Housing: Coed, all-female, all-male, apartments for single students, housing for disabled students, housing for international students. **Library Holdings:** 200,000 bound volumes. 900 periodicals. 155,000 microforms. 17,500 audiovisuals. **Special Academic Facilities/Equipment:** Berman Art Museum; International Language Center; 6 new telescopes; electron microscope; newly opened $16 million Pfahler chemistry, mathematics, and computer building; new field house; new 143-bed dormitory. **Computers:** *Recommended operating system:* Windows NT/2000. School-owned computers available for student use.

EXTRACURRICULARS

Activities: Choral groups, concert band, dance, drama/theater, jazz band, literary magazine, music ensembles, pep band, radio station, student government, student newspaper, student-run film society, television station, yearbook. **Organizations:** 116 registered organizations, 27 honor societies, 6 religious organizations, 9 fraternities (15% men join), 5 sororities (25% women join). **Athletics (Intercollegiate):** *Men:* baseball, basketball, cross-country, football, golf, lacrosse, soccer, swimming, tennis, track & field, wrestling. *Women:* basketball, cross-country, field hockey, golf, gymnastics, lacrosse, soccer, softball, swimming, tennis, track & field, volleyball.

ADMISSIONS

Selectivity Rating: 80 (of 100). **Freshman Academic Profile:** Average high school GPA 3.5. 40% in top 10% of high school class, 80% in top 25% of high school class, 94% in top 50% of high school class. 68% from public high schools. Average SAT I Math 598, SAT I Math middle 50% range 550-650. Average SAT I Verbal 595, SAT I Verbal middle 50% range 540-640. TOEFL required of all international applicants, minimum TOEFL 550. **Basis for Candidate Selection:** *Very important factors considered include:* class rank, extracurricular activities, secondary school record. *Important factors considered include:* alumni/ae relation, essays, minority status, recommendations, standardized test scores, talent/ability, volunteer work, work experience. *Other factors considered include:* character/personal qualities, geographical residence, interview. **Freshman Admission Requirements:** High school diploma or GED is required. *Academic units required/recommended:* 16 total required; 20 total recommended; 4 English required, 3 math required, 4 math recommended, 1 science required, 3 science recommended, 1 science lab required, 2 foreign language required, 4 foreign language recommended, 1 social studies required, 3 social studies recommended, 5 elective required. **Freshman Admission Statistics:** 1,547 applied, 78% accepted, 36% of those accepted enrolled. **Transfer Admission Requirements:** *Items required:* high school transcript, college transcript, essay, standardized test scores. Minimum college GPA of 3.0 required. Lowest grade transferable C. **General Admission Information:** Application fee $40. Priority application deadline February 15. Early decision application deadline January 15. Regular application deadline February 15. Nonfall registration accepted. Admission may be deferred for a maximum of 1 year. Credit and/or placement offered for CEEB Advanced Placement tests.

COSTS AND FINANCIAL AID

Tuition $26,200. Room & board $6,600. Required fees $0. Average book expense $600. **Required Forms and Deadlines:** FAFSA, institution's own financial aid form and CSS/Financial Aid PROFILE. Financial aid filing deadline February 15. Priority filing deadline February 15. **Notification of Awards:** Applicants will be notified of awards on or about April 1. **Types of Aid:** *Need-based scholarships/grants:* Pell, SEOG, state scholarships/grants, private scholarships, the school's own gift aid. *Loans:* FFEL Subsidized Stafford, FFEL Unsubsidized Stafford, FFEL PLUS, Federal Perkins, college/university loans from institutional funds. **Student Employment:** Federal Work-Study Program available. Institutional employment available. Off-campus job opportunities are excellent. **Financial Aid Statistics:** 78% freshmen, 75% undergrads receive some form of aid. Average income from on-campus job $1,200. **Financial Aid Phone:** 610-409-3600.

URSULINE COLLEGE

2550 Lander Road, Pepper Pike, OH 44124-4398
Phone: 440-449-4203 **E-mail:** admission@ursuline.edu **CEEB Code:** 1848
Fax: 440-684-6138 **Web:** www.ursuline.edu

This private school, which is affiliated with the Roman Catholic Church, was founded in 1871. It has a 110-acre campus.

STUDENTS AND FACULTY

Enrollment: 1,008. **Student Body:** Male 9%, female 91%, out-of-state 2%, international 1% (8 countries represented). **Ethnic Representation:** African American 22%, Asian 1%, Caucasian 72%, Hispanic 1%. **Retention and Graduation:** 68% freshmen return for sophomore year. 25% freshmen graduate within 4 years. **Faculty:** Student/faculty ratio 9:1. 62 full-time faculty, 64% hold PhDs. 88% faculty teach undergrads.

ACADEMICS

Degrees: Bachelor's, master's. **Academic Requirements:** General education including some course work in arts/fine arts, humanities, mathematics, philosophy, sciences (biological or physical), social science, religious studies and ursuline studies. **Classes:** 10-19 students in an average class. 10-19 students in an average lab/discussion section. **Majors with Highest Enrollment:** Nursing/registered nurse training (RN, ASN, BSN, MSN); business administration/management; education, general. **Disciplines with Highest Percentage of Degrees Awarded:** Health professions and related sciences 30%, business/marketing 29%, visual and performing arts 11%, education 9%, social sciences and history 4%. **Special Study Options:** Accelerated program, cooperative (work-study) program, cross registration, distance learning, double major, independent study, internships, teacher certification program, weekend college.

FACILITIES

Housing: Coed, all-female. **Library Holdings:** 126,491 bound volumes. 332 periodicals. 1 microform. 6,929 audiovisuals. **Special Academic Facilities/Equipment:** Fritsche Gallery (art), fitness center, swimming pool. **Computers:** *Recommended operating system:* Windows 98 SE. School-owned computers available for student use.

EXTRACURRICULARS

Activities: Drama/theater, literary magazine, student government. **Organizations:** 28 registered organizations, 3 honor societies, 1 religious organization. **Athletics (Intercollegiate):** *Women:* basketball, golf, soccer, softball, volleyball.

ADMISSIONS

Selectivity Rating: 63 (of 100). **Freshman Academic Profile:** Average high school GPA 3.0. 16% in top 10% of high school class, 43% in top 25% of high school class, 86% in top 50% of high school class. 81% from public high schools. Average SAT I Math 474, SAT I Math middle 50% range 420-530. Average SAT I Verbal 488, SAT I Verbal middle 50% range 450-540. Average ACT 20, ACT middle 50% range 17-22. TOEFL required of all international applicants, minimum TOEFL 500. **Basis for Candidate Selection:** *Very important factors considered include:* essays, recommendations, secondary school record, standardized test scores. *Other factors considered include:* alumni/ae relation, character/personal qualities, class rank, extracurricular activities, interview, minority status, talent/ability, volunteer work, work experience. **Freshman Admission Requirements:** High school diploma or GED is required. *Academic units required/recommended:* 19 total recommended; 4 English recommended, 3 math recommended, 3 science recommended, 2 science lab recommended, 2 foreign language recommended, 3 social studies recommended. **Freshman Admission Statistics:** 314 applied, 65% accepted, 48% of those accepted enrolled. **Transfer Admission Requirements:** *Items required:* college transcript, essay. Minimum college GPA of 2.5 required. Lowest grade transferable C. **General Admission Information:** Application fee $25. Nonfall registration accepted. Admission may be deferred for a maximum of 1 year. Credit and/or placement offered for CEEB Advanced Placement tests.

COSTS AND FINANCIAL AID

Average book expense $800. **Required Forms and Deadlines:** FAFSA and institution's own financial aid form. No deadline for regular filing. Priority filing deadline March 15. **Notification of Awards:** Applicants will be notified of awards on a rolling basis beginning on or about April 1. **Types of Aid:** *Need-based scholarships/grants:* Pell, SEOG, state scholarships/grants, private scholarships, the school's own gift aid. *Loans:* FFEL Subsidized Stafford, FFEL Unsubsidized Stafford, FFEL PLUS, Federal Perkins, college/university loans from institutional funds. **Student Employment:** Federal Work-Study Program available. Off-campus job opportunities are good. **Financial Aid Statistics:** 80% freshmen, 71% undergrads receive some form of aid. Average freshman grant $10,097. Average freshman loan $3,475. **Financial Aid Phone:** 440-646-8309.

UTAH STATE UNIVERSITY

0160 Old Main Hill, Logan, UT 84322-0160
Phone: 435-797-1079 **E-mail:** admit@cc.usu.edu
Fax: 435-797-3708 **Web:** www.usu.edu **ACT Code:** 4276

This public school was founded in 1888. It has a 400-acre campus.

STUDENTS AND FACULTY

Enrollment: 19,736. **Student Body:** Male 48%, female 52%, out-of-state 30%, international 2% (88 countries represented). **Ethnic Representation:** African American 1%, Asian 1%, Caucasian 94%, Hispanic 2%, Native American 1%. **Faculty:** 719 full-time faculty, 87% hold PhDs. 95% faculty teach undergrads.

ACADEMICS

Degrees: Associate's, bachelor's, certificate, doctoral, master's, terminal, transfer. **Academic Requirements:** General education including some course work in arts/fine arts, computer literacy, English (including composition), history, humanities, mathematics, sciences (biological or physical), social science, American institutions—collaborative learning and group decision making, depth in specified areas outside the major, interdisciplinary courses. **Classes:** 10-19 students in an average lab/discussion section. **Majors with Highest Enrollment:** Elementary education and teaching; psychology, general; business/commerce, general. **Disciplines with Highest Percentage of Degrees Awarded:** Business/marketing 15%, education 17%, home economics and vocational home economics 8%, computer and information sciences 7%, engineering/engineering technology 7%. **Special Study Options:** Accelerated program, cooperative (work-study) program, cross registration, distance learning, double major, dual enrollment, English as a second language, student exchange program (domestic), honors program, independent study, internships, liberal arts/career combination, student-designed major, study abroad, teacher certification program, weekend college.

FACILITIES

Housing: Coed, all-female, all-male, apartments for married students, apartments for single students, housing for disabled students, housing for international students, fraternities and/or sororities, mobile home park. **Library Holdings:** 1,457,649 bound volumes. 13,971 periodicals. 2,582,409 microforms. 17,008 audiovisuals. **Special Academic Facilities/Equipment:** Art gallery, agricultural and engineering experiment station, water research lab, wildlife and fishery research unit, on-campus school, intermountain herbarium, electron microscope, space dynamics lab. **Computers:** School-owned computers available for student use.

EXTRACURRICULARS

Activities: Choral groups, concert band, drama/theater, jazz band, marching band, music ensembles, musical theater, opera, pep band, student government, student newspaper, symphony orchestra. **Organizations:** 250 registered organizations, 32 honor societies, 8 religious organizations, 5 fraternities (2% men join), 3 sororities (2% women join). **Athletics (Intercollegiate):** *Men:* basketball, cross-country, football, golf, indoor track, tennis, track & field. *Women:* basketball, cross-country, gymnastics, indoor track, soccer, softball, tennis, track & field, volleyball.

ADMISSIONS

Selectivity Rating: 68 (of 100). **Freshman Academic Profile:** Average high school GPA 3.5. 22% in top 10% of high school class, 46% in top 25% of high school class, 80% in top 50% of high school class. Average SAT I Math 550, SAT I Math middle 50% range 480-610. Average SAT I Verbal 546, SAT I Verbal middle 50% range 490-600. Average ACT 23, ACT middle 50% range 20-26. TOEFL required of all international applicants, minimum TOEFL 500. **Basis for Candidate Selection:** *Very important factors considered include:* secondary school record, standardized test scores. *Other factors considered include:* class rank. **Freshman Admission Requirements:** High school diploma or GED is required. *Academic units required/recommended:* 4 English required, 3 math required, 3 science required, 1 science lab required, 2 foreign language recommended, 1 history required, 4 elective required. **Freshman Admission Statistics:** 5,689 applied, 89% accepted, 53% of those accepted enrolled. **Transfer Admission Requirements:** *Items required:* college transcript. Minimum college GPA of 2.2 required. Lowest grade transferable D. **General Admission Information:** Application fee $35. Nonfall registration accepted. Admission may be deferred for a maximum of 1 year. Credit and/or placement offered for CEEB Advanced Placement tests.

COSTS AND FINANCIAL AID

In-state tuition $1,947. Out-of-state tuition $6,816. Room & board $4,040. Required fees $456. Average book expense $830. **Required Forms and Deadlines:** FAFSA, institution's own financial aid form, and federal tax forms. No deadline for regular filing. **Notification of Awards:** Applicants will be notified of awards on a rolling basis beginning on or about April 1. **Types of Aid:** *Need-based scholarships/grants:* Pell, SEOG, state scholarships/grants, private scholarships, the school's own gift aid. *Loans:* FFEL Subsidized Stafford, FFEL Unsubsidized Stafford, FFEL PLUS, Federal Perkins, college/university loans from institutional funds. **Student Employment:** Federal Work-Study Program available. Institutional employment available. Off-campus job opportunities are good. **Financial Aid Statistics:** 33% freshmen, 49% undergrads receive some form of aid. **Financial Aid Phone:** 435-797-0173.

UTICA COLLEGE—OFFERING THE SYRACUSE UNIVERSITY DEGREE

1600 Burrstone Road, Utica, NY 13502-4892
Phone: 315-792-3006 **E-mail:** admiss@utica.ucsu.edu
Fax: 315-792-3003 **Web:** www.utica.edu **ACT Code:** 2973

This private school was founded in 1946.

STUDENTS AND FACULTY

Enrollment: 2,177. **Student Body:** Male 42%, female 58%, out-of-state 10%, international 2%. **Ethnic Representation:** African American 8%, Asian 2%, Caucasian 68%, Hispanic 4%, Native American 1%. **Retention and Graduation:** 71% freshmen return for sophomore year. 37% freshmen graduate within 4 years. 2% grads go on to further study within 1 year. 1% grads pursue business degrees. 1% grads pursue law degrees. 1% grads pursue medical degrees. **Faculty:** Student/faculty ratio 17:1. 102 full-time faculty, 67% hold PhDs. 100% faculty teach undergrads.

ACADEMICS

Degrees: Bachelor's, master's. **Academic Requirements:** General education including some course work in English (including composition), mathematics, sciences (biological or physical). **Classes:** 10-19 students in an average class. 10-19 students in an average lab/discussion section. **Majors with Highest Enrollment:** Biology/biological sciences, general; psychology, general; criminal justice/law enforcement administration. **Disciplines with Highest Percentage of Degrees Awarded:** Health professions and related sciences 24%, psychology 15%, business/marketing 14%, social sciences and history 9%, protective services/public administration 9%. **Special Study Options:** Accelerated program, cooperative (work-study) program, cross registration, distance learning, double major, dual enrollment, English as a second language, student exchange program (domestic), external degree program, honors program, independent study, internships, liberal arts/career combination, study abroad, teacher certification program, weekend college.

FACILITIES

Housing: Coed, all-female, all-male, apartments for single students, off-campus college-owned housing for some students, women's floor, men's floor. **Library Holdings:** 181,265 bound volumes. 2,148 periodicals. 60,583 microforms. 1,550 audiovisuals. **Special Academic Facilities/Equipment:** Edith Barrett Art Gallery. **Computers:** School-owned computers available for student use.

EXTRACURRICULARS

Activities: Choral groups, concert band, dance, drama/theater, literary magazine, music ensembles, pep band, radio station, student government, student newspaper, student-run film society, yearbook. **Organizations:** 70 registered organizations, 6 honor societies, 3 religious organizations, 6 fraternities (7% men join), 7 sororities (7% women join). **Athletics (Intercollegiate):** *Men:* baseball, basketball, diving, football, golf, ice hockey, lacrosse, soccer, swimming, tennis, volleyball. *Women:* basketball, diving, field hockey, golf, ice hockey, lacrosse, soccer, softball, swimming, tennis, volleyball, water polo.

ADMISSIONS

Selectivity Rating: 64 (of 100). **Freshman Academic Profile:** Average high school GPA 3.0. 11% in top 10% of high school class, 33% in top 25% of high school class, 64% in top 50% of high school class. Average SAT I Math 507, SAT I Math middle 50% range 440-550. Average SAT I Verbal 501, SAT I Verbal middle 50% range 440-540. ACT middle 50% range 18-23. TOEFL required of all international applicants, minimum TOEFL 525. **Basis for Candidate Selection:** *Very important factors considered include:* essays, secondary school record. *Important factors considered include:* interview. *Other factors considered include:* character/personal qualities, extracurricular activities, recommendations, standardized test scores. **Freshman Admission Requirements:** High school diploma or GED is required. *Academic units required/recommended:* 16 total recommended; 4 English recommended, 3 math recommended, 3 science recommended, 2 foreign language recommended, 4 social studies recommended. **Freshman Admission Statistics:** 2,007 applied, 79% accepted, 28% of those accepted enrolled. **Transfer Admission Requirements:** *Items required:* college transcript, statement of good standing from prior school. Minimum college GPA of 2.5 required. Lowest grade transferable C. **General Admission Information:** Application fee $35. Nonfall registration accepted. Admission may be deferred for a maximum of 1 year.

COSTS AND FINANCIAL AID

Tuition $18,848. Room & board $7,580. Required fees $270. Average book expense $700. **Required Forms and Deadlines:** FAFSA and state aid form. No deadline for regular filing. Priority filing deadline February 15. **Notification of Awards:** Applicants will be notified of awards on a rolling basis beginning on or about March 1. **Types of Aid:** *Need-based scholarships/grants:* Pell, SEOG, state scholarships/grants, private scholarships, the school's own gift aid. *Loans:* Direct Subsidized Stafford, Direct Unsubsidized Stafford, Direct PLUS, Federal Perkins. **Student Employment:** Federal Work-Study Program available. Institutional employment available. Off-campus job opportunities are good. **Financial Aid Statistics:** 92% freshmen, 90% undergrads receive some form of aid. **Financial Aid Phone:** 315-792-3179.

VALDOSTA STATE UNIVERSITY

1500 North Patterson Street, Valdosta, GA 31698
Phone: 229-333-5791 **E-mail:** admissions@valdosta.edu **CEEB Code:** 5855
Fax: 229-333-5482 **Web:** www.valdosta.edu **ACT Code:** 874

This public school was founded in 1906. It has a 200-acre campus.

STUDENTS AND FACULTY

Enrollment: 8,419. **Student Body:** Male 39%, female 61%, out-of-state 7%, international 1% (52 countries represented). **Ethnic Representation:** African American 22%, Asian 1%, Caucasian 74%, Hispanic 1%. **Retention and Graduation:** 74% freshmen return for sophomore year. 15% freshmen graduate within 4 years. **Faculty:** Student/faculty ratio 16:1. 468 full-time faculty, 73% hold PhDs. 85% faculty teach undergrads.

ACADEMICS

Degrees: Associate's, bachelor's, doctoral, master's, post-bachelor's certificate, post-master's certificate. **Academic Requirements:** General education including some course work in computer literacy, English (including composition), foreign languages, history, humanities, mathematics, sciences (biological or physical), social science, perspectives. **Classes:** 20-29 students in an average class. 20-29 students in an average lab/discussion section. **Disciplines with Highest Percentage of Degrees Awarded:** Business/marketing 24%, education 21%, social sciences and history 9%, visual and performing arts 7%, English 7%. **Special Study Options:** Accelerated program, cooperative (work-study) program, distance learning, double major, dual enrollment, English as a second language, honors program, independent study, internships, liberal arts/career combination, study abroad, teacher certification program.

FACILITIES

Housing: Coed, all-female, all-male, apartments for single students, housing for disabled students, housing for international students. **Library Holdings:** 290,295 bound volumes. 3,097 periodicals. 1,014,656 microforms. 19,400 audiovisuals. **Special Academic Facilities/Equipment:** Planetarium, herbarium, art gallery. **Computers:** *Recommended operating system:* Windows NT/2000. School-owned computers available for student use.

EXTRACURRICULARS

Activities: Choral groups, concert band, dance, drama/theater, jazz band, literary magazine, marching band, music ensembles, musical theater, pep band, radio station, student government, student newspaper, symphony orchestra, television station. **Organizations:** 111 registered organizations, 20 honor societies, 10 religious organizations, 11 fraternities (3% men join), 10 sororities (5% women join). **Athletics (Intercollegiate):** *Men:* baseball, basketball, cross-country, football, golf, tennis. *Women:* basketball, cheerleading, cross-country, softball, tennis, volleyball.

ADMISSIONS

Selectivity Rating: 63 (of 100). **Freshman Academic Profile:** Average high school GPA 3.1. 70% from public high schools. Average SAT I Math 510, SAT I Math middle 50% range 460-560. Average SAT I Verbal 520, SAT I Verbal middle 50% range 470-560. Average ACT 22, ACT middle 50% range 19-23. TOEFL required of all international applicants, minimum TOEFL 523. **Basis for Candidate Selection:** *Very important factors considered include:* secondary school record, standardized test scores. *Other factors considered include:* character/personal qualities, extracurricular activities, interview, talent/ability. **Freshman Admission Requirements:** High school diploma is required and GED is not accepted. *Academic units required/recommended:* 16 total required; 4 English required, 4 math required, 3 science required, 3 science lab required, 2 foreign language required, 3 social studies required. **Freshman Admission Statistics:** 4,844 applied, 71% accepted, 46% of those accepted enrolled. **Transfer Admission Requirements:** *Items required:* college transcript. Minimum high school GPA of 2.5 required. Minimum college GPA of 2.0 required. Lowest grade transferable D. **General Admission Information:** Application fee $20. Regular application deadline August 1. Nonfall registration accepted. Credit and/or placement offered for CEEB Advanced Placement tests.

COSTS AND FINANCIAL AID

In-state tuition $2,010. Out-of-state tuition $8,040. Room & board $4,680. Required fees $624. Average book expense $750. **Required Forms and Deadlines:** FAFSA. No deadline for regular filing. Priority filing deadline May 1. **Notification of Awards:** Applicants will be notified of awards on a rolling basis beginning on or about June 1. **Types of Aid:** *Need-based scholarships/grants:* Pell, SEOG, state scholarships/grants, private scholarships, the school's own gift aid, Federal Nursing. *Loans:* Direct Subsidized Stafford, Direct Unsubsidized Stafford, Direct PLUS, state loans. **Student Employment:** Federal Work-Study Program available. Institutional employment available. Off-campus job opportunities are excellent. **Financial Aid Statistics:** 47% freshmen, 48% undergrads receive some form of aid. Average freshman grant $2,000. Average freshman loan $3,000. Average income from on-campus job $2,000. **Financial Aid Phone:** 912-333-5935.

VALLEY CITY STATE UNIVERSITY

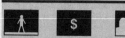

101 College St. SW, Valley City, ND 58072
Phone: 701-845-7101 **E-mail:** enrollment_services@mail.vcsu.nodak.edu
Fax: 701-845-7299 **Web:** www.vcsu.edu **ACT Code:** 3216

This public school was founded in 1890. It has a 55-acre campus.

STUDENTS AND FACULTY

Enrollment: 1,005. **Student Body:** Male 43%, female 57%, out-of-state 24%, international 5% (8 countries represented). **Ethnic Representation:** African American 2%, Caucasian 94%, Hispanic 1%, Native American 2%. **Retention and Graduation:** 57% freshmen return for sophomore year. 18% freshmen graduate within 4 years. 5% grads go on to further study within 1 year. 2% grads pursue business degrees. **Faculty:** Student/faculty ratio 15:1. 58 full-time faculty, 43% hold PhDs. 100% faculty teach undergrads.

ACADEMICS

Degrees: Bachelor's. **Academic Requirements:** General education including some course work in computer literacy, English (including composition), humanities, mathematics, sciences (biological or physical), social science, physical education (fitness/wellness). **Majors with Highest Enrollment:** Elementary education and teaching. **Disciplines with Highest Percentage of Degrees Awarded:** Education 63%, business/marketing 13%, liberal arts/general studies 8%, interdisciplinary studies 4%, computer and information sciences 3%. **Special Study Options:** Cooperative (work-study) program, double major, dual enrollment, internships, student-designed major, teacher certification program.

FACILITIES

Housing: Coed, all-female, all-male, apartments for married students, housing for disabled students, apartments for students with dependent children. **Library Holdings:** 103,174 bound volumes. 2,982 periodicals. 59,400 microforms. 15,069 audiovisuals. **Special Academic Facilities/Equipment:** Planetarium. **Computers:** School-owned computers available for student use.

EXTRACURRICULARS

Activities: Choral groups, concert band, drama/theater, jazz band, music ensembles, pep band, student government, student newspaper, yearbook. **Organizations:** 16 registered organizations, 5 honor societies, 3 religious organizations, 1 fraternity (2% men join), 1 sorority (2% women join). **Athletics (Intercollegiate):** *Men:* baseball, basketball, cross-country, football, indoor track, track & field. *Women:* basketball, cheerleading, cross-country, indoor track, softball, track & field, volleyball.

ADMISSIONS

Selectivity Rating: 63 (of 100). **Freshman Academic Profile:** Average high school GPA 3.1. 5% in top 10% of high school class, 25% in top 25% of high school class, 58% in top 50% of high school class. 98% from public high schools. Average ACT 21, ACT middle 50% range 19-23. TOEFL required of all international applicants, minimum TOEFL 500. **Basis for Candidate Selection:** *Very important factors considered include:* secondary school record. *Other factors considered include:* class rank, standardized test scores. **Freshman Admission Requirements:** High school diploma or GED is required. *Academic units required/recommended:* 13 total required; 4 English required, 3 math required, 3 science required, 3 science lab required, 3 social studies required. **Freshman Admission Statistics:** 279 applied, 95% accepted, 79% of those accepted enrolled. **Transfer Admission Requirements:** *Items required:* college transcript, statement of good standing from prior school. Lowest grade transferable D. **General Admission Information:** Application fee $25. Priority application deadline August 15. Nonfall registration accepted. Admission may be deferred. Neither credit nor placement offered for CEEB Advanced Placement tests.

COSTS AND FINANCIAL AID

In-state tuition $2,067. Out-of-state tuition $5,519. Room & board $3,020. Required fees $1,239. Average book expense $600. **Required Forms and Deadlines:** FAFSA. Priority filing deadline April 15. **Notification of Awards:** Applicants will be notified of awards on a rolling basis beginning on or about June 1. **Types of Aid:** *Need-based scholarships/grants:* Pell, SEOG, state scholarships/grants, private scholarships, the school's own gift aid. *Loans:* FFEL Subsidized Stafford, FFEL Unsubsidized Stafford, FFEL PLUS, Federal Perkins. **Student Employment:** Federal Work-Study Program available. Institutional employment available. Off-campus job opportunities are good. **Financial Aid Statistics:** 61% freshmen, 57% undergrads receive some form of aid. Average income from on-campus job $1,640. **Financial Aid Phone:** 701-845-7412.

VALPARAISO UNIVERSITY

Office of Admissions, Kretzmann Hall, 1700 Chapel Drive, Valparaiso, IN 46383-6493
Phone: 219-464-5011 **E-mail:** undergrad.admissions@valpo.edu **CEEB Code:** 1874
Fax: 219-464-6898 **Web:** www.valpo.edu **ACT Code:** 1256

This private school, which is affiliated with the Lutheran Church, was founded in 1859. It has a 310-acre campus.

STUDENTS AND FACULTY

Enrollment: 2,910. **Student Body:** Male 47%, female 53%, out-of-state 66%, international 3% (37 countries represented). **Ethnic Representation:** African American 3%, Asian 2%, Caucasian 90%, Hispanic 3%. **Retention and Graduation:** 88% freshmen return for sophomore year. 58% freshmen graduate within 4 years. 21% grads go on to further study within 1 year. 2% grads pursue law degrees. 2% grads pursue medical degrees. **Faculty:** Student/faculty ratio 13:1. 225 full-time faculty, 87% hold PhDs. 100% faculty teach undergrads.

ACADEMICS

Degrees: Associate's, bachelor's, certificate, first professional, master's, post-bachelor's certificate, post-master's certificate, terminal. **Academic Requirements:** General education including some course work in arts/fine arts, English (including composition), foreign languages, history, mathematics, philosophy, sciences (biological or physical), social science, theology. **Classes:** 10-19 students in an average class. 10-19 students in an average lab/discussion section. **Majors with Highest Enrollment:** Elementary education and teaching; biology/biological sciences, general; nursing/registered nurse training (RN, ASN, BSN, MSN). **Disciplines with Highest Percentage of Degrees Awarded:** Business/marketing 17%, social sciences and history 13%, engineering/engineering technology 10%, education 7%, physical sciences 7%. **Special Study Options:** Accelerated program, cooperative (work-study) program, cross registration, distance learning, double major, dual enrollment, English as a second language, student exchange program (domestic), honors program, independent study, internships, liberal arts/career combination, student-designed major, study abroad, teacher certification program.

FACILITIES

Housing: Coed, all-female, apartments for single students, fraternities and/or sororities, dormitory for German-language students. **Library Holdings:** 521,907 bound volumes. 5,282 periodicals. 1,864,382 microforms. 13,413 audiovisuals. **Special Academic Facilities/Equipment:** Art museum, galleries, language lab, planetarium, electron microscope, observatory, TV studio, psychology "rat" lab. **Computers:** School-owned computers available for student use.

EXTRACURRICULARS

Activities: Choral groups, concert band, dance, drama/theater, jazz band, literary magazine, music ensembles, musical theater, pep band, radio station, student government, student newspaper, student-run film society, symphony orchestra, yearbook. **Organizations:** 100 registered organizations, 33 honor societies, 8 religious organizations, 8 fraternities (24% men join), 7 sororities (20% women join). **Athletics (Intercollegiate):** *Men:* baseball, basketball, cheerleading, cross-country, diving, football, soccer, swimming, tennis, track & field. *Women:* basketball, cheerleading, cross-country, diving, soccer, softball, swimming, tennis, track & field, volleyball.

ADMISSIONS

Selectivity Rating: 79 (of 100). **Freshman Academic Profile:** 34% in top 10% of high school class, 68% in top 25% of high school class, 93% in top 50% of high school class. 81% from public high schools. Average SAT I Math 596, SAT I Math middle 50% range 530-650. Average SAT I Verbal 583, SAT I Verbal middle 50% range 530-630. Average ACT 26, ACT middle 50% range 23-29. TOEFL required of all international applicants, minimum TOEFL 550. **Basis for Candidate Selection:** *Very important factors considered include:* secondary school record. *Important factors considered include:* class rank, extracurricular activities, standardized test scores, talent/ability. *Other factors considered include:* alumni/ae relation, character/personal qualities, essays, interview, minority status, recommendations, religious affiliation/commitment, volunteer work. **Freshman Admission Requirements:** High school diploma or GED is required. *Academic units required/recommended:* 4 English required, 3 math required, 4 math recommended, 2 science required, 3 science recommended, 2 science lab required, 3 science lab recommended, 2 foreign language required, 2 foreign language recommended, 3 social studies required, 3 social studies recommended, 3 elective required, 3 elective recommended. **Freshman Admission Statistics:** 3,117 applied, 91% accepted, 25% of those accepted enrolled. **Transfer Admission Requirements:** *Items required:* college transcript, essay, statement of good standing from prior school.

Minimum college GPA of 2.0 required. Lowest grade transferable C-. **General Admission Information:** Application fee $30. Priority application deadline January 15. Regular application deadline August 15. Nonfall registration accepted. Admission may be deferred for a maximum of 1 year. Credit and/or placement offered for CEEB Advanced Placement tests.

COSTS AND FINANCIAL AID

Tuition $19,000. Room & board $5,130. Required fees $632. Average book expense $600. **Required Forms and Deadlines:** FAFSA. Priority filing deadline March 1. **Notification of Awards:** Applicants will be notified of awards on a rolling basis beginning on or about March 1. **Types of Aid:** *Need-based scholarships/grants:* Pell, SEOG, state scholarships/grants, private scholarships, the school's own gift aid. *Loans:* Direct Subsidized Stafford, Direct Unsubsidized Stafford, Direct PLUS, Federal Perkins, college/university loans from institutional funds. **Student Employment:** Federal Work-Study Program available. Institutional employment available. Off-campus job opportunities are good. **Financial Aid Statistics:** 69% freshmen, 64% undergrads receive some form of aid. Average freshman grant $12,533. Average freshman loan $5,661. Average income from on-campus job $1,000. **Financial Aid Phone:** 219-464-5015.

VANDERBILT UNIVERSITY

2305 West End Avenue, Nashville, TN 37203
Phone: 615-322-2561 **E-mail:** admissions@vanderbilt.edu **CEEB Code:** 1871
Fax: 615-343-7765 **Web:** www.vanderbilt.edu **ACT Code:** 4036

This private school was founded in 1873. It has a 323-acre campus.

STUDENTS AND FACULTY

Enrollment: 6,146. **Student Body:** Male 48%, female 52%, out-of-state 80%, international 2% (52 countries represented). **Ethnic Representation:** African American 6%, Asian 6%, Caucasian 77%, Hispanic 4%. **Retention and Graduation:** 94% freshmen return for sophomore year. 78% freshmen graduate within 4 years. 32% grads go on to further study within 1 year. 1% grads pursue business degrees. 7% grads pursue law degrees. 4% grads pursue medical degrees. **Faculty:** Student/faculty ratio 9:1. 690 full-time faculty, 96% hold PhDs.

ACADEMICS

Degrees: Bachelor's, doctoral, first professional, master's. **Academic Requirements:** General education including some course work in English (including composition), foreign languages, humanities, mathematics, sciences (biological or physical), social science. **Classes:** Under 10 students in an average class. 10-19 students in an average lab/discussion section. **Majors with Highest Enrollment:** Engineering science; psychology, general; sociology. **Disciplines with Highest Percentage of Degrees Awarded:** Social sciences and history 33%, engineering/engineering technology 14%, psychology 8%, biological life sciences 6%, mathematics 6%. **Special Study Options:** Accelerated program, cooperative (work-study) program, cross registration, distance learning, double major, dual enrollment, English as a second language, honors program, independent study, internships, student-designed major, study abroad, teacher certification program.

FACILITIES

Housing: Coed, all-female, all-male, apartments for married students, apartments for single students, housing for disabled students, housing for international students, Mctyeire International House (foreign languages), McGill Dorm (philosophy students). **Library Holdings:** 1,812,869 bound volumes. 26,885 periodicals. 2,902,729 microforms. 153,450 audiovisuals. **Special Academic Facilities/Equipment:** Art galleries, center for research on education and human development, multimedia classrooms, teaching center, observatories, free-electron laser, electron microscope. **Computers:** School-owned computers available for student use.

EXTRACURRICULARS

Activities: Choral groups, concert band, dance, drama/theater, jazz band, literary magazine, marching band, music ensembles, musical theater, opera, pep band, radio station, student government, student newspaper, student-run film society, symphony orchestra, yearbook. **Organizations:** 329 registered organizations, 20 honor societies, 18 religious organizations, 19 fraternities (34% men join), 12 sororities (50% women join). **Athletics (Intercollegiate):** *Men:* baseball, basketball, cross-country, football, golf, soccer, tennis. *Women:* basketball, cross-country, golf, lacrosse, soccer, tennis, track & field.

ADMISSIONS

Selectivity Rating: 94 (of 100). **Freshman Academic Profile:** 74% in top 10% of high school class, 93% in top 25% of high school class, 99% in top 50% of high school class. 60% from public high schools. SAT I Math middle 50% range 640-720. SAT I Verbal middle 50% range 610-700. ACT middle 50% range 27-31. TOEFL required of all international applicants, minimum TOEFL 570. **Basis for Candidate Selection:** *Very important factors considered include:* character/personal qualities, class rank, essays, extracurricular activities, recommendations, secondary school record, standardized test scores, talent/ability. *Other factors considered include:* alumni/ae relation, geographical residence, minority status, volunteer work, work experience. **Freshman Admission Requirements:** High school diploma or equivalent is not required. *Academic units required/recommended:* 17 total required; 24 total recommended; 4 English required, 4 English recommended, 3 math required, 4 math recommended, 2 science required, 3 science recommended, 2 science lab required, 3 science lab recommended, 2 foreign language required, 3 foreign language recommended, 2 social studies required, 3 social studies recommended, 2 history required, 2 history recommended, 2 elective recommended. **Freshman Admission Statistics:** 9,836 applied, 46% accepted, 35% of those accepted enrolled. **Transfer Admission Requirements:** *Items required:* high school transcript, college transcript, essay, standardized test score, statement of good standing from prior school. Lowest grade transferable C. **General Admission Information:** Application fee $50. Priority application deadline January 3. Early decision application deadline November 1. Regular application deadline February 15. Nonfall registration accepted. Admission may be deferred for a maximum of 1 year. Credit and/or placement offered for CEEB Advanced Placement tests.

COSTS AND FINANCIAL AID

Tuition $26,400. Room & board $9,060. Required fees $687. Average book expense $950. **Required Forms and Deadlines:** FAFSA, CSS/Financial Aid PROFILE and noncustodial (divorced/separated) parent's statement. Priority filing deadline February 1. **Notification of Awards:** Applicants will be notified of awards on or about April 1. **Types of Aid:** *Need-based scholarships/grants:* Pell, SEOG, state scholarships/grants, private scholarships, the school's own gift aid. *Loans:* FFEL Subsidized Stafford, FFEL Unsubsidized Stafford, FFEL PLUS, Federal Perkins, Federal Nursing, college/university loans from institutional funds. **Student Employment:** Federal Work-Study Program available. Institutional employment available. Off-campus job opportunities are excellent. **Financial Aid Statistics:** 40% freshmen, 42% undergrads receive some form of aid. **Financial Aid Phone:** 615-322-3591.

See page 1272.

VANDERCOOK COLLEGE OF MUSIC

3140 South Federal Street, Chicago, IL 60616-3886
Phone: 312-225-6288 **E-mail:** admissions@vandercook.edu **CEEB Code:** 1872
Fax: 312-225-5211 **Web:** www.vandercook.edu **ACT Code:** 1156

This private school was founded in 1909. It has a 1-acre campus.

STUDENTS AND FACULTY

Enrollment: 132. **Student Body:** Male 61%, female 39%, out-of-state 29%, international 2%. **Ethnic Representation:** African American 15%, Caucasian 73%, Hispanic 12%. **Retention and Graduation:** 68% freshmen return for sophomore year. 38% freshmen graduate within 4 years.

ACADEMICS

Degrees: Bachelor's, master's. **Academic Requirements:** General education including some course work in arts/fine arts, computer literacy, English (including composition), history, humanities, mathematics, sciences (biological or physical). **Disciplines with Highest Percentage of Degrees Awarded:** Education 100%. **Special Study Options:** Independent study, teacher certification program.

FACILITIES

Housing: Coed, all-female, all-male, fraternities and/or sororities. **Library Holdings:** 9,494 bound volumes. 80 periodicals. 2,713 audiovisuals. **Computers:** School-owned computers available for student use.

EXTRACURRICULARS

Activities: Choral groups, concert band, jazz band, music ensembles, musical theater, student newspaper. **Organizations:** 2 registered organizations, 19 fraternities, 1 sorority.

ADMISSIONS

Selectivity Rating: 64 (of 100). **Freshman Academic Profile:** 80% from public high schools. Average ACT 22, ACT middle 50% range 20-24. TOEFL required of all international applicants, minimum TOEFL 500. **Basis for Candidate Selection:** *Very important factors considered include:* interview, talent/ability. *Important factors considered include:* essays, extracurricular activities, secondary school record. *Other factors considered include:* alumni/ae relation, character/personal qualities, class rank, recommendations, standardized test scores, volunteer work, work experience. **Freshman Admission Requirements:** High school diploma or GED is required. *Academic units required/recommended:* 15 total required; 3 English required, 2 math required, 2 science required, 2 foreign language required, 3 social studies required, 3 elective required. **Freshman Admission Statistics:** 36 applied, 81% accepted, 83% of those accepted enrolled. **Transfer Admission Requirements:** *Items required:* high school transcript, college transcript, essay, interview, standardized test scores. Minimum college GPA of 2.5 required. Lowest grade transferable C. **General Admission Information:** Application fee $35. Regular application deadline June 1. Nonfall registration accepted. Admission may be deferred. Credit offered for CEEB Advanced Placement tests.

COSTS AND FINANCIAL AID

Tuition $14,120. Room & board $5,945. Required fees $370. Average book expense $900. **Required Forms and Deadlines:** FAFSA. **Types of Aid:** *Need-based scholarships/grants:* state scholarships/grants. *Loans:* FFEL Subsidized Stafford, FFEL PLUS. **Student Employment:** Federal Work-Study Program available. Institutional employment available. Off-campus job opportunities are good. **Financial Aid Phone:** 312-225-6288.

VANGUARD UNIVERSITY OF SOUTHERN CALIFORNIA

55 Fair Drive, Costa Mesa, CA 92626
Phone: 714-556-3610 **E-mail:** admissions@vanguard.edu **CEEB Code:** 4701
Fax: 714-966-5471 **Web:** www.vanguard.edu **ACT Code:** 432

This private school was founded in 1920. It has a 38-acre campus.

STUDENTS AND FACULTY

Enrollment: 1,227. **Student Body:** Male 39%, female 61%, out-of-state 21%, international 1% (14 countries represented). **Ethnic Representation:** African American 2%, Asian 3%, Caucasian 75%, Hispanic 16%, Native American 1%. **Retention and Graduation:** 68% freshmen return for sophomore year. 34% freshmen graduate within 4 years. **Faculty:** Student/faculty ratio 16:1. 71 full-time faculty, 64% hold PhDs. 100% faculty teach undergrads.

ACADEMICS

Degrees: Bachelor's, master's. **Academic Requirements:** General education including some course work in arts/fine arts, English (including composition), history, mathematics, sciences (biological or physical), social science, English proficiency exam, religion, multicultural. **Classes:** 10-19 students in an average class. 20-29 students in an average lab/discussion section. **Majors with Highest Enrollment:** Business administration/management; psychology, general; education, general. **Disciplines with Highest Percentage of Degrees Awarded:** Business/marketing 30%, psychology 15%, philosophy/religion/theology 14%, education 11%, social sciences and history 7%. **Special Study Options:** Accelerated program, cooperative (work-study) program, cross registration, double major, dual enrollment, external degree program, independent study, internships, study abroad, teacher certification program, weekend college.

FACILITIES

Housing: All-female, all-male, apartments for married students, apartments for single students, housing for disabled students, apartments for students with dependent children. **Library Holdings:** 144,952 bound volumes. 1,066 periodicals. 16,800 microforms. 4,668 audiovisuals. **Computers:** School-owned computers available for student use.

EXTRACURRICULARS

Activities: Choral groups, concert band, drama/theater, jazz band, music ensembles, musical theater, pep band, student government, student newspaper, yearbook. **Organizations:** 50 registered organizations, 25 religious organizations. **Athletics (Intercollegiate):** *Men:* baseball, basketball, cross-country, soccer, tennis, track & field. *Women:* basketball, cross-country, soccer, softball, tennis, track & field, volleyball.

ADMISSIONS

Selectivity Rating: 70 (of 100). **Freshman Academic Profile:** Average high school GPA 3.4. 26% in top 10% of high school class, 53% in top 25% of high school class, 85% in top 50% of high school class. 75% from public high schools. Average SAT I Math 500, SAT I Math middle 50% range 400-550. Average SAT I Verbal 500, SAT I Verbal middle 50% range 450-550. Average ACT 23, ACT middle 50% range 19-24. TOEFL required of all international applicants, minimum TOEFL 550. **Basis for Candidate Selection:** *Very important factors considered include:* character/personal qualities, essays, recommendations, religious affiliation/commitment, secondary school record. *Other factors considered include:* class rank, extracurricular activities, interview, standardized test scores, talent/ability, volunteer work. **Freshman Admission Requirements:** High school diploma or GED is required. *Academic units required/recommended:* 4 English recommended, 2 math recommended, 2 science recommended, 3 social studies recommended. **Freshman Admission Statistics:** 798 applied, 79% accepted, 52% of those accepted enrolled. **Transfer Admission Requirements:** *Items required:* college transcript, essay. Minimum high school GPA of 2.0 required. Minimum college GPA of 2.0 required. Lowest grade transferable C-. **General Admission Information:** Application fee $45. Priority application deadline March 3. Nonfall registration accepted. Admission may be deferred for a maximum of 1 year. Credit offered for CEEB Advanced Placement tests.

COSTS AND FINANCIAL AID

Average book expense $1,206. **Required Forms and Deadlines:** FAFSA and state aid form. No deadline for regular filing. Priority filing deadline March 2. **Notification of Awards:** Applicants will be notified of awards on a rolling basis beginning on or about April 1. **Types of Aid:** *Need-based scholarships/grants:* Pell, SEOG, state scholarships/grants, private scholarships, the school's own gift aid. *Loans:* FFEL Subsidized Stafford, FFEL Unsubsidized Stafford, FFEL PLUS, Federal Perkins. **Student Employment:** Federal Work-Study Program available. Institutional employment available. Off-campus job opportunities are excellent. **Financial Aid Statistics:** 73% freshmen, 64% undergrads receive some form of aid. Average freshman grant $10,106. Average freshman loan $1,658. Average income from on-campus job $2,500. **Financial Aid Phone:** 714-556-3610.

VASSAR COLLEGE

124 Raymond Avenue, Poughkeepsie, NY 12604
Phone: 845-437-7300 **E-mail:** admissions@vassar.edu **CEEB Code:** 2956
Fax: 845-437-7063 **Web:** www.vassar.edu **ACT Code:** 2982

This private school was founded in 1861. It has a 1,000-acre campus.

STUDENTS AND FACULTY

Enrollment: 2,472. **Student Body:** Male 39%, female 61%, out-of-state 72%, international 4% (41 countries represented). **Ethnic Representation:** African American 5%, Asian 9%, Caucasian 78%, Hispanic 6%, Native American 1%. **Retention and Graduation:** 95% freshmen return for sophomore year. 81% freshmen graduate within 4 years. 20% grads go on to further study within 1 year. 5% grads pursue business degrees. 19% grads pursue law degrees. 8% grads pursue medical degrees. **Faculty:** Student/faculty ratio 9:1. 258 full-time faculty, 98% hold PhDs. 100% faculty teach undergrads.

ACADEMICS

Degrees: Bachelor's, master's. **Academic Requirements:** General education including some course work in foreign languages. **Classes:** 10-19 students in an average class. 10-19 students in an average lab/discussion section. **Majors with Highest Enrollment:** English language and literature, general; psychology, general; political science and government, general. **Disciplines with Highest Percentage of Degrees Awarded:** Social sciences and history 32%, visual and performing arts 18%, psychology 8%, interdisciplinary studies 8%, English 8%. **Special Study Options:** Cooperative (work-study) program, cross registration, double major, student exchange program (domestic), independent study, internships, liberal arts/career combination, student-designed major, study abroad, teacher certification program.

FACILITIES

Housing: Coed, all-female, apartments for married students, apartments for single students, housing for disabled students, housing for international students, cooperative housing. **Library Holdings:** 830,235 bound volumes. 5,028 periodicals. 607,243 microforms. 19,396 audiovisuals. **Special Academic Facilities/Equipment:** Art center, theatres, nursery school, environmental field station, geology museum, electron microscope, observatory, Skinner Music Hall, fitness center. **Computers:** School-owned computers available for student use.

EXTRACURRICULARS

Activities: Choral groups, concert band, dance, drama/theater, jazz band, literary magazine, music ensembles, musical theater, opera, radio station, student government, student newspaper, student-run film society, symphony orchestra, television station, yearbook. **Organizations:** 85 registered organizations, 6 honor societies, 7 religious organizations. **Athletics (Intercollegiate):** *Men:* baseball, basketball, crew, cross-country, diving, fencing, lacrosse, soccer, squash, swimming, tennis, volleyball. *Women:* basketball, crew, cross-country, diving, fencing, field hockey, lacrosse, soccer, squash, swimming, tennis, volleyball.

ADMISSIONS

Selectivity Rating: 95 (of 100). **Freshman Academic Profile:** 65% in top 10% of high school class, 95% in top 25% of high school class, 99% in top 50% of high school class. 60% from public high schools. Average SAT I Math 664, SAT I Math middle 50% range 630-700. Average SAT I Verbal 685, SAT I Verbal middle 50% range 640-730. ACT middle 50% range 28-32. TOEFL required of all international applicants, minimum TOEFL 600. **Basis for Candidate Selection:** *Very important factors considered include:* secondary school record. *Important factors considered include:* character/personal qualities, class rank, essays, recommendations, standardized test scores. *Other factors considered include:* alumni/ae relation, extracurricular activities, geographical residence, interview, minority status, talent/ability, volunteer work, work experience. **Freshman Admission Requirements:** High school diploma or GED is required. *Academic units required/recommended:* 16 total recommended; 4 English recommended, 4 math recommended, 3 science recommended, 2 science lab recommended, 4 foreign language recommended, 3 social studies recommended, 2 history recommended. **Freshman Admission Statistics:** 5,733 applied, 26% accepted, 43% of those accepted enrolled. **Transfer Admission Requirements:** *Items required:* high school transcript, college transcript, essay, standardized test scores. Minimum college GPA of 3.0 required. Lowest grade transferable C. **General Admission Information:** Application fee $60. Early decision application deadline November 15. Regular application deadline January 1. Admission may be deferred for a maximum of 1 year. Credit offered for CEEB Advanced Placement tests.

COSTS AND FINANCIAL AID

Tuition $24,600. Room & board $6,940. Required fees $330. Average book expense $740. **Required Forms and Deadlines:** FAFSA, institution's own financial aid form, CSS/Financial Aid PROFILE, state aid form, noncustodial (divorced/separated) parent's statement and business/farm supplement. Financial aid filing deadline February 1. **Notification of Awards:** Applicants will be notified of awards on or about April 3. **Types of Aid:** *Need-based scholarships/grants:* Pell, SEOG, state scholarships/grants, private scholarships, the school's own gift aid. *Loans:* FFEL Subsidized Stafford, FFEL Unsubsidized Stafford, FFEL PLUS, Federal Perkins, college/university loans from institutional funds. **Student Employment:** Federal Work-Study Program available. Institutional employment available. Off-campus job opportunities are fair. **Financial Aid Statistics:** 55% freshmen, 53% undergrads receive some form of aid. Average freshman grant $19,917. Average freshman loan $2,797. Average income from on-campus job $1,100. **Financial Aid Phone:** 845-437-5230.

VILLA JULIE COLLEGE

1525 Greenspring Valley Road, Stevenson, MD 21153
Phone: 410-486-7001 **E-mail:** admissions@vjc.edu
Fax: 410-602-6600 **Web:** www.vjc.edu

This private school was founded in 1952. It has a 60-acre campus.

STUDENTS AND FACULTY

Enrollment: 2,437. **Student Body:** Male 26%, female 74%, out-of-state 3%, international students represent 4 countries. **Ethnic Representation:** African American 12%, Asian 3%, Caucasian 82%, Hispanic 1%. **Retention and Graduation:** 79% freshmen return for sophomore year. 9% grads go on to further study within 1 year. 2% grads pursue business degrees. 2% grads pursue law degrees. **Faculty:** Student/faculty ratio 12:1. 80 full-time faculty, 62% hold PhDs. 100% faculty teach undergrads.

ACADEMICS

Degrees: Associate's, bachelor's, certificate, master's, terminal, transfer. **Academic Requirements:** General education including some course work in arts/fine arts, computer literacy, English (including composition), history, humanities, mathematics, philosophy, sciences (biological or physical), social science. **Classes:** 10-19 students in an average class. **Majors with Highest Enrollment:** Nursing/registered nurse training (RN, ASN, BSN, MSN); information science/studies; legal assistant/paralegal. **Disciplines with Highest Percentage of Degrees Awarded:** Computer and information sciences 43%, interdisciplinary studies 20%, health professions and related sciences 11%, biological life sciences 8%, law/legal studies 7%. **Special Study Options:** Accelerated program, cooperative (work-study) program, double major, dual enrollment, honors program, independent study, internships, liberal arts/career combination, student-designed major, study abroad, teacher certification program, weekend college.

FACILITIES

Housing: Apartments for single students. **Library Holdings:** 124,417 bound volumes. 720 periodicals. 141,646 microforms. 2,288 audiovisuals. **Special Academic Facilities/Equipment:** Art gallery and theatre. **Computers:** School-owned computers available for student use.

EXTRACURRICULARS

Activities: Choral groups, dance, drama/theater, jazz band, literary magazine, music ensembles, pep band, student government, student newspaper, symphony orchestra. **Organizations:** 30 registered organizations, 7 honor societies, 4 religious organizations, 1 sorority (2% women join). **Athletics (Intercollegiate):** *Men:* baseball, basketball, cheerleading, cross-country, golf, lacrosse, soccer, tennis, track & field. *Women:* basketball, cheerleading, cross-country, field hockey, lacrosse, soccer, softball, tennis, track & field, volleyball.

ADMISSIONS

Selectivity Rating: 63 (of 100). **Freshman Academic Profile:** Average high school GPA 3.4. 23% in top 10% of high school class, 51% in top 25% of high school class, 82% in top 50% of high school class. 78% from public high schools. Average SAT I Math 523, SAT I Math middle 50% range 460-580. Average SAT I Verbal 513, SAT I Verbal middle 50% range 450-570. TOEFL required of all international applicants, minimum TOEFL 550. **Basis for Candidate Selection:** *Very important factors considered include:* secondary school record, standardized test scores. *Important factors considered include:* class rank, essays, extracurricular activities, interview, talent/ability. *Other factors considered include:* alumni/ae relation, character/personal qualities, recommendations, volunteer work. **Freshman Admission Requirements:** High school diploma or GED is required. *Academic units required/recommended:* 17 total recommended; 4 English recommended, 3 math recommended, 3 science recommended, 2 science lab recommended, 2 social studies recommended, 1 history recommended, 4 elective recommended. **Freshman Admission Statistics:** 1,494 applied, 83% accepted, 40% of those accepted enrolled. **Transfer Admission Requirements:** *Items required:* high school transcript, college transcript, essay, statement of good standing from prior school. Minimum college GPA of 2.5 required. Lowest grade transferable C. **General Admission Information:** Application fee $25. Priority application deadline March 1. Nonfall registration accepted. Admission may be deferred for a maximum of 1 year. Credit and/or placement offered for CEEB Advanced Placement tests.

COSTS AND FINANCIAL AID

Tuition $11,978. Required fees $820. Average book expense $1,000. **Required Forms and Deadlines:** FAFSA and institution's own financial aid form. Financial aid filing deadline March 1. **Notification of Awards:** Applicants will be notified of awards on a rolling basis beginning on or about March 15. **Types of Aid:** *Need-based scholarships/grants:* Pell, SEOG, state scholarships/grants, private scholarships, the school's own gift aid. *Loans:* FFEL Subsidized Stafford, FFEL Unsubsidized Stafford, FFEL PLUS, Federal Perkins. **Student Employment:** Federal Work-Study Program available. Institutional employment available. Off-campus job opportunities are excellent. **Financial Aid Statistics:** 71% freshmen, 57% undergrads receive some form of aid. Average freshman grant $12,062. Average freshman loan $15,591. Average income from on-campus job $1,774. **Financial Aid Phone:** 410-486-7000.

VILLA MARIA COLLEGE OF BUFFALO

240 Pine Ridge Road, Buffalo, NY 14225
Phone: 716-961-1805 **E-mail:** admissions@villa.edu
Fax: 716-896-0705 **Web:** www.villa.edu

This private school, which is affiliated with the Roman Catholic Church, was founded in 1960.

STUDENTS AND FACULTY

Enrollment: 416. **Student Body:** Male 25%, female 75%. **Ethnic Representation:** African American 25%, Asian 1%, Caucasian 70%, Hispanic 1%. **Faculty:** Student/faculty ratio 7:1. 24 full-time faculty, 20% hold PhDs. 100% faculty teach undergrads.

ACADEMICS

Degrees: Associate's, certificate, terminal, transfer. **Classes:** Under 10 students in an average class. 10-19 students in an average lab/discussion section. **Majors with Highest Enrollment:** Interior design; graphic design; early childhood education and teaching. **Special Study Options:** Cross registration, dual enrollment, internships, liberal arts/career combination, study abroad.

FACILITIES

Library Holdings: 32,000 bound volumes. 200 periodicals. 17,300 microforms. 5,000 audiovisuals. **Special Academic Facilities/Equipment:** Art gallery, music building. **Computers:** School-owned computers available for student use.

EXTRACURRICULARS

Activities: Choral groups, drama/theater, jazz band, literary magazine, music ensembles, musical theater, student government, student newspaper. **Organizations:** 1 honor society.

ADMISSIONS

Selectivity Rating: 63 (of 100). **Freshman Academic Profile:** 4% in top 10% of high school class, 15% in top 25% of high school class, 21% in top 50% of high school class. 95% from public high schools. SAT I Math middle 50% range 340-460. SAT I Verbal middle 50% range 380-480. TOEFL required of all international applicants, minimum TOEFL 450. **Basis for Candidate Selection:** *Important factors considered include:* interview, secondary school record. *Other factors considered include:* alumni/ae relation, character/personal qualities, class rank, essays, extracurricular activities, recommendations, standardized test scores, talent/ability, volunteer work, work experience. **Freshman Admission Requirements:** High school diploma or GED is required. *Academic units required/recommended:* 1 math required, 2 math recommended, 1 science required, 2 science recommended, 4 social studies required. **Freshman Admission Statistics:** 233 applied, 85% accepted, 58% of those accepted enrolled. **Transfer Admission Requirements:** *Items required:* high school transcript, college transcript, interview. Lowest grade transferable C. **General Admission Information:** Application fee $35. Nonfall registration accepted.

COSTS AND FINANCIAL AID

Tuition $9,200. Required fees $400. Average book expense $1,000. **Required Forms and Deadlines:** FAFSA and state aid form. No deadline for regular filing. **Notification of Awards:** Applicants will be notified of awards on or about May 1. **Types of Aid:** *Need-based scholarships/grants:* Pell, SEOG, state scholarships/grants, private scholarships, the school's own gift aid. *Loans:* FFEL Subsidized Stafford, FFEL PLUS. **Student Employment:** Federal Work-Study Program available. Off-campus job opportunities are fair. **Financial Aid Phone:** 716-961-1849.

VILLANOVA UNIVERSITY

800 Lancaster Avenue, Villanova, PA 19085-1672
Phone: 610-519-4000 **E-mail:** gotovu@villanova.edu **CEEB Code:** 2959
Fax: 610-519-6450 **Web:** www.villanova.edu **ACT Code:** 3744

This private school, which is affiliated with the Roman Catholic Church, was founded in 1842. It has a 254-acre campus.

STUDENTS AND FACULTY

Enrollment: 7,375. **Student Body:** Male 49%, female 51%, out-of-state 66%, international 2%. **Ethnic Representation:** African American 3%, Asian 5%, Caucasian 85%, Hispanic 6%. **Retention and Graduation:** 93% freshmen return for sophomore year. 80% freshmen graduate within 4 years. 14% grads go on to further study within 1 year. 1% grads pursue business degrees. 5% grads pursue law degrees. 3% grads pursue medical degrees. **Faculty:** Student/faculty ratio 13:1. 511 full-time faculty. 100% faculty teach undergrads.

ACADEMICS

Degrees: Associate's, bachelor's, doctoral, first professional, master's, post-bachelor's certificate, post-master's certificate. **Academic Requirements:** General education including some course work in English (including composition), foreign languages, history, humanities, mathematics, philosophy, sciences (biological or physical), social science, and core humanities including philosophy, ethics, religious studies. **Classes:** 10-19 students in an average class. 10-19 students in an average lab/discussion section. **Majors with Highest Enrollment:** Biology/biological sciences, general; psychology, general; finance, general. **Disciplines with Highest Percentage of Degrees Awarded:** Business/marketing 37%, engineering/engineering technology 11%, communications/communication technologies 10%, social sciences and history 10%, liberal arts/general studies 5%. **Special Study Options:** Accelerated program, cross registration, distance learning, double major, dual enrollment, English as a second language, honors program, independent study, internships, study abroad, teacher certification program.

FACILITIES

Housing: Coed, all-female, all-male, apartments for single students, housing for disabled students. **Library Holdings:** 860,000 bound volumes. 5,400 periodicals. 12,200 audiovisuals. **Special Academic Facilities/Equipment:** Augustinian historical museum, two observatories, art gallery, Center for Instructional Technologies, Math-Learning Resource Center, Writing Center. **Computers:** *Recommended operating system:* Windows 98. School-owned computers available for student use.

EXTRACURRICULARS

Activities: Choral groups, concert band, dance, drama/theater, jazz band, literary magazine, music ensembles, musical theater, pep band, radio station, student government, student newspaper, television station, yearbook. **Organizations:** 130 registered organizations, 31 honor societies, 23 religious organizations, 7 fraternities (6% men join), 8 sororities (25% women join). **Athletics (Intercollegiate):** *Men:* baseball, basketball, cheerleading, cross-country, diving, football, golf, indoor track, lacrosse, soccer, swimming, tennis, track & field, volleyball. *Women:* basketball, cheerleading, crew, cross-country, diving, field hockey, indoor track, lacrosse, soccer, softball, swimming, tennis, track & field, volleyball, water polo.

ADMISSIONS

Selectivity Rating: 83 (of 100). **Freshman Academic Profile:** Average high school GPA 3.6. 41% in top 10% of high school class, 57% in top 25% of high school class, 96% in top 50% of high school class. 55% from public high schools. Average SAT I Math 633, SAT I Math middle 50% range 610-680. Average SAT I Verbal 605, SAT I Verbal middle 50% range 580-650. Average ACT 27. TOEFL required of all international applicants, minimum TOEFL 550. **Basis for Candidate Selection:** *Other factors considered include:* alumni/ae relation, character/personal qualities, class rank, essays, extracurricular activities, geographical residence, minority status, recommendations, secondary school record, standardized test scores, volunteer work, work experience. **Freshman Admission Requirements:** High school diploma or GED is required. *Academic units required/recommended:* 18 total required; 20 total recommended; 4 English required, 4 math required, 4 science required, 2 science lab required, 3 science lab recommended, 2 foreign language required, 4 foreign language recommended. **Freshman Admission Statistics:** 10,897 applied, 47% accepted, 31% of those accepted enrolled. **Transfer Admission Requirements:** *Items required:* high school transcript, college transcript, essay, standardized test score, statement of good standing from prior school. Lowest grade transferable C. **General Admission Information:** Application fee $60. Regular application deadline January 7. Admission may be deferred for a maximum of 1 year. Credit and/or placement offered for CEEB Advanced Placement tests.

COSTS AND FINANCIAL AID

Average book expense $800. **Required Forms and Deadlines:** FAFSA and institution's own financial aid form. Financial aid filing deadline February 15. **Notification of Awards:** Applicants will be notified of awards on or about April 1. **Types of Aid:** *Need-based scholarships/grants:* Pell, SEOG, state scholarships/grants, private scholarships, the school's own gift aid. *Loans:* Direct Subsidized Stafford, Direct Unsubsidized Stafford, Direct PLUS, FFEL Subsidized Stafford, FFEL Unsubsidized Stafford, FFEL PLUS, Federal Perkins, state loans. **Student Employment:** Federal Work-Study Program available. Institutional employment available. Off-campus job opportunities are excellent. **Financial Aid Statistics:** 47% freshmen, 47% undergrads receive some form of aid. **Financial Aid Phone:** 610-519-4010.

VIRGINIA COMMONWEALTH UNIVERSITY

821 West Franklin Street, PO Box 842526, Richmond, VA 23284
Phone: 804-828-1222 **E-mail:** vcuinfo@vcu.edu **CEEB Code:** 5570
Fax: 804-828-1899 **Web:** www.vcu.edu

This public school was founded in 1838. It has a 131-acre campus.

STUDENTS AND FACULTY

Enrollment: 18,069. **Student Body:** Male 42%, female 58%, out-of-state 6%, international 1% (61 countries represented). **Ethnic Representation:** African American 22%, Asian 8%, Caucasian 64%, Hispanic 3%, Native American 1%. **Retention and Graduation:** 79% freshmen return for sophomore year. **Faculty:** Student/faculty ratio 13:1. 1,078 full-time faculty.

ACADEMICS

Degrees: Bachelor's, doctoral, first professional, master's, post-bachelor's certificate, post-master's certificate. **Academic Requirements:** General education including some course work in arts/fine arts, English (including composition), humanities, mathematics, sciences (biological or physical). **Classes:** 10-19 students in an average class. 20-29 students in an average lab/ discussion section. **Majors with Highest Enrollment:** Communications, journalism, and related fields; biological and physical sciences; psychology, general. **Disciplines with Highest Percentage of Degrees Awarded:** Visual and performing arts 16%, business/marketing 11%, psychology 11%, health professions and related sciences 11%, computer and information sciences 8%. **Special Study Options:** Accelerated program, cooperative (work-study) program, cross registration, distance learning, double major, dual enrollment, English as a second language, student exchange program (domestic), honors program, independent study, internships, student-designed major, study abroad, teacher certification program, weekend college.

FACILITIES

Housing: Coed, all-female, all-male, housing for disabled students, honors program, engineering, life sciences. **Library Holdings:** 1,738,178 bound volumes. 13,886 periodicals. 3,083,153 microforms. 44,434 audiovisuals. **Special Academic Facilities/Equipment:** Anderson Gallery, Kiosks Student Art Gallery, Larrick Student Center. **Computers:** School-owned computers available for student use.

EXTRACURRICULARS

Activities: Choral groups, concert band, dance, drama/theater, jazz band, literary magazine, music ensembles, opera, radio station, student government, student newspaper. **Organizations:** 207 registered organizations, 30 honor societies, 24 religious organizations, 11 fraternities (2% men join), 9 sororities (3% women join). **Athletics (Intercollegiate):** *Men:* baseball, basketball, cheerleading, cross-country, fencing, golf, rugby, soccer, softball, tennis, track & field, water polo. *Women:* basketball, cheerleading, cross-country, fencing, field hockey, soccer, softball, tennis, track & field, volleyball, water polo.

ADMISSIONS

Selectivity Rating: 64 (of 100). **Freshman Academic Profile:** Average high school GPA 3.1. 14% in top 10% of high school class, 38% in top 25% of high school class, 79% in top 50% of high school class. Average SAT I Math 520, SAT I Math middle 50% range 460-580. Average SAT I Verbal 531, SAT I Verbal middle 50% range 470-590. Average ACT 21, ACT middle 50% range 19-23. TOEFL required of all international applicants, minimum TOEFL 550. **Basis for Candidate Selection:** *Very important factors considered include:* secondary school record, talent/ability. *Important factors considered include:* standardized test scores. *Other factors considered include:* class rank, essays, extracurricular activities, interview, recommendations, volunteer work, work experience. **Freshman Admission Requirements:** High school diploma or GED is required. *Academic units required/recommended:* 20 total required; 23 total recommended; 4 English required, 4 English recommended, 3 math required, 4 math recommended, 2 science required, 4 science recommended, 1 science lab required, 1 science lab recommended, 3 foreign language recommended, 1 social studies recommended, 3 history required, 3 history recommended. **Freshman Admission Statistics:** 8,540 applied, 73% accepted, 49% of those accepted enrolled. **Transfer Admission Requirements:** *Items required:* college transcript. Minimum high school GPA of 2.0 required. Minimum college GPA of 2.0 required. Lowest grade transferable C. **General Admission Information:** Application fee $30. Early decision application deadline November 1. Nonfall registration accepted. Admission may be deferred for a maximum of 1 year. Credit and/or placement offered for CEEB Advanced Placement tests.

COSTS AND FINANCIAL AID

In-state tuition $3,016. Out-of-state tuition $13,986. Room & board $5,750. Required fees $1,202. Average book expense $830. **Required Forms and Deadlines:** FAFSA. Priority filing deadline April 1. **Notification of Awards:** Applicants will be notified of awards on or about April 1. **Types of Aid:** *Need-based scholarships/grants:* Pell, SEOG, state scholarships/grants, private scholarships, the school's own gift aid, United Negro College Fund, Federal Nursing. *Loans:* Direct Subsidized Stafford, Direct Unsubsidized Stafford, Direct PLUS, Federal Perkins, Federal Nursing, state loans, college/university loans from institutional funds. **Student Employment:** Federal Work-Study Program available. Institutional employment available. Off-campus job opportunities are excellent. **Financial Aid Statistics:** 55% freshmen, 54% undergrads receive some form of aid. Average freshman grant $4,083. Average freshman loan $3,283. **Financial Aid Phone:** 804-828-6669.

VIRGINIA INTERMONT COLLEGE

1013 Moore Street, Campus Box D-460, Bristol, VA 24201-4298
Phone: 276-466-7856 **E-mail:** viadmit@vic.edu **CEEB Code:** 5857
Fax: 276-466-7855 **Web:** www.vic.edu **ACT Code:** 4416

This private school, which is affiliated with the Baptist Church, was founded in 1884. It has a 27-acre campus.

STUDENTS AND FACULTY

Enrollment: 918. **Student Body:** Male 25%, female 75%, out-of-state 36%, international 3%. **Ethnic Representation:** African American 4%, Caucasian 95%. **Retention and Graduation:** 50% freshmen return for sophomore year. 22% freshmen graduate within 4 years. 20% grads go on to further study within 1 year. 6% grads pursue business degrees. 4% grads pursue law degrees. 2% grads pursue medical degrees. **Faculty:** Student/faculty ratio 11:1. 43 full-time faculty, 44% hold PhDs. 100% faculty teach undergrads.

ACADEMICS

Degrees: Associate's, bachelor's. **Academic Requirements:** General education including some course work in arts/fine arts, computer literacy, English (including composition), history, humanities, mathematics, philosophy, sciences (biological or physical), social science, physical education. **Classes:** Under 10 students in an average class. Under 10 students in an average lab/ discussion section. **Majors with Highest Enrollment:** Business administration/management; equestrian/equine studies; photography. **Disciplines with Highest Percentage of Degrees Awarded:** Business/marketing 32%, education 17%, agriculture 13%, visual and performing arts 12%, interdisciplinary studies 7%. **Special Study Options:** Cooperative (work-study) program, double major, English as a second language, independent study, internships, liberal arts/career combination, study abroad, teacher certification program, weekend college.

FACILITIES

Housing: Coed, all-female, all-male. **Library Holdings:** 59,525 bound volumes. 276 periodicals. 9,205 microforms. 4,650 audiovisuals. **Special Academic Facilities/Equipment:** Museum/gallery, 129-acre riding center for equestrian program, newly constructed Fine Arts Center, fully equipped modern fitness center. **Computers:** School-owned computers available for student use.

EXTRACURRICULARS

Activities: Choral groups, dance, drama/theater, literary magazine, musical theater, student government, yearbook. **Organizations:** 26 registered organizations, 4 honor societies, 2 religious organizations, 10% women join sororities. **Athletics (Intercollegiate):** *Men:* baseball, basketball, equestrian, golf, soccer, tennis. *Women:* basketball, equestrian, soccer, softball, tennis, volleyball.

ADMISSIONS

Selectivity Rating: 69 (of 100). **Freshman Academic Profile:** Average high school GPA 3.0. 5% in top 10% of high school class, 17% in top 25% of high school class, 60% in top 50% of high school class. 85% from public high schools. Average SAT I Math 455, SAT I Math middle 50% range 410-500. Average SAT I Verbal 490, SAT I Verbal middle 50% range 430-550. Average ACT 20, ACT middle 50% range 17-22. TOEFL required of all international applicants, minimum TOEFL 400. **Basis for Candidate Selection:** *Very important factors considered include:* secondary school record. *Important factors considered include:* class rank, standardized test scores. *Other factors considered include:* alumni/ae relation, character/personal qualities, essays, extracurricular activities, interview, recommendations, talent/ability, volunteer work, work experience. **Freshman Admission Requirements:** High school diploma or GED is required. *Academic units required/recommended:* 15 total required; 4 English required, 2 math required, 1 science required, 1 science lab required, 2 social studies required, 6 elective required. **Freshman Admission Statistics:** 661 applied, 67% accepted, 36% of those accepted enrolled. **Transfer Admission Requirements:** *Items required:* college transcript. Minimum college GPA of 2.0 required. Lowest grade transferable C. **General Admission Information:** Application fee $15. Nonfall registration accepted. Admission may be deferred for a maximum of 1 year. Credit and/or placement offered for CEEB Advanced Placement tests.

COSTS AND FINANCIAL AID

Tuition $11,890. Room & board $5,300. Required fees $320. Average book expense $800. **Required Forms and Deadlines:** FAFSA, institution's own financial aid form and state aid form. Financial aid filing deadline June 30. Priority filing deadline April 15. **Notification of Awards:** Applicants will be notified of awards on a rolling basis beginning on or about March 15. **Types of**

Aid: *Need-based scholarships/grants:* Pell, SEOG, state scholarships/grants, private scholarships, the school's own gift aid. *Loans:* FFEL Subsidized Stafford, FFEL Unsubsidized Stafford, FFEL PLUS, Federal Perkins. **Student Employment:** Federal Work-Study Program available. Institutional employment available. Off-campus job opportunities are good. **Financial Aid Statistics:** 53% freshmen, 70% undergrads receive some form of aid. Average freshman grant $7,526. Average freshman loan $3,207. Average income from on-campus job $1,500. **Financial Aid Phone:** 276-669-6101.

VIRGINIA MILITARY INSTITUTE

VMI Office of Admissions, Lexington, VA 24450-0304
Phone: 540-464-7211 **E-mail:** admissions@mail.vmi.edu **CEEB Code:** 5858
Fax: 540-464-7746 **Web:** www.vmi.edu **ACT Code:** 4418

This public school was founded in 1839. It has a 140-acre campus.

STUDENTS AND FACULTY

Enrollment: 1,299. **Student Body:** Out-of-state 49%, international 3% (12 countries represented). **Ethnic Representation:** African American 6%, Asian 3%, Caucasian 87%, Hispanic 3%, Native American 1%. **Retention and Graduation:** 87% freshmen return for sophomore year. 16% grads go on to further study within 1 year. 2% grads pursue law degrees. 2% grads pursue medical degrees. **Faculty:** Student/faculty ratio 11:1. 102 full-time faculty, 95% hold PhDs. 100% faculty teach undergrads.

ACADEMICS

Degrees: Bachelor's. **Academic Requirements:** General education including some course work in English (including composition), foreign languages, history, mathematics, sciences (biological or physical), ROTC, physical education. **Classes:** 10-19 students in an average class. **Majors with Highest Enrollment:** Business/managerial economics; history, general; mechanical engineering. **Disciplines with Highest Percentage of Degrees Awarded:** Social sciences and history 49%, engineering/engineering technology 23%, psychology 10%, computer and information sciences 5%, biological life sciences 5%. **Special Study Options:** Accelerated program, double major, student exchange program (domestic), honors program, independent study, internships, study abroad, teacher certification program, Summer Transition Program (optional for incoming freshmen).

FACILITIES

Housing: Barracks (3-5 students/room). **Library Holdings:** 162,053 bound volumes. 785 periodicals. 18,137 microforms. 4,896 audiovisuals. **Special Academic Facilities/Equipment:** VMI Museum, George C. Marshall Museum. **Computers:** *Recommended operating system:* Windows 95. School-owned computers available for student use.

EXTRACURRICULARS

Activities: Choral groups, concert band, drama/theater, jazz band, literary magazine, marching band, music ensembles, musical theater, pep band, student government, student newspaper, yearbook. **Organizations:** 47 registered organizations, 11 honor societies, 3 religious organizations. **Athletics (Intercollegiate):** *Men:* baseball, basketball, cross-country, football, golf, indoor track, lacrosse, rifle, soccer, swimming, tennis, track & field, wrestling. *Women:* cross-country, indoor track, rifle, soccer, swimming, track & field.

ADMISSIONS

Selectivity Rating: 77 (of 100). **Freshman Academic Profile:** Average high school GPA 3.3. 14% in top 10% of high school class, 28% in top 25% of high school class, 44% in top 50% of high school class. 84% from public high schools. Average SAT I Math 564, SAT I Math middle 50% range 530-660. Average SAT I Verbal 570. Average ACT 23, ACT middle 50% range 20-27. TOEFL required of all international applicants, minimum TOEFL 500. **Basis for Candidate Selection:** *Very important factors considered include:* character/personal qualities, class rank, secondary school record, standardized test scores. *Important factors considered include:* extracurricular activities, interview, minority status, state residency, volunteer work. *Other factors considered include:* alumni/ae relation, geographical residence, recommendations, talent/ability. **Freshman Admission Requirements:** High school diploma is required and GED is not accepted. *Academic units required/recommended:* 4 English required, 3 math required, 4 math recommended, 3 science required, 3 science lab required, 3 foreign language required, 4 foreign language recommended. **Freshman Admission Statistics:** 1,479 applied, 55% accepted. **Transfer Admission Requirements:** *Items required:* high school transcript, college transcript, standardized test scores. Minimum college GPA of 2.0 required. Lowest grade transferable C. **General Admission Information:** Application fee $35. Early decision application deadline November 15. Regular application deadline March 1. Credit and/or placement offered for CEEB Advanced Placement tests.

COSTS AND FINANCIAL AID

In-state tuition $2,924. Out-of-state tuition $13,992. Room & board $4,838. Required fees $2,206. Average book expense $650. **Required Forms and Deadlines:** FAFSA. Financial aid filing deadline March 1. Priority filing deadline March 1. **Notification of Awards:** Applicants will be notified of awards on a rolling basis beginning on or about March 15. **Types of Aid:** *Need-based scholarships/grants:* Pell, SEOG, state scholarships/grants, private scholarships, the school's own gift aid. *Loans:* Direct Subsidized Stafford, Direct Unsubsidized Stafford, Direct PLUS, Federal Perkins. **Student Employment:** Federal Work-Study Program available. Institutional employment available. Off-campus job opportunities are poor. **Financial Aid Statistics:** 44% freshmen, 41% undergrads receive some form of aid. Average freshman grant $10,243. Average freshman loan $3,012. Average income from on-campus job $825. **Financial Aid Phone:** 540-464-7208.

VIRGINIA STATE UNIVERSITY

One Hayden Street, PO Box 9018, Petersburg, VA 23806
Phone: 804-524-5902 **E-mail:** admiss@vsu.edu **CEEB Code:** 5860
Fax: 804-524-5055 **Web:** www.vsu.edu **ACT Code:** 4424

This public school was founded in 1882. It has a 246-acre campus.

STUDENTS AND FACULTY

Enrollment: 3,853. **Student Body:** Male 44%, female 56%, out-of-state 36%. **Ethnic Representation:** African American 97%, Caucasian 2%, Hispanic 1%. **Retention and Graduation:** 73% freshmen return for sophomore year. 19% freshmen graduate within 4 years. **Faculty:** Student/faculty ratio 18:1. 207 full-time faculty, 79% hold PhDs. 100% faculty teach undergrads.

ACADEMICS

Degrees: Bachelor's, doctoral, master's, post-master's certificate. **Academic Requirements:** General education including some course work in arts/fine arts, English (including composition), foreign languages, history, humanities, mathematics, sciences (biological or physical), social science. **Classes:** 20-29 students in an average class. 20-29 students in an average lab/discussion section. **Majors with Highest Enrollment:** Business administration/management; physical education teaching and coaching; psychology, general. **Disciplines with Highest Percentage of Degrees Awarded:** Business/marketing 20%, social sciences and history 18%, education 14%, liberal arts/general studies 10%, psychology 6%. **Special Study Options:** Cooperative (work-study) program, double major, dual enrollment, student exchange program (domestic), honors program, independent study, internships, teacher certification program.

FACILITIES

Housing: Coed, all-female, all-male, apartments for single students. **Library Holdings:** 880,742 bound volumes. 82,110 periodicals. 689,736 microforms. 892 audiovisuals. **Computers:** *Recommended operating system:* Mac. School-owned computers available for student use.

EXTRACURRICULARS

Activities: Choral groups, concert band, dance, drama/theater, jazz band, literary magazine, marching band, music ensembles, pep band, radio station, student government, student newspaper, television station, yearbook. **Organizations:** 99 registered organizations, 6 honor societies, 4 religious organizations, 5 fraternities (10% men join), 4 sororities (10% women join). **Athletics (Intercollegiate):** *Men:* baseball, basketball, cross-country, football, golf, indoor track, tennis, track & field. *Women:* basketball, cheerleading, cross-country, golf, indoor track, softball, tennis, track & field, volleyball.

ADMISSIONS

Selectivity Rating: 63 (of 100). **Freshman Academic Profile:** Average high school GPA 2.6. 4% in top 10% of high school class, 13% in top 25% of high school class, 49% in top 50% of high school class. Average SAT I Math 387, SAT I Math middle 50% range 350-440. Average SAT I Verbal 402, SAT I Verbal middle 50% range 360-450. Average ACT 15, ACT middle 50% range 14-19. TOEFL required of all international applicants, minimum TOEFL 500. **Basis for Candidate Selection:** *Very important factors considered include:* essays, recommendations, secondary school record, standardized test scores. *Other factors considered include:* alumni/ae relation, character/personal qualities, class rank, extracurricular activities, geographical residence, state residency, talent/ability, volunteer work, work experience. **Freshman Admission Requirements:** High school diploma or GED is required. *Academic units required/recommended:* 11 total required; 4 English required, 3 math required, 2 science required, 1 science lab required, 2 foreign language recommended, 2 social studies required. **Freshman Admission Statistics:** 3,780 applied, 66% accepted, 46% of those accepted enrolled. **Transfer Admission Requirements:** *Items required:* college transcript. Minimum college GPA of 2.0 required. Lowest grade transferable C. **General Admission Information:** Application fee $25. Priority application deadline March 31. Regular application deadline May 1. Nonfall registration accepted. Credit offered for CEEB Advanced Placement tests.

COSTS AND FINANCIAL AID

In-state tuition $2,030. Out-of-state tuition $8,624. Room & board $5,694. Required fees $1,774. Average book expense $700. **Required Forms and Deadlines:** FAFSA and institution's own financial aid form. Financial aid filing deadline March 31. Priority filing deadline May 1. **Notification of Awards:** Applicants will be notified of awards on a rolling basis beginning on or about May 1. **Types of Aid:** *Need-based scholarships/grants:* Pell, SEOG, state scholarships/grants, private scholarships, the school's own gift aid. *Loans:* Direct Subsidized Stafford, Direct Unsubsidized Stafford, Direct PLUS, college/university loans from institutional funds. **Student Employment:** Federal Work-Study Program available. Institutional employment available. Off-campus job opportunities are fair. **Financial Aid Statistics:** 86% freshmen, 85% undergrads receive some form of aid. Average freshman grant $5,315. Average freshman loan $2,232. Average income from on-campus job $2,000. **Financial Aid Phone:** 804-524-5990.

VIRGINIA TECH

Undergraduate Admissions, 201 Burruss Hall, Blacksburg, VA 24061
Phone: 540-231-6267 **E-mail:** vtadmiss@vt.edu **CEEB Code:** 5859
Fax: 540-231-3242 **Web:** www.vt.edu **ACT Code:** 4420

This public school was founded in 1872. It has a 2,600-acre campus.

STUDENTS AND FACULTY

Enrollment: 21,468. **Student Body:** Male 59%, female 41%, out-of-state 27%, international 3%. **Ethnic Representation:** African American 6%, Asian 7%, Caucasian 82%, Hispanic 2%. **Retention and Graduation:** 87% freshmen return for sophomore year. 40% freshmen graduate within 4 years. 19% grads go on to further study within 1 year. **Faculty:** Student/faculty ratio 15:1. 1,295 full-time faculty, 89% hold PhDs. 75% faculty teach undergrads.

ACADEMICS

Degrees: Associate's, bachelor's, doctoral, first professional, master's, post-master's certificate, terminal. **Academic Requirements:** General education including some course work in arts/fine arts, English (including composition), foreign languages, mathematics, sciences (biological or physical), social science. **Majors with Highest Enrollment:** Communications studies/speech communication and rhetoric; engineering, general; biology/biological sciences, general. **Disciplines with Highest Percentage of Degrees Awarded:** Business/marketing 24%, engineering/engineering technology 21%, home economics and vocational home economics 9%, social sciences and history 7%, biological life sciences 6%. **Special Study Options:** Accelerated program, cooperative (work-study) program, distance learning, double major, English as a second language, student exchange program (domestic), honors program, independent study, internships, student-designed major, study abroad, teacher certification program.

FACILITIES

Housing: Coed, all-female, all-male, housing for international students, fraternities and/or sororities, housing for Corps of Cadets and athletes, The World (a cross cultural environment), The W.E.L.L. (a personal health/development community), The Wing (a transitional/orientation community for freshmen), Residential Leadership Community, Biological & Life Sciences Learning Community, Virginia Tech Design Collaborative. **Library Holdings:** 2,098,075 bound volumes. 17,562 periodicals. 6,182,267 microforms. 19,206 audiovisuals. **Special Academic Facilities/Equipment:** Art gallery, digital music facilities, multimedia labs, Black Cultural Center, television studio, anaerobic lab, CAD-CAM labs, observatory, wind tunnel, farms, Math Emporium, the CAVE (virtual reality learning facility). **Computers:** School-owned computers available for student use.

EXTRACURRICULARS

Activities: Choral groups, concert band, dance, drama/theater, jazz band, literary magazine, marching band, music ensembles, musical theater, pep band, radio station, student government, student newspaper, symphony orchestra, television station, yearbook. **Organizations:** 600 registered organizations, 35 honor societies, 26 religious organizations, 34 fraternities (13% men join), 16 sororities (15% women join). **Athletics (Intercollegiate):** *Men:* baseball, basketball, cheerleading, cross-country, diving, football, golf, lacrosse, soccer, swimming, tennis, track & field, wrestling. *Women:* basketball, cheerleading, cross-country, diving, lacrosse, soccer, softball, swimming, tennis, track & field, volleyball.

ADMISSIONS

Selectivity Rating: 84 (of 100). **Freshman Academic Profile:** Average high school GPA 3.6. 40% in top 10% of high school class, 80% in top 25% of high school class, 99% in top 50% of high school class. 95% from public high schools. Average SAT I Math 650, SAT I Math middle 50% range 570-650. Average SAT I Verbal 600, SAT I Verbal middle 50% range 540-630. TOEFL required of all international applicants, minimum TOEFL 550. **Basis for Candidate Selection:** *Very important factors considered include:* secondary school record, standardized test scores. *Important factors considered include:* class rank. *Other factors considered include:* alumni/ae relation, essays, extracurricular activities, geographical residence, minority status, recommendations, state residency, talent/ability, volunteer work, work experience. **Freshman Admission Requirements:** High school diploma or GED is required. *Academic units required/recommended:* 18 total required; 4 English required, 3 math required, 2 science required, 3 science recommended, 2 science lab required, 3 foreign language recommended, 1 social studies required, 1 history required, 3 elective required. **Freshman Admission Statistics:** 17,770 applied, 68% accepted, 39% of those accepted enrolled. **Transfer Admission Requirements:** *Items required:* college transcript, essay. Minimum college GPA of 2.0 required. Lowest grade transferable C. **General Admission Information:** Application fee $40. Early decision application deadline November 1. Regular application deadline January 15. Nonfall registration accepted. Admission may be deferred for a maximum of 1 year. Credit and/or placement offered for CEEB Advanced Placement tests.

COSTS AND FINANCIAL AID

In-state tuition $3,444. Out-of-state tuition $13,060. Room & board $4,070. Required fees $892. Average book expense $900. **Required Forms and Deadlines:** FAFSA and general scholarship. Financial aid filing deadline March 11. Priority filing deadline February 1. **Notification of Awards:** Applicants will be notified of awards on or about April 15. **Types of Aid:** *Need-based scholarships/grants:* Pell, SEOG, state scholarships/grants, private scholarships, the school's own gift aid, cadet scholarships/grants. *Loans:* Direct Subsidized Stafford, Direct Unsubsidized Stafford, Direct PLUS, FFEL PLUS, Federal Perkins, college/university loans from institutional funds. **Student Employment:** Federal Work-Study Program available. Institutional employment available. Off-campus job opportunities are good. **Financial Aid Statistics:** 43% freshmen, 45% undergrads receive some form of aid. Average freshman grant $9,030. Average freshman loan $11,625. Average income from on-campus job $1,500. **Financial Aid Phone:** 540-231-5179.

VIRGINIA UNION UNIVERSITY

1500 North Lombardy Street, Richmond, VA 23220
Phone: 804-257-5881 **E-mail:** admissions@vuu.edu
Fax: 804-257-5808 **Web:** www.vuu.edu

This private school is affiliated with the Baptist Church.

STUDENTS AND FACULTY

Enrollment: 1,307. **Student Body:** Out-of-state 51%, international 1%. **Ethnic Representation:** African American 98%, Caucasian 1%, Hispanic 1%.

ACADEMICS

Degrees: Bachelor's, doctoral, master's.

ADMISSIONS

Selectivity Rating: 60 (of 100). **Freshman Academic Profile:** Average high school GPA 2.5. 22% in top 25% of high school class, 85% from public high schools. Average SAT I Math 416. Average SAT I Verbal 420. Average ACT 18. TOEFL required of all international applicants, minimum TOEFL 500. **General Admission Information:** Regular application deadline June 1. Credit and/or placement offered for CEEB Advanced Placement tests.

COSTS AND FINANCIAL AID

Room & board $3,950. Average book expense $500. **Student Employment:** Federal Work-Study Program available. Off-campus job opportunities are good. **Financial Aid Statistics:** Average freshman grant $1,189. Average freshman loan $1,376. Average income from on-campus job $1,400. **Financial Aid Phone:** 804-257-5882.

VIRGINIA WESLEYAN COLLEGE

1584 Wesleyan Drive, Norfolk/Virginia Beach, VA 23502-5599
Phone: 757-455-3208 **E-mail:** admissions@vwc.edu **CEEB Code:** 5867
Fax: 757-461-5238 **Web:** www.vwc.edu **ACT Code:** 4429

This private school, which is affiliated with the Methodist Church, was founded in 1961. It has a 300-acre campus.

STUDENTS AND FACULTY

Enrollment: 1,396. **Student Body:** Male 32%, female 68%, out-of-state 20%, international 1%. **Ethnic Representation:** African American 15%, Asian 2%, Caucasian 78%, Hispanic 3%, Native American 1%. **Retention and Graduation:** 27% grads go on to further study within 1 year. 5% grads pursue business degrees. 3% grads pursue law degrees. 2% grads pursue medical degrees. **Faculty:** Student/faculty ratio 13:1. 74 full-time faculty, 85% hold PhDs. 100% faculty teach undergrads.

ACADEMICS

Degrees: Bachelor's. **Academic Requirements:** General education including some course work in arts/fine arts, English (including composition), foreign languages, history, humanities, mathematics, sciences (biological or physical), freshman seminar (1-credit course providing orientation to education, cultural, and social opportunities), senior integrative experience (capstone experience designed to employ insights and methods of various disciplines toward understanding issues and problems of the modern world). **Classes:** 10-19 students in an average class. **Majors with Highest Enrollment:** Business, management, marketing, and related support services; multi/interdisciplinary studies; social sciences. **Disciplines with Highest Percentage of Degrees Awarded:** Business/marketing 24%, social sciences and history 20%, interdisciplinary studies 11%, communications/communication technologies 9%, psychology 6%. **Special Study Options:** Cross registration, distance learning, double major, honors program, independent study, internships, liberal arts/career combination, student-designed major, study abroad, teacher certification program, externships; PORTfolio, a 4-year competitive honors program designed to integrate liberal arts and experiential learning.

FACILITIES

Housing: Coed, all-female, all-male, housing for disabled students, fraternities and/or sororities. **Library Holdings:** 130,352 bound volumes. 617 periodicals. 15,789 microforms. 3,521 audiovisuals. **Special Academic Facilities/ Equipment:** Greenhouse, language lab, teleconferencing facility, social science teaching and learning lab, radio station, TV studio, Barclay Sheaks Art Gallery, computerized classroom, Internet access all classrooms, 24-hour computer lab, Lambuth M. Clarke Hall with state-of-the-art teaching technologies, three academic villages combining residences and campus offices and services. **Computers:** *Recommended operating system:* Windows NT/2000. School-owned computers available for student use.

EXTRACURRICULARS

Activities: Choral groups, concert band, dance, drama/theater, literary magazine, music ensembles, musical theater, radio station, student government, student newspaper, yearbook. **Organizations:** 60 registered organizations, 16 honor societies, 2 religious organizations, 2 fraternities (9% men join), 4 sororities (8% women join). **Athletics (Intercollegiate):** *Men:* baseball, basketball, cheerleading, cross-country, golf, lacrosse, soccer, tennis. *Women:* basketball, cheerleading, cross-country, field hockey, lacrosse, soccer, softball, tennis, volleyball.

ADMISSIONS

Selectivity Rating: 67 (of 100). **Freshman Academic Profile:** 65% from public high schools. TOEFL required of all international applicants, minimum TOEFL 550. **Basis for Candidate Selection:** *Very important factors considered include:* secondary school record. *Important factors considered include:* class rank, essays, extracurricular activities, recommendations, standardized test scores. *Other factors considered include:* alumni/ae relation, character/personal qualities, interview, talent/ability, volunteer work, work experience. **Freshman Admission Requirements:** High school diploma or GED is required. *Academic units required/recommended:* 12 total required; 19 total recommended; 4 English required, 3 math required, 2 science required, 3 science recommended, 2 science lab required, 3 science lab recommended, 3 foreign language recommended, 2 social studies recommended, 1 history required. **Freshman Admission Statistics:** 977 applied, 79% accepted, 37% of those accepted enrolled. **Transfer Admission Requirements:** *Items required:* college transcript, essay, statement of good standing from prior school. Minimum high school GPA of 2.5 required. Minimum college GPA of 2.0 required. Lowest grade transferable C. **General Admission Information:** Application fee $40. Priority application deadline March 1. Nonfall registration accepted. Credit and/or placement offered for CEEB Advanced Placement tests.

COSTS AND FINANCIAL AID

Tuition $19,200. Room & board $6,150. Required fees $0. Average book expense $750. **Required Forms and Deadlines:** FAFSA and state aid form. No deadline for regular filing. Priority filing deadline March 1. **Notification of Awards:** Applicants will be notified of awards on a rolling basis beginning on or about February 15. **Types of Aid:** *Need-based scholarships/grants:* Pell, SEOG, state scholarships/grants, private scholarships, the school's own gift aid. *Loans:* FFEL Subsidized Stafford, FFEL Unsubsidized Stafford, FFEL PLUS, Federal Perkins. **Student Employment:** Federal Work-Study Program available. Off-campus job opportunities are excellent. **Financial Aid Statistics:** 75% freshmen, 77% undergrads receive some form of aid. Average freshman grant $17,281. Average freshman loan $3,121. Average income from on-campus job $1,200. **Financial Aid Phone:** 757-455-3345.

VITERBO UNIVERSITY

815 9th Street South, La Crosse, WI 54601
Phone: 608-796-3010 **E-mail:** admission@viterbo.edu **CEEB Code:** 1878
Fax: 608-796-3020 **Web:** www.viterbo.edu **ACT Code:** 4662

This private school, which is affiliated with the Roman Catholic Church, was founded in 1890. It has a 13-acre campus.

STUDENTS AND FACULTY

Enrollment: 1,734. **Student Body:** Male 24%, female 76%, out-of-state 25%, international 1%. **Ethnic Representation:** African American 1%, Asian 2%, Caucasian 85%, Hispanic 2%. **Retention and Graduation:** 67% freshmen return for sophomore year. 30% freshmen graduate within 4 years. 9% grads go on to further study within 1 year. 2% grads pursue business degrees. 1% grads pursue law degrees. 3% grads pursue medical degrees. **Faculty:** Student/faculty ratio 16:1. 99 full-time faculty, 55% hold PhDs. 100% faculty teach undergrads.

ACADEMICS

Degrees: Bachelor's, master's. **Academic Requirements:** General education including some course work in arts/fine arts, computer literacy, English (including composition), history, humanities, mathematics, philosophy, sciences (biological or physical), social science. **Classes:** 10-19 students in an average class. 10-19 students in an average lab/discussion section. **Disciplines with Highest Percentage of Degrees Awarded:** Health professions and related sciences 42%, business/marketing 17%, education 11%, visual and performing arts 6%, social sciences and history 6%. **Special Study Options:** Cooperative (work-study) program, cross registration, double major, dual enrollment, independent study, internships, student-designed major, study abroad, teacher certification program.

FACILITIES

Housing: Coed, apartments for single students. **Library Holdings:** 100,000 bound volumes. 2,000 periodicals. 170,000 microforms. 4,037 audiovisuals. **Special Academic Facilities/Equipment:** Music library, nursing center with labs and simulated medical records department. **Computers:** School-owned computers available for student use.

EXTRACURRICULARS

Activities: Choral groups, dance, drama/theater, literary magazine, musical theater, opera, student government, student newspaper. **Organizations:** 30 registered organizations, 1 honor society, 3 religious organizations. **Athletics (Intercollegiate):** *Men:* baseball, basketball, soccer. *Women:* basketball, soccer, softball, volleyball.

ADMISSIONS

Selectivity Rating: 66 (of 100). **Freshman Academic Profile:** Average high school GPA 3.2. 73% from public high schools. Average SAT I Math 500. Average SAT I Verbal 550. Average ACT 22, ACT middle 50% range 21-25. TOEFL required of all international applicants, minimum TOEFL 550. **Basis for Candidate Selection:** *Very important factors considered include:* secondary school record, standardized test scores. *Important factors considered include:* talent/ability. *Other factors considered include:* alumni/ae relation, class rank, extracurricular activities, interview, recommendations. **Freshman Admission Requirements:** High school diploma or GED is required. *Academic units required/recommended:* 16 total recommended; 4 English required, 4 English recommended, 2 math required, 2 math recommended, 2 science required, 2 science recommended, 2 science lab recommended, 2 foreign language recommended, 2 social studies required, 2 social studies recommended. **Freshman Admission Statistics:** 1,246 applied, 89% accepted, 30% of those accepted enrolled. **Transfer Admission Requirements:** *Items required:* high school transcript, college transcript. Minimum college GPA of

2.0 required. Lowest grade transferable C-. **General Admission Information:** Application fee $15. Priority application deadline August 1. Nonfall registration accepted. Admission may be deferred for a maximum of 2 years. Credit and/or placement offered for CEEB Advanced Placement tests.

COSTS AND FINANCIAL AID

Tuition $13,350. Room & board $4,710. Required fees $280. Average book expense $600. **Required Forms and Deadlines:** FAFSA. No deadline for regular filing. Priority filing deadline March 15. **Notification of Awards:** Applicants will be notified of awards on a rolling basis beginning on or about March 1. **Types of Aid:** *Need-based scholarships/grants:* Pell, SEOG, state scholarships/grants, private scholarships, the school's own gift aid. *Loans:* FFEL Subsidized Stafford, FFEL Unsubsidized Stafford, FFEL PLUS, Federal Perkins, Federal Nursing. **Student Employment:** Federal Work-Study Program available. Institutional employment available. Off-campus job opportunities are excellent. **Financial Aid Statistics:** 68% freshmen, 81% undergrads receive some form of aid. Average freshman grant $5,000. Average freshman loan $2,500. Average income from on-campus job $900. **Financial Aid Phone:** 608-796-3900.

VOORHEES COLLEGE

PO Box 678, Denmark, SC 29042
Phone: 803-703-7111 **E-mail:** white@voorhees.edu **CEEB Code:** 5863
Fax: 803-793-1117 **Web:** www.voorhees.edu **ACT Code:** 3882

This private school, which is affiliated with the Episcopal Church, was founded in 1897. It has a 350-acre campus.

STUDENTS AND FACULTY

Enrollment: 738. **Student Body:** Male 36%, female 64%, out-of-state 28%, international 1%. **Ethnic Representation:** African American 99%, Caucasian 1%. **Retention and Graduation:** 70% freshmen return for sophomore year. 100% freshmen graduate within 4 years. 25% grads go on to further study within 1 year. 5% grads pursue business degrees. 2% grads pursue law degrees. 4% grads pursue medical degrees. **Faculty:** Student/faculty ratio 20:1. 43 full-time faculty, 44% hold PhDs. 100% faculty teach undergrads.

ACADEMICS

Degrees: Bachelor's, terminal. **Academic Requirements:** General education including some course work in arts/fine arts, computer literacy, English (including composition), foreign languages, history, humanities, mathematics, philosophy, sciences (biological or physical), social science. **Disciplines with Highest Percentage of Degrees Awarded:** Organizational management 50%, social sciences and history 13%, business/marketing 12%, law/legal studies 8%, biological life sciences 7%. **Special Study Options:** Cooperative (work-study) program, honors program, internships, weekend college.

FACILITIES

Housing: All-female, all-male, fraternities and/or sororities, faculty and staff apartments, housing for single mothers. **Library Holdings:** 117,248 bound volumes. 462 periodicals. 24,642 microforms. 1,192 audiovisuals. **Computers:** School-owned computers available for student use.

EXTRACURRICULARS

Activities: Choral groups, drama/theater, literary magazine, pep band, radio station, student government, student newspaper, yearbook. **Organizations:** 33 registered organizations, 2 honor societies, 3 religious organizations, 4 fraternities (30% men join), 4 sororities (22% women join). **Athletics (Intercollegiate):** *Men:* baseball, basketball, cheerleading, cross-country track. *Women:* basketball, cheerleading, cross-country, softball, volleyball.

ADMISSIONS

Selectivity Rating: 66 (of 100). **Freshman Academic Profile:** Average high school GPA 2.0. 1% in top 10% of high school class, 44% in top 25% of high school class, 50% in top 50% of high school class. 95% from public high schools. Average SAT I Math 430. Average SAT I Verbal 410, SAT I Verbal middle 50% range 300-400. Average ACT 17, ACT middle 50% range 11-18. TOEFL required of all international applicants, minimum TOEFL 500. **Basis for Candidate Selection:** *Very important factors considered include:* class rank, secondary school record, standardized test scores. *Important factors considered include:* alumni/ae relation, character/personal qualities, recommendations, talent/ability. *Other factors considered include:* extracurricular activities. **Freshman Admission Requirements:** High school diploma or GED is required. *Academic units required/recommended:* 20 total required; 21 total recommended; 4 English required, 4 English recommended, 3 math required, 3 math recommended, 2 science required, 3 science recommended, 2 foreign language required, 2 foreign language recommended, 1 social studies required, 1 social studies recommended, 1 history required, 1 history recommended, 7 elective required, 7 elective recommended. **Freshman Admission Statistics:** 2,627 applied, 41% accepted, 15% of those accepted enrolled. **Transfer Admission Requirements:** *Items required:* college transcript, statement of good standing from prior school. Minimum high school GPA of 2.0 required. Minimum college GPA of 2.0 required. Lowest grade transferable C. **General Admission Information:** Application fee $25. Nonfall registration accepted. Admission may be deferred for a maximum of 2 years. Credit offered for CEEB Advanced Placement tests.

COSTS AND FINANCIAL AID

Tuition $6,460. Room & board $3,516. Required fees $170. Average book expense $2,500. **Required Forms and Deadlines:** FAFSA and institution's own financial aid form. Priority filing deadline April 15. **Notification of Awards:** Applicants will be notified of awards on a rolling basis beginning on or about May 1. **Types of Aid:** *Need-based scholarships/grants:* Pell, SEOG, state scholarships/grants, private scholarships, the school's own gift aid, United Negro College Fund. *Loans:* FFEL Subsidized Stafford, FFEL Unsubsidized Stafford, FFEL PLUS, Federal Perkins. **Student Employment:** Federal Work-Study Program available. Institutional employment available. Off-campus job opportunities are poor. **Financial Aid Statistics:** 95% freshmen, 96% undergrads receive some form of aid. Average freshman grant $4,325. Average freshman loan $2,036. **Financial Aid Phone:** 803-703-7109.

WABASH COLLEGE

PO Box 352, 301 W. Wabash Avenue, Crawfordsville, IN 47933
Phone: 765-361-6225 **E-mail:** admissions@wabash.edu **CEEB Code:** 1895
Fax: 765-361-6437 **Web:** www.wabash.edu **ACT Code:** 1260

This private school was founded in 1832. It has a 55-acre campus.

STUDENTS AND FACULTY

Enrollment: 912. **Student Body:** Out-of-state 26%, international 3% (13 countries represented). **Ethnic Representation:** African American 7%, Asian 3%, Caucasian 84%, Hispanic 6%. **Retention and Graduation:** 86% freshmen return for sophomore year. 64% freshmen graduate within 4 years. 39% grads go on to further study within 1 year. 1% grads pursue business degrees. 12% grads pursue law degrees. 8% grads pursue medical degrees. **Faculty:** Student/faculty ratio 11:1. 82 full-time faculty, 96% hold PhDs. 100% faculty teach undergrads.

ACADEMICS

Degrees: Bachelor's. **Academic Requirements:** General education including some course work in arts/fine arts, English (including composition), foreign languages, history, humanities, mathematics, sciences (biological or physical), social science, freshman tutorial, cultures and traditions course. **Classes:** 10-19 students in an average class. 10-19 students in an average lab/discussion section. **Majors with Highest Enrollment:** History, general; English language and literature, general; political science and government, general. **Disciplines with Highest Percentage of Degrees Awarded:** Social sciences and history 31%, psychology 11%, philosophy/religion/theology 10%, English 10%, biological life sciences 9%. **Special Study Options:** Double major, independent study, internships, study abroad, teacher certification program. Student-designed majors, minors, or areas of concentration.

FACILITIES

Housing: All-male, fraternities and/or sororities, International House (not limited to international students), Language Houses (French, German, Spanish), college-owned apartments. **Library Holdings:** 420,906 bound volumes. 1,634 periodicals. 10,359 microforms. 10,557 audiovisuals. **Special Academic Facilities/Equipment:** Malcolm X Institute of Black Studies, two art galleries, language lab, electron microscope, atomic absorption, nuclear and infrared spectrometers, Beowulf Supercomputer, Center of Inquiry in the Liberal Arts, Wabash Center for Teaching & Learning in Theology & Religion. **Computers:** School-owned computers available for student use.

EXTRACURRICULARS

Activities: Choral groups, concert band, drama/theater, jazz band, literary magazine, music ensembles, pep band, radio station, student government, student newspaper, student-run film society, symphony orchestra, yearbook. **Organizations:** 45 registered organizations, 6 honor societies, 5 religious organizations, 10 fraternities (65% men join). **Athletics (Intercollegiate):** *Men:* baseball, basketball, cross-country, diving, football, golf, indoor track, soccer, swimming, tennis, track & field, wrestling.

ADMISSIONS

Selectivity Rating: 87 (of 100). **Freshman Academic Profile:** Average high school GPA 3.6. 32% in top 10% of high school class, 68% in top 25% of high school class, 95% in top 50% of high school class. 92% from public high schools. Average SAT I Math 609, SAT I Math middle 50% range 560-655. Average SAT I Verbal 576, SAT I Verbal middle 50% range 530-620. Average ACT 26, ACT middle 50% range 23-28. TOEFL required of all international applicants, minimum TOEFL 550. **Basis for Candidate Selection:** *Very important factors considered include:* class rank, secondary school record. *Important factors considered include:* recommendations, standardized test scores. *Other factors considered include:* alumni/ae relation, character/personal qualities, essays, extracurricular activities, geographical residence, interview, minority status, state residency, talent/ability, volunteer work, work experience. **Freshman Admission Requirements:** High school diploma or GED is required. *Academic units required/recommended:* 17 total recommended; 4 English recommended, 4 math recommended, 3 science recommended, 2 science lab recommended, 2 foreign language recommended, 2 social studies recommended, 2 history recommended. **Freshman Admission Statistics:** 1,287 applied, 50% accepted, 42% of those accepted enrolled. **Transfer Admission Requirements:** *Items required:* high school transcript, college transcript, essay, standardized test score, statement of good standing from prior school. Lowest grade transferable C. **General Admission Information:** Application fee $30. Priority application deadline December 15. Early decision application deadline November 15. Nonfall registration accepted. Admission may be deferred for a maximum of 1 year. Credit and/or placement offered for CEEB Advanced Placement tests.

COSTS AND FINANCIAL AID

Tuition $19,837. Room & board $6,397. Required fees $368. Average book expense $600. **Required Forms and Deadlines:** FAFSA, CSS/Financial Aid PROFILE and federal tax returns and W-2 statements. Financial aid filing deadline March 1. Priority filing deadline February 15. **Notification of Awards:** Applicants will be notified of awards on or about April 1. **Types of Aid:** *Need-based scholarships/grants:* Pell, state scholarships/grants, private scholarships, the school's own gift aid. *Loans:* FFEL Subsidized Stafford, FFEL Unsubsidized Stafford, FFEL PLUS, college/university loans from institutional funds. **Student Employment:** Institutional employment available. Off-campus job opportunities are excellent. **Financial Aid Statistics:** 77% freshmen, 68% undergrads receive some form of aid. Average freshman grant $18,668. Average freshman loan $3,301. Average income from on-campus job $1,000. **Financial Aid Phone:** 765-361-6370.

WAGNER COLLEGE

1 Campus Road, Staten Island, NY 10301-4495
Phone: 718-390-3411 **E-mail:** admissions@wagner.edu **CEEB Code:** 2966
Fax: 718-390-3105 **Web:** www.wagner.edu **ACT Code:** 2984

This private school, which is affiliated with the Lutheran Church, was founded in 1883. It has a 110-acre campus.

STUDENTS AND FACULTY

Enrollment: 1,810. **Student Body:** Male 43%, female 57%, out-of-state 55%, international 2% (21 countries represented). **Ethnic Representation:** African American 6%, Asian 3%, Caucasian 77%, Hispanic 6%. **Retention and Graduation:** 88% freshmen return for sophomore year. 71% freshmen graduate within 4 years. 44% grads go on to further study within 1 year. 15% grads pursue business degrees. 8% grads pursue law degrees. 4% grads pursue medical degrees. **Faculty:** Student/faculty ratio 16:1. 95 full-time faculty, 73% hold PhDs. 100% faculty teach undergrads.

ACADEMICS

Degrees: Bachelor's, master's, post-master's certificate. **Academic Requirements:** General education including some course work in arts/fine arts, computer literacy, English (including composition), history, humanities, mathematics, sciences (biological or physical), social science. **Majors with Highest Enrollment:** Biological science; business; psychology. **Disciplines with Highest Percentage of Degrees Awarded:** Business/marketing 21%, health professions and related sciences 19%, education 12%, visual and performing arts 12%, social sciences and history 12%. **Special Study Options:** Double major, student exchange program (domestic), honors program, independent study, internships, study abroad, teacher certification program.

FACILITIES

Housing: Coed, fraternities and/or sororities. **Library Holdings:** 310,000 bound volumes. 1,000 periodicals. **Special Academic Facilities/Equipment:** Art gallery, early childhood center, nursing resource center, planetarium, two electron microscopes, solar energy project, computer labs. **Computers:** School-owned computers available for student use.

EXTRACURRICULARS

Activities: Choral groups, concert band, dance, jazz band, radio station, literary magazine, music ensembles, musical theater, opera, pep band, student government, student newspaper, symphony orchestra, yearbook. **Organizations:** 66 registered organizations, 5 honor societies, 3 religious organizations, 9 fraternities, 3 sororities. **Athletics (Intercollegiate):** *Men:* baseball, basketball, cross-country, football, golf, indoor track, lacrosse, tennis, track & field, wrestling. *Women:* basketball, cross-country, golf, indoor track, lacrosse, soccer, softball, swimming, tennis, track & field, volleyball, water polo.

ADMISSIONS

Selectivity Rating: 72 (of 100). **Freshman Academic Profile:** Average high school GPA 3.5. 16% in top 10% of high school class, 47% in top 25% of high school class, 88% in top 50% of high school class. 59% from public high schools. Average SAT I Math 560, SAT I Math middle 50% range 510-610. Average SAT I Verbal 550, SAT I Verbal middle 50% range 510-620. Average ACT 26. TOEFL required of all international applicants, minimum TOEFL 550. **Basis for Candidate Selection:** *Very important factors considered include:* secondary school record, standardized test scores. *Important factors considered include:* class rank, essays, interview, recommendations, talent/ability. *Other factors considered include:* alumni/ae relation, character/personal qualities, extracurricular activities, geographical residence, minority status, volunteer work. **Freshman Admission Requirements:** High school diploma is required and GED is not accepted. *Academic units required/recommended:* 18 total required; 21 total recommended; 4 English required, 3 math required, 4 math recommended, 2 science required, 3 science recommended, 2 foreign language required, 3 social studies required, 4 social studies recommended, 1 elective required. **Freshman Admission Statistics:** 2,156 applied, 65% accepted, 31% of those accepted enrolled. **Transfer Admission Requirements:** *Items required:* college transcript, essay. Minimum college GPA of 2.8 required. Lowest grade transferable C. **General Admission Information:** Application fee $50. Priority application deadline February 15. Early decision application deadline December 1. Regular application deadline March 15. Nonfall registration accepted. Admission may be deferred for a maximum of 1 year. Credit and/or placement offered for CEEB Advanced Placement tests.

COSTS AND FINANCIAL AID

Tuition $21,500. Room & board $7,000. Average book expense $625. **Required Forms and Deadlines:** FAFSA. Financial aid filing deadline April 15. Priority filing deadline March 15. **Types of Aid:** *Need-based scholarships/grants:* Pell, SEOG, state scholarships/grants, private scholarships, the school's own gift aid, Lutheran scholarships. *Loans:* FFEL Subsidized Stafford, FFEL Unsubsidized Stafford, FFEL PLUS, Federal Perkins, Federal Nursing. **Student Employment:** Federal Work-Study Program available. Institutional employment available. Off-campus job opportunities are good. **Financial Aid Statistics:** 75% freshmen, 68% undergrads receive some form of aid. Average freshman grant $6,965. Average freshman loan $5,660. Average income from on-campus job $1,000. **Financial Aid Phone:** 718-390-3183.

See page 1274.

WAKE FOREST UNIVERSITY

Reynolda Station, Winston-Salem, NC 27109
Phone: 336-758-5201 **E-mail:** admissions@wfu.edu **CEEB Code:** 5885
Fax: 336-758-4324 **Web:** www.wfu.edu **ACT Code:** 3168

This private school was founded in 1834. It has a 340-acre campus.

STUDENTS AND FACULTY

Enrollment: 4,045. **Student Body:** Male 49%, female 51%, out-of-state 71%, international 1%. **Ethnic Representation:** African American 7%, Asian 3%, Caucasian 88%, Hispanic 2%. **Retention and Graduation:** 94% freshmen return for sophomore year. 76% freshmen graduate within 4 years. 31% grads go on to further study within 1 year. 7% grads pursue law degrees. 5% grads pursue medical degrees. **Faculty:** Student/faculty ratio 10:1. 430 full-time faculty, 90% hold PhDs. 100% faculty teach undergrads.

ACADEMICS

Degrees: Bachelor's, doctoral, first professional, master's. **Academic Requirements:** General education including some course work in arts/fine arts, English (including composition), foreign languages, history, mathematics, philosophy, sciences (biological or physical), social science, health and exercise science, religion. **Classes:** 10-19 students in an average class. 10-19 students in an average lab/discussion section. **Majors with Highest Enrollment:** Communications studies/speech communication and rhetoric; psychology, general; business/commerce, general. **Disciplines with Highest Percentage of Degrees Awarded:** Social sciences and history 25%, business/marketing 19%, communications/communication technologies 12%, psychology 9%, biological life sciences 7%. **Special Study Options:** Cross registration, double major, dual enrollment, student exchange program (domestic), honors program, independent study, internships, study abroad, teacher certification program, weekend MBA program.

FACILITIES

Housing: Coed, apartments for single students, housing for disabled students, fraternities and/or sororities, theme housing, substance-free housing, off-campus foreign language houses. **Library Holdings:** 1,734,305 bound volumes. 16,246 periodicals. 2,195,658 microforms. 24,856 audiovisuals. **Special Academic Facilities/Equipment:** American art and anthropology museums, art gallery, laser and electron microscope labs. **Computers:** *Recommended operating system:* Windows 98/XP. School-owned computers available for student use.

EXTRACURRICULARS

Activities: Choral groups, concert band, dance, drama/theater, literary magazine, marching band, music ensembles, pep band, radio station, student government, student newspaper, student-run film society, symphony orchestra, television station, yearbook. **Organizations:** 134 registered organizations, 15 honor societies, 16 religious organizations, 14 fraternities (37% men join), 9 sororities (50% women join). **Athletics (Intercollegiate):** *Men:* baseball, basketball, cheerleading, cross-country, football, golf, indoor track, soccer, tennis, track & field. *Women:* basketball, cheerleading, cross-country, field hockey, golf, indoor track, soccer, tennis, track & field, volleyball.

ADMISSIONS

Selectivity Rating: 95 (of 100). **Freshman Academic Profile:** 62% in top 10% of high school class, 91% in top 25% of high school class, 98% in top 50% of high school class. 67% from public high schools. SAT I Math middle 50% range 620-710. SAT I Verbal middle 50% range 600-680. TOEFL required of all international applicants, minimum TOEFL 550. **Basis for Candidate Selection:** *Very important factors considered include:* character/personal qualities, class rank, secondary school record, standardized test scores. *Important factors considered include:* alumni/ae relation, essays, extracurricular activities, minority status, recommendations, religious affiliation/commitment, talent/ability, volunteer work. *Other factors considered include:* geographical residence, state residency. **Freshman Admission Requirements:** High school diploma or GED is required. *Academic units required/recommended:* 16 total required; 20 total recommended; 4 English required, 4 English recommended, 3 math required, 4 math recommended, 1 science required, 4 science recommended, 2 foreign language required, 4 foreign language recommended, 2 social studies required, 4 social studies recommended. **Freshman Admission Statistics:** 5,995 applied, 41% accepted, 41% of those accepted enrolled. **Transfer Admission Requirements:** *Items required:* high school transcript, college transcript, essay, standardized test scores. Minimum college GPA of 2.0 required. Lowest grade transferable C. **General Admission Information:** Application fee $40. Early decision application deadline November 15. Regular application deadline January 15. Nonfall registration accepted. Admission may be deferred for a maximum of 1 year. Credit and/or placement offered for CEEB Advanced Placement tests.

COSTS AND FINANCIAL AID

Tuition $23,530. Average book expense $700. **Required Forms and Deadlines:** FAFSA, CSS/Financial Aid PROFILE, state aid form and noncustodial (divorced/separated) parent's statement. No deadline for regular filing. Priority filing deadline March 1. **Notification of Awards:** Applicants will be notified of awards on or about April 1. **Types of Aid:** *Need-based scholarships/grants:* Pell, SEOG, state scholarships/grants, private scholarships, the school's own gift aid. *Loans:* FFEL Subsidized Stafford, FFEL Unsubsidized Stafford, FFEL PLUS, Federal Perkins, state loans, college/university loans from institutional funds, alternative loans. **Student Employment:** Federal Work-Study Program available. Institutional employment available. Off-campus job opportunities are excellent. **Financial Aid Statistics:** Average freshman grant $17,343. Average freshman loan $4,674. **Financial Aid Phone:** 336-758-5154.

WALLA WALLA COLLEGE

Office of Admissions, 204 South College Avenue, College Place, WA 99324-1198
Phone: 509-527-2327 **E-mail:** info@wwc.edu **CEEB Code:** 4940
Fax: 509-527-2397 **Web:** www.wwc.edu **ACT Code:** 4486

This private school, which is affiliated with the Seventh-Day Adventist Church, was founded in 1892. It has a 77-acre campus.

STUDENTS AND FACULTY

Enrollment: 1,610. **Student Body:** Male 51%, female 49%, out-of-state 60%, international 1% (30 countries represented). **Ethnic Representation:** African American 2%, Asian 5%, Caucasian 83%, Hispanic 6%. **Retention and Graduation:** 67% freshmen return for sophomore year. 14% freshmen graduate within 4 years. **Faculty:** Student/faculty ratio 11:1. 116 full-time faculty, 62% hold PhDs. 100% faculty teach undergrads.

ACADEMICS

Degrees: Associate's, bachelor's, master's. **Academic Requirements:** General education including some course work in English (including composition), history, humanities, mathematics, sciences (biological or physical), social science, religion. **Classes:** Under 10 students in an average class. 10-19 students in an average lab/discussion section. **Disciplines with Highest Percentage of Degrees Awarded:** Health professions and related sciences 20%, engineering/engineering technology 17%, business/marketing 14%, education 11%, biological life sciences 6%. **Special Study Options:** Cooperative (work-study) program, cross registration, double major, dual enrollment, honors program, independent study, internships, liberal arts/career combination, study abroad, teacher certification program.

FACILITIES

Housing: All-female, all-male, apartments for married students, apartments for single students. **Special Academic Facilities/Equipment:** Marine station on Puget Sound. **Computers:** School-owned computers available for student use.

EXTRACURRICULARS

Activities: Choral groups, concert band, drama/theater, music ensembles, radio station, student government, student newspaper, television station, yearbook. **Organizations:** 33 registered organizations, 7 honor societies, 5 religious organizations. **Athletics (Intercollegiate):** *Men:* basketball, golf, soccer, volleyball. *Women:* basketball, softball, volleyball.

ADMISSIONS

Selectivity Rating: 81 (of 100). **Freshman Academic Profile:** Average high school GPA 3.1. 11% from public high schools. Average ACT 22, ACT middle 50% range 20-31. TOEFL required of all international applicants, minimum TOEFL 550. **Basis for Candidate Selection:** *Very important factors considered include:* character/personal qualities, recommendations, secondary school record, standardized test scores. **Freshman Admission Requirements:** High school diploma or GED is required. *Academic units required/recommended:* 10 total required; 4 English required, 2 math required, 1 science required, 1 science recommended, 1 science lab required, 2 foreign language recommended, 1 social studies recommended, 2 history required. **Freshman Admission Statistics:** 457 applied, 86% accepted, 87% of those accepted enrolled. **Transfer Admission Requirements:** *Items required:* high school transcript, college transcript, standardized test score, statement of good standing from prior school. Minimum high school GPA of 2.0 required. Minimum college GPA of 2.0 required. **General Admission Information:** Application fee $30. Priority application deadline September 1. Nonfall registration accepted. Admission may be deferred for a maximum of 2 years. Credit and/or placement offered for CEEB Advanced Placement tests.

COSTS AND FINANCIAL AID

Tuition $16,779. Room & board $4,605. Required fees $165. Average book expense $810. **Required Forms and Deadlines:** FAFSA and institution's own financial aid form. No deadline for regular filing. **Notification of Awards:** Applicants will be notified of awards on a rolling basis beginning on or about March 15. **Types of Aid:** *Need-based scholarships/grants:* Pell, SEOG, state scholarships/grants, private scholarships, the school's own gift aid. *Loans:* FFEL Subsidized Stafford, FFEL Unsubsidized Stafford, FFEL PLUS, Federal Perkins, Federal Nursing, college/university loans from institutional funds. **Student Employment:** Federal Work-Study Program available. Institutional employment available. Off-campus job opportunities are good. **Financial Aid Statistics:** 72% freshmen, 73% undergrads receive some form of aid. Average freshman grant $8,045. Average freshman loan $4,121. Average income from on-campus job $1,800. **Financial Aid Phone:** 800-656-2815.

WALSH UNIVERSITY

2020 Easton Street, Northwest, North Canton, OH 44720-3396
Phone: 800-362-9846 **E-mail:** admissions@walsh.edu **CEEB Code:** 1926
Fax: 330-490-7165 **Web:** walsh.edu **ACT Code:** 3349

This private school, which is affiliated with the Roman Catholic Church, was founded in 1958. It has a 58-acre campus.

STUDENTS AND FACULTY

Enrollment: 1,480. **Student Body:** Male 42%, female 58%, out-of-state 2%, international 1%. **Ethnic Representation:** African American 6%, Caucasian 86%, Hispanic 1%. **Retention and Graduation:** 75% freshmen return for sophomore year. **Faculty:** Student/faculty ratio 15:1. 67 full-time faculty, 71% hold PhDs.

ACADEMICS

Degrees: Associate's, bachelor's, master's. **Academic Requirements:** General education including some course work in arts/fine arts, English (including composition), foreign languages, history, humanities, mathematics, philosophy, sciences (biological or physical), social science. **Classes:** 10-19 students in an average class. Under 10 students in an average lab/discussion section. **Majors with Highest Enrollment:** Education, general; biology/biological sciences, general; business administration/management. **Disciplines with Highest Percentage of Degrees Awarded:** Business/marketing 43%, education 19%, biological life sciences 10%, social sciences and history 7%, communications/communication technologies 6%. **Special Study Options:** Accelerated program, cooperative (work-study) program, cross registration, double major, dual enrollment, student exchange program (domestic), external degree program, honors program, independent study, internships, study abroad, teacher certification program.

FACILITIES

Housing: Coed, all-female, all-male, apartments for single students, housing for disabled students. **Library Holdings:** 103,012 bound volumes. 605 periodicals. 8,536 microforms. 1,428 audiovisuals. **Computers:** School-owned computers available for student use.

EXTRACURRICULARS

Activities: Choral groups, drama/theater, music ensembles, radio station, student government, student newspaper. **Organizations:** 28 registered organizations, 4 honor societies, 2 religious organizations. **Athletics (Intercollegiate):** *Men:* baseball, basketball, cheerleading, cross-country, football, golf, soccer, tennis, track & field. *Women:* basketball, cheerleading, cross-country, golf, soccer, softball, tennis, track & field, volleyball.

ADMISSIONS

Selectivity Rating: 73 (of 100). **Freshman Academic Profile:** Average high school GPA 3.2. 24% in top 10% of high school class, 42% in top 25% of high school class, 71% in top 50% of high school class. 81% from public high schools. Average ACT 21, ACT middle 50% range 19-24. TOEFL required of all international applicants, minimum TOEFL 510. **Basis for Candidate Selection:** *Very important factors considered include:* secondary school record, standardized test scores. *Important factors considered include:* character/personal qualities, class rank, essays, recommendations, volunteer work. *Other factors considered include:* extracurricular activities, interview. **Freshman Admission Requirements:** High school diploma or GED is required. *Academic units required/recommended:* 4 English recommended, 3 math recommended, 3 science recommended, 2 foreign language recommended, 3 social studies recommended, 1 elective recommended. **Freshman Admission Statistics:** 920 applied, 79% accepted, 41% of those accepted enrolled. **Transfer Admission Requirements:** *Items required:* high school transcript, college transcript. Minimum college GPA of 2.0 required. Lowest grade transferable C. **General Admission Information:** Application fee $25. Regular application deadline August 15. Nonfall registration accepted. Admission may be deferred for a maximum of 1 year. Credit offered for CEEB Advanced Placement tests.

COSTS AND FINANCIAL AID

Average book expense $1,000. **Required Forms and Deadlines:** FAFSA and institution's own financial aid form. No deadline for regular filing. **Notification of Awards:** Applicants will be notified of awards on a rolling basis beginning on or about March 15. **Types of Aid:** *Need-based scholarships/grants:* Pell, SEOG, state scholarships/grants, private scholarships, the school's own gift aid. *Loans:* FFEL Subsidized Stafford, FFEL Unsubsidized Stafford, FFEL PLUS, Federal Perkins, state loans. **Student Employment:** Federal Work-Study Program available. Institutional employment available. Off-campus job opportunities are good. **Financial Aid Statistics:** 80% freshmen, 69% undergrads receive some form of aid. Average freshman grant $11,013. Average freshman loan $2,862. Average income from on-campus job $760. **Financial Aid Phone:** 800-362-9846.

WARNER PACIFIC COLLEGE

 $$  

Office of Admissions, 2219 SE 68th, Portland, OR 97215
Phone: 503-517-1020 **E-mail:** admiss@warnerpacific.edu **CEEB Code:** 4595
Fax: 503-517-1352 **Web:** www.warnerpacific.edu

This private school was founded in 1937. It has a 15-acre campus.

STUDENTS AND FACULTY

Enrollment: 645. **Student Body:** Male 34%, female 66%, out-of-state 20%, international 2% (8 countries represented). **Ethnic Representation:** African American 3%, Asian 3%, Caucasian 74%, Hispanic 3%, Native American 1%. **Retention and Graduation:** 76% freshmen return for sophomore year. **Faculty:** Student/faculty ratio 14:1. 38 full-time faculty, 52% hold PhDs.

ACADEMICS

Degrees: Associate's, bachelor's, certificate, master's. **Academic Requirements:** General education including some course work in arts/fine arts, English (including composition), humanities, mathematics, sciences (biological or physical), social science, religion. **Disciplines with Highest Percentage of Degrees Awarded:** Psychology 50%, business/marketing 34%, religion & music 7%, health professions and related sciences 5%, social sciences and history 2%. **Special Study Options:** Cooperative (work-study) program, double major, internships, student-designed major, study abroad, teacher certification program, weekend college.

FACILITIES

Housing: Coed, all-female, all-male, apartments for married students, apartments for single students. **Library Holdings:** 42,210 bound volumes. 233 periodicals. 1,195 microforms. 110 audiovisuals. **Special Academic Facilities/Equipment:** Early learning center, electron microscopes. **Computers:** School-owned computers available for student use.

EXTRACURRICULARS

Activities: Choral groups, dance, drama/theater, jazz band, music ensembles, musical theater, student government, student newspaper, yearbook. **Organizations:** 20 registered organizations, 2 religious organizations. **Athletics (Intercollegiate):** *Men:* basketball, cross-country, soccer. *Women:* basketball, cross-country, volleyball.

ADMISSIONS

Selectivity Rating: 64 (of 100). **Freshman Academic Profile:** 78% from public high schools. Average SAT I Math 507. Average SAT I Verbal 518. Average ACT 22. TOEFL required of all international applicants, minimum TOEFL 525. **Freshman Admission Requirements:** High school diploma or GED is required. *Academic units required/recommended:* 4 English recommended, 2 math recommended, 2 science recommended, 2 science lab recommended, 3 social studies recommended. **Freshman Admission Statistics:** 159 applied, 79% accepted, 100% of those accepted enrolled. **Transfer Admission Requirements:** *Items required:* college transcript, essay. Minimum high school GPA of 2.5 required. Minimum college GPA of 2.5 required. Lowest grade transferable D. **General Admission Information:** Application fee $25. Early decision application deadline June 1. Nonfall registration accepted. Admission may be deferred for a maximum of 1 year. Credit offered for CEEB Advanced Placement tests.

COSTS AND FINANCIAL AID

Tuition $14,410. Room & board $4,600. Required fees $260. Average book expense $500. **Required Forms and Deadlines:** FAFSA. No deadline for regular filing. **Notification of Awards:** Applicants will be notified of awards on a rolling basis. **Student Employment:** Federal Work-Study Program available. Institutional employment available. Off-campus job opportunities are good. **Financial Aid Statistics:** 92% freshmen, 77% undergrads receive some form of aid. Average freshman grant $10,000. Average freshman loan $3,000. Average income from on-campus job $2,400. **Financial Aid Phone:** 503-517-1017.

WARNER SOUTHERN COLLEGE

13985 Hwy. 27, Lake Wales, FL 33859
Phone: 863-638-7212 **E-mail:** admissions@warner.edu **CEEB Code:** 5883
Fax: 863-638-7290 **Web:** www.warner.edu **ACT Code:** 777

This private school, which is affiliated with the Church of God, was founded in 1968. It has a 320-acre campus.

STUDENTS AND FACULTY

Enrollment: 1,087. **Student Body:** Male 42%, female 58%, out-of-state 10%, international 2% (4 countries represented). **Ethnic Representation:** African American 18%, Caucasian 67%, Hispanic 9%, Native American 1%. **Retention and Graduation:** 66% freshmen return for sophomore year. 14% freshmen graduate within 4 years. 1% grads pursue business degrees. 10% grads pursue law degrees. **Faculty:** Student/faculty ratio 16:1. 44 full-time faculty, 43% hold PhDs. 100% faculty teach undergrads.

ACADEMICS

Degrees: Associate's, bachelor's, certificate, master's. **Academic Requirements:** General education including some course work in arts/fine arts, computer literacy, English (including composition), history, humanities, mathematics, sciences (biological or physical), social science, Bible & theology courses. **Classes:** 10-19 students in an average class. 10-19 students in an average lab/discussion section. **Majors with Highest Enrollment:** Business administration/management; communications studies/speech communication and rhetoric; education, general. **Disciplines with Highest Percentage of Degrees Awarded:** Business/marketing 71%, education 13%, philosophy/religion/theology 5%, psychology 2%, protective services/public administration 2%. **Special Study Options:** Accelerated program, distance learning, double major, dual enrollment, English as a second language, independent study, internships, teacher certification program.

FACILITIES

Housing: All-female, all-male. **Library Holdings:** 85,700 bound volumes. 212 periodicals. 15,100 audiovisuals. **Special Academic Facilities/Equipment:** Exhibit of Native American Artifacts. **Computers:** *Recommended operating system:* Windows 95. School-owned computers available for student use.

EXTRACURRICULARS

Activities: Choral groups, music ensembles, pep band, student government. **Organizations:** 2 registered organizations, 2 honor societies, 2 religious organizations. **Athletics (Intercollegiate):** *Men:* baseball, basketball, cheerleading, cross-country, golf, soccer, tennis, track & field. *Women:* basketball, cheerleading, cross-country, golf, soccer, softball, tennis, track & field, volleyball.

ADMISSIONS

Selectivity Rating: 63 (of 100). **Freshman Academic Profile:** Average high school GPA 3.1. 8% in top 10% of high school class, 21% in top 25% of high school class, 65% in top 50% of high school class. 85% from public high schools. Average SAT I Math 472, SAT I Math middle 50% range 400-500. Average SAT I Verbal 473, SAT I Verbal middle 50% range 420-520. Average ACT 20, ACT middle 50% range 17-22. TOEFL required of all international applicants, minimum TOEFL 450. **Basis for Candidate Selection:** *Very important factors considered include:* class rank, secondary school record, standardized test scores. *Important factors considered include:* recommendations. **Freshman Admission Requirements:** High school diploma or GED is required. *Academic units required/recommended:* 15 total recommended; 4 English recommended, 3 math recommended, 2 science recommended, 3 foreign language recommended, 1 social studies recommended, 2 history recommended. **Freshman Admission Statistics:** 289 applied, 71% accepted, 58% of those accepted enrolled. **Transfer Admission Requirements:** *Items required:* college transcript. Minimum college GPA of 2.0 required. Lowest grade transferable D. **General Admission Information:** Application fee $20. Nonfall registration accepted. Admission may be deferred. Credit offered for CEEB Advanced Placement tests.

COSTS AND FINANCIAL AID

Tuition $10,450. Room & board $5,060. Required fees $90. Average book expense $796. **Required Forms and Deadlines:** FAFSA, state aid form and verification form. No deadline for regular filing. Priority filing deadline May 1. **Notification of Awards:** Applicants will be notified of awards on a rolling basis beginning on or about February 1. **Types of Aid:** *Need-based scholarships/grants:* Pell, SEOG, state scholarships/grants, private scholarships, the school's own gift aid. *Loans:* FFEL Subsidized Stafford, FFEL Unsubsidized Stafford, FFEL PLUS, Federal Perkins. **Student Employment:** Federal Work-Study Program available. Institutional employment available. Off-campus job opportunities are fair. **Financial Aid Statistics:** 57% freshmen, 63% undergrads receive some form of aid. Average freshman grant $14,182. Average freshman loan $2,186. Average income from on-campus job $1,200. **Financial Aid Phone:** 863-638-7202.

WARREN WILSON COLLEGE

PO Box 9000, Asheville, NC 28815
Phone: 828-771-2073 **E-mail:** admit@warren-wilson.edu **CEEB Code:** 5886
Fax: 828-298-1440 **Web:** www.warren-wilson.edu **ACT Code:** 3170

This private school, which is affiliated with the Presbyterian Church, was founded in 1894. It has a 1,100-acre campus.

STUDENTS AND FACULTY

Enrollment: 781. **Student Body:** Male 39%, female 61%, out-of-state 79%, international 5%. **Ethnic Representation:** African American 2%, Asian 1%, Caucasian 95%, Hispanic 1%, Native American 1%. **Retention and Graduation:** 69% freshmen return for sophomore year. 30% grads go on to further study within 1 year. 1% grads pursue business degrees. **Faculty:** Student/faculty ratio 12:1. 56 full-time faculty. 100% faculty teach undergrads.

ACADEMICS

Degrees: Bachelor's, master's. **Academic Requirements:** General education including some course work in arts/fine arts, English (including composition), history, humanities, mathematics, philosophy, sciences (biological or physical), social science. **Classes:** 10-19 students in an average class. 10-19 students in an average lab/discussion section. **Majors with Highest Enrollment:** Environmental science; English language and literature, general; fine/studio arts, general. **Disciplines with Highest Percentage of Degrees Awarded:** Social sciences and history 35%, natural resources/environmental sciences 21%, interdisciplinary studies 11%, biological life sciences 8%, education 5%. **Special Study Options:** Cross registration, double major, dual enrollment, English as a second language, student exchange program (domestic), honors program, independent study, internships, liberal arts/career combination, student-designed major, study abroad.

FACILITIES

Housing: Coed, all-female, all-male. **Library Holdings:** 99,000 bound volumes. 29,000 periodicals. 25,000 microforms. 5,500 audiovisuals. **Special Academic Facilities/Equipment:** Two child development centers, 300-acre farm, 700-acre forest, archaeological dig on campus. **Computers:** *Recommended operating system:* Windows 95. School-owned computers available for student use.

EXTRACURRICULARS

Activities: Literary magazine, radio station, student government, student newspaper, yearbook. **Organizations:** 25 registered organizations, 5 religious organizations. **Athletics (Intercollegiate):** *Men:* basketball, cross-country, diving, soccer, swimming. *Women:* basketball, cross-country, diving, soccer, swimming.

ADMISSIONS

Selectivity Rating: 79 (of 100). **Freshman Academic Profile:** Average high school GPA 3.3. 18% in top 10% of high school class, 42% in top 25% of high school class, 77% in top 50% of high school class. 77% from public high schools. Average SAT I Math 544, SAT I Math middle 50% range 490-620. Average SAT I Verbal 579, SAT I Verbal middle 50% range 520-670. Average ACT 24, ACT middle 50% range 22-28. TOEFL required of all international applicants, minimum TOEFL 550. **Basis for Candidate Selection:** *Very important factors considered include:* character/personal qualities, essays, interview, secondary school record, standardized test scores, volunteer work, work experience. *Important factors considered include:* class rank, recommendations. *Other factors considered include:* alumni/ae relation, extracurricular activities, state residency, talent/ability. **Freshman Admission Requirements:** High school diploma or GED is required. *Academic units required/recommended:* 12 total required; 4 English required, 3 math required, 2 science required, 2 science lab required, 2 foreign language recommended, 1 history required. **Transfer Admission Requirements:** *Items required:* high school transcript, college transcript, standardized test scores. Minimum high school GPA of 2.5 required. Minimum college GPA of 3.0 required. Lowest grade transferable C. **General Admission Information:** Early decision application deadline November 15. Regular application deadline March 15. Nonfall registration accepted. Admission may be deferred for a maximum of 1 year. Credit and/or placement offered for CEEB Advanced Placement tests.

COSTS AND FINANCIAL AID

Tuition $16,674. Room & board $5,120. Required fees $200. Average book expense $724. **Required Forms and Deadlines:** FAFSA and institution's own financial aid form. Priority filing deadline April 2. **Notification of Awards:** Applicants will be notified of awards on a rolling basis beginning on or about March 2. **Types of Aid:** *Need-based scholarships/grants:* Pell, SEOG, state scholarships/grants, private scholarships, the school's own gift aid. *Loans:* FFEL Subsidized Stafford, FFEL Unsubsidized Stafford, FFEL PLUS, Federal Perkins, college/university loans from institutional funds. **Student Employment:** Federal Work-Study Program available. Institutional employment available. Off-campus job opportunities are good. **Financial Aid Statistics:** 48% freshmen, 50% undergrads receive some form of aid. Average freshman loan $2,325. Average income from on-campus job $2,472. **Financial Aid Phone:** 828-298-3325.

See page 1276.

WARTBURG COLLEGE

100 Wartburg Blvd., PO Box 1003, Waverly, IA 50677-0903
Phone: 319-352-8264 **E-mail:** admissions@wartburg.edu **CEEB Code:** 6926
Fax: 319-352-8579 **Web:** www.wartburg.edu **ACT Code:** 1364

This private school, which is affiliated with the Lutheran Church, was founded in 1852. It has a 118-acre campus.

STUDENTS AND FACULTY

Enrollment: 1,695. **Student Body:** Male 44%, female 56%, out-of-state 20%, international 4% (32 countries represented). **Ethnic Representation:** African American 4%, Asian 1%, Caucasian 89%, Hispanic 1%. **Retention and Graduation:** 77% freshmen return for sophomore year. 65% freshmen graduate within 4 years. 20% grads go on to further study within 1 year. 6% grads pursue business degrees. 12% grads pursue law degrees. 22% grads pursue medical degrees. **Faculty:** Student/faculty ratio 14:1. 101 full-time faculty, 79% hold PhDs. 100% faculty teach undergrads.

ACADEMICS

Degrees: Bachelor's. **Academic Requirements:** General education including some course work in arts/fine arts, English (including composition), foreign languages, humanities, mathematics, philosophy, sciences (biological or physical), social science. **Classes:** 20-29 students in an average class. 20-29 students in an average lab/discussion section. **Majors with Highest Enrollment:** Business, management, marketing, and related support services; elementary education and teaching; biology/biological sciences, general. **Disciplines with Highest Percentage of Degrees Awarded:** Education 23%, business/marketing 15%, biological life sciences 11%, communications/communication technologies 9%, protective services/public administration 8%. **Special Study Options:** Accelerated program, double major, dual enrollment, independent study, internships, student-designed major, study abroad, teacher certification program.

FACILITIES

Housing: Coed, all-female, all-male, townhouses for single senior students. **Library Holdings:** 171,852 bound volumes. 826 periodicals. 7,519 microforms. 3,754 audiovisuals. **Special Academic Facilities/Equipment:** International museum, art gallery, fine arts center, institute for leadership education, planetarium, prairie preserve, state-of-the-art new library. **Computers:** *Recommended operating system:* Windows 95. School-owned computers available for student use.

EXTRACURRICULARS

Activities: Choral groups, concert band, drama/theater, jazz band, literary magazine, music ensembles, musical theater, opera, pep band, radio station, student government, student newspaper, symphony orchestra, television station, yearbook. **Organizations:** 90 registered organizations, 11 honor societies, 5 religious organizations. **Athletics (Intercollegiate):** *Men:* baseball, basketball, cross-country, football, golf, indoor track, soccer, tennis, track & field, wrestling. *Women:* basketball, cross-country, golf, indoor track, soccer, softball, tennis, track & field, volleyball.

ADMISSIONS

Selectivity Rating: 73 (of 100). **Freshman Academic Profile:** Average high school GPA 3.5. 29% in top 10% of high school class, 60% in top 25% of high school class, 87% in top 50% of high school class. 95% from public high schools. SAT I Math middle 50% range 510-640. SAT I Verbal middle 50% range 500-660. ACT middle 50% range 21-26. TOEFL required of all international applicants, minimum TOEFL 480. **Basis for Candidate Selection:** *Very important factors considered include:* class rank, recommendations, secondary school record, standardized test scores. *Important factors considered include:* character/personal qualities, interview. *Other factors considered include:* extracurricular activities, minority status, talent/ability, volunteer work, work experience. **Freshman Admission Requirements:** High school diploma or GED is required. *Academic units required/recommended:* 15 total recommended; 4 English recommended, 3 math recommended, 3 science recommended, 2 foreign language recommended, 2 social studies recommended. **Freshman Admission Statistics:** 1,713 applied, 84% accepted, 36% of those accepted enrolled. **Transfer Admission Requirements:** *Items required:* high school transcript, college transcript, standardized test scores. Minimum college GPA of 2.0 required. Lowest grade transferable C-. **General Admission Information:** Application fee $20. Priority application deadline May 1. Nonfall registration accepted. Admission may be deferred for a maximum of 1 year. Credit and/or placement offered for CEEB Advanced Placement tests.

COSTS AND FINANCIAL AID

Tuition $17,150. Room & board $4,900. Required fees $380. Average book expense $600. **Required Forms and Deadlines:** FAFSA. No deadline for regular filing. Priority filing deadline March 1. **Notification of Awards:** Applicants will be notified of awards on a rolling basis beginning on or about March 1. **Types of Aid:** *Need-based scholarships/grants:* Pell, SEOG, state scholarships/grants, private scholarships, the school's own gift aid. *Loans:* FFEL Subsidized Stafford, FFEL Unsubsidized Stafford, FFEL PLUS, Federal Perkins, alternative. **Student Employment:** Federal Work-Study Program available. Institutional employment available. Off-campus job opportunities are good. **Financial Aid Statistics:** 79% freshmen, 80% undergrads receive some form of aid. **Financial Aid Phone:** 319-352-8262.

WASHBURN UNIVERSITY

1700 SW College Avenue, Topeka, KS 66621
Phone: 785-231-1030 **E-mail:** zzdpadm@washburn.edu **CEEB Code:** 6928
Fax: 785-296-7933 **Web:** www.washburn.edu **ACT Code:** 1474

This public school was founded in 1865. It has a 160-acre campus.

STUDENTS AND FACULTY

Enrollment: 5,098. **Student Body:** Male 38%, female 62%, out-of-state 4%, international students represent 45 countries. **Ethnic Representation:** African American 6%, Asian 2%, Caucasian 67%, Hispanic 4%, Native American 1%. **Retention and Graduation:** 67% freshmen return for sophomore year. 27% freshmen graduate within 4 years. **Faculty:** Student/faculty ratio 15:1. 227 full-time faculty, 88% hold PhDs. 100% faculty teach undergrads.

ACADEMICS

Degrees: Associate's, bachelor's, certificate, first professional, first professional certificate, master's, post-bachelor's certificate. **Academic Requirements:** General education including some course work in arts/fine arts, English (including composition), foreign languages, humanities, mathematics, sciences (biological or physical), social science, physical education. **Classes:** 10-19 students in an average class. 10-19 students in an average lab/discussion section. **Majors with Highest Enrollment:** Business administration/management; nursing/registered nurse training (RN, ASN, BSN, MSN); criminal justice/law enforcement administration. **Disciplines with Highest Percentage of Degrees Awarded:** Business/marketing 19%, protective services/public administration 15%, health professions and related sciences 14%, education 8%, communications/communication technologies 7%. **Special Study Options:** Cooperative (work-study) program, cross registration, distance learning, double major, English as a second language, honors program, independent study, internships, student-designed major, study abroad, teacher certification program.

FACILITIES

Housing: Coed, fraternities and/or sororities, off-campus referral service. **Library Holdings:** 538,124 bound volumes. 6,660 periodicals. 708,709 microforms. 17,731 audiovisuals. **Special Academic Facilities/Equipment:** Mulvane Art Museum, White Concert Hall, University Theatre, observatory, planetarium, language lab, mediated classrooms, Living Learning Center. **Computers:** School-owned computers available for student use.

EXTRACURRICULARS

Activities: Choral groups, concert band, drama/theater, jazz band, literary magazine, marching band, music ensembles, musical theater, pep band, student government, student newspaper, television station, yearbook. **Organizations:** 71 registered organizations, 8 honor societies, 4 religious organizations, 4 fraternities (7% men join), 4 sororities (6% women join). **Athletics (Intercolle-

giate): *Men:* baseball, basketball, cheerleading, football, golf, tennis. *Women:* basketball, cheerleading, softball, tennis, volleyball.

ADMISSIONS

Selectivity Rating: 63 (of 100). **Freshman Academic Profile:** Average high school GPA 3.2. 20% in top 10% of high school class, 32% in top 25% of high school class, 65% in top 50% of high school class. 99% from public high schools. Average ACT 21, ACT middle 50% range 19-25. TOEFL required of all international applicants, minimum TOEFL 520. **Basis for Candidate Selection:** *Other factors considered include:* alumni/ae relation, character/personal qualities, class rank, extracurricular activities, secondary school record, standardized test scores, talent/ability, volunteer work, work experience. **Freshman Admission Requirements:** High school diploma or GED is required. *Academic units required/recommended:* 4 English recommended, 4 math recommended, 4 science recommended, 3 foreign language recommended, 2 social studies recommended, 2 history recommended. **Freshman Admission Statistics:** 1,238 applied, 100% accepted, 60% of those accepted enrolled. **Transfer Admission Requirements:** *Items required:* college transcript, statement of good standing from prior school. Minimum college GPA of 2.0 required. Lowest grade transferable D. **General Admission Information:** Application fee $20. Priority application deadline July 1. Nonfall registration accepted. Admission may be deferred for a maximum of 4 years. Credit offered for CEEB Advanced Placement tests.

COSTS AND FINANCIAL AID

In-state tuition $3,300. Out-of-state tuition $7,440. Room & board $4,300. Required fees $56. Average book expense $690. **Required Forms and Deadlines:** FAFSA and institution's own financial aid form. Financial aid filing deadline March 1. Priority filing deadline March 1. **Notification of Awards:** Applicants will be notified of awards on a rolling basis beginning on or about January 1. **Types of Aid:** *Need-based scholarships/grants:* Pell, SEOG, state scholarships/grants, private scholarships, the school's own gift aid. *Loans:* FFEL Subsidized Stafford, FFEL Unsubsidized Stafford, FFEL PLUS, Federal Perkins. **Student Employment:** Federal Work-Study Program available. Institutional employment available. Off-campus job opportunities are excellent. **Financial Aid Statistics:** 44% freshmen, 65% undergrads receive some form of aid. Average freshman grant $1,000. Average freshman loan $2,400. Average income from on-campus job $1,600. **Financial Aid Phone:** 785-231-1151.

WASHINGTON & JEFFERSON COLLEGE

60 South Lincoln Street, Washington, PA 15301
Phone: 724-223-6025 **E-mail:** admission@washjeff.edu **CEEB Code:** 2967
Fax: 724-223-6534 **Web:** www.washjeff.edu **ACT Code:** 3746

This private school was founded in 1781. It has a 51-acre campus.

STUDENTS AND FACULTY

Enrollment: 1,209. **Student Body:** Male 52%, female 48%, out-of-state 19%, international 1% (7 countries represented). **Ethnic Representation:** African American 2%, Asian 2%, Caucasian 95%, Hispanic 1%. **Retention and Graduation:** 82% freshmen return for sophomore year. 69% freshmen graduate within 4 years. 37% grads go on to further study within 1 year. 1% grads pursue business degrees. 13% grads pursue law degrees. 9% grads pursue medical degrees. **Faculty:** Student/faculty ratio 12:1. 89 full-time faculty, 84% hold PhDs. 100% faculty teach undergrads.

ACADEMICS

Degrees: Associate's, bachelor's. **Academic Requirements:** General education including some course work in arts/fine arts, computer literacy, English (including composition), foreign languages, history, humanities, mathematics, philosophy, sciences (biological or physical), social science. **Classes:** 10-19 students in an average class. 10-19 students in an average lab/discussion section. **Majors with Highest Enrollment:** Business administration/management; accounting; English language and literature, general. **Disciplines with Highest Percentage of Degrees Awarded:** Business/marketing 42%, social sciences and history 14%, English 11%, biological life sciences 10%, psychology 9%. **Special Study Options:** Accelerated program, double major, dual enrollment, honors program, independent study, internships, student-designed major, study abroad, teacher certification program, advanced placement credit.

FACILITIES

Housing: Coed, all-female, all-male, apartments for single students, housing for disabled students, housing for international students, fraternities and/or sororities. **Library Holdings:** 184,258 bound volumes. 8,124 periodicals. 14,688 microforms. 4,112 audiovisuals. **Special Academic Facilities/Equipment:** Language lab, spectrometers, isolator lab, X-ray diffraction unit, neuropsychology lab, atomic absorption unit, refrigerated centrifuge. **Computers:** *Recommended operating system:* Windows XP and 2000. School-owned computers available for student use.

EXTRACURRICULARS

Activities: Choral groups, concert band, dance, drama/theater, jazz band, literary magazine, music ensembles, musical theater, pep band, radio station, student government, student newspaper, student-run film society, yearbook. **Organizations:** 78 registered organizations, 18 honor societies, 4 religious organizations, 7 fraternities (45% men join), 4 sororities (48% women join). **Athletics (Intercollegiate):** *Men:* baseball, basketball, cross-country, diving, football, golf, lacrosse, soccer, swimming, tennis, track & field, water polo, wrestling. *Women:* basketball, cross-country, diving, field hockey, golf, soccer, softball, swimming, tennis, track & field, volleyball, water polo.

ADMISSIONS

Selectivity Rating: 79 (of 100). **Freshman Academic Profile:** Average high school GPA 3.2. 28% in top 10% of high school class, 54% in top 25% of high school class, 84% in top 50% of high school class. 85% from public high schools. Average SAT I Math 552, SAT I Math middle 50% range 500-610. Average SAT I Verbal 545, SAT I Verbal middle 50% range 500-600. Average ACT 24, ACT middle 50% range 21-26. TOEFL required of all international applicants, minimum TOEFL 500. **Basis for Candidate Selection:** *Very important factors considered include:* class rank, secondary school record. *Important factors considered include:* character/personal qualities, essays, extracurricular activities, interview, recommendations, standardized test scores, volunteer work, work experience. *Other factors considered include:* alumni/ae relation, geographical residence, state residency, talent/ability. **Freshman Admission Requirements:** High school diploma or GED is required. *Academic units required/recommended:* 15 total required; 3 English required, 3 math required, 1 science required, 2 foreign language required, 6 elective required. **Freshman Admission Statistics:** 1,874 applied, 51% accepted, 35% of those accepted enrolled. **Transfer Admission Requirements:** *Items required:* high school transcript, college transcript, essay, standardized test score, statement of good standing from prior school. Minimum high school GPA of 2.5 required. Minimum college GPA of 2.5 required. Lowest grade transferable C. **General Admission Information:** Application fee $25. Priority application deadline January 15. Early decision application deadline December 1. Regular application deadline March 1. Nonfall registration accepted. Admission may be deferred for a maximum of 1 year. Credit and/or placement offered for CEEB Advanced Placement tests.

COSTS AND FINANCIAL AID

Tuition $21,258. Room & board $5,992. Required fees $400. Average book expense $600. **Required Forms and Deadlines:** FAFSA and state aid form. Priority filing deadline February 15. **Notification of Awards:** Applicants will be notified of awards on a rolling basis beginning on or about March 1. **Types of Aid:** *Need-based scholarships/grants:* Pell, SEOG, state scholarships/grants, private scholarships, the school's own gift aid. *Loans:* FFEL Subsidized Stafford, FFEL Unsubsidized Stafford, FFEL PLUS, Federal Perkins, college/university loans from institutional funds. **Student Employment:** Federal Work-Study Program available. Institutional employment available. Off-campus job opportunities are good. **Financial Aid Statistics:** 73% freshmen, 83% undergrads receive some form of aid. Average freshman grant $12,178. Average freshman loan $3,534. Average income from on-campus job $1,200. **Financial Aid Phone:** 724-223-6019.

WASHINGTON AND LEE UNIVERSITY

Letcher Avenue, Lexington, VA 24450-0303
Phone: 540-458-8710 **E-mail:** admissions@wlu.edu **CEEB Code:** 5887
Fax: 540-458-8062 **Web:** www.wlu.edu **ACT Code:** 4430

This private school was founded in 1749. It has a 322-acre campus.

STUDENTS AND FACULTY

Enrollment: 1,750. **Student Body:** Male 53%, female 47%, out-of-state 82%, international 4% (47 countries represented). **Ethnic Representation:** African American 4%, Asian 2%, Caucasian 92%, Hispanic 1%. **Retention and Graduation:** 96% freshmen return for sophomore year. 84% freshmen graduate within 4 years. 24% grads go on to further study within 1 year. 1% grads pursue business degrees. 9% grads pursue law degrees. 5% grads pursue medical degrees. **Faculty:** Student/faculty ratio 11:1. 191 full-time faculty, 92% hold PhDs. 100% faculty teach undergrads.

ACADEMICS

Degrees: Bachelor's, first professional. **Academic Requirements:** General education including some course work in computer literacy, English (including composition), foreign languages, humanities, mathematics, sciences (biological or physical), social science, physical education including a swimming test. **Classes:** 10-19 students in an average class. Under 10 students in an average lab/discussion section. **Majors with Highest Enrollment:** Business administration/management; journalism; economics, general. **Disciplines with Highest Percentage of Degrees Awarded:** Social sciences and history 28%, business/marketing 22%, communications/communication technologies 7%, physical sciences 7%, English 7%. **Special Study Options:** Double major, student exchange program (domestic), honors program, independent study, internships, liberal arts/career combination, student-designed major, study abroad, teacher certification program, international study agreements.

FACILITIES

Housing: Coed, housing for international students, fraternities and/or sororities, Outing Club House, Spanish House. **Library Holdings:** 1,036,280 bound volumes. 6,170 periodicals. 993,362 microforms. 13,104 audiovisuals. **Special Academic Facilities/Equipment:** History and porcelain museums, performing arts center, communications labs, nuclear science lab, scanning electron microscope. **Computers:** *Recommended operating system:* Windows XP Pro. School-owned computers available for student use.

EXTRACURRICULARS

Activities: Choral groups, concert band, dance, drama/theater, jazz band, literary magazine, music ensembles, radio station, student government, student newspaper, student-run film society, symphony orchestra, television station, yearbook. **Organizations:** 90 registered organizations, 3 honor societies, 12 religious organizations, 15 fraternities (80% men join), 5 sororities (72% women join). **Athletics (Intercollegiate):** *Men:* baseball, basketball, cross-country, equestrian, football, golf, indoor track, lacrosse, soccer, swimming, tennis, track & field, wrestling. *Women:* basketball, cheerleading, cross-country, equestrian, field hockey, indoor track, lacrosse, soccer, swimming, tennis, track & field, volleyball.

ADMISSIONS

Selectivity Rating: 99 (of 100). **Freshman Academic Profile:** Average high school GPA 4. 80% in top 10% of high school class, 96% in top 25% of high school class, 100% in top 50% of high school class. SAT I Math middle 50% range 640-720. SAT I Verbal middle 50% range 640-720. ACT middle 50% range 28-30. **Basis for Candidate Selection:** *Very important factors considered include:* character/personal qualities, extracurricular activities, secondary school record, standardized test scores. *Important factors considered include:* class rank, recommendations. *Other factors considered include:* alumni/ae relation, essays, geographical residence, minority status, state residency, talent/ability, volunteer work, work experience. **Freshman Admission Requirements:** High school diploma is required and GED is not accepted. *Academic units required/recommended:* 16 total required; 4 English required, 3 math required, 4 math recommended, 1 science required, 3 science recommended, 1 science lab required, 2 foreign language required, 3 foreign language recommended, 1 social studies required, 1 history required, 2 history recommended, 4 elective required. **Freshman Admission Statistics:** 3,188 applied, 31% accepted, 46% of those accepted enrolled. **Transfer Admission Requirements:** *Items required:* high school transcript, college transcript, essay, standardized test score, statement of good standing from prior school. Minimum college GPA of 2.0 required. Lowest grade transferable C. **General Admission Information:** Application fee $40. Early decision application deadline December 1. Regular application deadline January 15. Admission may be deferred for a maximum of 1 year. Credit and/or placement offered for CEEB Advanced Placement tests.

COSTS AND FINANCIAL AID

Tuition $21,000. Room & board $5,913. Required fees $175. Average book expense $1,480. **Required Forms and Deadlines:** FAFSA, CSS/Financial Aid PROFILE, noncustodial (divorced/separated) parent's statement and business/farm supplement. Priority filing deadline February 1. **Notification of Awards:** Applicants will be notified of awards on or about April 3. **Types of Aid:** *Need-based scholarships/grants:* Pell, SEOG, state scholarships/grants, private scholarships, the school's own gift aid. *Loans:* FFEL Subsidized Stafford, FFEL Unsubsidized Stafford, FFEL PLUS, Federal Perkins, college/university loans from institutional funds. **Student Employment:** Federal Work-Study Program available. Institutional employment available. Off-campus job opportunities are fair. **Financial Aid Statistics:** 26% freshmen, 27% undergrads receive some form of aid. **Financial Aid Phone:** 540-458-8715.

WASHINGTON COLLEGE

$$$ III

300 Washington Avenue, Chestertown, MD 21620
Phone: 410-778-7700 **E-mail:** adm.off@washcoll.edu **CEEB Code:** 5888
Fax: 410-778-7287 **Web:** www.washcoll.edu **ACT Code:** 1754

This private school was founded in 1782. It has a 120-acre campus.

STUDENTS AND FACULTY

Enrollment: 1,302. **Student Body:** Male 38%, female 62%, out-of-state 44%, international 5%. **Ethnic Representation:** African American 3%, Asian 1%, Caucasian 86%, Hispanic 1%. **Retention and Graduation:** 83% freshmen return for sophomore year. 65% freshmen graduate within 4 years. 50% grads go on to further study within 1 year. 8% grads pursue business degrees. 4% grads pursue law degrees. 3% grads pursue medical degrees. **Faculty:** Student/faculty ratio 12:1. 80 full-time faculty, 88% hold PhDs. 98% faculty teach undergrads.

ACADEMICS

Degrees: Bachelor's, diploma, master's. **Academic Requirements:** General education including some course work in arts/fine arts, English (including composition), foreign languages, history, humanities, mathematics, sciences (biological or physical), social science. All students are required to meet writing requirements by completing an intensive writing course in both the sophomore and junior years. **Classes:** 10-19 students in an average class. 10-19 students in an average lab/discussion section. **Majors with Highest Enrollment:** Business administration/management; environmental studies; English/language arts teacher education. **Disciplines with Highest Percentage of Degrees Awarded:** Social sciences and history 28%, business/marketing 16%, English 12%, biological life sciences 11%, psychology 10%. **Special Study Options:** Double major, English as a second language, student exchange program (domestic), independent study, internships, student-designed major, study abroad, teacher certification program.

FACILITIES

Housing: Coed, all-female, all-male, housing for disabled students, housing for international students, fraternities and/or sororities. **Library Holdings:** 2,436,030 bound volumes. 4,667 periodicals. 247,626 microforms. 6,114 audiovisuals. **Special Academic Facilities/Equipment:** Language lab, computer classroom, C.V. Starr Center for the Study of the American Experience, Center for the Environment and Society. **Computers:** School-owned computers available for student use.

EXTRACURRICULARS

Activities: Choral groups, concert band, dance, drama/theater, jazz band, literary magazine, music ensembles, student government, student newspaper, student-run film society, symphony orchestra, yearbook. **Organizations:** 50 registered organizations, 13 honor societies, 4 religious organizations, 3 fraternities (20% men join), 3 sororities (20% women join). **Athletics (Intercollegiate):** *Men:* baseball, basketball, crew, lacrosse, soccer, swimming, tennis. *Women:* basketball, crew, field hockey, lacrosse, soccer, softball, swimming, tennis, volleyball.

ADMISSIONS

Selectivity Rating: 78 (of 100). **Freshman Academic Profile:** Average high school GPA 3.4. 36% in top 10% of high school class, 68% in top 25% of high school class, 93% in top 50% of high school class. 71% from public high schools. Average SAT I Math 555, SAT I Math middle 50% range 500-610. Average SAT I Verbal 571, SAT I Verbal middle 50% range 510-620. ACT middle 50% range 20-26. TOEFL required of all international applicants, minimum TOEFL 500. **Basis for Candidate Selection:** *Very important factors considered include:* interview, secondary school record. *Important factors considered include:* character/personal qualities, class rank, essays, recommendations, standardized test scores. *Other factors considered include:* alumni/ae relation, extracurricular activities, minority status, talent/ability, volunteer work, work experience. **Freshman Admission Requirements:** High school diploma or GED is required. *Academic units required/recommended:* 15 total required; 20 total recommended; 4 English required, 4 English recommended, 3 math required, 4 math recommended, 3 science required, 4 science recommended, 2 science lab required, 3 science lab recommended, 2 foreign language required, 4 foreign language recommended, 3 social studies required, 4 social studies recommended. **Freshman Admission Statistics:** 2,032 applied, 64% accepted, 28% of those accepted enrolled. **Transfer Admission Requirements:** *Items required:* high school transcript, college transcript, essay, statement of good standing from prior school. Minimum high school GPA of 2.5 required. Minimum college GPA of 2.5 required. Lowest grade transferable C. **General Admission Information:** Application fee $40. Early decision application deadline November 15. Regular application deadline February 15. Nonfall registration accepted. Admission may be deferred for a maximum of 1 year. Credit and/or placement offered for CEEB Advanced Placement tests.

COSTS AND FINANCIAL AID

Tuition $23,740. Room & board $5,740. Required fees $560. Average book expense $1,500. **Required Forms and Deadlines:** FAFSA and institution's own financial aid form. Financial aid filing deadline February 15. Priority filing deadline April 1. **Notification of Awards:** Applicants will be notified of awards on a rolling basis beginning on or about March 1. **Types of Aid:** *Need-based scholarships/grants:* Pell, SEOG, state scholarships/grants, private scholarships, the school's own gift aid. *Loans:* FFEL Subsidized Stafford, FFEL Unsubsidized Stafford, FFEL PLUS, Federal Perkins, college/university loans from institutional funds. **Student Employment:** Federal Work-Study Program available. Institutional employment available. Off-campus job opportunities are excellent. **Financial Aid Statistics:** 59% freshmen, 51% undergrads receive some form of aid. Average freshman grant $14,707. Average freshman loan $3,825. Average income from on-campus job $1,200. **Financial Aid Phone:** 410-778-7214.

See page 1278.

WASHINGTON STATE UNIVERSITY

370 Lighty Student Services, Pullman, WA 99164-1067
Phone: 509-335-5586 **E-mail:** admiss2@wsu.edu **CEEB Code:** 4705
Fax: 509-335-4902 **Web:** www.wsu.edu **ACT Code:** 4482

This public school was founded in 1890. It has a 620-acre campus.

STUDENTS AND FACULTY

Enrollment: 18,024. **Student Body:** Male 47%, female 53%, out-of-state 13%, international 3% (112 countries represented). **Ethnic Representation:** African American 3%, Asian 5%, Caucasian 79%, Hispanic 4%, Native American 1%. **Retention and Graduation:** 83% freshmen return for sophomore year. 31% freshmen graduate within 4 years. **Faculty:** Student/faculty ratio 17:1. 1,082 full-time faculty, 87% hold PhDs.

ACADEMICS

Degrees: Bachelor's, doctoral, first professional, master's, post-bachelor's certificate. **Academic Requirements:** General education including some course work in English (including composition), foreign languages, history, humanities, mathematics, sciences (biological or physical), social science. **Classes:** 10-19 students in an average class. **Disciplines with Highest Percentage of Degrees Awarded:** Business/marketing 20%, social sciences and history 12%, health professions and related sciences 9%, education 8%, engineering/engineering technology 7%. **Special Study Options:** Cooperative (work-study) program, cross registration, distance learning, double major, English as a second language, student exchange program (domestic), external degree program, honors program, independent study, internships, liberal arts/career combination, study abroad, teacher certification program.

FACILITIES

Housing: Coed, all-female, all-male, apartments for married students, apartments for single students, housing for international students, fraternities and/or sororities, single undergrad freshmen under age 20 required to live on campus. **Library Holdings:** 2,045,438 bound volumes. 30,292 periodicals. 4,628,813 microforms. 383,146 audiovisuals. **Special Academic Facilities/Equipment:** Art, natural history, and anthropology museums and special collections, performing arts center, mycological herbarium, energy research center, primate research center, observatory and planetarium, electron microscopy center, nuclear radiation center, state-of-the-art Center for Undergraduate Education Building. **Computers:** School-owned computers available for student use.

EXTRACURRICULARS

Activities: Choral groups, dance, drama/theater, jazz band, literary magazine, marching band, music ensembles, pep band, radio station, student government, student newspaper, student-run film society, television station, yearbook. **Organizations:** 225 registered organizations, 23 honor societies, 23 religious organizations, 24 fraternities (13% men join), 16 sororities (13% women join). **Athletics (Intercollegiate):** *Men:* baseball, basketball, cross-country, football, golf, track & field. *Women:* basketball, crew, cross-country, golf, soccer, swimming, tennis, track & field, volleyball.

ADMISSIONS

Selectivity Rating: 75 (of 100). **Freshman Academic Profile:** Average high school GPA 3.4. 96% from public high schools. Average SAT I Math 533, SAT I Math middle 50% range 480-590. Average SAT I Verbal 522, SAT I Verbal middle 50% range 470-580. TOEFL required of all international applicants, minimum TOEFL 520. **Basis for Candidate Selection:** *Very important factors considered include:* secondary school record, standardized test scores. *Other factors considered include:* essays, extracurricular activities, recommendations, talent/ability. **Freshman Admission Requirements:** High school diploma or GED is required. *Academic units required/recommended:* 15 total required; 4 English required, 3 math required, 2 science required, 1 science lab required, 2 foreign language required, 2 social studies required, 1 history required, 1 elective required. **Freshman Admission Statistics:** 8,986 applied, 77% accepted, 41% of those accepted enrolled. **Transfer Admission Requirements:** *Items required:* college transcript. Minimum high school GPA of 2.0 required. Minimum college GPA of 2.0 required. Lowest grade transferable D. **General Admission Information:** Application fee $35. Priority application deadline March 1. Nonfall registration accepted. Credit offered for CEEB Advanced Placement tests.

COSTS AND FINANCIAL AID

Required Forms and Deadlines: FAFSA. No deadline for regular filing. Priority filing deadline March 1. **Notification of Awards:** Applicants will be notified of awards on a rolling basis beginning on or about April 15. **Types of Aid:** *Need-based scholarships/grants:* Pell, SEOG, state scholarships/grants, private scholarships, the school's own gift aid, Federal Nursing. *Loans:* FFEL Subsidized Stafford, FFEL Unsubsidized Stafford, FFEL PLUS, Federal Perkins, Federal Nursing, college/university loans from institutional funds, alternative loans. **Student Employment:** Federal Work-Study Program available. Institutional employment available. Off-campus job opportunities are good. **Financial Aid Statistics:** 42% freshmen, 45% undergrads receive some form of aid. Average freshman grant $5,306. Average freshman loan $8,533. Average income from on-campus job $4,000. **Financial Aid Phone:** 509-335-9711.

WASHINGTON UNIVERSITY IN ST. LOUIS

Campus Box 1089, One Brookings Drive, St. Louis, MO 63130-4899
Phone: 314-935-6000 **E-mail:** admissions@wustl.edu **CEEB Code:** 6929
Fax: 314-935-4290 **Web:** www.wustl.edu **ACT Code:** 2386

This private school was founded in 1853. It has a 169-acre campus.

STUDENTS AND FACULTY

Enrollment: 7,219. **Student Body:** Male 47%, female 53%, out-of-state 89%, international 4% (104 countries represented). **Ethnic Representation:** African American 8%, Asian 10%, Caucasian 69%, Hispanic 3%. **Retention and Graduation:** 96% freshmen return for sophomore year. 33% grads go on to further study within 1 year. **Faculty:** Student/faculty ratio 7:1. 811 full-time faculty, 98% hold PhDs. 90% faculty teach undergrads.

ACADEMICS

Degrees: Bachelor's, certificate, doctoral, first professional, master's, post-bachelor's certificate. **Academic Requirements:** General education including some course work in English (including composition), humanities, mathematics, sciences (biological or physical), social science; varies by school. **Classes:** Under 10 students in an average class. 10-19 students in an average lab/discussion section. **Majors with Highest Enrollment:** Finance, general; biology/biological sciences, general; psychology, general. **Disciplines with Highest Percentage of Degrees Awarded:** Social sciences and history 17%, business/marketing 16%, engineering/engineering technology 15%, psychology 10%, computer and information sciences 7%. **Special Study Options:** Accelerated program, cooperative (work-study) program, cross registration, double major, dual enrollment, English as a second language, student exchange program (domestic), independent study, internships, liberal arts/career combination, student-designed major, study abroad, teacher certification program, University Scholars Program.

FACILITIES

Housing: Coed, apartments for married students, apartments for single students, fraternities and/or sororities, special-interest suites, upperclass housing, single-sex floors in coed buildings, small group housing for students who share common interests and goals. **Library Holdings:** 1,565,626 bound volumes. 18,316 periodicals. 3,226,960 microforms. 69,422 audiovisuals. **Special Academic Facilities/Equipment:** Art gallery, business/economics experimental lab, botanical garden, NASA planetary imaging facility, TAP reactor system, triple monochromator, computer automated radioactive particle tracking and gamma ray computed tomography, observatory, EADS learning center, student enterprise zone, Edison Theatre, lab science building, outdoor Tyson Research Center. **Computers:** School-owned computers available for student use.

EXTRACURRICULARS

Activities: Choral groups, concert band, dance, drama/theater, jazz band, literary magazine, music ensembles, musical theater, opera, pep band, radio station, student government, student newspaper, student-run film society, symphony orchestra, television station, yearbook. **Organizations:** 200 registered organizations, 18 honor societies, 16 religious organizations, 11 fraternities (27% men join), 5 sororities (21% women join). **Athletics (Intercollegiate):** *Men:* baseball, basketball, cross-country, diving, football, soccer, swimming, tennis, track & field. *Women:* basketball, cross-country, diving, soccer, softball, swimming, tennis, track & field, volleyball.

ADMISSIONS

Selectivity Rating: 97 (of 100). **Freshman Academic Profile:** 62% from public high schools. SAT I Math middle 50% range 670-750. SAT I Verbal middle 50% range 640-730. ACT middle 50% range 28-32. TOEFL required of all international applicants, minimum TOEFL 550. **Basis for Candidate Selection:** *Very important factors considered include:* character/personal qualities, class rank, essays, extracurricular activities, recommendations, secondary school record, standardized test scores, talent/ability, volunteer work, work experience. *Other factors considered include:* alumni/ae relation, interview, minority status. **Freshman Admission Requirements:** High school diploma or equivalent is not required. *Academic units required/recommended:* 18 total recommended; 4 English recommended, 4 math recommended, 4 science recommended, 4 science lab recommended, 2 foreign language recommended, 4 social studies recommended, 4 history recommended. **Freshman Admission Statistics:** 19,514 applied, 24% accepted, 29% of those accepted enrolled. **Transfer Admission Requirements:** *Items required:* college transcript, essay, statement of good standing from prior school. Lowest grade transferable C. **General Admission Information:** Application fee $55. Early decision application deadline November 15. Regular application deadline January 15. Admission may be deferred for a maximum of 2 years. Credit and/or placement offered for CEEB Advanced Placement tests.

COSTS AND FINANCIAL AID

Tuition $28,300. Room & board $9,240. Required fees $753. Average book expense $960. **Required Forms and Deadlines:** FAFSA, CSS/Financial Aid PROFILE, noncustodial (divorced/separated) parent's statement and student and parent 1040 tax return or signed waiver if there is no tax return. Financial aid filing deadline February 15. **Notification of Awards:** Applicants will be notified of awards on or about April 1. **Types of Aid:** *Need-based scholarships/grants:* Pell, SEOG, state scholarships/grants, private scholarships, the school's own gift aid, United Negro College Fund. *Loans:* FFEL Subsidized Stafford, FFEL Unsubsidized Stafford, FFEL PLUS, Federal Perkins, state loans, college/university loans from institutional funds. **Student Employment:** Federal Work-Study Program available. Institutional employment available. Off-campus job opportunities are excellent. **Financial Aid Statistics:** 41% freshmen, 45% undergrads receive some form of aid. Average income from on-campus job $2,000. **Financial Aid Phone:** 888-547-6670.

WAYLAND BAPTIST UNIVERSITY

1900 West 7th Street, CMB 712, Plainview, TX 79072
Phone: 806-291-3508 **E-mail:** admityou@mail.wbu.edu
Fax: 806-291-1960 **Web:** www.wbu.edu **ACT Code:** 4246

This private school, which is affiliated with the Southern Baptist Church, was founded in 1908. It has an 80-acre campus.

STUDENTS AND FACULTY

Enrollment: 943. **Student Body:** Male 41%, female 59%, out-of-state 13%, international 1% (14 countries represented). **Ethnic Representation:** African American 2%, Caucasian 48%, Hispanic 15%. **Retention and Graduation:** 65% freshmen return for sophomore year. 18% freshmen graduate within 4 years. **Faculty:** Student/faculty ratio 12:1. 61 full-time faculty, 68% hold PhDs. 100% faculty teach undergrads.

ACADEMICS

Degrees: Associate's, bachelor's, master's, transfer. **Academic Requirements:** General education including some course work in arts/fine arts, computer literacy, English (including composition), foreign languages, history, humanities, mathematics, sciences (biological or physical), social science. **Classes:** 10-19 students in an average class. **Majors with Highest Enrollment:** Business administration/management; elementary education and teaching; religion/religious studies. **Disciplines with Highest Percentage of Degrees Awarded:** Education 35%, business/marketing 17%, philosophy/religion/theology 12%, biological life sciences 8%, psychology 6%. **Special Study Options:** Accelerated program, distance learning, double major, dual enrollment, external degree program, honors program, internships, teacher certification program.

FACILITIES

Housing: All-female, all-male, apartments for married students. **Library Holdings:** 107,285 bound volumes. 541 periodicals. 301,287 microforms. 10,937 audiovisuals. **Special Academic Facilities/Equipment:** Llano Estacado Museum. **Computers:** *Recommended operating system:* Windows 95. School-owned computers available for student use.

EXTRACURRICULARS

Activities: Choral groups, concert band, drama/theater, marching band, music ensembles, musical theater, pep band, radio station, student government, student newspaper, television station, yearbook. **Organizations:** 37 registered organizations, 3 honor societies, 9 religious organizations, 4% men join fraternities, 2% women join sororities. **Athletics (Intercollegiate):** *Men:* baseball, basketball, cross-country, golf, track & field. *Women:* basketball, cross-country, soccer, track & field, volleyball.

ADMISSIONS

Selectivity Rating: 66 (of 100). **Freshman Academic Profile:** Average high school GPA 3.4. 18% in top 10% of high school class, 46% in top 25% of high school class, 73% in top 50% of high school class. Average SAT I Math 504, SAT I Math middle 50% range 430-580. Average SAT I Verbal 494, SAT I Verbal middle 50% range 420-570. Average ACT 20, ACT middle 50% range 17-22. TOEFL required of all international applicants, minimum TOEFL 500. **Basis for Candidate Selection:** *Very important factors considered include:* class rank, standardized test scores. *Important factors considered include:* secondary school record. **Freshman Admission Requirements:** High school diploma or GED is required. *Academic units required/recommended:* 9 total required; 3 English required, 2 math required, 3 math recommended, 2 science required, 3 science recommended, 2 social studies required. **Freshman Admission Statistics:** 264 applied, 98% accepted, 73% of those accepted enrolled. **Transfer Admission Requirements:** *Items required:* college transcript, statement of good standing from prior school. Minimum college GPA of 2.0 required. Lowest grade transferable D. **General Admission Information:** Application fee $35. Priority application deadline August 1. Nonfall registration accepted. Credit offered for CEEB Advanced Placement tests.

COSTS AND FINANCIAL AID

Tuition $8,100. Room & board $3,420. Required fees $350. Average book expense $1,400. **Required Forms and Deadlines:** FAFSA and institution's own financial aid form. No deadline for regular filing. Priority filing deadline May 1. **Notification of Awards:** Applicants will be notified of awards on a rolling basis beginning on or about February 15. **Types of Aid:** *Need-based scholarships/grants:* Pell, SEOG, state scholarships/grants, private scholarships, the school's own gift aid. *Loans:* FFEL Subsidized Stafford, FFEL Unsubsidized Stafford, FFEL PLUS, Federal Perkins, state loans, college/university loans from institutional funds. **Student Employment:** Federal Work-Study Program available. Institutional employment available. Off-campus job opportunities are good. **Financial Aid Statistics:** 76% freshmen, 74% undergrads receive some form of aid. Average freshman grant $5,490. Average freshman loan $4,105. **Financial Aid Phone:** 806-291-3520.

WAYNE STATE COLLEGE

1111 Main Street, Wayne, NE 68787
Phone: 402-375-7234 **E-mail:** admit1@wsc.edu **CEEB Code:** 6469
Fax: 402-375-7204 **Web:** www.wsc.edu **ACT Code:** 2472

This public school was founded in 1909. It has a 128-acre campus.

STUDENTS AND FACULTY

Enrollment: 2,743. **Student Body:** Male 42%, female 58%, out-of-state 15%, international 1% (22 countries represented). **Ethnic Representation:** African American 3%, Asian 1%, Caucasian 91%, Hispanic 2%, Native American 1%. **Retention and Graduation:** 65% freshmen return for sophomore year. **Faculty:** Student/faculty ratio 18:1. 126 full-time faculty, 79% hold PhDs. 100% faculty teach undergrads.

ACADEMICS

Degrees: Bachelor's, master's, post-master's certificate. **Academic Requirements:** General education including some course work in arts/fine arts, computer literacy, English (including composition), history, humanities, mathematics, philosophy, sciences (biological or physical), social science, technology and society, health and physical education. **Classes:** 10-19 students in an average class. 10-19 students in an average lab/discussion section. **Majors**

with Highest Enrollment: Business administration/management; elementary education and teaching. **Disciplines with Highest Percentage of Degrees Awarded:** Business/marketing 23%, education 22%, parks and recreation 9%, communications/communication technologies 7%, psychology 6%. **Special Study Options:** Cooperative (work-study) program, distance learning, double major, dual enrollment, honors program, independent study, internships, student-designed major, teacher certification program.

FACILITIES

Housing: Coed, all-female. **Library Holdings:** 147,205 bound volumes. 656 periodicals. 650,000 microforms. 5,300 audiovisuals. **Special Academic Facilities/Equipment:** Art gallery, fine arts center, planetarium, recreation center, telecommunications network. **Computers:** School-owned computers available for student use.

EXTRACURRICULARS

Activities: Choral groups, concert band, dance, drama/theater, jazz band, literary magazine, marching band, music ensembles, musical theater, pep band, radio station, student government, student newspaper, television station. **Organizations:** 89 registered organizations, 16 honor societies, 9 religious organizations, 2 fraternities, 3 sororities. **Athletics (Intercollegiate):** *Men:* baseball, basketball, cross-country, football, golf, indoor track, track & field. *Women:* basketball, cross-country, golf, indoor track, soccer, softball, track & field, volleyball.

ADMISSIONS

Selectivity Rating: 64 (of 100). **Freshman Academic Profile:** Average high school GPA 3.1. 8% in top 10% of high school class, 23% in top 25% of high school class, 57% in top 50% of high school class. 90% from public high schools. Average ACT 21, ACT middle 50% range 18-24. TOEFL required of all international applicants, minimum TOEFL 550. **Basis for Candidate Selection:** *Very important factors considered include:* secondary school record. *Important factors considered include:* standardized test scores. *Other factors considered include:* class rank. **Freshman Admission Requirements:** High school diploma or GED is required. *Academic units required/recommended:* 4 English recommended, 3 math recommended, 2 science recommended, 3 social studies recommended. **Freshman Admission Statistics:** 1,253 applied, 71% accepted, 69% of those accepted enrolled. **Transfer Admission Requirements:** *Items required:* college transcript. Minimum college GPA of 2.0 required. Lowest grade transferable C. **General Admission Information:** Application fee $20. Nonfall registration accepted. Admission may be deferred for a maximum of 1 year. Credit and/or placement offered for CEEB Advanced Placement tests.

COSTS AND FINANCIAL AID

Required Forms and Deadlines: FAFSA and institution's own financial aid form. Priority filing deadline June 1. **Notification of Awards:** Applicants will be notified of awards on a rolling basis beginning on or about April 1. **Types of Aid:** *Need-based scholarships/grants:* Pell, SEOG, state scholarships/grants, private scholarships, the school's own gift aid. *Loans:* FFEL Subsidized Stafford, FFEL Unsubsidized Stafford, FFEL PLUS, Federal Perkins. **Student Employment:** Federal Work-Study Program available. Institutional employment available. Off-campus job opportunities are fair. **Financial Aid Statistics:** 67% freshmen, 61% undergrads receive some form of aid. **Financial Aid Phone:** 402-375-7230.

WAYNE STATE UNIVERSITY

Office of Admissions, Detroit, MI 48202
Phone: 313-577-3577 **E-mail:** admissions@wayne.edu **CEEB Code:** 1898
Fax: 313-577-7536 **Web:** www.wayne.edu **ACT Code:** 2064

This public school was founded in 1868. It has a 203-acre campus.

STUDENTS AND FACULTY

Enrollment: 18,408. **Student Body:** Male 40%, female 60%. **Ethnic Representation:** African American 30%, Asian 6%, Caucasian 51%, Hispanic 3%. **Faculty:** 62% faculty teach undergrads.

ACADEMICS

Degrees: Bachelor's, doctoral, first professional, master's, post-bachelor's certificate, post-master's certificate. **Academic Requirements:** General education including some course work in arts/fine arts, computer literacy, English (including composition), foreign culture, foreign languages, history, humanities, mathematics, oral communication, philosophy, sciences (biological or physical), social science. **Classes:** Under 10 students in an average class. Under 10 students in an average lab/discussion section. **Majors with Highest Enrollment:** Elementary education and teaching; multi/interdisciplinary studies; fine/studio arts, general. **Disciplines with Highest Percentage of Degrees Awarded:** Education 15%, business/marketing 15%, health professions and related sciences 15%, engineering/engineering technology 9%, psychology 7%. **Special Study Options:** Accelerated program, cooperative (work-study) program, cross registration, distance learning, double major, dual enrollment, English as a second language, student exchange program (domestic), honors program, independent study, internships, liberal arts/career combination, study abroad, teacher certification program, weekend college, external degree program.

FACILITIES

Housing: Coed, apartments for married students, apartments for single students, housing for disabled students. **Special Academic Facilities/Equipment:** Detroit Institute of Arts, Detroit Historical Museum, Detroit Science Museum. **Computers:** School-owned computers available for student use.

EXTRACURRICULARS

Activities: Choral groups, concert band, dance, drama/theater, jazz band, marching band, music ensembles, pep band, student government, student newspaper, student-run film society, symphony orchestra, yearbook. **Organizations:** 125 registered organizations, 4 honor societies, 12 religious organizations, 7 fraternities, 8 sororities. **Athletics (Intercollegiate):** *Men:* baseball, basketball, cross-country, diving, fencing, football, golf, ice hockey, swimming, tennis. *Women:* basketball, cross-country, diving, fencing, ice hockey, softball, swimming, tennis, volleyball.

ADMISSIONS

Selectivity Rating: 67 (of 100). **Freshman Academic Profile:** Average ACT 21, ACT middle 50% range 17-24. TOEFL required of all international applicants, minimum TOEFL 550. **Basis for Candidate Selection:** *Very important factors considered include:* secondary school record, standardized test scores. *Other factors considered include:* class rank, extracurricular activities. **Freshman Admission Requirements:** High school diploma or GED is required. *Academic units required/recommended:* 18 total recommended; 4 English recommended, 4 math recommended, 3 science recommended, 2 foreign language recommended, 3 social studies recommended, 2 elective recommended. **Transfer Admission Requirements:** *Items required:* college transcript. Minimum college GPA of 2.0 required. Lowest grade transferable C. **General Admission Information:** Application fee $20. Regular application deadline August 1. Nonfall registration accepted. Admission may be deferred for a maximum of 1 year. Credit and/or placement offered for CEEB Advanced Placement tests.

COSTS AND FINANCIAL AID

In-state tuition $4,242. Out-of-state tuition $9,720. Room & board $6,100. Required fees $481. **Required Forms and Deadlines:** FAFSA, income tax forms and W-2 forms. Priority filing deadline March 1. **Notification of Awards:** Applicants will be notified of awards on a rolling basis beginning on or about April 1. **Student Employment:** Federal Work-Study Program available. Institutional employment available. Off-campus job opportunities are excellent. **Financial Aid Statistics:** 59% freshmen, 55% undergrads receive some form of aid. Average freshman grant $3,398. Average freshman loan $2,378. Average income from on-campus job $2,840. **Financial Aid Phone:** 313-577-3378.

WAYNESBURG COLLEGE

51 West College Street, Waynesburg, PA 15370
Phone: 724-852-3248 **E-mail:** admissions@waynesburg.edu **CEEB Code:** 2969
Fax: 724-627-8124 **Web:** www.waynesburg.edu **ACT Code:** 3748

This private school, which is affiliated with the Presbyterian Church, was founded in 1849. It has a 30-acre campus.

STUDENTS AND FACULTY

Enrollment: 1,442. **Student Body:** Male 45%, female 55%, out-of-state 15%, (5 countries represented). **Ethnic Representation:** African American 5%, Caucasian 95%. **Retention and Graduation:** 72% freshmen return for sophomore year. 47% freshmen graduate within 4 years. 7% grads pursue business degrees. 2% grads pursue law degrees. 1% grads pursue medical degrees. **Faculty:** Student/faculty ratio 14:1. 65 full-time faculty, 70% hold PhDs. 100% faculty teach undergrads.

ACADEMICS

Degrees: Associate's, bachelor's, master's. **Academic Requirements:** General education including some course work in arts/fine arts, computer literacy,

English (including composition), history, mathematics, philosophy, sciences (biological or physical), social science, life skills, service learning, religion. **Classes:** 10-19 students in an average class. 10-19 students in an average lab/discussion section. **Majors with Highest Enrollment:** Business, management, marketing, and related support services; communications, journalism, and related fields; criminal justice/law enforcement administration. **Disciplines with Highest Percentage of Degrees Awarded:** Health professions and related sciences 25%, business/marketing 24%, protective services/public administration 10%, education 8%, communications/communication technologies 7%. **Special Study Options:** Accelerated program, cooperative (work-study) program, distance learning, double major, dual enrollment, English as a second language, honors program, independent study, internships, liberal arts/career combination, student-designed major, study abroad, teacher certification program.

FACILITIES

Housing: All-female, all-male. **Library Holdings:** 100,000 bound volumes. 492 periodicals. 65 microforms. 0 audiovisuals. **Special Academic Facilities/Equipment:** Geology, biology, archaeology, and ceramics museum, arboretum, 174-acre farm. **Computers:** School-owned computers available for student use.

EXTRACURRICULARS

Activities: Choral groups, drama/theater, literary magazine, music ensembles, radio station, student government, student newspaper, television station, yearbook. **Organizations:** 30 registered organizations, 16 honor societies, 7 religious organizations. **Athletics (Intercollegiate):** *Men:* baseball, basketball, football, golf, soccer, tennis, wrestling. *Women:* basketball, cross-country, golf, soccer, softball, tennis, volleyball.

ADMISSIONS

Selectivity Rating: 67 (of 100). **Freshman Academic Profile:** 16% in top 10% of high school class, 37% in top 25% of high school class, 67% in top 50% of high school class. TOEFL required of all international applicants, minimum TOEFL 550. **Basis for Candidate Selection:** *Very important factors considered include:* class rank, interview, secondary school record, standardized test scores. *Other factors considered include:* character/personal qualities, essays, extracurricular activities, recommendations, work experience. **Freshman Admission Requirements:** High school diploma or GED is required. *Academic units required/recommended:* 16 total required; 4 English required, 3 math required, 2 science required, 2 foreign language recommended, 2 social studies required, 5 elective required. **Freshman Admission Statistics:** 1,251 applied, 79% accepted, 31% of those accepted enrolled. **Transfer Admission Requirements:** *Items required:* high school transcript, college transcript, statement of good standing from prior school. Minimum college GPA of 2.0 required. Lowest grade transferable C. **General Admission Information:** Application fee $20. Nonfall registration accepted. Credit offered for CEEB Advanced Placement tests.

COSTS AND FINANCIAL AID

Tuition $12,870. Room & board $5,280. Required fees $330. Average book expense $1,000. **Required Forms and Deadlines:** FAFSA and institution's own financial aid form. No deadline for regular filing. Priority filing deadline March 15. **Notification of Awards:** Applicants will be notified of awards on a rolling basis beginning on or about February 15. **Types of Aid:** *Need-based scholarships/grants:* Pell, SEOG, state scholarships/grants, private scholarships, the school's own gift aid. *Loans:* FFEL Subsidized Stafford, FFEL Unsubsidized Stafford, FFEL PLUS, Federal Perkins, Federal Nursing, private alternative loans. **Student Employment:** Federal Work-Study Program available. Institutional employment available. Off-campus job opportunities are good. **Financial Aid Statistics:** 94% freshmen, 86% undergrads receive some form of aid. Average freshman grant $7,359. Average freshman loan $2,779. Average income from on-campus job $636. **Financial Aid Phone:** 724-852-3208.

WEBB INSTITUTE

Crescent Beach Road, Glen Cove, NY 11542
Phone: 516-671-2213 **E-mail:** admissions@webb-institute.edu **CEEB Code:** 2970
Fax: 516-674-9838 **Web:** www.webb-institute.edu **ACT Code:** 20228

This private school was founded in 1889. It has a 26-acre campus.

STUDENTS AND FACULTY

Enrollment: 67. **Student Body:** Out-of-state 78%. **Ethnic Representation:** African American 1%, Asian 3%, Caucasian 96%. **Retention and Graduation:** 77% freshmen return for sophomore year. 50% freshmen graduate within 4 years. 25% grads go on to further study within 1 year. **Faculty:** Student/faculty ratio 7:1. 8 full-time faculty, 37% hold PhDs. 100% faculty teach undergrads.

ACADEMICS

Degrees: Bachelor's. **Academic Requirements:** General education including some course work in computer literacy, English (including composition), history, humanities, mathematics, philosophy, sciences (biological or physical), social science, engineering. **Classes:** 10-19 students in an average class. **Disciplines with Highest Percentage of Degrees Awarded:** Engineering/engineering technology 100%. **Special Study Options:** Double major, internships.

FACILITIES

Housing: Coed, all-female, all-male. **Library Holdings:** 43,104 bound volumes. 262 periodicals. 1,633 microforms. 1,860 audiovisuals. **Special Academic Facilities/Equipment:** Towing tank for model testing, marine engineering lab. **Computers:** *Recommended operating system:* Windows NT/2000. School-owned computers available for student use.

EXTRACURRICULARS

Activities: Choral groups, drama/theater, student government, symphony orchestra, yearbook. **Organizations:** 2 registered organizations. **Athletics (Intercollegiate):** *Men:* basketball, cross-country, sailing, soccer, tennis, volleyball. *Women:* basketball, cross-country, sailing, soccer, tennis, volleyball.

ADMISSIONS

Selectivity Rating: 96 (of 100). **Freshman Academic Profile:** Average high school GPA 3.9. 83% in top 10% of high school class, 100% in top 25% of high school class. 88% from public high schools. Average SAT I Math 720, SAT I Math middle 50% range 700-740. Average SAT I Verbal 670, SAT I Verbal middle 50% range 620-710. **Basis for Candidate Selection:** *Very important factors considered include:* class rank, interview, secondary school record, standardized test scores. *Important factors considered include:* character/personal qualities, recommendations, talent/ability. *Other factors considered include:* extracurricular activities, minority status, volunteer work, work experience. **Freshman Admission Requirements:** High school diploma is required and GED is not accepted. *Academic units required/recommended:* 16 total required; 4 English required, 4 math required, 2 science required, 2 science lab required, 2 social studies required, 4 elective required. **Freshman Admission Statistics:** 82 applied, 41% accepted, 50% of those accepted enrolled. **Transfer Admission Requirements:** *Items required:* high school transcript, college transcript, interview, standardized test scores. Minimum high school GPA of 3.5 required. Minimum college GPA of 3.5 required. **General Admission Information:** Application fee $25. Priority application deadline October 15. Early decision application deadline October 15. Regular application deadline February 15. Neither credit nor placement offered for CEEB Advanced Placement tests.

COSTS AND FINANCIAL AID

Room & board $6,950. Average book expense $600. **Required Forms and Deadlines:** FAFSA. Financial aid filing deadline July 1. Priority filing deadline July 1. **Notification of Awards:** Applicants will be notified of awards on or about August 1. **Types of Aid:** *Need-based scholarships/grants:* Pell, state scholarships/grants, private scholarships. *Loans:* FFEL Subsidized Stafford, FFEL Unsubsidized Stafford, FFEL PLUS. **Student Employment:** Off-campus job opportunities are good. **Financial Aid Statistics:** 53% freshmen, 28% undergrads receive some form of aid. Average freshman grant $2,750. Average freshman loan $2,625. **Financial Aid Phone:** 516-671-2213.

WEBBER INTERNATIONAL UNIVERSITY

PO Box 96, Babson Park, FL 33827
Phone: 863-638-2910 **E-mail:** admissions@webber.edu **CEEB Code:** 5893
Fax: 863-638-1591 **Web:** www.webber.edu **ACT Code:** 773

This private school was founded in 1927. It has a 110-acre campus.

STUDENTS AND FACULTY

Enrollment: 521. **Student Body:** Male 60%, female 40%, out-of-state 8%, international 19%. **Ethnic Representation:** African American 23%, Asian 1%, Caucasian 67%, Hispanic 10%. **Retention and Graduation:** 71% freshmen return for sophomore year. 38% freshmen graduate within 4 years. 15% grads go on to further study within 1 year. 18% grads pursue business degrees. 2% grads pursue law degrees. **Faculty:** Student/faculty ratio 22:1. 16 full-time faculty, 50% hold PhDs. 100% faculty teach undergrads.

ACADEMICS

Degrees: Associate's, bachelor's, master's. **Academic Requirements:** General education including some course work in computer literacy, English (including composition), humanities, mathematics, sciences (biological or physical), social science, business core (Webber is a business university). **Classes:** 10-19 students in an average class. **Majors with Highest Enrollment:** Business administration/management; sports and fitness administration/management; marketing/marketing management, general. **Disciplines with Highest Percentage of Degrees Awarded:** Business/marketing 82%, parks and recreation 8%, law/legal studies 1%. **Special Study Options:** Double major, English as a second language, internships.

FACILITIES

Housing: All-female, all-male. **Library Holdings:** 25,000 bound volumes. 89 periodicals. 0 microforms. 210 audiovisuals. **Computers:** School-owned computers available for student use.

EXTRACURRICULARS

Activities: Student government, student newspaper. **Organizations:** 6 registered organizations, 1 honor society. **Athletics (Intercollegiate):** *Men:* baseball, basketball, cross-country, football, golf, soccer, tennis, track & field. *Women:* basketball, cross-country, golf, soccer, softball, tennis, track & field, volleyball.

ADMISSIONS

Selectivity Rating: 66 (of 100). **Freshman Academic Profile:** Average high school GPA 3.0. 4% in top 10% of high school class, 27% in top 25% of high school class, 54% in top 50% of high school class. 85% from public high schools. Average SAT I Math 462, SAT I Math middle 50% range 410-510. Average SAT I Verbal 433, SAT I Verbal middle 50% range 390-480. Average ACT 18, ACT middle 50% range 16-19. TOEFL required of all international applicants, minimum TOEFL 500. **Basis for Candidate Selection:** *Very important factors considered include:* essays, recommendations, secondary school record, standardized test scores. *Important factors considered include:* alumni/ae relation, character/personal qualities, interview, volunteer work. *Other factors considered include:* work experience. **Freshman Admission Requirements:** High school diploma or GED is required. *Academic units required/recommended:* 16 total recommended; 4 English required, 4 English recommended, 2 math required, 3 math recommended, 1 science required, 3 science recommended, 1 foreign language recommended, 1 social studies required, 1 social studies recommended, 2 history recommended, 4 elective recommended. **Freshman Admission Statistics:** 377 applied, 40% accepted, 99% of those accepted enrolled. **Transfer Admission Requirements:** *Items required:* college transcript, essay, statement of good standing from prior school. Minimum college GPA of 2.0 required. Lowest grade transferable C. **General Admission Information:** Application fee $35. Priority application deadline May 1. Regular application deadline August 1. Nonfall registration accepted. Admission may be deferred. Credit offered for CEEB Advanced Placement tests.

COSTS AND FINANCIAL AID

Tuition $11,500. Room & board $4,500. Required fees $100. Average book expense $650. **Required Forms and Deadlines:** FAFSA. Financial aid filing deadline August 1. Priority filing deadline May 1. **Notification of Awards:** Applicants will be notified of awards on a rolling basis beginning on or about March 15. **Types of Aid:** *Need-based scholarships/grants:* Pell, SEOG, state scholarships/grants, private scholarships, the school's own gift aid. *Loans:* FFEL Subsidized Stafford, FFEL Unsubsidized Stafford, FFEL PLUS, Federal Perkins. **Student Employment:** Federal Work-Study Program available. Institutional employment available. Off-campus job opportunities are good. **Financial Aid Statistics:** 62% freshmen, 59% undergrads receive some form of aid. Average freshman grant $10,523. Average freshman loan $2,617. Average income from on-campus job $750. **Financial Aid Phone:** 941-638-2929.

See page 1280.

WEBER STATE UNIVERSITY

1137 University Circle, Ogden, UT 84408-1137
Phone: 801-626-6744 **E-mail:** admissions@weber.edu **CEEB Code:** 4941
Fax: 801-626-6747 **Web:** www.weber.edu **ACT Code:** 4282

This public school was founded in 1889. It has a 526-acre campus.

STUDENTS AND FACULTY

Enrollment: 17,794. **Student Body:** Male 48%, female 52%, out-of-state 6%, international 1% (35 countries represented). **Ethnic Representation:** African American 1%, Asian 2%, Caucasian 79%, Hispanic 3%, Native American 1%. **Retention and Graduation:** 71% freshmen return for sophomore year. 12% freshmen graduate within 4 years. **Faculty:** Student/faculty ratio 23:1. 450 full-time faculty, 90% hold PhDs. 98% faculty teach undergrads.

ACADEMICS

Degrees: Associate's, bachelor's, certificate, master's, post-bachelor's certificate, terminal, transfer. **Academic Requirements:** General education including some course work in arts/fine arts, computer literacy, English (including composition), history, humanities, mathematics, sciences (biological or physical), social science. **Classes:** 20-29 students in an average class. Under 10 students in an average lab/discussion section. **Majors with Highest Enrollment:** Liberal arts and sciences/liberal studies; nursing/registered nurse training (RN, ASN, BSN, MSN); elementary education and teaching. **Disciplines with Highest Percentage of Degrees Awarded:** Business/marketing 21%, education 14%, health professions and related sciences 13%, protective services/public administration 9%, computer and information sciences 7%. **Special Study Options:** Accelerated program, cooperative (work-study) program, distance learning, double major, dual enrollment, English as a second language, student exchange program (domestic), external degree program, honors program, independent study, internships, student-designed major, study abroad, teacher certification program, First Year Experience.

FACILITIES

Housing: All-female, all-male, apartments for single students, housing for disabled students. **Library Holdings:** 686,681 bound volumes. 2,331 periodicals. 563,362 microforms. 17,499 audiovisuals. **Special Academic Facilities/Equipment:** Art gallery, language lab, TV studio, communication arts/technologies facilities, natural science museum, herbarium, planetarium, aerospace technology equipment for developing satellite projects, dental hygiene clinic. **Computers:** *Recommended operating system:* Windows NT. School-owned computers available for student use.

EXTRACURRICULARS

Activities: Choral groups, concert band, dance, drama/theater, jazz band, literary magazine, marching band, music ensembles, musical theater, opera, pep band, radio station, student government, student newspaper, student-run film society, symphony orchestra, television station. **Organizations:** 100 registered organizations, 1 honor society, 5 fraternities (2% men join), 5 sororities (3% women join). **Athletics (Intercollegiate):** *Men:* basketball, cheerleading, cross-country, football, golf, indoor track, tennis, track & field. *Women:* basketball, cheerleading, cross-country, golf, indoor track, soccer, tennis, track & field, volleyball.

ADMISSIONS

Selectivity Rating: 68 (of 100). **Freshman Academic Profile:** Average high school GPA 3.3. 56% in top 25% of high school class, 89% in top 50% of high school class. 95% from public high schools. SAT I Math middle 50% range 450-590. SAT I Verbal middle 50% range 450-580. Average ACT 22, ACT middle 50% range 18-25. **Basis for Candidate Selection:** *Important factors considered include:* secondary school record, standardized test scores. *Other factors considered include:* character/personal qualities, extracurricular activities, interview. **Freshman Admission Requirements:** High school diploma or GED is required. *Academic units required/recommended:* 15 total recommended; 4 English recommended, 2 math recommended, 2 science recommended, 2 foreign language recommended, 1 history recommended, 4 elective recommended. **Freshman Admission Statistics:** 5,663 applied, 100% accepted, 50% of those accepted enrolled. **Transfer Admission Requirements:** *Items required:* college transcript. Minimum college GPA of 2.0 required. Lowest grade transferable C. **General Admission Information:** Application fee $30. Regular application deadline August 23. Nonfall registration accepted. Admission may be deferred for a maximum of 1 year. Placement offered for CEEB Advanced Placement tests.

COSTS AND FINANCIAL AID

In-state tuition $1,786. Out-of-state tuition $6,252. Room & board $4,645. Required fees $466. Average book expense $900. **Required Forms and Deadlines:** FAFSA and institution's own financial aid form. Priority filing deadline March 1. **Notification of Awards:** Applicants will be notified of awards on a rolling basis beginning on or about March 15. **Types of Aid:** *Need-based scholarships/grants:* Pell, SEOG, state scholarships/grants. *Loans:* FFEL Subsidized Stafford, FFEL Unsubsidized Stafford, FFEL PLUS, Federal Perkins, Short-term Tuition Loan. **Student Employment:** Federal Work-Study Program available. Institutional employment available. Off-campus job opportunities are excellent. **Financial Aid Statistics:** 57% freshmen, 63% undergrads receive some form of aid. Average freshman grant $5,500. Average freshman loan $2,380. **Financial Aid Phone:** 801-626-6581.

WEBSTER UNIVERSITY

470 East Lockwood Avenue, Saint Louis, MO 63119-3194
Phone: 314-968-6991 **E-mail:** admit@webster.edu **CEEB Code:** 6933
Fax: 314-968-7115 **Web:** www.webster.edu **ACT Code:** 2388

This private school was founded in 1915. It has a 47-acre campus.

STUDENTS AND FACULTY

Enrollment: 3,458. **Student Body:** Male 38%, female 62%, out-of-state 20%, international 4% (104 countries represented). **Ethnic Representation:** African American 11%, Asian 2%, Caucasian 79%, Hispanic 2%. **Retention and Graduation:** 79% freshmen return for sophomore year. 43% freshmen graduate within 4 years. 22% grads go on to further study within 1 year. **Faculty:** Student/faculty ratio 13:1. 146 full-time faculty, 80% hold PhDs. 100% faculty teach undergrads.

ACADEMICS

Degrees: Bachelor's, certificate, doctoral, master's, post-bachelor's certificate, post-master's certificate. **Academic Requirements:** General education including some course work in arts/fine arts, English (including composition), history, humanities, mathematics, sciences (biological or physical), social science, critical thinking and values. **Classes:** 10-19 students in an average class. **Majors with Highest Enrollment:** Business administration/management; computer science; education, general. **Disciplines with Highest Percentage of Degrees Awarded:** Business/marketing 36%, computer and information sciences 12%, communications/communication technologies 12%, visual and performing arts 11%, education 6%. **Special Study Options:** Accelerated program, cooperative (work-study) program, cross registration, distance learning, double major, dual enrollment, English as a second language, independent study, internships, student-designed major, study abroad, teacher certification program, certificate programs, combination bachelor's/master's degree in many subject areas, independent study, Student Leadership Development Program. In addition to the programs offered at its five St. Louis area campuses, Webster University offers undergraduate degree completion programs at the following extended campus locations in the United States: Kansas City, MO (www.webster.edu/kc/); Los Angeles, CA, at Marymount Webster Weekend College (www.marymountpv.edu/weekend/); Orlando, FL (www.webster.edu/multicampus/orlandod.html); and San Diego, CA (www.webster.edu/multicampus/sandiego.html). Undergraduate students may also study at Webster's international campuses, where they may complete their entire degree at the following locations: Geneva, Switzerland (www.webster.ch); Leiden, The Netherlands (www.webster.nl); London, UK, at Webster at Regent's College (www.bacl.ac.uk); Vienna, Austria (www.webster.ac.at); and Cha-am, Thailand (www.webster.ac.th).

FACILITIES

Housing: Coed, apartments for married students, apartments for single students, housing for international students. **Library Holdings:** 268,000 bound volumes. 1,480 periodicals. 137,000 microforms. 14,800 audiovisuals. **Special Academic Facilities/Equipment:** Loretto-Hilton Center for Performing Arts (houses St. Louis Repertory Company, Opera Theatre of St. Louis, and Webster Symphony). **Computers:** School-owned computers available for student use.

EXTRACURRICULARS

Activities: Choral groups, dance, drama/theater, jazz band, literary magazine, music ensembles, musical theater, opera, radio station, student government, student newspaper, student-run film society, symphony orchestra, yearbook. **Organizations:** 37 registered organizations, 1 honor society, 2 religious organizations. **Athletics (Intercollegiate):** *Men:* baseball, basketball, golf, soccer, tennis. *Women:* basketball, cross-country, soccer, softball, swimming, tennis, volleyball.

ADMISSIONS

Selectivity Rating: 76 (of 100). **Freshman Academic Profile:** Average high school GPA 3.4. 27% in top 10% of high school class, 52% in top 25% of high school class, 84% in top 50% of high school class. 70% from public high schools. Average SAT I Math 563, SAT I Math middle 50% range 510-630. Average SAT I Verbal 578, SAT I Verbal middle 50% range 530-640. Average ACT 24, ACT middle 50% range 22-28. TOEFL required of all international applicants, minimum TOEFL 550. **Basis for Candidate Selection:** *Very important factors considered include:* secondary school record, standardized test scores, talent/ability. *Important factors considered include:* class rank, essays, interview, minority status, volunteer work. *Other factors considered include:* character/personal qualities, extracurricular activities, geographical residence, recommendations, work experience. **Freshman Admission Requirements:** High school diploma or GED is required. *Academic units required/recommended:* 19 total recommended; 4 English recommended, 3 math recommended, 3 science recommended, 2 science lab recommended, 2 foreign language recommended, 3 social studies recommended, 4 elective recommended. **Freshman Admission Statistics:** 1,118 applied, 58% accepted, 59% of those accepted enrolled. **Transfer Admission Requirements:** *Items required:* college transcript, essay. Minimum college GPA of 2.5 required. Lowest grade transferable C. **General Admission Information:** Application fee $25. Priority application deadline March 1. Regular application deadline July 1. Nonfall registration accepted. Admission may be deferred for a maximum of 1 year. Credit offered for CEEB Advanced Placement tests.

COSTS AND FINANCIAL AID

Tuition $14,600. Room & board $6,120. Average book expense $800. **Required Forms and Deadlines:** FAFSA and institution's own financial aid form. No deadline for regular filing. Priority filing deadline April 1. **Notification of Awards:** Applicants will be notified of awards on a rolling basis beginning on or about February 1. **Types of Aid:** *Need-based scholarships/grants:* Pell, SEOG, state scholarships/grants, private scholarships, the school's own gift aid. *Loans:* FFEL Subsidized Stafford, FFEL Unsubsidized Stafford, FFEL PLUS, Federal Perkins. **Student Employment:** Federal Work-Study Program available. Institutional employment available. Off-campus job opportunities are excellent. **Financial Aid Statistics:** Average freshman grant $5,800. Average freshman loan $3,000. **Financial Aid Phone:** 800-983-4623.

See page 1282.

WELLESLEY COLLEGE

Board of Admission, 106 Central Street, Wellesley, MA 02481-8203
Phone: 781-283-2270 **E-mail:** admission@wellesley.edu **CEEB Code:** 3957
Fax: 781-283-3678 **Web:** www.wellesley.edu **ACT Code:** 1926

This private school was founded in 1870. It has a 500-acre campus.

STUDENTS AND FACULTY

Enrollment: 2,300. **Student Body:** Out-of-state 83%, international 7%. **Ethnic Representation:** African American 6%, Asian 28%, Caucasian 50%, Hispanic 5%. **Retention and Graduation:** 95% freshmen return for sophomore year. 87% freshmen graduate within 4 years. 26% grads go on to further study within 1 year. 1% grads pursue business degrees. 16% grads pursue law degrees. 17% grads pursue medical degrees. **Faculty:** Student/faculty ratio 9:1. 217 full-time faculty, 96% hold PhDs. 100% faculty teach undergrads.

ACADEMICS

Degrees: Bachelor's. **Academic Requirements:** General education including some course work in arts/fine arts, English (including composition), foreign languages, humanities, mathematics, sciences (biological or physical), social science, writing program. **Classes:** 10-19 students in an average class. 10-19 students in an average lab/discussion section. **Majors with Highest Enrollment:** English language and literature, general; psychology, general; economics, general. **Disciplines with Highest Percentage of Degrees Awarded:** Social sciences and history 30%, foreign languages and literature 12%, psychology 11%, biological life sciences 10%, area and ethnic studies 9%. **Special Study Options:** Cross registration, double major, student exchange program (domestic), honors program, independent study, internships, student-designed major, study abroad, teacher certification program.

FACILITIES

Housing: Coed, all-female, apartments for single students, housing for disabled students, cooperative housing. **Library Holdings:** 765,530 bound volumes. 4,945 periodicals. 488,721 microforms. 22,777 audiovisuals. **Special Academic Facilities/Equipment:** Margaret Clapp Library, Knapp Media and Technology Center, Davis Museum and Cultural Center, Jewett Art Museum, Ruth Nagel Jones Theatre, Nannerl Overholser Keohane Sports Center, science center, Whitin Observatory, NMR spectrometers. **Computers:** School-owned computers available for student use.

EXTRACURRICULARS

Activities: Choral groups, dance, drama/theater, jazz band, literary magazine, music ensembles, radio station, student government, student newspaper, student-run film society, yearbook. **Organizations:** 160 registered organizations, 17 religious organizations. **Athletics (Intercollegiate):** *Women:* basketball, crew, cross-country, diving, equestrian, fencing, field hockey, golf, ice hockey, lacrosse, sailing, soccer, softball, squash, swimming, tennis, volleyball.

ADMISSIONS

Selectivity Rating: 98 (of 100). **Freshman Academic Profile:** 59% in top 10% of high school class, 92% in top 25% of high school class, 100% in top 50% of high school class. 63% from public high schools. Average SAT I Math 666, SAT I Math middle 50% range 630-720. Average SAT I Verbal 679, SAT I Verbal middle 50% range 620-720. Average ACT 29, ACT middle 50% range 27-31. TOEFL required of all international applicants, minimum TOEFL 600. **Basis for Candidate Selection:** *Very important factors considered include:* essays, recommendations, secondary school record, standardized test scores. *Important factors considered include:* character/personal qualities, class rank, extracurricular activities. *Other factors considered include:* alumni/ae relation, geographical residence, interview, minority status, state residency, talent/ability, volunteer work, work experience. **Freshman Admission Requirements:** High school diploma or equivalent is not required. *Academic units required/recommended:* 4 English recommended, 4 math recommended, 3 science recommended, 2 science lab recommended, 4 foreign language recommended, 4 social studies recommended, 4 history recommended. **Freshman Admission Statistics:** 2,877 applied, 47% accepted, 44% of those accepted enrolled. **Transfer Admission Requirements:** *Items required:* high school transcript, college transcript, essay, interview, standardized test score, statement of good standing from prior school. Lowest grade transferable C. **General Admission Information:** Application fee $50. Early decision application deadline November 1. Regular application deadline January 15. Admission may be deferred for a maximum of 1 year. Credit and/or placement offered for CEEB Advanced Placement tests.

COSTS AND FINANCIAL AID

Tuition $25,022. Room & board $7,890. Required fees $482. Average book expense $800. **Required Forms and Deadlines:** FAFSA, institution's own financial aid form, CSS/Financial Aid PROFILE, noncustodial (divorced/separated) parent's statement, business/farm supplement and parents' and student's tax returns and W-2s. Priority filing deadline January 15. **Notification of Awards:** Applicants will be notified of awards on or about April 1. **Types of Aid:** *Need-based scholarships/grants:* Pell, SEOG, state scholarships/grants, private scholarships, the school's own gift aid. *Loans:* FFEL Subsidized Stafford, FFEL Unsubsidized Stafford, FFEL PLUS, Federal Perkins, state loans, college/university loans from institutional funds. **Student Employment:** Federal Work-Study Program available. Institutional employment available. Off-campus job opportunities are excellent. **Financial Aid Statistics:** 56% freshmen, 56% undergrads receive some form of aid. Average freshman grant $21,366. Average freshman loan $2,325. Average income from on-campus job $1,800. **Financial Aid Phone:** 781-283-2360.

See page 1284.

WELLS COLLEGE

170 Main Street, Aurora, NY 13026
Phone: 315-364-3264 **E-mail:** admissions@wells.edu **CEEB Code:** 2971
Fax: 315-364-3327 **Web:** www.wells.edu **ACT Code:** 2971

This private school was founded in 1868. It has a 365-acre campus.

STUDENTS AND FACULTY

Enrollment: 437. **Student Body:** Out-of-state 27%, international 2% (8 countries represented). **Ethnic Representation:** African American 5%, Asian 4%, Caucasian 76%, Hispanic 5%. **Retention and Graduation:** 75% freshmen return for sophomore year. 59% freshmen graduate within 4 years. 20% grads go on to further study within 1 year. 1% grads pursue business degrees. 4% grads pursue law degrees. 3% grads pursue medical degrees. **Faculty:** Student/faculty ratio 7:1. 40 full-time faculty, 97% hold PhDs. 100% faculty teach undergrads.

ACADEMICS

Degrees: Bachelor's. **Academic Requirements:** General education including some course work in arts/fine arts, computer literacy, English (including composition), foreign languages, history, humanities, mathematics, philosophy, sciences (biological or physical), social science, senior seminar (a capstone course that ties together various elements of undergraduate study and leading ideas from the student's major), a physical education requirement/component, first-year seminar multi/interdisciplinary course. **Classes:** 10-19 students in an average class. 10-19 students in an average lab/discussion section. **Majors with Highest Enrollment:** Psychology, general; English language and literature, general; biology/biological sciences, general. **Disciplines with Highest Percentage of Degrees Awarded:** Psychology 28%, social sciences and history 17%, English 14%, biological life sciences 10%, visual and performing arts 10%. **Special Study Options:** Accelerated program, cross registration, double major, English as a second language, independent study, internships, student-designed major, study abroad, teacher certification program. Cross registration available with Cornell University, Ithaca College, and Cayuga Community College.

FACILITIES

Housing: All-female. **Library Holdings:** 140,598 bound volumes. 407 periodicals. 14,023 microforms. 924 audiovisuals. **Special Academic Facilities/Equipment:** Two greenhouses, environmentally regulated animal room, the college theatre (Phillips Auditorium), recital hall, electronic music studio, 15 pianos, a Dowd harpsichord, an early instrument collection, a sculpture and ceramics studio, darkrooms, painting and drawing studio, lithography presses, an extensive art library, art gallery, general and specialized clusters for the social sciences, foreign languages, and natural and mathematical sciences. **Computers:** School-owned computers available for student use.

EXTRACURRICULARS

Activities: Choral groups, dance, drama/theater, literary magazine, music ensembles, student government, student newspaper, yearbook. **Organizations:** 36 registered organizations, 2 honor societies, 2 religious organizations. **Athletics (Intercollegiate):** *Women:* field hockey, lacrosse, soccer, softball, swimming, tennis.

ADMISSIONS

Selectivity Rating: 80 (of 100). **Freshman Academic Profile:** Average high school GPA 3.5. 30% in top 10% of high school class, 67% in top 25% of high school class, 94% in top 50% of high school class. 90% from public high schools. Average SAT I Math 550, SAT I Math middle 50% range 500-590. Average SAT I Verbal 580, SAT I Verbal middle 50% range 530-650. Average ACT 25, ACT middle 50% range 22-26. TOEFL required of all international applicants, minimum TOEFL 550. **Basis for Candidate Selection:** *Very important factors considered include:* extracurricular activities, recommendations, secondary school record, standardized test scores. *Important factors considered include:* essays, interview. *Other factors considered include:* alumni/ae relation, character/personal qualities, class rank, talent/ability, volunteer work, work experience. **Freshman Admission Requirements:** High school diploma or GED is required. *Academic units required/recommended:* 16 total required; 23 total recommended; 4 English required, 4 English recommended, 3 math required, 4 math recommended, 2 science required, 3 science recommended, 2 science lab required, 3 science lab recommended, 3 foreign language required, 4 foreign language recommended, 2 social studies required, 3 social studies recommended, 2 elective required, 3 elective recommended. **Freshman Admission Statistics:** 404 applied, 86% accepted, 31% of those accepted enrolled. **Transfer Admission Requirements:** *Items required:* high school transcript, college transcript, essay, standardized test score, statement of good standing from prior school. Minimum college GPA of 2.0 required. Lowest grade transferable C. **General Admission Information:** Application fee $40. Priority application deadline December 15. Early decision application deadline December 15. Regular application deadline March 1. Admission may be deferred for a maximum of 1 year. Credit and/or placement offered for CEEB Advanced Placement tests.

COSTS AND FINANCIAL AID

Tuition $13,070. Room & board $6,450. Required fees $680. Average book expense $600. **Required Forms and Deadlines:** FAFSA and CSS/Financial Aid PROFILE for early decision applicants only. No deadline for regular filing. Priority filing deadline February 15. **Notification of Awards:** Applicants will be notified of awards on a rolling basis beginning on or about March 1. **Types of Aid:** *Need-based scholarships/grants:* Pell, SEOG, state scholarships/grants, private scholarships, the school's own gift aid. *Loans:* FFEL Subsidized Stafford, FFEL Unsubsidized Stafford, FFEL PLUS, Federal Perkins. **Student Employment:** Federal Work-Study Program available. Institutional employment available. Off-campus job opportunities are fair. **Financial Aid Statistics:** 80% freshmen, 78% undergrads receive some form of aid. Average freshman grant $9,978. Average freshman loan $3,066. Average income from on-campus job $1,200. **Financial Aid Phone:** 315-364-3289.

See page 1286.

WENTWORTH INSTITUTE OF TECHNOLOGY

550 Huntington Avenue, Admissions Office, Boston, MA 02115-5998
Phone: 617-989-4000 **E-mail:** admissions@wit.edu **CEEB Code:** 3958
Fax: 617-989-4010 **Web:** www.wit.edu

This private school was founded in 1904. It has a 35-acre campus.

STUDENTS AND FACULTY

Enrollment: 3,235. **Student Body:** Male 82%, female 18%, out-of-state 29%, international 5%. **Ethnic Representation:** African American 5%, Asian 4%, Caucasian 77%, Hispanic 4%. **Retention and Graduation:** 69% freshmen return for sophomore year. **Faculty:** Student/faculty ratio 25:1. 129 full-time faculty, 42% hold PhDs. 100% faculty teach undergrads.

ACADEMICS

Degrees: Associate's, bachelor's, certificate, post-bachelor's certificate, terminal. **Academic Requirements:** General education including some course work in computer literacy, English (including composition), mathematics, sciences (biological or physical), social science. **Classes:** 20-29 students in an average class. 10-19 students in an average lab/discussion section. **Majors with Highest Enrollment:** Engineering technology, general; computer science; architecture (BArch, BA/BS, MArch, MA/MS, PhD). **Disciplines with Highest Percentage of Degrees Awarded:** Engineering/engineering technology 47%, computer and information sciences 13%, architecture 9%, visual and performing arts 8%. **Special Study Options:** Cooperative (work-study) program, cross registration, honors program, independent study, student-designed major, study abroad, weekend college.

FACILITIES

Housing: Coed, apartments for single students. **Library Holdings:** 77,000 bound volumes. 500 periodicals. 177 microforms. 1,020 audiovisuals. **Computers:** School-owned computers available for student use.

EXTRACURRICULARS

Activities: Drama/theater, music ensembles, radio station, student government, student newspaper, student-run film society, yearbook. **Organizations:** 40 registered organizations, 2 honor societies. **Athletics (Intercollegiate):** *Men:* baseball, basketball, golf, ice hockey, lacrosse, rifle, soccer, tennis, volleyball. *Women:* basketball, rifle, soccer, softball, tennis, volleyball.

ADMISSIONS

Selectivity Rating: 67 (of 100). **Freshman Academic Profile:** Average SAT I Math 535. Average SAT I Verbal 485. TOEFL required of all international applicants, minimum TOEFL 525. **Basis for Candidate Selection:** *Very important factors considered include:* secondary school record. *Important factors considered include:* standardized test scores. *Other factors considered include:* essays, extracurricular activities, interview, recommendations, volunteer work, work experience. **Freshman Admission Requirements:** High school diploma or GED is required. *Academic units required/recommended:* 8 total required; 16 total recommended; 4 English required, 4 English recommended, 3 math required, 4 math recommended, 1 science required, 3 science recommended, 1 science lab required, 2 science lab recommended. **Freshman Admission Statistics:** 2,892 applied, 90% accepted, 37% of those accepted enrolled. **Transfer Admission Requirements:** *Items required:* high school transcript, college transcript. Minimum high school GPA of 2.0 required. Minimum college GPA of 2.0 required. Lowest grade transferable C. **General Admission Information:** Application fee $30. Priority application deadline May 1. Nonfall registration accepted. Admission may be deferred for a maximum of 1 year. Credit and/or placement offered for CEEB Advanced Placement tests.

COSTS AND FINANCIAL AID

Tuition $14,300. Room & board $7,800. Required fees $350. Average book expense $1,000. **Required Forms and Deadlines:** FAFSA. No deadline for regular filing. Priority filing deadline March 1. **Notification of Awards:** Applicants will be notified of awards on a rolling basis beginning on or about March 15. **Types of Aid:** *Need-based scholarships/grants:* Pell, SEOG, state scholarships/grants, the school's own gift aid. *Loans:* Direct Subsidized Stafford, Direct Unsubsidized Stafford, Direct PLUS, Federal Perkins, state loans. **Student Employment:** Federal Work-Study Program available. Institutional employment available. Off-campus job opportunities are excellent. **Financial Aid Statistics:** 59% freshmen, 62% undergrads receive some form of aid. Average freshman grant $5,927. Average freshman loan $3,887. **Financial Aid Phone:** 617-989-4020.

WESLEY COLLEGE (DE)

120 North State Street, Dover, DE 19901-3875
Phone: 302-736-2400 **E-mail:** admissions@wesley.edu **CEEB Code:** 1433
Fax: 302-736-2301 **Web:** www.wesley.edu **ACT Code:** 636

This private school, which is affiliated with the Methodist Church, was founded in 1873. It has a 40-acre campus.

STUDENTS AND FACULTY

Enrollment: 1,508. **Student Body:** Male 45%, female 55%, out-of-state 58%, international 1%. **Ethnic Representation:** African American 23%, Asian 1%, Caucasian 71%, Hispanic 3%. **Retention and Graduation:** 88% freshmen return for sophomore year. 44% freshmen graduate within 4 years. 30% grads go on to further study within 1 year. 10% grads pursue business degrees. 1% grads pursue law degrees. 1% grads pursue medical degrees. **Faculty:** Student/faculty ratio 17:1. 59 full-time faculty, 74% hold PhDs. 100% faculty teach undergrads.

ACADEMICS

Degrees: Associate's, bachelor's, certificate, master's, post-bachelor's certificate, terminal, transfer. **Academic Requirements:** General education including some course work in arts/fine arts, English (including composition), history, humanities, mathematics, philosophy, sciences (biological or physical), social science. **Classes:** 10-19 students in an average class. Under 10 students in an average lab/discussion section. **Majors with Highest Enrollment:** Mass communications/media studies; psychology, general; business administration/management. **Disciplines with Highest Percentage of Degrees Awarded:** Business/marketing 46%, education 16%, psychology 12%, social sciences and history 7%, communications/communication technologies 5%. **Special Study Options:** Double major, English as a second language, independent study, internships, liberal arts/career combination, teacher certification program.

FACILITIES

Housing: Coed, all-female, all-male. **Library Holdings:** 95,719 bound volumes. 232 periodicals. 163,904 microforms. 936 audiovisuals. **Computers:** *Recommended operating system:* Windows NT/2000. School-owned computers available for student use.

EXTRACURRICULARS

Activities: Choral groups, drama/theater, literary magazine, music ensembles, student government, student newspaper, yearbook. **Organizations:** 15 registered organizations, 2 honor societies, 2 religious organizations, 2 fraternities (6% men join), 3 sororities (6% women join). **Athletics (Intercollegiate):** *Men:* baseball, basketball, cheerleading, cross-country, football, golf, lacrosse, soccer, tennis. *Women:* baseball, basketball, cheerleading, cross-country, field hockey, golf, lacrosse, soccer, softball, tennis.

ADMISSIONS

Selectivity Rating: 63 (of 100). **Freshman Academic Profile:** Average high school GPA 2.9. 17% in top 10% of high school class, 34% in top 25% of high school class. 80% from public high schools. Average SAT I Math 496, SAT I Math middle 50% range 450-530. Average SAT I Verbal 490, SAT I Verbal middle 50% range 450-520. TOEFL required of all international applicants, minimum TOEFL 550. **Basis for Candidate Selection:** *Important factors considered include:* alumni/ae relation, secondary school record, standardized test scores, talent/ability, volunteer work. *Other factors considered include:* essays, extracurricular activities, interview, minority status, recommendations, work experience. **Freshman Admission Requirements:** High school diploma or GED is required. *Academic units required/recommended:* 16 total required; 4 English recommended, 3 math recommended, 2 science recommended, 2 science lab recommended, 2 foreign language recommended, 2 social studies recommended. **Freshman Admission Statistics:** 1,700 applied, 72% accepted, 33% of those accepted enrolled. **Transfer Admission Requirements:** *Items required:* high school transcript, college transcript. Minimum college GPA of 2.0 required. Lowest grade transferable C. **General Admission Information:** Application fee $20. Early decision application deadline December 15. Nonfall registration accepted. Credit and/or placement offered for CEEB Advanced Placement tests.

COSTS AND FINANCIAL AID

Tuition $13,000. Room & board $6,200. Required fees $705. Average book expense $600. **Required Forms and Deadlines:** FAFSA and institution's own financial aid form. No deadline for regular filing. Priority filing deadline April 15. **Notification of Awards:** Applicants will be notified of awards on a rolling basis beginning on or about February 1. **Types of Aid:** *Need-based scholarships/grants:* Pell, SEOG, private scholarships, the school's own gift aid. *Loans:* Direct Subsidized Stafford, Direct Unsubsidized Stafford, Direct PLUS, FFEL

Subsidized Stafford, FFEL Unsubsidized Stafford, FFEL PLUS, Federal Perkins, college/university loans from institutional funds. **Student Employment:** Federal Work-Study Program available. Off-campus job opportunities are excellent. **Financial Aid Statistics:** 91% freshmen, 72% undergrads receive some form of aid. Average freshman grant $8,000. Average freshman loan $8,000. **Financial Aid Phone:** 302-736-2338.

WESLEY COLLEGE (MS)

PO Box 1070, Florence, MS 39073
Phone: 800-748-9972 **E-mail:** wccadmit@aol.com
Fax: 601-845-2266 **Web:** www.wesleycollege.com **ACT Code:** 2253

This private school, which is affiliated with the Methodist Church, was founded in 1944. It has a 40-acre campus.

STUDENTS AND FACULTY

Enrollment: 81. **Student Body:** Male 59%, female 41%, international 5% (4 countries represented). **Ethnic Representation:** African American 16%, Asian 1%, Caucasian 82%. **Faculty:** 100% faculty teach undergrads.

ACADEMICS

Degrees: Bachelor's, certificate. **Academic Requirements:** General education including some course work in arts/fine arts, English (including composition), history, mathematics, sciences (biological or physical), social science.

FACILITIES

Housing: All-female, all-male, apartments for married students, apartments for single students.

EXTRACURRICULARS

Activities: Choral groups, drama/theater, music ensembles, student government, student newspaper, yearbook. **Athletics (Intercollegiate):** *Men:* basketball.

ADMISSIONS

Selectivity Rating: 60 (of 100). **Freshman Academic Profile:** TOEFL required of all international applicants, minimum TOEFL 550. **Freshman Admission Requirements:** High school diploma or GED is required. **Transfer Admission Requirements:** *Items required:* high school transcript, college transcript, essay, standardized test scores. Minimum college GPA of 2.0 required. Lowest grade transferable C. **General Admission Information:** Application fee $20. Regular application deadline rolling. Nonfall registration accepted. Admission may be deferred.

COSTS AND FINANCIAL AID

Tuition $3,500. Room & board $2,150. Required fees $150. Average book expense $200. **Required Forms and Deadlines:** FAFSA. **Types of Aid:** *Loans:* Direct Subsidized Stafford, Direct Unsubsidized Stafford. **Student Employment:** Federal Work-Study Program available. Off-campus job opportunities are excellent. **Financial Aid Statistics:** 100% freshmen, 100% undergrads receive some form of aid. **Financial Aid Phone:** 601-845-2265.

WESLEYAN COLLEGE

4760 Forsyth Road, Macon, GA 31210-4462
Phone: 478-757-5206 **E-mail:** admissions@wesleyancollege.edu **CEEB Code:** 5895
Fax: 478-757-4030 **Web:** www.wesleyancollege.edu **ACT Code:** 876

This private school, which is affiliated with the Methodist Church, was founded in 1836. It has a 200-acre campus.

STUDENTS AND FACULTY

Enrollment: 679. **Student Body:** Out-of-state 19%, international 16%. **Ethnic Representation:** African American 35%, Asian 2%, Caucasian 58%, Hispanic 3%, Native American 1%. **Retention and Graduation:** 70% freshmen return for sophomore year. 37% freshmen graduate within 4 years. 26% grads go on to further study within 1 year. 5% grads pursue business degrees. 2% grads pursue law degrees. 3% grads pursue medical degrees. **Faculty:** Student/faculty ratio 11:1. 48 full-time faculty, 91% hold PhDs. 100% faculty teach undergrads.

ACADEMICS

Degrees: Bachelor's, master's. **Academic Requirements:** General education including some course work in arts/fine arts, English (including composition), foreign languages, humanities, mathematics, sciences (biological or physical), social science, first-year seminar course. **Classes:** 100+ students in an average class. 10-19 students in an average lab/discussion section. **Disciplines with Highest Percentage of Degrees Awarded:** Business/marketing 19%, psychology 16%, communications/communication technologies 13%, social sciences and history 11%, visual and performing arts 10%. **Special Study Options:** Cross registration, double major, dual enrollment, honors program, independent study, internships, student-designed major, study abroad, teacher certification program, weekend college, and dual-degree engineering (3/2) with Georgia Tech, Auburn University, and Mercer University.

FACILITIES

Housing: All-female, apartments for single students. **Library Holdings:** 141,818 bound volumes. 506 periodicals. 33,216 microforms. 4,259 audiovisuals. **Special Academic Facilities/Equipment:** Art and history museums, special collection of Georgiana and Americana, on-campus equestrian center. **Computers:** *Recommended operating system:* Windows NT/2000. School-owned computers available for student use.

EXTRACURRICULARS

Activities: Choral groups, dance, drama/theater, literary magazine, music ensembles, musical theater, student government, student newspaper, yearbook. **Organizations:** 40 registered organizations, 10 honor societies, 5 religious organizations. **Athletics (Intercollegiate):** *Women:* basketball, equestrian, soccer, softball, tennis, volleyball.

ADMISSIONS

Selectivity Rating: 69 (of 100). **Freshman Academic Profile:** Average high school GPA 3.5. 36% in top 10% of high school class, 60% in top 25% of high school class, 93% in top 50% of high school class. 90% from public high schools. Average SAT I Math 562, SAT I Math middle 50% range 480-610. Average SAT I Verbal 574, SAT I Verbal middle 50% range 500-610. Average ACT 25, ACT middle 50% range 19-25. TOEFL required of all international applicants, minimum TOEFL 550. **Basis for Candidate Selection:** *Very important factors considered include:* secondary school record. *Important factors considered include:* character/personal qualities, class rank, extracurricular activities, recommendations, standardized test scores, talent/ability, volunteer work. *Other factors considered include:* alumni/ae relation, essays, geographical residence, interview, minority status, religious affiliation/commitment, state residency, work experience. **Freshman Admission Requirements:** High school diploma or GED is required. *Academic units required/recommended:* 15 total required; 20 total recommended; 4 English required, 4 English recommended, 3 math required, 4 math recommended, 3 science required, 4 science recommended, 2 science lab required, 3 science lab recommended, 2 foreign language required, 3 foreign language recommended, 3 social studies required, 3 social studies recommended, 1 elective recommended. **Freshman Admission Statistics:** 449 applied, 72% accepted, 47% of those accepted enrolled. **Transfer Admission Requirements:** *Items required:* college transcript, essay. Minimum college GPA of 2.0 required. Lowest grade transferable C. **General Admission Information:** Application fee $30. Priority application deadline March 1. Early decision application deadline November 15. Regular application deadline June 1. Nonfall registration accepted. Admission may be deferred for a maximum of 1 year. Credit and/or placement offered for CEEB Advanced Placement tests.

COSTS AND FINANCIAL AID

Tuition $9,570. Room & board $7,450. Required fees $850. Average book expense $600. **Required Forms and Deadlines:** FAFSA, institution's own financial aid form, state aid form and noncustodial (divorced/separated) parent's statement. No deadline for regular filing. Priority filing deadline March 1. **Notification of Awards:** Applicants will be notified of awards on a rolling basis beginning on or about February 1. **Types of Aid:** *Need-based scholarships/grants:* Pell, SEOG, state scholarships/grants, private scholarships, the school's own gift aid. *Loans:* Direct Subsidized Stafford, Direct Unsubsidized Stafford, Direct PLUS, Federal Perkins, college/university loans from institutional funds, CitiAssist, Wells Fargo, collegiate loans, Key alternative loans. **Student Employment:** Federal Work-Study Program available. Institutional employment available. Off-campus job opportunities are good. **Financial Aid Statistics:** 58% freshmen, 58% undergrads receive some form of aid. Average freshman grant $11,943. Average freshman loan $4,094. Average income from on-campus job $1,224. **Financial Aid Phone:** 800-447-6610.

WESLEYAN UNIVERSITY

Office of Admission, 70 Wyllys Avenue, Middletown, CT 06459-0265
Phone: 860-685-3000 **E-mail:** www-admiss@wesleyan.edu **CEEB Code:** 3959
Fax: 860-685-3001 **Web:** www.wesleyan.edu **ACT Code:** 614

This private school was founded in 1831. It has a 240-acre campus.

STUDENTS AND FACULTY

Enrollment: 2,733. **Student Body:** Male 48%, female 52%, out-of-state 90%, international 6%. **Ethnic Representation:** African American 9%, Asian 8%, Caucasian 67%, Hispanic 7%. **Retention and Graduation:** 95% freshmen return for sophomore year. 86% freshmen graduate within 4 years. **Faculty:** Student/faculty ratio 9:1. 311 full-time faculty, 94% hold PhDs. 100% faculty teach undergrads.

ACADEMICS

Degrees: Bachelor's, doctoral, master's, post-master's certificate. **Classes:** 10-19 students in an average class. 10-19 students in an average lab/discussion section. **Disciplines with Highest Percentage of Degrees Awarded:** Social sciences and history 27%, visual and performing arts 15%, area and ethnic studies 14%, English 13%, psychology 8%. **Special Study Options:** Cross registration, double major, dual enrollment, student exchange program (domestic), honors program, independent study, internships, student-designed major, study abroad.

FACILITIES

Housing: Coed, apartments for married students, apartments for single students, housing for disabled students, housing for international students, fraternities and/or sororities, cooperative housing, special-interest housing. **Library Holdings:** 1,224,750 bound volumes. 4,281 periodicals. 255,164 microforms. 43,808 audiovisuals. **Special Academic Facilities/Equipment:** Art center, art galleries, center for Afro-American studies, East Asian studies center, cinema archives, music hall, public affairs center, language lab, electron microscope, observatory, nuclear magnetic resonance spectrometers. **Computers:** School-owned computers available for student use.

EXTRACURRICULARS

Activities: Choral groups, concert band, dance, drama/theater, jazz band, literary magazine, music ensembles, musical theater, pep band, radio station, student government, student newspaper, student-run film society, symphony orchestra, yearbook. **Organizations:** 170 registered organizations, 2 honor societies, 3 religious organizations, 9 fraternities (5% men join), 4 sororities (1% women join). **Athletics (Intercollegiate):** *Men:* baseball, basketball, crew, cross-country, diving, fencing, football, ice hockey, indoor track, lacrosse, rugby, soccer, squash, swimming, tennis, track & field, wrestling. *Women:* basketball, crew, cross-country, diving, field hockey, golf, ice hockey, indoor track, lacrosse, rugby, soccer, softball, squash, swimming, tennis, track & field, volleyball.

ADMISSIONS

Selectivity Rating: 98 (of 100). **Freshman Academic Profile:** 73% in top 10% of high school class, 94% in top 25% of high school class, 99% in top 50% of high school class. 56% from public high schools. Average SAT I Math 690, SAT I Math middle 50% range 650-730. Average SAT I Verbal 700, SAT I Verbal middle 50% range 640-740. Average ACT 29. TOEFL required of all international applicants, minimum TOEFL 600. **Basis for Candidate Selection:** *Very important factors considered include:* class rank, secondary school record. *Important factors considered include:* alumni/ae relation, character/personal qualities, essays, extracurricular activities, minority status, recommendations, standardized test scores, talent/ability, volunteer work. *Other factors considered include:* geographical residence, interview, work experience. **Freshman Admission Requirements:** High school diploma is required and GED is not accepted. *Academic units required/recommended:* 16 total required; 20 total recommended; 4 English required, 3 math required, 4 math recommended, 3 science required, 4 science recommended, 3 science lab recommended, 3 foreign language required, 4 foreign language recommended, 3 social studies required, 4 social studies recommended. **Freshman Admission Statistics:** 6,474 applied, 28% accepted, 40% of those accepted enrolled. **Transfer Admission Requirements:** *Items required:* high school transcript, college transcript, essay, standardized test score, statement of good standing from prior school. Lowest grade transferable C-. **General Admission Information:** Application fee $55. Early decision application deadline November 15. Regular application deadline January 1. Admission may be deferred for a maximum of 1 year. Credit and/or placement offered for CEEB Advanced Placement tests.

COSTS AND FINANCIAL AID

Required Forms and Deadlines: FAFSA, CSS/Financial Aid PROFILE, noncustodial (divorced/separated) parent's statement and business/farm supplement. Financial aid filing deadline February 1. **Notification of Awards:** Applicants will be notified of awards on or about April 1. **Types of Aid:** *Need-based scholarships/grants:* Pell, SEOG, state scholarships/grants, private scholarships, the school's own gift aid. *Loans:* FFEL Subsidized Stafford, FFEL Unsubsidized Stafford, FFEL PLUS, Federal Perkins. **Student Employment:** Federal Work-Study Program available. Institutional employment available. Off-campus job opportunities are good. **Financial Aid Statistics:** 47% freshmen, 47% undergrads receive some form of aid. Average freshman grant $23,992. Average freshman loan $2,770. Average income from on-campus job $1,900. **Financial Aid Phone:** 860-685-2800.

WEST CHESTER UNIVERSITY OF PENNSYLVANIA

Messikomer Hall, 100 W. Rosedale Avenue, West Chester, PA 19383
Phone: 610-436-3411 **E-mail:** ugadmiss@wcupa.edu **CEEB Code:** 3328
Fax: 610-436-2907 **Web:** www.wcupa.edu

This public school was founded in 1871. It has a 388-acre campus.

STUDENTS AND FACULTY

Enrollment: 10,467. **Student Body:** Male 39%, female 61%, out-of-state 12%. **Ethnic Representation:** African American 8%, Asian 2%, Caucasian 88%, Hispanic 2%. **Retention and Graduation:** 86% freshmen return for sophomore year. 26% freshmen graduate within 4 years. 19% grads go on to further study within 1 year. 2% grads pursue business degrees. 1% grads pursue law degrees. 3% grads pursue medical degrees. **Faculty:** Student/faculty ratio 17:1. 589 full-time faculty, 77% hold PhDs. 90% faculty teach undergrads.

ACADEMICS

Degrees: Bachelor's, certificate, master's, post-bachelor's certificate. **Academic Requirements:** General education including some course work in arts/fine arts, English (including composition), humanities, mathematics, sciences (biological or physical), social science, physical education. **Classes:** 20-29 students in an average class. **Majors with Highest Enrollment:** Elementary education and teaching; early childhood education and teaching; psychology, general. **Disciplines with Highest Percentage of Degrees Awarded:** Education 24%, business/marketing 17%, English 9%, parks and recreation 7%, health professions and related sciences 7%. **Special Study Options:** Accelerated program, cross registration, distance learning, double major, student exchange program (domestic), honors program, independent study, internships, student-designed major, study abroad, teacher certification program.

FACILITIES

Housing: Coed, all-female, apartments for single students. **Library Holdings:** 788,478 bound volumes. 2,874 periodicals. 1,423,614 microforms. 66,337 audiovisuals. **Special Academic Facilities/Equipment:** Art gallery, center for governmental and community affairs, herbarium, music library. **Computers:** *Recommended operating system:* Windows 95. School-owned computers available for student use.

EXTRACURRICULARS

Activities: Choral groups, dance, drama/theater, jazz band, literary magazine, marching band, music ensembles, radio station, student government, student newspaper, symphony orchestra, television station, yearbook. **Organizations:** 199 registered organizations, 26 honor societies, 12 religious organizations, 13 fraternities (9% men join), 12 sororities (9% women join). **Athletics (Intercollegiate):** *Men:* baseball, basketball, cross-country, diving, football, golf, lacrosse, soccer, swimming, tennis, track & field. *Women:* basketball, cross-country, diving, field hockey, gymnastics, lacrosse, soccer, softball, swimming, tennis, track & field, volleyball.

ADMISSIONS

Selectivity Rating: 63 (of 100). **Freshman Academic Profile:** Average high school GPA 3.3. 7% in top 10% of high school class, 33% in top 25% of high school class, 77% in top 50% of high school class. 60% from public high schools. Average SAT I Math 526, SAT I Math middle 50% range 480-570. Average SAT I Verbal 519, SAT I Verbal middle 50% range 480-560. TOEFL required of all international applicants, minimum TOEFL 550. **Basis for Candidate Selection:** *Very important factors considered include:* class rank, secondary school record. *Important factors considered include:* standardized test scores. *Other factors considered include:* alumni/ae relation, character/personal qualities, essays, extracurricular activities, minority status, recommendations, talent/ability, volunteer work, work experience. **Freshman Admission Requirements:** High school diploma or GED is required. *Academic units required/recommended:* 16 total required; 21 total recommended; 4 English required, 3 math required, 4 math recommended, 2 science required, 3 science recommended, 1 science lab required, 2 science lab recommended, 2 foreign language recommended, 4 history required, 4 elective recommended. **Freshman Admission Statistics:** 9,100 applied, 50% accepted, 39% of those accepted enrolled. **Transfer Admission Requirements:** *Items required:* college transcript, essay. Minimum college GPA of 2.0 required. Lowest grade transferable D. **General Admission Information:** Application fee $30. Priority application deadline January 1. Regular application deadline April 1. Nonfall registration accepted. Admission may be deferred for a maximum of 1 year. Credit and/or placement offered for CEEB Advanced Placement tests.

COSTS AND FINANCIAL AID

In-state tuition $4,378. Out-of-state tuition $10,946. Room & board $5,146. Required fees $1,090. Average book expense $800. **Required Forms and Deadlines:** FAFSA. No deadline for regular filing. Priority filing deadline March 1. **Notification of Awards:** Applicants will be notified of awards on a rolling basis beginning on or about April 15. **Types of Aid:** *Need-based scholarships/grants:* Pell, SEOG, state scholarships/grants, private scholarships, the school's own gift aid. *Loans:* Federal Perkins, Federal Nursing, state loans. **Student Employment:** Federal Work-Study Program available. Institutional employment available. Off-campus job opportunities are excellent. **Financial Aid Statistics:** 55% freshmen, 49% undergrads receive some form of aid. Average freshman grant $1,604. Average freshman loan $3,068. Average income from on-campus job $1,500. **Financial Aid Phone:** 610-436-2627.

WEST LIBERTY STATE COLLEGE

PO Box 295, West Liberty, WV 26074
Phone: 304-336-8076 **E-mail:** wladmsn1@wlsc.edu **CEEB Code:** 5901
Fax: 304-336-8403 **Web:** www.wlsc.edu **ACT Code:** 4534

This public school was founded in 1837. It has a 290-acre campus.

STUDENTS AND FACULTY

Enrollment: 2,566. **Student Body:** Male 45%, female 55%, out-of-state 28%, international 1%. **Ethnic Representation:** African American 3%, Caucasian 96%, Hispanic 1%. **Retention and Graduation:** 79% freshmen return for sophomore year. 15% freshmen graduate within 4 years. 43% grads go on to further study within 1 year. 1% grads pursue business degrees. 1% grads pursue law degrees. 1% grads pursue medical degrees. **Faculty:** Student/faculty ratio 19:1. 111 full-time faculty, 43% hold PhDs. 100% faculty teach undergrads.

ACADEMICS

Degrees: Associate's, bachelor's. **Academic Requirements:** General education including some course work in arts/fine arts, computer literacy, English (including composition), history, humanities, mathematics, philosophy, sciences (biological or physical), social science. **Classes:** 20-29 students in an average class. 20-29 students in an average lab/discussion section. **Majors with Highest Enrollment:** Business administration/management; elementary education and teaching; criminal justice/safety studies. **Disciplines with Highest Percentage of Degrees Awarded:** Education 31%, business/marketing 22%, protective services/public administration 8%, liberal arts/general studies 8%, health professions and related sciences 8%. **Special Study Options:** Accelerated program, double major, external degree program, honors program, independent study, internships, student-designed major, teacher certification program.

FACILITIES

Housing: Coed, all-female, all-male, apartments for married students. **Library Holdings:** 194,715 bound volumes. 485 periodicals. 123,233 microforms. 13,128 audiovisuals. **Special Academic Facilities/Equipment:** Book museums, language lab, clinical lab sciences and dental hygiene labs. **Computers:** School-owned computers available for student use.

EXTRACURRICULARS

Activities: Choral groups, concert band, drama/theater, jazz band, literary magazine, marching band, music ensembles, musical theater, pep band, radio station, student government, student newspaper, television station. **Organizations:** 50 registered organizations, 10 honor societies, 4 religious organizations, 5 fraternities (5% men join), 4 sororities (9% women join). **Athletics (Intercollegiate):** *Men:* baseball, basketball, cheerleading, cross-country, football, golf, swimming, tennis, track & field, wrestling. *Women:* basketball, cheerleading, cross-country, golf, softball, swimming, tennis, track & field, volleyball.

ADMISSIONS

Selectivity Rating: 65 (of 100). **Freshman Academic Profile:** Average high school GPA 3.0. 26% in top 25% of high school class, 57% in top 50% of high school class. 88% from public high schools. Average SAT I Math 467, SAT I Math middle 50% range 400-500. Average SAT I Verbal 467, SAT I Verbal middle 50% range 420-510. Average ACT 19, ACT middle 50% range 17-22. TOEFL required of all international applicants, minimum TOEFL 500. **Basis for Candidate Selection:** *Very important factors considered include:* secondary school record, standardized test scores. **Freshman Admission Requirements:** High school diploma or GED is required. *Academic units required/recommended:* 11 total required; 13 total recommended; 4 English required, 2 math required, 2 science required, 2 science lab required, 2 foreign language recommended, 2 social studies required, 1 history required. **Freshman Admission Statistics:** 1,201 applied, 98% accepted, 41% of those accepted enrolled. **Transfer Admission Requirements:** *Items required:* college transcript. Minimum high school GPA of 2.0 required. Minimum college GPA of 2.0 required. Lowest grade transferable D. **General Admission Information:** Nonfall registration accepted. Credit offered for CEEB Advanced Placement tests.

COSTS AND FINANCIAL AID

In-state tuition $2,748. Out-of-state tuition $7,098. Room & board $4,180. Required fees $0. Average book expense $800. **Required Forms and Deadlines:** FAFSA. Priority filing deadline March 1. **Notification of Awards:** Applicants will be notified of awards on a rolling basis beginning on or about February 15. **Types of Aid:** *Need-based scholarships/grants:* Pell, SEOG, state scholarships/grants, private scholarships, the school's own gift aid. *Loans:* Direct Subsidized Stafford, Direct Unsubsidized Stafford, Direct PLUS, Federal Perkins, Federal Nursing. **Student Employment:** Federal Work-Study Program available. Institutional employment available. Off-campus job opportunities are fair. **Financial Aid Statistics:** 64% freshmen, 68% undergrads receive some form of aid. Average freshman grant $2,108. Average freshman loan $2,745. Average income from on-campus job $1,100. **Financial Aid Phone:** 304-336-8016.

WEST TEXAS A&M UNIVERSITY

PO Box 60907, Canyon, TX 79016-0001
Phone: 806-651-2020 **E-mail:** lvars@mail.wtamu.edu **CEEB Code:** 3665
Fax: 806-651-5268 **Web:** www.wtamu.edu **ACT Code:** 4250

This public school was founded in 1909. It has a 135-acre campus.

STUDENTS AND FACULTY

Enrollment: 5,410. **Student Body:** Male 45%, female 55%, out-of-state 8%, international 2% (38 countries represented). **Ethnic Representation:** African American 4%, Asian 1%, Caucasian 81%, Hispanic 14%, Native American 1%. **Retention and Graduation:** 66% freshmen return for sophomore year. 13% freshmen graduate within 4 years. **Faculty:** Student/faculty ratio 23:1. 225 full-time faculty, 72% hold PhDs. 90% faculty teach undergrads.

ACADEMICS

Degrees: Bachelor's, master's. **Academic Requirements:** General education including some course work in arts/fine arts, computer literacy, English (including composition), history, humanities, mathematics, philosophy, sciences (biological or physical), social science, lifetime fitness. **Classes:** 20-29 students in an average class. 20-29 students in an average lab/discussion section. **Majors with Highest Enrollment:** Business administration/management; multi/interdisciplinary studies; general studies. **Disciplines with Highest Percentage of Degrees Awarded:** Business/marketing 18%, interdisciplinary studies 17%, liberal arts/general studies 11%, health professions and related sciences 10%, visual and performing arts 5%. **Special Study Options:** Accelerated program, cooperative (work-study) program, distance learning, double major, English as a second language, honors program, internships, teacher certification program.

FACILITIES

Housing: Coed, all-female, all-male, housing for disabled students, fraternities and/or sororities. **Library Holdings:** 1,078,526 bound volumes. 5,464 periodicals. 974,691 microforms. 1,561 audiovisuals. **Special Academic Facilities/Equipment:** Regional History Museum, research center, Panhandle Plains Historical Museum, Killgore Research Center. **Computers:** School-owned computers available for student use.

EXTRACURRICULARS

Activities: Choral groups, concert band, dance, drama/theater, jazz band, literary magazine, marching band, music ensembles, musical theater, opera, radio station, student government, student newspaper, student-run film society. **Organizations:** 120 registered organizations, 13 honor societies, 12 religious organizations, 6 fraternities (7% men join), 4 sororities (5% women join).

Athletics (Intercollegiate): *Men:* basketball, cheerleading, football, golf, soccer, softball, tennis, volleyball. *Women:* basketball, cheerleading, equestrian, golf, soccer, softball, tennis, volleyball.

ADMISSIONS

Selectivity Rating: 71 (of 100). **Freshman Academic Profile:** 17% in top 10% of high school class, 40% in top 25% of high school class, 81% in top 50% of high school class. 96% from public high schools. Average SAT I Math 489, SAT I Math middle 50% range 440-550. Average SAT I Verbal 499, SAT I Verbal middle 50% range 450-570. Average ACT 22, ACT middle 50% range 18-23. TOEFL required of all international applicants, minimum TOEFL 525. **Basis for Candidate Selection:** *Very important factors considered include:* class rank. *Important factors considered include:* secondary school record, standardized test scores. *Other factors considered include:* recommendations. **Freshman Admission Requirements:** High school diploma or GED is required. *Academic units required/recommended:* 17 total recommended; 4 English recommended, 3 math recommended, 2 science recommended, 2 science lab recommended, 2 foreign language recommended, 2 social studies recommended, 2 history recommended. **Freshman Admission Statistics:** 1,863 applied, 72% accepted, 63% of those accepted enrolled. **Transfer Admission Requirements:** *Items required:* college transcript. Minimum college GPA of 2.0 required. Lowest grade transferable C. **General Admission Information:** Application fee $25. Nonfall registration accepted. Admission may be deferred. Credit offered for CEEB Advanced Placement tests.

COSTS AND FINANCIAL AID

In-state tuition $2,175. Out-of-state tuition $10,890. Room & board $4,309. Required fees $1,131. Average book expense $750. **Required Forms and Deadlines:** FAFSA and Scholarship application form. No deadline for regular filing. Priority filing deadline May 1. **Notification of Awards:** Applicants will be notified of awards on a rolling basis beginning on or about March 1. **Types of Aid:** *Need-based scholarships/grants:* Pell, SEOG, state scholarships/grants, the school's own gift aid. *Loans:* FFEL Subsidized Stafford, FFEL Unsubsidized Stafford, FFEL PLUS, Federal Perkins, state loans, college/university loans from institutional funds. **Student Employment:** Federal Work-Study Program available. Institutional employment available. Off-campus job opportunities are excellent. **Financial Aid Statistics:** 55% freshmen, 49% undergrads receive some form of aid. Average freshman grant $3,678. Average freshman loan $2,702. Average income from on-campus job $2,500. **Financial Aid Phone:** 806-651-2055.

WEST VIRGINIA STATE COLLEGE

PO Box 1000, Campus 187, Institute, WV 25112-1000
Phone: 800-987-2112 **CEEB Code:** 5903
Fax: 304-766-3308 **Web:** www.wvsc.edu **ACT Code:** 4538

This public school was founded in 1891. It has an 88-acre campus.

STUDENTS AND FACULTY

Enrollment: 4,530. **Student Body:** Out-of-state 7%. **Ethnic Representation:** African American 13%, Asian 1%, Caucasian 86%. **Retention and Graduation:** 6% grads go on to further study within 1 year. 1% grads pursue business degrees. 1% grads pursue law degrees. 1% grads pursue medical degrees. **Faculty:** 100% faculty teach undergrads.

ACADEMICS

Degrees: Associate's, bachelor's. **Special Study Options:** Cooperative (work-study) program, off-campus study in Washington, DC.

FACILITIES

Housing: Coed, all-female, all-male, apartments for married students. **Library Holdings:** 10,793 bound volumes. 631 periodicals. 29,409 microforms. **Special Academic Facilities/Equipment:** On-campus day-care center, art gallery, ROTC Hall of Fame, Sports Hall of Fame. **Computers:** *Recommended operating system:* Mac. School-owned computers available for student use.

EXTRACURRICULARS

Organizations: 4 honor societies, 2 religious organizations, 6 fraternities (1% men join), 3 sororities (1% women join). **Athletics (Intercollegiate):** *Men:* baseball, basketball, cross-country, football, softball, tennis, track & field, volleyball. *Women:* basketball, cross-country, softball, tennis, track & field, volleyball.

ADMISSIONS

Selectivity Rating: 63 (of 100). **Freshman Academic Profile:** 99% from public high schools. TOEFL required of all international applicants, minimum TOEFL 500. **Freshman Admission Requirements:** High school diploma is required and GED is not accepted. *Academic units required/recommended:* 14 total required; 4 English required, 2 math required, 2 science required, 2 foreign language required, 3 social studies required, 1 history required. **Transfer Admission Requirements:** Minimum college GPA of 2.0 required. Lowest grade transferable C. **General Admission Information:** Early decision application deadline March 1. Regular application deadline August 11. Nonfall registration accepted. Credit and/or placement offered for CEEB Advanced Placement tests.

COSTS AND FINANCIAL AID

In-state tuition $2,116. Out-of-state tuition $5,150. Room & board $3,550. Required fees $125. Average book expense $500. **Required Forms and Deadlines:** FAFSA and institution's own financial aid form. **Types of Aid:** *Loans:* FFEL Subsidized Stafford, FFEL PLUS. **Student Employment:** Federal Work-Study Program available. Institutional employment available. Off-campus job opportunities are excellent. **Financial Aid Statistics:** Average income from on-campus job $1,300. **Financial Aid Phone:** 304-766-3131.

WEST VIRGINIA UNIVERSITY

Admissions Office, PO Box 6009, Morgantown, WV 26506-6009
Phone: 304-293-2121 **E-mail:** wvuadmissions@arc.wvu.edu **CEEB Code:** 5904
Fax: 304-293-3080 **Web:** www.wvu.edu **ACT Code:** 4540

This public school was founded in 1867. It has a 913-acre campus.

STUDENTS AND FACULTY

Enrollment: 16,692. **Student Body:** Male 54%, female 46%, out-of-state 38%, international 2% (90 countries represented). **Ethnic Representation:** African American 4%, Asian 2%, Caucasian 92%, Hispanic 1%. **Retention and Graduation:** 78% freshmen return for sophomore year. 27% freshmen graduate within 4 years. **Faculty:** Student/faculty ratio 19:1. 796 full-time faculty, 83% hold PhDs.

ACADEMICS

Degrees: Bachelor's, doctoral, first professional, master's. **Academic Requirements:** General education including some course work in English (including composition), humanities, mathematics, sciences (biological or physical), social science. **Classes:** 20-29 students in an average class. 20-29 students in an average lab/discussion section. **Majors with Highest Enrollment:** Engineering, general; psychology, general; business administration/management. **Disciplines with Highest Percentage of Degrees Awarded:** Business/marketing 12%, engineering/engineering technology 11%, social sciences and history 10%, liberal arts/general studies 10%, communications/communication technologies 9%. **Special Study Options:** Accelerated program, cooperative (work-study) program, distance learning, double major, English as a second language, student exchange program (domestic), external degree program, honors program, independent study, internships, student-designed major, study abroad, teacher certification program, weekend college.

FACILITIES

Housing: Coed, all-female, all-male, apartments for married students, apartments for single students, housing for disabled students, housing for international students, fraternities and/or sororities, special-interest floors available. Operation Jump Start places faculty residence hall leaders adjacent to residence halls allowing frequent opportunities for faculty-student interaction outside classroom. This program is mandatory for freshmen. **Library Holdings:** 1,694,414 bound volumes. 11,114 periodicals. 2,831,923 microforms. 45,126 audiovisuals. **Special Academic Facilities/Equipment:** Art galleries, creative arts center, arboretum, herbarium, planetarium, concurrent engineering research center, discovery lab (for inventors), Appalachian hardwood center, small business development center, pharmacy museum, coal and energy museum, center for economic research, fluidization center, center for software development. **Computers:** *Recommended operating system:* Windows 2000. School-owned computers available for student use.

EXTRACURRICULARS

Activities: Choral groups, concert band, dance, drama/theater, jazz band, literary magazine, marching band, music ensembles, musical theater, opera, pep band, radio station, student government, student newspaper, symphony orchestra, television station, yearbook. **Organizations:** 270 registered organizations, 43 honor societies, 25 religious organizations, 17 fraternities (9% men join), 14 sororities (9% women join). **Athletics (Intercollegiate):** *Men:* baseball, basketball, cross-country, diving, football, indoor track, rifle, soccer, swimming, tennis, track & field, wrestling. *Women:* basketball, crew, cross-country, diving, gymnastics, indoor track, rifle, soccer, swimming, tennis, track & field, volleyball.

ADMISSIONS

Selectivity Rating: 75 (of 100). **Freshman Academic Profile:** Average high school GPA 3.2. 19% in top 10% of high school class, 43% in top 25% of high school class, 74% in top 50% of high school class. Average SAT I Math 528, SAT I Math middle 50% range 470-580. Average SAT I Verbal 514, SAT I Verbal middle 50% range 460-560. Average ACT 23, ACT middle 50% range 20-25. TOEFL required of all international applicants, minimum TOEFL 550. **Basis for Candidate Selection:** *Very important factors considered include:* secondary school record, standardized test scores. *Other factors considered include:* alumni/ae relation, minority status. **Freshman Admission Requirements:** High school diploma or GED is required. *Academic units required/recommended:* 12 total required; 4 English required, 3 math required, 2 science required, 2 science lab required, 2 foreign language recommended, 3 social studies required. **Freshman Admission Statistics:** 9,147 applied, 94% accepted, 46% of those accepted enrolled. **Transfer Admission Requirements:** *Items required:* college transcript. Minimum high school GPA of 2.2 required. Minimum college GPA of 2.0 required. Lowest grade transferable D. **General Admission Information:** Application fee $25. Priority application deadline March 1. Regular application deadline August 1. Nonfall registration accepted. Admission may be deferred for a maximum of 1 year. Credit and/or placement offered for CEEB Advanced Placement tests.

COSTS AND FINANCIAL AID

In-state tuition $3,240. Out-of-state tuition $9,710. Room & board $5,572. Average book expense $727. **Required Forms and Deadlines:** FAFSA. Financial aid filing deadline March 1. Priority filing deadline February 15. **Notification of Awards:** Applicants will be notified of awards on a rolling basis. **Types of Aid:** *Need-based scholarships/grants:* Pell, SEOG, state scholarships/grants, private scholarships, the school's own gift aid. *Loans:* Direct Subsidized Stafford, Direct Unsubsidized Stafford, Direct PLUS, Federal Perkins, Federal Nursing, state loans, college/university loans from institutional funds. **Student Employment:** Federal Work-Study Program available. Institutional employment available. Off-campus job opportunities are good. **Financial Aid Statistics:** 38% freshmen, 46% undergrads receive some form of aid. Average income from on-campus job $1,000. **Financial Aid Phone:** 304-293-5242.

WEST VIRGINIA UNIVERSITY INSTITUTE OF TECHNOLOGY

Box 10 Old Main, Montgomery, WV 25136
Phone: 304-442-3167 **E-mail:** admissions@wvutech.edu **CEEB Code:** 3825
Fax: 304-442-3097 **Web:** www.wvutech.edu **ACT Code:** 4536

This public school was founded in 1895. It has a 200-acre campus.

STUDENTS AND FACULTY

Enrollment: 2,435. **Student Body:** Male 60%, female 40%, out-of-state 6%, international 3%. **Ethnic Representation:** African American 8%, Asian 1%, Caucasian 90%, Hispanic 1%. **Retention and Graduation:** 62% freshmen return for sophomore year. 14% freshmen graduate within 4 years. **Faculty:** Student/faculty ratio 16:1. 119 full-time faculty, 47% hold PhDs.

ACADEMICS

Degrees: Associate's, bachelor's, certificate, master's. **Academic Requirements:** General education including some course work in computer literacy, English (including composition), humanities, mathematics, sciences (biological or physical), social science. **Classes:** 10-19 students in an average class. 20-29 students in an average lab/discussion section. **Disciplines with Highest Percentage of Degrees Awarded:** Engineering/engineering technology 23%, interdisciplinary studies 13%, health professions and related sciences 12%, business/marketing 8%, trade and industry 6%. **Special Study Options:** Cooperative (work-study) program, distance learning, double major, dual enrollment, internships, student-designed major.

FACILITIES

Housing: Coed, all-female, all-male, fraternities and/or sororities. **Library Holdings:** 166,967 bound volumes. 510 periodicals. 438,232 microforms. 0 audiovisuals. **Computers:** *Recommended operating system:* Windows 95. School-owned computers available for student use.

EXTRACURRICULARS

Activities: Choral groups, concert band, drama/theater, jazz band, marching band, music ensembles, pep band, student government, student newspaper. **Organizations:** 52 registered organizations, 9 honor societies, 2 religious organizations, 5 fraternities (11% men join), 2 sororities (9% women join). **Athletics (Intercollegiate):** *Men:* baseball, basketball, football, golf, tennis. *Women:* basketball, cheerleading, soccer, softball, tennis, volleyball.

ADMISSIONS

Selectivity Rating: 63 (of 100). **Freshman Academic Profile:** Average high school GPA 3.2. 20% in top 10% of high school class, 21% in top 25% of high school class, 43% in top 50% of high school class. 95% from public high schools. Average SAT I Math 495, SAT I Math middle 50% range 400-580. Average SAT I Verbal 475, SAT I Verbal middle 50% range 380-530. Average ACT 20, ACT middle 50% range 17-23. TOEFL required of all international applicants, minimum TOEFL 500. **Basis for Candidate Selection:** *Very important factors considered include:* secondary school record, standardized test scores. *Other factors considered include:* alumni/ae relation, character/personal qualities, class rank, extracurricular activities, interview, recommendations, state residency, talent/ability, volunteer work. **Freshman Admission Requirements:** High school diploma or GED is required. *Academic units required/recommended:* 17 total required; 4 English required, 4 English recommended, 2 math required, 3 math recommended, 2 science required, 2 science recommended, 2 science lab required, 2 science lab recommended, 2 foreign language recommended, 3 social studies required, 3 social studies recommended. **Freshman Admission Statistics:** 1,191 applied, 74% accepted, 47% of those accepted enrolled. **Transfer Admission Requirements:** *Items required:* college transcript. Minimum college GPA of 1.7 required. Lowest grade transferable D. **General Admission Information:** Priority application deadline August 3. Nonfall registration accepted. Admission may be deferred. Credit offered for CEEB Advanced Placement tests.

COSTS AND FINANCIAL AID

In-state tuition $3,200. Out-of-state tuition $8,400. Room & board $4,896. Required fees $0. Average book expense $800. **Required Forms and Deadlines:** FAFSA and institution's own financial aid form. Financial aid filing deadline April 3. Priority filing deadline February 3. **Notification of Awards:** Applicants will be notified of awards on a rolling basis beginning on or about March 3. **Types of Aid:** *Need-based scholarships/grants:* Pell, SEOG, state scholarships/grants, private scholarships, the school's own gift aid. *Loans:* Direct Subsidized Stafford, Direct Unsubsidized Stafford, Direct PLUS, FFEL Subsidized Stafford, FFEL Unsubsidized Stafford, FFEL PLUS, Federal Perkins. **Student Employment:** Federal Work-Study Program available. Off-campus job opportunities are fair. **Financial Aid Statistics:** 60% freshmen, 54% undergrads receive some form of aid. Average freshman grant $2,401. Average freshman loan $2,100. Average income from on-campus job $1,250. **Financial Aid Phone:** 304-442-3228.

WEST VIRGINIA WESLEYAN COLLEGE

59 College Avenue, Buckhannon, WV 26201
Phone: 304-473-8510 **E-mail:** admission@wvwc.edu **CEEB Code:** 5905
Fax: 304-473-8108 **Web:** www.wvwc.edu **ACT Code:** 4544

This private school, which is affiliated with the Methodist Church, was founded in 1890. It has a 100-acre campus.

STUDENTS AND FACULTY

Enrollment: 1,560. **Student Body:** Male 45%, female 55%, out-of-state 47%, international 3% (26 countries represented). **Ethnic Representation:** African American 5%, Asian 1%, Caucasian 92%, Hispanic 1%. **Retention and Graduation:** 76% freshmen return for sophomore year. 41% freshmen graduate within 4 years. **Faculty:** Student/faculty ratio 15:1. 85 full-time faculty, 75% hold PhDs. 100% faculty teach undergrads.

ACADEMICS

Degrees: Bachelor's, master's. **Academic Requirements:** General education including some course work in arts/fine arts, computer literacy, English (including composition), history, humanities, mathematics, philosophy, sciences (biological or physical), social science. **Classes:** 10-19 students in an average class. 10-19 students in an average lab/discussion section. **Disciplines with Highest Percentage of Degrees Awarded:** Business/marketing 18%, social sciences and history 14%, education 13%, health professions and related sciences 7%, communications/communication technologies 6%. **Special Study Options:** Accelerated program, distance learning, double major, English as a second language, student exchange program (domestic), honors program, independent study, internships, student-designed major, study abroad, teacher certification program.

FACILITIES

Housing: Coed, all-female, all-male, apartments for single students, housing for disabled students, fraternities and/or sororities. **Library Holdings:** 91,061 bound volumes. 23,142 periodicals. 2,462 microforms. 7,605 audiovisuals. **Computers:** *Recommended operating system:* Windows 95.

EXTRACURRICULARS

Activities: Choral groups, concert band, dance, drama/theater, jazz band, literary magazine, music ensembles, musical theater, radio station, student government, student newspaper, yearbook. **Organizations:** 75 registered organizations, 31 honor societies, 6 religious organizations, 6 fraternities (25% men join), 5 sororities (25% women join). **Athletics (Intercollegiate):** *Men:* baseball, basketball, cross-country, football, golf, soccer, softball, swimming, tennis, track & field. *Women:* basketball, cross-country, soccer, swimming, tennis, track & field, volleyball.

ADMISSIONS

Selectivity Rating: 74 (of 100). **Freshman Academic Profile:** Average high school GPA 3.3. 23% in top 10% of high school class, 56% in top 25% of high school class, 83% in top 50% of high school class. Average SAT I Math 525, SAT I Math middle 50% range 460-580. Average SAT I Verbal 526, SAT I Verbal middle 50% range 470-570. Average ACT 23, ACT middle 50% range 20-26. TOEFL required of all international applicants, minimum TOEFL 500. **Basis for Candidate Selection:** *Very important factors considered include:* secondary school record, standardized test scores. *Important factors considered include:* character/personal qualities, class rank, essays, interview. *Other factors considered include:* alumni/ae relation, extracurricular activities, recommendations, talent/ability, volunteer work, work experience. **Freshman Admission Requirements:** High school diploma or GED is required. *Academic units required/recommended:* 4 English required, 3 math required, 3 science required, 2 science lab required, 2 foreign language recommended, 2 social studies required, 3 social studies recommended, 2 history required, 2 history recommended, 3 elective required. **Transfer Admission Requirements:** *Items required:* college transcript, essay, statement of good standing from prior school. Minimum high school GPA of 2.2 required. Minimum college GPA of 2.2 required. **General Admission Information:** Application fee $25. Priority application deadline March 3. Early decision application deadline December 2. Regular application deadline August 3. Nonfall registration accepted. Admission may be deferred for a maximum of 1 year. Credit offered for CEEB Advanced Placement tests.

COSTS AND FINANCIAL AID

Tuition $18,200. Room & board $5,200. Required fees $1,400. Average book expense $600. **Required Forms and Deadlines:** FAFSA. No deadline for regular filing. Priority filing deadline February 15. **Notification of Awards:** Applicants will be notified of awards on a rolling basis beginning on or about March 30. **Types of Aid:** *Need-based scholarships/grants:* Pell, SEOG, state scholarships/grants, private scholarships, the school's own gift aid, Federal Nursing. *Loans:* Direct Subsidized Stafford, Direct Unsubsidized Stafford, Direct PLUS, Federal Perkins, Federal Nursing, college/university loans from institutional funds. **Student Employment:** Federal Work-Study Program available. Institutional employment available. Off-campus job opportunities are poor. **Financial Aid Statistics:** 72% freshmen, 76% undergrads receive some form of aid. Average income from on-campus job $1,500. **Financial Aid Phone:** 304-473-8080.

WESTBROOK COLLEGE

Stevens Avenue, Portland, ME 04103
Phone: 207-797-7261
Fax: 207-797-7318

This private school was founded in 1831.

STUDENTS AND FACULTY

Enrollment: 458. **Student Body:** Out-of-state 28%.

FACILITIES

Housing: Coed, apartments for single students.

ADMISSIONS

Selectivity Rating: 68 (of 100). **Freshman Academic Profile:** 10% in top 10% of high school class, 35% in top 25% of high school class, 75% in top 50% of high school class. TOEFL required of all international applicants, minimum TOEFL 500. **General Admission Information:** Regular application deadline rolling.

COSTS AND FINANCIAL AID

Tuition $14,320. Room & board $5,820. Required fees $1,065. Average book expense $550. **Types of Aid:** *Need-based scholarships/grants:* Pell, SEOG, state scholarships/grants, private scholarships, the school's own gift aid. *Loans:* FFEL Subsidized Stafford, FFEL Unsubsidized Stafford, FFEL PLUS, Federal Perkins, college/university loans from institutional funds. **Student Employment:** Federal Work-Study Program available. **Financial Aid Statistics:** Average freshman grant $4,400. Average income from on-campus job $1,500.

WESTERN BAPTIST COLLEGE

5000 Deer Park Drive Southeast, Salem, OR 97301
Phone: 503-375-7005 **E-mail:** admissions@wbc.edu
Fax: 503-585-4316 **Web:** www.wbc.edu **ACT Code:** 477

This private school, which is affiliated with the Baptist Church, was founded in 1935. It has a 100-acre campus.

STUDENTS AND FACULTY

Enrollment: 729. **Student Body:** Male 38%, female 62%, out-of-state 33%, international 1% (7 countries represented). **Ethnic Representation:** African American 1%, Asian 1%, Caucasian 93%, Hispanic 3%, Native American 1%. **Retention and Graduation:** 65% freshmen return for sophomore year. 47% freshmen graduate within 4 years. **Faculty:** Student/faculty ratio 15:1. 34 full-time faculty, 41% hold PhDs. 100% faculty teach undergrads.

ACADEMICS

Degrees: Associate's, bachelor's. **Academic Requirements:** General education including some course work in arts/fine arts, computer literacy, English (including composition), history, humanities, mathematics, philosophy, sciences (biological or physical), social science, biblical/theological studies. **Classes:** Under 10 students in an average class. 10-19 students in an average lab/discussion section. **Majors with Highest Enrollment:** Business administration/management; elementary education and teaching; family systems. **Disciplines with Highest Percentage of Degrees Awarded:** Business/marketing 25%, psychology 21%, education 19%, liberal arts/general studies 11%, philosophy/religion/theology 7%. **Special Study Options:** Accelerated program, cross registration, distance learning, double major, honors program, independent study, internships, study abroad, teacher certification program, weekend college.

FACILITIES

Housing: All-female, all-male, apartments for married students, apartments for single students. **Library Holdings:** 85,000 bound volumes. 600 periodicals. 2,600 microforms. 4,500 audiovisuals. **Special Academic Facilities/ Equipment:** Prewitt-Allen Archeological Museum. **Computers:** School-owned computers available for student use.

EXTRACURRICULARS

Activities: Choral groups, concert band, drama/theater, jazz band, music ensembles, pep band, student government, student newspaper, yearbook. **Organizations:** 1 honor society. **Athletics (Intercollegiate):** *Men:* baseball, basketball, cross-country, soccer. *Women:* basketball, cross-country, soccer, softball, volleyball.

ADMISSIONS

Selectivity Rating: 77 (of 100). **Freshman Academic Profile:** Average high school GPA 3.5. 27% in top 10% of high school class, 55% in top 25% of high school class, 82% in top 50% of high school class. 40% from public high schools. Average SAT I Math 525, SAT I Math middle 50% range 420-641. Average SAT I Verbal 542, SAT I Verbal middle 50% range 449-652. Average ACT 24, ACT middle 50% range 20-30. TOEFL required of all international applicants, minimum TOEFL 500. **Basis for Candidate Selection:** *Very important factors considered include:* essays, recommendations, religious affiliation/ commitment. *Important factors considered include:* character/personal qualities, secondary school record, standardized test scores. *Other factors considered include:* alumni/ae relation, class rank, extracurricular activities, interview. **Freshman Admission Requirements:** High school diploma or GED is required. *Academic units required/recommended:* 13 total recommended; 4 English recommended, 3 math recommended, 2 science recommended, 1 foreign language recommended, 3 social studies recommended. **Freshman Admission Statistics:** 554 applied, 79% accepted, 33% of those accepted enrolled. **Transfer Admission Requirements:** *Items required:* high school transcript, college transcript, essay. Minimum high school GPA of 2.5 required. Minimum college GPA of 2.0 required. Lowest grade transferable C. **General Admission Information:** Application fee $35. Priority application deadline March 1. Regular application deadline August 1. Nonfall registration accepted. Credit offered for CEEB Advanced Placement tests.

COSTS AND FINANCIAL AID

Tuition $15,875. Room & board $5,725. Required fees $200. Average book expense $700. **Required Forms and Deadlines:** FAFSA. No deadline for

regular filing. Priority filing deadline February 15. **Notification of Awards:** Applicants will be notified of awards on or about March 1. **Types of Aid:** *Need-based scholarships/grants:* Pell, SEOG, state scholarships/grants, private scholarships, the school's own gift aid. *Loans:* Direct Subsidized Stafford, Direct Unsubsidized Stafford, Direct PLUS, Federal Perkins, state loans, alternative bank loans. **Student Employment:** Federal Work-Study Program available. Institutional employment available. Off-campus job opportunities are good. **Financial Aid Statistics:** 78% freshmen, 81% undergrads receive some form of aid. Average freshman grant $2,000. Average freshman loan $2,000. Average income from on-campus job $1,000. **Financial Aid Phone:** 503-373-7006.

WESTERN CAROLINA UNIVERSITY

242 HFR Administration, Cullowhee, NC 28723
Phone: 828-227-7317 **E-mail:** cauley@email.wcu.edu **CEEB Code:** 5897
Fax: 828-227-7319 **Web:** www.wcu.edu **ACT Code:** 3172

This public school was founded in 1889. It has a 265-acre campus.

STUDENTS AND FACULTY

Enrollment: 5,665. **Student Body:** Male 49%, female 51%, out-of-state 8%, international 2% (31 countries represented). **Ethnic Representation:** African American 6%, Asian 1%, Caucasian 90%, Hispanic 1%, Native American 2%. **Retention and Graduation:** 71% freshmen return for sophomore year. 22% freshmen graduate within 4 years. **Faculty:** Student/faculty ratio 16:1. 323 full-time faculty, 78% hold PhDs. 95% faculty teach undergrads.

ACADEMICS

Degrees: Bachelor's, doctoral, master's, post-master's certificate. **Academic Requirements:** General education including some course work in arts/fine arts, English (including composition), history, humanities, mathematics, philosophy, sciences (biological or physical), social science, oral communications, wellness. **Classes:** 20-29 students in an average class. 10-19 students in an average lab/discussion section. **Majors with Highest Enrollment:** Marketing/marketing management, general; elementary education and teaching; management information systems, general. **Disciplines with Highest Percentage of Degrees Awarded:** Business/marketing 22%, education 20%, health professions and related sciences 11%, protective services/public administration 7%, social sciences and history 6%. **Special Study Options:** Accelerated program, cooperative (work-study) program, distance learning, double major, dual enrollment, English as a second language, honors program, independent study, internships, student-designed major, study abroad, teacher certification program, satisfactory/unsatisfactory grading option.

FACILITIES

Housing: Coed, all-female, all-male, apartments for married students, fraternities and/or sororities. Sorority housing available within residence halls. **Library Holdings:** 675,929 bound volumes. 2,472 periodicals. 1,506,835 microforms. 24,514 audiovisuals. **Special Academic Facilities/Equipment:** Two art galleries, Mountain Resource Center, Mountain Heritage Center, Reading Center, State Center for the Advancement of Teaching, Speech/Hearing Center, High Technology Workplace Development Building (under construction), CATA Lab (high technology computer lab). **Computers:** School-owned computers available for student use.

EXTRACURRICULARS

Activities: Choral groups, concert band, dance, drama/theater, jazz band, literary magazine, marching band, music ensembles, musical theater, pep band, radio station, student government, student newspaper, student-run film society, yearbook. **Organizations:** 100 registered organizations, 22 honor societies, 5 religious organizations, 12 fraternities (15% men join), 9 sororities (11% women join). **Athletics (Intercollegiate):** *Men:* baseball, basketball, cheerleading, cross-country, football, golf, track & field. *Women:* basketball, cheerleading, cross-country, golf, soccer, tennis, track & field, volleyball.

ADMISSIONS

Selectivity Rating: 65 (of 100). **Freshman Academic Profile:** Average high school GPA 3.3. 9% in top 10% of high school class, 26% in top 25% of high school class, 61% in top 50% of high school class. 95% from public high schools. Average SAT I Math 510, SAT I Math middle 50% range 460-560. Average SAT I Verbal 502, SAT I Verbal middle 50% range 450-550. TOEFL required of all international applicants, minimum TOEFL 550. **Basis for Candidate Selection:** *Very important factors considered include:* secondary school record, standardized test scores. *Important factors considered include:* class rank. *Other factors considered include:* character/personal qualities, essays, extracurricular activities, interview, recommendations, state residency, talent/ability, volunteer work, work experience. **Freshman Admission Requirements:** High school diploma or GED is required. *Academic units required/recommended:* 20 total required; 24 total recommended; 4 English required, 3 math required, 3 science required, 3 science lab required, 2 foreign language recommended, 2 social studies required, 1 history required. **Freshman Admission Statistics:** 4,121 applied, 72% accepted, 41% of those accepted enrolled. **Transfer Admission Requirements:** *Items required:* high school transcript, college transcript, standardized test score, statement of good standing from prior school. Minimum college GPA of 2.0 required. Lowest grade transferable C. **General Admission Information:** Application fee $40. Priority application deadline February 1. Regular application deadline August 1. Nonfall registration accepted. Credit and/or placement offered for CEEB Advanced Placement tests.

COSTS AND FINANCIAL AID

Required Forms and Deadlines: FAFSA and institution's own financial aid form. No deadline for regular filing. Priority filing deadline March 31. **Notification of Awards:** Applicants will be notified of awards on a rolling basis beginning on or about April 1. **Types of Aid:** *Need-based scholarships/grants:* Pell, state scholarships/grants, private scholarships. *Loans:* Direct Subsidized Stafford, Direct Unsubsidized Stafford, Direct PLUS, Federal Perkins. **Student Employment:** Federal Work-Study Program available. Institutional employment available. Off-campus job opportunities are fair. **Financial Aid Statistics:** 46% freshmen, 44% undergrads receive some form of aid. Average freshman grant $2,172. Average freshman loan $5,501. Average income from on-campus job $2,482. **Financial Aid Phone:** 828-227-7290.

WESTERN CONNECTICUT STATE UNIVERSITY

Undergraduate Admissions Office, 181 White Street, Danbury, CT 06810-6855
Phone: 203-837-9000 **CEEB Code:** 3350
Web: www.wcsu.edu **ACT Code:** 558

This public school was founded in 1903. It has a 400-acre campus.

STUDENTS AND FACULTY

Enrollment: 5,274. **Student Body:** Male 45%, female 55%, out-of-state 12%, international 2% (20 countries represented). **Ethnic Representation:** African American 7%, Asian 3%, Caucasian 78%, Hispanic 5%. **Retention and Graduation:** 69% freshmen return for sophomore year. 13% freshmen graduate within 4 years. 23% grads go on to further study within 1 year. 2% grads pursue business degrees. 2% grads pursue law degrees. **Faculty:** Student/faculty ratio 17:1. 188 full-time faculty, 82% hold PhDs. 100% faculty teach undergrads.

ACADEMICS

Degrees: Associate's, bachelor's, master's. **Academic Requirements:** General education including some course work in English (including composition), humanities, mathematics, sciences (biological or physical), social science. **Classes:** 20-29 students in an average class. 10-19 students in an average lab/discussion section. **Majors with Highest Enrollment:** Nursing/registered nurse training (RN, ASN, BSN, MSN); elementary education and teaching; criminal justice/police science. **Disciplines with Highest Percentage of Degrees Awarded:** Business/marketing 26%, protective services/public administration 11%, education 10%, health professions and related sciences 10%, visual and performing arts 9%. **Special Study Options:** Accelerated program, cooperative (work-study) program, cross registration, distance learning, double major, dual enrollment, English as a second language, honors program, independent study, internships, student-designed major, study abroad, teacher certification program.

FACILITIES

Housing: Coed, all-female, apartments for single students. On-campus housing assigned on a first-come basis. **Library Holdings:** 144,532 bound volumes. 1,273 periodicals. 471,099 microforms. 8,654 audiovisuals. **Special Academic Facilities/Equipment:** Language lab, observatory, electron microscope, nature preserve, computer-enhanced classrooms, business library, Jane Goodall Institute. **Computers:** School-owned computers available for student use.

EXTRACURRICULARS

Activities: Choral groups, concert band, dance, drama/theater, jazz band, literary magazine, music ensembles, musical theater, opera, pep band, radio station, student government, student newspaper, symphony orchestra, yearbook. **Organizations:** 50 registered organizations, 7 honor societies, 2 religious organizations, 3 fraternities, 5 sororities. **Athletics (Intercollegiate):** *Men:* baseball, basketball, football, soccer, tennis. *Women:* basketball, lacrosse, soccer, softball, swimming, tennis, volleyball.

ADMISSIONS

Selectivity Rating: 63 (of 100). **Freshman Academic Profile:** 3% in top 10% of high school class, 14% in top 25% of high school class, 52% in top 50% of high school class. 91% from public high schools. Average SAT I Math 479, SAT I Math middle 50% range 420-520. Average SAT I Verbal 482, SAT I Verbal middle 50% range 430-520. TOEFL required of all international applicants, minimum TOEFL 550. **Basis for Candidate Selection:** *Very important factors considered include:* secondary school record, standardized test scores, talent/ability. *Important factors considered include:* class rank, extracurricular activities. *Other factors considered include:* alumni/ae relation, essays, interview, minority status, recommendations, state residency, volunteer work, work experience. **Freshman Admission Requirements:** High school diploma or GED is required. *Academic units required/recommended:* 13 total required; 4 English required, 3 math required, 2 science required, 2 science lab required, 2 foreign language required, 3 foreign language recommended, 1 social studies required, 1 history required. **Freshman Admission Statistics:** 3,131 applied, 61% accepted, 43% of those accepted enrolled. **Transfer Admission Requirements:** *Items required:* college transcript. Minimum college GPA of 2.0 required. Lowest grade transferable C-. **General Admission Information:** Application fee $40. Priority application deadline May 1. Nonfall registration accepted. Admission may be deferred for a maximum of 1 year. Credit offered for CEEB Advanced Placement tests.

COSTS AND FINANCIAL AID

In-state tuition $2,648. Out-of-state tuition $8,570. Room & board $6,580. Required fees $2,397. Average book expense $1,000. **Required Forms and Deadlines:** FAFSA and institution's own financial aid form. Financial aid filing deadline April 15. Priority filing deadline March 15. **Notification of Awards:** Applicants will be notified of awards on a rolling basis beginning on or about March 15. **Types of Aid:** *Need-based scholarships/grants:* Pell, SEOG, state scholarships/grants, private scholarships, the school's own gift aid. *Loans:* Direct Subsidized Stafford, Direct Unsubsidized Stafford, Direct PLUS, FFEL Subsidized Stafford, FFEL Unsubsidized Stafford, FFEL PLUS, Federal Perkins. **Student Employment:** Federal Work-Study Program available. Institutional employment available. Off-campus job opportunities are good. **Financial Aid Statistics:** 43% freshmen, 39% undergrads receive some form of aid. Average freshman grant $4,188. Average freshman loan $3,876. Average income from on-campus job $1,117. **Financial Aid Phone:** 203-837-8580.

WESTERN ILLINOIS UNIVERSITY

1 University Circle, 115 Sherman Hall, Macomb, IL 61455-1390

Phone: 309-298-3157 **E-mail:** wiuadm@wiu.edu **CEEB Code:** 1900

Fax: 309-298-3111 **Web:** www.wiu.edu **ACT Code:** 1158

This public school was founded in 1899. It has a 1,050-acre campus.

STUDENTS AND FACULTY

Enrollment: 11,033. **Student Body:** Male 50%, female 50%, out-of-state 5%, international 2% (54 countries represented). **Ethnic Representation:** African American 7%, Asian 1%, Caucasian 86%, Hispanic 3%. **Retention and Graduation:** 76% freshmen return for sophomore year. 29% freshmen graduate within 4 years. 21% grads go on to further study within 1 year. 6% grads pursue business degrees. 1% grads pursue law degrees. 1% grads pursue medical degrees. **Faculty:** Student/faculty ratio 17:1. 613 full-time faculty, 67% hold PhDs. 97% faculty teach undergrads.

ACADEMICS

Degrees: Bachelor's, master's, post-bachelor's certificate, post-master's certificate. **Academic Requirements:** General education including some course work in English (including composition), humanities, mathematics, sciences (biological or physical), social science. **Classes:** 20-29 students in an average class. **Disciplines with Highest Percentage of Degrees Awarded:** Education 16%, protective services/public administration 13%, liberal arts/general studies 13%, business/marketing 11%, social sciences and history 7%. **Special Study Options:** Distance learning, double major, dual enrollment, English as a second language, external degree program, honors program, independent study, internships, student-designed major, study abroad, teacher certification program, weekend college.

FACILITIES

Housing: Coed, apartments for married students, fraternities and/or sororities. Single rooms in the residence halls are the predominant lifestyle choice. **Library Holdings:** 998,041 bound volumes. 3,200 periodicals. 1,342,630 microforms. 3,445 audiovisuals. **Special Academic Facilities/Equipment:** Art gallery, electron microscope. **Computers:** School-owned computers available for student use.

EXTRACURRICULARS

Activities: Choral groups, concert band, dance, drama/theater, jazz band, marching band, music ensembles, musical theater, radio station, student government, student newspaper, television station, yearbook. **Organizations:** 235 registered organizations, 13 honor societies, 6 religious organizations, 12 fraternities (11% men join), 7 sororities (9% women join). **Athletics (Intercollegiate):** *Men:* baseball, basketball, cross-country, diving, football, golf, indoor track, soccer, swimming, tennis, track & field. *Women:* basketball, cheerleading, cross-country, diving, golf, indoor track, soccer, softball, swimming, tennis, track & field, volleyball.

ADMISSIONS

Selectivity Rating: 71 (of 100). **Freshman Academic Profile:** 6% in top 10% of high school class, 25% in top 25% of high school class, 60% in top 50% of high school class. 87% from public high schools. Average ACT 22, ACT middle 50% range 19-24. TOEFL required of all international applicants, minimum TOEFL 550. **Basis for Candidate Selection:** *Very important factors considered include:* class rank, secondary school record, standardized test scores. **Freshman Admission Requirements:** High school diploma or GED is required. *Academic units required/recommended:* 15 total recommended; 4 English recommended, 3 math recommended, 3 science recommended, 3 social studies recommended. **Freshman Admission Statistics:** 9,682 applied, 64% accepted, 31% of those accepted enrolled. **Transfer Admission Requirements:** *Items required:* college transcript. Minimum college GPA of 2.0 required. Lowest grade transferable D. **General Admission Information:** Application fee $25. Regular application deadline August 3. Nonfall registration accepted. Admission may be deferred. Credit offered for CEEB Advanced Placement tests.

COSTS AND FINANCIAL AID

In-state tuition $3,165. Out-of-state tuition $6,330. Room & board $5,062. Required fees $1,344. Average book expense $800. **Required Forms and Deadlines:** FAFSA. No deadline for regular filing. Priority filing deadline February 15. **Notification of Awards:** Applicants will be notified of awards on a rolling basis beginning on or about February 15. **Types of Aid:** *Need-based scholarships/grants:* Pell, SEOG, state scholarships/grants, private scholarships, the school's own gift aid. *Loans:* FFEL Subsidized Stafford, FFEL Unsubsidized Stafford, FFEL PLUS, Federal Perkins. **Student Employment:** Federal Work-Study Program available. Institutional employment available. Off-campus job opportunities are fair. **Financial Aid Statistics:** 52% freshmen, 52% undergrads receive some form of aid. Average freshman grant $5,003. Average freshman loan $2,492. Average income from on-campus job $1,055. **Financial Aid Phone:** 309-298-2446.

WESTERN INTERNATIONAL UNIVERSITY

9215 North Black Canyon Highway, Phoenix, AZ 85021

Phone: 602-943-2311 **E-mail:** karen.janitell@apollogrp.edu

Fax: 602-943-3204 **Web:** www.wintu.edu

This private school was founded in 1978.

STUDENTS AND FACULTY

Enrollment: 820. **Student Body:** Out-of-state 22%.

ACADEMICS

Degrees: Associate's, bachelor's, master's, post-master's certificate, terminal.

EXTRACURRICULARS

Activities: Student newspaper. **Organizations:** 6 registered organizations.

ADMISSIONS

Selectivity Rating: 63 (of 100). **Freshman Academic Profile:** TOEFL required of all international applicants, minimum TOEFL 500. **General Admission Information:** Regular application deadline February 1.

COSTS AND FINANCIAL AID

Required fees $50. Average book expense $500. **Types of Aid:** *Need-based scholarships/grants:* Pell, SEOG, state scholarships/grants, private scholarships, the school's own gift aid. *Loans:* FFEL Subsidized Stafford, FFEL Unsubsidized Stafford, FFEL PLUS, Federal Perkins, college/university loans from institutional funds. **Student Employment:** Federal Work-Study Program available. **Financial Aid Statistics:** Average freshman grant $1,500. Average freshman loan $2,625. Average income from on-campus job $1,500.

WESTERN KENTUCKY UNIVERSITY

Potter Hall 117, 1 Big Red Way, Bowling Green, KY 42101-3576
Phone: 270-745-2551 **E-mail:** admission@wku.edu **CEEB Code:** 1901
Fax: 270-745-6133 **Web:** www.wku.edu **ACT Code:** 1562

This public school was founded in 1906. It has a 200-acre campus.

STUDENTS AND FACULTY

Enrollment: 14,135. **Student Body:** Male 41%, female 59%, out-of-state 16%, international 1%. **Ethnic Representation:** African American 8%, Asian 1%, Caucasian 89%, Hispanic 1%. **Retention and Graduation:** 75% freshmen return for sophomore year. **Faculty:** Student/faculty ratio 18:1. 599 full-time faculty, 80% hold PhDs. 100% faculty teach undergrads.

ACADEMICS

Degrees: Associate's, bachelor's, certificate, master's, terminal, transfer. **Academic Requirements:** General education including some course work in English (including composition), foreign languages, history, humanities, mathematics, sciences (biological or physical), social science. **Classes:** 20-29 students in an average class. 10-19 students in an average lab/discussion section. **Majors with Highest Enrollment:** Elementary education and teaching; general studies; psychology, general. **Disciplines with Highest Percentage of Degrees Awarded:** Business/marketing 17%, education 16%, communications/communication technologies 10%, social sciences and history 10%, liberal arts/general studies 9%. **Special Study Options:** Cooperative (work-study) program, distance learning, double major, dual enrollment, English as a second language, student exchange program (domestic), honors program, independent study, internships, student-designed major, study abroad, teacher certification program.

FACILITIES

Housing: Coed, all-female, all-male, housing for disabled students, housing for international students, fraternities and/or sororities. **Library Holdings:** 1,061,241 bound volumes. 4,564 periodicals. 2,651,784 microforms. 93,955 audiovisuals. **Special Academic Facilities/Equipment:** Kentucky museum, university farm, planetarium. **Computers:** *Recommended operating system:* Windows 95. School-owned computers available for student use.

EXTRACURRICULARS

Activities: Choral groups, concert band, dance, drama/theater, jazz band, literary magazine, marching band, music ensembles, musical theater, pep band, radio station, student government, student newspaper, student-run film society, symphony orchestra, television station. **Organizations:** 217 registered organizations, 35 honor societies, 22 religious organizations, 14 fraternities (10% men join), 11 sororities (10% women join). **Athletics (Intercollegiate):** *Men:* baseball, basketball, cross-country, diving, football, golf, rifle, soccer, swimming, tennis, track & field. *Women:* basketball, cross-country, diving, golf, rifle, softball, swimming, tennis, track & field, volleyball.

ADMISSIONS

Selectivity Rating: 72 (of 100). **Freshman Academic Profile:** Average high school GPA 3.1. 20% in top 10% of high school class, 41% in top 25% of high school class, 71% in top 50% of high school class. Average SAT I Math 520, SAT I Math middle 50% range 460-570. Average SAT I Verbal 519, SAT I Verbal middle 50% range 460-570. Average ACT 21, ACT middle 50% range 18-24. TOEFL required of all international applicants, minimum TOEFL 525. **Basis for Candidate Selection:** *Very important factors considered include:* secondary school record, standardized test scores. *Important factors considered include:* class rank. *Other factors considered include:* character/personal qualities, interview, recommendations, talent/ability. **Freshman Admission Requirements:** High school diploma or GED is required. *Academic units required/recommended:* 20 total required; 4 English required, 3 math required, 4 math recommended, 2 science required, 3 science recommended, 1 science lab required, 2 foreign language recommended, 2 social studies required, 3 social studies recommended, 1 elective recommended. **Freshman Admission Statistics:** 5,105 applied, 85% accepted, 63% of those accepted enrolled. **Transfer Admission Requirements:** *Items required:* college transcript. Minimum college GPA of 2.0 required. Lowest grade transferable D. **General Admission Information:** Application fee $30. Regular application deadline Aug. 1. Nonfall registration accepted. Credit and/or placement offered for CEEB Advanced Placement tests.

COSTS AND FINANCIAL AID

In-state tuition $2,290. Out-of-state tuition $6,870. Room & board $3,990. Required fees $554. Average book expense $600. **Required Forms and Deadlines:** FAFSA. No deadline for regular filing. Priority filing deadline April 1. **Notification of Awards:** Applicants will be notified of awards on a rolling basis beginning on or about March 1. **Types of Aid:** *Need-based scholarships/grants:* Pell, SEOG, state scholarships/grants, private scholarships. *Loans:* FFEL Subsidized Stafford, FFEL Unsubsidized Stafford, FFEL PLUS, Federal Perkins, college/university loans from institutional funds. **Student Employment:** Federal Work-Study Program available. Institutional employment available. Off-campus job opportunities are good. **Financial Aid Statistics:** 49% freshmen, 48% undergrads receive some form of aid. Average freshman grant $3,124. Average freshman loan $3,231. Average income from on-campus job $2,098. **Financial Aid Phone:** 270-745-2755.

WESTERN MICHIGAN UNIVERSITY

1903 W. Michigan Avenue, Kalamazoo, MI 49008
Phone: 269-387-2000 **E-mail:** ask-wmu@umich.edu **CEEB Code:** 1902
Fax: 616-387-2096 **Web:** www.wmich.edu **ACT Code:** 2066

This public school was founded in 1903. It has a 1,200-acre campus.

STUDENTS AND FACULTY

Enrollment: 23,643. **Student Body:** Male 49%, female 51%, out-of-state 7%, international 4% (102 countries represented). **Ethnic Representation:** African American 5%, Asian 1%, Caucasian 91%, Hispanic 2%. **Retention and Graduation:** 76% freshmen return for sophomore year. 18% freshmen graduate within 4 years. **Faculty:** Student/faculty ratio 16:1. 985 full-time faculty, 86% hold PhDs. 100% faculty teach undergrads.

ACADEMICS

Degrees: Bachelor's, doctoral, master's, post-master's certificate. **Academic Requirements:** General education including some course work in arts/fine arts, computer literacy, English (including composition), humanities, mathematics, sciences (biological or physical), social science. **Majors with Highest Enrollment:** Health professions and related sciences; communications, journalism, and related fields; marketing. **Disciplines with Highest Percentage of Degrees Awarded:** Business/marketing 26%, education 21%, engineering/engineering technology 7%, social sciences and history 6%, communications/communication technologies 5%. **Special Study Options:** Accelerated program, cooperative (work-study) program, cross registration, distance learning, double major, dual enrollment, English as a second language, student exchange program (domestic), honors program, independent study, internships, student-designed major, study abroad, teacher certification program, weekend college.

FACILITIES

Housing: Coed, all-female, all-male, apartments for married students, apartments for single students, housing for disabled students, housing for international students, fraternities and/or sororities, health and wellness dorm. **Library Holdings:** 4,227,891 bound volumes. 6,707 periodicals. 1,878,273 microforms. 32,535 audiovisuals. **Special Academic Facilities/Equipment:** Pilot plant for manufacturing and printing of paper and for fiber recovery, behavior research and development center, nuclear accelerator, center for electron microscopy, particle accelerator lab, women's poetry collection, Meade Rare Book Room. **Computers:** School-owned computers available for student use.

EXTRACURRICULARS

Activities: Choral groups, concert band, dance, drama/theater, jazz band, marching band, music ensembles, musical theater, opera, pep band, radio station, student government, student newspaper, symphony orchestra. **Organizations:** 275 registered organizations, 18 honor societies, 43 religious organizations, 19 fraternities (8% men join), 13 sororities (8% women join). **Athletics (Intercollegiate):** *Men:* baseball, basketball, cross-country, football, ice hockey, soccer, tennis, track & field. *Women:* basketball, cross-country, golf, gymnastics, soccer, softball, tennis, track & field, volleyball.

ADMISSIONS

Selectivity Rating: 73 (of 100). **Freshman Academic Profile:** Average high school GPA 3.3. 16% in top 10% of high school class, 34% in top 25% of high school class, 72% in top 50% of high school class. 90% from public high schools. Average ACT 22, ACT middle 50% range 20-25. TOEFL required of all international applicants, minimum TOEFL 550. **Basis for Candidate Selection:** *Very important factors considered include:* secondary school record. *Important factors considered include:* alumni/ae relation, minority status, standardized test scores, talent/ability. *Other factors considered include:* character/personal qualities, essays, extracurricular activities, interview, recommendations, volunteer work, work experience. **Freshman Admission Requirements:** High school diploma or GED is required. *Academic units required/recommended:* 16 total required; 18 total recommended; 4 English required, 3 math required, 4 math recommended, 2 science required, 1 science lab required, 1 foreign language required, 2 foreign language recommended, 2 social studies required, 1 history required, 2 elective required. **Freshman Admission Statistics:** 15,832 applied, 80% accepted, 35% of those accepted enrolled. **Transfer Admission Requirements:** *Items required:* college transcript. Minimum college GPA of 2.0 required. Lowest grade transferable C. **General Admission Information:** Application fee $25. Nonfall registration accepted. Admission may be deferred. Neither credit nor placement offered for CEEB Advanced Placement tests.

COSTS AND FINANCIAL AID

Required Forms and Deadlines: FAFSA. No deadline for regular filing. Priority filing deadline February 1. **Notification of Awards:** Applicants will be notified of awards on a rolling basis beginning on or about March 15. **Types of Aid:** *Need-based scholarships/grants:* Pell, SEOG, state scholarships/grants, private scholarships, the school's own gift aid. *Loans:* Direct Subsidized Stafford, Direct Unsubsidized Stafford, Direct PLUS, Federal Perkins, alternative loans. **Student Employment:** Federal Work-Study Program available. Institutional employment available. Off-campus job opportunities are excellent. **Financial Aid Statistics:** 40% freshmen, 38% undergrads receive some form of aid. Average income from on-campus job $4,400. **Financial Aid Phone:** 269-387-6000.

WESTERN NEW ENGLAND COLLEGE

1215 Wilbraham Road, Springfield, MA 01119
Phone: 413-782-1321 **E-mail:** ugradmis@wnec.edu **CEEB Code:** 3962
Fax: 413-782-1777 **Web:** www.wnec.edu **ACT Code:** 1930

This private school was founded in 1919. It has a 215-acre campus.

STUDENTS AND FACULTY

Enrollment: 3,151. **Student Body:** Male 63%, female 37%, out-of-state 57%, international 1%. **Ethnic Representation:** African American 3%, Asian 2%, Caucasian 83%, Hispanic 3%. **Retention and Graduation:** 75% freshmen return for sophomore year. 41% freshmen graduate within 4 years. 10% grads go on to further study within 1 year. **Faculty:** Student/faculty ratio 17:1. 154 full-time faculty, 87% hold PhDs. 100% faculty teach undergrads.

ACADEMICS

Degrees: Associate's, bachelor's, certificate, first professional, master's, terminal. **Academic Requirements:** General education including some course work in arts/fine arts, computer literacy, English (including composition), history, humanities, mathematics, sciences (biological or physical), social science. **Classes:** 20-29 students in an average class. 10-19 students in an average lab/discussion section. **Majors with Highest Enrollment:** Business/commerce, general; criminal justice/law enforcement administration; psychology, general. **Disciplines with Highest Percentage of Degrees Awarded:** Protective services/public administration 42%, business/marketing 26%, engineering/engineering technology 8%, computer and information sciences 6%, social sciences and history 6%. **Special Study Options:** Cross registration, double major, dual enrollment, honors program, independent study, internships, liberal arts/career combination, student-designed major, study abroad, teacher certification program.

FACILITIES

Housing: Coed, all-female, all-male, apartments for single students, housing for disabled students. **Library Holdings:** 151,896 bound volumes. 352 periodicals. 363,166 microforms. 2,989 audiovisuals. **Special Academic Facilities/Equipment:** Art gallery; math, writing, and science centers. **Computers:** School-owned computers available for student use.

EXTRACURRICULARS

Activities: Choral groups, concert band, dance, drama/theater, jazz band, literary magazine, music ensembles, pep band, radio station, student government, student newspaper, yearbook. **Organizations:** 60 registered organizations, 6 honor societies, 1 religious organization. **Athletics (Intercollegiate):** *Men:* baseball, basketball, cross-country, football, golf, ice hockey, lacrosse, soccer, tennis, wrestling. *Women:* basketball, cross-country, field hockey, lacrosse, soccer, softball, swimming, tennis, volleyball.

ADMISSIONS

Selectivity Rating: 68 (of 100). **Freshman Academic Profile:** Average high school GPA 3.1. 8% in top 10% of high school class, 31% in top 25% of high school class, 72% in top 50% of high school class. Average SAT I Math 535, SAT I Math middle 50% range 480-580. Average SAT I Verbal 516, SAT I Verbal middle 50% range 470-560. TOEFL required of all international applicants, minimum TOEFL 500. **Basis for Candidate Selection:** *Very important factors considered include:* recommendations, secondary school record, standardized test scores. *Other factors considered include:* character/personal qualities, class rank, essays, extracurricular activities, interview, minority status, talent/ability, volunteer work, work experience. **Freshman Admission Requirements:** High school diploma or GED is required. *Academic units required/recommended:* 10 total required; 18 total recommended; 4 English required, 4 English recommended, 2 math required, 4 math recommended, 1 science required, 2 science recommended, 1 science lab required, 2 science lab recommended, 2 foreign language recommended, 1 social studies required, 2 social studies recommended, 1 history required, 2 history recommended. **Freshman Admission Statistics:** 4,180 applied, 73% accepted, 26% of those accepted enrolled. **Transfer Admission Requirements:** *Items required:* high school transcript, college transcript, statement of good standing from prior school. Minimum college GPA of 2.3 required. Lowest grade transferable C-. **General Admission Information:** Application fee $50. Priority application deadline March 15. Nonfall registration accepted. Admission may be deferred for a maximum of 1 year. Credit and/or placement offered for CEEB Advanced Placement tests.

COSTS AND FINANCIAL AID

Average book expense $660. **Required Forms and Deadlines:** FAFSA, student and parent 1040 and W-2s. No deadline for regular filing. Priority filing deadline April 1. **Notification of Awards:** Applicants will be notified of awards on a rolling basis beginning on or about March 15. **Types of Aid:** *Need-based scholarships/grants:* Pell, SEOG, state scholarships/grants, private scholarships, the school's own gift aid. *Loans:* Direct Subsidized Stafford, Direct Unsubsidized Stafford, Direct PLUS, Federal Perkins, state loans, private loan programs. **Student Employment:** Federal Work-Study Program available. Institutional employment available. Off-campus job opportunities are good. **Financial Aid Statistics:** 72% freshmen, 61% undergrads receive some form of aid. Average freshman grant $10,408. Average freshman loan $2,722. **Financial Aid Phone:** 413-796-2080.

WESTERN NEW MEXICO UNIVERSITY

100 College Avenue, Silver City, NM 88062
Phone: 800-222-9668
Fax: 505-538-6155

This public school was founded in 1893.

STUDENTS AND FACULTY

Enrollment: 1,758. **Student Body:** Out-of-state 24%.

FACILITIES

Housing: Coed, all-female, all-male, apartments for single students.

EXTRACURRICULARS

Organizations: 17 honor societies, 21 religious organizations. **Athletics (Intercollegiate):** *Men:* baseball, basketball, football, softball, track & field, volleyball. *Women:* basketball, softball, track & field, volleyball.

ADMISSIONS

Selectivity Rating: 63 (of 100). **Freshman Academic Profile:** 5% in top 10% of high school class, 25% in top 25% of high school class, 58% in top 50% of high school class. Average ACT 17. TOEFL required of all international applicants, minimum TOEFL 550. **General Admission Information:** Regular application deadline August 2.

COSTS AND FINANCIAL AID

Room & board $2,260. Average book expense $500. **Types of Aid:** *Loans:* FFEL Subsidized Stafford, FFEL PLUS. **Student Employment:** Federal Work-Study Program available. **Financial Aid Statistics:** Average income from on-campus job $1,824.

WESTERN OREGON UNIVERSITY

345 North Monmouth Avenue, Monmouth, OR 97361
Phone: 503-838-8211 **E-mail:** wolfgram@wou.edu **CEEB Code:** 4585
Fax: 503-838-8067 **Web:** www.wou.edu **ACT Code:** 3480

This public school was founded in 1856. It has a 157-acre campus.

STUDENTS AND FACULTY

Enrollment: 4,463. **Student Body:** Male 42%, female 58%, out-of-state 11%, international 2% (18 countries represented). **Ethnic Representation:** African American 2%, Asian 3%, Caucasian 84%, Hispanic 5%, Native American 1%. **Retention and Graduation:** 75% freshmen return for sophomore year. 15% freshmen graduate within 4 years. 12% grads go on to further study within 1 year. **Faculty:** Student/faculty ratio 20:1. 178 full-time faculty, 83% hold PhDs. 99% faculty teach undergrads.

ACADEMICS

Degrees: Associate's, bachelor's, master's, post-bachelor's certificate. **Academic Requirements:** General education including some course work in arts/fine arts, computer literacy, English (including composition), humanities, mathematics, philosophy, sciences (biological or physical), social science, health/physical education. **Classes:** 10-19 students in an average class. 20-29 students in an average lab/discussion section. **Majors with Highest Enrollment:** Business administration/management; psychology, general; corrections. **Disciplines with Highest Percentage of Degrees Awarded:** Social sciences and history 15%, business/marketing 14%, psychology 12%, interdisciplinary studies 12%, education 10%. **Special Study Options:** Distance learning, double major, English as a second language, honors program, independent study, internships, student-designed major, study abroad, teacher certification program.

FACILITIES

Housing: Coed, apartments for married students, apartments for single students. Special-interest communities (wellness, honors, multicultural, quiet) and single-parent/family housing available. **Library Holdings:** 157,186 bound volumes. 3,680 periodicals. 682,067 microforms. 3,169 audiovisuals. **Special Academic Facilities/Equipment:** Jensen Arctic Museum. **Computers:** School-owned computers available for student use.

EXTRACURRICULARS

Activities: Choral groups, concert band, dance, drama/theater, jazz band, literary magazine, music ensembles, musical theater, pep band, student government, student newspaper, television station. **Organizations:** 50 registered organizations, 4 honor societies, 6 religious organizations. **Athletics (Intercollegiate):** *Men:* baseball, basketball, cheerleading, cross-country, football, track & field. *Women:* basketball, cheerleading, cross-country, soccer, softball, track & field, volleyball.

ADMISSIONS

Selectivity Rating: 81 (of 100). **Freshman Academic Profile:** Average high school GPA 3.2. 11% in top 10% of high school class, 35% in top 25% of high school class, 66% in top 50% of high school class. 95% from public high schools. Average SAT I Math 490, SAT I Math middle 50% range 430-550. Average SAT I Verbal 485, SAT I Verbal middle 50% range 430-540. Average ACT 21, ACT middle 50% range 17-24. TOEFL required of all international applicants, minimum TOEFL 500. **Basis for Candidate Selection:** *Very important factors considered include:* secondary school record, standardized test scores. *Important factors considered include:* class rank. *Other factors considered include:* alumni/ae relation, minority status, recommendations, talent/ability. **Freshman Admission Requirements:** High school diploma or GED is required. *Academic units required/recommended:* 14 total required; 4 English required, 3 math required, 2 science required, 1 science lab recommended, 2 foreign language required, 2 social studies required, 1 history required. **Freshman Admission Statistics:** 1,541 applied, 93% accepted, 55% of those accepted enrolled. **Transfer Admission Requirements:** *Items required:* college transcript. Minimum college GPA of 2.0 required. Lowest grade transferable D-. **General Admission Information:** Application fee $50. Nonfall registration accepted. Admission may be deferred for a maximum of 1 year. Credit and/or placement offered for CEEB Advanced Placement tests.

COSTS AND FINANCIAL AID

In-state tuition $2,700. Out-of-state tuition $10,752. Room & board $5,724. Required fees $1,020. Average book expense $1,080. **Required Forms and Deadlines:** FAFSA. Priority filing deadline March 1. **Notification of Awards:** Applicants will be notified of awards on a rolling basis. **Types of Aid:** *Need-based scholarships/grants:* Pell, SEOG, state scholarships/grants, private scholarships, the school's own gift aid. *Loans:* Direct Subsidized Stafford, Direct Unsubsidized Stafford, Direct PLUS, Federal Perkins. **Student Employment:** Federal Work-Study Program available. Institutional employment available. Off-campus job opportunities are good. **Financial Aid Statistics:** 57% freshmen, 60% undergrads receive some form of aid. Average freshman grant $6,164. Average freshman loan $6,125. **Financial Aid Phone:** 503-838-8684.

WESTERN STATE COLLEGE OF COLORADO

600 N. Adams St., Gunnison, CO 81231
Phone: 970-943-2119 **E-mail:** discover@western.edu **CEEB Code:** 4946
Fax: 970-943-2212 **Web:** www.western.edu **ACT Code:** 536

This public school was founded in 1911. It has a 228-acre campus.

STUDENTS AND FACULTY

Enrollment: 2,320. **Student Body:** Male 58%, female 42%, out-of-state 28%. **Ethnic Representation:** African American 1%, Asian 1%, Caucasian 87%, Hispanic 5%, Native American 1%. **Retention and Graduation:** 58% freshmen return for sophomore year. 12% freshmen graduate within 4 years. 15% grads go on to further study within 1 year. **Faculty:** Student/faculty ratio 20:1. 97 full-time faculty, 82% hold PhDs. 100% faculty teach undergrads.

ACADEMICS

Degrees: Bachelor's. **Academic Requirements:** General education including some course work in arts/fine arts, English (including composition), history, humanities, mathematics, sciences (biological or physical), social science. **Classes:** 20-29 students in an average class. 20-29 students in an average lab/discussion section. **Majors with Highest Enrollment:** Business/commerce, general; biology/biological sciences, general; parks, recreation and leisure studies. **Disciplines with Highest Percentage of Degrees Awarded:** Business/marketing 28%, social sciences and history 17%, parks and recreation 17%, visual and performing arts 10%, psychology 8%. **Special Study Options:** Cooperative (work-study) program, distance learning, double major, dual enrollment, student exchange program (domestic), honors program, independent study, internships, liberal arts/career combination, study abroad, teacher certification program.

FACILITIES

Housing: Coed, all-female, all-male, apartments for married students, apartments for single students, fraternities and/or sororities. Theme housing: honors, art, wilderness/outdoor activities. **Library Holdings:** 158,698 bound volumes. 719 periodicals. 1,173,804 microforms. 1,539 audiovisuals. **Special Academic Facilities/Equipment:** Botanical garden, dinosaur museum, archaeological site. **Computers:** School-owned computers available for student use.

EXTRACURRICULARS

Activities: Choral groups, concert band, drama/theater, jazz band, literary magazine, music ensembles, pep band, radio station, student government, student newspaper, symphony orchestra, television station. **Organizations:** 56 registered organizations, 1 honor society, 5 religious organizations, 6 fraternities, 1 sorority. **Athletics (Intercollegiate):** *Men:* basketball, skiing (cross-country), cross-country, football, skiing (alpine), skiing (Nordic), track & field, wrestling. *Women:* basketball, skiing (cross-country), cross-country, skiing (alpine), skiing (Nordic), track & field, volleyball.

ADMISSIONS

Selectivity Rating: 66 (of 100). **Freshman Academic Profile:** Average high school GPA 2.9. 5% in top 10% of high school class, 19% in top 25% of high school class, 44% in top 50% of high school class. Average SAT I Math 482, SAT I Math middle 50% range 430-540. Average SAT I Verbal 500, SAT I Verbal middle 50% range 450-560. Average ACT 21, ACT middle 50% range 18-23. TOEFL required of all international applicants, minimum TOEFL 550. **Basis for Candidate Selection:** *Very important factors considered include:* class rank, secondary school record, standardized test scores. *Important factors considered include:* character/personal qualities, extracurricular activities, talent/ability. *Other factors considered include:* alumni/ae relation, essays, interview, recommendations. **Freshman Admission Requirements:** High school diploma or GED is required. *Academic units required/recommended:* 4 English required, 4 English recommended, 3 math required, 4 math recommended, 2 science required, 3 science recommended, 2 science lab required, 2 foreign language recommended, 2 social studies required, 3 social studies recommended, 2 history required, 3 history recommended, 3 elective required. **Freshman Admission Statistics:** 1,985 applied, 81% accepted, 38% of those accepted enrolled. **Transfer Admission Requirements:** *Items required:* college transcript. Minimum high school GPA of 2.5 required. Minimum college GPA of 2.0 required. Lowest grade transferable C. **General Admission Information:** Application fee $25. Priority application deadline May 1. Regular application deadline August 1. Nonfall registration accepted. Admission may be deferred for a maximum of 1 year. Credit and/or placement offered for CEEB Advanced Placement tests.

COSTS AND FINANCIAL AID

Average book expense $800. **Required Forms and Deadlines:** FAFSA. No deadline for regular filing. Priority filing deadline March 1. **Notification of Awards:** Applicants will be notified of awards on a rolling basis beginning on or about April 1. **Types of Aid:** *Need-based scholarships/grants:* Pell, SEOG, state scholarships/grants, private scholarships, the school's own gift aid. *Loans:* FFEL Subsidized Stafford, FFEL Unsubsidized Stafford, FFEL PLUS, Federal Perkins. **Student Employment:** Federal Work-Study Program available. Institutional employment available. Off-campus job opportunities are good. **Financial Aid Statistics:** 38% freshmen, 30% undergrads receive some form of aid. Average freshman grant $600. Average freshman loan $3,000. Average income from on-campus job $1,000. **Financial Aid Phone:** 970-943-3085.

WESTERN WASHINGTON UNIVERSITY

Mail Stop 9009, Bellingham, WA 98225-9009
Phone: 360-650-3440 **E-mail:** admit@cc.wwu.edu **CEEB Code:** 4947
Fax: 360-650-7369 **Web:** www.wwu.edu **ACT Code:** 4490

This public school was founded in 1893. It has a 300-acre campus.

STUDENTS AND FACULTY

Enrollment: 11,647. **Student Body:** Male 44%, female 56%, out-of-state 6%, international 1% (36 countries represented). **Ethnic Representation:** African American 2%, Asian 7%, Caucasian 85%, Hispanic 3%, Native American 2%. **Retention and Graduation:** 81% freshmen return for sophomore year. **Faculty:** Student/faculty ratio 20:1. 455 full-time faculty, 85% hold PhDs.

ACADEMICS

Degrees: Bachelor's, master's, post-bachelor's certificate. **Academic Requirements:** General education including some course work in English (including composition), humanities, mathematics, sciences (biological or physical), social science, and comparative, gender, and multicultural studies. **Classes:** Under 10 students in an average class. **Majors with Highest Enrollment:** English language and literature, general; psychology, general; political science and government, general. **Disciplines with Highest Percentage of Degrees Awarded:** Social sciences and history 15%, business/marketing 14%, education 6%, visual and performing arts 6%, psychology 6%. **Special Study Options:** Distance learning, double major, English as a second language, student exchange program (domestic), honors program, independent study, internships, liberal arts/career combination, student-designed major, study abroad, teacher certification program.

FACILITIES

Housing: Coed, apartments for married students, apartments for single students, housing for disabled students. **Library Holdings:** 1,322,050 bound volumes. 4,834 periodicals. 1,896,673 microforms. 26,095 audiovisuals. **Special Academic Facilities/Equipment:** Outdoor art museum, planetarium, electronic music studio, air pollution lab, motor vehicle research lab, marine lab, wind tunnel, electron microscope, neutron generator lab. **Computers:** School-owned computers available for student use.

EXTRACURRICULARS

Activities: Choral groups, concert band, dance, drama/theater, jazz band, literary magazine, music ensembles, musical theater, opera, radio station, student government, student newspaper, symphony orchestra, television station. **Organizations:** 125 registered organizations, 12 honor societies, 16 religious organizations. **Athletics (Intercollegiate):** *Men:* basketball, cheerleading, crew, cross-country, football, golf, soccer, track & field. *Women:* basketball, cheerleading, crew, cross-country, golf, soccer, softball, track & field, volleyball.

ADMISSIONS

Selectivity Rating: 82 (of 100). **Freshman Academic Profile:** Average high school GPA 3.5. 24% in top 10% of high school class, 61% in top 25% of high school class, 93% in top 50% of high school class. 90% from public high schools. Average SAT I Math 550, SAT I Math middle 50% range 500-600. Average SAT I Verbal 550, SAT I Verbal middle 50% range 490-610. Average ACT 23, ACT middle 50% range 20-26. TOEFL required of all international applicants, minimum TOEFL 550. **Basis for Candidate Selection:** *Very important factors considered include:* secondary school record. *Important factors considered include:* character/personal qualities, class rank, essays, extracurricular activities, standardized test scores, state residency, talent/ability, volunteer work, work experience. *Other factors considered include:* geographical residence, recommendations. **Freshman Admission Requirements:** High school diploma or GED is required. *Academic units required/recommended:* 15 total required; 4 English required, 3 math required, 2 science required, 1 science lab required, 2 foreign language required, 3 social studies required, 1 elective required. **Freshman Admission Statistics:** 7,464 applied, 74% accepted, 40% of those accepted enrolled. **Transfer Admission Requirements:** *Items required:* college transcript, statement of good standing from prior school. Minimum college GPA of 2.0 required. Lowest grade transferable D-. **General Admission Information:** Application fee $36. Regular application deadline March 1. Nonfall registration accepted. Admission may be deferred for a maximum of 1 year. Credit and/or placement offered for CEEB Advanced Placement tests.

COSTS AND FINANCIAL AID

In-state tuition $3,408. Out-of-state tuition $11,607. Room & board $5,648. Required fees $294. Average book expense $750. **Required Forms and Deadlines:** FAFSA. Priority filing deadline February 15. **Notification of Awards:** Applicants will be notified of awards on a rolling basis beginning on or about March 20. **Types of Aid:** *Need-based scholarships/grants:* Pell, SEOG, state scholarships/grants, private scholarships, the school's own gift aid. *Loans:* Direct Subsidized Stafford, Direct Unsubsidized Stafford, Direct PLUS, FFEL PLUS, Federal Perkins, college/university loans from institutional funds, private loans. **Student Employment:** Federal Work-Study Program available. Institutional employment available. Off-campus job opportunities are good. **Financial Aid Statistics:** 35% freshmen, 38% undergrads receive some form of aid. Average freshman grant $4,049. Average freshman loan $2,975. Average income from on-campus job $1,915. **Financial Aid Phone:** 360-650-3470.

WESTFIELD STATE COLLEGE

Westfield State, Westfield, MA 01086
Phone: 413-572-5218 **E-mail:** admission@wsc.ma.edu **CEEB Code:** 3523
Fax: 413-572-0520 **Web:** www.wsc.ma.edu **ACT Code:** 1912

This public school was founded in 1838. It has a 227-acre campus.

STUDENTS AND FACULTY

Enrollment: 4,415. **Student Body:** Male 44%, female 56%, out-of-state 7%, international students represent 1 country. **Ethnic Representation:** African American 3%, Asian 1%, Caucasian 82%, Hispanic 2%. **Retention and Graduation:** 77% freshmen return for sophomore year. 42% freshmen graduate within 4 years. 5% grads pursue business degrees. 1% grads pursue law degrees. **Faculty:** Student/faculty ratio 19:1. 159 full-time faculty, 82% hold PhDs. 100% faculty teach undergrads.

ACADEMICS

Degrees: Bachelor's, master's, post-bachelor's certificate, post-master's certificate. **Academic Requirements:** General education including some course work in arts/fine arts, English (including composition), mathematics, sciences (biological or physical), social science, literature or philosophy, diversity, American history or government. **Classes:** 20-29 students in an average class. 10-19 students in an average lab/discussion section. **Disciplines with Highest Percentage of Degrees Awarded:** Protective services/public administration 23%, education 14%, business/marketing 12%, psychology 11%, communications/communication technologies 7%. **Special Study Options:** Cooperative (work-study) program, cross registration, distance learning, double major, dual enrollment, student exchange program (domestic), honors program, independent study, internships, student-designed major, study abroad, teacher certification program.

FACILITIES

Housing: Coed, apartments for single students, housing for disabled students, living/learning unit (honors/academic intensive), quiet-living section, all-women section, designated smoking section (other housing smoke-free). **Library Holdings:** 124,363 bound volumes. 819 periodicals. 547,002 microforms. 2,379 audiovisuals. **Special Academic Facilities/Equipment:** Art gallery, language lab, electron microscope. **Computers:** School-owned computers available for student use.

EXTRACURRICULARS

Activities: Choral groups, concert band, drama/theater, jazz band, literary magazine, music ensembles, musical theater, pep band, radio station, student government, student newspaper, television station, yearbook. **Athletics (Intercollegiate):** *Men:* baseball, basketball, cross-country, football, golf, soccer, track & field. *Women:* basketball, cheerleading, cross-country, field hockey, soccer, softball, swimming, volleyball.

ADMISSIONS

Selectivity Rating: 63 (of 100). **Freshman Academic Profile:** Average high school GPA 3.0. Average SAT I Math 490, SAT I Math middle 50% range 480-550. Average SAT I Verbal 500, SAT I Verbal middle 50% range 470-550. TOEFL required of all international applicants, minimum TOEFL 550. **Basis for Candidate Selection:** *Very important factors considered include:* secondary school record, standardized test scores. *Important factors considered include:* extracurricular activities, talent/ability. *Other factors considered include:* character/personal qualities, class rank, essays, minority status, recommendations, volunteer work, work experience. **Freshman Admission Requirements:** High school diploma or GED is required. *Academic units required/recommended:* 16 total required; 4 English required, 3 math required, 3 science required, 2 science lab required, 2 foreign language required, 1 social studies required, 1 history required, 2 elective required. **Freshman Admission Statistics:** 3,858 applied, 64% accepted, 37% of those accepted enrolled. **Transfer Admission Requirements:** *Items required:* college transcript. Minimum high school GPA of 2.0 required. Minimum college GPA of 2.0 required. Lowest grade transferable C-. **General Admission Information:** Application fee $25. Regular application deadline March 1. Nonfall registration accepted. Admission may be deferred. Credit and/or placement offered for CEEB Advanced Placement tests.

COSTS AND FINANCIAL AID

In-state tuition $970. Out-of-state tuition $7,050. Room & board $4,762. Required fees $2,785. Average book expense $650. **Required Forms and Deadlines:** FAFSA. Priority filing deadline March 1. **Notification of Awards:** Applicants will be notified of awards on a rolling basis. **Types of Aid:** *Need-based scholarships/grants:* Pell, SEOG, state scholarships/grants, private scholarships, the school's own gift aid. *Loans:* FFEL Subsidized Stafford, FFEL Unsubsidized Stafford, FFEL PLUS, Federal Perkins, state loans. **Student Employment:** Federal Work-Study Program available. Off-campus job opportunities are good. **Financial Aid Statistics:** Average freshman grant $1,051. Average freshman loan $3,000. Average income from on-campus job $1,000. **Financial Aid Phone:** 413-572-5407.

WESTMINSTER CHOIR COLLEGE OF RIDER UNIVERSITY

101 Walnut Lane, Princeton, NJ 08540-3899
Phone: 800-962-4647
Fax: 609-921-8829

This private school was founded in 1926.

STUDENTS AND FACULTY

Enrollment: 280. **Student Body:** Out-of-state 59%, international students represent 25 countries. **Ethnic Representation:** African American 7%, Asian 8%, Caucasian 80%, Hispanic 4%, Native American 1%. **Retention and Graduation:** 15% grads go on to further study within 1 year.

FACILITIES

Housing: Coed, apartments for single students.

EXTRACURRICULARS

Activities: Student government, student newspaper, yearbook. **Organizations:** 8 registered organizations, 4 honor societies.

ADMISSIONS

Selectivity Rating: 74 (of 100). **Freshman Academic Profile:** Average SAT I Math 517. Average SAT I Verbal 539. TOEFL required of all international applicants, minimum TOEFL 550. **General Admission Information:** Regular application deadline rolling.

COSTS AND FINANCIAL AID

Room & board $6,610. Required fees $380. Average book expense $700. **Types of Aid:** *Need-based scholarships/grants:* Pell, SEOG, state scholarships/grants, private scholarships. *Loans:* FFEL Subsidized Stafford, FFEL Unsubsidized Stafford, FFEL PLUS, Federal Perkins, Federal Nursing, state loans. **Student Employment:** Federal Work-Study Program available. Off-campus job opportunities are good. **Financial Aid Statistics:** Average freshman grant $7,500. Average income from on-campus job $1,200. **Financial Aid Phone:** 609-921-7100.

WESTMINSTER COLLEGE (MO)

501 Westminster Avenue, Fulton, MO 65251-1299
Phone: 573-592-5251 **E-mail:** admissions@jaynet.wcmo.edu **CEEB Code:** 6937
Fax: 573-592-5255 **Web:** www.westminster-mo.edu **ACT Code:** 2392

This private school, which is affiliated with the Presbyterian Church, was founded in 1851. It has a 65-acre campus.

STUDENTS AND FACULTY

Enrollment: 785. **Student Body:** Male 55%, female 45%, out-of-state 27%, international 5%. **Ethnic Representation:** African American 3%, Asian 1%, Caucasian 92%, Hispanic 1%, Native American 2%. **Retention and Graduation:** 75% freshmen return for sophomore year. 38% freshmen graduate within 4 years. 21% grads go on to further study within 1 year. 2% grads pursue business degrees. 7% grads pursue law degrees. 1% grads pursue medical degrees. **Faculty:** Student/faculty ratio 12:1. 58 full-time faculty, 84% hold PhDs. 100% faculty teach undergrads.

ACADEMICS

Degrees: Bachelor's. **Academic Requirements:** General education including some course work in arts/fine arts, English (including composition), foreign languages, history, humanities, mathematics, philosophy, sciences (biological or physical), social science, nonwestern culture. **Classes:** 10-19 students in an average class. **Majors with Highest Enrollment:** Biology/biological sciences, general; psychology, general; business administration/management. **Disciplines with Highest Percentage of Degrees Awarded:** Business/marketing 43%, education 13%, biological life sciences 13%, social sciences and history 8%, psychology 8%. **Special Study Options:** Cooperative (work-study) program, cross registration, double major, dual enrollment, student exchange program (domestic), honors program, independent study, internships, student-designed major, study abroad, teacher certification program.

FACILITIES

Housing: Coed, all-female, all-male, apartments for single students, fraternities and/or sororities, theme houses. **Library Holdings:** 111,932 bound volumes. 3,081 periodicals. 18,984 microforms. 9,082 audiovisuals. **Special Academic Facilities/Equipment:** Winston Churchill Memorial Museum, language lab, NMR spectrometer, laser equipment. **Computers:** *Recommended operating system:* Windows NT/2000. School-owned computers available for student use.

EXTRACURRICULARS

Activities: Choral groups, drama/theater, jazz band, literary magazine, music ensembles, musical theater, student government, student newspaper, yearbook. **Organizations:** 49 registered organizations, 15 honor societies, 2 religious organizations, 6 fraternities (61% men join), 3 sororities (56% women join). **Athletics (Intercollegiate):** *Men:* baseball, basketball, cheerleading, football, golf, soccer, tennis. *Women:* basketball, cheerleading, golf, soccer, softball, tennis, volleyball.

ADMISSIONS

Selectivity Rating: 78 (of 100). **Freshman Academic Profile:** Average high school GPA 3.4. 21% in top 10% of high school class, 47% in top 25% of high school class, 76% in top 50% of high school class. 70% from public high schools. Average SAT I Math 549, SAT I Math middle 50% range 490-640. Average SAT I Verbal 531, SAT I Verbal middle 50% range 460-580. Average ACT 24, ACT middle 50% range 21-27. TOEFL required of all international applicants, minimum TOEFL 550. **Basis for Candidate Selection:** *Very important factors considered include:* class rank, secondary school record, standardized test scores. *Important factors considered include:* essays, interview, recommendations. *Other factors considered include:* alumni/ae relation, character/personal qualities, extracurricular activities, talent/ability, volunteer work, work experience. **Freshman Admission Requirements:** High school diploma or GED is required. *Academic units required/recommended:* 16 total required; 4 English required, 3 math required, 2 science required, 2 science lab required, 2 foreign language recommended, 2 social studies recommended, 2 elective recommended. **Freshman Admission Statistics:** 941 applied, 66% accepted, 34% of those accepted enrolled. **Transfer Admission Requirements:** *Items required:* high school transcript, college transcript, standardized test scores. Minimum college GPA of 2.0 required. Lowest grade transferable C. **General Admission Information:** Application fee $25. Priority application deadline February 1. Nonfall registration accepted. Admission may be deferred for a maximum of 1 year. Credit and/or placement offered for CEEB Advanced Placement tests.

COSTS AND FINANCIAL AID

Tuition $16,130. Room & board $5,430. Required fees $240. Average book expense $800. **Required Forms and Deadlines:** FAFSA. No deadline for

regular filing. Priority filing deadline February 28. **Notification of Awards:** Applicants will be notified of awards on a rolling basis beginning on or about February 14. **Types of Aid:** *Need-based scholarships/grants:* Pell, SEOG, state scholarships/grants, private scholarships, the school's own gift aid. *Loans:* FFEL Subsidized Stafford, FFEL Unsubsidized Stafford, FFEL PLUS, Federal Perkins. **Student Employment:** Federal Work-Study Program available. Institutional employment available. Off-campus job opportunities are fair. **Financial Aid Statistics:** 68% freshmen, 62% undergrads receive some form of aid. Average freshman grant $12,026. Average freshman loan $3,008. Average income from on-campus job $730. **Financial Aid Phone:** 800-475-3361.

See page 1288.

WESTMINSTER COLLEGE (PA)

319 South Market Street, New Wilmington, PA 16172
Phone: 724-946-7100 **E-mail:** admis@westminster.edu **CEEB Code:** 2975
Fax: 412-946-6171 **Web:** www.westminster.edu **ACT Code:** 2975

This private school, which is affiliated with the Presbyterian Church, was founded in 1852. It has a 350-acre campus.

STUDENTS AND FACULTY

Enrollment: 1,340. **Student Body:** Male 34%, female 66%, out-of-state 21%. **Ethnic Representation:** African American 1%, Caucasian 83%, Hispanic 1%. **Retention and Graduation:** 89% freshmen return for sophomore year. 66% freshmen graduate within 4 years. 21% grads go on to further study within 1 year. 2% grads pursue business degrees. 3% grads pursue law degrees. 3% grads pursue medical degrees. **Faculty:** Student/faculty ratio 13:1. 97 full-time faculty, 83% hold PhDs. 100% faculty teach undergrads.

ACADEMICS

Degrees: Bachelor's, master's. **Academic Requirements:** General education including some course work in arts/fine arts, computer literacy, English (including composition), foreign languages, history, humanities, mathematics, philosophy, sciences (biological or physical), social science, inquiry, speech, writing: core courses. **Classes:** 10-19 students in an average class. 10-19 students in an average lab/discussion section. **Disciplines with Highest Percentage of Degrees Awarded:** Education 17%, business/marketing 16%, social sciences and history 15%, biological life sciences 11%, communications/communication technologies 10%. **Special Study Options:** Double major, student exchange program (domestic), honors program, independent study, internships, liberal arts/career combination, student-designed major, study abroad, teacher certification program.

FACILITIES

Housing: All-female, all-male, housing for disabled students, fraternities and/or sororities. **Library Holdings:** 244,707 bound volumes. 933 periodicals. 21,302 microforms. 13,058 audiovisuals. **Special Academic Facilities/Equipment:** On-campus preschool, Moeller pipe organs, planetarium, observatory, electron microscopes, X-ray diffractor, spectrometer. **Computers:** *Recommended operating system:* Windows 98. School-owned computers available for student use.

EXTRACURRICULARS

Activities: Choral groups, concert band, dance, drama/theater, jazz band, literary magazine, marching band, music ensembles, musical theater, pep band, radio station, student government, student newspaper, television station, yearbook. **Organizations:** 60 registered organizations, 21 honor societies, 3 religious organizations, 5 fraternities (50% men join), 5 sororities (50% women join). **Athletics (Intercollegiate):** *Men:* baseball, basketball, cheerleading, cross-country, football, golf, indoor track, soccer, swimming, tennis, track & field. *Women:* basketball, cheerleading, cross-country, soccer, softball, swimming, tennis, volleyball.

ADMISSIONS

Selectivity Rating: 75 (of 100). **Freshman Academic Profile:** Average high school GPA 3.3. 20% in top 10% of high school class, 55% in top 25% of high school class, 87% in top 50% of high school class. 90% from public high schools. Average SAT I Math 543, SAT I Math middle 50% range 480-590. Average SAT I Verbal 544, SAT I Verbal middle 50% range 480-580. Average ACT 24, ACT middle 50% range 19-26. TOEFL required of all international applicants, minimum TOEFL 500. **Basis for Candidate Selection:** *Very important factors considered include:* interview, secondary school record, standardized test scores. *Important factors considered include:* character/personal qualities, class rank, essays, recommendations. *Other factors considered include:* alumni/ae relation, extracurricular activities, minority status, talent/ability, volunteer work, work experience. **Freshman Admission Requirements:** High school diploma or GED is required. *Academic units required/recommended:* 16 total required; 4 English required, 3 math required, 2 science required, 2 science lab required, 2 foreign language required, 2 social studies required, 1 history required, 3 elective required. **Freshman Admission Statistics:** 1,191 applied, 78% accepted, 38% of those accepted enrolled. **Transfer Admission Requirements:** *Items required:* high school transcript, college transcript, essay, interview, standardized test scores. Minimum college GPA of 2.5 required. Lowest grade transferable C. **General Admission Information:** Application fee $20. Regular application deadline April 15. Credit and/or placement offered for CEEB Advanced Placement tests.

COSTS AND FINANCIAL AID

Tuition $18,100. Room & board $5,590. Required fees $860. Average book expense $1,700. **Required Forms and Deadlines:** FAFSA, institution's own financial aid form. Priority filing deadline May 1. **Notification of Awards:** Applicants will be notified of awards on a rolling basis. **Types of Aid:** *Need-based scholarships/grants:* Pell, SEOG, state scholarships/grants, private scholarships, the school's own gift aid. *Loans:* FFEL Subsidized Stafford, FFEL Unsubsidized Stafford, FFEL PLUS, Federal Perkins. **Student Employment:** Federal Work-Study Program available. Off-campus job opportunities are good. **Financial Aid Statistics:** 82% freshmen, 78% undergrads receive some form of aid. Average freshman grant $7,500. Average freshman loan $3,100. Average income from on-campus job $1,300. **Financial Aid Phone:** 412-946-7102.

WESTMINSTER COLLEGE (UT)

1840 South 1300 East, Salt Lake City, UT 84105
Phone: 801-832-2200 **E-mail:** admispub@westministercollege.edu **CEEB Code:** 4948
Fax: 801-484-3252 **Web:** www.westminstercollege.edu **ACT Code:** 4284

This private school was founded in 1875. It has a 27-acre campus.

STUDENTS AND FACULTY

Enrollment: 1,915. **Student Body:** Male 43%, female 57%, out-of-state 8%, international 2% (19 countries represented). **Ethnic Representation:** African American 1%, Asian 3%, Caucasian 79%, Hispanic 4%, Native American 1%. **Retention and Graduation:** 77% freshmen return for sophomore year. 33% freshmen graduate within 4 years. **Faculty:** Student/faculty ratio 11:1. 112 full-time faculty, 89% hold PhDs. 100% faculty teach undergrads.

ACADEMICS

Degrees: Bachelor's, master's, post-bachelor's certificate. **Academic Requirements:** General education including some course work in arts/fine arts, computer literacy, English (including composition), foreign languages, history, mathematics, philosophy, sciences (biological or physical), social science, public speaking. **Classes:** Under 10 students in an average class. **Majors with Highest Enrollment:** Nursing/registered nurse training (RN, ASN, BSN, MSN); business administration/management; education, general. **Disciplines with Highest Percentage of Degrees Awarded:** Business/marketing 29%, education 11%, protective services/public administration 9%, health professions and related sciences 9%, biological life sciences 7%. **Special Study Options:** Accelerated program, cooperative (work-study) program, double major, honors program, independent study, internships, liberal arts/career combination, student-designed major, teacher certification program, weekend college.

FACILITIES

Housing: Coed, all-female, all-male, apartments for single students. **Library Holdings:** 119,212 bound volumes. 437 periodicals. 241,443 microforms. 6,165 audiovisuals. **Special Academic Facilities/Equipment:** Jewett Center for the Performing Arts. **Computers:** *Recommended operating system:* Windows XP. School-owned computers available for student use.

EXTRACURRICULARS

Activities: Choral groups, dance, drama/theater, jazz band, literary magazine, music ensembles, musical theater, student government, student newspaper, student-run film society, symphony orchestra. **Organizations:** 45 registered organizations, 3 honor societies, 4 religious organizations. **Athletics (Intercollegiate):** *Men:* basketball, golf, soccer. *Women:* basketball, golf, volleyball.

ADMISSIONS

Selectivity Rating: 71 (of 100). **Freshman Academic Profile:** Average high school GPA 3.6. 27% in top 10% of high school class, 55% in top 25% of high school class, 86% in top 50% of high school class. 84% from public high schools. Average ACT 25, ACT middle 50% range 24-26. TOEFL required of all international applicants, minimum TOEFL 550. **Basis for Candidate Selection:** *Very important factors considered include:* secondary school record.

Important factors considered include: class rank, interview, standardized test scores. *Other factors considered include:* essays, extracurricular activities, recommendations, talent/ability. **Freshman Admission Requirements:** High school diploma or GED is required. *Academic units required/recommended:* 4 English required, 3 math required, 4 math recommended, 3 science required, 4 science recommended, 2 foreign language recommended, 3 social studies recommended, 3 history recommended. **Freshman Admission Statistics:** 775 applied, 87% accepted, 49% of those accepted enrolled. **Transfer Admission Requirements:** *Items required:* college transcript. Minimum high school GPA of 3.0 required. Minimum college GPA of 2.8 required. Lowest grade transferable C-. **General Admission Information:** Application fee $30. Nonfall registration accepted. Admission may be deferred for a maximum of 1 year. Credit and/or placement offered for CEEB Advanced Placement tests.

COSTS AND FINANCIAL AID

Tuition $15,700. Average book expense $900. Required fees $290. Room and board $4,820. **Required Forms and Deadlines:** FAFSA. No deadline for regular filing. Priority filing deadline April 15. **Notification of Awards:** Applicants will be notified of awards on a rolling basis beginning on or about March 30. **Types of Aid:** *Need-based scholarships/grants:* Pell, SEOG, state scholarships/grants, private scholarships, the school's own gift aid, United Negro College Fund, Federal Nursing. *Loans:* FFEL Subsidized Stafford, FFEL Unsubsidized Stafford, FFEL PLUS, Federal Perkins. **Student Employment:** Federal Work-Study Program available. Institutional employment available. Off-campus job opportunities are excellent. **Financial Aid Statistics:** 70% freshmen, 69% undergrads receive some form of aid. Average freshman grant $8,997. Average freshman loan $3,940. Average income from on-campus job $870. **Financial Aid Phone:** 801-832-2500.

WESTMONT COLLEGE

955 La Paz Road, Santa Barbara, CA 93108
Phone: 805-565-6200 **E-mail:** admissions@westmont.edu **CEEB Code:** 4950
Fax: 805-565-6234 **Web:** www.westmont.edu **ACT Code:** 478

This private school, which is affiliated with the Christian (Nondenominational) Church, was founded in 1937. It has a 130-acre campus.

STUDENTS AND FACULTY

Enrollment: 1,374. **Student Body:** Male 37%, female 63%, out-of-state 34%. **Ethnic Representation:** African American 1%, Asian 5%, Caucasian 85%, Hispanic 7%, Native American 2%. **Retention and Graduation:** 85% freshmen return for sophomore year. 61% freshmen graduate within 4 years. **Faculty:** Student/faculty ratio 13:1. 85 full-time faculty, 87% hold PhDs. 100% faculty teach undergrads.

ACADEMICS

Degrees: Bachelor's, post-bachelor's certificate. **Academic Requirements:** General education including some course work in arts/fine arts, computer literacy, English (including composition), foreign languages, history, humanities, mathematics, philosophy, sciences (biological or physical), social science, religious studies, physical education, world civilization. **Classes:** 10-19 students in an average class. 10-19 students in an average lab/discussion section. **Majors with Highest Enrollment:** Communications studies/speech communication and rhetoric; biology/biological sciences, general; economics, general. **Disciplines with Highest Percentage of Degrees Awarded:** Social sciences and history 23%, communications/communication technologies 14%, biological life sciences 12%, liberal arts/general studies 9%, English 9%. **Special Study Options:** Accelerated program, cooperative (work-study) program, double major, student exchange program (domestic), honors program, independent study, internships, liberal arts/career combination, student-designed major, study abroad, teacher certification program.

FACILITIES

Housing: Coed, apartments for married students, apartments for single students, housing for disabled students. The coed dorms are segregated by floors and/or suites. Men and women do not share hallways and bathrooms. There are selected visiting hours for members of the opposite sex. **Library Holdings:** 165,512 bound volumes. 651 periodicals. 19,175 microforms. 8,032 audiovisuals. **Special Academic Facilities/Equipment:** Reynolds Art Gallery features the gallery, art studios and classrooms; Carroll Observatory houses a 6" refracting telescope and a 16.5" reflecting telescope; Mericos Whittier Science facility includes state-of-the-art technical equipment such as ultracentrifuge, Fouriertransform NMR spectrometer, etc., as well as the pre-med center; Voskuyl Library holds over 150,000 bound volumes; the physics department is developing advanced experiments for the lab; Ellen Porter Hall of Fine Arts showcases ten to twenty live musical and theatrical performances each year; Physiology Lab and Fitness Center for Kinesiology Studies. **Computers:** School-owned computers available for student use.

EXTRACURRICULARS

Activities: Choral groups, concert band, dance, drama/theater, jazz band, literary magazine, music ensembles, musical theater, pep band, radio station, student government, student newspaper, student-run film society, symphony orchestra, yearbook. **Organizations:** 50 registered organizations, 7 honor societies, 40 religious organizations. **Athletics (Intercollegiate):** *Men:* baseball, basketball, cross-country, soccer, tennis, track & field. *Women:* basketball, cross-country, soccer, tennis, track & field, volleyball.

ADMISSIONS

Selectivity Rating: 76 (of 100). **Freshman Academic Profile:** Average high school GPA 3.7. 44% in top 10% of high school class, 76% in top 25% of high school class, 96% in top 50% of high school class. 71% from public high schools. Average SAT I Math 600, SAT I Math middle 50% range 550-650. Average SAT I Verbal 610, SAT I Verbal middle 50% range 560-650. Average ACT 26, ACT middle 50% range 24-28. TOEFL required of all international applicants, minimum TOEFL 560. **Basis for Candidate Selection:** *Very important factors considered include:* character/personal qualities, essays, religious affiliation/commitment, secondary school record, standardized test scores. *Important factors considered include:* class rank, extracurricular activities, interview, minority status, recommendations. *Other factors considered include:* alumni/ae relation, talent/ability, volunteer work, work experience. **Freshman Admission Requirements:** High school diploma or GED is required. *Academic units required/recommended:* 16 total recommended; 4 English recommended, 3 math recommended, 3 science recommended, 2 science lab recommended, 2 foreign language recommended, 1 social studies recommended, 2 history recommended, 4 elective recommended. **Freshman Admission Statistics:** 1,335 applied, 75% accepted, 37% of those accepted enrolled. **Transfer Admission Requirements:** *Items required:* high school transcript, college transcript, essay, statement of good standing from prior school. Minimum college GPA of 2.5 required. Lowest grade transferable C. **General Admission Information:** Application fee $50. Priority application deadline February 15. Regular application deadline February 15. Nonfall registration accepted. Credit and/or placement offered for CEEB Advanced Placement tests.

COSTS AND FINANCIAL AID

Tuition $20,378. Room & board $7,068. Required fees $586. Average book expense $810. **Required Forms and Deadlines:** FAFSA. Priority filing deadline March 1. **Notification of Awards:** Applicants will be notified of awards on or about April 1. **Types of Aid:** *Need-based scholarships/grants:* Pell, SEOG, state scholarships/grants, private scholarships, the school's own gift aid. *Loans:* FFEL Subsidized Stafford, FFEL Unsubsidized Stafford, FFEL PLUS, Federal Perkins, Institutional. **Student Employment:** Federal Work-Study Program available. Institutional employment available. Off-campus job opportunities are excellent. **Financial Aid Statistics:** 52% freshmen, 55% undergrads receive some form of aid. Average freshman grant $11,156. Average freshman loan $3,848. Average income from on campus job $852. **Financial Aid Phone:** 888-963-4624.

WHEATON COLLEGE (IL)

501 College Avenue, Wheaton, IL 60187
Phone: 630-752-5005 **E-mail:** admissions@wheaton.edu **CEEB Code:** 1905
Fax: 630-752-5285 **Web:** www.wheaton.edu **ACT Code:** 1160

This private school was founded in 1860. It has an 80-acre campus.

STUDENTS AND FACULTY

Enrollment: 2,395. **Student Body:** Male 49%, female 51%, out-of-state 77%, international 1% (44 countries represented). **Ethnic Representation:** African American 2%, Asian 6%, Caucasian 88%, Hispanic 3%. **Retention and Graduation:** 94% freshmen return for sophomore year. 75% freshmen graduate within 4 years. 25% grads go on to further study within 1 year. 5% grads pursue business degrees. 5% grads pursue law degrees. 18% grads pursue medical degrees. **Faculty:** Student/faculty ratio 11:1. 183 full-time faculty, 94% hold PhDs. 90% faculty teach undergrads.

ACADEMICS

Degrees: Bachelor's, doctoral, master's, post-bachelor's certificate. **Academic Requirements:** General education including some course work in arts/fine arts, English (including composition), foreign languages, history, humanities, mathematics, philosophy, sciences (biological or physical), social science, biblical studies. **Classes:** 10-19 students in an average class. 10-19 students in an average lab/discussion section. **Majors with Highest Enrollment:** English language and literature, general; business/managerial economics; elementary education and teaching. **Disciplines with Highest Percentage of Degrees Awarded:** Social sciences and history 17%, English 14%, philosophy/religion/theology 11%, education 9%, business/marketing 9%. **Special Study Options:** Cross registration, double major, student exchange program (domestic), independent study, internships, liberal arts/career combination, student-designed major, study abroad, teacher certification program.

FACILITIES

Housing: All-female, all-male, apartments for married students, apartments for single students, cooperative housing. **Library Holdings:** 429,892 bound volumes. 2,751 periodicals. 643,223 microforms. 38,591 audiovisuals. **Special Academic Facilities/Equipment:** World evangelism museum, language lab, observatory, collection of works/papers of seven British authors. **Computers:** School-owned computers available for student use.

EXTRACURRICULARS

Activities: Choral groups, concert band, drama/theater, jazz band, literary magazine, music ensembles, musical theater, opera, pep band, radio station, student government, student newspaper, symphony orchestra, television station, yearbook. **Organizations:** 64 registered organizations, 13 honor societies, 9 religious organizations. **Athletics (Intercollegiate):** *Men:* baseball, basketball, cross-country, football, golf, indoor track, soccer, swimming, tennis, track & field, wrestling. *Women:* basketball, cross-country, golf, indoor track, soccer, softball, swimming, tennis, track & field, volleyball.

ADMISSIONS

Selectivity Rating: 92 (of 100). **Freshman Academic Profile:** Average high school GPA 3.7. 54% in top 10% of high school class, 84% in top 25% of high school class, 97% in top 50% of high school class. 64% from public high schools. Average SAT I Math 658, SAT I Math middle 50% range 610-700. Average SAT I Verbal 661, SAT I Verbal middle 50% range 620-710. Average ACT 29. ACT middle 50% range 26-31. TOEFL required of all international applicants, minimum TOEFL 550. **Basis for Candidate Selection:** *Very important factors considered include:* character/personal qualities, essays, minority status, recommendations, religious affiliation/commitment, secondary school record, standardized test scores, talent/ability. *Important factors considered include:* alumni/ae relation, class rank, extracurricular activities, interview. *Other factors considered include:* geographical residence, volunteer work. **Freshman Admission Requirements:** High school diploma or GED is required. *Academic units required/recommended:* 15 total required; 4 English recommended, 3 math recommended, 3 science recommended, 2 foreign language recommended, 3 social studies recommended. **Freshman Admission Statistics:** 1,968 applied, 54% accepted, 53% of those accepted enrolled. **Transfer Admission Requirements:** *Items required:* high school transcript, college transcript, essay. Minimum college GPA of 3.0 required. Lowest grade transferable C-. **General Admission Information:** Application fee $40. Priority application deadline November 1. Regular application deadline January 15. Admission may be deferred for a maximum of 1 year. Credit and/or placement offered for CEEB Advanced Placement tests.

COSTS AND FINANCIAL AID

Tuition $16,390. Room & board $5,544. Required fees $0. Average book expense $660. **Required Forms and Deadlines:** FAFSA and institution's own financial aid form. Priority filing deadline February 15. **Notification of Awards:** Applicants will be notified of awards on a rolling basis beginning on or about March 1. **Types of Aid:** *Need-based scholarships/grants:* Pell, SEOG, state scholarships/grants, the school's own gift aid. *Loans:* FFEL Subsidized Stafford, FFEL Unsubsidized Stafford, FFEL PLUS, Federal Perkins, state loans, college/university loans from institutional funds. **Student Employment:** Federal Work-Study Program available. Institutional employment available. Off-campus job opportunities are excellent. **Financial Aid Statistics:** 47% freshmen, 46% undergrads receive some form of aid. Average freshman grant $7,266. Average freshman loan $3,842. Average income from on-campus job $1,000. **Financial Aid Phone:** 630-752-5021.

See page 1290.

WHEATON COLLEGE (MA)

Best 351

Office of Admission, Norton, MA 02766
Phone: 508-286-8251 **E-mail:** admission@wheatoncollege.edu **CEEB Code:** 3963
Fax: 508-286-8271 **Web:** www.wheatoncollege.edu **ACT Code:** 1932

This private school was founded in 1834. It has a 385-acre campus.

STUDENTS AND FACULTY

Enrollment: 1,521. **Student Body:** Male 36%, female 64%, out-of-state 67%, international 2% (29 countries represented). **Ethnic Representation:** African American 3%, Asian 2%, Caucasian 85%, Hispanic 3%. **Retention and Graduation:** 88% freshmen return for sophomore year. 66% freshmen graduate within 4 years. 28% grads go on to further study within 1 year. 2% grads pursue business degrees. 5% grads pursue law degrees. 3% grads pursue medical degrees. **Faculty:** Student/faculty ratio 11:1. 122 full-time faculty, 96% hold PhDs. 100% faculty teach undergrads.

ACADEMICS

Degrees: Bachelor's. **Academic Requirements:** General education including some course work in arts/fine arts, English (including composition), foreign languages, history, humanities, mathematics, social science. **Classes:** 10-19 students in an average class. 10-19 students in an average lab/discussion section. **Majors with Highest Enrollment:** Psychology, general; English language and literature, general; fine/studio arts, general. **Disciplines with Highest Percentage of Degrees Awarded:** Social sciences and history 33%, psychology 17%, English 11%, visual and performing arts 10%, area and ethnic studies 10%. **Special Study Options:** Accelerated program, cross registration, double major, dual enrollment, student exchange program (domestic), external degree program, honors program, independent study, internships, liberal arts/career combination, student-designed major, study abroad, teacher certification program.

FACILITIES

Housing: Coed, all-female, all-male, housing for disabled students, housing for international students, special-interest houses. **Library Holdings:** 378,594 bound volumes. 2,046 periodicals. 82,258 microforms. 12,603 audiovisuals. **Special Academic Facilities/Equipment:** Art gallery, language lab, on-campus nursery school, media center, observatory. **Computers:** School-owned computers available for student use.

EXTRACURRICULARS

Activities: Choral groups, dance, drama/theater, jazz band, literary magazine, music ensembles, musical theater, pep band, radio station, student government, student newspaper, student-run film society, symphony orchestra, yearbook. **Organizations:** 60 registered organizations, 8 honor societies, 2 religious organizations. **Athletics (Intercollegiate):** *Men:* baseball, basketball, cross-country, diving, indoor track, lacrosse, soccer, swimming, tennis, track & field. *Women:* basketball, cross-country, diving, field hockey, indoor track, lacrosse, soccer, softball, swimming, tennis, track & field, volleyball.

ADMISSIONS

Selectivity Rating: 82 (of 100). **Freshman Academic Profile:** Average high school GPA 3.4. 43% in top 10% of high school class, 76% in top 25% of high school class, 93% in top 50% of high school class. 65% from public high schools. Average SAT I Math 610, SAT I Math middle 50% range 550-650. Average SAT I Verbal 630, SAT I Verbal middle 50% range 590-670. Average ACT 27, ACT middle 50% range 26-29. TOEFL required of all international applicants, minimum TOEFL 550. **Basis for Candidate Selection:** *Very important factors considered include:* character/personal qualities, essays, extracurricular activities, secondary school record, talent/ability. *Important factors considered include:* alumni/ae relation, class rank, interview, recommendations, volunteer work, work experience. *Other factors considered include:* geographical residence, minority status, standardized test scores, state residency. **Freshman Admission Requirements:** High school diploma or GED is required. *Academic units required/recommended:* 16 total recommended; 4 English recommended, 3 math recommended, 3 science recommended, 2 science lab recommended, 4 foreign language recommended, 2 social studies recommended. **Freshman Admission Statistics:** 3,534 applied, 44% accepted, 27% of those accepted enrolled. **Transfer Admission Requirements:** *Items required:* high school transcript, college transcript, essay. Minimum college GPA of 3.0 required. Lowest grade transferable C. **General Admission Information:** Application fee $50. Early decision application deadline November 15. Regular application deadline January 15. Nonfall registration accepted. Admission may be deferred for a maximum of 1 year. Credit and/or placement offered for CEEB Advanced Placement tests.

COSTS AND FINANCIAL AID

Tuition $27,105. Room & board $7,260. Required fees $225. Average book expense $1,060. **Required Forms and Deadlines:** FAFSA, CSS/Financial Aid PROFILE, noncustodial (divorced/separated) parent's statement, business/farm supplement, and parent and student federal tax returns and W-2s. Financial aid filing deadline February 1. **Notification of Awards:** Applicants will be notified of awards on or about April 1. **Types of Aid:** *Need-based scholarships/grants:* Pell, SEOG, state scholarships/grants, private scholarships, the school's own gift aid. *Loans:* FFEL Subsidized Stafford, FFEL Unsubsidized Stafford, FFEL PLUS, Federal Perkins, state loans, college/university loans from institutional funds, MEFA, TERI, CitiAssist, other private educational loans. **Student Employment:** Federal Work-Study Program available. Institutional employment available. Off-campus job opportunities are good. **Financial Aid Statistics:** 51% freshmen, 58% undergrads receive some form of aid. Average freshman grant $14,416. Average freshman loan $3,602. Average income from on-campus job $942. **Financial Aid Phone:** 508-286-8232.

WHEELING JESUIT UNIVERSITY

316 Washington Avenue, Wheeling, WV 26003
Phone: 304-243-2359 **E-mail:** admiss@wju.edu **CEEB Code:** 5906
Fax: 304-243-2397 **Web:** www.wju.edu **ACT Code:** 4546

This private school, which is affiliated with the Roman Catholic Church, was founded in 1954. It has a 70-acre campus.

STUDENTS AND FACULTY

Enrollment: 1,530. **Student Body:** Out-of-state 60%, international 4%. **Ethnic Representation:** African American 1%, Asian 1%, Caucasian 96%, Hispanic 2%. **Retention and Graduation:** 73% freshmen return for sophomore year. 32% grads go on to further study within 1 year. 8% grads pursue business degrees. 3% grads pursue law degrees. 4% grads pursue medical degrees.

ACADEMICS

Degrees: Bachelor's, master's. **Special Study Options:** Student exchange program (domestic), study abroad, off-campus study in Washington, DC.

FACILITIES

Housing: Coed, all-female, all-male, apartments for single students. **Library Holdings:** 135,000 bound volumes. 485 periodicals. 91,800 microforms. **Special Academic Facilities/Equipment:** Center for Educational Technologies (NASA). **Computers:** *Recommended operating system:* Mac. School-owned computers available for student use.

EXTRACURRICULARS

Activities: Literary magazine, student government, student newspaper, yearbook. **Organizations:** 9 honor societies, 6 religious organizations. **Athletics (Intercollegiate):** *Men:* basketball, cross-country, golf, lacrosse, soccer, softball, swimming, track & field. *Women:* basketball, cross-country, golf, soccer, softball, swimming, track & field, volleyball.

ADMISSIONS

Selectivity Rating: 71 (of 100). **Freshman Academic Profile:** 20% in top 10% of high school class, 45% in top 25% of high school class, 80% in top 50% of high school class. 62% from public high schools. Average SAT I Math 515. Average SAT I Verbal 530. TOEFL required of all international applicants, minimum TOEFL 550. **Freshman Admission Requirements:** High school diploma or GED is required. *Academic units required/recommended:* 17 total required; 4 English required, 2 math required, 3 math recommended, 1 science required, 2 science recommended, 2 foreign language recommended, 2 social studies required, 6 elective required. **Transfer Admission Requirements:** Minimum college GPA of 2.0 required. Lowest grade transferable C. **General Admission Information:** Regular application deadline rolling. Nonfall registration accepted. Credit and/or placement offered for CEEB Advanced Placement tests.

COSTS AND FINANCIAL AID

Tuition $15,000. Room & board $5,200. Average book expense $500. **Required Forms and Deadlines:** FAFSA and state aid form. **Types of Aid:** *Need-based scholarships/grants:* Pell, SEOG, state scholarships/grants, private scholarships, the school's own gift aid, Federal Nursing. *Loans:* FFEL Subsidized Stafford, FFEL Unsubsidized Stafford, FFEL PLUS, Federal Perkins, Federal Nursing, college/university loans from institutional funds. **Student Employment:** Federal Work-Study Program available. Institutional employment available. Off-campus job opportunities are fair. **Financial Aid Statistics:** Average freshman grant $5,461. Average freshman loan $3,193. Average income from on-campus job $1,000. **Financial Aid Phone:** 304-243-2304.

WHEELOCK COLLEGE

200 The Riverway, Boston, MA 02215
Phone: 617-879-2206 **E-mail:** undergrad@wheelock.edu **CEEB Code:** 3964
Fax: 617-566-4453 **Web:** www.wheelock.edu **ACT Code:** 1934

This private school was founded in 1888. It has a 6-acre campus.

STUDENTS AND FACULTY

Enrollment: 616. **Student Body:** Out-of-state 48%, international 1% (6 countries represented). **Ethnic Representation:** African American 5%, Asian 2%, Caucasian 85%, Hispanic 4%, Native American 1%. **Retention and Graduation:** 84% freshmen return for sophomore year. 52% freshmen graduate within 4 years. 25% grads go on to further study within 1 year. 1% grads pursue law degrees. **Faculty:** Student/faculty ratio 11:1. 57 full-time faculty, 84% hold PhDs. 47% faculty teach undergrads.

ACADEMICS

Degrees: Bachelor's, master's. **Academic Requirements:** General education including some course work in arts/fine arts, computer literacy, English (including composition), history, humanities, mathematics, sciences (biological or physical), social science, human growth and development. **Classes:** 10-19 students in an average class. **Majors with Highest Enrollment:** Elementary education and teaching; human development, family studies, and related services; social work. **Disciplines with Highest Percentage of Degrees Awarded:** Education 54%, health professions and related sciences 17%, protective services/public administration 14%, liberal arts/general studies 9%, visual and performing arts 6%. **Special Study Options:** Cross registration, double major, independent study, internships, liberal arts/career combination, study abroad, teacher certification program.

FACILITIES

Housing: Coed, all-female, all-male, cooperative housing, wellness floor. **Library Holdings:** 96,273 bound volumes. 547 periodicals. 107 microforms. 3,756 audiovisuals. **Special Academic Facilities/Equipment:** Art studio, resource center with fully equipped workshop for creating and developing original curriculum tools. **Computers:** *Recommended operating system:* Windows 95. School-owned computers available for student use.

EXTRACURRICULARS

Activities: Choral groups, drama/theater, musical theater, student government, yearbook. **Organizations:** 20 registered organizations, 1 honor society, 1 religious organization. **Athletics (Intercollegiate):** *Women:* basketball, diving, field hockey, soccer, softball, swimming.

ADMISSIONS

Selectivity Rating: 67 (of 100). **Freshman Academic Profile:** Average high school GPA 2.9. 8% in top 10% of high school class, 35% in top 25% of high school class, 70% in top 50% of high school class. 85% from public high schools. Average SAT I Math 505, SAT I Math middle 50% range 430-550. Average SAT I Verbal 516, SAT I Verbal middle 50% range 450-580. TOEFL required of all international applicants, minimum TOEFL 500. **Basis for Candidate Selection:** *Very important factors considered include:* essays, secondary school record. *Important factors considered include:* character/personal qualities, class rank, extracurricular activities, recommendations, volunteer work. *Other factors considered include:* alumni/ae relation, interview, minority status, standardized test scores, talent/ability, work experience. **Freshman Admission Requirements:** High school diploma or GED is required. *Academic units required/recommended:* 16 total required; 4 English required, 3 math required, 2 science required, 1 science lab required, 2 social studies required. **Freshman Admission Statistics:** 447 applied, 81% accepted, 39% of those accepted enrolled. **Transfer Admission Requirements:** *Items required:* high school transcript, college transcript, essay. Minimum college GPA of 2.0 required. Lowest grade transferable C-. **General Admission Information:** Application fee $30. Early decision application deadline December 1. Regular application deadline March 1. Nonfall registration accepted. Admission may be deferred for a maximum of 1 year. Credit offered for CEEB Advanced Placement tests.

COSTS AND FINANCIAL AID

Tuition $18,195. Room & board $7,325. Required fees $0. Average book expense $445. **Required Forms and Deadlines:** FAFSA and institution's own financial aid form. Financial aid filing deadline May 1. Priority filing deadline February 15. **Notification of Awards:** Applicants will be notified of awards on a rolling basis beginning on or about March 1. **Types of Aid:** *Need-based scholarships/grants:* Pell, SEOG, state scholarships/grants, the school's own gift aid. Merit scholarships are available for all freshmen and transfer applicants with a 3.0 GPA (or higher) or SAT scores of 1000 (or higher). Scholarships range from $3,000 to full tuition. *Loans:* FFEL Subsidized Stafford, FFEL Unsubsidized Stafford, FFEL PLUS, Federal Perkins, college/university loans from institutional funds. **Student Employment:** Federal Work-Study Program available. Institutional employment available. Off-campus job opportunities are excellent. **Financial Aid Statistics:** 79% freshmen, 72% undergrads receive some form of aid. Average freshman grant $9,810. Average freshman loan $3,807. Average income from on-campus job $1,253. **Financial Aid Phone:** 617-879-2206.

WHITMAN COLLEGE

515 Boyer Avenue, Walla Walla, WA 99362-2046
Phone: 509-527-5176 **E-mail:** admission@whitman.edu **CEEB Code:** 4951
Fax: 509-527-4967 **Web:** www.whitman.edu **ACT Code:** 4492

This private school was founded in 1883. It has a 117-acre campus.

STUDENTS AND FACULTY

Enrollment: 1,454. **Student Body:** Male 43%, female 57%, out-of-state 55%, international 2% (23 countries represented). **Ethnic Representation:** African American 1%, Asian 7%, Caucasian 80%, Hispanic 3%, Native American 1%. **Retention and Graduation:** 93% freshmen return for sophomore year. 77% freshmen graduate within 4 years. **Faculty:** Student/faculty ratio 10:1. 113 full-time faculty, 92% hold PhDs. 100% faculty teach undergrads.

ACADEMICS

Degrees: Bachelor's. **Academic Requirements:** General education including some course work in arts/fine arts, computer literacy, English (including composition), foreign languages, history, humanities, mathematics, philosophy, sciences (biological or physical), social science. Each student takes a minimum of six credits in each of the following areas: social sciences, humanities, fine arts, and science (including at least one science course with a lab). In addition, one course of three or more credits in quantitative analysis and two courses designated as fulfilling the requirements in alternative voices must be taken. **Classes:** 10-19 students in an average class. 20-29 students in an average lab/discussion section. **Majors with Highest Enrollment:** Biology/biological sciences, general; psychology, general; political science and government, general. **Disciplines with Highest Percentage of Degrees Awarded:** Social sciences and history 32%, visual and performing arts 14%, biological life sciences 13%, physical sciences 10%, English 9%. **Special Study Options:** Double major, dual enrollment, student exchange program (domestic), honors program, independent study, internships, liberal arts/career combination, student-designed major, study abroad, teacher certification program, undergraduate research conference.

FACILITIES

Housing: Coed, all-female, apartments for single students, fraternities and/or sororities, Theme houses: Asian Studies House; Community Service House; Writing House; Environmental House; Fine Arts House; French House; German House; Global Awareness House; Casa Hispana; MultiEthnic House; Tekisuijuku; school-owned rentals. **Library Holdings:** 350,699 bound volumes. 2,175 periodicals. 16,534 microforms. 4,500 audiovisuals. **Special Academic Facilities/Equipment:** Art gallery, Asian art collection, anthropology museum, planetarium, outdoor observatory, two electron microscopes, outdoor sculpture walk, technology/video-conferencing center, indoor and outdoor rock-climbing walls, organic garden. **Computers:** School-owned computers available for student use.

EXTRACURRICULARS

Activities: Choral groups, concert band, dance, drama/theater, jazz band, literary magazine, music ensembles, musical theater, opera, pep band, radio station, student government, student newspaper, student-run film society, symphony orchestra. **Organizations:** 70 registered organizations, 5 honor societies, 2 religious organizations, 4 fraternities (30% men join), 4 sororities (30% women join). **Athletics (Intercollegiate):** *Men:* baseball, basketball, skiing (cross-country), cross-country, golf, skiing (alpine), skiing (Nordic), soccer, swimming, tennis. *Women:* basketball, skiing (cross-country), cross-country, golf, skiing (alpine), skiing (Nordic), soccer, swimming, tennis, volleyball.

ADMISSIONS

Selectivity Rating: 95 (of 100). **Freshman Academic Profile:** Average high school GPA 3.8. 64% in top 10% of high school class, 90% in top 25% of high school class, 100% in top 50% of high school class. 30% from public high schools. Average SAT I Math 655, SAT I Math middle 50% range 610-700. Average SAT I Verbal 659, SAT I Verbal middle 50% range 610-710. Average ACT 28, ACT middle 50% range 26-31. TOEFL required of all international applicants, minimum TOEFL 560. **Basis for Candidate Selection:** *Very important factors considered include:* character/personal qualities, essays, secondary school record. *Important factors considered include:* extracurricular activities, recommendations, standardized test scores, talent/ability. *Other factors considered include:* alumni/ae relation, class rank, geographical residence, interview, minority status, state residency, volunteer work, work experience. **Freshman Admission Requirements:** High school diploma or GED is required. *Academic units required/recommended:* 18 total recommended; 4 English recommended, 4 math recommended, 3 science recommended, 3 science lab recommended, 2 foreign language recommended, 2 social studies recommended, 2 history recommended. **Freshman Admission Statistics:** 2,411 applied, 50% accepted, 31% of those accepted enrolled. **Transfer Admission Requirements:** *Items required:* high school transcript, college transcript, essay, statement of good standing from prior school. Minimum college GPA of 3.0 required. Lowest grade transferable C-. **General Admission Information:** Application fee $45. Early decision application deadline November 15. Regular application deadline January 15. Nonfall registration accepted. Admission may be deferred for a maximum of 1 year. Credit and/or placement offered for CEEB Advanced Placement tests.

COSTS AND FINANCIAL AID

Tuition $24,070. Room & board $6,550. Required fees $204. Average book expense $1,000. **Required Forms and Deadlines:** FAFSA, CSS/Financial Aid PROFILE and parent tax return. Financial aid filing deadline February 1. Priority filing deadline November 15. **Notification of Awards:** Applicants will be notified of awards on a rolling basis beginning on or about December 20. **Types of Aid:** *Need-based scholarships/grants:* Pell, SEOG, state scholarships/grants, private scholarships, the school's own gift aid. *Loans:* FFEL Subsidized Stafford, FFEL Unsubsidized Stafford, FFEL PLUS, Federal Perkins, alternative student loans. **Student Employment:** Federal Work-Study Program available. Institutional employment available. Off-campus job opportunities are fair. **Financial Aid Statistics:** 43% freshmen, 43% undergrads receive some form of aid. Average freshman grant $16,850. Average freshman loan $2,650. Average income from on-campus job $1,372. **Financial Aid Phone:** 509-527-5178.

See page 1292.

WHITTIER COLLEGE

13406 Philadelphia Street, PO Box 634, Whittier, CA 90608
Phone: 562-907-4238 **E-mail:** admission@whittier.edu **CEEB Code:** 4952
Fax: 562-907-4870 **Web:** www.whittier.edu **ACT Code:** 480

This private school was founded in 1887. It has a 74-acre campus.

STUDENTS AND FACULTY

Enrollment: 1,206. **Student Body:** Male 42%, female 58%, out-of-state 40%, international 5% (12 countries represented). **Ethnic Representation:** African American 5%, Asian 9%, Caucasian 50%, Hispanic 28%, Native American 2%. **Retention and Graduation:** 74% freshmen return for sophomore year. 45% freshmen graduate within 4 years. 28% grads go on to further study within 1 year. **Faculty:** Student/faculty ratio 11:1. 93 full-time faculty, 93% hold PhDs. 100% faculty teach undergrads.

ACADEMICS

Degrees: Bachelor's, first professional, master's. **Academic Requirements:** General education including some course work in arts/fine arts, English (including composition), history, humanities, mathematics, sciences (biological or physical), social science, writing. **Classes:** 10-19 students in an average class. 10-19 students in an average lab/discussion section. **Majors with Highest Enrollment:** Business administration/management; child development; biology/biological sciences, general. **Disciplines with Highest Percentage of Degrees Awarded:** Social sciences and history 25%, business/marketing 18%, psychology 17%, liberal arts/general studies 8%, English 8%. **Special Study Options:** Double major, independent study, internships, liberal arts/career combination, student-designed major, study abroad, teacher certification program, Whittier Scholars Program.

FACILITIES

Housing: Coed, all-female, substance-free residence halls, multicultural residence hall. **Library Holdings:** 248,888 bound volumes. 1,440 periodicals. 5,041 microforms. 4,300 audiovisuals. **Special Academic Facilities/Equipment:** Performing arts center, on-campus preschool/ elementary school, image processing lab. **Computers:** School-owned computers available for student use.

EXTRACURRICULARS

Activities: Choral groups, dance, drama/theater, jazz band, literary magazine, music ensembles, musical theater, pep band, radio station, student government, student newspaper, yearbook. **Organizations:** 60 registered organizations, 11 honor societies, 3 religious organizations, 4 fraternities (19% men join), 5 sororities (15% women join). **Athletics (Intercollegiate):** *Men:* baseball, basketball, cross-country, diving, football, golf, lacrosse, soccer, swimming, tennis, track & field, volleyball, water polo. *Women:* basketball, cross-country, diving, lacrosse, soccer, softball, swimming, tennis, track & field, volleyball, water polo.

ADMISSIONS

Selectivity Rating: 76 (of 100). **Freshman Academic Profile:** Average high school GPA 3.1. 14% in top 10% of high school class, 30% in top 25% of high school class, 52% in top 50% of high school class. Average SAT I Math 539, SAT I Math middle 50% range 490-600. Average SAT I Verbal 547, SAT I Verbal middle 50% range 490-590. Average ACT 23, ACT middle 50% range 20-26. TOEFL required of all international applicants, minimum TOEFL 550. **Basis for Candidate Selection:** *Very important factors considered include:* essays, secondary school record. *Important factors considered include:* class rank, interview. *Other factors considered include:* alumni/ae relation, character/personal qualities, extracurricular activities, minority status, recommendations, standardized test scores, state residency, talent/ability, volunteer work, work experience. **Freshman Admission Requirements:** High school diploma is required and GED is not accepted. *Academic units required/recommended:* 11 total required; 16 total recommended; 4 English required, 3 math required, 1 science required, 3 science recommended, 2 science lab recommended, 2 foreign language required, 3 foreign language recommended, 1 social studies required, 2 social studies recommended, 3 history recommended. **Freshman Admission Statistics:** 1,485 applied, 76% accepted, 27% of those accepted enrolled. **Transfer Admission Requirements:** *Items required:* high school transcript, college transcript, essay. Minimum high school GPA of 2.0 required. Minimum college GPA of 2.5 required. Lowest grade transferable C-. **General Admission Information:** Application fee $35. Priority application deadline February 1. Admission may be deferred for a maximum of 1 year. Credit and/or placement offered for CEEB Advanced Placement tests.

COSTS AND FINANCIAL AID

Tuition $21,878. Room & board $7,366. Required fees $960. Average book expense $500. **Required Forms and Deadlines:** FAFSA and CSS/Financial Aid PROFILE. No deadline for regular filing. Priority filing deadline February 1. **Notification of Awards:** Applicants will be notified of awards on a rolling basis beginning on or about April 1. **Types of Aid:** *Need-based scholarships/grants:* Pell, SEOG, state scholarships/grants, private scholarships, the school's own gift aid. *Loans:* FFEL Subsidized Stafford, FFEL Unsubsidized Stafford, FFEL PLUS, Federal Perkins, college/university loans from institutional funds. **Student Employment:** Federal Work-Study Program available. Institutional employment available. Off-campus job opportunities are good. **Financial Aid Statistics:** 71% freshmen, 73% undergrads receive some form of aid. Average freshman grant $16,098. Average freshman loan $7,228. Average income from on-campus job $1,250. **Financial Aid Phone:** 562-907-4285.

WHITWORTH COLLEGE

 $$$  

300 West Hawthorne Road, Spokane, WA 99251
Phone: 509-777-4786 **E-mail:** admission@whitworth.edu **CEEB Code:** 4953
Fax: 509-777-3758 **Web:** www.whitworth.edu **ACT Code:** 4494

This private school, which is affiliated with the Presbyterian Church, was founded in 1890. It has a 200-acre campus.

STUDENTS AND FACULTY

Enrollment: 1,971. **Student Body:** Male 41%, female 59%, out-of-state 45%, international 2%. **Ethnic Representation:** African American 1%, Asian 5%, Caucasian 90%, Hispanic 2%, Native American 1%. **Retention and Graduation:** 85% freshmen return for sophomore year. 58% freshmen graduate within 4 years. 50% grads go on to further study within 1 year. **Faculty:** Student/faculty ratio 14:1. 100% faculty teach undergrads.

ACADEMICS

Degrees: Bachelor's, master's. **Academic Requirements:** General education including some course work in arts/fine arts, English (including composition), foreign languages, history, humanities, mathematics, philosophy, sciences (biological or physical), social science. **Classes:** 10-19 students in an average class. 10-19 students in an average lab/discussion section. **Majors with Highest Enrollment:** Elementary education and teaching; business administration/management; psychology, general. **Disciplines with Highest Percentage of Degrees Awarded:** Business/marketing 18%, education 15%, social sciences and history 8%, English 8%, psychology 7%. **Special Study Options:** Cooperative (work-study) program, cross registration, double major, dual enrollment, English as a second language, student exchange program (domestic), honors program, independent study, internships, liberal arts/career combination, student-designed major, study abroad, teacher certification program.

FACILITIES

Housing: Coed, all-female, all-male, theme houses within walking distance to the campus. **Library Holdings:** 250,001 bound volumes. 1,731 periodicals. 130,000 microforms. 200 audiovisuals. **Special Academic Facilities/Equipment:** Language laboratory, art gallery, computer labs. **Computers:** *Recommended operating system:* Windows NT/2000.

EXTRACURRICULARS

Activities: Choral groups, concert band, dance, drama/theater, jazz band, music ensembles, musical theater, pep band, radio station, student government, student newspaper, symphony orchestra, yearbook. **Organizations:** 50 registered organizations, 5 honor societies. **Athletics (Intercollegiate):** *Men:* baseball, basketball, cheerleading, football, golf, soccer, swimming, tennis, track & field. *Women:* basketball, cheerleading, golf, soccer, softball, swimming, tennis, track & field, volleyball.

ADMISSIONS

Selectivity Rating: 81 (of 100). **Freshman Academic Profile:** Average high school GPA 3.6. 42% in top 10% of high school class, 65% in top 25% of high school class, 97% in top 50% of high school class. 85% from public high schools. Average SAT I Math 610, SAT I Math middle 50% range 510-620. Average SAT I Verbal 550, SAT I Verbal middle 50% range 520-630. TOEFL required of all international applicants, minimum TOEFL 525. **Basis for Candidate Selection:** *Very important factors considered include:* class rank, essays, recommendations, secondary school record, standardized test scores. *Important factors considered include:* alumni/ae relation, character/personal qualities, extracurricular activities, geographical residence, interview, talent/ability. *Other factors considered include:* minority status, religious affiliation/commitment, volunteer work. **Freshman Admission Requirements:** High school diploma or GED is required. *Academic units required/recommended:* 4 English recommended, 3 math recommended, 3 science recommended, 2 foreign language recommended, 3 social studies recommended, 3 history recommended. **Freshman Admission Statistics:** 1,816 applied, 73% accepted, 33% of those accepted enrolled. **Transfer Admission Requirements:** *Items required:* high school transcript, college transcript, essay, standardized test score, statement of good standing from prior school. Minimum college GPA of 2.8 required. Lowest grade transferable C-. **General Admission Information:** Regular application deadline March 1. Nonfall registration accepted. Admission may be deferred for a maximum of 1 year. Credit offered for CEEB Advanced Placement tests.

COSTS AND FINANCIAL AID

Tuition $18,550. Room & board $6,050. Required fees $248. Average book expense $720. **Required Forms and Deadlines:** FAFSA. No deadline for regular filing. Priority filing deadline March 1. **Notification of Awards:** Applicants will be notified of awards on a rolling basis beginning on or about April 1. **Types of Aid:** *Need-based scholarships/grants:* Pell, SEOG, state scholarships/grants, private scholarships, the school's own gift aid. *Loans:* Direct Subsidized Stafford, Direct Unsubsidized Stafford, Direct PLUS, Federal Perkins, college/university loans from institutional funds. **Student Employment:** Federal Work-Study Program available. Institutional employment available. Off-campus job opportunities are excellent. **Financial Aid Statistics:** 71% freshmen, 69% undergrads receive some form of aid. Average freshman grant $8,500. Average freshman loan $4,000. Average income from on-campus job $1,750. **Financial Aid Phone:** 509-777-3215.

WICHITA STATE UNIVERSITY

1845 Fairmount, Wichita, KS 67260
Phone: 316-978-3085 **E-mail:** admissions@wichita.edu **CEEB Code:** 6884
Fax: 316-978-3174 **Web:** www.wichita.edu **ACT Code:** 1472

This public school was founded in 1895. It has a 330-acre campus.

STUDENTS AND FACULTY

Enrollment: 11,886. **Student Body:** Male 43%, female 57%, out-of-state 3%, international 5%. **Ethnic Representation:** African American 7%, Asian 8%, Caucasian 73%, Hispanic 5%, Native American 1%. **Retention and Graduation:** 71% freshmen return for sophomore year. 11% freshmen graduate within 4 years. **Faculty:** Student/faculty ratio 17:1. 480 full-time faculty, 71% hold PhDs. 100% faculty teach undergrads.

ACADEMICS

Degrees: Associate's, bachelor's, certificate, diploma, doctoral, master's, post-master's certificate, terminal, transfer. **Academic Requirements:** General education including some course work in arts/fine arts, computer literacy, English (including composition), foreign languages, history, humanities, mathematics, philosophy, sciences (biological or physical), social science. **Classes:** Under 10 students in an average class. **Majors with Highest Enrollment:** Business administration/management; computer science;

elementary education and teaching. **Disciplines with Highest Percentage of Degrees Awarded:** Business/marketing 27%, education 11%, health professions and related sciences 11%, protective services/public administration 9%, engineering/engineering technology 8%. **Special Study Options:** Accelerated program, cooperative (work-study) program, cross registration, distance learning, double major, dual enrollment, English as a second language, student exchange program (domestic), honors program, independent study, internships, student-designed major, study abroad, teacher certification program, weekend college.

FACILITIES

Housing: Coed, apartments for married students, apartments for single students, fraternities and/or sororities. **Library Holdings:** 1,590,705 bound volumes. 15,169 periodicals. 1,102,728 microforms. 47,558 audiovisuals. **Special Academic Facilities/Equipment:** Art museum, performance hall, media resource center, observatory, national institute of aviation research, supersonic wind tunnels, 24-hour study room in library. **Computers:** School-owned computers available for student use.

EXTRACURRICULARS

Activities: Choral groups, concert band, dance, drama/theater, jazz band, literary magazine, music ensembles, musical theater, opera, pep band, radio station, student government, student newspaper, student-run film society, symphony orchestra, television station. **Organizations:** 158 registered organizations, 12 honor societies, 12 religious organizations, 7 fraternities (6% men join), 9 sororities (4% women join). **Athletics (Intercollegiate):** *Men:* baseball, basketball, cheerleading, crew, skiing (cross-country), cross-country, diving, golf, lacrosse, rugby, swimming, tennis, track & field. *Women:* basketball, cheerleading, crew, skiing (cross-country), cross-country, diving, golf, lacrosse, softball, swimming, tennis, track & field, volleyball.

ADMISSIONS

Selectivity Rating: 72 (of 100). **Freshman Academic Profile:** Average high school GPA 3.3. 17% in top 10% of high school class, 41% in top 25% of high school class, 74% in top 50% of high school class. Average ACT 21, ACT middle 50% range 19-25. TOEFL required of all international applicants, minimum TOEFL 530. **Basis for Candidate Selection:** *Very important factors considered include:* class rank, secondary school record, standardized test scores. **Freshman Admission Requirements:** High school diploma or GED is required. *Academic units required/recommended:* 16 total recommended; 4 English recommended, 3 math recommended, 3 science recommended, 2 foreign language recommended, 3 social studies recommended. **Freshman Admission Statistics:** 3,971 applied, 62% accepted, 53% of those accepted enrolled. **Transfer Admission Requirements:** Minimum high school GPA of 2.0 required. Minimum college GPA of 2.0 required. Lowest grade transferable C. **General Admission Information:** Application fee $25. Nonfall registration accepted. Admission may be deferred for a maximum of 2 years. Credit and/or placement offered for CEEB Advanced Placement tests.

COSTS AND FINANCIAL AID

In-state tuition $2,150. Out-of-state tuition $8,765. Room & board $4,120. Required fees $609. Average book expense $800. **Required Forms and Deadlines:** FAFSA, state aid form and WSU scholarship application. No deadline for regular filing. Priority filing deadline March 15. **Notification of Awards:** Applicants will be notified of awards on a rolling basis beginning on or about April 1. **Types of Aid:** *Need-based scholarships/grants:* Pell, SEOG, state scholarships/grants, private scholarships, the school's own gift aid, Bureau of Indian Affairs grants/scholarships. *Loans:* FFEL Subsidized Stafford, FFEL Unsubsidized Stafford, FFEL PLUS, Federal Perkins, college/university loans from institutional funds, various alternative loan programs. **Student Employment:** Federal Work-Study Program available. Institutional employment available. Off-campus job opportunities are excellent. **Financial Aid Statistics:** 45% freshmen, 52% undergrads receive some form of aid. Average freshman grant $3,649. Average freshman loan $4,365. **Financial Aid Phone:** 316-978-3430.

WIDENER UNIVERSITY

One University Place, Chester, PA 19013
Phone: 610-499-4126 **E-mail:** admissions.office@widener.edu **CEEB Code:** 2642
Fax: 610-499-4676 **Web:** www.widener.edu **ACT Code:** 3652

This private school was founded in 1821. It has a 105-acre campus.

STUDENTS AND FACULTY

Enrollment: 2,235. **Student Body:** Male 55%, female 45%, out-of-state 35%, international 1%. **Ethnic Representation:** African American 10%, Asian 3%, Caucasian 84%, Hispanic 1%. **Retention and Graduation:** 81% freshmen return for sophomore year. 43% freshmen graduate within 4 years. 12% grads go on to further study within 1 year. 5% grads pursue business degrees. 6% grads pursue law degrees. **Faculty:** Student/faculty ratio 12:1. 212 full-time faculty, 85% hold PhDs. 70% faculty teach undergrads.

ACADEMICS

Degrees: Associate's, bachelor's, certificate, doctoral, first professional, master's, terminal, transfer. **Academic Requirements:** General education including some course work in computer literacy, English (including composition), history, humanities, mathematics, sciences (biological or physical), social science. **Classes:** 10-19 students in an average class. Under 10 students in an average lab/discussion section. **Disciplines with Highest Percentage of Degrees Awarded:** Health professions and related sciences 22%, business/marketing 21%, psychology 9%, engineering/engineering technology 7%, communications/communication technologies 3%. **Special Study Options:** Accelerated program, cooperative (work-study) program, distance learning, double major, dual enrollment, English as a second language, student exchange program (domestic), honors program, independent study, internships, liberal arts/career combination, student-designed major, study abroad, teacher certification program, open major.

FACILITIES

Housing: Coed, all-female, all-male, apartments for single students, housing for disabled students, housing for international students, fraternities and/or sororities, wellness housing. **Library Holdings:** 159,346 bound volumes. 2,286 periodicals. 165,686 microforms. 12,663 audiovisuals. **Special Academic Facilities/Equipment:** Art gallery, restaurant lab, child development center education lab, recording studio, commercial graphics lab, physical therapy lab, science labs, engineering labs, nursing labs, multimedia classrooms. **Computers:** *Recommended operating system:* Windows 98. School-owned computers available for student use.

EXTRACURRICULARS

Activities: Choral groups, drama/theater, jazz band, literary magazine, music ensembles, musical theater, radio station, student government, student newspaper, television station, yearbook. **Organizations:** 60 registered organizations, 24 honor societies, 11 fraternities (20% men join), 4 sororities (12% women join). **Athletics (Intercollegiate):** *Men:* baseball, basketball, cross-country, diving, football, golf, ice hockey, indoor track, lacrosse, rugby, soccer, swimming, tennis, track & field. *Women:* basketball, cheerleading, cross-country, diving, field hockey, indoor track, lacrosse, soccer, softball, swimming, tennis, track & field, volleyball.

ADMISSIONS

Selectivity Rating: 70 (of 100). **Freshman Academic Profile:** Average high school GPA 3.2. 26% in top 10% of high school class, 50% in top 25% of high school class, 95% in top 50% of high school class. 51% from public high schools. Average SAT I Math 500, SAT I Math middle 50% range 450-570. Average SAT I Verbal 495, SAT I Verbal middle 50% range 450-560. TOEFL required of all international applicants, minimum TOEFL 500. **Basis for Candidate Selection:** *Very important factors considered include:* class rank, secondary school record. *Important factors considered include:* alumni/ae relation, character/personal qualities, extracurricular activities, recommendations, standardized test scores. *Other factors considered include:* essays, interview, talent/ability, volunteer work, work experience. **Freshman Admission Requirements:** High school diploma is required and GED is not accepted. *Academic units required/recommended:* 19 total required; 23 total recommended; 4 English required, 3 math required, 4 math recommended, 3 science required, 4 science recommended, 2 science lab required, 3 science lab recommended, 2 foreign language required, 4 foreign language recommended, 4 social studies required, 1 history required, 3 elective required. **Freshman Admission Statistics:** 2,148 applied, 76% accepted, 34% of those accepted enrolled. **Transfer Admission Requirements:** *Items required:* college transcript, essay, statement of good standing from prior school. Minimum college GPA of 2.0 required. Lowest grade transferable C. **General Admission Information:** Application fee $35. Priority application deadline February 15. Early decision application deadline December 1. Nonfall registration accepted. Admission may be deferred. Credit offered for CEEB Advanced Placement tests.

COSTS AND FINANCIAL AID

Tuition $19,300. Room & board $7,620. Required fees $0. Average book expense $750. **Required Forms and Deadlines:** FAFSA and institution's own financial aid form. No deadline for regular filing. Priority filing deadline February 15. **Notification of Awards:** Applicants will be notified of awards on a rolling basis beginning on or about March 1. **Types of Aid:** *Need-based scholarships/grants:* Pell, SEOG, state scholarships/grants, private scholarships, the school's own gift aid. *Loans:* Direct PLUS, FFEL Subsidized Stafford, FFEL Unsubsidized Stafford, FFEL PLUS. **Student Employment:** Federal Work-Study Program available. Institutional employment available. Off-campus job opportunities are fair. **Financial Aid Statistics:** 80% freshmen, 74% undergrads receive some form of aid. **Financial Aid Phone:** 610-499-4174.

WILBERFORCE UNIVERSITY

1055 North Bickett Road, Wilberforce, OH 45384
Phone: 800-376-8568 **E-mail:** kchristm@shorter.wilberforce.edu **CEEB Code:** 1906
Fax: 513-376-2627 **Web:** www.wilberforce.edu **ACT Code:** 3360

This private school was founded in 1856. It has a 125-acre campus.

STUDENTS AND FACULTY

Enrollment: 775. **Student Body:** Out-of-state 64%, international 1% (2 countries represented). **Ethnic Representation:** African American 100%.

ACADEMICS

Degrees: Bachelor's. **Special Study Options:** Cooperative (work-study) programs in arts, business, computer science, engineering, humanities, natural science, social-behavioral science.

FACILITIES

Housing: Coed, apartments for married students. **Library Holdings:** 58,000 bound volumes. 335 periodicals. 200 microforms. **Special Academic Facilities/Equipment:** African Methodist Church archives.

EXTRACURRICULARS

Organizations: 4 religious organizations, 4 fraternities (20% men join), 4 sororities (20% women join).

ADMISSIONS

Selectivity Rating: 63 (of 100). **Freshman Academic Profile:** 24% in top 10% of high school class, 54% in top 25% of high school class, 85% in top 50% of high school class. TOEFL required of all international applicants, minimum TOEFL 500. **Freshman Admission Requirements:** High school diploma is required and GED is not accepted. *Academic units required/recommended:* 15 total required; 4 English required, 2 math required, 2 science required, 1 social studies required, 1 history required, 4 elective required. **Transfer Admission Requirements:** Minimum college GPA of 2.0 required. Lowest grade transferable C. **General Admission Information:** Regular application deadline June 1. Nonfall registration accepted. Credit and/or placement offered for CEEB Advanced Placement tests.

COSTS AND FINANCIAL AID

Tuition $7,760. Room & board $4,260. Required fees $480. Average book expense $600. **Required Forms and Deadlines:** FAFSA, institution's own financial aid form and state aid form. **Types of Aid:** *Need-based scholarships/grants:* United Negro College Fund. *Loans:* FFEL Subsidized Stafford, FFEL PLUS. **Student Employment:** Federal Work-Study Program available. Off-campus job opportunities are good. **Financial Aid Statistics:** Average income from on-campus job $2,000. **Financial Aid Phone:** 800-367-8565.

WILEY COLLEGE

711 Wiley Avenue, Marshall, TX 75670
Phone: 903-927-3311 **E-mail:** admissions@wileynrts.wileyc.edu **CEEB Code:** 6940
Fax: 903-938-8100 **Web:** www.wileyc.edu

This private school, which is affiliated with the Methodist Church, was founded in 1873. It has a 63-acre campus.

STUDENTS AND FACULTY

Enrollment: 463. **Student Body:** Out-of-state 38%, international 2%. **Ethnic Representation:** African American 98%, Caucasian 2%. **Retention and Graduation:** 11% freshmen return for sophomore year. 11% grads go on to further study within 1 year. 1% grads pursue medical degrees.

ACADEMICS

Degrees: Associate's, bachelor's.

FACILITIES

Housing: Coed. **Library Holdings:** 80,000 bound volumes. **Computers:** *Recommended operating system:* Windows 95. School-owned computers available for student use.

EXTRACURRICULARS

Activities: Radio station, student government, student newspaper, yearbook. **Organizations:** 12 registered organizations, 5 honor societies, 5 religious organizations, 4 fraternities (50% men join), 3 sororities (60% women join).

ADMISSIONS

Selectivity Rating: 63 (of 100). **Freshman Academic Profile:** 99% from public high schools. TOEFL required of all international applicants, minimum TOEFL 400. **Freshman Admission Requirements:** High school diploma is required and GED is not accepted. *Academic units required/recommended:* 3 English recommended, 3 math recommended, 2 science recommended, 1 foreign language recommended, 2 social studies recommended, 1 history recommended. **Transfer Admission Requirements:** Minimum college GPA of 2.0 required. Lowest grade transferable C. **General Admission Information:** Regular application deadline August 10. Nonfall registration accepted.

COSTS AND FINANCIAL AID

Tuition $4,080. Room & board $3,230. Required fees $596. Average book expense $256. **Required Forms and Deadlines:** FAFSA. **Types of Aid:** *Need-based scholarships/grants:* state scholarships/grants, United Negro College Fund. *Loans:* FFEL Subsidized Stafford, FFEL PLUS. **Student Employment:** Federal Work-Study Program available. Off-campus job opportunities are good. **Financial Aid Phone:** 903-927-3217.

WILKES UNIVERSITY

171 South Franklin, Wilkes-Barre, PA 18766
Phone: 570-408-4400 **E-mail:** admissions@wilkes.edu **CEEB Code:** 2977
Fax: 570-408-4904 **Web:** www.wilkes.edu **ACT Code:** 3756

This private school was founded in 1933. It has a 27-acre campus.

STUDENTS AND FACULTY

Enrollment: 1,916. **Student Body:** Male 51%, female 49%, out-of-state 16%. **Ethnic Representation:** African American 2%, Asian 2%, Caucasian 95%, Hispanic 1%. **Retention and Graduation:** 78% freshmen return for sophomore year. 34% freshmen graduate within 4 years. 20% grads go on to further study within 1 year. 5% grads pursue business degrees. 2% grads pursue law degrees. 5% grads pursue medical degrees. **Faculty:** Student/faculty ratio 13:1. 106 full-time faculty, 88% hold PhDs. 100% faculty teach undergrads.

ACADEMICS

Degrees: Bachelor's, first professional, master's. **Academic Requirements:** General education including some course work in arts/fine arts, computer literacy, English (including composition), history, humanities, mathematics, sciences (biological or physical), social science, oral presenting, writing intensive, interdisciplinary courses, physical education. **Classes:** 20-29 students in an average class. 10-19 students in an average lab/discussion section. **Majors with Highest Enrollment:** Pharmacy (PharmD, BS/BPharm); psychology, general; biology/biological sciences, general. **Disciplines with Highest Percentage of Degrees Awarded:** Business/marketing 17%, psychology 16%, liberal arts/general studies 12%, engineering/engineering technology 8%, social sciences and history 8%. **Special Study Options:** Cooperative (work-study) program, cross registration, distance learning, double major, dual enrollment, honors program, independent study, internships, student-designed major, study abroad, teacher certification program, weekend college.

FACILITIES

Housing: Coed, all-female, all-male. **Library Holdings:** 236,942 bound volumes. 848 periodicals. 39,098 microforms. 159 audiovisuals. **Special Academic Facilities/Equipment:** Art gallery, performing arts center, electron microscope, television studio. **Computers:** School-owned computers available for student use.

EXTRACURRICULARS

Activities: Dance, drama/theater, jazz band, literary magazine, musical theater, pep band, radio station, student government, student newspaper, television station, yearbook. **Organizations:** 65 registered organizations, 12 honor societies, 4 religious organizations. **Athletics (Intercollegiate):** *Men:* baseball, basketball, football, golf, soccer, tennis, wrestling. *Women:* basketball, field hockey, lacrosse, soccer, softball, tennis, volleyball.

ADMISSIONS

Selectivity Rating: 70 (of 100). **Freshman Academic Profile:** 20% in top 10% of high school class, 46% in top 25% of high school class, 71% in top 50% of high school class. Average SAT I Math 523, SAT I Math middle 50% range 460-590. Average SAT I Verbal 514, SAT I Verbal middle 50% range 460-560. TOEFL required of all international applicants, minimum TOEFL 500. **Basis for Candidate Selection:** *Very important factors considered include:* class rank, secondary school record. *Important factors considered include:* character/personal qualities, extracurricular activities, interview, recommendations, standardized test scores. *Other factors considered include:* alumni/ae relation, essays, talent/ability, volunteer work, work experience. **Freshman Admission Requirements:** High school diploma or GED is required. *Academic units required/recommended:* 16 total required; 17 total recommended; 4 English required, 4 English recommended, 3 math required, 3 math recommended, 2 science required, 3 science recommended, 2 science lab required, 2 science lab recommended, 2 foreign language recommended, 3 social studies required, 2 social studies recommended, 2 history recommended. **Freshman Admission Statistics:** 1,938 applied, 83% accepted, 30% of those accepted enrolled. **Transfer Admission Requirements:** *Items required:* college transcript. Minimum college GPA of 2.0 required. Lowest grade transferable C. **General Admission Information:** Application fee $30. Nonfall registration accepted. Admission may be deferred for a maximum of 1 year. Credit and/or placement offered for CEEB Advanced Placement tests.

COSTS AND FINANCIAL AID

Tuition $17,956. Room & board $8,092. Required fees $904. Average book expense $900. **Required Forms and Deadlines:** FAFSA and institution's own financial aid form. No deadline for regular filing. Priority filing deadline March 1. **Notification of Awards:** Applicants will be notified of awards on a rolling basis beginning on or about February 21. **Types of Aid:** *Need-based scholarships/grants:* Pell, SEOG, state scholarships/grants, private scholarships, the school's own gift aid. *Loans:* FFEL Subsidized Stafford, FFEL Unsubsidized Stafford, FFEL PLUS, Federal Perkins, Federal Nursing, state loans, college/university loans from institutional funds. **Student Employment:** Federal Work-Study Program available. Institutional employment available. Off-campus job opportunities are good. **Financial Aid Statistics:** 84% freshmen, 81% undergrads receive some form of aid. **Financial Aid Phone:** 570-408-4345.

WILLAMETTE UNIVERSITY

900 State Street, Salem, OR 97301
Phone: 503-370-6303 **E-mail:** undergrad-admission@willamette.edu **CEEB Code:** 4954
Fax: 503-375-5363 **Web:** www.willamette.edu **ACT Code:** 3504

This private school, which is affiliated with the Methodist Church, was founded in 1842. It has a 72-acre campus.

STUDENTS AND FACULTY

Enrollment: 1,750. **Student Body:** Male 46%, female 54%, out-of-state 54%, international 1%. **Ethnic Representation:** African American 2%, Asian 7%, Caucasian 62%, Hispanic 5%, Native American 1%. **Retention and Graduation:** 91% freshmen return for sophomore year. 73% freshmen graduate within 4 years. 26% grads go on to further study within 1 year. **Faculty:** Student/faculty ratio 10:1. 187 full-time faculty, 71% hold PhDs. 100% faculty teach undergrads.

ACADEMICS

Degrees: Bachelor's, first professional, first professional certificate, master's, post-bachelor's certificate. **Academic Requirements:** General education including some course work in arts/fine arts, English (including composition), foreign languages, history, humanities, mathematics, sciences (biological or physical), social science, quantitative & analytical reasoning, freshman seminar: world views, writing-centered courses. **Classes:** 10-19 students in an average class. 10-19 students in an average lab/discussion section. **Majors with Highest Enrollment:** English language and literature, general; economics, general; political science and government, general. **Disciplines with Highest Percentage of Degrees Awarded:** Social sciences and history 28%, English 12%, visual and performing arts 9%, psychology 8%, foreign languages and literature 8%. **Special Study Options:** Double major, student exchange program (domestic), independent study, internships, student-designed major, study abroad, teacher certification program.

FACILITIES

Housing: Coed, all-female, apartments for single students, housing for international students, fraternities and/or sororities. Themed housing options include substance-free residence, environmental residence (Terra House), intensive study (24-hour quiet study). **Library Holdings:** 348,574 bound volumes. 1,436 periodicals. 333,275 microforms. 9,643 audiovisuals. **Special Academic Facilities/Equipment:** Art gallery, history museum, U.S. Senator Mark Hatfield's collected papers, herbarium, Japanese and botanical gardens, electron microscope, telescope. **Computers:** School-owned computers available for student use.

EXTRACURRICULARS

Activities: Choral groups, concert band, dance, drama/theater, jazz band, literary magazine, music ensembles, musical theater, opera, pep band, radio station, student government, student newspaper, symphony orchestra, yearbook. **Organizations:** 98 registered organizations, 9 honor societies, 9 religious organizations, 5 fraternities (32% men join), 3 sororities (32% women join). **Athletics (Intercollegiate):** *Men:* baseball, basketball, crew, cross-country, football, golf, soccer, swimming, tennis, track & field. *Women:* basketball, crew, cross-country, golf, soccer, softball, swimming, tennis, track & field, volleyball.

ADMISSIONS

Selectivity Rating: 85 (of 100). **Freshman Academic Profile:** Average high school GPA 3.6. 43% in top 10% of high school class, 73% in top 25% of high school class, 94% in top 50% of high school class. 79% from public high schools. Average SAT I Math 610, SAT I Math middle 50% range 560-660. Average SAT I Verbal 620, SAT I Verbal middle 50% range 560-680. Average ACT 27, ACT middle 50% range 25-30. TOEFL required of all international applicants, minimum TOEFL 550. **Basis for Candidate Selection:** *Very important factors considered include:* class rank, recommendations, secondary school record, standardized test scores. *Important factors considered include:* character/personal qualities, essays, extracurricular activities, interview, talent/ability. *Other factors considered include:* alumni/ae relation, geographical residence, minority status, volunteer work, work experience. **Freshman Admission Requirements:** High school diploma or GED is required. *Academic units required/recommended:* 4 English recommended, 4 math recommended, 3 science recommended, 3 foreign language recommended, 3 social studies recommended. **Freshman Admission Statistics:** 1,640 applied, 83% accepted, 26% of those accepted enrolled. **Transfer Admission Requirements:** *Items required:* high school transcript, college transcript, essay. Minimum college GPA of 2.0 required. Lowest grade transferable C. **General Admission Information:** Application fee $50. Priority application deadline February 1. Regular application deadline February 1. Nonfall registration accepted. Admission may be deferred for a maximum of 1 year. Neither credit nor placement offered for CEEB Advanced Placement tests.

COSTS AND FINANCIAL AID

Average book expense $800. **Required Forms and Deadlines:** FAFSA and CSS/Financial Aid PROFILE. Priority filing deadline February 1. **Notification of Awards:** Applicants will be notified of awards on or about April 1. **Types of Aid:** *Need-based scholarships/grants:* Pell, SEOG, state scholarships/grants, private scholarships, the school's own gift aid, United Negro College Fund. *Loans:* FFEL Subsidized Stafford, FFEL Unsubsidized Stafford, FFEL PLUS, Federal Perkins, state loans, private loans. **Student Employment:** Federal Work-Study Program available. Institutional employment available. Off-campus job opportunities are good. **Financial Aid Statistics:** 64% freshmen, 65% undergrads receive some form of aid. Average freshman grant $12,000. Average freshman loan $4,414. Average income from on-campus job $1,885. **Financial Aid Phone:** 503-370-6273.

WILLIAM CAREY COLLEGE

498 Tuscan Avenue, Hattiesburg, MS 39401-5499
Phone: 601-318-6103 **E-mail:** admissions@wmcarey.edu **CEEB Code:** 1907
Fax: 601-318-6765 **Web:** www.wmcarey.edu **ACT Code:** 2254

This private school, which is affiliated with the Baptist Church, was founded in 1906. It has a 64-acre campus.

STUDENTS AND FACULTY

Enrollment: 1,562. **Student Body:** Male 32%, female 68%, out-of-state 22%, international 2% (10 countries represented). **Ethnic Representation:** African American 31%, Caucasian 66%, Hispanic 1%, Native American 1%. **Retention and Graduation:** 69% freshmen return for sophomore year. 27% freshmen graduate within 4 years. **Faculty:** Student/faculty ratio 15:1. 96 full-time faculty, 64% hold PhDs. 100% faculty teach undergrads.

ACADEMICS

Degrees: Bachelor's, master's. **Academic Requirements:** General education including some course work in arts/fine arts, computer literacy, English (including composition), foreign languages, history, humanities, mathematics, philosophy, sciences (biological or physical), social science, religion. **Classes:** 10-19 students in an average class. **Majors with Highest Enrollment:** Elementary education and teaching; business administration/management; nursing/registered nurse training (RN, ASN, BSN, MSN). **Disciplines with Highest Percentage of Degrees Awarded:** Education 20%, health professions and related sciences 20%, liberal arts/general studies 17%, psychology 12%, business/marketing 7%. **Special Study Options:** Cooperative (work-study) program, distance learning, double major, dual enrollment, honors program, independent study, internships, study abroad, teacher certification program. Affiliation with Gulf Coast Research Lab, Ocean Springs, Mississippi.

FACILITIES

Housing: Coed, all-female, all-male, apartments for married students, apartments for single students, housing for disabled students. **Library Holdings:** 76,233 bound volumes. 379 periodicals. 33,185 microforms. 147 audiovisuals. **Special Academic Facilities/Equipment:** Historic Tatum Court, Lucille Parker Gallery. **Computers:** School-owned computers available for student use.

EXTRACURRICULARS

Activities: Choral groups, concert band, drama/theater, jazz band, literary magazine, music ensembles, musical theater, pep band, student government, student newspaper, yearbook. **Organizations:** 26 registered organizations, 7 honor societies, 1 religious organization, 8 fraternity, 2 sororities (5% women join). **Athletics (Intercollegiate):** *Men:* baseball, basketball, cheerleading, golf, soccer. *Women:* basketball, cheerleading, golf, soccer, softball.

ADMISSIONS

Selectivity Rating: 71 (of 100). **Freshman Academic Profile:** 90% from public high schools. Average SAT I Math 480, SAT I Math middle 50% range 430-540. Average SAT I Verbal 459, SAT I Verbal middle 50% range 370-540. Average ACT 21, ACT middle 50% range 18-23. TOEFL required of all international applicants, minimum TOEFL 525. **Basis for Candidate Selection:** *Very important factors considered include:* class rank, secondary school record, standardized test scores. *Important factors considered include:* alumni/ae relation, character/personal qualities, extracurricular activities, talent/ability. *Other factors considered include:* recommendations, volunteer work. **Freshman Admission Requirements:** High school diploma or GED is required. *Academic units required/recommended:* 15 total required; 15 total recommended; 4 English recommended, 3 math recommended, 3 science recommended, 2 social studies recommended. **Freshman Admission Statistics:** 232 applied, 59% accepted, 93% of those accepted enrolled. **Transfer Admission Requirements:** *Items required:* college transcript. Minimum college GPA of 2.0 required. Lowest grade transferable D. **General Admission Information:** Application fee $20. Regular application deadline July 15. Nonfall registration accepted. Credit offered for CEEB Advanced Placement tests.

COSTS AND FINANCIAL AID

Tuition $7,350. Room & board $3,150. Required fees $315. Average book expense $1,350. **Required Forms and Deadlines:** FAFSA. No deadline for regular filing. Priority filing deadline April 1. **Notification of Awards:** Applicants will be notified of awards on a rolling basis beginning on or about February 1. **Types of Aid:** *Need-based scholarships/grants:* Pell, SEOG, state scholarships/grants, private scholarships, the school's own gift aid. *Loans:* FFEL Subsidized Stafford, FFEL Unsubsidized Stafford, FFEL PLUS, Federal Perkins, college/university loans from institutional funds. **Student Employment:** Federal Work-Study Program available. Off-campus job opportunities are excellent. **Financial Aid Statistics:** 93% undergrads receive some form of aid. Average freshman grant $4,000. Average freshman loan $2,625. Average income from on-campus job $1,000. **Financial Aid Phone:** 601-318-6153.

WILLIAM JEWELL COLLEGE

500 College Hill, Liberty, MO 64068
Phone: 816-781-7700 **E-mail:** admission@william.jewell.edu **CEEB Code:** 6941
Fax: 816-415-5040 **Web:** www.jewell.edu **ACT Code:** 2394

This private school, which is affiliated with the Baptist Church, was founded in 1849. It has a 149-acre campus.

STUDENTS AND FACULTY

Enrollment: 1,168. **Student Body:** Male 42%, female 58%, out-of-state 20%, international 2% (12 countries represented). **Ethnic Representation:** African American 2%, Asian 1%, Caucasian 90%, Hispanic 2%. **Retention and Graduation:** 90% freshmen return for sophomore year. 48% freshmen graduate within 4 years. 24% grads go on to further study within 1 year. 2% grads pursue business degrees. 18% grads pursue law degrees. 10% grads pursue medical degrees. **Faculty:** Student/faculty ratio 12:1. 75 full-time faculty, 85% hold PhDs. 100% faculty teach undergrads.

ACADEMICS

Degrees: Bachelor's. **Academic Requirements:** General education including some course work in arts/fine arts, computer literacy, English (including composition), foreign languages, history, humanities, mathematics, philosophy, sciences (biological or physical), social science, responsible self plus 3-4 interdisciplinary general education courses, religious studies. **Classes:** Under 10 students in an average class. Under 10 students in an average lab/discussion section. **Disciplines with Highest Percentage of Degrees Awarded:** Business/marketing 18%, psychology 13%, visual and performing arts 10%, biological life sciences 9%, health professions and related sciences 9%. **Special Study Options:** Cooperative (work-study) program, double major, dual enrollment, honors program, independent study, internships, liberal arts/career combination, student-designed major, study abroad, teacher certification program.

FACILITIES

Housing: Coed, all-female, all-male, apartments for married students, housing for international students, fraternities and/or sororities. **Library Holdings:** 260,119 bound volumes. 868 periodicals. 207,784 microforms. 27,617 audiovisuals. **Special Academic Facilities/Equipment:** Radio station, art gallery, observatory, language and computer labs, teleconferencing center. **Computers:** School-owned computers available for student use.

EXTRACURRICULARS

Activities: Choral groups, concert band, dance, drama/theater, jazz band, literary magazine, music ensembles, pep band, radio station, student government, student newspaper, symphony orchestra, yearbook. **Organizations:** 51 registered organizations, 13 honor societies, 5 religious organizations, 3 fraternities (39% men join), 4 sororities (37% women join). **Athletics (Intercollegiate):** *Men:* baseball, basketball, cheerleading, cross-country, football, golf, indoor track, soccer, tennis, track & field. *Women:* basketball, cheerleading, cross-country, golf, indoor track, soccer, softball, tennis, track & field, volleyball.

ADMISSIONS

Selectivity Rating: 73 (of 100). **Freshman Academic Profile:** Average high school GPA 3.6. 31% in top 10% of high school class, 64% in top 25% of high school class, 93% in top 50% of high school class. 95% from public high schools. Average SAT I Math 560, SAT I Math middle 50% range 500-640. Average SAT I Verbal 580, SAT I Verbal middle 50% range 530-650. Average ACT 24, ACT middle 50% range 21-27. TOEFL required of all international applicants, minimum TOEFL 550. **Basis for Candidate Selection:** *Very important factors considered include:* class rank, secondary school record, standardized test scores. *Important factors considered include:* essays, recommendations. *Other factors considered include:* alumni/ae relation, character/personal qualities, extracurricular activities, interview, talent/ability, volunteer work, work experience. **Freshman Admission Requirements:** High school diploma or GED is required. *Academic units required/recommended:* 20 total recommended; 4 English recommended, 3 math recommended, 3 science recommended, 1 science lab recommended, 2 foreign language recommended, 3 social studies recommended, 2 history recommended, 4 elective recommended. **Freshman Admission Statistics:** 811 applied, 96% accepted, 45% of those accepted enrolled. **Transfer Admission Requirements:** *Items required:* college transcript, statement of good standing from prior school. Minimum college GPA of 2.0 required. Lowest grade transferable D. **General Admission Information:** Application fee $25. Nonfall registration accepted. Admission may be deferred for a maximum of 1 year. Credit and/or placement offered for CEEB Advanced Placement tests.

COSTS AND FINANCIAL AID

Tuition $14,600. Room & board $4,390. Required fees $150. Average book expense $650. **Required Forms and Deadlines:** FAFSA and William Jewell Scholarship application. Priority filing deadline March 1. **Notification of Awards:** Applicants will be notified of awards on a rolling basis beginning on or about March 1. **Types of Aid:** *Need-based scholarships/grants:* Pell, SEOG, state scholarships/grants, private scholarships, the school's own gift aid. *Loans:* FFEL Subsidized Stafford, FFEL Unsubsidized Stafford, FFEL PLUS, Federal Perkins, Federal Nursing, alternative loans (nonfederal). **Student Employment:** Federal Work-Study Program available. Institutional employment available. Off-campus job opportunities are good. **Financial Aid Statistics:** 69% freshmen, 64% undergrads receive some form of aid. Average freshman grant $9,404. Average freshman loan $6,629. Average income from on-campus job $765. **Financial Aid Phone:** 816-781-7700.

WILLIAM PATERSON UNIVERSITY

Office of Admission, 300 Pompton Road, Wayne, NJ 07470
Phone: 973-720-2125 **E-mail:** admissions@wpunj.edu **CEEB Code:** 2518
Fax: 973-720-2910 **Web:** www.wpunj.edu **ACT Code:** 2584

This public school was founded in 1855. It has a 370-acre campus.

STUDENTS AND FACULTY

Enrollment: 9,198. **Student Body:** Male 41%, female 59%, out-of-state 2%, international 1% (55 countries represented). **Ethnic Representation:** African

American 13%, Asian 4%, Caucasian 65%, Hispanic 15%. **Retention and Graduation:** 76% freshmen return for sophomore year. 12% grads go on to further study within 1 year. 1% grads pursue business degrees. 1% grads pursue law degrees. 1% grads pursue medical degrees. **Faculty:** Student/faculty ratio 12:1. 359 full-time faculty, 90% hold PhDs. 100% faculty teach undergrads.

ACADEMICS

Degrees: Bachelor's, master's, post-bachelor's certificate, post-master's certificate. **Academic Requirements:** General education including some course work in arts/fine arts, English (including composition), foreign languages, history, humanities, mathematics, philosophy, sciences (biological or physical), social science. Students must also take a course in health or movement science, one course in racism and/or sexism, and a course in some aspect of nonwestern culture. **Classes:** 20-29 students in an average class. **Majors with Highest Enrollment:** Business administration/management; communications studies/speech communication and rhetoric; sociology. **Disciplines with Highest Percentage of Degrees Awarded:** Social sciences and history 18%, business/marketing 17%, communications/communication technologies 14%, education 13%, psychology 9%. **Special Study Options:** Accelerated program, cross registration, distance learning, double major, dual enrollment, English as a second language, student exchange program (domestic), honors program, independent study, internships, study abroad, teacher certification program, cluster courses (a program that provides opportunities for students and faculty to study and learn together in courses grouped in interdisciplinary clusters of three; three faculty members teach these courses that meet together once every week to help students see the interdisciplinary connections), university honors program (honors majors tracks are available, and honors general education courses are offered), international exchange program.

FACILITIES

Housing: Coed, apartments for single students, housing for disabled students. A floor for women is available in one of the residence halls. Apartment-style housing is available in groups of single students who are 21 or older or are 20 with 52 or more credits. Academic interest housing is available; for example, one floor of a residence hall is reserved for nursing, biology, and community health students with a 2.5 GPA or better. Other floors combine majors; all must have 2.5 GPA or over. One residence hall is reserved for students who are 21 or older. **Library Holdings:** 305,155 bound volumes. 4,112 periodicals. 1,081,668 microforms. 19,661 audiovisuals. **Special Academic Facilities/Equipment:** Art gallery; collection of New Jersey state documents; collection of William Paterson's private papers; interactive television classroom; neurobiology facility; campus network with ATM technology; Center for Computer Art and Animation; state-of-the-art electron microscopy facility; teleconference center with uplink and downlink capabilities; 44,000-square-foot, state-of-the-art studio art facility; Center for Electro-Acoustic Music (CEM); E-Trade Financial Learning Center, a real-time simulated trading and financial educational facility. **Computers:** School-owned computers available for student use.

EXTRACURRICULARS

Activities: Choral groups, concert band, dance, drama/theater, jazz band, literary magazine, music ensembles, musical theater, opera, pep band, radio station, student government, student newspaper, student-run film society, symphony orchestra, television station, yearbook. **Organizations:** 45 registered organizations, 19 honor societies, 5 religious organizations, 11 fraternities (2% men join), 12 sororities (2% women join). **Athletics (Intercollegiate):** *Men:* baseball, basketball, cheerleading, cross-country, diving, football, indoor track, soccer, swimming, track & field. *Women:* basketball, cheerleading, cross-country, diving, field hockey, indoor track, soccer, softball, swimming, track & field, volleyball.

ADMISSIONS

Selectivity Rating: 78 (of 100). **Freshman Academic Profile:** 8% in top 10% of high school class, 26% in top 25% of high school class, 68% in top 50% of high school class. 88% from public high schools. Average SAT I Math 531, SAT I Math middle 50% range 450-550. Average SAT I Verbal 521, SAT I Verbal middle 50% range 440-540. TOEFL required of all international applicants, minimum TOEFL 550. **Basis for Candidate Selection:** *Very important factors considered include:* secondary school record, standardized test scores. *Important factors considered include:* class rank. *Other factors considered include:* alumni/ae relation, character/personal qualities, essays, extracurricular activities, minority status, recommendations, talent/ability, volunteer work. **Freshman Admission Requirements:** High school diploma or GED is required. *Academic units required/recommended:* 16 total required; 4 English required, 3 math required, 2 science required, 2 science lab required, 2 social studies required. **Freshman Admission Statistics:** 5,490 applied, 64% accepted, 40% of those accepted enrolled. **Transfer Admission Requirements:** *Items required:* college transcript. Minimum college GPA of 2.0 required. Lowest grade transferable C. **General Admission Information:** Application fee $35. Priority application deadline April 1. Regular application deadline May 1. Nonfall registration accepted. Admission may be deferred for a maximum of 1 semester. Credit and/or placement offered for CEEB Advanced Placement tests.

COSTS AND FINANCIAL AID

In-state tuition $6,400. Out-of-state tuition $10,200. Room & board $7,030. Required fees $0. Average book expense $800. **Required Forms and Deadlines:** FAFSA. Financial aid filing deadline April 1. Priority filing deadline April 1. **Notification of Awards:** Applicants will be notified of awards on a rolling basis beginning on or about March 1. **Types of Aid:** *Need-based scholarships/grants:* Pell, SEOG, state scholarships/grants, the school's own gift aid. *Loans:* Direct Subsidized Stafford, Direct Unsubsidized Stafford, Direct PLUS, Federal Perkins. **Student Employment:** Federal Work-Study Program available. Institutional employment available. Off-campus job opportunities are excellent. **Financial Aid Statistics:** 53% freshmen, 46% undergrads receive some form of aid. Average freshman grant $6,068. Average freshman loan $3,410. Average income from on-campus job $863. **Financial Aid Phone:** 973-720-2202.

See page 1294.

WILLIAM PENN UNIVERSITY

 $$  

201 Trueblood Avenue, Oskaloosa, IA 52577
Phone: 641-673-1012 **E-mail:** admissions@wmpenn.edu **CEEB Code:** 6943
Fax: 641-673-2113 **Web:** www.wmpenn.edu **ACT Code:** 1372

This private school, which is affiliated with the Quaker Church, was founded in 1873. It has a 53-acre campus.

STUDENTS AND FACULTY

Enrollment: 1,499. **Student Body:** Male 52%, female 48%, out-of-state 28%, international 1%. **Ethnic Representation:** African American 8%, Caucasian 88%, Hispanic 3%. **Faculty:** Student/faculty ratio 14:1. 35 full-time faculty, 48% hold PhDs. 100% faculty teach undergrads.

ACADEMICS

Degrees: Associate's, bachelor's, transfer. **Academic Requirements:** General education including some course work in arts/fine arts, computer literacy, English (including composition), history, humanities, mathematics, philosophy, sciences (biological or physical), social science, wellness and fitness, leadership, religion. **Classes:** Under 10 students in an average class. **Majors with Highest Enrollment:** Education, general; psychology, general; business administration/management. **Disciplines with Highest Percentage of Degrees Awarded:** Business/marketing 70%, education 7%, psychology 5%, social sciences and history 4%, communications/communication technologies 3%. **Special Study Options:** Cooperative (work-study) program, double major, English as a second language, independent study, internships, study abroad, teacher certification program, school for working adults.

FACILITIES

Housing: Coed, all-female, apartments for married students, apartments for single students. **Library Holdings:** 72,311 bound volumes. 354 periodicals. 2,718 microforms. 738 audiovisuals. **Special Academic Facilities/Equipment:** Foyer Gallery, Mid-East art and artifact collection. **Computers:** School-owned computers available for student use.

EXTRACURRICULARS

Activities: Choral groups, drama/theater, jazz band, literary magazine, music ensembles, musical theater, radio station, student government, student newspaper, yearbook. **Organizations:** 34 registered organizations, 3 honor societies, 4 religious organizations, 3 fraternities (5% men join), 3 sororities (5% women join). **Athletics (Intercollegiate):** *Men:* baseball, basketball, cheerleading, cross-country, football, golf, soccer, track & field, wrestling. *Women:* basketball, cheerleading, cross-country, soccer, softball, track & field, volleyball.

ADMISSIONS

Selectivity Rating: 63 (of 100). **Freshman Academic Profile:** Average high school GPA 2.8. 7% in top 10% of high school class, 25% in top 25% of high school class, 60% in top 50% of high school class. 97% from public high schools. Average ACT 19. TOEFL required of all international applicants, minimum TOEFL 500. **Basis for Candidate Selection:** *Very important factors considered include:* secondary school record. *Important factors considered include:* character/personal qualities, class rank, standardized test scores. *Other factors considered include:* alumni/ae relation, essays, extracurricular activities, interview, recommendations, talent/ability, volunteer work, work experience. **Freshman Admission Requirements:** High school diploma or GED is required. *Academic units required/recommended:* 15 total recommended; 3 English recommended, 2 math recommended, 2 science recommended, 2 foreign language recommended, 2 social studies recommended, 2 history recommended, 2 elective recommended. **Freshman Admission Statistics:** 781 applied, 62% accepted, 48% of those accepted enrolled. **Transfer Admission Requirements:** *Items required:* college transcript. Minimum college GPA of 2.0 required. Lowest grade transferable D. **General Admission Information:** Application fee $20. Priority application deadline July 1. Nonfall registration accepted. Credit offered for CEEB Advanced Placement tests.

COSTS AND FINANCIAL AID

Tuition $11,924. Room & board $4,140. Required fees $356. Average book expense $675. **Required Forms and Deadlines:** FAFSA. No deadline for regular filing. Priority filing deadline July 1. **Notification of Awards:** Applicants will be notified of awards on a rolling basis beginning on or about January 1. **Types of Aid:** *Need-based scholarships/grants:* Pell, SEOG, state scholarships/grants, private scholarships, the school's own gift aid. *Loans:* FFEL Subsidized Stafford, FFEL Unsubsidized Stafford, FFEL PLUS, Federal Perkins. **Student Employment:** Federal Work-Study Program available. Institutional employment available. Off-campus job opportunities are excellent. **Financial Aid Phone:** 641-673-1060.

WILLIAM TYNDALE COLLEGE

35700 W. Twelve Mile Road, Farmington Hills, MI 48331-3147
Phone: 800-483-0707 **E-mail:** admissions@williamtyndale.edu **CEEB Code:** 1167
Fax: 248-553-5963 **Web:** www.williamtyndale.edu **ACT Code:** 2252

This private school was founded in 1945. It has a 28-acre campus.

STUDENTS AND FACULTY

Enrollment: 488. **Student Body:** Male 49%, female 51%, out-of-state 7%, international 2% (8 countries represented). **Ethnic Representation:** African American 29%, Asian 1%, Caucasian 67%, Hispanic 1%. **Retention and Graduation:** 54% freshmen return for sophomore year. 12% freshmen graduate within 4 years. **Faculty:** Student/faculty ratio 6:1. 4 full-time faculty, 25% hold PhDs. 100% faculty teach undergrads.

ACADEMICS

Degrees: Associate's, bachelor's, certificate. **Academic Requirements:** General education including some course work in arts/fine arts, computer literacy, English (including composition), foreign languages, history, humanities, mathematics, philosophy, sciences (biological or physical), social science, Christian thought. **Classes:** Under 10 students in an average class. **Majors with Highest Enrollment:** Religion/religious studies; counseling psychology; business administration/management. **Disciplines with Highest Percentage of Degrees Awarded:** Business/marketing 64%, philosophy/religion/theology 18%, psychology 7%, visual and performing arts 4%, English 4%. **Special Study Options:** Accelerated program, distance learning, double major, dual enrollment, independent study, internships.

FACILITIES

Housing: Coed. **Library Holdings:** 60,000 bound volumes. 230 periodicals. 2,125 microforms. 3,300 audiovisuals. **Computers:** School-owned computers available for student use.

EXTRACURRICULARS

Activities: Choral groups, drama/theater, music ensembles, student government. **Organizations:** 2 registered organizations, 2 honor societies.

ADMISSIONS

Selectivity Rating: 73 (of 100). **Freshman Academic Profile:** Average high school GPA 3.2. 8% in top 10% of high school class, 25% in top 25% of high school class, 50% in top 50% of high school class. 76% from public high schools. Average SAT I Math 500. Average SAT I Verbal 542. Average ACT 23, ACT middle 50% range 17-25. TOEFL required of all international applicants, minimum TOEFL 500. **Basis for Candidate Selection:** *Very important factors considered include:* secondary school record, standardized test scores. *Other factors considered include:* character/personal qualities, essays, interview, recommendations, religious affiliation/commitment. **Freshman Admission Requirements:** High school diploma or GED is required. *Academic units required/recommended:* 17 total recommended; 4 English recommended, 3 math recommended, 3 science recommended, 2 foreign language recommended, 2 social studies recommended, 2 history recommended. **Freshman Admission Statistics:** 64 applied, 73% accepted, 55% of those accepted enrolled. **Transfer Admission Requirements:** *Items required:* high school transcript, college transcript, statement of good standing from prior school. Minimum high school GPA of 2.2 required. Minimum college GPA of 2.0 required. Lowest grade transferable C. **General Admission Information:** Nonfall registration accepted. Admission may be deferred for a maximum of 1 year. Credit and/or placement offered for CEEB Advanced Placement tests.

COSTS AND FINANCIAL AID

Tuition $8,550. Room & board $3,520. Required fees $100. Average book expense $1,328. **Required Forms and Deadlines:** FAFSA and institution's own financial aid form. No deadline for regular filing. Priority filing deadline February 15. **Notification of Awards:** Applicants will be notified of awards on a rolling basis. **Types of Aid:** *Need-based scholarships/grants:* Pell, SEOG, state scholarships/grants, private scholarships, the school's own gift aid. *Loans:* FFEL Subsidized Stafford, FFEL Unsubsidized Stafford, FFEL PLUS. **Student Employment:** Federal Work-Study Program available. Institutional employment available. Off-campus job opportunities are good. **Financial Aid Statistics:** 74% freshmen, 39% undergrads receive some form of aid. Average freshman grant $5,300. Average freshman loan $2,625. Average income from on-campus job $1,500. **Financial Aid Phone:** 800-483-0707.

WILLIAM WOODS UNIVERSITY

Office of Enrollment Services, One University Avenue, Fulton, MO 65251
Phone: 573-592-4221 **E-mail:** admissions@williamwoods.edu
Fax: 573-592-1146 **Web:** www.williamwoods.edu **ACT Code:** 2396

This private school, which is affiliated with the Disciples of Christ Church, was founded in 1870. It has a 170-acre campus.

STUDENTS AND FACULTY

Enrollment: 912. **Student Body:** Male 27%, female 73%, out-of-state 25%, international 4%. **Ethnic Representation:** African American 2%, Caucasian 95%, Hispanic 1%, Native American 1%. **Retention and Graduation:** 70% freshmen return for sophomore year. 48% freshmen graduate within 4 years. **Faculty:** Student/faculty ratio 9:1. 43 full-time faculty, 62% hold PhDs. 100% faculty teach undergrads.

ACADEMICS

Degrees: Associate's, bachelor's, master's. **Academic Requirements:** General education including some course work in arts/fine arts, English (including composition), foreign languages, history, humanities, mathematics, philosophy, sciences (biological or physical), social science, communications. **Classes:** Under 10 students in an average class. 20-29 students in an average lab/discussion section. **Majors with Highest Enrollment:** Education, general; business administration/management; animal sciences, general. **Disciplines with Highest Percentage of Degrees Awarded:** Business/marketing 43%, agriculture 15%, computer and information sciences 12%, education 6%, visual and performing arts 6%. **Special Study Options:** Accelerated program, cross registration, double major, dual enrollment, honors program, independent study, internships, liberal arts/career combination, student-designed major, study abroad, teacher certification program, Hollywood semester.

FACILITIES

Housing: Coed, all-female, all-male, apartments for single students, housing for disabled students, housing for international students, fraternities and/or sororities. **Library Holdings:** 99,801 bound volumes. 419 periodicals. 10,841 microforms. 28,204 audiovisuals. **Special Academic Facilities/Equipment:** Weitzman Court Room, Mildred Cox Gallery, Gladys Woods Kemper Center for the Arts, ASL interpreting lab, equestrian facilities. **Computers:** *Recommended operating system:* Windows NT/2000. School-owned computers available for student use.

EXTRACURRICULARS

Activities: Choral groups, dance, drama/theater, literary magazine, musical theater, radio station, student government, student newspaper. **Organizations:** 30 registered organizations, 3 honor societies, 1 religious organization, 2 fraternities (40% men join), 4 sororities (46% women join). **Athletics (Intercollegiate):** *Men:* baseball, equestrian, golf, soccer, volleyball. *Women:* basketball, equestrian, golf, soccer, softball, volleyball.

ADMISSIONS

Selectivity Rating: 63 (of 100). **Freshman Academic Profile:** Average high school GPA 3.2. 15% in top 10% of high school class, 35% in top 25% of high school class, 71% in top 50% of high school class. Average SAT I Math 509, SAT I Math middle 50% range 410-570. Average SAT I Verbal 523, SAT I Verbal middle 50% range 430-580. Average ACT 22, ACT middle 50% range 20-25. TOEFL required of all international applicants, minimum TOEFL 525. **Basis for Candidate Selection:** *Very important factors considered include:* class rank, secondary school record, standardized test scores. *Important factors considered include:* character/personal qualities, extracurricular activities, interview, recommendations. *Other factors considered include:* volunteer work, work experience. **Freshman Admission Requirements:** High school diploma or GED is required. *Academic units required/recommended:* 16 total required;

20 total recommended; 3 English required, 4 English recommended, 3 math required, 3 math recommended, 3 science recommended, 1 foreign language recommended, 3 social studies recommended, 2 history recommended, 4 elective recommended. **Freshman Admission Statistics:** 534 applied, 94% accepted, 40% of those accepted enrolled. **Transfer Admission Requirements:** *Items required:* college transcript, statement of good standing from prior school. Minimum college GPA of 2.5 required. Lowest grade transferable C. **General Admission Information:** Application fee $25. Priority application deadline March 1. Nonfall registration accepted. Admission may be deferred for a maximum of 1 year. Credit and/or placement offered for CEEB Advanced Placement tests.

COSTS AND FINANCIAL AID

Tuition $14,000. Room & board $5,700. Required fees $420. Average book expense $700. **Required Forms and Deadlines:** FAFSA and institution's own financial aid form. No deadline for regular filing. Priority filing deadline March 1. **Notification of Awards:** Applicants will be notified of awards on a rolling basis beginning on or about March 15. **Types of Aid:** *Need-based scholarships/grants:* Pell, SEOG, state scholarships/grants, private scholarships, the school's own gift aid. *Loans:* FFEL Subsidized Stafford, FFEL Unsubsidized Stafford, FFEL PLUS, Federal Perkins, college/university loans from institutional funds. **Student Employment:** Federal Work-Study Program available. Institutional employment available. Off-campus job opportunities are fair. **Financial Aid Statistics:** 69% freshmen, 71% undergrads receive some form of aid. Average income from on-campus job $800. **Financial Aid Phone:** 573-592-4357.

WILLIAMS BAPTIST COLLEGE

PO 3665, Walnut Ridge, AR 72476
Phone: 870-886-6741 **E-mail:** admissions@wbcoll.edu
Fax: 870-886-3924 **Web:** www.wbcoll.edu **ACT Code:** 140

This private school, which is affiliated with the Southern Baptist Church, was founded in 1941. It has a 180-acre campus.

STUDENTS AND FACULTY

Enrollment: 686. **Student Body:** Male 46%, female 54%, international 3% (8 countries represented). **Ethnic Representation:** African American 2%, Caucasian 88%, Hispanic 1%. **Retention and Graduation:** 69% freshmen return for sophomore year. 16% freshmen graduate within 4 years. **Faculty:** 100% faculty teach undergrads.

ACADEMICS

Degrees: Associate's, bachelor's. **Academic Requirements:** General education including some course work in arts/fine arts, English (including composition), history, humanities, mathematics, sciences (biological or physical), social science. **Special Study Options:** Cooperative (work-study) program, double major, independent study, internships, teacher certification program.

FACILITIES

Housing: All-female, all-male, apartments for married students, apartments for single students. **Computers:** *Recommended operating system:* Windows 95. School-owned computers available for student use.

EXTRACURRICULARS

Activities: Choral groups, drama/theater, student government. **Organizations:** 29 registered organizations, 6 honor societies, 5 religious organizations, 2 fraternities, 2 sororities. **Athletics (Intercollegiate):** *Men:* baseball, basketball, cross-country, golf, soccer. *Women:* basketball, cross-country, softball, volleyball.

ADMISSIONS

Selectivity Rating: 63 (of 100). **Freshman Academic Profile:** 62% from public high schools. TOEFL required of all international applicants, minimum TOEFL 500. **Basis for Candidate Selection:** *Very important factors considered include:* standardized test scores. *Important factors considered include:* class rank, interview, secondary school record. *Other factors considered include:* character/personal qualities, essays, extracurricular activities, recommendations, talent/ability, volunteer work. **Freshman Admission Requirements:** High school diploma or GED is required. *Academic units required/recommended:* 4 English recommended, 3 math recommended, 2 science recommended, 2 foreign language recommended, 3 history recommended. **Freshman Admission Statistics:** 385 applied, 78% accepted. **Transfer Admission Requirements:** *Items required:* college transcript. Minimum high school GPA of 2.3 required. Minimum college GPA of 2.0 required. **General Admission Information:** Application fee $20. Regular application deadline September 3. Nonfall registration accepted.

COSTS AND FINANCIAL AID

Tuition $6,000. Room & board $3,200. Required fees $270. Average book expense $850. **Required Forms and Deadlines:** FAFSA. Priority filing deadline May 1. **Notification of Awards:** Applicants will be notified of awards on a rolling basis beginning on or about April 1. **Types of Aid:** *Need-based scholarships/grants:* Pell, SEOG, state scholarships/grants, private scholarships, the school's own gift aid. *Loans:* Direct Subsidized Stafford, Direct Unsubsidized Stafford, Direct PLUS, college/university loans from institutional funds. **Student Employment:** Federal Work-Study Program available. Institutional employment available. Off-campus job opportunities are good. **Financial Aid Statistics:** 88% freshmen, 93% undergrads receive some form of aid. Average freshman grant $4,568. Average freshman loan $2,407. Average income from on-campus job $1,142. **Financial Aid Phone:** 800-722-4434.

WILLIAMS COLLEGE

PO Box 487, Williamstown, MA 01267
Phone: 413-597-2211 **E-mail:** admission@williams.edu **CEEB Code:** 3965
Fax: 413-597-4052 **Web:** www.williams.edu **ACT Code:** 1936

This private school was founded in 1793. It has a 450-acre campus.

STUDENTS AND FACULTY

Enrollment: 1,983. **Student Body:** Male 51%, female 49%, out-of-state 80%, international 6% (52 countries represented). **Ethnic Representation:** African American 8%, Asian 9%, Caucasian 74%, Hispanic 8%. **Retention and Graduation:** 97% freshmen return for sophomore year. 92% freshmen graduate within 4 years. 16% grads go on to further study within 1 year. 3% grads pursue law degrees. 3% grads pursue medical degrees. **Faculty:** Student/faculty ratio 8:1. 243 full-time faculty, 95% hold PhDs. 100% faculty teach undergrads.

ACADEMICS

Degrees: Bachelor's, master's. **Academic Requirements:** General education including completion of coursework in each of three basic areas: arts and humanities, social studies, and math and sciences. In addition, students must satisfy a one-course peoples and cultures requirement, a one-course quantitative/formal reasoning requirement, and a two-course intensive writing requirement. **Classes:** 10-19 students in an average class. 10-19 students in an average lab/discussion section. **Disciplines with Highest Percentage of Degrees Awarded:** Social sciences and history 37%, English 12%, psychology 11%, visual and performing arts 9%, biological life sciences 8%. **Special Study Options:** Accelerated program, cross registration, double major, student exchange program (domestic), honors program, independent study, internships, student-designed major, study abroad, teacher certification program.

FACILITIES

Housing: Coed. **Library Holdings:** 888,504 bound volumes. 1,904 periodicals. 488,433 microforms. 37,456 audiovisuals. **Special Academic Facilities/Equipment:** Hopkins Observatory; Williams College Museum of Art; Adams Memorial Theatre; Chapin Rare Books Library; Spencer Studio Art Building. **Computers:** *Recommended operating system:* Windows 95. School-owned computers available for student use.

EXTRACURRICULARS

Activities: Choral groups, dance, drama/theater, jazz band, literary magazine, marching band, music ensembles, musical theater, radio station, student government, student newspaper, student-run film society, symphony orchestra, yearbook. **Organizations:** 110 registered organizations, 3 honor societies, 13 religious organizations. **Athletics (Intercollegiate):** *Men:* baseball, basketball, crew, skiing (cross-country), cross-country, diving, football, golf, ice hockey, indoor track, lacrosse, skiing (alpine), soccer, squash, swimming, tennis, track & field, wrestling. *Women:* basketball, crew, skiing (cross-country), cross-country, diving, field hockey, ice hockey, indoor track, lacrosse, skiing (alpine), soccer, softball, squash, swimming, tennis, track & field, volleyball.

ADMISSIONS

Selectivity Rating: 99 (of 100). **Freshman Academic Profile:** 54% from public high schools. Average SAT I Math 694, SAT I Math middle 50% range 660-750. Average SAT I Verbal 701, SAT I Verbal middle 50% range 660-760. Average ACT 30. **Basis for Candidate Selection:** *Very important factors considered include:* essays, recommendations, secondary school record, standardized test scores. *Important factors considered include:* class rank, extracurricular activities, talent/ability. *Other factors considered include:* alumni/ae relation, character/personal qualities, geographical residence, minority status, volunteer work, work experience. **Freshman Admission Requirements:** High school diploma or equivalent is not required. *Academic units required/*

recommended: 4 English recommended, 4 math recommended, 3 science recommended, 3 science lab recommended, 4 foreign language recommended, 3 social studies recommended. **Freshman Admission Statistics:** 4,931 applied, 23% accepted. **Transfer Admission Requirements:** *Items required:* high school transcript, college transcript, essay, standardized test score, statement of good standing from prior school. Minimum college GPA of 3.5 required. Lowest grade transferable C-. **General Admission Information:** Application fee $50. Early decision application deadline November 15. Regular application deadline January 1. Admission may be deferred for a maximum of 1 year. Placement offered for CEEB Advanced Placement tests.

COSTS AND FINANCIAL AID

Tuition $26,326. Room & board $7,230. Required fees $194. Average book expense $800. **Required Forms and Deadlines:** FAFSA and CSS/Financial Aid PROFILE. Financial aid filing deadline February 1. **Notification of Awards:** Applicants will be notified of awards on or about April 1. **Types of Aid:** *Need-based scholarships/grants:* Pell, SEOG, state scholarships/grants, private scholarships, the school's own gift aid. *Loans:* Direct Subsidized Stafford, Direct Unsubsidized Stafford, Direct PLUS, Federal Perkins, college/university loans from institutional funds. **Student Employment:** Federal Work-Study Program available. Institutional employment available. Off-campus job opportunities are fair. **Financial Aid Statistics:** 45% freshmen, 41% undergrads receive some form of aid. Average freshman grant $18,187. Average freshman loan $2,533. Average income from on-campus job $1,646. **Financial Aid Phone:** 413-597-4181.

WILLISTON STATE COLLEGE

PO Box 1326, Williston, ND 58802-1326
Phone: 701-774-4210 **E-mail:** Lacey.Madison@wsc.nodak.edu
Fax: 701-774-4211 **Web:** www.wsc.nodak.edu

This public school was founded in 1961. It has an 80-acre campus.

STUDENTS AND FACULTY

Enrollment: 770. **Student Body:** Male 37%, female 63%, out-of-state 15%, international 2% (2 countries represented). **Ethnic Representation:** Caucasian 93%, Hispanic 1%, Native American 5%. **Faculty:** Student/faculty ratio 13:1. 31 full-time faculty. 100% faculty teach undergrads.

ACADEMICS

Degrees: Associate's, certificate, diploma, terminal, transfer. **Academic Requirements:** General education including some course work in computer literacy, English (including composition), humanities, mathematics, sciences (biological or physical), social science. **Special Study Options:** Cooperative (work-study) program, distance learning, dual enrollment, external degree program, independent study, internships, liberal arts/career combination, student-designed major.

FACILITIES

Housing: Coed, all-female, all-male, housing for disabled students, athletes' housing units, married/family housing units. **Computers:** School-owned computers available for student use.

EXTRACURRICULARS

Activities: Choral groups, drama/theater, literary magazine, music ensembles, musical theater, pep band, student government. **Organizations:** 18 registered organizations, 1 honor society, 1 religious organization. **Athletics (Intercollegiate):** *Men:* baseball, basketball, golf. *Women:* basketball, golf, volleyball.

ADMISSIONS

Selectivity Rating: 63 (of 100). **Freshman Academic Profile:** TOEFL required of all international applicants, minimum TOEFL 330. **Freshman Admission Requirements:** High school diploma or GED is required. *Academic units required/recommended:* 4 English recommended, 3 math recommended, 3 science recommended, 3 science lab recommended, 1 foreign language recommended, 3 social studies recommended. **Transfer Admission Requirements:** *Items required:* college transcript, statement of good standing from prior school. Lowest grade transferable D. **General Admission Information:** Application fee $35. Nonfall registration accepted. Credit and/or placement offered for CEEB Advanced Placement tests.

COSTS AND FINANCIAL AID

Required Forms and Deadlines: FAFSA and International Student Tuition Waiver. No deadline for regular filing. Priority filing deadline April 15. **Notification of Awards:** Applicants will be notified of awards on a rolling basis beginning on or about May 15. **Types of Aid:** *Need-based scholarships/grants:* Pell, SEOG, state scholarships/grants, private scholarships, the school's own gift aid. *Loans:* FFEL Subsidized Stafford, FFEL Unsubsidized Stafford, FFEL PLUS, Federal Perkins. **Student Employment:** Federal Work-Study Program available. Institutional employment available. Off-campus job opportunities are good. **Financial Aid Phone:** 701-774-4244.

WILMINGTON COLLEGE (DE)

320 Dupont Highway, New Castle, DE 19720
Phone: 302-328-9401 **E-mail:** mlee@wilmcoll.edu **CEEB Code:** 5925
Fax: 302-328-5902 **Web:** www.wilmcoll.edu **ACT Code:** 635

This private school was founded in 1967. It has a 15-acre campus.

STUDENTS AND FACULTY

Enrollment: 4,399. **Student Body:** Male 47%, female 53%, out-of-state 3%. **Ethnic Representation:** African American 14%, Asian 1%, Caucasian 64%, Hispanic 2%. **Retention and Graduation:** 87% freshmen return for sophomore year. 50% grads go on to further study within 1 year. 80% grads pursue business degrees. 10% grads pursue law degrees. 1% grads pursue medical degrees. **Faculty:** Student/faculty ratio 18:1. 100% faculty teach undergrads.

ACADEMICS

Degrees: Associate's, bachelor's, certificate, doctoral, master's, post-master's certificate. **Academic Requirements:** General education including some course work in arts/fine arts, computer literacy, English (including composition), humanities, mathematics, sciences (biological or physical), social science. **Majors with Highest Enrollment:** Education, general; business administration/management. **Special Study Options:** Accelerated program, cooperative (work-study) program, distance learning, double major, independent study, internships, teacher certification program, weekend college.

FACILITIES

Housing: All housing is off campus. **Library Holdings:** 114,000 bound volumes. 400 periodicals. 6,700 microforms. 0 audiovisuals. **Computers:** School-owned computers available for student use.

EXTRACURRICULARS

Activities: Student government. **Organizations:** 1 honor society, 3% men join fraternities, 2% women join sororities. **Athletics (Intercollegiate):** *Men:* baseball, basketball, cross-country, soccer. *Women:* basketball, softball.

ADMISSIONS

Selectivity Rating: 60 (of 100). **Freshman Academic Profile:** Average high school GPA 2.5. 70% from public high schools. TOEFL required of all international applicants, minimum TOEFL 500. **Basis for Candidate Selection:** *Important factors considered include:* recommendations, secondary school record. **Freshman Admission Requirements:** High school diploma is required and GED is not accepted. **Transfer Admission Requirements:** *Items required:* college transcript. Minimum high school GPA of 2.0 required. Minimum college GPA of 2.0 required. Lowest grade transferable C. **General Admission Information:** Application fee $25. Nonfall registration accepted. Admission may be deferred for a maximum of 1 year. Credit offered for CEEB Advanced Placement tests.

COSTS AND FINANCIAL AID

Tuition $6,060. Required fees $50. Average book expense $500. **Required Forms and Deadlines:** FAFSA. **Student Employment:** Federal Work-Study Program available. Off-campus job opportunities are excellent. **Financial Aid Statistics:** Average freshman grant $2,400. Average freshman loan $2,625. Average income from on-campus job $1,000. **Financial Aid Phone:** 302-328-9437.

WILMINGTON COLLEGE (OH)

Pyle Center Box 1325, 251 Ludovic Street, Wilmington, OH 45177
Phone: 937-382-6661 **E-mail:** admission@wilmington.edu **CEEB Code:** 1909
Fax: 937-382-7077 **Web:** www.wilmington.edu **ACT Code:** 3362

This private school, which is affiliated with the Quaker Church, was founded in 1870. It has a 65-acre campus.

STUDENTS AND FACULTY

Enrollment: 1,265. **Student Body:** Male 46%, female 54%, out-of-state 7%, international 1%. **Ethnic Representation:** African American 7%, Caucasian

75%, Hispanic 1%. **Retention and Graduation:** 71% freshmen return for sophomore year. **Faculty:** Student/faculty ratio 18:1. 69 full-time faculty, 66% hold PhDs. 100% faculty teach undergrads.

ACADEMICS

Degrees: Bachelor's, certificate, master's. **Academic Requirements:** General education including some course work in arts/fine arts, English (including composition), history, humanities, mathematics, sciences (biological or physical), social science. **Classes:** 10-19 students in an average class. 10-19 students in an average lab/discussion section. **Disciplines with Highest Percentage of Degrees Awarded:** Business/marketing 34%, education 17%, protective services/public administration 8%, agriculture 7%, psychology 6%. **Special Study Options:** Cross registration, double major, dual enrollment, honors program, independent study, internships, student-designed major, study abroad, teacher certification program.

FACILITIES

Housing: Coed, all-female, all-male, apartments for single students, fraternities and/or sororities. **Library Holdings:** 103,706 bound volumes. 408 periodicals. 41,151 microforms. 1,280 audiovisuals. **Special Academic Facilities/ Equipment:** Hiroshima-Nagasaki memorial collection and peace resource center, education lab, language lab, three farms, observatory, electron microscope. **Computers:** School-owned computers available for student use.

EXTRACURRICULARS

Activities: Choral groups, drama/theater, jazz band, literary magazine, music ensembles, musical theater, student government, student newspaper, yearbook. **Organizations:** 48 registered organizations, 3 honor societies, 3 religious organizations, 6 fraternities (25% men join), 5 sororities (25% women join). **Athletics (Intercollegiate):** *Men:* baseball, basketball, cheerleading, cross-country, football, golf, soccer, swimming, tennis, track & field, wrestling. *Women:* basketball, cheerleading, cross-country, golf, soccer, softball, swimming, tennis, track & field, volleyball.

ADMISSIONS

Selectivity Rating: 68 (of 100). **Freshman Academic Profile:** Average high school GPA 3.2. 14% in top 10% of high school class, 38% in top 25% of high school class, 76% in top 50% of high school class. Average ACT 22, ACT middle 50% range 18-25. TOEFL required of all international applicants, minimum TOEFL 500. **Basis for Candidate Selection:** *Very important factors considered include:* class rank, secondary school record, standardized test scores. *Important factors considered include:* alumni/ae relation, character/ personal qualities, extracurricular activities, geographical residence, interview, recommendations. *Other factors considered include:* essays, minority status, talent/ability, volunteer work, work experience. **Freshman Admission Requirements:** High school diploma or GED is required. *Academic units required/recommended:* 16 total required; 16 total recommended; 4 English required, 2 math required, 3 math recommended, 2 science required, 3 science recommended, 2 science lab required, 2 science lab recommended, 2 foreign language recommended, 2 social studies required, 2 social studies recommended, 4 elective required. **Freshman Admission Statistics:** 994 applied, 83% accepted, 41% of those accepted enrolled. **Transfer Admission Requirements:** *Items required:* high school transcript, college transcript, statement of good standing from prior school. Minimum college GPA of 2.0 required. Lowest grade transferable C. **General Admission Information:** Application fee $25. Priority application deadline May 1. Regular application deadline July 16. Nonfall registration accepted. Admission may be deferred for a maximum of 1 year. Credit and/or placement offered for CEEB Advanced Placement tests.

COSTS AND FINANCIAL AID

Tuition $16,128. Room & board $6,240. Required fees $436. Average book expense $1,000. **Required Forms and Deadlines:** FAFSA. Financial aid filing deadline June 1. Priority filing deadline March 31. **Notification of Awards:** Applicants will be notified of awards on a rolling basis beginning on or about March 1. **Types of Aid:** *Need-based scholarships/grants:* Pell, SEOG, state scholarships/grants, private scholarships, the school's own gift aid. *Loans:* Direct Subsidized Stafford, Direct Unsubsidized Stafford, Direct PLUS, Federal Perkins. **Student Employment:** Federal Work-Study Program available. Institutional employment available. Off-campus job opportunities are excellent. **Financial Aid Statistics:** 87% freshmen, 84% undergrads receive some form of aid. Average freshman grant $5,464. Average freshman loan $4,380. **Financial Aid Phone:** 800-341-9318.

WILSON COLLEGE

$$$

1015 Philadelphia Avenue, Chambersburg, PA 17201
Phone: 717-262-2002 **E-mail:** admissions@wilson.edu **CEEB Code:** 2979
Fax: 717-262-2546 **Web:** www.wilson.edu

This private school, which is affiliated with the Presbyterian Church, was founded in 1869. It has a 262-acre campus.

STUDENTS AND FACULTY

Enrollment: 739. **Student Body:** Male 14%, female 86%, out-of-state 29%, international 4% (11 countries represented). **Ethnic Representation:** African American 5%, Asian 2%, Caucasian 87%, Hispanic 1%. **Retention and Graduation:** 69% freshmen return for sophomore year. 44% freshmen graduate within 4 years. 34% grads go on to further study within 1 year. **Faculty:** Student/faculty ratio 9:1. 37 full-time faculty, 86% hold PhDs. 100% faculty teach undergrads.

ACADEMICS

Degrees: Associate's, bachelor's. **Academic Requirements:** General education including some course work in arts/fine arts, computer literacy, English (including composition), foreign languages, humanities, mathematics, sciences (biological or physical), social science. **Classes:** Under 10 students in an average class. 20-29 students in an average lab/discussion section. **Majors with Highest Enrollment:** Business administration/management; animal sciences, general; ecology, evolution, and systematics. **Disciplines with Highest Percentage of Degrees Awarded:** Biological life sciences 32%, business/marketing 19%, agriculture 15%, education 9%, English 6%. **Special Study Options:** Cooperative (work-study) program, cross registration, double major, English as a second language, independent study, internships, student-designed major, study abroad, teacher certification program.

FACILITIES

Housing: All-female, women with children housing, maximum of 2 children. **Library Holdings:** 172,205 bound volumes. 312 periodicals. 10,772 microforms. 1,664 audiovisuals. **Special Academic Facilities/Equipment:** Art gallery, natural history museum, electron microscope. **Computers:** School-owned computers available for student use.

EXTRACURRICULARS

Activities: Choral groups, dance, drama/theater, literary magazine, music ensembles, radio station, student government, student newspaper, yearbook. **Organizations:** 20 registered organizations, 1 religious organization. **Athletics (Intercollegiate):** *Women:* basketball, equestrian, field hockey, gymnastics, soccer, softball, tennis, volleyball.

ADMISSIONS

Selectivity Rating: 68 (of 100). **Freshman Academic Profile:** Average high school GPA 3.4. 13% in top 10% of high school class, 41% in top 25% of high school class, 80% in top 50% of high school class. 88% from public high schools. Average SAT I Math 506, SAT I Math middle 50% range 450-570. Average SAT I Verbal 527, SAT I Verbal middle 50% range 470-570. Average ACT 20, ACT middle 50% range 17-23. TOEFL required of all international applicants, minimum TOEFL 500. **Basis for Candidate Selection:** *Very important factors considered include:* secondary school record. *Important factors considered include:* character/personal qualities, class rank, essays, interview, recommendations, standardized test scores. *Other factors considered include:* alumni/ae relation, extracurricular activities, talent/ability, volunteer work, work experience. **Freshman Admission Requirements:** High school diploma or GED is required. *Academic units required/recommended:* 15 total recommended; 4 English recommended, 3 math recommended, 2 science recommended, 2 science lab recommended, 2 foreign language recommended, 4 social studies recommended. **Freshman Admission Statistics:** 213 applied, 68% accepted, 49% of those accepted enrolled. **Transfer Admission Requirements:** *Items required:* high school transcript, college transcript, essay. Minimum high school GPA of 2.7 required. Minimum college GPA of 2.0 required. Lowest grade transferable C. **General Admission Information:** Application fee $30. Priority application deadline April 30. Nonfall registration accepted. Admission may be deferred for a maximum of 1 year. Credit and/or placement offered for CEEB Advanced Placement tests.

COSTS AND FINANCIAL AID

Tuition $15,106. Room & board $6,790. Required fees $524. Average book expense $800. **Required Forms and Deadlines:** FAFSA, institution's own financial aid form and state aid form. Priority filing deadline April 30. **Notification of Awards:** Applicants will be notified of awards on a rolling basis beginning on or about February 15. **Types of Aid:** *Need-based scholarships/ grants:* Pell, SEOG, state scholarships/grants, private scholarships, the school's own gift aid. *Loans:* FFEL Subsidized Stafford, FFEL Unsubsidized Stafford, FFEL PLUS, Federal Perkins, college/university loans from institutional funds. **Student Employment:** Federal Work-Study Program available. Institutional employment available. Off-campus job opportunities are fair. **Financial Aid Statistics:** 60% freshmen, 70% undergrads receive some form of aid. Average freshman grant $10,855. Average freshman loan $3,929. Average income from on-campus job $1,339. **Financial Aid Phone:** 717-262-2016.

WINGATE UNIVERSITY

Campus Box 3059, Wingate, NC 28174
Phone: 704-233-8200 **E-mail:** admit@wingate.edu **CEEB Code:** 5908
Fax: 704-233-8110 **Web:** www.wingate.edu **ACT Code:** 3176

This private school, which is affiliated with the Baptist Church, was founded in 1896. It has a 390-acre campus.

STUDENTS AND FACULTY

Enrollment: 1,328. **Student Body:** Male 45%, female 55%, out-of-state 43%, international 3% (14 countries represented). **Ethnic Representation:** African American 11%, Asian 1%, Caucasian 83%, Hispanic 2%. **Retention and Graduation:** 73% freshmen return for sophomore year. 30% freshmen graduate within 4 years. 30% grads go on to further study within 1 year. 10% grads pursue business degrees. 2% grads pursue law degrees. 1% grads pursue medical degrees. **Faculty:** Student/faculty ratio 13:1. 83 full-time faculty, 90% hold PhDs. 100% faculty teach undergrads.

ACADEMICS

Degrees: Bachelor's, master's. **Academic Requirements:** General education including some course work in arts/fine arts, English (including composition), foreign languages, history, humanities, mathematics, sciences (biological or physical), social science. **Classes:** Under 10 students in an average class. Under 10 students in an average lab/discussion section. **Disciplines with Highest Percentage of Degrees Awarded:** Business/marketing 34%, communications/communication technologies 12%, education 8%, parks and recreation 8%, liberal arts/general studies 6%. **Special Study Options:** Cross registration, double major, dual enrollment, honors program, independent study, internships, study abroad, teacher certification program.

FACILITIES

Housing: All-female, all-male, apartments for married students, apartments for single students, fraternities and/or sororities. **Library Holdings:** 89,268 bound volumes. 15,325 periodicals. 440,680 microforms. 6,925 audiovisuals. **Special Academic Facilities/Equipment:** Art gallery, outdoor recreation lab. **Computers:** *Recommended operating system:* Windows 3x. School-owned computers available for student use.

EXTRACURRICULARS

Activities: Choral groups, concert band, drama/theater, jazz band, literary magazine, music ensembles, student government, student newspaper, television station. **Organizations:** 38 registered organizations, 10 honor societies, 6 religious organizations, 4 fraternities (7% men join), 2 sororities (10% women join). **Athletics (Intercollegiate):** *Men:* baseball, basketball, cheerleading, cross-country, football, golf, lacrosse, soccer, tennis. *Women:* basketball, cheerleading, cross-country, golf, soccer, softball, swimming, tennis, volleyball.

ADMISSIONS

Selectivity Rating: 66 (of 100). **Freshman Academic Profile:** Average high school GPA 3.3. 18% in top 10% of high school class, 48% in top 25% of high school class, 74% in top 50% of high school class. 85% from public high schools. Average SAT I Math 499, SAT I Math middle 50% range 470-570. Average SAT I Verbal 498, SAT I Verbal middle 50% range 450-560. Average ACT 22, ACT middle 50% range 19-25. TOEFL required of all international applicants, minimum TOEFL 550. **Basis for Candidate Selection:** *Very important factors considered include:* class rank, secondary school record, standardized test scores. *Important factors considered include:* essays, recommendations. *Other factors considered include:* character/personal qualities, extracurricular activities, talent/ability. **Freshman Admission Requirements:** High school diploma or GED is required. *Academic units required/recommended:* 18 total recommended; 4 English recommended, 3 math recommended, 2 science recommended, 1 science lab recommended, 2 foreign language recommended, 2 social studies recommended. **Freshman Admission Statistics:** 1,210 applied, 79% accepted, 39% of those accepted enrolled. **Transfer Admission Requirements:** *Items required:* high school transcript, college transcript, essay, statement of good standing from prior school. Minimum college GPA of 2.0 required. Lowest grade transferable C. **General Admission Information:** Application fee $25. Priority application deadline April 1. Early decision application deadline December 1. Nonfall registration accepted. Admission may be deferred for a maximum of 1 year. Credit and/or placement offered for CEEB Advanced Placement tests.

COSTS AND FINANCIAL AID

Tuition $13,550. Room & board $5,460. Required fees $1,000. Average book expense $750. **Required Forms and Deadlines:** FAFSA. Priority filing deadline May 1. **Notification of Awards:** Applicants will be notified of awards on a rolling basis beginning on or about March 15. **Types of Aid:** *Need-based scholarships/grants:* Pell, SEOG, state scholarships/grants, private scholarships, the school's own gift aid. *Loans:* FFEL Subsidized Stafford, FFEL Unsubsidized Stafford, FFEL PLUS. **Student Employment:** Federal Work-Study Program available. Institutional employment available. Off-campus job opportunities are excellent. **Financial Aid Statistics:** 95% freshmen, 91% undergrads receive some form of aid. Average freshman grant $5,655. Average freshman loan $2,625. Average income from on-campus job $1,200. **Financial Aid Phone:** 800-755-5550.

WINONA STATE UNIVERSITY

Office of Admissions, Winona State University, Winona, MN 55987
Phone: 507-457-5100 **E-mail:** admissions@winona.edu **CEEB Code:** 6680
Fax: 507-457-5620 **Web:** www.winona.edu **ACT Code:** 2162

This public school was founded in 1858. It has a 40-acre campus.

STUDENTS AND FACULTY

Enrollment: 7,130. **Student Body:** Male 36%, female 64%, out-of-state 30%, international 4% (53 countries represented). **Ethnic Representation:** African American 1%, Asian 1%, Caucasian 63%, Hispanic 1%. **Retention and Graduation:** 76% freshmen return for sophomore year. 27% freshmen graduate within 4 years. 15% grads go on to further study within 1 year. 6% grads pursue business degrees. 1% grads pursue law degrees. 1% grads pursue medical degrees. **Faculty:** Student/faculty ratio 21:1. 315 full-time faculty, 68% hold PhDs. 95% faculty teach undergrads.

ACADEMICS

Degrees: Associate's, bachelor's, master's, post-master's certificate. **Academic Requirements:** General education including some course work in arts/fine arts, English (including composition), history, humanities, mathematics, sciences (biological or physical), social science. **Classes:** 20-29 students in an average class. **Majors with Highest Enrollment:** Elementary education and teaching; nursing/registered nurse training (RN, ASN, BSN, MSN); business administration/management. **Disciplines with Highest Percentage of Degrees Awarded:** Education 18%, business/marketing 18%, health professions and related sciences 13%, communications/communication technologies 7%, parks and recreation 7%. **Special Study Options:** Accelerated program, cross registration, distance learning, double major, dual enrollment, external degree program, honors program, independent study, internships, student-designed major, study abroad, teacher certification program.

FACILITIES

Housing: Coed, all-female, all-male, apartments for single students, housing for disabled students. **Library Holdings:** 419,000 bound volumes. 1,940 periodicals. 950,000 microforms. 16,000 audiovisuals. **Computers:** School-owned computers available for student use.

EXTRACURRICULARS

Activities: Choral groups, concert band, dance, drama/theater, jazz band, literary magazine, music ensembles, musical theater, pep band, radio station, student government, student newspaper, student-run film society, symphony orchestra, television station. **Organizations:** 130 registered organizations, 20 honor societies, 6 religious organizations, 3 fraternities (3% men join), 3 sororities (3% women join). **Athletics (Intercollegiate):** *Men:* baseball, basketball, cross-country, football, golf, tennis. *Women:* basketball, cross-country, golf, gymnastics, soccer, softball, tennis, track & field, volleyball.

ADMISSIONS

Selectivity Rating: 77 (of 100). **Freshman Academic Profile:** Average high school GPA 3.3. 15% in top 10% of high school class, 50% in top 25% of high school class, 96% in top 50% of high school class. 68% from public high schools. Average SAT I Math 560. Average SAT I Verbal 540. Average ACT 23, ACT middle 50% range 21-26. TOEFL required of all international applicants, minimum TOEFL 550. **Basis for Candidate Selection:** *Very important factors considered include:* class rank, secondary school record, standardized test scores. *Other factors considered include:* recommendations. **Freshman**

Admission Requirements: High school diploma or GED is required. *Academic units required/recommended:* 16 total required; 4 English required, 3 math required, 3 science required, 3 science lab required, 2 foreign language required, 2 social studies required, 1 history required, 1 elective required. **Freshman Admission Statistics:** 4,248 applied, 82% accepted, 44% of those accepted enrolled. **Transfer Admission Requirements:** *Items required:* college transcript. Minimum college GPA of 2.4 required. Lowest grade transferable C. **General Admission Information:** Application fee $20. Priority application deadline March 1. Regular application deadline rolling. Nonfall registration accepted. Admission may be deferred for a maximum of 1 year. Credit and/or placement offered for CEEB Advanced Placement tests.

COSTS AND FINANCIAL AID

In-state tuition $3,490. Out-of-state tuition $7,370. Room & board $4,140. Required fees $1,675. Average book expense $500. **Required Forms and Deadlines:** FAFSA. No deadline for regular filing. **Notification of Awards:** Applicants will be notified of awards on a rolling basis beginning on or about March 1. **Types of Aid:** *Need-based scholarships/grants:* Pell, SEOG, state scholarships/grants, private scholarships, the school's own gift aid. *Loans:* FFEL Subsidized Stafford, FFEL Unsubsidized Stafford, FFEL PLUS, Federal Perkins, state loans, college/university loans from institutional funds. **Student Employment:** Federal Work-Study Program available. Institutional employment available. Off-campus job opportunities are good. **Financial Aid Statistics:** 62% freshmen, 53% undergrads receive some form of aid. Average freshman grant $1,500. Average freshman loan $2,000. Average income from on-campus job $1,800. **Financial Aid Phone:** 800-342-5978.

WINSTON-SALEM STATE UNIVERSITY

601 MLK, Jr. Drive, Winston-Salem, NC 27110
Phone: 336-750-2070 **E-mail:** admissions@wssu1.adp.wssu.edu **CEEB Code:** 5909
Fax: 336-750-2079 **Web:** www.wssu.edu **ACT Code:** 3178

This public school was founded in 1892. It has a 94-acre campus.

STUDENTS AND FACULTY

Enrollment: 2,865. **Student Body:** Male 33%, female 67%, out-of-state 6%. **Ethnic Representation:** African American 80%, Asian 1%, Caucasian 18%, Hispanic 1%. **Retention and Graduation:** 72% freshmen return for sophomore year. 13% freshmen graduate within 4 years. **Faculty:** 100% faculty teach undergrads.

ACADEMICS

Degrees: Bachelor's. **Academic Requirements:** General education including some course work in arts/fine arts, computer literacy, English (including composition), history, humanities, mathematics, sciences (biological or physical), social science. **Special Study Options:** Cooperative (work-study) program, double major, dual enrollment, student exchange program (domestic), honors program, independent study, internships, liberal arts/career combination, study abroad, teacher certification program.

FACILITIES

Housing: Coed, all-female, all-male. **Library Holdings:** 132,356 bound volumes. 1,694 periodicals. 860 microforms. 12 audiovisuals. **Special Academic Facilities/Equipment:** Art gallery. **Computers:** *Recommended operating system:* Mac. School-owned computers available for student use.

EXTRACURRICULARS

Activities: Choral groups, jazz band, marching band, music ensembles, radio station, student government, student newspaper, yearbook.

ADMISSIONS

Selectivity Rating: 66 (of 100). **Freshman Academic Profile:** Average high school GPA 2.7. 1% in top 10% of high school class, 13% in top 25% of high school class, 31% in top 50% of high school class. Average SAT I Math 420. Average SAT I Verbal 432. Average ACT 17. **Basis for Candidate Selection:** *Very important factors considered include:* class rank, secondary school record, standardized test scores. *Other factors considered include:* alumni/ae relation, character/personal qualities, extracurricular activities, interview, talent/ability. **Freshman Admission Requirements:** *Academic units required/recommended:* 16 total recommended; 4 English recommended, 3 math recommended, 3 science recommended, 2 foreign language recommended, 4 social studies recommended. **Freshman Admission Statistics:** 1,353 applied, 80% accepted, 46% of those accepted enrolled. **Transfer Admission Requirements:** *Items required:* college transcript. Minimum college GPA of 2.0 required. Lowest grade transferable C. **General Admission Information:** Application fee $20. Regular application deadline rolling. Nonfall registration accepted.

COSTS AND FINANCIAL AID

In-state tuition $1,575. Out-of-state tuition $7,868. **Required Forms and Deadlines:** FAFSA. Priority filing deadline April 1. **Notification of Awards:** Applicants will be notified of awards on or about May 15. **Types of Aid:** *Need-based scholarships/grants:* Pell, SEOG, state scholarships/grants, private scholarships, the school's own gift aid, Federal Nursing. *Loans:* FFEL Subsidized Stafford, FFEL Unsubsidized Stafford, FFEL PLUS, Federal Perkins, state loans, college/university loans from institutional funds. **Student Employment:** Federal Work-Study Program available. Institutional employment available. Off-campus job opportunities are good. **Financial Aid Statistics:** Average income from on-campus job $800. **Financial Aid Phone:** 910-750-3280.

WINTHROP UNIVERSITY

Rock Hill, SC 29733
Phone: 803-323-2191 **E-mail:** admissions@winthrop.edu **CEEB Code:** 5910
Fax: 803-323-2137 **Web:** www.winthrop.edu **ACT Code:** 3884

This public school was founded in 1886. It has a 418-acre campus.

STUDENTS AND FACULTY

Enrollment: 5,056. **Student Body:** Male 30%, female 70%, out-of-state 12%, international 2%. **Ethnic Representation:** African American 27%, Asian 1%, Caucasian 70%, Hispanic 1%. **Retention and Graduation:** 74% freshmen return for sophomore year. 34% freshmen graduate within 4 years. 11% grads go on to further study within 1 year. 25% grads pursue business degrees. 3% grads pursue law degrees. 5% grads pursue medical degrees. **Faculty:** Student/faculty ratio 17:1. 262 full-time faculty, 80% hold PhDs. 98% faculty teach undergrads.

ACADEMICS

Degrees: Bachelor's, master's, post-master's certificate. **Academic Requirements:** General education including some course work in computer literacy, English (including composition), foreign languages, history, humanities, mathematics, sciences (biological or physical), social science. **Classes:** 20-29 students in an average class. 20-29 students in an average lab/discussion section. **Majors with Highest Enrollment:** Curriculum and instruction; biology/biological sciences, general; psychology, general. **Disciplines with Highest Percentage of Degrees Awarded:** Business/marketing 27%, education 24%, visual and performing arts 9%, social sciences and history 9%, psychology 6%. **Special Study Options:** Cooperative (work-study) program, cross registration, distance learning, double major, student exchange program (domestic), honors program, independent study, internships, study abroad, teacher certification program.

FACILITIES

Housing: Coed, all-female, all-male, apartments for married students, apartments for single students, fraternities and/or sororities. **Library Holdings:** 424,681 bound volumes. 1,856 periodicals. 1,209,273 microforms. 2,555 audiovisuals. **Special Academic Facilities/Equipment:** Art gallery, on-campus nursery and kindergarten. **Computers:** *Recommended operating system:* Windows XP. School-owned computers available for student use.

EXTRACURRICULARS

Activities: Choral groups, concert band, dance, drama/theater, jazz band, literary magazine, music ensembles, opera, pep band, radio station, student government, student newspaper, yearbook. **Organizations:** 115 registered organizations, 21 honor societies, 16 religious organizations, 8 fraternities (11% men join), 8 sororities (19% women join). **Athletics (Intercollegiate):** *Men:* baseball, basketball, cheerleading, cross-country, golf, soccer, tennis, track & field. *Women:* basketball, cheerleading, cross-country, golf, soccer, softball, tennis, track & field, volleyball.

ADMISSIONS

Selectivity Rating: 69 (of 100). **Freshman Academic Profile:** Average high school GPA 3.6. 20% in top 10% of high school class, 56% in top 25% of high school class, 89% in top 50% of high school class. Average SAT I Math 529, SAT I Math middle 50% range 470-580. Average SAT I Verbal 526, SAT I Verbal middle 50% range 470-580. Average ACT 22, ACT middle 50% range 19-24. TOEFL required of all international applicants, minimum TOEFL 520. **Basis for Candidate Selection:** *Very important factors considered include:* secondary school record. *Important factors considered include:* class rank, recommendations, standardized test scores. *Other factors considered include:* essays, extracurricular activities, interview, talent/ability, volunteer work, work experience. **Freshman Admission Requirements:** High school diploma or GED is required. *Academic units required/recommended:* 20 total required; 21

total recommended; 4 English required, 4 English recommended, 3 math required, 4 math recommended, 3 science required, 3 science recommended, 3 science lab required, 3 science lab recommended, 2 foreign language required, 2 foreign language recommended, 2 social studies required, 2 social studies recommended, 1 history required, 1 history recommended, 4 elective required, 4 elective recommended. **Freshman Admission Statistics:** 3,600 applied, 72% accepted, 42% of those accepted enrolled. **Transfer Admission Requirements:** *Items required:* college transcript, statement of good standing from prior school. Minimum college GPA of 2.0 required. Lowest grade transferable C. **General Admission Information:** Application fee $35. Nonfall registration accepted. Admission may be deferred for a maximum of 1 year. Credit offered for CEEB Advanced Placement tests.

COSTS AND FINANCIAL AID

In-state tuition $5,600. Out-of-state tuition $10,310. Room & board $4,470. Required fees $20. Average book expense $900. **Required Forms and Deadlines:** FAFSA. Priority filing deadline March 1. **Notification of Awards:** Applicants will be notified of awards on a rolling basis beginning on or about April 1. **Types of Aid:** *Need-based scholarships/grants:* Pell, SEOG, state scholarships/grants, private scholarships, the school's own gift aid. *Loans:* Direct Subsidized Stafford, Direct Unsubsidized Stafford, FFEL PLUS, Federal Perkins, state loans. **Student Employment:** Federal Work-Study Program available. Institutional employment available. Off-campus job opportunities are excellent. **Financial Aid Statistics:** 50% freshmen, 54% undergrads receive some form of aid. Average freshman grant $2,863. Average freshman loan $2,500. Average income from on-campus job $1,358. **Financial Aid Phone:** 803-323-2189.

WISCONSIN LUTHERAN COLLEGE

8800 West Bluemound Road, Milwaukee, WI 53226
Phone: 414-443-8811 **E-mail:** admissions@wlc.edu **CEEB Code:** 1513
Fax: 414-443-8514 **Web:** www.wlc.edu **ACT Code:** 4699

This private school, which is affiliated with the Lutheran Church, was founded in 1973. It has a 19-acre campus.

STUDENTS AND FACULTY

Enrollment: 669. **Student Body:** Male 39%, female 61%, out-of-state 19%, international 1% (4 countries represented). **Ethnic Representation:** African American 2%, Asian 1%, Caucasian 96%, Hispanic 1%. **Retention and Graduation:** 75% freshmen return for sophomore year. 55% freshmen graduate within 4 years. **Faculty:** Student/faculty ratio 11:1. 48 full-time faculty, 64% hold PhDs. 100% faculty teach undergrads.

ACADEMICS

Degrees: Bachelor's. **Academic Requirements:** General education including some course work in arts/fine arts, English (including composition), foreign languages, history, humanities, mathematics, sciences (biological or physical), social science, theology. **Classes:** 10-19 students in an average class. Under 10 students in an average lab/discussion section. **Majors with Highest Enrollment:** Elementary education and teaching; business/managerial economics; English language and literature, general. **Disciplines with Highest Percentage of Degrees Awarded:** Education 16%, visual and performing arts 12%, psychology 12%, business/marketing 11%, communications/communication technologies 10%. **Special Study Options:** Double major, dual enrollment, independent study, internships, student-designed major, study abroad, teacher certification program.

FACILITIES

Housing: All-female, all-male, apartments for single students. **Library Holdings:** 71,731 bound volumes. 614 periodicals. 9,211 microforms. 4,409 audiovisuals. **Computers:** School-owned computers available for student use.

EXTRACURRICULARS

Activities: Choral groups, concert band, dance, drama/theater, jazz band, music ensembles, student government, student newspaper, yearbook. **Organizations:** 31 registered organizations. **Athletics (Intercollegiate):** *Men:* baseball, basketball, cross-country, football, golf, soccer, track & field. *Women:* basketball, cross-country, golf, soccer, softball, tennis, track & field, volleyball.

ADMISSIONS

Selectivity Rating: 77 (of 100). **Freshman Academic Profile:** Average high school GPA 3.4. 24% in top 10% of high school class, 50% in top 25% of high school class, 76% in top 50% of high school class. 34% from public high schools. Average ACT 24, ACT middle 50% range 22-27. TOEFL required of all international applicants, minimum TOEFL 550. **Basis for Candidate Selection:** *Very important factors considered include:* secondary school record, standardized test scores. *Important factors considered include:* class rank, extracurricular activities, recommendations, religious affiliation/commitment. *Other factors considered include:* character/personal qualities, essays, geographical residence, interview, minority status, state residency, talent/ability, volunteer work. **Freshman Admission Requirements:** High school diploma or GED is required. *Academic units required/recommended:* 16 total required; 20 total recommended; 4 English required, 4 English recommended, 3 math required, 4 math recommended, 2 science required, 3 science recommended, 1 science lab required, 2 science lab recommended, 2 foreign language required, 4 foreign language recommended, 2 history required, 2 history recommended, 3 elective required, 3 elective recommended. **Freshman Admission Statistics:** 419 applied, 79% accepted, 49% of those accepted enrolled. **Transfer Admission Requirements:** *Items required:* college transcript, statement of good standing from prior school. Minimum college GPA of 2.5 required. Lowest grade transferable CD. **General Admission Information:** Application fee $20. Nonfall registration accepted. Credit and/or placement offered for CEEB Advanced Placement tests.

COSTS AND FINANCIAL AID

Required fees $126. Average book expense $650. **Required Forms and Deadlines:** FAFSA, institution's own financial aid form and business/farm supplement. No deadline for regular filing. Priority filing deadline March 1. **Notification of Awards:** Applicants will be notified of awards on a rolling basis beginning on or about March 15. **Types of Aid:** *Need-based scholarships/grants:* Pell, SEOG, state scholarships/grants, private scholarships, the school's own gift aid. *Loans:* FFEL Subsidized Stafford, FFEL Unsubsidized Stafford, FFEL PLUS, state loans, private alternative loans. **Student Employment:** Federal Work-Study Program available. Institutional employment available. Off-campus job opportunities are excellent. **Financial Aid Statistics:** 82% freshmen, 75% undergrads receive some form of aid. Average freshman grant $9,441. Average freshman loan $1,971. Average income from on-campus job $1,240. **Financial Aid Phone:** 414-443-8856.

WITTENBERG UNIVERSITY

PO Box 720, Springfield, OH 45501
Phone: 800-677-7558 **E-mail:** admission@wittenberg.edu **CEEB Code:** 1922
Fax: 937-327-6379 **Web:** www.wittenberg.edu **ACT Code:** 3364

This private school, which is affiliated with the Lutheran Church, was founded in 1845. It has a 71-acre campus.

STUDENTS AND FACULTY

Enrollment: 2,320. **Student Body:** Male 43%, female 57%, out-of-state 46%, international 2%. **Ethnic Representation:** African American 8%, Asian 1%, Caucasian 84%, Hispanic 1%. **Retention and Graduation:** 82% freshmen return for sophomore year. 61% freshmen graduate within 4 years. 35% grads go on to further study within 1 year. 8% grads pursue business degrees. 6% grads pursue law degrees. 4% grads pursue medical degrees. **Faculty:** Student/faculty ratio 14:1. 138 full-time faculty, 85% hold PhDs. 100% faculty teach undergrads.

ACADEMICS

Degrees: Bachelor's, master's. **Academic Requirements:** General education including some course work in arts/fine arts, computer literacy, English (including composition), foreign languages, history, humanities, mathematics, philosophy, sciences (biological or physical), social science. **Classes:** 20-29 students in an average class. **Majors with Highest Enrollment:** Business/commerce, general; biological and physical sciences; teacher education, multiple levels. **Disciplines with Highest Percentage of Degrees Awarded:** Social sciences and history 19%, business/marketing 13%, biological life sciences 12%, English 11%, psychology 10%. **Special Study Options:** Accelerated program, cross registration, double major, dual enrollment, student exchange program (domestic), honors program, independent study, internships, liberal arts/career combination, student-designed major, study abroad, teacher certification program.

FACILITIES

Housing: Coed, all-female, all-male, apartments for married students, apartments for single students, fraternities and/or sororities, university-owned houses around campus. **Library Holdings:** 259,678 bound volumes. 1,175 periodicals. 81,619 microforms. 24,032 audiovisuals. **Special Academic Facilities/Equipment:** Language lab, electron microscope, observatory. **Computers:** School-owned computers available for student use.

EXTRACURRICULARS

Activities: Choral groups, concert band, dance, drama/theater, jazz band, literary magazine, music ensembles, musical theater, pep band, radio station, student government, student newspaper, symphony orchestra, yearbook. **Organizations:** 130 registered organizations, 6 honor societies, 10 religious organizations, 6 fraternities (22% men join), 7 sororities (35% women join). **Athletics (Intercollegiate):** *Men:* baseball, basketball, cheerleading, crew, cross-country, diving, football, golf, indoor track, lacrosse, soccer, swimming, tennis, track & field. *Women:* basketball, cheerleading, crew, cross-country, diving, field hockey, golf, indoor track, lacrosse, soccer, softball, swimming, tennis, track & field, volleyball.

ADMISSIONS

Selectivity Rating: 80 (of 100). **Freshman Academic Profile:** Average high school GPA 3.4. 29% in top 10% of high school class, 52% in top 25% of high school class, 74% in top 50% of high school class. 78% from public high schools. Average SAT I Math 582, SAT I Math middle 50% range 478-683. Average SAT I Verbal 576, SAT I Verbal middle 50% range 463-677. Average ACT 26, ACT middle 50% range 24-27. TOEFL required of all international applicants, minimum TOEFL 550. **Basis for Candidate Selection:** *Very important factors considered include:* secondary school record. *Important factors considered include:* alumni/ae relation, character/personal qualities, class rank, essays, extracurricular activities, interview, minority status, recommendations, standardized test scores, talent/ability, volunteer work, work experience. *Other factors considered include:* geographical residence, religious affiliation/commitment, state residency. **Freshman Admission Requirements:** High school diploma or GED is required. *Academic units required/recommended:* 16 total required; 4 English required, 3 math required, 3 science required, 3 foreign language required, 3 social studies required. **Freshman Admission Statistics:** 2,524 applied, 85% accepted, 30% of those accepted enrolled. **Transfer Admission Requirements:** *Items required:* college transcript, statement of good standing from prior school. Minimum college GPA of 2.0 required. Lowest grade transferable C. **General Admission Information:** Application fee $40. Priority application deadline December 1. Early decision application deadline November 15. Regular application deadline March 15. Nonfall registration accepted. Admission may be deferred for a maximum of 1 year. Credit and/or placement offered for CEEB Advanced Placement tests.

COSTS AND FINANCIAL AID

Tuition $24,948. Room & board $6,368. Required fees $150. Average book expense $800. **Required Forms and Deadlines:** FAFSA and institution's own financial aid form. Financial aid filing deadline March 15. Priority filing deadline February 15. **Notification of Awards:** Applicants will be notified of awards on a rolling basis beginning on or about February 15. **Types of Aid:** *Need-based scholarships/grants:* Pell, SEOG, state scholarships/grants, private scholarships, the school's own gift aid. *Loans:* Direct Subsidized Stafford, Direct Unsubsidized Stafford, Direct PLUS, FFEL Subsidized Stafford, FFEL Unsubsidized Stafford, FFEL PLUS, Federal Perkins, state loans, college/university loans from institutional funds. **Student Employment:** Federal Work-Study Program available. Institutional employment available. Off-campus job opportunities are good. **Financial Aid Statistics:** 71% freshmen, 71% undergrads receive some form of aid. Average freshman grant $16,000. Average freshman loan $4,400. Average income from on-campus job $1,500. **Financial Aid Phone:** 800-677-7558.

See page 1296.

WOFFORD COLLEGE

429 North Church Street, Spartanburg, SC 29303-3663
Phone: 864-597-4130 **E-mail:** admissions@wofford.edu **CEEB Code:** 5912
Fax: 864-597-4147 **Web:** www.wofford.edu **ACT Code:** 3886

This private school, which is affiliated with the Methodist Church, was founded in 1854. It has a 155-acre campus.

STUDENTS AND FACULTY

Enrollment: 1,085. **Student Body:** Male 49%, female 51%, out-of-state 34%. **Ethnic Representation:** African American 8%, Asian 2%, Caucasian 89%, Hispanic 1%. **Retention and Graduation:** 87% freshmen return for sophomore year. 70% freshmen graduate within 4 years. 35% grads go on to further study within 1 year. 14% grads pursue business degrees. 9% grads pursue law degrees. 8% grads pursue medical degrees. **Faculty:** Student/faculty ratio 12:1. 80 full-time faculty, 91% hold PhDs. 100% faculty teach undergrads.

ACADEMICS

Degrees: Bachelor's. **Academic Requirements:** General education including some course work in arts/fine arts, computer literacy, English (including composition), foreign languages, history, humanities, mathematics, philosophy, sciences (biological or physical), social science. **Classes:** 10-19 students in an average class. **Majors with Highest Enrollment:** Business/managerial economics; English language and literature, general; biology/biological sciences, general. **Disciplines with Highest Percentage of Degrees Awarded:** Business/marketing 27%, social sciences and history 24%, biological life sciences 13%, English 9%, foreign languages and literature 8%. **Special Study Options:** Accelerated program, cross registration, double major, dual enrollment, independent study, internships, student-designed major, study abroad, teacher certification program, Presidential International Scholar Program, Milliken Research Corporation "summer challenge."

FACILITIES

Housing: Coed, fraternities and/or sororities. **Library Holdings:** 209,084 bound volumes. 551 periodicals. 35,239 microforms. 3,602 audiovisuals. **Special Academic Facilities/Equipment:** Art gallery, Franklin W. Olin Building (teaching technology center), Milliken Science Center. **Computers:** School-owned computers available for student use.

EXTRACURRICULARS

Activities: Choral groups, concert band, drama/theater, literary magazine, music ensembles, pep band, student government, student newspaper, yearbook. **Organizations:** 80 registered organizations, 10 honor societies, 8 religious organizations, 8 fraternities (54% men join), 4 sororities (61% women join). **Athletics (Intercollegiate):** *Men:* baseball, basketball, cross-country, football, golf, indoor track, soccer, tennis, track & field. *Women:* basketball, cross-country, golf, indoor track, soccer, tennis, track & field, volleyball.

ADMISSIONS

Selectivity Rating: 81 (of 100). **Freshman Academic Profile:** Average high school GPA 3.9. 53% in top 10% of high school class, 79% in top 25% of high school class, 97% in top 50% of high school class. 73% from public high schools. Average SAT I Math 624, SAT I Math middle 50% range 580-670. Average SAT I Verbal 612, SAT I Verbal middle 50% range 560-660. Average ACT 25, ACT middle 50% range 22-27. TOEFL required of all international applicants, minimum TOEFL 550. **Basis for Candidate Selection:** *Very important factors considered include:* secondary school record. *Important factors considered include:* character/personal qualities, class rank, essays, extracurricular activities, standardized test scores, talent/ability, volunteer work. *Other factors considered include:* alumni/ae relation, geographical residence, interview, minority status, recommendations, state residency, work experience. **Freshman Admission Requirements:** High school diploma or GED is required. *Academic units required/recommended:* 17 total recommended; 4 English recommended, 4 math recommended, 3 science lab recommended, 3 foreign language recommended, 2 social studies recommended, 1 elective recommended. **Freshman Admission Statistics:** 1,349 applied, 78% accepted, 28% of those accepted enrolled. **Transfer Admission Requirements:** *Items required:* high school transcript, college transcript, essay, statement of good standing from prior school. Minimum high school GPA of 3.0 required. Minimum college GPA of 2.5 required. Lowest grade transferable C. **General Admission Information:** Application fee $40. Early decision application deadline November 15. Regular application deadline February 1. Nonfall registration accepted. Admission may be deferred for a maximum of 1 year. Credit and/or placement offered for CEEB Advanced Placement tests.

COSTS AND FINANCIAL AID

Tuition $18,645. Room & board $5,780. Required fees $770. Average book expense $851. **Required Forms and Deadlines:** FAFSA. Priority filing deadline March 15. **Notification of Awards:** Applicants will be notified of awards on a rolling basis beginning on or about March 25. **Types of Aid:** *Need-based scholarships/grants:* Pell, SEOG, state scholarships/grants, private scholarships, the school's own gift aid. *Loans:* FFEL Subsidized Stafford, FFEL Unsubsidized Stafford, FFEL PLUS, Federal Perkins, state loans. **Student Employment:** Federal Work-Study Program available. Institutional employment available. Off-campus job opportunities are excellent. **Financial Aid Statistics:** 55% freshmen, 54% undergrads receive some form of aid. Average income from on-campus job $750. **Financial Aid Phone:** 864-597-4160.

WOODBURY UNIVERSITY

7500 Glenoaks Boulevard, Burbank, CA 91510-7846
Phone: 818-767-0888 **E-mail:** info@woodbury.edu **CEEB Code:** 4955
Fax: 818-767-7520 **Web:** www.woodbury.edu **ACT Code:** 481

This private school was founded in 1884. It has a 22-acre campus.

STUDENTS AND FACULTY

Enrollment: 1,182. **Student Body:** Male 42%, female 58%, out-of-state 10%, international 8% (25 countries represented). **Ethnic Representation:** African American 8%, Asian 15%, Caucasian 41%, Hispanic 35%. **Retention and Graduation:** 74% freshmen return for sophomore year. 31% freshmen graduate within 4 years. **Faculty:** Student/faculty ratio 11:1. 41 full-time faculty, 87% hold PhDs. 100% faculty teach undergrads.

ACADEMICS

Degrees: Bachelor's, master's. **Academic Requirements:** General education including some course work in arts/fine arts, computer literacy, English (including composition), history, humanities, mathematics, philosophy, sciences (biological or physical), social science. **Classes:** 10-19 students in an average class. **Majors with Highest Enrollment:** Business/managerial operations; architecture (BArch, BA/BS, MArch, MA/MS, PhD); graphic design. **Disciplines with Highest Percentage of Degrees Awarded:** Business/marketing 49%, architecture 22%, visual and performing arts 20%, computer and information sciences 5%, psychology 3%. **Special Study Options:** Accelerated program, double major, independent study, internships, liberal arts/career combination, student-designed major, study abroad, weekend college.

FACILITIES

Housing: Coed, off-campus overflow apartments. **Library Holdings:** 58,902 bound volumes. 6,344 periodicals. 92,433 microforms. 17,663 audiovisuals. **Special Academic Facilities/Equipment:** Art gallery; architecture gallery. **Computers:** School-owned computers available for student use.

EXTRACURRICULARS

Activities: Literary magazine, student government, student newspaper, yearbook. **Organizations:** 20 registered organizations, 3 honor societies, 1 religious organization, 2 fraternities (1% men join), 2 sororities (1% women join).

ADMISSIONS

Selectivity Rating: 69 (of 100). **Freshman Academic Profile:** Average high school GPA 3.3. 5% in top 10% of high school class, 45% in top 25% of high school class, 92% in top 50% of high school class. 75% from public high schools. Average SAT I Math 515, SAT I Math middle 50% range 435-550. Average SAT I Verbal 466, SAT I Verbal middle 50% range 415-500. Average ACT 21. TOEFL required of all international applicants, minimum TOEFL 500. **Basis for Candidate Selection:** *Very important factors considered include:* secondary school record, standardized test scores, talent/ability. *Important factors considered include:* character/personal qualities, class rank, extracurricular activities. *Other factors considered include:* essays, interview, recommendations. **Freshman Admission Requirements:** High school diploma or GED is required. *Academic units required/recommended:* 4 English recommended, 3 math recommended, 1 science recommended, 3 foreign language recommended, 2 social studies recommended. **Freshman Admission Statistics:** 505 applied, 80% accepted, 32% of those accepted enrolled. **Transfer Admission Requirements:** *Items required:* college transcript. Minimum college GPA of 2.5 required. Lowest grade transferable C. **General Admission Information:** Application fee $35. Nonfall registration accepted. Admission may be deferred for a maximum of 2 years. Credit offered for CEEB Advanced Placement tests.

COSTS AND FINANCIAL AID

Tuition $19,114. Room & board $6,874. Required fees $70. Average book expense $810. **Required Forms and Deadlines:** FAFSA and institution's own financial aid form. No deadline for regular filing. Priority filing deadline March 2. **Notification of Awards:** Applicants will be notified of awards on a rolling basis beginning on or about March 15. **Types of Aid:** *Need-based scholarships/grants:* Pell, SEOG, state scholarships/grants, private scholarships, the school's own gift aid. *Loans:* FFEL Subsidized Stafford, FFEL Unsubsidized Stafford, FFEL PLUS, Federal Perkins, college/university loans from institutional funds, alternative private loans. **Student Employment:** Federal Work-Study Program available. Institutional employment available. Off-campus job opportunities are excellent. **Financial Aid Statistics:** 70% freshmen, 75% undergrads receive some form of aid. Average freshman grant $6,038. Average freshman loan $2,625. Average income from on-campus job $2,000. **Financial Aid Phone:** 818-767-0888.

WORCESTER POLYTECHNIC INSTITUTE

100 Institute Road, Worcester, MA 01609
Phone: 508-831-5286 **E-mail:** admissions@wpi.edu **CEEB Code:** 3969
Fax: 508-831-5875 **Web:** www.wpi.edu **ACT Code:** 1942

This private school was founded in 1865. It has an 80-acre campus.

STUDENTS AND FACULTY

Enrollment: 2,767. **Student Body:** Male 77%, female 23%, out-of-state 48%, international 5% (68 countries represented). **Ethnic Representation:** African American 1%, Asian 7%, Caucasian 85%, Hispanic 3%. **Retention and Graduation:** 91% freshmen return for sophomore year. 59% freshmen graduate within 4 years. **Faculty:** Student/faculty ratio 12:1. 237 full-time faculty, 96% hold PhDs. 100% faculty teach undergrads.

ACADEMICS

Degrees: Bachelor's, doctoral, master's. **Academic Requirements:** General education including some course work in humanities, mathematics, sciences (biological or physical), social science. **Classes:** Under 10 students in an average class. 20-29 students in an average lab/discussion section. **Majors with Highest Enrollment:** Mechanical engineering; electrical, electronics, and communications engineering; computer science. **Disciplines with Highest Percentage of Degrees Awarded:** Engineering/engineering technology 54%, computer and information sciences 18%, biological life sciences 12%, business/marketing 7%, physical sciences 4%. **Special Study Options:** Accelerated program, cooperative (work-study) program, cross registration, double major, dual enrollment, English as a second language, student exchange program (domestic), independent study, internships, liberal arts/career combination, student-designed major, study abroad, teacher certification program.

FACILITIES

Housing: Coed, apartments for single students, housing for international students, fraternities and/or sororities, quiet floors, healthy alternatives. **Library Holdings:** 146,372 bound volumes. 982 periodicals. 109,648 microforms. 2,500 audiovisuals. **Special Academic Facilities/Equipment:** Several off-campus project centers, TV studio, robotics lab, CAD-CAM lab, laser labs, electron microscopes, wind tunnel, manufacturing engineering applications center, VLSI design lab, nuclear reactor. **Computers:** School-owned computers available for student use.

EXTRACURRICULARS

Activities: Choral groups, concert band, dance, drama/theater, jazz band, literary magazine, music ensembles, musical theater, radio station, student government, student newspaper, symphony orchestra, yearbook. **Organizations:** 112 registered organizations, 13 honor societies, 4 religious organizations, 12 fraternities (35% men join), 2 sororities (25% women join). **Athletics (Intercollegiate):** *Men:* baseball, basketball, crew, cross-country, diving, football, golf, ice hockey, soccer, swimming, tennis, track & field, wrestling. *Women:* basketball, crew, cross-country, diving, field hockey, soccer, softball, swimming, tennis, track & field, volleyball.

ADMISSIONS

Selectivity Rating: 86 (of 100). **Freshman Academic Profile:** Average high school GPA 3.4. 47% in top 10% of high school class, 82% in top 25% of high school class, 98% in top 50% of high school class. 79% from public high schools. Average SAT I Math 660, SAT I Math middle 50% range 610-710. Average SAT I Verbal 620, SAT I Verbal middle 50% range 540-660. TOEFL required of all international applicants, minimum TOEFL 550. **Basis for Candidate Selection:** *Very important factors considered include:* class rank, secondary school record, standardized test scores. *Important factors considered include:* essays, extracurricular activities, minority status, recommendations. *Other factors considered include:* alumni/ae relation, character/personal qualities, geographical residence, interview, state residency, talent/ability, volunteer work, work experience. **Freshman Admission Requirements:** High school diploma is required and GED is not accepted. *Academic units required/recommended:* 10 total required; 4 English recommended, 4 math required, 2 science required, 2 science lab required. **Freshman Admission Statistics:** 3,191 applied, 76% accepted, 29% of those accepted enrolled. **Transfer Admission Requirements:** *Items required:* high school transcript, college transcript, essay, statement of good standing from prior school. Minimum college GPA of 2.8 required. Lowest grade transferable C. **General Admission Information:** Application fee $60. Early decision application deadline November 15. Regular application deadline February 1. Nonfall registration accepted. Admission may be deferred for a maximum of 2 years. Credit offered for CEEB Advanced Placement tests.

COSTS AND FINANCIAL AID

Tuition $27,720. Room & board $8,900. Required fees $170. Average book expense $690. **Required Forms and Deadlines:** FAFSA, CSS/Financial Aid PROFILE, noncustodial (divorced/separated) parent's statement and parent's and student's prior year federal tax return and W-2s. Financial aid filing deadline March 1. Priority filing deadline March 1. **Notification of Awards:** Applicants will be notified of awards on or about April 1. **Types of Aid:** *Need-based scholarships/grants:* Pell, SEOG, state scholarships/grants, the school's own gift aid. *Loans:* FFEL Subsidized Stafford, FFEL Unsubsidized Stafford, FFEL PLUS, Federal Perkins, state loans, college/university loans from institutional funds. **Student Employment:** Federal Work-Study Program available. Institutional employment available. Off-campus job opportunities are good. **Financial Aid Statistics:** 77% freshmen, 51% undergrads receive some form of aid. Average freshman grant $12,121. Average freshman loan $4,620. **Financial Aid Phone:** 508-831-5469.

WORCESTER STATE COLLEGE

486 Chandler Street, Department of Admissions, Worcester, MA 01602-2597
Phone: 508-929-8040 **E-mail:** admissions@worcester.edu **CEEB Code:** 3524
Fax: 508-929-8183 **Web:** www.worcester.edu **ACT Code:** 1914

This public school was founded in 1874. It has a 53-acre campus.

STUDENTS AND FACULTY

Enrollment: 4,465. **Student Body:** Male 37%, female 63%, out-of-state 5%, international 2%. **Ethnic Representation:** African American 4%, Asian 3%, Caucasian 84%, Hispanic 3%, Native American 1%. **Retention and Graduation:** 75% freshmen return for sophomore year. 17% freshmen graduate within 4 years. **Faculty:** Student/faculty ratio 16:1. 168 full-time faculty, 69% hold PhDs. 100% faculty teach undergrads.

ACADEMICS

Degrees: Bachelor's, master's, post-bachelor's certificate. **Academic Requirements:** General education including some course work in arts/fine arts, English (including composition), history, humanities, mathematics, philosophy, sciences (biological or physical), social science, health studies. **Disciplines with Highest Percentage of Degrees Awarded:** Health professions and related sciences 27%, psychology 14%, education 10%, social sciences and history 10%. **Special Study Options:** Accelerated program, cross registration, double major, dual enrollment, student exchange program (domestic), honors program, independent study, internships, study abroad, teacher certification program. Off-campus studies: College Academic Program Sharing (CAPS) with the other eight Massachusetts state schools; students may spend a year at another school to take the special program; there is a special Washington, DC, experience for one semester; student exchange programs with universities in China, England, Puerto Rico, Costa Rica.

FACILITIES

Housing: All-female, all-male, housing for disabled students, housing for international students. **Library Holdings:** 143,887 bound volumes. 1,137 periodicals. 15,149 microforms. 11,963 audiovisuals. **Special Academic Facilities/Equipment:** Language lab, learning resources center, speech and hearing clinic. **Computers:** *Recommended operating system:* Windows 98. School-owned computers available for student use.

EXTRACURRICULARS

Activities: Choral groups, concert band, jazz band, radio station, student government, student newspaper, television station, yearbook. **Organizations:** 44 registered organizations, 15 honor societies, 3 religious organizations. **Athletics (Intercollegiate):** *Men:* baseball, basketball, crew, cross-country, football, golf, ice hockey, rugby, soccer, tennis, track & field, volleyball. *Women:* basketball, crew, cross-country, equestrian, field hockey, soccer, softball, tennis, track & field, volleyball.

ADMISSIONS

Selectivity Rating: 60 (of 100). **Freshman Academic Profile:** Average high school GPA 2.9. TOEFL required of all international applicants, minimum TOEFL 550. **Basis for Candidate Selection:** *Very important factors considered include:* secondary school record, standardized test scores. *Important factors considered include:* class rank. *Other factors considered include:* essays, extracurricular activities, interview, minority status, recommendations, talent/ability, volunteer work, work experience. **Freshman Admission Requirements:** High school diploma is required and GED is not accepted. *Academic units required/recommended:* 16 total required; 4 English required, 3 math required, 3 science required, 2 science lab required, 2 foreign language required, 2 social studies required, 2 elective required. **Freshman Admission Statistics:** 2,451 applied, 52% accepted, 36% of those accepted enrolled. **Transfer Admission Requirements:** *Items required:* high school transcript, college transcript, statement of good standing from prior school. Minimum high school GPA of 2.9 required. Minimum college GPA of 2.5 required. Lowest grade transferable C-. **General Admission Information:** Application fee $10. Priority application deadline June 1. Regular application deadline August 1. Nonfall registration accepted. Admission may be deferred for a maximum of 1 year. Credit and/or placement offered for CEEB Advanced Placement tests.

COSTS AND FINANCIAL AID

In-state tuition $1,090. Out-of-state tuition $7,050. Room & board $4,484. Required fees $1,368. Average book expense $648. **Required Forms and Deadlines:** FAFSA and institution's own financial aid form. No deadline for regular filing. Priority filing deadline March 1. **Notification of Awards:** Applicants will be notified of awards on a rolling basis. **Types of Aid:** *Need-based scholarships/grants:* Pell, SEOG, state scholarships/grants, private scholarships, the school's own gift aid. *Loans:* FFEL Subsidized Stafford, FFEL Unsubsidized Stafford, FFEL PLUS, Federal Perkins, state loans. **Student Employment:** Federal Work-Study Program available. Institutional employment available. Off-campus job opportunities are excellent. **Financial Aid Statistics:** Average freshman grant $1,170. Average freshman loan $1,916. Average income from on-campus job $191. **Financial Aid Phone:** 508-793-8056.

WRIGHT STATE UNIVERSITY

3640 Colonel Glenn Highway, Dayton, OH 45435
Phone: 937-775-5700 **E-mail:** admissions@wright.edu **CEEB Code:** 1179
Fax: 937-775-5795 **Web:** www.wright.edu **ACT Code:** 3295

This public school was founded in 1964. It has a 557-acre campus.

STUDENTS AND FACULTY

Enrollment: 12,531. **Student Body:** Male 43%, female 57%, out-of-state 3%, international 1% (69 countries represented). **Ethnic Representation:** African American 11%, Asian 2%, Caucasian 81%, Hispanic 1%. **Retention and Graduation:** 71% freshmen return for sophomore year. 12% freshmen graduate within 4 years. **Faculty:** Student/faculty ratio 20:1. 512 full-time faculty. 87% faculty teach undergrads.

ACADEMICS

Degrees: Associate's, bachelor's, certificate, doctoral, first professional, master's, post-master's certificate, terminal, transfer. **Academic Requirements:** General education including some course work in arts/fine arts, English (including composition), history, humanities, mathematics, sciences (biological or physical), social science. **Classes:** 20-29 students in an average class. Under 10 students in an average lab/discussion section. **Disciplines with Highest Percentage of Degrees Awarded:** Business/marketing 25%, education 19%, social sciences and history 9%, health professions and related sciences 8%, engineering/engineering technology 7%. **Special Study Options:** Cooperative (work-study) program, cross registration, distance learning, double major, English as a second language, honors program, independent study, internships, student-designed major, study abroad, teacher certification program.

FACILITIES

Housing: Coed, apartments for married students, apartments for single students, housing for disabled students, fraternities and/or sororities, honors dorm. **Library Holdings:** 491,339 bound volumes. 5,564 periodicals. 1,324,705 microforms. 13,812 audiovisuals. **Special Academic Facilities/Equipment:** Art gallery located in the Creative Arts Center. **Computers:** School-owned computers available for student use.

EXTRACURRICULARS

Activities: Choral groups, concert band, dance, drama/theater, jazz band, literary magazine, marching band, music ensembles, musical theater, opera, pep band, radio station, student government, student newspaper, symphony orchestra, television station. **Organizations:** 160 registered organizations, 21 honor societies, 3 religious organizations, 11 fraternities, 7 sororities. **Athletics (Intercollegiate):** *Men:* baseball, basketball, cheerleading, cross-country, diving, golf, soccer, swimming, tennis. *Women:* basketball, cheerleading, cross-country, diving, soccer, softball, swimming, tennis, track & field, volleyball.

ADMISSIONS

Selectivity Rating: 68 (of 100). **Freshman Academic Profile:** Average high school GPA 3.0. 15% in top 10% of high school class, 34% in top 25% of high

school class, 66% in top 50% of high school class. 85% from public high schools. Average SAT I Math 506, SAT I Math middle 50% range 450-580. Average SAT I Verbal 515, SAT I Verbal middle 50% range 450-580. Average ACT 21, ACT middle 50% range 19-25. TOEFL required of all international applicants, minimum TOEFL 500. **Basis for Candidate Selection:** *Very important factors considered include:* secondary school record, standardized test scores. *Important factors considered include:* class rank. *Other factors considered include:* recommendations, state residency. **Freshman Admission Requirements:** High school diploma or GED is required. *Academic units required/ recommended:* 15 total required; 4 English required, 3 math required, 3 science required, 3 science lab required, 2 foreign language required, 3 social studies required. **Freshman Admission Statistics:** 4,884 applied, 92% accepted, 53% of those accepted enrolled. **Transfer Admission Requirements:** *Items required:* college transcript. Minimum high school GPA of 2.0 required. Minimum college GPA of 2.0 required. Lowest grade transferable C. **General Admission Information:** Application fee $30. Nonfall registration accepted. Admission may be deferred. Credit and/or placement offered for CEEB Advanced Placement tests.

COSTS AND FINANCIAL AID

Average book expense $900. **Required Forms and Deadlines:** FAFSA. No deadline for regular filing. Priority filing deadline March 2. **Notification of Awards:** Applicants will be notified of awards on a rolling basis beginning on or about April 2. **Types of Aid:** *Need-based scholarships/grants:* Pell, SEOG, state scholarships/grants, private scholarships, the school's own gift aid, United Negro College Fund, Federal Nursing. *Loans:* FFEL Subsidized Stafford, FFEL Unsubsidized Stafford, FFEL PLUS, Federal Perkins, Federal Nursing, state loans, college/university loans from institutional funds. **Student Employment:** Federal Work-Study Program available. Institutional employment available. Off-campus job opportunities are excellent. **Financial Aid Statistics:** 55% freshmen, 63% undergrads receive some form of aid. Average income from on-campus job $1,900. **Financial Aid Phone:** 937-775-5721.

XAVIER UNIVERSITY (OH)

3800 Victory Parkway, Cincinnati, OH 45207-5311
Phone: 513-745-3301 **E-mail:** xuadmit@xavier.edu **CEEB Code:** 1965
Fax: 513-745-4319 **Web:** www.xavier.edu **ACT Code:** 3366

This private school, which is affiliated with the Roman Catholic Church, was founded in 1831. It has a 125-acre campus.

STUDENTS AND FACULTY

Enrollment: 3,942. **Student Body:** Male 42%, female 58%, out-of-state 34%, international 1%. **Ethnic Representation:** African American 10%, Asian 2%, Caucasian 86%, Hispanic 1%. **Retention and Graduation:** 90% freshmen return for sophomore year. 59% freshmen graduate within 4 years. 20% grads go on to further study within 1 year. **Faculty:** Student/faculty ratio 13:1. 268 full-time faculty, 80% hold PhDs. 98% faculty teach undergrads.

ACADEMICS

Degrees: Associate's, bachelor's, certificate, doctoral, master's, post-bachelor's certificate, post-master's certificate. **Academic Requirements:** General education including some course work in arts/fine arts, English (including composition), foreign languages, history, mathematics, philosophy, sciences (biological or physical), social science, theology, ethics, cultural diversity. **Classes:** 10-19 students in an average class. 10-19 students in an average lab/ discussion section. **Majors with Highest Enrollment:** Business/commerce, general; education, general; liberal arts and sciences/liberal studies. **Disciplines with Highest Percentage of Degrees Awarded:** Business/marketing 26%, liberal arts/general studies 16%, communications/communication technologies 10%, education 7%, social sciences and history 6%. **Special Study Options:** Cooperative (work-study) program, cross registration, double major, dual enrollment, English as a second language, honors program, independent study, internships, study abroad, teacher certification program, weekend college, Service Learning Semester.

FACILITIES

Housing: Coed, apartments for single students, housing for disabled students, special-interest housing. **Library Holdings:** 191,923 bound volumes. 1,633 periodicals. 716,740 microforms. 8,371 audiovisuals. **Special Academic Facilities/Equipment:** Student-run art gallery, Montessori Lab School. **Computers:** School-owned computers available for student use.

EXTRACURRICULARS

Activities: Choral groups, concert band, dance, drama/theater, jazz band, literary magazine, music ensembles, musical theater, pep band, radio station, student government, student newspaper, television station, yearbook. **Organizations:** 88 registered organizations. **Athletics (Intercollegiate):** *Men:* baseball, basketball, cross-country, golf, rifle, soccer, swimming, tennis. *Women:* basketball, cross-country, golf, rifle, soccer, swimming, tennis, volleyball.

ADMISSIONS

Selectivity Rating: 75 (of 100). **Freshman Academic Profile:** Average high school GPA 3.5. 31% in top 10% of high school class, 61% in top 25% of high school class, 88% in top 50% of high school class. 45% from public high schools. Average SAT I Math 583, SAT I Math middle 50% range 520-640. Average SAT I Verbal 576, SAT I Verbal middle 50% range 520-630. Average ACT 25, ACT middle 50% range 22-28. TOEFL required of all international applicants, minimum TOEFL 500. **Basis for Candidate Selection:** *Very important factors considered include:* secondary school record. *Important factors considered include:* character/personal qualities, class rank, essays, recommendations, standardized test scores. *Other factors considered include:* alumni/ae relation, extracurricular activities, talent/ability, volunteer work, work experience. **Freshman Admission Requirements:** High school diploma or GED is required. *Academic units required/recommended:* 21 total recommended; 4 English recommended, 3 math recommended, 3 science recommended, 2 foreign language recommended, 3 social studies recommended, 5 elective recommended. **Freshman Admission Statistics:** 3,514 applied, 83% accepted, 26% of those accepted enrolled. **Transfer Admission Requirements:** *Items required:* high school transcript, college transcript, statement of good standing from prior school. Minimum college GPA of 2.0 required. Lowest grade transferable C. **General Admission Information:** Application fee $30. Regular application deadline February 1. Nonfall registration accepted. Admission may be deferred for a maximum of 1 year. Credit and/or placement offered for CEEB Advanced Placement tests.

COSTS AND FINANCIAL AID

Required Forms and Deadlines: FAFSA. Priority filing deadline February 15. **Notification of Awards:** Applicants will be notified of awards on a rolling basis beginning on or about March 1. **Types of Aid:** *Need-based scholarships/ grants:* Pell, SEOG, state scholarships/grants, private scholarships, the school's own gift aid. *Loans:* FFEL Subsidized Stafford, FFEL Unsubsidized Stafford, FFEL PLUS, Federal Perkins. **Student Employment:** Federal Work-Study Program available. Institutional employment available. Off-campus job opportunities are excellent. **Financial Aid Statistics:** 57% freshmen, 47% undergrads receive some form of aid. **Financial Aid Phone:** 513-745-3142.

XAVIER UNIVERSITY OF LOUISIANA

One Drexel Drive, Att: Admissions Office, New Orleans, LA 70135-1098
Phone: 504-483-7388 **E-mail:** apply@xula.edu **CEEB Code:** 6975
Fax: 504-485-7941 **Web:** www.xula.edu **ACT Code:** 1618

This private school, which is affiliated with the Roman Catholic Church, was founded in 1915. It has a 29-acre campus.

STUDENTS AND FACULTY

Enrollment: 3,184. **Student Body:** Male 26%, female 74%, out-of-state 52%, international 2%. **Ethnic Representation:** African American 89%, Asian 3%, Caucasian 1%. **Retention and Graduation:** 78% freshmen return for sophomore year. 48% grads go on to further study within 1 year. **Faculty:** Student/faculty ratio 16:1. 226 full-time faculty, 90% hold PhDs. 98% faculty teach undergrads.

ACADEMICS

Degrees: Bachelor's, first professional, master's, post-master's certificate. **Academic Requirements:** General education including some course work in arts/fine arts, English (including composition), foreign languages, history, humanities, mathematics, philosophy, sciences (biological or physical), social science, African American studies. **Majors with Highest Enrollment:** Pharmacy (PharmD, BS/BPharm); business administration/management; biology/biological sciences, general. **Disciplines with Highest Percentage of Degrees Awarded:** Biological life sciences 45%, physical sciences 13%, psychology 12%, business/marketing 7%, communications/communication technologies 6%. **Special Study Options:** Accelerated program, cooperative (work-study) program, cross registration, double major, dual enrollment, student exchange program (domestic), honors program, internships, study abroad, teacher certification program.

FACILITIES

Housing: Coed, all-female, all-male. **Library Holdings:** 157,436 bound volumes. 1,868 periodicals. 755,596 microforms. 5,093 audiovisuals. **Computers:** School-owned computers available for student use.

EXTRACURRICULARS

Activities: Choral groups, concert band, dance, jazz band, literary magazine, music ensembles, opera, student government, student newspaper, symphony orchestra, television station, yearbook. **Organizations:** 88 registered organizations, 8 honor societies, 1 religious organization, 4 fraternities (2% men join), 4 sororities (6% women join). **Athletics (Intercollegiate):** *Men:* basketball, cross-country, tennis. *Women:* basketball, cross-country, tennis.

ADMISSIONS

Selectivity Rating: 72 (of 100). **Freshman Academic Profile:** Average high school GPA 3.0. 30% in top 10% of high school class, 55% in top 25% of high school class, 80% in top 50% of high school class. 84% from public high schools. Average SAT I Math 493, SAT I Math middle 50% range 430-550. Average SAT I Verbal 508, SAT I Verbal middle 50% range 440-540. Average ACT 21, ACT middle 50% range 18-23. TOEFL required of all international applicants, minimum TOEFL 550. **Basis for Candidate Selection:** *Very important factors considered include:* recommendations, secondary school record, standardized test scores. *Important factors considered include:* class rank. *Other factors considered include:* alumni/ae relation, character/personal qualities, essays, extracurricular activities, interview, minority status, talent/ability, volunteer work, work experience. **Freshman Admission Requirements:** High school diploma or GED is required. *Academic units required/recommended:* 4 English required, 2 math required, 4 math recommended, 1 science required, 3 science recommended, 1 foreign language recommended, 1 social studies required, 2 social studies recommended, 1 history recommended, 8 elective required. **Freshman Admission Statistics:** 3,862 applied, 87% accepted. **Transfer Admission Requirements:** *Items required:* college transcript. Lowest grade transferable C. **General Admission Information:** Application fee $25. Priority application deadline March 1. Regular application deadline July 1. Nonfall registration accepted. Credit and/or placement offered for CEEB Advanced Placement tests.

COSTS AND FINANCIAL AID

Tuition $10,000. Room & board $6,000. Required fees $900. Average book expense $1,000. **Required Forms and Deadlines:** FAFSA. Priority filing deadline January 1. **Notification of Awards:** Applicants will be notified of awards on a rolling basis beginning on or about April 1. **Types of Aid:** *Need-based scholarships/grants:* Pell, SEOG, state scholarships/grants, private scholarships, the school's own gift aid, United Negro College Fund. *Loans:* Direct Subsidized Stafford, Direct Unsubsidized Stafford, Direct PLUS, FFEL Subsidized Stafford, FFEL Unsubsidized Stafford, FFEL PLUS, Federal Perkins. **Student Employment:** Federal Work-Study Program available. Institutional employment available. Off-campus job opportunities are good. **Financial Aid Statistics:** 84% freshmen, 79% undergrads receive some form of aid. Average freshman grant $3,228. Average freshman loan $3,965. Average income from on-campus job $1,000. **Financial Aid Phone:** 504-483-7517.

YALE UNIVERSITY

PO Box 208234, New Haven, CT 06520-8234
Phone: 203-432-9300 **E-mail:** undergraduate.admissions@yale.edu **CEEB Code:** 3987
Fax: 203-432-9392 **Web:** www.yale.edu **ACT Code:** 618

This private school was founded in 1701. It has a 260-acre campus.

STUDENTS AND FACULTY

Enrollment: 5,286. **Student Body:** Male 51%, female 49%, out-of-state 92%, international 7%. **Ethnic Representation:** African American 8%, Asian 15%, Caucasian 56%, Hispanic 6%, Native American 1%. **Retention and Graduation:** 98% freshmen return for sophomore year. 28% grads go on to further study within 1 year. 7% grads pursue law degrees. 11% grads pursue medical degrees. **Faculty:** Student/faculty ratio 7:1. 994 full-time faculty, 88% hold PhDs.

ACADEMICS

Degrees: Bachelor's, doctoral, first professional, master's, post-master's certificate. **Academic Requirements:** General education including some course work in foreign languages, humanities, sciences (biological or physical), social science. **Classes:** 10-19 students in an average class. **Disciplines with Highest Percentage of Degrees Awarded:** Social sciences and history 42%, biological life sciences 10%, English 8%, visual and performing arts 7%, area and ethnic studies 7%. **Special Study Options:** Accelerated program, double major, English as a second language, student exchange program (domestic), honors program, independent study, liberal arts/career combination, student-designed major, study abroad, teacher certification program.

FACILITIES

Housing: Coed, housing for disabled students. Students are randomly assigned to 1 of 12 residential colleges where they live, eat, socialize, and pursue various academic and extracurricular activities. All undergraduate housing is provided through residential college system. **Library Holdings:** 10,500,000 bound volumes. 63,656 periodicals. 6,000,000 microforms. 2,900,000 audiovisuals. **Special Academic Facilities/Equipment:** Art and history museums, observatory, electron microscopes, nuclear accelerators, center for international and area studies, child study center, marsh botanical gardens, center for parallel supercomputing. **Computers:** School-owned computers available for student use.

EXTRACURRICULARS

Activities: Choral groups, concert band, dance, drama/theater, jazz band, literary magazine, marching band, music ensembles, musical theater, opera, pep band, radio station, student government, student newspaper, student-run film society, symphony orchestra, yearbook. **Organizations:** 200 registered organizations. **Athletics (Intercollegiate):** *Men:* baseball, basketball, crew, cross-country, diving, fencing, football, golf, ice hockey, indoor track, lacrosse, soccer, squash, swimming, tennis, track & field. *Women:* basketball, crew, cross-country, diving, fencing, field hockey, golf, gymnastics, ice hockey, indoor track, lacrosse, soccer, softball, squash, swimming, tennis, track & field, volleyball.

ADMISSIONS

Selectivity Rating: 99 (of 100). **Freshman Academic Profile:** 95% in top 10% of high school class, 99% in top 25% of high school class, 100% in top 50% of high school class. 53% from public high schools. SAT I Math middle 50% range 680-770. SAT I Verbal middle 50% range 680-770. ACT middle 50% range 28-33. TOEFL required of all international applicants, minimum TOEFL 600. **Basis for Candidate Selection:** *Very important factors considered include:* character/personal qualities, class rank, essays, extracurricular activities, recommendations, secondary school record, standardized test scores, talent/ability. *Other factors considered include:* alumni/ae relation, geographical residence, interview, minority status, state residency, volunteer work, work experience. **Freshman Admission Requirements:** High school diploma or equivalent is not required. **Freshman Admission Statistics:** 14,809 applied, 14% accepted, 64% of those accepted enrolled. **Transfer Admission Requirements:** *Items required:* high school transcript, college transcript, essay, standardized test score, statement of good standing from prior school. **General Admission Information:** Application fee $65. Early decision application deadline November 1. Regular application deadline December 31. Admission may be deferred for a maximum of 1 year. Placement offered for CEEB Advanced Placement tests.

COSTS AND FINANCIAL AID

Tuition $26,100. Room & board $7,930. Required fees $0. Average book expense $2,370. **Required Forms and Deadlines:** FAFSA, CSS/Financial Aid PROFILE, state aid form, noncustodial (divorced/separated) parent's statement, business/farm supplement, and tax returns. Financial aid filing deadline February 1. Priority filing deadline February 1. **Notification of Awards:** Applicants will be notified of awards on or about April 1. **Types of Aid:** *Need-based scholarships/grants:* Pell, SEOG, state scholarships/grants, private scholarships, the school's own gift aid, United Negro College Fund. *Loans:* FFEL Subsidized Stafford, FFEL Unsubsidized Stafford, FFEL PLUS, Federal Perkins, state loans, college/university loans from institutional funds. **Student Employment:** Federal Work-Study Program available. Institutional employment available. Off-campus job opportunities are good. **Financial Aid Statistics:** 42% freshmen, 39% undergrads receive some form of aid. **Financial Aid Phone:** 203-432-0360.

YESHIVA UNIVERSITY

500 West 185th Street, New York, NY 10033-3299
Phone: 212-960-5277 **E-mail:** yuadmit@yu.edu **CEEB Code:** 2990
Fax: 212-960-0086 **Web:** www.yu.edu **ACT Code:** 2992

This private school was founded in 1886. It has a 12-acre campus.

STUDENTS AND FACULTY

Enrollment: 2,820. **Student Body:** Male 56%, female 44%, out-of-state 55%, international 3% (53 countries represented). **Ethnic Representation:** Caucasian 100%. **Retention and Graduation:** 85% freshmen return for sophomore year. **Faculty:** 100% faculty teach undergrads.

ACADEMICS

Degrees: Bachelor's, doctoral, master's. **Majors with Highest Enrollment:** Political science and government, general; psychology, general; Jewish/Judaic studies. **Special Study Options:** Honors program, study abroad.

FACILITIES

Housing: All-female, all-male, apartments for married students, apartments for single students. **Library Holdings:** 995,312 bound volumes. 9,760 periodicals. 1,588 audiovisuals. **Special Academic Facilities/Equipment:** Archives and rare book collection, museum of Jewish art, architecture, history, and culture. **Computers:** *Recommended operating system:* UNIX. School-owned computers available for student use.

EXTRACURRICULARS

Activities: Choral groups, drama/theater, music ensembles, radio station, student government, student newspaper, yearbook. **Athletics (Intercollegiate):** *Men:* basketball, fencing, tennis, volleyball. *Women:* basketball, tennis.

ADMISSIONS

Selectivity Rating: 93 (of 100). **Freshman Academic Profile:** Average SAT I Math 621. Average SAT I Verbal 553. TOEFL required of all international applicants, minimum TOEFL 500. **Freshman Admission Requirements:** High school diploma is required and GED is not accepted. *Academic units required/recommended:* 16 total required; 4 English required, 2 math required, 2 science required, 2 foreign language required, 2 history required, 4 elective required. **Freshman Admission Statistics:** 1,768 applied, 78% accepted, 68% of those accepted enrolled. **Transfer Admission Requirements:** Minimum college GPA of 3.0 required. Lowest grade transferable C. **General Admission Information:** Application fee $40. Regular application deadline February 15. Nonfall registration accepted. Credit and/or placement offered for CEEB Advanced Placement tests.

COSTS AND FINANCIAL AID

Tuition $19,065. Room & board $6,426. Required fees $445. Average book expense $800. **Required Forms and Deadlines:** FAFSA, institution's own financial aid form, CSS/Financial Aid PROFILE, state aid form, noncustodial (divorced/separated) parent's statement and business/farm supplement. No deadline for regular filing. Priority filing deadline March 15. **Types of Aid:** *Need-based scholarships/grants:* Pell, SEOG, state scholarships/grants, private scholarships, the school's own gift aid. *Loans:* FFEL Subsidized Stafford, FFEL Unsubsidized Stafford, FFEL PLUS, Federal Perkins, college/university loans from institutional funds. **Student Employment:** Federal Work-Study Program available. Institutional employment available. Off-campus job opportunities are good. **Financial Aid Statistics:** 43% freshmen, 41% undergrads receive some form of aid. Average freshman grant $9,554. Average freshman loan $5,625. Average income from on-campus job $500. **Financial Aid Phone:** 212-960-5269.

YORK COLLEGE OF PENNSYLVANIA

Country Club Road, York, PA 17405-7199
Phone: 717-849-1600 **E-mail:** admissions@ycp.edu **CEEB Code:** 2991
Fax: 717-849-1607 **Web:** www.ycp.edu **ACT Code:** 3762

This private school was founded in 1787. It has a 118-acre campus.

STUDENTS AND FACULTY

Enrollment: 5,213. **Student Body:** Male 40%, female 60%, out-of-state 45%, international 1% (29 countries represented). **Ethnic Representation:** African American 1%, Asian 1%, Caucasian 96%, Hispanic 1%. **Retention and Graduation:** 83% freshmen return for sophomore year. 42% freshmen graduate within 4 years. 20% grads go on to further study within 1 year. **Faculty:** Student/faculty ratio 15:1. 141 full-time faculty, 78% hold PhDs. 100% faculty teach undergrads.

ACADEMICS

Degrees: Associate's, bachelor's, master's. **Academic Requirements:** General education including some course work in arts/fine arts, computer literacy, English (including composition), history, humanities, mathematics, sciences (biological or physical), social science. **Classes:** 20-29 students in an average class. 10-19 students in an average lab/discussion section. **Majors with Highest Enrollment:** Nursing/registered nurse training (RN, ASN, BSN, MSN); elementary education and teaching; criminal justice/law enforcement administration. **Disciplines with Highest Percentage of Degrees Awarded:** Business/marketing 25%, health professions and related sciences 12%, education 11%, protective services/public administration 11%, communications/communication technologies 10%. **Special Study Options:** Cooperative (work-study) program, distance learning, double major, dual enrollment, honors program, independent study, internships, liberal arts/career combination, student-designed major, study abroad, teacher certification program.

FACILITIES

Housing: Coed, all-female, all-male, apartments for single students, minidorms featuring units of 10 students, suites, sponsored houses and apartments. **Library Holdings:** 300,000 bound volumes. 1,400 periodicals. 500,000 microforms. 11,000 audiovisuals. **Special Academic Facilities/Equipment:** Museum, telecommunications center, science and foreign language labs. All of campus is wired to the computer network. **Computers:** School-owned computers available for student use.

EXTRACURRICULARS

Activities: Choral groups, concert band, drama/theater, jazz band, literary magazine, music ensembles, musical theater, radio station, student government, student newspaper, symphony orchestra, television station, yearbook. **Organizations:** 80 registered organizations, 7 honor societies, 3 religious organizations, 10 fraternities (10% men join), 7 sororities (10% women join). **Athletics (Intercollegiate):** *Men:* baseball, basketball, cheerleading, cross-country, golf, lacrosse, soccer, swimming, tennis, track & field, wrestling. *Women:* basketball, cheerleading, cross-country, field hockey, soccer, softball, swimming, tennis, track & field, volleyball.

ADMISSIONS

Selectivity Rating: 76 (of 100). **Freshman Academic Profile:** Average high school GPA 3.1. 28% in top 10% of high school class, 65% in top 25% of high school class, 93% in top 50% of high school class. 82% from public high schools. Average SAT I Math 541, SAT I Math middle 50% range 520-590. Average SAT I Verbal 548, SAT I Verbal middle 50% range 530-610. TOEFL required of all international applicants, minimum TOEFL 530. **Basis for Candidate Selection:** *Very important factors considered include:* secondary school record. *Important factors considered include:* character/personal qualities, class rank, standardized test scores. *Other factors considered include:* alumni/ae relation, essays, extracurricular activities, interview, recommendations, talent/ability, volunteer work, work experience. **Freshman Admission Requirements:** High school diploma or GED is required. *Academic units required/recommended:* 15 total required; 4 English required, 3 math required, 4 math recommended, 3 science required, 2 foreign language required, 3 social studies required. **Freshman Admission Statistics:** 3,993 applied, 72% accepted, 37% of those accepted enrolled. **Transfer Admission Requirements:** *Items required:* high school transcript, college transcript. Minimum college GPA of 2.0 required. Lowest grade transferable C. **General Admission Information:** Application fee $30. Nonfall registration accepted. Admission may be deferred for a maximum of 1 year. Credit and/or placement offered for CEEB Advanced Placement tests.

COSTS AND FINANCIAL AID

Tuition $7,500. Room & board $5,570. Required fees $500. Average book expense $500. **Required Forms and Deadlines:** FAFSA and institution's own financial aid form. No deadline for regular filing. **Notification of Awards:** Applicants will be notified of awards on a rolling basis beginning on or about February 15. **Types of Aid:** *Need-based scholarships/grants:* Pell, SEOG, state scholarships/grants, private scholarships, the school's own gift aid. *Loans:* Direct Subsidized Stafford, Direct Unsubsidized Stafford, Direct PLUS, Federal Perkins, Federal Nursing, state loans, college/university loans from institutional funds. **Student Employment:** Federal Work-Study Program available. Institutional employment available. Off-campus job opportunities are excellent. **Financial Aid Statistics:** 59% freshmen, 46% undergrads receive some form of aid. Average freshman grant $3,955. Average freshman loan $2,798. Average income from on-campus job $1,200. **Financial Aid Phone:** 717-849-1682.

YORK UNIVERSITY

140 Atkinson Building, Toronto, ON M3J 1P3
Phone: 416-736-5825 **E-mail:** intlenq@yorku.ca **CEEB Code:** 894
Fax: 416-650-8195 **Web:** www.yorku.ca

This public school was founded in 1959. It has a 550-acre campus.

STUDENTS AND FACULTY

Enrollment: 33,749. **Student Body:** Male 38%, female 62%. **Faculty:** Student/faculty ratio 18:1. 1,149 full-time faculty, 100% hold PhDs. 100% faculty teach undergrads.

ACADEMICS

Degrees: Bachelor's, certificate, doctoral, first professional, master's, post-bachelor's certificate. **Academic Requirements:** General education including some course work in humanities, sciences (biological or physical), social science. Number and nature of courses that a student might have to take to satisfy degree requirements in addition to their chosen major varies by program. For example, liberal arts students take a natural science course as one of their required courses (one particularly developed to serve nonscience majors). **Disciplines with Highest Percentage of Degrees Awarded:** Liberal arts/general studies 30%, psychology 13%, education 12%, business/marketing 9%, visual and performing arts 5%. **Special Study Options:** Accelerated program, distance learning, double major, English as a second language, student exchange program (domestic), honors program, independent study, internships, student-designed major, study abroad, teacher certification program.

FACILITIES

Housing: Coed, apartments for married students, housing for disabled students. Some dorm floors are women-only or men-only. **Library Holdings:** 2,300,000 bound volumes. 14,734 periodicals. 3,265,009 microforms. 52,925 audiovisuals. **Special Academic Facilities/Equipment:** 5 museums with more than 4.4 million items. Observatory with 2 telescopes. Robotics laboratory. 2 professionally staffed art galleries. 6 student-run art exhibition spaces. 3 theatres. Wide-variety professional standard film and video production facilities. **Computers:** School-owned computers available for student use.

EXTRACURRICULARS

Activities: Choral groups, concert band, dance, drama/theater, jazz band, literary magazine, music ensembles, musical theater, radio station, student government, student newspaper, student-run film society, symphony orchestra, yearbook. **Organizations:** 160 registered organizations, 21 religious organizations. **Athletics (Intercollegiate):** *Men:* basketball, cross-country, fencing, football, golf, ice hockey, rugby, soccer, swimming, tennis, track & field, volleyball, water polo. *Women:* basketball, cross-country, fencing, field hockey, ice hockey, lacrosse, rugby, soccer, swimming, tennis, track & field, volleyball, water polo.

ADMISSIONS

Selectivity Rating: 60 (of 100). **Freshman Academic Profile:** Average high school GPA 3.0. TOEFL required of all international applicants, minimum TOEFL 560. **Basis for Candidate Selection:** *Very important factors considered include:* essays, recommendations, secondary school record. *Important factors considered include:* standardized test scores. *Other factors considered include:* class rank. **Freshman Admission Requirements:** High school diploma is required and GED is not accepted. **Transfer Admission Requirements:** *Items required:* college transcript. Minimum high school GPA of 3.0 required. Minimum college GPA of 3.0 required. Lowest grade transferable C. **General Admission Information:** Application fee $60. Priority application deadline February 1. Regular application deadline June 1. Nonfall registration accepted. Admission may be deferred for a maximum of 1 year. Credit offered for CEEB Advanced Placement tests.

COSTS AND FINANCIAL AID

In-state tuition $4,544. Out-of-state tuition $4,544. Room & board $4,693. Required fees $702. Average book expense $800. **Required Forms and Deadlines:** FAFSA. **Types of Aid:** *Loans:* FFEL Subsidized Stafford, FFEL Unsubsidized Stafford, FFEL PLUS, Federal Perkins, institutionally administered bursaries, international work study positions available on a limited basis, Canadian student loans, provincial student loans (for Canadian citizens only). **Student Employment:** Institutional employment available. Off-campus job opportunities are poor. **Financial Aid Statistics:** Average freshman grant $2,700. **Financial Aid Phone:** 416-736-5825.

YOUNGSTOWN STATE UNIVERSITY

One University Plaza, Youngstown, OH 44555
Phone: 330-941-2000 **E-mail:** enroll@ysu.edu **CEEB Code:** 1975
Fax: 330-941-3674 **Web:** www.ysu.edu **ACT Code:** 3368

This public school was founded in 1908. It has a 150-acre campus.

STUDENTS AND FACULTY

Enrollment: 11,375. **Student Body:** Male 46%, female 54%, out-of-state 9%, international 1% (51 countries represented). **Ethnic Representation:** African American 10%, Asian 1%, Caucasian 81%, Hispanic 2%. **Retention and Graduation:** 72% freshmen return for sophomore year. **Faculty:** Student/faculty ratio 18:1. 402 full-time faculty, 83% hold PhDs.

ACADEMICS

Degrees: Associate's, bachelor's, certificate, diploma, doctoral, master's, post-bachelor's certificate, terminal, transfer. **Academic Requirements:** General education including some course work in English (including composition), humanities, mathematics, sciences (biological or physical), social science. **Classes:** 20-29 students in an average class. Under 10 students in an average lab/discussion section. **Majors with Highest Enrollment:** Early childhood education and teaching; nursing/registered nurse training (RN, ASN, BSN, MSN); business administration/management. **Disciplines with Highest Percentage of Degrees Awarded:** Education 23%, business/marketing 18%, protective services/public administration 9%, engineering/engineering technology 6%, social sciences and history 5%. **Special Study Options:** Accelerated program, cooperative (work-study) program, cross registration, distance learning, double major, dual enrollment, English as a second language, student exchange program (domestic), honors program, internships, student-designed major, study abroad, teacher certification program, weekend college, off-campus study with Lorain Country Community College.

FACILITIES

Housing: Coed, all-female, apartments for single students, fraternities and/or sororities. University Scholars Program honors facility available. **Library Holdings:** 991,501 bound volumes. 2,908 periodicals. 901,023 microforms. 16,976 audiovisuals. **Special Academic Facilities/Equipment:** Art museum, human services development center, engineering services center, planetarium, center for urban studies, industrial development center. **Computers:** School-owned computers available for student use.

EXTRACURRICULARS

Activities: Choral groups, concert band, dance, drama/theater, jazz band, literary magazine, marching band, music ensembles, musical theater, opera, pep band, radio station, student government, student newspaper, symphony orchestra. **Organizations:** 130 registered organizations, 36 honor societies, 8 fraternities (3% men join), 6 sororities (3% women join). **Athletics (Intercollegiate):** *Men:* baseball, basketball, cheerleading, cross-country, football, golf, tennis, track & field. *Women:* basketball, cheerleading, cross-country, golf, soccer, softball, swimming, tennis, track & field, volleyball.

ADMISSIONS

Selectivity Rating: 67 (of 100). **Freshman Academic Profile:** 11% in top 10% of high school class, 28% in top 25% of high school class, 56% in top 50% of high school class. Average ACT 21, ACT middle 50% range 17-24. TOEFL required of all international applicants, minimum TOEFL 500. **Freshman Admission Requirements:** High school diploma or GED is required. *Academic units required/recommended:* 16 total recommended; 4 English recommended, 3 math recommended, 3 science recommended, 1 science lab recommended, 2 foreign language recommended, 3 social studies recommended. **Freshman Admission Statistics:** 4,210 applied, 100% accepted, 52% of those accepted enrolled. **Transfer Admission Requirements:** *Items required:* high school transcript, college transcript. Minimum college GPA of 2.0 required. Lowest grade transferable D. **General Admission Information:** Application fee $30. Regular application deadline August 15. Nonfall registration accepted. Admission may be deferred for a maximum of 1 year. Credit and/or placement offered for CEEB Advanced Placement tests.

COSTS AND FINANCIAL AID

Required Forms and Deadlines: FAFSA and institution's own financial aid form. Priority filing deadline February 15. **Notification of Awards:** Applicants will be notified of awards on a rolling basis beginning on or about May 30. **Types of Aid:** *Need-based scholarships/grants:* Pell, SEOG, state scholarships/grants, private scholarships, the school's own gift aid. *Loans:* FFEL Subsidized Stafford, FFEL Unsubsidized Stafford, FFEL PLUS, Federal Perkins, state loans. **Student Employment:** Federal Work-Study Program available. Institutional employment available. Off-campus job opportunities are excellent. **Financial Aid Statistics:** Average freshman grant $2,625. **Financial Aid Phone:** 330-941-3505.

SCHOOL SAYS . . .

In this section you'll find hundreds of colleges with extended listings describing admissions, curriculum, internships, and much more. This is your chance to get in-depth information on colleges that interest you. The Princeton Review charges each school a small fee to be listed, and the editorial responsibility is solely that of the college.

ACADEMY OF ART COLLEGE

GENERAL INFORMATION

Ever since its founding in 1929, the Academy of Art College has enacted the philosophy of its founder, Richard S. Stephens, who was the advertising creative director of *Sunset* magazine: "Aspiring artists and designers, given proper instruction, hard work, and dedication, can learn the skills needed to become successful professionals." At the beginning, 46 students met in a single classroom in San Francisco's North Beach neighborhood and learned advertising art from practicing artists. In this tradition, top professionals continue to groom successive generations of artists for work-place success. To master the advertising components of illustration, photography, and copy, the Academy's first students studied art and design basics such as drawing, painting, color, light, layout, and typography. This curriculum grew to incorporate fine arts (such as sculpture and printmaking), graphic design, fashion (design, textiles, and merchandising), and interior design. The Academy received accreditation from the California Department of Education in 1966 and began granting Bachelor of Fine Arts degrees, with Masters of Fine Arts degrees added 10 years later. By 1992, the Academy enrolled 2,500 students and conducted classes in five more buildings with Elisa Stephens, the founder's granddaughter, at the helm. She promptly identified the burgeoning field of computer arts and expanded the department to equip students with the multimedia skills sought by leading companies, including Silicon Graphics, Pixar, Adobe, and Walt Disney Productions.

The Academy of Art College has grown to the point of being the biggest private institution of art and design in the country. Its 5,000 students come from across the country and globe—international students account for one-third of the population. Nineteen buildings in the thriving, picturesque city of San Francisco provide space for classes, studios, exhibitions, and residences, and Academy buses transport students between locations. Applicants are not required to submit portfolios because of the dearth of art classes now available in high schools. Once admitted, they can pursue a certificate or an AA, BFA, or MFA degree in any of the 10 majors. The Academy recruits experienced art and design professionals from diverse locales to contribute to the academic and arts setting of the Bay Area. Students participate in an internship during their senior year to prepare them for the transition into the working world.

STUDENT BODY

The Academy's Campus Activities Program organizes a wide array of cultural, recreational, and community events during the course of the year. Participating students build social ties that carry over to collaboration in the classroom. In addition, students work together in a variety of organizations and clubs that flourish at the Academy.

ACADEMICS

To complete a Bachelor of Fine Arts degree, students must earn 132 units, distributed as follows: 18 units of foundation courses, 60 units in the major, 12 units of art electives, and 42 units of liberal arts/art history courses. Students earn three units per class. In the first year, students are required to take foundation courses in English, art history, and computer applications. These classes are tailored according to a student's intended major, giving them the tools they will need for focused study in their field staring in the second year. Within the major, classes are arranged sequentially in order to ensure smooth skill acquisition and application. Students may choose to take certain major courses at the same time. Classes in the liberal arts complement studio work and teach students to think critically. Students who do not speak English as their first language enroll in as ESL class as well, placed according to the results of an English language proficiency test. The Academy's department heads are available to meet with students to discuss their coursework and academic development. Every student has his or her portfolio assessed after the first two years of study; continued work at the Academy is contingent upon meeting a baseline standard of quality and progress.

Students at the Academy of Art College can pursue an Associate of Arts, Bachelor of Fine Arts, or Master of Fine Arts degree. Certificate programs are also available. The Academy offers the following majors: advertising design (art direction, copywriting, and television commercials), computer arts (animation, special effects, video games, and web design), fashion (design, knitwear, merchandising, and textile), fine art (painting/drawing, printmaking, and sculpture), graphic design (corporate identity, packaging, and print), illustration (feature film animation), industrial design studios (transportation and automobile design), interior architecture and design (commercial and residential interior design), motion pictures and video (film and television production), and photography (advertising illustration, documentary/photojournalism, and fine art).

For the most part, the Academy employs instructors who work full time as professional artists and designers and part time as teachers. On average, 500 instructors lead classes in a given semester. Undergraduates benefit from the low student-instructor ratio of 18:1.

79 New Montgomery Street
San Francisco, CA 94105
Phone: 415-274-2222
Fax: 415-263-4130
Website: www.academyart.edu

CAMPUS LIFE

The Academy of Art College's urban location gives students access to the cultural and artistic resources of a world-class city. San Francisco's innumerable museums and galleries, lively performing arts scene, and cutting-edge technological development make it an ideal place to live and study. The ethnic and cultural diversity of the population correlates with a diversity of thought, artistic style, and global influences. The city attracts travelers and business people from all over the world. The picturesque vistas offer students in the landscape painting course plenty of subjects for their work. Students attending the Northpoint campus on Pier 39 even have a direct view of Alcatraz Island. Other classrooms are located near Union Square and in the Financial District, convenient to galleries, shops, and restaurants. San Francisco residents enjoy a mild, Mediterranean climate, alternating between sunshine and fog during most of the year. Students at the Academy take advantage of the city's opportunities and also give their talents and energy back to the community.

Students work closely with the Career Services department to find applicable internships and jobs while they are students at the Academy and as they launch their post-graduation careers. Career Services lists full- and part-time opportunities that draw on the skills learned in the various art and design majors, and they also assist students without formal design experience find entry-level positions. Many students participate in the study abroad program and gain valuable insight from studying art and art history in pertinent locations, including London, Florence, Rome, and Venice.

COST AND AID

Undergraduates pay $500 per credit unit, and typically, full-time students take 12 or 15 units each semester. One hundred dollars of the $120 registration fee may be applied to tuition payment. Students should budget for $25 to $400 in lab fees each semester. Applicants are reminded that tuition and fees may be changed. In addition, most students spend $250 to $500 on supplies each semester. Certain majors require more supplies and lab time than others. Students enrolled at the Academy are eligible for discounts at the campus art supply store. Rather than purchase expensive technical equipment, students may borrow most items or utilize them in the labs.

ADMISSIONS

A high school diploma or the GED equivalent is required of all BFA students. Students who do not speak English as their first language must be tested on their written and spoken proficiency in order to place them in the appropriate ESL courses, if necessary. ESL requirements can be filled concurrently with regular art and design coursework. Each of the foundation classes runs sections specifically for ESL students, led by instructors who are experienced in language assistance. Applicants may begin classes at the Academy at the start of the spring, fall, or summer sessions. Undergraduate applicants pay a $100 application fee. Please be advised that details of the information in this profile may change at any time. In order to receive the most current information, visit the website or use the contact information provided below.

Further information and a catalog may be obtained by contacting:

Academy of Art College
Prospective Student Services
79 New Montgomery Street
San Francisco, CA 94105
Phone: 415-274-2222 or 800-544-ARTS (toll free)
Fax: 415-263-4130
Website: www.academyart.edu

ANNA MARIA COLLEGE

GENERAL INFORMATION

Anna Maria College, a coeducational Catholic institution of higher education founded in 1946 by the Sisters of St. Anne, is dedicated to the liberal arts and professional studies. At Anna Maria College, students build the strong foundation they need to live meaningful lives and pursue productive careers. Liberal arts courses sharpen students' critical thinking skills, leading to lifelong personal and professional growth. In fulfillment of the College's Catholic mission, the faculty and staff integrate the importance of personal values, social responsibility, and spiritual growth into their teaching. Through internships, field experiences, and work, students apply what they've learned in the classroom to the real world. In the process, they discover that learning never ends and that fulfilling their potential is a lifelong journey.

STUDENT BODY

For its more than 500 full-time undergraduates, Anna Maria College offers a multitude of opportunities in a caring, close-knit community. The majority of Anna Maria students take part in intercollegiate and intramural sports. The College's small size also reinforces the value of co-curricular and residential life activities. Anna Maria College's 11 NCAA Division III varsity teams include men's basketball, baseball, cross-country, golf, and soccer, and women's basketball, cross-country, field hockey, soccer, softball, and volleyball. Through a variety of student clubs and organizations ranging from the student government association to the ski club, students develop leadership skills and make friends that last a lifetime.

ACADEMICS

The cornerstone of Anna Maria College's academic programs is the core curriculum, which integrates the College's Catholic character with its commitment to liberal arts education. Rather than seeing a college education as simply fulfilling a series of unrelated requirements, Anna Maria sees it as building an interdisciplinary foundation so strong that it will sustain students for life. There are four divisions within the academic departments. Division I is Humanities and International Studies; Division II is Business, Law, and Public Policy; Division III is Human Development and Human Services; and Division IV is Environmental, Natural, and Technological Sciences. Though each division has a particular focus, the program's ultimate goal is to illuminate the commonalties between each area of study. Students are encouraged to look outside their major discipline to find similarities of methodology, history, or theory in different materials. As a result, students receive a broad-based and interdisciplinary liberal arts foundation, which compliments the professional preparation in their major field. Anna Maria College is one of 13 colleges within the colleges of Worcester Consortium, Inc., which collectively enrolls more than 40,000 students each year. The benefits of affiliation with 12 nearby colleges and universities include cross registration, joint degree programs, collaborative career services, and sharing of recreational and research facilities.

50 Sunset Lane, Box O
Paxton, MA 01612-1198
Phone: 508-849-3360
Fax: 508-849-3362
Website: www.annamaria.edu

Anna Maria College

In addition to the established areas of study that follow, the College encourages students to explore their own areas of interest and design their own majors. Areas of study include art, art and business, art education, art therapy, biology, business administration, Catholic studies, chemistry, computer information systems, criminal justice, economics, education, English, English-language arts, English as a foreign language, environmental science, fire science, graphic design, history, humanities, international studies, legal studies/paralegal, management information systems, mathematics, modern languages, music therapy, music/music education, nursing (RN to BSN—transfers only), philosophy, physics, political science, pre-medical, psychology, public policy, social work, sociology and anthropology, theater, and theology and religious studies.

"Accomplished, excellent, student-focused, accessible, practicing professionals . . ."—these are some of the ways Anna Maria College students describe the faculty. The College maintains small classes, resulting in a dynamic learning environment in which students are active participants. The professors know more than just their students' names—they know the students and care about their success. It's that simple.

ADMISSIONS

The Admission Committee reviews each application individually and weighs high school curriculum and grades, SAT I or ACT scores, recommendations from teachers and guidance counselors, the applicant's essay, and extracurricular activities including work experience and awards. Applications for admission are reviewed on a rolling basis, but the priority deadline is March 1. The Office of Admission strongly encourages visits to the campus, tours of the campus, and one-on-one interviews. Students can schedule any or all of these by calling 800-344-4586, ext. 360. The College seeks candidates who are capable of benefiting from a career-oriented liberal arts education in the Catholic tradition, offered in a small community environment.

CAMPUS LIFE

Nestled in the hills of Paxton, Massachusetts, on a 180-acre campus, the Anna Maria College campus offers students a safe, rural setting just minutes from Worcester, Massachusetts, New England's third largest city and home to nine other colleges and universities. The picturesque town of Paxton offers students the best of both worlds: a relaxed country setting in which to live and study, and close proximity to a vibrant college town. Anna Maria College was recently ranked first by the APBnews.com and CAP Index, Inc. among the nearly 1,500 four-year colleges for the campus neighborhood with the lowest risk of violent crime.

Off-campus social and cultural life centers around the city of Worcester. Anna Maria College students, along with the thousands of nearby college students, take advantage of social, cultural, and recreational events at venues including the Worcester Centrum, Worcester Auditorium, Worcester Art Museum, Worcester Center for Crafts, and Mechanics Hall, to name a few. The city of Worcester also boasts many restaurants and shops. Boston; Hartford, Connecticut; and Providence, Rhode Island, are within an hour's drive. Daily train service to Boston is available from Worcester.

COST AND AID

Expenses for the 2002–2003 academic year include tuition, $16,410; fees, $1,450; and room and board, $6,550. Tuition for music majors is $18,660.

AQUINAS COLLEGE (MI)

GENERAL INFORMATION

Aquinas College, located in Grand Rapids, Michigan, is a Catholic, coeducational, liberal arts college with an enrollment of just over 2,500 students. The College enjoys all the advantages of its location in the second largest city in Michigan, and students seize the opportunities offered in one of the fastest growing cities in America. Internships abound, providing hands-on learning experiences for any major. Participating organizations range from FOX 17 WXMI for mass communications internships to the Grand Rapids headquarters of Steelcase Inc. for business internships.

At Aquinas we have laid the groundwork for the future. By pushing a few keys on a campus computer, you can open the doors to hundreds of libraries and databases all over the world without ever leaving campus. Our newest high-tech learning center is a model for classrooms of the future that provides network plug-ins every few feet. Our core curriculum was designed to give students the critical foundation needed to be successful in an ever-changing world. Faculty bring to the classroom portfolios of academic scholarship and real-world experience.

Of course, not all learning takes place in the classroom. Students travel overseas to countries such as France, Spain, Ireland, Japan, Germany, Costa Rica, and Peru. They are also involved in the many and varied service learning opportunities taking place in locations such as Oaxaca, Mexico; El Salvador; and Haiti. Students at Aquinas believe in giving back to the community in which they live. Professors at Aquinas believe who you are is just as important as what you choose to do. Scholarship awards are available to students who not only excel academically but who also are leaders, volunteers, activists, and athletes. A private education can be more affordable than you think.

STUDENT BODY

Aquinas College encourages all students to participate in the more than 40 extracurricular organizations that are available, ranging from intramural teams and academic clubs to performing arts activities, student-run publications, and service groups. One such group of note is Insignis, in which students of exceptional academic record participate in social activities in the form of lectures, receptions, and cultural outings based on intellectual interests.

The Student Senate is the governing body of the Aquinas students, which votes on issues that are brought before the College's Academic Assembly. The Senate brings many academic, social, recreational, and cultural activities to campus.

An on-campus coffeehouse, the "Moose," offers select coffees, a juice bar, and light snacks. Students and faculty congregate in the Moose to relax or carry on discussions that have continued long after class has ended.

Weekly, students are treated to live entertainment on campus ranging from eclectic acoustic performers to comedians. A spring theatre festival is also a popular event.

ACADEMICS

The academic program at Aquinas College follows a unique structure outside of the major/minor course study. This structure maintains certain requirements for each of the four years. Each course exposes students to a broad philosophical theory meant to provide all graduates with an understanding of the human condition. Our core curriculum and liberal arts distribution plan ensure academic competencies that are critical to our ever-changing world.

Freshmen are required to take an integrated skills course called Inquiry and Expression. The thematic content of this course is American Pluralism: The Individual in a Diverse America. This year-long course emphasizes writing and reading critically, oral communication skills, critical thinking, library/electronic research methods, computer utilization, and basic quantitative reasoning. Sophomores take a year-long Humanities course. The junior-year requirement consists of completing the three-hour course Religious Dimensions of Human Existence, with a choice of emphasis in Scripture, Catholic/Christian Thought, or Contemporary Religious Experience. Seniors participate in a capstone course called Global Perspectives.

All students are required to demonstrate proficiency in a foreign language through the "201" level. The general education plan covers The Individual in a Global Community; Myth, Mind, Body, and Spirit; Natural World; Artistic and Creative Studies; and Quantitative Reasoning and Technology.

During summer orientation students begin a career/professional development component, which lasts throughout the four years. Topics include assessment of students' strengths, skills, and interests; development of goals and a learning plan and setting a direction; focus on individual wellness, personal finances, and leadership/team skills; awareness of careers, professions, and graduate study; information on making and maintaining a professional portfolio and resume; participating in a professional/career mentor program; career fairs and networking; and experiential learning (choices include co-op, internship, service learning, service trips, and study abroad).

The College follows a two-semester calendar with a summer session. Aquinas also accepts credit through CLEP and Advanced Placement.

Aquinas College offers the following undergraduate degrees: Bachelor of Arts, Bachelor of Fine Arts, Bachelor Arts in General Education, Bachelor of Music Education, Bachelor of Science, Bachelor of Science in Business Administration, Bachelor of Science in Environmental Science, and Bachelor of Science in International Business.

The College offers majors/programs of study in the following: accounting, accounting/business administration, art, art/business administration, art history, biology, business administration, business administration/communication arts, business administration/sports management, chemistry, communication arts, community leadership, computer information systems, conductive education, drawing, economics, education, English, environmental science, environmental studies, foreign language, French, geography, German, health, history, international studies, Japanese, journalism/publications, Latin, learning disabilities, mathematics, medical technology, music, nuclear medicine technology, organizational communication, painting, philosophy, photography, physical education and recreation, physics, political science, pre-engineering, printmaking, psychology, religious studies, sculpture, social science, sociology, Spanish, studio art, urban studies, and women's studies.

1607 Robinson Road SE
Grand Rapids, MI 49506-1799
Phone: 616-732-4460
Fax: 616-732-4469
Website: www.aquinas.edu

Pre-professional courses are available in dentistry, law, and medicine. A Bachelor of Science in Nursing is offered in collaboration with University of Detroit Mercy and St. Mary's Mercy Medical Center.

Associate's degrees are also available, including the Associate of Arts and the Associate of Science.

The main goal of Aquinas faculty is to make sure that when their students enter the workforce or graduate school they are prepared with values as well as skills. In addition to teaching, faculty act as advisors, mentors, and on-campus club and organization consultants. The enviable 15:1 student/faculty ratio allows for individual attention, personal relationships, and small classes. Seventy-one percent of the faculty has doctorate or terminal degrees. All classes are taught by faculty. Aquinas does not use graduate assistants in any of their classes. In addition to their primary dedication to the students, Aquinas professors boast exciting research careers that allow for faculty development.

ADMISSIONS

The Aquinas College admissions committee admits students on the basis of several factors, including the following: academic preparation, scholarship, character, high school transcript, SAT or ACT score, curriculum, and extracurricular activities. Transfer students must have a minimum 2.0 grade point average on a 4.0 scale. Each application is reviewed on a case-by-case basis so that all factors can be considered in the final decision.

Applicants must remit a $25 application fee. Letters of recommendation are encouraged but not required. Freshman and transfer students are accepted on a rolling basis. Applications submitted via the Internet do not require an application fee. Submit at www.aquinas.edu.

CAMPUS LIFE

Aquinas College's campus buildings run the gamut from early-nineteenth-century structures to more modern facilities, but all intermingle nicely to create a charming atmosphere that some call the most beautiful small school in the state. The 107-acre campus is peppered with inviting natural beauties: small ponds, full-grown trees, winding wooded paths, and bubbling creeks. This peaceful campus is set on the edge of Grand Rapids, western Michigan's center of economic, educational, and cultural life and growth. This is a big city with a small-town feel that has amenities to fulfill anyone's interests, including restaurants, entertainment venues, recreational access, and sports stadiums. Other popular points of interest include festivals, special events, and arts attractions. With nearly half a million residents, Grand Rapids is Michigan's second largest city and just a three-hour drive from the state's largest city of Detroit and the Midwest's biggest city, Chicago.

Aquinas students have the opportunity to participate in many off-campus programs both in the United States and abroad. The Dominican College Campus Interchange Program allows students to study at any of the following cooperating institutions: Barry University in Miami, Florida; Dominican College in San Rafael, California; and St. Thomas Aquinas College in Spark Hill, New York. Another option for students who want to remain in the United States is the semester in Montana, where students live and study on a Native American reservation. Aquinas has a study center in Tully Cross, Ireland, where two Aquinas faculty members accompany 25 students for a study abroad program worth a full semester of credit. This program introduces students to life in a rural Irish community and allows them to experience traveling abroad.

Students are involved in service learning opportunities from as near as the inner city of Chicago to as far away as Haiti, Costa Rica, and Peru. The College also offers study abroad opportunities in France, Spain, Germany, and Japan.

Aquinas students are also encouraged to take advantage of a variety of co-op and internship programs. Opportunities are available in business, government agencies, local hospitals, accounting firms, social service agencies, art and cultural venues, and other organizations.

COST AND AID

The 2002–2003 tuition is $15,620; room and board is $5,436. Other expenses, including books, travel, and personal supplies, average $2,000.

ARCADIA UNIVERSITY

GENERAL INFORMATION

Arcadia University is a coeducational university located just outside Philadelphia. Founded in 1853, the school has a historical affiliation with the Presbyterian Church, though today it is independently operated. Arcadia University offers an excellent combination of strengths, offers the diversity and academic options typical to a large university in the context of a close-knit and supportive small college environment. There are 1,410 fulltime and 267 part-time undergraduates and 70 percent of full-time undergraduates live in campus housing. The diverse student body hails from 31 states, 15 foreign nations, and a variety of cultural and economic backgrounds. In addition, there are an additional 1,329 students in the graduate school, many international students who attend Arcadia's American Language Academy, and adult students in the Continuing Education Program, who add even greater diversity to the traditional undergraduate population. An active campus community, Arcadia University students participate in wide variety of clubs, organizations, sports, and social events. Outside of student life, students at Arcadia are actively involved in the greater community. Service is integral to student life and many participate in neighborhood improvement projects, literacy programs or gerontology centers, and through helping of disadvantaged or disabled youth. Arcadia College participates in the NCAA Division III, competing in women's field hockey, lacrosse, softball, and volleyball, men's baseball, and both men and women's basketball, cross-country, golf, soccer, swimming, and tennis. There is also an active intramural sports program. Graduate students can pursue a master's degree in the following subject areas: counseling, education, English, environmental education, forensic science, genetic counseling, health administration, health education, humanities, international peace studies and conflict management, health education, public health, physical therapy, and physician assistant studies.

STUDENT BODY

The student activities program complements the academic program and enhances the overall educational experience of students through development of, exposure to and participation in social, cultural, intellectual, recreational and governance programs. Through these activities, students are introduced to various cultures and experiences, ideas and issues, art and musical forms and styles of life that bring cultural, intellectual and social stimulation to the campus community.

ACADEMICS

Arcadia University's academic program strives to provide students with a solid foundation in the liberal arts and sciences while creating a deep understanding in the major area. Students are encouraged to explore different subject areas on and off campus, through research, cooperative education, or internships. Off campus programs give students the opportunity to hone relevant workplace skills and use their academic training in the real world. For example, many students participate in the Cooperative Education Program, in which they can earn course credit for off-campus employment, while concurrently earning income. There are more than 32 different major programs offered at Arcadia University, and students also have the option of designing an individually tailored major. The Honors Program gives academically accomplished freshmen, sophomores, and juniors access to special seminars, independent study courses, and exclusive cultural events. Students may receive course credit for a score of 3 or above on the College Board's Advanced Placement examinations. Students can also earn course credit through the College-Level Examination Program (CLEP) and examinations that are locally administered. Arcadia University operates on a two semester academic calendar. Between the two semesters, from May to early August, the school offers summer sessions. It is typical for students to take four courses each semester for a total of 128 semester hours upon graduation. Students have the option of taking a limited number of courses for pass-fail grade.

Students can pursue the Bachelor of Arts degree in the following subject areas: art, art history, biology, business administration, chemistry, communications, computer science, education (early childhood, elementary, secondary), English, health administration, history, interdisciplinary science, international business and culture, mathematics, modern languages, philosophy, political science, psychobiology, psychology, science illustration, sociology, Spanish, and theatre arts. The University confers the Bachelor of Science in accounting, business administration, chemistry and business, computer science, finance, health administration, management, management information systems, marketing, mathematics, and personal human resources administration. Students can also pursue the Bachelor of Fine Arts in studio arts with a concentration in ceramics, graphic design and illustration, interior design, metals and jewelry, painting, photography, and printmaking. The acting major is also a BFA. The University also offers a certification program in art education in conjunction with the BFA program, as well as undergraduate preparation for students who plan to do graduate work in art

450 South Easton Road
Glenside, PA 19038
Phone: 215-572-2910
Fax: 215-572-4049
Website: www.arcadia.edu

therapy. Students may also participate in a special program to complete the Bachelor of Arts in education and a Master of Education in special education over the course of five years. The Actuarial Science Program offers actuarial examination preparation. There are also programs in physical therapy (4+3 doctorate), physician assistant studies (4+2), genetic counseling (4+2), and international peace and conflict resolution (4+2). These programs allow you to complete four years of undergraduate study in a related field with three years of study towards the Doctorate of Physical Therapy (DPT) degree or two years of studies for the Master of Medical Science in Physician Assistant Studies (MMS), Master of Science in Genetic Counseling, or Master of Arts in International Peace and Conflict Resolution. Admissions priority in the above mentioned graduate programs is given to the University's undergraduates who are applying for entrance and meet admissions criteria. The school also offers a dual-degree (3+2) program in engineering in conjunction with Columbia University. The school offers an accelerated program for the Bachelor of Arts/Doctor of Optometry degree in conjunction with Pennsylvania College of Optometry. There are also pre-professional preparation programs in dentistry, law, medicine, optometry, physical therapy, and theology and other areas. There is an evening program for part-time students pursuing a Bachelor of Science or post baccalaureate certificate in business administration or in computer science. The evening program also confers the Bachelor of Arts in communications or English. The newest graduate degree program offered at Arcadia University is the Master of Science in Forensic Science. This program is offered full-time and is a two-year program.

The faculty at Arcadia University are dedicated to teaching. Professors, not teaching assistants, teach all classes at Arcadia and the average class size is no more than 15 to 20 students. With excellent student/faculty ratio of 12:1, students have ample opportunity to talk with and get to know their professors. The result is a vibrant, close-knit, and collaborative academic environment, characterized by informal discussions between teachers and students, field trips and research, and special activities. 85 percent of Arcadia University instructors have doctoral or terminal degrees in their subject areas.

ADMISSIONS

Prospective students are evaluated on the basis of their academic preparation, intellectual achievement, and potential for success. The admissions staff evaluates each application individually. The most important factors in an admissions decision are the student's academic transcript, the quality of their secondary school program, GPA, and class rank. The school also looks at standardized test scores, recommendations, and the student's involvement in extracurricular or community activities. Prospective freshmen must submit a secondary school transcript, official scores from the SAT I or ACT, a personal essay, and recommendations from a high school teacher and guidance counselor. Students are strongly encouraged to follow a strong high school program of at least 16 academic units. Arcadia offers programs in early admission and early decision, as well as deferred admission. Students may also apply through the Gateway to Success or Act 101 Program. Though not required, it is recommended that students visit the campus and schedule an admissions interview before applying. Students applying for transfer admission may apply for the fall or spring semester, and must submit college transcripts from each school they have attended. Transfer students with less than 30 college credits are also required to submit their high school transcript.

CAMPUS LIFE

Arcadia University is located on 60 acres in Glenside, a residential neighborhood just outside Philadelphia. While the immediate area is quiet and suburban, Philadelphia is a quick trip away, giving students all the advantages of urban living in the context of a tranquil college setting. The centerpiece of campus is the famous Grey Towers Castle, a National Historic Landmark. In addition to Arcadia's historic buildings, the school is constantly expanding and improving to better meet student needs. Over the past nine years, the University has added eight major facilities, including an athletic and recreation center, the sophisticated Health Sciences Center, a new dining hall, a new residence hall, and most recently, an impressive new library facility. Downtown Philadelphia is only 25 minutes from campus, offering students access to a multitude of museums, galleries, performing arts events, restaurants, social events, government sites, and shopping. In addition to the wide variety of resources in lively Philadelphia, the metropolitan areas of New York City and Washington, DC, are only a few hours from campus and accessible via train. Many students also plan trips to the nearby New Jersey shore and the Pocono Mountains to participate in year round recreational activities.

Arcadia University operates extensive overseas studies programs, among the best in the nation. Arcadia University sponsors and approves more than 100 international programs worldwide in Australia, Britain (including the universities in Aberdeen, Bristol, Edinburgh, London, and York), Greece, Ireland, Korea, Mexico, Italy, New Zealand, and Spain. In addition, first year students in good academic standing may participate in the unique London Preview program, a week-long study session in London, England, run every year during spring break. Students are also encouraged to pursue off campus opportunities in the greater Philadelphia area, such as internships and fieldwork. In addition, students may choose to spend a semester in Washington, DC, at American University, and juniors may enroll in advanced courses at the University of Pennsylvania.

COST AND AID

For 2003–2004, undergraduate tuition is $20,990 and room and board is $8,620. Student fees total $280 per year.

ART INSTITUTE OF ATLANTA

THE INSTITUTE AT A GLANCE

Founded in 1949, The Art Institute of Atlanta is a private college of creative professional studies. The college prepares students for careers in design, media arts, and culinary arts by providing a challenging and stimulating educational environment, with attention to changing technologies and the requirements of the global marketplace.

In June 1999, the college moved to a new, 5-story, 115,000-square-foot facility. The new campus offers computer labs with both Mac and PC platforms, camera studios, a wet photo lab and digital imaging photo lab, a video production studio, digital and linear video editing labs, art labs, figure drawing studios, drafting labs, an interior design resource room, an extensive library, an art gallery, professional teaching kitchens, and a dining lab, as well as classrooms, conference rooms, and student lounges. All classrooms, labs, offices, and the library are wired for Internet access. This contemporary facility provides an exciting, dynamic environment for creative work.

The new campus is built on a solid tradition of excellence, with emphasis on career-focused education. Founded as Massey Business College, the college became The Art Institute of Atlanta in 1975 and is celebrating more than 50 years of commitment to students and their success in their chosen career fields.

About 80 percent of the college's 2,200 students come from Georgia, with the remaining students representing 29 states and 44 foreign countries. Although most students are of traditional college age, a significant number are adult students returning to college or studying to earn a second degree. The college is proud of the diversity of its student body.

The college is accredited by The Commission on Colleges of the Southern Association of Colleges and Schools (SACS) to award the bachelor of fine arts degree and the associate in arts degree. The interior design bachelor's program is accredited by the Foundation for Interior Design Education Research (FIDER), and the culinary arts associate's program is accredited by the American Culinary Federation (ACF). The college is licensed by the State of Georgia and is eligible to accept the Georgia HOPE scholarship. It is also approved for the training of veterans and eligible veterans' dependents, and authorized under federal law to enroll nonimmigrant students from other countries.

Students engage in a rigorous program of study that includes art foundation and general education courses as well as technical courses in their chosen field. Majors include graphic design, media arts and animation, multimedia and Web design, interior design, photographic imaging, video production, and culinary arts.

The Art Institute of Atlanta is a member of The Art Institutes, with 23 locations nationwide and more than 125,000 alumni. The Art Institutes provide an important source of design, media arts, fashion, and culinary professionals.

Career success for graduates is an important goal for the college. Of all 1999 graduates available for employment, 92 percent were working in a field related to their program of study within six months of graduation. Average starting salaries ranged from $22,637 to $30,648 depending on the program. All students learn essential job search skills such as résumé writing, interviewing, and networking. In their last quarter, design and media arts students participate in a Portfolio Show where employers are invited to meet new graduates and view their work. The resources of the career services office, both in Atlanta and throughout The Art Institutes' family of schools, remain available to alumni throughout their careers.

LOCATION AND ENVIRONMENT

The Art Institute is located in the exciting New South city of Atlanta, Georgia, about 30 minutes by car or public transportation from downtown. Atlanta is the leading city of the Southeast, a vibrant and diverse place where tree-lined neighborhoods are just minutes away from skyscrapers housing Fortune 500 companies. Its thriving business environment includes high-tech businesses such as Macquarium, Earthlink and iXL as well as corporate giants like The Coca-Cola Company, CNN, Delta Air Lines, AT&T, and Georgia Pacific. As a leading provider of applied arts education, the college is a major player in the growth of Atlanta's high-technology business initiative to attract "industries of the mind."

Atlanta had its beginning in the 1830s when the railroad cut through north Georgia and a few streets were cleared along the Indian trails that crisscrossed the hilly region along the Chattahoochee River. Atlanta has been on the move ever since. Built by pioneering entrepreneurs of transportation and business, Atlanta has always been a city of vision. After General Sherman's army burned and pillaged the city during the Civil War, Atlantans took the mythical phoenix as their symbol and rose from the ashes to build what renowned nineteenth-century journalist Henry Grady called "a brave and beautiful city." Though many know Atlanta best for its fictional portrait in *Gone With the Wind*, the reality includes fame as the birthplace of Martin Luther King Jr. and praise from President John F. Kennedy for the nonviolent voluntary integration of its schools and public places.

The city's tradition of diversity is expanding to include new residents from all over the world, especially since the 1996 Centennial Olympic Games. Atlanta is a city of commerce, a city of hospitality, a city of neighborhoods, a city of dreams, and most of all, a city on the move. Students at The Art Institute of Atlanta become a part of this vital, energizing city while working toward realizing their own dreams.

STUDENT LIFE AND OFF-CAMPUS OPPORTUNITIES

From the moment students are accepted, they become part of an environment that supports their efforts to reach their goals. At the Art Institute, students enjoy small classes, hands-on learning, and close relationships with faculty and staff. But it's not all study, classes, and labs. On campus, students can grab lunch or a snack at the deli, catch the newest gallery exhibit, participate in a variety of student activities, or make a purchase at the Supply Store. Beyond the college, students enjoy everything a major metropolitan area can offer, from clubs and concerts to galleries and museums, Braves baseball games to rollerblading in Piedmont Park. The High Museum of Art and the Michael C. Carlos Museum are wonderful resources for students of the applied arts, as are the Atlanta Contemporary Art Center and the dozens of art galleries throughout the city. The burgeoning restaurant scene offers enrichment opportunities of a different kind. Students find that those who were strangers at orientation are soon friends to hang out with, laugh with, and share ideas with.

Students can grow both personally and professionally by participating in numerous organizations such as American Culinary Federation (ACF), American Institute of Graphic Artists (AIGA), American Society of Interior Designers (ASID), Atlanta ACM-SIGGRAPH (computer graphics), Creative Club of Atlanta (CCA), International Television Association (ITVA), the Special Projects Group (SPG), the Student Council, and the Student Ambassadors Program. Many upper-quarter students qualify to work for academic credit as interns with area employers, gaining valuable experience in their fields. Optional college-organized trips to Europe offer students a unique perspective on their academic studies; field trips closer to the college are a regular part of many classes or as an extracurricular student activity.

6600 Peachtree Dunwoody Road, 100 Embassy Row
Atlanta, GA 30328
Phone: 800-275-4242
Fax: 770-394-0008
Website: www.aia.artinstitute.edu

For practical advice, student services is ready to help with housing, counseling, organized activities, or finding a part-time job. Even after graduation, students remain part of the Art Institute family, with ongoing assistance from career services as they develop professionally.

Some students choose to live in college-sponsored apartments a short drive from the campus. Others prefer to live with family or in off-campus housing of their own choosing. In addition to its residence life program, student services offers a roommate and apartment referral service, as well as general advice about housing issues including information on apartment referral agencies, utility companies, and transportation.

ACADEMIC PROGRAMS, MAJORS, AND DEGREES OFFERED

The Art Institute of Atlanta offers bachelor of fine arts degrees in graphic design, interior design, media arts animation, multimedia and Web design, and photographic imaging, and associate in arts degrees in graphic design, photographic imaging, video production, multimedia & Web design, and culinary arts. Full-time students may attend day or evening classes in most majors. The Personal Track program offers students an opportunity to take classes for credit on a part-time basis without enrolling in a full degree program. Courses and majors are designed to stay current with the needs of a rapidly changing business environment.

With a student faculty ratio of 17 to 1, students are assured of personal attention. More than 125 full-time and adjunct faculty bring solid academic credentials, and often extensive experience in their fields, to the task of ensuring that students learn the competencies required for each course. Students benefit from close direct interaction with the faculty in their classes.

General education courses in English, math, psychology, history, and art history are part of the required program for all students. Students in programs other than culinary arts also study art foundations (drawing, visual expression, design, and color theory). For students who may lack the academic preparation needed for success at the college level, the Art Institute offers a transitional studies program when recommended by the admissions committee. More information on all aspects of the academic program is available by calling the admissions office.

COSTS AND FINANCIAL AID

The Art Institute of Atlanta understands the significant financial commitment that a college education requires. The student financial services department works one-on-one with students and their families to develop a personal financial plan that is based on each individual's particular financial needs and allows students to reach their educational and career goals. Financial planners guide families through the process of assessing educational costs, applying for financial aid programs, completing financial aid paperwork (including the Free Application for Federal Student Aid, or FAFSA), and developing a payment plan.

The Art Institute offers a comprehensive financial aid program for those who qualify. Each year the college oversees the administration of more than $14.9 million in financial aid including federal and state loans and grants, and institutional scholarships, both need-based and merit-based. Financial aid options for those who qualify include the Georgia HOPE scholarship, the Georgia Tuition Equalization Grant (GTEG), federal loans and grants, merit scholarships, alternative loan programs, and part-time employment. The college also provides customized, interest-free payment plans for those who wish to spread their financial commitment out over time.

As of May 2001, tuition for full-time students is $14,544 per academic year (three quarters). For their first quarter, all students purchase a starting kit ($595–$740, depending on the academic program). In subsequent quarters, additional books and materials need to be purchased, varying by program from approximately $360 to $750 per quarter. College-sponsored housing is an additional $4,990 per academic year. The college reserves the right to adjust tuition and fees as necessary. Information about the college's tuition lock-in program is available from the admissions office.

ADMISSION PROCEDURES AND REQUIREMENTS

Because The Art Institute of Atlanta has a rolling admissions policy, students may begin their studies at the start of any quarter. All students interested in the college are assigned to an assistant director of admissions, who works closely with the applicant and his or her family throughout the admissions process.

In addition to completing a personal interview, applicants must submit a completed application for admission; an official high school transcript (preference is given to students with an average of 3.0 or above) or General Equivalency Diploma (GED) test scores; an official report of SAT, ACT, ASSET; or COMPASS test scores; and a $50 application fee. The COMPASS test is administered at the Art Institute at no cost to the student. A portfolio is not required for admission, but is required for high school seniors entering the annual scholarship competitions. Slightly different requirements apply for transfer or international students. Students are generally advised of the decision of the admissions committee within two weeks after all application materials are received. The committee determines whether or not the applicant has a reasonable chance to be successful based on his or her academic record, essay, and how appropriate the applicant's stated career goals are as related to the chosen program of study. A tuition deposit of $100 is required within 10 days of acceptance or 30 days of application.

All interested students and their families are encouraged to visit the college. Personalized tours are part of the admissions interview. Students who live at a distance from Atlanta may complete a telephone interview.

Full information on scholarships, financial aid, and admissions policies, as well as faculty biographies, program requirements, sequences, and course descriptions is available in the college catalog and on the website. For more information, students should contact:

Director of Admissions
The Art Institute of Atlanta
6600 Peachtree Dunwoody Road
100 Embassy Row
Atlanta, GA 30328
Telephone: 770-394-8300
800-275-4242 (toll free)
Fax: 770-394-0008
Email: aiaadm@aii.edu
World Wide Web: www.aia.artinstitute.edu

ART INSTITUTE OF BOSTON AT LESLEY UNIVERSITY

THE INSTITUTE AT A GLANCE

The Art Institute of Boston (AIB) is a private visual arts college, offering academic programs that prepare students for successful careers in illustration, animation, graphic design, photography, Web design, and fine art. The academic environment at AIB is challenging but supportive, fostering artistic expression while teaching the practical skills necessary to succeed in the visual arts.

AIB's student body hails from 33 U.S. states and 27 foreign countries, making up a stimulating atmosphere of artists from diverse backgrounds and global perspectives. With only 500 full-time students, the community at AIB is close-knit, encouraging students to create close relationships with each other, as well as with the faculty and staff. The average size of a studio art class is no more than 13 students, allowing for ample personal attention from instructors and a focus on individual development and self-exploration. Through their course work, students are exposed to the most modern trends and current technology in their respective fields. This knowledge is augmented through the multitude of internships and work opportunities available through AIB, which help hone important professional skills and make real-world connections.

Though the atmosphere on campus is supportive and intimate, AIB is located in the world-class city of Boston, a prominent cultural and educational hub where students can take advantage of endless educational, and social opportunities. Students further benefit from AIB's association with Lesley University, a sizable research institution. As a result, students at AIB have more opportunities than those typically offered at many independent art schools, without sacrificing the small college atmosphere.

Additionally, AIB students have the opportunity to participate in art exhibitions, attend lectures and art auctions, and attend events in the Visiting Artist Program, a year-long series that invites renowned artists to lecture and teach workshops on campus.

Home to almost 225,000 students and 70 college and universities, Boston is an unparalleled college town. Beyond the rich collegiate atmosphere, Boston affords endless cultural, social, and educational opportunities, from sports and concerts to world-class museums, galleries, lectures, and theater. While Boston is a world-class city, its atmosphere is pleasantly provincial, boasting historic neighborhoods, city parks, and the attractive New England coast in close proximity.

In addition, the Museum of Fine Arts, Boston offers free admission to all full-time AIB students.

MAJORS AND DEGREES OFFERED

The Art Institute of Boston offers a Bachelor's of Fine Arts in graphic design, fine arts, illustration/animation, and photography. Students also have the option of pursuing an interdisciplinary degree in fine arts/illustration or illustration/design. The school offers a three-year diploma in fine arts, illustration, or photography as well as a professional certificate in illustration or design, which can be conferred after two years of study.

The graphic design program covers topics in advertising, corporate communications, publishing, book design, and Web design. The illustration program offers a focus in advertising, book, editorial, and animation illustration. Students in the fine arts department may choose to concentrate their studies in drawing, painting, printmaking, or sculpture, and may also take course work in ceramics, installation, and electronic arts. The photography program offers specializations in commercial, documentary, fine arts, or media photography.

During the academic year and throughout the summer, high school students are invited to join an intensive pre-college program.

The school offers two master's programs in conjunction with Lesley College in expressive therapies and art education.

ACADEMIC PROGRAMS

AIB's curriculum trains students in the process of visual expression and communication, while giving them a solid foundation in history and the social and cultural influences in the visual art world.

The faculty at AIB faculty comprises experienced artists, educators, and businesspeople from New England. Of the 103 faculty members, 95 percent hold advanced degrees in their field. In addition, 89 percent are practicing artists, professional designers, illustrators, and photographers. With an excellent student/faculty ratio of 10:1, students form close relationships with faculty members and receive ample individual attention. In addition to instruction, faculty members are open to helping students with career counseling and are a key resource for students seeking professional employment in the visual arts.

All first-year students are required to participate in an intensive curriculum in drawing and visual perception, designed to introduce students to the skills and insights necessary for the advanced study of art. Photography students follow a unique first-year foundation, in which they are immersed in the history, technique, and concept behind artistic photography.

After the first year, students select a major or combined major that usually includes a specialization within the field of study and incorporates interdisciplinary material and special workshops. In addition to core courses, students receive increasingly individualized instruction during their course of study, working closely with faculty to develop and meet their artistic and professional goals. Outside of class work, students are given professional studio assignments and are encouraged to participate in an internship, a valuable experience that prepares them for a career in the visual arts. Students can locate professional opportunities with the help of the campus Artist's Resource Center, which provides information about art competitions, fellowships, grants, internships, and jobs.

Other than required major work, degree and diploma candidates must take required and elective classes in the liberal arts. Liberal arts courses develop communication skills, strengthen the understanding of the history of their area of study, and encourage students to further their interests and wisdom.

AIB offers credit courses in the day and evening during the fall, spring, and summer. In addition to the undergraduate and graduate curriculums, the continuing and professional education program caters to professionals, artists, and educators who want to expand their skills through evening and weekend workshops and seminars in visual arts, liberal arts, and career development.

The AIB student government sponsors an annual program of social events, lectures, film series, and field trips for the student body. Students who wish to share ideas with the administration are invited to a monthly round table with the college dean.

700 Beacon Street
Boston, MA 02215-2598
Phone: 617-585-6700
Fax: 617-437-1226
Website: www.aiboston.edu

OFF-CAMPUS OPPORTUNITIES

Advanced students at The Art Institute of Boston may be selected to participate in a merit-based illustration program in Rotterdam, Holland. Students also have the option to study art and Italian at The Art Institute of Florence or spend a semester at Burren College of Art in Ireland. For photography students, AIB offers an exchange program in Paris, France.

In the U.S., AIB is a member of the Association of Independent College of Art and Design (AICAD). Through the association, AIB students also have the option to spend their junior year at one of the 30 schools in the AICAD association, located across the country. A year program of study and studio art in New York City is among the most popular. Boston Architectural Center and the Maine Photographic Workshop also have classes open to AIB students.

FACILITIES AND EQUIPMENT

AIB students have access to three on-campus Macintosh laboratories, an Oxberry master animation stand, video animation stands, a complete color and black-and-white photography lab, a printmaking studio with etching and lithography presses, a metals studio with welding facilities, a wood shop, and a ceramics studio with wheels and kilns. In their final year, fine arts students receive private studios.

Recently, the Institute was admitted to the New Media Centers Program, an association of colleges and digital technology companies dedicated to advancing learning through new media. Due to this affiliation, technology and resources will continue to improve at AIB. Plans are in the works for the AIB New Media center, which will give students even broader opportunity to incorporate state-of-the-art technology and first-rate equipment into the study of art.

The AIB library collection contains more than 9,000 books, 70 periodicals, 26,000 slides and 250 art-related videos, as well as a reference file of 10,000 photographs and illustrations. The library also contains the National Gallery of Art's American Art Collection on videodisc, an excellent visual reference that contains over 26,000 images.

AIB students have full access to Lesley University's Eleanor De Wolfe Ludcke Library, which, in addition to a state-of-the-art multimedia center, offers more than 62,000 books, 700 current periodicals, 2,200 computer software and CD-ROM titles, 650 film titles, and circulating media equipment. AIB students are also members of the Fenway Library Consortium, which extends borrowing privileges to six more libraries in Boston.

Student housing is located within walking distance of campus. Many students choose to locate their own apartment in Boston or live at home during their course of study. The Office of Admissions can provide housing assistance to students.

AIB's galleries are continually exhibiting contemporary and period work by established and emerging artists, as well as AIB alumni. In addition to exhibitions, AIB hosts a full series of lectures by visiting artists, giving students the unique opportunity to meet with distinguished professionals in the visual arts. Students get hands-on experience helping to prepare the gallery for exhibitions and talk personally with professional artists. In the past, AIB has had the honor to present shows by Chuck Close, Duane Michals, Edward Gorey, and Milton Glaser. In addition, there is a student gallery, always reserved for student exhibitions.

TUITION, ROOM AND BOARD, AND FEES

Tuition for the 1999–2000 year was $12,500 plus room and board costs of approximately $7,600–$8,300 for student housing. Material costs vary for each department. Students in foundation, fine arts, illustration, and design students may expect to spend about $1,500 annually for supplies, and photography students usually spend about $2,300 per year. Student fees are $670 for everyone, except photography and design students who pay a $770 fee. Students may incur further expenses depending on the equipment and materials they choose.

More than 70 percent of students receive financial aid through AIB's strong financial aid program. Aid is available in the form of student loans and part-time employment, based on the need determined by the United States Department of Education. The Financial Aid Office helps students meet education costs through a combination of Federal Pell Grants, Federal Stafford Student Loans, Federal Work-Study, as well as other federal grants, scholarships, and state programs.

In addition to federal and state assistance, AIB offers a number of merit-based scholarships and need-based scholarships. AIB distributes over $3.5 million in financial aid annually. Students seeking merit-based assistance for fall enrollment must submit completed publications before February 16. The deadline for need-based financial awards is March 17.

ADMISSIONS PROCESSES AND REQUIREMENTS

The Art Institute of Boston invites applicants with artistic potential and drive to succeed to apply for admission. In order to be considered for admission, applicants must submit an application form and personal essay, an application fee, an official transcript from secondary school, and SAT I scores. In addition, students are required submit a portfolio of original visual work. The portfolio is an extremely important aspect of the application; however, AIB also evaluates prospective students on the strength of their grades and test scores, letters of recommendation, and extracurricular activities. AIB encourages prospective students to visit the campus to present their portfolio and discuss their potential at AIB.

Admissions are made on a rolling basis; however, students who wish to start classes in the autumn semester should apply before February 16. We encourage transfer and international students to apply. For further information or questions about the application process, please contact the Office of Admissions.

ASSUMPTION COLLEGE

GENERAL INFORMATION

In 1904, Augustinians of the Assumption founded Assumption College, a Catholic institution that blends strong programs in liberal arts and sciences with the values of the Catholic tradition. Located in Worcester, Massachusetts, among New England's premiere cities, the College's 175-acre campus boasts excellent academic and housing facilities, an extensive library, and a world-class recreational center. A lively spiritual and intellectual environment, Assumption College provides a traditional liberal education while teaching the modern skills and ideas necessary to succeed professionally. Assumption confers 32 majors and offers 6 special academic programs. Students are encouraged to enroll in honors classes or work with faculty on individual research projects. With an excellent student/faculty ratio of just 14:1, Assumption's academic atmosphere is close-knit and community-oriented. There are 400 graduate students and more than 2,000 undergraduate students at Assumption College. More than 90 percent of undergraduates choose to live in one of the 14 residence halls on campus.

STUDENT BODY

The Student Government Association (SGA) is a student-run organization, responsible for overseeing and financing the school's various student clubs. The Student Senate of the SGA is made up of elected student representatives and is the official body that communicates the needs of the student body to the College administration.

ACADEMICS

Assumptionist founder Father Emmanuel d'Alzon dedicated Assumption College with this motto: "Until Christ be formed in you." The College remains committed to that pursuit through a strong liberal arts education, in which students and instructors explore the ideas and events that shaped the modern world. Assumption College aims to teach not just how to ask questions, but also how to find answers. In the classroom, the faculty encourage a hands-on approach to learning through group projects, writing assignments, and tasks that encourage students to think about materials, not just to memorize. Classes are generally discussions, not lectures. Assumption College follows a two-semester academic calendar, beginning in late August and ending in May. There are two summer programs run by the Continuing Education School and the Graduate School. In addition to major requirements, Assumption College requires all students to complete two courses in English composition, philosophy, and religious studies, and two courses in either mathematics, a laboratory science, or a third year of a foreign language. In addition, students must complete one course in literature, history, and social science, and one course in either art, music, or theater. In order to graduate, students must have 120 semester credits, with 9 to 12 in the upper division of the major. Assumption students have the option of participating in Army and Air Force ROTC programs.

Assumption College offers the following majors: accounting, biology/biological sciences, chemistry, classics, computer science, economics, economics with a business concentration, English, English/writing and mass communications, environmental sciences, foreign languages, French, global studies, history, international business, international economics, Latin American studies, management, marketing, mathematics, organizational communications, philosophy, political science, psychology, social and rehabilitation services, sociology, Spanish, theology, and visual arts. In addition, the College has special programs in elementary education, middle school education, secondary education, medical technology, pre-medical/pre-dental/pre-law, and engineering (offered in conjunction with Worcester Polytechnic Institute).

Assumption College faculty is an accomplished group of educators, deeply dedicated to their students. They bring diverse professional experience and education to the College community, and more than 93 percent hold terminal degrees in their subject area.

500 Salisbury Street
Worcester, MA 01609-1296
Phone: 508-767-7285
Fax: 508-799-4412
Website: www.assumption.edu

ASSUMPTION COLLEGE

ADMISSIONS

Assumption College admits men and women of intelligence and motivation from applicants who have completed all prescribed high school requirements. Assumption College encourages secondary school officials to pursue regional accredited status in order to provide assurance of the quality of education of its applicants. Assumption College strongly recommends that prospective students schedule an interview and campus visit prior to applying for admission. During the autumn semester, prospective students may attend group information sessions on Saturdays, or schedule a campus visit by appointment. To apply, students are required to submit an online or paper application, a $50 application fee, official high school transcripts, scores from the SAT I or ACT, and a letter of recommendation. Applications, including all supporting documents and recommendations, must be received in the Office of Admissions by March 1. Students who wish to seek early decision must apply by November 1. For more information, please contact:

Assumption College
Office of Admissions
500 Salisbury Street
Worcester, MA 01609
Phone: 888-882-7786 (toll free) or 508-767-7285
E-mail: admiss@assumption.edu
Website: www.assumption.edu

CAMPUS LIFE

Assumption College's beautiful 175-acre campus is located in the suburban neighborhood of Westwood Hills in Worcester, Massachusetts. Worcester is home to 10 colleges and is one of the largest cities in New England. A lively collegiate environment, Worcester provides students with many academic and social opportunities. Outside of university life, Worcester is culturally rich, boasting a renowned annual music festival and symphony orchestra, as well as the Worcester Art Museum and the Ecotarium. There are a multitude of outdoor and recreational activities in Worcester and its environs. The majority of well-known New England cities, including Boston and Providence, Rhode Island, are only 45 minutes away, while the Worcester Regional Airport opens up the rest of the country.

Assumption College is a member of the Colleges of Worcester Consortium, an association of the 13 higher learning institutions in the Worcester metropolitan area. Through the consortium, Assumption students can register for courses at the other nine colleges, as well as participate in social and cultural events. During their undergraduate education, Assumption College students may choose to spend a semester or year abroad. In recent years, Assumption College students have studied throughout the world, from France and England, to the Netherlands and the Czech Republic. Many students augment their education and hone professional skills by pursuing national and international internships. Assumption students have had the opportunity to work in diverse organizations across the globe, from the U.S. Department of Commerce, Central America Bureau, and the U.S. Department of State, NAFTA Agreement, to Smith Barney, Fidelity, Dean Witter Reynolds, AT&T, and the Alliance Francaise in Paris.

COST AND AID

Tuition for the 2002–2003 school year is $19,980 plus $7,820 room and board.

BABSON COLLEGE

GENERAL INFORMATION

This small New England school enrolls about 400 students each year into its freshman class—keeping the student population fewer than 1,800. Set in beautiful Wellesley, Massachusetts, on a campus that is huge in comparison to the number of students who live there, Babson College offers a strong business curriculum with a liberal arts foundation. The diversity of the student body makes this school a particularly attractive choice for those seeking a good education and a place to grow and interact with a small yet unique group of people. About 20 percent of undergraduates are international students who represent 70 countries; ethnic and socioeconomic diversity are also strong.

Babson is accredited by the New England Association of Schools and Colleges, the International Association for Management Education, and the American Assembly of Collegiate Schools of Business.

STUDENT BODY

Babson offers students an extensive variety of student activities. These extracurriculars include 22 NCAA Division III (11 men's and 11 women's) intercollegiate athletic teams. Intramural sports are also popular student activities. A variety of student-run clubs, organizations, and publishing opportunities are available across every interest spectrum.

The school also has three fraternities and two sororities. Approximately 12 percent of students are involved in Greek life.

ACADEMICS

Babson College operates on the semester system and has one six-week-long summer session.

Students are required to take 50 percent liberal arts courses and 50 percent business courses. Babson offers unique programs including First-Year Experience, Foundation Management Experience, field-based learning programs, independent study, and an honors program. All students start and operate their own businesses with money loaned by Babson during their freshman year as part of the Foundation Management Experience. Students also have the opportunity to work as consultants to nonprofit organizations as part of the Management Consulting Field Experience. Pre-professional programs are available in law and business management.

All students are encouraged to self-design their course of study. Rarely do students' goals exactly parallel a pre-designed major. This unique opportunity allows students to cultivate their own course of study to best prepare them to meet their immediate career goals upon graduation. Although all students will graduate Babson College with a Bachelor's Degree in Business Administration, most courses of study incorporate one or more of the following fields: accounting, economics, entrepreneurship, finance, international business, investment banking, management, management information systems, marketing and quantitative methods.

Babson College employs 155 full-time faculty, 90 percent of whom hold doctorates in their field. The student/faculty ratio is 11 to 1. All faculty set teaching as the top priority and many further expand their academic interest by conducting research in their subject.

Mustard Hall
Babson Park, MA 02457
Phone: 781-239-5522
Fax: 781-239-4006
Website: www.babson.edu

ADMISSIONS

Babson College bases its acceptance of students on both academic and nonacademic factors. The academic factors that are very important include high school record, recommendations, standardized test scores, and essays; class rank is considered but not essential. The nonacademic factors that are important include extracurricular activities, recommendations, and character/personal qualities. Other nonacademic factors include particular talent or ability, alumni relationships, geographical residence, multicultural affiliation, volunteer work, and work experience. A campus visit and on- or off-campus admissions interview are available, but not required.

Graduation from secondary school is required for admission; the GED is accepted. Applicants are expected to have fulfilled the following 16 units of college-prep courses: English (4 units), mathematics (4 units), science (2 units), science lab (1 unit), social studies (2 units), and academic electives (3 units). The admissions committee recommends, but doesn't require, that students complete 3 units of lab science and 3 units of foreign language. The SAT I or ACT is required for admission, the SAT II in writing and math level I or IIC are required for course placement. The TOEFL is required for international applicants; although the following applicants may elect to take the English Language Proficiency Test (ELPT) in place of the TOEFL: U.S. citizens/permanent residents who are nonnative speakers of English and currently attend a U.S. high school, and international students who have been enrolled in a U.S. high school for a minimum of two years and are in an ESL program. Transfer students may apply as well as those interested in the early decision program. Admission may be deferred for up to one year.

The nonrefundable application fee is $50 (for students with a permanent United States mailing address, and $100 for students with non-U.S. mailing address), but may be waived in cases of financial need. The application deadline is February 1 and acceptance notification is sent by April 1. Students applying for early action or early decision must apply by December 1.

Students may earn credit and placement for high scores on the CEEB, Advanced Placement, CLEP, or International Baccalaureate.

CAMPUS LIFE

This 370-acre suburban campus is located in Wellesley, Massachusetts (population 26,650). This is the ideal charming New England town, a classic setting for a college environment. A mere 14 miles outside of Boston, students here are sure to experience the best of both worlds: the quaintness of small town life bordering the cultural and social excitement of the big city. Although Boston is accessible by means of public transportation, approximately 70 percent of students have cars.

Babson College encourages students to expand their academic challenges by engaging in internship opportunities. Students can enroll in courses off campus through cross-registration programs with Brandeis University, Pine Manor College, Regis College, and Wellesley College.

Students who are interested in studying abroad may choose from among 30 different programs in 20 locations including Western Europe, Argentina, Australia, Chile, Czech Republic, Japan, New Zealand, Russia, and South Africa. The Semester at Sea program is a particularly exciting and interesting study abroad opportunity.

AFROTC, NROTC, and ROTC programs are available through Boston University.

COST AND AID

Tuition for the 2001–2002 academic year is $24,544, room and board is $9,226, and books and supplies are estimated at $658.

BARNARD COLLEGE

GENERAL INFORMATION

Founded in 1889, Barnard College was one of the first colleges to offer young women what had, until then, been just out of reach: the chance to earn a college degree. Today, Barnard College is still committed to the education of over 2,300 undergraduate women from over 30 countries and 49 states. Barnard College became affiliated with Columbia University in 1900 but maintains its own Board of Trustees, campus, faculty, staff, and admissions process. Barnard also works with its own endowment, and Columbia University confers Barnard students' degrees. Despite the independent nature of the two schools, students at Barnard can register for courses at Columbia, and vice versa. Barnard students have full access to an extensive Columbia library system that contains over 6 million volumes. The small, personal character of Barnard is supplemented by all the resources of a large university. Barnard is located in the Morningside Heights neighborhood of Manhattan. The school stretches from 116th Street to 120th Street on Broadway, and the four-acre campus has everything its students need. A gymnasium is tucked away on the first floor of Barnard Hall, which faces the College's main entrance. The dorm complex—Brooks, Reid, Hewitt, and Sulzberger Hall—is at the southern tip of campus, though there are other housing options including opportunities for coeducational living. The heart of student life is the Millicent McIntosh Student Center, where students have access to many amenities to augment their academic life.

ACADEMICS

Barnard requires students to complete 120 points of course work (including First-Year English, First-Year Seminar, and two semesters of physical education) for the AB degree; the degree structure is highly adaptable to students' interests and needs. Barnard believes that a successful liberal arts education revolves around central ways of knowing the world—this philosophy forms the basis of most of the general education requirements within the nine Ways of Knowing curriculum. The nine Ways of Knowing are: Reason and Value, Social Analysis, Cultures in Comparison, Language, Laboratory Science, Historical Studies, Literature, Visual and Performing Arts, and Quantitative Reasoning.

Barnard offers the Bachelor of Arts (AB) degree, and students have a wide selection of majors to choose from: American studies, ancient studies, anthropology, architecture, art history, Asian and Middle Eastern cultures, biochemistry, biological studies, biopsychology, chemistry, classics (Greek and Latin), comparative literature, computer science, dance, economic history, economics, education, English, environmental science, foreign area studies, French, German, history, human rights studies, Italian, linguistics, mathematics, medieval and renaissance studies, music, Pan-African studies, philosophy, physics and astronomy, political science, psychology, religion, Russian, sociology, Spanish, statistics, theater, urban affairs, and women's studies.

There are also opportunities for double and joint degrees, which students earn from both Barnard and other schools in the Columbia system. One option is the five-year (4-1) AB/MIA (Master in International Affairs) program where students earn their Master's from the School of International Affairs. Another five-year (4-1) option gives students the chance to earn an AB/MPA (Master of Public Administration) after studying in Columbia's public affairs and administration program. Columbia's law school offers an option where Barnard students can begin their legal studies after only three years of undergraduate work in a program of interdisciplinary legal education. Science and engineering students can earn both AB and BS degrees in a five-year (3-2) program with The School of Engineering and Applied Science, where students can specialize in various engineering fields including aerospace, civil, and electrical. Music students can take advantage of the Juilliard School's five-year (3-2) program: they can spend three years earning their AB from Barnard, then two years at Juilliard earning their MM degree. Finally, students have the chance to earn an AB and a seminary degree in conjunction with the Jewish Theological Seminary, which is only two blocks from Barnard.

3009 Broadway
New York, NY 10027
Phone: 212-854-2014
Fax: 212-854-6220
Website: www.barnard.edu

There are 185 full-time faculty members at Barnard and 107 part-time members for a student/faculty ratio of 10:1. The assigning of faculty advisors who advise students with scheduling and other academic matters ensures that Barnard students are given individual attention and guidance.

ADMISSIONS

High school transcripts, letters of recommendation, standardized test scores, and personal attributes and achievements all play a role in Barnard admission. The College seeks women with strong academic records who exhibit the capacity and desire to grow intellectually and personally. Barnard is very selective, and each student accepted has unique qualities that make her desirable-there is not a set group of criteria that an applicant must match. The only set requirement is that applicants must have completed a college-prep program or its equivalent, with a recommended 4 years of English, 3 of math, 3 or 4 of a foreign language, 3 of science and laboratory work, and 2 of history. Every applicant is evaluated on both the qualities that she personally espouses and the potential for success at Barnard that she exhibits. Barnard asks applicants for the following test scores: SAT I and three SAT II: Subject Tests including the SAT II: Writing Test or SAT II: Literature, or the ACT. Students whose first language is not English must submit the TOEFL. Interviews are recommended.

CAMPUS LIFE

Barnard is ideally situated in New York City—a place that offers students endless cultural, academic, and professional opportunities. Barnard views New York as an extension of the classroom, and students are encouraged to make use of its resources for study and exploration—a wide selection of over 2,500 internships, for example, is available for students throughout the whole of New York City. Institutions neighboring the Barnard campus include the Manhattan School of Music, Teachers College, Bank Street College of Education, Union Theological Seminary, and the Jewish Theological Seminary.

There are numerous opportunities for Barnard students to explore academics outside of Barnard. As previously stated, Barnard students have full access to Columbia resources and can often take graduate or professional-level courses with permission. The Jewish Theological Seminary offers credit for courses Barnard students take there, and Juilliard and the Manhattan School of Music allow qualified Barnard musicians to take lessons at their institutions. There are also many opportunities for Barnard students to explore academics beyond both New York and the United States. In Paris, Reid Hall, a Barnard-Columbia facility, offers programs for both semesters and full years. The Intercollegiate Center for Classical Studies offers Classics students the opportunity to study in Rome. Other institutions offering study abroad programs include Somerville College in Oxford; Newnham College in Cambridge; University College, London School of Economics, King's College, or Queen Mary College at the University of London; the University of Warwick; and other institutions in Japan, Berlin, and Madrid. Atlanta's Spelman College and Arizona's Biosphere II offer domestic exchange programs.

COST AND AID

Total tuition and fees are $25,270 for 2002–2003 at Barnard, and room and board is an additional $10,140.

BARRY UNIVERSITY

GENERAL INFORMATION

In 1940, Barry College opened its doors to an incoming class of only 30 students. A Catholic women's institution, Barry was dedicated to providing an excellent education and fostering the values of religion and service to the community. Since its inception, Barry has remained unwavering in its commitment to quality but has grown in size and prestige. In 1981, Barry College became a coeducational university. In 2001, the total enrollment had reached 8,650, drawing students from 49 states and 83 countries. Barry is characterized by a unique sense of community. Barry professors care about their students and aim to prepare them for a successful academic career and rewarding life. Barry University is fully accredited by the Commission on Colleges of the Southern Association of Colleges and Schools. The school awards bachelor's, master's, specialist, and doctoral degrees in more than 60 academic fields from computer science and e-commerce, to photography and golf management. In addition, Barry offers more than 50 graduate degrees through the Schools of Adult and Continuing Education, Arts and Sciences, Business, Education, Graduate Medical Sciences, Human Performance and Leisure Sciences, Law, Natural and Health Sciences, Nursing, and Social Work. In every course of study, quality academics are augmented with internship and community service experience.

Located in Miami Shores, Barry's beautiful campus is the ideal environment for study. Replete with Spanish-style buildings and Florida's perfect weather, Barry's campus is home to 700 undergraduates. In addition to dormitories and academic buildings, the campus has a snack bar and cafeteria, post office, student center, performing arts center, television studio, radio station, health and sports center, and outdoor recreation center. There are a wide range of health and student services on campus, such as career counseling, international student services, disability services, campus ministry, and health services. Barry University is a member of NCAA Division II, competing in men's baseball, basketball, golf, soccer, and tennis, and women's basketball, golf, rowing, soccer, softball, tennis, and volleyball. Besides varsity sports, students play a variety of intramural sports, from the traditional basketball, volleyball, and soccer, to modern versions of the originals, such as sand volleyball, street hockey, and wiffle ball.

STUDENT BODY

Barry's Student Government Association (SGA), which is responsible for overseeing the 92 student organizations on campus, was recently ranked number two in the state by *Florida Leader* magazine. Students also run the Campus Activities Board, which is responsible for planning and coordinating campuswide events such as barbecues, lectures, dances, and concerts, or crab races, sailing trips, and casino nights. Barry has an active campus ministry, a number of intramural sports, wellness classes, and intercollegiate athletics teams.

ACADEMICS

Barry University operates on a two-semester academic calendar. Between the spring and fall semesters, Barry offers two six-week summer sessions. To earn an undergraduate degree, students must complete 120 units and maintain a GPA of 2.0. Of the 120 required credits, students must complete 9 each in philosophy and theology, communication, the arts and humanities, physical or natural sciences, mathematics, and social and behavioral sciences. Students traditionally take 12 to 18 credits per semester and 6 credits during the summer term. Students may select a major or choose to study a broad liberal curriculum. All students must satisfy the requirements of their particular program, including professional preparation requirements. With the recommendation of the dean and department chair, select, qualified seniors can earn up to six graduate credits during undergraduate studies. Most majors require internship experience. To accommodate the needs of the international community, the ELS Language Center helps students increase English language proficiency. The Center for Advanced Learning has special services designed to help students with learning disabilities successfully complete a degree. The university also offers an active honors program designed to add breadth and depth to the educational experience.

Barry University offers the Bachelor of Arts degree in the following fields: advertising, art (ceramics, digital imaging, and painting and drawing), broadcast communication, communication studies, English (literature, professional writing), environmental studies, French, general studies, history, international studies, philosophy, photography (biomedical/forensic, digital imaging, creative, photo/communication), pre-law, public relations, Spanish, theater (acting, design/technical), and theology. The Bachelor of Science degree is conferred in accounting,

11300 North East Second Avenue
Miami Shores, FL 33161-6695
Phone: 305-899-3100
Fax: 305-899-2971
Website: www.barry.edu

athletic training (pre-medical option, pre-physical therapy), biology (biotechnology specialization, marine biology specialization, pre-dental, pre-medical, pre-optometry, pre-pharmacy, pre–physical therapy, pre–physician assistant, pre-podiatry, pre-veterinary, three-year accelerated option), cardiovascular perfusion, chemistry (environmental, pre-dental, pre-medical, pre-pharmacy, pre-veterinary), computer information sciences, computer science, criminology, cytotechnology, diagnostic medical ultrasound technology, e-commerce, economics/finance, elementary education, environmental science, pre-engineering, exceptional student education, exercise science (pre-medical, pre–physical therapy, five-year seamless BS to MS), international business, management, management information systems, marketing, mathematical sciences (actuarial science, applied, computational), medical technology, nuclear medicine technology, physical education (grades K–8 and grades 6–12), political science, pre-K primary education, pre-K primary Montessori education, psychology, sociology, sport management management (diving industry specialization, golf industry specialization). Undergraduates can pursue minors in most major fields of study, as well as peace studies, women's studies, and film studies. Barry offers a Bachelor of Science in Nursing, with an accelerated option, basic option, LPN to BSN option, RN to BSN option, RN/BS to MSN bridge option, and seamless RN to MSN option. Barry University offers the Bachelor of Fine Arts, the Bachelor of Music, and the Bachelor of Social Work. Programs in teaching certification are available for elementary education, exceptional student education, Montessori education, and pre-K primary education. Students may obtain secondary school teaching certification for a limited number of specific areas. Barry also offers a Spanish translation and interpretation certificate program. Barry offers degree programs through the School of Adult and Continuing Education. Working adults can pursue the Bachelor of Professional Studies, the Bachelor of Liberal Studies, the Bachelor of Public Administration, and the Bachelor of Science in health services administration, information technology, legal studies, and professional administration with a flexible schedule designed for continuing students.

Barry's academic environment is characterized by its commitment to personal attention and development. Academic advising is fundamental to undergraduate progress, and with a low 13:1 student/faculty ratio, students receive individualized attention from the school's accomplished professors. Of Barry's 324 full-time and 482 part-time faculty, 81 percent hold a doctoral or terminal degree in their field.

ADMISSIONS

In addition to a completed application, students must submit an official high school transcript, scores from the SAT I or ACT, and a $30 nonrefundable fee. Barry recommends that prospective students apply well in advance; applications can be accepted as early as after the junior year of high school. A completed application should be submitted to:

Barry University
Office of Admissions 11300 North East Second Avenue
Miami Shores, FL 33161-6695
Phone: 305-899-3100 or 800-695-2279 (toll-free)
Fax: 305-899-2971
E-mail: admissions@mail.barry.edu
Website: www.barry.edu (Students can also apply online.)

CAMPUS LIFE

Located in Miami Shores, just north of Miami and south of Fort Lauderdale, on- and off-campus recreational and cultural opportunities abound at Barry. In the surrounding environs, students can play golf, tennis, soccer, and swim, scuba dive, water-ski, and sail. The surrounding environs are also home to the Florida Keys, the Everglades, and many national, state, and marine parks. The numerous local pro sports teams include football's Miami Dolphins, the NBA's Miami Heat, baseball's Florida Marlins, hockey's Florida Panthers, and the WNBA' s Miami Sol. Every year, there is a full season of performances and events at the Miami Film Festival, the New World Symphony, the Florida Grand Opera, the Miami City Ballet, the Coconut Grove Playhouse, and the Broward Center for the Performing Arts. Barry sponsors several summer programs in Europe and is a member of the College Consortium for International Studies, giving students the option to study at colleges and universities in 25 countries. Barry University students can take Air Force ROTC courses at a nearby university.

COST AND AID

Full time tuition for the 2002–2003 school year is $18,900, including all student fees. Room and board averages an additional $6,600. Students may incur other expenses for books, supplies, laboratory fees, and transportation.

BAY PATH COLLEGE

GENERAL INFORMATION

Bay Path College is a private, four-year, women's college, dedicated to preparing students for careers after graduation. Offering a diverse and cutting-edge curriculum, the College has developed a total educational approach that integrates leadership, communication, and technological skills in response to real-world needs. Bay Path is the first women's college in New England to offer a bachelor's degree in information technology. The distribution of the more than 800 students enrolled at the College is diverse: Students come from throughout the United States and the College has a strong student-of-color and international representation.

In addition to the undergraduate program, the College offers a continuing education program, a Saturday one-day-a-week college, and a master's degree in communications and information management.

STUDENT BODY

More than half of the undergraduate students live in residence halls. There are more than 35 on-campus organizations available for student participation, including dance company, theatre workshop, literary club, Women in Technology, chorale, Women of Culture, and student government.

Bay Path is a charter member of the North Atlantic Conference (NCAA III) and participates in basketball, cross-country, soccer, softball, and volleyball.

ACADEMICS

Bay Path offers the BA degree and the BS degree in a variety of areas. BA programs are offered in liberal studies, American studies, biological sciences, fine and performing arts, early childhood education (pre-K–3), elementary education (grades 1–6), leadership in early childhood (preschool), communications, general psychology, child psychology, forensic psychology, gerontology, and industrial/organizational psychology. The BS degree is offered in business administration, information technology management (business), international business, management marketing, office information management, residential & commercial interior design, travel & hospitality, criminal justice, information technology, legal studies/paralegal, and occupational therapy.

Associate's degrees and certificate programs are available in more than 20 areas.

Bay Path College has approximately 70 faculty members and a student/faculty ratio of 13:1. Faculty members work closely with students and take an active role in developing a school-to-career pathway through special projects, independent research, and internships. Each student is assigned a faculty advisor to assist in course selection and academic counseling.

588 Longmeadow Street
Longmeadow, MA 01106-2292
Phone: 413-565-1331
Fax: 413-565-1105
Website: www.baypath.edu

ADMISSIONS

The Admissions Committee evaluates applicants on the basis of secondary school records, SAT I or ACT scores, letters of recommendation, interviews, and essays. The College requires 4 years of English, 3 years of math, 2 years of social studies, 2 years of a foreign language, and 2 years of laboratory sciences. The Office of Admissions encourages visits to the campus and arranges tours; students may call the Office of Admissions at 800-782-7284 for an appointment. For more information about Bay Path, check out the College website: www.baypath.edu.

For undergraduates, Bay Path has a rolling Admissions process and also offers an early action program.

CAMPUS LIFE

Located at the crossroads of New England, Bay Path's campus is in the beautiful and historic town of Longmeadow, Massachusetts. Minutes from Springfield, Massachusetts as well as in close proximity to Hartford, Connecticut and Northampton, Massachusetts, students have access to a multitude of artistic and cultural opportunities and events.

Bay Path encourages experiences beyond the boundaries of a standard college education. Internships and independent learning opportunities are available for all majors and areas of studies. Among the sites at which students have completed internships are: Aetna, Inc.; Sheraton Hotels; LEGO Systems, Inc.; Disney; MassMutual; Delta Airlines; United States Marshal Service; Boston EquiServe; Yale New Haven Hospital; American Red Cross; and more.

International experiences are also available. Students can participate in the annual Capitals of the World trip (past visits have included Paris, Athens, London, Rome, and Madrid), or take advantage of the study abroad program.

Culturally and artistically, Bay Path is conveniently within a day's trip to Boston or New York City. Locally, other leisure options include the Springfield Civic Center, Mullins Center (Amherst, Massachusetts), Springfield Symphony, Tanglewood, CityStage (Springfield), Jacob's Pillow, Historic Deerfield, Springfield Quadrangle, Mass MOCA, and the Basketball Hall of Fame.

COST AND AID

Estimated expenses for the 2001–2002 academic year include tuition of $14,745 and room and board of $6,897 or $7,554 (depending on meal plan).

BECKER COLLEGE

GENERAL INFORMATION

Situated in and around Worcester, the second-largest city in Massachusetts, Becker College offers a truly multifaceted college experience. Though Becker College did not take its current shape until the 1970s, its roots can be traced back to 1784, when an educational academy was started in Leicester, six miles from Worcester. Today, the Leicester campus is among the 20 oldest college campuses in the nation. In 1887, scholar E. C. A. Becker established the Worcester campus, and nearly a century after that—in 1974—the two campuses began an academic partnership. Three years later, in 1977, the Leicester and Worcester campuses officially merged into a modern Becker College. While each campus maintains its own dormitories, libraries, and academic halls, the cooperation between the Leicester and Worcester campuses allows Becker students to enjoy broad academic, recreational, and social experiences.

Becker College's centuries-old devotion to excellence thrives today through its co-ed student body of 1,100. Drawn from 18 states and a dozen countries, Becker students are educated in an academic environment that provides individual attention, support, and recognition to each student. Students at the Worcester campus reside in elegant houses that have been restored to suit college living; in Leicester, students may choose between restored historic homes or modern residence halls. Students sometimes opt to live off-campus, as well. Regardless of where students live, they become part of the strong community spirit that's one of Becker's trademarks.

At Becker, extracurricular activities are provided through a variety of student groups and the campus activities office. Becker recognizes that education, personal growth, and amusement should not end at the classroom door; the importance of recreational activities is vigorously emphasized. Student clubs range from the Black Student Union to the International Club, from the Ski Club to the *Becker Journal* (student newspaper). As a college with demonstrated dedication to student needs, Becker encourages students to create and maintain new campus organizations. Each year, new students bring new interests to the college. Among the most popular sources of extracurricular activity at Becker are varsity athletics. In fact, more than 50 percent of Becker's student body takes part in recreational or intramural athletics. Becker College is an NCAA Division III institution, and new member to the Eastern Colleges Athletic Conference (ECAC). The college offers a variety of varsity intercollegiate options, including five for men (baseball, basketball, soccer, golf, and tennis) and six for women (basketball, field hockey, soccer, softball, tennis, and volleyball). Equestrian riding is also available as a co-ed activity.

STUDENT BODY

Clubs, organizations, and all other activities sponsored by the student activity fee are overseen by the Student Government Association (SGA). The SGA's officers and participants are charged with monitoring and increasing the quality of student life at Becker by paying particular attention to the expressed expectations of the student body. Every residence hall elects representatives to the SGA. Commuter students and leaders from campus organizations are elected to the SGA as well.

ACADEMICS

To complete the Bachelor of Arts or Science degree programs, students must fulfill the following requirements: completion of at least 122 credits and a final, cumulative grade point average (GPA) of 2.0 or better. To qualify for the Associate of Science degree, students must complete at least 60 credits with a minimum GPA of 2.0. General studies credits must account for 30 percent of a student's total credits. In numerous programs, internships or clinical fieldwork must be completed prior to graduation.

Becker College offers programs leading to Bachelor of Science, Bachelor of Arts, and Associate of Science degrees. Bachelor of Science degrees can be earned in business administration, with concentrations in financial accounting, computer information systems, hospitality and tourism management, human resources, management, marketing, and sports management; criminal justice, with concentrations in criminal justice administration and policing; kinesiology, with concentrations in applied kinesiology, exercise science, and health and fitness; legal studies; and veterinary science, with options in clinical medicine and laboratory animal medicine. Bachelor of Arts degrees can be earned in design, with concentrations in graphic design, interior design, and internet communications design; and psychology, with concentrations in child studies, early-childhood education (pre-kindergarten through grade two), elementary education (grades one through six), human services, and liberal arts. Associate of Science degrees can be earned in accounting, animal care, business administration, criminal justice administration, early-childhood education, liberal arts, liberal studies, nursing (RN), paralegal studies, physical therapist assistant, speech-language pathology assistant, and veterinary technology.

With 126 faculty members, Becker College operates with a 15:1 student/faculty ratio. As these numbers attest, Becker is committed to a personalized style of education that provides the attention, recognition, and the tools to succeed to each individual student

61 Sever Street
Worcester, MA 01609
Phone: 508-791-9241
Fax: 508-890-1500
Website: www.beckercollege.edu

ADMISSIONS

Students who wish to be considered for admission to Becker College must submit the following: a completed application form, a $25 application fee, an official secondary-school transcript, and SAT I or ACT scores. Essays and recommendation letters are strongly encouraged. Applicants to health science programs must exhibit their proficiency in science and math, and complete prerequisite courses in algebra, biology and chemistry with labs with grades of C or better. As an institution that is interested in the individuality of its students, Becker College will consider the specific accomplishments and abilities of each applicant. Becker College accepts applications on a rolling basis. Applications will be reviewed when all required materials are received. In most cases, students will receive notification from the Becker College Office of Admissions within two weeks of submitting a complete application.

CAMPUS LIFE

Becker College's Worcester and Leicester campuses are perfectly located in the center of Massachusetts, providing convenient access to other major spots throughout New England. Boston, Hartford, and Providence are just an hour away, and New York City is only three hours south. Transportation by air, rail, and road links Worcester to other cities in New England and around the United States. The college's Worcester campus is located in Elm Park, a neighborhood appealing for its quaint streets and proximity to the city's business district. A citywide bus service operated by the Worcester Regional Transit Authority allows students to easily navigate the second-largest urban area in New England. The Leicester campus—six miles from its partner in Worcester, at the intersection of Routes 9 and 56—is situated around the town's village green. With historic roots that were laid before the American Revolution, Leicester grants students a small-town New England experience. At the same time, students have easy access to the cultural opportunities in nearby Worcester. College sponsored shuttle services provide transportation between the two campuses. The Worcester Regional Transit Authority provides transportation to Consortium schools.

As a participating member of the Colleges of Worcester Consortium–composed of 10 institutions from the area–Becker supplements its academic offerings with an inter-library loan service and cross-collegiate course registration. Cooperative social events occur as well. Each semester, full-time Becker students may enroll in one course at a member college at no cost (on the condition that the faculty advisors at the other institution approve). Consortium members are Anna Maria College, Assumption College, Clark University, College of the Holy Cross, Quinsigamond Community College, Tufts University School of Veterinary Medicine, University of Massachusetts Medical School, Worcester Polytechnic Institute, and Worcester State College.

COST AND AID

For the 2002–2003 academic year, the college's tuition and fees total $14,200. Room and board fees are $7,550. The estimated expenses for books and personal allowance are $1,500.

BENEDICTINE COLLEGE

GENERAL INFORMATION

Benedictine College (BC) offers a Catholic, residential, coeducational college for students pursuing four-year degrees. The College attracts a diverse pool of students with its liberal arts curriculum and its one-of-a-kind Discovery College program. In Discovery College, students conduct advanced projects and examine their own lives. The monastic communities of Mount St. Scholastica College (founded in 1924) and St. Benedict's College (founded in 1858) came together and set up Benedictine College in 1971.

With a strong foundation in spiritual ethics, the campus is a bastion of respect for the dignity of each person. The environment encourages students and instructors to pursue scholarship, independent research, and performance in order to add to the ever-growing body of human knowledge. Benedictine College promotes undergraduate research opportunities, where students work with top faculty members, even during the first two years of study. Professors form collaborative as well as teaching research relationships with students. The College's strong research component strives to develop students' skills in exploration, collaboration, problem-solving, decision-making, and investigative methods. The results of student research are often published in academic journals or presented at conferences, sometime on the national level. Benedictine College holds accreditation from the North Central Association of Colleges and Schools.

More than 800 students, arriving from 30 states and 13 other countries, comprise Benedictine's diverse student body. Benedictine College does not discriminate on the basis of sex, race, color, religion, or national origin. Approximately 75 percent of Benedictine students reside in campus dormitories, choosing the comfort, convenience, safety, and community they offer. Students have formed more than 35 student clubs and organizations that provide an outlet for interests ranging from business to poetry. Opportunities for leadership and friendship arise in organizations such as student government, Students in Free Enterprise (SIFE), departmental clubs, Pax Christi, Amnesty International, Hunger Coalition, Knights of Columbus, Chamber Singers, Hispanic Club, African American Club, *Loomings* literary magazine, *The Raven* yearbook, and *The Circuit* student newspaper. Students flock to the Student Union to see concerts, plays, and lectures, work out in the gymnasium and exercise rooms, study at the coffee shop, eat at the snack and pizza bar, have meetings, and hang out with friends.

Students also visit the Career Development Center, which provides services to prepare students for life after graduation. Students have access to individual counseling, career testing, workshops, and seminars. Qualified career counselors also offer advice regarding graduate and professional school applications, resume writing, interviewing skills, cover letter writing, and job search strategies. Benedictine is proud of the fact that 75 percent of graduates with degrees in natural science go on to graduate or professional schools; this number close to doubles the national average for liberal arts college graduates. The College also boasts one of the region's best medical school acceptance rates. All Benedictine graduates benefit from the Raven alumni network, in terms of career contacts and social events. Many high-profile organizations, including the Federal Reserve Bank, Hallmark Cards, and the Mayo Clinic, count BC alumni among their leaders.

Benedictine owns an impressive collection of antique books and documents from the nineteenth century. When students aren't studying, they can be found cheering on the College's athletic teams or making trips to nearby Kansas City.

STUDENT BODY

Students elected to the College's Student Government assume the role of identifying and addressing the needs of the students body, whether they are academic, social, cultural, or religious in nature. Class officers and executive offers work together to establish administrative policies and carry them out.

The Benedictine Ravens compete in NAIA and Heart of America Athletics Conference athletics with the following 13 teams: men's baseball, basketball, football, golf, soccer, tennis, and track; and women's basketball, soccer, softball, tennis, track, and volleyball. Recently the College has received national awards for the cheerleading and spirit squads. Athletic facilities include a gymnasium and tennis courts, completed in 1996, and a football stadium and outdoor track, completed in 1998.

All students may partake in intramural athletics, choosing from 15 sports, including coed basketball, flag football, soccer, softball, and volleyball. The Student Union provides facilities for students to take and break from the books and utilize the gymnasium, training equipment, and fitness machines.

1020 North Second Street
Atchison, KS 66002
Phone: 913-367-5340
Fax: 913-367-5462
Website: www.benedictine.edu

ACADEMICS

The academic calendar at Benedictine College consists of two 16-week semesters and a summer term. One hundred and twenty-eight units, earned in courses numbered 100 or higher, are necessary for graduation with a bachelor's degree. Students must take a minimum of 40 units in upper-division courses and complete all requirements for general education and their major. The College does not allow students to apply more than four independent study classes or more than four units from internships toward the total needed for degree completion.

Additional requirements include a 2.0 grade-point average, a passing score on standardized tests in the student's major area of study, and completion of two terms of work in residence. Benedictine's general education courses fall into three areas: core requirements, disciplinary requirements, and proficiency requirements. Entering students may be awarded credit for Advanced Placement scores, College-Level Examination Program (CLEP) scores, or life experiences gained by students who are 23 or older. Undergraduates at Benedictine may take courses at Missouri Western State College and participate in its Reserve Officers' Training Corps (ROTC) program.

Benedictine classes ensure that students have the chance to explore possible career options and gain practical knowledge and skills. For example, the biology department runs the well known Wetlands and Wildlife Restoration Project, which allows students to learn field study techniques while contributing to the health of environment along the Missouri River. Students studying business administration apply their classroom and book learning as they run their own small businesses. Faculty members in departments including history, business, chemistry, education, political science, and sociology are respected as top researchers and authors in their fields. This combination of hands-on experience and successful role models prepares Benedictine graduates to shape their communities with their leadership, creativity, and compassion.

Three quarters of Benedictine professors have earned their PhD or terminal degree in their field. The College prioritizes close interaction between students and their instructors, which is enabled by the low student/faculty ratio of 14:1. No classes are led by graduate students or teaching assistants. Benedictine selects faculty members on the basis of their teaching abilities and desire to connect with students as well as their professional qualifications.

ADMISSIONS

The Benedictine application requires SAT I or ACT scores and official transcripts from all high schools and/or colleges the student has attended. The admissions committee advises applicants to demonstrate 16 units of college-preparatory classes, with the following break-down: 4 units of English, 3 to 4 units of math, 2 to 4 units of foreign language, 2 to 4 units of natural science, 2 units of social science, and 1 unit of history.

Students are admitted on a rolling basis. Applicants must pay the $25 application fee. For additional information or to request an application packet, prospective students should contact:

Kelly J. Vowels
Dean of Enrollment Management
Benedictine College
1020 North Second Street
Atchison, KS 66002
Telephone: 913-367-5340 or 800-467-5340 (toll free)
E-mail: bcadmiss@benedictine.edu
World Wide Web: www.benedictine.edu

CAMPUS LIFE

Benedictine College's setting in Atchison, Kansas, offers tranquil and scenic surroundings to serve as a backdrop for study. The town, home to 12,000 residents, enjoys views of the Missouri River and offers a variety of shops, restaurants, and recreation sites. The campus is convenient to the Kansas City airport, and Kansas City awaits less than an hour away by car.

Students who speak Spanish can participate in Benedictine's study abroad opportunities in Cuernavaca, Mexico, or at the University of Grenada in Spain. Those hoping to hone their French may choose the Catholic University of the West in Angers, France, or the world-famous Sorbonne in Paris. Additional programs are available in China, England, Ireland, Germany, the Netherlands, and Wales.

COST AND AID

Nine out of 10 students at the College pay for their education with the help of financial aid. Benedictine grants in excess of $3.3 million annually in the form of academic, athletic, and other merit-based scholarships. Benedictine students may also be eligible for federal aid, work-study programs, government loans, ROTC funding, and state of Kansas financial assistance. Students seeking financial aid are encouraged to apply by the priority deadline of April 1.

BENNINGTON COLLEGE

GENERAL INFORMATION

Bennington College, a liberal arts institution established in 1932, has offered students an open invitation to learn since its inception 70 years ago. A Bennington education embodies the principle that instructors must have real-world experience in their fields of expertise and that their teaching should draw upon that experience. It is for this reason that the Bennington academic community is made up of scholars, artists, writers, and scientists with a unique devotion to teaching. Students here find themselves investigating world literature with published poets, conducting labs with research chemists, discussing international affairs with former diplomats, and learning music from recorded composers. Bennington professors frequently collaborate to design interdisciplinary courses that expose students to a variety of perspectives on a single subject. Bennington stresses a collaborative mentoring approach to instruction, one in which student and teacher are actively involved. Just as a coach guides an athlete's training, a Bennington professor directs a student's development until, as a result of this guidance, the student can approach the professor as a colleague. At Bennington, not only do students participate in faculty projects, faculty members also frequently participate in student work. Bennington runs a three-term academic calendar. Fall and spring terms consist of 14 weeks of intensive on-campus study; winter term, which lasts for 8 weeks, requires fieldwork off campus. Students undertake internships and jobs related to their areas of study during winter term; this experience helps prepare students for their post-college years. Students are assisted in their search for winter term experiences by the College's fieldwork term office; which has had great success placing students in a wide variety of fields. Employers' assessment of students' performances are added to the students' academic profile, as are students' written accounts of their experiences in the field. Winter term activities provide graduating students with resumes along with their diplomas. Bennington offers several graduate degrees: the Master of Fine Arts (MFA), Master of Arts in Liberal Studies (MALS), Master of Arts in Teaching (MAT), and Master of Arts in Teaching a Second Language (MATSL) degrees. The school offers a post-baccalaureate program—one year in duration—in allied health sciences and pre-medical studies; this program is designed to prepare students for graduate study in these fields. The MAT program is open to undergraduates, graduate students, and transfer students.

STUDENT BODY

The Bennington Student Body consists of 627 undergraduates and more than 160 graduate students. Nearly all Bennington undergraduates take advantage of available College housing. Self-governance is essential to the student experience here. A Bennington student must take responsibility not only for his or her studies but also for his or her extracurricular life. Bennington expects students to strike a balance between independence and responsible behavior; self-governance places a large measure of the responsibility for regulating student behavior with the students themselves.

ACADEMICS

Students at Bennington design unique study programs with the aid of their advisors. Whereas the traditional academic program is structured like a pyramid—starting broad, then narrowing—a Bennington program is constructed like an hourglass: first broad, then focusing, and finally broadening again. First-year students explore a plethora of possibilities, examining a cornucopia of intellectual and imaginative endeavors. Second-and third-year students immerse themselves in more specific areas of study: an academic discipline, a craft, or perhaps a multidisciplinary pursuit of an answer to a particular question. Fourth-year students broaden their scope, applying the specific knowledge and insight they gained during their second and third years to a study of the world at large. Bennington students receive regular faculty feedback in the form of written reports assessing their strengths and weaknesses. Faculty reports direct students toward new areas of study and gauge students' overall progress. The Bennington faculty is more concerned with providing students with the resources to fashion a life of self-education and independent thought than with designing majors. From instructors' perspective, a true education is created actively; it is not passively received. Throughout their Bennington education, students are encouraged to pursue questions that they determine to be of import. They are also taught the skills needed to pursue such questions no matter where they lead. Bennington does not presume that a student's journey is necessarily a progressive elimination of diverse interests in pursuit of a major; rather, our approach presumes that a student may decide to investigate in depth a wide range of disciplines. During their four years here, students regularly confer with their faculty advisor, both in person and in writing, to determine what courses to take and why. They formulate statements of purpose, which change throughout their Bennington tenure, in order to design, chart, and defend their course of study. These individualized statements—called the "plan"—replace the "major" favored by institutions more traditional than ours. Students' plans are discussed and reviewed continually by panels of faculty members. Students at Bennington learn how to develop and pursue their own intellectual identity by playing an active role in designing their educations. They learn to substitute self-discipline for imposed discipline and to manage a world in which demands arrive internally rather than externally. A Bennington education leads students to that most important of all academic questions: "What constitutes a real education?"

Office of Admissions and Financial Aid
Bennington, VT 05201
Phone: 800-833-6845
Fax: 802-440-4320
Website: www.bennington.edu

Liberal arts study is available in all traditional disciplines, including philosophy, mathematics, literature, history, science, and philosophy. The visual and performing arts (e.g. ceramics, computer graphics, sculpture, painting, drama, classical and jazz music, architecture) also have a home at Bennington. Also, Bennington offers a five-year bachelor's/master's degree in teaching. The teaching program certifies graduates in early childhood, elementary, or secondary education; graduates also receive a license to teach in Vermont, which is also recognized in 44 other states, including Massachusetts, California, and New York. Students must wait until after their freshman year to apply to this program.

Because teacher-practitioners are the norm at Bennington, our faculty members are active scholars, writers, and artists. A full 25 percent of the curriculum is comprised of tutorials. With the exception of tutorials, the average class size is 20; the student/faculty ratio is 9:1. All instructors teach first-year classes as well as upper-level classes.

ADMISSIONS

Bennington seeks students who are alive to the potential of a college education, and who demonstrate an equal measure of passionate curiosity and self-discipline. Bennington carefully considers all parts of a student's application. However, the Admissions interview is afforded particular importance. The school does not employ any formulas in making Admissions decisions. Bennington requires SAT I or ACT scores. Bennington welcomes early Admissions applicants who have not yet completed high school. The school accepts transfer students for enrollment in the fall and spring terms. Freshman applications must be received by the school by January 1; transfer applications must arrive by January 1 for the spring term and June 1 for the fall term. Early decision applications must arrive by November 15; the school notifies early decision applicants by December 15. Financial statements accompanying applications for financial aid should be filed as soon as possible, by March 1 at the latest for incoming freshmen and spring transfers, and by June 1 for fall transfers. For more information about Bennington College, students should contact:

Office of Admissions & the First Year Bennington College
One College Drive
Bennington, VT 05201
Telephone: 800-833-6845 (toll free) or 802-440-4312
Fax: 802-440-4320
E-mail: Admissions@bennington.edu
Web: www.bennington.edu.

CAMPUS LIFE

Tucked into the Green Mountains in the southwest corner of Vermont, Bennington's bucolic 550-acre campus is located less than one hour from Albany, New York. Two major metropolitan areas, Boston and New York City, are less than four hours away by car. Bennington students dine together in a room facing "the end of the world," a broad commons lined with colonial houses that function as dormitories. The commons extends toward the mountains on the horizon. The campus is home to gorgeous wooded trails that link campus buildings, soccer fields, and a lovely pond. Students here enjoy many opportunities for outdoor activity: Rock-climbing, cross-country and downhill skiing, hiking, and canoeing are all popular here.

Bennington belongs to The School for Field Studies (SFS) consortium, which provides opportunities to study field biology throughout the world. Bennington is proud of its role as a facilitator of a hands-on education designed to address critical and pressing environmental issues in the world today. Students who participate in SFS may apply their work toward the fulfillment of Bennington's degree requirements. Bennington provides numerous options for study abroad in collaboration with international institutions. Students earn academic credit for their work abroad.

COST AND AID

Total charges for the 2002–2003 academic year were $33,240 (this figure includes room and board, as well as the required health and activities services fees).

BENTLEY COLLEGE

GENERAL INFORMATION

As a business university, Bentley College has the resources to invest in the tools of the information age, put them in student's hands, and offer a remarkable depth of business-related majors and concentrations. Bentley blends the breadth and technological strength of a university with the values and student orientation of a small college. The Bentley academic experience combines a strong liberal arts foundation with the most advanced business education possible. This combination prepares students for success in our global, information-driven world. In courses and projects, students gain a solid understanding of technologies and have the opportunity to watch them come alive in several hands-on, high-tech learning laboratories—each among the first of its kind in higher education. In addition, through internships, jobs, campus activities, and study abroad opportunities, students gain the critical skills necessary to manage and analyze the nearly limitless amount of information that drives the business world. Bentley enrolls approximately 4,250 full-time and part-time undergraduates. Students come from 40 states and more than 80 countries. On-campus housing options include single-, double-, or triple-occupancy dorm rooms; apartments; or suites, comprising 13 residence halls and apartment-style buildings. Seventy-eight percent of students live on-campus.

STUDENT BODY

Bentley's small-college environment delivers plenty of opportunities for fun. Students can explore current interests or develop new ones by getting involved in a wide range of on-campus activities including athletic events, music and theater programs, and more than 70 clubs and student organizations. The student center is the heart of action outside the classroom. Students enjoy a large dining room, games room, the 1917 Tavern, campus radio station and newspaper, and office and meeting space for student organizations. Bentley fields more than 23 varsity sports teams, which compete at the NCAA Division I and II levels. The College is a member of the Northeast-10 Conference, and the Division I Metro Atlantic Athletic Conference Hockey League. Many teams have regularly qualified for post-season competition, and individual athletes have routinely earned honors. Recreational athletes may take part in Bentley's ever-growing list of intramural sports and activities, which include dance and fitness training.

ACADEMICS

Bentley combines the powerful resources of a business university with the strengths of a small college to help students develop the skills that employers are looking for. Students draw on a varied curriculum to shape an academic program that reflects their interests and goals. Bentley is widely known for its distinctive programs that meet at the intersection of business and technology. Students learn to use information technology the way business does, as an important tool for planning, producing, marketing, and managing. Through the Mobile Computing Program all Bentley freshman receive a laptop that is network-ready and fully loaded with software. Many courses require students to use their laptops in class, while most offer online access to syllabi, discussion groups, course assignments, and other materials. With computer ports located all over campus—classrooms, dining halls, dorm rooms, and the library—students have incredibly fast and convenient access to the Internet, Bentley network, and many other information sources. "Learn by doing" is a core philosophy at Bentley. Hands-on experience is a key to many courses and projects. Students get the opportunity to test drive concepts and theories learned in the classroom by working in one of Bentley's specialized learning labs, which include the financial trading room, Center for Marketing Technology, accounting lab, Design and Usability Testing Center, or Center for Language and International Collaboration. Students also apply classroom theory in real life situations through hands-on experience such as internships, group consulting projects, service learning assignments, and other opportunities. Bentley's service-learning program has consistently been recognized for leadership in the field of student character development. Recently, *U.S. News & World Report* America's Best Colleges 2003 ranked Bentley's Service-Learning Center number 10 nationwide. The Center helps students build valuable skills in business, communication, and teamwork while also contributing to society. Through projects such as computer workshops for the underprivileged or a spring break trip to Hungary to learn conflict management and mediation, hundreds of Bentley students have taken advantage of these business skill development opportunities. Through aggressive on-campus recruiting, an online job-listing service, an alumni database, career fairs and workshops, the Miller Center for Career Services helps students explore career options, gain hands-on work experience, and connect with top employers. Within six months of graduation, about 93 percent of students find professional employment or enroll in graduate school full time. An internship program allows students to fine-tune skills, explore interests, and make job connections, all while earning course credit. The program offers many opportunities at some of the leading companies in the United States. Past internship positions include those at organizations such as IBM, Reebok International, Big Five accounting firms, and Hewlett-Packard.

175 Forest Street
Waltham, MA 02452-4705
Phone: 781-891-2244
Fax: 781-891-3414
Website: www.bentley.edu

While focused on business, a Bentley education is broad in scope. Students have many options for creating an academic program that meets their needs and interests. Degree options include: Bachelor of Science in accountancy, accounting information systems, computer information systems, corporate finance and accounting, economics-finance, finance, information design and corporate communication, management, managerial economics, marketing, and mathematical sciences; Bachelor of Arts in English, history, international studies, liberal arts, philosophy, and public policy and social change. In addition, students can choose a BA in mathematics or design their own arts and sciences concentration in areas such as behavioral sciences, communication, or environmental studies. Students can combine their interests by choosing a minor or concentration that complements their major area of study. For example, accounting majors can minor in law if they are interested in a career in public service, while marketing majors can minor in information design and corporate communication to gain essential communication skills for a career in public relations. There is also an opportunity for students to apply to a special program that allows them to earn a bachelor's degree and a master's degree in five years.

Bentley professors are committed teacher-scholars known equally well for their skills in the classroom and for their leading-edge research. They stay closely connected to the business world and interject real-life perspectives into classroom lectures and projects. With an average class size of 25 and a student/faculty ratio of 16:1, students benefit from a collaborative approach to teaching. There are no teaching assistants or graduate assistants in the classroom. There are 422 full-time and part-time faculty members; 82 percent of full-time professors hold doctoral degrees.

ADMISSIONS

Admission to Bentley is selective, based on past accomplishments and future potential. Along with the application, Bentley requires a secondary school transcript, letters of recommendation from a teacher and a counselor, and official results of either the SAT or ACT test. Prospective students are encouraged to complete a solid college-preparatory program, which includes 4 years of English, 4 years of mathematics (preferably algebra I and II, geometry, and a senior-year math course), and 3 to 4 years each of history, laboratory science, and foreign language. For regular admission, students must submit all required documents by February 1 for September admission and by November 15 for January admission. Candidates are notified by April 1 for the fall semester and by December 5 for the spring semester. Designed for academic achievers for whom Bentley is the first choice, the Early Decision Program allows for an admission decision by January 1. If admitted, candidates must withdraw any applications to other colleges. Students may also participate in the Early Action Program if Bentley is among their top choices but they prefer not to make a commitment in January. The application deadline for both programs is December 1. Bentley College also accepts the Common Application. All international students must file an international student application. Applicants who are non-native speakers of English must also have official results of the Test of English as a Foreign Language (TOEFL) forwarded to the Office of Undergraduate Admission. For additional information, students should contact:

Office of Undergraduate Admission
Bentley College
175 Forest Street
Waltham, Massachusetts 02452-4705
Phone: 781-891-2244, 1-800-523-2354
Fax: 781-891-3414
E-mail: ugadmission@bentley.edu
Website: www.bentley.edu

CAMPUS LIFE

Bentley is located 10 miles west of Boston, in Waltham, Massachusetts. Situated on 163 acres, the suburban campus represents the best of New England college campuses and provides an inviting atmosphere for study and socializing. The city's many resources are within easy reach; the Bentley shuttle makes regular trips to Harvard Square in Cambridge. From theater to art exhibits, dance clubs to alternative rock concerts, championship sports to championship shopping, Boston has the proverbial "something for everyone."

Bentley students can choose to spend a semester or entire year abroad in countries on five continents, including Australia, Austria, Belgium, England, France, Hong Kong, Hungary, Italy, Mexico, and Spain.

COST AND AID

Tuition in 2002–2003 is $22,965. Room and board (double room, meal plan) costs $9,350. Additional costs include books, supplies, laptop computer, and personal and travel expenses.

BERKELEY COLLEGE

AT A GLANCE

Since its inception in 1931, Berkeley College has been committed to providing an exceptional undergraduate business education. Today, Berkeley College is recognized across the nation as a premier business school, preparing students for successful careers in the modern world. Berkeley College's strong academic program succeeds through a blend of traditional education, professional training, and real-world experience.

At Berkeley, students benefit from small class sizes, personal academic and career counseling, and the chance to individually develop their analytical and creative skills. Berkeley believes that teaching should bring a practical perspective to traditional material, and Berkeley's distinguished faculty brings academic preparation and professional experience to the classroom. Teachers are chosen for not just their academic achievements but for their applicable background in the business world.

The Middle States Commission on Higher Education accredits Berkeley College and the New York State Board of Regents authorizes the New York City and Westchester campuses. Academic programs in New York and New Jersey are registered by the New York State Education Department and The New Jersey Commission on Higher Education, respectively. The Paralegal studies program at all campuses is approved by the American Bar Association (ABA).

LOCATION AND ENVIRONMENT

Berkeley's five campus locations offer outstanding convenience and accessibility. Whether students are seeking an active city setting or a quieter suburban environment, they can find it at one of Berkeley's campuses. Whichever campus is chosen, students have the easy access to the invaluable resources of New York City, where unlimited opportunity awaits.

MAJORS AND DEGREES OFFERED

Berkeley offers Bachelor degrees in accounting, e-business, general business, international business, management, marketing, and information systems management. An Associate's degree program is offered in business administration, with specializations in accounting, management, marketing, and information systems management. Berkeley also offers Associate's degree programs in e-business, fashion marketing and management, interior design, international business, paralegal studies, network management, and Web design. Not all programs are offered at all campuses.

ACADEMIC PROGRAMS

Berkeley programs provide the comprehensive foundation necessary to start or progress in a career field. At Berkeley, the traditional undergraduate curriculum is enhanced with professional training and experience. Internships are integral to learning, and Berkeley students are expected to participate in real-world work experience during their course of study. The result is a highly effective business education. Upon graduation, 94 percent of students are employed in positions related to their field of study. The Academic Resource Centers and Learning provide students with a wide range of support services to help improve their study skills as well as their reading, writing and mathematical abilities. Academic, career, individual advisement and free tutorial services are also available.

OFF-CAMPUS OPPORTUNITIES

Off-campus jobs and internships are integral to a Berkeley education. Every degree program at Berkeley has an internship component, which requires students to pursue off campus work experience related to their field of study. The internship program helps Berkeley students get real-world experience and skills, as well as develop a network of business contacts before graduation.

CAREER PLANNING/PLACEMENT OFFICES

Berkeley's has extensive career placement services, which are available to students while studying at Berkeley and throughout their lives. The Career Placement Division has 20 full-time placement advisors who work with students to identify career goals, set up internship positions, write their resume and develop key interviewing skills.

FACILITIES AND EQUIPMENT

All Berkeley campuses maintain a library, which supports the academic programs of the College and provides for the general, intellectual, and cultural enrichment of the Berkeley community. Library Web pages provide 24/7 access to the online catalog of Berkeley's system wide holdings of books, video's, DVDs, and audiocassettes, electronic databases, reference tools, Internet search engines, library services and staff, and links to institution-wide portals.

TUITION, ROOM & BOARD AND FEES

For the 2003–2004 school year, full-time tuition is $15,135. Students that maintain continuous enrollment do not suffer from any tuition increase during their course of study. A variety of residence facilities are available. Rates vary according to the location and accommodations.

FINANCIAL AID

Berkeley College believes that all students should receive a quality education, regardless of their financial situation. Berkeley College offers a number of financial aid programs and financing options.

FULL AND PART-TIME FACULTY

Berkeley's accomplished instructors bring academic preparation and invaluable professional experience to undergraduate classes. In addition, several nationally recognized business education leaders, authors, lecturers, and consultants work as administrators at Berkeley.

STUDENT ORGANIZATIONS AND ACTIVITIES

Berkeley students participate in a variety of educational, cultural, and social clubs and activities. The Student Government Association plans campus activities and events, such as picnics, ski weekends, theater parties, charity drives, and dude ranch weekends. In addition, elected representatives of the Student Government Association meet with the administration on a regular basis and are responsible for communicating the student body's social and academic concerns. Students also serve on the Library and Student Services committees, which give students experience in responsible leadership.

TRANSFER CREDIT REQUIREMENTS

Transfer credits are evaluated by the Academic Office. Berkeley accepts transfer credits from regionally accredited post-secondary institutions for courses applicable to a student's program at Berkeley. Students must have earned a minimum grade of C to

earn transfer credits. Berkeley uses the World Educational Services, Inc. guidelines to evaluate courses from foreign universities. Transfer courses are not part of a student's GPA. Courses taken at another college may be substituted for Berkeley electives; in some cases, the length of the program may be shortened proportionately.

Advanced placement and appropriate academic credit will be granted to students who pass the challenge exam administered by the Dean and Chairperson of the appropriate academic department. Credit by examination is not part of the GPA calculation.

Incoming students take who passed College Board Advanced Placement (AP) exams will receive credit for courses applicable to their course of study.

Berkeley acknowledges that many adults have acquired learning experience that, in some cases, is at the college level. Berkeley may give course credit for documented college-level learning, including skills and competencies acquired from work. Adult students can consult with the academic advisor for prior learning to review previous experiences and discuss the possibilities for earning credit. Berkeley evaluates course credit according to standard assessment guides, including National PONSI (Program on Noncollegiate-Sponsored Instruction), ACE (The American Council on Education), and DANTES (Defense Activity for Non-Traditional Educational Support), as well as acceptable scores on standardized examinations such as AP, CLEP (College-Level Examination Program), and ACT-PEP (Proficiency Examination Program), and ACE professional certification exams. Berkeley College also may award credit for portfolios. To earn credit, students must submit a comprehensive experiential learning portfolio for evaluation. For more information on credit for portfolios, prospective students should consult academic advisor for prior learning.

ADMISSION REQUIREMENTS

All successful applicants must have completed high school or equivalent (GED) and taken the SAT or ACT. To be considered for admission, students must submit a completed application, a $40 application fee, and a high school transcript and a high school diploma or its equivalent. In addition, Berkeley strongly recommends that students schedule a personal interview. Students who attended or are attending a college or university may apply as transfer students. Prospective transfer students must submit a completed application, a $40 application fee, a transcript from all college or university course work, and a high school transcript or GED.

Students may be admitted to the upper division if they have completed a relevant associate's degree or at least 60 semester/90 quarter-credits in appropriate course work with a grade of C or better.

Applications are accepted on a rolling basis. Prospective students should contact the Director of Admissions at one of the following Berkeley College campuses:

New York City Campus
3 East 43rd Street
New York, NY 10017
Telephone: 212-986-4343
800-446-5400, ext. WPR (toll free)
Fax: 212-818-1079
Email: info@berkeleycollege.edu
World Wide Web: www.berkeleycollege.edu

Westchester Campus
99 Church Street
White Plains, NY 10601
Telephone: 914-694-1122
800-446-5400, ext. WPR (toll free)
Fax: 914-328-9469
E-mail: info@berkeleycollege.edu
World Wide Web: www.berkeleycollege.edu

Garret Mountain Campus
44 Rifle Camp Road
West Paterson, NJ 07424
Telephone: 973-278-5400
800-446-5400, ext. WPR (toll free)
Fax: 973-278-9141
E-mail: info@berkeleycollege.edu
World Wide Web: www.berkeleycollege.edu

Bergen Campus
64 East Midland Avenue
Paramus, NJ 07652
Telephone: 201-967-9667
800-446-5400, ext. WPR (toll free)
Fax: 201-265-6446
E-mail: info@berkeleycollege.edu
World Wide Web: www.berkeleycollege.edu

Middlesex Campus
430 Rahway Avenue
Woodbridge, NJ 07095
Telephone: 732-750-1800
800-446-5400, ext. WPR (toll free)
Fax: 732-750-0652
E-mail: info@berkeleycollege.edu
World Wide Web: www.berkeleycollege.edu

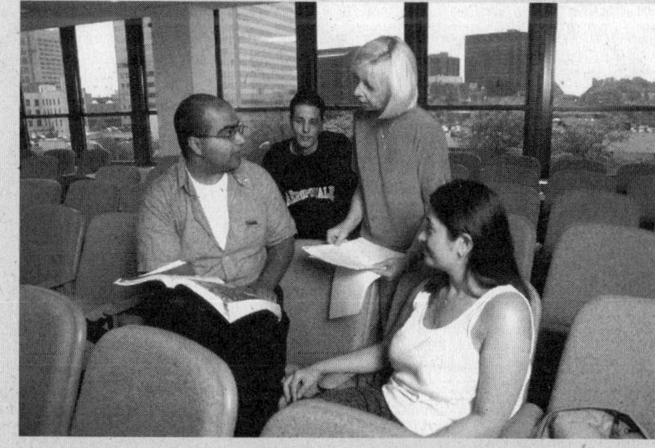

BLOOMFIELD COLLEGE

GENERAL INFORMATION

Bloomfield College, founded in 1868, is a four-year independent college historically related to the Presbyterian Church (United States). The College awards Bachelor of Arts and Bachelor of Science degrees. The curriculum is designed to provide students with a liberal arts education as well as specialized career training. More than 55 nationalities are represented on campus, reflecting the College's commitment to its distinctive mission: to prepare students to function at the peak of their potential in a multiracial, multicultural society. Programs of study are rooted in the liberal arts and assist students in obtaining the skills, knowledge, and values they need to become empowered, active individuals engaged in renewing themselves, their relationships, their work places, and their communities. One of the strengths of Bloomfield College is the rich diversity of its students. The College is committed to this richness because it provides an ideal context for personal growth and a basis for a better society. In joining Bloomfield College, each person assumes a personal responsibility to strive to achieve academic excellence, to take full advantage of the resources offered, and to contribute to the quality of the College community. Bloomfield College enrolls approximately 2,000 students per semester, about two-thirds of whom are full time.

STUDENT BODY

Athletics: Bloomfield's athletic teams compete in men's and women's basketball and soccer, women's softball and volleyball, and men's baseball and cross country as part of the Central Atlantic College Conference, NCAA Division II. Intramural programs include men's and women's basketball and volleyball.

Social Life: With more than 30 organizations to choose from, Bloomfield offers many extracurricular programs for students to enrich their educational experience. In addition to an active student government, student activities include a full program of intercollegiate and intramural athletics for men and women. Campus publications include *In Print*, the College newspaper; the College yearbook; and *Common Ground*, the literary magazine.

ACADEMICS

Bloomfield College offers major programs in the following disciplinary areas: Bachelor of Arts (BA) in creative arts and technology, education, English, history, philosophy, political science, psychology, religion, and sociology; Bachelor of Science (BS) in allied health technologies, accounting, applied mathematics, biology, business administration, chemistry, clinical laboratory science, computer information systems, and nursing. The College offers flexible class schedules that include weekend and evening sessions.

The faculty is currently comprised of almost 190 full- and part-time professors. Many of our faculty members are national leaders in scholarship, developing innovative ways to meet the intellectual, social, and demographic changes in society.

1 Park Place
Bloomfield, NJ 07003
Phone: 973-748-9000
Fax: 973-748-0916
Website: www.bloomfield.edu

ADMISSIONS

All applicants are encouraged to visit the College to discuss their academic and career plans with an admission counselor. Campus tours are given on a regular schedule and by appointment. Applicants are invited to spend a day on campus attending classes and talking with students, faculty members, and administrators regarding academic programs and student activities as well as admission and financial assistance. Applicants for admission to Bloomfield College are considered on the basis of their high school academic record, Scholastic Assessment Test (SAT-1) or American College Test (ACT) scores, recommendations, extracurricular activities, and post-secondary school transcripts where applicable. Preference is given to applications submitted by June 1 for the fall semester, January 1 for the spring semester, and May 1 for the summer sessions. Applications received after these dates will be considered on a space-available basis. Applicants are accepted throughout the school year through a rolling admission policy. Applicants are, however, encouraged to apply early. A nonrefundable fee of $35 must be sent with each application. Applicants are notified of their admission eligibility after their credentials have been received and evaluated. Send applications and requests for information to:

Bloomfield College
467 Franklin Street
Bloomfield, NJ 07003
Phone: (973) 748-9000, ext. 230 or 800-848-4555
Fax: 973-748-0916
E-mail: admission@bloomfield.edu www.bloomfield.edu

CAMPUS LIFE

Located 20 miles west of New York City, Bloomfield College enables students to take advantage of the educational, social, and cultural experiences offered in Manhattan and the region. The College's 12-acre campus reflects the area's history and architecture. The Robert V. Van Fossan Theatre is a 300-seat, state-of-the-art facility housed in Westminster Hall, a Romanesque, sandstone edifice also known for its magnificent stained glass windows. Seibert Hall, the oldest of the 28 buildings on the campus, was built in 1810. A new library providing material in both print and digital format opened in 2000.

Bloomfield College is a member of the College Consortium for International Studies (CCIS). Students are encouraged to take advantage of study abroad opportunities either for a semester or summer program.

COST AND AID

Full-time day student tuition is $12,100. Tuition for evening, weekend, summer, and part-time students is $1,220 per course. Room and board is $5,850.

BLUFFTON COLLEGE

GENERAL INFORMATION

Founded in 1899, Bluffton College is a Christian, liberal arts school in northwestern Ohio, nationally recognized for its high academic quality, supportive atmosphere, and reasonable price. Affiliated with the Mennonite Church and shaped by its tradition of peace, justice, and service, Bluffton College helps students pursue rewarding careers, while teaching the values of social responsibility and community service. Bluffton's campus community is close and supportive. The Student Life program encourages personal growth through numerous social, educational, and recreational activities, and campus chapel services and Sunday worship add a spiritual dimension to the collegiate atmosphere. Religious and community service groups are active on campus, including BASIC (Brothers And Sisters In Christ), and the Christian outreach groups Diakonia and Habitat for Humanity. The campus community adheres to the Honor System in all aspects of life, promoting an honest and open atmosphere. A model environment, Bluffton was one few Ohio institutions to be awarded the prestigious John Templeton Foundation Honor Roll of Character-Building Colleges.

Music and theater groups, academic and pre-professional clubs, the campus newspaper, and student government are among the most popular of Bluffton's many campus activities. Bluffton also boasts a strong varsity sports program, which includes Men's basketball, cross-country, football, golf, soccer, tennis, and track, and women's varsity basketball, cross-country, golf, soccer, softball, tennis, track, and volleyball. A member of the Heartland Collegiate Athletic Conference, Bluffton was the first Division III school to be included in the NCAA Life Skills Program, which helps student-athletes transition to life after college. Residential life is an integral part of the Bluffton experience and students are required to live on campus, unless they are married or choose to commute from their parents' home. There are no fraternities and sororities at Bluffton and new residential students are promised a "Satisfaction Guarantee" when they move in. In return, students are expected to comply with the school's established rules and spirit, which prohibits the use tobacco, alcohol, and drugs.

STUDENT BODY

The Bluffton College Student Senate, comprised of elected representatives from each undergraduate class, represents the student body and communicates its needs to the administration. With the help of Hall Associations, the Student Senate oversees and coordinates all co-curricular activities on campus.

ACADEMICS

In addition to major requirements, all Bluffton students must complete a core curriculum in the liberal arts and sciences, which integrates social science, humanities, fine arts, and natural sciences. Students are also required to take courses in Bible and theology, a unique cross-cultural course, "Christian Values in a Global Community," a First Year Seminar, and a cross-cultural requirement. Degree candidates must complete at least 122 semester hours with a minimum 2.0 GPA to earn a Bachelor's Degree.

Bluffton College confers the Bachelor of Arts degree, the Master of Arts in Education, and the Master of Arts in Organizational Management. Bachelor's degrees may be conferred in the following areas: accounting; adolescent/young adult, multi-age, vocational education; art; biology; business administration; chemistry; child development; apparel/textiles merchandising and design; communication; computer science; criminal justice; dietetics; economics; early childhood education; English; family and consumer sciences; food and nutrition-dietetics; food and nutrition-wellness; health; physical education and recreation (HPER); history; information systems; intervention specialist (special education); mathematics; middle childhood education; music; music education; physics; pre-medicine; psychology; recreation management; religion; social studies; social work; sociology; Spanish; Spanish/economics; sport management; writing; and youth ministries and recreation. In addition, Bluffton offers minors, pre-professional curriculums, and special programs, such as pre-law, peace and conflict studies, TESOL studies, and women's studies.

Of Bluffton's 68 full-time instructors, approximately 75 percent hold a doctorate or terminal degree in their field. Though many of Bluffton's distinguished faculty sustain independent projects in research and writing, they are committed to advising and teaching. Approachable and ready to help, Bluffton instructors promote an atmosphere of respect and learning throughout the school community.

Office of Admissions, 280 West College Avenue
Bluffton, OH 45817
Phone: 419-358-3257
Fax: 419-358-3232
Website: www.bluffton.edu

ADMISSIONS

Successful applicants to Bluffton College must have graduated from secondary school or obtained a GED. For acceptance, students must have satisfactorily completed all secondary school requirements. Bluffton gives priority to students in the top 50 percent of their graduating class. Bluffton recommends a strong secondary school preparation that includes 4 years of English and 3 years of mathematics, social studies, science, and foreign language. When making admissions decisions, Bluffton also considers high school GPA, performance on the ACT or SAT I, the student's involvement in extracurricular and community activities, their stated goals for college study, and letters of recommendation.

Prospective students should submit a completed application early in the senior year of high school. Applications for fall semester should be submitted before May 1 of that year. For other semesters, prospective students should submit an application no later than 30 days before enrollment. In addition to a completed application, students must submit a $20 application fee, letters of recommendation from a guidance counselor and a teacher, an official high school transcript, and scores to the ACT or SAT. Though not required, a campus visit and interview are strongly recommended.

The Office of Admissions makes admissions decisions on a rolling basis and notifies applicants shortly after receiving their application. Students may request additional information from the Office of Admissions. Please contact:

Office of Admissions
Bluffton College
280 West College Avenue
Bluffton, OH 45817-1196
Telephone: 800-488-3257 or 419-358-3257
Fax: 1-419-358-3081
E-mail: admissions@bluffton.edu
World Wide Web: www.bluffton.edu

CAMPUS LIFE

Set in the pleasant Allen County town of Bluffton, the College's lovely campus encompasses 60 acres adjacent the Bluffton College Nature Preserve. Downtown Bluffton is home to a few restaurants and a movie theater, all within walking distance of campus. While the immediate setting is quiet and rural, proximity to I-75 makes the towns of Findlay, Lima, Toledo, Dayton, and Columbus easily accessible by car.

Undergraduates at Bluffton College can earn course credit through exchange programs in the U.S. and overseas. The school sponsors several semester-long programs in a variety of international locations, including Northern Ireland. Additional overseas opportunities are available through the Council of Christian Colleges and Universities, which offers programs in Washington DC, the Middle East, Russia, Central America, and more. In May, students can participate in a cross-cultural exchange in various exciting locations, from Kentucky, Washington DC, Chicago, and San Antonio to Jerusalem, Jamaica, Spain, and Vietnam. Aside from college-sponsored programs, many Bluffton students work with independent organizations such as Habitat for Humanity and Witness for Peace. Bluffton students may earn up to four course units pursuing off campus, independent study courses.

COST AND AID

Total tuition for the 2003–2004 school year, including room and board, is $23,690. Academic tuition is $17,260 plus an additional $400 technology fee. Students pay an additional $3,272 for board and $2,758 for room. Students may incur other personal expenses.

BOSTON UNIVERSITY

GENERAL INFORMATION

Located along Boston's Charles River, Boston University is a coeducational, private, independent university with a stimulating learning environment. The University is a well-known and respected research institution, dedicated to cultivating innovation and ingenuity. Boston University boasts a faculty of elite world-renowned authorities who are wholly committed to educating the University's dedicated students. Most freshman- and sophomore-level classes have 29 students or fewer. Boston University's 11 undergraduate colleges and schools together offer 250 major and minor programs of study. Students have a wide variety of programs from which to choose, including biochemistry, broadcast journalism, business, computer engineering, elementary education, international relations, physical therapy, and theater arts. The student body at Boston University is one of the most geographically diverse in the nation; it includes students from more than 100 countries as well as from all regions of the United States. More than 400 campus organizations invite students to participate, including community service groups, ice broomball teams, performing arts groups, and student government, as well as academic, cultural, and professional clubs.

STUDENT BODY

Boston University students dare to excel every day, participating in academic clubs, cultural or religious organizations, cutting-edge research, community service groups, and professional internships. A separate student government exists at each College and School to manage student affairs, and the Student Union, the governing body that presides over all of the University's student governments, includes members who represent all branches of the University.

ACADEMICS

Boston University is committed to providing well-rounded instruction, merging the fundamentals of a conventional liberal arts program with preparation for the professional job market. Additionally, honors programs in both the College of Arts and Sciences and the School of Management are offered to outstanding freshmen and sophomores who wish to participate.

The University awards the BA, BS, BSBA, BSEd, BAS, BLS, BAA, MusB, and BFA undergraduate degrees. Eleven of Boston University's 16 colleges and schools have undergraduate study programs. The listing below shows the wide variety of study options available to undergraduates.

College of Arts and Sciences students may pursue degrees in American studies, Ancient Greek, Ancient Greek and Latin, anthropology, anthropology/religion, archaeology, art history, astronomy, astronomy/physics, biochemistry, biochemistry/molecular biology, biology, biology with an emphasis on ecology and conservation, biology with an emphasis in marine science, biology with an emphasis in neuroscience, chemistry, classical civilization, classics/philosophy, classics/religion, computer science, earth sciences, East Asian studies, economics, economics/mathematics, English, environmental analysis and policy, environmental earth science, environmental science, French/continental European literatures, French language and literature, geography, geography with specialization in human geography, geography with specialization in physical geography, geophysics and planetary sciences, German/continental European literatures, German language and literature, Hispanic/continental European literatures, Hispanic language and literature, history, independent concentration, international relations, Italian/continental European literatures, Italian studies, Latin, Latin American studies, linguistics, mathematics, mathematics/computer science, mathematics/philosophy, Modern Greek studies, music (nonperformance), philosophy, philosophy/anthropology, philosophy/physics, philosophy/political science, philosophy/psychology, philosophy/religion, physics, political science, psychology, religion, Russian language and literature, Russian/continental European literatures, Russian/Eastern European studies, sociology. Special curricula are also available, including a dual degree program; seven-year programs in liberal arts and dentistry, and liberal arts and medicine; the Modular Medical Integrated Curriculum; and a variety of combined BA/MA degree programs. Pre-medical, pre-veterinary, and pre-dental studies are supported through the College of Arts and Sciences with nearly any major.

Through the College of Communication, students can pursue concentrations in advertising, film, television, journalism (including broadcast journalism, magazine journalism, news-editorial print journalism, and photojournalism), mass communications, and public relations.

At the College of Engineering, students may choose from programs in aerospace, biomedical, computer systems, electrical, interdisciplinary, manufacturing, and mechanical engineering. Students may also pursue the Engineering/Medical Integrated Curriculum to begin medical school courses in their sophomore year. The School of Education allows students to pursue bilingual education, deaf studies, early childhood education, elementary education, English education, history and social science education, human movement (including physical education), mathematics education, modern foreign language education, science education, and special education.

The School of Hospitality Administration has an intense program that trains students in the management of hotels, restaurants, food and beverage service, travel and tourism, and entertainment.

The School of Management allows students to pursue concentrations in accounting, entrepreneurship, finance, general management, international management, management information systems, marketing, operations management, and organizational behavior.

At the College of Fine Arts, students may pursue studies in the School of Music (history and literature of music, music education, performance, and theory and composition), the School of Theatre Arts (acting; costume, lighting, and scenic design; directing; production; stage management; technical production; and theater studies), and the School of Visual Arts (art education, graphic design, painting, and sculpture).

121 Bay State Road
Boston, MA 02215
Phone: 617-353-2300
Fax: 617-353-9695
Website: www.bu.edu

At the Sargent College of Health and Rehabilitation Sciences, students may pursue concentrations in athletic training, communication disorders, exercise science, human physiology, nutritional sciences, and rehabilitation and human services. Also available are a five-year combined BS/MS degree program in occupational therapy and a six-year combined BS/DPT program in physical therapy.

The College of General Studies has a two-year liberal arts-based program centered on a core curriculum and rigorous team teaching. The program allows junior-level students to advance to the University's specific schools and colleges.

The University Professors Program provides a unique opportunity for students with outstanding abilities to pursue degrees in areas that either merge, or fall outside of, recognized University fields of study. Students study a core curriculum for the program's first two years, then devise their own study programs for their final two years, culminating with an original contribution to their field of study.

The Metropolitan College Science and Engineering Program is a five-semester program aimed at students requiring further preparation for the study of sciences or engineering.

Boston University's instructors distinguish themselves through their experience, published works, research, and excellent teaching skills. As well as skillfully performing classroom duties, each teaching staff member serves as a knowledgeable career advisor, who helps students to obtain internship and research positions.

ADMISSIONS

The Board of Admissions judges each prospective student individually. The Board's main focus centers on the merits of a student's high school record, but required standardized test scores (SAT I or ACT), personality and integrity, interests, teacher and counselor references, and other qualities relevant to qualification are also considered carefully. All candidates must have graduated from high school or earned an equivalency diploma to be considered. For acceptance to the College of Fine Arts, students must either perform an audition or submit a portfolio. A few select programs require interviews and submission of SAT II: Subject Test scores. Students should consult the Boston University Application for Admission or Undergraduate Bulletin for additional information. Both are available online at www.bu.edu. Boston University also considers students with transferable credit from other institutions for admission. Boston University considers applicants for September or January admission. Transfer students cannot be admitted to the accelerated liberal arts medical or dental programs, the College of General Studies, the Metropolitan College Science and Engineering Program, or Sargent College's physical therapy and nutritional science program. Transfer students also may not apply for January admission to the College of Fine Arts (Schools of Theatre and Visual Arts) and Sargent College's occupational therapy and nutritional sciences programs. Boston University offers early decision (which is binding on the applicant), early admission, and deferred admission options. All applications must be postmarked by January 1 (early decision applications are due by November 1; accelerated program and select scholarship applications must be submitted by December 1). Transfer students seeking September admission must submit application forms by April 1. Boston University accepts qualified applicants regardless of age, color, disability, national origin, race, or sex to all of its activities and programs.

CAMPUS LIFE

Boston provides an environment rich in intellectual and cultural stimuli; no other city in the world can compete with Boston's remarkable concentration of higher education facilities. Boston attractions include numerous excellent museums, major league baseball at Fenway Park, the Boston Symphony Orchestra, and a thriving theater district. The city has an atmosphere of excitement abetted by its many college students, who comprise 20 percent of Boston's population, making Boston the quintessential college town. The city of Boston provides University undergraduates with many opportunities for internship and research positions. The Undergraduate Research Opportunities Program (UROP) office helps students locate research positions both within and beyond the University. Moreover, the Martin Luther King Jr. Center works to provide students with internships (either paid or not paid) in any number of fields.

Boston University also has one of the world's most extensive study abroad programs, offering opportunities to study in Auckland, New Zealand; Beijing; Dublin; London; Oxford; Madrid; Moscow; Paris; Quito, Ecuador; and Sydney. Fieldwork programs in Belize and Ecuador are available to students wishing to pursue academic research projects. Students may participate in foreign language programs in France, Germany, Israel, Italy, Japan, Niger, and Spain. Furthermore, students have the option to take part in summer study courses in Australia, China, England, France, Italy, and Spain. Communication students may also spend a semester in Washington, D.C., or Los Angeles as part of their curriculum.

COST AND AID

Tuition for the 2003–2004 academic year is $28,512; room and board amounts to $9,288. Additional University and College fees equal $394. These figures do not take into account the cost of books, supplies, travel, and other incidentals.

BREVARD COLLEGE

GENERAL INFORMATION

Nestled in the beautiful Blue Ridge Mountains of North Carolina, Brevard College is a four-year comprehensive liberal arts college affiliated with the United Methodist Church. *U.S. News & World Report* ranks Brevard College second in the nation for its First Year Experience program for first year students. The ranking places Brevard College ahead of institutions like Princeton University, Duke University and Stanford University in its ability to make freshmen feel connected to their college through regular small group interactions between students, faculty and staff and peers. Through the First Year Forum (FYF) advising program, Brevard College orients new and transfer students toward academic and intellectual success through a special one-semester course. A faculty, staff and student team introduces students to an array of resources, including academic counseling, campus services, and opportunities for social involvement, leadership and responsibility. The Forum also allows entering students to set goals and to develop strategies to meet those goals. Brevard College overall ranks among the best comprehensive colleges in the southern United States that focus on undergraduate education and offer a range of degree programs both in the liberal arts and professional fields. *U.S. News & World Report* also ranks Brevard College 14th in Best Value among comprehensive colleges in the South for the quality of its academic programs compared to net cost of attendance at the institution. Brevard College is also recognized among Southern Comprehensive Colleges for its campus diversity and high proportion of classes with fewer than 20 students. Caring faculty and staff and a 10:1 student/faculty ratio allow students to be known, their interests and activities to be supported and their voices heard.

A range of majors including fine arts, business & organizational leadership, wilderness leadership & experiential education, environmental studies, religion studies and integrated studies is available to its diverse student population (from 37 states and 20 foreign countries). The College provides a variety of opportunities for leadership and service in numerous co-curricular organizations, including an active student government association. It balances nationally competitive athletic programs with a range of intramural activities and outdoor leadership opportunities. Brevard College's programs in music and art afford talented students exceptional educational and performance opportunities and enliven the arts on campus. Its outreach and academic internship programs directly involve students in real-world problem solving. The College's Wilderness Leadership & Experiential Education program, Center for Campus and Community Service, Appalachian Center for Environmental Solutions, Institute for Sacred Music, and Center for Transformational Leadership reach out to the professional community and engage students in making a practical difference outside the classroom. Upon graduation, students are ready to embark on their careers or go on to graduate school. The College's Career Services staff is dedicated to pursuing creative and innovative ways of developing and maintaining relationships and resources, while assisting students and graduates in their pursuit of satisfying and rewarding careers.

STUDENT BODY

Brevard College's student clubs and organizations reflect the energy and interests of a vibrant, involved and creative student body. Whether on campus, out on the rugged mountain trails, or in the surrounding communities, students are active in government, the College's newspaper, athletics, dance, drama, musical productions, volunteer service, whitewater sports, hiking, mountain biking, rock climbing, concerts, special events and exploring the area. The College's Outing Club offers off campus excursions, while the student-run Twister Productions brings concerts, games and other entertainment to campus. Brevard College's Division of Campus Life is "totally committed to students" (TC2S). Campus Life works with students to create and maintain a campus environment that enables the development of the "whole" student—intellectual, spiritual, vocational, emotional, physical and social. Campus Life accomplishes this through a range of activities, services and programs. Brevard College's student clubs and organizations create energy for environmental causes, spiritual awakenings, fellowship and fun. They include: Student Government Association (SGA), Campus Crusade for Christ, Circle K, Commuter Student Association (CSA), Debate Society, Fellowship of Christian Athletes (FCA), Omicron Delta Kappa Society, and Beta Beta Beta Honor Societies, Pastimes (History Club), Outing Club, Twister Productions Dimensions (Mathematics Society), Photography Club, BC Recycles, and Student Ambassadors.

ACADEMICS

Founded in 1853, Brevard College is the oldest college or university in western North Carolina. It uses a semester calendar and offers Bachelor of Arts, Associate in Arts, and Associate in Fine Arts degrees. The College's core curriculum provides a strong interdisciplinary base in literature and languages, religion, humanities, mathematics and analytical reasoning, history, natural and social sciences, fine arts, physical activity, and environmental studies. In addition to traditional disciplines, Brevard incorporates the surrounding natural resources into course work, bringing students to study in the Pisgah National Forest, the Davidson and French Broad River ecosystems, the Great Smoky Mountain National Park, and the Cradle of Forestry in America. A special, selective academic program called "Voice of the Rivers" blends wilderness leadership skills with environmental studies. The College also offers strong programs in music and art, in which students benefit from performance and exhibition opportunities on and off campus, in settings such as the Porter Center for Performing Arts at Brevard College, the Brevard Music Center, the Brevard Chamber Orchestra, and the Asheville Art Museum. Brevard College incorporates community service into the academic curriculum through a variety of service-oriented classes. The Center for Campus & Community Service helps students locate service opportunities.

Special Programs & Opportunities: Honors programs; study abroad; internships; study abroad internships; experiential studies (Pisgah National Forest, Great Smoky Mountains National Park, Cradle of Forestry, regional museums, area orchestras); immersion semesters in wilderness leadership and interdisciplinary and environmental studies, including the Voice of the Rivers Expeditions; Institute for Sacred Music; Appalachian Center for Environmental Solutions; and Center for Transformational Leadership, Pisgah Forest Institute

Majors:

- Art, with optional emphases in art history, archaeology, graphic design, painting, photography, sculpture
- Business & organizational leadership, with emphases (one required) in computer information systems, entrepreneurship and small business leadership, management and organizational leadership, sport and event management
- Ecology, with optional emphasis in computer science
- English/interdisciplinary studies, with emphases (one required) in art, creative writing, environmental journalism, history, literary studies, music, natural sciences, pre-law, religion, theatre arts
- Environmental studies, with optional emphasis in archaeology
- Exercise science, with emphases (one required) in exercise gerontology and allied medical fields, fitness leadership, teaching/coaching
- Health science studies
- History, with optional emphases in art history and archaeology, environmental history, modern American history, modern European history, music history
- Integrated studies, with emphases in pre-law, pre-medicine, psychology and counseling, theatre arts
- Mathematics
- Music, with optional emphases in church music, composition, jazz studies, music teaching, music theory/history, performance
- Religion studies, with optional emphases in outdoor ministries, counseling and educational ministries, youth ministries, music ministries
- Wilderness leadership & experiential education

Minors: art, biology, chemistry, coaching, computer information systems, computer science, ecology, English, environmental art and design, environmental studies, fitness leadership, geology, history, management and organizational leadership, mathematics, music, personal fitness, pre-law, religion, sport and event management, theatre, wilderness leadership & experiential education

Pre-professional Studies: pre-law, pre-dentistry, pre-medicine, and pre-veterinary

400 North Broad Street
Brevard, NC 28712-3306
Phone: 800-527-9090
Fax: 828-884-3790
Website: www.brevard.edu

Brevard College is accredited by the Commission on Colleges of the Southern Association of Colleges and Schools and the University Senate of The United Methodist Church to award degrees at the baccalaureate and associate levels. The College's music programs are accredited by the National Association of Schools of Music.

Brevard College's faculty is a unique group of 63 full time and 36 part time instructors, characterized by their accomplishments and strong personal character. The College's faculty is dedicated to undergraduate teaching and takes pride in all aspects of their job, from instruction and lecturing, to advising and mentoring. This dedication, along with the excellent 10:1 student/faculty ratio and consistently small class sizes, gives students the opportunity to form lasting and meaningful student/teacher relationships.

ADMISSIONS

Brevard College seeks to admit students who distinguish themselves by their talents, creativity, adventurous spirit, motivation, and concern for others. At Brevard, students will have every opportunity to take advantage of our educational programs, small classes, and caring faculty in order to realize their potential as students and as leaders among their peers. The College is interested in enrolling students who give proof of academic curiosity, creativity, and community concern. We actively seek those who add diversity to the student body and welcome students of any race, national origin, religious belief, gender, or physical ability. We seek students who will contribute their energies to the campus community and display a willingness to place themselves in situations that call for personal initiative and leadership. An admissions staff of energetic and caring people invites all interested students to visit and learn about our special community. The application process is candidate-oriented, so that the admissions staff serves as the applicant's advocate. For the latest admissions information, visit the College's website at www.brevard.edu.

The Application Process: When the applicant's file is complete, an admissions counselor reviews the file and notifies the candidate of the decision. Decisions are made on a rolling basis, every week. An applicant's file is complete when the following has been received: (1) A completed application and nonrefundable $30 application fee. (2) Official transcripts showing all high school work, grades, and test scores. Transfer students must also submit transcripts showing all college work attempted, grades, and test scores if applicable. (3) Official scores from the SAT or the ACT may be sent directly to the College (fill in code 5067 for the SAT and code 3074 for the ACT). All achievement test scores are welcome and will be considered in the candidate's favor but are not required. For international students to whom English is a second language, the TOEFL (Test of English as a Foreign Language) scores are required if SAT/ACT not available. *Note:* Students who have successfully completed an associate degree, the SAT or ACT is not required. (4) For students wishing to be considered for degree programs in music or studio art, an audition with a member of the Brevard College music faculty or submission of a portfolio of ten slides of the student's artwork for review is required.

Since not all persons are suited for membership in our academic community, the College has the sole right to make admissions decisions, including the right to cancel an offer of admission once extended if, on the basis of new information, it appears that such cancellation is in the best interest of the student and/or the College.

Freshmen: For those who have not successfully completed at least a semester of collegiate work, the high school transcript should show successful completion of college preparatory work, including four units of English, three units of mathematics, and courses in social studies, laboratory sciences, foreign language, and the arts. The program at Brevard College requires completion of Core Requirements that include studies in the above fields. Students planning to major in music or art should show competencies in their selected field and will be asked to audition for music or to submit a portfolio of ten slides of their work for art.

Transfer Students: Applicants who have attended other institutions of higher learning or taken courses online will be considered for admission as transfer students provided: they are eligible, both socially and academically, to return to the college last attended, and they present a grade point average equal to that expected for continuation at Brevard College. In the evaluation of transcripts, the following principles shall apply: (1) Credit will be accepted only from colleges and universities that are accredited as university-parallel institutions. (2) Credit will be given only for college-level courses in which the grade is at least a C-. (3) No credit shall be recorded until an official transcript has been received. (4) Equivalent credit will be awarded for courses similar in content to courses offered at Brevard College. (5) Elective credit will be awarded only for courses appropriate to the student's educational program. (6) Transfer courses not offered at Brevard College may be used to satisfy core, major, and/or minor requirements, provided the courses meet the same level and similar content; approval is required from the advisor, major coordinator, and the division chair, with written documentation from the division chair approving the substitute course. (7) At least 32 hours of work must be taken at Brevard College in order to earn the Bachelor of Arts degree and no more than 92 credit hours from other institutions may be applied toward graduation. (8) Transfer students must meet all current requirements for graduation.

International Students: Brevard College seeks to add diversity to our student body through the acceptance of eligible international candidates. All students who are neither citizens nor legal residents of the United States must submit the following information: (1) A completed application and application fee of U.S. $30. (2) Results (500 or above) of the Test of English as a Foreign Language (TOEFL), if English is not the native language, sent directly to Brevard College. SAT or ACT scores are acceptable, if the examination is available to the student. (3) Certificate of Financial Support. (4) Official transcripts showing in detail all secondary and post-secondary study. Certified English translations must accompany all documents not presented in English. Photostats must be notarized as true copies of the original documents. (5) Transfer/Visa Certification Form for students currently attending a college or university in the United States.

Brevard College Admissions
400 North Broad Street
Brevard, NC 28712
Phone: 828-884-8300 or 800-527-9090, ext. 003 (toll free)

CAMPUS LIFE

Set on 120 acres of woods and rolling hills with majestic views of the Great Smokey Mountains, Brevard College's campus is a beautiful setting for study and personal growth. Nearby, the Pisgah National Forest, the Blue Ridge Parkway and the Great Smoky Mountains National Park, offer recreation as well as research opportunities for students. The College offers a wide variety of programs, resources, and services to enhance the college experience for students, from participating in religious life retreat, to being a leader of a campus organization. The beautiful City of Brevard is often ranked among the safest cities in the nation. Though the setting is rural, Brevard is a culturally rich and sophisticated town. Downtown is just up the hill from campus. The City of Brevard offers numerous restaurants, coffee shops, a movie theatre and shops that cater to college students. The county is home to Pisgah National Forest and more than 100 natural waterfalls, and is situated in close proximity to the Great Smoky Mountains National Park and many famous rivers, such as the Nantahala, the Oconee, and the French Broad. Brevard is only 30 minutes from the Asheville Regional Airport and an hour and a half from Greenville-Spartanburg, South Carolina. Other important Southern cities, such as Charlotte, and Atlanta are only a few hours by car.

COST AND AID

While the College makes a sincere effort to project the actual cost of attendance, the Board of Trustees reserves the right to make necessary adjustments in fees at any time.

2002–2003 Tuition And Fee Schedule For Full-Time Students (Fall and Spring Semesters)

For commuting students, tuition is $11,980, general fees are $930, the parking fee is $60, the student government fee is $20, and the total cost is $12,990.

For residential students, tuition is $11,980, room is $2,200 for older residence halls and $3,120 per year for the Residential Village, board is $3,200, the general fee is $930, the telecommunications fee is $650, the parking fee is $120, the student government fee is $20, and the total cost is $19,100.

For North Carolina residents, total costs are reduced by the NC Legislative Tuition Grant. For the 2001–2002 academic year, the rate was $1,800.

BRIDGEWATER STATE COLLEGE

GENERAL INFORMATION

In 1840, Bridgewater State College opened its doors to a freshman class of just 21 students. Since then, the College has been steadily growing in size and prestige, and today, it is a comprehensive, liberal arts school with a total enrollment of more than 9,000 students. Academic programs at Bridgewater State College are augmented by the school's lively and social atmosphere. Every year, students benefit from a wide variety of cultural and recreational programs on campus, such as lectures, guest speakers, movie screenings, concerts, and art exhibits. In addition to programs and entertainment, students participate in more than 100 extracurricular clubs and organizations, many of which operate from the Rondileau Campus Center, the hub of student life. Bridgewater State College is a member of the NCAA Division III, competing in men's baseball, basketball, cross-country, football, soccer, swimming, tennis, track and field, and wrestling, and women's basketball, cross-country, field hockey, lacrosse, soccer, softball, swimming, tennis, track and field, and volleyball. There is also an active club sports program, including the popular men's lacrosse club, as well as Ultimate Frisbee, karate, cheerleading, men's ice hockey, and men's and women's rugby. Situated on 255 picturesque acres in Bridgewater, Massachusetts, the College campus contains 8 student residence halls and 20 classroom and administrative buildings. A friendly and informal academic atmosphere, the College is a true community, with shared interests and goals. The College offers all major student support services, such as career counseling, academic counseling, personal counseling, disability services, health services, and housing assistance. There are 28 graduate programs leading to master's degrees or to certificates of advanced graduate studies.

STUDENT BODY

Bridgewater State College views students, instructors, administrators, staff, and alumni as active and important members of the campus community. Everyone affiliated with Bridgewater is included in the educational program and expected to foster a community of academic excellence. With this philosophy in mind, all Bridgewater students are members of the Student Government Association, the primary body responsible for representing student views to the greater school community. The Student Government Association's officers, elected by the student body, are responsible for communicating with instructors and administrators. In addition to this role, elected officers organize all-campus activities and service projects.

ACADEMICS

Bridgewater State College offers 28 major fields in a variety of disciplines. In addition to providing an in-depth understanding in the major field, the College aims to educate students in a broad range of liberal arts, sciences, and professional fields through general education courses. To earn an undergraduate degree, students must satisfactorily complete at least 120 units, of which 30–36 semester hours must completed in the major area. In addition, students in every subject area must fulfill the core requirements in the general education courses. Accomplished students have the opportunity to enroll in honors programs through the College or through their major department. All incoming students receive individual academic counseling through the Academic Achievement Center. Bridgewater State College operates on a traditional two-semester academic calendar and offers two optional summer sessions.

Bridgewater State College awards the Bachelor of Arts, Bachelor of Science, and Bachelor of Science in Education degrees. Undergraduate students may choose to major in the following subject areas: anthropology, art, aviation science (aviation management and flight training), biology, business (see "management science"), chemistry, communication arts and sciences (dance education, speech communication, speech education, theater arts, and theater education), computer science, criminal justice, early childhood education, earth sciences, economics, elementary education, English, geography, history, management science (accounting, energy and environmental resources management, finance, general management, global management, information systems management, marketing, and transportation), mathematics, music, philosophy, physical education, physics, political science, psychology, social work, sociology, Spanish, and special education (communication disorders).

Of the College's 262 full-time and 229 part-time faculty, 81 percent hold doctoral or terminal degrees in their subject area. With a student/faculty ratio of just 18:1, students are assured ample opportunity for personal interaction with the school's accomplished instructors. Faculty at Bridgewater State College is committed to undergraduate instruction and only professors—not graduate students—teach undergraduate courses. Bridgewater instructors regard every student as an individual and are committed to helping them achieve academic success.

Gates House
Bridgewater, MA 02325
Phone: 508-531-1237
Fax: 508-531-1746
Website: www.bridgew.edu

ADMISSIONS

Bridgewater State College seeks students of strong intellectual capacity who have demonstrated motivation, character, and sound academic preparation. Applicants are considered for admission without regard for race, religion, national origin, sex, age, color, ethnic origin, or handicap. The most important factors in an admissions decision are the student's high school coursework, SAT or ACT scores, and personal qualifications. Students may submit a personal essay along with their application materials. Admissions interviews and recommendations are not required. Transfer students are required to submit a transcript from all previous work at an accredited college or university. Accomplished high school students may apply through the early admission program as soon as they have finished their third year of secondary school. The school also offers an early action program. Qualified international students are invited to apply to the College. International students should submit all application materials at least nine months previous to the desired enrollment date. In addition, international students must submit official Test of English as a Foreign Language (TOEFL) scores. Prospective freshman must submit application materials before March 1. Applications for on-campus housing must also be submitted before March 1. Transfer students who wish to enter in the spring semester must apply before December 1. Transfer students who wish to enter in the fall semester must apply by April 1. Early admission applicants should take the SAT I or ACT at the end of their junior year. Students applying through the early action program must submit all application materials by November 15. All early action applicants will be notified of their admissions by December 15. To request an application form or more information about Bridgewater State College, please contact:

Steve King, Director of Admissions
Bridgewater State College
Bridgewater, MA 02325
Phone: 508-531-1237
Fax: 508-531-1746
E-mail: admission@bridgew.edu
Website: www.bridgew.edu

CAMPUS LIFE

Located in Bridgewater, Massachusetts, Bridgewater State College is only 30 miles from the world-class city of Boston and 25 miles from the historic Cape Cod seashore. A town of more than 200,000 people, Bridgewater offers ample social and recreational opportunities in the immediate vicinity. In addition to the town's many resources, there is daily train service to Boston from the MBTA Commuter Rail station on campus.

While at Bridgewater State College, students are encouraged to take courses or spend a semester at other colleges and universities. The College Academic Program Sharing (CAPS) allows full-time students to take courses at any other Massachusetts state school. The College is also a part of the Southeastern Association for Cooperation of Higher Education in Massachusetts (SACHEM), which allows the College's students to take classes at any other member institutions, which include Bristol Community, Cape Cod Community, Dean, Massasoit Community, Stonehill, and Wheaton colleges; Massachusetts Maritime Academy; and the University of Massachusetts at Dartmouth. Bridgewater recently joined the National Student Exchange Program, which affords students the opportunity to study at other national, public colleges and universities. In addition to coursework, students can earn academic credit for off-campus internships. Internships give students the opportunity to learn valuable real-world skills while pursuing their degree. Faculty is available to help students locate internships in their field of study. In recent years, Bridgewater students have participated in internships in many different aspects of business, education, and government.

COST AND AID

Tuition for the 2000–2001 was $970 for in-state residents and $7,050 for out-of-state residents. Student fees total $2,108 annually. Books and supplies generally cost about $600 per year. Resident students pay an additional $2,500 for room, plus $1,800 for board, annually.

BRYANT COLLEGE

GENERAL INFORMATION

Bryant College is a four-year, private, New England College that focuses on helping each individual student build the knowledge and character needed to achieve success. Founded in 1863, Bryant offers a student-centered learning environment, state-of-the-art facilities, and academic and co-curricular programming for diverse interests. Bryant engages students with challenging academic programs in applied psychology, business administration, communication, information technology, and liberal studies. Courses are designed to prepare students for the competitive global market by developing critical-thinking and problem-solving skills and providing a solid base for a professional career. As part of their tuition, state-of-the-art IBM laptops, network-ready and fully loaded with software, are provided to all incoming freshmen to ensure that they will have the technology skills that are essential to success in life and business. The 2,600 full-time, undergraduate students come from 32 states and 37 countries. Bryant has all the advantages of a small community with close relationships among students, faculty, and college administrators. Opportunities abound for the exchange of ideas and dialogue between students and faculty members. Students learn how business decisions impact society and the relationship between business functions and the larger spectrum of human need and well-being. Students have many opportunities to participate in a wide variety of intellectual and experiential activities such as internships and student-faculty research. The John H. Chafee Center for International Business links Bryant directly to New England businesses. Students can utilize the Center's resources for research and reference and gain practical experiences through internships and assistantships.

STUDENT BODY

Bryant's 60 student clubs and organizations benefit many social causes and provide recreational enjoyment. From the Marketing Association to the Global Entrepreneurship Program to the Performing Arts Committee, Bryant provides activities for many areas of interest. The Student Senate, the student governing body, serves as a channel of communication among students and faculty and administrators. The Student Programming Board organizes cultural and social programs for the Bryant community. The size of Bryant's campus allows easy access to all campus services, and there are many places for students to gather and enjoy bands, poetry, and comedians. Housing at Bryant is guaranteed for four years and more than 80 percent of students live on campus. There is a variety of housing arrangements to choose from, including the First-Year Complex, suite-style residence halls, and the townhouse villages for seniors.

ACADEMICS

Academic programs focus on the intellectual and professional development of each student in preparation for leadership positions in a wide range of careers. Bryant graduates are successful businesspeople and community leaders in corporate, nonprofit, and entrepreneurial organizations throughout the country and the world. Career exploration and planning begin as early as the freshman year. Operating on a semester plan, Bryant College requires students to complete a minimum of 122 semester hours to graduate. For students pursuing a four-year baccalaureate degree, these hours must include core liberal arts and business courses. Students will blend course work in the liberal arts with career-specific skills and business philosophies for success in their professional careers. Entering students may receive credit through the Advanced Placement (AP) program or the College-Level Examination Program (CLEP) administered by the College Board. Credit is also awarded for International Baccalaureate (IB) Higher Level exams.

Bryant College offers a Bachelor of Arts in Applied Psychology; a Bachelor of Science in Business Administration with concentrations in accounting, accounting information systems, applied actuarial mathematics, computer information systems, finance, financial services, management, and marketing; a Bachelor of Arts in Communication; a Bachelor of Science in Information Technology; and a Bachelor of Arts in Liberal Studies, with concentrations in economics, English, history, and international studies. Students can pursue a minor in one of 18 business and/or liberal arts disciplines.

Teaching is the prime responsibility of Bryant's full-time faculty. Bryant's focus is on the learning experience and the faculty's focus is on teaching. Professors make a special effort to turn the classroom into a forum for the presentation and exchange of ideas. They are scholars, business professionals, and teachers, and they serve as role models and mentors. Among the faculty at Bryant you'll find a practicing clinical psychologist, a nationally respected expert in advertising effectiveness and public policy, and the State Poet Laureate of Rhode Island. Bryant faculty members are also active in original research projects, publishing, consulting, and community service. Eighty-six percent of full-time tenured and tenure-track faculty have the highest degrees in their fields. Several faculty members are current or former Fulbright scholars.

1150 Douglas Pike
Smithfield, RI 02917
Phone: 401-232-6100
Fax: 401-232-6741
Website: www.bryant.edu

ADMISSIONS

Bryant College seeks students who are motivated learners and have a history of academic achievement. Acceptance is based on the quality of scholastic achievement shown by the individual applicant. Scores earned on the SAT I or on the ACT must be submitted. The Admission Committee considers recommendations from the secondary school guidance office and faculty members concerning character and personal qualifications not shown in the academic record. Interviews, though not required, may be scheduled in advance of a campus visit. Applications must be submitted to the Office of Admission, with a nonrefundable fee of $50. It is the responsibility of the applicant to request that the secondary school guidance office send a copy of the student's school record directly to Bryant and to have SAT I or ACT scores sent to the College. International applicants must also submit TOEFL scores and a completed Certification of Finances form. The Early Decision and Early Action deadline is November 15. The regular application deadline is February 15. For further information, students should contact:

Director of Admission
Bryant College
1150 Douglas Pike
Smithfield, RI 02917-1285
Telephone: 401-232-6100 or 800-622-7001 (toll free)
Fax: 401-232-6741
E-mail: admission@bryant.edu

CAMPUS LIFE

Bryant College is situated on 392 acres of beautiful New England countryside. Bryant is only 15 minutes from Providence, which offers access to a variety of restaurants, professional sports events, concerts, and a nationally acclaimed repertory theater. Rhode Island's geographic, historic, and cultural attractions include Newport's world-class sailing, jazz festivals, stunning mansions, and panoramic beaches. Bryant is only one hour from Boston and three hours from New York City and all of the cultural and social amenities in these major metropolitan areas.

Bryant College offers students various opportunities to expand their learning beyond the classroom. Students can gain practical experience in their field of study through the College internship program. Each year, over 400 students get a head start on their careers through internships or practica at companies such as Walt Disney World, Fidelity Investments, PricewaterhouseCoopers, the New England Patriots, and a variety of nonprofit organizations. By studying abroad for a semester, students gain exposure to new cultures as well as intellectual knowledge. Bryant students have to studied in Eastern and Western Europe, Asia, Japan, Canada, Australia, and many other countries. Bryant participates in the Army ROTC Program.

COST AND AID

For the 2003–2004 academic year freshman tuition and fees are $22,458 including the use of a personal IBM Pentium 4 laptop computer. Residential housing is guaranteed for all students, and 80 percent choose to live on campus in residence halls (freshmen live in the first-year complex), where room and board is $8,546. Upper-classmen may live in townhouses, where the fee is $6,450 for a single-occupancy room and $6,012 for a double. There are special fees for the summer sessions.

BUTLER UNIVERSITY

GENERAL INFORMATION

In 1855, two professors, several assistant teachers and 20 students walked through the doors of Butler University to begin years of academic excellence and visionary innovations. Butler admitted women on an equal basis with men—only the second in the nation to do so—and has admitted all minorities throughout its history.

Today, Butler is an independent, coeducational, nonsectarian university with a total undergraduate enrollment of approximately 3,500 students. The scenic campus is set within Indianapolis, a major metropolitan city—an advantage distinguishing Butler from many other universities. Nestled in a historic northside neighborhood, about two-thirds of the student body lives in on-campus housing.

Students discover Butler's challenging learning environment, a wide range of academic programs steeped in the liberal arts and excellent career and graduate school preparation. A core curriculum encourages students to gain knowledge in humanities, arts, social sciences, natural sciences and mathematics. Butler offers more than 60 major academic fields of study in five colleges: the College of Liberal Arts and Sciences; the College of Business Administration; the College of Pharmacy and Health Sciences; the College of Education; and the Jordan College of Fine Arts. Graduate programs are also available within these colleges.

Student life has also benefited from additions to student housing with upperclassmen apartments; Hampton House, a servant-learning house; and Residential College, a co-ed living-learning residence hall. Atherton Union has expanded twice in the last 10 years to include numerous amenities such as a 24-hour computer lab, a Starbucks Coffee shop, a fitness center, a bookstore, e-mail stations, a food court, a dining hall and a convenience store.

Butler students represent almost every state in the nation and more than 40 countries, reflecting diversity of cultures, interests, aspirations, personalities and experiences. They get involved in many ways through the 100 student organizations, including student government; intramural sports; NCAA Division I varsity athletics; social, religious, and volunteer organizations; service clubs; honorary societies; performance groups; and fraternities and sororities. Students take advantage of Broadway shows on campus at Butler's Clowes Memorial Hall, the city's premier performing arts center. Basketball fans cheer on the Bulldogs at the 11,000-seat historic Hinkle Fieldhouse, where the final game in the movie Hoosiers was filmed.

Butler University is accredited by the North Central Association of Colleges and Schools. A solid foundation was laid in 1855 and that legacy will continue with Butler achieving excellence long into the future.

STUDENT BODY

Student organizations and activities include: Academy of Students of Pharmacy, Accounting Club, AIDS Awareness Association, Alliance, Alpha Kappa Alpha, Alpha Kappa Psi, Alpha Lambda Delta, Alpha Phi, Alpha Chi Omega, Alpha Phi Omega, Alpha Psi Omega, American Chemical Society, American Choral Directors, Amnesty International, AMSA Pre-Med Club, Anthropology Club, Atherton Union Board, BACCHUS, Ballroom Dance Association, Best Buddies, Biology Club, Black Student Union, Blue Key, Butler Student Foundation, BUMPA (Butler University Methodist Hospital Physicians Assistant Program), Campus Crusade, Campuswide, C.A.R.E., Chi Sigma Iota, Christian Science Organization, Circle K, College Mentors for Kids, College Republicans, Collegian, Commuter Association, Crew Club, Cycling Club, Dance Team, Dawgnet, Debate Team, Delta Gamma, Delta Tau Delta, Demia, Drift, Economics Club, Entrepreneurship Club, ECO (Environmental Concerns Organization), Equestrian Team, F.A.C.E.S., Fall Alternative Break, Fellowship of Christian Athletes, Finance Club, Flag Line, Global Business Club, Greek Affairs, Greek Council, Habitat for Humanity, Hillel at Butler University, Hockey Club, Interfraternity Council, International Club, Japanese Karate-Do Club, Jewish Student Union, Journey of Understanding, Kappa Alpha Theta, Kappa Delta Pi, Kappa Kappa Gamma, Kappa Kappa Psi, Kappa Psi, Lambda Chi Alpha, Lambda Kappa Sigma, Lutheran Campus Ministry, Manuscripts, Butler Marketing Association, Mathematical Sciences, MBA Association, Mock Trial, Model United Nations, Mortar Board, Mu Phi Epsilon, Music Educators National Conference, National Residence Hall Honorary, National Student Speech-Language-Hearing Association, Omicron Delta Epsilon, Order of Omega, Panhellenic Association, Phi Alpha Theta, Phi Delta Chi, Phi Eta Sigma, Phi Kappa Psi, Phi Lambda Sigma, Phi Mu Alpha Sinfonia, Phi Sigma Iota, Pi Beta Phi, Political Science Organization, Pre-Law, Pre-Med (See AMSA Pre-Med), Psi Chi, Psychology Club, Public Relations Student Society of America, Recreation Department, RHA (Residence Hall Association), Rho Chi, Rugby Club, S.A.B.L. (Students for the Advancement of Business Leadership), Shokotan Karate Club, Sigma Alpha Iota, Sigma Chi, Sigma Delta Pi, Sigma Gamma Rho, Sigma Tau Delta, Society of Physics Students, Society of Professional Journalists, Sociology Club, Spanish Club, Student Education Association, Student Government Association, Student Health Advisory Committee, Student National Pharmaceutical Association, Student Society of Hospital Pharmacists, Students for Animal Welfare, Tau Beta Sigma, Tau Kappa Epsilon, TRUST, Voices of Deliverance, Volleyball (men's) Club, YMCA, Young Democrats, and Young Life.

ACADEMICS

All candidates for the baccalaureate degree must complete the university core requirements and at least 45 semester hours of work at Butler. At least 30 of the 45 hours must be in the college granting the degree. Eligible students may participate in the Honors Program, taking courses such as, Paris: City and Imagemakers, Jazz: A Listener's Perspective and Life in the Universe. By the end of the sophomore year honors course work is generally completed. Students then begin the next phase, an independent study to help them research, write and eventually present their honors thesis. Butler is a sponsoring institution for the National Merit Scholarship Program. Butler also offers advanced placement with appropriate academic credit in most subjects covered by either the Advanced Placement (AP) examinations or the College-Level Examination Program (CLEP) tests. Students may choose to enroll in Air Force and Army ROTC programs.

The opportunity to participate in research is something rarely offered to undergraduate students at most universities. At Butler, students not only have the chance to participate in research with faculty members, they also originate research projects and develop them into professional presentations and publications. In particular, hundreds of Butler students present their projects at the Undergraduate Research Conference, hosted by Butler every April. In addition, the Butler Summer Institute awards students a $2,000 grant plus housing while they work on summer research projects with faculty members.

Baccalaureate degrees are offered through Butler's five colleges. Unique programs include the Engineering Dual-Degree Program, offered jointly by Butler University and the Purdue School of Engineering and Technology at Indiana University-Purdue University Indianapolis. Students receive both a Butler Bachelor of Science degree in a selected liberal arts and sciences major (biology, chemistry, computer science, economics, mathematics, physics, or science, technology, and society) and a Purdue Bachelor of Science degree in computer, electrical, or mechanical engineering.

For students who are undecided about their major field of study, there is an Exploratory Studies Program, where students develop a personalized academic plan to help choose the major that best suits their interests and abilities. Butler also offers an individualized major which allows students to create their own major such as women's studies.

The College of Liberal Arts and Sciences creates lifelong learners. The college affirms the central role of liberal arts education while offering opportunities for specialization. Majors include: actuarial science, actuarial sciences/management (five-year BS/MBA), anthropology, biological sciences, chemistry, chemistry and pharmaceutical sciences, communication studies, computer science and software engineering, economics, English, French, French and business studies, German, German and business studies, Greek, history, international studies, journalism, Latin, mathematics, philosophy, physics, political science, psychology, public and corporate communication, religion, science technology and society, sociology, sociology and criminology, Spanish, Spanish and business studies, speech language pathology and urban studies.

4600 Sunset Avenue
Indianapolis, IN 46208
Phone: 317-940-8100
Fax: 317-940-8150
Website: www.butler.edu

The College of Business Administration prepares students to be tomorrow's business leaders through classroom work and two required semester-long cooperative education experiences. Majors include: accounting, economics, finance, international management, management information and marketing.

The Jordan College of Fine Arts integrates intensive conservatory training with broad objectives and a strong academic curriculum. The college is well respected for its tradition of educating students as emerging professionals in the arts. Majors offered: arts administration, dance, dance performance, music, music business, music education, music performance, music piano pedagogy, telecommunication arts and theatre arts.

The College of Education is dedicated to preparing outstanding teachers. The faculty, staff and administration of the college are committed to providing the best possible learning experience for students. For the past six years, the college has experienced a 100 percent placement rate for its students—an indicator that Butler students place first in education. Majors offered: elementary education/early childhood with concentrations in middle grades, reading or special education, and middle/secondary education with concentrations in any academic area (English, history, math, etc.) or in physical education, reading or special education.

College of Pharmacy and Health Sciences graduates serve society as caring, ethical health professionals and community leaders. The college's professional programs combine intensive classroom education with clinical experiences in the professional phases of the degrees. Majors offered are pharmacy (PharmD) and physician assistant (BSPA).

Butler also offers pre-professional programs in dentistry, forestry, law, medicine, physical therapy, seminary and veterinary medicine. Graduate programs include MBA, MS in school counseling, education administration or education, MA in English or history, MM in composition, conducting, music education, music history, performance, piano pedagogy or theory.

Teaching is top priority for Butler's 257 full-time faculty members; 83 percent hold the highest (terminal) degree in their fields. Many are active in national research programs, write for publications, counsel in government and business, and participate in the arts. With a comfortable teaching load, Butler's faculty members have time to work with students individually. The student/faculty ratio is 14:1. All classes are taught by professors; there are no teaching assistants.

ADMISSIONS

Applicants are expected to complete a minimum of 17 academic units in high school, including four years of English, three years of laboratory sciences and mathematics, two years each of history or social studies and two years of foreign language. A candidate for admission typically ranks in the upper third of his or her high school class and should submit satisfactory results of the SAT I or the ACT. The Jordan College of Fine Arts requires an audition. In addition to these factors, the Admission Committee considers the applicant's leadership skills, motivation and writing sample. Students who wish to transfer from another regionally accredited college or university are considered if they are in good standing and have a grade point average of 2.0 or better in their previous academic work. Transfer students must submit official transcripts of all college work.

Although regular admission is on a rolling basis, students may choose to apply for early admission. Butler offers two nonbinding early admission programs (not early decision) with specific benefits associated with each program. The application priority date for Early Admission I is December 1 of the senior year and its benefits include: early consideration for freshman academic scholarships and departmental scholarships, early course registration, priority housing and optional living-learning center participation. The application priority date for Early Admission II is February 1 and it carries the following benefits: early consideration for freshman academic scholarships, early course registration and priority housing. Scholarship notification is on a rolling basis and begins December 15. Campus visits and interviews are strongly recommended, though not required, and are arranged on a daily basis. Several open-house programs are also scheduled throughout the year. Interested students and their families are encouraged to call the Office of Admission to make arrangements for campus visits.

For more information, contact:

Office of Admission
Butler University
4600 Sunset Avenue
Indianapolis, IN 46208-3485
Telephone: 317-940-8100 or 888-940-8100 (toll free)
Fax: 317-940-8150
E-mail: admission@butler.edu
Website: www.butler.edu/admissions/

CAMPUS LIFE

Located just six miles from the heart of the thriving city of Indianapolis and surrounded by well-established residential communities, Butler's 290-acre campus remains a serenely beautiful area with its playing fields, a formal botanical garden and a nature preserve. Its urban location offers students a wide range of internship opportunities, providing excellent preparation both for graduate professional schools and careers.

Indianapolis, Indiana's state capital and the 13th largest city in the nation, has a wide range of recreational and cultural activities, including the Indianapolis Symphony Orchestra, the Indiana Repertory Theater, the Indianapolis Museum of Art (just two blocks from campus), the Eiteljorg Museum, and the world's largest Children's Museum. Indianapolis also hosts numerous citywide celebrations, including ethnic festivals, art fairs and outdoor music festivals. The Indianapolis Motor Speedway is the anchor of Indianapolis' professional sports, while basketball, football, hockey and baseball have homes in three major sports arenas. Indianapolis, "the amateur sports capital," has hosted more than 360 national and international amateur sporting events. It's home to the NCAA headquarters and its Hall of Champions. Butler has been the proud co-host of the NCAA Final Four Championship in 1991, 1997 and 2002 and will co-host again in 2006.

One of the largest study abroad programs in the United States is hosted by Butler University's Institute for Study Abroad (IFSA), which sends students from American colleges and universities to Australia, Ireland, Scotland, New Zealand, England, Argentina, etc. In addition, Butler offers a Directed Study Abroad Program, a flexible program tailored to the needs and interests of the students. Butler is also a member of the International Student Exchange Program (ISEP), in which students can study at one or more than 100 member universities in 40 countries.

COST AND AID

2002–2003

Tuition: $19,990
Room and board: $6,710

CALDWELL COLLEGE

GENERAL INFORMATION

Caldwell College is a Catholic, coeducational, four-year liberal arts institution with a proud 700-year Dominican tradition of rigorous scholarship, committed teaching, and ethical values. Founded in 1939 by the Sisters of Saint Dominic, Caldwell College's most popular programs include undergraduate degrees in business, communication arts, and education. The College offers an individualized major for students seeking a concentrated major to design their own coursework with administrative approval. Caldwell College has 27 undergraduate degrees, 12 graduate programs, and a Caldwell Scholars Program. Also offered are an adult undergraduate program and a uniquely structured distance-education external degree program for adult learners. The College offers accelerated options that combine the curricular opportunities of the distance education program with traditional on-campus offerings. In addition, the College provides master's degrees in accounting, counseling psychology, curriculum and instruction, educational administration, contemporary management, and pastoral ministry. A specialization in art therapy is open to students in the counseling psychology program. Post-master's programs in art therapy, professional licensing for counselors, and supervisor's certificate are also offered. Post-baccalaureate teacher certificate and special education certification programs are also available. Caldwell College's website—www.caldwell.edu—makes information about the College easily available.

The Office of Career Development provides career counseling, career education, interest testing, and graduate study information to help students in identifying personal goals and considering academic and career opportunities. A career library and a career-planning course provide additional resources. Caldwell College supports work-based internship and cooperative education opportunities through the Office of Experiential Learning. These programs allow students to integrate work experience with classroom learning. Approximately 40 percent of the students who participate in internship and cooperative education programs are offered full-time positions upon graduation. The office also helps students and alumni who are seeking full- and part-time employment. The College's Business Advisory Council was formed in 1994. Through lectures by business leaders, mentoring programs, and interaction during business conferences, students acquire a sense of how to be successful in today's workplace. Businesses benefit from the expertise of the College's business faculty and through College-sponsored conferences related to current business trends. The Business Advisory Council includes about 40 members from major corporations throughout New Jersey.

Caldwell College enrolls 2,218 full-time, part-time, and graduate students each year. The College enrolled its largest full-time undergraduate population ever in 2002 and continues its fantastic growth while maintaining its liberal arts character. Fully qualified faculty members and a 13:1 student/faculty ratio provide students with close, personal attention. Approximately 91 percent of full-time students are from New Jersey. In addition, the College's rich cultural diversity draws individuals from northeastern and mid-Atlantic states and from more than 26 countries. The cultural mix of full-time, part-time, and graduate students includes white, 68 percent; African-American, 15 percent; Hispanic, 8 percent; Asian-American, 2 percent; international, 4 percent; and approximately 3 percent unknown. About 41 percent of full-time students live on campus. Single, double, triple, and a few quad rooms are available. All students, both commuters and residents, including incoming freshmen, can have automobiles on campus.

A full program of student activities involves both residents and commuters in campus life. An assortment of clubs and organizations as well as publications are available. Guest artists, musicians, authors, and speakers appear on campus regularly. Student social life features dances and other open activities. An on-campus fitness center provides students with health and exercise opportunities. The center is equipped with cardiovascular equipment, including treadmills, stationary bicycles, steppers, and combination weight machines. The College is a full member of the National Collegiate Athletic Association Division II (NCAA II.) Caldwell fields intercollegiate teams in men's baseball, basketball, soccer, and tennis; women's basketball, soccer, softball, and tennis; and coed golf. The College also sponsors a variety of intramural sports.

STUDENT BODY

Caldwell College's students, through the Student Government Association and Resident Council, form many nonacademic policies and regulations. Students also help establish total College policy through representation on several College standing committees.

ACADEMICS

Eligibility for a degree requires completion of a minimum of 122 credits and a GPA of at least 2.0 (C). Students must also complete major courses with a minimum grade of C and satisfy all other departmental requirements. All programs require that students successfully pass a form of outcomes assessment in the senior year. To complete the liberal arts requirements, students must choose courses from computer literacy, English, fine arts, foreign language, history, mathematics, natural sciences, philosophy, physical education, public speaking, religious studies, and social sciences. In 1997, the Writing Across the Curriculum program was introduced to systematically develop a student's ability to write well regardless of his or her major. Opportunities for independent study, internships, co-ops, double majors, minors, and certificate programs are available. The Caldwell Scholars Program challenges outstanding students with both interdisciplinary studies and a directed honors project and is supplemented by guest lectures. Students must score a 3, 4, or 5 on the College Board's Advanced Placement test to receive advanced placement or credit for completed work. Students may receive credit for knowledge gained through independent study or experience through the College-Level Examination Program (CLEP). The English as a Second Language Program helps students with limited English proficiency master American English for academic success. Offerings include leveled courses in composition, grammar, communication skills, and reading. A TOEFL score is required with the application for international students. Course selection is determined by placement test results. The adult undergraduate program encourages adults to return to college to complete their degree, earn a new degree, or enjoy learning for pleasure. Through day, evening, Saturday, and distance learning courses, the College highlights the significance of lifelong learning. The College offers accelerated options that combine the curricular opportunities of the distance education program with traditional on-campus offerings. Adult students can earn credit through Caldwell's Prior Learning Assessment Policy, provided they can display acquired knowledge that corresponds with course requirements.

9 Ryerson Avenue
Caldwell, NJ 07006-6195
Phone: 973-618-3500
Fax: 973-618-3600
Website: www.caldwell.edu

Caldwell College offers 27 undergraduate Bachelor of Arts (BA), Bachelor of Science (BS), and Bachelor of Fine Arts (BFA) degrees. The BA is offered in art, biology, chemistry, communication arts, criminal justice, elementary education, English, French, history, an individualized major, mathematics, music, political science, psychology, religious studies, social studies, sociology, and Spanish. The BS is offered in accounting, business administration, computer information systems, computer science, international business, management, marketing, and medical technology. The BFA is offered in art. The education department offers teacher certification programs in elementary education (nursery through grade 8) and for teaching grades K–12 in art, biology, English, French, mathematics, music, social studies, and Spanish. A certification program in school nursing is also available to registered nurses.

There are 76 full-time faculty members, with 85 percent having earned their doctoral/terminal degree, and 14 part-time faculty. There are five full-time English As A Second Language (ESL) and Learning Center instructors and 100 adjunct faculty members.

ADMISSIONS

The admission office reviews each applicant's high school record, class rank, high school performance, and SAT I or ACT scores and determines the student's ability to succeed at Caldwell College. A student must complete at least 16 high school academic units, including 4 years of English, 2 years of foreign language, 2 years of mathematics, 2 years of science, and 1 year of history. Caldwell College does not discriminate against applicants on the basis of race, color, creed, age, national or ethnic origin, or handicap. Applicants are accepted throughout the school year based on a rolling admissions policy; however, applicants are encouraged to apply early. A nonrefundable $40 fee must accompany each application. Applicants are informed of their admission eligibility after their credentials have been received and evaluated. For further information, students should contact:

Director of Admission
Caldwell College
9 Ryerson Avenue
Caldwell, NJ 07006-6195
Phone: 973-618-3500 or 888-864-9516 (toll-free outside New Jersey)
Fax: 973-618-3600
E-mail: admissions@caldwell.edu
Website: www.caldwell.edu

CAMPUS LIFE

Located on a beautiful, secure 70-acre campus 20 miles west of New York City, Caldwell College enables students to share in numerous educational, cultural, and social experiences while still enjoying a comfortable atmosphere of campus life. The center of Caldwell, with a variety of shops and restaurants, is within walking distance. Area attractions include theaters, museums, parks, ski resorts, malls, the New Jersey Performing Arts Center, the Meadowlands sports complex, and the New Jersey shore. Many corporate headquarters are readily accessible from Caldwell and provide a variety of internship opportunities. The College is convenient to major highways—including Routes 280, 80, and 287; the Garden State Parkway; and the New Jersey Turnpike—and can be reached by public transportation.

The College signed its first exchange program agreement in 1995 with Duksung Women's University in Korea. Since then, three female students have attended Duksung, and the College has hosted six female students. In fall 1998, the College signed an exchange program agreement with the Catholic University of Korea that for the first time allowed male students with broad international educational opportunities to better prepare themselves for the global marketplace. The latest articulation agreement now makes it possible for both male and female students to earn credits for business, education, music, science, and other courses while learning the Korean culture, economy, and language. In addition, the College has established both undergraduate and graduate affiliation programs for students in health-related majors to accelerate their career goal of becoming health professionals.

COST AND AID

For the 2002–2003 academic year, full-time tuition and fees are $16,000, and campus room and board is $6,800. Undergraduate tuition for part-time students is $378 per credit hour.

CALIFORNIA COLLEGE OF ARTS AND CRAFTS

GENERAL INFORMATION

Founded in 1907, the California College of Arts and Crafts (CCAC) offers a comprehensive approach to art education, training students in a variety of disciplines and fostering collaboration between artists and designers. The College is committed to providing an interdisciplinary curriculum, educating students in a wide range of fine arts, architecture, and design. With an undergraduate population of about 1,400, CCAC offers world-class resources and facilities in a small, private college environment. CCAC maintains close connections with the Bay Area arts community and the greater community. The CCAC Wattis Institute for Contemporary Arts offers leading-edge programs including exhibitions, lectures, artist residencies, performances, and symposia. CCAC's Center for Art and Public Life focuses on issues in community development, service learning, new models of practice in community-based art and design, and cultural diversity and youth development through the arts. In addition, the College offers continuing education courses for adults, middle school, and high school students.

CCAC comprises two campuses in the neighboring cities of Oakland and San Francisco, California. The San Francisco campus is a large, newly renovated light-filled structure in the city's design district; it houses the school's programs in architecture, design, selected fine arts programs, and graduate programs. The Oakland campus is set on four acres of lush landscaped grounds in a residential neighborhood just three miles from the University of California, Berkeley. First-year students may choose to live in the new residence hall on the Oakland campus; transfer students are offered housing in Webster Hall, located two miles from campus in downtown Oakland. CCAC is fully accredited by the Western Association of Schools and Colleges and the National Association of Schools of Art and Design. The interior design program is accredited by the Foundation for Interior Design Education Research. The five-year architecture program is accredited by the National Architectural Accrediting Board.

STUDENT BODY

The CCAC Student Council is made up of student representatives from both campuses and is responsible for organizing extracurricular activities and special events for the student community. Select students have the opportunity to serve on the CCAC board of trustees.

ACADEMICS

CCAC believes that a superior art education has its foundation in a well-rounded academic curriculum of arts and humanities. The College allows a flexible course of study that encourages students to explore a variety of media and develop programs related to their individual interests. The academic program at CCAC helps students explore many aspects of visual art and communication, critical thinking, and problem solving. To graduate, Bachelor of Fine Arts (BFA) candidates must successfully complete at least 126 semester units, comprising 75 units in studio work and 51 units in the humanities and sciences. Undergraduates begin their education in a Core curriculum, which introduces students to a variety of media, principles, and processes. In Core courses, students begin mastering problem solving and critical thinking skills. The Core curriculum also offers courses in writing, literature, and art history, as well as courses that incorporate community service. CCAC runs on a two-semester academic calendar. The College offers a six-week summer session and a pre-college program. There are continuing education programs throughout the year.

Students at CCAC may pursue the BFA degree in the following subjects: ceramics, fashion design, film/video, glass, graphic design, illustration, industrial design, interior design, jewelry/metal arts, painting/drawing, photography, printmaking, sculpture, textiles, and wood/furniture. In addition, the College offers the Bachelor of Arts (BA) degree in creative writing and visual studies and a five-year program leading to the Bachelor of Architecture (BArch) degree. BA students must successfully complete 51 units of humanities and sciences courses, 15 units of Core studio courses, 36 units in the major, and 24 units of studio electives. Architecture students must successfully complete at least 162 units including the first-year Core program. In addition to undergraduate programs, CCAC offers five graduate programs: the MFA in design, the MFA in fine arts, the MFA in writing, the MA in curatorial practice, and the MA in visual criticism. Concentrations in the fine arts program include ceramics, drawing/painting, film/video, glass, jewelry/metal arts, photography, printmaking, sculpture, textiles, and wood/furniture. Prospective students may request more information from the Assistant Director of Graduate Admissions.

The CCAC faculty consists of 326 professional artists, designers, and scholars (31 full-time and 295 part-time instructors) who imbue teaching with a healthy mix of theory and practice.

1111 Eighth Street
San Francisco, CA 94107
Phone: 415-703-9523
Fax: 415-703-9539
Website: www.ccac-art.edu

ADMISSIONS

Undergraduate applicants must have a high school diploma or the equivalent. The Admissions Committee evaluates prospective students on the strength of previous academic work, the statement of purpose, standardized test scores, recommendations, and portfolio of art. CCAC recognizes that not all prospective students have had equal opportunity to study art and that some successful applicants arrive at CCAC with limited experience in art. In all cases, CCAC considers all aspects of the applicant's previous achievements, including artistic achievement, academic success, and personal goals.

Undergraduate students applying for merit scholarships must complete applications by February 15. Applicants for fall semester programs are encouraged to apply before the priority deadline of March 1. Spring semester applicants should submit their application before October 1. Students who meet the admissions priority deadlines receive priority consideration for housing, financial aid, and course selection. Admissions decisions are made on a rolling admission basis; applications are reviewed in the order they are received. Students receive their acceptance and financial aid package after the priority dates. In addition to the application, students must submit a nonrefundable application fee of $50. It is possible to register for one or more courses as a nondegree student (on a space-available basis).

To request the application forms, the college catalog, or additional information about the school or admissions procedures, contact:

Office of Enrollment Services
California College of Arts and Crafts
1111 Eighth Street
San Francisco, CA 94107
Telephone: 800-447-1ART (toll free)
World Wide Web: www.ccac-art.edu
E-mail: enroll@ccac-art.edu
Students may apply online at www.ccac-art.edu.

CAMPUS LIFE

CCAC's Montgomery campus in San Francisco spans half a city block. This light, open building contains classrooms and studios, the Timken Lecture Hall, the Simpson Library, six computer labs, designated studio space for upper-division students, and three large studios for model making and wood/furniture, as well as studio space for 75 graduate students. In addition, the San Francisco campus is home to the Logan Galleries and the Long/Pollack Graduate Student Gallery.

CCAC students have the option of registering for courses to supplement their curriculum through cross-registration at nearby Mills College or Holy Names College in Oakland. CCAC is a member of the Association of Independent Colleges of Art and Design, which offers students the opportunity to study at other campuses through their mobility program. Students also have the option of studying overseas through several exchange programs sponsored by CCAC. Through this program, students can attend universities in Australia, France, Germany, Italy, the Netherlands, and Sweden.

COST AND AID

Tuition for the 2003–2004 academic year is $22,970 for full-time, undergraduate students and $957 per unit for part-time students. Tuition is the same for California and out-of-state residents. Students who reside in college housing in 2003–2004 will pay an additional residence hall fee of $4,620 to $6,063 for a full year of housing, or $2,800 for a single semester. Students should expect to spend approximately $35,050 per year, which includes tuition and fees of $23,220; $8,030 for room and board; $1,300 or books and supplies; and $2,500 in miscellaneous expenses. Students looking for off-campus housing can get assistance from the Student Affairs Office, which maintains a local housing list.

CASE WESTERN RESERVE UNIVERSITY

GENERAL INFORMATION

The institution of Case Western Reserve University (CWRU) has been educating students for well over 150 years. Created as CWRU in 1967 by the merger of Case Institute of Technology (founded in 1880 as Case School of Applied Science) and Western Reserve University (founded in 1826), today CWRU offers outstanding undergraduate, graduate, and professional degree programs in more than 60 fields of study. Currently, we have more than 90,000 living alumni.

Our interdisciplinary admission policy enables all CWRU undergraduates to pursue interests in the arts and sciences, engineering, and management schools regardless of their intended major.

Our students create unparalleled double majors, triple majors, and major and minor combinations. Some recent examples include the double majors of systems engineering and theater, and computer science and history; a triple major of Asian studies, Spanish, and international studies; and a biomedical engineering major with a minor in anthropology. When a student is admitted to CWRU, that student is admitted to the entire University.

Enrollment Profile (Fall 2000): 3,450 undergraduates (830 freshmen); 6,003 graduate and professional students; 9,601 total. Admission Profile, Class of 2004: 4,760 applied; 3,135 admitted; 766 enrolled.

Academic Interests: Arts and sciences, 31 percent; engineering, 49 percent; undecided, 12 percent; management, 4 percent; nursing, 4 percent.

STUDENT BODY

With more than 100 student organizations and groups to choose from at CWRU, it is simple to find the right group for you. All groups are student-driven and student-run, and the activities of any one organization are based on student interests.

CWRU has academic groups, athletic groups, engineering groups, fraternities and sororities, honorary groups, international/ethnic groups, student media organizations, performance groups, philanthropy/service groups, political groups, religious groups, groups representing all residence halls, and special interest groups.

Undergraduate student activities include the University Programming Board, Undergraduate Student Government, Media Board, Interfraternity Congress and Panhellenic Council, and intramural and sports clubs.

ACADEMICS

Through a combination of core curricula, major requirements, and minors or approved course sequences, all undergraduates receive a broad educational base as well as specialized knowledge in their chosen field.

The University offers students opportunities for independent research and internships or professional practicums in business, health care, government, arts, or service fields. The College Scholars Program allows a small number of highly motivated, responsible students to pursue individually tailored baccalaureate programs. A five-year Cooperative Education Program (Co-Op) provides two seven-month work periods in industry or government and is available for majors in engineering, science, management, and accounting.

The Pre-professional Scholars Programs (PPSP) in medicine, dentistry, and law grant to a few outstanding freshmen applicants conditional commitments of admission to the appropriate professional school at CWRU. For more information, refer to information on the application for admission.

Our interdisciplinary admission policy enables all CWRU undergraduates to pursue their academic interests, regardless of their intended major. Major areas of concentration: Accounting, American studies, anthropology, applied mathematics, art education*, art history, Asian studies, astronomy, biochemistry, biology, chemistry, classics (Latin and Greek), communication sciences (communication studies, communication disorders), comparative literature, computer science, economics, engineering (aerospace++, biomedical++, chemical++, civil++, computer++, electrical++, fluid and thermal sciences++, materials science and engineering++, mechanical++, polymer science and engineering++, systems and control++, undesignated+++), engineering physics, English, environmental geology, environmental studies+, French, French studies, geological sciences, German, German studies, gerontological studies+, history, history and philosophy of science and technology, international studies, management (business), mathematics, music**, music education**, natural sciences+, nursing, nutrition, nutritional biochemistry and metabolism, philosophy, physics, political science, pre-architecture+, psychology, religion, sociology, Spanish, statistics, theater arts (drama and dance), undergraduate scholars/dean's approved major***, women's studies. Minor areas of concentration: Most majors listed above and the following: art studio, artificial intelligence, Chinese, education, electronics, environmental engineering, history of technology and science, human development, industrial engineering, Japanese, management information and decision systems, photography, public policy, Russian, sports medicine.

*Joint program with Cleveland Institute of Art.

**Joint program with Cleveland Institute of Music.

***Individually designed major; joint program with Cleveland Museum of Art; joint program with John Carroll University for teacher certification (grades 7-12) in biology, chemistry, earth science, English, French, history, mathematics, and physics.

+Available as a second major only.

++Accredited by Accreditation Board for Engineering and Technology, Inc. (ABET)

+++Not reviewed by ABET for accreditation.

103 Tomlinson Hall, 10900 Euclid Avenue
Cleveland, OH 44106-7055
Phone: 216-368-4450
Fax: 216-368-5111
Website: www.cwru.edu

Ninety-five percent of CWRU's more than 2,000 full-time faculty hold a PhD or appropriate terminal degree. More than 93 percent of the undergraduate credit hours are taught by faculty, not students.

While some introductory classes are large, 67 percent of our classes have fewer than 30 students, and 53 percent have fewer than 20 students. As material becomes more specialized, small class sizes allow students and faculty to interact and exchange ideas more intensively.

ADMISSIONS

The University requires at least 16 units of full-credit high school work in solid academic subjects, including 4 years of English or its equivalent. All applicants are expected to have completed 3 years of high school mathematics, and students interested in mathematics, science, or engineering majors should have 4. At least 2 years of laboratory science are required of all applicants, and prospective mathematics and science majors must present 3 years. For all engineering candidates, physics and chemistry are required. Two years of foreign language study are recommended for students considering majors in the humanities, arts, and social and behavioral sciences.

CWRU does not admit by formula: we evaluate each application carefully and select students based on their combination of academic, personal, and intangible qualities. An interview is not required but is strongly recommended as the best way to learn about the University.

Admission to CWRU is highly selective. More than 90 percent of admitted freshmen rank in the top 20 percent of their high school graduating class. We accept either the SAT or ACT scores. The middle 50 percent composite SAT I scores of admitted students is 1260–1450. The middle 50 percent composite ACT scores of admitted students is 27–32. For a detailed description of admission requirements refer to the application for admission.

CAMPUS LIFE

Some have called Cleveland the "Comeback City," but frankly, we never thought it had left! Prentice Hall's *Places Rated Almanac* recently rated Cleveland 14th of 343 most-livable cities in North America. The Rock and Roll Hall of Fame, Great Lakes Science Center, Omnimax Theater, Gund Arena, Jacobs Field, state parks that dot the shoreline of Lake Erie, and many more Cleveland attractions are only five miles from campus.

Our Career Planning and Placement Program helps students take advantage of CWRU's strong connections with the city's Fortune 500 companies, world-famous medical centers, local corporations, and government offices.

CWRU is in the center of University Circle, a park-like setting for some of the finest cultural, intellectual, and scientific institutions in the United States. With eight museums, three performing arts centers, and a botanical garden, some of our esteemed neighbors include the Cleveland Museum of Art; Severance Hall, home of the world-renowned Cleveland Orchestra; the Cleveland Museum of Natural History; the Cleveland Institute of Art; and the Cleveland Institute of Music. Coursework and research introduce many of our students into this vibrant intellectual community.

We also have a diverse assortment of nearby restaurants, music clubs, and other hangouts that speckle the University Circle landscape, offering our students a wealth of activity throughout the week. Ambitious student explorers can take full advantage of all that our urban location has to offer.

Selected students in history and political science may enroll as juniors and seniors in the Washington Semester, which is conducted each spring at American University's School of Social Science and Public Affairs.

Students with a B average or higher may participate in the junior-year abroad program. Up to 30 hours of credit may be granted for study at a foreign university.

Students may also cross register at other Cleveland-area colleges and universities for one course per semester.

COST AND AID

Typical undergraduate costs 2001–2002 academic year: tuition $21,000; room and board $6,250; required fees $168; books $750; personal expenses and loan fees $1,210. Total $29,378

CASTLETON STATE COLLEGE

GENERAL INFORMATION

Founded in 1787, Castleton State College is the 18th oldest higher-learning institute in the United States and the oldest in the state of Vermont. The historic village of Castleton in western Vermont is home to the college's 160-acre campus. Of the 1,500 undergraduates who attend Castleton full time, nearly 1,000 hail from the state of Vermont. Other students come to Castleton from Vermont's New England neighbors and the mid-Atlantic states. Castleton State College is dedicated to providing an education that embraces the principles of liberal arts and the fundamentals of career preparation. Among the innovative aspects of Castleton's curriculum is a program called Soundings, in which first-year students must attend a series of events in order to earn their academic credits. The Soundings events range from theatre and dance to debates and speeches by renowned leaders. Freshmen also enroll in First-Year Seminar, a normal general education course with an additional component designed to teach them the skills they'll need to thrive in a collegiate environment.

Castleton's six residence halls house a total of 710 students. Every room in the residence halls includes two (or more) Internet connections, which guarantees that all students with computers will have access to e-mail and the Web. Students can use these connections at no charge. Phone lines and television cable outlets are connected to each room. On-campus students enjoy meals at the Huden Dining Hall. Students who live off-campus find housing in the village of Castleton, as well as nearby Fair Haven and Rutland. All students may bring automobiles to campus. The array of student activities at Castleton is wide. With over 40 student groups to choose from, Castleton's undergrads are involved in club sports, the student newspaper, the campus radio station, the outing club, rugby, and dozens of other recreations. Other clubs focus on majors or prospective careers. And yet others strive to service the college or surrounding communities. Men can choose from nine varsity sports: baseball, basketball, cross-country, ice hockey, lacrosse, skiing, snowboarding, soccer, and tennis. Women choose from ten: basketball, cross-country, field hockey, ice hockey, lacrosse, skiing, snowboarding, soccer, softball, and tennis. A large portion of Castleton's undergrads participate in intramural or recreational sports. And skiing, snowboarding, and other snow sports are favorite pastimes all around.

STUDENT BODY

The Student Association serves as the primary body of student government on campus. Each student who is enrolled in at least eight credit hours is considered a member of the association. The association's elected representatives are granted membership in many College committees as well. Beyond the Student Association, students develop skills in leadership and decision-making through participation in student organizations.

ACADEMICS

Castleton's academic programs allow students to build a firm foundation in liberal arts at the same time that they prepare for particular careers. By graduation, all four-year undergraduates must fulfill a core curriculum of 42 liberal arts credits. Many students use their freshman year to explore various academic opportunities and majors. Students who arrive at Castleton with specific career paths in mind may opt to begin work in the chosen major immediately. By the end of sophomore year, each four-year student must declare an academic major. Typically, each student takes five courses per semester. Fall and spring semester are 15 weeks long; courses are also offered in three four-week blocks during the summer. Castleton employs traditional methods of grading, including pass/fail options. While internships and fieldwork can strengthen many academic degrees, they are required for students in the following programs: communication, criminal justice, education, and social work. Two-year students already enrolled at Castleton may transfer to four-year tracks if they are pursuing degrees in business, communications, computer information systems, criminal justice, or general studies. Castleton will recognize as many as 64 credits (or the amount needed to earn the associate's degree) from students who arrive at the college with a two-year degree from another accredited institution. First-year students who earn a GPA of 3.5 or higher will be inducted into Castleton's chapter of the national freshman honor society, Phi Eta Sigma. Similarly, the Castleton Chapter of Alpha Chi acknowledges the academic achievements of outstanding juniors and seniors. Education, psychology, Spanish, and theater arts majors are eligible for discipline-related honors societies as well. The Dean's List consists of students who achieve at least a 3.5 GPA; the President's List of Outstanding Students recognizes undergraduates who achieve a 4.0.

Bachelor Degrees: art, biology, business administration (accounting, e-commerce management, marketing), communication (digital media, journalism, mass media, public relations), computer information systems, criminal justice, environmental science, geology, health science, history, literature, mathematics (statistics), multidisciplinary studies, music, natural science, physical education (teaching licensure), sports administration, psychology (developmental, forensic), social sciences, social studies, social work, sociology, criminology, Spanish language and literature, sports medicine (athletic training, exercise science), theatre arts.

Office of Admissions
Castleton, VT 05735
Phone: 802-468-1213
Fax: 802-468-1476
Website: www.castleton.edu

Associate Degrees: business, chemistry, communication, computer programming, criminal justice, general studies, nursing.

Education Licensure Programs: elementary education, secondary education, special education.

Graduate Programs: Master of Arts in Education (curriculum and instruction, education leadership, language arts and reading, special education), Master of Arts (forensic psychology), Certificate of Advanced Graduate Study.

Castleton's full-time faculty comprises 86 members. Ninety-four percent of the full-time professors have earned terminal degrees. Adjunct professors include local professionals who provide in-depth and practical insights for students pursuing the study of specific careers. The College's 13:1 student/faculty ratio guarantees students personal attention. Furthermore, each student works with a faculty advisor.

ADMISSIONS

Applicants are assessed according to their prior achievement in high-school classrooms and on standardized tests. Additionally, recommendations are strongly considered. Applicants will be admitted to Castleton based on their demonstrated capacity to excel in a post-secondary education atmosphere. Application forms can be obtained via the College website listed below. Incoming students may enroll in either the fall or spring semester. Applications are considered on a rolling basis. Applicants will receive notification from the admissions office after their folders have been completed. To learn more about Castleton State College or to set up a visit, please contact:

Dean of Enrollment
Bill Allen
Castleton State College
Castleton, VT 05735
Telephone: 802-468-1213 or 800-639-8521 (toll free)
Fax: 802-468-1476
E-mail: info@castleton.edu
World Wide Web: www.castleton.edu

CAMPUS LIFE

Castleton's campus is located on the western edge of Vermont. Rutland, the second most populated city in Vermont, is 12 miles east. Albany, Boston, Burlington, Hartford, Montreal, and New York City can all be reached by car or via the public transportation options in Rutland. Outdoor enthusiasts regularly take advantage of the college's proximity to the ski slopes at Pico, Killington, Okemo, and Bromley Mountain. Lake Bomoseen and the Green Mountains also offer excellent outdoor recreation, not to mention pristine environments for living as well as learning.

Castleton offers great opportunities in community service, internships, and service-learning through the Stafford Center for the Support and Study of the Community. Two annual Career Fairs allow all students to make job contacts and begin networking. Off-campus employment is available in nearby Rutland and at Killington, the largest ski area in the East.

COST AND AID

2002–2003

Vermont-resident tuition: $4,624

Nonresident tuition: $10,836

Room and board: $5,782

Room only: $3,382

Board only: $2,400

Fees for new student: $1,030

Fees for continuing student: $880

Nonresident total: $17,648

Resident total: $11,430

CAZENOVIA COLLEGE

GENERAL INFORMATION

Founded in 1824, Cazenovia College is one of the 30 oldest, continuously operating colleges in the nation. Since its inception, the College has grown from a small seminary school to a two-year women's college, to the coeducational, four-year college it is today. Cazenovia College offers an array of unique baccalaureate degrees and continues to offer some two-year associate's degree programs. Most Cazenovia students, of which 30 percent are male, come from New York State and are of traditional college age. Most students who come from outside New York are from the greater New England area. Cazenovia College has a strong campus community and residential life program. Fewer than 150 students choose to live off campus. First year students receive housing assignments based on a questionnaire and in the following years, students receive residence assignments via lottery. Campus dining facilities are open every day of the week and operate up to 12 hours daily. There are 24 classroom, administrative, and residential buildings on the main campus. All five residence halls have been recently renovated. All residence halls are equipped for fiber-optic communications, giving students full access to the campus network and the Internet from their rooms. The College athletic complex has two gyms, a competition size pool, a fitness center, outdoor fields, and tennis courts. South Campus, which is just a few blocks from the main facilities, is home to the arts and design programs, offering modern computer facilities and cutting edge software for environmental design, commercial illustration, and advertising/graphic design. In addition, the College owns a 240-acre farm, which serves as training ground for the school's accomplished equestrian program and riding teams. While Cazenovia is situated in a tranquil small town environment, there is a wide range of recreational, athletic, and cultural opportunities in close proximity. Social life is centered in the residence halls and extracurricular clubs. On campus activities abound, from dances and theme weekends, to student performances sporting events, intramural sports. Cazenovia College seeks to prepare students academically, as well as for professional, real-world situations. During their first year, students may take a blend of major courses and traditional liberal arts classes. Integral to course work in the liberal arts, as well as within each major, is practical training and development workplace skills. The Middle States Association of Colleges and Schools accredits Cazenovia College.

STUDENT BODY

Elected officials of the Student Government Association (SGA) are responsible for representing the student body in various aspects of educational and extracurricular life. All students are considered to be members of the SGA and elect officials for the positions of executive and class officers, residential communities representatives, representatives of the commuter population, and Community Judicial Board's student chair. SGA officials are responsible for allocating money to student clubs, representing students in the campus government and administration, planning campus events, and helping administrate and advise the campus disciplinary process. There are currently 32 student clubs and organizations on campus representing a wide range of student interests.

ACADEMICS

Cazenovia offers a flexible undergraduate curriculum, which features a number of distinctive major programs. The College offers a range of degrees in art and design, business, early childhood education, equine studies, and human services. The school also offers degree programs interdisciplinary liberal studies and professional studies. All students are required to complete a core program in the traditional liberal arts, which includes course work in literacy, writing, and communication. In addition, students must complete a major course of study. In their final year, seniors are expected to submit a culminating final project, which demonstrates a wide-breadth of understanding as well as strong knowledge of the major field. The excellent Center for Teaching and Learning provides special student support services, such as Title IV student-support services, job placement aid, transfer counseling, and the Higher Education Opportunity Program, a learning acceleration program. The Center's quality has been noted in the National Directory of Exemplary Programs. The Counseling Center also offers a variety of student services, including confidential professional counseling. Incoming students may earn college credit through advanced placement or through examination. Qualified students may also chose to participate in select honors courses or design an independent study program in their major field. Bachelor's degree candidates must satisfy all major program requirements and complete 120 credits with a GPA of 2.0 or better. Students must complete at least sixty credits before the junior year. Cazenovia operates on a traditional two-semester academic calendar, with two 14-week terms in the fall and spring, and optional summer programs.

Majors include:

- English (BA BS) with concentrations in literature & culture, theatre arts, communication studies
- Liberal studies (BA, BS, AA)
- Inclusive elementary education (BS)
- Early childhood education and program administration (BS)
- Early childhood teacher education (BS)
- Environmental studies (BS)
- Business management (BS)
- Management (BPS) with specializations in accounting, business management, equine business management, sport management, fashion merchandising
- Social science (BA, BS) with concentrations in history & government or sociology
- Psychology (BS)
- Human services (BS) with specializations in generalist, counseling/mental health, criminal justice, and social services for children and youth
- Interior design (BFA)
- Fashion sesign studies (AAS)
- Studio art (AS, AAS, BFA)
- Photography (AAS, BFA)
- Visual communications (BFA) in advertising/graphic design, commercial art

Also pre-law advising is available to all majors

13 Nickerson St.
Cazenovia, NY 13035
Phone: 315-655-7208
Fax: 315-655-4860
Website: www.cazenovia.edu

Cazenovia has 55 full-time and 35 part-time instructors. Cazenovia faculty is highly accomplished their field, and all full-time faculty have a PhD or relevant degree. Many of the College's part-time instructors continue to work in professional careers, adding real world knowledge to the College's academic programs. The College is committed to undergraduate teaching and instructors prioritize students over research. With a student/faculty ratio is 14:1, students have the opportunity to personally interact with their instructors. Professors are active in student life and often advise program-related clubs. In addition, faculty members fill the role of academic advisor and counselor.

ADMISSIONS

Cazenovia seeks motivated and intelligent students whose previous academic achievement, test scores, and recommendations suggest that they will succeed in college. Candidates for admission must submit an application form, an official secondary school transcript, standardized test scores, and a summary of extracurricular activities. Cazenovia recommends that students also schedule a campus tour and admissions interview. Applicants for the freshman class are encouraged to take the SAT I or ACT, though it is not required. Before applying, prospective students should have completed at least six semesters at an accredited high school. Students have the option of deferring entrance after admission. Students may also be promoted to advanced standing. Students applying for transfer admission must have maintained a GPA of 2.0.

Application and Information

Admissions decisions are made on a rolling basis. Applicants are generally notified within 30 days of receipt of all application materials. Though there are no official deadlines, the College recommends that students submit application materials before March 1 to ensure space in the incoming freshman class. All students must submit an application fee of $25 along with their materials.

For more information, contact:

Dean of Admissions and Financial Aid
Cazenovia College
Cazenovia, NY 13035
Telephone: 315-655-7208 or 800-654-3210 (toll free)
Fax: 315-655-4860

CAMPUS LIFE

Located in the charming village of Cazenovia in central New York State, Cazenovia College is an ideal environment for work and study. The town of Cazenovia has a distinctive, nineteenth-century feel and many of its historic buildings are listed on the National Register of Historic Places. Despite a small population of 4,000, the community offers a number of charming specialty shops, inns, and fine restaurants. Nearby Cazenovia Lake provides opportunity for summer and winter sports, as does the beautiful surrounding countryside, which is filled with hiking and ski trails. The larger city of Syracuse is just 18 miles from campus and offers even further cultural and entertainment options, including a symphony orchestra, a regional theater group, museums, restaurants. In addition, Syracuse University's domed stadium attracts major athletic events on a regular basis.

In recent years, Cazenovia College has been placing increased emphasis on the importance of experiential education, encouraging students to participate in service learning projects and internships. Through these programs, students can integrate career development and practical experience into their academic curriculum. Internships help students explore the practical side of their major field, and prepare them for success in the modern marketplace. Cazenovia students have participated in internships at corporations, banks, and government agencies, as well as newspapers, hospitals, and radio and television stations. In addition, students may choose to study abroad via Cazenovia College's affiliation with the American College in London.

COST AND AID

2003–2004

Tuition $16,730

Room $3,740

Board $3,220

CHAMINADE UNIVERSITY OF HONOLULU

GENERAL INFORMATION

Chaminade University of Honolulu is an independent, comprehensive, teaching University conducted in the Catholic, Marianist tradition. The University offers undergraduate and graduate programs in a Pacific Island environment rich in diversity. Chaminade's culture is characterized by small classes, values-based education, a strong sense of community, and commitments to student academic success and the development of the whole person.

STUDENT BODY

The Chaminade Student Government Association (CSGA) is the official representative organization of the student body. CSGA focuses on improving the quality of life of undergraduate students and represents the needs, interests, and concerns of its constituents.

Clubs and organizations offer all students a chance to pursue interests and extend their activities beyond the classroom. They also offer great opportunities to develop and hone leadership skills.

Chaminade University is at the Division II level of NCAA play. The institution is a member of the Pacific West Conference, a six-team league representing institutions from Hawai'i, Montana, and New Mexico. Intercollegiate sports include men's basketball, women's volleyball, women's softball, men's water polo, men's and women's tennis, and men's and women's cross-country. Chaminade hosts the popular Maui Invitational Basketball Tournament each November on Maui. Athletic scholarships are available.

Chaminade University also has a popular program of intramural sports and recreation open to all students. The program offers coeducational intramural sports in a noncompetitive atmosphere.

ACADEMICS

Undergraduate study at Chaminade University is structured in three parts:

1) A general education core of basic skills development and liberal arts inquiry
2) Intensive study in a chosen field of concentration (the major)
3) Elective courses, three of which must be upper division and taken from outside the major

All baccalaureate degrees require a minimum of 124 credit hours of course work with a minimum of 45 hours in upper division courses. Within these basic guidelines, the individual student, with the help of an advisor, selects a program of studies appropriate to personal needs and interests.

Chaminade University is committed to a broad liberal education for its students because such an education provides the foundation for lifelong personal growth, the foundation for a career that may include many job changes as the workplace changes, and the background that will allow students to rise to leadership positions in their chosen professional fields and in their communities. Outstanding professional training at Chaminade is supplemented by continued reflection on questions of meaning, purpose, and value.

Chaminade University of Honolulu offers 21 undergraduate majors as well as two associate degree programs. The Bachelor of Arts degree is available in biology, chemistry, communication, English, environmental studies, historical and political studies, humanities, international studies, management, philosophy, psychology, religious studies, and social studies. The Bachelor of Science degree is offered in accounting, behavioral sciences, biology, chemistry, computer information systems, criminology and criminal justice, early childhood education, elementary education, forensic science, and interior design.

Pre-professional programs are offered in engineering, health sciences, law, medicine, nursing, and physical therapy.

Students may elect to pursue a minor in most of the major programs as well as in anthropology, Hawaiian and Pacific studies, history, mathematics, physics, political science, sociology, and studio art.

The Associate in Arts degree is available in management, and Associate Degrees in Science are offered in computer information systems and criminology and criminal justice.

Graduate degrees are offered in business administration, counseling psychology, criminal justice administration, pastoral leadership, public administration, and education.

Chaminade University employs 60 full-time faculty members and 4 part-time professors. Chaminade classes do not employ any teaching assistants, and even science laboratory courses are taught by professors.

3140 Waialae Avenue
Honolulu, HI 96816-1578
Phone: 808-735-4735
Fax: 808-739-4647
Website: www.chaminade.edu

ADMISSIONS

Chaminade University welcomes applications from all students who have the ability, motivation, and preparation to benefit from the various programs offered. All applicants should have earned a high school diploma or the equivalent. Adequate preparation typically includes 4 years of English, 3 years of social studies, 3 years of mathematics, 2 years of science, and 4 years of college-preparatory electives.

An application for admission must be completed by each candidate seeking admission to any credit course or program offered. Applications may be obtained from the office of admissions by telephone at 808-735-4735 (toll free at 800-735-3733), by e-mail at admissions@chaminade.edu, or on the Web at www.chaminade.edu.

While the admissions office operates on a rolling admission basis, the following dates are recommended to ensure adequate time for receipt and processing of all admissions documents:

Fall semester: May 1

Spring semester: December 1

The Admissions Committee reviews each application individually and weighs high school curriculum and grades, SAT I or ACT scores, the applicant's essay, and extracurricular activities.

CAMPUS LIFE

Chaminade University is located on a hillside with a spectacular view sweeping across downtown Honolulu to Waikiki, Diamond Head, and the Pacific Ocean. Although Chaminade is located only minutes from the city and Waikiki, the campus offers a safe setting to our students. On campus, students become part of a diverse student body made up of various ethnic backgrounds.

The students of Chaminade University may spend their junior year at one of the two sister schools: The University of Dayton in Ohio or St. Mary's University in San Antonio, Texas.

Chaminade students also have the opportunity to spend their summers in Summer Study Abroad Programs, sponsored by the University of Dayton. Students may earn academic credits in these programs, which are taught entirely in English, or may elect full immersion in a foreign language. These Study Abroad programs are held in Australia, England, France, Germany, Ireland, Italy, Mexico, Morocco, Quebec (Canada), and Spain.

COST AND AID

Full-time undergraduate tuition (12 to 19 hours) on campus for 2002–2003 is $6,475 per semester.

Part-time tuition for students in the day program is $430 per semester hour.

Housing costs per semester range from $1,700 to $2,730 depending on the accommodations. Meal plans range from $1,270 to $1,770 per semester, depending on the number of meals selected by the student.

CHAMPLAIN COLLEGE

GENERAL INFORMATION

Champlain College, a private, coeducational institution founded in 1878, offers professional education for careers in today's complex world, plus enriching experiences in the humanities/social sciences. The 19-acre campus, home to more than 1,500 full-time students from 31 states and 29 countries, is located in Burlington's historic Hill Section, overlooking Lake Champlain and the Adirondack Mountains. Champlain values personal attention and provides a strong foundation upon which to excel in the professional world. The College remains responsive to changing workplace environments, developing innovative curricula and delivery. Champlain embraces the Vermont tradition of hard work, entrepreneurship and commitment to community. Students who appreciate a small-college learning environment and who respond to a culture of concerned and challenging faculty will thrive at Champlain. We encourage actual visits on campus any time of the year, and offer individual interviews with a professional admissions counselor and campus tours with current students. Request a copy of our video or take a virtual tour at www.champlain.edu. The characteristics that distinguish Champlain include: 97 percent job placement over the last eight years; 2+2 curricular format-an embedded associate's degree within the bachelor's degree; internships in 96 percent of majors offered locally, nationally or internationally; unique Victorian-era residence halls; and a safe and stunning location in one of America's best college towns.

STUDENT BODY

Champlain College is committed to involving its entire student body in extracurricular activities, including the Champlain College Players, Music Makers and literary magazine. The Readers Series brings poets, authors and historians to campus. The Intercollegiate Writers' Exchange provides an opportunity to share writing with other college students in the Burlington area. Intramural programs include basketball, indoor soccer, ice hockey, outing club, skiing/snowboarding and more. Unique partnerships with nearby businesses offer indoor climbing, nautilus/free weight facilities, swimming pools, indoor track, basketball, and aerobics/spinning classes.

ACADEMICS

Champlain is accredited by the New England Association of Schools and Colleges and the Commission on Accreditation of Allied Health Education Programs

Champlain offers 24 career-building majors, all front-loaded with major-specific courses to be taken in the first two years of study. Majors include accounting, business, computer information systems, computer networking, criminal justice, e-business & commerce, elementary education, global networks & telecommunications, hospitality industry management (hotel restaurant management and tourism event management), international business, management, marketing management, multimedia/graphic design, paralegal, professional writing (media/creative writing and business/technical writing), public relations & media communications, radiography, respiratory therapy, social work, software development, software engineering, sport management, and website management & development. Students may also enter as an "undeclared" major and decide on a career concentration by the end of their sophomore year. All majors emphasize oral and written communication, critical thinking, development of ethical judgment, and global awareness.

Champlain's professors bring the requisite academic credentials to their classrooms but also enrich them with extensive practical professional experience. In addition to a core of 76 full-time professors, Champlain looks for adjunct professors with relevant professional experience to enhance the learning environment and professional contacts for our undergraduates.

163 South Willard Street Box 670, PO Box 670
Burlington, VT 05402-0670
Phone: 802-860-2727
Fax: 802-860-2767
Website: www.champlain.edu

ADMISSIONS

The College operates on "rolling admissions," admitting students for fall or January term. Greatest emphasis is placed on the strength of a student's high school curriculum. Suggested college preparatory curriculum should include: 4 years writing- and reading-intensive English, 4 years writing- and reading-intensive history/social sciences, 3 years math (through at least Algebra II), 3 years science, 2 years foreign language, and a full academic course load senior year.

The Admissions Committee looks on average grades in highest-level courses (Honors or AP) as favorably as above-average grades in regular college prep courses. Most admitted students rank at least within the top 50 percent of their class. Admission decisions are "need blind."

- Enrollment: 1,500 students
- Typical Academic Profile: 2.5/80 GPA or better
- Midrange combined SAT: 1020–1220
- College prep curriculum with full course load senior year
- International students need minimum TOEFL score of 500/173

CAMPUS LIFE

Burlington is a small city (46,000 people) on the shore of Lake Champlain, sometimes called the "sixth Great Lake." One of Vermont's most progressive cities, Burlington also has a national reputation as one of the healthiest and happiest cities in the country. A&E Television has ranked Burlington as the nation's "Best Place to Live." Home to six institutions of higher learning, the city also has one of the leading medical centers on the East Coast. Montreal, Quebec, is within an hour and a half driving distance. An international airport and Amtrak passenger train route make the city accessible.

Champlain has established study abroad programs in England, France, Sweden, and Switzerland. Champlain offers a Master's of Science in Innovation and Information Technology, and a 4+1 BS/MBA option with Clarkson and Southern New Hampshire Universities.

COST AND AID

For 2002–2003, tuition, fees, and room and board total $20,695.

CHAPMAN UNIVERSITY

GENERAL INFORMATION

Since its inception in 1861, Chapman University has been steadily gaining size and prestige. Founded by members of the First Christian Church, Chapman has grown from a small, traditional school into a midsize, nationally recognized university with renowned programs in film and television production, business and economics, music, education, communication arts, and the natural and applied sciences. Chapman's beautiful campus features historic buildings, tranquil gardens, world-class recreational facilities, and "smart" classrooms. With wireless technology throughout the campus, Chapman was recently named one of the top 50 "Best Wired" campuses by Yahoo! The Argyros Forum, the heart of the school community, is home to the largest campus dining area, numerous conference and classroom facilities, and student offices. Other first-rate facilities include Bertea Hall and the School of Music, and the beautiful 1,000-seat Memorial Auditorium, noted on the National Register of Historic Places. Chapman offers a dynamic and comprehensive athletic program, and the Hutton Sports Center includes a 3,000-seat indoor arena, a large outdoor stadium, championship tennis courts, and fitness facilities. Thurmond Clarke Library has more than 250,000 volumes and modern computer labs with full Internet services. Recently constructed, Beckman Hall features state-of-the-art "smart" classroom facilities, is home to the Argyros School of Business and Economics, and has several endowed centers, including the A. Gary Anderson Center for Economic Research, the Ralph W. Leatherby Center for Entrepreneurship and Business Ethics, and the Walter Schmid Center for International Business. The School of Communication Arts facilities feature the Guggenheim Art Gallery and Waltmar Theatre, and science students benefit from the resources of Hashinger Science Center, which contains nuclear science, radiation, crystallography, genetics, food science, and physical therapy laboratories. There are five residence halls and six apartment buildings on campus. In addition, the University recently added a five-story parking structure, a new School of Law facility, and Liberty Plaza, which features portions of the Berlin Wall.

Chapman's academic preparation and wide breadth of excellence is evidenced by the University's accomplished alumni, who include the Honorable Loretta Sanchez ('88), member of Congress; the Honorable David Bonior ('85), member of Congress and current house minority whip; John Copeland ('73), a television and film producer; Steve Lavin ('88) head basketball coach at the University of California, Los Angeles; former San Diego Padre stars Tim Flannery ('80) and Randy Jones ('72); and George L. Argyros ('65), U.S. ambassador to Spain.

STUDENT BODY

Intercollegiate athletics are a big part of undergraduate life at Chapman, and almost 20 percent of students compete in varsity sports. Chapman is an independent in the NCAA Division III, often qualifying for championships. Last year, 4 students were named All-American and 14 received the title Academic All-Americans. Chapman competes in men's baseball, basketball, water polo, crew, cross-country, football, golf, lacrosse, soccer, softball, and tennis, and in women's basketball, crew, cross country, soccer, swimming, tennis, track and field, volleyball, and water polo. More than 75 campus clubs and organizations offer myriad opportunities for involvement and community service and stewardship. Five national fraternities and five national sororities are active. A complete offering of intramural sports and activities also help Chapman to offer students an involving and electric outdoor-oriented environment.

ACADEMICS

Chapman University strives to provide every student with an excellent, individualized course of study, which will result in a well-rounded, successful life and career. Academic departments are divided into the Wilkinson College of Letters and Sciences, the AACSB-accredited Argyros School of Business and Economics, the School of Communication Arts, the School of Education, the School of Film and Television, the NASM-accredited School of Music, and the School of Law. Chapman is also home to the IFT-accredited program in food science and nutrition, and the APTA-accredited graduate program in physical therapy. The A. Gary Anderson Center for Economic Research is recognized throughout the world for its excellence in economic forecasting. Chapman was recently named a "Character-Building College" by the Templeton Foundation. As testament to Chapman's commitment to offer its students "smart" classrooms and a state-of-the-art wireless campus, Yahoo! recently included Chapman in its list of "The Top 50 Best Wired Campuses."

Chapman University confers degrees in the following fields of study: accounting, art, athletic training, biology, business administration, chemistry, communications, computer information systems, computer science, dance, economics, English, environmental science, film and television, food science and nutrition, French, history, leadership and organizational studies, legal studies, liberal studies (teaching), mathematics, music, peace studies, philosophy, physical education, political science, psychology, psychobiology, public relations and advertising, religion, sociology, Spanish, and theater.

Total instructional faculty: 222 full-time, 288 part-time. Total minority faculty: 30. Total women faculty: 84. Total with doctorate/terminal degree: 182

ADMISSIONS

Chapman University seeks accomplished students who will be successful in a challenging academic program. Admission to the school is selective with only 58 percent of the 2002 applicant pool being offered admission to the University. Prospective students are evaluated on the strength of their secondary school coursework and GPA, and SAT I or ACT scores. Applicants are encouraged to visit the campus and to schedule an interview with a member of the admissions staff. Students can arrange an interview and campus tour through the Office of Admission. Chapman offers a nonbinding Early Action Deadline for freshman

One University Drive
Orange, CA 92866
Phone: 714-997-6711
Fax: 714-997-6713
Website: www.chapman.edu

applicants. To apply in the Early Action program, students must submit the application before November 30. The regular application deadline is January 31. The deadline for transfer application is March 15. Students may request more information by contacting:

Director of Admission
Chapman University
One University Drive
Orange, CA 92866
Phone: (714) 997-6711 or 888-CUAPPLY (toll free)
Fax: 714-997-6713
E-mail: admit@chapman.edu

CAMPUS LIFE

Chapman University is located in Orange County's beautiful south coast, famous for its ideal climate, cultural and recreational opportunities, and varied natural resources. With the San Diego and Los Angeles metropolitan areas in close proximity, students can attend concerts, see professional sports, or go to world famous theme parks like Disneyland and Knott's Berry Farm. There are outdoor activities throughout the year, with Pacific beaches only 10 miles away and winter ski resorts only a 90-minute drive from campus. Add to these benefits an average year-round temperature of 71° F, and its no surprise that *Places Rated Almanac* recently named Orange County, California, "the #1 place to live in North America." On campus, Chapman students take part in the dynamic Student Activities Program. There are more than 70 student-run clubs, including community service organizations, five national fraternities and sororities, an active intramural sports program, and music, art, and theater productions. Though Chapman students are predominantly from California, the student body is diverse, with students hailing from 40 states and 34 foreign countries. Chapman students have distinguished themselves in a variety of forums. In the preceding five years, Chapman students have been recognized as Truman Scholars, Coro Fellows, USA Today All-USA College Academic Team members, NCAA All-Americans, and NCAA Academic All-Americans.

Chapman's Career Development Center provides a variety of services to students, graduates, and former students. These include: internship opportunities, an on-campus recruiting program, full-time job postings and computer-networked job listings, individual career counseling and career assessment, a career resource library, job-search and resume-writing skills development, interview coaching, and an Alumni Mentor Program. The center will assist teachers in establishing a self-managed educational placement file. Chapman students are encouraged to participate in study abroad programs in many academic fields in almost every part of the world. Students studying abroad through Chapman-approved programs are enrolled in a full course of study at the host institution but receive academic credit from Chapman. The study abroad program directly supports Chapman's emphasis on encouraging students to recognize and develop their roles as global citizens in an increasingly interdependent world. The Chapman London Center at the University of Greenwich offers additional study and travel opportunities, with a focus on British culture and history.

COST AND AID

Undergraduate tuition (annual, 12–18 semester credits), room and board, and fees for the 2003–2004 academic year are as follows: annual tuition $23,950; accident/sickness plan $340; associated students fee $120; Wellness Center fee $180; total tuition/fees: $24,590. Average room and board cost for academic year 2003–2004: room $4,692, telecommunications fee $220, activity fee $40, board plan $3,576; total room and board (average) $8,528.

CHESTNUT HILL

THE COLLEGE AT A GLANCE

Founded in 1924, Chestnut Hill College is a Catholic women's institution overlooking Wissahickon Creek in Philadelphia. Chestnut Hill College has remained a women's college since its inception, committed to providing a strong, values-oriented education that helps prepare women for success in the modern world. Chestnut Hill helps women make a positive difference in society, fostering important personal skills such as leadership and self-expression. The 372 full-time and 116 part-time undergraduate students come diverse backgrounds and hail from 15 states and 13 countries. In addition to the undergraduate program, there are 426 women and men in the continuing education evening and weekend program. Chestnut Hill awards undergraduate degrees as well as the MEd, MA, and MS in elementary education, counseling psychology and human services, holistic spirituality, and technology in education.

An active campus community, Chestnut Hill College students are involved a wide range clubs and participate in various recreational activities such as aerobics, horseback riding, golf, and archery. Chestnut Hill is a member of the NCAA Division III, competing in basketball, field hockey, lacrosse, softball, tennis, and volleyball. On-campus athletic facilities include a swimming pool, a gym, a hockey field, a weight room and fitness center, and eight tennis courts.

STUDENTS

Students are encouraged to think creatively and independently at Chestnut Hill. CHC encourages students to take leadership roles in the community and students are involved in the administration of student affairs. For example, students, faculty, and administration serve jointly on the Curriculum Committee and the College Council. In addition, the Student Organization has Academic, Social-Cultural, and Student Affairs committees, which seek to represent student interests and meet student academic and social needs.

ACADEMICS

Chestnut Hill's academic calendar runs two 15-week semesters. In between the fall and spring semesters, there are two 6-week sessions during the summer. In addition to intensive study in a major field, CHC seeks to provide students with a strong foundation in the fine arts, humanities, and sciences, as well as an awareness of modern social problems.

To qualify for a BS or BA degree, students must complete 120 semester hours and satisfy basic academic requirements. Outside of a major course of study, all students are required to complete 11 semester hours in natural sciences (of which 8 must be in laboratory science), 9 semester hours in social sciences, and 21 semester hours in the humanities. In addition, students must take 6 semester hours of religious studies, 6 hours at the advanced level in a foreign language, and 3 hours in a writing course. Students may complete up to 45 semester hours of the required 120 within their major area.

Student may be approved to pursue a degree two major fields. Students who wish to double major must discuss their proposed course of study with the chair of each department and submit a proposal to the dean of the College. To earn a dual degree, students must satisfy the individual requirements of both department programs.

Select freshmen and sophomores have the opportunity to participate in the CHC's challenging interdepartmental honors program. The honors program gives students the chance study independently with a professor or in a small seminar. Students participating in the honors program can fulfill all distribution requirements by completing the four honors courses and an honors paper, plus two elective courses and two laboratory science courses. To be considered for admission to the honors programs, students must apply at the beginning of their freshman or sophomore year.

Accomplished sophomores may be invited to participate in an independent study program in their major department during junior and senior year. Students then use the research produced during the independent study to write an honors thesis. Students who complete an independent study and honors thesis receive honors at graduation.

Chestnut Hill College offers Bachelor of Arts and Bachelor of Science degrees in the following subject areas: accounting, art history, art studio, biochemistry, biology, business administration, chemistry, communications and technology, computer and information science, computer and information technology, computer and mathematical sciences, early childhood education (with a Montessori certification option), early childhood and elementary education, economics, elementary education, English, environmental science, fine arts and technology, French, history, management, marketing, mathematical sciences, molecular biology, music, music education, political science, psychology, secondary education certification in various disciplines, sociology (with professional option in criminal justice), and Spanish.

Students in any major discipline may choose to augment their course of study through the school's certificate programs in art therapy, environmental studies, gerontology, international studies, and women in management.

Chestnut Hill provides several pre-professional programs in allied health fields, dentistry, law, medicine, and veterinary sciences. Students may participate in cooperative studies at LaSalle University.

Chestnut Hill's faculty is accomplished in research, publication, and travel, but are first and foremost teachers. There are 109 faculty members, 57 of whom are full-time; over 75 percent of faculty members hold doctoral or terminal degrees in their subject area. Chestnut Hill instructors take teaching seriously, and with an excellent student/faculty ratio of 12:1, students have ample opportunity to work individually with professors. Chestnut Hill's distinguished instructors have earned degrees from such premiere institutions as the University of Oxford in England, the University of Paris, the University of Budapest, Catholic University of America, Middlebury College, Bryn Mawr College, Columbia University, the University of Notre Dame, the University of Pennsylvania, Duke University, New York University, the New School for Social Research, Purdue University, Temple University, and the University of Minnesota.

9601 Germantown Avenue
Philadelphia, PA 19118-2693
Phone: 215-248-7001
Fax: 215-248-7082
Website: www.chc.edu

CAMPUS LIFE

Located in a historic area of Philadelphia, Chestnut Hill's beautiful campus is bordered by Fairmount Park, yet is a quick train or car ride away from bustling downtown Philadelphia. One of New England's premiere cities, Philadelphia offers a wide variety of restaurants, sports, and cultural and recreational activities. In particular, Philadelphia is home to a number of world-class museums, including the Art Museum, the Rodin Museum, the Living History Museum, and the Franklin Institute. A historic city, the atmosphere and architecture around Independence Hall, Society Hill, and Penn's Landing are gems of colonial architecture and atmosphere. In addition to the city's cultural resources, Philadelphia is home to 25 colleges and universities, creating a vibrant collegiate environment for study and social life.

While students at Chestnut Hill have access to cosmopolitan Philadelphia, CHC is set in a lovely suburban neighborhood in the northwest corner of the city. The charming colonial area of Chestnut Hill is just a mile from campus. Well known in and beyond Philadelphia, Chestnut Hill gives students easy access to shopping and cultural events, as well as convenient transportation downtown.

Chestnut Hill College has forged an association with La Salle University, a local coeducational institution, easily accessible via public transportation. Through the agreement, students from either college can register for courses at the other for full course credit. Therefore, Chestnut Hill students have use of two campuses and can choose classes from two complete course catalogs without paying additional tuition.

CHC students are encouraged to use the month between semesters to travel or pursue independent study. With the guidance of professors, students can plan an off-campus program of study. Students may also travel or study off campus during the summer, should they prefer a program longer than the interim. In the past, Chestnut Hill students have designed programs such as studying French culture in Paris, women in English literature in London, and marine biology in Florida.

Chestnut Hill College is a member of a national 10-college consortium founded by the Sisters of St. Joseph. As a member of the consortium, Chestnut Hill students can enroll at any other of the 10 member colleges for a semester or a year. Therefore Chestnut Hill students have the option of studying in locations across the nation without losing their status as a Chestnut Hill student.

Upper-class students who maintain an average of B or better and obtain the approval of the academic dean may choose to study abroad. To receive academic credit, the student's major department has to pre-approve the curriculum. Through this program, Chestnut Hill College students have studied in prominent European cities, including London, Rome, Madrid, Vienna, and Salzburg.

In recent years, many departments have developed internship programs in response to students' growing interest in acquiring real-world experience while in college. Through these programs, students can earn course credit for pursuing professional internships in a field related to their major. In addition, Chestnut Hill has an office of cooperative education, which assists students seeking salaried jobs in line with their interests and academic preparation. Cooperative education students alternately work and attend classes; they earn course credit for their job experience.

COSTS & AID

Over 75 percent of students at Chestnut Hill College receive financial aid. Chestnut Hill College offers financial aid in the form of scholarships, loans, work-study, federal grants, and Chestnut Hill College grants. The majority of awards are made according to a student's financial need and usually combine several types of aid. Each package is tailored to suit a student's needs and abilities. All prospective students applying for aid must file the Free Application for Federal Student Aid (FAFSA). In addition to need-based awards, Chestnut Hill awards several merit-based scholarships annually.

To be considered for admission, students must submit an application, a nonrefundable application fee, an official high school transcript, and scores from the SAT I or ACT. Though usually not required, a personal interview is recommended.

Tuition for 2001–2002 was $16,990 plus additional room and board fees of roughly $7,000 to $8,000.

ADMISSIONS

CHC seeks accomplished students prepared to benefit from a challenging undergraduate curriculum. The Admissions Committee reviews all the applications and evaluates students on their intellectual ability and academic achievement, taking into consideration the student's performance in high school and SAT I or ACT scores. Chestnut Hill College offers prospective students the option of applying through Early Decision, Early Admission, and Advanced Placement programs.

Prospective transfer students are required to submit an official transcript of all college or university work.

Admissions decisions are made on a rolling basis. To set up an interview or request more information about academics or admissions, students may contact:

Director of Admissions
Chestnut Hill College
9601 Germantown Avenue
Philadelphia, PA 19118-2693
Telephone: 215-248-7001
800-248-0052 (toll free)
E-mail: chcapply@chc.edu
Website: www.chc.edu

CHRISTIAN BROTHERS UNIVERSITY

AT A GLANCE

Christian Brothers University (CBU) is a private, Catholic, coeducational university whose purpose is to prepare students for the workplace and for success in life. On this friendly campus, in the heart of a thriving city, you'll find room to grow without getting lost. With 2,000 men and women coming from more than 20 states and 25 countries and representing 35 different faiths, you'll have the opportunity to become your best self-intellectually, professionally, and spiritually-because the classes are small, the faculty care, and our attention is focused on you.

CBU is a comprehensive university with the resources to stretch your intellect, ignite your technological skills, and build your appreciation for art and culture. We emphasize excellence in teaching and individualized attention to the whole person in a values-oriented, interfaith educational community. Our mission is to prepare students for professional careers and advanced study in the arts and sciences, engineering, and business, and for lives of moral responsibility and constructive community involvement.

LOCATION AND ENVIRONMENT

Christian Brothers University is located in the center of the friendly southern city of Memphis, Tennessee, and is situated on the banks of the majestic Mississippi River. Memphis is the home of rock and roll, the blues, and barbecue, and is characterized by graceful southern architecture, lingering summers, and lush gardens. CBU's 75-acre, wooded and landscaped campus is set in the heart of midtown

Memphis, about four miles east of downtown, near interstates 40,240, and 55. Sporting events, concerts, plays, galleries and parks are all easily accessible because of CBU's central location in the city.

MAJORS AND DEGREES OFFERED

Bachelor of Arts

Bachelor of Science in Business Administration

Bachelor of Science in Engineering

Bachelor of Arts in Science and Mathematics

Bachelor of Science in Science and Mathematics

Master of Business Administration

Master of Arts in Teaching

Master of Education

Master of Science in Educational Leadership

Master of Engineering Management

ACADEMIC PROGRAMS

Whether you are undecided about your future or clearly focused on a goal, CBU has programs that lead to successful careers in the twenty-first century. A student can choose from more than 50 programs in business, engineering, liberal arts, and science. The School of Business offers a Bachelor of Science degree in Business Administration with majors available in accounting, information technology management, economics, finance, marketing, and management. Also offering BS degrees, the School of Engineering is ABET-accredited and offers programs in chemical engineering, civil and environmental engineering, electrical and computer engineering, and mechanical engineering. In the School of Liberal Arts, Bachelor of Arts degrees are offered in English, English for corporate communication and management, history, human development, liberal studies, psychology, applied psychology, and religion and philosophy. The School of Science offers both a BS and a BA in biology, and a BS in chemistry, computer science, engineering physics, mathematics, natural science, and physics. In addition to chosen majors, a student can elect to concentrate on a pre-professional area including dentistry, elementary education, law, medicine, nursing, optometry, pharmacy, physical therapy, secondary education, and veterinary medicine. CBU also offers a Master of Education, a Master of Business Administration, an Executive Master of Business Administration, and a Master of Engineering Management.

OFF-CAMPUS OPPORTUNITIES

Located in the heart of bustling Memphis, CBU is minutes away from many international companies, such as Federal Express and International Paper, and is close to major medical centers, including St. Jude Children's Research Hospital. Memphis offers unlimited opportunities for partnerships with progressive business and technological enterprises such as Andersen Consulting, Smith and Nephew, Shell, and Exxon. Internship opportunities exist both in Memphis and throughout the nation. With large alumni bases in Dallas, Chicago, St. Louis, and Houston, among other cities, opportunities exist nationwide and are not limited to the Memphis area.

While Memphis is a city of festivals generally centered on the musical and cultural heritage of the Mid-South community, the annual celebrations actually begin with a month-long salute to the arts, customs, and food of a selected foreign country, better known as Memphis in May. Other events to attend include Arts in the Park, the Cooper-Young festival, and the Wonders Exhibit. Memphis is also host to a Triple A baseball team, the Memphis Redbirds, who play at Autozone Park located downtown. Memphis's central location and its access to plane, bus, or train transportation provides an easy route to travel throughout the United States and abroad. There is also ample opportunity for nature activities and outdoor sports.

Admissions, Box T-6, 650 East Parkway South
Memphis, TN 38104-5519
Phone: 901-321-3205
Fax: 901-321-3202
Website: www.cbu.edu

FACILITIES AND EQUIPMENT

Plough Memorial Library has more than 156,000 volumes and more than 560 periodical subscriptions and microfilm items. Access to the library's collections is provided through an online catalog and an automated circulation system available electronically on campus, on the Internet, and by dial-in access. Students can also search a variety of electronic and CD-ROM databases. All residence hall rooms are networked, allowing access to e-mail and full Internet access. Hundreds of computers-primarily PC's but also some Macs and UNIX workstations-are available in various campus labs. In addition, each residence hall room is wired for free local telephone service and cable television.

Students in the School of Sciences have access to the most specialized equipment, including research-quality microscopes, UV visible spectrophotometer, PCR thermoclyclyer and computer interfaced microscopes, just to name a few.

Students in the School of Engineering as well as in the School of Sciences will soon enjoy a remodeled state of the art classroom and lab facility thanks to a $3 million grant from the Assisi Foundation of Memphis.

School of Business students spend most of their time in Buckman Hall,

an advanced and "wired" facility with networked computer labs, the latest business software, extensive multi media capabilities and theatre-style classrooms.

TUITION, ROOM & BOARD, AND FEES

CBU is an outstanding value, costing 25 percent less than the average selective private university in the United States. Estimated expenses for the 2003–2004 academic year include tuition, $16,740; fees, $450; and room and board, $5,100. This adds up to a yearly estimated cost of $22,290.

FINANCIAL AID

Scholarships: Priority date for scholarships is December 1. The application for admission serves as the application for scholarship. Students applying by the Regular Application Deadline of March 1 will receive full consideration for scholarships. After that date, scholarships will be awarded based on available funds. These scholarships are competitive, awarded without regard to need, and available to new students only. CBU scholarships require that the student exhibit strong academic qualities with a cumulative GPA of 3.2 or higher and an ACT of 23 or higher or the SAT equivalent. Other criteria reviewed for scholarship awarding include level of difficulty of high school courses, essay, scholastic honors and academic awards, interview, community service, leadership and involvement, and extracurricular activities.

Financial Aid: The priority deadline for applying for financial assistance is March 1, at which time all admission and financial aid forms should have been submitted to the University. All students with complete credentials as of March 1 will be among the first to receive any offer of assistance from CBU, usually by April 1. Forms submitted after March 1 will be processed as quickly as possible. Resources from the University and those from donors provide funds available to students that, combined with resources through the state and federal governments, help to build the bridge between costs at CBU and the ability of the student and family to finance a CBU education. The University's financial assistance usually takes the form of a package, which combines gift aid (grants and/or scholarships) with self-help (loans and/or work programs) and is awarded with regard to a family's financial situation. The University also provides an extensive merit-based scholarship program regardless of financial need. In addition, several deferred payment plans are available through the CBU Business Office to assist with the costs not met by financial aid.

FULL- AND PART-TIME FACULTY

Approximately 162 faculty, including 32 Christian Brothers, continue our tradition of excellence in teaching. Because teaching is the priority, 100 percent of faculty teach undergraduates. With a 14:1 student/faculty ratio, students develop personally as well as academically. Offering personalized attention in small classroom settings, faculty work during the academic year, the summer, and sabbaticals on special projects that complement and enhance their classroom instruction. Faculty members regularly conduct research; author papers, articles, and books; consult in the corporate world; and perform community service.

STUDENT ORGANIZATION AND ACTIVITIES

At Christian Brothers University, 65 percent of new students live on campus in traditional halls. Freshmen choose from three halls and returning students have the option to live in a three-building complex of fully furnished, student resident apartments.

With over 40 clubs and organizations, the Office of Student Life makes it the number-one priority to ensure that all students have a chance to become involved in the larger life of this Lasallian community. Honor societies, professional fraternities, social sororities and fraternities, and clubs fall under the reign of the Student Government Association. In the fall, the SGA sponsors a club fair that allows students to become familiar with the various organizations on campus. A club membership drive follows a few weeks later. Students have the opportunity to sign up for organizations that match their interests. In the athletic arena, CBU competes at the NCAA Division II level and offers the following sports for men and women: basketball, soccer, cross-country, and tennis. Men also compete in baseball and golf, and women also compete in softball and volleyball. There is also an extensive intramural athletic program.

ADMISSIONS PROCESS AND REQUIREMENTS

Entering students are encouraged to apply through our Early Scholars Program, an Early Action program. All applications must be postmarked by December 1. If accepted through the ESP Option, you are guaranteed a place in CBU's entering class, scholarship notification by Christmas, if eligible, room in the residence halls, and invitation only events in January and February.

Entering students may apply during the Regular Application period. The Regular Application deadline is March 1 (postmarked). Notification of admission decisions will be mailed on a rolling basis after January 15. Applications submitted after March 1 will be handled on a space-available basis.

To apply, student must submit a completed application, a high school transcript, ACT or SAT I, an essay, and an academic recommendation. Interviews are recommended. The middle 50 percent of the entering class scores 22–27 on the ACT and has between a 3.2 and 3.5 GPA.

CLARION UNIVERSITY OF PENNSYLVANIA

GENERAL INFORMATION

Founded in 1867 and set on two campuses in Clarion and Oil City, Clarion University is one of 14 state-owned schools in Pennsylvania. Clarion University is fully accredited by the Middle States Association of Colleges and Schools. The National Council for Accreditation of Teacher Education (NCATE) and the National Academy of Early Childhood Programs accredits the education programs, the American Chemical Society approves the chemistry program, the Association to Advance Collegiate Schools of Business (AACSB) accredits all programs under the College of Business Administration. Clarion University of Pennsylvania participates in the American Association of Colleges for Teacher Education, the American Association of State Colleges and Universities, and is an Educational Associate of the Institute of International Education. The Bachelor and Associate of Science in Nursing programs are accredited by the National League for Nursing. The prominent American Library Association accredits the graduate program in library science and the Education Standards Board of the American Speech-Language-Hearing Association accredits the pathology and audiology graduate programs. The American Bar Association approves the legal business program at the Venago campus.

There are 12 advanced degree programs offered through the Graduate School: biology (MS), business administration (MBA), communication (MS), English (MA), library science (MSLS), nursing (MSN), special education (MS), and speech pathology and audiology (MS), and the Master in Education (MEd), with focus programs in elementary education, mathematics, reading education, and science education. The University is comprised of two campuses, with a combined enrollment of about 6,500 students. The main campus in Clarion is set on 130 acres, and contains 7 residence halls and more than 40 buildings. The smaller Venango campus is made up of 4 buildings set on 64 acres.

STUDENT BODY

There are more than 125 student run clubs and organizations at Clarion University including intramural sports, Greek organizations, and music and drama programs. Cultural and recreational activities abound on campus, from the famous Autumn Leaf Festival and Homecoming Weekend, to movie nights, concerts, theatre, and art exhibits on campus. In addition to student performances, the school invites many renowned orchestras, theatre groups, and speakers to campus. Clarion offers the following in Division II women's sports: basketball, cross country, soccer, softball, swimming & diving, tennis, track & field, and volleyball. Division II men's sports include baseball, basketball, cross country, football, golf, swimming & diving, and track & field. Clarion University is Division I in men's wrestling.

ACADEMICS

Clarion is committed to a well rounded, interdisciplinary approach to learning. With this philosophy in mind, Clarion's academic program is flexible and allows for double majors, specializations, and minors. To earn a bachelor's degree, students must satisfactorily complete 120 credits. To earn an associate degree, students must complete 64 credits. The school also operates an honors program for accomplished students and further recognizes academic excellence through awards and honorary societies. Clarion's academic calendar operates on a two-semester system. Incoming freshmen may receive college credit for high school course work through the Advanced Placement program or through examination. Prospective students may also earn credit by enrolling in courses taught in select, local high schools by Clarion instructors.

Students at Clarion University may choose to major in more than 70 baccalaureate degree programs for the Bachelor of Arts (BA), the Bachelor of Science (BS), the Bachelor of Science in Business Administration (BSBA), the Bachelor of Music (BM), the Bachelor of Fine Arts (BFA), the Bachelor of Science in Nursing (BSN), and the Bachelor of Science in Education (BSEd).

The College of Arts and Sciences confers the Bachelor of Arts in the following fields of study: anthropology, art, biology, chemistry, communication, computer science, cooperative engineering, earth science, economics, English, environmental biology, environmental geoscience, French, geography, geology, history, humanities, industrial mathematics, information systems, liberal studies, mathematics, medical technology, molecular biology/biotechnology, music-elective studies in business, natural science, philosophy, physics, political science, psychology, social sciences, sociology, sociology/psychology, Spanish, speech communication, and theatre.

Admissions Office, 840 Wood Street
Clarion, PA 16214
Phone: 814-393-2306
Fax: 814-393-2030
Website: www.clarion.edu

Students in the College of Business Administration may choose to pursue an undergraduate degree in accounting, economics, finance, industrial relations, international business, management, marketing, and real estate.

The College of Education and Human Services offers degree programs in early childhood education, elementary education, library science, music education, rehabilitative science, secondary education (with certification available in 11 areas), special education, and speech pathology and audiology. The school also offers a program in athletic training.

Students may choose to augment their major field through minors, concentrations, pre-professional programs, and dual certificate programs.

The Venago campus is home to the School of Nursing, which confers the Associate of Science and the Bachelor of Science in nursing, as well as the Associate of Science in allied health. The Bachelor's degree is offered at the School of Nursing at the Pittsburgh Site/West Penn Hospital. Students at the Venango campus also may pursue the Associate of Science (AS) degree in business administration, the Associate of Science in Rehabilitative Services, the Bachelor of Science in Radiologic Sciences, the Associate of Science in Legal Business Studies (Paralegal), the Associate of Science in Early Childhood Education, and the Associate of Arts in Liberal Studies.

Clarion's accomplished faculty hails from diverse backgrounds and experiences, holding degrees from the top national and international universities. Current faculty join Clarion from the Universities of Heidelberg, Baghdad, Leningrad, Paris, and Bombay. In addition, Clarion has the honor of counting a number of Fulbright lecture appointees among its instructors. With a low student/faculty ratio of 18:1, Clarion students benefit from smaller class sizes and generous interaction with distinguished faculty members. Clarion University counselors are accredited through the International Association of Counseling Services and are always available to help students with academic and personal matters. The school also offers free career counseling to all students.

ADMISSIONS

Prospective students are evaluated on the strength of their high school curriculum, their GPA, their class rank, SAT or ACT scores, and extracurricular jobs and activities. In particular, Clarion University looks favorably on students who took a challenging high school curriculum, which includes college-prep courses, honors programs, and AP courses. Last year, nearly 4,000 prospective students applied to Clarion University, of which about 2,800 were accepted. The resulting incoming class for the fall semester was more than 1,500 students. The school also offers academic support and summer start admissions. Clarion encourages prospective students to apply early and to visit the campus. Clarion University offers numerous visit opportunities and can tailor a campus visit to specifically to address a prospective student's interests.

CAMPUS LIFE

Located in the beautiful countryside atop the Allegheny plateau, the Clarion campus is an ideal environment for work and study. Surrounded by mountains and away from the distractions of a city, the lovely small town of Clarion has a population of about 6,500. Nearby mountain ranges, Cook Forest, and the Clarion River are known throughout the region, and offer ample opportunity for camping, hiking, boating, fishing, and water sports. The spectacular Autumn Leaf Festival is a major local attraction, drawing more than 100,000 visitors annually. Though hometown Clarion is small, there are restaurants, stores, and other conveniences a few blocks off campus. Just off Interstate 80, Clarion is only a two-hour drive from Erie and Pittsburgh.

Students who wish to pursue a course of study overseas or gain professional experience outside the classroom have the option of participating in exchange programs, cooperative education, and internship programs for course credit. In the past years, students have studied in such international locations as Malta, Costa Rica, France, Spain, England, and Korea.

COST AND AID

For the 2002–2003 academic year Pennsylvania residents paid $10,073 for tuition, room, board and fees. Out of state students paid $12,313 for tuition, room, board and fees. Students generally spend an additional $1,500 on books, transportation, entertainment, and personal expenses every year.

CLARKSON UNIVERSITY

GENERAL INFORMATION

Clarkson University is an independent, coeducational institution with a strong focus in technology. It offers innovative programs in business, engineering, liberal arts, the sciences, and health sciences. The academic environment is collaborative and interdisciplinary. A rigorous curriculum emphasizes team project-based learning to develop technical expertise, collaboration and communication skills, versatility, and hands-on management experience. Clarkson alumni have earned a growing national reputation as leaders in technological fields. (One graduate in 12 is CEO, president, vice president, or owner of a company.)The school is also known for having a friendly campus, where students easily form personal relationships with their professors and one another.

There are 2,700 undergraduates at Clarkson and 25 percent are women. The Graduate School offers 24 master's degree and 9 doctoral programs, with a combined enrollment of 350 students. Clarkson is nationally recognized for the effectiveness of its team project-based learning programs. It won the 2001 Boeing Outstanding Educator Award, was first runner-up for the 2002 National Undergraduate Entrepreneurship Education Award, won the Corporate and Foundation Alliance Award for and won the 2002 IBM Linux Scholar Challenge, an international open-source computer programming contest.

STUDENT BODY

Clarkson's active campus boasts a wide variety of extracurricular activities. There are more than 100 campus clubs and interest groups, which range from the outing club, pep band, and amateur radio, to auto, chess, photo, trail biking, drama, equestrian, table tennis, rugby, and ski clubs. Students publish a lively campus newspaper, a humor magazine, and a literary publication, and run a radio and television station. In addition, there are active professional and honor societies, and an elected student government.

The neighboring 6 million acre Adirondack Park offers year-round recreational opportunities, including hiking, mountain and rock climbing, bicycling, boating, downhill and cross-country skiing, swimming, camping, fishing and hunting. An Adirondack Lodge is campus headquarters for outdoor recreation activities. Intercollegiate and intramural sports are popular. Recreational facilities include a field house and gym with racquetball, basketball, and indoor tennis courts, a fitness center, and swimming pool. The student center includes fast food facilities, the campus post office, an international reading room, the student newspaper office, music practice rooms, student meeting rooms and lounges, as well as a hockey arena. The beautiful 640-acre campus has numerous outdoor playing fields, a designated wetland nature preserve, and miles of woodland trails for hiking, biking, or cross-country skiing.

Student Government comprises the Clarkson University Student Association (CUSA) Senate, Interfraternity Council, and Panhellenic Council. The Student Senate is responsible for funding extracurricular activities and student clubs. The Clarkson Union Board is a student-run group that organizes cultural and social events on campus. The Interfraternity and Panhellenic Councils set standards and rules for the ten fraternities and two sororities on campus. Through these student government organizations, students work closely with faculty.

ACADEMICS

Clarkson encourages students to explore their individual interests and goals. Many students have multiple academic interests and pursue specializations, double majors, minors, and concentrations. Students also gain hands-on career experience through co-ops and internships. Across the curriculum, Clarkson emphasizes a team project-based approach to learning, with an emphasis on solving real-word, open-ended problems. Clarkson pioneered interdisciplinary learning. Its innovative engineering and management curriculum, established in 1954, integrates technology with business leadership. Today the University's interdisciplinary programs also include bio-molecular science, environmental science and policy, industrial hygiene-environmental toxicology (environmental and occupational health), Project Arete (a double major in business and liberal arts), and software engineering. Clarkson classes are designed to foster critical thinking and problem-solving abilities across disciplines.

Every year, almost 400 Clarkson undergraduates participate in faculty-mentored research or intercollegiate multidisciplinary team competitions. Such teams are made up of students from different fields who combine their skills and perspectives. There are 15 different teams at Clarkson, organized through the Student Projects for Engineering Experience and Design (SPEED). The University won the 2001 Boeing Outstanding Educator Award as a result of SPEED's incredible effectiveness and ability to develop skills in collaboration, communication, leadership and problem solving. All Clarkson business majors participate in real-world entrepreneurial projects during their first year. In 2002 the effectiveness of Clarkson's entrepreneurial programs led to the University being named first runner-up for the National Undergraduate Entrepreneurship Education Award. The school's hands-on approach to learning also brought first-place honors in the IBM Linux Scholar Challenge, an international programming competition, when Clarkson students took home three of six prizes awarded in all of North America.

Clarkson offers undergraduate degree programs in the following subject areas: aeronautical engineering, applied mathematics and statistics, biology, bio-molecular science, business and technology management, chemical engineering, chemistry, civil engineering, computer engineering, computer science, e-business, electrical engineering, engineering and management, environmental science and policy, financial information and analysis, history, humanities, industrial hygiene-environmental toxicology (environmental and occupational health), information systems and business processes, mathematics, mechanical engineering, physics, political science, Project Arete (liberal arts/business), psychology, social sciences, software engineering, and technical communications. Incoming students who have not chosen a major may begin in a general program in business studies, engineering studies, science studies, or university studies.

Clarkson offers an honors program, a three-year bachelor's degree option, a five-year BS/MS in chemistry/biochemistry, a five-year BS/MBA, and pre-professional pre-law, pre-medicine, pre-dental, pre-veterinary, and pre-physical therapy (in preparation for a master's degree in physical therapy).

Clarkson's 168 full-time faculty members teach undergraduate and graduate classes, with graduate students assisting only in undergraduate lab sciences. With an excellent student/faculty ratio of 16:1, undergraduates benefit from regular interaction with the school's faculty. The University attracts teacher/scholars who enjoy mentoring students and who are accessible. And 94 percent of Clarkson faculty members hold a doctorate or other highest degree in their field.

Box 5605
Potsdam, NY 13699
Phone: 315-268-6479
Fax: 315-268-7647
Website: www.clarkson.edu

ADMISSIONS

Clarkson recommends that prospective students follow a challenging secondary school curriculum, which includes mathematics, science, and English. Candidates for the School of Engineering or the School of Science must successfully complete high school physics and chemistry as well. Previous academic achievement is the most important component of any application. Prospective students must submit SAT I or ACT scores. SAT II achievement tests are optional. International students who are not native English speakers must submit a TOEFL score of at least 550 for the paper-based test or 213 for the computer-based test. Students may receive course credit for a score of 4 or better on the College Board's Advanced Placement examinations. Students can receive advanced placement and course credit in any subject area; however, advanced standing is usually granted in English, mathematics, and science.

Clarkson offers an Early Decision admission program for students who have identified Clarkson as their first-choice. Students may submit applications to other schools when they submit an Early Decision application to Clarkson; however, they must withdraw other applications if they are accepted by Clarkson. Another special option is The Clarkson School. This is a unique program for talented high school students who have completed eleventh grade or are otherwise accelerated and ready to begin college studies. Clarkson School students enroll as fully matriculated University undergraduates and earn approximately 30 college credit hours during one academic year. Subsequently they may continue as sophomores at Clarkson University or enroll at another institution.

Though not required, it is highly recommended that students schedule a personal interview with the Admission Office. Interviews are especially encouraged for Early Decision candidates. Students who complete an interview also receive a waiver of their $30 application fee. Prospective students may schedule interviews by contacting the Admission Office. Hours are Monday through Friday from 9 A.M. to 4 P.M. The office is also open by appointment on Saturdays. The University welcomes visitors and can make arrangements for prospective students and their families to tour campus or to meet with specific academic departments. In addition, admission staff members also schedule appointments with prospective students off campus in major cities throughout the Northeast. For more information about interviewing, please contact the Admission Office.

For more information, contact:

Office of Undergraduate Admission
Clarkson University
PO Box 5605
Potsdam, NY 13699-5605
Telephone: 315-268-6479 or 315-268-6480 or 800-527-6577 (toll free)
Fax: 315-268-7647
E-mail: admission@clarkson.edu
World Wide Web: www.clarkson.edu

CAMPUS LIFE

Clarkson University is located in Potsdam, New York, a small town of 9,500, nestled in the foothills of the Adirondack Mountains. The community is situated in the beautiful northeast corner of New York State, home to Adirondack Park, and bordered by the St. Lawrence River and Thousand Islands region. Surrounded by natural beauty, Clarkson students can enjoy outdoor activities and sports throughout the year. Within two hours of campus are Lake Placid, two-time host of the Winter Olympics, and the cosmopolitan Canadian cities of Montreal and Ottawa. This scenic area is also home to the State University of New York (SUNY) at Potsdam. The village of Potsdam has a distinct collegiate feel and Clarkson hosts numerous social and cultural events in conjunction with its nearest collegiate neighbor. SUNY College of Technology at Canton and St. Lawrence University are just 10 miles away, providing even more opportunities for social and cultural interaction. Clarkson students enjoy easy access to library and other facilities on all four campuses, and can cross register in up to two courses per year at the other schools without paying extra tuition.

Students are encouraged to pursue off-campus opportunities such as include study abroad at international universities and internship and co-op experiences. Students may participate in formalized exchange programs with universities in Australia, Austria, England, France, Germany, Italy, New Zealand, and Sweden, or they may pursue customized individual plans to study in other countries. Clarkson's Career Center helps students benefit from valuable on-the-job real-world experiences through co-ops and internship work, while they are still in college. The University has established numerous professional connections in business and industry, making it easy for students to locate career and internship positions.

COST AND AID

Tuition is $23,100 for the 2003–2004 school year. For a double room in campus housing, students pay an additional $4,550 annually and a board bill of $4,176, for 19 meals a week. Student fees total $400. In addition, students usually spend about $2,000 annually on books and supplies, and travel and personal expenses.

COLBY-SAWYER COLLEGE

GENERAL INFORMATION

Founded in 1837, Colby-Sawyer College grew from the tradition of the New England academy, and today is a coeducational, residential, undergraduate college. Colby-Sawyer's commitment to higher education began in 1928, and its curriculum integrates liberal arts and sciences with professional preparation. All of Colby-Sawyer's programs promote students' intellectual and personal growth, no matter what their backgrounds or abilities. The College hopes they obtain a better understanding of not only themselves and others but also the varied elements that influence and shape the world around them. Over the past several years, Colby-Sawyer has gradually increased and enhanced the College. There are currently around 940 students at the College, and these students come not only from all over the United States, but also from five other countries, and 69 percent of the students come from places outside of New Hampshire. The steadily growing student population has prompted Colby-Sawyer to build apartment-style and two suite-style residence halls over the recent years. We have also added more faculty, two academic programs, a new Liberal Education model, a varsity sport, a fully renovated Exercise and Sport Science facility, and will begin construction on a new Science Center. With these enhancements, Colby-Sawyer can offer more to its students while still providing an attentive, enriching, and personally challenging education.

STUDENT BODY

Students make things happen at Colby-Sawyer College by participating in and collaborating with faculty, staff, and other students in the development of a wide variety of campus activities. Students are encouraged to become involved through existing student organizations and clubs, athletic and recreational activities, departmental organizations, and through programs such as Mountain Day, Family Weekend, Spring Weekend, and volunteer opportunities. Students may be come active in such student and developmental organizations as the *Courier* student newspaper, Dance Club, CSC Players, Student Government Association, WSCS Radio Station, and Key Association. Student athletic involvement occurs at the varsity, club, intramural, and recreational levels.

There are 10 varsity sports for women (NCAA Division III basketball, diving, lacrosse, soccer, swimming, tennis, track and field, and volleyball; ECSC Alpine ski racing; and IHSA riding) and 9 for men (NCAA Division III baseball, basketball, diving, soccer, swimming, tennis, and track and field; ECSC Alpine ski racing; and IHSA riding). Athletic successes include a nationally ranked men's basketball team that competed in the NCAA tournament in 2001, 2002, and 2003; a track and field team that sent individual qualifiers to the NCAA Championships in 2000, 2001, and 2002; and conference championships for men's baseball in 1998 and 1999, men's basketball in 2001, 2002, and 2003, women's volleyball in 1999, and women's basketball in 1997, 1998, and 1999. The women's basketball team has also competed in the 2001, 2002, and 2003 ECAC tournament as well as the NCAA tournament in 1997, 1998, 1999. The women's volleyball also made an appearance in the NCAA tournament in 1999. Colby-Sawyer's equestrian team was the reserve national champion in 1998 and has sent riders to the IHSA National Team every year since 1987. The Alpine ski racing team has competed in the USCSA National Championships the past six seasons, sent one individual on to NCAA Division I Championships in 1998, and produced All-Americans in 2001, 2002, and 2003. The Colby-Sawyer Chargers compete as a member of the Commonwealth Coast Conference.

Opportunities for athletic participation also exist at the club, intramural, and recreational level. Club sports offer intercollegiate competition against other regional colleges. Some our club sports include men's and women's rugby, men's lacrosse, softball, and hockey. Some of our intramural sports include soccer, water polo, floor hockey, flag football, and wiffleball. Our location also provides excellent opportunity for such recreational activities as hiking, Alpine and Nordic skiing, kayaking, and biking.

ACADEMICS

All students begin their liberal education at Colby-Sawyer by selecting a Pathway Seminar. Students choose a topic they are interested in learning more about, pose questions that are personally relevant, and search for answers through experiences in several liberal arts areas. They return to these themes in a seminar in their sophomore year, applying all they have learned to answer their own questions and share insights with classmates on such topics as "Money and the Meaning of Life," "Photography and Reality," and "Animals in Culture and Nature." Colby-Sawyer's Honors Program offers an environment conducive to intellectual exploration and creativity beyond that available in the general curriculum. This program is carefully designed to advance and polish critical skills of each participating student. Students in Honors courses experience an environment of lively discussion and guided independent research. The Honors Program also includes enrichment events outside of class such as "Pizza and Politics" and Restless Minds road-trips. Study abroad programs are available at Colby-Sawyer, and students are urged to take advantage of them for a semester or even a year. There is a study abroad advisor who helps students choose an experience and a school that fits their needs and interests. Students have journeyed to England, Australia, Spain, France, Italy, Ireland, Scotland, and Switzerland.

Colby-Sawyer is part of the 12-college New Hampshire College and University Council (NHCUC), which gives students the ability to enroll in other NHCUC institutions for either a course or an entire semester. The New England Association of Schools and Colleges accredits the College, and professional programs have earned the appropriate accreditations as well. Colby-Sawyer College is proud to have been consistently ranked as one of the top colleges in its category.

Bachelor of Arts Degrees

Biology

Communication studies

English

History, society & culture

Psychology

Studio art

Bachelor of Fine Arts Degrees

Graphic design

Studio art

Bachelor of Science Degrees

Business administration

Child development

Community & environmental studies

Nursing

Exercise and sport sciences (with specialization offered in athletic training, exercise science, or sport management)

Teacher Certification

Art education (K–12)

Early childhood education (K–3)

English education (5–12)

Social studies education (5–12)

Student-designed and double majors are also available, as well as 16 minors.

100 Main Street
New London, NH 03257
Phone: 603-526-3700
Fax: 603-526-3452
Website: www.colby-sawyer.edu

Colby-Sawyer's faculty and staff are committed to teaching undergraduates. Students can be certain of individual attention, as the student/faculty ratio is 12:1 and class sizes average 18 students. Furthermore, senior faculty members teach not only upperclassmen but also first-year students.

There are 55 full-time and 113 total faculty members. Seventy-nine percent of classes are taught by full-time faculty and staff.

ADMISSIONS

A minimum of 15 units of college-preparatory work is required of prospective students. Typically, this includes 4 years of college prep English, 3 years of mathematics, 2 or more years of social studies, 2 years of the same foreign language, and 2 or more years in a laboratory science. Interested students are urged to schedule a visit to the College for a tour and interview. Interviews are not required, but they often make a difference in the final admissions decision and are strongly encouraged. Students are welcome to submit applications throughout the year. Starting in December, the College reviews completed applications on a rolling basis and applicants are notified as soon as a decision is reached by the admissions office. The required components of an application are: a transcript of the candidate's high school work (including first-quarter grades of the senior year), SAT I or ACT scores, two letters of recommendation (ideally one from a teacher and one from a guidance professional), a personal essay, and a $40 nonrefundable application fee. Application forms and additional information may be obtained by contacting:

Office of Admissions
Colby-Sawyer College
541 Main Street
New London, NH 03257
Telephone: 603-526-3700 or 800-272-1015 (toll free)
Fax: 603-526-3452
E-mail: csadmiss@colby-sawyer.edu
World Wide Web: www.colby-sawyer.edu

CAMPUS LIFE

New London, New Hampshire is home to Colby-Sawyer's picturesque 200-acre campus. Situated on the top of a hill, the carefully cared for campus combines spectacular, panoramic views with classic Georgian architecture. The campus environment is welcoming and active, making it easy for students to open their minds to learning and exploration. Colby-Sawyer is in the middle of the Dartmouth-Lake Sunapee region, which offers recreational and cultural activities year-round and is known for its beautiful lakes and mountains. The College is only an hour and a half north of Boston, two hours south of Burlington, and three and a half hours south of Montreal. The College's van or the public bus provides easy access to these and other major cities. The nearby seacoast and the surrounding lakes, mountains, and state parks give students the opportunity to bike, camp, canoe, golf, hike, ice skate, Nordic and Alpine ski, swim, and play tennis. Art and culture abound: New London, nearby Concord, the state capital, and Hanover, the home of Dartmouth College, all offer plenty of cultural resources.

COST AND AID

The fees for 2003–2004 are as follows:

Tuition: $22,200

Board: $4,740

Room: $3,780

Total: $30,720

COLGATE UNIVERSITY

GENERAL INFORMATION

Colgate is a small liberal arts college that "thinks big" and succeeds on the highest level. Whether in fields of academic distinction, international programs, student research, the scope of our student activities program, or the success of our Division I varsity athletics, Colgate tradition defies the odds. Visitors quickly sense the energy, enthusiasm, and talent that abounds in this community of just 2,700 students. In this highly personalized setting, individual contribution is essential and rewarded.

Colgate's undergraduate students come from 47 states, the District of Columbia, Puerto Rico, and 31 foreign countries. They have excelled in classroom and extracurricular involvement throughout high school. Almost all graduated in the top 20 percent of their high school class-most in the top 10 percent-and were leaders in many activities outside the classroom. New students to Colgate quickly learn they have joined a talented group of students from many diverse backgrounds. These differences let them learn from each other as well as from their close interactions with the faculty.

STUDENT BODY

Time and again, students and faculty refer to the "participatory nature" of Colgate students. Most of the 100-plus campus organizations were started by students and remain active each year. They include departmental clubs, music and drama groups, religious organizations, service clubs, and various student run publications. Though most students find plenty of options within the existing clubs, it is also easy to start your own. A few are added every year, reflecting Colgate's "entrepreneurial" character.

ACADEMICS

All undergraduates complete the Liberal Arts Core Program, four interdisciplinary courses pursued in the first two years, plus a First-Year Seminar. The Core covers issues and ideas in western culture, cultural studies, and scientific perspectives on contemporary concerns. Core seminars and "distinction" or honors-level work is an option. Elective courses, as well as the Core, help students shape their choice of academic major or concentration. Students declare their field of concentration at the end of sophomore year.

The academic interests of Colgate students span the full range of 50 concentration programs. On average, 42 percent major in the social sciences, 27 percent in the humanities, 26 percent in the natural sciences, and 5 percent in interdisciplinary programs. Seventeen percent will complete a double major, and 26 percent a minor program. Many students add a second concentration, or work toward a minor to complement their primary field of study. Colgate offers honors or high honors distinctions in all concentrations. Students may also design their own concentration.

Some of the most popular majors are English, economics, psychology, biology, political science, and history. Many students, however, say they chose to attend Colgate for the variety of academic programs that reach beyond these traditional liberal arts subjects. Options include astrogeophysics, neuroscience, four different areas of environmental studies, nine different languages, Native American studies, and many more. Most students pursue some interdisciplinary electives.

Learning is not restricted to the classroom. Undergraduate research opportunities are available each semester and throughout the summer, allowing students to work closely with professors on hundreds of different projects. Colgate students enjoy a flexibility in the curriculum and opportunities normally reserved for students at much larger universities.

Colgate offers the Bachelors of Arts degree in 50 different academic concentrations (majors) within the arts and sciences. Colgate also awards the Masters in Teaching (MAT) in the fields of English, mathematics, social studies, and natural science.

All Colgate classes are taught by faculty; there are no teaching assistants. Senior faculty often teach first-year and core classes, and students have many opportunities to collaborate with faculty on research. Nearly all of the 279 members of the faculty have received the highest degree expected in their fields. While teaching is their primary responsibility, they are also active researchers, authors, artists, performers, and contributors to their professional disciplines. At Colgate, research brings faculty and students together. The average class size at Colgate is 19 students and the student/faculty ratio is 11:1. Class size varies according to the level and type of course, but there are more than three times as many courses with 20 or fewer students as there are with 30 or more.

13 Oak Drive
Hamilton, NY 13346
Phone: 315-228-7401
Fax: 315-228-7544
Website: www.colgate.edu

ADMISSIONS

All students applying in the fall of 2001 will use the Common Application form and a short supplement specific to Colgate. Students can find the Common Application and Colgate Supplement on the Colgate Office of Admission website at: http://offices.colgate.edu/admission/, by linking to www.commonapp.org, or inside the Colgate Application packet mailed to prospective students. The application deadline for all students is January 15. Colgate also offers two early decision plans. The deadline for Early Decision Option I is November 15, with decisions mailed to students one month later. Students who apply by January 15 may declare themselves Early Decision Option II candidates until March 1 and receive a decision within three to four weeks. Both early decision plans are binding agreements, in that students agree to withdraw all applications to other colleges upon receiving a letter of acceptance from Colgate.

Colgate does not use a preset formula in determining which applicants will gain admission. Accepted students have a powerful combination of academic achievement, extracurricular involvement and strength of character that sets them apart. Our review of candidates reflects the priorities and values of Colgate, focusing on academic excellence and a willingness to contribute in academics and in the community.

We welcome you to contact the Office of Admission by phone or e-mail to be added to our mailing list, or to learn more about our options and procedures.

CAMPUS LIFE

Colgate is located in Hamilton, New York in upstate New York, about one hour southeast of Syracuse. Set on a hillside overlooking a small lake, Colgate's campus is spectacular. The setting and surroundings attract students who love the outdoors and love contributing to an active campus-based community. As a residential college in a small town, Colgate generates much of its own activity. The people of the village take part in many of the on-campus activities and the students benefit from the close community. Since most of the faculty, staff and university employees live in Hamilton, there is a strong connection that lets students feel at home almost immediately on campus and in the village.

Colgate provides students with 22 semester-long off-campus study programs, with nearly 60 percent of the students choosing to participate. Most of the Colgate programs are one semester and are completed during a student's junior year. Three are based in the United States, while the others take students to every corner of the globe. The programs are led by Colgate faculty who accompany the students for the semester, teach some of the courses, and serve as a liaison during the time spent away from campus. The faculty-designed programs reflect the international expertise and professional connections of Colgate faculty. Colgate students are also allowed to attend approved study abroad programs offered through other schools.

COST AND AID

The cost of attending for the 2001–2002 school year will be:

Tuition: $26,845

Room and board: $6,455

Fees : $180

Total cost: $33,480

COLLEGE OF CHARLESTON

GENERAL INFORMATION

The College of Charleston is a highly respected student-centered public liberal arts and sciences university located in historic Charleston, South Carolina. Founded in 1770, the College offers its approximately 10,000 undergraduate students an exceptional educational experience—one that emphasizes intellectual growth through research opportunities, co-curricular activities, and study abroad. For over two centuries, the College of Charleston has adhered to its commitment to the liberal arts as the strongest foundation for life and career. Graduates of the College receive valuable preparation for further academic study or entry into the professional world through a combination of a comprehensive general education program, intensive study within a major field, faculty/student collaboration in research, and internships. First and foremost a teaching institution, the College provides its students the opportunity to work closely with nationally recognized faculty—an experience usually associated with a small liberal arts college—and at a public school price. Students are treated as valued participants of the College's close-knit community of scholars. The College is divided into five schools: School of the Arts, School of Business and Economics, School of Education, School of Humanities and Social Sciences, and School of Sciences and Mathematics. Students select from 41 majors and also have the opportunity to enhance their academic record and broaden their knowledge by choosing from 80 minors and 36 concentrations within a variety of majors. Students, faculty, and alumni agree that the College furnishes a learning experience without equal—a creative and intellectually stimulating environment led by a committed and caring faculty within a superb setting and at an incredible value.

STUDENT BODY

The College of Charleston is a state-supported liberal arts and sciences university located in Charleston, South Carolina. Although home to approximately 10,000 undergraduate students, the College of Charleston retains an intimate feel usually associated with a small, private liberal arts college. Classes are kept small, so students enjoy close relationships and one-on-one interaction with their professors. Students, when not occupied with their studies, participate in a wide range of activities, from running a television show to jumping out of an airplane. Because the campus population is diverse, students have the chance to meet new people, explore new ideas, and pursue new interests. The College encourages all of its students to be involved in its many clubs, organizations, and co-curricular programs, whether for recreation, fellowship, or scholastic enrichment. Students also benefit from the many choices—social outlets, jobs, and internships—that the city of Charleston and surrounding areas offer. Situated in historic downtown, the College is only a few steps away from numerous historic sites, streets lined with shops and art galleries, and a vibrant nightlife. Or, if a student is interested in a less cosmopolitan setting, there are world-class beaches, a national forest, and the pristine landscape along the Lowcountry's marshes and rivers just a few minutes away. For the College of Charleston student, each day is the beginning of a new adventure.

ACADEMICS

The College of Charleston offers a first-rate student-centered experience, at the heart of which is an individualized liberal arts and sciences education. Recognizing that learning is not confined to the classroom, the College encourages intellectual growth through research opportunities, experiential learning, co-curricular activities, and study abroad.

Education at its best is an exciting collaboration between teacher and student. The College's excellent faculty have chosen to teach in order to share the adventure of learning, discovery, and achievement with the leaders of tomorrow. "For those students who prefer smaller, more intimate classes where there can be a lot of discussion, group activities, and a better professor/student relationship, then this is the school for them" is one student's advertisement for the College's unique private college atmosphere.

Every academic program at the College that has been reviewed by the South Carolina Commission on Higher Education has received a Commendation for Excellence, which cites the program's overall quality, quality of instruction, student-faculty research activities, number of graduates, success in job placement of graduates, facilities and equipment, and uniqueness. The College of Charleston has received more Commendations for Excellence for its academic offerings than any other institution of higher learning in the state.

To earn a College of Charleston Bachelor of Arts or Bachelor of Science degree, students are required to successfully complete a core curriculum of 14 to 18 courses designed to introduce the students to the principal areas of intellectual inquiry, and to teach him or her basic intellectual skills. These courses are designed to provide students with a solid foundation for further study and are an essential part of their undergraduate education. Narrowing the focus of their academic interests, students choose from 41 majors and also have the opportunity to complement their major course of study by selecting from 80 minors and 36 concentrations within a variety of majors. The College is proud to foster a close student-teacher community that is dedicated to engaging in original inquiry and creative expression in an atmosphere of intellectual freedom. Whether students choose to attend graduate school or embark on a career following graduation, their undergraduate experience at the College of Charleston places them at a distinct advantage.

66 George Street
Charleston, SC 29424
Phone: 843-953-5670
Fax: 843-953-6322
Website: www.cofc.edu

The College of Charleston offers the following areas of study in the five undergraduate schools. The School of the Arts offers art history, arts management, dance, historic preservation & community planning, music, studio arts, and theatre. The School of Business offers marketing and management, economics, finance, hospitality and tourism management, and global logistics and transportation. The School of Education offers health, secondary education, and secondary education certification in biology, chemistry, Classics/Latin, English, French, German, history, mathematics, physical education, physics, political science (social studies), sociology (social studies), and Spanish. The School of Humanities and Social Sciences offers Ancient Greek, anthropology, Classics, communication studies, creative writing , criminal justice, English, French, German, Hispanic studies, history, Italian, Latin, media studies, philosophy, political science, psychology, religious studies, sociology, and Spanish. The School of Sciences and Mathematics offers astronomy, biology, chemistry, computer science, geology, information systems, mathematics, physics, engineering physics, and meteorology. The College of Charleston also offers a wide variety of interdisciplinary minors: African American studies, pre-actuarial studies, African studies, arts management, American studies, Asian studies, British studies, criminal justice, environmental studies, European studies, film studies, French studies, German studies, international studies, Italian studies, Japanese studies, Jewish studies, languages and international business, Latin American and Caribbean studies, linguistics, Russian studies, and women's studies.

ADMISSIONS

Application fee: $35 electronic, $45 paper

Priority application: November 15

Early Action closing date: November 15

Early Action notification date: February 1

Regular application deadline: April 1

Regular application notification date: Rolling

Admissions for nonfall terms: Yes (spring)

Separate application (deadline of January 15) is required for the Honors Program. No application fee required. Essay required for Honors Program application may also be used for the Admissions Office. Early planning and visit to campus is strongly encouraged.

For more information, please contact:

College of Charleston
Office of Admissions
66 George Street
Charleston, SC 29424
Phone: 843-953-5670
Fax: 843-953-6322
Website: www.cofc.edu/admissions

THE COLLEGE OF NEW JERSEY

GENERAL INFORMATION

At the College of New Jersey (TCNJ), undergraduates study in a personal, supportive environment. In the first two years, almost every class has a size limit of 28; on average, classes have 23 students. This reflects the College's commitment to facilitating interaction between professors and students. Many students extend their classroom work by participating in research with faculty members. Often, professors and students co-author papers published in academic journals. The mentor relationship helps students discuss career options and land pertinent fellowships, internships, and summer research positions. TCNJ admits a class each year full of ambitious students, eager to build on their earlier education and plunge into new topics. The most successful students are prepared to steer their own academic pursuits towards post-graduation goals of graduate school, professional training, or satisfying careers. Prestigious graduate schools, including the University of Pennsylvania, Georgetown Law School, Maxwell School at Syracuse University, NYU Law School, and Harvard, Yale, and Northwestern Universities, routinely welcome TCNJ alumni into their ranks. Eighty-five percent of TCNJ students who apply to medical school are accepted. Many top corporations recruit TCNJ graduates, providing avenues into rewarding jobs directly after graduation. Other barometers of student success include the 95 percent passing rate of education majors taking the state teacher preparation test and the 95 percent passing rate for nursing students applying for a license. The variety of learning opportunities at the College prepare students to prosper in any arena after leaving the campus.

STUDENT BODY

Classroom learning at TCNJ is complemented by an extensive and acclaimed Leadership Development Program. Student can participate in any of the more than 150 TCNJ clubs, catering to interests as diverse as the theater, professional training, honors courses, journalism, fraternities and sororities, and athletics. TCNJ teams play in the NCAA Division III, open to non-scholarship student athletes. The men field teams in 11 sports, while women compete in 10. The College holds the record for championship and runner-up titles since Division III was started in 1979. For those looking for something a little less competitive, intramural sports, including flag football, volleyball, softball, floor hockey, and basketball have thriving coed leagues of their own. Intramural teams play in state, regional, and national tournaments. The College was proud to send its top-ten flag football team to the recent championship in New Orleans. TCNJ students administer both the Student Finance Board and College Union Board. They organize popular student events, bringing to the campus such people as Tonic, Jim Breuer, and Sugar Ray.

ACADEMICS

All students at TCNJ acquire a solid background in the liberal arts through the courses in the core curriculum. The small classes facilitate dialogue between students, and every class at TCNJ is taught by a full professor, not a graduate student. The goal is to challenge students to open their minds and retain what they learn. By the time students complete their four years at TCNJ, they will have honed the following skills: the ability to read and listen critically; the ability to write and speak clearly and effectively; the ability to collect, analyze, and interpret information and communicate the results to others; critical reasoning skills and the use of analogy, deduction, and induction; the ability to solve widely varied problems; and the ability to make informed judgments concerning ethical values. The College also incorporates a program called the First-Year Experience into the core curriculum. First-year students partake in service projects and residence-based courses to solidify the concepts from their other classes. One of TCNJ's guiding tenets is to value of both in-class and out-of-class learning. Top students may enroll in TCNJ's honor program, designed to provide a core curriculum with additional challenges and opportunities for individualized work. Most honors classes take an interdisciplinary approach to the history of civilization, its accomplishments, and its problems. Independent study arrangements fall easily within the parameters of the honors program.

The College of New Jersey hosts seven schools: Art, Media, and Music; Business; Culture and Society; Education; Engineering; Nursing; and Science. The College offers programs leading to the Bachelor of Arts, Bachelor of Fine Arts, Bachelor of Music, Bachelor of Science, and Bachelor of Science in Nursing. TCNJ grants degrees in the following majors (° denotes programs in which students may prepare for teacher certification): accountancy, art°, fine arts, graphic design, biology°, business administration (specializations in finance, general business, information systems management, international business, management, and marketing), chemistry°, communication studies, computer science, economics, early childhood education°, education of the deaf and hard of hearing°, elementary education°, health and physical education°, special education for the developmentally handicapped°, engineering (computer engineering, electrical engineering, mechanical engineering, and engineering science), English° (options in liberal arts, journalism, and professional writing), history°, international studies, law and justice, mathematics° (option in statistics), music°, nursing, philosophy, physics° (options in scientific computer programming and earth science), political science, psychology, sociology (option in pre-social work), Spanish°, technology education°, and women's and gender studies. Students may also choose to complete a minor, in any of the major fields or another subject area, such as African American studies, classical studies, comparative literature, religion, public administration, French, and Italian.

PO Box 7718
Ewing, NJ 08628-0718
Phone: 609-771-2131
Fax: 609-637-5174
Website: www.tcnj.edu

Joint degrees are also available at TCNJ. In conjunction with the University of Medicine and Dentisty of New Jersey, students can pursue a seven-year combined BS/MD degree. A seven-year combined BS/OD degree program is also available through the State University of New York College of Optometry. There is also a four-year combined BS/MA degree in law and justice with Rutgers University. Students can study for five years to receive their dual certification in the education of the deaf and hard of hearing and elementary education/Master of Arts in teaching.

The College's 322 full-time faculty members are both dedicated teachers and active participants in their professional and academic fields. When they are not focused on their students, faculty members are working as researchers, authors, artists, and performers, among many other things. Many of the College's professors have been responsible for writing textbooks and serving as leaders in their respective fields on the regional and national level. Faculty members prove their prestige by winning grants and fellowships including the Bancroft Prize in history, the Sloan Fellowship, Fulbright Fellowships, and grants from the National Science Foundation, the National Institute for Advanced Study, the Guggenheim Foundation, the Templeton Foundation, and the National Endowment for the Humanities. Some top-notch part-time instructors add their expertise to the College's classes, often teaching at the school for many consecutive years.

ADMISSIONS

The admissions committee at TCNJ accepts a class of motivated, ambitious, and talented students. Most successful applicants have taken 16 college-preparatory units in high school. They also show impressive class ranks and SAT I scores. The committee also considers extracurricular involvement, individual pursuits, and community participation. Students applying to the art, music, and health and exercise science departments are evaluated on additional criteria specific to their intended course of study. Those applying for September admission must submit their applications by February 15. TCNJ offers an early decision program to those who know the College is their first choice; applications received by November 15 will receive a response by December 30. A small number of students begin classes in January, and they must apply by November 1. For further information, please contact:

Office of Admissions
The College of New Jersey
PO Box 7718
Ewing, NJ 08628-0718
Telephone: 800-624-0967
E-mail: admiss@vm.tcnj.edu

CAMPUS LIFE

Students at TCNJ enjoy a campus with 289 acres of trees, lakes, and open spaces within the suburban setting of Ewing Township, New Jersey. Two out of three undergraduate students live in campus residence halls. The dormitories vary in configuration from the freshman towers to suites and townhouse arrangements for older students. The College ensures that on-campus housing is available to all students in their first two years. More that 150 student organizations flourish at the College. Students can easily find an intramural sports team, Greek organization, cultural club, or academic group to suit their interests. Many students make friends and enjoy their leisure time participating in one of these groups. In addition, the College Union Board organizes events, including concerts, performances, and comedy nights. Nearby cities, such as Trenton, Philadelphia, and New York, allow for abundant entertainment, employment, and social options. Many courses incorporate field trips to New York City or Washington DC.

TCNJ administers an extensive international study program, featuring exchange programs in locations as diverse as London and Santiago, Chile. Some students choose to attend one of the 131 available institutions in the U.S., while others venture to one of the 33 countries offering full-year or semester-long programs. Some of the most important off-campus opportunities are the internships, fellowships, and research opportunities open to students. Many students partake in these activities during the school year, and others arrange to work over breaks. Faculty members lend their advice and help students to locate and obtain appropriate opportunities. Students may also utilize resources at the Office of Career Services to find positions in New York, Philadelphia, or any of the corporations, government agencies, or research organizations closer to campus.

COST AND AID

Because TCNJ is a public institution, costs are lower than some equivalent private institutions. The tuition and fees for undergraduates in the 2001–2002 academic year are as follows: in-state tuition and fees, $6,661; out-of-state tuition and fees, $10,409; room and board (all students), $6,764.

THE COLLEGE OF NEW ROCHELLE

GENERAL INFORMATION

Founded in 1904 as the first Catholic college for women in New York State, The College of New Rochelle has grown to a Student Body of 7,000 in four schools: the all-female School of Arts & Sciences, the coeducational School of Nursing, the School of New Resources (offering an adult degree program at seven campus locations), and the Graduate School. The College of New Rochelle (CNR) offers undergraduate and graduate programs in the liberal arts and several professionally oriented fields, an internationally recognized faculty, an environment where students receive individual attention. The College has a large variety of extracurricular activities to choose from, including student government, publications, and intercollegiate sports. Our 35,000 graduates who have made their mark in virtually every field of endeavor attest to our success in educating women for nearly a century. We count among our alumnae company presidents, judges, lawyers, doctors, nurses, journalists, artists, teachers, scientists, and those who have devoted their lives to family, religious vocations, and public service. The information that follows applies to the College's School of Arts & Sciences and School of Nursing basic undergraduate programs.

STUDENT BODY

Participating in the wealth of campus activities available at CNR will help you sharpen vital leadership and communication skills while having fun in the process. Intramural and intercollegiate sports, the student theater group, student government, the yearbook, clubs, dances, and special events provide opportunities to interact with fellow students and socialize with male students from other institutions. In addition, many of our students perform volunteer service in a variety of local community organizations ranging from serving meals in the local soup kitchen to tutoring elementary school children in reading and math. The many clubs and organizations students can participate in include CNR clubs and organizations, Business Board, Madison Society, Psi-Chi, Nursing Students Taking Action for Tomorrow, Student National Education Association, Science and Math Society, Resident Council, Commuter Council, Activities Council, Student Government Association, International Students Club, Latin American Women's Society, Black Student Union, Caribbean Student Organization, Gaelic Society, Environmental Club, CLP LIFE, *Annales* (yearbook), *Phoenix* (literary magazine), *Tatler* (student newspaper), *Femmes d'Esprit* (honors program newsletter), Props and Paint (student theater group), Dance Ensemble, NP Film Productions, Karate Club, Ski Club, basketball team, swimming team, softball team, tennis team, volleyball team, cheerleading, and track.

ACADEMICS

At CNR, you will receive an excellent undergraduate education from an internationally recognized faculty. The small classes and student/faculty ratio of 10:1 will enable you to know your professors and vice versa. Your freshman year at CNR will be a coherent experience extending throughout the year: You will be oriented to life at CNR, prepared for a satisfying and successful experience at the College, and aided in effectively using your college experience to formulate your career goals. Whether you are already clear about your major or are still unsure, CNR provides a solid foundation on which to build. The Core Curriculum is designed to expose you to a broad spectrum of areas including art, music, science, literature, language, philosophy, and religion while enabling you to develop writing, mathematical, and reasoning skills. In addition, through our internship, study abroad, and honors programs, you will complement your work in and outside the classroom and be better prepared for the job market after graduation.

CNR offers over 20 undergraduate degree programs. Majors: art education, art history, art therapy, studio art, biological sciences, business, chemistry, classics, communication arts, economics, English, environmental studies, French, history, mathematics, modern foreign languages, nursing, philosophy, political science, psychology, religious studies, social work, sociology, and Spanish. Pre-professional programs: art therapy, health professions, law, medicine, and physical therapy. Special programs: community leadership program, co-op education, honors, internship, and study abroad. Interdisciplinary studies: American studies, comparative literature, international studies, and women's studies. Professional programs: community-school psychology (combined bachelor's and master's degrees in five years), elementary education, secondary education, and special education.

During your years at CNR, you will be guided by a caring and dynamic faculty who have chosen teaching as their vocation. With a student/faculty ratio of 10:1, classes are small—ranging from 16 to 20 students—so you and your professors are able to get to know each other both academically and professionally. In addition to challenging you to grow and excel academically, our faculty strive to promote critical thinking and to help you apply what you learn in the classroom to life in general.

29 Castle Place
New Rochelle, NY 10805-2339
Phone: 914-654-5452
Fax: 914-654-5464
Website: www.cnr.edu

ADMISSIONS

The admission process is a simple, straightforward one, designed to determine if you will be successful at CNR. A strong, well-balanced program in high school is the best preparation for success in college studies. A minimum of 16 academic units should be taken. Regular admission: High school seniors interested in applying to CNR must submit a CNR application for admission, an official copy of their transcript, SAT or ACT scores, and a recommendation. The College operates on a rolling admission system, which usually allows a decision to be reached within two weeks of the completion of an applicant's admission folder. Early decision admission: If CNR is your first choice, you may apply for an early decision on admission and financial aid. Applications must be received by November 1. Notification of acceptance will be sent no later than December 15. Early Admission: A decision will be reached as soon as your application is complete and you will be notified immediately. Generally, we require that students complete 16 units in the high school academic curriculum. Nursing students must have completed at least three years of mathematics including Algebra I, Algebra II, and Geometry, as well as three years of science, including laboratory science courses in chemistry and biology.

CAMPUS LIFE

Imagine a tree-lined suburban campus nestled in a residential neighborhood. Now imagine the United Nations, the Metropolitan Museum of Art, Broadway, and Wall Street, all just minutes from where you go to school. CNR offers all of these advantages. Located in southeastern Westchester County, CNR is situated on a 20-acre suburban campus nestled in a residential neighborhood just 16 miles north of midtown Manhattan and less than a mile from Long Island Sound.

CNR's location will allow you to benefit from the many professional internship opportunities at outstanding business, cultural, medical, and scientific institutions in Westchester County and New York City. Recent internship placements include IBM, the New York Stock Exchange, NBC, MTV, CBS, Rye Psychiatric Hospital, American Craft Museum, Gannett Suburban Newspapers, Merrill-Lynch, Buena Vista Pictures, Guardian Records, Lord & Taylor, the U.S. State Department, *Time* magazine, the Bank of New York, Hothouse Productions, Hebrew Home for the Aged, Memorial Sloan-Kettering Institute for Cancer Research, New Rochelle Office of Probation, and much more. As a nursing student you will gain excellent clinical experience in hospitals, clinics, and nursing agencies throughout the New York metropolitan area, including Our Lady of Mercy Medical Center, Visiting Nurse Association, United Hospital Home Health Agency, Kateri Residence, and Columbia Presbyterian Hospital. You may also take advantage of New York City's many attractions, including the Bronx Zoo, New York Botanical Garden, the Metropolitan Museum of Art, and Broadway, or just relax on one of the beaches of Long Island Sound, less than a mile from the College.

COST AND AID

For 2002–2003, tuition is $13,000, room and board is $6,850, and fees are $250.

COLLEGE OF NOTRE DAME OF MARYLAND

GENERAL INFORMATION

The College of Notre Dame of Maryland, a four-year liberal arts women's college, was established in 1873 by the School Sisters of Notre Dame, an international congregation of women religious. The College is renowned worldwide for its emphasis on values-based education, its contemporary outlook, and its rich and abiding traditions. In 1896, it became the first Catholic women's college in the United States to be chartered to award the baccalaureate degree.

STUDENT BODY

Notre Dame has more than 30 clubs and organizations that foster leadership and teamwork. The diversity of organizations reflects the diverse interests of students. Student organizations at the College include Art Society, Association of Women in Communications, Black Student Association, *Columns* (student newspaper), Community Service Organization, Hispanic Society, Honor Board, Student Environmental Organization, Student Senate, WCND Radio Station, and WCND-TV, among many others. Part of the NCAA Division III Atlantic Women's Colleges Conference, Notre Dame Athletic teams compete in basketball, field hockey, lacrosse, soccer, swimming, tennis, and volleyball. In addition, intramural sports programs are established each semester in response to student interest.

ACADEMICS

The College of Notre Dame of Maryland's values-centered education emphasizes the student's total development: intellectual, social, moral, spiritual and physical. As a liberal arts college, the Notre Dame curriculum is designed to acquaint students with the key areas of learning, to provide in-depth study in their chosen fields, and, through the wide choice of electives, to provide opportunities to explore an array of interests. The College of Notre Dame offers 27 majors, with great opportunities for minors or concentrations within certain majors that help students build the perfect academic background to reach their personal and professional goals. The following majors and concentrations are offered: art (art history, photography/graphic design, pre-museum studies, studio art); biology (cell and molecular, ecology, pre-professional); biology/psychology; business (accounting, computer information systems, finance, human resource management, management, marketing); chemistry (pre-professional); classical studies; communication arts (advertising and public relations, film and video, human communication, journalism); computer information systems (internet systems); computer science (internet systems); criminology/social deviance (forensic psychology, women and social deviance); economics (environmental, financial, international); education (early childhood, elementary, secondary, special education); engineering (five-year dual degree program); English (drama); history (pre-museum studies); human services (administrative, direct service); international studies (international business , international relations); liberal arts; mathematics; modern foreign languages (French, Spanish); music (education, music history, performance, theory/composition); nonprofit management; nursing (dual degree program); philosophy; physics; political science (pre-law, public service); psychology; radiological sciences (business, clinical, computer systems management, organizational management); religious studies; and pre-professional programs (four-year programs in dentistry, law, medicine, and veterinary medicine).

The College has 83 full-time faculty and 146 part-time faculty. The undergraduate student/faculty ratio is 13:1.

ADMISSIONS

The Admissions Office at Notre Dame considers each student individually, assessing her unique abilities, experiences, and personal qualities. The Admissions Office considers a variety of factors to ascertain the intellectual promise and the potential maturity and responsibility of each woman who applies. Academic record, quality of high school curriculum, and standardized test scores are all considered; however, the College's review ranges well beyond a simple computation of averages and scores. The College gives careful consideration to such personal qualities as compassion, creativity, and leadership. It also looks at goals, special interests, and talents. The student's application essay, letters of recommendation, and personal interview all contribute to the assessment of her potential.

The application priority deadline for the fall semester is February 15 and the priority deadline for the spring semester is December 15. Students interested in applying for academic and achievement scholarships should attempt to file completed applications by these dates for scholarship consideration. Late applications are assessed on a space available basis. Freshman applicants should submit the following: Completed admissions application and nonrefundable $25 fee, official high school transcript, SAT and/or ACT scores, recommendation letter from guidance counselor, recommendation letter from an English teacher, student essay and resume. International applicants should submit TOEFL scores, transcripts (both the original and a copy translated into English), and a completed financial affidavit. The College requires transfer students to submit both high school and college transcripts along with a completed application, a resume, an essay, one letter of recommendation, and a nonrefundable $25 application fee. For admissions information, contact:

College of Notre Dame of Maryland
Office of Admissions
4701 North Charles Street
Baltimore, MD 21210
Telephone: 410-532-5330 or 800-435-0200 (toll free in MD) or 800-432-0300 (toll free outside MD)
Fax: 410-532-6287
E-mail: admiss@ndm.edu
Website: www.ndm.edu

4701 North Charles Street
Baltimore, MD 21210
Phone: 410-532-5330
Fax: 410-532-6287
Website: www.ndm.edu

CAMPUS LIFE

Notre Dame's beautiful 58-acre wooded campus is located in one of Baltimore's most prestigious and secure residential communities, but it is only 15 minutes from popular downtown attractions. Baltimore's Inner Harbor boasts a vast array of cultural, social, and entertainment possibilities. Popular attractions include: The Hard Rock Café, Oriole Park at Camden Yards, Raven's Stadium, The National Aquarium, and historic Fell's Point. The Baltimore Museum of Art, Lyric Opera House, Mechanic and Center Stage Theaters, and Baltimore Symphony Orchestra provide cultural enrichment within 10 minutes of campus. The College is also part of the Collegetown Network—a consortium of 13 colleges and universities—that offers great opportunities for students to meet, study and have fun with others from nearby campuses. Washington, DC, and historic Annapolis, MD, are within an hour's drive of the campus. Philadelphia, PA, and New York City are easily accessible by plane, train or car.

Exchange Programs: College of Notre Dame of Maryland students may supplement their studies with course work at seven nearby schools including Loyola College and Johns Hopkins University.

Career Planning/Internships: Notre Dame's Career Center provides assistance in career planning with a respected internship program that combines academics and real-world experience. Students have interned at companies and organizations including: McCormick & Company, Inc., Baltimore Symphony Orchestra, Discovery Channel, Magellan Health Services, The History Factory, and local law firms, television and radio stations.

Study Abroad: The wide selection of study abroad programs demonstrates Notre Dame's commitment to global education. The College currently offers 34 study abroad programs in 21 countries. Programs are designed for every major and financial aid can be applied for study abroad.

COST AND AID

Tuition for the 2003–2004 academic year is $18,700; room and board totals $7,600; and the student activities fee is $375. The College offers a variety of tuition payment options.

COLUMBUS COLLEGE OF ART AND DESIGN

GENERAL INFORMATION

CCAD is one of the largest and oldest private art colleges in the country, with more than 1,500 students from 40 states and 30 foreign countries. Artwork by students, alumni, and faculty and impressive traveling exhibitions are on display in six galleries and throughout the campus. A dramatic 100-foot-tall, 31-ton steel sculpture spelling out the word "ART" was installed at the heart of the campus in 2001. Campus facilities include the Schottenstein Residence Hall, the Packard Library (with more than 46,000 volumes), extensive studio space, computer and fine arts labs and equipment, and a 400-seat auditorium used by both CCAD and the community. A student center houses a lounge, a student-run gallery, and meeting spaces for student organizations. College programs include internships, job placement, international visiting artist lectures and presentations, industry-sponsored class projects, and community outreach and volunteer opportunities. In addition to the students enrolled in the degree program, Saturday Morning Art Classes have offered visual art education to tens of thousands of central Ohio children since 1880-more than 1,000 children in grades 1 through 12 are enrolled in Saturday classes throughout the school year. College PreView–a two- or three-week residential program–is offered each July for high school students interested in art and design.

STUDENT BODY

Opportunities are available for students to participate in student government, campus events, art-related organizations (i.e., Ceramics Club, Glass Guild) special-interest organizations (i.e., Environmental Awareness Society, International Student Association, Anime Club), and team and individual sports (i.e., basketball, soccer, karate, yoga).

ACADEMICS

The 130 semester credit hours necessary for a Bachelor of Fine Arts degree are split between roughly 88 credits in art classes and 42 in liberal arts. New students are required to take a sequence of core courses in anatomy, color, concept, computer fundamentals, design, drawing, painting, and perspective drawing, along with liberal arts classes in English and art history, as part of CCAD's renowned Foundation Studies program. Students choose a major in their sophomore year and begin receiving instruction in the fundamentals within their specific major. In their third and fourth years, students develop as professionals within their prospective fields. The Columbus College of Art & Design strives to produce graduates who are consummate professionals, displaying resourcefulness, versatility, creativity, and skillfulness in their field. The course of study is designed to ensure a logical sequence of learning that reveals connections between concurrent classes and builds skills productively. Practical knowledge is key; courses teach modern techniques utilized in professional art studios, agencies, and businesses. At the same time, instructors cultivate deep appreciation of historical artistic concepts and methods to facilitate the pursuit of aesthetic ideals. Students may register for a double major. Independent study is available in studio courses within the fine arts. CCAD is responsive to contemporary issues in art and design and frequently incorporates new classes of special interest in the curriculum.

CCAD offers a four-year program of study leading to the Bachelor of Fine Arts degree in seven majors: advertising and graphic design, fashion design, illustration, industrial design, interior design, media studies, and fine arts, which includes painting, drawing, ceramics, sculpture, printmaking, and glassblowing. In addition to the majors, CCAD offers specialized concentrations in animation, art therapy, computer graphics, fashion illustration, package design, photography, and product design. Liberal arts courses-imperative for the development of well-rounded visual artists-are integrated within all areas of study.

CCAD's faculty consists of 175 working professionals and artists and designers who have extensive professional experience and hold appropriate degrees in the areas of art taught by CCAD. Faculty members are professionally oriented, practicing artists/designers with broad teaching experience. Liberal Arts faculty are experienced teachers with doctoral or master's degrees in the humanities and sciences. Faculty who serve in the Advising Office take an active interest in the welfare of students and advise on a one-on-one basis regarding curricular concerns and career decisions. CCAD's student/faculty ratio is 12:1. Faculty biographies are available on the CCAD website, www.ccad.edu.

107 North Ninth Street
Columbus, OH 43215-3875
Phone: 614-222-3261
Fax: 614-232-8344
Website: www.ccad.edu

ADMISSIONS

Students applying to CCAD need a high school diploma or equivalency certificate. High school transcripts should show a grade point average of at least 2.0. In addition to the application form, students much submit recommendations from an art teacher and guidance counselor in addition to 10 to 15 art samples, demonstrating drawing ability, and SAT I or ACT scores. An interview at the college is encouraged but not mandatory. It is necessary that transfer students have transcripts, with a 2.0 GPA or higher, sent directly from their previous institutions. Applications should be received significantly before the applicant wishes to begin taking classes. Visit www.ccad.edu or phone 614-224-9101 for more information about CCAD and its programs. Phone the Admissions Office toll free, 877.997.CCAD, to request a viewbook.

CAMPUS LIFE

Located in the heart of Ohio's largest city amid an impressive array of cultural opportunities and institutions of higher education in downtown's "Discovery District," CCAD's 17-building campus is within walking distance to the Columbus Museum of Art, the Columbus Metropolitan Library, the Ohio Statehouse, parks, theaters, shopping, and a multitude of historic buildings and landmarks. CCAD's downtown campus is well served by the city's bus system (COTA), so students have access to employment and internship opportunities as well as shopping and entertainment options elsewhere in Columbus. Columbus is the 15th largest city in America.

CCAD offers many exciting opportunities to enrich the educational experience out of the classroom. Imagine drawing in the south of France or painting on the limestone flats of Ireland. A semester in New York can energize creativity and jump-start future career plans. Currently, CCAD offers study abroad in Ireland, France, Italy, and Chile; the Mobility Program, which permits students to participate in a one-term exchange program at any of the Association of Independent Colleges of Art and Design institutions, after which course credits are transferred back to CCAD; and The New York Studio Program.

COST AND AID

For the 2002–2003 academic year, tuition is $17,160 ($8,580 per semester); room and board is $6,300 ($3,150 per semester). Supplies and books are approximately $1,000 for the first year.

CONCORD COLLEGE–ATHENS

GENERAL INFORMATION

Concord College, a growing state-supported college committed to undergraduate instruction, was founded in 1872. Concord features an accredited career-oriented education with a strong liberal arts base and focuses on the needs of the individual student as its fundamental concern. The beautiful 95-acre campus stands on a ridge of the Appalachian Mountains. Four residence halls and adult studio apartments house up to 1,100 students from 28 states—predominately from the East, South, and Midwest. Concord also has a large international student population with 30 nations represented. With a total student population of 3,015, Concord serves the needs of an active commuter population, who join the residential students in following courses of study in the arts and sciences, business administration, teacher education, as well as such fields as advertising/graphic design, and social work. Preparation for advanced and professional study is a Concord hallmark. Each year, the Alexander Fine Arts Center presents the Artist-Lecture Series, which includes recitals, plays, art exhibitions, and guest speakers. Special events have included the North Carolina Dance Theatre; the West Virginia Symphony; lecturers such as Dr. Homer Hickam, NASA scientist and author of the book *Rocket Boys* (which was later made into the hit movie *October Sky*); Dr. Cornel West, preeminent African American scholar from Harvard; and professional art exhibitions. Theatrical productions range from Shakespeare and Chekhov to Woody Allen. Students enjoy special-interest organizations, honor societies, five fraternities, four sororities, yearbook, newspaper, and many other student activities and events, including comedians, musicians, magicians, and other entertainers. Concord was recently awarded the Great Lakes Regional Award for Outstanding Comprehensive Programming at the NACA conference. In addition, students participate in intramural and intercollegiate sports. Intercollegiate sports for men include baseball, basketball, cross-country, football, golf, tennis, track and field, and soccer. Women compete in basketball, softball, tennis, track and field, soccer, and volleyball. Counseling and tutoring are strongly supported through Student Support Services; faculty-supervised developmental labs in English, reading, and mathematics; and twice-a-year individual counseling with faculty advisors. The Student Needs and Assistance Program offers extensive academic support ranging from time management to reducing stress anxiety to testing at your best.

STUDENT BODY

Concord's Student Government Association (SGA) budgets the student activity fee and plans entertainment. The SGA names students to voting membership on administrative councils and committees. Students also fund the SGA Memorial Scholarship. The College Center Board provides on-campus movies, dances, and special programs, and the Concord Office of Student Residential Life offers numerous programs and activities in the residence halls.

ACADEMICS

All students must complete a minimum of 128 semester hours with a grade-point average of 2.0 (C) or better in order to receive a degree. A program of general studies, required of all students, includes courses in communication and literature, fine arts, social sciences, natural sciences, mathematics, foreign languages (optional in most majors), and physical education. Credit is awarded for satisfactory scores on the College-Level Examination Program (CLEP), Advanced Placement (AP), and the International Baccalaureate (IB) tests. An outstanding honors program is also available to qualifying students. Honors courses and independent study projects are available in most departments. Semesters begin in late August and mid-January, and summer terms are also offered.

Concord offers more than 80 majors, minors, and programs. The degrees offered at Concord are the Bachelor of Science in computer information systems and athletic training; the Bachelor of Arts in communication arts; the Bachelor of Arts/Bachelor of Science in interdisciplinary studies; the Bachelor of Social Work; the Bachelor of Science in education (with a wide selection of teaching fields); the Bachelor of Science in medical technology; the Bachelor of Science in business administration; the Bachelor of Science with majors in biology, comprehensive chemistry, GIS and cartography, mathematics (mathematics/comprehensive, mathematics/computer science), pre-professional biology, and chemistry. Pre-professional studies in medicine and law offer an excellent pre-professional mentoring program. The Bachelor of Arts offers majors in advertising/graphic design, English (with emphases in journalism, literature, and writing), geography, history, history with a concentration in philosophy, political science, psychology, sociology, and studio art. Concord offers the Regents Bachelor of Arts degree for adults who cannot interrupt their normal activities to attend college but have gained comparable knowledge outside the classroom. Concord also offers a two-year degree, the Associate of Arts in office supervision, and five structured interdisciplinary options including environmental geosciences, health care management, leadership and entrepreneurial studies, public administration, and sports management.

All full-time members of the faculty teach courses in the program of general studies, and all counsel and advise students. Terminal degrees are held by approximately two-thirds of the College's full-time faculty members. In addition, the College employs adjunct instructors who are experts in their fields. The average class size is 18.

1000 Vermillion Street, PO Box 1000
Athens, WV 24712
Phone: 304-384-5248
Fax: 304-384-9044
Website: www.concord.edu

ADMISSIONS

Concord College has a rolling Admissions policy, which means that we can accept you for admission until the beginning of classes for that semester. We also accept students for admission in between Fall and Spring semesters. You may apply online at www.concord.edu. The steps listed below are necessary for you to be considered for admission and are to be completed by December 31 of your senior year in high school.

Step 1: File your free Concord Application for Admission, and tell your counselor that you are applying to Concord College. To obtain an application, call 1-888-384-5249 or e-mail Admissions@concord.edu. Send all applications to:

Concord College Office of Admissions
PO Box 1000
Athens, WV 24712
Or apply online (no application fee).

Step 2: Send your high school transcript to the Concord College Office of Admissions.

Step 3: Send your ACT or SAT scores to Concord College Office of Admissions.

Step 4: File your Freshman Scholarship Application. Send form request and application to the Concord College Office of Admissions or apply online (no application fee). To be considered for financial aid at Concord, file your Free Application For Student Aid (FAFSA) between January 1 and January 31 of your senior year. You will be able to obtain this form at any high school or you may request one from the Concord College Office of Admissions and Financial Aid by mail or by logging on to www.fafsa.ed.gov.

CAMPUS LIFE

Athens is a small town in southern West Virginia, near the Virginia border. Located near Princeton and Bluefield, West Virginia, Athens is six miles from I-77 and not far from I-64 and I-81. Athens has easy access to thriving population centers such as Roanoke, Virginia; Charleston, West Virginia; and Charlotte, North Carolina. Shopping malls and entertainment are also available nearby, and Pipestem State Park Resort offers many recreational opportunities. WinterPlace ski resort is approximately 20 minutes north of the campus, and whitewater rafting is also nearby.

The Concord College Beckley Center offers a wide range of academic opportunities to students in and around Raleigh County, West Virginia, from freshman-level courses to the four-year degree in business administration. Summer internships, which provide valuable professional contacts and experience, are part of the program of study for students majoring in communication arts and advertising/graphic design. Professional fieldwork placements form part of the social work program, and an internship program is available for travel industry management students. Concord's most comprehensive internship program is in the area of medical technology. Students in this program must complete a 12-month internship at an approved hospital. Additionally, Concord's pre-med mentoring program includes paid summer projects, one-on-one mentoring with physicians, special advocacy for medical school applications, and MCAT preparation. The pre-law mentoring program provides one-on-one mentoring, internships in law firms, special advocacy for law school applications, LSAT preparation, and visits to area law schools. Concord provides study abroad opportunities for students in various majors. For Presidential Scholars, study abroad opportunities are included in the award package. Concord is the only public institution of 24 institutions that participate in the Bonner Scholarship program, which is based on "changing the world through service." Students who are chosen as Bonner Scholars or receive Community Service Covenant Grants volunteer at either on- or off-campus locations depending on need.

COST AND AID

For the 2002–2003 academic year, the tuition, fees, and room and board for West Virginia residents was $7,750. For out-of-state students, annual costs were $11,436. Books and supplies cost approximately $500, and personal expenses were about $1,000. These figures are subject to change.

CONCORDIA COLLEGE (MOORHEAD, MN)

GENERAL INFORMATION

Concordia College, as a private Lutheran liberal arts college with an enrollment of approximately 2,900 students, offers a high-quality education for young people. The college was founded in 1891 by Norwegian immigrants who sought to preserve their values of church and family while preparing young people for effective citizenship. The college has maintained a reputation for academic excellence over its 112-year history. With small classes, innovative programs, and a faculty dedicated to teaching, Concordia produces graduates who are leaders in their communities, businesses, and churches. The College places a high value on ethical, values-based decision-making, and encourages students to explore individual moral reasoning and to develop in their spiritual growth so they will become active participants in whatever path they choose in life. The John Templeton Foundation has named Concordia one of America's leading character-building colleges. The College asks students to think globally—Concordia ranks sixth among all liberal arts colleges for the number of students studying abroad. There are students from 41 other countries and 37 states on campus. More than 40 percent of graduates enroll in post-graduate study; 93 percent of graduates applying to law schools are accepted, and placement in medical schools is twice the national average. Many people come to know Concordia through its renowned music groups, which frequently tour across the United States and around the world. The acclaimed Concordia Christmas Concert, featuring more than 450 student musicians, attracts nearly 20,000 people each year to performances on campus and at Orchestra Hall in Minneapolis, and is nationally televised on public television and cable stations. The highly regarded Concordia Language Villages annually hosts more than 8,500 young people ages 7–18 who study 12 world languages in an outdoor setting, and is a recognized leader in cultural immersion learning.

STUDENT BODY

Most Concordia students live on campus or in nearby rental housing, so the campus is a vibrant place hosting a variety of activities, including lectures, recitals, concerts, and athletic events. Concordia encourages students to participate in a co-curricular activity, and there are literally hundreds of participation opportunities. There are 100 student clubs and organizations, including Sources of Service in which some 400 students annually volunteer their time to community organizations. Music is very popular–more than 650 students are involved in one or more of 5 voice choirs, 2 bands, 2 orchestras, 2 jazz ensembles, and a marimba choir and percussion ensemble. Some 325 students annually are involved in theatre productions. Mock Trial and Forensics are especially strong at Concordia and in recent years the college has produced several individual national champions. There are 20 NCAA Division III intercollegiate sports, 10 each for men and women, including soccer and hockey, with the 1999–2000 men's hockey team advancing to the national championship playoffs. Concordia has placed among the top three teams nationally in women's golf in the last six years, routinely produces All-Americans in track and cross-country, and has won national championships in women's basketball and men's football.

901 Eighth Street South
Moorhead, MN 56562
Phone: 218-299-3004
Fax: 218-299-4720
Website: www.goconcordia.com

ACADEMICS

Concordia offers 82 majors in 40 academic areas and courses in 18 pre-professional programs, including pre-law, pre-medicine, and church professions. The College is exceptionally strong in world languages and study abroad programs. The Bachelor of Arts and Bachelor of Music degrees are awarded. Major programs include art, biology, business and economics, business education and office administration, chemistry, classical studies, communication, environmental studies, education, English, English writing and print journalism, family and nutrition sciences, French, Russian, German, Spanish, Latin and Norwegian, history, humanities, international business and international relations, mathematics and computer science, medical technology, music, nursing, philosophy, physical education and health, physics, political science, psychology, religion, Scandinavian studies, sociology and social work, speech communication and theatre art, and women's studies.

Concordia has approximately 280 faculty members and a student/faculty ratio of 14:1. A high percentage of faculty have PhDs or the highest degree in their field. Senior faculty teach courses at all levels. Faculty members often work closely with students on research projects and frequently develop mentoring relationships with students. Every student is assigned a faculty advisor for assistance in course selection and academic and career counseling.

ADMISSIONS

Concordia College in Moorhead, Minnesota, has rolling admission, which means there are no deadlines for applying. The average SAT combined is 1000 and the average ACT composite is 24. Requirements include high school transcript, ACT or SAT test scores, academic and character(coach or music director) reference. The admission committee looks at the student as a whole and makes a decision based on all the requirements not just the SAT or ACT scores. Types of classes taken are also key in the admission process.

CAMPUS LIFE

Concordia College is located in a peaceful neighborhood section of Moorhead, Minnesota, across the Red River from Fargo, North Dakota. Together the two communities form a population of 170,000 and are regional centers for education, performance and visual arts, government, banking, industry, medical services, and transportation. Fargo-Moorhead regularly appears on national lists of great places to live. The communities are commended for their excellent school systems, high quality of life, clean, safe environment, and sound business climate.

Fargo-Moorhead is the largest regional center between Minneapolis and Seattle, so opportunities for activities abound. As a leading business center, there are many choices for internships and cooperative education programs available with global firms like leading software producer Microsoft Great Plains, and Rosenbluth International, the world's largest travel company, There are many cultural opportunities, including opera, theatre, and the Fargo-Moorhead Symphony Orchestra, whose core is formed by faculty and students at Concordia. The area has an active art community and several galleries mount major exhibitions several times a year. With three major colleges in the community, there is an exciting array of concert performances ranging from classical to blues to folk to rock. The 20,000-seat Fargodome has hosted such well-known touring acts as Bruce Springsteen, the Dixie Chicks, the Rolling Stones, and Garth Brooks. The dome also hosts college and professional football and IBL professional basketball. The FM Redhawks, a minor league baseball franchise, and hockey's FM Ice Sharks play before sellout crowds.

COST AND AID

For more than a century Concordia has built a reputation for high-quality education and moderate cost. In fact, Concordia maintains the lowest tuition cost of the Minnesota private colleges. Expenses for the 2003–2004 year include tuition, $16,420; student activity fees, $140; and room and board, $4,540; for a total comprehensive fee of $21,100.

CONCORDIA UNIVERSITY, RIVER FOREST

THE UNIVERSITY AT A GLANCE

Nestled in a secure neighborhood of tree-lined streets and stately homes just 10 miles west of downtown Chicago, Concordia University, River Forest is a unique and special place. Building on a strong tradition of Lutheran Christian education, Concordia University graduates people who are intellectually, socially, spiritually, and physically prepared to lead and serve in this complex world.

EMPOWERING THE MIND TO MAKE A DIFFERENCE

At Concordia University, you will find excellent academic programs with a strong Christian heritage. All are focused on empowering your mind and enriching your ability to recognize and respond to the needs of others. Personal attention from an excellent teaching faculty in small classes, opportunities for spiritual development, and a close-knit campus community combine to nourish your spirit and shape your future.

In addition, a high four-year graduation rate, a tuition that is below comparable private colleges and universities in the Midwest, and a variety of financial assistance opportunities make Concordia University an excellent value.

But we are not for everyone. Our students understand that accomplishment coupled with Christian values results in a life well lived. Success is measured not by how much one can accumulate for oneself, but by how much one can contribute to making the world a better place. That's why Concordia University stresses service as part of the University experience.

If you are ready to apply your Christian faith to scholarship and action, you are ready for Concordia University.

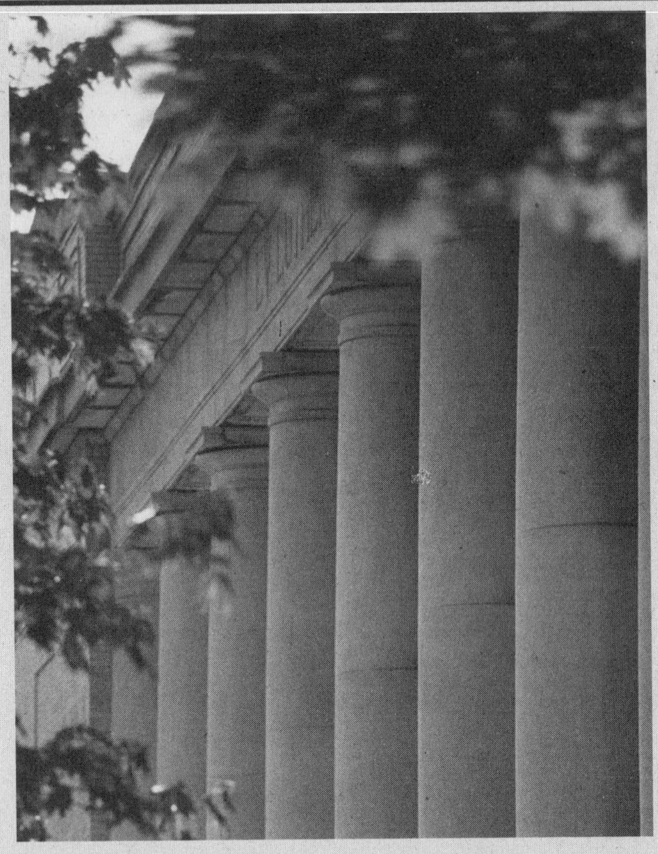

EMPOWERING THE MIND IN A SUPPORTIVE ATMOSPHERE

"I can sit down for 45 minutes after my classes with a professor . . . and we can talk, one-on-one."

This student's comment sums it up. At Concordia, you will enjoy small classes taught by warm and caring professors who love to teach and are committed to your growth. Students benefit from classroom discussion that puts their challenging curriculum into the context of the wider world.

CAMPUS FACILITIES THAT MEET YOUR NEEDS

Our students have unlimited access to one of the most sophisticated computer systems to be found in institutions of our size. In fact, Concordia was the first institution of its type in Illinois to offer Internet access on all campus computers.

Concordia's $5 million Education Communication Center underscores our commitment to providing you with an unparalleled educational experience. It includes a television studio and control rooms, a production area for a campus radio station, and a photography studio. Or take the university's unique Human Performance Laboratory. Students in the exercise science and fitness management program use the latest fitness equipment to study and research exercise physiology, biomechanics, strength and conditioning, and injury prevention.

7400 Augusta Street
River Forest, IL 60305-1499
Phone: 708-209-3100
Fax: 708-209-3473
Website: www.curf.edu

BEYOND THE CLASSROOM

From the start, our students are encouraged to develop relationships with professors, our campus pastor, academic advisors, and their peers. By the time they graduate, Concordia University students are skilled at placing problems in perspective and working with others to achieve a common goal. Many Concordia graduates can be found providing direction, promoting equality, and making long-lasting contributions to the communities they serve and the professions they are called to pursue.

Even before that important commencement day, Concordia students are in demand at companies, schools, agencies, and institutions around the country and in the "learning laboratory" of one of America's most dynamic cities. The diversity of nearby Chicago offers a wide range of practicum and internship opportunities that are just 15 minutes or less from campus. Our reputation for preparing students of high moral and intellectual character makes employers eager recruiters.

EMPOWERING THE MIND THROUGH EXCELLENT ACADEMIC PROGRAMS

Who are Concordia graduates? They are successful educators, psychologists, exercise physiologists, broadcasters, nurses, pastors, systems analysts, musicians, stage managers, social workers, physicians, deaconesses, lawyers, librarians, and business professionals, to name just a few. You'll find 32 major fields of study in the College of Arts and Sciences alone. In addition, there's the College of Education, the Concordia University and West Suburban College of Nursing, the Graduate School, the University College and the Concordia Organizational Management Program.

No matter what your chosen field of study, your education begins with an emphasis on the liberal arts and sciences and expands to include comprehensive professional preparation. The result? Our graduates are strong communicators who excel in their professions.

When nursing is your calling, our baccalaureate nursing program is built on the strength of two institutions: Concordia University and West Suburban College of Nursing. It successfully integrates a liberal arts education with a solid nursing curriculum.

ENRICHING THE SPIRIT THROUGH A CALLING TO SERVE

The moment you walk onto the Concordia University campus, you'll feel the difference. It's an intensity that comes from people finding creative ways to put their Christian faith into action and give something back to the community.

Concordia is a Lutheran university. As a result, community involvement is an important part of student life. You may find yourself rehabbing apartments in a Chicago housing project or reaching out to international students through an on-campus program called Conversation Partners.

Concordia students discover that when you reach out to others, your actions enrich your own spirit. In other words, there's great satisfaction in making life a little more meaningful for another person.

CAMPUS VISITS

To experience Concordia first hand you will want to participate in one of several open houses scheduled throughout the year. Or you may visit whenever it is convenient for you.

Please call us at 1-800-285-2668 or 708-209-3100 to make an appointment so we can give you personal attention as you make your college plans. We look forward to meeting you.

CORCORAN COLLEGE OF ART AND DESIGN

THE COLLEGE AT A GLANCE

There is a long tradition of partnership between art schools and museums; a logical relationship when one considers the extraordinary opportunity shared by students and faculty in a museum environment. Surrounded by great art and frequently by the contemporary masters whose work is regularly exhibited, the atmosphere of a museum art school is charged by the excitement of direct contact with the world of art. The Corcoran College of Art and Design is special, for it remains one of America's very few examples of a "pure" museum art school by maintaining its original relationship to one of Washington's greatest museums. Officially founded in 1890, some 15 years after William Wilson Corcoran established Washington's first museum, the Corcoran ranks among America's oldest and most distinguished colleges of the visual arts. Less than one block from the White House, the Corcoran's collections and College are housed in one of America's greatest examples of neo-classical architecture, with wings designed by Ernest Flagg and Charles Platt. The Corcoran recently commisioned architect Frank O. Gehry to design its second and final wing.

As our nation's capital grew, the Corcoran complemented the development of its city, acquiring one of the finest collections of American art in the world. The collection is supplemented by holdings in European painting and sculpture, classical antiquities, and the decorative arts. As Washington's first museum of art, the Corcoran has played a central role in the development of American culture for more than 125 years.

Where else can student exhibitions be held regularly in the galleries of a museum of international stature, open to visitors from all parts of the country and every nation, who can "discover" the art or design talents of emerging young professionals? And where else can students leave their studios and wander only a few blocks to the National Gallery, visit the many branches of the Smithsonian Institution, take in the best of American performing arts, or see the great monuments of our national history?

LOCATION AND ENVIRONMENT

Washington is a city of monuments, set off by the classical architecture of government buildings, parks, trees, and greenery, all enhanced by a climate of long, balmy fall and spring seasons. With 16 major colleges and universities in the metropolitan area, there exists a feeling of a giant "campus" in which restaurants, coffee shops, movie theaters, and night spots are intermingled with bookstores, clothing boutiques, and academic facilities. A short walk from the Corcoran brings us to the world famous Mall, ringed by museums, galleries, and the country's most distinguished monuments. Not only is the mall the physical center of our nation's cultural history, it is one of the world's largest playgrounds—an ideal spot for jogging, biking, picnicking, kite-flying, or a simple morning stroll. Within a mile, there exist numerous beacons of quality and innovation in the performing arts, such as the Kennedy Center, Ford's Theater, and the National Theater. Washington remains the center of world power as well as a cultural and intellectual capital.

MAJORS AND DEGREES OFFERED

The College offers the Bachelor of Fine Arts degree in four full-time majors: fine art, graphic design, photojournalism, and photography. Studio art courses comprise 65 percent of the BFA degree requirements, with the remaining degree credits earned in academic disciplines such as art history, writing, and humanities.

The Corcoran College of Art and Design is accredited by the Middle States Association of Colleges and Schools, and is an accredited institutional member of the National Association of Schools of Art and Design (the nation's only recognized body for the accreditation of art colleges).

ACADEMIC PROGRAMS

In the first year of study, students follow a unified and structured Foundation Program developing essential visual and technical skills in a wide variety of media. A distinctive aspect of the Corcoran's Foundation program is team-teaching in several studio courses, encouraging maximum participation, interchange, and dialogue between students and faculty. Students are exposed to multiple points of view to promote independent thinking, expand perceptual phenomena, and build an artistic vocabulary.

Students select a major in the second year choosing between fine art, graphic design, photojournalism, and photography. Fine art majors may concentrate in ceramics, digital art, drawing, painting, printmaking, and sculpture. Photography students may major in fine arts photography or photojournalism. Graphic design majors may elect to follow the digital media design or graphic design concentrations. Sophomore studio courses are designed to bridge the ongoing development of technical skills and the increasing personal knowledge of artistic expression. Conceptual abilities are also challenged by academic requirements in art history and humanities.

In the junior and senior year, the focus shifts towards one's personal vision, individual initiative, and professional development. Internships, individual projects, directed studies, and advanced academic and studio electives hone each student's specific career goals. The degree studies culminate in formal exhibitions of senior thesis projects in the Hemicycle Gallery of the Corcoran Museum of Art.

OFF-CAMPUS OPPORTUNITIES

Student life at the Corcoran is closely linked to the life of the Washington, D.C. community. The city becomes an extended campus and offers limitless opportunities for cultural, social, artistic, academic, and professional growth. With numerous internships and jobs for college students available in the metropolitan area, this community is a magnet for young people from across the country and the world.

500 17th Street NW
Washington, DC 20006-4804
Phone: 202-639-1814
Fax: 202-639-1830
Website: www.corcoran.edu

FACILITIES AND EQUIPMENT

The Corcoran College of Art and Design is located a block from the White House in the heart of Washington, D.C., with additional facilities in close proximity. The Georgetown campus is home to the graphic design department and the state-of-the-art computer laboratories of the Corcoran Computer Graphics Institute. The H Street campus hosts the library, tutoring resource center, classrooms, and faculty offices. All students will spend most of their first year in the classrooms, studios, and workshops in the downtown campus that houses both the College and Museum, as well as the fine art and photography departments.

The Corcoran library provides students with access to a collection of over 20,000 volumes; 45,000 slides; and a large periodical and artists' book collection. Resource equipment includes televisions, video cassette recorder, video camera, slide equipment, typewriter, copier, and a variety of computer equipment for word processing, scanning, printing, and Internet access.

TUITION, ROOM AND BOARD, AND FEES

Tuition (including fees) for the 2001–2002 academic year is $16,970 for all full-time students taking 12 to 18 credits per semester. Expenses for books and art supplies are estimated at $2,000 annually but will vary with personal preference.

The College is within easy walking distance of several desirable Washington neighborhoods. The Office of Student Services actively assists students in obtaining suitable housing options in the community. Housing Day, held during the summer, provides students with the opportunity to meet potential roommates, discuss affordable housing with staff, and in many cases, find appropriate housing that day. The OSS works with area apartment building and real estate management companies to secure College-leased apartments, discounts, and other incentives for Corcoran students.

FINANCIAL AID

Admission to Corcoran is need-blind, and we are committed to assisting students with their educational expenses throughout their undergraduate careers. Over 60 percent of our students receive some form of financial aid, including need- and merit-based scholarships. Corcoran participates in all of the major financial aid programs offered by the U.S. Department of Education and provides institutional funds to supplement federal or state financial aid. We provide a payment plan through Academic Management Services as well as information about other options for our students to meet their educational expenses. Please contact the Director of Financial Aid at 202-639-1816 with questions.

FULL- AND PART-TIME FACULTY

Washington is home to one of the country's finest and most active communities of artists and designers. These creative professionals form the faculty of the College and bring real-world values, concerns, and techniques to the classroom. With 110 faculty members, the Corcoran boasts an exceptional student/faculty ratio of 10:1, assuring personal attention and a close working relationship within the College community.

STUDENT ORGANIZATIONS AND ACTIVITIES

The staff of the Office of Student Services helps students to take advantage of this unique city-campus and career life as a student-artist. A wide variety of educational, social, cultural, and fundraising activities are held throughout the year in conjunction with the Corcoran Student Council. A weekly newsletter, the *Corcoran Canvas*, is published to inform the community of current and future events as well as other items of interest. As museum members from the outset, students are able to take advantage of numerous special opportunities in the arts offered by the Corcoran Museum of Art.

CAREER SERVICES

The Career Resource Center is committed to helping artists with their career development by providing a variety of resources and information, including an up-to-date listing of art-related jobs, internships, grants, scholarships, competitions, résumé-writing workshops, and career seminars with alumni and guest artists. Each year, the Center hosts visits from various companies and organizations wishing to recruit Corcoran students. The Smithsonian Institution, the world's largest museum complex, grants several internships a year to Corcoran students. Students may intern at the National Portrait Gallery, Air and Space Museum, Freer Gallery of Art, Hirshhorn Museum and Sculpture Garden, and at the many other museums and offices associated with the Smithsonian. The Center also maintains a listing of organizations actively recruiting students for employment in fine arts, photography, and graphic design.

MOBILITY AND STUDY ABROAD PROGRAMS

Corcoran is a member of the Association of Independent Colleges of Art and Design (AICAD), a consortium of 35 art colleges from across the country (www.aicad.org). AICAD's mobility program allows students from any of the member schools to spend a semester at another AICAD college of their choice. Students in good standing who have met the academic requirements may apply for mobility for the fall semester of their junior year. Enrollment is based on space availability at the host institution.

The Corcoran is actively pursuing partnerships with colleges in other countries where students may study abroad for short periods of time. Current affiliations include The University of Georgia Studies Abroad Program in Cortona, Italy; the Studio Art Centers International (SACI) in Florence, Italy; and the Canberra School of Art, The Australian National University, in Canberra, Australia.

In addition, opportunities are available through the Corcoran Museum to travel across the country and abroad as well as to nonaffiliated institutions. Current opportunities include a joint faculty/student trip to Altzella, Germany for the Batuz Foundation/Société Imaginaire Residency program.

ADMISSIONS PROCESS AND REQUIREMENTS

The Corcoran College of Art and Design enrolls approximately 350 full-time students in the four-year BFA program. Students from more than 18 countries and 25 states attend the Corcoran, contributing to the cultural, ethnic, and artistic diversity of the College community. We seek applications from candidates who are committed to the professional study of the visual arts and demonstrate artistic, as well as intellectual talent. The Admissions Committee prioritizes their review of applications beginning with the candidate's academic record (high school and college/university); a portfolio of artwork; personal attributes (interview, recommendations, essays, extracurricular activities); and official results of standardized tests such as the SAT I, ACT, or the TOEFL. All applicants are encouraged to contact our office to arrange for a campus tour, personal interview, and portfolio review. Portfolios may be submitted on slides and will be returned upon request. Candidates may also meet with our representatives for portfolio reviews during National Portfolio Days that are held nationally, or by appointment as we travel across the country for high school visits and college fairs.

CUMBERLAND COLLEGE

GENERAL INFORMATION

For more than 100 years, Cumberland College has been committed to providing a superior education in an exceptional Christian atmosphere at an affordable cost. Emphasis is placed on the growth of the individual student. The College strives to instill in students the desire to be agents of change in the world and to use knowledge for the benefit of others, as well as themselves. Cumberland is a four-year, coed liberal arts college offering a broad curriculum with more than 40 programs of study from which to choose. A graduate program leading to the Master of Arts in Education is also offered. The student body consists of 1,743 students representing 38 states and 14 countries. Most students live on campus in the College's ten residence halls. A director assisted by student staff members supervises each hall. Students benefit from such special services as the Career Services Center, Center for Leadership Studies, Student Health Center, Academic Resource Center, and free tutorial assistance. Cumberland College is accredited by the Commission on Colleges of the Southern Association of Colleges and Schools (telephone: 404-679-4501) to award the Bachelor of Arts, Bachelor of General Studies, Bachelor of Music, Bachelor of Science, and Master of Arts in Education degrees.

STUDENT BODY

Movies, dances, concerts, drama productions, departmental clubs, honor societies, intramurals, athletics, student government, Christian outreach ministries, and more keep the student active and involved.

ACADEMICS

Cumberland seeks to provide academic specialization within the broad framework of a liberal arts education. To supplement the in-depth knowledge acquired within each major, 45 semester hours of general studies from the areas of Christian faith and values, cultural and aesthetic values, the English language, humanities, leadership and community service, natural and mathematical sciences, physical education, and social sciences are required. Students must earn 128 semester hours to graduate with a bachelor's degree. The academic year begins in late August, with the first semester ending in mid-December. The second semester runs from early January to early May. Two five-week undergraduate summer session and two four-week graduate summer sessions are also offered. Orientation, pre-registration, and academic advising by faculty members begin in the summer preceding entrance. Students may receive credit for passing the College Board, the College-Level Examination Programs (CLEP), and special departmental tests. Through the honors program, highly qualified students have the opportunity to undertake advanced independent study.

Cumberland College confers the Bachelor of Arts, Bachelor of Science, Bachelor of General Studies, and Bachelor of Music. Major and minor fields of study include accounting, art°, athletic training, biblical languages, biological science°, biology, business administration, business and marketing education°, chemistry, church music, communication arts, communication and theatre arts°, computer information systems, early elementary education°, English°, French°, geography, health, health education°, history, history and political science, mathematics°, medical technology, middle school education°, movement and leisure studies°, music°, office administration, philosophy and religion, physical science°, physics, political science, psychology, public health, religion, social studies°, social work, Spanish°, special education°, theatre arts. Pre-professional and special curricula are offered in medical technology, military science, pre-dentistry, pre-engineering, pre-law, pre-medicine, pre-nursing, pre-optometry, pre-pharmacy, pre-physical therapy, pre-veterinary medicine, and religious vocations.

°Denotes teacher certification available

There are 95 full-time and 6 part-time faculty members who are respected scholars and whose primary responsibility is to teach. Graduate assistants do not teach courses. The student/faculty ratio is 16:1 enabling students to receive ample attention and assistance from professors. Faculty members also serve as advisors to help students in planning their academic programs.

6178 College Station Drive
Williamsburg, KY 40769
Phone: 606-539-4241
Fax: 606-539-4303
Website: www.cumberlandcollege.edu

ADMISSIONS

Cumberland admits students on a rolling basis.

Required items include:

Application and $30 application fee

Essay

Teacher recommendation

High school information form

CAMPUS LIFE

Williamsburg is located in southern Kentucky, 185 miles south of Cincinnati, Ohio, and 70 miles north of Knoxville, Tennessee. The campus is easily accessible from Interstate 75, about one mile from Exit 11. Williamsburg is one of Kentucky's older towns and is known for the hospitality of its people. Cumberland offers a picturesque campus with stately buildings and rolling green lawns nestled in the foothills of the Appalachian mountain range. Within a few miles of campus are Laurel Lake, Cumberland Falls State Park, Cumberland Gap National Park, and the Daniel Boone National Forest.

COST AND AID

For 2003–2004, the basic academic year expenses are $11,458 for tuition and fees and $4,926 for room and board. There are no additional fees for out-of-state students. The average cost for books and supplies is approximately $350 per semester.

DAEMEN COLLEGE

GENERAL INFORMATION

Located in the beautiful suburbs north of Buffalo, New York, Daemen College is a private, liberal arts school, committed to undergraduate education. Daemen is distinguished by a low student/faculty ratio and consistently small classes sizes, which encourage students to interact with professors and grow as individuals.

STUDENT BODY

The Student Governing Board is composed of elected student officials, responsible for the oversight of extracurricular and student affairs on campus. In addition to the Student Governing Board, there are student committees that represent students to the college president, the academic dean, and other campus administrators. An active school community, there are a number of student clubs and organizations at Daemen, including men's and women's basketball teams, women's volleyball, *A Step Ascending* (literary publication), Accounting Club, Art Club, *Ascent* (newspaper), Business Club, Campus Ministry, Cheerleading, Commuter Council, Drama Club, Education Club, English Club, Greek and Social Clubs, Honor Societies, Humanities Association, Indoor Soccer Club, Multi-Cultural Association, New York Students for Effective Education, Physician Assistant Student Society, Psychology Club, Resident Council, Ski Club, Social Work Alliance, Special Olympics, Sports Fitness and Wellness Club, Student Association, Student Physical Therapy Association, and *Summit* (yearbook).

ACADEMICS

Daemen College is committed to complimenting the depth of study in a major field with a well-rounded academic understanding in the liberal arts. The College's new core curriculum, which will be instituted in Fall 2003, will ensure that every student graduates with the following seven core competencies: critical thinking and creative problem solving; oral, written and visual communication; information and multi-media technologies; civic responsibility; contextual understanding; affective judgment; and moral and ethical discernment.

Daemen College offers BA, BFA, and BS programs in the following subject areas: accounting, art, art education, biochemistry, biology, business administration, business education, business weekend program, communications/public relations, drawing/illustration, early childhood, elementary education, English, environmental studies, French, global economics, graphic design, health care studies, history and government, human resource management, human services, humanities, international business, management information systems, marketing, mathematics, natural sciences, nursing, operations management, painting/sculpture, physical therapy, physician assistant, political science, pre-dentistry, pre-law, pre-medicine, pre-veterinary, printmaking, psychology, religious studies, secondary education, social work, Spanish, special education, sport management, international business, and individualized studies.

Graduate programs include MS programs in adult nurse practitioner, special education, physician assistant, palliative care, global business and a Doctorate program in physical therapy.

Classes usually have no more than 15 to 30 students. Small class sizes allow instructors to gain individual insight into every student. There are 145 full- and part-time faculty at Daemen College, of which 90 percent hold doctoral or terminal degrees in their field.

4380 Main Street
Amherst, NY 14226-3592
Phone: 716-839-8225
Fax: 716-839-8229
Website: www.daemen.edu

ADMISSIONS

Successful applicants to Daemen College must have completed college-preparatory studies in high school. Daemen occasionally considers accepting students who are in their third year of high school and who have demonstrated academic promise and personal maturity.

CAMPUS LIFE

Daemen's beautiful 39-acre campus is located in Amherst, New York, a safe, peaceful suburb of Buffalo. Money magazine has reported Amherst, New York as America's safest city for the fifth time in the last six years. Due to its proximity to Buffalo—New York's second largest city—Daemen's campus is close to many major rail, plane, and motor routes. While the campus setting is tranquil and residential, Buffalo is a vibrant cultural city, bustling with world-class entertainment, such as the Philharmonic Orchestra, the Albright-Knox Art Gallery, and the Studio Arena Theater. The greater Buffalo area is rich with sports and recreational activities all year round, whether it be skiing and swimming, or watching NFL football. The surrounding Niagara Frontier boasts numerous historic and scenic locations. For example, Niagara Falls is only 30 minutes away and the attractive, international city of Toronto is just two hours by car. On campus, the numerous trees and open spaces create a lovely environment to work and study, and compliment the nearby urban environment.

Daemen's Cooperative Education Program gives students a chance to gain professional experience in their field of study during their undergraduate career. Through the Cooperative Education Program, students may receive academic credit for off campus work, in addition to receiving a salary. At the same time, students foster essential workplace skills and preparation while still in college. In that vein, Daemen offers numerous workshops to help students write high quality resumes and cover letters, and practice interviewing and job hunting techniques.

COST AND AID

Tuition for the 2002–2003 academic year is $14,270, with additional room and board fees of $7,000.

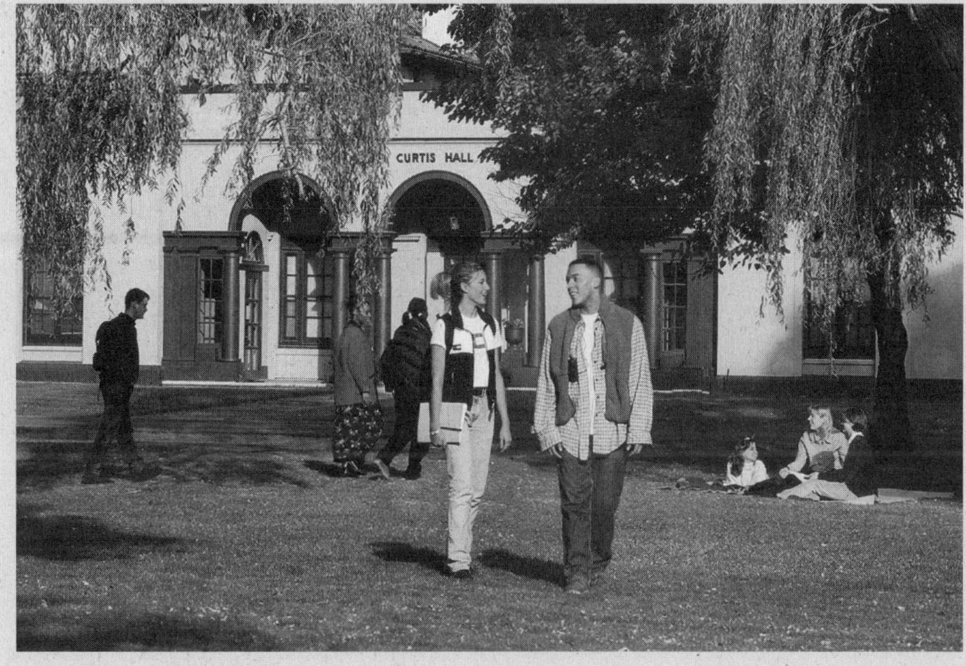

DARTMOUTH COLLEGE

GENERAL INFORMATION

Dartmouth College, founded in 1769, is one of the foremost universities in the world. A member of the Ivy League, Dartmouth has a long history of dedication to the highest educational ideals. The College community comprises a breadth of cultures, traditions, and ideas. The diversity of backgrounds, talents, and accomplishments among our students, faculty, and staff enrich our community and create a campus that is alive with ongoing debate and exploration. Hanover, New Hampshire, is an idyllic New England town located just over two hours northwest of Boston. Set upon the intersection of the Connecticut River and the Appalachian Trail, and flanked by the White Mountains of New Hampshire and the Green Mountains of Vermont, Dartmouth's location is striking in its natural beauty. At the same time, Dartmouth's status as a major research institution brings tremendous academic and extracurricular opportunities. The resources at Dartmouth are one of the distinguishing features of the school. From the extensive library system and top-flight laboratory facilities to the outstanding faculty, the College provides its students with everything they need to fully explore their intellectual interests. Yet, most importantly, Dartmouth accomplishes that feat without sacrificing its dedication to the individual learning experiences of each student. Dartmouth has an unrivaled commitment to the liberal arts education.

STUDENT BODY

Dartmouth students come from all 50 states and more than 70 foreign countries. The student body, with 4,300 undergraduates and 1,200 graduate students, represents a diverse set of backgrounds, perspectives, and life experiences reflecting American society and an increasingly intertwined world. The Dartmouth student's life is not confined to the classroom. A blend of academic, cultural, social, and extracurricular pursuits contribute to the Dartmouth residential learning experience. Educational, cultural, community-service, and social activities are organized by students and staff in each residence. Upon matriculation, first-year students can take advantage of Dartmouth's natural resources by participating in three-day trips led by the Dartmouth Outdoor Club.

Extracurricular activities are also an important component of every student's education. Dartmouth undergraduates participate in more than 250 organizations, clubs, and teams ranging from the Dartmouth Symphony Orchestra to the Ski Patrols, from Women in Politics to the Daniel Webster Society. Included are religious organizations, ethnic and cultural groups, numerous publications, preprofessional societies, and political, economic, social, sports, and recreational organizations. In keeping with Dartmouth's encouragement of student-initiated projects, new organizations and programs are constantly evolving to fill special interests and kindle new enthusiasms. Currently, Dartmouth students participate in more than 250 organizations, clubs, and teams. Among the list are religious organizations; ethnic, social, and cultural groups; publications; pre-professional societies; and political, economic, sports, volunteer, and recreational organizations. The Hood Museum of Art hosts a collection of more than 60,000 pieces, while the Hopkins Center for the Creative and Performing Arts maintains a calendar of more than 500 events each year. The College's 34 varsity teams (Division I-AA, Ivy League) and athletic clubs participate in more than 500 intercollegiate competitions annually.

ACADEMICS

More than 2,000 courses are offered in 29 departments and 10 interdisciplinary programs. There are 44 standard majors and limitless possibilities for combined, specialized, and self-designed programs of study. Dartmouth's unique and flexible calendar system provides students with unparalleled opportunities to design an educational program that is most closely suited to their individual needs, interests, and aspirations. The "Dartmouth Plan" is possible through the use of a year-round calendar consisting of four 10-week academic terms (fall, winter, spring, and summer). Students use this flexibility to include terms of off-campus study in Dartmouth programs around the world or at other institutions, and vacation terms scheduled to best meet their internship or other interests. More than half of all Dartmouth students participate in at least one of the more than 50 off-campus options.

Dartmouth awards the Bachelor of Arts (BA) and Bachelor of Engineering degrees.

Majors and academic programs include the following areas of study: African and African American studies; anthropology; art history; Asian and Middle Eastern studies; Arabic; Chinese; Hebrew; Japanese; East Asian languages and literature; biology; biochemistry and molecular biology; genetics, cell, and developmental biology; environmental and evolutionary biology; chemistry; biophysical chemistry; classical archaeology; classics (emphasis on Latin/Greek/both); ancient history; comparative literature; computer science; drama; earth sciences; environmental earth sciences; economics; education; engineering sciences; engineering physics; English; English and creative writing; environmental studies; film and television studies; French; geography; German; government; history; Italian; Latin American, Latino, and Caribbean studies; linguistics; cognitive science; mathematics; mathematics and social sciences; music; Native American studies; philosophy; astronomy; physics/astronomy; psychology; religion; romance languages; Russian area studies; Russian language and literature; sociology; Spanish literatures; Spanish language, culture, and society; Latino studies; Iberian studies; studio art; and women's studies.

In addition, students may incorporate the following minors into a Dartmouth degree: applied mathematics for biological and social sciences; applied mathematics for physical and engineering sciences; education; epistemology and metaphysics; Greek; history of philosophy; Jewish studies; Iberian Studies; Latin; Latin American and U.S. Hispanic literatures; logic and philosophy of science; markets, management, and the economy; moral philosophy; neuroscience; operations research; Portuguese and Brazilian literatures; public policy; social inequalities; Spanish literature; statistics; and war and peace studies.

Professors at the College are among the leaders in their fields, yet they remain fully committed to teaching. True exemplars of the phrase "teacher-scholar," faculty teach 100 percent of the classes at Dartmouth and actively support the independent research interests of their students. Graduate students do not teach any courses. Through course-related discussions, research collaborations, and casual conversation, students get to know their professors as instructors, mentors, colleagues, and friends.

6016 McNutt Hall
Hanover, NH 03755
Phone: 603-646-2875
Fax: 603-646-1216
Website: www.dartmouth.edu

ADMISSIONS

Dartmouth is a highly selective institution. This is a function of not only the sheer number of applicants, but also the quality therein. There is no set formula or prescription for admission. We consider the range of different opportunities and educational experiences of our applicants to be a strength, and therefore take an open-minded and flexible approach to our review process. An understanding of the applicant's academic background is supplemented by essays, recommendations, and interviews. Dartmouth believes a diverse student body enhances the intellectual environment and encourages students from all backgrounds to apply.

In addition to completing the admissions application itself, Dartmouth requires all applicants, including foreign students, to take either the SAT I or the ACT and any three SAT II: Subject Tests. All tests must be taken no later than January of the senior year in high school. Applicants to the College are offered two interview options. High school seniors may call the Admissions Office to arrange an on-campus interview during the summer or fall. In addition, most applicants will have the opportunity to interview with graduates of the College in their hometowns after the admissions application has been submitted.

Students who have Dartmouth as a clear first-choice may apply under the College's Early Decision program. Applying as an Early Decision candidate involves a commitment to matriculate at Dartmouth if admitted. Early Decision candidates must submit their applications by November 1 (testing must be completed by November 1); by mid-December, candidates are notified that they have been accepted, denied, or that a final decision has been deferred until early April. Candidates applying under the Regular Decision program must submit application materials by January 1. All Regular Decision applicants, as well as those deferred from Early Decision, will receive notification in early April.

CAMPUS LIFE

The College's beautiful campus combines the educational opportunities of one of the nation's most prestigious institutions with an ideal New England setting. While the College itself provides many of the intellectual and cultural advantages usually found in more urban areas, Dartmouth's proximity to the mountains and rivers of Vermont and New Hampshire allows for a range of outdoor activities.

Each year, off-campus study is available through approximately 40 Dartmouth programs in approximately 20 countries. The programs are led by Dartmouth faculty, and students earn full academic credit for their participation. Foreign language programs are offered in Argentina, Brazil, France, Germany, Greece, Italy, Japan, Mexico, Morocco, the People's Republic of China, Russia, and Spain. Examples of other off-campus academic programs are the study of religion in Scotland; classics in Greece or Italy; earth sciences in the western United States; English literature in Ireland, Scotland, or Trinidad; geography in the Czech Republic; government in England or Washington, DC; philosophy in Scotland; earth sciences in Mexico; biology in the Caribbean; art history in Florence, Italy; environmental studies in Zimbabwe; and drama, economics, history, and music in England.

Dartmouth also offers approximately a dozen domestic exchange programs. Students can study at historically black colleges like Morehouse College and Spelman College or focus on an academic area, like biology at the University of California—San Diego or Native American Studies at Stanford University.

COST AND AID

Tuition, room, board, and fees for the 2002–2003 academic year total $37,770. Dartmouth guarantees meeting 100 percent of a student's demonstrated financial need. The average scholarship for those students receiving scholarship aid from the College is approximately $22,800.

DAVIDSON COLLEGE

GENERAL INFORMATION

With a strong dedication to undergraduate teaching and learning, Davidson, founded in 1837, has been recognized consistently as one of the country's most outstanding private liberal arts colleges. Davidson's 1,611 students, chosen not only for their academic promise but also for their character, bring curiosity, initiative, and an enthusiasm for learning to every aspect of campus life. They challenge each other with experiences such as researching the link between DNA and mental retardation, tutoring small children at an inner-city elementary school, competing in Division I athletics, and studying South Asian culture and history in India. In and out of class, Davidson students respect each other and learn from their differences. Through a broad education across many different academic disciplines, Davidson encourages students to engage in an academic exploration that leads to a lifelong appreciation of learning. The Davidson honor system forms a foundation for the campus community. The honor code represents a declaration by the entire College community-students, faculty, staff, and alumni-that an honorable course is the most just, and therefore the best. The honor code at Davidson is much more than just a pledge, it is a way of life. As a result, take-home tests are common. Students are allowed to self-schedule exams, and library stacks are open.

STUDENT BODY

Davidson students lead well-balanced lives, through opportunities to be involved daily in a myriad of activities that reflect a diversity of interests and talents. By participating in more than 100 campus organizations, students can influence college policy and campus life, organize campus events, and promote social causes and multicultural interests. Knobloch Campus Center (Alvarez College Union & Duke Family Performance Hall) opened in spring 2001, and has quickly become the focal point of campus social and cultural life. Inside the center, Alvarez College Union houses a café and grill, convenience store, the campus bookstore, a full-service U.S. Post Office, a fitness center, and the Smith 900 Room, a venue for concerts, lectures, and socials. Alvarez is also home to student government offices; The Davidsonian and Libertas publications; the Career Services office; and Davidson Outdoors, which sponsors excursions throughout the year to sites like the Florida Everglades and the Rio Grande. Knobloch also houses the critically acclaimed Duke Family Performance Hall, which opened in winter 2002 with a residency and performances by the Royal Shakespeare Company. The other important center of social life on campus is Patterson Court. Six national fraternities, three women's eating houses, a coed eating house, and the Black Student Coalition are located on Patterson Court. Each house has both dining and social facilities, and serves as a place where members eat meals and socialize. In addition to sponsoring large and small parties open to the entire campus community, members of each house are actively involved in a variety of community service projects. Davidson has a strong tradition of contributing to the local community through service projects. More than 800 students each year get involved in community outreach programs in Davidson and the greater Charlotte community. Davidson offers a range of athletic programs for serious athletes or just for fun. Approximately 85 percent of students participate in intramural or club sports, and about 25 percent play on one of the varsity teams, which average about a 50 percent walk-on rate. As one of the smallest colleges competing in the Division I of the NCAA, Davidson enrolls true scholar-athletes to play 11 different varsity sports for men and 10 for women.

Box 7156
Davidson, NC 28035-7156
Phone: 704-894-2230
Fax: 704-894-2016
Website: www.davidson.edu

ACADEMICS

Davidson encourages students to gain a lifelong appreciation of learning. At Davidson, you will be engaged in exploring the life of the mind. This exploration begins in the classroom, but you will be challenged and directed down pathways of learning well beyond the bounds of the campus. Davidson's liberal arts curriculum is dedicated to allowing students to explore their interests while at the same time challenging students to discover new interests, strengths, and talents. Davidson's core curriculum requires that each student take courses across all disciplines–humanities, social sciences, fine arts, and science and mathematics. Students can choose from among 20 majors, 10 minors, and 8 concentrations. In addition, students have the option of designing their own majors through the Center for Interdisciplinary Studies. Davidson offers pre-professional programs in medicine, dentistry, law, medical humanities, neuroscience, education, and engineering. Davidson incorporates a level of faculty-student research that is remarkable at a four-year, undergraduate college, with students presenting research papers at national professional conferences.

Great teaching reflects the heart and soul of the Davidson experience. With a student/faculty ratio of 10.5:1, the capstone of the Davidson academic experience is the close relationships that Davidson enables students to develop with professors. All classes are taught by full professors, 98 percent of whom hold terminal degrees in their fields. Classes are small, with the average class size of no more than 20 students. Small classes allow Davidson's 156 full-time faculty members to have engaging and thought-provoking discussions within the classroom-a time when students are encouraged to share their ideas and opinions and to actively participate in the learning process. Rounding out on-campus perspectives, nearly 70 percent of Davidson students study abroad during their college career.

ADMISSIONS

In selecting a first-year class, Davidson seeks students who will contribute to the life of the College both inside and outside of the classroom. Thus, as they shape a first-year class, the members of the Office of Admission and Financial Aid review each application with great care, looking at the high school record, application essays, personal activities and achievements, recommendations, and test scores. The rigor of the student's high school curriculum is of prime importance in the admission decision. Therefore, Davidson encourages students to take advantage of the most challenging curriculum available to them in their high schools. Three-quarters of Davidson students graduated in the top tenth of their high school classes. The middle 50 percent of those accepted had combined SAT I scores of 1320–1460, and of those students who submitted ACT scores, the middle 50 percent scored between 28 and 32.

CAMPUS LIFE

Located in the town of Davidson, 20 miles from Charlotte, North Carolina, Davidson students enjoy the best of two worlds-the freedom and safety of living in a small college community, and access to one of America's fastest growing cities. Davidson students are an active part of the town, frequenting coffee shops and restaurants and volunteering in the community at local schools and retirement homes. In Charlotte, students explore internships with businesses, hospitals, and law firms and enjoy access to cultural, arts, and sporting events.

About 60 percent of the student body takes advantage of Davidson's extensive study abroad options, studying literature in England and Germany, art history in Italy and France, culture in India and Ghana, and environmental issues in Kenya, Australia, and the Virgin Islands. Students can also participate in exchange programs with Howard University and Morehouse College, cross register with other Charlotte-area colleges and universities, study marine biology on the North Carolina coast, or spend a semester in Philadelphia or Washington, DC.

COST AND AID

Thanks to careful financial management and a strong endowment that supports academic programs, Davidson is able to keep its costs moderate in comparison to other colleges and universities of similar quality and national stature. Tuition and fees pay only about 59 percent of the actual cost of educating each Davidson student, and funds of the College make up the difference. Fees for the 2002–2003 academic year are as follows:

Required charges (tuition, laundry, and activity fee): $24,930

Room: $3,746

Board: $3,348

Total: $32,024

DENISON UNIVERSITY

GENERAL INFORMATION

You'll feel a sense of momentum and vitality as you arrive at Denison University's picturesque 1,200-acre campus in Granville, Ohio. An independent, residential college of liberal arts and sciences for men and women, Denison was founded in 1831. It is steeped in tradition and focused on the success of its approximately 2,000 students who can select from more than 43 courses of study and 9 preprofessional programs. Denison has an alumni body of 26,000 and an endowment of $430 million that places it among the top colleges and universities in the United States. U.S. Senator Richard Lugar and Walt Disney Co. President/CEO Michael Eisner are among its well-known alumni.

Denison is situated atop a ridge overlooking Granville, a quaint, New England-like village with shopping, restaurants, and services conveniently located adjacent to campus. Columbus—Ohio's capital and a metropolitan area with a population of 1.5 million—is just 35 minutes from campus.

The University has begun work on a $60 million construction project, its most ambitious in more than a quarter-century. Scheduled for completion in 2003, the project will include a two-acre Campus Common framed by the state-of-the-art Samson Talbott Hall of Biological Science and the Burton D. Morgan Center for student, faculty, and alumni-related activities.

STUDENT BODY

Through the Denison Campus Government Association, students budget and direct such campus organizations as the Student Senate, FM radio station, Denison Film Society, and campus newspaper. Students are strongly represented on the governance councils of the University.

ACADEMICS

Denison expects its students to profit from exposure to a broad liberal arts education and to achieve proficiency in a major field. Degree requirements include successful completion of approximately 35 courses (127 semester hours) with a 2.0 or better average, both overall and in the major and minor fields; fulfillment of all general education requirements; achievement of passing scores on comprehensive examinations if required in the major; and fulfillment of minimum residence requirements.

About one-third of a student's coursework (13 courses) must be chosen from core course offerings in the humanities, sciences, social sciences, and fine arts. Another one-third is taken in the major field of study, and the remainder is fulfilled in electives. Denison offers opportunities for directed study and independent study. Students may receive advanced placement or credit through College Board's Advanced Placement (AP) tests or proficiency examinations. Credit is automatically given for an AP score of 4 or 5. Denison's academic calendar consists of two semesters and an optional May term that includes internships and travel seminars. The academic year begins in late August and ends in early May.

Denison offers the degrees of Bachelor of Arts, Bachelor of Science, and Bachelor of Fine Arts. Departmental, interdepartmental, and individually designed majors, as well as concentrations within the departments, are available within the degree programs. The BA can be earned through departmental programs in art (history or studio), biology, chemistry, cinema, communication, computer science, dance, economics, education, English, environmental studies, geology, history, international studies, mathematical sciences, modern languages (Chinese, French, German, and Spanish), music, philosophy, physical education, physics, political science, psychology, religion, sociology/anthropology, and theater, and through interdepartmental programs in black studies, classical studies, East Asian studies, educational studies, and women's studies. Interdisciplinary programs leading to a BA in philosophy, politics, and economics (PPE) and media technology and arts (MTA) have recently been added. The BS is offered in biochemistry, biology, chemistry, computer science, geology, mathematical sciences, physics, and psychology. The BFA majors are art (studio) and theater. Concentrations can be arranged in astronomy, geophysics, Latin American and Caribbean studies, and neuroscience. Certification is available in secondary education and organizational studies.

1 Southridge Road, Box H
Granville, OH 43023
Phone: 740-587-6276
Fax: 740-587-6306
Website: www.denison.edu

DENISON UNIVERSITY

Pre-professional preparation is available in business, dentistry, engineering, forestry, law, medicine, nursing, occupational therapy, and veterinary medicine. Denison offers 3–2 programs in engineering with Rensselaer Polytechnic Institute, Washington University, Case Western Reserve University, and Columbia University; in forestry and environmental studies with Duke University; in natural resources management with the University of Michigan; and in medical technology with Rochester General Hospital.

Denison's 187 full-time and 7 part-time faculty members are deeply committed to teaching and to students. Many have national reputations in their fields; each year faculty members win national awards for teaching excellence. Ninety-eight percent of faculty members have an earned doctorate or terminal degree in their field. The student/faculty ratio is 12:1. Small classes (the average class size is 20) and unique opportunities for one-on-one research with a faculty member encourage active learning. All incoming first-year students are assigned a faculty advisor to assist with course selection and to ease the transition to college life.

ADMISSIONS

Entering first-year students should have earned at least 16 academic credits in secondary school, including 4 years of college-preparatory English. Strongly recommended are 3 years each of mathematics, science, foreign language, and social studies. A candidate for admission must file a formal application and submit scores on either the SAT I or ACT. The Admissions Committee is particularly interested in the quality of the academic program, the grade point average, and test results from the SAT I or ACT. The other selection criteria are written references from a college advisor and an academic teacher, extracurricular and personal accomplishments, and the student's essay on the application. An interview is recommended but not required. It is Denison's goal to enroll a broad cross section of students. Denison University admits students of any race, color, religion, age, personal handicap, sex, sexual orientation, veteran status, and national or ethnic origin.

CAMPUS LIFE

The 1,200-acre Denison campus is located on a hill overlooking the village of Granville, in central Ohio. Founded in 1805 by settlers from Massachusetts, Granville bears a marked resemblance to a New England village. Columbus, the state capital, 27 miles to the west, is the nearest large city and is served by numerous national airlines. Newark, seven miles to the east, is an industrial city of 50,000 people. Granville has several fine restaurants and shopping facilities, but those seeking the larger department stores go to Newark or Columbus. The University is a cultural and recreational center for the local community, and the Denison Community Association encourages student participation in community service activities, providing nearly 10,000 hours of volunteer fieldwork each year. State parks, lakes, bike trails, and ski areas are nearby.

Denison cooperates in off-campus study programs sponsored and supervised by recognized American colleges and universities and by the Great Lakes Colleges Association. Qualified students may take a semester or a year of international study in Africa, Asia, Europe, Latin America, or the Middle East. Domestic programs, offered on a one- or two-semester basis, include the Washington Semester, the Philadelphia Semester, the Fine Arts Program in New York City, the Oak Ridge Science Semester, the Newberry Library Program in Chicago, the Border Studies Program, and linkages with historically black universities.

COST AND AID

Annual charges for the 2002–2003 academic year are as follows: tuition $23,680; room and board $6,880; and student fees $500. An estimated $1,800 for books, travel, and personal expenses brings the total annual cost to $32,860.

DEVRY UNIVERSITY

AT A GLANCE

DeVry University provides a high-quality, career-oriented education through campuses nationwide. Today DeVry University is one of the largest private higher education networks in North America, offering students undergraduate and graduate degree programs in business, technology and management.

DeVry has long recognized the need for flexible, career-based programs offered in a variety of formats to suit the needs of a diverse student population. Since the school opened in 1931, the DeVry system has grown to serve annually some 52,000 students building solid careers by taking advantage of DeVry's onsite and online learning opportunities.

Keller Graduate School of Management of DeVry University offers master's programs in business administration, accounting and financial management, human resource management, information systems management, project management, public administration and telecommunications management.

Recently DeVry launched its DeVry University Centers to enable students who are balancing job, family and school commitments to more easily pursue their educational goals, as well as to accommodate those living in geographic areas not served by a DeVry campus.

DeVry campuses in the U.S. are accredited by The Higher Learning Commission and are members of the North Central Association (NCA), 30 N LaSalle St, Chicago, IL 60602, 800-621-7440.

DeVry University undergraduate campus locations include:

Addison, IL

Alpharetta, GA

Arlington, VA

Chicago, IL

Colorado Springs, CO

Columbus, OH

Decatur, GA

Federal Way, WA

Fort Washington, PA

Fremont, CA

Houston, TX

Irving, TX

Kansas City, MO

Long Beach, CA

Long Island City, NY

Miramar, FL

North Brunswick, NJ

Orlando, FL

Phoenix, AZ

Pomona, CA

Tinley Park, IL

West Hills, CA

Westminster, CO

Calgary, AB, Canada

Mississauga, ON, Canada

MAJORS AND DEGREES OFFERED

DeVry University offers bachelor's, associate and diploma programs that enable you to pursue the academic path that meets your goals and needs. Below are degree programs offered by DeVry University (program availability can vary by location):

Business administration (also offered online)

Business operations

Computer engineering technology

Computer information systems (also offered online)

Computer technology

Electronics & computer technology

Electronics engineering technology

Information technology (also offered online)

Network systems administration

Technical management (also offered online)

Telecommunications management

ACADEMIC PROGRAMS

DeVry's on-campus undergraduate programs give you the flexibility and convenience of morning, afternoon, evening, and weekend schedules at locations close to work or home. Class schedules are designed to benefit both full-time and part-time workers. DeVry's programs give you the technical knowledge and hands-on experience you'll need to secure the future's most promising careers.

DeVry Online's distance learning programs integrate today's high-tech Internet capabilities with DeVry's proven educational methodologies. This innovative "anywhere, anytime" educational delivery system extends the offering of DeVry programs to students whose schedules preclude their conveniently attending classes on campus, and to students who live beyond commuting distance to a DeVry campus.

DRAKE UNIVERSITY

GENERAL INFORMATION

Students are drawn to Drake University for its diverse course offerings, emphasis on teaching, and thriving intellectual environment. Drake offers more than 70 majors, covering subjects from the liberal arts to professional and pre-professional programs. The University employs professors who demonstrate a dedication to students along with academic prowess. Students benefit from the low 13:1 student/faculty ratio, and they never take classes from graduate students or teaching assistants. Drake enrolls a heterogeneous group of 5,100 students, who arrive from 48 U.S. states and approximately 60 foreign countries. The 1,700 students who live in campus residence halls enjoy high-speed Internet access from their dorm rooms. Drake prides itself on alumni success, noting that more than 97 percent of Drake graduates embark on careers or start graduate programs during their first six months out of school.

Drake grants master's degrees in the following areas: accounting, business administration, education, and public administration. Students may also pursue their Doctor of Pharmacy, Doctor of Jurisprudence, and Doctor of Education degrees. Joint degrees are also available in MBA/JD, MPA/JD, MBA/PharmD, MPA/PharmD, and PharmD/JD.

STUDENT BODY

With more than 160 organizations operating on campus, students can always find activities that suit their interests. Elected student representatives run the Student Senate, which represents student opinions and interests regarding campus policies. Students also hold seats on committees in the Faculty Senate. Another student organization, the Student Activities Board, is charged with putting on special events, including cultural celebrations, social functions, guest speakers, and concerts. Drake also maintains the Residence Hall Association, composed of students who manage the logistics and activities surrounding residential life.

ACADEMICS

From their first classes on the Drake campus, students have the chance to learn in an individualized, challenging, and supportive environment. Research opportunities abound; students work closely with their professors and often publish their findings. With more than 160 student-run organizations on campus, there is an outlet for every interest. Students complement their class work with participation in student teaching programs, performing arts projects, the campus newspaper and other publications, or on the Drake radio and television station. Internships allow students to investigate career paths and network with professionals in their field. Graduates join the distinguished ranks of the 45,000 Drake alumni, who provide contacts in all industries across the country and globe. Students at Drake benefit from a combination of liberal arts training and professional preparation.

Through the Drake Curriculum, all students take interactive classes that develop their critical thinking and expressive skills. Students also receive personalized academic advising. At the end of their four years, students undertake the Senior Capstone, which is a research project, thesis, or other major work that shows the concepts and skills the student has acquired at Drake. To complete an undergraduate degree, students must earn at least 124 semester hours. Drake's Honors Program is open to top students who wish to undertake a rigorous, interdisciplinary course of study. Many students tailor their education to their personal interests with internships, undergraduate research, independent study, and combined bachelor's and master's degree programs. Drake awards credit for participation in the College Board's Advanced Placement Program, the International Baccalaureate, and the College-Level Examination Program. The academic calendar is made up of two semesters and additional summer sessions.

Those studying in the College of Arts and Sciences receive a classic liberal arts education, preparing them for futures in science, mathematics, politics, or the arts. Students may earn their Bachelor of Arts and Bachelor of Science degrees in the following areas: anthropology and sociology; astronomy; biochemistry, cell and molecular biology; biology; chemistry; computer science; English; English/writing; environmental policy; environmental science; ethics; history; international relations; law, politics, and society; mathematics; mathematics education (secondary); philosophy; physics; politics; psychology; religion; rhetoric and communication studies; and sociology. Some students design their own majors, while others opt for "open enrollment" and do not immediately declare a major.

The University also administers pre-professional study and combined degree programs in church vocations, dentistry, law, medicine and allied fields, and physics/engineering.

Approved concentrations include aging studies, cultural studies, geography, Latin American studies, multicultural studies, neuroscience, and women's studies.

Students who attend the School of Fine Arts pursue their Bachelor of Arts, Bachelor of Fine Arts, Bachelor of Music, and Bachelor of Music Education degrees. The available fields include art, music, and theatre arts with a dual focus on teaching excellence and artistic creativity. Holding accreditation from by the National Association of Schools of Art and Design, Drake's Department of Art and Design offers instruction in art history, drawing, graphic design, painting, printmaking, and sculpture. Students in the Department of Music select from degrees in church music, music education, music performance, and piano pedagogy. Other alternatives exist, such as a Bachelor of Arts degree with a music major, a Bachelor of Music degree with elective studies in business, and a Bachelor of Music with a jazz studies concentration. Those who wish to study theatre, acting, directing, theatre design, musical theatre, and theatre education enroll in the Department of Theatre Arts. Students may also choose to study art, music, and theatre arts under the undeclared option.

Students enrolled in Drake University's College of Business and Public Administration complete their undergraduate degree of Bachelor of Science in Business Administration in four years. The available majors include accounting, accounting/other business major, actuarial science, actuarial science/finance, economics, finance, general business, information systems, insurance concentration, international business, management, and marketing. The College allows interdisciplinary majors, combinations of majors, and open business (undeclared) status. The College is accreditation by the AACSB-The International Association for Management Education.

Students attending the College of Pharmacy and Health Sciences complete a two-year pre-pharmacy program then begin a four-year PharmD program. The College is accredited by the American Council on Pharmaceutical Education and belongs to the American Association of Colleges of Pharmacy.

Students who wish to pursue a Bachelor of Arts majors in advertising (management and creative tracks), electronic media (broadcast news and radio/television), magazines, news/Internet, and public relations study in the School of Journalism and Mass Communication. The School allows an open enrolled (undeclared) option and holds accreditation from the Accrediting Council on Education in Journalism and Mass Communication.

In addition, the College of Arts and Sciences, the College of Business and Public Administration, and the School of Journalism offer combined 3+3 programs with the Drake Law School. Students in this program can obtain their undergraduate degrees in three years in one of the aforementioned schools, then pursue a law degree for the next three years at the Law School.

2507 University Avenue
Des Moines, IA 50311-4505
Phone: 515-271-3181
Fax: 515-271-2831
Website: www.choose.drake.edu

Programs at the School of Education lead to degrees in elementary education, secondary education, and rehabilitation services. Students may earn a Bachelor of Science or Bachelor of Arts degree that are tailored to prepare graduates for employment in elementary or secondary schools. Other options include adding middle school and coaching endorsements to teaching credentials. Drake University has belonged to the American Association of Colleges for Teacher Education since the association's founding.

Drake employs professors who prioritize teaching while remaining active in their fields. The 267 full-time faculty members make for a low 13:1 student/faculty ratio. Students work closely with their instructors; even top professors teach lower-division courses, and every student receives guidance from an advisor.

ADMISSIONS

While admission is selective, Drake University considers the full record of each candidate for admission. Since the University prefers students with varied talents and interests, there is no single and inflexible set of admission standards applied to all candidates for admission. The admission process involves a comprehensive review of a student's academic background (courses and grades), standardized test scores (ACT or SAT I), personal essay, recommendations, and activities both in high school and the community. Drake University does not discriminate on the basis of age, sex, sexual orientation, race, religion, color, national or ethnic origin, or disability. A complete application file for first-year admission contains the following items: a completed application form, the $25 nonrefundable application fee, the High School Report and Counselor Recommendation Form, an official high school transcript, and ACT or SAT I scores. While it is not mandatory, applicants are strongly encouraged to write a personal essay as well. Online applications are available; students who submit their materials online do not pay the application fee.

Students applying to transfer to Drake are required to submit official transcripts for all previous college-level course work. Drake begins accepting applications for the fall, spring, or summer terms on October 1. After that date, students can expect to receive a decision within three weeks of receipt of their applications. March 1 is the priority deadline for consideration for admission and merit- and need-based financial aid.

Candidates should contact:

Drake University
Office of Admission
2507 University Avenue
Des Moines, IA 50311
Phone: 800-44-DRAKE, ext. 3181 or 515-271-3181 locally and outside the U.S.
Fax: 515-271-2831
Website: www.choose.drake.edu

CAMPUS LIFE

Students take advantage of Drake's location in Des Moines, Iowa, the state capital and a thriving business center. Internships are available in fields such as government, banking, insurance, publishing, nonprofit organizations, and health care, and nearly three-quarters of students participate in at least one internship during their four years at the University. Students venture off campus to visit facilities such as the convention center, the renowned art center, or the civic center. They can also catch professional sporting events, hit the bike trails, relax in the park, or walk around the downtown skywalk system.

Many students take advantage of overseas studies options offered by the Center for International Programs and Services. Through the Center's work with international institutions and consortia, semester- and year-long programs are offered in Argentina, Australia, Austria, Belgium, Belize, Bolivia, Botswana, Brazil, Cameroon, Canada, Central America, Chile, China, Costa Rica, Cuba, Czech Republic, Dominican Republic, Ecuador, England, France, Germany, Ghana, Greece, Guatemala, Hong Kong, Hungary, India, Indonesia, Ireland, Italy, Jamaica, Japan, Jordan, Kenya, Latin America, Madagascar, Mali, Malta, Mexico, Morocco, Namibia, Nepal, the Netherlands, New Zealand, Nicaragua, Northern Ireland, Poland, Russia, Samoa, Scotland, South Africa, Spain, Sweden, Switzerland, Taiwan, Tanzania, Thailand, Tibet, Tunisia, Turkey, Uganda, Venezuela, Vietnam, Wales, and Zimbabwe. In addition, students can participate in the Semester at Sea program.

COST AND AID

Tuition and fees totaled $18,510 in 2002–2003. Room and board cost $5,490 annually.

D'YOUVILLE COLLEGE

GENERAL INFORMATION

Focused on professional studies and the liberal arts, D'Youville College is a private institution with a coed student body of 2,400. Founded in 1908, D'Youville has a proud history: The College was the first in western New York to grant undergraduate degrees to female students. Today, D'Youville offers degrees in 30 different undergraduate and graduate programs. The College's holistic approach to education, as well as the 14:1 student/faculty ratio, encourages personal development alongside of academic pursuits. D'Youville hosts one of the nation's biggest four-year, private nursing programs. The multiple-option Nursing Degree Program allows students to choose between BSN, BSN/MS (five years), and RN to BSN courses of study. Students can also undertake a five-year program resulting in a combined bachelor's/master's (BS/MS) degree in the areas of education, occupational therapy, international business, and dietetics. Those seeking master's degrees may apply in elementary, secondary, special education, community health nursing, physical therapy, dietetics, occupational therapy, international business, and health services administration. Upon graduating from D'Youville, 96 percent of students either secure jobs in their chosen field or go on to graduate school.

The College's location by the Niagara River and Lake Erie provides breathtaking vistas, enjoyed by students living in Marguerite Hall. The Koessler Administration Building houses the president's offices as well as the offices of admissions, financial aid, student accounts, and the registrar. The Learning Center and Kavinoky Theatre also share that building. When it's time to relax, students head to the Student Center, outfitted with a gymnasium, swimming pool, weight-training room, dance studio, general recreation center, pub, and dining facilities. Campus life thrives thanks to student organizations including social groups, academic clubs, and the College newspaper. For athletes of any persuasion, the ski club, intramural teams, and NCAA Division III intercollegiate sports (baseball, basketball, volleyball, golf, cross-country, soccer, and softball) provide athletic activities.

STUDENT BODY

Student representatives elected to the Student Association (SA) work with the administration and faculty to make decisions regarding the College's academic, social, and moral life. The SA comprises the Executive Council and Student Senate, and any D'Youville attendees can run for a position or participate in any of the 17 related academic and social organizations.

ACADEMICS

Students select a major based on their interests and career goals. Any area of study provides a solid background for post-college pursuits. In order to graduate, students must fulfill the requirements of their department, complete the core requirements, pass a total of 120 credit hours, and maintain a minimum grade point average of 2.0. The core requirements cover humanities, 24 hours; social science, 12 hours; science, 7 hours; mathematics/computer science, 6 hours; and electives, 9 hours. Most students take five or six classes, approximately 16 credit hours, each semester. Internships can compliment classroom experiences in any course of study. Students who are undecided regarding their major can benefit from participation in the Career Discovery Program. Over the course of two years, students explore career options through classes and internships. The academic year is divided into two 15-week semesters. Students complete the final exams for the first semester prior to winter break. Summer programs, lasting eight weeks, are also available for certain classes. In order to better prepare for D'Youville courses, students can find assistance at the College Learning Center. For help in a specific subject, the Tutor Bank provides trained peer tutors.

One D'Youville Square, 320 Porter Avenue
Buffalo, NY 14201
Phone: 716-881-7600
Fax: 716-881-7790
Website: www.dyc.edu

D'Youville students can pursue the degrees of Bachelor of Arts (BA), Bachelor of Science (BS), Bachelor of Science in Nursing (BSN), and five-year, two-degree BS+MS programs. They choose from majors including accounting, biology, biology, business management, education, career discovery program, creative writing, dietetics, education (elementary, secondary, and special), English, English education, global studies, health services, history, history education, international business, informational technology, nursing, occupational therapy, philosophy, psychology, physical therapy, physician assistant studies, pre-professional studies (dental, law, medicine, and veterinary studies), and sociology. For the BS+MS programs, achieved over five years, the courses of study include dietetics, international business, nursing, occupational therapy, informational technology (BS) plus international business (MS), and education. Additionally, students may elect to pursue a six-year combined bachelor's and master's degree in physical therapy. We are now offering a doctoral degree, EdD, in health policy and health education.

Students receive personal attention thanks to the 14:1 student/faculty ratio and the faculty's commitment to individual advising. Full-time professors all have their doctorate or other advanced degree. No teaching assistants serve on the faculty.

ADMISSIONS

In order to enroll, students must graduate from high school or pass the GED. Applicants are encouraged to demonstrate coursework in college-preparatory classes: English, history, and a series of classes in math or science. Applicants must also submit their SAT I or ACT scores. The Admissions Committee considers applicants' high school grade point average, rank in class, and scores on the SAT I or ACT. Those who have earned Advanced Placement units from high school coursework may apply it at D'Youville. Applicants who fall slightly below standard admissions requirements may attend the College with a less intensive class load.

CAMPUS LIFE

Located in Buffalo, the D'Youville campus enjoys a residential setting. The downtown shopping center, the Kleinhans Music Hall, the Albright–Knox Art Gallery, two museums, and several theaters are all nearby. Toronto, a mere 90 miles away, offers additional metropolitan attractions, and Niagara Falls can be reached in just 25 minutes. Skiers can make it to Holiday Valley in about an hour. Buffalo can be reached via the New York State Thruway, Amtrak, Greyhound and Trailways bus lines, and most major airlines. D'Youville connects itself to the community by forging relationships with local schools, hospitals, and social groups. Buffalo is home to more than 60,000 college students in all. Specific departments affiliate with the appropriate area organizations. For instance, the nursing program works with 13 local hospitals and public health agencies. Nearby elementary, junior high, and secondary schools, as well as special education centers, are available for student-teaching assignments for those in the education program. D'Youville students pursuing degrees in occupational therapy, physical therapy, and the physician assistant program can get hands-on experience at clinics across the country.

COST AND AID

In 2002–2003, tuition totaled $6,568 each semester, with another $3,280 charged for room and board. A mandatory College fee is assessed according to the number of credit hours a student enrolls in. The $40 Student Association feed defrays the costs of concerts, yearbooks, guest lectures, and other activities. Accepted students are required to pay a $100 deposit ($150 for dietetics, physician assistant studies, occupational therapy, and physical therapy programs), which is credited to tuition.

EARLHAM COLLEGE

GENERAL INFORMATION

Located in Richmond, Indiana, Earlham College is a four-year, coeducational liberal arts college, founded in 1847 by the Religious Society of Friends (Quakers). Today Earlham sits on 800 wooded acres along beautiful National Road US 40. Undergraduate enrollment is 1,080 students, hailing from 47 states and 28 foreign countries. Earlham offers Bachelor of Arts degrees in more than 30 academic fields and allows students to design their own, individually tailored major. The school also offers cooperative programs in business, engineering, and teaching, and pre-professional programs in law, medicine, and ministry. Students can choose to minor in almost every major field as well as in Jewish studies, legal studies, and Quaker studies. Earlham College is also home to the renowned Lilly Library, acknowledged to be the foremost undergraduate teaching library in the nation. Earlham boasts strong academic programs, distinguished faculty, and a unique sense of community. With an excellent student/faculty ratio of 11:1, Earlham students enjoy generous interaction with their instructors, who encourage an active, involved approach to learning.

The creativity, research, and academic excellence displayed by the college's students and faculty has been noted through a number of grants and fellowships from such prominent sources as the Ford Foundation, Danforth Foundation, IBM, Woodrow Wilson Foundation, Fulbright-Hayes Foundation, Kellogg Foundation, Japan Foundation, Lilly Endowment Inc., National Endowment for the Humanities, National Science Foundation, Carnegie-Mellon Foundation, and the Howard Hughes Medical Institute. Earlham is distinguished by its commitment to undergraduate education and its unique international orientation. Earlham College believes that an international, cultural education is essential in the modern global society.

As a member of the "International 50," Earlham is nationally renowned for superb international education programs. Earlham has been on the cutting edge of international education since 1897, when it first began developing international programs. Today, Earlham remains on the forefront, offering extensive national and international opportunities, and a cutting edge program in Japanese studies. The College offers 25 off-campus study programs in the United States, Asia, Latin America, Europe, Africa, and the Middle East. Currently, only 1 percent of undergraduates in the U.S. choose to study abroad during college; at Earlham, 65 percent of students study on an off-campus program before graduating.

Earlham seeks to create a diverse college community, and aims to support and encourage Latino/a, African American, and Asian American students. More than 25 percent of the current student population is nonwhite. The College advisor on multicultural issues, The Associate Dean for Multicultural Affairs, is always available to act as a counselor for individual students. There are many on campus housing facilities and cultural centers, such as Beit Kehillah (Jewish Cultural Center), Cunningham African American Cultural Center, International Cultural Center, and Latino and Asian American Cultural Center.

Over 90 percent of undergraduates live in the 7 campus residence halls and 27 student houses. There are also several theme residences on campus: Casa Hispana, Deutsches Haus, Inter-Faith House, Japan House, Maison Francaise, Miller Farm (Agriculture), Peace House, Service Learning House, and Wellness House. Earlham College is described in Loren Pope's book, Colleges that Change Lives. He says: "If every college and university sharpened young minds and consciences as effectively as Earlham does, this country would approach Utopia. . . . Earlham has made great contributions to education and quietly sets the standard."

STUDENT BODY

An active campus, the wide variety of student run associations and organizations at Earlham can meet every student's taste, interest or pastime. Student participate in music, theater, dance, social and political action, ethnic and international awareness, as well as intramural and varsity athletics. Students run an FM radio station, manage a food co-op, publish a campus newspaper, and produce a literary magazine, among other things. Earlham's Student Government makes decisions through consensus, rather than majority voting. Through consensus governance, group discussion and active listening are the tools through which decisions are made. Students are represented on virtually every committee or administrative group that makes decisions regarding student life and the business of the College. Earlham boasts a number of student run clubs and organizations, such as Women of Color, International Club, Action Against Rape, Committee for Justice in the Middle East, Committee in Solidarity with Latin America, Black Leadership Action Coalition, and Earlham Environmental Action Coalition. There are also many religious groups, such as Questing Catholics, Ecumenical Communion Group, Earlham Young Friends, Jewish Cultural Center, Bahai Club, and Fellowship of Christian Athletes.

ACADEMICS

Earlham College believes that success in the modern world depends on an ability to understand and make connections between distinct subject areas. With this philosophy, the undergraduate curriculum at Earlham is devised to prepare students for a life of critical knowledge and informed action. The College revised its general education program in 2002–2003, adapting its long-term mission to the changing needs of the present. The new requirements introduce students to ways of knowing rather than to specific disciplinary or divisional requirements. Through the core courses, students develop a deep understanding of one or more disciplines in their major of academic concentration. Majors are usually 8 to 10 courses in a single subject area, a research project or seminar in the final year of study, and a comprehensive examination given by the department. To graduate, students must complete 120 semester units and complete the two-year residency requirement. Earlham operates on a two semester academic calendar. In addition to the fall and spring semester, Earlham offers an optional May term. The College also sponsors a two-week summer program called Explore-A-College for high school students.

Earlham College Admissions, Drawer #192
Richmond, IN 47374
Phone: 765-983-1600
Fax: 765-983-1560
Website: www.earlham.edu

EARLHAM

Earlham confers the Bachelor of Arts (BA) degree in the following subject areas: African and African American studies, art, biochemistry, biology, business and nonprofit management, chemistry, classical studies, computer science, economics, education, English, environmental science, French, geoscience, German, history, human development and social relations, international studies, Japanese studies, Latin American studies, mathematics, music, peace and global studies, philosophy, physics/astronomy, politics, psychology, religion, sociology/anthropology, Spanish, theatre arts, and women's studies.

Students may choose to minor in most major areas, as well as in Japanese language, Jewish studies, journalism, legal studies, museum studies, outdoor education, Quaker studies, and Teaching English to Speakers of Other Languages (TESOL). There are also cooperative programs in business, engineering, and teacher education, and pre-professional programs in law, medicine, and ministry. Additional educational programs that are part of Earlham's broad general education program include living and learning in community, interpretative and comparative practices, and wellness and physical education. Students are encouraged to design their own major, and have the opportunity of completing a degree in three years, if possible.

Earlham's distinguished faculty is dedicated to teaching. The school has 92 fulltime teaching faculty members, 97 percent of whom hold a doctoral or terminal degree in their field. Faculty members are not just teachers, but advisors and mentors, research partners and friends. A large number of professors live close to campus and often invite students to their home.

ADMISSIONS

Admission is selective. Earlham considers the complete profile of every student when making admission decisions. In addition to the student's GPA and standardized test scores, Earlham considers the quality of the academic program followed in secondary school, teacher and counselor recommendations, the personal essay, and the interview. Strong candidates should follow a strong, college-preparatory program in high school. Earlham recommends that students take the SAT I, but accepts scores from the ACT. Though not required, interviews are strongly recommended. Students can request an Earlham application in September of their final year of high school. Students also have the option of downloading the college's application in PDF format, or applying online on the Earlham website. Earlham does accept the Common Application, and students who want to apply using the Common Application must submit the Supplemental Application Form.

Earlham offers Early Decision and Early Action programs. Students applying early decision must submit their application by December 1 and will be notified by December 15. Students applying through the early action (nonbinding) program must submit their application by January 1 and will be notified on February 1. All other applications must be received by February 15 and the school will inform candidates of their status by March 15. The application deadline for transfer students is April 1, with admission notification by April 15. The deadline for all students who are not U.S. citizens is February 1. Students may be accepted after the application deadline as long as there is space available in the incoming class.

CAMPUS LIFE

Nestled on the southwestern edge of Richmond, Indiana, Earlham is situated on a beautiful, 800-acre campus. Earlham takes an active part in the Richmond community and students often participate in local activities and events. A progressive city of 40,000, Richmond boasts a beautiful arboretum and parks, a symphony orchestra, several theater and opera groups, and the art association. In addition, the city is located in close proximity to other urban areas, such as Dayton, Ohio and Indianapolis, Indiana.

Earlham aims to educate students outside the classroom, adding real-world experience to academic studies. Over 65 percent of undergraduates participate on an off-campus program during their undergraduate career. Through off campus programs, students earn academic credit at no extra cost. Earlham sponsors or approves programs in Austria, China, the Czech Republic, England, France, Germany, Greece, Hong Kong, India, Japan, Kenya, Martinique, Mexico, the Middle East, Northern Ireland, Russia, Scotland, Senegal, and Spain. There are also a number of College-sponsored national programs in the southwest, Philadelphia, New York, Chicago, Woods Hole in Massachusetts, and Oak Ridge, Tennessee. New students have the opportunity to participate in a one-month backpacking trip in the Uinta Mountains of Utah or canoeing in Canada. Students also take courses throughout the U.S. during the optional May term. Every program is different and students in every field of study are encouraged to participate.

COST AND AID

Expenses for the 2003–2004 academic year total $29,976, including tuition, room, board, and student fees. As part of their tuition, students get admission to the Earlham Artist Series, athletic events, speakers, and on-campus lectures, concerts, and dances.

EMBRY RIDDLE AERONAUTICAL UNIVERSITY (FL)

GENERAL INFORMATION

At Embry-Riddle Aeronautical University, what we do—and do best—is teach the science, practice, and business of the world of aviation and aerospace. Since it was founded just 22 years after the Wright brothers' first flight, the University and its graduates have built an enviable record of achievement in every aspect of aviation and aerospace. Embry-Riddle is the world's most well-known, largest, and most prestigious university specializing in aviation and aerospace. The curriculum at Embry-Riddle covers the operation, engineering, research, manufacturing, marketing, and management of modern aircraft and the systems that support them. The University engages in extensive research, consulting, and related activities that address the unique needs of aviation, aerospace, and related industries. Residential campuses in Daytona Beach, Florida, and Prescott, Arizona, provide education in a traditional setting, while an extensive network of more than 120 teaching centers throughout the United States and Europe and a web-based distance learning program serve civilian and military working adults.

STUDENT BODY

The Office of Student Activities works to develop an active campus life by providing programs and activities for students to realize their academic and personal potential. The Student Activities office helps students feel connected to the university through leadership development programs, student organizations, and other programs. Student organizations continue to grow and thrive on campus. With approximately 120 organizations, there are many opportunities to become involved. Being part of a club enables students to enhance leadership skills through workshops, retreats, leadership programs and just plain fun! Campus organizations are categorized into 11 areas: aviation/aerospace, ethnic/cultural, fraternity/sorority life, honor society, military, professional/academic, religious, service, special interest, sports, and the student government association. The Office of Student Activities also offers a broad range of social and entertainment events. Weekly movies, concerts, speakers and sports provide a calendar of activities that appeals to virtually everyone!

ACADEMICS

If you want to fly, design or fix aircraft or space craft . . . If you want to manage or write about the aviation and aerospace industries . . . If you want to develop and analyze systems in aviation and aerospace . . . If you want to control air traffic or predict the weather . . . Embry-Riddle has the degree program for you! The Daytona Beach campus offers bachelor of science degrees in the following majors: Aeronautical Science, Aeronautical Systems Maintenance, Aerospace Electronics, Aerospace Engineering, Aerospace Studies, Air Traffic Management, Aircraft Engineering Technology, Applied Meteorology, Aviation Business Administration, Aviation Maintenance Management, Aviation Management, Avionics Engineering Technology, Civil Engineering, Communication, Computer Engineering, Computer Science, Engineering Physics, Human Factors Psychology, Management of Technical Operations, Professional Aeronautics, Safety Science, and Software Engineering.

The faculty at Embry-Riddle share a common interest with the students: a passion for aviation and aerospace. The faculty are career professionals who have years of practical experience in their professional fields and make themselves available to meet the needs of the students.

ADMISSIONS

There are three ways to apply for admission to Embry-Riddle Aeronautical University. You can apply online, download the application, or give us a call and we will gladly mail you an application and any information you may need. Please know that no matter how you submit it, your application will always be treated with professionalism and confidentiality. Our Directors of Admissions look forward to receiving and reviewing your application. New students are eligible for admission at the beginning of the fall, spring, and summer terms. Applications are accepted throughout the year, but we recommend that you apply as early as possible before the desired enrollment date. U.S. residents must apply 60 days prior to semester start. International students must apply 90 days prior to semester start.

600 South Clyde Morris Boulevard
Daytona Beach, FL 32114-3900
Phone: 386-226-6100
Fax: 386-226-7070
Website: www.embryriddle.edu

CAMPUS LIFE

The Daytona Beach campus is located next to the Daytona Beach International Airport. High-technology industries in the Daytona Beach and Orlando areas, as well as the Kennedy Space Center, provide the University with an outstanding support base. The 178-acre campus serves more than 4,900 undergraduate and graduate students in 43 buildings. The campus offers state-of-the-art facilities, including the 75,000-square-foot College of Aviation building; the Lehman Engineering and Technology Center, which houses the technology for distance learning, videoconferencing, decision support systems, and three-dimensional modeling; and the Airway Science Simulation Laboratory, which simulates the elements of the National Airspace System. The Advanced Flight Simulation Center, which contains an FAA Level-D Beech 1900D full-motion simulator, serves as a focal point for the University's relationships with airlines, governments, and corporations. The Student Village is the newest student housing complex on campus and is equipped with Internet and satellite-TV connectivity.

Embry-Riddle's cooperative education program is considered to be one of the best in the nation. Co-ops offer students an opportunity to gain practical work experience, earn college credit and develop valuable industry contacts and marketable skills. Companies like NASA, American Airlines, and Sikorsky have provided co-op students with real-world challenges including developing flight routes, scheduling flight crews, and participating in safety investigations.

COST AND AID

Daytona Beach campus undergraduate tuition and fees for fall 2003/spring 2004 are as follows:

Tuition:

1-11 credit hours: $865 per credit hour

12-16 credit hours: $10,350 per semester

More than 16 credit hours: $ 865 per credit hour

Flight instruction: average annual flight costs of $9,300

Average housing costs: $1,720 per semester for room, $1,305 per semester for board

Other miscellaneous mandatory fees apply.

EMERSON COLLEGE

GENERAL INFORMATION

The flagship programs at Emerson College are those in the fields of communications or the arts. Established in 1880, the College offers 20 undergraduate degrees and 12 graduate degrees. Modern facilities combined with an internationally recognized faculty make for an ideal learning environment. Emerson extends the study of communications and the arts to real experiences. The College is proud to host WERS 88.9 FM, New England's first noncommercial radio station, as well as the productions that take place in the Emerson Majestic Theatre. *Ploughshares*, the well-known literary journal, is run from the Emerson campus. Emerson has always been at the forefront of instruction in communications and performing arts. The pioneering children's theater program was initiated in 1919, and the undergraduate degree in broadcasting started in 1937. Other forward-looking program inceptions have included speech pathology and audiology (1935), educational FM radio (1949), closed circuit television (1955), and the BFA degree in film (1972). The nation's first graduate program in professional writing and publishing began at Emerson in 1980. Emerson's diverse student body of 3,700 (2,800 undergraduates) includes people from 60-plus foreign countries and 45 U.S. states and territories.

STUDENT BODY

Emerson students compliment their classroom studies with extra-curricular activities, choosing from numerous student clubs, performance organizations, 12 NCAA Division III intercollegiate teams, student publications, and honor societies. Many students in the communications field tie their studies to the on-campus radio stations, TV and video studios, campus cable network, and publications. In addition, students organize around cultural issues, nationality, spiritual practices, community service projects, professional goals, and performances.

ACADEMICS

Emerson's academic calendar is made up of two semesters. The College has accreditation from the New England Association of Schools and Colleges. In order to graduate, students must fulfill requirements in general education, liberal arts, and their major. Students may also earn credits for most majors through internships. Freshman seminars, honors classes, independent study opportunities, and interdisciplinary courses are available through the Institute for Liberal Arts and Interdisciplinary Studies. The College's School of the Arts and School of Communication administer 20 undergraduate and 12 graduate programs with internship opportunities offered in each. Further class variety can be accessed through the offerings within the six-member Boston ProArts Consortium.

Emerson College grants the BA, BFA, BS in Sp, MA, MFA, and MS in Sp. The School of the Arts and School of Communication runs undergraduate programs in acting, audio/radio, broadcast journalism, communication sciences and disorders, communication studies, dance/theatre, film, marketing communication: advertising and public relations, media studies, musical theatre, new media, political communication, print and multimedia journalism, production/stage management, television/video, theatre design/technology, theatre education, theatre studies, and writing, literature, and publishing.

Emerson has worked hard to assemble a dynamic and knowledgeable faculty, 70 percent of whom hold a PhD or their field's terminal degree. Most instructors continue their work as playwrights, editors, producers, writers, directors, entertainment lawyers, speech-language pathologists, journalists, and Web designers. Roughly 900 courses are available in a given semester. Students benefit from the low student/teacher ratio of 15:1. Along with the full-time instructors, qualified visiting lecturers and part-time faculty bring their expertise. They are often prestigious authors, producers, consultants, and researchers.

120 Boylston Street
Boston, MA 02116-4624
Phone: 617-824-8600
Fax: 617-824-8609
Website: www.emerson.edu

ADMISSIONS

Admitted students generally display a combination of academic and personal achievement. Applications submitted to the Office of Undergraduate Admission must include a completed application form, recommendations from a high school counselor and teacher, SAT I or ACT scores, and the student's official transcript from secondary school. Applicants are encouraged to put thought into their admission essay. Students may arrange an interview, but they are not mandatory. For acceptance to the Honor's Program, students must write an additional Honors Program Essay. Those seeking admission to programs in the Department of Performing Arts may have to audition or submit a portfolio. Competition for admission to Emerson is apparent in the fact that each year approximately 4,000 applicants vie for 650 spots in the incoming class.

Admissions decisions are based on candidates' personal qualifications and academic record. Applicants' transcripts must show 4 years of English and 3 years each of mathematics, science, social science, and foreign language. The deadline for early action applications is November 15. Those applying to start in September should meet the February 1 regular admission deadline. Transfer students have until March 1. The deadline for January admission is November 15; November 1 for transfer students. Tours are available for students who wish to visit the campus. To make arrangements, please call 617-824-8600 or go to: www.emerson.edu/undergraduate_admission.cfm.

CAMPUS LIFE

Situated directly on Boston Common, Emerson's Theatre District location allows for easy access to the Massachusetts State House, Freedom Trail, the Boston Public Garden, Newbury Street shops, the financial district, and a variety of restaurants and museums. Student life thrives in Boston thanks to the concentration of colleges and universities. Emerson students have the chance to partake in scenic harbor cruises, Boston Pops concerts, neighborhood festivals, Red Sox games, and the Boston Marathon. The campus is located right on the "T," providing easy public transportation to all parts of the city. A high percentage of Emerson attendees participate in internships, in Boston and around the nation. Those who want to hone their resumes for a career in entertainment head to the College's Los Angeles Center for a semester of work.

Emerson offers two overseas programs. The first takes place in Prague and focuses on film. The other is a semester spent in Holland's Kasteel Weel, a renovated thirteenth-century castle that serves as a jumping off point for trips across the Continent. Students at Emerson are also eligible to take classes at the other institutions involved in the Boston ProArts Consortium. These schools are Berklee College of Music, Boston Conservatory, Boston Architectural Center, Massachusetts College of Art, and the School of the Museum of Fine Arts.

COST AND AID

In 2002–2003, tuition was $21,120, room cost $5,680 for double occupancy, and board ran $3,862. Approximately $2,500 should be allotted for books, supplies, fees, health insurance, and personal expenses, including travel.

EMORY UNIVERSITY

GENERAL INFORMATION

Emory College combines the personal concern of a small, liberal arts college with the rich diversity of a major, urban university. The oldest and largest division of Emory University, Emory College has provided instruction in the arts and sciences to talented, highly motivated students for more than 165 years. Today its faculty of some 400 offers more than 1,200 courses to nearly 5,000 students drawn from every section of the United States and many foreign countries. The college offers students a wide range of off-campus programs, including the opportunity to participate in internship programs and to study abroad at institutions that include St. Andrews University in Scotland, the Pushkin Institute in Moscow, and Oxford University in England. In addition, a number of other study abroad programs are offered during the summer.

Emory College's resources are enriched by those of Emory University, a research university comprising Oxford College, a two-year college located in Oxford, Georgia; the Graduate School of Arts and Sciences; and the schools of business, law, medicine (including the allied health programs), nursing, public health, and theology. Emory University is a community of scholars where undergraduates, graduate and professional students, faculty, and staff benefit from the presence of each other as well as from the presence on or near campus of the U.S. Centers for Disease Control and Prevention, The Carter Center of Emory University and the Jimmy Carter Library and Museum, Yerkes National Primate Research Center, and the national headquarters of both the American Cancer Society and the American Academy of Religion.

To encourage full participation in its programs, Emory College requires that first-year students live on campus and urges other students to live on or near campus. The college's commitment to campus residence reflects its conviction that largeness of mind and spirit may be learned in dormitories and concert halls, on stages and playing fiends, as well as in classrooms, laboratories, and libraries. Students are, therefore, encouraged to participate in cocurricular activities that range from lectures, colloquia, and symposia, to concerts, exhibits, and plays, to intercollegiate and intramural sports, to scores of social clubs, civic organizations, and religious groups.

For more than half a century, academic integrity has been maintained at Emory through the student-initiated and student-regulated Honor Code. The responsibility for maintaining a standard of unimpeachable honor in all academic work falls on every individual who is a part of Emory University. Every student who chooses to attend Emory College agrees, as a condition of attendance, to abide by all provisions of the Honor Code as long as he or she remains a student in the college. By continued attendance in Emory College, students reaffirm their pledge to adhere to and uphold the provision of the Honor Code.

ACADEMICS

Both the Bachelor of Arts degree and the Bachelor of Science degree combine liberal studies with advanced studies. To earn the BA degree or the BS degree, a student must complete successfully 128 semester hours in approved academic courses plus four semester hours in physical education. No rigid program for either degree is prescribed by Emory College. Each student must design a program of study suited to individual interests and needs. To aid the student in this task and to ensure that no program is either too narrow or too diffuse, the college assigns advisors who work with students in planning their programs. The undergraduate education in Emory College comprises three overlapping components: general education requirements that provide a common core of substance and methodology; more intensive and advanced study in a major field; and free-ranging exploration by means of elective courses.

BA programs are offered in African American Studies, anthropology, anthropology and religion, art history, art history and history, Asian and Asian American Studies, biology, chemistry, classical civilization, classical studies, classics, classics and English, classics and history, classics and philosophy, comparative literature, computer science, dance and movement studies, economics, economics and history, economics and mathematics, educational studies, English, English and creative writing, English and history, environmental studies, film studies, French studies, German studies, Greek, history, history and religion, interdisciplinary studies in society and culture, international studies, Italian studies, Jewish studies, Latin, Latin American and Caribbean studies, mathematics, medieval and Renaissance studies, Middle Eastern studies, music, philosophy, philosophy and religion, physics, political science, psychology, psychology and linguistics, religion, religion and classical civilization, religion and Judaic studies, religion and sociology, Russian area studies, Russian language and cultures, Russian and linguistics, sociology, Spanish, theater studies, and women's studies. A co-major is offered in journalism.

BS programs are offered in anthropology and human biology, biology, chemistry, computer science, environmental science, mathematics, mathematics-computer science, neuroscience and behavioral biology, physics, and applied physics.

The Bachelor of Business Administration and the Bachelor of Science in Nursing degrees usually require that students spend two years in Emory College followed by either two years in the Roberto C. Goizueta Business School or the Nell Hodgson Woodruff School of Nursing of Emory University.

Boisfeuillet Jones Center
Atlanta, GA 30322
Phone: 404-727-6036
Fax: 404-727-4303
Website: www.emory.edu

EMORY

ADMISSIONS

Each year Emory College enrolls a first-year class of approximately 1,200 students. For admission, an applicant must be a secondary school graduate (unless applying under the Early Admission Program) with at least 16 acceptable units of academic work; must be recommended by the high school as possessing good character and strong academic potential; and must present satisfactory scores on the examinations of the College Entrance Examination Board (CEEB/SAT) or American College Testing Program (ACT). Emory strongly recommends a secondary school course of study that includes 4 years of English, 3 or 4 years of mathematics, at least 2 years of a foreign language, 2 or more years of history or social studies, 2 years of a laboratory science, and an introduction to music and art. Although the college regards the program above as highly desirable, it understands that some secondary schools provide limited opportunities, and it is more concerned with a student's overall achievement and promise than with the specific accumulation of credits. However, admitted students typically complete a program of study more challenging than these guidelines suggest, often exhausting the most rigorous courses offered at their secondary school.

The middle 50 percent of accepted students score between 640–720 on the Verbal portion of the SAT, and between 660–740 on the Math portion. On the ACT, the middle 50 percent of accepted students score between 29–33. Admitted candidates usually graduate from high school with at least a B+ average. The admission committed also looks for students who have demonstrated leadership and commitment in extracurricular activities and who will contribute to the dynamic community of Emory University. In addition, the Office of Admission encourages students to learn more about Emory College by visiting campus, ordering a Video Visit, talking with an admission counselor at a college fair, or attending an information session in your city.

Applicants may apply to Emory College through one of two early decision plans or regular decision. Students who have selected Emory as their first choice and who wish to receive an admission decision early in the year may choose one of two early decision options. To be considered in the first round of early decision, candidates must apply and all standardized testing must be completed by November 1. To be considered in the second round, candidates must complete all standardized testing by December 1 and must apply by January 1. Candidates in both rounds may be admitted, deferred to regular decision, or denied. Candidates will be notified by December 15 if applying early decision one, and February 1 if applying early decision two. Regular decision candidates should apply in the fall of their senior year, but no later than January 15. Standardized testing must be completed by January 1. Regular decision applicants may be admitted, waitlisted, or denied. Candidates for regular decision will be notified by April 1.

CAMPUS LIFE

Surrounded by a hilly residential section of Atlanta called Druid Hills, the Emory campus combines natural beauty with historic interest. Peavine Creek, a branch of Peachtree Creek, winds through the campus, Flowering shrubs-azaleas, dogwoods, and redbuds-abound; and towering trees-magnolias, maples, oaks, and pines-provide shade. Several buildings on the main quadrangle are listed in the National Register of Historic Places, and several markers on the campus commemorate historic events. A few miles south and west of the campus, the center of Atlanta bustles with activities stimulated by government, business, and transportation as well as research, education and culture. A contemporary city of energy and charm, Atlanta has increasingly gained national and international prominence. This was highlighted by its selection as the host of the 1996 Olympic Games. It is the home of some 20 colleges and universities. Several professional sports teams are based in the city. Opera and theatre have been strong since the opening of DeGive's Opera House in 1893. Today Atlanta's Woodruff Arts Center includes the High Museum of Art and the Alliance Theatre as well as the Atlanta Symphony and Chorus. Located more than one thousand feet above sea level, Atlanta offers four distinct seasons. A few hours north of the city, students hike on the Appalachian Trail, canoe and raft on the Chattanooga, Chestatee, and Hiawassee rivers, or ski on Sugar Mountain. East and south, they swim and sun on the coasts of South Carolina, Georgia, and Florida.

The college offers students a wide range of off-campus programs, including the opportunity to participate in internship programs and to study abroad at institutions that include St. Andrews University in Scotland, the Pushkin Institute in Moscow, and Oxford University in England. In addition, a number of other study abroad programs are offered during the summer.

COST AND AID

Estimated expenses for the 2002–2003 academic year include $26,600 for tuition, $332 for fees, $9,9198 for room and board, $700 for books, and $600 for travel. Estimated expenses total $37,430.

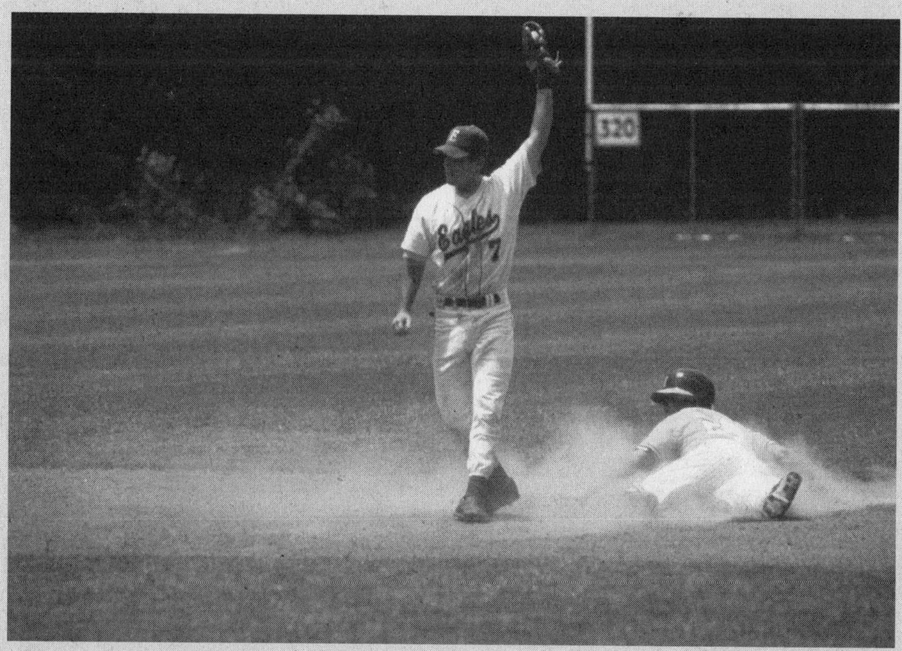

EUGENE LANG COLLEGE/NEW SCHOOL UNIVERSITY

GENERAL INFORMATION

Eugene Lang College, a division of New School University, focuses on the study of liberal arts. The College is marked by its urban setting and progressive attitude toward scholarship. Specifically, students and faculty are united by their thirst for freedom in intellectual pursuits. Also, students take responsibility in steering their own course of study. Students get the intimacy of a small school with the resources of a larger institution. Lang's 630 students form a diverse group. Close to half of the student body is not from the New York City area. In fact, 13 countries and 43 states are represented; 3 percent of students are foreign citizens. Women outnumber men three to one. Nearly one-quarter of students identify as minorities. Some students live on campus while others commute. University-run housing is available close to the campus, allotted first to those in their first year at Lang. Students participate in a wide variety of extracurricular activities, based around the literary journal, performances, political organizations, social groups, and cultural clubs. The Office of Student Development helps to facilitate many of these organizations. Activities take place on campus and throughout the city. Since the 1919 inception of the New School for Social Research, the campus has drawn forward-thinking scholars and artists. The founders, John Dewey, Alvin Johnson, and Thorstein Veblen, created an environment for groundbreaking scholarship, bringing W.E.B. DuBois to teach classes in black culture and race and Sandor Ferenezi (who worked with Freud) to teach psychoanalysis. Other instructors in this illustrious tradition have included Martha Graham, Aaron Copland, and Thomas Hart Benton. Currently, Robert Heilbroner, Eric Hobsbawm, Jerome Bruner, and Rayna Rapp are a few of the faculty members, renowned in their fields, that lend their guidance to Lang College students. The University comprises additional divisions to suit particular pursuits. Students in The New School division choose from more than 2,000 classes each term. The Graduate Faculty of Political and Social Science, known at its 1933 founding as the University in Exile, offers MA and PhD degrees. Students may work toward their MA or MPS degree at the Robert J. Milano Graduate School of Management and Urban Policy. The Parsons School of Design is a major component in the national art school arena. The university operates a classical conservatory in the Mannes College of Music. Classes at the School of Dramatic Arts may lead to an MA. In the 2001–2002 academic year, all of these divisions combined had roughly 7,000 students enrolled.

STUDENT BODY

Students at Lang have an active role in steering College policies regarding academics and student life. The student union brings students together to express their views and run their events.

ACADEMICS

Personal development and goals form the foundation of planning a course of study at Eugene Lang. Advisors assist students in making clear-headed and individual decisions regarding their academics. Students benefit from the interdisciplinary seminar format of many classes. With an 18-person limit, these classes are intimate enough to allow discussions to flourish, primary texts to be tackled, and real relationships to be formed among students and professors. First-year students must enroll in four seminars, one of which focuses on writing, in their freshman year. Outside of this, there are few general requirements. In subsequent years, students can combine seminars with classes from The New School adult division, Graduate School of Management and Urban Policy, Parsons School of Design, and the Graduate Faculty. Two semesters make up the academic year, running from September to mid-May. The typical load is 16 units each semester. Graduation requires 120 units total.

With guidance from an advisor, students design their own concentrations within 12 general areas to earn their Bachelor of Arts degree at Eugene Lang. Students achieve a depth of knowledge in their concentration by taking approximately 10 related classes. Internships can round out classroom learning in many subject areas. Five-year joint degrees are also available. Students can pursue a BA/BFA in jazz studies or in areas taught at Parsons School of Design. Qualified students undertake a five-year BA/MA, working within the College's graduate school programs.

Classes at Eugene Lang are small, 10 to 18 students, and the student/faculty ratio is a low 15:1, ensuring close working relationships that are also reflected in the quality of advising. Ninety percent of instructors have their PhDs, typically earned at top institutions. Professors from the entire university come to Lang, as well as visiting scholars, writers, and lecturers, all of whom bring their individual expertise.

65 West 11th Street, Office of Admission
New York, NY 10011
Phone: 212-229-5665
Fax: 212-229-5166
Website: www.lang.edu/admissions.cfm

ADMISSIONS

Eugene Lang College encourages students from diverse racial, ethnic, religious, and political backgrounds to apply. The Admissions Committee looks for students who demonstrate an ability to make the best use of college-level resources and contribute to the Lang community. Particular qualities that the College looks for include an ability to question, a seriousness of purpose, and the capacity for intensive yet progressive liberal arts study. The Admissions Committee takes the whole student into account when making admissions decisions. A student's personal convictions and creative work, exhibited in the personal essay and required interview, are weighed alongside of scholastic achievement, represented by transcripts, recommendations, and SAT I or ACT scores. Most successful candidates have completed a college-preparatory course load in high school. Applicants are encouraged to take a tour and sit in on a seminar. The early decision application option is highly recommended for those who know that Eugene Lang is their first choice. High school juniors who display a high level of achievement may apply for early entrance, turning in two teacher recommendations with their application materials. Transfer students with a minimum of one year of college work behind them may apply and enroll in upper-level seminars upon acceptance. Those applying internationally follow regular application procedures. Non-native English speakers should submit their TOEFL scores. Students attending other institutions have a chance to come to Eugene Lang and participate in an internship through the New York Connection program. Certain programs have special application requirements. To enter the jazz studies program, students need to audition. Fine arts applicants submit a portfolio and take a home exam. Those students pursuing the BA/BFA in either jazz studies or fine arts should strongly consider applying to the five-year programs initially. All categories of admits may begin their time at Eugene Lang in the fall (September) or spring (January) semester. A $50 application fee is required. Waivers may be issued under the College Board's Fee Waiver Service. All required materials must be submitted by the following deadlines: November 15 for spring semester or for fall semester early decision, and February 1 for freshman general admission and freshman early entrants (April 1 notification). May 15 is a rolling deadline for transfers and visiting students.

CAMPUS LIFE

The university's New York City location offers access to world-class cultural opportunities. Greenwich Village in particular has the benefits of tree-lined streets, beautiful architecture, and a tradition of artistic activity.

Students at Eugene Lang College are encouraged to take their classroom learning into the world outside of school. Internships provide the chance to apply academic theories in practical situations. Students in their third year may opt to participate in an exchange with Sarah Lawrence College, the University of Amsterdam, or other programs that can be arranged within the United States or overseas.

COST AND AID

In 2002–2003, tuition and fees totaled $22,500, with room and board costing roughly $10,500 more, varying according to residence and meal plan options. University fees run $115 annually, and students pay $180 each year for the Health Services Center fee.

THE EVERGREEN STATE COLLEGE

GENERAL INFORMATION

The Evergreen State College is a public, four-year college of liberal arts and sciences. From the moment its doors opened in 1971, Evergreen established itself as one of the most innovative colleges in the country, and its national reputation continues to grow. Evergreen's curriculum is built on five key principles: emphasizing interdisciplinary studies, collaborative learning, learning across significant differences, personal engagement in one's education, and linking theory with practical applications. Evergreen's community of students, faculty, and staff represent diverse talents, cultures, ages, ethnicities, sexual orientations, physical ability levels, and socioeconomic backgrounds. Nearly 4,100 undergraduates from almost every state are enrolled at Evergreen; 18 percent are students of color.

STUDENT BODY

The numerous student organizations on campus enhance the college community with social, cultural, recreational, spiritual, and educational activities sponsored throughout the year. Public radio, political and environmental organizations, and performing arts groups are among the many activities from which students can choose. Evergreen students have also chosen to actively serve on campus committees and task forces rather than form a more traditional student government. Approximately 1,000 students live on campus in apartment-style units. Accommodations include single and double studios, two-person apartments, four- and six-bedroom apartments, and two-bedroom/four-person duplexes.

Evergreen's intercollegiate teams compete in basketball, soccer, and cross country running, for both men and women. Volleyball for women is another intercollegiate sport. Numerous intramural sports are also available. The College Recreation Center, surrounded by 20 acres of playing fields, offers a gymnasium, an 11-lane swimming pool and a separate diving well, indoor and outdoor climbing walls, indoor racquetball courts, a weight room, and saunas. An outdoor program features mountaineering, kayaking, skiing, rafting, and a challenge course.

ACADEMICS

Evergreen's curriculum is innovative, flexible, and challenging. Students enroll in a single, comprehensive program rather than a series of separate courses. These coordinated programs bring a group of students and faculty together into a learning community where a theme or issue may be explored from the perspectives of several different academic disciplines. Evergreen programs emphasize seminars, small groups in which students learn to reflect on their learning, present their ideas and positions, and consider the ideas and positions of others. Additionally, faculty schedule a variety of activities\labs, lectures, workshops, and field trips\designed to enhance student learning. Academic progress is assessed through detailed written evaluations of the student's work by faculty. The narrative evaluations describe each student's academic activities, objectives, and level of success in the program. Students also prepare self-evaluations, addressing their accomplishments, new understandings, and goals for the future. Students are asked to think creatively, to listen to others' ideas and defend their own, and to apply their knowledge. They are invited to identify their own goals and then find ways to achieve them.

Evergreen offers two undergraduate degrees, the Bachelor of Arts and the Bachelor of Science. Undergraduate studies at Evergreen are interdisciplinary. Students may self-design, with faculty advisement, a personalized area of concentration to meet their own unique educational goals. Common areas of study include agriculture, American studies, anthropology, biology, chemistry, communications, community studies, computer science, cultural studies, ecology, economics, education, energy studies, environmental studies, ethnic studies, film and video, history, human services, humanities, languages (French, Japanese, Russian, and Spanish), literature, management, marine studies, mathematics, music, Native American studies, performing arts, physics, political economy, pre-law, pre-medicine, psychology, public administration, social sciences, sociology, theater, visual arts, women's studies, writing, and zoology. Evergreen also offers three advanced degrees:

Master of Environmental Studies

Master of Public Administration

Master in Teaching

Office of Admissions
Olympia, WA 98505
Phone: 360-867-6170
Fax: 360-867-6576
Website: www.evergreen.edu

Evergreen has approximately 216 faculty members and an instructional student/faculty ratio of 25:1. Forty-nine percent of Evergreen's faculty are women and 24 percent are people of color. Seventy-three percent of faculty have earned a PhD or the equivalent in their field. Faculty members teach in one full-time program at a time, enabling them to maintain close contact with a small group of students. Faculty members strive to foster a learning environment where working across cultural and personal differences and making the abstract real and applicable to true-life situations happens on a regular basis. Evergreen students spend an average of 12 to 16 hours a week in direct contact with their faculty members.

CAMPUS LIFE

Located in the midst of 1,000 acres of forested land just outside of Olympia, Washington's capital, Evergreen's campus provides a beautiful location for students to live and study. The campus is heavily forested and has extensive trails for walking, jogging, and bicycling. The 3,300-foot waterfront on Puget Sound provides a delightful place for relaxation or marine research. Olympia, with a population of about 70,000, provides students opportunities for entertainment and exploration and is easily accessible via public transportation or biking. Beyond Olympia and all within a one- or two-hour drive are the rainforests and mountains of the Olympic Peninsula, Mount Rainier, Mount St. Helens, the Pacific Ocean, and the dynamic cities of Seattle and Portland.

Advanced students are afforded numerous opportunities to put theory into practice through Evergreen's extensive internship program. More than 800 students each year earn some of their academic credit through faculty sponsored internships. Additionally, many of the on-campus interdisciplinary programs include a "hands on" component that allows students to take skills and concepts learned in the classroom and apply them in local communities to address real-world problems. Evergreen also has a student exchange program with Miyazaki and Kobe Universities in Japan and offers a number of coordinated programs that enable students to spend a portion of their year overseas.

COST AND AID

Estimated expenses for the 2002–2003 academic year include Washington State resident tuition of $3,441; nonresident tuition, $12,264; room and board, $5,610; books and supplies, $780; and travel and personal expenses, $3,441. The total estimated cost of attendance for Washington State residents is $13,272. The estimated cost of attendance for nonresidents is $22,095.

FAIRFIELD UNIVERSITY

GENERAL INFORMATION

Fairfield University was founded in 1942 by the Jesuits, a Roman Catholic order renowned for its 450-year-old tradition of excellence in education and service to others. This Jesuit tradition inspires a commitment to educating the whole person for a life of leadership in a constantly changing world. Fairfield University welcomes students of all faiths and beliefs who value its mission of scholarship, truth, and justice, and it values the diversity their membership brings to the university community. The current undergraduate enrollment is approximately 3,200 students, hailing from 37 states and 40 countries. Students of color represent approximately 12 percent of the undergraduate population.

The University is comprised of four undergraduate schools: the College of Arts and Sciences, the Dolan School of Business, the School of Engineering, and the School of Nursing. Graduate and/or certificate programs are offered in business, engineering, education, nursing, American studies and math. A Fairfield education is characterized by its breadth in the core curriculum and the depth of study attained in the major(s), enhanced by the application of classroom theory into real-world settings offered in guaranteed internships and research opportunities as well as community-based service projects. Faculty members are in the classroom at all times and are unusually accessible to students as mentors and advisors. (There are no teaching assistants at Fairfield.) The relationship between faculty and students leads to creative collaborations on independent study, hands-on research in funded science projects, and one-on-one mentoring as students seek fellowships, research grants, and graduate school admission.

STUDENT BODY

Fairfield students are fully engaged outside of the classroom. Depending upon interests, student social life can focus on cultural clubs, the arts, residence hall events, community service, or informal gatherings in campus facilities and student townhouses. The sponsored clubs and organizations number more than 80, ranging from the many multicultural clubs, to the performing arts, to the Frisbee Golf Team, to Debate Team, to the Student Environmental Club. The Fairfield University Student Association (FUSA) also sponsors activities throughout the year. Athletics is a popular focal point for student life, with 19 varsity sports at Division I level; numerous club sports; and an extensive array of intramural programs for all levels of play. Student participation—both as scholar-athletes and as fans—is enthusiastic to say the least! In addition, the renovated Recreational Complex offers a multitude of aerobic/fitness classes.

ACADEMICS

The University uses a semester calendar, and also offers day and evening summer sessions as well as a limited number of intercessions. The core curriculum provides all students—regardless of major or future profession—with a firm foundation for engaging in the world. Sixty credit hours are taken in the five core areas: natural sciences and mathematics; history and social sciences; philosophy, religious studies and applied ethics; English and visual and performing arts; and modern or classical languages and literature. Through the flexible offerings in each of these areas, students can create their minor, explore a new area of interest, or pull together a common thread of academic pursuit in one of many "course clusters" available. Recent cluster themes have included Russia and the West: History and Culture, Global Perspectives on Economic and Political Behavior, and Understanding and Writing about American Politics. An interdisciplinary approach is also the hallmark of the Honors Program, which is open by invitation to freshmen and sophomores. Honors courses and seminars include team-taught classes in such courses as "Ideas that Shaped the West," "Genius and Creativity," and "Challenges to The Western Tradition."

The AACSB-accredited Dolan School of Business curriculum takes "interdisciplinary" to the cutting edge, offering team-taught, cross-functional classes in the major business areas to fully prepare students (from sophomore year onward) in all areas of the business world. Project-based learning is another essential component to the business program, often in collaboration with area corporations. Fairfield University is a member of Phi Beta Kappa.

The College of Arts and Sciences offers degrees in American studies, biology, chemistry, communications, computer science, economics (BA and BS), English literature and English writing, history, international studies (joint with the School of Business), mathematics, modern languages and literature, philosophy, physics, politics, psychology (BA and BS), religious studies, sociology and anthropology, visual and performing arts (art history, music, studio art, theater). Master's degrees are offered in American studies and mathematics. In the Dolan School of Business, majors include accounting, finance, information systems, marketing, management, and international studies (joint with the College of Arts and Sciences). A five-year BA-MBA is also available. The School of Nursing offers a BS and MS in Nursing. The School of Engineering offers degrees in electrical, mechanical, computer, and software engineering, as well as a 3/2 option with Columbia, RPI, University of Connecticut, and Stevens Institute. Pre-professional programs include 3/2 engineering, pre-medical (including preparation of graduate level in allied medical professions such as physical therapy), pre-dental, pre-veterinary, and pre-law. Fairfield also has an array of interdisciplinary minors, including applied ethics, Asian studies, biochemistry, Black studies, education (with certification at the secondary level), environmental science or environmental studies, Greek and Roman studies, Judaic studies, Italian studies, Latin American and Caribbean studies, marine science, peace and justice, Russian and Eastern European studies, and women's studies. Minors are available in most undergraduate departments listed above, and in most cases students may minor or double major outside of their school.

The University has 206 full-time and 161 part-time faculty. Ninety-three percent have a doctoral or terminal degree. The student/faculty ratio is 13:1. There are no teaching assistants. Average class size is 24 for freshmen, 20 for upper-division.

ADMISSIONS

There are several different ways to apply to Fairfield. For those students who know that Fairfield is their top choice, we offer an Early Decision option. This decision is binding and students admitted under early decision are expected to enroll. This application deadline is November 15. For student who are interested in being considered for a university merit-based scholarship, our deadline for application is December 1. Only students who meet this deadline will be considered for scholarship. Fairfield's regular application deadline is February 1. Students can anticipate being notified of a decision around April 1. May 1 is our confirmation deadline. The application fee is $55.

Fairfield University uses the Common Application for admission. You can get a copy at your high school guidance office or apply online by visiting our website at www.fairfield.edu. Fairfield also asks for a Common Application Supplement which can be downloaded and printed from our website. Admission to Fairfield University is selective. The admission process, however, is not a simple review of test scores and grades but a deliberate consideration of each individual's strengths and prospects for success.

1073 North Benson Road
Fairfield, CT 06824-5195
Phone: 203-254-4100
Fax: 203-254-4199
Website: www.fairfield.edu

Here's a look at our typical incoming class: **Class Rank:** The majority of students rank in the top 20 percent of their class. **Grades:** The majority of students maintain a B+ average or better in a college prep/honors curriculum. **Standardized Tests:** The middle 50 percent range for SAT scores is 1170–1300 (ACT range is 26–29). **Activities:** The typical Fairfield applicant is quite involved in a variety of high school activities and athletics, and many hold leadership positions in one or more.

CAMPUS LIFE

Set on 200 acres of woods and rolling lawns with views of the nearby Long Island Sound, Fairfield's campus is a beautiful setting for study and personal growth. Nearby, the beaches of the Sound offer recreation as well as research opportunities for marine biology and environmental science students, while the woods and trails of New England offer hiking, biking and other outdoor activity. Metro North railroad, also in town, takes students to New York City for all the diverse cultural and career opportunities available. Excursions to New York are frequently built into the class curriculum, as well as into social opportunities for students. Fairfield County itself is a Mecca for small and large corporations. With one of the largest concentrations of Fortune 500 companies in the nation, it offers outstanding internship, career placement, and mentoring possibilities for undergraduate students of all majors.

Students who take full advantage of on- and off-campus resources find a wealth of opportunity at their disposal. From week-long "urban plunge" experiences, to service projects in rural Appalachia, to mission programs abroad, to literacy projects as part of a psychology course, Fairfield fully incorporates the world around it to the great benefit of its students. Formal study abroad options are also quite popular, with up to 25 percent of students going abroad for one or two semesters. Fairfield programs are available in Florence, Italy; Harlaxton, England; and St. Petersburg, Russia. Summer programs are also offered in India, Jerusalem, Costa Rica, Germany and the Netherlands. Through affiliated programs students can also select countries around the globe. The emphasis on global opportunities, in combination with student performance and solid faculty mentoring has led to a tremendous success in student Fulbrights, with 15 students in the past three years winning Fulbrights for continued research abroad after graduation.

Fairfield's location—in the heart of Fairfield County, just one hour from New York City—as well as its established reputation among organizations both regionally and nationally, have created an unusual level of opportunity for our students to explore their career options. Internships are virtually guaranteed, regardless of major, and range from banking, insurance, and financial services to positions with prestigious national magazines, public relations and media firms, art galleries, and governmental agencies. Most students take advantage of at least one internship experience, often two. The Career Planning Center has a rich array of resources and substantial programming throughout the four undergraduate years to fully explore each student's potential career paths. Services include resume writing and interview workshops; a library of both print and online resources on corporations and organizations; one-on-one counseling; a considerable Alumni Network for mentoring; mock interviewing and job shadowing; and a full schedule of on-campus recruiting by more than 100 corporations and organizations. Fortune 500 corporations return to campus annually, pleased with both the career-related competencies of Fairfield graduates as well as the well-rounded preparation provided by the core academic curriculum.

COST AND AID

Tuition for the 2002–2003 academic year is set at $24,100, with fees of $455. Room and board is $8,560.

FELICIAN COLLEGE

GENERAL INFORMATION

Felician College is a liberal arts, coeducational, Catholic college located in northern New Jersey. Founded in 1942 by the Franciscan Sisters, Felician College currently enrolls 1,700 students in 40 undergraduate and graduate programs in the arts and sciences, health sciences, and teacher education. Felician College's NCAA Division II athletic teams compete in basketball, soccer, baseball, softball, cross country, and track and field. Cheerleading and dance teams root the athletes on and show off their own skills in competitions throughout the year.

With a mission to provide a values-oriented education based in the liberal arts, Felician College prepares students for meaningful lives and careers in today's competitive marketplace. Day, evening, and weekend programs are offered to meet the needs of Felician's diverse student body, and students may take coursework through semester or accelerated trimester formats. Two summer sessions are also available each year for nonmatriculated students.

Felician College is accredited by the Middle States Association of Colleges and Schools and carries program accreditation from the National League for Nursing Accrediting Commission, the National Accrediting Agency for Clinical Laboratory Sciences, and the International Assembly for Collegiate Business Education.

In addition to undergraduate degree programs, Felician College offers a Master of Science in nursing (MSN), a Master of Arts in religious education, a Master of Arts in English, and a Master of Arts in teacher education. A three-plus-three doctoral degree program in physical therapy is also offered in collaboration with the University of Medicine and Dentistry of New Jersey (UMDNJ).

STUDENT BODY

Felician College offers a competitive athletic program. The College is a member of the National Collegiate Athletic Association (NCAA) Division II. The Golden Falcons athletic teams compete in men's baseball, soccer, basketball, cross-country, and track, as well as women's softball, soccer, basketball, cross-country, and track. The athletic department also sponsors cheerleading and dance teams as well as numerous intramural sports activities.

With residence halls on the Rutherford campus, students may elect to reside in one of the spacious suites in Elliot Hall or Milton Court, which accommodate as many as 600 students. The campuses offer comfortable student lounge areas, meeting rooms, dining halls, a gymnasium, a fitness center, and a campus green for outdoor recreation.

With student events and activities dotting the calendar throughout the year, campus life bounds with energy. There are more than 23 clubs and organizations on campus to meet the special interests of the students. At orientation, new students are introduced to college life through a broad program that begins with pre-admission interviews followed by an orientation day and ongoing orientation sessions. A special theme, chosen by students, sets the tone for the year's orientation program.

ACADEMICS

A candidate for the BA in liberal arts is required to complete an organized program of study comprising 120 semester hours distributed among prescribed and elective courses. Four interdisciplinary courses are required in the Core Curriculum focusing on "The College Mission." In addition, students must complete 46 to 48 credits of General Education courses beyond the 12-credit Core. Each baccalaureate degree student in arts and sciences is required to prepare a written and oral senior research project. A minimum of 45 credit hours must be earned at the College. A student who pursues an AA degree is required to complete 64 to 68 credits in an approved program of study.

A candidate for the BA in elementary or special education is required to complete a program of 126 to 130 semester hours, including credits in general education, professional education, and a major in the arts and sciences. Students begin field experience in their freshman year, participate in a practicum in the junior year, and conduct supervised teaching during the senior year in a public elementary school. The education programs are approved by the National Association of State Directors of Teacher Education and Certification (NASDTEC).

Clinical experiences in the medical laboratory techniques begin during the first semester, continue throughout each semester, and include a summer internship. The Associate in Applied Science program requires 70 to 71 credit hours.

Felician College offers programs of study in the arts and sciences, health sciences, and teacher education.

Departmental majors for a Bachelor of Arts degree include art with a concentration in fine or graphic art; biology with a concentration in biochemistry; business administration with a concentration in accounting, marketing/management, or sports management; computer science; English; history; liberal arts; mathematics; natural sciences, including environmental science, general science, mathematical sciences; philosophy; psychology with a concentration in gerontology; religious studies; social and behavioral sciences, including international education and foreign language, political science, and sociology.

Bachelor of Arts degree programs in early childhood education, elementary education, special education, and teaching math K–12 enable students to seek New Jersey certification.

The health sciences division offers a generic Bachelor of Science in Nursing degree program for high school graduates and an upper division Bachelor of Science in Nursing degree program for registered nurses. Students who complete the four-year generic nursing degree program are eligible to take the examination for licensure as a registered nurse (RN) given by the New Jersey Board of Nursing. A bachelor's degree in clinical laboratory science is also available in conjunction with UMDNJ School of Health Related Professions. For this degree, a student may concentrate in cytotechnology, medical technology, or toxicology. Also offered in conjunction with UMDNJ is a Bachelor of Science program in allied health technology. Students may study medical sonography, nuclear medicine technology, respiratory care, or vascular technology.

262 South Main Street
Lodi, NJ 07644
Phone: 201-559-6131
Fax: 201-559-6138
Website: www.felician.edu

Associate's degrees are available in liberal arts. Also, the Associate in Applied Science degree is available in medical laboratory technology, and the Associate in Science degree is available in psychosocial rehabilitation. A student who completes the medical laboratory technology program is eligible to take the nationally administered examination for certification by the Board of Registry of the American Society of Clinical Pathologists.

With a "students first" philosophy, Felician College provides a number of services designed to meet a variety of needs. Housed on campus are the Center for Learning, a nursing skills laboratory, and a child care center. To help students plan for their futures, a career services center coordinates field experiences, career seminars, internships, and job placements. The Honors Program provides an opportunity for students with strong academic records to conduct scholarly research and develop leadership skills through service learning.

Felician College has a fully qualified faculty with advanced degrees who teach and advise students. A student/faculty ratio of 15:1 and an average class size of 15 to 20 students assure a personalized and individualized approach to each student's education.

ADMISSIONS

Applicants for admission are considered for the fall semester (late August/early September) and the spring semester (January) on a rolling basis. Students are informed of an admission decision within two weeks of the completion of their file. A completed file includes a transcript from an accredited high school (with date of graduation) or a high school equivalency certificate, satisfactory SAT I or ACT scores, a 500-word personal statement, and a physician's certificate of health. A personal interview with the College's admission staff is recommended.

Students are eligible to transfer to Felician. Transcripts of previous college work from recognized junior or four-year colleges are required, and an evaluation will be made upon receipt of official college transcripts. Admission requirements may be adjusted for adults on the basis of maturity and experience. Felician College offers credit for acceptable scores on the College Board Advanced Placement tests and College-Level Examination Program (CLEP) tests.

Open houses and tours of all facilities are available through the Office of Admission. For more information on admissions, contact:

Felician College—Lodi Campus
262 South Main Street
Lodi, NJ 07644
Phone: 201-559-6131
Website: www.felician.edu

CAMPUS LIFE

Felician College is located on two beautifully landscaped campuses in Lodi and Rutherford, New Jersey. Both campuses, set in suburban towns, are a 30-minute bus or train ride from New York City and a few miles from the New Jersey Meadowlands sports complex. With classes offered on both campuses, free shuttle buses transport students between the campuses, which are located just a few miles apart.

The College houses an impressive library collection with more than 120,000 books, professional journals, periodicals, microforms, CD-ROMs, and PCs for online learning. A curriculum library serves as a resource center for the teacher education programs.

COST AND AID

The cost of undergraduate tuition for 2003–2004 is $14,500 for full-time students. The annual cost of room and board is $7,200.

FIVE TOWNS COLLEGE

GENERAL INFORMATION

Nestled in the rolling hills of Long Island's North Shore, Five Towns College offers students the opportunity to study in a suburban environment that is within easy access of New York City. Founded in 1972 by a group of educators and community leaders who wished to provide students with an alternative to the large university atmosphere, Five Towns College is a nonsectarian, coeducational institution that places its emphasis on the student as an individual. Many students are drawn to Five Towns College because of its strong programs in music and music-related fields. As an institution of higher learning that offers two-year, four-year, and master's degree programs, the College is the only school on Long Island with the authority to offer the prestigious Bachelor of Music degree (MusB). From as far away as England and Japan and from as close as Long Island and New York City, the 800 full-time students who attend the College reflect a rich cultural diversity. The College's enrollment is currently 60 percent men and 40 percent women; there is a minority population of approximately 25 percent. The College's music programs are contemporary in nature and therefore easily distinguished from classical-oriented programs. The most popular programs are audio recording technology, music business, mass communication, performing music, teacher education, theater, and film/video. In addition, the College offers graduate degree programs leading to a Master of Music (MusM) in jazz/commercial music or music education and Elementary education. Coeducational living accommodations are available just a short distance from the Five Towns College campus at the State University of New York at Farmingdale. On-campus dormitories are currently under construction with two buildings finished and another two expected to be completed shortly.

ACADEMICS

Five Towns College awards the Bachelor of Music degree in jazz/commercial music, with concentrations in audio recording technology, composition/songwriting, music business, performing music, musical theater, and film/ video music. Students may also take a degree program in music teacher education. Five Towns College awards a Bachelor of Professional Studies (BPS) degree in business management, with concentrations in audio recording technology, music business, and video arts. The college also awards a Bachelor of Fine Arts (BFA) degree in theater, with concentrations in acting, film/video, and theater technology. Two teacher education programs are offered, The Bachelor of Science (BS) in childhood education (1–6) and the Bachelor of Music (MusB) in music education (K–12). Furthermore, a Bachelor of Science (BS) in Mass Communication with concentrations in broadcasting or journalism is available. Five Towns College awards the AA, AS, and AAS degrees in 18 subject areas. These include business administration, business management, jazz/commercial music, and liberal arts. Business management students may select a concentration in accounting, audio recording technology, broadcasting, marketing/retailing, music business, or film/video arts. Liberal arts students may select a concentration in literature, dramatic arts, or communications.

The teacher education programs include childhood education leading to a BS degree and music education leading to a MusB degree. The music education program is designed for students interested in a career as a teacher of music in a public or private school (K–12). The program leads to New York State certification and prepares students for the New York State Examination for Teacher Certification. The course work provides professional training and includes a student-teaching experience in a cooperating public school district under the supervision of the music education coordinator.

Music majors are required to complete at least 40 credits with a minimum grade point average of 3.0, and pass a piano qualifying exam before admission to the music education program. The audio recording technology concentration is designed to provide students with tools needed to succeed as professional engineers and producers in the recording industry. Students receive intensive instruction in audio recording, a comprehensive music education, and the opportunity to participate in supervised internships. The College's proximity to New York City allows many students the opportunity to intern in world-class studios. The music business concentration is designed for students interested in a career in music-related business fields such as the recorded music industry. The course work covers the various aspects of this exciting and rapidly growing field, including the technical, legal, production, management, and merchandising aspects of the music business. The composition/songwriting concentration provides professional training for students who intend to pursue careers as composers, arrangers, and songwriters. Students receive intensive instruction in core technical studies that include courses such as harmony, orchestration, counterpoint, MIDI, songwriting, keyboard techniques, form and analysis, commercial arranging, and composition. The performance concentration is designed for students planning to pursue careers as professional performers. It provides a common core of technical studies and a foundation of specialized courses such as music history, harmony, counterpoint, improvisation, ensemble performance, and private instruction. The video music concentration provides professional training in music scoring and compositional techniques and in the artistic and technical skills required for the creation of video music. Student compositions are performed and recorded in the College's new 72 channel SL9000J console and 48- and 24-track recording studios. They are then adapted and synchronized to videotape in the College's professional film/video production studio. To earn a Bachelor of Music degree, a student must complete 128 credits. Music education majors must complete 64 credits in applied music, 30 credits in liberal arts, 22 credits in music education (including 9 credits of student teaching), and 12 credits in music history. All other music majors must complete 57 credits in applied music, 30 credits in liberal arts, 24 credits in a major area of concentration, 12 credits in music history, and 5 credits of electives.

To earn a Bachelor of Professional Studies degree in business management, a student must complete 120 credits, with 42 credits in liberal arts, 45 credits in business, 24 credits in a major area of concentration, and 9 credits of electives. To earn a Bachelor of Fine Arts degree in theater, a student must complete 120 credits. Bachelor of Science candidates must complete 130 credits.

305 North Service Road
Dix Hills, NY 11746
Phone: 631-424-7000
Fax: 631-424-7008
Website: www.fivetowns.edu

The BS in Mass Communication permits students to become broadcast professionals or enter into the field of journalism. Scholarships are available for those who qualify. The campus radio station, school newspaper and yearbook serve as hands-on applications of the trade, coupled with mandated internship programs.

To earn an associate's degree, a student must complete 60 to 64 credits of course work. Distribution of credits varies according to degree and concentration sought. To graduate from any degree program, students must earn a grade point average of 2.0 (C). The academic year is divided into two traditional semesters of at least 15 weeks each and summer sessions.

The College's growing faculty currently consists of almost 75 full- and part-time members. Five Towns College students enjoy a faculty/student ratio of 1:14. The College partially attributes its strong student retention rate to this factor. While the faculty is more strongly committed to teaching than to research, many members continue to be active in their respective areas of expertise. Thus, the faculty members, who also serve as the academic advisors, are able to provide students with guidance about the academic requirements of the College and also with practical guidance regarding students' career objectives.

ADMISSIONS

Five Towns College seeks students who are generally able to benefit from the programs of study available at the College and who will enrich the lives of their fellow students by actively participating in the academic process and debate. Although all applicants are considered, the College encourages applications from students who have attained a minimum high school grade point average of 78 percent. Prospective students must submit a completed application and an official high school transcript. An interview is required. A GED score of 280 is required. The SAT I or A is required for students entering the College after the spring 2003 semester. Transfer students must also submit official transcripts of all college-level work attempted. International students must present a TOEFL score of at least 520 or its equivalent. Students may be admitted for deferred entrance or advanced standing. The College does not accept students on an early admissions basis, although early decision is available.

Admission into the Bachelor of Music program is contingent on passing an audition demonstrating skill in performance on a major instrument or vocally. Bachelor of Music degree applicants are also required to take written and oral examinations in harmony, sight-singing, and ear training in order to demonstrate talents, well-developed musicianship, and artistic sensibilities. Applicants for a Bachelor of Fine Arts program are also auditioned. An interview may be required. Students are accepted on a rolling admission basis and are notified shortly after all required documents have been filed with the admissions office. New students may begin their studies at the start of either the fall semester or the spring semester. There is an application fee of $25. For further information, students should contact:

Five Towns College
Director of Admissions
305 North Service Road
Dix Hills, NY 11746-5871
Telephone: 631-424-7000, ext. 2110
World Wide Web: www.fivetowns.edu

CAMPUS LIFE

The College's serene 40-acre campus, located in the wooded countryside of Dix Hills in the town of Huntington, New York, provides students with a parklike refuge where they can pursue their studies. Just off campus is Long Island's bustling Route 110 corridor, the home of numerous national and multinational corporations. New York City, with everything from Lincoln Center to Broadway is just a train ride away and provides students with some of the best cultural advantages in the world. Closer to campus, the many communities of Long Island abound with the cultural and recreational opportunities. The sandy shores of Jones Beach State Park and the Fire Island National Seashore are world renowned for their white sandy beaches.

Off-campus internship opportunities are available for all Five Towns College students who have fulfilled the necessary prerequisites, including a cumulative GPA of at least 3.0, with a 2.5 in their major. In recent semesters, students have obtained valuable field experience interning for major corporations such as MTV, Atlantic Records, Polygram Records, CBS Records, EMI Records, MCA Records, Cablevision, Channel 12 News, The Power Station, SONY Records, Pyramid Recording Studios, and many others.

COST AND AID

For the 2003–2004 academic year, the tuition at Five Towns College is $12300. Miscellaneous fees are approximately $300, and books are about $700. Private instruction fees for performing music students are $575 per semester. For information regarding on-campus room and board charges, contact the Five Towns College Admissions Office.

FRANKLIN PIERCE COLLEGE

GENERAL INFORMATION

Franklin Pierce College is a traditional liberal arts college with an entrepreneurial spirit. We seek to combine the history and values of a liberal arts education with the expectations of a change-oriented, technology-based contemporary society. Our students are "experiencers." They learn best as active partners in an educational structure that allows them to participate with hands-on experience. We are best known for our award-winning Individual and Community curriculum that encourages involvement and service on campus and in the communities beyond. The powerful themes of "individual" and "community" are explored throughout our 42-credit general education curriculum, and students are encouraged to consider the individual's responsibility to the community, and in turn, the community's relationship to the individual. In addition to our 26 academic majors, several programs offer a new environment or culture in which our students can choose to be immersed for a unique learning experience: The Walk Across Europe; the Marine Awareness Research Expedition; the London program; and the Washington Internship Center. Three academically oriented institutes, directed by Franklin Pierce faculty members, engage in research, education, and outreach to the campus and wider community. The college recently dedicated the new Marlin Fitzwater Center for Communication. This state-of-the-art teaching facility offers industry-standard studios and equipment to provide our students with a living laboratory in which to study radio, television, and journalism. At Franklin Pierce College, our highest priorities are the development of intellect and character. In all that the College does, we endeavor to provide an academic home in which our students are encouraged to achieve more than they could have imagined when they first arrived on campus.

STUDENT BODY

Approximately 35 student organizations contribute to the wide variety of social, educational, recreational, and cultural activities that are offered throughout the year. Students also gain valuable experience by taking active leadership roles in the planning of those activities. Since Franklin Pierce is a small college, there are many opportunities to join an existing club or organization or to form a new one.

Franklin Pierce is a member of the National Collegiate Athletic Association (NCAA), Division II, the Eastern Collegiate Athletic (ECAC), and the Northeast 10. Intercollegiate sports include men's baseball, basketball, crew, cross-country, golf, ice hockey, lacrosse, soccer, and tennis, and women's basketball, crew, cross-country, field hockey, golf, lacrosse, soccer, softball, tennis, and volleyball.

ACADEMICS

Majors: accounting, advertising, American studies, anthropology, art, arts management, biology/pre-med, business management, communications, computer science, criminal justice, dance, drama, elementary education, English, environmental science, financial management, graphic communications, history, pre-law, information technology, journalism, marketing, mass communication, mathematics, music, political science, psychology, radio and television, secondary education, sociology, social work and counseling, sports and leisure management, student-designed majors, and technical theatre arts.

The Honors Program: The Honors Program is intended to reflect the value the College places on academic achievement by its students and faculty. It is meant to provide students of exceptional academic ability with an opportunity to work closely with their peers and faculty members to explore a wide range of subjects.

Through the Academic Services Center, a variety of learning support services are available. The Center is staffed by a team of professionals dedicated to assisting students in developing the skills, strategies, and attitudes necessary for academic success at FPC. All students are encouraged to avail themselves of the services offered.

The College offers the degrees of Bachelor of Arts and Bachelor of Science at the Rindge campus. An MBA, MS in IT Management, and Master of Physical Therapy programs are offered through the Division of Graduate and Professional Studies at the satellite campuses.

Students may major in any of 26 subject areas. Minors may be chosen from among 32 subject areas. Students may also design their own major in conjunction with a faculty advisor.

Given the student-centered nature of the Franklin Pierce mission, the primary responsibility of the faculty is to teach well. The Rindge campus employs 61 full-time faculty members, 75 percent of whom hold terminal degrees. Part-time faculty also teach classes, but no interns or graduate assistants teach undergraduates.

Admissions Office, Box 60, 20 College Road
Rindge, NH 03461
Phone: 603-899-4050
Fax: 603-889-4394
Website: www.fpc.edu

ADMISSIONS

Students may apply to enter in the fall, spring, or summer sessions. Applicants are evaluated on an individual basis with the student's potential and seriousness of purpose of primary concern. The trend toward improved grades, more difficult course work, and greater school involvement are weighed heavily in the student's behalf. Applications are considered on a rolling basis until the class is filled.

Admissions Checklist:

1. The completed application form (no fee required)
2. Official secondary school transcript or GED
3. Official transcript from each college attended
4. Official secondary school recommendation (guidance counselor, principal, or teacher)
5. Results of the SAT I or ACT tests (the SAT II is not required)
6. A sample of the students writing graded by a teacher, or an essay
7. An on-campus interview is recommended but not required

Transfer Students: Transfer students are welcome at Franklin Pierce. Applicants must submit transcripts of all previous college work. Transfer students who hold the AA or AS degrees from accredited colleges will enter FPC with junior standing.

International Students: A diverse Student Body enriches the College community. Students of all nationalities are welcome at FPC. Applicants must submit acceptable TOEFL (or SAT/ACT) scores and the Declaration of Finances along with their application, transcripts, and recommendation. Qualified international students may be eligible for scholarships (maximum $8,000).

CAMPUS LIFE

FPC is located in southwestern New Hampshire, in the heart of New England. It is one and a half hours from Boston, four and a half hours from New York City, and 30 minutes from Keene, New Hampshire. It is accessible by air from Manchester, New Hampshire or Boston, Massachusetts, or by bus. The campus is set on 1,200 acres, with its waterfront on Pearly Lake and spectacular views of Mount Monadnock. In addition, six satellite campuses located throughout New Hampshire provide graduate and professional studies programs.

The London Program: Franklin Pierce holds affiliate status with Richmond College in London, England. The campus in Kensington is centrally located in one of London's most fashionable neighborhoods, and museums, shops, and parks are all within easy walking distance.

The Walk Across Europe: The Walk Across Europe is a unique opportunity for FPC juniors to immerse themselves in the culture of Europe. By walking approximately 15 miles a day, the students have time for deep, personal reflection as well as time for appreciation of the country through which they walk and the people they meet. A tradition at FPC for more than 30 years, students who participated in previous walks found that the experience changed their lives.

The Washington Center: The Washington Center for Internships and Academic Seminars believes that the key to student success is active involvement in the educational process. Through the programs, students can earn academic credit while they gain practical experience. Sample internship placements include congressional offices, think tanks, museums, advocacy organizations, government agencies, newspapers, television stations, and trade and professional associations.

The Marine Awareness Research Expedition Center: The M.A.R.E. Center provides multidisciplinary marine education programs for college and high school students. Each summer the Center offers accredited 14-day programs on the coast of Maine in activity groups known as the Mariners, the Explorers, and the Global Voyagers. Mariners and Global Voyagers join the 131-foot schooner *Harvey Gamage* for a voyage of discovery on the coast of Maine or Nova Scotia, and the Explorers is an expedition by sea kayak into the marine environment of Maine's Muscongus Bay.

COST AND AID

Tuition and Fees for 2003-2204 (per year)

Tuition: $20,790

Room: $4,000

Board: $3,300

Programming fee: $240

Technology/Voice Mail: $350

Comprehensive: $28,680

GEORGIAN COURT COLLEGE

GENERAL INFORMATION

Since its founding by the Sisters of Mercy of New Jersey in 1908, Georgian Court College (GCC) has grown from a women's liberal arts college to its present enrollment of 1,258 female undergraduates and an additional 617-student population in the coeducational Undergraduate Evening Division, founded in 1979. The graduate school began offering courses in 1976. While preparing students for their roles in the professional world, the College also pays close attention to personal development and fostering a sense of responsibility and agency in our culture. The GCC curriculum balances the breadth necessary in a liberal arts education with the specialization required to excel in graduate school or the job market. Georgian Court strives to nurture free-thinking and capable leaders with a foundation of strong moral, spiritual, and intellectual values.

Seventeen buildings set on 150 acres comprise the College's pristine campus, on the former estate of George Gould. Students live in private or semiprivate rooms in one of the College's two residence halls, St. Joseph Hall and Maria Hall. Both dormitories are equipped with kitchenettes on every floor. Most students at GCC are from New Jersey, though some arrive from nearby states or foreign countries. Just more than one fifth of student's at the women's college live on campus. Resident students and commuters come together for many different activities, such as cultural events and parties. Students also participate in College-run outings to New York City and Philadelphia to enjoy the museums, plays, and shopping opportunities. Students at neighboring colleges are invited to GCC social events. Georgian Court students often congregate in the Patrick and Julia Gavan Student Lounge for parties, performances, and special events. Of the 35 student-run clubs and organizations on campus, many are geared towards cultural, educational, honorary, and service-oriented interests. Those who wish to exercise their writing or photography skills can contribute to the two student publications. Students interested in music can participate in the Court Singers, Court Notes, or the Georgian Court College Concert Band or Jazz Band. In the athletic arena, women compete in basketball, cross-country, soccer, tennis, volleyball, and softball. GCC's teams are part of the National Collegiate Athletic Association, the Central Atlantic College Conference, and the Jersey Nine Association. All students have access to the College's heated swimming pool, tennis courts, and areas for running and biking.

The Counseling Center is available for students who want guidance in adapting to college life, managing their schedule, or developing their leadership skills. The Center also offers referral services as well as group counseling and individual sessions. Current students and alumni can take advantage of the career counseling and placement programs. Tutorial support, managed by Student Support Services, is perfect for students seeking additional help in a particular class or subject. For medical attention and overall health care, students go to the registered nurses available at Health Center. For spiritual guidance, students turn to the campus ministers. Students can attend the Eucharistic Liturgy on campus. Those seeking other forms of worship have their choice of many churches and synagogues close by in Lakewood. Students with mild to moderate learning disabilities are served by The Learning Center. This assistance programs teaches students effective independent learning strategies and study habits.

STUDENT BODY

Students elected to the Student Government Association are responsible for running campus events. Student officials develop their leadership skills by making decisions regarding student life and working alongside of faculty and administrators on College committees.

ACADEMICS

Students must complete 132 credit hours, with the correct distribution to meet general education requirements, in order to receive their BA, BFA, BS, or BSW degree. The breadth requirements, covering nine approved semester courses in the humanities, five in the social sciences, and three in the natural sciences/mathematics, ensure that all graduates have a comprehensive liberal arts background. Students may pursue a second major with the permission of their department. Certain departments allow students to pursue minors, certificates, or concentrations. The available programs include anthropology, bilingual/bicultural studies, commercial art, computer science, economics, English as a second language, gerontology, holistic health, marketing, medical technology, nuclear medicine technology, philosophy, and political science. Course work in pre-professional areas is offered in chiropractic, dentistry, law, medicine, and veterinary. Also, students may complete interdisciplinary minors in American studies, international area studies, Latin American studies, and women's studies. Experiences such as internships, externships, and practicums may compliment work in most majors. Additionally, students can pilot independent study work.

Georgian Court College grants Bachelor of Arts degrees in art, art history, biology, chemistry, computer information systems, English, French, history, humanities, mathematics, music, physics, psychology, religious studies, sociology, Spanish, and special education. Bachelor of Fine Arts degree are available in general fine arts and graphic design/illustration. Students pursuing a Bachelor of Science degree choose from accounting, allied health technologies (a joint degree program with the University of Medicine and Dentistry of New Jersey), biochemistry, biology, business administration, chemistry, computer science, and physics. Aspiring social workers enroll in the Bachelor of Social Work program. Students striving to be teachers can earn their teaching certificates in elementary education, subject areas (N–12), special education, and English as a second language.

Students enjoy the student/faculty ratio of 14:1 and an average class size of roughly 15. Seventy-one percent of full-time professors have their PhD Upper-level instructors, including department chairs, are available to students throughout their GCC career. Georgian Court emphasizes the advising relationship between faculty members and students, ensuring a personalized learning process.

900 Lakewood Avenue
Lakewood, NJ 08701-2697
Phone: 732-364-2200
Fax: 732-364-4442
Website: www.georgian.edu

ADMISSIONS

Successful applicants to Georgian Court College demonstrate their interest in a liberal arts education and the background needed to get the most out of their undergraduate studies. The admissions committee weighs the high school transcript heavily, looking for success in a college-preparatory course load. Applicants need to have 16 academic (Carnegie) units and must take the SAT I or ACT, hopefully by December of their final year of high school. The application evaluation also takes participation in extracurricular activities and recommendations into account. The College encourages applicants to take a tour of the campus and come in for a campus interview.

An early decision option is available to applicants who know that GCC is their first choice. They should have top qualifications and apply by November 15. Early entrance may be offered to students who display a high degree of achievement and maturity after three years of high school. Transfer students in good standing at their current institution may apply to come to GCC in the fall or spring semester of their freshman, sophomore, or junior year. Those arriving at the College with fewer than 24 credits will need to meet admissions standards for the freshman class.

International students with a minimum TOEFL score of 550 on the paper test of 213 on the computer test can be granted assistance with their I-20 forms. They should initiate their application procedures six months before the beginning of the semester. International students are required to submit a GCC financial support form and financial documentation. They should be able to cover their educational and personal costs in the United States. This school is authorized under Federal law to enroll nonimmigrant students.

Applications, complete with transcripts, recommendations, and the $40 application fee, should be received by the College by August 1 for fall admission and January 1 for spring admission.

CAMPUS LIFE

Georgian Court's home of Lakewood, New Jersey, provides a tranquil college setting on the north shore of Lake Carasaljo. This convenient location is accessible by to the Route 9 corridor, the Garden State Parkway, and Interstate 195. Students enjoy proximity to New York City, Philadelphia, and Atlantic City. Plus, the beach is only 10 miles away.

The College recognizes credits earned in international programs for Autumn Semester in Quebec and study abroad in a Spanish-speaking country. Undergraduates may also choose to participate in study abroad programs sponsored by other accredited colleges or universities.

COST AND AID

Undergraduate Costs for 2003–2004

Full-time tuition: $15,872 per year, $7,936 per semester

Part time tuition: $428 per credit

Room and board (7-day plan): $6,600 per year, $3,300 per semester

Room and Board (5-day plan): $6,450 per year, $3,225 per semester

Fees: approximately $400 per year

Annual cost for 2003–2004: $22,872

GONZAGA UNIVERSITY

AT A GLANCE

Gonzaga University, founded in 1887, is an independent, comprehensive university with a distinguished background in the Catholic, Jesuit, humanistic tradition. Gonzaga emphasizes the moral and ethical implications of learning, living, and working in today's global society. Through the University Core Curriculum, each student develops a strong liberal arts foundation, which many alumni cite as a most valuable asset. In addition, students specialize in any of more than 75 academic programs and majors. Gonzaga enrolls approximately 3,800 undergraduate and 1,700 graduate and law students.

Gonzaga's 110-acre campus combines the old and new: the original administration building and DeSmet Residence Hall with the modern architectural structures of Foley Library, Jundt Art Center and Museum, and the Rosauer Center for Education. A multi-phase renovation to the Hughes Hall for Life Sciences provides additional research and teaching laboratories as well as the addition of the Inland Northwest Natural Resources Research Center. A 13,000-square-foot fitness center has also been added to the Martin Athletic Centre. The campus is characterized by sprawling green lawns and majestic evergreen trees. Towering above the campus are the stately spires of St. Aloysius Church, the well-recognized landmark featured in the University logo.

Gonzaga encompasses five undergraduate schools: Arts and Sciences, Business Administration, Education, Engineering, and Professional Studies. The University offers the BA, BBA, BE, BEd, BGS, BS, BSCE, BSCpE, BSGE, BSEE, BSME, and BSN degrees.

Gonzaga offers several unique options for students. The Honors Program provides a rigorous liberal arts curriculum for intellectually curious students who thrive in a competitive academic environment as well as study abroad option at Oxford University. Students in the Hogan Entrepreneurial Leadership Program take a challenging curriculum designed to foster interest and ability in an entrepreneurial setting. Business leaders mentor the students, and internships are an integral part of the program. The award-winning Gonzaga Alumni Mentor Program (GAMP) connects current students and recent graduates with alumni in their professional areas of interest. The Army ROTC unit prepares select women and men as leaders in service for their communities and their country. Gonzaga's nationally ranked debate team includes all skill levels, from beginners to some of the nation's best forensic competitors. The Mock Trial Team competes nationally and involves students majoring in many different areas of study. Internships, research with faculty, and community service learning enhance class time while providing students first-hand experience.

LOCATION AND ENVIRONMENT

As the second largest city in Washington, Spokane plays a vital role in shaping the University's character. While offering urban advantages such as museum exhibits, shopping, symphony, Broadway and ballet performances, Spokane still maintains an intimate, friendly, and safe atmosphere. The 30-mile Centennial Trail for running and cycling runs through campus to Coeur d'Alene, Idaho. Within a short distance of campus, students snow and water ski, hike, cycle, rock climb, swim, camp, and golf. With an average rainfall of only 16.7 inches per year, outdoor activities are easily accessible.

The 16 residence halls on campus, both single-sex and coed, house 15 to 361 students each. Freshmen and sophomores are required to live on campus. The ZagNet network provides students round-the-clock electronic access to e-mail, Internet, campus intranet, and library holdings, all directly from residence hall rooms. Resident Directors and Assistants, along with a Resident Chaplain, provide a fun, secure, and nurturing environment.

MAJORS AND DEGREES OFFERED

Gonzaga offers the following areas of study in the five undergraduate schools. The School of Arts and Sciences offers applied communication studies, applied physics, art, biochemistry, biology, broadcast and electronic media studies, chemistry, classical civilization, computer science, criminal justice, economics, English, exercise science, French, history, integrated studies, international studies (including international relations and Asian, European, and Latin American studies), Italian studies, journalism, literary studies, mathematics, mathematics/computer science, music (including composition, education, literature, and performance), philosophy, physics, political science, psychology, public relations, religious studies, sociology, Spanish, and theatre arts. Students interested in the following areas take tracks of classes respectively in Pre-dentistry, pre-law, pre-medicine, pre–physical therapy, pre-allied health, and pre-veterinary studies.

The School of Business Administration offers majors in accounting or business administration (with concentrations in e-commerce, economics, entrepreneurship, finance, human resource management, individualized study, international business, law and public policy, management information systems, marketing, operations management, and supply chain management).

As well as granting teacher certification on both the elementary and secondary levels, the School of Education offers degrees in physical education, special education, and sports management.

The School of Engineering offers civil, computer, electrical, and mechanical engineering degrees, as well as a general engineering degree and a BSGE/MBA option.

The School of Professional Studies offers general studies and nursing degrees. Advanced degrees in accounting, business, education, philosophy, religious studies, law, and nursing are also offered.

OFF-CAMPUS OPPORTUNITIES

Recognizing the importance of an international perspective for learning, Gonzaga offers study abroad programs in Australia, British West Indies, Canada, Costa Rica, Kenya, Mexico, China, England, France, Germany, Ireland, Japan, and Spain. Gonzaga also has a campus in Florence, Italy. Students are encouraged to volunteer their services at any of the area nonprofit organizations. Gonzaga University is the leading provider of service hours in the entire city of Spokane. University Ministry, the Gonzaga Student Body Association, and the Center for Community Action and Service Learning (CCASL) provide organized projects for students to become involved in the greater Spokane community. Additionally, students have opportunities to attend Mission Possible in a variety of chosen cities over Spring Break. During this Alternative Spring Break week, students work in nonprofits in low-income neighborhoods combating and learning more about social injustices.

502 E. Boone Avenue
Spokane, WA 99258
Phone: 509-323-6572
Fax: 509-324-5780
Website: www.gonzaga.edu

FACILITIES AND EQUIPMENT

The Foley Library contains more than 782,000 volumes and microform titles, with two special collections of material especially rich in the areas of philosophy and classical civilization, as well as the nation's most extensive collection of works about the famous Jesuit poet Gerard Manley Hopkins. The historic administration building houses the student-operated FM radio station (KAGU), a television broadcasting studio, an arts lab for the *Bulletin* (the weekly student-published newspaper), Russell Theater, a 24-hour computer lab, the newly remodeled University Chapel, and numerous classrooms and faculty offices.

Students are able to produce sophisticated multimedia presentations and research hundreds of libraries across the country from their own residence hall rooms or from one of the 10 labs on campus. Additionally, the University has more than 250 PC, Macintosh computers, and sun Workstations throughout campus. The Herak Engineering Center houses state-of-the-art CAD/CAM, electronic, digital, microwave, and calibration labs, and a new addition to Hughes Hall for Life Sciences will create space for the Inland Northwest Natural Resources Research Center.

The Martin Athletic Center is home to the Gonzaga Bulldog Club, intramural, and varsity teams. A new 13,000-square-foot fitness center offers all students the most modern cardiovascular and weight equipment available. The athletic department sponsors an extensive intramural program; more than 85 percent of students participate in sports at some point during their four years at GU. Gonzaga is a NCAA Division I School and a member of the West Coast Conference.

TUITION, ROOM & BOARD AND FEES

Tuition for the 2002–2003 academic year is $19,400; room and board is $6,150. Over 90 percent of students receive financial aid. The average package for 2001–2002 was $15,566, awarded in the form of grants, scholarships, loans, and campus employment. A number of merit-based and merit/need-based and athletic scholarships are awarded to students each year. Students should file the Free Application for Federal Student Aid (FAFSA) by the priority date of February 1. Through the Gonzaga Guarantee, all University-funded scholarships and grants will not decrease over a student's four-year enrollment, provided he or she remains in good academic standing. Gonzaga is committed to working with students and families to finance their investment in a quality education.

FULL AND PART-TIME FACULTY

GU's faculty is a diverse group of scholars with degrees from all over the world. Professors teach 100 percent of the classes offered, and around 81 percent of them hold the highest degree in their respective fields. Interactions with professors during office hours and through individual research projects help create a setting that is conducive to learning while building on concepts studied in the classroom. Professors at Gonzaga University know their students!

STUDENT ORGANIZATIONS AND ACTIVITIES

GU students enjoy a wide variety of activities on and off campus. The Gonzaga Student Body Association (GSBA) oversees over 75 academic, social, and cultural clubs and provides the structure of student government. GSBA organizes service and conservation projects, dances, and countless other activities to channel and challenge the talents and passions of motivated men and women who seek to make a difference. Division I sports include baseball (men), basketball, crew, cross-country/track, golf, soccer, tennis, and volleyball (women).

ADMISSION PROCESSES AND REQUIREMENTS

The University seeks diligent, inquisitive applicants with diverse backgrounds who will benefit from the rigorous Jesuit instruction at Gonzaga as well as enhance the University environment. A Gonzaga Application for Admission or the Common Application, SAT I or ACT scores, two letters of teacher recommendations, a counselor/dean's report, an activities list or resume, and an essay are required. Transfer students or students with any college credit must submit official transcripts from all colleges. International students must also submit official transcripts from all colleges attended. International students must submit official results of their TOEFL examination.

Gonzaga offers entering freshmen students a nonbinding Early Action Program. The Early Action application deadline is November 15 (postmarked). Students for whom Gonzaga is a top college choice may wish to apply under the Early Action Program. The main advantages of the Early Action Program are early communication of admission (by January 15), early financial aid information, early information about housing possibilities, and early information about registration. Students who apply Early Action may also expect more comprehensive communications from current Gonzaga students and faculty. The Regular Decision application date is February 1 (postmarked). Students applying Regular Decision by this date will receive an admission decision in the middle of March. After February 1, applications will be accepted only if space is available.

GOUCHER COLLEGE

GENERAL INFORMATION

Since its founding in 1885, Goucher has been firmly committed to excellence in liberal arts and sciences education. The 1,250 undergraduates come from 42 states and 20 foreign countries. Goucher is an independent, coeducational liberal arts college located on 287 wooded acres just north of the city of Baltimore. Goucher offers a wide variety of majors and encourages students to create individualized, interdisciplinary programs of study. Undergraduates are required to participate in at least one international study program, internship, or community service project, testing and enhancing their classroom learning through real, firsthand experience in the field. Close interaction with faculty is another cornerstone of a Goucher education, as is Goucher's strong belief in the importance of staying connected to the world outside campus through community action, intercultural awareness, and international exploration.

STUDENT BODY

Students looking for more ways to be involved on campus, more opportunities to get to know other Goucher community members, or for an avenue to express their interests may choose to join one of more of over 50 student clubs or organizations. The activities fall into the following general categories: academic/departmental, recreational, performing and visual arts, publications, special interest, governance, and student mentors. Examples of clubs include: Amnesty International, a Career Development Board, Goucher Chamber Symphony, Hillel, International Club, UMOJA-The African Alliance, Community Auxiliary for Service (CAUSE), and Seekers, a Christian Fellowship group. The Student Government Association (SGA) regulates and enforces social policies and the honor code. A yearbook, newspaper, and literary magazine are among the student publications.

ACADEMICS

Goucher's core curriculum exposes students to both the diversity of human thought and the connections among the disciplines. Students will choose a sequence of two courses from each of four Goucher divisions: arts, humanities, natural sciences and mathematics, and social sciences. Proficient writing is expected of all Goucher students, and is measured twice during each student's college career: on a general college level and in a student's major area of study. Competence in a language other than one's own is an integral part of the liberal arts. All students are required to complete the intermediate level of a foreign language. A computer proficiency requirement in the major area of study is also required. A series of seminars taught by faculty from across the disciplines and organized around a common theme, is taught to all freshmen and is called "frontiers." Each class is small like a senior seminar and emphasizes student participation. The Goucher degree requires 120 semester hours of credit, with the departmental major consisting of at least 30 credits. In addition, a 5-credit off campus experience, either as an internship, independent study, or study abroad, is required. The academic calendar follows the semester system.

Goucher offers majors in 18 departments and five interdisciplinary areas, and gives students the option to design their own majors. Goucher students may create double, combination, or individualized majors or majors with minors. A 3+2 engineering program with Johns Hopkins University is also offered. Areas of study and concentration include: American studies, art, arts administration, biological sciences, chemistry, cognitive studies, communication, computer science, dance, economics, education, English, historic preservation, history, international relations, international and intercultural studies (British, European, Latin American, and Russian), management, mathematics, modern languages (French, German, Russian, and Spanish), music, peace studies, philosophy, physics, politics and public policy, pre-law studies, pre-medical studies, psychology, religion, sociology-anthropology, special education, theater, and women's studies.

The 122 men and women who make up Goucher's faculty include Danforth, Fulbright, Guggenheim, Newberry, and Woodrow Wilson Fellows. More than 90 percent of faculty have earned the doctorate or the highest degree attainable in their fields. Most classes have 20 or fewer students, and the student/faculty ratio is 10:1. Collaboration with professors focuses students on real-world issues and needs. Goucher undergraduates have been involved in nationally recognized and federally funded research on a variety of subjects, including superconductivity, the design of computer software, and gender biases in middle schools. Faculty members are known for their accessibility both in and out of the classroom.

1021 Dulaney Valley Road
Baltimore, MD 21204-2794
Phone: 410-337-6100
Fax: 410-337-6354
Website: www.goucher.edu

GOUCHER

ADMISSIONS

The Admissions Committee seeks applications from students who have the ability to succeed academically at Goucher College and who, as individuals, feel they can contribute positively to the college's diverse community of scholars. Chosen from over 2,750 applicants, the most successful students bring with them a commitment to their academic development, along with a wide variety of talents, interests and extracurricular activity. The applicants' personal qualities are weighed along with academic potential. Consequently, secondary school transcripts and recommendations, are critically important. Test scores are but one measurement in this context. No one is accepted or rejected solely on the basis of test results. The SAT middle 50 percent range is 550–650 on the Verbal portion and 520–640 on the Math portion. An application essay is required. Applicants are encouraged to apply as early in the fall as possible. The Early Action application deadline, which is nonbinding, is December 1; these candidates are notified by January 15. The Regular Decision closing deadline is February 1, with notification by April 1. Candidate reply date is May 1. Applications from transfer students filed by May 1 are given priority. Those filed after that date are considered on a rolling admissions basis.

CAMPUS LIFE

Located on a 287-acre wooded campus nestled in a sprawling northern suburb of Baltimore, Goucher is eight miles from Baltimore city. Immediately surrounding the campus is a lively business and residential community with a wide variety of shopping, dining, and entertainment opportunities. From campus, students can easily walk to a movie complex, one of the area's largest and most popular malls, shops, churches, and a choice of restaurants and night spots. Downtown Baltimore is accessible by bus, and Washington, DC, is 45 minutes by train.

An off campus experience is an essential component of a Goucher education: students take part in internships, study abroad or do independent study and research to complete their off campus requirement. Nearby Baltimore and Washington, DC, are rich resources for internships, field work, and other hands-on learning. Goucher was one of the first colleges in the country to recognize the importance of integrating real-world experience into a liberal arts education: the internship program has been in continuous operation for over 75 years. Students can intern during the school year; over the summer or during a break, in the U.S. or abroad. Study abroad options have grown significantly in recent years, with more than a dozen programs on four continents. Goucher is a member of the "International 50," a select group of colleges whose graduates have made special contributions to the international arena.

COST AND AID

Tuition for the 2003–2004 academic year is $24,150 for two semesters. The cost per credit hour for part-time students is $865. For two semesters, the cost for room is $5,350, and the cost for board (average week plan) is $2,850. Students pay a $150 student activity fee and a $150 health center fee.

GRAND VALLEY STATE UNIVERSITY

GENERAL INFORMATION

Founded in 1960, Grand Valley State University is a comprehensive, public university located in Allendale, Michigan, 12 miles west of downtown Grand Rapids. Grand Valley has established a reputation for preparing students to excel in virtually every field. The academic programs are as challenging as they are personal, interactive, and focused on individual student achievement. GVSU has seven academic divisions: Arts and Humanities, Kirkhof School of Nursing, Science and Mathematics, School of Education, School of Social Work, Seidman School of Business, and Social Sciences. We offer more than 200 areas of study, including 67 undergraduate majors and 20 master's programs giving students a higher degree of choice when selecting a major or minor. Our students benefit from small class sizes, and personalized instruction from faculty dedicated to teaching. Professors collaborate with students on advanced research projects, gaining knowledge and skills more commonly associated with graduate-level study. Grand Valley has been named one of the "100 Best College Buys in the United States" for five consecutive years, combining academic excellence and affordability. With enrollment of more than 20,000 students, Grand Valley is the seventh-largest university in Michigan and operates campuses in Grand Rapids and Holland.

Every detail of the Grand Valley experience is designed to support academic achievement and career success. GVSU owns a public broadcasting television station WGVU-TV 35 and WGVK-TV 52, as well as two radio stations WGVU-FM (88.5) and WGVU-AM (1480). Facilities are located at the Meijer Broadcasting Studios at the Eberhard Center in Grand Rapids. The Cooke-DeVos Center for Health Professions, scheduled to open in the Spring of 2003 in Grand Rapids, will create unique opportunities for student/faculty research, internships, employment and clinical study. Our academic buildings are equipped with wireless technology that offers maximum convenience to the library systems, degree audits, and transfer equivalencies. Students are provided with exceptional high-speed computing and network accessibility as soon as they apply to the University. Advance network/IT support, including high-end workstations, UNIX computers, and Enterprise servers, allows for the integration of cutting-edge technology into instructional programs. Professors utilize Web-based instructional activities, provide online course posting, even host chat groups that include students and faculty from around the world. Grand Valley's Web page offers many features, including class schedules, course equivalencies, online registration, tuition information, online application, scholarship search, student diaries, and information regarding academic programs, student life activities, and athletics. Our on-campus residential housing is among the newest and most contemporary in Michigan. Living on campus puts students just steps away from classes, professors, campus dining, and extracurricular activities. More than 150 clubs, societies, groups, and organizations make it simple to connect with other students who share common interests, academic goals, hobbies, ethnic backgrounds, and religious beliefs. Grand Valley competes in 19 collegiate sports at the NCAA Division II level and our football team won the 2002 national championship title. We invite students to visit our campus and discover for themselves the "Grand Valley Advantage."

STUDENT BODY

GVSU has more than 150 clubs and organizations that offer opportunities for student development outside of the classroom. Volunteer GVSU coordinated more than 150,000 hours of volunteer time by the Grand Valley community last year. Fraternities and sororities offer students social and service opportunities. Campus Ministry activities include alternative spring breaks, group study opportunities, and many club programs. Students may progress to differing levels of leadership training through the Leadership Program. The Student Senate represents the interests of students both on-campus and with legislative issues at the state and federal level. Concerts and lectures are scheduled regularly and provide learning and entertainment experiences. Diversity is celebrated through activities coordinated by the Multicultural Center and the Minority Affairs Office. Opportunities for musical and theater performance abound including the jazz band, university orchestra, festival chorus, madrigal singers, S.T.A.G.E. theater group, and the Shakespeare Festival.

Grand Valley is a member of NCAA Division II in athletics and is a member of the Great Lakes Intercollegiate Athletic Conference. Additionally, GVSU is a member of the Midwest Intercollegiate Football Conference. Athletic scholarships are offered in all sports which include baseball (M), basketball (M, W), cross country (M, W), football (M), golf (M, W), soccer (W), softball (W), swimming and diving (M, W), tennis (M, W), track (M, W), and volleyball (W). Intramural athletics are coordinated in more than 35 activities each year. The GVSU Fitness Center is open for all students, faculty, and staff and includes weight training circuits, cardiovascular machines, an elevated indoor running track, three basketball/volleyball courts and a climbing wall.

Housing is available on campus, but is not mandatory for any student. New freshman students who wish to guarantee a space are encouraged to apply for housing by March 1 of their senior year in high school. Options for freshman students include traditional residence halls, and suite-style and apartment-style living center suites. Upper-class students may also choose from three different apartment complexes on campus and two-bedroom apartment-style living centers.

ACADEMICS

The academic program at Grand Valley State is built around our general education curriculum. The purpose of general education is to strengthen students' abilities to think critically, communicate effectively, and creatively solve problems. Students take courses in a broad spectrum of disciplines, including the arts, the humanities, mathematical sciences, natural sciences, social sciences, world perspectives and U.S. diversity.

GVSU offers undergraduate programs in the following fields: accounting, advertising and public relations, anthropology, art and design, athletic training, behavioral science, biology, biomedical sciences, biopsychology, broadcasting, business, cell and molecular biology, chemistry, city and regional planning, classics, communica-

1 Campus Drive
Allendale, MI 49401
Phone: 616-331-5000
Fax: 616-331-2000
Website: www.gvsu.edu

tions, computer science, criminal justice, dance, earth science, east Asian studies, economics, education, engineering, English, film and video, finance, French, geochemistry, geography, geology, German, Greek, health communication, health sciences, history, hospitality and tourism management, information systems, international business, international relations, journalism, Latin, legal studies, liberal studies, management, marketing, mathematics, music, natural resources management, nursing, occupational safety and health, philosophy, photography, physics, political science, pre dental, pre medical, pre veterinarian, psychology, public administration, Russian Studies, social work, sociology, Spanish, special-education psychology, statistics, theatre, therapeutic recreation, and writing.

Master's degrees are offered in these fields: accounting, biology, business—general, communications, computer information systems, criminal justice, education—general, engineering, health sciences, nursing, occupational therapy, physical therapy, physician assistant studies, public administration, reading/language arts, social work, special education, and taxation.

Grand Valley is a destination point for professors who want teach, sharing their knowledge in a highly interactive, personal learning environment. GVSU is known as a premier teaching institution where professors have a passion for sharing their expertise, their time, and their knowledge with students. These talented people come to Grand Valley from some of the country's leading institutions—including Harvard, Yale, and Northwestern, just to name a few—in order to teach at a university where students come first. It may sound simple but it sets Grand Valley apart. It's why classes are always taught by faculty members, not graduate assistants. And, why professors often collaborate with students on research and literary projects, creating learning experiences for undergraduate students that are typically reserved for master's and doctoral candidates.

ADMISSIONS

A complete application for admission to the freshman class will include a signed application, official high school transcripts, scores from ACT or SAT, and nonrefundable $20 application fee (check or money order payable to GVSU). Although not required, letters of recommendation from teachers or counselors and personal essays may be included. Admission to Grand Valley State University is based on a combination of factors, including a college preparatory curriculum consisting of 4 years of English (including 1 composition), 3 years of mathematics (including 2 years of algebra), 3 years of social studies, and 3 years of science (including 1 laboratory science). A fourth year of math, additional science, computer science, and foreign language are strongly recommended.

A transfer student is someone who has attended another college or university. The application will be evaluated based on previous course work at the college level. High school performance will also be considered for those who have earned fewer than 30 semester credit hours of college-level course work. Transfer students are normally admitted based upon the completion of 30 semester credit hours and a cumulative grade point average of 2.0 or higher. Transfer applicants must submit a signed application, official transcripts from each post-secondary institution attended, and nonrefundable $20 application fee (check or money order payable to GVSU). Applicants with less than 30 semester credit hours must also furnish official high school transcripts.

CAMPUS LIFE

Grand Valley State University's main campus is located almost midway between downtown Grand Rapids and Lake Michigan, near the town of Allendale. The natural land structure of Grand Valley's 1,078-acre campus is formed by deep wooded ravines penetrating a high bluff overlooking the Grand River to the east and gently rolling open fields to the west. The campus is designed to take advantage of the area's scenic wooded ravines as well as its open meadowlands. Automobile traffic is routed along a main campus drive to parking lots at the edge of the academic areas. Winding walkways between buildings connect with a series of natural trails along the riverbank.

The Richard M. DeVos Center on the 29-acre Pew campus in downtown Grand Rapids has 22 classrooms, 3 distance education classrooms, 5 Pentium computer labs, 1 Macintosh lab, a student project area, and a 242,000-volume library with a computer-operated robotic retrieval system and New York-style reading room. The Seidman School of Business, the Kirkhof School of Nursing, the School of Social Work, the School of Public and Nonprofit Administration, the School of Criminal Justice, and the Development Office are housed in the DeVos Center. The Eberhard Center has 43 classrooms and labs, a tutoring center, high-technology teleconference and conference facilities, and two interactive television rooms. The School of Education and the Padnos School of Engineering are housed in the Eberhard Center. Classes are offered in certain graduate and upper-level undergraduate programs. The Keller Engineering Laboratories Building, located adjacent to the Eberhard Center, is a newly constructed, three-story, 27,000-square-foot facility built with its structural, mechanical, and electrical systems exposed to provide students with a living laboratory. Two double-height design bays facilitate student project work and a rooftop deck allows students to conduct experiments outside. The building houses laboratories for instruction and research in electronics, instrumentation and controls, manufacturing processes and control, materials, vibrations, and fluid and thermal systems. The building includes extensive shops for students to implement their designs.

Some of the most important learning at Grand Valley happens outside the classroom. Our office of Career Services has teamed up with hundreds of businesses and organizations to offer student internships in nearly every field. Each year, more than 2,000 students participate, gaining valuable experience while often laying the groundwork for employment after graduation. Grand Valley offers many different ways for student to explore the diversity and complexity of the world around them.

In addition to the many classes on foreign languages and cultures, most academic programs offer courses that address international issues related to the major. In addition, students can choose to live in the language house to take their study of language and culture beyond the classroom. Grand Valley offers a language house on campus for students studying Spanish, French, or German. Students in Every major have opportunities to study in another country. The Padnos International Center sponsors summer, semester and yearlong study abroad programs through partnerships with universities in Europe, Asia, South America, and Australia.

COST AND AID

For the 2002–2003 academic year, estimated expenses for Michigan residents are:

Tuition and fees: $5,056

Room and board: $5,656

Books/Supplies: $800

Miscellaneous: $1,200

For non-Michigan residents:

Tuition and fees: $10,936

Room and Board: $5,656

Books/Supplies: $800

Miscellaneous: $1,200

GREENSBORO COLLEGE

THE COLLEGE

Greensboro College, a four-year, coeducational, liberal arts undergraduate institution affiliated with the United Methodist Church, was founded in 1838. The school is situated in the College Hill Historic District in the city of Greensboro, North Carolina. With an enrollment of just over 1,200 students and a 14:1 student/faculty ratio, Greensboro College emphasizes a small community environment.

Greensboro College recently completed a $10 million building and renovation project resulting in new classrooms and laboratories. The project also transformed the grounds and gardens in a way that enhances the campus setting while preserving its traditional Georgian architecture. The 40-acre campus offers both academic and recreational opportunities in abundance. Campus buildings include classroom buildings, an auditorium, a chapel, three residential halls, a student center, a student services center, a library, and a main administrative building.

At the James G. Hanes gymnasium, students have access to an indoor pool, athletic training room, weight-training room, basketball court, and dance gymnasium. Full-time students may visit the nearby YMCA and use, free of charge, the facility's racquetball courts, basketball courts, weight rooms, indoor pool, sauna, and Jacuzzi. The College fields NCAA Division III intercollegiate teams in men's baseball, basketball, cross-country, football, golf, lacrosse, soccer, and tennis; and women's basketball, cross-country, lacrosse, soccer, softball, swimming, tennis, and volleyball. The College also belongs to the Dixie Intercollegiate Athletic Conference. A broad selection of intramural sports is available to students.

Greensboro College is proud of the ethnic and religious diversity of its student body; more than 30 states and 24 foreign nations are represented. Greensboro College graduates have proceeded to prestigious professional and graduate schools throughout the country and around the world; among the graduate schools that have recently accepted our graduates are the College of William and Mary; Duke; Emory; Georgetown; Johns Hopkins; North Carolina State; Princeton; the Universities of Chicago, Hawaii, North Carolina at Chapel Hill, and Virginia; St. Andrews University in Scotland; and Temple, Vanderbilt, and Wake Forest Universities. The majority of College graduates pursuing advanced degrees continue their studies in the arts, business, education, and health care.

Numerous extracurricular activities complement and support the College's academic program. Over 100 student leadership posts are available in nearly 50 distinct student organizations, allowing most students to pursue an active campus life to whatever degree they desire. The College's pioneering Co-curricular Portfolio Program, a component of the Greensboro College leadership development program, is offered to all students.

LOCATION

The city of Greensboro, located in central North Carolina, offers a cornucopia of resources. The city is home to major insurance companies, textile manufacturers, and other major industries. Greensboro also provides many cultural, athletic, and social opportunities. The Triad region, of which Greensboro is part, has a population exceeding 1 million and is home to six colleges and universities serving more than 24,000 undergraduates. Greensboro College is integral to the life of this growing, dynamic city.

MAJORS

Greensboro College confers the Bachelor of Arts and Bachelor of Science degrees. Majors are offered in the following disciplines: accounting, art, biology, birth-through-kindergarten teacher education, business administration and economics, chemistry, communications, education or special education, English, French, history, history and political science, mathematics, middle school education, music, physical education, political science, psychology, religion and philosophy, secondary education, sociology, Spanish, sports and exercise studies, and theater. Minors are offered in child and family studies, computer science, dance, ethics, interdisciplinary studies, legal administration, women's studies, and areas in which majors are offered. Combined-degree programs are available in medical technology and radiological technology

ACADEMIC

All undergraduates are complete courses in the arts, the humanities, the natural sciences, and the social sciences. A total of 52 semester hours constitute the general education requirements for both the BA and BS degrees; 124 semester hours are required for graduation.

Outstanding students may qualify for Greensboro College's honors program; SAT I or ACT scores, AP examination results, and high school grade point average are all considered in the honors program admissions decision. Completion of the honors program entails requirements in addition to those necessary for the completion of a regular BA and BS degree.

A comprehensive freshman-year program is available to first-year students who choose to participate. The program includes the Précis, a three-day outing intended to help new students meet their new classmates; it also includes focused opportunities to enroll in many campus clubs and organizations.

Greensboro College acknowledges that students must learn professional as well as academic skills; accordingly, the liberal arts curriculum and the school's locale impart the context for an assortment of professional programs (accounting, business, and legal administration among them) and pre-professional programs (in law, medicine, and theology) as well. The College offers career and academic counseling; it also seeks to make certain that its graduates attain all the skills necessary to manage the shifting requirements of a specific career or the volatility of work opportunities. The College also attempts to instill in its students a coherent life philosophy and a grasp of Judeo-Christian values that will enrich their spiritual lives.

Greensboro College seeks to foster the leadership skills inherent in each of its undergraduates. The primary element of the College's Leadership Program is the Co-curricular Portfolio. This program allows students to gauge their skills, establish goals, and design and log achievements and activities in a professionally printed portfolio for their use after graduation. During the junior and senior years, an internship program places undergraduates in settings related to their major and career aspirations.

OFF-CAMPUS OPPORTUNITIES

Greensboro College participates in the Greater Greensboro Consortium and the Piedmont Independent Colleges Association, which allow College students to take courses (pending permission from the academic dean) at Bennett College, Elon College, Guilford College, Guilford Technical Community College, High Point College, North Carolina Agricultural and Technical State University, Salem College, and the University of North Carolina at Greensboro. Students also have access to the libraries of all participating schools.

815 West Market Street
Greensboro, NC 27401-1875
Phone: 800-346-8226
Fax: 336-378-0154
Website: www.gborocollege.edu

ACADEMIC FACILITIES

The James Addison Jones Library contains roughly 103,000 volumes, periodicals, CD-ROMs, and microfilm reels. Students may access the collections of other area colleges through a computerized card catalog system. They may also borrow volumes from the libraries of other colleges through the Interlibrary Loan program. The library's open stacks extend to four levels and include large collections in religion and juvenile literature. The library also houses periodical and browsing rooms, reading rooms, and the Sternberger Cultural Center, a multi-use conference room for College and community events.

The College aims to ensure that each student graduates with a wide range of technical skills applicable to twenty-first-century work and study. Computer labs featuring state-of-the-art equipment are available to all undergraduates; Internet and World Wide Web access is available throughout the campus as well. All dorm rooms are wired for e-mail and Internet service. The College's facilities also include a modern computer laboratory; a computerized writing laboratory; natural science laboratories; the Parlor Theater; and the state-of-the-art Gail Brower Huggins Performance Center, which is among the Triad's most elegant performance venues. Music facilities include practice rooms, 39 pianos (including a 9-foot concert grand), two recital areas, a concert stage, and a computerized music laboratory. Greensboro College is one of only three colleges in North Carolina that has a Fisk organ. The College also has two large art studios, one dedicated to two-dimensional media and one dedicated to three-dimensional media. The education department offers it students support through the Curriculum Materials Center, which contains textbooks, teaching kits, audiovisual equipment, and many other special supplies.

COSTS

The cost of tuition, fees, and room and board for 2002–2003 was approximately $20,410. Students selecting a private room are charged an additional $1,500 on average. Students must typically budget an additional $800 to $1,500 for books, clothing, and other discretionary spending.

FINANCIAL AID

Federally funded financial aid is available to Greensboro College students through the Federal Pell Grant, Federal Work-Study, Federal Perkins Loan, Federal Supplemental Educational Opportunity Grant, Federal Parent Loan for Undergraduate Students, and Federal Stafford Student Loan programs. State funding includes North Carolina Legislative Tuition Grants, the State Contractual Scholarship Fund, North Carolina Prospective Teacher's Scholarships/Loans, and North Carolina Student Incentive Grants. The College funds additional aid in the form of a College work-study program, grants, scholarships, and loans. Merit scholarships, both full- and partial-tuition, are available. Need-based and merit-based grants and scholarships are also available through the United Methodist Church. The school offers full merit-based Presidential Scholarships, valued at more than $81,000 each, to exceptional students. Overall, about 90 percent of Greensboro College undergraduates receive financial assistance in some form. The College encourages all students to apply for financial aid by submitting a Free Application for Federal Student Aid (FAFSA). Students must apply separately for United Methodist Church scholarships and grants; applications are available from the financial planning office. All students, regardless of financial need, may use the career development office on campus to acquire a part-time job while attending the College.

FACULTY

Greensboro College employs 105 full- and part-time faculty. Every member of the full-time faculty holds the highest degree in his or her area of expertise. While a number of our instructors have achieved distinction through their creativity, scholarship, and research projects, all are fundamentally committed to teaching and mentoring undergraduate students. A faculty advisor is assigned to each student. The student/faculty ratio is a favorable 14:1.

STUDENT GOVERNMENT

The student-run College Council of Greensboro College, acting in accordance with the regulations and policies of the College, is the principal representative of the student body. The College Council acts as the students' surrogate in the administration of the College, addressing policy decisions that impact the student body and acting as a platform for student opinions. The College Council serves as liaison to student organizations, the student body, the administration, the staff, and the faculty. The College Activities Board (CAB) organizes student events on campus.

ADMISSION REQUIREMENTS

The Admissions Committee considers all aspects of an applicant's record. High school record is the single most important factor; standardized test scores are also considered. No quantifiable formula is applied to an applicant's record; acceptable scores on the SAT I or ACT, rank in class, grade point average, and quality of high school program all figure into the committee's decision. The College recommends that applicants demonstrate successful completion of a challenging academic program that demonstrates intellectual curiosity and emotional and social maturity. A sample curriculum that would adequately prepare a student for Greensboro College might consist of 4 units of English, 3 units of college-preparatory math (algebra I and II and geometry), 2 units of science (including one laboratory science), 2 units of history, 2 units of the same foreign language, and electives chosen from art, music, physical education, and social science. An on-campus interview is not required but can be extremely helpful to both the student and the Admissions Committee. Applicants are free to schedule interviews at their convenience.

Greensboro College reviews application for transfer credit on a case-by-case basis. Credit is awarded for work successfully completed at accredited junior colleges, technical colleges, community colleges, senior colleges, and universities.

APPLICATION

Once they have decided to apply to the College, applicants should request transcripts be sent to Greensboro by all high schools colleges they have attended; they should make every effort to ensure that transcripts are delivered as quickly as possible. Applicants should also have SAT I or ACT scores forwarded to Greensboro College by the testing agency or by their high school. The Admissions Committee may choose to ask for reference letters. Applications are reviewed on a rolling basis; applicants are notified as soon as the committee reaches its decision. Applications arriving before March 31 receive priority treatment. The College has no closing date for applications. Direct inquiries and application materials to:

Director of Admissions
Greensboro College
815 West Market Street
Greensboro, NC 27401-1875
Telephone: 800-346-8226 (toll free nationwide)
Fax: 336-378-0154
E-mail: admissions@gborocollege.edu
World Wide Web: http://gborocollege.edu

HAMPSHIRE COLLEGE

GENERAL INFORMATION

Hampshire College was founded to allow students to direct their own education and focus on interdisciplinary fields. In 1965, people from four of the country's top institutions came together to develop this unique learning environment. The Hampshire faculty helps students evaluate their experiences in diverse fields and combine the subjects that most intrigue them. Interdisciplinary topics formed in the past include neuropsychology and the creative process, conflict resolution and international studies, and film and physics. To culminate their studies, students complete a senior project, such as an academic essay, research paper, scientific experiment, body of creative writing, film, invention, art exhibition, or performance-based project. Hampshire students have access to all of the resources of Five Colleges, Inc., an education consortium with Amherst, Hampshire, Mount Holyoke, and Smith Colleges, and the University of Massachusetts as members. Between all of these schools, there are 6,400 courses, 8 million library volumes, and a wide array of cultural events. The coed student body of 1,100 arrives at Hampshire from most states and around the world. The members of this diverse group are united by their thirst for knowledge and appreciation of Hampshire's unique educational style.

STUDENT BODY

The Outdoors/Recreational Athletics Program administers the College's athletic classes. It also facilitates the following team sports: soccer, basketball, softball, and fencing. Finally, the Program organizes backpacking, rock-climbing, bicycle, and canoe trips for all skill and experience levels. All students have access to the swimming pool, playing floor, games area, rock-climbing wall, bouldering cave, and weight-training equipment in the extensive Robert Crown Center. To participate in indoor tennis, jogging, weight training, soccer, volleyball, or aerobics, students head to the Multisport Center. Student-run clubs cover the gamut of social and cultural interests. Some of the 85 organizations are listed here: Students For A Free Tibet, Ultimate Frisbee-Red Scare, Slam Poetry Collective, Soapbox, Spontaneous Combustion (*a capella*), Latin Dance Group, Improv Comedy, Hip (Hampshire Independent Productions), Czech Cuisine, Free Press, Hampshire Anime Group, Earth!, and Collective Action.

ACADEMICS

The College's innovative approach to teaching and learning ensures that students enjoy small class sizes, one-on-one contact with instructors, personalized programs, and an education that crosses subject boundaries. Courses are divided into three overarching groups. Division I, Basic Studies, allows students to investigate the disciplines of humanities, arts, social sciences, or cognitive or natural sciences through classes, research, or creative work. Through Division II, Concentration, students gain a depth of knowledge in a subject by participating in their choice of internships, individual projects, overseas study, and additional classes. Division III, Advanced Studies, has two parts. Primarily, students work to finish a substantial project, such as a thesis, creative piece, or scientific experiment, to tie together and culminate their previous studies. They also have the choice of attending an advanced, interdisciplinary seminar centered on helping an instructor facilitate a class. In addition to Division coursework, all students participate in community service. A final requirement asks students to think about their chosen concentration in relation to the developing world. Faculty members give students detailed written comments, rather than letter grades, as evaluations. As a record of their achievements, students compile a portfolio, which features projects, evaluations, and grades from any Five College courses they have taken. This type of transcript stands Hampshire graduates in good stead: close to 60 percent of alumni go on to complete at least one graduate degree.

Students earn their Bachelor of Arts degrees by excelling in the course of study they design with the help and support of their instructors.

ADMISSIONS

For September admissions, the deadline is February 1 for first-year students and March 1 for transfer students; all applicants are notified of their admission status by April 1, and those admitted must reply to Hampshire by May 1. November 15 is the deadline for early decision, and December 15 is the date of notification. Students who submit their applications by January 1 may receive early action notification by January 21; however, they do not need to respond until the May 1 date. To begin in the spring term (February), the application deadline is November 15 with notification on December 15. International first-year and transfer students seeking financial assistance are only considered for the fall start date. Their application deadline is February 1. High school juniors who demonstrate both academic and personal maturity may be accepted as part of the Early Entrance Plan based on application materials and a mandatory interview.

Admissions Office, 893 West Street
Amherst, MA 01002
Phone: 413-559-5471
Fax: 413-559-5631
Website: www.hampshire.edu

CAMPUS LIFE

Hampshire's setting in the Pioneer Valley of western Massachusetts puts the campus close to a variety of cultural and recreational opportunities. For nearby shopping and restaurants, students head to Amherst and Northampton; Boston and New York City are also nearby for urban diversion. A variety of concerts, films, lectures, theater and dance performances, and gallery shows are put on by the Five Colleges. Those who enjoy the outdoors find a paradise in New England's picturesque landscape.

The resources at Hampshire are supplemented by those available at the other institutions involved in Five Colleges, Inc. Hampshire students take the free shuttle to the other campuses and get involved in extracurricular activities organized by these neighboring schools at no additional cost. The concentration of colleges and universities in the area make for a lively intellectual and cultural environment. Additionally, the nearby Holyoke mountain range provides an arena for hiking, mountain biking, and wildlife viewing. The College's Outdoors Program sponsors kayaking, rock-climbing, and ski trips as well as opportunities to develop outdoor leadership skills.

COST AND AID

Every year, Hampshire distributes $10 million in financial aid, covering an average of two-thirds of costs for roughly half of the College's attendees. The following merit-based scholarships are also available: the Harold F. Johnson Scholarship, which awards renewable amounts of $5,000 to $7,500; the Arturo Schomburg Scholarship, which gives $7,500 each year for up to three years to top minority students; and renewable National Merit Scholarships of $1,000. Financial aid applications are submitted simultaneously with admissions applications.

HARTWICK COLLEGE

GENERAL INFORMATION

Hartwick College enjoys a picturesque location at the northern rim of New York's Catskill Mountains. Established in 1797, Hartwick was the first of America's Lutheran seminaries. In 1928, an updated charter converted Hartwick into a private, four-year coeducational institution guided by the principles of a liberal arts and sciences education. Today, Hartwick College enrolls nearly 1,400 undergraduate students. The ratio of male to female students is 45:55. About two-thirds of Hartwick's students hail from the state of New York, with another 30 percent coming from other Northeastern states. In total, the Student Body has been drawn from 30 states and almost 40 nations. Most students live in coeducational residence halls on campus, sharing meals in the college commons. Special-interest houses are available as well. The College maintains 20 townhouses on the Hartwick campus that can house 80 students and that provide an alternative to off-campus living. Townhouses include three bedrooms (two singles and a double), a pair of bathrooms, a common area, a study section, and kitchen facilities. Ten Greek houses provide residence for approximately 75 students. Hartwick's 720-acre Pine Lake Environmental Campus offers another option for off-campus living. Hartwick's full menu of student-life options includes more than 60 student organizations. Student organizations and the College provide a range of extracurricular events each year, including a number of annual weekend events both on-campus and in New York and other cities. After arriving on campus, freshmen are introduced to the services of the Career Planning Center, which helps them focus their career objectives. The Center's Guaranteed Placement Program pledges that if any student who completes the Center's list of required activities and cross-disciplinary experiences without falling below a 3.0 GPA has not found a job in the first six months following graduation, Hartwick's Board of Trustees will guarantee a funded internship in the student's field of study. The Center's success is apparent with a 99 percent job-placement rate for Hartwick graduates.

STUDENT BODY

Hartwick offers a wide range of extracurricular opportunities for its students. Nationally renowned bands, comedians, and other entertainers are brought to campus by the Office of Student Activities. The Student Senate—the Student Body's primary voice—serves in legislative and executive capacities in the College's student government. Funding for all student organizations is determined by the Student Senate. More than 75 percent of Hartwick students take part in athletics on some level, whether it's intercollegiate, recreational, or intramural. The College's men's Division I soccer program, which has been a national power for many years, won the NCAA championship in 1977. The women's water polo team, also Division I, is the premier program in the East. The field hockey, basketball, lacrosse, and swimming teams are also highly competitive at the Division III level. Hartwick fields 24 intercollegiate programs. The fine and performing arts make their home at the Anderson Center for the Arts, a building that comprises both studios and classrooms, practice rooms, a theater, and an art gallery. The expansive Yager Hall houses the library (300,000 volumes), the College archives, a computer lab, classrooms, labs, offices, and the Yager Museum, whose holdings include a collection of thousands of artifacts from Native American culture spanning more than ten millennia. The Yager Collection has been acknowledged as among the most definitive collections of Native American artifacts in the state of New York. Classrooms, offices, and a laboratory theatre can be found in Arnold and Bresee Halls. Clark Hall is the location of the writing center, the media center, and the departments of English, foreign languages, and psychology. And the Binder Physical Education Center is at the heart of Hartwick's intercollegiate and recreational programs. Binder houses an eight-lane swimming pool, a fitness center, two gyms, and racquetball and squash courts.

ACADEMICS

The goals of a Hartwick College education are embodied in Curriculum XXI, an innovative academic plan that grew from the careful consideration of Hartwick's faculty members. In essence, Curriculum XXI restructures the basic shape of higher education by acknowledging that today's students will need to succeed in an ever-changing twenty-first century. The plan consists of core requirements, including classes in history, literature, mathematics, nonwestern culture, science, and social and behavioral analysis. Combined, these core requirements demand that students come to terms with their own culture, cultures foreign to them, and larger constructs of humanity and of nature. Beyond the core curriculum, students must engage in a focused study in a major discipline, capping their majors with a senior thesis or a culminating project. Students must also complete seminars that promote student interaction and cooperation. During their first year, students enroll in a seminar geared at introducing them to the principles espoused by a liberal education. In the seminar, students become immersed in the exploration of a fundamental social issue and approach it through critical and analytical methods. This process is continued in junior or senior seminars in which interdisciplinary investigations into contemporary topics demonstrate how complicated issues can be addressed logically and responsibly by people with liberal educations. By instructing, advising, and demonstrating effective methods of approaching issues, the members of Hartwick's staff and faculty help students recognize and achieve their academic ambitions. In many cases, out-of-classroom experiences such as internships and independent studies become integral aspects of a student's education. All students must demonstrate writing competency to graduate. Students who earn a 3 or better on Advanced Placement exams (4 or 5 on music and French exams) can receive both accelerated placement and course credit. Hartwick also offers advanced placement to students who demonstrate proficiency through the College-Level Examination Program, a series of exams that accounts for applicable knowledge gained outside the walls of a traditional classroom. Hartwick operates on a traditional fall/spring calendar (15 weeks each semester), with a four-week January term.

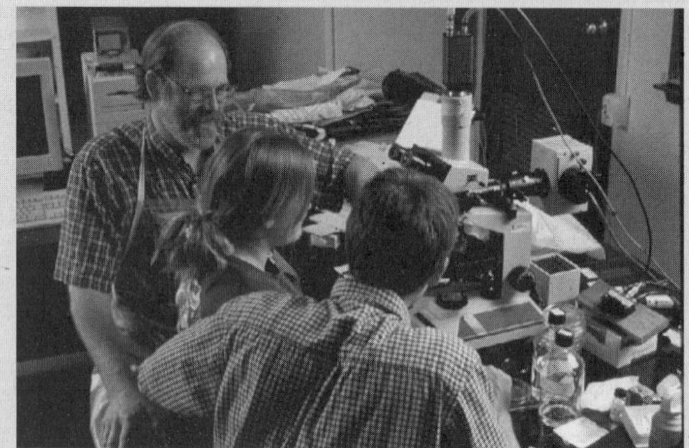

PO Box 4020
Oneonta, NY 13820-4020
Phone: 607-431-4000
Fax: 607-431-4102
Website: www.hartwick.edu

Hartwick College offers 30 programs of study administered by 19 academic departments. In addition, the College allows independent study and student-designed major tracks. Partner institutions, off-campus programs, and special on-campus options provide further opportunities. Hartwick's established majors are accounting, biochemistry, chemistry, economics, English, French, geology, German, history, management, mathematics, music, philosophy, philosophy/religious studies, physics, political science, psychology, religious studies, sociology, Spanish, and theater arts. Interested students may opt for an accelerated BA or BS program. In partnership with Clarkson University and the Columbia University School of Engineering and Applied Science, Hartwick offers pre-professional programs in engineering. Participating students complete their work at Hartwick in three years, followed by two years of study at the cooperating institution; after all requirements are complete, Hartwick grants a BA and the other institution grants a BS. Other cooperative programs at Hartwick include a joint MBA/MS with Clarkson and a 3-3 law-degree partnership with the Albany Law School. After graduation, nursing students qualify for the State Board Examination, which allows them to become registered nurses. Students who earn degrees in medical technology are eligible for the National Registry Examination, which provides professional certification.

At Hartwick, faculty members see themselves as teachers, principally committed to assisting each individual student—a commitment reflected in the 11:1 student/faculty ratio. Aside from acting as advisors to students and student organizations, faculty members serve with students on campus committees. The percentage of faculty with terminal degrees is greater than 90 percent.

ADMISSIONS

Successful Hartwick College applicants are those with high school diplomas, have demonstrated academic proficiency in the past, and show potential to learn from and contribute to the community at Hartwick. While class standing and standardized test scores are considered, applicants also are evaluated on individual qualities, prior participation in activities, unique talents, and official recommendations. Though not mandatory, in-person interviews and SAT I or ACT scores are highly recommended. The application deadline is February 15 for the year of anticipated enrollment. Early decision applications must be filed by January 15; early decision notifications are usually sent out two weeks after the completed file is received by the Admissions office. Regular decision candidates receive notification around March 15. All applications must include a $35, nonrefundable fee. If students fill out the application online or officially visit campus, the College waives the application fee. Hartwick recognizes the College's application form, the Common Application Form, and the online application form. For more information or to request application materials, please contact:

Hartwick College Admissions Office
One Hartwick Drive
Oneonta, NY 13820
Telephone: 1-888-HARTWICK (toll free) or 1-607-431-4150
E-mail: Admissions@hartwick.edu
Website: www.hartwick.edu

CAMPUS LIFE

"College town" is a phrase often used to describe Oneonta. Aside from its 14,000 permanent residents, Oneonta is home to the students of Hartwick College and the SUNY College of Oneonta. Students from either college may gain access to the library system at the other. Additionally, students may cross register for courses. Hartwick has long been an important aspect of the town's community, inviting local residents to participate in campus events while members of the campus community take advantage of Oneonta's fine shopping, dining, and entertainment. The town's sources of culture and recreation include everything from ski centers, golf courses, and parks to the Catskill Symphony Orchestra, the Catskill Choral Society, and the Orpheus Theater. Soccer fans enjoy the National Soccer Hall of Fame, located in Oneonta; and it's a quick drive for baseball fans to the National Baseball Hall of Fame in Cooperstown.

Hartwick prides itself on the off-campus study options it offers its students. In fact, a recent survey named Hartwick fourth among nationwide liberal arts schools for the percentage of its students who take part in programs abroad. During the past several years, students have spent semesters in Argentina, Australia, Austria, Chile, Colombia, England, India, Ireland, Italy, Kenya, Mexico, the Netherlands, Peru, and Spain, as well as participating in domestic off-campus programs in Arizona, Colorado, Hawaii, Massachusetts, and New York. Programs during the College's January term have taken students to Australia, Austria, the Bahamas, Banaras, China, Costa Rica, Cuba, the Czech Republic, England, the Florida Keys, France, Guatemala, the Grand Canyon, Greece, Hawaii, India, Ireland, Israel, Jordan, New York City, South Africa, Spain, and Thailand. Year-long programs and independent-study options are available as well. Freshmen can participate in the Early Experience Program, which provides first-year students with possibilities for study abroad in January.

COST AND AID

In 2001–2002, tuition was $25,715, and room and board was approximately $10,000. Books, transport, and personal expenses were estimated at $1,500.

HAVERFORD COLLEGE

GENERAL INFORMATION

Haverford is a coeducational, undergraduate, liberal arts college founded in 1833 by members of the Religious Society of Friends (Quakers). While the College is not formally affiliated with any religious body today, the values of individual dignity, academic strength, and tolerance on which it was founded remain central to its character.

Haverford's 1,100 students represent a wide variety of interests, backgrounds, and talents. They come from independent and public schools across the United States, Puerto Rico, and more than 20 countries around the world.

Extensive cooperation with nearby Bryn Mawr College adds an important dimension to the resources available at Haverford. Educational opportunities are further enhanced by cooperation with Swarthmore College and the University of Pennsylvania.

Although students choose Haverford because of its academic excellence, a sense of community participation informs the Haverford College experience both inside the classroom and out. Students work together through the arts and cultural activities, self-government and service programs, athletic programs, and day-to-day campus life.

The Honor Code, affirmed by the student body each year, represents the philosophy of conduct within the College. Students are expected to maintain a strong sense of individual responsibility as well as intellectual integrity, honesty, and genuine concern for others.

Haverford College offers an atmosphere of intellectual challenge, excitement, and growth in a close-knit community that is dedicated to encouraging humane values during the undergraduate years and for a lifetime.

STUDENT BODY

There are more than 100 student organizations on campus. Musicians, athletes, writers, actors, rock climbers, gourmet cooks, feminists, political activists . . . everyone finds ways to pursue their extracurricular passions at Haverford. There are 10 varsity sports for men and 11 for women. In addition, the students support a host of club sports and intramural teams. Visit www.haverford.edu/students/students.html/ for more insight into extracurricular life at Haverford.

The Honor Code is a fundamental part of life at Haverford College. All students at Haverford agree to uphold the standards and ideals of the Honor Code. The following excerpts help to demonstrate these ideals:

"The Honor Code depends for its effective operation on both our personal concern for each other and our collective concern for the maintenance of the community standards reflected in the Code. Both concerns are central to the functioning of the Code, and both have meaning only as they form the basis for conduct of our daily lives. The Code makes it possible for members of a diverse student body to live together, interact, and learn from one another in ways that protect both personal freedom, and community standards. It makes it possible for a climate of trust, concern and respect to exist among us, a climate conducive to learning and growing, and one without which community would soon deteriorate."

The idea of dialogue is central to the Honor Code. Challenging ourselves (and others) to understand different experiences and perspectives is never easy. At the same time, our potential for learning and growth is severely limited by self-censorship and unwillingness to put oneself in situations that may be uncomfortable."

The Honor Code affects both social and academic life at Haverford:

The Social Sphere: "Our social relationships should be based on mutual respect and concern. We must consider how our words and actions may affect the sense of acceptance essential to an individual's or groups' participation in the community. We strive to foster an environment which genuinely encourages respectful expression of values rather than unproductive self-censorship. On encountering actions or values which we find degrading to ourselves an to others, we should feel comfortable initiating dialogue with the mutual goal of increasing our understanding of each other."

The Academic Sphere: "As students we are responsible for proper conduct and integrity in all of our scholastic work. We must follow a professor's instructions as to the completion of tests, homework, and laboratory reports, and must ask for clarification if the instructions are not clear. In general students should not give or receive aid when taking exams, or exceed the time limitations specified by the professor."

Ratification: The Honor Code is entirely student-written and student-run. Each year the student body re-ratifies the Code at a community wide "Plenary," where students also have the opportunity to make changes to the Honor Code. In this way, the Honor Code is a living, evolving part of the community at Haverford.

ACADEMICS

Haverford offers the following academic programs in addition to majors and minors; these are Concentrations: Africana studies, biochemistry and biophysics, computer science, East Asian studies, education, feminist and gender studies, Latin American and Iberian studies, mathematical economics, neural and behavioral sciences, peace studies, 3/2 liberal arts and engineering. Students may pursue pre-medical, pre-law or pre-business intentions through any major; special advising is offered in these areas.

Natural Sciences: astronomy, biology, chemistry, geology, mathematics, physics.

Social Sciences: anthropology, economics, growth and structure of cities, history, political science, psychology, sociology.

Humanities: archaeology, classics, comparative literature, English, fine arts, French, German, history of art, Italian, Japanese, music, philosophy, religion, Russian, Spanish.

The Bachelor of Arts is offered in all majors; science majors have the option of choosing the Bachelor of Science.

There are 105 full-time and 6 part-time faculty at the College.

- 97 percent of the full-time faculty have their PhDs
- 92 percent of the part-time faculty have their PhDs
- The student/faculty ratio is 8:1
- 70 percent of faculty live on campus

370 Lancaster Avenue
Haverford, PA 19041
Phone: 610-896-1350
Fax: 610-896-1338
Website: www.haverford.edu

ADMISSIONS

Criteria for Admission: The primary criteria for admission are the student's academic and personal qualities as shown by the school record and recommendations, College Board test results, and extracurricular and personal accomplishments both in and out of school. The College is primarily concerned with the candidate's motivation and preparation for rigorous academic work, but is also concerned with the qualities of character and personality that indicate that the student will be an effective member of a community that emphasizes integrity and concern for others.

Campus Visit and Interview: A visit to the Haverford campus is strongly encouraged. Plan visits in advance by writing, e-mailing or calling the Admission Office (admission@haverford.edu or 610-896-1350). Interviews are required of all students living within 150 miles of the College.

Application Procedures: Students may begin their studies in the fall semester only. Applications should be filed as early as possible in the student's senior year; the deadline is January 15. The College uses the Common Application solely, along with a Supplement which can be obtained online or by mail. All applications should be accompanied by a nonrefundable $50 application fee payable to Haverford College. Decisions are announced before April 15. Applications are available through Haverford's website. Students are required to submit all forms and supporting documents included in the application. In addition, they must also have their official SAT or ACT scores and three SAT II (one of which must be Writing) test scores sent to Haverford.

CAMPUS LIFE

Originally landscaped by the English gardener William Carvill, the park-like, 204-acre campus includes more than 400 species of trees and shrubs, a nature walk, and a duck pond. The varied architectural styles of campus buildings, representing more than 150 years of architectural evolution, give the campus a unique character and charm. Just 10 miles away from Haverford are the cultural and educational resources of Philadelphia. Frequent train service to and from the city add to campus resources and enhance student opportunities.

In addition to the course offerings at Swarthmore, Bryn Mawr, and the University of Pennsylvania, there are numerous opportunities for internships and volunteer service in the surrounding communities and in Philadelphia. If students want to go farther afield they may participate in one of the 50 study abroad programs supported by Haverford. Domestic study away programs include exchanges with Claremont McKenna, Spelman and Fisk.

COST AND AID

2003–2004 School Year

Tuition: $28,612

Room: $5,050

Board: $3,970

Activity fee: $268

Orientation fee: $160 (new students only)

Total for new students: $38,060

Total for returning students: $37,900

HAWAII PACIFIC UNIVERSITY

GENERAL INFORMATION

Students seeking a liberal arts education that emphasizes small class sizes and career-building skills find it in Hawai'i Pacific University (HPU). A private, coeducational institution, HPU grants bachelors and masters degrees in close to 50 fields of study. The HPU environment is unique in that there is no majority population among the student body. The University fosters diversity and the breadth of knowledge, experience, and sensitivity it brings. Because HPU students arrive from every state in the nation as well as 100 foreign countries, students have the immediate opportunity to learn from other cultures and their values, customs, traditions, and principles. Friendships at HPU cut across racial, ethnic, and national lines, forming a global network of collaboration and support.

The following graduate programs are available at HPU: the Master of Business Administration (MBA) with 12 concentrations; the Master of Science in Information Systems (MSIS) and Nursing (MSN); and the Master of Arts in Communication (MA/COM), Diplomacy and Military Studies (MA/DMS), Global Leadership (MA/GL), Human Resource Management (MA/HRM), Organizational Change (MA/OC), and Teaching English as a Second Language (MA/TESL). HPU varsity athletic teams participate in NCAA Division II in intercollegiate sports. The men compete in baseball, basketball, cheerleading, cross-country, soccer, and tennis. The women field teams in cheerleading, cross-country, soccer, softball, tennis, and volleyball. Students have a variety of choices regarding their housing at HPU. Many attendees decide to live in the Hawai'i Loa campus' residence halls, complete with cafeterias. Others reside in off-campus apartments in Honolulu/Waikiki.

STUDENT BODY

Student representatives are elected to lead the Associated Students of Hawai'i Pacific University (ASHPU), to which all students automatically belong. This organization sponsors student clubs, organizations, and activities. Many students choose to participate in the literary magazine, student newspaper, pep band, service organizations, pre-professional groups, cultural clubs, athletics, or social events.

ACADEMICS

A minimum of 124 semester hours is required for baccalaureate graduation. The core liberal arts requirements comprise 45 of these units, providing a solid background for advanced study. Students earn the rest of their units completing their major requirements and taking electives. At HPU, the academic calendar consists of two semesters separated by a five-week winter intersession. It is possible to earn an undergraduate degree in just three years by staying on for the summer session. Students may also enroll in the five-year joint BS/, BA/MBA program.

Undergraduates at HPU may pursue the degrees of Bachelor of Arts and Bachelor of Science. Those working toward their Bachelor of Arts (BA) choose from the following majors: advertising, anthropology, applied sociology, communication (concentrations in speech or visual communication), East-West classical studies, economics, English, environmental studies, history, human resource development, human services, international relations, international studies (concentrations in American, Asian, comparative, European, or Pacific studies), journalism, justice administration, political science, psychology (community and human services, human development and education, personal growth and counseling), public relations, social sciences, and teaching English as a second language. Students seeking a Bachelor of Science (BS) may select a major in applied mathematics, biology, computer science, diplomacy and military studies, environmental science, marine biology, nursing, oceanography, or pre-medical studies. Business-oriented undergraduates may earn a BS in business administration from the School of Business. Available majors include accounting, business economics, computer information systems, corporate communication, entrepreneurial studies, finance, human resource management, international business, management, marketing, public administration, and travel industry management. In addition, the University grants the Bachelor of Social Work. Students may also pursue dual degrees, double majors, and minors.

Students at HPU are never instructed by teaching assistants; rather, considering the low 18:1 student/faculty ratio, students have the opportunity to form close academic relationships with highly qualified professors. Of the 145 full-time and 281 part-time instructors, more than three-quarters hold their PhD or terminal degree. Teaching is more important than research, and the average class size of 25 allows for discussion and interaction. Many faculty members are well known in their respective fields and share their real-world experience with students. Students also benefit from assistance from academic advisors. Before registering for a semester's courses, students meet with advisors to plot their academic direction and discuss personal goals.

1164 Bishop Street
Honolulu, HI 96813
Phone: 808-544-0238
Fax: 808-544-1136
Website: www.hpu.edu

ADMISSIONS

Hawai'i Pacific solicits applications from students who demonstrate that they are academically and personally prepared to undertake university-level study. Applicants should submit their high school transcripts and SAT or ACT scores along with the application form. Transfer students are required to send transcripts from all previously attended colleges, as well. The University requires SAT or ACT results to be submitted. First-year candidates should have at least a 2.5 high school GPA and a solid record of college-preparatory classes. The suggested course of study includes 4 years of English, 3 years of math and social studies, and at least 1 year of history and 2 years of science. Students who have less than a 2.5 must turn in three letters of recommendation and an essay outlining their academic goals in order to be reviewed by the Admissions Committee. Students applying to the marine science and environmental science programs should have a 3.0 high school GPA with classes in biology, chemistry, physics, and math through pre-calculus. Transfer students who wish to enter these programs should show proficiency in college-level science and math. If applicants do not meet these criteria, they can still enroll as undeclared students and, after passing HPU science and math classes, enter the desired program. A 2.0 GPA is mandatory for transfer students with 24 or more postsecondary credits. Students with fewer than 24 credits will be evaluated according to both their college and high school grades.

CAMPUS LIFE

Hawai'i Pacific maintains two campuses, one in downtown Honolulu and the other set amid the picturesque foothills of the Ko'olau mountains. In Honolulu, students are immersed in a thriving business and financial environment. Just a few minutes by car out of the city, the Hawai'i Loa campus provides resources for studying nursing, marine science, and other disciplines. Students take a shuttle between these locations, choosing classes at either campus and enjoying the advantages of both an urban life and a natural retreat. HPU prioritizes an education that applies to career goals. Thus, cooperative education and internship programs, easily arranged with local businesses, complement much of classroom work at the University's. The healthy island economy offers plenty of opportunity for students to participate in the business world. When students aren't studying or working, the outdoors await: the state's renowned weather and natural beauty allow for endless outdoor recreation and exploration.

Studying at HPU always entails a real-world component, furnished by the extensive cooperative education/internship program. By participating in an internship, students receive career experience, academic credit, and pay—a practical and educational combination. Advanced students often land internships with premier Honolulu companies, including Aloha Airlines; the Bank of Hawai'i; the city and county of Honolulu; the state of Hawai'i; Hilton Hawai'ian Village Hotel; IBM; KGMB-TV and Radio; Merrill Lynch; New York Life; Ogilvy & Mather; Pricewaterhouse; Sears, Roebuck and Company; Sheraton; Starr, Siegle, McComb; and U.S. agencies and departments.

COST AND AID

In 2002–2003, tuition was $9,850 annually. Marine science majors pay $5,925 per semester in tuition, while nursing majors who are in their last two years pay $7,100 per semester. Approximately $1,455 should be allotted for books, supplies, and health insurance. Room and board for Hawai'i Loa Campus residents runs $6,910 annually. Students who choose to live in off-campus apartments (operated by Cadmus Properties Corporation) pay between $2,295 to $2,495 per semester. A $500 refundable security deposit must be paid for residence halls and Cadmus-run apartments.

HILBERT COLLEGE

GENERAL INFORMATION

Hilbert College is an independent, coeducational four-year institution in the Catholic/Franciscan tradition. Since its founding in 1957, the College has made close individual attention and challenging academic programs the cornerstones of a Hilbert education. Hilbert College has an enrollment of approximately 1,000 students in its bachelor and associate degree programs.

Academically, Hilbert College has program offerings in the areas of law and justice, social sciences, business/accounting, English, and human services. The College is also home to the Institute for Law and Justice, which is a local, regional, and national resource for law enforcement, crime prevention, and community well-being.

In harmony with its Franciscan spirit and commitment to the individual, the College provides counseling and support services for students whose diversified needs are best met in this small college setting.

Its small size and intimate atmosphere provide its students with numerous activities and avenues for involvement on campus. Hilbert College fields 11 athletic teams in NCAA Division III intercollegiate competition. These are: baseball (m), basketball (m/w), cross-country (mixed), golf (mixed), lacrosse (w), soccer (m/w), softball (w), and volleyball (m/w).

STUDENT BODY

Student involvement on campus extends far beyond the classroom. Numerous academic and social clubs provide a positive atmosphere for social growth and intellectual exploration. The small-college atmosphere provides its students with a greater voice. The Student Government Association is the largest student-run organization on campus and is an advocate for the students' needs. It sponsors, plans, and runs a long list of events each year. This includes speakers, concerts, dances, and workshops. In addition, the Office of Student Life maintains an active calendar of annual campus-wide, traditional and seasonal, festivals and activities.

ACADEMICS

Hilbert College has established itself as a center for learning in the areas of law and justice. Its criminal justice department is one of the largest and most respected in the region. The economic crime investigation program is one of two in the nation and provides students the opportunity to study in the areas of computer and white-collar crime. The paralegal studies program is one of a few ABA-approved programs in the state. The liberal studies program provides the theoretical foundations for students wishing to pursue advanced careers in law and government. Hilbert College's business administration, human services, and accounting programs offer the personal attention, practical hands-on internships, and individualized career focus that many larger programs lack. Its psychology and English departments offer both the solid educational foundation needed for graduate school and the flexibility to address each individual student's academic interests. The Honors Program spans all the disciplines and offers exceptional students the opportunity to pursue advanced work in their areas of study. Hilbert College also offers many minors and concentrations in various areas of study ranging from Forensic Investigations to Sports Management. These elective areas allow students to further define themselves and specialize in their interest areas.

Common to all these programs is Hilbert College's belief in a core curriculum in the liberal arts, the purpose of which is to develop the habits of thought, methods of critical investigation, and ethical perspectives that enable students to make sound judgments and increase their capacity for leading fuller lives. All students must complete common course work in basic skill areas, interdisciplinary studies, and prescribed and elective liberal arts components prior to graduation.

Hilbert College has developed a series of transfer articulation agreements with most two-year colleges in New York State and some proprietary and Canadian institutions. These agreements allow two-year graduates to move directly into a related four-year program as full juniors and with no course duplication. The College is accredited by the Commission on Higher Education of the Middle States Association of Colleges and Schools. Therefore, its credits are readily transferable nationwide to other four-year colleges and universities.

Hilbert College offers programs of study leading to a Bachelor of Arts degree in English, liberal studies (law & government), and psychology. A Bachelor of Science degree is offered in accounting, business administration, criminal justice, economic crime investigation, human services, and paralegal studies. In addition to its four-year offerings, the College also maintains associate degree programs in accounting, banking, business administration, criminal justice, human services, liberal arts, management information systems, and paralegal studies.

Hilbert College has a full-time teaching faculty of 36 men and women. Sixty-one percent of its full-time faculty have doctoral or terminal degrees in their disciplines. In addition, the College employs 57 part-time faculty members, many of whom are directly employed in their fields and bring their practical experience into the classroom.

5200 South Park Avenue
Hamburg, NY 14075-1597
Phone: 716-649-7900
Fax: 716-649-0702
Website: www.hilbert.edu

ADMISSIONS

Hilbert College is open to men and women regardless of faith, race, age, physical handicap, or national origin. All accepted students have an equal opportunity to pursue their educational goals through programs available at the College. Students can request an application be sent to them or they can apply online at www.hilbert.edu. A $20 application fee is required and all official transcripts (high school and college) must be received prior to registration.

The Admissions Committee reviews applications on a rolling basis; there is no set date for receiving applications prior to the start of classes. Students are encouraged to apply early in order to be considered for the College's merit-based scholarships and limited institutional grant money. The College considers for admissions to regular degree study only those students who have been awarded a high school diploma or a recognized high school equivalency diploma. SAT and ACT scores, although not required, are strongly recommended. Admission decisions are based on an evaluation of academic ability and skills based on a study of submitted transcripts, recommendations, and test scores. Math and English placement tests are required of most freshmen.

CAMPUS LIFE

Hilbert College's 47-acre campus is located in the Town of Hamburg in western New York. It is near the shore of Lake Erie and approximately 10 miles south of the City of Buffalo. The campus consists of nine buildings, athletic fields, and well-maintained campus grounds. Hilbert College also provides student housing for more than 130 students. Its proximity to Buffalo makes all the cultural and recreational resources of a large city readily accessible to students.

Hilbert College's academic programs offer individually tailored internship opportunities to students in their senior year of study. These placements are the result of close departmental mentoring and student/faculty interaction. Internship sites have ranged from private companies to governmental agencies, both in state and out of state. In addition to academic opportunities, Student Life and Campus Ministry offers many opportunities for students off campus in terms of community service and extracurricular outings. Hilbert College, in conjunction with another institution, also offers study abroad opportunities to students wishing to spend a semester in another country in order to enhance a global perspective.

COST AND AID

For 2003–2004, annual tuition and fees are $13,500, and average room and board is $5,670. Hilbert College is among the most affordable private college choices in western New York.

HILLSDALE COLLEGE

GENERAL INFORMATION

Hillsdale College was founded in 1844, built on a gratefulness for God's "inestimable blessings" and a desire to spread knowledge in order to ensure the "perpetuity of these blessings." Since then, the private, nonsectarian, coeducational institution has focused on liberal arts education. Hillsdale has preserved its unalloyed dedication to the Judeo-Christian and Greco-Roman tradition by remaining independent of any federal funding. The widespread private support enables a private financial aid program, as well. The small undergraduate population of 1,100 is half women and half men. Students arrive from 47 states and 10 countries other than the United States, though nearly half of attendees are Michigan residents. In class of 2001 typically entered Hillsdale with a 3.5 high school GPA behind them, along with strong SAT or ACT scores. High student-satisfaction levels are shown in the fact that 90 percent of the freshman class returns for their second year. Most students (70 percent) complete their degree in four years, and 74 percent are finished after five years. Students live in single-sex dormitories staffed by a resident director and upperclassmen. All first-year students who are not commuting must live on campus. As alternatives to dormitories, older students live in Greek housing or find off-campus residences. The College makes career counseling, job placement assistance, academic mentoring and tutoring, and health services available to all students.

STUDENT BODY

Hillsdale College fields teams in the Great Lakes Intercollegiate Athletic Conference of the NCAA's Division II. Men participate in baseball, basketball, cross-country, football, golf, tennis, soccer, swimming, and indoor and outdoor track. The women compete in basketball, cross-country, softball, swimming, tennis, soccer, indoor and outdoor track, and volleyball. Hillsdale College is proud of the academic awards granted to many of the school's student-athletes. Aside from varsity competition, students organize intramural leagues and club sports, including hockey, lacrosse, and skiing. Students get involved in a variety of extracurricular activities, joining organizations such as fraternities, sororities, InterVarsity Christian Fellowship, College Republicans, and Charis. Other clubs and groups focus on community service, academics, or social activities. Students interested in the performing arts can join the drama troupe, jazz band, pep band, wind ensemble, concert choir, chorale, and/or the College-community orchestra. Eighteen students are elected by their peers to serve on the Student Federation, which makes decisions on behalf of the student body. The Student Federation allocates fund, organizes events, and responds to student needs and opinions. Additional social events are thrown each month by the Activities Board. The Men's Council and Women's Council work with the administration to function as legislative and judicial bodies. Participation in these organizations allows students to hone their leadership skills, which are applicable at Hillsdale and in the work force.

ACADEMICS

The academic year runs on two semesters, one from late August to mid-December and the other from mid-January to mid-May. Students may also attend three-week sessions during the summer. All students complete core class requirements in the humanities, natural sciences, and social sciences, ensuring a well-rounded education. Majors must be selected by the end of students' second year. A minimum of 124 credits are necessary for graduation. These credits must include the course requirements for a particular major. The BA course of study focuses on language skills, foreign language proficiency, literature, the arts, and social sciences. Students working on their BS concentrate on math, natural science, and social science. Top students may enroll in the Honors Program. During their first two years, students in the honors program work together in honors classes; in their junior and senior years, participants undertake advanced colloquia. During their four years at Hillsdale, students are also required to attend two week-long seminars run by the Center for Constructive Alternatives (CCA). Guest speakers facilitate the seminars, addressing topics as diverse as politics, religion, or culture. The goal is to connect classroom learning with real-world applications and issues. Students can choose from four seminars offered each year.

Students can pursue their Bachelor of Arts or Bachelor of Science degree in accounting, art, biology, business economics, chemistry, classical studies, computational mathematics, economics, education, elementary education, English, French, German, history, mathematics, music, philosophy, physical education, physics, political science, psychology, religion, sociology, Spanish, and theater and speech. The following majors incorporate interdisciplinary work: American studies, Christian studies, comparative literature, European studies, international business, and political economy. The College also grants pre-professional degrees in dentistry, engineering, forestry, law, medicine, optometry, osteopathy, pharmacy, theology, and veterinary medicine.

Of the 89 full-time faculty members, 88 percent have their PhD or terminal degrees. Thirty-eight additional instructors round out the teaching staff. All faculty members prioritize teaching and student contact, and graduate students never teach Hillsdale classes. Instructors remain active in their fields, researching and publishing continuously. Students receive individual attention from their professors, including the advisor assigned to support them in academic and career decisions.

33 East College Street
Hillsdale, MI 49242
Phone: 517-607-2327
Fax: 517-607-2223
Website: www.hillsdale.edu

ADMISSIONS

The Admissions Committee looks for students who are prepared to get the most out of college life and share their talents with the Hillsdale community. Successful applicants demonstrate intellectual curiosity, motivation, and social awareness. Students should present strong grades, test scores, class rank, and extracurricular activities. Other factors include strength of curriculum, interviews, self-evaluations, and recommendations from high school counselors or teachers. Admissions decisions are based on a combination of all of these criteria. Transfer students need to send in the following materials: the application form, high school transcripts, ACT or SAT scores, transcripts from all previously attended colleges, and a transfer form from the dean of students of the last college attended. Hillsdale accepts applications from students who have completed at least their junior year of high school. Applicants should submit an application form, a $15 application fee, an academic letter of recommendation, ACT/SAT scores, and a high school transcript. The College receives applications on a rolling basis. Students can expect a decision from the Admissions Committee within three weeks of submitting their application. Hillsdale College has adhered to its nondiscriminatory admissions policy—"to furnish all persons who wish, irrespective of nation, color, or sex, a literary and scientific education"—since long before the government passed nondiscrimination laws. To make a request or submit records or forms, please use the following contact information:

Hillsdale College
Admissions Office
33 E. College Street
Hillsdale, MI 49242-1298
Phone: 517-437-7341 ext. 2327
Fax: 517-437-7241
E-mail: admissions@ac.hillsdale.edu

CAMPUS LIFE

Hillsdale College, set amid the idyllic setting of south-central Michigan, is conveniently reached by the Ohio or Indiana Turnpikes. The College's hometown of Hillsdale is home to 10,000 people and plenty of businesses, churches, and places to eat. Students can easily travel to cities including Detroit, Chicago, Cleveland, Toledo, and Indianapolis.

Students often compliment their classroom studies with internship experiences. One such program is the Washington-Hillsdale Intern Program (WHIP), which places students at the ERI National Journalism Center or in congressional and government offices, during the school year or summer. Many students also elect to study abroad. They may take advantage of Hillsdale's affiliation with Keble College of Oxford University and attend as associate members. Other students travel to Spain, France, or Germany. The College works with students to design a course of study that will allow them to advance their Hillsdale degree work while studying overseas and experiencing a different culture.

COST AND AID

For the 2000–2001 academic year, tuition cost $14,400. An additional $2,886 was paid for room and $3,000 for board. Student fees totaled $300. Students should allot an additional $1,100 (approximately) for books, supplies, and personal expenses such as travel, recreation, and clothing.

HIRAM COLLEGE

GENERAL INFORMATION

Located in the rolling hills of Northeast Ohio, about 30 minutes from Cleveland, Hiram College has dared to be distinctive ever since our founding in 1850. Our pioneering freshman-year program, plus our study abroad and writing-across-the-curriculum programs, helped set the standard for other institutions and made us a national liberal arts college. We're always seeking new ways to meet the changing needs of our students while preserving the rich traditions of liberal arts learning.

STUDENT BODY

Hiram has 900 students from 28 states and 18 foreign countries. Ninety-six percent of our students live on campus, forming a unique community. Hiram has over 90 student organizations, from concert band and newspaper staff to club volleyball and Model United Nations. Annual events on campus include the Chili Cook-Off and Happy Hour in February, Springfest in May, and the madrigal musical performance in December. In addition, Hiram has 17 varsity sports and competes in arguably one of the toughest Division III conferences in the country, the North Coast Athletic Conference.

ACADEMICS

Hiram College awards the Bachelor of Arts (BA) degree. The major areas of study at Hiram College include: art, biology, biomedical humanities, chemistry, classical studies, communication, computer science, economics, education (elementary and secondary), English, environmental studies, French, German, history, international economics & management, management, mathematical sciences, music, philosophy, physics, political science, pre-law, pre-medicine, psychobiology, psychology, religious studies, sociology & anthropology, Spanish, theatre arts. Pre-professional programs offer preparation for study in a wide variety of fields, including dentistry, engineering, law, medicine, physical therapy, and veterinary medicine. For more information about our academic programs, consult our website at www.hiram.edu/acad/.

Since 1850, Hiram College has been a distinctive place to study the liberal arts and sciences. Hiram's academic calendar, the Hiram Plan, is unique among colleges and universities. Each 15-week semester is divided into a 12-week and a 3-week session. During the 3-week session, students take only one intensive course. The plan provides two formats for learning, which increases opportunity for small-group study with faculty, study in special topics, hands-on learning through field trips and internships, and study abroad. Our unique academic calendar; the study abroad program; and our commitment to practical, hands-on education are three reasons why we've been named a national liberal arts college and received recognition from Loren Pope in his book *Colleges That Change Lives*.

Concern for the student's personal as well as academic welfare is one of the qualities that makes Hiram such a warm and happy place and such an exceptional college. It is one of the reasons why young people find their power and their confidence burgeoning and why they talk about realizing potentials they didn't know they had when they came there. More than a wonderful place, Hiram is a national asset. Hiram has a teaching faculty of 81 full-time members, 95 percent of whom hold doctorates or the appropriate terminal degree. The student/faculty ratio is 12:1. The ideal of a "community of scholars" thrives at Hiram, where students engage in research side by side with their professors, enjoy extracurricular activities with their teachers, and reach out with the faculty to serve the community.

Cambridge. Israel. Costa Rica. Australia. Greece. Guatemala & El Salvador. Zimbabwe. Paris. Spain. Trinidad & Tobago. These are just some of the trips Hiram students have taken recently as part of the College's innovative study abroad program. Hiram College's study abroad program has 45 years of experience behind it, and the result is a program that is distinctly different from those offered by many colleges; Hiram's programs are affordable. Rather than buying into expensive, packaged tours, the Center for International Studies staff coordinates all travel arrangements. Many students find they can study abroad several times while at Hiram, and 40 percent of Hiram students go on at least one of these trips. Hiram's programs are led by Hiram faculty. The resulting benefits are numerous—professors bring to the classroom the most current international aspects of their fields; the courses taken abroad are designed to fit into the regular curriculum; and the experiences shared with faculty and classmates create lasting friendships. Study abroad programs vary in length from three weeks to an entire term. Students may also take advantage of the College's affiliation with the Institute for European Studies, the Institute for Asian Studies, and exchange programs with the Mithibai College of the University of Bombay, India; Bosporus University in Istanbul, Turkey; and Kansai University of Foreign Studies in Osaka, Japan. Most of Hiram's academic departments offer EMS programs. Foreign language students in particular are urged to participate in EMS and, whenever possible, to spend a year studying abroad. Each year, 8 to 10 programs are available. About 40 percent of all Hiram students take advantage of study abroad through the Extra Mural Studies Program. In addition to study abroad opportunities, internships with corporations and agencies are also available in all academic departments, and arrangements are made for students on an individual basis.

PO Box 96
Hiram, OH 44234
Phone: 800-362-5280
Fax: 330-569-5944
Website: www.hiram.edu

ADMISSIONS

Hiram's Admission Committee prizes students who combine solid academic credentials with an open mind, a sense of adventure, and a creative flair. Admission to Hiram is competitive. Your record should show a strong college preparatory program in high school, including a minimum of 17 academic units in the humanities, mathematics, natural sciences, and foreign language. Consideration is given to students who have not taken the recommended program but who demonstrate that they can be successful at Hiram. Your application must include a secondary school report, the results of the SAT I or ACT, recommendations (including one from a teacher), and an essay. International students must submit TOEFL scores. A personal interview with a member of the admission staff is highly recommended for all applicants and required for academic scholarship candidates.

The application deadline is March 15 for entrance in August. Applications received after that date are evaluated on a space-available basis. Generally, we will notify you of our decision within four weeks of receiving your completed application. If you wish to be considered for an academic scholarship, you should apply by February 1. Admission decisions are made without regard to financial circumstances. For more information about applying to Hiram, consult our website at www.hiram.edu/admission/.

CAMPUS LIFE

Hiram's location gives students a range of educational and entertainment opportunities outside the classroom. The College itself is part of a historic village, with restored houses and a profusion of public gardens, set in the midst of the lush rolling hills of the Western Reserve. According to one student, the Village of Hiram "is one of the safest places on earth. Where else can you take a walk at 3 A.M. and never have to worry?" Five minutes from Hiram is the town of Garrettsville, with grocery stores, fast-food restaurants, video rentals, a movie theatre, drug stores, and other amenities. Less than an hour away are three major metropolitan areas (Cleveland, Akron, and Youngstown) with all the excitement you would expect to find in large cities. Hiram regularly takes advantage of the area's cultural and recreational opportunities, the most recent addition being the Rock and Roll Hall of Fame and Museum in Cleveland. Excursions are planned to events like performances by the world-renowned Cleveland Orchestra (an area foundation provides Hiram students with free tickets), Cleveland Opera, Cleveland Playhouse, the Ohio Ballet, and touring shows like Phantom of the Opera, Les Miserables, and Miss Saigon. Outings are planned regularly to professional sporting events (Cleveland has professional baseball, basketball, soccer, and hockey). The star of downtown Cleveland is Jacobs Field, home of the Indians. Professors frequently make use of resources in the surrounding cities for their courses-a class excursion to one of several major museums in the area or Cleveland's International Film Festival, for example. The region's natural areas also play a part in Hiram's academic life. As the culminating experience in a collegium on economics and the environment, for example, the class spends the weekend camping in a state park.

Hiram opened a new, five-level, state-of-the-art library in 1995 and a $7.5 million science facility in 2000. Other distinctive facilities include a 260-acre scientific field station for biological research, an observatory, a writing center, and recently renovated residence halls. The computer facilities include a fiber-optic network, two microcomputer laboratories, a computer classroom, and four cart-based computer projection systems. Students have 24-hour access to the Hiram network from their residence hall rooms.

COST AND AID

For the 2000–2001 school year, tuition, room and board, and fees will be $25,015.

HOBART AND WILLIAM SMITH COLLEGES

GENERAL INFORMATION

Hobart and William Smith are coordinate liberal arts colleges—Hobart for men founded in 1822 and William Smith for women founded in 1908. All classes are coed, there is one faculty, one curriculum, one president, one campus. However, each college grants its own degree, maintains its own student government, and has its own dean and athletic programs. In short, it offers the advantages of both coed and single-sex schools.

STUDENT BODY

The Hobart Student Association (HSA) and the William Smith Congress (WSC) are the elected student governments for each college. They work together to determine allocation of funds, to address concerns of the student body, and to stage various charitable and social events. There are more than 60 clubs based on interests ranging from activist/social concerns to the arts, media, religious affiliations, intercultural concerns, and sports and recreation. Hobart and William Smith students involve themselves in a wide range of community service activities. A weekly newspaper, literary magazines, and the Colleges' radio station (WEOS-FM, an affiliate of National Public Radio), offer many students the opportunity to become involved in communications. Intercollegiate teams compete in nearly 20 sports at the NCAA Division III level (with the exception of Hobart lacrosse in Division I). Hobart fields teams in soccer, tennis, golf, football, basketball, squash, cross-country, sailing, crew, and lacrosse. William Smith fields teams in tennis, field hockey, cross-country, crew, sailing, basketball, swimming and diving, lacrosse, and squash. Club sports with intercollegiate schedules include skiing and rugby.

ACADEMICS

At the heart of Hobart and William Smith's curriculum is the requirement that each student complete a major and a minor, or two majors, one of which must be disciplinary, the other interdisciplinary. The first gives a student depth of knowledge, the latter gives breadth by reaching across traditional disciplines. Working closely with an advisor, each student's program must also address the Colleges' educational goals and objectives: critical reading and listening; effective speaking and writing; developing skills for critical thinking and argumentation; experience with scientific inquiry; the ability to reason quantitatively; an appreciation of artistic expression based on experience; an intellectually grounded understanding of race, gender, and class; critical knowledge of the multiplicity of world cultures; and an intellectually grounded foundation for ethical judgment and action. Each First-Year student must also complete a First-Year Seminar.

Hobart and William Smith awards the Bachelor of Arts and Bachelor of Science degrees. Departmental majors include anthropology, art (studio and history), biochemistry, biology, chemistry, classics, computer science, comparative literature, dance, economics, English, French, geoscience, history, mathematics, modern languages, music, philosophy, physics, political science, religious studies, sociology, and Spanish.

Interdisciplinary and individual majors have been developed in Africana studies; American studies; architectural studies; European studies; international relations; Latin American studies; lesbian, gay, and bisexual studies; media and society; public policy studies; Russian area studies; theater; urban studies; and women's studies.

Approximately 13 percent of students design their own majors. Programs leading to provisional New York State certification in elementary, secondary, and special education are offered.

The full-time faculty numbers 148 with 135 holding the terminal degree or PhD; part-time, 18. The student/faculty ratio is 12:1.

629 South Main Street
Geneva, NY 14456
Phone: 315-781-3472
Fax: 315-781-3471
Website: www.hws.edu

ADMISSIONS

Admissions is based on achievement and demonstrated potential to undertake college-level work and to contribute to campus life. Students must submit their high school transcript(s) as well as scores from either the SAT I or ACT. Students submitting the SAT I are also encouraged to submit the results of any SAT II: Subject Tests. In addition, two teacher recommendations are required, one of which must be from the student's 11th or 12th grade English teacher. Personal interviews are not required, but are encouraged and may be arranged by contacting the Offices of Admission. Applications should be made no later than February 1 of the senior year. A nonrefundable fee of $45 must accompany each application. First-year candidates will be notified by the end of March and must reply by May 1. Two early decision plans are offered for students who have selected Hobart or William Smith as their first-choice college. Under these plans, students who apply by November 15 will be notified by December 15; students applying by January 1 will be notified by February 1.

CAMPUS LIFE

The Colleges are located in Geneva, New York, a city of 15,000 on the north shore of Seneca Lake, the largest of New York's Finger Lakes. Within an hour's drive are Rochester, Syracuse, and Ithaca, each home to major research universities and extending the cultural reach of our 1,850 students.

Hobart and William Smith offer students an extraordinary range of opportunities to study off campus, both overseas and within the U.S. Our overseas programs are offered on six continents with programs in Australía (Melbourne, Perth, Brisbane); China (Beijing, Nanjing); Denmark (Copenhagen); Dominican Republic (Santiago de los Caballeros); Ecuador (Quito); England (Bath, London); France (Aix-en-Provence); Germany (Tuebingen); Iceland (Reykjavik); India (Jaipur); Ireland (Galway); Israel (Beer Shiva); Italy (Rome); Japan (Osaka, Tokyo); Korea (Seoul); Mexico (San Cristobal de las Cases); Poland (Krakow); Scotland (Edinburgh); Senegal (Dakar); Spain (Madrid); Switzerland (Geneva); and Vietnam (Hanoi). In the U.S., programs are offered in Los Angeles; Washington, DC; and New York. Many off-campus programs include internships. The Colleges also participate in cooperative programs in engineering, architecture, and a 4+1 MBA.

COST AND AID

For 2001–2002, tuition was $26,818, room was $3,812, and board was $3,418. Fees total $540.

ILLINOIS INSTITUTE OF TECHNOLOGY

COLLEGE AT A GLANCE

In 1890, the Armour Institute of Technology and Lewis Institute united to become the Illinois Institute of Technology (IIT). Today, IIT is a comprehensive, full-scale university, situated in a suburban area near Chicago. The 120-acre campus is internationally noted for its architecture, designed by noted architect Ludwig Mies van der Rohe, among the most important architects of the century. In addition to designing the campus master plan, Rohe is the former director of the Institute's College of Architecture. IIT is composed of the College of Architecture, the Armour College of Engineering, the Institute of Psychology, the Stuart School of Business, the Institute of Design, and the Chicago-Kent College of Law.

IIT participates in the Association of Independent Technological Universities (AITU), along with Carnegie-Mellon, Case Western, Clarkson, Cooper Union, Drexel, Kettering, Harvey Mudd, MIT, Milwaukee School of Engineering, Polytechnic University, RPI, RIT, Rose-Hulman, Stevens Institute of Technology, and Worcester Polytechnic.

There are a total of 1,736 undergraduate students, 2,994 graduate students, and 1,143 law students at IIT, of which 32 percent are female. Forty-four percent of IIT's diverse undergraduate population is from outside Illinois and 30 percent come from foreign countries.

LOCATION AND ENVIRONMENT

IIT is located in close proximity to Lake Michigan and the White Sox ballpark, in a rapidly developing community near Chicago. The campus is just three miles from the Chicago Loop, giving students access to a wide range of art, music, drama, movies, museums, and entertainment. The rest of Chicago is easily accessible from campus via expressway. There are bus stops and elevated rail lines on campus, and the Institute offers free bus service between the main campus and Chicago's West Loop area, home to the University's Downtown Center.

MAJORS AND DEGREES

Students can pursue a Bachelor of Science in Engineering through the Armour College of Engineering in the following subject areas: aerospace, architectural, chemical, civil, computer, electrical, environmental, mechanical, and metallurgical and materials engineering. The Armour College of Engineering also offers a Bachelor's of Science in computer science and the Bachelor of Science degree in applied mathematics, biology, chemistry, computer information systems, molecular biochemistry and biophysics, physics, political science, psychology, and professional technical communication, and Internet communication. Students in the College of Architecture can receive a Bachelor of Architecture degree through a five-year professional program.

Students in every major can choose minors and specializations, such as bioengineering, business, computer-aided drafting, ethics and morality, law, management, manufacturing technology, military science, psychology, public policy, and technical communications. Students may also design their own individual specialization with the dean's approval. Students may choose to pursue a combined undergraduate/graduate degree in conjunction with business administration (BS/MBA), law (BS/JD), and public administration (BS/MPA).

In addition to the traditional pre-med curriculum, IIT offers an honors combined program in engineering and medicine (BS/MD) in conjunction with Finch University of Health Sciences/Chicago Medical School. There is also a combined honors program in law (BS/JD) in conjunction with Chicago-Kent College of Law. Students who would like to participate in either combined program are required to submit a supplemental application in addition to the standard undergraduate application. The Office of Admission will provide students with further details about undergraduate, graduate, and combined degree programs upon request.

ACADEMIC PROGRAMS

Graduation requirements vary by program; however, all undergraduates must fulfill general education requirements, composed of at least 7 units of mathematics and computer science, 11 units of natural science or engineering, 9 units of humanities, 9 units of social sciences, and 6 units of professional projects. Students in the Bachelor of Science in Engineering program and the physical sciences are also required to complete a more comprehensive core program in mathematics, computer science, chemistry, and physics. In addition to core courses, students must complete all major program requirements, which usually consist of about 30 to 40 units of course work. Except for architecture students, all students must complete 124 to 136 units to confer an undergraduate degree.

Most disciplines allow students to participate in cooperative education programs. Students in cooperative education begin their career with a full-year of study then alternate between a semester of study and a semester of employment for an additional year. The University has placement services to help students locate internship and work opportunities. Upon graduation, 92 percent of recent IIT graduates begin working in a field related to their major or go directly to graduate or professional school.

IIT students may earn course credit for study at colleges and universities overseas. Currently, the school approves programs in England, Italy, Germany, Belgium, Mexico, People's Republic of China, Poland, Scotland, France, and Spain.

10 West 33rd Street
Chicago, IL 60616
Phone: 312-567-3025
Fax: 312-567-6939
Website: www.iit.edu

OFF-CAMPUS OPPORTUNITIES

The vibrant town of Chicago is home to 4,473 restaurants, 129 art galleries, 24 cinema complexes, 30 museums, and 6 professional sports teams. A world-class city, Chicago is the daily host to theater, performances, and concerts and is the birthplace of the world's best pizza. In addition to the many resources available in the Chicago metropolitan area, the campus is close to many recreational areas, such as McCormick Place exhibition hall, Soldier Field, Grant Park, and Lincoln Park Zoo as well as many bicycle paths and lakefront beaches.

FACILITIES AND EQUIPMENT

The IIT library system has an extensive collection of titles on economics, engineering, science, and business. There are a total of 32 research centers at IIT, including the Center for Synchrotron Radiation Research, the Fluid Dynamics Research Center, and the Research Laboratory in Human Biomechanics. The Institute also has 11 wind tunnel facilities, of which one is the largest wind tunnel at any university in the nation, supporting study of high subsonic aerodynamics. The majority of research centers have opportunities for IIT undergraduates to take part in ongoing research projects.

TUITION

Tuition for the 2001–2002 academic year is $18,600. Room and board is $5,592 annually. Students should expect to spend an additional $1,000 on books and supplies, $2,100 in personal expenses, and $1,200 on transportation to and from college. Student activities fees are $100 per year. Given these expenses, the total cost for a first-year student is approximately $28,592 annually.

FINANCIAL AID

IIT has an extensive scholarship program. The Institute awards numerous merit-based scholarships every year, some of which can cover the full cost of tuition and room and board for up to five years of undergraduate study. Engineering students have the opportunity to receive from $67,000 to $120,000 in scholarship money through the NEXT Initiative. All students are considered for Heald scholarships upon admission, which cover half the cost of tuition. More than 1,200 students are awarded the Heald scholarship annually. Qualified student athletes also have the opportunity to receive athletic scholarships. In addition, IIT has many proprietary scholarships and loans and many students receive funding from outside companies and organizations. Students may work to supplement their financial package through campus employment or as a member of the cooperative education program. Aside from IIT's resources, students may qualify for state and federal grants and loans.

Students may choose to participate in Army, Naval, and Air Force ROTC. ROTC scholarship winners are also eligible to receive scholarships from IIT.

Applicants seeking any form of financial assistance must file the Free Application for Federal Student Aid (FAFSA) after January 1. The FAFSA code for IIT is 001691.

FACULTY

IIT has 280 full-time faculty members, of which 97 percent have a doctoral or terminal degree in their field. IIT has an excellent student/faculty ratio of about 12:1 and senior faculty teach upper- and lower-division courses, ensuring students generous interaction with the school's accomplished instructors. IIT's part-time faculty is comprised of skilled professionals in their field.

STUDENT ORGANIZATIONS AND ACTIVITIES

There are over 80 student-run clubs and organizations at IIT, such as the campus newspaper, a student-run radio station, theater groups and music ensembles, intramural and varsity athletics, fraternities and sororities, honor societies, professional societies, student government, residence hall organizations, and the student-run Union Board.

On campus, the union building has its own bowling alley and recreation area, a convenience store, a bookstore, a gym, and seven residence halls, as well as seven fraternity houses. IIT offers academic counseling, job placement services, and student health services.

ADMISSIONS INFORMATION

Students are admIITed to IIT on rolling basis for the fall and spring semesters. IIT thoroughly reviews every application, and evaluates each student's potential and performance in a wide range of contexts. The most important factor in any admissions decision is the student's performance in secondary school, especially in relation to the student's future field of study. IIT recommends a strong high school preparation that includes at least 16 units of credit, with 4 courses in English, 4 courses in mathematics, and 2 courses in laboratory sciences. IIT requires that students take physics and mathematics through pre-calculus. Though not required, calculus is strongly encouraged. In addition, chemistry and physics are highly recommended. Admissions to IIT is exclusive. Roughly 70 percent of incoming IIT students were in the top 10 percent of their high school class. The median SAT I score of admits is generally between 1200 and 1380, and the median ACT score was between 28 and 31.

Students must submit the application form along with recommendations, official test scores of either SAT I or ACT, and an official high school transcript. Interviews are not required. There are supplemental application forms for the Honors Program in Engineering and Medicine, for the Honors Law Program, and for the NEXT Initiative Scholarship Program. Please note that these programs also have special application deadlines.

ITHACA COLLEGE

THE COLLEGE AT A GLANCE

Coeducational and nonsectarian, Ithaca is a nationally recognized college of 6,400 students. As a comprehensive institution, Ithaca offers an excellent foundation in the liberal arts as well as strong professional programs at the undergraduate level. Moreover, all of our degree programs are supplemented by independent and interdisciplinary studies, dual majors, minors, and elective courses in other academic fields.

Nearly every state and more than 80 countries are represented in the student population; 2,800 men and 3,600 women are currently enrolled. Some 300 of those students are enrolled in graduate programs.

Founded in 1892 as the Ithaca Conservatory of Music, the school eventually grew into a private college offering academic programs in several professional fields. At mid-century, the institution's curricula in liberal arts were unified, and the large and diversified School of Humanities and Sciences now forms the core of the Ithaca educational experience.

In 1960, the College moved from downtown Ithaca to its current home on South Hill. Here, the College's 750 acres command a majestic vista of the city of Ithaca and Cayuga Lake.

STUDENTS

Campus life is sparked by more than 140 student organizations, 25 intercollegiate sports teams, and hundreds of lectures, films, and other events each year. Our NCAA Division III teams enjoy frequent success: Our teams hold 12 national titles in football (3), women's soccer (2), wrestling (3), baseball (2), field hockey, and gymnastics. Music and theater performances by students are frequent, and national acts visit campus often; during the last two school years, for example, Rusted Root, Fuel, Eve 6, and Ben Folds Five performed here.

ACADEMICS

Whether you know exactly what you want to do after graduation or need to explore your options, Ithaca has a program to suit you. In our Schools of Business, Communications, Health Sciences and Human Performance, Humanities and Sciences, and Music, we offer the breadth of a university with the intimate feel of a college.

First-year students in the Schools of Business, Health Sciences and Human Performance, Humanities and Sciences, and Music can choose from among several small, seminar-style classes that combine rigorous study with transition-to-college topics.

Students in our School of Music are part of one of the nation's most highly regarded music programs. From your first year at Ithaca, you'll be learning with the best and performing on a regular basis in our modern recital halls.

Our School of Business offers a wide range of courses covering the world of business. With features such as a real-time stock ticker in our trading room and a new e-commerce "smart" classroom, you'll have the tools at your fingertips to shape a successful start to your career. Our new master's program in business administration can help further that career as well.

If your interests are not encapsulated by a single major, you can turn to our planned studies program, which affords the opportunity to craft your own major across several programs.

Other options include five-year programs in physical and occupational therapy, each leading to certification; New York State teacher certification programs in several fields; and joint agreements with other schools that provide opportunities to study engineering or optometry or to attain a Master in Business Administration degree.

No matter what you choose, all of our programs are imbued with an intensive, hands-on approach to education. Close contact with advisors and frequent opportunities to take learning beyond the classroom are Ithaca's hallmarks. That approach pays off; surveys show that 97 percent of our alumni either find employment or attend graduate school within a year of graduation.

Ithaca College offers more than 2,000 courses and 100 degree programs in five schools. The College confers the Bachelor of Arts, Bachelor of Science, Bachelor of Fine Arts, Bachelor of Music, Master of Business Administration, Master of Science, and Master of Music degrees.

Ithaca College employs 418 full-time and 169 part-time faculty members, resulting in a 12:1 student/faculty ratio. About 88 percent of faculty members have a doctorate or a terminal degree in their field.

100 Job Hall
Ithaca, NY 14850-7020
Phone: 607-274-3124
Fax: 607-274-1900
Website: www.ithaca.edu

CAMPUS LIFE

Ithaca is located in the center of upstate New York's Finger Lakes region; approximately 90,000 people live in the surrounding county. Major air and bus lines serve the city, which is 60 miles south of Syracuse, 60 miles north of Binghamton, and an hour's flight from New York City.

You'll have access to extensive opportunities for internships in business, communications, music, athletic training, speech-language pathology and audiology, health policy studies, community health education, humanities, natural sciences, and more. If you attend the School of Communications, you might apply to spend a semester at our communications program in Los Angeles. Ready access to internships and industry experts make this program a fast-paced working and learning experience.

Study abroad is also popular. Programs are available at the College's own London Center or through our study centers and exchange programs in Scotland, Ireland, Spain, the Czech Republic, Australia, Singapore, Japan, and elsewhere. There are also opportunities for study at more than 45 other affiliated programs throughout the world.

COSTS

About 80 percent of incoming students receive some form of financial assistance. Applicants seeking financial aid must submit the FAFSA (Free Application for Federal Student Aid), available from high school guidance offices, directly to the appropriate processor for the U.S. Department of Education listed on the back of the form. The form should be submitted by February 1 to ensure arrival by March 1. Early decision candidates seeking institutional aid should submit the PROFILE application, available from the College Scholarship Service, by November 1 and the FAFSA by February 1. Please contact the Office of Admission for more information.

The College recognizes outstanding academic achievement and demonstrated talent and considers all applicants for merit-based aid. The College offers President's and Dean's Scholarships ranging from $3,000 to $10,000 per year for four years. A separate application is not required for consideration for these scholarships. As a sponsor in the National Merit Scholarship Corporation (NMSC) program, Ithaca College makes available Merit Scholarships of up to $2,000 to students who list Ithaca as their first-choice institution to NMSC in accordance with NMSC guidelines. In addition, Ithaca College provides these students with a $10,000 Ithaca College President's Scholarship.

Tuition and fees: $21,102
Room: $4,476
Board: $4,484
Health and accident insurance (optional): $300

Charges quoted are for the 2002–2003 academic year and are subject to change in subsequent years. Students are expected to live on campus, with some exceptions. Please contact the Office of Admission for more information.

ADMISSIONS

Admission to Ithaca College is based on high school record, personal recommendations, SAT I or ACT scores, and for some programs, audition or portfolio. Admission is selective and competitive; individual talents and circumstances are always given serious consideration by the admission committee. Typically, some 10,500 men and women apply for 1,550 places in the freshman class; applicants are notified of their status as soon as possible after all admission materials are received. We advise you to submit your application early in your senior year of high school, and no later than March 1. Ithaca College also accepts the Common Application; contact the Office of Admission or your high school's guidance office for more information. Applications must be submitted by March 1, and applicants will receive a decision no later than April 15. Students offered admission are asked to respond by May 1, the candidate reply date established by the College Board.

Early decision candidates should submit their application for admission no later than November 1. Candidates will receive notification of the committee's decision no later than December 15. Please contact the Office of Admission for details.

Transfer applicants generally follow the same admission procedures as freshmen, and their applications are reviewed as soon as they are complete.

JOHN CARROLL UNIVERSITY

GENERAL INFORMATION

John Carroll University adheres to the Jesuit tradition of faith, service, and leadership, providing undergraduates with a demanding liberal arts curriculum focused on the ethical and moral questions of yesterday and today. The University aims to train tomorrow's leaders in whichever field they choose to pursue. It offers undergraduate degrees in 54 fields covering the arts and sciences, business, and pre-professional fields.

John Carroll is one of only 28 Jesuit colleges and universities in the United States. John Carroll originated as St. Ignatius College in 1886; it changed its name briefly to Cleveland College in 1925. John Carroll, the school's namesake, was the first Catholic bishop of the United States. The University relocated from Cleveland's west side to its current site in University Heights in 1934. The school, which originally admitted men only, officially embraced coeducation in 1968. In 1999–2000, 3,297 full-time undergraduates and 874 graduates attended John Carroll. The student body represents 32 states, the Virgin Islands, Puerto Rico, and 7 other nations. There is roughly the same number of men and women at the University; about 10 percent of the students represent minorities. University housing has a capacity of 1,850.

Learning does not end at John Carroll when the student exits the classroom. Co-curricular activities and leadership opportunities abound within the campus community. Volunteerism and community service are popular among the majority of undergraduates. Other co-curricular outlets include varsity and intramural sports for men and women, and academic honor societies. Thorn Acres, a 30-acre state park-like facility is an excellent resource for those interested in canoeing, fishing, retreats, and student-group meetings. More than 80 student clubs and organizations make their home on campus. The Student Center offers a wide variety of facilities, including a natatorium, two gymnasiums, racquetball and tennis courts, and weight-training and fitness centers. The Student Center also houses offices for the school radio station, yearbook, newspaper, fraternities, and sororities, Student Union, and numerous student organizations. Students may take advantage of free therapy, personal and psychological counseling, and in-depth review of academic and vocational issues through University Counseling Services. The Jesuit spirit of engagement and service are evident in the student body's commitment to the surrounding community. Student volunteers feed the homeless, minister to the sick, and paint the homes of the underprivileged and the elderly. Students run Project Gold, a charitable program that contributes to such University-operated community service projects as Christmas in April and Meals on Wheels.

The Graduate School at John Carroll confers the Master of Science in biology, chemistry, mathematics, and physics; the Master of Arts in communications management, counseling and human resources, English, history, humanities, and religious studies; the Master of Education; and the Master of Business Administration degree. The campus is also home to Economics America (the Cleveland Center for Economic Education), a nonprofit educational organization that offers advanced economics coursework to teachers.

STUDENT BODY

The Student Union is the instrument of student self-government at John Carroll. Elected Student Union officers represent all students—undergraduate, graduate, full and part time, and day and evening—and actively champion their interests in academic, social, religious, and disciplinary matters. The Student Union is made up of 56 men and women, all elected to one-year terms.

ACADEMICS

The Jesuit approach to liberal arts education demands that students graduate with a broad understanding of the world around them. The core curriculum ensures this result. It includes a first-year seminar that focuses on a single theme; four courses in humanities; four courses in science; two courses in religious studies; one course in English composition and rhetoric; and one in speech communication. In order to complete the core, all students spend their first two years in the College of Arts and Sciences. At the completion of their second year, students choose a major and are admitted to the appropriate degree program. Students must complete at least 128 credit hours and earn a minimum GPA of 2.0 (a C average) in order to earn a degree. They must also earn at least a 2.0 GPA in their major field as well as in any fields of concentration or minors. Students must complete their final 30 hours of coursework at John Carroll. The school offers ROTC, student exchange, and other special programs. John Carroll operates on a semester calendar; it also offers three 5-week summer sessions.

John Carroll confers the Bachelor of Arts degree in art history, classical languages (Greek and Latin), communications, education and allied studies (pre-kindergarten, elementary education, secondary education, and certain disabilities), English, French, German, Greek, history, humanities, mathematics teaching, modern languages (French, German, Spanish), philosophy, physical education, political science (with optional concentration in public administration and policy studies), religious studies (with an optional concentration in religious education), sociology, and world literature. The University confers the Bachelor of Science degree in biology, chemistry, computer science, engineering physics, mathematics, physics (with optional concentrations in computer engineering, electrical engineering, and engineering physics), and psychology. The Bachelor of Science in Business Administration degree is offered (through John Carroll's Boler School of Business) in accounting, business logistics, economics, finance, management, and marketing. Students may pursue minors in the American political system, art history, business, chemistry, communications, computer science, economics, engineering physics, English, foreign affairs, French, German, Greek, history, humanities, Latin, mathematics, philosophy, physical education, physics, probability and statistics, psychology, public administration and public policy, religious education, religious studies, sociology, and Spanish. John Carroll excels in pre-professional preparatory study; programs include those in dentistry, engineering, law, and medicine. Students may pursue interdisciplinary concentrations in such areas as East Asian studies, economic and mathematics, environmental studies, gerontology, humanities, international economics and modern language, international studies, neuroscience, perspectives on sex and gender, and public administration and policy studies.

20700 North Park Boulevard
University Heights, OH 44118-4581
Phone: 216-397-4294
Fax: 216-397-3098
Website: www.jcu.edu

Most of John Carroll's 481 professors teach undergraduate classes; some teach graduate programs as well, while others teach graduate students exclusively. Ninety percent of University instructors hold doctorates or the equivalent terminal degree in their field; approximately two-thirds of the faculty is tenured. Faculty members engage in research but also dedicate considerable time to students and community, providing counseling and performing community service. The faculty includes 15 resident Jesuit priests. The student/faculty ratio is 15:1.

ADMISSIONS

The Admissions Office carefully considers applications from all serious candidates. John Carroll welcomes students of all economic, geographic, racial, and religious backgrounds. The school regards the quality of an applicant's high school curriculum and grade point average as the most important factors in its admissions decision. Also important are standardized test scores (SAT I or ACT), record of extracurricular activities, and letter of recommendation from a high school counselor or teacher. The school recommends that candidates sit for personal interviews; the results of the interview (which is not required) is considered during the admissions decision process. Students must apply to John Carroll by February 1. The school makes admissions decisions on a rolling basis; it usually contacts candidates within four weeks of receiving their application. Those admitted to John Carroll are required to declare their intentions by May 1. A deposit (including a room deposit, for those who plan to live on campus) is required at the time the student notifies the school of his/her intention to attend. Deposits are refundable up to May 1; refund requests must be submitted in writing. To receive an application, a viewbook, or other information, please contact:

Thomas P. Fanning, Director of Admission
John Carroll University
University Heights, OH 44118-4581
Phone: 216-397-4294

CAMPUS LIFE

John Carroll is set in the middle of the tranquil residential Heights neighborhood, only a half-hour from downtown Cleveland. The area is surrounded by Cleveland Heights, Shaker Heights, and University Heights. The campus earns justifiable praise for its lovely greenery and stately walkways; Gothic and contemporary architecture successfully commingle to create a lovely, unified campus "look." The campus is well served by public transportation and can be easily reached by automobile. Better still, the campus is within walking distance of two shopping centers that house banks, department stores, grocery stores, specialty shops, movie theaters, and restaurants. University Circle—home of the Cleveland Symphony Orchestra; Cleveland's museums of art, natural history, and health education; and the Garden Center of Greater Cleveland—is only 10 minutes from campus. Downtown Cleveland offers a tremendous variety of cultural, educational, and commercial diversions, including comedy clubs, the Rock and Roll Hall of Fame, the Flats (a sprawling entertainment district situated along the Cuyahoga River), the Great Lakes Science Center, theaters, shopping, Jacobs Field (home of the Cleveland Indians), Gund Arena (where the Cleveland Cavaliers, Rockers, and Lumberjacks play), and the new Cleveland Stadium (home to the Cleveland Browns).

John Carroll offers exchange programs with two universities in Japan. Students annually take part in archeological explorations in two locations in Israel, Tel el-Hesi and Ashkelon. The school offers a number of other approved study abroad programs. John Carroll University is a member of the Northeast Ohio Commission on Higher Education, which allows full-time students to take one course each semester at one of the other 16 area member universities. Students may take any course not offered at John Carroll; there is no additional charge for courses taken off campus through this consortium. Many students use this option to take courses in the performance-based arts or in specific engineering fields.

COST AND AID

During the 2000–2001 academic year, tuition was $16,334. Room and board cost an additional $6,128. Students typically spend $800 per year on books and supplies.

JOHNSON AND WALES UNIVERSITY—PROVIDENCE

GENERAL INFORMATION

Founded in Providence in 1914, Johnson & Wales University (J&W) is a private, career-oriented institution offering programs that are geared to the success of a range of students. The University's 14,945 students attend classes at campuses in Providence, Rhode Island; Charleston, South Carolina; Norfolk, Virginia; North Miami, Florida; and Denver, Colorado. The University will be opening a new campus in Charlotte, North Carolina in fall 2004. Most are recent graduates of high school business, college-preparatory, and vocational/technical programs, representing 50 states and 96 countries.

The academic focus of the University is on two- and four-year degree programs in business, culinary arts, food service, hospitality, and technology. MBA programs include global business leadership (with a concentration in accounting, financial services management, international trade, organizational leadership, or marketing) and hospitality and tourism global business leadership (with concentrations in event leadership, finance, marketing and tourism planning). MA programs in teaching (with or without certification) include business and food service. The University also offers a doctoral program in educational leadership.

Students are involved in a variety of extracurricular activities. The Student Activities Office and fraternities and sororities are among the many groups that schedule social functions throughout the academic year. Sports and fitness programs include aerobics, baseball, basketball, soccer, tennis, and volleyball. The University maintains 24 residence halls throughout its five campuses. Student services include academic counseling and testing, a tutorial center, and health services.

The University's Career Development Office provides extensive career planning and placement services. Within 60 days of graduation, 98 percent of J&W students from the 50 states have jobs in their chosen career field. Johnson & Wales is accredited by the New England Association of Schools and Colleges. The hospitality programs in Providence are accredited by the Accreditation Commission for Programs in Hospitality Administration.

STUDENT BODY

Student Government Association (SGA) representatives serve as the link among students, faculty, and administration to bring student body concerns to the awareness of the University community. Students are involved in a variety of extracurricular activities. Nearly 20 percent of the University's population are members of National Student Organizations such as Business Professionals of America, Future Business Leaders of America (Phi Beta Lambda), Family, Career, Community Leaders of America (FCCLA), The National FFA, Junior Achievement, SkillsUSA-VICA, and Technology Association of America. The Student Activities Office and fraternities and sororities are among the many groups that schedule social functions throughout the academic year. Sports and fitness programs include aerobics, baseball, basketball, sailing, soccer, tennis, golf, wrestling, ice hockey, and volleyball.

ACADEMICS

Johnson & Wales University offers programs in business, culinary arts, food service, hospitality, and technology within an academic structure of three 11-week terms. Classes generally meet four days a week, Monday through Thursday. The "upside-down" curriculum of the University provides immediate concentration in the student's chosen major. The associate degree is awarded after two years of successful study, at which time the student may continue studies toward the baccalaureate degree or seek immediate employment. Two degrees, the associate and the bachelor's, can result from a complete four-year course of study. Learning by doing is an important part of career training at J&W, and many programs include laboratory studies as well as formal internship requirements. Special advanced placement programs are featured for high school seniors with exceptional skills in culinary arts or baking and pastry arts. In addition, the University awards credit for certain courses based on the successful completion of Challenge, CLEP or Portfolio Assessments. All degree candidates must successfully complete the required number of courses and/or quarter credit hours, as prescribed in the various curricula, with a minimum average of 2.0.

Johnson & Wales University's Providence campus offers Bachelor of Science degree programs in accounting, baking and pastry arts, computer graphics and new media, criminal justice, culinary arts, culinary nutrition, electronics engineering, engineering design and configuration management, entrepreneurship, equine business management, equine business management/riding, financial services management, food marketing, food service entrepreneurship, food service management, hospitality management, hotel management, information science, international business, international hotel and tourism management, management, marketing, marketing communications, network engineering, paralegal studies, retail marketing and management, sports/entertainment/event management, technology services management, travel-tourism management, and Web management and Internet commerce.

The Associate in Science degree is awarded in accounting, advertising communications, applied computer science, baking and pastry arts, business administration, computer/business applications, computerized drafting, computer graphics and new media, computing technology services, criminal justice, culinary arts, entrepreneurship, equine business management, equine studies (riding program), fashion merchandising, financial services management, food and beverage management, hotel management, management, marketing, paralegal studies, restaurant management, travel-tourism management, and website development.

In its Continuing Education division, Johnson & Wales's Providence campus also offers diploma programs in baking and pastry arts and culinary arts; certificate programs are offered in computer-aided drafting, paralegal studies, and legal nurse (a bachelor's degree is required for acceptance into the paralegal studies certificate program, and student must be a Registered Nurse or at least hold an associate degree for acceptance into the legal nurse certificate program).

The University's campus in Charleston, South Carolina, offers the Associate in Applied Science degree in baking and pastry arts, culinary arts, food and beverage management, hotel management, restaurant management, and travel-tourism management.

The campus at Norfolk, Virginia, offers an Associate of Science degree in culinary arts and a one-year certificate program in culinary arts.

The North Miami, Florida, campus offers Bachelor of Science degrees in accounting, criminal justice, culinary arts, food service management, hospitality management, hotel management, management, marketing, and sports/entertainment/event management. Associate of Science degrees are offered in accounting, baking and pastry arts, business administration, criminal justice, culinary arts, fashion merchandising, food and beverage management, hotel management, management, marketing, restaurant management, and travel-tourism management.

8 Abbott Park Place
Providence, RI 02903-3703
Phone: 401-598-2310
Fax: 401-598-2948
Website: www.jwu.edu

The Denver, Colorado campus offers bachelor's degrees in accounting, financial services management, food service management, hotel management, international business, management, marketing, and sports/entertainment/event management. Associate of Science degrees are offered in accounting, advertising communications, baking and pastry arts, business administration, culinary arts, fashion merchandising, food and beverage management, hotel management, and marketing.

The University's newest campus in Charlotte, North Carolina campus will open in fall 2004 and planned majors include Bachelor of Science degrees in accounting, food service management, hotel management, international hotel & tourism management, management, marketing, marketing communications, and sports/ entertainment/event management. Associate of Science degrees will include accounting, advertising communications, baking and pastry arts, business administration, culinary arts, fashion merchandising, food & beverage management, hotel management, management, marketing and restaurant management.

The University's 428 full-time and 195 part-time undergraduate faculty members (all campuses) are oriented toward instruction rather than research. Many are chosen for their professional experience in business, culinary arts, hospitality services, and technology. The student/faculty ratio is 30:1.

ADMISSIONS

Johnson & Wales University seeks students who are career-focused and who have a true desire to succeed. Academic qualifications are important, but an applicant's motivation and interest in doing well are given special consideration. Graduation from high school or equivalent credentials are required for admission. It is recommended that students applying for admission into the culinary arts and baking and pastry arts programs have some prior education or experience in food service.

Although no tests are required, all applicants are encouraged to submit scores from the SAT I or ACT. Students who wish to apply for the Honors Program must have either a score of 500 math and 500 verbal on the SAT or a score of 21 math and 21 verbal on the ACT. High school juniors may apply for early admission under the ACCESS Program. Transfer students are required to submit official high school and college transcripts and to have a minimum GPA of 2.0. Credits to be transferred from other institutions are evaluated on the basis of their equivalent at Johnson & Wales. Johnson & Wales does not require an application fee.

After submitting the application, the student is responsible for requesting that appropriate transcripts be forwarded to the Admissions Office of the University. While there is no deadline, students are advised to apply as early as possible before the intended date of enrollment to ensure full consideration of their application. Applications are accepted for terms beginning in September, December, and March and for the summer sessions. Inquiries and applications should be addressed to:

Kenneth DiSaia
Vice President of Enrollment Management
Johnson & Wales University
8 Abbott Park Place
Providence, RI 02903
Telephone: 401-598-1000 or 800-DIAL-JWU (toll free)
Fax: 401-598-4901
E-mail: www.jwu.edu

CAMPUS LIFE

The location of each of the University's campuses enables students to take advantage of internship and part-time work activities offered by many nearby businesses, community groups, and government agencies. All of Johnson & Wales's city campuses retain a small-town feel and easy accessibility to students. The urban setting of the Providence, Rhode Island, campus provides students proximity to the city's many cultural and recreational facilities. The Charleston, South Carolina, campus is located in the Port City Center of that historic city, which is home to numerous special events each year. The Norfolk, Virginia, campus is in the heart of the Hampton Roads area. Norfolk is one of Virginia's most accessible cities, near to the many yearly festivals and activities of the region. In North Miami, Florida, the J&W campus is a short trip from the sun and fun of Fort Lauderdale and the culture and diversity of Miami. Denver, Colorado, offers students great opportunities as the nation's sixth leading tourist destination and *Fortune* magazine's "second best city in America to work and live." The new Charlotte, North Carolina, campus is located in a vibrant urban setting that combines commercial and residential life. More than 300 Fortune 500 companies have offices in the Charlotte area, which is known as the second largest financial center in the U.S.

Learning at Johnson & Wales University is not limited to the classroom. Many of our majors offer internships at University-owned facilities. The hotel-restaurant management program features an internship at the Johnson & Wales Inn, Radisson Airport Hotel, or the Bay Harbor Inn and Suites—all are full-service hotel complexes owned and operated by the University (the Radisson is a corporate franchise). Fashion merchandising and retailing majors may spend their eleven-week internships at Gladding's, a women's specialty store also owned by the University. Students majoring in travel-tourism management may participate in an internship at the University's travel agency. For all majors optional selective career co-ops are available with cooperating businesses for students throughout the U.S. and world-wide, such as Marriott International; Hyatt Regency Hotels; Food Network; FleetBoston Financial; Foxwoods Resort and Casino; and Putnam Investments. Most internships and co-ops are one term in duration and carry 13.5 quarter hours of credit. Foreign exchange and term-abroad programs are also offered.

COST AND AID

The Guaranteed Tuition Plan guarantees students no tuition increases while they are continuously enrolled at the University. Tuition at all campuses for 2003–2004 ranges from $15,438 to $18,444, depending on the program of study. The basic room-and-board plans range from $6,621 to $8,433. Each student is also charged a general fee of $750, and there is an orientation fee of $200 for new students. Books and supplies are estimated at $600 to $800 per year, depending upon the program. Tuition, room, and board fees may vary at each campus. Students should consult the respective campus catalogs for further details.

KANSAS CITY ART INSTITUTE

GENERAL INFORMATION

Kansas City Art Institute is a private and fully accredited four-year college of art and design founded in 1885. KCAI combines intensive time in the classroom, extensive experience in the studio, a broad liberal arts emphasis, focused learning opportunities, and a dynamic campus community. It is this rich combination that develops both the artist and the person. Ranked among the nation's top 10 art schools by *U.S. News & World Report*, the Kansas City Art Institute is comprised of nearly 600 students (representing more than 45 states and 7 foreign countries) and a faculty of approximately 75 talented artists and educated scholars.

ACADEMICS

The First-Year Foundation program is the initial year of the undergraduate curriculum and brings freshmen into the studio for an intensive exploration of new creative perspectives. It is a year in which students experiment with various media and investigate areas of interest. Foundation fosters interaction with a diverse range of people who share many ideas and experiences. For most students, it is their first experience working in an environment where a disciplined approach to "art-making" and "art-thinking" is the focus.

The Foundation program is critical to developing new artistic viewpoints and challenging preconceived ideas and attitudes toward creativity. Full-time faculty encourage students to experiment; explore, and develop problem-solving skills as they define their interests. Foundation students work in one of the largest freshman studio spaces available. The facility houses studios, offices, and conference areas.

The curriculum at KCAI complements the studio concentration with course work in the liberal arts guiding each student in the developing of critical-thinking and problem-solving abilities, fostering communication skills, and building a lifelong interest in learning. Study of the liberal arts can bring to the student a framework for artistic explorations and the understanding of human society. An art history major and a creative writing major are available.

Through global information and communication systems, both the diversity and the homogeneity of our worlds become more apparent. For the student at KCAI, the liberal arts program addresses contemporary philosophical, social, and political concerns with faculty who are scholars of diverse points of view and disciplines. At every level of liberal arts study, faculty members engage students in discussion, analysis, and interpretation of events, uses, trends, and historical precedents. Students can develop an emerging awareness of the complexity of human existence as they develop their individual creative voices. Liberal arts courses at KCAI range from literature and history to philosophy and the sciences. Studies in the humanities and sciences allow KCAI students to raise questions and develop knowledge about the fundamental problems and possibilities of human life. This knowledge will provide an invaluable foundation as student artists explore their roles in contemporary society and the effect their art has on the world.

The curriculum allows for exploration with three BFA options:

- New: The Interdisciplinary Studies degree
- New: The Major Plus program
- The single-focus BFA sequence

The faculty of nationally and internationally known scholars comes from a broad range of viewpoints and is challenged to find new ways to purposefully investigate the relationships between intellectual and perceptive powers in both the creation and enjoyment of art.

Students pursue the Bachelor of Fine Arts. The curriculum is offered within the following four schools: The School of the Foundation year consists of the communal set of course experiences that all freshmen at the Institute share. The Foundation School provides students with the essential technical and conceptual competencies important as cornerstones for young artists as well as an exploration of the upper-class opportunities at the Institute. The School of Design seeks to educate artists who can adapt to the changing nature of the professional design and illustration fields. The program underscores the integrated nature of graphic, digital, three-dimensional, and environmental design and illustration as well as design process and "the architecture of experience" as a philosophical premise.

The School of Fine Arts is comprised of the departments of ceramics, fiber, painting/printmaking, photography/new media, and sculpture. The programs in this School emphasize the tradition of self-expression as the motivation for artmaking while providing learning opportunities across traditional artmaking boundaries.

The School of Liberal Arts provides the general education course work KCAI deems to be critical to the education of young artists, from the freshman through the senior year. Additionally, the School offers majors in creative writing and art history as a Liberal Arts counterpart to the studio experience.

The approximately 75 faculty members at KCAI are a distinguished group. They are recognized scholars, sought-after consultants, talented artists, and professional mentors. They bring impressive degrees from Cranbrook Academy of Art, Pratt Institute, Alfred University, Yale University, and other prestigious programs. Their work has been exhibited the world over and it resides in the permanent collections of places such as the Metropolitan Museum of Art, MoMA, The National Museum of Wales, The Nelson Atkins Museum of Art, and the Smithsonian. They have professional experience through employment and consulting with the likes of Atlantic Records, Hallmark Cards Inc., Perry Ellis, and Time/Life Books.

4415 Warwick Boulevard
Kansas City, MO 64111-1762
Phone: 816-474-5225
Fax: 816-802-3309
Website: www.kcai.edu

ADMISSIONS

All serious students with a passion for art are encouraged to apply. And while it is not mandatory that applicants follow a preparatory program in high school with courses in studio and art history where possible, it is highly recommended to assure competitiveness with other applicants.

The criteria for admissions include evaluation of the student's portfolio, academic transcripts, standardized test scores, statement of purpose, letters of recommendation, and other indicators of potential success as a professional artist.

Applicants must have successfully completed a recognized secondary school program (high school) or its equivalent with a good academic record to be eligible for admission to KCAI. While there is no specific high school program of study required, students are advised to follow a college preparatory curriculum similar to the following: 4 years of English, 3 years of social sciences, and as many art courses as is practical. Considerable emphasis is placed on abilities in the areas of drawing, color, and design.

KCAI students' backgrounds are diverse but they share a desire to pursue an education in the arts. Students are admitted on the quality of work in their portfolios and their academic profile as determined by high school grades or previous college transcripts. The most important criterion for admission is a student's potential for success.

The Admissions Committee looks for serious and motivated students who are willing to work hard and take risks. The committee evaluates each application with a great deal of sensitivity and open-mindedness before reaching an admission decision because the Committee knows each student's level of imagination, innovation, and academic achievement is highly individual.

CAMPUS LIFE

KCAI's scenic 15-acre campus provides a caring, cohesive setting in which to live and learn. Students benefit from proximity to the Nelson Atkins Museum of Art (one of the top art museums in America) and the Kemper Museum of Contemporary Art. Galleries and studios, restaurants and cafes, the Country Club Plaza, and other entertainment spots are only a short distance from campus.

Kansas City Art Institute students are working within the Kansas City community and the community is working with them. Opportunities to work off campus include working with Chameleon Inc, a youth art development agency; Destination Creation, a summer arts program operated through the YWCA; and KCAI Corporate Partners, an exhibition program through which KCAI students work is displayed in dozens of Kansas city businesses. Students at KCAI have every opportunity to go out into the world and make their mark. KCAI offers international exchange programs in Australia, Canada, Ecuador, England, Italy, the Netherlands, New Zealand, and Japan. Also offered are exchange programs at nearly three-dozen acclaimed art schools across the country, in locations such as Boston, Los Angeles, Atlanta, San Francisco, Chicago, Cleveland, Philadelphia, New York, and many others. To gain additional real-world experience, many KCAI students complete internships and other art-related work experiences while at KCAI.

COST AND AID

Estimated tuition and fees are $20,310 per year. Room and board costs are $8,500 for a single room, $6,450 for a double room, and $5,880 for a triple room. Each includes a 19-meal plan. Books and supplies are estimated at $2,000, and personal and transportation expenses are estimated to be $2,500.

KEAN UNIVERSITY

GENERAL INFORMATION

Kean University has grown steadily since its founding in 1855. The school relocated to the current campus in 1958 and has been enjoying the benefits of modern facilities and vast tracts of land ever since. Tucked away from the city environment, students can roam the 122 acres of grass and woodlands or relax by the stream. The East Campus, providing another 28 acres, is utilized for intercollegiate and intramural athletics as well as student events. The University's student body comprises 12,000 students, pursuing undergraduate or graduate degrees either full- or part-time. The diverse student body includes students from a wide range of cultural heritages. Roughly 90 percent of the full-time undergraduate population lives off-campus and commutes. Outside of the classroom, students partake in various cultural, social, and athletic activities. Recent programs have included guest lecturers, classical and contemporary music performances, plays, dance performances, jazz concerts, and art exhibitions. A large number of participants turn out for varsity, intramural, and lifelong sports events, as well.

STUDENT BODY

Students elected to the Student Organization operate autonomously to make decisions pertaining to the student body. They are responsible for the allocation of money collected from student fees. They also organize cultural programming, co-curricular activities, entertainment, and athletics. Kean University values the students' right to self-governance. Students are always incorporated in the process of making university-wide decisions.

ACADEMICS

To complete a degree, students must complete the general education requirements, totaling 52 units. Eighteen of these credits are earned in the humanities-based core curriculum. The remaining 34 are distributed between departments to lay a broad liberal arts background on which to base later, specialized study. Each department specifies major requirements, with a minimum of 30 units, and students also take elective courses. Most departments can arrange internships for juniors and seniors. Some subject areas also provide course options that students can complete from off-campus locations. Two semesters make up the academic year, along with two summer sessions.

Kean University grants bachelor degrees in 45 majors and more than 70 options and collateral programs. Students can pursue Bachelor of Arts degrees in art history, biology, chemistry, communications, early childhood education, earth science, economics, elementary education, English, fine arts, foreign languages (Spanish), history, mathematics, music, music education, philosophy and religion, physical education, political science, psychology, public administration, recreation administration, sociology, special education, speech and hearing, and theater. The University has recently added Bachelor of Arts programs in industrial education, visual communication, interior design, finance, studio art, marketing, graphic communications, criminal justice administration, speech, and theatre arts. Bachelor of Science degrees can be earned in accounting, computer science, health information management, industrial technology, management science, medical technology, occupational therapy, and psychology/psychiatric rehabilitation. Students may also work toward their Bachelor of Fine Arts, Bachelor of Social Work, and Bachelor of Science in Nursing (for RNs only) degrees. Undergraduates may undertake the dual MS program in physical therapy. The program is available through an alliance with the University of Medicine and Dentistry of New Jersey (UMDNJ).

The instructors at Kean include 353 full-time faculty members, 13 part-time faculty members, and roughly 426 adjunct faculty members. The faculty interacts with students in office hours, campus committees, and through their involvement in university operations. Classes remain connected to the community thanks to part-time instructors, who may be entrepreneurs, politicians, or prominent industry people. No graduate students are the main instructors for undergraduate classes.

PO Box 411
Union, NJ 07083-0411
Phone: 908-737-7100
Fax: 908-737-7105
Website: www.kean.edu

ADMISSIONS

The admissions committee evaluates students' apparent capacity to succeed at Kean. Decisions are not based on age, sex, race, color, creed, or national origin. High school transcripts should display a minimum cumulative GPA of 2.5 and a minimum of 16 units completed. Many accepted applicants have an SAT I score of 1000. These guidelines may be revised to meet certain specific circumstances. Accompanied by a recommendation from a guidance counselor, students may apply as juniors in high school. Students may enter Kean with advanced standing considering CLEP scores or substantial life experience. Most transfer students must have a 2.0 GPA for admission. Certain departments, such as physical therapy, demand a higher GPA. Those applying to enter their freshman year must submit their application by May 31 for fall admission and November 1 for spring admission. Kean émploys a rolling admissions system. International students should apply for their F-1 visas by are March 1 for fall admission and November 1 for spring admission. Complete application packets include the following items: the Kean University application, a $35 application fee, high school and college transcripts, and SAT I results (for first-year candidates only). For those wishing to visit the campus, tours are run every Friday at 10 in the morning from October through April. For other times, please arrange an appointment. For additional information and application forms, students should contact:

Director of Admissions
Kean University
Union, NJ 07085
Telephone: 908-527-2195
Fax: 908-351-5187
E-mail: admitme@turbo.kean.edu
World Wide Web: www.kean.edu.

CAMPUS LIFE

Kean University's hometown of Union, New Jersey, has been designated an All-America City by the National Municipal League. Just 10 miles outside of New York City, the campus is conveniently reached by road, sea, or air.

Students may enroll in Kean University's study abroad programs, located around the world and lasting for a semester or less. Course credit is available in these programs, or students may choose to travel simply for personal development. Students also have the opportunity to learn in nontraditional settings, through service projects or by enrolling in distance learning programs.

COST AND AID

Tuition for full-time undergraduates with New Jersey residency for 2000–2001 was $4,384. Out-of-state students paid $6,395. (These figures may be adjusted for 2001–2002.) The price for on-campus housing was $4,500 for the school year. Up to 1,250 students can be accommodated in on-campus apartments. Two hundred and fifty students live in the dormitories, paying $600 per semester for food. Variable-cost food plans are available to students not living in the dorms. Commuters are charged $15 each year for parking registration.

KENYON COLLEGE

GENERAL INFORMATION

Kenyon College was the first private college established in Ohio. Since 1824, Kenyon has maintained its rank among the first-rate colleges in Ohio and in the country. The College is often described as the ideal liberal arts and sciences college because of our strong belief in the tradition of the liberal arts, emphasis on teaching, size of the student body, and emphasis on the development of critical-thinking, problem-solving, analytic-reasoning, and communication skills.

Kenyon students are a lively, talented, and intellectually curious group. They are drawn from all 50 states and more than two dozen countries. Bright, motivated students who wish to be active in campus organizations, athletics, student government, and other activities find Kenyon an attractive and satisfying experience.

The Carnegie Foundation for the Advancement of Teaching has recognized several faculty for outstanding teaching, and one faculty member holds a Macarthur Fellowship, the so-called "genius prize." Faculty are first and foremost teachers, and their scholarship, research, and artistic creation invigorate teaching and include students in exciting intellectual endeavors.

Kenyon students graduate well prepared to move into a wide range of vocations. Typically, two-thirds will enter the job market upon graduation. The most popular career paths include banking and finance, business, journalism and the media, education, public and government service, science research, and health care. While one-third will enter graduate or professional school directly upon graduation, 80 percent will earn an advanced degree within 10 years.

Kenyon has concluded a $116 million capital campaign that further enhances teaching, academic facilities, and financial aid programs. Among the significant results are completely new or renovated laboratory and classroom facilities for science, a significant addition to music facilities, several teaching positions, and expanded scholarship programs.

STUDENT BODY

Kenyon has a lively and diverse array of organizations and activities. More than 100 student organizations are recognized and funded through Student Council. These include groups with large memberships and broad reach, such as the Kenyon College Drama; WKCO, the campus radio station; or *The Collegian*, the weekly student newspaper. There are also special interest groups with smaller membership and narrower appeal such as the Kenyon Barbecue and Grill Club, the Hip Hop Society, or the Chess Club. The most popular student activities include drama, music (particularly vocal music), media and writing, student government, and sports and athletics.

The College sponsors 22 varsity sports, 11 each for men and women. The phrase "scholar-athlete" truly describes Kenyon's varsity players. No other college in the country has won more NCAA post-graduate fellowships, just as no other college in the country has won more Division III national championships than Kenyon. Club or intramural sports are offered as well and include the equestrian team, men's and women's rugby teams, soccer, basketball, and others.

The College also offers religious activities that include services or groups for Protestant and Catholic students, Jewish students (Hillel), Quaker students, and Muslim students.

ACADEMICS

Kenyon offers the Bachelor of Arts degree. Students may elect to major in more than one department or interdisciplinary area, and may also create their own majors through the synoptic major option. Majors include the following: American studies, anthropology, art (studio), art history, biochemistry, biology, chemistry, classics, Greek, Latin, dance, drama, economics, English, history, international studies, mathematics, modern languages and literatures, molecular biology, neuroscience, French, German, Spanish, music, philosophy, physics, political science, psychology, religious studies, and sociology. In addition to departmental and interdisciplinary majors, students may also elect to take on an interdisciplinary concentration such as African and African American studies, Asian studies, environmental studies, integrated program in humane studies, law and society, neuroscience, public policy, women's and gender studies, or scientific computing.

Admissions Office, Ransom Hall
Gambier, OH 43022-9623
Phone: 740-427-5776
Fax: 740-427-5770
Website: www.kenyon.edu

We endeavor to maintain a high level of quality throughout the curriculum, so that every major and program offered is recognized for its excellence. Nonetheless, the College offers a number of academic programs that enjoy especially strong recognition. The English department has long been considered one of the finest for its study of literature and creative writing. The College is the home of *The Kenyon Review*, one of the most highly acclaimed literary magazines in the world. Kenyon's science departments are noted for student research programs. The Summer Science Scholars Program provides funding for about 40 students each year to pursue sophisticated research. The success of science graduates in gaining admission to research or medical universities underscores our strong reputation. The Kenyon Center for Environmental Studies offers a unique combination of science research, public policy, and community outreach. For students interested in foreign language, Kenyon offers beginning through advanced instruction in Chinese, French, German, Italian, Japanese, Russian, and Spanish. All are taught using the intensive method developed at Dartmouth College.

Kenyon's faculty numbers 165 professors, of whom more than 92 percent hold the PhD or other terminal degree. The student/faculty ratio is 10:1. Of the total number of faculty, 142 are full-time, 23 are part-time; 92 members are tenured. Male faculty number 61 percent, with 39 percent female.

ADMISSIONS

Kenyon offers both regular decision and early decision admission plans. Application deadlines for early decision are December 1 and January 15, and for regular decision, January 15. Kenyon uses a two-part application. Part I is a brief request for biographical information. Part II is the Common Application and a Kenyon-specific supplement to the Common Application. Students are encouraged to use the online applications available through the Kenyon website.

Kenyon is a highly selective college admitting students with strong, demonstrated academic achievement, intellectual curiosity, and motivation. We recognize the importance of both academic and personal qualities in our selection process, so students who produce evidence of success and promise in both classroom and extracurricular endeavors will present the strongest cases. The recommended high school curriculum includes 4 years of English and mathematics, 3 years of language and science, and 3 years of social science. Students are encouraged to go beyond these minimum recommendations, and also encouraged to include honors or advanced courses in their programs. Students must submit the official high-school transcript as well as official results from the SAT I or ACT. The application includes several written responses including an essay.

CAMPUS LIFE

Set atop the picturesque hills of central Ohio, Kenyon's campus is one of the most beautiful in the country. The Gothic design of our buildings resembles that of Oxford and Cambridge and reflects the English origins of the College. A campus that exceeds 1,000 acres allows for much open green space as well as special academic opportunities such as environmental studies. While there are many small colleges located in small college towns, none of these towns has quite the ambiance of Gambier.

Social, cultural, and extracurricular life at Kenyon are campus-centered. All students live in College housing and take meals in the College dining halls. Most faculty members also reside in Gambier, their homes a short walking distance from their classrooms, studios, and laboratories. This close proximity contributes to the distinctively strong sense of community that characterizes Kenyon life. This is a college where students and faculty take interest in each others' activities and experiences.

Gambier is five minutes from the small town of Mount Vernon; an hour's drive from Columbus, Ohio's capital city; and two hours' drive from Cleveland, home of the Indians, a world-renowned art museum, and the Rock and Roll Hall of Fame.

Approximately 40 percent of Kenyon students include off-campus study in their academic program. The College views off-campus study as an extension of the curriculum, hence the high number of students who elect to participate. Through affiliations with other colleges and international educational organizations, the College offers approximately 160 programs in more than 50 countries. Full academic credit is awarded for all work completed successfully. Students receiving financial aid to attend Kenyon can apply their financial aid to off-campus study.

COST AND AID

For the 2003–2004 academic year, mandatory fees are as follows:

Tuition: $29,500

Average room and board: $5,040

Mandatory fees: $830

Fees will increase each year approximately 4 percent.

KETTERING UNIVERSITY

GENERAL INFORMATION

Kettering University (formerly GMI Engineering and Management Institute) has taken college education and put a spin on it. Billed as "America's premiere co-op university" this college based in Flint, Michigan, has more than 700 corporate partners, corporations, and agencies throughout 800 locations in North America, Europe, and Asia.

The philosophy of this fully accredited school is that college students work while they earn their college education, and in essence the corporate partners "grow their own" engineers and managers. The program is four and a half years long with students' time split evenly between classroom training (in processes, products, corporate culture, and technology, with an emphasis in engineering, the sciences, and business) and paid, full-time professional co-op work experience off site.

The corporate partners represent major industries that include leaders in business innovation and manufacturing technology. The list of current co-op companies reads like an honor roll of America's top corporations, representing automotive, aerospace, medical, chemical, computer, plastics, and delivery systems industries, just to name a few. Graduates have the skills and experience to succeed in key executive leadership positions, as many have done. Year after year nearly 100 percent of Kettering graduates have a full-time job offer or are accepted into a top graduate program by the time they receive their diploma.

STUDENT BODY

Kettering offers students the best of both worlds: graduates actually have a solid two and a half years of work experience to put on their resume, but during the other two and a half years spent on campus, Kettering students enjoy the activities and participate in the organizations that make college exciting and unique.

Kettering has the largest student chapter of the Society of Automotive Engineers (SAE), and our Delta Epsilon Chi Chapter (college version of DECA) annually wins top awards in state and national competitions. Students compete in an intense intramural athletic program and are involved in clubs and professional organizations. More than half of Kettering students join the 14 national fraternities and 6 sororities that are represented on campus. The school's active student government produces programs to develop peers' leadership skills, self-confidence, interpersonal relations, and organizational operations. Because enrolled students represent approximately 48 states and 18 countries, they have a lot to share with and learn from one another.

ACADEMICS

The unique structure of the Kettering program allows students to fulfill the academic requirements of 160 credit hours throughout a four-and-a-half-year period. This is completed over 9 academic semesters and up to 11 co-op work semesters. Many students complete a capstone thesis project on behalf of their co-op employer for credit toward the 160 required hours. The academic year consists of two 11-week academic terms on-campus in Flint and two 12-week academic terms working for the corporate employer; students alternate their time between Flint and the employer's site. On average, a freshman student who spends 24 weeks during the academic year working for the professional co-op employer earns $11,000.

The four-and-a-half-year professional cooperative education program allows students to earn designated Bachelor of Science degrees in computer engineering, electrical engineering (specialties in electronics, communication systems, control systems, and power systems), industrial engineering (specialties in computer systems integration, human factors & work design, quality assurance & reliability, production control systems, and manufacturing systems design), and mechanical engineering (specialties in bioengineering, applications, automotive powertrain, automotive body & chassis, mechanical systems design, design for durability, and plastic product design).

A designated Bachelor of Science degree is available in business management (concentrations in accounting/finance, information systems, manufacturing management, marketing, materials management), applied mathematics (minors in applied & computational mathematics, and applied statistics), applied physics (concentrations in acoustics, applied optics, and materials science), computer science, and environmental chemistry.

Minors are available in applied chemistry, applied mathematics, applied optics, computer science, liberal arts, and management. Kettering University offers Master of Science degree programs in engineering, engineering management, manufacturing management, manufacturing operations, and operations management.

A staff of 150 full-time professors, 80 percent of whom hold a doctoral degree, makes up the Kettering faculty. Because of the unique structure of the program, only about half of the 2,400 Kettering undergraduate students are on campus at a time, allowing for smaller classes and personalized attention. Most professors have industrial work experience to complement their academic credentials, and maintain contact with the industrial environment through consulting, sponsored research, and by advising students on their senior theses. The Kettering faculty is comprised of people who enjoy the professional industrial world as well as academia and are therefore stimulated and challenged by the students' experiences in both the classroom and those gained training with their corporate employers.

1700 West Third Ave.
Flint, MI 48504
Phone: 810-762-7865
Fax: 810-762-9837
Website: www.kettering.edu

ADMISSIONS

Admission to Kettering University is competitive and based on scholastic achievement and extracurricular interests, activities, and achievements. Applicants are required to have completed the following courses (one credit represents two semesters or one year of study): 2 credits algebra, 1 credit geometry, .5 credits trigonometry, 2 credits laboratory science (1 of these credits must be from physics or chemistry, and both are strongly recommended), and 3 credits English. A minimum of 16 credits is required, but 20 credits is strongly encouraged. Applicants must submit SAT I or ACT scores. Most Kettering University students rank at or near the top 10 percent of their high school class.

After students are accepted, the Kettering staff assists students until they secure a professional cooperative employment position. Students interview with co-op employers and many students accept co-op positions before classes begin. Corporate employers seek out students who demonstrate an interest in activities, career goals, experiences, leadership, and other positive personal qualities.

Although applications are accepted all year long, prospective students are encouraged to file their application early in their senior year. Early application significantly improves students' chances for early co-op employment. Kettering University also accepts transfer students. Admission decisions for transfer applicants are based on college record for those who completed at least 30 credits. Application fee is $35. Interested students can apply on line at www.admissions.kettering.edu.

CAMPUS LIFE

Although the professional co-op aspect of this program sets it apart from the traditional college experience, students at Kettering do enjoy the things that make college life unique and exciting, including on-campus housing for freshmen, a state-of-the-art recreation center, a variety of competitive athletic opportunities, fraternities and sororities, and an active residence life. Flint is located in east-central Michigan, just 60 miles west of Lake Huron and the Canadian boarder and 60 miles north of Detroit. Flint is a small city of 155,000 residents and has a metropolitan area of 450,000. Just a mile and a half from campus is the College Cultural Center Complex, which houses a museum, a performing arts auditorium, a planetarium, and the Flint Public Library. The proximity to outdoor activities, city culture, and Flint's own distinctive resources provides students with access to a wide range of activities and opportunities.

More than half of a Kettering student's time is spent off campus, fulfilling professional co-op work requirements outside the Flint area. On average students spend 11 academic semesters working for their co-op employer and 9 academic semesters in the classroom. The 700 corporate partners, corporations, and agencies that employ Kettering students are located throughout North America, Europe, and Asia, although approximately 70 percent of students work for a corporation located in their hometown, which allows them to live at home during the work experience portion of their education. On average, students earn between $40,000 and $65,000 over the entire professional co-op program.

COST AND AID

Tuition for the 2003–2004 academic year is $21,184. Room and board, including 19 meals per week totals $4,924. The technology fee is $100 per term.

LABORATORY INSTITUTE OF MERCHANDISING

GENERAL INFORMATION

The Laboratory Institute of Merchandising (LIM) is headquartered in an exquisite townhouse in central Manhattan, the world's undisputed fashion capital. LIM graduates populate the ranks of the fashion industry. The school's exacting academic standards have earned it accreditation from the Middle States Association of Colleges and Schools. Students at LIM receive highly individualized attention as they study the fashion industry. Most are traditional (i.e., age 18–22) students, but LIM also attracts a number of nontraditional undergraduates. Our student body of 400 is drawn from across the country and around the world. Students become not only colleagues but also close friends and, in many cases, lifelong business associates. The LIM curriculum stresses both professional and academic preparation. Our placement office is one of LIM's chief assets. All students, prior to graduation, receive extensive career counseling that helps direct them to a position in their field of study. LIM is extremely proud of its placement record; more than 90 percent of its graduates are employed in their fields of study within three months of graduation. Support services are also critical to the fulfillment of the LIM mission. The school provides not only academic and career counseling, but also personal counseling (through the Student Services Office).

The LIM curriculum requires students to complete a core set of courses in business and the liberal arts but also stresses the importance of hands-on training and diversification. This unique approach opens numerous options to graduates, whom the school prepares for work in communications, management, marketing, executive training, and merchandising in both the fashion world and fashion-related businesses. The unusually small size of the school means that students have near-universal access to instructors, staff, and administrators up to and including the president. Each junior and senior is assigned a mentor from the school's advisory board; all board members are successful executives in the fashion industry. Co-curricular organizations include the Student Government, the Fashion Club, and various clubs formed by students to serve special needs and interests. Students produce the annual yearbook (called *LIMLIGHT*), run fashion shows, and organize other cultural and social activities. LIM housing is located at the de Hirsch Residence at the 92nd Street Y. Single and double rooms are available to students on a "first-come, first-served" basis. LIM welcomes all interested prospects to its unique open-house program, Student for a Day. This program invites prospects and their families to tour the school with current students, learn about career opportunities in the fashion industry, explore academic programs and financing options, meet with faculty or administrators, and enjoy a complimentary breakfast. After lunch, visiting students may sit for a personal interview, which is a required part of the application process.

STUDENT BODY

Co-curricular activities generally originate with the Student Life Office, which houses the student government office and both funds and oversees student clubs and organizations.

ACADEMICS

Students at LIM learn in a variety of settings. Classroom instruction is supplemented by fieldwork performed under the supervision of industry professionals. The entire program is aimed at preparing students for entry-level executive positions throughout the fashion industry. LIM offers coursework in four divisions: fashion, business, visual, and arts and communications. The curriculum includes frequent field trips to various centers of the fashion industry as well as guest lectures by important figures in fashion. All students receive extensive work experience as part of their LIM education.

During freshman and sophomore year, students complete two 5-week work projects; each is worth three academic credits. Work Project I places students in full-time retail positions; this experience teaches students the fundamental processes of fashion retailing. Students are paid for their work. Work Project II also involves retail sales, usually through placements in fashion publishing, designer showrooms, cosmetics, and fashion forecasting companies. The increased level of responsibility that accompanies Work Project II qualifies it as a true internship experience. The third and final work project is the semester-long Senior Co-op, a required 6-credit placement in an area that complements the student's chosen area of specialization. Co-op jobs take students to fashion magazines, public relations firms, buying offices, and numerous other essential areas of fashion merchandising. Senior Co-op prepares undergraduates for the challenge and excitement of the business world. A two-year associate's degree is also available. Students in this program complete the first two years of the bachelor's program, including Work Projects I and II.

For the bachelor's degree, 126 credit hours are required; 64 credit hours are required for the associate's degree, and 33 credit hours are required for one-year ACCESS students. Furthermore, students must earn a minimum GPA of 2.0 and successfully complete all required work projects.

12 East 53rd Street
New York, NY 10022
Phone: 212-752-1530
Fax: 212-421-4341
Website: www.limcollege.edu

Transfer students are welcome at LIM. Transfers who have earned an associate's degree in fashion merchandising or an associated field may be accepted as juniors; so too are transfers who have earned 60 college credits from an accredited institution. To earn an LIM degree, transfers must earn at least 46 semester hours of credit at the College and must also satisfy the co-op requirement.

LIM operates on a two-semester calendar; students may enter in either semester. The College offers a summer program in July; it is open to high school and college students. Summer courses, which include Display Workshop, Fashion Magazines, Fashion Coordination, and Intro to Cosmetics, combine traditional coursework with hands-on activities. Each course is worth three college credits.

LIM offers two four-year degrees in fashion merchandising and marketing, the Bachelor of Business Administration (BBA) and the Bachelor of Professional Studies (BPS). The Associate in Applied Sciences (AAS) is a two-year degree. Qualified transfers may apply for a one-year associate's degree (through the ACCESS program). Most students major in fashion merchandising; a visual merchandising major is also available.

LIM's exceptional faculty have extensive experience in the fashion industry. More than one-third of the College's instructors (including all liberal arts professors) hold advanced degrees. Many classes involve guest lectures and discussion sessions with industry leaders. The student/faculty ratio is an unusually low 8:1. Each student works closely with an advisor who is also a member of the faculty or administration. The Career Services Office provides work-study assignments and career counseling. Placement counselors meet with each student before, during, and after cooperative work experiences; another series of meetings precedes the beginning of job placement interviews. Students are free to meet with placement counselors at any time.

CAMPUS LIFE

An amazing location is one of the many assets enjoyed by LIM undergraduates. World-famous works of architecture, such as St. Patrick's Cathedral, the Museum of Modern Art, Trump Tower, and Rockefeller Center are all within a short walk of the College. The fashion universe literally waits just beyond the school's front door. Nearby stores include Saks Fifth Avenue, Armani, Henri Bendel, Bloomingdale's, and Ralph Lauren. New York City is the center of many fashion and fashion-related industries, including cosmetics, garment, textiles, and fashion publishing; the school's location and prestige guarantee that students will interact with many principals in these areas. In fact, the curriculum frequently incorporates the city's numerous resources; the Fashion Magazines class, for example, includes field trips to modeling agencies, photography studios, advertising firms, and magazine publishing offices. No city can offer the breadth of experiences and fashion-related opportunities that New York offers.

Students may study overseas in a number of locations, including London, Paris, Milan, Barcelona, and China.

COST AND AID

Tuition for the 2002–2003 academic year is $14,000. On average, students spend an additional $750 per year on books, supplies, and fees. All other expenses, such as room and board, vary according to individual circumstances. Commuters spend between $330 to $1,500 for transportation. Off-campus room and board was approximately $6,000 in 2000–2001. Students should budget $1,000 per year for personal expenses.

LAKE FOREST COLLEGE

GENERAL INFORMATION

Since 1857, Lake Forest College has worked to bring its students to their highest personal and academic level. About 1,200 women and men make up the undergraduate community, and the beautiful campus is enhanced by the many wonderful resources that nearby Chicago has to offer. It is a point of pride for Lake Forest that its students come from so many places: 45 states and 44 countries. Fifteen percent of students are from minority groups. And students are given plenty of time to get to know each other because more than 90 percent of them live on campus. Students share their experiences throughout their time at Lake Forest as they learn many important life skills.

STUDENT BODY

Students at Lake Forest have more than 90 extracurricular activities from which to choose. Student-run organizations and clubs augment the classroom side of college life, helping to bring students to even higher levels of academic and personal achievement. Lake Forest strives to give each student the leadership and service experiences that will lead to greater personal fulfillment. Athletes at Lake Forest compete in the NCAA Division III program. Students can get involved with sports on three levels: varsity, club, and intramural. Men can participate in football, hockey, swimming, basketball, cross-country, handball, soccer, and tennis on a varsity level. Women's varsity choices include volleyball, softball, swimming, soccer, cross-country, tennis, and ice hockey.

ACADEMICS

Each semester at Lake Forest is 15 weeks long, and the semesters span late August to mid-December and mid-January to early May. Students are involved with general education courses throughout their four years, and these courses create the breadth and depth so vital to a liberal arts education. Courses in cultural diversity and college-level writing are two requirements. However, there is still plenty of flexibility for students to design academic programs that interest them. To graduate, students should pass 32 classes, complete the required general education courses, and fulfill the requirements for their chosen major.

The Bachelor of Arts (BA) degree is offered at Lake Forest, and students can choose from more than 500 classes in 19 academic disciplines and 7 interdisciplinary majors. Majors include: art, biology, business, chemistry, communications, computer science, economics, education (to be combined with a second major), English, French, German, history, mathematics, music, philosophy, physics, politics, psychology, sociology and anthropology, and Spanish. Students interested in an interdisciplinary major can choose from American studies, area studies, Asian studies (including Japanese language), comparative literature, environmental studies, and international relations. There are also classes in the fields of religion and theater. Students also may choose to be independent scholars, a program through which they can design a major of their choice. The program is open to students with the proper qualifications and motivation, and the majors students pursue are rooted in specific topics instead of in broader academic disciplines. Students can also choose to minor in any field, whether departmental or nondepartmental, that offers a major. Minors can also be declared in religion, theater, African American study, French civilization, metropolitan studies, and women's studies. Six to eight classes constitute a minor. Engineering students have the chance to take advantage of a cooperative degree program offered with the School of Engineering of Washington University (St. Louis, Missouri) and the University of Illinois—Urbana-Champaign. The program is 3-2, and qualified students can earn a BA from Lake Forest and a BS from Washington University.

Lake Forest culls its faculty from more than 40 universities, and these faculty—94 percent of whom have a PhD—are the people teaching and advising students. Lake Forest does not use teaching assistants. These accomplished faculty challenge students and get them thinking in new ways, and many teachers supplement a course's reading and classroom work with trips to Chicago or other nearby areas. Most importantly, the Lake Forest faculty are devoted to giving students one-on-one guidance and instruction.

555 North Sheridan Road
Lake Forest, IL 60045
Phone: 847-735-5000
Fax: 847-735-6271
Website: www.lakeforest.edu

LAKE FOREST College

ADMISSIONS

High achievement in academics and a good record of extracurricular activities are the most important factors when it comes to Lake Forest's competitive admission. Those at Lake Forest assessing applicants take into consideration the students' high school studies, their level of academic success, their proven potential for learning, their demonstrated curiosity, their character and personality, and their school and community activities. Admissions decisions are made without regard to social background, religious affiliation, race, natural origin, gender, handicap, or financial position. Lake Forest's diverse student body demonstrates this admission policy. High school seniors should begin applying early in the year. Though there is no actual deadline for general applications, there is a deadline of January 1 for early decision. By the third week of March, the admission selections have been reported for the first-year applicants who turned in their applications before March 1. The suggested secondary school academic program includes at least 4 years of English; 3 or more years of mathematics, including trigonometry; in-depth study in at least one foreign language; and 2 to 4 years of study in natural and social sciences. Applicants must also submit ACT or SAT scores, and though an interview is optional, the admissions staff encourages students to arrange a visit to the school with their families. Students also have the option of submitting the Common Application and other application programs that can be found online. One option is Apply! The start of each semester is when transfer students are admitted into the College. Requirements for transfer applicants are: an overall college average of at least a C or the equivalent, and the eligibility to return to their original schools. Transfer students can transfer a maximum of 60 semester hours. Applications for transfer students must include: admission application, secondary school transcript, transcripts of all college work completed to date, and a letter of recommendation from the academic dean or a professor at the current college. Interested students can explore Lake Forest on the Internet and take advantage of resources such as the online application, the College viewbook with links to Chicago sites, the College video, and the admitted-students site.

CAMPUS LIFE

Chicago is just 30 miles south of Lake Forest, but the campus feels very far from urban: from its position on a bluff, students have a view of the 321-mile-long Lake Michigan. Ravines, woods, and large fields naturally divide the 107-acre College into three campuses. The town is suburban and safe, with fewer than 20,000 residents; in fact, it is considered the safest "smaller" town in Illinois. Access to Chicago is easy: trains from the North Shore commuter rail line head to Chicago almost hourly. And the beach and downtown are an easy five-minute walk from campus.

Students come from far and wide to Lake Forest, and they also study far and wide. Paris, France; Santiago, Chile; and Greece and Turkey are some of the destinations for Lake Forest study abroad programs. Internships are the basis for the programs in France and Chile, and these give students the opportunity to gain work experience in a variety of fields. Midwestern college consortiums offer other opportunities for study outside of Lake Forest. The Associated Colleges of the Midwest (ACM) and the Great Lakes College Association (GLCA) jointly sponsor 14 programs for study, and destinations include the Czech Republic, Florence, and Chicago. A professor from the school involved serves as the leader of the program. All students from the participating schools can apply, and they can use the credits obtained from the ACM/GLCA program to satisfy some of their graduation requirements. Lake Forest's Off-Campus Studies Office can help students find other programs beyond the College or the ACM/GLCA group. To get credit for courses taken outside of Lake Forest, the Registrar must give approval.

COST AND AID

Lake Forest tuition is $21,190, along with $5,290 for room, board, and fees.

LAWRENCE TECHNOLOGICAL UNIVERSITY

GENERAL INFORMATION

Lawrence Technological University was founded in 1932 by two brothers, Russell and E. George Lawrence, its original name was the Lawrence Institute of Technology. Today, the University claims more than 22,000 alumni around the world. The University offers a diverse curriculum with a strong emphasis on practical applications and theory. The school has always been (and continues to be) committed to making a Lawrence Tech education affordable without compromising the quality of instruction. The North Central Association of Colleges and Schools accredits the school, which maintains graduate programs in architecture, business, and engineering (professional degree programs receive additional accreditation from the appropriate professional agencies in administration and management, architecture, chemistry, engineering, illustration, and interior architecture/design). Graduate degree programs are offered in architecture, automotive engineering, business administration, civil engineering, computer science, industrial operations, information systems, manufacturing systems, and science education.

About 5,000 students attend Lawrence Tech, of whom approximately 450 live on campus. Women make up 23 percent of the student body. Students at the University have many opportunities to enjoy on-campus events sponsored by Greek organizations (fraternities and sororities) as well as professional and social organizations. About one-fourth of all students participate in the intramural sports program; campus athletic facilities include the 38,000-square-foot Don Ridler Field House (featuring a gymnasium, racquetball courts, a running track, saunas, and a weight and conditioning room). The campus is comprised of eight major buildings, all less than 50 years old. Since 1981, the campus has expanded by more than 100 percent. A new 85,000-square-foot Technology and Learning Center, which opened in 2001, is currently the largest facility on campus.

STUDENT BODY

Lawrence is home to an active Student Government that funds and manages numerous diverse campus activities. It supervises expenditures, plans events, and levies fines for lesser on-campus violations. The school is home to more than 40 student organizations and clubs; these include honor societies, fraternities, sororities, and student chapters of professional groups.

ACADEMICS

Over 40 majors or areas of concentration are available at the University. Most programs can be completed through both day and evening programs. The school offers dual degree programs that combine the associate's and baccalaureate programs. The University prepares students for postgraduate study with programs in pre-biomedical engineering, pre-dentistry, pre-law, and pre-medicine. Students in the College of Architecture and Design may pursue the Bachelor's of Science degree in architecture and interior architecture/design. The school also offers a Bachelor's of Fine Arts degree in architectural illustration. The College of Arts and Sciences confers the Bachelor's of Science degree in the following fields: administration, chemistry, computer science, environmental chemistry, humanities, mathematics, mathematics and computer science, physics, physics and computer science, and technical communication. The school also offers an associate's degree in chemical technology. The College of Engineering offers the Bachelor's of Science degree in the following areas: civil engineering, computer engineering, electrical engineering, engineering technology, industrial management, mechanical engineering, and technology management. Also available are evening associate programs in construction, electrical, manufacturing, and mechanical engineering technology. The College of Management confers graduate degrees.

The Lawrence Tech faculty consists of approximately 350 members (full time and part time). A number of part-time instructors work full time in industry; their teaching provides students with real-world perspectives. Approximately three-fifths of all full-time instructors hold a terminal degree (e.g. the PhD) in their area of expertise. Students interact with instructors in class and through on-campus professional organizations, which faculty members sponsor. A number of faculty members are professional architects or engineers working in the states. The majority of undergraduate classes have fewer than 20 students; only 2 percent have more than 50 students.

21000 West Ten Mile Road
Southfield, MI 48075-1058
Phone: 248-204-3160
Fax: 248-204-3188
Website: www.ltu.edu

ADMISSIONS

Students must have achieved a high school diploma or its equivalent to gain entry into the University's baccalaureate or associate's degree programs. Most applicants to the baccalaureate program must demonstrate a minimum overall GPA of 2.5 in academic subjects and a minimum GPA of 2.0 in subjects related to their intended program of study. Applicants to associate's degree programs must demonstrate a combined minimum GPA of 2.0 in the humanities, mathematics, and science. All applicants must provide official score reports for the ACT exam. Different University programs require different preparatory high school curricula. Lawrence Tech offers a variety of courses designed to address potential shortfalls in an incoming student's academic background. Lawrence's academic programs commence in August and January. The University also offers an optional summer term, which commences in May or July. The school recommends that students enter in the fall. Applicants must provide official transcripts from all schools they have attended. Applications must be accompanied by a nonrefundable $30 application fee. Contact the admissions office at the address below to obtain an application form or a University catalog:

Admissions Office
Lawrence Technological University
21000 West Ten Mile Road
Southfield, MI 48075-1058
Telephone: 800-CALL-LTU (toll free)
E-mail: admissions@ltu.edu
Website: www.ltu.edu

CAMPUS LIFE

Lawrence Tech makes its home in Southfield, a Detroit suburb of approximately 76,000 people. Southfield is an industrial and corporate center that offers a satisfying balance between urban amenities and residential peacefulness. It is located in Oakland County, which boasts the nation's third-highest per capita income. More than a quarter million people work in the Southfield area. The University campus is close to major highways; downtown Detroit can be reached by car in a half-hour. Southfield and its surroundings offer a wide range of cultural and recreational options; public transportation allows all students, even those without cars, to take advantage of these opportunities. Parks, recreational facilities, restaurants, and shopping centers are all within a few miles of the Lawrence Tech campus. The area is ideal for co-op students, offering numerous opportunities in business, manufacturing, research, and science. More than 200 Fortune 500 companies operate in the immediate area.

Cooperative learning opportunities are available to Lawrence Tech engineering and technology students. Co-op students alternate semesters of classes and work.

COST AND AID

Tuition and fees for the 2002–2003 academic year are as follows:

For freshmen and sophomores majoring in arts and sciences, management, or engineering technology, $450 per credit hour; for juniors in these areas, $470 per credit hour; and for seniors, $418 per credit hour.

Freshmen and sophomores studying architecture and design are charged $470 per credit hour; juniors and seniors, $486 per credit hour.

Charges for engineering majors are: freshmen and sophomores, $470 per credit hour; juniors, $486 per credit hour; seniors, $434 per credit hour.

Students normally take 12–17 credit hours per semester. An additional registration fee of $100 per semester is charged. International students in the country on a temporary visa must pay full tuition and fees for their first semester when they register.

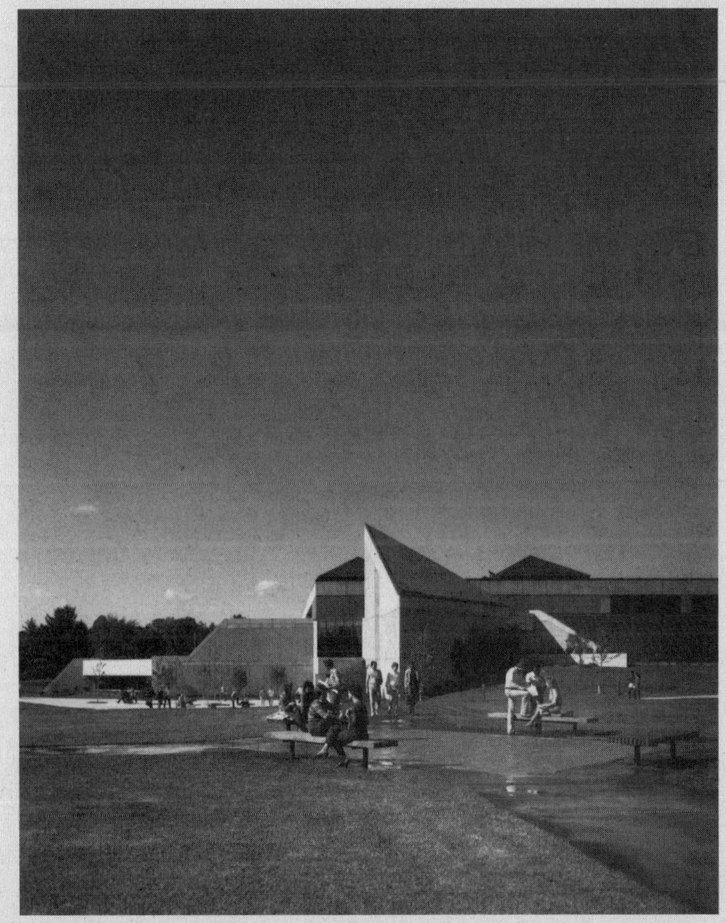

LESLEY COLLEGE

GENERAL INFORMATION

Lesley College, the undergraduate women's college of Lesley University, is a small residential, four-year college of approximately 550 students. Lesley College students benefit tremendously from the resources and breadth of opportunities that come from being part of Lesley University, a coeducational university of more than 7,500 students, at the same time enjoying the warmth and informality of a close-knit community. Lesley College offers professional majors in art therapy, child studies, communication technology, counseling, education, human services, and management. Central to the mission at Lesley is a commitment to excellent and creative instruction offered in an intimate college environment in which each student is valued, significant, and a contributing member. An education at Lesley combines theoretical and practical approaches to learning, blending a strong liberal arts foundation with substantial professional preparation. Beginning with freshman year, Lesley students have direct exposure to their chosen fields. The result is a balanced integration of theory and practice. Lesley College students are able to cross register for courses in the other schools at Lesley University, including the Art Institute of Boston, and accelerated bachelor's/master's programs have been developed in conjunction with the School of Education and the Graduate School of Social Sciences. In addition, the Lesley Dividend offers qualified Lesley College students a year of free graduate tuition when they continue with a master's degree program at Lesley University. The University is accredited by the New England Association of Schools and Colleges. The teacher-certification programs have been approved by the NASDTEC (National Association of State Directors of Teacher Education and Certification) Interstate Contract, a reciprocity agreement in which more than 40 states have established standards for granting teacher certification.

STUDENT BODY

Lesley College students have the best of both worlds. They are part of a close-knit undergraduate women's college of 550 students, but at the same time they are part of Lesley University, a coeducational institution of more than 7,500 students . . . which only enhances Campus Life. In fact, Lesley College students regularly join with Art Institute of Boston students in various campus activities, attend gallery openings at AIB, or take advantage of lectures sponsored by one of the graduate programs or the Lesley University Mind, Body, Spirit Institute. Lesley College students are involved in a variety of clubs and organizations from Student Senate to a literary magazine, a drama club to Amnesty International. Lesley also fields five NCAA Division III athletic teams: basketball, crew, soccer, softball, and volleyball. A variety of on-campus events are sponsored throughout the year by various student organizations as well as the Office of Student Development. And then there are all the happenings on other college campuses in the area . . . not to mention the events at coffeehouses, theaters, concert halls, and museums in Cambridge and Boston.

ACADEMICS

All of Lesley's academic programs are designed to integrate study in the liberal arts with professional course work and significant "hands on" internship experience. Internship experiences begin in the freshman year and are developmentally sequenced to complement classroom instruction throughout the undergraduate program. Internships are designed to show students what the workplace is like, challenge assumptions they may have about themselves and the world, and give the kind of experience that creates exceptional resumes. In fact, by the end of four years Lesley students have spent between 400 and 650 hours out in the field. What's more, internships are integrated with seminar classes in which students discuss and evaluate their fieldwork—learning also from fellow students' experiences about workplace issues and emerging trends. It is this careful integration of theory and practice that we believe really distinguishes the Lesley curriculum from that at other colleges. Through a comprehensive general education program, all students also build a strong liberal arts foundation by taking courses in the arts, humanities, sciences, and social sciences. Through this liberal arts course work, students develop their ability to think critically, strengthen writing skills, as well as ensure that they have a breadth of knowledge and skills that will lead to success in graduate school and an interest in a life of learning.

Lesley College offers a Bachelor of Science degree in the following areas: art therapy, child studies, communication technology, counseling, education, human services, and management. Although most students do major in a professional area, there are also seven liberal arts majors that are designed to work especially well with the education programs. Liberal arts majors include American studies, the arts, English, environmental studies, global studies, human development and family studies, and natural science: mathematics and science. Students interested in teaching may choose from the following majors: early childhood education, elementary education, middle school education, secondary education, or day care leadership (a noncertificate program). Students majoring in one of these areas are also required to elect a double major in one of seven liberal arts areas listed above. Completion of a major in education qualifies a student to be recommended for initial licensure in Massachusetts and 40 other states that belong to the NASDTEC (National Association of State Directors of Teacher Education and Certification) Interstate Contract. Students pursuing a major in other professional areas (art therapy, child studies, communication technology, counseling, human services or management) combine a liberal arts minor with their professional studies. Like all Lesley students, those who choose to major in one of the liberal arts areas integrate professional course work and internship experiences through an individualized professional minor. This creates a liberal arts program that is designed for the real world—for real careers and real success. In addition, the following accelerated bachelor's/master's degree programs are offered in conjunction with Lesley's graduate programs: a BS/MA in counseling psychology or clinical mental health counseling; and a BS/MEd in early childhood education, elementary education, middle school education, or special education.

Office of Admissions, 29 Everett Street
Cambridge, MA 02138
Phone: 617-349-8800
Fax: 617-349-8810
Website: www.lesley.edu/prospective/uwc.html

Lesley College faculty hold teaching undergraduates as their highest priority. Even more important to a student's classroom experience, however, is the fact that many of the faculty are trained practitioners, classroom educators, counselors, social workers, business professionals, etc. In fact, many continue to work in the field, or as consultants, and bring a wealth of "real world" experience into their classroom teaching. Of the 70 full- and part-time Lesley College faculty, more than two-thirds hold a doctorate or other terminal degree. Faculty serve as academic advisors for students, and the student to faculty ratio of 16:1 allows for a close relationship to develop between students and their professors.

ADMISSIONS

Throughout the application process, great attention is paid to the individual. We want to get to know each applicant as a person. We begin the process by gathering as much information as possible about each interested student, in the form of various credentials and other pertinent pieces of information that includes: the high school transcript, transcripts of any college course work, teacher recommendation, personal recommendation, and standardized tests (SAT I or ACT scores). Academic performance; level of motivation; as well as volunteer, community, and/or work experiences form the basis of all Admissions decisions. Admissions decisions for the fall semester are sent out on a rolling basis beginning December 1, and applicants can expect a decision within three weeks of having completed the application. There is a preferred deadline of March 15 for freshman applications and June 1 for transfers. Also, we strongly encourage students to visit the campus and have a personal interview with an Admissions counselor. This gives each student a valuable opportunity to see the campus, experience the atmosphere of the community, and get direct answers to all her questions. Equally important, it gives us a chance to sit down with each woman considering Lesley and create a full picture of each applicant—a true context in which we can best evaluate the more impersonal part of the process, test scores and transcripts.

CAMPUS LIFE

Lesley College students live on a 5-acre campus, an urban academic village, set in the heart of the Cambridge, Massachusetts, intellectual community just across the river from downtown Boston. Lesley is located in a residential neighborhood, just outside of Harvard Square, an area filled with cafés, theaters, bookstores, concert halls, museums, shops and restaurants. Harvard Law School is across the street, Harvard, MIT, and Tufts are close by, and Boston is only a short subway ride away. Cambridge and Boston are famous for their historical, cultural, and business resources and has one of the most concentrated enclaves of high-tech industry in the nation. In particular, Lesley students take full advantage of these resources when selecting internship experiences that are an integral part of the Lesley College curriculum. But more than anything, Boston/Cambridge is the ultimate "college town" with more than 45 colleges and 230,000 college students living in the area. Cultural life in the Boston area is rich and varied. More than 100 museums—dedicated to virtually every artistic, cultural, and scientific discipline—provide ample opportunities for student involvement on many levels. There are shops and restaurants of every ethnic variety, first-run films, theater, and famed professional sports teams. In addition, the Boston area has an efficient public transportation system for travel within the metropolitan area and easy, direct transportation to and from all regions of the United States.

Lesley College offers students the opportunity to participate in a number of Lesley-affiliated programs for off-campus study in the U.S. and abroad, through which they may obtain Lesley College credit. In addition, each year a number of students choose to study abroad in nonaffiliated programs, and the director of international studies provides guidance regarding transfer of credit as well as advice about researching available programs. Lesley-affiliated programs include: Orebro University Exchange Program in Sweden, The American University and Washington and World Capitals Semester Program in Washington, D.C., as well as several Lesley-sponsored study/travel opportunities. Current study/travel opportunities include: The British Experience, Field Study in Europe: The Holocaust; Traditions and Cultures: Ireland; Traditions and Cultures of the Southwest: Santa Fe; and New England Field Studies: The Tall Ship *Ernestina*.

COST AND AID

Fees for the 2003–2004 academic year include: tuition, $19,525; room and board, $8,800; a health services fee, $1,100; and a student activities fee, $175.

LEWIS UNIVERSITY

GENERAL INFORMATION

Lewis University, a comprehensive Catholic University, continues the tradition of educational and social responsibility established by its sponsors, the Christian Brothers, and the founder of the Brotherhood, St. John the Baptist de La Salle. The Christian Brothers currently maintain 60 high schools and 7 institutions of higher learning in the United States; throughout the world, the Brotherhood teaches in 80 nations.

Lewis focuses its efforts on the individual needs of its students by providing a wide choice of curricular and social options. Small classes allow for plenty of individual attention and student-teacher interaction; the availability of more than 50 majors and graduate programs means that students need not limit their intellectual curiosity to just a few disciplines. A 15:1 student/faculty ratio ensures that a Lewis student never becomes "just another Social Security number." Faculty members counsel students in both academic and career pursuits. Approximately 4,300 men and women attend Lewis University. The majority are Illinois residents, although the student body includes representatives of more than 25 states and 30 countries. About 75 percent of Lewis undergraduates commute to campus. Even so, nearly 1,000 students live in the school's eight residence halls. Residents enjoy an especially close rapport and a strong sense of campus community.

Students interested in co-curricular activity can choose from more than 40 student organizations and clubs representing a broad range of interests. Four fraternities and five sororities provide other social opportunities. The University competes in 18 intercollegiate sports and maintains a popular intramural sports program (four-fifths of our undergraduates play intramural sports). Lewis fields men's teams in baseball, basketball, cross-country, golf, soccer, swimming, tennis, track, and volleyball. Women compete in basketball, cross-country, golf, soccer, softball, swimming, tennis, track, and volleyball. All 18 teams compete in Division II of the NCAA. Lewis is extremely competitive on and off the field; the school has earned the Great Lakes Valley Conference's All Sports Trophy 12 times in the past 19 years and boasts a high percentage of successful scholar-athletes. Ninety-five percent of our intercollegiate athletes complete their bachelor's degree; a large number make the Deans' List. Lewis University offers the following graduate degrees: the Master of Business Administration (MBA); the Master of Arts (MA) in counseling psychology, education, leadership studies, and school counseling and guidance; the Master of Science in Nursing (MSN); the Master of Education; and the Master of Science (MS) in criminal/social justice.

STUDENT BODY

The governmental mechanism of the Lewis student body is the Student Governing Board (SGB). Ten campus groups have their own councils: the Black Student Union, commuters, the interfraternity council, the interorganizational council, the International Student Association, the Latin American Student Organization, the Pan Hellenic council, the scholars' council, the student athletic advisory board, and the residence hall council. Each council is represented on the SGB. The SGB organizes campus activities, funds and oversees students clubs and organizations, regulates the conduct of student organizations (through its student court), and represents students' concerns to administrators.

ACADEMICS

All Lewis students must complete a curriculum consisting of three modules: general education requirements, major requirements, and electives. General education, which ensures that all students receive a well-rounded education, includes pre-selected courses in the humanities and the social or natural sciences. Major requirements guarantee that students receive in-depth instruction in an area of their choosing. Electives offer students the chance to dig deeper into their major areas, explore related academic disciplines, or simply indulge their curiosity. The undergraduate curriculum stresses communication arts and humanities in an effort to acquaint students with the historical foundations of modern social and political issues. The school awards academic credit to those who demonstrate achievement through CLEP or AP (Advanced Placement) exams, as well as to those with appropriate life experience.

Majors in the College of Arts and Sciences are designed to sharpen critical thinking skills, encourage openness to new ideas, and introduce students to a wide variety of intellectual traditions. The College of Business develops functional business skills and fosters responsible approaches to the economic, political, and social elements of business practice. Business students must take a number of classes in the liberal arts, as must students at the College of Nursing & Health Professions. Nursing students focus on the humanities and the sciences during their first two years, then undertake advanced nursing course work and on-site clinical training during their final two years. The nursing program is designed to prepare students to deliver healthcare services in a wide variety of situations.

Lewis follows a semester calendar. Fall classes begin the Monday preceding Labor Day; spring classes begin in the middle of January. A variety of summer sessions are available; they vary in duration from six to ten weeks.

Students pursuing the Bachelor of Arts degree may major in accountancy, American studies, athletic training, biochemistry, biology, broadcast journalism, business administration, business studies, chemistry, communications technology, computer science, criminal/social justice, drawing, economics, education, English, environmental science, finance, graphic arts, history, human communications, human resources management, illustration, journalism, liberal arts, management information systems, marketing, mathematics, multimedia production, music, music merchandising, painting, philosophy, physics, political science, private security/loss prevention management, psychology, public relations, broadcast production, religious studies, social work and human services, sociology, special education, speech, sport management, and theater.

One University Parkway, Box 297
Romeoville, IL 60446-2200
Phone: 815-836-5250
Fax: 815-836-5002
Website: www.lewisu.edu

Students pursuing the Bachelor of Science degree may major in airway science, aviation majors, biochemistry, biology, chemistry, computer science, math, physics, political science, and public administration.

Pre-professional programs are offered in dentistry, engineering, law, medical dietetics, medicine, meteorology, optometry, pharmacy, physical therapy, physician's assistant studies, and veterinary science. Interdisciplinary study in such areas as ethnic studies and women's studies is available at the University. Working adults may pursue accelerated degree completion programs. The College of Nursing & Health Professions offers the Bachelor of Science in Nursing (BSN) degree.

Lewis maintains a solid program in aviation. The school offers Bachelor of Science degrees with majors in aviation administration, aviation maintenance, or professional pilot. Minors are available in avionics, nondestructive inspection, aircraft dispatch, airport management, and airline station management. Lewis' programs prepare undergraduates to qualify for the FAA Airframe and Powerplant Certificate (required of aircraft mechanics).

Students seeking a broad or self-designed curriculum may wish to pursue the Bachelor of Elected Studies (BES) degree and a liberal arts degree. The BES degree allows students to create a major by selecting a concentration from any University department. The liberal arts degree allows student to combine two minors into a single, self-designed major.

Research and teaching are equally important responsibilities of the University faculty. About three-fifths of the faculty hold PhDs or equivalent terminal degrees in their field; every member of the aviation faculty possesses an FAA-approved license. A low student/faculty ratio (15:1) results in cohesive classes and close student-teacher interaction in and out of the classroom.

ADMISSIONS

Lewis University seeks students who are motivated to succeed. It gives preference to those who show a past record of academic achievement. Applicants for freshman admission must submit standardized test scores (ACT or SAT I), as well as an official high school transcript. Students whose first language is not English must take the Test of English as a Foreign Language (TOEFL) and score at least 500. Applicants for the nursing program must meet all the above requirements and must also complete 1 year of chemistry, 1 year of biology, and at least 1 year of algebra in high school.

Transfer students with at least 12 college credits should contact the Office of Admissions' transfer coordinator to learn more about transfer application. The school accepts most college credits for transfer, up to a maximum of 72 credit hours. Transfer applicants must provide transcripts from every college and university attended. Transfer students who have earned fewer than 12 credits should follow the same application procedure as freshman applicants.

Contact the Office of Admission to request application forms for admission and financial aid.

CAMPUS LIFE

Romeoville, Illinois, is the hometown of Lewis University. The suburban area is only 30 minutes outside Chicago, which can be easily reached by expressway. The 350-acre campus provides a serene setting for study with convenient access to one of the nation's premier cities. Buses run between campus and commuter trains (to Chicago); recreational and shopping areas in Joliet, Lockport, and Plainfield can also be reached easily by bus.

LINCOLN UNIVERSITY (PA)

GENERAL INFORMATION

Lincoln University is the nation's oldest college founded for the express purpose of delivering higher education to youth of African descent. This state-related, coeducational, nonsectarian, four-year liberal arts school was founded in 1854; today it serves exceptional students of all races.

CAMPUS LIFE

Modern architecture seamlessly blends with older design styles on Lincoln's manicured campus. Facilities include 18 residence halls (7 for men, 11 for women); a student union building that houses a bookstore, activity rooms, and a snack bar; Manuel Rivero Hall, an up-to-date athletic facility that includes a 2,400-seat gymnasium, an Olympic-size swimming pool, a dance studio, a bowling alley, and a large game room; and John Miller Dickey Hall, a humanities complex and $5.4 million computer facility; and the $17 million up-to-the-minute Thurgood Marshall Living and Learning Center. In the near future, the school will open its $13 million International Cultural Center, equipped with a 2,000-seat auditorium. Twelve computer labs for students mean that Lincoln boasts a 6:1 student/computer ratio. A state-of-the-art television station and radio station are also available to students. Currently 2,000 students attend Lincoln University.

Lincoln's intercollegiate teams compete in Division III of the NCAA; teams compete in baseball, basketball, cross-country, soccer, tennis, and track. Lincoln University also sponsors a student dance troupe, a drama group, a student newspaper, a student radio station, and a vigorous music program encompassing numerous choral groups and a jazz band. The campus often hosts lectures, concerts, and many other recreational and cultural programs.

The campus is located in rural southern Chester County amid the rolling hills and farmland of Pennsylvania. The University is located on Old U.S. Route 1, about 45 miles south of Philadelphia; 55 miles north of Baltimore, Maryland; and 25 miles west of Wilmington, Delaware. All three are major cities that provide exceptional cultural and recreational opportunities. Closer to campus (four miles south) is the town of Oxford, Pennsylvania, which offers banks, churches, restaurants, and shopping areas. Graduate students attend classes at the Center for Continuing Education and Graduate Studies (Urban Center) in Philadelphia, Pennsylvania.

ACADEMICS

Lincoln University confers four-year Bachelor of Arts and Bachelor of Science degrees. Majors are available in the following areas: accounting, biology, business administration and economics, chemistry, computer science, criminal justice, education, English, finance, history, human services, international relations, journalism and communications (offered in conjunction with Temple University), mathematics, modern languages, music, philosophy, physical education, physics, political science, psychology, public affairs, recreational leadership, religion, sociology/anthropology, studio arts, and therapeutic recreation. The University also offers pre-professional programs in dentistry, engineering, law, medicine, nursing, and veterinary science.

Accelerated degree programs are also available. Lincoln offers a 3-3 engineering program in cooperation with Drexel University and 3-2 programs in engineering in cooperation with Howard University, Lafayette College, New Jersey Institute of Technology, Pennsylvania State University, Rensselaer Polytechnic Institute, and the University of Delaware. All of these program lead to a Lincoln BA and a BS from the participating engineering school.

The University runs a semester calendar. Accreditation is conferred by the College and University Council of the State of Pennsylvania and by the Middle States Association of Colleges and Schools. The University's health-related programs receive accreditation from the American Medical Association.

Graduate students may pursue any of five master's degree programs, offered in administration, education, human services, mathematics, and reading, with concentrations in educational administration, human resource management, and budget and financial management. Lincoln also offers a certification program in reading as well as a teacher certification program.

All Lincoln undergraduates are required to undertake in-depth study in a single area of concentration. Faculty advisors are assigned to entering students at the time of enrollment; the student's declared career goal is used to select the appropriate advisor. Students typically carry 15 credit hours per semester, plus one physical education course. Full-time students must register for a minimum of 12 credit hours per semester. Students wishing to carry more than 18 credit hours or 5.5 courses must receive the approval of their advisor and the University registrar. An undergraduate degree is conferred following the satisfactory completion of 120 to 128 credit hours.

The T.I.M.E. (Talent Improvement and Motivational Experience) Program, which receives funding through the Commonwealth of Pennsylvania Legislative Act 101, provides counseling and tutorial support in mathematics, reading, writing, and content courses. It is one of Lincoln University's many supportive services programs.

The University is home to the Lincoln Advanced Science and Engineering Reinforcement program (LASER), which is among the most successful science and engineering training programs in the United States.

Lincoln Hall
Lincoln University, PA 19352-0999
Phone: 610-932-8300
Fax: 610-932-1209
Website: www.lincoln.edu

COSTS AND AID

For the 2003–2004 academic year, tuition and fees total $6,378 for Pennsylvania residents and $9,816 for out-of-state students. Tuition, fees, and other costs—including room and board—total approximately $11,962 for Pennsylvania residents and $15,400 for out-of-state students. Tuition and fees are subject to change without notice.

The University distributes financial aid on the basis of demonstrated need. Aid applicants must submit the Free Application for Federal Student Aid (FAFSA) and mail the application to the Central Processor. Remember to include Lincoln University's federal code, which is 003290. The deadline for financial aid applications is March 15.

More than 90 percent of Lincoln students receive financial assistance in some form. Scholarships, federal grants, state grants, Federal Perkins Loans, Federal Stafford Student Loans, Federal Work-Study Program awards, and institutional aid all may be included in any financial aid package.

The University also offers merit scholarships to applicants who demonstrate exceptional academic potential. Applicants for merit-based aid must have a minimum combined SAT score of 900 and a minimum 3.0 (the equivalent of a letter grade of B) average. They must also demonstrate significant involvement in both school and their community. Contact the director of admissions for additional information.

ADMISSIONS

The University prefers students who are graduates of accredited high schools. Applicants who rank in the top half of their graduating class, have a minimum 2.8 average, demonstrate leadership abilities, and have completed 21 Carnegie units, including 4 of English, 3 of mathematics, 3 of social science, and 3 of science, will be admitted. Applicants typically submit a combined SAT score of at least 870 and two letters of recommendation. All applications are reviewed individually.

Lincoln University has a rolling admissions policy. Students seeking application forms and additional information should contact:

Office of Admissions
MSC 147
Lincoln University
PO Box 179
Lincoln University, PA 19352-0999
Telephone: 610-932-8300 or 800-790-0191 (toll free)
E-mail: admiss@lu.lincoln.edu
World Wide Web: www.lincoln.edu

LOCK HAVEN UNIVERSITY OF PENNSYLVANIA

GENERAL INFORMATION

Lock Haven University (LHU) began as the Central State Normal School in 1870. Currently, as a key component of Pennsylvania's State System of Higher Education, the university enrolls 4,100 students, allowing for an intimate educational setting. Between the College of Arts and Sciences and the College of Education and Human Services, LHU presents more than 75 academic courses of study. Some of the top programs include education, health science, recreation, psychology, criminal justice, and the biological sciences. Students can pursue master's degrees in education (curriculum and instruction), health science (physician assistant in rural primary care), and liberal arts.

The University holds accreditation from the Middle States Association of Colleges and Schools, the National Council for Accreditation of Teacher Education, the National Athletic Training Association, the Council for Social Work Education, the National League of Nursing, and the Accreditation Review Commission on Education for the Physician Assistant.

A total of 1,700 students live in the University's seven dormitories. All of these facilities have computer clusters, study lounges, laundry facilities and recreational equipment. Students compliment their classroom learning with participation in any of the school's 80 clubs and organizations.

STUDENT BODY

The Student Cooperative Council (SCC) serves as the governing body of the student population. All students are automatically members upon paying their activity fee every term. The Parson Union Building, the student bookstore, the campus snack bar, and the new and modern fitness center all fall under SCC jurisdiction. The Council also makes decisions regarding the finances of athletic teams and student organizations. The SCC manages the money behind many campus improvements and schoolwide cultural events. Popular social organizations include the Residence Hall Association and the six national fraternities, four sororities, and various academic- and service-based Greek organizations. Student-athletes lead LHU teams to success in NCAA Division I men's wrestling as well as Division II men's and women's basketball, soccer, track and field, and cross country; men's football and baseball; and women's field hockey, lacrosse, softball, swimming, and volleyball. A total of more than 80 clubs and organizations are offered.

ACADEMICS

Graduation requires 120 credits, approximately 52 of which are earned in general education classes. The University calendar comprises two semesters. Students may choose to attend a summer term as well. Students are encouraged to round out their course work with internships and independent study. Students may transfer credits from other regionally accredited schools as long as they have achieved at least a 2.0 grade point average. The Office of Enrollment Services determines whether classes attended while serving in the armed forces can be applied. The university runs a Veteran's Affairs Office to offer guidance regarding financial aid, among other topics. Students may participate in the Army Reserve Officers' Training Corps' program in military science.

LHU grants Bachelor of Arts degrees in art, economics, engineering (a cooperative five year dual-degree program with Pennsylvania State University), English, environmental geology, French, German, history, humanities (English, philosophy, and speech/theater), international studies, journalism and mass communications, Latin American studies, mathematics, natural sciences (biology, chemistry, and physics), philosophy, political science, psychology, social sciences (economics, history, political science, and sociology/anthropology), sociology, Spanish, communication studies, and theater.

Students may also pursue a Bachelor of Fine Arts in music or in studio art.

The Bachelor of Science degree is available in accounting, applied geology, biology, biology/chemistry, biology/chemistry with a medical technology emphasis, business administration, chemistry, computer science, computer information science, criminal justice, geography, paralegal studies, physics, pre-professional preparation (dentistry, medicine, pharmacy, and veterinary medicine), recreation, social work and sport administration.

Students may work towards their Bachelor of Science in Education in early childhood education, elementary education, health and physical education, secondary education (with concentrations in biology, biology/general science, chemistry, citizenship studies, earth and space science, English, French, general science, geography/social science, German, mathematics, physics, and Spanish), and special education.

Those students seeking a Bachelor of Science in Health Science choose between concentrations in athletic training/sports medicine, community health, pre-professional, pre-physical therapy, and pre-physician assistant. The University's sports medicine/athletic training program stands as one of only 90 programs in the country approved by the National Athletic Training Association.

Students benefit from LHU's low student/faculty ratio of 19:1. The full- and part-time faculty members number 270. This diverse and accomplished pool of professors offers extensive experience in teaching and their various professional fields. Nearly all instructors hold an advanced degree; more than half of the tenure-track professors have their PhD.

Akeley Hall
Lock Haven, PA 17745
Phone: 570-893-2027
Fax: 570-893-2201
Website: www.lhup.edu

ADMISSIONS

Students should take their applications along with a $25 application fee to their high school guidance office. The guidance counselors will forward the application in addition to the necessary transcripts and SAT I or ACT score. In the case of transfer students, the basic materials should be sent to LHU along with official transcripts showing all high school and college work. SAT I or ACT scores are required only if students will be applying with fewer than 24 previously earned credits. International students need to submit application materials 6 to 12 months in advance of their intended start date. They also must pass the Test of English as a Foreign Language (TOEFL) with a minimum score of 213, if English is not their first language. Those students applying from high school should have their application to LHU by January of their senior year to begin in the fall semester. Those who want to begin in the spring should have their materials in by December 1. June 1 is the recommended deadline for transfer students for the fall and December 1 for spring. For more information, please contact the Office of Admission toll free at 800-332-8900 (in state), 800-233-8978 (outside PA), or admissions@lhup.edu.

CAMPUS LIFE

Based in Lock Haven, Pennsylvania, a town of population 10,000, the University enjoys a 165-acre campus perched on a hill with a view of the Susquehanna River. Students have convenient access to outdoor activities including skiing, swimming, fishing, hiking, hunting, camping, and hang gliding. The University's Ross Library is home to an impressive collection of art by Lock Haven native John Sloan. The fine arts building is named after him. Also, LHU students can take in summer-stock theater at the nearby Millbrook Playhouse. The cities of Pittsburgh, Philadelphia, New York City, and Washington, DC, are all close enough for visits. Those coming to Lock Haven may drive via Interstate Route 80 and U.S. Routes 15 and 220, fly into Williamsport or State College airports, or take the bus to the Trailways station.

COST AND AID

In 2002–2003, in-state students paid $4,378 in tuition and $4,744 for room and board. The total for out-of-state enrollees was $8,946 for tuition and $4,744 for room and board. Fees totaled $1,278, covering the student activity fee, health service fee, the educational services fee, a student center fee, and a technology fee.

LOYOLA UNIVERSITY NEW ORLEANS

GENERAL INFORMATION

What makes Loyola University New Orleans Unique?

Rich Jesuit Tradition: Loyola's rich history and Jesuit influence date back to the early eighteenth century when the Jesuits first arrived among the earliest settlers in New Orleans and Louisiana. The Jesuits are renowned for liberal arts, value-centered education of the whole person, and a commitment to lifelong learning, social justice, and service.

Ideal Size: More than 60 academic programs provide choices available at larger universities, while giving the student more opportunities to succeed individually. Students relish the opportunity to work in teams on research projects, to publish jointly with faculty members, and to experience the benefit of having faculty members testify to their triumphs inside and outside of the classroom.

Academic Excellence: Loyola's tradition of academic excellence had been built upon the quality of faculty, students, and programs, and is enhanced by the many academic resources available to students. Recognized with British Marshall and Rhodes Scholars winners, a nationally recognized advertising team, and a renowned student newspaper, Loyola is focused on becoming one of the preeminent universities in the country.

Special Programs: Accredited by the AACSB, acknowledged with the 2001 Louisiana Quality Award, and recognized by *U.S. News & World Report* as one of the Best Business Programs in the country, the College of Business Administration is equally proud of its win at the American Marketing Association competition for the 2001–2002 year.

The Department of Chemistry houses one of the few undergraduate programs in forensic science in the Southeast and the only program in the state of Louisiana.

The Loyola School of Law offers the Early Admission Program to Loyola students interested in attending law school. This program allows qualified Loyola undergraduates the opportunity to matriculate to the School of Law after their junior year.

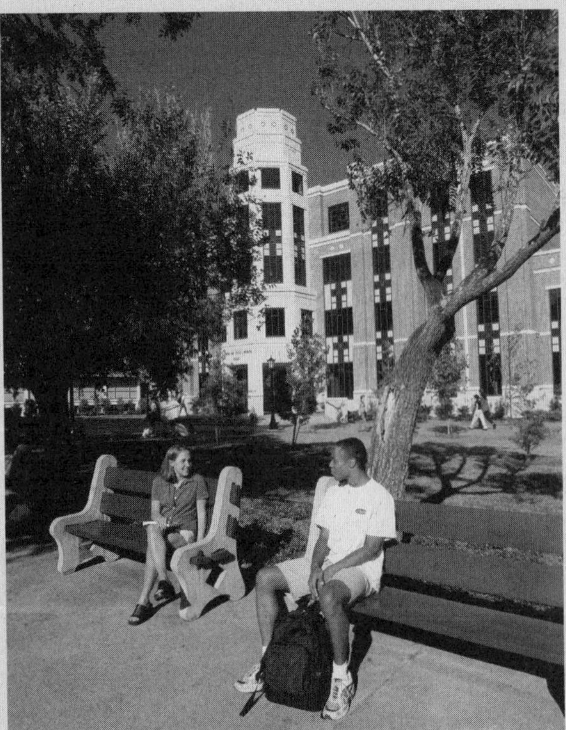

STUDENT BODY

More than 120 on-campus organizations provide a variety of activities for all students. They include academic and professional societies, social and honorary fraternities and sororities, service organizations, special interest groups, sports clubs, and media organizations.

The Loyola Wolfpack intercollegiate athletic program competes in the NAIA Division I as a member of the Gulf Coast Athletic Conference (GCAC). Loyola has intercollegiate men's and women's basketball, cross-country, and track (distance); women's volleyball and soccer; and men's baseball. Students can also participate in a host of intramural recreational sports or club sports, such as crew, rugby, dance team, and lacrosse. Loyola does not provide athletic scholarships.

ACADEMICS

Loyola offers approximately 60 undergraduate programs of study. Some of the most popular majors include communications, business, pre-medicine, psychology, music, political science, and history.

Once enrolled at Loyola, students are introduced to the Common Curriculum, designed to give them a well-rounded preparation in the liberal arts and sciences. Core courses include English, history, philosophy, and religious studies. The curriculum is divided into four categories: major, minor, common curriculum, and elective courses. Students must meet the requirements of their degree program as specified by their particular college.

Loyola has four colleges as well as the School of Law.

The College of Arts and Sciences is the largest of the four colleges and offers the following degrees: Bachelor of Arts, Bachelor of Fine Arts, and Bachelor of Science. The College also offers the Master of Science in counseling, reading, elementary education, and secondary education as well as the Master of Arts in communications and communications/Juris Doctor.

The Joseph A. Butt, S.J., College of Business Administration is fully accredited through the AACSB and offers the Bachelor of Accountancy and the Bachelor of Business Administration. The College also offers the Master of Business Administration and the Master of Business Administration/Juris Doctor.

Loyola's College of Music offers the following undergraduate degrees: Bachelor of Music, Bachelor of Arts in Music, Bachelor of Music Education, and Bachelor of Music Therapy. The College also offers the Master of Music, Music Education, and Music Therapy.

6363 St. Charles Avenue, Box 18
New Orleans, LA 70118
Phone: 504-865-3240
Fax: 504-865-3383
Website: www.loyno.edu

City College is the evening division for working adult students which offers the following degrees: Bachelor of Applied Science, Bachelor of Criminal Justice, Bachelor of Liberal Studies, and Bachelor of Science-Nursing. The College also offers the Master of Religious Education, Pastoral Studies, the Master of Arts in Religious Studies, as well as the Master of Arts in Religious Studies/Juris Doctor, the Master of Science in Nursing, and the Master of Criminal Justice. The School of Law awards the Juris Doctor degree.

Behind every program at Loyola is a faculty of Jesuit and lay professors who are especially well-qualified in their particular fields. The Jesuit Order, recognized throughout the world for its educational contributions over the centuries, administers the University's faculty of 277 full-time professors, 92 percent of whom hold the terminal degree in their field. Loyola also employs 160 part-time instructors. There are no graduate students or teaching assistants teaching courses at Loyola. The student/faculty ratio of 12:1 emphasizes the University's special quality of personal involvement and concern for each student and his or her particular needs.

ADMISSIONS

Loyola bases admissions decisions on several factors including academic record, ACT or SAT I scores, counselor/teacher recommendation, essay, and resume of extracurricular involvement/leadership activities. Admissions is on a rolling basis; however, the priority deadline for academic scholarships is December 1.

CAMPUS LIFE

Loyola University New Orleans is located in New Orleans, Louisiana. Our campuses sit conveniently on the route of the famous St. Charles Avenue streetcar, only a 20-minute ride to downtown New Orleans and the French Quarter, in the heart of one of the most prestigious neighborhoods in the Crescent City.

All venues of New Orleans jazz and Cajun and Creole cuisine from the finest restaurants are close at hand. In addition, New Orleans offers a wide variety of educational and cultural attractions, from the Aquarium of the Americas to the New Orleans Museum of Art to the historic French Quarter. New Orleans is also home to the annual Jazz and Heritage Festival, which takes place in early spring. The Loyola campus is located directly across from the Audubon Zoo and Park, the city's premier recreation center for walking, jogging, golf, and other outdoor sports.

COST AND AID

The 2002–2003 annual costs are as follows:

Tuition: $18,700

Fees: $692

Room and board: $6,916

LOYOLA UNIVERSITY OF CHICAGO

GENERAL INFORMATION

Loyola University of Chicago, founded by priests of the Society of Jesus in 1870, continues the long Jesuit tradition of educational excellence. The University, the most comprehensive Jesuit institute of higher learning in the United States, employs a curriculum that stresses a solid grounding in the liberal arts. Quality teaching and cutting-edge research go hand in hand at Loyola. Students come to Loyola's nine schools and colleges (the College of Arts and Sciences, the Graduate School, the School of Business Administration, the School of Education, the Stritch School of Medicine, the School of Law, the Niehoff School of Nursing, the School of Social Work, and Mundelein College [for adult and lifelong learning]) from all 50 states and from 74 countries. Nearly 1,000 freshmen and 400 transfers enter Loyola University each year. Students select Loyola because it offers personal attention in an excellent academic environment: they also appreciate its stellar reputation for career training. The city of Chicago provides Loyola's students with an additional educational resource. Students here often combine study with part-time employment and internships. The University strives to create an environment that enhances the academic, spiritual, and social growth of its undergraduates. The school sustains more than 125 student organizations (these include 15 national fraternities and sororities) and wide-ranging recreational facilities and sports programs. Loyola competes in Division I of the NCAA, fielding teams in basketball, cross-country, golf, soccer, track, and volleyball for men; and in basketball, cross-country, golf, soccer, softball, track, and volleyball for women. The Lake Shore Campus includes 12 undergraduate residence halls; among them are two learning communities. The University maintains both single-sex and coed residence halls. Loyola expects freshmen and sophomores to live in campus residences. Upperclass students may wish to take advantage of the convenient, reasonably priced housing immediately off campus.

STUDENT BODY

Loyola's student government functions as a liaison between students and administrators. The Student government provides a medium for discussion, suggestion, and action on issues relating to students and student rights. Students may also participate in University governance by participating in policy and advisory committees and by serving as elected representatives of their residence halls.

ACADEMICS

The core curriculum at Loyola is designed to provide a broad foundation in the liberal arts and sciences, which the Jesuits have always considered essential to any education. Core requirements differ from college to college, but they typically include courses in history, expressive arts, literature, mathematical and natural sciences, philosophy, social sciences, and theology. The core introduces students who have not decided on majors to many of the options available at the University. The University requires 128 semester hours for graduation in most majors. Exceptional students may wish to apply to the Honors Program. Undergraduates may receive credit through the AP (Advanced Placement) Program tests. Loyola accepts the International Baccalaureate (IB) and certain College-Level Examination Program (CLEP) tests. Army and Naval ROTC programs are available to Loyola students through nearby universities.

The four undergraduate colleges of Loyola University offer the following degrees: Bachelor of Arts (BA); Bachelor of Science (BS); Bachelor of Business Administration (BBA), Bachelor of Science in Education (BSEd); and the Bachelor of Science in Nursing (BSN).

Students at the College of Arts and Sciences may pursue majors in anthropology, biology, chemistry (biochemistry), classical civilization, communication (communication and social justice, journalism, and organization communication/business), computer science, criminal justice, economics, English (creative writing), environmental studies, fine arts (art history, studio art, and visual communication), French, German, Greek (ancient), history, international studies, Italian, Latin, mathematics, mathematics and computer science (operations research), music, philosophy, physics, physics and engineering (theoretical physics and applied mathematics), political science, psychology (applied social psychology), social work, sociology and anthropology, Spanish, statistical science (actuarial science), theology, and women's studies.

Students at the School of Business Administration may pursue majors in accounting (public), economics, finance, human resource management, information systems management, international business, managerial accounting, marketing, and operations management.

Students at the School of Education may pursue a major in elementary education; the school also offers secondary school certification in 14 majors.

Students at the Niehoff School of Nursing may pursue the Bachelor of Science in Nursing. The school also offers a major in food and nutrition/dietetics and a baccalaureate completion program for registered nurses.

820 North Michigan Avenue
Chicago, IL 60611
Phone: 312-915-6500
Fax: 312-915-7216
Website: www.luc.edu

The University offers five-year dual degree (bachelor's/master's) programs in applied social psychology, biology/MBA, computer science, criminal justice, information systems management, mathematics, political science, and sociology. Students may pursue minors in most fields listed above. Minors are also available in Asian and Asian American studies, black world studies, international studies, Latin American studies, medieval studies, neuroscience, peace studies, psychology of crime and justice, Rome studies, and women's studies. Loyola offers pre-professional programs in dentistry, law, medicine, optometry, osteopathic medicine, pharmacy, podiatry, and veterinary medicine. The University's 3+3 Law Program, offered in tandem with the Loyola University School of Law, permits talented students to commence graduate study in law at the end of their third year of college. Some students are eligible for an articulated admission to the Loyola Stritch School of Medicine through our early assurance program. Some engineering students are eligible to enter a 3+2 Engineering Program offered in tandem with the University of Illinois at Urbana-Champaign, Washington University in St. Louis, and other universities.

More than 95 percent of Loyola's full-time faculty hold a terminal degree in their field of expertise. Most faculty members teach both undergraduates and graduate students. Senior faculty often teach Loyola's core curriculum courses. Students at Loyola enjoy the benefits of a student/faculty ratio that is well below the national average. As a result, faculty members are accessible to students seeking instruction and academic advising.

ADMISSIONS

Loyola University of Chicago evaluates applicants' complete academic record, including standardized test (ACT or SAT I) scores. The majority of undergraduates rank in the top 25 percent of their graduating class; the University will consider students who graduate in the upper half. Applicants should be on track to graduate with at least 15 academic units from an accredited high school; coursework should include study in English, math, social studies, and science. Foreign language study is also highly recommended. Complete applications must include an application form, test scores, a high school transcript, and a letter of recommendation from a counselor. Applicants may meet individually with University admissions counselors both before and after submitting their applications. Transfer students must demonstrate at least 20 semester hours of acceptable credit. Transfer candidates are assessed solely on the basis of their work at college. Transfers must have achieved a minimum grade point average of 2.0 (C) for the College of Arts and Sciences and the School of Education; for transfer to the Schools of Business Administration and Nursing, a minimum GPA of 2.5 (C+) is required. Candidates must leave the college they attended previously in good standing. Loyola notifies applicants of its admission decision three to four weeks after receiving the application, supporting credentials, letter of recommendation from the secondary school counselor, and the $25 application fee. Loyola encourages all prospective students to visit the University's campus. Students may schedule individual appointments and tours of the campus. They are also welcome to participate in a wide variety of campus programs presented throughout the academic year. To request an application, receive further information, or to arrange a visit, please contact:

Undergraduate Admission Office
Loyola University Chicago
820 North Michigan Avenue
Chicago, IL 60611
Phone: 312-915-6500 or 800-262-2373 (toll free)
E-mail: admission@luc.edu
Website: www.luc.edu/

CAMPUS LIFE

Loyola's Lake Shore Campus sits only eight miles north of the center of Chicago. It is located along the Lake Michigan shore in the Rogers Park/Edgewater area, a popular residential area that is home to many Loyola faculty and staff members. Undergraduates enjoy the advantages of the peaceful lakeside setting, yet are within minutes of the busy and vibrant downtown area. The University runs a shuttle bus that makes regular trips downtown; public transportation is also convenient to the campus. The Lake Shore Campus is home to the Martin D'Arcy Gallery of Medieval and Renaissance Art as well as the Fine Art Department's gallery and studios. The University's Water Tower Campus can be found on the near northeast side along Chicago's fashionable "Magnificent Mile." The campus is close to museums, theaters, major corporate headquarters and financial institutions, and a number of Chicago's chicest boutiques and shops. The Water Tower Campus is home to the School of Business, headquartered in a $38 million complex.

Study abroad options include a semester or year at Loyola's Rome Center of Liberal Arts in Rome, Italy. Students may opt for one of the University's study abroad programs in Australia, Chile, France, Israel, Mexico, Spain, Thailand, and the United Kingdom.

COST AND AID

Tuition for full-time undergraduates during the 2001–2002 academic year was $18,814. Room and board (based on double occupancy) averaged $7,400. The average student spends $1,580 per year on books and fees.

LYNDON STATE COLLEGE

GENERAL INFORMATION

Founded in 1911, Lyndon State College is committed to offering liberal arts and professional programs that challenge students to develop their full potential. Students may choose from 19 undergraduate majors supported by state-of-the-art facilities and dedicated faculty and staff. Some of Lyndon's unique and nationally recognized degree programs are: design & graphic communications, interactive digital media, meteorology, recreation resource and ski resort management, and television studies.

Located in the Northeast Kingdom of Vermont, Lyndon State's combination of strong, challenging, and unique academic curricula with the inspiring, pristine view draws our 1,200 undergraduate students from throughout Vermont, New England, the country, and the world.

STUDENT BODY

There are 29 student clubs and organizations at Lyndon State College, which encourage widespread student involvement. In addition to the academic, media, social, and service clubs, there are 10 NAIA Division II men's and women's intercollegiate teams, student publications, radio broadcasting opportunities, and a large variety of intramural sports.

ACADEMICS

Lyndon State College is accredited by the New England Association of Schools and Colleges. Undergraduate programs are offered in accounting, business administration, computer information systems (business, meteorology), design and graphic communications, education (early childhood education, elementary education, reading teacher, secondary education, special education), English (journalism and writing, literature, license to teach secondary education), environmental science, health science (pre-professional study in health science, physical education licensure program, self-designed program), human services, interactive digital media, liberal studies, mathematics (mathematics, license to teach secondary education), meteorology (American Meteorological Society/graduate school, National Weather Service, broadcasting, private industry), natural science (license to teach secondary education), psychology, recreation resource and ski resort management (adventure-based program management, recreation resource management, ski resort management), small-business management and entrepreneurship, social sciences (history, philosophy, political science, social science/interdisciplinary, license to teach secondary education), and television studies (broadcast news, broadcast design and production)

Lyndon State has more than 60 full-time faculty, each with the highest degree in his or her field, and a student/faculty ratio of 17:1. While it's Lyndon's outward appearance that first captures the eye, it's the faculty/student relationship that sets it apart. Lyndon places a special emphasis on faculty members and students developing friendships in and out of the classroom. The students will be first to comment on the devotion of Lyndon State's faculty. Many students say they will never forget the lessons learned and the friendships forged during their years at LSC.

ADMISSIONS

Lyndon State College welcomes applications from all qualified high school students. Students must submit a completed application form with a $30 application fee, an official secondary school transcript, a recommendation from their guidance counselor or teacher, and SAT I or ACT scores. Interviews are recommended, not required.

Admissions staff considers each applicant for admission using three main criteria: ability, character, and motivation. Lyndon State requires 4 years of English and 2 to 3 years each of mathematics (up to Algebra II), science, and social science. Candidates for early acceptance should apply by November 1. The College employs rolling Admissions, so that you may apply at any time. However, it's highly recommended that students submit applications by February 1 to put themselves in the most beneficial position for receiving financial aid. All applications are given prompt attention; candidates may expect a decision two weeks after the date the application process is complete. Lyndon State highly recommends that students visit our campus. Tours and interviews may be arranged by calling 802-626-6413 or 800-225-1998 (toll free, in New England) or via e-mail at Admissions@lyndonstate.edu.

CAMPUS LIFE

Lyndon State's Academic Center—located atop the Samuel Read Hall Library—features state-of-the-art academic and computer classrooms and laboratories, including a fully equipped computer lab that is linked to the College's expanding information network. The computer facilities include a 24-hour general purpose lab, multipurpose PC and Mac labs, and seven labs with industry-specific software for business, graphic design, GIS/GPS, interactive digital media, meteorology, physics, recreation, and writing.

The Samuel Read Hall Library maintains a collection of more than 100,000 circulating volumes as well as periodicals, audio and video materials, and microfiche collections. The library also participates in the Interlibrary loan system, which allows students more extensive access to reference materials. Last year Lyndon's library received the honor of New England's Best Interlibrary Loan Program.

Language and science laboratories and music rooms are available to students for study, experimentation, and practice.

The meteorology department has a fully-equipped meteorology lab. The lab is designed for classroom instruction, research, course assignments, and personal interest. It consists primarily of 21 Pentium workstations for student use and an instructor's workstation at the front of the lab. The instructor's computer is connected to an overhead projection system. More than 60 percent of the classes in the meteorology curriculum are held in the lab. The department has also recently acquired a WeatherProducer system from Weather Services International (WSI).

1001 College Road, PO Box 919
Lyndonville, VT, 05851
Phone: 802-626-6413
Fax: 802-626-6335
Website: www.lsc.vsc.edu

WeatherProducer is a state-of-the-art weather graphics production system used at more than 60 percent of the television stations around the country. LSC Meteorology Broadcast students prepare their own television weather briefings with this equipment. Their briefings are aired live on a local cable access channel to more than 10,000 viewers. This experience gives our Broadcast Meteorology students a competitive advantage in the workplace, as very few Meteorology schools around the country have such a system on campus.

Television studies majors enjoy a state-of-the-art studio that rivals many professional broadcast studios. LSCTV/News 7 is a noncommercial, public-service television facility that provides local news and educational, cultural, and public-service programs. News 7 is a CNN affiliate. Radio station WWLR-FM, is staffed by student volunteers who provide local communities with programs of news, music, and interviews.

Every room in Lyndon's residence halls offers both an Ethernet connection to the College's local area network and a T-1 line for Internet access. With two jacks per room, both roommates can be online simultaneously. Each room is also equipped with cable, a phone, and two voicemail accounts.

All of Lyndon State's degree programs place great emphasis on experiential, hands-on learning. By tying the hands-on experience into responsive programs, students stay abreast of industry trends, market realities, and the latest knowledge in their fields. Lyndon offers a variety of opportunities for off-campus study for credit throughout Vermont, New England, and the country. Students work closely with LSC faculty and the Career Services Office for internship/co-op placement.

COST AND AID

Expenses for the 2002–2003 academic year include tuition (in-state $4,624; out-of-state $10,836; NEBHE $6,956) and room and board (double occupancy) $5,782. Books and supplies, activity fee, development fee, comprehensive fee, orientation fee, health insurance, and travel are estimated at an additional $2,400.

Each year, more than 75 percent of the students at Lyndon State College receive some sort of financial assistance. The Lyndon Financial Aid Office is dedicated to helping students finance their education and provides need-based support packaged in awards that combine grants, scholarships, loans, and work-study. To apply for financial aid, students must complete the FAFSA (Free Application for Federal Student Aid). Filing deadlines are important. For more information, contact the Admissions Office by calling 802-626-6413 or 800-225-1998 (toll free, in New England) or via e-mail at Admissions@lyndonstate.edu.

LYNN UNIVERSITY

GENERAL INFORMATION

Founded in 1962, Lynn University is a private, coeducational institution located in Boca Raton, Florida. The University, small by design, provides an environment within and outside the classroom in which a community of learners can pursue academic excellence. Faculty, staff, and students contribute to an atmosphere that nurtures creativity, fosters achievement, and values diversity. Accredited in 1967 by the Southern Association of Colleges and Schools, Lynn University has steadily grown to become a comprehensive university offering undergraduate and graduate programs in more than 35 disciplines.

Lynn leads the country in offering majors in many of the world's fastest-growing professions, thus preparing its students to meet the career demands of the twenty-first century. The 2,000 students who are currently enrolled come from all parts of the United States and nearly 89 nations.

Lynn is a residential institution with five air-conditioned residence halls that house 65 percent of the undergraduates. The residence halls include study lounges and recreation areas, as well as health and fitness facilities offering free weights, exercise machines, and cardiovascular equipment. The Lynn Student Center, the "living room" of the University, houses the dining room and the auditorium. Students study or relax outside on the patio or on big comfortable sofas in the lounge. Also in the student center are the University Grill-a popular "snacking spot" for students, faculty members, and staff. Laundry facilities, mailboxes, the University bookstore, and a variety of athletic facilities are all located on campus.

University life is designed to provide a learning situation through which students are guided toward responsible decision-making and leadership. An extensive program of activities complements the academic program at Lynn, ensuring the development of the whole person. Students may choose from a variety of campus organizations and activities, including student government, the newspaper or yearbook, co-curricular clubs, leadership groups such as The Knights of the Roundtable, and fraternities or sororities. Lynn University holds membership in the National Collegiate Athletic Association (NCAA) Division II and the Sunshine State Conference. Lynn has won 16 national championship titles in a number of sports. The intercollegiate athletic program includes men's and women's basketball, golf, soccer, tennis, and crew; men's baseball; and women's softball and volleyball. An even wider range of athletic opportunities is available for students through the intramural athletic program.

STUDENT BODY

The Office of Student Activities seeks to complement the academic mission of Lynn University by providing structured opportunities for students to be involved in campus-life outside of the classroom. Specifically, the Office of Student Activities offers recreational, social, cultural, intellectual, and community service programs and activities that address a wide variety of students needs and interests. In addition, the office supports leadership development by offering a formal leadership training program for students; promoting involvement and creating opportunities to participate in and assume leadership roles in student organizations; and encouraging students to take an active role in departmental decision-making through committee membership. Student Activities also strives to work collaboratively with other offices and programs on campus to encourage our students to be as dynamic as possible. The staff maintains an open door policy that encourages students to seek advisement and make an administrative connection with the University. The ultimate goal of Student Activities is to promote the development of well-rounded individuals who have the knowledge, skills, and interest to make a significant contribution to the community in which they are apart.

ACADEMICS

The University is committed to student-centered learning, where faculty and staff members provide personalized attention to students who have varying levels of academic proficiency with a motivation to excel. A full range of academic and support programs is coordinated to serve the increasingly diverse needs of all students. These are enhanced by the favorable 19:1 student/faculty ratio.

The Freshman Seminar is the cornerstone to freshman advising at Lynn and provides an introduction to college life for all new students. The course includes academic success strategies, time management, communication skills, study and test-taking techniques, academic advisement, and career development. Select members of the faculty and staff who serve as mentors to new students throughout their freshman year teach the course.

The Honors Program strives to create a dynamic academic environment that will serve to heighten intellectual curiosity, promote free and active inquiry, and stimulate creative discovery among students with particularly strong academic promise. The innovative curriculum, team-taught by faculty members, encompasses the full breadth of the liberal arts and sciences while promoting both an in-depth exploration and a broad intellectual synthesis of the ideas and concepts that have shaped the dilemmas and choices of the past, present, and future.

The Freshmen Frontiers Program provides a smooth transition to college life for incoming students. Specialized assistance and support enable a student to be successful in the first and most critical semester of their college careers. Students become involved in tutorials that provide the academic foundation of good study habits and meet weekly with mentors who deal with any problems that arise. the dean of freshmen reviews the academic background and preparation of all incoming students in order to individualize learning by selecting a blend of university-level courses designed to address identified needs.

The Academic Center for Achievement is designed for students with specific learning differences who have the motivation and intellectual capacity for college-level work-students whose skill and performance levels indicate that without support, their chances of success at the college level would be at risk. Various accommodations are available, including content area tutorials given in specific subjects by tutors with advanced degrees. Untimed and verbal examinations, taped lectures, and textbooks on tape are also available. All students admitted to the Academic Center for Achievement are required to take a 3-credit course titled Language and Learning.

Lynn University's approach to the development of academic programs has been one that focuses on the balance of a carefully selected core of liberal arts subjects within the framework of a curriculum that is career-oriented and provides both theoretical and practical preparation. Upon this solid liberal arts foundation, students build special competence in their chosen fields of concentration. The practical application of knowledge is a vital component of Lynn's academic program; therefore, residencies, student teaching, community service projects, and internships are required for many degrees. The University follows a semester calendar and offers a summer session. Graduate programs are scheduled on 8-week term cycles.

Major: A major consists of a minimum of 30 credits within a well-defined discipline or group of disciplines. The major allows students to develop a significant degree of expertise in an area of study. The exact courses, credit requirements, prerequisites and electives for each major will vary. An outline of these requirements is included in the departmental program areas in the University catalog. In some majors, the opportunity for a concentration in the discipline is accommodated via a specialization, as explained below.

Dual Major: In addition to satisfying all admission, progression, and graduation requirements of the program offering the first major in a baccalaureate degree program, students may enroll in a second major. In order to do so the student must (1) earn a minimum of 30 credit hours at Lynn University beyond those required for the first baccalaureate degree or a minimum of at least 150 credit hours and (2) satisfy the admission, progression, and graduation requirements of the program or College offering the second major. Students may be enrolled in both major programs simultaneously.

Related Requirements: With the core requirements, these related courses support the major. Related courses are in a discipline or group of disciplines other than the field of study or may be a specialized area within the discipline. The number of related courses varies with each major but should not outweigh the number of courses in the major.

Minor: A minor consists of a minimum of 15 credit hours outside of the major. The minor enables a student to develop a secondary degree of expertise in an area of study in addition to his or her major academic program of study. While a minor program is intended to enable students to develop some degree of expertise in one area of study, it may be interdisciplinary. The completion of a minor is

3601 North Military Trail
Boca Raton, FL 33431-5598
Phone: 561-237-7900
Fax: 561-237-7100
Website: www.lynn.edu

optional. The minor may be chosen to support the major, to offer greater job opportunities to the student on graduation, or to provide recognition of study in a second academic area. To receive a minor, a student must also complete the requirements of a major of a baccalaureate degree concurrently from the University. Course work should be at the upper divisional level (300+) and be specified by the appropriate College or department in which the minor courses will be acquired. The student's transcript shall indicate the minor.

Specialization: Some majors may include an area of specialization. A specialization would consist of a sequence of no less than 15 credit hours of course work within the major. Where appropriate, the transcript shall indicate the major and the specialization (i.e. Major: Business Administration and specialization in Accounting). The following degrees are offered by Lynn University upon completion of degree requirements:

College of Arts and Sciences: Biology, Graphic design, Visual design with minor options in computer graphics or illustration, International relations with specializations in Asian affairs, European affairs, international business, international communications, Latin American affairs. Liberal arts major with specializations in English or history, Psychology. **College of Business and Management:** Business administration major/specializations in: Aviation management, Computer management systems, Fashion management, International business, Marketing, General management. **College of Hospitality, Tourism, and Recreation Management:** Hospitality Administration major/specialization in: International Golf Management, International Hotel and Tourism Management, Sports and Recreation Management, Hotel, Resort, and Food Service Management. **College of Education, Health, and Human Services:** Criminal justice, Elementary education, Human services, Secondary education with major/specialization in social sciences, English/humanities. **College of International Communications:** Communications, Broadcasting, Film Studies, International communications, Journalism. **Conservatory of Music:** Music performance major/specialization in: Piano, Strings, Winds, Brass, Percussion.

Master of Business Administration with specializations in: International business, Marketing, Health care administration, Sports and athletics administration, Communication and media management, Managerial electronic business, Aviation management. **Master of Education with specializations in:** Varying exceptionalities, Educational leadership. **Master of Science in Administration:** Criminal justice, Criminal justice/technical intelligence operations, Emergency planning and administration, Health care administration, Sports and athletic administration. **PhD in Global Leadership:** Educational leadership, Corporate leadership—This specialization is designed for individuals who desire advanced training in research, culminating in a terminal degree, which would enable them to serve as professors, consultants or higher level corporate executives.

Faculty members are thoroughly committed to teaching and are readily accessible to students. The University has a very favorable student/faculty ratio of 19:1. Seventy percent of full-time faculty members hold doctoral degrees. Individualized attention is emphasized, and students are challenged as well as nurtured. A freshman mentoring program ensures a solid transition to University life.

ADMISSIONS

The following are the steps necessary for admission to Lynn University as a freshman:

- Complete an application. You may use the online application or you may request one through the Office of Admission.
- Arrange to have all official transcripts sent to Lynn University. If you are currently a high school student, the transcript should include grades for the first term (marking period) of your senior year.
- Ask your guidance counselor, college advisor or academic dean to complete a letter of recommendation and send it to:

    Office of Admission
    Lynn University
    3601 North Military Trail
    Boca Raton, FL 33431

- Please send us your SAT or ACT scores.
- Complete the personal statement/essay. Describe an experience or achievement that has influenced a belief or value that you hold. Explain your long-range educational and professional goals. If you could interview a significant historical figure, past or present, who would it be and why? Select a topic of your choice that gives us insight into you and your personal interests, or submit a recent writing sample (i.e., short paper, essay, creative piece) that is indicative of your writing ability. Please include a brief statement as to the content and purpose of this paper.

CAMPUS LIFE

The University is located in Boca Raton, one of the most vibrant communities in the state of Florida. Its location provides a wide variety of cultural and recreational opportunities to students. Boca Raton is a progressive community with tremendous economic potential and is quickly becoming one of the nation's leading centers of commerce. Facilities of IBM, Siemens, MNBA Marketing Systems, Sony, Pratt and Whitney, Motorola, Sensormatic, and other similar companies are located just a few miles from the University. The picturesque 123-acre campus is positioned three miles from the Atlantic Ocean and two miles from the heart of Boca Raton, providing excellent opportunities for internships and employment after graduation. The campus is set among freshwater lakes, palms, and lush tropical foliage, providing the peace and quiet necessary to concentrate on academics.

At Lynn University, great importance has been placed on bringing together students of various nationalities and cultures in an effort to foster a greater understanding of diversity. Through a commitment to international education, students are empowered with the knowledge and understanding to effectively and efficiently deal with the challenges that face them in today's world.

Recently, the University broadened it's global perspective through the development of a number of study abroad programs and the new School of International Studies. Study abroad is an integral part of the Lynn University education. The American College Dublin in Ireland, an affiliate of Lynn University, welcomes students for a semester or a full year of study abroad. Both campuses provide quality international education to Lynn University students interested in expanding their horizons. Through faculty-lead academic study tours, students are able to experience many different opportunities to enhance their education with unique cultural and social experiences.

The College of International Communications, established in 1996, has as its dean Mr. Irving R. Levine, the renowned NBC News Chief Economics Correspondent. Under the school's umbrella, the seven undergraduate departments share a common core curriculum and the development of internationalized field experiences. Community service educational experiences, symposia, workshops, lectures by visiting scholars, and international internship opportunities are also offered within this degree.

COST AND AID

All student charges must be paid in full before the student is allowed to register or attend classes. All statements of account are due and payable in full on or before the date shown on the statement. Since the University incurs many expenses of a continuing nature, such as salaries and maintenance, it is essential that the annual income from tuition and fees be assured in order to plan and maintain these services over the entire year. For this reason, it is understood that students are enrolled for the entire academic year or such portion as remains after the date of entrance. Furthermore, the University will not grant a degree, issue transcripts, or release semester grades until all financial obligations have been satisfied.

Tuition, room & board, and fees for the 2003–2004 academic year for full-time undergraduates are as follows:

Tuition: $22,000. **Room & board:** $7,000 (triple occupancy) to $11,000 (private room with private bathroom). **Service & activity fee:** $500. **Technology fee for dormitory students:** $250. **Technology fee for commuter students:** $100.

Deposits are applied against tuition and/or room and board. Deposits are nonrefundable. However, a new student may request a refund prior to May 1 before the beginning of the academic year. The tuition deposit for 2002–2003 is $200 per semester and the residence hall deposit is $300 per semester.

MAINE COLLEGE OF ART

GENERAL INFORMATION

Maine College of Art (MECA) is a professionally accredited, independent four-year college of art and design located in the heart of Portland's lively Arts District. Founded in 1882, MECA offers Bachelor's of Art degrees in eight studio majors and minors in art history, illustration, and drawing and a Master's of Fine Arts degree in studio arts.

MECA is home to 450 student-artists from across the nation as well as other countries. MECA offers students an intimate learning atmosphere with a student faculty ratio of 10:1. MECA's faculty members are accomplished artists who can often be found working alongside their students. At MECA, professors take a keen interest in cultivating students' artistic energy and potential.

The Institute of Contemporary Art, MECA's professional gallery, is Maine's premier showcase for contemporary art by nationally and internationally recognized artists. The ICA@MECA also showcases work by students and faculty in its professional gallery spaces.

The College calendar is packed with activity from Orientation Week in September to Senior Thesis Exhibition in May and includes visiting artist lectures, student and faculty shows, field trips, and various student-run social events. First-year students begin their MECA education with a workshop at Haystack Mountain School of Crafts on scenic Deer Isle—the ideal setting in which to spark new friendships.

STUDENT BODY

The MECA Student Center (the Living Room) offers a comfortable environment for student gatherings, all-school meetings, social activities, and relaxation. Students can contribute to the school newspaper, a student-run periodical that is a forum for opinions, ideas, and creative collaboration. Other student-run groups include the Film Society and Yoga and Tae Kwon Do classes. The MECA Outing Club takes various trips to Maine's ski slopes as well as concerts and festivals.

The Student Representative Association (SRA) is made up of one representative from each department and oversees the distribution of student funds. Students are also encouraged to sit on the College's many committees including the Curriculum Committee, the Dean's Advisory Council, the Multicultural Committee, the Gallery, and the Library Advisory Committee.

ACADEMICS

The structured four-year BFA program seeks to develop students' abilities in perception, organization, and expression and increases their self-understanding, oral and written skills, and sense of personal place in human thought and cultural accomplishment. MECA's academic year consists of two 15-week semesters. The Senior Thesis Exhibition takes place at the end of the student's fourth year and showcases work in their selected area of study.

Maine College of Art is nationally recognized for its intensive two-year foundation program in drawing and two- and three-dimensional design. After this strong foundation students are free to choose a major based on their experiences in a wide range of mediums. Throughout the four years students take additional courses in the liberal arts and art history-elements that are critical to artistic development. The BFA program is designed to equip students with the skills, visual insights, self-confidence, and self-discipline necessary to live and work as a professional artist or designer.

The College belongs to the Greater Portland Alliance of Colleges and Universities, which allows qualified students to take courses at four area colleges at no additional cost. MECA also takes part in an exchange program with Bowdoin College, which is just 20 miles north of Portland. Students are free to take additional courses at Bowdoin with no additional tuition charge. Prior to taking such courses, interested students must fulfill their English composition and art history survey requirements at MECA and must have obtained approval from the appropriate department head. MECA is also the first art college to take part in an exchange program with the Hanoi Fine Arts College in Vietnam. Advanced MECA students are eligible to take part in this very unique exchange program.

The College offers a residential summer early college art program for high school students during the month of July. Early College carries three college credits and consists of an intensive foundation program taught by faculty members and visiting artists. Planned activities such as field trips and visits to area museums add to the enjoyment of this summer program. Students get a firsthand college experience as they live in dorms and take part in the college's activities for the entire month. Scholarships for qualified high school students are available.

Maine College of Art's year-round Continuing Studies Program offers credit courses in a variety of disciplines for adults. All classes are taught by practicing artists, including members of the faculty in the BFA program. Noncredit workshops are also offered in the evenings and on weekends for adults seeking enrichment programs. Classes for students in grades 4–12 are offered on Saturdays during the academic year as well as on weekdays in the summer. Emerging and professional graphic designers expand their design vocabulary with workshops led by internationally acclaimed designers during July and August. MECA also sponsors a week long summer studio fellowship for high school art teachers.

97 Spring Street
Portland, ME 04101
Phone: 207-775-3052
Fax: 207-772-5069
Website: www.meca.edu

Maine College of Art offers the Bachelors of Fine Arts degree in ceramics, graphic design, metalsmithing and jewelry, new media, painting, photography, printmaking, sculpture, and self-designed studies. Students may also minor in art history, illustration, and drawing and pursue K–12 teacher certification. MECA also offers a Master of Fine Arts degree in studio arts.

The MECA faculty is made up of 35 full-time and 34 part-time faculty members of the BFA program. Both educators and artists, MECA faculty members are accomplished in their field and have a great deal of personal dedication to their students serving as student advisors. MECA prides itself in creating a close learning environment between student and professor. The student/faculty ratio is 10:1.

ADMISSIONS

A complete package of application information and materials may be obtained by contacting:

Admissions Office
Maine College of Art
97 Spring Street
Portland, ME 04101
Telephone: 207-775-3052 or 800-639-4808 (toll free)
E-mail: admissions@meca.edu
World Wide Web: www.meca.edu

CAMPUS LIFE

Rated one of the nation's top art destinations and places to live by *American Style* and *Outdoor Magazine*, Portland offers all the benefits of an urban city without the congested traffic, smog, or crime. MECA is located in the city's Arts District and is surrounded by coffee shops, boutiques, museums, and cafes. MECA is only a five-minute walk to Portland's historic Old Port. The Old Port, with its waterfront cobblestone streets, is home to a lively music scene, brew pubs, bookstores, art galleries, unique shops, and a multitude of restaurants. The Old Port would not be complete without its active harbor. Here students find fishing and lobster boats, scenic cruises, and ferries to any one of the islands off the Casco Bay coast in a matter of minutes.

Portland is the perfect location for the outdoor enthusiast. Just outside the city students find accessibility to hiking trails, rock climbing, kayaking, canoeing, Olympic-level skiing/snowboarding, and camping. Portland is also surrounded by numerous pristine beaches and breathtaking ocean vistas.

All MECA college students receive free admission to the Portland Museum of Art and swimming privileges at the YWCA. Within walking distance students can also find a number of gyms, health clubs, bike/roller-blade paths, tennis courts, and playing fields.

Students become involved in the community through Art in Service internships that place students in local schools and health agencies. Students may also participate in credit-earning internships with area businesses and service agencies ranging from film studios to museums.

The Gallery Outreach program allows students the opportunity to show their work in local galleries, businesses, storefront windows, and area restaurants.

COST AND AID

Costs per year for BFA students:

Tuition: $19,400

Dormitory: $4,502–$5,246

Meal plan: $2,810

MANNES COLLEGE OF MUSIC

GENERAL INFORMATION

A small, distinguished conservatory in the heart of New York City, Mannes College of Music features faculty who are members of New York City's most prominent and internationally known ensembles. Students receive rigorous professional training as members of a friendly, supportive community dedicated to the highest artistic achievement.

STUDENT BODY

There are many opportunities for students to become involved at both Mannes and the main campuses of the New School University. At Mannes College of Music, the dean's Student Advisory Council and the Pan-African Cultural Organization welcome student involvement. Also, many New School University committees have seats available to interested students. The New School also has active student organizations dedicated to issues and activities of interest to people of color, women, gays and lesbians, and international students, as well as other extracurricular activities. Students are also encouraged to form new organizations as needed.

ACADEMICS

Mannes is one of seven academic divisions of the New School University. Its musical strengths are therefore linked to a university known for its progressive outlook and deep commitment to the arts. Mannes students may take advantage of a complete range of course offerings at the New School, and Mannes's position within the University provides academic and cultural resources that are unobtainable at most independent colleges of music.

Within the music profession, Mannes is especially noted for its intensive training. All students take rigorous and extensive courses in theory, ear training, harmony, analysis, and counterpoint. Mannes's pioneering curriculum in these areas is heavily influenced by Heinrich Schenker's analytic approach and is now being emulated by many music schools throughout the world.

Mannes College awards a Bachelor of Music (BM) and a Bachelor of Science (BS) degree in the following areas: all orchestral instruments (violin, viola, cello, double bass, flute, oboe, clarinet, bassoon, horn, trumpet, trombone, tuba, harp, and percussion), piano, harpsichord, guitar, voice, composition, conducting, and theory.

Mannes also awards a Master of Music (MM) degree in the following areas: all orchestral instruments (violin, viola, cello, double bass, flute, oboe, clarinet, bassoon, horn, trumpet, trombone, tuba, harp, and percussion), piano, harpsichord, guitar, voice, composition, conducting, theory, and vocal accompanying.

An Undergraduate Diploma (UDPL) is offered in all majors and is equivalent to the Bachelor of Music degree minus the liberal arts courses.

A Professional Studies Diploma (PSD), which is an advanced course of study to enhance performance or compositional skills, is offered in all majors. The Professional Studies Diploma is generally pursued following an earned master's degree or the equivalent. Individual programs are designed in coordination with the assistant/associate dean. Orchestral instruments participate in orchestra during each semester of residency. Additionally, chamber music is a curricular component of some instrumental majors.

Throughout its history, Mannes has attracted the world's foremost teaching artists to its faculty. Faculty members today include Vladimir Feltsman, Richard Goode, Ruth Falcon, Caroline Levine, Hsin-Yun Huang, Timothy Eddy, Regina Resnik, Renata Scotto, Marji Danilow, Jordan Frazier, Cristina Stanescu, Michael Werner, Keith Underwood, Elanie Douvas, Charles Neidich, Leonard Hindell, Patricia Rogers, David Jolley, Per Brevig, David Taylor, and many other principals and associates from the New York Philharmonic, Metropolitan Opera, and New York City Opera and Ballet orchestras. Some of the master classes scheduled for the 2001–2002 school year included Vladimir Feltsman, Cho-Liang Lin, Glenn Dicterow, Fred Sherry, Peter Wiley, Heidi Castleman, and Claude Frank.

ADMISSIONS

All entering students must be high school graduates and are required to pass live entrance auditions in their major fields of study. Placement tests in theory, ear training, dictation, and piano are also required. Application deadlines are December 1 and April 1.

150 West 85th Street
New York, NY 10024
Phone: 212-580-0210
Fax: 212-580-1738
Website: www.mannes.edu

CAMPUS LIFE

Mannes College of Music, a division of New School University, is a degree-granting classical music conservatory with majors in all orchestral instruments, voice and opera, piano, vocal accompanying, guitar, conducting, composition, and theory. Scholarships are available. Distinguished by a world-class faculty and an internationally acclaimed curriculum, Mannes's small classes allow for personalized attention.

Mannes's location is particularly well suited for both students and musicians. Manhattan's Upper West Side is one of the most vibrant areas of the city's major musical and other cultural activities. Within blocks of the College are Lincoln Center for the Performing Arts (home to the New York Philharmonic, the Metropolitan Opera, and other world-renowned orchestras and opera and ballet companies) and the Museum of Natural History as well as recreational centers such as Central Park and Riverside Park. Easily accessible by public transportation of every kind, the College is also near restaurants of many cuisines and price ranges.

Mannes Community Services provides opportunities to gain public exposure through solo recitals, chamber concerts, and small ensemble performances throughout the New York metropolitan area—experience that creates future playing opportunities and develops career skills.

COST AND AID

Mannes Bachelor of Music (BM), Bachelor of Science (BS), Master of Music (MM), and Undergraduate Diploma (UDPL) programs tuition and fees for the 2001–2002 school year:

Tuition: $19,800

General fees: $230

Health insurance and health center fee: $1,300

Total tuition and fees: $21,330

Mannes Professional Study Diploma tuition and fees for the 2001–2002 school year:

Tuition: $12,500

General fees: $230

Health insurance and health center fee: $1,300

Total tuition and fees: $14,030

Estimated living expenses 2001–2002 school year:

Apartment share ($780 per month): $9,360

Board ($300 per month): $3,600

Public transportation ($65 per month): $780

Books and supplies: $1,950

Personal: $2,400

Total estimated living expenses: $17,090

MARLBORO COLLEGE

THE COLLEGE AT A GLANCE

Marlboro College is a liberal arts college unlike any other in the country. Marlboro is known for the rigor of its academic program, its philosophy of self-governance, and students who value learning for its own sake. Marlboro's curriculum combines wide exploration in many courses within the first two years with more focused research and independent study in the second two years. Marlboro College also offers numerous opportunities to study abroad through its partnership with Huron University in London, the World Studies Program, and a variety of faculty-led trips to places like London and Cuba.

STUDENTS

One particularly unique feature of Marlboro College is the collegewide Town Meeting held every three weeks during each semester. On these Wednesday afternoons, the whole College community, including students, faculty, and staff, gathers after lunch to discuss and debate any variety of college issues. Town Meeting's all-inclusive nature distinguishes it from more traditional student body governments.

Marlboro College is not the type of college that has a football team, unless you count a pick-up game of tag football. Instead, one of the most heavily used student activities is the Outdoor Program, OP for short. The OP offers a variety of activities from week-long orientation trips for new students to weekend mini trips, to winter- and spring-break trips in tropical climates. Some of the popular activities have been rock climbing, hiking, rafting, kayaking, camping, yoga, intramural soccer, and Ultimate Frisbee.

Marlboro College has no fraternities or sororities. Students enjoy a wide range of social, artistic, and cultural activities. A sampling of student activities in one semester would include performances by rock, folk, jazz, and ethnic bands; dances; lectures; poetry readings; recitals; plays; and concerts. Annual events that are considered traditions are Convocation, Fall and Spring Rites, Cabaret, Broomball Tournament, Community Dinners, Baccalaureate, and Commencement.

ACADEMICS

The first two years at Marlboro are designed to give students the opportunity to study many different courses. With the approval of their faculty advisors, students choose their own course schedules incorporating course work from all four areas of the curriculum: arts, humanities, sciences, and social sciences. In addition to this broad exploration of liberal arts courses, students must also pass the Clear Writing Requirement within the first two semesters. When a student moves from the sophomore to the junior year, it is referred to as going "on Plan."

The Plan of Concentration is what sets Marlboro's curriculum apart from other colleges and is Marlboro's answer to traditional majors. Plans are often interdisciplinary and self-designed with faculty sponsors. In the junior year, Plan students spend time strengthening their knowledge in the particular areas of study on which they are focusing. In the senior year, students complete a great deal of independent study and research. Throughout the whole process of working on their Plan, students benefit from the close academic sponsorship they receive from faculty members.

Marlboro College awards three undergraduate degrees: Bachelor of Arts, Bachelor of Science, and Bachelor of Arts in International Studies.

Students draw from the following formal areas of study to design their plans:

American studies

Anthropology

Art history

Astronomy

Biochemistry

Biology

Ceramics

Chemistry

Classics

Computer science

Cultural history

Dance

Economics

Environmental studies

Film/Video studies

History

Languages

Literature

Mathematics

Music

Painting

Philosophy

Photography

Physics

Political science

Psychology

Religion

Sociology

Theater

Visual arts

World studies

Writing

While not formal areas of study, students have also studied from the following fields: African studies, ethnic and cultural studies, gender studies, pre-med, pre-law, and pre-vet.

With a student/faculty ratio of 7:1, Marlboro College remains committed to the idea that small classes with lively discussions offer the best way to learn. The faculty choose to work at Marlboro because they value the intellectual interaction with their students; in fact, many claim they have learned more in their fields by working with their students. At Marlboro, there are no teaching assistants or lecture hall classes.

Faculty are also involved in the life of the college community. It is a common sight to see faculty and students eating lunch together, working side by side on college committees, and forming friendships that last long after students graduate.

PO Box A, South Road
Marlboro, VT 05344
Phone: 800-343-0049
Fax: 802-257-4154
Website: www.marlboro.edu

CAMPUS LIFE

Nestled in the foothills of southern Vermont, Marlboro College offers the benefits of living in the country, with more urban areas nearby. The campus itself is situated on the side of Potash Hill in the town of Marlboro, Vermont. Most of the 350-acre campus is deliberately preserved as natural forest with trails and streams running through the property.

With Brattleboro, a town of 12,000, 10 miles away and Northampton, Massachusetts, 45 minutes away, Marlboro students have access to many resources, activities, and cultural life in central New England. Vans run from the College into Brattleboro five times a day and trips to Northeastern cities such as Boston, New York, and Montreal happen several weekends each semester.

The World Studies Program (WSP) is an especially popular aspect of Marlboro's curriculum. Formed in 1984, the World Studies Program integrates the best traditions of liberal arts learning and international studies with a six-to-eight-month working internship in a foreign culture. Students use their experiences abroad in their Plan of Concentration work. Students in the WSP design and carry out their internships in numerous fields, including photojournalism, business, education, relief work, development, anthropology, and scientific research, to name just a few. Graduates of the program have been accepted to many prestigious graduate schools, and more than two-thirds of the program's graduates now work or study in international fields. The World Studies Program operates in conjunction with the School for International Training in Brattleboro, Vermont, about 15 miles away from Marlboro's campus.

In March 1998 Marlboro, with approval from the New England Association of Schools and Colleges, extended its accreditation to Huron University in London, effectively forming an academic partnership. This allows for many studying and teaching opportunities for students and professors at both campuses. Huron's ideal location in the heart of the Kensington neighborhood (near Hyde Park, Victoria and Albert Museum, and Royal Albert Hall) provides students with the chance to study everything from art history to business. Huron offers an American-style liberal arts education with a particular focus on business education and undergraduate international area studies.

A recent $136,000 grant from the Department of Education has allowed Marlboro to expand its international studies and languages programs. New courses in environmental studies and Spanish have been implemented and include a substantial international focus. Another tangible result of the grant is a semester abroad program based in Mexico and Central America, which occurs on a biannual basis.

COSTS

Students should not refrain from applying to Marlboro College because of perceived inability to meet costs. Marlboro College is committed to helping every student who qualifies for financial aid assemble the resources necessary to attend. More than 80 percent of all Marlboro students receive at least some financial help. Applicants should contact the Financial Aid Office directly to request a financial aid packet, which includes step-by-step instructions. The deadline for qualifying for financial aid is March 1. After that date the College cannot promise a full financial aid package. The financial aid office can be reached at 800-343-0049 or finaid@marlboro.edu.

For 2002–2003 academic year:

Tuition: $18,800

Room & board: $6,750

Fees: $860

ADMISSIONS

Students may apply to Marlboro under three different application plans.

Early Decision: Deadline—November 15. Notification—December 15.

Early Action: Deadline—January 15. Notification—February 1.

Regular Admission: Priority Deadline—March 1. Notification—Rolling.

Please note that if you are applying for financial aid it is important to apply by March 1.

Application Checklist:

Application and $50 nonrefundable application fee
High school and college transcript(s)
SAT or ACT scores
An autobiographical statement
A graded academic writing sample
Interview
Two letters of recommendation (teacher and general)

MCGILL UNIVERSITY

GENERAL INFORMATION

James McGill is the namesake for McGill University, which was founded over 180 years ago. James McGill was a fur trader from Scotland who eventually became a well-known merchant and philanthropist in Montreal. King George IV gave McGill College its royal charter in 1821. In 1829, the teaching wing of Montreal General Hospital became part of the College, and classes started. In 1843, the Faculty of Arts had its beginning. Modern languages, commercial studies, and sciences were all added over the next 10 years. Until 1884 there had been no female students; once they were admitted, classes that had been divided by gender eventually merged. Ste. Anne de Bellevue is a small village around 25 miles west of Montreal, and this is where, in 1906, a college earned the endowment of Sir William Macdonald. The Faculty of Agricultural and Environmental Sciences is now housed in these Macdonald Campus buildings, and this faculty includes the school of dietetics and human nutrition and the school of environment. These students have an abundance of opportunities for fieldwork and hands-on research: The Macdonald Farm, the Morgan arboretum, the St. Lawrence Valley Ecomuseum, and the Avian Science and Conservation Centre provide livestock, facilities, and other materials for teaching and learning in an actual agricultural environment.

McGill is a publicly funded university, and its comprehensive offerings attract a very diverse student body. There are 22,822 full-time students at McGill, and they come from a wide variety of places: 54 percent are from Quebec, 27 percent are from other Canadian provinces, and 19 percent come from the United States and approximately 150 other countries. Classes are taught in English, but as French is the first language of one out of every five students, students have the option of writing term papers and tests in French. There are 11 faculties, 10 schools, and 4 institutes at McGill. These are: the Faculties of Agricultural and Environmental Sciences, Arts, Dentistry, Education, Engineering, Law, Management, Medicine, Music, Religious Studies, and Science; the Schools of Architecture, Communication Sciences and Disorders (graduate), Computer Science, Dietetics and Human Nutrition, Environment, Library and Information Studies (graduate), Nursing, Physical and Occupational Therapy, Social Work, and Urban Planning (graduate); and the Institutes of Air and Space Law, Comparative Law, Islamic Studies, and Parasitology. Bachelor's and master's degrees are available, and McGill offers doctorates in major subject areas as well. Students can also choose from the professional degrees of law, dentistry, and medicine. Nontraditional students can explore the Centre for Continuing Education, through which courses, diploma programs, and certificate programs are available.

Housing options for students include apartments, shared facilities/houses, and co-ed and women's dormitory-style residences. There are about 1,750 places available for students who are eligible. Most McGill students who live in residence for their first academic year move into apartments of their own for their following years of study. McGill offers a wide variety of extracurricular activities, and believes that these activities are key in offering students leadership opportunities, relaxation, entertainment, and independence. There are over 170 clubs run by McGill students, covering a wide spectrum of interests. One of the most popular clubs—and the largest—is the McGill Outdoors Club, which offers members opportunities for skiing, canoeing, climbing, and hiking trips. McGill athletes, both women and men, can participate in both indoor and outdoor sports. The intercollegiate teams compete against teams from other universities, while the intramural teams at McGill compete against each other. There are also instructional programs available for students who want to improve their performance and abilities in many different activities.

STUDENT BODY

McGill values student participation in University governance and administration, and students can exert their influence by getting involved in the Senate and the Board of Governors. Undergraduate societies, which are offered by various academic departments, are another way for students to assume leadership roles. The Undergraduate Students' Society, for example, is responsible for running its own building, including facilities and food services.

ACADEMICS

The McGill school year consists of two semesters. The fall semester runs from September to December, while the winter semester lasts from January until May. In May, June, July, and August, students can register in summer sessions. If prospective students have completed an acceptable educational level outside of Quebec, they can be considered for entrance into a McGill program of at least eight semesters (four years), or 120 credits, of study. Some programs at McGill require additional semesters or credits. Students who have completed a Quebec Diploma of Collegial Studies, Advanced Level Examinations, or the French or International Baccalaureate are eligible for admission to a three-year, 90-credit program.

McGill offers a Bachelor of Arts degree in African studies, anthropology, art history, Canadian studies, classics, computing (foundations of), East Asian studies, economics, English (literature, drama and theatre, and cultural studies), environment (faculty program only, many domains available), French language and literature (linguistics, literature, literature and translation), geography (geography/urban systems), German (contemporary studies, language and literature, literature and culture), Hispanic literature and culture/languages, Hispanic studies (honors only [honors]), history, humanistic studies, industrial relations (faculty program only, many domains available), international development studies, Italian studies (Italian studies—literature [honors]), Jewish studies, Latin American studies (and Caribbean Studies [honors]—area and thematic), linguistics, mathematics, Middle East studies, music, North American studies, philosophy, political science, psychology, Quebec studies, religious studies (scriptures and interpretations/world religions/Western religions [honors]/Asian religions [honors]), Russian, sociology, and women's studies.

McGill offers a Bachelor of Science degree in anatomy and cell biology; atmospheric science; atmospheric science and physics; biochemistry; biology; biology and mathematics (faculty program only); chemistry (bioorganic, environmental, and materials options); chemistry and biological sciences (faculty program only); chemistry and mathematics (faculty program only); computer science; earth sciences [honors]; earth and planetary sciences; environment (many domains available); geography; immunology [honors]; mathematics; mathematics/applied [honors]; mathematics and computer science (faculty program only); mathematics, statistics, and computer science (faculty program only); mathematics, chemistry, and physics (faculty program only); microbiology and immunology; physics; physics and computer science, physics and geophysics; physiology; physiology and mathematics; physiology and physics; planetary sciences [honors]; probability and statistics [honors]; psychology; science for teachers; and software engineering.

McGill also offers a BSc/Bed program.

The University offers a Bachelor of Science (agriculture) degree in agricultural economics (agribusiness, agricultural systems, and natural resource economics options), agricultural science (many domains available), animal biology, animal science, applied zoology, botanical sciences (ecology and molecular options), environmental biology, microbiology, plant science, resource conservation, and wildlife biology.

Students can also pursue Bachelor of Science degrees in agricultural engineering, architecture, food science, nursing, nutritional science (dietetics and nutrition options), occupational therapy, and physical therapy.

McGill offers a Bachelor of Commerce degree in accounting, economics, economics and accounting [honors], economics and finance [honors], entrepreneurship, finance, information systems, international business, international management (faculty program only in East Asia; Latin America and the Caribbean; Western Europe-France, Germany, Italy, or Spain; Canada; the United States), labor-management relations, management science, marketing, mathematics, operations management, organizational behavior and human resource management, psychology, and strategic management.

McGill offers a Bachelor of Education degree in kindergarten and elementary education (also Jewish studies option), general secondary two-subject option, vocational secondary education (one subject), inclusive education, kinesiology, physical education, and teaching of English as a second language (ESL) or French as a second language (FSL). Students can also pursue combined BEd/BMus and BEd/BSc degrees.

McGill offers a Bachelor of Engineering degree in chemical engineering, civil engineering, computer engineering, electrical engineering, mechanical engineering, metals and materials engineering, and mining engineering (co-op). There is also a Bachelor of Software Engineering.

845 Sherbrooke Street West
Montreal, QC H3A 2T5
Phone: 514-398-3910
Fax: 514-398-8939
Website: www.mcgill.ca

McGill offers a joint Bachelor of Laws/Bachelor of Civil Law degree in common and civil law.

The University offers a Bachelor of Music degree in composition, music education, music history, music technology [honors], performance, performance—church music/early music/keyboard studies/or jazz, and theory. Music students also have the option of a simultaneous BMus/BEd.

McGill students can pursue a Bachelor of Social Work (BSW) degree, and a year-long BSW degree program is available for those who already hold a degree (the application deadline for this program is December 1, for May entrance).

McGill offers a Bachelor of Theology degree in religious studies.

The University also offers the professional degrees of Doctor of Dental Medicine and Doctor of Medicine/Master of Surgery.

The Centre for Continuing Education offers courses and/or diploma and certificate programs in graduate and undergraduate career and management studies, education, general studies, information technology, and languages and translation.

Teaching and learning at McGill have always been augmented by research. Hands-on learning through laboratory and library work brings theoretical classroom discussions into broader, real-life contexts. Most of the full-time professors at McGill have a PhD, and full-time, regular staff members teach nearly every class.

ADMISSIONS

Prospective students are evaluated on the strength of their entire academic dossier. Academic performance over the past three years, the level of programs taken, class rank, and standardized test scores (if applicable) are all given the proper consideration. Applicants should have at least a B+ average or the equivalent, depending on where they have completed their studies. McGill University is very selective. For transfer applicants, the university/college record is reviewed in addition to the above criteria.

First-year applicants who wish to enroll in September must meet the following deadlines: January 15 for international and U.S. institution first-year and transfer applicants and non-Canadian/non-permanent resident transfer applicants from Canadian institutions; February 1 for first-year applicants from Canadian provinces other than Quebec; May 1 for exchange and Canadian/permanent resident transfer applicants from Canadian institutions and non-Canadian/non-permanent resident special and visiting applicants; and July 1 for Canadian/permanent resident special and visiting applicants. Confirmation of deadlines is available at www.mcgill.ca/applying. A few January admission slots are open to non-Quebec applicants. Refer to McGill's website for program availability and deadlines.

McGill welcomes all applications, and does not discriminate on the basis of race, religion, age, handicap, nationality, or sex. More information on admissions and the University calendar is available on the website. Also available is an online application which can be retrieved, filled out, and submitted at www.mcgill.ca/applying. Interested students are welcome to schedule a visit to McGill's main campus in downtown Montreal, or to the Macdonald Campus, in Ste-Anne-de-Bellevue (30 minutes away). Hour-long tours, given by McGill students, are available in the morning or afternoon. Prospective students are also welcome to attend a variety of classes in most faculties in October, November, February, and March. Course calendars, faculty and departmental brochures, and information about Montreal are available in the Welcome Centre. Students interested in visiting and/or touring McGill should contact:

The Welcome Centre
Burnside Hall, Room 115
805 Sherbrooke Street
West Montreal, Quebec H5A 2K6
Canada
Telephone: 514-398-6555
Fax: 514-398-2072
E-mail: welcome@mcgill.ca
World Wide Web: www.mcgill.ca

Prospective students can access (and submit) the application form at www.mcgill.ca/applying. Paper copies of the application form and additional information can be obtained by contacting:

Admissions, Recruitment, and Registrar's Office
McGill University
845 Sherbrooke Street
West Montreal, Quebec H5A 2T5
Canada
Telephone: 514-398-3910
Fax: 514-398-8939
E-mail: admissions@mcgill.ca
World Wide Web: www.mcgill.ca/applying

CAMPUS LIFE

Montreal has the best of both worlds: while it is undeniably North American, it is also very European. The world of Montreal is literally just beyond the University gates. From these gates, students spill out onto a major downtown avenue, with restaurants, cafés, office buildings, shops, and underground shopping malls at their feet. A mountain park on the north end of campus, just past the student housing and athletic buildings, brings nature home to students. Winter, spring, summer, and fall each hold different charms for those living in Montreal, and each season offers unique possibilities for indoor and outdoor activities.

There is a wide selection of exchange programs with over 500 universities around the world, and students also have the option of making arrangements on their own for spending a semester or a year outside of Montreal.

COST AND AID

In 2002–2003 tuition fees for full-time students (those enrolled for 30 credits) were $1,668 for Quebec residents; $4,012 for other Canadian citizens and permanent residents; and $9,500 to $15,000, for visa students, depending on the program (fees are quoted in Canadian funds). Other fees (University Students Services, Student Society, course materials, etc.) come to approximately $1,050 to $1,450 (again, depending on program). The approximate cost of books and instruments is $1,000. Visa students are also obligated to purchase health insurance. Room and board come to about $7,500. Costs for transportation, clothing, and other personal expenses are individual to each student. All figures are in Canadian dollars, and keep in mind that fees may increase in 2003–2004.

MERCER UNIVERSITY—MACON

GENERAL INFORMATION

A Baptist coeducational private university, Mercer University (founded in 1833) offers more than 20 undergraduate, graduate and professional degree programs in more than 60 areas of study. The University consists of 10 colleges and schools: the College of Liberal Arts, the Eugene W. Stetson School of Business and Economics, the Georgia Baptist College of Nursing, the James & Carolyn McAfee School of Theology, the School of Engineering, the School of Medicine, the Southern School of Pharmacy, the Tift College of Education, the College of Continuing and Professional Studies, and the Walter F. George School of Law. Mercer University, with campuses in both Macon and Atlanta, Georgia, and regional centers around the state, receives its accreditation from the Commission on Colleges of the Southern Association of Colleges and Schools. *U.S. News & World Report* has ranked Mercer among the leading universities in the South, both for value and quality of education, for 13 consecutive years. Mercer's exceptional reputation springs from its sound academic programs, excellent faculty, and modern facilities. Tradition, however, is also a central component of this institution's unique identity. Mercer's commitment to Judeo-Christian values and its dedication to intellectual and religious freedom truly distinguish the University. Mercer enrolls more than 7,000 students in its 10 schools. With only 2,500 undergraduates studying at the main campus, undergraduates enjoy small classes (average class size is 25) made possible by the 15: 1 student/faculty ratio (an unusually low ratio for a university of its size). While a majority of Mercer students come from the Southeast, the student body is representative of at least 35 states and 75 countries. All students gain from Mercer's friendly atmosphere, excellent teaching (by faculty members only, never by teaching assistants), and small classes. Mercer instructors hold degrees from some of the most prestigious institutions in the world; they excel in both their research and teaching abilities. Nearly all hold PhDs or the equivalent terminal degree in their fields. Undergraduates may choose from a range of housing options, including conventional dormitories, apartment-style residences, and Greek houses.

Mercer is an active campus, home to more than 80 clubs and organizations; among their number are academic clubs, honor societies, performing arts organizations, special interest groups, and religious groups. Ten fraternities and six sororities play a central role in the community, providing social outlets and performing a wide assortment of community services. ROTC is another option available to Mercer undergraduates. Mercer's athletic teams compete in Division I of the NCAA and the Atlantic Sun Conference. The University fields teams in men's baseball, basketball, cross-country, golf, tennis, soccer, and rifle, and in women's basketball, cross-county, golf, soccer, softball, tennis, and volleyball. The school also offers a variety of intramural athletic competition.

STUDENT BODY

The Student Government Association sponsors and manages numerous student activities at the University. Each year, elections are held in the spring to select the SGA president, vice president, secretary-treasurer, and freshman advisor, as well as representatives of each of the four classes plus one at-large representative. Students also elect the editors of major student publications and members of the Student Union Activities Board. Most important school committees include student representatives from the liberal arts, business, engineering, and education divisions. Student life is enhanced by a diverse array of fraternities and sororities, organizations, clubs, professional societies, honorary societies, special interest groups, and religious groups.

ACADEMICS

Undergraduates at Mercer may choose between two academic tracks. The first, the General Education Program, requires study in a number of areas and leads to a broad-based education. General Education students investigate the major fields of human accomplishment and learning. This track, which is completed by the end of sophomore year, establishes a base from which students can continue a lifetime of study in many fields. General Education students spend their junior and senior years specializing in a major field and completing upper-division courses. The second track, the Great Books Program, immerses students in the classic works of western civilization. Students probe the writings of Plato, Socrates, Milton, and Freud in order to learn more about our society and its intellectual lineage. The Great Books Program is an eight-course sequence that is not completed until the first semester of the student's final year. Exceptional students are eligible to participate in Mercer's Honors Program, which helps academically superior students reach their maximum learning potential by undertaking more challenging assignments and coursework. Qualified students in the College of Liberal Arts, School of Business and Economics, College of Education, and School of Engineering are eligible to enter the Honors Program. All students at Mercer University must complete a major. However, the University also encourages undergraduates to investigate fields outside their majors. Options for independent reading, independent research, and coursework in special topics exist in many departments. The University also allows undergraduates to design independent majors, with the consultation of an academic advisor and the approval of the college dean and a faculty committee. Most students in the College of Liberal Arts, the Stetson School of Business and Economics, and the Tift College of Education undertake 15 hours of coursework (five courses) per semester. Students in the School of Engineering generally undertake 15 to 18 hours of coursework (five to six courses) per semester. Students who wish to take an extra course must have a GPA of 3.0 or better and receive permission from their academic advisor. Up to 30 hours of course credit can be earned through the College-Level Examination Program (CLEP) or International Baccalaureate (IB). Students who take Advanced Placement exams (College Board) and receive scores of 3 or better usually receive credit for the equivalent coursework.

The College of Liberal Arts offers the following undergraduate degrees: Bachelor of Arts; Bachelor of Science; Bachelor of Music Education; Bachelor of Music in Performance; and Bachelor of Music in Sacred Music. Available majors and concentrations include: African American studies, art, biology, biochemistry, chemistry, Christianity, communication and theater arts, computer science, drama and theater, economics, English, environmental science, French, German, history, information science and technology, international affairs, journalism, Latin, leadership and community service, mathematics, media studies, music, music education, philosophy, physics, political science, psychology, sociology, and Spanish. The Eugene W. Stetson School of Business and Economics offers the Bachelor of Business Administration degree; its students must complete a pioneering curriculum called MAPS (Managed Academic Path to Success). MAPS allows undergraduates, along with their advisor, to design the business program that best suits their professional and academic interests. Examples include: accounting information systems, arts administration, international finance, marketing and advertising, music business, and political management. The School of Engineering offers programs leading to the Bachelor of Science in Engineering degree. Students may specialize in biomedical, computer, electrical, industrial, mechanical, and environmental engineering. The School also offers the Bachelor of Science degree, with majors available in industrial management and technical communication. The Tift College of Education offers the Bachelor of Science in Education degree in both early childhood and middle grades education. The school offers secondary/grade certification in art, English, foreign languages, history, mathematics, music, broad field science, and broad field social science. The certification programs are offered in conjunction with the College of Liberal Arts.

Admissions Office, 1400 Coleman Avenue
Macon, GA 31207-0001
Phone: 478-301-2650
Fax: 478-301-2828
Website: www.mercer.edu

Mercer's low student/faculty ratio promotes a nurturing academic atmosphere where professors know their students' personal ambitions and professional goals. The Mercer faculty is a community of 500 distinguished scholars, professionals, and researchers, most of whom have achieved the terminal degree in their field of expertise. Mercer's experienced professors teach all of the undergraduate courses at all levels, not teaching assistants.

ADMISSION

The Mercer Office of Admissions seeks candidates whose academic records and personal qualities suggest that they will benefit from and succeed in a Mercer education. Students seeking admission to the freshman class should be on track to complete (or have already completed) a college preparatory high school curriculum including at least 4 units each of English and mathematics, 3 units each of laboratory science and social science, and 2 units of foreign language. For this work, they should have received a minimum B average (3.0 GPA). Applicants should submit standardized test scores reflecting a minimum combined SAT I score of 1000 or its equivalent ACT composite score. Furthermore, students seeking admission to computer science, engineering, mathematics, pre-health sciences (medicine, pharmacy, nursing, dentistry, etc.) or natural sciences programs must score at least a 550 on the SAT I math test (or its equivalent on the ACT). Applicants must be in good academic and disciplinary standing at the school currently, or most recently, attended. Students seeking admission to Mercer should submit an application and nonrefundable $50 application fee, an official high school transcript that clearly identifies academic coursework (admitted students must submit a completed transcript at the end of their senior year to finalize their admission to Mercer), and an official standardized test score report (SAT I or ACT; scores on official high school transcripts are accepted). Students seeking admission in the fall should submit applications before June 30. Students who demonstrate financial need may receive a waiver on the application fee. Relatives of Mercer alumni also receive a waiver on the application fee. Enrollment at the University is limited, so applicants should submit all necessary materials as early as possible. Contact the Office of University Admissions with all inquiries. More information is available by contacting:

Office of University Admissions
Mercer University
1400 Coleman Avenue
Macon, GA 31207
Phone: 478-301-2650 or 800-840-8577 (toll free)
E-mail: admissions@mercer.edu
Website: www.mercer.edu

CAMPUS LIFE

The 130-acre Macon campus is a blend of tradition and innovation. Students walk among 100-year-old trees, yet state-of-the-art learning technology is at their fingertips. Opening in Fall 2003 will be the 230,000-square-foot University Center. From enjoying a lingering cup of mocha at the coffee shop to jogging laps around the indoor track to attending a concert or Division I basketball game in the arena, students will make memories in this facility that will enhance their college experience. Macon is home to professional football and hockey teams, the annual Cherry Blossom Festival and great restaurants and shopping. Centrally located in the heart of the state, the campus allows easy access to the Georgia coast, Florida beaches, and the Blue Ridge Mountains. Grand antebellum homes along the tree-lined streets contrast with the new convention center and one of the largest shopping malls in Georgia. Downtown Macon, site of the renovated Douglass Theatre, the Grand Opera House, the Georgia Music Hall of Fame, and the Georgia Sports Hall of Fame, is a vibrant shopping and visitors district located not far from the campus.

COST AND AID

Tuition for the 2002–2003 school year is $19,200; room and board is an additional $5,840. On average, students spend $600 on books and supplies each year.

MERCY COLLEGE

GENERAL INFORMATION

Mercy College is a premier college in New York for undergraduate and graduate programs in business, education, behavioral sciences, and health sciences areas. As a result of attracting a skilled, professional faculty and combining it with innovative and progressive programs, the College has been widely recognized for the accomplishments of its students. The College's history goes back to 1950, when the Sisters of Mercy founded a college that was based on traditional educational foundations. Since 1960 the school has become a private, coed, nonsectarian institution dedicated to educational excellence and community service. Mercy College boasts a uniquely dynamic curriculum that caters to a multicultural student body of more than 10,000.

On campus, nonacademic activities reflect the interests of this student body that reflects a cross section of ages, ethnic origins, social backgrounds, and goals. Extracurricular activities include a diverse choice of student publications, social and political organizations, athletics, performing arts, and lecture series. The administration works closely with its student body, creating programs that consider all students in all situations: it offers degrees in nontraditional subjects; academic, personal, and career counseling; and distance-learning, online degree programs. The new computer center on the main campus is aimed at advancing students' computer skills.

Mercy College has nine locations throughout Westchester County and New York City. The main campus is located in Dobbs Ferry on 60 acres along the Hudson River. Other campuses are located in White Plain, Yorktown, Bronx, and midtown Manhattan. Mercy is accredited by the Middle States Association of Colleges and Secondary Schools and the Board of Regents of the University of the State of New York. Programs in paralegal studies, nursing, accounting, acupuncture and oriental medicine, film studies, computer arts and technology, social work, veterinary technology, and physical and occupational therapy have additional academic accreditations. Overall, Mercy offers students more than 90 different undergraduate and graduate degree programs.

STUDENT BODY

In addition to having facilities available for recreational purposes, the College sponsors NCAA Division II teams for men and women in baseball, basketball, golf (men's team), soccer, softball (women's team), tennis, and volleyball (women's team). In past years, Mercy teams have won conference and regional championships in soccer, golf, women's softball, and women's volleyball.

The Mercy College athletic teams are a member of the following: Eastern Collegiate Athletic Association (ECAC) Division II, Metropolitan Collegiate Tennis Conference, NCAA Division II, Intercollegiate Soccer Association of America (ISAA), New York Collegiate Athletic Conference (NYCAC), and Collegiate Track Conference.

The Student Association (SA) represents the voice of the student body, acting as a liaison between the students and the faculty. In conjunction with the College Council for Student Affairs, the SA sets policy, administers the activities funds, authorizes organizations and clubs, and approves their budgets.

ACADEMICS

Mercy's academic calendar consists of fall and spring 16-week semesters, comprised of two 8-week terms each, and a summer semester consisting of one 12-week term and two 6-week terms. A 10-week weekend program is also available at the White Plains and Dobbs Ferry campuses.

To graduate with a bachelor's degree students must complete 120 academic credits and must fulfill all requirements in one major. Students may earn a double major or minor. To earn an associate's degree, a student must complete 60 academic credits and satisfy the required curricular distribution.

Mercy College offers a program for students with learning disabilities, a program in English as a second language, and courses taught in Spanish and Korean through the Bilingual Education Program.

Students who earn satisfactory scores on the CLEP, New York State Regents College Examinations, or Advanced Placement exams are eligible for advanced placement. Up to 30 credits for life achievement may also be awarded to qualified students. Entering students selected on the basis of past achievement and motivation may be invited to participate in the Mercy College Honors Program, which offers stimulating activities.

Mercy College offers programs leading to the Master of Arts, MBA, Master of Professional Studies, Master of Science, Bachelor of Arts, Bachelor of Science, Associate in Arts, and Associate in Science degrees and certificate programs. The major degree program offerings include accounting, behavioral science (specialization in community health, gerontology, and health services management), biology, business administration, banking, direct marketing, finance, general business administration, international business, management, marketing, computer arts and technology, communication disorders, computer information systems, computer science, corporate communication, criminal justice, English literature, environmental health and safety, film studies, history, human resource management, Internet business management, interdisciplinary studies, journalism and media, mathematics, medical technology, music, music industry and technology, nursing (post-RN) Occupational therapy, organizational leadership, organizational management, paralegal studies, physical therapy, physician assistant, pre-chiropractic, psychology (specialization in computer research applications), public accounting, social work, sociology (specialization in computer applications), School supervision and administration, therapeutic recreation, and veterinary technology (specialization in pre-veterinary medicine). Interdisciplinary programs are available in American studies and business leadership. Pre-professional programs are offered in chiropractic, law, medical technology, medicine, optometry, nursing, and pharmacy.

Teacher certification and the Master of Science degree are offered in childhood education, early childhood, middle childhood, adolescence, students with disabilities, bilingual, teaching English to speakers of other languages, learning technology and school administration and supervision.

555 Broadway
Dobbs Ferry, NY 10522
Phone: 914-674-7324
Fax: 914-674-7382
Website: www.mercy.edu

Career-oriented certificate programs include accounting, animal-assisted therapy, child care, criminal justice, direct marketing, fire science, general business administration, gerontology, human behavior, information technology, journalism and media, liberal studies, management, marketing, office computer systems, occupational safety and health administration, personal computer applications, and personnel management, private security and public safety and substance abuse counseling.

Mercy's innovative majors with unique class scheduling also include physician assistant, BS/MPS program in acupuncture and Oriental medicine, and BS/MS program in occupational therapy, and physical therapy. Bilingual programs in Spanish and Korean are also available.

Mercy College employs 860 full- and part-time faculty, more than 60 percent of whom hold doctorates. Professors both teach students and advise them on academic and career decisions. Their main goal is to prepare men and women to be constructive, employable, and productive people. The 17:1 student/faculty ratio allows for an atmosphere that encourages personal relationships and individual attention, which helps students realize and reach their goals. Faculty help students by being accessible and by providing mentoring relationships.

ADMISSIONS

Mercy College provides access to higher education for all applicants who demonstrate motivation, desire, and the potential to benefit from programs of study in the liberal arts, health sciences, and professional studies. The College welcomes applications from high school seniors and transfer students as well as adult students returning to study. The SAT is recommended but not required. All applicants are encouraged to visit the College campus and meet with an admissions counselor or to participate in a phone interview. Early admission or advanced study at Mercy are available to qualified high school students who wish to start college courses before they complete high school. All applicants accepted to Mercy College must earn a satisfactory score on Mercy's placement examination. The College uses a rolling admissions process for admitting new students.

Prospective freshmen must submit the following to be considered for enrollment: an application, an application fee of $35, and an official high school transcript. Transfer students must submit the following; an application, the $35 application fee, an official transcript from all colleges or universities they previously attended, and if they have completed fewer than 15 college credits they must also submit an official high school transcript. Some students may be required to take placement examinations to determine their initial level of courses.

CAMPUS LIFE

Mercy College offers both a lush suburban and an urban landscape as backdrops to its five campuses. When you want to escape and enjoy life beyond the halls of learning you can take in the sheer beauty of Dobbs Ferry, New York, the home of Mercy's main campus. The Hudson River is a spectacular natural treasure that borders on the beautifully landscaped College campus. The area around the Hudson is rich in outdoor recreation, including places to sail, hike, bike, canoe, camp, and ski. Dobbs Ferry plus its campuses in White Plains and Yorktown are part of Westchester County, which is known for its beautiful recreational areas and historical sites.

New York City and all of its culture and social opportunities are a 40-minute train ride away. The campus is easily accessible from New York; Westchester, Rockland, Putnam, and Orange counties; northern New Jersey; and southern Connecticut.

The Bronx and Manhattan campuses are located in urban settings and are close to the fast-paced life of New York City. The Bronx campus is near several major highways and public transportation. The new Manhattan campus in across the street from Macy's main department store in Herald Square, offering more than 55,000 square feet of educational and student interaction space.

Whether you are seeking the tranquility of the lush suburbs with its river, landscapes, and walking trails or the visual excitement of The Big Apple, Mercy College offers it all in its five campus locations.

Mercy College offers students the opportunity to learn through joint ventures with private businesses, industries, and research facilities including The Westchester Consortium of Colleges, The Westchester Conservatory of Music, The Institute of Continuing Biomedical Education, The NY Medical College Graduate School, and The Karol Marchinkowski University of Medical Science in Poznan, Poland.

Juniors and seniors are eligible to participate in the College's cooperative education program. This program allows students to be paid while they work in a professional environment, gaining experience that parallels classroom work in their major.

Students may complete degrees through Mercy College's distance learning program, called Merlin, which allows students take courses and earn degrees online. Mercy awards degrees through the distance learning program in the following areas: psychology, computer science, business, direct marketing, banking, Internet business systems, and liberal arts.

COST AND AID

For the 2003–2004 academic year, undergraduate tuition is $10,700 for a full-time student (12–18 credits per semester) or $450 per credit for part-time students. There is also a technology fee of $144 per year for full-time and $6 per credit for part-time students. Graduate tuition is $510 for all programs, except banking which has a tuition of $575 per credit and acupuncture and oriental medicine, which cost $430 per credit. Graduate education, learning technology and school administration programs cost $495 per credit.

MESSIAH COLLEGE

GENERAL INFORMATION

Messiah College is an independent, liberal arts and sciences college committed to providing a rigorous education in the context of the Christian tradition. The College aims to develop each student's intellect, character, and faith, preparing them for successful lives in the church and in society. There are 2,800 students at Messiah College, hailing from 38 states and 22 foreign countries. Collectively, students represent 60 religious denominations, and 6 percent of students are ethnic minorities. Messiah has a distinctive residential atmosphere and a strong sense of community; more than 90 percent of undergraduates live on campus.

STUDENT BODY

A lively campus community, Messiah students participate in more than 75 groups and organizations, including theater groups, a campus newspaper, and a student-produced radio station. More than 35 percent of undergraduates participate in student government elections. Messiah does not have any fraternities or sororities, at either the national or local level. The College operates a number of campus safety services for students, such as an after-hours transport and escort service, 24-hour emergency telephone alarm devices, day-and-night professional security patrol, and student security patrols. In addition, all entrances to the residence halls are electronically operated. Messiah College maintains one of the most overall successful athletics programs in the nation, competing in the NCAA Division III. Messiah competes in men's baseball, basketball, cross-country, golf, lacrosse, soccer, tennis, track and field, and wrestling, as well as women's basketball, cross-country, field hockey, lacrosse, soccer, softball, tennis, track and field, and volleyball.

ACADEMICS

Messiah students must complete 126 units to graduate. In addition to courses required by their major field, all students must complete a set of required courses in writing, the arts and sciences, language and culture, Christian faith, and physical education. Students fill the remaining required units through elective courses. The College operates on a two-semester academic calendar, with a January term between the fall and spring terms. During January term, students take one intensive, month-long course of study. Qualified students are also encouraged to participate in the Honors Program, to design an individual major or an independent study program, or participate in service-learning programs and internships.

Messiah offers the Bachelor of Arts and the Bachelor of Science degrees in more than 50 major fields. Undergraduates may pursue a degree in the following areas of study: accounting; art history; athletic training; Bible; biochemistry; biology; broadcasting, telecommunications, and mass media; business administration; business information systems; chemistry; Christian ministries; communication; computer science; economics; education; English; environmental science; family studies; French; German; history; humanities; human resource management; international business; journalism; marketing; mathematics; music; nursing; nutrition and dietetics; philosophy; physical education; physics; political science; psychology; religion; social work; sociology; Spanish; Spanish business; special education; sport and exercise science; studio art; theater; and therapeutic recreation. Messiah also runs pre-professional programs in dentistry, law, medical technology, medicine, ministerial, pharmacy, physical therapy, and veterinary. In addition to the main campus, Messiah operates a satellite campus in Philadelphia. The Philadelphia campus offers degree programs in conjunction with Temple University in art education; art history; broadcasting, telecommunications, and mass media; civil engineering; French; German; journalism; physics; social work; and therapeutic recreation. Messiah also offers 50 minors programs, from coaching, criminal justice, and horticulture, to peacemaking and urban studies.

Messiah employs faculty who demonstrate scholastic accomplishment and commitment to the Christian faith, as well as exemplary teaching ability. The College is committed to undergraduate teaching, and all classes are taught by professors, not by graduate assistants. With a student/faculty of 15:1, students have ample opportunity to form individual relationships with professors, and the full-time faculty also serve as academic advisors to students. There are 139 full-time professors at Messiah College, 73 percent of whom hold a doctoral or terminal degree in their field, as well as 104 part-time faculty.

One College Avenue
Grantham, PA 17027
Phone: 717-691-6000
Fax: 717-796-5374
Website: www.messiah.edu

MESSIAH COLLEGE

ADMISSIONS

Messiah seeks students with demonstrated academic promise who wish to share in the College's ardent commitment to Christ. Messiah encourages transfer, international, and minority students to apply. In addition to a completed application, prospective students must submit a personal essay, official scores from the SAT I or ACT, a secondary school transcript, and two official recommendations from secondary school officials. Successful applicants will have completed a strong high school curriculum, which includes 4 years of English, 2 years of both math and science, 2 or more years of a foreign language, and 2 years of social studies. Admissions to the College is selective. Roughly 60 percent of the current freshman class were in the top 20 percent of their class and one-fifth ranked in the top 5 percent. There were 69 students named valedictorian or salutatorian, 13 who won the title of National Merit Scholar, and 170 with a composite SAT I score of over 1300 or ACT scores of over 28.

CAMPUS LIFE

Messiah College is situated on 400 beautiful acres, just 10 miles south of Harrisburg, Pennsylvania. In addition to the numerous internship and service opportunities available in the city of Harrisburg, the College is just two hours from the major urban centers of Philadelphia, Baltimore, and Washington, D.C. There are many recreational and outdoor activities in the immediate vicinity, including the Yellow Breeches Creek, which runs through the campus, and the Susquehanna River.

Messiah offers a variety of opportunities for students to study off campus. Messiah is a member of the Council of Christian Colleges and Universities, which gives students the opportunity to study at the American Studies Program (Washington, D.C.), AuSable Institute of Environmental Studies (Michigan), Central American Study and Service, Global Stewardship Study Program, Jerusalem University College, Latin American Studies Program (Costa Rica), Los Angeles Film Studies Center, Oxford Semester (England), Russian Studies Program, Middle East Studies Program, and Oregon Extension and International Business Institute (Europe and Russia). Messiah also participates in the Brethren Colleges Abroad program, which gives students access to even more international locations, including China, Ecuador, England, France, Germany, Japan, and Spain. In addition, Messiah operates a student-faculty exchange program with Daystar University College in Kenya. Students also have the opportunity to study abroad during January term or the summer term. In recent years, students have traveled to Greece, Guatemala, Israel, and the Bahamas.

COST AND AID

For the 2001–2002 academic year, tuition and fees were a combined $16,860, with additional room and board costs of approximately $5,970. In addition, students spend roughly $500 on books, $550 in transportation costs, and roughly $1,100 in personal expenses annually.

METROPOLITAN COLLEGE OF NEW YORK (FORMERLY AUDREY COHEN)

GENERAL INFORMATION

The unique experiential Purpose-Centered System of Education is what students will experience when they begin their studies at Metropolitan College of New York, which was founded in 1964. Recognizing the country's shift from a manufacturing to a service economy, the College has developed a curriculum that focuses on the practical use of skills and knowledge in workplace settings, throughout the educational process. Classes at MCNY are often animated conversations between instructors and students—small-sized "roll-up-your-sleeves" exchanges of ideas and experiences. A lesson taught Monday gets put into action at work on Tuesday and is back in class Wednesday for analysis. The College's purpose-centered educational approach requires each student to create a specific, real-world solution to an issue needing attention within the student's workplace each semester.

Working with MCNY staff and faculty, students design and implement the initiative within their work setting. This could include everything from a plan for transitional housing for the homeless, to a market survey in ethnic cosmetics. The unique MCNY learning experience often leads to promotions and other advancements, even before a student graduates. Because enrolled students receive credit for both classes and workplace experience, it is possible for able, highly motivated students to maintain full-time employment while completing three semesters a year.

Students who pursue their studies without a break can complete their associate's in less than one and a half years, their bachelor's in just under three years, and their master's degree program in one year. Additionally, tuition is fixed for students who stay continuously enrolled until graduation.

MCNY encompasses the Audrey Cohen School for Human Services and Education, the School for Business, and the Graduate School for Public Affairs and Administration. MCNY offers both full-time and part-time programs at the undergraduate level and full-time programs at the graduate level. The academic year consists of three semesters. Around 1,665 students enrolled in the fall 2002 semester, and of these approximately 80 percent were women. The Middle States Association of Colleges and Schools has accredited the College, and the College has been approved for training veterans and other eligible persons by the New York State Education Department.

Most Metropolitan College of New York students pursue their studies full-time while working full-time. This allows for the accelerated degree program. Students also have the option of part-time study on the undergraduate level. The College has fostered close relationships with local New York City organizations employing its students—some are Fortune 500 firms and leading social service agencies, while others are smaller business firms and nonprofit organizations. Students who are not presently employed will be helped by the College's Career Services Office, which will assist in securing a challenging internship site.

In addition to offering an Associate of Arts degree in human services and an Associate of Science in business to complement its Bachelor of Professional Studies (human services) and Bachelor of Business Administration degrees, Metropolitan College of New York offers six three-semester master's programs: the Master of Public Administration, the MBA in general management, the MBA in media management, the MBA in multimedia and e-commerce, the MBA in sports management, and the MBA in sports, recreation, and leisure management.

STUDENT BODY

Drawing upon the creativity and vitality of the metropolitan New York area, MCNY appeals to highly motivated learners who are adamant about transforming their lives. The vast majority of MCNY students hail from the metropolitan area, but the College's educational programs are available to out-of-state and international students too. While 14 hours of interning or working are required of full-time students each week, opportunities exist for extracurricular involvement, such as student government, mentoring other students, and journalistic activities. For low-key social interaction and networking, there is a comfortable student lounge.

ACADEMICS

Each semester's learning experience or performance area at Metropolitan College of New York is called a Purpose. This Purpose is essential to success in a student's chosen field. In the Audrey Cohen School for Human Services and Education, for example, the sixth Purpose is devoted to serving as a community liaison, while during the same semester, the School for Business is concerned with managing economic resources. Each semester, full-time students take five or more Dimension classes—15 credits or more—that explore the wide range of human knowledge drawn from the liberal arts, social sciences, and professional studies. The generic dimensions remain consistent throughout your college career and generally include courses in the following areas: Constructive Action seminar, values and ethics, self and others, systems, skills,I and internship/work experience. Over the course of every semester, students also plan and implement a Constructive Action (CA), a sustained effort carried out in a work situation to identify and achieve a significant initiative related to the semester's performance area. In the CA seminar, students learn to integrate knowledge from all their classes and are assessed on their effectiveness in planning, implementing, and analyzing their Constructive Actions. The CA serves as a source of learning, an opportunity to achieve something that has positive social value, and as the basis for a comprehensive assessment of a student's academic performance. The CA involves research, planning, action, and evaluation. It is the heart of the MCNY educational experience and a key vehicle in enabling the College to achieve its mission. While students are not required to attend the three semesters of courses offered each calendar year without interruption, most students do, which enables them to finish their degrees in two years and eight months. (An even shorter length of time is possible for transfer students or students who are accepted into the Advanced Standing Option.)

75 Varick Street
New York, NY 10013
Phone: 212-343-1234
Fax: 212-343-8470
Website: www.metropolitan.edu

Metropolitan College of New York offers the following programs:

School for Business: Associate of Science in business; Bachelor of Business Administration; Master of Business Administration (in general management; media management; multimedia industry and e-commerce; sports, recreation, and leisure service management; or sports management); Master of Science (in culture and commerce; media industry and e-commerce; or sports, recreation, and leisure service management); MS in sports, recreation, and leisure service management/MBA in media management; MS in multimedia industry and e-commerce/MBA in media management; MS in culture and commerce/MBA in sports, recreation, and leisure service management; MS in culture and commerce/MBA in general management; MS in culture and commerce/MBA in media management; MS in culture and commerce/MBA in multimedia industry and e-commerce; MS in multimedia industry and e-commerce/MBA in general management; MS in sports, recreation, and leisure service management/MBA in general management; MS in sports, recreation, and leisure service management/MBA in multimedia and e-commerce; MS in multimedia and e-commerce/MBA in sports, recreation, and leisure service management; MS in multimedia and e-commerce/MBA in sports management.

Audrey Cohen School for Human Services and Education: Associate of Arts in human services, Bachelor of Professional Studies in human services.

Graduate School for Public Affairs and Administration: Master of Public Administration.

There are 28 full-time faculty and 126 adjunct faculty in the Audrey Cohen School for Human Services and Education. The School for Business is made up of 6 full-time faculty members and 123 adjuncts. More than 70 percent of full-time faculty members have doctoral degrees. MCNY faculty are affiliated with leading human service organizations and international corporations. The full-time faculty members act as students' mentors and advisors. They also monitor students' performances as interns, and they help students plan and succeed in every step of their program.

ADMISSIONS

Prospective undergraduate students must complete and return the application with a $30 application fee, undergo a personal interview with an admissions counselor, submit two letters of reference, provide official transcripts for secondary and any postsecondary schools attended, and (for recent high school graduates) submit the results of SAT I or (for adult applicants) arrange to take the TABE (Test of Adult Basic Education), which the College administers as its entrance exam. There is also an assigned essay. Students must also submit proof of immunizations for measles, mumps, and rubella. Applicants will be notified of admissions decisions on a rolling basis. For additional information, please contact:

Admissions Office
Metropolitan College of New York
75 Varick Street
New York, NY 10013
Phone: 212-343-1234, ext. 5001
Fax: 212 343-8470
Website: www.metropolitan.edu

CAMPUS LIFE

Lower Manhattan is home to the College. The main campus is located at 75 Varick Street, right next to Greenwich Village, the financial district, and the exciting media and art communities in SoHo and TriBeCa. Public transportation is easily accessible, as are major thoroughfares. For students in the Bronx, Flushing, and Staten Island, there are convenient extension centers.

COST AND AID

Undergraduate tuition charges per semester are $4,960 for the School for Human Services and $5,250 for the School for Business at MCNY's main campus; lower rates apply at extension centers. An additional $1,840 is required of students who participate in the Advanced Standing Program. Tuition fees will not increase for students who stay continuously enrolled. Most students at Metropolitan College of New York commute from home, so there is no on-campus housing. Students who need housing can find many student residences in New York that are not restricted to a specific institution.

MILWAUKEE SCHOOL OF ENGINEERING

GENERAL INFORMATION

Milwaukee School of Engineering (MSOE) offers a combination of academic excellence and personal experiences that prepare you for work and life. The University's applications-oriented educational philosophy has earned national praise. For nearly a century, MSOE has brought theory to life through extensive integration of laboratory experimentation. Understanding theoretical concepts and knowing how to apply them is key to the success of MSOE graduates in their first jobs and throughout their careers.

MSOE graduates have a reputation for being problem solvers and leaders. MSOE graduates typically are a step ahead of their peers, whether they are attending graduate school, creating new products, starting or heading companies, or working to better their communities. MSOE's innovative curriculum has resulted in a 98 percent placement rate for the University's bachelor's degree graduates over the past five years, at average annual salaries of more than $40,000. Representatives of firms from across the country, including representatives from Fortune 500 companies, visit MSOE during the academic year to interview graduating students for employment and to discuss career opportunities.

"I am attending a college with an excellent reputation, and it makes me proud to say, 'I go to MSOE!' Every day, I am experiencing more and increasing my knowledge." —Thomas Zemek, MSOE student

Learning by Doing

MSOE believes that for a graduate to succeed in today's global market, wide-ranging, practical experience is required. That is why MSOE students experience an average of more than 600 laboratory hours before they graduate, assist with projects in the University's Applied Technology Center, participate in internships, and take advantage of international study options.

Graduation in Four Years

Guaranteed. MSOE formally guarantees its full-time undergraduate students that they will graduate in four years, provided they stay on track within their major and meet the conditions of graduation.

Governance

MSOE is governed by a Board of Regents of more than 50 members elected by leaders in business and industry nationwide and who are also members of the more than 200-member MSOE Corporation.

Students

The Student Body of 3,000 men and women comes from throughout the United States and numerous countries. Since its founding, the University has encouraged the enrollment of students of any race, color, creed, or gender. Approximately half the full-time students live in three modern high-rise residence halls.

Accreditation

MSOE is accredited by the Commission of Institutions of Higher Education of the North Central Association of Colleges and Schools. Individual program accreditation is identified in MSOE's academic catalog.

STUDENT BODY

MSOE offers you more than 50 recognized professional societies, Greek organizations, and other student- and special-interest groups. MSOE is a member of the NCAA Division III Lake Michigan Conference, where our 18 intercollegiate athletic teams compete in men's baseball, basketball, cross-country, golf, hockey, soccer, tennis, track and field, volleyball, and wrestling; women's basketball, cross-country, golf, soccer, softball, tennis, track and field, and volleyball; and a variety of intramural and club sports. These co-curricular activities are invaluable in helping prepare you for life. (And they're also a lot of fun.)

The Student Life and Campus Center provides on-campus recreational activities. This facility houses student activity rooms, student organization offices, a TV viewing area, a cafeteria, game rooms, and the Koss Listening Center. Additional recreational areas can be found in the residence halls and MSOE Sports Center. MSOE currently is planning a state-of-the-art recreation, fitness, health, and wellness facility called the Kern Center. The $25 million facility broke ground in mid-2002.

ACADEMICS

The degree programs at MSOE combine study in degree specialty courses with basic study in science, communication, mathematics, and humanities in a high-technology, applications-oriented environment. Students who are admitted with advanced credit to a program leading to a bachelor's degree must complete at least 50 percent of the curriculum in residence at MSOE. MSOE operates on a quarter system. Students generally take 16 to 19 credits per quarter, representing a combination of lecture and laboratory.

MSOE offers students the opportunity to participate in the Air Force, Army and Navy Reserve Officer Training Corps (ROTC) programs, which are offered in conjunction with Marquette University.

MSOE offers 16 Bachelor of Science programs, one Bachelor of Arts program, six Master of Science degree programs, several dual degree combinations, and international study opportunities.

Bachelor's degrees are offered in architectural engineering; biomedical engineering; business; computer engineering; construction management; electrical engineering; electrical engineering technology*; industrial engineering; international business; management*; management information systems; mechanical engineering; mechanical engineering technology*; nursing; software engineering; and technical communication.

**Transfer programs only*

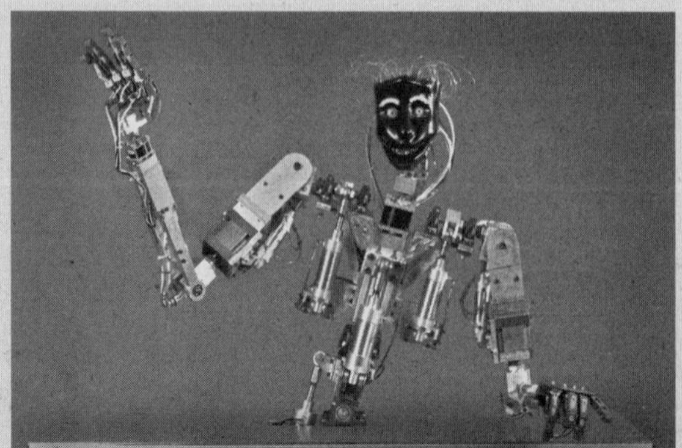

1025 North Broadway
Milwaukee, WI 53202-3109
Phone: 414-277-6763
Fax: 414-277-7475
Website: www.msoe.edu

Master's degrees are offered in engineering, engineering management, environmental engineering, medical informatics (offered in conjunction with the Medical College of Wisconsin), perfusion, and structural engineering.

A dual degree, five-year option is available in a combination of engineering, business, and technical communication programs. An engineering/environmental engineering degree (BS/MS) combination is also available.

You'll benefit from the fact that MSOE's professors stay current because of their industrial associations, many made as a result of faculty consulting. MSOE professors bring years of their own experience in business and industry to the classroom. This emphasis on practical application of theory also means that MSOE does not use teaching assistants.

With an average class size of 19 and a student/faculty ratio of only 11:1, MSOE offers students individual attention. Full-time faculty number 117, with an additional 143 part-time faculty providing very specific expertise as needed. Many are registered professional engineers, architects, or nurses in Wisconsin and other states.

"MSOE's small class sizes provide an unrestricted learning environment. Students feel at ease asking questions in class and know professors are readily available to answer questions outside of class as well." —Daniel Wittrock, MSOE student

ADMISSIONS

Each applicant to MSOE is reviewed individually on the basis of his or her potential for success as determined by academic preparation. Admission may be gained by submitting an application for admission and the appropriate transcripts indicating graduation from an approved high school or high school equivalency. In addition, transfer students are required to submit transcripts from all prior institutions attended. An applicant's prior course work is reviewed to determine eligibility for admission. Required course work varies depending on the desired course of study. Students are encouraged to complete math through pre-calculus (including algebra and geometry), chemistry, biology (for nursing), physics, and four years of English. All entering freshmen are also required to provide results from the ACT or the SAT I unless they have completed 15 or more college credits or have been out of high school for two or more years. Entering freshmen are given placement tests to determine their exact standing in mathematics and science.

Transfer opportunities exist for placement into the junior year of the Bachelor of Science in Management Systems and the Bachelor of Science/Bachelor of Arts in Technical Communication programs, with the appropriate associate degree or equivalent credits.

Classes start in September, November, March, and June. Freshmen and transfer students may enter at the beginning of any quarter; however, entry in the fall quarter is recommended. An application for admission may be obtained by contacting MSOE directly or by visiting MSOE's website at www.msoe.edu. Procedures for admission are included with the application.

CAMPUS LIFE

Milwaukee, one of the country's 20 largest cities, provides an ideal backdrop for developing extracurricular interests. The MSOE campus is only a few blocks from the shores of Lake Michigan—the world's second-largest inland lake—and is 90 miles north of Chicago.

The area boasts nearly 15,000 acres of county parks, 240 miles of bike trails, an IMAX theater, a horticultural conservatory, a symphony orchestra, a ballet, several opera companies, art museums, theater companies, a nationally acclaimed zoo, one of the country's largest museums of natural history, and the world-famous Summerfest music festival.

Several major- and minor-league sports teams call Milwaukee home. The city also stages more than 50 major festivals annually as well as other public get-togethers. An all-weather, all-season city, there is plenty to see and do in Milwaukee year-round.

Graduate programs in engineering and engineering management are available in Appleton, Wisconsin. Select graduate courses are offered at several southeast Wisconsin locations including Brookfield, Kenosha, Port Washington, Racine, Sheboygan, and Waukesha, in addition to the main MSOE campus in Milwaukee.

COST AND AID

For 2002–2003, tuition is $21,855 per year, plus $1,140 for the Technology Package (notebook computer, software, insurance, maintenance, Internet access, and user services). The cost of room and board in the residence halls is approximately $5,115 per year. Books and supplies average $350 per quarter but may be somewhat higher the first quarter.

MINNEAPOLIS COLLEGE OF ART AND DESIGN

GENERAL INFORMATION

Since 1886, the Minneapolis College of Art and Design has offered students the opportunity to study at one of the biggest art centers in the country. Together, the Minneapolis Institute of Arts, the Children's Theatre Company, and the College occupy several square blocks close to downtown Minneapolis. The resnlt is a thriving arts community that enjoys access to top-quality facilities. Of the approximately 600 undergraduates currently attending MCAD, 35 percent live in modern, furnished apartments owned by the College. Presently, more men than women attend MCAD. MCAD is an independent, accredited institution offering a four-year curriculum integrating the liberal arts into 14 professional BFA degree majors in fine arts, media arts and design; a four-year BS degree program in visualization; a two-year MFA degree program in visual studies; and a one-year Post-Baccalaureate certificate program. The College also offers educational opportunities for the general public through continuing studies, distance learning, and exhibition programs. All MCAD programs challenge students to progress to the highest levels of artistic expression and intellectual investigation.

The Continuing Studies Office runs programs for students wishing to attend classes in the evenings, on the weekends, or during the summer. Additional events include art-related films, lectures, performances, and conferences. All students can benefit from seeing the work of significant modern artists and designers shown at the MCAD Gallery. The College invites renowned artists, designers, and critics to come to the campus to share their expertise with the students and faculty. While students do make time for social events and recreation, the focus at MCAD is on academics. Undergraduates are expected to show dedication to the College's standards of professionalism and accomplishment.

STUDENT BODY

Elected student representatives serve in the roles of chairperson, secretary, treasurer, and committee members on many of the College's standing committees. In their weekly meetings, the student government hears student concerns and organizes campus activities. In the past, they have coordinated film series, social events, lectures, events, student gallery showings, and memberships to the Walker Art Center and the Minneapolis YMCA.

ACADEMICS

BFA Undergraduates pursuing a BFA degree also must earn 120 semester credits. More than half of these are allotted to studio classes. Thirty-nine credits come from liberal arts courses, and 18 are complete in the Foundation Studies Program during the freshman year. MCAD believes that the development of critical thinking skills, artistic inquiry methods, professional responsibility ethics, and interdisciplinary connections stand as the foundation of a rewarding creative life. Therefore, the Foundation Studies Program challenges first-year students to integrate verbal and visual communication skills and hone their individual aesthetic as they learn the basics of their fields. As students work within their major field, they gain the technical know-how and conceptual familiarity they need to excel as artists. Electives allow students to explore other media and techniques. To round out the MCAD education, the liberal arts curriculum covers history, criticism, literature, philosophy, religion, and the social and behavioral sciences.

Candidates for the BS degree in visualization at MCAD must earn 120 semester credits. Classes related to visualization, including Communication Theory and Marketing: History, Strategies, Forms and Perceptions; Media Analysis; and Hypermedia, account for 36 of these credits. Another 18 credits come from studio classes. In addition, students must present group projects and a senior project or exhibit. Finally, an externship or overseas study is required. Students who graduate with this degree typically use the skills they have learned in visual persuasion and information techniques in careers in advertising/marketing, science/technology, entertainment, education, and corporate communications.

Minneapolis College of Art and Design also offers the Bachelor of Fine Arts degree in the following majors: advertising design, animation, comic art, drawing, filmmaking, fine arts studio, furniture design, graphic design, illustration, interactive multimedia, painting, photography, printmaking, and sculpture.

The Minneapolis College of Art and Design's Master of Fine Arts degree in visual studies provides individuals seeking advanced study in the arts an opportunity to secure the recognized terminal degree in the studio arts. The MCAD MFA serves students of high personal motivation, independent thinking, and significant prior studio experiences.

The one-year post-baccalaureate program at MCAD is an intensive educational experience for students seeking opportunity to acquire advanced communication and art and design skills in a structured, academic program. The objective of this new post-baccalaureate is to prepare individuals who have already accomplished a baccalaureate degree to apply for graduate study in art and design or to enter jobs requiring knowledge and skills in art and design or visualization.

Ninety-two professional artists and designers make up the MCAD faculty, with 36 serving full time. Two-thirds of these instructors hold a terminal degree in their field. Alongside of teaching, faculty members in the fine arts and media arts continue to produce work and hold exhibits in Minneapolis, across the country, and around the world. Instructors bring practical knowledge to the classroom, based on their experiences in corporations, agencies, and design firms. Owing to the low student/faculty ratio of 11:1, students get personal attention from their professors and develop strong working relationships.

2501 Stevens Avenue
Minneapolis, MN 55404
Phone: 612-874-3760
Fax: 612-874-3701
Website: www.mcad.edu

ADMISSIONS

The admissions committee looks for applicants who demonstrate academic success, creative talent, and a strong motivation to learn. To be admitted, students must have a high school diploma or its equivalent. A complete application includes the following materials: application form, application fee, letters of recommendation, SAT or ACT scores, a statement of interest, a high school transcript, and an essay (for the BS in visualization only). It is recommended that hose applying to the BFA programs send a letter from an art teacher along with a portfolio showing their creative best. Applicants who do not have a background in art may send a recommendation from a counselor or a teacher in any subject.

Students applying to transfer to MCAD are required to send both their high school and college transcripts in addition to a portfolio if they wish to transfer studio credits. Applicants who have already earned a four-year college degree do not need to submit high school grades. The College has a strong commitment to a diverse student body and actively works to create a community representing a wide variety of cultural, racial, religious, economic, and geographical backgrounds.

CAMPUS LIFE

The Twin Cities of Minneapolis and St. Paul are home to 2 million people and the cultural and recreational facilities they support. Students at MCAD enjoy outings to the Guthrie Theatre, the Walker Art Center, the Minnesota Orchestra, the Hennepin Center for the Arts, and the University of Minnesota. For sports fans, it is convenient to attend professional baseball, basketball, hockey, and football games. Outdoor activities, including biking, skiing, hiking, boating, and swimming, are also available nearby.

Many MCAD students choose to participate in internships/externships or organize courses of independent study. The College also facilitates mobility programs, which allow students to take classes at any of the 35 schools involved in the Association of Independent Colleges of Art and Design. The Minneapolis College of Art and Design has a number of existing off-campus study opportunities, both in America and around the world. To be eligible for most programs, a student must have a cumulative GPA of 3.0 and have earned junior standing during the semester off-campus. Overseas study programs in Denmark, England, France, Germany, Ireland, Italy, Scotland, Japan, Holland, and Mexico are available, as is a studio semester in New York City. MCAD also accommodates students who are not enrolled in degree programs with the Student-at-Large program, which opens day classes when space is available.

COST AND AID

The following costs and fees apply to all students enrolled for the 2002–2003 academic year:

Undergraduate tuition per semester (12–18 credits): $10,650

Graduate program tuition: $710 per credit

Student-at-Large tuition: $710 per credit

Student activity fee: $42

Health insurance per semester (waived if proof of personal insurance on file for current school year): approximately $130

On-campus apartment rental per semester per student: $1,410–$2,680

Rental charges for student apartments vary based on type of unit, number of occupants, and whether the unit is furnished or unfurnished. Contact the Housing Office at 612-874-3780 for more information. Apartment rental charge includes all utilities except long distance phone service.

MOLLOY COLLEGE

THE COLLEGE AT A GLANCE

A little background on Molloy brings this school to life. It was founded in 1955 with 44 students, 15 faculty, and 5,000 books. A commitment to academic excellence and a desire to start a new tradition in higher education on Long Island was a commonality among these 44 and 15; their spirit remains alive today among current faculty and students.

Molloy's youth and exponential growth (today it is home to 2,500 students and 300 faculty) gives the school a perspective and vibrancy that few colleges know. It has changed so radically so quickly that it can easily create an effective and active learning environment no matter the circumstance. Today these circumstances happen to be quite good; Molloy stands among the most respected four-year, private, coed institutions of higher learning in the area. It offers an intimate and nurturing environment that fosters personal relationships between students and faculty. Molloy enrolls an ethnically and socioeconomically diverse student body that finds an academically alive environment in Rockville Centre.

Molloy is accredited by the Board of Regents of the University of the State of New York and the Middle States Association of Colleges and Schools. Its programs in nursing and social work are accredited by the National League for Nursing Accreditation Commission and the Council on Social Work Education, respectively.

STUDENTS

Molloy students are involved in a highly active life outside the classroom, something that the college administration supports and encourages. Whether you are an athlete, an aspiring journalist, someone with a strong opinion, or just someone with a desire to expand your horizons, you will find a group to join here. Such organizations provide students with the opportunity to interact with fellow students as leaders, as part of a team, or in a social environment.

Student-run publications include the yearbook, a literary magazine, a newspaper, and a weekly newsletter. Molloy women compete in varsity-level sports, including basketball, cross-country, lacrosse, soccer, softball, tennis, and volleyball. These teams compete in the NCAA, the ECAC, and the NYSAIAW. The women's equestrian team belongs to the Intercollegiate Horse Show Association. Men's baseball, basketball, cross-country, lacrosse, tennis and soccer compete in the NCAA Division II.

The student government is elected from the Molloy Student Association, made up of every member of the student body. Members of the Molloy Student Government provide their classmates with a leadership that keeps extracurricular activities alive, productive, and practical.

ACADEMICS

A minimum of 128 credit hours is required for a baccalaureate degree; these courses include a strong liberal arts core curriculum for every major field of study. Students may choose a double major, and many minors are available. Molloy has a 4-1-4 academic calendar.

Students may earn CLEP and CPE credit, and advanced placement credit is granted for a score of 3 or better on the AP exam. Qualified full-time students may participate in the Army ROTC program at Hofstra University or St. John's University on a cross enrolled basis. Molloy students may also elect Air Force ROTC on a cross enrolled basis with New York Institute of Technology.

Molloy College offers the AA degree in liberal arts; the AAS degree in cardiovascular technology, health information technology, nuclear medicine technology, and respiratory care; and the BA or BS degree in accounting, art, biology, business management, communications, computer science, computer information systems, criminal justice, English, environmental studies, French, history, interdisciplinary studies, international peace and justice studies, mathematics, music, music therapy, nursing, philosophy, political science, psychology, social work, sociology, Spanish, speech language pathology/audiology, and theology. Teacher certification programs are available in childhood (1–6), adolescence (7–12), and special education.

Students interested in pre-dental, pre-law, pre-medical, or pre-veterinary programs are offered special advisement.

With 307 full- and part-time faculty and only 2,500 students, Molloy College enjoys a student/faculty ratio of 9:1, thus providing small classes and individual attention. Faculty members are experts in their fields who have chosen to make teaching their top priority. They act not only as educators to students, but also as career and academic advisors.

CAMPUS LIFE

Rockville Centre, Long Island, is located on the outskirts of New York City, which allows Molloy students to access all of the cultural and social opportunities in Manhattan, just an easy train ride away from the 30-acre campus. Long Island itself is just as it sounds: an island surrounded by the beauties and activities of the Atlantic Ocean. It is home to vast beaches, quaint towns, and an endless array of conveniences and opportunities.

Molloy College offers students the opportunity to combine job experience and classroom exposure through the internship program. Internships are available in accounting, art, business management, communications, computer science, criminal justice, English, history, IPJ studies, mathematics, music therapy, political science, psychology, social work, and sociology.

1000 Hempstead Avenue
Rockville Centre, NY 11570
Phone: 516-678-5000
Fax: 516-256-2247
Website: www.molloy.edu

COSTS

Financial aid, which is based on academic achievement and financial need, is awarded to more than 85 percent of the student body. Aid is awarded in the form of scholarships, grants, loans, and Federal Work-Study Program employment. Non-need scholarships and grants are also available. Students are required to complete the FAFSA. Students who graduate from high school with a 95 percent average and a minimum combined score of 1250 on the SAT I are considered for the Molloy Scholars' Program, which awards full tuition scholarships. Partial scholarships are available through the following: the Board of Trustees Scholarships, Dominican Scholarships, Fine and Performing Arts Scholarships, and Community Service Awards. The Transfer Scholarship Program awards partial tuition scholarships to students transferring into Molloy College with at least a 3.0 cumulative GPA. Athletic grants (Division II only) are awarded to full-time students who show superior athletic ability in baseball, basketball, cross-country, equestrian, lacrosse, soccer, softball, tennis, or volleyball.

Tuition and fees are $13,690 for the 2001–2002 academic year. Part-time students pay $420 per credit.

ADMISSIONS

Molloy College's admissions committee recommends that applicants meet the following admission qualifications: graduation from a four-year public or private high school or equivalent (GED test) with a minimum of 18.5 units, including 4 in English, 4 in social studies, 3 in a foreign language, 3 in mathematics, and 3 in science. Nursing applicants must have completed biology and chemistry courses. Mathematics applicants must have taken 4 units of math and 2 of science (including chemistry or physics). Biology applicants must have credits in biology, chemistry, and physics and 4 units in math. Art applicants must submit a portfolio; music students must audition. The committee selects candidates based on the following: high school record, SAT I or ACT scores, class rank, and the school's recommendation. Personality and character are considered in admissions decisions, as are talent or ability in a noncurricular field, as well as alumni relationships.

The St. Thomas Aquinas Program, which includes both HEOP and the Albertus Magnus Program, may be an option for students not normally eligible for admission.

Early admission is available. Molloy admits students on a rolling basis and students are advised of the admission decision within a few weeks of completion of the application filing process.

Prospective students should submit the following to the admissions office to be considered for enrollment: a completed application for admission, a nonrefundable $30 application fee, an official high school transcript or GED score report, official SAT I or ACT score, and official college transcripts (transfer students only).

MOUNT MERCY COLLEGE

THE COLLEGE AT A GLANCE

You can see your future from here. Planning, building, and living your future starts today at Mount Mercy College. Here you'll find engaging students, a strong academic program, supportive faculty, the energy of Cedar Rapids, and a tree-lined hilltop campus. We're a Catholic college grounded in the welcoming spirit of our founders, the Sisters of Mercy—the perfect starting point for your vision, your future.

Located just two miles from downtown Cedar Rapids (population 130,000), our 40-acre hilltop campus is tucked in an attractive residential neighborhood. More than 1,400 students attend Mount Mercy College and are working toward degrees in our 36 majors.

Our faculty focus their energy on teaching. They are accomplished in their professions as researchers, authors, Fulbright scholars, and nationally recognized artists. The student/faculty ratio is 14:1.

In addition to weekly social events such as Club Friday and annual events such as Hill Fest and Spring Fling, students participate in more than 30 clubs and organizations, 13 intercollegiate sports and intramural activities, the college newspaper, drama productions, choir, and community service.

Mount Mercy athletic teams are part of the Midwest Classic Conference and compete at the NAIA Division II level in men's baseball, basketball, cross-country, golf, soccer, and track and field and women's basketball, cross-country, golf, soccer, softball, track and field, and volleyball.

The Mount Mercy Career Development Office provides a career libary, graduate school information, regular job bulletins, career search assistance, development opportunities, mock interviews, and a resume referral program. Students have access to prime internship opportunities, annual on-campus career fairs, and mentoring and networking programs.

Nearly 100 percent of new full-time freshmen receive institutional financial aid. This is in the form of Mount Mercy scholarships and/or grants, federal and state grants, and work-study opportunities.

STUDENTS

At Mount Mercy you can transition your talents and interests from your earlier years—or develop new ones. Our campus has an energetic theater program and choir, an active Student Government Association, and a bi-weekly student newspaper. Student activities include more than 30 clubs and organizations.

Mount Mercy College is a member of the National Association of Intercollegiate Athletics (NAIA) and the Midwest Classic Conference. The College offers intercollegiate competition in men's basketball, baseball, cross-country, golf, soccer, and track and field. In women's sports, the College offers basketball, cross-country, golf, soccer, softball, track and field, and volleyball.

These programs have combined for more than 20 conference championship Mount Mercy teams, and individuals that regularly qualify for regional and national championships events. In addition, Mount Mercy student athletes are recognized annually as NAIA Academic all-Americans.

Intramural activities include basketball, cross-country, flag football, golf, softball, and volleyball.

ACADEMICS

Small classes are a start. Another key is a faculty whose primary role is teaching. A commitment to active learning helps complete the teaching and learning picture. Mount Mercy's active learning environment helps you gain confidence in discussing your views and opinions. Our talented and caring faculty members are here to guide you and share their experiences from work as authors, Fulbright scholars, published researchers, and nationally recognized artists.

Mount Mercy College requires 123 semester hours for graduation, with a cumulative grade point average of at least 2.0 on a 4.0 scale. Additional graduation requirements may vary according to the major field of study.

General education requirements include two courses each in English and social sciences and one each in fine arts, history, mathematics, multicultural studies, natural science, philosophy, religious studies, and speech.

Special academic opportunities are offered to outstanding students through special honors sections of general education courses and upper-level courses. Students graduating in the honors program receive special recognition at commencement.

Mount Mercy's academic year consists of fall and spring semesters, plus a winter term. This four-week term offers required courses as well as exploratory electives, allowing students to make more rapid progress toward their degrees. Two five-week summer sessions are also held.

Mount Mercy awards the Bachelor of Arts, Bachelor of Science, Bachelor of Business Administration, Bachelor of Applied Science, and the Bachelor of Applied Arts degrees.

The Bachelor of Arts degree is awarded to graduates who major in art, biology, criminal justice, English, history, interdisciplinary majors (applied philosophy, international studies, and urban and community studies), mathematics, music, political science, psychology, public relations, religious studies, social work, sociology, and speech/drama.

The Bachelor of Science degree is awarded to graduates who major in biology, computer information systems, computer science, elementary education, mathematics, medical technology, nursing, and secondary education. (Majors in biology and mathematics may elect either the Bachelor of Science or the Bachelor of Arts degree.)

1330 Elmhurst Drive Northeast
Cedar Rapids, IA 52402-4797
Phone: 319-368-6460
Fax: 319-363-5270
Website: www.mtmercy.edu

The Bachelor of Business Administration is awarded to graduates who major in accounting, management, marketing, and the pre-structured interdisciplinary business administration majors (criminal justice administration, English administration, health services administration, political science administration, psychology administration, sociology administration, and visual arts administration).

The following majors offer endorsements for secondary education: American history, art, biology, business, English, mathematics, multicategorical resource room, music, social science, speech/drama, and world history.

The Bachelor of Applied Science and Bachelor of Applied Arts degree programs are designed for technically trained students who wish to broaden their specialized background to include a liberal arts education.

Mount Mercy College has 66 full-time and 65 part-time faculty members, most of whom hold the terminal degree in their fields. Many have received recognition from their respective professional organizations for their achievements, and the faculty includes Fulbright Scholars and grant recipients from the National Endowment for the Humanities and the National Endowment for the Arts. With a student/faculty ratio of 14:1, Mount Mercy offers students the opportunity to know their teachers well and to learn from them in an informal, friendly, and supportive environment.

CAMPUS LIFE

Tucked into a tree-lined residential neighborhood, the inviting Mount Mercy campus is well-lit, comfortable, and secure. With larger rooms than those at a lot of other places, all Mount Mercy campus living spaces are equipped with an Internet connection for each resident and basic cable television included in your room cost. In addition to traditional single, double, or triple residence hall accommodations, the campus features a new suite-style buiding as well as a traditional apartment living complex for junior and senior students.

Just about everything you need on a daily basis is right here. Just steps away from any spot on our 40-acre campus are a dining room with 12-hour continuous dining, the Lundy Commons student center, the bookstore, the Chapel of Mercy, and the Hennessey Recreation Center. Plus, an underground tunnel system connects the entire campus.

Your future begins here when you tap into the business life and economy of Cedar Rapids, one of the most vibrant cities in the Midwest. Mount Mercy's Mentoring program pairs students one-on-one with local alumni who work in a profession in the student's field of interest. Readily available internships and part-time jobs help you connect with the job market and gain experience by meeting and working with established professionals in your field.

Of course you don't study and work all the time. The "City of Five Seasons" also is a great resource for your leisure hours. Cedar Rapids has a symphony, Theatre Cedar Rapids, Liars Theatre, the Paramount Theatre performance hall, the Cedar Rapids Museum of Art, minor league baseball and hockey, a downtown arena that hosts popular concerts and shows, and the Science Station with an IMAX theater.

Mount Mercy College has an exchange program with the University of Palacky in the Czech Republic. This program allows students to study abroad without any additional expense for tuition, room, and board.

COSTS

Nearly all of our new, full-time freshmen receive some type of institutional assistance in the form of Mount Mercy scholarships or grants, federal or state grants, loans, on-campus employment, or a combination of these sources. Additionally, financial assistance is available for transfer students.

To apply for Mount Mercy scholarships and grants, students must first be admitted to the College. Early application is advised, as the priority deadline for filing the FAFSA (Free Application for Federal Student Aid) is March 1.

Full-time tuition for the 2002–2003 academic year is $15,300, which is at the midpoint among Iowa private colleges. Majors fees are included in this figure. Room costs are $2,060 based on double occupancy, and board is $3,014 based on a 19-meal plan. Estimated annual costs for a resident student, including books, supplies, and personal expenses is $21,300.

ADMISSIONS

Mount Mercy College admits students whose academic preparation, abilities, interests, and personal qualities give promise of success in college. Applicants are considered on the basis of academic record, class rank, test scores, and recommendations and should have at least a 2.5 grade point average on a 4.0 scale, a 19 on the ACT or 980 on the SAT, and rank in the top half of their class. The applications of students meeting minimum qualification requirements are reviewed by an Admission Committee. Students may apply online.

Prospective students are encouraged to visit the campus and meet with a faculty member in their area of interest. Special campus visit days are scheduled each year, and individual appointments are welcome. Overnight accomodations in residence halls can be arranged.

MOUNT SAINT MARY COLLEGE (NY)

GENERAL INFORMATION

Mount Saint Mary College is a private, four-year liberal arts college for men and women with an enrollment of 2,500 students. With a favorable student/faculty ratio of 16:1, the Mount provides a warm and personal atmosphere. Mount Saint Mary College is a young, vibrant, growing school where group commitment is made to the individual student. The Mount has set the goal of preparing its students, within the environment of a small, independent, undergraduate college, to assume, by choice and preparation, their roles in an ever-changing cultural, intellectual, psychological, and social climate. A wide variety of choices make it possible for all students to find activities that fit their own interests. Intercollegiate athletics programs include baseball, basketball, soccer, softball, swimming, tennis, and volleyball. The 47,000-square-foot Kaplan Recreational Facility features two NCAA basketball/volleyball courts, a cardiovascular fitness center, a weight room, an aerobics/dance studio, a swimming pool, a raised running track, training rooms, study lounges, a TV lounge, a snack bar, a game room, and four classrooms.

STUDENT BODY

Students at Mount Saint Mary College participate in a very active system of student governance. Student representatives are members of every College committee. The Resident Living Council governs and represents the resident students of the College, while the Commuter Council focuses on the commuting population. Most student activities are generated by Student Government organizations, and the Student Government plays a leading role in the development of College policy; it is the main outlet for student participation in the College's decision making process and in the planning of events. The Student Government manages its own student activities budget.

ACADEMICS

Mount Saint Mary College is dedicated to providing a diversity of programs to accommodate people with individual needs and specific objectives, while developing a total learning environment for all students. Each individualized program is geared to the complex and varied needs of each student seeking to become a whole person, ready for a rewarding career and ready to make full use of his or her leisure hours. A minimum of 120 credit hours is required for degrees granted by the Mount, including 90 credit hours in the liberal arts and sciences for the Bachelor of Arts degree and 60 credit hours in the liberal arts and sciences for the Bachelor of Science degree. A core curriculum of 39 credit hours is also required. Major requirements consist of 28 to 40 credit hours. Advanced placement, credit for life experience, accelerated courses, and an honors program are available. Students are encouraged to take part in the Mount's study abroad program. All students have the opportunity to gain practical experience within their major through cooperative education and internships.

Mount Saint Mary College awards Bachelor of Arts (BA) and Bachelor of Science (BS) degrees in such programs as accounting, biology, business management, chemistry, computer science, English, Hispanic Studies, history, history/political science, human services, information technology, interdisciplinary studies, mathematics, media studies, medical technology, nursing, psychology, public relations, social science, sociology, and undeclared. Concentrations include counseling and client services, criminal justice, educational computing, finance, general concentration in human services, human resource management, international business, management information systems, marketing, networking, social and community services, and Web technologies. Certification programs are available in childhood education, childhood education and teaching students with disabilities (grades 1–6), childhood education with middle school extension (grades 7–9) and adolescence education, adolescence education and teaching students with disabilities (grades 7–12) and adolescence education with middle school extension (grades 5–6). Pre-professional studies are available in dentistry, law, medicine, and veterinary medicine. The College offers a 3-3 or 4-3 physical therapy program with New York Medical College, a 3-2 mathematics/engineering program with Catholic University and a 3-2 social work program with Fordham University.

Mount Saint Mary College offers its students an environment that fosters close student-teacher interaction with the aid of a very committed faculty. The student/teacher ratio is 16:1, which allows for individualized advisement and instruction. The average class size is 25, and classes emphasize seminar and discussion-based learning.

330 Powell Avenue
Newburgh, NY 12550
Phone: 845-569-3248
Fax: 845-562-6762
Website: www.msmc.edu

ADMISSIONS

Mount Saint Mary College welcomes students whose potential for academic and social success is in keeping with the objectives of the College. Applicants are evaluated primarily on their past academic performance, SAT I scores and class rank are also considered. Transfer applicants should be in good academic standing at their previous college. Campus visits and interviews are strongly recommended. Early admission to the College is available. Students who wish to apply to the Mount should submit a completed application and a $30 application fee to the Admissions Office. Students should also make arrangements for their high school transcript and SAT I scores to be forwarded to the same office. Letters of recommendation, while not required, are strongly advised. Mount Saint Mary College operates on a rolling admission policy. Once a student's file is complete, he or she is usually notified of the admission decision within two to four weeks.

CAMPUS LIFE

Mount Saint Mary College is located in a residential section of Newburgh, New York, on the banks of the scenic Hudson River, approximately halfway between Albany and New York City. The accessibility of New York City makes it possible for students to take advantage of a variety of cultural and social activities as well as the many attractions of the Mid Hudson Valley. Recreational areas nearby provide facilities for skiing, boating, hiking, golfing, riding, and swimming. Shopping facilities are near the College. Many students are involved in some aspect of community service, often combining their academic interests with a community activity.

Cooperative Education is an optional experiential education program that promotes academic, personal, and professional development. This enrichment program adds a professional dimension to the traditional college curriculum by enabling students to combine practical work experiences with academic majors and career goals. Participation in Cooperative Education is recorded on students' transcripts. Many businesses, schools, health-care facilities, social service agencies, scientific laboratories, information systems companies, public relations and media companies employ students in career-related work experiences that reinforce knowledge learned in the classroom and prepare students with life skills and career choices. Students may work in paid co-op positions or unpaid internships. During the internship experience, students earn academic credit that satisfies degree requirements. Occasionally, students may earn academic credit for the learning that occurs during a paid co-op experience. Cooperative education affords students in all academic disciplines the opportunity to:

- Gain practical career related experience before graduation
- Develop professional work habits and interpersonal skills
- Apply skills learned in the classroom
- Explore potential career interests
- Develop employer contacts
- Earn college credit for internships and selected co-op experiences
- Defray educational costs

COST AND AID

Tuition for the 2002–2003 academic year was $12,930 for most full time students. Room and board costs were $6,550, including a room and full weekly meal plan. Additional fees total approximately $420 annually.

NAROPA COLLEGE AT NAROPA UNIVERSITY

GENERAL INFORMATION

In 1974, Chögyam Trungpa, a Tibetan meditation master and scholar, founded The Naropa Institute, which eventually became Naropa University. Trungpa dreamed of an environment where "East meets West and sparks will fly." Naropa University's mission is rooted in an educational philosophy that originated at Nalanda University, an important learning institution in India that was run by the famous Buddhist scholar Naropa in the eleventh century. Naropa College is continually inspired by its Buddhist heritage. The academic curriculum at Naropa is challenging, and the programs are meant for innovative, resourceful students. Students at Naropa can focus on a specific field of study while at the same time immersing themselves in an environment that encourages and develops precision, gentleness, spontaneity, and critical intellect. The environment at Naropa is one of vitality and dignity. The community atmosphere at Naropa is an important part of the academic experience, and relationships between faculty members and students form a vital part of this community.

Naropa University strives to train its students to be active, effective people through the development of wisdom, compassion, and intellectual ability. Students at Naropa get a "contemplative education," which takes into account the essences of contemplative traditions from around the globe and strives to introduce its practitioners to a lifestyle of focusing on the present moment. Under the guidance of this contemplative education, students learn the differences between intellect and wisdom, as well as how to combine them. They are also introduced to the value of working altruistically, thinking less of the self and more of others. A private, nonsectarian, accredited liberal arts university, Naropa offers a four-year undergraduate degree in a variety of majors, all in a unique atmosphere. The undergraduate program is administered by Naropa College. A BFA in performance is also available. MA, MDiv, MFA, and MLA degrees are offered through Naropa University. Naropa has been accredited by the North Central Association of Colleges and Schools since 1986.

STUDENT BODY

Though Naropa students cover a wide spectrum of personalities, most have a vibrant curiosity, an adventurous spirit, a creative way of thinking, a lively independence, an individual point of view, and a desire to improve the world. Naropa students come from 45 states and 19 countries, and represent a variety of life experiences, backgrounds, and ages. There are over 1,000 students on degree tracks at Naropa, and nearly 50 percent of these are undergraduates at Naropa College. The Student Union of Naropa (SUN), founded in 1989, gives students a voice. Through the program, students can work with faculty and administration to vocalize student concerns and to help create school policies that are most beneficial to students. SUN makes sure that the Naropa environment always protects dignity and self-expression. Students who want to get involved with organizations at Naropa have a wide selection from which to choose. Students participate in contemplative practice, diversity awareness, GBLT issues, sustainability and conservation, theatrical productions, dance and musical performances, outdoor activities, publications, literary readings, and coffeehouses.

ACADEMICS

The BA degree requires 120 semester credits for completion. Students begin their studies in the College Core Program. During their first two years, students select courses from the wide variety of offerings, including Writer's Craft, Chinese Energetics, Gender Savvy in Contemporary Religion, and Peace Studies: Conflict Resolution and Restorative Justice. These courses fulfill graduation requirements in eight subject areas: contemplative practices, world wisdom traditions, cultural and historical studies, artistic processes, leadership and service, healing arts, communication arts, and complex systems. While completing these courses, students are given tremendous support and individual advising.

When students have earned 45-60 credits, a major must be declared. Naropa College offers the following nine majors: contemplative psychology, early childhood education, environmental studies, music, interdisciplinary studies, religious studies, traditional eastern arts, visual arts, and writing and literature. Naropa also offers an ensemble-based BFA in performance. Students may enter the BFA in their freshman year or transfer later in their college career.

Contemplative psychology consists of two main parts, a contemplative core and an area of concentration. Areas of concentration include Buddhist and western psychology, expressive arts and well-being, psychology of health and healing, somatic psychology, and transpersonal and humanistic psychology.

The early childhood education major is inspired and influenced by the holistic and spiritual traditions of Montessori, Waldorf, and Shambhala. The state of Colorado grants graduates of this program its pre-approval and certification as pre-school teachers, private kindergarten teachers, and child care center directors.

Environmental studies majors apply ecocentric, holistic, and systems science perspectives to ecological and cultural systems. The concentrations from which students can select are anthropology, ecology, ecopsychology, horticulture, sustainable built environments, and American Indian studies.

The music major gives students the chance to study composition, improvisation, and performance in a supportive and creative atmosphere. Students learn from the leading innovators and musicians in their field and can focus on jazz, world music, recording, and technical skills.

Interdisciplinary studies majors do not have to declare a minor. This program gives students a chance to design a curriculum chosen on their own and selected from the College's major offerings. The result is a personally directed educational experience.

Religious studies focuses on the living traditions of major world religions, through nonsectarian, scholarly, and critical examination. Religions studied include Buddhism, Hinduism, Christianity, Judaism, Islam, Native American traditions, and the religions of East Asia.

Traditional eastern arts is a degree program unique to Naropa. It offers a program of training and study in the traditional arts of tai-chi chuan, aikido, and yoga, combined with sitting meditation.

Visual arts allows students to take a studio approach to their work. Students gain knowledge of the traditional and contemporary artistic techniques from many world cultures. Meditative disciplines, art history, and portfolio/gallery presentations are the main areas of emphasis.

The writing and literature program emphasizes the importance of creating original writing in tandem with study, contemplation, and astute criticism. Writing workshops, literature classes, and preparation for oral presentations of creative work are all components of the program. The Jack Kerouac School of Disembodied Poetics was founded in 1974 by the poets Allen Ginsberg and Anne Waldman, and many innovative writers come to the program as both teachers and visitors.

2130 Arapahoe Avenue
Boulder, CO 80302
Phone: 303-546-3572
Fax: 303-546-3583
Website: www.naropa.edu

Naropa also offers a BFA in performance that students enter into as freshmen or transfers. This degree features conservatory-style ensemble training in dance, theater, and voice. The BFA in performance integrates contemplative practices and traditional eastern arts, along with extensive community-based workshops, trainings, and teaching opportunities.

Besides the main degree programs, Naropa offers several special programs. The Naropa Summer Writing Program gathers students, poets, scholars, fiction writers, performance artists, activists, Buddhist teachers, musicians, printers, and small press publishers from around the world. Each summer for four weeks, students have the opportunity to interact with a selection of our most distinguished and provocative contemporary writers. The Summer Writing Program arose from the Jack Kerouac School of Disembodied Poetics. The School of Extended Studies hosts a wide variety of weekend workshops, short courses, evening lectures, and professional training programs year-round. Presenters have covered a wide spectrum of personalities, including Mickey Hart, Julia Butterfly Hill, and Thich Nhat Hahn. Students have many opportunities for learning and volunteering at Naropa University's Hedgerow Farm, a working 20-acre organic farm. The farm serves as both a center for education in sustainable living and a real-world, real-life laboratory for students interested in environmental studies.

Faculty members of Naropa College have backgrounds rich in professional, artistic, and academic experiences within their specific fields. They are dedicated to nurturing each student's unique insights and intelligence. Beyond Naropa's strong core faculty, scholars and artists from around the world are consistently attracted to the school's powerful vision and leadership. There are between 8 and 45 students in each class, and the student/teacher ratio is 13:1.

ADMISSIONS

Naropa College looks for students with a voracious appetite for learning and a desire for experiential education. Other elements the Admissions Committee evaluates are curiosity, engagement, and previous academic achievement. The statement of interest, interview, and recommendation letters are also important. Naropa recommends but does not require SAT or ACT scores. Undergraduates who have earned fewer than 45-60 semester credits apply to Naropa's College Core Program (the lower division) or the BFA in Performance. Those students who have earned at least 45 semester credits can apply directly to one of the nine upper-division majors. No more than 60 semester credits are accepted for transfer students. Students from other institutions also have the option of spending a semester or a year at Naropa as visiting students.

To apply to Naropa College, students must submit: a completed application form, a $35 application fee (waived for international students), a two to four-page statement of interest, two letters of recommendation, high school transcripts for all applicants with fewer than 30 semester college credits, and official transcripts for all previous college-level study. Some departments also request supplemental application materials, and often a telephone or on-campus interview will be required. Transfer students with more than 45-60 semester college credits should apply directly to the department of their desired major. Interested students are encouraged to schedule a visit. There is an open house each semester hosted by the Office of Admissions, and there are guided tours of campus all year, Monday through Friday. Although there is no stringent deadline for applications, the suggested deadline is February 15 for the fall semester and October 15 for the spring semester. After these suggested deadlines have passed, applications will be evaluated on a space-available basis. For further information, interested students should contact:

Admissions Office
Naropa College
2130 Arapahoe Avenue
Boulder, CO 80302-6697
Telephone: 303-546-3572 or 800-772-6951 (toll free)
Fax: 303-546-3583
E-mail: admissions@naropa.edu
World Wide Web: www.naropa.edu

CAMPUS LIFE

The Rocky Mountain foothills of Boulder, Colorado, are home to Naropa College. Boulder has a population of 100,000; Denver is just 25 miles to the southeast. In 1997, *Outdoor Magazine* rated Boulder as one of the top 10 places in the U.S. to live for health and recreation. The city offers a wide variety of theater, dance, and music companies and is home to the University of Colorado. Transportation in Boulder is varied and convenient: there are numerous bike paths, and public buses run frequently all day. The Arapahoe campus of Naropa is dotted with trees, and its spacious grounds include a performing arts center, a meditation hall, the Allen Ginsberg Library, a computer center, Naropa Gallery, a student lounge, a bookstore, and Naropa Café.

Students have even more learning opportunities outside of Naropa, through study abroad programs. These programs give students an in-depth introduction to the lifestyles and traditions of Sikkim, Bali, South India, and Prague. There are lectures, field trips, and classes, but students gain even more direct cultural experience through community gatherings and events. Interested degree-seeking students must have a minimum grade point average of 2.5. Undergraduate and graduate students from other colleges are also welcome to apply. Financial aid is available for Naropa students for these programs; students from other schools should investigate financial aid options from their own institutions. The public can also apply for these study abroad programs. For students who want the flexibility of online courses, Naropa has developed a distance education option. Naropa Online offers a selection of courses on the Internet, using the latest technologies. Threaded discussions, chat rooms, journals, e-mail, and collaborative workspaces give Naropa Online students plenty of opportunities to interact with faculty and other students.

COST AND AID

Undergraduate tuition for 2002–2003 is $15,300 ($510 per semester credit for a 30-credit load). There is also a $283 registration fee each semester, which includes a pass for bus transportation in the Boulder-Denver area. Students spend approximately $600 each year on books and an average of $3,150 each year for personal and miscellaneous expenses. There are limited options for student housing in the Sangha House residence hall, where rooms cost from $2,091 to $2,483 each semester (2002–2003), depending on size. Meal plans are also available. On average, off-campus room and board begins at $8,300 per year, and the Office of Student Affairs can help students find a housing situation that suits them.

NAZARETH COLLEGE OF ROCHESTER

GENERAL INFORMATION

Nazareth College is a coeducational, independent, comprehensive college offering career-related programs built upon a solid liberal arts foundation. The College is located in Pittsford, a Rochester suburb in western upstate New York. Since its founding in 1924, Nazareth has awarded more than 12,000 undergraduate and master's degrees. More than 1,900 of Nazareth's 3,200 students are undergraduates; they hail from 23 states and 8 foreign nations. The College's bucolic 150-acre campus features 23 buildings of contemporary and Gothic design. The center of student life is the Otto A. Shults Community Center, which houses an immense gymnasium, a 25-meter swimming pool, a newly expanded fitness center, a multi-faith religious center, the student union, and student personnel offices.

About 59 percent of the full-time student body lives on campus; Nazareth's 10 residence halls include both coed and single-sex options. Singles, doubles, suites and apartments are all available. The College opened two new apartment-style dormitories in 1998 and a third in the autumn of 2001. Foreign language majors have the option of rooming at La Maison Francaise. Nazareth also maintains Casa Hispana and Casa Italiana, as well as the German Cultural Center, which serve as social, academic, and cultural centers for students wishing to immerse themselves in Spanish, Italian, and German customs. Nazareth competes in Division III of the NCAAA. Its intercollegiate teams include those in men's and women's basketball, cross-country, golf, lacrosse, soccer, swimming and diving, tennis, and track and field. Women also have teams in field hockey and volleyball. Co-ed teams include equestrian and cheerleading

STUDENT BODY

Nazareth offers a wealth of co-curricular choices for students of all interests and backgrounds. Campus clubs and organizations include Amnesty International, Art Club, Association of Student Social Workers, Campus Ministry Council, Cultural Affairs/CALEB, Dance Team, Economics Club, Environmental Club, French Club, German Club, *Gleaner* (the student newspaper), Italian Club, Inter-ethnic Nazareth Coalition, Lambda Association, Math Club, Music Therapy Club, Nazareth Commuter Association, Nazareth Speech Hearing and Language Association, Physical Therapy Club, Pre-Med Club, Residence Hall Association, Science Club, *Sigilium* (yearbook), Spanish Club, Student Activities Council, Theatre League, *Verity* (literary magazine), WNAZ (radio station), and Wilderness Club. The students' political voice is heard through the Undergraduate Association.

ACADEMICS

Nazareth's core curriculum stresses the liberal arts and sciences; its goal is to improve students' analytical and critical thinking skills. The core also exposes undergraduates to interesting areas of study that they might not otherwise encounter on their own. Undergraduates must successfully complete at least 120 class hours and pass a comprehensive exam in their major field during their final year of undergraduate study. Students must fulfill all curriculum requirements of their major department and the College at large to earn an undergraduate degree from Nazareth.

Nazareth College offers the Bachelor of Arts, Bachelor of Music, and Bachelor of Science degrees in the following areas: accounting, American studies, anthropology, art (studio), art education, art history, biochemistry, biology, business administration, business education, chemistry, communication sciences and disorders (speech pathology), economics, English, environmental science, French, German, history, information technology, international studies, Italian, mathematics, music, music education, music theory, music therapy, nursing, philosophy, physical therapy, political science, psychology, religious studies, social science, social work, sociology, Spanish, and theatre arts.

Nazareth offers pre-professional programs in dentistry, law, medicine, and veterinary medicine. Students may combine education certification with their declared major to earn certification in elementary, middle, and special education (grades 1–9), or secondary education (grades 7–12). Nazareth offers certification in art, music, and speech and hearing for grades K–12. Most majors are also available as academic minors. Students may pursue interdisciplinary minors in gerontology, multicultural studies, and women's studies.

The Nazareth College faculty is composed of 132 full-time members and more than 85 part-time instructors. Teachers hold advanced degrees from more than 100 academic institutions around the world. More than 92 percent of all full-time instructors have earned a terminal degree in their area of expertise. Students enjoy small, intimate classes (average size, 25 students) made possible by the 13:1 student/faculty ratio.

4245 East Avenue
Rochester, NY 14618-3790
Phone: 585-389-2860
Fax: 585-389-2826
Website: www.naz.edu

ADMISSIONS

A complete application to Nazareth includes an application form, a letter of recommendation from a teacher or guidance counselor, an official transcript of high school academic achievement, official standardized test scores (SAT I or ACT), and a nonrefundable $40 application fee. Both early decision, early action, and regular decision applications are welcome. The deadline for early decision applications is November 15; applicants are notified starting December 15; the due date for enrollment deposit is January 15. Those applying for Early Action must have their application in by December 15; notification for early action applicants begins January 15; students have until May 1st to make a decision about attending Nazareth. Those applying for regular decision are encouraged to file before the final deadline of February 15. Regular admission applicants receive notification of the school's decision starting on February 15. Those admitted must make a final decision on whether they will attend Nazareth by May 1.

The school recommends that applicants complete a college-preparatory curriculum including English, mathematics, social studies, science, and foreign language. Academic achievement is the primary consideration in admissions decisions, but the Admissions Committee also considers special talent in drama, music, and art; it also looks at students' co-curricular activities. We also recommend a personal interview to familiarize yourself with the campus and all that it offers; an interview is not, however, a required part of the application. You can plan a visit or ask for more information by contacting:

Office of Admissions
Nazareth College
4245 East Avenue
Rochester, NY 14618
Telephone: 585-389-2860 or 800-462-3944
E-mail: admissions@naz.edu
World Wide Web: www.naz.edu

CAMPUS LIFE

The Nazareth campus is only a short walk from the center of Pittsford, a lovely village offering a selection of restaurants and specialty shops, as well as bike trails and boat rides along the Erie Canal. The campus is only seven miles from Rochester, a city of more than 300,000 (making it the third largest in New York State) that is rich in culture and entertainment. The city serves as world headquarters two major corporations, Eastman Kodak and Bausch and Lomb; a major Xerox facility is also located in Rochester. The city offers a broad array of museums, annual festivals, shopping malls, tourist attractions, professional sporting events, and ski resorts.

Students at Nazareth College have access to study abroad programs in France, Italy, Spain, and Germany, among many others. Rochester's sister city in France, Rennes, is home to the Universite de Haute-Bretagne and the Franco-American Institute, hosts of Nazareth's French program. The Universita degli Studi "G.D' Annunzio" in Pescara is Nazareth's partner in its Italian program. The Spanish program takes students to Valencia to study at the Institute of Spanish Studies; there they engage in intensive study of the Spanish language and culture. Nazareth also partners with the Studien Forum Berlin to accommodate students who wish to study in Germany. Nazareth College belongs to the Rochester Area College Consortium; other members include Rochester Institute of Technology, State University of New York at Geneseo, and the University of Rochester. The consortium allows Nazareth students to take one course per semester at a consortium member, class space permitting. Nazareth offers its students numerous chances to gain valuable work-related experience as part of their studies. Student teaching assignments, physical therapy clinicals, social work placements, and internships are just a few of the many opportunities available. The school offers internships associated with all majors.

COST AND AID

Estimated costs for the 2003–2004 academic year are $24,565 ($16,800 for tuition; $7,300 for room and board; $465 for college fees). Books, transportation, and personal expenses are not included in this estimate. Fees may change at any time; for the most current information, contact the Admissions Office.

NEW COLLEGE OF FLORIDA

GENERAL INFORMATION

New College began as a small, very distinctive private college. It quickly achieved national prominence for its academic innovations and excellence. Eleven years after opening, the college affiliated with the University of South Florida, gaining greater resources without sacrificing its unique character. Today, New College enjoys both state and, in the manner of an independent college, substantial private funding. Some 30 years ago, a small group of citizens in Sarasota, Florida, found themselves in a position to create a college that could address the dissatisfaction they felt with American higher education-dissatisfaction with putting bright students to trivial tasks, with the gulf between teacher and student, and with a collegiate culture that tolerated amateur academics while promoting professional sports. From the group's discussions came four principles, principles that, if put into practice, would change the way an undergraduate education happens. The principles became part of New College, and they continue to guide students and professors at New College today. Each Student is responsible for his or her own education. New College students take responsibility for learning, entering into an academic contract each semester with a professor that defines the courses, tutorials, and projects to be undertaken and the criteria for success. The best education demands a joint search for learning by exciting teachers and able students. In this context, professors serve as facilitators and mentors, not just purveyors of information. Students' progress should be based on demonstrated competence and real mastery rather than on the accumulation of grades and credits. Professors write narrative evaluations of students' work. Students comment: "You find yourself competing with yourself, not with other students. I don't just get a score, but an analysis of my answers." Students should have from the outset opportunities to explore in depth areas of interest to them. Tutorials, seminars, independent studies, laboratories, student research and travel grants, community service, and study abroad lead to knowledge and mastery.

STUDENT BODY

Just as students design their academic programs with faculty, they design their social world with other students. Activities are largely student-initiated and include theatrical performances, publications, service organizations and religious groups, film series, and more. The student government provides student representation not only in the student-life arena, but in academic policy making as well. Voting student representatives participate in faculty meetings and academic division meetings, and serve on various faculty standing committees. Student government has authority over funding for recreation, social events, and student organizations. Athletic facilities include basketball, racquetball, and tennis courts; a multi-purpose field; a running path; a volleyball pit; a 25-meter swimming pool; and a fitness center. Nautilus equipment and free aerobics, yoga, and dance classes are available through the fitness center. Students can use student-owned equipment for canoeing, sailing, and SCUBA diving.

ACADEMICS

The curriculum is based on the academic contract, enabling students, in close consultation with faculty, to develop programs of seminars, tutorials, independent research, and off-campus experiences. In January, students undertake independent study projects, which they design and complete under faculty sponsorship. New College does not give grades. Students receive detailed narrative evaluations of their work. To graduate, students satisfactorily complete seven contracts (one per semester), three independent study projects (one per year), a senior thesis, and an oral baccalaureate exam.

At New College, students choose from more than 20 undergraduate majors in the liberal arts and sciences: anthropology, art history, biology, chemistry, classics, economics, English and American literature, environmental studies, fine arts, French language and literature, German language and literature, history, humanities, mathematics, medieval and renaissance studies, music, natural sciences, philosophy, physics, political science, psychology, public policy, religion, Russian language and literature, social sciences, sociology, Spanish language and literature, theater, and urban studies. Theater is available only in conjunction with another major. Students also develop special topic and interdisciplinary majors. New College awards a Bachelor of Arts degree and provides an excellent foundation for post-baccalaureate study in business, law, and medicine.

Ninety-six percent of the faculty hold the PhD; most publish or show their work frequently. All are at New College full-time. Professors do lecture, but learning at New College never ends with just listening. A New College professor is a mentor whose goal is to help you gain independent mastery, so that you can pose the questions, gather the data, and evaluate answers on your own. The 11:1 student/faculty ratio is a key factor in the College's individualized approach to learning.

5700 North Tamiami Trail
Sarasota, FL 34243-2197
Phone: 941-359-4269
Fax: 941-359-4435
Website: www.ncf.edu

ADMISSIONS

New College seeks students with outstanding academic aptitude and a serious interest in disciplined inquiry, students for whom intense study with faculty in seminars and tutorials will have rich personal meaning. New College is among the most selective colleges in the nation. An applicant's high school program must include 4 years of English, 3 years of math, 3 years of natural sciences, 3 years of social sciences, 2 years of the same foreign language, and 4 additional academic electives. All applicants must submit SAT I or ACT scores, nonrefundable $20 application fee, official transcript(s), a teacher recommendation, and a counselor recommendation. The New College Application requires two essays.

Applications for fall semester are reviewed on a rolling basis, from September through May 1. The class will close before May 1 if enrollment goals have been met. All applicants may apply for fall semester enrollment; only transfer students may apply for spring semester enrollment. If fall enrollment exceeds projections, the College reserves the right to cancel the spring transfer enrollment cycle.

CAMPUS LIFE

New College is located on Sarasota Bay in Sarasota, Florida, 55 miles south of Tampa. Attracting visitors and new residents from throughout the world, Sarasota has some of America's most beautiful free public beaches; professionally-led symphonic, opera, choral, and ballet companies; and three professional theaters (one, the Asolo, is adjacent to campus). Sarasota also attracts contemporary artists. The city has more than 30 art galleries. Several New College fine arts majors have had their careers launched by Sarasota-based galleries. Next door to our bayfront campus is the Ringling Museum of Art, recognized internationally for its collection of Baroque art. Marie Selby Botanical Gardens and Mote Marine Laboratory are important environmental research institutions, where students often conduct senior thesis research. New College is in a residential neighborhood near the airport, 15 minutes from the beach and 10 minutes from downtown Sarasota.

As a New College student, you can expand your analytical skills, broaden your cultural horizons, and test career interests through off-campus study and travel, including course work at other colleges and universities, internships, apprenticeships, field work, and independent research. Because off-campus study can make a major contribution to your education, New College actively encourages such experiences. The academic contract allows you to include in your academic program not only classes elsewhere, but nonclassroom activities such as archaeological field work or a legislative internship. Programs identified as being particularly well-suited and cost-effective for New College students include: The School for International Training, USF International Exchange Program; Florida State University Study Centers in London and Florence; Educational Programs Abroad; Independent Study Semesters; Budapest Semester in Mathematics; and The Capital Experience. At New College, you can also be off campus while on campus. Opportunities exist for field studies as a component of your contract. Some examples include conducting research at Myakka State Park or Mote Marine Laboratory; acting as curator for new displays at Selby Botanical Gardens, and participating in land-use planning at the Sarasota County Department of Planning.

COST AND AID

For the 2000–2001 academic year, in-state tuition and fees are $2,663, and out-of-state tuition and fees are $11,464. Room and board is $4,977. (Tuition and fees are determined by the Florida legislature around August 1.)

NEW YORK SCHOOL OF INTERIOR DESIGN

GENERAL INFORMATION

The New York School of Interior Design (NYSID) is a coeducational, independent, nonprofit school accredited by the National Association of Schools of Art and Design. Architect Sherrill Whiton founded the School in 1916, and it was chartered by the Board of Regents of the University of the State of New York in 1924. Since its establishment, the School has been fully dedicated to the study of interior design and has significantly contributed to the growth and advancement of the interior design field. Roughly 700 students are enrolled in the School. NYSID continually modifies its curriculum in an effort to keep abreast of new developments in the interior design field. In addition to learning about design basics such as the appropriate colors, textiles, and other materials associated with specific eras of residential interior design, undergraduates also learn how to design restaurants, hospitals, and offices with barrier-free access. Whether learning the value of preserving historic design elements or studying state-of-the-art computer-aided design programs, NYSID undergraduates are taught a wide variety of skills and methods by instructors who are active in the design field.

The New York area's antique shops, art galleries, design studios, museums, and showrooms are stimulating features of the campus environment. The school possesses a cosmopolitan air, not only because of its prime location, but also because it draws undergraduates from all regions of the country and overseas. About 10 percent of undergraduates at the School come from outside the United States. Furthermore, many undergraduates transfer from other schools in an effort to build a more specialized educational background. Because of its elite faculty and impeccable reputation, the School maintains a strong, active bond with the interior design world. This creates opportunities for undergraduates to form business relationships that establish career prospects in the design field upon completion of the NYSID degree program. Sherrill Whiton, founder of the New York School of Interior Design, included the following in the school's mission statement: "The value in studying the decorative arts is not limited to its contribution toward creative effort or to the development of the imagination. A greater benefit is the cultural information that is acquired in the process. The roots of these arts entwine themselves around nearly all branches of human thought and activity, and an understanding of them will aid greatly in the development of one's ability to analyze, reason, and judge human affairs." In addition to three interior design major programs, NYSID also has an interior design post-professional Master of Fine Arts degree.

STUDENT BODY

The school has an active undergraduate branch of the American Society of Interior Designers (ASID). Over the course of the school year, ASID coordinates a variety of events such as workshops, lectures, and tours, allowing students the opportunity to view the inner workings of the interior design field.

ACADEMICS

A single-major institution, the New York School of Interior Design is dedicated to providing undergraduates with a broad interior design education. The meticulously structured curriculum is frequently assessed and updated by design industry professionals. The academic programs offered make up an integrated course of study covering all aspects of interior design, including architecture, furniture, history of art, interiors, communication and technical skills, methods and materials, philosophy, theory, professional design techniques, and problem-solving measures. Undergraduates may pursue three interior design programs at New York School of Interior Design: a four-year Bachelor of Fine Arts degree accredited by the Foundation for Interior Design Education Research, a two-year Associate of Applied Science degree, and a nondegree 24-credit Basic Interior Design certificate program. The Basic Interior Design Program is a 24-credit sequence of foundation classes in which all undergraduates enroll. This required curriculum provides a general, professional, and cultural framework to the interior design industry. Although completion of the Basic Interior Design program is the ultimate goal for some undergraduates, the majority of students use the program as a springboard for advancing to the degree programs.

107 East 70th Street
New York, NY 10021
Phone: 212-472-1500
Fax: 212-472-1867
Website: www.nysid.edu

The AAS degree program offers the minimum educational essentials needed to become a New York State certified interior designer. The 66-credit program consists of design, liberal arts, and professional courses. The BFA degree is a 132-credit program that, when coupled with practical experience, prepares the graduate to sit for interior design certification qualifying exams in many states and to gain membership in local and national professional organizations. Studies concentrate on the development of a wide range of technical skills, creative problem-solving, and conceptual analysis, as well as on significant cultural developments. In addition to a selection of design courses, undergraduates must take liberal arts classes in architectural and art history. Program scheduling is flexible and allows undergraduates to take day, evening, and weekend classes on a part-time basis at any point in their education. The School also provides students with job placement assistance. The job placement program allows students to experience a broad range of employment opportunities representing the multitude of career options available in the interior design industry.

The School's curriculum is supported by an outstanding and committed 80-member faculty. Besides teaching, instructors maintain successful professional careers in appraising, architecture, decorative arts, fine arts, furniture and fabric design, history, interior design, law, lighting design, and psychology.

ADMISSIONS

All prospective students are required to file an application, an official high school transcript, SAT I or ACT scores, and two recommendation letters. Students seeking admission to degree programs are required to submit a portfolio as specified in the catalog. Transfer students are required to supply college transcripts. Applicants from outside the United States should contact the School's International Student Adviser for application assistance. The School makes admission decisions on a rolling basis. The Admission Committee notifies applicants of its decision by mail shortly after the receipt of all necessary documents and the fulfillment of visual requirements. Inquiries and applications should be directed to:

Director of Admissions
New York School of Interior Design
170 East 70th Street
New York, NY 10021-5110
Telephone: 212-472-1500 ext. 204 or 800-336-9743 (toll free)
Fax: 212-472-1867
E-mail: admissions@nysid.edu
World Wide Web: www.nysid.edu

CAMPUS LIFE

The New York School of Interior Design is situated on Manhattan's Upper East Side, in close proximity to numerous well-known interior design studios. Also nearby are an abundance of the world's most renowned galleries, museums, and showrooms; most are within walking distance. The city is justly famous for its architecture, cultural activities, historic areas, and the cosmopolitan urban lifestyle it offers. The school is easily accessible by bus, car, subway, and train.

COST AND AID

Tuition for the 2002–2003 school year is $560 per credit, with an added $75 registration/technology fee per semester. There are added costs for textbooks and other supplies. Standard full-time expenses for the freshman year (excepting room and board, which the School does not offer, and incidental expenses) are as follows: tuition, $17,920 (16 credits each semester); registration fees, $150; and textbooks and supplies, $1,000.

NEW YORK UNIVERSITY

GENERAL INFORMATION

Located in Greenwich Village, New York University (NYU) is unlike any other U.S. institution of higher education. The energy and resources of New York City serve as an extension of our campus, providing unique opportunities for research, internships, and job placement. On campus, NYU's intellectual climate is fostered by a faculty of world-famous scholars, researchers, and artists, among them Nobel laureates and Pulitzer Prize winners. Faculty teach both undergraduate and graduate courses, and students have the opportunity to work on individual projects with these outstanding professors. NYU draws exceptional students from every state and more than 120 countries. They enroll in one of seven schools and choose from 2,500 courses in 160 majors.

STUDENT BODY

The traditions of Campus Life—more than 250 student-run clubs, 22 fraternities and sororities, athletics, and other activities—are very much a part of the University. Students have the opportunity to write for the student newspaper and to work with NYU's own radio station, WNYU. The Center for Music Performance encourages students to join one of NYU's many choral or instrumental ensembles. Every year, hundreds of NYU students devote their time and energy to community service and choose from hundreds of volunteer organizations through the NYU Community Service Center. Student services include the University Health Center; the Office of African American, Latino, and Asian American Student Services; the Office of Student Activities; and the Henry and Lucy Moses Center for Students with Disabilities.

ACADEMICS

Seven of the University's 14 schools are devoted to undergraduate education. Each school has its own distinctive character and small-college atmosphere. The College of Arts and Science offers an extensive curriculum in liberal arts and science, including pre-professional programs in law, medicine, and dentistry. The Leonard N. Stern School of Business ranks among the top 10 nationally, and it combines a liberal arts core with an outstanding business curriculum. The School of Education is focused on the human-service professions, including education, health, nursing, communications, and the arts. The Tisch School of the Arts, for the media and performing arts, combines a liberal arts education with conservatory training. The Gallatin School of Individualized Study allows highly motivated students to design their own curriculum and includes an extensive internship program. The Shirley M. Ehrenkranz School of Social Work combines a liberal arts education with a firm grounding in social work, including on-site fieldwork. The School of Continuing and Professional Studies offers four-year degree programs in hotel and tourism management, communication technologies, and sports management and leisure studies and a two-year general studies program leading to an associate's degree. NYU offers a superior undergraduate curriculum, taught by some of the country's leading intellectuals. NYU's intensely intellectual climate is fostered by world-famous scholars and researchers who have received Nobel, Crafoord, and Pulitzer Prizes; MacArthur, Guggenheim, and Fulbright Fellowships; and Oscar and Emmy Awards. Faculty members teach both graduate and undergraduate courses, making it possible for undergraduate students to become directly involved in research projects with internationally known scholars.

The overall student/faculty ratio is 12:1, the average class size is 30 students, and many classes are seminars and small discussion groups. More 70 percent of the faculty live on the Washington Square campus, and a number of professors live in the residence halls, providing students and faculty members with an opportunity for informal interaction.

22 Washington Square North
New York, NY, 10011
Phone: 212-998-4500
Fax: 212-995-4902
Website: www.nyu.edu

ADMISSIONS

Admission is highly selective. The admission process involves a comprehensive review of one's academic background, standardized test scores (SAT I or ACT), activities, essays, and recommendations. Three SAT II tests are recommended, one of which should be Writing. Emphasis in the admission process is placed on academic preparation. Sound preparation should include 4 units of English with heavy emphasis on writing, 3–4 units of history/social studies, 2–3 units of foreign language, 3–4 units of mathematics, and 2–3 units of laboratory sciences. Special consideration is given to honors or advanced placement courses. Some majors require students to submit portfolios, creative materials, or to audition. Participation in meaningful school and community activities and evidence of maturity and character are important factors. Freshman and transfer students are admitted for the fall, spring°, or summer° semester. For fall entrance, the application deadline is November 15 (early decision freshman candidates), January 15 (freshmen), or April 1 (transfer students). For spring entrance, the application deadline is November 1 for both freshman and transfer students. The application deadline for the summer session is April 1. A campus tour or an appointment for an information session can be arranged by calling 212-998-4524 or online at www.nyu.edu/ugAdmissions/.

°*certain programs may not be available for spring and summer enrollment*

CAMPUS LIFE

All undergraduate study takes place at the University's Washington Square campus in the heart of Greenwich Village. One of the city's most creative and energetic communities, the Village is a historic neighborhood that has attracted generations of writers, musicians, artists, and intellectuals. Beyond the Village, New York City becomes an extension of NYU's campus. New York City is the integral backdrop to NYU's undergraduate experience. The very lifeblood of this urban university—its spirit of innovation, renewal, and excitement—is sustained by the vitality of the city that surrounds it. Rather than building walls to separate the campus from the community, NYU embraces the city as an essential element of academic life. Because NYU is located in New York City, a world center of finance, media, and the arts, internships and part-time jobs give students the opportunity to experience firsthand the rewards of a career in their field. The city offers students the best in theater, dance, music, film, libraries, museums, and galleries. Studying in New York City also gives students access to a variety of internships, part-time jobs, and research experiences that complement course work with practical experience. NYU undergraduates can be found presenting academic papers at annual undergraduate conferences; entering their student films and winning prizes at film festivals; working on scientific research projects in innovative laboratories; interning at Wall Street financial firms; and completing fieldwork in some of the world's best hospitals, schools, and human service agencies.

Undergraduates also take advantage of study abroad opportunities at NYU centers in Florence, London, Paris, Madrid, and Prague. In addition, many international exchange programs and summer abroad programs are available. After graduation, 80 percent of NYU students go on to post-baccalaureate work within three years. Of those who apply for admission to medical and dental schools, 80 percent—twice the national average—are accepted.

COST AND AID

For 2002–2003, average tuition and fees total $26,646. Room and board is $10,430.

NIAGARA UNIVERSITY

GENERAL INFORMATION

Founded in 1856 by the Vincentian fathers and brothers, Niagara University (NU) is a Catholic, comprehensive, co-educational, independent institution. Located minutes from Niagara Falls, Niagara University's suburban campus is set on 160 acres and is a blend of historic ivy-covered structures and elegant modern buildings. There are over 2,500 undergraduates and about 800 graduate students at Niagara. NU is comprised of four academic divisions: the College of Arts and Sciences, College of Education, College of Business Administration, and the College of Hospitality & Tourism Management.

While at NU, students have access to a range of important support services that help them develop academically and chose a major. In fact, incoming students who have not decided on a field of study may enroll in the Academic Exploration Program (AEP). In addition, all students are assigned a faculty advisor from their academic major or one of the counselors from the Academic Exploration Program. Select students have the opportunity to participate in the honors program, a special academic program designed to stimulate and challenge accomplished students. Students also have access to medical care at the Health Center, free academic tutoring through the Learning Center, and professional career counseling at the Career Development Office.

Students may earn university credit through Advanced Placement tests, College-Level Examination Program tests, and course work taken at other colleges and universities. Many of NU's academic programs allow students to earn course credit through internships, research projects, independent study programs, service learning projects, and cooperative education programs. Students may also participate in Army ROTC. NU students may choose to spend a semester or summer studying abroad. Niagara is a member of the Western New York Consortium of higher learning institutions, through which NU students can enroll in courses at other participating colleges and receive course credit at NU.

The Middle States Association of Colleges and Schools accredits Niagara University. The follow organizations accredit NU's academic programs: National Council for Accreditation of Teacher Education, the Association to Advance Collegiate Schools of Business (AASCB International), the Council on Social Work Education, and the American Chemical Society. The Commission for Programs in Hospitality Administration accredits the Hospitality & Tourism Management curriculum. NU's faculty is dedicated to teaching and takes an active interest in their students' academic and personal growth. With a student/faculty ratio of just 16:1 and an average class size of just 22, students have ample opportunity for personal interaction with their professors.

STUDENT BODY

NU has an active, diverse, and social campus culture, with over 70 student-operated clubs and organizations. Ranging from academic and cultural groups, to social and athletic clubs, NU has an activity to suit every taste. Niagara is a member of the NCAA Division I, competing in the Eastern College Athletic Conference and the Metro Atlantic Athletic Conference. NU competes in men's and women's basketball, cross-country, ice hockey, swimming and diving, tennis, and soccer, men's baseball and golf, and women's volleyball and softball. There is also an active intramural and recreational athletic program.

ACADEMICS

Students can pursue undergraduate degrees through the College of Arts and Sciences, College of Business Administration, College of Education, and the College of Hospitality & Tourism Management. For students who enter NU with undeclared major, the University offers the Academic Exploration Program to help them explore fields and hone their individual interests.

Through the College of Arts and Sciences, students can pursue a Bachelor of Arts in the following areas of study: chemistry, with concentration in chemistry or environmental studies; communications studies; English; French; history; international studies; life sciences; mathematics; philosophy; political science with concentration in political science or environmental studies; psychology; religious studies; social sciences; sociology; and Spanish.

NU also offers the Bachelor of Fine Arts degree in theatre studies and the Associate in Arts in liberal arts.

NU offers the Bachelor of Science in biochemistry; biology with concentration in biology, biotechnology, or environmental studies; chemistry with concentration in chemistry or environmental studies; computer and information sciences; criminology and criminal justice; mathematics; and social work.

NU also offers the Associate in Science degree in pre-engineering.

Through the College of Business Administration, students can pursue a Bachelor of Business Administration, accounting, or a Bachelor of Science degree in commerce, with concentrations in economics, general business, human resources, international business, management, marketing, or transportation and logistics. The school also confers the Associate in Applied Science in business.

The College of Education offers Bachelor's degree programs for the New York State initial certification in early childhood and childhood (birth–grade 6), childhood (grades 1–6), childhood and middle childhood (grades 1–9), adolescence (grades 7–12), special education & childhood (grades 1–6), and special education and adolescence (grades 7-12). Education majors must choose an academic concentration in English, mathematics, social studies, French, Spanish, biology, chemistry, or business. Education students who choose a concentration in business education can only pursue certification for grades 5–12. In addition to eligibility in New York State, NU education graduates automatically receive the Letter of Eligibility to teach in the Canadian province of Ontario.

Students in the College of Hospitality & Tourism Management may receive a Bachelor of Science in hotel & restaurant management with concentrations in hotel & restaurant planning and control and foodservice management, restaurant entrepreneurship; tourism and recreation management with concentrations in tourism marketing and recreation & sports management.

NU also offers several pre-professional programs in pre-medical; pre-dental; pre-legal; pre-veterinary; and Army-ROTC.

Bailo Hall, PO Box 2011
Niagara Falls, NY 14109
Phone: 716-286-8700
Fax: 716-286-8710
Website: www.niagara.edu

There are over 50 academic programs and majors at NU housed within the College of Arts & Science, College of Business Administration, College of Education, and College of Hospitality and Tourism Management. The University confers Bachelor of Arts, Bachelor of Science, Bachelor of Business Administration, Bachelor of Fine Arts, Associate in Arts, Associate in Science, Associate in Applied Science, Master of Arts, Master of Science, Master of Science in Education, and Master of Business Administration Degrees. The programs and majors offered are: academic exploration program, accounting, biochemistry, biotechnology, business, chemistry, commerce, communication studies, computer & information science, criminology & criminal justice, education (elementary, early childhood and childhood, childhood & middle, middle & adolescence, special education & childhood, and special education & adolescence), economics, English, environmental studies, foodservice management, general business, history, hotel & restaurant management, hotel & restaurant planning and control, human resources, international studies, international business, liberal arts, life sciences, logistics & transportation, management, marketing, mathematics, philosophy, political science, pre-engineering, psychology, religious studies, restaurant entrepreneurship, social sciences, social studies, social work, spanish, sports & recreation management, theater, tourism marketing, tourism & recreation management, pre-professional programs (Army ROTC, pre-dental, pre-legal, pre-medical, pre-veterinary).

The spirit of collaboration is alive at Niagara University. The University's academic program is characterized by the lively exchange of ideas between students and faculty, a resource as valuable to students as books or research. At NU, students and faculty work as a community, not as individual parts in an impersonal institution. NU's faculty is composed of diverse and accomplished individuals, joining the University from a variety of backgrounds. All professors share a dedication to teaching and students at NU enjoy a spirited and educational blend of teaching styles and attitudes.

ADMISSIONS

Niagara University encourages all men and women whose aptitude and demonstrated academic achievement in high school or college give evidence of their ability to successfully complete the various university programs to apply for admission. Niagara welcomes all students, regardless of race, sex, age, national origin, religious preference, status as a veteran, or physical disability.

To apply for admission, students must submit an official high school transcript and official scores from the SAT I or ACT. International students must submit scores from the TOEFL examination. NU also recommends that prospective students schedule an admissions interview. Transfer students may apply to enter any semester. The dean of each academic division evaluates transfer credit. Students who complete a strong high school curriculum in three years can apply for early admission. New York State residents who come from an economically and educationally disadvantaged background may apply through the Higher Educational Opportunity Program (HEOP).

CAMPUS LIFE

Niagara University's suburban campus is located just outside the city of Niagara Falls, within minutes of the scenic falls and the quaint village of Lewiston. The campus is about 20 minutes from Buffalo, New York, and 90 minutes from Toronto, Canada. The area boasts a wide variety of resources and attractions, including the famous Niagara Falls. In addition, the Canadian border and the vibrant cities of Toronto and Buffalo are easily accessible from NU.

The campus community is an ideal size, combining a strong community spirit with a friendly campus setting. This size provides a wide range of activities and events in the context of a close-knit, intimate environment. At NU, no one is a stranger, and students, faculty, and staff say "hello" to each other when passing by. There are five residence halls, both single-sex and coed, as well as a cluster of residence cottages and new student apartments, for on-campus students housing. Residence life at NU is a creative, social, and educational experience, with a wide range of programs and activities designed to help new students become a part of the NU's community. Student rooms have comfortable furniture, telephone hookups, cable television, and computers. A beautiful mix of architecture, NU's 147-year history is reflected in the school's ivy-covered residence buildings. Modern buildings such as the Castellani Art Museum, Dwyer Ice Complex, Bailo Hall, and Kiernan Center, are a symbol of the University's dynamic and exciting future.

NU students are encouraged to pursue off-campus study programs and learning opportunities during their undergraduate career. Among the options available through the University are Washington semester and a semester in Albany. In addition, students can earn course credit for internships in most majors and many academic areas support cooperative education programs. Students also have the option of studying at a university overseas or to cross register for courses at other U.S. colleges through the Western New York consortium. Many students volunteer off campus through the Niagara University Community Action Program or through the Learn and Serve Niagara program, which grants students academic credit for volunteer work.

COST AND AID

For the 2002–2003 academic year, tuition is $15,900 plus room and board charges of $7,300. Student fees total an additional $650.

OBERLIN COLLEGE

THE COLLEGE AT A GLANCE

Oberlin College is a liberal arts college with a wealth of resources and programs, the highest academic standards, and recognition as one of the handful of truly distinctive colleges in America. It is impossible to sum up Oberlin in a few paragraphs, since all the students here have their own unique experiences. Each student charts his or her own course from our wide array of offerings. But there are a few common themes to the Oberlin experience:

Oberlin is for thinkers. Ours is a genuinely intellectual community, where students explore ideas because they are inspired to learn, not simply to pass a test. Obies are independent and they are risk takers. They frequently undertake double majors or independent-study projects in close collaboration with faculty mentors.

Oberlin professors are simultaneously scholars and teachers. Like the professors at major research universities, they devote their entire careers to making important contributions to their disciplines through writing and research. Unlike the major research universities, however, Oberlin has no graduate students to distract professors from the task of teaching undergraduates. All faculty members, even the most renowned, can be found in the classroom, teaching everything from first-year courses to advances seminars. All keep regular and frequent office hours. All coordinate and suprvise independent study projects. All view the education of undergraduates as central to their calling.

Oberlin is socially involved. Oberlin introduced coeducation to America and was the first, and for many years the only, institution that made the education of African Americans and whites together central to its mission. This historical commitment to socially engaged learning and social and cultural diversity persists today. Fully 70 percent of our students participate in service projects during their college experience and many of these projects result in fascinating career directions for our graduates.

Oberlin is artistically alive. You may know of the fame of our music conservatory; it is world renowned for producing generations of stars of the international concert stage. The Conservatory, though small (total enrollment: 619 students), fosters an artistic environment that enriches our entire community. Oberlin enjoys a dazzling array of musical activities throughout the year. Of course great music is something you would expect at a school with one of the finest conservatories in the nation. Each year, Oberlin hosts more than 500 concerts, from classical to jazz, rock to funk, bluegrass to blues. These include numerous concerts and recitals by Conservatory students and faculty members, as well as appearances by world-renowned musicians. The Artist Recital Series brings some of the world's best classical musicians to Oberlin each year. Last year's Recital Series included the pianist Richard Goode, the American Brass Quintet, the Tokyo String Quartet, soprano Barbara Bonney, and cellist Janos Starker. The Cleveland Orchestra performs at Oberlin each year as part of the series. Other groups on campus host performances by a wide range of musical artists. Many of these concerts are free, and most others are moderately priced. Each year sees a new group of bands hit campus. Recent years' hot bands include BullFrog, Rufus Wainwright, and 8th Wonder. An established presence on campus is the Can Consortium, which plays its own unique style of steel drum music at special events. But Oberlin's artistic environment is not limited to music. We feature a superb art museum—one of the nation's best—and a nonstop program of performances in dance, theater, film, and performance arts. An average year at Oberlin features more than 200 film showings, two operas, and more than 25 theater and dance productions (that's about a movie a night and a theater or dance production every weekend of the school year for those of you counting).

There's also plenty to do at Oberlin if you are not interested in the Arts. In the past semester the College has welcomed American Indian activist, novelist, poet, and screenwriter Sherman Alexie; social activist Barbara Smith; Xicana activist, poet, and author Cherrie Moroga; and dozens of other speakers on topics from the mathematics of crystals to the racial divisions in America. There are more than 100 chartered student organizations at Oberlin, ranging from juggling to our student co-op association, community service groups, political organizations, radio station, newspaper, and more. It is rare to find a student at Oberlin who does not participate in one or more extracurricular activities. The Oberlin lifestyle is to participate on multiple fronts. Sampling is encouraged. Students sometimes commit to a single activity for all four years, but more often they experiment—sports at one time, politics at another, and a musical production at another. Opportunities for leadership abound. Extracurricular activities provide the valuable lessons that come through interaction with likeminded and not-so-likeminded people.

THE CONSERVATORY OF MUSIC AT A GLANCE

Since 1867 the Oberlin Conservatory of Music has been considered one of the nation's leading professional music schools. More than 75 distinguished faculty members teach 619 students in an atmosphere supportive of artistic and intellectual growth. Housed in a multimillion-dollar complex, the Conservatory's extensive facilities include more than 150 practice rooms, nearly all with Steinway pianos, a library of 95,000 scores and books and 33,500 sound recordings, concert and recital halls, and outstanding electronic and computer music facilities.

Oberlin enjoys a rich musical environment, with more than 400 concerts and recitals taking place yearly. In addition to performances by faculty and guest artists, there are numerous performances offered by student ensembles: The Oberlin Orchestra, Chamber Orchestra, Opera Theater, Wind Ensemble, Brass Ensembles, Early Music Ensembles, large and small jazz groups, Indian Music Ensemble, and Contemporary Music Ensembles.

Oberlin is distinguished from most other professional music schools in that it shares its campus with a superb college of arts and sciences. Although some students come to Oberlin to study music exclusively, others, concerned with the narrow educational scope of most professional music programs, find the special relationship between the College and the Conservatory very attractive. Conservatory students may take as much as 40 percent of their course work in the College of Arts and Sciences. Some, preferring an even stronger academic involvement, pursue both a Bachelor of Arts and a Bachelor of Music degree through the five-year double degree program.

STUDENTS

Students on Oberlin's campus are presented with a rich diversity of extracurricular options. There are almost 120 student clubs and organizations funded through the Student Union. Over 400 concerts and recitals are presented annually by students, along with almost 100 theater, musical theater, and opera performances. A large number of visiting artists perform at Oberlin, as do many lecturers and speakers. Oberlin also sponsors an excellent film series, and there are numerous campus parties, dorm and co-op picnics, and special events sponsored by the Student Union.

101 North Professor Street
Oberlin, OH 44074
Phone: 440-775-8411
Fax: 440-775-6905
Website: www.oberlin.edu

ACADEMICS

In addition to the traditional academic offerings listed above, Oberlin offers a winter term, in which students complete independent and often self-designed projects, either on or off campus. Projects include, but are not limited to, research projects, internships, reading projects, arts projects, and community service. Oberlin is also home to the Experimental College, a series of classes in a huge variety of traditional and nontraditional subjects. Experimental College classes are taught by all members of the Oberlin community, including students.

The College of Arts and Sciences and the Conservatory of Music are both on the same campus. The College offers a Bachelor of Arts; the Conservatory offers a Bachelor of Music and some Master of Music degrees as well. Oberlin also offers a unique five-year "Double Degree" program in which a student attends both the College and the Conservatory and graduates with both the BA and BMus degrees.

The College of Arts and Sciences has 263 full-time and 10 part-time faculty members. The Conservatory of Music has 82 full-time and 20 part-time faculty. More than 95 percent of Oberlin's faculty have earned doctoral or terminal degrees in their field. The student/faculty ratio is 12:1 in the College and 8:1 in the Conservatory.

CAMPUS LIFE

Oberlin College is located in the center of Oberlin, Ohio, a town of about 8,000 residents, about a 35-minute drive from Cleveland. Oberlin is an idyllic residential town, which is made lively and exciting by the presence of the College. Though there is a multitude of bicycles in Oberlin, everything a student needs is within walking distance of campus. The campus also provides weekend bus trips to Cleveland.

Oberlin offers an extensive study away program, including several programs sponsored by Oberlin, programs sponsored by the Great Lakes College Association, and a large variety of programs from other sources. Oberlin's Career services office helps students to find a variety of summer internships, and research opportunities can be found through the Career Services office and also through academic departments. Oberlin's Center for Service and Learning helps coordinate a multitude of community service opportunities.

COSTS

Oberlin meets the full evaluated need of all admitted students. In 2001-2002, approximately 66 percent of students received need-based aid. The average package was about $23,355, of which $18,000 or so was grant money. Oberlin requires financial aid applicants to complete both the FAFSA and the PROFILE.

Tuition for the 2001–2002 academic year is $26,580. Room and board fees total $6,560. The student activity fee is $170. Costs for the College of Arts and Sciences and the Conservatory of Music are the same.

ADMISSIONS

Admission to both the College of Arts and Sciences and the Conservatory of Music is highly selective. In the Arts and Sciences class entering in 2001, the middle 50 percent of enrolled students scored between 630 and 730 on the Verbal portion of the SAT I and between 610 and 700 on the Math section. The median unweighted GPA was 3.60 and the middle 50 percent had unweighted GPAs between 3.3 and 3.8 in rigorous high school curriculums.

The Conservatory seeks talented music students who have demonstrated records of achievement, potential for further growth and development, the ability to meet Oberlin's demanding standards, and the dedication required to become professional musicians. The most important factor in admission to the Conservatory is the performance audition, or in the case of certain programs, the compositions, tapes, and supporting materials submitted.

OGLETHORPE UNIVERSITY

GENERAL INFORMATION

Oglethorpe University gives you what virtually no other small, liberal arts college anywhere in the country can, an excellent academic program in tune with one of the nation's most exciting, dynamic, international cities, Atlanta. Our combination of academic excellence and metropolitan excitement connects you with the best students from more that 30 states and 30 countries. It also connects you with some of the best professors in the country, professors devoted to teaching in small class environments with bright and motivated students. But it's not just the location that makes Oglethorpe different. It's our approach. You won't get an "ivory tower" education here. Instead, you'll enjoy unparalleled opportunities for growth. Whatever your academic or career interests, you can take advantage of Oglethorpe-sponsored internships with leading business, political, broadcast, arts, and professional groups for real-world experience you can't get anywhere else. Oglethorpe does more than connect you with new ideas, it connects you with the world. As Oglethorpe University continues to grow, academically and materially, it is ever mindful of its distinguished heritage and will still remain, in the affectionate words of poet and alumnus Sidney Lanier, "a college of the heart."

STUDENT BODY

This is just a sampling of the many organizations available: Accounting Club, International Club, Student Government, Black Student Caucus, College Republicans and College Democrats, Environmentally Concerned Oglethorpe Students, International Club, Oglethorpe Academic Team, Oglethorpe Cycling Club, the Playmakers, University Singers and Stage Band, Young Professionals Club, fraternities and sororities. Oglethorpe is a member of the SCAC and NCAA Division III. Varsity sports for men and women are basketball, baseball (men only), cross country, golf, soccer, tennis, track, and volleyball (women only). Intramural sports are basketball, flag football, softball, tennis, and volleyball.

ACADEMICS

Academic opportunities are numerous and include pre-professional programs, an honors program, experiential educational programs, and an urban leadership program. Dual degree programs in Art with the Atlanta College of Art and in Engineering with Georgia Tech, Auburn University, the University of Southern California, and the University of Florida offer further options. Fresh Focus, a seminar for freshmen, allows students to interact and explore their academic and career interests while becoming familiar with resources on campus. Sophomore Choices, a six-week seminar offered to sophomores, assists students in choosing majors and careers which suit their interests, talents, and goals. It includes comprehensive individual self-assessment, opportunity to learn and practice techniques for gathering career information, resume writing, and a week-long "shadowing" experience in the workplace.

International exchange partnerships/study abroad programs offer students the opportunity to study abroad at a recognized, accredited university or through a program sponsored by an American college or university. Oglethorpe advisors acquaint students with programs at partner institutions and a wide variety of additional overseas study abroad programs. Currently, Oglethorpe has 10 partner institutions throughout Europe, Asia, Mexico and South America. Our sister institutions are located in:

Argentina: Universidad de Belgrano and Universidad del Salvador, both in Buenos Aires

France: Lycee J.A. Margueritte in Verdun and Universite Catholique de Lille

Germany: Universitat Dortmund

Japan: Seigakuin University in Tokyo

Mexico: Instituto Tecnologico y de Estudios Superiores de Occidente in Guadalajara Monaco: University of Southern Europe

Netherlands: Haagse Hogeschool

Russia: Moscow State Linguistic University of Russia

4484 Peachtree Road NE
Atlanta, GA 30319
Phone: 404-364-8307
Fax: 404-364-8500
Website: www.oglethorpe.edu

The Bachelor of Arts degree is offered in American studies, art, business administration and behavioral science, communications, economics, education, English, French, history, individually planned major, international studies, philosophy, politics, psychology, sociology, and Spanish.

The Bachelor of Science Degree is offered in accounting, biology, business administration/computer science, chemistry, economics, mathematics, and physics.

The Bachelor of Business Administration is offered in accounting and business administration.

The strength of our academic program lies in the strength of our faculty. Ninety-six percent hold the highest degree in their field. Many received their advanced degrees from prestigious graduate schools. And because of our greater Atlanta location, Oglethorpe draws from a rich pool of talented political, legal, arts, medical, and science leaders for associate faculty positions. New students are assigned a faculty advisor who assists in academic planning and other matters. One-on-one advising sessions provide for the development of close relationships between students and faculty. Through these ties, students and faculty are able to create lively and stimulating discussions both inside and outside the classroom.

ADMISSIONS

The Admission policy of Oglethorpe University is based on an individual selection process. Early application and timely deposits are the best way to secure a space in the incoming class. Deadlines: Early Action, December 1. Regular Decision, Applicants are accepted after February 1 on a "space-available" basis. Along with the application form and required essay, submit an official copy of your high school transcript, a reference from your counselor, principal, or a teacher, and official score reports from either the SAT or ACT. Additional letters of recommendation and student resumes are welcome.

CAMPUS LIFE

Atlanta is a magnet for some of the best minds in business, art, communications, health and education. As an Oglethorpe student, you can tap into the excitement, energy and drama of this major international city which captured the attention of the world as host city of the 1996 Olympic Games. This is the "new American City," a place where you can apply what you learn in class to the real world in order to make a life and make a living. A place where you can test out your growing leadership and intellectual skills in classes that are uniquely intertwined with the rhythm of the city. Here, your options are endless. Backed by a solid core curriculum, you could be in for the educational experience of a lifetime. It's no accident that two-thirds of all Oglethorpe University alumni stay in Atlanta after graduation. You can tap into this considerable network of successful graduates to enhance your college experience, as well as your career prospects.

"Atlanta is happening." More and more Fortune 500 companies are relocating their corporate headquarters here. The city is a beacon for accomplished arts and entertainment talent. With a robust economy and thriving commercial and artistic life, Atlanta gives Oglethorpe students a real-world experience in addition to rigorous academic work. Opportunities abound for exciting internships, including: IBM, Delta Airlines, Atlanta Botanical Gardens, The New York Times, CNN, Atlanta Braves, CDC, Federal Reserve Bank of Atlanta, Canadian Consulate, Carter Presidential Center, Yerkes Regional Primate Research Center, Southern Center for International Studies, and many more. There is an endless array of entertainment options, professional athletics, (baseball, football, basketball, hockey), concerts by artists well-known around the world, cultural centers, and recreational facilities, all within minutes of the campus. MARTA, the rapid rail transportation system, is within walking distance.

COST AND AID

Tuition: $17,500 per year

Room and board: $5,500 per year

Total comprehensive fees: $22,800 per year

OHIO NORTHERN UNIVERSITY

GENERAL INFORMATION

A dynamic educational experience awaits students at Ohio Northern University, whose four undergraduate colleges, liberal arts and professional programs, and College of Law offer a vast array of academic options. The University, which was founded in 1871, is associated with the United Methodist Church and sees its mission as promoting spiritual growth as well as academic achievement. With nearly 3,000 undergraduates, ONU draws students of many different academic pursuits. ONU undergraduates have numerous opportunities to explore a broad assortment of academic, physical, spiritual, and social activities. Life in the 10 on-campus residence halls plays an essential role in the complete ONU educational experience. Facilities, residence-based programs, and the professional staff who serve the halls all play an integral part in students' development. The residence halls are also important study centers. Students dine together in a large hall at the student union. Eight national fraternities and four national sororities make their home at Ohio Northern, as do 32 scholastic and service-based honor societies. ONU competes in the Ohio Athletic Conference. Intercollegiate teams include men's baseball, basketball, cross-country, football, golf, indoor and outdoor track, soccer, swimming and diving, tennis, and wrestling, as well as women's basketball, cross-country, fast-pitch softball, golf, indoor and outdoor track, soccer, swimming and diving, tennis, and volleyball.

STUDENT BODY

Self-governance in many areas is made possible by the Student Senate; this student-elected legislative body, which meets weekly, also seeks to promote student service and principled behavior within the University community. The Student Senate is the official representative of the Student Body as a whole in matters concerning the administration and various offices of ONU.

ACADEMICS

Students in the College of Arts and Sciences typically devote their first two years of study to a general education program. Students proceed to advanced level work in their majors during their final two undergraduate years. Students at Ohio Northern University may pursue the following degrees: Doctor of Pharmacy, Bachelor of Arts, Bachelor of Fine Arts, Bachelor of Music, and Bachelor of Science. Students may major in accounting, art (graphic design and studio arts), athletic training, biochemistry, biology, chemistry, civil engineering, communication arts (musical, theater, professional and organizational communication, public relations, telecommunications, and theater), computer engineering, computer science, criminal justice, early childhood education, electrical engineering, English creative writing, English language arts, English literature, English professional writing, environmental studies, French, health education, history, international business and economics, international studies, journalism, management, mathematics, mathematics/statistics, mechanical engineering, medical technology, medicinal chemistry, middle childhood education, molecular biology, music, music composition, music education, music performance, music with elective studies in business, pharmacy, philosophy, philosophy/religion, physical education, physics, political science, psychology, religion, social studies, sociology, Spanish, sport management, technology, and wellness.

ONU offers special programs in pre-dentistry, pre-law, pre-medicine, pre-physical therapy, pre-seminary, and pre-veterinary medicine. Those who successfully complete the pre-law program with a minimum GPA of 3.2 are guaranteed admission to the Petit College of Law. Students may opt for interdisciplinary degree programs in arts/engineering and arts/pharmacy. The University also offers programs in athletics coaching, athletics training, driver's education, and reading validation. The school offers teacher licensing programs at the early childhood, middle childhood, and adolescent levels in 32 different program areas.

To earn a Bachelor of Arts, Bachelor of Fine Arts, or Bachelor of Science degree, undergraduates must complete at least 182 quarter hours. Students may enroll in any of ONU's undergraduate colleges. Coursework must include required general education courses and completion of major requirements; to graduate, students must maintain a minimum 2.0 grade point average. To earn a Bachelor of Music Degree, students must complete at least 182 quarter hours and concentrate in either music performance or music education. All undergraduates must spend their last three quarters at ONU and earn at least 45 quarter hours with at least 90 quality points (with coursework focused primarily on the student's chosen major field) in order to earn a degree from the University. Students seeking the Bachelor of Science in medical technology must meet a different set of requirements.

Students in the College of Business Administration typically devote the first two years of study to completing general education requirements and to undertaking introductory courses in basic business principles and disciplines. To earn an undergraduate degree in business, students must complete at least 182 quarter hours. Coursework must include required general education courses and completion of major requirements; students must maintain a minimum 2.0 grade point average to graduate. All business undergraduates should undertake an internship program in either their third or fourth year of study.

Students in the College of Engineering may pursue degrees in civil engineering, computer engineering, electrical engineering, and mechanical engineering. All engineering students follow the same basic program during their freshman and sophomore years; this allows students to choose their intended field of concentration relatively late in their academic experiences. Engineers must maintain a GPA of at least 2.0 in all areas and in the subset of academic courses relating specifically to engineering, math, and science. All engineering students who maintain at least a 2.5 GPA may pursue an optional five-year co-op program. Students who maintain a minimum 2.5 GPA may also take up a minor in computer science and options in business administration and environmental studies.

525 South Main Street
Ada, OH 45810
Phone: 419-772-2260
Fax: 419-772-2313
Website: www.onu.edu

Students in the College of Pharmacy may undertake the six-year Doctor of Pharmacy program; students may apply for admission to the program while still in high school. Students in the program spend their first three years completing coursework in the physical sciences, humanities, professional areas, and social sciences. They then spend two years studying pharmacology through a curriculum that focuses on patient care and includes disease-based modules, body system modules, practice-based modules, and administrative modules. The final, experimental year places students in different clinical settings across the country. ONU also offers a nontraditional Doctor of Pharmacy program to pharmacists who hold the BS degree. Much of this program can be completed over the Internet. Students who study on campus have access to an excellent undergraduate research program. Dual majors in biochemistry and medicinal chemistry are available.

ONU maintains a faculty of 161 full-time and 58 part-time instructors, all of whom are employed exclusively to teach undergraduates. The professors' primary responsibility is to teach, although many pursue research as well; the University considers research an important component of effective, up-to-date teaching. Most faculty members reside within walking distance of the campus, and many participate in one or more co-curricular activities with students. ONU places special emphasis on the importance of close academic and personal advising. The student/faculty ratio is 13:1.

ADMISSIONS

Applicants should provide high school transcripts reflecting completion of a minimum of 16 units. Specific requirements vary by school. The College of Arts and Sciences requires 12 academic units: 4 in English, 2 in mathematics (algebra and geometry), and 6 in history, social studies, language, and/or natural science. For the College of Business Administration, the requirement is 13 academic units: 4 in English, 3 in mathematics (including algebra and geometry), and 6 in history, social studies, language, and/or natural sciences. For the College of Engineering, 10 academic units are required: 4 in English, 4 in mathematics (algebra I and II, geometry, and at least a half-unit in trigonometry or its equivalent), and 2 in science (1 in physics and preferably 1 in chemistry). The College of Pharmacy requires 11 academic units: 4 in English, 4 in mathematics (algebra I and II, geometry, and trigonometry or pre-calculus), and 3 in science (biology, chemistry, and physics). Applicants must submit standardized test scores (ACT or SAT I). The school recommends but does not require an interview.

CAMPUS LIFE

The Ohio Northern campus is set in the middle of the town of Ada, a friendly and peaceful community of 5,000. The interstates that pass through northwestern Ohio can be easily accessed from campus. The cities of Columbus, Dayton, and Toledo are all within reasonable driving distance. Students can thus enjoy the quiet hospitality of Ada and also take advantage of urban amenities whenever they wish.

Students in most majors have the option of studying abroad; many students plan such study experiences with the help of professors. Students in most majors may also pursue internships and field experiences. Pharmacy students must complete externships in retail and clinical venues. Students seeking a teaching license must complete at least one quarter of primary or secondary classroom teaching, supervised by practicing teachers. Students earn credit for all of these off-campus learning experiences.

COST AND AID

Tuition, room, and board for the 1999–2000 year totaled $25,680 for the Colleges of Arts and Sciences and Business Administration, $27,090 for the College of Engineering, and $28,260 for the College of Pharmacy. The average student spends $600 per year on books and fees.

OHIO WESLEYAN UNIVERSITY

GENERAL INFORMATION

An Ohio Wesleyan University education is distinguished by its unique combination of liberal arts study and pre-professional training. OWU is one of only five independent undergraduate schools in the nation whose graduates rank in the top 20 both in the number of PhDs earned and in the number of business leaders. The University, which was founded in 1842 by the United Methodist Church, is dedicated to instilling the service ethic in undergraduates, to wedding theory and practical applications, and to tackling those issues that will frame the major debates of the future. Approximately 1,850 men and women undergraduates attend OWU. The Student Body is drawn from 44 states and 52 countries; proportionally, OWU has the sixth highest international student population of schools in its class. The majority of students live on the lovely 200-acre campus. Residences include six large halls that feature special interest corridors, a variety of smaller special interest domiciles (such as the Tree House and the Peace and Justice House), and 11 fraternity houses (the school's five sorority houses are not residential).

Students may choose from a large selection of co-curricular activities. Service projects, discussion groups, and intramural competitions are organized by students for students. Students also publish an independent student newspaper, produce five major theater pieces and numerous smaller studio pieces each year, and stage concerts featuring OWU's seven large ensembles as well as other, smaller musical groups. Cultural and ethnic-interest groups are represented by such diverse organizations as the Student Union on Black Awareness and the Christian Fellowship. Other groups perform crisis intervention work, engage in local and national politics, and serve the needs of the school's many pre-professional students. Student life focuses on the $12 million Campus Center.

OWU has 21 varsity athletic teams:10 men's teams, 10 women's teams, and a coed sailing team. Several teams are nationally ranked in Division III of the NCAA: men's baseball, golf, lacrosse, soccer, swimming, and track; and women's soccer, whose team won its third national championship in 2001 (four members of the team were named to the Division III Championship All-Tournament Team). Men's soccer earned the national crown in 1998; men's basketball accomplished the same feat in 1986. In 2001, the women's basketball team reached the national semifinals, and coach Nan Carney-DeBord won the Russell Athletic/WBCA Division III Coach of the Year award. OWU's intramural programs enjoy wide support throughout the Student Body. Students will also find ample facilities for swimming, weight-training, and racquet sports in the contemporary Branch Rickey Physical Education Center. The surrounding area provides many opportunities for backpacking, boating, camping, golf, skiing, and swimming.

STUDENT BODY

The Student Body of OWU is deeply involved in all aspects of campus life. It is a matter of pride among students, alumni, faculty, and administrators that undergraduates play a major role within the entire University community. Major departments incorporate the contributions of student academic boards in planning coursework and requirements. The School president and other upper-level administrators meet frequently with the student Archway Committee to discuss issues of importance to the campus. Student organizations report to student-run oversight groups such as the Small Living Unit Board and the Interfraternity and Panhellenic councils. The school provides both the encouragement and the necessary resources for students to start new organizations to meet the needs and interests of any group. The level of student involvement and responsibility at OWU is typified by the student government. Students serve on a legislature, the WCSA (Wesleyan Council on Student Affairs), which helps set policy on campus. The WCSA, whose members include faculty and administrators as well as students, convene open meetings to discuss academic issues, residential life, the university judicial system, and the distribution of student activity fees.

OWU is home to over 85 student clubs and organizations; new groups form every year to meet the ever-changing needs of our students. Each organization is managed by its officers, committees, and treasurer; thus, each organization offers a variety of leadership opportunities. Students may serve as Residence Assistants and Small Living Unit Moderators. The campus is extremely active in community service, and the fraternity and sorority scene is lively, both socially and within the community. Those seeking co-curricular options will find all they could hope for at OWU. Students here take the mantle of leadership as a matter of course.

ACADEMICS

Ohio Wesleyan stresses the importance of acquiring a broad general education that fosters insight into our cultural and historical past. The curriculum also emphasizes the value of specialization through its major requirements. OWU does not teach students in a vacuum; material is presented in the context of ethics and values. The curriculum is designed to encourage independent thought through the development of logic, problem-solving skills, and communication. OWU ensures that students improve these skills through competency requirements in English composition and foreign language (the requirements can be met through coursework or through placement examination) and distribution requirements in the natural and social sciences, the humanities, and the arts. Nearly all majors require students to complete between 8 and 15 courses. The school encourages students to pursue double majors and minors. Students must complete 34 courses in order to graduate. Students can earn Advanced Placement both with and without credit. The University's four-year honors program designates select freshmen as Merit Scholars and allows them to work one-on-one with faculty advisors on original creative work, self-designed reading programs, and research. Independent study is encouraged for juniors and seniors. The school is home to chapters of more than 20 scholastic honor societies, including Phi Beta Kappa.

The Sagan National Colloquium exemplifies the goals of education at Ohio Wesleyan. Each year the colloquium focuses on a single issue of major societal importance. Recent topics have included "Decoding Gender: Rules, Roles, and Identity," and "The Silver Bullet: Can Technology Protect Liberty and Security at the Same Time?" The colloquium includes weekly guest lectures on the chosen subject as well as semester-long seminars. The program encourages discussion across the campus and invites students from all disciplines to contribute their unique perspectives while learning from their peers in other departments. The goal is not only to help students formulate an opinion on the topic but also to help them understand how and why they reached their opinion.

Admissions Office, 61 South Sandusky Street
Delaware, OH 43015
Phone: 740-368-3020
Fax: 740-368-3314
Website: web.owu.edu

Ohio Wesleyan confers the Bachelor of Arts degree in accounting, astronomy, biological sciences (botany, microbiology, and zoology), chemistry, computer science, economics (including accounting, international business, and management), education (elementary and secondary licensing in 17 areas), English literature and writing, environmental science, fine arts, French, geography, geology, German, history, humanities-classics, journalism and broadcast journalism, mathematics, music (applied or history/literature), neuroscience, philosophy, physical education, physics, politics and government, psychology, religion, sociology/anthropology, Spanish, and theater and dance. The school offers 15 interdisciplinary majors, including black world studies, East Asian studies, environmental studies, international studies, urban studies, and women's studies, as well as pre-law and pre-medicine. Students have the option to design majors in topical, period, or regional studies. The University awards two professional degrees: the Bachelor of Fine Arts in art history, arts education, pre-art therapy, and studio art; and the Bachelor of Music in music education, performance, and pre-music therapy. It also offers combined-degree programs (usually on a 3-2 schedule) in engineering, medical technologies, optometry, and physical therapy.

OWU has 126 full-time faculty numbers; the student/faculty ratio is approximately 13:1. All full-time faculty members have earned the terminal degree (e.g., the PhD) in their field of expertise. Instructors are dedicated to teaching and advising undergraduates; most also remain active and significant contributors to ongoing research in their fields. The faculty includes a number of practicing artists who create original works to be exhibited in campus galleries and theaters.

ADMISSIONS

Admission to OWU is competitive. The school considers each candidate on an individual basis. The applicant's academic record is the most important factor in admissions decisions; however, teacher and counselor recommendations, SAT I or ACT scores, and many other factors are also carefully considered. The school looks for evidence of creativity, community service, and leadership, all considered indicators that a candidate may contribute positively to the University community. The school requires a 16-course preparatory high school curriculum, recommending 4 units of English and 3 each of mathematics, social studies, science, and foreign language; variations of this program are considered. SAT II: Subject Tests may be used for advanced placement but are not required for admission. Students pursuing the BMus degree must audition; audition tapes are acceptable in lieu of a live audition.

OWU offers early action, early decision, and transfer admission options. The University strongly recommends but does not require campus interviews. OWU admitted 1,740 of the 2,227 applicants it reviewed in 2001. The University encourages students to apply as early as possible in the senior year of high school, particularly if they wish to be considered for financial aid. Admissions decisions are made on a rolling basis once all application materials (application, transcript, recommendations, and SAT I or ACT scores) are received; the first decisions are delivered after January 1. Students must notify the school of their intent by May 1. Those seeking early action and early decision must apply by December 1; the school responds to such applications within two weeks. Applications arriving after April 1 are considered on a space-available, rolling admission basis.

CAMPUS LIFE

Hometown Delaware (population 25,000) offers OWU students a quaint, quiet, small-town setting in which to pursue their studies. The city is only a half-hour north of the state capital, Columbus, America's sixteenth largest city. Columbus provides OWU undergraduates with numerous opportunities for internships, access to international research projects, and a wide range of cultural events, shopping centers, and restaurants. Founded in 1808, Delaware features post-Colonial architecture and design in many neighborhoods. The campus is conveniently located in town. Approximately 50 percent of the faculty live within walking distance of the University.

Most academic departments offer opportunities for advanced research, internships, and apprenticeships. The Great Lakes Colleges Association (GLCA), a respected consortium of 12 independent institutions, sponsors many of these opportunities. Available programs include the GLCA Arts Program in New York, the Philadelphia Urban Semester, and the Oak Ridge National Laboratory Science Semester. The University participates in other cooperative projects, including the Drew University United Nations Semester, the Newberry Library Program, and Wesleyan in Washington. The U.S. Department of Agriculture (USDA) conducts research locally at its Delaware laboratories, the Columbus Zoo, and other nearby sites.

The Ohio Wesleyan curriculum strengthens students' awareness of international cultures and issues. A large portion of the undergraduate population arrives from outside the United States. The school offers significant opportunities for study overseas. Formal study abroad programs are available in over 20 countries, including Ohio Wesleyan's affiliation program in Strasbourg, France, as well as programs in Africa, China, Colombia, England, India/Nepal, Japan, Russia, and Scotland. Students are encouraged to develop study abroad plans anywhere in the world that their curiosity leads them.

COST AND AID

The cost of attending OWU for the 2002–2003 academic year is $30,010. This amount includes tuition ($24,000), room ($3,530), and board ($3,480). Students must also pay a $200 technology fee. Books and personal expenses cost, on average, $1,100 per year. In addition, nominal fees are charged for some studio art courses, off-campus study, student teaching programs, and private music lessons for students who are not music majors.

OLD DOMINION UNIVERSITY

GENERAL INFORMATION

Old Dominion University is a young and vital institution leading Virginia into the twenty-first century by embracing new technology and providing the educational environment of the future. The university offers a wide range of programs of study in engineering, science, health sciences, business and public administration, education, and arts and letters. More than 65 undergraduate programs are available and nearly as many graduate programs. Physical therapy, coastal physical oceanography, and nuclear physics have gained national ranking. In the university's dynamic 70-year history, it has produced numerous award-winning faculty, Rhodes and Truman scholars, and a USA Today Academic All-American.

THE STUDENTS

Old Dominion University students come from all 50 states and more than 110 foreign countries. Nearly 80 percent of the student population is from Virginia, and about 1,400 are from foreign countries. The average incoming first-year student has achieved a 3.2 high school grade point average, ranks in the top 25 percent of his or her graduating class, and scored 1080 on the SAT. Transfer students account for nearly half of all new students and have greater than a 2.2 transfer grade point average while completing more than 25 credit hours at other institutions. The University also leads the nation in distance learning for adult, place-bound students via the nationally recognized program teletechnet, which beams live classes from campus to community colleges, places of business, and military installations throughout Virginia, the nation, and the world. Distance learners make up nearly a third of all students enrolled at Old Dominion University.

UNIVERSITY UNIQUENESS

Old Dominion University is the only doctoral institution to guarantee a co-op or internship to every undergraduate student. Many of these positions are paid, and students receive academic credit for all such experiences. This real-world experience provides an edge to Old Dominion graduates as they compete for jobs with graduates from other institutions. More than 60 percent of students who have held such positions while attending Old Dominion University have been offered full-time employment from their co-op or intern employer.

Old Dominion University is a nationally recognized research institution in the U.S. that prides itself on the caliber of its faculty. Students find their faculty accessible both in the classroom and for one-on-one consultations. Our faculty is on the leading edge of technology and real-world knowledge. This atmosphere creates a dynamic undergraduate environment where faculty members teach most classes, and students attain the most current education.

To attract the best and brightest, the University offers nearly $4.5 million in merit scholarships based on students' academic achievement in high school and community college. This includes the $16,000 Governor's Technology Scholarships awarded to deserving undergraduates pursuing technology disciplines, such as engineering and sciences.

The ultimate gateway to learning more about Old Dominion University is our "Learn more about ODU" page.

ACADEMIC CLIMATE

All classes are taught by faculty members and have an average size of 30 students. Students are challenged to write, make presentations, utilize technology, and formulate ideas in settings that will prepare them for their future career fields. The University boasts an Honors College where selected students attend classes with less than 20 students, and learn from the most respected faculty members. Students are encouraged to participate in outside-the-classroom learning experiences such as research, study abroad, and professional organizations. In an environment with a faculty to student ratio of 1:16, Old Dominion students gain valuable insight not available at most institutions.

As part of its commitment to technological education, Old Dominion provides each student with free e-mail and Internet access to facilitate learning and discovery. Beginning in January 2000 all of the residence halls will be wired for computer access. Currently the campus maintains computer labs with hundreds of computers for student use.

108 Rollins Hall, 5215 Hampton Boulevard
Norfolk, VA 23529-0050
Phone: 757-683-3685
Fax: 757-683-3255
Website: www.odu.edu

ACADEMICS

Old Dominion University has a number of programs our students enjoy.

For example, with the Career Advantage Program, all undergraduates are guaranteed a practical experience, or classroom experience working in a "real-world" setting. All interns receive academic credit toward their major and over 70 percent of the opportunities are paid.

Also, being a member of the Honors College means that you can enjoy several special benefits. Among them are that Honors College students receive an annual $500 scholarship ($250 each semester), and juniors and seniors may compete for $1,000 undergraduate research awards. Of course, you can learn more about our exciting majors and academic programs at our website, www.admissions.odu.edu.

Old Dominion University offers more than 65 undergraduate programs, and nearly that many graduate ones. Please see our complete listing of majors and programs at: www.odu.edu/ao/admissions/mp/majors_programs.html.

ADMISSIONS

Old Dominion is a selective institution, but we base our admit decisions on the total student—that's why we require at least two letters of recommendation, an activity resume, and an essay—not just on SAT and GPA alone.

CAMPUS LIFE

Old Dominion University is located in Norfolk, Virginia, the city *Money* magazine ranked as the best large city in the South. A few miles north of downtown Norfolk, the campus is less than an hour from historic Williamsburg, Yorktown, and Jamestown, and about 20 minutes from the Virginia Beach oceanfront. Norfolk affords tremendous opportunities for students to enjoy festivals, professional sports, world-class theater, and numerous business and industry employers for co-op, internships, and post-graduate employment. The local climate has been rated as one of the best in the nation by the National Weather Service, allowing for year-round outdoor activities. Washington, DC, and the Blue Ridge Mountains are only a few hours away. Located near the world's largest naval base, Old Dominion University maintains a close relationship with the military and offers excellent opportunities for Navy ROTC and Army ROTC students. The University has begun construction of the new University Village that will be the home of athletics, academics, and living and social activities for the campus in the near future. This will add to the world-class campus environment which features a newly renovated and nationally respected library, and new facilities including an oceanography and physics building, a performing arts center, a university center and student union, athletic fields and recreational facilities, and the recently opened distance learning center.

Some off-campus opportunities you will enjoy at Old Dominion University are:

- Guaranteed internships—called the Career Advantage Program and handled through our Career Management Center, Old Dominion guarantees an internship in your major *and* field of study.
- ODU students use Hampton Roads Transit public transportation system for free.
- Old Dominion is less than three miles from downtown Norfolk, so it's conveniently close to shopping, restaurants, and jobs. Also, Norfolk is the epicenter of the greater Hampton Roads region, and is close to the cities of Virginia Beach, Chesapeake, Portsmouth, Suffolk, Newport News, and Hampton.

To learn more about these or other programs offered at Old Dominion, please visit us on the Web at: www.admissions.odu.edu.

COST AND AID

Tuition rates are subject to change, so please visit our Rates, Fees, and Financial Aid page for up-to-date information.

OLIVET NAZARENE UNIVERSITY

THE UNIVERSITY AT A GLANCE

Founded in 1907, Olivet Nazarene University is a private, Christian, liberal arts university—a service of the Church of the Nazarene, theologically grounded in the Wesleyan tradition. The beautiful 200-acre, park-like campus is located in the historic village of Bourbonnais, Illinois—just 45 minutes from Chicago's loop. With the perfect blend of ivy-covered residence halls and leading-edge academic classrooms and facilities, Olivet stands tall as one of the Midwest's premier private universities.

We believe higher education should have a higher purpose. Here, students not only learn how to make a living; they learn how to live. Since Olivet's founding in 1907, more than 22,000 students have earned the bachelor's or master's degree. Whether their chosen field has been in medicine, business, education, theology, or a myriad of other professions, Olivet's alumni are making a difference in every corner of the globe.

With a student body of 3,300 (2,100 undergraduate) from 15 countries, representing more than 30 religious denominations, Olivet Nazarene University offers diversity within a climate of rigorous academics where professors and students alike are open about their faith.

For those students who are interested, Olivet offers numerous opportunities to travel or study abroad. From four weeks to an entire semester, students can choose from more than a dozen programs, including the Au Sable Institute for Environmental Science, the Russian Studies Program in Moscow, Eduventure Indonesia, the American Studies Program or the Summer Institute of Journalism (both in Washington, D.C.), the Los Angeles Film Studies Program, the International Business Institute in Finland, the Romanian Studies Program, studies at Tokyo Christian University, the Focus on the Family Institute in Colorado Springs, the Oxford Honours Programme, and the Middle East or China Studies Program.

Many students choose to spend their vacations on short-term, missions-oriented trips to various parts of the world. Recent trips have included Denver, San Francisco, Miami, New York City, Nicaragua, and Guyana and Zimbabwe in Africa.

Athletics thrive at Olivet Nazarene University, with more than 18 varsity men's and women's sports. Recently, Olivet was chosen from 13 Illinois colleges and universities as the new summer home of the NFL Chicago Bears, giving a rousing endorsement of the athletic facilities and playing fields.

Olivet's first-quality academic programs combine a foundation of liberal arts study with a variety of career-focused majors, minors, and concentrations. An emphasis on career preparation equips students for productive personal and professional lives of service to God and humanity.

Students have access to state-of-the-art technology that Olivet's impressive faculty of more than 100 men and women use to create programs of study that are well beyond typical university standards. The University's focus on integrating the best of both learning and faith encourages students to look beyond the facts in their disciplines to more critical life applications. Olivet students blend the liberal arts with professional preparation into what might be called "The Living Arts."

Olivet Nazarene University is accredited by The Higher Learning Commission of the North Central Association of Colleges and Schools (NCA), the Council on Social Work Education (CSWE), the American Dietetics Association (ADA), the International Assembly for Collegiate Business Education (IACBE), the Accreditation Board of Engineering & Technology (ABET), the National League for Nursing (NLN), the Commission on Collegiate Nursing Education (CCNE), the National Association of Schools of Music (NASM), and the National Council for Accreditation of Teacher Education (NCATE) (Candidate) and is approved by the Illinois State Board of Education–Teacher Training for baccalaureate and graduate degrees and the Board of Nursing Department of Professional Regulation of the State of Illinois.

STUDENTS

Student activities include The Olivet Nazarene University Associated Student Council, more than a dozen instrumental and choral ensembles, Spiritual Life Ministries, the Aurora yearbook, *The GlimmerGlass* student newspaper, Men's and Women's Residential Life, Social Committee, The Academy, Capitol Hill Gang, Computer Club, Christian Music Society (CMS), Diakonia (Social Work Club), Dialog: The Theology Club, Engineering Club, Fellowship of Christian Athletes (FCA), Green Room (Drama), International Club, Kappa Delta Pi (National Education Honor Society), Kappa Omicron Nu (Family and Consumer Sciences Honor Society), Kappa Sigma Chapter of Sigma Theta Tau (International Nursing Honor Society), Nursing Students in Action (NSA), Off-Campus Olivetians, Olivet Geological Society (OGS), Olivetians for Life, Phi Alpha Theta (History Club), Psi Chi (Psychology Club), Student Association of Family and Consumer Sciences (SAFCS), Sigma Tau Delta (English Honor Society), Student Education Association (SEA), and Students in Free Enterprise (SIFE).

ACADEMICS

Degrees are offered in accounting, art, art history, athletic training, biblical studies, biochemistry, biology, business administration, chemistry,* Christian education, church music, clinical laboratory science, commercial graphics, communication studies,* computer science, corporate communication, counseling, criminal justice, cross-cultural ministries, dietetics, digital production, drawing, early childhood education, earth and space science, economics and finance, elementary education, electrical engineering, engineering, English,* environmental science, exercise science, family and consumer sciences, fashion merchandising, film studies, finance, French, general studies, geochemistry, geoengineering, geology, graphics, Greek, history,* housing and environmental design, international business, journalism,* literature, management, marketing, mathematics,* music education, music performance, nursing, nutrition, painting, personnel psychology, philosophy and religion, photography, physical education,* physical science,* physics, political science, practical ministries, pre-dentistry, pre-law,

One University Avenue
Bourbonnais, IL 60914
Phone: 815-939-5203
Fax: 815-935-4998
Website: www.olivet.edu

pre-medicine, pre-optometry, pre-pharmacy, pre-physical therapy, pre-physician's assistant, pre-veterinary, psychology,* public policy, radio, religion, religious studies, romance languages, ROTC, secondary education, social justice, social science,* social work, sociology, Spanish,* sports management, systems programming, television/video production, theatre, writing, youth ministry, and zoology.

**Teaching major and minor available*

Olivet Nazarene University grants the Bachelor of Arts and the Bachelor of Science Degrees. Baccalaureate degrees offered by the University are awarded upon completion of the appropriate curriculum and upon recommendation of the faculty.

The Olivet Nazarene University School of Graduate and Adult Studies offers programs leading to master's degrees. Degrees offered include the Master of Arts, Master of Arts in Education, Master of Arts in Teaching, Master of Education, Master of Church Management, Master of Pastoral Counseling, Master of Business Management, and Master of Practical Ministries. Adult studies programs lead to bachelor's degree completion for those entering with 60 hours of college work or an associate's degree.

CAMPUS LIFE

Olivet Nazarene University offers all the small-town safety and comfort of a historic village, yet is only a short drive from one of the country's greatest cities—Chicago. Students choose between residence halls and apartment living, all nestled on campus. Campus dining is in the Ludwig Center, boasting a dynamic, newly remodeled dining hall; the Red Room for burgers, fries, and pizza; and Common Grounds, where you can sip a latte or cappuccino by the fire indoors, or outside on the porch in warmer weather.

Weekday and weekend events include many varsity NAIA athletic events, from football to soccer to tennis, campus plays and musicals, movie nights, Party with Jesus at the Warming House, Disco Late Skate, variety shows, Mr. ONU, Tiger Championship Wrestling, Karaoke Night, FallFest, recitals and concerts, bible studies and all-campus competitions, like Ollie's Follies and Gotcha!. Many students also participate in local and global volunteer efforts. Students attend Chapel Convocation twice weekly, hearing such keynote speakers as Supreme Court Justice Sandra Day O'Connor, popular author William Bennett, and the campus chaplain.

Academic facilities rival those of most midwestern private schools. With the new 56,700-square-foot Weber Center for Social Sciences and Education; the Larsen Fine Arts Center; Strickler Planetarium; Parrott Athletic Center; McHie Arena; the Reed Hall of Science; and the Benner Library with more than 400,000 books, microforms, periodicals, and audio-visual materials, Olivet maintains its commitment to academic resources.

Community life encourages individual spiritual, physical, and social growth. Every dorm room and apartment is wired with at least two network computer ports, linking in to Olivet's own fiber-optic network. Students use an all-campus phone system, which provides voicemail with security and efficiency.

COSTS

Olivet believes funding a student's education is a partnership between each family, Olivet, and the state and federal governments. Cost is below average for private colleges nationwide, and more than 90 percent of Olivet students receive financial aid. Numerous scholarships, grants, loans, and other financial aid help make an Olivet education affordable.

When choosing Olivet, you get not only a great education, but also a friendly, knowledgeable, and accessible staff of Financial Aid Professionals. They are happy to help in finding the best financial assistance for you and are committed to going above and beyond to make an Olivet education affordable to every young person.

The Olivet Nazarene University Leadership Scholarship for Freshmen provides a significant award for those students who qualify through an application and essay process.

Tuition for 2001–2002, based on 12-18 credit hours, is $13,464. Room and Board based on double occupancy and the 21-meals-per-week plan is $5,266.

ADMISSIONS

Students considering Olivet Nazarene University are encouraged to visit the campus to meet with admissions personnel, faculty, students, and financial aid representatives. While a personal interview is not required, the campus visit is essential in choosing a college.

Admission involves both academic achievement at the high school level and a commitment to a lifestyle consistent with the objectives and values of the University. Emphasis is placed on the whole person, as the student is expected to have concentrated on college preparatory program in high school. A student with a good background in English and literature, mathematics, and natural and social science should succeed at the college level.

Students are expected to have completed a minimum of 15 units of academic work for high school grades 9 though 12 with a grade average of C or better. The student should rank in the upper three-fourths of the graduating class. Some majors require specific prerequisites at the high school level.

Every student is required to complete and submit the application for admission, two character reference forms, the ACT transcript, and official high school transcripts before final admission to the University. Both ACT and SAT scores are accepted for scholarship eligibility, but the ACT is required for placement in some general education course work. Transfer students follow a similar procedure, plus an evaluation of prior course work. International students are required to submit TOEFL scores.

OTIS COLLEGE OF ART & DESIGN

GENERAL INFORMATION

Otis College of Art and Design, founded in 1918, offers an interdisciplinary education for artists and designers who will shape the future. Its programs embrace new technologies and emerging disciplines, uniting these practices with established strengths in fine arts, design, and fashion. Otis's reputation attracts students from 39 states and 26 countries, making it the most diverse private art college in the U.S. The College's diversity is its strength; it prepares students to imagine what lies ahead and benefits employers who know the value of creativity. Otis graduates shape our visual world, from museum and exhibition design to the Hollywood screen, from the clothes we wear to the toys with which our children play. Otis alumni are cultural and economic leaders, in high-level positions at companies such as Disney, Mattel, Paramount Pictures, Nike, Guess?, DKNY, Sony Pictures, the Los Angeles County Museum of Art, Industrial Light and Magic, and Warner Brothers. Among Otis alumni are costume designer Edith Head and artists John Baldessari, Philip Guston, Robert Irwin, Billy Al Bengston, and Alison Saar.

Otis began when Los Angeles Times founder and editor Harrison Gray Otis bequeathed his property in MacArthur Park to create an art institute. Today, Otis has three campuses and state-of-the-art facilities for its programs in fashion design, toy design, digital media, communication arts, environmental design, and fine arts. Also offered are graduate level programs in fine arts and writing. Otis's newest building, the Galef Center for Fine Arts, is an "art factory" in which students research painting, sculpture, photography, and new genres in light-filled loft spaces. It also houses two large museum-quality art galleries. Otis's 1,000 students earn degrees accredited by both WASC (Western Association of Schools and Colleges) and NASAD (National Association of Schools of Art and Design). The College also enrolls 1,000 weekend and evening students through its continuing education programs.

STUDENT BODY

Students in the Student Government Association (SGA) represent every program of study on campus. As an organization actively involved in promoting student life on campus, the SGA sponsors an array of lectures and events for the Student Body.

ACADEMICS

Otis reinforces creativity through integrated learning; students take advantage of a coordinated set of offerings and disciplines to gain deep training in each discipline. They graduate with cross-boundary thinking and the ability to formulate transdisciplinary solutions to problems that may not even exist at the time of their matriculation. In the foundation year, new students master an array of studio skills, including life drawing, form and space, color and design, drawing and composition. Liberal studies and art history courses are carefully designed to complement the studio curriculum. At the end of the year, having developed both a creative vocabulary and a grounding in liberal arts, students select a major.

Otis offers the BFA degree in six areas: communication arts, digital media, environmental design, toy design, fashion design, and fine arts. In the School of Design, students chose among four majors. Communication arts (graphic design and illustration) focuses on the connections between applied art and design concepts and current and emerging technologies. Students gain an essential understanding of drawing, painting, typography, narrative sequence, storytelling, visual literacy, and history. The digital media major includes several components: two-dimensional (image creation and manipulation, text as image, and typography), three-dimensional (character design and animation, props, vehicles, and virtual sets), motion graphics, interactive design, and web design. The environmental design program creates the spaces that people inhabit, both external and internal, through the exploration of architecture, landscape, interiors, and environmental graphics. The toy design major combines product design, marketing, and engineering. Each year focuses on a specific category such as plush, action figures, preschool, vehicles, dolls, and games.

In the School of Fashion Design, the year follows the professional seasons calendar, allowing students to work on three collections annually. In the final two years, students interact with professional designers through the mentor program. The School of Fine Arts offers three areas of concentration: painting, photography, and sculpture/new genres, encouraging students to discover their own artistic vision. Faculty members and visiting artists work with students in a cross-disciplinary approach, so that painters work with photographers, and video artists with sculptors.

There are two MFA programs in creative writing and fine arts which allow for advanced independent work. Writing students participate in critical practice seminars, and concentrate on poetry or fiction. Fine arts students focus on methodology and art making skills through critiques with their peers and resident and guest faculty members. In both graduate programs, the emphasis is on an interdisciplinary approach to developing artistic vision.

The faculty at the Otis College of Art and Design is composed of active artists and designers dedicated to using their expertise to foster the talents of rising artists and designers. At present, the faculty includes 32 full-time and 150 part-time members.

9045 Lincoln Boulevard
Los Angeles, CA 90045
Phone: 310-665-6820
Fax: 310-665-6821
Website: www.otis.edu

ADMISSIONS

To be considered for the BFA program, applicants must have completed (or be in the process of completing) high school or the equivalent. A strong academic record can have a significant impact on the admissions decision. Prospective students must submit the Otis Application for Admission along with a non-refundable application fee of $50. Apply online at www.otis.edu. Paper applications can be requested from the College's Admissions Office. Supporting documents may be sent separately. All applicants must submit high-school transcripts, with the exception of students with bachelor's degrees. Students who have previously attended college should have all post-secondary transcripts forwarded to the Admissions Office. Current high-school students must file SAT I or ACT scores. While letters of recommendation are not mandatory, they are encouraged.

All applicants must also submit an essay that discusses their decision to pursue art or design, as well as a portfolio consisting of 10-20 samples of original art. Observational drawing should comprise approximately 50 percent of a student's portfolio. The rest of the portfolio should highlight the applicant's interests and abilities; these works need not be in the student's intended major. Slides are preferred although electronic submissions or flat pieces will be considered. A committee reviews all applications and gives equal consideration to each section of the application. . Otis' priority deadline is February 15. Otis operates under a policy of rolling admissions. Otis College of Art and Design encourages all prospective students to visit the campus. To schedule a visit or to learn more about Otis, please contact:

Admissions Office
Otis College of Art and Design
9045 Lincoln Boulevard
Los Angeles, CA 90045-9785
Telephone: 310-665-6820 or 800-527-6847 (toll free)
E-mail: otisinfo@otis.edu
World Wide Web: www.otis.edu

CAMPUS LIFE

Otis's main five-acre campus is on Los Angeles' west side, in the heart of Southern California's most dynamic film, digital imagery, and toy design industries. The proximity of art museums, studios, and galleries allows students to experience some of the most significant fine art in the country. The School of Fashion Design is in the heart of downtown L.A.'s garment district. The third campus, in the beach community of El Segundo, houses individual studios for graduate fine arts majors.

Otis's Mobility Program provides juniors the opportunity to spend a semester studying at another art institution, in cooperation with the Association of Independent Colleges of Art and Design (AICAD). Participating colleges include premier AICAD art colleges in the United States, as well as selected colleges in Europe (such as Paris, Stockholm, and London) and Canada. The Registration Office can provide further information.

COST AND AID

During the 2003–2004 academic year, tuition and fees will total $23,368. Housing, living costs, and other expenditures vary according to personal circumstances; these costs generally range from $4,900 to $9,600 annually. The Office of Admissions maintains updated information on all costs.

PITZER COLLEGE

GENERAL INFORMATION

Pitzer is a distinctive liberal arts and sciences college founded in 1963 as the sixth member of The Claremont Colleges. Our emphasis on interdisciplinary learning, intercultural understanding and social responsibility distinguishes us from most other American colleges and universities. Interdisciplinary learning encourages you to explore how different academic fields intersect and draw on each other's wisdom and ideas; intercultural understanding enables you to see issues and events from cultural perspectives different from your own; and social responsibility shows you how to transform knowledge into action as you strive to make the world a better place to live for yourself and future generations.

What's more, Pitzer requires fewer general education courses than most other colleges, so you get to take more of the courses that appeal to your individual interests. You can also choose among a range of courses that connect classroom learning to real-world experience—whether it's working inside a labor union, assisting with a faculty member's research, advising a neighboring city about economic development, or helping underprivileged children prepare for a future that includes college. Such experiences help you grasp the deeper implications of your actions and how your education at Pitzer prepares you to make a difference in society.

Lastly, Pitzer offers an intimate academic and social community alongside access to the resources of a larger university through membership in The Claremont Colleges, and students are allowed to cross register at the other Claremont Colleges. This opportunity greatly enhances the range of courses available to students. The total enrollment of all the colleges is about 6,000 students.

STUDENT BODY

The spirit of involvement extends well beyond the classroom, and is the essence of a Pitzer education. Opportunities abound within the College to participate in more than 50 student organizations, intramural sports, community service programs, and social activities. Students participate in all College committees, and play a key part in the governance of the College.

Pitzer joins Pomona College to field NCAA Division III teams in baseball, basketball, cross-country, football, golf, soccer, softball, swimming and diving, tennis, track and field, volleyball, and water polo. In addition, there are numerous club sports to participate in, including cycling, lacrosse, badminton, fencing, and rugby.

ACADEMICS

To earn the Bachelor of Arts degree, students are required to complete 32 courses, about one-third of which are in the field of major. Students work with faculty advisors to organize a curriculum that meets the educational objectives of the College.

Pitzer co-sponsors a science program with Claremont McKenna and Scripps Colleges. The Keck Science Center has state-of-the-art laboratories for teaching and research and a large biological field station. In cooperation with The Claremont Graduate University, Pitzer provides 3-2 programs in business (MBA), mathematics, and public administration. Pitzer joins with Western University of Health Sciences in nearby Pomona to offer a seven-year program culminating in the BA and DO degrees. A 3-2 program in management engineering is offered in cooperation with universities throughout the U.S.

Pitzer grants the Bachelor of Arts degree in 41 fields of study. At Pitzer you may complete a major in the following fields:

Anthropology
Art
Asian American studies
Asian studies
Biology
Biology-chemistry
Black studies
Chemistry
Chicano studies
Classics
Dance
Economics
English and world literature
Environmental science
Environmental studies
European studies
French
Gender and feminist studies
History
Human biology
International and intercultural studies
Latin American and Caribbean Studies
Linguistics
Mathematical economics
Mathematics
Media studies
Music
Neuroscience
Organizational studies
Philosophy
Physics
Political economy
Political studies
Psychology
Religious studies
Science and management
Science, technology, and society
Sociology
Spanish
Theater
Third World studies

1050 North Mills Avenue
Claremont, CA 91711-6101
Phone: 909-621-8129
Fax: 909-621-8770
Website: www.pitzer.edu

PITZER

A Member of The Claremont Colleges

All courses are taught by faculty members; Pitzer does not utilize teaching assistants. Ninety-eight percent of the faculty hold their doctorate or terminal degree in a specialized area. The faculty/student ratio is 1:12. Faculty pride themselves in being accessible to students. At the same time many of them conduct research in their own academic area. Pitzer has been identified as one of 11 selective, residential, liberal arts and sciences colleges in the country that have best achieved a balance between teaching and research.

ADMISSIONS

Early Action: First-year applicants who have a strong academic record and rank Pitzer among their top two or three college choices are encouraged to apply for Early Action. This application deadline is December 1. Applicants are notified by January 1.

Regular Admission: First-year applicants seeking regular admission should have their admission applications submitted by January 15. Applicants are notified by April 1.

Pitzer has adopted a new admission policy for first-year students applying for admission for fall 2004, and continuing for a trial period of three years. Pitzer is adopting this policy to provide applicants with greater flexibility in presenting application materials that accurately reflect their diverse academic abilities and potentials.

First-year applicants are required to submit the following:

1) The Common Application
2) Pitzer's supplement to the Common Application
3) $50 application fee
4) High school transcript(s)
5) Transcripts of any college attended, if any
6) Standardized tests or alternatives:

Note: You are not required to submit any of the items mentioned below if your cumulative grade point average in high school is 3.5 or higher in academic subjects, or if you are in the top 10 percent of your graduating class.

You may choose one or more of the following options:

a) ACT (if it includes a writing section), or
b) SAT I, or
c) Two SAT II tests (one in writing and one in mathematics), or
d) Two or more Advanced Placement (AP) tests with scores of at least 4 (one must be the AP English or AP English language, and one must be in mathematics or a natural science), or
e) Two International Baccalaureate (IB) tests: one must be English 1A (higher level) and one must be the Mathematics Methods (Standard Level), or a higher level course in mathematics, or
f) One recent junior or senior year graded, analytical writing sample from a humanities or social science course, plus one recent graded exam from an advanced mathematics course (algebra II or above). The samples must include teachers' comments, grades, and the assignment.

Pitzer expects that students seeking admission would have selected a rigorous academic program in high school. Your senior year is very important and should include a variety of solid academic courses.

The recommended college preparatory program includes 4 years of English (including as many courses as possible which require students to write extensively), at least 3 years of social and behavioral sciences (including history), and 3 years each of the same foreign language, laboratory science, and mathematics.

Pitzer College adheres to the May 1 National Candidate's Reply Date Agreement.

CAMPUS LIFE

We are located in the city of Claremont (population 35,000) at the base of the San Gabriel Mountains, about 35 miles east of Los Angeles and 78 miles west of Palm Springs. Pitzer is a short distance from rock climbing at Joshua Tree National Park; the Getty, Norton Simon, and other L.A. County museums; skiing at Mt. Baldy and Big Bear; and the beaches of Southern California. Claremont's quaint village, a short walk from campus, has a wide variety of restaurants, galleries, and shops.

About 60 percent of our students participate in study abroad programs at more than 100 sites throughout the world. Pitzer administers its own language and culture programs in China, Ecuador, Italy (Parma and Modena), Nepal, Turkey, Venezuela, and Wales. The College also offers an innovative program in the neighboring city of Ontario, Canada. This program is modeled, in part, on the study sites abroad, and emphasizes community involvement. The program features homestays with local families, internships with a wide range of city and nongovernmental agencies, and a program center in the community that serves as a base for classes and community service projects.

COST AND AID

The cost of attending Pitzer for 2003–2004 is tuition, $26,646; room, $4,880; board, $2,916; and fees, $3,158. Books and personal expenses are estimated to be about $1,900. Travel expenses will vary. Costs are subject to change for 2004–2005.

POINT PARK COLLEGE

GENERAL INFORMATION

Point Park College is located in the center of downtown Pittsburgh, Pennsylvania, one of America's most dynamic cities. Once known primarily for its steel industry, Pittsburgh has emerged in the twenty-first century as a revitalized and thriving metropolis. Yet, despite the sweeping changes, Pittsburgh has managed to retain the charm and friendliness of a small town. Point Park College has participated actively in the city's renaissance. As such, we consider our city our campus. The campus has expanded from the partial use of one building to four buildings downtown and the Pittsburgh Playhouse of Point Park College in Oakland. Presently the College's buildings include the new Library Center, housing the Point Park College Library, the Business Library and the Downtown Branch of the Carnegie Library of Pittsburgh; Academic Hall, with classrooms, laboratories, a newsroom, television studio, computer center and administrative offices; Lawrence Hall, a 21-story building with dance studios, classrooms, student lounges, snack bar, recreational center, cafeteria, administrative offices and dormitory rooms; and Thayer Hall, home of the Point Park Children's School and additional dormitory rooms. The Playhouse of Point Park College is a multi-theatre complex, which serves as the educational arm for the College's Conservatory of Performing Arts Department. The Pittsburgh Playhouse offers outstanding dramatic, musical, children's theatre and dance productions to diverse audiences from throughout the region. Students who attend Point Park College can walk to such cultural attractions as the Pittsburgh Symphony, the Three Rivers Arts Festival, the Three Rivers Regatta, the Pittsburgh Ballet, the Pittsburgh Folk Festival, and the Pittsburgh Opera. Professional sports venues are also within a short walk of campus. Major League Baseball's Pittsburgh Pirates and the National Football League's Pittsburgh Steelers both play their home games just across the Allegheny River on the North Shore at PNC Park and Heinz Field respectively. The Penguins, Pittsburgh's National Hockey League franchise, play uptown at Mellon Arena, also within easy reach. Just across the river from the College is historic Station Square with its wide selection of boutiques, restaurants, and shops. Other local attractions include the Pittsburgh Zoo, the Duquesne and Monongahela Inclines, the Pittsburgh Aviary, and the Phipps Conservatory. Notable museums in the area include the Carnegie Museums of Art and Natural History, the Carnegie Science Center, the Andy Warhol Museum, and the Senator John Heinz Pittsburgh Regional History Center.

ACADEMICS

Conservatory of Performing Arts: Point Park College confers Bachelor of Arts and Bachelor of Fine Arts degrees in theatre and dance. Students accepted into the Conservatory program can expect a rigorous curriculum which includes hands-on performance experience at The Pittsburgh Playhouse, a three-theatre performing arts center owned and operated by Point Park College. Our high-caliber training ensures that our graduates are prepared to achieve professional excellence. Distinct among college and universities, Point Park's dance program offers equal concentrations in Classical Ballet, Modern and Jazz dance as well as a wide spectrum of classes designed to create the total artist. Each year, our dancers interact with guest artists of international stature. Guest have included: Claire Bataille and Ginger Farley of the Hubbard Street Dance Company; Maxine Sherman of the Martha Graham Dance Company; Patricia Wilde, former Artistic Director of the Pittsburgh Ballet Theatre; as well as Bebe Miller, Lar Lubovitch, Jennifer Muller, Edward Villella, Pattie Obey; and Tony Award winners Chita Rivera and Michael Rupert.

The Bachelor of Arts degree program with a major in dance consists of 125 credits, of which 63–64 credits are in dance. Students select one of the three dance 23–24-credit concentrations: ballet, jazz or modern. Students may pursue a double major, or one or more minors.

Those students who, in the judgment of the faculty, have the potential to succeed in professional dance or theatre may pursue the Bachelor of Fine Arts degree program after completion of the first year. Students who wish to be considered for a Bachelor of Fine Arts degree must make application to the faculty before February 1 of their sophomore year. In the case of transfer students, the application must be made by February 1 of their second term at Point Park College. All other students in the dance program qualify for the Bachelor of Arts program. For the BFA degree, the department requires 139 credits, of which 88 credits are in dance. A concentration of 36 credits in ballet, jazz or modern is included. Acceptance into the Bachelor of Fine Arts program is dependent on the requisite Quality Point Average (QPA) and the approval of the dance faculty.

The Point Park College dance program is a member of the National Association of Schools of Dance (NASD) and the American College Dance Festival Association (ACDFA). On seven separate occasions, our dancers earned the honor of performing at the National College Dance Festival at the Kennedy Center in Washington, DC.

The Bachelor of Arts degree program with a major in theatre arts consists of 130 credits, of which 66 credits are in the theatre arts. Students select one of the four theatre 38- or 39-credit concentrations: musical theatre, technical theatre/design, acting or stage management. By carefully choosing from the available elective courses and consulting with the appropriate department chair and/or academic advisors, students may pursue a double major, or one or more minors.

The College also offers those students who, in judgement of the faculty, have the potential to succeed in professional theatre may pursue the Bachelor of Fine Arts degree program after completion of the first year. For the BFA degree, the department requires 135 credits, of which 91–103 credits are in theatre arts. A concentration of 61–73 credits in acting, musical theatre, stage management, or technical theatre/design is included. Acceptance into the Bachelor of Fine Arts program is dependent on the requisite Quality Point Average (QPA) and the approval of the theatre arts faculty.

All programs feature opportunities for students to cross-select classes in dance, music and/or theatre—all taught by creative, experienced, working artists as well as internationally recognized master teachers, directors and choreographers.

The Department of Film and Electronics Arts will be an innovative department within the Conservatory of Performing Arts of Point Park University. Dedicated to a conservatory approach to training, the Department of Film and Electronic Arts will emphasize professional education and liberal arts, both in theory and in practice. Exploring the integration of media and the arts in our society and the impact of technology on our culture, the curriculum will be designed to provide practical, professional training while developing a sound foundation in the arts and humanities. Theory and aesthetics will be taught as an integral part of developing communication and production skills. The mission of the department will be to educate, train, and artistically equip students with the skills necessary to compete in the commercial media industry. The Department of Film and Electronic Arts will offer a four-year, 120-credit Bachelor of Arts degree in film and electronic arts with concentrations in cinematography, directing, editing and sound, producing and screenwriting.

School of Business: The curricula for all department majors reflect a contemporary view of business and technology combined with a solid liberal arts foundation. Bachelor of science degrees are offered in accounting, business management, information technology, sport, arts and entertainment management services, the management services capstone program, and the public administration program. Special courses highlighting new developments in various career fields are frequently offered to keep students abreast of changing technology and management techniques. In addition, students have many opportunities to participate in internships related to their field of study. This experience allows them to apply the management and problem-solving skills developed in the classroom to day-to-day situations occurring in business.

School of Arts and Sciences: The Mission of the Department of Education and Community Services is to prepare students to successfully enter teaching professions of early childhood, elementary, and secondary education. The Department's goal is to develop a quality, innovative, holistic, humanistic program in which students majoring in education can acquire knowledge of subject areas and specific pedagogical methodologies appropriate for teaching those subjects. The Department subscribes to the view that the effective teacher teaches the whole child in a humanistic way with special emphasis on the interconnections among all subjects as well as facts, skills and attitudes.

All education students are required to apply for admission to the teacher certification program after having completed 48-semester credit hours at the standards required by the Pennsylvania Department of Education for teacher certification as well as taking and passing the three Pre-Professional National Teachers Examinations. Point Park monitors the progress of teacher certification candidates through performance in the following areas: content mastery; planning; class-

201 Wood Street
Pittsburgh, PA 15222
Phone: 412-392-3430
Fax: 412-391-1980
Website: www.ppc.edu

room management; organization; monitoring student progress; leadership; sensitivity to students' needs; problem analysis; strategic and tactical decision making; oral and written communication and presentation; professional standards; and practice and mastery of instructional technology.

Education majors who meet all of the requirements of approved teacher preparation programs must also complete the remaining 2-3 National Teachers before applying for student teaching. Please see Education Department for additional information and applications. All Education and Community Services Department requirements are subject to change in state and federal regulations.

The Department of Humanities and Human Sciences provides an interdisciplinary approach to the study of human behavior, experience, and expression. It draws on insights derived from anthropology, history, legal studies, linguistics, literary studies, philosophy, political science, psychology, and sociology and directs its efforts toward developing a critical understanding of human nature, language, thought, and the relationship of the individual and society. The Department is committed to the idea that genuine intellectual growth requires a stimulating and challenging environment. Students are encouraged to think clearly and analytically, to read with insight and understanding, and to write with clarity and precision. The subject matter and methods of inquiry fundamental to the various disciplines of the Department are presented and explored in detail in order to provide students with the specialized education needed to pursue advanced degrees or prepare for a career. Simultaneously, there is a strong emphasis on the development of a common core of knowledge and skills that will provide graduates with a solid educational foundation in a rapidly changing world.

The Department offers programs leading to the Bachelor of Arts degree with majors in applied history, behavioral sciences, citizenship/secondary education, English, English/secondary education, political science and psychology. Programs leading to the Bachelor of Science degree are offered in criminal justice and human resources management. The Department offers Capstone programs leading to the Bachelor of Arts degree in Legal Studies and the Bachelor of Science degree in criminal justice, general studies and human resources management for students with associate degrees. In addition, the Department offers post-baccalaureate degree programs leading to the Bachelor of Arts degree in citizenship/secondary education and English/secondary education and the Bachelor of Science degree in general studies and human resources management.

Journalism and mass communication majors are encouraged to participate in the production of campus media as early as their freshman year. The independent student newspaper, *The Globe*, provides students with experience in newspaper publication, including news-editorial and layout and design. Students also produce *The Pioneer*, a news magazine, in a regularly scheduled class. Broadcasting students create programs and edit in the department's TV facilities and at WPPJ Radio. *The Cavalcade*, the college's literary magazine, provides students with the opportunity to explore other literary venues for their writing talents. Students in journalism and mass communication also have the opportunity to apply skills learned in the classroom through internships. With the college's downtown location, Point Park students are within a short walk of some of the finest internship opportunities in the nation. The department offers two other degrees. Students with associate's degrees can earn a bachelor's in applied corporate communications in an accelerated format through the School of Professional Studies. They attend classes on Saturdays and complete the program in two years. A Master of Arts degree in journalism and mass communication is also offered through the School of Professional Studies.

The Department of Natural Sciences and Engineering Technology at Point Park College offers Bachelor of Science degrees for natural sciences in biological sciences, biological sciences/secondary education, biotechnology, environmental health science and protection, funeral services, health services, and mathematics/secondary education. The curricula for all majors reflect a diverse liberal arts background in conjunction with the natural sciences requirements. In addition to developing a solid foundation in their specialized fields of interest, graduates may pursue careers or advanced degrees relative to their technical and scientific knowledge. Fully equipped, modern laboratories provide students with practical experience necessary before they graduate. The overall success of our graduates can directly be attributed to four particular features of the program: the personal attention of accessible and caring professors provides students with every opportunity for success, the curriculum builds a strong foundation from which graduates can develop or advance their careers, experienced faculty members are aware of the needs of the health, science and environmental fields and prepare students accordingly, our urban location is key to the availability of a variety of career and graduate study opportunities for our natural science graduates, providing access to a multitude of industries from which to choose.

The department also offers Bachelor of Science degrees in engineering technology. The program offers a diverse liberal arts background in conjunction with three majors in engineering technology: civil, electrical and mechanical. Engineering technologists work with engineers and architects to transform concepts and ideas into real working systems. Their primary responsibility is to work in conjunction with engineers in research development, production, design, testing and quality control. They are also concerned with management and improvements of existing technologies. The Engineering Technology program has fully equipped, modern laboratories that provide students with practical experience. Surveying, soil and fluid testing, materials testing, computer-assisted drafting and design, electronics, microwave theory, auto control and robotics, microprocessors, and instrumentation all have laboratory settings. Graduates of the program work in many different areas of engineering technology, from development to production to design. They are also involved with product testing and quality control. The Engineering Technology program focuses on application and hands-on experience in traditional and cutting-edge technologies. Students in their junior year are eligible to sit for the Fundamentals of Engineering (FE) Exam in the state of Pennsylvania. This examination leads to eventual registration as a professional engineer with the State Registration Board for Professional Engineers of the Commonwealth of Pennsylvania.

ADMISSIONS

Students interested in entering Point Park College as freshmen are considered for admission from three perspectives. First, academic abilities of the applicant are evaluated on the basis of secondary school performance, the types of courses taken, the grades earned and the class rank. Second, standardized national tests, such as the SAT and the ACT, provide a means of predicting academic success at Point Park College. The third area is concerned with personal qualities and achievements which include participation in extracurricular activities, community involvement and the recommendation of guidance counselors, teachers and others who know the applicant well. Students in their final year of secondary school should submit their applications as early as possible. Applications are reviewed as soon as they are complete and students are informed of the decision at that time. While most students seeking admission as freshmen apply for the fall academic term, Point Park College also admits students to freshman status for the spring and summer academic terms. The documents required for a completed application include an application form, a secondary school transcript and SAT or ACT test scores. The application fee is $20. The application fee is waived if you apply online. A personal interview, while not required, is encouraged. Students who desire an interview should contact the Office of Admission approximately one week in advance to arrange an appointment. All freshman admission candidates must have completed an academic program in secondary studies or, in the judgment of the Admission Committee, have achieved an equivalent competence prior to matriculation.

CAMPUS LIFE

The Student Activities Center is Point Park's hub for student communications, activities information and support services for all students and organizations. Located on the second floor of Lawrence Hall, the Student Activities Center contributes to the mission of Point Park College by helping to create a positive out-of-classroom environment for our students which supports and enhances their academic experiences. Specifically, Student Activities aims to create and support opportunities for: student leadership in the College; student involvement with and connection to the College and to the College community; co-curricular learning experiences which build on students' academic experiences; and, broadening or students' life experiences through cultural, recreational, educational and social activities.

COST AND AID

For the 2002–2003 school year, undergraduate tuition is $13,888 and $14,682 for Conservatory students. Room and board is $6,098 and student fees add up to $460.

QUINNIPIAC UNIVERSITY

GENERAL INFORMATION

Quinnipiac, private and nonsectarian, founded in 1929, offers its 4,500 undergraduate and 2,000 graduate and part-time students a residential atmosphere on a uniquely attractive campus of 300 acres in south central Connecticut. Quinnipiac is committed to providing quality academic programs in a student oriented environment on a campus with a strong sense of community.

STUDENT BODY

Division I athletics are offered in 19 sports—men's basketball, baseball, cross country and track, lacrosse, ice hockey, golf, tennis, and soccer and women's basketball, softball, cross country and track, field hockey, ice hockey, lacrosse, soccer, tennis, and volleyball. Quinnipiac is a member of the Northeast Conference and an associate member of the MAAC Conference.

Facilities include a 1,500-seat main gymnasium, locker rooms, training rooms, steam room, and a 24,000-square-foot, fully-equipped fitness center, outdoor lighted tennis, and racquetball courts.

More than 50 clubs and organizations, including student government, newspaper, yearbook, radio station, service organizations, community activities, religious fellowships, diversity awareness, dance and drama productions, and Greek life, along with numerous recreation activities, provide a balanced college experience. Intramural teams compete in more than 20 sports.

Special activities during the year include Homecoming, Parents' Weekend, the annual Holiday party, Sibling Weekend, and May Weekend.

ACADEMICS

School of Business majors: accounting, advertising, computer information systems (dual majors available), economics, finance, health administration, international business, management (human resources management, production and operations management, and strategic/entrepreneurial management), marketing (international marketing and marketing management).

School of Health Sciences majors: athletic training/sports medicine, biochemistry, biology, chemistry, clinical laboratory science, diagnostic imaging, health/science studies, medical laboratory sciences, microbiology/biotechnology, nursing, occupational therapy, and physical therapy (both 5-year freshman entry-level programs), physician assistant (6-year freshman entry-level program), psychobiology, respiratory care, veterinary technology.

The pre-med program is designed to provide the undergraduate student interested in a career as a health professional the appropriate background necessary to meet the entrance requirements of a variety of different medical schools. Eligible students who display maturity, dedication, and sensitivity may be paired with a health professional at one of our local hospitals or health care practices for a 12-week internship. Students can also participate in several local volunteer programs in conjunction with the Hospital of St. Raphael, Gaylord Hospital for Rehabilitation, or Yale New Haven Hospital.

College of Liberal Arts majors: English, computer science, criminal justice, gerontology, history, independent major, legal studies, mathematics, political science, psychology (child development, human services), social services, sociology, Spanish. Students who are interested in pre-law have the advice of an on-campus faculty member who is a lawyer, and the benefit of an on-campus Law School. There is a guaranteed baccalaureate/JD degree with the Quinnipiac Law School for highly qualified entering freshmen.

School of Communications majors: undergraduate majors in media production, e-media, media arts, journalism, and public relations, and graduate programs in journalism and e-media for writing and design in the journalistic community.

Education: For those interested in teaching, completion of an undergraduate major in an area in the liberal arts or natural sciences, combined with junior and senior year courses in education, ending with a fifth-year full-time graduate education program, culminates in the Master of Arts in Teaching degree and eligibility for certification to teach at the elementary, middle, or secondary levels.

Undergraduate students can choose from more than 50 majors in business, liberal arts, mass communications, and health sciences. Freshmen entry-level master degree programs are available in education, physical therapy, occupational therapy, e-media, and physician assistant.

Graduate students specialize in law, business, health administration, journalism, education, and health science programs in physician assistant, physical therapy, pathologist's assistant, medical and laboratory sciences, molecular and cell biology, forensic nursing, and nurse practitioner. The Quinnipiac School of Law occupies a $20 million state-of-the-art Law Center building on campus.

Mount Carmel Avenue, 275 Mount Carmel Avenue
Hamden, CT 06518
Phone: 203-582-8600
Fax: 203-582-8906
Website: www.quinnipiac.edu

With an average class size of less than 20, and fewer than 5 percent of class sections having 40 or more students, there is strong interaction between students and faculty. All classes are taught by college faculty-no teaching assistants or graduate students teach classes. A 16:1 student/faculty ratio assures students of easy access to faculty members, who also function as their advisors. More than 80 percent of the faculty have earned the highest possible degrees in their field.
With an average class size of less than 20, and fewer than 5 percent of class sections having 40 or more students, there is strong interaction between students and faculty. All classes are taught by college faculty-no teaching assistants or graduate students teach classes. A 16:1 student/faculty ratio assures students of easy access to faculty members, who also function as their advisors. More than 80 percent of the faculty have earned the highest possible degrees in their field.

ADMISSIONS

High school students can begin applying for admissions early in their senior year. A completed application consists of the application form, an official high school transcript, SAT I test scores (Quinnipiac's SAT code is 3712) or ACT scores (Quinnipiac's ACT code is 0582) senior year, first-quarter grades, a personal statement, and one letter of recommendation.

Recommended deadline is February 15 for all programs *except* physical and occupational therapy and physician assistant, which have a December 31 deadline. Notification of decisions usually occurs about four weeks after receiving all application materials. Decisions for the PT, OT, and PA programs are mailed in February. All programs subscribe to the nationally recognized candidate reply date of May 1.

Transfer students who have, or will receive, an associate's degree prior to entrance do not need to provide high school transcripts and SAT results. We must receive transcripts of all courses taken at other colleges. Physical therapy and physician assistant programs are closed to transfer students.

Questions? Please call Quinnipiac at 800-462-1944 or 203-582-8600, e-mail the University at admissions@quinnipiac.edu, or check the website at www.quinnipiac.edu.

CAMPUS LIFE

Hamden, Connecticut is located eight miles north of New Haven and 20 miles south of Hartford, and is midway between Boston and New York City. While in a suburban environment, the campus is adjacent to Sleeping Giant State Park, with 1,700 acres of hills and trails for hiking and walking. A picturesque setting and quiet surroundings provide an enjoyable campus experience, with easy access to theater, shopping, museums, sports, recreation, and a variety of dining and entertainment options.

Driving time to Quinnipiac from Boston or New York City is about two hours. Metro-North railroad from Grand Central Terminal in New York City and Amtrak Northeast Corridor trains also arrive in New Haven. The campus is a 10-minute taxi ride from the terminal. Bradley Airport, north of Hartford is the nearest international airport, about 40 minutes from campus. Students can also arrive at John F. Kennedy, Newark, or LaGuardia airports in the New York area and travel via Connecticut Limousine to New Haven.

All programs at Quinnipiac offer an excellent combination of classroom learning with internships or clinical affiliations. Students in the health sciences are placed in clinical affiliations as part of their course work. Students in business, communications, and liberal arts have nearby corporations, health care agencies, or media outlets available for internships.

Our Career Services Office can provide excellent assistance in resume writing and job placement. A survey of recent graduates shows that 90 percent were either employed or in graduate school within six months of graduation. Each year about 50 percent of students in internships are offered permanent jobs as a result of their work.

Students in all majors can also take advantage of study abroad opportunities either during the summer months or during the academic year.

COST AND AID

Tuition and Fees for 2001–2002 are $18,840, with $8,530 for room and board. Seventy percent of the freshman class comes from outside of Connecticut, and close to 90 percent of the incoming class lives on campus. Residence accommodations range from traditional style rooms to suites, apartments, and multi-level townhouses.

RADFORD UNIVERSITY

GENERAL INFORMATION

Students come to Radford University for the small class sizes, residential community, dedicated professors, and academic excellence. Since its founding in 1910, the University has grown to encompass the following Colleges: College of Arts and Sciences, the College of Business and Economics, the College of Education and Human Development, the College of Information Science and Technology, the Waldron College of Health and Human Services, the College of Visual and Performing Arts, and the College of Graduate and Extended Studies. Currently, 87 percent of the approximately 9,000 students attending the University are pursuing one of the 112 undergraduate degrees. The 36 graduate programs grant the MS, MA, MBA, MFA, MSN, MSW, or EdS degrees. More than one-third of students, including all freshmen, live on campus in one of the 15 residence halls, all configured as two-room suites. A variety of learning/residential communities are available to suit the interests and needs of students. Students who choose to live off-campus typically rent an apartment within walking distance of the University.

The student body is composed of students from many parts of Virginia in addition to 47 other states and 43 foreign countries. The University offers students ample opportunity to participate in overseas study programs. Radford organizes activities including guest speakers, theater performances, concerts, film screenings, Greek events, student publications, radio and television stations, and intramural sports competition. People congregate in the Heth Student Center to utilize the lounge, recreation facilities, study rooms, and meeting areas. Dalton Hall houses the food court including Chick-Fil-A, dining hall, bookstore, and post office. The $10.8 million Dedmon Center is home to the University's 19 NCAA Division I athletic teams; it also provides students with comprehensive sports and fitness facilities.

STUDENT BODY

All Radford undergraduates are part of the Student Government Association, and elected representatives voice student opinions as part of the following committees: the Executive Council, Cabinet, Senate, House of Representatives, Off-Campus Student Council, Graduate Student Council, Class Representatives Council, Black Student Affairs Council, International Student Affairs Council, And Diversity Promotions Council. RU has over 300 clubs and organizations available. Examples are the Radford Redcoats equestrian team, RU Outdoors, the social sorority and fraternities, and academic, service, sport and religious organizations. All are popular options for students.

ACADEMICS

Radford requires 120 units of credit to complete an undergraduate degree. Fifty of these units are earned in general education classes. The Highlander Scholars Program administers honors courses for top students. The University assists students in adjusting to college life with specially designed new-student programs, including the University 100 class and Success Starts Here. During Quest, the orientation that takes place over the summer, incoming freshmen meet with advisors, sign up for classes, and meet their classmates. Radford offers the Army ROTC program to students pursuing a career in the military. The academic calendar is made up of fall (September to December) and spring (January to May) semesters.

At Radford, students may work toward their BA, BS, BFA, BM, BBA, BSN, BSW, or BGS degree. For undergraduates, the following majors are offered: accounting; anthropology; art; biology; chemistry; communication; communication sciences and disorders; computer science and technology; criminal justice; dance; economics; English; exercise sport and health education; fashion; finance; foods and nutrition; foreign languages; geography; geology; history; human development; information science and systems; interdisciplinary studies (education); interior design; management; marketing; mathematics and statistics; media studies; medical technology; music; music therapy; nursing; philosophy and religious studies; physical science; political science; psychology; recreation, parks, and tourism; social science; social work; sociology; and theater.

PO Box 6903, RU Station
Radford, VA 24142-6903
Phone: 540-831-5371
Fax: 540-831-5038
Website: www.radford.edu

Radford attracts top professors from 45 states and 11 foreign countries. More than 80 percent of the faculty hold their PhD or terminal degree in their field. The University facilitates close academic relationships between instructors and students by maintaining a low 19:1 student/faculty ratio. Fewer than 5 percent of undergraduate classes are led by graduate students. Professors focus on their roles as teachers and student advisors while continuing their professional research and publication efforts.

ADMISSIONS

The Admissions Committee at Radford evaluates each applicant's academic record, looking for signs of scholastic and personal potential. Factors include high school course difficulty, GPA, class rank, SAT I or ACT scores, and extracurricular pursuits. It is recommended that students take the following classes in high school: 4 units of English, 4 units of college-preparatory mathematics, 3-4 units of foreign language, 4 units of lab science, and 4 units of social science (including American history). Applicants intending to pursue a degree in nursing should have both biology and chemistry on their transcripts. The University does not discriminate on the basis of race, sex, handicap, age, veteran status, national origin, religious or political affiliation, or sexual preference.

Students must submit all of the following materials in their completed application: the official application form, the nonrefundable application fee, an official high school transcript, and official SAT I or ACT scores. Transfer applicants are required to send the application form along with transcripts from their previously attended accredited college or university. The deadline for applications for fall admission is April 1. Applications that arrive later than the deadline will be evaluated as space is available. Campus visits can be arranged between 8 A.M. and 5 P.M., Monday through Friday, or between 9 A.M. and noon on Saturday, from September to May. Prospective students may also attend a campus tours at 10 A.M., noon, and 2 P.M. on Monday and Friday, 10 A.M. and 2 P.M. on Tuesday, Wednesday, and Thursday, and at 10 A.M., 11 A.M., and noon on Saturday during the school year.

CAMPUS LIFE

The University's hometown of Radford, Virginia, about half an hour outside of Roanoke in the western half of the state, is set amid the scenic Blue Ridge Mountains. The town's population of 16,200 supports a variety of restaurants and shops. Students who enjoy the outdoors take advantage of the campus's proximity to The Blue Ridge Parkway, the Appalachian Trail, New River, and Claytor Lake. Available activities include skiing, hiking, canoeing, biking, and camping. The campus is convenient to I-81 for motorists and close to the Roanoke airport for those arriving by plane.

COST AND AID

In the 2002–2003 school year, in-state undergraduates paid $3,344 for tuition and fees. Out-of-state students paid $9,792. An additional $5,442 was charged for room and board. In addition, students spend roughly $650 on books and supplies.

RANDOLPH-MACON WOMAN'S COLLEGE

GENERAL INFORMATION

Randolph-Macon Woman's College (R-MWC) is an independent, selective, liberal arts and sciences college situated in the foothills of the Blue Ridge Mountains in Lynchburg, Virginia. Founded in 1891 and affiliated with the United Methodist Church, R-MWC is noted for the strength of its academic programs. The College ranks among the top 10 percent of all colleges and universities in the United States in the percentage of its graduates who go on to earn PhDs. With 721 undergraduates from 45 states as well as Washington, DC, and 44 countries, R-MWC boasts a low student/faculty ratio of 9:1.

The Honor System is a vital part of college life at R-MWC and allows students to live and study in an atmosphere of integrity and trust. Each student is a member of Student Government, which provides a voice for student opinion, oversees student activities, and makes policy through the elected representatives. Students serve on most College committees.

National Recognition

U.S. News & World Report ranked R-MWC 66th out of 159 national liberal arts colleges in the country in its 2001 Best Colleges edition covering more than 1,400 accredited colleges and universities. R-MWC was also listed among the top 20 national liberal arts colleges for the percentage of international students on campus and in the top 12 for the number of classes offered with fewer than 20 students.

Barron's Best Buys (sixth edition) selected R-MWC as one of the nation's "best buys" and described the College as having "tough academics, great leadership opportunities, and close faculty/student relationships."

The Princeton Review's *The Best 331 Best Colleges,* 2002 Edition, ranked R-MWC 9th in the nation for Dorms like Palaces, 16th for Great Food, and 19th for Got Milk?

The 2001 *Fiske Guide to Colleges* ranked R-MWC among the top 21 private institutions in the United States as a best buy.

The Insider's Guide to the Colleges 2001 selected R-MWC, based on academic quality, as one of the 311 institutions to be profiled in their latest edition.

In the April 2000 edition of *Yahoo! Internet Life* magazine, R-MWC was ranked 17th among the nation's "most wired" colleges and universities in a recent Internet survey.

R-MWC is a member of the International 50, a group of selective liberal arts colleges recognized for international programs and global awareness.

R-MWC was the first women's college in the South to be granted a Phi Beta Kappa charter and the first to be accredited by the American Chemical Society and the Southern Association of Colleges and Schools.

STUDENT BODY

R-MWC offers more than 50 clubs and organizations, from academic and honor societies to service and leadership groups. Our students also plan and participate in events with some of the more than 25,000 other college students living within a one-hour radius of campus. A sampling includes BIONIC (Believe It Or Not, I Care-volunteer service); Black Woman's Alliance; *Hail, Muse, etc.!* (literary magazine); *Helianthus* (yearbook); Sock & Buskin (theatre group); Student Government, *The Sundial* (campus newspaper);Modern United Nations; Pan World Club; Psychology Club; and Society of Physics Students.

Classified NCAA Division III, R-MWC is a member of the Old Dominion Athletic Conference and offers 8 intercollegiate sports: basketball, field hockey, riding, soccer, softball, swimming, tennis, and volleyball.

ACADEMICS

A broad liberal arts and sciences curriculum offers a wide range of knowledge and skills to prepare students for a successful future. The primary goal is to train students to think critically and independently and to be able to communicate their conclusions effectively in both written and oral forms.

All students must meet the College's general education requirements, which encompass three areas: skills (composition, math, and a foreign language), distribution (courses in literature, artistic expression, history, philosophy or religion, and the social sciences), and dimensions (a women's studies course and three cultural diversity courses). A unique program called The Macon Plan provides the framework for students to make deliberate choices about their futures. Through guidance from faculty, students create their own four-year plan that combines course work, internships, study abroad, and co-curricular activities. To document their progress, students maintain an Electronic Portfolio, which will serve as a resume of skills and accomplishments gleaned from their college experience.

R-MWC offers 25 major programs, emphases within majors, and 40 departmental and 18 interdisciplinary concentrations leading to a Bachelor or Arts or Bachelor of Science degree.

Majors and Emphases

American culture

Art

—art history

—art history and museum studies

—studio art

Biology

—environmental biology

—general biology

—health-related biology

—molecular and cell biology (biotechnology)

—organismal biology

Chemistry

Classics

—classical archaeology

Classical civilization

—classical languages

Communication

Curricular studies

Dance

Economics

Engineering physics

English

—creative writing

—English literature

Environmental studies

French

—literature

—language and civilization

German studies

Health services

History

International studies

Mathematics

Music
—music history
—music performance
—music theory
Philosophy
Physics
Politics
Psychology
Religion
Russian studies
Sociology/anthropology
Spanish
Theatre
—pre-professional preparation
Teacher licensure/certification
—elementary
—secondary
Pre-law
Pre-med
Pre-vet

Other health-related study: 3/2 Cooperative Career Programs in nursing and engineering

The student/faculty ratio is 9:1. All classes are taught by professors rather than by teaching assistants. Most classes have 18 or fewer students. Average class size is 12. Fifty-three percent of the College's 94 faculty members are women. Seventy-two faculty are full-time, approximately 92 percent of whom hold the highest degree in their fields.

ADMISSIONS

Early Decision applicants should apply by November 15. Regular Decision candidates should submit their applications and supportive credentials by March 1.

SAT I or ACT scores, two recommendations, and a $35 application fee are required in addition to the high school transcript. Campus visits are strongly encouraged. During the visit, students can attend a class, speak with current students and faculty, tour campus with a student tour guide, and ask lots of questions.

During the academic year tours and interviews can be scheduled from 9 A.M. to 4 P.M. weekdays and 10 A.M. to 12 P.M. Saturdays. Tours may also be scheduled on Saturday and Sunday afternoons on request. From May 15 to August 31 the Admissions Office schedules appointments on weekdays only. Please contact the Admissions Office at 434-947-8100 or 800-745-7692 to schedule a visit. For more information, contact:

Randolph-Macon Woman's College
2500 Rivermont Ave.
Lynchburg, VA 24503
Telephone: 434-947-8100 or 800-745-RMWC (7692)
E-mail: Admissions@rmwc.edu
World Wide Web: www.rmwc.edu

CAMPUS LIFE

The College's 100-acre campus is located in a gracious residential area of Lynchburg at the foot of the Blue Ridge Mountains. The old and majestic buildings, arranged in a semicircle, are surrounded by grand trees that provide a picturesque setting. Glass corridors called trolleys link nearly all campus buildings.

Lynchburg, a city of 80,000, was named as the second "most livable" small city in the southeast by *Money* magazine in 1998. Higher education institutions (there are five in the city) and high-tech companies have brought a cosmopolitan population and broad range of amenities to the city, but it is small enough to offer safe streets and a small-town atmosphere. Founded in 1786 by John Lynch, a Quaker, Lynchburg is located along the James River and is within minutes of the Blue Ridge Parkway. The town's history is closely tied to Thomas Jefferson, whose summer retreat at Poplar Forest is minutes away. Centrally located in the state, Lynchburg is within driving distance of Charlottesville, Roanoke, Richmond, and Washington, DC.

International Study

More than one-fourth of R-MWC's juniors study abroad. Approximately 30 juniors majoring in all fields participate in the College's Junior Year Abroad program at the University of Reading, England. In addition, students have studied recently in Argentina, Australia, the Czech Republic, France, Japan, Russia, Scotland, and Spain. Students may also participate in programs sponsored by other colleges.

American Culture Program

This dynamic learning opportunity explores what it means to be an American by taking a thematic and hands-on approach to studying American images and voices both on campus and at key locations in Virginia and across the nation. The American Culture Program takes two forms: a semester-long program in the spring and a shorter early-summer experience. In each format students are able to immerse themselves in program themes through related literature, art, music, and history. Founded in 1991, the program has already visited 39 states, Canada, and Mexico.

COST AND AID

Tuition: $20,150

Room and board: $7,900

Telecommunications fee (TV, telephone): $200

Student activity fee: $180

Annual charge: $28,430

REED COLLEGE

GENERAL INFORMATION

As former Stanford president Donald Kennedy once put it, "If you're a genuine intellectual, live the life of the mind, and want to learn for the sake of learning, the place most likely to empower you is . . . the most intellectual college in the country—Reed, in Portland, Oregon." To its 1,360 students and 128 faculty members, Reed College embodies the intellectual ideal: a community of inquisitive independent thinkers drawn to study by their natural curiosity. For nearly 100 years, the typical Reed student has had both a sincere passion for academic inquiry and the self-discipline necessary to achieve great things. The Reed student body is drawn from across the country and around the world. Only 15 percent of Reed students are native Oregonians. About one-fifth of the students arrive from the Northeast; approximately 5 percent are international students. Reed adheres to a traditional curriculum designed to reward hard work and rigorous analytical thinking, but its students are anything but conventional. "Reedies," the term Reed undergraduates use to refer to themselves, are a diverse and quirky lot liberated by the lack of a social norm on campus. "Live and let live" is the watchword of the Reed community, in which geeks, geniuses, and glamour queens happily coexist.

STUDENT BODY

Reed shuns exclusive organizations and activities, so the College has no Greek organizations and no NCAA or NAIA athletic teams (more about sports below). All campus organizations are student-created and student-run. The student activity fund of approximately $85,000 is administered by the Student Senate. Student organizations must lobby the Student Senate for funding annually, after which the Senate oversees a vote in which the entire student body decides which organizations should be funded. Thus, the number and nature of campus organizations at Reed changes every year to meet current student interests. Reed may not compete at the NCAA or NAIA level, but most students participate in sports on an informal basis. Intramural sports and club sports proliferate in basketball, fencing, rugby, sailing, soccer, and ultimate Frisbee. A three-semester physical education requirement demonstrates that the school recognizes the importance of physical fitness and the salutary effects of exercise, if not the necessity of stressful intercollegiate competition. Students at Reed work hard but also have many outlets for letting off steam. A Reed-managed ski cabin on Mt. Hood allows students to escape campus for a night or weekend of hiking, skiing, or just relaxing in a gorgeous setting. The Reed Outdoor Club and backpack co-op facilitate students' abilities to take advantage of Reed's location in the rugged Northwest. Reed's Gray Fund endows a number of cultural, recreational, and social activities, including guest lecturers and exploratory trips to Portland and throughout the Pacific Northwest.

ACADEMICS

The curriculum at Reed is both demanding and wide-ranging. Through required studies, Reed students receive a solid grounding in the liberal arts and sciences. All freshmen must complete "Hum 110," a survey of Greek and Roman scholars from Homer to St. Augustine, in order to acquaint themselves with the foundations of western culture. The course entails both weekly lecture classes and small discussion groups of fewer than 20 students. Professors utilize the Socratic method to direct the all-important student discussions at the core of the Hum 110 experience.

Distribution requirements set a substantial portion of a student's curriculum for the first two years at Reed. Freshmen and sophomores must complete a year-long course in each of the four major divisions of the College. No specific courses are required; students are free to pursue their interests within the strictures of the requirements, which force many to broaden their intellectual purviews. Reed juniors must pass a comprehensive exam in their major; the purpose of the exam is to allow faculty members the chance to determine the student's readiness for his or her senior thesis project.

The required senior thesis is the capstone experience of a Reed education. Every senior must produce an original independent research project over the course of the final year. The project may be creative, critical, or experimental in nature. Students typically spend the first half of the year researching their subject, then spend the second half of the year shaping their work into a finished written product. The thesis process is completed when the student successfully defends his or her thesis before a faculty panel.

Reed strongly believes that learning should be undertaken for its own sake, not for the sake of letter grades. Accordingly, students do not receive grade reports unless they wish to. A student's transcript does include letter grades for all courses taken, but students can better gauge their progress through professors' written evaluations of their work and one-on-one meetings with faculty. Most prefer this system, which greatly eases competition among students and thus allows them to focus entirely on the content of their academic work. A Reed education opens virtually all doors to those who complete it successfully. The curricular focus on critical thinking and oral and written communication nurture a full complement of skills applicable to nearly all of life's endeavors. Reed students acquire an array of experiences, perspectives, and interpretive methods that enable them to tackle any problem within any career.

Reed confers the Bachelor of Arts degree in a wide selection of fields, both in traditional academic departments and in interdisciplinary combinations. The following traditional majors are offered: American studies, anthropology, art, biochemistry and molecular biology, biology, chemistry, chemistry-physics, Chinese literature, classics, classics-religion, dance-theatre, economics, English literature, French literature, general literature, German literature, history, history-literature, international and comparative policy studies, linguistics, literature-theatre, mathematics, mathematics-economics, mathematics-physics, music, philosophy, physics, political science, psychology, religion, Russian literature, sociology, Spanish literature, and theatre.

3203 SE Woodstock Boulevard
Portland, OR 97202-8199
Phone: 503-777-7511
Fax: 503-777-7553
Website: www.reed.edu

Undergraduates are encouraged to design interdisciplinary majors; such majors must be planned with the approval of faculty advisors from each department involved. In recent years, students have developed such interdisciplinary majors as art/political science and history/mathematics. Reed offers a number of 3-2 (dual degree) programs; these allow undergraduates to earn a three-year bachelor's degree from Reed, then earn a professional degree from a cooperating institution in two additional years. Dual degree programs include: applied physics and electronic science (offered through the Oregon Graduate Institute), computer science (University of Washington), engineering (California Institute of Technology, Columbia University, and Rensselaer Polytechnic Institute), and forestry and environmental sciences (Duke University). The College also offers a dual-degree program in the visual arts through the Pacific Northwest College of Art..

Professors, not graduate students, teach all classes at the College. Eighty-four percent of faculty members have received the terminal degree in their areas of expertise. Reedies appreciate the close working and personal relationships they maintain with their professors; to many, it is the most beneficial aspect of a Reed education. Likewise, the faculty values the unique opportunity to work with a truly engaged and extremely accomplished student body dedicated to learning for its own sake. The faculty constantly undertakes important research but considers its primary responsibility the teaching of undergraduates. Professors frequently involve students in the creation of papers and scientific research; in many cases, students receive credit as co-authors and co-investigators on the work produced. A low 10:1 student/faculty ratio allows for small classes and frequent one-on-one meetings.

ADMISSIONS

Reed seeks students who demonstrate a commitment to hard work and to the ideals embodied by a liberal arts education. Freshman and transfer applications are welcome. The admissions committee attempts to determine which candidates will benefit most from a Reed education as well as who is most likely to succeed at Reed. The ideal incoming class is diverse in its range of talents, interests, backgrounds, and perspectives, yet constituted of students who share a common passion for academic inquiry.

The admissions committee places most emphasis on an applicant's record of previous academic accomplishment. A rigorous secondary school curriculum that includes honors and advanced courses affords the applicant a great advantage; such a program typically includes 4 years of English, at least 3 years of a foreign or classical language, 3 to 4 years of mathematics, 3 to 4 years of science, and 3 to 4 years of history or social studies. Because secondary school curricula vary widely in quality and content, the school sets no fixed requirements in this area. With rare exceptions, incoming students have obtained a secondary school diploma prior to enrollment. The admissions committee sets no "cutoff points" for high school grades, college grades (for transfer students), or standardized test scores. Reed seeks candidates who demonstrate excellence of character, particularly in areas of motivation, intellectual curiosity, individual responsibility, and social consciousness. These qualities often help the chances of admission for candidates whose academic records might not otherwise meet Reed's standards.

The admission committee recognizes the importance of creating a diverse community in which individual differences contribute to the vitality of the campus. The school strongly recommends a personal interview, especially for early decision candidates, but an interview is not required. Early decision applications should arrive at Reed by November 15 (Option 1) or January 2 (Option 2). Early decision at Reed is binding; students who are accepted under early decision are expected to matriculate. The deadline for regular freshman admission applications is January 15. Transfer candidates should apply no later than March 1.

CAMPUS LIFE

Perched on the suburban edge of a major city, only five miles from downtown, a Reed education affords undergraduates both peaceful, verdant surroundings and easy access to urban culture and entertainment. Portland is among the nation's most pleasant urban environments, a paradise for nonconformists who just happen to enjoy world-class coffee. Students can reach nearly any part of the city with a short bicycle or bus ride. Mt. Hood and the Oregon Coast, and their attendant recreational options, are both easily accessible. The lovely Willamette River bisects the city into east and west. Portland is a city rich in culture, entertainment, and west coast charm. Like many west coast cities, it is wide open, lush with greenery, and generally laid-back in demeanor. The 4,600-acre Forest Park, located in the northwest section of the city, is widely regarded as the largest municipal park in the United States. The city is home to a multitude of theatre troupes; African dance, ballet, and opera companies; several symphonies; museums; and a growing gallery district that locals call "the Pearl." It's the type of city where revival and art movie houses still thrive; indeed, they outnumber the multiplexes that have overtaken much of rest of the country. Used book hunters will love scavenging the city's dozens of independent bookstores.

Rain, as you've probably heard, is a fact of life in the Pacific Northwest, although the amount and negative impact of regional rainfall are vastly overestimated. Most of our rain falls during the winter. Its beneficial effects include year-round greenery and unusually clean air. Spring, summer, and fall are predominantly temperate with clear, deep blue skies. Blistering summer days and bitterly cold winter mornings are truly a rarity. Reed is no cloistered academy set apart from its surroundings. Neighbors freely enjoy the campus, walking their dogs and jogging its tree-lined paths. Local community members are welcome to enjoy lectures and performances on campus. Reedies are similarly integrated into the life of Portland, contributing to and benefiting from the city's large artistic and intellectual communities. Of course, Reed students are also active in community service.

Reed undergraduates may participate in a number of domestic exchange and study abroad opportunities. Domestic exchange programs are run in conjunction with Howard University in Washington, DC; Sarah Lawrence College in New York; and Sea Semester, based in Woods Hole, Massachusetts. Study abroad programs are established at University of East Anglia, University of Sussex, Oxford University, and the British Academy of Dramatic Arts in England; University of Rennes and University of Paris (among others) in France; Beijing Foreign Studies University, Capital Normal University, Fujian Normal University, and East China Normal University in China; Hebrew University of Jerusalem; University of Munich and Tobingen University in Germany; University of Florence and Intercollegiate Center for Classical Studies in Italy; Trinity College Dublin in Ireland; Universidad San Francisco de Quito and Universidad Catolica in Ecuador; Hertzen University, Irkutsk University, Moscow State University, and Moscow Art Theatre School in Russia; the University of Costa Rica and the Organization for Tropical Studies in Costa Rica; Budapest Semester in Mathematics in Hungary; and universities in Getafe, Segovia, and La Rioja in Spain. Reed encourages students to pursue independent study off-campus. Such plans must be developed with the assistance of appropriate Reed faculty members, the director for off-campus studies, and the registrar.

COST AND AID

Tuition (and fees) for the 2003–2004 academic year are $29,000. Room and board is an additional $7,750, bringing the yearly total cost to $36,950.

RENSSELAER POLYTECHNIC INSTITUTE

GENERAL INFORMATION

Founded in 1824 to train students to "apply science to the common purpose of life," Rensselaer Polytechnic Institute is the nation's oldest technological university. Located in New York's historic Hudson Valley, Rensselaer pursues its mission today just as fervently as it did 179 years ago. Without question, Rensselaer is among the world's foremost research universities. Rensselaer offers over 100 programs (and more than 1,000 courses) leading to bachelor's, master's, and doctoral degrees. Undergraduates may enroll in Schools of Architecture, Engineering, Humanities and Social Sciences, Management and Technology, or Science; they may also undertake our interdisciplinary program in information technology. Rensselaer has long championed a real-world, multidisciplinary, industry-oriented approach to education and research. The university offers a number of cross-school programs, such as product design and innovation. Students may pursue majors in such unique areas as bioinformatics and molecular biology; electronic media, arts, and communication; and information technology. Rensselaer is home to 18 major interdisciplinary research centers that have produced significant breakthroughs in advanced computing, composite materials, microelectronics, and simulation-based engineering. The university is justly famous for the cutting-edge research it steadily produces. The school maintains extensive ties to a wide assortment of businesses, ranging from multinationals to small, cutting-edge entrepreneurs. These relationships guarantee that a Rensselaer education focuses on state-of-the-art technology and contemporary issues. They also facilitate a vast array of co-op, internship, and employment options for students. The Rensselaer student body is made up of 5,139 undergraduates and 1,739 graduate students. The highly accomplished, motivated student body represents all 50 states, the District of Columbia, Puerto Rico, the Virgin Islands, and 71 foreign countries.

STUDENT BODY

The Rensselaer student government plays a major role in directing student life. With a budget of approximately $8.5 million, the student government funds and manages numerous student organizations, clubs, and sports. Rensselaer students have a large assortment of extracurricular activities from which to choose. Nearly all are run by the students themselves. Rensselaer is home to 28 men's fraternities, 2 co-ed fraternities, and 4 sororities. Student media include a weekly newspaper and a 10,000-watt FM stereo station. Theater groups, musical ensembles, and over 170 clubs, professional societies, special interest groups, sports leagues, and organizations provide for a full slate of options beyond the classroom. Over 5,000 RPI students compete in 18 intramural sports. Rensselaer also engages in intercollegiate sports, fielding a Division I men's ice hockey team and 22 Division III men's and women's teams in 13 sports. An indoor track, an all-weather track and field facility, weight rooms, several indoor tennis courts, handball and squash courts, and two swimming pools are among the school's recreational facilities. All forms of outside entertainment, from performers to guest lecturers, visit the school's Student Union, Chapel and Cultural Center, and Houston Field House.

ACADEMICS

Rensselaer is on the cutting edge of educational innovation and reform. Rensselaer's interactive, studio-based approach to teaching won the prestigious National Electrical Engineering Department Heads Association (NEEDHA) Innovative Program Award in 2001. The Rensselaer approach supplements lectures with discussion sessions, team problem-solving assignments, and one-on-one faculty mentoring. Each year, the school has striven to reduce the amount of class time devoted to traditional lectures. Rensselaer has also revamped its approach to better suit the material taught. Instead of a conventional semester system in which students take five or more 3-credit courses, Rensselaer employs a "4x4" curriculum of four 4-credit-hour courses. Students may access faculty, the university's information systems, the Internet, and each other from practically anywhere on campus, thanks to the school's mobile computing network. All Rensselaer students are required to have a laptop computer meeting Renssleaer specifications. A Rensselaer education is notable for the close working relationships it fosters between students and their instructors. The university encourages all students to take part in faculty research, cooperative education, independent projects, and study abroad. Hands-on experience in a wide variety of areas is available to all full-time undergraduates through the Undergraduate Research Program; the program offers both paying and credited opportunities. Students earn practical experience through their cooperative work assignments. Despite the work-study demands of a Rensselaer education, most students graduate in the class with which they entered Rensselaer. Students have the option of joining Air Force, Army, and Naval/Marine ROTC programs.

Rensselaer offers the Bachelor of Science (BS) degree in aeronautical engineering; applied physics; biochemistry/biophysics; bioinformatics and molecular biology; biology; biomedical engineering; building sciences; chemical engineering; chemistry; civil engineering; communication; computer and systems engineering; computer science; economics; electrical engineering; electric power engineering; electronic arts; electronic media, arts, and communication; engineering physics; environmental engineering; environmental science; geology; hydrogeology; industrial and management engineering; information technology; interdisciplinary science; management; materials engineering; mathematics; mechanical engineering; nuclear engineering; philosophy; physics; psychology; and science, technology, and society. Rensselaer offers professionally accredited degree programs in the fields of architecture and engineering. The Bachelor of Architecture (BArch) degree concludes a five-year program; the Master of Architecture (MArch) degree can be earned in six years. Students may choose to complete the five-year professional engineering curriculum, leading to both the Bachelor of Science and Master of Engineering (MEng) degrees, in four years. Rensselaer offers a seven-year physician-scientist program, earning a BS degree in biology from Rensselaer and an MD from Albany Medical College. Accelerated law programs are also available to management or science, technology, and society majors; the six-year program results in a BS degree from Rensselaer and a JD from Albany Law School. Other accelerated programs for undergraduates yield a BS in three years, or a BS/MS in four or five years. Rensselaer offers a combined BA/BS to students at 44 elite liberal arts colleges. Students complete three years at their original college, then transfer to Rensselaer for their final two years. They earn a BA from their original institution and a BS from Rensselaer.

Students at Rensselaer have unusually easy access to their professors because of the school's studio-style classrooms, the academic advising program, and the numerous opportunities for undergraduate research with faculty. Under faculty supervision, the duties of a graduate teaching assistant may include providing lectures on a limited basis; conducting discussions; and preparing materials for faculty-guided classroom or laboratory instruction. Teaching assistants are not responsible for the intellectual or instructional content of a course. The graduate teaching assistant serves as an instructional apprentice under the supervision of a faculty member. The school monitors professors' teaching and rewards those who are most effective in the classroom. About 350 full-time professors teach at Rensselaer; all hold the terminal degree in their field. The faculty include a Nobel laureate, National Science Foundation National Young Investigators and Early Career Awards, and fellows of the national academies.

110 Eighth Street
Troy, NY 12180-3590
Phone: 518-276-6216
Fax: 518-276-4072
Website: www.rpi.edu

ADMISSIONS

All applications are reviewed individually by Rensselaer's Admissions committee. It is important to note that some differences in preparation and academic background may be considered. In order to insure their success in Rensselaer's demanding curricula, all qualified applicants' academic preparation should include: 4 years of English, 4 years of mathematics through pre-calculus, 3 years of science including chemistry and physics, 2 years of social studies/history.

Students must provide standardized test scores for the SAT I or ACT. SAT II: Subject Tests in Math, Writing, and Science are required for Accelerated Program applicants only (or ACT in lieu of SAT I and II). Those seeking admission to the architecture or electronic arts programs must submit a portfolio by January 1. Applicants who speak English as a second language must provide Test of English as a Foreign Language (TOEFL) scores or some other proof of English proficiency. Applicants must have a minimum score of 570 on the paper-based test (PBT) or a minimum score of 230 on the computer-based test (CBT). Please note that applicants may have this requirement waived if they have an SAT Verbal score of 580 or above. *Note:* Please include Rensselaer's institutional code of 2757 for the SAT and TOEFL exams, and include the college code of 2866 for the ACT Assessment. This will ensure that your scores arrive at Rensselaer's Admissions Office.

Candidates for the fall term must submit applications by January 1 of the year in which they wish to be admitted. Those seeking early decision must apply by November 15; those seeking entry into accelerated programs must apply by December 1. The school offers a limited number of January admissions to freshmen and transfer students. The university has transfer arrangements with nearly 100 institutions, and all 107 campuses of the California state community college system. Rensselaer encourages all prospective students to visit campus. Tours led by Rensselaer students and admissions information sessions are available year-round. For more information, please contact:

Rensselaer Admissions
Rensselaer Polytechnic Institute
110 8th Street
Troy, NY 12180-3590
Phone: 518-276-6216
E-mail: admissions@rpi.edu
World Wide Web: http://admissions.rpi.edu

CAMPUS LIFE

Rensselaer is located in Troy, New York, in northeastern New York state. Other area cities include Schenectady and Albany (the capital of New York). All told, New York's Capital District is home to almost 900,000 people. Government, industry, business, and education are all major contributors to the area's economy. 14 area institutions of higher learning bring over 40,000 undergraduates to the area each year. Rensselaer makes its home on a 260-acre campus overlooking the Hudson River. Most observers liken the campus grounds to a quiet, well-tended park. The architectural core of the campus consists of century-old, classical-style brick buildings covered in ivy—all of which have been renovated to reflect twenty-first-century technology. The school has a number of modern facilities as well, and has begun construction of a center for biotechnology research and interdisciplinary studies, scheduled to open in the spring of 2004. Next on the construction horizon is a magnificent venue to celebrate and support experimental media and performing arts on the Rensselaer campus and in the surrounding area. The school's cutting-edge teaching techniques are visible everywhere, however, the historical commitment to Rensselaer's older buildings and area legacy have been carefully preserved. Rensselaer is conveniently located within several hours of some exciting major cities. New York City is only two-and-a-half hours' drive from campus. Boston can be reached in three hours; Montreal, four. Numerous recreational facilities are within an hour of the school; the Adirondacks, the Berkshires, and the Catskills, all offer opportunities to ski, hike, camp, and boat. Dozens of student clubs serve those whose interests lead them to the outdoors.

Rensselaer maintains formal exchange programs with Williams College in Massachusetts and Harvey Mudd College in California. The university also sponsors study abroad programs in Australia, China, Denmark, England, France, Germany, India, Italy, Japan, Spain, Switzerland, and Turkey. Additional cooperative programs with local two- and four-year institutions allow students to supplement the Rensselaer curriculum with courses at other schools, at no additional cost. Over 200 Rensselaer students take advantage of this cross-registration program annually.

COST AND AID

Tuition for the 2003–2004 academic year is $27,700; room and board, on average, total $9,083 (depending on room and meal plan); additional fees total $796. With the advent of a program requiring laptop computers of all students, an option to purchase the laptop is available on campus. Students may, however, bring their own if it meets the published specifications.

Many of Rensselaer's turn-of-the century buildings house ultra-modern classrooms and laboratories.

RIDER UNIVERSITY

GENERAL INFORMATION

Rider University, established in 1865, is a co-ed, independent institution with no religious affiliation. Rider's two campuses are located in Lawrenceville, New Jersey, and Princeton, New Jersey. The university is an accredited member of the Middle States Association of Colleges and Schools. The university is comprised of four academic colleges. The College of Business Administration; the College of Liberal Arts, Education, and Sciences and the College of Continuing Studies are in Lawrenceville. The Westminster Choir College is in Princeton. Rider is fundamentally a teaching institution, and its faculty members all share a devotion helping students develop the knowledge and skills needed to succeed in their disciplines. Doctorates or equivalent degrees have been earned by greater than 95 percent of the University's full-time faculty. There are no teaching assistants at Rider; instead, faculty members lead all classrooms and laboratories. Rider's 353-acre campus in Lawrenceville combines vast outdoor spaces with up-to-date building. Not one of Rider's 38 buildings is more than 35 years old. More than two-thirds of Rider's 3,100 undergrads live in campus residence halls or fraternity and sorority houses. All students who meet application and deposit deadlines will receive campus housing. The university's athletic teams all compete in NCAA Division I. Women may participate in basketball, cross-country, field hockey, indoor track, soccer, softball, swimming and diving, tennis, track and field, and volleyball. Men's may participate in baseball, basketball, cross-country, golf, indoor track, soccer, swimming and diving, tennis, track and field, and wrestling.

STUDENT BODY

The campus's active Student Government Association (SGA) sponsors a variety of events, including lectures, plays, and concerts. Students devise, amend, and enforce all regulations pertaining to social rules. The SGA includes representatives from each class, residence hall, the Panhellenic Society, the Interfraternity Council, and the commuting student population.

ACADEMICS

Each college at Rider mandates that students must complete at least 120 credit hours to receive a degree. In all cases, students must complete, at minimum, their final 30 credit hours at Rider. In the College of Business Administration, students must complete the last 45 credit hours while at Rider. Students in all disciplines are eligible to participate in the Baccalaureate Honors Program. Consideration may be given to any incoming freshmen students who are ranked in the highest 10 percent of their high-school classes and have a combined score of 1150 or more on the SAT I. Furthermore, current and incoming transfer students with a 3.25 GPA or higher are eligible. The Baccalaureate Honors Program Committee interviews each applicant to the program. Rider University acknowledged scores on Advanced Placement (AP) exams. For most tests, scores of 3 or higher will earn students credit and/or accelerated placement. Students who meet minimum required standards on tests through the College-Level Examination Program (CLEP) may receive course credit as well, depending on their score.

Through the College of Business Administration students can earn Bachelor of Science in Business Administration (BSBA) degrees in accounting, actuarial science, advertising, business administration, computer information systems, economics, finance, global business, human resource management, management and leadership, and marketing. Rider is an accredited member of the AACSB International—The Association to Advance Collegiate Schools of Business. The College of Liberal Arts, Education, and Sciences, or CLAES, offers a Bachelor of Arts (BA) in elementary education and secondary education. The College offers a Bachelor of Science (BS) in business education and marketing and distributive education. The National Council for the Accreditation of Teacher Education (NCATE) has approved the College's education programs. Other BA degrees awarded by CLAES include American studies, communications, economics, English, fine arts, French, German, history, global and multinational studies, journalism, mathematics, philosophy, physics, political science, psychology, Russian, sociology, and Spanish. Additional BS degrees are available in biochemistry, biology, biopsychology, chemistry, environmental science, geoscience, and marine science. Pre-professional degrees in allied health, dentistry, law, and medicine are offered as well. Among graduates of the pre-med program who seek admittance to medical schools, approximately 75 percent are accepted. And approximately 92 percent of those students applying to law school are accepted. At Rider, career preparation is continued outside of the classroom. Services such as group and individual career counseling, job-hunt workshops, resume creation, and video interview opportunities are available to students through the Office of Career Services. Other career-oriented opportunities include internships, a referral service, and a steady docket of on-campus visits by recruiters from regional, national, and global companies. Nearly 95 percent of Rider's graduates find employment or pursue advanced degrees.

Rider's faculty consists of 226 full-time and 187 part-time members. Ninety-five percent of Rider's faculty has earned a doctorate or equivalent degree. Undergraduates and graduates share the same faculty. Teaching assistants are not used at Rider. The University's 13:1 student/faculty ratio is testament to its dedication to granting students individual guidance. In addition, faculty hold seats on student affairs committees and advise student organizations.

2083 Lawrenceville Road
Lawrenceville, NJ 08648
Phone: 609-896-5042
Fax: 609-895-6645
Website: www.rider.edu

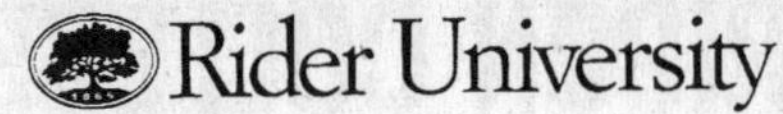

ADMISSIONS

To be admitted to Rider University, candidates must have completed at least 16 units of college-preparatory study by the completion of high school. This requirement includes 4 units in English and 12 in other traditional disciplines, such as foreign languages, history, literature, mathematics, science, and social studies. The college-preparatory requirement may not be fulfilled by vocational or business classes. A mathematics prerequisite (at least, algebra I, algebra II, and geometry) exists for all applicants to pre-med, pre-dentistry, business, mathematics, and science programs. All students must provide official SAT I or ACT results. Most students admitted to the University have finished in the top 50 percent of their graduating class in high school. Rider University promotes diversity among its student body and invites applications from candidates of all economic, ethnic, geographic, racial, and religious backgrounds. While on-campus interviews are not required, they are strongly encouraged. Student ambassadors host candidates during campus visits, including taking them to a class, to lunch, and introducing them to various students and faculty members. In other words, student ambassadors give prospective students "a day in the life" at Rider. Rider University accepts applications on a rolling basis, though fall-semester candidates are recommended to file applications no later than February 15 to ensure campus housing. Spring semester candidates should submit by December 15. Students may also apply via the Early Action Option. A $40 fee must be included with the submission of an application. Admissions decisions are usually sent three to four weeks after an application is submitted. To find out more about Rider University contact:

Director of Undergraduate Admissions
Rider University
2083 Lawrenceville Road
Lawrenceville, NJ 08648-3099
Telephone: 609-896-5042 or 800-257-9026
E-mail: admissions@rider.edu
World Wide Web: www.rider.edu

CAMPUS LIFE

Lawrenceville, New Jersey, is the suburban home of Rider University. Lawrenceville is located about halfway between Princeton and Trenton, with Philadelphia about 45 minutes southwest and New York City a little more than an hour northeast. While students have easy access to the abounding opportunities in these surrounding communities, they are able to concentrate on their studies in a quiet, suburban environment.

The University offers study abroad programs in countries such as Austria, England, France, Israel, Puerto Rico, and Spain and many more. Semester and year-long programs are available.

COST AND AID

Annual tuition in 2003–2004 will be $20,590. A $200 student activity charge and a once-only $200 orientation fee are added. Room and board costs equal $8,060 per year. Books, transportation, and other personal expenses run approximately $1,900.

RIPON COLLEGE

GENERAL INFORMATION

Ripon offers an intensely personal undergraduate education. Ask any senior who has done research with a faculty member, any junior who has gone jogging with her biology professor, any sophomore who has been over to his English professor's home for dinner, or any first-year student who spent two hours going over a paper in a faculty member's office, and they'll tell you-we take your education very personally. Since 1851, Ripon has been providing a personal education that makes a remarkable difference in the lives of students. And because a personal education is fundamentally a better education, we warmly invite you to learn more about Ripon.

STUDENT BODY

Take advantage of all the opportunities to participate at Ripon. You'll do more than you ever imagined, and learn so much about yourself in the process. You can broadcast a jazz show on the campus radio station, chair a Student Senate committee, or plan a Martin Luther King Day celebration. While experience might be required at a large school, it's not at Ripon. The amateur and the expert alike can participate in an extracurricular environment that is, as David Sarnowski, director of student activities, says, "as comfortable as your favorite pair of shoes. Anyone can try Ripon on."

A Sampling of Activities: Black Student Union, Chamber Music Ensemble, Choral Union, *College Days* (campus newspaper), Forensics, Jazz Ensemble, Multi-Cultural Club, music and dramatic theatre productions, Student Senate, WRPN-FM (campus radio station).

Men's Varsity: Baseball, basketball, cross-country, football, golf, soccer, swimming, tennis, track.

Women's Varsity: Basketball, Cross-Country, Golf, Soccer, Softball, Swimming, Tennis, Track, Volleyball.

ACADEMICS

You need to think critically, speak convincingly, and write clearly to be prepared for the world of work. Companies are looking for college graduates who can write, use modern technology with confidence, communicate, and make a contribution to a team. These are skills you will learn—and learn well—at Ripon College. We have initiated a Communicating Plus program, which emphasizes the development of written and oral communication and problem-solving skills. While other colleges have become increasingly specialized, Ripon has remained steadfast in its belief that the liberal arts are the key for a life of both personal and professional success.

Our new business administration program is fully integrated with our liberal arts philosophy, preparing business leaders who are socially responsible, independent and creative thinkers, who have an interest in business that may or may not follow mainstream society.

A Ripon education could take you anywhere. You could study psychology and play basketball at Ripon and then become a five-time Grammy winner like jazz singer Al Jarreau '62. You could guide the space shuttle into orbit like Jeff Bantle '80, chief flight director office, NASA, or become an international opera star like Gail Dobish '76. Perhaps you'll set records in medical science like neonatologist Dr. John Muraskas '78, who is on record for saving the world's smallest premature baby, or cover world events, like Richard Threlkeld '59, former Moscow correspondent for CBS News. Or perhaps you'll end up in *Inc.* magazine like Larry Laux '78, whose software firm was identified as one of the nation's fastest growing companies. As a Ripon student you will define your dream. As a Ripon graduate, you will have the skills you need to make your dream a reality.

Majors: Anthropology, art, biology, business administration, chemistry, chemistry-biology, communication, computer science, economics, educational studies, exercise science, foreign languages (French, German), global studies, history, Latin American area studies, mathematics, music, philosophy, physical science, politics and government, psychobiology, psychology, religion, sociology-anthropology, Spanish, theatre.

Pre-professional Programs: Dentistry, journalism, law and government, library and information science, medicine, ministry, optometry, physical therapy, veterinary medicine.

Dual Degree Programs: Engineering, forestry, nursing & allied health sciences/medical technology, social welfare.

Certification Programs: Education certification, early childhood, elementary, elementary/middle school, secondary, secondary/middle, music K-12, physical education K-12.

Unique Programs: Leadership studies, women's studies, Army ROTC, sports medicine/athletic training.

Ripon has 47 full-time and 27 part-time faculty members. Ninety percent of the full-time faculty have PhDs.

300 Seward Street, PO Box 248
Ripon, WI 54971
Phone: 920-748-8337
Fax: 920-748-8335
Website: www.ripon.edu

ADMISSIONS

Ripon College enrolls students who will contribute to and benefit from the academic and residential programs we provide. Ripon does not discriminate on the basis of gender, sexual orientation, race, color, age, religion, national and ethnic origin, or disability in the administration of its educational policies, admission practices, scholarship and loan programs, athletic and other college-administered programs.

The faculty committee on academic standards establishes the criteria for admission. Among the factors considered are the student's secondary school record, scores on standardized tests (SAT or ACT), recommendations from the applicant's school, and extracurricular or community service activities. The Ripon College admission process reflects the personal attention students can expect to receive during their college careers, and applicants are encouraged to provide any additional information that they consider helpful.

For more information on Ripon College, contact:

Admission Office
Ripon College
300 Seward Street
PO Box 248
Ripon, WI 54971
Telephone: 800-94RIPON

CAMPUS LIFE

A residential college really makes a difference. The nearly 1,000 students here do more than go to class: they live, work, play, and learn in the same setting. Ninety percent of the students at Ripon live on campus. Here, you'll launch a club with English classmates, have dinner at a chemistry professor's home, maybe even play a game of softball with the president. There is an openness that extends from the warmth of the city of Ripon to the college's operation and governance. If a personal, challenging liberal arts and sciences education in a small and caring community of students and professors is what you're looking for, then put Ripon on your list of schools to visit.

Small classes matter. There's a strong relationship between the size of your classes and how much you learn. Ripon's classes average 20 students. There are no teaching assistants, no pencil-coded exams, no cavernous auditoriums. Instead, you'll discover a personal community of students and faculty members, often on a first-name basis, exchanging ideas with people they know. Personal education—that's the way students learn at Ripon College. Seventy percent of the classes at Ripon have fewer than 20 students.

International Exchanges: Central Europe, China, Costa Rica, Czech Republic, England, France, Germany, Hong Kong, Hungary, India, Italy, Japan, Puerto Rico, Russia, Spain, Tanzania, United Kingdom.

Domestic Exchanges: Chicago Semester in the Arts, Fisk University-Ripon Exchange Program, Newberry Library Program in the Humanities, Oak Ridge Science Semester (Knoxville, Tennessee), ROTC Basic Camp, Urban Education (Chicago), Urban Studies (Chicago), Washington Semester, Woods Hole.

COST AND AID

Ripon College is a smart investment worth making now. Your future depends on the choices you make today. Choosing a college is an emotional and an economic decision. You want to go where it feels right-but you also want to choose a college that provides a high return on your investment. In 2002, *U.S. News & World Report* labeled Ripon a Best Value including the College in its national list of Great Schools at Great Prices. Additionally, Ripon ranks high for having graduates who accumulate the least amount of debt.

Tuition is $19,700, room and board is $5,055, and fees are $240, for a comprehensive cost of $24,995.

RIVIER COLLEGE

GENERAL INFORMATION

Rivier College is a Catholic, coeducational, private liberal arts college founded in 1933. Over the years, the academic world has consistently acknowledged the quality of Rivier's academic offerings. The College emphasizes the need for both a solid grounding in the liberal arts and hands-on training in career-related study. In this way, Rivier optimally prepares its undergraduates for a wide variety of post-graduation options. Approximately 1,550 students attend the School of Undergraduate Studies, with about 700 attending full-time during the day. Undergraduates benefit from a low student/faculty ratio (18:1) that results in small classes; the small student population allows all who are interested to become extremely active in Rivier's academic and social spheres. While Rivier continues to expand, it maintains its commitment to providing a small-college education that stresses great teaching and a support network for students that reaches well beyond the classroom. The typical full-time undergraduate at Rivier is between 18 and 22 years old and a resident of New England. A number of students come from New Jersey and New York, while a few arrive from such far-flung locales as Texas, Florida, and countries in Africa, Asia, Europe, and South America.

Rivier maintains four modern residence halls; most rooms are double-occupancy. A little less than half the school's full-time day students commute. The Dion Student Center includes a dining room, bookstore, mailroom, meeting rooms, a commuter lounge, and student development office. Undergraduates may have cars on campus. The Office of Student Development sponsors an orientation period for incoming students. Undergraduate support services are provided throughout the year by several agencies. Rivier employs a chaplain full-time who, with Campus Ministry, organizes spiritual activities. Rivier maintains a full-service career development program to prepare students for life upon leaving the College. A campus clinic attends to students' health needs, and a campus counseling center provides services.

Student organizations and clubs offer a wide assortment of cultural, recreational, and social activities, including live performances, sporting events, and films. These organizations are funded and overseen by the Student Government Association. Rivier fields athletic teams that compete in Division III of the NCAA. Men's teams include baseball, basketball, cross-country, soccer, and volleyball (nationally ranked in 2001 and 2002). Women's teams include basketball, cross-country, soccer, softball, and volleyball. A broad assortment of intramural sports and fitness options are available, including aerobics, floor hockey, skiing (cross-country and downhill), tennis, volleyball, and weight training. There are frequent outings to Boston to enjoy the city's many cultural and recreational outlets, as well as organized trips to other destinations. The Rivier Theater Company mounts productions throughout the year.

STUDENT BODY

All full-time undergraduates are members of the Student Government Association (SGA), which aims to enliven the campus by organizing activities, to communicate student needs and aspirations to the administration, and to foster a spirit of cooperation that allows students and the administration to work together for the benefit of undergraduates and Rivier College. The SGA manages the student activity fee, which is used to oversee and supervise student organizations and clubs. Students' views on institutional policies are communicated to the administration through the SGA Executive Board.

ACADEMICS

Rivier College offers an exceptional curriculum that includes both professional studies and a solid grounding in the liberal arts. The goal of the curriculum is to prepare students to adapt to the fast-changing world of the future. The curriculum emphasizes the importance of general knowledge and is designed to promote personal growth, challenge students, and prepare undergraduates for successful and rewarding careers. Different degrees carry different core curriculum requirements, but nearly all include coursework in English, mathematics and/or natural sciences, modern languages and literature, philosophy, religious studies, social science, and western civilization. Students must complete at least 10 courses in their major field. Undergraduates must earn at least 120 credits and maintain a grade point average of at least 2.0 to receive a bachelor's degree. Students must complete at least 60 credits and earn a grade point average of at least 2.0 to receive an associate's degree.

Rivier College undergraduates may earn Bachelor of Arts, Bachelor of Fine Arts, and Bachelor of Science degrees in the following areas of concentration: art (drawing and painting, graphic design, illustration, photography and digital imaging, and studio art), biology and biology education, business (business administration, information technology management, and management), communications (broadcast/print journalism, desktop publishing, and public relations), computer science, education (early childhood/special, elementary/special, and secondary), English, English education, history, human development, government, liberal studies, mathematics, mathematics education, modern languages (modern-language education and Spanish), nursing, psychology, social science education, and sociology. Students can also receive associate's degrees in art, business (business administration, management and information technology management), computer science, early childhood education, liberal arts, and nursing. The College offers pre-professional programs in dentistry, law, medicine, and veterinary medicine.

420 Main Street
Nashua, NH 03060
Phone: 603-897-8507
Fax: 603-891-1799
Website: www.rivier.edu

All qualified juniors and seniors are encouraged to seek internships related to their fields of study. Those studying education serve as student-teachers in local schools as early as their freshman year, while nursing students undertake clinical rotations in a variety of area health-care facilities. Communications and English students often find internships in broadcasting and public relations. Art majors have opportunities to work in graphic design, advertising, or galleries. Students of government have a wide variety of options: law firms, legal-assistance agencies, government, and local businesses. Psychology and sociology majors often intern with local social service organizations and agencies. Special offerings in career education include the associate's and bachelor's degree programs in nursing.

The school offers exceptional students the opportunity to make the dean's list, join Kappa Gamma Pi, earn a degree designated "with honors," and receive listing in *The National Dean's List* and *Who's Who Among Students in American Universities and Colleges*. Rivier offers a four-year Honors Program to students with exceptional academic talents. The Rivier academic calendar consists of two 15-week semesters. The first semester ends with an examination period prior to Christmas recess. Students typically take five courses per semester. Incoming students may earn academic credit by demonstrating their achievement level through Advanced Placement and CLEP examinations. Students may also request a special examination to determine whether they can receive credit for a course offered at Rivier.

Eighty full-time instructors make up the Rivier faculty, resulting in a 13:1 ratio of full-time students to faculty. The school hires part-time instructors from among area professionals whose real-world expertise adds new, cutting-edge elements to classroom instruction. Faculty members, not graduate students, teach all classes. Department chairs provide undergraduate academic advising to students in their departments.

ADMISSIONS

Rivier suggests that applicants complete at least 16 academic units by the end of their senior year of high school, including 4 in English, 2 in a modern foreign language (waived in certain cases), 3 in mathematics, 2 each in social science and science, and 3 in electives. Students most likely to be admitted have been ranked in the upper half of their graduating class and have maintained a minimum 3.0 GPA in academic courses. Art students must include a portfolio as part of their application. Rivier welcomes transfer applications and applications from students outside the United States. Transfer students are required to provide official transcripts of all work at all previous colleges as well as a high school transcript. International students may be asked provide official TOEFL (Test of English as a Foreign Language) scores and must meet all other requirements for general admission. Rivier will defer admission to applicants it accepts for one year, provided the student does not undertake full-time post-secondary study in the interim period. All applications must include a non-refundable $25 application fee, SAT I scores, a letter of recommendation, and an official high school transcript.

Rivier admits applicants on a rolling basis; applicants generally are notified of the school's admission decision a month after submitting a completed application. Transfer applications should arrive no later than June 1 (for admission in the following fall semester) or December 1 (for the spring semester). Financial aid applications are due by February 1. The College strongly suggests that candidates schedule a personal interview, but this is not required. Contact the Admissions Office to arrange an interview. To receive more specific information or an application form, contact:

Director of Undergraduate Admissions
Rivier College
420 Main Street
Nashua, NH 03060
Telephone: 603-897-8507 or 800-44-RIVIER (toll free)
Fax: 603-891-1799
E-mail: rivadmit@rivier.edu
World Wide Web: www.rivier.edu

CAMPUS LIFE

Rivier's hometown of Nashua (population 84,000) is located just north of the Massachusetts border, about 15 miles northeast of Lowell. Boston is only 40 miles to the southeast and can be easily reached by public transportation or car. The region is flush with lakes and ski areas that allow for many wonderful recreational opportunities year-round. The White Mountains are just to the north of Nashua; the ocean can be reached by car in one hour.

The College is a member of the New Hampshire College and University Council, a consortium of 12 senior colleges. Membership in the Council allows Rivier students to take courses at any member college; Rivier confers credit for courses completed at any of the member institutions.

COST AND AID

For 2002–2003, tuition and fees were $17,730; room and board was $6,916; and books and supplies, on average, cost about $700. A $100 activities fee and a $25 registration fee are charged each semester.

ROCKFORD COLLEGE

GENERAL INFORMATION

Founded as the Rockford Female Seminary in 1847, Rockford College is a private, coeducational, fully accredited independent institution of higher learning. Undergraduate study in more than 40 fields as well as graduate programs in business and education are offered at Rockford, which is located approximately 90 miles northwest of Chicago. A Rockford education is grounded firmly in the liberal arts and sciences; communication skills are stressed throughout the curriculum. Excellence in scholarship and dedication to undergraduate teaching are both emphasized within the Rockford faculty. *U.S. News & World Report* has named Rockford a top-tier regional university. The school is one of only 11 Illinois undergraduate institutions with a Phi Beta Kappa chapter.

Rockford is home to 1,200 students, drawn from more than 25 states and 20 countries. The school offers a wide assortment of residential options. Rockford College encourages students to engage in a full slate of co-curricular activities. Community service plays a large role in the lives of many Rockford students. Many also find time for departmental clubs, honorary academic societies, and intramural sports programs. Career services, recreational programming, health and counseling, and international student support are available through the Student Affairs Division. Roughly one in four full-time students are involved in Rockford's intercollegiate athletic program. The Rockford College Regents compete in Division III of the NCAA and in the Northern Illinois and Iowa Conference (NIIC). Women field teams in basketball, soccer, softball, tennis, and volleyball. Men compete in baseball, basketball, football, golf, soccer, and tennis.

STUDENT BODY

Students participate in the administration of the College through the Rockford College Student Government. Through the SGA, students run the student court, enforce the honor code, oversee campus media, serve on College committees, and consult with administrators on campus policy changes. Through the Entertainment Council, the SGA organizes campus events, including concerts, dances, lectures, and other social activities.

ACADEMICS

Rockford develops students as generalists, and as experts in their chosen field. The liberal arts curriculum requires both broad-based learning and concentration in a major area. To graduate, students must complete a minimum of 124 credit hours. Rockford operates on a two-semester calendar, and also offers summer courses. The College admits elite students to its Honors Program in Liberal Arts, whose extensive core curriculum and thorough distribution requirements place particular emphasis on the humanities. Students must apply separately for admission to the Honors Program. All students may participate in the Forum Series, which focuses on great ideas, significant scholars, and influential artists. Rockford hosts a chapter of Phi Beta Kappa as well as other scholastic honor societies. The Archaeological Institute of America, academic internships, art exhibits, faculty seminars, opportunities for independent study, and a broad-ranging study abroad program are among the other features of the College. All new students must complete a freshman seminar program.

Rockford awards the Bachelor of Arts degree in accounting, anthropology/sociology, art (with concentrations in ceramics, drawing, painting, photography, printmaking, and sculpture), art history, biology, business administration (with tracks in management and marketing), chemistry, classics, computer science (management information systems), criminal justice (program in anthropology/sociology), economics (with tracks in finance, international economics, and public policy), education, English, French, German, history, Latin, mathematics, music history and literature, philosophy, physical education (with tracks in business and teaching), political science, psychology, science and mathematics, social sciences, Spanish, theater arts, and urban studies. Rockford awards the Bachelor of Fine Arts degree in art (with concentrations in ceramics, drawing, painting, photography, printmaking, and sculpture) and performing arts (musical theater performance). Rockford awards the Bachelor of Science degree in accounting, anthropology/sociology, biochemistry, biology, business administration (with tracks in management and marketing), chemistry, computer science (management information systems), economics (with tracks in finance, international economics, and public policy), education, English, history, mathematics, physical education (with tracks in business and teaching), political science, pre-social work (program in anthropology/sociology), psychology, science and mathematics, social sciences, and urban studies. The College also offers a four-year NLNAC-accredited Bachelor of Science in Nursing program. Registered nurses may take a BSN completion program specifically designed to meet their academic and professional needs. Rockford offers meticulously designed pre-professional programs for those interested in dentistry, engineering (3-2 program), health professions (optometry and physical therapy), law, medicine, pharmacy, and veterinary medicine. Rockford College students may also minor in any of the following areas: British studies, communication, dance, Greek, human development, military science, peace and conflict studies, physics, and religious studies.

Office of Admission, 5050 East State Street
Rockford, IL 61108-2393
Phone: 815-226-4050
Fax: 815-226-2822
Website: www.rockford.edu

More than 80 men and women of distinguished academic achievement make up the full-time faculty; the student/faculty ratio is 12:1. Nearly three-fourths of the faculty hold PhDs or the equivalent terminal degree in their fields of expertise. Professionals who work in the Rockford and Chicago areas are often invited to teach at Rockford College so that students can learn first-hand of up-to-the-minute developments in various businesses and industries. The College maintains a faculty development program to keep professors abreast of the latest teaching techniques. Students interact with faculty members as advisors and mentors; the faculty also advise student organizations and clubs. Incoming freshmen are matched with advisors and mentors from the full-time faculty.

ADMISSIONS

The Rockford Office of Admission considers each application individually with the goal of assessing candidates' potential for academic success at the College. The school looks primarily at an applicant's record of academic and personal achievement, including class rank, GPA, quality of high school curriculum, and standardized test scores (ACT or SAT I). Applicants must demonstrate at least a 2.65 high school GPA, placement in the top half of their class, and minimum standardized test scores of 19 for the ACT (with no subscore below 17) or a combined 910 on the SAT I. All applications must include official transcripts and standardized test score reports. Students may submit applications any time after the completion of their junior year in high school. Transfer students are assessed based on their college course work (once they have completed at least 12 hours of college-level study) and must provide transcripts from all colleges and universities they have attended. Transfer students must show a minimum college GPA of 2.30. Applications must be accompanied by a nonrefundable $35 application fee; students who visit the campus, however, receive a waiver of this fee. The College strongly recommends on-campus interviews and the inclusion of a personal statement in the application. In some cases, the College may request letters of recommendation. The Director of International Student Admission handles all applications from international students. Applicants must earn a minimum TOEFL score of 550. Contact the Office of Admission for more information.

The College expects degree applicants to complete a college-preparatory high school curriculum of 15 academic units including 4 years of English and at least three of the following: 2 years of mathematics (algebra and geometry), 1 year of history, 1 year of foreign language, and 1 year of lab science. Those wishing to study nursing should complete chemistry and biology while in high school. Rockford College admits applicants on a rolling basis. Students are typically notified of the school's decision within two weeks of submitting completed applications (with all required accompanying documents). To receive additional information, please contact:

Office of Admission
Nelson Hall
Rockford College
5050 East State Street
Rockford, IL 61108-2393
Telephone: 815-226-4050 or 800-892-2984 (toll free in the U.S. and Canada)
Fax: 815-226-2822
E-mail: admission@rockford.edu
Website: www.rockford.edu

CAMPUS LIFE

The city of Rockford is conveniently located near two major metropolises; Chicago and Milwaukee are 90 miles away. Rockford is a substantial city in its own right, the second-largest in Illinois. It is home to the MetroCentre, the Coronado Theater, the New Amsterdam Theater, the Rockford Dance company, more than 500 restaurants, museums, shopping centers and malls, and a justly famous park district. The city can be easily reached by car, plane, or bus. Many Rockford College students interact frequently with the urban community by performing volunteer service and engaging in internships and part-time jobs. The College views its home city and its surrounding community as integral to the Rockford educational experience.

Students seeking study abroad opportunities will discover several options at Rockford. For about the same cost as studying at the Rockford campus, students can spend a semester or a full year at Regent's College in London, England. Regent's College offers a wide assortment of fully accredited academic options as well as internship opportunities. It is a residential college set in a culturally rich area; theaters, galleries, and museums are all nearby. Students residing at Regent's College should have no trouble traveling throughout Britain and the rest of the European continent. Other study abroad programs send Rockford undergraduates to Australia, France, Germany, Spain, and other countries. Rockford participates in the Washington and United Nations semesters here in the United States.

COST AND AID

Tuition for the 2002–2003 academic year is $18,320 for tuition; room, for a double occupancy, is $3,600 annually. Board plans start at $2,330 per year. Students should expect to spend about $900 per year on books and $2,000 on additional expenses (transportation, discretionary spending, etc.).

SAINT ANSELM COLLEGE

GENERAL INFORMATION

Saint Anselm was established by Benedictine monks in 1889. It is one of the three original Catholic colleges established in New England. There are 1,964 students (1,078 women and 886 men) enrolled at Saint Anselm; the school is and will remain committed to maintaining its status as a small college. Saint Anselm feels that the small college atmosphere allows it to choose applicants selectively, ensuring that all students enrolled are fully dedicated to academic excellence. In addition, its small enrollment enables Saint Anselm to maintain the distinctive spirit of long-standing family spirit for which Benedictine institutions are known. Saint Anselm offers specialized major courses of study in business, liberal arts, nursing, pre-professional preparation, and the sciences. The College's main objective, however, is to offer learning opportunities that will help students blossom into innovative and open-minded individuals with well-rounded educational backgrounds. Saint Anselm looks upon each of its students as a unique individual and highly respects each student's life aspirations.

STUDENT BODY

Student government helps to create an atmosphere of camaraderie and unity on campus. Saint Anselm's student government consists of three branches: the Campus Activities Board, the Class Councils, and the Student Senate. The student government's primary goal is to ensure that all students have as many educational opportunities open to them as possible. Student government coordinates academic, cultural, and social functions, all of which are essential to a broad liberal arts education. Student government provides students with the opportunity to hone such crucial life skills as cooperation, resourcefulness, and leadership.

There are over 80 organizations at Saint Anselm's, catering to a wide variety of interests. Among these are the Abbey Players (theater group), choral groups, the debate group, an economics club, a jazz band, a local Knights of Columbus chapter, a music society, an outing club, a pre-law society, a pre-med society, and a volunteer center. Anselm offers men's intercollegiate sports in baseball, basketball, cross-country, football, golf, hockey, lacrosse, skiing, soccer, and tennis, and women's sports in basketball, cross-country, field hockey, lacrosse, skiing, soccer, softball, tennis, and volleyball. Intramural sports at the College include basketball, ice hockey, indoor and outdoor soccer, racquetball, softball, tennis, and volleyball. There are men's and women's club sports in alpine skiing, crew, cycling, rugby, ski and snowboard, swimming, and track. There is also a cheerleading club for women and a volleyball club for men.

ACADEMICS

Students at Saint Anselm College are provided with a sound liberal arts education to supplement their primary field of study. Students normally take between 10 and 15 courses directly related to their major; the remainder of the 40 courses needed to graduate consist of liberal arts core curriculum and a variety of electives. Students in the Honors Program take additional courses in order to earn their Honors Degree. As freshmen and sophomores, all students take part in Saint Anselm's humanities program, which is recognized throughout the nation. This rigorous program, known as "Portraits of Human Greatness," focuses on a series of group seminars and lectures that explore various facets of western civilization. Saint Anselm takes part in the College Board's Advanced Placement program. Students who earn a score of 3 or greater on the AP examinations may gain credit and advanced placement in the related course of study. Students who have taken examinations through the College-Level Examination Program may be awarded credit and advanced placement if they earn satisfactory scores.

At Saint Anselm College, students may pursue the Bachelor of Arts degree in accounting, biochemistry, biology, business, chemistry, classics, computer science, computer science with business, computer science with mathematics, criminal justice, economics, English, environmental science, financial economics, fine arts, French, history, liberal studies in the great books, mathematics, mathematics with economics, natural science, philosophy, physics, politics, psychology, sociology, Spanish, and theology. A program leading to the Bachelor of Science in Nursing degree is also offered. Saint Anselm students may pursue pre-professional programs in dentistry, secondary education, law, medicine, and theology. A 3-2 engineering program is offered in partnership with the University of Notre Dame, University of Massachusetts-Lowell, Catholic University of America, and Manhattan College.

Saint Anselm's teaching staff is comprised of 122 full-time instructors and 42 part-time instructors. Ninety-five percent of Saint Anselm's full-time instructors have earned the highest degrees possible in their fields. The College's 14:1 student/teacher ratio ensures that students and professors interact closely. In addition to performing their teaching duties, faculty members work as academic advisors for students within their department. Graduate students are never appointed as course instructors.

100 Saint Anselm Drive
Manchester, NH 03102-1310
Phone: 603-641-7500
Fax: 603-641-7550
Website: www.anselm.edu

ADMISSIONS

In reviewing applications to the freshman class, the admissions board considers each prospective student individually and carefully. The board assesses each applicant's secondary school performance, SAT I or ACT scores, recommendation letters, and the written essay included in the application for admission. Of highest priority is the applicant's secondary school transcript, with a specific focus on both the rigor of course study and the marks received. Saint Anselm invites transfer and international students to apply. The same basic admission measures are necessary, as well as a minimum of a C average in all courses transferred and, for international applicants, an adequate TOEFL score. Saint Anselm College employs rolling admissions; students who apply by March 1 receive priority consideration. It is highly suggested that students visit the Saint Anselm campus for a tour and interview to fully appreciate the multitude of benefits this fine College has to offer. For more information, students should contact:

Director of Admissions
Saint Anselm College
100 Saint Anselm Drive
Manchester, NH 03102-1310
Telephone: 603-641-7500 or 888-426-7356 (toll-free)
Fax: 603-641-7550
E-mail: admissions@anselm.edu
World Wide Web: www.anselm.edu

CAMPUS LIFE

Nestled in its breathtaking New Hampshire surroundings, the Saint Anselm campus melds traditional and contemporary architecture to create a beautiful academic environment. Students from 16 countries and 27 states attend the College. Roughly 88 percent of Saint Anselm's students enjoy on-campus housing in apartments, dormitories, suites, and townhouses. Situated on the outer edge of Manchester, New Hampshire's largest city, Saint Anselm College provides the advantages of a chiefly residential neighborhood in a suburban locale. Manchester has a great deal to offer, including a variety of movie theaters, restaurants, and shopping malls. Furthermore, public transportation runs hourly between Manchester and the campus. Southern New Hampshire provides a perfect atmosphere for students desiring a dynamic college lifestyle. The exciting city of Boston, the majestic mountains, and Hampton Beach on the Atlantic Ocean are all within an hour's drive from campus.

The majority of departments throughout Saint Anselm College offer internship positions to students who wish to apply their classroom knowledge to a real-life work experience. Students normally acquire internship positions as juniors or seniors. Internships are offered in Boston, in and around Manchester, in New York City, and in Washington, D.C. Saint Anselm has several programs that allow students to study abroad. The College frequently helps students participate in programs outside the school. Study abroad programs can be incorporated into most majors and provide students with tremendous opportunities to study a foreign language and culture.

COST AND AID

The 2002–2003 school year tuition is $20,390, and room and board costs $7,700, for a total of $28,090. Books and other expenses amount to roughly $1,000.

SAINT EDWARD'S UNIVERSITY

GENERAL INFORMATION

Located in Austin, Texas, a diverse and thriving city, St. Edward's University provides an ideal combination of highly qualified teachers, individual attention, and local vibrancy in a community focused on service. As a private, liberal arts university affiliated with the Catholic church, St. Edward's is committed to providing challenges within the intimate context of a small college. The Congregation of the Holy Cross established the University, and this Catholic heritage persists in the forms of high academic achievement and personal devotion to educating and being educated. St. Edward's endeavors to guide students not only toward solving problems and thinking critically, but toward developing the convictions and abilities to confront the ever-evolving challenges of today's society. The Student Body's 3,600 members come from about 40 states and upwards of 50 countries. The undergraduate population is approximately 57 percent female. The diversity among this undergraduate Student Body breaks down to 33 percent Hispanic, 3 percent African American, 2 percent Asian/Pacific Islander, and 6 percent international. The University's College of Professional and Graduate Studies includes 700-plus graduate students pursuing degrees in business administration and human services.

STUDENT BODY

Despite the small size of the campus, St. Edward's offers a large variety of student organizations – more than 70 in all. Students at the University share extracurricular interests in academic and professional pursuits, in cultural and community service activities, in social and special interest topics. The Student Body is encouraged to be vocal, and the Student Government Association, consisting of elected members of the Student Body and representatives from constituencies around campus, is the primary vehicle for the student voice. The Association holds general meetings every two weeks to organize and implement campus activities. The president of the Association regularly attends the meetings of the Board of Trustees. Aspiring writers often contribute to the University's student-run newspaper, creative-writing journal, academic journal, and yearbook. Students taking part in the University Programming Board and the Residence Hall Association coordinate campus-wide events. St. Edward's hosts popular comedians, independent film screenings, poetry readings, and well-known local bands. The University's volunteer fair provides service-oriented students with a large number of possibilities to get involved in the surrounding community. As an NCAA Division II member, St. Edward's offers plenty of opportunities for its athletes. Men's teams include baseball, basketball, golf, soccer, and tennis. Women have teams in basketball, soccer, softball, tennis, and volleyball. On the club level, soccer and lacrosse are available. The University also offers a range of intramural sports.

ACADEMICS

During their four years at St. Edward's, all students are required to complete an intensive, 57-credit-hour general education program, which covers three fundamental aspects of learning: foundational skills (college math, computational skills, English writing, foreign language, and oral communication), cultural foundations (a six-course cluster including American Dilemma, Rise of the West, and Contemporary World Issues), and foundation for values and decision (a five-course cluster that includes Ethics and Science in Perspective). A course called Capstone, which focuses on oral and written examination, analysis, and problem solving of controversial topics, is the culmination of the gen-ed program. Each student's intensive work within a major reinforces the skills in logic, communication, and social understanding that are fostered through general education courses. Students must complete 120 credit hours to graduate. St. Edward's operates on a two-semester basis. Day and evening class are available during the summer.

A vital aspect of the St. Edward's experience is a focus on career exploration, preparation (through workshops and advising), and experience (through internships). Graduate school guidance is also available. More than 60 percent of the majors at St. Edward's include an internship or research requirement. Because opportunities are so prevalent, interested students can participate in more than one internship or research experience. Adventurous students can learn about the University's study abroad and work abroad opportunities by contacting the Office of International Education Services.

St. Edward's offers Bachelor of Arts, Bachelor of Science, and Bachelor of Business Administration degrees. Students in the School of Behavioral and Social Science can earn undergraduate degrees in criminal justice, history, international relations, political science, psychology, social work, and sociology. School of Business Administration students can earn degrees in accounting, business administration, economics, finance, management, and marketing. Through the School of Natural Science, degrees are available in biochemistry, biology, chemistry, computer information science, computer science, and mathematics. The School of Humanities offers degrees in art, communication, English literature, English writing and rhetoric, liberal studies, philosophy, photocommunications, religious studies, Spanish, Spanish and international business, and theatre arts. The School of Education confers degrees in English, kinesiology, language arts, social studies, and Spanish/bilingual education (for students pursuing certification in elementary or secondary teaching). Pre-professional programs are available in dentistry, engineering, law, medicine, and physical therapy.

Approximately 70 percent of full-time faculty members hold doctorates or other terminal degrees. The University has a 15:1 student/faculty ratio and an average of 18 students in each class. All faculty members maintain regular office hours, which allow students to meet often with faculty outside of the classroom. As freshmen, all students receive full-time advisors who offer assistance, advice, and counseling as students shape and navigate their academic careers. Students are linked with faculty advisors after 30 hours of coursework have been completed and a major has been declared.

3001 South Congress Avenue
Austin, TX 78704-6489
Phone: 512-448-8500
Fax: 512-464-8877
Website: www.stedwards.edu

ADMISSIONS

All applicants to St. Edward's are reviewed individually and evaluated according to demonstrations of academic accomplishment, a challenging curriculum, extracurricular participation, and results on standardized tests. Candidates for admission should have finished among the top 50 percent of their high school class and earned standardized test results that meet or exceed the nationwide average. The University accepts applications on a rolling basis. A student will be notified of admissions decisions two or three weeks after the Office of Admission has received the student's completed file. A file is not complete until each of the following has been submitted: the application form, the nonrefundable fee of $30, results from the SAT I or ACT test, and official transcripts from high school. Students are encouraged to submit personal statements and recommendation letters, though they are not mandatory. For more specific information on the policies and procedures of admission, visit the University website at www.stedwards.edu. For additional information, please contact:

Office of Admission
St. Edward's University
3001 South Congress Avenue
Austin, TX 78704-6489
Telephone: 512-448-8500 or 800-555-0164 (toll free)
Fax: 512.464.8877
E-mail: seu.admit@admin.stedwards.edu
World Wide Web: www.stedwards.edu

CAMPUS LIFE

Austin, the capital of Texas, is a regional center for politics, education, and culture that lies in the state's hill country along the Colorado River. With the fifth-highest population in the state, Austin offers unlimited opportunities to enjoy culture and recreation, including a variety of galleries, museums, and theaters that highlight the vibrant artistic community in the city. National and local music acts find the spotlight at venues along Sixth Street, the most popular stretch of nightspots in town. Dubbed the "Live Music Capital of the World," Austin is the annual host of the renowned South by Southwest Music and Film Festival, an event that draws increasing attention as Austin evolves into a center for major film production. With an average age of 28, the people of Austin have plenty of energy to enjoy city events, such as Mardi Gras, the Pecan Street Festival, the Bob Marley Fest, and more. Outdoor enthusiasts, who can take advantage of more than 200 parks in the city and many regional lakes, find a wealth of opportunity for boating, canoeing, rowing, tubing, swimming, wind surfing, water skiing, cycling, mountain biking, hiking, rock climbing, Frisbee, golf, and camping. And after working up an appetite, it's nice to know that Austin has the highest per capita restaurant population in the state – higher than Houston, Dallas, or San Antonio. It's not surprising that Austin is regularly listed as one of the 10 most livable cities in the country.

COST AND AID

The tuition for the 2001–2002 academic year was $12,728. Room and board costs ranged from $4,850 to $6,992, with variations according to selection of residence hall and meal plan.

SAINT FRANCIS UNIVERSITY (PA)

GENERAL INFORMATION

Saint Francis is private, Catholic, co-ed liberal arts university. Established in 1847, the University is among America's first Franciscan institutions and is the nation's 12th-oldest Catholic institution. Saint Francis operates under the conventions of the Franciscan Friars of the Third Order Regular. The University is dedicated to providing each student with top-rated academics, a vibrant student life, opportunities for leadership, and unflagging attention from a distinguished faculty. For the past century and a half, Saint Francis University's commitment to academics and student life has embodied two important values: high-quality education and respecting students as individuals. Saint Francis contends that an education in the liberal arts-consisting of a broad core of courses and a major track-provides students with the strongest preparation for successful lives. Core courses, which all students must complete, comprise Saint Francis's award-winning General Education Program.

STUDENT BODY

The University provides students many opportunities to exercise their interests and talents. For instance, 50-plus on-campus clubs and organizations are active. These range from departmental clubs to volunteer organizations, and include social and service sororities and social, service, and business fraternities. Student-run activities on campus include the Bell Tower yearbook, KSFU-FM radio, New Theatre drama group, the SFU singers, and the Troubadour newspaper. Each year, the Student Activities Organization brings a lively docket of comedians, concerts, films, and lectures to campus. The University is a member of NCAA Division I athletics and maintains a comprehensive program that consists of 21 men's and women's teams. Men may compete in basketball, cross-country, football (Division I-AA), golf, soccer, tennis, track (indoor and outdoor), and volleyball. Women may compete in basketball, cross-country, field hockey, golf, lacrosse, soccer, softball, swimming, tennis, track (indoor and outdoor), and volleyball. Men and women may also participate in cheerleading. Scholarships may be granted to athletes in all sports except football.

ACADEMICS

Bachelors degrees are typically earned within eight semesters. To graduate, each student is required to complete a course of study that meets with approval from the vice president for academic affairs. Each student must earn a minimum of 128 credits through a combination of general education, major, collateral, and elective courses. All students in every major must complete the 58-credit general education program. The University operates on a two-semester academic calendar, with three sessions in the summer.

The University offers bachelor of arts degrees in American studies, biology, computer science, criminal justice, engineering (3-2 program), English, English/communications, history, mathematics, philosophy, political science, psychology, public administration/government service, religious studies, and sociology. Bachelor of science degrees are available in accounting, biology, chemistry, computer science, criminal justice, economics and finance, elementary/special education, environmental management (3-2 program), information systems management, management, marketing, mathematics, medical technology, nursing, occupational therapy (five-year masters), physical therapy (six-year masters), physician assistant science (five-year masters), psychology, public administration/government service, secondary education, social work, and sociology. Pre-professional programs are also available in dentistry, engineering (3-2 program), law, medicine, optometry, podiatry, and veterinary medicine. Additionally, students may minor in the following areas of concentration: anthropology, biochemistry, bioinformatics, environmental politics, environmental science, forensics, international studies, marine biology, molecular biology, political communications, public management, and public relations. In cooperation with Duke University, Saint Francis offers a 3-2 program in forestry and environmental management. Students have the option of selecting a single major and a single minor, declaring a double major, or self-designing a major that suits individual goals. Select students opt to complement their academic careers by participating in the competitive honors program.

The faculty members at Saint Francis University have been selected based on their prowess in their fields of study and their abilities as educators and communicators. Seventy-six percent of the University's faculty members have earned PhDs or equivalent degrees in their academic subjects. At Saint Francis University, classes are not taught by graduate students or teaching assistants.

PO Box 600
Loretto, PA 15940
Phone: 814-472-3000
Fax: 814-472-3335
Website: www.sfu.edu

ADMISSIONS

Admission to Saint Francis University is granted on rolling basis. All applicants must submit a completed admissions application, an official high school transcript, ACT or SAT I scores, and a minimum of one recommendation letter. A January 15 deadline applies to the physician assistant, physical therapy, and occupational therapy programs. To learn more about Saint Francis University, students and families are encouraged to call the Office of Admissions at 866-DIAL-SFU (toll free).

CAMPUS LIFE

Saint Francis University in Loretto, Pennsylvania, occupies 600 wooded acres at the crest of a mountain. From a recently completed residence hall to a nine-hole golf course and from a lake to an athletics complex, the University's campus caters to comfortable student living. Saint Francis is six miles east of the county seat, Ebensburg. The mid-sized cities of Altoona and Johnstown are nearby, each offering a wide range of entertainment and activities. Pittsburgh is 90 miles to the west.

Students who obtain permission from Saint Francis University's administration are able to participate in junior-year study abroad or receive credit for completion of summer programs in foreign countries that are operated by other accredited colleges or universities from the United States. Numerous academic departments offer specific off-campus study opportunities; some departments require off-campus experience. Student in all majors are encouraged to fill some of their elective credits with an internship.

COST AND AID

In 2002–2003, costs included $17,024 for tuition; $7,346 for room and board; and a $1,050 laptop computer fee. The tuition for full-time undergraduates is determined on a basis of 32 credits a year. Part-time students pay tuition at a rate of $532 a credit.

ST. JOHN'S UNIVERSITY (NY)

GENERAL INFORMATION

For 130 years, St. John's University has excelled at preparing young men and women for personal and professional success. Founded in 1870 by the Vincentian Fathers, the University has flourished since its early days in downtown Brooklyn. Today, St. John's is one of America's leading Catholic universities.

St. John's occupies five handsome sites: a tree-lined, 100-acre residential campus in Jamaica, Queens, New York; a charming, 16.5-acre residential campus in Grymes Hill, Staten Island, New York; a Manhattan campus with strong ties to New York City's financial district; the 175-acre Eastern Long Island Campus in Oakdale, New York; and a campus in Rome, Italy. Each campus combines superb academic and technological resources with a supportive, close-knit atmosphere.

Chartered by the State Education Department of New York, St. John's is accredited by the Middle States Association of Colleges and Schools. Its varied programs are accredited by such organizations as the International Association for Management Education, American Association for Accreditation of Laboratory Animal Care, the American Bar Association, the American Chemical Society, the American Council on Pharmaceutical Education, the American Library Association, the American Psychological Association, the American Speech-Language-Hearing Association, and the Association of American Law Schools.

St. John's enrolls more than 14,000 full and part-time undergraduates, yet its low 18:1 student/faculty ratio ensures personal attention in the classroom. Many of the University's 130,000 alumni hold top-level positions in government, industry, and the private sector.

The Queens campus comprises St. John's College of Liberal Arts and Sciences, the Peter J. Tobin College of Business, the School of Education and Human Services, the College of Pharmacy and Allied Health Professions, the College of Professional Studies, and the School of Law. The Staten Island campus also includes St. John's College of Liberal Arts and Sciences, the Peter J. Tobin College of Business, the School of Education and Human Services, and the College of Professional Studies. The Manhattan campus includes the School of Risk Management, Insurance, and Actuarial Science, a unit of the Tobin College of Business. The Rome campus offers an MBA program and an MA in government and politics.

STUDENT BODY

At St. John's, the Student Government represents and serves the Student Body through effective and responsible leadership. It also functions as a liaison between students and the administration and faculty. Student Government funds and coordinates the more than 180 student organizations and clubs on both the Queens and Staten Island campuses.

ACADEMICS

St. John's offers more than 100 academic majors in its five acclaimed undergraduate colleges. At the Queens campus, St. John's College of Liberal Arts and Sciences offers programs leading to the Bachelor of Arts in American studies, anthropology, economics, English, environmental studies, French, government and politics, history, Italian, mathematics, philosophy, psychology, public administration and public service, sociology, Spanish, speech (general and public address), speech pathology and audiology, and theology. The Bachelor of Fine Arts is offered with majors in art (painting, printmaking, and sculpture), creative photography, graphic design, and illustration. The Bachelor of Science is available in biology, chemistry, environmental studies, mathematical physics, mathematics, physical science, and physics.

St. John's College of Liberal Arts and Sciences also offers a five-year BA/MA program in English, government and politics, history, mathematics, sociology, Spanish, and theology. Students may also choose five-year BS/MS programs in biology and chemistry, a BA/JD or BS/JD degree combining any undergraduate degree with a law degree from St. John's School of Law, a BS/DDS degree combining an undergraduate biology degree with a Doctor of Dental Surgery degree from Columbia University's School of Dental and Oral Medicine, and a BS/OD degree combining an undergraduate degree in biology with a Doctor of Optometry degree from SUNY Optometry. Bachelor's-degree students in St. John's College are eligible for the pre-MBA program.

The Institute of Asian Studies, under the auspices of St. John's College, offers a BA in Asian studies and a five-year BA/MA in East Asian studies. The College of Business Administration offers programs leading to the BS in accounting, economics, finance, management, and marketing. A five-year BS/MS in accounting is also available.

In the School of Education and Human Services, programs lead to the Bachelor of Science in education, including childhood education grades (1-6) and childhood education/special education (grades 1-6), as well as to the BS/MS degree in childhood education/special education. In cooperation with St. John's College, the School of Education and Human Services also offers the BSEd degree in adolescent education, with concentrations in English, mathematics, physics, social studies, and Spanish, all grades 7-12. The BS in human services is also offered.

The College of Pharmacy and Allied Health Professions grants the Doctor of Pharmacy (six years), the Bachelor of Science in cytotechnology, and the Bachelor of Science in medical technology. There is a five-year BS/MS degree program in toxicology, as well as programs of study leading to the BS in pathologist assistant studies, physician assistant studies, and toxicology.

Programs in the College of Professional Studies lead to the BS degree in administrative studies, communication arts, computer science, criminal justice, funeral-service administration, health-care administration, hospitality management, journalism, microcomputer systems, paralegal studies, real estate management, safety and corporate security, sports management, telecommunications, and television and film production. The BA is available with majors in social science and literature and speech. Also offered are five-year BS/MA programs in communication arts/government and politics, communication arts/sociology, criminal justice/government and politics, criminal justice/sociology, health-care administration/government and politics, health-care administration/sociology, journalism/government and politics, and paralegal studies/sociology.

Pre-professional programs include dentistry, engineering, law, medicine, osteopathy, social work, veterinary medicine, and other health-related fields. A combined BA/JD or BS/JD degree program is available with any undergraduate major.

8000 Utopia Parkway
Jamaica, NY 11439
Phone: 718-990-2000
Fax: 718-990-5728
Website: www.stjohns.edu

In addition, the College of Professional Studies offers an AA degree in liberal arts, as well as AS degrees in business (accounting and general business), criminal justice, electronic data processing, microcomputer technology, paralegal studies, paraprofessional school service, and telecommunications. Certificate programs are available in business administration, computer science, health-care administration, international criminal justice, paralegal studies, sports management, and telecommunications. Most programs also are offered on evenings and weekends.

At the Staten Island campus, St. John's College of Liberal Arts and Sciences offers programs leading to the BA or BS degree in English, government and politics, history, mathematics, psychology, social studies, sociology, and speech (general). St. John's College also offers BA degrees in economics, philosophy, and theology, as well as a BS in computer science and speech language pathology and audiology. Students may choose a five-year BA/MA program in government and politics. Also available are a BA/JD or BS/JD degree combining any undergraduate degree with a law degree from St. John's School of Law. Students pursuing a liberal arts degree may pursue a pre-professional concentration in business. The AA in liberal arts also is available.

The Peter J. Tobin College of Business at Staten Island offers programs of study leading to the BS in accounting, economics, finance management, and marketing. Also offered is a five-year BS/MS in accounting. In the School of Education and Human Services, students may pursue programs of study leading to the BSEd degree in childhood education grades 1-6 or childhood education/special education grades 1-6, as well as the BS/MS degree in childhood education/special education. In addition, the School of Education offers the BS degree in adolescent education with concentrations in English, mathematics, and social studies.

The Staten Island campus also offers a number of degree and certificate programs through the College of Professional Studies. Programs of study lead to the BS in communication arts, computer science, criminal justice, funeral-service administration, health-care administration, hospitality management, paralegal studies, real estate management, safety and corporate security, sports management, telecommunication, and television and film production. There is a combined BA/JD or BS/JD program. Also available are AS degree programs in business (accounting and general business), criminal justice, paralegal studies, and telecommunications. Pre-professional programs include dentistry, engineering, law, medicine, osteopathy, social work, veterinary medicine, and other health-related fields.

To graduate, students in St. John's College of Liberal Arts and Sciences are expected to complete a minimum of 126 semester hours for the BA or the BS and 144 semester hours for the BFA. The School of Education and Human Services requires completion of 126-139 semester hours. The College of Professional Studies requires completion of 126-127 semester hours for the BS or BA degree. Students in the Tobin College of Business must complete 130-134 semester hours. In the College of Pharmacy and Allied Health Professions, students in the six-year pharmacy program are expected to complete a minimum of 201 semester hours. The BS program in cytotechnology requires 128 semester hours. For the physician assistant program, 134 semester hours must be completed. The requirements are 133 semester hours in the toxicology or pathologist assistant program and 132 semester hours in the medical technology program. Students in associate's degree programs are required to complete 60-63 semester hours. All students are expected to fulfill University core curriculum requirements, along with completing their major sequence and free-elective groupings.

Professors at St. John's enjoy international recognition for their scholarship and commitment to teaching. There are 1,111 faculty (561 full-time, 550 part-time); 89 percent of full-time faculty hold doctoral or other terminal degrees in their fields.

ADMISSIONS

Admission to St. John's is determined by the applicant's previous academic performance, satisfactory achievement on appropriate standardized tests, recommendations, and other factors that suggest academic potential and personal motivation. A minimum of 16 academic units earned at an accredited secondary institution or an appropriate score on the GED test is required. The units should include 4 English, 2 mathematics (elementary algebra, plane geometry, or 10th-year mathematics), 2 foreign language, 1 history, 1 science, and 6 electives, of which at least 3 must be in academic subjects. These requirements may vary, depending on the program.

Students may apply by submitting an official high school transcript, official scores on the SAT I or ACT, and a completed and signed application for admission. Transfer students are encouraged to apply and form a large part of the undergraduate population. St. John's advises transfer students to have all records of previous high school and college work forwarded to the Office of Admission. On-campus interviews are conducted through the Office of Admission. Students may apply anytime under St. John's rolling admission policy for all but the pharmacy degree programs, which have a February 1 deadline. For further information, contact:

Office of Admission
St. John's University
8000 Utopia Parkway
Jamaica, NY 11439
Telephone: 888-9STJOHNS (toll free) or 718-990-2000
Fax: 718-990-2096

Office of Admission
St. John's University
300 Howard Avenue
Staten Island, NY 10301
Telephone: 888-9STJOHNS (toll free) or 718-390-4500
Fax: 718-390-4298

CAMPUS LIFE

The park-like Queens campus is conveniently located in a peaceful, residential neighborhood just off the Grand Central Parkway. The Staten Island campus, on a wooded hill overlooking scenic New York Harbor, is a few miles from the Verrazano-Narrows Bridge. By car or public transportation, these two campuses are a short ride from Times Square, Greenwich Village, and other New York City attractions. The Manhattan campus is within easy walking distance of dynamic Wall Street. The Eastern Long Island Campus is on Suffolk County's south shore. The Rome campus is located at the Pontificio Oratorio San Pietro, off Via Aurelia on Via Santa Maria Mediatrice.

COST AND AID

Tuition for a full-time student (12-18 credits a semester) is $16,900 per academic year. Tuition may vary by program and class year. Mandatory fees total $430. St. John's offers a Fixed Rate Tuition Option for students who want to lock in a set cost for all four years. Room and board is $8,330.

SAINT JOSEPH COLLEGE (CT)

GENERAL INFORMATION

Saint Joseph College was founded in 1932 by the Sisters of Mercy to provide higher education opportunities for women. Over the years, the College has remained true to this vision, offering students solid professional training grounded in a tradition rich in the liberal arts. Consistently cited on the national level for the quality of its academic programs, Saint Joseph College is committed to responding to the needs of an ever-changing society. Today, the College serves the needs of a diverse, intergenerational Student Body while remaining true to its original mission. Saint Joseph College serves the higher educational needs of the region through three academic divisions: The Women's College, The Coeducational Weekend College, and the Graduate School. The total enrollment of the three divisions exceeds 2,000 students. The majority of the students are Connecticut residents, and more than half are from the Greater Hartford region. Minority enrollments comprise 15 percent of the total student population in the Women's College, and 40 percent of these minority students hail from the Greater Hartford region. Saint Joseph College works to provide access to all students of merit, thereby fulfilling its mission of developing a "diverse student population."

STUDENT BODY

Beyond its vast academic offerings, Saint Joseph College sponsors a variety of educational outreach programs that enrich the lives of area residents, exemplifying its extensive reach into the community. The College's Adventures in Science program cultivates an interest in science for urban and suburban middle school students. Similarly, the Academy for Young Writers unites youngsters from divergent backgrounds while enhancing their literary skills. Other programs work in close accord with community organizations to improve educational opportunities for minority students while addressing the complex needs of urban education. Special focus is placed on encouraging young women, especially those from Hartford, to pursue college degrees. The impact of Saint Joseph College resonates throughout the community. In fostering service and leadership as critical aspects of education, the College inspires its Student Body to participate in the world outside the campus. Currently, 85 percent of the student population willingly performs community service as a means to better themselves and society. This is a trait that carries beyond graduation into the professional lives of alumnae. With 70 percent of Saint Joseph College graduates working and living in Connecticut, chances are that most in the community will one day be taught, treated, or cared for by an alumna. The impact of a Saint Joseph College education is not solely regional, however. The remaining third of the College's graduates can be found throughout the United States and as far away as England, Italy, France, and Japan. On the cultural front, events such as workshops, lectures, conferences, concerts, and art exhibitions provide opportunities to local professionals, as well as to the general public. The College's new athletic facility has also proven to be a tremendous community resource. The O'Connell Athletic Center meets the recreation and fitness needs of individuals throughout the community. Additionally, it hosts a broad range of sports competitions, programs, workshops and summer camps. The Ivan Lendl Wheelchair Tennis Day Camp, The Nutmeg Games, and The Hartford Youth League Basketball Clinics are just some of the programs that utilize the facilities.

ACADEMICS

Focused on providing "a rigorous liberal arts education," the College offers a wide range of majors. Small classes and an intimate campus allow for a high level of individual attention. Students can opt to pursue degrees in the sciences, the human services, or the humanities. In accordance with the Founding Sisters' vision of combining professional program applications with broader humanistic studies, the curriculum incorporates themes such as the social/historical contexts of science and technology, global awareness, women's studies, and ethical analysis. Most major fields of study incorporate practical experience and professional opportunity as part of the curriculum. Students are provided internships, mentorships, study abroad programs, and professional networking opportunities.

1678 Asylum Avenue
West Hartford, CT 06117
Phone: 860-231-5216
Fax: 860-233-5695
Website: www.sjc.edu

Along with 30 undergraduate programs, Saint Joseph College offers a Master of Arts degree, a Master of Science degree, and a Master of Business Administration degree; teacher, nursing, and social work certification programs; programs in pre-law and pre-med; and a new minor in information technology (IT). The College awards the BA or BS in the following majors: American studies; art history; biology; biology/chemistry; business administration (accounting and management); chemistry; child study; dietetics; economics; English; environmental science; family studies; foods and nutrition; French; history; history/political science; home economics; mathematical and computer sciences; mathematics/economics; natural sciences; nursing; philosophy; political science; psychology; religious studies; social science and history; social work; sociology; Spanish; and special education. Teaching certification is offered in five areas: early childhood education, elementary education, middle school education, secondary education, and special education. Research, clinical, and work placements are factored into all majors as an important component of each student's program. For instance, nursing majors begin their clinical training early in the sophomore year.

CAMPUS LIFE

The beautiful, 84-acre, suburban West Hartford campus houses The Women's College, The Coeducational Weekend and Graduate Schools, and The Gengras Center. Located one block from campus is the renowned School for Young Children, one of the oldest early childhood centers in the state. The School for Young Children also serves as an on-site laboratory for preschool teacher training. The College's newest facility, The Carol Autorino Center for the Arts and Humanities, opened its doors in 2000.

Saint Joseph College students from all majors are invited to participate in the College's extensive study abroad program. Participants in this program live, work, study, and experience life in a foreign country. Recent international studies majors have studied in Germany, Italy, and France. Students from other majors utilize the program to meet academic requirements and to fulfill personal goals.

COST AND AID

The tuition and fees for freshmen entering in 1999 totaled $15,900. Room and board was $6,610. The cost per credit for part-time students was $405.

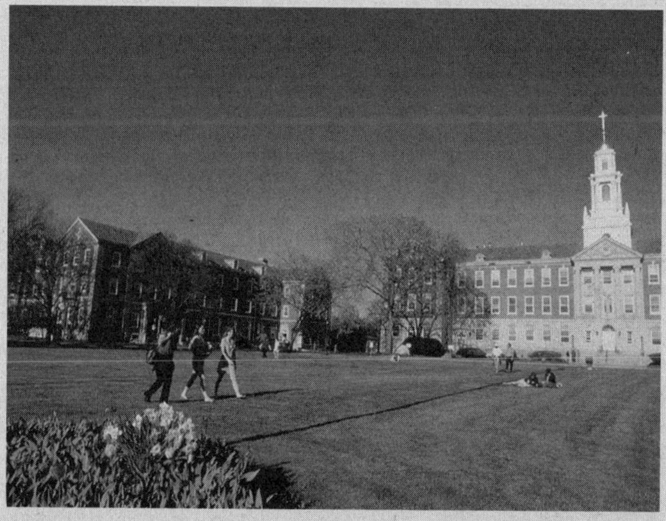

SAINT JOSEPH'S COLLEGE (ME)

GENERAL INFORMATION

Saint Joseph's College of Maine offers academic excellence in a magnificent setting on Maine's second-largest lake. The only Catholic college in Maine, it offers a liberal arts education to men and women of all ages and faiths. Founded in 1912 and sponsored by the Sisters of Mercy, the College focuses on the intellectual, spiritual, and social growth of its students within a values-centered environment. The school offers more than 40 majors and concentrations. The sustained growth in student population has led to the opening of a new residence hall, with another opening in summer 2003. A new 50,000 square foot Academic Center featuring 30 classrooms, an auditorium, and offices for 50 faculty members will open in 2004. The Harold Alfond Center, which opened in summer 1999, houses a swimming pool, basketball courts, an elevated jogging track, a rock-climbing wall, fitness equipment, and a dance/aerobics studio. Recently, an academic building has been renovated and expanded, and the College's dining hall has been doubled in size.

The College's full-time undergraduate enrollment consists of 970 students. More than 80 percent of full-time students live on campus. The 10 residence halls include a choice of single-sex, coed-by-floor, and substance-free housing options. Saint Joseph's College of Maine looks to its students to take an active role in campus leadership. Opportunities to become involved in student government, athletics, and cultural and social organizations are numerous. The College has a close-knit family atmosphere that permeates campus life. Social life revolves around clubs and organizations and the many events held in the Chalet and the Alfond Center. Intercollegiate athletic competition is actively sponsored by the College. Men compete in basketball, soccer, golf, baseball, and cross-country. Women compete in basketball, cross-country, field hockey, soccer, softball, and volleyball. Recreational facilities include a private sandy beach on Sebago Lake, as well as cross-country running and ski trails. The College is just 18 miles from Portland, Maine's largest city and is located in a four-season recreational area.

STUDENT BODY

At Saint Joseph's College of Maine, clubs and activities offer students a variety of things to do. Students can swim at the pool, take a yoga class, or climb the rock wall. They can catch a movie, check out the stand-up comic or the poetry reading, join the cast of a theater production, play intramural basketball, or just hang out with friends at the Chalet. In addition to studying and having fun, one in four students takes a significant role in campus leadership. St. Joseph's College believes in actively supporting students in becoming leaders and offers leadership training in consensus building and communication, invaluable skills that students take with them to the world beyond campus. Saint Joseph's College builds confidence along with knowledge. Students have many opportunities to get involved as leaders at Saint Joseph's; they can become resident advisors, orientation advisors, AmeriCorps volunteers, peer educators, community service volunteers, student senators, or class officers. The many and varied student clubs include Campus Ministry, SEAM (Student Education Association of Maine), SOURCE (Students of Universal Races, Colors and Ethnicities), Superkids, *Shield* (yearbook), *Fortitudo et Spes* (newspaper), Student Nurses Association, WSJB/91.5 FM, Commuter Association, Interhall Council, Habitat for Humanity, Campus Activities Board, Cheerleading, *e.g.* (literary magazine), Feeney Players (theater troupe), High Adventure, Liturgical Choir, Political Student Union, Ski Club, Student Senate, The Producers (Media), International Club, Business Club, Peer Educators, Red Cross, and SJC Emergency Medical Services.

ACADEMICS

For all of its students, Saint Joseph's College requires 28 credits in the Inner Core of Knowledge, Understanding, and Insight for the Twenty-first Century. In conjunction with the major, the core curriculum is the basis for lifelong learning and an enduring liberal education. This curriculum enhances the foundation skills of writing and quantitative reasoning; explores different ways of asking questions and approaching knowledge; develops social, civic, and environmental understanding for the world of the twenty-first century; grounds self-knowledge and builds values; and commits faculty and students to the search for truth and justice. The courses of the core curriculum study the principal civilizations of the world and their basic contributions to the development of western civilization; explore the interrelationships among persuasive writing, thinking, and speaking; probe the challenging and significant themes of twentieth-century literature; explore the metaphysical and epistemological foundations of human life; apply ethical theories to contemporary ethical problems; investigate the phenomenon of religious faith as an enduring concern of the human community; and consider contemporary issues in science.

Saint Joseph's College offers the Bachelor of Arts, Bachelor of Science, Bachelor of Science in Nursing, and Bachelor of Science in Business Administration degrees. Student can choose from the following majors: applied computer science, biology, business administration (with concentrations in accounting, advertising, finance, international business, management, and marketing), chemistry, communications (with concentrations in journalism, multimedia, and public relations/advertising), criminal justice, elementary education, English, environmental science/studies, history, liberal arts and sciences, marine science, mathematics, nursing, philosophy, physical education (with concentrations in exercise science, sports management, and teacher preparation), psychology, secondary education certification, sociology (with a concentration available in social work), and theology. A pre-pharmacy program is also offered. Academic minors are available in applied computer science, biology, business administration, chemistry, classics, communications, English, environmental science, fine arts, history, journalism, marine science, mathematics, philosophy, political science, psychology, secondary education, sociology, theology, and writing.

Vibrant energy between faculty and students is an important aspect of academics at Saint Joseph's College of Maine. The lively exchange is evident as faculty stop to chat with students or students stay after class to continue talking with the professor. In the 2002–2003 academic year, Saint Joseph's College celebrated 90 years of academic excellence, steeped in tradition that values each student. The College takes pride in its distinctive faculty and strong liberal arts curriculum. While nearly 95 percent of the faculty hold a doctorate or the highest degree in their field, their expertise is often based on real-world experience as well as academic rigor, which means they know how to educate students in a well-rounded way. Small classes are essential to a Saint Joseph's education. With an average of just 20-25 students per class, professors know students and their goals individually. When it comes time for a reference letter upon graduation, they don't have to wonder if the student sat in the first row or the eighth. The student to faculty ratio at Saint Joseph's is 12 to 1, and there are 59 full-time and 48 part-time faculty members.

278 Whites Bridge Road
Standish, ME 04084-5263
Phone: 207-893-7746
Fax: 207-893-7862
Website: www.sjcme.edu

ADMISSIONS

Saint Joseph's College of Maine seeks to enroll qualified men and women of all religious faiths. Students who have challenged themselves academically, who are committed to learning through involvement, who participate in community service, and who believe in their potential for success are encouraged to apply. Decisions on admission to the College are made on an individual basis, taking into account the following factors: challenge, depth, and number of college-preparatory courses in high school; grade point average in these courses; rank in class; writing skills; community service; special talents and achievements; recommendations; leadership skills; SAT or ACT scores; and demonstrable interest in attending Saint Joseph's College. The College recommends that students take a full set of college-preparatory courses in high school, including 4 years of English, at least 3 years of mathematics (algebra I and II and geometry), at least 2 years of laboratory science (biology and chemistry), at least 2 courses in history or social sciences, at least 2 years of foreign language, and other college-preparatory courses. Students interested in nursing or the sciences should be sure to take a more challenging curriculum in mathematics and science. For any intended major a typical transcript from a candidate for admission should include 16 or more college-preparatory courses.

Regular admission plan notification for September entry begins in mid-December and continues on a rolling basis through early summer. Notification for January entry begins in mid-October. The College encourages students to apply as early as possible in order to receive full consideration. Candidates for admission under the early action plan attend one of the College's Early Action Days programs in November. Attendance is limited. Students should call the admission office for information regarding this program. Students are required to have a B or higher average and competitive SAT or ACT scores. Students accepted under the early action plan retain the right to respond to the College's offer of acceptance up to May 1. Admitted students reserve their places in the entering class by sending a $200 deposit. Students expecting to live on campus are required to submit an additional $100 to serve as a room deposit. Deposits are refundable for the fall semester if notice is given prior to May 1; deposits are refundable for the spring semester if notice is given prior to January 1. The college anticipates an application fee of $35 for students applying for the fall 2004 semester.

CAMPUS LIFE

Saint Joseph's College is located on a 331-acre campus on the shore of Sebago Lake in Standish, Maine, on what was once a large estate owned by the Verrill family of Portland. It is located 18 miles from Portland and two hours from Boston. With its easy access to beaches, mountains, and cities, southern Maine is one of the most desirable areas in New England. Sophisticated yet quaint, nearby Portland is Maine's largest city, with a metropolitan population of 215,000. Portland is well-known for its fine restaurants and shops, along with its variety of music and concert venues, professional theater, acclaimed art museum, symphony orchestra, public market, and two professional sports teams. Rich in maritime history, the city's Old Port district features boutiques, galleries, cobblestone streets, and red-brick storefronts. And then there's the seafood, caught fresh from Casco Bay.

The College has developed excellent relationships with businesses, schools, social service agencies, and health care agencies in the Greater Portland area—all places that welcome Saint Joseph's students as interns, part-time employees, and volunteers. Professors and the College career offices help students begin their professional networking by assisting them in finding internships that can steer them in the right direction or lead to eventual employment. Students also gain valuable experience volunteering for leadership positions in campus groups and through work-study opportunities.

COST AND AID

Tuition for full-time students (12-19 credits per semester) is $17,430 per year. Fees totaling $640 per year are assessed to full-time students. If two or more members of the same family attend the College, the second member is entitled to a 10 percent reduction in tuition. Room and board totals $7,350 per year.

ST. LAWRENCE UNIVERSITY

GENERAL INFORMATION

St. Lawrence University is a private, independent, nondenominational university that seeks to provide a stimulating and rigorous liberal arts education to undergraduate students chosen for their intellectual potential and seriousness of purpose. Chartered in 1856, it is New York State's oldest continuously coeducational college or university. St. Lawrence's 2,100 students come from 40 states and 20 countries. The school is situated in Canton, New York (population 6,500), midway between the Adirondack Mountains and Ottawa, Canada's national capital. The University provides unmatched access to social and cultural opportunities, international government, and outdoor recreation.

STUDENT BODY

Undergraduates commence their studies with the First-Year Program, which places 30 to 45 first-year students in communities that live and learn together. Professors serve as first-year advisors. Once they attain upperclass status, students may choose to live in traditional residence halls, interest-based theme suites, theme cottages, or Greek houses. St. Lawrence provides a full range of services to students, including extensive career planning, as well as graduate and professional school guidance.

Students seeking co-curricular activities can choose from nearly 100 organizations, including everything from student government to interest groups to arts and culture. St. Lawrence boasts 32 teams in 19 varsity sports, including NCAA Division I teams in men's and women's ice hockey. All other teams compete in the NCAA's Division III. Club sports are also available, as is a broad range of intramural sports. The University is home to numerous recreational facilities, including a complete 133-station fitness center, cross-country ski and running trails, and indoor and outdoor tennis courts. Students enjoy access to two gymnasium/fieldhouse complexes; one has a 9-lane, 400-meter track and five basketball/tennis courts, while the other has a 200-meter track, recently completed squash courts, and three tennis courts. The new fieldhouse complex also includes a three-story climbing wall. Other facilities include an Astroturf field; new baseball, softball, and soccer fields; an equestrian center; a golf course; an indoor golf school; an ice arena; and a pool.

ACADEMICS

St. Lawrence University provides a distinctive learning environment, offering the Bachelor of Arts and Bachelor of Science degrees in 34 majors, as well as three graduate programs in education. The St. Lawrence core curriculum requires coursework in six areas as well as concentrated study in a major field. Students have the option of declaring a double major. The University offers 12 interdepartmental programs and 36 optional minors. Qualified students may pursue combined five-year programs in business administration (leading to the MBA) and engineering. Specialized advising is available for postgraduate work in dentistry, law, medicine, and veterinary medicine. All students are expected to demonstrate writing competence before graduating. The University provides extensive opportunities for honors projects and independent work. Its First-Year Program is nationally recognized.

Students may major in African studies, anthropology, Asian studies, biochemistry, biology, biology/physics, Canadian studies, chemistry, computer science, economics, economics/mathematics, English, environmental studies, fine arts, French, geology, geology/physics, German, global studies, government, history, mathematics, mathematics/computer science, multi-field (self-designed), multi-language, music, neuroscience, philosophy, physics, psychology, religious studies, sociology, Spanish, and speech and theatre.

Students may pursue an optional minor in African studies, anthropology, applied statistics, Asian studies, biology, Canadian studies, Caribbean and Latin American studies, chemistry, computer science, cultural encounters, economics, education, European studies, film studies, fine arts, gender studies, geology, German, global studies, government, history, international literature, literature (English), mathematics, multi-field, music, Native American studies, outdoor studies, philosophy, physics, psychology, religious studies, sociology, speech and theatre, sports studies and exercise science, and writing (English).

St. Lawrence employs 202 faculty members; the student/faculty ratio is 12:1. The faculty teach all courses. Graduate students do not teach undergraduate courses at St. Lawrence. While faculty members are working scholars, they are first and foremost teachers.

Payson Hall
Canton, NY 13617
Phone: 315-229-5261
Fax: 315-229-5818
Website: www.stlawu.edu

ADMISSIONS

St. Lawrence seeks undergraduates with the capacity to manage a demanding academic regimen successfully. In addition, the ideal student contributes substantially to the quality of community life. The University strives to enroll students who represent the broadest possible range of economic, ethnic, geographic, and social backgrounds. The admissions committee values academic achievement, but ability in athletics, community service, or the creative arts is also considered a strong indicator of a student's capacity to benefit from his or her time at St. Lawrence. The University requires scores on the SAT I or ACT for admission. Students are strongly encouraged to plan a campus visit; interviews may be scheduled on campus. In certain areas, off-campus interviews are also an option. The University makes no requirement of applicants' high school curricula; however, successful applicants generally demonstrate extensive preparation in the humanities, mathematics, the natural sciences, and the social sciences. Advanced Placement and Honors work are looked upon favorably, as they demonstrate the applicant's intellectual curiosity and maturity. These are qualities that are highly sought by the admission committee.

Applicants may request applications directly from the University. Students may also use the Common Application. The University charges a $50 fee to process applications. Applicants pursuing regular decision should submit all materials by February 15; they will be notified by late March. Students whose first choice is St. Lawrence may apply for early decision; the deadlines for early decision applications are November 15 or January 15. Early Decision applicants are notified one month after the deadline. Applicants for transfer to St. Lawrence should submit all application materials by November 1 for the spring semester or April 1 for the fall semester. To request an application or for more information, students should contact:

Office of Admissions and Financial Aid
St. Lawrence University
Canton, NY 13617
Telephone: 315-229-5261 or 800-285-1856 (toll free)
E-mail: admissions@stlawu.edu
World Wide Web: www.stlawu.edu

CAMPUS LIFE

St. Lawrence is currently undergoing an educational renaissance; bold academic initiatives are underway to maximize the learning potential of each and every student. A major facilities upgrade, fueled by a $130 million capital campaign, is providing expanded resources to undergraduates.

St. Lawrence University offers international programs in 14 countries: Australia, Austria, Canada, China, Costa Rica, Denmark, England, France, India, Italy, Japan, Kenya, Spain, and Trinidad & Tobago. Students can also direct-enroll in foreign universities in more than 20 additional countries through the International Student Exchange Program. The University also runs three off-campus study programs within the United States. These are located at: American University, Washington, D.C.; Fisk University, Nashville, Tennessee; and the Adirondack Semester, near Tupper Lake, New York.

COST AND AID

For the 2002–2003 academic year, the comprehensive fee (including tuition, fees, and typical room and board) is $34,235. On average, annual personal costs and book expenditures cost an additional $1,450.

SAINT MICHAEL'S COLLEGE

GENERAL INFORMATION

Saint Michael's College is a residential Catholic liberal arts college committed to creating a life-changing educational experience for 1,900 undergraduate students from throughout the U.S. and the world.

Situated on 440 scenic acres just outside Burlington—Vermont's largest city, between Lake Champlain and the majestic Green Mountains—Saint Michael's campus strikes the perfect balance between a busy college town and a spectacular natural wilderness. Ranked among the 15 finest master's universities in the North by *U.S. News and World Report* for 13 consecutive years, Saint Michael's offers 29 majors in the traditional arts and sciences, and it offers contemporary and pre-professional fields of study, all grounded in a strong liberal arts core. About 600 graduate students pursue degrees in business, education, clinical psychology, theology, and teaching English as a foreign language.

With more than 92 percent of students living on campus, Saint Michael's "24/7" living and learning environment enables exceptional teaching to continue beyond the classroom and traditional class hours, building lifelong bonds among students, faculty and college staff. A vibrant campus experience encompasses everything from academic enrichment to leadership and community service opportunities to athletics and recreation to the fine and performing arts to the unique international character of the college.

Global perspectives enrich the campus both through an increasingly international, multicultural faculty and Student Body, and the presence of our School of International Studies, one of the nation's oldest English language institutes. Known as "the international college in Vermont," Saint Michael's is a favored venue for visiting international businesspeople, government leaders and student groups and is headquarters to the Vermont Council on World Affairs. The College was named Vermont's "Exporter of the Year" in 2000 for exemplary exportation of educational services.

With top-ranking in the *USA Today*/NCAA Academic Achievement awards, Saint Michael's offers 21 intercollegiate Division II sports, most in the Northeast-10 Conference. A wide variety of club and intramural sports such as snowboarding, rugby, basketball, softball, and even table tennis are available. And, our acclaimed wilderness programs bring students into the great Vermont outdoors for adventure sports and survival training, from beginner to advanced certification levels.

Service to humankind and the broader community is not just a value, but a vibrant part of most students' lives as they embrace the heritage of service begun by the Edmundite priests who founded Saint Michael's in 1904. Saint Michael's student-led MOVE (Mobilization of Volunteer Efforts) program was named the nation's 34th "Point of Light" by President George Bush in 1982.

STUDENT BODY

Saint Michael's College operates on the principle that the students who get the most out of college are the students who give the most. Because nearly all undergraduates live on campus, students have unlimited opportunity to stretch their own boundaries and explore new frontiers through activities as diverse as an award-winning online student magazine, a weekly student newspaper, 21 intercollegiate sports, numerous club and intramural teams, student government, our student-led volunteer corps, the Martin Luther King Jr. Society, a variety of Edmundite campus ministry activities, the all-student fire and rescue squad, and our groundbreaking wilderness program, which certifies leaders in survival skills and also introduces novices to their first hiking, climbing, skiing or kayaking outings.

ACADEMICS

Through small classes, strong advising relationships, and an emphasis on faculty-student research and faculty involvement in Campus Life, students at Saint Michael's can't help but become engaged in a rigorous learning environment that transcends the boundaries of traditional classrooms and class meetings.

Exceptional teaching at the undergraduate level is our goal in maintaining a student/faculty ratio of 13:1. Of the 145 full-time faculty members at Saint Michael's, four out of five hold PhDs or the terminal degree in their field.

All students complete a liberal studies requirement that includes work in humanities, natural and mathematical sciences, philosophy, religious studies, social sciences and organizational studies, and artistic experience. Students also must demonstrate proficiency in writing and a foreign language. In addition to fulfilling these requirements, students complete the degree requirements for one of the College's majors or an approved combination of those majors. Saint Michael's College offers bachelor's degrees in the following areas: accounting, American studies, biochemistry, biology, business administration, chemistry, classics, computer science, economics, elementary education, English, environmental science, fine arts (art, music, theatre), French, history, information systems, journalism, mathematics, philosophy, physical science, physics, political science, psychology, religious studies, sociology, and Spanish. In addition, advising and pre-professional preparation for medicine, dentistry, law, and veterinary science are available for all interested students. Secondary school licensure is also available in several subject areas. A special 3+2 engineering program is offered in conjunction with Clarkson University (Potsdam, New York) and the University of Vermont (Burlington, Vermont), for students interested in combining a liberal arts background with engineering. A 4+1 MBA program is offered in conjunction with Clarkson University. A highly regarded English as a Second Language program is available for international students. Saint Michael's academic year consists of two semesters and one summer session.

One Winooski Park
Colchester, VT 05439
Phone: 802-654-3000
Fax: 802-654-2591
Website: www.smcvt.edu

For Saint Michael's 144 full-time and 51 part-time faculty, teaching undergraduates is always the first priority. Indeed, our professors' commitment to their students often goes above and beyond the call of duty as many enjoy getting involved in our 24/7 living and learning environment on campus. As just one example, many of our faculty participate in our Faculty Visitor program where professors develop a relationship with a first-year residence hall on campus, visiting residents on a regular basis during the first semester to help them acclimate to college life. Notably, 83 percent of our full-time professors have a doctorate or terminal degree in their field, and all faculty enjoy getting to know their students (and always by name). Our faculty/student ratio of 13:1 allows for high student engagement and many opportunities to get involved with faculty research projects.

ADMISSIONS

Admission to Saint Michael's College is selective. As we review each application, we look for students who are enthusiastic about learning, want to take an active part in their education, are energized by ideas, have made an impact, and will contribute to the campus community.

Generally applicants should have a solid high school record that includes some AP or honors-level courses. Admitted students typically rank in the top 25 percent of their high school class. The middle 50 percent of students accepted last year scored between 1040 and 1230 on the SAT. An interview is not required but is highly recommended, and alumni interviews are available in many locations.

Saint Michael's has two early action application deadlines (November 15 and December 15) and a regular deadline of February 1.

CAMPUS LIFE

Saint Michael's College strikes the perfect balance between the bustle of a busy college town and the splendor and challenge of Vermont's natural wilderness.

Three miles from Lake Champlain and Burlington—Vermont's largest city and the epitome of a great college town—Saint Michael's is conveniently located in Colchester (exit 15 off I-89), in view of Mount Mansfield, the tallest of the Green Mountains. Called "the Number One Small City to Have It All" by Arts and Entertainment television, Burlington has every reason to cater to students' needs and interests; besides Saint Michael's, it is home to four other colleges, including the University of Vermont. Students flock to the thriving downtown area for shopping, a vibrant music scene, theater and fine arts presentations, and, of course, Ben & Jerry's ice cream—a Vermont tradition. The area combines a culturally rich, yet livable and safe small city with the recreational benefits of Vermont's lakes and mountains.

Situated on the shores of Lake Champlain, Burlington has a natural beauty that attracts many. The Adirondacks to the west and the Green Mountains to the east serve as constant reminders of the great skiing, riding, and hiking available nearby. Saint Michael's students take full advantage of the many recreational and social opportunities provided in this region, bringing some of their own great talents to the local slopes (as witnessed in Saint Michael's alumna Tricia Byrnes' 2002 Olympic snowboarding performance).

The area is served by train, air, and bus transportation on a daily basis. The Burlington International Airport, served by several major airlines, is just three miles from campus.

Saint Michael's students are lucky to have Burlington—Vermont's largest city and the cultural hub of the state—at their doorstep. Abundant internship and academic enrichment opportunities in Burlington and beyond range from scientific research laboratories, brokerage houses, political offices, newspapers, and accounting firms to several "uniquely Vermont" opportunities like working with Burton snowboards; Rossignol ski equipment company; and Ben & Jerry's. Saint Michael's internship coordinator works one-on-one with each student interested in pursing an internship to find an experience that matches his or her academic and career goals.

Nearly 30 percent of our students also choose to take advantage of our extensive study abroad opportunities, with the help and support of our full-time study abroad advisor. Saint Michael's commitment to study abroad shows in our direct tuition-exchange policy: Regardless of the study abroad destination, students pay their normal Saint Michael's fees for the semester, covering their tuition, room, and board expenses overseas. Saint Michael's works with more than 100 different study abroad programs, giving students a wide variety of countries and universities from which to select.

COST AND AID

For 2003–2004, tuition and fees are $22,420, a standard double room is $4,775, and a standard meal plan is $2,905.

SALEM COLLEGE

GENERAL INFORMATION

Founded by the Moravian church in 1772, Salem College strives to set its signature upon its students by encouraging them to recognize and strengthen their human faculties and their capacity for service, professional life and leadership. Salem women have ample opportunities to profit from extracurricular events and activities on campus. Intercollegiate and intramural athletics, performing groups in the arts, publications, social organizations, and academic organizations related to specific subjects all play a central role in campus life. Salem's athletic facilities are outstanding. The Center for Student Life and Fitness includes a gymnasium and a 25-meter competition indoor swimming pool; the facility also has space for fitness, athletic, and recreational activities. Twelve tennis courts and two outdoor playing fields supplement the Center's offerings. The Salem Commons student center is a four-story structure with lounges for parties and dances, performance space, a dance studio, and meeting rooms. The Career Planning and Placement Office helps Salem's 900 women develop and begin their pursuit of career goals.

STUDENT BODY

The Student Government Association aims to achieve a strong sense of community and unity within the Student Body and to enforce standards for behavior and achievement commensurate with Salem's tradition of student honor. The Student Government enacts the regulations that govern student life, subject to approval by the Faculty Advisory Board. Faculty committees and the Board of Trustees include students as consultants or voting members.

ACADEMICS

Requirements vary among the different degree programs offered at Salem. Each program entails distribution requirements, major requirements, and a prescribed number of elective courses. Distribution requirements allow students considerable leeway in designing their programs while guaranteeing a well-rounded education. Salem encourages its students to pursue independent study. In addition to major fields of study, Salem offers minors in 23 areas. All students are required to complete the Salem Signature Program, a unique sequence of courses covering personal development and leadership skills. The sequence includes a mandatory 30-hour commitment to community service as well as a major-related internship. Exceptional students are eligible for Salem's four-year College Honors Program, which pushes students to dig deeper into their fields of study. Salem operates on a 4-1-4 calendar that includes a January term. Many students use this short term to pursue independent study projects, pre-professional internships, in-depth mini-courses, or off-campus study (including study abroad).

Salem College offers the Bachelor of Arts, Bachelor of Science, and Bachelor of Music degrees. Majors are available in accounting, American studies, art history, arts management, biology, business administration, chemistry, communication, economics, English, French, German, history, interior design, international business, international relations, mathematics, medical technology, music, music performance, philosophy, psychology, religion, sociology, Spanish, and studio art. Students who plan their curricula carefully can build the intellectual foundation to nurture a vast array of professions, including business, communication, law, library work, medicine, and social service. Salem confers teacher certification in elementary education, secondary school subjects, and learning disabilities; the program is rated as the best in North Carolina. A 3-2 program in engineering is offered in conjunction with Duke University (Durham, North Carolina) and Vanderbilt University (Nashville, Tennessee).

Salem maintains a faculty of 84 professors. About 90 percent of the full-time faculty hold terminal degrees in their fields. Teaching is the primary responsibility of Salem professors, who teach everything from freshman classes to advanced seminars and labs. Students enjoy a 13:1 student/faculty ratio.

ADMISSIONS

Salem seeks out applicants whose records demonstrate academic aptitude, personal integrity, and the ambition to succeed as individuals and community members. The College welcomes students from all ethnic, racial, and religious backgrounds. Salem College suggests that applicants complete 16 academic units at the secondary-school level: 4 in English, 3 in mathematics (2 in algebra and 1 in geometry), 3 in science, 2 to 4 in foreign languages, 2 in history, and 4 academic electives. The College also requires standardized test scores (SAT I or ACT) and two letters of recommendation from teachers. The Admissions Committee considers the entire application package, weighing most heavily the applicant's high school curriculum, academic course grades, test scores, and recommendations. The Committee also considers community activity and participation in extracurricular activities. Prospective music majors must audition; the audition may be submitted on tape. An interview is recommended.

PO Box 10548
Winston-Salem, NC 27108
Phone: 336-721-2621
Fax: 336-917-5572
Website: www.salem.edu

1772
SALEM
COLLEGE

Applicants are encouraged to submit application materials during the fall of their senior year in high school. Salem practices rolling admissions, evaluating applications as they arrive. The College may admit a student conditionally or defer an admission decision until the applicant's first-semester senior year grades and standardized test scores (SAT I or ACT) are available. The school sets no deadline for transfer applications, but most successful transfer applications arrive before March 1. Those accepted to Salem must state whether they plan to attend the school by May 1. Contact the admissions office to arrange a campus tour, interview, or class visit. To request informational brochures, a college catalog, and an application form visit the website at www.salem.edu or contact:

Dean of Admissions
Salem College
Winston-Salem, NC 27108
Telephone: 336-721-2621 or 800-32-SALEM (toll free)
E-mail: admissions@salem.edu

CAMPUS LIFE

The 57-acre campus of Salem College is situated in Winston-Salem's historic, nationally known Old Salem restoration area. The campus is only 10 minutes from downtown Winston-Salem by foot. The city of Winston-Salem, home to nearly 170,000 people, has one of the most vibrant artistic and cultural communities in the southeastern states. Two airports, Piedmont Triad International Airport near Greensboro and Smith Reynolds Airport in Winston-Salem, serve the region. Several major airlines fly regularly in and out of Piedmont Triad International.

Undergraduates may register at Wake Forest University for classes not available at Salem. Salem students pursuing professional training in medical technology and similar fields may study at Wake Forest University Medical School and Forsyth Memorial Hospital. Salem students have numerous study abroad options. Those interested in government may wish to participate in the American University Washington Semester and the Drew University United Nations Semester. The community of Winston-Salem affords Salem undergraduates many opportunities to work closely with business firms, churches, the police department, public schools, and social and health agencies.

COST AND AID

Salem charges a comprehensive fee (covering tuition, room, board, laboratory fees, and some infirmary services) for students who attend full-time and reside on campus. In 2001–2002, this fee was $23,650. Students living off-campus paid a comprehensive fee of $14,780. All traditional-age (17 to 21 years old) students must live on campus or with family near campus. On average, students spend between $400 and $500 per year on books and supplies. An additional student government fee of about $215 pays for the yearbook and other student publications, class dues, and organizational dues. Nontraditional students in the Adult Degree Program pay $675 per course.

SAVANNAH COLLEGE OF ART AND DESIGN

GENERAL INFORMATION

The Savannah College of Art and Design is a private college whose mission is to prepare tomorrow's visual and performing artists, designers, professionals in the building arts, and art and architecture historians. The school is coeducational. Individual attention to each student, offered in a constructive environment, is the hallmark of a Savannah College education. The curriculum is designed to foster creativity, strengthen thinking skills, and provide a thorough grounding on which students can build careers. A balanced fine arts and liberal arts curriculum attracts students from every state and from more than 80 countries, making SCAD one of the largest art and design colleges in the United States. Current enrollment is approximately 5,500 students. The College welcomes both resident and nonresident students. Students who reside on campus enjoy eye-catching residence halls. The school encourages students to strongly consider campus residence; the immersion in the college community provided by residence is, for many, the highlight of the undergraduate experience. Space is allotted on a first-come, first-served basis. All rooms include drafting tables; utility charges are covered by the housing fee. Space is limited, so early reservations are strongly recommended. Meal plans are available to both residents and nonresidents. Savannah College of Art and Design fields men's and women's athletic teams competing in NCAA Division III. Intramural sports run throughout the school year. The college confers several graduates degrees: the Master of Fine Arts degree, the Master of Arts degree, and professional and post-professional Master of Architecture degrees. Accreditation is granted by the Commission on Colleges of the Southern Association of Colleges and Schools; the school is accredited to award bachelor's and master's degrees. The Bachelor of Fine Arts/Master of Architecture degree (BFA/MArch) is also accredited by the National Architectural Accrediting Board (NAAB). The College has received numerous distinctions, including an Honor Award from the National Trust for Historic Preservation. This award recognized the College for creating its campus from 40 historic buildings; the College adapted the buildings to the school's purpose while maintaining many significant architectural and design features.

STUDENT BODY

Student government at the College takes several forms. The United Student Forum is made up of representatives of various campus leadership groups. The Inter-Club Council includes delegates representing over 40 official student organizations. The Student Activities Council plans such campus events as concerts, film screenings, lectures, and plays, as well as recreational and social activities. Savannah fields intercollegiate athletic teams competing in Division III of the NCAA. Teams include men's and women's basketball, crew, cross-country, equestrian, golf, soccer, and tennis; women's softball and volleyball; and men's baseball. Club sports include men's and women's sailing and archery, and women's lacrosse. The College also supports a cheerleading squad. Students participate in the production of a weekly newspaper and help run the campus radio station (learn more about it at www.scadradio.org); both outlets help prepare students for careers in media.

ACADEMICS

Savannah operates on a quarterly academic calendar. The school year begins in mid-September with the fall quarter; the traditional academic year runs through May. The College offers summer classes running from late June through August. The Savannah curriculum balances the benefits of a thorough liberal arts education with class work that teaches essential professional skills. Modern facilities with state-of-the-art equipment allow undergraduates to master the high-tech skills valued in today's arts market. Double majors and multidisciplinary study are options open to Savannah undergraduates. Independent study is an option for those interested in a specific area not currently offered as a major. All undergraduates must complete 35 to 50 credit hours in the foundation studies program, 55 to 65 credit hours in the liberal arts program (including a concentration in art history), 60 to 70 credit hours in the major area of study, and 10 to 20 credit hours in electives. A total of 180 quarter credit hours (36 courses) is required for to complete the BFA program. Students may also pursue a five-year professional BFA/MArch degree, which requires 225 credit hours. Successful completion of this program requires 35 foundation hours, 60 hours of liberal arts study, 95 hours in the major program, and 35 hours of electives.

The Savannah College of Art and Design confers the following degrees: the Bachelor of Fine Arts, Master of Arts, and Master of Fine Arts. Degree programs are available in the following areas: architectural history, art history, computer art, fashion, fibers, furniture design, graphic design, historic preservation, illustration, interior design, media and performing arts, metals and jewelry, painting, photography, product/industrial design, sequential art, and video/film. The College also confers an accredited, professional Master of Architecture degree. Students may pursue minors in all major areas, as well as in dance, decorative arts, drawing, electronic design, interaction design, museum studies, printmaking, sculpture, sound design, and writing.

Close work between students and professors is ensured by a low student/faculty ratio. Classes are small; professors hold terminal degrees in their fields or are otherwise distinguished by professional achievement. All faculty members must, as a matter of school policy, offer regularly scheduled meetings with students and, when necessary, extra help sessions.

PO Box 3146
Savannah, GA 31402-3146
Phone: 912-525-5100
Fax: 912-525-5986
Website: www.scad.edu

ADMISSIONS

The College welcomes online applications; to learn more, point your Web browser to www.scad.edu. All applications must include an official report of standardized test scores (SAT I or ACT), official transcripts from each high school or college attended, at least two letters of recommendation (three are preferred), a completed application form, and an application fee, which is nonrefundable. The school encourages applicants to supply a portfolio and statement of purpose and to sit for an interview; none of these, however, is required. The school welcomes applications from students in special circumstances—e.g. those schooled at home, those not seeking a degree, and transient students. Admission to the architecture program requires a minimum SAT math score of 540 or ACT math score of 23. Savannah admits students for full-time study at the end of their junior year provided that they have earned a GPA of 3.5 (B+) or better through the 11th grade, have scored SAT I or ACT scores above the national average, and have received a letter of recommendation for early admission from an art teacher or counselor; students meeting these criteria may also attend part-time during their senior year of high school. The Rising Star program is a five-week summer program that allows promising high school seniors the chance to experience life and study at an arts college. Transfer students may have no more than 90 credit hours of previous work applied toward a Savannah BFA degree. All students must complete their final 45 hours of course work at the College in order to receive a Savannah degree. The College welcomes international applicants. Students whose first language is not English must submit scores on the Test of English as a Foreign Language; they must also show proof of having adequate funds for one year. International students need not submit SAT I or ACT scores. International students are eligible for scholarships. The College seeks candidates whose special talents and contributions enhance the academic community; it makes special exceptions to general admission criteria for applicants of unique ability or exceptional motivation. The Savannah College of Art and Design does not discriminate on the basis of race, color, national or ethnic origin, religion, age, sex, handicap, or marital status in administering its educational policies, admission policies, scholarship and loan programs, athletics, and other institutionally administered programs or activities generally made available to students at the college.

CAMPUS LIFE

Located in the middle of Georgia's oldest city, Savannah College of Art and Design offers students the charm of an historic Southern city as well as the luxury of oceanside dwelling (the school is situated mere minutes from the Atlantic). The city of Savannah boasts one of the largest urban National Historic Landmark districts in the nation. All students should find the city a stimulating environment in which to create and grow. The climate is mild year-round, a great boon to outdoor activity. Culture flourishes in Savannah, a city that is home to a symphony orchestra, theater and dance companies, museums, and many ethnic and arts festivals. The city is well-known for its fine dining, clubs, and shopping districts, all easily reached from campus by foot, bicycle, or bus. Day trips to Charleston and Hilton Head, South Carolina; Orlando, Florida; and Atlanta are all facilitated by Savannah's convenient location. An international airport connects Savannah to destinations across the country and around the world.

The College offers numerous educational opportunities outside the classroom, including lectures, seminars, and workshops led by renowned artists, professionals, and scholars. The school sponsors study-related trips to major arts centers to further enrich students' educational experiences. Professional and faculty advisement ensure that students receive proper guidance in designing their curricula and preparing to enter the working world. Special programs are available, at no charge, to first-year students. No-charge tutoring is available to all students, as are the facilities and staff of the Writing Assistance Center. Students wishing to pursue off-campus study and study abroad will find numerous options at the Savannah College of Art and Design. Students may pursue short sessions in New York City or overseas, or they may spend a credited quarter (or more) at The Lacoste School of the Arts in Lacoste, France. Opportunities vary among departments, as some (but not all) programs relate to specific academic and studio disciplines. Off-campus study can be especially beneficial to students of architectural history, photography, art history, graphic design, illustration, video, computer art, architecture, interior design, the fine arts, and theater. Off-campus study and study abroad are available to students in all majors. Some programs combine internships and/or independent study with traditional course work. Financial assistance is available to fund these exceptional opportunities.

COST AND AID

For 2002–2003, undergraduate tuition is $17,955. This figure includes all laboratory and activity fees but does not include the cost of books and art materials. Annual housing costs vary from $4,800 (dormitory) to $4,900 (apartment); this figure includes a $750 nonrefundable deposit. The school offers a number of different meal plans; each provides a fixed number of meals per week plus some amount of flexible spending credit which can be used at college eateries of the student's choice. The basic rate per quarter for meal plans is $940. Students living in apartment-style housing facilities may simply choose to prepare their own meals.

SCHOOL OF THE ART INSTITUTE OF CHICAGO

GENERAL INFORMATION

The School of the Art Institute of Chicago (SAIC) has been providing students with a top-quality interdisciplinary art education for the past 134 years. Independent students flourish in the studio environment, which offers ample outlets for their creative ambition. A wide range of tools and resources are available, allowing these budding artists to experiment with many different media and expand their vision. A variety of aesthetic styles are encouraged by the faculty and course offerings at SAIC. The students and instructors take an active part in steering the philosophies and practices of the School. Faculty members remain available to students and share the knowledge they have gained working as professional artists, designers, and academics. The School's location next to the well-known Art Institute of Chicago museum gives students access to this incomparable collection. Students may visit the Art Institute exhibits, the Ryerson and Burnham Library, and the Glore Print Study Room free of charge. The city of Chicago sustains a thriving arts scene, considering that it has the second highest number of artists per capita in the nation. The undergraduate population of 1,819 includes students from 49 states and 40 countries. They may pursue a Bachelor of Fine Arts (BFA), Bachelor of Fine Arts with Professional Certification in Art Education, or Bachelor of Interior Architecture (BIA) degree. The School also offers strong graduate programs. SAIC is accredited by the North Central Association of Colleges and Schools and the National Association of Schools of Art and Design.

ACADEMICS

The SAIC academic calendar is made up of two semesters, a six-week interim session in the winter, and an eight-week summer program. During the interim session and the summer, faculty members take students on two- or three-week trips to study art in locations such as China, Ireland, South Africa, Italy, France, and England. Students must earn 132 credits to receive their BFA or BIA degree. The BFA with Professional Certificate in Art Education requires 138 hours, two-thirds of which are done in studio classes and the remaining third in academic classes. All first-year students with fewer than 18 credits of studio art work at the college level must take part in the First Year Program, which covers 2-D drawing, 3-D sculpture, and 4-D time arts (film, video, performance, and sound), art history, and English in the first two semesters. Freshmen take one elective studio art course in addition to the First Year Program. Once they have finished the First Year Programs, students steer their own course work with the guidance of a faculty advisor. SAIC does not confine students within specific majors; they are free to focus on a narrow subject area or explore a wider variety of courses. Studio classes last six hours and meet for 16 weeks. Many students complement their classroom and studio learning with the Cooperative Education Program. This program allows students to gain career experience while earning SAIC credit. Other off-campus opportunities include overseas study in Europe, Asia, and South America or the Mobility Program, which connects SAIC to partner schools across the country and in Canada. Students may also enroll in the New York Studio semester. The Off-Campus Programs Office helps students decide how to spend their out-of-class time.

The 347 full- and part-time faculty members at SAIC are all devoted teachers as well as active professionals in their respective fields. The School is proud to employ recipients of many prestigious grants, including 10 Guggenheim winners.

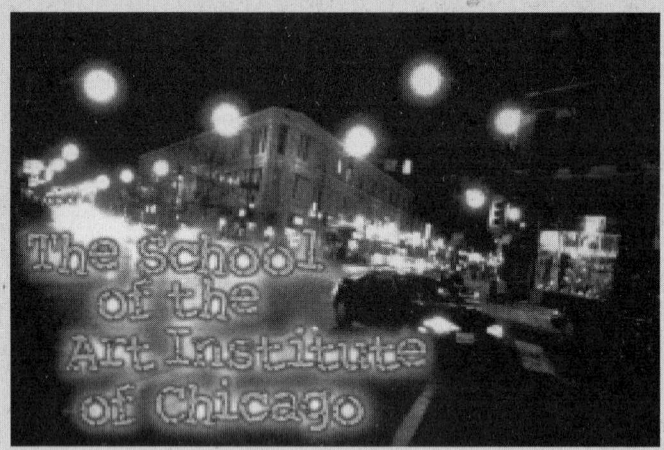

37 South Wabash Avenue
Chicago, IL 60603
Phone: 312-899-5219
Fax: 312-899-1840
Website: www.artic.edu

ADMISSIONS

The School admits students who demonstrate dedication to their visual arts pursuits and the intellectual curiosity necessary to make the most of the academic opportunities at SAIC. Applications are accepted from those with high school diplomas or the equivalent, as well as transfer students. A complete application to the BFA program includes the following materials: a completed application form, a $45 application fee, a portfolio representing the applicant's work, a personal statement, high school transcripts or an equivalency certificate, a reference letter, SAT I or ACT scores, and TOEFL scores for international students. Transfer students who have earned more than 18 credits at another institution are asked to turn in 30 slides that reflect their creative direction and background. Students applying to the Bachelor of Interior Architecture program should gear their portfolios toward plans, sections, elevations, drawings, and other materials that exhibit knowledge of interior spaces. The School offers an Immediate Decision Option (IDO) in addition to the regular admissions process. Students choosing the IDO bring all required materials to the School on specific days and get a response to their application by the end of the day. It is recommended that students bring samples of their actual work instead of slides for IDO consideration. While their work is being reviewed, IDO applicants may tour the campus, meet with students, learn about financial aid, and visit the career office. All other applicants send their materials to the Admissions Committee for review and receive notification by mail on a rolling basis. Applicants seeking financial aid are advised to submit all forms by the March 1 priority deadline. To receive an application or further information, please contact:

Office of Admissions
The School of the Art Institute of Chicago
37 South Wabash Avenue
Chicago, IL 60603
Telephone: 312-899-5219 or 800-232-7242 (toll free)
E-mail: admiss@artic.edu
World Wide Web: www.artic.edu/saic/saichome.html

Tours of the School are given daily Monday through Friday, by appointment only.

CAMPUS LIFE

The six buildings of SAIC stand against the background of the Chicago skyline. Two of the buildings are dormitories, which house roughly 200 students. Another residence hall, scheduled to open in the fall of 2000, will offer accommodations to an additional 467 students. All students affiliated with SAIC may use the off-campus housing resources offered by the Office of Residence Life. The Office also builds the sense of community on campus with special activities and programs. The Visiting Artist Program, which invites more than 100 visual artists, writers, and political activists to campus each year, gives students the opportunity to attend workshops and have their work critiqued. Other activities, including the Holiday Art Sale and "Schoolapalooza," a school-wide social event, are run by the Student Activities/Student Galleries group. The School's gallery space is allotted to groups and individuals by the Student Union Galleries (SUGS). Elected representatives of the student body serve on the Student Union and influence policy regarding student needs. At the present time, 15 student organizations thrive on campus, including cultural groups and art-oriented clubs. Students may also participate in the school newspaper, *F Magazine*, or the television station.

COST AND AID

In the 1999–2000 academic year, tuition cost $19,140 for undergraduates taking 15 credit hours each semester. The cost per credit hour was $638. Tuition includes all lab and activity fees. A single room in student housing runs from $6,540 to $7,320 annually, and a double room is $6,070. Students should allot an additional $12,000 to $13,000 per year to cover books, supplies, room and board, travel expenses, and personal items.

SCHOOL OF VISUAL ARTS

GENERAL INFORMATION

The School of Visual Arts, well-positioned in the heart of New York City, offers students the opportunity to become involved in one of America's largest and most vibrant cities, the art capital of the world. The energy, spirit, and desire to be the best that characterizes New York is embodied in SVA's renowned faculty of more than 700 working professionals, who challenge and inspire their students.

Bachelor of Fine Arts degrees are offered in advertising, animation, cartooning, computer art, graphic design, illustration, interior design, film and video, fine arts and photography.

Master of Fine Arts degrees are offered in computer art, design, fine arts, illustration as visual essay and photography and related media.

A Master of Professional Studies degree is offered in art therapy.

A Master of Arts in Teaching degree is offered in art education.

SVA also offers workshops, continuing education classes, concentrated studio residencies, an international student program, summer programs abroad, and a pre-college program for high school students.

STUDENT BODY

The Office of Student Activities provides a diverse range of programming designed to enrich the SVA student's experience. Students have the opportunity to tap into a multitude of activities, including theatrical events, poetry readings, concerts, and gallery openings. Students are encouraged to take advantage of all New York City has to offer through Campus Life–sponsored tours and events. The student government also sponsors activities.

Developing a life outside of the classroom is an important part of a student's growth at SVA. Several activities are planned to maximize the extracurricular experience. On weekends, the New York City metro area offers a wide range of fun day trips that provide scenic sites away from the hustle and bustle of the city.

A sampling of clubs at the college includes Dance Team, Judo Club, Sunday Painting Club, *SVA VOICE* (SVA's literary magazine), and WSVA (the College's radio station).

ACADEMICS

The four-year curriculum remains responsive to the needs and demands of the industry and is designed to allow students greater freedom of choice in electives and requirements with each succeeding year. The first year of each program, a foundation year, ensures the mastery of basic skills in each chosen discipline, as well as in writing and art history. After the first year, students focus on specific areas of concentration and, under the guidance of academic advisors and faculty members, pursue their own individual goals. The college provides students with studios that continually mirror the standards of the professional art world, and boasts one of the largest and most well-equipped computer art campuses in the country.

SVA is proud to boast one of the largest faculties of art professionals in the world. The faculty at SVA is composed of over 700 practicing artists and designers who represent an array of fields in the fine and applied arts. Each faculty member has chosen to commit to the professional art world as well as to teaching the next generation of artists. As a result of the college's policy of using working professionals to teach, the college has been able to attract to the faculty some of the most prominent artists in New York.

209 East 23rd Street
New York, NY 10010
Phone: 212-592-2100
Fax: 212-592-2116
Website: www.schoolofvisualarts.edu

ADMISSIONS

Deadlines:

- Deadline for freshmen and transfers: rolling (deadline for animation, computer art, film and video, and photography: March 15, 2004)
- Deadline for Early Decision: December 1, 2003
- Deadline for applying to the Silas H. Rhodes Scholarship Program: February 2, 2004 for first-time freshman applicants and March 15, 2004 for transfer applicants

Requirements:

- Application for Undergraduate Admission Form
- A nonrefundable $50 application fee ($80 for international applicants)
- Official transcripts from all high schools and colleges attended
- Results of the SAT or ACT
- Statement of intent
- Portfolio
- Letters of recommendation (optional)
- Interview (optional, recommended)
- Demonstration of English proficiency (required of all applicants whose primary language is not English)
- Declaration of Finances form and Verification of Finances letter from bank (international applicants only)

CAMPUS LIFE

There are few places as perfect to study art than New York City, the extended campus of SVA. Living and learning happens throughout Manhattan and the other boroughs, exposing you to all the culture and life of the intellectual energy center of the planet.

The official SVA campus is placed near the city's photography, art and advertising centers. SVA life is New York City life. Students come here to be immersed in real-world experience, not the insulated experience of other schools. They get a whole other chunk of learning from this, which eases the transition from student to working adult.

SVA students have the opportunity of participating in art programs abroad during the summer semester. SVA offers Painting in Barcelona, Paint and Photography in Florence, and Art, Myths, and History of Ancient Greece. Third-year students in fine arts, graphic design, illustration, interior design, and photography have the opportunity to study abroad for one semester at an AIAS (Association of Independent Art Schools) affiliate in Europe.

The College also has an Internship for Credit Program, which allows qualified juniors and seniors to work part-time for studio credit. Internships are a great way to establish contact with prospective employers. In many cases interns have been offered full-time, part-time or freelance positions after completing internships.

COST AND AID

Expenses For 2003–2004

Application fee: $50 ($80 for international applicants)

Tuition: $18,200 per year full-time

Departmental fees: $150 to $1,100 per semester depending on major

Estimated supplies: $1,050 to $3,150

Housing charges: range from $7,200 to $9,800 per year

SCRIPPS COLLEGE

GENERAL INFORMATION

From its founding in 1926 as one of the few institutions in the West dedicated to educating women for professional careers as well as personal growth, Scripps College has championed the qualities of mind and spirit described by its founder, newspaper entrepreneur and philanthropist Ellen Browning Scripps. Scripps remains a women's college because it believes that having women at the core of its concerns provides the best environment for intellectually ambitious women to learn from a distinguished teaching faculty and from each other. Scripps emphasizes a challenging core curriculum based on interdisciplinary humanistic studies, combined with rigorous training in the disciplines, as the best possible foundation for any goals a woman may pursue. The interdisciplinary emphasis of the curriculum has always been a hallmark of a Scripps education. Because Scripps women learn to see the connections not only among academic subjects, but also among the major areas of their own lives, alumnae often remark that Scripps prepared them for life. Everyone affiliated with the College, from the students and faculty to the alumnae and staff, are expected to continue to contribute to the Scripps community, as well as their own communities in both professional and personal capacities. Above all, Scripps gives women an intensive, challenging education that will help them to lead, in the words of its founder, "lives filled with confidence, courage, and hope."

STUDENT BODY

Over 200 clubs and organizations are available at the Claremont Colleges. Many others exist, from the politically based to the activity-based to the culturally based. Students can also choose from a variety of five-college and Scripps campus events, 10 NCAA Division III sports teams, and intramural and club sports teams.

ACADEMICS

At least 32 courses are required for the Bachelor of Arts degree at Scripps. There are three groups of courses: core curriculum requirements, coursework for the chosen major, and elective courses or courses for a minor. The core curriculum courses serve as a framework for the academic experience, and the electives give students the chance to study the social sciences, humanities, fine arts, natural sciences, and mathematics. There are two semesters to each academic year, which runs from early September to mid-May.

The following majors are available at Scripps or through cross registration with other Claremont Colleges: accounting; American studies; anthropology; art history; Asian studies; Asian American studies; biology; biology-chemistry; black studies; chemistry; Chicano studies; Chinese; classical language and literature; classical studies; computer science; dance; economics; engineering; English; environment, economics and politics; environmental science; environmental studies; European studies; foreign languages; gender and women's studies; geology; German literature; German studies; Hispanic studies; history; human biology; humanities/interdisciplinary studies in culture; Italian; Italian studies; Japanese; Jewish studies; Latin American studies; legal studies; linguistics; management engineering; mathematical economics; mathematics; media studies; molecular biology; music; neuroscience; organizational studies; philosophy; philosophy, politics, and economics; physics; politics and international relations; psychology; public policy analysis; religious studies; Russian; science and management; science, technology, and society; sociology; and studio arts theatre.

Scripps College has 58 full-time and 31 part-time faculty members. All faculty members teach undergraduates, and the student/faculty ratio is 11:1. Ninety-seven percent of the full-time faculty hold doctorates of equivalent terminal degrees.

1030 Columbia Avenue, Mailbox #1265
Claremont, CA 91711
Phone: 909-621-8149
Fax: 909-607-7508
Website: www.scrippscollege.edu

ADMISSIONS

The desired Scripps applicant is energetic, intellectually curious, and interested in exploring an intensive liberal arts curriculum. High academic achievement is expected, as is personal success. Scripps also values leadership, motivation, honesty, and creativity. Every part of a student's application is important to the Admission Committee. The quality of a student's academic work is key, and a recommended course of study includes five academic subjects in each year of high school, for a total of 4 years of English, 4 years of mathematics, 3 years of social studies, 3 years of laboratory science (biology, chemistry, or physics), and either 3 years of a foreign language or 2 years each of two different languages. Honors, Advanced Placement, or International Baccalaureate courses are highly regarded by the Committee. Applicants are encouraged to take the SAT II: Subject Tests and to schedule an interview. Also required are an essay and a graded writing assignment from the junior or senior year of high school. Applicants are welcome to submit their materials on computer disk and online. For the class entering in the fall of 2002, the middle 50 percent had SAT verbal scores of 620-720 and math scores of 600-690. The average GPA for the class entering in the fall of 2002 was 3.8. Scripps has two early decision application deadlines: November 1 and January 1. The academic scholarship application deadline is November 1. The regular decision application deadline is February 1.

CAMPUS LIFE

Scripps is listed on the National Register of Historic Places. Its home is Claremont, California, a college town with a population of 35,000. Los Angeles and Pasadena are 40 miles and 20 miles west, respectively. Within driving distance are mountains, beaches, and deserts, all of which can be enjoyed in the beautiful southern California climate. The winters are dry and cool, while the temperature rises in the late spring.

Scripps students can take courses at any Claremont College. Students also have a variety of other programs to choose from, including internships, a selection of work-study programs, study abroad in any of 36 countries, and a semester in Washington. Arts and business administration students have the option of 3-2 accelerated degree programs. Engineering students have the opportunity to participate in a 3-2 program (BA-BS) in conjunction with Harvey Mudd College, Washington University in St. Louis, USC, UC-Berkeley, and Columbia, Stanford, and Boston Universities.

COST AND AID

For the 2003–2004 academic year, tuition and fees will cost $27,063 and room and board, $8,651, for a total cost of $35,714 (pending approval by the Board of Trustees).

SEATTLE UNIVERSITY

AT A GLANCE

Seattle University, founded in 1891, is one of 28 Jesuit colleges and universities in the United States. The undergraduate student body numbers 3,561 and includes representatives from 49 states and 46 nations. Seattle University provides an ideal environment for motivated students interested in self-reliance, awareness of different cultures, social justice, and the fulfillment that comes from making a difference. Our location in the center of one of the nation's most diverse and progressive cities attracts a student body, faculty, and staff rich in diversity. Our urban setting promotes the development of leadership skills and independence and provides the opportunity for students to apply what they learn through internships, clinical experiences, and volunteer work.

The student life program includes over 80 extracurricular clubs and organizations. Three residence halls and an on-campus apartment complex house 1,500 students, and undergraduate housing is available all four years. Approximately 85 percent of the freshmen and sophomores live on campus. The Connolly Athletic Center serves as the major facility for varsity and intramural athletics and recreation. It features two swimming pools, two gymnasiums, and saunas. A six-acre complex provides fields for outdoor sports.

Seattle University is accredited by the Northwest Association of Schools and Colleges, the Accrediting Board for Engineering and Technology, the International Association for Management Education (formerly AACSB-IAME), the American Chemical Society, the Commission on Accreditation of Allied Health Education Programs, the National Council for Accreditation of Teacher Education, Association of Theological Schools, the National League for Nursing Accrediting Commission, and the American Bar Association.

LOCATION AND ENVIRONMENT

Seattle University is located in a port city of unsurpassed natural beauty. As the Pacific Northwest's largest city (and the 14th largest metropolitan area in the United States), Seattle is a scenic and cultural center in a setting that includes breathtaking mountain views of the Cascades to the east and the Olympics to the west. In addition to being situated along Puget Sound, Seattle also contains Lakes Union and Washington.

The campus is located in the center of the city. Seattle's sights and sounds, rich ethnic diversity, celebrated restaurants, first-run entertainment, major-league athletics, theater, opera, and ballet enhance campus life.

MAJORS AND DEGREES OFFERED

Seattle University offers the following undergraduate degrees: Bachelor of Arts, Bachelor of Science, Bachelor of Science in Nursing, Bachelor of Social Work, and the Bachelor of Arts in Business Administration. The University offers 45 majors and 31 minors in five academic units: The Albers School of Business and Economics; The College of Arts and Sciences; The School of Nursing; The School of Science and Engineering; and The Matteo Ricci College, a consortium in cooperation with The Seattle Preparatory School, which offers a six-year BA degree that begins with ninth grade.

Undergraduate Programs include accounting; art history; biochemistry; biology; business administration; business economics; chemistry; communications; computer engineering, computer science; criminal justice; diagnostic ultrasound; e-commerce, ecological studies; economics; electronic commerce; engineering (civil, computer, electrical, environmental, and mechanical); English/creative writing; finance; fine, applied, and performing arts; French; general science; German; history; humanities; international business; international studies; journalism; liberal studies; management; marketing; mathematics; medical technology; military science/ROTC; nursing; philosophy; physics; political science; pre-law; pre-medical/pre-dental; psychology; public affairs; sociology; Spanish; theology/religious studies; and women's studies.

ACADEMIC PROGRAMS

Students at Seattle University take a basic program of liberal studies called the core curriculum. The university core curriculum has several distinguishing characteristics: it provides an integrated freshman year; gives order and sequence to student learning; provides experience in the methods and content of the range of liberal arts, sciences, philosophy, and theology; calls for active learning in all classes, for practice in writing and thinking, and for an awareness of values; and fosters a global perspective and a sense of social and personal responsibility. Our academic offerings provide leadership opportunities and enable graduates to serve society through a demanding liberal arts and social sciences foundation. In the Jesuit educational tradition we teach students how to think, not what to think.

Seattle University also offers a special two-year honors program. This seminar-oriented study of the humanities provides intensive work in philosophy, theology, literature, history, art, and science. The honors program fulfills all core requirements. Admission is competitive and requires a separate application.

Admissions Office, 900 Broadway
Seattle, WA 98122-4340
Phone: 206-296-2000
Fax: 206-296-5656
Website: www.seattleu.edu

OFF-CAMPUS OPPORTUNITIES

SU offers three international study programs—programs for French in France, Latin American Studies in Mexico, German in Germany, and three reciprocal exchange programs with the University of Graz in Austria, Sophia University in Japan, and Taejon University in Korea. Additional study abroad programs in other nations, in conjunction with other colleges' overseas programs, are also offered.

Seattle University is affiliated with the Council for International Educational Exchange, a consortium of colleges and universities which sponsor a variety of academic programs around the world.

FACILITIES AND EQUIPMENT

The University is located on 58 acres in the First Hill neighborhood in the center of Seattle. There are 28 buildings recently enhanced by $157 million in additions, renovations, and new construction.

TUITION, ROOM & BOARD AND FEES

For the 2003–2004 academic year, full-time tuition is $20,070; room and meals are $6,858. The estimate for books, supplies, fees, and personal expenses is an additional $3,156. Travel costs vary among students. Costs are subject to change. Seattle University operates on a quarter calendar with fall term beginning in late September.

FINANCIAL AID

Approximately 87 percent of new freshmen receive an average financial aid award of $17,313 per year. These awards usually include scholarships, grants, loans, and Federal Work-Study. Last year Seattle University awarded more than $50.6 million in aid to undergraduates—nearly $19.3 million of that came from the university's own funds. Students are required to apply for financial aid by February 1, as awards are made early each spring for the following fall quarter. Applications that are received after this deadline will be evaluated in the order received for any remaining aid. Students must submit the Free Application for Federal Student Aid (FAFSA) and be accepted for admission to be considered for financial assistance. There are a number of scholarships for freshmen that are awarded on the basis of academic achievement, extracurricular involvement, and community service. Transfer scholarships are also available.

FULL AND PART-TIME FACULTY

There are 460 faculty members; 87 percent of whom possess doctoral or terminal degrees. The mission of faculty members who choose Seattle University is teaching. Most classes average 20; the student/faculty ratio is 14:1. All classes are taught by faculty members, who provide extra assistance, help students with their research, and assist in the arranging of internships. Faculty advisors provide guidance, direction, and encouragement throughout the year.

STUDENT ORGANIZATION AND ACTIVITIES

All undergraduates belong to the Associated Students of Seattle University (ASSU), the central student organization on campus, which is organized around an elected president, an executive vice president, and an activities vice president. Additionally, a 12-member representative council oversees every facet of the student body and is responsible for policy making, a diverse activities program, and the communication of student needs to the administration and faculty.

ADMISSIONS PROCESS AND REQUIREMENTS

Seattle University is committed to qualitative decision making based on evaluations of students as a whole. Decisions are based primarily on individual course selection, performance, and trends. The expected academic program comprises 16 units of course work, including 4 years of English, 3 years of social studies or history, 2 years of a foreign language, 3 years of college-preparatory mathematics, and 2 units of lab science (3 are preferred). Laboratory physics and chemistry, as well as 4 units of college-preparatory mathematics are required for engineering; we require laboratory chemistry and biology for admission to the nursing program. Also required for all programs are official scores from either the ACT or the SAT I. The middle 50 percent of enrolling freshmen have secondary school averages of 3.2 to 3.8 (on a 4.0 scale).

Essays or personal statements are required for admission and are carefully considered during application review. College credit is awarded to those who have successfully earned minimum scores on Advanced Placement or International Baccalaureate examinations.

Applications and information can be obtained by contacting the Admissions Office. Secondary school students who have completed at least six semesters are encouraged to complete the application process by February 1 of their senior year. Transfer students must submit official transcripts from all post-secondary institutions attended, regardless of whether course work was completed. The recommended financial aid/admission deadline for transfers is March 1. Applications are accepted after these dates but financial aid funds may no longer be available. Campus visits can be scheduled Monday through Friday and most Saturdays. Guests can attend a class, meet with faculty, participate in a campus tour, and speak individually with representatives from admissions and financial aid. Students can apply directly or online via our website, www.seattleu.edu. Seattle University is also a member of the Common Application.

SETON HALL UNIVERSITY

GENERAL INFORMATION

Seton Hall University, established in 1856 by James Roosevelt Bayley, was named after St. Elizabeth Ann Seton, who established the first Sisters of Charity community in the United States. Sharing his Aunt St. Elizabeth Ann Seton's pioneering spirit, James Roosevelt Bayley served as Newark's first Catholic bishop. The first diocesan undergraduate institution in the United States, Seton Hall University advanced to university status in 1950. Today, the school remains affiliated with Newark's Roman Catholic Diocese. Although Seton Hall is a Catholic institution, it is not exclusively sectarian and invites undergraduates of all faiths. The University accentuates Judeo-Christian intellectual values and customs. About 4,700 men and women make up the present undergraduate student body.

The University is comprised of nine schools: on the South Orange university grounds are the College of Arts and Sciences, the College of Education and Human Services, the College of Nursing, Immaculate Conception Seminary and School of Theology, the School of Diplomacy and International Relations, the School of Graduate Medical Education, the W. Paul Stillman School of Business, and University College; the School of Law is located in Newark. Seton Hall receives its accreditation from the Middle States Association of Colleges and Schools. The College of Education and Human Services receives its accreditation from the National Council for Accreditation of Teacher Education and is authorized by the State Department of Education in New Jersey in accordance with standards of the National Association of State Directors of Teacher Education and Certification. The W. Paul Stillman School of Business receives its accreditation from the American Assembly of Collegiate Schools of Business. The College of Nursing receives its accreditation from the New Jersey State Board of Nursing and the National League for Nursing. The Seton Hall University campus spans 58 acres. University-managed apartments and coeducational residence facilities house about 1,950 students. The University's seminary facilities include the School of Theology classrooms and residential housing for faculty members and graduate seminarians.

Undergraduates may participate in a variety of activities, including the Black Students Union; choral, drama, and radio groups; community service organizations; a debate team with national ranking; fraternities and sororities; the International Students Organization; a musical theater; a pep band; the Puerto Rican Institute; and student publications including a magazine, newspaper, and a yearbook. In addition, members of all denominations may participate in the Seton Hall campus ministry. The University has men's varsity teams in baseball, basketball, cross-country, golf, indoor and outdoor track, soccer, swimming and diving, tennis, and wrestling. There are women's varsity teams in basketball, cross-country, indoor and outdoor track, soccer, softball, swimming, tennis, and volleyball. An intramural sports program is also offered. Walsh Auditorium-Gymnasium has a 3,400-person main arena capacity, and is also the location of Seton Hall's 2,000-watt FM radio station. The University offers students such services as aptitude testing, career counseling, career services, health services, personal counseling, and special services. The campus is designed to allow the disabled access to all areas.

STUDENT BODY

The Student Government Association, a bicameral undergraduate entity, serves the dual purpose of representing the University's students and offering programs that benefit the campus community. Undergraduates are elected to University Senate, which handles all legislative issues that apply to the University. The Resident Student Association, the student's other governmental body, works to uphold the rights and interests of undergraduate residents, and the Commuter Council acts on behalf of commuter students.

ACADEMICS

The University operates on a semester-based calendar. A daytime-and-evening summer program is also offered. The University's largest division is the College of Arts and Sciences. Students must maintain a minimum GPA of 2.0 in the major field and earn a minimum of 130 credits in order to achieve a BA or BS. The W. Paul Stillman School of Business undergraduate program is grounded in a broad liberal arts curriculum. During their first and second years of study, undergraduates learn the behavioral, economic, quantitative, and scientific fundamentals of the business world and society as a whole. During their third and fourth years of study, a business-related core curriculum in finance, management, and marketing is covered. Undergraduates must complete a minimum of 128 credits in order to earn a BS degree.

The College of Education and Human Services offers a preparatory program for elementary and secondary school teaching certification valid in 29 states. Students pursuing an education degree complete a program that deeply rooted in liberal arts study. The program is designed to integrate educational technique studies with supplementary academic disciplines, and to allow undergraduates the opportunity to experience classroom teaching situations. The goal of this program is to develop the future instructor's creative, humanistic, and intellectual potential. Undergraduates must maintain a 2.5 minimum GPA and complete 126–131 credits to earn their BS degree.

The College of Nursing program merges liberal arts study with professional instruction in nursing to ready undergraduate nursing students for careers in a wide range of health-care fields. Students are given the opportunity to experience the clinical procedures followed by hospitals, industrial organizations, nursing homes, public health agencies, schools, and other community organizations. Students who successfully complete the program are qualified to take the state examination leading to certification as a registered nurse. Undergraduates must complete a minimum of 130 credits to earn their BSN degree.

The School of Diplomacy and International Relations works jointly with the United Nations of the USA, offering a Bachelor of Science program in international relations. Through this program, undergraduates will gain knowledge of international relations, and develop the abilities needed to utilize their knowledge and management skills. The program enables students to prepare for positions in governmental and nongovernmental organizations, international commerce, and international organizations.

Students may seek internships in many programs, cooperative education programs through the W. Paul Stillman School of Business and the College of Arts and Sciences, and independent study programs. Undergraduates may also pursue a four-year honors program for exceptional students, offered by the College of Arts and Sciences. Credit is usually awarded to students who score 3 or higher on AP tests or for satisfactory scores on CLEP examinations (both general and subject). Applicants may earn no more than 30 hours worth of course credit though such exams.

Enrollment Services, 400 South Orange Avenue
South Orange, NJ 07079
Phone: 973-761-9332
Fax: 973-275-2040
Website: www.shu.edu

At the College of Arts and Sciences, students may pursue the BA in African American studies, anthropology, art, Asian studies, classical studies, communication, criminal justice, economics, English, French, history, Italian, liberal studies, modern languages, music, philosophy, political science, psychology, religious studies, social and behavioral sciences, social work, sociology, and Spanish. Students may also pursue the BS in biology, biochemistry, chemistry, computer science, mathematics, and physics. At the W. Paul Stillman School of Business, students may pursue the BS in accounting, economics, finance, management, management information systems, marketing, and sports management and the BA in business administration. At the College of Education and Human Services, students may pursue the BS in early childhood education, elementary education, secondary education, and special education and. The College also offers teacher certification programs. At the College of Nursing, students may pursue the Bachelor of Science in Nursing (BSN). The University offers pre-professional programs in dentistry, law, medicine, and optometry. Engineering is offered in cooperation with the New Jersey Institute of Technology. Six-year physician's assistant and physical therapy programs are offered in cooperation with the University of Medicine and Dentistry of New Jersey (BS/MS). Students may also pursue a six-year occupational therapy program (BA/MS). A seven-year, dual-admission law program is offered in cooperation with the Seton Hall School of Law.

Seton Hall has 343 full-time instructors and 390 part-time instructors. Nearly 70 percent of the full-time instructors have earned a doctoral degree. The University has a 14:1 student/faculty ratio (based on full-time undergraduates and full-time instructors). Members of the faculty act as advisors to undergraduate members of their department.

ADMISSIONS

In selecting new students, Seton Hall University takes into account secondary school performance record, SAT I or ACT scores, and counselor and instructor references. Applicants must have graduated from an accredited secondary school or have received satisfactory marks on the GED test. The University requires that applicants have completed 16 high school credits: 4 in English, 2 in foreign language, 1 in laboratory science, 3 in mathematics, 2 in social studies, and 4 in accepted academic electives. The University has separate admission guidelines for nontraditional applicants (i.e. those who have not been in high school for many years). Applicants requesting a transfer to the University must have at least a 2.5 GPA (at least a 2.75 GPA for business, computer science, math, and science programs) and must have performed satisfactorily at the previous school attended. Credit is generally awarded for grades of 2.0 or greater in University-level curriculum taken at recognized institutions; students may transfer no more than 100 semester hours to apply toward a bachelor's program at Seton Hall.

Freshman applicants must provide high school transcript, SAT I or ACT scores, and a $45 application fee. Applicants may also opt to include instructor and/or counselor references, and an essay. They may also wish to take part in a personal interview. Admission to the University is granted on a rolling basis; beginning January 1, Seton Hall announces admission decisions as they are reached. It is suggested that freshman applicants submit applications by March 1, and transfer students submit applications by June 1. For more information, contact:

Office of Enrollment Services
Seton Hall University
400 South Orange Avenue
South Orange, NJ 07079
Telephone: 800-THE-HALL (toll free outside New Jersey)
E-mail: thehall@shu.edu

CAMPUS LIFE

Just 14 miles outside of New York City, the University is situated in a suburb of South Orange, New Jersey. Convenient bus, car, or train transportation allows students access to the multitude of entertainment and cultural activities that New York City has to offer. Students may find all manner of recreational activities, including resorts and state parks, within a 100 mile radius of South Orange. In the northern New Jersey area, students may pursue many employment prospects, internships, and learning opportunities.

Seton Hall University undergraduates may participate in study abroad opportunities in the Dominican Republic, Japan, Korea, People's Republic of China, the and Puerto Rico. Through the University's International Student Exchange Program, undergraduates may opt to study at any of 101 universities in 35 nations for one school year. Undergraduates have a variety of options to pursue internships and cooperative learning in the University's surrounding metropolitan area. Many co-op opportunities are with Fortune 500 corporations, other positions are with leading charitable, cultural, government, and scientific organizations. Students may also pursue one-semester internships and classes in Washington, DC, at exchange universities.

COST AND AID

Tuition includes an access charge for a laptop computer that the University issues to all new undergraduates.

SETON HILL UNIVERSITY

GENERAL INFORMATION

Seton Hill University was founded in 1918 by the Sisters of Charity. Their goal was to empower the Student Body with the tools of education. Seton Hill has built a reputation at the forefront of liberal arts education ever since. Seton Hill University's location in the Laurel Highlands area of southwestern Pennsylvania provides breathtaking scenery and endless opportunities for enjoying the outdoors. Popular activities include hiking, canoeing, whitewater rafting, and downhill and cross-country skiing. Buildings designed by architect Frank Lloyd Wright also surround the campus. Professional sporting events, shopping, nightlife, concerts, and other urban attractions await students just 35 miles away in Pittsburgh. The 1,500 students of Seton Hill participate in a wide variety of extra-curricular activities. Student-athletes participate in sports including tennis, basketball, golf, softball, cross-country, equestrian team competition, soccer, and volleyball on both the varsity and intramural levels. Additionally, lacrosse and field hockey will be available beginning in 2003. Student-run clubs cover professional interests including education, communication, chemistry, and business, as well as academic pursuits, such as honors coursework. The literary magazine and award-winning newspaper also provide opportunities for involvement.

Those wishing to pursue graduate studies have their choice of the following programs at Seton Hill: the Master of Education in technologies-enhanced learning; the Master of Business Administration; and the Master of Arts in marriage and family therapy, elementary education, special education, art therapy, or writing popular fiction. Seton Hill demonstrates its commitment to fostering future entrepreneurs with the National Education Center for Women in Business. Students from any major are invited to take classes in all facets of running a business at this groundbreaking facility.

STUDENT BODY

Student representatives serving on the Seton Hill Government Association are entrusted with decisions that drive campus life. Students hold voting positions on many faculty committees. Representatives are also responsible for organizing activities, including cultural outings to nearby cities. In order to facilitate communication between student leaders and the general Student Body, each residence hall floor selects a senator to relay opinions and needs to the Government Association. Participation in student government is a valuable experience that develops leadership skills and a working understanding of government in general.

ACADEMICS

In addition to the 30 academic disciplines of the five divisions of Seton Hill, students can also design their own majors. All degrees share the basis of the University's liberal arts core curriculum, recognized with past awards. Students who have not selected a major receive the support of special programs. Students who graduate at the top of their high school class have the opportunity to enroll in Seton Hill's Honors Program. During their four years at the University, students compile a portfolio presenting the best of their classroom and extracurricular work. The portfolio stands as a testament to their learning and represents their achievements as they begin their careers.

Seton Hill offers courses of study leading to the Bachelor of Arts, Bachelor of Fine Arts, Bachelor of Science, Bachelor of Music, and Bachelor of Social Work degrees. In the sciences, Seton Hill awards degrees in biochemistry, biology, chemistry, computer science, engineering, mathematics (including actuary science), and physics. The university's social science majors include economics, political science, psychology, social work, pre-law, and sociology (including criminal justice). Students in the field of communication can choose among corporate communication, instructional design, and political communication classes. Health care-related degrees are granted in medical technology, nutrition/dietetics, physician assistant, and pre-professional health sciences programs in optometry, physical therapy, podiatry, dentistry, veterinary medicine, and occupational therapy. Students heading into business may choose to study business administration (including finance), accounting, or hospitality and tourism. The study of family and consumer sciences includes work in childcare administration. Those students earning a degree in another area may tailor their programs to include education certification in art, biology, chemistry, dual elementary/special, early childhood, elementary, English, French, home economics, mathematics, music, social studies, Spanish, or special education. The art department offers programs in art and technology, art education, art history, art therapy, graphic design, studio art, and visual arts management. The theater department encompasses musical theater, technical theater, theater arts, theater management, and theater performance. Undergraduates pursuing degrees in music can study music theatre, music education, performance, and sacred music. The English department offers courses in creative writing, journalism, and literature. Other humanities programs include Spanish, history, international studies, religious studies/theology, and women's studies.

Seton Hill employs 60 full-time faculty members, and more than 81 percent of all faculty members hold PhDs or other terminal degrees. All instructors display a dedication to teaching and personal interaction with students. This mentoring relationship is enabled by the low student/faculty ratio of 13:1. Faculty members make themselves available outside of class to offer individual guidance to students.

1 Seton Hill Drive
Greensburg, PA 15601
Phone: 724-838-4255
Fax: 724-830-1294
Website: www.setonhill.edu

Your chance to shine.℠

ADMISSIONS

Successful applicants to Seton Hill have a strong college preparatory background. Their high school transcripts show a minimum of 15 academic units, comprising 4 units of English, 2 units of college-preparatory mathematics, 2 units of social science, 2 units of the same foreign language, 1 unit of laboratory science, and 4 academic electives. Transfer applications are welcome; after a transfer student has been accepted, the University will consider transferring credits from other institutions by examining transcripts and evaluating each course separately. Applications to Seton Hill are accepted on a rolling basis, and students are notified of their admissions status in a timely manner after receipt of materials. The complete application packet for incoming freshmen includes the following: a completed application form, a $30 application fee, an official secondary school transcript that displays the applicant's rank and overall grade point average, and SAT I or ACT scores. A "write option" plan is possible for students who do not wish to send SAT or ACT scores—this should be arranged with the Admissions staff. For further information, please contact:

Mary Kay Cooper
Director of Admissions and Adult Student Services
Office of Admissions
Seton Hill University
Seton Hill Drive Box 991
Greensburg, PA 15601-1599
Telephone: 724-838-4255 or 800-826-6234 (toll free)
Fax: 724-830-1294
E-mail: admit@setonhill.edu
World Wide Web: www.setonhill.edu

CAMPUS LIFE

Seton Hill University, a private institution, maintains a safe, secure campus in Greensburg, Pennsylvania. The University's 200 acres of picturesque woodland provide students with an idyllic setting for focusing on their academic pursuits. Greensburg, located 35 miles east of Pittsburgh, benefits from access to a large city while preserving its small-town appeal. The Westmoreland Museum of American Art, the Westmoreland Symphony Orchestra, hospital, and plenty of shopping centers are located in Greensburg, the seat of Westmoreland County. Seton Hill is easily reached by plane, train, or car.

Seton Hill encourages students to cultivate ideas and learn new skills outside of the classroom. The University facilitates opportunities such as internships, fieldwork projects, and experiences in cooperative education. With the help of faculty mentors and the Office of Career Development, students can find off-campus positions to enhance their course of study and develop post-graduation job prospects. Many undergraduates also choose to balance their on-campus learning with time studying overseas.

COST AND AID

Full-time tuition in the 2002–2003 academic year totaled $17,370. Fees for room and board ranged from $5,800-$6,010. Another $1,000-$2,000 should be allotted for personal expenses and books annually.

A picturesque landmark. The campus view of Seton Hill College is simply breathtaking.

SIENA COLLEGE

GENERAL INFORMATION

Siena College is a liberal arts college of 2,700 men and women that offers undergraduate degrees in liberal arts, business, and science. Student-focused professors are at the heart of a supportive learning environment that prepares students for careers and for an active role in their community. Siena College provides a personal, values-oriented education—one student at a time.

Siena was founded by the Franciscan Order of the Catholic Church, and the teachings of St. Francis of Assisi are the cornerstone of Siena's philosophy. The Franciscan Tradition—a tradition of concern for others and dedication to the local and global community—is very much alive at Siena today.

STUDENT BODY

Siena students know how to work hard, but they also know how to relax and have fun! Intramural sports are very popular, and Siena's 18 Division I athletic teams are a focus for players and fans alike. Clubs range from the Model United Nations to the Ski Club, and there are many academic honor societies. Performers can get involved in Stage Three, the theater club that puts on several plays every year.

Students are active in Big Brothers/Big Sisters, Habitat for Humanity, local soup kitchens and homeless shelters, and a host of other outreach programs. By being involved in their community, our students are able to share the gift of their education and talents with others. In return, they grow in compassion, find a new commitment to service in society, and gain confidence in themselves and their own abilities. Often they feel that they gain as much from their experiences in these roles as those they help do!

ACADEMICS

Siena College bases its education of each of its students on a strong liberal arts foundation. A liberal arts education will serve you for a lifetime of career choices and changes. Liberal arts classes teach more than facts and figures–through them, students develop an ability to analyze and evaluate the world around them. Sometimes knowing what questions to ask is more important than knowing answers. Siena's professors encourage their students to think critically-to examine problems from all sides, and to use the knowledge they have gained throughout their studies to understand and explore the issues that face them in the classroom and in the world outside.

At Siena, classes are small and interactive; no class is larger than 35 students, and most are between 10 and 20.

This atmosphere allows each student to be active in discussion, work in teams, and ask questions. Our 16:1 student/faculty ratio means that professors get to know their students and have time to spend inside and outside the classroom with students.

Siena students can augment their major studies with certificate programs or minors; they can complete a secondary education certificate and be ready to teach upon graduation. In conjunction with an appropriate major, students can engage in pre-professional preparation for law, medicine, and engineering.

Siena offers bachelor's degrees in 26 different majors.

Bachelor of Arts Degrees are offered in American studies, creative arts, classical languages, economics, English, environmental studies, French, history, mathematics, philosophy, political science, psychology, religious studies, social work, sociology, and Spanish.

Bachelor of Science Degrees are offered in biology, biochemistry, chemistry, computer science, economics, finance, marketing and management, mathematics, physics, and environmental studies.

Bachelor of Business Administration and Master of Business Administration Degrees are offered in accounting.

Full-time faculty: 186

Part-time faculty: 89

515 Loudon Road
Loudonville, NY 12211
Phone: 518-783-2423
Fax: 518-783-2436
Website: www.siena.edu

ADMISSIONS

There is no one formula by which Siena's admissions decisions are made. Our Admissions Committee considers your whole record—your curriculum, grades, activities, class rank, standardized test scores, and counselor comments. You should submit a completed Application for Admission by March 1 of your senior year (including transcript, SAT I or ACT scores, and a counselor recommendation).

All students seeking admission to Siena should have a solid foundation in the full range of college preparatory courses: four years of English and social science courses, at least three courses each in the sciences (with labs), mathematics, and a foreign language.

Siena offers both Early Decision and Early Action application options.

Siena College offers Presidential Scholarships to outstanding high school seniors. Students must apply by January 15, and those students who are nominated for the scholarship must attend an on-campus interview program.

We strongly recommend that all applicants visit Siena. The Admissions Office hosts Open House and Group Visit programs, as well as interviews Monday through Friday and many Saturdays when school is in session. With all campus visits we provide a tour of campus. The only way to decide if Siena is the school for you is to visit!

Our Admissions Counselors are happy to speak with you to discuss Siena and arrange a visit that best meets your needs. To speak with an Admissions Counselor or to arrange a visit to campus, please call 888-AT-SIENA.

You can make visit arrangements by calling the Siena Admissions Office at 518-783-2423 or 888-AT-SIENA.

Visit Siena on the Web at www.siena.edu.

CAMPUS LIFE

Siena is located in Loudonville, New York, a suburb of the state capital Albany, and the location provides our students with the best of two worlds-a comfortable and safe suburban community just minutes from the excitement and opportunities of a vital city. The Capital region is home to 14 colleges and universities (and more than 50,000 college students), so there's a lot to do. Siena is just three hours from New York and Boston, and four hours from Montreal.

The fall of freshman year is the beginning of four years of growth and learning-not just in the classroom, but in the residence halls, in clubs and sports, and through interpersonal relationships. Siena alumni greatly value the friendships they made here-not just with other students, but with friars and faculty members as well.

Internships: Each semester, more than 300 Siena juniors and seniors gain valuable hands-on work experience through internships. Some have chosen a career, and are using their internship as the first step to a professional position. Others are still undecided as to their career path, and use their internship to discern what sort of work they are looking for, and where their interests lie. Whatever their reasons for taking an internship, all students are developing essential qualities that will make them attractive to employers in the future: good communication skills, a knowledge of business practices, a personal style of working with others, and the self-confidence to present themselves and their ideas effectively.

What kind of internships are available? Through Siena's standing in the Capital District, internships in almost every field have been cultivated. There are internships in every facet of public service, from the governor's office and the state legislature, to criminal justice fields, to the state education department. Local laboratories and research companies offer research-based internships in the science industries. Banks, financial management firms, and many other private-sector employers offer valuable business experience.

Study Abroad: Siena juniors and seniors have a wealth of opportunities to broaden their horizons and see the world. Some attend classes at Regent's College in the heart of London, combining study with an international internship. Others go to Ireland, France, or Spain, and some even venture "Down Under" at any of two dozen Australian universities. Through study abroad, you can go almost anywhere your imagination will take you!

COST AND AID

For 2001–2002

Tuition: $15,330

Fees: $540

Room: $4,275

Board: $2,540

Orientation fee: $180

Because of its relatively low cost and high quality education, Siena is rated the best buy for a private education in New York State and second best buy for a private college in the Northeast.

SKIDMORE COLLEGE

GENERAL INFORMATION

Skidmore College is an independent, coeducational liberal arts college located in Saratoga Springs, New York. With a student body of 2,200 and a faculty of 200 dedicated teacher-scholars, the college offers a wide array of academic majors in the liberal arts as well as in career-specific fields such as business, social work, education, and the fine and performing arts. Skidmore's history underscores a nimble spirit and adaptability to changing student needs that is still apparent. Founded in 1903 as a school for women, it was chartered as a four-year degree-granting college in 1922. As it grew and evolved, the college made the bold decision in the 1960s to build an entirely new campus. In the 1970s, Skidmore began admitting men, was chartered by Phi Beta Kappa, and launched its highly regarded University Without Walls, a nonresidential program for adult students. A program for the master of arts degree in liberal studies was added in 1993.

Skidmore's academic program is designed to promote creative thinking across the disciplines. The curriculum emphasizes strong foundations in the liberal arts and interdisciplinary study, and builds upon the college's founding principle of linking theoretical and applied learning. It is not unusual for students to design cross-disciplinary double majors such as art history and business, or education and Spanish, and the curriculum's flexibility allows for self-determined majors as well.

The beautiful 650-acre campus has been upgraded and enhanced in the past decade with key renovations to the library, science center, athletic facilities, student center, and technology infrastructure. The spectacular Tang Teaching Museum and Art Gallery, opened in 2000, enriches the campus scene with experimental programming closely allied with the college's interdisciplinary focus. Co-curricular life on campus offers many options. The college's 89 student clubs and organizations run the gamut and include student government, a cappella singing groups, *The Skidmore News* (student newspaper), WSPN Radio, comedy and cabaret troupes, and a number of cultural awareness groups. Skidmore athletes compete at the NCAA Division III level, and the college fields 19 intercollegiate teams. The riding and women's tennis teams have won national championships in recent years. Students are very active in the intramural sports program and enjoy abundant opportunities for personal fitness and recreation, both on campus and in the nearby Adirondack Mountains.

STUDENT BODY

Skidmore students participate in all aspects of academic and social life on campus. They play a major role in governing the College through the Student Government Association (SGA) and numerous major College committees on which students serve as members. The SGA is authorized by the Board of Trustees; it is committed to the goals of responsible behavior and democratic self-government. The SGA concerns itself with a broad range of issues, including educational policy, freshman orientation, SGA elections, social events, student publications, and student organizations and clubs. Elected faculty members and students serve side-by-side on three panels: the Academic Integrity Board, the All-College Council, and the Social Integrity Board.

ACADEMICS

Skidmore College is renowned for its unique blending of traditional liberal arts study with opportunities to delve deeply into pre-professional disciplines. Skidmore's liberal studies core curriculum, which requires students to complete two or more interdisciplinary courses, is widely respected. Skidmore's core requirements cover a wide range of disciplines, requiring at least one course in each of the following disciplines: the arts; humanities; foreign language; nonwestern culture; science; and social science. Students must select a major by the end of their sophomore year; they may choose from 64 options, including self-designed majors, interdepartmental concentrations, and minors. The College observes a two-semester academic calendar. Internship opportunities follow directly after the second semester ends in May. Students typically take four or five courses per semester. Summer study is available through PASS, a six-week program that allows high school students to earn college credit for two courses. Skidmore offers a nonresidential, nontraditional baccalaureate degree program called University Without Walls (UWW). Students in the program confer one-on-one with a faculty advisor to specify the content of their degree programs. UWW students are also encouraged to pursue nontraditional means to obtain the information necessary to their studies, including independent study, self-directed study, and real-world experiences gained through paid and volunteer work. The College implemented a similar Master of Arts in Liberal Studies program in 1993.

Skidmore College offers a Bachelor of Arts degree in the following disciplines: American studies, anthropology, Asian studies, biology, chemistry, classical studies, computer science, economics, English, environmental studies, foreign languages and literatures (French, German, and Spanish), geology, government, history, history of art, mathematics, music, neuroscience, philosophy, physics, political economy, psychology, religion, sociology, and women's studies. The Bachelor of Science degree is granted in areas of a more professional nature, including business, dance, dance theater, education, exercise science, social work, studio art, and theater. The school offers 33 interdepartmental majors. Students may also opt to pursue double majors, self-determined majors, and minors. 3-2 programs are available in conjunction with either the Thayer School of Engineering at Dartmouth College or Clarkson University. Through its School of Management, Clarkson joins Skidmore in offering a 4-1 MBA program. Other accelerated multi-degree options include a 3-2 MBA program at Skidmore and Rensselaer Polytechnic Institute, and a 4-1 Master of Arts in Teaching program,

815 North Broadway
Saratoga Springs, NY 12866-1632
Phone: 518-580-5570
Fax: 518-580-5584
Website: www.skidmore.edu

offered through Union College. Students may receive both a bachelor's degree and a law degree in six years through a program offered by Skidmore and the Cardozo Law School, Skidmore also has certification programs in social work and teaching, as well as pre-professional programs in medicine and law.

Skidmore College employs 199 full-time instructors and 10 part-time faculty members, including some with special appointments. Over 90 percent of Skidmore's faculty members in the liberal arts have earned doctoral degrees. The students/full-time faculty ratio is about 11:1, the average class size is 16. Skidmore's faculty is actively involved in both research and publication in their areas of expertise; however, instructors here look upon teaching as their principal responsibility. Faculty advisors assist students in choosing courses and in planning their comprehensive academic programs.

ADMISSIONS

Those seeking admission to Skidmore's freshman class should complete a secondary school curriculum that includes at least 16 credits in college-preparatory courses. The Admissions Committee is also pleased to consider applications from qualified high school juniors who plan to accelerate and enter college early. Applicants typically have completed 4 years each of English, 4 years of a foreign language, 4 years of mathematics, 4 years of social studies, and 4 years of science. Applicants must provide a secondary school transcript, standardized test scores (SAT I or ACT), letters of recommendation from two teachers of academic subjects, and a report from their guidance counselor. Skidmore recommends that applicants submit scores for three SAT II: Subject Tests, the Writing Test among them. The school also strongly recommends a campus visit and interview. Through its participation in the Higher Education Opportunity Program (HEOP), Skidmore enrolls capable, energetic, and ambitious New Yorkers who, because of their academic and financial situations, would not otherwise gain admission to the College under traditional requirements.

CAMPUS LIFE

Set on 650 acres in Saratoga Springs, New York, Skidmore College offers undergraduates the beauty and serenity of a rural setting as well as convenient access to a historic town of 30,000. New Yorkers have long flocked to Saratoga Springs to take advantage of its resorts; horse-racing and culture of many varieties have well-established homes in this cosmopolitan town. Each summer, performing arts ensembles such as the Philadelphia Orchestra, New York City Ballet, and Harlem Boys Choir take up residence at the Saratoga Performing Arts Center.

Lovers of the outdoors find Skidmore an ideal location; it is within an hour's drive of state parks, lakes, and major ski areas throughout eastern New York, western Massachusetts, and Vermont. Saratoga Springs is a mere 30 miles north of New York's state capital of Albany. Buses link Saratoga Springs to New York City, Boston, Montreal, and other regional major cities. Train service to New York City and Montreal is also available seven days a week. Albany International Airport is served by major airlines; rental cars are also available at the airport. The College is located near Exit 15 of I-87 (the Northway).

Skidmore belongs to the Hudson-Mohawk Association of Colleges and Universities, a consortium that allows undergraduates to cross register at any of fourteen area colleges and universities. Skidmore students may take advantage of the Washington Semester to spend a term in our nation's capital at American University; the program consists of course work, research projects, government internships, and seminars that cumulatively create a rigorous workshop experience. Skidmore undergraduates pursue their studies in China, England, France, India, and Spain through Skidmore's Study Abroad program. Affiliations with other study abroad programs allow students to spend a semester or a full year in locations in Asia, Australia, Europe, Latin America, and Africa. Skidmore's Office of Career Planning and Field Experience Programs arranges for student internships in such varied fields as the arts (dance, museum, and theater work), business, government, medicine, scientific research, and social work.

COST AND AID

Financial assistance at Skidmore is awarded on the basis of demonstrated need. Aid applicants must file the Free Application for Federal Student Aid (FAFSA), a copy of the federal income tax form, and the CSS/Financial Aid PROFILE each year. Entering freshmen must submit applications by January 15. Skidmore awards a number of merit-based scholarships as well. The annual Filene Music Scholarship Competition awards four $36,000 ($9,000 per year) scholarships to students with exceptional musical ability; financial need is not considered in the awarding of these scholarships. Likewise, Skidmore awards five $10,000 merit scholarships in math and science each year. Students seeking more information about grants, loans, and/or work awards should contact the Office of Student Aid and Family Finance. For the 2002–2003 academic year, tuition and fees for all students were an estimated $27,980. Room and board for students living in Skidmore residence halls was an estimated $7,835.

SOUTHERN NEW HAMPSHIRE UNIVERSITY

GENERAL INFORMATION

Formerly New Hampshire College (the name was changed in 2001) Southern New Hampshire University is a private, coeducational, nonprofit, accredited university specializing in professional training combined with a liberal arts education. The school's small size, coupled with its newly acquired University status, allows the institution to offer the community feel of a small college with the status and power of a university. Approximately 1,700 students attend the University full-time during the day; with a total enrollment in all divisions (undergraduate, graduate, continuing education, and distance education) that stands at 6,000 students. The University offers over 30 undergraduate programs covering business, education, hospitality management, and the liberal arts. The campus truly facilitates learning on all fronts, offering small classes (20 students on average), an idyllic setting, and university resources. Because of its small-school feel, the University allows undergraduates ample opportunities to participate in classroom discussion and to undertake leadership roles within the campus community. Southern New Hampshire University boasts a magnificent 275-acre wooded campus. The University's hometown, Manchester, is among the most pleasant small cities in the United States. Twenty-six buildings house campus facilities, which include state-of-the-art classrooms, a student center with a dining hall, an athletic complex with a 5,000-square-foot fitness center, a library, and computer labs. The University recently completed a $13 million construction project that added Newcastle Hall, a 200-bed residence hall; the Robert Frost Academic Center (60,000 square feet); and the new fitness center. Southern New Hampshire University is ideally located, with easy access to urban amenities and all the recreational options that the ocean, rural New England, and the mountains have to offer.

STUDENT BODY

Students have a wide assortment of clubs and organizations available to them. Social clubs (including fraternities and sororities), professional associations, service- and special-interest related clubs, and athletics all thrive on the Southern New Hampshire University campus. The Student Government Association is a 26-student body led by 5 officers; it represents students in administrative decisions (one member sits on the Board of Trustees, which governs the University) and manages the student activity fund. Intercollegiate teams compete in Division II of the NCAA, the Eastern College Athletic Conference, and the Northwest-10 Athletic Conference; the school fields teams in baseball, basketball, cross-country, golf, ice hockey, lacrosse, soccer, softball, tennis, and volleyball. Intramural sports are also extremely popular among undergraduates.

ACADEMICS

All undergraduates at Southern New Hampshire University receive a solid grounding in the liberal arts with a special curricular focus on developing written and oral communication skills. Core courses in public speaking, writing, computing, arts and humanities, mathematics, science, and social science are required of all students. Additional, more specialized requirements are imposed by each of our three schools (business, hospitality, and liberal arts) to ensure that all graduates leave with a broad understanding of their major areas. Students also receive ample opportunities to take elective courses in whatever areas capture their curiosity. Students may, if they so choose, concentrate their electives in one area to earn a minor in any of 30 subjects. The University curriculum offers both structure and flexibility; the school feels this is the best approach to preparing its graduates for their real-world adventures. Southern New Hampshire University also offers study abroad at the University of North London; the Sepang Institute of Technology in Malaysia; and the Christelijke Hogeschool in Leeuwarden, the Netherlands.

2500 North River Road
Manchester, NH 03108
Phone: 603-645-9611
Fax: 603-645-9693
Website: www.snhu.edu

Southern New Hampshire University houses three schools—business; liberal arts; and hospitality, tourism, and culinary management—all of which afford students a strong liberal arts foundation and thorough professional training, and the University Center for Teacher Education, which offers education degrees at the undergraduate and graduate levels. The School of Business offers degrees in: accounting, accounting/finance, advertising, business administration, business administration three-year degree, business studies, economics/finance, fashion merchandising, information technology, international business, management advisory services, marketing, retailing, sport management, and technical management. The School of Liberal Arts offers degrees in: advertising, communication, digital media, English language and literature, humanities, political science, psychology, public relations, social science, and. The School of Hospitality, Tourism, and Culinary Management offers degrees in club management, convention and event management, culinary arts, destination management, food and beverage management, hospitality administration, hotel and resort management, and travel management. Undergraduate education programs include: early childhood education, elementary/general special education; and secondary education programs in business, marketing, English and social studies.

The faculty of Southern New Hampshire University includes 99 full-time and 153 part-time instructors. Nearly three-quarters of the faculty hold a PhD or the equivalent terminal degree in their area of expertise. Many instructors have valuable work experience in the industries they teach; some continue to serve as business consultants. Many of those who teach accounting are registered CPAs. All classes are taught by professors, not by graduate students. The student/faculty ratio is 18:1.

ADMISSIONS

Southern New Hampshire University strives to select incoming students who will best utilize the school's many academic and co-curricular resources. Applicants must successfully complete high school or earn a GED certificate prior to entering the University. Those seeking entry to the two-year and four-year programs must submit the following: a completed application form, an official high school transcript, a letter of recommendation, and a personal essay. Freshman applicants must also provide official standardized test results (SAT1 or ACT). Those wishing to pursue the three-year honors program in business administration must submit all of the above and have an interview with the program director, or an admission representative. Students whose first tongue is other than English must submit TOEFL scores to demonstrate English proficiency. Those seeking to transfer must provide official transcripts from all schools attended to date. The school strongly recommends a campus visit and an interview. The University admits students on a rolling basis; candidates are generally informed of admissions decisions within one month of completing their applications. Early action applications must arrive before November 15. Applicants can have their $25 application fee waived by applying through the school's website.

CAMPUS LIFE

The University is located in Manchester, which sits at northern New England's crossroads. One hour's drive takes students to the finest ski areas on the East Coast, the ocean beaches of Maine and New Hampshire, or the numerous cultural and entertainment options that Boston offers. More than 115,000 people make Manchester their home; the city has a very active social and cultural life. *Money* magazine recently named Manchester the "most livable city," in the East. Students at the University are active within the Manchester community.

Nearly one-half of Southern New Hampshire University undergraduates participate in cooperative education (also known as internships), work experiences that tie into a student's academic program. Co-op jobs are typically undertaken during junior or senior year. Students work with faculty members and career counselors to find appropriate co-op assignments, which can earn participants between 3 and 12 academic credits.

COST AND AID

Undergraduate tuition for the 2002–2003 academic year is $17,376. Room and board totals an additional $7,340. Students must pay $280 in fees each year, and must budget funds for books, supplies, and personal expenses. Culinary Arts students are also required to purchase uniforms and a knife set.

SOUTHERN VERMONT COLLEGE

GENERAL INFORMATION

Southern Vermont College's philosophy begins with a deep belief in the potential of every individual. The College is committed to offering a student-centered, career-oriented liberal arts education to a student body from diverse backgrounds. Just over 500 students from 26 states and 6 countries call Southern Vermont College home. The small size of our College, intimate setting and the personalized nature of our learning environment allow students to develop critical thinking, excellent communication skills and a sense of community and responsibility. The College fosters a dynamic learning environment by encouraging class participation and through hands-on experiential learning. Graduates of Southern Vermont College are prepared to be lifelong learners and citizen leaders able to face the challenges presented by a complex, global society.

Located on 371 spectacular Vermont acres, our campus is situated at the base of Mount Anthony in Bennington, Vermont. Southern Vermont College offers motivated students an opportunity to be part of an exciting learning experience and receive the personalized attention every student deserves. In addition to gaining a solid liberal arts foundation, our students take advantage of the great outdoors of Vermont by going skiing and snowboarding at some of the best ski mountains in the northeast, biking, kayaking, swimming and hiking on the Appalachian trail. The College is situated in the southwest corner of Vermont, located within driving distance from Boston, New York City and Montreal.

STUDENT BODY

Student involvement is apparent in all facets of campus life at Southern Vermont. The College offers a wide array of athletics, student-run activities, and organizations. NCAA Division III athletic teams compete during both fall and spring semesters. NCAA teams include men's and women's basketball, cross-country, soccer, track, baseball, and softball, and women's volleyball. Organizations and activities include a very active Student Government Association (SGA), Everyone's Earth Nature Club, *Mountain Press* student newspaper, Music/Alchemy Club, Madhatter's Drama Group, Community Service, Ski/Snowboard Club, Wit's End Journal Writing Club, Student Nurse's Association, Men's Rugby, Alpha Chi Honors Society, Multi-Cultural Club, SVC Cheerleading Squad, and *Summit* yearbook. Students also compete intramurally in sports like flag football, volleyball, ice hockey, and billiards. The SGA sponsors weekend activities and trips to museums and nearby cities and hosts on-campus events like lecture series, dances and musical groups.

ACADEMICS

Southern Vermont College offers a total of 20 bachelor's and associate degree programs. The College's academic programs are divided into five divisions of study: The McCormick Division of Business, the Division of Humanities, Division of Nursing, Science and Technology, and Social Sciences. The majors offered are business administration, child development, creative writing & literature, criminal justice, English, communications, environmental studies, human services, liberal arts, liberal arts/management, nursing, pre-law, and psychology. An extensive list of minors and concentrations are also offered to complement the student's major, and students can elect to pursue a double major. Students also have the option of developing an Individualized Degree Program with help from their faculty advisor. Southern Vermont College is accredited by the New England Association of Schools and Colleges.

Southern Vermont College has approximately 43 faculty, of whom 15 are full time, and an 11:1 student/faculty ratio. Fifty percent of the full-time faculty hold terminal degrees. Freshmen, including those who have not declared a major, are assigned a faculty advisor who will assist them throughout their time at Southern Vermont College.

ADMISSIONS

Southern Vermont College uses a portfolio approach in assessing an applicant's file. A student's personal character and motivation are important to the Admissions Committee and are considered in conjunction with the academic background of the student. To complete the Admissions Requirements, a student must submit the following: an application for admission, the $30 application fee, official high school transcripts, SAT or ACT test scores, two letters of recommendation, and a personal essay. While Southern Vermont College operates on a rolling admissions policy (students may apply up to two weeks before the start of a semester), applications received by March 1 are automatically reviewed for merit scholarships.

A personal interview with an admissions counselor is recommended. Interested students are asked to tour the campus with a current Southern Vermont College student and meet with an admissions representative. For more information please contact the Admissions Office at admis@svc.edu or 800-378-2782, ext. 6304.

982 Mansion Drive
Bennington, VT 05201
Phone: 802-447-6304
Fax: 802-447-4695
Website: www.svc.edu

CAMPUS LIFE

Southern Vermont College is located in Bennington, Vermont, a historic New England town in the heart of the Green Mountains with a population of about 30,000 people. Our 371-acre campus is about one mile from downtown Bennington, which is full of shops, restaurants and coffee shops, allowing our students accessibility while maintaining a secure sense of privacy. Overlooking the Appalachian Trail, the main college building is the converted 27 room historic Everett Mansion with spectacular views in all directions. The Mansion is now the heart of the Southern Vermont College learning environment and houses our classrooms and administrative and faculty offices. Students seeking a nurturing and comfortable environment and intimate community, find that this unique setting is an ideal place to pursue their college career. The five on-campus residence halls offer suite-style housing for all freshmen and transfer students and other students who wish to live on campus. Besides the plethora of activities in the immediate area, students can take advantage of exploring one of the numerous cities within close proximity for a little taste of urban life.

Students participate in a wide variety of internships throughout the state of Vermont as well as in other Northeast cities. Recent internships include the Vermont Department of Corrections, the Bennington County Family Court, St. Peter's Alcohol Recovery Center, Merrill Lynch, Mount Snow Ski Resort, and the Vermont Department of Fish and Wildlife, to name a few. Faculty-sponsored study abroad courses are occasionally sponsored as well.

COST AND AID

The College has the lowest comprehensive fees of any private residential college in the state of Vermont, equaling $17,685 per year. Tuition for the 2002–2003 academic year is $11,695. Room and board is an additional $5,990 per year, which includes a 19-meal/week meal plan. Health insurance is required for students who are not covered under any other plan.

SPELMAN COLLEGE

GENERAL INFORMATION

Founded in 1881, Spelman College is an historically black, private, independent, four-year liberal arts school for women. From its austere origins of five frame barracks on 9 acres of drill ground previously utilized by post-bellum federal troops, the school has grown to occupy its current 32-acre, 24-building campus. Spelman maintains a distinct identity, providing exceptional opportunities for students aspiring to leadership positions, while benefiting from its participation in the Atlanta University Center, a consortium of area schools.

CAMPUS LIFE

Manley College Center, home to Spelman's faculty and student lounges, dining hall, food court, student government offices, and some administrative offices, serves as a nexus of activity for the campus' 2,070 women. A wide variety of professional, cultural, and student events take place regularly on campus. Many such activities are sponsored and organized by the Student Government Association. Others are offered by the school's jazz and classical music ensembles, exceptional dance groups, and various departmental clubs and honor societies. Spelman has a long history of nurturing the fine arts; the fruits of its efforts can be seen in the work of the renowned Spelman Glee Club, the Spelman-Morehouse Chorus, and the Spelman-Morehouse Players. The College's physical education and health facilities include a gymnasium, a swimming pool, a weight room, tennis courts, dance studios, and bowling lanes.

Several notable publications are produced by the student body, including the yearbook (*Reflections*), a newspaper (*Spotlight*), and a literary magazine (*Focus*). Religious services and devotion are central to the lives of many Spelman students. The College provides opportunities for meaningful fellowship experiences, such as special convocations and counseling.

Spelman's hometown of Atlanta is often referred to as "The Gateway to the South." Atlanta is quickly becoming one of the nation's premier urban centers. Spelman's proximity to Atlanta's other institutions of higher learning augment the College's ample academic, cultural, and social offerings. Spelman belongs to the six-member Atlanta University Center (AUC) consortium.

Atlanta offers unique and exciting learning prospects to Spelman's undergraduate population. Opportunities to meet and work with local, national, and world political leaders abound. Community programs involve students in the efforts to solve the crucial social challenges present in so many urban centers around the world. Spelman coordinates with local community agencies to find placement for Spelman students interested in community service.

ACADEMICS

Spelman confers the Bachelor of Arts and the Bachelor of Science degrees. Majors are offered in art, biochemistry, biology, chemistry, child development, comparative women's studies, computer science, drama and dance, economics, engineering (through participating schools), English, environmental science, French, history, mathematics, music, philosophy, physics, political science, psychology, sociology/anthropology, and Spanish. Students may also pursue an independent major. Special minors are offered in dance, international studies, management and organization, teacher certification, women's studies, and writing. Pre-professional tracks in pre-medical, pre-dentistry, and pre-law are offered.

Spelman offers a dual-degree engineering program in cooperation with the following institutions: Auburn University, Boston University, California Institute of Technology, Columbia University, Dartmouth College, University of Florida, Georgia Institute of Technology, Rochester Institute of Technology, Rensselaer Polytechnic Institute, North Carolina A&T, and the University of Alabama in Huntsville. Students in the program undertake liberal arts course work at Spelman for three years, then spend two years studying engineering at the partner school. The program confers a pair of bachelor's degrees, one from each institution.

The Spelman academic year is divided into two semesters. The College requires a core curriculum in order to introduce undergraduates to the primary branches of academia: natural sciences, social sciences, mathematics, fine arts, language and literature, and the humanities. Courses designed to foster reading skills, writing skills, logical thinking, and imaginative thinking are also required. Exceptional students are eligible for enrollment in the honors program.

Different majors carry different credit-hour requirements. Core curriculum courses include a sequenced, two-semester interdisciplinary survey, foreign language, English composition, the African Diaspora in the World, history, mathematics, literature, health education, and physical education. All students must also complete at least 4 credits in each of the following disciplines: fine arts, humanities, natural sciences, and social sciences.

The most recent addition to the Spelman campus, the Albro Falconer Manley Science Center, opened in 2000. This state of-the-art facility is a nexus of scientific creativity and intellectual discourse; it accommodates ongoing research and classroom instruction, and provides the technological tools necessary for modern science teaching. The Camille O. Hanks Cosby Academic Center houses laboratories and classrooms for humanities students. It is home to a number of interdisciplinary programs and departments, as well as offices for faculty in English, history, modern foreign languages, philosophy, and religion. The Cosby Center also houses an art museum, an auditorium, the Spelman College archives, educational media, the Ennis Cosby Reading Room, and the Women's Research and Resource Center. The Fine Arts Building includes a small, state-of-the-art proscenium theater, practice rooms, and art and music studios. Two living-learning centers accommodate residence hall facilities and conference rooms that provide workspace outside the classroom. Spelman students also have access to the Robert Woodruff Library of the Atlanta University Center, home to more than 500,000 volumes and a microfilm depository.

350 Spelman Lane, South West
Atlanta, GA 30314
Phone: 800-982-2411
Fax: 404-215-7788
Website: www.spelman.edu

COSTS AND AID

In 2002–2003, tuition equaled $10,660 per year; room and board equaled $7300 per year; fees amounted to an additional $2015. The total cost to on-campus residents was $19,975; the cost to those living off campus was $12,675. Students must also anticipate transportation costs, plus approximately $750 per year for books and $1,550 for personal expenses. All costs are subject to change.

The College pursues all avenues in its efforts to aid students who demonstrate financial need. Scholarships, grants, loans, and work-study programs all contribute to the College's financial assistance strategies. All aid applicants must submit the Free Application for Federal Student Aid (FAFSA), which is used to determine need. The College suggests that applicants begin the financial aid process much earlier than the April 1 deadline; funding is limited and awards are granted on a first-come, first-served basis. Those who file all necessary information by March 1 receive priority processing and consideration. Unfortunately, Spelman does not have adequate funding to meet the full documented need of every aid applicant.

Scholarships are available to applicants who demonstrate academic excellence and outstanding achievement. Such scholarships are competitive and are awarded both to entering first-year and continuing students. The Scholarship Committee considers academic and personal accomplishments as demonstrated by academic records, standardized test scores, special talent, leadership, community service, character, and in certain cases, financial need. All students who complete the Spelman College Application for Admission are considered for Spelman scholarships. Certain scholarships—the Women in Science and Engineering (WISE) Program Scholarship and the Bonner Scholar Program—require the submission of additional materials.

ADMISSIONS

The Admissions Committee considers applicants on the basis of their academic records, SAT I or ACT scores, recommendations, and personal information submitted with the application. First-year students may enter only in the fall term.

Spelman can accommodate a limited number of transfer students each year. The Admissions Committee considers each transfer applicant's complete academic records, recommendations, and personal information submitted with the application for admission. The Committee also considers the amount of available space in the transfer's intended academic majors. In some cases, applicants who have reached the equivalent of senior status are not considered.

Spelman selects qualified female candidates without regard to race, color, physical challenge, religious preference, or national, ethnic, or regional origin. The ideal candidate presents credentials that show potential for academic success at Spelman as well as personal traits of integrity, purpose, and high motivation. The College does not require an interview. Tours and individual information sessions are available to those considering application to Spelman. Contact the Office of Admissions and Orientation Services for more information.

Applications for Spelman's Early Action Plan must be postmarked and mailed by November 15 of the applicant's senior year; applicants are notified of Early Action decisions by December 31. The deadline for standard admission to Spelman is February 1 of the applicant's senior year; notification is made by April 1. Transfer applications for fall admission must be postmarked and mailed by February 1; applicants are notified of the school's decision by April 1. Transfer applications for spring admission must be postmarked and mailed by November 1; applicants are notified of the school's decision by December 1. Those seeking application forms and additional information should contact:

Office of Admissions and Orientation Services
Box 277
Spelman College
Atlanta, GA 30314
Telephone: 404-681-3643, ext. 2188 or 800-982-2411 (toll free)
E-mail: admiss@spelman.edu
World Wide Web: www.spelman.edu

STEVENS INSTITUTE OF TECHNOLOGY

GENERAL INFORMATION

Founded in 1870 as the first American college to devote itself exclusively to engineering education based on scientific principles, Stevens Institute of Technology is a prestigious independent university for study and research. Standard and Poor's has ranked Stevens 11th among the top 550 college and universities that have produced presidents, vice presidents, and directors of U.S. companies. It is a leading national university according to *U.S. News & World Report*.

At the undergraduate level, Stevens' broad-based education leads to prestigious degrees in business, the sciences, computer science, engineering, or the humanities. Master's and doctoral degrees are awarded in a variety of areas within the sciences, computer and information sciences/systems, engineering, management, and technology management. Research activities are vital to the university's educational mission; thus Stevens attracts world-renowned faculty to complement its exceptional on-campus facilities. In addition, Stevens maintains an Honor System that has been in existence since 1908. Stevens' 1,700 undergraduates come from more than 30 states and 68 countries, creating a diverse, dynamic environment.

STUDENT BODY

There are more than 70 student organizations on campus, including Student Government; *Stute*, the weekly campus newspaper; *Link*, the yearbook; WCPR radio; Glee Club; Drama Society; brass and jazz ensembles; ethnic and religious groups; and national, honor, and professional societies. Offices are located in Jacobus Hall, the Stevens student center, and all organizations utilize areas on campus to host events, sponsor guest speakers, and organize social activities or volunteer work.

To encourage competitive and recreational activities students have use of a number of facilities. The $13.2 million Schaefer Athletic and Recreation Center features a NCAA competition-size pool with Jacuzzi, four-court basketball gymnasium, racquetball courts, and a fitness center. Newly renovated DeBaun Field has been surfaced in NexTurf, a state-of-the-art, durable, year-round playing surface for varsity and intramural competition. Walker Gym has an elevated indoor track plus a new weightlifting facility and dance studios. There are also six outdoor tennis courts and a sand volleyball court.

Stevens competes in NCAA Division III. There are 11 sports for men, comprising baseball, basketball, cross-country, fencing, indoor/outdoor track and field, lacrosse, soccer, swimming, tennis, and volleyball; and 10 for women, comprising basketball, cross-country, fencing, indoor/outdoor track and field, lacrosse, soccer, swimming, tennis, and volleyball. Students may also join a club team or play an intramural sport.

ACADEMICS

The Stevens mission is to educate students as leaders and innovators and to expand the frontiers and applications of technology. The entire community helps stimulate the intellectual enrichment and educate each student as a whole person. Computer fluency and usage is also essential; in 1982 Stevens became the first institution to require undergraduates to own and use a personal computer. As technology changed, all entering freshmen began using a notebook computer.

The learning process at Stevens is fulfilled by having students learn theory in the classroom, solve problems in the laboratories, and undertake internships and participate in research projects in conjunction with faculty. Stevens also offers a number of unique educational programs.

Research opportunities and summer internships are available for all major fields of study. The Cooperative Education program alternates semesters of on-campus study with semesters of paid, professional work experience. Currently, 40 percent of the undergraduate body elects to co-op and many earn more than $50,000 by the end of the five-year period.

The Stevens Scholars Program allows truly talented students to accelerate their course work and graduate with a bachelor's and master's degree in four years at no additional cost. The Undergraduate Projects in Technology and Medicine (UPTAM) is a summer program for selected students interested in medical engineering or biomedical sciences. Stevens Technical Enrichment Program (STEP) helps broaden the access of minority and economically disadvantaged students to careers in engineering, science, and technology through pre-college and in-college programs and support services. The Personalized Self-Paced Instruction (PSI) program provides an alternative to the conventional lecture-recitation method of instruction, enabling students to work at their own pace. Stevens Reduced Course Load allows undergraduates to spread four years of course work over a five-year period at no additional tuition cost.

No matter which path a student chooses, eight humanities subjects and six physical education courses carefully balance the rigorous education in technical, scientific, and management subjects at Stevens. Stevens also provides a wide range of academic support services to all students outside of the classroom. This includes faculty advising, private tutoring, personal counseling, and mentoring and career development services.

Stevens' undergraduate academic calendar consists of two semesters, fall and spring, and two optional summer sessions.

Stevens Institute of Technology consists of three schools that award the Bachelor of Engineering (BE), Bachelor of Science (BS), and Bachelor of Art (BA) degrees.

1 Castle Point on Hudson
Hoboken, NJ 07030
Phone: 201-216-5194
Fax: 201-216-8348
Website: www.stevens.edu

STEVENS
Institute of Technology

Areas of study for a BE degree include chemical engineering, biomedical engineering, civil engineering, computer engineering, electrical engineering, engineering management, environmental engineering, and mechanical engineering.

Stevens awards BS degrees in applied physics, chemical biology, chemistry, computer science, and mathematics. Students can also earn a BS in business, which provides a comprehensive background in principles of management and entrepreneurship, from finance and marketing to product development.

To earn the BA students may pursue English and American literature, history, philosophy, or science and technology studies. Stevens students may pursue a dual degree or a pre-professional program in dentistry or medicine (seven years) or law (six years). Students may also choose to minor in one of a variety of subjects.

Stevens has 171 full-time faculty members and 129 special faculty and research staff. Approximately 100 percent of full-time academic faculty hold doctoral degrees. The student/faculty ratio is 9:1.

ADMISSIONS

Stevens is highly competitive. Undergraduate applicants must submit an Application for Admission; an official high school transcript including 4 years of English, 4 years of mathematics, and a minimum of 3 years of science; and official SAT I or ACT scores and meet with an admissions representative for a personal interview. SAT II scores are required for those applying to an accelerated program and are encouraged for all other applicants. Two recommendations (one by a guidance counselor and one by a faculty member) are required and a personal statement is encouraged. Stevens typically accepts less than 50 percent of its applicants and enrolls 440 to 450 students each fall; SAT scores (from the 25th–75th percentile) range from 1200–1370; average high school GPA is 3.8. The application deadline for the fall semester is February 15 (early decision November 1).

Transfer applicants must submit an Application for Admission, an official college transcript (and a high school transcript noting SAT I or ACT scores if less than 30 post-secondary credits have been earned), and meet with an admissions representative for a personal interview. The deadline for the fall semester is July 1; spring semester is November 1.

Prospective students are encouraged to visit Stevens to meet with an admissions counselor and to take a student-guided campus tour. Organized visit days and open houses are also held throughout the year and posted on the website.

For more information about Stevens and to receive a viewbook and application and/or schedule an appointment to visit campus, contact Stevens at:

Stevens Institute of Technology
Office of Undergraduate Admissions
Castle Point on Hudson
Hoboken, NJ 07030
Telephone: 800-458-5323
201-216-5194
Fax: 201-216-8348
E-mail: admissions@stevens-tech.edu
World Wide Web: www.stevens-tech.edu

CAMPUS LIFE

Stevens is in one of the most exciting small towns in America, known for, among its other distinctions, as the home of the first baseball game. Hoboken, New Jersey, is a quaint one-mile-square town with old Victorian brownstones and tree-lined streets dotted with great restaurants and trendy shops. Located on a high bank of the majestic Hudson River, the 55-acre campus, with stretches of deep green lawns, old-growth elms and maples, and historic classroom buildings, offers the best view of the New York City skyline. Stevens students take advantage of being just minutes away from the Big Apple by car, bus, train, and cab, and the Office of Student Life also plans various trips to Broadway plays, museums, and cultural and sporting events throughout the year.

Residential, athletic, and library and computing facilities are sprinkled throughout the academic buildings, laboratories, and research facilities. Approximately 80 percent of Stevens students live on campus; housing is guaranteed for undergraduates for all four years. Eight national fraternities and three sororities have chapters on campus and most maintain houses where members may live. Approximately 30 percent of undergraduates join a Greek organization.

In addition to the popular internship, research, and co-op opportunities, Stevens offers other off-campus programs. Juniors may spend the year abroad at the University of Dundee in Scotland or choose from a variety of institutions through the International Exchange Program.

COST AND AID

Stevens tuition for 2002–2003 is $24,500. Room and board total $8,100. First-year fees amount to $750.

STOCKTON COLLEGE OF NEW JERSEY

THE COLLEGE AT A GLANCE

Location: Pomona, New Jersey
Enrollment: 6,298
Tuition & Fees (NJ Res): $4,400
Room & Board: $5,368
Admission: rolling and selective
Application Deadline: generally May 1 for freshmen, June 1 for transfers. Call Admissions for specialty program deadlines.

State-supported, four-year coed college founded in 1969. Located 12 miles from Atlantic City, Stockton is a public liberal arts college within the New Jersey State system offering both undergraduate and graduate programs. Special educational experiences are encouraged, including study abroad, internships, field studies, and independent study. Admission is selective.

Undergraduates: Full-time: 4,833 students, 56 percent women, 44 percent men. Part-time: 1,142 students, 61 percent women, 39 percent men. Diversity: students come from 22 states and territories, 23 other countries, 2 percent from out-of-state, 0.2 percent Native American, 5 percent Hispanic, 8 percent black, 5 percent Asian American or Pacific Islander, 1 percent international, 24 percent 25 or older, 39 percent live on campus, 13 percent transferred in. Retention: 83 percent of 2000 full-time freshmen returned. Areas of study chosen: 14 percent business, 15 percent social sciences, 8 percent health professions 8 percent natural sciences, 9 percent biological sciences/life sciences, 7 percent psychology, 5 percent computer and information sciences, 4 percent English language/literature, 4 percent physical sciences, 2 percent communications and journalism, 2 percent education, 2 percent fine arts, 2 percent foreign language and literature, 2 percent liberal arts/general studies, 2 percent mathematics, 1 percent interdisciplinary studies, 1 percent pre-law, 1 percent pre-medicine, 1 percent performing arts, 1 percent philosophy.

Freshmen: 755 total; 3,255 applied, 50 percent were admitted, 48 percent of whom enrolled. 26 percent from top 10 percent of their high school class, 63 percent from top quarter, 96 percent from top half. Thirty-six class presidents, three valedictorians, 205 student government officers. Student/undergrad faculty ratio is 18:1; average class size is 23 in required courses; tutorials available.

Special Academic Options: College credit for advanced placement, accelerated degree program, distance learning, self-designed majors, summer session for credit, part-time degree program (daytime), adult/continuing education programs, internships, a few graduate courses open to undergrads.

Career Planning and Placement Office: Three full-time professional staff, 2 full-time clerical support staff. Services include career counseling and assessment, automated career library, resume preparation, employability skills and graduate/professional school workshops, online job bank and resume referrals, on-campus interviews, career and internships fairs. 270 organizations recruited on-campus in 1999–2000. After graduation: 83 percent of class of 1997 had job offers within 6 months. 39 percent of class of 1997 went directly to graduate and professional school: 15 percent graduate arts and sciences, 3 percent medicine, 6 percent business, 9 percent education, 3 percent law, 1 percent dentistry, 1 percent engineering, 1 percent veterinary medicine.

Campus Culture: drama-theater group, choral group, student-run newspaper, radio station, TV station. Social organizations: 81 open to all; nine national fraternities, eight national sororities; 3 percent of eligible men and 3 percent of eligible women are members. Campus security: 24-hour emergency response devices and patrols, late-night transport-escort service, on-campus police force. Student Focus: health center, personal-psychological counseling. Most popular recent majors: business administration; environmental science; criminal justice/law enforcement administration, biology, and psychology.

LOCATION AND ENVIRONMENT

State-supported, comprehensive, coed. Part of New Jersey State College System. Awards bachelor's and master's degrees. Founded 1969. Setting: 1,600-acre suburban campus very close to the Jersey shore with easy access to Philadelphia and New York City. Total enrollment: 6,298.

ACADEMIC PROGRAMS

Core, interdisciplinary curriculum. Graduation requirements: 128 credit hours; internship (some majors); senior project for honors program students and some majors. Calendar: traditional semesters. 1,325 courses offered in 1998–1999.

Jimmie Leeds Road, PO Box 195
Pomona, NJ, 08240
Phone: 609-652-4261
Fax: 609-748-5541
Website: www.stockton.edu

OFF-CAMPUS OPPORTUNITIES

Study Abroad: Australia, China, England, Germany, Israel, Japan, Mexico, Spain. Independent study. Unusual degree programs: 3-2 engineering with New Jersey Institute of Technology, Rutgers, The State University of New Jersey, public administration with Rutgers, The State University of New Jersey, seven-year BS/MD with University of Medicine and Dentistry of New Jersey, New York College of Podiatric Medicine, Pennsylvania College of Podiatric Medicine, Robert Wood Johnson Medical School.

MAJORS AND DEGREES OFFERED

Undergraduate (BA, BS, BSN): accounting, anthropology, applied art, applied mathematics, art, biology, biochemistry, molecular biology, business administration, business marketing and marketing management, chemistry, communications, computer/information sciences, computer programming, computer science, criminal justice/law enforcement administration, dance, pre-dentistry, ecology, economics, education certification programs, English, environmental science, finance, fine/studio arts, geology, health education, history, information sciences/systems, interdisciplinary studies, pre-law, liberal arts and studies, literature, marine biology, communications, mathematics (including actuarial science track), pre-medicine, nursing (BSN completion), oceanography, philosophy, photography, pre–physical therapy, physics, political science, psychology, public health, social work, sociology, Spanish, speech pathology and audiology.

Graduate (MA, MSOT, MPT, MSN): business studies, Holocaust and genocide studies, instructional technology, nursing, occupational therapy, physical therapy.

FACILITIES AND EQUIPMENT

Library: The Richard Stockton College of New Jersey Library with 287,769 books, 23,152 microform titles, 4,122 serials, 13,780 audiovisual materials.

Student Computers: 514 computers available for general student use. Computer purchase/lease plans available. A computer is recommended for some students. A campuswide network can be accessed from student residence rooms and from off campus. Students can contact faculty members and/or advisers through email. Computers for student use in computer center, computer labs, classrooms, learning resource center, library, student center, and dorms provide access to the Internet/World Wide Web, and on- and off-campus email addresses. Twenty-four-hour computer labs on campus provides training in use of computers, software, and the Internet.

Housing: 2,080 college housing spaces available; 100 percent occupancy in 2000–2001.

TUITION, ROOM AND BOARD, AND FEES

Application Fee: $35. State resident tuition and fees: $4,400 full-time (32 credit hours), $137 per credit hour part-time. Nonresident tuition and fees: $6,432 full-time (32 credit hours), $201 per credit hour part-time. College room and board: $5,368.

FINANCIAL AID

Of all full-time matriculated undergraduates who enrolled in 2000, 68 percent applied for aid, 78 percent of those were judged to have need, 70 percent of those had their need fully met. Average percent of need met: 86 percent. Average amount awarded: $8,330. 224 Federal Work-Study (averaging $1,592), 770 part-time jobs. In 2000, 273 non-need-based awards were made. Required form: FAFSA. Priority deadline: March 1.

FULL- AND PART-TIME FACULTY

Faculty: 355 (206 full-time, 97 percent with terminal degrees, 149 part-time).

STUDENT ORGANIZATIONS AND ACTIVITIES

Most popular organizations: Student Senate, Stockton Action Volunteers for the Environment, Board of Activities, Stockton Television, Unified Black Student Society, Stockton Residents Association.

Athletics: Member NCAA Division III. Intercollegiate: baseball (M), basketball (M/W), crew (W), cross-country (M/W), lacrosse (M), soccer (M/W), softball (W), synchronized swimming (W), tennis (W), track and field (M/W), volleyball (W). Intramural/Club: archery, baseball, basketball, bowling, crew, fencing, football, golf, racquetball, skiing (cross-country), skiing (downhill), swimming and diving, table tennis, tennis, volleyball, weight lifting, wrestling. Contact: Mr. Larry James, Director of Athletics and Recreation, 609-652-4217; Ms. Susan Newcomb, Assistant Director of Athletics and Recreation, 609-652-4875.

ADMISSIONS PROCESSES AND REQUIREMENTS

Freshman Applicants: Required: essay, official high school transcript, SAT I or ACT, TOEFL for international students. Recommended: "B" high school GPA, recommendations. Application deadline: May 1. Notification: rolling

Transfer Applicants: Required: essay, official college transcript(s). Recommended: recommendations, C+ college GPA. Required for some: standardized test scores, official high school transcript. Application deadline: June 1. Notification: rolling.

For more information, conyact:

Mr. Salvatore Catalfamo
Dean of Enrollment Management
The Richard Stockton College of New Jersey
PO Box 195
Pomona, NJ 08240-0195
Telephone: 609-652-4261
Fax: 609-748-5541
Email: admissions@stockton.edu
World Wide Web site: www.stockton.edu.

STONY BROOK UNIVERSITY
STATE UNIVERSITY OF NEW YORK

GENERAL INFORMATION

Founded in 1957, Stony Brook University has quickly developed into one of the premier education and research centers in the United States. A study recently published by Johns Hopkins University Press ranked Stony Brook among the nation's best research institutions, an assessment confirmed by Stony Brook's recent entry to the Association of American Universities (AAU); this major organization of research universities includes only 63 schools, among them Harvard, Princeton, Yale, Johns Hopkins, and Stanford. The Carnegie Foundation has classified Stony Brook a Research I University, a classification granted to fewer than 2 percent of the nation's undergraduate institutions. Stony Brook is among the top 25 institutions in the amount of funding received from the National Science Foundation. Stony Brook excels at incorporating research into undergraduate education. In fact, the University has recently received special recognition in this field from the National Science Foundation; only 9 other schools were so honored. Stony Brook's ever-evolving approach to undergraduate Academics means that the University is always on the cutting edge of new educational practices. Many universities around the country look to Stony Brook as a model for integrating research and undergraduate study. Stony Brook maintains strong departments in the sciences, mathematics, engineering, humanities, fine arts, social sciences, and health professions. According to the 1998 Gourman Report, both the University as a whole and a considerable number of its individual programs rank among the nation's 50 best. Stony Brook's reputation is such that students from all across the country and around the world flock to its campus in central Long Island. The Student Body consists of 14,224 undergraduates (arriving from all 50 states and 80 foreign countries) and a total of 21,989 full- and part-time students. The Stony Brook campus occupies 1,100 wooded acres on Long Island's north shore. The surrounding area is rich in natural splendor and offers a tremendous variety of co-curricular activities and off-campus diversion. University life offers much excitement of its own, including NCAA Division I athletic competition and numerous on-campus performances (nearby New York City ensures a steady stream of international performing stars). All elements of Campus Life at Stony Brook combine to create an optimal setting for intellectual and personal growth.

STUDENT BODY

Undergraduates are served by an elected student government that funds and oversees more than 100 clubs and organizations. These diverse groups include the Commuter Student Association, the Committee on Cinematic Arts (COCA), the Cycling Club, the Pre-Med Society, Stony Brook at Law, the Chess Masters, the Science Fiction Forum, and a number of cultural clubs, such as the African Student Union, the Asian Students' Alliance, the Caribbean Students Organization, Club India, and the Latin American Student Organization. The campus radio station (WUSB) and newspaper (*The Statesman*) are staffed largely by students. Stony Brook students inherit a rich tradition of co-curricular fun. Annual events, such as Midnight Madness and the Roth Quad Regatta, rally and unite the campus. Athletics loom large in the thoughts of most students, whether they are participating in one of the University's 19 varsity teams or simply cheering them on. Seawolves squads include teams in men's baseball and football, women's softball and volleyball, and men's and women's basketball, cross-country, lacrosse, soccer, swimming, tennis, and both indoor and outdoor track and field.

ACADEMICS

Stony Brook's vast resources and exceptional faculty open a universe of study options, both traditional and pioneering, to undergraduates. Within their majors, students develop a level of expertise through course work with world-renowned scholars. All study at the University commences with the Diversified Education Curriculum, a broad-ranging set of core courses designed to develop writing and quantitative skills and to hone students' ability to analyze and assess important issues. Stony Brook developed the concept of the learning community, which brings students together in groups in order to reap the benefits of a small-college experience within the university setting. Stony Brook's newest learning-communities initiative, Undergraduate Colleges, provides entering freshmen with a cohesive social and academic foundation. Academically talented freshmen may apply for admission through the Honors College or Women in Science and Engineering. Upperclassmen are invited to join one of eight living/learning centers, residential units shared by students with common interests. Research plays an integral role in the day-to-day workings of the Stony Brook academic community. Undergraduates find numerous opportunities to work with faculty researchers and to develop their own research projects. Independent study is encouraged throughout the curriculum, as is hands-on experiential learning. As a university, Stony Brook is able to offer a vast assortment of undergraduate and graduate degree programs. The school's academic units include the College of Arts and Sciences, College of Engineering and Applied Sciences, the W. Averell Harriman School for Management and Policy, the Marine Sciences Research Center, and the Health Sciences Center (which consists of the schools of medicine, health technology and management, dental medicine, nursing, and social welfare).

Stony Brook confers the BA, BS, and BE degrees in the following areas: Africana studies, American studies, applied mathematics and statistics, anthropology, art history and criticism, astronomy and planetary sciences, athletic training, atmospheric and oceanic sciences, biochemistry, bioengineering, biology, business management, chemistry, cinema and cultural studies, comparative literature, clinical laboratory sciences, computer engineering, computer science, cytotechnology, earth and space sciences, economics, electrical engineering, engineering chemistry, engineering science, English, environmental studies, French, geology, German, health science, history, humanities, information systems, Italian, linguistics, mathematics, mechanical engineering, multidisciplinary studies, music, nursing, pharmacology, philosophy, physician's assistant studies, physics, political science, psychology, religious studies, respiratory care, Russian, social sciences, social work, sociology, Spanish, studio art, theatre arts, and women's studies. More than 60 minors are also available. The University offers programs leading to New York State provisional certification for secondary school teaching in biology, chemistry, earth science, English, French, German, Italian, mathematics, physics, Russian, social studies, Spanish, and teaching English as a second language. Bachelor's/master's dual degree programs are offered in all of the engineering departments, applied mathematics and statistics, geological oceanography, health sciences/occupational therapy, mathematics secondary teacher preparation, nursing, and political science/public affairs.

The Stony Brook faculty includes a Nobel laureate, 4 MacArthur Fellows, a Pulitzer Prize winner, a Fields prize winner, National Medal of Technology and the Benjamin Franklin Medal winners, 15 members of the National Academy of Sciences, 12 members of the American Academy of Arts and Sciences, and 3 members of the National Academy of Engineering. Stony Brook professors are committed teachers who also define the cutting edge of contemporary research. Our faculty includes 73 recipients of the Chancellor's Awards for Excellence in Teaching. The student/faculty ratio is 18 to 1; Stony Brook employs a faculty of 1,902 professors. All full-time faculty (1,343 professors) hold the terminal degree in their field; more than 90 percent are currently involved in research leading to publication. The Stony Brook faculty ranks second among all U.S. institutions in the number of articles published in prestigious academic journals.

Office of Admissions
Stony Brook, NY 11794-1901
Phone: 631-632-6868
Fax: 631-632-9898
Website: www.stonybrook.edu

ADMISSIONS

Admission to Stony Brook is selective; the Office of Admissions evaluates candidates on an individual basis. The Admissions Committee aims to compile incoming classes that are academically strong and diverse in talents and backgrounds. Stony Brook strongly encourages those with special talent or exceptional ability in a particular area to apply. The Admissions Committee looks most closely at the quality of an applicant's high school curriculum, grades, and scores on standardized tests. The Committee also considers class rank, extracurricular activities, and letters of recommendation. Typically, successful applicants submit transcripts reflecting a strong high school academic program that includes 3–4 units of mathematics (4 units required for engineering), 4 units of English, 4 units of social studies, 3 units of science (4 units required for engineering), and 2–3 units of a foreign language. Standardized test scores should indicate that the candidate has a good chance of successfully pursuing a demanding undergraduate curriculum. Stony Brook also welcomes applicants with special talents or exceptional ability in a particular area; students may demonstrate these talents by submitting SAT II scores in writing, mathematics, and a third area of the student's choice.

The school encourages freshman applicants for the fall semester to apply by December 1; those seeking entry for the spring semester should apply by November 1. Applications for early action are due by November 15; candidates are notified of early action decisions by January 1. Upon receipt of the standard application, all freshmen applicants will be mailed additional required supplemental application. Interviews are recommended but not required.

Stony Brook welcomes transfer applicants. Anyone who has previously attended a college or university after graduating from high school may apply as a transfer. Stony Brook expects transfer applicants to demonstrate success at their previous institutions. Those wishing to transfer to upper-division programs in the Health Sciences Center must have previously completed at least 57 credits in liberal arts and sciences; certain specific courses are also required. Transfers who have earned fewer than 24 credits at their previous undergraduate institution must also provide an official high school transcript. Transfer applicants are encouraged to apply by March 1 for fall admission; November 1 for spring.

Applicants may make an appointment to meet with an admission counselor at any time during the year. Campus tours, led by student guides, are also offered year-round. Please call ahead to schedule a tour. To request an application form, schedule an interview, arrange a campus tour, or receive additional information, please contact:

Office of Undergraduate Admissions
State University of New York at Stony Brook
Stony Brook, NY 11794-1901
Telephone: 631-632-6868
Fax: 631-632-9898
E-mail: ugAdmissions@notes.cc.sunysb.edu
TDD: 631-632-6859
Website: www.stonybrook.edu

CAMPUS LIFE

Stony Brook University sits at Long Island's midpoint, approximately 60 miles east of New York City and 60 miles west of scenic Montauk Point. The University provides easy access to both the nation's greatest city and the quiet farmland and shorelines of eastern Long Island. The campus and its surroundings offer a nature lover's paradise of wildlife sanctuaries, nature preserves, woodlands, and foliage. Bike trails crisscross the site, which is conveniently located to the north shore beaches and, consequently, to some of the East Coast's finest windsurfing. Stony Brook Village can be reached on foot; this historic town dates back to pre-Revolutionary times and played a crucial role in the war for America's independence. The Long Island Rail Road stops on campus, providing an affordable and convenient means of reaching midtown Manhattan (the rail trip is approximately two hours long).

Study abroad opportunities are plentiful. Stony Brook sponsors study in England, France, Germany, Italy, Japan, Korea, Madagascar, Tanzania, and Spain. Furthermore, the State University system to which Stony Brook belongs sponsors separate programs in western Europe, the Middle East, the Far East, Canada, and Latin America. Students may also choose to study for up to one year at one of more than 150 state undergraduate institutions in the United States and its territories; this option is made possible through the National Student Exchange. Students can earn academic credit while earning money and gaining valuable work experience through Stony Brook's many internship and field research opportunities. Stony Brook undergraduates have been placed with research laboratories, hospitals, clinics, businesses, and government, legal, and social agencies on Long Island and in New York City, Washington, DC, and Albany.

COST AND AID

Tuition and fees for the 2002–2003 academic year are $4,310 for New York state residents. For nonresidents, tuition and fees are $9,210. On average, room and board cost $6,940. The cost of books and supplies is approximately $750 annually.

SWEET BRIAR COLLEGE

GENERAL INFORMATION

Since its founding in 1901, Sweet Briar College has been deeply committed to the education of women. It is consistently ranked as one of the top liberal arts colleges for women in the country. In 2003, Sweet Briar was selected by Project DEEP (Documenting Effective Educational Practices) as one of 20 schools who best engage students in and out of the classroom. Its excellent academic reputation, beautiful campus, and attention to the individual, attract smart, confident women who want to excel. Students can expect that their Sweet Briar experience—connecting academic work to the wider world—will allow them to fulfill their promise as scholars and leaders, while enjoying the close-knit friendships and camaraderie that come with a small, residential community. The College has a wide geographic, ethnic, and socioeconomic representation. About 600 women from more than 40 states and 18 countries are enrolled at Sweet Briar's Virginia campus; another 100 students are enrolled in Sweet Briar's coed Junior Year in France and Junior Year in Spain Programs. Additionally, Sweet Briar's Turning Point Program attracts women of nontraditional age to begin or continue their college education. A Sweet Briar education sets in motion the conviction that any goal is achievable. Classes average twelve students, and a student/faculty ratio of 8:1 ensures academic interaction and personal attention.

STUDENT BODY

Students who benefit the most from the Sweet Briar experience are those who contribute the most, striking a balance between academic work and co-curricular activities. A majority of students enter Sweet Briar having already been involved in extracurricular activities; they recognize that one of the advantages of a women's college is the opportunity for them to participate and assume leadership roles in many types of organizations and activities. More than sixty-two campus organizations are available, including honor societies, a literary journal, community service groups, a multicultural club, political groups, a student newspaper, drama and dance clubs, a radio station, and singing groups. Students plan and participate in an extensive array of concerts, films, and dance and theater productions as well as workshops and master classes by visiting scholars and performers. Recent visitors have included the National Theater of the Deaf; dancer (and alum), Sarah Skaggs; writer, Maya Angelou; violinist, Judith Ingolfsson; and performance artist Meredith Monk. Varsity athletes compete in NCAA Division III field hockey, lacrosse, soccer, swimming, tennis, and volleyball. Club sports include fencing, equestrian (riding), and softball. Sweet Briar's riding program, both competitive and instructional, has consistently garnered national recognition. Students participate in the governance of the College through offices and committee positions of the Student Government Association. The Association and its committees are largely responsible for the self-governance of the student body.

ACADEMICS

Sweet Briar College supports its mission to prepare women to be active, responsible members of a world community by integrating the liberal arts and sciences with opportunities for internships, research, campus and community leadership, and career planning. The curriculum emphasizes comprehensive understanding, analysis, reflection, creation, and communication across disciplines. The general education requirements include composition, oral communication, quantitative reasoning, western and nonwestern culture, literature, modern language, value assessment, creative artistic expression, world systems, scientific theory and experimentation, research, self-assessment, and physical activity. Independent studies, available at all levels, and seminars, are included in most majors, with a culminating senior course or exercise required in most majors. Sweet Briar has ten honorary societies including a chapter of Phi Beta Kappa. The four-year Honors Program is nationally recognized for its innovative partnering of interdisciplinary academic and co-curricular programs. Honors students take special tutorials, known as honors variants and honors seminars. Seniors may choose to complete a year-long research project culminating in an honors thesis on an original topic in the major department. Sweet Briar's two-semester calendar allows students to participate in intensive courses, independent research projects, and internships on campus or throughout the world. A Sweet Briar education sets in motion the conviction that any goal is achievable. Classes average twelve students, and a student to faculty ratio of 8:1 ensures academic interaction and personal attention.

Sweet Briar awards the Bachelor of Arts, Bachelor of Science, or Bachelor of Fine Arts degree in 40 majors: anthropology, art history, biochemistry and molecular biology, biology, business management, chemistry, classical studies: civilization, classical studies: Greek & Latin languages, communications, computer science, dance, economics, education (liberal studies major leading to teacher licensure preK–6), engineering (3-2 dual degree), English, English and creative writing, environmental science, environmental studies, fine arts, French, German, German studies, government, history, international affairs, Italian studies, liberal studies, mathematical physics, mathematics, modern languages and literatures, music, philosophy, physics, psychology, religion, sociology, Spanish, Spanish/business, studio art, and theatre arts. Additional area studies, minors, and certificate programs include archaeology, arts management, equine management, Italian, film studies, law & society, musical theatre, pre-law, pre-med, pre-vet, and women and gender studies. Students may design interdisciplinary majors focusing on a topic of special interest or may construct individualized majors.

Sweet Briar's faculty have been commended by numerous regional and national educational groups for their exceptional excellence in teaching. Faculty members are actively engaged in teaching, research, publication, and other forms of creative activity. More than 95 percent of full-time faculty members have a doctorate or an appropriate terminal degree in their fields. About half are women. Classes average 12 students, and a student/faculty ratio of 8:1 ensures academic interaction and personal attention. Students work one-on-one with faculty members and visiting scholars and artists to engage in meaningful creative activity, scholarship, and research.

PO Box B
Sweet Briar, VA 24595
Phone: 434-381-6142
Fax: 434-381-6152
Website: www.sbc.edu

SWEET BRIAR COLLEGE

ADMISSIONS

Sweet Briar seeks talented women who are adventurous, enthusiastic about learning, and want to take an active part in their education. In addition to academic achievement, the Admissions Committee looks for qualities such as independent thinking, upholding of ethical principles, creativity, and an appreciation of diversity. Sweet Briar welcomes students of all economic, ethnic, geographic, religious, and social backgrounds. Requirements normally include a minimum of 4 units in English, 3 in mathematics, 3 in social studies, 2 sequential years in a foreign language, and 3 units in science, as well as additional units in these subjects to total 16. Most candidates have 20 such academic units. Additional units may be earned in other subjects but will not count as academic units. Special attention is given to the difficulty of the applicant's curriculum, her class rank, and the school attended; scores on the SAT I or ACT are required. An interview at the College is strongly recommended but not required. Candidates who are unable to visit the campus are urged to meet with representatives of the College in their community such as alumnae or visiting admissions officers, or to request the Sweet Briar College video.

Regular candidates should apply by February 1 of the senior year. Early decision applications are due by December 1 of the senior year, and notifications are sent December 15; the reservation deposit is due January 15. Transfer applications are due by July 1. A completed application includes a transcript of the candidate's course work, scores on the required tests, recommendations from a guidance counselor and a teacher, and essays written by the candidate. There is a $25 application fee, but it may be waived at the request of the student and her guidance counselor if it is deemed to be a financial burden. Sweet Briar also accepts the Common Application and online applications. All materials should be sent to the address given below; information may be requested from the same office.

Dean of Admissions
Sweet Briar College
Sweet Briar, VA 24595
Telephone: 434-381-6142 or 800-381-6142 (toll free)
Fax: 434-381-6152
E-mail: admissions@sbc.edu
World Wide Web: www.sbc.edu

CAMPUS LIFE

Sweet Briar is located in central Virginia in the foothills of the Blue Ridge Mountains. The spacious campus of nearly 3,300 acres contains hiking trails, nature preserves, and spectacular views. The core buildings, designed by Ralph Adams Cram, form the Sweet Briar College National Historic District. Recent additions to campus include a modern conference center and student commons that opened in 2002. Sweet Briar is also the only college in the United States with a residential artists' colony on its campus, the Virginia Center for the Creative Arts. The on-campus riding center, one of the largest and best-designed college facilities in the country, attracts both competitive and recreational riders. The community atmosphere of the College is enhanced by the large proportion of faculty and administrators who also live on campus. The College is centrally located on the outskirts of Lynchburg, Virginia, and southwest of Washington, DC, and Charlottesville. Students also enjoy activities in nearby Roanoke and Richmond.

Sweet Briar participates in the Tri-College Consortium along with Randolph-Macon Woman's College and Lynchburg College. In addition to taking courses at the other colleges, students can also participate in social and cultural activities. More than a third of Sweet Briar's junior class spends either a semester, or more commonly, a full year studying abroad at multiple destinations. Sweet Briar sponsors two study abroad programs, in France and in Spain, either for full-year or semester.

The Sweet Briar Junior Year in France Program (JYF) is the oldest coeducational intercollegiate American program in Paris. Classes are offered at the Sorbonne and other institutions of higher learning such as, the Institute Catholique, the Alliance francaise and the Faculte Libre d'Economie et de Droit. Students consistently rate the program highly in terms of value, wide selection of classes, and facilities. Over 5,500 students from 269 schools have participated in this prestigious program to date, which is now celebrating its 55th year.

Sweet Briar College's Junior Year in Spain (JYS) students study at the University of Seville, one of Spain's most prestigious universities. The University of Seville itself occupies a huge, eighteenth-century baroque building, formerly the Real Tabacalera, or tobacco factory, the setting for Bizet's "Carmen." The program provides an academic experience designed to increase students' competency in the Spanish language while permitting the selection of courses in disciplines for which students qualify, including classes in the University of Seville's Business School. Beginning in the fall of 2004, JYS will open a new program in Madrid which will provide university classes in addition to other opportunities for students to exchange ideas and build awareness of contemporary issues, including women's contributions to all areas of human endeavor. For more information visit our web site at www.jys.sbc.edu.

The College has special arrangements with St. Andrew's University in Scotland, Heidelberg University in Germany, Doshisha Women's College in Japan, and the University of Urbino in Italy. In addition, Sweet Briar works with students to select destinations throughout the world for study during the academic year or for a summer session. Summer programs include those at Oxford University, Directed Studies Program in Urbino, German Summer Program in Munster, and the American School of Classical Studies Summer Program at Athens.

COST AND AID

For 2003–2004, tuition is $19,700 and room and board are $8,040. Books, supplies, and fees cost about $600. Personal expenses average $750. All students may have cars.

TEMPLE UNIVERSITY

GENERAL INFORMATION

Temple University attracts top students from all 50 states and 130 foreign countries. Students come for the blend of large-school resources and small-school feel. Based in Philadelphia, Pennsylvania, Temple prides itself on achievements in teaching and research. Attendees choose between suburban and city campuses depending on their location preferences. Additionally, students have the opportunity to study at Temple's campuses in Tokyo, Japan, and Rome, Italy. The Temple faculty includes instructors at the top of their fields. Professors excel in the teaching, research, and professional aspects of their careers. Students have true access to the faculty thanks to an average class size of 24. The University organizes Freshman Learning Communities, groups of 20 to 30 first-year students taught by two to four professors in several classes. Groups form according to shared interests and goals and help to ease the transition to university life and study. Upon graduation, students are ready to embark on their careers or go on to graduate school. Philadelphia and the surrounding area provide students the opportunity for career development and professional networking opportunities, such as internships and co-ops. Temple alumni have an education held in high esteem by employers everywhere. Students are never at a loss for things to do at Temple. If they are not participating in recreational, cultural, and athletic on campus, they have all the attractions of Philadelphia close by.

STUDENT BODY

Student life thrives on all Temple campuses. Students have constant opportunities to attend movies, concerts, guest lectures, and performances of all kinds. More than 100 clubs and organizations provide outlets for socializing, political debate, community service, and more. Student-athletes compete in intercollegiate and intramural athletics. The Independence Blue Cross Student Recreation Center provides 59,000 square feet of fitness facilities. Students get their exercise by utilizing cardiovascular machines, free weights and weight machines, racquetball courts, a martial arts center, and an aerobics room. The Rec Center is just one component of the Liacouras Center. Liacouras, the home court of perennially successful Temple basketball, also houses entertainment venues and a recreation center. In addition, the Student Pavilion, a multipurpose, 4-court field house provides students with additional recreational space for volleyball, basketball, badminton, floor hockey, indoor soccer, tennis, golf, and much more. The Ambler campus is a hub of activity in its own right. From there, students run the campus radio station and newspaper and participate in various other student clubs and organizations. Athletic facilities include basketball and tennis courts, an in-line skating area, a fitness center, and a pool. Resident students, totaling nearly 5,000, live mainly in the high-rise dormitories and apartment-style residences on the Main Campus. However, students also live on the Ambler and Tyler campuses. Both coed and single-sex floors are available to accommodate student preferences. Additionally, wellness floors have taken off, asking students to vow to a healthy lifestyle.

ACADEMICS

Temple's high-quality yet affordable education both gets students ready for the rigors of the workplace and cultivates their understanding of the world around them. The core curriculum puts all students through a broad, liberal arts course of study, allowing the entire student body to share part of their academic experience. Full-time professors typically lead core courses. First-year students can participate in courses designed to meet their unique needs. Specifically, freshman seminars are tailored to ease the adjustment to college-level courses. The Honors Program provides an arena for top students to stretch their intellectual capacity. Students take one out of four of their courses in smaller, more challenging classes. Those wishing to attend the Temple University Schools of Medicine and Dentistry or School of Law can, as undergraduates, participate in the TempleMed Scholars, Temple Dental School, and TempleLaw Scholars programs, thus securing provisional admission to the graduate programs depending on their performance. Temple's pharmacy school sponsors a comparable program.

Temple University grants undergraduate degrees in 119 majors in the areas of liberal arts, sciences, business, communications, fine and performing arts, engineering, education, allied health, architecture, sports, management/recreation, social work, and landscape architecture/horticulture.

Temple employs more than 1,200 full-time professors. They are selected both for their achievements in their field and their ability to communicate their expertise to students. Many high-ranking faculty members teach introductory courses and serve as academic advisors. Students do not have to wait until later years and higher-level classes to interact with the most sought-after instructors. Every year, students pay tribute to teaching excellence by choosing five professors to be honored with the Temple University Great Teacher Award.

1801 North Broad Street
Philadelphia, PA 19122-6096
Phone: 215-204-7200
Fax: 215-204-5694
Website: www.temple.edu

ADMISSIONS

The admissions committee at Temple looks for signs of motivation and accomplishment in students that demonstrate their ability to benefit from the academic opportunities and challenges at the University. High school grades, class rank, standardized test scores, and co-curricular activities are all considered. The application essay gives students the chance to express their intentions and qualifications in their own words. It is also helpful to tour the campuses before applying. Requirement for admission include a high-school diploma from an accredited school showing at least 16 academic units. SAT or ACT scores are also necessary. To inquire about visiting, to receive more information or to apply online go to our website at www.temple.edu, or write or call:

Temple University Admissions
1801 North Broad Street
Philadelphia, PA 19122
Telephone: 888-340-2222

CAMPUS LIFE

The surrounding city of Philadelphia is a cornerstone of Temple life. Second only to New York City in size on the east coast, Philadelphia is the home of forward-looking businesses, progressive work in technology and science, and a thriving art scene. The city is the product of its rich history, but it also stays on the cutting edge, with plenty of opportunities to go to of plays, concerts, museums, major league sporting events, stores, clubs, and restaurants. As an alternative to the urban setting, students can attend Temple University Ambler or the Tyler School of Art. Ambler, set on 187 acres 30 minutes outside of the city, offers introductory courses for all majors and entire degree programs in 22 departments. Fine arts majors head to Elkins Park, Pennsylvania, to take courses at The Tyler School of Art.

Temple students have a variety of options for incorporating travel and study into their academic experience. Courses covering architecture, business, liberal arts, and visual arts are available at the Rome campus. Both Japanese and American students partake in classes in Asian studies and Japanese at Temple University Japan's Tokyo campus. Students may also elect to attend summer programs studying French literature in Paris, British mass media in London, or West African cultures in Ghana. Temple's Office of International Programs administers these programs. Furthermore, Temple facilitates exchange programs with institutions in Puerto Rico, Germany, and Paris.

COST AND AID

Pennsylvania residents paid full-time undergraduate tuition of $7,602 in 2002–2003. Those arriving from out of state pay approximately $13,856 in tuition. The cost of room and board for the year runs roughly $6,500, and student fees are an additional $460. Specific schools and colleges within the university, including the Esther Boyer College of Music, the Tyler School of Art, and the College of Allied Health Professions, may charge slightly different tuitions.

TEXAS TECH UNIVERSITY

AT A GLANCE

Texas Tech University, founded in 1923, is a residential state university with a population of 25,000 students who come from all 50 states and 99 countries. Students at Texas Tech have the opportunity to study from more than 300 graduate and undergraduate degree programs.

No other state university in Texas rivals Texas Tech in offering such diverse academic programs on one campus. The University is built around eight Colleges: Agricultural Sciences and Natural Resources, Architecture, Arts and Sciences, Business Administration, Education, Engineering, Honors, and Human Sciences. A law school, which often boasts the highest number of students passing the bar exam in Texas, is conveniently located on the main campus. Students will also find the Texas Tech University Health Sciences Center with its Schools of Medicine, Nursing, Pharmacy, and Allied Health.

Chancellor John T. Montford oversees the University System and its $500 million capital campaign. David J. Schmidly, PhD serves as University president and believes that academic diversity coupled with high educational standards is the key that has placed Texas Tech among the most notable universities in the state.

Academics are the top priority at Texas Tech and students will find admission standards to be comparable with those of other state institutions.

Texas Tech has become a leader in academic programs ranging from pioneering research with the U.S. Department of Agriculture to improving alternative fuel capabilities for the nation's leading automakers. Wind engineering research at the University has lead to the creation of shelters that withstand the nation's most deadly tornadoes. In addition, students will also find opportunities to master the arts with instruction from classically trained musicians as well as unique study abroad programs. A new addition to the academic programs includes the creation of the Institute for Environmental and Human Health. The institute offers graduate and undergraduate education in environmental science, toxicology, and environmental health.

The University joined the Big XII Conference for intercollegiate athletics in 1996. Women participate in basketball, track and field, golf, tennis, volleyball, soccer, and softball while men participate in football, basketball, tennis, track and field, golf, and baseball. In addition, the University offers 22 club sports such as lacrosse, polo, swimming, rugby, men's soccer, and wrestling.

LOCATION AND ENVIRONMENT

The 1,839-acre campus is located in Lubbock, a west Texas city of 200,000 people. Within a few hours' drive, students will find snow skiing in the pine-covered mountains of northern New Mexico, the lush scenery of the Texas hill country and the vast canyons of Palo Duro and Big Bend. Temperatures are mild in the winter and warm in the summer, with an average of 267 days of sunshine each year.

MAJORS AND DEGREES OFFERED

The College of Agricultural Sciences and Natural Resources at Texas Tech offers programs in agribusiness, agricultural communications, agricultural economics, agricultural education, agronomy, animal production, animal science, crop and soil sciences, entomology, environmental conservation, food technology, horticulture, landscape architecture, pre–veterinary medicine, range management, and wildlife and fisheries management.

The College of Architecture offers architectural design, delineation, design-business administration, history and historic preservation, structures, structures-civil engineering, and urban design.

The College of Arts and Sciences provides programs in advertising, aerospace studies, anthropology, art (studio), art education, art history, Asian Pacific Rim studies, atmospheric science, biochemistry, biology, botany, broadcast journalism, cell and molecular biology, chemistry, communication studies, community and urban studies, comparative literature, creative writing, dance, design communications, economics, English, environmental studies, ethnic studies, exercise and sports sciences, French, geography, geology, geophysics, geosciences, German, health, history, international economics, international studies, Italian, Japanese, journalism, Latin, Latin American area studies, liberal arts, linguistics, literature, mathematics, microbiology, military science, music composition, music education, music history and literature, music performance, music theory, philosophy, photocommunications, physics, political science, pre–clinical laboratory science, pre–communication disorders, pre-dentistry, pre-law, pre–medicine, pre-nursing, pre–occupational therapy, pre-optometry, pre-pharmacy, pre–physical therapy, psychology, public relations, recreation and leisure services, Russian, Russian language and area studies, social work, sociology, Spanish, statistics, technical communication, telecommunications, theater arts, and zoology.

The College of Business Administration offers accounting, business economics, finance, finance-real estate, international business, management, management information systems, marketing, and petroleum land management.

The College of Engineering provides programs in chemical engineering, civil engineering, engineering physics, engineering technology, environmental engineering, industrial engineering, mechanical engineering, and petroleum engineering.

Students in the College of Human Sciences study programs in early childhood education, family financial planning, family studies, fashion design, food and nutrition/dietetics, home economics, human development, interior design, merchandising, restaurant, hotel, and institutional management, and substance abuse studies.

ACADEMIC PROGRAMS

Texas Tech's undergraduate curriculum provides a broad range of courses in more than 150 majors. Recently, students at Texas Tech have seen an increase in competitive academic scholarships as well as the creation of the University's Honors College. Students accepted into the college will find unparalleled undergraduate research opportunities for students in all major disciplines. As a result, Texas Tech students are consistently awarded the prestigious Barry M. Goldwater Scholarship for science, engineering, and mathematics. In the 1997–1998 academic year, Texas Tech led the state's public universities with two Goldwater Scholars; in the 1996–1997 year, three students received the honor; and in the 1995–1996 academic year, Texas Tech was the only university to have four students receive the Goldwater Scholarship.

PO Box 45005
Lubbock, TX 79409-5005
Phone: 806-742-1480
Fax: 806-742-0980
Website: www.ttu.edu

OFF-CAMPUS OPPORTUNITIES

Texas Tech University operates a 400-acre south Texas center in Junction, where summer classes and May intersessions are held. Just minutes from campus, the Lubbock Lake Landmark State Historical Park is an excavation site where Texas Tech researchers have documented a 12,000-year record of continuous human habitation. In addition, numerous study abroad opportunities are available for college credit in most countries around the world.

FACILITIES AND EQUIPMENT

The University Library, the Medical Library, the Southwest Collection archival library, the Law Library, and the Architecture Library are linked by a common online catalog, TechPAC. Additional access is provided to numerous bibliographic and full-text databases as well as catalogs from libraries throughout the nation. The University Library collection includes 1.3 million volumes, 15,000 subscriptions, and almost 1 million microforms. The library is one of only two regional depositories in the state for U.S. government documents, which now number 1.4 million. The library also houses the Advanced Technology Learning Center, a multiroom lab with a wide variety of computers and programs. There are also computer facilities located in each college and residence hall throughout campus.

TUITION, ROOM & BOARD AND FEES

Texas Tech is listed in The 100 Best College Buys for 2000 and 2001, which is a directory of the top colleges and universities in the country whose costs are below the national average, but whose academics are above the national average. In 2000–2001, the average cost for 30 undergraduate credit hours including books and nine-month room and board was $8,574 for Texas residents. Residents from Arkansas, New Mexico, and Oklahoma living in bordering counties to Texas paid in-state tuition; residents of nonbordering counties paid an additional $900 per year. Students from other states paid an additional $6,450 per year for out-of-state tuition. It is important to note that students who receive a $1,000 scholarship from Texas Tech will be exempt from paying out-of-state tuition. Costs are subject to change.

FINANCIAL AID

A variety of student financial aid is offered in the form of scholarships, loans, and grants. The University awards competitive scholarships based on academic merit, SAT I or ACT scores, high school class rank, and organizational or athletic involvement. More than 350 Presidential Endowed Scholarships are available to students with outstanding academic ability and leadership potential. Need-based assistance is also available in the form of scholarships, government and private loans, grants, and work-study. All financial aid is determined by the Free Application for Federal Student Aid (FAFSA). For a guide to scholarships and deadlines, students should write to:

Office of Financial Aid/Scholarships
Texas Tech University
Box 45011
Lubbock, TX 79409-5011

FULL AND PART-TIME FACULTY

Full-time faculty members number 830, while there are 806 part-time faculty members and teaching assistants. Among faculty members are distinguished professionals serving as visiting and adjunct professors. Faculty members' research has gained international attention and has been published in leading academic journals. The University's average student/faculty ratio is 18:1.

STUDENT ORGANIZATION AND ACTIVITIES

At Texas Tech, students actively participate in 350 student organizations. Students will find an opportunity to join academic/professional groups, honorary clubs, international student organizations, multicultural groups, recreational activities, religious groups, residence hall government, service organizations, social fraternities and sororities, and special interest groups.

The Texas Tech Student Government Association includes a Student Senate whose elected members serve as official student representatives and act as liaisons to the Lubbock community and University administration. In addition, a freshman council of first-year students works specifically on issues relating to the freshman experience.

ADMISSIONS

Admission criteria for all students are designed to ensure academic success. For freshmen, admission decisions are based primarily on test scores and class rank. Additional factors such as leadership experience and extracurricular activities, community or volunteer service, talents and special honors, and awards and achievements, as well as employment and internship activities, are considered.

Students in the top 10 percent of their graduating class are guaranteed admission to the University. For assured admission, students who rank in the first quarter of their class must score at least 1140 on the SAT I or 25 on the ACT. Students who rank in the second quarter must score at least 1230 on the SAT I and 28 on the ACT. Those in the lower half must score at least 1270 on the SAT I and 29 on the ACT.

Applicants not meeting the assured admission criteria will be reviewed. Students who are not admitted with a favorable review may apply for the Provisional Program. Provisionally admitted students may attend Texas Tech in the summer after high school graduation or the following spring. Before fall enrollment, provisionally admitted students must achieve a prescribed number of college hours and grade point average.

Admission requirements for transfer students differ depending on the number of college hours a student has earned. Transfer students will be admitted to Texas Tech by transferring 24 or more hours from an accredited institution with at least a 2.25 grade point average or by transferring 12 to 23 hours with at least a 2.50 grade point average and at least 12 hours of required basic courses. Students with less than 12 transfer hours must meet the requirements for freshmen and have at least a 2.0 grade point average. All students must be eligible to return to the institution from which they are transferring.

The University will admit all students who hold scholarships awarded by an official Texas Tech University scholarship committee.

All students should submit the State of Texas Common Application, a high school transcript, SAT I or ACT test scores, and the $25 application fee. Requests for applications and other information should be directed to:

Office of Admissions and School Relations
Texas Tech University
Box 45005
Lubbock, TX 79409-5005
Telephone: 806-742-1480
Fax: 806-742-0980
E-mail: admissions@ttu.edu
World Wide Web: www.ttu.edu

TOWSON STATE UNIVERSITY

AT A GLANCE

Towson University (TU), a regional comprehensive university founded in 1866, offers degrees in the liberal arts and sciences as well as in pre-professional and professional disciplines. Towson's beautiful 328-acre campus is situated in Towson, Maryland, a suburban community eight miles north of Baltimore's popular downtown area. The University offers the bachelor's degree in 60 areas, the master's degree in 35, and three doctorates. Superior teaching and continuous scholarly growth are both hallmarks of the Towson faculty. The University is nationally acclaimed for its outstanding offerings in business, communications, computer science, fine arts, health professions, teacher education, and women's studies.

Towson University offers academic programs through eight colleges: the College of Business and Economics, the College of Education, the College of Fine Arts and Communication, the College of Health Professions, the College of Liberal Arts, the College of Science and Mathematics, the College of Graduate Education and Research, and the College of Extended Programs.

Nearly 17,000 full-time and part-time students are enrolled at the University. Their numbers include over 800 international students from 100 nations. TU is home to more than 14,000 undergraduates; more than 13 percent are minority students. About 77 percent of the freshman class, and over 3,900 students among all four classes, resides on campus. The University has 13 residence halls, which include apartment complexes, modern high-rise towers, and more traditional two- and three-story residential buildings. Campus life offers exciting opportunities in many areas; academic, athletic, cultural, and social life all thrive here. TU is home to over 100 campus organizations and student clubs. Fraternities, sororities, and social and professional clubs all find a home at TU. Students love to gather at the University Union, which houses the school bookstore, dining facilities, the post office, a recreation center, ATM machines, and more. Students have access to a counseling center, an academic advising center, a health center, and a career center.

Towson University is represented by teams in 11 men's and 12 women's sports. The University completes in Division I of the National Collegiate Athletic Association (NCAA). The Tigers also participate in the Colonial Athletic Association in 21 sports, as well as the East Atlantic Gymnastics League, while the Tiger football squad is a member of the Patriot League. Towson boasts a 24-acre athletic complex that includes University Stadium, home to Tiger football, track, field hockey, and lacrosse teams. The Towson Center, with capacity seating of over 5,000, is home to Tiger basketball teams as well as the volleyball and gymnastics squads. Athletic facilities at TU include an NCAA-regulation swimming pool, 23 tennis courts, 6 racquetball courts, 6 squash courts, 3 gymnasiums, 2 weight training rooms, a sand volleyball court, and a fitness center. Towson also offers an intramural program for men and women.

LOCATION AND ENVIRONMENT

Towson University is situated in Baltimore County, in the pleasant suburb of Towson. Towson Town Center, the area's prime upscale shopping center, is located a mere 10 minutes from campus. Bookstores, movie theaters, libraries, and restaurants are but a brief walk from campus. Just 20 minutes to the south are the cultural and educational resources of downtown Baltimore. The city is home to Federal Hill, the Maryland Science Center, the world-famous National Aquarium, Oriole Park at Camden Yards, and the Walters Art Museum. Towson is centrally located within the mid-Atlantic region, conveniently close to the Appalachian Mountains; the Atlantic beaches; Washington, DC; Philadelphia; and New York City.

MAJORS AND DEGREES OFFERED

Undergraduates at Towson University may earn a Bachelor of Arts or Bachelor of Science degree in: accounting; art; art education; athletic training; biology; business administration; chemistry; communication studies; computer information systems; computer science; cultural studies; dance performance and education; deaf studies; electronic business; early childhood education; earth-space science; economics; electronic media and film; elementary education; English; environmental science and studies; exercise science; family studies; French; geography and environmental planning; geography and land surveying; geology; German; gerontology; health-care management; health science; history; interdisciplinary studies; international studies; law and American civilization; mass communication; mathematics; medicinal chemistry; metropolitan studies; molecular biology, biochemistry and bioinformatics; music; music education; nursing; occupational therapy; philosophy; physical education; physics; political science; psychology; religious studies; secondary education; social science; sociology–anthropology; Spanish; special education; speech-language pathology and audiology; sport management; sport studies; theatre; and women's studies. Also offered are the Bachelor of Fine Arts degree in dance and the Bachelor of Technical and Professional Studies in chemical dependency counseling and education.

ACADEMIC PROGRAMS

Towson operates on a semester system with spring and fall terms. The school offers an optional January minimester as well as three 5-week summer sessions and one 7-week summer session. The University's primary goal is to provide a strong education in the liberal arts and sciences to all its students. To achieve this goal, Towson University requires the completion of a General Education (GenEd) program, which is designed to provide a fundamental introduction to all major concepts in the arts and sciences. To receive a bachelor's degree, undergraduates must complete at least 120 hours of college-level course work. They must also achieve a grade point average of at least 2.0 (C) in their major field and a cumulative grade point average for all course work of 2.0 or higher. All students must complete 44 to 46 credit hours in General Education–related course work and fulfill the requirements of their major as set by their major department. Academic advising plays an essential role in fulfilling Towson's entire mission.

Qualified students are invited to join the Honors College. Honors College classes offer undergraduates opportunities for course work, mentoring, and research in a wide variety of academic areas. Honors College students have access to honors scholarships and receive priority in class scheduling. The College also offers extracurricular programs and seminars.

The University offers more than 900 courses during the academic year. Full-time and part-time students are welcome; classes are offered during the day, in the evening, and on Saturday.

OFF-CAMPUS OPPORTUNITIES

The University provides opportunities for off-campus study in more than 40 countries in Asia, Australia, Canada, Central and South America, Europe, and the Middle East. Each year nearly 250 students engage in a wide assortment of disciplines taking advantage of Towson's exchange and study abroad programs.

The University's Internship Program offers students the chance to earn college credit while gaining valuable work experience and exploring career choices. Towson places over 700 undergraduates in internships across the country each year.

FACILITIES AND EQUIPMENT

The University's Albert S. Cook Library, which is centrally located on campus, gathers more than 580,000 books, 2,180 periodicals, and a variety of other media, including audiocassettes, microforms, DVDs and videos. An online catalog system allows Towson undergraduates to access materials available from all 11 University System of Maryland libraries. MdUSA, a valuable Web resource, provides a virtual library with abstracting, indexing, and full-text articles. The Center for the Arts is home to the departments of art, dance, music, and theatre arts. It houses a 346-seat theater; a 520-seat concert auditorium; and two art galleries. Van Bokkelen Hall, home to the Department of Communication Sciences and Disorders and the Department of Mass Communication and Communication Studies, provides students access to modern communication equipment. Van Bokkelen Hall contains a clinic that provides services to individuals with hearing and speech disorders. Science departments make their home in Smith Hall, which contains up-to-date research facilities as well as a planetarium. The College of Business and Economics is headquartered in historic Stephens Hall, which includes the Stephens Hall Auditorium (700 seats). The University's Media Center houses WMJF-TV, the student-run television station, as well as the campus radio station.

8000 York Road
Towson, MD 21252-0001
Phone: 410-704-2113
Fax: 410-704-3030
Website: www.towson.edu

TUITION, ROOM & BOARD, AND FEES

The anticipated 2003–2004 tuition and fees for Maryland residents are $2,827 per semester and $6,650 for out-of-state students. Room and board charges are an estimated $3,161 per semester.

FINANCIAL AID

Approximately 66 percent of full-time undergraduates at Towson University receive financial assistance of some kind. Assistance is available to qualified students through grants, loans, scholarships, and employment, both on and off campus. The University takes part in major federal and state aid programs. The University also offers academic scholarships to qualified applicants.

FULL AND PART-TIME FACULTY

Towson provides many opportunities for one-on-one contact between students and faculty. The University also promotes a nurturing environment designed to satisfy the personal and professional goals of its undergraduates. The student/faculty ratio is 18:1; small classes (25 to 35 students, on average), allow undergraduates to interact directly with professors.

Eighty-four percent of the University's full-time teachers have earned the PhD or a terminal degree in their fields of expertise; many attended the finest academic institutions in the world. A substantial number of the 520 full-time faculty members are renowned for their published works and for the honors granted them.

STUDENT ORGANIZATIONS AND ACTIVITIES

All undergraduates are officially represented by the Student Government Association, which plans, arranges, and directs student programs, organizations, and clubs on campus. The SGA also works together with the faculty and administrators in governing certain aspects of university life.

ADMISSION PROCESSES AND REQUIREMENTS

Freshmen: Towson considers applicants who have taken college-preparatory courses in high school. The Admissions Committee looks at the applicant's high school grade point average in academic courses, standardized test scores (SAT I or ACT), letters of recommendation from appropriate academic officials, and other indications of the applicant's ability to succeed at the college level. All entering freshmen must take placement exams in mathematics, reading, and writing unless SAT I scores allow an exemption. Fifty-eight percent of all freshman applicants for fall 2002 were offered admission. The middle 50 percentile of students admitted scored between 500 to 590 Verbal and 510 to 590 Math on the SAT I. The mean high school GPA for this group was 3.48.

Transfer Students: Transfer students from a Maryland community college who have earned at least 56 transferable credits, are in good academic standing, and have maintained a GPA that meets the policies set by the Maryland Higher Education Commission and University System of Maryland will receive priority admission. Students who have earned fewer than 56 transferable credits or who are transferring from an institution other than a Maryland community college, will be admitted based on combined cumulative GPA of transferable credits and space availability. Students wishing to transfer must provide transcripts from all previously attended colleges. Transfer students with fewer than 30 transferable credits must comply with the requirements for incoming freshmen and possess the minimum transfer GPA.

International Students: International applicants who are not native English speakers must provide an official report of Test of English as a Foreign Language (TOEFL) scores. Applicants must earn a minimum score of 500 on the paper-based TOEFL; a score of 173 is required for those taking the computer-based TOEFL. Towson is a selective undergraduate institution. Towson admits applicants on a continuous basis (rolling admissions). Applicants seeking fall admission should submit all required application materials and academic credentials by March 1; those seeking admission in the spring must submit applications by December 1. However, the University reserves the right to close applications when space is no longer available.

Each applicant is responsible for submitting all required materials (application forms, recommendations, test scores, and transcripts) to the Admissions Office in compliance with official deadlines. Applications that are incomplete or improperly filled out may be cancelled. A nonrefundable $35 application fee or an authorized form granting fee deferment must accompany all applications. You may apply online, or by downloading a PDF file, or by requesting an application from the website at www.discover.towson.edu (click on "Prospective Students"), or by requesting an application from the Admissions Office. To receive more information, contact:

Admissions Office
Towson University
8000 York Road
Towson, MD 21252-0001
Telephone: 410-704-2113 or 888-4TOWSON (toll free)
World Wide Web: www.discover.towson.edu.

TRANSYLVANIA UNIVERSITY

GENERAL INFORMATION

Constantly rated among the nation's best schools of its type, Transylvania University is a small private liberal arts school attended by about 1,100 men and women. The school derives its name from the heavily wooded area in which it was founded in 1780 (Transylvania is Latin for "across the woods"). Transylvania was the nation's sixteenth college and the westernmost institution of higher learning at the time of its founding. The first law school and medical school on what was then the nation's western frontier were established at Transylvania; its graduates went on to shape the political, legal, medical, and religious history of the early United States. Transylvania's literary magazine, *The Transylvanian*, which is still published today, was the first publication of its kind in the West. The University administration building, Old Morrison, is a registered National Historic Landmark that is featured prominently on the official seal of the City of Lexington.

Today Transylvania is on the cutting edge of higher education, fulfilling its mission to train tomorrow's leaders in government, business, the sciences, the arts, and education. Transylvania undergraduates benefit from small classes (many have fewer than 10 students) that allow close work with professors. A large number of Transylvania students proceed to selective law, medical, and professional graduate programs. Twenty-eight states and 11 countries are represented in the Student Body. Students at Transylvania engage in over 50 available co-curricular activities. The school fields varsity teams in seven men's and eight women's sports; intramural competition covers 12 sports. Four national fraternities and four national sororities make their home at Transylvania. The Lampas Circle of Omicron Delta Kappa, a national honorary leadership society, recognizes undergraduates who demonstrate leadership and academic excellence.

STUDENT BODY

The Transylvania administration and the University's governing board are extremely accessible to all undergraduates. The Student Government Association allows students the opportunity to participate in representative government and to influence school policy. Students serve on the Board of Trustees and on standing faculty committees.

ACADEMICS

Transylvania operates on a 4-4-1 academic calendar. Two 14-week terms are held in the fall (September to December) and winter (January to April); a short term is held in May. The short term allows students to engage in a wide assortment of on-campus and off-campus projects. Most students take four courses during each of the 14-week terms and one course during the short term. Students must complete 36 courses in order to graduate. All freshmen must complete the two-term Foundations of Liberal Arts sequence. In these courses, students sharpen their communication, study, and critical thinking skills; attend films, concerts, lectures, and other cultural events; and engage in faculty-led discussions with small groups of their fellow freshmen. Students have the option of participating in additional study-skill workshops and clinics. Distribution requirements ensure that students receive a broad grounding in the natural sciences, social sciences, logic, mathematics, humanities, fine arts, and languages. Students may earn course credit through Advanced Placement exams (scores of 4 or 5 are required) or the International Baccalaureate Program (scores of at least 5 are required). Students interested in this option should contact the Office of the Registrar for more details.

Undergraduates may pursue the Bachelor of Arts degree in the following majors: accounting, art, biology, business administration (with specializations in finance, management, marketing, and hotel, restaurant, and tourism administration), chemistry, computer science, drama, economics, education, English, exercise science, French, history, mathematics, music, philosophy, physical education, physics, political science, psychology, religion, sociology, sociology/anthropology, and Spanish. Students may fashion their own majors, and they may pursue minors in most major areas as well as in anthropology; classical studies; communication; European studies; German; hotel, restaurant, and tourism administration; international affairs; multicultural studies; and women's studies. The school offers advising and special undergraduate pre-training in dentistry, engineering, law, medicine, ministry, pharmacy, physical therapy, and veterinary medicine. Students interested in engineering may pursue a physics or liberal studies BA at Transylvania (which they complete in three years), then spend two years earning a BS in engineering from the University of Kentucky, Vanderbilt University, or Washington University. Accounting students may take advantage of a similar cooperative program with the University of Kentucky to earn an accounting BA from Transylvania in four years and an MS in accounting from UK in one additional year. Those who successfully complete this track are qualified to take the CPA exam.

Transylvania students reap the benefits of the school's small Student Body and low student/faculty ratio (13:1) in the close academic mentoring and advising they receive. Nearly all full-time instructors at the University hold the PhD or the equivalent terminal degree in their field; many have earned these degrees at the world's most prestigious graduate institutions. While many professors are renowned for their research and published work, the education of their students is the faculty's chief focus. Transylvania emphasizes the importance of teaching through its highly praised Bingham Program for Excellence in Teaching, which utilizes financial incentives and frequent evaluation to reward excellence in instruction.

300 North Broadway
Lexington, KY 40508-1797
Phone: 859-233-8242
Fax: 859-233-8797
Website: www.transy.edu

ADMISSIONS

Transylvania considers each applicant on his/her own merits. The school evaluates applicants' academic records, standardized test scores (SAT I and/or ACT), co-curricular activities, interests, essays, and letters of recommendation. The school welcomes applications for transfer students, international students, and nontraditional students. International applicants must submit standardized test scores (SAT I, ACT, or TOEFL). The school also considers candidates who plan to graduate at the end of their junior year. The freshman class of 2001–2002 consisted of 325 students. The middle 50 percent composite ACT score for the freshman class was 24-29; the middle 50 percent combined SAT I score was 1100-1290. Nearly two-thirds of incoming freshmen graduated in the top 10 percent of their high school class.

All applicants must submit a Transylvania Application for Admission and Scholarships; this form qualifies students for admission and most merit-based awards. Students should contact the admissions office to learn about specific application deadlines as they relate to scholarships and various types of financial assistance. Those seeking priority admission or special scholarships should submit their completed applications by December 1; priority admission candidates are notified of the school's decision by January 1. Students applying for general admission and those seeking all scholarships except the William T. Young and Pioneer scholarships need to submit applications by February 1. Applications that arrive before February 1 will be assessed on a rolling basis; those that arrive after this date will be assessed on a space-available basis. Applicants (including transfers) seeking admission for the winter term must submit applications by December 5. Students may submit applications electronically through our website, www.transy.edu.

The University urges prospective students to visit the campus. High school seniors may stay overnight; the school provides dormitory lodging with a student admissions assistant. Those who visit during the week can take a campus tour, sit in on classes, meet with professors, students, and administrators, and eat at the campus dining hall. Contact the Office of Admissions to arrange a visit. Plan your visit one to two weeks in advance, if possible. The University holds open houses in the fall and winter. High school sophomores and juniors are invited to a college planning workshop in the spring. To request application materials and additional information, contact:

Office of Admissions
Transylvania University
300 North Broadway
Lexington, KY 40508-1797
Telephone: 859-233-8242 or 800-872-6798 (toll free)
E-mail: admissions@transy.edu
Internet: www.transy.edu

CAMPUS LIFE

Lexington, Kentucky, home to Transylvania, is a growing city of nearly a quarter-million people. Commerce, culture, education, and research all play a major role in the life of the city. The area surrounding Lexington is often referred to as "the horse capital of the world"; its green pastures and rolling hills make this central Kentucky bluegrass region the ideal place to raise thoroughbreds. Nearly 30,000 undergraduates live in or just outside the city. The verdant Transylvania campus is just blocks from downtown, allowing students ready access to shopping, movies, live entertainment, and restaurants. Many students take advantage of the downtown area to find internships and part-time jobs in accounting firms, hospitals, law offices, and organizations. A shuttle bus transports Transylvania students between the modern Transylvania library and the University of Kentucky libraries every day; the Lexington Public Library is within walking distance of campus. Louisville and Cincinnati are a little more than an hour's drive away. Several major airlines travel in and out of Lexington.

Transylvania encourages its students to engage in international study. Many students choose to study abroad; some spend a summer overseas, others take a semester abroad, and still others spend an entire year studying outside the United States. A cooperative program with Regent's College in London allows Transylvania undergraduates to study in London for the same amount of money they would spend to study at our home campus. The school offers scholarships to help fund semester and summer study overseas. Transylvania is affiliated with the Kentucky Institute for International Studies; this affiliation allows for summer study in Austria, Brazil, China, Costa Rica, Ecuador, France, Germany, Italy, Japan, Mexico, and Spain. Another cooperative program, offered with the English-Speaking Union, offers exceptional students scholarships to study at Cambridge and Oxford Universities over the summer. The Washington Center helps send Transylvania undergraduates to our nation's capital to participate in seminars and undertake internships. Other internships—with national, state, city, and local government, as well as with local businesses—are readily available. Students may enroll in Air Force or Army ROTC (Reserve Officers Training Corps) through the University of Kentucky.

COST AND AID

Full-time students during the 2002–2003 school year pay tuition of $16,170; room and board (for a double-occupancy room) totals $5,940, and the general fee is $620. Tuition covers full-time coursework for the fall, winter, and May terms. Some classes, such as applied music, require additional special instruction fees.

TRINITY COLLEGE (CT)

GENERAL INFORMATION

Trinity College is an independent, nonsectarian liberal arts college located in the historic capital city of Hartford, Connecticut. Founded in 1823, Trinity is one of the oldest colleges in the United States. Our nearly 2,000 students, from 46 states and 41 countries, and a distinguished faculty are engaged in a quest for knowledge in the classical liberal arts tradition.

There are four elements central to the success of this quest: an outstanding and diverse faculty whose members excel in their dual vocation as teachers and scholars; a rigorous curriculum that is firmly grounded in the traditional liberal arts but also incorporates newer fields, an interdisciplinary approach, and our urban location; a talented, strongly motivated, and diverse body of students who are engaged with their studies, their professors, and one another; and an attractive and supportive campus community that provides students with an abundance of opportunities and exposure to a wide range of cultural, social, and volunteer experiences.

This quest is the lifeblood of a community of learning and is facilitated by a stimulating academic environment, small classes, and exceptional facilities, from our cutting-edge, fiber-optic computer network to secluded nooks that invite thought and contemplation.

Our students immerse themselves in a total educational environment in the classroom, in the studio, in the city, on the stage, and on the athletic fields. You will be challenged to hone and refine the skills that you bring to the College and, more importantly, you will be encouraged to explore new worlds, thoughts, and ideas while hopefully having some fun in the process. At commencement, we don't want you to be the same person you were when you arrived.

STUDENT BODY

While the number in our student body is relatively small, their interests are incredibly large. Because of our size, the opportunities for immediate involvement are wide open—whether doing something in which you've previously been involved or something that is completely new to you. And if you have an interest that isn't covered by an existing organization, then start one! It will probably be impossible for you not to find at least one activity that appeals to you, whether on campus or in the city. Academics are the most important part of your education, but they aren't the only part. We want you to have some fun and to get involved beyond the classroom. The opportunities are right at hand.

ACADEMICS

The curriculum features the First Year Seminar Program that emphasizes writing, discussion, and critical analysis. There are many special curricular options, which include the Guided Studies, Interdisciplinary Science and Cities Programs, the Trinity Action Project, CityTerm, the Rome Campus, the Trinity/La MaMa Performing Arts Program in New York, the Tutorial College, the . . . well, you get the idea. Trinity also has the only undergraduate Human Rights Program in America.

The key words here are variety and flexibility—if you don't see exactly what you want, that doesn't mean we don't have it. Independent study? Open semester? Engineering? Neuroscience? Law courses? How about an academic leave of absence to work on a political campaign or hike the Appalachian Trail? Many Trinity students pursue these and other existing opportunities. And it is very easy to work with faculty to create your own opportunities. Your motivation and imagination are your only limits.

The Bachelor of Arts is the degree normally conferred by Trinity on an undergraduate completing the necessary requirements. In some instances, undergraduates may elect to be awarded the Bachelor of Science degree. There is a five-year Trinity/Rensselaer at Hartford program in engineering and computer science, which leads to both a bachelor's degree and a master's degree.

In all, Trinity offers more than 970 courses in 37 majors. There are eight interdisciplinary majors, such as American studies, as well as self-designed majors, such as environmental studies. At Trinity, your education is student-centered, and our array of curricular options will provide you with the tools to help you to meet your goals.

Trinity has a total of 196 full-time and 53 part-time members, although one could argue that we have nearly 2,000 additional part-time faculty, since student-to-student and student-to-faculty learning is part of the process of education. Of the full-time faculty, over 90 percent hold the highest degree in their field.

Trinity is, first and foremost, a teaching institution. Consequently, that is the primary calling of our faculty. That is part of what prompts one faculty member to remark, "The relationship between student and teacher is special here."

Research and scholarship is also part of the faculty mission, frequently in collaboration with students. Our faculty have received numerous grants from organizations such as the National Science Foundation, the National Endowment for the Humanities, the Olin Foundation, and the National Aeronautics and Space Administration.

300 Summit Street
Hartford, CT 06016
Phone: 860-297-2180
Fax: 860-297-2287
Website: www.trincoll.edu

ADMISSIONS

Selecting candidates for admission to Trinity is a complex but personalized process. The components of your evaluation include your academic credentials—your grades, of course, are very important, but so is the strength of your academic programs, especially in the senior year. We require either the SAT 1 and SAT II: Writing Test, or three SAT IIs (one of which must be the Writing Test), or the ACT. For non-native speakers of English, the TOEFL may be substituted.

In addition, recommendations are important. Teachers give us insight into your scholarship, work habits, and classroom contributions. Personal qualities are considered, too. What talents, skills, or qualities can you bring to the life of the campus? What contributions have you made to your school and community? We aren't so concerned with the number of your activities as we are with the quality and depth of them.

Your application should reflect positively on you, your accomplishments, and your school. If we may be of assistance, please don't hesitate to call on us in the Office of Admissions at 860-297-2180 or e-mail admissions.office@trincoll.edu. You can also visit us at www.trincoll.edu.

CAMPUS LIFE

Trinity is situated on a beautiful, 100-acre hilltop campus near downtown Hartford, midway between Boston and New York. Hartford is a city with a rich past. Mark Twain lived here, as did Harriet Beecher Stowe. Dentist Horace Wells discovered anesthesia here. It is the home of the oldest continuously published newspaper in America as well as the oldest public art museum.

Our campus, in essence, is a tranquil park in the city, and the city, in essence, is a classroom and laboratory for the campus. As a result, Trinity has assets matched by few liberal arts colleges of our size. In a partnership with several institutions in the city and with the support of business, government, and major foundations, the College has launched a multifaceted neighborhood revitalization initiative. The heart of this initiative is the "Learning Corridor" that will include a public, Montessori-style elementary school; a middle school; a magnet math-science-art high school resource center; the first Boys and Girls Club in the country to be located on a college campus; and a Health and Technology Center. Trinity students will have numerous opportunities to engage in volunteer work, internships, and research projects in conjunction with this initiative.

Many professors incorporate aspects of city life into their courses—from art history to political science and from economics to neuroscience. There is even a program designed to study cities throughout history from a wide variety of humanities and social science perspectives. There are hundreds of internships, which will allow you to continue your education as well as explore career opportunities. And whatever your tastes are, there are cultural and entertainment events throughout the city. To help bring all of these elements of Hartford even more within your reach, the College provides a shuttle service.

To cite a recent advertising campaign, we, too, ask "Where do you want to go today?" Perhaps you want to remain in Hartford to do an internship, or take additional music courses at the Hartt School of Music, or obtain teaching certification through St. Joseph's College. Perhaps you want to go on Twelve College Exchange to Dartmouth or Smith? Have you thought about spending a semester at a large university to see what that's like? Perhaps you'd prefer an archaeological dig in Israel? Or how about the Washington Semester program? The National Theater Institute? The Williams-Mystic Seaport Program in Maritime Studies? Or maybe you would "settle" for being part of the 40 percent of your classmates at Trinity who will study abroad on nearly every part of the planet? "Where do you want to go today?"

COST AND AID

The schedule of college fees for 2002–2003 is as follows:

Tuition: $27,170

Room: $4,746

Board: $2,884

General fee: $842

UNION COLLEGE (NY)

GENERAL INFORMATION

Union College attracts talented and motivated students of high academic promise and strong personal motivation. Founded in 1795 as the first college to be chartered by the New York Board of Regents, Union today offers studies in the humanities, the social sciences, the sciences, and engineering. The College offers nearly 1,000 courses—a range that is unusual among America's highly-selective colleges—and places strong emphasis on undergraduate research and international study.

Each year, the Admissions Committee selects a diverse class of 520 out of the roughly 4,000 candidates. The student population of 2,000 full-time undergraduates, with nearly equal numbers of men and women, comes from 35 different U.S. states and 20 foreign countries. Roughly one out of three graduates go straight on to graduate or professional school.

STUDENT BODY

Union College encourages students to complement their classroom learning with extracurricular experiences. More than 100 student-run clubs and organizations provide venues for any interest. Many students attend on-campus cultural events, such as concerts, lectures, and movies. Union also offers athletic opportunities ranging from intercollegiate competition to intramural leagues, club sports, and casual recreational games.

By the beginning of the 2004 school year, Union will have the new House System in place. Each student will be assigned to a House, which provides a residential locus for social interaction as well as intellectual discussion. In general, students live on campus for at least two years.

ACADEMICS

All Union students undertake the General Education Program, including the Freshman Preceptorial, which lays a strong academic foundation in science, mathematics, and social science. In addition to these general requirements, students are encouraged to learn another language and study a nonwestern culture. Many programs orchestrate internship opportunities. Students can spend a 10-week term in Washington, DC, or participate in the legislative internship in Albany, New York.

Top students may enroll in the Union Scholars program, set up to allow in-depth study of subjects introduced in General Education. Participating students work closely with professors to design their own independent study projects during their freshman and sophomore years. In the junior year, Union Scholars study overseas or complete an off-campus internship, tailoring their education to their personal goals.

In order to graduate, students must successfully complete 36 courses (up to 40 for engineering degrees). All departmental and general education requirements need to be satisfied, as well. The academic calendar features three 10-week terms, starting in early September and running through early June. Students normally take three classes per term.

Union vigorously encourages student research in all disciplines and annually sends one of the largest contingents to the National Conference on Undergraduate Research. More than 350 students present the results of their scholarly activities at Union's own Steinmetz Symposium each year. The newest element in Union's academic program, called Converging Technologies (CT), is designed to address a major challenge facing our society—the discovery and application of scientific and technological advances that will shape the next century. This new interdisciplinary approach brings together students from engineering and liberal arts so that they graduate with a broad background that goes beyond that provided by the traditional major.

Grant Hall
Schenectady, NY 12308
Phone: 518-388-6112
Fax: 518-388-6986
Website: www.union.edu

Union grants the Bachelor of Arts degree in American studies, anthropology, art, classics, economics, English, history, modern languages, philosophy, political science, sociology, and women's studies. The Bachelor of Science is awarded in biochemistry, biology, chemistry, computer science, computer engineering, electrical engineering, geology, industrial economics, mathematics, mechanical engineering, physics, and psychology. Students may undertake one of the formal interdepartmental programs available in Africana studies, East Asian studies, environmental studies, Latin American and Caribbean studies, managerial economics, and Russia and East European studies. Union offers dual and student-designed majors, as well as the Leadership in Medicine program (eight-year BS, MS or MBA/MD joint program with Albany Medical College) and the Law and Public Policy program (six-year BA/JD with Albany Law School) and a five-year bachelor's/MBA program. Students interested in teaching can be certified to teach at the secondary level through Union's educational studies program.

The 200 full-time faculty members, 94 percent of whom hold the doctorate or terminal degree, work closely with students in order to ensure an environment centered on discussion and critical thinking. The student/faculty ratio is 11:1, and professors are readily available to answer questions or offer feedback. There are no teaching assistants. Faculty salaries are above the national average for colleges of comparable size. Students benefit from the small class sizes; 22 for the average introductory class, 14 for the average lab, and 15 for upper-class courses.

ADMISSIONS

Applications are assessed on the basis of four main elements. The first is the student's high school transcript, reflecting class rank and the difficulty of the course load. Second, students must submit recommendations from their high school teachers or counselors. Third, the College considers extracurricular activities and personal attributes. Finally, applicants must submit SAT I or ACT scores, or the results from three SAT II: Subject exams. If the student chooses to submit SAT II test scores, the Writing test must be one of the three. Successful applicants present a strong and varied curriculum covering English, a foreign language, mathematics, social studies, and science. Additional courses are encouraged, and honors and AP classes are seen as strong pluses on any application. Students may arrange an on-campus interview from May through January. Students desiring an alumni interview should request one by December 15.

CAMPUS LIFE

Union is located in the small upstate city of Schenectady, which is within 15 miles of Albany, the capital of New York. The Capital District area has a population of approximately 850,000, including 55,000 college and university students. The Union campus is three hours from New York City or Boston, and approximately four hours from Montreal. Nearby natural attractions include the Catskills, Adirondacks, Green Mountains, and the Massachusetts Berkshires. Students enjoy the gardens, natural woodland, and grassy areas that make up the 100-acre campus.

Union offers study abroad programs in more than two dozen countries and close to two-thirds of Union students choose to participate. Closer to home, students may cross-register for classes offered at any of the schools involved in the Hudson-Mohawk Association of Colleges and Universities, all located in the Capital District. The Association also enables Union students to enroll in the Reserve Officer Training Corps (ROTC) programs of the Army, Navy, and Air Force.

COST AND AID

The cost of tuition for 2002–2003 totaled $27,246. On average, room and board was an additional $6,738. An activities fee of $268 is charged to each student annually.

UNITED STATES AIR FORCE ACADEMY

GENERAL INFORMATION

The Air Force Academy was established in 1954 to train and motivate Air Force cadets pursuing careers in the military. The Academy emphasizes character building, military discipline, physical fitness, and academic excellence. An Academy education builds valuable leadership skills in all areas. Approximately 4,000 students attend the Academy, about 1,200 of whom are entering students (fourth-class). The makeup of the Student Body reflects that of the corps of Air Force officers: approximately 15 percent women and 18 percent minority. Cadets arrive from all 50 states and a number of other countries. They share a common bond: the aspiration to become military officers. All cadets are required to live on campus and wear uniforms.

The Academy is accredited by the North Central Association of Colleges and Schools. Engineering programs are approved by the Engineering Accreditation Commission of the Accreditation Board for Engineering and Technology. Computer courses are approved by the Computing Sciences Accreditation Board. The Commission on Professional Training of the American Chemical Society establishes the requirements made of biochemistry and chemistry majors.

Cadets are required to engage in club, intramural, intercollegiate athletics each semester. Options for intramural activity include basketball, cross-country, flag football, flickerball, racquetball, rugby, soccer, softball, team handball, tennis, ultimate Frisbee, volleyball, wallyball, water polo, and men's boxing. The Academy fields intercollegiate teams in Division I of the NCAA; its teams compete both regionally and nationally. The men compete in baseball, basketball, boxing, cross-country, fencing, football, golf, gymnastics, ice hockey, lacrosse, rifle, soccer, swimming, tennis, track, water polo, and wrestling teams. Women compete in basketball, cross-country, fencing, gymnastics, rifle, soccer, swimming, tennis, track, and volleyball. More than 80 extracurricular activities are available to cadets; they include competitive and recreational clubs, hobby clubs, mission support, professional organizations, and sports groups.

Qualified graduates of the Academy may commence flight training after graduating. About three-quarters of all cadets undertake graduate study within 10 years of completing their Academy studies. Every year, many graduates of the Academy are given graduate fellowships and scholarships; these awards include the Guggenheim, Marshall, National Collegiate Athletic Association, National Science Foundation, and Rhodes Scholar awards.

STUDENT BODY

Cadets learn important leadership skills through their duties in the Cadet Wing, an organization though which upper-class cadets take responsibility for enforcing the honor system and honor education, leading underclass cadets in military drills, and enforcing the human relations, ethics, and character development programs of the Academy. First-class cadets (fourth-year students) supervise the operations of the Cadet Wing; they hold the rank of cadet officer and command its groups, squadrons, flights, and elements.

ACADEMICS

The school year for entering students begins in late June or early July; incoming cadets commence their tenure at the Academy with a rigorous six-week summer training program designed to test their physical and mental abilities. This training is conducted by upper-class cadets; commissioned officers serve as advisors. Cadets who successfully complete this program are admitted as fourth-class cadets in the Cadet Wing. Academic courses begin in early August and run through May. Cadets in their first two years focus on core curriculum courses in engineering, humanities, science, and the social sciences. Cadets pursue a specialized academic major during their final two years. Core courses are designed to prepare cadets for a wide range of duties as Air Force officers. They include courses in academic subjects; military training and leadership; and athletics and physical education. All cadets must also complete the requirements of an academic major (30 are available at the Academy). Other graduation requirements include: demonstration of ability to serve and to lead; demonstration of character befitting a member of a professional military; maintenance of a minimum GPA of 2.0, with a minimum 2.0 GPA in core courses; and completion of at least 145 credit hours. Cadets have numerous options in selecting elective courses. All cadets must enter as freshmen. Cadets who have previously completed comparable core course work at other institutions may earn transfer credit or validation credit for their work. Those receiving transfer credit may take other courses at the Academy in place of their core courses. Advanced study classes are open to cadets who meet academic prerequisites, including a minimum grade point average. Cadets learn all operational procedures of the Air Force through the Academy's aviation program. Optional courses are available in basic flying, navigation, parachuting, and soaring. Students who complete these courses may earn pilot or glider certificates issued by the Federal Aviation Administration. Once they have graduated from the Academy, select cadets may enter Air Education and Training Command flight programs to train as pilots or navigators. Cadets may pursue summer studies in aviation and military training; these programs prepare students for the responsibilities of an Air Force officer. A number of optional assignments are available, both at the Air Force Academy and at other military installations.

Graduates receive a Bachelor of Science degree and are commissioned as second lieutenants in the Air Force. Students may pursue the BS in 30 majors: aeronautical engineering; astronautical engineering; basic sciences; behavioral sciences; biology; chemistry; civil engineering; computer engineering; computer science; economics; electrical engineering; engineering; engineering mechanics; English; environmental engineering; foreign area studies; geography; history; humanities; legal studies; management; mathematical sciences; mechanical engineering; meteorology; military doctrine, operations, and strategy; operations research; physics; political science; social sciences; and space operations. Cadets may minor in computer science, foreign languages, mathematics, military operations and strategy, and philosophy.

The faculty at the Academy comprises Air Force officers and civilians. Some officers representing other branches of the United States Armed Forces, as well as some officers from allied countries and a number of civilian visiting professors, augment the Academy's teaching staff. All classes are taught by full professors, not by graduate students. Many faculty members have earned the terminal degree in their field; all others have at least a master's degree. Instructors have earned degrees from many outstanding secondary and graduate educational institutions across the country and around the world. The faculty engages in the lives of cadets, sponsoring, refereeing, and coaching extracurricular athletic activities; sponsoring student groups and squadrons and attending their special events; and counseling students on academic, career, and personal matters.

HQ USAFA/RRS, 2304 Cadet Drive, Suite 200
USAF Academy, CO, 80840-5025
Phone: 719-333-2520
Fax: 719-333-3012
Website: www.usafa.edu

ADMISSIONS

Every year, young U.S. citizens—both men and women—receive appointment to the Academy. They arrive from all of the nation's states and territories. A limited number of foreign nationals are also admitted. Applicants must be between the ages of 17 and 22 as of July 1 of their projected year of admission. Applicants must be unmarried and without dependents. They must be principled individuals; they must also be physically fit. An official nomination is a required part of any application to the Academy. Most nominations come from members of Congress and are submitted for students living in their districts and states. Representatives and senators nominate high school juniors who have demonstrated academic excellence, possess leadership qualities (as demonstrated by academic and extracurricular record), are physically fit, have the respect of their peers and associates, and desire a career in the military. It is not necessary for applicants to know their congressional representatives personally in order to receive their nomination. Other categories than congressional exist; interested applicants should consult their guidance counselor or local Air Force Admissions Liaison Officer to learn more about other available nomination categories. Students wishing to enter the Academy upon completion of high school should submit applications as soon after January 31 of their junior year as possible. Applicants who receive a nomination must pass a physical fitness exam and a medical exam; they must also submit standardized test scores (SAT I or ACT). Applicants should carefully read the instructions that accompany the application package. These instructions clearly detail the proper procedure for submitting an application. The application package includes, among other materials, sample letters to members of Congress, senators, and the President requesting nomination to the Academy. Applicants seeking help with application requirements should contact an Air Force Admissions Liaison Officer; there is at least one in every state. See the Academy catalog for a list of Liaison Officer Directors and their locations. Applications are available to high school juniors; to request an application, write to:

HQ USAFA/RRS
2304 Cadet Drive
Suite 200
USAF Academy, CO, 80840
Telephone: 719-333-2520
Website: www.usafa.edu/rr/

CAMPUS LIFE

Located among the foothills of the Rocky Mountains' Rampart Range, the Academy is truly surrounded by natural beauty. The campus sits upon a 7,000-foot mesa; the campus and its immediate area are among the state's most popular tourist attractions. Contemporary architecture is featured on campus; the space-age Cadet Chapel, with its seventeen 150-foot aluminum spires, set the tone for the entire cadet area. This modern setting aptly reflects the campus's mission: to train tomorrow's Air Force leaders and officers. The campus is located just north of Colorado Springs, a city of nearly 360,000; the city sits at the foot of Pikes Peak (alt. 14,100 feet). The state capital, Denver, is just 55 miles to the north; this metropolis of more than 2 million offers a plethora of cultural, educational, and recreational opportunities. Cadets also enjoy horseback riding, hunting, skiing, whitewater rafting, and many other outdoor activities facilitated by the nearby mountains and its resorts.

Cadets chosen to participate in exchange programs may visit the Military Academy, Naval Academy, Coast Guard Academy, or any of 15 Air Force academies around the world. International programs are usually one to two weeks in duration; exchange programs with other U.S. service academies generally run for a single semester, as do exchange programs with Air Force academies in Germany and France.

COST AND AID

The government of the United States bears the entire cost of a United States Air Force Academy education. There are no charges for tuition, room, board, or medical and dental care. Academy cadets earn a monthly salary, with which they are expected to purchase clothing, supplies, and personal items. Cadets who manage their money carefully will meet all obligations and have a small sum left over for personal expenses.

UNITED STATES MILITARY ACADEMY

THE ACADEMY AT A GLANCE

As the nation's oldest service academy, the United States Military Academy offers young men and women a first-rate and highly respected college education program. West Point offers cadets a variety of exciting career opportunities while serving as commissioned officers in the U.S. Army.

LOCATION AND ENVIRONMENT

West Point is located approximately 50 miles north of New York City in the picturesque Hudson Valley region. Flanked by the Hudson River and the Storm King Mountain, the U.S. Military Academy maintains some of the finest educational and military training facilities in the nation on its 16,000 acres. That includes nearby Camp Buckner, the sight of summer military training for first- and second-year cadets.

MAJORS AND DEGREES OFFERED

Every West Point graduate earns a Bachelor of Science degree and a commission as a second lieutenant in the U.S. Army. West Point graduates serve at least five years of active duty as commissioned officers. The Military Academy curriculum complements the core program by providing the opportunity for in-depth study through the elective program. There are 21 optional majors and 24 fields of study available for cadets. These fields and majors cover virtually all the liberal arts, science, and engineering disciplines one would expect to find in a high-quality, selective college or university of comparable size. At the Military Academy cadets may enter most fields of study or majors without restriction. No special grade point averages are established for entry, but there may be a limitation as to the number of cadets in a particular major or field of study. Over 75 percent of the Corp of Cadets choose to major in a specialized subject. Those include the American legal system, chemistry and life science, civil engineering, computer science, electrical engineering, computer engineering, electronic systems engineering, engineering management, engineering physics, environmental engineering, geography and environmental science, information systems engineering, mathematical sciences, mechanical engineering, operations research, systems engineering, art, philosophy and literature, behavioral science, economics, foreign languages, general management, history, and political science.

ACADEMIC PROGRAM

A broad background in the arts and sciences is the focal point of the academic program at the United States Military Academy. The program also prepares cadets for future graduate study. The curriculum develops essential character, competence, and intellectual abilities in an officer. There are 31 core courses that provide the essential broad base of knowledge required for success as a commissioned officer in addition to supporting a subsequent choice of an academic concentration. Cadets who choose to major must take 10–13 electives in the area of concentration and complete a senior thesis or design project.

West Point academic classes are small, averaging 12 to 18 cadets. Consequently, cadets receive individual attention, and may request tutorial sessions if needed. Cadets with exceptional ability also may take advanced and honors courses.

West Point's Centers of Excellence serve to enhance the quality of the Academic program. They coordinate professional expertise and concentrate technical resources in order to enrich cadet education, enhance cadet academic performance, improve faculty teaching, promote faculty and cadet research, and provide outreach and support to the Army.

Cadets study military science and participate in class instruction on the principles of small-unit tactics and leadership during a two-week intersession period between the first and second semesters. Field training is concentrated on during the summer as each cadet gains opportunities to learn and practice the military skills and principles that are learned in the classroom.

OFF-CAMPUS OPPORTUNITIES

All cadets take Christmas, spring, and summer leave, along with the four-day Thanksgiving break. When academics begin, first classmen or seniors get twice as many weekend leaves as second classmen or juniors. A plebe or freshman will have only a few weekend passes. Plebes may also leave West Point for extracurricular or cultural trips and athletic competition.

FACILITIES AND EQUIPMENT

Cadets and faculty at West Point enjoy the benefits of a first-class information technology environment. With a personal computer at every desk, and everyone connected both to a large array of powerful academic computing services at West Point and with unlimited access to the Internet, West Point has carefully crafted an electronic environment in which virtually every course offered has integrated computer use. This developmental "computer thread" fosters cadet use of their personal computer in the place where most learning occurs: in the barracks room.

Computer-aided math, design, and simulation, dynamic news sources, worldwide electronic mail, spreadsheets, statistical analysis, database access, library bibliographic research, and electronic bulletin boards, document preparation and printing all contribute to an academic environment rich with information resources and electronic media tools. Cadets also register for classes, get grades and counseling reports, and receive and send homework assignments using the USMA network.

TUITION, ROOM AND BOARD, AND FEES

The cost of a four-year education at West Point, including tuition, room, board, medical and dental expenses, is paid by the U.S. government. As members of the Army, cadets also receive an annual salary of approximately $7,200. This helps to pay for uniforms, books, a personal computer, supplies, and incidental living expenses. An initial deposit of $2,400 is required to cover uniform costs and initial expenses during the first year.

FINANCIAL AID

There are no financial aid programs at West Point because the U.S. government pays most expenses. Scholarship awards may offset the cost of the required initial deposit.

FULL- AND PART-TIME FACULTY

About 75 percent of the West Point faculty are military personnel who have completed graduate work at the most respected universities in the nation. There are senior military personnel who serve as professors and department heads. There are also civilian professors and associate professors. All faculty members have their master's degrees and more than 30 percent have doctoral qualifications.

STUDENT ORGANIZATIONS AND ACTIVITIES

Cadets are busy, but there is still time for fun and relaxation. There is an intercollegiate athletic program with 25 sports and numerous competitive club teams such as rugby, crew, and sailing. There is an active intramural sports program with cadet companies competing against other cadet companies year round. The Cadet Activities Office coordinates more than 100 extracurricular activities. Among those are the Cadet Fine Arts Forum, the Cadet Glee Club, and the Cadet Drill Team. A cadet can be a disk jockey at the FM radio station and also learn to fly. There are dances and other social functions that bring students from neighboring colleges to West Point.

ADMISSIONS PROCESSES AND REQUIREMENTS

Eligibility Requirements: You must be a citizen of the United States, at least 17 and not yet 23 on July 1 of the year you seek admission. You must not be married, pregnant, nor have a legal obligation to support a dependent. If you are a naturalized citizen you must provide documentation.

Other Qualifications Necessary for Admission: You must receive a nomination from an authorized source to be considered for an appointment to West Point. You will be evaluated in the areas of academics, leadership potential, and physical aptitude. You must also meet medical qualification standards and Army appearance standards regarding tattoos and brands. In academics your complete scholastic transcript and extracurricular record, the results of your ACT or SAT examinations, your high school rank in class, and the recommendations of your faculty are used to determine academic qualification.

How to become competitive for admission:

- English: 4 years with a strong emphasis on composition, grammar, literature, and speech.

600 Thayer Road, West Point, NY 10096-1797
Telephone: 914-938-4041 • Fax: 914-938-3021
Email: 8dad@exmail.usma.army.mil • World Wide Web: www.usma.edu

CEEB Code: 2924 • ACT Code: 2976

- Mathematics: 4 years of college preparatory mathematics, to include algebra, geometry, intermediate algebra, and trigonometry as a minimum; if your school includes a course in pre-calculus and calculus those courses will be beneficial.
- Foreign Language: 2 years of a foreign language.
- Science: 2 years of a laboratory science such as chemistry and physics.
- History: 1 year of U.S. history. Courses in geography, government, and economics also will be helpful.
- Keyboarding: a basic computer course will also be beneficial.

Leadership potential is evaluated on your participation in athletics, clubs, and, other extracurricular activities as well as community, church, and scouting activities. Leadership success in those activities is demonstrated by serving as a team captain on an athletic team or a student council officer in student government. In scouting an Eagle Scout or Gold Award is viewed highly.

Physical development is measured by taking a physical aptitude examination. This examination includes five events: pull-ups (for men) or flexed arm hang (for women); standing broad jump; basketball throw from kneeling position; 300-yard shuttle run; and a two-minute span of push-ups.

To prepare for the Physical Aptitude Examination and for the physical demands that will be placed upon you as a cadet, you should reach the level of physical conditioning required for participation in a strenuous team sport. Vigorous conditioning exercises, cross-country running, and swimming are recommended. Emphasis should be placed on a variety of strenuous activities rather than on one sport.

Steps toward gaining admission:

1. You should first determine whether or not you meet all of the basic requirements. You should then begin the application process by contacting the Admissions Office in the spring of your junior year of high school. To do so write to the Director of Admissions, U.S. Military Academy, 606 Thayer Road, West Point, NY 10996-1797. You can visit the West Point website at www.usma.edu/admissions or send an email to admissions@www.usma.edu. You can also call the Admissions Office at 845-938-4041 if you have additional questions. Juniors and seniors will be sent a Prospectus and a Candidate Questionnaire. When you fill out the questionnaire and return it to the Admissions Office an admissions file will be opened.
2. Apply for a nomination. A nomination is the legal authority for the U.S. Military Academy to consider a candidate for admission. You should apply for nominations at the same time you open your applicant file at West Point. All candidates are eligible to apply for nominations from your two United States Senators, your local member of Congress and the Vice President. Other candidates may be eligible for a service-connected nomination. The Prospectus explains the requirements for those nominations.
3. Open an Admissions file at West Point by filling out the Candidate Questionnaire and returning it to us. Competitive candidates will also receive an additional packet of forms to fill out in order to complete their admissions files.
4. Follow up the nomination process. Many members of Congress form committees to evaluate candidates who request nominations. Make sure you provide all of the information that is required for those committees.
5. Complete all admissions testing including:
   - ACT or SAT

   These examinations are given at various times throughout the academic year. Check with your guidance counselor for the testing dates. Follow the instructions for forwarding the results of those tests to the Admissions Office and members of Congress. The Admissions Office accepts the highest score on the SAT I or the ACT.
   - Qualifying Medical Examination

   If you are a competitive candidate, you will receive instructions for taking the qualifying medical examination directly from the Department of Defense Medical Examination Review Board (DODMERB), 8034 Edgerton Drive, Suite 132, U.S.A.F. Academy, CO 80840-2200. You may be scheduled at an Army, Air Force, Naval, or civilian facility near your home. Medical test results will be forwarded to you. Questions on your medical status should be directed to DODMERB at 719-333-3562.
   - Physical Aptitude Examination

   Have a coach or physical education instructor administer the Physical Aptitude Examination and forward the score sheet to the Admissions Office in the envelope provided.
6. Monitor the evaluation and the status of your application. West Point uses a rolling admissions process so it is advantageous to complete your admissions file early. If West Point is your first choice among your college options, then consider applying for the Early Action Plan. Under provisions of the Early Action Plan applicants will be notified of their admission status by the second Monday in January. To be considered under the Early Action Plan you must notify West Point in writing by the third Monday in October and have a completed file ready for evaluation by the first Monday in December. Applicants under this plan need not have a nomination or the results from the medical examination in order to apply.
7. Await application status. A formal offer of admission is possible as early as November for fully qualified candidates who have completed all admissions requirements and receive a nomination. Admissions decisions are made on a rolling basis with the majority of offers of admission announced by mid-April. Files not completed by the third Monday in March will be closed from further consideration.
8. Visit West Point. Candidate Orientation visits are offered Monday through Friday during the academic year (September 1–December 1 and January 25–April 30). Members of the Corps of Cadets volunteer to escort each candidate individually. The orientation includes class attendance, a visit to the barracks, lunch in the Cadet Mess and admissions briefing. A West Point visit offers an invaluable insight into cadet life and can assist in the college decision-making process. To arrange for a visit call 845-938-5760. Two weeks notice is required for a visit to be scheduled.
9. Prepare for entrance to West Point. Candidates should prepare for the academic, physical, and leadership demands facing them at West Point. If you have met the academic qualifications for admission, you will be ready for the challenges of the West Point curriculum. Candidates are urged to become physically conditioned before entering the Military Academy. Vigorous conditioning exercises, swimming, and cross-country running are recommended.
10. The Admissions Office enjoys the assistance nationwide of liaison officers who provide service to candidates. They include graduates of West Point both in and out of the Active Army and U.S. Army Reserve Officers who have been trained at West Point for this specific program. These volunteers are available to assist candidates in the admissions process and in answering questions about specific West Point programs.

UNIVERSITY OF ARKANSAS—FAYETTEVILLE

GENERAL INFORMATION

Founded in 1871, the University of Arkansas, located in Fayetteville, is both the major land-grant university for Arkansas and the state university. It has a proud legacy of internationally significant scientific and intellectual achievements in many academic fields. It also enjoys a reputation of being a great teaching university, producing 120,567 graduates over its 132-year history who have provided leadership in all walks of life. In addition, the University creatively harnesses its intellectual capital to reach out to Arkansans and others through myriad outreach and public service programs, making life better for everyone. The year 2002 marked a great inflection point in the University's history. Thanks to the generosity of the Walton Family Charitable Support Foundation, the University of Arkansas received a $300 million gift—the largest in the history of American public higher education. $200 million is being used to establish and endow what is poised to become the nation's finest undergraduate public honors college. The remaining $100 million is being used to endow the University of Arkansas Graduate School. These two initiatives will fuel a rapid rise in academic quality and reputation, which in turn will allow the university to fulfill its potential for serving as a powerful engine of economic development and cultural change. The University of Arkansas is small among major research institutions, with 16,035 students (12,929 undergraduates), but includes a diverse student population, with 931 international students representing 102 countries. The University offers more than 208 degree programs in a comprehensive range of fields.

STUDENT BODY

The University offers a vibrant campus life for its mainly full-time, residential undergraduate student population. University residence halls accommodate approximately 3,200 students, and the rest live in and about the city of Fayetteville. Students have 230 registered student organizations at their disposal, including special interest organizations, religious organizations, international and cultural organizations, honorary and professional service organizations, student government, and more. Greek life is robust as well: In 2001–2002, 14 percent of male and 19 percent of female undergraduates belonged to the 15 fraternities and 12 sororities on campus.

Culturally and intellectually, the academic semesters overflow with faculty and student musical performances, theatre productions, art exhibits, concerts, poetry readings and visiting speakers—both on campus and at the adjacent Walton Arts Center. In fall 2002, for example, the University Speakers series brought together for the first time the former prime minister of Pakistan, Benizir Bhutto, and the former prime minister of Israel, Erud Barak, for a discussion on the United States and world affairs. The Arkansas Union Society stirs lively student debate on topical issues several times a semester.

The Division of Student Affairs enhances the University of Arkansas experience by helping students to become intellectually engaged, more self-aware, and strongly bonded to the institution, particularly through an extensive First-Year Experience Program for new students. Through its various departments—General Student Services, the Arkansas Union, University Health Services, Career Services, University Housing, and Special Projects and Services—Student Affairs provides leadership in the development of programs and services that supplement the classroom experience, shape student leadership skills and enrich the quality of campus life.

The Associated Student Government represents the student constituents in the University decision-making process. ASG seeks to provide needed services for the students and delegates funding for registered student organizations. The Graduate Student Association performs a similar function for students engaged in advanced studies.

ACADEMICS

The U of A operates on a traditional two-semester academic year schedule, with two regular summer sessions and some special concurrent summer sessions. Requirements for graduation include a minimum University-wide core along with core requirements in each college. The majority of undergraduate degree offerings follow a four-year plan requiring from 124 to 136 course hours for graduation; there are some exceptions to this requirement, such as the five-year, design-oriented architecture program, which requires 163 hours. A course in English as a second language is offered in five 9-week sessions throughout the year. Classes focus on all language skills: grammar, reading, writing, and listening/speaking. The newly endowed Honors College provides opportunities for students to pursue honors programs in any college or department. Requirements vary among programs and schools, but the latest information is available at http://honorscollege.uark.edu.

Degree programs are offered in the following fields (arranged by college or school):

Dale Bumpers College of Agricultural, Food and Life Sciences: agricultural business; agricultural and extension education; agricultural economics and agribusiness; animal science; biological and agricultural engineering; crop, soil, and environmental science; food, human nutrition, and hospitality; entomology; food science; horticulture; human development, family sciences, and rural sociology; human environmental sciences; plant pathology; poultry science; turf and landscape horticulture.

School of Architecture: architecture, landscape architecture, architectural studies.

J. William Fulbright College of Arts and Sciences: African American studies (minor), American studies, anthropology, art, art history (concentration), Asian studies (concentration), biological sciences, chemistry and biochemistry, classical studies, communication, computer science, drama, economics, English, European studies, French, gender studies (minor), geosciences, German, history, international relations, journalism, Latin American studies, mathematical sciences, music, philosophy, physics, political science, psychology, religious studies (minor), Russian and Soviet studies, school of social work, sociology and criminal justice, Spanish, statistics (minor).

Sam M. Walton College of Business: accounting, economics, enterprise computing, finance, industrial marketing, information systems, information systems with area emphasis, marketing management, management, quantitative analysis, retail marketing, transportation and logistics, graduate school of business.

College of Education and Health Professions: curriculum and instruction; educational leadership, counseling, and foundations; health science, kinesiology, recreation and dance; rehabilitation, human resources, and communication disorders; Eleanor Mann School of Nursing.

College of Engineering: biological and agricultural engineering, chemical engineering, civil engineering, computer engineering, electrical engineering, industrial engineering, mechanical engineering.

The Honors College: All academic majors (students are enrolled concurrently in the "home" college or school of their academic major).

School of Law: JD degree program, LLM degree program.

The Graduate School: 85 master's degree programs, 34 doctoral degree programs.

The University of Arkansas has 849 faculty members, 94 percent of which are full-time. 92 percent of the faculty hold a doctorate or other terminal degree in their field. The faculty to student ratio is 16 to 1, and more than 70 percent of undergraduate classes have 29 or fewer students.

200 Silas Hunt Hall
Fayetteville, AR 72701
Phone: 479-575-5346
Fax: 479-575-7515
Website: www.uark.edu

ADMISSIONS

Entering freshmen are advised to prepare for admission to the U of A while in high school by taking 4 years of English, 3 years each of math, social studies, and natural sciences, as well as 3 academic electives. A minimum of a 3.0 high school GPA and an ACT composite score of 20 (or 930 on the SAT) is required for automatic admission, but other students may be admitted after an individual review. The ACT code for the U of A is 0144, and the SAT I code is 6866. Transfer students need a cumulative GPA of at least 2.0 on all college courses taken, and must be in good academic standing when applying for admission. We calculate a GPA on all course work including developmental courses. If you have completed fewer than 24 transferable hours, you will need to meet all requirements for freshman admission in addition to those for transfer students.

International students must have above-average secondary school records, and those who are not native speakers of English must submit a minimum TOEFL score of 550 (paper) or 213 (computer), or an IELTS score of 6.5. The University of Arkansas offers qualified applicants conditional admission to the Spring International Language Center, with academic admission granted upon reaching a satisfactory English language level. International students must submit an application for admission with a $50 application fee. A financial statement, a TOEFL score, and official secondary and post-secondary academic recorded are also required. For the fall term, the application deadline is May 31; the summer term deadline is March 1; and the spring term deadline is October 1. International students should visit the international admissions website at http://international.uark.edu and can contact us at uaiao@uark.edu or (+1) 479-575-6246.

To enroll in the University, students must submit a completed Application for Undergraduate Admission and an application fee of $30. An online admission form can be found at the University's website listed below. The application deadline for the fall semester is August 15; the spring deadline is January 1. To be considered for scholarships, applications must be received by February 15. The student must also request that official transcripts be mailed to the Office of Admissions. A preliminary admission is provided for those high school seniors who have a transcript of six or seven semesters, but a final transcript is needed to certify high school graduation. Official ACT or SAT scores no more than 4 years old must be submitted by all entering freshmen and transfer students with fewer than 24 transferable hours. For further information, students should contact:

Office of Admissions
200 Silas H. Hunt Hall
University of Arkansas
Fayetteville, AR 72701
Telephone: 800-377-UOFA (toll free)
Fax: 479-575-7515
E-mail: uofa@uark.edu
Website: www.uark.edu/application

CAMPUS LIFE

The University of Arkansas is located in Fayetteville, a city of nearly 60,000 residents. Fayetteville is at the southern tip of a metroplex that runs northward for 25 miles along I-540 through Washington and Benton counties in Northwest Arkansas and ends in Bella Vista, an upscale retirement community near the state's northern border. The Northwest Arkansas metroplex, from Fayetteville northward, also includes Springdale (home of Tyson Foods, the world's largest meat producer), Lowell (home of J. B. Hunt Trucking), Rogers and Bentonville (home of Wal-Mart Stores Inc., the world's largest corporation). The two Northwest Arkansas counties (Washington and Benton) that contain this metroplex are growing rapidly, due to a booming regional economy. The Fayetteville-Springdale-Rogers metropolitan area is ranked by the U.S. Census Bureau as being the sixth fastest-growing metro area in the nation. From 1990 to 2000, the metropolitan area grew 47.5 percent, from 210,908 to 311,121. In 2002, Northwest Arkansas was ranked 23rd among the top 269 metro areas considered as the Best Places for Business and Career, according to *Forbes* magazine and the Milken Institute. The rankings were based on job growth, salary growth, plus high-tech growth.

Situated on the Ozark Mountain Plateau, Northwest Arkansas offers friendly people, beautiful scenery, a moderate climate, excellent school districts, and a robust economy in which the unemployment rate runs well below national averages. Fayetteville itself presents the vibrant cultural life that would be expected in any major university town. Since the 1960s, the area has been a haven for writers, artists, poets and musicians. In 2002, *Business Week* magazine ranked Fayetteville as one of the "Dazzling Dozen" small cities in the United States, on the basis of low unemployment and the ability to create jobs during the past year. In 2001, Fayetteville was one of only 23 locales and the only Arkansas location to be included in the book The Most Beautiful Villages and Towns of the South (New York: Thames and Hudson). In 2000, The Searchers, a St. Louis-based data research company, ranked Fayetteville as one of the 157 best places to retire in the United States.

The University of Arkansas campus proper comprises 130 buildings on 345 acres. It rests on a former hilltop farm that overlooks the Ozark Mountains to the south; at the time of the University's founding, the site was described as "second to none in the state of Arkansas." Old Main, the University's signature building designed in Second Empire architectural style, has come to symbolize higher education in Arkansas. Old Main is one of 11 campus buildings that have been placed on the National Register of Historic Places. The campus also is graced by the unique, much-loved tradition of Senior Walk. Since the University's founding, the names of all 120,567 graduates have been etched into more than five miles of campus sidewalks, their names arranged by year of graduation.

The University of Arkansas' study abroad office works hard to create the possibility for students to study in virtually any country around the world. Students in any major are eligible to go abroad and can start as early as the summer after their freshman year. It is not even necessary to know a foreign language, as students can study in English speaking countries or on programs where classes are taught in English in other countries. Studying abroad does not have to slow down progress toward a degree, and the study abroad office advises students to ensure that they receive both major and elective credit on their programs. Some programs run in the summer, while others run for a semester or even an entire year. The University of Arkansas allows most scholarships to apply to study abroad programs and federal financial aid (including Pell grants and Stafford loans) can be applied. There are numerous additional scholarships available for study abroad. The recent Walton gift included $4 million endowing international study for undergraduates. Students can study abroad more than once, with several students undertaking multiple trips during the course of their degrees.

COST AND AID

The University of Arkansas is among the most affordable of major research universities. Tuition and fees for 2002–2003 average $4,456 for Arkansas residents, and $10,828 for out-of-state residents. Room and board rates average $4,810 annually. For undergraduate students, the resident tuition rate is $141 per credit hour and nonresident tuition is $353 per credit hour. For graduate students, the resident tuition rate is $257 per credit hour and the nonresident tuition is $534 per credit hour.

UNIVERSITY OF DALLAS

THE UNIVERSITY AT A GLANCE

The University of Dallas is a private, independent, Catholic university dedicated to the study of the liberal arts.

The 750-acre campus houses the Constantin College for Liberal Arts, the Braniff Graduate School, and the Graduate School of Management.

Since its beginning in 1956, UD's undergraduate program has emphasized the great ideas, deeds, and works of Western civilization through its core curriculum. This is central to all 22 majors.

Undergraduate students at UD benefit from classes taught only by faculty members; a sophomore semester on UD's campus in Rome, Italy; academic programs relevant to the real world; and career-oriented electives.

A plethora of student organizations offer lecture and film series, art exhibitions, plays and musical events, Charity Week, intramural sports, campus ministry, and more. The University competes intercollegiately in NCAA Division III.

UD is one of only eight universities in Texas and among only 13 Catholic universities to earn a Phi Beta Kappa chapter. We are one of the youngest universities to earn this honor.

College guides noting UD's excellence include Peterson's *Top Science Colleges*, National Review College Guide's *America's Top 50 Liberal Arts Colleges*, *Fiske Guide to Colleges*, John Templeton Foundation's *Honor Roll for Character Building Colleges* and *Money* magazine's *Best Buy College Guide*.

The Braniff Graduate School offers liberal arts graduate degrees. The liberal arts curriculum includes American studies, art, English, humanities, literature, philosophy, politics, religious studies, and theology. It offers degrees through the PhD. The Graduate School of Management offers the MBA and Master's of Management degrees, and is one of the largest programs in the Southwest.

UD is accredited by the Southern Association of Colleges and Schools, and the American Academy for Liberal Education.

LOCATION AND ENVIRONMENT

UD is located in Irving, Texas, a city of 150,000 in the middle of the Dallas/Fort Worth metroplex.

MAJORS AND DEGREES OFFERED

The Constantin College offers programs leading to a Bachelor of Arts and Bachelor of Science. Majors include: art (studio and art history), biochemistry, biology, chemistry, computer science, economics, classics (Latin and Greek), drama, education, English, history, mathematics, modern languages (French, German, and Spanish), philosophy, philosophy and letters, physics, politics, psychology, and theology. Uniquely qualified students may have the opportunity to shape an interdisciplinary curriculum through the Constantin Scholars Program.

The Braniff Graduate School's Liberal Arts Division program supports the doctoral program in the Institute of Philosophic Studies, the Master of Fine Arts, Master of Art, and the Master's program in art, American studies, English, humanities, philosophy, politics, and theology. The School's Graduate School of Management offers the Master of Business Administration and Master of Management.

ACADEMIC PROGRAMS

The core curriculum is the center of undergraduate education at UD. The organization and content of the core are determined by the premise that these goals can best be achieved through a curriculum founded on the Western heritage of liberal education. Within this heritage, the Christian intellectual tradition is an essential element, and the American experience merits special consideration.

The curriculum includes: English, 12 credits; philosophy, 12 credits; mathematics and fine arts, 9 credits; science, 6–8 credits; classics and modern language 3–14 credits; American civilization, 6 credits; Western civilization, 6 credits, politics, 3 credits; economics, 3 credits; and theology, 6 credits.

Study Abroad: In the fall of 1970, the University instituted The Rome Program. All sophomores are encouraged to spend one semester on UD's Rome campus. Approximately 80 percent of UD graduates participate in the program. The Rome curriculum is a coherent and integral part of UD's undergraduate education, regardless of major. Study abroad courses are taught by UD faculty. The courses are selected from the core curriculum requirements, which concern the development of Western civilization and are most appropriate to the Rome semester experience. UD students also may elect to spend a summer or semester abroad studying Spanish in Latin America, Mexico, or Spain. Approximately 30–40 students participate each year. The program is sponsored by the Modern Languages and Literatures Department.

Internships: The University works with interested students, usually sophomores and juniors, to secure internships at the many Fortune 500 company headquarters and other leading businesses throughout the Dallas/Fort Worth metroplex.

Dallas Year Program: Designed to educate new students about the Dallas/Fort Worth metroplex, the program fosters out-of-classroom relationships between the faculty, staff, and students while exploring the cultural offerings of the community.

Honors: Phi Beta Kappa (liberal arts), Kappa Delta Pi (education), Omicron Delta Epsilon (economics), Phi Alpha Theta Kappa Rho (history), and Sigma Pi Sigma (physics).

TUITION, ROOM AND BOARD AND FEES

Application fee: $40

General deposit: $100

Undergraduate tuition: $7,464 per semester

Undergraduate part-time tuition: $625 per credit hour

Room and board per semester:

The University offers eight residence halls on the main campus and one on the Rome campus, which can house up to 766 students. Dorms are single-sex or coed by floor. UD also offers one- and two-bedroom apartments for upper-division and graduate students.

Charges for the basic categories of dormitory rooms and apartment housing are listed below. The telephone service fee is included in room rates. Food service is required for dormitory students and is also available for apartment residents and other nondormitory students upon request.

Meal plan only: 14-meal plan $1,326; 19-meal plan $1,399

Single in double room: 14-meal plan $3,391; 19-meal plan $3,464

Single in single room: 14-meal plan $3,244; 19-meal plan $3,317

Double room: 14-meal plan $2,708; 19-meal plan $2,781

Triple/quad room: 14-meal plan $2,676; 19-meal plan $2,749

Housing deposit: $100 refundable, one-time charge for all campus residents

University apartment housing: one bedroom (two students) to two bedroom (four students) $1,658 to $1,306.

Anslem Hall: single apartment (one student) to double apartment (two students) $2,427 to $2,038.

1845 East Northgate Drive
Irving, TX 75062
Phone: 972-721-5266
Fax: 972-721-5017
Website: www.udallas.edu

FINANCIAL AID

The University administers many "need-blind" scholarship programs for entering students who have been fully admitted to the University. Scholarships are offered through the primary, departmental, National Merit, and Phi Theta Kappa programs. First-time freshman applicants who wish to be considered for merit-based scholarships must submit an application by the December 1 priority consideration deadline, or by the January 15 regular scholarship deadline. Detailed information about requirements and deadlines is available from the Office of Admission and Financial Aid 972-721-5266 or 800-628-6999.

FULL- AND PART-TIME FACULTY

Full-time faculty: 118

Part-time faculty: 114

Only faculty teach classes.

Ninety-seven percent of full-time faculty hold terminal degree in their field.

STUDENT ORGANIZATION AND ACTIVITIES

Sports

- **Divisions:** NCAA Division III and American Southwest Conference
- **Intercollegiate:** Men and women: basketball, cross-country running, golf, soccer, and tennis. Men: baseball. Women: volleyball.
- **Intramural:** Men and women: badminton, basketball, football, sailing, soccer, softball, tennis, and volleyball. Men: rugby.

STUDENT ORGANIZATIONS

Most popular student organization events: Charity Week, Oktoberfest, Christmas Progressive dinner, Spring Musical, fall and spring drama productions, Spring Formal, Family Weekend, International Day, Dinner & Discourse, Senior Art Openings, Constitution Day Dinner, Cotillion, Mallapalooza, and Intramural Finals.

Most active student organizations: Student Government and its Program Board, Student Foundation, and Crusaders for Life.

Student organizations: African American Culture Committee, American Chemical Society/Student Affiliates, Association of Texas Professional Educators, Best Buddies, Chinese Student Association, Classics Club, College Democrats, College Republicans, The Crusader (annual yearbook), Crusaders for Life, DRAGON (Dallas Role-playing and Gaming Organization), German Club, Indonesian Student Organization, International Student Association, Intramurals, Italian Club, Japanese Student Association, Korean Student Association, Latin American Student Organization, Latin Liturgy Society, Math Club, Orientation Leaders, Prehealth Professions Society, The Rostrum, Society of Physics Students, Student Foundation, Thai Student Association, Turkish Student Association, University News, Vietnamese Association, Young Conservatives of Texas, Chess Club, Rugby Football Club, Sailing Club, Soccer Club, and Tactical Operations Club.

ADMISSIONS PROCESSES AND REQUIREMENTS

The University is open to applicants without regard to ethnic or national origin, creed, or sex. Applicants for admission must furnish evidence of good character and of sufficient academic preparation and ability to do the work.

Interested students must submit a completed application, required application essay, academic letter of recommendation completed by an instructor or counselor, and $40 application fee.

Freshman candidates (high school seniors and students with fewer than 24 transferable hours) also must submit an official high school transcript, high school class rank, and official results of the SAT or ACT.

Transfer applicants also must submit official transcripts from all colleges attended, whether or not credit was earned, an official high school transcript showing final class rank, and SAT or ACT scores.

International candidates must also submit official transcript (with certified English translations) showing all secondary and post-secondary courses and grades, "O" and "A" levels (or other national examination results), if applicable, official results of the TOEFL, the University of Dallas Educational History Form, the Confirmation of Financial Resources, certified by a bank official, and a copy of their passport, if applicable.

Important Deadlines:

- December 1: Early Action deadline
- January 15: Scholarship deadline
- February 15: Regular Admission deadline
- August 1: Transfer Student deadline

Admissions Contact:

Larry Webb
Enrollment
1845 East Northgate Drive
Irving, TX 75062
Telephone: 800-628-6999 (toll free)

UNIVERSITY OF HARTFORD

GENERAL INFORMATION

The University of Hartford, a fully accredited, independent, nonsectarian institution, is composed of the College of Arts and Sciences; the College of Engineering; the College of Education, Nursing, and Health Professions; Hillyer College; the Barney School of Business and Public Administration; the Hartford Art School; the Hartt School; S.I. Ward College of Technology; and Hartford College for Women.

Students from most of the states and 61 countries make up the full-time undergraduate group of approximately 4,200 men and women. Students participate in about 100 organized student groups, including clubs devoted to special interests or political, professional, religious, or civic activities. Athletics include intercollegiate (NCAA Division I) and intramural sports. These activities, as well as the recreational and fitness needs of the University, are served by the modern 130,000-square-foot Sports Center. Students are also involved in school publications and AM and FM radio stations, and the Hartt School, the Hartford Art School, and the University Players present a variety of concerts, exhibitions, and theatrical productions each year.

The University's Career Development and Placement Center provides vocational counseling and information on occupations, employers, testing, and graduate schools; serves as a reference and credential source; and provides graduating students with an on-campus recruiting program. Courses, programs, and educational counseling are provided by the Office of Graduate and Adult Academic Services for part-time adult students

STUDENT BODY

The Student Government Association (SGA) represents all full-time students at the University. Through SGA, students and faculty work together to develop and coordinate the co-curriculars of the University. In addition, students are represented on all major administrative committees, including the Board of Regents.

ACADEMICS

The University of Hartford is known nationally for the breadth and depth of its program. Hartford's nine schools and colleges offer more than 80 undergraduate majors. The University encourages students to sample a variety of academic areas and enroll in courses in any of the colleges on campus. Students interested in interdisciplinary majors can combine courses from the different schools within the University. Students are assigned academic advisors who help guide them in curriculum choices, career exploration, and the transition to university life. The All-University curriculum was developed in order to help students learn more about how different academic disciplines approach related problems. Courses in different fields of expertise are team taught, and topics are examined from the perspective of several academic disciplines. Students who are undecided on their majors are assisted by a special program at the University. Individual students will also find help in the areas of writing proficiency, reading comprehension, and research and test-taking skills at the reading and writing center, which is available to the entire Student Body. The Math Tutoring Lab, which is staffed by full-time faculty members and math majors, offers further help for students in math. Selected students are encouraged to participate in the Honors Program, which gives students the opportunity to graduate with an Honors degree.

The Bachelor of Arts is offered in art history, biology, chemistry, cinema, communication, computer science, criminal justice, drama, economics, English, foreign languages and literatures, history, information technology, international studies, Judaic studies, mathematics, music, philosophy, physics, political economy, politics and government, professional and technical writing, psychology, and sociology.

The Bachelor of Science in secondary education is offered in the College of Education, Nursing, and Health Professions with a major in English.

Students can earn the Bachelor of Fine Arts in ceramics, dance, drawing, illustration, music theater, painting, photography, printmaking, professional theater training, sculpture, video, and visual communication design.

The Bachelor of Music is offered at the Hartt School with majors in performance (guitar, orchestral instrument, organ, piano, and voice), composition, jazz studies, music education, music history, music management, music production and technology, opera, performing arts management, piano accompaniment and ensemble, and theory.

The Bachelor of Science is awarded in biology, clinical lab science/lab tech, chemistry, chemistry/biology, computer science, early childhood education, elementary education, health sciences (upper division only), human services, mathematics, mathematics/management science, nursing (for registered nurses only), occupational therapy, physics, radiological technology, respiratory therapy, and special education (offering dual certification and covering emotional disabilities, learning disabilities, and mental retardation).

The Bachelor of Science in Business Administration is offered in accounting, economics and finance, entrepreneurial studies, finance and insurance, management, marketing, and management information systems.

Additional BS programs are offered in the College of Engineering and include ABET-accredited BSEE, BSME, BSCE, BSCompE, and interdisciplinary BSE options. The most popular BSE options are acoustics/music, biomedical engineering, and environmental engineering.

Bachelor of Science degrees offered at the Ward College of Technology are architectural engineering technology, chemical engineering technology, computer engineering technology, electronic engineering technology, and mechanical engineering technology. Students can also earn the Associate in Applied Science (AS) in electronic technology and computer engineering technology. Also available is the fall-semester noncredit pre-technology program designed to prepare students for the degree program.

200 Bloomfield Avenue
West Hartford, CT 06117
Phone: 860-768-4296
Fax: 860-768-4961
Website: www.hartford.edu

The Hartford College for Women grants the Associate of Arts in liberal studies, Associate of Science in legal studies, Bachelor of Arts in women's studies, and Bachelor of Science in legal studies.

Additional special programs include the five-year music education program; five-year double-major programs; Bachelor of Music with an emphasis in management, offered by the Hartt School in conjunction with the Barney School of Business and Public Administration; and the Bachelor of Science in Engineering with a music-acoustics major, offered by the College of Engineering.

The faculty consists of 721 full-time and adjunct members. The undergraduate and graduate faculties make up essentially the same group. Eighty-one percent of full-time faculty hold the terminal degree in their field. Academic and personal advisory service is readily available. Each new student is assigned to a faculty advisor during summer orientation.

ADMISSIONS

The admissions decision is based on a combination of the following: quality of the secondary school curriculum, academic performance in secondary school, recommendations of the secondary school principal or guidance counselor, ACT or SAT I scores, evidence of a desire to succeed, and leadership qualities shown by academic and extracurricular activities. Music and art applicants are required to audition, show portfolios, and take other tests depending upon the program to which they are applying. The University has a rolling admission policy. For more information, students should contact:

Richard A. Zeiser
Dean of Admission
University of Hartford
West Hartford, CT 06117-0395
Phone: 860-768-4296 or 800-947-4303 (toll free)
Fax: 860-768-4961
E-mail: admission@uhavax.hartford.edu
World Wide Web: www.hartford.edu

CAMPUS LIFE

The University, located in the residential suburb of West Hartford, is comprised of two campuses. The West Hartford area provides many opportunities for students to discover new cultural and intellectual experiences. With museums, theaters, libraries, the Hartford Civic Center, the Hartford Coliseum, other colleges, a symphony orchestra, shopping, great restaurants, an international airport, and local and intercity transportation systems, the opportunities are limited only by the individual's imagination.

Through the Hartford Consortium for Higher Education, Hartford students have the opportunity to register for select courses at the Connecticut School of Dance, Saint Joseph College, and Trinity College. Opportunities are available to teaching and human services majors in the College of Education, Nursing, and Health Professions for field and/or clinical experiences where applicable. The cooperative education office is available to custom-tailor work experiences within many of the University's programs.

COST AND AID

Tuition for the 2000–2001 academic year was $18,626. On-campus room and board was $7,840. Student service fees were $1,104. Approximately 3,300 students can be accommodated in a variety of on-campus housing.

UNIVERSITY OF MAINE–FARMINGTON

THE UNIVERSITY AT A GLANCE

As Maine's most selective public liberal arts college, the University of Maine at Farmington provides the tradition, setting and friendly atmosphere of a small New England college. U. Maine Farmington focuses exclusively on undergraduates and offers quality programs in the arts and sciences, business, teacher education, professional studies, health, and human services. The University's enrollment cap of just 2,000 students enables UMF to offer a 15:1 student/faculty ratio and an average class size of 19. Students and faculty work together closely to help students meet their individual educational goals. Students are encouraged to participate in internships, field experiences, community service, professional associations, symposiums, and national and international exchange programs. An active Honors Program provides enrichment for those students seeking additional academic challenges.

U. Maine Farmington's programs in education are nationally accredited by the prestigious National Council for the Accreditation of Teacher Education (NCATE). For the past five years, the UMF has been named the #1 public college in New England in its category by *U.S. News & World Report* (1998, 1999, 2000, 2001, 2002). And, *Kiplinger's Personal Finance Magazine* recently named UMF one of the 100 best values in public colleges as well as the best value in Maine.

STUDENTS

At U. Maine Farmington students make a difference; they are involved in just about everything and anything happening on campus. Students make up the student government, which, through the Student Senate, administers the activity fees and oversees the clubs and organizations on campus. Students assist in running the residence halls through the Campus Residence Counsel. In addition, students sit on administrative standing committees, help hire new faculty and staff, participate in advisory groups, and provide input as they work in all sorts of offices on campus.

The student-run Program Board regularly sponsors on-campus activities such as dances, concerts, comedians, films, and lectures. The Latte Landing coffeehouse has events scheduled every night of the week and fitness activities are available in the Health and Fitness Center seven days a week. The Art Gallery, Nordica Auditorium, and Alumni Theater make UMF the cultural center of west central Maine. Students and community members participate together in the UMF Community Chorus and Band and the Sandy River Players, a local theater group. The Center for Human Development offers seminars on career development and graduate school as well as organizing several job fairs through out the year to assist students in locating jobs on campus, summer jobs, and internships and to assist graduating students with their job or graduate school search.

UMF fields nine varsity sports and several club sports as well as running a robust intramural program. There are more than 40 active clubs and organizations on campus. These organizations sponsor many on-campus activities as well as off-campus trips. Many students participate in community service activities in nearby schools and health organizations.

ACADEMICS

Students are encouraged to connect classroom study with career opportunities by incorporating practical experience into their college life. More than 70 percent of U. Maine Farmington's students participate in academic practica, internships, service learning, the campus work initiative, or student exchange programs. The Math Clinic and the Writing Clinic help students develop their mathematics and writing skills. The Learning Assistance Center can provide tutors, on request, for any class offered at UMF. The Honors Program creates a focused community of students and faculty dedicated to inquiry and discussion. It offers highly motivated students small, interdisciplinary seminar courses and the option of completing a senior thesis or honors project.

246 Main Street
Farmington, ME 04938
Phone: 207-778-7050
Fax: 207-778-8182
Website: www.umf.maine.edu

As Maine's most selective public liberal arts college, UMF offers high quality undergraduate programs in a challenging and supportive educational environment. Academic programs are built on a strong interdisciplinary, liberal arts foundation. Students can earn Bachelor of Arts, Bachelor of Science, and Bachelor of Fine Arts degrees at UMF.

Students can major in art, biology, business economics, community health/school health education, computer science, creative writing, early childhood education, early childhood special education, elementary education, English, environmental planning and policy, environmental science, geology/chemistry, geology/geography, geography, history, international studies, mathematics, music/arts, philosophy/religion, political science/social science, psychology, rehabilitation, secondary education (with concentrations in biology, English, language arts, mathematics, mathematics/computer science, physical science, science, social science), sociology/anthropology, special education (with concentrations in emotional disturbance, learning disabilities, mental retardation), theater/arts, or women's studies.

With the approval of the Arts and Sciences Committee, students may choose to design their own academic program through Interdisciplinary Studies or an Individualized Major. Pre-professional advising is available for students planning to enter graduate programs in allied health, dentistry, medicine, optometry, veterinary science, or law.

Academic minors are available in arts, biology, business, coaching, chemistry, computer science, economics, English, exercise science, French, geography, geology, history, mathematics, music, nutrition, philosophy, physics, political science, psychology, rehabilitation services, religion, sociology, theater, and women's studies. Certificate programs are offered in exercise instruction and ski industries.

UMF is small on purpose, because the college values faculty and student interaction. Communication between faculty and students is encouraged both inside and outside the classroom. Our student/faculty ratio of 15:1 and our average class size of 19 make it easier for faculty to get to know their students. Most UMF students will tell you that it is their ability to get to know both their faculty and their fellow classmates that makes UMF such a friendly and supportive place. Of the 153 faculty, 108 are full-time, 94 hold terminal degrees in their fields, and 43 are women. At UMF full professors regularly teach first- and second-year classes.

CAMPUS LIFE

UMF is located in the town of Farmington, Maine, in the foothills of the Longfellow mountains. Downtown, with its shops, restaurants, banks, and movie theater, is a three-minute walk away and gives the campus a hometown, friendly, community atmosphere. The surrounding mountains, lakes, and rivers provide lots of opportunities to enjoy the great outdoors. The Appalachian Trail, white water rafting, camping, and world class skiing at Sugarloaf, USA, and Sunday River are only a short distance away. Skiing, biking, and hiking areas are available in Farmington, which is the county seat and home to about 7,500 people. The campus is a few hours drive from Boston, Massachusetts and Quebec City, Canada, and within a half day's drive from Montreal, Canada.

COSTS

As a public liberal arts college, UMF tuition is substantially lower than private colleges of about the same size. Early application for financial aid is suggested. UMF requires only the FAFSA form. Last year UMF students received more than $13.1 million in aid through grants, scholarships, loans, and work-study programs. The Office of Financial Aid is committed to helping working students and their families receive as much assistance as they are eligible for. Interest-free payment plans and other cost-saving programs are available through the financial aid office.

As a small, public institution, UMF is proud of its ability to provide a high quality education at a reasonable cost. UMF participates in the New England Regional Program that offers reduced tuition for certain majors to residents of other New England states. See our Web page for up-to-date tuition, fees, and room and board costs and information.

ADMISSIONS

UMF offers an early admission process for students applying before December 1 for fall admission and a rolling admission process for those applying after December 1. Applicants applying for January admission should complete their applications early in the fall. First-year students are encouraged to apply as soon as possible after their first set of senior grades are available, and transfers should apply early in the semester preceeding the semester in which they wish to start to ensure that there is still space available in their program of interest. UMF encourages applicants to apply electronically. Paper applications are available on request from the Office of Admission.

First-year applicants are considered for admission based on the following: the number and sequence of college-preparatory courses completed (extra weight is given to AP or Honors-level courses), the overall secondary school record (see the website or catalog for a list of required and recommended college preparatory courses) and class rank, an official high school recommendation, a personal essay, and school and community activities. Personal interviews are not required but are recommended and will be considered. SATs are not required, but if they are submitted by the student or if they are included on the high school transcript, they will be considered and they can make a difference in the admission decision. Students who choose not to submit SAT scores or whose SAT scores are below certain cutoffs will be asked to take placement tests in writing and mathematics. Students not graduating from a recognized high school are asked to submit their results on the GED examination with the rest of their academic records. Transfer students are asked to submit official transcripts of all college course work completed at the time of application, which will be an important factor in the admission decision.

UNIVERSITY OF MASSACHUSETTS—DARTMOUTH

GENERAL INFORMATION

In 1895, the Massachusetts legislature chartered the New Bedford Textile School and the Bradford Durfee Textile School, laying the foundation for the modern University of Massachusetts—Dartmouth. Since then, the base of local economy slowly changed from textiles to manufacturing and service, and the University's programs grew along with the economy, continually expanding to meet modern needs. In 1988, the Swain School of Design was incorporated into the University of Massachusetts—Dartmouth's College of Visual and Performing Arts. In 1962, the Southeastern Massachusetts Technological Institute was founded, later to become the more comprehensive Southeastern Massachusetts University in 1969. In 1991, the University of Massachusetts Amherst, Boston, and Dartmouth campuses joined with the University of Lowell, Southeastern Massachusetts University, and the Medical Center in Worcester to create a new University of Massachusetts educational system. Today, UMass Dartmouth is a comprehensive teaching and research university, offering a variety of educational programs, research opportunities, and extension and continuing education programs in the liberal arts, creative arts, sciences, and professional fields. Undergraduate enrollment is roughly 5,700 and graduate enrollment is about 600. Currently, about 90 percent of students are from Massachusetts; however, every year, the University attracts a growing number of students from other U.S. states and foreign countries.

STUDENT BODY

At UMass Dartmouth, there are a wide variety of extracurricular clubs, organizations, and events on campus, giving students of every background and interest the opportunity to participate in campus life. There are over 60 student-run organizations, including the Outing Club, Theatre Company, Society of Women Engineers, and the student-produced radio station WSMU. The University also competes in 25 intercollegiate athletic teams. The Student Senate, the Campus Center Board of Governors, Residence Hall Congress, and Student Judiciary are elected students organizations that have a direct hand in the formation of campus policy and procedure. In addition to clubs and activities, the University brings a multitude of events to campus, such as famous entertainers and musicians, noted lecturers, movie screenings, and art exhibits.

ACADEMICS

The academic year consists of two semesters, beginning in September and ending in mid-May. Between the conclusion of the fall semester in December and the start of the spring semester in late January, the University offers a three-week January term. From the end of May through the end of August, the University offers summer sessions through the Division of Continuing Education. To earn an undergraduate degree, students must complete at least 120 credits of course work. Students generally earn three credits for each semester course and take four or five courses per semester. In some major fields, students must complete 133 credits to graduate. In addition to course work required by their major field, students must complete General Education Requirements in the following six academic areas: ethics and social responsibility; mathematics, natural science, and technology; global awareness and diversity; written and oral communications; cultural and artistic literacy; and information and computer literacy.

The University is divided into five colleges: The Colleges of Arts and Sciences, which offers 16 major fields, the College of Business, which offers 5 major fields, The College of Engineering, which offers 8 major fields, the College of Visual and Performing Arts, which offers 7 major fields, and the College of Nursing. Students may also study in the Graduate School of Marine Sciences and Technology, a program jointly operated by several local universities. Students at UMass Dartmouth may pursue a Bachelor of Arts, Bachelor of Fine Arts, or Bachelor of Science degree. The University also operates an undergraduate honors program, supports interdisciplinary studies, offers pre-law and pre-med curriculums as well as numerous minor programs, and offers undergraduate academic advising. Students may also earn course credit through independent study, directed study courses, and contract learning programs.

In the University's 5 colleges and 32 academic departments, there are a combined 335 full-time faculty members. Of the full-time faculty, nearly 90 percent hold doctoral or terminal degrees in their field. The school maintains an excellent student/faculty ratio of just 14:1 and an average class size of just 23 students. All University faculty members are committed to undergraduate education and also serve as academic advisors, helping students make successful academic decisions.

ADMISSIONS

Admission to the University is selective and every prospective student is evaluated by the general University standards, as well as by the standards of the academic departments in which they intend to study. In some departments, there are a limited number of spaces available each year. Candidates are evaluated on the strength of their secondary school academic program, weighted GPA, class rank, SAT I or ACT scores, and their personal essay. Transfer students must also submit transcripts from all previous college or university work. Prospective students are encouraged to visit the campus for a tour and to schedule a personal interview with an admissions counselor. Students are admitted to the University on a rolling basis until each program is filled. The University is committed to providing equal admissions opportunity to all qualified students through standard and alternative admission programs. The University offers an alternative admissions program, College Now, specially designed for students from a low-income family, who have limited English speaking ability, or who are an ethnic minority.

To apply for freshman admission, candidates must submit a completed application along with an application fee. The application fee is $25 for in state applicants and $45 for out of state applicants. In addition to these materials, the University requires a secondary school transcript, official scores from the SAT I or ACT, and any other supporting documents the Admissions Committee should consider. Transfer students make up about one-third of all incoming students annually. To apply for transfer status, students must submit the preceding materials as well as official records of all work at the college or university they attended previously. Transfer candidates are evaluated by the same standards as freshman applicants, with a stronger emphasis on their college or university achievement. Students may apply for admission to the January or September semester. The application procedures are the same for either term.

285 Old Westport Road
Dartmouth, MA 02747-2300
Phone: 508-999-8605
Fax: 508-999-8755
Website: www.umassd.edu

The University recommends that all international students submit their credentials no later than June 1 for September entrance and no later than November 1 for January entrance. In addition to its own standards, the University evaluates students by the Massachusetts State Board of Higher Education admission standards. Massachusetts State Board of Higher Education evaluates applicants based on the strength of their secondary school curriculum, the level of course work, and standardized test results. Undergraduate students may be admitted as freshman, transfer, or College Now students.

CAMPUS LIFE

University of Massachusetts—Dartmouth is located on 710 acres in southeastern Massachusetts, near the historic cities of Fall River and New Bedford. The renowned architect Paul Rudolph, former dean of the Yale University School of Art and Architecture, designed the University's extraordinary, modern campus. In addition to the main campus, the University's arts programs are located in a renovated retail store in downtown New Bedford. There are a variety of shops and restaurants within walking distance of the University and ample public transportation servicing areas outside the immediate vicinity. Massachusetts State beaches, hiking trails, and neighboring cities offer a variety of social, cultural, and recreational activities in the surrounding region. Beyond local resources, the world-class cities of Boston and Providence are an hour from campus, offering multitude museums, libraries, performances, concerts, and sporting events. In addition, New York City, New Hampshire, and Vermont's famous mountain ranges are only four hours away. Boston and Providence both offer extensive, national air, bus, and rail lines.

As a member of SACHEM (Southeastern Association for Cooperation in Higher Education in Massachusetts), students at UMass Dartmouth can cross register for courses at neighboring public and private colleges for full course credit. In addition, the University operates exchange programs with the University of Grenoble (France), the Lycee du Gresivaudanat Meylan and the Lycee Aristide Berges, Nottingham Trent University (England), the Baden-Wurttemburg Universities (Germany), Centro de Arte eCommunicacao (Portugal), Nova Scotia College of Art and Design, Ben Gurion University of the Negev (Israel), and the Ecole Nationale Superieure des Industries Textiles, Universite de Haute Alsace (France). In addition to the formal exchange programs, students often earn course credit through individually arranged overseas programs.

COST AND AID

Tuition and fees for in-state residents is roughly $4,200 annually. Tuition for out-of-state students is about $11,800 annually. Room and board costs are between $4,895 and $5,403, depending on the meal plan a student selects. Students should also expect to spend approximately $700 on books and supplies, though this cost that varies by major.

UNIVERSITY OF NEW HAVEN

GENERAL INFORMATION

Founded in 1920, the University of New Haven is a private, coeducational institution that offers a wide range of major fields in a small, intimate college environment. The academic programs at University of New Haven are designed to help students prepare for success in the modern business world and are continuously growing to meet the challenges of contemporary society. The University maintains consistently small class sizes, allowing students work closely with the school's distinguished faculty. The University's main campus is located in West Haven, Connecticut, a residential community adjacent the city of New Haven. The campus sits on a hillside with a view of the Long Island Sound and overlooking downtown New Haven. The main campus has the University's primary administration and classroom buildings for the School of Business, the School of Engineering and Applied Science, the School of Hospitality & Tourism, the School of Public Safety and Professional Studies, the Graduate School. The main campus also houses six student residence halls, the University library, the bookstore, the student center and the Computer Center, the psychology building, the College of Arts and Sciences, and the Admissions Building. Two blocks from the main campus, the North Campus contains the Charger Gymnasium and athletic playing fields. The University also operates a branch in New London, Connecticut. University of New Haven runs a strong, intercollegiate sports program, competing in baseball, basketball, golf, cross-country, football, lacrosse, soccer, softball, tennis, track, and volleyball. There is also an active men's and women's intramural athletics program.

STUDENT BODY

There are over 40 campus clubs and organizations, including chapters of several professional societies, religious groups, social clubs, student councils, cultural clubs, and national fraternities and sororities. The Day Student Government and Evening Student Council oversee all aspects of undergraduate life, organizing campus social and cultural activities, supporting the student-run radio station and student-produced publications, and overseeing the budget for all undergraduate organizations. In addition, select students are elected to serve on the University's Board of Governors every year.

ACADEMICS

Students can pursue a Bachelor of Arts degree through the College of Arts and Sciences in the following fields of study: art, chemistry, communications, English (with concentrations in literature and writing), graphic design, history, interior design, liberal studies, mathematics, music, music industry, music and sound recording, political science, and psychology (with concentrations in community-clinical or general psychology). The College also confers the Bachelor of Science degree in biology (with concentrations in general biology, biochemistry, and pre-medical/pre-dental/pre-veterinary), biotechnology, dental hygiene, general dietetics, environmental science, marine biology, mathematics (with concentrations in computer science, natural sciences, and statistics), and music and sound recording. Students can pursue the Bachelor of Science degree through School of Business in accounting, business administration, business economics, communication, finance, international studies, management of sports industries and marketing, and electronic commerce and the Associate of Science degree in business administration and communication. The Taglietella School of Hospitality and Tourism confers the Bachelor of Science in hotel and restaurant management with a concentration in tourism administration and a certificate in gastronomy and culinary arts. Through the School of Engineering and Applied Sciences, students may pursue the Bachelor of Science degree in chemical engineering, chemistry, civil engineering, computer science, electrical engineering, industrial engineering, and mechanical engineering. Students can also pursue the Associate of Science degree in chemistry, civil engineering, computer science, electrical engineering, industrial engineering, and mechanical engineering. The School of Public Safety and Professional Studies confers the Bachelor of Science degree in the following fields: arson investigation, criminal justice, fire protection engineering, fire science administration, fire science technology, forensic science and legal studies, occupational safety and health administration, and occupational safety and health technology. The School of Public Safety and Professional Studies also confers the Associate of Science degree in aviation science, corrections, fire and occupational safety, law enforcement administration, and occupational safety and health.

300 Orange Avenue
West Haven, CT 06516
Phone: 203-932-7319
Fax: 203-931-6093
Website: www.newhaven.edu

University of New Haven employs competent and accomplished faculty who demonstrate a commitment to teaching, leadership, and commitment to the community. There are 175 full-time professors at University of New Haven, of which 90 percent hold a doctoral or terminal degree in their field. In compliance with University policy and in attempt to maintain a high quality of education throughout the colleges, all professors teach both undergraduate and graduate students. Furthermore, all undergraduate classes are taught by full professors, not teaching assistants. In addition to full-time faculty, University of New Haven employs 58 practitioner-in-residence and 223 part-time instructors. The overall student/faculty ratio is an excellent 11:1.

ADMISSIONS

Successful admissions candidates must have completed high school or the equivalent. Students are evaluated on the strength of their secondary school record, class rank, SAT I or ACT scores, and participation in extracurricular activities, personal essay, recommendations. University of New Haven encourages prospective students to visit campus for an admissions interview and a campus tour. Qualified athletes may be referred the coaching staff for a personal interview. Every year, the admissions staff visits local high schools and junior colleges to offer information sessions about the University and the admissions process. Students from other states are evaluated by the same standards as Connecticut residents. To be considered for admission, candidates must complete the application form and submit it along with a nonrefundable $50 application fee. In addition to the completed application, students must send secondary school transcripts and SAT I or ACT scores, a personal essay and recommendations. For further information about the University and admissions, students may contact:

Undergraduate Admissions Office
Telephone: 203-932-7319 or 800-DIAL-UNH ext. 7319 (toll free)
Fax: 203-931-6093
E-mail: adminfo@newhaven.edu
Website: www.newhaven.edu

CAMPUS LIFE

New Haven is among Connecticut's most prominent cities, offering a wide variety of theaters and performances, fine restaurants, museums and galleries, and a world-class coliseum that attracts famous entertainment and sporting events. There are six other colleges and universities in the New Haven metropolitan area, which often host social and cultural events, open to the community. The surrounding region is also home to a deepwater harbor and a number of nearby state beaches. In addition the resources in the local area, New Haven is in close proximity to New York, Boston, and Cape Cod, as well as the famous mountain ranges in north and central New England. Two national airlines provide service to the local airport. The city is also located on a major rail line and is at the junction of two interstate highways.

COST AND AID

For the 2003–2004 academic year, tuition is $29,000 including all student fees and room and board costs.

UNIVERSITY OF NOTRE DAME

GENERAL INFORMATION

The University of Notre Dame, founded in 1842 by Rev. Edward F. Sorin, a priest of the Congregation of the Holy Cross, is an independent, national Catholic university located adjacent to the city of South Bend, Indiana.

Admission to Notre Dame is highly competitive, and the University has five applicants for each freshman class position. The University's minority student population has doubled in the past 10 years, and women, first admitted to undergraduate studies at Notre Dame in 1972, now account for 47 percent of undergraduate and overall enrollment. The University is organized into four undergraduate colleges (Arts and Letters, Science, Engineering, and Business Administration), the School of Architecture, the Law School, the Graduate School, five major research institutes, several centers and special programs, and the University Library system. Fall 2002 enrollment is approximately 11,300 students, with approximately 8,200 of those at the undergraduate level.

One indicator of the quality of Notre Dame's undergraduate programs is the success of its students in post-baccalaureate studies. The medical school acceptance rate of the University's pre-professional studies (pre-medicine) graduates is more than 70 percent, twice the national average, and Notre Dame ranks 18th among private universities (first among Catholic institutions) in the number of doctorates earned by its undergraduate alumni, a record compiled over some 70 years.

The Graduate School, established in 1918, encompasses 46 master's, 2 first professional, and 25 doctoral degree programs in and among 27 University departments and institutes. While its graduate student body is small in comparison to many research institutions, Notre Dame nonetheless ranks among the nation's top 50 universities in number of doctorates awarded annually.

The source of the University's academic strength is its faculty, which since 1982 has seen the addition of more than 100 new members and the establishment of some 60 new endowed professorships.

At Notre Dame, education always has been linked to values, among them living in community and volunteering in community service. Residence hall life, shared by more than four of five undergraduates, is both the hallmark of the Notre Dame experience and the wellspring of the University's rich tradition. A younger tradition, the University's Center for Social Concerns, serves as a catalyst for student volunteerism. Almost 90 percent of Notre Dame students engage in some form of voluntary community service during their years at the University, and approximately 10 percent devote a year or more after graduation to serving the less fortunate in the U.S. and around the world.

No description of Notre Dame would be complete without mentioning the mystique of Fighting Irish athletics. Among college football teams, Notre Dame has compiled the highest winning percentage and the most national championships and Heisman Trophy winners. In recent years, Notre Dame also has developed one of the strongest overall athletic programs in the nation, with perennially powerful teams in women's soccer, fencing, volleyball, basketball, cross-country, softball, tennis, and swimming, and in men's fencing, baseball, lacrosse, cross-country, tennis, and hockey. In addition, Notre Dame ranks among the top three universities in the overall graduation rate of its student-athletes.

With 1,250 tree-lined acres containing two lakes and 166 buildings with an insured replacement value of more than $1.4 billion, Notre Dame is equally renowned for the quality of its physical plant and the beauty of its campus. Sacred Heart Basilica, the 14-story Hesburgh Library with its 132-foot-high mural depicting Christ the Teacher, and the University's 120-year-old Main Building with its famed Golden Dome are among the most widely known university landmarks in the world.

STUDENT BODY

At Notre Dame, a great deal of student life is centered in the residence halls; each residence hall community has commissions that organize liturgies, service projects, hall-wide dances, inter-hall sports teams, and other dorm events. There is also a wealth of clubs and organizations on campus—over 260 at last count. Some clubs have an academic orientation, such as the American Institute of Architects. Other groups, such as the Black Cultural Arts Council, relate to ethnic groups. Students who enjoy music may choose a number of different groups, including the renowned Notre Dame Glee Club, Folk Choir, and marching band. The Center for Social Concerns also provides a wide array of opportunities for service, social action, and experiential learning.

220 Main Building
Notre Dame, IN 46556
Phone: 574-631-7505
Fax: 574-631-8865
Website: www.nd.edu

ACADEMICS

Graduate studies and research are vital and significant at Notre Dame, but it is the undergraduate teaching program for which the University is best known and most respected. The undergraduate program is comprised of four colleges (Arts and Letters, Business, Engineering, and Science), the School of Architecture, and the First Year of Studies. An innovative program in which all first-year students are enrolled, the First Year of Studies, allows students to sample a wide variety of academic disciplines and provides them with a firm foundation for advancing into their major area of study. The First Year of Studies also provides academic counselors and a comprehensive, free tutoring program to all first-year students. The program is one reason why 94 percent of Notre Dame students earn their degree, a graduation rate bettered only by Harvard, Yale, Princeton, and Dartmouth. The high freshman-to-sophomore-year retention rate of 98 percent is also attributed, in large part, to the First Year of Studies and the support network at Notre Dame.

The academic year is divided into two semesters, with the fall term beginning in late August and the spring term ending the first week in May. Students generally take five courses per semester.

The College of Arts and Letters offers Bachelor of Fine Arts degrees in art studio, art history, and design. It also offers the Bachelor of Arts degrees in American studies; anthropology; classics (classical civilization, Arabic, Greek, and Latin); East Asian languages and literatures (Chinese and Japanese); economics; English; film, television, and theatre; German and Russian languages and literatures; political studies; history; mathematics (honors); medieval studies; music; philosophy; philosophy/theology joint major; program of liberal studies; psychology; Romance languages and literatures (French, Italian, and Spanish); sociology; and theology. The College also offers a variety of concentrations, special programs, and supplementary majors.

The College of Business Administration offers the degree of Bachelor of Business Administration in accountancy, finance, management, management information systems, and marketing.

The College of Engineering offers Bachelor of Science degrees in aerospace engineering, chemical engineering, civil engineering, computer engineering, computer science, electrical engineering, engineering and environmental sciences, environmental geosciences, and mechanical engineering.

The College of Science offers Bachelor of Science degrees in applied physics, biochemistry, biological sciences, chemistry, chemistry/option, environmental sciences, mathematics, physics, physics/computing, physics in education, physics in medicine, pre-professional studies (pre-medicine), science-business, science-computing, and science-education.

The School of Architecture offers a five-year program of study leading to the Bachelor's of Architecture degree, including a required third year in Rome.

In 2002–2003, Notre Dame's instructional faculty numbered 760 full-time and 395 part-time members. Other faculty, such as administrative, professional specialists, librarians, and research fellows numbered 379 full-time and 72 part-time members. Ninety-eight percent of the full-time instructional faculty have terminal degrees, 93 percent have doctorates. Ninety-seven percent of the full-time instructional faculty are lay persons. The student/faculty ratio is 12:1.

ADMISSIONS

Admission to the University of Notre Dame is highly competitive and each application is evaluated on the following criteria: the high school record and rigor of curriculum, standardized testing (SAT I or ACT), extracurricular accomplishment and personal qualities, essay and personal statement, and teacher's evaluation. For the class of 2006, the middle 50 percent of admitted students had a rank in class of 1 percent to 6 percent, SAT I total scores of 1310 to 1440, and ACT composite scores of 30 to 33.

The University requires at least 16 units of full-credit high school work in solid academic subjects: English, mathematics, science, foreign language, history, as well as choice academic electives. Pre-calculus or calculus and chemistry and physics are required of all architecture, engineering, and science intents.

To apply as a transfer student, you must have at least one year at an accredited college, 27 semester hours of transferable credit, and a cumulative B (3.0) average.

CAMPUS LIFE

Centrally situated in the middle of the Midwest, Notre Dame is adjacent to the city of South Bend, Indiana, the center of a metropolitan area with a population of some 250,000. Downtown Chicago and its multiple cultural and entertainment options are just 90 miles by car or commuter railroad, the beautiful beaches of Lake Michigan are 30 miles to the west, and Indianapolis is 130 miles to the south. Other major Midwestern cities are within easy driving distance and South Bend Regional Airport offers a variety of convenient airline options. In addition to the many cultural, athletic, and recreational opportunities available at Notre Dame, the South Bend area includes the newly renovated Morris Performing Arts Center, the South Bend Regional Museum of Art, the Northern Indiana Historical Society Museum, the East Race Waterway, a minor league professional baseball franchise, the College Football Hall of Fame, more than a dozen golf courses, and some 45 movie screens.

Notre Dame has the largest proportion of students studying abroad of any major American university, according to a survey in the Chronicle of Higher Education. The far-flung international studies programs include semester and year-long opportunities in Angers, France; Athens; Dublin; Fremantle, Australia; Innsbruck, Austria; London; Monterrey and Puebla, Mexico; Nagoya and Tokyo Japan; Rome; Santiago, Chile; Shanghai, China; Toledo, Spain. The University also offers a semester of classes and internships in Washington, DC.

COST AND AID

Tuition and fees for the 2002–2003 academic year are $25,850. Room and board total $6,510. Other expenses, including books, supplies, and transportation are variable, depending on academic program, travel, and personal expenses.

UNIVERSITY OF OREGON

GENERAL INFORMATION

The University of Oregon—located in Eugene, Oregon, in the Willamette Valley, approximately 50 miles from the Pacific Ocean to the west and the Cascade Mountain Range to the east—offers students a world-class education in an unparalleled environment. More than 20,000 students call this campus home, attending classes by day and films, lectures, and concerts by night. Here you can spend your weekend immersed in the book stacks of the UO library system—the largest in the state—or in the whitewater of the McKenzie river flowing from the Cascades just northeast of town.

As a UO undergraduate student, you'll choose a course of study from 116 comprehensive programs, many of them ranked among the best in the world. Majors are offered in the colleges of arts and sciences, architecture and allied arts, business, education, journalism and communication, and music. At the UO, you'll receive personal attention from premier faculty in classes of 25 or fewer students during your freshman year. Our Learning Communities, such as Freshman Interest Groups, allow you to take a block of fall-term courses with a group of less than 25 students who have interests similar to your own. Freshman Seminars are a unique set of courses designed each year by UO faculty especially for new students. And, if you're interested in an honors program, The Robert Donald Clark Honors College offers exceptional students the best of both worlds: the benefits of a small liberal arts college and the rich resources of a major university. The Society of College Scholars also allows students to explore the possibilities of honors programs in their majors.

STUDENT BODY

The University has been named by *Mother Jones* magazine among the nation's most activist campuses in two of the last seven years. In 2000, the UO had the highest voter turnout of any school our size in the nation, and we are the fifth largest producer of Peace Corps volunteers in the United States. But you can decide for yourself the issues and your level of involvement. The Associated Student of University of Oregon offer more than 250 student organizations to choose from, including cultural organizations, fraternities and sororities, student government, campus ministries, professional organizations, political and environmental action groups, performing arts groups, international student clubs, and honor societies. These organizations draw from an $8.2 million annual budget. A complete list of student organizations is available on the Admissions website at: http://students.uoregon.edu/studentgroups.htm.

ACADEMICS

The University of Oregon is one of only 63 public and private institutions in the United States and Canada selected for membership in the exclusive Association of American Universities. *The Fiske Guide to Colleges* and Kaplan-Newsweek's College Catalog 2002 list the University of Oregon as one of the best buys among the nation's colleges and universities. The UO ranks 15th in the nation among public institutions and 6th nationally among "rising" public universities. And the Robert Donald Clark Honors College ranks first in the nation for the greatest increase in demand for admission among public universities with honors programs. The UO's undergraduate programs in architecture, communication disorders and sciences, and journalism are ranked in the top 25 in the nation. The "green" chemistry program, which uses nontoxic materials in experiments, is the first and only program of its kind in the nation. The Freshman Interest Group program is one of the nation's top character-building programs for first-year students, offering, in the words of *The Templeton Guide: Colleges That Encourage Character Development*, the "tools to develop a moral compass to navigate between increased personal freedom and new responsibilities."

The 116 undergraduate academic majors, minors, certificates, and preparatory programs offered are architecture and allied arts architecture, art, art history, community arts, ceramics, fibers, historic preservation, interior architecture, landscape architecture, metalsmithing and jewelry, multimedia, multimedia design, painting, photography, planning, public policy and management, printmaking, sculpture, and visual design.

College of Arts and Sciences: anthropology, Asian studies, biochemistry, biology (with concentrations including marine biology), chemistry, Chinese, classical civilization, classics, comparative literature, computer and information science, computer and information technology, dental hygiene°, dentistry°, East Asian studies, economics (with concentrations including business economics), engineering°, English, environmental sciences, environmental studies, ethnic studies, European studies, exercise and movement science, film studies, folklore, forensic science°, French, general science, geography, geological sciences, German, German area studies, Greek, health sciences°, history, humanities, independent study, international studies, Italian, Japanese, Judaic studies, Latin, Latin American studies, law°, linguistics, mathematics, mathematics and computer science, medical technology°, medicine°, medieval studies, nursing°, occupational therapy°, optometry°, peace studies, pharmacy°, philosophy, physical therapy°, physician assistant°, physics (with an emphasis in astronomy), podiatry°, political science, psychology, religious studies, Romance languages, Russian, Russian and East European studies, Scandinavian, second-language acquisition and teaching°, social work°, sociology, Southeast Asian studies, Spanish, theater arts, veterinary medicine°, women's and gender studies.

Charles H. Lundquist College of Business: accounting, business administration (with concentrations in entrepreneurship and small businesses, finance, management, marketing, sports marketing).

College of Education: communication disorders and sciences, educational studies, family and human services, special education, teacher education°.

1217 University of Oregon
Eugene, OR 97403-1217
Phone: 541-346-3201
Fax: 541-346-5815
Website: www.uoregon.edu

School of Journalism and Communication: journalism (with concentrations in advertising, communication studies, electronic media, journalism, magazine, news-editorial, public relations).

School of Music: dance, jazz studies, music (with concentrations in music composition, music education, music education: elementary education, music history, music performance, music theory).

°preparatory program

At the UO, you'll learn from research-active scholars who publish and make contributions in their fields. Because faculty members believe that good teaching flows out of good research, resident and visiting scholars are dedicated to their work both in and out of the classroom. Faculty members teach students to become scholars through the habits of good research. You'll have access to teachers recognized for their outstanding teaching skills and renowned for original research. Among them are winners of every major UO teaching award and every major recognition given for research and scholarship, including the Fulbright, Woodrow Wilson, Guggenheim, National Science Foundation, American Council of Learned Societies, and National Endowment for the Humanities awards, as well as membership in the National Academy of Sciences.

ADMISSIONS

To best prepare for your freshman year in college, we challenge you to concentrate on earning good grades through your senior year and recommend that you take at least four college-preparatory courses as a senior. The early notification deadline for fall 2004 is November 1, 2003. The standard admission deadline for fall 2004 is January 15, 2004. To be eligible for freshman admission, you must have a high school GPA of at least 3.00, be a graduate of a standard or accredited high school, and submit SAT or ACT scores. A cumulative GPA of 3.25 or better on a 4.00 scale and completion of at least sixteen units of academic course work qualifies you for guaranteed admission.

We require the following college-preparatory courses: English—4 years: English language, literature, speaking and listening, writing. Mathematics—3 years: first-year algebra, two additional years of college-preparatory mathematics. Science—2 years. Social science—3 years: 1 year of U.S. history, 1 year of global studies such as world history or geography, 1 elective. Second language—2 years of study in one language. If you meet the minimum admission standards, we next look at such factors as the quality of course work taken in high school, your grade trend, class rank, and senior-year course load. Academic potential and special talents are also considered. To apply, submit a completed application for admission, transcripts, SAT or ACT scores and nonrefundable $50 application fee to the Office of Admissions.

CAMPUS LIFE

For good reason, one of the UO's faculty members calls our location "Oz on earth." Eugene, Oregon, is a classic college town, with more than 100 city parks, 250 miles of bicycle trails, rock climbing areas, and incredible public gardens, set in the middle of a vast recreation area. You can travel less than an hour by car in any direction and find ancient national forests, wilderness areas, lakes, breathtaking waterfalls, streams, snow-capped mountains, glaciers, world-class skiing, lava fields, hot springs, sand dunes, and the Pacific Ocean.

The campus is located in the center of Eugene (population 136,490), which offers the cultural opportunities of a large city with the accessibility and friendly feel of a small town. Cultural opportunities abound, as the Hult Center for the Performing Arts and the nationally renowned Oregon Bach Festival lure a variety of nationally acclaimed musical acts. On campus, the excitement of intercollegiate athletics begins in the fall, when students cheer on the Ducks football team from their own seating section at Autzen Stadium. In the winter, the men's and women's basketball teams thrill the crowds at McArthur Court, and in the spring, the UO's men's and women's track stars compete at Hayward Field, often the site for NCAA championships and U.S. Olympic Track and Field Trials. Four museums on campus are valuable resources in the sciences and visual arts. Three theaters offer students an opportunity to produce and perform, regardless of major. Films, lectures, and cultural events are an everyday part of campus life.

Internships are available to all majors and include Global Graduates, the Oregon International Internship Program, which offers students the chance to earn academic credit while gaining career-related work experience overseas. Career and internship fairs and the Career Development Internship Program (CDIP) help you find off-campus internships in fields related to your academic majors or extracurricular interests. The Office of International Education and Exchange offers more than 70 overseas study programs in 25 countries. While overseas, you can experience the history, arts, social institutions, customs, and beliefs of a new culture, all while earning credit toward your UO degree. Approximately 680 UO students participate each year in overseas exchanges that range in length from one term to one year.

COST AND AID

2003–2004 Estimated Costs of Undergraduate Attendance

Tuition and fees are $4,527 for residents and $15,961 for nonresidents. On-campus residence halls including room and board are $6,875, books and supplies are $876, and personal expenses, are $2,350. Cost of attendance therefore totals $14,628 for residents and $26,062 for nonresidents.

UNIVERSITY OF PITTSBURGH—BRADFORD

GENERAL INFORMATION

Founded in 1963, the University of Pittsburgh at Bradford is committed to providing undergraduates with a top-flight education. Students at Pitt-Bradford benefit from an individualized undergraduate experience in a small liberal arts school setting, coupled with the school's affiliation with a world-famous university and the impressive Pitt degree. The University is dedicated to training tomorrow's professionals while imparting a broad liberal arts education. Pitt-Bradford is well known for its excellent faculty and staff, its solid professional and academic programs, and the individual attention its students receive. These elements combine to create a strong sense of community at Pitt-Bradford.

Up-to-the-minute computers and modern facilities are the hallmarks of this friendly, safe campus. A Pitt-Bradford degree is affordable; its 1,200 students earn their degrees at a cost that is roughly 10 percent of what their peers at private colleges pay. Active learning is encouraged through debates, discussions, group research projects, computer-assisted learning projects, field trips, participation in the arts (e.g. drama and music) and numerous internships and independent study ventures. Campus residents must take part in a University dining hall board plan. Housing is guaranteed to first and second year students, and cars are permitted on campus for all students. The Pitt-Bradford Sport and Fitness Center houses facilities for recreational activity as well as for both intercollegiate and intramural athletic events. The complex was just expanded; this $9.3 million construction project was completed in August of 2002. Pitt-Bradford competes in Division III of the NCAA it fields five men's and six women's teams. Pitt-Bradford's commons building is currently undergoing major renovation. Scheduled for completion in 2003, this $9 million-plus upgrade will enhance campus life by providing upgraded dining facilities, a new campus bookstore and new facilities for the campus newspaper and radio station. Also underway is the first half of construction of Blaisdell Hall, which will house communications, arts, and theatre and music the facility should be completed by fall 2003.The second half will house a new auditorium and orchestra pit and is scheduled for completion in 2004

STUDENT BODY

The Student Government Association (SGA) is central to the life of the Pitt-Bradford campus. The SGA charters and funds more than 30 college organizations and clubs. A diverse selection of entertainment comes to the Pitt-Bradford campus each year through the efforts of the Student Activities Council. Among Pitt-Bradford's students groups are three social fraternities and three social sororities, *Bailey's Beads* (the literary magazine), the Black Action Committee, CHISPA international (international organization), the Dance Club, Greek Council, Habitat for Humanity Club, *The Source* (newspaper), WDRQ (radio station), and numerous other academic organizations and clubs. The Student Activities Council schedules comedy performances, lectures, art exhibits, movies, and trips to such places as Toronto, Niagara Falls, Cooperstown, and New York City.

ACADEMICS

The academic programs at Pitt-Bradford are intended to prepare undergraduates for successful and rewarding careers. Our curricula stress critical-thinking skills and communication; they also encourage hands-on learning through field experience, internships, and faculty-student collaboration on research. A Pitt-Bradford bachelor's degree requires 120–128 credit hours (requirements differ slightly among programs). Students must complete between 60 and 70 credit hours to earn an associate's degree. The business management program at the University places a strong emphasis on teaching practical applications; courses often focus on cases taken from real business situations. Students may concentrate in accounting, finance, international business, management information systems, or marketing. Students in the communications, English, public relations, and writing programs learn by doing as they work on the staff of the student newspaper, *The Source*; broadcast over the college radio station, WDRQ; and publish original works in the student literary magazine, *Baily's Beads*. Students in the communication arts have access to outstanding on-campus facilities that include an electronic newsroom, a radio studio, a television studio, and a video editing room with analog and digital technology.

Education students may attain certification in elementary education and secondary education while pursuing a double major. Secondary education certification is available in the following areas: biology, chemistry, earth and space science, English, general science, mathematics, social studies, and speech communications.

The mathematics, computer science, and engineering department offers numerous prospects for Pitt-Bradford undergraduates. Mathematics students may study applied mathematics and secondary education; concentrations in actuarial science and physics are also available. A wide assortment of two-year and four-year programs is available in computer science. All receive support from the Pitt network as well as from the computer science lab.

Majors in the natural sciences are available in athletic training, biology, chemistry, environmental studies, geology and environmental science, physical sciences, psychology, radiological sciences, sport and recreation management, and sports medicine. Students in these programs have had phenomenal success rates in gaining entry to, and succeeding in, postgraduate programs in medical, dental, and other health-related fields. The Allegheny Institute of Natural History also makes its home at Pitt-Bradford.

Pitt-Bradford offers many different nursing programs. The Associate of Science in Nursing (ASN) can be completed in two years; the Bachelor of Science in Nursing (RN-BSN completion) requires an additional two years (students may commence this program on completion of the ASN). The University also offers a School Nurse Certification program for registered nurses who wish to work in the school system.

Office of Admissions, Hanley Library, 300 Campus Drive
Bradford, PA 16701
Phone: 814-362-7555
Fax: 814-362-7578
Website: www.upb.pitt.edu

Pitt-Bradford offers a wide array of academic opportunities in the social sciences. Students may prepare for careers in nonprofit organizations and the government. They may also prepare for law school or graduate study in the social sciences. Students who major in the administration of justice open opportunities to serve in law, the courts, and the corrections system. Students in the human relations program benefit from a cross-disciplinary approach to the behavioral sciences; our program combines study of anthropology, psychology and sociology.

Students may relocate to another University campus in order to complete academic programs not offered at Pitt-Bradford; they may earn no more than 70 credits before transferring. All students in the arts and sciences may relocate provided they are students in good standing. Engineering students may relocate if they maintain quality point average of at least 2.5.

Students at Pitt-Bradford may pursue a four-year major in administration of justice, athletic training, biology, business management, chemistry, communications (radio and television), computer science (BA & BS), economics, education, English, environmental studies, geology and environmental science, history/political science, human relations, mathematics, nursing, physical sciences, psychology, public relations, radiological science, social sciences, sociology, sport and recreation management, sports medicine, and writing. A number of these majors are useful in preparing students for graduate work in dental medicine, law, medicine, occupational therapy, optometry, physical therapy, and veterinary medicine. Elementary and secondary education certifications are available to students in a number of majors. Pitt-Bradford students may study engineering (chemical, civil, computer, electrical, industrial, manufacturing, mechanical, and petroleum) for two years. Engineers must complete the rest of the program at the Pittsburgh campus. Students in information systems and nursing (RN) may pursue associate's degrees.

Students may pursue 3-4 programs offered in conjunction with the University of Pittsburgh School of Dental Medicine and the Pennsylvania College of Optometry; undergraduates begin their studies at Pitt-Bradford and, after three years, transfer to the appropriate graduate school to complete a further four years' study. Pitt-Bradford also offers the first two years study leading to the Doctorate in Pharmacy; students must complete their final four years at the Pittsburgh campus (admission to this campus is competitive). The Pittsburgh School of Pharmacy pre-admits some qualified high school seniors, pending completion of the first two years of the pre-professional program at Pitt-Bradford.

Pitt-Bradford has 75 full-time faculty members; all hold doctorates and master's degrees from such prestigious institutions as Cornell, Harvard, Stanford, and the University of Pittsburgh. Professors take their teaching duties seriously, regarding them as their primary responsibility at the University. Our student/faculty ratio of 13:1 allows instructors to place a premium on personal attention both in and out of the classroom (average class size is a scant 17 students).

ADMISSIONS

The Admissions committee looks primarily at three factors in evaluating applicants: the applicant's record of high school achievement; standardized test results (SAT I or ACT), and letters of recommendation from teachers and/or a counselor at their high school. Class rank, extracurricular activities, personal qualifications, and potential role in the school community are also considered. Pitt-Bradford accepts applicants on a rolling basis. Applications are welcome at any time. The Admissions committee notifies candidates as soon as a decision has been made on their application. Applicants must complete and submit the application form and a nonrefundable $35 fee. An official high school transcript and an official standardized test score report (SAT I or ACT) are also required. Transfer applicants must also submit official copies of all college transcripts; those transcripts must reflect a GPA of at least 2.0.

Students and their families are welcome to visit our campus; campus visits often help students come to a final decision about the University. The Office of Admissions schedules interviews and tours Monday through Friday, 9 A.M. to 4 P.M. all year long, as well as on selected Saturdays during the school year. Contact the Office of Admissions to arrange a visit. Students seeking more information should contact:

The Office of Admissions
The University of Pittsburgh at Bradford
300 Campus Drive
Bradford, PA 16701-2898
Telephone: 814-362-7555 or 800-872-1787 (toll free)
Fax: 814-362-7578
Website: www.upb.pitt.edu
E-mail: admissions@www.upb.pitt.edu

CAMPUS LIFE

The University of Pittsburgh at Bradford is situated in the town of Bradford, nestled in an area with a population of roughly 22,000. Bradford lies on the edge of the Allegheny National Forest in the northwestern corner of Pennsylvania. Buffalo is located 80 miles to the north; Pittsburgh is 160 miles to the southeast. Bradford is home to many national and international businesses, including Dresser Manufacturing and Zippo Manufacturing. The 155-acre campus is ideally located for outdoor enthusiasts; opportunities for boating, camping, fishing, hiking, snowboarding, hunting, fishing, and downhill and cross-country skiing are plentiful in the area. Pitt-Bradford can be reached easily by ground and air transportation.

COST AND AID

Full-time tuition for a 15-week term in 2002–2003 was $3,934 for Pennsylvania residents, $8,338 for nonresidents. Tuition for the nursing program was $5,062 (per term) for Pennsylvania residents and $10,656 for nonresidents. Room and board for a double room occupancy and 19-meal-per-week plan were $2,735 per term. Students must also pay a $75 activity fee per term, a $130 computer fee per term, a $17 health fee per term, a $70 recreation fee per term and a one-time freshman orientation fee of $90. On average, students spend about $400 per term on books and supplies.

UNIVERSITY OF ROCHESTER

GENERAL INFORMATION

The University of Rochester is among the nation's premier private universities. Founded in 1850, the University is one of 63 member schools of the eminent Association of American Universities. It is also one of eight members of the University Athletic Association, a consortium of national research institutions that share a unique approach to academics and athletics. A population of 4,435 undergraduates and 2,570 graduates attend Rochester (including students of the Eastman School of Music). Rochester's moderate size and the range of its academic and research programs allow for both individual attention and uncommon flexibility in designing undergraduate studies. The unique Rochester Curriculum allows students to maximize the potential of their undergraduate experience. Undergraduates have access to courses offered at six colleges and professional schools: the College (Arts and Sciences; School of Engineering and Applied Sciences), the Eastman School of Music, the William E. Simon Graduate School of Business Administration, the Margaret Warner Graduate School of Education and Human Development, the School of Medicine and Dentistry, and the School of Nursing.

STUDENT BODY

Among the more than 170 organizations at the University of Rochester are groups dedicated to community service, student governance, political action, pre-professional and academic interests, international and multicultural issues, religion, music and performing arts, and a wide range of special interests and hobbies. Nearly 20 percent of all undergraduates join a fraternity or sorority during their tenure. Athletics are paramount at Rochester, home to 22 varsity teams, 35 club teams, an active intramural sports community, and recreational athletic classes. Rochester competes in the University Athletic Association, which covers the greatest geographic area of all NCAA Division III conferences; it also competes in the Upstate Collegiate Athletic Association. The school's athletic facility, the Robert B. Goergen Athletic Center, was recently renovated. It includes a two-story fitness center; an indoor track; pools for swimming and diving; multi-use rooms; squash and racquetball courts; courts for indoor soccer, basketball, volleyball, and tennis; and a sizeable basketball arena.

ACADEMICS

The unique Rochester Curriculum allows undergraduates to choose their major from among the three branches of learning: the natural sciences, the social sciences, and the arts and humanities. Students must then select two "clusters" of three courses each outside their major; the clusters add breadth to the curriculum by exposing students to the other two branches. Rochester's distinctive Quest courses offer freshmen the benefits of small classes, mentorship and collaboration, and the opportunity to conduct original research. Students learn the value and skills of independent study through Quest courses, a lesson that serves them both during their undergraduate careers and after. Through the "Take Five" Scholars Program, selected students may undertake a tuition-free fifth year so that they may pursue their diverse interests. Exceptional undergraduates interested in studying medicine may pursue the Rochester Early Medical Scholars (REMS) program, an eight-year BA/BS-MD program. Enrollees enter the University of Rochester with a guarantee of admission to the School of Medicine and Dentistry, dependent upon successful completion of undergraduate studies. Among other available special opportunities are: off-campus employment, including paid internships and a national summer jobs program; 3-2 programs, which permit selected students to earn both a bachelor's and master's degrees in five years; and the Senior Scholars Program.

The University of Rochester offers Bachelor of Arts and/or Bachelor of Science programs through the College. Available majors include American Sign Language, anthropology, art history, biological sciences (biochemistry, cell and developmental biology, ecology and evolutionary biology, microbiology, molecular genetics, or neuroscience), biology, brain and cognitive sciences, chemistry, classics, computer science, economics, English, environmental science, environmental studies, film and media studies, French, geological sciences, geomechanics, German, health and society, history, integrated sciences, interdepartmental studies, Japanese, linguistics, mathematics, mathematics-applied, mathematics-statistics, music, philosophy, physics, physics and astronomy, political science, psychology, religion, Russian, Russian studies, Spanish, statistics, studio arts, and women's studies.

Box 270251
Rochester, NY 14627-0251
Phone: 585-275-3221
Fax: 585-461-4595
Website: www.rochester.edu

The College offers certificate programs in actuarial studies, Asian studies, biotechnology, international relations, management studies, and Polish and Central European studies. These programs complement traditional majors. The School of Engineering and Applied Sciences offers study in biomedical, chemical, electrical and computer, and mechanical engineering; geomechanics; optics; engineering and applied sciences; and engineering science. Rochester not only offers a BA in music through the college, but also a Bachelor of Music degree through the Eastman School of Music; available majors include applied music, jazz studies and contemporary media, music composition, music education, and music theory. Private instruction through the Eastman School is available to students in the College; students there may also take part in any of 14 music ensembles.

Rochester students benefit from a 9:1 student/faculty ratio, which allows many opportunities to work closely with an inspiring faculty of internationally prominent scholars. All Rochester professors teach at the undergraduate level; all engage in advanced research as well. Rochester's faculty is highly regarded by peers at sister institutions; many departments at the University rank among the nation's elite.

ADMISSIONS

Applications for admission to the fall semester freshman class should be submitted by January 20; those applying for spring admission should submit applications no later than October 1. The deadline for Early Decision applications is November 15; applicants are notified in December. The University welcomes applications from transfer students for either semester. Students wishing to apply online will find an application at the University's website; there is no fee for online application. The Common Application may be used instead of the school's own application. Applicants must submit either SAT I or ACT scores; SAT II scores are not required, but the committee does consider those results that are provided. The Higher Education Opportunity Program (HEOP) provides support services and financial aid to New York State residents from lower-income families; qualified applicants are encouraged to consider this option. The application committee evaluates applicants' high school records (cumulative average, class rank, quality of courses taken, etc.), standardized test performance, participation in co-curricular activities, letters of recommendation, and application essays. Other factors are also considered. The University of Rochester is committed to providing equal opportunity to all persons regardless of age, color, disability, ethnicity, marital status, national origin, race, religion, sex, sexual orientation, or veteran status. In addition, the University abides by all nondiscrimination laws applicable to the administration of its programs, policies, and activities.

CAMPUS LIFE

The River Campus, which is situated along the Genesee River, is home to most of the undergraduates at University of Rochester. An ample variety of dormitories, special interest housing, and fraternity houses are available. The University recently renovated most of its original buildings; all residence halls are now fully wired for cable television and computer access. The Rochester region is home to more than 1 million people. This appealing area is bordered by Lake Ontario to the north and the picturesque Finger Lakes to the south; unsurprisingly, it has been ranked among America's most livable cities. Rochester offers a profusion of recreational and cultural opportunities through its parks, professional sports teams, planetarium, museums, orchestras, and theater companies.

Rochester students may take advantage of full-year and semester-long opportunities for study abroad; summer and winter trips are also available. In all, Rochester offers more than 50 study abroad programs. Destinations include Australia, Austria, Belgium, China, Egypt, France, Germany, Ireland, Italy, Japan, Mexico, Poland, Russia, Spain, Sweden, and Taiwan. Internships are available in Brussels, London, Paris, Berlin, Bonn, and Madrid. For those interested in an exciting and enlightening domestic field experience, the Department of Political Science directs the Washington Semester Program; this program allows selected undergraduates to participate actively in the national legislative process.

COST AND AID

For the 2002–2003 academic year, costs for freshmen are: tuition, $25,430; room, $5,054; board, $3,450–$3,870 (depending on meal plan); and fees, $832 (including health fee, activity fee, and freshman orientation).

UNIVERSITY OF SAN FRANCISCO

GENERAL INFORMATION

When the Jesuits founded the University of San Francisco in 1855, it was a one-room schoolhouse. Now, it is one of the West Coast's largest Catholic universities. Some things haven't changed: class size is still small, and student/faculty ratio is still low. USF has been dedicated to helping students learn the skills they need to improve their world for 148 years. USF's Jesuit education is committed to providing all students with individual attention. Both love of learning and the willingness to face the challenge of serving society are fostered in programs in the arts, the sciences, business, education, nursing, and the law.

San Francisco itself is a laboratory for USF students. The city and its university have interconnected histories, and today, this vibrant partnership gives student the wonderful opportunity to bring classroom theory into real, twenty-first-century life. There are 3,800 undergraduates on the 54-acre residential campus, and these students come from all 50 states and 76 countries. Freshman and sophomore students must live on campus unless they live with their parents, and USF is located in a lovely residential neighborhood. Within the University, students have access to facilities including libraries, gymnasiums, a health and recreation center with an Olympic-size swimming pool, a pub, a coffeehouse, and a games room. But right outside is the city of San Francisco and "facilities" of its own: the ballet, opera, museum exhibits, concerts, theater, and sports events.

Students have the opportunity to live with their peers in a cozy, laid-back environment within the residence halls. There are traditional residence halls and also University apartment-style facilities on campus. Coed Gillson Hall is mainly for freshmen. Only women live in Hayes-Healy Hall. Coed upperclassmen live in Phelan Hall. Students over the age of 21 live in the coed Lone Mountain Hall and Loyola Village. Double rooms are standard, but there are a few single rooms for upperclassmen. There are laundry facilities, study/computer rooms, and television lounges in every residence hall. There are several dining facilities on campus that are convenient to (i.e. within walking distance of) the residence halls and classrooms. The World Fare has a dining environment similar to a food court. Other options include two student-run coffeehouses, a fast-food restaurant, an ice cream shop, Jamba Juice, and a bookstore.

There are more than 50 student-run associations for undergraduates at USF, including sororities, honor societies, and social organizations such as the USF Rugby Club and the USF Dons Club. These associations include the oldest continuously performing theater group west of the Mississippi River, an award-winning FM radio station, a weekly newspaper, and a literary magazine. The Career Services Center is one of the most active offices, aiding students in choosing a career path and learning about work opportunities available both now and later. The exciting Koret Health and Recreation Center is new to campus and houses facilities for exercise, racquetball, swimming, court games, and socializing. There are graduate programs in the arts and sciences, business, education, law, and nursing.

STUDENT BODY

Every undergraduate student is a member of the Associated Students of the University of San Francisco (ASUSF). There are three purposes to the ASUSF: to represent the official student viewpoint, to recommend policies, and to fund activities and services. There are three branches: the executive branch, the Student Senate, and the Student Court. The main representative body of the undergraduate day students is the Senate, and it monitors the expenditures of the $200,000-plus student budget.

ACADEMICS

It is hoped that students leave USF with a well-rounded education. A curriculum of 128 units is required for the degree. General education from six particular categories of knowledge make up 51 units of the curriculum, including a nine-unit block of basic skills courses and 80 to 83 units divided between major requirements and electives. Superior students may be selected for an honors program that provides a high academic challenge. USF urges qualified high school students to study subjects traditionally reserved for colleges as early as possible. To this end, advanced placement courses, as certified by the College Board's Advanced Placement Program tests, are honored. USF also cooperates with the College-Level Examination Program (CLEP). Students interested in obtaining this credit are required to take the CLEP tests before registering for their freshman courses. A special program is available through the St. Ignatius Institute. The institute has a core curriculum that is based on the Western civilization's great books, with an emphasis on the great works of Christianity. General education course requirements can be met through courses at the institute, no matter what the student's major. Army ROTC is also available at USF, and qualified applicants and continuing students have access to ROTC scholarships. Two semesters make up the academic year, and there are also summer sessions and a January intersession.

BA and BS degrees are available through USF. The College of Arts and Sciences offers majors in biology, chemistry, communication studies, computer science, economics, English, environmental science, environmental studies, exercise and sports science, fine arts, French, history, Latin American studies, mathematics, media studies, performing arts, philosophy, physics, physics/engineering, politics, psychological services, psychology, sociology, Spanish, theology/religious studies, undeclared arts/science, and visual arts. The McLaren College of Business offers degrees in accounting, business administration, finance, hospitality management, international business, and marketing. Qualified high school graduates and second-baccalaureate candidates can pursue a four-year baccalaureate program through the School of Nursing. Students can receive teacher certification at the elementary or secondary level by completing a fifth year of study.

2130 Fulton Street
San Francisco, CA 94117
Phone: 415-422-6563
Fax: 415-422-2217
Website: www.usfca.edu

The Pre-Professional Health Committee at USF advises and recommends students to medical and dental professional health schools, as well as to schools for pharmacy, optometry, veterinary medicine, and podiatry. The pre-medical or other pre-health science requirements can be taken as part of, or in addition to, the requirements of an academic major. The Pre-Professional Health Committee helps students with the application process, creates a professional file for each student, gathers and sends recommendations to professional schools, gives interviews in preparation for application, and endorses approved candidates through a committee letter of recommendation that is sent to all professional schools the student selects.

There are close to 240 full-time and 350 part-time faculty, and 91 percent of the full-time faculty have a doctoral degree. The undergraduate divisions employ about 250 faculty. Traditionally, students and faculty enjoy a close relationship, which is reflected in small class size, low student/faculty ratio, and the accessibility of faculty members for counseling. USF does not use student teachers or teachers' assistants.

ADMISSIONS

Students with a desire to obtain a well-rounded education are sought after by USF. Admission is selective, and each application receives an individual review. USF desires a high-quality and diverse student body, and so encourages applications from men and women of all races, nationalities, and religious beliefs. Prospective students are evaluated on many criteria, including high school grade point average, the application essay, a personal recommendation, and satisfactory test scores. All applicants must take the SAT I or the ACT, and international applicants must take the TOEFL. A completed application file is made up of the application form, an essay, all academic transcripts, SAT I or ACT scores, and one letter of recommendation. For the fall semester, November 15 is the deadline for early action and February 1 is the deadline for regular action. For additional information, please contact:

Office of Admission
University of San Francisco
2130 Fulton Street
San Francisco, CA 94117-1046
Telephone: 415-422-6563 or 800-CALL-USF (toll free outside California)
Fax: 415-422-2217
E-mail: admission@usfca.edu
World Wide Web: www.usfca.edu

CAMPUS LIFE

The beautiful University of San Francisco campus is 54 acres, and is located in a residential neighborhood. Downtown San Francisco and the Pacific Ocean are just minutes away, and the 1,000-acre Golden Gate Park is only a block away. There are many benefits of an urban campus, and San Francisco's diversity and compact geography allow students to discover research facilities, community involvement options, and work opportunities found in few other cities.

USF students have many opportunities for university-sponsored study abroad programs, such as ones to Sophia University (Tokyo), Oxford (England), and Innsbruck (Austria), through USF's St. Ignatius Institute, a program at Universidad Iberoamericana in Mexico City, and a joint program with Hungary's University in Budapest. USF is connected to Gonzaga University's study abroad program in Florence (Italy) and to Loyola University of Chicago's program in Rome. The Institute of European and Asian Studies, of which USF is an associate member, offers programs in Durham and London, England; Paris, Dijon, and Nantes, France; Berlin and Freiburg, Germany; Vienna, Austria; Madrid and Salamanca, Spain; Milan, Italy; Tokyo and Nagoya, Japan; Moscow, Russia; Adelaide and Canberra, Australia; Beijing, China; and Singapore. There are many other study abroad opportunities as well. Students receive assistance from USF in all aspects of the program: choosing a location, completing applications, arranging financial matters, registering for academic credit, obtaining a passport and visa, and organizing travel plans.

COST AND AID

Tuition for the 2003–2004 school year is $23,220. Room and board are $9,790 for the academic year. An additional $3,300 per year is generally required for books, fees, travel, and other expenses.

THE UNIVERSITY OF SCRANTON

GENERAL INFORMATION

A Jesuit institution in Pennsylvania's Pocono northeast region, The University of Scranton is known for many things, especially its outstanding academics, state-of-the art campus and technology, and exceptional sense of community. Founded in 1888, the University offers more than 80 undergraduate and graduate academic programs of study through five colleges and schools. For nine consecutive years, *U.S. News & World Report* ranked Scranton among the 10 finest master's universities in the North—4th in the 2003 edition, and 11th among Great Schools at a Great Price. *Yahoo! Internet Life* has ranked Scranton among the nation's 100 most wired colleges and universities for three straight years—39th in the 2001 edition. The Princeton Review counts Scranton among *The Best 345 Colleges* in the nation, according to its 2003 edition. The University is profiled in the 2003 edition of Kaplan Publishing's *The Unofficial, Unbiased, Insider's Guide to the 320 Most Interesting Colleges*. In addition, Scranton is one of only 100 schools in the nation on Templeton's Honor Roll of Character-Building Colleges. Medical and related schools accepted 100 percent of the University's 30 graduating seniors who applied in 2002—more than twice the national average. The acceptance rate for the 35 Scranton students applying to law schools in 2002 was 75 percent—about 15 percent above the national average. In 2001 and 2002 alone, Scranton students earned a remarkable eight Fulbrights, a Truman Scholarship, a Jack Kent Cooke Scholarship, four Freeman Awards, two NCAA Post-Graduate Scholarships, two Rotary Ambassadorial Scholarships, two State Farm Fellowships, and a DeRance Scholarship. Scranton has always had high rates of both graduation and retention. Graduation rates are monitored at intervals of four and six years. The graduation rate is 67 percent for four-year students (21 percent higher than the national average) and 78 percent for six-year students (18 percent higher than the national average). The retention rate (the percentage of students who come back after the first year) averages 90 percent.

STUDENT BODY

Because learning does not stop at the classroom door, we provide opportunities to participate in an array of social, educational, wellness, and retreat activities. You will be able to participate in more than 80 clubs and organizations. If your interests are journalism or writing you can become involved in *The Aquinas* (student newspaper), *Esprit* (literary journal), *Windhover* (yearbook), or Royal Network News (campus electronic news). You can become active in the arts through the University Players, University Bands, and University Singers. You can develop as a leader through student government or explore politics with the Campus Democrats and College Republicans. You can even choose clubs that link to academic majors or that celebrate ethnic and cultural roots. And you can experience the satisfaction of helping others through Students for Social Justice, Habitat for Humanity, and Collegiate Volunteers. Historically, the University of Scranton has had athletic success in NCAA Division III. The men's and women's basketball teams have both won national championships, and the 10 men's and 9 women's teams regularly compete for and win Middle Atlantic Conference (MAC) titles. There are also many intramurals, recreational sports, and club sports, including rugby, men's volleyball, equestrian, skiing, crew, and track.

ACADEMICS

We offer a full range of undergraduate programs of study to match your interests and prepare you to meet the future with confidence. The newest additions to the University's 58 undergraduate majors include electronic commerce, enterprise management technology, accounting information systems, exercise science, and media and information technology. Scranton also offers 44 minors, 29 concentrations and tracks, and 23 master's degree programs. You can choose our highly successful pre-law and pre-medical programs. You can even enhance study in a particular field through double majors, bachelor's/master's degree combinations, ROTC, foreign study, internships, clinicals, research, and three programs of advanced study. Each year we select between 50 and 60 of the most qualified freshmen to join the Special Jesuit Liberal Arts Program (SJLA), a program that allows them to fulfill their general education credits in a community atmosphere encouraging excellence and service to others. Open to all majors, the Honors Program each year accepts between 40 and 50 of our most able sophomores, giving them the opportunity to take seminars together and to work one-on-one with professors both in tutorials and on projects. Open to students from all majors, our Business Leadership Program helps students develop the talents and skills necessary to succeed in a variety of leadership settings, especially in the world of business. This highly selective program accepts 15 sophomores each spring to explore basic theories and concepts of leadership through special seminars and courses in management, ethics, strategy, and analysis. The Office of Fellowship Programs builds on Scranton's remarkable success in securing Fulbrights by supporting students who wish to compete for the nation's other top fellowships and scholarships.

Majors are available in: accounting, accounting information systems, biochemistry, biology, biomathematics, biophysics, chemistry, chemistry/business, chemistry/computers, classical languages, communication, computer engineering, computer information systems, computer science, criminal justice, early childhood education, economics, electrical engineering, electronic commerce, electronics/business, elementary education, English, enterprise management technology, environmental science, exercise science, finance, French, German, gerontology, health administration, history, human resources studies, human services, international business, international language/business, international studies, management, marketing, mathematics, media & information technology, medical technology, neuroscience, nursing, occupational therapy, operations management, philosophy, physical therapy, physics, political science, pre-engineering, psychology, secondary education, sociology, Spanish, special education, theatre, theology/religious studies. These majors lead to Bachelor of Science and Bachelor of Arts degrees. On the graduate level, students can earn the Master of Business Administration, Master of Science, Master of Arts, and Master of Health Administration degrees. Additionally, physical therapy and occupational therapy are offered in a five-year, direct-entry, Master of Physical Therapy degree program open only to first-time freshmen. Applicants are allowed to enroll as undecided and choose a major in their sophomore year.

800 Linden Street
Scranton, PA 18510-4699
Phone: 570-941-7540
Fax: 570-941-5928
Website: www.scranton.edu

With a student/faculty ratio of just 13:1 and an average class size of 23, our professors get to know our students. Our more than 250 faculty members hold degrees from 135 different universities in 30 countries on five continents. Cambridge and the University of London in England; Louvain and the Gregorian on the Continent; the University of Calcutta in India; the Sophia University in Japan; Soochow University in China; Berkeley, Yale, MIT, Notre Dame, Harvard, and Georgetown in America—all are represented among the faculty. They are the most cosmopolitan element in the community. Hindu and Muslim, Christian and Jew, ministers and rabbis—scholars and teachers all.

ADMISSIONS

Scranton welcomes men and women of all races, national origins, and religious beliefs. We look for high-achieving students who have shown that they are prepared for a challenging college program through their high school course selection and level, grades, class rank, and SAT/ACT scores. Also important are involvement in activities, athletics, and service, and work experience. Physical therapy and occupational therapy students must submit documentation of experience in their field. A campus visit with an informational interview or small group presentation is encouraged. The University of Scranton offers an Early Action program with a November 15 deadline. Students who apply early will receive notification of admission on December 15. The application deadline for students interested in applying for the physical therapy program is November 15. For students who choose not to apply for Early Action, we operate on a rolling admissions basis, with an application deadline of March 1 and a confirmation deadline of May 1.

CAMPUS LIFE

Easily reached by major highways, The University of Scranton is about two hours from New York City, Philadelphia, Syracuse, and Danbury (Connecticut) and only about four hours from Baltimore and Washington. An urban campus, The University of Scranton offers all of the opportunities of a city location. Students can also take advantage of the University's Conference and Retreat Center at Chapman Lake, just 25 minutes from campus. One visit to our 50-acre campus is enough to experience the friendliness and enthusiasm that is the cornerstone of the Scranton community. A safe campus in one of the nation's safest cities, our students have a comfortable environment in which to study and grow. Located in the City of Scranton (population 76,000), The University of Scranton is within walking distance of internships, cultural opportunities, a downtown mall and movie theaters, and the Steamtown National Historic Site. Students can intern at one of three hospitals within a mile of campus, law offices, businesses, local television stations and newspapers, service agencies and other organizations. Just a 10-minute drive away is Montage Mountain with its winter ski area and summer water slides and concert amphitheater. The nearby 12,000-seat Lackawanna County Stadium is the place to cheer on both the University of Scranton Royals baseball team and the Philadelphia Phillies' AAA Red Barons. The Luzerne County Arena, 15 minutes away from Montage, offers professional ice hockey featuring a minor league affiliate of the Pittsburgh Penguins and arena football. Other attractions include the Pocono Motor Speedway, Elk Mountain ski resort, several state parks, and two museums.

COST AND AID

Annual tuition for the 2002–2003 academic year is $20,248, with mandatory fees of $200. Room Charges range from $4,818 to $5,948. Meal plans range from $2,874 to $3,662.

UNIVERSITY OF TAMPA

GENERAL INFORMATION

The University of Tampa is a private, comprehensive university offering challenging learning experiences in two colleges: the College of Liberal Arts and Sciences and the College of Business. Fully accredited by the Southern Association of Colleges and Schools and the Association to Advance Collegiate Schools of Business, the University offers undergraduate and graduate courses in more than 60 fields of study. In all programs, students work with experts in their fields, and there is a shared belief in the value of a liberal arts–centered education, practical work experience, and the ability to communicate effectively. Situated on a beautiful, parklike campus on the Hillsborough River, the University is just two blocks from downtown Tampa. Plant Hall, once a luxurious hotel for the rich and famous, is the center of the campus. Its ornate Victorian gingerbread features and Moorish minarets, domes, and cupolas remain a symbol of the city. Although Plant Hall receives most of the attention, the campus has 45 other buildings, including a student union, a library, art galleries, modern science labs, a computer resource center, a television studio, a theater, seven residence halls, and complete athletic facilities. Both coed and single-sex residence halls have mostly double rooms and suites with private baths. More than 4,250 students, including 3,200 full-time undergraduates, representing 50 states and nearly 100 countries, are enrolled at the University. The environment outside the classroom is supportive, stimulating, and fun. Students choose from more than 100 student organizations, including honor societies, social clubs, and Greek life. The University of Tampa has one of the top NCAA Division II sports programs in the nation. The UT Spartans have won five national championships in recent years, three in baseball and two in soccer. Intercollegiate sports for men and women include basketball, crew, cross-country, soccer, and swimming. Men's baseball and golf and women's softball, tennis, and volleyball are also offered. All students may have cars on campus.

STUDENT BODY

Students choose from more than 100 student clubs and organizations including honors societies, social clubs, and student government activities. Fifteen percent of UT students are members of a fraternity or sorority. Students produce seven award-winning publications, including *The Minaret* (newspaper), *Moroccan* (yearbook), *Quilt* (literary magazine), and *Respondez!* (honors journal). Student-run television and radio stations also broadcast from campus. The McNiff Fitness Center, tennis courts, a track, and an outdoor heated pool offer students places to relax and exercise year-round. In addition to an academic transcript, graduating students may elect to send a co-curricular transcript of all extracurricular activities and leadership positions held to prospective employers and graduate schools.

ACADEMICS

The undergraduate curriculum is designed to give students a broad academic and cultural background as well as a concentrated study in a major. The "Baccalaureate Experience" begins with a special freshman seminar program designed to help students assess their skills and research their interests. All students participate in a special "Gateways" orientation and career exploration program during the freshman year. During the first two years, students pursue an integrated core program of 13 courses consisting of two in English, one in math, one in computer science, and three in humanities. Prior to graduation, students are also required to take three writing-intensive courses, one course that deals with nonwestern/Third World concerns, and an international/global awareness course. International experience is a celebrated focus of study and Campus Life. International academic opportunities begin with a global issues course required of all first-year students. Students go on to develop international expertise in a variety of ways, including majors in international studies and international business, certificate programs in European studies and Latin American studies, or participation in the Summit of the Americas, the Harvard Model United Nations, Global Village, and European Union Simulation programs. For qualifying students, the University offers an honors program of expanded instruction and student research. The program features honors classes, honors floors in residence halls, a senior thesis, and study in London or at Oxford University. Students also compete for annual honors research fellowships to work with faculty on research projects. The Saunders Writing Center offers free tutorial assistance to students working on writing projects in all courses. The Academic Center for Excellence (ACE) provides support and reinforces and supplements classroom work. Through a peer-tutoring program, upper-level students are assigned to courses as mentors and conduct weekly tutoring sessions. The ACE is one of the few internationally certified by the College Reading and Learning Association. Army and Air Force ROTC programs are offered.

The University of Tampa offers Bachelor's degrees in accounting, art, athletic training, biochemistry, biology, chemistry, communication, computer graphics, computer information systems, criminology, economics, education (elementary and secondary certification), English, environmental science, exercise science and sport studies, finance, government and world affairs, graphic design, history, international business, liberal studies, management, marine science (biology and chemistry), marketing, mathematical programming, mathematics, music, nursing, performing arts, psychology, social sciences, sociology, Spanish, sports management, and writing. Minors and concentrations are offered in adult fitness, advertising, aerospace studies, arts administration and management, biology-business, business administration, computer information systems, chemistry (pre-professional), dance/theater, French, international studies, law and justice, military science, molecular biology, philosophy, physical education, recreation, sports medicine, theater and speech, urban studies, and women's studies. Pre-professional programs offered include pre-dentistry, pre-law, pre-medicine, allied health, and pre–veterinary science. Certificate programs include art therapy, European studies, gerontology, and Latin American studies. An undergraduate evening college offers 10 degree programs designed for adults who want to study part-time. Three summer sessions also offer excellent learning and professional advancement opportunities. On the graduate level, the University offers the Master of Business Administration degree and the Master of Science in Nursing degree.

401 West Kennedy Boulevard
Tampa, FL 33606-1490
Phone: 813-253-6211
Fax: 813-258-7398
Website: www.ut.edu

The University Of
TAMPA

The University is proud of its outstanding faculty. Members hold degrees from the most prestigious universities, and 97 percent hold the highest degree in their field. With a student-to-faculty ratio of 17:1, the average class size is only 20 students. All classes are taught by professors, not graduate assistants, who prize the relationships that a small class size affords them. Faculty members also pursue scores of research projects each year, often with students as assistants. There are 167 full-time faculty and 176 part-time faculty.

ADMISSIONS

For freshmen, 15 high school units are recommended from the following areas: 4 units in English, 2 units in college-preparatory mathematics, 2 units in science, 2 units in social studies, and 5 units of academic electives. A foreign language is not required, but 2 units are recommended. The results of the SAT I or the ACT are required. A personal essay and at least one recommendation from a high school counselor are requested. Early admission may be granted to students who have completed 14 academic units by the end of their junior year and who have a minimum 3.0 average (on a 4.0 scale), good SAT I or ACT scores, and their counselor's or principal's recommendation. Students receive advanced placement by earning acceptable scores on Advanced Placement exams, the College-Level Examination Program tests, or by completing the International Baccalaureate diploma. As much as one year's credit may be awarded. Transfer students should have an overall 2.25 average or better (on a 4.0 scale) for college or university work attempted. They must be in good academic and social standing with the institution of prior attendance. Transfer students who have an associate's degree may be given full junior status. All international students for whom English is not a native or first language should take the Test of English as a Foreign Language (TOEFL). For intensive English study, the American Language Academy (ALA) is located on campus. ALA students may audit one or two classes at the University of Tampa until adequate English proficiency is reached to study full-time. The University evaluates applications on a rolling basis, which means students are notified of their Admissions status promptly once all required documentation is received. If students bring admission documents with them on the day of their campus visit, the Admissions staff will review qualifications and inform students of their status before they leave that day. Campus visits may be arranged Monday through Friday, 9 A.M. to 3 P.M. throughout the year and many Saturday mornings during the academic year. Open-house programs for prospective students and their parents are also held on selected weekends throughout the year. High school students may apply online after the end of their junior year. To request information or apply online go to: University of Tampa's website: www.ut.edu

CAMPUS LIFE

Located on the west-central coast of Florida, Tampa is more than just beautiful beaches and pleasant year-round temperatures. Home to 1.3 million people, Tampa Bay is one of the fastest-growing areas in the United States. The city is a leading center for the arts, banking, real estate, law, transportation, international business, education, communications, and health and scientific research. According to Newsweek Magazine, Tampa Bay will be one of the 10 best areas of the country for jobs during the next 25 years. Students attend concerts, art exhibitions, theater productions, dance performances, and special lectures on campus and nearby. Just across the river are the Museum of Art, the St. Petersburg Times Forum, the Performing Arts Center, the Convention Center, the aquarium, and an outstanding public library. Busch Gardens, the second-largest tourist attraction in Florida, is just a few miles from campus. Within 90 minutes' drive are Disney World and Universal Studios, Florida. Tampa International Airport conveniently connects students with every major city in the world. Six major shopping malls and dozens of restaurants are nearby. Latin American, African, Caribbean, and European influences all add spice to the area's cultural heritage.

Practical experience is an integral aspect of every course. Off-campus learning activities help students integrate academic theory with real-world practices. UT was founded by the Chamber of Commerce in 1931 and still enjoys close working relationships with local and international business communities. More than 600 community and business leaders serve on the University's boards as academic support groups and as classroom advisors, providing students with real-world voices of experience, internships, and invaluable networking opportunities. Students study in universities around the world to develop expertise in foreign languages, international business, international studies, government and world affairs, European or Latin American studies, or other areas. Faculty-led study/travel courses also complement an internationally rich curriculum.

COST AND AID

The total estimated cost for the 2002–2003 academic year, excluding summer sessions, is $23,164. This cost includes tuition and all mandatory fees of $882 and average room and board costs of $6,132. Board includes 15 meals per week. Evening College tuition is $235 per credit hour. Graduate tuition is $352 per credit hour.

UNIVERSITY OF VERMONT

GENERAL INFORMATION

Standing in the shadows of the Green Mountains on Lake Champlain, the University of Vermont blends the close faculty-student relationship most commonly found in a small liberal arts college with the dynamic exchange of knowledge associated with a major research university. For UVM students that means 2,500 course offerings representing more than 90 majors; hands-on research opportunities supported by state-of-the-art facilities and the expertise of leading scientists and scholars; and a vibrant campus community in which 80 percent of our students are involved in athletics, clubs, and volunteer service. It's no secret that our setting is also an attraction.

STUDENT BODY

Getting involved comes naturally to most UVM students. Almost 100 student organizations (from the campus radio station, WRUV, to the UVM Rescue Squad), 22 Division I varsity teams, several intramural and club sports programs, countless community service opportunities, and a packed schedule of cultural events fill in where the classroom leaves off. First- and second-year students are required to live on campus, an arrangement that helps create strong connections with academic pursuits, co-curricular activities, and fellow students. The University offers an array of housing alternatives, each with its own amenities and character, such as the Living Learning Center, in which residents live in suites and share common academic, cultural, or recreational interests; or Wright Hall, which boasts its own fitness center and houses students who share a commitment to promoting academic excellence; or Slade Hall, where those interested in biology, nutrition, and environmental studies manage their own meals and grow food year-round in the Slade greenhouse.

ACADEMICS

Seven distinct academic schools and colleges are the foundation of the University of Vermont. While one of them will best match your needs, you will be encouraged to engage in courses throughout the University. Regardless of major, every student pursues course work in the liberal arts aimed at developing a global perspective and communication skills essential to life-long learning and success. While it's true that your college experience will be largely what you make it, the UVM community takes very seriously its supporting role. First-year students are assigned a faculty advisor, someone to turn to for advice and counsel on course selection and other aspects of university life. Other resources include the Learning Co-op, UVM's Counseling Center, and the Career Services Office.

Most programs result in a Bachelor of Arts or Bachelor of Science degree: animal sciences, anthropology, area and international studies, art education, art history, art studio, Asian studies, biochemical science, biological sciences, biology, biomedical technology, botany, business administration, Canadian studies, chemistry, civil engineering, classical civilization, communication science, community development and applied economics, computer science, computer science information systems, dental hygiene (2-year), dietetics, early childhood and preschool programs, economics, electrical engineering, elementary education (K-6), engineering management, English, environmental sciences, environmental studies, European studies, family and consumer sciences, education, forestry, French, geography, geology, German, Greek, history, human development and family studies, individually designed major, Latin, Latin American studies, mathematics, mechanical engineering, medical laboratory science microbiology, molecular genetics, music, music education, natural resources, nuclear medicine technology, nursing, nutrition and food sciences, philosophy, physical education, physics, plant and soil science, political science, psychology, radiation therapy, recreation management, religion, resource economics, Russian, Russian/European studies, secondary education, social work, sociology, Spanish, theatre, urban forestry and landscape horticulture, wildlife and fisheries biology, women's studies, zoology.

UVM faculty are practicing scientists, scholars, and artists, dedicated both to the advancement of knowledge and to teaching and inspiring others. Internationally known scholars instruct not only juniors and seniors, but first-year students as well. Faculty involved in research bring commitment and passion, depth of understanding, and cutting-edge knowledge to the classroom. Only 3 percent of classes are taught by graduate teaching assistants.

Office of Admissions, 194 South Prospect Street
Burlington, VT 05401-3596
Phone: 802-656-3370
Fax: 802-656-8611
Website: www.uvm.edu

ADMISSIONS

Admission to the University of Vermont is selective. First-year students are evaluated primarily on high school performance and standardized examinations; transfer students are judged on college-level course work, standing at previous institutions, and/or other educational credentials. Rigor of course work and preparation for the major are considered. Beyond academic credentials, other characteristics and experiences are reviewed; essays, recommendations, and other evidence of life experience assist in understanding a student's potential to succeed and contribute at the University. The University offers both Early Decision (binding) and Early Action (nonbinding), both with November 1 application deadlines and notification in late December. January 15 is the regular decision deadline, with notification by late March. Transfers for fall apply by April 1, for spring by November 1; notification is rolling. The University of Vermont application is on the web at: www.uvm.edu/admissions. The University also accepts the Common Application. For a full listing of requirements, consult www.uvm.edu/admissions.

CAMPUS LIFE

The Green Mountain landscape has shaped the University and does the same for its students, challenging mind, body, and spirit in work and play. On a three-day backpacking trip or a ten-minute walk across the campus, the natural beauty of Vermont is part of everyday life. UVM's location in Burlington, a lively city with a broad appeal, offers an array of cultural and recreational options. Church Street Marketplace, a half-mile from campus, is the heart of downtown Burlington. Shops, restaurants, coffeehouses, and sidewalk cafes line the pedestrian mall, creating a streetscape with a friendly, European air. Burlington's waterfront bikepath is great for walkers, bladers, runners, and cyclists. Boston and New York are both within a half-day's drive, and the French-Canadian culture of Montreal is waiting to be explored just 100 miles north of campus.

COST AND AID

Estimated Costs for 2003–2004

In-state tuition: $8,696

Out-of-state tuition: $21,748

Room and board: $6,680

Fees: $940

UNIVERSITY OF WYOMING

GENERAL INFORMATION

More than any other university of its kind, the University of Wyoming is a reflection of the state it serves. The broad range of outstanding academic programs mirrors the broad expanse of the dynamic Wyoming landscape. Its research goals, which benefit Wyoming and the world, are as lofty as the Snowy Range Mountains or the Grand Tetons.

Wyoming's people have been most influential in shaping the University. The distance between places, the beauty of the terrain, and the interdependence of neighbors have created a people who care about the land and who care about each other. UW is an institution of higher learning that combines the academic ambitions of the nation's finest extensive research universities with a deep love for the state and a tremendous regard for the values of Wyoming's people. That has been UW's philosophy since it was founded in 1886 when Wyoming was still a territory four years from statehood.

From the beginning, the land-grant mission has been to provide high-quality undergraduate and graduate education, research, and service. UW has remained true to the goal of serving the educational needs of students today and preparing them for a complex world tomorrow while preserving Wyoming's rich western heritage.

Unique among the 50 states, Wyoming has only one university, which enjoys tremendous statewide support. More than 11,700 students from all parts of the U.S. and 57 other countries attend UW classes in Laramie and at sites around the state. UW offers bachelor's, master's, and doctoral degrees in six undergraduate colleges, including the Doctor of Pharmacy in the College of Health Sciences. In the Colleges of Agriculture, Arts and Sciences, Business, Education, Engineering, and Health Sciences, students gain a broad range of classroom, laboratory, and co-curricular experiences that are the educational building blocks for a successful career or graduate study. Undergraduate education is a high priority at UW. The best and brightest of the faculty members teach undergraduate classes.

More that 180 campus clubs and organizations are recognized by the University, including 14 national fraternities and sororities. UW competes in Mountain West Conference Division I NCAA athletics in 17 men's and women's sports.

Campus recreational facilities include two indoor swimming pools, racquetball and tennis courts, an 18-hole golf course, weight rooms, rifle and archery ranges, indoor and outdoor tracks, softball and baseball fields, and a hockey rink. The student union hosts a variety of facilities, including eating establishments, a convenience store, student common areas, the bookstore, and meeting rooms.

The University houses 2,400 students in six residence halls. Living environments include coed or single-sex floors, special interest floors, honors floors, and other academic environments.

STUDENT BODY

UW students play a significant role in the governance of the University. The Associate Students of the University of Wyoming considers legislation that touches on all aspects of student life. The student body president sits as an ex officio member of the University Board of Trustees.

ACADEMICS

UW's commitment to student success is underscored by the large number of courses offered each semester, ensuring that students have an opportunity to graduate in four years in most majors.

UW's University Studies program requires all UW students to complete a set of common education requirements before receiving degrees. Reflecting UW's commitment to providing an education for complete living, the program is designed to develop the basic skills students need in areas such as writing and problem solving and to acquaint them with the realities of a global society. The academic calendar consists of two semesters and a complete summer session. Baccalaureate programs require 120 to 164 credit hours of course work. The University Honors Program provides distinctive learning experiences for a select group of students who show promise of academic excellence at the university level. The Senior Research Project is the hallmark of this program and prepares students for graduate and professional school. Freshman interest groups offer clustered classes and common living areas that allow participants to develop close relationships with other students who share common interests.

The University of Wyoming opened its doors in September 1887, with 1 building, 5 professors, 2 tutors, and 42 students. Programs of study available to those students included philosophy, arts, literature, and science. Today, UW offers 84 undergraduate programs and 92 graduate and professional degree programs within the Colleges of Agriculture, Arts and Sciences, Business, Education, Engineering, Health Sciences, and Law and the Graduate School.

The College of Agriculture offers agricultural business, agricultural communications, agroecology, animal science, farm and ranch management, food science, general agriculture, home economics (with options in child and family studies, dietetics, fashion and interior merchandising, home economics education, and human nutrition and food management), international agriculture, molecular biology (with options in biochemistry, biotechnology, and microbiology), range management, and vocational agriculture.

The College of Arts and Sciences offers degrees in the biological sciences—biology, botany, environmental and natural resources, physiology, psychology, wildlife and fisheries biology and management, and zoology; in the fine arts—art, music, music education (instrumental and vocal), music performance, music theory and composition, and theater and dance; in the humanities—English, English/theater, French, German, philosophy, Russian, and Spanish; interdisciplinary majors in administration of justice, American studies, humanities/fine arts, international studies, natural science/mathematics, self-designed major, social science, and women's studies; in the mathematical sciences—applied mathematics, mathematics, and statistics; in physical science—astronomy/astrophysics, chemistry, environmental geology/geohydrology, geology, and physics; and in social sciences—anthropology, communication, economics, geography, history, journalism, political economy, political science, and sociology.

Admissions Office, PO Box 3435
Laramie, WY 82071
Phone: 307-766-5160
Fax: 307-766-4042
Website: www.uwyo.edu

The College of Business offers accounting, business administration, economics, finance, management, marketing, and small business management.

In the College of Education, degrees may be earned in business education, distributive education, elementary and special education, elementary education, industrial technology education, secondary education, special education, trades and industrial education, vocational agriculture, and vocational homemaking.

The College of Engineering offers degrees in architectural engineering, chemical engineering (with options in petroleum engineering and environmental engineering), civil engineering, electrical engineering (with options in bioengineering and computer engineering), mechanical engineering, computer science, and management information systems (with options in accounting, business, and computer science).

The College of Health Sciences offers dental hygiene, health education (with options in teaching and health behavior promotion), nursing, physical education (with options in teaching and exercise and sport science), and speech, language, and hearing sciences. UW also offers pre-professional programs in dentistry, forestry, law, medicine, occupational therapy, optometry, physical therapy, and veterinary medicine.

More than 600 professors have come to teach at UW from the world's most respected colleges and universities. Recognized nationally and internationally as experts in their fields, they are deeply committed to the success of their students. UW's professors have as their primary responsibility the education of undergraduate students. Fewer than 10 percent of all credit hours are taught by graduate assistants. Many of the most accomplished professors teach first-year courses, enabling students to begin a mentoring process from the first day of class. Because Wyoming maintains a low student/faculty ratio (15:1) that allows for individual instruction and attention, the professors truly get to know their students. This relationship transcends teaching to include academic advising and inclusion of undergraduates in cutting-edge research projects. Over 90 percent of all UW instructors hold a PhD or the highest degree in their chosen fields.

ADMISSIONS

A variety of factors are used to determine eligibility for admission to UW. Students who are high school graduates with fewer than 30 transferable college credit hours must have taken and passed 13 core courses (4 years of English, 3 years of mathematics, 3 years of science, and 3 years of cultural context). A minimum grade point average of 2.75 and an ACT score of 20 or an SAT I score of 960 are also required. Admission with conditions is available to student who do not meet these standards, but who have a minimum 2.25 grade point average and an ACT composite score of 20 or an SAT I score of 960.

To be considered for admission, students must submit a completed UW application for admission, an official high school transcript, ACT or SAT I scores, and the $30 application fee. The priority deadline for financial aid is March 1.

UW encourages all prospective students and their parents to visit the campus. For more information or to schedule a campus tour, students should contact:

Admission Office
University of Wyoming
Box 3435
Laramie, WY 82071-3435
Telephone: 307-766-5160 or 800-DIAL-WYO (342-5996) (toll free)
E-mail: undergraduate.admissions@uwyo.edu
World Wide Web: www.uwyo.edu/

CAMPUS LIFE

UW's 785-acre campus is located in Laramie, a small city of 30,000 in southeastern Wyoming. Laramie is conveniently located 45 miles west of Wyoming's capital, Cheyenne, and 130 miles northwest of Denver, Colorado. Laramie sits between two mountain ranges and offers outstanding outdoor recreation. The campus and the community mesh into a friendly and supportive university town.

Education at the University of Wyoming is not confined to the buildings that comprise the main campus in Laramie. Bringing educational opportunities to students in all 23 Wyoming counties continues to be a top University priority. Since UW's inception, courses have been taught throughout the state using today's leading technology. Courses are taught through video technology that allows professors in Laramie and students in counties throughout Wyoming to hear and see each other in classrooms hundreds of miles apart.

Selected undergraduate and graduate programs are also extended to Wyoming communities through traditional independent study approaches, face-to-face instruction, and correspondence.

Study abroad and National Student Exchange opportunities are available to students in all academic programs.

COST AND AID

The University of Wyoming's tuition and fees were $8,729 for nonresident students and $2,807 for Wyoming residents in 2001–2002. The cost of room and board in the UW residence halls for one year was $4,744. Other expenses for the year were estimated at $700 for books and supplies and $1,700 for personal expenses.

VANDERBILT UNIVERSITY

GENERAL INFORMATION

In 1873, Commodore Cornelius Vanderbilt endowed Vanderbilt University with the hope that it would "contribute to strengthening the ties which should exist between all sections of our common country." Today, Vanderbilt is a selective, medium sized university with a total enrollment of just over 10,000. In line with the Commodore's dream, students join the campus community from a wide variety of regions, backgrounds, and disciplines. A recent incoming class of 1,558 drew students from all 50 U.S. states and more than 40 foreign countries. There are 5,885 undergraduates at Vanderbilt, of which 83 percent live on campus. Undergraduates live in residence halls, which are shared by students in all four undergraduate schools.

The University has a strong residential character, and the housing staff works with the InterResidence Hall Association (Interhall) to organize social, cultural, and educational events on campus. As residents, students are responsible for determining many of the rules under which they must live. In addition to traditional student housing, the McTyeire International House is reserved for students who speak Chinese, French, German, Japanese, and Spanish. About 42 percent of undergraduates are members of the 17 fraternities and 12 sororities on campus. Though fraternities and sororities do not have residential houses, Greek organizations play an active role in undergraduate life.

The Sarratt Student Center is the hub of student life, boasting recreational facilities such as a movie theater, a pub, a game room, and a music-listening center, as well as meeting rooms, an art gallery, and craft and darkroom facilities. The Sarratt Student Center is also home to a student-produced FM radio station. Vanderbilt University Theatre programs and the intercollegiate debate program are open to all undergraduate students. The state of the art Student Recreation Center is a 130,000-square-foot complex, comprised of gyms, handball courts, a swimming pool, racquetball courts, a climbing wall, an indoor track, and a weight room. There are also indoor and outdoor tennis courts, baseball and softball fields, and a sand volleyball court.

STUDENT BODY

The Student Government Association is responsible for maintaining a lively educational atmosphere on campus. Elected representatives of the Student Government Association work in conjunction with the 250 student-run groups to bring noted lecturers and events to campus. Vanderbilt operates under the honor system, a backbone of the undergraduate academic experience. Students elected to serve on the Honor Council are responsible for upholding and governing the honor system. There are students seats on the majority of administrative committees. Every year, one senior has the honor of serving as the Young Alumni Trustee of the University's Board of Trust.

ACADEMICS

Undergraduate academic programs are divided into four schools: the College of Arts and Science, the School of Engineering, Peabody College for education and human development, and the Blair School of Music. All four schools allow students to earn Advanced Placement credit or pursue independent study programs. Vanderbilt operates on a traditional, two-semester calendar, running from late August to early May. Between the spring and fall semesters, Vanderbilt offers a wide range of summer programs.

Students may pursue a BA, BS, BE, or BM degree in the following fields of study: anthropology, biological sciences, biomedical engineering, chemical engineering, chemistry, child development, civil engineering, classical languages, classics, cognitive studies, communication studies, computer engineering, computer science, education (with majors in early childhood education, elementary education, secondary education, and special education), ecology/evolution/organismal biology, economics, electrical engineering, elementary education, engineering science, English, fine arts, French, French and European studies, geology, German, German and European studies, history, human and organizational development, mathematics, mechanical engineering, molecular and cellular biology, musical arts, musical arts/teacher education, music composition/theory, music performance, neuroscience, philosophy, physics, physics and astronomy, political science, Portuguese, psychology, religious studies, Russian, sociology, Spanish, and theater. Vanderbilt also offers interdisciplinary majors in African-American studies, American and Southern studies, comparative literature, East Asian studies, European studies, Latin American and Iberian studies, public policy studies, and science communications. Students also have the option of designing an individual major. In recent years, students have designed programs in film studies, medieval studies, Slavic studies, and women's studies.

There are 1,787 full-time and a 300 part-time faculty at Vanderbilt, all highly accomplished in their field. Many faculty members have often been elected to high offices in their professional associations and many hold distinguished scholarship awards. Though they display excellence in research and study, Vanderbilt faculty is committed to teaching. All Vanderbilt instructors teach to both graduates and undergraduates. With student/faculty ratio of 9:1 and an average class size of just 19, undergraduates are assured the opportunity to build close relationships with their professors.

2305 West End Avenue
Nashville, TN 37203
Phone: 615-322-2561
Fax: 615-343-7765
Website: www.vanderbilt.edu

ADMISSIONS

Vanderbilt seeks accomplished students who are prepared to benefit from a serious undergraduate program. The Admissions Committee evaluates every aspect of a candidate's application and previous achievement, both academic and extracurricular. The Admissions Committee selects students whose previous performance indicates that they will be successful in a challenging college environment, and looks out for students who will add diversity of culture and background to the student body.

The majority of incoming students have completed 20 or more units in high school, and successful applicants must have completed at least 15 academic units upon entering college. Students applying to the College of Arts and Science and the Blair School of Music must complete a strong academic program that includes at least 2 years of foreign language. School of Engineering applicants must have completed at least 4 units of mathematics. The Admissions Committee evaluates every candidate on the strength of the high school transcript, extracurricular activities, official recommendations, and personal goals and achievements. In addition, prospective students must submit SAT I or ACT scores. Vanderbilt recommends that students also submit scores from three SAT II Subject Tests, including Writing and Math I, IC, or IIC, which the school uses for course placement and advising. In addition to standard application materials, candidates for the Blair School of Music must audition in an instrument or voice. The Blair School of Music recommends that students schedule a personal audition; however, candidates who live more than 400 miles from Nashville may submit a high quality cassette tape in lieu of a personal appearance. All percussion players must schedule a personal audition.

Students may contact the Office of Admissions to request information about group information sessions and campus tours, local accommodations for visitors, and opportunities to visit undergraduate classes. Vanderbilt strongly encourages students to take a campus tour. Vanderbilt operates an Early Decision program for students who have already selected Vanderbilt as their first choice. Early Decision I applications are due by November 1 and Early Decision II applications are due by January 5. Vanderbilt notifies Early Decision I candidates of the result by December 15 and notifies Early Decision II candidates by February 15. The priority deadline for regular applications is January 5. Auditions for the Blair School of Music may be scheduled throughout December, January, and February. Applications received after January 5 will be evaluated as long as there is space in the incoming class. Students applying via the regular admissions process will receive a decision by April 1. Prospective transfer students must submit a completed application before February 1 to enter in the following fall semester, and no later than November 15 to enter in the spring semester.

CAMPUS LIFE

Vanderbilt University is located in the city of Nashville, home to a diverse population of more than a million and marked by a special touch of Southern charm. As the capital of Tennessee, Nashville is an important cultural and commercial hub in the mid-South. Located equidistant from the northern and southern U.S. borders, Nashville sits at the intersection of three major interstate highways and 18 airlines serve the city. Beyond the city limits, the surrounding area contains 81 parks and recreation areas, and more than 30,000 acres of lakes, offering ample opportunity for sports year round.

During their undergraduate career, students are encouraged to study overseas, giving them the opportunity to develop language skills and a deeper cultural awareness. Vanderbilt offers academic programs in Argentina, Australia, Brazil, Chile, China, the Dominican Republic, England, France, Germany, Israel, Italy, Japan, Russia, and Spain. Students receive course credit for overseas study and do not pay extra tuition to participate in programs abroad. Most programs allow students to participate without extending their graduation date.

COST AND AID

For the 2000–2001 academic year, tuition is $24,080 plus student fees of $620. Residential students pay an additional $5,368 for room and $2,960 for board. In addition, students should expect to spend roughly $1,120 in personal expenses, and $860 for books and supplies. In total, students should expect to spend a combined $35,018. Costs may change in the upcoming year.

WAGNER COLLEGE

GENERAL INFORMATION

Wagner College, a four-year residential college located in Staten Island, has a long and proud tradition of excellence in the liberal arts. Wagner's location presents unique opportunities; the campus is a scant 25 minute ferry ride from the near-limitless cultural, professional, and social resources of Manhattan (and the ferry ride is free!). Starting in the fall semester of freshman year, Wagner students take full advantage of New York City's resources via field experiences coordinated to supplement three of their classes. A number of Manhattan's most prominent companies and cultural institutes provide internships and upper-class mentorships to Wagner students throughout the academic year. Wagner undergrads enjoy the benefits of a large, supportive alumni base throughout the greater New York region; the alumni network is instrumental in helping students find internships as well as jobs after graduation. "Learning by doing" is not just a slogan at Wagner. Approximately 1,750 undergraduates and 400 graduate students attend Wagner each year; they hail from all regions of the United States and 20 other countries.

Students select Wagner because it provides optimal access to outstanding cultural and professional opportunities, all within a traditional college framework. Approximately 85 percent of undergraduate students live in one of Wagner's three residence halls, all of which overlook the New York Harbor. Wagner offers a tremendous assortment of social events and activities, many organized by the Student Life office. Among these activities are clubs, Greek organizations, performances and concerts, museum outings, Broadway shows, sporting events, and other regional attractions. Wagner also participates in the Academic and Cultural Enrichment Program; the program sponsors numerous speakers, films, seminars, and other events throughout the year. Wagner is committed to its exceptional athletic programs and enjoys NCAA Division I standing in 22 sports. The College is home to a wide assortment of intramural and club sports, as well as an outstanding coaching staff.

STUDENT BODY

Wagner's intimate size makes it easy for students to involve themselves meaningfully in campus organizations. Wagner recognizes the importance of student life in the educational experience and encourages undergraduates to become involved with campus organizations. The campus is home to more than 70 organizations and clubs, including intramural leagues, honor societies, religious and leadership groups, Greek organizations, a campus newspaper, a literary magazine, and student government. Volunteerism is a required component of any student organization's activities at Wagner; in this way, Wagner students become involved in the surrounding community. Wagner sponsors a full assortment of student activities both on campus and off; these activities provide students with important educational and social experiences. Wagner is home to 22 Division I NCAA intercollegiate athletics teams. Men's teams include baseball, basketball, football (Division IAA), golf, lacrosse, tennis, track/cross-country, and wrestling. Women's teams include basketball, golf, lacrosse, soccer, softball, swimming, tennis, track/cross-country, volleyball, and water polo.

ACADEMICS

The "Wagner Plan for the Practical Liberal Arts" is Wagner's unique undergraduate program; it highlights "Learning by Doing" by connecting students' classroom experiences with fieldwork. The academic program, which provides a broad education within the liberal arts tradition, requires students to complement classroom learning with active engagement in real-world activities. Wagner students must complete three Learning Communities (LCs) prior to graduation: one is undertaken during freshman year, the second in sophomore or junior year, and the final one is completed during senior year. Learning Communities include three courses linked by a shared theme and a common group of students. LCs are cross-disciplinary; they include field experiences throughout the New York metropolitan area. Freshmen spend time visiting a designated site throughout the semester to observe the organization, its procedures, and its culture. Seniors undertake an internship or full-semester practicum with an organization related to their major. Each candidate must complete 36 units in order to earn the baccalaureate degree. Students at Wagner can study in 33 majors, 28 minors, and 9 pre-professional programs. Wagner also has five graduate divisions. All students must choose a major no later than the end of their second year. Wagner runs a two-term schedule; a fall semester (August to December) and a spring semester (January to May). Several summer session options are also available. Advanced placement and advanced credit standing is available to qualified entering and current students at Wagner College. Advanced Placement examinations are used to determine qualification.

Wagner College offers the Bachelor of Arts, Bachelor of Science and Bachelor of Science in Education. Undergraduate study (majors, minors, or fields of concentration) is available in accounting, anthropology, art, arts administration, art history, biology, biopsychology, business administration, chemistry, computer science, dance, economics, education, English, foreign languages (French, German, Spanish), gender studies, history, international affairs, journalism, mathematics, microbiology, music, nursing, philosophy, physician assistant, physics, political science, psychology, public policy and administration, religious studies, sociology, and theatre.

Wagner benefits from both its location and its long history of academic excellence; nowhere is this clearer than in its gifted faculty. Ninety-five percent of the full-time faculty has earned a doctoral degree or its equivalent in their field. Student-faculty relationships at Wagner are close and are grounded in mutual respect. Faculty members take part in all areas of College life because they are deeply involved in their students' development. Instructors consider New York City an unrivaled resource for both course work and field experience. The student/faculty ratio at Wagner is 16:1.

1 Campus Road
Staten Island, NY 10301-4495
Phone: 718-390-3411
Fax: 718-390-3105
Website: www.wagner.edu

ADMISSIONS

Admission is competitive at Wagner; academic qualifications are considered the most important factor in the admissions decision. The admission committee also takes into account personal qualities that might enable a student to benefit most from the complete Wagner educational experience. Wagner seeks undergraduates who can contribute substantially both to the school and the surrounding community; for this reason, applicants' talents in performance, athletics, and leadership areas are highly valued. The admission committee considers the applicant's secondary school academic record, class rank, ACT or SAT I, letters of recommendation from teacher(s) and/or a guidance counselor, and a personal statement or essay. Furthermore, the student's activities outside the classroom (participation in the community or extracurricular organizations) and character (as reflected by recommendations) are assessed. Wagner strongly recommends a personal interview but does not require one. SAT II: Subject Tests are also recommended. The admissions committee weighs all factors together in order to form a clear picture of the applicant and his or her potential place in the Wagner community. An applicant to Wagner should have completed at least 18 academic units in the following areas: 4 English, 3 mathematics, 3 history, 2 science, and 2 foreign language. The school recommends another four units from among the following electives: 1 computer science, 1 art, 1 religion, 1–3 history, 1–3 mathematics, 1–3 natural sciences, 2–4 foreign language, 1–2 music, and 1–2 social studies.

Prospective students are strongly encouraged to visit our campus; the Office of Admissions provides tours throughout the year, as well as interviews and informative presentations. Prospects who visit campus may meet with an admissions official to discuss admissions requirements and academic offerings at Wagner. Upon request, the Office of Admissions will happily arrange meetings with faculty members, athletic coaches, and financial aid counselors. Students should call 718-390-3411 or 800-221-1010 to arrange a campus visit. Wagner accepts application for both early decision and regular decision. Candidates for early decision must submit applications by December 1. The deadline for regular decision is February 15. Those applying to the theatre or physician assistant programs must apply by January 1; they may not apply for early decision. Those interested in pursuing a theatre major or music scholarship must audition. The school begins sending out early decision notifications on January 2; regular decision notifications are sent out in early March; decisions on applications to the physician assistant program are sent in late February. All applications must include secondary school transcripts, SAT I or ACT scores, letters of recommendation, personal statement or essay, and an application fee of $50.

CAMPUS LIFE

Students at Wagner get to enjoy the best of two worlds. Wagner's park-like, wooded 105-acre campus overlooks New York Harbor and the breathtaking Manhattan skyline. The Grymes Hill section of Staten Island, with its turn-of-the-century mansions and estates, provides a lovely and homey environment that Wagner students appreciate. From campus, Manhattan can be reached easily by ferry, car, or bus. Students may reach the Staten Island ferry terminal quickly via a Wagner-run shuttle bus; the shuttle also makes stops at other Staten Island locales. Wagner is uniquely situated to accommodate those seeking the many assets of New York City while pursuing their studies in a lovely suburban setting. Because Wagner is located in New York City, students have access to exceptional resources in countless professional and educational fields. The requirement that all students complete an internship and field experience means all enjoy the windfall of these resources. More than 700 students each year participate in internship and field experiences throughout the metropolitan area. Among the field sites for first-year students are: Ellis Island, S. I. University Hospital, New York Urban League, Museum for African Art, Alice Austen House, Fort Wadsworth, S. I. Zoological Society, and the Better Business Bureau. Past internship sites include: the United Nations, Oppenheimer Fund, J. P. Morgan, Dupont, the American Stock Exchange, Christie's Auction House, Disney Theatrical Productions, Saturday Night Live, and the Museum of Modern Art.

Wagner also offers numerous opportunities for world travel. The College belongs to the oldest, most selective study abroad program in the U.S., the esteemed Institute for the International Education of Students program (IES). Wagner students who qualify for the program may elect to study abroad for a semester, summer, or an entire year. The program takes students to such diverse locales as Beijing, Berlin, Canberra, Dublin, LaPlata, London, Madrid, Paris, Tokyo, and Vienna. Studies abroad are pursued through classes designed specifically for U.S. students and through standard classes offered by universities in the host city; these classes fully integrate the U.S. students with their peers in the host nation. The Wagner Semester Exchange Program with the American University in Paris annually provides 12 students a chance to study in Paris and live with a French family; participants immerse themselves thoroughly in French culture. Wagner offers summer programs in London and Bologna as well. Those interested in public administration and political science can take advantage of semester-long programs in Washington, DC, and Albany; both include internship opportunities.

COST AND AID

For the 2002–2003 academic year, tuition was $21,500; room and board was $7,000.

WARREN WILSON COLLEGE

GENERAL INFORMATION

Since its founding in 1894, Warren Wilson College has educated students with a unique "triad" of a strong liberal arts program, work for the College, and service to those in need, which makes Warren Wilson unlike any other college. This triad teaches students, in a way no other program can, to make connections, solve problems, and grasp ideas. With 775 students from 42 states and 25 countries and an average class size of 15, each individual is a significant part of our diverse and vibrant academic community. More than 90 percent of all students live on campus in one of 11 residence halls.

The Academic Program includes hundreds of courses, which continue to grow in scope and popularity in response to student interest. You may earn your BA or BS in any of 31 majors and concentrations and 21 minors. The Work Program requires 15 hours of work per week with your assigned work crew, one of more than a hundred crews that are essential to the daily operation of the College. In return, students receive a grant of more than $2,400 in credit toward the cost of tuition. The Service Program requires at least 100 hours of service during your four years, with 25 of those hours focused on one issue or group. Service projects can take you into the community, across the country, or even abroad.

Ambitious, idealistic, independent—Warren Wilson students are passionate about social justice and believe in taking risks. They're hard workers and loyal friends. Always questioning and looking for new challenges, they are a community of self-made individuals who thrive on inquiry and change.

STUDENT BODY

There are some things you won't encounter on campus: sororities, fraternities, a football team. What you will find: a student-run food co-op, music coffeehouses, yoga, a Denebe Drum Club, poetry readings, forums on campus issues, and a Student Caucus, which is the representative voice of the student body.

We are a member of the United States Collegiate Athletic Association (USCAA). The USCAA is composed of colleges and universities throughout the country with enrollments of 1,000 undergraduates or less. As a member of the USCAA, Warren Wilson College's student-athletes are eligible for post-season play, national team rankings, and various post-season awards. Our athletic department also follows NCAA Division III guidelines as directed by the NCAA. We are beginning the process of applying for NCAA Division III membership. Varsity sports include basketball, cross-country, soccer, and swimming. Our club sports include indoor soccer, women's softball, mountain biking, triathlon, ultimate Frisbee, kayaking, whitewater rafting, and rock climbing.

ACADEMICS

Our curriculum provides the foundation for bringing Warren Wilson's triad to life in a way that is uniquely tailored to you. Students will consider the ways humans acquire and use knowledge, the importance of global and international issues, and the meaning of work and service to others.

There is a required freshman seminar, designed to provide new students the opportunity to explore various fields. At least one class within each of the school's eight liberal arts areas (language and global issues, literature, history and political science, natural science, mathematics, social science, philosophy and religion, and artistic expression) is required to give you a rich base of experience while allowing the freedom to explore and apply your strengths to a certain major. A senior seminar is designed as a capstone experience, as is a senior letter to evaluate the student's college experiences.

All Warren Wilson students must demonstrate competence in writing and mathematics, either through testing or by completing core courses. Each semester in the academic calendar is broken into two eight-week terms. A student traditionally takes only two courses per term.

The bachelor's degree may be awarded in any of 31 majors and concentrations, 21 minors, and 8 special programs.

Major programs and concentrations include:

Art

Biology

Chemistry (biochemistry)

Creative writing

Economics and business administration

Education (elementary and secondary)

English (theater/English)

Environmental studies (analysis, education policy, forest resource conservation, sustainable agriculture, wildlife biology) History and political science

Humanities

Human studies (American, global, individual and society, Latin American studies, women's studies)

Integrative studies

Mathematics and computer science

Outdoor leadership

Psychology

Social work

Sociology/Anthropology

Minors include:

Appalachian studies

Art

Biology

Chemistry

Computer science

Economics and business administration

English

Environmental studies

History and political science

Human studies

Mathematics

Intercultural studies

Modern language

Music

Outdoor leadership

Philosophy

Physics

Psychology

Religion

Theater

Women's studies

Writing

Special programs include:

Pre-medical studies

Pre-Peace Corps

Pre-veterinary studies

Pre-law

3-2 engineering

PO Box 9000
Asheville, NC 28815
Phone: 828-771-2073
Fax: 828-298-1440
Website: www.warren-wilson.edu

3-2 forestry

Honors English

Honors math

Honors science

MFA in creative writing

Our faculty are drawn here by a teaching philosophy that emphasizes the integration of theory and practice as well as a focus on the individual. They come from some of the nation's top graduate programs: Cornell, Duke, Stanford, UC-Berkeley, Northwestern, Harvard, UNC-Chapel Hill, and Yale. Of our 46 full-time members, 84 percent hold doctoral degrees. All classes and labs are taught by faculty members, not graduate students. With a student/faculty ratio of 12:1, our professors get to know you as an individual; they can offer the support you need to excel and to reach your potential. Approximately 50 percent of all faculty and staff live on campus, so there are plenty of opportunities for interaction.

ADMISSIONS

Admission to Warren Wilson College is a selective process based on both the potential and academic qualifications of the applicant. All available information is considered, including previous academic records, evidence of academic and social maturity, extracurricular activities, community service, SAT or ACT scores, essay, recommendations, grade trends, and an optional interview.

A college preparatory curriculum is required (4 years of English, 2 years of algebra, 1 year of geometry, 2 years of laboratory science, and 1 year of history).

Each candidate must apply by March 15 of their senior year. There is no fee to apply. The College notifies students about admission beginning on February 1.

CAMPUS LIFE

Warren Wilson College, beneath the high peaks of the Craggy Range of the Blue Ridge mountains, is settled in a valley that the Native Americans called Swannanoa. Located just outside the city of Asheville, North Carolina, the 1,100-acre campus includes a 300-acre working farm, 600 acres of forest, 25 miles of hiking trails, and a whitewater kayaking course. A haven for outdoor enthusiasts, Asheville itself is a city of nearly 100,000 people and is considered one of the most livable cities in the United States. Surrounded by more than a million acres of national forest, Asheville is located in an ideal setting, presenting views of outstanding beauty throughout all four seasons. In the spring and summer, variations in altitude combined with warm southern sun favor the native vegetation; dogwood, wildflowers, rhododendron, mountain laurel, and azaleas cover the mountains. The arresting beauty of the autumn colors attracts photographers, artists, and sports enthusiasts from the world over. During the winter, natural snow is enhanced by machine-made snow, producing excellent downhill skiing and snowboarding.

A short drive from the Warren Wilson College campus are the Great Smoky Mountains National Park, Pisgah National Forest, and the Blue Ridge Parkway, offering panoramic views, excellent camping facilities, and a perfect setting for class field trips.

At Warren Wilson College, we're continually reaching outside our immediate resources to offer students an even wider range of experience. The College maintains an active partnership with the North Carolina Outward Bound School, part of the internationally known Outward Bound wilderness adventure organization. Its location on the edge of campus allows for innovative cooperative programming. The Environmental Leadership Center on campus works to raise awareness of environmental realities and inspire citizens to act as responsible caretakers of the earth. The Center provides a portfolio of internships with outstanding institutions such as the Boyce Thompson Institute for Plant Research at Cornell, the Tropical Forest Initiative in Costa Rica, and the Audubon Society's Puffin Project in Maine.

Warren Wilson World Wide is a program that connects our students with work, service, and study opportunities in the world. Experiential Adventures are offered as individual internships or group excursions to African cities and villages, Central American rain forests, Indian ashrams, Caribbean homes, and on the deck of a boat in Gulf waters. Study abroad partnerships are as diverse as the students who attend the College. Whether at a university in Great Britain, Japan, Central America, Spain, or Korea, the student is challenged in the triad tradition right in the heart of a foreign culture. An Academic Honors Option is offered to qualified students at Oxford University, England.

COST AND AID

Students who are accepted and decide to enroll must send their $300 nonrefundable deposit by May 1. Tuition and fees for the 2002–2003 school year are $15,848. Room and board is $4,994. The total cost is $20,842, minus the work compensation of $2,472. Thus, the actual cost is $18,370.

WASHINGTON COLLEGE

THE COLLEGE AT A GLANCE

Chartered in 1782, Washington College is the 10th oldest college in the United States. Named after its primary benefactor, Washington College is a selective liberal arts college with a current enrollment of 1,100 undergraduate students from 35 states and 40 foreign countries.

STUDENTS

Washington College has 35 student clubs and organizations. NCAA III varsity sports include baseball, softball, field hockey, men's and women's lacrosse, men's and women's soccer, men's and women's basketball, men's and women's rowing (crew), men's and women's swimming, men's and women's tennis, and both women's and co-ed sailing.

Club sports are offered in men's and women's rugby, men's lacrosse, and men's ice hockey.

The Equestrian Club at Washington College is open to all students, regardless of riding ability. Students can participate in educational field trips, monthly trail rides, riding lessons, and/or competitions within the Intercollegiate Horse Show Association.

ACADEMICS

Programs of study are offered in elementary and secondary teacher certification, pre-medical/pre-vet studies, pre-law studies, creative writing, behavioral neuroscience, gender studies, Chesapeake regional studies, 3+2 engineering, 3+2 nursing, and 3+4 pharmacy.

Washington College offers undergraduate degrees in the following areas:

American studies

Anthropology

Art

Biology

Business management

Chemistry

Computer science

Drama

Economics

English

Environmental studies

French

German

History

Humanities

International studies

Mathematics

Music

Philosophy

Physics

Political science

Psychology

Sociology

Spanish

Graduate degrees are offered in the following areas:

English

History

Psychology

Washington College has a 12:1 student/faculty ratio. Most professors are full-time members of the faculty, and 95 percent hold a terminal degree. The average class size at WC is 17 students.

300 Washington Avenue
Chestertown, MD 21620
Phone: 410-778-7700
Fax: 410-778-7287
Website: www.washcoll.edu

FIRST COLLEGE CHARTERED IN THE NEW NATION
WASHINGTON
COLLEGE
300 Washington Avenue • Chestertown, Maryland 21620-1197

CAMPUS LIFE

The College is located in the historic community of Chestertown on Maryland's Eastern Shore. The 120-acre campus is situated in the middle of a residential community that is safe and scenic. WC has excellent waterfront facilities on the Chester River, one mile from the main campus. Washington, DC; Baltimore; and Philadelphia are each a 90-minute drive from campus.

Washington College has established study abroad programs in Australia, Costa Rica, Cuba, Ecuador, Mexico, Turkey, Denmark, England, France, Finland, Germany, Hungary, Ireland, Italy, Russia, Spain, Scotland, Slovenia, The Netherlands, South Africa, Thailand, and Japan.

Summer and/or academic-year internships are offered in all undergraduate majors.

COSTS

Eighty-five percent of all Washington College students receive some form of either need-based or merit-based student aid. Need-based aid applicants are required to file both the FAFSA and Washington College applications. Merit-based awards range in amount from $5,000 to $20,000 per year and are available to admitted applicants either on the basis of GPA and SAT scores or as a result of membership in the National Honor Society or Cum Laude Society. All NHS and CLS members who are admitted to the College are offered $10,000 annual tuition scholarships.

Tuition for the 2002–2003 academic year is $22,740. Room and board charges total $5,740.

ADMISSIONS

Washington College is a selective institution. In order to assess an applicant's "fit" with the College, the Admission Committee requires the submission of all relevant academic records and test scores, an activity profile, an essay/personal statement, and two letters of recommendation. In some cases, an on-campus interview may also be required.

Prospective applicants are strongly encouraged to come to campus for an information session and tour. These visits should be scheduled in advance by calling 800-422-1782, ext. 7700.

WEBBER INTERNATIONAL UNIVERSITY

GENERAL INFORMATION

Webber International University was established in 1927 by world-renowned economist Roger Babson. This four-year nonaffiliated coeducational institution is situated on a stunning 110-acre campus perched along the Lake Caloosa shoreline. Webber International University's location offers students convenient access to popular attractions such as Disney World and Cypress Gardens, among others. Webber receives its accreditation from the Southern Association of Colleges and Schools. The University prides itself on its strong tradition of high moral standards and exemplary academic achievement. Webber has cultivated an atmosphere that promotes success through hard work and scholastic merit. Roughly 300 women and 325 men are enrolled in Webber's undergraduate program. About 70 percent of those students are Florida residents; the remaining 30 percent come from 21 states across the nation and nearly 30 countries around the world. The University's off-campus placement programs provide students with practical, on-the-job business experience. Webber also offers field trips designed to enhance undergraduates' business education pursuits.

The University fields intercollegiate sports teams in baseball, basketball, cross-country, football, golf, soccer, tennis, and track and field for men and in basketball, cheerleading, cross-country, golf, soccer, softball, tennis, track and field, and volleyball for women. Students may also participate in Webber's intramural athletics program. The University's sports complex includes a beach volleyball court, a fitness room, two gymnasiums, racquetball courts, a soccer field, a junior Olympic-size swimming pool, and tennis courts. Undergraduates may also participate in lakeside and water sports such as beach volleyball, canoeing, fishing, and kayaking.

Webber International University offers a large assortment of social clubs and organizations including athletic boosters, Eta Sigma Delta and the Society of Hosteurs, FCA, an international club, a marketing club, Phi Beta Lambda, SIFE, a sport management club, a student government association, a tourism society, and Webber ambassadors. These organizations, among others, help to fund the numerous social events at Webber.

LOCATION

Webber International University is located in the small rural community of Babson Park, which lies at the center of Florida's citrus groves near a variety of freshwater lakes. The area has a welcoming and tranquil atmosphere. Babson Park is convenient to the many popular recreational amenities and tourist attractions of Florida's central region.

MAJORS AND DEGREES

Webber International University students may pursue bachelor's and associate degrees in business administration. The school offers nine majors: accounting, finance, global business, hospitality business management, international tourism management, management, marketing, pre-law, and sport management.

ACADEMIC PROGRAM

Webber International University follows a semester calendar with 15-week semesters, and two 6-week summer terms. Webber requires its students to complete 60 credit hours for the Associate of Science degree and 120 credit hours for the Bachelor of Science degree with a 2.0 minimum GPA. Students typically carry a 15 hour course load per semester. Undergraduates pursuing the Bachelor of Science degree must complete roughly 30 hours in the major, 36 hours in the business core, 36 hours in the general education core, and 18 hours of tailored electives. Undergraduates pursuing the Associate of Science degree must complete 27 hours in the business core, 18 hours in the general education core, and 15 hours in the major and tailored elective. Students pursuing the Bachelor of Science degree in general business studies must complete 45 hours in the general business studies core, 39 hours in the general education core, and 36 hours of tailored electives. All undergraduates are required to complete 30 of the last 33 hours at Webber International University to earn a degree. Students who earn exemplary scores on Advanced Placement (AP) and College-Level Examination Program (CLEP) general tests are awarded credit.

OFF-CAMPUS ARRANGEMENTS

Webber International University offers study abroad opportunities to undergraduates pursuing a bachelor's degree. Students may complete either one or two semesters in Paris, France, or Barcelona, Spain.

The hospitality, marketing, and tourism departments offer internship programs with major restaurants and hotels in the Orlando region. In-state and out-of-state internships with prominent retail outlets are also available.

The finance department offers internship opportunities in a variety of financial organizations and in the financial divisions of regional corporations. Internship positions in the international tourism business provide undergraduates with practical tourism industry experience.

Additional off-campus opportunities include elective programs in which undergraduates survey and evaluate business procedures and operations of area companies, then report their conclusions in a presentation. In this way, students gain valuable experience in the field of business consultancy.

A special departmental program is available that allows undergraduates in all 9 majors to spend the summer semester abroad and to observe business methods in an international setting.

ACADEMIC FACILITIES

Situated at the center of the campus is the Roger Babson Learning Center, a state-of-the-art business library. The facility presently holds approximately 35,500 volumes, a wide variety of audiovisual resources, and a CD-ROM computer reference program. The library has computers available for undergraduate use. Numerous research databases are on hand for students to use as well.

Webber's computer resources centers are data processing hubs and teaching facilities whose equipment offers the most up-to-date technology, encouraging outstanding student performance in business, communication, and creativity.

Webber College, PO Box 96
Babson Park, FL 33827
Phone: 863-638-2910
Fax: 863-638-1591
Website: www.webber.edu

COSTS AND AID

For the 2002–2003 academic year, the annual fee (including room and board, the student activities fee, and tuition) was $17,050. The annual fee for commuting students totaled $11,330. These costs are adjusted periodically. Webber International University projects that $1,200 is sufficient for books and supplies. Laboratory fees are not included in this amount.

The Student Financial Aid Department is available to guide and assist students in meeting educational costs. Financial aid is distributed on the basis of academic performance, applicant need, and potential. Roughly 80 percent of undergraduates at the University are awarded financial assistance. Students applying for need-based assistance must file the Free Application for Federal Student Aid (FAFSA). Numerous forms of aid, such as Federal Work-Study awards, grants, loans, and scholarships are employed to meet undergraduate needs. A small number of non-need-based scholarships are also offered; these are awarded based on academic achievement, on college and community service, or on athletic performance in basketball, cross-country, golf, soccer, softball, tennis, track and field, or volleyball. Students seeking aid must resubmit applications annually. Webber International University participates in the Federal Perkins Loan, Federal Supplemental Educational Opportunity Grant, and Federal Work-Study programs. Prospective applicants must apply for any government-funded grant for which they are qualified, such as the Federal Pell Grant; Florida residents are required to apply for a Florida Student Assistance Grant and the Florida Tuition Voucher Program. Federal Stafford Student Loans are offered as well. Students seeking financial aid should submit their applications prior to April 1 in order to qualify for specific financial aid opportunities.

FACULTY

Over three-fifths of Webber's full-time professors hold doctoral degrees. The University has a faculty/undergraduate ratio of 1:19, and all undergraduates work with a faculty advisor. All professors are available to meet with students during posted office hours. Most of Webber's professors have at least five years of practical professional experience in their field of expertise in addition to their extensive classroom experience. This combination of field work and instructional experience provides Webber professors with the unique ability to comprehend the interests of their undergraduates.

STUDENT GOVERNMENT

The Student Government Association, Webber's primary governing organization, is comprised of elected undergraduate representatives and a staff advisor. The SGA addresses nonacademic aspects of campus life. It oversees the activities of student organizations and involves undergraduates in campus procedures and policies. Representatives from many different undergraduate organizations participate in the Student Government Association, as do elected representatives from the University's student body.

ADMISSION REQUIREMENTS

Prospective students must be high school graduates. It is recommended that applicants have completed at least 4 years of English and 2 to 3 years of mathematics as well as preparation in seven other academic subjects. The majority of prospective students rank in the top half of their graduating class. Applicants must present their SAT I or ACT scores before being considered for admission. International applicants are required to present scores on the Test of English as a Foreign Language (TOEFL).

Early admission is an option for exceptional juniors with test scores near the top 15th percentile in the state or country, a grade point average of at least 3.0 (on a 4.0 scale), a favorable letter of reference from a counselor or principal, and a letter of permission from their parents or legal guardian. Applicants are required to interview with the dean of student development.

Transfer student applications are welcome, as well as applications from students resuming their education as nontraditional adult students. Transfer students must have satisfactory records at their previous institution.

Applicants who fall short of regular entrance requirements may be considered individually as candidates for the Fresh Start program by the Fresh Start admissions committee. All Fresh Start applicants must appear for a personal interview.

Application and Information<BT>The Admissions Committee formally considers an application once it has received the $35 domestic student application fee or the $75 international student application fee, all necessary test scores and recommendations, and transcripts from all learning institutions attended. The University operates on a rolling admissions basis. It is strongly suggested that application forms be submitted at the earliest possible date, as on-campus housing is in high demand. (Freshmen must reside in the dormitory unless they share a residence with a parent, guardian, or spouse.)

To receive application forms, catalogs, and other information, applicants should contact:

Webber International University
1201 North Scenic Highway
PO Box 96
Babson Park, FL 33827-9990
Telephone: 863-638-2910
E-mail: admissions@webber.edu
World Wide Web: www.webber.edu

WEBSTER UNIVERSITY

GENERAL INFORMATION

Founded in 1915, Webster University is a private, four-year, liberal arts university located in Webster Groves, Missouri, a suburb of St. Louis.

Enrollment: Undergraduate full-time: 2,000
Undergraduate part-time: 1,050
Graduate (total): 1,900

Average Class Size: 15–25

Student/Faculty Ratio: 16/1

Selectivity: Moderate

Average Entering Freshman GPA: 3.3 (on a 4.0 scale)

Average Entering Freshman ACT: 24

Average Entering Freshman Combined SAT: 1150

Student Body Represents: 46 states; 20 countries

Costs: Tuition: $15,500

Conservatory of Theatre tuition: $18,500

Room, board, and fees: approximately $6,500 (no difference for out-of-state students)

Financial aid: Over 90 percent of full-time freshman receive fiancial aid

Scholarships: Competitive academic awards range from $2,000 to full-tuition.

Average Financial Aid Package: $14,300

Housing: On-campus residence halls and apartments; all accomodations feature semi-private bathroom facilities.

Unique Majors Include: animation, film production, audio production, tech theatre, stage management, interactive media, scriptwriting, global journalism.

STUDENT ORGANIZATIONS

Art Council
Association for African-American Collegians
Behavioral and Social Sciences Club
Cheerleaders
Chinese Student Association
Commuter Involvement Association
Counterbalance
Dance Club
Debate/Forensics Team
Fellowship of Christian Athletes
Foreign Language Club
Habitat for Humanity
History, Politics, and Law Club
International Association for Jazz Education
International Student Association
Latin American Students Organization
Literature Club
Marketing Communications Club
Martial Arts Club
Media Association
Outdoors Club
Partners for Global Change
Residence Hall Association
Student Activities Council
Student Athlete Advisory Board
Student Government Association
Students for a Free Tibet
Webster Animal Rights Team
Webster Pride
Webster Swim Club

Majors Offered<BT>

Accounting
Acting
Advertising/marketing communications
Alternative media
American studies
Animation
Anthropology
Art
Art history
Audio production
Biology
Biotechnology
Broadcast journalism
Business administration
Ceramics
Communications (general)
Computer science
Costume construction
Costume design
Creative writing
Dance
Directing (for theatre)
Drama
Drawing
Early childhood education
Economics
Elementary education
English
Film studies
Film production
French
German
Global journalism
Graphic design
Health care administration
Human resource management
History
Interactive media
International business

470 East Lockwood Avenue
Saint Louis, MO 63119-3194
Phone: 314-968-6991
Fax: 314-968-7115
Website: www.webster.edu

International relations

International studies

Jazz studies

Journalism

Legal studies

Lighting design

Literature

Management

Marketing

Mathematics

Media literacy

Middle school education

Music composition

Music education

Music performance

Music technology

Musical theatre

Painting

Philosophy

Photography (art emphasis)

Photography (communications emphasis)

Political science

Pre-architecture

Pre-dentistry

Pre-engineering

Pre-law

Pre-medicine

Pre-occupational therapy

Pre-veterinary

Printmaking

Psychology

Public relations

Real estate

Religious studies

Scene design

Scriptwriting

Sculpture

Secondary education

Social science

Sociology

Sound design

Spanish

Special education

Speech communications studies

Stage management

Technical theatre

Video production

Vocal performance

Writing as a profession

FACULTY

160 full-time faculty

400 part-time faculty

ADMISSIONS

Applications are reviewed on a rolling basis. After all application materials are received, students are notified of their status within three weeks. ACT or SAT test is required. Selectivity is moderate

CAMPUS LIFE

Webster Groves, Missouri, is a residential suburb of St. Louis characterized by large trees, Victorian houses, and a small-town atmosphere. The campus is easy to get around, with no two spots farther than a five-minute walk away. Centrally located, Webster University is 15 minutes from downtown St. Louis, and 25 minutes from the airport.

Webster University offers a unique study-abroad opportunity for those interested.

Currently, the University offers five international locations where students can study: Cha'am, Thailand; Geneval, Switzerland; Leiden, The Netherlands; London, England; Vienna, Austria.

These campus owned and operated by Webster, which means you do not have to transfer schools, or convert grading schools. You're still at Webster, just in a different location. All classes are taught in English. In addition, you keep your financial aid package and pay is U.S. currency.

For students interested in studying overseas, Webster offers a program called "Freshman Fly Free," which means if you enter Webster as a freshman and remain in good standing, the University will pay your airfare to and from the overseas campus.

Other study abroad locations are available as well, inlcuding opportunities in Argentina, France, Germany, Japan, and Mexico.

COST AND AID

2003–2004

Full-time tuition: $15,500

Full-time tuition for theatre majors: $18,500

Room, board, and fees: $6,500

There is no difference for out-of-state tuition.

WELLESLEY COLLEGE

GENERAL INFORMATION

Wellesley is a small, independent women's college, located just 12 miles outside Boston, Massachusetts. Wellesley attracts serious, accomplished women who have a strong desire to grow personally, achieve academically, and succeed in the professional world. Wellesley's 2,300 undergraduates join the College from hundreds of national and international high schools, each bringing their unique background, culture, and experience to the campus community. The College is residential, and the majority of students choose to live in campus residence halls. Residence halls are an important part of the undergraduate experience and operate like smaller, close-knit communities within the larger campus community. Taking an active role in extracurricular education, residence halls sponsor social events, lectures, faculty dinners, and professional-in-residence programs, while also being a place to gather for informal chats and group dinners.

Among Wellesley's first-rate facilities is the College's Sports Center, which contains an 8-lane, 25-meter pool and diving well, a volleyball court, badminton, squash, and racquetball courts, exercise studios, weight rooms, and an athletic training facility. These facilities are augmented by the campus field house, which has a basketball stadium, tennis courts, a track, and a cardiovascular fitness area. At the on-campus Lake Waban, there is a boathouse with canoes, sailboats, and crew shells, as well as a beach for swimming. The campus also contains a 9-hole golf course, 24 tennis courts, and fields for soccer, field hockey, and lacrosse.

The Schneider College Center is the home base for a wide range of extracurricular clubs and events. Though Wellesley does not have any sororities, there are several national academic societies, including two traditionally black community service groups. The black student association, Ethos, has its own residence, Harambee House, which hosts an annual program of speakers, art exhibits, and cultural events. The Hispanic/Latin American student group, Alianza, and the Hispanic/Latina student group, Mezcla, were both student-founded and promote cultural solidarity and awareness through a varied cultural program. Alianza and Mezcla members are also active off campus, taking part in service projects and special events in Boston's Spanish-speaking communities. The various student groups that comprise the Asian Student Union sponsor movie nights, seminars and informative workshops, and social and cultural events at Wellesley and at other local colleges. International students can congregate and relax at the Slater International Center. In addition to the many events organized by campus clubs, the College sponsors a complete annual events program that brings noted lecturers, artists, musicians, and public figures to campus.

Students are actively involved in the formation and governance of campus policy through the College Government Senate. Students also serve on the majority of College committees. There are student representatives on Board of Trustees committees, the Board of Admission, and departmental committees. Student-run House Councils oversee resident life and manage the activity funds distributed amongst the 160 student clubs and organizations. Wellesley operates on the honor system, a tradition that permeates the administration of the College. Under the honor system, instructors allow students to schedule exams at their convenience and take tests outside the classroom. In line with this philosophy, the College does not create or enforce stringent social rules.

ACADEMICS

To earn a degree from Wellesley, students must complete at least 32 units of academic work and maintain an average of C or better throughout their undergraduate career. In addition, students must complete general education courses in a range of disciplines. All students must take at least nine credits in each of the following general subject areas: language and literature; visual arts, music, video, film, and theater; social and behavioral analysis; epistemology and cognition; ethics, religion, and moral philosophy; historical studies; natural and physical science; and mathematical modeling and problem solving in the natural sciences, mathematics, and computer science. In addition, students must achieve proficiency in a foreign language and take courses in writing and quantitative reasoning. Finally, students are required to take one course with a multicultural focus, designed to expose them to a new culture or society.

Wellesley offers strong pre-med and pre-law programs and boasts an excellent rate of acceptance to law, medical, and other graduate school programs. In general, about 64 to 74 percent of Wellesley applicants are admitted to medical school and about 80 percent are accepted to law school. About 25 to 30 percent of Wellesley graduates enter advanced degree programs directly upon graduation.

Wellesley welcomes continuing students who are not of traditional college age through the Elisabeth Kaiser Davis Degree Program, a more flexible undergraduate program that allows women to pursue a BA on a part-time or full-time basis. The program strives to meet the special needs of adult students, giving them special consideration in the admissions process, academic advising, housing options, and financial aid packages. Wellesley also offers post-baccalaureate study for students who already hold a bachelor's degree and would like to pursue more undergraduate study for a specific purpose. In general, students in the post-baccalaureate program take courses in preparation for medical school or another graduate program. Post-baccalaureate study is open to both men and women. For more information on Wellesley's academic programs, prospective students may contact the Board of Admission.

Wellesley College offers the Bachelor of Arts degree in the following major departments: Africana studies, anthropology, astronomy, biological sciences, chemistry, Chinese, computer science, economics, English, French, geology, German, Greek, history, history of art, Italian, Japanese, Latin, mathematics, music, philosophy, physics, political science, psychology, religion, Russian, sociology, Spanish, studio art, and women's studies. Wellesley also offers 20 interdepartmental majors in American studies, architecture, biological chemistry, Chinese studies, classical and Near Eastern archaeology, classical civilization, cognitive science, comparative literature, French cultural studies, German studies, international relations, Italian culture, Japanese studies, Jewish studies, language studies, Latin American studies, medieval/renaissance studies, neuroscience, peace and justice studies, and Russian area studies. Students also have the option of designing an individual major. In recent years, students have created majors in astrophysics, environmental science, Islamic studies, media arts and sciences, theatre studies, and urban studies.

There are 230 full-time faculty members at Wellesley, 98 percent of whom hold a doctoral or terminal degree in their field of study. In addition to full-time faculty, Wellesley employs roughly 102 distinguished, part-time instructors. Fifty-four percent of tenured professors are women. All faculty members are accomplished in their field of study and are encouraged to continue their pursuits in research and publication. However, undergraduate instruction is of primary importance at Wellesley, and professors are committed to teaching, advising, and working closely with students.

Board of Admission, 106 Central Street
Wellesley, MA 02481-8203
Phone: 781-283-2270
Fax: 781-283-3678
Website: www.wellesley.edu

ADMISSIONS

Admission to Wellesley is highly selective. Candidates for admission must have a strong academic record and must have followed a challenging course of study throughout their four years of high school. Students who display considerable academic promise and social maturity may apply to Wellesley after three years of secondary school; however, most incoming students have completed all four years of high school. Wellesley encourages all prospective students to follow a strong academic preparation, which includes rigorous training in writing, verbal communication, and reading comprehension and interpretation, as well as a strong understanding of mathematics and history. Wellesley further recommends that students take at least two years of lab sciences and coursework that displays competency in a foreign language, either ancient or modern. Incoming students may earn course credit through Advanced Placement examinations. To apply for admission, students must submit scores from the ACT or SAT I, as well as three SAT II: Subject Tests, of which one must be the Writing Test. Though not required, Wellesley recommends that prospective students schedule a personal interview. International applicants for whom English is not their first language are encouraged to take the Test of English as a Foreign Language (TOEFL) or the SAT II: English Language Proficiency Test (ELPT). In addition to regular admissions, Wellesley offers an early decision program. Transfer students may apply for entrance in either the fall or spring semester.

CAMPUS LIFE

Wellesley is located in a beautiful, suburban community of 27,000, just outside the world-class city of Boston, Massachusetts. There are a variety of shops, fine restaurants, and bookstores within close proximity to the College and nearly endless cultural and entertainment opportunities in the greater metropolitan area. With many other local colleges and universities, Boston is an unparalleled college town, home to over 250,000 college students. In addition to the vibrant, collegiate atmosphere, Boston offers the opportunity to pursue internships in government or social service agencies, as well as cultural exhibitions and events at the Boston Ballet, the Boston Symphony, the Museum of Fine Arts, and the Museum of Science. The city is also home to several well-known professional sports teams, including the Boston Celtics, the Bruins, and the Red Sox. Near Boston, there are many famous recreation areas, including New England's mountain ranges and winter sports resorts, Atlantic coast beaches, and the Cape Cod seashore.

Students at Wellesley can cross register for classes at MIT, Babson, and Brandeis for full course credit and at no additional cost. Wellesley also participates in the Twelve College Exchange program, which gives students the opportunity to spend a semester or year studying at any of the other member institutions: Amherst, Bowdoin, Connecticut College, Dartmouth, Mount Holyoke, Smith, Trinity, Vassar, Wesleyan, Wheaton, and Williams. Students also have the option of attending the National Theater Institute at the Eugene O'Neill Theater Center, accredited by Connecticut College, or the Williams-Mystic Seaport Program in Maritime Studies. Wellesley also offers an exchange program with Spelman College, a historically black women's college in Atlanta, Georgia, and with Mills College, a women's college in Oakland, California. During their junior year, about 30 percent of students choose to study abroad for a semester or a year, through overseas programs sponsored by Wellesley or by other colleges and universities. Currently, Wellesley operates overseas programs in Aix-en-Provence, France; Konstanz, Germany; and Oaxaca, Mexico, and is consortium member at schools in Spain, Italy, and Japan. Wellesley also operates exchange programs in the United Kingdom, Japan, Argentina, and Korea. Every year, 18 to 20 juniors spend the summer in Washington, D.C. through the Washington Internship Program, in which they have the opportunity to work with Congress, at public-interest organizations, and at various cultural and scientific institutions in the Capital.

COST AND AID

For the 2001–2002 academic year, tuition was $25,022, plus $7,890 for room and board. There is also a student activity fee of $164 and a facilities fee of $318. In addition, students should expect to spend roughly $1,800 annually on books, laundry, and personal expenses. Transportation costs to and from Wellesley vary.

WELLS COLLEGE

GENERAL INFORMATION

Wells College is a private, residential, liberal arts college enrolling 450 women from across the United States and throughout the world. Founded in 1868, it was the second institution in the country to award the baccalaureate degree to women. Its founder, Henry Wells, who built his fortune with the creation of the Wells Fargo Express, believed that women would play a vital role in the future of America. Today, true to its heritage, Wells maintains a national reputation for academic excellence. The College prides itself on offering one of the most collaborative learning environments in higher education today.

Wells offers women education of the highest quality at an affordable price. This impressive combination makes us a best value among national liberal arts colleges. Ninety-eight percent of Wells faculty members have doctoral degrees. And all classes are taught by professors—not teaching assistants. Wells students prepare for careers and entrance into top graduate and professional schools through experiential learning: internships, research with faculty members, community service, and other options. Eighty-two percent of the members of the Class of 2002 held at least one internship during their college careers. All students at Wells benefit from an academic experience similar to honors programs available only to a small number of students at other institutions. Throughout their four years, they work toward a senior project or thesis that is comparable to graduate-level study. Wells prides itself on offering one of the most collaborative learning environments in higher education—small class size fosters a great sense of supportive, personal attention.

STUDENT BODY

Wells students enjoy all of the advantages of living in a closely-knit community. The environment is relaxed and congenial. A well-respected Honor Code shapes the educational and social atmosphere of the campus. Wells supports more than 42 clubs and organizations, in addition to student-sponsored events, lectures, and performances. Clubs and organizations include Amnesty International, Choir, Christian Fellowship, Dance Collective, French Club, Green Geese (environmental club), Henry's VIII (a capella singing group), Kastalia Honoree Society (dramatic arts club), L.B.Q.T.A (Lesbian, Bisexual, Questioning, Transgendered and Allies), Model U.N., *The Onyx* (student newspaper), Phoenix Literary Society, Wells Democrats, Wells Republicans, Wells Hillel, and the Women's Resource Center to name a few. Wells is also a Division III member of the NCAA, and members of the Atlantic Women's College Conference and the New York State Women's Collegiate Athletic Association. Wells' women compete in six intercollegiate sports: soccer, lacrosse, softball, field hockey, tennis, and swimming.

ACADEMICS

While education at many colleges and universities grows increasingly specialized and narrow, society needs women who can meaningfully interpret information and find creative solutions to complex problems. A Wells liberal arts education provides breadth of knowledge, refines your ability to think critically, and teaches the decision-making process. You develop strong skills, and gain an understanding of human dynamics and the liberal arts. Fundamental to Wells' curriculum is an interdisciplinary approach to the liberal arts with the opportunity to experience intimate classes and innovative teaching methods. At Wells, you will work closely with faculty members from various disciplines to create an educational experience that simultaneously integrates knowledge from many subject areas. This kind of thinking might involve using knowledge of both history and sociology to understand a literary text or dramatic production. You might find yourself solving human problems through quantitative analysis or by examining the political and ethical implications connected to breakthroughs in science.

Wells College offers the Bachelor of Arts degree with majors in the following areas (concentrations within the majors appear in parentheses): American studies (African-American studies, American cultures); arts and performance (music, theatre and dance); biological and chemical sciences (biochemistry and molecular biology, biology, chemistry); economics and management (economics, management); English (creative writing, literature); environmental studies; foreign languages, literatures, and cultures (French, German, Spanish); history; international studies; mathematical and physical sciences (computer science, mathematics, physics); psychology; public affairs: ethics, politics, and social policy (ethics and philosophy, government and politics); religious studies and human values (human nature and values, religious studies); sociology and anthropology (cultural/cross-cultural sociology), visual arts (art history, studio art); women's studies.

In consultation with the dean and faculty, students may also design their own concentrations and majors. In addition, Wells offers programs that lead to provisional certification in elementary and secondary education. The College offers a 3/2 program in engineering with Cornell University, Columbia University, Clarkson University, and Case Western Reserve University. In the dual degree programs, the student earns both a BA from Wells College and the professional degree from the affiliated university within five years. Finally, Wells offers a 3/4 program with the College of Veterinary Medicine of Cornell University, which leads to the DMV degree.

Learning at Wells College takes place in small, seminar-style classes where you are a collaborative partner in the educational process. Starting immediately in your first semester, you work directly with professors who are recognized experts in their fields—not teaching assistants. More than 98 percent of Wells professors hold terminal degrees in their area of expertise. They have been educated at the world's leading research universities such as Harvard, Yale, Princeton, Columbia, Cornell, Brown, and Stanford. Your professors know your name; they know you. What you will discover in Wells classes is your own voice and the importance of exploring ideas with others.

170 Main Street
Aurora, NY 13026
Phone: 315-364-3264
Fax: 315-364-3327
Website: www.wells.edu

WELLS

ADMISSIONS

Wells College admits students on the basis of the strength of their academic preparation. Since many of the classes at Wells are small and emphasize original, independent work, a student is expected to possess the intellectual curiosity, motivation, and maturity to profit from this experience. Wells seeks students from varied backgrounds, as diverse interests and talents provide a stimulating, intellectual environment. Wells College students come from widely different backgrounds. The common denominator of Wells students is enthusiasm for their academic pursuits and serious intent to use their education in the future to enhance both their personal and professional lives.

Candidates for admission are expected to complete a solid college preparatory program throughout their four years in secondary school. The college recommends a program which provides the best background for study at Wells, including 4 years of English grammar, composition, and literature; 3 years of a foreign language; 3 years of mathematics; 2 years of history; and 2 years of laboratory science. Students' records are enhanced by the addition of courses such as computer science, art, and music, when appropriate curricular choices are offered. It is further recommended that candidates pursue English and one other area for four years, so that they may have the stimulation and challenge of advanced level work.

To apply for admission to Wells College candidates must submit completed application forms to the Admissions Office by March 1 of the year of entrance. In addition, the following credentials are required: a transcript of all secondary school work, including the recommendation of the high school principal or guidance counselor; scores from either the College Entrance Examination Board Scholastic Aptitude Test (SAT I) or the American College Testing Program (ACT); two letters of recommendation from teachers in academic subject areas. A personal interview is strongly recommended.

ADMISSIONS DEADLINE OPTIONS

Early Decision: December 15. Students whose first choice is Wells College are encouraged to apply under the early decision option. This is a binding admissions option; if admitted, early decision applicants agree to accept Wells' offer of admission and agree to withdraw their applications to all other colleges.

Early Action: December 15. Students who would like to receive an early review of their application files are encouraged to apply under the early action option. This is a nonbinding admissions option.

Regular Admissions: March 1. All other applications to the college should be received by the regular admissions deadline. Applications are reviewed after this date and decisions are mailed by April 1.

CAMPUS LIFE

The beautiful 365-acre lakeside campus is situated in the heart of the Finger Lakes Region of New York State in the historical village of Aurora. The campus is 30 minutes from Ithaca, one hour from Syracuse and Rochester, and approximately five hours from New York City. Wells College is located in an area known for its high concentration of nationally renowned colleges and universities, including Cornell University, Colgate University, Hamilton College, Hobart and William Smith Colleges, Syracuse University, and the University of Rochester.

During their four years at Wells, students may also participate in study abroad or affiliated programs in the following countries and cities: Copenhagen, Denmark; Paris, Grenoble, and St. Victor Lacoste, France; Berlin, Bonn, and Heidelberg, Germany; Cork, Ireland; Florence and Rome, Italy; Kyoto, Japan; Puebla, Mexico; Dakar, Senegal; Seville, Spain; and London, Bath, and York, United Kingdom. Students may also pursue global study through the School for Field Studies in Australia, Africa, and the Caribbean, at the Salt Center in Portland, Maine, and other locations. The Washington Semester at American University in Washington, DC, is a popular option for those students interested in communications, economics, or government. Through a unique exchange program, Wells students may also take courses at nearby Cornell University or Ithaca College.

COST AND AID

For the 2002–2003 year, tuition is $13,070, room and board is $6,450, and fees are $480.

WESTMINSTER COLLEGE (MO)

GENERAL INFORMATION

Westminster College currently enrolls 800 students, 35 percent of whom come from outside Missouri. States strongly represented are Oklahoma, Arkansas, Texas, Kansas, and Illinois. Facilities include the Hunter Activity Center, which houses a gymnasium, an indoor running track, racquetball courts, student mailboxes, a recreation room, student activity offices, and the campus grill. The expanded Priest Athletic Complex includes varsity and practice facilities for soccer, softball, baseball, and football; the facility has new lights for night events. The Wetterau Field Sports Facility includes athletic offices, varsity locker rooms, training rooms, and a varsity weight room. The Mueller Student Center is a popular place for student parties, special college events, and athletic practice.

Westminster's Center for Leadership and Service promotes leadership development, character development, and community service on the campus and in the community. The Center works closely with the Center for Teaching Excellence to promote service-learning opportunities and excellent teaching throughout the Westminster campus. Whether students plan to enter the professional world immediately or pursue a graduate program, they are given encouragement, advice, and guidance in preparing for life after Westminster. Included in the placement effort is an important linking of current students with graduates who are now in influential positions in society. In addition, Westminster's formalized internship program is designed to extend the student's learning opportunities beyond the traditional classroom setting into professional work environments.

The Green Lecture Series, a distinguished series on economic, social, and international affairs, was established in 1936 as a memorial to John Findley Green, an 1884 Westminster graduate. The roster of past speakers includes former Presidents Bush, Reagan, and Truman; former British Prime Minister Edward Heath; former CIA Director William Casey; former U.S. Ambassador to Russia Robert S. Strauss; former President of the Soviet Union Mikhail Gorbachev; and Nobel laureate Lech Walesa, former President of Poland. The 1996 Green Lecture, presented by Lady Margaret Thatcher, commemorated the fiftieth anniversary of Winston Churchill's "Iron Curtain" address, held in the historic Westminster Gym. Westminster College uses as its chapel a seventeenth-century English Church, which was dismantled in London and rebuilt on the campus. The lower level of the church houses the Winston Churchill Memorial and Library, which contains memorabilia of Sir Winston Churchill and World War II. The church, originally designed by Sir Christopher Wren, is a national landmark that attracts 30,000 visitors annually.

STUDENT BODY

The Westminster College Student Government Association (SGA) is composed of all students at the College. Its officers are elected by the entire Student Body. The SGA serves the interests of individual students and student groups. The activity fee charged each student gives the Student Government Association a sizable budget ($200,000) to carry out such programs as intramurals, community relations, publications, entertainment, and other special events. Many of the student clubs and organizations receive their funding from the SGA, which sponsors and supports activities and events on behalf of students and groups. What makes the SGA so popular at Westminster is that its voting membership is based on living groups and clubs, so that all students have a "voice" and opportunities for leadership positions. Faculty advisors work closely with students in the publication of the campus newspaper, college yearbook, and literary magazine. Westminster College participates in the National Collegiate Athletic Association (Division III) and the St. Louis Intercollegiate Athletic Conference, competing in men's baseball, basketball, football, golf, soccer, and tennis, as well as women's basketball, golf, soccer, softball, tennis, and volleyball.

ACADEMICS

Westminster is a selective college with an innovative curriculum based on the liberal arts that emphasizes breadth as well as depth. The College's general education program reflects a commitment to liberal learning in the arts and sciences and to providing its students with opportunities to explore the aesthetic, cultural, ethical, historical, scientific, and social contexts in which they will live, work, and learn in the twenty-first century. Requirements for the baccalaureate degree are usually completed in four years. Students must satisfy general course requirements as well as departmental requirements in courses outside their major. Academic advisors guide all students through the four years of their enrollment. The Westminster Seminar Program is designed to bridge the gap between high school and college and introduce students to campus facilities, resources, faculty members, and other students. The program begins prior to the start of classes for all first-year students. The professor of this class is the student's faculty advisor until the student declares a major. Westminster operates on a traditional two-semester calendar. A three-week term is available after the spring semester for special travel and field study courses or internships.

Major programs of study offered at Westminster include accounting, biology, business administration (entrepreneurial studies, finance, management, and marketing), chemistry, computer science, economics, education (elementary, middle school, secondary, and physical education), English (creative writing, literature), environmental science, environmental studies, French, history, international business, international studies, management information systems, mathematical sciences, philosophy, physical education, physics, political science, psychology, religious studies, self-designed major, sociology and anthropology, and Spanish.

501 Westminster Avenue
Fulton, MO 65251-1299
Phone: 573-592-5251
Fax: 573-592-5255
Website: www.westminster-mo.edu

Minor programs of study offered at Westminster include: allied health (biology), American studies, Asian studies, biology, business administration, chemistry, classics with Latin component, classics without Latin component, coaching, economics, English, entrepreneurial studies, environmental sciences, environmental studies, European history, European studies, French, German, history, international business, leadership studies, mathematical sciences, music, philosophy, physics, political science, pre-engineering , pre-law, psychology, religious studies, self-designed minor, sociology and anthropology, Spanish, United States history, and women's and gender studies.

The 57 faculty members are part of a unique learning environment where students and teachers work together to discover answers to the complex problems faced in and out of the classroom and, in the process, establish life-long relationships. Approximately 75 percent of the distinguished faculty members hold the doctorate or equivalent terminal degree; many are published authors and others are engaged in advanced research and scholarly study. Although faculty members are involved in research and writing, they primarily constitute a teaching faculty whose main concern is the education of undergraduate students.

ADMISSIONS

Each application is considered individually by the Enrollment Services staff and the Admissions Committee, who evaluate a number of factors, including courses taken in secondary school, a counselor's recommendation, test scores, grade point average, and activities. To apply to Westminster College, a student should submit the application for admission, an official copy of the secondary school transcript, test scores on either the ACT or SAT I, and a recommendation from a high school official. Transfer students must submit a transcript from each college previously attended. International students must submit the TOEFL test score. While the College operates on a rolling admissions calendar, students are encouraged to apply early. Westminster College does not discriminate on the basis of race, sex, color, national or ethnic origin, sexual orientation, or physical handicap in the administration of its educational policies, admissions policies, scholarship and loan programs, or other school-administered programs. For further information regarding admissions, financial assistance, academic programs, and campus visits, students should write or call:

Office of Enrollment Services (Admissions & Financial Aid)
Westminster College
501 Westminster Avenue
Fulton, Missouri 65251-1299
Telephone: 573-592-5251 or 800-475-3361 (toll-free)
Fax: 573-592-5255
E-mail: admissions@jaynet.wcmo.edu
Web: www.westminster-mo.edu

CAMPUS LIFE

Westminster College is located in Fulton, Missouri, a safe, historic community of approximately 12,000 people, situated in the rolling hills and trees of central Missouri. Nearly 15 percent of the Fulton population are college students. Westminster is located a little more than an hour north of the Lake of the Ozarks, a beautiful recreational area. Within 25 minutes to the west is Columbia, a college town of more than 70,000 people. Just to the south of Fulton is Jefferson City, Missouri's state capital. Kansas City is 2 hours west, and St. Louis is located 2 hours east on Interstate 70.

The College's Center for Off-Campus and International Programs assists students seeking overseas study opportunities or pursuing exchange opportunities with sister institutions. Westminster participates in the Institutes of European and Asian Studies, which provide 20 campuses throughout the world for Westminster students to spend a semester or a year studying abroad. The College's strong historical relationship with England has led to several educational opportunities, including exchange programs with Queen Mary and Westfield College and the University of East Anglia School of English and American Studies in Norwich, two hours from London. Other overseas exchange programs are available at Kansai Gaidai University (Osaka, Japan) and L'Ecole Superieure des Sciences Commerciales (ESSCA, School for Business Study) in Angers, France; the latter allows French majors the opportunity to study abroad in a French-speaking environment. Other off-campus programs include the United Nations Semester, the Washington Semester, and the Chicago Urban Studies Semester.

COST AND AID

The basic cost for the 2003–2004 academic year is $17,970 for tuition, room, board, and the student activity fee. The College estimates that students should allow $2,400 annually for books, supplies, and personal expenses.

WHEATON COLLEGE (IL)

GENERAL INFORMATION

Wheaton College offers academic programs rooted in the classic liberal arts tradition, taught from an evangelical Christian perspective. It's a top-ranked college that challenges students to grow their intellect in the context of developing a whole life-a school that combines serious study and academic rigor with Christian distinctiveness. Ranked by *U.S. News & World Report* as one of the top national liberal arts colleges, Wheaton College attracts exceptional high school students from all 50 states and more than 40 countries.

Established in 1860 as a co-ed, interdenominational Christian liberal arts college, Wheaton takes the pursuit of faith and learning seriously. Seeking to create a diverse, service-oriented community, Wheaton College offers a rich curriculum that emphasizes global awareness and engagement. Students participate in a vibrant, growing multicultural community of talented, capable learners who are distinct in their desire to grow intellectually, to grow in relationship with one another, and to grow in Christ. Wheaton's concern for values is a long-standing tradition, not a trend. Wheaton College has consistently appeared on the Honor Roll of Character Building Colleges established by The John Templeton Foundation. Such recognition reflects Wheaton's commitment to character building programs such as its Center for Applied Christian Ethics, Urban Studies Program, the Human Needs and Global Resources Program (HNGR), the Honduras Project, HoneyRock's High Road Wilderness Programs, and the many services and ministries of the Office of Christian Outreach.

A profile of the Class of 2005 demonstrates the caliber of students that choose Wheaton. Of the 574 students who entered in the fall of 2001, 49 were National Merit Finalists. The group's average high school GPA was 3.67 and 60 percent graduated in the top 10 percent of their class. The middle 50 percent scored between 1240 and 1400 on the re-centered SAT and between 27 and 31 on the ACT; 12 percent are multi-cultural. More than 80 percent will graduate on time. Wheaton, with its emphasis on faith, learning, and service, is a place where students like this can thrive.

STUDENT BODY

Who says scholarship can't mix with fun? Chicago may beckon, but students don't have to catch the train when they're looking for things to do. Right here on campus there's the Talent Show, Homecoming, CU Concerts, Coffee Houses, Late Night Skates, Brother/Sister Floor activities in the dorms, Air Jam in the spring, plays and concerts throughout the year, Class Films, and an amazingly versatile place to play called the Sports and Recreation Complex. Wheaton offers men and women intercollegiate participation in 21 different sports as a member of the NCAA Division III. Its teams in eight different sports have won 14 conference titles over the past five years. More than 75 students have earned All-American recognition. Dozens of club and intramural sports are also offered.

ACADEMICS

Academically, Wheaton compares with the finest schools in the nation. It boasts a rigorous curriculum, a top-tier science department, a nationally regarded conservatory of music, and outstanding summer research programs. The college has been ranked among the top 50 liberal arts schools that produce the best science graduates and is ranked 11th in the nation in the percentage of graduates who go on to earn doctorates. Distinguished graduate schools such as those at Yale, Princeton, Harvard, and the University of Chicago regularly enroll Wheaton graduates in various fields.

With top quality faculty, sophisticated instrumentation, and abundant resources, Wheaton College's science department ranks today among the top 25 liberal arts science departments in the nation's "baccalaureate colleges." Here, careers in medicine, energy, natural resources, biological science, environmental science, engineering, law, and higher education get a strong start. Fully, one-quarter of our science graduates go on to complete doctorates.

Those with a flair for the visual arts, a gift for music, or a special way with words will find courses they are looking for within the Division of Arts, Media and Communication. This academic division sustains a creative environment that includes the plays of Arena Theater, fine art from the studios of Adams hall, original audio and video productions, and outstanding musical performances.

Wheaton's Conservatory of Music is one of the finest music schools in the nation. The reasons why? A talented faculty, an 80-member orchestra, several outstanding music ensembles, interesting workshops, opportunities for travel abroad, and a long list of renowned alumni.

501 College Avenue
Wheaton, IL 60187
Phone: 630-752-5005
Fax: 630-752-5285
Website: www.wheaton.edu

We offer 35 majors in the arts and sciences: ancient languages, anthropology, archaeology, art, biblical/theological studies, biology, business/economics, chemistry, Christian formation/ministry, communications, computer science, economics, education, English, environmental science, French, geology, German, history, history/social science, interdisciplinary studies (integrating course work in two or three fields), international relations, kinesiology, liberal arts-engineering, liberal arts-nursing, mathematics, music, philosophy, physical science, physics, political science, psychology, sociology, Spanish and world religions. In the Conservatory of Music we offer a Bachelors of Music in five fields: composition, education, history/literature, performance, and music with elective studies in an outside field of the student's choice.

Along with this rich academic program, Wheaton students enjoy matchless resources, the core of which is our faculty. One hundred percent of our professors teach their own classes. More than 90 percent of Wheaton's faculty members hold doctoral or other terminal degrees, more than one third graduated from the top 25 graduate schools as designated in *U.S. News & World Report*. One hundred and eighty one full time professors and 93 part time, together compromise our disciplined and productive group of scholars. The ratio of students to teachers is 11:1 and 97 percent of the classes have under 50 students enrolled. Wheaton encourages its faculty to engage in research, but not at the expense of strong teaching and mentoring.

ADMISSIONS

Wheaton selects candidates for admission from those who evidence a vital Christian experience, high academic ability, moral character, personal integrity, and social concern. The College seeks to enroll, from its more than 2,100 applicants, a well rounded freshman class; a class composed of about 575 dynamic individuals with a wide variety of attributes, accomplishments, backgrounds, and interests. Wheaton offers both regular admission and early action application options. The deadline for early action is November 1 and for regular decision January 15. The application includes biographical data and essays. The recommended high school curriculum includes 4 years of English, 3–4 years each of mathematics, science, and social studies, and 2–3 years of foreign language. Students are encouraged to include honors, advanced, and AP courses in their curriculums. Applicants must submit the official high school transcript as well as official results from the SAT I or ACT. Students are encouraged to use the online applications available through Wheaton's website.

CAMPUS LIFE

Wheaton, Illinois, population 54,000, is a family-oriented community known for its good schools, pleasant neighborhoods, and many churches. Major airports, O'Hare and Midway, are easily accessible for domestic and international travel. A 45-minute train ride links suburban Wheaton to downtown Chicago and all the excitement and wonder a world-class city offers, including a magnificent lakeshore. Chicago provides Wheaton students with a focus for their interests in art, music, science, and sports, and for a wide variety of their professional, academic, and ministerial aspirations.

In addition to the academic subjects taught in traditional classroom settings, there are many off-campus study, research, and internship opportunities. These popular programs include the Science Station at the Black Hills campus in South Dakota; HoneyRock campus in the north woods of Wisconsin; the American Studies Program in Washington, DC; the Human Needs and Global Resources Program focused on Third World Development; Urban Studies; and ROTC. There are study abroad programs in East Asia, England, France, Germany, the Holy Lands, Latin America, Russia, Spain, and Western Europe. Students can also pursue summer research and study projects with members of the faculty.

COST AND AID

For 2003–2004 the costs are:

Tuition: $18,500

Room: $3,570

Board: $2,530

The cost of a Wheaton College education is remarkably low compared to private institutions of similar quality. Of the 114 national liberal arts colleges classified with us in the top two tiers of National Liberal Arts Colleges in *U.S. News & World Report*'s Annual Best Colleges Book, Wheaton's tuition ranks 104th.

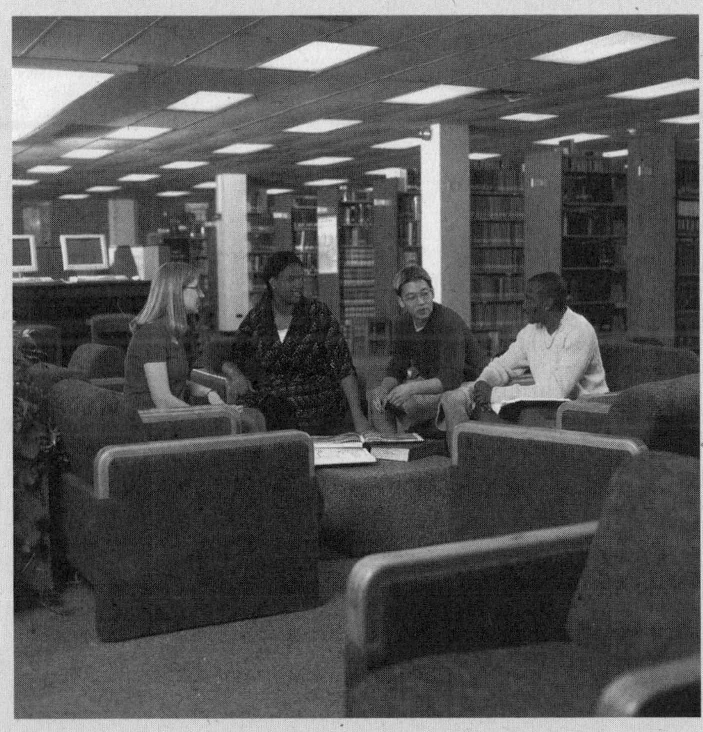

WHITMAN COLLEGE

GENERAL INFORMATION

Whitman College's programs in the arts, humanities, social sciences, and natural sciences have earned the college a national reputation for excellence. In the classroom and the laboratory, as well as through participating in the college's residential and extracurricular programs, Whitman's students acquire the knowledge and talents to succeed in whatever career and life paths they choose. What students from across the United States and from many other countries find at Whitman today, as students have since the college's founding in 1883, is a closely-knit community of dedicated teachers and students working together to achieve lives of intellectual vitality, personal confidence, social responsibility, and the flexibility to adapt to a rapidly changing world. With just 1,400 students, our average class size of 15 and student/faculty ratio of ten-to-one ensure a rigorous, personalized education. *U.S. News & World Report* has recognized Whitman's quality by ranking the college in the top tier among national liberal arts colleges. Believing that every moment should be a "learning moment," we offer extensive, impressive extracurricular and residential programs. Our student body is extremely active, with more than 100 interest groups and clubs that are almost entirely student-run. Three-quarters of Whitman students live on campus in a wide variety of living arrangements, including coeducational and apartment-style residence halls; 11 special interest houses, dedicated to foreign language study, environmental awareness, the arts, writing, and other interests; four fraternity houses; and an all-women's residence hall that provides living space and chapter rooms for the college's four national sororities.

STUDENT BODY

Students complement their classroom learning with extracurricular activities, which connect them to their peers and the surrounding community. Most people can find a group that shares their interests within one of the college's 100 students organizations. Students are welcome to found new clubs and groups. Those interested in communications may participate in KWCW, the student radio station, *The Blue Moon*, an award-winning literary magazine, or *The Pioneer*, Whitman's newspaper. Active students enjoy the outdoor program, the ultimate Frisbee team, and 12 other intramural and 10 club sports. Varsity athletes compete in the NCAA's Division III. The men field teams in alpine skiing, baseball, basketball, cross-country, golf, Nordic skiing, soccer, swimming, and tennis. The women compete in alpine skiing, basketball, cross-country, golf, Nordic skiing, soccer, swimming, tennis, and volleyball. Many undergraduates undertake volunteer work arranged by the Whitman College Center for Community Service. The college's forensics team excels on the national level, and the theatre program stages up to 10 major productions a year as well as numerous smaller performances. Students interested in music have 16 groups to choose from, and an opera or musical is staged annually.

ACADEMICS

Whitman strives to equip all students with the intellectual tools they need to become life-long learners. All students undertake the general studies program, which hones skills in reasoning, critical thinking, leaderships, and expository writing. The program exposes students to modern society's historical foundations and teaches them to make sound decisions based on ethics. In the first year, all undergraduates take Antiquity and Modernity an interdisciplinary seminar focused on reading, writing, and in-class discussion about many of the great books of Western intellectual thought. Whitman's distribution requirements mandate a minimum of six semester units in each of these five subjects: fine arts, social sciences, humanities, sciences, and alternate voices. In addition, students must complete a class in quantitative analysis. The capstone to each academic major at Whitman is a comprehensive oral examination, Whitman was the first college in the nation to require such exams. Most majors also require a written comprehensive exam. Top students receive honors distinctions in their respective majors. The academic calendar is made up of two semesters.

Whitman College grants Bachelor of Arts degrees in the following majors: anthropology, art, art history and visual culture studies, biology, biochemistry/biophysics & molecular biology, chemistry, classics, economics, English, foreign languages and literatures (French, German studies, German literature, or Spanish), geology, history, mathematics, music, philosophy, physics, politics, psychology, rhetoric and film studies, sociology, and theatre. Many students choose to combine majors or pursue interdepartmental majors in areas such as Asian studies, astronomy-geology, biology-geology, chemistry-geology, economics-mathematics, environmental studies (emphases in biology, chemistry, economics, geology, physics, politics, or sociology), geology-physics, mathematics-computer science, mathematics-physics, and physics-astronomy. Most departments also offer minors. Additional available minors include American ethnic studies, astronomy, Chinese, classics, computer science, education, gender studies, Japanese, religion, sports studies/recreation and athletics, and world literature. Students wishing to design their own major work closely with professors to ensure approval and proper course selection. Whitman arranges top-quality cooperative degree programs with partner institutions. Students may pursue engineering in conjunction with the University of Washington, Columbia, Duke, Cal Tech, and Washington University in St. Louis. An oceanography program is run with the University of Washington, while Duke facilitates environmental management and forestry programs. Whitman works with Columbia School of Law on law degrees and the Monterey Institute of International Studies on international studies and international business. Students may study education with the Bank Street College of Education, Whitworth College and the University of Puget Sound or computer science with the University of Washington.

515 Boyer Ave
Walla Walla, WA 99362-2046
Phone: 509-527-5176
Fax: 509-527-4967
Website: www.whitman.edu]

WHITMAN COLLEGE

Whitman College prioritizes teaching and chooses faculty members accordingly. Aside from their teaching duties, professors maintain active research and publication efforts and make noteworthy contributions to their respective fields. Faculty members are frequently honored with awards and grants from outside organizations. A full 98 percent of the faculty members have earned their PhD or terminal degree. Instructors also work with students in the role of academic advisors. With Whitman's low student/faculty ratio of 10:1, students get the individual attention they need to blossom as scholars. It is common for students to work alongside their instructors on research projects, but they also interact outside of academics, playing intramurals together, serving on committees, and sharing meals. Whitman ensures a high quality academic environment with this combination of dedicated professors and empowered students.

ADMISSIONS

Whitman's admissions committee seeks applicants who clearly show motivation, a dedication to learning, and the potential to contribute significantly to the college's community. Each admitted class includes students from diverse backgrounds who can meet the academic challenges presented in the Whitman curriculum. Gaining admission to Whitman is a highly competitive process. Almost 70 percent of admits graduated in the top 10 percent of their high school class. The middle 50 percent of enrolled students score between 620–710 on the verbal section of the SAT I and 610–710 on the math section. Whitman does offer an Early Decision option for students who know that Whitman is their top college choice. The deadline for Early Decision applicants in November 15 or January 1. Students applying Regular Decision must have their materials in by January 15. Those seeking spring admission must meet the November 15 deadline. Students may apply to Whitman online at www.whitman.edu/admission/apply.html. Students may also complete the Common Application, app.commonapp.org, as long as they also submit the additional essay found on the College's Personal Supplement form, or by paper form. Official scores from the SAT I or the ACT are mandatory. Candidates must submit the application fee of $45 with their materials. In addition, international students are required to send TOEFL scores, ELPT or APIEL scores, and the College Board's International Student Financial Aid Application and Certification form.

CAMPUS LIFE

Whitman's hometown of Walla Walla, Washington, has a rich history and welcoming local community of 30,000. The location in the foothills of the Blue Mountains gives students access to all of the outdoor activities available in the southeastern part of the state: skiing, backpacking, hiking, kayaking, rafting, and rock climbing. The sun shines 300 days a year in Walla Walla, providing an arid, bright climate throughout the various seasons. The campus attracts performers and intellectuals from many fields, so students have many opportunities to attend concerts, film screenings, art shows, lectures, and interactive panel discussions.

Whitman believes that overseas studies provide the opportunity for students to expand their minds and complement their on-campus learning. The College organizes programs in countries across the globe, and 4 out of 10 students embark on trips to Asia, South America, Africa, Europe, or even Australia before they complete their four years at Whitman. Semester- and year-long programs are available. Other valuable experiences await closer to home in the form of off-campus internships or urban-study programs in Chicago, Philadelphia, and Washington, DC.

COST AND AID

In the 2003–2004 school year, tuition totals $25,400. Room and board cost $6,880. Students spend approximately $1,250 more on books, supplies, and personal expenses. All students pay an annual associated student body fee of $226.

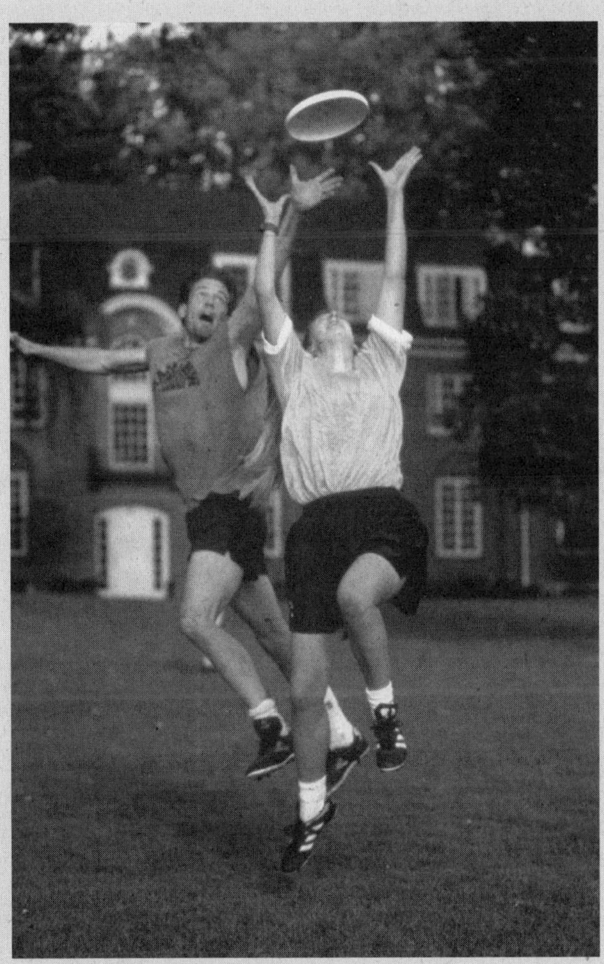

WILLIAM PATERSON UNIVERSITY

GENERAL INFORMATION

William Paterson University, a public school founded in 1855, has grown to become a comprehensive, liberal arts institution committed to academic excellence and student success. Accredited by the Middle States Association of Schools and Colleges, it offers 30 undergraduate and 19 graduate degrees and professional development programs through its five colleges: Arts and Communication, Christos M. Cotsakos College of Business, Education, Humanities and Social Sciences, and Science and Health. The 10,924 full and part-time students, who come from a diversity of backgrounds, enjoy the resources of a large university as well as the individual attention available at a smaller school. William Paterson is located in the hills of suburban Wayne, New Jersey, within an hour of the ocean, the mountains, the Meadowlands, and New York City. The 370-acre campus is the former estate of Garret Hobart, the country's 24th vice president. Students can relax and study amid the University's woods and waterfalls or take advantage of New York City's many opportunities. William Paterson offers a wide variety of student activities, modern on-campus housing, and the most up-to-date educational facilities. As a state-assisted institution, the University offers the value of a first-rate education at a fraction of the cost of private colleges and universities. Financial aid is also available to qualified students.

STUDENT BODY

Outside the classroom, students partake in a variety of social, cultural, and recreational activities. The activity calendar includes concerts, art exhibits, and theater performances. Greek organizations contribute to the social scene, while 50-plus student clubs provide outlets for a wide variety of interests. The University is proud to host the Jazz Room Series, a nationally acclaimed jazz event. Also, the Orchestra at William Paterson and the New Jersey Percussion Ensemble have both national and international reputations. Guest lecturers including Jesse Jackson, Henry Kissinger, Colin Powell, Margaret Thatcher, Jaime Escalante, and C. Everett Koop have come to campus as part of the Distinguished Lecturer Series. William Paterson athletic teams participate in the NCAA's Division III. Both men and women have teams in basketball, cross-country, soccer, swimming, and track. In addition, the men field baseball and football teams. Women also participate in field hockey, softball, and volleyball. Club sports are organized for bowling, horseback riding, volleyball, and ice hockey.

ACADEMICS

The baccalaureate degree requires 128 credits. Sixty of those credits are earned in general education classes. Another 30 to 60 come from work in the student's major, and 20 to 40 can be earned in electives. The general education specifications and major requirements vary depending on the degree. William Paterson students can pursue BA, BS, BFA, and BM degrees in any of the University's five colleges. Bachelor of Arts degrees are granted in African, African American, and Caribbean studies; anthropology; art; communication; English; French and Francophone studies; geography; history; Latin American studies; mathematics; music; philosophy; political science; psychology; sociology; Spanish; special education; and women's studies. Bachelor of Science degrees include accounting, applied chemistry, biology, biotechnology, business administration, community health/school health education, computer science, environmental science, nursing, and physical education. The Bachelor of Fine Arts degree is awarded in fine arts. In the Bachelor of Music program, students can choose between performance, jazz, and music management. Students may also pursue certification in elementary, secondary, and special education.

Counseling and advising are available to students who are undecided as to their major, and students seeking guidance on their career choices can take advantage of the University's Career Development Center. Honor programs, which offer students further challenges, include biopsychology, cognitive science, humanities, life science and environmental ethics, music, nursing, and performing and literary arts. There are also pre-professional progams in dentistry, engineering, law, medicine, pharmacy, physical therapy, speech-language pathology, and veterinary medicine. Alumni of the university's pre-medical program routinely gain entrance to the country's medical schools. Those who complete the pre-engineering degree have the know-how acquired in the first half of a four-year collegiate engineering program: After two years of study at the University, students can transfer to the New Jersey Institute of Technology. The required scores on Advanced Placement tests and/or College-Level Examination Program tests can earn college-level credit. Military experience may also be evaluated for credit.

The 366 full-time and 595 part-time members of the University's faculty bring both academic and real-world knowledge and expertise to the classroom. More than 88 percent of full-time faculty hold the highest degree in their field, and 26 have won Fulbright fellowships, the U.S. government's flagship international exchange program for scholars. Students benefit from the low 12:1 student-teacher ratio and average class size of only 22 students. Small class size encourages the informal, one-on-one interaction between faculty and students for which the University is known. Faculty members and students also interact closely on matters of class choices and career paths. Students are also encouraged to extend their classroom learning into research work; roughly 30 percent of students do.

Admissions Hall, 300 Pompton Road
Wayne, NJ 07470
Phone: 973-720-2125
Fax: 973-720-2910
Website: www.wpunj.edu

WILLIAM PATERSON UNIVERSITY

ADMISSIONS

In order to gain entrance to William Paterson, applicants should display a strong academic record in at least 16 Carnegie units and SAT I or ACT scores. Those seeking admission to the art department should provide a portfolio; students applying to the music department (aside from musical studies) are asked to audition. Transfer students need a 2.0 GPA and 12 college-level credits; those with fewer credits should send their high school transcript as well. Applicants to the nursing or computer science programs should have a 2.5 GPA. Those seeking special education degrees or teaching certification must have a 2.75 GPA. The deadline for all application forms, transcripts, and the $35 application fee for both first-year applicants and transfer students is May 1 for the fall term and November 1 for the spring semester. Candidates should bear in mind that the cut-off dates may be earlier if the combination of continuing students and new applications begins to exceed space availability. For information or the online application, please visit the undergraduate admissions website at www.wpunj.edu or contact:

Office of Admissions
William Paterson University of New Jersey
Wayne, NJ 07470
Telephone: 973-720-2125
Toll-free: 877-WPU-EXCEL
Fax: 973-720-2910
E-mail: admissions@wpunj.edu
World Wide Web: www.wpunj.edu

CAMPUS LIFE

Students participate in internships that help them clarify career goals and forge relationships that can result in post-graduation jobs. Study abroad programs are also available to sophomores and juniors who maintain a minimum GPA of 2.5. Students have the opportunity to earn 15 units while studying in Europe (Great Britain, Denmark, Hungary, Spain, Austria, Ireland, and France, among other countries), Latin America (Mexico, Ecuador, Chile, Costa Rica, Argentina, and Brazil), Australia, and certain countries in Asia and Africa. Students may also elect to study in the University's distance learning programs or at the centers affiliated with regional New Jersey community colleges.

COST AND AID

Full-time students from New Jersey paid $6,400 for tuition and fees in 2002–2003. Tuition for out-of-state students was $10,200. Room and board runs roughly $7,030 annually, which means the total is $13,430 for in-state residents and $17,230 for out-of-state residents. These totals may vary subject to decisions by the University's Board of Trustees.

WITTENBERG UNIVERSITY

THE UNIVERSITY AT A GLANCE

Founded in 1842 in Springfield, Ohio, Wittenberg is a private, coeducational, liberal arts and sciences college affiliated with the Evangelical Lutheran Church of America. Wittenberg's mission is to strive to develop the intellectual, spiritual, aesthetic, social, and physical qualities that characterize the wholeness of person. The five goals of a Wittenberg education are that each student have the ability to respond with understanding to the depth and complexity of the human experience; have the ability to recognize, define, and solve problems; develop a sense of vocation; have the ability to assume leadership; and take moral responsibility. The University encourages an environment of respect for all people and diverse beliefs, while at the same time supporting critical assessment of personal faith, beliefs, and ethics. Wittenberg is committed to providing a nurturing and challenging living and learning environment, which strives to teach moral responsibility and social consciousness while also creating an atmosphere that enhances the academic reputation. All students must engage in community service in the local area.

Wittenberg enrolls 2,200 full-time students, representing more than 43 states, the Virgin Islands, Puerto Rico, and more than three dozen countries around the world. The greatest concentration of students is from the Midwest and Northeast, although the student body includes students from coast to coast.

Ninety-eight percent of Wittenberg's students live on or near campus, making the campus a full-time, 24-hour-a-day, 7-day-a-week campus. All first- and second-year students reside in the residence halls; juniors and seniors have the option to remain in the residence halls, move off campus into a house or apartment, or live in a fraternity or sorority house.

Wittenberg's strong arts and sciences programs and community service make its graduates attractive to prominent medical, law, and graduate programs. More than 20 percent of Wittenberg graduates begin graduate programs immediately after graduation, and 70 percent eventually pursue an advanced degree at some point in their careers. Wittenberg ranks in the top 10 percent of private liberal arts and sciences colleges nationwide in the number of doctoral degrees earned by alumni. Graduates have enjoyed successful careers in a variety of fields, including education, business, science, fine and performing arts, politics, medicine, ministry, dentistry, and law.

Wittenberg competes in the nationally renowned Division III North Coast Athletic Conference (NCAC), which consists of 10 academically selective colleges and universities in Ohio, Pennsylvania, and Indiana. The NCAC features championship competition in 22 sports—11 for men and 11 for women. Men's teams include baseball, basketball, cross-country, football, golf, lacrosse, soccer, swimming and diving, tennis, and indoor and outdoor track. Women's teams include basketball, cross-country, field hockey, lacrosse, soccer, softball, swimming and diving, tennis, indoor and outdoor track, and volleyball. There is also a full list of club sports for men and women, including crew, ice hockey, golf, rugby, volleyball, and cricket. Wittenberg is accredited by the North Central Association of Colleges and Schools, the American Association of University Women, the American Chemical Society, and the National Association of Schools of Music.

STUDENTS

With more than 125 organizations and clubs, students can easily foster their academic and personal interests and develop management and leadership skills. Student groups are formed on topics ranging from cultural and social awareness to recreational to religious involvement and communication.

Current groups include American International Association, Circle K, College Democrats, College Republicans, Concerned Black Students, Conservation Club, Habitat for Humanity, Model United Nations, Outdoor Club, Caving Club, Martial Arts Club, Newman Club, Jewish Student Association, Wittenberg Christian Fellowship, Residence Hall Association, Residence Hall Government, Student Senate, *The Torch* (weekly newspaper), Union Board (student activity planning), *The Wittenberg Review of Literature and Art*, and WUSO (radio station).

Theatre productions, a dance company, and music groups such as the Wittenberg Choir, Kalliope (early music), Opera Studio, Brass Choir, Jazz Ensemble, orchestra, and symphonic band are available.

Approximately 30 percent of the students are involved in Greek Life. Many academic departments have honor societies and clubs for specific majors. Weekend activities include lectures, art exhibits, concerts, dances, movies, coffeehouses, and comedians.

New organizations and activities are created regularly to meet the changing interests of students.

ACADEMICS

To experience an education possessing both breadth and depth, students complete courses of study in two broad categories—a comprehensive education in the liberal arts & sciences and a major program of study. The comprehensive program is based on 16 learning goals that involve developing skills and competencies in writing, research, foreign language, speaking, mathematics, and computing. Students also perform community service and take courses in religion and philosophy, fine and performing arts, natural sciences, social sciences, other cultures, and physical activity.

Opportunities exist for independent studies, honors theses or projects, and experiential learning.

The Wittenberg Honors Program, which offers special seminars, honors theses or projects, and a variety of academic and cultural activities, is available for outstanding students who want to challenge themselves and enhance their academic program.

Wittenberg offers five undergraduate degrees: Bachelor of Arts (BA), Bachelor of Science (BS), Bachelor of Music (BMus), Bachelor of Music Education (BME), and Bachelor of Fine Arts (BFA). Wittenberg also offers a Masters in Education degree.

We offer 28 majors: America studies, art, biochemistry & molecular biology, biology, chemistry, communication, computer science, East Asian studies, eonomics, education, English, French, geography, geology, German, history, management, mathematics, music, philosophy, physics, political science, psychology, religion, Russian area studies, sociology, Spanish, and theatre and dance.

In addition to the above, Wittenberg offers these additional minors: dance, environmental studies, global studies, urban studies, women's studies, and writing.

Finally, Wittenberg has cooperative education programs with other colleges and universities to help students complete their majors. These special programs are: accounting, engineering, environmental studies, marine/aquatic biology, nursing, and occupational therapy.

Pre-professional programs include accounting, education, law, theology, and the pre-health fields of pre-medicine, pre-denistry, pre-veterinary, and pre-optometry. With approval, students may plan interdepartmental majors composed of courses selected from several departments that reflect a unified purpose or theme.

The faculty consists of 145 full-time teaching members, 97 percent of whom hold a PhD or the highest degree in their field. Professors are active on campus, in the community, and with their professional associations. They regularly receive teaching awards and research grants to pursue cutting-edge scholarship.

With a student-faculty ratio of 14:1, small classes are the norm. Professors can quickly assess their students' strengths and weaknesses and will offer the necessary support and encouragement.

An innovative advising system designed to facilitate mentoring relationships between students and faculty pairs each student with a faculty member who will serve as an academic advisor. Each student meets one-on-one with their faculty advisor until they graduate; the faculty advisor typically teaches one of the student's first semester classes.

Most faculty members have open-door policies. Students can also work with a faculty member on a research project or independent study, often leading to publishable research papers.

PO Box 720
Springfield, OH 45501
Phone: 800-677-7558
Fax: 937-327-6379
Website: www.wittenberg.edu

Wittenberg UNIVERSITY

CAMPUS LIFE

Located in Springfield, Ohio, Wittenberg's campus rests on 100 wooded, rolling acres in a residential neighborhood. Springfield is both a "living laboratory" and a "college town." With a population of 68,000, Springfield offers the cultural events and internship opportunities found in larger urban areas, as well as the friendliness and sense of community typical of small towns.

Students have access to a wide range of real learning opportunities that include the advantages, challenges, and realities of small-city life. Students intern with local businesses, social service agencies, hospitals, and schools and volunteer in a variety of community settings. They also attend many types of concerts at Kuss Performing Arts Center, explore the Springfield Museum of Art, and relax at area parks and golf courses.

Many shops, restaurants, and parks are within walking distance, but public transportation is available to the mall, airport, and other major cities. Springfield's proximity to Dayton (25 miles), Columbus (45 miles), and Cincinnati (75 miles) gives students convenient access to concerts, shopping, parks, museums, and sporting events. The University is easily reached by Interstate 70 and U.S. Highways 40 and 68.

Wittenberg offers a variety of off-campus opportunities in Springfield for community service, internships, and part-time jobs. Classroom education is also put to work through off-campus educational opportunities and study abroad programs.

The unique Community Partnership Program allows students to work in a variety of businesses and social service agencies in Springfield. Through the Community Workshop students serve at many local agencies for children, the elderly, the environment, literacy, youth mentoring, or the physically disabled. Students have volunteered at the Springfield Museum of Art, Mercy Hospital, Springfield Local Schools, the Humane Society, Kuss Performing Arts Theatre, and more.

Among many others, students have held internships with the Springfield Museum of Art, the Springfield Symphony, the Urban League, Project Woman, WDTN-TV2 (Dayton), Community Hospital, Glen Helen Nature Preserve, the Public Defender's Office, and Wright Patterson Air Force Base.

The economic diversity of Springfield allows students to maintain a variety of part-time jobs.

Off-campus academic opportunities include an extensive student-teaching program, a marine biology/freshwater ecology program in the Bahamas, the City Government Internship Program in Florida, and the Lutheran College Washington D.C. Semester Program. Students have also held internships across the country, including the U.S. Library of Congress, ABC Primetime Live, The Children's Museum of Indianapolis, and the National Institutes of Health.

The University maintains a full-time Office of International Education to assist students with selecting study abroad programs and to counsel them on integrating international study with their academic and career goals. Through memberships in several consortia, Wittenberg students can participate in study abroad programs at 40 sites in more than 20 countries in Europe, Asia, and Latin America.

COSTS

Wittenberg is committed to providing financial assistance to eligible and deserving students and offers both need-based and merit-based assistance.

Need-based assistance includes grants, loans, and work-study programs. More than 75 percent of Wittenberg students qualify for financial assistance, and the average financial assistance award is $19,000 per year. To be considered, applicants must file the Free Application for Federal Student Aid (FAFSA) by March 15.

All accepted students are automatically considered for academic scholarships and special awards. The most prestigious awards include the full-tuition Smith Scholarships and the half-tuition Wittenberg University Scholar Awards and Broadwell Chinn Awards (for African American students).

Wittenberg Alumni Scholarships and Lutheran Scholarships are worth up to $10,000 per year. There are additional Lutheran Scholarships for children of Pastors and Lutheran Lay Workers, and the Lutheran Scholarship Partners Program matches up to $500 of congregational scholarship money awarded to Wittenberg students.

The Community Service Award, with an annual $8,500 scholarship and $1,500 student-employment stipend, rewards superior achievements in community service. There is a special application for this award. Wittenberg also offers scholarships recognizing leadership skills and talent in art, dance, music, and theatre. There are also merit scholarships for involvement in Hugh O'Brian Youth Leadership and Boys and Girls State.

Basic costs for the 2002–2003 academic year are:
Tuition: $23,610
Room: $3,134
Board: $2,932
Activity fee: $150
Books (approximate): $600
Total: $30,426

ADMISSIONS

Admission to Wittenberg is selective and is based on the following information: high school record, including the strength of the high school and its curriculum, and trends in the students academic work; SAT or ACT scores; co-curricular activities and community participation; recommendations; and an essay. International students and transfer students are encouraged to apply. An on-campus interview is not required, but it is highly recommended. Students may apply using the Wittenberg application, the Common Application, or the online application at www.wittenberg.edu.

The deadlines for applying are as follows for incoming freshman:

Early Decision: November 15
Early Action I: December 1
Early Actiion II: January 15
Regular Action: March 15

Students must apply by February 15 to be considered for merit-based scholarships. Transfer applications deadlines are December 1 for spring semester and July 1 for fall semester. The international student application deadline is March 15.

INDEXES

ALPHABETICAL INDEX

C

M

N

O

S

T

U

V

W

INDEX BY LOCATION

UNITED STATES

ALABAMA

ALASKA

ARIZONA

ARKANSAS

CALIFORNIA

COLORADO

CONNECTICUT

DELAWARE

DISTRICT OF COLUMBIA

FLORIDA

INDIANA

IOWA

KANSAS

KENTUCKY

NEBRASKA

NEVADA

NEW HAMPSHIRE

NEW JERSEY

NEW MEXICO

NEW YORK

NORTH CAROLINA

NORTH DAKOTA

OHIO

OKLAHOMA

OREGON

PENNSYLVANIA

TEXAS

UTAH

VERMONT

THE VIRGIN ISLANDS

VIRGINIA

WASHINGTON

WEST VIRGINIA

WISCONSIN

WYOMING

CANADA

INDEX BY SIZE
(in descending order)

MORE THAN 10,000 STUDENTS

10,000 TO 4,000 STUDENTS

UP TO 4,000 STUDENTS

INDEX BY ENVIRONMENT

RURAL

SUBURBAN

URBAN

INDEX BY COST
(in ascending order)

$10,000 TO $15,000

MORE THAN $15,000

INDEX BY SELECTIVITY

64

68

69

75

76

77

78

79

NOTES

NOTES

Countdown to the SAT:
The Week Before the Test

Studying Tips

- Make sure that you get enough sleep every night. Try going to bed earlier and waking up earlier.
- Get up early on the weekend and take a practice test. You need to train your mind to be alert in the morning and able to think for three hours. Treat the practice test as the "real thing."
- Get into a pattern of doing 30-45 minutes' worth of SAT problems each day from now until the test day. You're probably really busy, but think of it this way: you can make this tiny sacrifice now, or go through the entire process all over again.
- When you practice at home, do so under timed conditions. You need to get the feeling of what it will be like on the day of the test. As always, don't do your homework in front of the television or with the radio playing.
- Review all of the formulas and strategies that you've learned so far.

Got What You Need?

- Make sure you have your admission ticket. If you lose it or if it hasn't arrived at least one week before the test, call ETS at (609) 771-7600.
- Put new batteries in your calculator.
- Buy some No. 2 pencils, an eraser, and a sharpener.
- Confirm the location of the test center and make sure you know exactly where it is. If you haven't been there before, take a test run. How long does it take to get there? What's traffic like on Saturdays? Where should you park?
- Make sure you have a picture ID (e.g., driver's license, school ID with photo, passport). If you don't have one, see your counselor. Have him or her write a brief physical description of you on school stationery, and then both you and your counselor should sign it.

Extra Study Tip

Get a 5" x 7" index card; write math strategies on one side and verbal strategies on the other. Keep this card with you all week. Study it whenever you have free time: in study hall, in between classes, or on the ride home.

Countdown to the SAT:
The Day Before the Test

Studying Tips

- DON'T STUDY!!! Cramming just won't help. Put your books away on a high shelf where you can't see them.
- Take it easy and let your brain relax. Catch an early movie or have dinner with friends.

At Night

- Go to bed at a reasonable hour. However, don't try to go to sleep at 7:00 p.m. It won't work.
- Set your alarm clock.

"Don't Forget" Checklist

Prepare everything that you'll need for the morning of the test:

- Admission ticket
- Photo ID
- No. 2 pencils
- Eraser
- Sharpener
- Calculator
- Watch or clock (one that doesn't beep)
- Morning warm-up problems

Countdown to the SAT:
The Morning of the Test

At Home

- Eat a healthy breakfast. It will give you the energy you need to make it through three hours of testing. However, don't give your body what it's not used to. For example, don't eat steak and eggs if you normally have toast and a glass of juice.
- Wear comfortable clothes. Also, dress in layers. You never know whether the test center will be unusually hot or cold.
- Take everything from the "Don't Forget" Checklist with you.
- Leave yourself 20 minutes more than you think you'll need to get to the test center. Be sure to arrive at least 20 minutes before the scheduled test time.

At the Test Center

- Use the bathroom before the test starts. You'll also have a chance to go to the bathroom during the first break (after Section 2). However, you will not have a chance to go during the second break (after Section 4).
- Do your warm-up problems. A great time to work on these questions is before you're seated.
- Try to maintain your focus. Do not listen to what other people say about the test, including which section they think is the experimental one.

Hit Parade

Want to improve your scores?

Start with your vocabulary. The Princeton Review's exclusive *Hit Parade* workbook includes several hundred words that appear most frequently on the SAT. The workbook is available only in our SAT courses, but here's a sampling:

abstract general; not concrete
aesthetic having to do with the appreciation of beauty
alleviate to ease a pain or a burden
ambivalent simultaneously feeling opposing feelings
apathetic feeling or showing little emotion
auspicious favorable; promising
benevolent well-meaning; generous
candor sincerity; openness
cogent convincing; reasonable
comprehensive large in scope or content
contemporary current, modern; from the same time
conviction a fixed or strong belief
diligent marked by painstaking effort; hard-working
dubious doubtful; of unlikely authenticity
eclectic made up of a variety of sources or styles
egregious conspicuously bad or offensive
exculpate to free from guilt or blame
florid describing flowery or elaborate speech
gratuitous given freely; unearned; unwarranted
hackneyed worn-out through overuse; trite
idealize to consider perfect
impartial not in favor of one side or the other; unbiased
imperious arrogantly domineering or overbearing
inherent inborn; built-in
innovative introducing something new
inveterate long established; deep-rooted; habitual
laudatory giving praise
maverick one who resists adherence to a group
mollify to calm or soothe
novel strikingly new or unusual
obdurate stubborn; inflexible
objectivity treating facts uninfluenced by emotion
obstinate stubbornly adhering to an opinion
ornate elaborately decorated
ostentatious describing a pretentious display
paramount of chief concern or importance
penitent expressing remorse for one's misdeeds
pervasive dispersed throughout
plausible seemingly valid or acceptable; credible
profound having great depth or seriousness
prosaic unimaginative; dull
quandary a state of uncertainty or perplexity
rancorous hateful; marked by deep-seated ill will
spurious not genuine; false; counterfeit
stoic indifferent to pleasure or pain; impassive
superfluous extra; unnecessary
tenuous having little substance or strength; unsure; weak
timorous timid; fearful about the future
transitory short-lived; temporary
vindicated freed from blame

SAT vs. ACT

To help you decide which test is right for you, take a side-by-side glance at these important exams.

	SAT	ACT
Preferred by?	Private schools, and schools on the east and west coasts.	Public schools, and schools in the middle of the country. ACT is preferred by more U.S. colleges than the SAT.
Accepted by?	Nearly all U.S. colleges and universities.	Nearly all U.S. colleges and universities.
When is it administered?	Seven times per year.	Six times per year.
Test structure	Seven-section exam: Three Verbal, three Math, and one Experimental. The Experimental section is masked to look like a regular section.	Four-section exam: English, Math, Reading, and Science Reasoning. An Experimental section is added to tests on certain dates only, and is clearly experimental.
Test content	Math: up to 9th grade basic geometry. No science section. Reading: one passage with roughly one minute to answer each question. Stresses vocabulary. A test of strategy and testmanship.	Math: up to trigonometry. Science section included. Reading: four passages with less than one minute to answer each question. Stresses grammar. A test of time management and studiousness.
Is there a penalty for wrong answers?	Yes	No
How the test is scored/highest possible score	200-800 for each subject, added together for a combined score. A 1600 is the highest possible combined score.	1-36 for each subject, averaged together for a composite score. A 36 is the highest possible composite score.
Are all scores sent to schools?	Yes. If a student requests a score report be sent to specific colleges, the report will include the scores the student received on every SAT taken.	No. There is a "score choice" option. Students can choose which schools will receive their scores AND which scores the schools will see.
Other uses for the exams	Scholarship purposes.	Scholarship purposes. Certain statewide testing programs.
When to register	At least six weeks before the test date.	At least four weeks before the test date.
For more information	Educational Testing Service (ETS) (609) 771-7600 www.ets.org The College Board www.collegeboard.com	ACT, Inc. (319) 337-1270 www.act.org

The Princeton Review Admissions Services

At The Princeton Review, we care about your ability to get accepted to the best school for you. But, we all know getting accepting involves much more than just doing well on standardized tests. That's why, in addition to our test preparation services, we also offer free admissions services to students looking to enter college or graduate school. You can find these services on our website, *www.PrincetonReview.com*, the best online resource for researching, applying to, and learning how to pay for the right school for you.

No matter what type of program you're applying to—undergraduate, graduate, law, business, or medical—**PrincetonReview.com has the free tools, services, and advice you need to navigate the admissions process.** Read on to learn more about the services we offer.

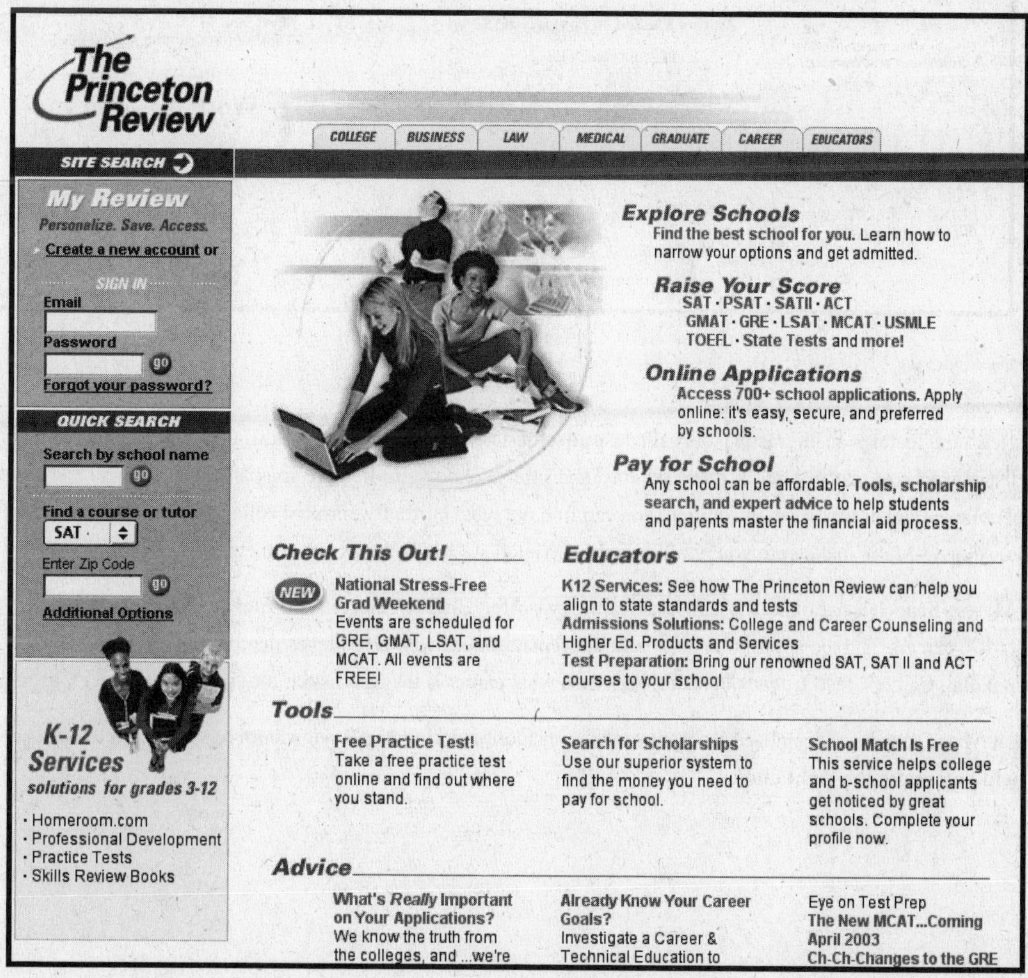

Research Schools
www.PrincetonReview.com/Research

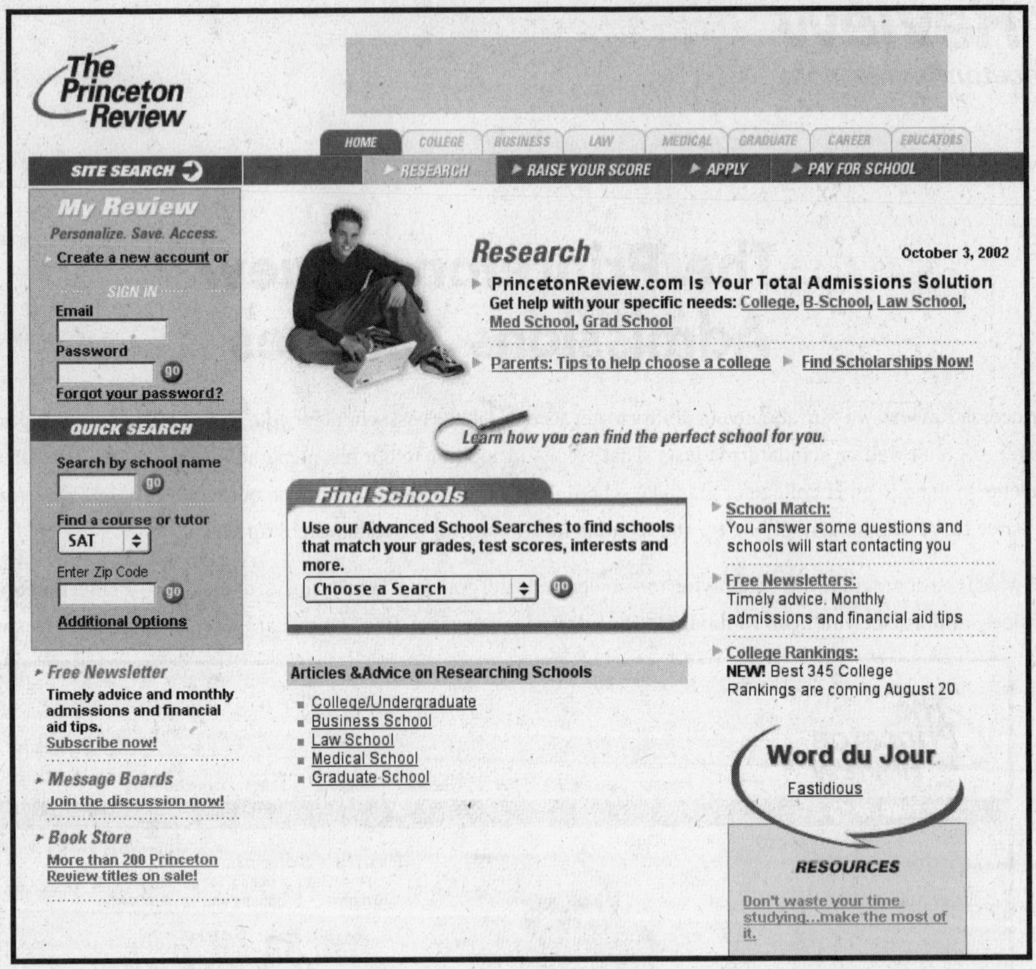

PrincetonReview.com features an interactive tool called **Counselor-O-Matic.** When you use this tool, you enter stats and information about yourself to find a list of your best match schools, reach schools, and safety schools. From there you can read statistical and editorial information about thousands of colleges and universities. In addition, you can find out what currently enrolled college students say about their schools. Once you complete Counselor-O-Matic make sure you opt in to School Match so that colleges can come to you.

Our **College Majors Search** is one of the most popular features we offer. Here you can read profiles on hundreds of majors to find information on curriculum, salaries, careers, and the appropriate high school preparation, as well as colleges that offer it. From the Majors Search, you can investigate corresponding Careers, read **Career Profiles**, and learn what career is the best match for you by taking our **Career Quiz**.

No matter what type of school or specialized program you are considering, **PrincetonReview.com has free articles and advice, in addition to our tools, to help you make the right choice.**